PEDIATRICS

Fifteenth Edition

This volume represents the Fifteenth Edition of Holt's DISEASES OF INFANCY AND CHILDHOOD, originally written in 1896 by the late L. Emmett Holt, Professor of Diseases of Children at Columbia University from 1901 to 1923. Associated with him in several revisions was John Howland, Professor of Pediatrics at Johns Hopkins University from 1912 to 1926. From 1927 until 1962 L. Emmett Holt, Jr. and Rustin McIntosh were responsible for its revision. In 1962 they shared this responsibility with Henry L. Barnett, who, since 1968, has carried it alone.

PEDIATRICS

Fifteenth Edition

EDITOR

HENRY L. BARNETT, M.D.

PROFESSOR AND CHAIRMAN
DEPARTMENT OF PEDIATRICS
ALBERT EINSTEIN COLLEGE OF MEDICINE OF YESHIVA UNIVERSITY
BRONX, NEW YORK

CO-EDITOR

ARNOLD H. EINHORN, M.D.

PROFESSOR OF PEDIATRICS
ALBERT EINSTEIN COLLEGE OF MEDICINE OF YESHIVA UNIVERSITY;
DEPUTY DIRECTOR OF PEDIATRICS
BRONX MUNICIPAL HOSPITAL CENTER
BRONX, NEW YORK;
VISITING PROFESSOR OF PEDIATRICS
UNIVERSITY CHILDREN'S HOSPITAL
UNIVERSITY OF BERN, SWITZERLAND

APPLETON-CENTURY-CROFTS / New York
A Publishing Division of Prentice-Hall, Inc.

To colleagues and students at the
Albert Einstein College of Medicine
and elsewhere who seek new medical
knowledge and new ways to use it for
improving the lives of infants and
children and their parents.

Associate Editors

LEONARD APT, M.D.
Associate Professor of Ophthalmology, The University of California at Los Angeles School of Medicine; Staff, The UCLA Center for the Health Sciences, Departments of Pediatrics and Ophthalmology, Cedars of Lebanon Hospital, Los Angeles, California

IRWIN M. ARIAS, M.D.
Professor of Medicine and Director, Division of Gastroenterology-Liver Diseases, Albert Einstein College of Medicine of Yeshiva University, Bronx, New York

FREDERICK C. BATTAGLIA, M.D.
Professor of Pediatrics and of Obstetrics and Gynecology, and Director, Division of Perinatal Medicine, University of Colorado Medical Center School of Medicine, Denver, Colorado

M. DONALD BLAUFOX, M.D., Ph.D.
Associate Professor of Radiology, Assistant Professor of Medicine; Director, Division of Nuclear Medicine, Albert Einstein College of Medicine of Yeshiva University, Bronx, New York

GOODWIN M. BREININ, M.D.
Kirby Professor of Ophthalmology and Chairman, Department of Ophthalmology, New York University School of Medicine; Director of Ophthalmology, Bellevue Hospital Center, University Hospital-New York University Medical Center, New York, New York

SIDNEY CARTER, M.D.
Dwight D. Eisenhower United Cerebral Palsy Professor of Neurology, and Chief, Division of Pediatric Neurology, Columbia University College of Physicians and Surgeons; Attending Neurologist, Neurological Institute, Presbyterian Hospital, New York, New York

DAVID H. CARVER, M.D.
Associate Professor of Pediatrics and of Microbiology, and Director, Division of Infectious Diseases, Department of Pediatrics, The Johns Hopkins University School of Medicine, The Johns Hopkins Hospital, Baltimore, Maryland

MURRAY DAVIDSON, M.D.
Clinical Professor of Pediatrics, Albert Einstein College of Medicine of Yeshiva University; Director of Pediatrics, Bronx-Lebanon Hospital Center, Bronx, New York

CHESTER M. EDELMANN, JR., M.D.
Professor of Pediatrics and Director, Division of Pediatric Nephrology, Albert Einstein College of Medicine of Yeshiva University, Bronx, New York

Contributors

CHARLES F. ABILDGAARD, M.D.
Professor of Pediatrics, University of California, Davis School of Medicine, Davis, California

MARK ABRAMOWICZ, M.D.
Assistant Professor of Pediatrics, Albert Einstein College of Medicine of Yeshiva University, Bronx, New York

KARLIS ADAMSONS, M.D., Ph.D.
Professor of Obstetrics and Gynecology, Professor of Pharmacology, The Mount Sinai School of Medicine of the City University of New York, New York, New York

HATTIE E. ALEXANDER, M.D.
Late Professor Emeritus of Pediatrics, Columbia University College of Physicians and Surgeons; Late Consultant in Pediatrics, Babies Hospital and Presbyterian Hospital, New York, New York

CHESTER A. ALPER, M.D.
Harvard Medical School, Blood Grouping Laboratory, The Children's Hospital Medical Center, Boston, Massachusetts

SEYMOUR ALPERT, M.D.
Clinical Assistant Professor in Surgery, Department of Surgery, Albert Einstein College of Medicine of Yeshiva University, Bronx, New York

RAYMOND A. AMOURY, M.D.
Professor of Surgery and Professor of Pediatrics, The University of Missouri School of Medicine; Surgeon-in-Chief, The Children's Mercy Hospital; Attending Surgeon, Kansas City General Hospital and Medical Center; Associate Attending Surgeon, St. Luke's Hospital of Kansas City, Kansas City, Missouri

LEONARD APT, M.D.
Associate Professor of Ophthalmology, The UCLA School of Medicine; Staff, The UCLA Center for the Health Sciences; Departments of Pediatrics and Ophthalmology, Cedars of Lebanon Hospital, Los Angeles, California

IRWIN M. ARIAS, M.D.
Professor of Medicine, Director, Division of Gastroenterology-Liver Disease, Albert Einstein College of Medicine of Yeshiva University, Bronx, New York

FREDERICK C. BATTAGLIA, M.D.
Professor of Pediatrics and of Obstetrics and Gynecology, Director, Division of Perinatal Medicine, University of Colorado Medical Center, Denver, Colorado

KURT BENIRSCHKE, M.D.
Professor of Reproductive Biology, Departments of Obstetrics and Gynecology and of Pathology, University of California School of Medicine, San Diego, La Jolla, California

WILLIAM R. BERGREN, Ph.D.
Professor of Biochemistry, University of Southern California School of Medicine; Acting Director of Research, Head, Division of Biochemistry Research, Children's Hospital of Los Angeles, Los Angeles, California

JAY BERNSTEIN, M.D.
Visiting Associate Professor, Albert Einstein College of Medicine of Yeshiva University, Bronx, New York; Director, Anatomic Pathology, William Beaumont Hospital, Royal Oak, Michigan

M. DONALD BLAUFOX, M.D., Ph.D.
Associate Professor of Radiology, Assistant Professor of Medicine, Director, Division of Nuclear Medicine, Albert Einstein College of Medicine of Yeshiva University, Bronx, New York

ROBERT M. BLIZZARD, M.D.
Professor of Pediatrics, The Johns Hopkins University School of Medicine, The Johns Hopkins Hospital, Baltimore, Maryland

SIDNEY BLUMENTHAL, M.D.
Professor of Pediatric Cardiology, Associate Dean of Continuing Education, University of Miami School of Medicine, Miami, Florida

LARS BOREUS, M.D.
Head of Department of Clinical Pharmacology, Karolinska Hospital, Stockholm, Sweden

ALFRED M. BONGIOVANNI, M.D.
William H. Bennett Professor and Chairman, Department of Pediatrics, University of Pennsylvania School of Medicine; Physician-in-Chief, Children's Hospital of Philadelphia, Philadelphia, Pennsylvania

JOHN MAXWELL BOWMAN, M.D.
Associate Professor of Pediatrics, Clinical Director Rh Laboratory, The University of Manitoba Faculty of Medicine; Assistant Pediatrician, Children's Hospital of Winnipeg, Winnipeg General Hospital, Grace General Hospital, Winnipeg, Manitoba, Canada

WILLIAM BRADFORD, M.D.
Professor Emeritus of Pediatrics, The University of Rochester School of Medicine and Dentistry, Rochester, New York

ROSCOE O. BRADY, M.D.
Assistant Chief, Laboratory of Neurochemistry, National Institute of Neurological Diseases and Stroke, National Institutes of Health, Bethesda, Maryland

JAMES B. BRAYTON, M.D., D.V.M., M.P.H.
Assistant Professor of Pediatrics and Laboratory Animal Medicine, The Johns Hopkins University School of Medicine, The Johns Hopkins Hospital, Baltimore, Maryland

GOODWIN M. BREININ, M.D.
Kirby Professor of Ophthalmology and Chairman, Department of Ophthalmology, New York University School of Medicine; Director of Ophthalmology, Bellevue Hospital Center, University Hospital-New York University Medical Center, New York, New York

EDWIN A. BRONSKY, M.D.
Assistant Professor of Pediatrics, University of Colorado Medical Center School of Medicine; National Jewish Hospital and Research Center, Denver, Colorado

A. JOSEPH BROUGH, M.D.
Adjunct Assistant Professor (FT), Affiliated Program in Pathology, Wayne State University School of Medicine; Associate Pathologist, Associate Director of Laboratories, Children's Hospital of Michigan, Detroit, Michigan

ERIKA BRUCK, M.D.
Professor of Pediatrics, The State University of New York at Buffalo School of Medicine; Attending Physician, Children's Hospital of Buffalo, Buffalo, New York

PHILIP A. BRUNELL, M.D.
Associate Professor of Pediatrics, New York University School of Medicine; Associate Attending Physician, University Hospital-New York University Medical Center; Associate Visiting Physician, Bellevue Hospital Center, New York, New York; Consultant, Pediatrics, United States Military Academy, West Point, New York

JOSEPH W. BURNETT, M.D.
Associate Professor of Medicine in Dermatology, University of Maryland School of Medicine, Baltimore, Maryland

CHARLES C. J. CARPENTER, M.D.
Professor of Medicine, The Johns Hopkins University School of Medicine; Physician-in-Chief, Baltimore City Hospital, Baltimore, Maryland

SIDNEY CARTER, M.D.
Dwight D. Eisenhower United Cereral Palsy Professor of Neurology, Chief, Division of Pediatric Neurology, Columbia University College of Physicians and Surgeons; Attending Neurologist, Neurological Institute, Presbyterian Hospital, New York, New York

DAVID H. CARVER, M.D.
Associate Professor of Pediatrics and of Microbiology, Director, Division of Infectious Diseases, Department of Pediatrics, The Johns Hopkins University School of Medicine, The Johns Hopkins Hospital, Baltimore, Maryland

ROBERT F. CASTLE, M.D.
Professor of Pediatrics, University of New Mexico School of Medicine, Director of Pediatric Cardiology, University of New Mexico Hospitals, Albuquerque, New Mexico

DORA CHAO, M.D.
Clinical Assistant Professor, Baylor College of Medicine, Houston, Texas

J. JULIAN CHISHOLM, M.D.
Professor of Pediatrics, The Johns Hopkins University School of Medicine, Baltimore, Maryland

GERALD CHOTINER, M.D.
Chief Resident, Department of Dermatology, Medical College of Georgia School of Medicine, Augusta, Georgia

ABE M. CHUTORIAN, M.D.
Associate Professor of Clinical Neurology, Columbia University College of Physicians and Surgeons, Associate Attending Neurologist, Columbia-Presbyterian Medical Center, Consultant in Neurology, Blythedale Children's Hospital, Harlem Hospital Medical Center, New York, New York

DAVID B. CLARK, M.D., Ph.D.
Professor and Chairman, Department of Neurology, Professor of Pediatrics, University of Kentucky College of Medicine of the Albert B. Chandler Medical Center, Lexington, Kentucky

HERBERT J. COHEN, M.D.
Associate Professor of Pediatrics and Rehabilitation Medicine, Albert Einstein College of Medicine of Yeshiva University; Director, Children's Evaluation and Rehabilitation Clinic, Rose F. Kennedy Center; Director, Bronx State Hospital Developmental Services, Bronx, New York

MICHAEL I. COHEN, M.D.
Associate Professor of Pediatrics, Albert Einstein College of Medicine of Yeshiva University; Director, Division of Adolescent Medicine, Department of Pediatrics, Montefiore Hospital and Medical Center, Bronx, New York

LOUIS Z. COOPER, M.D.
Associate Professor of Pediatrics, New York University School of Medicine; Associate Attending Pediatrician, Bellevue Hospital Center, New York, New York

MARVIN CORNBLATH, M.D.
Professor and Head, Department of Pediatrics, University of Maryland School of Medicine, Baltimore, Maryland

JOANN M. CORNET, M.D.
Assistant Professor of Pediatrics, The University of Illinois College of Medicine, Chicago, Illinois

DAVID BAIRD COURSIN, M.D.
Director, Research Institute, St. Joseph Hospital, Lancaster, Pennsylvania

ROBERT G. CROUNSE, M.D.
Professor of Dermatology and Cell and Molecular Biology; Associate Dean, Office of Instructional Systems, Medical College of Georgia School of Medicine, Augusta, Georgia

EDWARD C. CURNEN, JR., M.D.
Carpentier Professor of Pediatrics, Columbia University College of Physicians and Surgeons; Attending Pediatrician, Babies Hospital and Vanderbilt Clinic, Presbyterian Hospital, New York, New York

B. SHANNON DANES, M.D., Ph.D.
Associate Professor, Cornell University Medical College; Associate Attending Physician, The New York Hospital, New York, New York

MURRAY DAVIDSON, M.D.
Clinical Professor of Pediatrics, Albert Einstein College of Medicine of Yeshiva University; Director of Pediatrics, Bronx-Lebanon Hospital Center, Bronx, New York

WILLIAM DE MYER, M.D.
Professor of Neurology, Indiana University School of Medicine, Indianapolis, Indiana

GEORGE N. DONNELL, M.D.
Professor and Acting Chairman, Department of Pediatrics, University of Southern California School of Medicine; Acting Physician-in-Chief, Head, Division of Medical Genetics, Department of Medicine, Children's Hospital of Los Angeles, Los Angeles, California

EUGENIE F. DOYLE, M.D.
Professor of Pediatrics, New York University School of Medicine; Director of Pediatric Cardiology, University Hospital-New York University Medical Center, New York, New York

ARTHUR L. DREW, M.D.
Director of Pediatric Neurology, Indiana University School of Medicine, Indianapolis, Indiana

HERBERT DU PONT, M.D.
Assistant Professor of Medicine, University of Maryland School of Medicine, Baltimore, Maryland

VU VAN DZI, M.D.
Captain, Medical Corps, Army of the Republic of Vietnam, Saigon, Republic of Vietnam

WALTER R. EBERLEIN, M.D.
Professor of Pediatrics, The University of Pennsylvania School of Medicine; Endocrinologist, Senior Physician, Children's Hospital of Philadelphia, Philadelphia, Pennsylvania

CHESTER M. EDELMANN, JR., M.D.
Professor of Pediatrics, Director, Division of Pediatric Nephrology, Albert Einstein College of Medicine of Yeshiva University, Bronx, New York

HEINZ EICHENWALD, M.D.
William Buchanan Professor, Chairman, Department of Pediatrics, University of Texas Southwestern Medical School at Dallas, Dallas, Texas

ARNOLD EINHORN, M.D.
Professor of Pediatrics, Albert Einstein College of Medicine of Yeshiva University; Deputy Director of Pediatrics, Bronx Municipal Hospital Center, Bronx, New York; Visiting Professor of Pediatrics, University Children's Hospital, University of Bern, Switzerland

ELLIOT F. ELLIS, M.D.
Associate Professor of Pediatrics, University of Colorado Medical Center School of Medicine; Chief of Pediatrics, National Jewish Hospital and Research Center, Denver, Colorado

MARY ALLEN ENGLE, M.D.
Professor of Pediatrics, Cornell University Medical College; Director of Pediatric Cardiology, Attending Pediatrician, The New York Hospital, New York, New York

FRED J. EPSTEIN, M.D.
Assistant Professor of Neurosurgery, New York University School of Medicine, New York, New York

SIBYLLE ESCALONA, Ph.D.
Professor of Psychiatry (Psychology), Albert Einstein College of Medicine of Yeshiva University, Bronx, New York

FRANK FALKNER, M.D., M.R.C.P.
Fels Professor of Pediatrics, University of Cincinnati College of Medicine, Cincinnati, Ohio; Director, Fels Research Institute, Yellow Springs, Ohio

JOSE M. FERRER, M.D., F.A.C.S.
Professor of Surgery, Columbia University College of Physicians and Surgeons; Director of Surgery, Harlem Hospital Medical Center; Attending Surgeon, Babies Hospital and Vanderbilt Clinic, Presbyterian Hospital, New York, New York

LAURENCE FINBERG, M.D.
Professor and Chairman, Department of Pediatrics, Albert Einstein College of Medicine of Yeshiva University (Montefiore Hospital and Medical Center), Bronx, New York

PHILIP FIREMAN, M.D.
Associate Professor of Pediatrics, University of Pittsburgh School of Medicine; Director, Allergy-Immunology, Children's Hospital of Pittsburgh, Pittsburgh, Pennsylvania

ALFRED L. FLORMAN, M.D.
Professor of Pediatrics, New York University School of Medicine; Attending Physician, Bellevue Hospital Center, New York, New York

CLAUDE A. FRAZIER, M.D., F.A.C.A.
The Medical College of Virginia of Virginia Commonwealth University; Chief-of-Allergy, Memorial Mission Hospital, Richmond, Virginia

PIERCE GARDNER
Assistant Professor of Medicine, Harvard Medical School; Associate in Infectious Diseases, The Children's Hospital Medical Center; Associate in Medicine, Beth Israel Hospital, Boston, Massachusetts

LAWRENCE M. GARTNER, M.D.
Associate Professor of Pediatrics, Albert Einstein College of Medicine of Yeshiva University, Bronx, New York

SYDNEY S. GELLIS, M.D.
Professor and Chairman, Department of Pediatrics, Tufts University School of Medicine, Boston, Massachusetts

SALOME GLUECKSOHN-WAELSCH, Ph.D.
Department of Genetics, Albert Einstein College of Medicine of Yeshiva University, Bronx, New York

SUMIO GO, M.D.
Assistant Professor of Pediatrics, University of Colorado Medical Center School of Medicine, National Jewish Hospital and Research Center, Denver, Colorado

ARNOLD P. GOLD, M.D.
Associate Professor, Clinical Neurology (Pediatrics), Columbia University College of Physicians and Surgeons; Associate Attending Neurologist, Presbyterian Hospital, New York, New York

ELI GOLD, M.D.
Professor of Pediatrics, Case Western Reserve University School of Medicine, Cleveland Metropolitan General Hospital, Cleveland, Ohio

SIDNEY GOLDFISCHER, M.D.
Associate Professor, Department of Pathology, Albert Einstein College of Medicine of Yeshiva University; Attending Pathologist, Bronx Municipal Hospital Center, Bronx, New York

ROBERT W. GOLTZ, M.D.
Professor and Head, Department of Dermatology, The University of Minnesota Health Science Center, Minneapolis, Minnesota

GEORGE G. GRAHAM, M.D.
Professor of International Health (Human Nutrition), The School of Hygiene and Public Health, The Johns Hopkins University; Associate Professor of Pediatrics, The Johns Hopkins University School of Medicine, Baltimore, Maryland; Director of Research, British-American Hospital, Lima, Peru

MELVIN GREER, M.D.
Professor and Chief, Neurology Section, University of Florida College of Medicine, Gainesville, Florida

ROBERT H. GREGG, M.D.
Associate Professor of Pediatrics, Wayne State University School of Medicine; Director of Pulmonary Services, Children's Hospital of Michigan, Detroit, Michigan

MOSES GROSSMAN, M.D.
Professor of Pediatrics, University of California San Francisco Campus School of Medicine; Chief of Pediatrics, San Francisco General Hospital, San Francisco, California

PETER GRUENWALD, M.D.
Associate Professor of Pathology, Hahnemann Medical College and Hospital of Philadelphia, Philadelphia, Pennsylvania

MELVIN M. GRUMBACH, M.D.
Professor and Chairman, Department of Pediatrics, Director of Pediatric Services, University of California San Francisco Campus School of Medicine, San Francisco, California

WARREN G. GUNTHEROTH, M.D.
Professor of Pediatrics, Head, Division of Pediatric Cardiology, The University of Washington School of Medicine, Seattle, Washington

JAMES F. HAMMILL, M.D.
Associate Professor of Clinical Neurology, Columbia University College of Physicians and Surgeons; Associate Attending Neurologist, Neurological Institute, Presbyterian Hospital, New York, New York

SUSAN R. HARRIS, M.D.
Instructor in Medicine, Albert Einstein College of Medicine of Yeshiva University; Assistant Attending Physician, Bronx Municipal Hospital Center, Bronx, New York

HAROLD E. HARRISON, M.D.
Professor of Pediatrics, The Johns Hopkins University School of Medicine; Pediatrician-in-Chief, Baltimore City Hospitals, Baltimore, Maryland

THOMAS A. HELMRATH
Assistant Professor, Department of Human Development, Michigan State University College of Human Medicine, East Lansing, Michigan

KEITH S. HENLEY, M.D.
Department of Internal Medicine, Section of Gastroenterology, The University of Michigan Medical Center; Ann Arbor, Michigan

WALTER L. HENLEY, M.D.
Department of Pediatrics, Mount Sinai School of Medicine of the City University of New York, New York, New York

HORACE L. HODES, M.D.
Professor and Chairman, Department of Pediatrics, Mount Sinai School of Medicine of the City University of New York, New York, New York

JULIEN I. E. HOFFMAN, M.D.
Associate Professor of Pediatrics and Member of Cardiovascular Research Institute, University of California San Francisco Campus School of Medicine, San Francisco, California

L. EMMETT HOLT, JR., M.D.
Professor of Pediatrics, New York University School of Medicine, New York, New York

GEORGE R. HONIG, M.D.
Associate Professor of Pediatrics, University of Illinois, Abraham Lincoln School of Medicine; Attending Pediatrician, University of Illinois Hospital, Chicago, Illinois

DOROTHY M. HORSTMANN, M.D.
Professor of Epidemiology and Pediatrics, Yale University School of Medicine, New Haven, Connecticut

ERNST R. JAFFE, M.D.
Professor of Medicine, Albert Einstein College of Medicine of Yeshiva University; Attending Physician, Bronx Municipal Hospital Center, Bronx, New York

L. STANLEY JAMES, M.D.
Professor of Pediatrics, College of Physicians and Surgeons, Columbia University; Attending Pediatrician, Pediatric Services, Director, Division of Perinatology, Babies Hospital, New York, New York

SAMUEL L. KATZ, M.D.
Professor and Chairman, Department of Pediatrics, Duke University School of Medicine, Durham, North Carolina

HERBERT J. KAYDEN, M.D.
Professor of Medicine, New York University School of Medicine; Visiting Physician, Bellevue Hospital Center; Attending Physician, University Hospital-New York University Medical Center, Manhattan Veterans Administration Hospital, New York, New York

C. HENRY KEMPE, M.D.
Professor and Chairman, Department of Pediatrics, The University of Colorado Medical Center School of Medicine; Pediatrician-in-Chief, Colorado General Hospital, Denver, Colorado

MARSHALL H. KLAUS, M.D.
Associate Professor of Pediatrics, Case Western Reserve University School of Medicine; Director, Neonatal Center, University Hospitals, Cleveland, Ohio

HAROLD P. KLINGER, M.D., Ph.D.
Associate Professor of Genetics, Department of Genetics, Albert Einstein College of Medicine of Yeshiva University, Bronx, New York

ARTHUR F. KOHRMAN, M.D.
Associate Professor, Department of Human Development, Michigan State University College of Human Medicine, East Lansing, Michigan

NECHAMA S. KOSOWER, M.D.
Associate Professor of Medicine, Albert Einstein College of Medicine of Yeshiva University; Associate Attending Physician, Bronx Municipal Hospital Center, Bronx, New York

NORMAN KRETCHMER, M.D., Ph.D.
Harold K. Farbor Professor of Pediatrics, Chief, Division of Developmental Biology, Stanford University Medical Center, Stanford, California

SAUL KRUGMAN, M.D.
Professor and Chairman, Department of Pediatrics, New York University School of Medicine; Director of Pediatrics, Bellevue Hospital Center, New York, New York

HOWARD E. KULIN, M.D.
Senior Investigator, Reproduction Research Branch, National Institute of Child Health and Human Development, National Institutes of Health, Bethesda, Maryland

WILLIAM S. LANGFORD, M.D.
Professor of Psychiatry, Columbia University College of Physicians and Surgeons; Attending Pediatrician, Babies Hospital and Vanderbilt Clinic; Attending Psychiatrist, New York State Psychiatric Institute, New York, New York

LYNNE L. LEVITSKY, M.D.
Assistant Professor of Pediatrics, University of Illinois, Abraham Lincoln School of Medicine, Chicago, Illinois

SELWYN B. LEVITT, M.D.
Assistant Professor of Urology, Director of Pediatric Urology, Albert Einstein College of Medicine of Yeshiva University, Bronx, New York

IRIS F. LITT, M.D.
Assistant Professor of Pediatrics, Albert Einstein College of Medicine of Yeshiva University; Director, Junior Center Service, Division of Adolescent Medicine, Department of Pediatrics, Montefiore Hospital and Medical Center, Bronx, New York

NIELS L. LOW, M.D.
Associate Clinical Professor of Neurology, Columbia University College of Physicians and Surgeons; Associate Attending Physician, Presbyterian Hospital; Clinical Director, Blythedale Children's Hospital, New York, New York

CHARLES U. LOWE, M.D.
National Institute of Child Health and Human Development, National Institutes of Health, Bethesda, Maryland

LULA O. LUBCHENCO, M.D.
University of Colorado Medical Center, Denver, Colorado

MARCUS H. MA, M.D.
Staff Physician, Royal Prince Albert Hospital, Sydney, New South Wales, Australia

PAUL C. MAC DONALD, M.D.
Professor and Chairman, Department of Obstetrics and Gynecology, The University of Texas Southwestern Medical School at Dallas, Dallas, Texas

ANDREW M. MARGILETH, M.D.
Professor and Vice-Chairman, Department of Pediatrics, The George Washington University School of Medicine; Senior Attending Physician, Children's Hospital, Washing, D. C.

MILTON MARKOWITZ, M.D.
Professor and Head, Department of Pediatrics, University of Connecticut School of Medicine, Hartford, Connecticut

ROBERTO MASELLI, M.D.
Assistant Professor of Pediatrics, University of Colorado Medical Center School of Medicine, National Jewish Hospital and Research Center, Denver, Colorado; Associate Professor of Microbiology, Facultad de Ciencias Medicas, Guatemala, Central America

ERNEST S. MATHEWS, M.D.
Associate Professor of Clinical Neurosurgery; Chief, Pediatric Neurosurgery, Mount Sinai School of Medicine of the City University of New York; Associate Attending Neurosurgeon, Mount Sinai Hospital, New York, New York

ANGUS M. MC BRYDE, M.D.
Professor of Pediatrics, Duke University School of Medicine; Director of Nurseries, Duke Medical Center, Durham, North Carolina

GEORGE MC CRACKEN, M.D.
Assistant Professor of Pediatrics, The University of Texas Southwestern Medical School at Dallas, Dallas, Texas

JOSEPH MC GUIRE, M.D.
Associate Professor, Department of Dermatology, Yale University School of Medicine, New Haven, Connecticut

DONALD S. MC LAREN, M.D.
Professor of Clinical Nutrition, American University of Beirut School of Medicine, Beirut, Lebanon

GIACOMO MESCHIA, M.D.
Department of Physiology, University of Colorado Medical Center School of Medicine, Denver, Colorado

ROBERT W. MILLER, M.D.
Chief, Epidemiology Branch, National Cancer Institute, National Institutes of Health, Bethesda, Maryland

J. GORDON MILLICHAP, M.D.
Professor of Neurology and Pediatrics, Northwestern University Medical School; Pediatric Neurologist, Children's Memorial Hospital and Passavant Memorial Hospital, Chicago, Illinois

RALPH E. MOLOSHOK, M.D.
Clinical Professor of Pediatrics, Mount Sinai School of Medicine of the City University of New York; Attending Pediatrician, Mount Sinai Hospital, New York, New York

JAMES MOSLEY, M.D.
Associate Professor of Medicine, University of Southern California School of Medicine, Los Angeles, California

LUIS L. MOSOVICH, M.D.
Assistant Professor of Pediatrics, State University of New York at Buffalo School of Medicine, Buffalo, New York

MARTIN A. NASH, M.D.
Assistant Professor of Pediatrics, Division of Pediatric Nephrology, Albert Einstein College of Medicine of Yeshiva University, Bronx, New York

ERWIN NETER, M.D.
Professor of Microbiology, The State University of New York at Buffalo School of Medicine; Director of Bacteriology, Children's Hospital, Buffalo, New York

HAROLD M. NITOWSKY, M.D.
Professor of Pediatrics, Associate Professor of Genetics, Albert Einstein College of Medicine of Yeshiva University; Attending Pediatrician, Bronx Municipal Hospital Center, Bronx, New York

WILLIAM L. NYHAN, M.D., Ph.D.
Professor and Chairman, Department of Pediatrics, University of California, San Diego School of Medicine, La Jolla, California

MILTON H. PAUL, M.D.
Professor of Pediatrics, Northwestern University Medical School; Director, Division of Cardiology, Willis J. Potts Children's Heart Center, Children's Memorial Hospital, Chicago, Illinois

ELSA PROEHL PAULSEN, M.D.
Associate Professor, Department of Pediatrics, University of Virginia School of Medicine, Charlottesville, Virginia; Visiting Associate Professor, Department of Pediatrics, Albert Einstein College of Medicine of Yeshiva University, Bronx, New York

DAVID S. PEARLMAN, M.D.
Associate Professor of Pediatrics, University of Colorado Medical Center School of Medicine; Director, Pediatric Allergy Clinics, University of Colorado Medical Center; Consultant in Pediatric Allergy, National Jewish Hospital and Research Center, Denver, Colorado

ROGER PEARSON, M.D.
Associate Professor of Dermatology, Rush-Presbyterian-St. Luke's Medical Center, Chicago, Illinois

EDWARD J. QUILLIGAN, M.D.
Chairman, Department of Obstetrics and Gynecology, University of Southern California School of Medicine; Chief of Professional Services, Women's Hospital, Los Angeles County-USC Medical Center, Los Angeles, California

HELEN M. RANNEY, M.D.
Professor of Medicine, Department of Medicine, The State University of New York at Buffalo School of Medicine, Buffalo, New York

JOSEPH RANSOHOFF, M.D.
Professor and Chairman, Department of Neurosurgery, New York University School of Medicine; Director of Neurosurgery, University Hospital-New York University Medical Center; Director of Neurological Services, Bellevue Hospital Center, New York, New York

MARK M. RAVITCH, M.D.
Professor of Surgery, The University of Pittsburgh School of Medicine; Surgeon-in-Chief, Montefiore Hospital, Pittsburgh, Pennsylvania

R. GERALD RICE, M.D.
Chief, Bureau of Maternal and Child Health, Michigan Department of Public Health, Lansing, Michigan

JOSEPH RICHMAN, Ph.D.
Senior Psychologist and Associate Professor, Department of Psychiatry, Albert Einstein College of Medicine of Yeshiva University, Bronx, New York

JOHN B. ROBBINS, M.D.
Clinical Director, National Institute of Child Health and Human Development, National Institutes of Health, Bethesda, Maryland

JUAN RODRIGUEZ-SORIANO, M.D.
Director, Hospital Infantil de la Seguridad Social, Bilbao, Spain

FRED S. ROSEN, M.D.
Harvard Medical School, The Children's Hospital Medical Center, Boston, Massachusetts

MILTON ROSENBAUM, M.D.
Visiting Professor, Department of Psychiatry, Albert Einstein College of Medicine of Yeshiva University, Bronx, New York

SOLOMON N. ROSENSTEIN, D.D.S.
Professor of Dentistry and Director, Division of Pedodontics, Columbia University School of Dental and Oral Surgery; Attending Dental Surgeon (Pedodantics), Presbyterian Hospital, New York, New York

ROBERT J. RUBEN, M.D.
Professor and Chairman, Department of Otolaryngology, Albert Einstein College of Medicine of Yeshiva University; Director of Service, Hospital of the Albert Einstein College of Medicine, Lincoln Hospital, Bronx Municipal Hospital Center, Bronx, New York

ABRAHAM M. RUDOLPH, M.D.
Professor of Pediatrics, University of California San Francisco Campus School of Medicine; Senior Staff Member, University of California Cardiovascular Research Institute; Director of Pediatric Cardiology, University of California Medical Center, San Francisco, California

THOMAS V. SANTULLI, M.D.
Professor of Surgery, Columbia University College of Physicians and Surgeons; Attending Surgeon, Columbia-Presbyterian Medical Center; Chief, Pediatric Surgical Service, Babies Hospital, New York, New York

IRVING SCHULMAN, M.D.
Professor and Head, Department of Pediatrics, University of Illinois, Abraham Lincoln School of Medicine; Chief of Pediatrics, University of Illinois Hospital, Chicago, Illinois

WILLIAM E. SEGAR, M.D., Ph.D.
The University of Wisconsin Medical Center, Madison, Wisconsin

MERRY RUBIN SHERMAN, Ph.D.
The Sloan-Kettering Institute for Cancer Research, New York, New York

HENRY R. SHINEFIELD, M.D.
Clinical Professor of Pediatrics, The University of California San Francisco Campus School of Medicine; Chief of Pediatrics, Kaiser Hospital, San Francisco, California

KENNETH SHULMAN, M.D.
Professor of Neurological Surgery and of Pediatrics, Albert Einstein College of Medicine of Yeshiva University, Bronx, New York

HOWARD SHOOKOFF, M.D.
Visiting Associate Professor of Community Health, Albert Einstein College of Medicine of Yeshiva University, Bronx, New York; Adjunct Associate Professor of Medicine, Columbia College of Physicians and Surgeons; Chief of the Division of Tropical Disease, Bureau of Preventable Disease, New York City Department of Health, New York, New York

JAMES B. SIDBURY, JR., M.D.
Professor of Pediatrics, Duke University School of Medicine, Durham, North Carolina

JOSE E. SIFONTES, M.D.
Dean and Professor of Pediatrics, University of Puerto Rico School of Medicine; Associate Attending Pediatrician, University Hospital, San Juan, Puerto Rico

MERVIN SILVERBERG, M.D.
Associate Clinical Professor of Pediatrics, Chief, Pediatric Gastrointestinal-Liver Research Program, Bronx-Lebanon Hospital Center, Bronx, New York

FREDERIC N. SILVERMAN, M.D.
Professor of Pediatrics and of Radiology, University of Cincinnati College of Medicine; Director, Division of Roentgenology, Attending Pediatrician, Children's Hospital, Cincinnati, Ohio

JOHN C. SINCLAIR, M.D.
Professor, Department of Pediatrics, McMaster University Faculty of Medicine, Hamilton, Ontario, Canada

DAVID H. SMITH, M.D.
Associate Professor of Pediatrics, Harvard Medical School, Boston, Massachusetts

DONALD C. SMITH, M.D., D.P.H.
Professor of Maternal and Child Health, The University of Michigan, Ann Arbor, Michigan

J. GRAHAM SMITH, JR., M.D.
Professor of Dermatology and Medicine, Chairman, Department of Dermatology, Medical College of Georgia School of Medicine; Chief of Staff, Eugene Talmadge Memorial Hospital, Augusta, Georgia

MADISON S. SPACH, M.D.
Department of Pediatrics, Duke University Medical Center, Durham, North Carolina

ADRIAN SPITZER, M.D.
Associate Professor of Pediatrics, Division of Pediatric Nephrology, Albert Einstein College of Medicine of Yeshiva University, Bronx, New York

ALEX J. STEIGMAN, M.D.
Professor of Pediatrics, Mount Sinai School of Medicine of the City University of New York; Attending Pediatrician, Mount Sinai Hospital, New York, New York

GENE H. STOLLERMAN, M.D.
Professor and Chairman, Department of Medicine, The University of Tennessee College of Medicine; Physician-in-Chief, City of Memphis Hospitals, Memphis, Tennessee

L. JOSEPH STONE, Ph.D.
Professor of Psychology, Vassar College, Poughkeepsie, New York

PHILIP SUNSHINE, M.D.
Associate Professor, Pediatric Director of Nurseries at Stanford, Stanford University School of Medicine, Stanford, California

LAWRENCE T. TAFT, M.D.
Professor of Pediatrics, Associate Director for Clinical Services and Training Program of the Rose Fitzgerald Kennedy Center for Research in Mental Retardation and Human Development, Albert Einstein College of Medicine of Yeshiva University, Bronx, New York

IGOR TAMM, M.D.
Professor of Virology, The Rockefeller University; Senior Physician, The Rockefeller University, Hospital, New York, New York

WILLIAM H. TOOLEY, M.D.
Associate Professor of Pediatrics, Member, Cardiovascular Research Institute, University of California San Francisco Campus School of Medicine, San Francisco, California

JUDSON J. VAN WYK, M.D.
Professor of Pediatrics, The University of North Carolina School of Medicine, Chapel Hill, North Carolina

CLAUDE A. VILLEE, JR., Ph.D.
Andelot Professor of Biological Chemistry, Harvard Medical School, Boston, Massachusetts

MARY L. VOORHESS, M.D.
Professor of Pediatrics, State University of New York Upstate Medical Center College of Medicine; Attending Pediatrician, State University Hospital and Crouse Irving-Memorial Hospital, Syracuse, New York

ALAN A. WANDERER, M.D.
Assistant Professor of Pediatrics, University of Colorado Medical Center School of Medicine; Director, Pediatric Allergy Out-Patient Service, National Jewish Hospital and Research Center, Denver, Colorado

MYRON E. WEGMAN, M.D., M.P.H.
Professor of Pediatrics and Communicable Diseases, The University of Michigan Medical School; Dean and Professor of Public Health, The University of Michigan School of Public Health, Ann Arbor, Michigan

WILLIAM B. WEIL, M.D.
Professor and Chairman, Department of Human Development, Michigan State University College of Human Medicine, East Lansing, Michigan

JONATHAN H. WEISS, Ph.D.
Director, Behavior Science Division, Children's Asthma Research Institute and Hospital, Denver, Colorado

STUART WEISS, M.D.
Assistant Professor of Clinical Neurology, Washington University School of Medicine, St. Louis, Missouri

CLARK D. WEST, M.D.
Professor of Pediatrics, University of Cincinnati College of Medicine; Associate Director, Children's Hospital Research Foundation, Cincinnati, Ohio

ROBERT T. WINTERS, M.D.
Professor of Pediatrics, Columbia University College of Physicians and Surgeons; Attending Pediatrician, Babies Hospital and Vanderbilt Clinic, New York, New York

MURRAY WITTNER, M.D., Ph.D.
Associate Professor of Pathology and Parasitology, Albert Einstein College of Medicine of Yeshiva University; Director of Parasitology Laboratories and Clinics, Bronx Municipal Hospital Center, Hospital of the Albert Einstein College of Medicine, and Lincoln Hospital, Bronx, New York

EMANUEL WOLINSKY, M.D.
Professor of Medicine, Case Western Reserve School of Medicine, Cleveland, Ohio

T. WOODWARD, M.D.
Professor and Chairman, Department of Medicine, University of Maryland School of Medicine, Baltimore, Maryland

RICHARD JAY WURTMAN, M.D.
Professor of Endocrinology and Metabolism, Laboratory of Neuroendocrine Regulation, Department of Nutrition and Food Sciences, Massachusetts Institute of Technology, Cambridge, Massachusetts

SUMNER J. YAFFE, M.D.
Professor and Associate Chairman, Department of Pediatrics, The State University of New York at Buffalo School of Medicine; Attending Pediatrician, Children's Hospital, Buffalo, New York

MITCHELL R. ZAVON, M.D.
Assistant Professor of Industrial Medicine, University of Cincinnati College of Medicine, Cincinnati, Ohio

Preface

The goals sought in this edition of Pediatrics are those described in the Preface to the 14th Edition, and the policy of sharing responsibility with Associate Editors has been continued and extended to include all chapters. New Associate Editors of the chapters on Perinatal Pediatrics, Nutrition, Physical Growth, Genetic Principles in Pediatrics, Anomalies of Metabolism, Immunologic Principles in Pediatrics, Allergy, Systemic Arterial Hypertension, the Nose and Pharynx, the Ears, and the Appendix have produced major rewriting of a large portion of the text. All other chapters have been revised extensively and new subjects have been added, including entire sections on the Epidemiology of Congenital Malformations, Cholera, Drowning, and, sadly, on Suicide and Drug Abuse in children.

Grateful appreciation is extended again to many people, especially to the Associate Editors and particularly to Arnold H. Einhorn, M.D., whose contributions to the book are now acknowledged by his designation as Co-editor. Thanks are given again to Shirley B. Barnett for her editorial assistance and psychologic support.

HENRY L. BARNETT, M.D.

New York
April, 1972

Preface to the
Fourteenth Edition

This 14th Edition of Pediatrics was planned and prepared * during a period when pediatrics, "the branch of biology which concerns itself with the life of infants and children" (Pediatrics, 13th Edition), was undergoing a number of changes in the United States. Two of these changes influenced considerably both the organizational arrangements and the subject matter of the book; these were, first, the inevitable trend toward increasing specialization within pediatrics; and, second, changes in patterns of delivery of child health services.

The development of pediatric nephrology as a specialty provides an example of the trend toward increasing specialization within pediatrics; it was the subject of the editor's Still Memorial Lecture (*Arch. Dis. Child.*, 41:229, 1966) given before the British Paediatric Association in 1965 in which he stated that we are uneasy "about the developments of more and more specialization within paediatrics. On the one hand we seek to preserve the concepts of the unity of the child and to understand his interrelationships with his family and with society. On the other, the complexities of paediatric cardiology, neurology, haematology—and nephrology, among others —have become so great that productive research, mechanistic teaching, and optimal consultative clinical care of the specialty's complicated patients all require ever increasing specialization. Acceptance of paediatric nephrology acknowledges the scientific necessity for such specialization, and, indeed, welcomes the advances which have made it necessary. Its effect on general paediatrics is a very important but separate matter."

This attitude toward specialization has influenced the present edition of Pediatrics in two ways: It determined the policy of inviting outstanding pediatrics specialists to serve as Associate Editors to share responsibility for most of the major chapters. The Associate Editors selected contributors for their sections and in most instances did extensive preliminary editing. In addition, the importance of specialization in pediatrics was responsible for the increased emphasis in the present edition on mechanisms underlying both human development and disease in infants and children. The presentations retain clinical descriptions and basic therapeutic procedures, but the very advances in knowledge of mechanisms which have made specialization necessary have also dictated that to be of value for present-day medical students and practitioners a textbook of pediatrics must include extensive and sophisticated discussion of these underlying mechanisms.

Anticipated changes in patterns of child health services in the United States with foreseeable modifications in the role of the pediatrician also suggest the neces-

* The early stages of preparation of this 14th Edition of Pediatrics were done during a sabbatical leave supported in part by a fellowship from the Commonwealth Fund of New York while enjoying the hospitality of the Department of Medical Statistics and Epidemiology of the London School of Hygiene and Tropical Medicine.

sity for a textbook of pediatrics to include detailed discussion of mechanisms. If, as seems likely, many child health services performed by pediatricians are to be shared more extensively with other health personnel including pediatric nurses, psychologists, social workers, and their "helpers," the pediatrician must become increasingly professional in the one unique role in which only he can function: the diagnosis and treatment of illness in infants and children. If, in the process, he becomes increasingly what might be considered a "specialist in general pediatrics," he needs a textbook of pediatrics which provides pertinent basic as well as applied information about his subject.

This 14th Edition of Pediatrics will, it is hoped, fulfill these new needs. It is an almost entirely new textbook of pediatrics offering more extensive discussions not only of clinical pediatrics, but also of psychological, physiological, and biochemical aspects of diseases of infants and children. As any "first" edition, it will require subsequent editions to achieve the fine concise editorial qualities developed through thirteen previous editions of Holt's original Diseases of Infancy and Childhood.

Designations of authorship require some explanation. In chapters having Associate Editors, sections not attributed to other contributors have been written by the Associate Editors whose name is not repeated unless a section was written jointly with another author. It should be explained also that although every effort was made to preserve both the content and interpretation of the primary authors and of the Associate Editors, the final form in which material appears was determined by and is the responsibility of the Editor.

Grateful acknowledgment of help is due to many people but above all to the Associate Editors and to Arnold H. Einhorn, M.D., who with the highest devotion brought his extensive knowledge of all phases of pediatrics and his fine linguistic skills to every phase of the preparation of this 14th Edition of Pediatrics including the index. Thanks are due also to Lewis Fraad, M.D., and Mark Abramowicz, M.D., for advice on many matters, to Mathilda Page and Shirley B. Barnett for their valuable editorial assistance at work and at home, and finally, to Mr. David Stires, Miss Pat McAteer, Mrs. Rosemarie Johnson, Miss Adele Spiegler, and Mr. Daniel Shapiro of Appleton-Century-Crofts for their skillful guidance of an inexperienced, but appreciative editor.

HENRY L. BARNETT, M.D.

New York
May, 1968

Contents

Associate Editors   vii

Contributors   xi

Preface   xix

Preface to the 14th Edition   xxi

CHAPTER 1—PREVENTIVE PEDIATRICS AND PUBLIC HEALTH   1

1.1	Introduction	1
1.2	Community Aspects of Pediatric Practice	1
1.3	Epidemiology of Congenital Malformations	11

CHAPTER 2—PERINATAL MEDICINE   15

2.1	Introduction	15

Before Birth: (The Fetus)

2.2	Obstetric Management of the Mother and Fetus	15
2.3	Fetal Growth and Differentiation	21
2.4	Chemical Composition	28
2.5	Biochemistry	34
2.6	Physiology	43
2.7	Pharmacology	51
2.8	Intrauterine Diagnosis	56

The Transition from Fetus to Newborn

2.9	Labor, Delivery, and the Beginning of the Independent Life	66

The Newborn Infant

2.10	Physical Examination	77
2.11	Low-Birth-Weight Infant	88
2.12	Multiple Births	117
2.13	The High-Birth-Weight Infant	124

CHAPTER 3—NUTRITION   129

Maintenance of Health and Growth

3.1	Energy Requirement	129
3.2	Essential Human Nutrients	131
3.3	Feeding Techniques and Diets	148

Disorders of Nutritional Homeostasis

3.4	Deficiencies of Specific Nutrients	170
3.5	Calcium Metabolism	195
3.6	Obesity in Children and Adolescents	214
3.7	Water and Electrolyte Physiology	221
3.8	Diarrhea in Infancy	226

CHAPTER 4—PHYSICAL GROWTH   232
    Abnormal Physical Growth   248

CHAPTER 5—NORMAL DEVELOPMENT: PERSONALITY AND BEHAVIOR   253

CHAPTER 6—ABNORMALITIES OF PSYCHOLOGIC GROWTH AND
    DEVELOPMENT   265
    Suicide in Children and Adolescents   290

CHAPTER 7—GENETIC PRINCIPLES IN PEDIATRICS   295
    7.1   Introduction   294
    7.2   Molecular Genetics   294
    7.3   The Behavior of Genetic Disease in Families and Population 298
    7.4   Developmental Genetics   304
    7.5   Human Cytogenetics   308
    7.6   Dermatoglyphic Analysis   313

CHAPTER 8—ANOMALIES OF METABOLISM   319
    8.1   Biochemical Aspects of Gene Action   319

    Anomalies of Amino Acid, Purine, and Pyrimidine Metabolism

    8.2   Disorders of Amino Acid Metabolism   321
    8.3   Disorders of Amino Acid Transport   336
    8.4   Disorders of Purine and Pyrimidine Metabolism   338

    Anomalies of Carbohydrate Metabolism

    8.5   Diabetes Mellitus in Children   343
    8.6   Mellituria   356
    8.7   Hypoglycemia   360
    8.8   The Glucogenoses   367

    Anomalies of Lipid Metabolism

    8.9   Plasma Lipids and Lipoproteins   373
    8.10 Lipidoses   381

    Anomalies of Protein Metabolism

    8.11 Serum and Metal-Binding Proteins   386
    8.12 Deficiencies of Erythrocyte and Leucocyte Enzymes   391
    8.13 Mucopolysaccharidoses   398
    8.14 The Porphyrias   405

CHAPTER 9—CYSTIC FIBROSIS OF THE PANCREAS   413

CHAPTER 10—IMMUNOLOGIC MECHANISMS   431

CHAPTER 11—ALLERGY   443
    11.1 Pathophysiology of Allergic Disease   443
    11.2 Diagnostic Methods in Allergic Disease   448
    11.3 Principles of Treatment of Allergic Disorders   450
    11.4 Allergic Rhinitis and Serous Otitis Media   459
    11.5 Asthma   464
    11.6 Psychologic Aspects of Asthma   468
    11.7 Atopic Dermatitis   471
    11.8 Contact Dermatitis   475
    11.9 Urticaria and Angioedema   477

CHAPTER 11—ALLERGY (cont.)

11.10	Drug Allergy	478
11.11	Insect Allergy	483
11.12	Serum Sickness	485
11.13	Hypersensitivity Reactions to Physical Factors	487

CHAPTER 12—CONNECTIVE TISSUE DISEASES — 491

12.1	Rheumatic Fever	491
12.2	Juvenile Rheumatoid Arthritis	503
12.3	Systemic Lupus Erythematosus	508
12.4	Polymyositis	510
12.5	Progressive Systemic Sclerosis	512
12.6	Polyarteritis Nodosa	513
12.7	Suggested Work-up of Acute Arthritis	514

CHAPTER 13—ACCIDENTS, POISONING, AND OTHER ENVIRONMENTAL HAZARDS IN CHILDHOOD — 517

13.1	Accidents	517
13.2	Burns in Childhood	519
13.3	Drowning	524
13.4	Poisonings in Childhood	527
13.5	Iron Poisoning	537
13.6	Kerosene Poisoning	538
13.7	Lead Poisoning	540
13.8	Mercury Poisoning	548
13.9	Organic Phosphate Ester Poisoning	550
13.10	Salicylate Intoxication	552
13.11	Poisoning Due to Snake Bites	555
13.12	Intentional Accidents	556
13.13	Drug Abuse	558
13.14	Neonatal Narcotic Addiction	573
13.15	Sudden and Unexpected Death	575

CHAPTER 14—INFECTIOUS DISEASES — 579

14.1	Antimicrobial Therapy of Bacterial Diseases	579
14.2	Sepsis Neonatorum	596
14.3	Bacterial Meningitis	598
14.4	Botulism	609
14.5	Brucellosis	610
14.6	Cholera	612
14.7	Diphtheria	614
14.8	Influenza Bacillus Infections	618
14.9	Leptospirosis	621
14.10	Meningococcal Infections	622
14.11	Mycoplasma Infections	625
14.12	Pertussis and Parapertussis	627
14.13	Rat-Bite Fever	634
14.14	Salmonella, Shigella and Enteropathogenic E. coli Infections	635
14.15	Staphylococcal Colonization and Disease	644
14.16	Staphylococcal Enterocolitis and Staphylococcal Food Poisoning	646
14.17	Streptococcal Infections	647
14.18	Syphilis	652
14.19	Tetanus	658
14.20	Tuberculosis	662
14.21	Diseases Caused by Other Mycobacteria	690
14.22	Tularemia	691

CHAPTER 14—INFECTIOUS DISEASES (cont.)

Viral Diseases

14.23	Selective Inhibition of Viral Replication	694
14.24	Cat Scratch Disease	697
14.25	Chicken Pox	700
14.26	Cytomegalic Inclusion Disease	703
14.27	Exanthum Subitum	705
14.28	Viral Hepatitis	706
14.29	Herpesvirus Hominus Infections	712
14.30	Infectious Mononucleosis	717
14.31	Influenza and Other Viral Infections of the Respiratory Tract	719
14.32	Lymphocytic Choriomeningitis	728
14.33	Measles	729
14.34	Mumps	737
14.35	Picornaviruses Including Poliomyelitis	740
14.36	Coxsackie Viruses	749
14.37	Echo Viruses	752
14.38	Rabies	755
14.39	Rubella	759
14.40	Smallpox	769
14.41	Psittacosis—Lymphogranuloma—Trachoma and Inclusion Conjunctivitis and Agents	775
14.42	Human Rickettsioses	777

Mycotic Diseases

14.43	Actinomycosis	785
14.44	Aspergillosis	786
14.45	Blastomycosis	787
14.46	Coccidioidomycosis	788
14.47	Histoplasmosis	791
14.48	Cryptococcosis	793
14.49	Phycomycosis	795
14.50	Candidiasis	795

Parasitic Diseases

14.51	Helminthic Diseases	797
14.52	Protozoan Diseases	825
14.53	Disease Caused by Arthropods	844

Unclassified Diseases

14.54	Hemorrhagic Fevers	846

CHAPTER 15—THE NERVOUS SYSTEM   849

15.1	Diagnosis of Neurologic Disease	849
15.2	Prenatal and Developmental Defects	857
15.3	The Static Encephalopathies	879
15.4	The Degenerative and Demyelinating Diseases of the Nervous System	905
15.5	Tumors of the Central Nervous System	937
15.6	Pseudotumor Cerebri	957
15.7	Cerebrovascular Diseases	960
15.8	Trauma to the Nervous System	966
15.9	Paroxysmal Disorders	980
15.10	The Peripheral Neuropathies	1006
15.11	Infections of the Nervous System	1009
15.12	Diseases of the Muscles	1025
15.13	Disorders of the Nervous System Specific to Children	1040

CHAPTER 16—THE ENDOCRINE SYSTEM 1045

16.1   Neural and Endocrine Communications   1045
16.2   The Anterior Pituitary   1046
16.3   The Thyroid   1058
16.4   Adrenal Cortex   1090
16.5   Adrenal Cortical Hormones   1102
16.6   Adrenal Medulla and Sympathetic Nervous Tissue   1107
16.7   The Pineal Organ   1113
16.8   The Ovaries   1115
16.9   Endocrine Changes at Puberty   1120
16.10 Sexual Precocity   1122
16.11 Abnormalities of Sex Differentiation   1130
16.12 Primary Disturbances of Water Homeostasis   1148

CHAPTER 17—THE BLOOD AND BLOOD-FORMING ORGANS 1155

17.1   Fetal and Neonatal Erythropoiesis   1155

The Anemias

17.2   Anemias Due to Impaired Production of Red Cells and Hemoglobin   1160
17.3   Anemias Due to Accelerated Destruction of Red Cells   1169
17.4   Anemias Due to Blood Loss   1201
17.5   Polycythemia and Erythrocytosis   1202

Diseases of the White Blood Cells   1203

17.6   Leucopenias   1204
17.7   Acute Infectious Lymphocytosis   1206
17.8   Acute Leukemia   1208
17.9   The Spleen   1215
17.10 The Lymph Nodes   1221

Disorders of Hemostasis   1228

17.11 Mechanisms of Hemostasis   1228
17.12 Diagnosis of Hemorrhagic Disorders   1229
17.13 Clinical Aspects of Hemorrhagic Disorders   1232

CHAPTER 18—THE RETICULOENDOTHELIOSES AND SARCOIDOSIS 1245

18.1   The Nonlipid Reticuloendothelioses   1245
18.2   Sarcoidosis   1250

CHAPTER 19—THE PULMONARY SYSTEM 1255

Respiratory Function and Pulmonary Diseases and the Newborn   1255

19.1   Respiratory Function in the Newborn   1255
19.2   Pulmonary Diseases of the Newborn   1261

Respiratory Function and Pulmonary Diseases in Older Infants and Children   1273

19.3   The Airways   1274
19.4   Specific Diseases Causing Obstruction   1284
19.5   The Parenchyma   1299
19.6   Diseases Causing Reduction of the Parenchyma   1303
19.7   Pneumonitis   1310
19.8   The Chest Wall   1322
19.9   Diseases of the Chest Wall and Pleural Diseases   1324

CHAPTER 20—THE CIRCULATORY SYSTEM   1333

20.1   The Fetal Circulation and Circulatory Adjustments After Birth   1333
20.2   The Signs and Symptoms of Cardiovascular Diseases
        in Infants and Children   1334
20.3   Cardiovascular Sound   1338
20.4   Radiography and Fluoroscopy   1344
20.5   The Electrocardiogram and Vectorcardiogram   1346
20.6   Cardiac Catheterization   1355
20.7   Disorders of the Heartbeat   1363
20.8   Pathophysiology of Congenital Heart Disease   1370
20.9   Obstructive Lesions of the Circulation   1379
20.10   Left-to-Right Shunts   1393
20.11   Cyanotic Congenital Heart Disease   1401
20.12   Abnormalities of Chamber and Great Vessel Localization   1418
20.13   Congestive Heart Failure in Infancy and Childhood   1419
20.14   Infections of the Heart   1425
20.15   Myocardial Disorders   1432

CHAPTER 21—SYSTEMIC ARTERIAL HYPERTENSION   1437

21.1   Regulation of Blood Pressure   1437
21.2   Measurement of the Blood Pressure   1437
21.3   Prevalence of Childhood Hypertension   1438
21.4   Evaluation of the Hypertensive Child   1439
21.5   Essential Hypertension   1441
21.6   Renovascular Hypertension   1442
21.7   Renal Hypertension   1444
21.8   Pheochromocytoma   1444
21.9   Primary Hyperaldosteronism   1445
21.10   Coarctation of the Aorta   1446
21.11   Miscellaneous Causes of Hypertension   1446
21.12   Therapy   1447

CHAPTER 22—THE KIDNEYS AND URINARY TRACT   1451

22.1   Morphologic Development   1451
22.2   Physiology and Functional Development of the Kidney   1453
22.3   Clinical Evaluation of Renal Function   1459
22.4   Uremia: Pathophysiology and Treatment   1463
22.5   Renal Abnormalities in the Newborn   1471
22.6   Abnormalities of Renal Development: Hypoplasia
        and Dysplasia; Cystic Disorders and Polycystic Disease   1474
22.7   Postural Proteinuria   1478
22.8   Glomerulonephritis   1480
22.9   Glomerulonephritis in Systemic Disease   1492
22.10   The Idiopathic Nephrotic Syndrome of Childhood
        (Lipoid Nephrosis)   1499
22.11   Miscellaneous Nephropathies   1506
22.12   Hereditary Nephropathies   1514
22.13   Disorders of Renal Tubular Function   1516
22.14   Circulatory Disturbances   1533
22.15   Urolithiasis   1535
22.16   Infections of the Urinary and Genital Tracts   1539
22.17   Urology   1546

CHAPTER 23—THE GASTROINTESTINAL TRACT   1565

23.1   Anatomy, Physiology, and Biochemistry of the
        Gastrointestinal Tract   1565

CHAPTER 23—THE GASTROINTESTINAL TRACT (cont.)

Symptomatic Conditions of the Gastrointestinal Tract: Diagnosis and Treatment   1573

23.2   Vomiting   1573
23.3   Rumination Syndrome (Merycism or Merycasm)   1576
23.4   Gastrointestinal Bleeding   1578
23.5   Diarrhea   1580
23.6   Abdominal Pain   1599
23.7   Constipation   1600
23.8   Rectal Incontinence and Pruritis Ani   1603

Malformations of the Gastrointestinal Tract   1603

23.9   Abnormalities of Development Causing Obstruction   1603
23.10   Esophageal Malformations   1604
23.11   Gastric Malformations   1608
23.12   Malformations of the Small Intestine   1612
23.13   Congenital Aganglionic Megacolon (Hirschsprung's Disease)   1621
23.14   Anorectal Malformations   1625
23.15   Malformations of the Abdominal Parietes   1630

Inflammatory Diseases   1635

23.16   Esophagus   1635
23.17   Stomach   1637
23.18   Peptic Ulcer   1638
23.19   Intestines   1640
23.20   Regional Enteritis   1642
23.21   Ulcerative Colitis   1644
23.22   Anorectal Conditions   1648
23.23   Peritonitis   1648

Miscellaneous Surgical Topics   1650

23.24   Foreign Bodies of the Gastrointestinal Tract   1650
23.25   Esophageal Varices   1652
23.26   Dilation of the Stomach; Gastric Perforations   1652
23.27   Intestinal Obstruction After the Neonatal Period   1653
23.28   Rectum and Anus   1659
23.29   Ascites   1660
23.30   Neoplasms of the Alimentary Tract   1661

CHAPTER 24—THE LIVER   1663

24.1   Subcellular Anatomy of the Liver Parenchymal Cell   1663
24.2   Clinical-Laboratory Evaluation of Hepatic Function   1670
24.3   Bilirubin Metabolism   1673
24.4   Jaundice in the Newborn   1676
24.5   Conjugated Neonatal Hyperbilirubinemia   1682
24.6   Jaundice in Older Children   1685
24.7   Metabolic Disorders of the Liver   1687
24.8   Hepatitis   1689
24.9   Cirrhosis   1690
24.10   Portal Hypertension   1691
24.11   Hepatic Failure   1692
24.12   Tumors of the Liver   1693

CHAPTER 25—THE BONES AND JOINTS   1695

25.1   The Skull   1695
25.2   The Extremities   1706

CHAPTER 25—THE BONES AND JOINTS (cont.)

25.3	The Axial Skeleton	1714
25.4	Systemic Affections of the Skeleton	1719
25.5	Juvenile Osteochondroses	1737
25.6	The Joints	1746

CHAPTER 26—THE SKIN   1753

26.1	Introduction	1753
26.2	Diseases of Keratinization	1755
26.3	Diseases of the Dermis	1763
26.4	Blistering Diseases	1770
26.5	Infections of the Skin	1781
26.6	Disorders of Pigmentation	1799
26.7	Eczema (Atopic Dermatitis)	1806
26.8	Other Diseases of the Skin	1808

CHAPTER 27—THE EYES   1817

27.1	Examination of the Eye	1817
27.2	Anomalies of the Globe and Related Structures	1817
27.3	The Lids	1818
27.4	The Conjunctiva	1819
27.5	The Cornea	1822
27.6	The Lacrimal Apparatus	1824
27.7	The Sclera	1824
27.8	Congenital Glaucoma	1825
27.9	Phakomatoses	1826
27.10	The Lens	1826
27.11	The Uvea	1827
27.12	The Retina and Optic Nerve	1828
27.13	The Orbit	1830
27.14	Strabismus (Squint)	1832
27.15	Refractive Errors	1835

CHAPTER 28—THE MOUTH   1837

28.1	The Mouth of the Newborn	1837
28.2	Soft Tissue Lesions of the Alveolar Ridge and Floor of the Mouth	1839
28.3	Malformations of the Lips, Palate, and Jaw	1841
28.4	Tongue	1848
28.5	Lesions of the Gums and Oral Mucosa	1851

CHAPTER 29—TEETH   1857

29.1	Growth and Development of the Teeth	1857
29.2	Developmental Disorders of Teeth	1862
29.3	Common Acquired Disorders of the Teeth	1867
29.4	Dentistry for Handicapped Children	1869

CHAPTER 30—THE NOSE, PARANASAL SINUSES, AND PHARYNX   1871

30.1	Nose and Paranasal Sinuses	1871
30.2	Nasopharynx and Oropharynx	1877

CHAPTER 31—THE EAR   1881

31.1	Physiology	1881
31.2	Growth and Development	1882
31.3	Examination	1882

CHAPTER 31—THE EAR (cont.)

31.4   Malformations   1884
31.5   Inherited Diseases   1884
31.6   Growths   1886
31.7   Infections   1886
31.8   Trauma   1889
31.9   Special Problems   1889

CHAPTER 32—GENERAL PEDIATRIC PRACTICES   1893

General Care of Healthy Infants and Children

32.1   General Health Supervision   1893
32.2   Hygiene and General Care   1893
32.3   Immunization Against Infectious Diseases   1896

Appraisal and Care of the Sick Child

32.4   Symptomatology and Diagnosis   1896
32.5   General Therapeutic Measures   1908

The Child's Environment

32.6   Pediatric Practice, an Ecology of the Family Unit   1912

Appendix   **1915**

Index   **1931**

chapter 1

PREVENTIVE PEDIATRICS AND PUBLIC HEALTH

MYRON E. WEGMAN, Associate Editor

1.1 INTRODUCTION

Since Emmett Holt, Sr., produced the first edition of this text, the concern of physicians and of society for their responsibility to the country's children has changed profoundly. Physicians in the 1970's are more acutely aware of the community's responsibility to its children. Society now accepts readily the thesis that individual health care of uniformly high quality is a right which is not dependent on income or other attributes, and that every child is entitled to a wholesome environment—water, air, and housing.

This text is devoted to childhood diseases and disabilities, and their backgrounds. Thoughtful coverage is also given to normal growth and development of the child, which needs to be promoted. The text can deal in limited fashion only with the physical environment as it affects health, and it can barely mention the social and economic factors which bear so directly on the health of children. One of the latter, of basic concern to all physicians, is appreciation of the wide disparity in health and disease between children of different ethnic and socioeconomic backgrounds. Overwhelming also is the evidence that socioeconomic factors due to discrimination are behind the reasons that ghetto children are at a serious disadvantage. The same table for black infants would be quite different. In the United States the majority of the poor are white but the proportion of blacks afflicted by poverty is far greater: Table 10 in the Appendix presents data by state and region for white and nonwhite infants. The latter are predominately black, and the contrast is striking. The second half of this century is witnessing a titanic struggle as, for the first time in its history, a nation is consciously trying to compensate for a racist heritage and to abolish prejudice and discrimination. The effect on health of such progress would be enormous.

This chapter sets the stage for the larger context in which pediatrics and all of child care is carried out. It needs to be read less as a special subject than a question of attitude and awareness to cover every aspect of pediatric practice.

In delivering the first Parisot Lecture to the World Health Assembly on 16 July 1969, René Dubos said:

Of course the environment continues unceasingly to transform the organism. However, the first years of life have effects so profound and irreversible that they are the most important part of human ecology. I am emphasizing this fact because it seems to me that it should influence the general policy of WHO and encourage scientists to devote more effort to the problems of childhood. It is beyond doubt that the establishment of an atmosphere favourable to the biological and mental development of the child is the most economical way of improving world health.

1.2 COMMUNITY ASPECTS OF PEDIATRIC PRACTICE

DONALD C. SMITH and R. GERALD RICE

The evolution of child care is the story of the evolution of civilization itself (Henderson). In many primitive societies the welfare of children receives little attention, and under unfavorable circumstances the child is the first to suffer. Developing societies should regard their children as a most valuable natural resource, deserving the best care and protection that money and human effort can provide, yet too often this is not the case. Even in affluent countries, moreover, there may be wide gaps between the goal and its achievement.

The community provides the milieu in which the child grows, develops, and matures. Its adult members can do much to promote healthy child growth and development through organized health and hospital services, well-planned educational and recreational programs, and elimination of hazardous environmental conditions. These community measures for the promotion of health and the prevention of illness are of particular significance in childhood because it is during the growing years that they are most likely to be successful.

Basic responsibility for health care of the child rests with his parents and with his physician. The wise physician will utilize to the fullest extent those community facilities and services which will help make the care he provides and secures for all children more effective. To do this he must appreciate how social, economic, and environmental factors influence

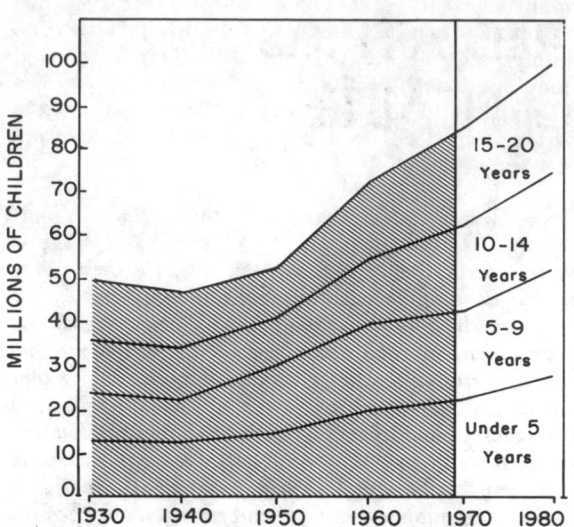

Fig. 1.   Projected growth of U.S. child populations.

importance of the use of community facilities increases proportionately. The primary purpose of this chapter is to discuss the ways this knowledge may be used by the physician as he works with families and with children.

Growth of the Child Population

Population growth obviously depends on an excess of births over deaths. In much of the world, high birth rates, previously offset by high death rates, have continued as mortality has decreased with public health measures, Decline of mortality in the United States, while not as rapid as in some countries, has been associated, until recently, with a sustained high birth rate, resulting in consistent population growth.

Since 1960, however, there has been a slow but steady decline in birth rate. Births in the United States during 1968 totaled 3,470,000, the smallest number since 1946, and preliminary data indicate an even lower figure for 1969. In the same year there were approximately 1,923,000 deaths. Excess of births over deaths thus added some 1.55 million persons to the population, a rate of natural increase of 7.8 persons per 1,000 population. Future trends are not easy to predict since the number of marriages continued to rise totaling 2,059,000 in 1968. How-

health and behavior, and he must be familiar with the functions and roles of the various official and voluntary health agencies which exist in his community. When parents are less able to meet their responsibilities for health care of their children, the

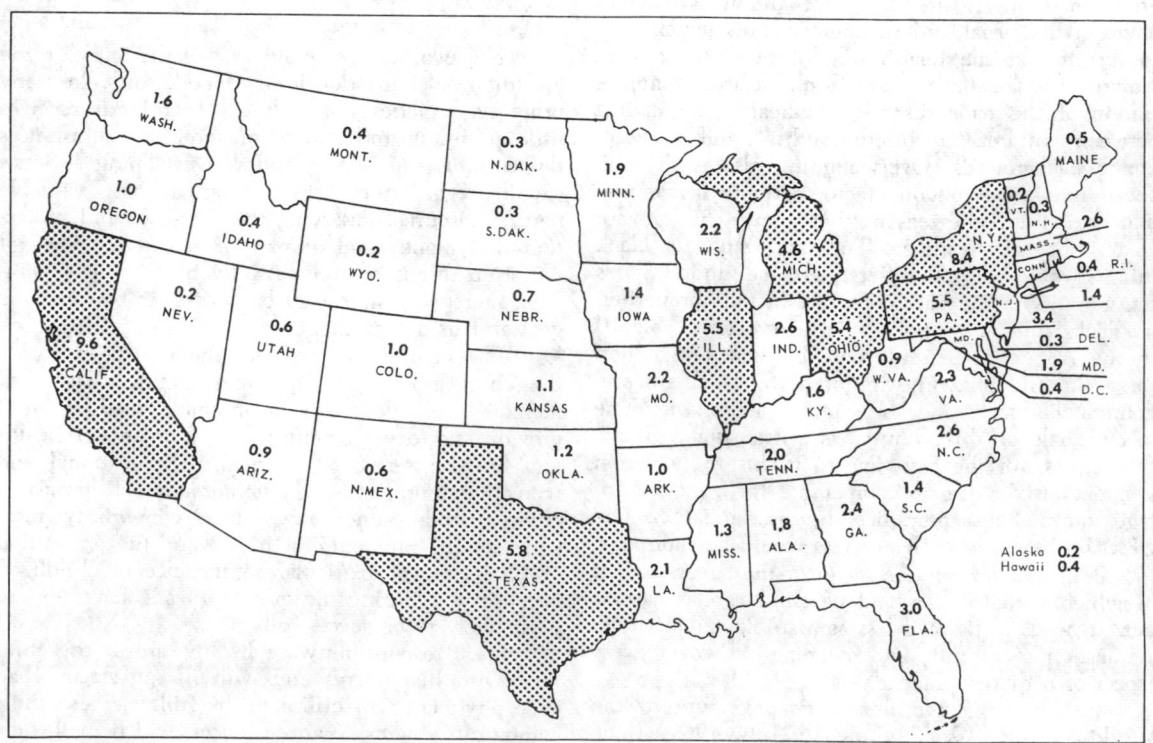

Fig. 2.   Map showing 44.8 percent of the total resident child population concentrated in seven states, as of July 1, 1968. (Children under 18 years: 70,809,000.) (Bureau of the Census Series P-25 No. 420, April 17, 1969. Percentages computed.)

ever, this increase appears to be accompanied by a greater tendency to postpone childbearing.

A major effect of the high birth rate experienced during the postwar years has been a steady increase in both the absolute and relative size of the child population (Fig. 1). In 1940 there were 45,000,000 young people under 20 years of age in the United States, 34.4 percent of the total population; by 1968 this figure had grown to 77,748,000, which represents 38.9 percent of the population. The parallel increase in the population over 65 accounts for the statement that the population is growing younger and older at the same time.

Along with this rapid increase, the child population has become concentrated in relatively few geographic areas of this country. Seven states now contain 45 percent of the total child population (Fig. 2).

Changing Patterns of Mortality and Morbidity in Childhood

Two measures, limited to be sure, in which child health problems may be expressed are mortality and morbidity.

Infant Mortality

A remarkable decline in mortality rates in both infancy and childhood has taken place in widespread areas of the world. Changes in the infant mortality rate, expressed as deaths occurring prior to the first birthday per 1,000 live births, have a special significance. Because the same factors causing high infant death rates affect adversely all public health, the infant mortality rate is commonly regarded as one of the most sensitive indices of the health of a community. In the United States this rate decreased from approximately 100 in the year 1915 to less than 30 in 1950, fell by only 12 percent during the period from 1950 to 1956, by less than 3 percent between 1956 and 1962, then by 14 percent between 1962 and 1968 (Fig. 3). A large portion of the total decline has been due to an impressive reduction in death from infectious disease. However, better medical care for mothers and children, new medical and social programs, and higher standards of living have also contributed to these recent improvements in the infant mortality rate. Nevertheless, despite dramatic improvement, the present situation is far from satisfactory. A number of other countries, some less well off economically than the United States, but with equally precise and accurate vital data, have substantially lower infant mortality rates. For example, in 1968, the state with the lowest rate, Utah, was 50 percent higher than Sweden. There remains also a persistent, albeit decreasing gap, between white and nonwhite infant mortality rates. The probability of a nonwhite infant dying during the first year of life is some 80 percent greater than that for a white infant. In vital statistics most of those included in the nonwhite category are black children. Such children are exposed to greater socio-economic and environmental hazards than white children and it is particularly welcome that in recent years a more rapid decline in the mortality of black infants is evident. For the country as a whole, the age-specific death rate for nonwhite children under 1 year in 1968 (33.1) was 6.5 percent below 1967, while the rate for white children (19.6) did not change. There are also wide variations in

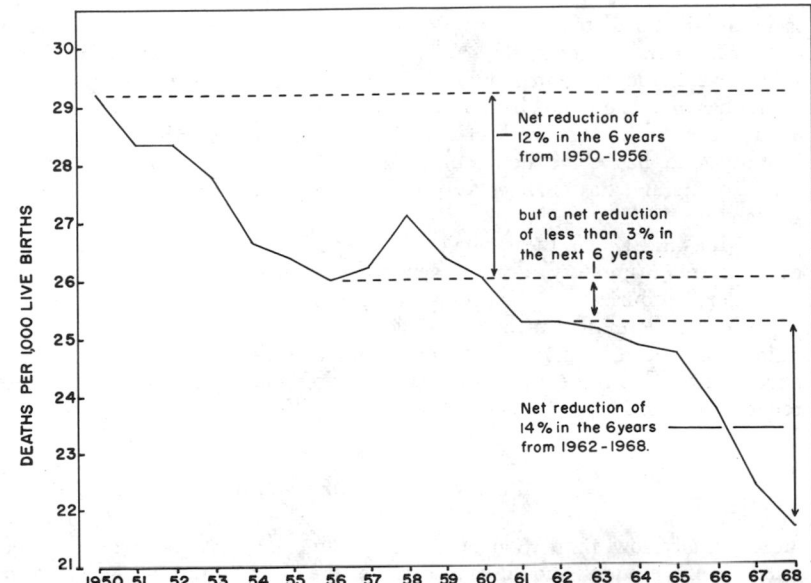

Fig. 3. Infant mortality rate in the United States from 1950 to 1968.

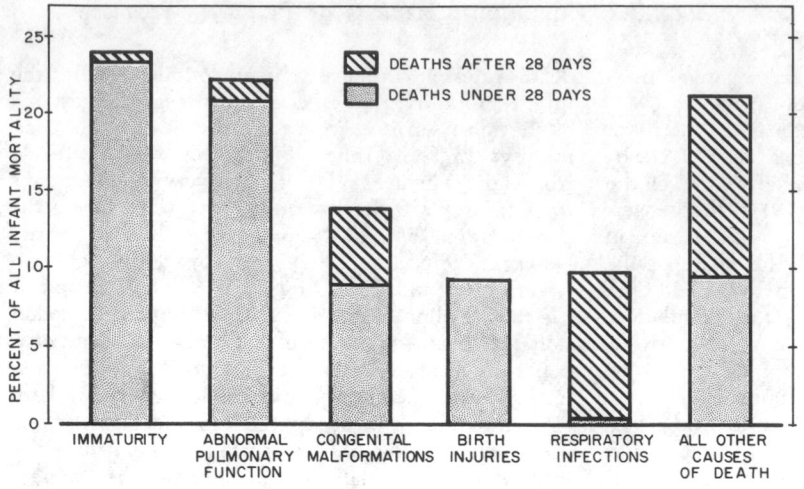

Fig. 4. Leading causes of death in the first year of life.

infant mortality rates among states and communities (See Appendix).

Perinatal Mortality and Morbidity

In a country like the United States the bulk of mortality in early childhood is related to those problems most likely to cause death in the period around the time of birth. Out of this concern has developed the concept of *"perinatal mortality."* The "perinatal" period is defined in two overlapping ways:

"Perinatal I" This includes deaths of fetuses weighing 1,001 g or more (28 weeks gestation) and deaths of live-born infants occurring in the first seven days of life.

"Perinatal II" This includes deaths of fetuses weighing 501 g or more (20 weeks gestation) and deaths of liveborn infants occurring in the first 28 days of life.

Each rate is calculated on the basis of total births in the period chosen for study.

The overall decrease in mortality in the first year of life has not been matched by a similar decrease in mortality in the first week of life. The first week mortality rate has come down quite slowly in the past 40 years and has changed very little in the past 10 years.

In the mid-1960's the major causes of perinatal deaths were respiratory distress syndrome, immaturity, birth injuries, and congenital malformations (Fig. 4). For the most part these conditions have their origin before birth, and efforts to prevent them must be concentrated on the mother's health during the prenatal and natal period and prior to conception.

Postneonatal Mortality

The relatively low proportion of deaths in the age period 1–11 months should not obscure the fact that these deaths are more easily prevented than neonatal deaths and still total some 21,000 a year. Environmental factors—housing, infection, and nutrition—have particular significance in this age group, as they do throughout the rest of childhood and youth.

Mortality in the Preschool and School Years

Mortality rates reach their minimum level during the preschool and school years. Nevertheless, a significant number of deaths which do occur between the first and nineteenth years of age are preventable and therefore deserve special attention in the community's child health program.

Leading causes of death in preschool and school years in the United States are summarized in Table 1. Accidents and congenital malformations are significant causes throughout the childhood years, accounting for approximately half of all deaths among school age children; malignant disease has been clearly established as an important cause of death in children as well as in adults; homicide and suicide have emerged as serious and frightening problems in the middle and late adolescent years. It is noteworthy that in the 15–19 age group, almost three out of four (71 percent) of the deaths are related to social and environmental factors rather than purely biologic processes.

Childhood Morbidity

Morbidity is much more difficult to measure than mortality. Special studies, such as the National Health Survey, give a fairly accurate picture of those illnesses which are most common in childhood and most likely to interfere with the child's normal activities. These illnesses constitute a large part (45 percent) of all those experienced by the community. While a majority of these events represent acquired injuries and acute infectious diseases which are short-

TABLE 1. *Leading Causes of Death in Childhood: U.S. 1967* *

Rank	1-4 years of age	%	Rank	5-9 years of age	%
1.	Accidents	37.6	1.	Accidents	45.5
2.	Congenital Malformations	11.2	2.	Malignant Neoplasms	17.0
3.	Influenza and Pneumonia	10.7	3.	Congenital Malformations	6.9
4.	Malignant Neoplasms	9.5	4.	Influenza and Pneumonia	4.4
TOTAL DEATHS 13,506		100.0	TOTAL DEATHS 8,809		100.0
Rank	10-14 years of age	%	Rank	15-19 years of age	%
1.	Accidents	47.8	1.	Accidents	60.7
2.	Malignant Neoplasms	15.0	2.	Malignant Neoplasms	7.4
3.	Congenital Malformations	4.6	3.	Homicide	5.9
4.	Influenza and Pneumonia	3.8	4.	Suicide	4.6
TOTAL DEATHS 8,084		100.0	TOTAL DEATHS 18,168		100.0

*Source: Vital Statistics of U.S. Vol. II, Mortality Part B, Section 7, Table 7-5. Ranked according to national methods.

term in nature and which respond readily to appropriate medical measures, a significant percentage are chronic and require highly specialized, costly care.

Only a small portion of these childhood illnesses —possibly one in ten—will lead to hospitalization. Among these children who are hospitalized, the most frequent diagnostic categories are tonsillectomies, which may account for 25 percent or more of all hospital admissions for children; acute respiratory tract infections (15 percent); and trauma of all kinds (15 percent). Other important categories include prematurity, congenital anomalies, gastrointestinal infections, and appendicitis, each responsible for some 3 to 5 percent of all child admissions. The remaining third of admissions are distributed among the numerous, less common diagnoses. It is a cause of some concern that despite repeated and careful studies over the years, indicating that in a majority of cases the benefits of tonsillectomy are dubious to say the least, the procedure is still widely used.

The average hospital stay of patients varies with the differing admitting diagnoses. The average hospitalization for tonsillectomy is one and a half days; for premature infants it is 13 to 15 days; and for the other conditions it ranges between 5 and 8 days.

In addition, there are significant numbers of children and youth who require long-term residential care. In the United States in 1960 there were some 306,325 (4.3 per 1,000 children under age 21) in such institutions. More than one-half of these (58 percent) were in correctional institutions and institutions for neglected and dependent children; slightly over one-quarter (25.6 percent) were in institutions for the mentally retarded; the remainder were divided between institutions for children with psychotic illnesses and physical disabilities (Fig. 5). The number of children in these institutions continues to rise; the greatest increase has been in the admission of children to institutions for the mentally retarded.

There were many more boys than girls in institutions in 1960. In institutions for physically handicapped children, the proportion of boys was 55 percent; in institutions for the retarded, 60 percent; and in correctional institutions, 83 percent.

There is reason to believe that there are in most large child care institutions a number of children who, with additional intensive care, could be discharged to their homes. In a substantial group of children, growth and development could be better promoted within the institution. A certain percentage of children could probably be kept at home if ambulatory facilities included a more comprehensive and skillful diagnostic evaluation and if certain community services (including skilled counseling) were made available to the child and his family. The practicing

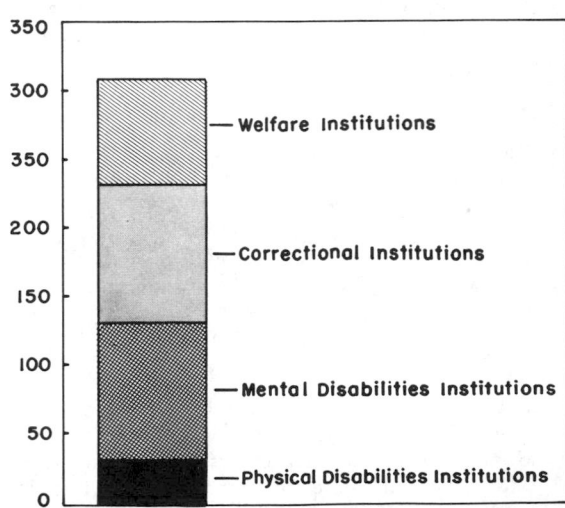

Fig. 5. Children in institutions.

physician is in a unique position to mobilize needed community services and to insure that they are utilized by families at a time when they are most likely to be beneficial.

Disadvantaged Children

Human growth and development may be hindered by many factors other than disease. These factors may operate at any age but are most influential in early childhood. It is during infancy and the preschool years that attempts to promote healthy growth and development by improving the physical and social environment are most likely to be successful.

Physical factors of importance include inadequate housing, overcrowding, malnutrition, noise, and pollution. Social factors which, to a considerable extent, determine the individual child's pattern of growth and development are found within his own family and also in the community at large. Influential factors are missing parents, severe illlness or addiction in another member of the family, marital discord, blatant promiscuity, and emotional disturbances which interfere with normal family relationships. In the community, a variety of social conditions may seriously limit the child's opportunities for healthy growth and development. These include prejudice as well as inadequate educational, health, recreational, and cultural facilities.

For a significant number of children the most important factors which lead to disadvantage are economic in nature. Cultural deprivation has its roots in poverty, which may be defined as inability to purchase minimal levels of health care, housing, food, and education.

Broken homes, poor family relationships, emotional and social disturbances, economic pressures, migration, and overcrowding, as well as physical disease, are all factors which often lead to indifference, alienation, low aspirations, below average achievement, delinquency, and illness. In this way they may seriously limit the child's ability to participate in and contribute to society.

Children in Adoption

During the six-year period 1963–1968 the number of adoptions increased by approximately 5 percent yearly. Today there are about 2 million adopted children in the United States. In 1968, an estimated 166,000 children were placed for adoption as compared to 96,000 children adopted in 1958, and of these 52 percent were adopted by nonrelatives. The most important increase over the last 10 years has been in the number of adoptions arranged by social agencies. Social agencies in 1958 handled 53 percent of adoptions by nonrelatives, while in 1968, 74 percent of adoptions were handled by social agencies.

Although the number of adopted children and the number of applicants continue to rise, the ratio of adoptive parents to adoptable children is declining. This relative decrease may be attributed to many out-of-wedlock births, to the fact that there are now proportionately fewer couples in the age group (30 to 39) most likely to choose to adopt a child, and to improved methods of treating infertility which give married couples a greater chance of producing their own children. In response to these trends most adoption agencies are utilizing more flexible policies in an attempt to promote the placement of "hard to place" children such as handicapped or racially mixed children, and to accommodate applications from prospective parents who have varied social and economic backgrounds.

Most adoption agencies retain the full-time or part-time services of a pediatric consultant. His responsibilities will vary from agency to agency. Ideally his contributions to the adoption process should include: medical appraisal of the child prior to placement in adoption, assistance in the selection of adoptive parents, consultation with adoptive parents, guidance in the use of community facilities by the staff of the adoption agency, participation in staff development programs, providing liaison with practicing physicians in the community, and lending technical assistance in the evaluation of current adoption procedures. In order to meet these responsibilities in an effective manner the pediatrician must be fully conversant with the adoption process and with current trends in the field.

Comprehensive Health Care for Children and Youth

There is no generally accepted definition of the term comprehensive health care: the term has different meanings for different persons. To some health care is comprehensive if it reaches a large number of families scattered over a wide geographical area. Others consider a health program to be comprehensive if it brings services to families at all social and economic levels in a designated geographical area. Still others consider the word comprehensive as referring to the spectrum of services provided. Actually, all of these ingredients need to be considered in the planning and provision of adequate health care. What is important to individual families is that they have ready access to a wide array of preventive, diagnostic, treatment, and rehabilitation services. These services must be available on a continuing basis, must be of high quality, and focused upon the individual in his own ecologic setting.

The kinds of health services needed by children and youth are multiple and varied. They include:

1. Individual preventive services: Prenatal care; family planning services; care at time of delivery; postnatal care; and continuing health supervision with particular attention to development and nutrition, throughout childhood and adolescence.
2. Care of the sick child: Continuing, personalized medical and dental care; comprehensive diagnostic services; specialist and auxiliary services; hospital and nursing home services; home care services, including nursing, physical therapy, and home aides; and all those rehabilitation services which are needed by the handicapped child if he is to attain his maximum potential.
3. General community services: Organized health education services, utilizing both individualized and group approaches; general environmental health services, including accident prevention services, fluoridation of water, and pollution control.

These health services, then, may be regarded as essential elements in a comprehensive health care program for children and youth. To be effective they must be organized, financed, and available.

Health Services During the Prenatal Period

Extension of health services for mothers during the prenatal period has been associated with a reduction in mortality and morbidity from toxemia, hemorrhage, and infection; concomitantly, the lives of many infants have been saved. Prenatal care has provided opportunities for the study, detection, and early treatment of blood incompatibilities, maternal infections, fetal malnutrition, and genetic disorders, thus reducing fetal and neonatal wastage.

All mothers and unborn infants should have access to adequate and comprehensive prenatal care. Unfortunately, certain high-risk groups, including very young mothers, unwed mothers, older multiparas, and mothers from economically deprived families, who have particular need of prenatal care, often do not receive it. Newer knowledge of the long-term effects of maternal undernutrition constitutes an inescapable demand for direct and comprehensive attack on this problem.

The pediatrician must have access to the prenatal record which has been compiled by the obstetrician. Under ideal circumstances, he will have the opportunity of meeting and talking with the prospective parents prior to the delivery of the infant. The pediatrician must also be concerned with the quality of obstetric care provided at the time of labor and delivery. Some of the most urgent problems which occur during the perinatal period, such as incompatibilities or fetal distress, demand the closest cooperation between the obstetrician and the pediatrician.

Services to the Newborn, Including the Premature

Skilled medical supervision and care during the newborn period is exceptionally important. For newborn care to be efficient and safe (see Chap. 2), all hospitals must be organized and equipped so as to meet acceptable standards with regard to both facilities and staff. *Standards and Recommendations for Hospital Care of Newborn Infants*, published by the American Academy of Pediatrics, is an excellent guide for the development of such standards.

Infancy and Preschool Years

Many of the important health problems experienced by older children and adults have their origin in the first five years of life. A significant percentage of these can be prevented or their seriousness minimized if they are identified at an early age and treatment given promptly.

While the specific content of health supervision provided for an individual child will depend upon his particular health needs, it should always include three basic components:

1. Periodic evaluation of the child's health and nutritional status
2. Parent counseling
3. Immunization against infectious disease

PERIODIC EVALUATION OF THE CHILD'S HEALTH STATUS. Because the child is growing, developing, and changing, it is important that a careful evaluation of the health status be made at periodic intervals. Meaningful appraisal of the child's health status requires both time and skill. It can be achieved only against the background of a carefully taken medical history, which must include a review of family, prenatal, and perinatal factors. Particular attention should be given to the child's overall developmental and nutritional status, as well as to the recognition of correctable defects.

The conference with parents and the physical examination should be complemented by certain selected laboratory studies. Hemoglobin estimations should be carried out whenever there is reason to believe that anemia is present. Tuberculin testing, which is a valuable case-finding technique, should be started at about 6 months of age and repeated annually thereafter. Toward the middle of the preschool period, screening tests for vision and hearing defects become important. They should be performed between 3½ and 4 years of age and again at the time the child enters school. All of the tests mentioned are reasonably inexpensive and can be performed in the office of the physician. In an effort to bring the benefits to these screening procedures to larger numbers of children, an increasing number of local health departments are carrying them out as part of their community's maternal and child health program. None of these tests, however, can replace the knowledge gained by skilled observation and by the careful questioning of the parent as to the child's progress and behavior at home and in the community.

A significant proportion of infants and young children receiving well-child supervision and presumed to be healthy will, upon careful assessment, be found to have some physical or emotional disorder requiring medical attention. Periodic health appraisal of the child will be useful only when necessary follow-up measures are taken; conversely, effectiveness of the follow-up will depend upon adequacy of the health appraisal itself. Institution of appropriate remedial measures may depend upon securing support from a community facility or program such as Medicaid or the state's crippled children's program.

PARENT COUNSELING. Young parents especially need help with the multiple and varied health problems which arise in the course of normal child growth and development. Perhaps the principal reasons, in addition to immunization, which motivate mothers to bring their children for periodic health supervision are the need for reassurance and the desire for specific information regarding child-rearing practices. Effective counseling depends upon the physician's awareness of these motivating influences as well as the particular needs of each mother. A carefully taken medical history will serve to define the current status of the problem, indicate what the family has already done about this problem, and, at the same time, express the physician's cognizance of its importance to the family. Appreciation of the mother's capabilities and an understanding of the relationship which has been established between parent and child will make it possible for the physician to provide help with such developmental and behavior problems as patterns of sleeping, bowel and bladder control, sibling relations, and needs for limits and discipline.

The schedule of immunizations provides a basis for working out an overall plan of health supervision, with additional visits for health appraisal and parent counseling being arranged in relation to the child's age and stage of development and to the needs of the parents.

IMMUNIZATION AGAINST INFECTIOUS DISEASE. This subject is considered in Chapter 32. A standard reference is the *Report of the Committee on the Control of Infectious Diseases*, published by the American Academy of Pediatrics.

The provision of meaningful medical supervision for the growing child requires both skill and time but can be a most rewarding part of the physician's work with children.

Health Services for Children of School Age

School age brings new dimensions to the continuing problems of the young child. Mortality is at a comparatively low level, but for most children school also involves intensification of risk of contagious disease and the stress of competition in all forms. At the same time, the school provides at least two remarkable opportunities to help the schoolchild, who will be tomorrow's adult. As a community unit, a center for community action, the school has no equal. Furthermore, in this environment the child has, if well provided, a chance to learn about health and to form good health habits for a lifetime. In this sense, health education means far more than classroom instruction in hygiene. Theoretical concepts of health mean little unless supported by actual examples of a truly healthful school environment and services by the nurse and physician which will create respect for, and give meaning to, the growing child's concern for his health.

When the child approaches adolescence, and during adolescence, the physician's approach to health supervision and care must change. Ultimately, he will deal directly with the adolescent himself without the presence of the parents. The general scope of care remains the same, but emphasis will shift to the physical, emotional, and social problems related to the physiologic changes taking place.

Planning and Organization of Community Services for Children and Their Families

Development of Health and Welfare Services for Children

Organized public concern for the health and welfare of children has, for the most part, developed in the last 100 years. So much progress has been made that it is difficult to realize that, as reported by Shattuck, a child born in 1850 to a group representing a large segment of the population in Boston had less than a 50 percent chance of living to be 10 years of age. Also, as late as the first two decades of this century, thousands of young children were forced to work long hours each day in factories and sweatshops under appalling conditions.

The tremendous mortality among infants and the exploitation of children as labor first became the concern of a few and, then, of many. In the 1870's the Society for the Prevention of Cruelty to Children was formed; the medical profession, recognizing the special health needs of children, established a section on the diseases of children in the American Medical Association; and the New York Legislature passed the first Child Welfare Law to protect children from abuse. The first children's hospital in this country was opened in Philadelphia in 1855.

Based upon the pioneering work of Budin and Dufour in France, the idea of arranging to distribute clean milk to prevent the highly fatal "summer complaint" infant diarrhea, soon caught on in the United Kingdom and in the United States. The "pure milk" stations established in New York in 1893 developed into the well-baby clinics of later years.

Increased professional and citizen concern led to the formation of the American Society for the Study and Prevention of Infant Mortality in 1909, and these activities reflected a general upsurge of interest in child health. The United States Children's Bureau was formed in 1912 with a mandate to investigate and report to Congress and the people on the adverse conditions affecting the lives of children. In its early years most of its efforts were in the field of social welfare. Much of the legislation protecting children from forced labor is a result of the dedication of the small and efficient staff of the Bureau. In 1921, Congress provided the Children's Bureau with funds for grants-in-aid to states for the development of public health services for mothers and children. These grants were discontinued after a few years, but with the passage of the Social Security Act in 1935, a new era was ushered in with substantial, continuing, and expanding federal aid to the states for maternal and child health, crippled children, and child welfare services.

In each state health department there is a unit which is responsible for the community health programs for mothers and children. These maternal and child health agencies are supported by state funds and by federal grants-in-aid, and they foster the provision of prenatal services, maternity and newborn care, hospital care of the premature infant, well-child conferences, school health services, diagnostic and treatment services for the mentally retarded, and a variety of other preventive health services for mothers and children.

Handicapped children have special needs for community services and support. In each state there is also a unit of state government responsible for a crippled children's program. All states provide services for the orthopedically handicapped, and the majority also operate services for children with cleft lip and cleft palate and for children with cardiac disease. An increasing number of states provide or support provision of care for children with a wide variety of handicapping conditions. In general, diagnostic services in the crippled children's program are free; parents are expected to pay what they can for treatment services.

Child welfare grants are made to state welfare departments for the care of children in institutions and foster homes, for adoption services, and for other services to children in trouble.

A unique feature of American public life has been the creation of a large number of voluntary agencies in the health field. These agencies have been effective in focusing concern on children with specific handicaps who previously were overlooked except by a few. In recent years rather marked proliferation of voluntary agencies has tended to confuse the public, since many of them limit their services to a specific disease category. Some progress in the coordination of efforts to secure voluntary funds for the support of these agencies has been made; the next logical step will be unification of the services and programs provided by these agencies.

Current Concerns

The 14th edition of this textbook noted with satisfaction progress that had been made in meeting the health and welfare needs of children. The decrease in infant and maternal mortality, the services of state and community agencies, and the accomplishments of the Children's Bureau of the federal government in improving the conditions under which children live were evidence of such progress.

In 1970 satisfaction has been replaced by apprehension. The urban crises, the fact that 25 to 33 percent of our children still live in families whose income is such that they dwell in poverty, the fact that the infant mortality rate in America is higher than that in some 14 other developed countries, give cause for real concern.

The urban crises have forced us to look at our cities. In many of our largest metropolitan areas, the major medical facility for the poor is a city-administered hospital. The outpatient departments of these hospitals are crowded, waiting times are long, and staffs are overworked. It is often difficult for these institutions to provide high quality, total, comprehensive health care for all children. The medical care is also apt to be episodic rather than continuing and may not be accompanied by necessary supportive services.

A great deal of major social legislation affecting the lives of children and youth was passed in the 1960's by Congress. Some examples with particular influence on child health include: the Title XIX Amendments to the Social Security Act, which authorized establishment of the Medicaid Program; the Economic Opportunity Act, which made possible development of the Head Start Program; and the legislation creating state comprehensive health planning programs and regional medical programs. Large sums of money are being expended in support of these programs, but there is still reasonable doubt as to their ultimate effect on the quality of child life and health in America.

The Medicaid Program initiated by Title XIX of the Social Security Amendments of 1965, was intended to make comprehensive medical services available, within a period of 10 years, to all persons regarded as unable to pay for them, according to federal and state standards and definitions of "medical indigency." States were required to have a Medicaid Program in operation by January 1, 1971, or to forfeit the federal funds previously available to them under a variety of previous programs.

The Medicaid Program is a federal-state enterprise. Each state drafts a medical assistance program for its plan and assumes major responsibility for its administration. This has produced great variation in standards and skyrocketing costs which have diverted attention from the goal of assuring every American of access to a single high standard of care. In most instances the program is essentially limited to those who are "on welfare," and the concept of meeting high medical costs for an otherwise self-supporting family has largely been lost. Thus, unfortunately, Medicaid has not yet been successful in bringing health services to many children in greatest need. Two further serious limiting factors have been shortage of health manpower, and the unwillingness of many states to include preventive and case-finding services in their Medicaid programs.

The Head Start Program was instituted under the Economic Opportunity Act. It was designed to provide intensive early educational experiences to disadvantaged young children in an effort to prepare them better to take advantage of educational opportunities at school. Recognizing the interrelation between health and learning, every Head Start project had a health component. Although not well correlated with other community services, a limited number of children have received health care through this mechanism.

Two new child health programs of special importance have their authority in amendments to the Social Security Act. The first, authorized in 1963, allowed the Children's Bureau to give grants to states, communities, or directly to cities for the improvement of maternity and infant care in core city areas. The second, under a 1965 amendment, authorized similar grants to develop comprehensive health services for preschool, school, and adolescent children. Hospital and satellite clinics have been developed or expanded, and medical and paramedical staffs including social workers, public health nurses, and nutritionists have striven to improve care and provide it on a more comprehensive basis.

The Maternity and Infant Care Projects and the Children and Youth Projects are aimed at the most vulnerable segment of the population. They attempt to build services where none exist, and to provide continuous care of high quality and of a comprehensive nature. The demand for services under these programs has far exceeded funds available for their support.

Comprehensive Care

Health care in the United States is usually characterized as pluralistic, since there is no "system." Services are provided under a melange of auspices—public and private, individual and group, unevenly distributed, often broken up into specialties, varying widely in quality, and, most significant, bearing only the most casual of relationships among themselves. This fragmentation can produce, nevertheless, as has been clearly demonstrated, medical care of the highest order. At the same time a growing proportion of the population is dissatisfied with unpredictability, lack of standards, and, too often, care too poor to be acceptable.

To remedy this unsatisfactory situation a number of steps are being taken. Under the Comprehensive Health Planning Acts (1965) and the Partnership for Health Act (1967) federal stimulus is producing development of state and regional ("areawide") planning councils. These have as their aim the involvement of both consumers and providers of health services—the former must, by law, be in the majority—in planning of health services and facilities. The proportion of the country's gross national product going into health has doubled in the last generation. There is probably less need for additional money for the "health system" (or nonsystem!) than for more sensible allocation of public as well as private resources. Hopefully, the comprehensive health planning efforts of the state and regional councils can help accomplish a more effective utilization and distribution of available funds.

Also in 1965 the Regional Medical Programs came into service. These are in a different dimension since they aim at facilitating distribution of knowledge from the country's great medical centers throughout the regions they normally serve, regardless of state lines. Although designed primarily for education, research, and demonstration, it is inevitable that some overlap with comprehensive health planning will occur. Mutual consultation and exchange of information should minimize any encroachments and permit the two programs to complement each other, as originally intended.

Perhaps most important is the necessity to re-examine and redesign our systems of delivery of health care to determine how they can be made most responsive to the needs of children and families. There is obvious need to combine preventive and curative services, whether they be offered in an individual private physician's office or in some other locale. There must be greater attention to mechanisms which will insure quality of care. A significant effect on costs will result from greater emphasis on ambulatory care and more supportive services in homes. The manifest advantages of group arrangements, permitting physicians to support each other and to utilize specialized knowledge, needs far more intensive development. The concept of the health team is changing rapidly. Many of the current tasks of the pediatrician can be accomplished equally well by pediatric nurses, pediatric assistants, nutritionists, or technicians, who are members of the allied health professions. As this book goes to press this whole subject is being widely explored. Open-minded study and critical experimentation can develop new patterns of care which will produce not only higher quality of service to the patient but greater satisfaction to the physician.

While recognizing the special needs of children and youth, pediatric care in the future must be developed within the larger context of health and social services for families, with genuine and extensive citizen participation and support. The goal is the provision of comprehensive care for all young persons regardless of family income, race, and place of residence.

REFERENCES

American Academy of Pediatrics. Committee on Adoptions. Adoption of Children, 2nd ed. Evanston, Amer. Acad. Pediat., 1967.
—————— Committee on Fetus and Newborn. Standards and Recommendations for Hospital Care of Newborn Infants. Revised. Evanston, Amer. Acad. Pediat., 1966.
—————— Committee on Hospital Care. Care of Children in Hospitals. Evanston, Amer. Acad. Pediat., 1960.
—————— Council on Pediatric Practice. Standards of Child Health Care. Evanston, Amer. Acad. Pediat., 1967.
—————— Report of the Committee on the Control of Infectious Diseases, 16th ed. Evanston, Amer. Acad. Pediat., 1970.
American Public Health Association. Committee on Child Health. Health Supervision of Young Children. A Guide for Practicing Physicians and Child Health Conference Personnel. New York, Amer. Public Health Assoc., 1955.
—————— Services for Handicapped Children. A Guide to General Principles and Practices for Public Health Personnel. New York, Amer. Public Health Assoc., 1955.
Anderson, Nancy. Emerging patterns of comprehensive health planning. Inquiry, 6:39, December, 1969.
Comprehensive Health Care. A Challenge to American Communities. National Commission on Community Health Services. Report of the task force on Comprehensive Personal Health Services. Wash., D.C., Public Affairs Press, 1967.
Lewis, Charles. The thermodynamics of regional planning. Amer. J. Public Health, 59:773, May, 1969.
Low, S. America's Children and Youth in Institutions, 1950-1960-1964, A Demographic Analysis. U.S. Children's Bureau. Publ. No. 435, 1965.
Massachusetts Sanitary Commission. Report of the Sanitary Commission of Massachusetts. By Lemuel Shattuck et al. Cambridge, Harvard University Press, 1948.
Bi-Regional Conference on Comprehensive Health Care for Children and Families: Proceedings. Dearborn, Michigan, January 17-19, 1967. Sponsored by the schools of Public Health of the University of Minnesota and the University of Michigan. Ann Arbor, Michigan, 1967.
Smith, Donald C. Pediatrics Consultation in Adoption Practice. Pediatrics, 41:519, No. 2, February, 1968.
Stewert, W. H. Medicine and the Community. Physician, pp. 30-33, January, 1969.
Wallace, H. M. et al. Comprehensive Health Care of Children. Amer. J. Public Health, 58:1839, October, 1968.
Wegman, M. E. Annual Summary of Vital Statistics— 1968. Pediatrics, Vol. 44, No. 6, December, 1969.
—————— Pediatrics in Public Health. New Physician, 11:7, 1962.
White, K. L. Medical Care for Children. Amer. J. Dis. Child., 116:456-457, November, 1968.
U.S. Children's Bureau. Publication No. 460. The Nation's Youth. 1968.
U.S. Department of Commerce. Current Population Reports. Population Estimate. No. 420, April 17, 1969, and No. 416, February 17, 1969.
U.S. Department of Health, Education and Welfare. Vital Statistics of the U.S., Vol. 1: Natality, 1967, Mortality. Parts A and B, Vol. 2, 1967.
—————— Monthly Bi-Statistical Report. Provisional Statistics. Annual Summary for the U.S. 1968. Births, Deaths, Marriages, and Divorces. Vol. 17. No. 13, August 15, 1969.
—————— Adoptions in 1968. Supplement to Child Welfare Statistics 1968. National Center for Social Statistics. Report CW-1 (68), Suppl.

1.3
EPIDEMIOLOGY OF CONGENITAL MALFORMATIONS

ROBERT W. MILLER

It is not generally appreciated that the discovery of German measles as a cause of congenital defects in man was made through an epidemiologic study. By studying retrospectively the histories of mothers of affected children, Gregg identified rubella infection during pregnancy as the cause of congenital cataracts.

Epidemiology can either test or generate hypotheses. In contrast to laboratory research, such studies are usually observational rather than experimental. Epidemiologists must take facts as they are and not as they may want them to be. They must wait for natural circumstances to create opportunities and then make the most of them.

There are two main phases of epidemiology: descriptive and analytic. The *descriptive* approach—a source of hypotheses—can be extremely informative by providing clues to the origins of disease. It seeks peculiarities in the distribution of illness according to such variables as age, sex, race, geography, or socioeconomic status. Of particular value with regard to the etiology of congenital defects are studies of case-clustering in time or space (geography), and changing risks with maternal age.

Through the *analytic* approach one may test ideas about etiology. These ideas may come from the laboratory, from a single clinical observation, or from other epidemiologic studies. The source of suggestions is large. Illustrative examples from days past include the legendary account of a farm girl who pointed out that cowpox protects against smallpox, and the little known report that an inebriated bystander first correctly identified the burning of battery casings as a cause of lead poisoning among Baltimore children.

Clinical Observations

The human teratogens known to date were in general *initially* recognized, not through large-scale surveys, but by alert clinicians. Rubella embryopathy was detected by an Australian ophthalmologist; thalidomide-induced limb deformities were observed by a young obstetrician—again in Australia—and by a German geneticist; radiogenic microcephaly with mental retardation was reported by obstetricians in Europe and the United States; and cerebral palsy due to inorganic mercury was traced by Japanese pediatricians to the ingestion of fish from polluted waters. It should be noted that the agents implicated were viral, chemical, or physical in nature. In three instances the situation was man-made, two being iatrogenic.

Establishing Causality

In the establishment of a causal relationship, statistical association alone is not enough. Implications of causality will be greatly aided by demonstrating a specificity of effect (i.e., for certain rather than for all causes of morbidity); a dose-related response; absence of an influence of concomitant variables; results that are consistent with other information—especially with regard to animal experimentation; and disappearance of the effect when the cause is removed. These criteria are met, for example, in the study of the teratogenic effects among the atomic bomb survivors.

RUBELLA. Correlation of cause to effect is strikingly illustrated by the history of rubella embryopathy. Once suspicion had fallen on the virus by retrospective study of a small cluster of cases, attempts were made to define, by the prospective approach, the spectrum of anomalies produced and the interval of susceptibility during gestation. Cohorts of women were identified as they developed rubella during pregnancy, and then kept under study until the child could be evaluated at delivery and afterwards. This prospective approach provided denominators essential for the calculation of rates. The data revealed that the effect was small when infection occurred later than the twelfth week of gestation. Infection before that time increased not only the frequency of severe anomalies in various combinations among the liveborn, but also the risk of miscarriage. These and more subtle effects such as deafness in the absence of other anomalies, were found when laboratory tests to detect rubella infection were made on blood specimens obtained routinely during pregnancy or from cord blood in more than 50,000 pregnancies.

Such a study was conducted by the National Institute of Neurological Diseases and Blindness in the large prospective Collaborative Perinatal Study. In consequence of these studies physicians are now able to advise women accurately as to the risk involved when rubella infection occurs during pregnancy.

IONIZING RADIATION. Understanding of the teratogenicity of ionizing radiation has followed a similar course. The initial case reports were followed by reports of case series and then by an imperfect but very useful multihospital survey. These studies were retrospective and the denominators (the population at risk) were unknown or very uncertain. Yet they revealed unmistakably that microcephaly with mental retardation was related to pelvic radiotherapy during pregnancy. Finally, explosion of the atomic bombs in Japan provided the basis for a prospective study. Cohorts of women in various stages of pregnancy could be studied to determine the effects of a wide range of radiation dosage on the unborn child. The effect was found to have occurred almost entirely among children whose mothers had last menstruated 7 to 15 weeks before exposure. Within this group the frequency and severity of malformation increased in proportion to the radiation dose; among those within 1,200 meters of the hypocenter 8 of 11 were affected. Although the doses involved in radiotherapy and in atomic explosion were large, the importance of minimizing exposure to x-rays during pregnancy is obvious.

OTHER ENVIRONMENTAL AGENTS. *Microorganisms.* Discovery of the teratogenicity of rubella virus led to an intensive search for other viruses that produce congenital malformations in man. To date only cytomegalovirus (CMV) has been implicated in this regard. Because symptoms are so mild in the infected adult, the clinical illness can usually not be recognized, and the relationship of CMV to neonatal microcephaly has been difficult to establish. The clue to its teratogenicity came through laboratory studies. Intranuclear inclusion bodies observed at autopsy were related to CMV through serologic and virus-isolation studies, and to microcephaly through epidemiologic techniques. Other microorganisms such as the *Treponema pallidum* and *Toxoplasma gondii* are not truly teratogenic since they do not disrupt embryogenesis but damage normal organs after they have formed.

Drugs. Accumulated case reports clearly indicate that certain drugs are powerfully teratogenic. Among them are aminopterin (cranial defects), warfarin sodium (hypoplasia of the nose), Tetracycline (yellow fluorescence of the teeth), goitrogens (congenital goiter), and specific androgens and progestins (masculinization of the external genitalia of female infants).

The array is impressive, yet in the aggregate these agents can be implicated only in a small proportion of all congenital malformations. They illustrate, however, the need for alertness in the recognition of teratogenic agents, particularly drugs introduced recently. An essential concept of epidemiology is distinguishing excessive from normal occurrence and its random variation. To implicate an agent, one must show that the frequency of a specific anomaly following its use exceeds normal expectation.

Associated Diseases

Mention has been made of retrospective and of prospective studies in a search for the cause of disease. It is logical that there should also be "laterospective" studies which means looking "sideways" for collateral or associated diseases. No such term is used in textbooks of epidemiology, but the approach is valid, inexpensive, and extremely effective. In this way the association of leukemia with Down's syndrome was found to be about 200 times more frequent than in the general population. The question then arose: Are other specific congenital malformations excessively associated with specific childhood neoplasms? Wilms' tumor was a good prospect for study in this regard. Its peak occurrence soon after birth suggested that the tumor has its origins during intrauterine life. Case reports indicated that it was associated with several rare congenital malformations. By the simple procedure of reviewing 440 hospital records of children with Wilms' tumor, it was easily established that this neoplasm was found far more often in children with congenital aniridia than could be attributed to chance. The frequency of concurrence of aniridia with Wilms' tumor was 1:73 as compared with 1:50,000, the at-birth incidence of aniridia in the general population. The study also established that Wilms' tumor occurred excessively in association with defects of the urinary tract and in a constellation involving four different manifestations of disproportionate cellular, tissue, or visceral *overgrowth*. (Fig. 6.) Sharing in these relationships are adrenal cortical neoplasia and primary liver cancer. These three malignant neoplasms are associated with *hamartomas*, such as benign vascular or pigmented nevi, with *congenital hemihypertrophy*, and with (Beckwith's) *visceral cytomegaly* syndrome, in which there are unusually large cells in the kidney, adrenal cortex, and liver—the same organs that are prone to neoplasia in children with hemihypertrophy. Thus, from relatively crude data seemingly dissimilar, clinical entities are shown to have common origins.

This observation opens new avenues of research: Any one of the disorders can now be evaluated in terms not only of what is known about it, but also what is known about the etiology of the diseases with which it is associated. Teratogenesis can thus provide clues to oncogenesis. Knowledge of associations between diseases is also of clinical benefit because it can lead to the early detection and prompt treatment of neoplasms in children with congenital anomalies known to carry a high risk of cancer.

The same approach has led to the realization that personal traits and environmental exposures associated with a high risk of leukemia are characterized by chromosomal abnormalities, though not of a single type. Thus, in Bloom's syndrome and Fanconi's aplastic anemia there is chromosomal fragility on culture; in Down's syndrome there is an extra chromosome, and exposure to ionizing radiation or benzene produces long-persisting chromosomal breaks.

These cytogenetic abnormalities do not carry a high risk of lymphoma, a neoplasm associated with inherited immunologic defects (Wiskott-Aldrich syndrome, congenital X-linked agammaglobulinemia, and ataxia-telangiectasia), and apparently with immunosuppressive therapy following renal transplantation. Once again, from simple observations complex relationships have been defined.

The Future

What are the prospects for epidemiologic research into the origins of congenital malformations? Much depends on more complete identification of children with specific defects and improved reporting to a central registry of such anomalies as soon as they are diagnosed. State and other agencies for the aid of crippled children can serve as sources of case material.

When recognition is adequate, the influence of infectious and other environmental agents may be investigated through studies of geographic clusters of specific anomalies in parallel with the distribution of these agents. Statistical techniques developed for the detection of clusters of rare diseases in time and space lend themselves quite appropriately to this purpose.

The capacity of chemicals to induce malformations can be determined through the study of offspring of workers occupationally exposed to sus-

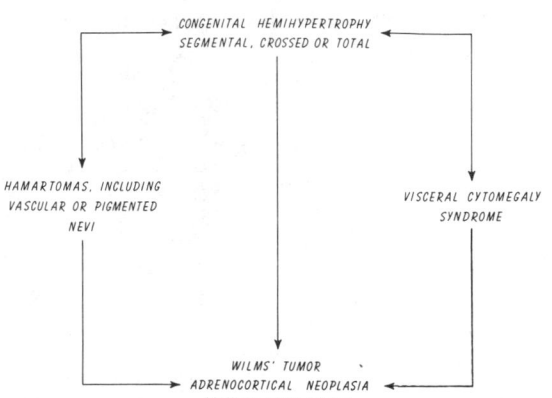

Fig. 6. Relationships among four types of growth excess.

pected agents. A relation to common medication during or before pregnancy (e.g., oral contraceptives) may be ascertained through data routinely recorded in large prepaid medical programs.

How can the individual practitioner contribute to clarifying the origins of congenital malformations? In the hospital or in office practice an attempt should always be made to put historical data of the family, pregnancy, and child into etiologic perspective for this purpose. The physician should take into account what is already known about the relationship of the findings to one another, which new hypotheses are suggested by the present case, and how they might be tested epidemiologically and by appropriate laboratory studies. Major illness in the family should be recorded in the form of a pedigree, which may sometimes lead the identification of syndromes, elements of which are scattered among several family members rather than concentrated in a single individual. Thus, leukemia and Down's syndrome occur excessively not only within the same child, but also as individual diseases which affect different children in the same sibship. It is also important to inquire into occupational and other environmental exposures during and just before the time that the child under study was in utero.

The computer offers intriguing possibilities for the massive linkage of health records. However, machines cannot replace physicians in posing questions and interpreting results on the basis of clinical experience and knowledge. Despite the advances expected from the use of computers, exciting discoveries can still be made by hand-tabulations of data. Bedside observations and hospital charts can be a rich source of new information in this regard. The clinician today, with no more information than he can obtain by history and physical examination, may have as much opportunity to gain new insight into etiology from a small series of cases as Gregg had in 1941.

REFERENCES

Cohlan, S. Q. Teratogenic agents and congenital malformation. J. Pediat., 63:650, 1963.

Elizan, T. S., Ajero-Froehlich, L., Fabiyi, A., Ley, A., and Sever, J. L. Viral infection in pregnancy and congenital CNS malformations in man. Arch. Neurol., 20:115, 1969.

Grumbach, M. M., Ducharme, J. R., and Moloshok, R. E. On the fetal masculinizing action of certain oral progestins. J. Clin. Endocr., 19:1369, 1959.

Henderson, J. L. Evolution of child care. Lancet, 2:265, 1953.

Kerber, I. J., Warr, O. S., and Richardson, C. Pregnancy in a patient with a prosthetic mitral valve, associated with a fetal anomaly attributed to warfarin sodium, J.A.M.A., 203:223, 1968.

Kline, A. H., Blattner, R. J., and Lunin, M. Transplacental effect of tetracyclines on teeth. J.A.M.A., 188:178, 1964.

Lenz, W. Chemicals and malformations in man. In Second International Conference on Congenital Malformations. New York, International Medical Congress, Ltd., 1964.

MacMahon, B., and Sowa, J. M. Physical damage to the fetus. Milbank Mem. Fund. Quart., 39:14, 1961.

Manson, M. M., Logan, W. P. D., and Loy, R. M. Rubella and Other Virus Infections during Pregnancy. London. Her Majesty's Stationery Officer, Ministry of Health Publ. No. 101, 1960.

Miller, R. W. Delayed radiation effects in atomic-bomb survivors. Science, 166:569, 1969.

———— Prenatal origins of mental retardation: epidemiological approach. J. Pediat., 71:455, 1967.

———— Relation between cancer and congenital defects: an epidemiologic evaluation. J. Nat. Cancer Inst., 40:1079, 1968.

———— Origins of congenital heart disease: an epidemiologic perspective. Teratology, 2:77, 1969.

Milunsky, A., Graef, J. W., and Gaynor, M. F., Jr. Methotrexate-induced congenital malformations with a review of the literature. J. Pediat., 72:790, 1968.

Sever, J. L. Perinatal infections affecting the developing fetus and newborn. In Conference on the Prevention of Mental Retardation Through Control of Infectious Diseases. U.S. Dept. of Health, Education and Welfare, Public Health Service Publ. No. 1692, Washington, D.C., U.S. Government Printing Office, 1968.

Warkany, J. Environmental Teratogenic Factors. In First International Conference on Congenital Malformations. Philadelphia, J. B. Lippincott Company, 1961.

chapter 2

PERINATAL MEDICINE

FREDERICK C. BATTAGLIA, Associate Editor

2.1
INTRODUCTION

The dividing lines separating pediatrics, obstetrics, and internal medicine have traditionally been drawn more on the basis of the physician's particular skills and talents than on the basis of sound knowledge of human development. Perinatal medicine is concerned with human development centering around birth. It aims to bring together for the benefit of patient care the knowledge, talents, and goals of obstetrics and pediatric newborn medicine. A more natural division for a medical specialty would be to consider the development of each individual from conception through intrauterine and early postnatal life, including preschool development. However, currently the perinatal period is generally understood to mean the time from the beginning of the second half of pregnancy to the end of the neonatal period. One outstanding characteristic of development during this time is the specialization of organ function. In order to provide optimal postnatal care to the infant it is essential to have a sound understanding of normal intrauterine development. In this chapter we shall try to review an orderly progression from intrauterine development to early postnatal life. At the core of this chapter, then, are the introductory sections on obstetrics, fetal physiology, and fetal biochemistry. Perinatal medicine is one of the areas of medicine changing most rapidly, in great part due to the creation of regional perinatal medical centers devoted to optimal care of *both* the mother and infant. Recognition of the importance of such centers has given an impetus to current clinical research in obstetrics aimed at earlier definition of high-risk pregnancies, for referral to intensive care obstetric and newborn services.

Before Birth: (The Fetus)

2.2
OBSTETRIC MANAGEMENT
OF THE MOTHER AND FETUS

EDWARD J. QUILLIGAN

To assure optimum chances for survival as a fetus, as a neonate, and indeed even as an adult, attempts have been made to sort out in the past history of a pregnant patient factors helpful in determining whether or not it is a high-risk pregnancy, both from the viewpoint of the mother and the conceptus. A significant amount of information can be obtained from the pregnant patient at her initial interview which aids in the prediction of the perinatal mortality rate applicable to this pregnancy. However, the past history of the mother obtained at the first prenatal visit must be regarded as only the first stepping stone in the evaluation of pregnancy outcome. Even if one includes all known diseases associated with an increased perinatal risk, one is left with a large group of unknown causes. Any pregnancy which by past history may be considered at low risk of maternal or fetal morbidity may have to be reassigned to a high-risk group by some development late in pregnancy. Some factors in the past history which are associated most clearly with a given perinatal outcome are listed in Table 1, taken from a recent study of Nesbitt et al. Their data suggest that, using the criteria in Table 1, approximately 10 to 20 percent of pregnant patients would be recognized on the initial prenatal clinic visit as being at high risk, and these would account for over 50 percent of the poor pregnancy outcomes.

Prenatal Care

Initial Visit

Even the best prenatal care is no assurance of an excellent pregnancy outcome. However, more and more clinical tools are being developed which, by permitting early recognition of specific obstetric complications and, in many instances, early active treatment during pregnancy, increase the chances for optimal fetal development. Several studies have documented a better perinatal outcome in women who seek

TABLE 1.   *Maternal-Child Health Care Index**

Name:_____ Date:_____ EDC:_____ Hospital: _____
                                                                    & Number: _____

The scoring system below is an attempt to categorize the degree of maternal and fetal risk based on the information available at the initial history and physical upon registration in our obstetric clinics. Please circle the numbers under each of the 8 categories which you feel apply and, at the bottom of this sheet, add up these numbers and subtract from a perfect score of 100.

I. Maternal Age

Under 15	20
15-19	10
20-29	0
30-34	5
35-39	10
Over 40	20

II. Race and Marital Status

White	0
Nonwhite	5
Single	5
Married	0

III. Parity

0	10
1-3	0
4-7	5
Over 8	10

IV. Past Obstetric History

Abortions		Prematures		Fetal Death		Neonatal Death		Congenital Anomaly		Damaged Infants	
1	5	1	10	1	10	1	10	1	10	Physical	10
2	15	2+	20	2+	30	2+	30	2+	20	Neurologic	20
3+	30										

V. Medical-obstetric Disorders and Nutrition

Systemic Illnesses

Acute, mild	5
Acute, serious	15
Chronic, nondebilitating	5
Chronic, debilitating	20

Specific Infections

Urinary:	
acute	5
chronic	25
Syphilis:	
treated	0
untreated	20
at term	30

Diabetes

Pre	20
Overt	30

Chronic Hypertension

Mild	15
Severe	30
Nephritis	30

Heart Disease

Class I or II	10
Class III or IV	30
History prior failure	30

Endocrine Disorders

Definite adrenal, pituitary, or thyroid problem	30
Recurrent menstrual dysfunction	10
Involuntary sterility: Less than 2 years	10
More than 2 years	20

Anemia

Hgb, 10-11 g	5
Hgb, 9-10 g	10
Hgb, less than 9 g	20

Rh Problem

Sensitized	30
Prior infant affected	30
Prior ABO incompatibility	20

Nutrition

Malnourished	20
Very obese	30
Inadequate diet but not malnourished	10

VI. Generative Tract Disorders

Prior fetal malpresentations	10
Prior cesarean section	30
Known anomaly or incompetent cervix	20
Myomas:	
Over 5 cm	20
Submucous	30
Contracted pelvis:	
Borderline	10
Any contracted plane	30
Ovarian masses:	
Over 6 cm	20
Endometriosis	5

VII. Emotional Survey (Grade 0-20 based on)

Fears, attitudes, biases, hostilities, motivations, and behavioral patterns; prior pregnancies without supervision; time of registration; standard of child care and responsibilities; family unit, marital relationship; history of psychiatric illness in family

VIII. Social and Economic Survey (Grade 0-10 based on)

Employment—husband, patient; annual income adequacy, public assistance;
Education—husband, patient;
Housing—location, quality, facilities, and neighborhood environment

Total score of all 8 categories   _____

100 less above score equals MCH Care Index   _____

*From Nesbitt and Aubry. *Amer. J. Obstet. Gynec.*, 103:972, 1969.

and receive good prenatal care. For example, in the District of Columbia the incidence of low-birth-weight infants was 22.7 percent in women with no prenatal care and 10.4 percent in women with prenatal care.

HISTORY. Ideally, prenatal care should begin 2 to 4 weeks after the first missed menstrual period. During the initial visit a carefully taken history should include a detailed reproductive history, any problems during prior pregnancies, length of labor, type of delivery, weight of babies at birth, postpartum complications in either mother or infant, and the health status of other living children. A fetus at term estimated to weigh 5 pounds when the mother has previously delivered three 8-pound infants demands investigation as a suspected placental insufficiency. The knowledge of a past medical history of maternal systemic disease, such as diabetes, nephritis, and hypertension, will be of help in anticipating problems both to mother and fetus in the current pregnancy. If there is a history of diabetes in the family, the chances of developing diabetes during pregnancy increase by a factor of three, from about 5 to 15 per cent. Similarly, a history of twinning in the family should alert the obstetrician to the possibility of a multiple gestation in the present pregnancy.

A *careful* menstrual history taken at the first prenatal visit is essential and should include the date of the patient's last normal menstrual period, any bleeding since that normal menstrual period, and the periodicity of the patient's cycles over the past several years. If a patient has a 45-day cycle rather than a 28-day cycle, her expected date of confinement (EDC) would be 2 weeks later than that calculated in the usual way, i.e., 280 days from the first day of the last menstrual period.

PHYSICAL EXAMINATION. During this initial prenatal visit, a careful physical examination should include a pelvic examination which is done to determine the presence or absence of pregnancy, the size of the uterus, and the capacity of the bony pelvis. An evaluation of uterine size in relation to the length of gestation should be made, which later in pregnancy may be very important in evaluating abnormal uterine size or length of gestation. During the initial pelvic examination a Papanicolaou smear of the cervix should be performed to rule out cervical neoplasia.

LABORATORY TESTS. A hematocrit determination, blood typing, and a complete urinalysis including a urine culture to rule out asymptomatic bacteriuria should be done during the initial visit.

INSTRUCTION. The patient should receive some guidelines on proper prenatal care, particularly if she is a primigravida. Ideally one would like to limit the weight gain during pregnancy to approximately 20 pounds, which is the combined weight of the fetus, placenta, amniotic fluid, plus the increase in weight of the uterus, breasts, and retained water. In general this weight gain can be achieved with a 2,500-calorie diet including at least 100 g of protein and 4 to 6 g of NaCl. Assuming that the patient has normal iron

stores, a daily iron supplement of 0.6 g of ferrous sulfate should be prescribed. There are virtually no restrictions on travel or bathing, and instructions about these matters are usually unnecessary. Advice to get ample exercise should be given. Finally, one should attempt to answer any questions which preoccupy the patient about this pregnancy. Usually the symptoms of early pregnancy, such as mild nausea, breast enlargement and tenderness, lethargy, and constipation, can be treated quite conservatively. Occasionally it is necessary to give antiemetics for more severe nausea and vomiting of early pregnancy; however, any drug should be prescribed with caution. There is experimental evidence in animals that antiemetics such as meclizine can cause congenital anomalies.

Subsequent Prenatal Care

The frequency of prenatal visits following the first prenatal visit must depend on the course of the pregnancy. Assuming a normal pregnancy, the woman should be seen every month during the first six months, every two weeks during the seventh and eighth months, and every week during the ninth month of pregnancy. Each prenatal visit should include a history, measurements of blood pressure and fundal height, auscultation of fetal heart tones, an attempt to palpate the position of the fetus, and an estimate of fetal weight. Progressive growth of the uterus usually indicates progressive growth of the fetus. A uterus which is too large for the estimated gestational age should raise a suspicion of (1) multiple gestation, (2) hydramnios, or (3) an infant large for his gestational age. A uterus which appears small for the duration of pregnancy suggests intrauterine growth retardation. In any case, a uterus of discrepant size for the gestational age alerts the obstetrician to treat this as a high-risk pregnancy. The date at which the patient first feels the fetus move (quickening) and the date at which the obstetrician first hears the fetal heart rate provide additional clinical information upon which to fix the EDC. Quickening usually occurs about the 16th week of gestation, and fetal heart tones should be heard around the 18th week of gestation. The patient must be weighed at each prenatal visit. Optimal weight gain is approximately half a pound per week. If there is excessive weight gain due to water retention, as shown by edema, salt intake should be limited appropriately to 2 g per day. In most cases such a dietary restriction will be sufficient; if not, diuretics can be added. They must, however, be given cautiously, particularly around labor and delivery if a pitocin induction is used, because severe dilutional hyponatremia can develop in both the infant and the mother. Listlessness and hypotonia in the first few hours after birth are the most common signs in the infant.

An oral glucose tolerance test should be performed, preferably towards the end of the first or at the beginning of the second trimester, in pregnant women with a family history of diabetes, a history of large babies delivered previously (over 9 pounds in the Caucasian; over 8½ pounds in the Negro), or a history of unexplained fetal loss. The existence of diabetes, either gestational or overt, requires that the 24-hour urinary estriols, which give some indication of fetoplacental function, be measured frequently. The fetal adrenal produces dehydroepiandrosterone, which is hydroxylated in the fetal adrenal gland and liver. The placenta converts 16-hydroxydehydroepiandrosterone to estriol. The test is also useful in placental insufficiency, preeclampsia and eclampsia, intrauterine growth retardation, maternal hypertension, and fetal demise. It is, however, not helpful in the rhesus-sensitized patient. In a high-risk patient during the third trimester the total urinary estriol may need to be measured on alternate days, and a persistent decrease in the urinary estriol excretion alerts the obstetrician to consider immediate delivery.

The Rh-negative patient should have an initial antibody titer drawn on the first or second prenatal visit. If the patient has a titer of Rh antibodies greater than 1 to 16, her amniotic fluid should be examined spectrophotometrically at repeated intervals throughout the pregnancy. Transabdominal amniocentesis should be begun at approximately 20 to 24 weeks of gestation (see section on intrauterine diagnosis). If the fetus is severely affected *prior* to the 34th week of gestation, intrauterine transfusions with packed red cells should be considered. If the fetus is severely affected *after* the 34th week of gestation, he should be delivered promptly.

In any high-risk clinical situation such as maternal diabetes and fetal erythroblastosis, the pediatrician should play an integral role in the care of the patient beginning in the latter part of the second trimester of pregnancy. It is only with complete cooperation between the obstetrician, the pediatrician, and the internist that optimal results can be obtained in terms of management of both the mother and fetus during complications of pregnancy. For example, whenever an erythroblastotic infant is to be delivered, the pediatrician must be prepared for immediate postdelivery exchange transfusion. He should know the fetal size and gestational age as estimated by the obstetrician, and the time of elective delivery either vaginally or by cesarean section.

Many of the complications of pregnancy, such as diabetes, hypertensive toxemia of pregnancy, and erythroblastosis, require preterm delivery. In many of these situations the fetus is either larger or smaller than the dates would indicate. Obstetric and pediatric teams must then base their decisions concerning management of the mother and infant in part upon their assessment of fetal maturity. Until recently, radiographic studies of the mother's abdomen revealing the fetal distal femoral epiphyses (36 weeks of gestation) or proximal tibia epiphyses (38 weeks of gestation) were the only laboratory assistance available. Determinations in the amniotic fluid of the amount of

creatinine and of the number of fat-containing cells have proved of more significant help to obstetricians and pediatricians in establishing the length of gestation. Creatinine values exceeding 2 mg and the presence of 20 percent or more fat-containing cells in the amniotic fluid indicate a gestational stage of 36 weeks or more.

Intrauterine Infection

Intrauterine infection can be either bacterial or viral. The viral infections associated primarily with severe fetal disease are rubella (particularly in the first trimester), cytomegalovirus, and herpes simplex vaginalis.

The clinical diagnosis of rubella can now be confirmed by the demonstration of a rising titer of rubella antibodies or positive throat culture washings. If the patient has contracted the disease in the first trimester of her pregnancy, and the diagnosis of rubella has been confirmed, therapeutic abortion should be strongly considered. The patient should be told that rubella infection is associated with a high incidence of congenital malformations especially during the first 8 weeks of gestation but continuing through the 16th week (see Sec. 14.38).

Herpes simplex vaginalis has been found to be a more common infection in the maternal reproductive tract than previously thought. This diagnosis can be made by special cultures of vaginal and cervical secretions, and its characteristic inclusion bodies can be seen on a routine Papanicolaou smear. If active herpetic infection is present in the genital region at the time of labor, delivery by cesarean section is indicated. Extremely high perinatal mortality or severe central nervous system degeneration threaten the newborn infected with this virus.

Bacterial infection generally occurs following premature rupture of the membranes, that is, membranes which have ruptured prior to the onset of labor. Several studies have indicated a sharp rise in the incidence of bacterial infection of the newborn, associated with an increased perinatal mortality, after the membranes have been ruptured for 24 hours or longer. Antibiotics administered to the mother have not protected the fetus. Therefore, if labor has not started, the decision which faces the pediatrician and the obstetrician is whether or not to initiate delivery of the infant. Beyond 38 weeks of gestation the answer is relatively simple and affirmative. Labor should be induced and the child delivered within the first 24 to 48 hours following rupture of the membranes. Earlier than 38 weeks of gestation the pediatrician and the obstetrician must balance the risk between prematurity with its subsequent problems and the potential for fetal loss due to infection. After the membranes have been ruptured 24 hours, perinatal mortality approaches 10 percent in the premature infant; therefore, labor should be induced at the estimated fetal size and gestational age at which perinatal mortality due to prematurity alone approximates 10 percent. This will vary in different centers and among different populations.

Obstetric Care During Labor and Delivery

Once recognized, all high-risk pregnancies should be monitored during labor and delivery. Two types of monitoring are currently available. The first relates fetal heart rate and uterine contractions; the second assesses the acid-base status of the infant during labor. It has been known for many years that the infant whose heart rate falls below 100 beats per minute has a higher perinatal mortality. However, in many instances conclusions erroneous in either direction have been drawn from auscultatory findings. Infants who had low fetal heart rates by auscultation were perfectly normal at birth while infants with normal fetal heart rates were very depressed at delivery. With continuous fetal heart rate monitoring, the interpretation of fetal heart rate changes has been put on a sounder basis. The procedure requires a fetal scalp electrode and an intraamniotic catheter. By using continuous recordings, Hon has suggested that three patterns of fetal heart rate changes associated with uterine contractions can be recognized. They are those of head compression, uteroplacental insufficiency, and cord compression (Fig. 1). The distinguishing features of these patterns have to do with the timing of the onset of fetal bradycardia in relation to uterine contractions and the rate at which bradycardia develops. In general, the head compression pattern and moderate cord compression patterns appear innocuous to the fetus; however, severe cord compression patterns and any uteroplacental insufficiency patterns indicate fetal distress.

The second method of attempting to recognize fetal distress during labor and delivery consists of obtaining fetal blood samples from the fetal scalp through a dilated cervix. The blood should be an arterialized specimen, treated anaerobically, and analyzed as quickly as possible for its pH and base deficit. In general, a fetal pH less than 7.25 or base deficit greater than −10 is indicative of fetal distress and raises the question of the desirability of immediate interruption of pregnancy. This decision, of course, is not made on the basis of pH measurements alone but requires culling all the clinical information.

Another index of fetal distress during labor is meconium staining of the amniotic fluid in a vertex presentation. Perinatal mortality increases roughly by a factor of three or four when meconium staining is present.

It is important that the obstetrician and anes-

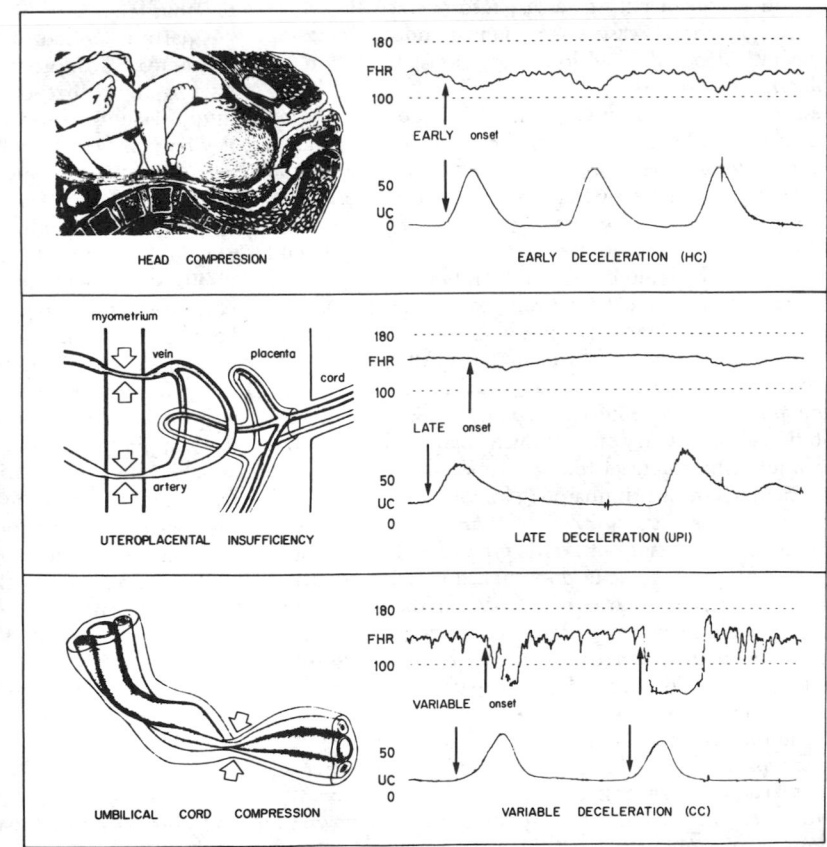

Fig. 1. Three patterns of fetal heart rate changes (FHR) associated with uterine contractions (UC). (From Quilligan. *J. Gynec. Invest.,* in press.)

thesiologist do everything possible during labor to minimize interference with oxygen transfer to the fetus. This principle is particularly true in high-risk pregnancies in which labor must frequently be either induced or augmented. Induction of labor is best achieved by a slow, continuous infusion of intravenous oxytocin at a rate of from 0.5 to 20 milliunits per minute. Whenever oxytocin therapy is being used, intrauterine pressures should be monitored on a continuous basis. Only in this way can the physician determine if there is excessive uterine tonus (resting pressure) or excessive uterine contractility. Both are detrimental, since they may reduce uterine blood flow. Diminished intervillous space blood flow lasting for more than one minute seems to be harmful to the fetus. It is associated with an increased incidence of fetal bradycardia of the uteroplacental insufficiency type and results in a higher fetal mortality.

Similarly, maternal hypotension increases the incidence of uteroplacental insufficiency patterns. Maternal hypotension is most frequently seen following conduction anesthesia when the patient is supine. One can treat this type of hypotension by manually lifting the uterus off the vena cava, by shifting the patient to the lateral position, by elevating the patient's legs to approximately 60° from horizontal, or by rapid infusion of 5 percent glucose and water to increase blood volume. Vasopressors should be given only as a last resort, since they may cause peripheral vasoconstriction without increasing uterine blood flow. More hazardous reduction of blood pressure may follow overzealous use of hypotensive agents in reducing the blood pressure of preeclamptic or hypertensive women during pregnancy. It has been repeatedly demonstrated that the fetal mortality is higher when vigorous antihypertensive therapy is used. The blood pressure of the mother should be lowered only to the level which will tend to protect the mother against cerebral vascular accidents (systolic to 160, diastolic to 100 or 110).

Obstetric analgesia, particularly in the high-risk patient, is a formidable challenge. All analgesic as well as anesthetic agents in clinical use will cross the placenta and enter the fetus. In general, the obstetrician must try to balance pain relief in the mother with potential fetal depression. Early in labor, particularly in a primiparous patient, short-acting barbiturates (Seconal, 100 to 200 mg) may be given to combat apprehension. This type of sedation should only be given if one does not anticipate delivery within the next 4 to 6 hours. When the patient enters the phase of active labor (cervical dilation 2 to 4 cm and contractions occurring every 3 minutes, lasting 45 to 60 seconds), the patient may require more than simple sedation, and here Demerol (in combination with Thorazine or Phenergan) is the drug of choice. The dosage is 75 to 100 mg of Demerol with 25 mg of Thorazine given intramuscularly. This medication should not be given if delivery is anticipated within 2 hours. If delivery is anticipated within 2 hours and narcotics are to be used, it is best to give small doses of Demerol intravenously, 12½ to 25 mg. During the latter stages of labor (7 cm in a nulliparous patient and 5 to 6 cm in a multiparous patient), caudal or epidural anesthesia can be used, while following maternal blood pressure carefully. The contraindication to caudal or epidural anesthesia at this point is a hypertensive mother, as these patients frequently have a very profound drop in blood pressure with the consequences mentioned above. If caudal or epidural anesthesia is contraindicated or if no anesthetist is available, pain relief can be obtained with paracervical block.

There are some studies which suggest that for cesarean section some form of inhalation anesthesia, namely, induction with Pentothal and maintenance with a curariform drug plus nitrous oxide, yields the best results. However, it should be emphasized that no one form of obstetric anesthesia has been shown to be clearly superior and free of risk.

Obviously, a pediatrician should join the anesthesiologist and obstetrician in the delivery room whenever a high-risk infant is anticipated. (For delivery room care, see section on labor and delivery.)

The Puerperium

Cooperation between the pediatrician and obstetrician should not end in the delivery room. It is essential that teamwork between the two continue into the postpartum period. For many mothers it is a time of increased apprehension, particularly for women having their first child. Daily reassurance is absolutely essential concerning the condition of their newborn infant as well as their own progress. Many of the problems which may arise in the postpartum period can be allayed by proper antenatal instruction. Informing the mother about the baby's anticipated reactions during its first few days, and a thorough discussion of whether the mother wishes to nurse or bottle feed the infant, should be the responsibility of both pediatrician and obstetrician during the antenatal period. If the mother has decided to breast feed, it is important that she make the necessary preparations before the baby arrives. Toughening of the nipple by daily massage will prevent cracking and bleeding of the nipple, which is one of the most frequent complications in the nursing mother. During the postpartum period, particularly in the nursing mother, reassurance that the baby is doing well is absolutely essential. In general, the milk will enter the breasts on the third postpartum day. The nursing mother will find that her milk production and the baby's demands are not synchronous for the first week or two of nursing. There will be times when she will have an excessive supply of milk and thus will be uncomfortable due to overproduction, and other times when the child will be uncomfortable due to underproduction of milk. With help from her pediatrician and obstetrician, adjustments can be made and breast feeding can be successful. It is important for the obstetrician to remember that, if the patient is nursing, many of the drugs given to the mother will eventually find their way into breast milk.

REFERENCES

Baird, D. Social factors in obstetrics. *In* Greenhill, J. P., ed. Yearbook of Obstetrics and Gynecology. Chicago, Year Book Medical Publishers, Inc., 1969, p. 16.

Bishop, E. N. Symposium on prematurity. Clin. Obstet. Gynec., 7, 1964.

Hon, E. H. An Atlas of Fetal Heart Rate Patterns. New Haven, Conn., Harty Press Incorporated, 1968.

Nesbitt, R. E. L., and Aubry, R. H. High risk obstetrics. II. Value of semi-objective grading system in identifying the vulnerable group. Amer. J. Obstet. Gynec., 103:972, 1969.

Weingold, A. B. Symposium on evaluation of fetal environment. Clin. Obstet. Gynec., 11, 1968.

2.3

FETAL GROWTH AND DIFFERENTIATION

PETER GRUENWALD

During approximately 280 days of intrauterine life the conceptus undergoes extensive changes in structure and function. In an effort to organize the vast amount of information, observers have subdivided the subject matter into such arbitrary categories as the period of organogenesis (embryonic period) vs. that of growth (fetal period), growth vs. maturation, and in the field of pathology, malformation vs. fetal disease. As useful as these approaches are when broad aspects are considered, they cannot be applied to every facet and it is important to keep in mind the basic continuity of changes in structure and function.

The intricate processes of early development and their regulation will not be described here. Several texts of embryology designed for the medically oriented reader are available. To those interested in basic principles of development, *Analysis of Development* by Willier et al., *Principles of Embryology* by Waddington, and *Organogenesis* edited by De-Hann and Ursprung are recommended. There is also an exhaustive compilation of numerical data edited by Altman and Dittmer. Recent reference books on the late fetus include Dawes' *Foetal and Neonatal Physiology* and several symposia: Dawkins and Mac-Gregor's *Gestational Age, Size and Maturity,* Adamsons' *Diagnosis and Treatment of Fetal Disorders,* and the Pan American Health Organization's *Perinatal Factors Affecting Human Development.*

Growth and Maturation

Development encompasses two basic types of processes which are interdependent to some extent, *differenta-*

tion or *maturation* producing qualitative changes, and *growth,* leading to increase in bulk. Maturation is controlled mostly by mechanisms inherent in the fetus and is largely independent of the environment; growth depends heavily on the adequacy of the supply line. Maturation determines the functional state of the fetus, and with it the ability to adjust to extrauterine life; it is therefore a very basic parameter and its evalutaion is of the greatest importance in assessing a neonate. Growth, on the other hand, is of less immediate significance; it is, however, easily measured by determining weight achieved after a given length of gestation* and is a more sensitive indicator of the adequacy of the intrauterine environment than maturation would be. This justifies our preoccupation with weights and measurements.

In perinatal pathology it is easy to demonstrate that in a mature but severely growth-retarded neonate the maturity of the lungs, kidneys, and brain corresponds fairly closely to the gestational age rather than body weight (Gruenwald, 1963). Assessment of maturity during neonatal life depends heavily on cerebral function which, because of its great diversity and complex timetable, provides the clearest landmarks. It, too, shows a closer relation to conceptional age than to birth weight (Parmelee and Schulte).

GROWTH AND CELL MULTIPLICATION. Early embryonic growth is accomplished largely through cell division. As cells differentiate, increase in size, and lay down large amounts of intercellular substance, the role of cell multiplication decreases. The development of genetically determined variations of body size has been studied in several species; it was found that in some instances differences appear during embryonic life and are the result of differing rates of cell division rather than cell size. The role of cell multiplication in growth has been studied by relating the DNA content of tissues (representing cell number) to RNA or protein (representing cell mass) and by histometry. Increase in cell number stops in most tissues early in life; in the human brain this occurs about one-half year after birth. This time is rigidly set by the inherent regulatory mechanisms; if under unfavorable circumstances the normal number of cells has not formed by that time, it probably cannot be produced later even under the most favorable conditions. Later in life growth occurs by enlargement of cells and deposition of intercellular substance.

Intrauterine growth as determined by body weight or length depends on factors inherent in the fetus, the placenta, and the mother. Since most of the factors relate in some way to the mother, an arbitrary classification will be used, particularly with reference to the last trimester of pregnancy.

* Throughout this section "gestational age" refers to "menstrual age" (weeks or lunar months from the beginning of the last menstrual period). Embryologists frequently use "conception age" (counting from the known or presumed time of fertilization) which, assuming a regular 28-day cycle, is two weeks less than the former.

FETAL FACTORS. Included are those which are inherent in the fetus at the end of the second trimester, and thus constitute the growth potential of the fetus from then on. These factors may be either genetic or imparted to the fetus earlier than the second trimester; for instance growth retardation of malformed infants may arise from either genetic or environmental factors. This trend appears early in fetal life when limitation by deprivation is unlikely, and has been documented in chromosomal abnormalities (Schutt) and for unselected malformations among perinatal deaths (Gruenwald, 1969).

Fetal disease may retard growth even in the absence of significant maternal disease, for instance in cytomegalic inclusion disease or in fetal rubella (Naeye and Blanc). There are data suggestive of growth retardation in malaria, although information relating birth weight to gestational age is lacking (Jelliffe).

PLACENTAL FACTORS. The placenta, which is at first much larger than the embryo, grows at a slower rate than the latter. Its weight alone is not an indication of functional capacity, since the placenta becomes more efficient per unit weight as it matures. It is, however, fair to assume that during the first half of gestation the functional reserve of the placenta is very great. Only extreme degeneration or catastrophic retroplacental hemorrhage is likely to produce placental insufficiency during this period, and it is improbable that a placenta damaged to this extent can support even curtailed fetal growth to term.

It is virtually certain that the increase of the supply line is not proportional to fetal growth, but falls behind it. This placental decline may explain, in part, why the rate of growth of the fetus decreases near term. These events take place at a specific average time, usually between 34 and 36 weeks, and shortly thereafter deceleration of ponderal growth becomes apparent. When this phenomenon and its pathologic exaggerations were first recognized, they were ascribed to placental insufficiency without much evidence. Now, with increasing knowledge of maternal factors, it becomes clear that true placental insufficiency may not be the leading cause of suboptimal fetal growth. It is actually dangerous from the heuristic point of view to ascribe all fetal deprivation to placental insufficiency since little can be done about the placenta, and investigation of maternal factors might be neglected.

The placenta is a fetal organ: its fixed cells, including the layers through which the exchange of substances takes place, are fetal. Only the maternal circulation in the intervillous space which surrounds the villi is subject to maternal regulations and metabolic conditions. Therefore, if a small fetus has a proportionally small placenta, this does not justify the conclusion that the fetus is small because the placenta is small; the placenta may be small because it is an organ of a fetus which is small for other reasons. During the third trimester the proportion of placental to fetal weight declines from 1:5 to 1:7, but this may be offset to some extent by maturation of the placenta, with an increasing area and efficiency of metabolic exchange change per unit of weight. Yet after the placenta is structurally mature its growth decelerates before that of the fetus (Gruenwald, 1963). On the other hand, Aherne and Dunnill found that villous surface area increases sharply until term. They found a highly significant correlation between villous surface area and fetal weight in normal pregnancies. They suggested with appropriate caution that stunting of the fetus may occasionally be caused by primary placental hypoplasia.

True insufficiency doubtless occurs in placentas with extensive pathologic change such as infarcts or angiomas and interferes with the exchange between fetus and mother. Premature separation sufficiently extensive to cause placental insufficiency is infrequently associated with continuation of pregnancy. These severe pathologic changes, to which excessively small size of the placenta might be added, are quite infrequent. One may conjecture that, in addition, insufficiency of a structurally normal placenta may occur, particularly if pregnancy lasts well past term.

MATERNAL FACTORS. Many maternal characteristics or abnormalities have been found to be associated with poor fetal growth and well-being, as demonstrated by low birth weight in relation to gestational age. Well-known maternal factors include primiparity, heavy smoking, short stature, small heart volume, living at high altitude, chronic or preeclamptic hypertensive disease, and other maternal diseases. It has been known for a long time that the average birth weight of some population groups is significantly lower than that of Caucasian populations with high living standards. This has been ascribed to ethnic—that is, genetic—differences. Actually, there is mounting evidence that socioeconomic factors account for much of the difference. The mother's health and nutrition at the time of the current pregnancy is not the only determining factor; mothers having grown up under unfavorable circumstances are likely to have smaller babies than those who grew up under favorable conditions, even if both now live in similar circumstances. The full effect of improved socioeconomic status may thus take more than one generation to make itself evident to the full extent. The increase in birth weight of many population groups during the last century, presumably as a result of improved socioeconomic, nutritional, and medical conditions, has been reviewed by Bakwin. A striking example occurred in Japan during a 20-year period following World War II. The entire increase in mean birth weight was due to more rapid fetal growth; duration of pregnancy remained the same. This illustrates the usefulness of studies of fetal growth in assessing the biologic effects of socioeconomic changes (Gruenwald, 1968).

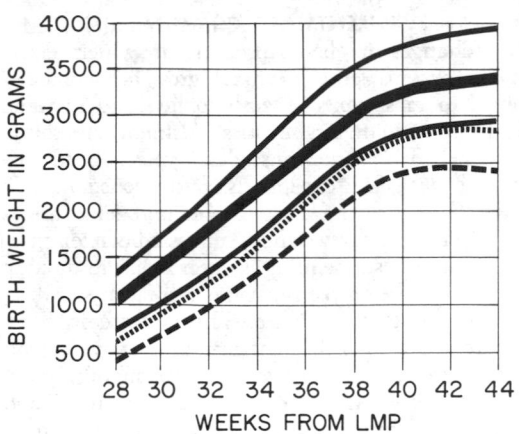

Fig. 2. Birth weight in relation to gestational age: mean (heavy line) ± standard deviation (thin line), 10th percentile (dotted line), and mean minus 2 standard deviations (broken line). (Data from Gruenwald, 1966.)

Normal Growth of the Human Fetus

Since it is impossible to weigh or measure the same fetus repeatedly during normal gestation, our knowledge is based on examination of infants born at various gestational ages. This is not necessarily representative of the normal state, but we have reason to believe that it comes reasonably close to it. According to these data, growth of the fetus follows the S-shaped curve characteristic of most growth processes, from its lower curvature into a period of straight-line growth which then continues through most of the remainder of intrauterine life (Fig. 2). These curves are misleading if they suggest slow growth during the early phases. From the data of Streeter, it can be demonstrated that during the third lunar month fetal weight increases thirteenfold, during the fourth month eightfold, during the fifth month threefold, and during the sixth month twofold.

Figure 2 gives one example of birth weight curves derived from a mixed population of a hospital in Baltimore (Gruenwald, 1966). Many others have recently become available. It has been mentioned that human growth follows the usual S-shaped curve when considered over its entire span. However, it is erroneous to consider the slowing of fetal growth, which begins shortly before term, as the true decelerating limb of the sigmoid curve. This deceleration is not due to a declining growth *potential*, since the neonate resumes more active growth after adjusting to extrauterine existence (McKeown and Record) (Fig. 3). The reasons for the apparent decline in fetal growth rate near term are still unknown.

If "normal growth" is defined as that occurring in the average fetus at a given gestational age, then empirical curves are appropriate and one may use them to judge whether a given fetus is keeping up with the expected average values. If, on the other hand, one is interested in optimal performance or perfect well-being, then these curves may not be appropriate. It has been suggested that the growth of postterm fetuses be judged by two different standards: one obtained in the usual manner from an actual population, and in addition an extrapolated

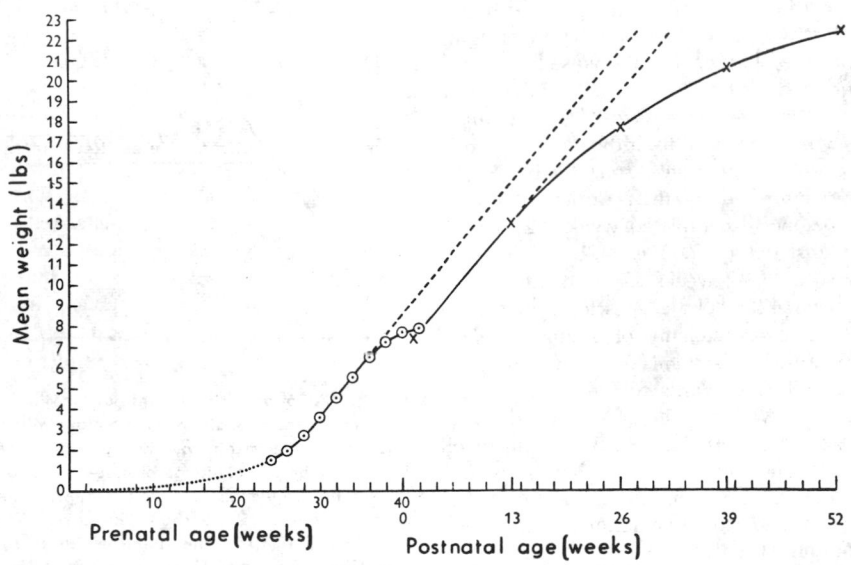

Fig. 3. Growth of the fetus and infant. The decline of fetal growth about term is not due to a decreasing growth potential since the more rapid rate is resumed after birth. (From McKeown and Record. *J. Endocr.,* 9:418, 1953.)

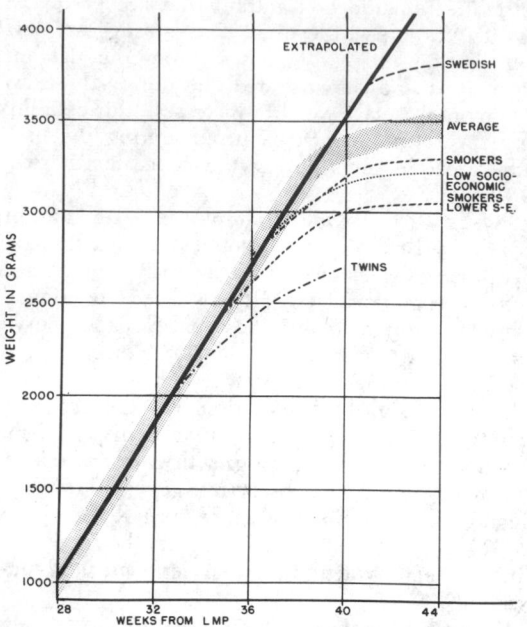

Fig. 4. Prenatal growth of several population groups. Depending on the time of onset of limitation of supply, fetal growth departs from the straight course at different times in gestation.

growth curve which continues at the same slope as between 28 and 38 weeks of gestation (Fig. 4).

Concern over recognition of abnormal intrauterine growth is reflected in terminology: in 1961 an expert committee of the World Health Organization realized that many infants are born small for reasons other than true prematurity, and suggested to supplant the old usage of the term *premature* by *infant of low birth weight* based solely on weight. The term *premature,* having been misused so long, is to be abandoned. The American Academy of Pediatrics found that the term *infant of low birth weight* is also being misused to indicate "small-for-date" infants, and has suggested that birth weight classifications be identified by their limits in grams. Gestational age below 38 completed weeks (266 days from the last menstrual period) is to be designated as preterm, from 38 to 42 weeks (267 to 294 days) as term, and above 42 weeks as postterm birth. In addition, the American Academy of Pediatrics suggested classifying infants as small, adequate, or large for gestational age by standards for the appropriate week of gestation. No one set of standards was recommended, and the 10th and 90th percentile of the data of Lubchenco et al. were shown as examples. Other workers have used ±2 standard deviations as the limit. In the final analysis, repeated clinical examinations (see section on Physical Examination) will provide the basis for clinical decision as to whether a particular patient has had significant intrauterine growth retardation, regardless of whether

his birth weight is just above or below an arbitrary limit.

OTHER MEASUREMENTS IN COMMON USE. The striking changes in body proportions which occur during embryonic and postnatal growth have been portrayed in most texts of embryology, and in some detail by Scammon in *Morris' Human Anatomy.* However, body proportions during the third trimester are, with few exceptions, fairly constant.

Length. It is not easy to obtain reliable measurements of total body length (crown-heel length); yet these are most frequently recorded, presumably because they are directly comparable to standing height measured in later life. The increase in body length from one month to the next is close to the error of measurement for one given month, even when special precautions are taken to obtain reliable data. It is, therefore, suggested that for evaluation of an infant at birth, body weight is more valuable and easier to use. A meaningful way of relating body weight to length is the Rohrer index (weight over third power of length). This is shown in Figure 5. Its rise up to 35 weeks, and a slower rate up to 39 weeks, suggests that the fetus grows stouter. At 39 to 41 weeks there is no change, and after that time the average fetus (only those within standard deviation of the mean for gestational age are included) gets thinner.

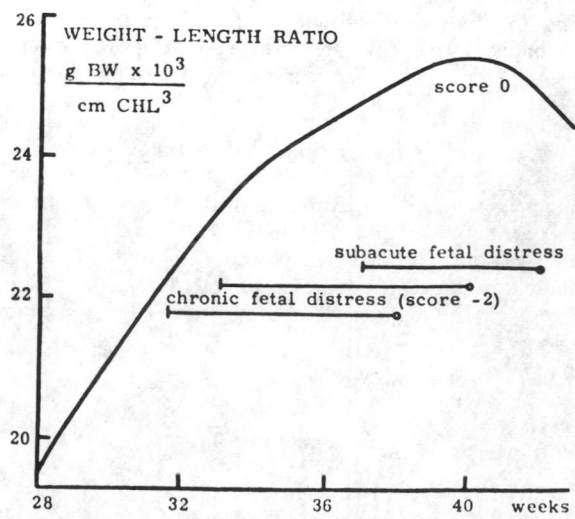

Fig. 5. Ratio of birth weight to the third power of crown-heel length for neonates with a weight within 1 standard deviation from the mean for the respective week of gestation. From data of the National Birthday Trust. Data for groups of fetuses in chronic distress, and a representative case of subacute fetal distress are shown by circles. The horizontal lines extend to the left to the points which these would occupy if gestational age were commensurate with the actual birth weights. (From Gruenwald. In Jonkis, S. H. P., et al., eds., *Nutricia Symposium: Aspects of Praematurity and Dysmaturity,* 1968. Courtesy of H. E. Stenfert Kroese N. V.)

TABLE 2. *Body Length and Head Circumference in Relation to Birth Weight**

In normally grown infants (N) and severely growth-retarded ones (R) with a birth weight below mean minus 2 standard deviations, all survivors.

Birth Weight (g)	Body Length N	Body Length R	Head Circumference N	Head Circumference R
1251-1500	39		21	
1501-1750	42	42	29	30
1751-2000	43	43	29	31
2001-2250	44	45	31	32
2251-2500	46	46	32	32
2501-2750	48		33	
2751-3000	49		33	
3001-3250	50		34	
3251-3500	51		35	
3501-3750	51		35	
3751-4000	52		35	

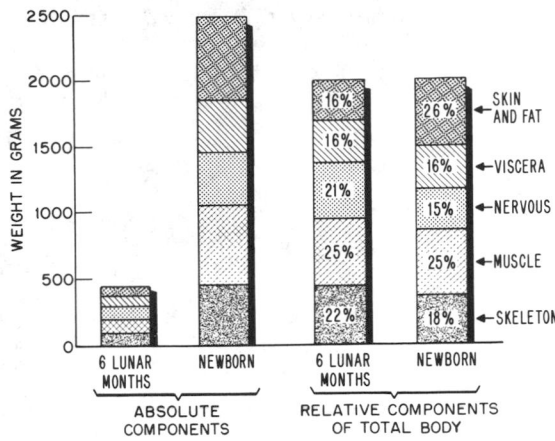

Fig. 6. Change in body composition during the second half of fetal life. (From Wilmer. *Proc. Soc. Exp. Biol. Med.,* 43:545, 1940.)

Head Circumference. In instances in which there is a question of brain abnormality, head measurement serves as a baseline which may be used to follow possible growth abnormalities of the brain and head through infancy. Data on head circumference in relation to birth weight have been obtained by several investigators, and most of these agree reasonably well. The relationship between head circumference, body length, and birth weight in normally grown infants and in infants with severe growth retardation is shown in Table 2.

Growth of Fetal Organs. Only a few data are available on the partition of the body into such components as skin, viscera, nervous tissue, muscle, and skeleton. This partition has been estimated by Wilmer on the basis of his own studies and others reported in the literature, and is demonstrated in the form of diagrams shown in Figure 6. Although the trends depicted here are probably valid, there is some question about the exact measurement, since details of the methods used to obtain this information

are lacking. The most conspicuous change during the third trimester is the beginning accumulation of adipose tissue (mostly subcutaneous).

Information concerning growth of the viscera of the human fetus is on a firm basis because these organs may readily be weighed at autopsy. As is also true for studies reported by Wilmer, all this information has the disadvantage of being derived from dead infants, who may not be representative of the normal state. In Gruenwald's data (1963) an attempt was made to circumvent part of the bias introduced by examining dead infants by including only those infants whose body weight was within one standard deviation of the mean for all births of the same gestational age (Tables 3, 4).

During most of the period in which viable infants are born, namely from 28 to 38 weeks of gestation, there are few striking changes in the relative weights of the viscera compared to each other. Beyond 38 weeks, and particularly past term, the trends differ somewhat and take a course resembling changes observed with moderate deprivation; the brain, for in-

TABLE 3. *Organ Weights (Mean and Standard Deviation) in Relation to Gestational Age*

Only newborn infants with a birth weight within one standard deviation from the mean for survivors were included.

Weeks from LMP	Heart	Lungs Combined	Spleen	Liver	Adrenals Combined	Kidneys Combined	Thymus	Brain
28	8.1 ± 2.1	27 ± 7	3.3 ± 1.9	49 ± 13	3.9 ± 1.5	10.9 ± 3.2	3.6 ± 1.5	150 ± 33
29-30	10.2 ± 3.3	34 ± 11	4.2 ± 1.9	60 ± 21	4.3 ± 1.7	14.7 ± 5.1	5.4 ± 2.4	189 ± 45
31-32	12.5 ± 3.1	39 ± 11	4.9 ± 2.0	72 ± 22	4.6 ± 2.0	16.4 ± 4.6	8.2 ± 3.3	234 ± 41
33-34	14.6 ± 2.9	47 ± 12	6.7 ± 2.5	86 ± 22	6.1 ± 2.4	18.3 ± 5.7	8.7 ± 3.5	275 ± 39
35-36	18.1 ± 4.2	58 ± 11	8.2 ± 3.4	108 ± 28	7.6 ± 3.0	22.3 ± 5.9	9.0 ± 3.9	325 ± 29
37-38	20.2 ± 4.9	63 ± 14	10.4 ± 3.6	127 ± 27	9.0 ± 3.0	24.8 ± 4.8	11.5 ± 4.8	367 ± 37
39-40	20.7 ± 4.7	59 ± 16	10.5 ± 3.8	142 ± 35	9.0 ± 2.5	25.9 ± 6.0	10.9 ± 3.7	400 ± 50
41-42	22.6 ± 5.8	62 ± 16	10.9 ± 4.0	146 ± 34	9.4 ± 3.2	26.0 ± 6.2	10.1 ± 3.7	425 ± 48
43-44	23.9 ± 3.4	60 ± 15	10.7 ± 3.7	146 ± 28	9.9 ± 3.3	27.8 ± 9.2	8.0 ± 3.7	433 ± 46

TABLE 4.   *Organ Weights (Mean and Standard Deviation) in Relation to Body Weight*

Only newborn infants with a birth weight within one standard deviation
from the mean for survivors were included.

Median Body Weight (g)	Heart	Lungs Combined	Spleen	Liver	Adrenals Combined	Kidneys Combined	Thymus	Brain
1,000	7.4 ± 1.6	29 ± 9	3.1 ± 1.2	40 ± 13	3.9 ± 1.9	11.8 ± 1.9	3.3 ± 1.5	150 ± 26
1,250	9.3 ± 2.3	32 ± 8	3.7 ± 1.9	53 ± 15	4.0 ± 1.4	13.2 ± 3.8	5.3 ± 2.4	173 ± 24
1,500	10.9 ± 2.7	32 ± 11	4.4 ± 1.9	64 ± 17	4.6 ± 1.8	14.8 ± 4.2	6.2 ± 2.4	202 ± 34
1,750	12.3 ± 3.2	43 ± 9	5.0 ± 2.0	73 ± 19	4.5 ± 1.9	15.6 ± 4.7	6.9 ± 2.9	234 ± 29
2,000	14.9 ± 3.1	45 ± 8	6.2 ± 2.1	84 ± 21	5.3 ± 2.0	19.0 ± 5.1	8.8 ± 3.4	259 ± 37
2,250	15.8 ± 2.7	51 ± 11	6.7 ± 2.6	89 ± 16	6.3 ± 1.6	19.0 ± 3.9	8.4 ± 3.2	290 ± 25
2,500	17.2 ± 1.9	55 ± 8	7.4 ± 2.3	105 ± 15	7.6 ± 2.6	21.4 ± 3.2	9.4 ± 4.3	330 ± 32
2,750	19.0 ± 2.5	60 ± 14	9.6 ± 3.1	112 ± 27	7.9 ± 2.4	23.6 ± 4.0	9.8 ± 3.1	355 ± 32
3,000	19.2 ± 4.3	57 ± 16	10.6 ± 4.7	133 ± 30	8.4 ± 2.7	24.0 ± 5.4	10.4 ± 4.2	379 ± 47
3,250	21.6 ± 4.9	61 ± 16	10.4 ± 3.5	140 ± 31	9.1 ± 2.9	27.6 ± 6.4	10.8 ± 4.6	398 ± 49
3,500	22.9 ± 5.7	64 ± 16	11.6 ± 4.3	151 ± 32	9.9 ± 3.3	28.1 ± 7.6	11.8 ± 4.8	413 ± 39
3,750	25.0 ± 3.6	68 ± 16	12.2 ± 3.8	176 ± 26	11.0 ± 3.7	30.1 ± 3.4	12.2 ± 3.5	426 ± 58

stance, continues to grow at nearly the same rate as before 38 weeks, whereas the liver is disproportionately small and the thymus even decreases in size (Gruenwald, 1964).

Variations and Abnormalities of Fetal Growth

Birth weight curves obtained by various investigators show marked differences early in the third trimester. These are due in part to small numbers of cases, in part to inconsistent policies of dealing with grossly discrepant cases—especially with weight grossly higher than expected, and partly to understated gestational age (most likely by 4 weeks; Gruenwald, 1966). Yet some of the large infants of low stated gestational age may be truly immature, which may account, in part, for their high mortality (Battaglia et al.).

Differences late in pregnancy are presumably indicative of true trends. They must be considered in several categories which differ not only in the degree of abnormality, but also in the manner in which they manifest themselves.

What may be called *group variation* seldom exceeds 300 g at term, an amount which is well within the range of individual variation and can be meaningful only in the statistical assessment of populations. In contrast, sporadic cases of *pathologic growth retardation* may result in a much greater weight deficit, up to half or more of the normal weight. Thirdly, *fetal wasting* without significant deficit of longitudinal growth may be recognized by certain bodily characteristics in the absence of a weight deficit characteristic of growth retardation.

VARIATION AMONG POPULATIONS. These variations become apparent during the last few weeks of intrauterine life at which time the functional reserve of the fetal supply line (mother and placenta) is decreasing; consequently, unfavorable circumstances manifest themselves more readily as pregnancy advances, as was discussed above under maternal factors. Ounsted and Ounsted have studied the association with maternal factors in a small but carefully analyzed sample.

PATHOLOGIC GROWTH RETARDATION. As has been mentioned, criteria of growth retardation have been set arbitrarily as either the mean minus 2 standard deviations or the 10th percentile, for the respective week of gestation. When information on the last menstrual period is absent or questionable, growth retardation may be suggested from the level of functional maturity or (at autopsy) histologic maturity, including the pattern of organ weights, and the development of cerebral convolutions. A weight deficit of sufficient magnitude to place a neonate below the 10th percentile cannot result from wasting alone. It must be due to chronic fetal distress of several weeks' duration, beginning before the time when normal panniculus adiposus forms. Thus, growth in weight and length slows simultaneously, and this explains the nearly normal external body proportions of neonates with severe retardation of growth.

Among sporadic cases of chronic fetal distress, several groups stand out. These include infants derived from pregnancies associated with hypertension, and twins (Gruenwald, 1968). In the majority of cases, however, no association with any known factors can be established. In some of these, some unknown factor, presumably maternal, is responsible for the repeated birth of small-for-dates infants to the same mother. As was mentioned, the small size of many malformed infants is presumably not due to deprivation.

In chronic deprivation, organ growth, in contrast to external measurements, shows characteristic trends which resemble those described in experimentally deprived animal fetuses. Most conspicuous is the proportionately slight effect on the brain,

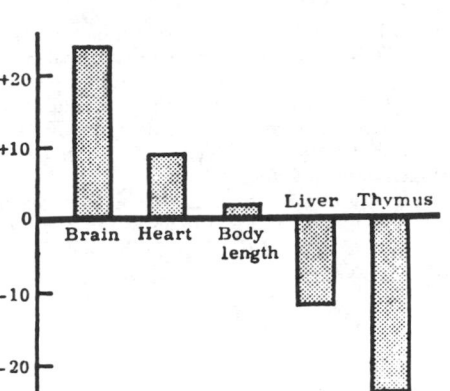

Fig. 7. Body length and organ weights of cases of chronic fetal distress (birth weight below mean minus 2 standard deviations for gestational age) expressed as percent of values for normally grown, preterm infants (within 1 standard deviation from the mean) of similar weight. (From Gruenwald. *In* Jonkis, S. H. P., et al., eds., *Nutricia Symposium: Aspects of Praematurity and Dysmaturity,* 1968. Courtesy of H. E. Stenfert Kroese N. V.)

which is small for gestational age but strikingly large for body weight. The effect on the thymus, on the other hand, is different: owing to involution in chronic or subacute fetal distress it is small even in relation to the reduced body weight (Gruenwald, 1963). Surprisingly, head circumference as usually measured does not reflect the relatively large size of the brain in chronic fetal distress: it is consistently, but only slightly, greater than in true premature infants of similar weight. These and other characteristic changes in chronic fetal distress are shown in Figure 7. Larroche and Haggi have also documented the relatively slight growth deficit of the brain in small-for-date infants.

Fetal Wasting. If a fetus has developed normally, formed a panniculus adiposus, and then suffered deprivation for a few days or perhaps a week or two (subacute fetal distress), it is born wasted, with a wrinkled skin: the well known "long, thin" baby. This appearance occurs more frequently and conspicuously the longer subacute fetal distress has continued after a nearly complete period of growth, and is, therefore, seen most prominently in prolonged pregnancy. Figure 5 shows one of the possible relationships between weight and length in chronic and in subacute fetal distress. The points representing two groups of cases of chronic distress fall close to normal when transposed where they would be if their gestational age were commensurate with their weight. This confirms a relationship of weight and length close to that of normally grown fetuses of similar weight. In contrast, a representative case of subacute distress (a long, thin baby born near term) remains far from normal when similarly treated, showing the disturbed ratio of weight to length.

Comment

It has become clear in recent years that fetal growth, approaching that shown in the extrapolated curve in Figure 4, is indicative of favorable circumstances of living. To that extent, and not because bigger babies are necessarily better, this is a desirable trend. Observed variations in fetal growth, presumably influenced by socioeconomic factors, suggest improving conditions in many parts of the world.

Severe, pathologic growth retardation is associated with handicaps of its own, distinct from those of the other leading cause of low birth weight, namely, preterm birth. Present-day knowledge of late sequelae in survivors is fragmentary because until recently all infants of low birth weight were lumped in studies of cerebral damage. Twins, and particularly those weighing considerably less than their partners, form a well defined group with severe fetal deprivation, and their intellectual performance is significantly impaired (Babson et al.; Holley and Churchill). This emphasizes the need to study infants of low birth weight with regard to the cause of their small size at birth. Also, the effect of such superimposed neonatal factors as asphyxia and hyperbilirubinemia (particularly in preterm infants) and hypoglycemia (in small-for-date ones) needs to be separated from damage already present at birth.

REFERENCES

Adamsons, K. ed. Diagnosis and Treatment of Fetal Disorders. New York, Springer-Verlag, 1968.

Aherne, W., and Dunnill, M. S. Quantitative aspects of placental structure. J. Path. Bact., 91:123, 1966.

Altman, P. L., and Dittmer, D. S., eds. Growth Including Reproduction and Morphological Development. Washington, D.C., Fed. Amer. Soc. Exp. Biol., 1962.

American Academy of Pediatrics. Committee on Fetus and Newborn. Nomenclature for duration of gestation, birth weight and intra-uterine growth. Pediatrics, 39:935, 1967.

Babson, S. G., Kangas, J., Young, N., and Bramhall, J. L. Growth and development of twins of dissimilar size at birth. Pediatrics, 33:327, 1964.

Bakwin, H. The secular change in growth and development. Acta Paediat. Scand., 53:79, 1964.

Battaglia, F. C., Frazier, T. M., and Hellegers, A. E. Birth weight, gestational age, and pregnancy outcome, with special reference to high birth weight-low gestational age infant. Pediatrics, 37:417, 1966.

Butler, N. R., and Bonham, D. G., eds. Perinatal Mortality. Edinburgh and London, Livingstone, 1963.

Churchill, J. A. Summary of maternal factors affecting the offspring-theory of intrauterine impoverishment. *In* Perinatal Factors Affecting Human Development. Washington, D.C., 1969. Pan American Health Organization.

Dawes, G. S. Foetal and Neonatal Physiology. Chicago, Year Book Medical Publishers, 1968.

Dawkins, M., and MacGregor, B., eds. Gestational age, size and maturity. Clin. Develop. Med., 19, 1965.

DeHaan, R. L., and Ursprung, H., eds. Organogenesis. New York, Holt, Rinehart and Winston, 1965.

Gruenwald, P. Chronic fetal distress and placental insufficiency. Biol. Neonat., 5:215, 1963.

——— The fetus in prolonged pregnancy. Amer. J. Obstet. Gynec., 89:50, 1964.

——— Growth of the human fetus. I. Normal growth and its variation. Amer. J. Obstet. Gynec., 94:1112, 1966.

——— Growth of the human foetus. Advances Reprod. Physiol., 2:279, 1967.

——— Fetal growth as an indicator of socioeconomic change. Pub. Hlth. Rep. 83:867, 1968.

——— Growth pattern of the normal and the deprived fetus. In Jonkis, S. H. P., Visser, H. K. A., and Trodsta, J. A., eds., Nutricia Symposium: Aspects of Praematurity and Dysmaturity. Neiden, The Netherlands, H. E. Stengert Kroese, N.V., 1968.

——— Growth and maturation of the foetus and its relationship to perinatal mortality. In Butler, N. R., and Alberman, E. D., eds., Perinatal Problems. Edinburgh and London, Livingstone, 1969.

Holley, W. L., and Churchill, J. A. Physiological and mental deficits of twinning. In Perinatal Factors Affecting Human Development. Washington, D.C., Pan American Health Organization, 1969.

Horn, R., Grävinghoff, C., and Wolf, H. Ergebnisse psychologischer Nachuntersuchungen von ehemals frühgeborenen und ehemals hypotrophen Neugeborenen. Monatschr. Kinderheilk., 117:442, 1969.

Jelliffe, E. F. P. Low birth-weight and malarial infection of the placenta. Bull. Wld. Hlth. Org., 38:69, 1968.

Larroche, J.-C., and Haggai, E. Maturation cérébrale et hypodeveloppement pondéral du nouveau-né. J. Neurol Sci., 5:39, 1967.

Lubchenco, L. O., Hansman, C., Dressler, M., and Boyd, E. Intrauterine growth as estimated from liveborn birthweight data at 24 to 42 weeks of gestation. Pediatrics, 32:793, 1963.

McDonald, A. Retarded foetal growth. Clin. Develop. Med., 19:14, 1965.

McKeown, T., and Record, R. G. The influence of placental size on foetal growth in man, with special reference to multiple pregnancy. J. Endocr., 9:418, 1953.

Naeye, R. L., and Blanc, W. Pathogenesis of congenital rubella. J.A.M.A., 194:1277, 1965.

——— and Kelly, J. A. Judgment of fetal age: III. The pathologist's evaluation. Ped. Clin. North Amer., 13:849, 1966.

Ounsted, M., and Ounsted, C. Maternal regulation of intrauterine growth. Nature, 212:995, 1966.

Pan American Health Organization. Perinatal Factors Affecting Human Development. Washington, D.C., 1969. Pan American Health Organization.

Parmelee, A. H., Jr., and Schulte, F. J. Developmental testing of pre-term and small-for-date infants. Pediatrics, 45:21, 1970.

Scammon, R. E. Developmental anatomy. In Morris' Human Anatomy, 11th ed. New York and Toronto, Blakiston, 1953.

Schutt, W. Foetal factors in intrauterine growth retardation. Clin. Develop. Med., 19:1, 1965.

Streeter, G. L. Weight, sitting height, head size, foot length, and menstrual age of the human embryo. Contrib. Embryol., 11:143, 1920.

Waddington, C. H. Principles of Embryology. New York, Macmillan, 1956.

Willier, B. H., Weiss, P. A., and Hamburger, V. Analysis of Development. Philadelphia and London, Saunders, 1955.

Wilmer, H. A. Changes in structural components of human body from six lunar months to maturity. Proc. Soc. Exp. Biol. Med., 43:545, 1940.

Winick, M. Cellular growth of the placenta as an indicator of abnormal growth. In Adamsons, K., ed. Diagnosis and Treatment of Fetal Disorders. New York, Springer-Verlag, 1968.

World Health Organization. Expert Committee on Maternal and Child Health. Public health aspects of low birth weight. Wld. Hlth. Org. Tech. Rep. Ser., 217:1, 1961.

2.4

CHEMICAL COMPOSITION

WILLIAM B. WEIL, JR. and
THOMAS A. HELMRATH

The chemical composition of the intact human body has defied exact description. There are now many methods for indirect determination of the total body composition of various substances during life. These determinations, however, are all approximations calculated from certain basic assumptions concerning the composition of the fat-free body, or lean body mass. These indirect methods have shown large variations among individual subjects.

General Body Composition

The traditional concept of body composition is illustrated in Figure 8, in which the major change during intrauterine life is seen as an absolute increase in size, changes in compositional makeup being less obvious in such a schema. Presenting the same data in the manner illustrated in Figure 9, expressed as a percent of body weight, brings out more clearly the considerable change in body composition during intrauterine life, the greatest change being the increase in body fat and the relative decrease in body water.

FAT.   As understanding of the biologic variation in separate components of the body increased, it became recognized that body fat could increase or decrease without producing marked alteration in the relationship between other constituents of the body. This concept led to the method of representation shown in Figure 10. The quantity of fat present in the body was considered much as a fifth appendage, and was thought to have limited physiologic significance. Only in recent years has it been appreciated that the quantity of fat as well as its fatty acid composition may have great importance in the ultimate

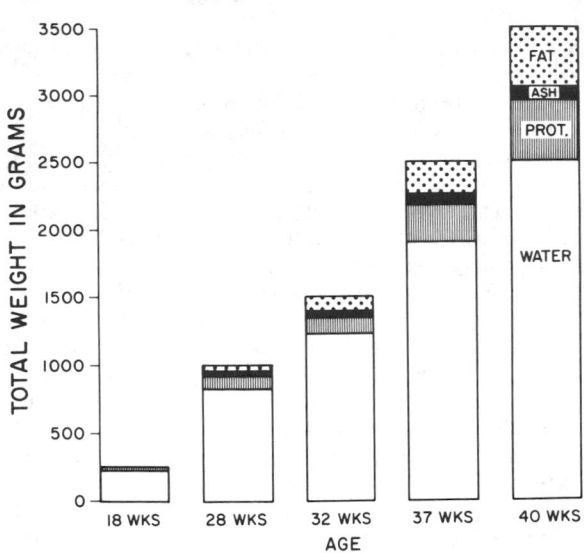

Fig. 8. Composition of fetus at various ages expressed in absolute values.

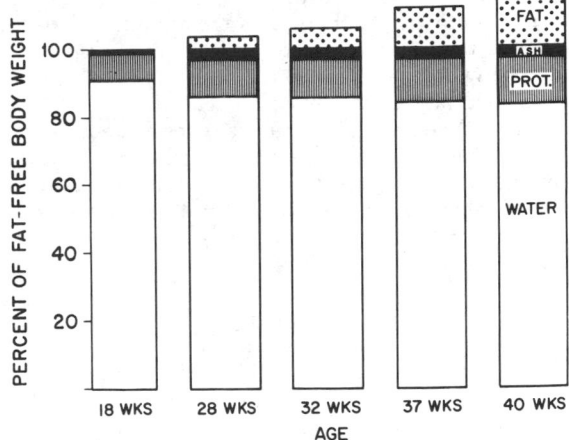

Fig. 10. Composition of fetus at various ages with values expressed as percent of fat-free body weight.

fate of the individual. Moreover, there is evidence that metabolism of adipose tissue in the neonate may be of particular importance in thermogenesis (p. 97). In Figure 10 the basic unit of composition is a kilogram of fat-free body, alternately termed a kilogram of "lean body mass." The majority of investigations in recent years have been concerned with variations in lean body mass which either occur developmentally or which can be produced by modification of the environment.

WATER. Considering the chemical development of the lean body element of the fetus, there is still a gradual increase in the proportions of protein and ash. Although the proportion of total ash increases with fetal age, more detailed analysis indicates that the sodium and chloride contents are decreasing on

a percentage basis. From this observation it has been assumed that the relative decrease in water content is primarily a reduction in the extracellular fluid. From the increasing protein content, it has also been assumed that there is a relative increase in the intracellular fluid compartment.

It has been the impression of physicians that dehydrating processes have more serious implications for premature infants than for full-term ones. If this were true, the mechanism must result either from a greater rate of expenditure of water or a smaller reservoir or insufficient compensatory mechanisms.

Thus, the smaller the premature infant, the greater the percentage of total water in the body and also the greater the relative size of the extracellular fluid volume in comparison to the intracellular. This difference in body composition alone should allow the premature infant to withstand a specific volume deficit (dehydration) more effectively than the full-term infant, especially since most dehydrating processes affect the extracellular volume first. In addition, available data suggest that the prematurely born infant has a *lower* metabolic rate per unit of body weight than the full-term infant. On the basis of general physiologic information, the rate of water expenditure or loss is directly related to metabolic rate. Therefore, one must conclude from the data on the body water pool size and metabolic rate that the premature infant should have less difficulty than the full-term neonate with those processes producing dehydration.

However, if one extends these concepts further to the comparison between infants and adults, one must keep in mind that although the infant has 10 percent greater water content per unit of weight than an adult, the infant also has a metabolic rate per unit of weight that is almost twice that of the adult. Therefore, the rate of water expenditure will more than wipe out the infant's slight advantage in having

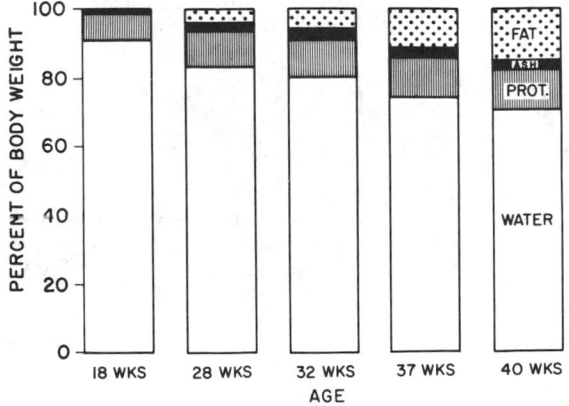

Fig. 9. Composition of fetus at various ages with values expressed as percent of body weight.

a greater water reservoir, and the infant will be much more sensitive to dehydrating events than the adult. Returning to the premature infant, it is conceivable that the premature could have a disproportion between the rate of water loss and metabolic rate, e.g., larger stool volumes per unit of weight than predicted from metabolic considerations, but there is no data to substantiate such a hypothesis. Another possibility is that the premature infant is less efficient in compensating for fluid losses, and thus becomes symptomatic with a smaller fluid volume deficit. Again, there are no data available to confirm or deny this hypothesis. Finally, there is also the subjective problem that the physician faces when working with the small absolute volumes of fluid involved: a 150 ml deficit of water in a 1,500 g infant is comparable to a 350 ml deficit in a 3,500 g neonate. For this reason, one can tolerate much smaller absolute errors in recording fluid intake and output in the very small newborn infant.

GLYCOGEN. Human fetal liver glycogen concentrations of approximately 10 to 20 mg/g of tissue are found at midgestation, and then rapidly increase over the last 4 weeks of the pregnancy to levels of 40 to 60 mg/g of tissue. The prenatal accumulation and postnatal decrease in liver glycogen are depicted in Figure 11.

Studies of the fetal pituitary-adrenal axis have revealed the necessity of an intact system for liver glycogen to accumulate. The corticosteroids induce the necessary enzymes for glycogen deposition. The role of insulin in this deposition is not as clear, although exogenous insulin administered to the rat fetus increased glycogen content in the liver.

Following birth, liver glycogen concentrations decrease rapidly in infants of all gestational ages, indicating that the birth process and subsequent events are responsible rather than a gestational-dependent process. All evidence to date would suggest that the hydrolysis of liver glycogen is essential for stabilization of the neonate's blood glucose at levels which allow continued cerebral activity. In a term fetus, there is enough liver glycogen present to stabilize the blood sugar for 18 to 24 hours, as long as moderate to severe cold stress is prevented. A recent study in term infants placed in a neutral thermal environment immediately after birth revealed that the plasma glucose concentration remained above 70 mg/100 ml over the first 24 hours, even with fasting. The limitations on the ability of the premature infant to stabilize his blood sugar from liver glycogen storage is obvious when the liver content at 30 to 32 weeks is compared to that of 40 weeks.

Cardiac and skeletal muscle glycogen accumulation and subsequent hydrolysis with birth is also depicted in Figure 11. Glycogen in muscle is unavailable directly as blood glucose, but is hydrolyzed via anaerobic glycolysis, with subsequent release of lactic acid. Thus increased physical activity of the newborn would, as an end product, provide more substrate for glucose formation and increase production of heat through the activities of the relatively inefficient muscular system.

IRON. The fetal accumulation of iron has been shown by Widdowson and Spray to follow a straight-line relationship with fetal weight. When the data were expressed on a fat-free body weight basis, the heavier and older infant was found to have more iron per unit weight than the smaller fetus. It is recognized that the iron deficiency anemia in premature infants has a multiple etiology, but it is apparent that one factor is their decreased supply of body iron.

Rate of Change in Composition

The changes in composition depicted in Figure 10 are most rapid in the early part of pregnancy and

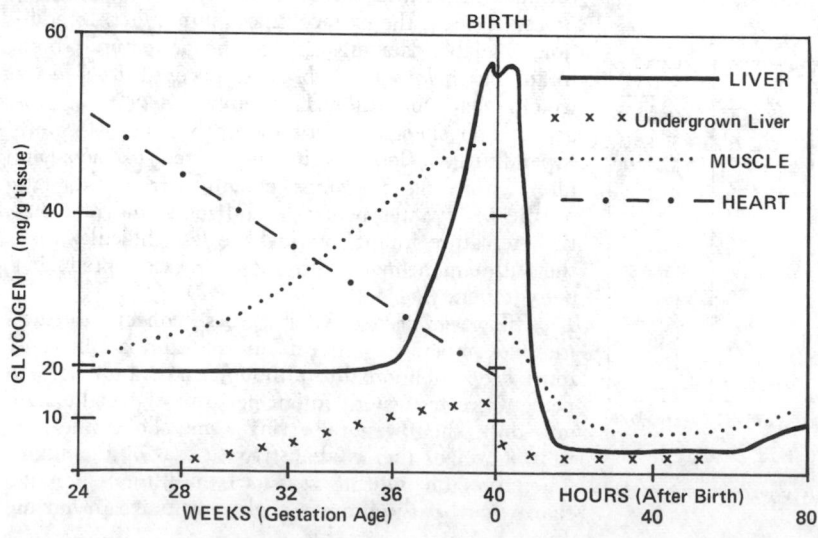

Fig. 11. Glycogen accumulation and hydrolysis in relationship to gestation and time of birth. (Redrawn from data of Shelley.)

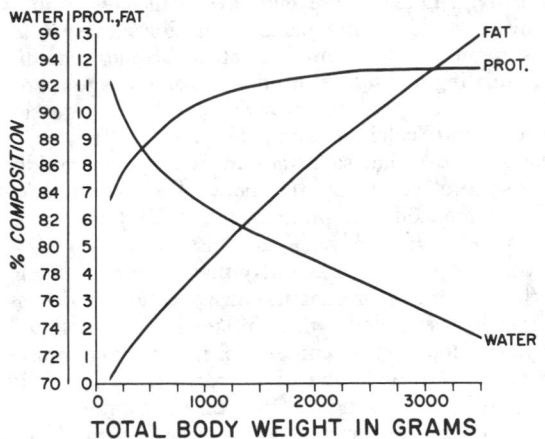

Fig. 12. Composition of fetus with values expressed as percent of total weight.

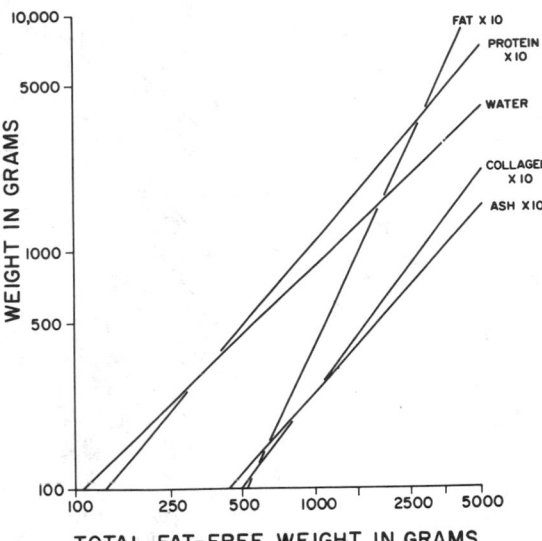

Fig. 13. Total weight of the various components of body composition with total fat-free weight expressed as $Y = bX^k$: an allometric relationship.

become less pronounced as pregnancy approaches term. This may also be illustrated by a series of hyperbolic curves, as shown in Figure 12. The tendency of the slope to become flattened with time was interpreted in the past as indicating that chemical composition has stabilized at some point. The term "chemical maturity" was coined to indicate the composition of the body once this stable condition was attained. A variety of interpretations were given to the fact that different species of animals reached "chemical maturity" at different periods after conception. It was also concluded that "chemical maturity" occurred at a point in *time* in the growth process rather than at some level of weight or size. In either case, this term is no longer applicable for describing the composition of an organism until all growth has ceased.

In the 1930's, a concept of relative growth was introduced by J. F. Huxley and G. Teissier. This concept, later termed "allometry," has come to refer to the straight-line relationships between the logarithmic expressions of any two substances involved in growing organisms.* These relationships may be expressed in terms of length, weight, or volume. Characteristically, allometry indicates that the rela-

* These relationships can be expressed by several formulas:
 1. $Y = bX^k$ where Y is the amount of one substance present at some time, b is a constant, X is the amount of the second substance present at this time, and the exponent k is a constant.
 2. $\log Y = \log b + k \log X$ is another way of expressing the same relationship. In this form the equation can readily be seen to be one dsecribing a straight-line relationship between the logarithms of two variables, and k represents the slope of the line.
 3. $k = \dfrac{(dy/y)}{(dx/x)}$ is the same relationship expressed in differential form. From this equation, it can be appreciated that although the rate of change of either variable need not be constant, the ratio of the rates of change is.

tionship between two increasing quantities will be linear when each of the measurements is expressed logarithmically. Inherent in this concept is the fact that growth is a multiplicative process and that the increase in a quantity is related to the amount of the quantity present at the time the increase is taking place.

Early studies on allometric relationships in growth were confined primarily to various types of larvae and other lower forms. However, in 1955, this concept was applied to the increase in water, sodium, potassium, and chloride content in the human fetus. By combining the known analytical data on the chemical composition of the fetus, one can demonstrate, as shown in Figures 13 and 14, that there is an allometric relationship between each of the major chemical components and the total weight of the human fetus. Total fat-free wet weight of the fetus is shown on the abscissa, and weights of the various components are given on the ordinate. In Figure 13, the rapid rate of increase in body fat in relationship to the increase in components of fat-free weight is dramatically illustrated. In addition, the changing relationship between water and protein content is also apparent. Figure 14 illustrates that the same allometric relationships hold true for the major inorganic elements in the body.

In order to examine the relationship between the slopes or k values for the major components of the body, Figure 15 was drawn so that the term b was constant for all substances, the difference in the lines being due then to their different k values. If a substance had a k value of 1, shown as a dashed line, it would indicate that its rate of increase is the same as the simultaneous rate of increase in the

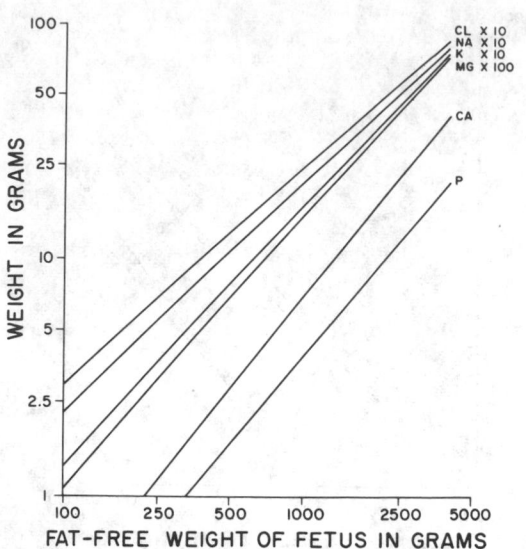

Fig. 14. Weight of inorganic components of fetus and total fat-free weight expressed as $Y = bX^k$: an allometric relationship.

fat-free weight. None of the substances in these analyses has such a slope; the substances group themselves into two categories: those with k values greater than 1, which are substances increasing at a rate more rapid than the fat-free weight of the individual; and those with a k value less than 1, which are increasing at a rate less than that for the total fat-free weight of the individual. It follows that, with increasing body size, substances with k values

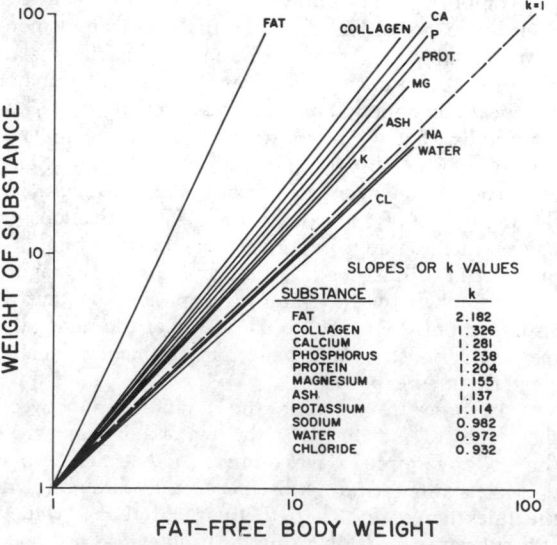

Fig. 15. Relative values for k in $Y = bX^k$. No units of weight are appropriate since the lines have been given a common origin for purposes of demonstrating the relative values of k.

greater than 1 constitute a greater percentage of the body, whereas those with a k value less than 1 constitute a decreasing percentage. From these relationships it can be seen that fat is the most rapidly accumulating substance in the fetus. Collagen protein, the basic matrix on which bone salts are deposited, and calcium and phosphorus, the major ions in these bone salts, are the next most rapidly increasing elements of the body. Protein includes both the noncollagen protein of cells and the collagen protein. If one were to illustrate a curve for noncollagen protein, it is likely that it would tend to overlap the line for magnesium, a cation which is intimately associated with intracellular solids. Finally, the total water content of the body decreases proportionately with age. This decrease is primarily extracellular, as indicated by the comparable decrease in sodium and chloride ions. Intracellular water tends to remain constant or increase slightly, as indicated by the relative increase in the content of potassium, the major cation of intracellular water.

The relationships shown in Figures 13 and 14 encompass the majority of analyses available in the literature. From these expressions one can derive the composition of a fetus of any given weight. Examples of such calculations are given in Table 5.

TABLE 5. *Average Composition for Fetuses of Varying Size*

Weight (g)	250	500	1000	1500	2500	3500
Age (weeks)	18	22	28	32	37	40
Grams						
Fat	2	10	40	90	240	450
Fat-free	248	490	960	1410	2260	3050
Water	223	435	830	1210	1915	2550
Protein	20	45	105	165	285	410
Ash	5	10	25	35	60	90
Millimoles						
Na	24	47	90	131	207	278
Cl	19	37	68	96	150	197
K	9	20	42	64	108	151
Mg	1	3	6	10	16	23
Ca	29	70	166	272	500	736
P	23	53	121	194	332	500
Percent Total Weight						
Fat	1	2	4	6	10	13
Water	89	87	83	81	77	73
Protein	8	9	10	11	11	12
Ash	2	2	3	2	2	3
Percent Fat-Free Wet Weight						
Water	90	89	86	86	84	84
Protein	8	9	11	12	13	13
Ash	2	2	3	2	3	3
Millimoles per Kilogram (Fat-Free)						
Na	96	96	94	93	92	91
Cl	77	76	71	68	66	65
K	36	41	44	45	48	50
Mg	4	6	6	7	7	8
Ca	118	143	173	193	221	241
P	93	108	126	138	147	164

Several other concepts are made clear by these allometric relationships. First, the fat-free composition of the body is primarily dependent on the size of the body rather than its age. Furthermore, there is an obvious tendency for the composition of the body to follow a specific pattern of development. This tendency has been termed "compositional homeostasis," and such a term seems justified from other experimental work. Extreme nutritional modification in postnatal growth results in marked decrease in total size; the resultant alteration in body composition is determined almost entirely by this change in size. The major exception to this size- or weight-dependent determinant of body composition in such experiments occurs in the connective tissue elements, primarily the collagen and ash of bone.

CLINICAL IMPLICATIONS. During intrauterine existence, there does not ordinarily appear to be sufficient variation in the human fetus' level of nutrition to result in any detectable disturbance in compositional homeostasis for protein, water, and ash. The marked growth alterations produced in the offspring of women with diabetes result only in an increase in fat content which is out of proportion to the fat-free weight, and a small decrease in the extracellular components, sodium and chloride. The relationship between water, protein, and ash, however, remains what one would predict from the fat-free weight of the total body.

The fact that the fat-free composition of the body of the fetus is apparently not altered by certain nutritional aberrations does not imply that total size or fat content may not be markedly affected. Experimental studies in rabbits suggest that chronic reduction in nutrition to the fetus may result in an overall limitation in growth. Although there are insufficient data to be certain, it would be reasonable to suspect that the actual composition of such a fetus might be appropriate to its size rather than its age. However, the distribution of substances in organs may be grossly altered in a growth-retarded fetus as compared with a more immature individual of comparable total size. Undernutrition occurring after the 28th week of gestation might result in reduced fat content but might not affect the relationship of the other chemical moieties.

Energy Expenditure in Relation to Intrauterine Growth

The oxygen and glucose requirements of sustained fetal growth are not known. There have been many difficulties in measuring the oxygen consumption of the fetus, separate from other products of conception and the uterus (see section on fetal physiology). A study of uterine arteriovenous oxygen differences at term shows that approximately 22 to 34 ml/minute of oxygen are taken up by the uterus. The oxygen consumption of the placenta has been found to be about 8 ml/minute, leaving the fetus at term with approximately 20 ml/minute of oxygen for its needs.

To obtain in a general way the range of possible fetal oxygen consumptions, we have analyzed the O_2 consumption data from newborn infants of gestational ages ranging from 27 to 41 weeks. The infants were stated to be in a neutral thermal state and not in distress. The mean postpartum age of the group was two days. The oxygen consumptions of this group may differ to some extent from the intrauterine state because of activity, cold exposure, and a necessity for respiratory activity. The oxygen data are plotted against the infants' calculated fat-free body weight on a logarithmic scale in Figure 16. From this graph, we can derive a k value for the slope of the derived line and compare it to the k values obtained for water, protein, and minerals in the growing fetus. The k value for this relationship is 1.37, which is similar to that of protein and collagen (see Fig. 15). This would suggest that the increasing oxygen consumed by the growing fetus is proportional to the enlarging protein mass of the fetus. At any point in time, then, for the lean body mass to continue to grow, the oxygen supply must also continue to increase. If the placenta's ability to transfer oxygen is compromised, but not to the extent of acute hypoxia, then alterations of fetal weight and composition would logically result.

Examination again of Figure 12 shows the rapid accumulation of body fat from 32 to 40 weeks, while the changes in protein content are more gradual. If then at 36 weeks, the oxygen and glucose supply of the fetus were only sufficient to meet basal needs, the most obvious effect would be seen in the segment normally showing the greatest change, that is fat. An infant delivered at term, who had experienced 4 weeks of such marginal nutrition, would be classified as demonstrating intrauterine malnutrition when his physical measurements were plotted on

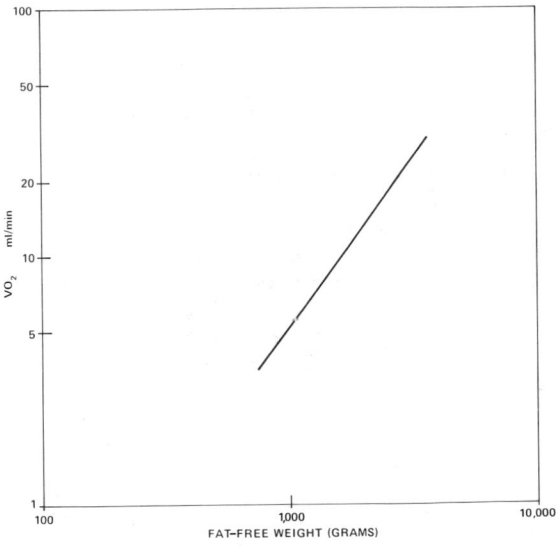

Fig. 16. Relationship of oxygen consumption to fat-free body weight on logarithmic scale.

intrauterine growth grids. His total lean body mass, though, might not be appreciably lower than that of a normal term infant, and consequently, his oxygen consumption should be similar to that found in a term infant. While there is some conflict in the literature on this point, some investigators have shown that when the oxygen consumption data on undergrown infants is compared to similar weight infants, a "hypermetabolic state" is present. However, when the data are compared to that of infants of the same gestational age (having the same lean body mass), the infants are no longer hypermetabolic but are eumetabolic. A similar extension from current data can be made for the frequent occurrence of hypoglycemia in idiopathic undergrown or intrauterine-malnourished infants. With a normal size lean body mass, and decreased substrate stores, as seen in Figure 11, current nursery management would stimulate the rapid consumption of available glycogen stores, and thus the infant would be unable to stabilize the blood glucose level within an acceptable range.

It must be emphasized that the relationships defined in these figures apply only to intrauterine growth. There are insufficient data on man to define these relationships for the period of extrauterine growth.

Summary

In summary, the chemical composition of the fetus is continually changing, and these changes occur in a predictable and regular fashion. Chemical maturity does not appear to be reached at any time during the growth process and has little meaning when composition is considered in the context of allometric relationships. The major component of the body by weight is water, which declines proportionately throughout pregnancy. This relative reduction is primarily in the extracellular, rather than the intracellular, water. Other significant changes which occur during gestation include: a more rapid increase in the cellular constituents than in total weight; an increase in the skeletal elements which is more rapid than that for the soft tissue structures; and a still more rapid increase in body fat, liver, and skeletal muscle glycogen, which becomes quantitatively significant only in the final trimester of pregnancy. A derived relationship between oxygen consumption and body consumption has been described with particular reference to the undergrown infant.

REFERENCES

Battaglia, F. C. Some theoretical aspects of placental metabolism. J. Pediat., 62:926, 1963.
Fee, B. A., and Weil, W. B., Jr. Body composition of infants of diabetic mothers by direct analysis. Ann. N.Y. Acad. Sci., 110:869, 1963.
Forbes, G. B. Inorganic chemical heterogony in man and animals. Growth, 19:75, 1955.
Huxley, Julian S. Problems in Relative Growth. New York, The Dial Press, 1932.
Jackson, C. M. On the prenatal growth of the human body and the relative growth of the various organs and parts. Amer. J. Anat., 9:119, 1909.
Miller, I., and Weil, W. B., Jr. Some problems in expressing and comparing body composition determined by direct analysis. Ann. N.Y. Acad. Sci., 110:153, 1963.
Moulton, C. R. Age and chemical development in mammals. J. Biol. Chem., 57:79, 1923.
Needham, J. Biochemistry and Morphogenesis. University Press, 1950.
Reeve, E. C. R., and Huxley, Julian S. Some problems in the study of allometric growth. In Clark, W. E. LeGros, and Medawar, P. B. eds., Essays on Growth and Form, Oxford, Clarendon Press, 1945.
Shelley, H. J. Glycogen reserves and their changes at birth and in anoxia. Brit. Med. Bull., 17:137, 1961.
——— and Leligan, G. A. Neonatal hypoglycemia. Brit. Med. Bull., 22:34, 1966.
Sinclair, J. C., Scopes, J. W., and Silverman, W. A. Metabolic reference standards for the neonate. Pediatrics, 39:724, 1967.
——— Intrauterine growth in active tissue mass of human fetus with particular reference to the undergrown baby. Pediatrics, 38:48, 1966.
Teissier, G. La relation d'allometri, sa signification statistique et biologique. Biometrics, 4:14, 1948.
Weil, W. B., Jr., and Wallace, W. M. The effect of variable food intakes on growth and body composition. Ann. N.Y. Acad. Sci., 110:358, 1963.
Widdowson, E. M., and Spray, C. M. Chemical development in utero. Arch. Dis. Child., 26:205, 1951.

2.5
BIOCHEMISTRY

CLAUDE A. VILLEE

Enzymatic Development—
Control Processes

The nature of the biochemical mechanisms controlling the development of a specific enzyme in a specific tissue of the fetus at some definite time in development is one of the most challenging questions of present-day biology. Advances in biochemical genetics have provided a reasonable hypothesis as to the mechanism by which biologic information is transferred from one generation of cells to the next. It has also provided an explanation as to how the biologic information in the genes may be transcribed in each cell to produce its constituent proteins. However, it is not yet possible, within the framework of this hypothesis, to explain how a gene may determine the quantity of an enzyme to be produced, or the time in development at which the enzyme will appear, or how certain cells in the tissues of a multicellular organism may have a particular enzyme or protein, whereas other cells of the same organism do not. The mitotic process ensures the exact distribution of genes to the daughter cells so that each cell of an organism has exactly the same pattern of genes as every other cell. Consequently the differences in enzymes and other proteins in different cells must arise by differences in the activity of the same set of genes operating in different cells. Thus the riddle of cellular differentiation can now be stated in somewhat more precise terms than previously, but it still remains unsolved.

The present-day central dogma of biology states that each gene has a specific sequence of deoxyribonucleotides which is different from that of every other gene. Each gene has two primary functions: to undergo replication so that one of the two replicates may be transmitted to each daughter cell, and to undergo one or more transcriptions so that the genic information becomes available to direct the synthesis of a specific protein within the cell. A considerable body of experimental evidence supports the hypothesis that this transcription involves the formation of messenger RNA with information coded in a particular sequence of purine and pyrimidine ribonucleotides. Messenger RNA, synthesized enzymatically in the nucleus in close association with the DNA, has a ratio of purines and pyrimidines which is similar to that of DNA. The specific sequence of the ribonucleotides in messenger RNA is determined in some way by the specific sequence of deoxyribonucleotides in the genic DNA. The exact mechanism of the transcription process is not yet completely clear. The messenger RNA formed by this process in the nucleus passes through the nuclear membrane to the ribosomes in the cytoplasm. In the cells of most higher organisms, the ribosomes are attached to the membranes of the endoplasmic reticulum. The messenger RNA combines with the ribosomal RNA and provides a template for the synthesis on the ribosome of a specific protein. The sequence of amino acids in the peptide chain which dictates the molecular configuration of the protein and its enzymatic or other properties is determined by the sequence of nucleotides in the messenger RNA, which in turn is determined by the sequence of deoxyribonucleotides in the DNA. The gene is a linear polynucleotide molecule and a protein is a linear polypeptide, a linear sequence of amino acids. The essence of the genetic code is that the sequence of the amino acids in the peptide chain is dictated by the order of the corresponding nucleotide bases in one of the two polynucleotide chains of the DNA molecule. Thus the DNA molecule and the resulting polypeptide chain are said to be colinear.

The synthesis of a protein begins with the activation of the amino acids by an enzyme which catalyzes the reaction of the amino acid with ATP to form an amino acid adenylate. This reacts in turn with a specific transfer RNA to form an amino acid–transfer RNA complex. Each kind of amino acid is activated and transferred by a specific enzyme to a specific kind of transfer RNA. There is at least one kind of transfer RNA specific for each kind of amino acid. For some amino acids there are four or six different transfer RNA's. The transfer RNA's are comparatively small molecules made up of a chain of some 70 ribonucleotides folded in a cloverleaf pattern. The three terminal nucleotides at the end to which the amino acid is attached are identical in all of the kinds of transfer RNA that have been analyzed to date. There is a specific sequence of three nucleotides at some other point in the transfer RNA which serves as a code, called an anticodon, to determine where that amino acid–transfer RNA molecule will fit onto the complementary triplet of nucleotides in the messenger RNA, called a codon. Thus this specific pairing of complementary nucleotides, A-U (adenylic-uridylic) and G-C (guanylic-cytidylic), in codon and anticodon lines up the appropriate amino acids in a specific order on the template so that protein synthesis may proceed.

Experiments over the past decade have shown that the genetic code in DNA and in messenger RNA is a triplet code—that is, a sequence of three nucleotides in the DNA or messenger RNA determines a single amino acid. The codons, composed of three nucleotides which specify a given amino acid, are adjacent, but do not overlap. In other words adjacent codons do not share a given nucleotide. Furthermore, it appears that the genetic code is universal—the sequence of nucleotides that specifies a given amino acid in man, specifies that same amino acid in bacteria and viruses as well as in plants and other animals. Combinations of the four nucleotides, A, C, G, and U, taken three at a time, will provide for 64 different combinations—64 different triplet codons. It is now possible to assign a specific triplet codon for each of the amino acids and to assign an amino acid to each of the 64 triplet codons.

How a gene may determine the amount of enzyme per cell is still unknown. In the inheritance of galactosemia, for example, individuals with two normal genes (homozygous normal individuals) have approximately twice as much of the specific enzyme galactose-1-phosphate uridyl transferase as do individuals with a single gene, the heterozygous carriers. The individuals that are homozygous for the disease have only an insignificant amount of the enzyme. This finding suggests that there may be quantitative as well as qualitative relationships between genes and the enzymes for which they code.

It is not yet possible to relate the process of cellular differentiation to this model system for the synthesis of specific proteins. The control of enzyme formation could conceivably occur in the gene, at the level of messenger RNA, at the level of the process occurring on the ribosome, or in some way at the ultimate protein product. It appears that differentiation does not occur by any differential assortment of genes into the daughter cells during mitosis. Rather each cell in a multicellular organism has the same complement of genes, the same quota of biologic information, as every other cell. There are several lines of investigation that support this concept; for example, in plants a single somatic cell is able to give rise to an entire plant. Several species of animals have been examined, and no variations in the morphology or number of the chromosomes cultured from various organs can be observed. The DNA content of normal diploid nuclei of many different cell types from the same organism is constant. Further, the DNAs isolated from a variety of tissues in the mouse showed no distinguishing characteristics in their average nucleotide composition, their chromatographic behavior, or their density. All of these observations are consistent with the idea that all somatic cells of an organism have identical sets of genes, that is, have identical polynucleotide sequences in their DNA.

The problem of how a cell would contain the various kinds of DNA represented by its entire genic complement and not produce the corresponding variety of messenger RNA's is, indeed, a vexing one. It would clearly be an advantage if a cell's ribosomes were not encumbered with nonfunctional molecules of messenger RNA and if it were able to produce at any given moment only those kinds of messenger RNA required for the synthesis of certain proteins. Biologically, the most economical control of protein synthesis would be some mechanism that would determine which kinds of DNA are to be transcribed at a particular time, within a particular cell. Genes may be bound to histones or other proteins, and the bound genes may be unavailable for transcription. This hypothesis, for which there is some experimental evidence, moves the problem of differentiation back one step and raises the question of what determines which molecules of DNA, that is, which genes, are combined with histone, which are free, and what controls this presumably reversible relationship.

On the basis of experiments with microbial systems, Jacob and Monod postulated that, in addition to the structural genes containing information for the assembly of specific proteins, there are operator genes that turn the structural genes on and off. Each operator gene and the contiguous structural genes under its control compose a genetic unit termed an "operon." The structural gene is normally repressed and does not produce its specific protein, but the normal substrate of the enzyme or substances related to it may activate the operator gene, turn on the structural gene, and lead to the production of the enzyme. The operator gene in turn is controlled by a regulator gene. This produces a regulator molecule that interacts with the operator gene. This model system, originally proposed to explain the phenomenon of induction of an enzyme in bacteria by its substrate, has been extended and modified as a possible model for the process of differentiation.

A somewhat more complex model was proposed by Roy Britten and Eric Davidson in 1969. This model has the advantage of providing an explanation of how the activities of noncontiguous genes can be coordinated. In higher organisms the appropriate integration of the cellular functions requires that the activity of a great many genes located far from one another in a genome be integrated. The Britten-Davidson model is based on the premise that two different regulatory genes, which they call integrators and receptors, may have the same sequences of nucleotides; that is, they are "redundant." It is known that in higher organisms there are many such repeated DNA sequences. Such redundancy has not been observed in the bacterial genomes studied by Jacob and Monod. The Britten-Davidson model suggests that some control agent, such as a hormone, first binds to a specific "sensor" gene, and that this initiates or activates a series of integrator genes which synthesize a so-called "activator" RNA. The activator RNA molecules then complex by complementary base pairings with each of a series of receptor genes, and the complexed receptor genes then trigger the transcription of the producer (structural) genes. Thus in this model the regulation of gene activity is controlled by the specific binding of an RNA species to the receptor genes, whereas in the Jacob-Monod model the expression of the gene is controlled by the binding of histone repressors to the DNA.

TISSUE DIFFERENCES. The properties and the constituents of each type of cell in a multicellular organism are ultimately determined by its complement of enzymes. There are clear examples of both qualitative and quantitative differences in the enzymatic content of cells from the same individual. Mammalian liver cells contain a glucose-6-phosphatase and can produce free glucose from glycogen and other precursors. Mammalian muscle cells lack this enzyme and cannot secrete glucose into the bloodstream. Enzymes, such as the phosphorylases of liver and skeletal muscle, which carry out the same reaction in different tissues may differ in their molecular size and amino acid composition, in their immununologic properties, and in their responses to hormones.

The course of development may be characterized by the sequential appearance of specific enzymes in a single tissue, by an increase in the amount of a specific enzyme in a single tissue, or by the sequential appearance of the same enzyme in different tissues. In the serum of fetal rats at successive stages of development there is not only an increase in the total amount of protein but an increase in the number of immunoelectrophoretically distinct proteins. There are five such proteins at 17 days of gestation, and more than 15 at 22 days of gestation, as in the adult.

The rate of glycolysis in human cerebral cortex increases linearly with time during weeks 18 to 25 of gestation. This suggests that the rate-limiting enzyme in that sequence of reactions increases in activity during this period of development. In the human fetus, glucose-6-phosphatase appears in the liver at 10 weeks of gestation, in the lung at 11 weeks, and in the kidney at 14 weeks. Thus, the tissue must be specified in making any statement about the time of appearance of some specific enzyme.

There is an interesting reciprocal relationship between the activity of the enzyme glucose-6-phosphatase in fetal tissues and in the placenta during human development. Early in development the human fetal tissues lack this enzyme and are unable to secrete glucose and thus to regulate the content of glucose in fetal serum. However, the fetal placenta does have marked glucose-6-phosphatase activity as well as a sizable store of glycogen and other precursors of glucose-6-phosphate. Experiments with tissue slices in vitro show that placental cells can secrete glucose at this stage in development. As the enzyme begins to develop in fetal tissues, first in fetal liver and then in fetal lung, the fetus can take over this activity. The enzyme activity in the placenta gradually decreases and has usually been lost completely by the time of parturition.

ISOENZYMES. Even within a single tissue or a single cell, there may be multiple molecular forms of a given enzyme, all of which catalyze the same overall reaction but have distinct physical and chemical properties which permit their separation. They may differ in their kinetic properties, in their rates of reaction with certain substrates or cofactors, and in their inhibition by other substances. Such multiple molecular forms were first described for lactic dehydrogenase and have been termed isoenzymes. Many other enzymes have since been shown to exist in multiple molecular forms, and it is now believed that many, if not all, enzymes exist in such forms.

Studies of the multiple forms of lactic dehydrogenase in mammalian tissues suggest that each is a tetramer of two different kinds of polypeptide chains, somewhat analogous to the hemoglobin molecule which is composed of two α and two β chains. The five isoenzymes of lactic dehydrogenase typically found in tissues are believed to differ in the relative number of the two kinds of chains present in the tetramer. The lactic dehydrogenase tetramer may be composed of any combination of the two subunits— AAAA, AAAB, AABB, ABBB, or BBBB. Only two genes would be required, one for each kind of polypeptide. The problem of differentiation remains unanswered, for different types of tissues have characteristically different ratios of the kinds of isoenzymes, presumably reflecting the relative rates of synthesis of the two kinds of subunits. Even more curious is the observation that chicken breast muscle undergoes a change during embryonic development from pure "heart" lactic dehydrogenase, BBBB, through a series of intermediate types to pure "muscle" lactic dehydrogenase, AAAA, in the adult. Recently the discovery of a sixth type of lactic dehydrogenase, found only in mature sperm, has indicated the need for some revision of this genetic theory.

Human fetal tissues tend to have more of their lactic dehydrogenase activity in the intermediate hybrid forms than in pure AAAA or BBBB forms. In contrast, the tissues of the adult tend to have the pure types; liver has predominantly AAAA and heart has predominantly BBBB lactic dehydrogenase. This difference between fetal and adult tissues may be fortuitous, but it is conceivable that the hybrid lactic dehydrogenases are in some way more suited to the metabolic requirements of fetal tissues than are the pure forms of the enzymes.

SPECIES DIFFERENCES. There are notable differences in the course of enzymatic development in different species. The enzymes for the synthesis of glycogen and for the production of glucose appear in human fetal liver about one-third of the way through gestation, whereas they appear in the livers of fetal rats only in the last few days before birth. The enzyme histidase appears during the first week of postnatal life in rat liver but is present at 15 weeks of gestation in the human. The enzyme which converts uridine-diphosphoglucose to uridine-diphosphoglucuronic acid appears after birth in rats, but is present in detectable amounts in the human fetal liver at 15 weeks of gestation. Thus, in a number of different enzymatic pathways, key enzymes appear in human fetal liver before they appear in the livers of rats and other common laboratory animals. In making inferences for man from experiments in animals, suitable care must be taken to ensure that the situations are indeed comparable.

Enzyme Systems in Fetal Tissues

CARBOHYDRATE METABOLISM. Many biochemical characteristics of cells appear to be established very early in the course of development. The enzymes of carbohydrate metabolism—those involved in glycolysis and the tricarboxylic acid cycle—are so fundamental to the production of biologically useful energy that it would be difficult to imagine any animal cell surviving without them. These enzymes are probably present in the unfertilized egg and continue to be present in all cells subsequently derived from the fertilized egg. Certain tissues may show quantitative differences in the activity of one or another of these enzymes during development, but other tissues have rates of carbohydrate metabolism which undergo little or no change during the course of intrauterine development. The rates of oxygen consumption and of lactate production of slices from a variety of different tissues of the human fetus remain relatively constant over the period of development from week 6 to week 24 (Table 6). An exception to this generalization is cerebral cortex, in which lactate production increases from 15 μmoles lactate per gram tissue per hour at 15 weeks to 29 μmoles per gram tissue per hour at term. With all substrates tested, the heart produces more lactate than any other tissue, and the amount produced is less dependent on the kind of substrate present than in other tissues. This and other evidence suggests that most of the lactate

TABLE 6.   *Metabolic Rates of Human Fetal Tissues in Vitro**

	Age in Weeks	7.5-10	11-12	13-15	16-19	20-24	40
Liver	Oxygen utilized	5.3	5.3	5.1	3.6	4.6	3.2
	Lactate produced	24	20	19	22	18	24
Heart	Oxygen utilized	3.4	3.5	3.4	3.5	3.9	5.3
	Lactate produced	59	59	49	44	50	99
Lung	Oxygen utilized	2.8	2.9	3.5	3.6	—	2.0
	Lactate produced	16	12	15	18	—	20
Kidney	Oxygen utilized	2.8	4.6	4.1	4.3	4.4	4.5
	Lactate produced	20	25	21	18	17	22
Diaphragm	Oxygen utilized	1.9	2.2	2.1	2.2	2.0	2.0
	Lactate produced	22	21	16	16	13	27
Cerebral Cortex	Oxygen utilized	4.9	4.8	4.7	5.2	5.8	4.6
	Lactate produced	15	21	17	16	26	29

*Oxygen utilization expressed as microliters oxygen per milligram (dry weight) tissue per hour; lactate production expressed as micromoles lactate per gram (wet) tissue per hour. Tissue slices incubated in medium containing 11.1 mmoles glucose and 10 mmoles pyruvate per liter.

comes from the large store of glycogen present in the fetal heart. There is clear evidence that lactic dehydrogenase is functional in all of these tissues as early as it has been possible to test them.

Tissue slices of lung, liver, and kidney incubated in vitro in a medium containing glucose will carry out the net synthesis of glycogen, but slices of heart muscle were characterized by a net glycogenolysis when incubated in vitro.

The production of glucose by the fetal liver begins at the tenth week of development and reaches a level of some 20 μmoles per gram tissue per hour by 20 weeks. The lung begins to produce glucose at about the 11th week of development and the kidney about the 15th week. The other fetal tissues tested—heart, skeletal muscle, and brain—did not secrete glucose at any time. The presence of diabetes in the mother had no effect on the production of glucose by fetal tissues. The utilization of glucose shows no consistent change with developmental age in the human fetal tissues tested, except in cerebral cortex. The rates of glucose utilization by tissues from fetuses of diabetic mothers are usually

less than the rates of glucose utilization of comparable tissues from the fetuses of nondiabetic mothers. The number of observations for most ages and tissues is too small to permit the calculation of appropriate standard errors, and this conclusion can be advanced only tentatively. When slices of heart or diaphragm were incubated with a glucose substrate, both showed increases in the uptake of glucose and its metabolism to carbon dioxide when insulin was added to the incubation medium.

The overall rate of glycolysis can be measured by incubating tissue slices with labeled glucose and isolating labeled pyruvate at the end of the incubation period. Such experiments show that diaphragm and liver have remarkably constant rates of pyruvate production from glucose whereas in kidney, lung, and heart this aspect of metabolism increases slightly with time. The ability of brain slices to convert glucose to pyruvate increased fivefold over the period 9 weeks to 21 weeks.

The rate of utilization of pyruvate provides an indirect estimate of the activity of the tricarboxylic acid cycle, which yields most of the energy produced

TABLE 7.   *Percentage of Respiratory Carbon Dioxide Derived from Labeled Carbon of Substrate* *

	Glucose-U-^{14}C	Pyruvate-2-^{14}C	Alanine-2-^{14}C	Glycine-1-^{14}C
Liver	4.6	29.2	2.3	16.8
Heart	6.6	17.2	0.13	0.3
Lung	2.4	21.8	0.5	0.7
Kidney	3.8	16.8	0.9	1.3
Diaphragm	1.4	11.7	0.2	1.2
Cerebral cortex	9.0	26.6	1.4	—

*Tissue slices were incubated in phosphate-buffered saline containing 11.1 mM glucose, 10 mM pyruvate, 10 mM alanine, or 10 mM glycine.

biologically. The constancy of pyruvate utilization in these tissues is probably a reflection of a fairly constant rate of energy production and utilization with growth. The utilization of pyruvate was remarkably constant in all fetal tissues tested from 7½ weeks to term. An even more direct estimate of the activity of the tricarboxylic acid cycle is obtained by measuring the percentage of respiratory carbon dioxide derived from carbon-2 of pyruvate (Table 7). There appeared to be little or no change with gestational age in the rate at which pyruvate is converted to carbon dioxide in liver, lung, kidney, heart, cerebral cortex, or diaphragm. There was a suggestion that the percentage of respiratory carbon dioxide derived from pyruvate was slightly less in tissues from fetuses of diabetic mothers than in fetuses from normal mothers. When both glucose and pyruvate were present in the incubation medium, the tissue slice derived three to ten times as much of its carbon dioxide from pyruvate as from glucose.

AMINO ACID METABOLISM AND TRANSAMINATION. When tissue slices were incubated with alanine-2-^{14}C, only a small amount of carbon dioxide was derived from the carbon-2 of alanine. To be metabolized, alanine is first transaminated to yield pyruvate; thus alanine-2-^{14}C becomes pyruvate-2-^{14}C. Since pyruvate-2-^{14}C was converted to carbon dioxide readily, whereas alanine-2-^{14}C was not, this would indicate that transamination of alanine occurs in fetal liver only at a very slow rate. In contrast, the carboxyl carbon of glycine (glycine-1-^{14}C) is converted to carbon dioxide at a very rapid rate by the fetal liver as early as the sixth week of development. Adult rat liver is known to be rich in glycine oxidase, and these experiments show that this enzyme is present at an early age in human fetal liver.

LIPID SYNTHESIS AND OXIDATION. Lipid synthesis has been studied in tissue slices of fetal liver incubated with alanine, glycine, or acetate. Carbon-2 of alanine is incorporated into lipid more rapidly than the carboxyl carbon of glycine, but the rates of both incorporations are rather low. The rate of incorporation is much greater in liver than in heart or brain, with lung and kidney occupying an intermediate position. The respiratory quotient (RQ) of slices of fetal liver incubated in oxygen with either glucose or acetate as substrate was considerably greater than that of slices of adult human liver incubated under identical conditions. This is consistent with a high rate of lipogenesis in fetal liver. The rate of incorporation of acetate into lipids in the fetal liver is much higher than in the adult liver; the rate of oxygen was 1.42 μmoles per gram tissue per hour in fetal liver and 0.042 μmoles per gram tissue per hour in adult livers. In the fetal liver more than twice as much acetate is converted to lipid than is metabolized to carbon dioxide, whereas in the adult liver some six times as much acetate is converted to carbon dioxide than to lipid. There is thus a very pronounced difference in the rate of lipid synthesis in fetal, as opposed to adult, liver. The high rate of lipid synthesis by the fetal liver is demonstrable with acetate and pyruvate as substrates; the carbon atoms of glucose, fructose, glycerol, and citrate are incorporated into lipid by fetal liver at somewhat lower rates. With each of these, the rate of lipid synthesis in fetal liver was at least twice that in adult liver when using the same substrate. When fetal liver is incubated under anaerobic conditions, the rate of lipid synthesis is greatly depressed, to about one-twentieth the rate occurring in oyxgen.

Radioactive lipid that had been synthesized in one incubation by fetal liver was isolated and purified, and served as substrate for a second experiment with liver slices. With this radioactive fat as a sole substrate, the liver slice was able to metabolize it to labeled carbon dioxide quite rapidly. When the lipid synthesized was fractionated and the neutral fat was used as substrate, it was again found that the fetal liver slice could convert this to carbon dioxide. Thus, the enzymes for both the biosynthesis and the oxidation of lipids are present in the fetal liver at 15 weeks of gestation. The lungs, brain, kidney, heart, and diaphragm carry out lipogenesis from acetate at much lower rates than the liver. Lung has about 10 percent of the activity of the liver, and heart and diaphragm have about 10 percent of the rate in the lung.

As the brain develops, the metabolic rate of the cerebral cortex increases more rapidly than that of the brainstem. Although the brainstem initially has a higher rate of metabolism than the cortex, by the time the fetus measures 20 cm crown-to-rump, the rate in the cortex exceeds that in the brainstem. The aspects of metabolism measured were oxygen consumption, production of carbon dioxide and of lactate, and the conversion of acetate to carbon dioxide in lipid. The brainstem converts acetate to lipid more rapidly than the cortex does. The brain is more dependent on exogenous substrates than the lung or other tissues, for when slices of cerebral cortex are incubated, three times more lactic acid is produced when glucose is present in the medium than when it is absent. With other tissues, the production of lactic acid is increased only a small extent when glucose is added to the incubation medium. The brain contains a very small glycogen content and depends largely on exogenous glucose for its metabolism. However, cerebral cortex and brainstem can metabolize other substances such as acetate or pyruvate to carbon dioxide or to fats.

Slices of lung incubated in vitro revealed some interesting characteristics. Lung has a high content of glycogen and can carry out the net synthesis of glycogen when incubated in glucose. The glycogen content of fetal lung is as high as that in liver or heart, when related to the wet weight of the tissue, and is even higher than in those two organs when calculated on a dry weight basis. This fact, plus the finding that the lung contains a glucose-6-phosphatase and can secrete glucose after the 11th week of development, suggests that the fetal lung may play a role in the carbohydrate economy of the fetus as a site of the storage of glycogen and as a regulatory organ which supplements the liver.

STEROID SYNTHESIS. Experiments using tissue slices or homogenates of fetal adrenal glands revealed that very early in development, at eight weeks or less, the adrenal gland can carry out the 16, 17, 21, and 11 hydroxylation of progesterone and thus can form, among other things, both corticosterone and cortisol from progesterone. However, the activity of the enzyme (Δ^5-3β-hydroxysteroid dehydrogenase) converting pregnenolone to progesterone or dehydroepiandrosterone to androstenedione is very low during fetal life but is high at birth. Thus it appears that, during fetal life, the adrenal gland could synthesize corticosteroids from progesterone but not from pregnenolone, cholesterol, or earlier precursors. The fetal adrenal could produce its adrenal corticoids from the progesterone synthesized in the placenta and transferred to it through the fetal bloodstream. In view of the large amount of progesterone that is produced by the placenta, it is possible that the low level of Δ^5-3β-hydroxysteroid dehydrogenase in the fetal adrenal gland represents an example of the inhibition of enzyme formation by the product of the enzymatic reaction. The increase in the enzyme at birth might represent synthesis of the enzyme in response to release of inhibition, or simply in response to some intrinsic differentiation process. Although the fetal testis has a moderate amount of steroid metabolic activity, the fetal ovary has very little. The fetal testis of 10 to 15 weeks of gestation can synthesize testosterone and androstenedione from progesterone or pregnenolone.

Endocrine Interrelationships of Placenta and Fetal Tissues

The human fertilized ovum develops into the blastocyst which in turn gives rise in part to the human embryo and fetus, while the remainder of the blastocyst develops into the trophoblast which becomes incorporated into the placenta. Most of the tissue of the human placenta is derived from fetal trophoblast rather than from maternal chorion. Though derived from a common genetic origin, the fetal tissues and the placenta develop unique constellations of enzymes and provide an interesting model for cellular differentiation.

The synthesis and metabolism of steroids has been studied perhaps more intensively than the metabolism of other compounds in this system, and an interesting pattern has come to light. Several of the key enzymes for the synthesis of estriol are found exclusively in fetal tissues, and others are found exclusively in the placenta. Thus both fetal and placental tissues are required for the synthesis of estriol, and consideration of this has led to the concept of a "fetoplacental unit" for the synthesis of estriol. In contrast, the synthesis of progesterone does not require the intervention of any enzymes in fetal tissues, for the placenta can carry out all of the steps in the synthesis of progesterone alone and unaided. Human term placenta and the placentas earlier in gestation can synthesize, from acetate and mevalonic acid, the intermediates squalene, lanosterol, cholesterol, and pregnenolone, in the course of the synthesis of progesterone.

In a series of experiments the rate of each enzymatic step in the synthesis of cholesterol was studied and compared with the rate of the comparable enzyme in rat liver. Under these experimental conditions, placental enzymes carried out the conversion of mevalonate to squalene at a rate comparable to that in liver, but the rate of cyclization of squalene to lanosterol was considerably less in the placenta than in the liver. Similarly the system of placental enzymes that carry out the demethylation of lanosterol to form cholesterol had only about half the activity of the comparable system in liver microsomes. This is borne out by analyses of the metabolic products of squalene in the placenta in which the amount converted to lanosterol greatly exceeds the conversion to cholesterol, whereas comparable incubations with liver microsomes yield more cholesterol and less lanosterol. Human placental mitochondria contain a very active enzyme system for the conversion of cholesterol to pregnenolone. In addition, the placenta contains a very active 3β-hydroxysteroid dehydrogenase which converts pregnenolone to progesterone. Thus the human placenta at term has been shown to have all of the enzymes necessary to convert small precursor molecules, such as acetate or mevalonate, to progesterone. There is no need to postulate that the placenta must receive partially synthesized intermediates for the production of progesterone. However, there is no reason to dismiss the possibility that the placenta may take in from the maternal bloodstream pregnenolone, cholesterol, or some earlier intermediate and use that material in the synthesis of progesterone.

The placenta, however, is unable to carry out the overall synthesis of any estrogen from acetate or mevalonate because it lacks certain enzymes, especially the steroid $C_{17, 20}$ desmolase which converts C_{21} steroids to C_{19} steroids. Thus the placenta is unable to convert pregnenolone to dehydroepiandrosterone or to convert progesterone to androstenedione. In addition, the placenta has very little, if any, 16-hydroxylase. The enzymes lacking in the placenta are present in the fetal adrenal in ample amounts. Similarly the enzymes lacking in fetal tissues, the Δ^5-3β-hydroxysteroid dehydrogenase and the steroid sulfatase, are present in the placenta (Table 8).

The enzyme for the 17-hydroxylation of steroids was present in even the youngest fetal adrenals tested, as was the 16-hydroxylase. The enzymes for the 21-hydroxylation and the 11-hydroxylation of steroids appear after the tenth week of development, and reach maximal activity after 15 weeks. In contrast, there is very little Δ^5-3β-hydroxysteroid dehydrogenase in the adrenal early in development. It begins to appear between the 20th and 25th week, and is present in ample activity at birth. Without this enzyme the fetal adrenal early in development would be unable to produce adrenal corticoids unless supplied with progesterone. The human placenta does produce progesterone and secretes it into the fetal circulation. Zander and others have shown that progesterone is utilized by the perfused fetus and presumably by the fetus in situ as well. It is conceivable that the lack of the 3β-hydroxysteroid dehydrogenase activity in the fetal adrenal is an example of the inhibition or repression of the enzyme by its product.

The fetal liver has enzymes to convert progesterone to pregnanediol and to 20α-hydroxy-4-pregnen-3-one. It can also convert progesterone to estradiol and estradiol to estriol, in very small amounts. The fetal liver, as well as the fetal adrenal, has enzymes to convert steroids to their respective steroid sulphates, whereas the fetal lung has very little of such activity.

From the pattern of enzymatic locations that have been found, one could postulate that pregnenolone or progesterone synthesized in the placenta passes to the fetus and within the fetal tissues is converted from C_{21} to C_{19} steroids. This is catalyzed by the steroid $C_{17, 20}$ desmolase present in fetal tissue but absent from the placenta. The C_{19} steroids are then sulfurylated and perhaps undergo 16-hydroxylation in the fetal adrenal and fetal liver, then are transported as the steroid sulfates back to the placenta. There the sulfate group is removed by the potent steroid sulfatase present, and the steroid nucleus is aromatized to yield estradiol and estriol. It has been inferred that steroids are sulfurylated in the fetal adrenal to increase their solubility for transport to the placenta. However, it has been shown that only the human fetus secretes significant amounts of dehydroepiandrosterone sulfate in its blood, and that many other animals manage to complete gestation without synthesizing dehydroepiandrosterone sulfate. Because of the distribution of enzymes between maternal, placental, and fetal compartments, the steroids shuttle back and forth from one compartment to another for successive steps in the biosynthesis of estriol. Consequently the excretion of estriol in the maternal urine measures some combination of placental and fetal functions. There may be other examples of integration of fetal, placental, and maternal tissues to carry out physiologic and biochemical processes, but future research will be needed to clarify them. At present the concept of the fetoplacental unit rests entirely on evidence from steroid metabolism and specifically from the biosynthesis of estriol. In contrast, the placental protein hormones, chorionic gonadotropin and placental lactogen, are synthesized entirely by the placenta, and present evidence suggests that they do not enter the fetal circulation to any extent and have little or no effect on fetal metabolism, although they do have important effects on maternal metabolism.

TABLE 8. *Distribution of Enzymes Between Placenta and Fetus*

Placenta	Fetus (adrenal)
Enzymes present	
Δ^5-3β-Hydroxysteroid dehydrogenase	$C_{17,20}$ Desmolase
17β-Hydroxysteroid dehydrogenase	16α-Hydroxylase
Aromatizing system	17-Hydroxylase
Steroid 3β-sulfatase	21-Hydroxylase
	11β-Hydroxylase
	Sulfokinase
Enzymes absent or present in very small amount	
$C_{17,20}$ Desmolase	Δ^5-3β-Hydroxysteroid dehydrogenase
Sulfokinase	Sulfatase
16α-Hydroxylase	

Changes in Enzymes at Birth

CARBOHYDRATE METABOLISM AND "RESISTANCE" TO HYPOXIA. The ability of most newborn mammals to withstand severe hypoxia is well established. Newborn rats, mice, kittens, and dogs may survive as long as 45 to 50 minutes in an atmosphere of pure nitrogen. In contrast, the newborn guinea pig is killed by 7 minutes of anoxia. This ability to survive prolonged deprivation of oxygen declines rapidly after birth, and disappears in the first few weeks. The classic experiments of Himwich established that accelerated glycolysis is an important factor in providing for the survival of the newborn animal during hypoxia. Studies in our laboratory with tissue slices from both rats and human fetuses corroborated Himwich's finding that fetal tissues can increase the rate of glycolysis to a greater extent under anaerobic conditions than can adult tissues.

Several theories regarding the ability of the fetus to survive hypoxia have postulated the presence of unique pathways of anaerobic metabolism which enable the newborn to survive. A careful search for such pathways using a variety of in vitro techniques yielded no evidence for their existence. It was clear, however, that fetal tissues do respond to anaerobiosis with a much greater increase in glycolysis than do adult tissues.

Fetal and adult human livers have comparable rates of oxygen consumption, but fetal liver has a much higher respiratory quotient with either glucose or acetate as substrate. This indicates that the synthesis of fatty acids is occurring at a rapid rate (Table 9). When metabolizing acetate-2-^{14}C, fetal liver converts more than twice as much radioactive carbon to lipid as to carbon dioxide. In the adult liver, in contrast, some six times as much carbon was converted to carbon dioxide as to lipid. There is thus more than a twelvefold difference in the relative rates of lipogenesis in fetal and adult livers. Lactic acid is produced in oxygen at simlar rates by both fetal and adult liver. This is true in both human and rat tissues. Fetal liver is thus not characterized by a high rate of aerobic glycolysis but by a high rate of production of lactic acid under anaerobic conditions. Under anaerobic conditions the fetal liver produces three to four times as much lactic acid as it does under aerobic conditions. The increase in adult liver is something less than 100 percent. The most direct measure of the rate of glycolysis is, perhaps, the rate of conversion of ^{14}C-glucose to ^{14}C-pyruvic acid. Using this method, it can be estimated that the fetal liver increases glycolysis fourfold as the system becomes anaerobic, whereas in adult liver the increase is much less. The synthesis of fatty acids by the fetal liver is less under anaerobic than aerobic conditions at 15 to 20 weeks of gestation, Pyruvate and acetate were the most active precursors of lipid and were converted to fatty acids at a twentyfold greater rate in oxygen than in nitrogen.

When tissue slices of liver or cerebral cortex were incubated under anaerobic conditions for an hour and then washed, placed in fresh incubation medium, gassed with oxygen, and incubated for a

TABLE 9.   *Metabolism of Human Liver Slices in Vitro*

	Fetal Liver Incubated in		Adult Liver Incubated in	
	Oxygen	Nitrogen	Oxygen	Nitrogen
Substrate: Glucose-^{14}C, Uniformly Labeled				
RQ	1.31	—	0.95	—
Oxygen consumption	28.4	—	28.4	—
Glycogen utilization	−54	−68	−114	−155
Glucose production	+13	+14	+50	+73
Glucose utilization	0	−12	−15	−17
Lactate production	+17	+52	+21	+38
Conversion of carbon of glucose to lipid	0.23	0.03	0.15	0.11
Conversion of carbon of glucose to carbon dioxide	0.41	0.08	0.20	0.10
Substrate: Acetate-2-^{14}C				
RQ	1.19	—	0.96	—
Oxygen consumption	28.4	—	30.1	—
Glycogen utilization	−40	−52	−114	−116
Lactate production	+16	+40	+18	+34
Conversion of carbon of acetate to lipid	1.42	0.08	0.042	0.0065
Conversion of carbon of acetate to carbon dioxide	0.66	0.065	0.245	0.074

Initial content of glycogen: Fetal liver, 110 μmoles/g wet tissue. Adult liver, 200 μmoles/g wet tissue. All values except RQ are expressed as μmole/g tissue/hour.

second hour, the experiments demonstrated that one hour of anoxia causes no irreparable damage to the enzymes. Oxygen consumption by the slices that had been in nitrogen the previous hour was about 80 percent as great as that of slices that had been in oxygen the previous hour. Slices that had been under anaerobic conditions for an hour were able to utilize oxygen and pyruvate, produce lactate, and convert acetate to carbon dioxide and lipid at rates that were comparable to those of slices that had spent the previous hour under aerobic conditions.

AMINO ACID METABOLISM. The premature but not the full-term infant excretes in the urine a substance identified as p-hydroxyphenylpyruvic acid, a metabolite of tyrosine. Tyrosine is also present in increased amounts in the urine of the premature infant. The administration of ascorbic acid to the premature infant decreases the concentration of tyrosine and p-hydroxyphenylpyruvic acid in the urine. The rate at which tyrosine is oxidized by homogenates of liver from premature, full-term, and adult human beings undergoes a marked increase with development. Similar differences are demonstrable in the rate of tyrosine oxidation by liver preparations from fetal, newborn, and adult rats. The rate-limiting step appears to be tyrosine transaminase which has very low activity in the fetal liver. This may be compared to the low rate of alanine transamination noted in incubation with fetal tissue slices.

The activity of the enzyme which converts phenylalanine to tyrosine increases markedly during the first 4 to 12 days after birth in the human. The livers of the fetus and the newborn have only a small amount of the enzyme that oxidizes homogentisic acid, but this appears shortly after birth. Tryptophan pyrrolase is another enzyme that increases rapidly from nearly zero activity to nearly the adult level within a short time after birth in the rabbit. In the rat, the enzyme activity increases more slowly, and the adult rate is not reached until about three weeks after birth. The amount of the enzyme histidase increases markedly in the liver of the rat within the first week of life. In the light of our current hypotheses of protein biosynthesis, this rapid increase should mean that the specific DNA for that enzyme is activated, and a burst of messenger RNA, coding for the enzyme, passes from the nucleus to the ribosomes and leads to its synthesis. However, it has not yet been possible to demonstrate any such burst of specific messenger RNA in fetal or newborn rat liver.

ENZYMATIC "IMMATURITY." Some of the many physiologic problems that beset the premature infant have been ascribed to an "immaturity" of one or more of its organs or organ systems. This term has also been applied to "immature" enzyme systems, in which enzyme activity is insufficient to carry out required enzyme functions at an adequate rate. A tissue may be considered immature if it does not have an adequate number of enzyme molecules to carry on its metabolic processes efficiently, but this does not imply that the enzyme molecules themselves are immature. In a strict sense, this would imply that the enzyme molecule had not been completely assembled, that some of its amino acid residues were missing, or that the folding of the protein molecule was incomplete. The evidence available at present suggests that the synthesis of an enzyme is essentially an all-or-none process and that a given enzyme molecule is either completely active or completely inactive. Although there are some exceptions to this rule, it would appear that differences in the activity of an enzyme at different times in development may most readily be explained as differences in the number of enzyme molecules per mass of tissue, rather than as differences in the specific activity of a constant number of enzyme molecules.

REFERENCES

Cold Spring Harbor Symp. Quant. Biol., 19, 1954.

Hermann, H., and Tootle, M. L. Specific and general aspects of the development of enzymes and metabolic pathways, Physiol. Rev., 44:289, 1964.

Lanman, J., ed., Josiah Macy, Jr. Conference on the Physiology of Prematurity, 2, 1957; 3, 1958.

Wolstenholme, G. E. W., and O'Connor, M., eds. Somatic Stability in the Newly Born, CIBA Symposium Series, 1961.

2.6
PHYSIOLOGY

GIACOMO MESCHIA

Since the publication in 1931 of Needham's Chemical Embryology there has been no attempt to collect and organize the vast amount of information about fetal physiology which is scattered in hundreds of different publications. The recent trend has been to collect in monographs a few selected research topics in the hope of forming nuclei of systematized knowledge that might eventually expand. Some of these topics form the substance of this section. For additional information, the reader is referred to recent books on fetal physiology (Assali, Dawes).

Basic Physiology of Transplacental Exchange

Uterine blood flow, the placental membrane, and umbilical blood flow represent the three basic components of the placental exchange unit. We shall describe them separately and then indicate how they work together as a functional unit.

UTERINE BLOOD FLOW. The nonpregnant uterus is a relatively small organ that receives a small fraction of cardiac output. The blood flow to the nonpregnant uterus can be increased manyfold by the injection of estrogens and rises spontaneously to a peak level at estrus in sheep (Greiss and Anderson) (Fig. 17). During pregnancy uterine blood flow grows enormously, most of it going to the placental cotyledons (Makowski et al., 1968a). The physiologic factors that produce this increased blood flow are unknown. It is not yet clear whether the administration of additional estrogens can further increase the already large uterine blood flow of late pregnancy. The blood flow to the pregnant uterus can be reduced acutely by hypotension (Ladner et al.). Similarly, injections of norepinephrine and epinephrine (Ladner et al.; Greiss) cause vasoconstriction of the uterine vascular bed. In sheep, acute maternal hypoxia and hyperoxia, induced by breathing gas mixtures that give a 40 to 400 mm Hg range of arterial Po_2, have virtually no effect on the uterine blood flow (Greiss).

The maternal blood that flows through the placenta represents the external environment of the fetus. Under optimum conditions this environment has remarkably constant physicochemical characteristics. However, changes in this environment are rather common for two reasons: (1) homeostatic mechanisms are not always able to prevent change (e.g., maternal hypoglycemia due to starvation) and

(2) the maternal homeostatic mechanisms may not attempt to prevent change (e.g., constancy of uterine blood flow in acute moderate hypoxia) or may even change selectively in a direction which is unfavorable to the fetus (e.g., uterine vasoconstriction by catecholamines). Most of the adaptive mechanisms in the mother are geared to her own survival, a sine qua non of fetal survival.

THE PLACENTAL MEMBRANE. The tissue layers interposed between maternal and fetal blood plasmas constitute the placental membrane. A section of the human placental membrane at term is shown in Figure 18. The surface of the human trophoblast (microvilli excluded) has been estimated by histometric techniques to be approximately 11 m^2 at term (Aherne and Dunnill). According to Wilkin, the trophoblastic surface grows during gestation proportionally to fetal weight. In the second half of pregnancy, the area to fetal weight ratio is approximately 3 to 4 m^2/kg. The thickness of the membrane has been estimated to be roughly 3.5 μ at full term (Aherne and Dunnill). In comparison to the alveolar membrane of the human lungs the placental membrane has a larger surface to body weight ratio and is much thicker. The greater thickness reflects the fact that the placenta is far more active metabolically than the lungs. The thickness and metabolic activity of the membrane represent hindrances to the respiratory function of the placenta. These hindrances are partially offset by the larger surface. Quantitative studies concerning the characteristics of the placental membrane in vivo are scanty. It is generally assumed that some molecules of physiologic importance (e.g., O_2, CO_2, urea) cross the placenta by simple diffusion. The permeability of the sheep placenta to urea (Meschia et al., 1965) and carbon monoxide (Longo et al.) has been evaluated by measuring the "diffusing capacity" of the placental membrane. Diffusing capacity is the rate of placental transfer of a substance per unit concentration difference between maternal and fetal plasmas. During gestation, the diffusing capacity of the sheep placenta to urea rises proportionally to the fetal weight (Fig. 19). As shown elsewhere in this chapter, in man, placental weight and fetal weight are linearly related in the second half of pregnancy. Thus, both data on trophoblastic surface and placental weight in man, and physiologic measurements in sheep indicate a close relationship between placental changes and fetal growth. It has been suggested that amino acids cross the placental membrane by active transfer, because the concentration of amino acids in fetal plasma is higher than in maternal plasma. It has also been suggested that glucose crosses the placenta by facilitated diffusion (Widdas). These suggestions deserve further study, for they have important implications in the regulation of fetal metabolism.

UMBILICAL BLOOD FLOW. There is a progressive increase of umbilical blood flow with fetal age. Approximately 94 percent of the umbilical blood

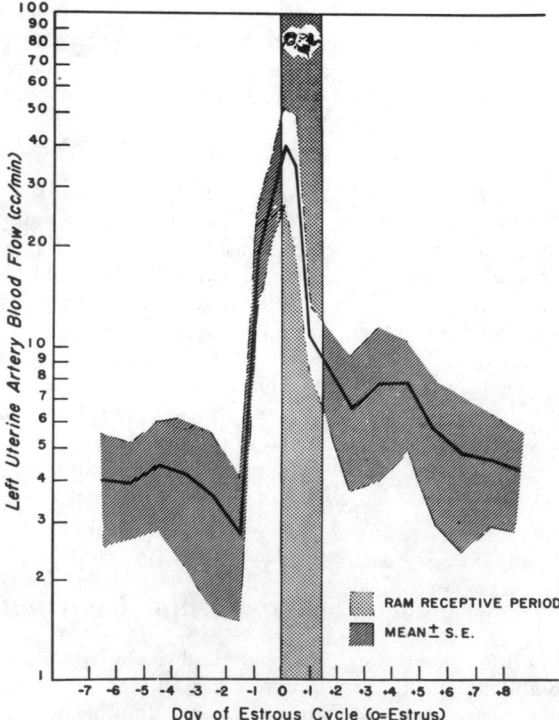

Fig. 17. Semilogarithmic graph of uterine blood flow during the ovine estrous cycle. (From Greiss and Anderson. *Amer. J. Obstet. Gynec.*, 103:637, 1969.)

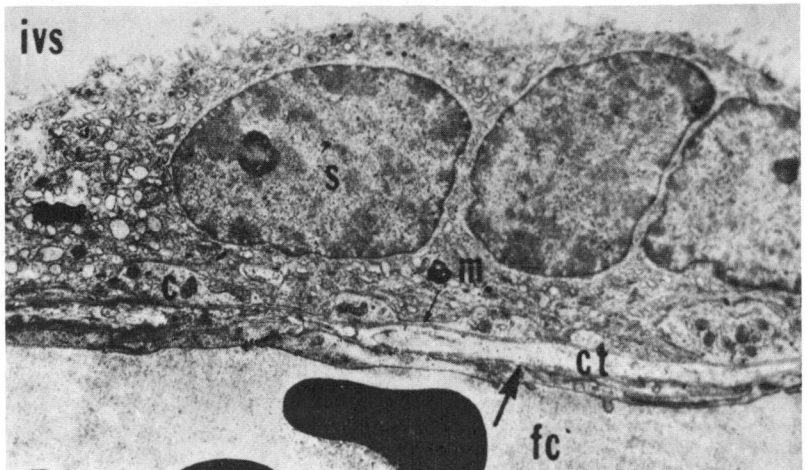

Fig. 18. Electronmicrograph of the human placental membrane at term. Intervillous space (ivs). The heavy arrow points to the basement membrane of a fetal capillary (fc). (From Wynn. *In* Eastman, N. J., and Hellman, L. M., eds., *Williams Obstetrics*, 13th ed., 1966. Courtesy of Appleton-Century-Crofts.)

flow is to the placental cotyledons (Makowski et al., 1968b). This increase appears to be the combined effect of a rise in fetal blood pressure and growth of the placental vascular bed (Dawes). The physiologic factors responsible for this growth are unknown. It is not yet clear whether umbilical blood flow rises proportionally to fetal weight. The reason for this uncertainty, as for so many others concerning data in fetal physiology, is that umbilical blood flows have been measured in anesthetized animals under acute experimental conditions. Just as in the uterine circulation, changes in the partial pressures of the respiratory gases appear to have almost no effect on the umbilical vascular bed (Dawes).

PLACENTAL CLEARANCE. The simplest process of transplacental exchange, useful also in illustrating some essential characteristics of placental physiology, is the placental clearance of substances that are not rapidly metabolized and are not protein bound. By definition, placental clearance of a given substance is the quantity crossing the placenta per unit concentration difference between umbilical arteries and maternal arteries (Meschia et al., 1967a). The placental clearance of a given substance depends upon the *permeability* of the placental membrane to that substance and the magnitude of the fetal and maternal placental *blood flows*.

If the placental permeability to a given substance is very low, the clearance will also be very low, irrespective of the magnitude of the placental flows. In this instance the clearance is said to be primarily *diffusion limited*. The clearance becomes progressively higher for substances to which the placental membrane is progressively more permeable and tends to a *maximum value* in which the permeability is no longer rate limiting. This maximum clearance is called *flow limited* because the magnitude and pattern of the placental flows are the only factors that determine the rate of transplacental diffusion at a given concentration difference between the arteries. Experimental evidence (Meschia et al., 1967a; Battaglia et al., 1968a) indicates that in both sheep and rhesus monkeys the placental clearances of antipyrine and tritiated water represent the maximum flow-limited clearance, whereas the clearance of urea is to a significant degree diffusion limited.

The experimental setup used in studying the transplacental diffusion of highly diffusible substances is schematically represented in Figure 20. The test molecule (antipyrine in the example of Fig. 20) is infused at a constant rate into a fetal vein. In a stable preparation, approximately 40 minutes after starting the infusion, the system attains dynamic equilibrium between infusion and excretion rates. Characteristic of this dynamic equilibrium is the steady pattern of concentrations in the uterine and umbilical vessels exemplified in Figure 21. Of great interest is the fact that the venous concentra-

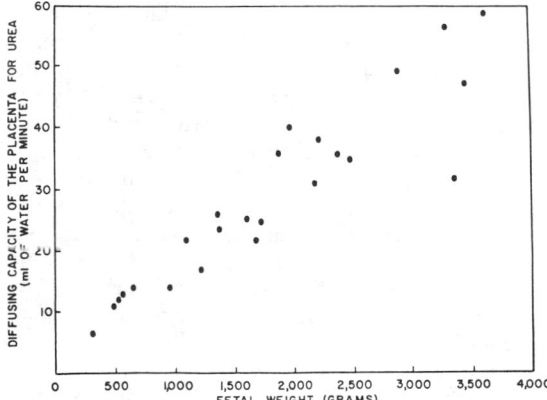

Fig. 19. The amount of urea (in milligrams) that crosses the sheep placenta in 1 minute for a transplacental difference of concentration of 1 mg/ml of water is plotted against the fetal body weight. (From Meschia et al. *Quart. J. Exper. Physiol.*, 50:23, 1965.)

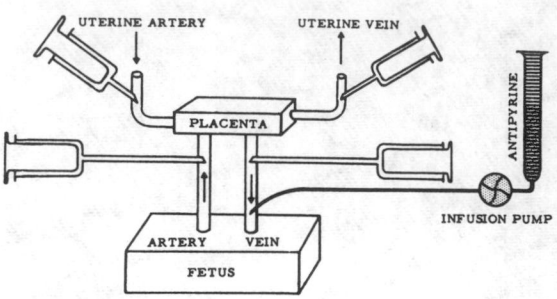

Fig. 20. Scheme representing the position of the infusion and sampling catheters for studying the transplacental diffusion of highly diffusible molecules under steady state conditions. (From Meschia et al. *Quart. J. Exper. Physiol.*, 52:1, 1967.)

tion in the donor stream (umbilical vein) is higher than the venous concentration in the recipient stream (uterine vein). This fact, which is true over a large range of uterine to umbilical blood flow ratios, cannot be attributed to a low permeability of the placenta to antipyrine, for the antipyrine clearance, as we have seen, is flow limited. It represents rather a fundamental property of the placental exchanger, namely that the venous output of the umbilical stream tends to equilibrate with the venous output of the uterine stream. Exact equilibration is not observed for several reasons. The uterine venous output is a mixture of venous drainage from the uterine muscle, the endometrium, and the placental cotyledons. The umbilical venous output is a mixture of

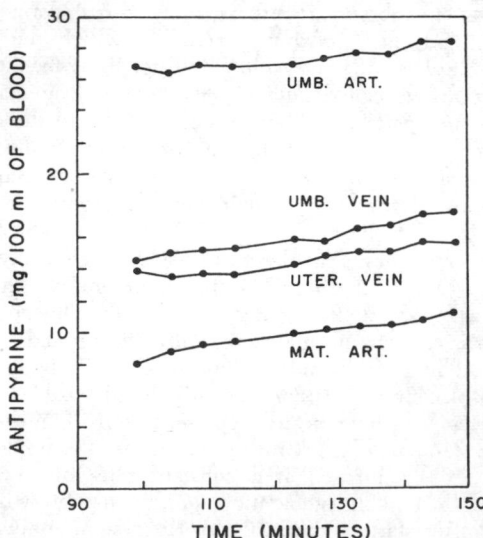

Fig. 21. Pattern of antipyrine concentrations in fetal and maternal blood when antipyrine is infused at constant rate in the fetal vein of a stable preparation. The infusion began at time zero. (From Meschia et al. *Quart. J. Exper. Physiol.*, 52:1, 1967.)

blood from chorion laeve and chorion villosum. When the effect of these "shunts" is taken into consideration, the concentration difference between the venous outputs of the placental cotyledons is reduced to a smaller, but still significant, difference. Thus the placenta is somewhat less efficient than an ideal concurrent exchanger in which the two venous outputs attain concentration equilibrium. Uneven placental perfusion could be causing this inefficiency, but there is no convincing experimental evidence to support this hypothesis. The transplacental flow-limited clearance in sheep and goat fetuses is approximately 100 ml of blood per minute per kg of fetal body weight. With these clearance values a step change in the composition of maternal fluids would lead to a rapid change in the fetal fluids, since the half-time of the equilibrium process of inert molecules with flow-limited clearances is approximately 7 minutes. Thus, relatively low permeability of the placental membrane to some components of the fetal plasma is a necessary requirement for fetal control of these components.

Fetal Respiration

The normal O_2 consumption in utero is estimated to be approximately 6 to 8 ml STP of O_2 per kg of fetal body weight per minute (Meschia et al., 1967b). It compares with similar O_2 consumptions in newborn infants in a thermal neutral environment once adequate ventilation is established. If the placenta fails to deliver the required amount of O_2, the fetus becomes anoxic in a few minutes, for the amount of O_2 present in the fetal body at any one time is quite small in comparison to the normal consumption rate. A well-documented characteristic of fetal respiration is the low O_2 pressure in umbilical blood. The primary reason for this phenomenon is that the placenta, as we have shown, simulates a somewhat inefficient concurrent exchanger. Thus, the *most arterialized blood of the fetus* (umbilical venous blood) is blood that falls short of equilibration with *maternal placental venous blood*. An illustration of this fact is given in Figure 22, which shows the P_{O_2} values in the uterine and umbilical veins of a sheep sampled at daily intervals via chronically indwelling catheters. The large uterine vein-umbilical vein P_{O_2} difference poses the question whether the transplacental O_2 uptake is predominantly flow limited or there is some degree of diffusion limitation (the velocities of reaction of O_2 with adult and fetal hemoglobin and placental O_2 consumption may be part of the diffusion limitation). According to the available evidence, it would appear that transplacental diffusion of O_2 during maternal O_2 inhalation is primarily flow limited, whereas during hypoxia, when the maternal arterial O_2 pressure is low, as for example at high altitude, diffusion limitation plays a major role.

Acute maternal O_2 inhalation improves fetal

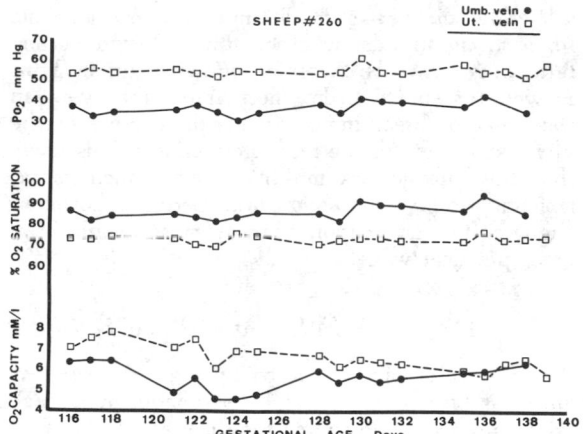

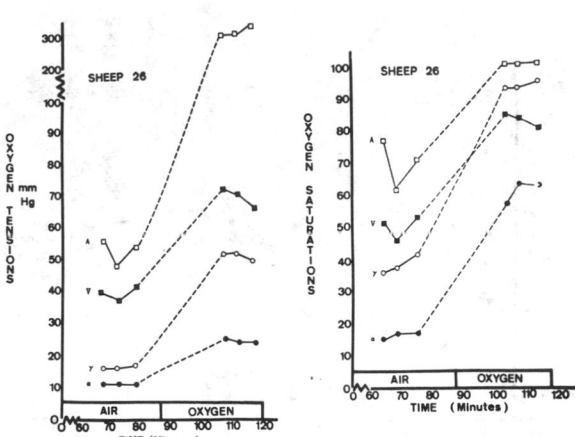

Fig. 22. The O_2 capacity, percent O_2 saturation, and Po_2 in the uterine and umbilical veins of a sheep in the last month of gestation. Note that the O_2 saturation in the umbilical vein is higher than in the uterine vein despite a much lower Po_2. This phenomenon is due to the higher O_2 affinity of fetal blood. (From Meschia et al. *Yale J. Biol. Med.,* 42:154, 1970.)

Fig. 23. Oxygen tensions and saturations in maternal artery (A), uterine vein (V), umbilical vein (γ), and umbilical artery (α) during periods of air and oxygen inhalation. (From Battaglia et al. *J. Clin. Invest.,* 47:548, 1968.)

oxygenation by raising the O_2 pressure of umbilical vein blood (Battaglia et al., 1968b). If fetal oxygenation is impaired by maternal hypoventilation, low uterine blood flow, or maternal anemia, maternal O_2 inhalation may improve dramatically the O_2 saturation of umbilical blood (see Figure 23). It should be emphasized that due to the characteristics of the placental exchanger and of fetal circulation there is no danger that maternal O_2 inhalation at normal atmospheric pressure might raise the Po_2 of fetal blood to the relatively high levels required to produce constriction of some fetal arteries in vitro (e.g., ductus arteriosus, umbilical artery).

Fetal oxygenation is impaired by:

1. All the conditions that lower the Po_2 in the maternal placental veins, i.e., low O_2 saturation in the maternal arterial system, anemia, low uterine blood flow, alkalosis (by shifting the maternal O_2 dissociation curve to the left; maternal acidosis, everything else being equal, improves fetal oxygenation).
2. At normal levels of maternal uterine venous Po_2, fetal oxygenation may be impaired because of some impairment in the transplacental diffusion of O_2 (e.g., placental detachment) or the transport of O_2 to the fetal tissues (e.g., compression of the umbilical cord, fetal anemia).

The term "fetal hypoxia" has been used in the past with two different meanings: (1) to describe the low O_2 pressure characteristic of normal intrauterine life and (2) to designate the pathologic situation in which placental O_2 supply is less than fetal O_2 requirement. The normal O_2 pressure in fetal blood, although low by adult standards, is above the critical level at which the aerobic metabolic rate of the

fetus becomes Po_2-dependent. This has been demonstrated by the fact that raising the Po_2 of fetal blood by maternal O_2 inhalation does not raise significantly the normal rate of fetal O_2 consumption (Battaglia et al., 1968b). Thus, from the fundamental point of view of metabolism, the *normal fetus in utero* is *not hypoxic* and the term of "fetal hypoxia" should be used with reference to pathologic conditions only. A clear distinction should also be made between acute and chronic fetal hypoxia. Fetuses of sheep living at high altitude may show blood O_2 contents similar to those at sea level, and much higher than those observed by exposing unacclimatized animals acutely to high altitude (Barron et al.). Therefore, there are important mechanisms of compensation to chronic maternal hypoxic conditions which are not available acutely. The exact nature of these chronic mechanisms must still be clarified.

A well-known characteristic of intrauterine life is the high O_2 affinity of fetal red cells (see Fig. 22). Exchange transfusion of adult red cells in the fetal circulation produces a marked drop of O_2 saturation in the umbilical vessels (Battaglia et al., 1969). Thus, the high O_2 affinity of fetal red cells has the functional advantage of providing a high level of O_2 saturation in the umbilical vein blood. This advantage is lost in infants whose predominant cell type becomes adult Rh-negative cells after repeated intrauterine transfusions.

ONSET OF BREATHING. At birth, a normal baby switches from placental to pulmonary respiration in seconds. Since the primary function of respiration is the consumption of oxygen and the excretion of CO_2, it seems reasonable to postulate that the onset of breathing is determined by hypoxia and CO_2 accumulation. Against this hypothesis is the fact that in the fetus, the blood perfusing the respiratory

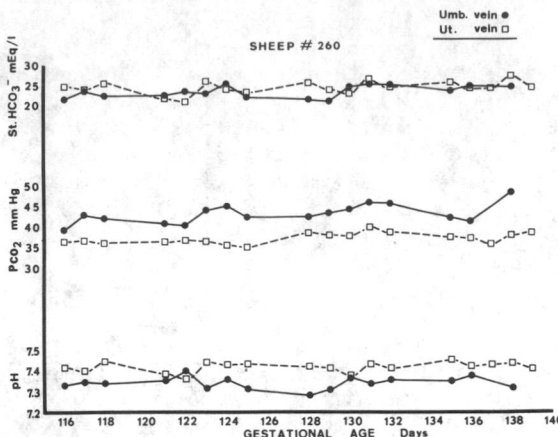

Fig. 24. The standard bicarbonate, Pco₂, and pH in the uterine and umbilical veins of a sheep in the last month of gestation. Same animal as in Figure 22. (From Meschia et al. *Yale J. Biol. Med.*, 42:154, 1970.)

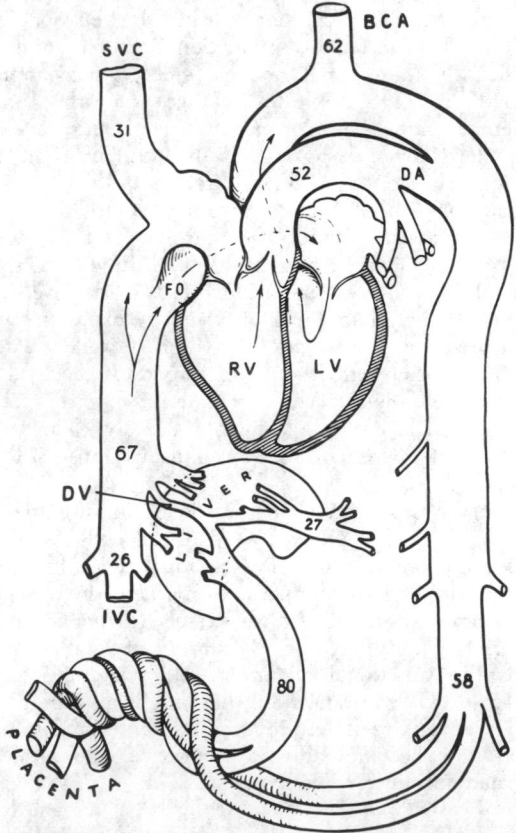

Fig. 25. Diagram of the circulation in the mature fetal lamb. The numerals indicate the mean O_2 saturation (percent) in the great vessels of six lambs: *RV*, right ventricle; *LV*, left ventricle; *SVC*, superior vena cava; *BCA*, brachiocephalic artery; *FO*, foramen ovale; *DA*, ductus arteriosus; *DV*, ductus venosus. (From Born et al. *Cold Spring Harbor Symp. Quant. Biol.*, 19:102, 1954.)

center and the chemoreceptors already has, by postnatal standards, a very low Po_2, a high Pco_2, and a slightly acid pH—a condition that seems adequate for a strong stimulation of breathing. Yet, a normal fetus does not make breathing efforts in utero. Thus it would seem that the most important event in the onset of breathing is an abrupt change in the physiologic state of the respiratory center. It is likely that this change has multiple causes, such as peripheral sensory stimulation and, perhaps, hormonal changes. The elucidation of these causes would have great practical value.

Fetal Acid-Base Balance

The best information concerning fetal acid-base balance has been derived from experiments in animals with chronically indwelling fetal catheters. The Pco_2 of umbilical vein blood is significantly higher than the Pco_2 of uterine vein blood (Fig. 24). This result is in agreement with the data concerning the transplacental diffusion of inert molecules and O_2. The standard bicarbonate concentration of normal fetal plasma is within the normal adult range (Fig. 24). The "normal" pH of umbilical vein blood is generally slightly more acid (approximately 0.05 pH units) than the "normal" pH of uterine vein blood. Thus, by adult standards, the normal fetal acid-base balance could be described as a mild, noncompensated respiratory acidosis. Previous studies which purported to find a metabolic acidosis as a normal characteristic of fetal blood were in error, probably reflecting the effect of operative stress on the fetus.

The relationship between fetal and maternal Pco_2 is a consistent finding, whereas under abnormal conditions the fetal bicarbonate concentration and pH may be much higher or much lower than corresponding maternal values. These facts are explained by the properties of the placental membrane. The placenta is much more permeable to CO_2 than to bicarbonate and chloride ions. Consequently the Pco_2 in fetal blood changes rapidly in response to changes of Pco_2 in maternal blood, but marked changes in bicarbonate concentration of maternal or fetal extracellular fluids do not lead to rapid equilibration of the two compartments. Because of these characteristics of the placental membrane, changes of maternal blood pH may be followed by similar or opposite changes in the fetal blood, depending upon the mechanism of these changes. Thus, acute maternal respiratory acidosis or alkalosis will produce a rapid decrease or increase respectively of fetal pH, but maternal metabolic acidosis with compensatory hyperventilation will move maternal and fetal pH in opposite directions (Blechner et al.).

Fetal Circulation

The anatomic characteristics of fetal circulation are schematically represented in Figure 25. A point that needs comment is that the inferior vena cava

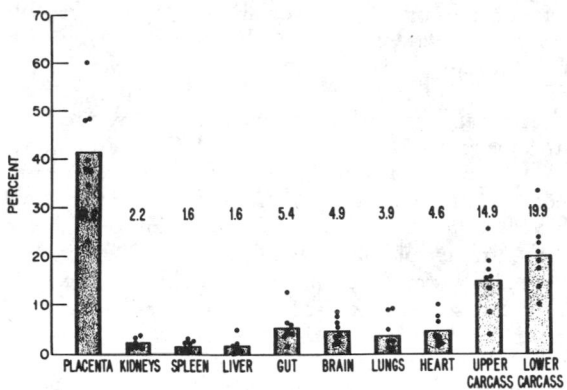

Fig. 26. The range and average of the percent of the cardiac output distributed to each of the fetal organs in eight fetal lambs. (From Rudolph and Heymann. *Circ. Res.,* 21:163, 1967.)

communicates directly with the left atrium through the foramen ovale. Thus the blood flowing from the inferior vena cava into the heart is divided into two columns: (1) inferior vena cava—foramen ovale—left auricle—left ventricle (via sinistra) and (2) inferior vena cava—right auricle—right ventricle (via dextra). In normal extrauterine life, virtually all of the systemic venous return goes to the right ventricle, and the only input to the left ventricle is represented by the pulmonary venous return. Thus, postnatally, the two ventricles work in series and have equal outputs, and the term "cardiac output" refers to the output of *either* ventricle. In normal fetal life, the major input to the left ventricle is represented by inferior vena caval blood which bypasses the right heart and enters the left atrium via the foramen ovale. The rest of the systemic venous return enters the right ventricle and is ejected into the pulmonary artery. Most of the output of the right heart bypasses the lungs and enters the descending aorta via the ductus arteriosus. Thus, in fetal life, the right and left ventricles work in parallel and the term "cardiac output" refers to the output of *both* ventricles. In the fetal lamb close to term, the fetal cardiac output has been estimated to be approximately 300 ml per kg of body weight per minute (Rudolph and Heymann). The approximate distribution of fetal cardiac output is presented in Figure 26. The large proportion of cardiac output that supplies the placenta and the small proportion that supplies lungs and kidneys represent the most outstanding characteristics of this distribution.

An important aspect of the fetal circulation is its effect on the oxygen saturation and O_2 pressure of the blood that perfuses different fetal organs. The liver receives a mixture of blood from the umbilical vein, the hepatic artery, and the portal vein. Each of these three bloodstreams contributes blood with quite different O_2 saturations in unknown proportions, which could be significantly different for the left and right hepatic lobes. If the umbilical flow were a large fraction of the hepatic flow, the liver

might be the only fetal organ exposed to approximately the same O_2 pressure before and after birth. All other fetal organs are perfused by blood with a Po_2 which is extremely low in comparison to normal extrauterine life. There are two main reasons for this low Po_2. The first, as we have seen, is due to the characteristics of placental exchange; that is, equilibration of umbilical venous blood with uterine venous blood. The second is due to the fact that the blood in fetal arteries is a mixture of arterialized blood from the placenta and venous blood from the fetal body. In order of decreasing O_2 saturation and Po_2 there are three distinct arterial systems: (1) the arteries that originate from the aorta above the ductus arteriosus; (2) the arteries that originate from the aorta below the ductus arteriosus; and (3) the pulmonary arteries (see Fig. 25). Thus the onset of breathing at birth represents a sudden and marked increase of O_2 pressure in the systemic and pulmonary arteries. There is good evidence (Assali, Dawes) that this change represents one of the important stimuli that promote the transition from the fetal to adult circulatory pattern. (High O_2 pressure tends to dilate the pulmonary vascular bed and to constrict the umbilical arteries and ductus arteriosus. Thus smooth muscle of different arteries reacts differently to the same stimulus.)

The normal heart rate of the human fetus at term is approximately 140 beats per minute. The interpretation of heart rate changes is discussed elsewhere in this book.

Fetal blood volume (i.e., volume of blood in the fetal vascular space, including placenta) is approximately 10 percent of fetal body weight. Despite the very low Po_2 of fetal blood, the hematocrit and O_2 capacity in fetuses free from stress are within the normal range of the adult animal. Fetal systemic arterial blood pressure at term is approximately 50 mm Hg, and compares with a similar mean arterial pressure for term newborn infants. However, the maintenance of a systemic arterial blood pressure of ~50 mm Hg is achieved by the fetus through the combined work of both ventricles, whereas this work load is carried by the left ventricle alone in the newborn infant.

Renal Physiology

WATER AND ELECTROLYTE BALANCE. Ordinarily, the sheep fetus produces markedly hypotonic urine. However, if the same fetus is exposed to a stressful experimental procedure, its urine tends to become more concentrated to the point of being moderately hypertonic. In agreement with these findings in the experimental animal, a wide range of osmolality has been found in human fetal urine at term, with a range from ~100 to 400 mOsm/kg H_2O. Although accurate measurements of urinary production rate in the unstressed fetus in utero are not available, it seems fairly well documented (Alexander and Nixon) that the fetal urinary output is very high and comparable to that of an animal with diabetes insipidus. This large volume of urine is excreted into the allantoic and/or amniotic fluids depending upon the species and, within the same species, the gestational age. Since the volume of urine produced by the fetus over several days exceeds the volume of these fluids, there must be reabsorption of water from the amniotic and allantoic sacs.

The hypotonicity and large output of fetal urine and the relatively low renal blood flow (see Fig. 26) indicate profound differences between fetal and postnatal renal function. Some of these differences can be attributed to the immaturity of the organ. For example, in the developing kidney, the newly formed nephrons have a short loop of Henle. This characteristic makes the nephron inherently less capable of concentrating the glomerular ultrafiltrate. On the other hand, the excretion of metabolic end products across the placenta from fetus to mother rather than into the amniotic sac via the fetal kidneys requires a high placental clearance/renal clearance ratio. Thus a kidney incapable of excreting some metabolites at the normal postnatal rate may represent an important functional advantage for the fetus.

Unfortunately, very little can be said about the regulation of fetal water and electrolyte balance. The changes in body proportions and particularly of extracellular and intracellular fluid volumes as a proportion of body weight have been discussed in the previous section. The osmolarities of maternal and fetal plasmas are virtually identical under normal circumstances (Meschia et al., 1957). Fetal dehydration can be produced by infusion in the mother of substances that do not cross the placenta at rapid rate. These substances increase osmotic pressure of maternal plasma and draw water from the fetus by osmosis (Bruns et al.). We have seen that fetal urine production tends to expand amniotic fluid volume rapidly. Reabsorption of water across the amniotic membrane and fetal swallowing tend to decrease the volume of amniotic fluid. The problems of polyhydramnios and oligohydramnios represent an imbalance of this dynamic equilibrium, which can be produced in several ways. The obstetrical literature contains detailed and elaborate descriptions of the exchange of radioactively tagged water molecules between maternal blood and amnion and between fetal blood and amnion. These descriptions are supposed to clarify the problems of fetal water balance. In reality, processes such as fetal glomerular filtration rate, swallowing of amniotic fluid, and osmotic flow of water across the placental and the amniotic membrane, are *bulk* movements of water which have no quantitative relationship with the rate of appearance or disappearance of labeled water molecules injected in a given compartment.

Regulation of Glucose Metabolism

Glucose is one of the main substrates of fetal metabolism. According to preliminary observations in our laboratory on ewes with chronically indwelling catheters in the umbilical circulation, glucose normally crosses the placenta from mother to fetus at a steady rate. In sheep, this rate can account for approximately 50 percent of fetal aerobic metabolism. It is not yet clear what other substances besides glucose are used in large quantities to sustain fetal O_2 consumption.

Two important facts about fetal glucose regulation are: (1) glucose can be raised or lowered in fetal blood by raising or lowering respectively the glucose concentration of maternal blood; and (2) it is substantially lower than the maternal blood concentration. The second of these facts can be easily explained by assuming that fetal glucose uptake requires the existence of a large transplacental gradient. In sheep, the transplacental glucose difference becomes larger at high concentrations of maternal and fetal glucose. Widdas has interpreted this finding as evidence for the presence of a glucose carrier in the placental membrane. It seems clear from these observations that the placenta normally imposes on the fetus a physiologic hypoglycemia and that the fetus has a limited control over its own blood glucose level. Most likely, this situation requires homeostatic mechanisms which are set quite differently than in postnatal life. For example, despite the hypoglycemia, the fetus consumes glucose in large quantities and is able to store glycogen in the liver and other tissues during the latter part of gestation (Shelley and Neligan). These glycogen stores can be depleted by maternal starvation. Storage of fetal liver glycogen is under hormonal control (Jost and Jacquot), and the fetal pancreas is capable of producing insulin. Many of the enzymes involved in glycogen storage and breakdown have different activities in the fetal and postnatal liver (Dawkins). Presumably, these differences are related to the peculiar requirements of fetal glucose regulation, but there is neither evidence to substantiate this hypothesis, nor are there any clues as to the hormonal mechanisms that might be responsible.

REFERENCES

Aherne, W., and Dunnill, M. S. Morphometry of the human placenta. Brit. Med. Bull., 22:5, 1966.

Alexander, D. P., and Nixon, D. A. The foetal kidney. Brit. Med. Bull., 17:112, 1961.

Assali, N. S. Biology of Gestation, 1st ed. New York, Academic Press, 1968.

Barron, D. H., Metcalfe, J., Meschia, G., Huckabee, W., Hellegers, A., and Prystowsky, H. Adaptations of pregnant ewes and their fetuses to high altitude. *In* The Symposium on the Physiological Effects of High Altitude. New York, Pergamon Press Ltd., 1963, pp. 115-125.

Battaglia, F. C., Behrman, R. E., Meschia, G., Seeds, A. E., and Bruns, P. D. Clearance of inert molecules, Na and Cl ions across the primate placenta. Amer. J. Obstet. Gynec., 102:1135, 1968a.

—— Meschia, G., Makowski, E. L., and Bowes, W.

The effect of maternal oxygen inhalation upon fetal oxygenation. J. Clin. Invest., 47:548, 1968b.

——— Bowes, W., McGaughey, H. R., Makowski, E. L., and Meschia, G. The effect of fetal exchange transfusions with adult blood upon fetal oxygenation. Pediat. Res., 3:60, 1969.

Blechner, J. N., Meschia, G., and Barron, D. H. A study of the acid-base balance of fetal sheep and goats. Quart. J. Exp. Physiol., 45:60, 1960.

Bruns, P. D., Hellegers, A. E., Seeds, A. E., Behrman, R. E., and Battaglia, F. C. Effects of osmotic gradients across the primate placenta upon fetal and placenta water contents. Pediatrics, 34:407, 1964.

Dawes, G. S. Foetal and Neonatal Physiology. 1st ed. Chicago, Year Book Medical Publishers, 1968.

Dawkins, M. J. R. Biochemical aspects of developing function in newborn mammalian liver. Brit. Med. Bull., 22:27, 1966.

Greiss, F. C. The uterine vascular bed: effect of adrenergic stimulation. Obstet. Gynec., 21:295, 1963.

——— and Anderson, S. G. Uterine vascular changes during the ovarian cycle. Amer. J. Obstet. Gynec., 103:629, 1969.

Jost, A., and Jacquot, R. Recherches sur les facteurs endocriniens de la charge en glycogène du foie foetal chez le lapin. Ann. Endocr., 16:849, 1955.

Ladner, C., Brinkman, III, Weston, P., and Assali, N. S. Dynamics of uterine circulation in pregnant and nonpregnant sheep. Amer. J. Physiol., 218:257, 1970.

Longo, L. D., Power, G. G., and Forster, R. E., Jr. Respiratory function of the placenta as determined with carbon monoxide in sheep and dogs. J. Clin. Invest., 46:812, 1967.

Makowski, E. L., Meschia, G., Droegemueller, W., and Battaglia, F. C. Distribution of uterine blood flow in the pregnant sheep. Amer. J. Obstet. Gynec., 101:409, 1968a.

——— Meschia, G., Droegemueller, W., and Battaglia, F. C. Measurement of umbilical arterial blood flow to the sheep placenta and fetus in utero. Circ. Res., 23:623, 1968b.

Meschia, G., Breathnach, C. S., Cotter, J. R., Hellegers, A., and Barron, D. H. The diffusibility of urea across the sheep placenta in the last two months of gestation. Quart. J. Exp. Physiol., 50:23, 1965.

——— Battaglia, F. C., and Bruns, P. D. Theoretical and experimental study of transplacental diffusion. J. Appl. Physiol., 22:1171, 1967a.

——— Cotter, J. R., Makowski, E. L., and Barron, D. H. Simultaneous measurement of uterine and umbilical blood flows and oxygen uptakes. Quart. J. Exp. Physiol., 52:1, 1967b.

——— Battaglia, F. C., and Barron, D. H. A comparison of the freezing points of fetal and maternal plasmas of sheep and goat. Quart. J. Exp. Physiol., 42:164, 1957.

Needham, J. Chemical Embryology. New York, The Macmillan Company, 1931.

Rudolph, A. M., and Heymann, M. A. The circulation of the fetus in utero. Circ. Res., 21:163, 1967.

Shelley, H. J., and Neligan, G. A. Neonatal hypoglycaemia. Brit. Med. Bull., 22:34, 1966.

Widdas, W. F. Inability of diffusion to account for placental glucose transfer in the sheep and consideration of the kinetics of a possible carrier transfer. J. Physiol., 118:23, 1952.

Wilkin, P. La perméabilité placentaire. In Snoeck, G., ed., Le Placenta Humain. Paris, Masson et C., 1958, pp. 194-241.

2.7
PHARMACOLOGY

SUMNER J. YAFFE and LARS O. BOREUS

For many years, drugs have been prescribed to the pregnant woman for maternal indications. The realization that the fetus simultaneously serves as a target for the maternally administered drug is a recent concept, appreciation of which has been greatly stimulated by the thalidomide tragedy of the early sixties. This resulted in a marked decrease in drug utilization during pregnancy in those countries in western Europe in which thalidomide had been in use. On the other hand, there has been no apparent change in drug consumption in the United States, where thalidomide was not marketed and where it is estimated that the pregnant female consumes an average of four medications during each pregnancy. In addition to the prescription items which can be recorded, there are innumerable unrecognized contacts with drugs and chemicals in the environment. High rates of congenital malformation and neonatal mortality continue despite considerable advances in obstetric and pediatric knowledge. It is highly probable that maternal drug ingestion plays a role in these untoward effects. More recently, drugs have been prescribed to the gravid female to treat *fetal* disease, with varying success. Knowledge concerning fetal pharmacology is a prerequisite in helping the pediatrician understand how certain agents may produce deleterious effects while others may be employed for their therapeutic effects upon the fetus.

General Considerations

Numerous factors govern the action of a drug within an organism. These include mechanisms that determine the duration of action of the chemical agent and factors which control the concentration of the substance at a receptor site. Irrespective of route of administration, a drug must usually traverse one or several semipermeable membranes before the required receptor is reached. On both sides of each membrane the net effects of storage, excretion, and inactivation tend to decrease the effective concentration of the drug. In administering a drug to a pregnant woman, either for her benefit or to treat the fetus, the physician must consider: (1) maternal pharmacologic mechanisms; (2) effects on the placenta, including its pharmacodynamic capability; and finally, (3) effects on the fetus as an additional recipient of the drug. Fetal pharmacology must, therefore, examine the interplay between the fetus and the mother, with the placenta mediating this dual relationship. Most attention in the past has been focused on the teratogenic effects of drugs as they relate to the developing embryo (Sec. 1.3). In the present section, the effects of drugs on the developing organism *beyond* the stage of organogenesis will be considered.

THE ROLE OF THE PLACENTA. The placenta as an organ of transport is discussed elsewhere (p. 45). Its role in the transmission of drugs is essentially to permit passage (usually by passive diffusion) of all compounds with molecular weights less than 1,000, with only an occasional exception. This is in keeping with current concepts of the placenta as a filter instead of a barrier. What happens to placental transmission of drugs during toxemia and other abnormalities of pregnancy is not at all clear; nor are data available concerning variations in rates of transmission at different stages of placental development during pregnancy. There has long been evidence that the placenta functions as a metabolic organ, and its role in drug transformation must be considered. Lipid soluble drugs easily pass across the placenta to gain access to the fetus, and the possibility exists that they may be metabolically altered during the transport process. Recent investigations have demonstrated that hydrolytic and reductive reactions are most active in homogenates of term placentae. Conjugating activity is very low in placental tissue and, if present, is likely to be overwhelmed by hydrolytic enzymes whose activity probably serves to facilitate the bidirectional transfer of drug substrates between mother and fetus. Exceptions with respect to conjugation reactions appear to be acetylation and glycine coupling. Oxidation of drugs also appears to be minimal in placenta unless the mother has *smoked cigarettes* during pregnancy or received doses of inducing agents such as phenobarbital. While these studies were carried out at the end of pregnancy, it is likely that other reactions may be mediated by the placenta in early gestation. It has been hypothesized that the placenta supplements the fetal liver and that the placenta should be able to metabolize drugs maximally early in gestation, when the developing fetal liver is metabolically most incompetent (cf. section on drug metabolism in the fetus). The significance of drug biotransformation by the placenta has not been fully clarified. However, the metabolic conversions effected by the placenta could influence the developing fetus (and pregnant mother) in a number of ways: e.g., metabolites could act directly upon fetal tissues to produce abnormal effects; drug substrates could compete for enzyme systems within the placenta which are normally used for the metabolism of endogenous substances such as hormones, thus disturbing the internal environment of the fetus; or drug metabolites could inhibit the biochemical functions of the placenta which are important in the energy-requiring transport mechanisms of this unique organ.

DRUG DISTRIBUTION IN THE FETUS. The exposure of fetal tissues to maternally administered drugs is dependent upon the kinetics of equilibration between maternal and fetal blood as well as on the special features of distribution within the fetus.

The rate of elimination of the drug in the mother is the major determinant of the time needed to achieve equal concentrations in the mother and fetus. For example, it has been estimated that for a drug whose rate of transfer is flow-limited, and at a constant arterial drug concentration in the mother, 50 percent of that concentration will be achieved in fetal arterial blood in about 5 minutes but equilibration to 90 percent will require about 40 minutes. If the drug has a short half-life in the mother, approximately equal concentrations (90 percent) will be reached earlier, since less of the drug has to be transferred and the concentration at that time in maternal and fetal arterial blood is low. It has also been shown that the drug level in fetal blood may eventually be higher than in maternal blood, which will result in a net flow from fetus to mother. This has no apparent clinical significance, since it occurs at low drug levels. It demonstrates, however, that a single maternal/fetal ratio value is entirely unsatisfactory to characterize the complicated process of distribution.

The comparatively slow rates of equilibration between maternal and fetal tissues on the one hand and maternal and fetal plasma concentrations on the other may be the main explanation for the fact that a mother can be deeply anesthetized with barbiturates while her newborn baby is alert and has a good Apgar score. However, other factors, such as higher lipid solubility in the brain of the mother than of the fetus, or an extracellular reduction of Pco_2 after birth resulting in a shift of barbiturates out of the cells, have also been suggested as contributing to this difference in degree of CNS depression.

Little is known about the rates of membrane permeation of drugs in the fetus as compared to adult individuals. It is generally believed that the blood-brain barrier is less effective in the immature organism, allowing substances like morphine to penetrate more easily.

Receptor Function in the Fetus. The initiation of the pharmacologic response usually results from the interaction between the drug molecules and active sites (receptors) in the tissues. It has been demonstrated that autonomic receptor function is well developed in human fetal tissues at the end of the first trimester of pregnancy. At this age, both cholinergic and adrenergic receptors display the same affinity and specificity for agonists and antagonists as in adult tissues. The fetal myocardium, for example, will respond with an increase in rate and force of contraction to beta-adrenergic stimulants. This capacity of the fetus to respond to maternally administered drugs which cross the placenta must be taken into consideration as one plans for drug therapy during pregnancy.

Drug Metabolism in the Fetus. The termination of drug action in man is mainly accomplished by chemical change, with urinary excretion of the native drug being of little quantitative importance. The biochemical mechanisms for transforming a myriad of drugs appear to involve only a few chemical pathways, the most common of which are oxidation, reduction, conjugation, and hydrolysis. Examination of these mechanisms in the liver of the mammalian (nonprimate) fetus at or near term has generally revealed minimal to absent activity. A notable exception is the activity of the enzymatic systems concerned with the transfer and hydrolysis of sulfate. Except for those concerned with sulfation, most of the drug-metabolizing enzymes are isolated in the microsomal fraction, and deficient activity correlates well with histologic evidence of a decreased amount of endoplasmic reticulum, from which drug-metabolizing enzymes and microsomes are derived. Generalizations based upon in vitro experiments with liver tissue cannot be extended to all fetal organs; for example, although hepatic conjugating ability may be low in the term fetus, activity in the gastrointestinal mucosa of the rat is greater in the fetus than in the adult. The mucosa, however, probably contributes little to the overall drug-metabolizing capabilities, the bulk of which is carried out in the liver.

While the general view exists that fetal tissues are unable to metabolize foreign compounds, it should be emphasized that these investigations were conducted on nonprimate fetal tissues. Endocrinologists have provided ample evidence that human fetal tissue (especially liver and adrenal) obtained in early and midgestation is able to carry out a number of metabolic functions (with steroid substrates), including oxidation, reduction, demethylation, sulfation, and glucuronidation. In fact, human trophoblast cell suspensions grown in tissue culture have been shown capable of acetylating sulfonamides and hydroxylating other drug substrates. While the majority of these studies has been concerned with hormones as substrates, recent data have shown many similarities between the enzyme systems which hydroxylate steroids and those which oxidize drugs, suggesting that steroid hormones are the naturally occurring substrates for microsomal drug-metabolizing enzymes. Steroids appear to have a greater affinity for the enzyme systems, and for this reason may prevent drug substrates from gaining access to the active site on the microsomal enzyme. Final assessment of the drug-metabolic capability of the human fetus must await investigations with human tissue, employing conditions which take into consideration the role of hormones as natural substrates.

Studies during the last 10 years have shown that the chronic administration of many drugs to the intact organism causes a nonspecific increase in the metabolism of drugs by microsomal enzymes and thereby decreases the duration and intensity of drug action in vivo (induction). This approach has been applied to the fetus, and it has been demonstrated that agents such as phenobarbital administered to the pregnant animal late in gestation can stimulate the activities not only of the mixed-function oxidase system in fetal liver microsomes but also of glucuronyl transferase. These findings have applications to the clinical care of the human infant (see below). The lack of effect of these inducers early in gestation may indicate the insensitivity of a biochemical system which has yet to make its evolutionary appearance, or may be due to the inhibitory effect of high concentrations of steroid hormones.

Since pregnancy is associated with dramatic and profound physiologic and biochemical changes in the maternal organism, it would not be surprising if the drug-metabolizing capability of the mother was also altered during pregnancy. The available evidence suggests that microsomal drug metabolism by maternal hepatic microsomes is markedly reduced during pregnancy. This makes the metabolic contribution by fetal liver and placenta assume added importance. While the placenta and fetus have been discussed separately, mention should be made of the concept of the integration of the fetus and placenta as a functional unit. This realization has arisen from studies of steroid metabolism, where one or more key enzymes have been found to be absent in either the fetal liver or placenta. Since the enzymes lacking in one tissue are present in the other, the fetus and placenta together can carry out biochemical functions which neither could accomplish alone. This interdependence of the fetus and placenta is further suggested when one considers the common origin of both in the fertilized ovum. This concept has not been applied to fetal pharmacology but will undoubtedly prove to be a fruitful area for future investigation.

Clinical Considerations

Therapeutic use of pharmacologic agents during pregnancy has been mainly directed toward maternal disease. However, the fetus is also exposed to such drugs which may produce unexpected and occasionally tragic results in the developing fetus, for whom the drug was not intended. However, the fact that the fetus does function as a recipient of such drugs also suggests the possibility of producing desirable drug effects in the fetus by giving drugs to the pregnant women. Recent knowledge gained from animal experiments, in which treatment of the mother during the latter part of pregnancy induced the activities of a number of hepatic microsomal enzymes, has been applied to man.

DRUG THERAPY OF THE FETUS. Apart from the treatment of syphilis in the pregnant female with concomitant cure of fetal infection, intrauterine transfusion has been a much-needed stimulant for the development of the idea of intrauterine therapy of the fetus. The concept of pharmacologic induction of drug metabolic enzyme activity when applied to the human fetus is another example of fetal therapeutics which holds great promise for future success. The approach has been employed primarily to treat the unconjugated hyperbilirubinemia of the newborn and premature infant. For example, the administration of phenobarbital orally (30 to 120 mg per day) to the mother for two weeks prior to delivery has been shown to produce marked decrease in neonatal serum bilirubin concentrations as contrasted to a control group of infants born to untreated mothers. Retrospectively, it has been noted that infants born to mothers receiving phenobarbital as therapy for epilepsy are less jaundiced than control infants. The mechanism by which phenobarbital decreases serum bilirubin concentrations is not entirely clear, although induction of glucuronyl transferase activity plays a significant role. In this case, the risks of phenobarbital usage are unknown and may outweigh its benefits, since the phenobarbital inductive effect is nonspecific, and activities of other liver microsomal enzymes that, for example, metabolize steroid hormones and other endogenous substrates are also increased. Alterations in steroid concentrations at such a critical period of development may have long-lasting consequences which may not become apparent until later on in development. The use of phenobarbital is probably justified in treating a fetus known to have hemolytic disease where the benefits from induction may be greater than the risks mentioned above.

MATERNAL DRUG THERAPY. As discussed above, all pharmacologic agents (with rare exceptions) when administered to the mother will be transported across the placenta to the fetus. The concept of the placenta serving as a barrier has some usefulness in immunology but does not apply to considerations of therapeutic agents. In the following sections several classes of drugs commonly administered to the pregnant woman in mid- and late gestation are surveyed. Compounds have been chosen to exemplify principles of fetal pharmacology and not to catalog all the drugs used during pregnancy. All drugs sooner or later can produce adverse effects on the fetus, and it is worthless to present for the physician a list of drugs to avoid and to memorize.

Anesthetics. With the exception of patients who receive local anesthetics, nearly all primigravidas and most multiparas are given a general anesthetic in the latter part of the first stage and in the second stage of labor. Gaseous agents are commonly used, and anesthesia is usually maintained at the level of analgesia to minimize the severe pain as the head of the fetus passes through the vulva. With forceps delivery and for repair of lacerations or an episiotomy, anesthesia is deepened to stage three (surgical anesthesia). All agents used in inhalation anesthesia rapidly diffuse across the placenta. The degree of narcosis of the newborn is the resultant of many factors, including the amount of drug given to the mother, pattern of placental blood flow, and rate of equilibration of the anesthetic between mother and fetus. Since the gases, with the exception of trichloroethylene (Trilene), are primarily excreted by exhalation without prior metabolism, the duration of anesthetic effect in the newborn infant after delivery will depend upon the infant's ventilatory capacity and the amount of drug present. Ultrashort-acting barbiturates used under similar circumstances easily pass the placenta. Since this type of barbiturate undergoes nearly complete biotransformation by the liver into an inactive metabolite, the newborn may undergo prolonged depression owing to his inability to oxidize the intravenous anesthetic (thiopental or hexobarbital). Local anesthetics given either by regional infiltration or by the spinal, epidural, or caudal route have been used extensively during delivery without recognizable harmful effect on the fetus or infant unless maternal hypotension has occurred. However, paracervical block with the amide-type of local anesthetics has been associated with fetal bradycardia in as many as 30 percent of fetuses, probably as a result of placental transfer of the drug and its effect upon the fetal myocardium. The muscle relaxants, such as curare and succinyl choline, do not cross the placenta. Their use as muscle relaxants during cesarean section reduces the amount of inhalation anesthetic needed, and has been universally accepted.

Analgesics. The goals in obstetric analgesia are to provide pain relief for the mother without affecting the fetus or the delivery process. Opiates and their synthetic substitutes such as meperidine (Demerol) easily reach the fetus when given to the mother during delivery. Respiratory depression in the newborn infant is frequently seen, since glucuronidation, the major conjugating mechanism for morphine, functions at a low level in the fetus and newborn infant. All of the narcotic analgesics are competitively antagonized by nalorphine and levallorphan, congeners of morphine, which have been used effectively to combat the depressant effects. Since the antagonistic effect ocurs either when injected into the mother immediately prior to delivery or when given into the umbilical vein, transplacental passage must occur readily. Morphine and heroin addiction can occur in utero (see Chap. 13), but the diagnosis may be missed because of the possibility of late appearance of withdrawal signs several days after birth. So characteristic is the withdrawal picture that it can be the clue to the diagnosis of addiction in the mother. Early recognition and treatment is mandatory in order to minimize infant morbidity. Abstinence signs in utero, presenting as markedly increased fetal activity, have been observed in the pregnant addict at a time when she begins to crave a dose.

The nonnarcotic analgesics, of which salicylate is the major prototype, are used in a free and uncontrolled manner throughout pregnancy. Although mechanisms for conjugation (glucuronide formation and coupling with glycine) are low in activity in the fetus and newborn, and high concentrations of unaltered salicylate occur immediately following delivery, overt toxic effects on the fetus or newborn have rarely been noted. Occasionally maternal ingestion of salicylates may produce temporary coagulation defects in newborn infants, presumably by suppression of prothrombin synthesis. In mice, salicylates are teratogenic and in late pregnancy produce bleeding in fetal liver.

Hypnotics and Sedatives. All members of this class of drugs readily cross the placenta, but little is known about their metabolism and excretion by the fetus and newborn except for barbiturates, which are the most frequently used hypnotic agents. The duration of action of the various barbiturates is inversely proportional to their rate of metabolic degradation, with more of the long-acting compound appearing unchanged in the urine. Side-chain oxidation, the major metabolic event, occurs minimally in fetal and newborn liver, accounting for the markedly prolonged duration of action in the newborn infant. Renal excretion of the long-acting compounds such as phenobarbital has not been studied, but since the glomerular filtration rate in the newborn approximates 30 to 40 percent of adult values, a diminished rate of excretion presumably would contribute to a more prolonged hypnotic effect. While hypnosis is the intended therapeutic aim in the mother, inadequate excretory and metabolic mechanisms may lead to increased barbiturate concentrations in the fetus, who may become anesthetized and indeed may succumb postnatally from respiratory center depression.

Alcohol has been said to damage the fetus, but direct proof is elusive due to the association of other factors such as inadequate vitamin intake in mothers with chronic alcoholism. Ethanol administered to the mother just prior to delivery has been shown to be associated with decreased serum bilirubin concentration in the newborn. This effect is presumably the result of enhanced rate of conjugation of bilirubin due to enzyme induction. The deficiency of the newborn in metabolizing alcohol should be kept in mind, however, before this treatment is adopted.

Antihypertensive Drugs. Active management of toxemia of pregnancy and the associated hypertension has led to a profound decrease in maternal and fetal mortality. Antihypertensive drugs have played a major role in the treatment program and have not usually been accompanied by major adverse effects in the offspring. Thrombocytopenia has been reported in infants born to mothers receiving thiazides. This is apparently a rare event and is most likely due to a direct toxic effect on the fetal megacariocyte production, since maternal platelet counts were normal. Reserpine administration to the pregnant mother within two days prior to delivery has led to a clinical syndrome in the newborn infant characterized by severe noninfective nasal discharge, lethargy, anorexia, and respiratory depression. Symptoms usually subside spontaneously

with the first week of life. However, no pharmacologic investigations have been undertaken to explain the symptomatology, which is most likely due to prolonged blockage of norepinephrine uptake at neurotransmitter storage sites in the infant.

Antithyroid Drugs. The fetal thyroid gland begins to function during the fourth month of gestation and any antithyroid agent administered to the mother may affect the function and subsequent development of the infant's thyroid-pituitary axis, since antithyroid drugs readily cross the placenta.

The use of radioactive iodine during pregnancy may lead to congenital malformations in the fetus, and this radioisotope may produce destructive effects on the fetal thyroid. These findings have been verified in animal experiments and noted in human stillborn infants. The potential for transplacental initiation of malignant change in the infant thyroid at some later date should also serve to preclude the use of ^{131}I during pregnancy.

Thiouracil derivatives are transmitted across the placenta and inhibit thyroxin synthesis by the independently functioning fetal thyroid. This effect is probably responsible for many congenital goiters. In most instances the enlargement of the thyroid gland regresses spontaneously in the postnatal period, and no therapy is needed unless there is mechanical obstruction of the airway. Potassium perchlorate and potassium iodide have also been incriminated as fetal goitrogens when used during pregnancy, presumably by interfering with the iodide concentrating and binding function of the thyroid.

Hormones. Steroid hormones are used widely in clinical obstetrics primarily to prevent abortion, sustain placentation, and decrease uterine tone. Discussion of pharmacologic effects must begin with consideration of the *physiologic* role and significance of these agents during fetal development. There is ample experimental evidence to indicate that no fetal endocrine gland is indispensable for survival of the fetus, perhaps because of the presence of placental or maternal hormone. Homeostasis in the fetus can evidently be regulated by the maternal environment mediated through the placenta. Fetal hormones probably play a more important role in the physiologic and morphologic development of their target organs.

Permanent structural changes are a conspicuous effect of gonadal hormones, and fetal female masculinization may follow the use of testosterone or 17-substituted steroid hormones in certain pregnant women. The mechanism for this pharmacologic effect has been clearly elucidated by Jost, who demonstrated a critical period during development when masculinization of the female fetus can occur (end of first trimester), with resultant fusion of the urethral folds and development of a penislike phallus. Administration of the hormone after this critical period may only lead to an enlarged clitoris. The drug effect, in this case androgenic action, is exerted at the time during normal development when sex differentiation is taking place. The function of fetally-produced androgen is to prevent the genital tract of males from differentiating along the female line. Feminine differentiation is nonhormone dependent, and excess androgen in the maternal environment finds a sensitive receptor organ in the fetus when present at the time of differentiation of the female genital tract.

Steroid hormones appear to pass readily from mother to fetus and also in the reverse direction. Transport probably involves hydrolysis of the conjugated hormone by placental enzymes (sulfatases), since transfer of the unconjugated form proceeds much more easily than that of the conjugated drug.

Oxytocin preparations may contain antidiuretic activity, and water intoxication in the mother and fetus has been reported in a few cases after prolonged infusion given to stimulate contractility.

Insulin secretion by the fetal pancreas has been shown to occur by midgestation in rodents, but the exact time when this takes place in human development is not known. The blood glucose level of the fetus is probably controlled by that of the mother, but the fetal pancreas at term may respond to hyperglycemia by the secretion of insulin. The available evidence suggests that insulin does not cross the placenta in either direction in physiologically significant amounts.

Tolbutamide freely crosses the placenta and has been associated with hypoglycemia in the neonate, presumably due to stimulation of fetal insulin release. Teratogenic effects have been reported both in animals and man, but those in man are difficult to evaluate because of the higher malformation rate in infants of diabetic mothers.

Antimicrobial Agents. Antibacterial chemotherapeutic agents administered to the mother usually reach the fetus without observable side effects. Very little is known about the handling of this class of drugs by the fetus. Hearing loss in the infant has been reported following the administration of streptomycin to pregnant women with tuberculosis. This complication appears to be rare as judged by the small number of cases reported.

Tetracycline is deposited as a fluorescent complex in growing bone, and it has been shown that there is interference with skeletal growth when this agent is given to premature infants. Staining of deciduous teeth and enamel hypoplasia may follow transplacental acquisition of tetracycline.

Other antibiotics, such as chloramphenicol and novobiocin, have adverse effects when administered to the premature and newborn infant. Their effect upon the fetus has not been adequately studied.

Sulfonamides may have a hazardous pharmacologic effect when administered during pregnancy or to the newborn infant. Sulfonamides, like salicylates, have a propensity for dissociating bilirubin from albumin. No longer stored within the albumin space, the free bilirubin may diffuse more readily into the central nervous system to exert its damaging effects, while at the same time, with

greater volume for distribution within the organism, its concentration in the serum is decreased. This effect of sulfonamides is particularly important in the immediate postnatal period when critical relationships exist between bilirubin production and hepatic bilirubin metabolism.

REFERENCES

Baker, J. B. E. The effects of drugs on the foetus. Pharmacol. Rev., 12:37, 1960.

Brown, A. K., and Zuelzer, W. Studies on the neonatal development of the glucuronide conjugating system. J. Clin. Invest., 37:332, 1958.

Finster, M., et al. Plasma thiopental concentrations in the newborn following delivery under thiopental-nitrous oxide anesthesia. Amer. J. Obstet. Gynec., 95:621, 1966.

Fouts, J. R., and Adamson, R. H. Drug metabolism in the newborn rabbit. Science, 129:897, 1959.

Goldstein, A., Aronow, L., and Kalman, S. M. Passage of drugs across the placenta. In Goldstein, A., et al., eds., Principles of Drug Action. New York, Harper & Row, 1968, pp. 179-194.

Gordon, H. R. Fetal bradycardia after paracervical block; correlation with fetal and maternal blood levels of local anesthetic (Mepivacaine). New Eng. J. Med., 279:910, 1968.

Hagerman, D. D. Enzymatic capabilities of the placenta. Fed. Proc., 23:785, 1964.

Hart, L. G., Adamson, R. H., Dixon, R. L., and Fouts, J. R. Stimulation of hepatic microsomal drug metabolism in the newborn and fetal rabbit. J. Pharmacol. Exp. Ther., 137:103, 1962.

Hill, R. M., Desmond, M. M., and Kay, J. L. Extrapyramidal dysfunction in an infant of a schizophrenic mother. Pediatrics, 69:589, 1966.

Jost, A. The role of fetal hormones in prenatal development. Harvey Lectures, Series 55:201, 1960.

Lamb, J. M. Neonatal respiratory depression secondary to maternal analgesics, treated by exchange transfusion. Pediatrics, 43:94, 1969.

Levitz, M., and Dancis, J. Transfer of steroids between mother and fetus. Clin. Obstet. Gynec., 6:62, 1963.

Lucey, J. F. Hazards to the newborn infant from drugs administered to the mother. Pediat. Clin. N. Amer., 8:413, 1961.

Percy, A. K., and Yaffe, S. J. Sulfate metabolism during mammalian development. Pediatrics, 33:965, 1964.

2.8
INTRAUTERINE DIAGNOSIS

JOHN M. BOWMAN

Inadequacy of Clinical Examination Before Birth

Accurate knowledge of the physical condition of the fetus and his environment is important for all the reasons stressed in previous sections of this chapter. However, obtaining reliable data on the intra-uterine environment, with safety to the mother and infant, remains a difficult task. Even frequent, careful clinical examinations during the latter part of pregnancy and labor are often insufficient to determine the condition of the fetus. Many intrapartum deaths occur without apparent warning, which could be prevented if a more accurate estimate of the condition of the fetus could be made. Ancillary methods of examination developed to meet this need, do not supplant careful clinical examinations but serve as an essential adjunct to such examinations.

Diagnostic Amniocentesis

Examination of amniotic fluid removed transabdominally can provide valuable information and carries minimal risk to the fetus. Diagnostic amniocentesis was first put into widespread clinical use in the management of pregnancies complicated by Rh immunization. Subsequently, amniotic fluid examination has proved useful in determination of fetal maturity, in high-risk situations such as toxemia of pregnancy and diabetes mellitus, and in pregnancies at high risk of chromosomal or biochemical abnormalities in the fetus.

Amnioscopy, the direct examination of the amniotic fluid by introduction of a small endoscope through the undilated cervix of the unanesthetized mother, has been used in toxemic, postterm, and Rh-isoimmunized pregnancies. The presence of scant, yellow, or meconium-stained fluid is a sign that the fetus may be in jeopardy and induction of labor may be advisable. Although the procedure carries no risk to the mother, prompt labor ensues in one third of cases, limiting its use to pregnancies after 36 to 37 weeks' gestation.

AMNIOTIC FLUID EXAMINATION IN ERYTHROBLAS-TOSIS FETALIS. Amniotic fluid coproporphyrin, nonhematin iron, and protein levels, all rise as degree of severity of erythroblastosis fetalis increases. However, the correlation is not sufficiently reliable to make them of value in predicting severity of involvement or likelihood of intrauterine death. Falling amniotic fluid estriol levels have been noted in some cases of increasing severity of Rh disease, but correlate well only with a fetal death in utero. In other cases, severely affected liveborn erythroblastotic babies have been associated with normal amniotic fluid estriol levels. Estimations of amniotic fluid bilirubin, either quantitatively or spectrophotometrically, have provided the best correlation with severity of Rh hemolytic disease.

Quantitative amniotic fluid bilirubin levels can give a valuable correlation with severity of Rh disease. However, since the actual amounts of indirect bilirubin are small (usually less than 1.0 mg percent even in the presence of very severe Rh disease), spectrophotometric measurement of the increase in optical density at wavelength 450 mμ provides a

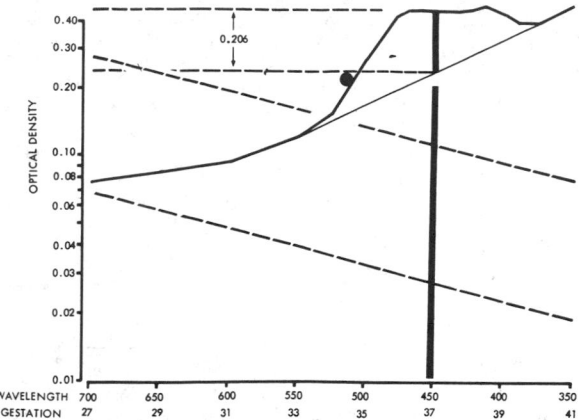

Fig. 27. Amniotic fluid optical density curve at 34½ weeks' gestation of a fetus severely affected with erythroblastosis. Prehydropic infant delivered at 35 weeks' gestation, salvaged after five exchange transfusions. (Cord Hb 4.7 g percent.)

The observed optical density of filtered centrifuged amniotic fluid is plotted from 700 to 350 mμ on semilogarithmic paper (continuous line). A rise in optical density is computed by determining the difference between the observed density at 450 mμ and the density at the same wave length of a tangent (thin continuous line) connecting 500 mμ with 365 mμ (the difference is 0.206 in the present example). This value is then plotted according to gestational age (0.206 at 34½ weeks—large black dot) and is related to severity of hemolytic disease (3 areas marked off by the diagonal dashed lines—lower zone, mildly affected; middle zone, moderate disease; and upper zone, impending stillbirth). In this example 0.206 at 450 mμ denotes impending stillbirth.

more accurate means of assessing severity of erythroblastosis. Various methods of measurement have been described; most are minor variations of that proposed by Liley. All depend upon the fact that indirect bilirubin absorbs visual light at 450 mμ and the amount of bilirubin present is directly proportional to the amount of light absorbed at 450 mμ. Spectrophotometric measurements allow differentiation between the severely affected fetus who is likely to die unless delivered early or transfused in utero (Fig. 27), and the mildly involved who should not be exposed to the unnecessary risks of early induction and delivery (Fig. 28).

Heavy contamination of amniotic fluid with blood produces characteristic high optical density peaks at 580, 540, and 415 mμ. It makes the fluid of no value for spectrophotometric examination. Chloroform extraction of the amniotic fluid bilirubin and spectrophotometric absorption studies of the chloroform supernatant (Brazie et al.) reduces the errors introduced by the presence of moderate amounts of maternal blood. However, if there is heavy contamination with blood, chloroform extraction will not avoid the errors produced by bilirubin present in maternal serum or in fetal serum. Small amounts of blood may be disregarded if removed promptly by centrifugation and filtration. Amniotic

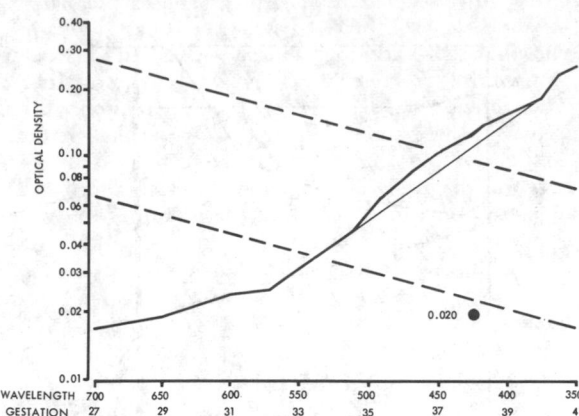

Fig. 28. Amniotic fluid optical density curve at 38 weeks' gestation of a fetus mildly affected with erythroblastosis. Optical density rise of 0.020 at 450 mμ (lower zone) denotes mild disease. Infant born spontaneously at term did not require treatment. Cord Hb 16 g percent, bilirubin 2.1 mg percent. (See Fig. 27 for data on severely affected infant.)

fluid must be protected from light, which rapidly decolorizes the yellow pigment. In amniotic fluid not contaminated by blood, a shift of wave length of maximal absorption from 450 mμ toward 405 mμ, or a second absorption peak at 405 mμ, indicates the presence of heme pigment, always a sign of very severe Rh disease.

In Rh-negative pregnancies immunized before 28 weeks' gestation, amniotic fluid spectrophotometric examinations should be repeated at 5- to 14-day intervals. Serial examinations which define the trend of the 450 mμ optical density rise (increasing, stationary, or decreasing) provide a more accurate index of the degree of Rh disease in the fetus than a single amniotic fluid examination.

The presence of meconium in amniotic fluid produces a turbid green color and a shift in the maximal wavelength of absorption between 405 and 415 mμ. It is an ominous sign, indicating an episode of fetal hypoxia and the likelihood of stillbirth. Occasionally, however, a normal fetus will pass meconium in utero.

Amniocentesis carries little risk to the mother. Rare cases of maternal bleeding and stillbirth due to abruptio placentae have been reported. If the placenta is traversed by the aspirating needle there is a risk of fetal hemorrhage into the mother's circulation. Although fetal blood loss is almost never severe enough to produce anemia, it will produce increasing isoimmunization and more severe Rh disease in the fetus. Placental localization studies, which should be carried out before every initial amniocentesis, minimize the risk of fetomaternal bleeding.

AMNIOTIC FLUID EXAMINATION IN CHROMO-SOMAL AND BIOCHEMICAL DISORDERS. *Cytogenetics.* The direct staining and examination of amniotic fluid cells of fetal origin for the presence

of a nuclear sex chromatin mass allows an accurate prediction of the sex of the fetus. This knowledge is of importance in pregnancies of women heterozygous for sex-linked recessive disorders such as hemophilia and muscular dystrophy. The demonstration of a male sex in the fetus does not establish that the fetus is affected but increases such probability from 25 to 50 percent.

The ABO, but not the Rh, constitution of the fetus can be determined by isohemagglutinin neutralization studies of amniotic fluid cells. Such knowledge may be of value in detecting genetic disorders linked to the ABO blood group locus.

Culture of amniotic fluid cells obtained by amniocentesis, with subsequent cytogenetic and biochemical examination, can now be carried out successfully as early as the 12th or 24th week of gestation. Successful amniotic fluid cultures have been reported as high as 78 percent. Cytogenetic examination of cells from such amniotic fluid cultures is important in women with chromosomal translocations who have produced babies with translocation defects (e.g., translocation Down's syndrome) or who are in their late reproductive years and at risk of producing trisomic infants. If the diagnosis of such chromosomal abnormalities is made early enough in gestation, appropriate measures, such as therapeutic abortion, may be considered.

Biochemistry. It is possible to reveal the existence of the adrenogenital syndrome in utero from increased levels of amniotic fluid 17-ketosteroids and pregnanetriol, on direct biochemical examination of amniotic fluid.

Biochemical studies of cultured amniotic fluid cells demonstrate as early as the 10th week of gestation, the presence of the following normal tissue enzymes: acid and alkaline phosphatase, α-glucosidase, α-keto-isocaproate decarboxylase, cystathione synthetase, galactose-1-phosphate uridyl transferase, glucocerebrosidase, glucose-6-phosphate dehydrogenase, hypoxanthine guanine phosphoribosyl transferase, lactate dehydrogenase, phytic acid hydroxylase, 6-phosphogluconic dehydrogenase, sphingomyelinase, and valine transaminase.

Theoretically it should be possible to establish the existence of fetal disease related to the absence of any of the above enzymes or to the presence of an abnormal intermediary product. This approach has been used already to determine whether or not a fetus was affected by both Hunter's and Hurler's variant of mucopolysaccharidosis, galactosemia, maple syrup urine and Type II glycogen storage diseases, and X-linked uric aciduria. As techniques improve, more cytogenetic and biochemical disorders will undoubtedly be revealed by amniotic fluid studies.

AMNIOTIC FLUID AND GESTATIONAL AGE. In many circumstances an exact knowledge of gestational age is essential, particularly when early delivery is contemplated because of fetal disease or when a discrepancy exists between uterine size and the stage of gestation elicited from menstrual history. In the

TABLE 10. *Tests Helpful in Estimating Gestational Age and High-Risk Pregnancies*

1. Amniotic fluid
   a. Creatinine concentration
   b. Bilirubin levels
   c. % Anucleate squames
2. Maternal enzymes and hormones
3. Ultrasound A or B scan measurements of fetal diameter

latter instance, the question of intrauterine growth retardation or acceleration arises. A reliable estimate of gestational age is essential for proper management of erythroblastosis fetalis. At least three different components of amniotic fluid change during gestation and are helpful in deciding gestational age (Table 10).

Amniotic fluid creatinine levels increase sharply after 34 weeks' gestation. After 37 weeks' levels are usually 1.8 mg percent or greater; before 34 weeks' gestation 1.5 mg or less; at 1.8 to 2.0 mg the fetus is sufficiently mature to be delivered. A significant number of fetuses at more than 35 weeks' gestation have amniotic fluid creatinine levels of 1.5 mg percent or less. Of the three tests, this has proven the most useful clinically, since it rarely gives an overestimate of gestational age.

Amniotic fluid bilirubin levels tend to decrease as gestation progresses except in Rh-immunized pregnancies, and the proportion of *amniotic fluid anucleate squames* which stain orange with Nile blue stain tends to increase as gestation advances. Neither the bilirubin concentration nor the percentage of fetal squames provides a reliable estimate of gestational age in preterm pregnancies. However, if the bilirubin concentration is zero and there is more than 50 percent of fetal squames, the fetus is probably at term. This information is particularly useful when uterine size is small in a pregnancy estimated to be at term by menstrual history, a situation which may occur with severe intrauterine growth retardation.

AMNIOTIC FLUID PRESSURE RECORDINGS. Insertion of an indwelling catheter into the amniotic cavity during labor allows continuous intrauterine pressure recording. In conjunction with continuous monitoring of fetal heart rate and serial fetal blood pH determinations, this test is of value in detecting early fetal distress during labor in high-risk pregnancies (see section on obstetrics).

Enzymes and Hormones in High-Risk Pregnancies

Determinations of maternal serum enzymes and maternal serum and urinary hormones, particularly estriol, are very valuable in high-risk pregnancies such

as maternal diabetes, toxemia of pregnancy, intrauterine growth retardation, and prolonged pregnancy.

MATERNAL ENZYMES. Diamine oxidase, alkaline phosphatase, and oxytocinase levels in maternal plasma rise progressively during normal pregnancy. The activity of diamine oxidase in amniotic fluid is two to three times greater than in normal plasma. An increase in this enzyme has been used to confirm the diagnosis of pregnancy, and a falling level to predict imminent abortion or stillbirth.

Alkaline phosphatase rises progressively in normal pregnancy from 1.5 to 4 Bodansky units initially to a mean of 16 units. The placental alkaline phosphatase, which increases as pregnancy progresses, is heat stable and reflects the functional state of the placenta. In toxemic pregnancies its level drops frequently during the ninth month. It has been suggested that a falling heat-stable alkaline phosphatase after 34 weeks' gestation is of bad prognostic significance and is an indication for delivery.

The maternal plasma level of oxytocinase relates also to placental function. Values increase from 0 to 25 units by the fourth week to 200 to 400 units at term. The enzyme can be used to provide a rough indication of fetal maturity, and, hopefully, to predict chronic fetal distress with risk of death in utero. Levels are very low following fetal death.

MATERNAL HORMONES. Serial quantitative determinations of the 24-hour urinary estriol excretion are of great value in monitoring high-risk pregnancies. Since the determination of estriol has not been adequately standardized, it is important to establish the normal range for each laboratory. Values consistently below 2 to 4 mg per 24 hours after 33 weeks' gestation indicate that fetal death is imminent and delivery should be induced. Conversely, if levels are in the range of 12 to 40 mg per 24 hours, the fetus is nearly always in good condition. The immunoassay of chorionic gonadotropin represents currently the only other hormone measurement which could serve as an indicator of fetal condition. However, levels are too high and too variable to be of assistance in the management of high-risk pregnancies.

X-Ray and Ultrasound Examinations of the Fetus and Adnexa

The development of refined ultrasound techniques has reduced the indications for radiography in obstetrics except in pregnancies which require operative manipulation of the fetus such as intrauterine fetal transfusion.

FETAL MATURITY. Radiologic determination of fetal maturity has the same shortcomings as maternal enzyme and hormone determinations. It is not precise enough before 36 weeks' gestation, when accurate knowledge of maturity is most important. If distal femoral epiphyses are visible, the fetus is usually at or beyond 37 weeks' gestation. However, in 50 percent of mature fetuses distal femoral epiphyses are not demonstrated. Hence, radiologic tech-

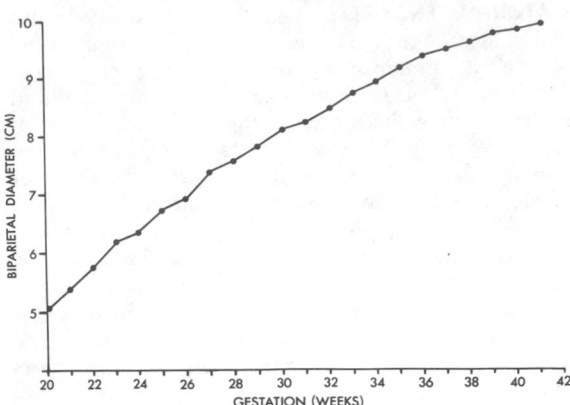

Fig. 29. Gestational age of the fetus related to biparietal diameter measured by ultrasound technique; compiled by Dr. Stuart Campbell. (From Donald. *J. Pediat.*, 75:326, 1969.)

niques for estimating fetal maturity are rarely indicated. Amniotic fluid creatinine determinations and ultrasound measurements of the biparietal diameter provide more reliable information about fetal maturity without subjecting mother and infant to radiation. A fairly accurate estimate of fetal size and biparietal diameter can be obtained with ultrasound techniques using both an A and B scan. However, ultrasound provides information on fetal size and maturity only where fetal growth rate is normal. With normal fetal growth the biparietal diameter correlates well with gestational age (see Fig. 29), and provides an estimation of fetal maturity within a range of 7 to 10 days. Unfortunately no clinical data are available on the rate of increase of biparietal diameter applicable to cases of intrauterine growth retardation or acceleration.

TWINNING AND ANOMALIES. Radiography is useful in diagnosing multiple births, but continuous ultrasound utilizing the Doppler effect will reveal the presence of two distinct fetal heartbeats as early as 11 to 12 weeks of gestation. A and B scans are also helpful in determining the presence of multiple gestations, fetal position, and presentation; however, they are not as precise as radiographs.

Gross anomalies of the head (hydrocephalus and anencephalus) may be diagnosed by either technique. Failure to detect a fetal heartbeat by continuous ultrasound is adequate proof of fetal death. This finding has supplanted x-ray evidence of intrauterine death such as a radiolucent "halo" around the fetal skull, or overlapping sutures (Spalding-Horner sign). On rare occasions, overriding sutures are seen in the living fetus.

HYDROPS FETALIS. The presence of a "halo" sign in a living fetus is usually due to hydrops fetalis, where edema produces elevation of the subcutaneous fat layer from the underlying bone. Radiograms may also demonstrate incomplete flexion of the upper

and lower extremities owing to extreme distension of the abdomen, the so-called Buddha position.

THE FETAL GASTROINTESTINAL TRACT AND PERITONEAL CAVITY. Special radiographic techniques have been devised for the investigation and management of the fetus with severe Rh erythroblastosis fetalis. Radiologic examination after injection of 76 percent meglumine diatrozoate (Renografin) into the amniotic fluid (amniography), outlines placental site, fetal position, and fetal hydrops, if present. Films taken 5 to 10 hours later reveal swallowed contrast material in the gastrointestinal tract (Fig. 30). The presence of the radiopaque substance serves as a target for accurate placement of needle and intraperitoneal catheter when fetal transfusion is undertaken in severe hemolytic disease of the newborn. Although the gut may not be visualized in the immature fetus, good concentration has been obtained as early as the 24th week of gestation. Failure to visualize the dye in the fetal bowel may indicate hydrops fetalis, where swallowing is prevented by edema of the lips. The intestinal tract is not visualized when the fetus is dead. Injection of contrast material into the fetal peritoneal cavity with subsequent radiographic examination is necessary for correct placement of the catheter prior to intra-

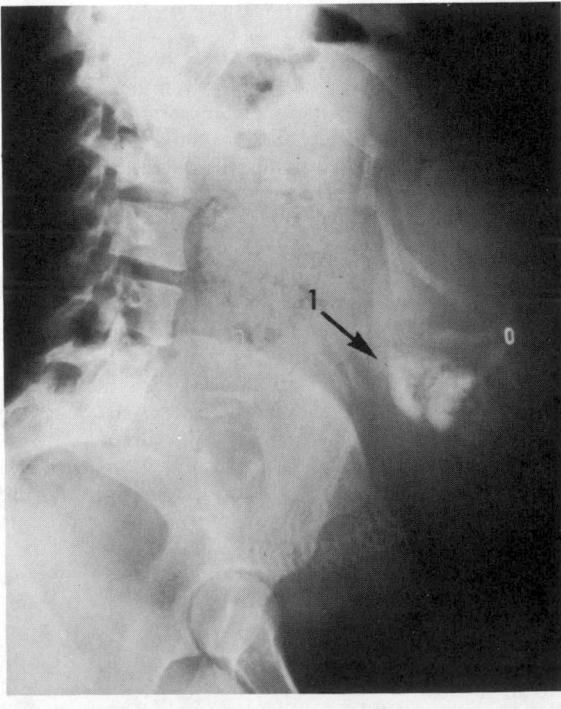

Fig. 30. Radiogram of erythroblastotic fetus at 28 weeks' gestation following injection of dye into the amniotic cavity. Note dye (Arrow 1) which the fetus has swallowed, concentrated in the bowel of the fetus. Dye and marker (o) serve as target for placement of needle and catheter in fetal peritoneal cavity prior to intraperitoneal transfusion of the fetus.

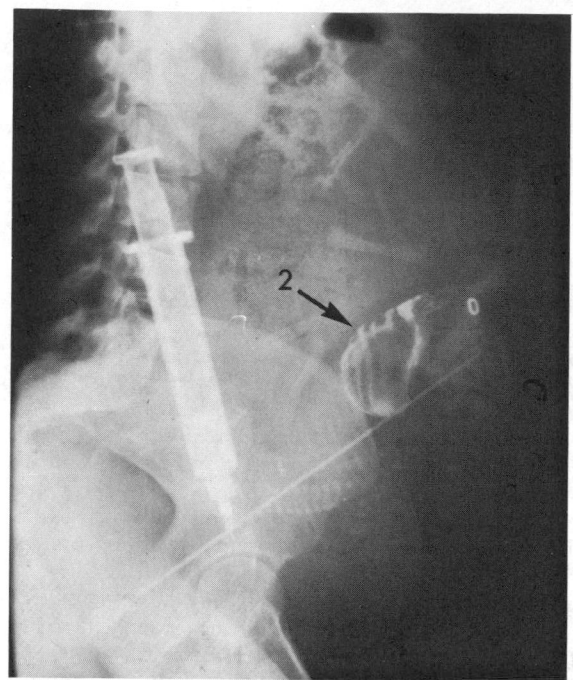

Fig. 31. Radiogram of same fetus as Figure 30 following injection of dye into fetal peritoneal cavity. Note dye present in crescents between loops of bowel and under the diaphragm (Arrow 2). This baby was salvaged after four intraperitoneal blood transfusions.

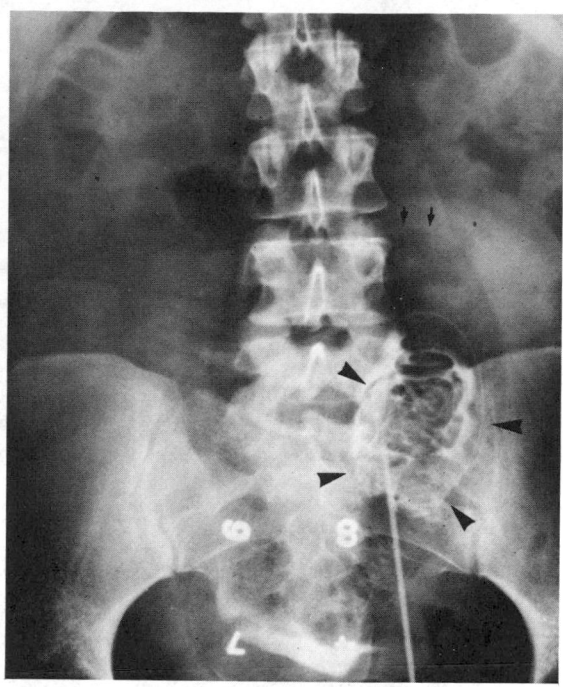

Fig. 33. A fetus in which the intrauterine diagnosis of congenital diaphragmatic hernia was made. At initial fetal transfusion, radiopaque dye (meglumine diatrazoate) outlines loops of bowel (large arrows) displaced cephalad. (Small arrows point to fetal buttock.) The diagnosis of congenital diaphragmatic hernia was confirmed at autopsy.

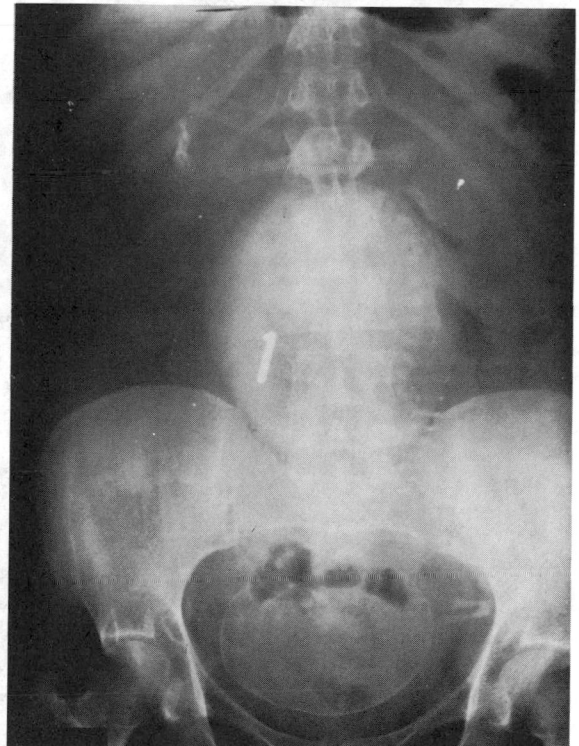

Fig. 32. Radiogram of hydropic fetus at 29 weeks' gestation. Note distended abdomen full of fluid (intraperitoneal injection of 15 ml 76 percent renografin). The fetus died three days later.

peritoneal transfusion (Fig. 31). Normally, the radiopaque substance is seen in crescents between loops of fetal bowel and under the diaphragm. Ascites, which may be the earliest and only sign of fetal hydrops, is readily demonstrated radiographically following intraperitoneal dye injection (Fig. 32).

Occasionally intraperitoneal injection of dye will provide evidence of a major congenital anomaly. On one occasion radiopaque contrast material outlining loops of bowel in the thoracic cavity led to the discovery of a left congenital diaphragmatic hernia in the fetus (Fig. 33).

PLACENTAL LOCALIZATION. Accurate localization of the placental site is of great importance when placenta previa is suspected. It is also essential prior to amniocentesis in Rh-immunized pregnancies. In 30 percent of pregnancies the placenta is implanted on the anterior uterine wall. If the amniocentesis needle penetrates the placenta, fetal red cells enter the maternal circulation, cause a rise in Rh antibody levels, and increase the severity of the erythroblastosis. In Winnipeg, prior to the use of placental localization techniques, fetomaternal hemorrhage occurred in 11.2 percent of 410 amniocenteses, and Rh antibody rose in 50 percent of such cases.

Both ultrasound and radioisotope techniques may be used to localize the placenta. With experience, the placenta, its thickness, and its relation to

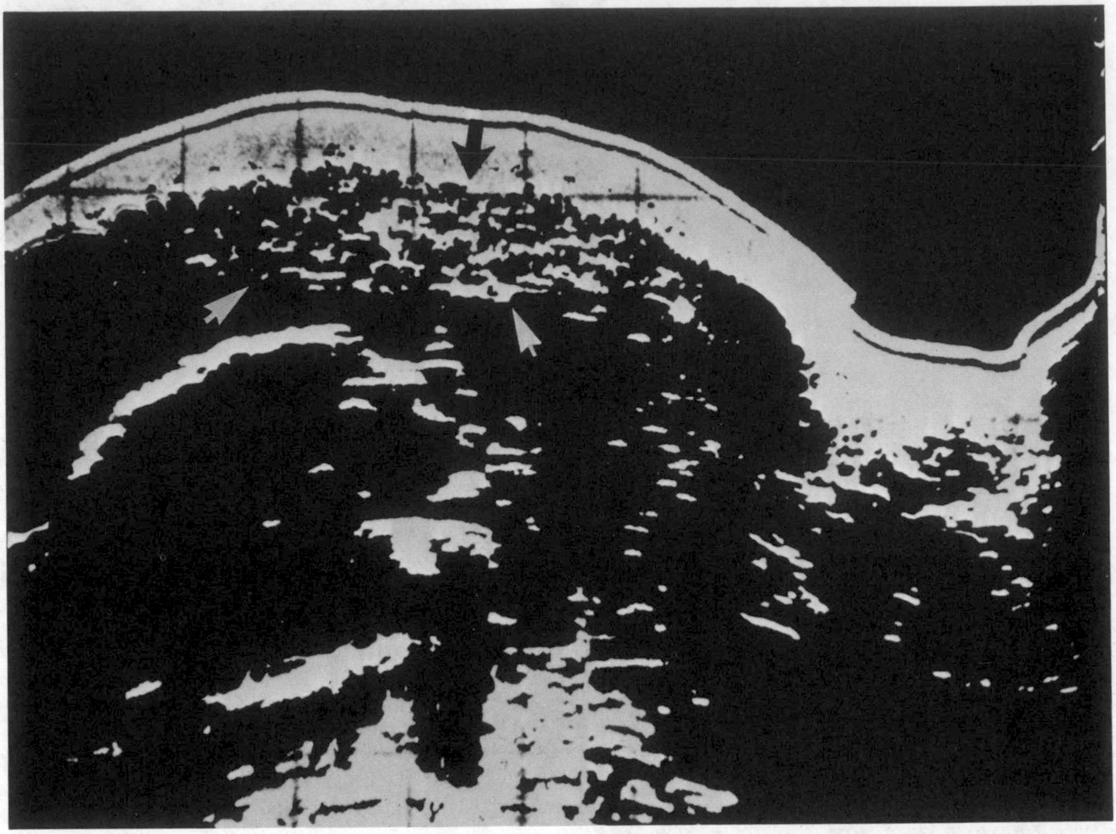

Fig. 34.   Ultrasound localization of placenta (arrows) situated on the anterior wall of the uterus. (Longitudinal scan, anterior surface of the abdomen at the top of the figure.)

the anterior uterine wall can be outlined quite accurately by an ultrasound B scan (Fig. 34).

Radioactive placental localization techniques include the use of chromium 51-tagged red cells, technetium 99 M-tagged human albumin, and indium 113 M-tagged albumin. With the development of tagged human serum albumin, chromium 51 is used less frequently. All three methods have the disadvantage of exposing mother and fetus to radiation. Scanning with a gamma detector following injection of technetium or indium radioisotopes produces an accurate picture of the placenta site (Fig. 35). When scanned in two dimensions the placental site can be mapped in relation to the uterine fundus, lower segment, and anterior and posterior walls. Although the amount of radiation is small, ultrasound localization when available is the preferred method.

Lateral and anteroposterior x-rays (amniogram) following injection of meglumine diatrozoate into the amniotic fluid before fetal transfusion will also reveal the site of the placenta and its size with considerable accuracy (Fig. 36).

Fetal Heart Monitoring

The fetal heart may be monitored electronically (fetal electrocardiogram), by ultrasound, or by pho-

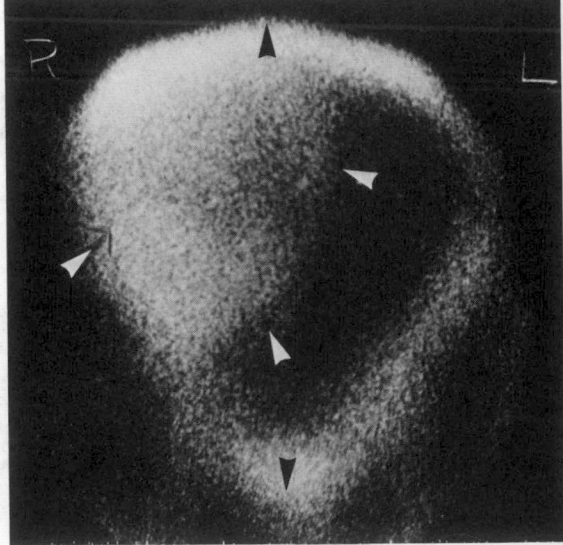

Fig. 35.   Gamma camera technetium 99 M localization of placenta (white arrows) situated in the right upper quadrant of the uterus. Uterine fundus at the top and cervix at the bottom of the figure (black arrows).

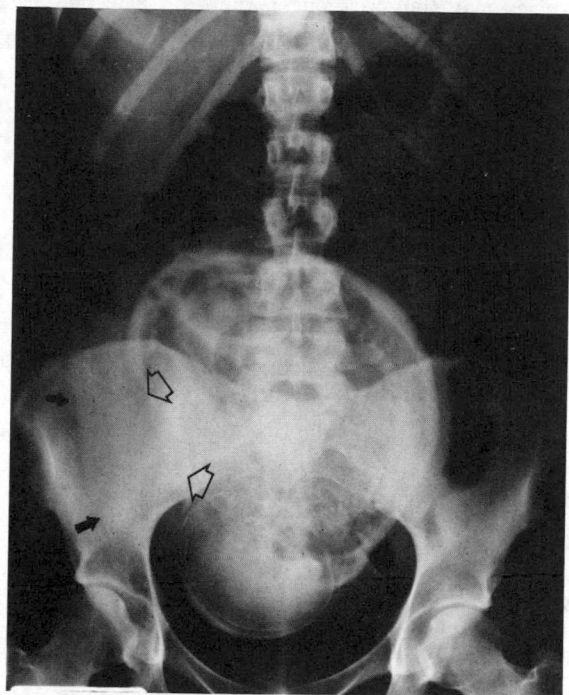

Fig. 36. Radiopaque dye (melglumine diatrazoate) injected into the amniotic fluid prior to fetal transfusion. Fetus well outlined as a vertex facing to the right. Open arrows point to a filling defect in the dye outline of the internal uterine wall localizing the placenta to the right lateral wall of the uterus. Dark arrows indicate the outer wall of the uterus. The placenta is thick and large (characteristic of severe erythroblastosis).

nography. The latter technique has not yet been perfected. Unlike ultrasound, and similar to electrocardiography, it requires no energy input. Fetal heart monitoring is of value in confirming the diagnosis of pregnancy, the position of the fetus (Figs. 37 and 38), and the presence of multiple fetuses (Fig. 39). Fetal heart impulses have been demonstrated by ultrasound as early as the tenth week and by electrocardiography by the twelfth week of gestation.

Methods which permit continuous fetal heart

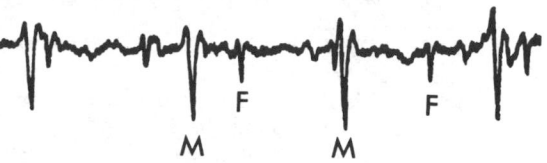

Fig. 38. Fetal electrocardiogram. Fetus is in breech position. (Fetal QRS is in same direction as maternal QRS.)

rate monitoring are of value in detecting early fetal distress. Although some argue that fetal EKG changes are significant, there is no convincing evidence to support the use of fetal electrocardiography except as a means of determining fetal heart rate.

FETAL HEART RATE. Following the fetal heart rate continuously during labor by any of the above techniques is of greater value than periodic auscultation. The previous section on obstetrics has described the significance of different patterns of fetal heart rate related to intraamniotic pressure changes. There is general agreement that persistent late deceleration or Type II dips should be regarded as an indication of fetal hypoxia.

Although late decelerations may be observed occasionally in fetuses who will be normal at birth, a progressive increase in the lag period between the

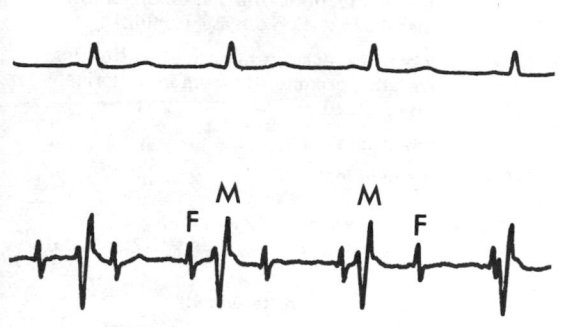

Fig. 37. Fetal electrocardiogram. Maternal and fetal complexes well seen. Fetus is in vertex position. (Fetal QRS in reverse direction to maternal QRS.)

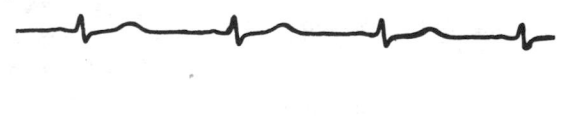

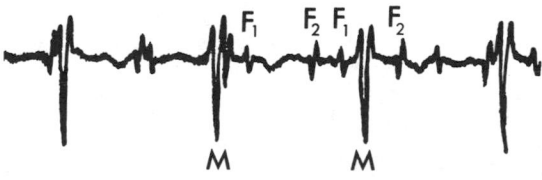

Fig. 39. Fetal electrocardiogram of twins. Two fetal QRS complexes readily seen. F_1 vertex (fetal QRS in reverse direction to maternal QRS), F_2 breech (fetal QRS in same direction as maternal QRS).

end of the contraction and the return of the fetal heart rate to normal is frequently associated with poor condition at birth.

FETAL HEART RATE AND PASSAGE OF MECONIUM. The presence of both fetal bradycardia and meconium-stained amniotic fluid is a particularly ominous sign. Fenton and Steer found the incidence of stillbirth, neonatal death, and brain damage to be twice as high when bradycardia and meconium were noted (5.4 percent of 766 babies) than when they were not (2.7 percent of 7,029 babies). Greatest risk occurred when the fetal heart rate was below 110 beats per minute and thick meconium was passed (21 percent of 42 babies in this group died). If the fetal heart rate remained between 110 and 180 per minute, passage of meconium was not associated with increased mortality rate, and fetuses with heart rates which dropped below 110 per minute showed no increase in mortality as long as meconium was not passed (1.7 percent).

Direct Blood Sampling of the Fetus

Direct examination of fetal blood pH, P_{CO_2}, and P_{O_2} is now possible (Saling). Blood is obtained by micropuncture of the presenting part during labor (scalp or buttock). The P_{CO_2} and P_{O_2} determinations on this blood are not always accurate indicators of central arterial P_{CO_2} and P_{O_2} in the fetus. The pH is more reliable in this respect. A "normal" pH range for such blood is 7.28 to 7.34, although during a uterine contraction transient pH drops to as low as 7.19 may occur in a fetus who is in good condition.

Serial pH estimations during labor in high-risk pregnancies may, on occasion, permit the detection of fetal distress not recognized either by conventional clinical signs or by continuous fetal heart rate monitoring and intrauterine pressure recording.

While endoscopy allows fetal blood to be obtained before labor begins, the high risk of precipitating labor limits its clinical use.

Cord Blood Examination

Cord blood should be saved from high-risk deliveries for possible future examination (see Table 11). The main value of cord blood examination is in the management of babies with Rh and other isoimmunization problems (see also Chap. 20). The Coombs' test (red cell antihuman globulin test) determines whether the red cells of the fetus have been coated with antibody and are being destroyed. A negative Coombs' test excludes all forms of hemolytic disease of the newborn due to isoimmunization except possibly that caused by ABO incompatibility. The number of nucleated cells per 100 white cells, and the concentrations of hemoglobin and bilirubin, give some index of the severity of erythroblastosis and provide criteria for possible exchange transfusions. Reticulocyte counts and heme pigment levels, although less frequently performed, also indicate the degree of hemolysis. In erythroblastotic infants who have had intrauterine transfusions, the percentage of cells containing adult hemoglobin, principally donor cells, can be determined by the Kleihauer technique. Most infants after several intrauterine transfusions

TABLE 11. *Cord Blood Tests*

Test	Indications
1. Direct Coombs' test	Erythroblastosis other than ABO
2. Hemoglobin and hematocrit	Erythroblastosis Acute or chronic fetal bleeding Intrauterine growth retardation Discordant identical twins
3. Reticulocyte and nucleated red cell count	Erythroblastosis Fetal bleeding
4. Indirect and total bilirubin levels	Erythroblastosis Intrauterine infections (rubella, toxoplasmosis, cytomegalic inclusion disease, syphilis)
5. Fetal/adult red cell ratio (Kleihauer)	Erythroblastosis after intrauterine transfusions Differentiating prematurity from intrauterine growth retardation
6. Heme pigment levels	Erythroblastosis
7. Cultures (bacterial and viral)	Intrauterine infection: 　Maternal fever 　Premature supture of membranes 　Known maternal infection (GU, respiratory, etc.)
8. Serum IgM levels	Intrauterine infections (elevated)
9. Toxicology studies (barbiturates, magnesium sulfate, total protein, serum sodium, etc.)	Suspected maternal intoxication (deliberate or iatrogenic)

will have predominantly or entirely Rh-negative adult cells.

Cord blood studies are also important in the growth-retarded infant. Hemoglobin and hematocrit levels are higher than in premature infants: these values are sometimes significantly higher, with mean capillary blood levels of 19.8 g percent versus 16.1 g percent, and 67.2 percent versus 54.4 percent respectively. The growth-retarded fetus also tends to have a greater percentage of red cells containing adult hemoglobin (10 to 15 percent by the Kleihauer technique) than does the premature infant (1 to 7 percent).

Examination of Umbilical Cord, Placenta, and Fetal Membranes

After birth, inspection of the umbilical cord, placenta, and fetal membranes may alert the physician to the possibility of disease in the baby.

SINGLE UMBILICAL ARTERY. A single umbilical artery, found in 0.2 to 1 percent of all deliveries, is frequently associated with major congenital anomalies. The incidence of all fetal abnormalities associated with a single umbilical artery has varied from 20 percent to 65 percent in different series and has involved many different organ systems.

AMNION NODOSUM. The presence of numerous gray-yellow plaques on the fetal surface of the placenta is due to the deposition of vernix on the surface of the amnion. It is always indicative of severe oligohydramnios, frequently associated with severe urinary tract anomalies in the fetus.

AMNIOTIC INFLAMMATION SYNDROME. Chorioamnionitis occurs in about 10 percent of all deliveries. Such inflammation is favored by premature rupture of the membranes and prolonged labor. When complicated by bacterial infection, common organisms involved are *E. coli, Aerobacter aerogenes,* and *Paracolobactrum.*

Although neonatal infection does not occur in the majority of instances where amniotic fluid and membranes are the site of bacterial contamination, the risk of such an infection in the newborn is nevertheless considerably greater than when membranes and fluid are not infected (see Sec. 14.2 on neonatal sepsis). When, from clinical signs in the mother (fever, early rupture of the membranes, foul amniotic fluid discharge), infection of the fetus is suspected, immediately after birth cultures should be taken of cord blood and from the cut surface of the cord and the fetal surface of the placenta and membranes. In addition the following two ancillary methods, although infrequently carried out, may be of value in directing attention to the infants at risk from infection acquired in utero:

Umbilical Cord. The first method is examination of frozen sections of the umbilical cord. Initially, margination of the vein wall is seen, followed by infiltration by polymorphonuclear leucocytes. Migra-tion into Wharton's jelly then occurs, with inflammatory cells surrounding all three vessels and finally reaching the surface of the cord.

Amnion. "Whole mount of the amnion" examination is based on the fact that neutrophils accumulate beneath the amnion in chorioamnionitis. A square inch of amnion is taken from the placental surface in an area overlying chorionic vessels. It is fixed in 95 percent alcohol, strained with cresyl violet, and mounted with the amniotic epithelium in contact with the slide. Neutrophils in the subamniotic tissue are evidence of amnionitis.

REFERENCES

Blanc, W. A. Vernix granulomatosis of amnion ("amnion nodosum") in oligohydramnios. New York J. Med., 61:1492, 1961.
—— Pathways of fetal and early neonatal infection. J. Pediat., 59:473, 1961.
Borell, U., Fernstrom, I., and Ohlson, L. The halo sign in living and dead fetus. Amer. J. Obstet. Gynec., 908:87, 1963.
Bowman, J. M., Friesen, R. F., Bowman, W. D., McInnis, A. C., Barnes, P. H., and Grewar, D. Fetal transfusion in severe Rh immunization. J.A.M.A., 207:1101, 1969.
—— and Pollock, J. M. Amniotic fluid spectrophotometry and early delivery in the management of erythroblastosis fetalis. Pediatrics, 35:815, 1965.
Boyd, J. J., Bowman, J. M., McInnis, A. C., and Kiernan, M. K. Fetal diaphragmatic hernia detected at intra-uterine transfusion. Canad. Med. Ass. J., 100:1105, 1969.
Brazie, J. V., Bowes, W. A., and Ibbott, F. A. An improved rapid procedure for the determination of amniotic fluid bilirubin and its use in the prediction of the course of Rh-sensitized pregnancies. Amer. J. Obstet. Gynec., 104:80, 1969.
Donald, I. Sonar as a method of studying prenatal development. J. Pediat., 75:326, 1969.
Droegmueller, W., Jackson, C., Makowski, E. L., and Battaglia, F. C. Amniotic fluid assessment as an aid in the assessment of gestational age. Amer. J. Obstet. Gynec., 104:424, 1969.
Fenton, A. N., and Steer, C. M. Fetal distress. Amer. J. Obstet. Gynec., 83:354, 1962.
Fratantoni, J. C., Neufeld, E. F., Uhlendorf, B. W., and Jackson, C. B. Intrauterine diagnosis of the Hurler and Hunter syndromes. New Eng. J. Med., 280:686, 1969.
Gordon, H., and Brosens, I. Cytology of amniotic fluid. A new test for maturity. Obstet. Gynec., 30:652, 1967.
Greene, J. W., Jr., and Tweeddale, D. N. Endocrine indices of fetal environment. Clin. Obstet. Gynec., 11:1106, 1968.
Hon, E. H., and Khazin, A. F. Biochemical studies of the fetus: I. The fetal pH measuring system. Obstet. Gynec., 33:219, 1969.
Humbert, J. R., Abelson, H., Hathaway, W. E., and Battaglia, F. C. Polycythemia in small for gestational age infants. J. Pediat., 75:812, 1969.
Kohorn, E. I., Secker Walker, R. H., Morrison, J., and Campbell, S. Placental localization. Amer. J. Obstet. Gynec., 103:868, 1969.

Kubli, F. W., Hon, E. H., Khazin, A. F., and Takemura, H. Observations on the heart rate and pH in the human fetus during labor. Amer. J. Obstet. Gynec., 104:1190, 1969.

Larks, S. D., and Anderson, G. V. The abnormal fetal electrocardiogram. Amer. J. Obstet. Gynec., 84:1893, 1962.

Lenoski, E. F., and Medovy, H. Single umbilical artery—incidence, clinical significance and relation to autosomal trisomy. Canad. Med. Ass. J., 87:1229, 1962.

Liley, A. W. Intrauterine transfusion of the fetus in haemolytic disease. Brit. Med. J., 1107, 1963.

Nadler, H. L. Prenatal detection of genetic defects. J. Pediat., 74:132, 1969.

Peddle, J. L. Increase of antibody titre following amniocentesis. Amer. J. Obstet. Gynec., 100:567, 1968.

Saling, E. Neues Vorgehen zur Untersuchung des Kindes unter der Geburt (A new method for examination of the child during labour). Arch. Gynaek., 197:108, 1962.

Schreiber, M. H., Nichols, M. M., and McGanity, W. J. Epiphysial ossification center visualization. Its value in the prediction of fetal maturity. J.A.M.A., 184:504, 1963.

Serr, D. M., Zakut, H., Rabau, E., and Mannor, S. M. Observations on the fetal electrocardiogram in postmaturity. Israel J. Med. Sci., 4:949, 1968.

Weingold, A. B. Enzymatic indices of fetal environment. Clin. Obstet. Gynec., 11:1081, 1968.

The Transition from Fetus to Newborn

2.9
LABOR, DELIVERY, AND THE BEGINNING OF INDEPENDENT LIFE

L. STANLEY JAMES and
KARLIS ADAMSONS, JR.

Normal Intrauterine Environment

The development of techniques for implanting catheters into fetal and maternal vessels for prolonged periods without interruption of pregnancy has made it possible to obtain serial samples from unrestrained, nonanesthetized animals. As a result, information has been provided for the first time on many aspects of normal intrauterine environment, and much of the controversy and mystery concerning the subject has been resolved (see Sec. 2.6).

Hemoglobin concentration and oxygen-carrying capacity of fetal blood during the third trimester are similar to those in the adult animal and do not change as pregnancy advances unless the animal is in stress. Oxygen-carrying capacity is higher immediately following operative procedures and also rises during labor. Although the oxygen tension is low by adult standards, oxygen consumption is similar to basal values obtained after birth and appears to remain constant during the third trimester. The gradients for hydrogen ion and carbon dioxide tension across the placenta are small, so that the fetus is neither acidotic nor hypercapnic under normal conditions. While minor species differences may exist, these statements appear to hold true in man.

Acidosis of Birth Asphyxia

In vigorous infants, oxygen levels in the umbilical arterial blood at birth range from 0 to nearly 70 percent saturation. The average value in these infants is approximately 22 percent but is 10 percent or less in nearly one quarter of them. These varying degrees of hypoxemia are accompanied by varying degrees of hypercapnia and acidosis, the average Pco_2 being 58 mm Hg and pH 7.28. In general, lower oxygen saturations are associated with a lower pH and higher Pco_2. Immediately following birth there is an increase in the acidosis which continues for several minutes despite good lung expansion and rapid reoxygenation.

These findings suggest that the final stages of labor and delivery are associated with a reduction in exchange of oxygen and carbon dioxide across the placenta, leading to various degrees of asphyxia * at birth. Direct proof of this concept has been provided by experimental observations and by capillary blood sampling from the human fetal scalp, which reveals a developing acidosis as labor advances. Many of the findings in the cord blood at birth are the result of a disturbance in the functional relationship between mother and fetus during delivery, whether this be per vaginam or by cesarean section, and do not reflect adaptations to an hypoxic environment in utero.

Animal experiments have shown that under conditions of asphyxia the concentrations of blood gases change rapidly, oxygen content of the arterial

* Asphyxia refers to a condition of hypoxemia, hypercapnia, and acidosis. Unresponsive infants are described as depressed rather than asphyxiated, although more severe degrees of asphyxia can reduce the responsiveness of the central nervous system.

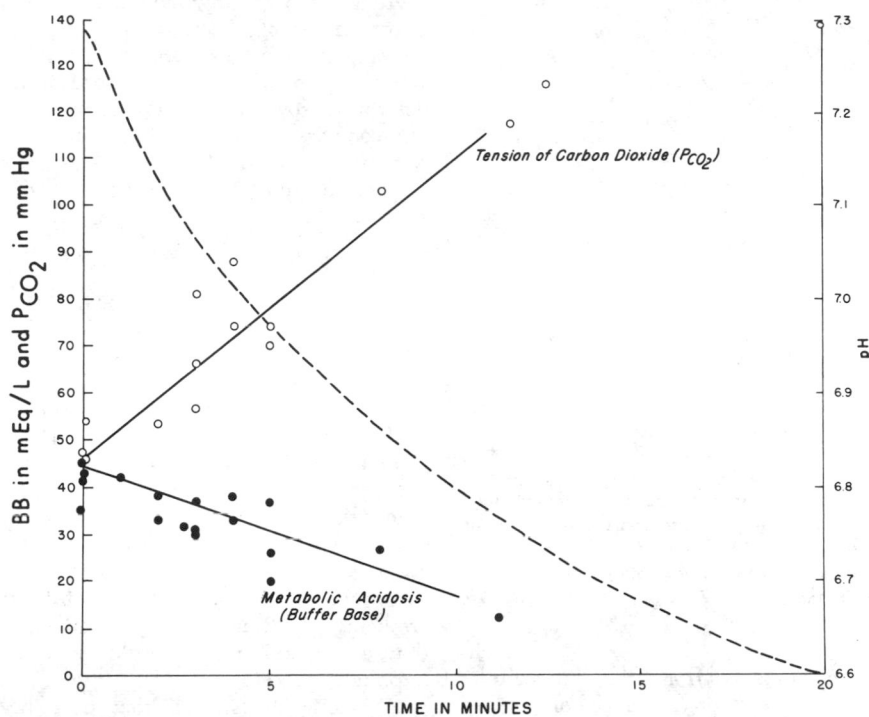

Fig. 40. Change in arterial pH (dashed line), carbon dioxide tension (Pco$_2$) (open circles), and buffer base (BB) (filled circles) in newborn puppies asphyxiated from the time of birth (0 time).

blood falling to near zero in 2.5 minutes and carbon dioxide tension rising at the rate of approximately 10 mm Hg per minute, while pH falls initially at approximately 0.1 pH units per minute and buffer base falls at the rate of 2 mEq/L per minute (Fig. 40). The rapidity of these processes indicates that in the healthy newborn the period of asphyxia may be quite brief.

Several factors can disturb the normal functional relationship between fetal and maternal circulations and cause fetal acidosis. Strong uterine contractions, inferior vena caval compression causing maternal hypotension, or aortic compression by the uterus can all lead to a reduction in intervillous blood flow. Maternal acid-base state and oxygenation can be altered by drugs and anesthesia through their effect on ventilation and tissue perfusion. Excessive muscular activity or dehydration during prolonged labor can lead to acidosis in the mother. Since hydrogen ions are exchanged readily across the placenta, maternal acidosis will be reflected in the fetus. Maternal alkalosis resulting from excessive hyperventilation can also lead to fetal acidosis, probably by reducing uterine blood flow. Cord compression, which occurs in approximately one third of all deliveries, represents the most common mechanism on the fetal side interfering with transplacental exchange.

Disturbances in the normal functional relationships between fetal and maternal circulation that inevitably occur during labor and delivery limit considerably the value of data relating to the composition of cord blood. This applies especially to respiratory gases but it is also true of most substances that are in continuous exchange between the mother and fetus.

Achievement of Normal Acid-Base Balance Postnatally

During the first minutes after birth the pH continues to fall while lactate concentrations rise. These changes occur even in the most vigorous infants in whom respiration is well established by one minute of age. Depressed infants are more acidotic initially, and the fall in pH after birth is greater and of longer duration. By one hour of age, pH and lactate concentrations in healthy infants are near normal adult values but are still abnormal in the depressed infants with low Apgar scores (see p. 72). Increase in acidosis immediately following birth is partly caused by a rise in the concentration of oxyhemoglobin, which dissociates more hydrogen ions than reduced hemoglobin; the concomitant rise in lactate concentration, however, indicates the influx of additional

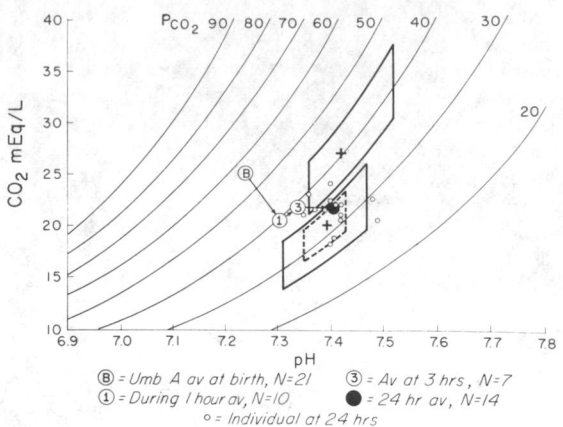

Fig. 41. The ordinate in mEq/L plasma CO_2. The abscissa is pH. The curved lines are Pco_2 isobars logarithmically spaced. The upper quadrilateral represents the range of normal adult arterial values. The lower quadrilateral represents the range of maternal arterial values, with one SD from the mean indicated by broken lines. Indicated values obtained from healthy full size newborn infants. (From Weisbrot. *J. Pediat.*, 52:395, 1958.)

hydrogen ions, presumably from the intracellular compartment, and is further evidence of oxygen insufficiency during delivery. Following lung expansion, arterial oxygen tension rises and Pco_2 falls rapidly, but a relatively normal acid-base state is not achieved for 1 to 3 hours. Recovery is accomplished primarily by pulmonary elimination of carbon dioxide and not by renal excretion of hydrogen ion. By 24 hours, the healthy newborn has reached the same acid-base state as the mother prior to labor (Fig. 41).

A number of factors influence the rate of recovery from birth asphyxia—analgesic and anesthetic drugs received prior to delivery and prematurity being the most important. Delay in recovery is seen also in the more asphyxiated infants, owing probably to circulatory impairment and central nervous system depression. Exposure of the naked newborn to usual room temperature also influences recovery, in that oxygen consumption of the vigorous infant increases, metabolic acidosis persists, and there is a further elevation in blood lactate concentration; a normal pH is maintained by increasing CO_2 elimination. The biochemical changes induced by cold stress in the depressed infants differ from those seen in the healthy ones in several respects; namely, pH falls, there is a greater increase in base deficit, a smaller increase in oxygen consumption, and an increase in the ratio of lactate to pyruvate. These observations suggest that depressed infants have inadequate circulatory and respiratory response to cold stress.

Several explanations have been offered for the low arterial Pco_2 (about 32 mm Hg) observed in healthy infants once normal acid-base balance has been achieved. Hyperventilation, due to anoxia or to increased levels of organic acids due to anaerobic metabolism, were first thought to be the cause. However, it has been suggested that the newborn's respiratory center has been made more sensitive to CO_2 by progesterone. It is also possible that the homeostatic responses of the newborn infant have been determined by the fetal environment, where Pco_2 is low compared with the adult. Finally, the ventilatory response to mild cold stress, as noted, could be implicated, the infant gradually becoming "cold adapted" to his new environment.

Onset of Breathing

There has been much speculation on factors responsible for initiation of breathing at birth, but only a limited amount of experimental work has dealt with this issue. The isolation of a proprioceptive stimulus for the first breath has been difficult because birth is accompanied by marked changes in fetal arterial Po_2 and acid-base state, in the thermal environment of the neonate, as well as by the tactile, auditory, and visual stimuli to which he is exposed. Examination of one variable while the remaining are being kept constant is quite difficult. It is unlikely that a single impulse would serve to initiate this important process.

Among the stimuli that have been implicated in the initiation of breathing, asphyxia has often been considered the principal driving force. There is no doubt that a fall in arterial Po_2 and pH, accompanied by a rise in Pco_2, may induce gasping in utero as well as postnatally. Rhythmic breathing may ensue as a result of improving oxygenation and normalization of acid-base state. In the severely asphyxiated newborn monkey, gasping always precedes the onset of rhythmic breathing by a considerable time interval. The respiratory drive during asphyxia depends upon the presence of carotid and aortic chemoreceptors which are known to be functional in the newborn, at least in the rabbit and lamb. However, neither hypoxia nor hypercapnia alone initiates breathing. These findings suggest two possibilities: either the chemoreceptors of the fetus do not respond to hypoxia in the presence of normal pH and Pco_2, or the state of activity of the respiratory neurons is such that the afferent stimuli from the carotid and aortic chemoreceptors do not lead to sufficient efferent discharge.

The time interval between birth and the first breath is normally only a few seconds. This favors the explanation that initial excitation of the respiratory centers is by neurally transmitted impulses from the peripherally located receptors, rather than by changes in the composition of blood, which are, by comparison, slow. Thermal perception appears to be of particular significance. The stimulating effects of cold upon respiration have been appreciated for centuries, and this has possibly reduced interest in establishing the relationship between thermal stimuli and postnatal lung expansion under controlled experimental conditions. Stimulation of peripheral thermal receptors immediately after birth must be intense. Calculations based on the rate of fall of skin temperature in the first minutes of extrauterine life have shown that at usual room temperature the newborn human infant may lose about 600 calories per minute. Cooling of the fetal lamb delivered by cesarean section initiates respiratory movements which cease upon removal of the stimulus.

Occlusion of the umbilical cord, which causes a prompt though transient rise in blood pressure, is considered by some to be of cardinal importance in the initiation of breathing. However, breathing can occur in the presence of intact umbilical circulation in the experimental animal and in the human, both in utero and following delivery. To establish the role of baroreceptors in postnatal excitation of the respiratory center, it would be necessary to produce circulatory alterations similar to those taking place following mechanical cord occlusion, without changing fetal oxygenation, Pco_2, and hydrogen ion activity. Such experiments have yet to be performed.

Tactile stimuli appear to be of secondary importance. Although strong stimulation of the fetal lamb produces gasping, rhythmic breathing is not initiated.

Excitability of the respiratory neurons in the adult is principally maintained by the state of activity of the reticular formation, which in turn is dependent upon a variety of afferent stimuli. At birth, the excitability appears to increase, probably because of the variety of new sensory impulses arriving from the periphery. Thus, without necessarily increasing in intensity, a given stimulus responsible for the initiation of breathing could evoke an effector organ response. On the other hand, excitability of the respiratory neurons may be decreased by depressant drugs, hypoxia, hypercarbia, or acidosis. The importance of extracellular pH and Pco_2 have been demonstrated in experiments where monkeys were asphyxiated at birth; gasping, which had ceased at a pH of approximately 6.77, was reinitiated when pH was rapidly elevated and Pco_2 lowered by intravenous infusion of *tris*-(hydroxymethyl) aminomethane (THAM). The onset of respiration at birth thus depends upon the relative contributions of facilitating and inhibiting factors to the respiratory neurons.

The First Breath

The majority of healthy infants start to breathe spontaneously within seconds of being born, even before separation from their mothers. This was not the case earlier in the century when heavy maternal medication and general anesthesia for delivery were widely employed. The onset of breathing was frequently delayed for several minutes, during which time painful and thermal stimuli were applied, often combined with the administration of analeptics.

Cineradiographic studies have shown that there is an elastic recoil of the chest wall as it emerges from the birth canal. This can draw in 7 to 42 ml of air to replace fluid squeezed out from the air passages during the final stages of delivery and provides an explanation for the cough which occasionally precedes the first inspiratory effort. Glossopharyngeal muscles may force down an additional 5 to 10 ml ("frog breathing"). Neither of these, however, is essential since uneventful lung expansion occurs in infants born by cesarean section or in whom "frog breathing" is prevented by the insertion of a pharyngeal airway.

The negative intrathoracic pressure during the first breath, measured by means of an esophageal catheter, ranges between 20 and 70 cm H_2O and is accompanied by an inflow of 20 to 80 ml of air. Much of this air remains in the lung as residual volume. Despite the high negative intrathoracic pressures which are sometimes observed, it is surprising how often the initial lung expansion appears to require little effort. The first inspiration is usually followed by a cry as the infant expires against a partially closed glottis; this creates a positive intrathoracic pressure of up to 40 cm H_2O. After the first few breaths, the lungs are almost completely and evenly expanded, and within a few minutes functional residual capacity reaches about three-quarters of that present by one to three days of age.

In the more asphyxiated infants, the first inspiratory effort is a gasp. It is characterized by the participation of accessory inspiratory muscles; the changes in intrathoracic pressure under these circumstances are both relatively greater and more rapid.

Little is known about the rate of absorption of the liquid present in the alveoli and air passages at the time of lung expansion. Its low protein content would facilitate rapid absorption as soon as pulmonary blood flow increases, and absorption probably occurs during the first few breaths. Under conditions of severe asphyxia, when pulmonary vascular resistance remains high, removal of fluid could be delayed. This might explain some of the difficulties encountered in lung expansion under such circumstances.

In addition to viscosity, surface tension forces will oppose movement of fluid into the finer peripheral portions of the lung because of an increase in cross-sectional area at branching sites. The presence of surface active substances would decrease the work required for lung expansion.

Although the work required for initial lung expansion is undeniably greater than that for quiet breathing, it is not greater than that performed many times a day during vigorous crying.

Circulatory Readjustments After Birth

Contrary to earlier notions, the transition from fetal to adult type of circulation is not an abrupt process but a gradual one; the foramen ovale and ductus arteriosus apparently remain open for varying periods of time. For the first hours of extrauterine life the flow through the ductus arteriosus is bidirectional. The shunt eventually becomes entirely left-to-right and by 15 hours of age is functionally insignificant.

The pulmonary arterial pressure is maintained at or near systemic levels for several hours, pressures similar to those in the systemic circulation being required to maintain adequate pulmonary perfusion. This is not unexpected because the lumina of the pulmonary arterioles and elastic arteries increase only gradually. A sudden fall in pulmonary vascular resistance immediately postpartum would cause a considerable imbalance in the output of left and right ventricles, owing to left-to-right shunting through the ductus arteriosus. The characteristic fetal features in the pulmonary arteries and arterioles are discernible for about 10 days. Postnatal rather than postconceptional age appears to be the principal determinant in this process of vascular alteration; the histologic appearance of pulmonary vessels in premature infants is similar to those of term infants of comparable postnatal age.

The left atrial pressure falls in the first few hours of life to levels below those in the normal adult; by 24 hours it may be less than 1 mm Hg above that in the right atrium. This small pressure difference probably accounts in part for the persistence of a right-to-left shunt through the foramen ovale for 24 hours or longer.

Constriction of the ductus arteriosus depends on an increase in arterial Po_2. It also constricts in response to sympathomimetic amines. Vasoconstriction induced by epinephrine and norepinephrine is obliterated by adrenergic blocking agents, whereas that caused by a high Po_2 is not. Hypoxemia is associated with constriction of the ductus arteriosus and reestablishment of the fetal pattern of circulation by increasing the pulmonary vascular resistance. This response of the ductus arteriosus to variations in oxygen tension is thus opposite to that of the pulmonary arterioles, enabling the right ventricle to contribute a variable fraction of its output to placental perfusion during fetal life. The different reactivity of these vessels during hypoxia, while an asset to the fetus, becomes a liability for the newborn. Hypoxic episodes in early neonatal life can lead to a rise in pulmonary vascular resistance and opening of the ductus arteriosus, increasing any residual right-to-left shunt. Diversion of a great portion of the right ventricular output directly into the systemic circulation will further reduce O_2 uptake by the lung. Mechanisms responsible for the different responses of these vessels to hypoxia have so far not been determined.

Resuscitation

In the past, assessment of resuscitative procedures has relied upon clinical impressions or data gathered from experiments on adult animals, in which many responses are known to be different from those of the newborn. Recently, it has been found that cardiovascular, respiratory, and biochemical changes occurring during asphyxia under controlled conditions are predictable. Information on this subject is fairly complete in the newborn monkey, and has allowed quantitative evaluation of various modalities of treatment.

Primary and Secondary Apnea

During the initial phase of asphyxia of the unanesthetized newborn monkey, respiratory efforts increase in depth and frequency for up to 3 minutes. This period is called primary hyperpnea. It is followed by primary apnea, which lasts for approximately 1 minute. Rhythmical gasping then commences and is maintained at a fairly constant rate of about six gasps per minute for several minutes. The gasps finally become weaker and slower. Their cessation marks the beginning of secondary apnea.

There is some variation in the duration of gasping (time to last gasp) in different species. The duration depends upon the initial acid-base state, drugs given to the mother, and environmental temperature. At a given environmental temperature, the principal determinant of duration of gasping in the nonanesthetized animal is the initial arterial pH. Narcotics and systemic anesthetic agents given to the mother can abolish the period of primary hyperpnea and prolong the primary apnea; large doses can suppress all respiratory efforts. Gasping is prolonged if body temperature is lowered.

During primary apnea a variety of stimuli can initiate gasping (pain, cold, analeptics). During secondary apnea, however, these stimuli are without effect. Artificial ventilation or rapid correction of pH by infusion of alkali, if given soon enough after the "last gasp," are the only ways presently known by which gasping can be reinitiated.

RELATIONSHIP BETWEEN DURATION OF APNEA AND ONSET OF BREATHING. There is a linear relationship between the duration of asphyxia and the recovery of respiratory function following resuscitation. In the newborn monkey, for each minute after the last gasp that artificial ventilation is delayed, there is a further delay of 2 minutes before gasping recommences, and 4 minutes before rhythmical breathing is established (Fig. 42). This indicates that the longer artificial ventilation is delayed during secondary apnea the longer it will take to resuscitate the infant.

Treatment and Initial Appraisal of the Newborn

The delivery room must always be prepared for adequate and prompt treatment of severe asphyxia at

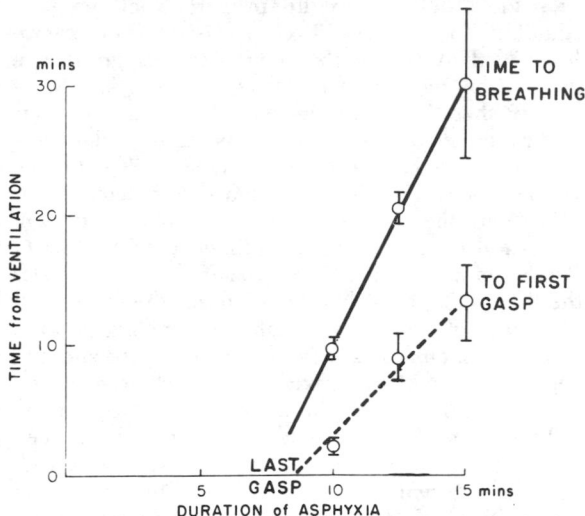

Fig. 42. Time from ventilation after the last gasp to first new gasp (dashed line) and to rhythmic breathing (solid line) in 16 newborn monkeys asphyxiated for 10, 12½, and 15 minutes at 30°C. The points represent the means of 5 or 6 animals ± 1 SE. The mean time from the onset of asphyxia until the last gasp was 8.42 ± 0.24 (SE) minutes. (From Adamsons. *J. Pediat.*, 65:807, 1964.)

birth. All members of the delivery room team should be trained in methods of resuscitation, for both mother and baby may be in difficulty at the same time. Indecision or ineffective therapy may cause the few moments during which the baby can be saved to be lost.

Every piece of apparatus necessary for emergency resuscitation should be carefully checked before each delivery. There should be suction equipment, a plastic oropharyngeal airway, a laryngoscope equipped with a pencil handle (containing two good batteries) and a premature blade, and a Cole plastic endotracheal tube with a stylet. Oxygen should also be available.

The early procedures, during and immediately after delivery, apply to all babies. The fetal heart should be monitored constantly to the moment of delivery. A heart rate below 100 or above 160 between contractions or the passage of meconium in a vertex presentation is an urgent warning sign of fetal distress. If these signs develop, the staff should be alerted for an emergency, and the baby delivered as soon as possible. Analysis of capillary samples from the fetal scalp for pH and blood gases may, in the future, permit a more precise evaluation of the fetal condition.

Immediately after delivery, the baby is held head down while the cord is clamped and cut. The infant is then placed supine on a table, and every effort should be made to minimize heat loss. The head is kept low with a slight lateral tilt. A nurse or assistant listens to the heartbeat immediately, indicating the rate by finger movement. A strong beat with a rate of over 100 per minute indicates that there is no immediate emergency. Distant and slow heart sounds indicate severe depression, calling for resuscitative measures. At the same time that the nurse is listening to the heart, the physician aspirates the mouth, the pharynx, and the nose with a catheter. This suction is brief. From birth to completion of suctioning should take about one minute. Lightly slapping the heels frequently aids in initiating a deep breath and crying. More severe methods of stimulation, such as dilating the anal sphincter, hot and cold tubbing, or vigorous back slapping, are traumatic, ineffectual, and a waste of time.

The initial appraisal of the newborn should start from the moment of birth, particular attention being paid to the first few breaths and the evenness and ease of respiration. A congenital laryngeal web or choanal atresia can cause complete airway obstruction. Both require immediate treatment. A diaphragmatic hernia with abdominal viscera in the chest, abdominal distension from ascites, or intrauterine pneumonia may all cause respiratory difficulty and may even prevent lung expansion.

TABLE 12.   *Acronym of the Apgar Score**

	Sign	Score		
		0	1	2
A	Appearance (color)	Blue; pale	Body pink; extremities blue	Completely pink
P	Pulse (heart rate)	Absent	Below 100	Over 100
G	Grimace (reflex irritability response to stimulation of sole of foot by glancing slap)	No response	Grimace	Cry
A	Activity (muscle tone)	Limp	Some flexion of extremities	Active motion
R	Respiration (respiratory effort)	Absent	Slow; irregular	Good strong cry

*Sixty seconds after complete birth of infant (disregarding cord and placenta), the five objective signs are evaluated and each given a score of 0, 1, or 2. Total score of 10 indicates an infant in best possible condition. (From Butterfield and Covey, *J.A.M.A.*, 181:353, 1962.)

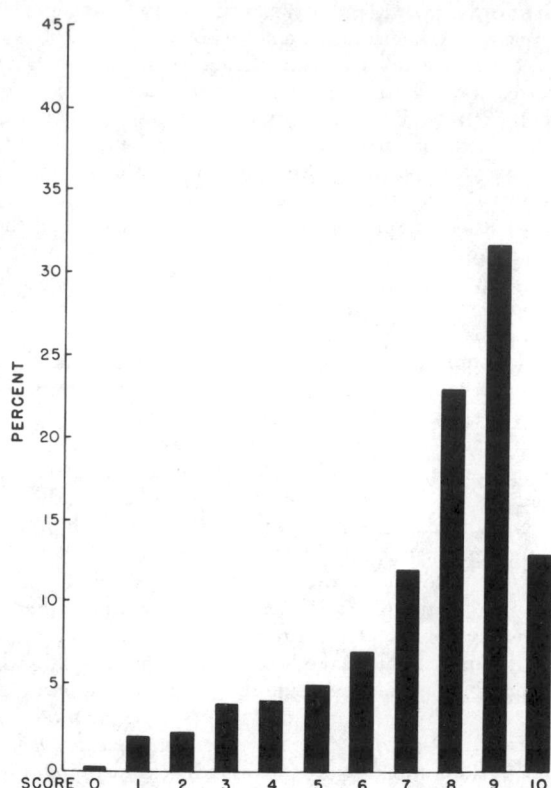

Fig. 43. Percent distribution (ordinate) of score (abscissa) at 1 minute among 27,715 liveborn infants.

THE APGAR SCORING SYSTEM.   The scoring system introduced by Virginia Apgar in 1952 is a useful aid for clinical evaluation of the baby. The score is based on heart rate, respiratory effort, muscle tone, reflex irritability, and color, as described in Table 12. The majority of infants are vigorous, with a summed score of 7 to 10 (Fig. 43); they cough or cry within seconds of delivery. No further resuscitation procedures are necessary for them. The largest group requiring some form of resuscitation at birth are the mildly to moderately depressed infants. These infants are pale or blue at one minute after delivery. They have not established sustained respiration and may be nearly flaccid. However, their heart rate and reflex irritability are good. The score in this group may be 4, 5, or 6.

INTUBATION AND VENTILATION.   If resuscitative measures have produced no response by one and a half minutes after delivery, the progressing asphyxia usually leads to diminished muscular tone and a fall in the heart rate. A small, plastic oropharyngeal airway should then be inserted into the infant's mouth. Next, oxygen is applied under pressure of 16 to 20 cm of water, for one to two seconds. Although this pressure is insufficient to expand the alveoli, some oxygen will reach the respiratory bronchioles. The rise in intrabronchial pressure stimulates pulmonary stretch receptors. This stimulus, added to that of the chemoreceptors, initiates a gasp in the majority of the cases.

If there is no respiratory effort and the heart rate continues to fall, the infant becoming completely flaccid, the larynx should be visualized with the laryngoscope. This is not a difficult procedure, but skill should be obtained by practice on the stillborn.

Intubation is best accomplished with the infant lying supine on a flat surface. A folded towel under the head and a slight extension of the neck will place him in a position resembling a sniffing posture. The head should be steadied with the right hand and kept in line with the body. With the laryngoscope held in the left hand, the blade is introduced at the right corner of the mouth and advanced between tongue and palate for about 2 cm. As it is advanced, the blade is swung to the midline. This moves the tongue to the left of the blade. The operator looks along the blade for the rim of the epiglottis. The laryngoscope is gently advanced into the space between the base of the tongue and the epiglottis (Fig. 44). Slight elevation of the tip of the blade will expose the glottis as a vertical dark slit bordered posteriorly by pink arytenoid cartilage.

If foreign material such as small blood clots, meconium-stained mucus, or vernix obstructs the larynx, quick brief suction is indicated. When the glottis is seen to be patent, a curved endotracheal tube is introduced at the right corner of the mouth and inserted through the cords until the flange of the tube rests at the glottis. Care must be taken not to intubate the esophagus instead of the glottis. The larnygoscope is then withdrawn. Rarely, the glottis is obstructed by a laryngeal web. If this is partial or

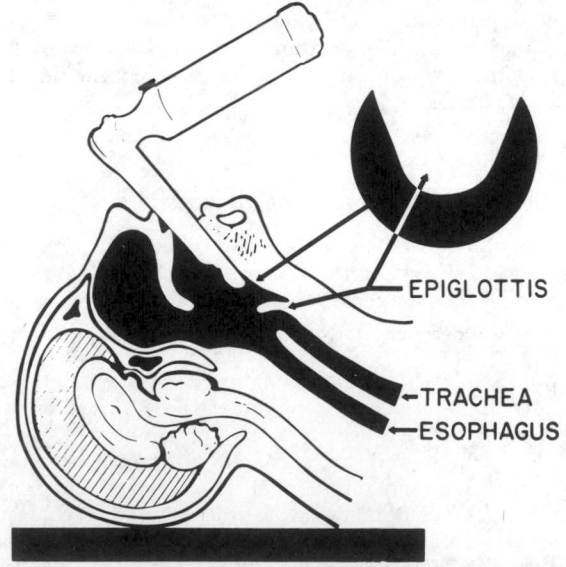

Fig. 44. Sagittal section through mouth and pharynx showing relationship of laryngoscope blade to epiglottis.

thin, it may be perforated with a stylet or enlarged with an endotracheal tube. The presence of a thick membrane requires immediate tracheostomy.

If stimuli from these procedures have not initiated a spontaneous gasp, positive pressure should be applied to the endotracheal tube. Brief puffs of air blown through the tube with enough force to cause the lower chest to rise gently will usually start spontaneous respiration. If the stomach rises, however, the esophagus has been intubated instead of the trachea, and the position of the tube must be corrected. Pressures between 25 and 35 cm of water are necessary to expand the alveoli initially and can be applied safely for one or two seconds. Oxygen-enriched air may be delivered to the infant by placing a tube carrying oxygen in the operator's mouth.

If the endotracheal tube is fitted with adaptors of appropriate size, it can be connected to a rubber bag of oxygen or oxygen-enriched air or to one of the mechanical devices for applying positive pressure.

The act of expanding the lungs appears to stimulate respiration. With the first or second application of positive pressure, these infants usually make an effort to breathe. The endotracheal tube may be withdrawn after the infant has taken five or six breaths.

SEVERELY DEPRESSED INFANTS. If, from the moment of birth, the infant is severely depressed, flaccid, unresponsive, and pale, his Apgar score is 0, 1, or 2. In such an infant, no time should be lost, and the glottis should be visualized immediately with the laryngoscope. If meconium or thick, meconium-stained mucus has been aspirated into the trachea, it must be suctioned out at once. Immediately thereafter the lungs should be inflated.

It is usually possible to accomplish these procedures within one minute after delivery. These severely depressed infants usually require 3 to 8 minutes of artificial ventilation before a spontaneous gasp is taken. Rarely, 25 or 30 minutes of assisted ventilation is necessary. The endotracheal tube can be removed as soon as quiet and sustained respiration is established. One of the most common errors in resuscitation is not allowing sufficient time for passive expiration during positive pressure ventilation. The result of this error is to end up with hyperinflated lungs and a barrel-chested infant with very little air exchange. For this reason, the rate of ventilation should not exceed 30 to 40 per minute, and this should be timed very carefully.

Under some circumstances lung expansion is impossible in spite of proper intubation. There are three principal conditions where this difficulty occurs: massive aspiration of meconium which cannot be removed by suctioning; intrauterine pneumonia with organization of the exudate; and large bilateral diaphragmatic hernias with hypoplastic lungs. Infants belonging to the first two categories are usually severely depressed at birth. However, those with hypoplastic lungs may be initially vigorous and score as high as 7 at one minute of age, making

strenuous but ineffective respiratory efforts. At present there is no available therapy for this condition.

CARDIAC MASSAGE. Blood pressure and heart rate fall during prolonged asphyxia. If the blood pressure is unduly low at the beginning of resuscitation, positive pressure ventilation is unlikely to be successful unless cardiac massage is employed. Cardiac massage has been successfully applied through the intact chest wall in human infants.

External manual compression of the heart between the chest wall and the vertebral column forces blood into the aorta. Relaxation of pressure allows the heart to fill with venous blood. When combined with proper ventilation, external manual heart compression often is able to maintain blood pressure and adequate oxygenation until spontaneous cardiac activity returns.

The technique consists of intermittent compression of the middle and lower third of the sternum 100 to 120 times per minute, with the index and middle fingers. Massage is interrupted every five seconds to permit two or three inflations of the lung. It should be employed only after the lungs have been well expanded and if a heartbeat cannot be detected or if the heart rate does not rise promptly.

The optimal case for cardiopulmonary resuscitation in infants is one in which there has been no clinical evidence of fetal distress, and where a normal fetal heart rate has been heard between the contractions up to the moment of birth. Figure 45, taken from a study by Hey and Kelly, illustrates the sequence of events during the successful resuscitation of a severely depressed infant. The combination of intubation, intermittent positive pressure ventilation, and external cardiac massage were all required to establish a normal heart rate and sustained independent respirations in this infant. It is worth pointing out that this resuscitation was achieved without the administration of buffers of any kind. This emphasizes the fact that in the severely depressed infant primary effort should be directed at maintaining an adequate circulation and establishing adequate ventilation before other aspects of therapy are begun.

RAPID CORRECTION OF pH. In experimental animals, maintenance of a normal pH during asphyxia by rapid intravenous infusion of alkali together with glucose prolongs gasping and delays cardiovascular collapse. Resuscitation is also facilitated if alkali and glucose are infused at the same time that artificial ventilation is started; oxygen consumption is greater and the time to establish spontaneous breathing is shorter. Cardiac massage is less frequently necessary in the treated animals. In severely asphyxiated newborn infants, when one attempts to correct a metabolic acidosis, $NaHCO_3$ should be used. The concentrated solution (44 mg/50 ml) should be diluted, 1 ml of buffer to 2 ml of 5 percent glucose, prior to injection to reduce its osmolality.

HYPERBARIC OXYGEN. It is claimed that severely asphyxiated and apneic infants can be resuscitated

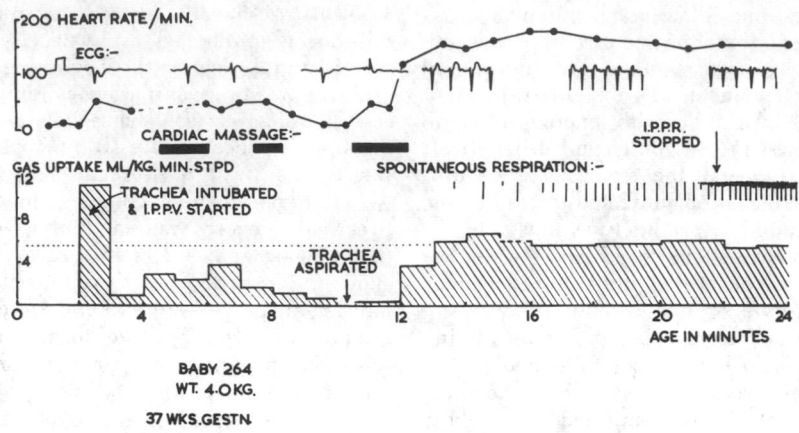

Fig. 45. Summary of the heart rate, electrocardiograph, respiratory response, and gas uptake recorded during the successful resuscitation of an infant who suffered severe asphyxia as a result of shoulder dystocia during vaginal delivery. (From Hey and Kelly. J. Obstet. Gynaec. Brit. Cmm., 75:414, 1968.)

merely by placing them in a hyperbaric oxygen chamber. These claims have not been substantiated in animal experiments. On theoretical grounds alone it is unlikely that a technique which considers only O_2 uptake and ignores CO_2 elimination could be effective in the treatment of either birth asphyxia or the respiratory distress syndrome (RDS).

Furthermore, even if an adequate amount of oxygen could diffuse through the skin, skin blood flow would have to be equal to the resting left ventricular output in order to transport sufficient oxygen to other body tissues. In the presence of circulatory collapse and intense peripheral vasoconstriction, these criteria could not possibly be met.

HYPOTHERMIA.   There are several reasons why hypothermia might be a valuable adjunct in the resuscitation of the asphyxiated newborn. Metabolic rate could be lowered, increased peripheral vasoconstriction could lead to maintenance of blood pressure, Pco_2 could be lowered owing to increased solubility of CO_2 at lower temperature, and pH could be elevated because of changes in the dissociation constants of water and other acids. However, the rate of cooling is slow, particularly in the presence of a collapsed circulation, and the rise in pH and fall in Pco_2 are small compared with the changes which accompany ventilation.

Experiments in which cooling starts at the same time as asphyxia have no bearing on asphyxia before birth, when the fetus is at a warmer temperature than the mother. The techniques have been tried under controlled, experimental conditions in newborn monkeys asphyxiated prior to cooling and do not appear to prevent brain damage.

ASPHYXIA AND BRAIN DAMAGE.   Animal experiments have established that rapid correction or maintenance of pH in the presence of hyperglycemia during asphyxia can reduce or prevent morphologi-

cally detectable brain damage. Asphyxiated newborn monkeys which are resuscitated before the last gasp (i.e., within 8.4 minutes) show little or no permanent cerebral damage. On the other hand, prolongation of asphyxia for four minutes beyond the last gasp is accompanied by widespread tissue damage and abnormal behavior in the surviving animals.

The question arises as to how long resuscitation can be safely delayed in the apneic newborn human infants. For the newborn monkey the "safe" period of anoxia is quite short if functional integrity is to be maintained. A relatively brief delay in resuscitation can have serious sequelae. Until it is possible to evaluate the duration of asphyxia before birth and to know whether the nonbreathing infant is in primary or secondary apnea, and until it is known whether or not drugs administered to the mother have a protective action against asphyxia, an answer cannot be provided.

Physical Examination in the Delivery Room

As soon as respiration is well established, a careful examination of the newborn baby should be carried out. The principal reason is to determine the presence of major abnormalities such as tracheoesophageal fistula, duodenal atresia, imperforate anus, choanal atresia, or arteriovenous fistula, which require prompt attention. It is also important that other minor anomalies or birth injuries be first discovered by the physician, in order that necessary explanations can be given to the parents. The subsequent complete physical examination of the newborn infant is described in another section (p. 77).

SKIN. The color is normally pale pink save for the hands and feet, which may remain cyanotic for more than an hour, even in vigorous infants. Some differential cyanosis of the lower part of the body due to persistence of right-to-left shunting through the ductus arteriosus is also often present for the first 30 minutes of life. This is demonstrated more clearly if the infant is given high concentrations of oxygen for 5 or 10 seconds. Persistence of this differential cyanosis indicates failure of ductus closure, high pulmonary vascular resistance, or a preductal coarctation. These changes are less apparent in infants with heavily pigmented skins. Generalized cyanosis after the onset of respiration is rare even with gross cardiac anomalies, presumably due to cutaneous vasoconstriction. It is seen in the first few minutes of life in infants who have difficulty in establishing ventilation.

Generalized pallor indicates either intense cutaneous vasoconstriction or anemia. The former is present in severely asphyxiated infants. The latter should be suspected in the presence of erythroblastosis, placenta previa, or multiple pregnancy, but can also occur as a result of fetomaternal hemorrhage. Pallor is less apparent in infants with heavily pigmented skins.

Yellow appearance of the skin and umbilical cord is usually the result of meconium staining and is accompanied by golden coloring of the vernix and meconium in the amniotic fluid. It is also seen in erythroblastotic infants who are severely anemic at birth. However, since fetal retention of bilirubin is unusual in erythroblastosis fetalis, jaundice at birth is rather rare.

HEAD AND NECK. There is considerable variation in the shape of the head as the result of molding during labor and delivery, particularly in primigravida and occipitoposterior presentations. Excessive elongation should be noted because of the possibility of tentorial tears. Vacuum extractors create a sharply demarcated circular edema which may reach up to 2 cm in thickness. It disappears more slowly than naturally occurring edema. Forceps marks consisting of depressions or edema with erythema and sometimes abrasions frequently signify a traumatic delivery and may be associated with cranial nerve injuries or fractures. These should be suspected particularly in cases of improper application of forceps (face-mastoid). Fortunately, modern obstetrics, by elimination of complicated vaginal deliveries in favor of cesarean section, has considerably reduced the incidence of these complications.

The eyes are usually closed but may be open in postmature infants; in severe asphyxia they may be wide open and staring. The size of the pupils, their reactivity to light, and the color of the sclera should be noted. Fixed dilated pupils, or anisocoria, indicate severe asphyxia or brain damage. Subconjunctival hemorrhage is occasionally seen following difficult breech or impacted shoulders delivery.

The umbilical cord should be examined for the absence of one umbilical artery and the infant closely observed for the passage of urine and for evidence of malformation in other organ systems.

THORAX. The chest must be observed and auscultated for evenness of aeration. By five minutes of age, adventitious sounds normally remain only over the precordial area. Sternal or intercostal retraction in mature infants is abnormal and indicates airway obstruction or incomplete lung expansion. In premature infants, some retraction is expected because of the softness of the chest wall and less compliant lungs. Prolongation of expiration with or without an audible grunt is also abnormal and frequently is the first sign of incipient respiratory distress syndrome (RDS).

Diminished or absent breath sounds on one side are indicative of pneumothorax or diaphragmatic hernia with abdominal viscera in the chest. Percussion will usually differentiate the two. Soft or distant heart sounds associated with an increase in heart rate are found with pneumomediastinum. If any of these conditions is suspected, a roentgenogram of the chest should be obtained.

The heart is nearly in the midline, and frequently there is marked precordial activity during the first 30 minutes of life, when bidirectional shunting through the ductus arteriosus is maximal. The heart rate following delivery is 160 to 170 beats per minute, which is about 15 percent higher than the rate during labor. By 20 to 30 minutes of age, the rate returns to the previous level. Although the reason for this transient acceleration of heart rate is not known, it probably represents a response to various tactile, auditory, and thermal stimuli. Furthermore, increased total cardiac output in the presence of bidirectional shunting is necessary if the rate of tissue perfusion is to remain constant.

A pansystolic crescendo murmur is present in approximately 15 percent of all infants during the first two hours of life. It is more common in premature infants and in those recovering from severe asphyxia. The cause of this murmur has not yet been determined. Two likely possibilities are shunting through the ductus arteriosus and regurgitation through the mitral or tricuspid valves. Only one third of infants with cardiac malformation have detectable murmurs in the immediate neonatal period.

ABDOMEN. Prior to palpating the abdomen for abnormal masses, the catheter used for oropharyngeal suction during resuscitation should be passed through the mouth and esophagus into the stomach. The proper position of the catheter tip can usually be appreciated by a bulge in the left upper abdominal quadrant. Even if this is not seen, suction is applied to the tube and the stomach emptied. Should no secretions be obtained, the position of the catheter is verified by injecting air through it while auscultating the epigastrium. Esophageal atresia and tracheoesophageal fistula must be suspected if difficulties are encountered in the passage

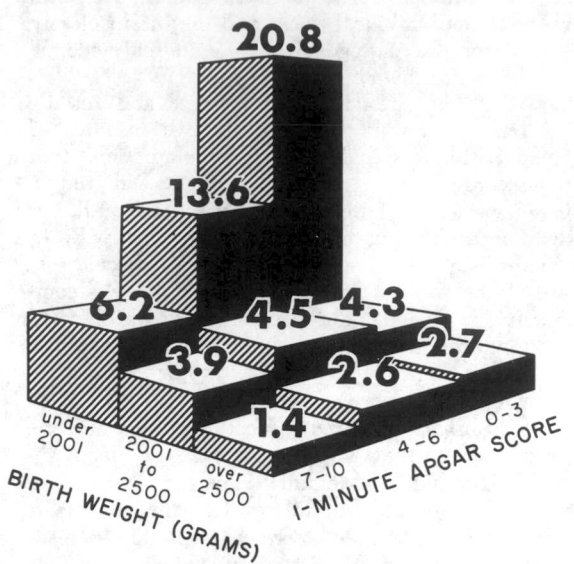

Fig. 46. Correlation between Apgar score (age 1 minute), birth weight, and incidence of neurologic deficit (percent affected) at 12 months of age. (From Collaborative Project for Cerebral Palsy, N.I.H., Bethesda, Maryland.)

of a catheter. The stomach of the newborn infant contains between 4 and 8 ml of fluid; the volume is usually greater in those born by elective cesarean section. Duodenal atresia or other types of upper gastrointestinal tract obstructions are likely to be present if larger quantities of fluid are obtained (more than 30 ml).

Emptying of the stomach is essentially a diagnostic procedure, but may be therapeutic if the volume of fluid in the stomach is large enough to interfere with movement of the diaphragm. If a soft rubber or plastic catheter is used, there is virtually no danger of visceral injury.

The anal region should be inspected and the patency of the anus and rectum tested by insertion of the previously used rubber catheter for 8 cm. If anal atresia is present, the bladder should be catheterized and the urine examined for meconium since there is usually an associated rectovesical fistula.

NEUROLOGIC EXAMINATION. This examination should be brief and usually limited to testing of the grasp and Moro reflexes. If the infant has had a low Apgar score and remains limp after establishing respiration, there is an increased possibility of neurologic impairment (Fig. 46).

PLACENTA AND MEMBRANES. The placenta should be weighed, and both fetal and maternal surfaces should be inspected. The presence of infarcts or adherent clots should be recorded. On the fetal side, the color of the membranes is pale gray. Brown or green discoloration indicates prolonged exposure to meconium in the amniotic fluid. Vesicular formation on the surface of the placenta is suggestive of a

renal anomaly. In multiple pregnancy, the number of amniotic sacs should be determined and the surface examined for vascular connections between fetal circulation (p. 118).

LABORATORY PROCEDURES. In all cases of blood incompatibility, blood is removed from the umbilical cord for direct antiglobulin (Coombs') test, bilirubin concentration, typing, and hematocrit (see Table 11). If the infant appears pale, a microhematocrit should be determined on a venous blood sample. Immediately after birth and for 12 to 16 hours thereafter a capillary hematocrit taken from a heel prick is inaccurate even after warming the limb. When the membranes have been ruptured for longer than 12 hours, a section of the cord and of the surface of the placenta should be removed for microscopic examination, and cultures should be taken from the amniotic surface of the placenta, cord blood, and nose and throat of the infant. If facilities are available, a blood sample, from either the umbilical vessels or a heel prick, should be obtained in severely asphyxiated infants with a persistent low Apgar score and examined for pH and Pco_2. This provides a measure of the degree of asphyxia before birth and during resuscitation and serves as a guide for therapy.

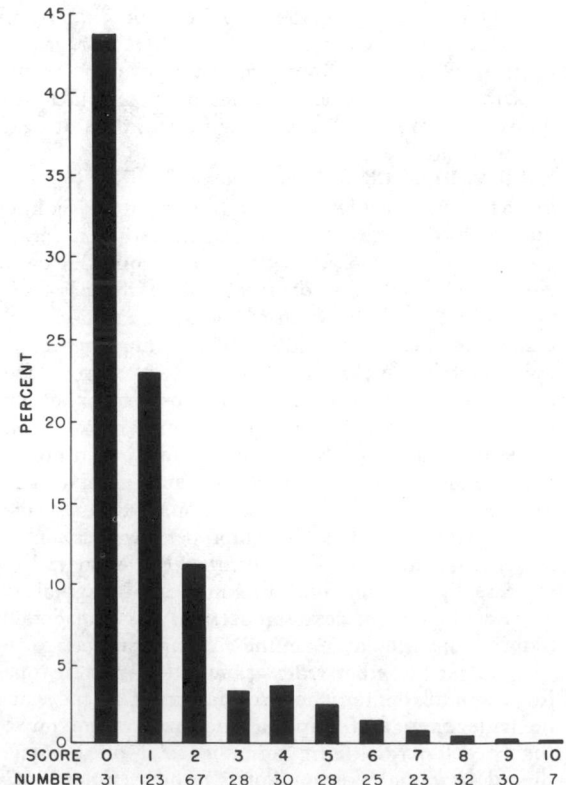

Fig. 47. Association between 28 days' mortality per 100 live births (ordinate) and score (abscissa) among 27,715 liveborn infants. (From Apgar and James. Amer. J. Dis. Child., 104:419, 1962.)

As stated, correction of acidosis facilitates recovery of the asphyxiated experimental animal.

SPECIAL CARE UNIT. The Apgar scoring system is a useful guide for selection of infants at high risk, since mortality correlates inversely with score (Fig. 47). Under ideal circumstances, such infants should be retained in a special unit where close observation and care by experienced personnel are available.

REFERENCES

Abramson, H., ed. Resuscitation of the Newborn Infant. St. Louis, The C. V. Mosby Co., 1960.

Adamsons, K., Jr., Behrman, R., Dawes, G. S., James, L. S., and Koford, C. Resuscitation by positive pressure ventilation and tris-hydroxymethyl-aminomethane of rhesus monkeys asphyxiated at birth. J. Pediat., 65:807, 1964.

Apgar, V., and James, L. S. Further observations on the newborn scoring system. Amer. J. Dis. Child., 104:419, 1962.

Benirschke, K. Examination of the placenta. Obstet. Gynec., 18:309, 1961.

Born, G. V. R., Dawes, G. S., Mott, J. C., and Rennick, B. R. Constriction of ductus arteriosus caused by oxygen and by asphyxia in newborn lambs. J. Physiol. (London), 132:304, 1956.

Gandy, G. M., Adamsons, K., Jr., Cunningham, N., Silverman, W. A., and James, L. S. Thermal environment and acid-base homeostasis in human infants during the first few hours of life. J. Clin. Invest., 43:751, 1964.

Harned, H. S., Jr., Rowshan, G., MacKinney, L. G., and Sugioka, K. Relationships of Po_2, Pco_2 and pH to onset of breathing of term lamb as studied by flow-through cuvette electrode assembly. Pediatrics, 33:672, 1964.

Hey, E., and Kelly, J. Gaseous exchange during endotracheal ventilation for asphyxia at birth. J. Obstet. Gynaec. Brit. Comm., 75:414, 1968.

James, L. S. Physiology of respiration in newborn infants and in the respiratory distress syndrome. Pediatrics, 24:1969, 1959.

———— and Adamsons, K., Jr. Respiratory physiology of the fetus and newborn infant. New Eng. J. Med., 272:1352 and 272:1403, 1964.

Karlberg, P., Cherry, R. B., Escardo, F. E., and Koch, G. Respiratory studies in newborn infants. II. Pulmonary ventilation and mechanics of breathing in first minutes of life, including onset of respiration. Acta Paediat. Scand., 51:121, 1962.

The Newborn Infant

2.10
PHYSICAL EXAMINATION

MOSES GROSSMAN

Following the delivery room examination and after admission of the infant to the nursery, a detailed physical examination should be done, which will serve several purposes: (1) to determine the general well-being of the infant; (2) to detect congenital anomalies or evidence of birth trauma; (3) to establish a base line for serial observations, examinations, and measurements essential for the early detection of morbidity; and (4) to determine a clinical estimate of gestational age of the newborn. The latter evaluation will enable the pediatrician to compare his own assessment of gestational age based on physical and neurologic examination, with estimates made earlier from obstetric signs, menstrual history, and laboratory tests. The appraisal of gestational age is particularly important in infants who have had abnormal intrauterine growth rates. However, the physical examination for the purpose of determining the infant's maturity is worthless in any infant with clinical problems likely to affect his performance, such as hypoglycemia, sepsis, or hypothermia.

The importance of a comprehensive physical examination cannot be overestimated; a number of anomalies require early therapy for optimal correction. Since congenital anomalies are frequently multiple, the finding of one abnormality should lead to a careful search for the existence of others. After the examination of the infant, the physician has the obligation to inform the parents immediately about his findings.

The initial physical examination should be followed by a series of observations including the time of the first urination, the first stool and its nature, excessive salivation, and the nature of the baby's sucking and swallowing. Periodic observations for the presence of jaundice are essential. Measurements of weight, length, head circumference, pulse and respiratory rates, and temperature should be performed meticulously. Blood pressure should be measured in all newborn infants, either by the usual indirect methods, or by direct measurement if an umbilical arterial catheter has been inserted in critically ill infants. Interim examinations, more limited in scope, should be performed on any infant who remains in the nursery for an appreciable length of time. How frequent and how detailed subsequent observations are, and whether they are made by physicians or other professional staff, will depend upon the physician's initial evalution and the infant's course. Of particular importance is the final examination performed before discharging the infant from the newborn nursery. Good record keeping has special significance in the newborn period when even normal findings, such as the presence of descended testes, may be of interest in future evaluations.

Inspection

Before handling the infant, inspection constitutes a very useful feature of the physical examination of a newborn. His respiration, color, position, spontaneous activity, and general behavior should be observed. The pattern of spontaneous activity of the infant can be very helpful in detecting conditions which affect the central nervous system and which may require further laboratory tests for diagnosis. The skin should also be observed for exanthemata, meconium staining, petechiae, or bruising. A variety of syndromes in the newborn, such as Down's syndrome, cretinism, and arthrogryposis, can be readily recognized by inspection.

Systemic Examination

SKIN. The skin of the term newborn infant is covered with a whitish fatty substance, the *vernix caseosa,* and with *lanugo,* a fine downy hair. The high cutaneous blood flow and the thinness of the skin make observation of its color particularly useful. Shortly after birth it should be quite red. The face, particularly the nose, is often covered with small whitish papules known as *milia;* these represent slightly distended sebaceous glands. In the first days of life, a term infant may exhibit *erythema toxicum* (Fig. 48), a scattered rash consisting of 3- to 4-mm papules with mild erythema; occasionally these papules are topped with minute vesicles. The rash is sometimes called "fleabite dermatitis" and occurs so frequently that it is regarded as "normal." However, in preterm infants, particularly in those weighing less than 1,500 g, it should not be regarded as normal but as an exanthema of unknown etiology.

Infants of Asian or African ancestry often exhibit bluish discolorations of the skin, varying in size and usually on the lower part of the back or buttocks. These *mongolian spots* (Fig. 49) are due to the presence of specific pigment cells in the dermis and disappear by 4 or 5 years of age. Telangiectasia-like markings may occur over the eyelids and the nape of the neck and disappear without a trace within the first two years of life.

Generalized *cyanosis* requires immediate investigation. However, localized cyanosis of the hands and feet, *acrocyanosis,* is frequently seen and is unimportant unless it persists after several days.

Mottling of the skin of the extremities and trunk is often seen in newborn infants, particularly preterm babies.

A mild degree of *jaundice* is commonly present after the second or third day of life in normal infants.

When the icterus is severe or present in the first 24 hours it should alert the physician to the possible existence of serious illness (e.g., hemolytic disease, septicemia, neonatal hepatitis, congenital or acquired viral infections, drugs or other chemical intoxications). Proper lighting is essential for early detection of jaundice—strong daylight or white fluorescent light of 100-candle power intensity.

If *petechiae* are present, their distribution should be noted. Infants born with a cord around the neck often have petechiae above the neck only; the distribution is more general when associated with systemic disease.

Impetiginous lesions present as vesicles filled with turbid fluid or pustules, especially in the diaper area. The vesicles break easily and leave a moist denuded area which often forms a crust. It can be confused with erythema toxicum. For this reason, especially in preterm babies, the fluid of any vesicular lesion should be collected and stained to demonstrate granulocytes and bacteria.

Cutaneous moniliasis appears as a maceration of the perianal skin and groin and may be accompanied by marked erythema. It is not present at birth but usually appears at about one week of age. The diagnosis can be readily confirmed by microscopic examination of skin scrapings.

Strawberry hemangiomas are seldom seen at birth, but the site of a later lesion may appear as a slightly depigmented area.

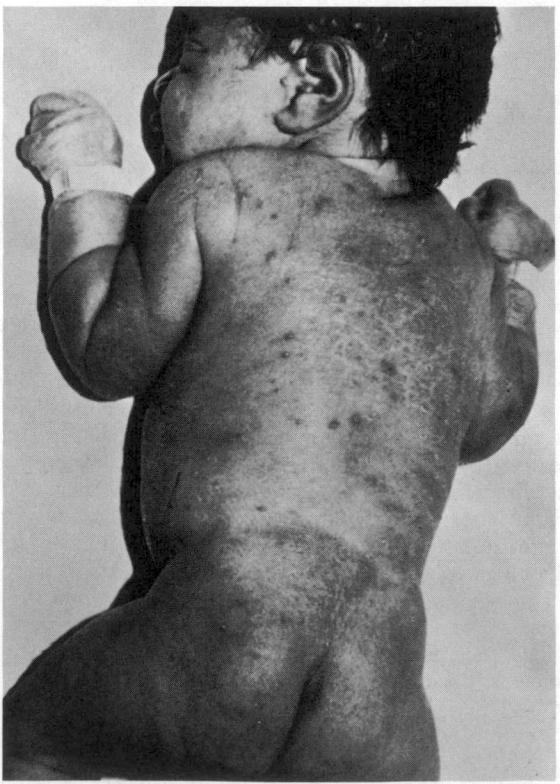

Fig. 48. Erythema toxicum.

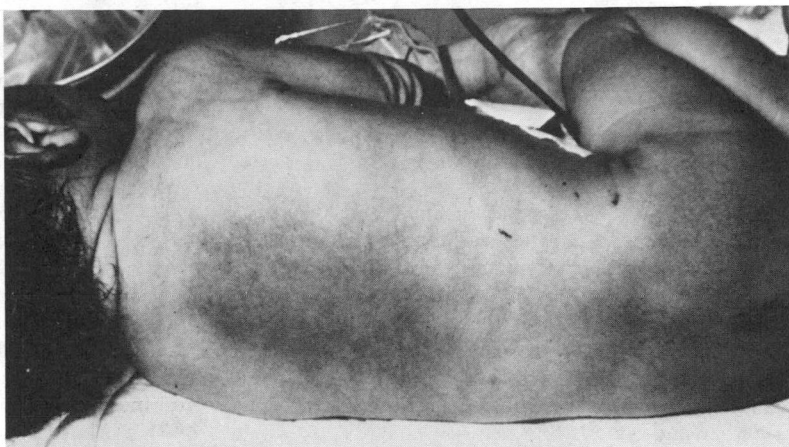

Fig. 49. Mongolian spots.

Sclerema neonatorum is found in association with major illnesses of the neonatal period. The infant's skin is first cool to touch, then the subcutaneous tissues of the buttocks, thighs, calves, and thorax harden. Eventually the skin feels woody to touch, and there is marked limitation of joint movement and respiratory excursion.

The absence of subcutaneous tissue is a characteristic of both the premature and intrauterine growth-retarded infant. In the postmature infant, finger and toe nails are especially well developed and often stained yellow.

Skin creases on the soles of the foot are helpful in estimating the degree of maturity (Fig. 50).

HEAD. Both the intrauterine position and the passage through the birth canal result in asymmetrical *molding* of the baby's head. The sutures may overlap, shrinking the fontanelle. The molding and asymmetry disappear over the first few days or weeks of life. In contrast, the head of the infant born by cesarean section and/or of a breech presentation is strikingly round and symmetrical.

Caput succedaneum is an edematous area of the scalp which may show petechiae, purpura, or ecchymoses. The caput forms on the portion of the head encircled by the dilated cervical ring during delivery. The deformity disappears within the first few days of life. Its margin is vague and undefined in contrast to a cephalohematoma.

Craniotabes, which is pathologic in an older child, is normal in the newborn infant. The sign is elicited by pressing lightly on the parietal bones

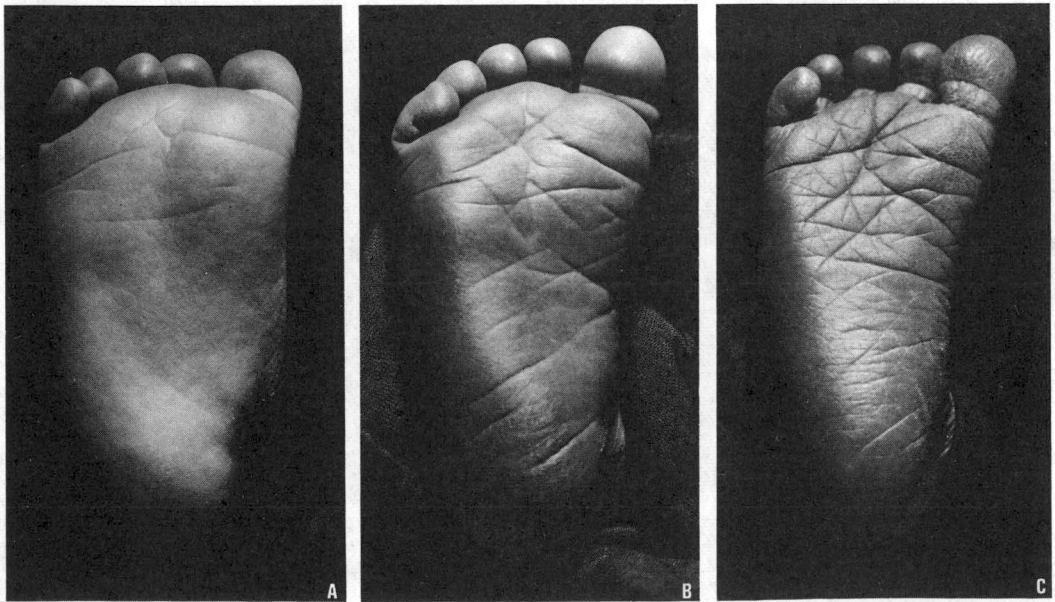

Fig. 50. A. Foot of an infant of 36 weeks' gestational age, showing posterior three quarters of the sole smooth. B. Foot of an infant of 38 weeks' gestational age, showing some sole creases. C. Foot of an infant of 40 weeks' gestational age, showing a complex series of creases extending the whole length of the sole. (From Usher et al. *Pediat. Clin. N. Amer.*, 13:842, 1966.)

and results in a slight indentation, producing the sensation of compressing a table tennis ball.

Cephalohematoma is produced by bleeding beneath the periosteum of the cranial bones. Most common over the parietal bones, it is limited by the periosteal attachments and does not extend across suture lines. The hematoma is often largest on the second or third day of life at which time the swelling feels fluctuant, demarcated sharply by a slightly elevated ridge, giving often the impression of a depressed skull fracture. A cephalohematoma should not be needled because of the hazard of introducing infection. It will usually disappear within two or three weeks; occasionally, calcium is deposited in the hematoma, and the swelling may persist for as long as a year and a half.

EYES.   Examination of the eyes of newborn infants is easier and is more satisfactory if the examiner waits for the baby to open his eyes spontaneously. Since some retinal hemorrhages occur in as many as 40 percent of vaginally delivered infants, there is no purpose in attempting a careful fundoscopic examination in normal term infants. The eye examination in a term infant should focus on: (1) pupil and corneal size; (2) pupillary light reflex; (3) the possible existence of lenticular opacities; and (4) the red reflex. However, a careful fundoscopic examination should be carried out prior to discharge in any high-risk infant with CNS signs or symptoms and in any preterm infant who has received O_2 therapy.

Nonpatency of the *lacrimal duct* is common at birth; tears usually are not copious until the second month of life. A *purulent discharge* is suspicious. Despite the almost universal practice of eye prophylaxis at birth, gonorrheal ophthalmia still occurs. Silver nitrate often produces a chemical irritation sometimes associated with purulence. *Inclusion blenorrhea* is an important cause of inflammatory discharge in the first postnatal days. The diagnosis is made by demonstrating inclusion bodies in conjunctival scrapings. *Subconjunctival hemorrhages* occur frequently and are of little significance. They result from pressures exerted during delivery and disappear within the first few days of life.

FACE.   Facial appearance may reveal pathologic conditions, such as Down's syndrome (Fig. 51), renal agenesis, or cretinism. Facial nerve paralysis can occur in the neonate. In addition, twitching at the corners of the mouth or at the eyelids, or jaw tremors are among the earliest signs of hyperirritability or jitteriness in a newborn infant.

EARS.   Malformed or *low-set pinnae* may be associated with kidney anomalies. *Preauricular fistulae* or *tubercles* are quite common. The degree of cartilaginous development of the ear lobe is one of the indicators of gestational age (Figs. 52 and 53).

NOSE.   The newborn baby is a preferential nose breather. In the newborn period complete bilateral nasal obstruction results in acute respiratory distress requiring immediate therapy. Bilateral *choanal atresia* causes such obstruction, and symptoms will be evident at birth. *Unilateral atresia* may be undetected or may present as a unilateral nasal discharge. Once suspected, this malformation can be demonstrated by closing the infant's mouth while alternately occluding one nostril. The definitive diagnosis is established by inability to pass a nasogastric tube.

MOUTH.   Careful examination in a good light is necessary to visualize the entire soft and hard palate and uvula. A *cleft lip* or a prominent *cleft palate* can be seen without difficulty; however, a small cleft

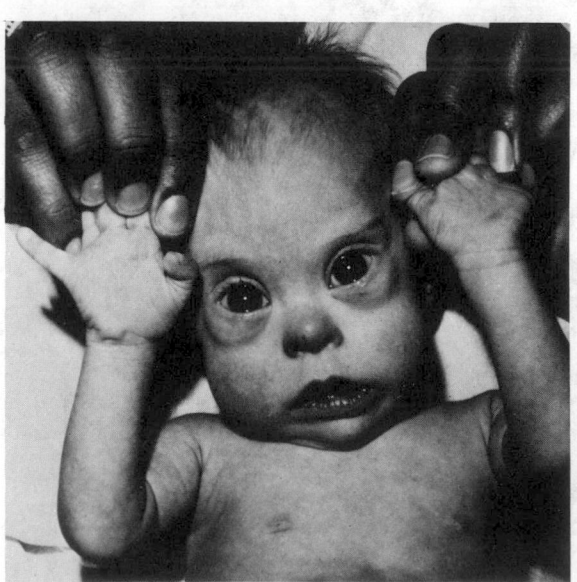

Fig. 51.   Down's syndrome.

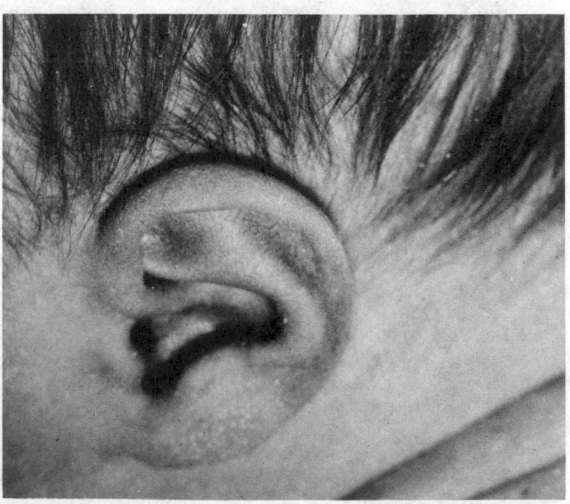

Fig. 52.   The ear of an infant of 36 weeks' gestational age, showing a relatively shapeless, pliable structure with little cartilaginous support. The fineness of the hair can also be seen. (From Usher et al. *Pediat. Clin. N. Amer.*, 13:844, 1966.)

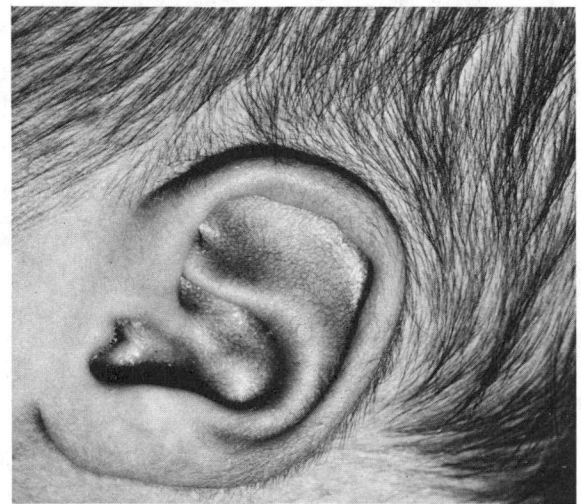

Fig. 53. The ear of an infant of 40 weeks' gestational age, showing a more rigid earlobe, stiffened with cartilage. The hair is rather coarse, each hair being separately visible. (From Usher et al. *Pediat. Clin. N. Amer.*, 13:844, 1966.)

of the soft palate is easily missed. A very high *arched palate* can occur without associated defect and may contribute to upper airway obstruction.

A *sucking pad* is present on the inner surface of each cheek, and after a day or two sucking corns develop on the lip surface. Individual *tooth bud compartments* are common, and occasionally an infant is born with erupted teeth. *Epithelial pearls* or *inclusion cysts* are firm white cysts found along gum margins or sometimes in the palate and are of no significance.

The *frenulum linguae* varies widely in length and width. An abnormally large tongue suggests the presence of hemangioma or lymphangioma. The enlarged tongue of the cretin is accompanied by other stigmata. An infant with Down's syndrome also has a slightly enlarged tongue, which he tends to suck continually. A normal tongue may appear to be large in the small oral cavity of micrognathia. The association of cleft palate, micrognathia, and glossoptosis is known as the *Pierre Robin syndrome*.

Moniliasis, or *thrush*, presents as a thick white coating of the tongue and buccal membranes. The coating is very adherent, in contrast to milk curd which can be wiped off with ease; its removal often causes bleeding. When this material is placed on a glass slide, cleared with potassium hydroxide, and examined under the microscope, the typical yeast structure of monilia is seen. The newborn has a negligible amount of tonsillar tissue.

The presence of an unusual amount of saliva or frothing suggests *esophageal atresia*. This malformation can be ruled out quickly by passing a gastric tube into the stomach.

NECK. The newborn infant generally has a short, squat neck, and the head appears to sit almost directly on top of the shoulders. A mass in the neck from an enlarged thyroid or other tumor may be life threatening in the neonatal period through airway compression. *Fistulous openings of branchial clefts* or *of the pharyngoglossal duct* may be discovered on close inspection of the neck. *Congenital torticollis* is generally not recognized until after the infant has left the newborn nursery. The presenting sign of a *fractured clavicle* is usually a unilateral absence of the Moro reflex; careful palpation of the clavicle may then reveal the actual site of fracture.

THORAX. A relatively common finding is the presence of *supernumerary nipples*, which may be unilateral or bilateral. These have only cosmetic significance. Sternal deformities include "pigeon breast," where the sternum is prominent and elevated. The lower portion may be depressed, resulting in a "funnel chest."

The size of the *mammary gland* in the newborn bears some relation to gestational age. Usually this tissue is not palpable before 33 weeks and increases thereafter. Shortly after birth the breast may become quite engorged. This swelling, due to the influence of maternal hormones, may be pronounced. The engorged breast may even secrete a few drops of "witches' milk." This fluid should not be expressed, since this increases the risk of staphylococcal infection of the breast. The normal breast engorgement is easily differentiated from the much less common finding of *mastitis*, generally due to staphylococcal infection.

LUNGS. The newborn's *respiration* is chiefly diaphragmatic, at a rate of 30 to 50 per minute. An elevated respiratory rate, respiratory grunt, and deep retractions of the sternum are signs of serious respiratory distress. Infants who have respiratory difficulties will often have *intercostal* as well as *suprasternal* retraction on inspiration. Evaluation and grading of these retractions is an important way of following respiratory distress in the newborn. Irregular respirations or weak, shallow respirations may be a sign of CNS dysfunction. *Percussion of the lungs* is helpful in detecting pneumothorax, pneumomediastinum, or diaphragmatic hernia. Asymmetric movements of the chest wall and abdomen point to similar clinical problems or unilateral phrenic nerve paralysis. Asynchronous movement of the chest and abdomen (see-saw respirations) are seen in severe upper airway obstruction.

Auscultation of the lungs in the newborn has limitations. Surprisingly good breath sounds may often be produced by a relatively small amount of ventilation. Careful auscultation is especially important after resuscitation and tracheal intubation. Immediately after intubation the air entry into both lungs should be specifically checked to insure that the endotracheal tube has not been introduced into one of the main stem branches. Peristaltic sounds heard in the thorax suggest the existence of a diaphragmatic hernia.

HEART. The position of the heart should be determined to rule out dextrocardia or major shifts of the mediastinal structures.

Auscultation of the heart must include determination of rate, rhythm, quality of sounds, and the presence of murmurs. The rate in the term newborn is usually 120 to 140 beats per minute. Preterm infants often have sinus arrhythmias, sometimes quite marked, especially during gavage feedings or extensive handling. A very slow rate may be associated with congenital heart block, intracranial hemorrhage, or anoxia. A very rapid rate often denotes a pathologic state, such as the respiratory distress syndrome, cardiac failure, myocarditis, or paroxysmal supraventricular tachycardia. An electrocardiogram should be obtained immediately in all anomalies of cardiac rate and/or rhythm.

Heart sounds and murmurs are not as helpful in the diagnosis of congenital heart disease on the first day of life as they are subsequently. Circulatory changes which occur during passage from the fetal to the extrauterine life are not complete and make evaluation of heart sounds and murmurs difficult. A significant number of newborn infants have a transient grade I to II systolic murmur during the first day of life, of no clinical significance. A harsh grade IV murmur, a murmur audible in the back, or a persisting murmur is more suggestive of organic disease.

VESSELS AND BLOOD PRESSURE. Systemic palpation of brachial and femoral arteries is mandatory. A poor pulse in all extremities suggests diminished left ventricular outflow; coarctation of the aorta is associated with absent or poor pulses in the lower extremities only. Blood pressure measurements should not be limited to sick infants only; they are part of the examination of any normal newborn.

UMBILICUS. At birth, the *umbilical cord stump* is moist and avascular. Very soon after birth it becomes colonized by bacteria and may provide a portal of entry for an ascending infection or cellulitis. Redness or inflammation should be noted. A *single umbilical artery* is frequently associated with congenital defects of the gastrointestinal and/or genitourinary tract; thus, the number of umbilical vessels should always be recorded.

A common finding is an *umbilical hernia,* a small midline defect measuring 0.5 to 2 cm in diameter, at the site where the cord penetrates the abdominal wall. It is unusual to have protrusion of abdominal structures through this defect during the immediate neonatal period. The defect almost invariably closes by two or three years of age. On the other hand, an *omphalocele,* a striking anomaly which consists of protruding intestinal contents covered by amnion, demands immediate surgical attention. The contents of the sac are likely to become injured or infected.

ABDOMEN. A flat empty abdomen suggests a *diaphragmatic hernia.* A distended abdomen arouses suspicion of intestinal obstruction (Fig. 54). *Diastasis recti abdominis,* a wide separation between the two rectus muscles cephalad to the umbilicus, is very commonly present in the newborn.

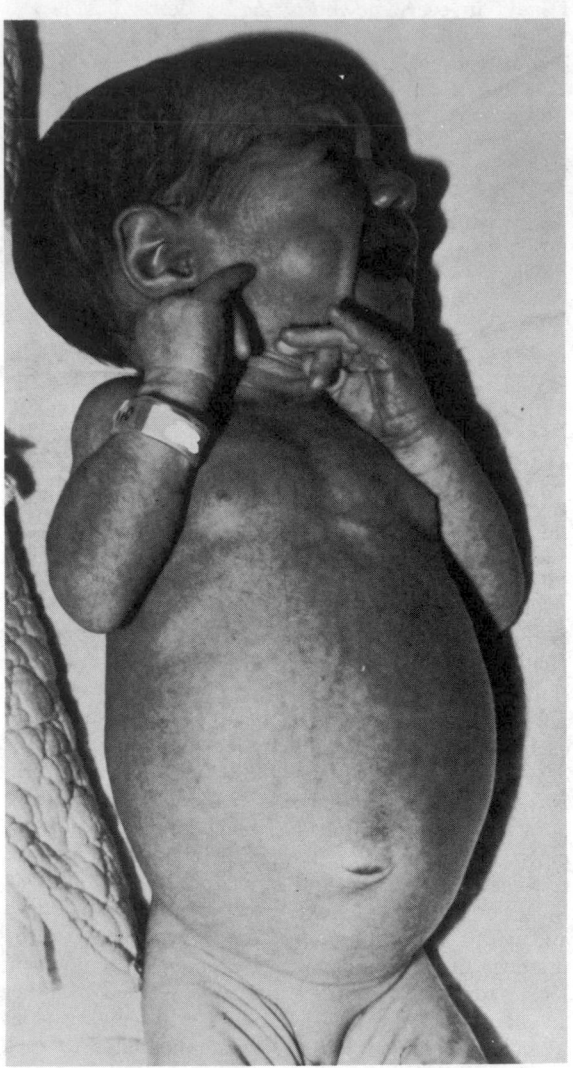

Fig. 54. Abdominal distension in a newborn with Hirschsprung's disease.

Congenital absence of abdominal musculature, a rare anomaly of the abdominal wall, produces the so-called *prune belly.* This defect may be associated with *fetal ascites,* most commonly due to a urologic anomaly. However, the ascites may be chylous in nature or may be associated with a large ovarian cyst.

Careful palpation is particularly useful in the newborn, since abdominal organs are generally easy to feel. It should be very light; organs are superficial and may be pushed out of the way by heavy palpation. The *liver* is relatively large. Its margin is sharp and easily palpable, about 2 cm below the right costal border. The left lobe of the liver is also palpable. An enlarging liver with a blunt, tender margin should suggest congestive heart failure. A soft *spleen tip* can be felt at the left costal margin in the anterior axillary line.

One should make a special effort to feel the *kidneys* in every newborn and to detect abdominal masses or other abnormal structures.

Patency of the *anus* and *rectum* should be established in the delivery room or upon admission to the nursery by the insertion of a catheter or a rectal thermometer. The normal position of the anus and the existence of a sphincter should be verified. A completely *imperforate anus* is readily apparent. Occasionally a fistulous tract which passes meconium is found opening into the perineum, vagina, or bladder. *Sacrococcygeal tumors* may occur in this area of the body.

GENITALIA. *In the male* there are normal variations in size of the penis, scrotum, and testes. The *glans penis* is covered by a prepuce which is so adherent that it is almost impossible to retract it without breaking the adhesions. However, the end of the prepuce can be peeled back to make sure that the urethral meatus is located at the tip of the glans.

Hypospadias is associated with a hooded prepuce which leaves the ventral portion of the glans penis uncovered. The prepuce should not be removed by circumcision, since extra skin may be necessary for subsequent hypospadias repair. In the most common type of hypospadias, the urethral opening is found ventrally, at the junction of the glans and the penile shaft.

In most newborns the *testes* can be palpated either in the scrotum or inguinal canal. Even if they are not palpable the diagnosis of cryptorchidism should not be made at this time, since they often descend and are felt on subsequent examination.

A unilateral or bilateral *hydrocele* is a common finding, has no clinical significance, and usually disappears spontaneously. *Inguinal hernia* is a rare problem in the newborn period.

There is considerable variation in normal *female genitalia* in the size of the labia majora, labia minora, and clitoris. A *large clitoris* suggests masculinization, due to either the adrenogenital syndrome or the influence of hormones taken during pregnancy. Exceptionally, the clitoris may be so large as to confuse the question of the true sex.

Most newborn girls have prominent *hymenal tags* and a small amount of *mucoid vaginal discharge* which lasts a week or 10 days. Occasionally, the secretion is blood tinged, in response to maternal hormone withdrawal. If vaginal secretions are retained, a moderate-sized mass may develop behind a bulging imperforate hymen (*hydrometrocolpos*).

EXTREMITIES. Gross anomalies of the limbs, mottling, and range of motion of all four extremities are to be noted. *Paralysis* of an upper extremity may be associated with a broken clavicle, a brachial or cervical plexus injury, or fracture of one of the long bones of the arm (Fig. 55). Weakness of both lower extremities points to a spinal cord anomaly or injury.

Polydactyly is a common anomaly. The extra digit is usually rudimentary and attached to a soft

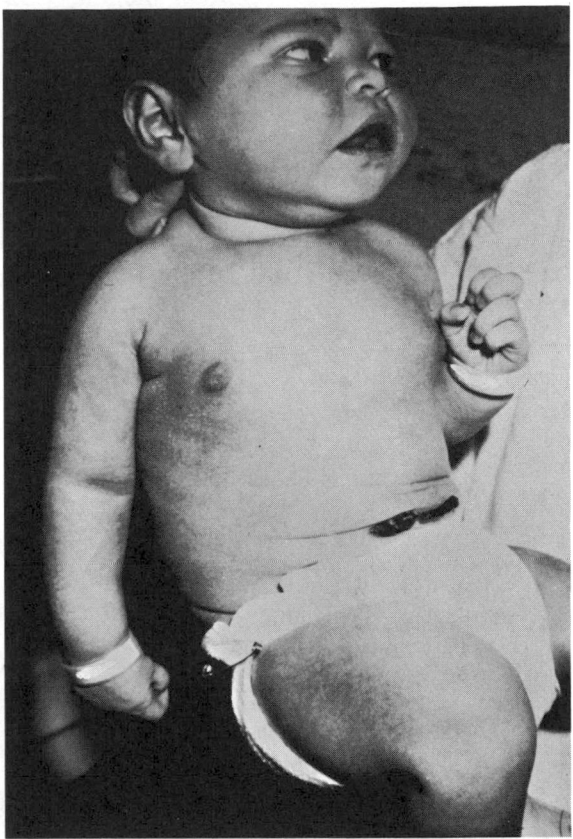

Fig. 55. Erb's palsy due to brachial plexus injury.

tissue tag which can be easily divided. It is less common to have fully developed extra fingers or toes. *Syndactyly* (Fig. 56) is more common in the lower than in the upper extremities and is often familial.

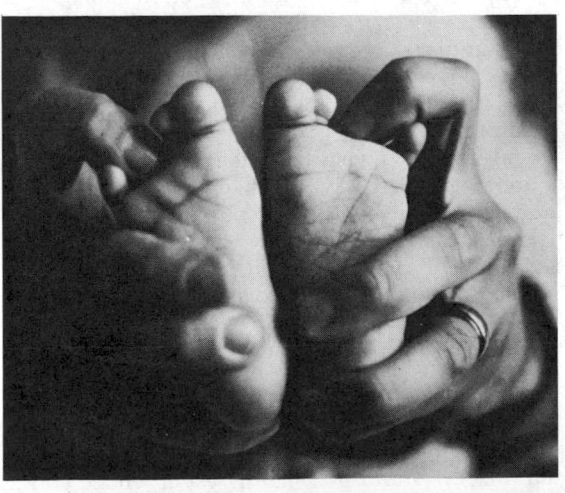

Fig. 56. Syndactyly.

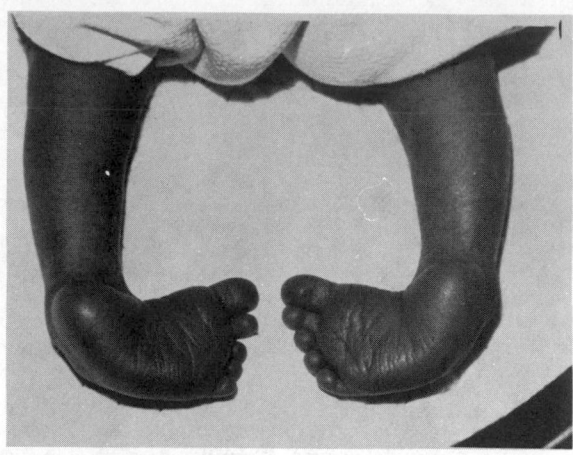

Fig. 57. Club feet or talipes equinovarus.

The position of the arms and legs at birth is somewhat dependent upon intrauterine position and mode of delivery. After a frank breech presentation the infant's lower extremities are apt to be abducted and externally rotated. Because of these positional variations, only gross abnormalities can be diagnosed shortly after birth. Clubfoot, or *talipes equinovarus* (Fig. 57), should be diagnosed promptly and requires prompt orthopedic attention. *Congenital hip dislocation* should be demonstrated during the first few days of life. Shortening of the lower extremity, inability to completely abduct the thigh, and a click on attempted abduction (Ortolani maneuver) are suggestive of dislocation. Many abnormal positions of the feet, such as *talipes calcaneus,* correct spontaneously shortly after birth.

NEUROLOGIC EXAMINATION OF THE NEWBORN. The neurologic examination immediately after birth is useful only in detecting immediate morbidity, since the infant is often recovering from CNS depression from obstetric anesthesia or from the stress of labor and delivery (Table 13). It should be repeated until stable signs are found consistent with the infant's postconceptual age. The neurologic examination of the newborn provides much of the data for a pediatric clinical estimate of gestational age. The central nervous system bears the brunt of the effects of intrauterine hypoxia, birth trauma, dystocia, and intrauterine infections, and abnormalities in the neurologic examination may reflect such situations. Serial neurologic examinations also provide the basis for the early recognition of those infants symptomatic from such causes as hypoglycemia, hypocalcemia, hypomagnesemia, or drug intoxications or withdrawals (Table 14).

Gross abnormalities such as *hydrocephalus, bulging fontanel, microcephaly,* or *meningomyelocele* are usually obvious on inspection. *Horner's syndrome* and massive fundal hemorrhages or chorioretinitis suggest the presence of central nervous system disorders.

TABLE 13. *Causes of Depression at Birth*

1. Asphyxia or severe hypoxia
    (i)   Cord complications
    (ii) Placental insufficiency
    (iii) Maternal hypotension
        (a) Postural due to IVC compression
        (b) Complication of spinal or caudal anesthesia
        (c) Placenta previa
    (iv) Fetal hypotension and shock
        (a) Fetomaternal transfusions
        (b) Parabiotic syndrome
        (c) Placenta previa
    (v)   Brain swelling from prolonged subacute asphyxia
    (vi) Hydrops—severe Rh incompatibility
            Intrauterine heart failure
                Cardiac arrhythmias
                Paroxysmal tachycardia

2. Drugs: analgesic, anesthetic or tranquilizing agents administered to mother or fetus
    (i)   Hypnotics:
        (a) Barbiturates
        (b) Alcohol
        (c) Magnesium
    (ii) Analgesics:
        (a) Meperidine
        (b) Morphine
    (iii) Narcotic antagonists
    (iv) Tranquilizers: hydroxazines
    (v)   Local anesthetics to mother (or by accident to fetus)
    (vi) Systemic anesthetics

3. Trauma
    (i)   Forceps delivery
    (ii) Abnormal presentation (face, breech)
    (iii) Prolonged labor, cephalopelvic disproportion
    (iv) Precipitous delivery

4. Infections
    (i)   Acute viral or bacterial
        (a) Congenital pneumonia
        (b) Septicemia
        (c) Meningitis
    (ii) Chronic
        (a) Rubella
        (b) Syphilis
        (c) CMI
        (d) Toxoplasmosis

5. Metabolic
    (i)   Hyponatremia following prolonged administration of diuretics to mother
    (ii) Hypothyroidism

It is difficult to be certain whether the infant can *see.* At birth, fixation and following objects with the eyes are variable and depend on the state of maturity and state of wakefulness. When pupils fail to react to light, or when their responses are disorganized and when purposeless eye movements exist, the suspicion of blindness should be entertained.

Hearing is also difficult to evaluate. Response to loud noise by a startle reaction or blink is reassuring, but failure to react may be due to a generally depressed state rather than to deafness.

Examination of the infant's *posture* and spontaneous movement is an important part of the neurologic examination.

TABLE 14.   *Causes of Irritability at Birth*

1. Recovery from asphyxia
   (depression and hypotonia is followed by hypertonia and finally convulsions develop)

2. Drugs
   Morphine or heroin withdrawal
   Phenothiazine giving Parkinsonian-like syndrome
   Local anesthetic agents via mother (carbocaine or lidocaine)
      (hypotonia at birth > hypertonia and convulsions after resuscitation and oxygenation)
   Hyperventilation—(salicylate intoxication via mother)

3. Trauma
   Intracranial hemorrhage

4. Metabolic
   Hyperthyroidism
   Pyridoxine dependency in the infant (may cause intra-uterine convulsions)

The nature of the infant's *cry* is significant; a *high-pitched cry* suggests brain damage or hypocalcemia.

Muscle tone may be tested by manipulation and resistance to passive motion. *Flaccidity* or *rigidity* should be noted. A comparison should be made between the muscle tone of the trunk and the extremities, between the left and right sides, and between lower and upper extremities. Involuntary abnormal movements of various degrees can occur in newborn infants, ranging from mild jitteriness in response to auditory or tactile stimuli to frank convulsions. It is sometimes difficult, and not particularly useful, to attempt to draw the line between frank convulsions and progressive hyperirritability. The important point is that jitteriness and hyperirritability at rest or in response to stimuli should always be regarded as abnormal and should stimulate careful repeated neurologic examinations. The extent of diagnostic workup will depend upon the physician's evaluation of the seriousness of the findings. Jitteriness should not be accepted as normal either in a preterm or a term infant.

Transillumination of the skull is another useful procedure and should be carried out in a totally

TABLE 15.   *Reflex. Development of Reflex Activity with Maturity, Illustrated for Sucking, Rooting, Grasp, Moro, Crossed Extension, and Automatic Walking Reflexes**

	6 Months 28 Weeks	6½ Months 30 Weeks	7 Months 32 Weeks	7½ Months 34 Weeks	8 Months 36 Weeks	8½ Months 38 Weeks	9 Months 40 Weeks
1. Sucking reflex	Weak and not really synchronized with deglutition		Stronger and synchronized with deglutition	Perfect ---▶		-------▶	-------▶
2. Rooting reflex	Long latency period. Response is slow and imperfect		Complete and more rapid. Hand-to-mouth attraction established	Brisk Complete --▶ Durable		-------▶	-------▶
3. Grasp reflex	Finger grasp is good and reaction spreads up whole upper limb but not strong enough to lift infant up off bed		Stronger	Stronger	The reaction of upper limb is strong enough to lift infant up off bed	---▶	-------▶
4. Moro reflex	Weak, obtained just once, and not elicited every time		Complete reflex ▶	-------▶		-------▶	-------▶
5. Crossed extension	Flexion and extension in a random pattern, purposeless reaction		Extension but no adduction	Still incomplete	Good response with: 1. Extension 2. *Adduction* ---▶ 3. Fanning of the toes	-------▶	
6. Automatic walking	—	—	Begins tip-toeing with good support on sole and a righting reaction of legs for a few seconds	Pretty good Very fast Tip-toeing	• A premature who has reached 40 weeks. Walks in a toe-heel progression or tip-toes • A full-term new born of 40 weeks. Walks in a heel-toe progression on whole sole of foot		

*From Amiel-Tison. *Arch. Dis. Child.*, 43:89, 1968.

dark room with a strong flashlight fitted with a tight rubber seal.

ASSESSMENT OF MATURITY. During the past decade a great deal of work has been done on the neurologic evaluation of the newborn infant and the correlation of neurologic maturation with gestational age. The development of the central nervous system is relatively less affected than body weight by the same intrauterine environmental conditions which produce deviations in intrauterine growth rate. For this reason the neurologic examination can be used in the clinical assessment of gestational age. As mentioned previously, the neurologic examination cannot be used for this purpose until after the effects of birth stress or morbidity have disappeared, usually after the third day of life. Eliciting these findings

requires practice, but they can be evaluated quite accurately. The examination includes the assessment of muscular tone, including posture and recoil, and testing for a variety of reflexes. A summary of the more useful features of the neurologic examination for the estimation of maturity is presented in Tables 15, 16, and 17.

Muscle Tone, Posture, and Recoil. In a general way muscle tone develops in the lower extremities first and proceeds cephalad; tone in extensor muscles precedes that of the flexors. *Posture* is observed by placing the infant in a supine position. The 24-week infant is completely hypotonic; at 30 to 32 weeks the lower extremities begin to assume a flexed position; flexion develops in the upper extremities at about 36 weeks. *Recoil* refers to the rapidity with

TABLE 16. *Passive Tone. Increase of Tone with Maturity Illustrated by Means of 6 Clinical Tests**

	6 Months 28 Weeks	6½ Months 30 Weeks	7 Months 32 Weeks	7½ Months 34 Weeks	8 Months 36 Weeks	8½ Months 38 Weeks	9 Months 40 Weeks
1. Posture	Completely hypotonic	Beginning of flexion of thigh at hip	Stronger flexion	Frog-like attitude	Flexion of the four limbs	Hypertonic	Very hypertonic
2. Heel to ear maneuver							
3. Popliteal angle	150°		110°	100°	100°	90°	80°
4. Dorsi-flexion angle of foot			40-50°		40-50°		Premature reached 40 wk 40° / Full term
5. 'Scarf' sign	'Scarf' sign complete with no resistance		'Scarf' sign more limited		Elbow slightly passes midline		Elbow almost reaches midline
6. Return to flexion of forearm	Upper limbs very hypotonic lying in extension			Flexion of forearms begins to appear, but very weak	Strong 'return to flexion'. Flexion tone inhibited if forearm maintained 30 sec in extension	Strong 'return to flexion'. Forearm returns very promptly to flexion after being extended for 30 sec	

*From Amiel-Tison. *Arch. Dis. Child.*, 43:89, 1968.

TABLE 17. *Active Tone. Increase of Tone with Maturity Illustrated by Means of 4 Tests of Righting Reactions**

	6 Months 28 Weeks	6½ Months 30 Weeks	7 Months 32 Weeks	7½ Months 34 Weeks	8 Months 36 Weeks	8½ Months 38 Weeks	9 Months 40 Weeks
1. LOWER EX-TREMITY	–	Beginning of extension of lower leg on thigh upon stimulation of soles in lying position	Good support when standing up but very briefly (see illustration below)	Excellent righting reaction of leg ----▶ --------▶ --------▶			
2. TRUNK	–	–	–	± transitory	Good righting of trunk with infant held in vertical suspension (see illustration below)	Good righting of trunk with infant held in walking position (see illustration below)	
3. NECK EX-TENSORS Baby pulled backward from sitting position	–	–	Head begins to right itself with great difficulty	Still difficult and incomplete	Good righting but cannot hold it	Begins to maintain head which doesn't fall back for few seconds	Keeps head in line with trunk for more than a few seconds
4. NECK FLEXORS Baby pulled to sitting position from supine	Head pendulant	Head pendulant	Contraction of muscles is visible but no movement of head	Head begins to right itself but still hanging back at end of movement	At first head is hanging back, then with sudden movement head goes forward onto chest	Head begins to follow trunk, keeps in line for few seconds in upright position	Difference between Extensors and Flexors has diminished (see illustration below)
			Straightening of legs		Straightening of trunk Stimulation arm support		Straightening of head and trunk together

*From Amiel-Tison. *Arch. Dis. Child.*, 43:89, 1968.

which an extremity returns to its previous position after stretching and release.

The *popliteal angle,* the *heel to ear maneuver,* and the *scarf maneuver* are illustrated graphically in the accompanying Table 16, taken from Amiel-Tison. The scarf maneuver is performed by grasping the infant's hand and drawing his arm across his chin toward the opposite shoulder.

Reflexes. The *Moro reflex* can be elicited by various maneuvers which cause extension of the head on the spine. The gentlest way to elicit this reflex is to lift the infant by the arms without lifting the head off the examining surface. The release of the limbs is followed by extension and abduction of the arms, extension of the hands and fingers, followed by an embrace-like motion. This reflex appears fairly early (26 weeks) but can be easily exhausted until about 32 weeks, after which time it is invariably present. Its absence denotes serious pathology. The *grasp reflex* refers to flexion of the fingers, and in 36-week-old infants of the whole arm, in response to touching the palm of the hand.

The *rooting reflex* is stimulated by touching the cheek; the face turns toward the stimulated side and moves up and down as though searching for a nipple.

The *sucking reflex* manifests itself in sucking movements when the lips are touched. At about 32 weeks of gestation this reflex begins to be synchronized with swallowing and by 34 weeks this synchrony is perfected enough so that bottle feeding can be confidently expected.

The *pupillary response* refers to the conventional constriction of the pupil when exposed to light.

Automatic walking is elicited by holding the infant erect by the trunk and placing the feet on a solid surface. At 32 weeks the infant begins to tiptoe, does it well by 37 weeks (still tiptoeing), and by 40 weeks places his heel down as well.

The *crossed extension reflex* involves holding one lower extremity firmly in extension and observing the response of the contralateral free extremity. Withdrawal of the extremity appears first, followed by extension, which may begin to appear at 32 weeks but is not complete until 37 weeks of gestation, and finally by adduction, which appears at 37 weeks and is fully present by 41 weeks.

REFERENCES

Amiel-Tison, C. Neurological evaluation of the maturity of newborn infants. Arch. Dis. Child., 43:89, 1968.

Desmond, M. M., et al. The clinical behavior of the newborn. I. The term baby. J. Pediat., 62:307, 1963.

Moss, A. J., and Adams, F. G. Problems of Blood Pressure in Childhood. Springfield, Ill., Charles C Thomas, Publisher, 1962.

Paine, R. S. Neurologic examination of infants and children. Pediat. Clin. N. Amer., 7:471, 1960.

——— Neurologic conditions of the neonatal period. Pediat. Clin. N. Amer., 8:577, 1961.

Parmelee, A. H. Management of the Newborn. Chicago, Year Book Medical Publishers, 1959.

Robinson, R. J. Assessment of gestational age by neurological examination. Arch. Dis. Child., 41:437, 1966.

Ross Conference on Pediatric Research. Report of the 46th Conference. Physical Diagnosis of the Newly Born. Houston, Texas, March, 1963.

Schaffer, A. Diseases of the Newborn. Philadelphia, W. B. Saunders Company, 1960.

Thomas, A., Chesni, Y., and Dargassies, S. The Neurological Examination of the Infant. London, The Medical Advisory Committee of the National Spastics Society, 1960.

Usher, R., McLean, F., and Scott, K. E. Judgment of fetal age. II. Clinical significance of gestational age and an objective method for its assessment. Pediat. Clin. N. Amer., 13:835, 1966.

2.11
LOW-BIRTH-WEIGHT INFANT

JOHN C. SINCLAIR

Physiology

DEFINITIONS. About 8 percent of infants born in the United States weigh 2,500 g or less at birth. These "low-birth-weight" infants have generally been called "premature." It is true that the majority of them are born early, before 37 weeks' completed gestation. However, in an appreciable number, about one-third, the small size is due primarily to a retarded rate of intrauterine growth, the resulting birth weight being significantly less than that expected for gestational age calculated from the maternal menstrual history. (See p. 17.)

The distinction between the early and the growth-retarded infant has not been made in many studies of the low-birth-weight infant. There are both size-related similarities and age-related differences between the two groups. Changes in body composition are more related to body size than to fetal age, so that small infants, whether born early or growth-retarded, tend to resemble one another in their scant subcutaneous fat and relatively large extracellular fluid volumes. On the other hand, structural and functional maturation of the central nervous system proceeds according to fetal age and is relatively unaffected by differences in rate of fetal growth. Thus, newborn infants of similar fetal age, but who may be of different body size, behave similarly in terms of muscle tone, posture, reflex activity, wake-sleep behavior, electroencephalographic patterns, and nerve conduction velocity.

PHYSICAL DIMENSIONS. In general, infants of low birth weight show a crown-heel length of less than 47 cm and a crown-rump length of less than 32 cm. The occipitofrontal head circumference is less than 33 cm. The chest circumference measures less than 30 cm.

Two dimensions, body length and head circumference, bear further comment. Both the infant ·born prematurely and the growth-retarded infant are short. The former has grown at a normal rate in utero and exhibits a length appropriate for gestational age. The latter suffers delayed appearance of ossification centers and retarded rate of longitudinal growth; thus birth length is less than expected for gestational age, being comparable to that of a normally grown infant of earlier postconceptional age.

The head of the small neonate usually appears disproportionately large in comparison to the rest of the body. In the infant born prematurely, this disproportion represents the late fetal relationship between the size of the head and the size of the body. Since intrauterine growth retardation associated with fetal malnutrition usually interferes less with brain growth than with growth of other organs, fetally malnourished infants commonly show a similar disproportion. On the other hand, fetal growth retardation due to chronic nonbacterial fetal infection or chromosome anomaly often retards the growth of the brain as well.

PHYSIOLOGIC CHARACTERISTICS. The placenta functions both as an organ of *assimilation,* for oxygen and other nutrients, and as an organ of *excretion,* for carbon dioxide, heat, and various metabolic waste products. (See section on Physiology.) In adapting to extrauterine life, the newborn infant must perform by himself the homeostatic functions that previously were largely performed by the placenta. Special problems often arise in the case of the low-birth-weight infant. These occur because preterm delivery or small body size impose serious restrictions on the baby's functional capacity for independent existence. In addition, the asphyxial effects of labor and delivery may be critical in this group.

Effect of Early Delivery. Preterm delivery may adversely affect adaptation to extrauterine life because various organ functions have not sufficiently matured. The functional capacity of the lung to substitute for the placenta as an organ of gas exchange may be used to illustrate this point. Although, in the fetus, formation of bronchi and bronchioles is well advanced by 16 weeks' gestation, alveoli and proliferating capillaries close to the developing alveoli do not appear until about 28 weeks' gestation. Both alveolar and capillary development continue until term. Thus, the infant born prematurely possesses an adverse disproportion between the nonrespiratory and respiratory components of the lung. In the most immature infants, there is probably an absolute insufficiency of gas-exchanging surface area to support extrauterine existence. Moreover, the lungs need to develop not only air spaces but also surface-active material before they can be adequately ventilated. Surfactant first appears in the air sacs of some human fetuses in quantities permitting adequate lung function at about 24 weeks' gestation; in others this is delayed until about 30 weeks. Surfactant deficiency predisposes to atelectasis, since at low lung volumes the tendency of terminal air spaces to collapse is very great. Many small premature infants die within a few days of birth with the pathologic finding of "atelectasis of prematurity."

Although functional development in some instances is timed from conception, in other instances it is triggered by birth. The separation of the baby from the placenta results in the accumulation of end products of metabolism which require for their biologic transformation or excretion in the infant mechanisms which they themselves induce. For example, the postnatal accumulation of unconjugated bilirubin, excreted by the placenta during fetal life, appears to induce mechanisms for hepatic uptake, conjugation, and excretion which become increasingly effective within the first days of life. Both low-birth-weight and full-size infants show this evidence of induction during the immediate postnatal period. Pharmacologic agents may sometimes substitute as inducers. The effect of phenobarbital as an inducer of glucuronyl transferase activity has been demonstrated.

Effect of Small Body Size. Small body size per se can limit homeostatic capacity in the neonatal period. The small baby, whether born prematurely or small for his gestational age, suffers a limited thermoregulatory range because of the limited thermal insulation that accompanies small body size. The smaller the baby, the less his thermal insulation and the more easily does he exchange heat with his environment for a given gradient of temperature between skin and environment (low surface-air insulation). More important, the absolute amount of tissue through which heat must be transferred, either by conduction from core to surface or by the flow of blood from hotter to cooler parts, is small (low tissue insulation). At body weights below 2 kg, tissue insulation decreases substantially. Although small babies can increase heat production in response to cold stress, their limited ability to defend themselves against heat loss results in a large fall in body temperature in environments providing thermal comfort for the adult.

Effect of Labor and Delivery. The moderate degree of asphyxia characteristic of the normal labor and delivery is likely to be less well tolerated by the infant of low birth weight because of his limited myocardial and hepatic glycogen stores. Normal hepatic glycogen stores are achieved primarily in the last weeks of gestation, probably less so in infants with intrauterine growth retardation. Asphyxia in the presence of prematurity is particularly dangerous in that it may lead to loss of pulmonary surfactant. The fetal lung in response to asphyxia shows marked pulmonary vasoconstriction and reduction in pulmonary blood flow. The hypoperfusion of the lung may lead to asphyxial damage to alveolar cells and to impairment of surfactant production. Since the half-life of surfactant is only a few hours, functional deficiency of this material may result. The development of hyaline membrane disease may be related to the combination of immaturity and perinatal asphyxia, where a relatively small insult may be effective in causing critical damage to the lungs.

Effect of Extrauterine Environment. Anatomic and functional development of organ systems in the fetus may proceed differently when the infant is born prematurely. Studies of the effect of minor manipulations of the environment on the extrauterine development of the premature infant have revealed that differences in the rate of development of certain homeostatic mechanisms can be produced, but do not yet provide answers as to the optimal or desirable rate at which these capacities should be induced. For example, there is evidence in premature infants that brown adipose tissue continues to develop for some weeks after birth, as does capacity for nonshivering thermogenesis. Glass et al. tested the effect of varying environmental temperature on this developmental process. They found that premature infants raised in slightly subthermoneutral conditions for between 1 and 3 postnatal weeks had improved cold resistance at the end of that interval whereas matched controls, fed isocalorically, did not. The improved cold resistance was associated with an increased capacity to increase oxygen consumption in response to a cold stress.

Extrauterine maturation of renal function provides a second example of environmental effect. In utero, where the kidney apparently does not need to function as an excretory or regulatory organ, renal blood flow, glomerular filtration, and tubular functions are all at low levels. After birth the kidney must replace the placenta as the organ primarily responsible for excretion of many waste products.

Edelmann and Wolfish studied the effect of diet on the rate of renal maturation after birth. Premature infants fed high-protein, high-solute diets from birth were compared with infants fed low-protein, low-solute diets. After 4 weeks the clearances of inulin and PAH and the capacity to excrete hydrogen ion were approximately double in the group on the high-protein intake.

We will now consider in more detail the functional characteristics of specific organ systems in low-birth-weight infants during the first days of extrauterine life. Those areas that are particularly important in extrauterine adaptation include respiration, circulation, and thermoregulation.

RESPIRATION. *Onset of Pulmonary Respiration.* The fetus ordinarily does not make rhythmic respiratory movements in utero, but can be stimulated to make gasping efforts either by physical stimulation or by partial asphyxia after 16 weeks' gestation.

Although partial asphyxia and tactile stimulation may produce gasping, they do not necessarily lead to rhythmic ventilatory efforts. A summation of afferent impulses from a variety of sources appears to be necessary to sustain rhythmic breathing. In the low-birth-weight infant, cold stimulation of cutaneous thermoreceptors may comprise a critical afferent input, in that rapid warming of such infants may induce apnea.

The stimuli which affect the establishment of pulmonary respiration after birth fail more frequently in low-birth-weight infants than in full-size babies. As a group, infants of low birth weight show a higher incidence of low Apgar scores (indicating depression) than do larger babies; about 20 percent of small neonates weighing less than 2,000 g can be expected to score less than 3.

Intrauterine growth-retarded babies often respond to the chronic asphyxial insult of placental insufficiency by passing meconium into the amniotic fluid and by gasping in utero. It is not unusual to find such babies covered with meconium at birth, or to find the presence of amniotic debris and meconium in the periphery of the tracheobronchial tree at autopsy after intrauterine asphyxia.

Clearance of Lung Fluid. The lung, in contrast to other fetal organs, contains more water with increasing gestational age. The fluid in the lung originates as an ultrafiltrate of plasma, with selective reabsorption or secretion of some components. Its composition differs also from that of amniotic fluid. For example, glucose concentration is lower and phospholipid concentration higher in lung fluid than in amniotic fluid. The onset of air breathing is associated with the reabsorption of fluid present in the fetal lung. The compression of the thorax during a vaginal delivery results in the expulsion of some of this fluid through the baby's mouth. It is also absorbed into the blood capillaries and into the lymphatics. An increase in lymph flow from the heart and lung has been observed after establishment of ventilation in both mature and immature lambs. The importance of delayed reabsorption of lung fluid in the pathogenesis of respiratory distress is uncertain. A group of newborn infants has been described in whom clinical and radiologic features suggest delayed reabsorption of lung fluid as the cause for respiratory distress.

Compliance. Pulmonary compliance is the volume change per unit pressure change at points of no air flow. Measurements of compliance of the lungs of term infants suggest that the distensibility of the infant lung approximates that of the adult in that both subjects generate about the same negative pleural pressure to achieve a tidal volume. When related to body length, the compliance of the lungs of full-size and low-birth-weight infants, determined in vivo, is similar in the first days of life. However, Gruenwald, using air to inflate lungs obtained at autopsy, found a difference in the pattern of inflation: higher pressures were needed to inflate the terminal air spaces in lungs of prematurely born infants than were needed for term infants. Typical patterns of expansion which he observed are shown in Figure 58. The terminal air spaces of excised lungs obtained postmortem, once inflated, tend to collapse on deflation, particularly in very small infants. Growth-retarded babies of low birth weight showed a pattern of expansion which followed gestational age rather than birth weight.

Surfactant. Gruenwald also found that lower pressures were needed when lungs were inflated with saline rather than with air. The difference is due to surface forces that act at an air-liquid interface to minimize the area of the surface, and so promote alveolar collapse. Surface tension is not a constant value, but varies with changing surface area. Normally, a reduction in area is associated with a reduction in surface tension. In 1959, Avery and Mead showed that the surface tension of lung extracts derived from very small premature infants (under 1,200 g birth weight) remained abnormally high at low area.

Pulmonary surfactant is a phospholipid whose principal surface-active component is lecithin. It is synthesized in or secreted by large alveolar cells which contain osmiophilic inclusion bodies. The half-life of the material is short (hours) and the reservoir is less in the preterm than the term infant. It is suspected that pulmonary hypoperfusion impairs surfactant production by causing asphyxial damage to alveolar cells. The clinical results include retraction of the chest wall on inspiration, decreased pulmonary compliance, and end-expiratory closure of terminal air spaces. The role of surfactant deficiency in the pathogenesis of hyaline membrane disease is considered in Section 19.2.

Resistance to Airflow. The newborn infant, including the infant of low birth weight, is an obligate nose breather. Resistance to airflow is contributed by the nose, lower airway, lung tissue, and chest wall. Low-birth-weight infants have higher values for total pulmonary resistance (nose, airway, and lung tissue) than do full-size infants. To date, the components of this total have not been individu-

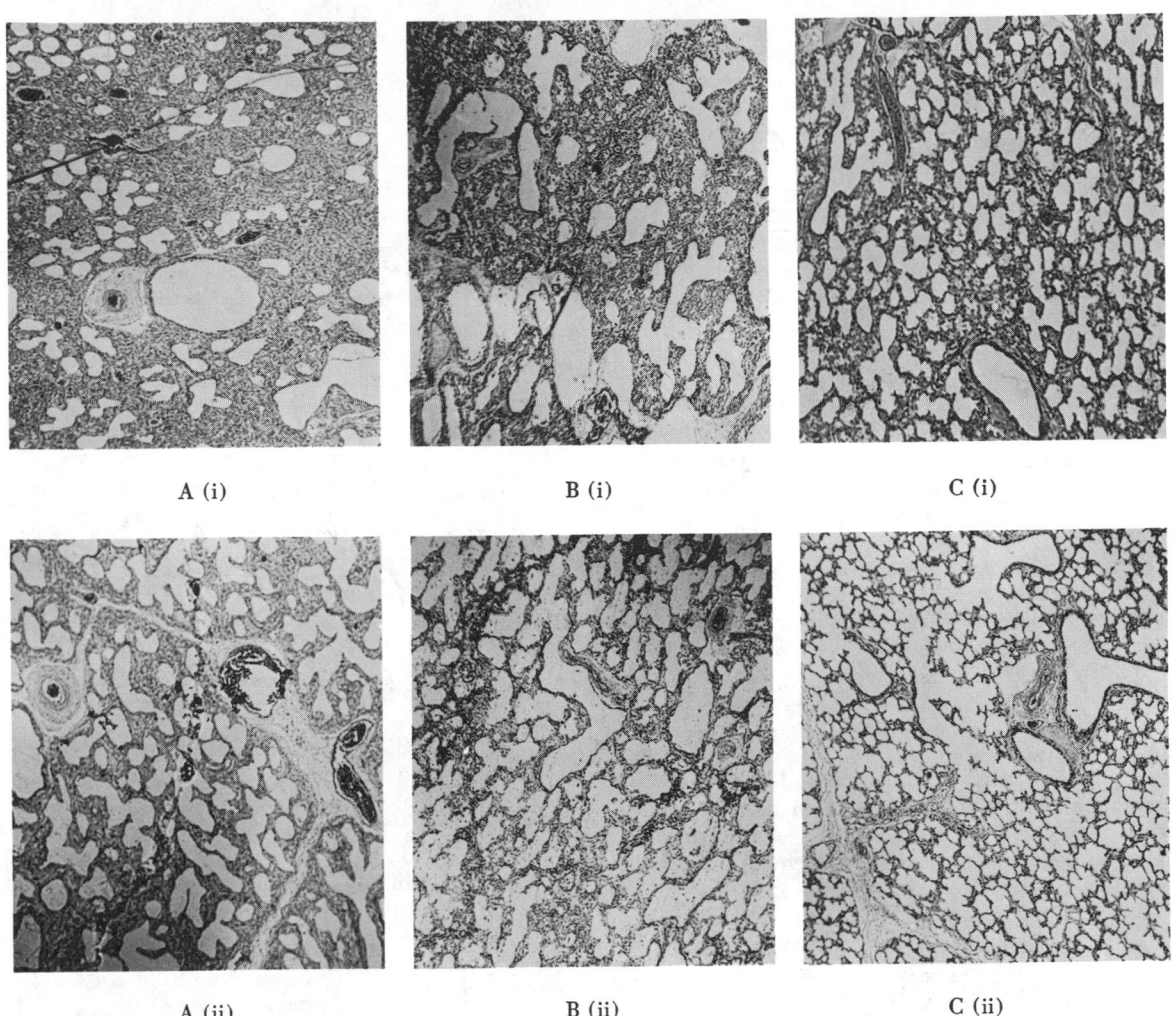

A (i)   B (i)   C (i)

A (ii)   B (ii)   C (ii)

Fig. 58. Infant lungs expanded by air and tied off at a lower pressure (top row) and at a higher pressure (bottom row); pressures in cm water are specified below. ×22. A. Twelve hours old, body weight 707 g; gestational age 25 weeks; 30, 60 cm. Air spaces consist only of branched tubes in which air is distributed at random. B. Stillborn, 1,260 g; 20, 75 cm. Beginning formation of alveolar ducts and alveoli. Distal parenchyma remains collapsed at moderate pressure, but alveoli open at higher pressure. C. Stillborn, 3,132 g; 38 weeks; 20, 60 cm. Alveoli are well developed. Diffuse aeration can be achieved at relatively low pressure. (From Gruenwald. *Anat. Rec.,* 146:337, 1963.)

ally measured in the low-birth-weight baby. However, both airway resistance and lung tissue resistance are probably increased, because resistance to airflow must be very high in airways of small radius and because the parenchymal and perhaps fluid contents of the immature lung tends to be high.

Burnard et al. found the resistance to airflow to be higher on expiration than on inspiration, due to partial collapse of airways on expiration. Moreover, the compliance of airways of small premature infants was particularly high, so that they tended to collapse on expiration. This defect may sometimes lead to gas trapping.

Postnatal Change in Compliance and Lung Volumes. Postnatally, lung function may deteriorate in many low-birth-weight infants. This deterioration is characterized by a fall in compliance, a fall in

thoracic gas volume and functional residual capacity, and persistence of abnormally large alveolar-arterial gradients for oxygen and carbon dioxide. Some of these changes can be reversed acutely by exerting negative pressure around the baby's chest. This deterioration is most common in the smallest infants (under 1,200 g); it is not known whether the small-for-date infant is equally susceptible to it. Tachypnea, retractions of the chest wall, hypoxia, and hypercapnea may occur. Some babies develop radiographic changes suggesting atelectasis and focal hyperaeration. The Wilson-Mikity syndrome (Sec. 19.2) represents the extreme form of this picture.

Spontaneous improvement in function occurs in mildly affected infants, beginning in the third or fourth week. Improvement is characterized by an increase in thoracic gas volume, decrease in alveolar-

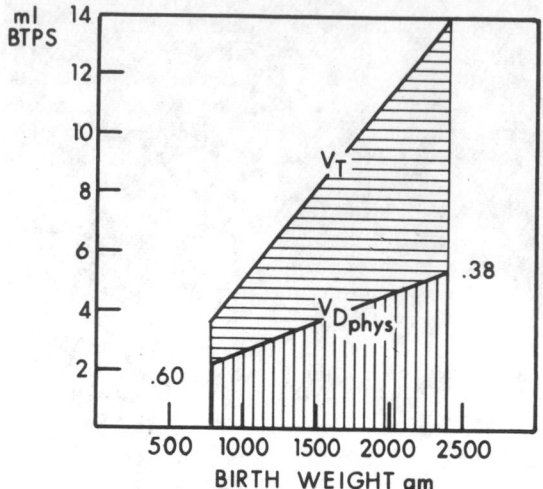

Fig. 59. Decrease in physiologic dead space (Vd$_{phys}$/tidal volume (Vt) ratio with birth weight in asymptomatic premature infants. BTPS-volume at body temperature, atmospheric pressure, saturated with water vapor. (Unpublished data of Sinclair and Silverman.)

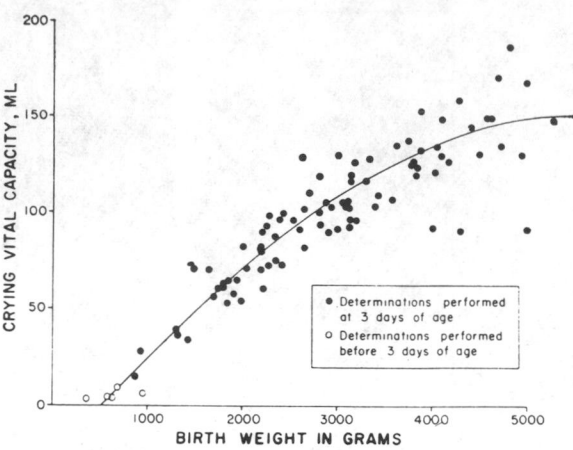

Fig. 60. Increase in crying vital capacity with birth weight, illustrated with calculated parabolic curve. (From Sutherland and Ratcliff. Amer. J. Dis. Child., 101:67, 1961.)

arterial oxygen gradient, and rise in arterial Po$_2$ toward normal.

This postnatal deterioration and subsequent improvement is thought to depend on underventilation or nonventilation of perfused areas of the lung, and their subsequent reexpansion. Mechanical disadvantages of the very compliant thorax and airways may contribute to the pathologic pattern of inflation.

Ventilation. The low-birth-weight infant commonly exhibits a respiratory rate of about 40 breaths per minute, but there is a wide variation among asymptomatic subjects. Higher rates are commonly observed in the first hour or two after birth.

Tidal volume (the amount of air taken in with each breath) averages 5.4 ml per kilogram. Of this volume, a large proportion (2.4 ml) is physiologic dead space, which does not undergo gaseous exchange with pulmonary capillary blood. Figure 59 shows the relationship between the physiologic dead space/tidal volume ratio, and birth weight. It is seen that the dead space/tidal volume ratio is highest in the infants of lowest birth weight, and tends to decrease as infants increase in birth size.

The volume of a cry (termed "crying vital capacity") has been measured in newborn infants and is shown, in relation to birth weight, in Figure 60. Values obtained in the first few minutes after birth average 77 percent of those obtained at three days.

Figures 61 and 62 show minute volume and alveolar ventilation achieved by resting low-birth-weight infants during the first weeks of life. In spite of a relatively large dead space, most healthy low-birth-weight infants are able to maintain an alveolar ventilation that is adequate in relation to

metabolic CO$_2$ production; consequently, arterial Pco$_2$ is maintained at approximately 30 to 40 mm Hg after the initial acid-base adjustment following birth.

An elevated arterial Pco$_2$ means that alveolar ventilation is inadequate in relation to metabolic CO$_2$ production. This situation, termed "alveolar hypoventilation," may result from either decreased total minute volume (decrease in amount of air breathed per minute) or from an increased proportion of the minute volume failing to ventilate pul-

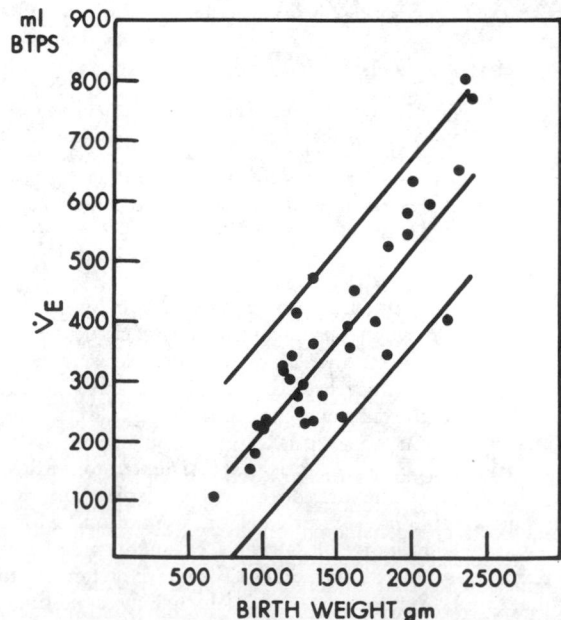

Fig. 61. Increase in minute volume (Ve) with birth weight in asymptomatic premature infants. (Unpublished data of Sinclair and Silverman.)

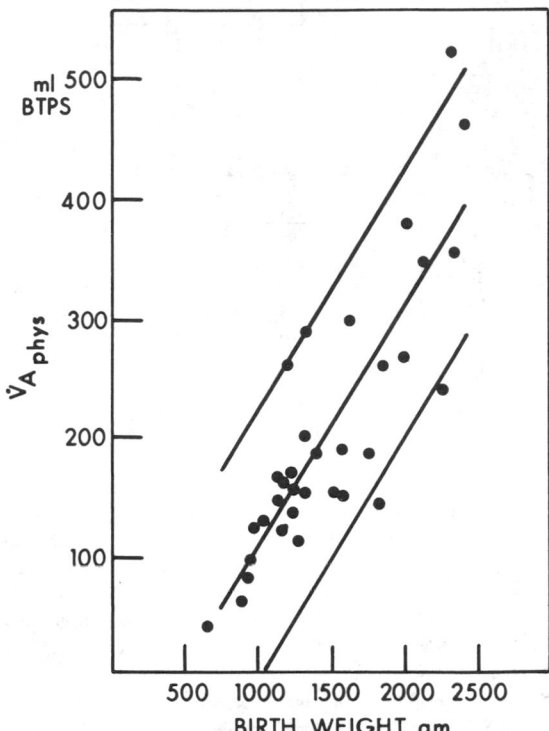

Fig. 62. Increase in alveolar ventilation (Va_{phys}) with birth weight in asymptomatic premature infants. (Unpublished data of Sinclair and Silverman.)

monary capillary blood (increase in physiologic dead space). A common cause of decreased minute volume is deranged central control of respiration, such as occurs in central nervous system trauma, drug depression, hemorrhage, or infection; in this situation, a serious elevation of arterial Pco_2 may result despite a relative absence of signs of respiratory distress. On the other hand, an increase in physiologic dead space, such as occurs with nonperfusion of ventilated alveoli (see below), when associated with intact ventilatory control usually results in marked compensatory increase in minute volume, tachypnea, retractions, and only moderate or minimal elevation of arterial Pco_2. Thus, it is incorrect to equate clinical signs of respiratory distress with alveolar hypoventilation, without measuring the arterial Pco_2, whenever the clinical setting suggests the possible existence of alveolar hypoventilation.

Ventilation-Perfusion Relationships. Factors which control pulmonary blood flow in the fetus and newborn are considered on page 48. Measurements of alveolar-arterial differences for oxygen and nitrogen indicate that underventilation of perfused alveoli occurs frequently, particularly in the first hours of life. This defect results in an oxygen deficit in arterial blood. Hypoxia and acidosis can result in an increase in pulmonary vascular resistance which

further compounds the physiologic shunt. Thus, venous admixture may also occur through the ductus arteriosus or foramen ovale, both of which are functionally patent in the first days of life.

Ventilation of nonperfused or underperfused alveoli has been detected in low-birth-weight infants by measuring an arterial-alveolar difference for CO_2. This defect is not a cause of hypoxemia but is a cause of wasted ventilation at the alveolar level (alveolar dead space).

Diffusion. Gaseous exchange depends not only on an optimal relationship between ventilation and perfusion but on diffusion as well. Although diffusion block does not appear to limit gaseous exchange in term infants, there is little information about this in prematurely born subjects, who may depend on a significant amount of gaseous diffusion across air-conducting passages.

Oxygen Consumption. When measured under resting, "thermoneutral" conditions (see below), oxygen consumption of preterm babies ranges between 4.3 and 5.4 ml/kg/minute on the first day of life. There is an increase in oxygen consumption postnatally in both preterm and term infants. Prematurely born babies may reach values as high as 8 or 9 ml/kg/minute by 4 to 6 weeks of age. Small-for-date babies tend to have higher rates of oxygen consumption than gestationally less mature babies of similar weight. This difference is discernible beyond 2 days' postnatal age, and may indicate a disproportionately large brain in relation to body weight.

The maintenance caloric expenditure of the low-birth-weight infant can be derived from his rate of oxygen consumption, and amounts to 40 to 50 cal/kg daily for the preterm infant, and 50 to 60 cal/kg for the small term infant. But additional expenditures for activity, thermal homeostasis, specific dynamic action, and growth, as well as the fecal loss of 5 to 10 percent of the calories ingested, require that the low-birth-weight infant consume approximately 120 cal/kg daily to achieve a normal rate of growth during the first weeks of life.

Regulation of Respiration. Various respiratory rhythms may be observed in infants of low birth weight, including regular rhythm, regular rhythm interrupted by sighs, and "period breathing." Periodic breathing is seen most commonly in healthy infants of short gestation. It consists of recurrent apneic episodes of at least 3 or 4 seconds followed by spontaneous resumption of respiration. Although heart rate may fall somewhat during the apneic interval, significant bradycardia does not occur. Periodic breathing can sometimes be converted to regular rhythm by increasing ambient oxygen concentration, by exerting negative pressure around the thorax, or by cutaneous cold stimulation. It has been proposed that periodic breathing results from defective integration of afferent stimuli by an immature central nervous system.

Low-birth-weight infants appear to regulate ventilation in response to both chemical and physical stimuli, but ventilatory responses are difficult to compare quantitatively with those of adults. The ventilatory response of the low-birth-weight infants to an increase in alveolar carbon dioxide tension achieved by increasing the amount of carbon dioxide in the inspired air is similar to that of adults. However, at any given alveolar Pco_2, the infants showed a greater ventilation per kilogram body weight than the adults. This is partly due to the infants' greater metabolism per kilogram body weight, but it is also true that the newborn infant, including the low-birth-weight infant, regulates arterial Pco_2 between 30 and 40 mm Hg, slightly below the adult normal. Normally, extracellular bicarbonate concentration is 19 to 21 mEq/L in the low-birth-weight infant, and arterial pH approximately 7.40.

Respiratory Function of Neonatal Blood. At birth, babies show a high oxygen affinity of whole blood, as demonstrated by a left shift in the oxyhemoglobin dissociation curve. Although most newborn infants possess high concentrations of fetal hemoglobin (hemoglobin F), this cannot be the sole explanation for the high affinity because dialyzed solutions of hemoglobin F and A have similar affinities. The reason for the high oxygen affinity of neonatal blood is still unknown, but may be related to the fact that red cell 2,3-diphosphoglycerate, which competes with oxygen for binding to hemoglobin, is itself bound less to fetal than to adult hemoglobin. The interaction between 2,3-DPG and hemoglobin A may thus comprise a mechanism whereby, with increasing concentration of hemoglobin A in the first weeks of life, the hemoglobin oxygen affinity can be gradually reduced postnatally below the high value characteristic of neonatal blood. The high oxygen affinity of fetal blood is beneficial to the fetus because it permits a greater oxygen uptake at the low Po_2 of umbilical venous blood. However, at the "loading" Po_2 (alveolar Po_2) obtained after birth, oxygen uptake is relatively unaffected by differences in position of the curve. Theoretically, the unloading of oxygen to the tissues may be hampered by a very high oxygen affinity in the blood. The clinical importance of the position of the oxyhemoglobin dissociation curve of neonatal blood remains to be demonstrated.

CIRCULATION. The Transitional Circulation. Circulatory changes occurring in the newborn infant at birth are described on page 48. Figure 63 is a diagram of the transitional circulation characteristic of the first days of life. Note that the pulmonary and systemic circuits are linked through patency of the foramen ovale and ductus arteriosus. The relative resistances in the pulmonary and systemic vessels will determine the direction and magnitude of shunt occurring through these channels. Left-to-right shunts can occur through the foramen ovale and ductus arteriosus. Right-to-left shunts can occur not only at these sites, but also in the lung.

The highest oxygen content anywhere in the circulation is the end pulmonary capillary oxygen

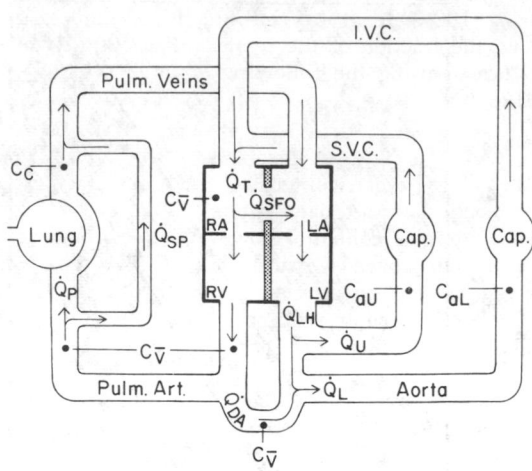

Fig. 63. Neonatal circulation, showing possible sites of right-to-left shunting. Q = blood flow (ml/min); C = oxygen content (ml/100 ml blood); Q_{LH} = output of left heart; Q_U = blood flow to upper segment of body; Q_L = blood flow to lower segment of body; Q_T = total systemic venous return (cardiac input); Q_{SFO} = foramen ovale right-to-left shunt; Q_{DA} = ductus arteriosus right-to-left shunt; Q_{SP} = intrapulmonary right-to-left shunt; C_{aU} = oxygen content of arterial blood flowing to upper segment of body; C_{aL} = oxygen content of arterial blood flowing to lower segment of body; $C_{\bar{V}}$ = mixed venous oxygen content; C_C = end pulmonary capillary oxygen content.

content. This value cannot be measured directly, but can be calculated by assuming equilibrium between alveolar and pulmonary capillary oxygen tensions, such as occurs when breathing 100 percent oxygen. Arterial oxygen content can be measured in samples of blood obtained from pulmonary vein, temporal artery, radial artery, or descending aorta via umbilical artery catheterization. Right-to-left shunts occurring at any of the three possible sites will produce an oxygen deficit in arterial blood as compared with the end pulmonary capillary oxygen content. *An oxygen deficit in pulmonary venous blood* reflects only intrapulmonary and/or venous admixture, due to blood flow past nonventilated alveoli. *An oxygen deficit in temporal arterial or radial arterial blood* reflects both intrapulmonary venous admixture and venous admixture through the foramen ovale. *An oxygen deficit in blood obtained from the aorta distal to the ductus arteriosus* reflects any one or any combination of venous admixtures occurring through the lung, through the foramen ovale, and through the ductus arteriosus. In the presence of a right-to-left shunt through the ductus arteriosus, oxygen content of postductal aortic blood is lower than the oxygen content and oxygen tension of blood flowing to the brain and retina. Thus neither the status of cerebral oxygenation nor the risk of retinal oxygen toxicity is precisely assessed by the postductal aortic blood sample.

The usual method for quantitating right-to-left shunts is to measure oxygen content of arterial blood during 100 percent oxygen breathing, and to calculate the fraction of the total cardiac output which is shunted using the following equation:

$$\frac{\dot{Q}s}{\dot{Q}t} = \frac{Cc - Ca}{Cc - C_v}$$

where Cc = oxygen content of end pulmonary capillary blood, Ca = arterial oxygen content, C_v = mixed venous oxygen content. However, the shunt equation shown above is valid only if Ca represents oxygen content of arterial blood distributed to the whole body. Because, with right-to-left ductal shunting, oxygen contents of pre- and postductal blood are different, there is no single Ca and the shunt equation in its usual form cannot be used. Moreover, in dealing with a newborn infant with a possible right-to-left ductal shunt, the physician should keep in mind the possibility that change in postductal aortic Po_2 can be caused not only by change in right-to-left shunt but also by change in distribution of cardiac output (i.e., change in cerebral blood flow).

Fall in Pulmonary Vascular Resistance. Normally, with successful expansion of the lungs at birth and adequate oxygenation of the infant, pulmonary vascular resistance falls and pulmonary blood flow is promptly increased. A variety of clinical and experimental data, including those obtained from catheterization of human infants, would suggest that this fall in pulmonary vascular resistance occurs in three stages: an initial rapid drop associated with expansion of the lungs, then a moderate drop over the first 1 to 2 weeks following birth, and finally a more gradual drop during the next 6 to 8 weeks.

Closure of Foramen Ovale and Ductus Arteriosus. As pulmonary blood flow increases following birth, left atrial pressure rises and right atrial pressure falls. These changes usually result in functional closure of the foramen ovale. The ductus arteriosus may remain patent for several hours following birth, but with oxygenation of the infant, it usually constricts. Pronounced reactivity to oxygen of the ductus arteriosus can be shown during the first few hours after birth. This reactivity, which can be detected on auscultation, is lost within a few hours, after which time relaxation in response to hypoxia can no longer be demonstrated.

Effects on Heart and Blood Vessels. Anatomic effects of the transition from the fetal to the neonatal circulation can be seen in blood vessels and in the heart.

Parallel growth in smooth muscle takes place in both systemic and pulmonary arterial beds during fetal life; but after birth, muscle mass in the systemic bed continues to increase while that in the pulmonary bed rapidly undergoes a relative decrease (Fig. 64).

Pulmonary arteries and arterioles retain narrow lumina up to the end of intrauterine life. After the third postnatal day, the lumina begin to widen; and after the tenth day of life the vessels are wide open. These findings apply to both term and prematurely

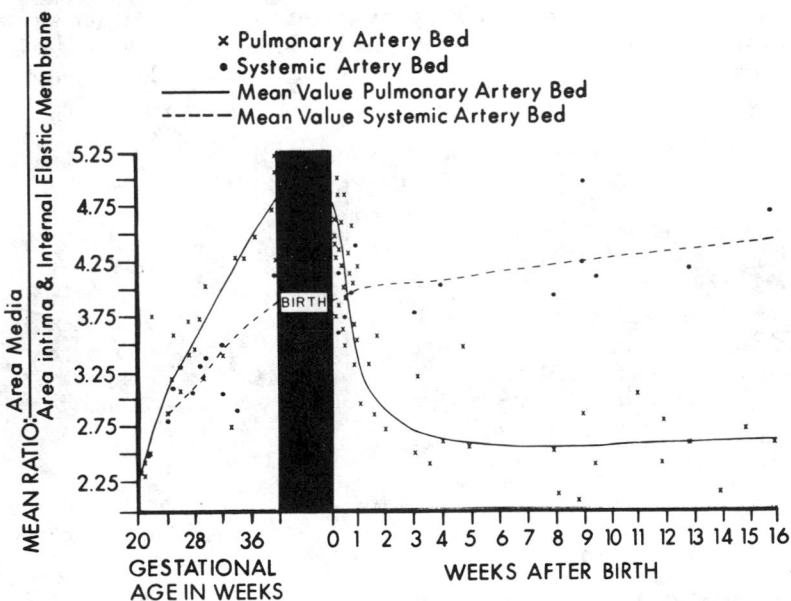

Fig. 64. A ratio reflecting arterial muscle mass plotted against gestational or postnatal age. Arterioles or arteries between 5 and 30 μ in luminal diameter were measured in each circulation. A line has been drawn through the average ratio at each period so the various periods may be compared. Arteries of medium size (30 to 50 μ) show a similar progression. (From Naeye. Arch. Path., 71:121, 1961.)

born infants, suggesting that gestational age is less important than duration of postnatal respiration for the development of a normal caliber of pulmonary vessels. Prolonged neonatal hypoxemia arrests the relative involution of smooth muscle about the pulmonary arterial bed. Hypoxemia-induced pulmonary vasoconstriction presumably occurs in these persistently muscular small pulmonary arteries.

The influence of birth is also evident in autopsy weights of right and left cardiac ventricles. Within five days following premature birth there is evidence of left ventricular (but not right ventricular) hypertrophy.

Cardiovascular Function in Asymptomatic Infants. *Heart rate.* Heart rate shows wide variation, ranging between 110 and 170 beats per minute, with a mean of 140.

Blood pressure. Blood pressure has been measured directly by umbilical artery catheterization. The values obtained in the first hour after birth, plotted against birth weight and gestational age are shown in Figures 65 and 66. Systemic blood pressure in low-birth-weight infants is positively correlated with birth weight, gestational age, and postnatal age. However, a mean arterial blood pressure of <30 mm Hg can be considered hypotension even in the smallest infants.

Blood Volume. Blood volume at birth is relatively high (108 ml/kg) in low-birth-weight infants. The plasma volume of these infants averages about 62 ml/kg, and the red cell mass 46 ml/kg. These volumes are determined in part by the practice of clamping the cord, since the ratio of placental to fetal blood volume is greatest in the most immature infant. Late cord clamping increases the blood volume of the newborn infant, and stripping of the cord before clamping may deliver an even larger transfusion. The relative risks associated with delivering a larger or smaller transfusion to the newborn infant at the time of delivery are presently being assessed.

Edema. Babies born prematurely often show pitting edema of the hands and feet; relatively immobile parts may exhibit dependent edema. Edema is usually barely detectable at birth, but becomes more prominent during the first day of life; it is more noticeable in the more immature subjects. The early transudation of fluid out of the vascular compartment accounts for the higher hematocrit commonly observed at 12 to 24 hours of age in premature infants as compared with that obtained at birth. The protein content of the edema fluid is very high, usually 3.0 to 3.5 g percent. In addition, the plasma colloid osmotic pressure is lower the more immature the infant. Thus the edema may be a manifestation of increased capillary permeability, which permits extravascular leakage of plasma constituents and a lower plasma colloid osmotic pressure. The capillary defect may play an important role in the production of hyaline membranes.

Vasomotor reflexes. Vasomotor regulatory mechanisms, as elicited by cold pressor tests and postural tilting, are present and functional at birth in prematurely born as well as in term infants. These vasomotor reflexes, as will be pointed out in the discussion on thermoregulation, have functional importance for temperature regulation as well as for cardiovascular homeostasis.

Peripheral blood flow. The technique of venous occlusion plethysmography has been successfully applied to obtain measurements of peripheral circulation in both term and preterm babies. Preterm babies, despite a lower arterial blood pressure, have a higher rate of limb blood flow per milliliter of tissue, indicating lower peripheral resistance. Pe-

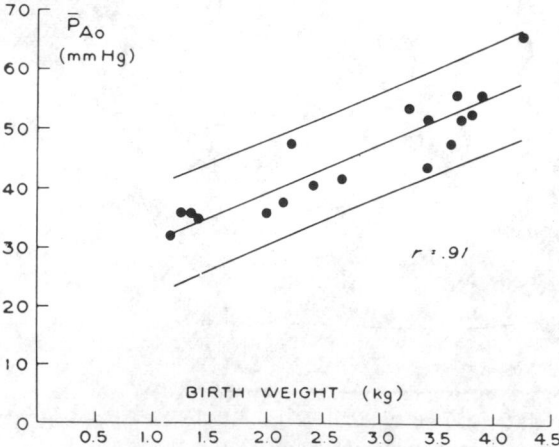

Fig. 65. Linear regression and 95 percent confidence limits of mean aortic blood pressure on birth weight in normal newborn infants during hours 2 to 12 of life (n = 300). The actual blood pressure readings are shown as dots. Correlation coefficient = r. (From Kitterman et al. *Pediatrics,* 44:959, 1969.)

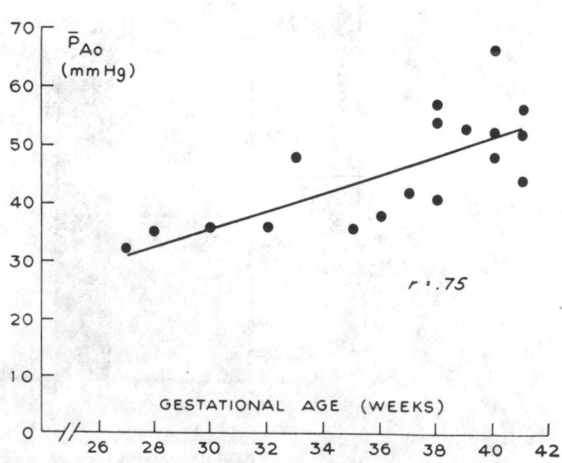

Fig. 66. Linear regression of mean aortic blood pressure on gestational age in normal newborn infants during the first year of life. Symbols are those used in Figure 65. (From Kitterman et al. *Pediatrics,* 44:959, 1969.)

ripheral blood flow is very responsive to change in environmental temperature.

Circulatory Derangements in Infants of Low Birth Weight. Incomplete lung expansion and deficient oxygenation, which often occur in preterm infants during the first few hours of postnatal life, might seriously compromise the normal postnatal circulatory adjustment. Under these conditions vascular resistance in the lung would remain high and the ductus would tend to remain open longer than usual. That these situations often occur in low-birth-weight infants is suggested by the finding, more frequent among small neonates than among larger ones, of crescendo systolic murmurs. These murmurs were decreased or obliterated by reduction in body temperature, by crying and expiratory grunting (which raise intrathoracic pressure), and by supplemental oxygen.

Cyanosis. Generalized cynanosis, which is relieved by raising the ambient oxygen concentration to 50 percent, is probably due to a ventilatory defect; but general cyanosis which persists despite a high ambient oxygen concentration suggests a right-to-left shunt. Most often these shunts are transient, occurring through the ductus arteriosus, foramen ovale, or atelectatic areas of lung; but the possibility of cyanotic congenital heart disease must always be kept in mind.

Bradycardia. Severe hypoxemia is associated with a slowing of the heart rate; in view of the relatively rapid heart rate shown by vigorous small neonates, the significance of heart rates under 100 per minute must be recognized.

Hypotension. Asphyxia at birth initially elevates the systemic blood pressure; babies who experience profound birth asphyxia show an increase in the radiologic cardiothoracic ratio. On the other hand, infants who develop severe respiratory distress syndrome show low systemic pressures, and an increase in heart size is not common.

Hypervolemia. Hypervolemia, as previously mentioned, may follow stripping of the umbilical cord. It is also seen in erythroblastosis, in the twin-to-twin transfusion syndrome in the transfused twin, and in the rare cases of maternofetal transfusion. Hypervolemia may also be produced iatrogenically; blood transfusion in the low-birth-weight infant should probably not exceed 10 ml/kg per transfusion, and vital signs should be followed carefully. Complications of hypervolemia include congestive heart failure, hyperbilirubinemia, and venous thrombosis. Infants with intrauterine growth retardation have significantly higher hematocrits than preterm infants of comparable size. This is reflected in the hyperviscosity of blood seen in some intrauterine growth-retarded infants.

Hypovolemia. Hypovolemia may occur in fetomaternal transfusion, twin-to-twin transfusion syndrome in the donor twin, or fetal blood loss from vasa previa or at cesarean section from the placenta. If acute, these processes may produce the clinical picture of shock in the newborn infant; if chronic, hypotension, small heart, and oliguria may be evident. There is a suggestion that atelectasis and hyaline membrane disease occur more frequently with hypovolemia.

Harlequin color change. A peculiar vasomotor phenomenon, known as the harlequin color change, is observed occasionally in immature infants during the first week of life. It is seen when the baby is lying on one side; the dependent half of the body remains pink, while the side which is uppermost becomes much paler than usual. A sharp line of demarcation occurs exactly in the midline. The phenomenon is believed to result from functional immaturity of the higher centers controlling peripheral vascular tone. No pathologic significance has been attached to it.

Oxygen, vascular tone, and immaturity. A final note should be made of the peculiar reactivity to oxygen of some components of the neonatal vasculature. Mention has already been made of constriction of the ductus arteriosus in response to high inspired oxygen concentration. This is presumably effected through elevation of arterial Po_2. A similar response to oxygen is exhibited by the retinal arterioles and, inferentially, by the umbilical arteries. Retinal arteriolar constriction in response to high oxygen environment is recognized as the first step in the development of retrolental fibroplasia, a disease peculiar to prematurely born infants. Prolonged pulsation of the umbilical arteries after birth is recognized as a sign of transitional distress in newborn infants. The response of the pulmonary arterioles to elevated Po_2 is paradoxical to that of the ductus, retinal arterioles, and umbilical arteries, in that dilation is produced. The reasons for these differences in response of smooth muscle to oxygen are unknown.

THERMOREGULATION. **Heat Production and Heat Loss.** Body temperature is dependent on the relationship between heat production and heat loss. Heat production depends on muscular activity and metabolic processes. The most important route of heat loss is from the body surface; heat loss also occurs from the lungs by the evaporation of water, by warming the inspired air, and, at high environmental temperature, by sweating.

Poikilothermy versus Homeothermy. A poikilothermic subject is unable to make thermoregulatory responses to stabilize deep body temperature; therefore, his body temperature changes with ambient temperature. A homeotherm exhibits homeostatic responses to thermal stimuli which serve to protect him from marked change in deep body temperature when environmental temperature changes. These homeothermic responses include the regulation of chemical heat production, in addition to vasoconstriction and shivering in response to a cold stimulus, and vasodilation and sweating following a warm stimulus.

At basal deep body temperature, oxidative metabolism is minimal and increases on each side of this point (Fig. 67). As body temperature rises above

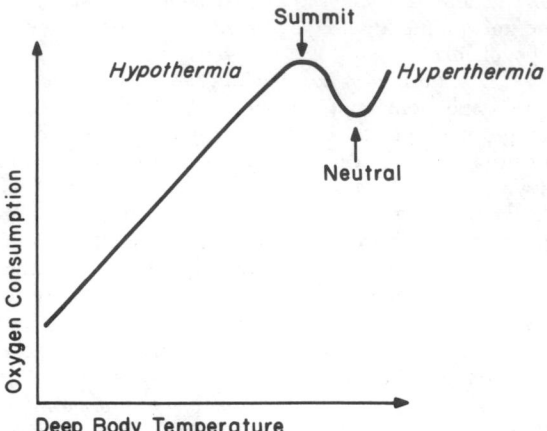

Fig. 67. Ideal homeothermic model. Oxygen consumption increases above and below the neutral zone. As deep body temperature falls, a summit metabolism is mounted before true hypothermia supervenes.

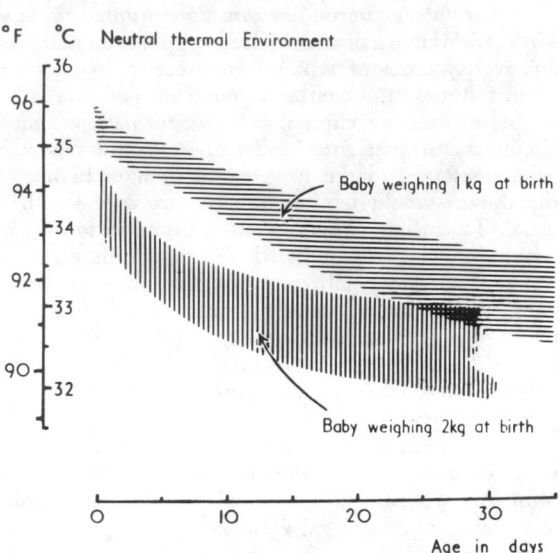

Fig. 68. The neutral operative temperature for a baby lying naked on a warm mattress in draft-free surroundings of moderate humidity (about 50 percent relative humidity) when mean radiant temperature is the same as air temperature. The hatched areas showed the average neutral temperature range for a healthy baby weighing 1 kg (≡) and 2 kg (⦀) at birth. (From Hey and Katz. *Arch. Dis. Child.*, 45:328-334, 1970.)

the neutral point, O_2 consumption also rises in accordance with van't Hoff's rule, which states that the velocity of chemical reactions is increased twofold or more for each rise of 10° C in temperature. As body temperature starts to fall below the neutral point, there is an increased chemical heat production; but if the homeothermic responses to cold should be overwhelmed by the magnitude of the heat loss, deep body temperature falls and the subject sinks into true hypothermia.

The main integrative center for temperature regulation appears to be the hypothalamus, which contains thermosensitive cells which respond to changes in blood temperature. The hypothalamus also receives afferent impulses from cutaneous thermoreceptors and, integrating the information from both central and peripheral sites, initiates the rather complex sequence of reactions which serve to maintain a relatively constant deep body temperature.

Fall in Body Temperature Following Birth. The newborn infant, particularly the low-birth-weight infant, exhibits a prompt fall in body temperature immediately after delivery. This results from the abrupt change in environmental temperature, from the mother's internal body temperature to that of the delivery room. The amount by which heat loss exceeds heat production during this immediate postnatal period will determine the magnitude of the fall in the infant's temperature.

The low-birth-weight subject is poorly equipped to conserve body heat because of a relatively large surface area for heat loss and meager subcutaneous fat. The magnitude of such losses is also influenced by conditions of air movement and relative humidity of the ambient air and the condition of the skin. Evaporative heat loss from skin wet with amniotic fluid is very great.

The Neutral Thermal Environment. Assuming that rectal temperature of an infant is to remain between 36.8 and 37.2° C, a range of operative temperatures was calculated by Hey and Katz which predicts the minimum and maximum environmental temperature to provide thermal neutrality for a baby being nursed naked in a draft-free commercial incubator at 50 percent relative humidity. The results of their calculations, shown in Figure 68, clearly indicate the modifying effects of body size and postnatal age. These thermoneutral ranges are specified in terms of "operative" temperature, and incubator air temperature has to be revised upward (about 1° C if room temperature is less than 27° C) to achieve "neutral" air temperature. For cot-nursed babies insulated against heat loss with clothes and blankets, neutral thermal conditions are provided by a room temperature of 24° C (or 30° C for babies under 1.5 kg).

Homeothermic Responses. There has been controversy as to whether newborn infants are able to make thermoregulatory responses to maintain deep body temperature. There is now convincing evidence that they can do so. However, the magnitude of heat losses experienced by the low-birth-weight infant in the immediate postnatal period is such that his cold limits are easily exceeded, and a fall in deep body temperature results. Heat losses may be minimized and deep body temperature maintained by placing the infant in an incubator immediately after birth and by appropriate heating equipment within the delivery room to minimize heat loss during prolonged resuscitations.

The homeothermic responses exhibited by the low-birth-weight infant exposed to cold include peripheral vasoconstriction and an increase in oxidative metabolism, but shivering is not observed.

Low-birth-weight subjects vary in their ability to withstand cold stress. The most successful maintain a relatively large temperature gradient between core and surface by vasoconstriction and mount a sustained increase in oxygen consumption. These responses appear to be better developed with increasing gestational age. In response to cold, the prematurely born infant increases heat production to a lesser degree than does the term infant. The magnitude of the metabolic response on cooling increases during the first days of life in both mature and immature neonates.

Mechanism of nonshivering thermogenesis. Nonshivering thermogenesis in the newborn appears to be mediated through norepinephrine. It has been shown that administration of norepinephrine to newborn kittens and rabbits and human neonates causes a rise in O_2 consumption. On exposure to cold, newborn infants increase their urinary output of norepinephrine and vanillyl mandelic acid. Norepinephrine stimulates brown fat metabolism by activating a lipase catalyzing triglyceride hydrolysis. Both the released fatty acids and glycerol (after its conversion to α-glycerophosphate) can be readily oxidized in vitro by the brown fat. The biochemical mechanism by which norepinephrine can induce a sustained elevation of the rate of brown fat oxygen consumption is not known. However, it has been proposed that norepinephrine indirectly uncouples oxidation and phosphorylation in brown fat mitochondria by elevating the intracellular level of fatty acids.

Sites of Metabolic Heat Production. The site of the neonate's metabolic response to cold to norepinephrine has been investigated in animals and indirectly in human infants. Although some observations suggest that the heat is produced by direct activation of an oxidative system in all tissues of the body, the search for possible major sites of heat production has continued. Extrapolating from various animal studies, major sites may include the liver and brown fat depots. The location of brown fat depots in the newborn infant is shown in Figure 69.

The chemical basis of heat production. The metabolic response to cold involves the oxidation of fat. Premature infants demonstrate a fall in respiratory exchange ratio on exposure to cold. The elevated oxygen consumption of newborn infants during mild cooling is associated with increased plasma glycerol levels but no change in plasma free fatty acids. Since triglyceride lipolysis in fat slices results in less free fatty acid being released from brown than from white fat, this may indicate brown fat thermogenesis. Heim et al. compared the brown adipose tissue from babies who died after having

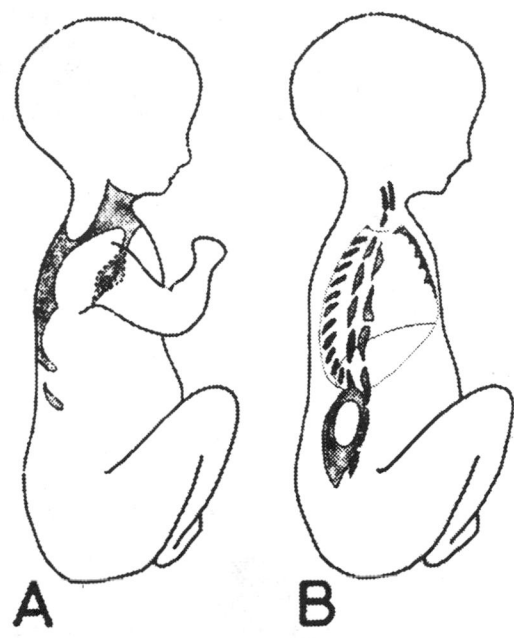

Fig. 69. Site and extent of brown adipose tissue in the newborn baby: A, superficial; B, deep. (From Aherne and Hull. *Proc. Roy. Soc. Med.,* 57:1172, 1964.)

been nursed either in incubators (34 to 35° C) or who were swaddled and nursed at room temperature (23 to 37° C). The tissues studied from the infants nursed in warmer conditions were replete with fat, whereas approximately 80 percent of the brown fat in the second group exhibited fat depletion.

Accidental Hyperthermia. Most clinical situations require the low-birth-weight infant to demonstrate his homeothermy by protecting himself against a fall in body temperature. On the other hand, overheating of the low-birth-weight infant may occur accidentally through improper control of incubator heating. In these situations the infant exhibits vasodilation and tachypnea. Sweat production is inadequate, however, particularly in babies born more than 6 weeks before term, and as a result body temperature may rapidly rise and death ensue unless the accident is detected and ambient temperature promptly lowered.

REFERENCES

Amiel-Tison, C. Neurological evaluation of the maturity of newborn infants. Arch. Dis. Child., 43:89, 1968.

Avery, M. E. The Lung and Its Disorders in the Newborn Infant. Philadelphia, W. B. Saunders Company, 1968.

——— and Mead, J. Surface properties in relation to atelectasis and hyaline membrane disease. Amer. J. Dis. Child., 97:517, 1959.

Battaglia, F. C., McGaughey, H., Makowski, E. L., and Meschia, G. Postnatal changes in oxygen affinity of sheep red cells: a dual role of diphosphoglyceric acid. Amer. J. Physiol., 219:217, 1970.

Bruck, K. Temperature regulation in the newborn infant. Biol. Neonat., 3:65, 1961.

Burnard, E. D. The cardiac murmur in relation to symptoms in the newborn. Brit. Med. J., 1:134, 1959.

—— Grathan-Smith, P., Picton-Warlow, C. G., and Granang, A. Pulmonary insufficiency in prematurity. Aust. Pediat. J., 1:12, 1965.

Cassels, D. E., ed. The Heart and Circulation in the Newborn and Infant. New York, Grune & Stratton, 1966.

Celander, O., and Marild, K. Regional circulation and capillary filtration in relation to capillary exchange in the foot and calf of the newborn infant. Acta Paediat. Scand., 51:385, 1962.

Chernick, V., Heldrich, F., and Avery, M. E. Periodic breathing of premature infants. J. Pediat., 64:330, 1964.

Cook, C. D., Sutherland, J. M., Segal, S., Cherry, R. B., Mead, J., McIllroy, M. B., and Smith, C. A. Studies of respiratory physiology in the newborn infant. III. Measurement of mechanics of respiration. J. Clin. Invest., 36:440, 1957.

Dawes, G. S. Foetal and Neonatal Physiology. Chicago, Year Book Medical Publishers, Inc., 1968.

Dawkins, M. J. R., and Hull, D. Brown adipose tissue and the response of new-born rabbits to cold. J. Physiol. (London), 172:216, 1964.

Day, R. Respiratory metabolism in infancy and in childhood. Regulation of body temperature of premature infants. Amer. J. Dis. Child., 65:376, 1943.

Delivoria-Papadopoulos, M., Battaglia, F. C., and Meschia, G. A comparison of fetal versus maternal plasma colloidal osmotic pressure in man. Proc. Soc. Exp. Biol. Med., 131:84, 1969.

Desmond, M. M., Kay, J. L., and Megarity, A. L. The phases of "transitional distress" occurring in neonates in association with prolonged postnatal umbilical cord pulsations. J. Pediat., 55:131, 1959.

Edelmann, C. M., Jr., and Spitzer, A. The maturing kidney. J. Pediat., 75:509, 1969.

—— and Wolfish, N. M. Dietary influence on renal maturation in premature infants. Pediat. Res., 2:421, 1968.

Glass, L., Silverman, W. A., and Sinclair, J. C. Effect of the thermal environment on cold resistance and growth of small infants after the first week of life. Pediatrics, 41:1033, 1968.

Gruenwald, P. Normal and abnormal expansion of the lungs of newborn infants obtained at autopsy. II. Opening pressure, maximal volume and stability of expansion. Lab. Invest., 12:563, 1963.

—— Normal and abnormal expansion of the lungs of newborn infants obtained at autopsy. III. The pattern of aeration as affected by gestational and postnatal age. Anat. Rec., 146:337, 1963.

—— Chronic fetal distress and placental insufficiency. Biol. Neonat., 5:215, 1963.

Heim, T., Kellermeyer, M., and Dane, M. Thermal conditions and the mobilization of lipids from brown and white adipose tissue in the human neonate. Acta Paediat. Acad. Sci. Hung., 9:109, 1968.

Hey, E. N., and Katz, G. Evaporative water loss in the new-born baby. J. Physiol. (London), 200:605, 1969.

—— and Katz, G. The range of thermal insulation in the tissues of the new-born baby. J. Physiol. (London), 207:667, 1970.

—— and Katz, G. The optimum thermal environment for naked babies. Arch. Dis. Child. (London), 1970 (in press).

Humbert, J. R., Abelson, H., Hathaway, W. E., and Battaglia, F. C. Polycythemia in small for gestational age infants. J. Pediat., 75:812, 1969.

Karlberg, P., Moore, R. E., and Oliver, T. K., Jr. The thermogenic response of the newborn infant to noradrenaline. Acta Paediat. Scand., 51:284, 1962.

Kidd, L., Levison, H., Gemmel, P., Aharon, A., and Swyer, P. R. Limb blood flow in the normal and sick newborn. Amer. J. Dis. Child., 122:402, 1966.

Kildeberg, P. Clinical Acid-Base Physiology: Studies in Neonates, Infants and Young Children. Baltimore, The Williams & Wilkins Co., 1968.

Lubchenco, L. O., Hansman, C., Dressler, M., and Boyd, E. Intrauterine growth as estimated from liveborn birthweight data at 24 to 42 weeks of gestation. Pediatrics, 32:793, 1963.

Moss, A. J., Duffie, R. R., and Emmanouilides, G. Blood pressure and vasomotor reflexes in the newborn infant. Pediatrics, 32:175, 1963.

Naeye, R. L. Arterial changes in the perinatal period. Arch. Path., 71:121, 1961.

Neligan, G. A., and Strang, L. B. A "harlequin" colour change in the newborn. Lancet, 2:1005, 1952.

Rudolph, A. M., Drorbaugh, J. E., Auld, P. A. M., Rudolph, A. J., Nadas, A. S., Smith, C. A., and Hubbell, J. P. Studies on the circulation in the neonatal period. The circulation in the respiratory distress syndrome. Pediatrics, 27:551, 1961.

Schulman, I., Smith, C. H., and Stern, G. C. Studies on the anemia of prematurity. II. The blood volume in premature infants. Amer. J. Dis. Child., 88:575, 1954.

Silverman, W. A., and Agate, F. J., Jr. Variation in cold resistance among small newborn infants. Biol. Neonat., 6:113, 1964.

—— Sinclair, J. C., and Agate, F. J., Jr. Oxygen cost of minor variations in heat balance of small newborn infants. Acta Paediat. Scand., 55:294, 1966.

Smith, C. A., and Nelson, N. M., ed. Physiology of the Newborn Infant, 4th ed. Springfield, Ill., Charles C Thomas, Publisher, 1970.

Sutherland, J. M., and Ratcliff, J. W. Crying vital capacity. Amer. J. Dis. Child., 101:67, 1961.

Thibeault, D. W., Poblete, E., and Auld, P. A. M. Alveolar-arterial O_2 and CO_2 differences and their relation to lung volume in the newborn. Pediatrics, 41:574, 1968.

Supportive Care

L. JOSEPH BUTTERFIELD

During the 1960's there was a steady decrease in the total number of live births in the United States from 4.2 million to 3.6 million annually. In the same decade the percentage of low-birth-weight infants increased from 7.5 to 8.2 percent. The net effect in the total number of low-birth-weight infants was a slight decrease from approximately 315,000 per year in 1960 to 295,000 in 1969. During the 1970's this total will probably rise due to the increasing number of women in the childbearing years (assumed to be 15 to 44 years). This anticipated increase in total number of low-birth-weight infants born yearly in the United States is a mounting challenge to health care in the perinatal period. In addition to the problem of increasing numbers there is also concern about the neurosensory sequelae of children who were small at birth. Thus, the care of the low-birth-weight infant has acquired new meaning as evaluations of eventual outcome are correlated with unfavorable events during gestation and the early days after birth. Mortality rate can no longer be regarded as the sole measure of comparison among nurseries that take care of low-birth-weight infants.

In selected circumstances, such as maternal diabetes, erythroblastosis fetalis, and intrauterine growth failure, the survival of an infant may depend on planned early delivery. Here, the care of the low-birth-weight infant is an extension of optimal obstetric management and must be considered in the decision to terminate a pregnancy.

HISTORY OF THE PREMATURE INFANT CENTER. The first special hospital unit for the care of the premature infant was established in Paris in 1893. French obstetricians, led by Tarnier and Budin, set down basic guidelines for care and devised techniques, such as gavage feeding and incubator care, that have not lost their place in the modern nursery. A student of Budin's, Martin Couney, traveled the exposition circuit from Berlin to Denver to Coney Island between the years 1896 and 1939. Wherever he went, he borrowed infants for whom little hope was held and set up exhibitions of the care of the premature infant. Though Couney, known as the "incubator doctor," may have been accused of preying upon the insatiable curiosity of the public, he nevertheless publicized the special needs of the low-birth-weight infant. In fact, with his meticulous attention to careful feeding and nursing measures, the survival rate of infants in his care was remarkable at a time when 1 of every 10 newborn infants died in the first year of life. Couney's selection of low-birth-weight infants over 1 week of age is testimony to his early appreciation of the excessive risks in the first week of life.

Soon after Couney displayed the little babies in Chicago in 1914, he attracted the interest and the friendship of Dr. Julius Hess. In 1922 Hess opened the first premature infant center in the United States at Michael Reese Hospital, not far from "White City" where the "incubator doctor" charged admission to see the smallest infants. Hess was fortunate to have the help of an exacting nurse, Miss Evelyn Lundeen, who dedicated the last 40 years of her life to the care of the "premies." Miss Lundeen insisted upon a careful "technique," which included fastidious hand washing, a measure that is no less important today. She demonstrated the unique importance of the nurse's role in the care of the low-birth-weight infant.

In the next 30 years, premature infant centers were established throughout the United States with the cooperation and support of state and federal agencies. These units in major community and university hospitals have served as intensive care facilities for patients, as well as centers for the education of nurses and physicians. These centers have been essential in the accumulation of information about the low-birth-weight infant which has led to a reformation in many areas of patient care as well as reassurance about some of the routine practices that were introduced nearly 75 years ago.

THE NEWBORN CENTER. In the past, emphasis was placed on the transportation of low-birth-weight infants needing specialized care to a "premature infant center." Today, the same emphasis is being placed on the transportation of all infants who require specialized care to a center that is staffed and equipped to manage the high-risk newborn, regardless of his size and without a rigid demarcation by postnatal age. Whenever possible the newborn infant should be cared for in the hospital where he was born. However, there is an obligation by the physician as well as the hospital and the community to provide a certain level of care for a sick baby; when nursing coverage, nursery facilities, and laboratory support are not satisfactory, the baby should be transferred to a newborn center where both the low-birth-weight infant and the problem-size baby can be given optimal care.

REGIONAL PERINATAL CENTER. With the increasing recognition that perinatal morbidity contributes excessively to later growth and developmental aberrations, both obstetricians and pediatricians are sharing the notion that a continuum of expert care is most important in the perinatal care of the high-risk mother and infant. Recent studies in Quebec have demonstrated a lower perinatal mortality in hospitals providing intramural neonatal intensive care facilities in addition to high quality obstetric services. From these early markers of the efficacy of concentrated perinatal care in reducing perinatal mortality—and presumably the sequelae of perinatal morbidity—it follows that responsible communities must consider a regional approach to perinatal care. The regional perinatal center will allow the most intensive care of the mother and fetus while serving as a rich source of teaching material and research potential. Paramedical personnel should receive part of their training here, since proper arrangements in the future of clinics, hospitals, and regional centers will depend on a fundamental understanding of the system of perinatal care. This might start at the physician's office or the neighborhood health center and culminate in the regional perinatal center in selected cases.

About 40 percent of problems in the perinatal period defy early recognition. Therefore, every hospital which delivers a baby must be prepared to offer temporary emergency care of the sick newborn and, if the minimal facilities for intensive care

are not at hand, be prepared to transfer the sick baby to the nearest intensive care facility.

TRANSPORTATION. When small or sick infants require transportation to another hospital, preplanning makes the operation run smoothly. For short distances an ambulance or private car is satisfactory. However, the use of helicopters for short trips in the community may soon become a more efficient means of emergency transportation. Arrangements for transportation of a low-birth-weight infant or a sick newborn should be made by the patient's physician with the personnel in the newborn center. Whenever possible, nursery personnel should accompany the ambulance on the trip to the newborn center. Contact with the parents of the baby and his nurses, and review of the maternal and infant histories make this trip very worthwhile. In addition, an experienced nurse can provide expert surveillance of the infant during the return trip.

With the concentration of population in urban areas, the great majority of transport cases will be done in surface vehicles. Several referral centers are utilizing "mobile care" vehicles such as the one pictured in Figure 70, which is in use in Denver, Colorado. These modified vans allow easier access to the infant who has been placed in one of the transport incubators, so that appropiate evaluation, monitoring, and procedures such as resuscitation and intravenous therapy can be initiated or maintained.

For longer trips a small airplane can be used.

Air transfer greatly reduces the time that the infant is in transit and is not much more costly than an ambulance. The practice of sending a sick newborn infant to a distant hospital in the family car, accompanied only by his anxious father, should be discouraged. A nurse or a specially trained attendant should accompany the father in such instances. The ideal transport incubator should allow easy access to the baby and constant visibility, and provide supplemental oxygen and heat. Resuscitation equipment is an essential part of the emergency supplies.

ORGANIZATION. A newborn center must be closely supervised. This requires organization and acceptance of authority, whether the nursery exists in a private hospital or a medical center. In the premature infant centers, the nursery should be the responsibility of one physician-in-charge who delegates responsibility to his associates but maintains control of procedures and passes on new therapeutic regimens. In the newborn center of a private hospital, organization is equally important. Private physicians using the service must be willing to share their responsibility with a physician-in-charge, and uniform procedures must be accepted. In such a nursery, strict observance of "aseptic technique" and the adoption of a uniform set of procedures are essential.

The design, management, and optimal services of the nursery of a hospital are outlined in *Standards and Recommendations for Hospital Care of Newborn Infants,* published by the American Academy of

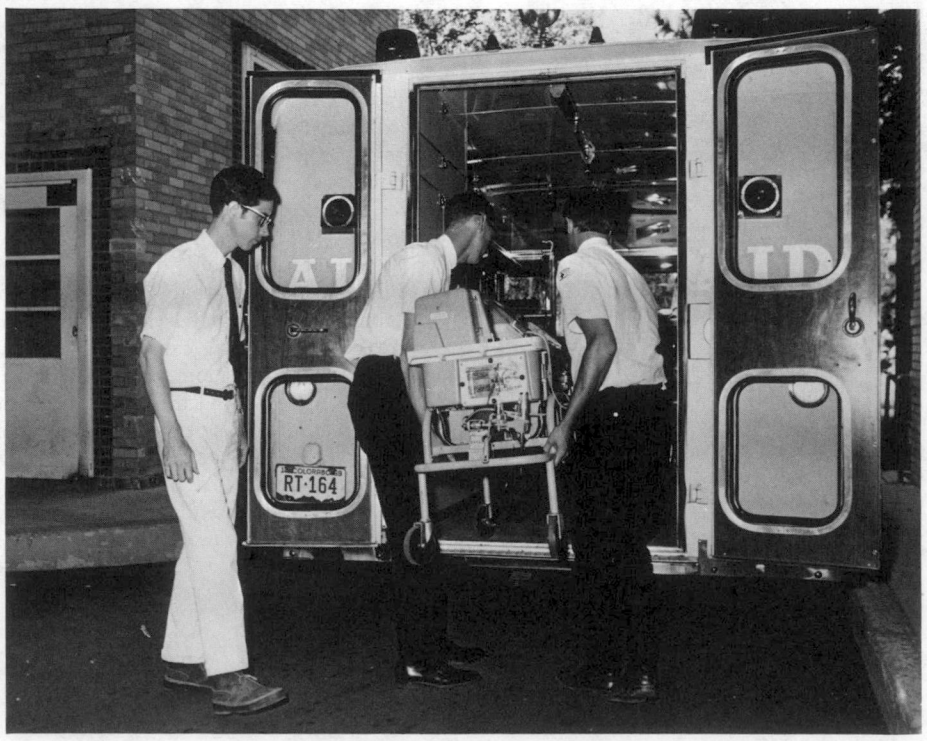

Fig. 70. Mobile care car.

Pediatrics (1970). A copy of this book should be included in the reference library of every hospital nursery.

Laboratory.   Great strides have been made in biomedical technology that allow the reporting of quantitative glucose, bilirubin, and blood gas determinations within minutes of the receipt of the blood sample in the laboratory. Facilities for microchemical determinations of essential electrolytes, glucose, acid-base status, blood gas tensions, and bilirubin should be available to every nursery which cares for sick or small newborn infants. The trauma of multiple phlebotomies and the excess volume of blood required for them make macrochemical techniques completely impractical for small newborn infants.

On occasion the cribside measurement of the serum glucose or total protein may be desired. A centrifuged tube of capillary blood can be tested with a Dextrostix or placed in a hand refractometer to provide glucose and total protein determinations with sufficient reliability for clinical management.

Except when special studies demand that an infant be taken to the radiology department, roentgenograms should be taken in the nursery. Most commonly, chest roentgenograms are requested, and the quality of portable films is satisfactory for diagnostic purposes.

Nurses.   The nurse who cares for the low-birth-weight infant must be specially trained. Her observations are more detailed than those of anyone else, and very often the alert nurse is the first to suspect trouble from the infant's behavior, especially during feedings. Ongoing educational programs for nurses in the hospital and in the community are essential. Nurses who work with low-birth-weight infants should not rotate to other wards in the hospital. By limiting their duties to the nursery, there is less lag in the recognition of the signs of illness in their patients and also less chance of introducing infections from other wards.

IMMEDIATE CARE OF THE LOW-BIRTH-WEIGHT INFANT.   **Perinatal Cooperation.**   Optimal care of the low-birth-weight infant begins before his birth (see section on obstetrics). This includes the selection of a hospital for delivery where nursery facilities are optimal. There is little sense in the deliberate delivery of a woman with a known complication of pregnancy in a hospital that is ill-equipped to deal with the immediate problems of the newborn infant. The previous reference to regional perinatal care centers represents an appeal for a community and regional approach to perinatal medicine.

Delivery Room.   Whenever the delivery of a low-birth-weight infant is anticipated, the nursery should be alerted so that an incubator can be warmed and the appropriate physician called. The smaller

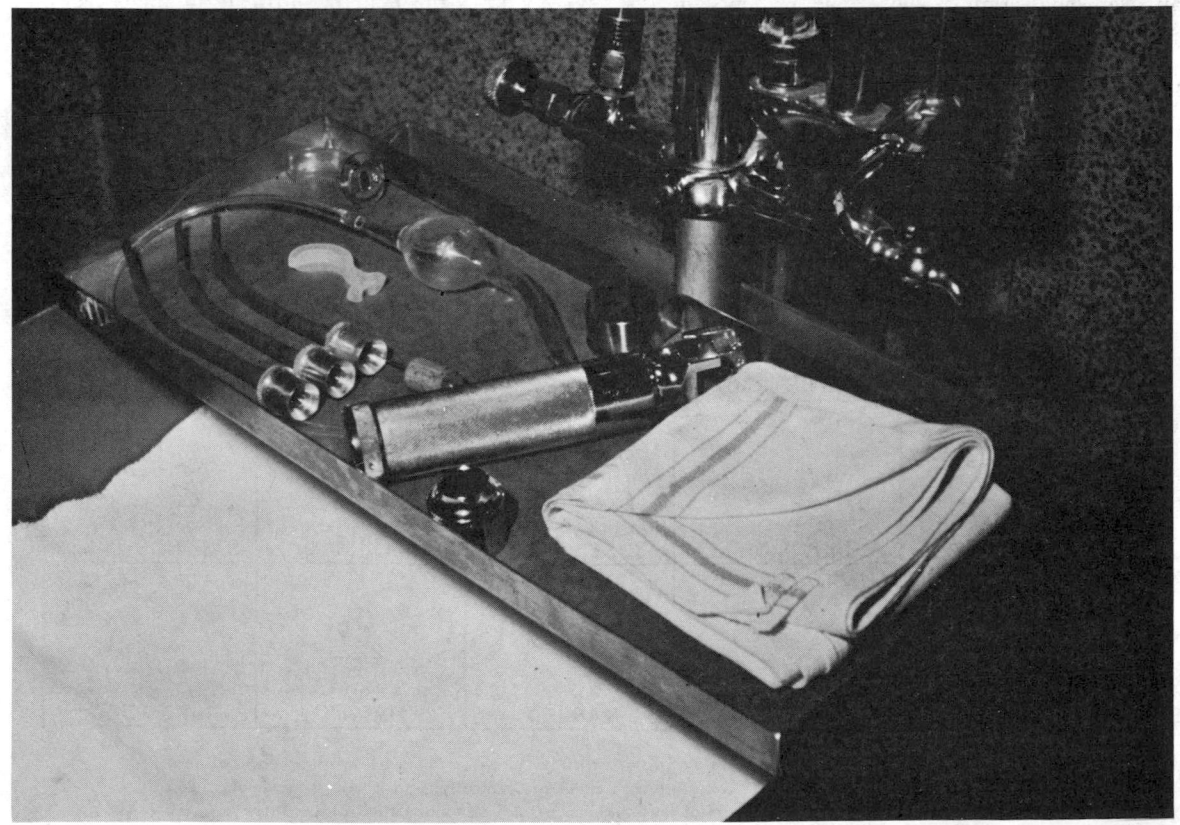

Fig. 71. Resuscitation tray.

the baby, the more likely it is that resuscitation will be needed.

Resuscitation procedures need review on a regular basis, either during a staff meeting or at the perinatal mortality conference, and at least every six months. A uniform set of resuscitation procedures (see p. 70) should be agreed upon by those who work in the delivery room, and a responsible person should be delegated to keep close contact with advances in resuscitative techniques and equipment as well as with problems that have arisen in the resuscitation of the newborn infant.

The resuscitation equipment must be in the delivery room before the delivery of the low-birth-weight infant, and the equipment must be checked for completeness and working order by the head nurse of the delivery room at least daily. To facilitate the availability of the resuscitation equipment, a stainless steel flanged tray has been designed (Fig. 71). This tray fits onto the resuscitation table that is found in most delivery rooms.

The importance of preventing heat loss from the newborn in the delivery room must constantly be stressed. Since most delivery rooms are maintained at a temperature which is comfortable for the mother and the staff, it is possible for a wet baby to lose several degrees of body temperature in a short time. Drying the infant soon after birth with a soft warmed blanket, and provision of a warming bed or an overhead warming device, will prevent unnecessary heat loss.

Admission Procedures. Infants with respiratory distress and the smaller infants are placed in incubators. This provides the dual advantages of easy observation and the ability to provide supplemental heat and oxygen. Two types of incubators in wide use are the forced-air, individually ventilated type (e.g., Isolette) and the convection type (e.g., older models of the Gordon-Armstrong incubator). The incubator should be prewarmed to 32° C with oxygen available but not used routinely. A bulb syringe is kept in the incubator for suction of the nose and mouth. The infant is placed on his back on a sterile sheet-covered mattress and left unclothed to permit better observation of respiration and cyanosis. Unless the infant has serious respiratory difficulty, he is weighed within the incubator during the first hour, using a suspension scale and a hammock. Body weight is an important measurement which must be obtained accurately.

Infants delivered at another hospital and admitted to a referral center should have bacterial cultures taken from the nose, mouth, cord, and rectum.

Body temperature is taken rectally until meconium is passed, and axillary temperatures are taken subsequently. The thermometer may stimulate the passage of meconium stools, and the patency of the anus is determined in this manner.

Prophylaxis of the eyes is carried out with 1 percent silver nitrate or an antibiotic ophthalmic ointment (see Chap. 27).

Within the hour of birth the infant is reevaluated with a physical examination that emphasizes inspection rather than handling. A thorough evaluation is possible without removing the baby from the

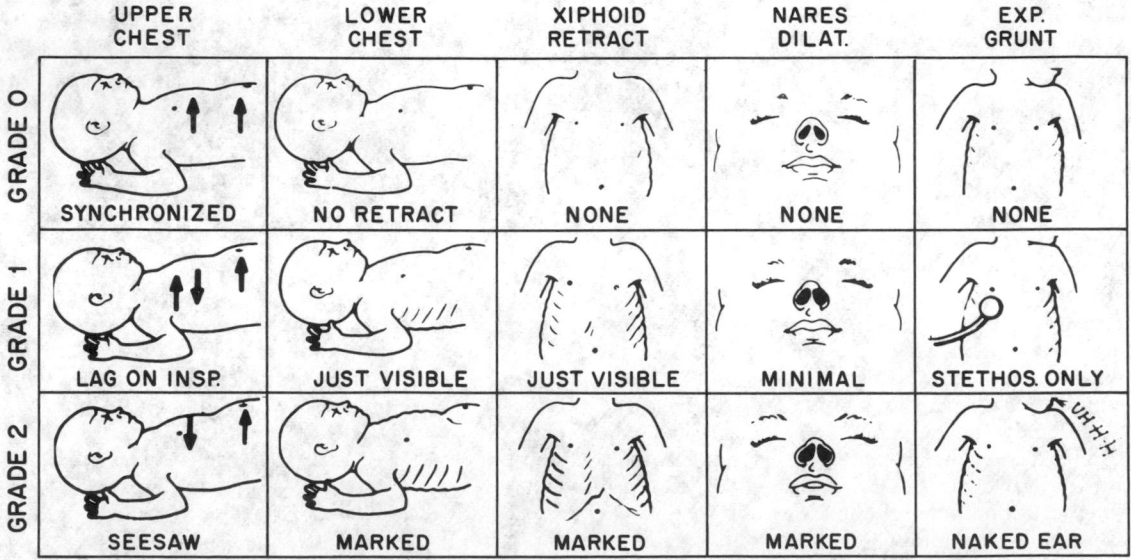

Fig. 72. Retraction scoring. An index of respiratory distress is determined by grading each of five arbitrary criteria: grade 0 indicates no difficulty, grade 1 moderate difficulty, and grade 2 maximum respiratory difficulty. The "retraction score" is the sum of these values; a total score of 0 indicates no dyspnea, whereas a total score of 10 denotes maximal respiratory distress. (From Silverman. *Dunham's Premature Infants*, 3rd ed., 1961. Courtesy of Paul B. Hoeber Inc.).

incubator. Of most importance are the signs and observations that may change with respiratory distress, cardiac failure, and infection. Attention is directed to the rate and the nature of the respirations. The retraction score represents an objective appraisal of respiratory distress, the most common problem in the first day of life (Fig. 72). The position of the liver is noted, and peripheral pulses are evaluated. A brief neurologic examination provides a base line for later comparison; however, the examination should be interrupted at the first sign of excessive fatigue or increasing respiratory difficulty.

During the first 12 hours, the nurse should make hourly observations and record the respiratory rate, the nature of the respirations, and whether the infant is grunting. The most recently admitted infants are kept closest to the nurses' station so that frequent visual checks are easier for the nurse and physician. This practice is a reversal of the older procedure of isolating the new infants until their culture reports return. The importance of a close watch of each new infant outweighs the unlikely possibility of introducing nursery infections from the delivery room.

NURSERY CARE. The cardinal principles of the care of low-birth-weight infants were outlined nearly 75 years ago by the French obstetrician Budin in his lectures to medical students:

Infants enfeebled by premature birth should be guarded with special solicitude. Not only do they share to a greater extent than full-term children the ordinary risks of infancy, but they labour under a danger which in its intensity is almost peculiar to them. I refer to the great readiness with which they become fatally chilled. With weaklings we shall then have to consider three points:
1. *Their temperature and their chilling*
2. *Their feeding*
3. *The diseases to which they are specially liable*

These goals have not changed since the beginnings of premature infant care.

Support of Body Temperature. Soon after the birth of the low-birth-weight infant, rapid cooling takes place and body temperature falls from the intrauterine level to 34° C or lower. The concepts of thermal regulation by the low-birth-weight infant were discussed earlier (p. 97). In the care of the low-birth-weight infant heat losses must be minimized; and for a naked infant in a modern incubator this can only be accomplished by supplemental heat. There is evidence that the survival of infants of low birth weight can be improved by adjusting the physical conditions of the incubator so that the temperature of the infant (not the incubator) is the end point of control. A normal deep body temperature (or axillary temperature) of 36° to 37.5° C does not reflect the intensity of metabolism which is being expended by the infant to maintain homeothermy. Superficial body temperature (abdominal skin) is

a reasonable site for control, and recent studies have demonstrated improved survival when abdominal skin temperatures are maintained at 36° C in the first days of life.

There is no evidence that very high humidity is necessary or desirable in the care of small infants in incubators if body temperature is carefully controlled. Moderate humidity (50 percent relative humidity) is recommended for routine care. When high concentrations of dry oxygen are used in the incubator, special efforts may be required to maintain moderate humidity.

As the small infant grows and he is clothed, his thermoregulatory range expands considerably, and precise control of the thermal environment is no longer necessary. When the superficial body temperature can be stabilized by clothing without supplemental heat, the infant can be moved into a bassinet.

Oxygen. Supplemental oxygen is not administered routinely to low-birth-weight infants. When supplemental oxygen is necessary, the concentration of the oxygen in the incubator in the region of the baby's nose is measured frequently with an oxygen analyzer at least every eight hours. Oxygen concentration rather than flow is recorded, since there may be variable leaks from the incubator to the room. Prolonged hyperoxia in the premature infant must be avoided because of the risk of causing retrolental fibroplasia. Measurement of oxygen tension in the arterial blood of a sick infant receiving supplemental oxygen is the only reliable method of determining whether the ambient oxygen concentration has resulted in hyperoxia in the patient.

Dry oxygen from a central supply or tank must be humidified rather than given directly by mask to the baby, particularly if the infant's upper respiratory tract has been bypassed by tracheostomy or intubation.

When the administration of oxygen to the sick newborn is indicated, measurement of the arterial oxygen tension is in order. Arterial samples may be obtained from the descending aorta via the umbilical artery or from the radial artery. These techniques must be performed by qualified personnel. The primary reason to avoid excessive arterial oxygen levels is the known association between excessive ambient oxygen and retrolental fibroplasia. Although the precise level of danger to the retinal vessels is unknown, it has been suggested that arterial oxygen tensions in excess of 150 mm Hg should be avoided, and from an appreciation of the shunting that may take place in the lungs and at the ductus arteriosus, it becomes apparent that the arterial oxygen tension measured in the descending aorta may be 10 to 20 percent lower than that in the blood reaching the retinal vessels.

Growth. Feeding the low-birth-weight infant properly has always been controversial because of the lack of a measure of success that was generally acceptable. This subject is presented in detail in another section (p. 108). Both technical and physiologic considerations must be kept in mind if one is to avoid mechanical feeding complications, which can cause serious morbidity and death.

Once an infant survives the first few days and has exhibited neither infection nor excessive jaundice, growth and development of the infant become paramount in importance. As mentioned, the subject of infant feeding is discussed at length elsewhere; the time of feedings and the measurement of growth will be discussed here.

There is suggestive evidence that feeding practices in the first month may have lasting effects on growth and development. Rats studied by McCance were retarded in growth after a period of early caloric deprivation. The children observed by Drillien had an increased incidence of physical and mental handicaps in later years when feedings had been delayed in the first days of life. These bits of evidence, however circumstantial, have prompted review of the feeding practices in nurseries for low-birth-weight infants. Early feeding of low-birth-weight infants may contribute to a more favorable outcome. But there remains an attendant risk: aspiration of feedings. The small baby with a small stomach and a weak gag reflex is at risk from overfeeding and may easily aspirate stomach contents as well as feedings themselves. Such an event can be fatal and must be weighed in the decision to feed early. Here the experience of the nurse is of great importance.

In general, the smallest infants require the longest time to regain birth weight. For babies weighing 1,000, 1,500, and 2,000 g, the average times below birth weight are usually 21, 14, and 7 days, respectively. Feeding small infants earlier and increasing the calories may shorten the time needed to regain birth weight. It remains to be seen whether efforts to minimize weight loss and encourage early weight gain are successful in improving immediate and eventual outcomes in very small infants.

Vitamin K$_1$. Vitamin K$_1$, 1 mg, is given on the day of birth. This small dose of K$_1$ is not toxic and may prevent hemorrhagic disease in susceptible babies.

Infection. Keeping the low-birth-weight infant "germ-free" is practically impossible. From the moment of birth, and frequently before, the infant begins to be colonized by microorganisms from the nose, throat, gastrointestinal tract, and skin of his mother and his attendants. The more important goal is the prevention of disease due to infection by minimizing the transmission of pathogenic organisms from infant to infant and from attendants to infant. The best defenses against nursery cross-infection are meticulous attention to hand washing and careful observation of "individual technique," the general measures of avoiding cross-contamination. Specific discussion of infections in the neonatal period will follow in a later section.

Parent Education. Parent education begins with the infant's admission. It is important for the parents to have an understanding of the nature and the seriousness of the baby's condition. If there is no complication other than low birth weight, it is still important to inform the parents of the baby's status and help them to an appreciation of the infant's risks. It is no longer acceptable to pass off the risk of premature birth with an allusion that the baby is small now but will "catch up" in time. As Lubchenco has shown (p. 115), the baby weighing less than 1,500 g is quite likely to have some eventual neurosensory handicap. Pamphlets on the care of the premature infant are helpful to the parents in reaching an early understanding of the care of their infant.

Daily Nursing Care. The details of daily nursing care should not be inflexible, and these should be kept in perspective by a periodic review of nursing practices and routines. When the baby is admitted to the nursery, excess vernix and blood are gently removed with oiled cotton balls. Until birth weight is regained, the baby is weighed daily. After that, he is weighed three times a week on Monday, Wednesday, and Friday, since weight gain is an important measure of progress. Bathing is not begun until the baby has a stable temperature in an open crib and is nearing 2,000 g. Before that, oil sponges and plain water are used for cleansing. The umbilical cord is allowed to dry.

Feeding. Daily feeding rounds are made with the head nurse. Careful consideration is given to the nurse's advice before the frequency or the volume of the feedings is changed. As a general rule, a single change is safer than two. This means that it is better to avoid both an increase in volume in feeding and a change in the number of nipple feedings or in the concentration of the milk in a single day.

Milk mixtures are ordered with a caloric designator to avoid confusion in the ratios of milk to water, particularly where a powdered milk is used. Thus, half-skimmed milk formula 16, simulated breast milk 20, and simulated breast milk 24 would refer to those milks in the concentration of 16, 20, and 24 calories per ounce.

Methods of Feeding. Smaller infants and those who have been seriously ill may need to be fed by "gavage." The classic technique of passing an oral gastric tube is easily learned and speedily executed by a trained nurse. Alternately, an indwelling nasogastric tube is placed by the physician and then taped in place for later feedings. This tube should be replaced at least weekly and carefully irrigated after each feeding to prevent clogging.

Larger and more vigorous infants can be fed by nippled bottle. Soft small nipples are necessary for easy feeding. At the time of discharge, it is better to send the baby home with a supply of soft nursery nipples than to attempt to instruct the mother in the purchase and preparation of good nipples.

Recently, disposable infant feeders with pre-mixed milk mixtures have become available. These systems of feeding have recognized the importance of a small soft nipple in feeding the weak or small infant and have provided a special nipple for this purpose.

Charting. The chart of the low-birth-weight infant is an important item in his care. The observations of both the physician and the nurse are more effective when their recording is concise and accurate. It is useful to have a blank page at the very front of the chart so that questions can be written and answered without becoming a part of the permanent record. In place of nurses' notes, a checklist of common signs of illness may be used for recording pertinent observations. Doctors' notes tell a story of the infant's progress. After the initial perinatal history is recorded, notes about the baby should be made frequently until the condition of the baby is stabilized. Doctors' notes are an indication of interest and an important part of the record.

Mothering-In. It is important for all those who care for the low-birth-weight infant to realize that the birth of a small, frail infant has a definite psychologic impact on a mother who was expecting a happy, vigorous baby. Studies of the maternal attitudes after a premature birth have shown that emotional stress occurs frequently. A mother may have strong guilt feelings and think of herself as an inadequate person. Some of these feelings may be reinforced when she is not permitted to get near her small baby for weeks or even months, as is the common practice in many hospitals. In an attempt to establish the mother-child relationship earlier, one hospital involves the mother in the care of her baby as soon as the baby can be moved from the intensive observation area. Scrubbed and gowned, the mother at first touches and holds the baby for brief periods. This is practical with infants weighing about 1,400 g. In time the mother is encouraged to participate further in the care of her baby until she is feeding, diapering, and bathing her child.

This experience, called "mothering-in," provides the mother with a chance to come to know her baby better and helps allay some of the worries that naturally accumulate in the weeks of forced separation. Fathers are also invited to participate in this more natural relationship. There is reason to believe that these experiences in mothering-in give the mothers a high level of confidence in caring for their babies.

2,000-Gram Check. When a baby reaches the 2,000-g level, it is time to plan his discharge. A checklist is put into the chart to facilitate the proper discharge procedures. The private physician is contacted and the case is discussed with him. A thorough physical examination is carried out, with emphasis on the neurologic examination and a careful fundoscopic examination after dilation of the pupils. If the infant has reached an appropriate weight, the first diphtheria-pertussis-tetanus immunization is given. The chart can be summarized and nearly completed at this time. All measures are taken to complete as much of the paper work as possible, and to arrange for extramural services. This minimizes the delay in taking the baby home on the day that the parents come for the baby, a day that has long been awaited.

The Time for Discharge. There is no set size a low-birth-weight infant must achieve before being sent home. While it is often stated that a baby is not sent home before he weighs 2,500 g, this is not necessary. It really depends on the baby and his family. In certain cases where the infant is taking nipple feedings well, is vigorous, and has done well during the mother's visits, he can go home weighing 2,000 g. Usually the conditions for discharge are met when the baby weighs about 2,300 g. The combined evaluation of the parents during visits to the nursery, the opinion of the visiting nurse, and the important suggestions of the family physician, all contribute to a more sensible decision on the time to discharge a given infant.

Home Visit. The mother of a low-birth-weight infant needs added attention during the first week that the baby is home. When possible, the physician should make a home visit a week after the baby is discharged. He can check on the baby's progress and answer the questions that nearly every mother quickly accumulates after the baby comes home.

In some communities a visiting nurse service will provide home visits to small infants. Some form of first-week home contact by a physician or a nurse is both comforting and helpful to many mothers of low-birth-weight infants. The telephone follow-up is less personal than a home visit but ensures contact with the family after the baby's discharge and serves as a detection system for problems that have arisen since discharge. Important symptoms may be overlooked by a mother whose baby is a relative stranger to her.

Follow-up. When graduate infants return to the special baby clinic for specific evaluation or well-baby care, certain mothers and the babies are encouraged to visit the nursery area. This is one way for the nurse who cared for the baby to see the results. Another method of providing the nursery personnel with a longitudinal viewpoint is to invite them to attend the follow-up clinics periodically. In these ways, the nurses are included in the care of the baby through a much longer period.

Whether a low-birth-weight infant returns to his private physician or to the clinic for subsequent care, follow-up evaluation is important. At six-month intervals for the first three or four years, the private physician should report back to the perinatal center on the growth and development of the low-birth-weight infant. Follow-up evaluation is essential in realizing the full effect of premature birth or intra-uterine growth retardation, as well as in the evaluation of earlier symptoms and signs. There is a great educational value for all concerned in such continued contact.

References

Abramson, H., ed. Resuscitation of the Newborn Infant. St. Louis, C. V. Mosby Co., 1960.

Desmond, M. M., Franklin, R. R., Blattner, R. J., and Hill, R. M. The relation of maternal disease to fetal and neonatal morbidity and mortality. Pediat. Clin. N. Amer., 8:421, 1961.

Drillien, C. M. The Growth and Development of the Prematurely Born Infant. Baltimore, The Williams & Wilkins Co., 1964.

Kaplan, D. M., and Mason, E. A. Maternal reactions to premature birth viewed as an acute emotional disorder. Amer. J. Orthopsychiat., 30:539, 1960.

Silverman, W. A. Dunham's Premature Infants, 3rd ed. New York, Paul B. Hoeber, Inc., 1961.

Feeding

MURRAY DAVIDSON

Low-birth-weight infants require nutrition at a time when their abilities to ingest, digest, and assimilate food may be limited. Although it is generally appreciated that they represent special problems in feeding, few specific questions have been entirely resolved.

Caloric Requirements. It is tempting to assume that the low-birth-weight infant has an increased "need" for growth and thus a higher caloric requirement than larger term infants. This is probably not so, however, since studies have shown the mammalian fetus to have an oxygen consumption in the same range as infants in the neonatal period (6 to 8 ml STP/kg/minute). Specific requirements for low-birth-weight infants may be approximated only indirectly, because we lack information on certain metabolic components and on the caloric needs of infants of the same birth-weight but different postconceptual ages. Observations on resting metabolism and caloric needs have been performed in normal term and in low-birth-weight infants by a number of workers with good general agreement. Measurements have also been made of additional caloric expenditures for physical activity and for losses incurred during feedings. However, allotments required for optimal continued growth are based only on assumptions, with the view of permitting resumption of the expected intrauterine rate of growth. Gordon et al. suggested an average *total* of 120 cal/kg/day. Measurements of gestational weights by Lubchenco et al. are somewhat higher than those used by earlier workers for their calculations and indicate that it may become necessary to revise caloric needs for growth upward. Current recommendations are not only based on the older, lower estimated growth requirements but they also provide smaller estimates for the first 10 to 14 days, on the assumption that physical activity and heat production are low at that time. This is especially true during the first 48 to 72 hours. Gordon measured resting metabolism in the initial 2 to 3 days of life at only 40 to 45 cal/kg/day in small infants and estimated that a total of approximately 50 cal/kg/day was sufficient for this age group. Recent concepts suggest that survival and ultimate well-being may be related to the speed with which an infant resumes his expected rate of intrauterine growth, and it is possible that greater allowances will be shown to be necessary in this early stage of life.

Fluid and Electrolyte Requirements. Particular attention must be given to the fluid and electrolyte requirements and to the volume and frequency of feedings of low-birth-weight infants because of (1) limitations in the volume of each feeding imposed by the functional delay in emptying the stomach, associated with lowered gastric acidity and increased mucus production and (2) the possibly increased metabolic requirements for growth of the infant. Levine and Gordon suggested daily water intakes of 130 to 150 ml/kg to maintain balance in these infants. Consideration of both the fluid and caloric requirements indicated the need to concentrate feeding mixtures beyond unmodified human or cow's milk; levels ranging between 0.8 to 1.1 cal/ml (24 to 34 cal/oz) have been tolerated and have yielded satisfactory growth. Higher concentrations may lead to dehydration, fever, anorexia, and gastrointestinal upsets.

It should be emphasized that all newborn infants handle the excretion of an excess water or solute load poorly. McCance showed some years ago that renal sodium clearance was only about one-fifth of the adult's, and maximum urine concentration was in the order of 400 to 500 mOsm/kg H_2O compared to about 1,400 mOsm/kg H_2O for thirsting adults. On the other hand, Ames documented the fact that even term newborn infants excrete intravenous or oral water loads poorly compared to older infants. Such observations emphasize the fact that the volumes and concentrations of feedings in the first days of life must be watched closely, since the margin of safety to the infant in handling excessive water or solute loads is limited. Some clinics begin with small volumes of feedings of approximately 0.5 cal/ml. However, limitations on volumes that can be tolerated and need for calories render this practice of dilution questionable. Whether this is advantageous to the infant is unclear. In addition, the work of Edelmann and Barnett indicates that early introduction of high osmolar concentration feedings may induce more rapid maturation of renal function. A convenient practical guideline combines Gordon's suggestion for total energy requirements of about 50 cal/kg/day for infants under 3 days of age with 0.8 cal/ml for all infants, to yield a net value of 60 to 65 ml/kg/day in the first few days of life.

Timing of Feeding. The disparity between the desirable amounts that should be fed and the volume that can be tolerated at each feeding by the small infant suggests that the frequency of feedings be increased. If intervals are too short, however, babies may utilize too much energy with excessive handling, and the time of skilled personnel may be used inefficiently. In most nurseries a three-hour schedule is used, though a number of institutions advocate feedings at two-hour intervals for the smallest infants. Prior to discharge, feedings are reduced to six or seven per day.

Timing of the first feeding is a subject of some controversy, due in part to a tendency to equate early feeding, either oral or gavage, with early *hydration.* Although the three-to-four-day fast once recommended has largely been eliminated, little agreement exists regarding how long the interval between birth and the initial oral feeding should be, mainly for lack of controlled studies and well-defined end points. Smallpiece and Davies reported that initiation of feedings of relatively large amounts of pooled mother's milk almost immediately after birth improved survival. Other authors indicate that early feedings may enhance glucose homeostasis and prevent neonatal symptomatic hypoglycemia. Wharton and Bowen examined this contention in a carefully controlled study and found increased mortality, mainly from aspiration, among infants receiving early feedings. In the preterm infants of 1,500 to 2,500 g birth weight the authors prefer a middle course of approximately 3 to 6 hours' delay before initiating feedings until more definitive data are available. Under certain circumstances—e.g., hypoglycemia, hyperbilirubinemia, or respiratory distress—either oral or parenteral administration of glucose solutions, with or without added electrolyte, may be desirable (Sec. 3.7).

Methods of Feeding. For the smallest infants (those below 1,650 g at birth) gavage feeding is safest at the outset owing to their limited ability to suck. Gavage feedings can be given as intermittent oral-gastric tube feedings. The chief advantage of this method is that a wide-caliber tube may be employed, allowing the milk to flow by gravity, while the major disadvantage is the requirement for experienced nursing at all hours. In other nurseries, indwelling nasogastric tubes are utilized. The major advantage of this method is convenience, since the tube may be passed by the physician and left in place for a period of four to five days before changing. Two disadvantages are reported. Tissue irritation from the indwelling tube is implicated in purulent rhinitis, otitis media, pharyngeal or esophageal erosions, and gastric perforations. This group of symptoms has been reported with decreasing frequency with improvements of materials and techniques in recent years. The second difficulty arises from the necessity to force milk through the narrower tubes utilized in this method. More mature (not necessarily larger) infants may

be fed with a bottle and special soft-rubber "premature" feeding nipples. Rubber-tipped medicine droppers are useful with small infants where gavage feeding is not possible. Breck feeders should never be used because of the danger of aspiration.

In a limited number of cases, gastrostomy for feeding has been performed in small infants with the intent of increasing efficacy in the introduction of larger volumes and greater safety from aspiration. This drastic procedure cannot be generally recommended. Its major use should be in infants who have undergone surgery for congenital defects and in whom feedings by mouth are impractical for extended periods. Similarly, implantations of catheters in the jugular veins for hyperalimentation, i.e., for intravenous feeding of adequate calories and nutriments to sustain positive nutritional balance and growth is occasionally life-saving among infants in whom extensive gastrointestinal resections have been carried out. However, both gastrostomy and intravenous hyperalimentation are associated with considerable morbidity in small infants and should be carried out only under conditions in which complications can be readily detected and corrected. These procedures should be reserved only for those patients in whom life could not be sustained by more traditional measures.

Minerals and Vitamins. The low-birth-weight preterm infant begins life with a total body deficit of many minerals that are stored mainly in the latter stages of gestation. Chief among these are iron, calcium, and phosphorus. Postnatal iron requirements and indications for supplementation are discussed elsewhere (Sec. 17.2). These infants are also born with diminished stores of fat-soluble vitamins, principally A and D. Supplements of 3,000 to 5,000 IU of vitamin A and 400 IU of vitamin D are started from the seventh day of life in most nurseries. There is special need for vitamin C in the diet of the prematurely born infant, since it activates the enzyme parahydroxyphenylpyruvate oxidase, necessary in the metabolic degradation pathway of tyrosine. Ascorbic acid is prescribed at 25 mg per day for the first week and 50 to 60 mg per day thereafter. Data are not available to indicate whether or not there is a need for B-complex supplementation of the diet of the low-birth-weight infant. In some clinics thiamine (vitamin B_1) is administered in doses approximating 1 mg daily, presumably because intermediate carbohydrate metabolism may be enhanced by this vitamin. On rare occasions infants may develop convulsions while receiving autoclaved formulas in which vitamin B_6 has been destroyed by heat.

Infants fed diets with high vegetable oil and unsaturated fatty acid content have lower serum vitamin E (tocopherol) levels than other infants. This may result in symptoms by accentuating effects of the low initial tissue stores and plasma levels among prematurely born infants. Red cells of low-birth-weight infants and of individuals with G6PD deficiency are susceptible to in vitro hemolysis in the presence of peroxide, a reaction preventable by addition of the antioxidant vitamin E to the in vitro system or by raising blood levels. In addition to clinically apparent hemolytic anemia, widespread edema has been attributed to deficiency of serum vitamin E levels in premature infants. However, there is not sufficient evidence of morbidity due to E deficiency to warrant a recommendation of routine vitamin E supplementation to all premature infants.

Protein. Immature infants are able to digest milk protein without difficulty. They have the capacity to absorb and retain nitrogen over a wide range of intake of human or cow's milk protein. Levine advised that small premature infants receive a daily allowance of 6.0 g per kilogram of body weight between 7 and 28 days of life with allowance of 4.4 to 5.0 g per kilogram for infants above 2,000 grams birth-weight in the same period. Other authors have been concerned about added electrolyte loads imposed on the kidneys with high-protein feedings, although the effect of protein intake on renal water requirements may be much less than thought previously. Small premature infants tend to develop uncompensated metabolic acidosis during the period between three days and three weeks of age, which Ranløv and Siggaard-Andersen have associated with feedings of more than 5.0 g protein/-kg/day. Though generally unaccompanied by clinical symptoms, the acidosis may be associated with slower weight gains. Others have demonstrated elevated blood levels of phenylalanine and tyrosine in prematurely born infants, raising the question of possible handicaps on brain development imposed by the increased aminoacidemia of high-protein feedings. The questions will remain unresolved until there is agreement on the yardsticks by which adequate or optimal nutritional allowances are to be judged. The authors advocate feeding 4.0 g of protein per kilogram per day for all prematurely born infants, until they reach 2,300 to 2,500 g.

Fat. Low-birth-weight infants have a decreased ability to absorb cow's milk fat. One approach widely used consists of partial skimming of cow's milk in preparing formulas for these infants. However, substitution of unsaturated fatty acid fats such as corn oil improves the absorptive ability and permits feeding a concentrated source of calories in the high-calorie mixtures for preterm infants.

Substitution of triglycerides made from fatty acids with chain lengths of 8 to 12 carbons (medium chain triglycerides) results in initially quantitative absorption, probably by direct entrance into the portal circulation. However, this fat source cannot currently be recommended for routine use. Sufficient clinical experience has not been accumulated with its prolonged administration as the sole fat source to a large number of low-birth-weight infants. It could potentially induce deficiency of essential fatty acids, and earlier experimental work has indicated that it might prove harmful when employed as an exclusive fat source in animals.

Carbohydrate. All newborn babies are able to digest and absorb carbohydrate extremely well. Except for suggestions from experimental and developmental observations that immature infants may have difficulty with lactose digestion or galactose metabolism, the general experience is that milk sugar, sucrose, and dextrin-maltose mixtures may be offered within wide limits without concern.

SPECIFIC RECOMMENDED REGIMEN. Infants are started on feedings of clear fluids (usually 5 percent dextrose in water) at three to six hours and are offered two feedings three hours apart in accordance with the following schedule of volumes:

Birth Weight (Grams)	ml/Feeding
less than 1,000	4–6
1,000–1,499	6–8
1,500–1,999	8–15
2,000–2,500	15–20

Attempts at early initiation of oral feedings with these small volumes are recommended for all infants, often with surprisingly good tolerance by the tiny but vigorous infant. However, the regimen must be modified for depressed babies, for those who suffer severe respiratory distress or from the effects of a traumatic delivery, and for those who are extremely immature. Among such infants three separate aspects of early "feeding" must be considered:

1. Hydration. Fluid requirements imposed by the initial catabolic state and the need to excrete prenatally accumulated solutes, rapidly induce water deficits in the small infant whose demands cannot be met by oral intake. Despite limited ability to handle excessive water loads, a salutary effect results from intravenous administration of 60 to 80 ml per kilogram per day of 10 percent D/W, frequently begun within the first hour or two after birth.

2. Serum Glucose and Acid-Base Levels. Among small infants who are in a precarious state during the first 48 to 72 hours of life, intravenous fluids may be necessary to treat hypoglycemia or metabolic acidosis. The composition of part or all of the 60 to 80 ml per kilogram per day of the 10 percent D/W solution should be modified in these circumstances in accordance with the recommendations discussed elsewhere in this chapter.

3. Calories and Nutriments. These may be supplied only in oral feedings of milk preparations. Provided hydration is maintained intravenously, initiation of the schedule outlined above may be delayed for 12 to 24 hours in some infants of the lowest birth weights, and in those who are severely ill. Among such babies earlier success is likely, when oral feedings are begun, if the smaller caliber indwelling nasogastric tube is routinely used in preference to intermittent gavage with larger caliber catheters. Repeated

insertions of the latter are more likely to stretch the esophagus and to stimulate vagal reflexes which may induce cardiac arrhythmias and apneic spells. It is often useful in very small or sickly infants to continue intravenous hydration for a number of days after oral feedings have been begun to insure adequate fluid intake. This is especially advisable in those infants in whom questions of tolerance of the recommended volumes may be raised, or among those in whom hemoconcentration is particularly undesirable, e.g., in infants with hyperbilirubinemia.

For larger and more vigorous infants who have no difficulty with the suggested early feeding scheme and among those who start more slowly, once the recommended initial feedings of a clear solution have been tolerated, 3-hourly feedings of a standard formula offering 120 calories, 4.0 g cow's milk protein, 5.2 g corn oil fat, and 14.5 g carbohydrate per 150 ml are started at the same volumes as have been fed during the first trials. This standard formula is increased daily or every other day by 1 or 2 ml per feeding, in accordance with the reports by nurses of the infant's ability to take more, until the infant reaches a total of 150 to 160 ml/kg/day. This period is usually 5 to 8 days for the largest infants and 10 to 14 days for those under 1,000 g birth weight. Once attained, formulas are usually kept in the range of 150 to 160 ml/kg/day to keep pace with weight gain, although each infant's management must be individualized.

REFERENCES

Ames, R. G. Urinary water excretion and neurohypophysial function in full term and premature infants shortly after birth. Pediatrics, 12:272, 1953.

Cox, W. M., and Filer, L. J. Protein intake for low-birth-weight infants. J. Pediat., 74:1016, 1969.

Davidson, M. The feeding of prematurely born infants—a critique of current status. J. Pediat., 57:604, 1960.

——— and Bauer, C. H. Patterns of fat excretion in feces of premature infants fed various preparations of milk. Pediatrics, 25:375, 1960.

——— Levine, S. Z., Bauer, C. H., and Dann, M. Feeding studies in low-birth-weight infants. I. Relationships of dietary protein, fat and electrolyte to rates of weight gain, clinical courses, and serum chemical concentrations. J. Pediat., 70:695, 1967.

Edelmann, C. M., Jr., and Barnett, H. L. Role of the kidney in water metabolism in young infants, physiologic and clinical considerations. J. Pediat., 56:154, 1960.

Gordon, H. H. Protein requirements of premature infants. J.A.M.A., 175:107, 1961.

——— Levine, S. Z., Deamer, W. C., and McNamara, H. Respiratory metabolism in infancy and childhood. Amer. J. Dis. Child., 59:1185, 1940.

Holt, L. E., Jr. Role of carbohydrates in infant feeding. Advances Carbohyd. Chem., 12:104, 1955.

——— Tidwell, H. C., Kirk, C. M., Cross, D. M., and Neale, S. Studies of fat metabolism: I. Fat absorption in normal infants. J. Pediat., 6:427, 1935.

Kretchmer, N., Levine, S. Z., McNamara, H., and Barnett, H. L. Certain aspects of tyrosine oxidizing system in human liver. J. Clin. Invest., 35:236, 1956.

Levine, S. Z. Protein nutrition in pediatrics. J.A.M.A., 128:283, 1945.

——— and Gordon, H. H. Physiologic handicaps of the premature infant: II. Clinical applications. Amer. J. Dis. Child., 64:297, 1942.

Lubchenco, L. O., Hansman, C., Dressler, M., and Boyd, E. Intrauterine growth as estimated from liveborn birth-weight data at 24 and 42 weeks of gestation. Pediatrics, 32:793, 1963.

Menkes, J. H., and Avery, M. E. The metabolism of phenylalanine and tyrosine in the premature infant. Bull. Hopkins Hosp., 113:301, 1963.

Ranløv, P., and Siggaard-Andersen, O. Late metabolic acidosis in premature infants. Prevalence and significance. Acta Paediat. Scand., 54:531, 1965.

Ritchie, J. H., Fish, M. B., McMasters, V., and Grossman, M. Edema and hemolytic anemia in premature infants. A vitamin E deficiency syndrome. New Eng. J. Med., 279:1185, 1968.

Smallpiece, V., and Davies, P. A. Immediate feeding of premature infants with undiluted breast milk. Lancet, 2:1349, 1964.

Smith, C. A., Yudkin, S., Young, W., Minkowski, A., and Cushman, M. Adjustment of electrolytes and water following premature birth (with special reference to edema). Pediatrics, 3:34, 1949.

Outcome

LULA O. LUBCHENCO

The outcome of the low-birth-weight infant depends on many factors, some of which are given below. The list is far from complete and the contribution of each of these items to long-term growth and development has not been settled. The relationship between birth weight and outcome has been best studied for obvious reasons. The smaller the infant the greater the chances of dying in the neonatal period and of having significant handicaps if he survives. Similarly, the shorter the gestational age the higher the mortality and long-term morbidity. Outcome is influenced by a number of maternal factors. The age and parity of the mother, her previous obstetrical record, and relative infertility all influence pregnancy outcome (see section on obstetrical management of the mother and fetus). Many of these are factors which act on the infant throughout pregnancy. Others are events which occur around labor and delivery (see section on labor, delivery, and the beginning of independent life). In addition, total outcome must be considered in terms of both mortality and morbidity, since one can expect that with better neonatal care and a lower neonatal mortality rate, the incidence of handicaps in surviving infants may rise. Since so many pre- and postnatal factors potentially can affect outcome, only a few factors whose roles have been most clearly defined will be examined. Early or neonatal outcome will be distinguished from later outcome.

EARLY OUTCOME (NEONATAL). Not surprisingly, there is evidence to show that neonatal mortality rates and later morbidity rates are associated with the same clinical groups. In groups where a high neonatal mortality rate exists, surviving infants are more likely to have residual handicaps, so that mortality rates do reflect to some extent later morbidity.

Neonatal Mortality. Infant mortality rates for the United States since 1930 have shown a downward trend, falling by approximately 5 percent per year. This has slowed considerably since 1950

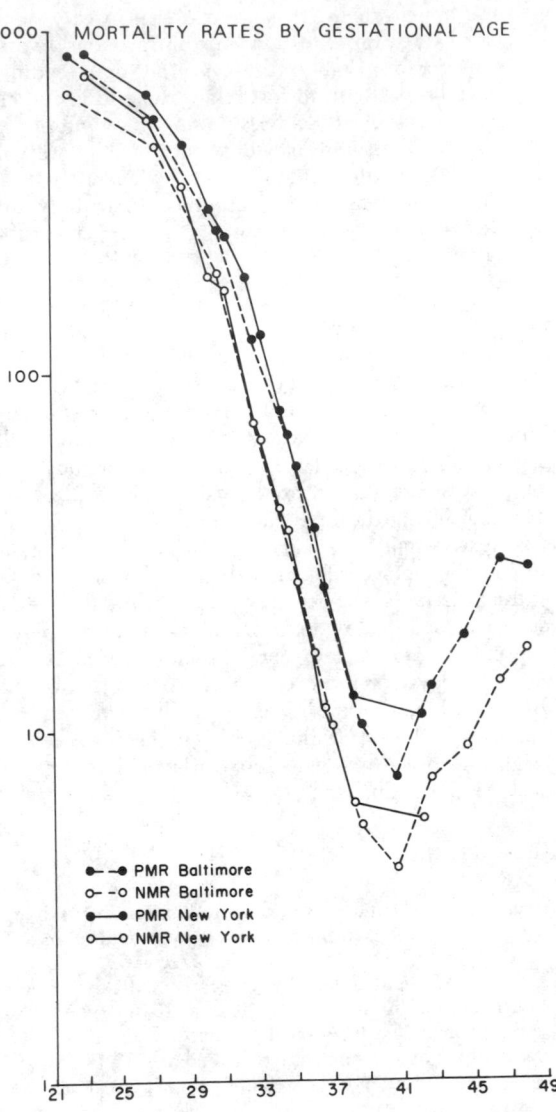

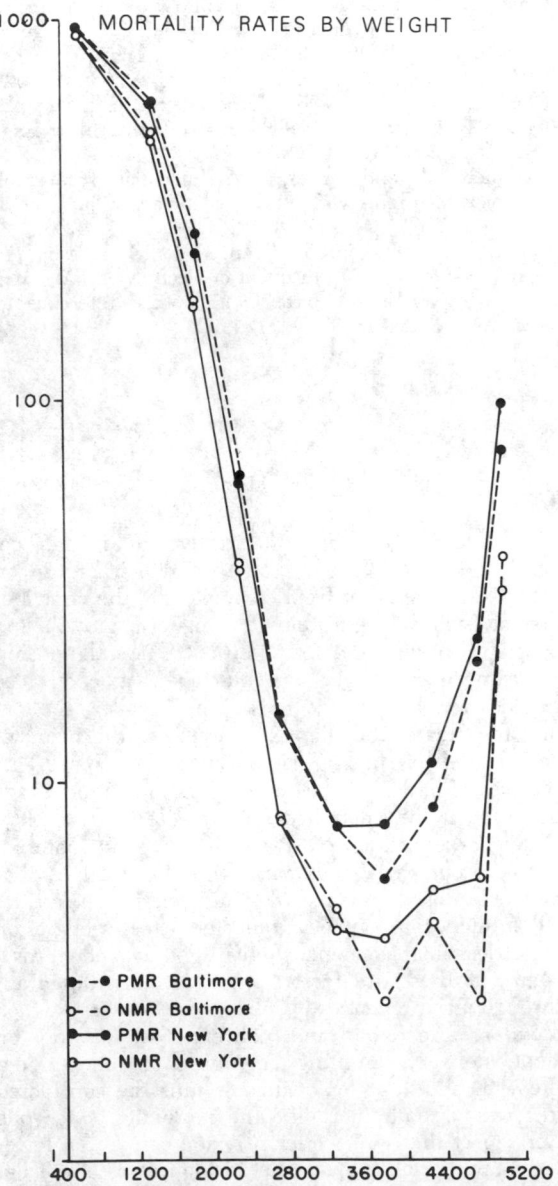

Fig. 73. Neonatal and perinatal mortality rates decrease abruptly as birth weight increases to 3,600 g. As birth weight increases above 4,000 g the death rate again rises.

Fig. 74. Neonatal and perinatal mortality rates decrease with each additional week of gestation in much the same manner as occurs with birth weight, Figure 73. There is also an increased death rate with gestations prolonged over 42 weeks.

(1 percent per year). The least improvement has occurred in deaths during the day of birth, in non-white populations, and in the low-birth-weight category. Perinatal mortality varies greatly in different parts of the country, from state to state, and from hospital to hospital. For example, some of the southern states had a perinatal mortality rate of 40 per 1,000 births, which contrasts with a 30 per 1,000 rate in New England. The white and nonwhite difference for the nation was 31 versus 52. These differences should not be interpreted as necessarily reflecting differences in the level of care,

since many other pre- and postnatal factors which affect outcome, such as parity and maternal age, may vary markedly from one population group to another.

Birth weight. The 1960 incidence of births in the low-birth-weight category (2,500 g or less) in the United States was 7.7 percent. These 7.7 percent of infants account for two-thirds of the infant deaths. The relationship between birth weight or gestational age and mortality can be seen in Figures 73 and 74.

Gestational age. The perinatal and neonatal mortality rates plotted against gestational age or birth weight are U-shaped; that is, there is an optimal birth weight and gestational age above which the mortality rate again increases. There are many such bits of data which emphasize that "the bigger the better" certainly does not apply to optimal growth and development. In general, perinatal mortality decreases approximately 50 percent for every two weeks' increase in gestational age up to 38 weeks; hence the rationale for the search in obstetrics for methods of prolonging pregnancy where premature onset of labor is threatened.

Mortality by birth weight and gestational age. From the data in Figures 73 and 74, it would appear that either birth weight or gestational age could serve to predict mortality rates; however, a better delineation of high-risk groups is obtained by considering both birth weight and gestational age, as Figure 75 shows. For any given weight group, the mortality rate improves as gestational age increases, and for any given gestational age, the mortality rate improves as the infant's weight increases to approximatey 4,000 g. The better survival rate of the small-for-gestational-age (SGA) infant, compared with a preterm infant of the same size, is impressive and holds true for infants with birth weights as low as 1,000 to 1,500 g.

Other factors. Birth weight and gestational age both reflect maturity to some extent. The reason for a higher mortality rate in association with other factors is not quite so clear. The nonwhite population and lower socioeconomic class are often combined; hence data supporting the role of one factor over the other in contributing to an increased mortality rate is difficult to obtain.

The male infant has a higher mortality rate than the female at almost every weight level. Neonatal mortality rates for females at weights between 1,001 and 4,000 g are one-half to three-fourths of those for males. The rate becomes lower for males only in the highest weight group (4,501 g or more). In some studies male survivors also have a higher handicap rate. Since male babies are heavier than female babies, some factor or factors other than birth weight and gestational age must be involved in the increased mortality of males.

Multiple births, on the other hand, result in a higher overall mortality rate, but in any given weight group they have a lower death rate than singletons. Some degree of intrauterine growth retardation results in more mature babies for their weights, and these babies have a better chance of survival than infants with a shorter gestation period (see below). Because so many twins are both small and preterm, the total result is a higher mortality rate.

Other factors related to neonatal mortality can be seen in Table 18.

Neonatal Morbidity. Neonatal morbidity tends to be highest in those infant groups where neonatal mortality rate is highest. Thus, one can expect

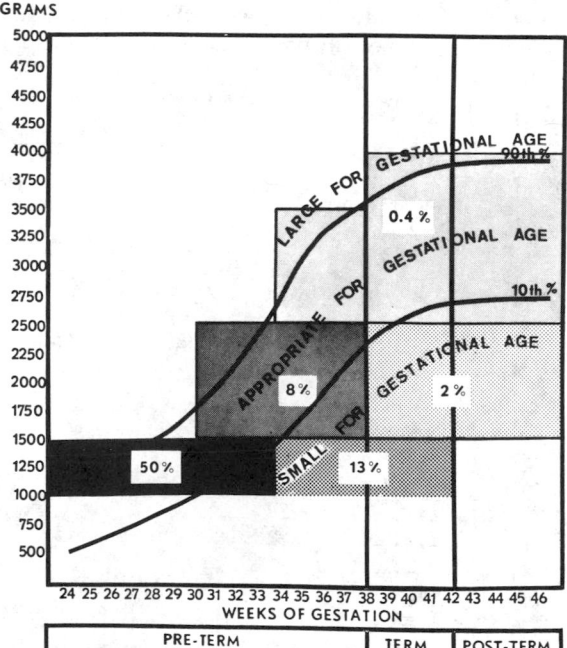

Fig. 75. Neonatal mortality rates per 100 by birth weight-gestational age blocks reveal the improved mortality for any given weight group as gestational age advances and likewise the improved mortality for any given gestational age as birth weight increases. The higher mortality in infants with birth weights over 4,000 g is also apparent. (Colorado General Hospital: 7/1/58–6/30/68.)

TABLE 18. *Perinatal Factors Contributing to Neonatal Mortality*

(listed in order of significance)

Birth Weight
Gestational Age
Previous Neonatal Death
Poor Condition of Infant at Delivery
  (1 minute Apgar score, 0-4; Endotracheal aspiration—positive pressure resuscitation)
Advanced Maternal Age
Maternal Toxemia
Previous fetal deaths (more than 2)
Fetal distress and 1 minute Apgar of 5-7

TABLE 19. *Neonatal Morbidity*

Preterm	Term
Appropriate for Gestational Age	Small for Gestational Age
Respiratory distress (Hyaline membrane)	Fetal distress leading to CNS depression
Nonhemolytic hyperbilirubinemia	Meconium aspiration
Neonatal infection	Hypoglycemia
Poor temperature control	Congenital anomalies
Poor feeding and prolonged weight loss	Chronic intrauterine infection
Bleeding (including intracranial)	Pulmonary hemorrhage
Anemia	Polycythemia
Apnea and cardiac arrhythmias	
Late metabolic acidosis	

morbidity to be related to birth weight and gestational age. In addition, certain maternal and fetal abnormalities may add additional risks to the chance of illness in the infant.

Information concerning the overall incidence of morbidity in low-birth-weight infants is of value in itself, but knowledge of the specific illness to be expected in a particular group of infants is of even more practical value. Some data are available which distinguish between the illnesses occurring in preterm infants and the illnesses likely to be seen in small, undergrown, but relatively mature infants.

In general, the preterm infant is subject to a variety of conditions reflecting immaturity of organ function. The intrauterine-growth-retarded infant has, among other problems, inadequate glycogen stores due to fetal undernutrition, which leaves him in a precarious position in maintaining a normal glucose level in his blood immediately after birth. He also is more likely to be small because of inherent disease in the fetus himself, e.g., congenital malformation or chronic infection. Table 19 outlines some of the more common management problems of preterm versus SGA infants.

LATE OUTCOME. *Mortality.* Even after the first postnatal year, there is a higher mortality in low-birth-weight infants than in infants with birth weights over 2,500 g. The cause of this increased mortality is difficult to evaluate. Some of it is due to infection and some to deaths associated with congenital anomalies and chronic infections acquired in utero.

The quantitative differences in later mortality between preterm infants and those who were small-for-gestational age have not been adequately determined; however, there are some data to suggest that preterm infants are more likely to succumb to acute infections, while the small-for-gestational age infants die from chronic intrauterine infections and complications of congenital anomalies.

Later Morbidity in Low-Birth-Weight Infants. In general, long-term sequelae in low-birth-weight infants can be related to birth weight and gestational age. Both factors are important, and the overall influence of each can be seen in Figure 76.

These data are limited to very small infants at birth, all of whom were preterm and only a few of

whom were small for gestational age in addition to being preterm. Follow-up studies on the larger birth weight groups indicate that the small-for-gestational-age infant has as high an incidence of handicaps as the preterm infant when birth weight groups are kept constant. These data include handicaps associated with congenital disease.

The long-term outlook probably should include neonatal mortality to reflect properly the total perspective necessary in dealing with problems of low birth weight. The SGA infant, with a lower neonatal mortality rate than the preterm infant, would then have a lower mortality-morbidity rate.

Environmental conditions assume a large role in determining later outcome. Socioeconomic status, illnesses and medical care, type of mothering and training, are especially important when the child is

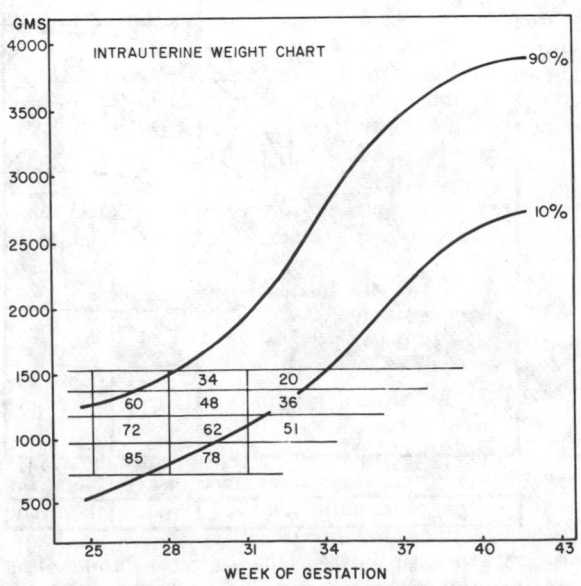

PERCENT INCIDENCE OF HANDICAP BY BIRTH WEIGHT AND GESTATIONAL AGE

Fig. 76. Percent of moderate to severe handicaps found in a sample of surviving infants with birth weights of 1,500 g or less. The outlook for normal development improves with birth weight for a given gestational age and similarly improves with advancing gestational age in any birth weight group. (From Lubchenco. *J. Pediat.,* in press.)

neurologically handicapped. A poor environment for such a child prevents him from attaining his full, though limited, potential.

The relationships between the mother's obstetrical history, the condition of the infant at birth, abnormal neurologic signs during the neonatal period, and later outcome of the infant are most important to know. Some available data relate a low Apgar score to neonatal mortality and morbidity. There is a strong association between low scores and low birth weight; however, in all birth weight groups only the low 5-minute score is predictive of later neurologic morbidity. The neurologic exam of the infant during the early days after delivery is also useful in predicting later outcome. If the signs which indicate normal neurologic maturity in the preterm infant are separated from the signs of neurologic damage, the neurologic examination is then useful in predicting later outcome. However, in careful longitudinal studies it has been observed that the early abnormal findings often decrease or disappear after the first year of life. Whether or not these infants will manifest evidence of minimal cerebral dysfunction or learning problems later remains to be documented.

The quality of postnatal care the infant receives must be important in later outcome, although the documentation of the value of special nurseries has been complicated by iatrogenic tragedies (retrolental fibroplasia, kernicterus, etc.). Reports from newborn centers on the later outcome of their populations vary greatly from one nursery to another and from year to year within the same nursery. Representative data on incidence of handicaps by birth weight can be seen in Figure 76.

SPECIFIC HANDICAPS FOUND IN PRETERM VERSUS SGA INFANTS. *Congenital Abnormalities.* Infants delivered before term may have congenital defects, and the incidence is somewhat higher than that found in the general newborn population. However, the incidence is much less than that found in SGA infants. When the fetus itself is abnormal, growth failure in utero is likely to occur. Infants with some syndromes are much more seriously affected than others. For example, infants who have Trisomy 16-18 are extremely small for their period of gestation, which also happens to be prolonged. Intrauterine growth retardation is associated with Seikel's syndrome (bird-headed dwarfism) and is almost invariable in Silver's syndrome. Infants who have osteogenesis imperfecta are both SGA and preterm. Twenty-five percent of newborn infants with Down's syndrome are classed as low birth weight, but the majority are full term and have an appropriate weight for their gestational age.

A few congenital defects result in infants who are large for gestational age; Beckwith's syndrome is one. Newborns with transposition of the great vessels tend to be above average in size, as do infants of diabetic mothers.

The later outcome of infants with congenital defects depends on the specific etiology, but in general there is a high infant mortality rate and a high incidence of mental retardation.

Chronic Antenatal Infection. Maternal syphilis generally leads to the preterm delivery of an infected infant. In other maternal antenatal infections pregnancy usually progresses to term, but the infant may have congenital defects and, occasionally, evidence of persistent acute infection. Maternal rubella acquired in the first trimester of pregnancy, toxoplasmosis, and cytomegalic inclusion disease are the best known of these infections. A disproportionate degree of intrauterine growth retardation in weight compared to length gives the infant a wasted appearance at birth. If encephalomyelitis accompanies the infection, head growth is discrepantly small; hence, these infants are predominantly SGA infants and constitute a special group in determining later outcome. Approximately 50 percent of infants with the extended rubella syndrome are neurologically damaged; the incidence of handicap in cytomegalic inclusion disease or toxoplasmosis is probably higher.

Intellectual Development. There is a significant incidence of decreased intellectual functioning in both SGA and preterm infants. A few cautious assumptions may be made regarding the difference in etiology of the mental retardation in the two categories. The preterm infant may have obvious signs of organic brain damage such as spastic diplegia, microcephaly, and EEG abnormalities in addition to mental retardation. In the SGA infants congenital anomalies and antenatal infections account for some, if not most, of the mental retardation. A likely cause of brain damage in the SGA infant who does not have evidence of congenital defect or infection is hypoglycemia, but the significance of this postnatal metabolic abnormality is not entirely clear. It has been suggested, but not documented, that hypoglycemia may be related to the learning difficulties seen in so many low-birth-weight infants at school age.

Neurologic Sequelae. Spastic diplegia appears to be a common neurologic sequel of very low-birth-weight preterm infants; about one-third of preterm infants with birth weights under 1,500 g are so affected. The neurologic findings are often accompanied by mental retardation and EEG abnormalities.

Not only do premature infants of low birth weight have a high incidence of mental retardation, they also have a high incidence of other neurologic deficits. The incidence of reported neurologic sequelae ranges from "very few" to as high as 50 percent in infants with birth weights of less than 1,500 g.

The neurologic findings peculiar to the low-birth-weight infant are spastic diplegia, microcephaly, and convulsions. There is a high incidence of electroencephalographic abnormalities. These findings, plus mental retardation and specific learning defects, are interpreted as brain damage. Neurologic abnormalities, including mild cases of spastic diplegia, occur in about one-third of the very low-birth-weight children (birth weights of 1,500 g or less). The clinical characteristics of spastic diplegia in the premature are classical. The children are slow to sit and stand, and walking is usually delayed until 18 months to 2 years. They are sometimes "stiff" babies. Once they begin to walk, they are clumsy, walk on their toes, stumble, and fall a great deal. As they become mobile, their motor control improves and many are taught to be normal by school age. However, these youngsters usually do not like gymnastics, dancing, or competitive sports. Physical examination reveals hyperactive reflexes, tight muscles with selective weakness mainly in the lower extremities. There is very little involvement in the upper extremities and shoulder girdle. Heel-cord shortening and pes cavus occasionally accompany the other signs. Athetosis is rare.

Children with the most severe form of mental retardation often show microcephaly; the size of the head is small both in actual measurement and in relation to other body proportions.

Minimal cerebral dysfunction is associated with low birth weight, but whether it occurs predominantly in the larger preterm infant or the SGA infant has not been clarified. The specific neurologic findings associated with birth defects and clinical syndromes mentioned earlier are to be found predominantly in SGA infants.

Encephalographic patterns show a variety of abnormalities in low-birth-weight infants. The incidence of abnormal EEG's is high, about 60 percent, in very low-birth-weight infants. Disorganization of the record, focal spikes, and seizure discharges are the most frequent findings. Six and 14 per second spikes are more common in children with normal intelligence.

Few children with EEG evidence of seizure patterns have clinical evidence of convulsions. SGA infants have as high an incidence of EEG abnormalities as do preterm infants, but specific patterns related to etiology have not yet been defined.

Vision and Hearing. Retrolental fibroplasia is a disease of prematurity. It rarely, if ever, occurs in the term infant. Although blindness from RLF is infrequent today, it nonetheless remains a constant threat to the preterm infant who has frequent attacks of apnea and who is treated with supplemental oxygen. Other eye disorders, especially myopia and convergent strabismus, are frequent in the preterm infant. SGA infants, except those with eye defects associated with congenital disease, are more likely to have normal eyes.

Hearing losses due to nerve damage are frequent in the low-birth-weight infant. Preterm infants are more likely to have anoxic nerve damage at birth and kernicterus, while SGA infants are more likely to have hearing losses due to maternal rubella.

Physical Growth. The majority of children of very low birth weight remain relatively small throughout their childhood years. One large survey showed that the average stature of low-birth-weight infants is less than that of the general population in adult years.

There appears to be a relationship between the pattern of intrauterine growth and later size. The preterm infant who is appropriate in weight for his gestational age is more likely to attain normal height and weight than the SGA infant. However, if the preterm infant incurs severe brain damage he does not grow well. The mechanism for growth failure in central nervous system damage is not understood.

Some SGA infants are simply well proportioned small infants. The congenitally handicapped group of SGA infants, like the preterm CNS-damaged infants, do not grow well. The SGA infant without congenital anomalies will grow postnatally according to the degree of undernutrition he experiences prior to birth. If weight alone is retarded he is likely to be a normal-sized individual. If height as well as weight is retarded at birth he is most likely to be short but have normal head size. However, when weight, height, and head circumference are all small at birth the child tends to remain small in these parameters throughout the childhood years.

Some SGA infants as toddlers are so small that diagnosis of dwarfism or postnatal failure-to-thrive is entertained. Occasionally they are considered microcephalic, based on actual head size. The SGA child who has a small head which is proportional to weight and height is frequently normal neurologically and intellectually.

Emotional Development. The events surrounding the birth of a premature infant to an unprepared family are sufficient to disturb a normal mother-child relationship and contribute to the development of emotional problems in the child. The mother who gives birth to such a child is understandably anxious about his survival, then concerned about the possibility of handicapping conditions later. Often, she is immediately separated from her child and usually feels inadequate to care for him. Later on, there is a natural tendency of the parents to overprotect him. The response of the mother to this situation is not specific for premature birth; it may occur with sick full-term babies, but prematurity contributes a large share of the sick children. Personnel in some nurseries recognize these emotional reactions, and the attention paid to the prevention or modification of the mothers' anxieties may well influence the behavior problems noted in the children later on.

Another frequent cause for emotional disturbance in a family, and also in the child, is the presence of a handicapping condition. The condition may be serious and appear early. It may add a financial burden to a family barely able to cope with ordinary expenses; or the parents may be unable to accept their child's deficiencies. The handicap may not be obvious until school age. When hearing losses are present, the child himself may become frustrated, easily distracted, or unruly in behavior. Unsuspected spastic diplegia or learning difficulties may result in undue school or family pressures to urge the child to perform beyond his ability. The incidence of behavior problems may vary with the type of handling, social class, family stress, obstetric complications, birth weight, sex, and degree of neurologic problems.

Iatrogenic Persistent Handicaps. Since the outcome of low-birth-weight infants is in part dependent on nursery procedures, the following hazards to normal outcome need to be mentioned: Whenever supplemental O_2 is being given in high concentrations the threat of retrolental fibroplasia is present even though arterial oxygen is being measured; the need to know the safe upper limit of oxygen tension in arterial blood is essential. Antimicrobial drugs continue to present a therapeutic dilemma; their need for combatting infection must be balanced against their potential for causing irreparable damage such as hearing losses, the grey syndrome, kernicterus, and possibly others not presently recognized. Umbilical vein or artery catheterization can result in various complications, ranging from portal vein obstruction and gangrene of an extremity secondary to embolic or thrombotic complications, to bacteremia. Sciatic nerve palsy has followed intramuscular injections into the buttocks of premature infants, and osteomyelitis of the hip may occur as a result of femoral vein puncture.

REFERENCES

Alm, I. The long term prognosis for prematurely born children. Acta Paediat., 42: Suppl. 94, 1953.

Amiel-Tison, C. Cerebral damage in full-term new-born. Aetiological factors, neonatal status and long-term follow-up. Biol. Neonat., 14:234, 1969.

Babson, S. G., et al. Growth and development of twins of dissimilar size at birth. Pediatrics, 33:327, 1964.

Burns, L. E., Hodgman, J. E., and Cass, A. B. Fatal circulatory collapse in premature infants receiving chloramphenicol. New Eng. J. Med., 261:1318, 1959.

Cochran, W. D., Davis, H. T., and Smith, C. A. Advantages and complications of umbilical artery catheterization in the newborn. Pediatrics, 42:769, 1968.

Coombs, J. T., et al. New syndrome of neonatal hypoglycemia: association with visceromegaly. New Eng. J. Med., 275:236, 1966.

Cornblath, M., Odell, G. B., and Levin, E. Y. Symptomatic neonatal hypoglycemia associated with toxemia of pregnancy. J. Pediat., 55:545, 1959.

——— et al. Symptomatic neonatal hypoglycemia: Studies of carbohydrate metabolism in the newborn infant. VIII. Pediatrics, 33:388, 1964.

Dann, M., Levine, S. Z., and New, E. The development of prematurely born children with birth weights or minimal postnatal weights of 1000 grams or less. Pediatrics, 22:1037, 1958.

Desmond, M. M., et al. Congenital rubella encephalitis. J. Pediat., 71:311, 1967.

Drillien, C. M. The Growth and Development of the Prematurely Born Infant. Baltimore, Maryland, The Williams & Wilkins Co., 1964.

——— Causes of Handicap in the Low Weight Infant. Aspects of Prematurity and Dysmaturity, Second Nutricia Symposium, H. E. Stenfert Kroese, N. V., Leiden, Holland, 1967. Springfield, Ill., Charles C Thomas, Publisher.

Gesell, A. The neonatal growth of prematurely born infants. J. Pediat., 2:676, 1933.

Hess, J. H., Mohr, G. J., and Bartelme, P. F. The Physical and Mental Growth of Prematurely Born Children. Chicago, University of Chicago Press, 1934.

Knoblock, H., and Pasamanick, B. Prematurity and development. J. Obstet. Gynaec. Brit. Comm., 66:729, 1959.

——— et al. Neuropsychiatric sequelae of prematurity. J.A.M.A., 161:581, 1956.

Lubchenco, L. O. Assessment of gestational age and development at birth. Pediat. Clin. N. Amer., 17:125, 1970.

——— et al. Sequelae of premature birth. Amer. J. Dis. Child., 106:101, 1963.

Shirley, M. Development of immature babies during their first two years. Child Develop., 9:347, 1938.

Silverman, W. A. Dunham's Premature Infants, 3rd ed. New York, Paul B. Hoeber, Inc., 1961.

U.S. Dept. of Health, Education and Welfare. Infant and Perinatal Mortality in the United States. Washington, D.C., National Center for Health Statistics, Series 3, No. 4, 1965.

Warkany, J., Monroe, B. B., and Sutherland, B. S. Intrauterine growth retardation. Amer. J. Dis. Child., 102:127, 1961.

Wiener, G. The relationship of birth weight and length of gestation to intellectual development at ages 8 to 10 years. J. Pediat., 76:694, 1970.

2.12
MULTIPLE BIRTHS

KURT BENIRSCHKE

Antenatal Considerations

Twinning is relatively frequent in Western populations, occurring in approximately 1 in 80 pregnancies, and it is associated with a variety of specific disturbances which concern the pediatrician. The occurrence of triplets and higher numbers of multiple births is much less common. For this reason and because conditions of prenatal and natal circumstances are much the same as in twins, only twins will be considered in this section. Twin pregnancies have many hazards, and newborn twins have a much higher mortality than singletons, in part because of their frequently premature delivery. Since some of the hazards are not shared equally by the two groups of twins—the fraternal and identical sets—it is pertinent to review the classification of twins and give reasons for this differential mortality.

CLASSIFICATION. Broadly speaking, one differentiates between identical (monovular, monozygous, MZ) and fraternal (biovular, dizygous, DZ) twins.

The former are derived from the "splitting" of the fertilized egg at early stages of development, usually into equal halves; the latter arises because of the simultaneous ovulation (and fertilization) of two ova. There is good evidence that the faculty of multiple ovulation, and therefore the tendency to fraternal twin births, is variable in ethnic groups, is dependent on inheritance, and increases with maternal age. It is least common in the Asiatic population and most prevalent in Negroes. Familial twinning is usually fraternal, and recent evidence indicates that it is related to the pituitary FSH levels of women. Thus, the clinical use of human FSH in the treatment of oligomenorrheic women has led to multiple births on the basis of multiple ovulation.

On the other hand, monovular twinning apparently occurs at random throughout all populations. Consequently, the variation in the incidence of twins in various geographic areas and, for that matter, in the collected series making up various twin studies, is a reflection of the frequency of fraternal twins. If in Asiatic countries only one set of twins results from 150 pregnancies, this indicates that absolutely fewer fraternal twins but relatively more identical twins are produced. As we will see, these considerations are of importance, since the prognosis of the two groups of twins differs appreciably.

The term "monozygous" twins is preferred over the common usage of "identical" for a variety of reasons. Theoretically, not only are these twins always of the same sex but also they have an identical genetic background; in practice this is almost universally the case. However, numerous reports have indicated that their development may differ appreciably at times. Indeed, numerous MZ twins with discordant severe congenital anomalies have been found. Moreover, in view of the frequency of genetically mosaic individuals now discovered, it is logical to suspect that mitotic aberrations occurring during early development and taking place around the time of "splitting" may lead to genetically dissimilar "identical" twins. This contradiction in terms is avoided when "monozygous" is used instead of "identical." Several such genetically discordant MZ twins have now been found, and some have even had different external genitalia (XY and XO).

Fraternal twins may be of the same sex or of different sexes. Genetically speaking, they are siblings and only incidentally share the same uterine environment. Inasmuch as fertilization can be construed as a random event, one would expect in a population of twins 50 male-female, 25 female-female, 25 male-male pairs, if all were fraternal twins. This distribution is not found in newborn twin studies; there are more like-sexed twins than would be expected from this assumption. The excess of like-sexed twins is considered to be the number of MZ twins in a population, and this calculation is the basis of the Weinberg * rule. This gives an estimate in a population, but what about the individual set of twins? How can one make an accurate diagnosis of zygosity? Parents often are anxious to know the answer.

This is a complex problem and it is not easily answered in every case. However, a few simple observations are of considerable help; they must be made at the time of birth and the results must find their way into the patients' records. One may rely chiefly on three findings: (1) The *sex* of the twins. If they are of different sex and normally developed, then fraternal twins can be diagnosed without further study. If they have the same sex, then (2) *blood grouping* is desirable. Blood is easily obtained for this purpose from the umbilical cords, and it should be typed at least for the ABO, CDEcde, and MN groups. If differences are found, then DZ twins are present. Ideally, the typing should be as extensive as local facilities permit. At the same time, (3) *the placental membrane relationship* is determined. The procedure for this is simple and should be followed in all multiple births, not only for the diagnosis of zygosity but also because during this examination one discovers the various causes for prenatal and perinatal disease states of twins. As a matter of fact, from a pathologist's point of view, it would be better to classify twins into two broad categories, the dichorial and monochorial twins, because of the better correlation of these factors with perinatal mortality than if zygosity alone is considered.

PLACENTATION OF TWINS. The two placentas of twins often have complex relationships which are easily understood if the embryology is recalled.

Fraternal twins develop from two separate blastocysts. Each makes its own placenta (i.e., villi, chorion, and amnion). Chance alone determines whether the two placentas develop at different sites in the uterus or side by side. Consequently, the placentas of DZ twins are either separate or fused. However, no matter how intimately fused these placentas are, DZ twins always have dichorial placental membranes.

Monovular twins on the other hand form a single blastocyst which may split at various times during development. If it splits before a placenta is formed, say at the two-cell stage, then two entirely separate placentas may develop. If splitting occurs after the blastocyst has implanted, then one chorion will envelop the twins. These may be within two amnions or one amnionic sac, depending on whether at the time of splitting the amnion had already formed.

Thus, fraternal twins always have a diamnionic, dichorionic (DiDi) placenta; fused or separated.

$$* \text{ \% MZ pairs} = \frac{\text{Number like-sex pairs} - \text{number opposite-sex pairs}}{\text{total number of twin pairs}} \times 100$$

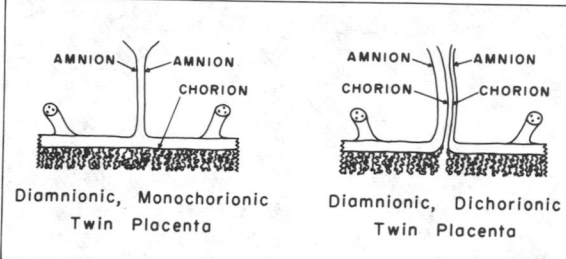

Fig. 77. Diagram of membrane relationship of monochorial twin placenta (left) and dichorial organ (right). The placental surface will not be disrupted when, in monochorial placentas, the amnions are peeled one from the other. A smooth chorionic membrane (Fig. 82) remains on the surface.

Monovular twins may have a DiDi fused or separate placenta in one-third of cases; in the other two-thirds of cases, they have a fused diamnionic, monochorionic (DiMo) organ. Rarely only one amnion is present in a monochorionic sac (MoMo). It follows, then, that if two chorionic sacs are found, the twins may be DZ or MZ. However, faced with a monochorionic placenta, the twins are surely monozygous; they cannot be fraternal (Fig. 77).

The monochorial versus dichorial membrane relationship is easily established at delivery by study of the membranous septa which separate the two twins' cavities. In the monochorial relationship, these "dividing membranes" are composed of two thin, translucent amnions only. When they are peeled apart, a procedure readily accomplished with the aid of two forceps, then the single chorionic plate of the placental surface becomes apparent. If the same procedure is employed in the presence of di-

Fig. 79. Diamnionic dichorionic twin placenta. The amnions of the "dividing membranes" are being peeled away from the two chorions which remain in the center. These twins may or may not be dizygous.

chorial dividing chorions, complete separation is impossible without disrupting the placental surface (Figs. 78 and 79).

Using these simple criteria (i.e., sex, minimal blood grouping, and membrane relationship of the placenta), Potter was able to assign zygosity at birth in 80 percent of a large twin study. The remaining 20 percent were like-sex twins, with identical blood groups and dichorial membranes. This percentage is also that expected for dichorial MZ twins, but much more extensive blood group studies and similarity tests in later life (e.g., hair color, eye color, fingerprints, etc.) would have to be undertaken before one could *prove* that these twins were indeed monozygous.

FETAL COMPLICATIONS. Twinning causes many problems in utero, only a few due to overdistension or crowding. Thus, toxemia of pregnancy, interlocking of twin heads at birth, etc., are recognized hazards; however, the two most important problems to the pediatrician are prematurity and the fetus-to-fetus transfusion syndrome.

In this latter and relatively common disorder, the two placental fetal vascular beds have become anastomosed early in development, and unequal amounts of blood are exchanged between the twins. The syndrome occurs only in monozygous twins, and of these, only in some of the monochorial sets, because only in this type of placentation are blood vessel communications formed between the placentas. Anastomoses cannot be detected among dichorial twins. The prototype of this condition is exemplified in Figure 80, a set of "identical" twins reported by Becker and Glass. In these twins, the most striking differences at birth existed in the blood picture: (A) hemoglobin 7.8 g, hematocrit 24 percent; (B) hemoglobin 27.6 g, hematocrit 76 percent.

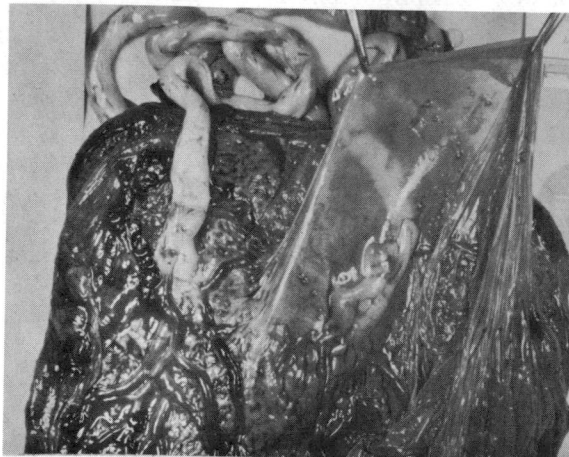

Fig. 78. Diamnionic monochorionic twin placenta. The "dividing membranes" of the two sacs are held up. They are translucent and peel apart readily, leaving a flat surface of chorion. Definitely monozygous twins. (From Benirschke. *Obstet. Gynec.*, 18:334, 1961.)

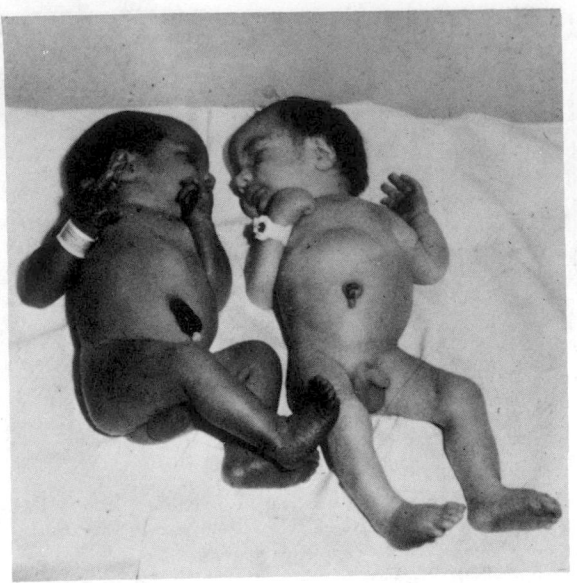

Fig. 80. Monozygous newborn twins with the transfusion syndrome. Severe plethora of twin on left who is also, characteristically, the larger infant. (From Becker and Glass. *Amer. J. Dis. Child.*, 106:624, 1963.)

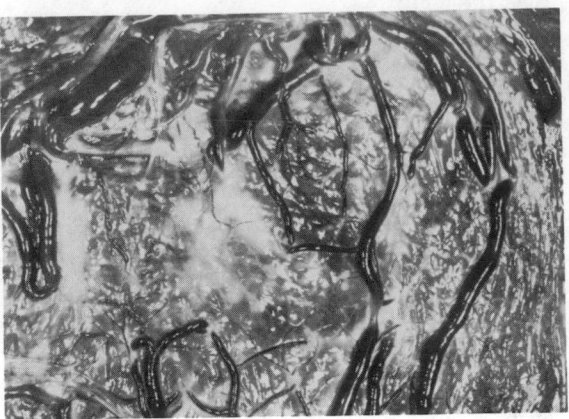

Fig. 82. Diamnionic monochorionic twin placenta. The amnions have been peeled; the chorionic surface remains with fetal vessels. This is the "vascular equator" between the two twins' chorionic vascular beds. Arteries always cross over veins. The complex anastomoses of this photograph are diagrammed in Figure 83.

Many other differences of development can be detected in such twins, which become clearer when the pathophysiology of the syndrome is considered. Careful injection studies of numerous placentas have shown that the basis for the unequal distribution of blood is the existence of an arteriovenous shunt (Figs. 81, 82, and 83). An artery from one fetus (A in this case) distributes blood into a fetal placental cotyledon. This, in turn, is drained by a vein leading to the other fetus (B). Consequently, fetus A loses some blood continuously into B. A becomes anemic and dehydrated, he is smaller, presumably he is hypotensive and usually lies in a relatively dry amnionic sac. On the other hand, B becomes plethoric, develops hypertension, cardiac hypertrophy, and polyuria; and there is usually an associated hydramnios. In fact, the development of hydramnios is so frequent in this syndrome, often so early and excessive (20 weeks, 2 to 3 gallons), that the diagnosis can be suspected prenatally. Likewise, it is the cause of premature delivery in many twins.

The severity of the transfusion syndrome varies a great deal. It depends not only on the size of the anastomosis but also on whether or not compensating artery-to-artery or vein-to-vein shunts are present in the placenta. At times, two AV fistulas go in one direction and one AV shunt proceeds in reverse, etc. Consequently, the size difference of the twins varies. They may be aborted because of gross inequalities and hydramnios, or they may show only minor differences in hydration and size, and the pregnancy may proceed to term. If marked inequalities exist, however, the twins present emergency problems at

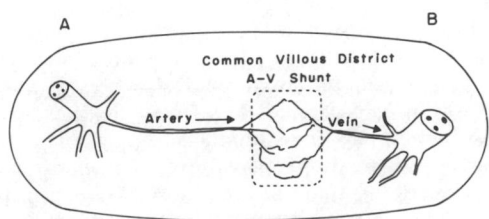

Fig. 81. Diagram of the mechanism of the transfusion syndrome (Fig. 80) in monochorial twins. The anastomoses which lead to a unidirectional flow of blood occur in the villi of one or more cotyledons of the placenta (dotted square). Twin B in this instance is the hypervolemic twin.

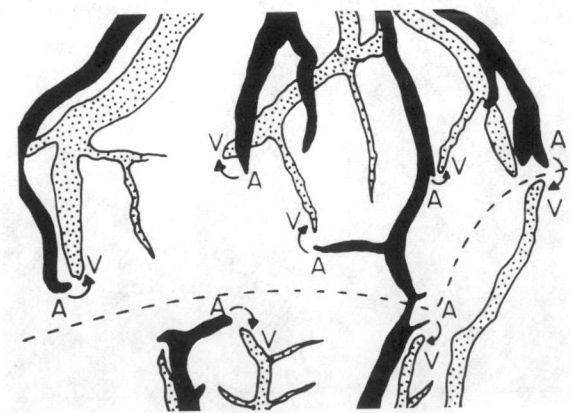

Fig. 83. Diagram of blood vessels of Figure 82. Dotted line represents "vascular equator." Arteries are black, veins dotted. Normal conditions at left. An A-V shunt, passing through a "common villous district," is shown at extreme right (see Fig. 82). A large A-A anastomosis is seen to the right of center.

birth, which the pediatrician must recognize and treat promptly.

The following measures have been employed successfully by several authors, and Conway makes a number of specific suggestions. The *anemic infant* is to be transfused with whole blood or packed red cells as soon as possible. This may have to be repeated in 12 to 24 hours, and appropriate fluid therapy for hydration is instituted soon after birth. The *plethoric twin* is often more critically ill at birth than his anemic partner despite apparently good color, larger size, etc. The larger, plethoric twin has a dual problem of an expanded blood volume and a disproportionate increase in red cell concentration in the blood which can lead to marked hyperviscosity with its attendant problems. Both the increased blood volume and the elevated hematocrit can be corrected by a limited exchange transfusion (50 ml in 10 ml aliquots over 30 minutes) while central venous pressure is carefully observed. In the next few days of life, the plethoric infant may exhibit marked jaundice and must be carefully followed with appropriate diagnostic and therapeutic procedures to prevent kernicterus. Digitalization for impending heart failure has also been employed at times, apparently with resulting improvement. It is important to be alert to these complications, as the clinical appearance of some twins may give a false sense of security.

When the critical perinatal period is overcome, the differences between the twins diminish during the next few months. However, long-term studies indicate that some growth retardation characterizes the donor, and cerebral palsy in one of the pair is more common than in dizygous twins. From autopsies on twins with this syndrome who succumb in the perinatal period, it is apparent that residual damage may be expected in some survivors. Degenerative changes in various parenchymal organs are common, and the quantitative studies of Naeye have shown

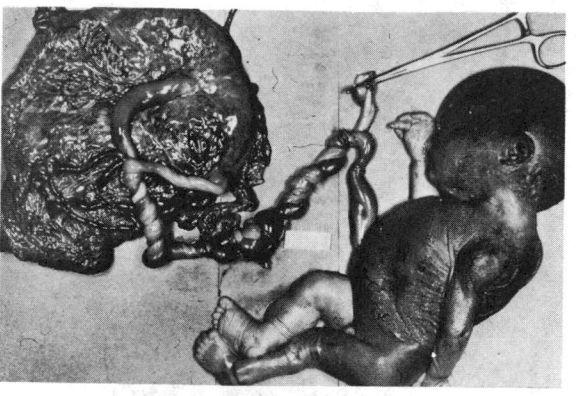

Fig. 85. Monoamnionic twins with one fetus macerated because of entangling and knotting of cords. The survivor, whose cord is clamped, died at age 3 months with extensive cerebral damage, presumably sustained from entangling of cords.

a variety of morphologic alterations which may have permanent sequelae. The pronounced and early cardiac hypertrophy of the recipient in this transfusion syndrome is shown in Figure 84. Other organs show similar, albeit less dramatic, size differences.

Other prenatal problems attend multiple pregnancy. In monoamniotic twins, double survival is relatively infrequent because of the entangling of cords and interruption of blood flow (Fig. 85). Marginal survival of one or both twins in such cases is often associated with brain damage. Moreover, irreversible destructive lesions may be produced in the survivor by a generalized coagulative process that is presumably engendered by the transfer of thromboplastin. It is envisaged that when one twin dies, the coagulation occurring in his vessels may spread via large anastomoses to his co-twin.

Velamentous insertion of the umbilical cord is quite frequent in twins. Its incidence in one infant of twins is 7 percent contrasted with 1 percent in singletons. From these abnormally inserted cords, blood vessels course over the membranes, and if they are in the way of the birth canal (vasa previa) and torn during delivery, rapid exsanguination may occur (Fig. 86). Therefore, this possibility must be anticipated in twins, and immediate transfusion may be indicated in some instances. The reason for the increased frequency of velamentous insertion of the cord is to be found in the competition for space by the two developing twin placentas; this is also the cause of a considerable increase in the incidence of the absence of one umbilical artery. This latter anomaly occurs in 1 percent of singletons and in 3.5 percent of twin fetuses. It may be present in both twins and, of course, is associated with a high incidence of anomalies in other organs. Malformations should be searched for with particular diligence in twins, because the incidence of congenital anomalies in twins is approximately twice as high as that in singletons. Of particular interest is the fre-

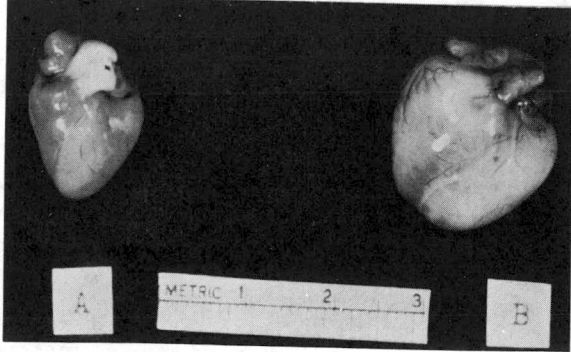

Fig. 84. Hearts of two monochorial twins with transfusion syndrome. In this severest degree of the unequal distribution of blood, marked hydramnios occurred at 20 weeks. Although the twins were not different in size (body weight: A, 249 g; B, 246 g), their hearts portray the hypovolemia and hypervolemia (heart weight: A, 1.2 g; B, 2.6 g).

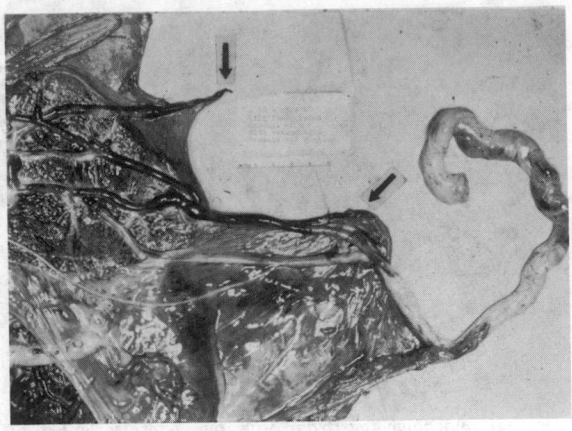

Fig. 86. Velamentous insertion of second twin's cord (bottom right) with fatal intrapartum exsanguination. The torn vasa previa are seen at arrows. (From Benirschke. *Obstet. Gynec.*, 18:334, 1961.)

quent finding that monozygous twins may be discordant for anomalies which are considered to have a hereditary basis, such as cleft palate and lip. To understand this phenomenon fully the pediatrician should be aware of current studies concerning traits that are based on "polygenic factors" (see Carter), for it may be that he can contribute in the ascertainment of those environmental factors that put one twin beyond that "threshold" where the anomalous phenotype will be expressed. The authors feel that the placental anomalies such as velamentous insertion and absence of one artery in the umbilical cord are potential teratogens in this respect.

PERINATAL MORTALITY. Despite expert attendance, the perinatal mortality of twins is approximately four times greater than that of singletons. The principal reasons for this high mortality are commonly sought in the higher prematurity rate. In obstetrics, attention has been paid to the possible differences in survival of first- versus second-born twins.

The type of placentation is the most important influence in perinatal deaths among twins. Figure 87 presents an analysis of the perinatal losses in 250 consecutive sets of twins delivered after 20 weeks of gestation. Monochorial twins have a much poorer prognosis than dichorial twins (26 versus 9 percent mortality). The greatest losses are in monoamnionic twins. This is followed by monochorial twins with the transfusion syndrome who are lost either because of the severe prematurity, induced by hydramnios, or because of inequalities of development.

Neonatal Complications

BIRTH ORDER. This subject has been analyzed extensively, and it is perhaps confusing to learn that no agreement has been reached among investigators whether one or the other twin suffers more severely from labor and its attending circumstances. It can be argued that the first twin might be handicapped because twins are so frequently delivered prematurely. On the other hand, most obstetricians have been concerned that the second twin is exposed to more anesthesia, more labor, and, since he is often delivered as a breech, to more trauma.

Possibly the majority are of the opinion that the second twin has a greater overall perinatal mortality. This is not true of our data on livebirths. It is important in this respect that macerated stillborns, usually delivered last in twins, be removed from the analysis of such series. In any event, if delivery is prompt and efficiently performed, the two twins have about an even chance of survival. Care must be taken that the cord of the first twin is securely ligated, as instances of exsanguination of the second twin, through large interfetal placental anastomoses, have been described.

As premature infants, twins have a greater likelihood of developing hyaline membrane disease, and this may affect only one or both (even of monozygous) twins. If ascending infection from prolonged rupture of the membranes occurs as a complication, it is usually confined to the first-delivered infant. It is of interest that transplacental infections (e.g., toxoplasmosis) have not always affected both twins.

BIRTH SIZE. Reliable data indicate that the average length of double gestations is 37 weeks. In other words, a great many twins are born prematurely, often as the result of the transfusion syndrome or because of toxemia of pregnancy. Moreover, for a given gestational age, twins are smaller than singletons. Thus, if one compares their mortality with that of singletons of the same weight, there is no great difference. If anything, it is lower in twins. This is true for infants under 3,000 g. Heavier twins have a greatly increased mortality when compared with singletons, and this is primarily due to mechanical and obstetric factors. In large twins, a detailed examination for trauma, particularly intracranial hemorrhage, is important.

TWIN MORTALITY AND PLACENTATION

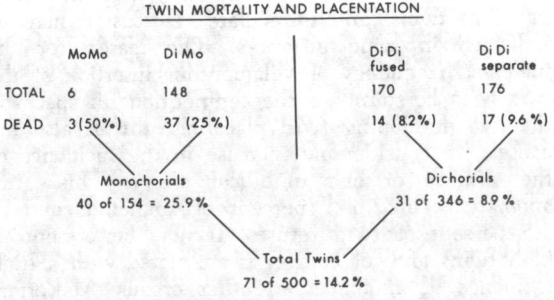

	MoMo	Di Mo		Di Di fused	Di Di separate
TOTAL	6	148		170	176
DEAD	3 (50%)	37 (25%)		14 (8.2%)	17 (9.6%)
		Monochorials 40 of 154 = 25.9%		Dichorials 31 of 346 = 8.9%	
			Total Twins 71 of 500 = 14.2%		

Fig. 87. Analysis of perinatal mortality of 250 sets of twins past 20 weeks' gestation and expressed with respect to placentation. Highest mortality in the monoamnionic monochorionic sets (MoMo); next most hazardous is the diamnionic monochorionic placentation (DiMo).

PROGNOSIS. As indicated, the prognosis for perinatal survival of twins is approximately four times poorer than that for singletons. The principal reason is premature delivery, and attempts have been made to improve these results by prolonged bed rest of mothers pregnant with twins. Subsequent physical growth of twins is discussed in the section of this chapter on Outcome. As a group, the surviving twins are known to have a somewhat lower mental development as measured by objective tests of intelligence. The average level of intelligence is lower in twins than in the general population or in comparable ex-prematures. It is lower still in triplets. Moreover, in studies of populations with cerebral palsy or mental deficiency, a disproportionately large number of twins is represented. If one attempts to determine the zygosity of such groups of twins (usually only possible by employing the Weinberg rule), a greater number of like-sex twins seems to be affected, suggesting again that monozygous twins seem to fare worst.

The reason for these findings is not easily determined. There will be instances of kernicterus, asphyxial cerebral hemorrhage, birth trauma, and similar defined entities in these damaged twins (see Neonatal Hypoglycemia, Chap. 12). In a majority, however, a cause cannot be assigned, and it is likely that retrospective data similar to those cited will add little to the future prevention of cerebral injury in twins. Natal circumstances are rarely known, and prenatal factors cannot be judged adequately in retrospect.

For all these reasons it is recommended that complete assessment and recording of the minimal diagnostic criteria of zygosity outlined previously must be obtained for all twin births.

Considerations of Intertwin Relationships

Recent experimental and analytic studies have led to clarification of many controversial aspects of twinning. Contrary to many other species, in human *fraternal* twins, interfetal placental blood vessel communications are exceedingly rare. In fact, they have not been demonstrated directly, and we know of their existence only through the discovery of seven sets of unlike-sex twins who were found to be blood chimeras. In these exceptional cases, the prenatal exchange of nucleated marrow elements has produced a mutual transplantation tolerance, and a permanent state of marrow and blood chimerism exists. Presumably, this exchange occurred through blood vessel communications as seen in monozygous twins. The reason for the apparently haphazard admixture of cells in these few reported instances is not understood at the moment. In a recent example described by Chown et al., both twins had 85 percent cells from the female twin, yet no indication was found that a one-way preferential anastomotic flow

had existed before birth. There was no hydramnios and the twins were about equal in development. It is likely that intense study of these exceptional twins will provide information of great interest in the future. The same state of chimerism among fraternal twins in cattle was the original observation leading to our present knowledge of transplantation immunology. Unlike cattle, however, these few exceptional human twin girls, with prenatal exposure to male co-twin androgens, were not sterilized. They did not develop into freemartins, as would be expected in cattle twins of the same relationship. The reason for this species difference is of considerable interest. At present it appears that it relates to the ability of the human placenta to convert androgenic steroids into estrogens, a normal pathway of human pregnancy.

Permanent admixture of foreign marrow elements may also have genetic implications. These will undoubtedly be explored in man, as they are now a subject of intense interest in other species. An important prerequisite for permanent transplantation tolerance among twins may depend on such a circumstance. The possibility of somatic cell mating, transformation, etc., is a challenge to future research. Moreover, it has also been learned that in animals other cells gain access to the co-twin via such anastomotic channels, e.g., germ cells. So far we do not know their ultimate fate; however, in an era when cytogenetic studies are beginning to blossom, cognizance must be taken of bizarre possibilities arising from prenatal parabiosis.

The care of twins presents many unique aspects. The primary problems encountered are similar to those of single premature infants, but they are more frequent among twins; and, as a group, twins present a high-risk population. In addition to prematurity per se, special hazards attend the perinatal period of twins, which can be anticipated and, as in the case of transfusion syndrome, treated successfully. For the pediatrician to take full advantage of the opportunities, he must have knowledge of the prenatal interrelationships of each set of twins under his care. He must cooperate with the obstetrician to fully assess the course of pregnancy and the status of the placenta, and he must record these findings. He is challenged by the complexities of advising parents on rearing twins, of differentiating fraternal from monovular twins, and, unfortunately often, of treating those whose perinatal experience has caused permanent damage. Finally, he can make enormous contributions to medical knowledge by the detailed study of the "exceptional twins," such as the genetically dissimilar monozygous pairs and the blood chimeras. Only if this study begins with an appreciation of prenatal circumstances and continues through childhood will Galton's hope come true, that through the study of twins, genetic versus environmental (nature/nurture) influences may be assessed critically.

It is pertinent also for the pediatrician to be cognizant of the fact that parents of twins face other problems, many of which are related to psychologic and socioeconomic adjustments. The great interest accorded twins is mirrored in the numerous books, for professional and lay audience, written on the subject. Moreover, the National Mothers of Twins Association has numerous local chapters throughout the country whose members are most willing to help new twin mothers with their many problems. They also provide a group of volunteers through whose cooperation many fine twin studies have been accomplished.

References

Becker, A. H., and Glass, H. Twin-to-twin transfusion syndrome. Amer. J. Dis. Child., 106:624, 1963.

Benirschke, K. Accurate recording of twin placentation. A plea to the obstetrician. Obstet. Gynec., 18:334, 1961.

——— and Driscoll, S. G. The Pathology of the Human Placenta. New York, Springer-Verlag, 1967.

Berg, J. M., and Kirman, B. H. The mentally defective twin. Brit. Med. J., 1:1911, 1960.

Carter, C. O. VI. Polygenic inheritance and common diseases. Lancet, 1:1252, 1969.

Chown, B., Lewis, M., and Bowman, J. M. A pair of newborn human blood chimeric twins. Transfusion, 3:494, 1963.

Conway, C. F. Transfusion syndrome in multiple pregnancy. Obstet. Gynec., 23:745, 1964.

Corner, G. W. The observed embryology of human single-ovum twins and other multiple births. Amer. J. Obstet. Gynec., 70:933, 1955.

Eastman, N. J., Kohl, S. G., Maisel, J. E., and Kavaler, F. The obstetrical background of 753 cases of cerebral palsy. Obstet. Gynec. Survey, 17:459, 1962.

Guttmacher, A. F., and Kohl, S. G. The fetus of multiple gestations. Obstet. Gynec., 12:528, 1958.

Moore, C. M., McAdams, A. J., and Sutherland, J. Intrauterine disseminated intravascular coagulation: A syndrome of multiple pregnancy with a dead twin fetus. J. Pediat., 74:523, 1969.

Naeye, R. L. Human intrauterine parabiotic syndrome and its complications. New Eng. J. Med., 268:804, 1963.

——— The fetal and neonatal development of twins. Pediatrics, 33:546, 1964.

Potter, E. L. Twin zygosity and placental form in relation to the outcome of pregnancy. Amer. J. Obstet. Gynec., 87:566, 1963.

Price, B. Primary biases in twin studies. A review of prenatal and natal difference-producing factors in monozygotic pairs. Amer. J. Hum. Genet., 2:293, 1950.

2.13
THE HIGH-BIRTH-WEIGHT INFANT

FREDERICK C. BATTAGLIA

Most of this chapter has been devoted to problems of low-birth-weight infants. This is justified, since the low-birth-weight infant group contributes most to neonatal mortality and morbidity; however, too little attention is usually given to the high-birth-weight infant. No arbitrary birth weight has been agreed upon to define this group of infants comparable to the 2,500 g dividing line for low-birth-weight infants, and it is only in the last few years that people have begun to look for causes, other than maternal diabetes, and to look for some of the immediate and long-term problems of high-birth-weight infants.

High-Birth-Weight Term Babies

In many respects, the difficulty in defining the problems of high-birth-weight infants is similar to that involving low-birth-weight infants. One complication associated with babies of very large size, regardless of their gestational ages, is an increased incidence of birth injuries, particularly around the head and neck. Adler et al., in reporting long-term results in 88 cases of Erb's palsy, point out the increased incidence of high-birth-weight infants in these cases. Injuries to the brachial plexus are by no means a minor obstetric catastrophe, since complete recovery occurs in only 10 to 15 percent of these patients. These injuries to the head and neck area in high-birth-weight infants are often multiple. Vassalos et al. found that 11.2 percent of infants with brachial plexus injuries had additional associated injuries such as fractured clavicles. Phrenic nerve damage with paralysis of the diaphragm is another complication sometimes seen with injuries to the cervical or brachial plexus but occurring rarely, if ever, as an isolated injury. Not surprisingly, perhaps, the perinatal and neonatal mortality rates plotted against birth weight are U-shaped, in that mortality decreases to an optimal weight range and then increases with the oversized infants (see Fig. 73). There are no reported clinical studies that have attempted to relate the incidence of abnormal fetal heart rate-uterine contraction patterns to infant size, particularly in the excessively large babies. One of the more interesting observations is that of Record et al., who noted an increased birth weight of babies with increasing parity (see Fig. 88). This may be due to changes in uterine vasculature with preceding preg-

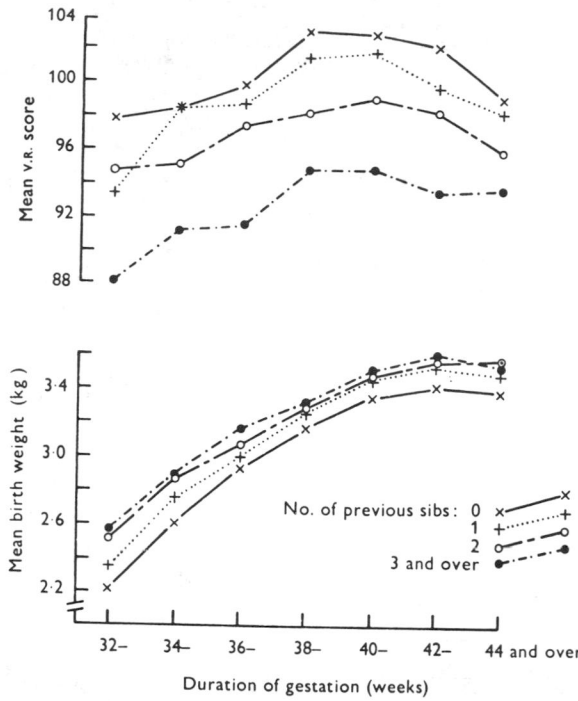

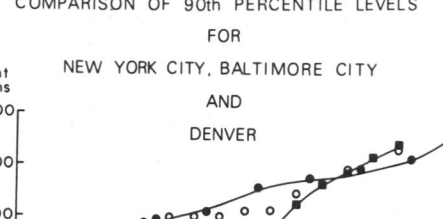

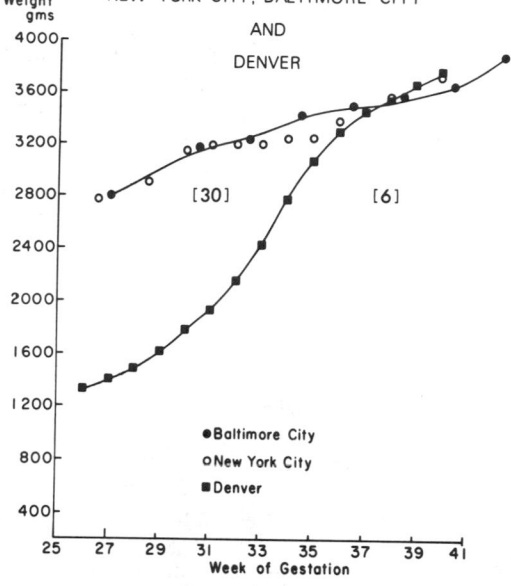

Fig. 88. Mean V.R. scores and mean birth weights (standard-ized to the sex distribution of the whole series) according to number of previous sibs and duration of gestation. (From Record et al. *Ann. Hum. Genet.*, 33:71, 1969.)

Fig. 89. Birth weight-gestational age distribution at 90th per-centile levels. Figures in brackets indicate approximate neo-natal mortality rate per 1,000 live births of 2,800 g-birth-weight infants at 31 weeks' gestation and at term. (From Battaglia et al. *Pediatrics*, 37:417, 1966.)

nancies which tend to make the uterus more respon-sive to the endocrinologic changes of pregnancy. At any rate, to emphasize further the fallacy of "the bigger the better," these same investigators found a lower verbal reasoning score at age 11 years in these larger babies born of multigravidas than in the smaller birth weight babies of primigravidas.

The reasons for this increased neonatal mortality rate are unknown. Further evidence that the high-birth-weight preterm infant should be considered at high risk stems from Weiner's recent study in which he found significant developmental retardation in these infants at 10 years of age.

High-Birth-Weight Preterm Babies

The recognition of high-birth-weight preterm infants has been difficult because it depends upon the es-tablishment of appropriate standards for birth weight-gestational age relationships. The marked variation in defining a 90th-percentile birth weight-gestational age distribution was clearly brought out in comparing published data on Baltimore and New York City, versus that reported for Colorado General Hospital (see Fig. 89). Superimposed on Figure 89 is an ap-proximate neonatal mortality rate per thousand of in-fants of 2,800 g and 31 weeks' gestational age versus an infant of the same size born at term. The mortality rate is approximately five times greater in the more immature infant. In that respect, it makes little difference that a 2,800 g, 31-week infant would be on the 75th percentile by one set of birth weight-gestational age data and above the 90th on another.

Infants of Diabetic Mothers

ANTENATAL CONSIDERATIONS. Modern manage-ment of diabetes mellitus permits more diabetic girls to grow up and more diabetic women to bear infants. Although poor control of maternal diabetes is asso-ciated with greater fetal wastage, fetal morbidity may be associated with gestational diabetes so mild that transient mild glucosuria or abnormal glucose toler-ance is noted only during pregnancy.

The two most obvious clinical manifestations prior to birth are intrauterine death and macrosomia. Unexpected intrauterine death is the crudest mani-festation of intrauterine metabolic disorder. The mechanism of its occurrence is not known. In hu-mans, fetal deaths occur more frequently in mothers with repeated bouts of keto-acidosis or a previous obstetric history of intrauterine death before the 36th week of gestation. This has led to a general recommendation to interrupt pregnancy at the 38th week of gestation, frequently by cesarean section.

Such recommendations may now need to be altered in light of the many tests available during a pregnancy for detecting fetal distress early in its devolpment while it is still easily reversible (see previous sections in this chapter on obstetrics and intrauterine diagnosis). For example, one may suggest that long-term results in infants of diabetic mothers might be significantly improved by allowing the pregnancy to continue till the spontaneous onset of labor, in the absence of any signs of fetal distress as determined by serial urinary estriol determinations.

THE PLACENTA IN DIABETIC PREGNANCIES. The development of severe vascular disease in the pregnant patient with diabetes can dominate the clinical picture in both the placenta and the fetus. In such cases the placenta may be small in weight, with multiple small infarcts. However, more commonly, both the placenta and the fetus are increased in weight. Winick et al. have presented data suggesting that total DNA in the diabetic placenta is increased in proportion to placental weight, and Aherne et al. have found an increased villous surface area in a diabetic placenta studied by histometric techniques. These observations are in general agreement with the studies on human placental lactogenic hormone levels (HPL) in maternal plasma, which are also increased in diabetic pregnancies (see Fig. 90).

BODY SIZE. As Figure 91 points out, macrosomia is a common finding in diabetic pregnancies. In this series, the weights of 75 percent of the infants were above the 50th percentile for infants of similar gestational ages. Except for the brain, the weights of various organs are also greater. However, just as in

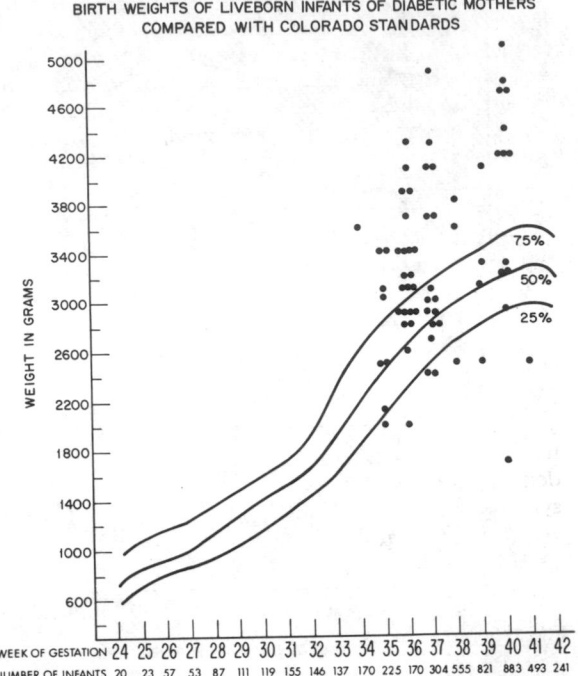

Fig. 91. Birth weights of liveborn infants of diabetic mothers compared with Colorado standards. (From Gordon. *Amer. J. Med. Sci.*, 224:35, 1962.)

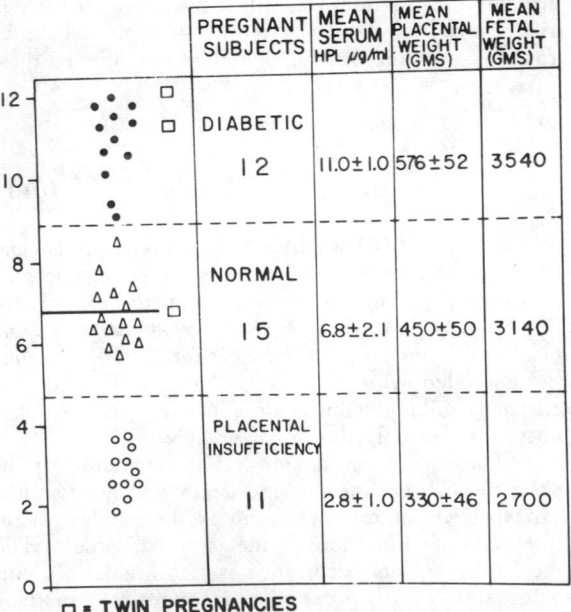

Fig. 90. Serum HPL levels in the third trimester (more than 32 weeks), showing the relation between HPL and placental and fetal weights. (From Saxena et al. *New Eng. J. Med.*, 281:225, 1969.)

other cases of discrepant intrauterine growth, the indices of maturity correlate best with the infant's gestational age, not with his weight. Thus, ossification centers of the distal femur and proximal tibia and general neurologic performance are in accord with the infant's gestational age. While these babies give the impression of being edematous, they are in fact obese, with increased body fat, decreased total body water, and an even more marked decrease in extracellular water as a percentage of body weight.

The plethoric, balloon-cheeked appearance has been called "cushingoid," but serum 17-hydroxycorticoids are not increased in the blood of infants of diabetic mothers. Some prematurely born infants of diabetic mothers, although not obviously fat, have round, full, plethoric faces. The macrosomia and plethoric facies are striking evidence of intrauterine metabolic disorder, and solution of this riddle might lead not only to prevention of infant morbidity and mortality but also to greater understanding of both diabetes and pregnancy. From a practical standpoint it must be recognized that these infants require at least the quality of care given to other immature babies rather than that given to babies of the same size born at term.

NEONATAL COURSE. A large number of infants exhibit the isolated sign of tachypnea during the first three to five days. Transient tachypnea, without progression to hyaline membrane disease or respiratory distress syndrome, may stem from any one of a number of factors. It may be a sign of hypoglycemia, hypothermia, polycythemia (or, more correctly, hyperviscosity), or it may be due to cerebral edema secondary to birth trauma, especially in an infant of excessive size. These factors should be born in mind in observing these babies, and one should not attribute all tachypnea to hyaline membrane disease in the absence of the full clinical picture, including radiologic evidence. Unexplained tachypnea, just like jitteriness, always warrants further investigation.

An increased incidence of renal vein thrombosis has been observed in infants of diabetic mothers. This complication should be suspected in the presence of a flank mass and gross hematuria. The proper management of this complication is still an open question.

A drop in blood sugar occurs in the first hours of life in all newborn infants. Infants of diabetic mothers have an increased incidence of hypoglycemia, defined as a blood sugar below 30 mg percent. The symptoms of hypoglycemia and its treatment are discussed in Section 8.6. However, it should be emphasized that many of the symptoms of hypoglycemia are seen in other metabolic complications of these infants. Hypocalcemia often accompanies hypoglycemia in these babies and may be another cause of jitteriness. Cerebral edema secondary to birth trauma, and hyperbilirubinemia may contribute to some of the CNS signs often attributed to hypoglycemia. **TREATMENT.** All pregnant women with overt or gestational diabetes should be followed carefully, using all the currently available tests for following a high-risk pregnancy; there should also be frequent prenatal clinic visits. These women should be delivered in hospitals where expert obstetric and pediatric care is available, both in the delivery room and in the nursery, since there is no predictable relationship between the severity of maternal diabetes and the clinical course of the offspring. All infants born to diabetic mothers should, regardless of size, receive close initial observation and intensive care, because their intrauterine environment may have been abnormal, their birth premature, and their delivery complicated. The course of the infant will then decide the steps to be taken for further diagnosis and treatment of specific conditions. If the infant is well enough, oral feedings of 10 to 20 percent glucose should be started within a few hours of birth. If the infant is not entirely well, oral feedings should not be forced, but rather the infant should be given 10 percent glucose by a peripheral intravenous infusion at a rate of 80 ml/kg/day, and close observation should be continued. Similarly, calcium should be given to all infants with serum calcium concentrations below 3 mEq/L and with signs of hyperirritability, jitteriness, or convulsions (see Sec. 3.5).

LONG-TERM PROGNOSIS. Infants of diabetic mothers have an increased incidence of congenital anomalies, particularly skeletal anomalies. The reported incidence has varied widely in different population groups from 8 to 80 percent. The reported incidence of diabetes mellitus in infants of diabetic mothers has ranged between 0.2 and 1.4 percent, which is higher than in the general population. Recent studies have shown that these babies, as older children, have an increase in body weight relative to height. While careful studies of total body fat and adipocyte number have not been made, these long-term observations suggest that children who start out as obese infants may retain this predilection to obesity in later life (Farquhar).

REFERENCES

Adler, J. B., and Patterson, R. L., Jr. Erb's palsy: Long-term results of treatment in eighty-eight cases. J. Bone Joint Surg., 49A:1052, 1967.

Aherne, W., and Dunnill, M. S. Quantitative aspects of placental structure. J. Path. Bact., 91:123, 1966.

Battaglia, F. C., Frazier, T. M., and Hellegers, A. E. Birth weight, gestational age, and pregnancy outcome, with special reference to high birth weight-low gestational age infant. Pediatrics, 37:417, 1966.

Farquhar, J. W. Prognosis for babies born to diabetic mothers in Edinburgh. Arch. Dis. Child., 44:36, 1969.

Record, R. G., McKeown, T., and Edwards, J. H. The relation of measured intelligence to birth order and maternal age. Ann. Hum. Genet. (London), 33:61, 1969.

——— McKeown, T., and Edwards, J. H. The relation of measured intelligence to birth weight and duration of gestation. Ann. Hum. Genet., 33:71, 1969.

Vassalos, E., Prevedourakis, C., and Paraschopoulou-Prevedouraki, P. Brachial plexus paralysis in the newborn. Amer. J. Obstet. Gynec., 101:554, 1968.

Weiner, G. The relationship of birthweight and length of gestation to intellectual development at ages 8 to 10 years. J. Pediat., 76:694, 1970.

Winick, M., and Noble, A. Cellular growth in human placenta. II. Diabetes mellitus. J. Pediat., 71:216, 1967.

chapter 3

NUTRITION

LAURENCE FINBERG, Associate Editor

Maintenance of Health and Growth

Nutrition in its broadest sense is one of the most important branches of pediatrics. Not only has the growing child exceptional requirements for nutrients; he is also peculiarly vulnerable to disturbances which interfere with his obtaining them. A knowledge of the fundamental principles of nutrition is essential to the physician. This chapter surveys the function of the essential nutrients and their requirements in health and disease. This section and the next deals with requirements in health. The succeeding sections will discuss diseases in which nutritional deficiency either causes or results from their presence.

3.1
ENERGY REQUIREMENTS

L. EMMETT HOLT, JR.

ENERGY METABOLISM. Like the adult, the child constantly expends energy, largely in the form of heat and work; the process goes on whether he is asleep or awake, although of course it is least rapid during quiet sleep, far greater in periods of muscular activity. To maintain energy balance he must assimilate energy from his food. The energy value of foods is usually expressed in calories, which in nutrition work refers to kilocalories. The different foodstuffs when burned in the body have approximately the following energy equivalents:

> 1 g of fat yields 9 calories
> 1 g of protein yields 4 calories
> 1 g of carbohydrate yields 4 calories

The caloric requirements of a growing child may be thought of in five categories: (1) basal metabolism, (2) bodily activity, (3) growth, (4) caloric loss in the excreta, and (5) specific dynamic action of foods. The energy intake of a growing child must provide for the obligatory losses and for the potential energy stored in the course of growth.

Efforts have been made to estimate these five components separately, principally by measurement of energy expenditure in a variety of circumstances. The cumbersome methods of direct calorimetry—

direct measurement of heat loss—have been largely superseded by the technically less exacting methods of indirect calorimetry. The subject is confined during relatively short observation periods in a respiration chamber while his oxygen consumption, carbon dioxide and water production, and nitrogen excretion are measured, permitting conversion of the chemical reactions involved into equivalent calories. The energy requirements for the various categories are summarized as follows.

Basal Metabolism. What is commonly referred to as basal metabolism in adults, the caloric expenditure during rest or sleep, differs in children since, in addition to maintenance, it includes the requirement for growth. It is highest during the period of most rapid growth, decreasing thereafter as the rate of growth declines. It is, however, fairly constant in children of the same age and weight. During the first year or 18 months of life the daily basal expenditure averages about 75 calories per kilogram (35 calories per pound). After this age it tends to diminish gradually, reaching the adult value (25 to 30 calories per kilogram) by the time growth has ceased. Since most of the observations were made on infants within a short time after feeding, the caloric expenditure measured also includes the specific dynamic action of the food consumed. In the adult, on the other hand, measurements of basal metabolism are commonly made after an overnight fast; specific dynamic action and growth do not enter the picture, and only maintenance is measured.

Requirements for Activity. The great variation seen in the food consumption of individual children results chiefly from differences in their muscular activity. While awake an infant expends more energy than when asleep, but the magnitude of the excess is highly variable. Vigorous crying may cause a temporary increase in metabolism of 100 percent. An average allowance for activity during the first year is 20 calories per kilogram (9 calories per pound) per day. Young or phlegmatic infants may require only half this amount, while unusually active ones may need four times as much. The energy expended in activity by individual children may vary considerably from day to day.

Growth Requirements. These are variable, since growth is not a constant process. Direct measurements have shown that about 2.5 calories are required for each gram of body weight gained throughout infancy. During the early months of life as much as 15 to 20 calories per kilogram (7 to 9 calories per pound) may be stored daily in the course of rapid normal growth. At the end of the first year the average is about 5 calories per kilogram (2 calories per pound) per day. The amount of energy stored gradually falls in relation to body weight during childhood, a conspicuous but temporary increase occurring at the time of the pubertal growth spurt.

Energy Lost in the Excreta. On a mixed diet, approximately 10 percent of the intake is normally lost in the excreta, mainly in the form of fat and protein. In infants this amounts to 8 to 11 calories per kilogram per day. In diarrhea and other conditions of disturbed digestion the caloric loss may be greatly increased.

Specific Dynamic Action of Food. This term refers to an increase in heat production, which may last 6 or 8 hours, following the administration of food. It is most marked after the intake of protein food, relatively small after the administration of fat or carbohydrate. The cause of specific dynamic action has been much disputed. It was at one time attributed to the "cost" of digestion and absorption, but it is now known to occur after intravenous alimentation. The increased oxidation is not accompanied by an increase in body work; only heat is produced, which is dissipated. According to Krebs et al. only reactions resulting in the synthesis of adenosine triphosphate are capable of performing body work; other oxidations liberate energy in the form of heat. The higher specific dynamic action of protein is attributed to the fact that the combustion of amino acids involves a number of steps which do not lead to the synthesis of ATP; some of these are concerned with the deamination of amino acids and others with the degradation of their carbon skeleton. The measurements of Levine and his co-workers indicate, on average diets, a need of 4 to 8 calories per kilogram to provide for specific dynamic action. On high-protein diets this requirement may be doubled.

Figure 1 shows somewhat schematically the general pattern of the caloric requirements for average infants during the first year.

A practical method of estimating the caloric needs of the individual child is based on his appetite. From a knowledge of the caloric value of the food consumed the average daily caloric intake can be calculated and then related to body weight, surface area, or some other parameter. The assumption is made that the appetite is a valid guide to the caloric requirements, an assumption that by and large seems to be reliable.

During the first week after birth the energy

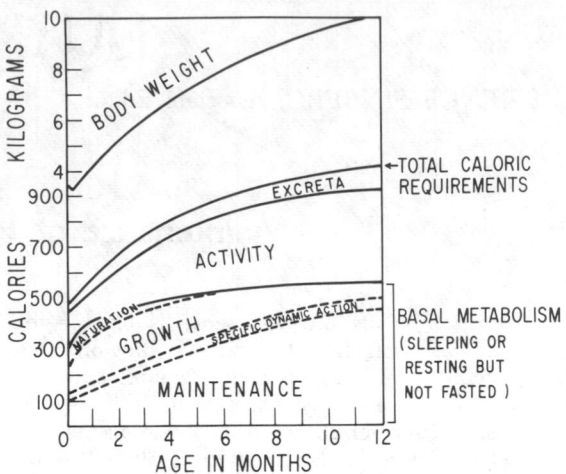

Fig. 1. Daily caloric requirements during the first year of life.

expenditure of an infant is often quite low, especially in one who spends nearly all of his time sleeping. Moreover, the growth process, active in intrauterine life, is temporarily suspended during the period of adjustment to an extrauterine environment. Indeed, during the first three days after birth, when the newborn infant takes little food either from breast or from bottle, he is expected to be for a time in negative caloric balance, drawing largely on his tissue stores for the energy required for basal metabolic needs and for physical activity. During the second and third weeks after birth the daily caloric requirements rise rapidly to about 100 to 120 per kilogram, after which they slowly fall.

The energy requirements during childhood in relation to body weight are shown schematically in Figure 2. There is a gradual decrease which continues until about 16 years in boys and 13 or 14 years in girls, followed by a more rapid decline to the adult level of 40 to 50 calories per kilogram.

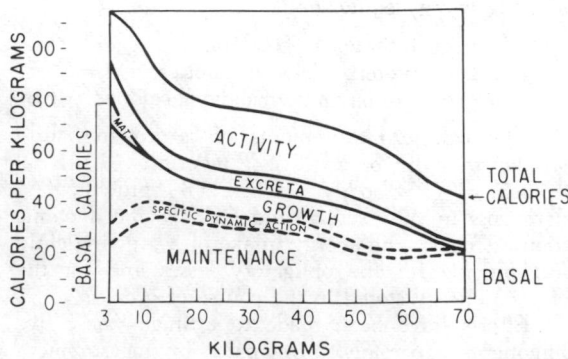

Fig. 2. Daily caloric requirements per kilogram throughout childhood.

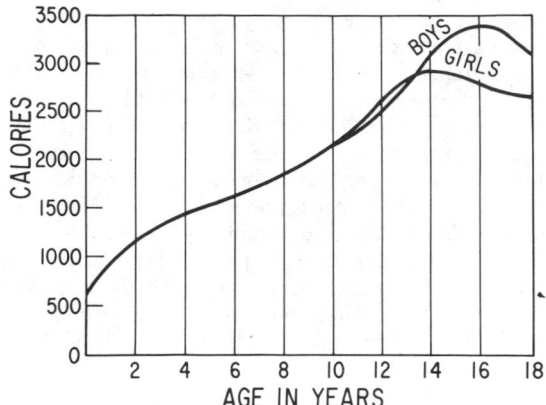

Fig. 3. Total daily calories for both sexes from birth to 18 years.

The foregoing data relating caloric requirements to body weight apply only to the *average* child. An obese child has an excess of relatively inert metabolic tissue and consequently needs less calories than his weight would indicate; conversely, a malnourished child with relatively more active metabolic tissue needs relatively more food, his requirements being more accurately approximated in terms of average weight for age rather than actual weight. Food requirements in disease vary widely. Although physical activity may be reduced, the basal requirement is increased by fever; in digestive disorders in which considerable portions of food are not absorbed the loss in the excreta may be greatly increased. Often the additional food, though needed, is not tolerated, and the individual must live on his body tissues; extra food must be supplied during convalescence to assist him in regaining lost weight.

Figure 3 gives average daily requirements for both sexes from the first to the eighteenth year. It will be noted that the food allowance during the period of adolescence is greater for both sexes than the standard allowance for adults of moderate activity. The reason for this is obvious and is in accord with general experience that the adolescent takes and needs more food than the adult. During the period of most active growth (14 to 17 years for boys, and 12 to 15 for girls) a large amount of food is needed. These charts represent averages only. They do not indicate the variations dependent on individual activity. Moreover, there are variations due to climate, clothing habits, etc., which are not represented. An exact estimation of the calories required for any individual child is not possible. The data presented are, however, of value in that they furnish a rough guide as to the amount of food needed. Calculation of the calories enables one to discover whether a child is being grossly underfed or overfed.

3.2
ESSENTIAL HUMAN NUTRIENTS

Until a few years ago it was generally assumed that the vast majority of people in the United States consumed diets of such a varied nature that detailed knowledge of all nutrients required by the growing human being was only of academic interest. Constant changes in eating patterns, with great reliance on manufactured items, and the numerous metabolic disorders becoming subject to dietary management, usually with carefully tailored semipurified diets, have created an awareness of potential and actual deficiencies of micronutrients in medical practice. Although it was generally recognized that severe malnutrition was prevalent in many parts of the world, it was believed to be a problem of calories, protein, iron, and a few vitamins, notably A and thiamin. We now recognize that malnutrition is most often a complex multiple deficiency state, and that complete fortification of foods is needed to cope with this problem.

Basic to an appreciation of nutrient requirements and the etiology of deficiency states is an understanding of the relationships between growth and the intakes and expenditures of energy, total nitrogen, essential and semiessential amino acids, essential fatty acids, vitamins, and minerals. Rates of growth and of weight gain, which are not synonymous, are determined primarily by calorie intake. Although not to the degree observed in small laboratory animals, the appetites of infants and children are affected by the caloric density of food, by the content of fat and nitrogen, and by the content and balance among essential amino acids. Small children, over a significant length of time, select diets which are balanced in regard to macronutrients. With the apparent single exception of sodium, however, they will not detect deficiencies of minerals and vitamins, continuing for a long time to consume diets which may lead to acute clinical deficiency states.

Protein and Amino Acids

GEORGE G. GRAHAM

After oxygen, water, and a source of energy, the nutrients most important for survival are the amino acids. Man, like all monogastric mammals, must consume enough protein to provide nitrogen and some 20 amino acids for the synthesis of new tissue during growth and to replace the nitrogen that is continuously lost from the body even when growth is complete. The ability of a protein to satisfy these requirements is determined primarily by its amino acid composition, for the body is able to synthesize from other compounds only about half of those needed for tissue protein synthesis; the rest must be provided preformed in the diet. Amino acids that can be synthesized are termed "dispensable" or "nonessential"; those that cannot, "indispensable" or "essential." For man the "essential" amino acids are valine, leucine, isoleucine, lysine, threonine, tryptophan, phenylalanine, and methionine; for the young infant histidine must be added to the list. Two additional amino acids, tyrosine and cystine, can only be synthesized from the "essentials" phenylalanine and methionine respectively. Since their presence in the diet reduces the need for the precursors, they are commonly called "semiessential." This classification applies only to dietary requirements for amino acids; they are all equally essential for protein synthesis. The "nonessential" amino acids can be synthesized by man from organic acids derived from intermediate carbohydrate metabolism, from nitrogen and surplus amino acids, or from such simple compounds as urea.

Many nitrogen-containing nonprotein compounds essential to body function are formed from amino acids: heme, creatine, choline, and glutathionine are examples. Tryptophan is the source of the pyridine nucleotides and of serotonin; phenylalanine and tyrosine are precursors of the thyroid hormones, the catecholamines, and melanin; methionine is the most important methyl donor of the body. Amino acids in excess of the needs for synthesis of protein and other compounds are deaminated, primarily in the liver, to yield either ammonia, which is converted to urea and excreted by the kidney, or α-keto acids, which may be used for synthesis of fat, glucose, and other substances. They may also be oxidized to carbon dioxide and water to yield energy in the form of phosphate bonds.

DIGESTIBILITY. Proteins cannot be absorbed intact but must undergo hydrolysis to their component amino acids. Hydrolysis is initiated in the stomach under the influence of pepsin, which facilitates the splitting of peptide bonds and the formation of shorter polypeptides. The stomach also controls the flow of partially digested food into the intestine, preventing overloading of digestive and absorptive capacities. In the intestine the partially digested protein is mixed with pancreatic and intestinal secretions and cells sloughed from the mucosa. It is estimated that these endogenous sources contribute at least as many amino acids as those coming from the dietary protein. Polypeptides undergo further hydrolysis under the influence of proteases and peptidases: trypsin, chymotrypsin, and carboxipeptidases from the pancreas and a mixture of peptidases from the intestine. Intestinal digestion is generally a rapid process.

The apparent digestibility of food protein is estimated by subtracting fecal nitrogen from the amount ingested and expressing the balance as a percentage of intake. For estimates of true digestibility, a correction must be made for endogenous fecal nitrogen, the amount excreted on a protein-free diet. Primarily because of their fiber content, most vegetable proteins are less well digested than those of egg and milk, the common standards of reference. This property adversely affects the net protein utilization of vegetable proteins. However, when isolated, their digestibility closely approximates that of milk or egg protein. It is believed, though not documented, that the molecular structure of proteins may alter their digestibility and the availability of their amino acids for protein synthesis in the body.

ABSORPTION. The naturally occurring L-amino acids are transported across the intestinal wall by an active process requiring energy. Different amino acids are transported against concentration gradients at different rates. At high concentrations some compete with others for common transport sites. There is also evidence for individual transport sites, probably of lesser capacity. It is unlikely that such competition is ever of importance in normal individuals; it may be in some inborn errors of metabolism. For example, the high levels of circulating phenylalanine in phenylketonuria interfere with tryptophan transport.

DISTRIBUTION. Some amino acids are removed during absorption for the synthesis of intestinal proteins, which have a rapid turnover; others, such as glutamic acid, may be transaminated to alanine, thereby changing their concentrations in the portal vein. However, the pattern of amino acids in the portal blood reaching the liver reflects rather faithfully the pattern in the dietary protein, as the amino acids removed for protein synthesis have a pattern nearly identical to those contributed from endogenous sources.

The liver withdraws amino acids for the synthesis of both liver and plasma proteins and for oxidation, particularly of those in surplus, converting the nitrogen to urea. It contributes those which are synthesized, including glycine, serine, alanine, aspartic and glutamic acids. Despite these alterations, free amino acids in the systemic blood will vary, for some time after a meal, according to the dietary pattern. Catabolism of excess amino acids is not a very active process, so it is some time before the levels of circulating amino acids return to the basal state. If an essential amino acid is deficient in the diet, its utilization in the intestine, liver, and elsewhere may markedly reduce its level in the systemic circulation, particularly at low levels of protein intake. Even when such an amino acid is not truly deficient but there is an excess of the remaining "essentials," its systemic level is reduced and appetite is adversely affected. This last situation is known as "amino acid imbalance."

Different tissues incorporate amino acids into protein at different rates. Secretory organs, notably the pancreas and small intestine, have the most rapid rates of uptake, followed by the liver. Muscle does so more slowly, but because it represents such a large fraction of body mass, it accounts for a great proportion of the amino acids utilized.

STORAGE. Unlike calories, amino acids are not stored in the form of glycogen and fat. Body protein content can be increased, but probably no more than 5 percent, by high protein intakes. This is hardly an efficient "store," since it is lost quite rapidly during periods of low intake. Normal body proteins which are lost first during starvation or low-protein consumption, and are made up promptly during refeeding, are at times referred to as "protein reserves." However, the term "labile body proteins" seems preferable, since their loss comprises function. These are lost primarily from liver, gastrointestinal tract, pancreas, and kidney. On prolonged depletion, muscle eventually contributes more than the viscera. The amino acids released under these circumstances are reutilized to maintain essential tissues and enzymes, with brain protein and oxidative enzymes particularly well conserved.

If all the amino acids are not available simultaneously in the proper proportions at protein synthetic sites, they will not be retained and the excesses will be disposed of within a few hours. It is thus not possible to consume at one meal a protein deficient in an essential amino acid and compensate for this by consuming the missing amino acid or a good source of it at the next meal. For efficient utilization of dietary protein it is essential that it be evenly distributed throughout the day and that each meal have a proper balance of amino acids. This requirement is of vital importance in infant nutrition.

The body does not distinguish between amino acids of dietary origin and those made available from the constant catabolism of body proteins. When the first are in short supply the second will be reused preferentially at sites which vary with the and size, but are determined by the total calorie intake and the efficiency of homeostatic mechanisms. These regulatory processes are accomplished through the endocrine and nervous systems, through their effects on transport and enzyme activity.

REQUIREMENTS. Much of the confusion about dietary requirements for nitrogen and essential amino acids can be resolved if it is recognized that these are not absolute for an individual of a given age and size but are determined by the total calorie intake, the rates of protein synthesis and of growth, and the physiologic state.

An estimate of the absolute requirement for total nitrogen can be made from the amounts for obligatory urine, stool, and skin losses and from changes in body composition with age. A general relationship holding for most mammals is the endogenous urinary excretion of 2 mg of nitrogen per basal kcal metabolized. On this basis, assuming a basal expenditure of 60 kcal/kg/day, a 10-kg infant would have a urine loss of 120 mg/kg/day. When measured urine losses on known protein intakes are extrapolated to a zero intake, this figure is approximated. On the other hand, when urine losses have been measured on a protein-free diet, these have been on the order of 40 to 60 mg/kg/day. Endogenous fecal nitrogen losses are generally estimated at 20 percent of the urine losses. On protein-free diets they have been measured at 10 to 20 mg/kg/day. Except under unusual conditions of heavy sweating, skin losses in infants and young children probably do not exceed 10 mg/kg/day. Thus the total obligatory losses lie between 60 and 150 mg/kg/day.

Nitrogen requirements during the first year of life are much higher per unit of body weight than at any other time. Besides rapid growth, with a tripling of body weight, an important process of "chemical maturation" is going on, with a change from approximately 2 percent nitrogen in the full-term newborn to 3 percent at one year. The premature, starting with a lower weight and lesser percentage of nitrogen, has even greater increment. For the full-term infant normal growth and maturation in the first year represent an average requirement of approximately 100 mg N/kg/day. Added to the obligatory losses, this becomes 160 to 250 mg, or roughly 0.5 to 0.8 g protein/kg/day. During the second year the requirement for growth falls to only 20 mg of N/kg/day and the total to 80 to 170 mg/kg/day. Since chemical maturation is nearly complete in the first four months and the rates of weight gain are progressively less during the course of the first year, the absolute requirement of nitrogen is much greater at the beginning than at the end of this year.

The figures given above assume 100 percent digestibility and utilization of dietary protein. However, even with human breast milk protein, this is never the case. Although digestibility may be over 95 percent, utilization for protein synthesis is not continuous, uniform, or perfectly efficient. Ingestion of food, as well as the availability of amino acids, occurs sporadically so that the synthetic ability is exceeded and amino acids are, in part, catabolized. Although protein-synthetic mechanisms are generally responsive to food intake, they have intrinsic rhythms of activity and limits to their capacity. Significant variations in physiologic state, even in quite normal infants, result in periods of poor appetite, increased caloric expenditure, reduced rates of protein synthesis, increased catabolism of protein, and consequent irregularities in the pattern of growth. In order to compensate for these variations in rates of protein utilization, dietary protein intake must of necessity exceed the calculated "requirement" by a large amount. The dietary requirement of the highest quality protein, determined from intakes known to be adequate for maximal growth during the first year, has been estimated to average around 1.5 g/kg/day, decreasing from approximately 2.2 g at birth to 1.2 g at one year, or roughly twice the calculated "requirement." Thereafter the dietary requirement of such a protein probably does not exceed 1.0 g/kg/day, even during the growth spurt of adolescence.

The breast-fed infant, or the one receiving a modified cow's milk formula at the same level of protein intake, retains approximately 45 percent of his nitrogen intake, an amount very near to that estimated on the basis of obligatory losses and the requirements for growth and maturation. With increasing age, as other sources of dietary protein gradually replace part or all of the milk protein, digestibility and biologic value became more important and a correction for these must be made in estimating the requirement.

When we relate the above estimates of dietary protein requirement to those of energy requirements, we can see that approximately 6 to 7 percent of dietary calories must be provided as high-quality protein. This is the range within which the protein/ calorie ratio of human breast milk falls. If dietary protein falls below 6 percent of calories for any length of time, manifestations of inadequacy appear, even though weight gain and linear growth continue. This subject is covered further in the section on protein deficiency (p. 170).

Human milk, cow's milk, and whole egg proteins, the usual standards of reference, provide approximately 50 percent of their nitrogen as "essential" and "semiessential" amino acids. In most vegetable proteins only 32 to 38 percent of nitrogen is present in this form. It has been shown that the high-quality proteins can have their essential amino acid content diluted with nonessential nitrogen without reducing their utilization by the human infant or child. It has also been shown that well-balanced vegetable proteins can be fed at levels which are critical for milk or egg protein and support equivalent rates of growth. These observations indicate that there is a "surplus" of essential amino acids in the high-quality animal proteins when they are fed at levels in which total nitrogen is the limiting factor for growth. This "surplus" is something on the order of 20 percent of the amount present. If essential amino acid requirements are estimated on this basis they come quite close to the estimates of Holt and Snyderman from studies with mixtures of pure amino acids. It is now generally conceded that the "pattern" of essential amino acids in human breast milk is ideal for the human infant, a revelation which is not too surprising. It is closely approximated by that of whole egg or of cow's milk as commonly modified to reduce its content of casein and increase the relative content of lactalbumin, approaching the proportions in breast milk. As the digestibility of these proteins is high, their net protein utilization is almost identical to that from breast milk.

The content of essential amino acids in the proteins of common cereals and other vegetable proteins is relatively low. Also, compared with breast milk protein, examination of the pattern of essentials and semiessentials reveals a markedly lower relative content of one or more essentials and occasionally an unusually high content of another. Lysine is markedly deficient in wheat protein; both lysine and threonine are deficient in rice protein; whereas in corn, lysine and tryptophan are deficient but leucine is present in excess. Most legumes have a high protein content, but generally there is a moderate excess of lysine and a marked deficiency of methionine. In commonly consumed mixed diets, such as rice and beans and corn and beans, the high protein and lysine contents of the legumes compensate for their low values in the cereals. The more generous methionine and cystine contents of the cereals only partially make up the deficiency in the beans, leaving the sulfur-containing amino acids as apparently first-limiting in the diets of most developing countries. In the diets of infants and small children in the same countries, however, the legumes are often not included or are given in very small amounts, leaving lysine as first-limiting in their almost exclusively cereal diets. For this reason the use of fish protein concentrates or a variety of soya products, both rich in protein and in lysine, and the synthetic amino acid itself, are receiving considerable attention as possible supplements to such diets. Diets based on the most abundant and inexpensive starchy roots and tubers, cassava and the sweet potato, are so low in protein that supplementation with a well-balanced protein takes precedence over attempts to correct their specific amino acid deficiencies. Attempts to compensate for this low protein content, or for a severe amino acid deficiency, by increasing the total consumption of such items, are forestalled by the inability to digest the tremendous excess of starch and by the calorie excess, relative to protein, which is automatically created.

The estimates of nitrogen and essential amino acid requirements which have been discussed are based on calorie intakes which support a steady rate of protein synthesis and growth at assumed "normal" rates. If calorie intake is significantly lower, or expenditure is increased, rates of protein synthesis decrease and so does the requirement. Provision of normal dietary intakes of protein under such circumstances results in its partial utilization as a source of energy and an excess of nitrogen to be excreted. In the management of renal failure this creates a hazard to health. It has been shown that in such circumstances the provision of essential amino acids alone is adequate for a considerable length of time, the accumulated excess of unessential nitrogen in the body, mostly as urea, serving as the nitrogen source for unessential amino acid synthesis.

When higher than usual calorie intakes are consumed, either during rehabilitation from undernutrition or during the accumulation of excess weight, the nitrogen and essential amino acid requirement is considerably higher than the usual. If such a relative excess of calories over protein is consumed for more than a few days, signs of protein deficiency will appear (see p. 175). With rare exceptions, a diet which provides approximately 8 percent of calories as high-quality protein will prove adequate at any level of caloric intake and rate of growth. In mixed protein diets, with poorer digestibility, with a lower ratio of essential amino acid to total nitrogen, and with a moderate deficiency of one or more essentials, 11 to 15 percent of calories as protein are usually adequate. Significant excesses of dietary protein, particularly in situations of limited water intake or excessive insensible losses, commonly result in chronic dehydration and "fever of unknown origin" by virtue of the increase in obligatory renal water excretion.

Natural dietary excesses of amino acids are not known to be of practical significance, with the possible exception of the role of excess leucine in the pathogenesis of pellagra. In the same condition a relative deficiency of tryptophan is of importance. A "specific" role for methionine deficiency in hepatic steatosis has long been debated. With these two exceptions, no specific lesions of single amino acid deficiency are documented or suspected from natural diets. In the management of inborn errors of amino acid metabolism it is necessary to create borderline deficiency states for the amino acids in question. When these deficiencies become excessive, the manifestations are basically indistinguishable from those of protein deficiency.

If parenteral nutrition is required for a few days in a previously well-nourished infant or child, it is seldom necessary to worry about nitrogen and amino acid intakes. It is also unnecessary and injudicious to attempt the provision of normal calorie intakes without protein, thus creating an acute protein-deficient state. If parenteral nutrition must be prolonged, or if it is necessary in the severely malnourished, the provision of at least 8 percent of calories as "protein" is certainly advisable. Protein hydrolysates or mixtures of synthetic amino acids are superior to intact proteins for parenteral nutrition since the former are immediately available at the sites of protein synthesis.

Fat

L. EMMETT HOLT, JR.

Fat is an integral constituent of all body tissues. The depot fat or adipose tissue serves primarily as an energy reserve and consists almost exclusively of neutral fat. A variable amount of glyceride is present in other tissues too, but much of their fat is combined as cholesterol esters and phospholipids; other fat complexes include the lipoproteins of the blood and the galactolipids of the brain and other tissues. The depot fat normally constitutes 10 percent or more of the body weight, but in states of inanition it may fall below 1 percent and in extreme obesity it may exceed 50 percent. Its characteristics are affected to a considerable extent by the dietary fat. In the adult the depot fat is relatively unsaturated, having an iodine value between 65 and 80, whereas in the newborn infant it is more saturated, having an iodine value between 30 and 45; the iodine value rises rapidly during the first year. There is evidence that the more saturated fat is less readily mobilized from the depots. The fat pads of the cheeks, the lipid of which remains relatively saturated throughout infancy, show a striking tendency to resist mobilization in inanition. The more saturated character of the fat in the neonatal period may explain the resistance to ketosis at this time of life.

The tissue lipids are less sensitive than the depot fat to alterations in the dietary fat. They are always more unsaturated than the ingested fat, and the extent to which they can be depleted in inanition is far more limited.

Fat is readily synthesized from the acetate residues derived from the breakdown of carbohydrate and protein. This is true of saturated fats and those with one unsaturated linkage. However, there appears to be difficulty in synthesizing the more highly unsaturated fatty acids, linoleic and arachidonic acid, which are needed by the body in minute amounts. Animal studies have shown that in the absence of these "essential fatty acids" a characteristic skin disease develops. It is probable that traces of the highly unsaturated fatty acids are essential to man also. The experimental studies of Hansen point to this conclusion. However, specific fatty acid deficiency is not to be feared in practical dietetics, since its development requires a more rigid exclusion of all traces of fat from the diet than would ever occur in practice. A new importance has been attached to the essential fatty acids in recent years with the observation that the level of blood cholesterol is affected by the intake of these highly unsaturated fatty acids. The substitution of vegetable fats such as corn oil, safflower oil, olive oil, and others which contain a higher proportion of these fatty acids than butter has a definite depressing effect on the serum cholesterol level, advantage of which is taken in current attempts to prevent atheromatous disease in adults. The importance of including more liberal intakes of these fatty acids in the diet of infants and young children has yet to be shown. It may be mentioned, however, that claims have been made that the seeds of atheromatous disease are planted in early life. Breast milk ordinarily contains more of the essential fatty acids than does cow's milk. However, it seems to result in higher cholesterol levels in the blood, a phenomenon which still cannot be explained.

Infants have been fed for months on virtually fat-free diets without obvious impairment of health, provided fat-soluble vitamins are supplied. The stools may be loose and mushy for a time, but this condition tends to disappear. A tendency toward eczema and toward asthma has been observed on complete withdrawal of fat from the diet. It seems possible that this phenomenon is associated with the increased hydration of the body when carbohydrate is substituted for the fat, a phenomenon which is discussed below.

Granting that fat can be withdrawn from the diet without serious consequences, there are good reasons for including it. It is the most concentrated source of energy available and is a vehicle for fat-soluble vitamins. There is literature indicating that the inclusion of some fat in the diet improves resistance against infections, an important question which deserves more critical study.

The dangers of a high-fat diet have, in our opinion, been greatly overestimated. Ketogenic diets are well tolerated for long periods barring the development of some intercurrent infection. The view that a high-fat diet per se may lead to fat intolerance does not bear critical analysis; in our experience such disturbances, when seen, can be attributed to factors other than the fat of the diet. There are, however, certain definite indications for reducing the fat intake: (1) certain cases of nausea and vomiting; (2) ketosis, unless induced for therapeutic purposes; (3) lipemia with or without a fatty liver; and (4) lymphatic obstructions leading to chylothorax or chylous ascites. The intake of fat which will lead to nausea and vomiting varies greatly with individuals and with conditioning; the phenomenon appears to be related in some way to the inhibition of gastric motility and secretion caused by fat. In the presence of these symptoms it may be desirable to reduce the fat intake. Ketosis occurs when more fat is presented for combustion than can be completely burned; this must be regarded as an unphysiologic state.* In the presence of lipemia or lymphatic obstruction dietary fat only adds to the severity of the process.

Steatorrhea, the loss of an abnormal amount of fat in the stools, has long been regarded as an indication for avoiding fat, a view which is open to question. It is clear that when fat assimilation is faulty, reducing the fat intake will reduce the fecal

* Ketosis. The older view that "fats burn in the flame of carbohydrates" and that antiketogenic factors derived from carbohydrate and protein are essential to the oxidation of ketone bodies has been reinterpreted. Metabolic products of all three calorigenic foodstuffs enter the citric acid cycle as acetyl CoA which combines with oxaloacetic acid to form citric acid. Fat, however, enters the cycle only at this point, whereas products of carbohydrate metabolism and those derived from some amino acids can enter the cycle directly at other points. The cycle is thus more readily fed by carbohydrate and protein than by fat and may become overtaxed when supplied only the acetyl CoA derived from fat, with the result that the ketone bodies accumulate. However, there is a marked ability to adapt to a ketogenic diet, decreasing quantities of ketones appearing as it is continued. According to Corcoran and Rabinowitch, Eskimos are extraordinarily resistant to ketosis.

fat and improve the appearance of the stools. However, it does not follow that fat restriction improves the patient or in any way shortens his disease. Metabolic observations in various types of steatorrhea have shown that the more fat given the more the patient absorbs, regardless of the loss in the stool, and that there is no resulting washing out of other nutrients or evidence of delayed recovery. This evidence suggests the desirability of liberal fat administration for the sake of maintaining a balanced assimilation of foodstuffs.

Fats differ in their ease of assimilation, depending on their constituent fatty acids. The short-chain fatty acids and those with unsaturated linkages are more readily assimilable. These differences are minimal in the case of the normal infant, but in conditions of steatorrhea, where assimilation is impaired, the substitution of vegetable fats, such as corn oil, olive oil, and soybean oil, for butter may be of practical value. Fine emulsification of the fat will also aid its assimilation in steatorrhea.

The inhibitory effects of fat upon gastric secretion and motility vary similarly with the composition of the fat, the more readily assimilable fats giving the greater inhibition.

Carbohydrate

L. EMMETT HOLT, JR.

This furnishes our most convenient source of energy. Although indispensable in the internal economy of the body, carbohydrate is not actually a dietary essential, for it can readily be synthesized from protein and to a considerable extent from fat. The eating habits of Eskimos and other exclusively carnivorous peoples show that a diet containing a minimum of carbohydrate is consistent with health and growth. Stefansson reports having seen infants successfully reared on a diet of seal meat chewed up by an adult and expectorated into the infant's mouth. Chwalibogowski fed an infant without mishap for the first 10 months of life on an exceedingly low carbohydrate diet. Such a regimen, however, has definite limitations. When considerable fat is given, ketosis is likely to develop.

The desirability of feeding infants with such a low carbohydrate intake as is present in unsupplemented cow's milk has been questioned. That such feedings can be successful is no longer disputed.

In older children the influence of high-carbohydrate, particularly high-sugar, ingestion on the development of dental caries appears to be well established. A high intake of carbohydrate was often blamed in the past for products which stimulated peristalsis. To combat this untoward development Finkelstein developed protein milk, a relatively low carbohydrate feeding which was widely used for infants by a generation of pediatricians. This concept has now been almost completely abandoned. Howland, Park, Marriott, and others showed that the addition of sugar to protein milk not only failed to exacerbate diarrhea but even benefited patients, presumably by supplying more calories. Only in cases of congenital disaccharidase deficiency and in exceptional instances of acquired deficiency of these enzymes does appreciable fermentative diarrhea occur.

A condition known in the German literature as *Mehlnahrschaden*—carbohydrate injury—was attributed to a diet in which cereal carbohydrate predominated. Infants so fed might gain in weight but not in strength; they were flabby and seemed to have little resistance to infection. It now seems clear that it was not the excess of carbohydrate but rather the deficiency of other nutrients, notably protein and vitamins, that explained the picture.

When an isocaloric shift is made, carbohydrate calories replacing fat calories, a sudden gain in weight may occur for a few days, after which the previous slope of the weight curve is resumed. The gain in weight is due to water retention accompanied by both extracellular and intracellular electrolyte and some nitrogen as well. These retained elements are loosely held and are readily lost in the presence of infection or when dietary carbohydrate is replaced by fat. The nitrogen partition in the urine is affected by this dietary shift; on the higher fat intake there is an increase in the excretion of total nitrogen and of all the nitrogenous ingredients of the urine with the exception of the purines, the excretion of which is diminished. Conversely, on the higher carbohydrate intake the total nitrogen of the urine falls, although the output of purines rises. The significance of these changes is not entirely clear. Munro has shown that it is the absolute change in carbohydrate intake rather than the change in fat or in the fat-carbohydrate ratio which is responsible. Retention of water and electrolytes on high-carbohydrate diets seems to be associated with the deposition of glycogen.

The question of whether resistance to infection can be appreciably enhanced or diminished by a predominance of one or another foodstuff in the diet cannot be answered at the present time. The available clinical evidence is conflicting. Efforts to reduce the frequency of intercurrent infections in clinically well-nourished infants and children by manipulation of the diet have on the whole produced disappointing results.

In infant feeding a carbohydrate supplement is commonly added to cow's milk. In former times great importance was attached to the type of carbohydrate used, but it is now realized that the differences in the behavior of the various carbohydrates are very minor ones and in the vast majority of instances are of no practical importance as far as health is concerned. The various carbohydrates used in infant feeding are described elsewhere.

Percentage Distribution of Calories

L. EMMETT HOLT, JR.

The energy content of a diet may be expressed best in terms of the percentage of calories derived from each of the primary sources of energy—protein, fat, and carbohydrate. Thus, once the optimal (or minimal) number of calories for intake is decided upon, the distribution allocated to these sources determines their content in the diet. Of the three, only the protein seems to have an important minimum. One must recognize the significance of this form of notation, because if the caloric value of a diet should be increased by the addition of carbohydrates, for example, the percentage of protein calories becomes lower and may fall below the minimum (6 to 8 percent) even though the absolute intake stays the same. The consequence will be protein undernutrition. The foregoing assumes that the higher caloric intake will be absorbed and fully utilized by the subject thus obligating more amino acids for protein synthesis.

The distribution of calories in breast milk—protein 8 percent, fat 50 percent, carbohydrate 42 percent—has certainly proved to be satisfactory when that food is used. Cow's milk feedings in which only a little more protein (10 percent of the calories) is given have been used for many years with success, as have feedings with more protein and less fat (protein 15 percent, fat 35 percent, carbohydrate 50 percent), carried over by tradition from the days when curd indigestion was a problem and when cow's milk fat was feared.

For older children figures for optimal caloric distribution are equally impossible to give. There are figures on what healthy children themselves take, but these are greatly influenced by habits and by what is offered to them. A wide range is apparently compatible with health. The American child in an upper or middle economic group takes, on the average, about 15 percent of his calories as protein, 35 percent as fat and 50 percent as carbohydrate, but there are wide individual variations. It is quite clear from the studies of McCance and others in postwar Germany that children do well on less protein and more carbohydrate. Further studies in this field are needed before one can be dogmatic about a desirable caloric distribution.

Vitamins

L. EMMETT HOLT, JR.

The term "vitamin" is applied to a group of organic accessory food factors that must be supplied to the body in small amounts to maintain health.

Many of them serve as constituents of body enzymes, and it may be that all of them function in this way. A large number of these factors have been described on the basis of observations in experimental animals, but only a few are of established importance in human nutrition. The human vitamins can be classified in three categories:

1. *Obligatory vitamins*—factors which must always be supplied in the diet if health is to be maintained.
2. *Conditional vitamins*—factors needed only in the presence of a deficit of some other nutrient.
3. *Questionable vitamins*—substances concerned in body metabolism which are not yet established as dietary essentials for the *normal human* subject. Until they are shown to be required, exception may be taken to the current practice of designating them as vitamins.

Obligatory Vitamins	Conditional Vitamins	Questionable Vitamins
Vitamin A (or its carotene equivalent)	Nicotinic acid	Biotin
	Choline	Inositol
	Vitamin K	Pantothenic acid
Thiamine		Vitamin E
Riboflavin		
Pyridoxine		
Folic acid		
Vitamin B$_{12}$		
Vitamin C (ascorbic acid)		
Vitamin D (or its equivalent in ultraviolet radiation)		

The Obligatory Vitamins

Vitamin A, a fat-soluble factor, plays an important part in maintaining the integrity of epithelial structures. It also is a constituent of the visual pigments of the retina. Natural vitamin A is found in most animal fats, with the exception of lard, but scarcely at all in vegetable fats. Several carotenoid pigments found in colored vegetables can, however, act as precursors of vitamin A, the most important of which is β-carotene. Deficiency will not occur unless both of these sources are cut off. In certain pathological conditions in which there is grossly defective fat absorption or failure of conversion of carotene to vitamin A, special attention should be given to this vitamin. The subject of vitamin A deficiency is considered in detail elsewhere.

Thiamine, a pyrimidine-thiazole compound, forms the prosthetic group of several respiratory enzymes. A deficiency of thiamine leads to beriberi, which is still an important deficiency disease in some parts of the world, notably where rice con-

stitutes a major portion of the diet. In the United States thiamine deficiency is exceedingly rare, being seen only as a result of dietary fads and in alcoholics. The function of thiamine and clinical aspects of thiamine deficiency are considered elsewhere.

Riboflavin, a greenish yellow pigment, an alloxazine ribose compound, forms the functional group of a large class of enzymes, the flavoproteins, which are present in every cell. Like thiamine, riboflavin is widely distributed in animal and vegetable foods, a deficiency becoming possible only when the diet consists largely of refined carbohydrates. The clinical features of riboflavin deficiency are considered on page 180.

Pyridoxine (vitamin B$_6$), a methoxy-pyridine derivative, is one of the most important cofactors in metabolic reactions. It is the prosthetic group of a great many enzymes concerned with the metabolism of amino acids and proteins and of some that are concerned with fat metabolism. Pyridoxine is well established as a dietary essential, a deficiency giving rise to anemia and to lesions of the skin and nervous system. However, because of its wide distribution, pyridoxine deficiency is rarely encountered in man. It has been observed only when some unusual heating procedure has damaged the pyridoxine of the food and in a rare condition known as pyridoxine dependency in which unusually large amounts of this vitamin are required.

Folic acid (pteroylglutamic acid) is widely distributed in natural foods. It is a constituent of many enzyme systems, notably those concerned with the transfer of single-carbon units. The reactions of folic acid and the circumstances under which deficiency may develop are described elsewhere.

Vitamin B$_{12}$ (cobalamine), the antipernicious anemia extrinsic factor, is a cobalt porphyrin compound in which the cobalt is linked coordinately to a benzimidazole-ribofuranase-phosphate complex. The terms cobalamine and B$_{12}$ refer to the group as a whole, its members having individual designations (the cyanide as cyanocobalamine or B$_{12a}$, the nitrite as nitritocobalamine or B$_{12b}$, etc.). The exact form present in the body is not known, but it appears to be intimately associated with the mitochondria.

Cobalamine is widely distributed in animal tissue but virtually absent in vegetable products, hence it is sometimes designated the animal growth factor. It is an essential metabolite for all higher animals but not necessarily a dietary essential. Herbivorous animals obtain it from bacterial synthesis in the gut. Whether B$_{12}$ is a dietary essential for man has been uncertain. Small amounts are synthesized by intestinal bacteria, but mostly in the large intestine from which little is absorbed. The most impressive evidence for its dietary essentiality comes from the study of vegans—complete vegetarians who rigorously exclude milk and eggs as well as animal tissues from their diet. Observations by Wokes et al. showed that in the course of years many of them developed evidence of B$_{12}$ deficiency. Hence it seems proper to class B$_{12}$ among the dietary essentials; it is of practical importance, however, only to vegetarians and to individuals who lack intrinsic factor and therefore have difficulty in absorbing B_{12}.

Absorption of B_{12} from the intestine is dependent on intrinsic factor, a heat-labile enzyme of mucoprotein nature which is defective in pernicious anemia, postgastrectomy anemia, and certain gastrointestinal malformations. Although most patients with pernicious anemia will respond to large doses of oral B_{12}, a few require parenteral therapy.

B_{12} is thought to function in respiratory metabolism. There is evidence that it is concerned with disulfide reductions, with formation of desoxyribose compounds, and with formation of succinate from methyl malonate. Its function is closely related to folic acid, which it may activate; a folic derivative, methyl tetrahydrofolic acid, is frequently found in the urine of untreated patients with pernicious anemia. B_{12} is concerned in some way with the transfer of single-carbon units and with the synthesis of purines and porphyrins. A deficiency of B_{12} induces maturation arrest of the red cells with macrocytosis and a megaloblastic marrow. The life-span of such red cells averages only 60 days. The degenerative changes in the nervous system in B_{12} deficiency have no counterpart in folic acid deficiency.

The administration of B_{12} is indicated in pernicious anemia, fish tapeworm anemia, postgastrectomy anemias, and for complete vegetarians. Reports that it stimulates the growth of premature and malnourished infants have not been substantiated, nor has it proved effective in degenerative disease of the central nervous system, other than that associated with pernicious anemia. The clinical management of pernicious anemia is discussed elsewhere (Sec. 17.2).

Ascorbic acid (vitamin C) is a hexuronic acid of lactone structure. It is a powerful reducing agent, but relatively little is known about its metabolic function. It is known to be concerned in the utilization of the aromatic amino acids, in the conversion of folic to folinic acid, and in the synthesis of steroids, but definite enzyme systems containing this factor have not been isolated. It is further discussed in connection with scurvy (p. 186) and megaloblastic anemia (Sec. 17.2).

Vitamin D. The body has a definite requirement for certain steroids possessing vitamin D activity. This factor is concerned particularly with calcification of the skeleton. This need can be met by providing a vitamin D-containing compound in the diet or by exposure of the body to ultraviolet radiation, which activates a precursor in the skin, 7-dehydrocholesterol, producing a steroid having vitamin D activity. In a sense vitamin D can be regarded as a conditional vitamin, since it is possible to meet the requirements by irradiation alone. By and large, however, we rely on ingested vitamin D to meet the demand, which is greatest in infancy when calcification of the skeleton is proceeding rapidly. The subject is discussed in detail elsewhere (p. 197).

The Conditional Vitamins

Nicotinic acid (pyridine carboxylic acid; niacin). The amide of nicotinic acid (niacinamide) is a constituent of the diphospho and triphospho pyridine nucleotides (DPN and TPN), the functional group of a number of important respiratory enzymes. A shortage of this factor is responsible for the development of pellagra (p. 181). However, nicotinic acid does not have to be supplied as such. It is readily formed from the degradation of tryptophan, provided pyridoxine (vitamin B_6) is present; in fact, tryptophan can supply all the body needs for nicotinic acid. The requirements for this factor are commonly expressed in terms of niacin equivalents rather than of niacin itself, a niacin equivalent being the quantity of niacin plus $\frac{1}{60}$ of the quantity of tryptophan in the diet, usually expressed in milligrams. Niacin is widely distributed in animal and vegetable foods, but the intake is likely to be low when the diet consists predominantly of refined carbohydrates. In the milling of cereals this factor, like thiamine and riboflavin, is in large part lost. Clinical pellagra is seen particularly in people subsisting on a diet of corn meal, for there is not enough tryptophan in corn to make up for the loss of niacin that occurs in milling. There is also some evidence suggesting that the niacin present in corn is not readily available.

Choline is a constituent of many important biologic compounds, notably acetylcholine and the lecithin-containing phospholipids. It is intimately concerned with the oxidation of fatty acids, with the turnover of phospholipids, and with fat transport. It also serves as a methyl donor in transmethylation reactions. A deficiency of choline in experimental animals leads to the accumulation of fat in the liver, and in the rat to hemorrhagic lesions in the kidney. Although choline is essential in the diet of certain animals there is good evidence that it can be synthesized in man from methionine. It cannot therefore be regarded as a human food essential except in states of methionine deficiency. The development of fatty liver in humans does not constitute specific evidence of a deficiency of choline or methionine, for a number of different types of imbalance can produce fatty liver. Administration of choline and methionine is rarely effective in the treatment of fatty liver in humans.

Vitamin K. A number of quinones, some natural and some synthetic, are known to possess vitamin K activity. Vitamin K is a fat-soluble factor normally present in the body which is concerned in the synthesis of prothrombin and certain other related blood coagulation factors in the liver. It is present in certain natural fats, but ordinarily the human requirement is effectively synthesized by the intestinal bacteria. Under exceptional circumstances, however, this synthesis is not adequate, and a deficiency of prothrombin develops. In the first few days of life, before the intestinal bacteria are well established, the production of vitamin K in the intestine is limited and a prolonged prothrombin time is the rule. Only rarely, however, is the degree of deficiency sufficient to lead to hemorrhagic manifestations (Sec. 17.13). Hemorrhagic disease of the newborn is somewhat more frequent in premature infants, in whom immaturity of the liver and defective formation of prothrombin from vitamin K play a part. Congenital atresia of the alimentary tract may also be associated with defective synthesis of vitamin K. Prothrombin deficiency is seen in older subjects as a result of liver disease or as a result of defective fat absorption in steatorrhea. We have seen it develop following prolonged administration of antibiotics. Under these circumstances the administration of vitamin K may be helpful. Most authorities recommend its routine administration to all newborn infants. Virtually all advise that it be given to premature infants.

The Questionable Vitamins

Biotin appears to function as a constituent of respiratory enzymes. Minute amounts are present in nearly all foods, and animal experiments have shown that it is readily synthesized in adequate amounts by the intestinal bacteria. A deficiency of biotin, which results in a characteristic dermatosis, results only when the biotin so formed is inactivated by eating raw egg white. Egg white contains a protein known as avidin, which combines with biotin and renders it unavailable. Biotin deficiency has been produced experimentally in adult volunteers by means of a diet containing liberal amounts of raw egg white, and in one instance at least it apparently developed in a dietary faddist who consumed such a diet. It has not been observed in children.

The discovery of biotin was followed by a number of uncritical reports of its efficacy in various dermatoses, but these have not been substantiated.

Inositol. One of the isomers of inositol—*meso-inositol* or *muscle sugar*—is closely related to glucose and appears to play an important part in metabolism. It is widely distributed in the body, being found in largest amounts in the heart, brain, and skeletal muscle. In unregulated diabetics and patients getting glucose infusions there is a marked loss of inositol in the urine. Inositol has been shown to be a dietary essential for rodents. The mouse on a diet devoid of this factor develops alopecia. In humans, however, it appears that inositol can be synthesized and cannot be regarded as a food essential.

Pantothenic acid, a compound of β-alanine and dihydroxy-dimethyl butyric acid, is an integral part of coenzyme A, other constituents being β-mercaptoethylamine, pyrophosphate, and phosphoadenosine. Coenzyme A plays a fundamental part in many metabolic reactions. Its active form, acetyl CoA, is concerned in the Krebs cycle and indeed with transfers of two-carbon units generally. It is concerned in the synthesis of fats, steroids, and porphyrins, with acetylation and glycine conjugation.

In experimental animals a variety of lesions has been produced by diets deficient in pantothenic acid. Dermatitis is prominent in the chick, alopecia is seen in the pig, and gray hair develops in black rats. Anemia, gastrointestinal symptoms, and degenerative changes in the nervous system occur in several species. Rats exhibit gonadal atrophy and adrenal hemorrhages, and there is evidence that they are particularly susceptible to stress; antibody formation may be impaired.

Evidence that humans suffer from pantothenic acid deficiency under any natural conditions is only suggestive. The *burning foot syndrome* observed in Japanese war prisoners was reported to respond to the administration of pantothenic acid. It is clear that pantothenic acid is not a human antigray-hair factor. A blind control study conducted by Bean and his co-workers on volunteer prisoners showed that rigid exclusion of this compound from the diet or the administration of an antagonist led to a variety of symptoms, which included fatigue, malaise, nausea and vomiting, abdominal cramps, paresthesias, and muscular incoordination. The eosinopenic response to ACTH was lost, perhaps because the stressful situation had already caused eosinopenia. It was not possible to demonstrate adrenal malfunction or impaired acetylation in these subjects. Improvement occurred when pantothenic acid was given, but it was incomplete. No evidence has been presented that infants and young children suffer from pantothenic acid deficiency or are benefited by a dietary supplement of this factor. Pantothenic acid is widely distributed in foods, and the possibility of a deficiency occurring on any natural diet is extremely remote.

Vitamin E. Vitamin E, a fat-soluble factor identified as α-tocopherol, is an effective antioxidant. It is a dietary essential for several animal species, but its mechanism of action is not known. In the rabbit, absence of E gives rise to progressive muscular dystrophy, in the chick a degenerative form of brain disease develops, and in the rat the reproductive organs are affected with degenerative changes in the testes in the male, and resorption of the fetus in the pregnant female. In the monkey, Dinning has observed the development, after some months, of a macrocytic anemia associated with multinucleated megaloblasts. Majaj, Dinning, and their co-workers have described in kwashiorkor patients an anemia similar to that in the monkey, responding to vitamin E and some related compounds. Whether this is a primary or a conditioned deficiency is not clear. Observations on human volunteers by Horwitt have also suggested the essentiality of vitamin E for man. Alpha-tocopherol can be measured in the blood and tissues, and there is definite evidence that it has a role in the human body. In steatorrhea, reduced absorption of this factor and lower blood levels have been demonstrated. György and his co-workers showed that in vitamin E-deficient animals the red cells were susceptible to hemolysis by hydrogen peroxide. This test has been found by Gordon to be positive in certain premature infants and in patients with cystic fibrosis of the pancreas, on the basis of which the administration of vitamin E to such subjects has been recommended. A positive peroxide hemolysis reaction can be reversed by vitamin E administration, but as yet no clinical benefit has been demonstrated. The administration of large amounts of polyunsaturated fat to animals appears to increase their requirement for vitamin E, perhaps because of its antioxidant properties.

In animal nutrition a curious relationship has been demonstrated between vitamin E and the element selenium. Some but not all of the manifestation of E deficiency can be counteracted by trace quantities of selenium in the diet. It is possible that traces of selenium present in human diets serve to protect humans from vitamin E deficiency.

Vitamin Supplementation of Human Diets

The discovery of the vitamins and the development of simple methods for their manufacture have been followed by their exploitation as food supplements. In the United States this has reached extraordinary proportions. Vitamins have become symbols of health and are ingested in quantities far beyond possible needs. This situation has been brought about by commercial pressures aided by enthusiastic nutrition workers whose attention has been focused on the prevention of deficiency diseases. Skillful advertising using fear techniques has created a public demand for vitamins, which in turn brings pressure to bear on the physician. The conscientious physician wishes to make sure that his patients do not suffer from deficiency, but he also feels the obligation to protect them from the expense and from the fear of deficits which they are in no danger of incurring. The Council on Foods of the American Medical Association has taken the position that administration of accessory factors as such or their incorporation in foods is justified when a need is demonstrated, a position in which we concur. The effort to render each article of human diet a complete and balanced food rather than to balance the diet by eating a variety of foods has little to recommend it. None of the deficiency diseases should be feared with customary American mixed diets. There is no more justification for giving unnecessary vitamins than for giving unnecessary medication. In both instances there are risks of overdosage which cannot be ignored.

In infancy some thought must be given to providing vitamin C and vitamin D. Cow's milk, unless reinforced, does not provide enough D to prevent rickets. Unless fed on evaporated milk or fresh milk with added vitamin D the infant may not receive the 400 international units per day which the normal infant requires during the period of rapid skeletal growth. The rare individual who requires more than this is a medical problem; the attempt to cover his requirements by giving more vitamin D to all infants has brought to the fore instances of hypercalcemia (p. 207), which are explained either by excessive intake or by unusual sensitivity to the action of vitamin D.

The possibility of vitamin A deficiency need occasion no concern except in the case of infants who are fed on skim milk. The fat of even half-skimmed milk is ample to meet the infant's needs.

The greatest exploitation has occurred in the case of the B vitamins, for which many unjustifiable claims about health and particularly mental health are made. The fact that many of these factors are found together in nature—in yeast and in the germ of cereals—has led to the view that they are functionally related and to their designation as the "B complex." This has been interpreted as an indication that a proper balance must be maintained in the intake of these factors.

There appears to be no reason for giving B complex as such. Some of the B factors, as has been pointed out, are readily synthesized and not needed in the diet. An imbalance caused by administering faulty proportions of the B factors has not been demonstrated. Infants who receive milk and older children on mixed diets are not in danger of acquiring any B deficiency, nor can their health or mentality by improved by supplements of these factors. Certain of the B factors have an important place in the diet of persons living in underdeveloped countries with a low standard of living. Some of these factors have a place in special pathologic states, but their administration to healthy subjects in the United States is superfluous. It is generally admitted that the abolition of pellagra in this country was brought about not by the administration of nicotinic acid but by socioeconomic factors which raised the standard of living in the South and led to a higher tryptophan intake.

Water

LAURENCE FINBERG

Water, constituting 70 percent of the lean body mass, represents an indispensable and prime constituent of the body. A daily water requirement occurs because of obligatory ongoing losses of water. These losses must occur because (1) energy expended in the form of heat removes water directly through evaporation from skin and lungs; and (2) the energy metabolism producing the heat creates changes in extracellular fluid composition, the adjustment of which obligates loss of water by the kidney. The

TABLE 1.   *Basal Water Requirements in Relation to Age, Weight, and Surface Area*

Age	Weight lbs	Weight kg	Surface Area m²	Basal Metabolism Cal/kg	Basal Metabolism Cal/24 hr	Minimal Basal Water Requirement ml/24 hr	Minimal Basal Water Requirement ml/m³	Minimal Basal Water Requirement ml/kg
Newborn	7.5	3.3	0.2	45	150	150	750	45
1 wk	7.5	3.3	0.2	60	200	200	1,000	60
2 mo	11	5	0.25	54	270	270	1,080	54
6 mo	17.5	8	0.35	50	400	400	1,140	50
12 mo	22	10	0.45	50	500	500	1,110	50
3 yr	33	15	0.60	47	700	700	1,170	47
5 yr	44	20	0.80	45	900	900	1,120	45
8 yr	66	30	1.05	37	1,100	1,100	1,050	37
13 yr	132	60	1.70	27	1,600	1,600	840	27

production and expenditure of heat goes on continuously as the principal mechanism for the maintenance of body temperature within a very narrow range. Most of the bodily energy produced in the resting or basal state goes for this purpose. Clearly, water requirements will vary with the energy produced or, stated in other terms, with the calories metabolized. Hence, requirements will be expressed in these terms. Others use the relationships between body surface area and heat loss to express losses as a function of surface area. The concept is similar and for clinical purposes, the choice is to some extent arbitrary. Inasmuch as the newborn represents an exception to the surface area calculation and because one may easily memorize a few points on the scale and readily interpolate between them, the caloric expenditure system has some practical advantage in addition to the pedagogic use of calling attention to the primary relationship. Table 1 permits use of either system and shows the relationships. In any event, neither calories expended nor surface area are measured directly; both are estimated from weight and age.

At basal conditions, obligatory water losses are approximately as follows:

Insensible (IWL)	45 ml/100 calories metabolized
(skin 30, lungs 15)	
Urine	50 ml/100 calories metabolized
Stool	5 ml/100 calories metabolized
Total	100 ml/100 calories metabolized

The calorie is the kilocalorie. The urine figure assumes no concentration or dilution of solutes by the kidney and thus a urine osmolality of 300 mOsm/l. For each 100 calories metabolized, 12 ml of water are available as "water of oxidation" which reduces the exogenous need. Infants and children on an ordinary diet with ordinary activity expend about 1½ times the basal energy. Further deviations occur with disease or other pathologic conditions, the most important of which relate to body temperature, activity, and hyperventilation. Total metabolism increases or decreases about 12 percent per degree centigrade change in central body temperature. Ac-

tivity may increase water loss by about 30 percent and hyperventilation may triple the loss from the lungs. Other factors such as the humidity of the environment may also play a role. For practical purposes of estimating obligatory water losses, the following four clinical states can be described:

1. Basal—as given in Table 1
2. Ordinary—diet, activity, and environment
   1½ times basal
3. Unusual fever, activity, or hyperventilation in some combination but not all maximal
   2 times basal
4. All of the above conditions simultaneously maximal (theoretical only)
   3 times basal

This simplified scheme gives limits useful to the clinician when treating disturbances of hydration which are discussed separately.

Minerals

L. EMMETT HOLT, JR.

At the present time seven macromineral nutrients are known: sodium, potassium, calcium and magnesium, chloride, phosphorus, and sulfur. Minimum requirements of these minerals for growth and maintenance are not accurately known. Tables 2 and 3 give retention figures obtained by Swanson on breast milk and on cow's milk. The figures are subject to correction because losses in sweat were not measured. The difference in mineral retention between the two feedings, retention being higher on the higher intake, is probably exaggerated. As Wallace has pointed out, the errors caused by incomplete collection of excreta and incomplete consumption of food are additive and tend to produce higher apparent retentions on higher intakes. Nevertheless it seems that chemical maturation, with respect to mineral as well as nitrogen, can be accelerated in infancy by an increased intake. Whether or not this so-called "superminerali-

TABLE 2.   *Total Daily Retention of Minerals by Young Infants*

	Na	K	Ca	Mg	Cl	P	S	N
				(In Millimoles)				
On breast milk	2.4	2.5	1.0	0.3	2.0	1.1	0.45	38.6
On cow's milk	5.2	4.9	5.0	0.7	5.5	3.7	0.27	66.3

TABLE 3.   *Retention of Minerals per Kilogram of Increase in Body Weight*

	Na	K	Ca	Mg	Cl	P	S	N
				(In Millimoles)				
On breast milk	104	108	39.6	12.2	88	49.4	19.9	1,690
On cow's milk	205	190	198	28.4	214	145	10.3	2,599

zation" of the growing infant is beneficial remains a question.

Essential as the macrominerals are, as dietary constituents they are not matters of practical concern in the feeding of normal infants and children in well developed countries, since they are adequately supplied by customary food. Deficiencies arise only in pathologic conditions. The chief electrolytes of the body fluids—sodium, potassium, and chloride—have low minimum requirements and a wide range of acceptable intake. In general, 2 to 3 mEq/100 calories metabolized on each represents about midrange.

Calcium is required for the formation of bones and teeth, about 99 percent of this element being present in the skeleton. Equally important are the functions of calcium in blood coagulation and in maintaining the integrity of heart and nerve. Calcium serves as an activator of a number of important enzymes, including adenosine triphosphatase, succinic dehydrogenase, lipase, and several proteolytic enzymes.

Only a fraction of the calcium intake is absorbed, the variation being from 10 to 40 percent. The amount of calcium that can be excreted in the urine is relatively small, and the body regulates its supply in large part by the amount absorbed; also a larger fraction is absorbed on a less generous intake. A number of other factors influence calcium absorption. Compounds which form insoluble calcium salts (phosphate, oxalate, phytate) tend to interfere with absorption, while increased acidity of the gut favors it. The introduction of ions which form soluble but poorly dissociated calcium salts—such as citrate, tartrate, and ascorbate—favors absorption. Of far greater importance are the influence of vitamin D and parathyroid hormone on calcium absorption.

In the past, considerable emphasis has been placed on maintaining a generous intake of calcium in the diet of growing children, an intake of 1 g per day being widely recommended. It is now realized that this figure is unnecessarily high. In the United States a deficient intake of calcium has not been clinically recognized; rickets and osteomalacia when they occur are not due to a deficient calcium intake. Even in countries without a dairy industry the diet supplies enough calcium, provided vitamin D or ultraviolet irradiation is adequate. For the rare infant who must be fed a milk substitute it is customary to provide as much calcium as in breast milk, but with this possible exception the intake of calcium need occasion no concern.

Of the small quantity of *magnesium* in the human body, about 70 percent is in the skeleton; a small but relatively constant amount is found in blood plasma and a somewhat larger amount in the tissue cells. In some respects the metabolism of magnesium resembles that of calcium; only a small moiety is absorbed in the intestine, and similar factors influence its absorption. Vitamin D does not appear to exert a controlling influence on magnesium metabolism, but the parathyroid hormone influences it to some extent; the administration of parathyroid hormone causes a sharp but very temporary rise in blood magnesium with increased excretion in the urine, whereas temporary retention of this element follows parathyroidectomy. In experimental animals a deficiency of magnesium leads to erythema of the extremities and to tetany. Magnesium-deficient tetany has also been reported in man.

Magnesium is a constituent of many enzyme systems; it also serves to catalyze various enzyme reactions. Magnesium is in some respects a calcium antagonist. Its administration may cause decalcification of bones and teeth. A similar antagonism is found in the nervous system; an excess of magnesium exerts a sedative action which can be neutralized by calcium. Hibernating animals, on the other hand, have been found to have an elevated blood magnesium.

Approximately three-fourths of the body *phosphorus* is found in the skeleton, the remainder consisting largely of organic phosphorus compounds in the cells; the inorganic phosphate of the plasma and interstitial fluids is a small moiety. Among the important organic phorphorus compounds are the nucleoproteins, the phospholipids present in plasma and in all cells, which are particularly abundant in the nervous system, and a variety of intermediate compounds concerned in cellular respiration, such as phosphocreatine, adenylic acid, the adenosine phosphates, hexose phosphates, the glycerophosphates, the pyridine nucleotides, thiamine phosphate, and the flavin phosphates. Phosphorylation—combination with phosphate—and the reverse process, dephosphorylation, are concerned in a large number of metabolic processes, notably those involved in energy transformation. The part played by inorganic phosphates in regulating acid-base equilibrium has been known for many years.

As far as is known the phosphorus needs of the body can be met entirely by inorganic phosphate in the diet. In milk a large part of the phosphorus is in organic combination as an integral part of the casein molecule, where it is combined with the amino acid serine; why this special form of phosphorus has been provided by nature is not clear. The requirement for phosphorus runs roughly parallel to that of calcium during the period of rapid skeletal growth; as the rate of growth diminishes, relatively more phosphorus is needed for other purposes, and the requirement exceeds that of calcium.

Intestinal absorption of phosphorus is far from complete, being as a rule between 20 and 50 percent of the quantity ingested. A small portion of the phosphorus ingested in cereals and vegetables is present in the form of phytate and other organic compounds which are poorly assimilated, but the chief factor limiting absorption is the formation of insoluble phosphates, chiefly calcium phosphate and to a lesser extent phosphates of magnesium and heavy metals. Acidity and the presence of other ions which can combine with calcium (such as oxalates and citrates) tend to promote phosphorus absorption; the reverse is also true. Vitamin D is of far greater importance in promoting phosphorus absorption. The parathyroid hormone has little effect on phosphorus absorption but increases its excretion in the urine.

Phosphorus deficiency due to inadequate intake has been observed in animals, but it is questionable whether an analogous state ever occurs in man. A moderate excess of phosphate in the diet is not harmful, but a great excess may interfere with calcium absorption. An excess of phosphate given by vein may lead to tetany. Retention of phosphate occurs with some types of renal insufficiency and may help to produce acidosis. The high concentrations of calcium and phosphorus in the blood which may result from overdosage with vitamin D or with parathyroid hormone may result in pathologic calcification if allowed to persist.

Sulfur is an essential body constituent. It is found in all body proteins in the form of the amino acids cysteine, cystine, taurine, and methionine. In the form of sulfate it occurs as heparin, as chondroitin sulfuric acid and mucoitin sulfuric acid in the mucoproteins of cartilage and mucus, and in the sulfolipids. Other important compounds are thiamine, lipoic acid, cystathionine, glutathione, and the ergothioneine of the red blood cells. It is an integral part of the coenzyme A molecule, and indeed sulfhydryl groups are concerned with the activity of a great many enzymes. Sulfur compounds play an important part in the detoxicating mechanisms of the body; certain aromatic compounds are excreted as ethereal sulfates, while others are detoxicated by combination with cystine, methionine, or glutathione. There is evidence that the intermediary metabolism of sulfur is greatly disturbed in certain diseases. Sullivan has found that a number of chronic diseases are associated with a diminished cystine content of the fingernails; with recovery the cystine content returns to normal.

The requirement for sulfur can be met only to a very limited extent by inorganic sulfates; these can provide for ethereal sulfate formation and for the various sulfate-containing compounds, but not for the amino acid sulfur, the sulfur-containing enzymes, and the other compounds containing reduced sulfur. For these compounds amino acid sulfur is needed. It appears that in man cystine will supply most of the latter needs, the absolute amount of methionine required being small. The small amount of thiamine required must be ingested as such. Although it can be synthesized in the human large intestine from simple sulfur compounds, such thiamine is, by and large, not absorbed.

Specific syndromes of sulfur deficiency are not recognized. In certain parts of the world sulfur amino acids are the limiting factor in the diet and their lack may cause impaired growth. In experimental animals methionine deficiency will cause fatty liver, but as already pointed out, a fatty liver will result from other types of imbalance and there is little evidence to indicate that fatty livers as seen in man respond to the administration of methionine.

Iron forms an integral part of the hemoglobin molecule. It also occurs in other porphyrin compounds, such as myoglobin, catalase, and the cytochrome pigments found in all cells. About 55 percent of the body iron is present as hemoglobin, from 10 to 20 percent as myoglobin, and the remainder in other tissues, either in the form of enzymes or as iron stores. Although the chief function of iron is that of oxygen transport, it also serves as a stimulus to red cell formation.

The factors controlling iron absorption are incompletely known, but there is good evidence that the proportion of ingested iron absorbed is greatly influenced by the need for this element. Commonly only about 10 percent of the intake is absorbed, but in states of iron deficiency the proportion may be considerably greater. Inorganic iron is more readily absorbed than organic, and ferrous iron more readily than ferric. Ascorbic acid favors absorption by its reducing action. Iron appears to be absorbed in the form of ferritin, an iron-rich protein. In the blood the iron is reduced and circulates for the most part in combination with a beta globulin known as transferrin. That which is not used is deposited chiefly in the liver and spleen, partly in the form of ferritin and partly as hemosiderin, the latter substance predominating when the stores are very large. Much of the iron liberated from destroyed red cells is re-utilized.

A deficiency of iron leads to a hypochromic, microcytic anemia (Sec. 17.2). This is not uncommon in infants fed exclusively on milk beyond the age of six or eight months. The milk-fed infant relies to a considerable extent on stores laid down in the liver in fetal life. Depending on the mother's diet during pregnancy these may vary from 30 to 500 mg at the time of birth. Premature infants are born with a low store and are peculiarly susceptible to iron-deficiency anemia. The synthesis of hemoglobin requires other factors besides iron—copper and pyridoxine are two recognized catalysts—but although a deficiency of either of these two factors may produce a hypochromic anemia, such deficiencies are exceedingly rare and hypochromic anemia is almost synonymous with iron deficiency.

An excessive intake of iron leads to black stools. In the absence of anemia, only a small amount of ingested iron is absorbed. The indiscriminate use of iron in anemias of all kinds is to be deplored; one must bear in mind that when some other cause is responsible for anemia the administration of iron will lead to its accumulation in the body. Extensive hemosiderin deposits in the liver and spleen may be seen after repeated transfusions for some congenital form of anemia. Acute iron poisoning commonly causes circulatory and cerebral symptoms. A number of fatalities in infants have been reported as a result of overenthusiastic iron therapy.

The requirement of the young child for iron is approximately known. During the first five or six weeks of life dietary iron is not readily utilized for hemoglobin formation, and the dietary requirement is almost negligible. Subsequently an intake of 0.3 mg per kilogram per day appears to be adequate for the early years of life. Thus a child of six months should be receiving 2.4 mg and a child of a year 3 mg. A child receiving only milk would receive no more than half these quantities, an intake known to be inadequate. The Food and Nutrition Board recommends 1 mg per kilogram per day for infants, a figure which does not appear to be excessive. Lesser amounts in terms of body weight are recommended for older subjects, the adult recommendation being 10 mg a day for males and 15 mg for menstruating females.

TRACE ELEMENTS. A great many elements are found in the body in trace amounts. Many of these, such as silicon, boron, aluminum, nickel, arsenic, and lead, have no known physiologic significance, their occurrence being presumably fortuitous. Unless toxic doses are ingested they need occasion no concern. Other trace elements, such as iodine, copper, manganese, molybdenum, zinc, cobalt, and fluorine, are essential in minute quantities, but these traces are ordinarily found in natural diets, and in most instances it is not necessary to make special provision for them. Deficiencies of cobalt, manganese, and molybdenum have not been observed in man.

The need for *iodine* for the synthesis of the thyroid hormones thyroxin and triiodothyronine is well established. Lack of this element even in goitrous districts rarely manifests itself before puberty, although it may occasionally do so. In goitrous regions of the civilized world the use of iodized salt is now so nearly universal that endemic goiter is a rarity.

Copper is present in minute traces in all cells, the highest concentrations being found in muscle, bone, and liver. The fetal liver contains stores of copper which appear to be of physiologic importance. Copper is a constituent of a number of enzymes, notably respiratory pigments and oxidases of tissues. It is present in the blood in large part as a blue protein complex, ceruloplasmin, the function of which is unknown. There is evidence that copper is needed for hemoglobin synthesis. Exceptional cases of hypochromic anemia are seen in infants which respond to copper and iron better than to iron alone. Hypocupremia is present in such cases in contrast to the usual iron-deficiency anemia in which the blood copper is found in excess. It is not clear whether these cases of hypocupremia are due to an unusually low intake or to some metabolic peculiarity. Exact data on the copper requirement in early life are not available. Copper given in moderate excess will cause gastrointestinal disturbance and eventually nervous symptoms. In Wilson's disease there is an accumulation of copper in the tissues associated with defective synthesis of ceruloplasmin.

Manganese is found as the metallic complex of the enzyme arginase, concerned in the urea cycle, as well as in bone phosphatase, leucine aminopeptidase, and several phosphorylating enzymes. This element is found in all tissues. In experimental animals manganese deficiency causes interference with growth and reproduction. In chicks a deformity of the ankle joint with slipping of the gastrocnemius tendon—a condition known as perosis—is in part caused by manganese deficiency. Manganese deficiency has not been recognized in man.

Zinc is found as the metallic complex of a number of important enzymes, among which are carbonic anhydrase, uricase, phosphatases, and carboxypeptidase. Its high concentration in the pancreas is due to its presence in the last-named enzyme. A deficiency of zinc leads to skin lesions in animals, alopecia and parakeratotic changes being conspicuous. Considerable zinc is present in the eye and in normal leucocytes. Leukemic leucocytes, however, have been found to contain only about one-tenth of the usual concentration of this metal. Zinc deficiency has been reported from Iran and from Egypt as a cause of anemia, dwarfism, and hypogenitalism in males who are for the most part dirt eaters. The pathogenesis of this condition is not altogether clear.

Cobalt deficiency has been recognized for years among ruminant animals in Australia and New Zealand as the cause of "enzootic marasmus," a condition characterized by progressive anemia, anorexia, and wasting. The ruminant appears to have a peculiar need for this element. That humans also need it to some extent has been established by its presence in vitamin B_{12} (p. 138). Cobalt has been reported as stimulating the formation of erythropoietin.

Molybdenum is one of the most recently established essential trace metals. It occurs as the metal complex of two flavoprotein enzymes—xanthine oxidase and aldehyde oxidase. A molybdenum supplement has been found to catalyze the formation of flavoproteins.

Fluorine is found in a small but constant concentration in bones and teeth, particularly in enamel. It appears to be an essential ingredient, in that a deficiency predisposes to dental caries. Minute amounts of fluorine in the drinking water exert a markedly protective effect against caries, and even the local application of fluoride is of some benefit. On the other hand, an excess of flourine in the drinking water such as occurs in some parts of the United States and elsewhere leads to mottling and discoloration of the enamel, a condition known as fluorosis (Chap. 29).

Selenium has not been established as a dietary essential for man, although there is some evidence that it is of nutritive importance in animals and can spare vitamin E in some respects.

Imbalances between the trace elements have been found to be important in animal husbandry and may eventually prove to be of significance in human nutrition. A definite antagonism between copper and molybdenum has been established: an excess of molybdenum will interfere with the utilization of copper and lead to copper deficiency; copper in turn will interfere with the absorption of molybdenum. Zinc likewise is known to depress copper absorption, leading to a copper-deficiency anemia. A high calcium intake given to swine may precipitate zinc deficiency. Antagonisms between essential and nonessential trace elements also exist. It appears to be quite as important for the animal organism to maintain homeostasis with these micronutrients as with the macronutrients.

Recommended Dietary Allowances

The modern era of nutrition with the discovery of the accessory food factors and their corresponding deficiency syndromes has led to an intensive and laudable effort to eliminate dietary deficiencies. The public as well as dietitians have been educated in regard to deficiencies and their prevention. Standard tables of dietary requirements and recommendations have been developed in many countries. In instances where requirements were not accurately known, a generous figure was supplied to insure adequacy. Dietary surveys using these standards, but for the most part unaccompanied by physical examinations, have reported a high incidence of dietary deficiency, and corrective measures have been applied on a large scale. The pharmaceutical industry has provided a variety of preparations to meet the daily requirements of the accessory factors, and the food industry has fortified a number of prepared foods with them.

In evaluating the net results of this effort we have on the positive side the almost complete disappearance of vitamin D deficiency rickets and scurvy; these represent notable achievements. The disappearance of pellagra is generally attributed to economic factors rather than to nutritional supplementation. On the negative side we have a very considerable expense to the public, a certain amount of poisoning from overdosage, particularly of the fat-soluble vitamins, and a large amount of apprehension raised in regard to deficiencies which were in no sense a menace. Very difficult to assess is the effect of this nutritional "enrichment" upon the changing pattern of disease in the United States. Possible remote effects of overnutrition, with specific nutrients as well as with calories, are now beginning to receive attention.

REFERENCES

PROTEIN AND AMINO ACIDS

Barness, L. A., Baker, D., Guilbert, P., Torres, F. E., and György, P. Nitrogen metabolism of infants fed human and cow's milk. J. Pediat., 51:29, 1957.

Fomon, S. J., DeMaeyer, E. M., and Owen, G. M. Urinary and fecal excretion of endogenous nitrogen by infants and children. J. Nutr., 85:235, 1965.

——— and Owen, G. M. Retention of nitrogen by normal full-term infants receiving an autoclaved formula. Pediatrics, 29:1005, 1962.

Food and Nutrition Board, National Research Council. Recommended Dietary Allowances, 7th ed. Publication 1694, Washington, D.C., National Academy of Sciences, 1968.

Graham, G. G., Placko, R. P., Acevedo, G., Morales, E., and Cordano, A. Lysine enrichment of wheat flour: evaluation in infants. Amer. J. Clin. Nutr., 22:1459, 1969.

Harper, A. E., and Rogers, Q. R. Amino acid imbalance. Proc. Nutr. Soc., 24:173, 1965.

Holt, L. E., Jr., and Snyderman, S. E. The amino acid requirements of infants. J.A.M.A., 175:100, 1961.

Joint FAO/WHO Expert Group. Protein Requirements. WHO Technical Report Series, No. 301, Rome, 1965.

Munro, H. N., and Allison, J. B. Mammalian Protein Metabolism. New York, Academic Press, Inc., 1964, Vol. 2.

Snyderman, S. E., Holt, L. E., Jr., Dancis, J., Roitman, E., Boyer, A., and Balis, M. E. Unessential nitrogen: a limiting factor for human growth. J. Nutr., 78:57, 1962.

FAT

American Medical Association Council on Foods and Nutrition. A symposium on fats in human nutrition with particular attention to fats, cholesterol, and atherosclerosis. J.A.M.A., 164:1890, 1957.

Corcoran, A. C., and Rabinowitch, I. M. A study of the blood lipoids and blood protein in Canadian eastern Arctic eskimos. Biochem. J., 31:343, 1937.

Deuel, H. J. The Lipids. New York, Interscience Publishers, 1951.

Fat Metabolism: A Symposium on Clinical and Biochemical Aspects of Fat Utilization in Health and Disease. V. A. Najjar, ed. Baltimore, Johns Hopkins University Press, 1954.

Hansen, A. E. Essential fatty acids and infant nutrition. Pediatrics, 21:494, 1958.

Hashim, S. A., Roholt, H. B., and Van Itallie, T. B. Pancreatogenous steatorrhea treated with medium chain triglyceride. Clin. Res., 10:394, 1962.

Holt, L. E., Jr., et al. Studies in fat metabolism. I. Fat absorption in normal infants. J. Pediat., 6:427, 1935.

Thomson, W. S. T., and Munro, H. N. The relationship of carbohydrate metabolism to protein metabolism. IV. Effect of substituting fat for dietary carbohydrate. J. Nutr., 56:139, 1955.

CARBOHYDRATE

Anderson, J. A., Ziegler, M. R., and Doeden, D. Banana feeding and urinary excretion of 5-hydroxyindoleacetic acid. Science, 127:326, 1958.

Carbohydrate Metabolism: A Symposium on the Clinical and Biochemical Aspects of Carbohydrate Utilization in Health and Disease. V. A. Najjar, ed. Baltimore, Johns Hopkins University Press, 1952.

Chwalibogowski, A. Experimentaluntersuchungen über kalorisch ausreichende, qualitativ einseitige Ernährung des Säuglings. Acta Paediat. Scand., 22:110, 1937.

Munro, H. N. Carbohydrate and fat as factors in protein utilization and metabolism. Physiol. Rev., 31:449, 1951.

Stefansson, V. The Friendly Arctic. New York, The Macmillan Co., 1921.

PERCENTAGE DISTRIBUTION OF CALORIES

Holt, L. E., and Fales, H. L. The food requirement of infants. V. Percentage distribution of calories. Amer. J. Dis. Child., 24:311, 1922.

McCance, R. A. Studies of Undernutrition. Wuppertal 1946-49, London, H.M. Stationery Office, 1951.

Powers, G. F. Comparison and interpretation on a caloric basis of the milk mixtures used in infant feeding. Amer. J. Dis. Child., 30:453, 1925.

VITAMINS

American Academy of Pediatrics. Report of Committee on Nutrition, Vitamin E in human nutrition. Pediatrics, 31:324, 1963.

Dinning, J. S., Majaj, A. S., Azzam, S. A., Darby, W. J., Shunk, C. H., and Folkers, K. Response of macrocytic anemia in children to the coenzyme Q4 chromanol. Amer. J. Clin. Nutr., 13:169, 1963.

Follis, R. H., Jr. Deficiency Disease. Springfield, Ill., Charles C Thomas Co., 1958.

György, P. Vitamin Methods. New York, Academic Press, Inc., 1951.

Hodges, R. E., Ohlson, M. A., and Bean, W. B. Pantothenic acid deficiency in man. J. Clin. Invest., 37:1642, 1958.

Majaj, A. S., Dinning, J. S., Azzam, S. A., and Darby, W. J. Vitamin E responsive megaloblastic anemia in infants with protein-calorie malnutrition. Amer. J. Clin. Nutr., 12:374, 1963.

Sebrell, W. H., and Harris, R. S. The Vitamins. New York, Academic Press, Inc., 1954.

Vitamins and Hormones. New York, Academic Press, Inc., 1965, Vol. 23.

West, E. S., and Todd, W. R. The vitamins. In Textbook of Biochemistry, 3rd ed. New York, The Macmillan Co., 1961, pp. 657-767.

Wokes, F., Badenoch, J., and Sinclair, H. M. Human dietary deficiency of vitamin B_{12}. Amer. J. Clin. Nutr., 3:375, 1955.

MINERALS

Calcium Requirements. Report of WHO/FAO Expert Group. Technical Report Series #230, World Health Organization, Geneva, 1962.

McCance, R. A., and Widdowson, E. M. Composition of the body. Brit. Med. Bull., 7:297, 1950-51.

Rominger, E., Meyer, H., and and Bomskov, C. Rachitisstudien. Langfristige Kalk- und Phosphorstoffwechseluntersuchungen bei gesunden und rachitischen Säuglingen. Ges. Exp. Med., 73:343, 1930.

Shohl, A. T. Mineral Metabolism. New York, Reinhold Publishing Corp., 1939.

Sullivan, M. X., and Hess, W. C. The cystine content of the finger nails in arthritis. J. Bone Joint Surg., 16:185, 1934.

Swanson, W. W. The composition of growth. II. The full-term infant. Amer. J. Dis. Child., 43:10, 1932.

Underwood, E. J. Trace Elements in Human and Animal Nutrition. New York, Academic Press, Inc., 1956.

Vallee, B. L. The metabolic role of zinc. J.A.M.A., 162:1053, 1956.

Wallace, W. M., Weil, W. B., and Taylor, A. The effect of variable protein and mineral intake upon the body composition of the growing animal. In Ciba Foundation Colloquia on Aging. Boston, Little, Brown & Co., 1958, Vol. 4, p. 116.

——— Nitrogen content of the body and its relation to retention and loss of nitrogen. Fed. Proc., 18:1125, 1959.

3.3
FEEDING TECHNIQUES AND DIETS

L. EMMETT HOLT, JR.

Breast Feeding

INCIDENCE. In many parts of the world the incidence of breast feeding approaches 100 percent. In the United States the incidence is much lower, and there is evidence that it is decreasing. A survey by Meyer in 1956 showed that 21 percent of American newborn infants were exclusively breast-fed as compared with 38 percent reported by Bain a decade earlier. Breast feeding was more common in rural than in uban areas. There were also marked regional differences; in Bain's survey 61 percent of infants in the Northeastern area were bottle-fed as compared with 18 percent in the Southwest and Southeast. The decline in breast feeding can be attributed largely to the present simplicity and success achieved with bottle feeding. With the exception of a few centers where great emphasis is put upon it, breast feeding is largely restricted to what has been termed "natural nursers"—women physiologically and psychologically so constituted that they achieve success without professional advice or assistance. Many mothers wish to nurse and they start out hopefully, but within a few days or a few weeks some minor difficulty, often one that might have been prevented or corrected, causes them to abandon the effort. The lack of hospital personnel interested and skilled in teaching the technique of breast feeding and early discharge of the mother and infant from the hospital are also factors responsible for the declining incidence.

ADVANTAGES ATTRIBUTED TO BREAST FEEDING. In considering the advantages of breast feeding, a clear distinction needs to be made between *breast milk* and *breast feeding,* the latter of which is discussed here. Aside from the frequently quoted but somewhat meaningless statement that breast feeding is the "natural" method of feeding infants, certain specific advantages over artificial feeding have been attributed to it which are worthy of review and reconsideration. These are:

1. Breast feeding is safer.
2. It provides a food superior from the nutritional point of view.
3. It is more convenient.
4. It is of psychologic value to the mother and to the infant.

The former beliefs that maternal nursing hastened involution of the uterus and improved the shape of the infant's jaw have not been supported by critical evidence.

The relative safety of maternal nursing is an important factor. This is probably not derived from maternal antibodies transmitted in milk, for these do not survive gastric digestion, but rather from the fact that breast milk is relatively free of microorganisms, whereas cow's milk contains large numbers. In addition, the chance for contamination with pathogens is greater with artificial feedings, the latter depending upon the cleanliness of the milk supply and the care with which feedings are prepared. In most regions of the United States the risk is negligible. However, in many parts of the world where the milk supply is open to question and where the preparation of formulas is less likely to be carefully done, the greater safety of breast feeding is of major importance.

The question of comparative nutritive value of breast milk and cow's milk, and the differences between these two milks, are discussed in detail elsewhere (p. 157). Our present information may be summarized by saying that extensive comparisons of these two foods given under similar conditions (e.g., by bottle) have not been carried out, but such studies as have been made have failed to establish the superiority of breast milk.

Some mothers consider the convenience of breast feeding one of its major advantages over artificial feeding which, even though it has been simplified, still requires preparation and sterilization of formulas. Others object to the fact that maternal nursing requires that they give all of the feedings with the exception of an occasional supplementary bottle.

It would appear that at least in the United States the advantages of breast feeding are not great in terms of either safety, the nutritional superiority of human milk, or necessarily convenience. The remaining factor, the psychologic value of breast feeding, would appear, therefore, to be the most important one and also the most difficult to evaluate.

There is no question that nursing is emotionally satisfying to many mothers. The influence on the child is much less clear. We do not believe there is any valid evidence to support the view that artificial feeding necessarily implies emotional deprivation for the infant. On the other hand, we would accept the possibility that the desire and the capacity of a mother to nurse her baby successfully may be a manifestation of an attitude which is favorable for his later psychologic development.

We believe that the most reasonable attitude on the part of the pediatrician should be to inquire honestly into the mother's attitude toward breast feeding, to encourage her to do so if she is willing to try, and to cooperate in efforts to make the atmosphere in the hospital more conducive to success. On the other hand, the pediatrician should accept a mother's considered decision not to breast-feed her infant and help minimize any feelings of guilt she might have.

WHEN MATERNAL NURSING SHOULD NOT BE ATTEMPTED. (1) No mother who has active clinical tuberculosis should nurse her infant; it exposes the infant to infection. (2) Nursing should seldom be allowed when serious complications have been connected with parturition, such as severe hemorrhage, sepsis, or eclampsia; women may, however, recover from these conditions so as to be able to nurse successfully. (3) If the mother is suffering from serious chronic disease or is markedly undernourished, breast feeding is best not attempted. (4) Mastitis is a contraindication for using the affected breast.

The response of individual mothers to nursing varies enormously; some find that it decreases their sense of well-being, while others appear to thrive on it. Some mothers are more likely to succeed with first or second children than with later ones, while others do as well with later infants as with the firstborn. Retracted nipples may render nursing impractical.

Syphilis is not a contraindication for nursing except in rare instances where the maternal infection is acquired shortly before the child's birth. If adequate antiluetic treatment has not been given during pregnancy and the child is infected, there is no menace from any further spirochetes which he may receive in the milk. And if the treatment has been adequate and the infant has escaped intrauterine infection, the possibility of an open lesion in the mother's breast which might infect him can be excluded.

The interesting observation of Bittner that the milk of mice from a strain susceptible to cancer of the breast contains an agent which conveys susceptibility to cancer to the suckling animal has caused concern lest a similar situation prevail in the human species. However, available data reveal no evidence for such a factor in human experience.

SECRETION OF BREAST MILK. The secretion of breast milk commences after parturition; only a few drops may be squeezed from the breasts before delivery. For the first few days the flow is scanty; usually it becomes well established by the third or fourth day, but it may be delayed until the tenth or twelfth day and yet come in abundance. One should not be too ready to decide that there will no milk but should persist in stimulating the breasts by suckling the child or by artificial means, such as manual expression or the use of an electrical breast pump.

DAILY QUANTITY. The following figures give the average daily quantities taken by healthy breast-fed infants.

Age	Approximate Quantity (ml)
At the end of the first week	300 to 500
During the second week	400 to 550
During the third week	430 to 720
During the fourth week	500 to 800
From the fifth to the thirteenth week	600 to 1,030
From the fourth to the sixth month	720 to 1,150

The caloric value of breast milk is about 0.67 calorie per milliliter. On the average, nursing infants consume approximately 100 to 120 calories per kilogram of body weight per day.

The amount of milk varies with the demands of the child in a very striking way. Complete emptying of the breast is the strongest stimulus to the production of milk; a hungry infant will therefore soon increase his milk supply. Conversely, when the supply is overabundant, as may happen when the milk first comes in, the breast is incompletely emptied and within a few days the quantity secreted falls off. The secretion of milk is a somewhat discontinuous process which goes on more actively during the periods of actual suckling than in the intervals of rest between nursings.

The quantity of milk obtained at one nursing shows a wider variation; it is greatly affected by the frequency of nursing. The following are average figures:

Age	Approximate Quantity (ml)
During the first week	18 to 45
During the second week	30 to 90
During the fourth week	45 to 140
During the sixth week	60 to 150
During the third month	75 to 160
During the fourth month	90 to 180
During the sixth month	120 to 220

Observations made by Smith and Merritt on the rate of emptying of the breast are given in Figures 4 and 5. The flow of milk is most rapid at

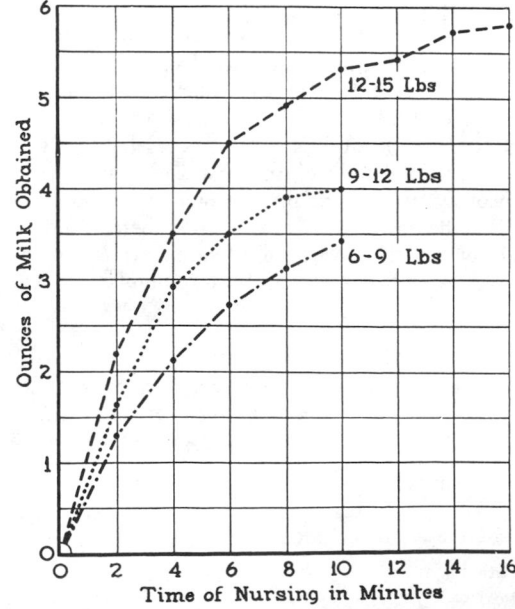

Fig. 4. Milk obtained by infants of different weights nursing at a single breast. (From Smith and Merritt. *Amer. J. Dis. Child.*, 24:413, 1922.)

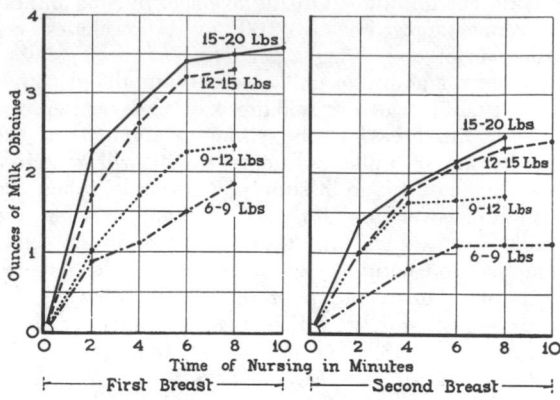

Fig. 5. Milk obtained by infants of different weights nursing 10 minutes at each breast. (From Smith and Merritt. *Amer. J. Dis. Child.*, 24:413, 1922.)

the onset of nursing and decreases rapidly thereafter. Half of the quantity obtainable from one breast is taken in the first two or three minutes; after 10 minutes, few babies get any milk whatever. Large and vigorous infants obtain more milk than do smaller infants in the average single nursing, whether from one breast or from both.

A mother's ability to nurse her infant is not affected by season of year, parity of the mother, her age, the size of her breasts, antepartum presence of secretion in the breasts, or the return of menstruation. It is affected unfavorably by obesity, the advent of pregnancy, the development of infection in the nipple or breast and also by adverse psychologic factors (p. 153).

COLOSTRUM. The secretion of the early days of lactation, to which the name "colostrum" has been given, differs quite markedly from the later milk. It is of creamy yellow color, with a specific gravity of 1.030 to 1.035, an alkaline reaction (average pH 7.7), and is readily coagulable by heat; sometimes the milk of the first day coagulates spontaneously. It contains more protein than does mature milk (the protein is from 3 to 5 percent), a large part of which consists of globulin. It is also richer in vitamin A activity and in minerals, particularly

TABLE 4.   *Average Values and Common Variations for the Chemical Composition of Mature Milk of Healthy Women*

	Normal Average (g/100 ml)	Common Healthy Variations (g/100 ml)		
Protein	1.1	0.9	to	1.6
Sugar	7.0	6.5	to	8.0
Fat	3.8	2.0	to	6.0
Ash	0.21	0.15	to	0.35
Water	88.0	87.0	to	89.0

TABLE 5.   *Typical Variations in Percentage Composition of Different Portions of a Single Nursing*

	1st	2nd	3rd
Protein	1.13	0.94	0.71
Fat	1.71	2.77	5.51

in sodium and potassium. It contains less sugar and fat than does the later milk. Many of the fat globules are of unusual size, and there are present large numbers of granular cells known as colostrum corpuscles. These are four or five times the size of the milk globules, and they are probably mononuclear phagocytes in which are contained numerous fat granules.

The characteristic features of colostrum continue for a period varying from 5 to 10 days, but it is not until about the end of the first month that the milk assumes its stable or mature character. The milk of the intermediate period is sometimes spoken of as "transition milk." This change is characterized by a gradual decrease in the protein and minerals and a moderate rise in the sugar and fat. When the composition of mature milk is reached, little variation is seen until near the close of lactation.

Cow's colostrum contains antibodies, notably those which protect the newborn calf against colon bacillus enteritis. These antibodies are found in a particular globulin fraction known as T-globulin, which is absorbed unsplit during the first 24 hours but not appreciably thereafter. Similar immune mechanisms are not known to exist in the human. Although antibodies are readily demonstrable in human colostrum as well as in mature milk, the observations of Vahlquist and his associates indicate that they do not survive digestion in significant quantities. Unlike the ruminant, the human infant is protected by antibodies transmitted by the placenta.

COMPOSITION OF BREAST MILK. A complete specimen of mature breast milk is similar to cow's milk in its appearance.* It is sweet to the taste; its reaction when fresh varies from pH 6.8 to 7.4, averaging close to 7.0. The specific gravity varies between 1.026 and 1.036, the average being 1.031. Microscopically there are seen great numbers of fat globules of variable sizes, with some granular matter and occasional epithelial cells.

Table 4 gives the average composition of the major constituents of mature milk and their common variations in health. Table 5 shows typical variations in percentage composition of different portions of a single nursing. The mineral constituents of breast milk are shown in Table 6.

* The first part of a nursing and such milk as may leak from a breast between nursing is, as pointed out elsewhere, low in fat and tends to resemble skim milk in appearance. The alteration from the yellowish creamy appearance of colostrum to what appears to be like skim milk is often a cause of concern and unnecessary weaning. A story that the milk "turned to water" at the third or fourth week is commonly obtained.

TABLE 6. *Mineral Constituents of Breast Milk*

Period	Total Ash	Na	K	Ca	Mg	Cl	P	Na	K	Ca	Mg	Cl	P
				(mg/100 ml)						(mEq/L)			
Colostrum (1-12 days)	308	34	78	33	6	57	18	14.8	20.0	16.5	2.5	16.3	5.8
Transition (12-30 days)	241	19	59	29	3	58	18	8.3	15.1	14.5	1.3	16.6	5.8
Early mature (1-4 mo)	206	11	45	35	5	35	15	4.8	11.5	17.5	2.1	10.1	4.8
Late mature (4-9 mo)	207	10	51	33	5	36	15	4.3	13.1	16.5	2.1	10.3	4.8
Late milk (10-20 mo)	198	10	48	28	4	44	13	4.3	12.3	14.0	1.7	12.6	4.2

Protein. The total protein of mature milk is usually between 1.0 and 1.4 percent. In abnormal specimens it may vary from 0.3 to 3.5 percent. The protein is highest in the colostrum period; after the first month it is relatively constant, but it tends to fall toward the end of lactation. Milk obtained from the early part of the nursing has a somewhat higher protein content.

The major proteins are casein, α-lactalbumin, and β-lactoglobulin, which are present in the ratio 2:2:1. The preponderance of the whey proteins—albumin and globulin—is in marked contrast to cow's milk in which most of the protein is casein. It is now known that casein is not a pure protein; it consists of a mixture of at least two and perhaps three distinct entities—α-, β-, and γ-casein. The caseins of human milk have been shown to differ from those of cow's milk, as is also true of the whey proteins. The chief globulins of human milk consist of a mixture of α- and β-lactoglobulin, of which the latter is by far the larger fraction. Up to the present the globulins have not been separated in pure form, although electrophoretic studies indicate that at least four such components exist. From the nutritional point of view the whey proteins have been regarded as superior to casein, a view which now seems questionable. Casein is peculiar in containing a considerable amount of phosphorus in combination with the amino acid serine. Casein possesses the property of being coagulated by acid or by the enzyme rennin. The difference in the curd of breast milk and cow's milk is due chiefly to the greater quantity of casein in the latter. Mellander has reported the presence of a peptide in breast milk which occurs to a lesser extent in cow's milk.

György and his co-workers have identified in human milk a mucopolysaccharide which is a specific growth factor for a variant of *L. bifidus* (var. *penn*). The activity of this factor in cow's milk was only $\frac{1}{30}$ to $\frac{1}{100}$ of that in human milk. There is no evidence thus far that the *bifidus* factor has significance in human nutrition.

Fat. This exists as a fine emulsion of particles rarely exceeding 10μ in diameter. The fat of breast milk consists almost enitrely of the neutral fats, palmitin, stearin, and olein, the last-mentioned predominating; small quantities of free fatty acids and of unsaponifiable matter are present. The fat of breast milk is relatively low in glycerides of the short-chain volatile fatty acids, as compared with that of cow's milk. It also commonly contains somewhat more of the polyunsaturated fatty acids. Insull et al. have shown that marked variations in the composition of the milk fat occur, depending upon the diet of the mother. In general the character of the milk fat tends to approach that of the dietary fat. The effect of a high-carbohydrate diet is to increase the proportion of lauric and myristic acids and to decrease that of the polyunsaturated fatty acids.

The quantity of fat shows a greater variation than that of any of the other constituents. The average is about 3.8 percent, but variations from 2.0 to 6.0 percent are not uncommon; the highest percentage we have known was 10.9. The concentration of fat in breast milk is influenced to a limited extent by the quantity of fat in the diet, but in part it is a characteristic of the individual mother. The proportion of fat is greatly affected by the time during nursing when the specimen is taken. The first milk drawn may contain only 1 percent fat, while at the end of nursing the "strippings," the last milk to be removed, may contain 7 or 8 percent.* No analysis is of value unless the specimen comprises practically the whole of the nursing. Table 5 illustrates typical variations in composition seen with different portions of a single nursing.

Sugar. The lactose is in solution. It is more nearly constant than the other ingredients, the usual limits being between 6.5 and 8.0 percent.

Minerals. The figures in Table 6 for the mineral constituents of women's milk were obtained by Holt et al. Figures are given in percent of whole milk.

The sulfur content is approximately 0.0016 percent; most of this is amino acid sulfur and should not properly be classed as one of the mineral constituents. All of the minerals are present in ample quantities with the exception of iron, which is present in a concentration of 1.5 to 2.0 mg per liter.

---

* The increase in the fat content of the milk during nursing is due to the fact that the mammary gland removes fat from the blood in appreciable quantities only after nursing has commenced. The preformed milk in the mammary gland before the onset of nursing is very low in fat, as Petersen et al. have shown by udder excision experiments on cows (*Amer. J. Physiol.*, 90:573, 582, 592, 1929).

The differences in the mineral content of cow's milk and breast milk will be considered later.

Buffer Value. The buffer content of breast milk is comparatively low; the significance of this fact in digestion is considered elsewhere (p. 161).

Enzymes. Lipase, amylase, and other enzymes have been demonstrated in breast milk. Their importance is questionable.

Vitamins. All the known vitamins are present in breast milk, the quantity being greatly influenced by the intake of the mother. Vitamin deficiencies other than vitamin D seldom occur in breast-fed infants in this country because maternal diets are generally adequate. Without vitamin D prophylaxis, rickets may be seen in nursing infants, particularly in those with dark skin or those not exposed to some sunlight.

EXAMINATION OF MILK. Chemical examination of milk is seldom of any assistance in solving the clinical problems of the nursing infant. It is a good general rule that if the milk is present in sufficient quantity, the quality, too, is adequate. The quantity of milk is best determined by weighing the child before and after nursing; sensitive scales should be used. Since the amount secreted varies somewhat at different times of the day, one should be cautious in drawing conclusions unless the secretion has been observed for at least a 24-hour period. Weighing should be done without removing the diaper in order to avoid the loss of weight due to passage of the excreta.

CONDITIONS AFFECTING THE COMPOSITION OF BREAST MILK. Age of the Mother. This has little influence; the milk of older mothers may be slightly lower in fat.

Number of Pregnancies. The fat and protein content are as a rule slightly higher in primiparas, while the sugar is slightly less.

Acute Illness. In minor ailments the milk may be somewhat reduced in quantity. In some illnesses the fat is often low and the protein high. Bacteria may be present in the milk in septic conditions.

Menstruation. The effect of this is exceedingly variable, depending upon the individual and the ease of menstruation. The most frequent changes are a slight diminution of the fat and an increase in the protein. Minor digestive disturbances occur in a small percentage of infants. The return of menstruation is not an indication for weaning.

Diet. Under conditions of normal nutrition, or even if the mother is receiving an inadequate amount of food, diet has little influence on the composition of the milk, with the exception of vitamins, which do not appear to be synthesized in the body, and the character of the fat, which is much influenced by the fat of the diet.

The nursing mother requires considerably more food than the average adult; not only must the calories secreted in the milk (400 to 1,200 a day)

be supplied, but in addition a certain amount of energy is probably consumed in the process of secretion itself. The water intake must be increased in order to take care of the additional fluid secreted. At the same time, the quantity of milk produced is largely independent of the mother's daily fluid intake within wide variations of water consumption. With abundant water intake her urine output is increased; with limited intake she suffers from thirst before the milk supply is affected.

Cow's milk is not to be considered a specific lactagogue, but it is a valuable and convenient food for the nursing mother. It is a good general rule to give a daily quantity of cow's milk similar to that of the breast milk which is being secreted. The milk need not be given as such; if it is distasteful it may easily be concealed in the cooking. The nursing woman should have a generous diet of simple food. One should not make the error of overfeeding, which may result in indigestion or merely in fattening the nurse.

Stimulants. The use of tobacco, tea, and coffee in moderation is not harmful; excesses should, of course, be avoided. Alcohol taken in small amounts does not appear in the milk, but the excessive use of alcohol by nursing women is to be condemned. An alcoholic debauch may produce severe toxic symptoms in the infant.

Drugs. A number of drugs may be eliminated in the milk, particularly when full doeses are given or after prolonged administration. Atropine, many of the opium derivatives, mercury, lead,[*] arsenicals, salicylates, iodides, bromides, and some of the alkaloid cathartics have all been found in the milk, sometimes in sufficient quantities to produce symptoms in the nursing child. Barbiturates, sulfonamides, and various antibiotics may also appear in the milk.

Pregnancy. The milk of a nursing woman who has become pregnant is generally scanty and poor in fat. The milk of a woman suffering with toxemia of pregnancy may be toxic to the infant.

Bacteria. Occasional organisms may be found in freshly pumped breast milk; they are chiefly cocci derived from the external milk ducts and are of no importance. In the presence of mastitis, pathogenic bacteria may be found. In septicemia, pathogenic organisms may reach the milk even in the absence of mastitis. Milk obtained from breast-milk dairies contains organisms similar in distribution and quantity to those of cow's milk.

Immune Bodies. Although numerous antibodies have been demonstrated in milk, they apparently do not survive digestion in significant quantities. Infants with erythroblastosis fetalis are not

---

[*] We have seen two instances of lead encephalitis in which the lead was acquired through the milk. In one case a lead acetate ointment was applied to the breast, but was wiped off before nursing. The other case resulted from the use of lead nipple shields; the excretion of lead continued in the milk more than a week after the shields had been discarded.

made worse by nursing, even when anti-Rh anti-bodies are shown to be present in the mother's milk.

Allergens. Allergic phenomena may appear in the nursing infant, presumably as a result of minute quantities of foreign protein transmitted through the milk.* The mother herself is often insensitive to the offending substance. Such instances are extremely rare; as a rule it is impossible to demonstrate the passage of food proteins into the milk.

Psychologic Factors. The effect of emotional stresses on the secretion of milk is very striking and much more important than the diet. Usually, though not invariably, worry, anxiety, fatigue, or any prolonged emotional stress tends to reduce the secretion of milk and in some instances to arrest it entirely. The psychologic state of the mother more than any other single factor appears to determine the success or failure of a mother to nurse her infant.

HORMONAL AND NERVOUS CONTROL OF LACTATION. In spite of a great deal of experimental work, the mechanisms concerned in lactation are still imperfectly known; species differences exist, and relatively few studies have been carried out on animals closely related to man. Mammary development is controlled largely by estrogens—in some species exclusively so, and in others progestin also plays a part. The effect of estrogens on the flow of milk depends on their concentration; small quantities stimulate the flow of milk, whereas larger quantities are inhibitory. The high concentrations of estrogen present during pregnancy prevent the flow of milk at that time, and the withdrawal of this influence after labor helps to initiate lactation. The inhibitory effect of high estrogen concentrations is utilized when sudden weaning is desired.

Lactation itself—i.e., the secretion of milk—is controlled primarily by prolactin formed in the anterior pituitary. The stimulus of suckling exerts its effect by increasing the production of prolactin. An important role is also played by the oxytocic factor of the posterior pituitary. This principle apparently controls the phenomenon known in the dairy industry as "letdown"—passage of milk from the alveoli into the ducts, caused by hormonal stimulation of smooth muscle in the walls of the milk ducts. Suckling initiates this phenomenon of letdown as a reflex through the posterior pituitary, and it is this mechanism which is interfered with by strong emotional stimuli. Waller has observed in nursing mothers a phenomenon analogous to letdown in cattle, which he designates as the "draught." A subjective sensation occurs spontaneously around nursing time and is inhibited by strong emotions.

Efforts to stimulate milk secretion in humans have met with very limited success. Some favorable results have been reported following the use of thyroid preparations, but the results are far from uniform. More consistent benefit can be obtained by increasing the suckling stimulus, as may be done by manual expression or with an electric breast pump, and by adjusting the environment. Douglas et al. have shown that injections of pituitrin will stimulate the flow of milk from the nipples, and purified oxytocic hormone and some of its synthetic derivatives prepared by du Vigneaud even more so, in some instances causing ejection of milk in a stream. The clinical usefulness of these preparations awaits further study. Methods for inhibiting lactation are discussed elsewhere (p. 156).

CARE OF THE BREASTS DURING LACTATION. Care should be given to the cleanliness of the breasts, particularly of the nipples; they should be washed carefully before and after nursing. A clean piece of cotton or gauze should cover the breasts between nursings; tight compression by the clothing should be avoided. If the nipples tend to become chafed, a bland ointment may be applied. Solutions of boric acid, used commonly in the past for this condition, should be avoided because of the danger of ingestion by the infant. With tender nipples, the use of a glass or rubber nipple shield during nursing may be tried, although it makes nursing difficult for the infant and usually is not altogether satisfactory.

The chief danger lies in fissured nipples which may result in infection of the breast and may lead eventually to abscess formation; nursing is inadvisable in these circumstances, for it tends to aggravate the condition. Healing of the nipples may be promoted by some bland ointment. The breast should be emptied by manual expression or by a breast pump. The milk may be fed to the infant unless evidences of infection of the breast are present.

Much can be done to prevent fissured nipples by proper care of the breasts during pregnancy. Daily gentle manipulation has been recommended as a hardening procedure. Retracted nipples, too, should receive attention at this time. Manual traction or traction with a breast pump during the last month of pregnancy may develop retracted nipples sufficiently so that successful nursing is possible.

Engorgement (caking) of the breasts may occur when the milk supply is overabundant. This sometimes occurs when the milk first comes in; it may happen when the child's appetite fails from acute illness or some other cause, or when, for any reason, sudden weaning is necessary. The practice of applying tight binders to the breast to decrease the milk supply is a relic of barbarism. Careful observations have shown that this does not hasten the diminution of the milk supply; it adds greatly to the discomfort of the mother. Within a day or two the supply of

---

* Lyon reported the case of a nursing infant who developed severe angioneurotic edema at the age of three weeks. Positive skin reactions were obtained to white navy beans and to sweet corn, both of which the mother had been eating. The infant gave a positive skin reaction to the mother's milk. The mother was herself insensitive to these substances. The angioneurotic edema was made to disappear by eliminating these articles from the mother's diet; it recurred when navy beans were again eaten (*Amer. J. Dis. Child.*, 36:1012, 1928).

milk tends to adjust itself to the decreased demand, even if no measures are used.

NURSING DURING THE FIRST DAYS OF LIFE. This serves to accustom the child and the mother to the procedure and may help in shaping the nipple before the milk comes in. Beginning 12 hours or so after delivery, the child should be put to the breast on the first day once every 6 hours, and on the second day once every 4 hours. Infants weighing more than 3,000 g at birth may be given five feedings a day after the first 24 hours. A nursing infant seldom gets more than 4 to 6 ounces a day for the first 2 or 3 days. Exceptionally large or active infants who cry vigorously may require additional fluid or food. A little water or a 5 percent sugar solution may be first given; 2 to 4 teaspoonfuls at a time are sufficient. If this does not satisfy the child, supplementary * bottle feeding may be begun after the fifth day. Should the milk be delayed beyond this time, it is probable that partial or complete bottle feeding will be required. The child should be put to the breast at regular intervals, but only for about 5 minutes; a bottle may then be offered.

If lactation is desired there is some disadvantage in early bottle feeding, since the infant quickly learns that it is easier to get food from the bottle than from the breast; his efforts at the latter may soon become only halfhearted. It is important not to cease efforts to induce milk secretion for several days longer. Should the child's sucking prove ineffectual, manual expression or a breast pump should be used.

NURSING HABITS. The value of regularity in nursing is a much disputed subject at the present time. An era in which great faith was placed in regularity has been followed by one in which psychologists have urged freedom of choice for the baby in his feeding times. It is regrettable that statistical information is not available to permit comparisons of the two methods and that decisions are based on preconceptions rather than on objective data. It is clear, however, that considerable latitude can be given to the mother in her nursing habits without obvious harm to the infant. Many mothers will find it convenient to regulate nursing hours and will appreciate the knowledge that a baby will readily and successfully adapt to a routine such as the following: After the third day five or six nursings in the 24 hours may be given. An infant at this age can usually be depended upon to take at least one long sleep of from 4 to 6 hours in the 24. For the rest of the day the child should be awakened, if necessary, at the regular nursing time and put to the breast, this plan being continued until 10 o'clock at night. He should then be allowed to sleep as long as he will, and but one nursing or none at all given

* A bottle feeding which immediately follows a nursing is sometimes designated as "complemental"; one which replaces an entire nursing being described as "supplemental" or "supplementary." We shall use the latter term in both senses.

between this hour and 6 in the morning. In the course of two or three weeks a healthy infant may nurse and sleep with almost perfect regularity, frequently going 8 hours regularly at night without feeding. Some young infants are unable to obtain sufficient milk at one nursing to enable them to go 4 hours without symptoms of hunger; they cry continually for an hour preceding nursings. When this is the case the interval may be shortened to 3 hours, but this practice should not be continued beyond the third month. If at the end of this time the child cannot be placed upon a 4-hour schedule, supplementary feeding should be given. Nursing with long intervals and relieving the mother of night nursing as soon as possible are of the greatest value and will often enable her to continue lactation when it would otherwise be terminated.

If the supply of milk is abundant, one breast only should be used at a nursing; the less frequent use of each breast decreases the likelihood of difficulties with sore or cracked nipples. When the supply of milk is scanty, both breasts should be used; the more frequent stimulus is of assistance in increasing the milk supply. Ordinarily the duration of nursing should not be more than 12 minutes if one breast is used, or more than 10 minutes on each breast when both are used at a nursing (p. 150). A longer period of nursing does not yield more milk except in the case of infants who nurse more slowly, and it may be an added burden to the mother. On the other hand, some mothers prefer to let even vigorously nursing infants nurse for longer periods if the infant gives indications of wanting to do so. Certain vigorous infants will obtain all they need at a single nursing within as little as 2 minutes.

After nursing, the infant should be held over the mother's shoulder for a few moments and patted gently to aid the expulsion of such air as may have been swallowed. He should then be returned to his crib and not disturbed for some time.

SYMPTOMS OF UNSUCCESSFUL NURSING. One should not hastily wean a child on account of symptoms which may have nothing to do with the food; nor should one wean when the causes of indigestion are remediable. On the other hand, nursing should not be continued simply because a conscientious mother desires it when every indication points to failure.

A parenteral infection will produce digestive disturbances in a breast-fed infant identical to those produced in the artificially fed infant. All too frequently these are blamed upon the milk supply and the infant is unnecessarily weaned. Organic causes of digestive symptoms should always be thought of; the vomiting of pyloric stenosis is not infrequently attributed to the milk.

UNDERFEEDING. The symptoms of underfeeding are readily confused with those of indigestion. There is failure to gain or even loss of weight. Constipation may appear with flatulence and what would appear to be colicky pain; at other times the stools may be thin, greenish, and numerous,* but small. There is usually fretfulness; at times vomiting may occur. Fever is notably absent. The symptoms of underfeeding result in part from the restlessness due to hunger, and in part from air which is swallowed during the ineffectual and often prolonged attempts to get sufficient nourishment from the breasts. There is nothing characteristic about these symptoms. Something may be learned from the manner in which the child takes the breast. When the milk is abundant, the infant will seldom nurse more than five or six minutes, sometimes less. If the milk is very scanty he will frequently nurse half an hour or more and then stop, more because he is exhausted than because he is satisfied. Sometimes when the breasts are practically empty the child will seize the nipple and nurse vigorously for a few moments, then drop it and refuse to make any further efforts. The only satisfactory way of determining the quantity of milk secreted is to weigh the child before and after nursing. This should be done at each nursing until all doubt is removed. A scanty milk supply usually means a milk of poor quality, low in fat, while an ample milk supply is for practical purposes a reliable indication that the quality is satisfactory.

In the presence of a scanty milk supply, the difficulties can often be overcome and nursing can be continued to advantage. Until a decided increase in the milk has occurred, the child should have, after taking both breasts, a supplementary bottle feeding sufficient in amount to insure his being properly nourished. In this way the stimulating effect of sucking upon the secretion of milk is secured. The child's effort may be reinforced by manual expression † or by an electric breast pump. The old-fashioned breast pump with a rubber bulb develops a relatively small negative pressure and is not likely to be of much help. The hygiene of the mother should be given careful attention. She should be given an undisturbed rest at night; if possible, she should be relieved of the care of the infant at this time, and if feeding is necessary, a bottle should be given. She should have a certain amount of exercise each day. Worry, anxiety, and emotional upsets should be kept to a

minimum. One should make sure that the diet and fluid intake are adequate. Sometimes a mother whose milk supply is inadequate while in the hospital responds with an abundant flow of milk after returning home.

In the large majority of instances it is possible by these measures to secure an adequate milk supply, but not in all. If after two or three weeks' trial the mother is unable to furnish more than 10 ounces of milk a day, weaning should be undertaken.

OVERFEEDING. This is less of a problem than underfeeding. When the milk first comes in, the supply may be excessive. The symptoms produced are usually gastric regurgitation or perhaps vomiting. Within 48 hours or so the supply adjusts itself to the demand; in the meantime the intake may be reduced by shortening the nursing time.

DIARRHEA. As in the case of artificially fed infants, digestive disturbances, particularly diarrhea, result from the presence of parenteral infections. Diarrhea per se is not a cause for weaning or changing the nursing regimen. Instances have been reported of diarrhea in the nursing infant caused by transmission in the milk of laxatives taken by the mother.

The treatment of other digestive disorders that may occur in nursing infants, such as vomiting, colic, constipation, severe diarrhea, and dehydration, will be taken up subsequently, since it is much the same as for artificially fed infants.

WET NURSING. When maternal nursing is impossible or undesirable, the milk of another lactating woman would seem to be the most natural and best substitute. Although wet nursing is still used in some parts of the world, at present it has been abandoned almost completely in the United States.

ADDITION OF OTHER FOODS. Vitamin D should be given after the first week; the dose is the same as that recommended for artificially fed infants (Sec. 3.5). Although scurvy is extremely rare in breast-fed infants, it is customary to start vitamin C from the age of about two weeks onward; here again, the quantity recommended is the same as for infants who are bottle-fed. The occasional substitution of a cow's milk feeding is often a great convenience to the mother. Addition of other foods to the diet will depend somewhat upon the supply of breast milk. The introduction into the diet of cereals, vegetable purees, and other nonmilk foods should follow the same principles as recommended for the artificially fed infant (p. 166). As a larger portion of the diet comes to be supplied by foods other than breast milk, the maternal supply will gradually decrease in response to a lessened demand until, some time during the second half year, it becomes negligible and is terminated.

WEANING. Weaning should be done gradually, if possible, substituting one bottle feeding a day for one nursing and so on until the child is taken from the breast altogether. Sudden weaning causes discomfort to the mother and may be followed by indigestion in the infant if an inappropriate food is

---

* This is sometimes referred to as "starvation diarrhea."

† The technique of manual expression is important. Simple massage or squeezing of the breast accomplishes little. The thumb and forefinger, separated as far as the width of the areola, should be pressed straight back, compressing the breast against the thorax. They are then brought together behind the nipple and drawn forward with a rather rapid motion. The fingers should not be allowed to slip over the skin. This cycle should be repeated 15 or 20 times a minute until no more milk is obtained. The milk may be collected in a sterile glass or other container. With skill and practice the breast may be emptied as completely as it is done by the average robust infant. Finkelstein reported the maintenance of a supply of 30 to 40 ounces a day for several months in a mother whose nipples were so retracted that nursing was impossible.

substituted. Even if the mother is physically capable of lactation beyond nine months, it is to be discouraged.

It is a common mistake to continue nursing too long owing to a dislike of making a change when things are going reasonably well. Prolonged breast feeding is one of the causes of iron-deficiency anemia. The child's weight often gives valuable information as to need of supplementing the diet or weaning him completely before the usual time.

When a nursing infant has been accustomed from an early age to take an occasional bottle feeding or has had other foods added to his diet, gradual weaning is generally an easy matter; otherwise it is sometimes very difficult, the child refusing all food except the breast and nothing but starvation can induce him to take food from either a bottle or a spoon.

Sudden weaning may be required at any time because of the development of serious acute or chronic disease, or because of the occurrence of pregnancy or disease of the breast. The administration of stilbestrol, 20 mg a day for three days, will cause the mother considerable relief from breast engorgement under these circumstances. Mothers frequently nurse their children through many of the minor ailments without seeming detriment to either. In some acute illnesses of short duration it is better, unless weaning is decided upon, to feed the child from a bottle and maintain the flow of milk by manual expression or by a breast pump. The previous flow can often be reestablished after a lapse of two weeks, and sometimes after a much longer time.

The difficulties in weaning a child of 9 or 10 months who has had nothing but the breast are occasionally great. To try to teach such older infants to take a bottle is unwise; feeding from a cup or spoon is usually quite as easy. Continued coaxing or forcing of foods is almost never effective and usually serves only to prolong the period of resistance. Instead, food should be offered at regular intervals and, if refused, taken away without coercion. A variety of things may be offered—cow's milk, cereals, broths, or bread and milk; usually the nature of the food makes little difference. Some determined infants will resist eating for 24 or 36 hours, occasionally for 48 hours. We have never seen serious symptoms in a child not eating under such circumstances. However, water should be given.

MIXED FEEDING. By mixed feeding is meant a combination of artificial feeding and nursing. Mixed feeding may be employed whenever the mother's milk supply is insufficient. If nursing appears to be an undue strain, a bottle may be substituted for the night nursing or for one or more day nursings. Mixed feeding is often necessary during the early weeks before the mother's milk supply becomes well established. Under these circumstances, it is better not to alternate the breast and bottle, but to put the child first to both breasts and to follow this with a bottle if an insufficient quantity of milk has been obtained. After nursing five minutes on each breast, he may be given a suitable cow's milk feeding and allowed five minutes at the bottle. The stimulating effect of nursing on the secretion of milk is thus better secured.

Artificial Feeding

The successful feeding of infants demands that the food be digestible, the nutritional requirements met, and contamination with pathogenic bacteria or other harmful substances prevented. Since cow's milk, our chief source for infant feeding, is an excellent culture medium, control of milk contamination is essential.

MICROORGANISMS IN MILK. The bacteriologic control of milk is now a public health problem, the production and processing of milk sold to the public being regulated by law in most parts of the civilized world. In the United States, inspection and testing of cattle have virtually eliminated bovine tuberculosis and have greatly reduced other sources of infection in the animals themselves, especially brucellosis and streptococcal mastitis. Epidemics of milk-borne disease occur from time to time from contamination in handling milk—infections with enteric organisms, streptococci and staphylococci—but even when these occur infants are seldom affected if terminal sterilization of infants' feedings is practiced.

A contentious question is the role of saprophytic bacteria of milk and their toxic products in producing diarrheal disease in the infant. The number of organisms in bottled milk, produced and distributed under the best conditions, is always large; as delivered, the bacterial count varies from 5,000 to 50,000 per milliliter according to season and may exceed 1,000,000 on standing in warm weather. These bacteria, which come from the udder, from the hands of employees, and from utensils, fall into two general groups: acidifying organisms and putrefying organisms. The *lactic acid producing group,* which causes the souring of milk by fermentation of lactose, includes many varieties of *Lactobacillus* and *Streptococcus lactis.* In unheated milk they constitute 95 percent of the milk bacteria and, as milk becomes sour, an even larger proportion, since these organisms are relatively resistant to acid. There is no question as to the harmlessness of this group, and various members of it are used in the preparation of commercial fermented milks. Putrefying organisms of the *colon* and *paracolon group* are also constantly found in milk, as are certain *spore-bearers, Bacillus subtilis* and *Clostridium perfringens* (*welchii*). Such organisms are ordinarily quite innocuous; nevertheless, they are somewhat more heat-resistant than are the lactic acid group, and their overgrowth in pasteurized milk may produce putrefaction. Pathogenic colon bacilli and staphylococci, while they may cause diarrhea in infants, are acquired by human contact, not from the milk.

Certain strains of staphylococcus, which are widely distributed, have been shown to elaborate a heat-stable, filtered product capable of evoking vomiting and diarrhea. The greater incidence of diarrheal disorders in infants fed on heavily contaminated milk, even when it is terminally sterilized, may well be related to elaboration of such toxic products, although proof of the pathogenic action of an exotoxin, as opposed to infection with pathogenic bacteria, has seldom been firmly established.

MILK STERILIZATION. Since even the most carefully handled milk occasionally produces disease when fed raw, some form of milk sterilization is now universally employed in feeding infants. Heat sterilization produces a number of changes in the milk aside from destroying the bacteria. The lactalbumin is altered in such a way that the milk acquires a slightly different taste, the casein coagulates in a finer curd * making the milk more digestible, partial caramelization of the sugar occurs at high temperatures, and there is some destruction of ascorbic acid and of thiamine. The nutritional value of the proteins is adversely affected only by severe thermal treatment which may involve some injury to several amino acids, notably to lysine. The extent of these alterations varies with the degree and the duration of thermal treatment.

Pasteurization as generally carried out (holding process—65° to 68° C for 30 minutes) destroys all pathogenic bacteria and roughly 99 percent of the saprophytes. Spores are not destroyed, and unless the milk is kept cool there may be an extensive growth of spore-bearers. In general, pasteurized milk should be kept below 50° F and used not more than 48 hours after delivery. The coagulability and taste of the milk are only minimally affected by pasteurization. About 20 percent of the vitamin C and about 10 percent of the thiamine are destroyed.

In *boiled milk* the taste is further altered, and the curd produced on acidification or after peptic digestion is even finer. About 50 percent of the vitamin C is lost and roughly 30 percent of the thiamine. The biologic value of the protein suffers to a minimal extent.[†]

---

* The finer character of the casein curd from heated milk is due to two factors: (1) an alteration in the state of the calcium produced by heating which may result in some precipitation of calcium phosphate and thus indirectly affect the deposition of calcium caseinate; and (2) the coagulation of the heat-denatured lactalbumin, which forms aggregates upon which casein particles are adsorbed. When subsequent coagulation of the casein occurs these aggregates tend to remain dispersed and a finer, smoother curd results. The mechanism appears to be quite similar to that which occurs when starch, gruels, and other protective colloids are added to milk.

† When the milk is heated in an open container, with little agitation, a scum forms which consists of coagulated lactalbumin with a certain amount of calcium phosphate and fat. This should be removed, for it is likely to clog the nipple of the feeding bottle.

Flowing steam sterilization effects changes comparable to those produced by actual boiling of the milk. This is carried out by exposing the feeding bottles to live steam at atmospheric pressure in a covered vessel for 15 minutes.

Autoclaving the milk for 10 minutes at 115° C causes complete destruction of bacteria and spores. The taste is altered considerably and the milk acquires a slightly yellowish tinge from caramelization of the sugar. The protein is more readily digested, although there is a slight loss of lysine.[‡] Roughly 60 percent of the vitamin C is lost and from 30 to 50 percent of the thiamine.

Since thiamine is ordinarily present in quantities more than double the minimal requirements, the destruction of this factor by heat need not occasion concern unless the treatment is unusually severe, as in the case of prolonged autoclaving. The destruction of lysine is negligible. The replacement of vitamin C is, however, a matter of great importance, since raw cow's milk contains barely enough to prevent scurvy. All infants fed on sterilized milk must be given a supplement of this factor.

FROZEN MILK. In cold weather milk is often unavoidably delivered partially or completely frozen. Only the water in the milk freezes, the fat undergoing separation in consequence; when such milk is thawed the fat globules coalesce, forming an oily layer on the surface. While older children are seldom affected by such milk, it may produce vomiting or diarrhea in infants. If, after thawing, the milk is skimmed and subsequently boiled, such digestive disturbances are usually avoided.[§]

EXPOSURE TO LIGHT. It should be appreciated that exposure to sunlight in delivery bottles causes a slight but not ordinarily significant loss of riboflavin.

DIFFERENCES BETWEEN COW'S MILK AND BREAST MILK. Physical differences between cow's milk and breast milk are altogether negligible. The specific gravity of both milks commonly lies between 1.028 and 1.033; a lower value should lead one to suspect adulteration.

The chemical composition of cow's milk varies to some extent with the breed of cow, that of Jerseys and Guernseys being richer in fat than that of Holsteins. In most of the milk that is marketed, however, the excess fat is removed, only the legal minimum (usually 3.3 to 3.5 percent) being left. The chief differences between average cow's milk and breast milk are given in Table 7, which does not, however,

---

‡ According to Mauron et al. (*Arch. Biochem. Biophys.*, 59:433, 1955), who made tests of "available" lysine as measured by pancreatic digestion in vitro, boiling caused inactivation of lysine to the extent of 5 percent of the quantity present, the inactivation in evaporated milk which is autoclaved being 11.2 percent. With dried milk prepared by the spray process the inactivation was less than 4 percent, but with drum drying it was approximately 20 percent. Spray drying is now universal practice in the United States.

§ The cause of altered digestibility of frozen milk is unsettled; it has been attributed to the action of certain bacteria which grow only at low temperatures, to unusual enzyme action, and to denaturization of the milk proteins. In all probability, however, purely physical changes are responsible; milk which has been quickly frozen and kept at a very low temperature retains its physical characteristics and its digestibility after thawing.

TABLE 7. *Average Percentage Composition of Mature Breast Milk and Cow's Milk* *

Constituents	Breast Milk		Cow's Milk	
Water	87.6		87.2	
Total Solids	12.4		12.8	
Protein	1.1		3.3	
Casein		0.4		2.7
Lactalbumin		0.4		0.4
Lactoglobulin		0.2		0.2
Fat	3.8		3.8†	
Lactose	7.0		4.8	
Ash	0.21		0.71	
Sodium		0.015		0.058
Potassium		0.055		0.138
Calcium		0.034		0.126
Magnesium		0.004		0.013
Iron		0.00021		0.00015‡
Chlorine		0.043		0.100
Phosphorus		0.016		0.099
Sulfur		0.014		0.330
Calories per ounce	22		21†	
Calories per 100 ml	71		69†	

*From Macy. *The Composition of Milks.* Nat. Res. Council Pub. 254, 1953.

†Much of the milk marketed in the United States contains only the legal minimum of 3.3 to 3.5 percent fat. Its caloric content then averages 20 calories per ounce (66 calories per 100 ml).

‡Consistently higher iron values were reported prior to the introduction of stainless steel dairy equipment.

show all of the differences between the two milks. The proteins of the two milks possess specific antigenic properties. The differences in the character of the casein coagulum are due chiefly to the difference in quantity of casein present rather than to chemical differences between the two caseins.

The assays of the nutritive quality of the protein by Tomarelli and his co-workers showed no differences of statistical significance between the protein of breast milk and cow's milk.

Table 8 gives the percentage of essential amino acids in the breast milk and cow's milk protein.

The fat of cow's milk differs in some respects from that of breast milk. Differences in the size of the fat globules are described, but in our experience these are inconstant and of no practical importance. Differences in the proportions of the fatty acids occur, as is shown on the accompanying table (Table 9). As a general rule breast milk contains somewhat more of the polyunsaturated fatty acids. The composition of the milk fat is, however, greatly influenced by the fat of the diet. There are wide variations in the fat of human milk, depending upon the type of fat ingested by the mother. Cow's milk, however, always contains a higher proportion of the volatile (short-chain) fatty acids than does breast milk. These are formed from carbohydrate rather than from dietary fat and are not appreciably affected

TABLE 8. *Essential Amino Acid Composition of Breast Milk Protein and Cow's Milk Protein* *

Amino Acid	Percent of Breast Milk Protein	Percent of Cow's Milk Protein	Ratio of Cow's Milk to Breast Milk
Histidine	1.9	2.4	1.26
Isoleucine	7.2	6.4	0.89
Leucine	13.4	10.8	0.81
Lysine	6.6	7.8	1.18
Methionine	1.9	2.6	1.37
Phenylalanine	5.3	5.2	0.98
Threonine	5.2	4.6	0.89
Tryptophan	1.8	1.5	0.83
Valine	7.5	6.9	0.92
Total aromatic amino acids (phenylalanine + tyrosine)	10.5	11.0	1.05
Total sulfur amino acids (methionine + cystine)	4.3	3.5	0.81

*From Macy. *The Composition of Milks.* Nat. Res. Council Pub. 254, 1953.

TABLE 9.   *Major Fatty Acids Contained in Breast Milk Fat, as Influenced by Maternal Diet*[*]

| | Composition of Breast Milk Fat | | | | Composition of Food Fat | | |
Fatty Acids	Diet Ad Lib, Average of 11 Mothers	Maintenance Diet, with Lard Providing 40% of Calories	Low Caloric, Low Fat Diet	Maintenance Diet, with Corn Oil Providing 40% of Calories	Lard	Corn Oil	Cow's Milk Fat (Stall and Pasture Fed)[†]
Butyric							3.3
Lauric	6.8[‡]	4.6	7.9	4.9	0.2	0.1	2.3
Myristic	8.5	4.3	9.0	4.3	1.7	0.3	8.8
Palmitic	20.9	23.8	23.5	12.7	22.3	12.6	21.8
Palmitoleic	2.4	3.1	6.8	1.5	2.7	0	12.7
Stearic	7.3	7.8	3.2	2.9	9.3	2.7	
Oleic	35.8	42.6	36.9	28.7	44.9	30.4	40.7
Linoleic and linolenic	7.9	10.3	7.3	42.0	13.5	52.9	5.8
Percent of total acids	89.6	96.5	94.6	97.0	94.6	99.0	95.4

*Table modified from Insull. *Biochem. J.*, 72:27, 1959, and *J. Clin. Invest.*, 38:443, 1959.
†From Hilditch. *The Chemical Constitution of Natural Fats*, 3rd ed. John Wiley & Sons Inc., 1956.
‡Data calculated as weight percentages of total methyl esters.

by the dietary fat intake. In years past these short-chain fatty acids were thought to be conducive to diarrhea, a view that is no longer held.

The carbohydrate of the two milks, lactose, is identical.

As may be seen in Table 7, the common minerals are found in cow's milk in concentrations from two to six times as great as in breast milk.

The buffer value of cow's milk is considerably greater than that of breast milk.

Average figures for the vitamin concentration of the two milks are given in Table 10.

Both the mineral and the vitamin concentrations

of milk may be considerably affected by the diet of the mother or the cow.

Enzymes are present in both milks, especially in cow's milk where they are probably associated with the bacteria. It is probable that such enzymes are of little importance, for as a rule they do not survive the acidity of the stomach. A variety of antibodies is present in both, but it has been shown that they are largely destroyed by the normal processes of digestion. Many attempts have been made to show that the breast-fed infant is more resistant to infections than the infant reared on cow's milk. Provided the nutrition of the artificially fed infant has been

TABLE 10.   *Vitamin Content of 100 ml Breast Milk and Cow's Milk (Fresh)*[*]

	Mature Breast Milk	Cow's Milk
Vitamin A	150 USP units	100 USP units
Carotenoids	27 µg	38 µg
B vitamins		
Thiamine	16 µg	42 µg
Riboflavin	43 µg	157 µg
Nicotinic acid	172 µg	85 µg
Pyridoxine	11 µg	48 µg
Pantothenic acid	196 µg	350 µg
Folic acid	0.18 µg	0.23 µg
Choline	9 mg	13 mg
Inositol	39 mg	13 mg
Biotin	0.4 µg	3.5 µg
B_{12}	0.04 µg	0.41 µg
Vitamin C	4.3 mg	1.8 mg
Vitamin D	0.4-10.0 USP units	0.3-4.0 USP units
Vitamin K	26 Dam-Glavind units	100 Dam-Glavind units

*From Macy. *The Composition of Milks*. Nat. Res. Council Pub., 254, 1953.

TABLE 11.   *Percentage Distribution of Calories*

	Protein	Fat	Carbo-hydrate
Breast milk	8	50	42
Cow's milk	20	51	29
Cow's milk (common modifications)*	10-15	30-35	50-60

*The figures given are only approximate.

properly maintained, it does not appear that he is more susceptible to infection.

THE MODIFICATION OF COW'S MILK. In the past, bacterial contamination of milk was unquestionably responsible for much of the difficulty in infant feeding. With the improvement in standards of cleanliness in milk production and the more general adoption of some form of milk sterilization, this menace has largely disappeared. Even pure cow's milk is, however, not a satisfactory food for many infants. The history of artificial feeding has been one long series of attempts to modify cow's milk in such a way as to make it more suitable for infants. As one or another difference between the two milks became appreciated, emphasis would be laid on correcting that particular factor. Such modifications were not always beneficial; sometimes they resulted in the reduction of some essential constituent of the diet which was not appreciated at the time. Efforts to render cow's milk more digestible not infrequently led to failure because the energy requirements were not met or because some essential constituent was inadequately supplied. With a wider knowledge of nutrition, such mistakes are more easily avoided, and, in such countries as the United States, for years it has been possible to feed the vast majority of infants successfully on modified cow's milk.

In modifying milk for infant feeding it is neither possible nor necessary to overcome all the differences between cow's milk and breast milk; in fact, some of the most successful artificial feedings have differed widely from breast milk in composition. Only certain essential differences need to be corrected. Of prime importance is modification of the character of the casein curd. Unmodified raw cow's milk produces tenacious curds in the stomach; these may give rise to symptoms of indigestion, but more important is the fact that a considerable proportion of the food escapes absorption. Tough, beanlike curds which consist of undigested casein and fat are found in the stools. Curd indigestion can be prevented in a number of ways—by heating the milk, by diluting it, by the addition of alkali, by the use of a protective colloid such as starch or cereal gruel, or by precoagulation of the casein in the form of fine curds by careful addition of acid or by fermentation of the

milk.* It is now common practice to accomplish this by some form of heat treatment. By this means curd difficulties can be completely overcome. It is also customary to dilute cow's milk, a maneuver which has the advantage of providing a greater margin of safety against dehydration. Such dilution decreases the protein and fat concentration of the original milk, the caloric deficit being made up by adding carbohydrate. The proportion of calories distributed as protein, fat, and carbohydrate in breast milk and in cow's milk, unmodified and as commonly fed in formulas, is shown in Table 11. A more detailed description of a variety of commonly used infant feedings is given on page 161.

An extensive literature deals with the desirability of reducing the fat intake when cow's milk is fed. The view that breast milk fat is more digestible and less likely to produce fat intolerance has led to various proprietary imitations of it. Personal observations have convinced us that the minor differences in assimilability of the two fats are of little or no practical importance. Convincing evidence is not available to support the once popular view that fat intolerance is induced by feeding fat.

It is possible to feed infants on undiluted cow's milk provided it is treated so as to avoid curd indigestion, but there is no advantage in doing so. A carbohydrate-supplemented feeding is more economical and delivers a lower solute load per calorie thereby adding water homeostasis. On the whole, we are inclined to believe that the traditional type of modification deserves to be continued.

Carbohydrate may be added to milk in the form of simple sugars, polysaccharides, or mixtures of the two. Except in rare instances of disaccharidase deficiency there appears to be no particular advantage in giving monosaccharides; the normal child is able to invert disaccharides without difficulty. Of the double sugars, lactose would seem the logical one to use since it is the natural carbohydrate of milk. Lactose is, however, relatively expensive and has not been shown to possess any superiority to cane sugar. It ferments somewhat more readily than other disaccharides and has achieved little popularity in infant

* *Coagulation by acid* results from the conversion of soluble caseinates to the insoluble isoelectric casein (isoelectric point pH 4.7). The process of coagulation is reversed by adding alkali.

Coagulation by rennin involves the conversion of casein into the protein, paracasein, by limited hydrolytic cleavage. The resulting paracaseinates are far less soluble than caseinates, and precipitation occurs without any change in pH. The change is irreversible and the curd so formed contains much mineral matter. Calcium salts favor coagulation, since the calcium caseinates are less soluble than caseinates of alkali metals and, conversely, substances which bind calcium (such as citrates and oxalates) tend to inhibit coagulation.

Heating milk favors subsequent coagulation by acid or rennin. Although some minimal chemical change in the casein is effected by heat, a more important factor is the coagulation of the lactalbumin at temperatures above 62° C, which affects the physical state of the casein.

feeding. Pure maltose is not used for infant feeding. Cane sugar (sucrose) is an entirely satisfactory product for use with infants; it is inexpensive and is always available in pure form.

Mixtures of dextrins and maltose have been widely used in infant feeding since their introduction during the last century by Liebig. The claim that the additional time required for their hydrolysis gives better opportunity for absorption is not well supported. These preparations are, however, altogether satisfactory; they have a pleasant taste and may possess some virtue when the time comes for introducing solid foods, for being somewhat less sweet than cane sugar, they do not condition the child to a sweet food. A number of preparations are on the market which differ somewhat in their properties. Some of the liquid extracts of malt contain impurities which are somewhat laxative and are therefore sometimes used in the treatment of constipation. Dextrimaltose and corn syrup are not laxative for most infants and are widely used for infant feeding.

Invert sugar (equal parts of dextrose and levulose) in the form of molasses or honey has been used abroad in infant feeding with considerable success, although it has attracted little interest in this country. Banana sugar, which is largely invert sugar, has also been employed. These invert sugar preparations are satisfactory but do not appear to possess particular virtues.

The addition of carbohydrate in the form of starch gruels was once widely used as a means of preventing the formation of tough curds encountered when raw milk was fed. With heated milk this is not necessary. At present starch is occasionally used to thicken the feeding in certain cases of vomiting. The starch should be thoroughly cooked for young infants, since their ability to digest raw starch is limited. An excess of starch appears in the stools unchanged; it is not harmful.

The extent to which cow's milk feeding should be diluted is no longer a matter of great concern. In times past dilute formulas were widely used to avoid curd indigestion. With present-day heat processing this problem has disappeared and there is no difficulty in giving formulas considerably more concentrated than the original milk. The difficulty with these concentrated formulas is their failure to provide for the water requirement with an adequate margin of safety, making it necessary to give supplementary water between feedings. Although there may be particular indications for giving a dilute or a concentrated formula, for routine feeding formulas approximately isocaloric with breast milk (containing 0.67 calories per ml) are most commonly employed.

Dietary of the Artificially Fed Infant

A variety of milk preparations is available for infant feeding. In an era in which symptoms of indigestion were commonly attributed to the food, great efforts were made to control these symptoms by altering the ingredients or the physical state of the formula. It is now generally appreciated that disturbances of digestion originate for the most part from causes other than food; by and large they are due to infections—enteric and parenteral. The concern of infant feeding today is not to search for a formula that will arrest digestive symptoms but rather to meet the nutritional requirements of the child.

The nutritional requirements of the infant may be adequately supplied by heat-processed cow's milk, evaporated milk, or dried milk, with or without a carbohydrate supplement. Special modifications designed to combat digestive disturbances are largely of historical interest. Many of them are, however, excellent foods and are still used.

Homogenized Milk. This was introduced in infant feeding early in the present century, the objective being to decrease the size of the fat globules in milk as an aid in fat assimilation. That a substantial gain in fat absorption resulted was, however, never conclusively demonstrated. Today milk is homogenized in the course of fortifying it with vitamin D. A secondary gain is the more even distribution of lipid; the fat of homogenized milk will no longer rise to the surface as cream.

Fermented and Acidified Milks. Fermented milks were used empirically for infant feeding in several countries before the development of scientific pediatrics. Their use received support from the concept that diarrhea resulted from carbohydrate fermentation. The proportion of carbohydrate fermented to lactic acid is, however, only a small fraction of the total. Fermented milks are more acid than fresh milk and, in addition, they are precurdled, the curd being precipitated in a very fine form. At one time the acidity was thought to be a matter of importance in gastric digestion, for cow's milk has a high buffer value and requires more acid to bring it to a given pH. It is now believed, however, that peptic digestion is almost negligible in the infant, in whom proteolytic digestion occurs largely in the intestine. The real virtue of fermented milk is that it produces fine friable curds which avoid curd indigestion.

Cultured milk—milk which has been sterilized by heat and then inoculated with a pure culture of some bacterium (usually *Lactobacillus bulgaricus* or *L. acidophilus* or *Streptococcus lactis*)—attained some popularity over naturally fermented milk, since it was safer from the point of view of pathogens and was a more uniform product. Addition of acids (usually lactic acid) also had a vogue. When acids were added cautiously, a fine coagulum could be secured, the product having much the same properties as fermented milk. All of these products have been falling into disuse in the United States since heat processing has solved the curd problem.

Skim Milk and Half-Skimmed Milk. These products came into use when it was noted that there was considerable fat loss in the stools in diarrhea and in certain other states, such as prematurity and celiac syndrome. Excessive loss of fat in the stools was attributed to the use of a feeding too rich in lipid. In some quarters this view is still maintained, though it is difficult to reconcile it with the observations of Schick and Wagner, Macrae and Morris, Chung, Snyderman, and others who have failed to find deleterious clinical effects from feeding fat in steatorrhea and who have shown by chemical measurements that, despite the absorptive defect, increasing fat intake increases fat absorption. Removal of all or part of the fat greatly increases the solute content of the feeding per calorie and in infants may compromise water balance.

Humanized Milks. This term is applied to a variety of proprietary milk feedings designed to imitate the composition of breast milk in one or more of the following respects: lower protein content, lower mineral content particularly with regard to calcium, and substitution of a vegetable-fat mixture containing more unsaturated fat for the milk fat. Carbohydrate, usually lactose, is added to make up for the reduced protein calories. A reduced protein intake was originally advocated by Rotch, who believed that the infant had a limited tolerance for this foodstuff, and in the days of raw milk feeding this policy doubtless served to avoid curd indigestion. Today, with heat processing, this is no longer a problem and one can feed with apparent impunity considerably more protein than cow's milk provides. The value of reducing the calcium intake is also questionable. Substitution of vegetable-fat mixtures for butter fat insures in some instances a slightly better fat absorption. In the case of normal infants the difference is negligible, but in situations of steatorrhea the difference may be significant. The effect of polyunsaturated fatty acids in reducing blood cholesterol to keep the serum cholesterol at moderate or even low concentrations has attracted attention in view of the possibility that, over the years, the tendency of arteries to show atheromatous change may thus be retarded. The conclusion that such diets are antiatherogenic cannot, however, be drawn at the present time. The chief value of the humanized milks lies in their convenience and ease of preparation. They are nutritionally adequate foods, a carbohydrate supplement has already been added, and they require only the addition of water. Several of them are marketed in both powdered and liquid form. Several are reinforced with vitamins.

The chief products of this group on the American market are Similac, S.M.A., Enfamil, and Bremil. The percentage distribution of calories in these products is as follows:

	Protein	Fat	Carbo-hydrate
Bremil	9	48	43
Enfamil	9	50	41
S.M.A.	9	48	43
Similac	11	47	42

Special Products. A variety of proprietary feedings are available for infants who are allergic to cow's milk, an allergy which has been infrequent in our experience. These feedings include goat's milk, the soya bean milks—Sobee, Mullsoy, and Soyalac—meat base formulas, and finally an enzymatic digest of casein containing no antigenic protein of any kind. These are all useful products and permit adequate nutrition. Some are available in both dry and liquid form.

Evaporated and Dried Milk. For the routine feeding of infants fresh pasteurized milk is still used to some extent, but in recent years it has been largely replaced by preserved milk—either evaporated or dried.

Dried milk, prepared now as a rule by the spray process, is a virtually sterile product. It does not support bacterial growth and can be kept for some time in opened tins. For this reason it is particularly useful in the absence of refrigeration, and in many countries where refrigeration facilities are limited it is the feeding of choice. The original milk is usually reconstituted by adding one part of the powder to eight parts of water by weight.

Evaporated milk has been subjected to autoclaving and is a completely sterile product. Its use requires refrigeration facilities, for it is subject to bacterial contamination after a can has been opened. Because of its convenience in preparing feedings it has become increasingly popular, and it is currently estimated that more than 80 percent of bottle-fed infants in the United States are fed either on evaporated milk or on some prepared milk feeding marketed in evaporated form. Evaporated milk is concentrated two and a quarter times and its composition as marketed is standardized by law:

	Protein %	Fat %	Carbo-hydrate %	Mineral %	Cals. per oz.
Evaporated milk	7	7.85	10	1.6	44
Evaporated milk diluted with equal parts of water	3.5	3.9	5.0	0.8	22
Percentage distribution of calories	20	51	29		

In the processing of both dried and evaporated milks a considerable fraction of the vitamin C is lost and must be replaced. Heat damage to other vitamins and to protein is, however, minimal.

Sweetened condensed milk was formerly used to some extent in infant feeding, because of superior bacteriostatic qualities owing to the very high sucrose content. When diluted with four parts of water it provides a mixture with a caloric value of 0.67 calories per ml and the following percentage distribution of calories: protein, 10 percent; fat, 22 percent; and carbohydrate, 68 percent. Vitamin supplementation is required. It appears to have no current advantage over evaporated milk, by which it has been largely replaced.

Carbohydrate Supplements. As pointed out, it appears to be immaterial what sugar is given to normal infants as a supplement. The exceptional problem of disaccharidase deficiency is discussed elsewhere (Sec. 23.5). Starch, too, is well digested after the first few months. In measuring the carbohydrate added the following table may be of value:

APPROXIMATE MEASURES OF DIFFERENT CARBOHYDRATES

Substance	Weight (g) Per 4 Tbsp	Equivalent
Corn syrup	79.4	1½ tbsp = 30 g
Cane sugar	52.3	2 tbsp = 26 g
Milk sugar	40.3	3 tbsp = 30 g
Dextri-maltose	35.2	4 tbsp = 35 g
Flour, wheat	33.5	4 tbsp = 33 g

APPARATUS FOR THE PREPARATION OF THE FEEDING. This includes a graduated pouring container, a standard tablespoon or 1 ounce measure, a bowl for mixing the formula, a funnel, a pitcher, feeding bottles, a bottle rack, nipples, metal or paper nipple protectors, bottle brushes, and some sort of heater. Bottles of Pyrex glass or of plastic capable of resisting sudden changes of temperature are a great convenience. The hole in the nipple should be large enough to permit the milk to drop readily when the bottle is inverted, but not so large that it will flow in a stream. When the liquid flows too slowly, the nipple may be improved by burning a larger hole in the rubber. An ordinary sewing needle, its eye stuck into a cork for a holder and its point heated in a flame, serves the purpose. A nipple through which liquid flows too fast may as well be discarded. Nipples should be rinsed in cold water after use, then cleaned with soap and hot water, rinsed, shaken dry, and kept in a covered jar. Bottles should first be rinsed with cold water, then washed with hot soapsuds and a bottle brush.

Disposable bottles and nipples are now available which are marketed with prepared formulas. They are convenient, but more expensive and they require more storage space.

DIRECTIONS FOR PREPARING FOOD. If facilities for refrigeration are adequate, all the food needed for 24 hours should be prepared at one time. The appropriate amount of water is placed in the graduated pitcher and the sugar or other carbohydrate supplement * added and stirred into solution. The lid of the can of evaporated milk is scalded with hot water and wiped dry with a clean dish towel or paper towel before being opened. After adding the desired amount of evaporated milk, the formula is poured into feeding bottles placed in the rack. Each bottle is capped with a nipple and the nipple covered with a pro-

* When liquid preparations like corn syrup are used, their measurement is considerably facilitated by warming.

tector. The loaded rack is then placed in the covered pail in 2 or 3 inches of water—enough to insure a free flow of steam for half an hour without risk of its boiling dry—and steam-sterilized for 15 minutes. It is important to wait until steam is escaping freely from the covered pail before starting to count the period of sterilization. The rack may then be removed and the feedings allowed to cool in room air before being stored in the refrigerator.

When dairy milk is used, unless the milk is homogenized, the bottle should be inverted several times in order to insure an even distribution of the fat. Whole milk feedings when subjected to terminal sterilization tend to produce a scum which easily plugs the nipple holes. To obviate this, the mixture may be boiled in a saucepan for at least a minute, cooled, the scum removed, and the formula poured into scalded or sterilized feeding bottles. The bottles are then capped or stoppered with cotton and stood in cold water until quite cool before they are put in the icebox.

Terminal sterilization is a traditional procedure in pediatrics and is still generally endorsed by authoritative bodies as a safety measure. The need for it has, however, been challenged under conditions in which the milk supply is beyond question and the water supply meets standard civilian requirements.

DIRECTIONS FOR FEEDING. It is common practice to warm the food to 100° F by placing the bottle in warm water for a few minutes. The temperature of the milk may be tested by pouring a few drops upon the inner surface of the wrist, where it should feel warm but not hot. Warming the feeding is not, however, a real necessity, for infants fed cold feedings seem to thrive quite as well. Iced feedings have been used for some years in France for the control of vomiting. A bottle should not be rewarmed for a second feeding.

Ordinarily an infant should not be more than 20 minutes in taking his food and should not sleep with the nipple in his mouth. The bottle should be placed or held in such a position that the nipple is kept full. At some time during the feeding, and again after it, the infant should be held upright over the nurse's shoulder and patted on the back to allow him to bring up such air as he may have swallowed. After the feeding he is placed in his crib and left alone.

Feeding of Healthy Infants During the Early Months

A suitable milk feeding for the majority of infants can be devised as follows:

1. Estimate the probable number of calories required in 24 hours, allowing 110 calories per kilogram of body weight (50 per pound).
2. The total caloric requirement, divided by 20, gives the needed number of ounces of a stand-

ard formula which provides 20 calories to the ounce,* such as the following:

Evaporated milk	3½ oz (or whole milk, 7 oz)
Cane sugar	½ oz (1 level tablespoonful)
Water, up to	10 oz

3. The formula is divided into the number of feedings desired.

The essential factor in feeding is the amount of food given in the 24 hours. The number of feedings into which this is divided and the interval between them is of secondary importance. Infants differ in their response to a schedule. Some do better with relatively large feedings at longer intervals, and others thrive best with smaller feedings given more often; no hard and fast rule can be laid down. The large majority of healthy infants can be readily trained to take their feedings at 4-hour intervals from the beginning. We have several times seen infants as young as six weeks of age thrive and be perfectly content on four feedings a day, with either a 4- or a 5-hour interval. The smaller number of feedings materially lessens the labor of the mother or nurse.

Schedules suitable for starting normal infants are given in Table 12.

For example, an infant three months old, weighing 12 pounds (5.5 kg), is to be artificially fed. On the basis of 50 calories per pound (110 calories per kilogram), it is apparent that he will require approximately (12 × 50 =) 600 calories per day. With the standard formula of 20 calories per ounce, 30 ounces a day (600/20) will be needed. This is best prepared by taking three times the quantities taken for making 10 ounces, namely:

To Make 10 Ounces

Evaporated milk	3½ oz
or whole milk	7 oz
Cane sugar	½ oz
Water, up to	10 oz

To Make 30 Ounces

Evaporated milk	10 oz
or whole milk	21 oz
Cane sugar	1½ oz *
Water, up to	30 oz

The formula may be divided into five bottles containing 5½ ounces each (or six bottles containing

---

* The use of such a standard formula, isocaloric with breast milk, makes a further calculation of fluid requirements unnecessary; if sufficient calories are provided, the fluid intake will be adequate.

In the interests of accuracy it is wisest to make up to 20, 30, or 40 ounces, even if some is to be discarded. If a 1-ounce measure is not available, a rounded tablespoon of cane sugar may be taken as the equivalent of ½ ounce.

4½ ounces each if a night feeding is still required) and fed at intervals of four hours.

The first attempt at artificial feeding is somewhat of an experiment. A feeding such as is given above may not be ideal for the particular child in question. One should observe carefully the weight of the child, the appetite, and the presence of untoward digestive symptoms to see if indications arise for changing the food.

Indications for Increasing the Food. If an infant appears healthy and contented and gains weight regularly, there is no reason for increasing his food even if he is taking somewhat less than the average caloric requirements. With some placid infants 80 calories per kilogram a day seem to be sufficient food. The two best indications that food should be increased are the weight curve and the presence of signs of hunger. The weight curve is important, but one should not be guided by it alone. When it is made the chief concern, there is a constant temptation to increase the food if the child is not gaining as rapidly as it is thought he should, regardless of his digestion and caloric intake. Gain in weight is seldom continuous; even healthy, breast-fed infants may have periods of a week or two, during the early months, when the weight remains stationary with no apparent cause. During the latter part of the first year and subsequently, there may be even longer periods of stationary weight. Evidences of hunger may be easy to detect, as when an infant finishes his bottle greedily and cries for more or becomes fretful considerably before his feeding time. At other times it may be difficult to distinguish symptoms of underfeeding from those of indigestion. Crying as a result of hunger may easily be mistaken for colic. An infant may, however, cry merely because he is spoiled. Underfeeding may lead to vomiting and even to diarrhea. An infant who remains hungry after finishing his bottle may continue to suck at the nipple and thus swallow considerable air, which may cause regurgitation; at other times the restlessness associated with hunger may lead to vomiting. The so-called starvation diarrhea, seen particularly in small infants who are underfed, consists in the frequent passage of small greenish stools composed chiefly of mucus and other secretions. The condition scarcely resembles true diarrhea except in the number of movements, for the total volume of material expelled is small. Cases of this kind respond promptly and favorably to the administration of more food. The therapeutic test should be appled if there is any suspicion of underfeeding. When underfeeding has been prolonged and has resulted in loss of weight, the appetite is as a rule lost. Such seriously underfed infants should not be placed at once on an adequate diet; the food should be gradually increased.

Indications for Decreasing the Food. Over feeding may result in loss of appetite; the infant does not finish his bottle. There may be regurgitation after meals if too much food is taken. In the latter event one should not be too ready to conclude that

TABLE 12.   *Food Requirements and Feeding Schedule for Normal Infants*

Age	Calories Per Day	Ounces of Formula Per Day	Number of Feedings in 24 Hours	Quantity Per Feeding
1 month	300-500	15-25 ⎫		3-4½ oz ⎧
2 months	400-580	20-29 ⎬	5 or 6	3½-6 oz ⎨
3 months	480-650	24-32 ⎫		4-7 oz ⎧
4 months	560-700	28-35 ⎬ *	4 or 5	5-8 oz ⎨
5 months	630-750	31-37 ⎭		6-8 oz ⎩

*It is not advisable to attempt to supply more than about 650 or 700 calories a day as milk formula. When more food is required, other articles should be added to the diet.

the total daily feeding is too large; it may be that too large a volume is given at one time. Prolonged overfeeding beyond the demands of the appetite is likely to result in digestive disturbances and eventually in failure to gain weight. It is apparent that somewhat similar symptoms may be produced by underfeeding and overfeeding. An examination of the caloric intake will enable one to avoid gross errors in either direction; at times it is necessary to try empirically the effect of increasing or decreasing the food.

When the caloric requirements of a particular child have been established empirically, and it has been found that he will gain satisfactorily and remain healthy on, let us say, 80 or 120 calories per kilogram as the case may be, one may then make regular increases in the food, as weight is gained, to maintain the caloric intake at the desired level with respect to body weight.

Feeding by Appetite.   The food intake of the breast-fed infant is automatically regulated by his appetite. With artificial feeding as well, appetite serves as a useful guide in determining the amount of food required, provided the composition of the formula food is a balanced one. The formulas described on page 164, as well as the prepared formulas of humanized milk, lend themselves admirably to such a scheme of regulation. No harm need be feared if at each feeding the infant is offered more formula than he requires and is allowed to take what he wants within a period of 15 or 20 minutes, the unconsumed excess being then discarded. Although the amount taken at each feeding may vary considerably in the course of a day, just as is the case with infants nursed at the breast, the 24-hour intake normally remains quite constant. If the appetite is impaired by illness, such as at the onset of an infection, the consumption of food will be correspondingly reduced and indigestion resulting from overfeeding will thereby be avoided.

Experience has shown that the more the feeding differs from what may be considered a complete and balanced diet for the infant, the less reliance can be placed upon the appetite. Thus, some infants given excessive amounts of fat may become nauseated and refuse food, taking less than their nutritional requirements, while others whose diet is lacking in some essential constituent may develop ravenous appetites and be grossly overfed. Infants given concentrated feedings with inadequate water may take more food than they need in order to satisfy their thirst, and conversely, with an overdiluted food, the stomach is likely to be distended and the appetite temporarily satisfied before sufficient food is taken.

Common Mistakes in Infant Feeding.   The mistake is sometimes made of changing feedings too frequently. Before changing an infant's food one should be certain that an indication exists. It is not possible to modify the food in such a way as to relieve every trivial discomfort or disturbance a child may have. Nurses are usually ready to ascribe every slight symptom to the food, particularly if they have strong opinions of their own on the subject of feeding and are not in full sympathy with the method employed. Often the cause is outside the food and even outside the digestive tract.

It is unwise to make too many changes in the feeding at one time. This does not apply to reductions of food, which must often be made suddenly in acute illness, but rather to increases in the amount of food or the addition of new foods. A change both in the food and in the feeding schedule should not be made at the same time, nor should more than one article of food be added at a time; otherwise, should untoward results follow, it is difficult to decide what caused them.

In deciding whether a change of food is beneficial one should usually allow not less than three days to elapse. To be sure, it may be self-evident within a few hours that acute indigestion has been produced and the food should then be discontinued at once. In judging improvement, however, a longer time is required.

Another common mistake is the introduction of solid food in quantity with no curtailment of the milk formula. This often results in refusal of food or in vomiting.

Indications for Changing the Food.   In *hot weather* the appetite is often impaired, and a temporary reduction in food intake may be desirable.

Since the need for fluid is increased, the volume of the formula should be maintained and additional water given between feedings. As soon as the period of excessive heat has passed, the usual food may be resumed.

The part played by *infections* in producing digestive disturbances is discussed in connection with vomiting and diarrhea. The response varies greatly with different infants and with different infections. Forcing of food under these circumstances should be avoided; the appetite is an excellent guide to follow.

A number of other conditions, such as vomiting, diarrhea, constipation, colic, and failure to gain weight, may require changes in feeding. These will be discussed in subsequent pages. After the age of three or four months, when additional carbohydrate is provided in the form of cereal, there is no need to add sugar or otherwise to modify the milk; plain boiled milk or diluted evaporated milk may be given.

THE USE OF FOOD OTHER THAN MILK DURING THE FIRST YEAR. *Vitamins.* Some form of vitamin D prophylaxis against rickets should be given to all infants after the first week of life. This is more fully discussed in connection with rickets. Orange juice or some other antiscorbutic should be given from the second week onward. One may commence with a teaspoonful a day and rapidly increase the quantity until the juice of one orange a day is taken. Pure ascorbic acid may be substituted for orange juice, 25 mg being given per day, dissolved in water or mixed with one of the feedings.

Solid Foods. The time at which solid foods are introduced varies greatly in American practice. As more and more prepared infant foods have become available the tendency has been to introduce them earlier. They have been successfully fed as early as the first week of life. Competition has developed between mothers and even among physicians in this respect. Granting that solid foods can be fed, if properly subdivided, even to the youngest infants the question remains whether there is any advantage or disadvantage in doing so.

The reasons given for starting solid foods are two: to provide iron, the one important element in which milk is deficient; and for their educational value, to accustom children to eating the type of food they will subsequently depend upon. As far as iron is concerned there is no advantage in starting it before the end of the second month. It is well established that iron administered before this time is not readily utilized for hemoglobin synthesis (Chap. 17). The young infant depends upon stores of iron which have accumulated in the liver during fetal life. As far as habit is concerned, it is also clear that when solid foods are postponed until the second half year difficulty is often encountered in getting infants to take them, the difficulty being greater the longer their introduction is postponed. Such difficulties are negligible during most of the first half year and cannot be said to constitute an argument for introducing solids before the age of four months.

The disadvantages of introducing solid foods before the fourth month are not serious. More time is consumed in feeding, which adds to the work of caring for the infant. In an appreciable number of small infants the tongue reflex which pushes the food to the back of the mouth in preparation for swallowing is imperfectly developed, and some difficulty in handling solid food is experienced unless the food is introduced well into the back of the mouth. The difficulty is said to be confined to the first two or three months. It has been postulated that the earlier administration of solid foods results in an increased incidence of allergy. Reliable evidence for this view is, however, not available. It was demonstrated by Schloss and his co-workers that infants regularly developed specific antibodies and often showed positive skin tests to each new food they received; these antibodies, however, were not associated with the development of allergic symptoms.

On the whole, the policy of exclusive milk feedings for the first three or four months of life appears to have no disadvantages and distinct advantages from the point of view of convenience. The earlier introduction of solid foods may be regarded as a fad, though in no sense a harmful one.

A great variety of precooked foods for infants is now available. It includes cereals, soups, vegetables, fruits, meat, fish, and egg yolk. For small infants, strained (homogenized) fruits, meats, and vegetables are marketed; and for older ones who can do some chewing, there are finely chopped ("junior") foods. The order in which these foods are introduced is not a matter of importance. A suggested schedule is given in Table 13.

New articles of diet should be introduced one at a time; two or three days should elapse before another change is made. One should always begin with a small quantity of the new food, not more than a teaspoonful; it is best given at the beginning of the meal. The feeding schedule should not be altered. As each new food is added, it may be expected that the infant will take somewhat less of his old food. It is advisable to reduce the amount of milk offered at the time a solid food is first introduced.

As solid foods constitute a more significant part of the diet and milk a less significant one, it is important to give a variety of solid foods in order to maintain a balanced diet. Most vegetable proteins are to some extent incomplete, and amino acid deficits

TABLE 13. *Suggested Age for Introduction of Various Foods into the Infant's Diet*

	Age
Vitamin D	2 weeks
Orange juice	2 weeks
Cereal, vegetable, fruit	2-4 months
Meat, fish, or egg	3-5 months
Breadstuffs (zwieback, toast, etc.)	5-6 months

in one are compensated by others. With increasing dependence on solid foods it becomes easier to adapt an infant to a schedule of three meals a day.

A caution against the early administration of egg to infants is often given, particularly to the administration of egg white on the ground that it may cause allergic symptoms. Some allergists have maintained that early administration of an antigen induces an allergy which would not otherwise have developed. There is no doubt that hypersensitiveness to egg albumin may occur and that it may be extreme, just as it may in the case of the lactalbumin of cow's milk and, less frequently, of wheat or other proteins. The experience with well-defined cases of hypersensitivity indicates that symptoms occur at the first contact with the food, regardless of whether this is early or late, and that decreasing sensitivity appears to result from repeated contact with small doses of the offending antigen rather than from some aging factor. It would thus appear that there is nothing to be gained by deferring contact with egg, and it is no more logical to do so than it would be to defer the administration of cow's milk. The administration of powdered egg yolk, a product marketed for its nonallergic properties, is not altogether without risk, for it has been found difficult in such products to control contamination with salmonella organisms.

Feeding During the Latter Part of the First Year

As soon as solid foods constitute any considerable portion of the diet, the calculation of the caloric intake becomes so inaccurate that it is of little value. Appetite assumes increasing importance not only in regulating the quantity of food but also in the selection of the food itself, as shown rather convincingly by the experiments in self-selection of diets carried out by C. M. Davis in Chicago. Infants of seven to nine months were offered a variety of food and allowed to select their own diets. The choice of food was often bizarre. From time to time an infant would show a marked preference for particular foods, of which large quantities would be taken for several days; as much as seven or eight eggs or four or five bananas might be consumed at a meal. These swings were, however, temporary, and the diet over a period of time was varied and well balanced. From the point of view of growth and gain in weight, as well as resistance to disease and freedom from symptoms of indigestion, the results were entirely satisfactory.

It is neither practical nor generally advisable to emulate these experiments in the average home, but one may safely allow an infant considerable leeway in the quantity of food, provided a suitable variety is taken. In practice, the only food likely to be taken in excess by an infant in his second six months is milk, and if this tendency appears, it is advisable to restrict the amount of milk offered, so

that there will be more encouragement to take other foods.

The following are typical of what may be fed to an average child of nine months:

DIETS * FOR INFANTS OF SIX TO NINE MONTHS

Breakfast	Strained juice or fruit
	Cereal
	Soft-cooked egg
	Toast, graham cracker, or zwieback
	Milk
Midmorning	Juice of an orange
Dinner	Ground meat or liver
	Mashed potatoes
	Strained or finely chopped vegetable
	Soft pudding, junket, custard, gelatine dessert, or strained fruit
	Milk
Supper	Milk toast, cottage cheese, or bacon
	Potato, spaghetti, or macaroni
	Strained or finely chopped green vegetable if desired
	Strained fruit, banana, or soft dessert
	Toast, graham cracker, or zwieback
	Milk

During the latter part of the first year the child should become accustomed to a variety of foods and should depend less on milk. *Weaning from the bottle* is a great help in attaining this end. This should be begun by the ninth or tenth month; by the end of the first year all milk should be taken from a cup. Children who are allowed to continue with the bottle after this time usually develop the bottle habit and often refuse all solid food as long as it is continued. It is also advisable to teach a child to feed himself as soon as possible; this can sometimes be done at the end of the first year.

Feeding of Healthy Infants During the Second Year

In the second year the diet of a healthy child should consist chiefly of milk, breadstuffs, farinaceous foods, vegetables, fruit juices or cooked fruit, meat, and eggs. The quantity of milk given need not exceed a pint a day. The notion that there are many children who cannot take milk is a mistaken one; the usual difficulty is that the quantity given is too large. There is, however, no actual necessity that a child at this age take milk at all, provided his diet is properly balanced.

An appropriate daily schedule during the second year is as follows:

Breakfast	Fruit juice or chopped fruit †
	Cereal with milk

* Vitamin D is the only vitamin that needs to be added to such diets.

† Orange, tomato, or grapefruit is given in some form every day.

	Egg
	Toast or bread
	Milk
Dinner	Ground meat, fowl, or fish without bones
	Potato
	Chopped vegetables
	Pudding, cake, ice cream, or chopped fruit
	Milk
Middle of the afternoon	A drink of milk or a cracker provided this does not disturb the appetite at mealtimes
Supper	Spaghetti with cheese, egg dish, soup or peanut butter sandwich
	Chopped vegetable if desired
	Chopped fruit or dessert
	Buttered toast or bread
	Milk or cocoa

It is not possible to prescribe the exact quantities of food to be given. One must rely on the child's appetite, which is a satisfactory guide, particularly if a child feeds himself. Many healthy children occasion surprise by eating almost as much as their parents. Dislike for a particular food may be overcome by giving this particular item of food first and withholding other food until it is eaten. The fact that the quantity of food eaten at different times is variable should occasion no concern, for appetite shows considerable variation. The attempt to standardize a child's intake is the cause of many feeding difficulties. Almost invariably the result is loss of appetite and a struggle on the part of parents to make him eat things it is believed he should have. Cajolery, bribery, and force are useless in such a situation; the child usually enjoys the struggle and the attention he receives. The wisest course is to put before the child a suitable meal and to set a time limit rather than a quantity limit. After 20 or 30 minutes the food is removed, no matter how little has been eaten. If the audience displays no interest in how little the child eats, with such a regimen it seldom requires more than a few days before the normal appetite is reestablished. Children of this age are peculiarly responsive to the emotional circumstances which attend the administration of food. The complaint of anorexia calls for study of the psychologic, as well as the somatic and dietetic, factors involved.

By the time a child is a year and a half old he should have a fairly efficient chewing apparatus, and finely chopped foods can be substituted for the strained infant foods. It may be advantageous to start the "junior" foods earlier if there is a tendency to constipation. Some discretion must be employed here, for certain children have a tendency to bolt their food and masticate poorly. A moderate amount of undigested food in the stool is not an indication for renewed sieving and grinding, but large quantities of unaltered solids may be so. Nuts are prohibited partly because they are likely to be poorly chewed, but chiefly because of the risk of their being aspirated. The danger of impacted fish bones calls for the avoidance of bony fish.

With increasing age of the child more latitude may be allowed in the child's diet and children past the age of two years may eat any of the usual adult foods according to their taste. Feeding problems in older children are discussed elsewhere (Chap. 6).

Parenteral Nutrition

LAURENCE FINBERG

Under circumstances where, for any reason, oral intake becomes temporarily interdicted, nutrition may be maintained by parenteral means. If the temporary period lasts no longer than a few days, water, glucose, and electrolytes are the only substances necessary and these are easily provided through standard intravenous techniques (p. 168). When a week or two must elapse before oral (or gastrostomy) feeding may be resumed, amino acid hydrolysates in a 5 percent solution plus necessary vitamins may be given to partially offset a catabolic state. For these relatively short periods, glucose, water, minerals, and, when indicated, amino acids in amounts adequate to offset losses and spare protein suffice to maintain the patient until ordinary feeding may be resumed.

Under special circumstances, such as major small intestinal surgical resection (short bowel syndrome) or other reason for intestinal malfunction, total parenteral nutrition may be accomplished. To do so requires a carefully devised solution delivering water, calories, protein, or amino acids and the necessary vitamins and minerals, including trace elements. Until recently, a practical dilemma arose because if one infused only solutions isotonic or slightly hypertonic to plasma into veins, the water load became very excessive resulting either in edema or an abnormal urinary output defeating the nutritional intent. On the other hand, if hypertonic solutions were used for long, veins became sclerotic and continuing treatment became impossible. With the availability of less irritating catheters and of low volume delivery and peristaltic pumps, Dudrick and his associates innovated the techniques of infusing a hypertonic solution (5 percent amino acid hydrolysate and 15 to 25 percent glucose plus vitamins and electrolytes) directly into a high flow region of the venous system. While there are problems with maintaining sterility and avoiding catheter clots, the technique can be made to work successfully for periods of many months. Further technical improvement should be anticipated.

REFERENCES

BREAST FEEDING

Aitkin, F. C., and Hytten, F. E. Infant feeding: Comparison of breast feeding and artificial feeding. Nutr. Abstr. Rev., 30:341, 1960.

Bain, K. Incidence of breast feeding in hospitals in the United States. Pediatrics, 2:313, 1948.

Berner, J. The milk factor in the transmission of mammary carcinoma. New Eng. J. Med., 243:375, 1950.

Bittner, J. J. Some possible effects of nursing on mammary gland tumor incidence in mice. Science, 84:162, 1936.

Boorman, K. E., Dodd, B. E., and Gunther, M. A consideration of colostrum and milk as sources of antibodies which may be transferred to the newborn baby. Arch. Dis. Child., 33:24, 1958.

Davies, V. Human milk studies. XXI. A simple technic for the manual expression of mother's milk. Amer. J. Dis. Child., 70:148, 1945.

Douglas, R. G., Kramer, E. E., and Bonsnes, R. W. Oxytocin, newer knowledge and present clinical usage. Amer. J. Obstet. Gynec., 73:1206, 1957.

Finkelstein, H. Säuglingskrankheiten 4th ed. Amsterdam, Elsevier, 1938.

Folley, S. J. The Physiology and Biochemistry of Lactation. London, Oliver and Boyd, 1956.

György, P. A hitherto unrecognized biochemical difference between human milk and cow's milk. Pediatrics, 11:98, 1953.

Holt, L. E., Courtney, A. M., and Fales, H. L. A chemical study of woman's milk, especially its inorganic constituents. Amer. J. Dis. Child., 10:229, 1915.

Hytten, F. E., and Thomson, A. M. Clinical and chemical studies on human lactation. Brit. Med. J., 2:232, 1955.

Insull, W., Jr., Hirsch, J., James, T., and Ahrens, E. H., Jr. The fatty acids of human milk. II. Alterations produced by manipulation of caloric balance and exchange of dietary fats. J. Clin. Invest., 38:443, 1959.

Kon, S. K., and Cowie, A. T. Milk: The Mammary Gland and Its Secretion. New York, Academic Press, 1961.

Lawrence, J. M., Herrington, B. L., and Maynard, L. A. Human milk studies. XXVII. Comparative values of bovine and human milks in infant feeding. Amer. J. Dis. Child., 70:193, 1945.

Macy, I. G. Composition of human colostrum and milk. Amer. J. Dis. Child., 78:589, 1949.

—— et al. Human milk studies. Amer. J. Dis. Child., 70:135, 142, 148, 150, 162, 171, 176, 182, 193, 1945.

Marrack, J. R. Antibodies in milk. Brit. Med. Bull., 5:187, 1947.

Mellander, O., et al. Breast feeding and artificial feeding; a clinical, serological, and biochemical study in 402 infants, with a survey of the literature. The Norrbotten study. Acta Paediat. Scand., 48:Suppl. 116, 1959.

Meyer, H. F. Infant feeding practices in hospital maternity nurseries; a survey of 1,904 hospitals involving 2,225,000 newborn infants. Pediatrics, 21:288, 1958.

Naish, F. C. Breast Feeding: A Guide to the Natural Feeding of Infants. New York, Oxford University Press, 1948.

Nickerson, K., Bonsnes, R. W., Douglas, R. G., Condlisse, P., and du Vigneaud, V. Oxytocin and milk ejection. Amer. J. Obstet. Gynec., 67:1028, 1954.

Nordbring, F. The failure of newborn premature infants to absorb antibodies from heterologous colostrum. Acta Paediat. Scand., 46:569, 1957.

—— The appearance of antistreptolysin and antistaphylolysin in human colostrum. Acta Paediat. Scand., 46:481, 1957.

Smith, C. H., and Merritt, K. K. The rate of secretion of breast milk. Amer. J. Dis. Child., 24:413, 1922.

Vahlquist, B. The Transfer of Antibodies from Mother to Offspring. In Advances in Pediatrics. Chicago, Year Book Publishers, 1958.

Waller, H. Some clinical aspects of lactation. Arch. Dis. Child., 22:193, 1947.

COW'S MILK

Kon, S. K., and Cowie, A. T. Milk: The Mammary Gland and Its Secretion. New York and London, Academic Press, 1961.

Macy, I. G., Kelly, H. J., and Sloan, R. E. The Composition of Milks. National Research Council Publication 254, Washington, D.C., National Academy of Sciences, 1953.

Webb, B. H. Fundamentals of Dairy Chemistry. Westport, Conn., Avi Publ. Co., 1965.

INFANT FEEDING

Aldrich, C. A., and Aldrich, M. M. Feeding Our Old-Fashioned Children. New York, The Macmillan Co., 1941.

Beal, V. A. On the acceptance of solid foods, and other food patterns of infants and children. Pediatrics, 20:448, 1957.

Davis, C. M. Self-selection of diet by newly weaned infants. An experimental study. Amer. J. Dis. Child., 36:651, 1928.

Fischer, C. C., and Whitman, M. A. Simplified method of infant feeding: Bacteriological and clinical study. J. Pediat., 55:116, 1959.

Gibson, J. P. Reaction of 150 infants to cold formulas. J. Pediat., 52:404, 1958.

Holt, L. E., Jr., Davis, E. A., Hasselmeyer, E. G., and Adams, A. A study of premature infants fed cold formulas. J. Pediat., 61:556, 1962.

—— and Snyderman, S. E. The feeding of premature and newborn infants. Ped. Clin. N. Amer., 13:1103, 1966.

Lanman, J. T. Modern Trends in Infant Nutrition and Feeding. New York, Sugar Research Foundation, 1952.

Lippard, V. W., Schloss, O. M., and Johnson, P. A. Immune reactions induced in infants by intestinal absorption of incompletely digested cow's milk protein. Amer. J. Dis. Child., 51:562, 1936.

Marriott, W. M., and Jeans, P. C. Infant Nutrition, 3rd ed. St. Louis, C. V. Mosby Co., 1941.

Mellander, O., et al. Breast feeding and artificial feeding; a clinical, serological, and biochemical study in 402 infants, with a survey of the literature. The Norrbotten study. Acta Paediat. Scand., 48:Suppl. 116, 1959.

Meyer, H. F. Infant Foods and Feeding Practice. Springfield, Ill., Charles C Thomas Co., 1960.

Tomarelli, R. M., Minnick, N., D'Amato, E., and Bernhart, F. W. Bioassay of the nutritional quality of the protein of human and cow's milk by rat growth procedures. J. Nutr., 68:265, 1959.

Vaughan, V. C., III, Dienst, R. B., Sheffield, C. R., and Roberts, R. W. A study of techniques of formulas for infant feeding. J. Pediat., 61:547, 1962.

PARENTERAL NUTRITION

Dudrick, S. J., Wilmore, D. W., Vars, H. M., and Rhoads, J. E. Can intravenous feeding as the sole means of nutrition support growth in the child and restore weight loss in an adult? An affirmative answer. Ann. Surg., 169:974, 1969.

Disorders of Nutritional Homeostasis

3.4
DEFICIENCIES OF SPECIFIC NUTRIENTS

GEORGE G. GRAHAM

Deficiencies of Calories and Protein

Significant variations in nutrition during early extrauterine existence result in profound changes which are not easily reversed. Excessive calorie intake results in a body composition which is different from the normal in both cell size and cell number. In addition, there are major changes in the hormonal mechanisms which control the utilization of nutrients, particularly insulin and growth hormone production. Prolonged undernutrition, conversely, cannot be presumed to result simply in delayed maturation and growth, correctible by an "optimal" diet. We must be concerned not only with the heavy death toll from malnutrition, but also with possible changes in body composition, performance, and resistance to stress of the survivors. Duration and severity of protein and calorie deficits determine major alterations in the rate and nature of growth in the human infant and child.

Prolonged failure to meet basal energy requirements eventually results in cessation of linear growth. At or about the same time, cellular multiplication in muscle, fat, and presumably most viscera ceases. Evidence for a similar arrest in the central nervous system is quite suggestive. Depending on the supply of amino acids and the severity of the calorie deficit, accompanying or preceding losses of intracellular protein occur. The clinical picture varies from hypocaloric dwarfism to extreme marasmus.

When calorie intake is excessive, adequate, or nearly adequate, but the supply of essential amino acids and total nitrogen is disproportionately low, or infection produces intestinal losses or failure of utilization of amino acids, the clinical picture of kwashiorkor may occur alone or superimposed on that of marasmus. Presumably the calorie intake has continued to favor cell multiplication, while protein deficiency results in decreased cell size in muscle and viscera, and fat accumulation in hepatic cells.

Hypocaloric dwarfism and marasmus probably represent states of appropriate adaptation to conserve life and vital functions, particularly those of the central nervous system and liver, at the expense of growth and function in other tissues. Kwashiorkor probably represents failure of adaptation or decompensation of a previously appropriate adaptation.

Although considerable overlap exists between them, and most cases have features of both calorie and protein deficiency, there are distinct differences between hypocaloric dwarfism, marasmus, and kwashiorkor with regard to age incidence, clinical characteristics, biochemical alterations, response to dietary therapy, and prognosis. Psychosocial dwarfism also deserves special consideration.

Hypocaloric Dwarfism

ETIOLOGY AND PATHOGENESIS. Hypocaloric dwarfism is common in medically developed countries as well as in the underdeveloped world. Characteristically it results from prolonged consumption of diets restricted in available energy but balanced in essential amino acids, nitrogen, vitamins, and minerals. In this country it results from numerous and varied causes, including errors in preparing infant formulas; insistence on breast feeding despite inadequate supplies of milk; irregular and infrequent feedings because of negligence or ignorance; intestinal malabsorption; chronic vomiting or regurgitation; anorexia as a result of disease, particularly congenital heart disease; chronic renal insufficiency and chronic infections; impaired utilization of nutrients; and from the increased caloric expenditure of infection or metabolic derangement. In the medically underdeveloped world there is a predominance of prolonged, inadequate, and unsupplemented breast feeding; excessive dilution of milk; repeated interruptions in normal feeding, usually as a result of frequent infections; and a misguided tendency to withhold food at the slightest provocation.

CLINICAL CHARACTERISTICS. The clinical appearance of hypocaloric "dwarfs," aside from their small size, is not particularly striking. As in most cases of malnutrition in early life, the approximately normal "dental age" may be the only clue to true age. Body composition and osseous maturation are appropriate for size, rather than age. Anemia is not prominent and serum proteins are usually normal, as is serum urea and the plasma amino acids, reflecting the appropriate protein/calorie ratio of the diet.

TREATMENT. Most hypocaloric dwarfs grow at an accelerated rate if there is no underlying pathology and they are given ordinary diets with calorie and protein intakes appropriate to their apparent age. Retentions of nitrogen and increases in protoplasm are commensurate with those of normal children of similar height and biologic age. Whether they recover their genetic potential depends on the adequacy and duration of rehabilitation, and on the possible loss of growth potential due to prolonged undernutrition.

Some, particularly those whose deprivation dates to the neonatal period and who have not grown until the second or third semester, do not respond well. When calorie intake is increased they may reject or vomit food; alternatively, they may just become fat. Linear growth is very slow, with little evidence of "catch-up," and their nitrogen retention is poor. In these patients it is seldom clear whether some unsuspected intrauterine difficulty or prolonged extrauterine severe caloric deprivation has compromised growth potential.

Marasmus

ETIOLOGY AND PATHOGENESIS. Infantile marasmus is characteristically a problem of slum areas, where urbanization of poor rural inhabitants has caused very early weaning from the breast, substitution by grossly inadequate feedings, a high incidence of infectious diarrhea, and repeated episodes of "therapeutic" starvation. The development of "hunger stools" and malabsorption, with additional infections, enteral or systemic, results in chronic diarrhea with acute exacerbations, prolonged "therapeutic" starvation, and gradual "decomposition." If breast feeding was successful for several months before weaning, significant linear growth may have occurred with a parallel advance in osseous maturation and growth of brain, lean body mass, supporting tissues, and fat cells.

As a result of subsequent starvation, linear growth stops with a parallel cessation of brain growth, osseous maturation, muscle and fat cell multiplication, and growth of supporting tissues and most visceral tissues. This effect is easily documented in the hair and the intestinal mucosa, which reveal no mitoses. Very early in starvation most fat cells are depleted and glycogen stores diminish in muscle and liver. In young infants two fat depots in the cheeks, the so-called sucking pads, are usually conserved. Muscle cells and most visceral cells lose soluble proteins, including many enzymes. Microscopically these tissues are characterized by atrophy,

cardiac muscle less so than skeletal and smooth muscles. Lymphoid tissues suffer early; the thymus, lymph follicles of the intestine, and the Malpighian bodies of the spleen shrink. The intestinal mucosa is flattened and the entire wall becomes paper-thin, making biopsy hazardous. The liver usually conserves its structural integrity, altering the direction and magnitude of its functions in order to conserve life. The supporting tissues of the body tend to conserve their structural proteins.

Severe losses of intracellular water are found, with maintenance or even relative expansion of the extracellular compartment. Wallace aptly described the marasmic infant as "shrinking around his extracellular water." Anemia is usually moderate and is in part an adaptation to decreased oxygen requirements. Serum albumin is normal or nearly so, and serum globulins are normal or elevated. No deficiency of the immunoglobulins has been documented. Serum urea is quite low except when elevated by dehydration. Plasma amino acids may reveal a normal pattern if starvation has been balanced, but may be altered as in kwashiorkor if the protein to calorie ratio of the diet was very low.

In the underdeveloped world, particularly in rural areas during famine conditions, it is not unusual to see a similar condition develop in preschool children, school children, and even adults. Many features are different in these older individuals because much growth has occurred prior to starvation, and because of differences in duration.

CLINICAL CHARACTERISTICS. The drawn features, wrinkled skin, and hollow temples of the marasmic infant give the appearance of a very old man. Absence of subcutaneous fat, atrophy of muscles, and potassium deficiency make the skin hang in loose folds (Fig. 6). Bones and joints are prominent, as are the superficial veins. The abdomen is usually scaphoid but may be distended if diarrhea and potassium deficiency are prominent. Body temperature and blood pressure are usually subnormal, while the pulse rate is quite variable, depending on the presence of associated conditions. Physical activity is almost nil, with a phlegmatic disposition. Broncho-

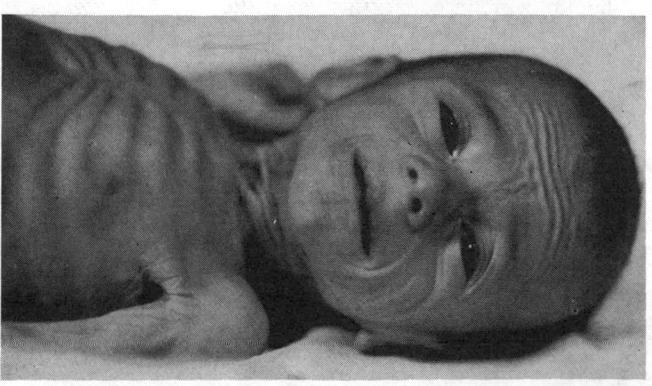

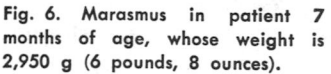

Fig. 6. Marasmus in patient 7 months of age, whose weight is 2,950 g (6 pounds, 8 ounces).

pneumonia and pyelonephritis are frequently present.
TREATMENT. In infantile marasmus the response to rehabilitation occurs slowly. If calorie intake is increased rapidly, even with an adequate proportion of protein, severe hypoalbuminemia and sodium retention with edema frequently develop. Nitrogen retention is poor, and many infants remain in negative balance for many days.

If calorie intake is increased cautiously over one or two weeks, there may be initial weight loss and a moderate fall in serum albumin, along with poor nitrogen retentions, but the hazards of sodium retention are less. In a few weeks, nitrogen retentions improve, serum albumin stabilizes, and rapid weight gain begins, soon followed by accelerated linear growth. Studies done in the course of rehabilitation, however, indicate a persistently decreased muscle cell size and relatively poor increases in intracellular water in young infants. A persistently blunted insulin response to a standard arginine infusion has also been documented.

Reports indicating prompt and avid nitrogen retention, and resumption of growth at an accelerated rate, usually deal with children in the second or even third or fourth year of life. In these patients, deficits in body length are considerably less severe than those in weight, indicating that their malnutrition was of recent onset. In most of them satisfactory nitrogen retentions are commonly observed along with prompt resumption of growth. Younger infants increase their muscle cell population very little during the first four months of rehabilitation, whereas older infants increase it at a relatively rapid rate. Increments in body fat and supporting tissues occur rapidly in both groups when calories are provided in generous amounts. The presence of systemic infection hinders recovery, making difficult the achievement of positive nitrogen balance.

Although intakes of nearly 200 kcal/kg/day are often necessary to establish satisfactory weight gain in young marasmic infants, these levels should be reached gradually and should be maintained for a relatively short time. There is no prognostic virtue in allowing excessive weight gain, particularly after appropriate weight for height is reached. At this point rehabilitation is far from complete, muscle mass is still reduced and body fat is now excessive. Calorie intake should be reduced at this point to levels adequate for maintenance of proportional growth; this often occurs voluntarily. At no time should less than 8 percent of calories be provided as high quality protein. An adequate diet for many months or years is necessary for maximal recovery. When very high calorie intakes are necessary, it is preferable to add pure fat and carbohydrate and the appropriate amount of protein to a standard infant formula than to give feedings with high solute loads. The marasmic infant has a generally reduced glomerular filtration rate and possibly an impaired concentrating and acidifying capacity.

During the initial stages, even when weight is not gained but is actually lost, correction of the altered body composition is going on and growth-regulating mechanisms are being normalized away from the adaptations made previously for survival. Early weight gain, if anything, should make the physician suspect water and sodium retention. The most cachectic-looking infant, often mistakenly felt to be dehydrated, may have 80 percent of his body weight as water, a value found in small premature infants.

If manifestations of lactose intolerance develop, a milk substitute of the highest possible quality should be used. In any special formula constructed from individual ingredients, particular attention should be paid to the content of the intracellular cations potassium and magnesium. As protein is synthesized and cellular composition returns toward normal these are tied down in cells, and signs of clinical deficiency may suddenly become apparent. During rehabilitation, deficiencies of other specific nutrients may develop. Clinical vitamin A or folic acid deficiency which is minimal or absent on admission may become quite severe in a few days if an adequate supply is not provided. Iron deficiency will become apparent in a few weeks if an adequate intake is not given. Copper deficiency has also developed during rehabilitation on exclusive milk diets and has occasionally been present at the outset of therapy making absorption of iron from the gut impossible.

Particular attention must be given to prompt diagnosis and treatment of infection. Many older marasmic infants will be found to have tuberculosis, pyelonephritis, or other chronic infections, which are often the cause, rather than the result, of malnutrition. Septicemia due to gram-negative bacteria may develop suddenly in an infant who is seemingly responding well to treatment. "Prophylactic" use of antibiotics seems if anything to increase the incidence. These agents should be used judiciously and only for specific reasons.

The mortality of untreated infantile marasmus is probably 100 percent. Depending on the promptness of diagnosis, the presence of complicating infections, and the degree of sophistication of the treatment facilities, this figure can probably be reduced to below 10 percent. If rehabilitation is not prolonged and if appropriate educational and other changes are not made in the household, the chances of a recurrence or of an early death at home are very high, particularly for those discharged below one year of age.

Kwashiorkor

ETIOLOGY AND PATHOGENESIS. In many areas of the world there is a significant incidence of kwashiorkor as originally described in the child weaned after one year of age in Africa. These children, usually breast-fed successfully for 6 to 18 months, are weaned to diets relatively generous in calories but deficient in nitrogen and in one or more essential amino acids. If previous growth was satisfactory, if calorie intake is maintained, and if protein deficiency is severe and acute, the manifestations of kwashiorkor may develop rapidly in a child with normal or nearly normal stature and considerable subcutaneous fat still present. These patients are the so-called "sugar babies" described in the literature. They have experienced severe losses of proteins in liver, muscle, and other organs, quite notably in the pancreas. Studies of the intestinal mucosa and hair indicate that cells continue to divide despite the severe shortage of protein.

More commonly kwashiorkor develops over a longer period of time, with prolonged consumption of a diet relatively adequate in total calories, but marginal or inadequate in total nitrogen and essential amino acids. Linear growth has slowed down and there has been loss of body fat and a severe loss of muscle and liver protein, with reduced amounts of total and circulating albumin. Further deterioration of the protein content and quality of the diet is usually precipitated by or associated with one or more episodes of infectious diarrhea or systemic infection. This results in the accumulation of liver fat and the insidious, sometimes precipitous, development of sodium and water retention. Serum albumin concentration may drop further, often to below 1 g/100 ml, because of failure of synthesis. Skin and hair changes are usually prominent. Depending on the duration and the previous nutritional state, loss of fat and muscle wasting is often severe enough to justify the term "marasmic kwashiorkor." Sudden access to a more generous calorie intake, or more commonly a severe infection in a marasmic infant may precipitate hepatic steatosis, hypoalbuminemia, and edema.

In fatal cases of kwashiorkor the prominent anatomic features include varying degrees of edema, but rarely with ascites; atrophy of skeletal, smooth, and cardiac muscle, particularly the first; atrophic changes in organs with high protein turnovers such as intestinal epithelium and pancreatic acini, in which fibrotic changes have been reported; and hepatic steatosis. This latter may vary from moderate to extremely severe. Added to these features may be the characteristic skin lesions and those of complicating infections, notably bronchopneumonia, pyelonephritis, and septicemia. Total body analyses reveal marked deficits of soluble protein and of potassium, the latter including the brain.

• Estimates of body composition reveal a marked increase in total body water as a percentage of body weight and of extracellular fluid as a fraction of total body water. Despite this, in cases with complicating acute diarrhea there may be a severe contraction of plasma volume. Intracellular fluid is reduced in absolute and relative terms. Biopsy of the liver reveals increased fat and glycogen and a decreased labile protein content, particularly at the expense

of enzymes. In muscle there is a marked decrease in cell size at the expense of water and protein, as well as potassium, magnesium, phosphorus, and zinc. There is an increase in intracellular sodium. There may at times be an increase in muscle fat content. Protein/DNA and RNA/DNA ratios are appreciably reduced. Alterations in intracellular enzymes have been described. Marked reductions in pancreatic exocrine secretions and intestinal disaccharidases have been documented.

CLINICAL CHARACTERISTICS. Physical activity is reduced; muscular weakness, apathy, and irritability are prominent. Many of these children elect to remain in the sitting position, even while sleeping. Edema may be gross and generalized (Fig. 7) or it may be inapparent, or slight and localized to the eyelids and feet. Skin changes, when present, are very similar to those of pellagra although generally more extensive. These consist of erythema followed by hyperpigmentation, desquamation, depigmentation, and at times ulceration. Some children spend their entire waking periods picking off the desquamating skin, increasing the possibility of infection. The hair is sparse and fine and breaks or pulls out easily. It may be totally absent over the temples and depigmented to a grayish or reddish tint. When adequate dietary protein is provided, newly formed

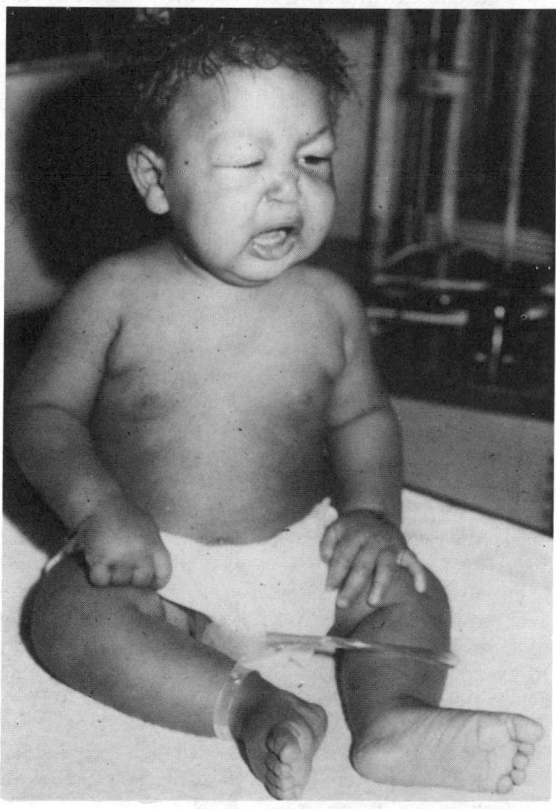

Fig. 7. Marked edema in patient with kwashiorkor. (From Taitz and Finberg. *Amer. J. Dis. Child.*, 112:76, 1966.)

hair is again pigmented and the discolored portion moves outward. Alternating periods of dietary adequacy and deficiency may result in the so-called flag sign, particularly in long-haired children.

The chronic "diarrhea" of malnutrition, with frequent, small, greenish stools, may be complicated by acute infectious diarrhea or disaccharide intolerance, particularly for lactose. In those children genetically predisposed to loss of their major lactase activity in childhood, an episode of severe malnutrition may precipitate permanent loss well ahead of schedule. Anorexia may be severe enough to require initial tube feeding, or parenteral feeding when this is not tolerated. As in marasmus, vitamin and mineral deficiencies may not be apparent on admission but may develop rapidly during rehabilitation.

Hypoalbuminemia without significant proteinuria immediately distinguishes these children from the occasional case of the nephrotic syndrome which might resemble kwashiorkor. Serum albumin concentration is typically between 1.5 to 2.5 g/100 ml but, in some instances, may be decreased to below 1 g or raised above 3 g due to changes in plasma volume. Isotope studies indicate that plasma albumin levels underestimate the deficit, since albumin which is normally extravascular and accounts for approximately 50 percent is more severely depleted. Despite this, serum albumin levels remain the most reliable clinical indicator of protein deficiency. After 10 to 15 days on a diet in which protein represents less than 6 percent of total calories, most infants and children, if they continue to gain weight, will suffer a drop of 0.5 to 1.0 g/100 ml in serum albumin level. In kwashiorkor the β-globulins and ceruloplasmin may also be reduced. Immunoglobulins are rarely reduced; if altered they are usually elevated.

Nearly all children with kwashiorkor, at least until they have received an adequate diet for 2 or 3 days, have characteristic elevations of most nonessential amino acids in plasma, particularly glycine, alanine, and serine. Most of the essential amino acids are severely depressed, particularly tyrosine, tryptophan, and the branched-chain amino acids. These changes are not specific for body protein deficiency, as indicated by their appearance in normal infants receiving a low-protein diet for one or two days. It would seem instead that they are indicative of dietary protein inadequacy. Since this is the hallmark of kwashiorkor, the plasma amino acid alterations are those expected. Very low serum and urine urea levels are typical, as are reduced levels of serum amylase, lipase, esterase, alkaline phosphatase, and cholinesterase. Serum cholesterol and triglycerides are lowered, whereas free fatty acids are generally elevated. A markedly decreased creatinine excretion reflects the reduced muscle mass. Disturbances of carbohydrate metabolism can lead to severe hypoglycemia. Elevation of serum bilirubin, if present, is due to sepsis or hepatic failure.

Much attention has been given to the anemia of protein malnutrition. When intestinal parasites are present, particularly hookworm, chronic blood loss may lead to severe anemia, which otherwise tends to be moderate with normochromia, macrocytosis, or a dimorphic picture. Protein deficiency is one of the causes; folic acid, iron, and copper deficiencies may also play a role. Serum vitamin B_{12} is usually elevated. Hypoprothrombinemia secondary to liver involvement and thrombocytopenia due to severe infection may lead to a hemorrhagic tendency.

Severe malnutrition probably does not lead to an increased incidence of infection but does alter the ability of the organism to cope with it; hence the greater severity and duration of diseases such as upper respiratory infections, diarrheal infections, tuberculosis, and the common childhood diseases, particularly measles. A generalized, fatal form of herpes simplex infection has been reported frequently. On the other hand, most infections aggravate the malnutrition, leading to a vicious cycle which accounts for the enormously excessive infant and preschool mortality rates in medically underdeveloped areas.

TREATMENT. Initial attention must be given to the restoration of circulation and glomerular filtration, if these are compromised by dehydration. For this purpose sodium-containing solutions must be given by vein, even though there may be a large surplus of sodium and water in the body. Potassium must be added much sooner than in the ordinary case of dehydration, as hypokalemia may be severe and may be aggravated fatally during hydration. Supplementary potassium must be continued for approximately 10 days. Oral, tube, or parenteral feeding of protein or amino acids must be begun on an urgent basis. However there is no need for large amounts of protein, which can and often do lead to hyperaminoacidemia, aminoaciduria, hypokalemia, hypomagnesemia, hypoglycemia, and to severe dehydration after diuresis.

In the usual case, if infection is not an important problem, the provision of a modest supply of high-quality protein, with or without an adequate calorie intake, is entirely adequate. If 2 g of protein and 75 kcal/kg/day are reached after 3 or 4 days and maintained for approximately 20 days, edema will disappear gradually, serum albumin will reach nearly normal levels, and much of the accumulated fat will be cleared from the liver. Retention of as much as 65 to 70 percent of the nitrogen ingested will begin promptly. In marasmic infants it is unusual to find 20 percent retention of such an intake within the first two weeks, even when 150 kcal/kg/day are consumed.

After delivery of edema, or even simultaneously with the diuresis, true weight gain will begin when an adequate calorie intake is provided. The energy requirement is determined by how much of a marasmic component existed originally. If significant subcutaneous fat is still present, it is not more than that usually appropriate for the age. Excessive calorie intakes lead to undesirable obesity and to persistence or reappearance of the hepatic steatosis.

Intakes of most vitamins and minerals do not

need to be higher than the ones appropriate to the protein and calorie intakes. Supplementary potassium has been mentioned, therapeutic doses of iron are usually indicated. Routine therapeutic doses of folic acid have been recommended, as have larger doses of vitamin A in certain areas.

Skin infections and bronchopneumonia are so frequently present that penicillin is probably indicated almost routinely. Other antibiotics should be used only for specific reasons and with caution, as they may well disturb the precarious balance of intestinal flora and favor the development of gram-negative sepsis, particularly with *Pseudomonas, Proteus,* and pathogenic *E. coli.* Heavy infestation with *Giardia lamblia* may interfere with intestinal absorption and call for early treatment. Most other parasites can be treated somewhat later unless they specifically interfere with recovery.

Many thousands of children recover spontaneously from episodes of mild to moderately severe kwashiorkor when their diet or family situation improves, and may have repeated seasonal recurrences. Of those sick enough to reach medical and hospital attention, anywhere from 10 to 40 percent will succumb, depending on the skill with which they are handled. Most deaths are due to acute electrolyte disturbances or to irreversible biochemical changes in the first 24 hours and to sepsis during the next 10 days. Enthusiastic overtreatment is a great danger throughout.

For every case of marasmus or kwashiorkor there are generally close to 100 patients with more moderate forms of malnutrition and probably 1,000 children growing at rates below their genetic potential. Any attack on the larger problem calls for sanitary measures, including mass immunization, provision of medical services, improved housing and education, child spacing, and the general availability of inexpensive and acceptable sources of good quality protein. Most basic to all of these, however, is economic development.

Psychosocial Dwarfism

During the past few years in the United States recognition of a condition now usually identified as "psychosocial dwarfism" has increased.

ETIOLOGY AND PATHOGENESIS. Mothering of children with psychosocial dwarfism has usually been grossly inadequate. They present with severe stunting of linear growth, correspondingly retarded bone ages, variation in weight from severe wasting to mild obesity, bizarre eating habits, and prodigious appetites when food is available. Their mothers claim that the prodigious eating is a daily and regular occurrence. A significant difference of opinion exists as to etiology: some believe that these children represent examples of prolonged intermittent starvation and others that there is interference with food utilization or with production of growth hormone. Regardless of etiology, many characteristics of these children distinguish them from those with other forms of malnutrition.

TREATMENT. If an adequate diet is provided regularly at home or in the hospital, the excessive eating soon slows to a normal rate and prompt acceleration of growth occurs.

General Considerations

The foregoing discussion may create the impression that children with malnutrition present very distinct clinical pictures. This is not intended. Just as older children may become marasmic, numerous infants in the first six months of life have been reported with kwashiorkor. Many children present without visible edema and yet have fatty livers, hypoalbuminemia, and skin changes. Just what precipitates sodium and water retention is not clear: Hansen has shown that potassium without protein can promote sodium diuresis in many cases of typical kwashiorkor. Loss of potassium or sudden contraction of plasma volume as the result of diarrhea may be the triggering event for the development of edema in a severely protein-deficient infant or child. A newborn who cannot be fed orally and is maintained on generous intravenous glucose feedings without protein for more than a few days will develop severe hypoalbuminemia and edema and may develop a fatty liver.

Although severe marasmus is more common before one year and kwashiorkor after it, this is probably not an age-related difference in response to similar diets. The young infant is more likely to be placed on a near-starvation regime, while the toddler is more likely to have access to common items rich in calories and poor in protein. He is also more likely to contract measles and infectious diarrhea, the two most common precipitating causes of kwashiorkor.

ADAPTATION. Given identical high-calorie, low-protein diets, infants and children may handle them quite differently. The typical bulkiness and unpalatability of many such diets, as well as their low-protein or specific amino acid content, may decrease appetite and lead gradually to the picture of marasmus. An infection may then precipitate kwashiorkor. Conversely, if generous amounts continue to be consumed for many weeks, the picture of the "sugar baby" may develop. When sweetened, condensed milk was commonly used for infant feeding, such a development was not unusual in prosperous families. Some, possibly most children consuming low-protein diets may be able to increase the heat production after meals, the so-called "specific dynamic action," maintain a high intake, and end up with a relatively well-balanced protein-to-calorie ratio. This must be a precarious situation and probably leads to slower growth rates and a persistent susceptibility to the development of a more severe deficiency state.

Reference has been made to the delicately balanced adaptation to grossly inadequate calorie and protein intakes. Although some of the changes in the pattern of enzymatic activity which help to conserve vital proteins at the expense of expendable tissues have been relatively well documented, the hormonal and neural mechanisms which bring them about remain relatively obscure. Fragmentary evidence, much of it in question, suggests increased adrenal steroid levels, if not production. The evidence for decreased thyroid hormone production is also weak. Although decreased growth hormone production has been postulated, most modern evidence suggests persistently elevated circulating levels, the more logical adaptation to calorie deprivation. Limited observations on insulin levels and their response to stimuli all tend to agree on a much blunted response, again appropriate. Under this combined influence, free fatty acids and glucose in blood should be elevated and this has been reported. However, it is more common, due to the exhaustion of substrate, for both to be low and for hypoglycemia to be easily precipitated. Growth hormone responses tend to normalize promptly. This is not true of the insulin responses, which may have prognostic significance. There is indirect evidence for a normal ability to secrete antidiuretic hormone.

In kwashiorkor the evidence for increased effective levels of cortisol and aldosterone in blood is incomplete. Elevated growth hormone and decreased insulin production, the latter possibly not as severe as in marasmus, have also been documented. Elevated plasma free fatty acids are the rule; hyperglycemia is not uncommon. The mixed nature of most cases of severe malnutrition makes interpretation more difficult, as does the almost inevitable presence of complicating infections and dietary manipulations occurring prior to the period of observation.

An understanding of the adaptive responses to severe malnutrition is of more than academic interest; it should be of value in planning programs for rehabilitation and in the interpretation of the responses to these. The fact that linear growth continues for some time, despite severe weight loss, suggests that adaptation is not immediate.

Of special importance, probably more than the type of malnutrition, is the age at which it began and its duration. The nature of growth in the first months of life and its control is undoubtedly different from that of the second semester and subsequently. An infant whose growth has been severely restrained from birth will respond initially much like a newborn, while another infant who has grown relatively well for many months and then suffers a setback is more likely to start where he left off and recover rapidly. The first one requires a much longer period of intensive rehabilitation.

LONG-TERM EFFECTS. In recent years much research effort in the field of nutrition has been devoted to the study of possible long-term effects of malnutrition in early life, intra- and extrauterine, on eventual body size, composition, and performance, particularly mental.

Most children who survive severe malnutrition in infancy are stunted in stature and perform poorly in mental tests, when compared to common reference standards. When they are compared to their siblings, however, no difference has been found, suggesting that the deficits of both are due to prolonged undernutrition and environmental deprivation and not to any finite period of more severe malnutrition. Healthy premature infants growing up in favorable environments match their full-term siblings in growth and mental performance; in poorer environments they do less well than full-term siblings. "Small-for-dates" infants have not been studied as thoroughly but some make complete recoveries while others do not, particularly those who carry stigmata of intrauterine infection.

Animal studies, particularly those in rodents, have produced more convincing evidence of permanent losses of growth potential and behavioral abnormalities following intrauterine or preweaning food restriction. Studies in pigs and dogs are less impressive, while there have been only very limited studies in nonhuman primates.

As physicians responsible for the well-being of children, we should naturally be concerned with the prevention and treatment of all forms of malnutrition, but we should not allow this concern to make us lose sight of the fact that physical and mental development are influenced by the total environment and that food is only one part of it. Long-lasting influences, such as chronic calorie restriction and frequent infections, almost certainly curtail eventual stature and muscle mass. In many poor environments this is most likely a convenient adaptation, favoring survival and longevity. A stable home, with healthy stimulation and learning experiences, is undoubtedly more important to mental capacity and behavior than a surfeit of food.

Vitamin Deficiency Diseases

Much of our knowledge of this group of diseases has been gained by animal experiments, and some of the well-established human deficiencies, such as those of vitamin A, vitamin K, and vitamin B$_6$, were first recognized in animals. The results of animal experiments must, however, be interpreted with great caution, for there are marked species differences in nutritive requirements. The rat, for example, has no difficulty in synthesizing vitamin C. Furthermore, a deficiency of the same factor may give totally different symptoms in different animal species. A lack of vitamin E in the rat affects primarily the reproductive system; in the rabbit it produces muscular dystrophy; in the chick, encephalomalacia; and in the monkey and perhaps in man also, a specific type of megaloblastic anemia. One cannot assume that the many deficiencies known in experimental animals will necessarily have counterparts in man. Human deficiencies also differ from those of experimental animals in that human diets, when defective at all, are likely to be lacking in several factors; the disease pictures are therefore more difficult to separate.

Deficiency of Vitamin A

DONALD S. MC LAREN

Vitamin A deficiency is virtually unknown in North America and western Europe today, although it is occasionally seen in infants fed skim milk and in malabsorption states. It is, however, a disease that is widespread throughout most of the developing regions of the world where it is an important cause of blindness. In India, Pakistan, and southeast Asia it has been estimated that more than 1 percent of all young children are affected. It is also common in the Middle East, North Africa, and Central America.

THE VITAMINS AND PROVITAMINS. Vitamin A (retinol) is a colorless, fat-soluble alcohol containing a β-ionone ring and a long aliphatic side chain. It is found in most animal fats, lard excepted, being most abundant in fish liver oils. Two chief forms are known: A_1, predominantly in the livers of salt water fish, and A_2 in livers of fresh water fish. Four carotenoid pigments of colored vegetables, notably β-carotene, serve as precursors of vitamin A in the diet, the conversion taking place in the intestinal mucosa. Deficiency occurs if both natural A and carotene are lacking. In general only about one-third of the β-carotene in foodstuffs is available for conversion, and the efficiency of conversion is about 50 percent. Thus 1 μg β-carotene may be taken to have the same activity as 0.167 μg retinol.

Preformed vitamin A or provitamin is esterified in the small intestine, absorbed by way of the thoracic duct, and transported to the liver, probably attached to β-lipoprotein. Vitamin A deficiency is often associated with protein deficiency. This is believed to result from impairment of transport and possibly storage. In the resting serum almost all of the vitamin is present in the alcohol form.

FUNCTION. The best known and very important function of the vitamin is its role in vision. In the rods of the retina vitamin A, in the form of 11-*cis*-retinol, is bound to a protein opsin, to form a photosensitive pigment, rhodopsin (visual purple). When vitamin A is deficient, there is impairment of dark adaptation and ultimately night blindness (nyctalopia). A different pigment containing vitamin A, combined with a different protein, is found in the cones, which function in bright light and in color vision; impairment of cone function is, however, less readily demonstrated in A-deficient states.

Apart from ocular function, vitamin A appears necessary for the maintenance of epithelial structures—the skin, the mucous membranes, the gastrointestinal tract. Evidence is accumulating that it exerts a regulatory influence on various membrane systems; in high doses it causes disruption of lysosomes with release of hydrolytic enzymes. Less well substantiated are suggestions that the vitamin plays a specific role in the biosynthesis of adrenal steroids and in synthesis of mucopolysaccharides.

PATHOLOGY. All vertebrate species tested have been shown to require vitamin A for normal rod function, maintenance of many epithelial structures, and growth of bones and teeth. The changes are most conspicuous during periods of active growth. A characteristic change is squamous metaplasia of epithelial tissues. In man this is most conspicuous in the conjunctiva and cornea, though other tissues may be affected. There is no good evidence that skeletal deformities or congenital malformations in man can be attributed to deficiency of vitamin A.

PATHOGENESIS. Because of the ability of the liver to store vitamin A, clinical deficiency results only after a long period of depletion. Liver stores have to be seriously depleted before serum levels begin to fall, and in turn the concentration in serum has to reach a low level before cell function and, later, structure are affected. Quite apart from the diet, important contributing factors to disease are disorders of the alimentary tract affecting absorption of the vitamin and, as has been mentioned, protein malnutrition, which affects its transport and possibly storage.

SYMPTOMS. Vitamin A deficiency can occur at any age. Congenital cases have been observed in China in infants whose mothers were deficient. Young children, between the ages of 6 months and 4 years, are, however, the group in which the disease is most commonly seen and the group which furnishes most fatalities. A defective diet for a period of weeks is ordinarily required before symptoms are detected. Night blindness is probably the earliest symptom of the disease. An ambulant child may be noted to stumble in the dark, but more often, unless a child is carefully examined, this is missed until more serious evidence of eye disease makes its appearance.

As the deficiency state advances, the bulbar conjunctiva becoms xerotic. It becomes dry, thickened, and wrinkled and loses its natural transparency and property of being wetted by tears. As part of the drying and thickening process, there may occur a heaping up of desquamated keratinized epithelium close to the limbus forming a silvery gray plaque with a foamy surface known as a Bitot's spot. This occurs most commonly on the temporal side.

Conjunctival xerosis is shortly followed by similar changes in the cornea, which loses its' luster, becoming dull and hazy. The precorneal film is poorly maintained; when the lids are held apart for about 15 seconds, an "oil on water" appearance is seen. The process is still reversible by therapy, but unless arrested the keratomalacia proceeds; there may be corneal vascularization and the stroma may undergo a process of rapid liquefaction known as "colliquative necrosis," followed by perforation and subsequent rapid destruction of the entire globe.

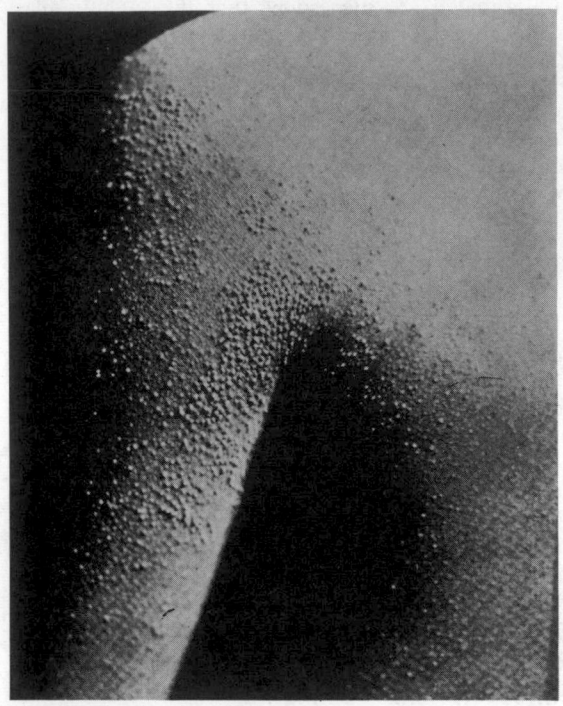

Fig. 8. Hyperkeratosis (phrynoderma) in vitamin A deficiency. (From Frazier and Hu.)

A follicular hyperkeratotic lesion of the skin known as phrynoderma is still a controversial topic. (See Fig. 8.) There is no doubt that vitamin A deficiency can cause a generalized hyperkeratosis, but such lesions are rare. Localized hyperkeratosis can also be caused by vitamin C deficiency, and in many instances it cannot be related to a dietary deficiency of any kind.

DIAGNOSIS. Special tests exist for measuring dark adaptation, even in infancy, including rod scotometry and electroretinography, but as a rule reliance must be placed on the clinical evaluation of ocular findings, on plasma vitamin A and carotenoid levels, and on responses to therapy. These, too, must be interpreted with caution. Night blindness is not necessarily due to vitamin A deficiency. Other causes—retinitis pigmentosa, glaucoma, high myopia—must be ruled out.

The characteristics of xerosis have been mentioned. Innocent lesions not unlike Bitot's spots are, however, encountered and offer difficulties even to the experienced observer. These tend to be smaller and smoother rather than foamy and to occur in older subjects. Their cause is unknown, and trauma may perhaps play a part in their formation.

Plasma levels of vitamin A below 25 international units per milliliter (1 IU = 0.33 μg retinol) may be regarded as significantly low, although the average is considerably higher. High carotenoids tend to produce falsely low figures for vitamin A. Sig-

nificant electroretinographic abnormalities are seen at plasma levels of 20 IU or below. Standards for hepatic stores, studied by liver puncture, are still being determined.

TREATMENT. Early diagnosis and prompt and adequate treatment may be sight-saving and, indeed, lifesaving. The most severe cases often succumb to complicating infections, perhaps because epithelial barriers are overwhelmed, perhaps because of damage to lysosomes and other membranes.

The symptoms of vitamin A deficiency respond with varying rapidity to treatment. Night blindness may show striking improvement within one hour of liberal oral dosage, but in other instances this may take two or three weeks. The lesions of xerophthalmia may show evidence of improvement in two or three days, but six to eight weeks may be required for complete healing. Even if corneal perforation has not occurred, opacities and scars may remain.

Deficiency states usually respond to 10,000 IU of vitamin A per kilogram given orally, usually as the palmitate, in a water-dispersible form. Oily preparations are less well absorbed by mouth and are slowly mobilized when given intramuscularly. Larger quantities may be indicated in the presence of a malabsorption syndrome. Intensive therapy should be continued for at least five days. Thereafter one may continue daily treatment with a reduced dose (25,000 IU per day), which may be provided by 30 ml of cod liver oil.

As pointed out, vitamin A deficiency rarely occurs alone, but is usually associated with protein calorie malnutrition and often with serious infections which of themselves demand urgent attention.

PROPHYLAXIS. Recommendations vary in different countries. Hume and Krebs demonstrated in experimental studies in adult volunteers that 1,300 IU per day permitted slow recovery from an induced deficiency. Current prophylactic recommendations are usually well above this. The U.S. Food and Nutrition Board recommends 1,500 IU per day for infants and 3,000 IU for adults. American children taking prophylactic vitamin D in the form of fish liver oils and concentrates which also contain A commonly receive in excess of 6,000 IU, and it is not surprising that the American problem in early life is not *hypo-* but *hyper*vitaminosis A. The problem in underdeveloped countries is quite different. The answer to the prophylaxis of vitamin A deficiency is the same as for all deficiency disease—economic growth and education. Hypervitaminosis A is discussed in detail elsewhere (Chap. 25).

Thiamine Deficiency (Beriberi)

L. EMMETT HOLT, JR.

Beriberi is a disease characterized by organic changes in the nervous system and heart and functional changes in other tissues. It is common in parts of the world where rice occupies a prominent place in the diet. In the United States it is rare, being confined almost exclusively to alcoholics and dietary faddists in adults and to children with chronic digestive disorders. Beriberi may occur at any age, even in nursing infants when the mother's diet is deficient.

THE VITAMIN. Thiamine, a pyrimidine-thiazole compound, is widely distributed in animal and vegetable foods. Although present in cereal grains it is frequently removed in milling, and it is only when milled cereals, particularly rice, predominate in the diet that deficiency is likely to be encountered.

Thiamine pyrophosphate constitutes the prosthetic group of three important decarboxylase enzymes. Together with lipoic acid and coenzyme A it is concerned with the decarboxylation of pyruvic acid to acetyl CoA, which then enters the citric acid cycle. A second reaction involving thiamine is the oxidative decarboxylation of α-ketoglutaric acid in the citric acid cycle. Thiamine is also a cofactor in the enzyme transketolase, an enzyme concerned in one step of the oxidative pathway of carbohydrate metabolism, the pentose phosphate shunt. In this reaction of oxidative decarboxylation, glucose-6-phosphate is split to form CO_2 and pentose-6-phosphate; the pentose so formed provides the ribose needed for the formation of nucleic acids and riboflavin. Further degradation of pentose by this same enzyme permits the formation of shorter carbon units. A thiamine-containing enzyme may also be concerned in the oxidation of alcohol.

Thiamine is present in most tissues, the highest concentrations being in liver and heart, next in brain and muscle. Nervous tissue, unlike others, is incapable of storing thiamine, a fact which may contribute to its vulnerability. In the tissues the thiamine is largely in enzyme form, combined with pyrophosphate, magnesium, and protein. Free thiamine is, however, found in the tissues and excreted in the urine.

PATHOLOGY. Early thiamine deficiency produces no characteristic anatomic changes. In frank beriberi the peripheral nerves and the central nervous system may show myelin degeneration. Degenerative changes have also been observed in beriberi hearts.

PATHOGENESIS. Thiamine deficiency may develop because of inadequate intake or abnormal loss. In severe and protracted diarrhea there is evidence that depletion of this vitamin may occur. Inadequate intakes are not likely to occur in children in this country. Such instances as we have observed have been in adolescent girls attempting to reduce weight.

Exceptionally, other conditions may lead to thiamine deficiency. An enzyme, thiaminase, is present in certain fish, including shellfish, and it is possible that a continuous diet of seafood might lead to thiamine deficiency, as has been observed in feeding foxes. A further complication that may lead to thiamine deficiency is the presence of an intestinal organism, *B. thiaminolyticus*, recently discovered in

Japan, which utilizes large quantities of thiamine, thereby increasing the dietary requirement. Up to the present, thiamine deficiency on this basis has not been observed in the United States.

SYMPTOMS. Because a *prodromal period* characterized by apathy, anorexia, and failure to gain weight is believed to precede frank manifestations, the thesis has been advanced that many American children with poor appetites are suffering from incipient thiamine deficiency. However, when Holt and Najjar induced thiamine deficiency in adolescent experimental subjects by a gradual reduction of their thiamine intake, appetite remained good until a day or two preceding the appearance of frank symptoms.

The *neuritis* of thiamine deficiency is in no way characteristic. It is both motor and sensory. In the experience of Holt and Najjar the motor and sensory disturbances appeared simultaneously, hyperesthesia and areflexia being the earliest neurologic manifestations. In experimental subjects studied in the United States the neuritis induced involved the extremities. However, reports from the Orient indicate that the cranial nerves are not infrequently involved; in infants the recurrent laryngeal has been said to be involved, with resulting hoarseness. This has also been observed in adults.

Wernicke's syndrome, ophthalmoplegia associated with cerebral disturbances, has been observed in adult alcoholics suffering from thiamine deficiency but is exceedingly rare in early life. Convulsions and coma are, however, described as not uncommon in infants and young children suffering from beriberi in the Orient.

Thiamine deficiency may cause *edema* unaccompanied by hypoproteinemia or cardiac or renal complications. The edema is often localized, involving an arm, a leg, or one side of the face. Its pathogenesis is not understood.

Cardiac involvement may begin with tachycardia and progress to cardiac enlargement and failure. It is not differentiated from other forms of cardiac disease by the electrocardiograph. Right heart failure, once thought characteristic, does not appear to be so.

The manifestations of thiamine deficiency vary greatly in individuals for reasons which are not clear. One subject will develop edema, another neuritis, and another cardiac involvement or psychologic disturbance, all maintained under comparable conditions of diet and exercise. The response to therapy in neuritis or myocardial involvement is slow, but anorexia, edema, and neurotic manifestations will usually disappear within 24 hours.

DIAGNOSIS. The history may be of help in recognizing thiamine deficiency, but caution is needed in interpreting dietary intakes. The diagnosis is often incorrectly made on the basis of intakes below the recommendations of the Food and Nutrition Board without appreciation of the fact that the recommendations include a generous margin of safety.

Laboratory diagnostic procedures are available but seldom employed. An elevated level of pyruvic acid is particularly valuable in subjects old enough to cooperate in venipunctures. Measurements of blood thiamine have been shown by Burch and her co-workers to reflect thiamine deficiency, but the procedure is technically difficult. Excretion tests in the urine, particularly the load test employed by Holt and Najjar in various stages of developing deficiency, will differentiate between clinical deficiency, a subnormal "reserve," and the normal well-fed individual. A deficiency of transketolase in the red cells has been employed by Brin as a diagnostic test. It appears to be a highly sensitive test which deserves further study. It should be pointed out that the chemical evidences of thiamine deficiency, including all the tests mentioned, may be corrected within 24 hours by an adequate thiamine intake, whereas the lesions of the heart and nervous system may persist. It is important to employ these diagnostic procedures before instituting therapy.

TREATMENT. A dose of 5 mg a day to an infant and twice this quantity to an adult will correct thiamine deficiency, although the results of damage may persist. There is no evidence that neuritis or carditis, behavior disorders, or loss of appetite other than that caused by thiamine deficiency is in any way benefited by the administration of this vitamin.

PROPHYLAXIS. The requirement of thiamine is commonly expressed in milligrams per 1,000 calories in the diet. The minimum requirement has been found to be from 0.14 mg to 0.20 mg per 1,000 calories, which for an infant may be regarded as the total daily requirement. Since thiamine is required primarily for purposes of carbohydrate metabolism and, indirectly, for such protein as is converted into carbohydrate, it follows and it has been definitely shown that fat exerts a sparing effect on the thiamine requirement. The requirement of breast-fed infants

is slightly less than of those on commonly employed cow's milk formulas. On high-carbohydrate formulas Holt and Snyderman observed an increase in the daily requirement from 0.20 to 0.28 mg per day. It is clear that the intakes of infants and the American dietary of older subjects furnish adequate amounts of thiamine at all ages; only in special circumstances is supplementation necessary, the chief indication being defective intestinal assimilation. It is our practice to add thiamine to parenteral infusions when the infusion is to be continued for some days.

Riboflavin Deficiency (Ariboflavinosis)

L. EMMETT HOLT, JR.

The incidence of this deficiency in the United States seems to be decidedly low, although some well-authenticated instances have been described at all ages, mostly in individuals living under marginal conditions in the South. In underdeveloped countries it appears to be not uncommon.

The characteristic clinical picture in man was first described by Sebrell and Butler and by Sydenstricker. The lesions affect the lips and tongue, the skin and the eyes. An angular stomatitis (*perlèche*) is characterized by redness, desquamation, and ulceration with fissures at the mucocutaneous junction. A glossitis, often with a magenta discoloration, is described, and there may be ulcerative changes with a necrotic exudate. Seborrheic lesions may appear on the face, usually in the nasolabial folds or between the lower lips and chin. The most prominent ocular lesion is a marginal vascularization of the cornea; later there may be cataract formation.

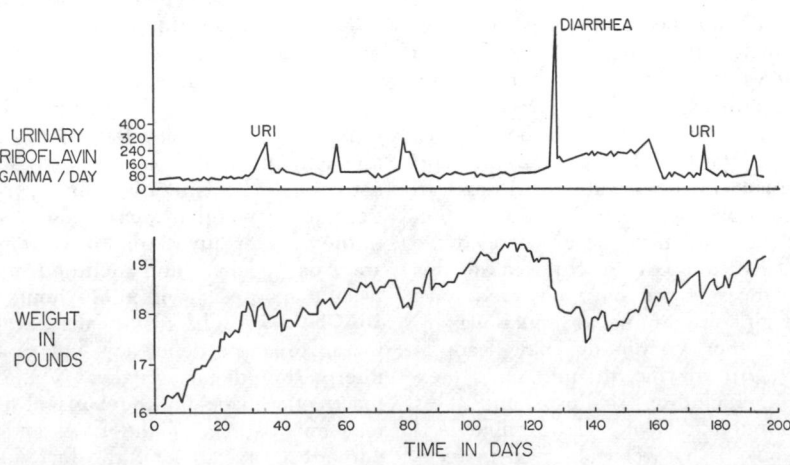

Fig. 9. The daily riboflavin excretion in the urine was followed in this infant who was maintained on a standard intake. When intercurrent infections occurred associated with loss of weight there was a marked increase in the urinary excretion of the vitamin. (From Holt. *Arch. Dis. Child.*, 31:427, 1956.)

The relation between these clinical symptoms and the function of riboflavin in the body is not clear. Riboflavin is the prosthetic group of a great many respiratory enzymes—the flavoproteins, which are present in all body cells.

The clinical diagnosis is rendered difficult by the fact that none of the symptoms observed in riboflavin deficiency is specific. Angular stomatitis may result from stretching of the lips from dental or medical procedures; it may also occur in B_6 deficiency and in other less clearly defined circumstances. Inflammatory lesions of the tongue may occur in other conditions; it is probable that secondary fungal infections play a part in some instances. The ocular lesions are inconstant and have been observed in other deficiency states, notably amino acid deficiencies. The clinical diagnosis must be made by the combination of these symptoms and by the response to riboflavin therapy. It may be confirmed by laboratory procedures, such as the retention of riboflavin following a standard load test or by a diminished concentration of the vitamin in the plasma or, preferably, in the red or white cells of the blood.

There is abundant riboflavin in the diet of the infant and older child as well as of the adult under conditions prevailing in the United States. Evidence showing a need for supplementing this diet has not been presented. In disease states accompanied by loss of weight a special need for additional riboflavin does not appear to exist; in fact, the contrary would appear to be the case, for the disintegration of tissue liberates riboflavin which must then be excreted (Fig. 9). The situation thus differs from that with certain other vitamins, notably vitamin C, for which there is evidence of an increased need during infections.

The daily requirement of the adult for riboflavin according to Horwitt and his co-workers is greater than 0.5 mg and less than 0.9 mg. Snyderman and her co-workers determined the requirement of infants which was found to be from 0.4 to 0.5 mg per day. Commonly employed milk formulas provide roughly three times this intake. In the case of breast milk the margin of safety is small but apparently adequate. The need for riboflavin does not seem to be significantly affected by the composition of the diet.

Niacin Deficiency (Pellagra)

GEORGE G. GRAHAM

A chronic, relapsing, generalized disorder, popularly characterized by three (or four) D's: dermatitis, diarrhea, dementia (and frequently death) has been known for over two centuries as pellagra, from the Italian *pelle* (skin) + *agra* (sour). Its association with poverty and excessive dietary dependence on maize led to conflicting theories as to etiology: that it was due to a toxic or infectious agent in spoiled corn or the remarkably accurate proposal, in 1856 by Lussana and Frua, that it was due to a diet of inadequate protein and sufficient energy. No other disorder requires such a thorough understanding of all aspects of nutrition.

For a period of 60 years following the Civil War, there were many thousands of cases of pellagra, with many deaths, in the southern United States. Although no longer a major public health problem, it is still seen occasionally in poor, maize-consuming people and is particularly frequent among chronic alcoholics; in persons with chronic obstructive or absorptive gastrointestinal disorders; with malignant carcinoid tumors; and in infants with Hartnup disease, an inborn error of tryptophan metabolism.

ETIOLOGY AND PATHOGENESIS. Goldberger's studies demonstrated conclusively that pellagra was due to an inadequate intake of high-quality protein and most probably to an inadequate intake of the essential amino acid tryptophan. When Elvehjem and his associates demonstrated that the vitamin nicotinic acid (niacin) could "cure" or prevent "black tongue," the experimental analogue of pellagra in dogs, as well as the natural disorder in man, another conflict, since resolved, seemed to exist.

Modern thinking attributes the multiple manifestations of this disorder to a deficiency of the essential coenzymes I and II, niacin adenine dinucleotide (NAD) and niacin adenine dinucleotide phosphate (NADP). These pyridine nucleotides are synthesized directly from dietary niacin or from tryptophan, with niacin or quinolinic acid as intermediates. A generous supply of energy and of the other essential amino acids can divert most of a limited supply of dietary tryptophan to protein synthesis, as well as create an increased requirement for the coenzymes. An excess of leucine in the diet, such as is present in corn, may interfere with tryptophan metabolism, as does a deficiency of pyridoxine.

The many vital functions of the hydrogen acceptors NAD and NADP make their deficiency result in a variety of manifestations and the danger of death. They are involved in the conversions of glucose-6-monophosphate to phosphogluconic acid, citric to α-ketoglutaric acid, lactic to pyruvic acid, alcohol to acetaldehyde, and at least 40 other oxidation-reduction reactions.

CLINICAL MANIFESTATIONS. The cutaneous lesions are usually the first to be noted, the characteristic symmetric dermatitis appearing on those parts of the body exposed to sunlight, heat, and other forms of mild trauma. Initially there is an erythema, resembling sunburn (or a diaper rash in infants) on the backs of the hands, wrists, forearms, and neck (Casal's necklace), as well as on the face of adults and children (Fig. 10). When no exposure to sunlight exists, the lesions may appear first on the elbows, knees, nape of the neck, eyelids, cheeks, perineum, and scrotum. The clearly demarcated, affected areas are initially red and infiltrated; they usually itch and burn, but may produce no discomfort. In the more acute cases these may progress to vesiculation, cracking, exudation, ulceration, and secondary infection.

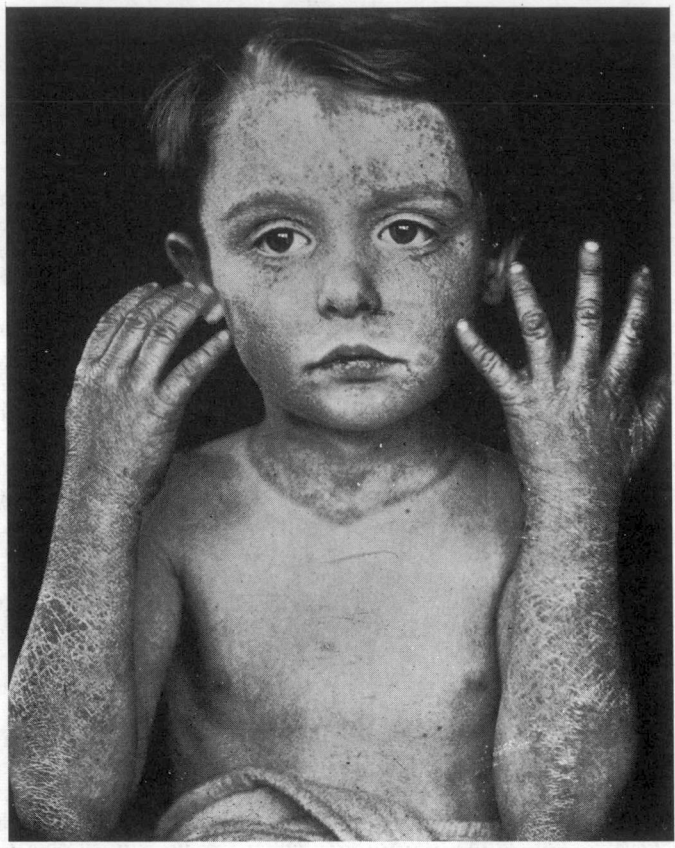

Fig. 10.   Pellagra in a boy 5 years old.

In the classical chronic case erythema progresses to roughening and keratosis with scaling. In almost all cases a brownish pigmentation develops and in the process of healing peels off, leaving healthy pink skin underneath. If still active, the entire cycle will be repeated, with healing in some areas and simultaneous progression in others.

The mouth is sore and may show angular stomatitis and cheilosis, possibly due to other associated deficiencies. The tongue has a "raw beef" appearance, red, swollen, and painful, though usually not depapillated; the rectum and anus are often inflamed as well, with extension to others parts of the digestive tract possibly accounting for the diarrhea and malabsorption which frequently accompany or follow the dermatitis, and result in weight loss.

Neurologic manifestations may appear without apparent involvement of the epithelial surface but usually follow it. These may be moderate with some weakness, malaise, anxiety, depression, and a short attention span; or severe with delirium. In the most chronic forms, amentia, posterolateral cord degeneration, pyramidal signs, and peripheral nerve lesions are also seen. Death may occur suddenly and unexpectedly. Only in the more severe examples of CNS involvement are permanent residuals likely to be present after proper treatment.

PATHOLOGY.   The skin reveals congestion of papillary blood vessels, edema of the papillae, lymphocytic infiltration of the corium, and most characteristically, notable thickening of the keratinized layer of the epidermis. Lesions of the mucous membranes and intestinal wall, particularly in the colon, resemble those of the skin. Demyelination of the posterolateral columns of the spinal cord and focal demyelination and ganglion cell degeneration of the cerebrum are seen in advanced cases.

LABORATORY FINDINGS.   In the urine of adults with pellagra the combined excretion of the two major metabolites of niacin, N_1-methyl nicotinamide and its 6-pyridone, is usually less than 2 mg in 24 hours. In milder deficiency states, slightly larger amounts are excreted but are still below the 5 to 8 mg of N_1-methyl nicotinamide and 7 to 10 mg of pyridone of normal subjects on a good diet. Although normal and deficient rates of excretion for infants and children have not been as accurately determined, they may be estimated from the relative caloric expenditures. Measurement of one or both metabolites in a 24- or 6-hour urine specimen is the most commonly used biochemical method for diagnosis of pellagra. The plasma tryptophan level is extremely low, even more so than in most cases of kwashiorkor.

DIAGNOSIS.   The characteristic skin lesions, with or without digestive and neurologic signs, should suggest the diagnosis, particularly when an abnormal dietary history is elicited or a disease is present which might cause an increased requirement of tryptophan or niacin.

Where kwashiorkor is frequent, it has been common to attribute its cutaneous manifestations to pellagra, which might well be true: they are more common and severe in maize-dependent areas. It is also true, however, that most of the other manifestations of kwashiorkor: depigmentation of the hair, edema, and hypoalbuminemia, are not part of the picture of pellagra. The oral lesions of pellagra, on the other hand, are not usually present in kwashiorkor, which is a more profound and general disturbance of protein metabolism and must be treated as such.

Lesions similar to those of pellagra have developed in infants and children consuming restricted semipurified diets and are believed to be due to complex, combined deficiencies of amino acids, vitamins, and trace minerals, particularly zinc. Their etiology is obscure and their possible relation to pellagra even more so. Nontropical sprue may produce skin lesions similar to those of mild pellagra.

When a history of a diet relatively rich in calories, very low in high-quality protein, particularly low in tryptophan, low in niacin, and relatively high in leucine is elicited, it forms a good basis for the diagnosis. Such a diet, based on maize in one of many forms combined with a generous intake of alcohol, molasses, or sugar, is not at all uncommon in many parts of the world, including the United States and parts of western Europe. Rice-based diets nearly meet these requirements, often being lower in tryptophan and niacin than corn-based diets, but much less often lead to pellagra. This is probably due to the fact that other essential amino acids, particularly leucine, are present in considerably lower concentration, and less tryptophan goes into protein synthesis, with more being available for conversion to pyridine nucleotides, without the presumed specific interference of leucine.

TREATMENT. In the acutely ill patient, 100 mg of nicotinamide (which lacks the unpleasant side-effects of nicotinic acid), given orally or parenterally three or four times daily will promptly relieve most of the manifestations, although much smaller doses of around 15 mg daily will often be just as effective. This is not the case, however, if a regular and adequate intake of tryptophan in the form of meat, milk, eggs, or another high-quality protein is not provided. If this is not established, high doses of niacin are needed and prompt relapse will occur when these are reduced to what should be an adequate prophylactic level. Experimental evidence suggests that only tryptophan, not niacin, will lead to storage of the pyridine nucleotides.

In milder cases, when oral ingestion and retention of food is possible, the simple curtailment of the excess calorie intake from alcohol or sugar, or the provision of a moderately generous supply of high-quality protein makes vitamin therapy unnecessary.

Attention must be paid to coexisting deficiencies of other vitamins, particularly thiamin, ascorbic acid, and vitamin A.

PREVENTION. Requirements are now commonly expressed in terms of mg niacin equivalents: the sum of the nicotinic acid ingested as such plus one-sixtieth the intake of tryptophan. This calculation is based on the observation that it takes 60 mg of dietary tryptophan to produce the same amount of niacin metabolites in the urine as 1 mg of niacin. While this was undoubtedly true under the conditions of the studies in question, variations in the diet and different physiologic states might result in different amounts of tryptophan being incorporated into protein or becoming available for pyridine nucleotide synthesis and storage.

A diet providing 4.0 mg niacin equivalents per 1,000 kcal is generally pellagrogenic, whereas one providing 4.4 equivalents per 1,000 kcal is protective. Human breast milk provides approximately 8 equivalents per 1,000 kcal. The 1968 recommended daily dietary allowances for children of the U.S. Food and Nutrition Board call for 6.4 to 7.0 equivalents per 1,000 kcal, slightly higher for the youngest infants. When a severely restricted protein and tryptophan intake is desirable for medical reasons, the entire amount should be provided as the vitamin on a very regular basis.

Pyridoxin (Vitamin B$_6$ Metabolism)

DAVID B. COURSIN

Vitamin B$_6$ includes the six interconvertible chemical structures of pyridoxin, pyridoxamine, pyridoxal, and their respective 5-phosphorylated forms. They are all metabolized through the pyridoxal-5-phosphate pathway with oxidation to 4-pyridoxic acid and excreted in the urine. Pyridoxal-5-phosphate is the most important member of the group, serving as the coenzyme for numerous enzyme systems that are responsible for the interconversion and metabolism of amino acids such as transamination, decarboxylation, and desulfuration. It is also an integral part of the molecular configuration of phosphorylases A and B. In these capacities, the vitamin is essential for the metabolism of amino acids, proteins, lipids, nucleic acids, and glycogen. It also has an important role in the formation of serotonin and other neurohumors from tryptophan. These numerous B$_6$-dependent enzyme systems are not uniform in their binding capacities for pyridoxal-5-phosphate, but are rank-ordered in this ability. Therefore, in B$_6$ deficiency, those with the least capability of retaining the vitamin in the holoenzyme will be most susceptible to its decreased availability. This causes related biochemical and physiologic abnormalities to occur sequentially in accordance with the severity and duration of the deprivation.

Experimental studies with B$_6$ deficiency in animals have resulted in reduced fertility, resorption of fetuses, congenital abnormalities, retardation of growth and development, dermatitis, convulsive seizures, reduction of active membrane transport of amino acids, depression of immune body responses, oxaluria, and a host of other disorders that reflect its multiplicity of metabolic roles.

LABORATORY DETERMINATIONS OF B$_6$ DEFICIENCY. Vitamin B$_6$ deficiency can be detemined directly by the measurement of its various forms, particularly pyridoxal-5-phosphate in biologic samples. Urinary pyridoxic acid excretion has also been shown to correlate well with decreases in the body stores of the vitamin.

Indirect evaluation of deficiency can be obtained through the determination of transaminase activity in serum and red blood cells, and by quantification of the urinary excretion patterns of metabolites following an L-tryptophan load test of 50 mg per kilogram to a maximum of 2 g for the adult. B$_6$ deficiency produces abnormalities in the urinary excretion of virtually all of these metabolites with diagnostically significant changes in kynurenine, 5-hydroxykynurenine, xanthurenic acid, N-1-methylnicotinimide, 2-pyridone, and 5-hydroxyindolacetic acid.

The electroencephalogram is also sensitive to established B$_6$ deficiency with nonspecific, grossly abnormal wave forms that contain alterations in frequency, amplitude, and evoked responses.

These abnormal laboratory findings, as well as the clinical symptoms of B$_6$ deficiency, are readily corrected with relatively small oral doses (5 to 10 mg) of pyridoxin, indicating that the disorders relate specifically to a lack of the coenzyme.

SOURCES AND REQUIREMENTS. Vitamin B$_6$ is widely found in plant and animal food sources with high concentrations occurring in meat, liver, kidney, whole grains, peanuts, and soybeans. It has been found that excessive heating of the vitamin will cause a number of chemical changes including formation of a disulfide complex that renders it inactive. The general availability of vitamin B$_6$ in foods is such that a normal individual receiving well-balanced dietary intake will ingest adequate quantities of the vitamin. Table 14 lists the daily requirements that have been established for various age groups and for pregnancy.

VITAMIN B$_6$ DEFICIENCY IN MAN. Early observations of B$_6$ deficiency in man documented the appearance of dermatitis, cheilosis, glossitis, peripheral neuritis, anemia, and convulsive seizures. In the early

1950's, a formula containing 60 µg/L of B$_6$ (compared to 100 µg/L in human milk) was inadvertently produced through the use of excessive measures of product sterilization. Infants maintained entirely on this formula developed hyperactivity, hyperacousis, behavioral changes, convulsive seizures, abnormal tryptophan load tests, and changes in their electroencephalograms. Patients' symptoms were aggravated by increases in the protein concentration of their diets. These phenomena were readily corrected by the administration of oral therapy of 5 to 10 mg of pyridoxin.

It was evident from these studies that borderline B$_6$ deficiency in man could produce definitive changes in the neurochemistry of the brain with derangements of neurophysiologic function that resulted in abnormalities of capabilities and performance. This stimulated widespread interest in the relationship of B$_6$ to the central nervous system and has resulted in a number of major advances in our understanding of this problem. To date, the mechanisms of convulsive seizures have not been completely clarified. One of the concepts that has been extensively explored relates to the reduction of gamma aminobutyric acid in the brain in B$_6$ deficiency. The two enzyme systems requiring pyridoxal-5-phosphate, decarboxylation and transamination, are involved in gamma aminobutyric acid metabolism and have different affinities for the coenzyme. Therefore, under conditions of deficiency, decarboxylation with its weaker binding capacity is unable to function normally. This causes a decrease in the concentration of gamma aminobutyric acid with a lowering of the threshold of central nervous system irritability that may result in convulsive seizures.

While the developing brain of the infant is especially sensitive to B$_6$ deficiency, a somewhat similar symptom complex of behavioral changes and convulsive disorders has been produced in healthy, young adult males. The subjects were maintained on an adequate diet that was very low in B$_6$ content and within weeks demonstrated that they also were susceptible.

Iatrogenic B$_6$ deficiency symptoms of the nervous system may also be produced by a number of drugs such as isonicotinic hydrazide and deoxypyridoxin. The former binds pyridoxal-5-phosphate to render it inactive, while the latter substitutes for pyridoxal-5-phosphate in its normal position resulting in the inactivation of the holoenzyme complex. In both instances, normal B$_6$-dependent enzyme activity is decreased. Hence, oral prophylactic pyridoxin in doses of 10 to 25 mg daily must be administered in conjunction with these drugs, as well as with others such as penicillamine and cycloserine, which may cause similar effects.

VITAMIN B$_6$ DEPENDENCY. In 1954, an inborn error of B$_6$ metabolism was discovered that was termed B$_6$ dependency. The patient had uncontrolled convulsive seizures shortly after birth and eventually proved to be mentally retarded. Despite a usually

TABLE 14. *Estimated Vitamin B$_6$ Requirements for Various Age Groups (mg/Day)*

Individual	Amount
Infant	0.10 - 0.5*
Child	0.5 - 1.5
Adolescent	1.5 - 2.0
Adult	1.5 - 2.0
Pregnancy	5.0 - 10.0

*20 µg/g protein. These ranges are related to normal ranges of protein intake.

adequate dietary intake of B_6, daily oral doses of 10 to 25 mg of pyridoxin were necessary in order to control the convulsive seizures, although there was no improvement in the patient's mental status. Incidentally, the tryptophan load test was normal and subsequent studies in other patients with B_6 dependency have shown that their levels of the vitamin and pyridoxic acid excretion were also normal.

B_6 dependency results from a genetic defect in B_6-requiring enzyme systems that initiate neurochemical changes in utero, despite the availability of adequate amounts of the vitamin. These are evidenced at birth by convulsive seizures and will eventuate in mental retardation, unless adequate pyridoxin therapy is instituted shortly after delivery. Present evidence suggests that this problem is caused by the abnormal molecular configuration of the involved apoenzymes, so that B_6 must be made available to them in large quantities (5 to 10 times the normal daily requirement) in order for them to function.

Homocystinuria, cystathioninuria, and familial xanthurenic aciduria are additional examples of inborn errors of metabolism that result from molecular abnormalities of single pyridoxal-5-phosphate–dependent apoenzymes (cystathionine synthetase, cystathioninase, and kynureninase, respectively). They also require 10 to 25 mg of pyridoxin daily to normalize their activities.

In addition to the two clearly defined entities of B_6 deficiency and B_6 dependency affecting the brain, the vitamin has also been implicated in a variety of other central nervous system disorders such as mongolism, phenylketonuria, and myoclonic epilepsy. Some patients with the latter disorder have shown partial improvement with oral therapy of 100 to 200 mg of pyridoxin daily. A somewhat similar experience with large doses of B_6 has been reported in a series of youngsters with a variety of convulsive disorders and mental retardation, abnormal electroencephalograms, and abnormal tryptophan load tests. These patients were found to require doses of pyridoxin in excess of 300 mg/day in order to correct their laboratory findings and to obtain even a small degree of clinical improvement.

Another form of B_6 dependency may occur in the hemopoietic system involving enzymes that participate in the normal production of hemoglobin. Patients with this hereditary defect generally develop their anemia in early adult life, despite the fact that their diets have contained usually adequate amounts of B_6. The anemia has been termed "pyridoxin-responsive anemia" and is different from that resulting from B_6 deficiency. It is characterized by microcytosis, hypochromia, erythroid hyperplasia of bone marrow, elevated plasma iron concentration with increased saturation of the total iron-binding capacity of the serum. The genetic defect responds to daily doses of 10 mg of B_6 with normalization of the syndrome.

FEMALE HORMONAL ACTIVITY AND VITAMIN B_6.
The hormonal changes that attend menstruation, pregnancy, and the use of anovulatory drugs have been shown to cause abnormal patterns in the tryptophan load test that are indicative of B_6 deficiency. The nausea and vomiting of the first trimester of pregnancy have been reported in some studies to respond well to pyridoxin with the interpretation that they may relate to a B_6 deficiency or increased need for the vitamin during that time. Recently, studies in patients with well-defined toxemia of pregnancy have shown that they have marked decreases in their placental pyridoxal-5-phosphate and pyridoxal phosphokinase. This adds new support to earlier observations of abnormal tryptophan metabolite excretion patterns that suggested marked B_6 deficiency in such patients. Examination of tryptophan metabolism in subjects receiving anovulatory agents containing estrogen has revealed patterns that are very similar to those seen in pregnancy. New information on these situations is now becoming available. The early onset of menstruation, the increased occurrence of pregnancy in adolescence, and the widespread use of anovulatory agents in younger age groups all call for an increased awareness and concern for their potentially important interrelationships with B_6.

Folic Acid Deficiency (Pteroylglutamic Acid Deficiency)

L. EMMETT HOLT, JR.

That folic acid is an important metabolite has been known for some years. Whether it can be synthesized by the body in adequate quantities has, however, been questionable. The observations of Herbert would seem to have settled the question. Its absence from the diet leads to bone marrow arrest; megaloblastic anemia develops which may be associated with pancytopenia. There is, however, evidence that at least a part of the requirement can be furnished by intestinal bacteria.

Folic acid is widely distributed in nature, notably in green vegetables. Its derivatives, which function as coenzymes in various reactions, are formed from an unstable reduction product, tetrahydrofolic acid, to which various single-carbon groups can be attached; the best known of these is the formyl derivative, known as folinic acid or the citrovorum factor. The requirement of folic acid, ordinarily extremely minute, is considerably affected by factors which convert folic acid into its reduced usable form. Antagonists such as aminopterin and amethopterin prevent this transformation, and ascorbic acid facilitates it; when ascorbic acid is deficient, large amounts of folic acid are needed. Folic acid coenzymes are concerned in the transfer of single-carbon units—methyl, methylene, methoxy, formyl, and formamino groups. They are also concerned with certain steps in the synthesis of purines and porphyrins, in the degradation of histidine, and in the hydroxylation of phenylalanine to form tyrosine.

Folic acid deficiency is rarely encountered in North American children. It has been observed in infants on diets deficient in ascorbic acid; it may result from deficient absorption in diseases of the small bowel or from the use of antifolic compounds in the treatment of leukemia. Occasional instances have been observed after the use of certain anticonvulsive drugs, namely Mysoline and Dilantin. There is now considerable evidence that a folic acid deficiency anemia is not an infrequent complication of kwashiorkor, resulting either from a deficient intake of the vitamin or the presence of some conditioning factor.

Folic acid will induce a hematologic response in various macrocytic anemias of adults, such as pernicious anemia, fish tapeworm anemia, the macrocytic anemia of pregnancy, and tropical and nontropical sprue. Its effect in the rare cases of pernicious anemia in children has not been extensively studied, and its use may not be without risk, since despite temporary hematologic remission the nervous lesions associated with Addisonian anemia may be made worse.

Folic acid deficiency can be measured by the level of folic acid in the blood, determined by microbiologic methods; impairment of folic absorption has been determined by measuring the radioactive material in blood following the administration of radioactive folic acid. A simpler and useful test of deficiency depends on the urinary excretion of an excess of formamino glutamic acid (FIGLU) after a histidine load; however, this test, which is also positive in B_{12} deficiency, is not altogether specific for folic acid deficiency.

Infants may be treated with 1 to 5 mg given orally, although smaller amounts may be effective. In cases of deficiencies induced by antifolic drugs, larger doses may be needed. Folinic acid is more effective in reversing the untoward effects of these drugs.

Scurvy (Deficiency of Vitamin C)

Scurvy is a disease caused by prolonged deprivation of ascorbic acid (vitamin C). Although it was known to the ancient Egyptians and was a familiar scourge of sailors throughout history, infantile scurvy was recognized by Barlow only in 1883. It is still often referred to as Barlow's disease. The most striking manifestations are changes in the bones, leading to pain on motion and a hemorrhagic tendency.

THE VITAMIN. The chemical properties and distribution of the vitamin have been described in Chapter 3. Ascorbic acid is present in all cells of the body but is particularly abundant in metabolically active tissues. High concentrations are found in the retina; in the endocrine glands, particularly the adrenal cortex; in intestinal epithelium; and in leucocytes. It accumulates in sites of connective tissue proliferation, such as in healing wounds. Specific enzyme systems of which ascorbic acid is a cofactor have not been isolated, and what is known of its function is derived from indirect evidence—the observed effects of withdrawal and administration. It is a powerful reducing agent and may serve as a regulator of oxidation and reduction in the cells. It is known to protect a number of enzymes from oxidative damage, among them folic acid reductase, which converts folic to folinic acid and parahydroxyphenylpyruvic oxidase. In ascorbic acid deficiency the tyrosyl compounds, p-OH-phenylpyruvic and p-OH-phenyllactic acid, appear in the urine. Ascorbic acid appears to be concerned in the hydroxylation of proline to hydroxyproline, a function in particular demand for connective tissue proliferation. It is also involved in the hydroxylation of tryptophan to form serotonin. It is concerned in some way with absorption of iron and with the formation and degradation of ferritin. It is also involved with cholesterol synthesis, which may be related to its high concentration in the adrenal cortex. Blood cholesterol levels are low in scurvy, and foods which are hypercholesterolemic fail to exhibit their effect until the scurvy is treated.

It is of interest that in several animal species which lack the enzyme gulanolactone oxidase and are hence unable to synthesize ascorbic acid the enzyme is present during embryonic life.

Just how the known chemical functions of the vitamin are related to the anatomical changes resulting from its deficiency is far from clear. The effects of ascorbic acid depletion include defective formation of intercellular cement substance, suspension of collagen production of fibroblasts, hemorrhagic phenomena, and defective formation of bones and teeth which are described later.

INCIDENCE. Scurvy is seen most frequently now in infants who have been fed for some months on heated milk formulas without adequate supplements of vitamin C. Healthy infants require 10 mg of ascorbic acid a day, and in the presence of infection double this amount may be required; hence 20 mg per day or more should be provided. Unless the mother's diet is inadequate, breast milk contains 4 to 7 mg per 100 ml, which provides adequate protection, scurvy being seen in breast-fed infants only in the presence of maternal malnutrition. Raw cow's milk contains only about 2 mg per ml, a marginal quantity, one-third to one-half of which is destroyed by the heating to which it is subjected—hence the necessity of supplementing the food if scurvy is to be prevented.

In exceptional instances scurvy is seen as a result of undue heat treatment of the vitamin or food supplement; we have known instances in which boiled orange juice was given. Scurvy is occasionally seen in a child placed on a highly restricted diet for the treatment of eczema or from prolonged cooking of foods to lower their allergenic properties. A few cases in older children have been attributable to food fads.

Most cases of scurvy encountered in the pediatric age group are seen during the latter part of the first year; before 6 months and after 15 months of age the disease is rare. The newborn infant starts life with an advantage in that the concentration of ascorbic acid in his plasma at birth is usually higher than that of his mother, so that he is protected to some extent by a store of vitamin acquired in intrauterine life. Moreover, he rarely suffers complete privation of dietary ascorbic acid, and the disease is consequently slow in manifesting itself. The onset of symptoms is usually delayed from four to nine months after the institution of the deficient diet. In rare instances a deficient maternal diet during pregnancy may cause the infant to be born with inadequate stores of ascorbic acid and thus shorten greatly the interval between birth and the development of scurvy. The youngest patient recorded was only 20 days old at the time of death; symptoms of scurvy had not been recognized during life, but the histologic picture of the bones was characteristic. In the New York City area, scurvy has largely disappeared from the pediatric scene since World War II; in some other areas it continues to appear despite the generally improved understanding of nutritional problems on the part of the public. The question of subclinical scurvy, an asymptomatic condition recognizable by laboratory criteria only, is still debated. Surveys based on ascorbic acid concentrations in plasma and on load tests indicate that stores of this vitamin are quite often low, but such findings do not mean that disease is present.

PATHOLOGY. The essential nature of the pathologic process in scurvy is not clearly understood. The susceptibility of scorbutic subjects to capillary hemorrhage without visible anatomic basis is an established clinical fact, as is also delayed wound healing, but the only histologic lesions pathognominic of scurvy are those found in growing bones and in teeth.

The characteristic bone changes are most pronounced in the region where endochondral ossification is proceeding (Fig. 11). The zone of proliferative cartilage becomes inconspicuous, with few mitoses and a disorderly arrangement of the cartilage cell column. The amount of cartilage matrix undergoing calcification, in contrast, is abnormally great; at the

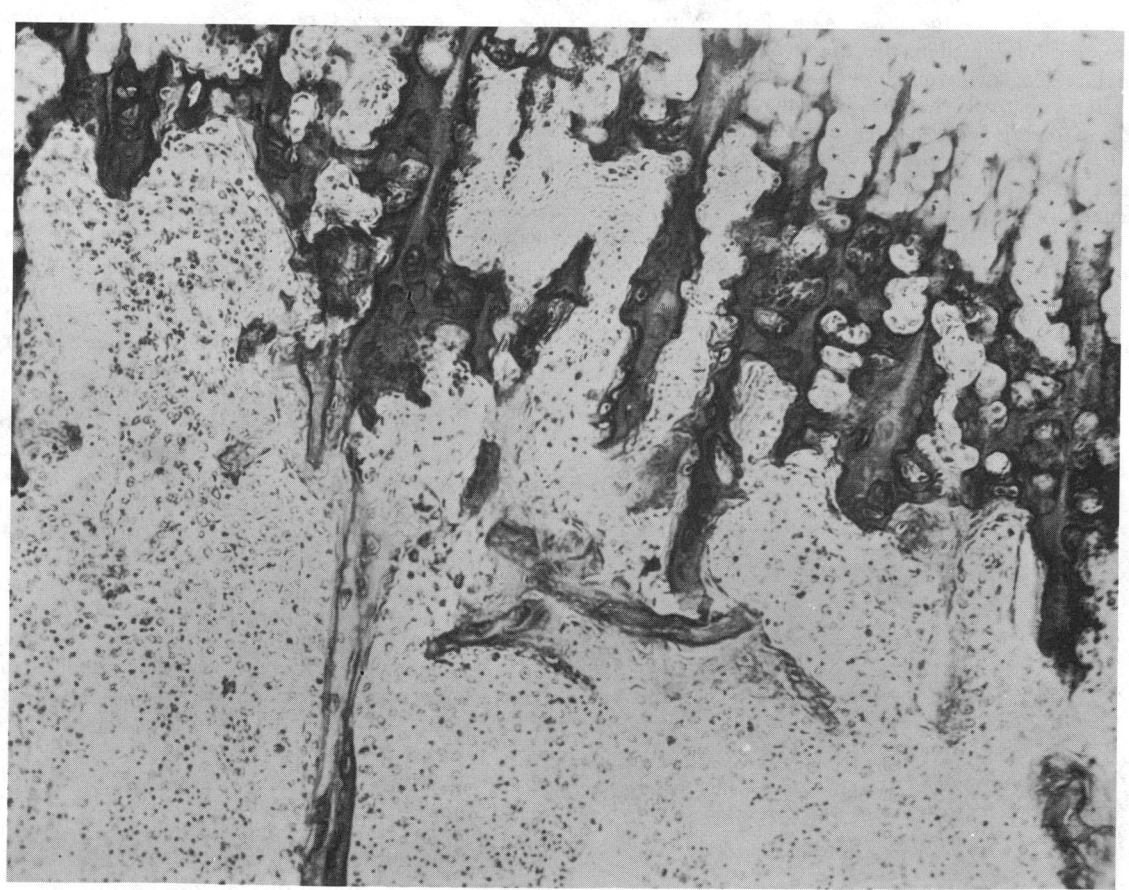

Fig. 11. Zone of preparatory calcification in scurvy. The masses of calcified cartilaginous matrix lying shaftward from the growing cartilage are imbedded in "framework marrow," the loose, relatively avascular and cell-poor scorbutic marrow. Several of the matrix elements have been pushed into bizarre alignment, others show fractures, and some of these fractured areas are surrounded by fibrin.

same time its conversion to bone is impaired, and the brittleness of the large, irregular masses of calcified matrix is often reflected in numerous microscopic fractures. Beneath this broad zone of provisional calcification the trabeculae are slender and scarce, and there are few evidences of osteoblastic activity. The marrow between the trabeculae has lost the appearance of normal hematopoietic marrow; it is known as "framework marrow" and consists chiefly of loose, embryonic-looking connective tissue, often containing hemorrhages. Periosteal ossification is also inactive, and hemorrhages may be found beneath the periosteum at any part of the shaft between the epiphyseal lines. Epiphyseal separation is common in scurvy, especially in incomplete degree (infraction). Cleavage usually takes place through the brittle zone of provisional calcification, sometimes with partial detachment of the epiphyseal fragment from the shaft, more often with comminution. The microscopic lesions in the skeleton are widely distributed and, as a rule, bilaterally symmetrical to a large degree. They are always more intense in places where bone is growing more rapidly. Macroscopic subperiosteal hemorrhages too are often found (Fig. 12); the most frequent sites are the lower end of the femur, the lower end of the tibia, the upper end of the femur, the bones of the arm (especially the upper end of the humerus), and the skull. Trauma not infrequently plays a part in determining the site of such lesions, as it does also in epiphyseal separation. Scurvy produces characteristic changes in tooth structure, identifiable by special techniques.

The buccal lesions will be described in the section on symptoms. Among the rare lesions of scurvy

Fig. 12. Femur showing subperiosteal hemorrhages in scurvy of seven weeks' duration.

may be mentioned hemorrhage into the orbit, giving rise to exophthalmos and sometimes to chemosis and edema of the lids; often there are subconjunctival hemorrhages as well. Visceral lesions are infrequent; there may be small hemorrhages beneath the pleura, pericardium, and peritoneum; hemorrhagic effusions into the serous cavities do not, however, occur. Despite the frequency of microscopic hematuria, the kidneys as a rule show nothing abnormal. The joints usually escape entirely, in spite of the striking lesions adjacent to them. Cutaneous ecchymoses or hemorrhages in any of the mucous membranes may be seen at times. Intracranial hemorrhage is rare.

The bleeding tendency in scurvy cannot be attributed to any defect of blood coagulation. It is regarded as due to alterations in the blood vessel walls.

Other deficiency diseases are not uncommonly associated with scurvy. The presence of rickets complicates the picture in the bones and sometimes makes its interpretation difficult.

SYMPTOMS.   In most cases, a period of indisposition, fretfulness, pallor, and loss of appetite precedes the local symptoms; as a rule this is not noticed at the time and is recalled only in retrospect. The first symptom to attract attention is usually tenderness of the legs. This may begin insidiously; at first it may be so slight as to cause the patient to cry only when the diaper is being changed or when he is lifted out of his bath. In other words, it is a sudden refusal to sit or stand. At first the tenderness is not definitely localized but is generally more marked about the knees and ankles. Some swelling may accompany it. Hemorrhage in regions other than the lower extremities may mark the onset of the disease. Changes in the arms are commonly found in the early stage, although they are rarely the first feature to attract attention.

The amount of constitutional disturbance is variable. There may be marked freftulness, poor sleep, pallor, anorexia, and loss of weight; in other cases symptoms of scurvy may continue for several weeks without making any perceptible impression upon the child's nutrition. Pain and disability may come and go, perhaps because of minor variations in vitamin intake. Severe scurvy develops only when the condition is unrecognized and allowed to progress or when the diet is completely devoid of ascorbic acid.

In severe cases fever is usually present, the temperature in some instances reaching 102° or 103° F (38.9° or 39.4° C). Tenderness in the legs becomes constant and is often exquisite, so that any movement or even the slightest touch causes the child to scream with pain or apprehension. The posture is characteristic. There is semiflexion of the thighs and legs and outward rotation of the hips (Fig. 13), the "pithed frog" position; the child often lies motionless, and voluntary movements of the extremities cannot be elicited (pseudoparalysis). The disability results chiefly from the pain which motion provokes and, when marked, usually denotes infraction of an

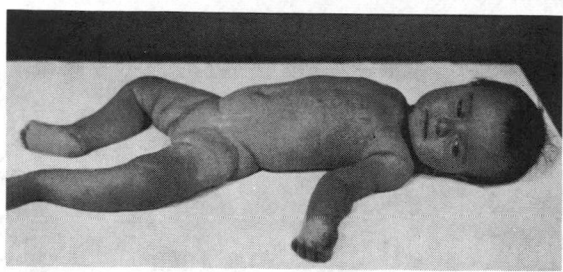

Fig. 13. Scurvy showing characteristic posture in an infant 10½ months old. (From McIntosh. In Brennemann. *Practice of Pediatrics*, vol. 1. Courtesy of W. F. Prior Co.)

epiphysis. Ecchymoses are occasionally seen about any of the large joints, resembling ordinary black-and-blue spots, and these often seem to confirm the opinion previously formed that the child has met with some accident. Swelling near the joints, particularly just above the knee, may be so great that the limb is nearly twice the size of its fellow. Although the swelling is principally due to subperiosteal hemorrhage, some brawny edema is commonly present in the extremities; it does not pit readily on pressure.

Evidence of epiphyseal infraction is seen in most of the severe cases, usually unaccompanied by gross displacement. It occurs most frequently either at the lower epiphysis of the femur or tibia, or at the upper epiphysis of the humerus; it is often bilateral. Although the condition of the bone is a predisposing factor, relatively mild trauma is usually the immediate cause. Crepitus is obtained only with complete separation and with unwarranted manipulations. The diagnosis can be readily made by roentgenography or by the persistence of local pain more than three or four days after institution of treatment.

Teeth which have recently erupted or which are about to erupt are often overlaid with redundant, hemorrhagic, or spongy gingiva. Often the gums of the upper jaw alone are involved, those about the upper central incisors being most commonly affected. In the most marked cases the gums may ulcerate, the appearance resembling that of mercurial stomatitis. Pain from sore gums may seriously interfere with taking of food.

Among the common sites of bone involvement in scurvy the ribs should be mentioned. One finds an angular mushrooming of the costochondral junctions with the production of a rosary quite comparable to that found in rickets. The typical scorbutic rosary is sharper and firmer than its rachitic counterpart and in some instances shows tenderness on pressure, but the clinical distinction between the two is not always possible.

Bleeding may occur from almost any of the mucous membranes; the hemorrhages are generally small but may be frequently repeated. Hematemesis is rare, as is also the passage of recognizable blood by rectum, but occult blood can often be demonstrated in the stools. Microscopic hematuria occurs

in about one-third of the cases; gross hematuria is less common. In some patients with blood in the urine, albumin and casts are present as well, suggesting the diagnosis of hemorrhagic nephritis; the abnormal findings disappear, however, shortly after treatment is started.

Petechiae and ecchymoses in the skin may be found in the vicinity of the gross bone lesions; widespread petechial eruptions are sometimes seen. If there is a superimposed skin disease associated with scurvy, such as measles, varicella, or furunculosis, the lesions are usually hemorrhagic. Other changes in the skin are seldom encountered in infants but are seen after the second or third year with increasing frequency, even in mild cases. The observation was made by Crandon and his associates that the earliest sign noted in experimentally induced human scurvy was a follicular hyperkeratosis indistinguishable from that associated with vitamin A deficiency (p. 177). In our own experience likewise, follicular hyperkeratosis in children has more often been explained on the basis of deficiency of ascorbic acid than of vitamin A.

The blood picture in early scurvy may be normal despite the presence of pallor. A macrocytic anemia appears quite commonly, and in many instances has been shown to result from a double deficiency of folic acid and ascorbic acid. In the presence of an abundance of vitamin C in the diet only a small amount of folic acid is needed, whereas when folic acid is abundantly supplied, little or no vitamin C is required to prevent anemia. Folic acid in massive doses will reduce the tyrosyl derivatives in the urine of scorbutic patients. Scurvy causes no characteristic changes in the leucocytes. Serum calcium and inorganic phosphorus concentrations are normal. The serum alkaline phosphatase activity is usually depressed.*

ROENTGENOGRAPHIC APPEARANCES. In cases of scurvy with extensive subperiosteal hemorrhages a striking x-ray picture is disclosed when the healing process causes bone formation to be resumed in the elevated periosteum. Of greater diagnostic importance are the changes met with in the early stages of the disease (Fig. 14). The features characteristic of early scurvy are (1) a *ground-glass appearance* of the shaft, due to atrophy of the trabeculae. The cortex is usually thinned out and, next to the epiphysial line, may consist of a mere pencil streak or may even vanish. (2) A *broadened epiphyseal line* (the zone of provisional calcification of cartilage matrix) is conspicuous, particularly at the lower end of the femur and at both ends of the tibia; it may be finely irregular. (3) Beneath the broad epiphyseal

* A recent study (Hoad et al.) has revealed that in experimental scurvy in man, the manifestations of Sjogren's syndrome (Chap. 27) appear along with the better known scorbutic symptoms and signs suggesting a common pathway for the action of ascorbic acid and the as yet unknown pathogenesis of a form of rheumatoid arthritis.

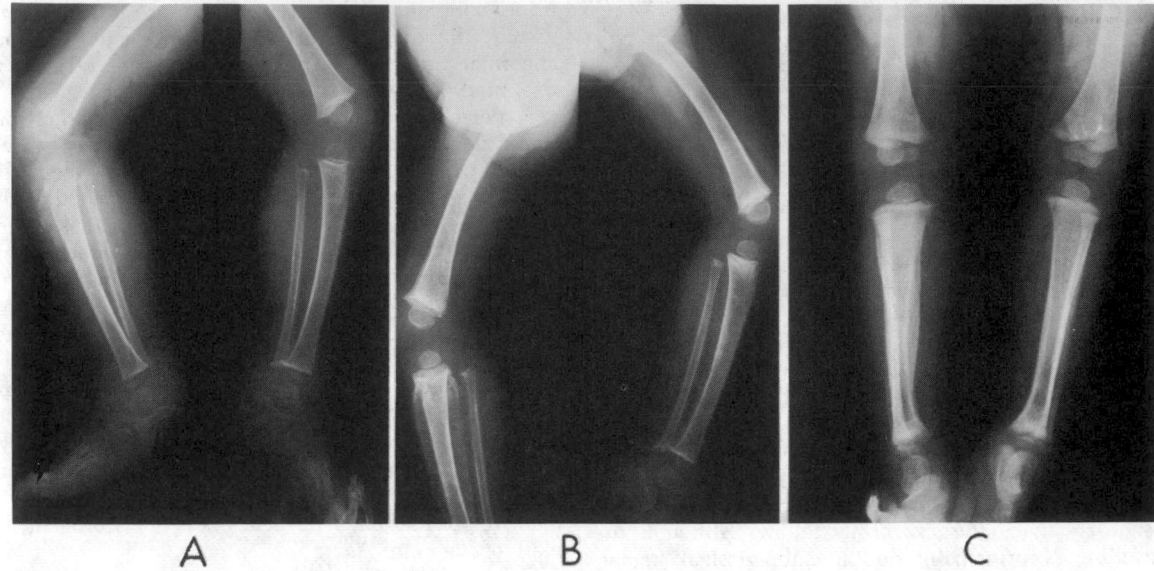

Fig. 14. Advanced scorbutic changes seen in a 16-month-old infant. A. The leg exhibits severe osteoporosis, with lucent centers of both epiphysis and shaft. The cortical bone is thinner. The proximal tibia shows a transverse lucent line under the epiphyseal plate, known as the "scurvy line." Fractures are present in the metaphyseal ends of the long bones, with exhibition of the "corner sign" seen best in the proximal fibula. There is periosteal elevation and beginning periosteal new bone production best demonstrated in the distal femur. B. After two weeks of therapy, healing with remineralization and calcification of subperiosteal hematomata along the shafts. C. After 12 weeks, further healing with ossification of the hematomata.

line is a *zone of rarefaction* corresponding to the region of greatest trabecular attrition (the scurvy line). This zone is often narrow and difficult to detect in early scurvy. The first two of these diagnostic features can be observed in the epiphyseal centers of ossification: the ground-glass appearance, with trabecular atrophy within the center, and the dense epiphyseal line appearing as a ring surrounding the epiphyseal center, most dense on the side toward the bone itself.

Displacement of the epiphysis is indicated by faulty alignment of the epiphyseal line with the shaft of the bone; there is lateral projection of the shadow caused by the epiphyseal line. Even more common is partial separation of the epiphysis occurring without displacement. This appears as a crack separating the epiphyseal line from the shaft and extending part way across the width of the bone. After hemorrhage has occurred, the first evidences of calcification in the elevated periosteum are seen as spurs of newly formed bone attached to the epiphyseal line, pointing toward the shaft of the bone or somewhat outward if the hemorrhage has been a large one.

As scurvy heals, the sites of subperiosteal hemorrhage take on a striking appearance. New bone is laid down in periosteum that has been detached from the underlying shaft, so that in the course of a week or two the full extent of periosteal stripping is dramatically revealed. Later, as the hematoma resorbs, the shell of new bone contracts and becomes more dense. Where considerable epiphyseal displacement has taken place, the restitution of normal contour may require as long as a year.

DIAGNOSIS. This seldom presents any obstacle when the essential features are kept in mind: the age incidence, the extreme tenderness of the legs, spongy swollen gums, swelling near the large joints, a tendency to hemorrhages, and usually a history of the prolonged use of heated or canned milk. One should not be too easily misled by a parent's statement that orange juice has been given; closer inquiry may reveal that it has been refused, vomited, or even heated.

Disability resulting from trauma alone seldom has the symmetrical distribution of scorbutic manifestations, and the evidences of physical injury usually include localized contusions and perhaps also breaks in the skin. With trauma from some blunt or padded object, however, roentgen examination may be required for differentiation. Cases with pseudoparalysis may be mistaken for poliomyelitis. Hyperesthesia is rarely as marked in poliomyelitis as in cases of scurvy, and painful stimulation of the extremities will usually indicate that actual paralysis is not present. The locomotor disability of scurvy may suggest rheumatic fever, but the resemblance is only superficial. We have known two patients with scurvy who were operated on by eminent surgeons, once with a diagnosis of malignant disease, and once with osteitis of both tibias. In cases with considerable fever, scurvy may be mistaken for acute suppurative arthritis or osteomyelitis.

As seen in roentgenograms, the bone changes of scurvy are widespread and tend to be symmetrical. Even when scorbutic disability is confined to the upper extremities, one may confidently anticipate characteristic roentgen changes in the bones of the lower extremities. In contrast, the roentgen features of traumatic or infectious lesions of bone are usually maximal at the sites of greatest pain and disability. The radiographic picture of infantile cortical hyperostoses (Chap. 25) bears some resemblance to that of gross scorbutic lesions in the healing stage, but other evidence of scurvy is lacking.

The osteochondritis of early congenital syphilis has many clinical features in common with scurvy; its x-ray appearances likewise present some similarity. Syphilitic osteochondritis, however, is found at an early age, almost always less than four months, while scurvy characteristically occurs after this time. Moreover, careful examination will usually reveal additional evidence confirmatory of one or the other condition.

Hematemesis from scurvy has led to a mistaken diagnosis of peptic ulcer; in one of our patients, an infant of six months, vomiting of blood was the presenting symptom. Loss of blood from the intestine may suggest intussusception. When hemorrhagic manifestations are absent, confirmatory evidence of scurvy may be obtained by the Rumpel-Leede phenomenon or other tests of capillary fragility. Such signs, while nearly always positive in scurvy, are never pathognomonic, being found also in other conditions.

Biochemical Diagnosis. The tests used include (1) measurement of ascorbic acid in plasma; (2) load tests in which plasma concentration or urinary excretion is followed after a specific load; (3) measurement of ascorbic acid in the buffy coat of centrifuged blood; and (4) a functional test based on the urinary excretion of certain tyrosine metabolites after administration of tyrosine. The significance of these various tests must be clearly appreciated. In normal subjects on a generous intake, ascorbic acid levels in the plasma usually range between 0.5 and 1.5 mg per 100 milliliters. In frank scurvy the concentration is usually zero. Unfortunately, the plasma level is considerably affected by recent intake. Thus, sudden withdrawal of the vitamin will cause the plasma concentration to fall to zero in a few weeks, although months may elapse before symptoms are detectable; conversely, administration of ascorbic acid to a depleted subject will raise the plasma level before the needs of the body have been met. The conclusion cannot be drawn that the subject with a plasma level less than 0.5 mg per 100 milliliters is suffering from subclinical scurvy; he may have merely a smaller margin of safety from ascorbic acid deficiency than has the individual with a higher plasma concentration.

Similar criticism applies to load tests in which a standard load is given to a child. A rise in plasma ascorbic acid concentration and in subsequent urinary output of the vitamin indicates that the stores are virtually filled, whereas failure to demonstrate a rise indicates that the stores are incompletely filled. In a scorbutic patient the daily oral administration of 200 mg of ascorbic acid may fail to evoke a distinct rise in the urinary level for three or four days, while in an adequately nourished subject the urine gives a strongly positive test within 24 hours. Roughly quantitative urinary tolerance tests of this kind can be satisfactorily carried out by analysis of single voided specimens and do not require the more difficult technique of complete collections. However, no load test thus far devised is capable of measuring accurately the degree of ascorbic acid depletion.

More closely correlated with symptoms is the ascorbic acid content of the buffy coat. In normal subjects the concentration is about 30 mg per 100 milliliters. On withdrawal of vitamin C from the diet the level falls at a fairly constant rate, reaching zero after about four months of depletion. Clinical manifestations of scurvy are usually detectable when ascorbic acid cannot be found in the leucocyte-platelet layer.

A sensitive test of scurvy and as simple as any is the functional test based on excretion of the so-called tyrosyl compounds, *para*-hydroxyphenylpyruvic acid and *para*-hydroxyphenyllactic acid, after administration of tyrosine itself or after a protein-containing meal. These acids are readily detected in the urine by the Millon reagent. In the normal subject tyrosyluria is absent, whereas in scurvy it is constantly present.

Another functional test devised by Gabuzda and co-workers consists in the administration of a test dose of folic acid. Its conversion to folinic acid is impaired in scurvy.

PROPHYLAXIS AND TREATMENT. To protect against the development of scurvy, every infant who is even partially dependent on boiled, pasteurized, dried, or evaporated milk should be given some anti-scorbutic food as early as the first two weeks. Orange juice is convenient; one teaspoonful daily should be given at first and the amount rapidly increased to the juice of one orange. Most canned and frozen orange juice preparations likewise provide an adequate source of vitamin C. Pure ascorbic acid is equally easy to administer; it may be given by itself, 25 or 50 mg being dissolved in a small amount of water and fed by spoon, or the tablet may be crushed and dropped into a feeding just before the bottle is offered, or it may be included in a polyvitamin supplement. One should not attempt to mix the day's dose of ascorbic acid in with the 24-hour feeding, lest the greater part of it be destroyed by oxidation. All fresh fruits have antiscorbutic properties, and the ascorbic acid content of vegetables is not as a rule completely destroyed in cooking. Consequently, by the time a child is taking a varied diet the necessity of giving ascorbic acid separately disappears.

The question whether additional vitamin C

should be given in infectious states is sometimes raised. It is known that in acute disease states the plasma ascorbic acid level may drop abruptly, sometimes even to zero. That there is an increased need for ascorbic acid in stressful states has been clearly established by the observations of Hamil and others. In a group of infants fed a fixed vitamin C intake, only those who developed infections developed scurvy. Although on marginal intakes of ascorbic acid an increase is thus clearly indicated, the tissue reserves on commonly-employed diets would seem to be adequate to meet what appears to be a mobilization of ascorbic acid to sites of stress in acute and even subacute conditions.

In treatment of frank scurvy large doses of vitamin C are required, and pure ascorbic acid in daily amounts of 500 or even 1,000 mg may be used to supplement the diet. The total requirement for replenishment of the depleted stores is often of the order of 2 g, and it has been shown that the entire quantity needed for maximal healing over a period of eight days may be administered at one time. Oral administration, permitting slower absorption, is ordinarily preferable to parenteral injection; with intravenous injection in particular, large amounts are lost in the urine. Concomitant diarrhea is not a contraindication to oral administration. Orange juice and other natural sources of the vitamin will generally effect equally rapid symptomatic improvement, though it is difficult when relying on them alone to obtain as prompt a saturation of the depleted stores.

Local treatment of the extremities is not generally required.

COURSE AND PROGNOSIS. Fatal scurvy is now rarely seen. It is only in neglected cases with severe malnutrition or other complications that the issue becomes doubtful. Secondary infections, like pneumonia, may cause death.

The results of treatment are usually prompt, often dramatic. Within the first 24 hours improvement in disposition and appetite is evident. The prompt disappearance of tenderness from the extremities is singularly striking and has never been satisfactorily explained. Persistence of tenderness suggests separation of an epiphysis. Hemorrhage is not likely to occur at new sites after the first few hours of treatment, but it is not uncommon for bleeding to continue for a few days from the gums or elsewhere. When the swelling of the gums subsides, a new tooth may be found to have erupted. Microscopic hematuria has been known to persist for as long as two weeks, but large hemorrhages either from the kidney or from the gastrointestinal tract usually cease promptly. Fever seldom persists more than two or three days. Sometimes malnutrition affords a serious problem; in such cases transfusion may be of help. Loss of weight during the first few days of treatment is by no means unusual, owing to disappearance of edema that may be present.

Repair of the bone lesions begins at once, although a week or more is required before improvement can be detected by x-ray. One of the earliest changes seen is new calcification as periosteal bone production is resumed. The elevated periosteum gradually contracts down as the hemorrhage beneath it is absorbed. Even after marked displacement of an epiphysis the alignment between the shaft and the epiphyseal fragment is gradually restored with growth of the bone. Roentgenologic evidences of scurvy may be recognizable years later in the form of a prominent transverse line buried in the shaft which once represented the broad epiphyseal line of acute scurvy; the circular or oval area of rarefied trabecular bone which once comprised the scorbutic center of ossification may persist, buried in the middle of a center which has grown much larger (Fig. 14C). Permanent deformities resulting from scurvy have not been observed.

REFERENCES

DEFICIENCIES OF CALORIES AND PROTEIN

Bowie, M. D., Brinkman, G. L., and Hansen, J. D. L. Acquired disaccharide intolerance in malnutrition. J. Pediat., 66:1083, 1965.

Bradfield, R. B., Cordano, A., and Graham, G. G. Hair-root adaptation to marasmus in Andean Indian children. Lancet, 2:1395, 1969.

Brinkman, G. L., Bowie, M. D., Friis-Hansen, B., and Hansen, J. D. L. Body water composition in kwashiorkor before and after loss of edema. Pediatrics, 36:84, 1965.

Brunser, O., Reid, A., Mönckeberg, F., Maccioni, A., and Contreras, I. Jejunal biopsies in infant malnutrition: With special reference to mitotic index. Pediatrics, 38:605, 1966.

Cheek, D. B., Hill, D. E., Cordano, A., and Graham, G. G. Malnutrition in infancy: Changes in muscle and adipose tissue before and after rehabilitation. Pediat. Res., 4:135, 1970.

Cohen, S., and Hansen, J. D. L. Metabolism of albumin and gamma globulin in kwashiorkor. Clin. Sci., 23:351, 1962.

Dean, R. F. A. Kwashiorkor. In Gairdner, D., ed., Recent Advances in Pediatrics. London, J. & A. Churchill, 1965.

Garrow, J. S., and Pike, M. D. Long-term prognosis of severe infantile malnutrition. Lancet, 1:1, 1967.

—— Smith, R., and Ward, E. E. Electrolyte Metabolism in Severe Infantile Malnutrition. London, Pergammon, 1968.

Gordillo, G., Soto, R. A., Metcoff, J., López, E., and Antillon, L. G. Intracellular composition and homeostatic mechanisms in severe chronic malnutrition. III. Renal adjustments. Pediatrics, 20:303, 1957.

Graham, G. G. The later growth of malnourished infants. Effects of age, severity and subsequent diet. In McCance, R. A. and Widdowson, E. M., ed., Calorie Deficiencies and Protein Deficiencies. London, J. & A. Churchill, 1968, p. 301.

—— Cordano, A., and Baertl, J. M. Studies in infantile malnutrition. II. Effect of protein and calorie intakes on weight gain. J. Nutr., 81:249, 1963.

—— Cordano, A., and Baertl, J. M. Studies in infantile malnutrition. III. Effect of protein and calorie intakes on nitrogen retention. J. Nutr., 84:71, 1964.

—— Cordano, A., and Baertl, J. M. Studies in infantile malnutrition. IV. The effect of protein and calorie intakes on serum proteins. Amer. J. Clin. Nutr., 18:11, 1966.

—— Cordano, A., Blizzard, R. M., and Cheek, D. B. Infantile malnutrition: Changes in body composition during rehabilitation. Pediat. Res., 3:579, 1969.

Holt, L. E., Jr., Snyderman, S. E., Norton, P. M., Roitman, E., and Finch, J. The plasma aminogram in kwashiorkor. Lancet, 2:1343, 1963.

Jackson, C. M. The Effects of Inanition and Malnutrition upon Growth and Structure. New York, McGraw-Hill Book Co., 1925.

Kerpel-Fronius, E., and Kovach, S. The volume of extracellular body fluids in malnutrition. Pediatrics, 2:21, 1948.

Keys, A., Brozek, J., Henschel, A., Michelson, O., and Taylor, H. L. Biology of Human Starvation. Minneapolis, University of Minnesota Press, 1950.

Metcoff, J., Frenk, S., Gordillo, G., Gómez, F., Ramos-Galván, R., Cravioto, J., Janeway, C. A., and Gamble, J. L. Intracellular composition and homeostatic mechanisms in severe chronic infantile malnutrition. Pediatrics, 20:317, 1957.

Snyderman, S. E., Holt, L. E., Jr., Norton, P. M., Roitman, E., and Phansalkar, S. V. The plasma aminogram. I. Influence of the level of protein intake and a comparison of whole protein and amino acid diets. Pediat. Res., 2:131, 1968.

Taitz, L. S., and Finberg, L. Kwashiorkor in the Bronx. Amer. J. Dis. Child., 112:76, 1966.

Truswell, A. S., Wannenburg, P., Wittmann, W., and Hansen, J. D. L. Plasma amino acids in kwashiorkor. Lancet, 1:1162, 1966.

Viteri, F., Béhar, M., Arroyave, G., and Scrimshaw, N. S. Clinical aspects of protein malnutrition. In Munro, H. N. and Allison, J. B., eds., Mammalian Protein Metabolism. New York, Academic Press, Inc., 1963, Vol. 2, p. 523.

Waterlow, J. C., Cravioto, J., and Stephen, J. M. L. Protein malnutrition in man. Advances Protein Chem., 15:131, 1960.

Whitehead, R. G., and Dean, R. F. A. Serum amino acids in kwashiorkor. II. An abbreviated method of estimation and its application. Amer. J. Clin. Nutr., 14:320, 1964.

Wittmann, W., and Hansen, J. D. L. Gastroenteritis and malnutrition. S. Afr. Med. J., 39:223, 1965.

VITAMIN A DEFICIENCY

Dingle, J. H. Action of vitamin A on the stability of lysosomes. Ciba Symposium on Lysosomes. Boston, Little, Brown & Co., 1963, p. 384.

—— and Lucy, J. A. Membrane phenomena in relation to vitamin A. Proc. Nutr. Soc., 24:170, 1965.

Hume, E. M., and Krebs, H. A. Vitamin A requirement of human adults. An experimental study of vitamin A deprivation in man. Spec. Rep. 264, Med. Research Council, London, 1949.

Hypovitaminosis A. Proceedings of a conference on beriberi, endemic goiter and hypovitaminosis A. Kinney, T. D., and Follis, R. H., Jr., eds. Fed. Proc., 17 (Suppl. 2):103, 1958.

Johnson, B. C., and Wolf, G. The function of vitamin A in carbohydrate metabolism. Vitamins and Hormones, 18:439, 457, 1960.

Lewis, J. M., Bodansky, O., Birmingham, J. R., and Cohlan, S. Q. Comparative absorption, excretion and storage of oily and aqueous preparations of vitamin A. J. Pediat., 31:496, 1947.

Maxwell, J. P. Vitamin A deficiency in the antenatal period; its effects on the mother and infant. J. Obstet. Gynaec. Brit. Comm., 39:764, 1932.

McLaren, D. S. Malnutrition and the Eye. New York, Academic Press, 1963.

—— et al. Xerophthalmia in Jordan. Amer. J. Clin. Nutr., 17:117, 1965.

—— Oomen, H. A. P. C., and Escapini, H. Ocular manifestations of vitamin A deficiency in man. Bull. WHO, 34:357, 1966.

Moore, T. Vitamin A. Amsterdam. Elsevier, 1957.

Oomen, H. A. P. C., McLaren, D. S., and Escapini, H. A global survey on xerophthalmia. Trop. Geogr. Med., 16:271, 1964.

Sweet, L. K., and Kang, H. J. Clinical and anatomic study of avitaminosis A among the Chinese. Amer. J. Dis. Child., 50:699, 1935.

Wald, G. The Visual Function of Vitamin A. In Vitamins and Hormones. New York, Academic Press, Inc., 1960, p. 417.

Vaughan, D. G. Xerophthalmia. Arch. Ophthalmol., 51:789, 1954.

THIAMINE DEFICIENCY

Andrews, V. L. Infantile beriberi. Philippine J. Sci., Sect. B, 7:67, 1912.

Brin, M. Erythrocyte as a biopsy tissue in the functional evaluation of vitamin adequacy. J.A.M.A., 187:762, 1964. Also correspondence. J. Nutr., 86:319, 1965.

Burch, H. B., et al. Nutrition survey and tests in Bataan, Philippines. J. Nutr., 42:9, 1950.

Conference on Beriberi, sponsored by World Health Organization and other organizations, Kinney, T. D., and Follis, R. H., Jr., eds. Fed. Proc., 17 (Suppl. 2):3, 1958.

Davis, R. A., and Wolf, A. Infantile beriberi associated with Wernicke's encephalopathy. Pediatrics, 21:409, 1958.

Holt, L. E., Jr. The thiamine requirement of man. Fed. Proc., 3:171, 1944.

—— and Najjar, V. A. The clinical diagnosis of deficiencies of thiamine, riboflavin and niacin. J. Lancet, 63:11, 1943.

—— et al. The thiamine requirement of the normal infant. I. Nutrition. 37:53, 1949.

—— and Snyderman, S. E. The influence of dietary fat on thiamine loss from the body. J. Nutr., 56:495, 1955.

Horwitt, M. K., et al. Investigations of Human Requirements for B Complex Vitamins. Bull. 116, National Research Council, Washington, D.C., 1948.

Vedder, E. B. The pathology of beriberi. J.A.M.A., 110:893, 1938.

RIBOFLAVIN DEFICIENCY

Foy, H. Effect of riboflavin deficiency on bone marrow function and protein metabolism of baboons. Brit. J. Nutr., 18:307, 1964.

Hills, O. W. Clinical aspects of dietary depletion of riboflavin. Arch. Int. Med., 87:682, 1951.

Holt, L. E., Jr. Studies of B Vitamin Requirements of Infants. Currents in Nutrition. New York, National Vitamin Foundation, 1950.

Horwitt, M. K., et al. Effects of dietary depletion of riboflavin. J. Nutr., 39:357, 1949.

——— et al. Correlation of urinary excretion of riboflavin with dietary intake and symptoms of ariboflavinosis. J. Nutr., 41:247, 1950.

Sebrell, W. H., and Butler, R. E. Riboflavin deficiency in man; preliminary note. Pub. Health Rep., 53: 2282, 1938.

Snyderman, S. E., et al. The minimum riboflavin requirement of the infant. J. Nutr., 39:219, 1949.

Sydenstricker, V. P. The clinical manifestations of nicotinic acid and riboflavin deficiency. Ann. Int. Med., 14:1499, 1941.

NIACIN DEFICIENCY

Belavady, B., Srikantia, S. G., and Gopalan, C. The effect of the oral administration of leucine on the metabolism of tryptophan. Biochem. J., 87:652, 1963.

Brown, R. R., Yess, N., Price, J. M., et al. Vitamin B_6 depletion in man: urinary excretion of quinolinic acid and niacin metabolites. J. Nutr., 87:419, 1965.

Elvehjem, C. A., Madden, R. J., Strong, S. M., and Woolley, G. W. Relation of nicotinic acid and nicotinic acid amide to canine black tongue. J. Amer. Chem. Soc., 59:1767, 1937.

Goldberger, J., and Tanner, W. F. Amino-acid deficiency is probably the primary etiological factor in pellagra. Pub. Health Rep., 37:462, 1922.

Goldsmith, G. A. Niacin: antipellagra factor, hypocholesterolemic agent. J.A.M.A., 194:167, 1965.

Krehl, W. A., Teply, L. J., Sarma, P. S., and Elvehjem, C. A. Growth-retarding effect of corn in nicotinic acid-low rations and its counteraction by tryptophane. Science, 101:489, 1945.

Nishizuka, Y., and Hayaishi, O. Studies on the biosynthesis of nicotinamide-adenine-dinucleotide. J. Biol. Chem., 238:3369, 1963.

Truswell, A. S., Hansen, J. D. L., and Wannenburg, P. Plasma tryptophan and other amino acids in pellagra. Amer. J. Clin. Nutr., 21:1314, 1968.

PYRIDOXIN

Harris, R. S., and Wool, I. G., eds. International Symposium on Vitamin B_6. Vitamins and Hormones. New York, Academic Press, Inc., 1964, Vol. 22, pp. 359-885.

Kelsall, M. A., ed. Vitamin B_6 in metabolism of the nervous system. Ann. N.Y. Acad. Sci., 166:1-364, 1969.

——— Report of the Committee on Nutrition. American Academy of Pediatrics. Vitamin B_6 requirements in man. Pediatrics, 38:1068-1076, 1966.

Sebrell, W. H., Jr., and Harris, R. S., eds. The Vitamins, 2nd ed. New York, Academic Press, Inc., 1968, Vol. 2, pp. 1-117.

FOLIC ACID DEFICIENCY

Flexner, J. M., and Hartmann, R. C. Megaloblastic anemia associated with anticonvulsant drugs. Amer. J. Med., 28:386, 1960.

Herbert, V. Experimental nutritional folate deficiency in man. Trans. Ass. Amer. Physicians, 75:307, 1962.

Luhby, A. L., Cooperman, J. M., and Teller, D. N. Histidine metabolic loading test to distinguish folic acid deficiency from vitamin B_{12} in megaloblastic anemias. Proc. Soc. Exp. Biol. Med., 101:350, 1959.

Vilter, R. W. Folic Acid. In Modern Nutrition in Health and Disease, 3rd ed., M. G. Wohl and R. S. Goodhart, eds. Philadelphia, Lea & Febiger, 1964, p. 409.

Welch, A. D., and Nichol, C. A. Water soluble vitamins concerned with one- and two-carbon intermediates. Ann. Rev. Biochem., 21:633, 1952.

Woodruff, C. W., Peterson, J. E., and Darby, W. J. Citrovorum factor and folic acid in treatment of megaloblastic anemia of infancy. Proc. Soc., Exp. Biol. Med., 77:16, 1951.

Zalusky, R., and Herbert, V. Failure of formamino glutamic acid (FIGLU) excretion to distinguish vitamin B_{12} deficiency from nutritional folic acid deficiency. J. Clin. Invest., 40:1091, 1961.

SCURVY

Barlow, T. On cases described as "acute rickets" which are probably a combination of scurvy and rickets, scurvy being an essential and rickets a variable element. Medico-Chirurgical tr. 66:159, 1883; reprinted in Arch. Dis. Child., 10:223, 1935.

Butler, A. M., and Cushman, M. Distribution of ascorbic acid in the blood and its nutritional significance. J. Clin. Invest., 19:459, 1940.

Crandon, J. H., Lund, C. C., and Dill, D. B. Experimental human scurvy. New Eng. J. Med., 223:353, 1940.

Dogramaci, I. Scurvy; a survey of 241 cases. New Eng. J. Med., 235:185, 1946.

Fabro, S., and Rinaldini, L. M. Loss of ascorbic acid synthesis in embryonic development. Develop. Biol., 11:468, 1965.

Follis, R. H., Jr., Park, E. A., and Jackson, D. The prevalence of scurvy at autopsy during the first 2 years of age. Bull. Hopkins Hosp., 87:569, 1950.

Gabuzda, G. J., Phillips, G. B., Schilling, R. F., and Davidson, C. S. Metabolism of pteroylglutamic acid and citrovorum factor in patients with scurvy. J. Clin. Invest., 31:756, 1952.

Hamil, B. M., Reynolds, L. Poole, M. W., and Macy, I. G. Minimal vitamin C requirement of artificially fed infants: A study of four hundred and twenty-seven children under a controlled dietary regimen. Amer. J. Dis. Child., 56:561, 1938.

Hess, A. F. Scurvy, Past and Present. Philadelphia and London, Lippincott, 1920.

Hoad, J., Burns, C. A., and Hodges, R. E. Sjogren's syndrome in scurvy. New Eng. J. Med., 282:1120, 1970.

Jackson, D., and Park, E. A. Congenital scurvy: a case report. J. Pediat., 7:741, 1935.

Jonxis, J. H. P., and Huisman, T. H. J. Aminoaciduria and ascorbic acid deficiency. Pediatrics, 14:238, 1954.

Laurin, I. Some ascorbic acid saturation tests on infants. Acta Paediat. Scand., 20:352, 1938.

McIntosh, R. Infantile scurvy (Barlow's Disease). Brennemann's Practice of Pediatrics. Hagerstown, Md., W. F. Prior Company, 1959, Vol. I, Ch. 35.

Morris, J. E., Harpur, E. R., and Goldbloom, A. The metabolism of 1-tyrosine in infantile scurvy. J. Clin. Invest., 29:325, 1950.

Park, E. A., Guild, H. G., Jackson, D., and Bond, M. The recognition of scurvy with especial reference to the early x-ray changes. Arch. Dis. Child. 10:265, 1935.

Symposium on Vitamin C. Ann. N.Y. Acad. Sci., 92:1-332, 1961.

Woodruff, C. W. Infantile scurvy; the increasing incidence of scurvy in the Nashville area. J.A.M.A., 161:448, 1956.

Zannoni, V. G., Jacoby, S. E., Malamasta, S. E., and LaDu, B. N. The effect of folic acid in tyrosine metabolism in guinea pigs. J. Biol. Chem., 237:3506, 1962.

3.5
CALCIUM METABOLISM

HAROLD E. HARRISON

Bone and the Metabolism of Calcium, Phosphate, and Magnesium

Bone is a complex solid system made up of an organic fibrillar matrix into which is incorporated a hard, crystalline mineral. This provides the combination of tensile and compressive strength which makes bone an excellent structural material for support of body weight and muscle pull. In addition there is a cellular component and bone is a growing, living tissue which remodels and reshapes itself by reaction to the forces which act upon it. The bone cells not only function to alter the size and shape of the bone but by their metabolic activity alter the rate of formation and dissolution of bone crystals. The skeleton thus can serve as a reservoir of calcium, magnesium, phosphate, and carbonate ions which through the influence of bone cell activity and in response to the composition of extracellular fluid can help to maintain stable concentrations of these ions in the body fluids.

Disorders of bone structure can result from abnormalities of the ionic composition of the extracellular fluid influencing directly the mineral phase of the bone; from disorders of the organic matrix, the collagen and protein-polysaccharide complex; and from abnormalities of bone cell metabolism. In the first category are the various forms of hypophosphatemic rickets whether due to vitamin D deficiency or to specific abnormalities of renal tubular transport of phosphate. In the second group are such diseases as osteogenesis imperfecta and scurvy in which collagen formation is impaired. Copper deficiency may also cause rarefaction of bone by impairment of collagen formation. Abnormalities of mucopolysaccharide metabolism also lead to structural changes in bone as in Hurler's syndrome. Metaphyseal dysostosis is also probably a disorder of bone matrix the nature of which is unknown. In the third group of abnormalities of bone cell metabolism could be grouped such disorders as hypoparathyroidism, hypophosphatasia, and possibly osteopetrosis, as well as the myriad of disorders in which growth is disturbed.

The three ions, calcium, phosphate, and magnesium, have in common the feature that a large proportion of the body content of these minerals is sequestered in the solid state in bone. In addition there is an interrelation between the homeostasis of these ions and bone growth and structure.

Calcium is the most abundant mineral in the body but only a tiny fraction of the calcium is in solution in the body fluids. Most of it is present as a crystalline deposit in the skeletal matrix. It has been estimated that the total calcium content of the body of the newborn infant is about 20,000 mg with only 160 mg, or less than 1 percent of the total, in solution in the body fluids. Each day during the first year of life more than 160 mg of calcium can be deposited in the skeleton so that in early infancy the calcium added to bone in one day may equal the total amount in solution in the body fluids at a given time. These values indicate the extent of the turnover of extraskeletal calcium in the body during this period. The relatively large store of calcium in bone is of course available to the body if calcium intake is reduced, so that normally serum calcium does not decrease below physiologic limits even on low intakes. However, hypocalcemia or hypercalcemia may occur in the face of apparently normal bone stores of calcium, since the deposition of calcium in bone or dissolution of calcium from bone is not a simple matter of chemical solubility but also requires metabolic activity of bone cells for the transport of calcium into and out of bone. Vitamin D and parathyroid hormone stimulate metabolic activity of bone cells so as to increase dissolution of bone mineral and matrix at the surface of these cells. The hormone calcitonin, on the other hand, apparently inhibits this function of bone cells leading to reduction of bone mineral solubilization and hypocalcemia. The importance of calcitonin in calcium homeostasis in the mammal is not yet established. The other tissue which plays a major role in the regulation of calcium metabolism is the intestinal mucosa. The absorption of calcium is in part dependent on the calcium intake and other factors in the diet, but the efficiency of calcium absorption is variable and is influenced by vitamin D, by the age of the subject, being greater in the young growing subject, and by other factors as yet undetermined. Kidney function plays only an indirect role in the control of serum calcium levels in contrast to the major role of the kidney in regulation of the concentrations of other ions in the body fluids. Renal tubular reabsorption of calcium is usually fairly complete, and urine calcium is ordinarily less than 2 percent of the filtered calcium. If the calcium load presented to the kidney is too great, renal injury may result due to hypercalciuria and precipitation of calcium in tubules and peritubular spaces or in the outflow tract. In addition, hypercalcemia produces renal vasoconstriction and glomerular damage. The important control of serum calcium levels is accomplished by intestinal absorption of calcium and by the balance between the uptake and feedback of calcium between the skeleton and the body fluids.

The concentration of calcium ion in extracellular fluid is of physiologic importance in systems other than those concerned with bone mineral deposition and resorption. Calcium ions participate in the reactions leading to fibrin formation; they are also essential in the maintenance of rhythmic cardiac muscle contraction, in the sequences of skeletal muscle contraction and relaxation, and in the initiation and transmission of the electrical impulse in nerve cells and fibers. For many of these functions, the concentration of calcium ion required is so low that these processes continue despite considerable reduction of extracellular calcium ion concentration. The increased excitability of the nervous system seen in tetany, results when the ionized calcium is decreased to about half the normal value. Changes in cardiac muscle function also may occur at this stage as shown by a prolonged QT interval in the ECG, and in rare instances partial heart block. Cardiac arrhythmia associated with hypocalcemia can be accentuated by increase of extracellular potassium.

Determination of the calcium ion concentration of serum is possible but not convenient. Most clinical laboratories determine only total serum calcium, which includes undissociated calcium proteinate and the small amount of calcium chelated with citrate and other organic acids. At normal levels of serum protein about 45 percent of the total calcium in serum is bound to protein, chiefly albumin. This fraction of protein-bound nondiffusible, and dissociated calcium is proportional to the concentration of serum protein. The total serum calcium can be reduced to 7.5 mg percent in the hypoalbuminemic patient, or elevated above 11 mg percent in a dehydrated patient with increased serum albumin concentration without abnormality of the ionized calcium level. The total serum calcium concentration under physiologic conditions is 10.0 ± 0.5 mg per ml which is approximately the same in the growing child as in the adult.

Plasma inorganic phosphate is almost entirely in the ionized diffusible form although a small fraction is bound, particularly in hyperphosphatemic states, presumably as an undissociated calcium phosphate protein complex. The concentration of intracellular phosphate, present chiefly as organic phosphoric esters, is much greater than that in the extracellular fluid. Intestinal uptake of phosphate, formation and resorption of the bone salt, and movement of phosphate into and out of cells are all factors in the control of plasma inorganic phosphate concentrations; however, a major homeostatic function is provided through renal tubular regulation of phosphate excretion in urine. In a child with a serum inorganic phosphate concentration of 5 mg/100 ml and a glomerular filtration rate of 70 ml/minute or approximately 100 liters/24 hours, the rate of excretion of phosphate in glomerular filtrate is 5,000 mg/24 hours which is greatly in excess of the amount available from the diet. Most of this phosphate must be retrieved by the renal tubules if the content of phosphate in the body is to be maintained and increased. If renal tubular reabsorption of phosphate is reduced, serum inorganic phosphate must drop until the rate of filtration of phosphate is reduced to that which the renal tubule can handle. Conversely, if glomerular filtration is reduced and renal tubular uptake of phosphate is unchanged, serum inorganic phosphate concentration will rise until a balance is again achieved. Renal hypophosphatemia or hyperphosphatemia result therefore from imbalance of glomerular filtration rate and rate of renal tubular reabsorption of phosphate. Depression of the glomerular filtration rate to less than 20 percent of the normal value will be associated with a rise of serum inorganic phosphate unless the intake or intestinal absorption of phosphate is severely limited. The normal range of serum phosphate concentrations varies with age and growth phase as shown in Table 15. The differences between values in the infant and adult depend upon the relative magnitudes of tubular reabsorption of phosphate and glomerular filtration rates at different ages. Pituitary growth hormone increases tubular transport of phosphate independently of parathyroid hormone. The effects of parathyroid hormone and vitamin D on serum phosphate concentration are discussed elsewhere.

Acute hypophosphatemia can occur during periods of starvation, especially in patients who are being maintained on intravenous fluids. Cell phosphate is maintained at the expense of extracellular phosphate under these conditions. Administration of glucose leads to uptake of phosphate by the cell causing further depression of serum phosphate which persists if no phosphate is available from the diet. This phenomenon is easily seen in the subject with diabetic ketosis treated with glucose and insulin. Although the serum inorganic phosphate may drop to exceedingly low levels there is no evidence of any physiologic abnormality directly associated with transient hypophosphatemia. Incorporation of inorganic phosphate into intravenous solutions has been recommended but the need for it has not been demonstrated. Chronic hypophosphatemia is of course of major physiologic significance since the rate of crystallization of bone mineral in matrix is depend-

TABLE 15. *Variation of Serum Phosphate and Magnesium with Age* [*]

Age Group	P	Mg
	mg/100 ml	
Premature infants	7.9 ± 0.28	1.70 ± 0.10
Newborns—full term	6.1 ± 0.33	1.81 ± 0.06
1-10 years	4.6 ± 0.16	2.25 ± 0.07
Adults	3.5 ± 0.19	2.41 ± 0.05

[*]From unpublished data of Harrison. All values mean ± SE of the mean.

ent upon the concentration of inorganic phosphate. The crystalline phase of bone mineral is hydroxyapatite with the basic formula $Ca_{10}(PO_4)_6(OH)_2$. The formation of bone mineral depends not only on the concentration of Ca^{++} but also that of inorganic phosphate (P_i). Formation of bone mineral can occur only when the product of $Ca^{++} \times P_i$ is sufficiently high to permit crystallization of hydroxyapatite from extracellular fluid on a template provided by the organic matrix of cartilage or bone. A high concentration of P_i therefore favors movement of Ca^{++} into the solid phase while a low concentration of P_i keeps Ca^{++} in body fluids. Chronic hypophosphatemia can result not only from renal tubular defects causing an excessive urinary excretion of phosphate but also from impaired absorption of phosphate. Iatrogenic hypophosphatemia has been observed as a result of excessive intake of antacids containing aluminum hydroxide, which forms insoluble aluminum phosphate and prevents intestinal absorption of phosphate. In adults this form of hypophosphatemia has been associated with muscle weakness.

Magnesium, like phosphate, is an important intracellular solute as well as a component of insoluble bone crystal. About 40 percent of body magnesium is in tissue cells and about 60 percent in bone mineral. The intracellular magnesium is an indispensable cofactor of cell enzyme systems and is not readily released to maintain serum magnesium concentrations. Skeletal magnesium, therefore, is the important buffer which releases or takes up magnesium in response to changes in extracellular concentration of this ion. About two-thirds of plasma magnesium is ionized, the remainder being protein-bound. The total serum magnesium concentration in normal subjects ranges between 1.8 to 2.5 mg per 100 ml. There is a slight age effect with somewhat lower average values in infants than in adults as indicated in Table 15. The evidence suggests that bone magnesium is present at the surface of the bone crystal like CO_3 and citrate and that bone magnesium is in equilibrium with extracellular Mg^{++} ion concentrations.

Rickets and Osteomalacia

Rickets and osteomalacia are disorders of bone mineralization in which osteoblastic activity and the production of bone matrix continue; however, a lag in the rate of mineralization of the matrix results in accumulation of unmineralized matrix. These physiologic disturbances produce rickets in the growing child; in the adult the same process results in osteomalacia. The most important physiologic alteration in rickets and osteomalacia is a deficiency of inorganic phosphate in the extracellular fluids with or without an associated deficiency of calcium.

VITAMIN D DEFICIENCY RICKETS. Vitamin D is a generic term for a group of steroids the most important of which are cholecalciferol, vitamin D_3, and ergocalciferol, vitamin D_2. The natural source of vitamin D for the human is the cholecalciferol produced in the skin by exposure to shortwave ultraviolet radiation of sunshine which activates 7-dehydrotachysterol. The conversion of ergosterol to vitamin D_2 by similar ultraviolet radiation is the source of the relatively inexpensive vitamin D used in enriched milk and vitamin concentrates. Neither cow's milk nor human milk ordinarily contains appreciable quantities of vitamin D (Table 16), which explains the once high incidence of rickets in infants living under climatic conditions in which the necessary exposure of the skin to the shortwave ultraviolet radiation of sunshine was limited. Rickets has become a rare disease in those areas in which oral administration of vitamin D, usually in the form of enriched milk, has effectively eliminated dependence of the infant on sunshine.

Whether it is in the form of endogenously produced cholecalciferol or of ingested cholecalciferol or ergocalciferol, vitamin D undergoes a metabolic transformation before it is physiologically active. The first step is hydroxylation at C-25 in the side chain resulting in 25-hydroxy vitamin D. In the rat and very likely in man this hydroxylation occurs chiefly if not exclusively in the liver. The 25-OH compound is taken up by intestinal mucosa and probably other target cells such as bone and renal tubular cells. In the intestinal mucosa there is further oxidation of the A ring resulting in a more polar compound which complexes with nuclear chromatin and results in the activation of DNA mediated mRNA synthesis and induction of a protein or proteins which mediate the action of vitamin D on transcellular movement of calcium and phosphate.

The various metabolic steps in the activation of vitamin D offer possibilities of inborn or acquired errors of vitamin D metabolism which might result in forms of rickets and osteomalacia refractory to ordinary vitamin D treatment. At present there is no definite genetically determined defect of vitamin D metabolism to explain primary hypophosphatemic vitamin D resistant rickets or vitamin D dependent (pseudovitamin D deficiency rickets). However, two acquired forms of increased vitamin D requirement

TABLE 16. *Amounts of Vitamin D Available in Foods, Including Fish Liver Oil*

Human milk	0 to 10 U/100 ml	Herring	1,500 U/100 g
Cow's milk	0.3 to 4 U/100 ml	Mackerel	1,800 U/100 g
Butter	35 U/100 g	Canned salmon	300 U/100 g
Egg yolk	25 U/average yolk	Canned tuna	250 U/100 g
Calf liver	15 U/100 g	Canned sardines	600 U/100 g
		Cod liver oil	175 U/100 g

may result from a block of 25-hydroxylation in the liver. One is that due to diffuse liver disease such as neonatal hepatitis or the liver injury of biliary atresia. The relative refractoriness to vitamin D of patients with severe renal insufficiency resulting in intestinal malabsorption of calcium might also be due to inhibition of 25-hydroxylation. When 25-hydroxycholecalciferol becomes available, it may be possible to answer these questions by observing its effect on the calcium metabolism of patients with hepatic and renal disease. It may also be of value in the prevention of rickets, hypocalcemia, and secondary hyperparathyroidism in such patients.

Physiology of Vitamin D. The active vitamin D metabolite is required for the efficient absorption of calcium and phosphate from the intestine and also for the efficient conservation of phosphate by the renal tubule. Whether the latter action is a direct effect of vitamin D or results indirectly from suppression of parathyroid hormone output is still being argued. The net result of lack of vitamin D is a decrease in the concentrations of both calcium and phosphate ion in extracellular fluids so that their ionic concentrations are inadequate for mineralization of bone matrix. The deficiency of phosphate ion is the more critical and if the hypophosphatemia is marked the serum calcium ion concentration may remain in the normal range because of markedly decreased uptake of calcium phosphate by bone. A secondary effect of the calcium and phosphate deficiency is an overproliferation of osteoblasts possibly in response to the deformation produced in the structurally weak bone. The elevated alkaline phosphatase activity in serum in vitamin D deficiency represents release of this enzyme from the osteoblasts. An additional manifestation of vitamin D deficiency is a generalized amino-aciduria due to abnormality of renal tubular reabsorption of amino acids. This renal amino-aciduria resembles that seen as a result of renal tubular injury in cystine storage disease, lead poisoning, or Wilson's disease. It has been suggested that the amino-aciduria of vitamin D deficiency is a manifestation of excess parathyroid hormone.

The hypocalcemia of vitamin D deficiency is due not only to poor absorption of calcium from the intestine but also to failure of response of the bone cells to parathyroid hormone. There is experimental evidence that full expression of the action of parathyroid hormone does not occur in the vitamin D deficient subject. In chronic vitamin D deficiency rickets, hypocalcemia is less pronounced as serum inorganic phosphate levels decrease to very low levels. However, a febrile illness or starvation with liberation of tissue phosphate and consequent increase of extracellular phosphate can precipitate hypocalcemia in the rachitic child. This explains the frequent association of tetany with infections in patients with vitamin D deficiency rickets.

Pathology. The morphologic changes in the rachitic bones have been described in detail by Park and by Follis. At the epiphyses of the growing long bones there is proliferation and maturation of the cartilage cells. The columns of cartilage cells are surrounded by matrix in which mineral is deposited resulting in a uniform zone of calcified cartilage at the junction of the bone and cartilage. Capillaries from the bony side invade the degenerating cartilage

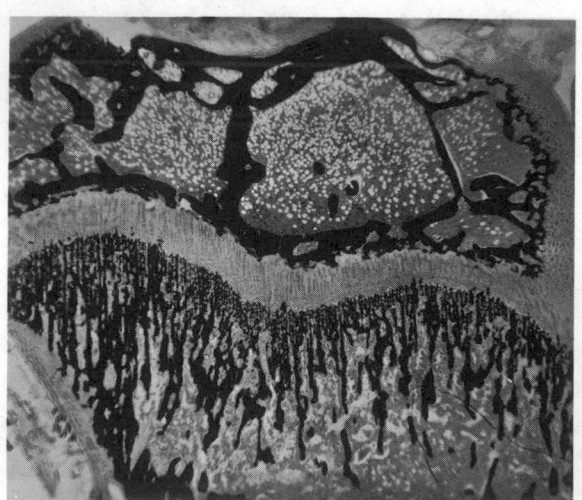
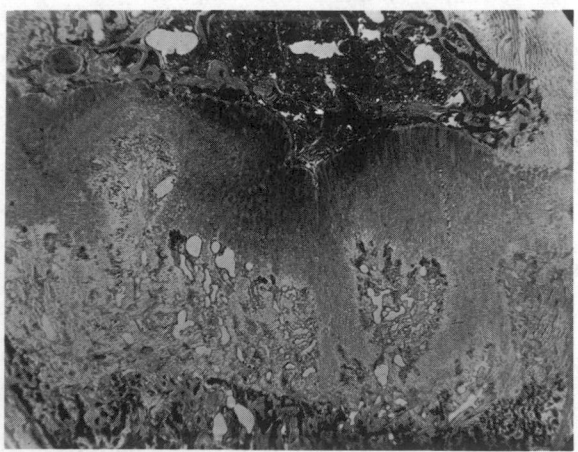

Fig. 15. Morphology of rachitic intermediate zone as seen in experimentally induced rickets of rat. The sections are stained by the Von Kosa method which stains the bone mineral black. Left, tibia of normal rat. The narrow regular zone of cartilage separating the epiphyseal plate of metaphysis from the center of ossification in the epiphysis is well demonstrated. The cartilage plate is composed of orderly rows of cartilage cells embedded in the matrix, and the epiphyseal plate is formed by a regular band of calcified matrix. Right, tibia of rachitic rat. The broad, irregular, rachitic intermediate zone is composed of degenerating cartilage, islands of capillaries, osteoblasts, and unmineralized osteoid. At the very bottom the bony trabeculae forming the irregular epiphyseal margin of the metaphysis are seen.

cells forming tunnels in the calcified matrix and osteoblasts which penetrate along with the capillaries deposit osteoid, i.e., the organic matrix of bone. The osteoid in turn is mineralized as the calcified cartilage matrix is resorbed. There is thus an orderly deposition of layer upon layer of new bone with continuous resorption and remodeling of the bone until the final stable structure is achieved. In rickets the sequence of events is disturbed starting with failure of calcification of the cartilage matrix. The capillaries invade the degenerating cartilage in a highly haphazard and irregular pattern and proliferating osteoblasts form osteoid which accumulates without being mineralized. A broad zone of proliferative cartilage and of osteoid develops in which bone mineral is irregularly deposited. This rachitic intermediate zone or metaphysis is a bulky mass consisting of cartilage, invading blood vessels, osteoblasts, fibroblasts, and marrow elements (Fig. 15). Islands of uncalcified cartilage covered with osteoid are found instead of the regular arrangement of chondroosseous trabeculae. This rachitic intermediate zone does not possess the rigidity of the normal bone cartilage junction. It is compressed and deformed by pressure and extends laterally producing the knobby ends of the bones characteristic of rickets. Much of the deformity of the long bones in rickets

can be explained in terms of the bending and twisting of the yielding rachitic metaphysis. The angulation of the lower end of the tibia, for example, results from the posterior displacement of the epiphysis by muscle pull due to the lack of structural resistance of the rachitic intermediate zone. In the shaft the bone trabeculae are covered with layers of unmineralized osteoid. The volume of bone is reduced while there is an increased volume of uncalcified organic matrix. Poorly mineralized layers of osteoid are also deposited subperiosteally. The bone shaft lacks rigidity and is bent by muscle pull or weight bearing and in severe rickets may be easily fractured. As the process becomes chronic, however, the bone shaft becomes considerably thickened by deposition of excessive matrix with partial mineralization. The failure of mineralization of the organic matrix is also seen in the membranous bones of the skull and the pelvis and bodies of the vertebrae causing the characteristic coarse almost cystic structure of these bones.

Roentgenographic Findings. The anatomic changes described above produce characteristic alterations in the gross structure of bone which can be visualized by radiographic examination. The structural abnormalities of bone which can be readily detected by roentgenogram are relatively late

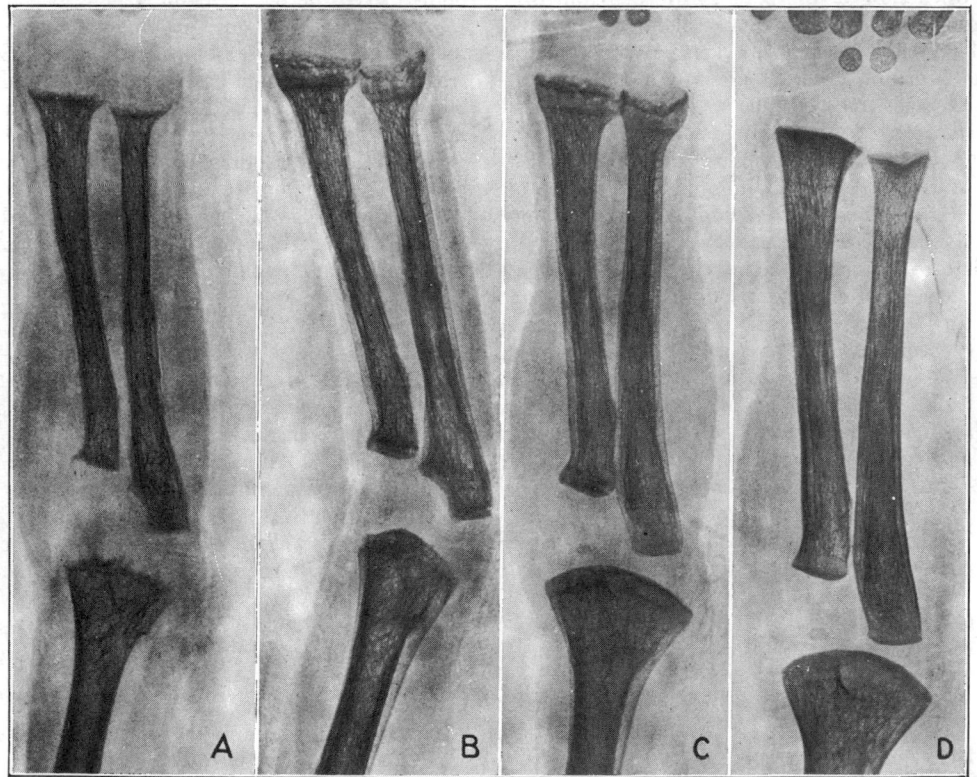

Fig. 16. Roentgen-ray appearance of the bones in advanced rickets, showing typical healing. A. Active rickets. B. Healing in progress after 27 days' treatment, showing new line of calcification in metaphyses. C. Healing after 34 days' treatment; dense lines of calcification; increase in periosteal calcification. D. Complete healing after three months. (From Special Report Series No. 77, Med. Res. Council, London, 1923. By permission of Her Britannic Majesty's Stationery Office.)

changes, however, and the histologic and biochemical disorders of rickets may exist before there is visible change in gross bone structure. Among the roentgenographic changes are: an increased width of the uncalcified portion of the bone between the center of ossification in the epiphyses and the end of the bony metaphysis; irregularity of the epiphyseal plate and its distortion by pressure so that there is cupping of the ends of the bone with projection of processes of mineralized tissue into the rachitic intermediate zone, forming spurs and an irregular fringe effect; a coarse trabecular structure of the shaft of the bone due to the increased volume of nonmineralized matrix surrounding the trabeculae; and often a layer of poorly mineralized matrix beneath the periosteum, producing the effect of apparent separation of the periosteum from the underlying cortex. These manifestations and the roentgenographic pattern which occurs with healing and mineralization of the osteoid are shown in Figure 16. When healing occurs, new bone is laid down in a more orderly pattern than that of the disorganized structure of rachitic bone, and the demarcation between new normal bone and old rachitic bone may be present for a considerable period of time after healing has been seemingly completed. In addition to the changes described, the deformities of the long bones due to bending and angulation will be visualized in the advanced cases. Marked thickening of the bone can result from overproliferation of osteoid especially along the concave aspect of the tibia in chronic rickets in which periods of partial healing and progression of the active rachitic changes may alternate. In cases of acute severe rickets, green stick fractures may be present.

Clinical Findings. Vitamin D deficiency has its genesis in the first few months of life but a considerable period of time is required before the skeletal changes are sufficiently far advanced to result in visible deformity. The biochemical changes, however, may be present after a few months of deprivation of vitamin D. Hypocalcemic tetany on a rachitic basis may occur as early as 2 to 3 months of age particularly in prematurely born infants. A few instances of so-called congenital rickets have been reported. These infants were born of mothers with osteomalacia who were themselves vitamin D deficient because of both dietary deprivation of vitamin D and lack of exposure to sunshine. Under ordinary living conditions, however, pregnant women receive enough vitamin D either in foods, vitamin supplements, or by skin exposure to sun to provide stores of vitamin D for the fetus. The newborn infant, therefore, has some reserves of vitamin D which may maintain adequate function for several months despite lack of dietary intake after birth.

At the present time most of the infants with nutritional vitamin D deficiency seen in Baltimore are babies who have been breast fed for most of the first year of life and who have not received vitamin D supplements because of the mothers' mistaken notion that breast milk is adequate to meet all nutritional requirements of the infant. The vitamin D content of nonenriched cow's milk is also inadequate but the vast majority of infants fed on cow's milk mixtures now receive milk enriched with vitamin D, either evaporated milk, enriched homogenized milk, or prepared infant feeding mixtures with added vitamin D. Thus vitamin D deficiency in infants fed cow's milk is infrequent at the present time in contrast to the high incidence prevalent before milk was enriched with vitamin D.

In a number of instances the diagnosis of rickets has been made incidentally when affected infants were admitted or seen in the outpatient department because of pneumonia or other infection. The febrile illness may precipitate hypocalcemic tetany with convulsive seizures as the presenting manifestation, or the early deformities of rickets may be noted on examination in the absence of specific complaints. In some instances x-rays of the chest may reveal enough of the bony structure of the humeri to suggest the diagnosis of rickets.

One of the early signs of rickets in the infant under 6 months of age is craniotabes. This phenomenon is the result of thinning of the inner tables of the skull by the pressure of the intracranial contents with failure of remineralization. This thinning is usually most pronounced in the posterolateral portions of the skull. The thin skull bone can be indented like a derby hat or ping pong ball by pressure of the finger, snapping back when the pressure is released. Rachitic craniotabes must be differentiated from physiologic craniotabes, which is usually limited to the bone close to the suture lines particularly the lambdoidal suture and is more likely to be found in infants under 3 months of age. Rachitic craniotabes can be more extensive and is present in somewhat older infants. As the rickets becomes more chronic, the skull bones become thicker with prominence of the frontal and parietal bosses. Growth of the skull bones is delayed so that the fontanelle and sutures remain open longer than usual.

The rachitic rosary is produced by the swelling of the rachitic intermediate zone at the junction of the costal cartilage and the calcified portion of the rib. When extensive, it can be seen as well as felt. Again slight prominence of the costochondral junctions can be felt in normal infants during the first year of life and a tentative diagnosis of rickets made on this basis alone may not be supported by biochemical or roentgenographic studies. In the later stage of rickets the chest deformity is more pronounced with pulling in of the costal cartilages and protrusion of the sternum, producing pigeon breast deformity. The lower portion of the rib cage is also flared out and a depression is produced by the pull of the diaphragm on the yielding rib structure (Harrison's groove). If the rachitic process progresses without treatment, deformity of the vertebral bodies results in scoliosis. This is a late manifestation of chronic progressive rickets.

The deformities of the long bones are initially

knobbing and prominence of the epiphyses particularly at the wrists and the ankles. The increased width of the proliferative cartilage separating the epiphyseal centers of ossification from the shaft of the bone may produce a characteristic abnormality of certain epiphyses such as those of the malleoli, giving the impression of a double epiphysis on palpation. Before weight bearing occurs, the lower end of the tibia may show angulation due to the posterior displacement of the distal epiphysis by a strong pull of the gastrocnemius-soleus muscle group. This angulation is aggravated by the posture of sitting with legs crossed. When weight bearing occurs the femora show lateral bowing with either genu valgus or varus deformity. In addition bowing and medial torsion of the tibiae can occur so that the femora are externally rotated to keep the feet from toeing in. This causes instability of the hip joints with a resulting waddling gait. A waddling gait may also result from a coxa vara deformity. Deformities of the pelvis also occur in rickets and these, of course, have in the past been responsible for serious problems of dystocia in women who had rickets in infancy. Severe vitamin D deficiency can interfere with growth of the tooth buds so that the appearance of deciduous teeth is delayed and the enamel may be hypoplastic when the teeth finally appear. Another manifestation of severe rickets is poor muscle tone. Abdominal distention, lordosis, and difficulty in walking result from this and from skeletal deformity.

The major deformities described above are now rarely seen except in cases of rickets not responsive to ordinary vitamin D therapy. The occasional infants with vitamin D deficiency rickets seen at the present time are usually diagnosed and treated before severe deformities have occurred, or, if undiagnosed, have had spontaneous healing due to increased exposure to sunshine or dietary sources of vitamin D as the infant grows older.

Impaired Intestinal Absorption of Vitamin D. Vitamin D deficiency rickets may develop in infants as the result of defective intestinal absorption of vitamin D despite ordinarily adequate dietary intakes. A variety of disturbances of fat absorption with increased fecal fat loss may be associated with failure of vitamin D absorption. We have observed two male siblings each of whom developed rickets along with signs of vitamin K deficiency at the end of the first year of life. Both infants were found to have increased loss of fatty acids in the stool presumably due to a congenital defect of lipase activity. Despite the evidence of impaired fat absorption neither infant was obviously malnourished nor showed any of the clinical characteristics of the celiac syndrome. In infants with fibrocystic disease of the pancreas, however, vitamin D deficiency has been exceedingly rare despite the disturbance of lipolysis and fat absorption. Exclusion of bile from the intestinal tract, as in biliary atresia, interferes with absorption of vitamin D. Rickets has also

occurred in young infants with infectious hepatitis. This was once thought to be due to impaired vitamin D absorption, but the newer knowledge of vitamin D metabolism suggests that impaired formation of the active metabolite 25-OH vitamin D might be responsible. This is of considerable interest since relatively mild liver disease may cause early rickets in young infants. An illustrative case history is as follows:

J.F. was a male infant admitted at 3 months of age because of jaundice of 2 weeks' duration associated with vomiting and epistaxis. The pertinent findings suggesting a diagnosis of infectious hepatitis were hepatosplenomegaly, jaundice, acholic stools, and the following laboratory data: serum bilirubin, direct 5.8, total 8.5 mg percent; serum glutamic pyruvate transaminase activity, 950 units; cephalin flocculation, 3+. The bilirubinemia and clinical findings gradually cleared over a period of several weeks and the serum glutamic pyruvate transaminase values returned toward normal. Study of the metabolism of the fat-soluble vitamins revealed low levels of carotene and tocopherol in the serum. The concentration of serum calcium was 11.2 mg percent and that of phosphorus was 3.6 mg percent. Roentgenograms of the long bones showed the early evidences of rickets, portrayed in Figure 17, with striking evidence of healing when 600,000 units of vitamin D were given orally. This infant had been fed enriched evaporated milk since the first few days of life so that it must be assumed that the vitamin D deficiency was related to the effects of hepatitis upon absorption or metabolism of vitamin D. In accord with this idea is the finding of evidences of impaired absorption of other fat-soluble vitamins in this infant.

Vitamin D Requirements. The vitamin D requirements of infants and children are satisfied by a daily intake of 400 units either as ergocalciferol (vitamin D_2) or cholecalciferol (vitamin D_3). Evaporated milk and the various modified milk preparations for infant feeding are fortified with vitamin D_2 in the amount of 400 units per can or equivalent quart of whole cow's milk. Homogenized, vitamin D enriched, pasteurized milk also contains 400 units of vitamin D_2 per quart. Infants fed these cow's milk preparations will usually be taking a quart of milk or its equivalent by 2 months of age and will therefore receive the required 400 units. The small, prematurely-born infant presents an exception, however, since his calorie and therefore milk intake will be much less than that of the full-term infant for several months. Low-birth-weight infants should be given a vitamin D supplement in addition to that moiety of vitamin D supplied by the milk so that their total intake is at least 400 units daily. It is not necessary to give premature infants larger amounts of vitamin D than the full-term infant, however, it is important that the breast-fed infant also receive a vitamin D preparation supplying 400 units of vitamin D daily.

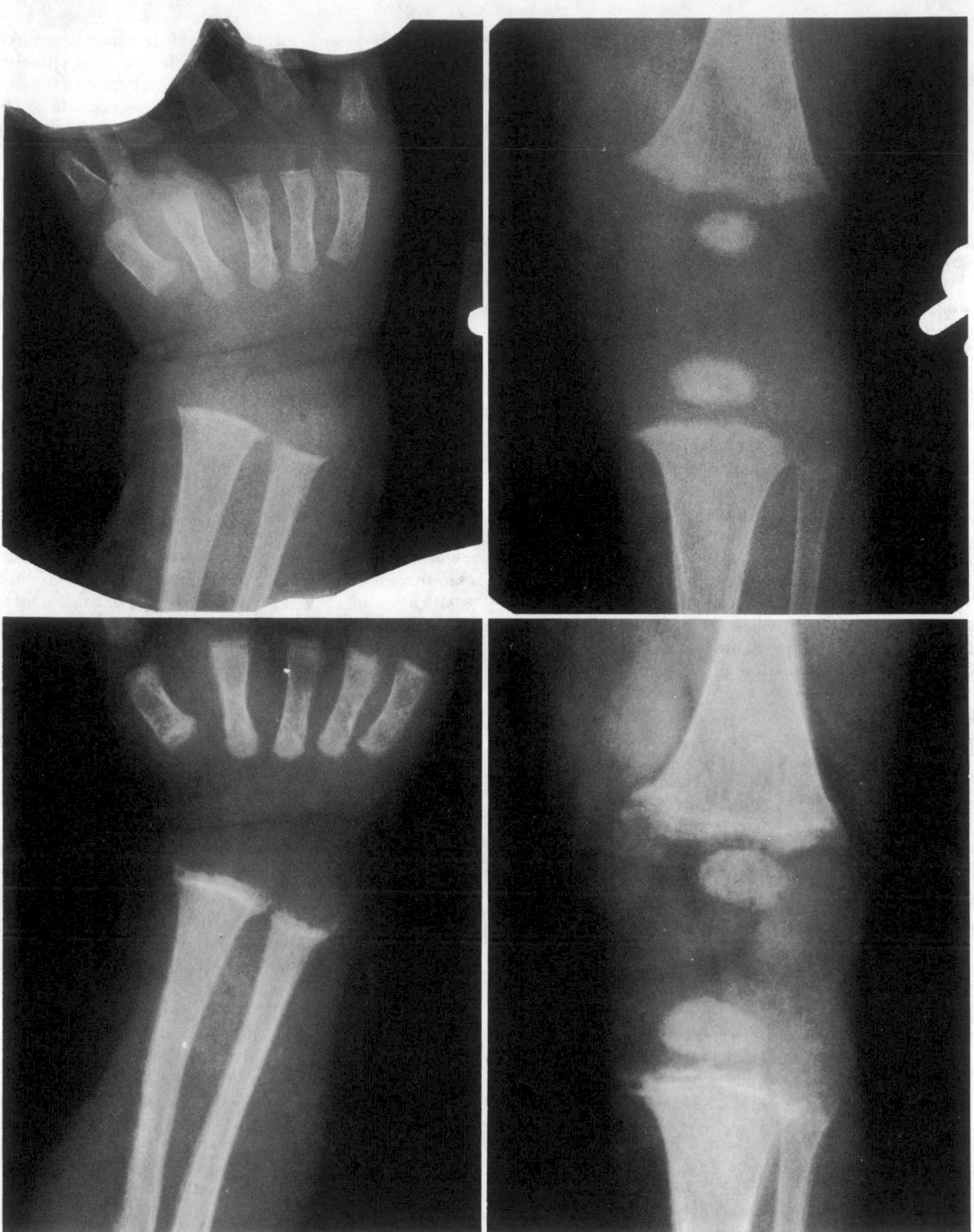

Fig. 17.   Roentgen-ray appearance of the bones in early rickets of infant 3 months of age. The pretreatment findings are minimal and might be overlooked, but following treatment the deposition of bone salt in the rachitic cartilage indicates the extent of the rachitic changes. Top left, wrist—before treatment, showing minimal irregularity of epiphyseal plate. Top right, knee—before treatment, showing increased distance between epiphyseal plate and center of ossification as only evidence of rickets. Bottom left, wrist—14 days after single dose of 600,000 units of vitamin D, showing rapid mineralization of rachitic intermediate zone. Bottom right, knee—14 days after vitamin D treatment. The increased width of the rachitic intermediate zone can be better appreciated now that its mineralization is visualized.

In Europe the practice of giving a young infant a single large dose of vitamin D, usually 600,000 units, has been recommended. Since vitamin D is slowly inactivated or excreted such a dose will provide protective levels for 3 to 6 months, making it unnecessary to provide daily doses of vitamin D. The infant is thus protected should the mother be indifferent or uncooperative in its care. The danger of such a regimen is that these large loads of vitamin D may be repeated, resulting in hypervitaminosis D. Since vitamin D enriched milk can be given to infants without the necessity of additional vitamin supplements, there is no need for the prophylactic use of highly concentrated preparations of vitamin D in large dosage.

The use of prophylactic doses of vitamin D greatly in excess of 400 units per day should be discouraged. In an eagerness to prevent rickets and to promote growth, multivitamin preparations or vitamin D concentrates providing several thousand units of vitamin D a day have sometimes been prescribed. Although there is a considerable variation in tolerance to vitamin D, some children develop evidences of hypervitaminosis D on daily doses which are only moderately in excess of the usual requirement. The entity of "idiopathic hypercalcemia" (see p. 207) possibly represents hypervitaminosis D due to accumulation of the vitamin D at doses of only a few thousand units a day.

Treatment of Vitamin D Deficiency Rickets.

Vitamin D deficiency rickets can be treated with moderately large doses of vitamin D, 10,000 units per day, for 30 to 60 days. This dose can be given in the form of vitamin D_2 in propylene glycol (Drisdol), which is miscible in milk, orange juice, and other fluids, or as an irradiated ergosterol concentrate in oil which can be given by dropper. An alternative method of treatment is to give a massive dose of vitamin D, namely 600,000 units at one time. For this purpose a vitamin D concentrate in oil is required since the propylene glycol solution is too dilute and the large volume of solvent would produce serious side effects, particularly depression and stupor. One advantage of treatment by large dose is that the earliest evidences of healing, elevation of the serum phosphorus level, may be seen within a few days, providing assurance that the problem is not one of increased requirement for vitamin D which would necessitate further study of the underlying problem. Another indication for the use of a large dose is hypocalcemia due to vitamin D deficiency. If a single large dose of vitamin D is given, calcium homeostasis is restored much more rapidly than when treatment consists of moderate daily amounts of vitamin D, thus reducing the period during which there is danger of hypocalcemic tetany. If this complication of rickets does occur it can be treated by the intravenous injection of calcium as the 10 percent solution of calcium gluconate. Five to 10 ml are injected slowly, with monitoring of the heart rate because too rapid elevation of plasma

calcium causes bradycardia and even cardiac arrest.

NONVITAMIN D DEFICIENCY RICKETS. The imbalance between growth of bone matrix and its mineralization which is characteristic of rickets and osteomalacia can also result from metabolic abnormalities which suppress or make impossible the normal function of vitamin D. A variety of forms of rickets may result, therefore, which are not due to lack of vitamin D or failure of its absorption.

Vitamin D Dependent Rickets (Pseudo-Vitamin D Deficiency; Increased Requirement for Vitamin D). It has long been recognized that occasional children require much greater amounts of vitamin D to prevent rickets than the standard 400 units daily preventive dose. Prader et al. collected several such cases in which there was a familial occurrence with a genetic pattern indicating transmission as an autosomal recessive. (In the original report an autosomal dominant gene was suggested but this was subsequently corrected.) Rickets appears late in these patients beyond the first year of life with characteristic deformities and radiographic changes. A striking feature is the frequent reduction of serum calcium concentration sometimes to tetany levels. The serum phosphate concentration is reduced but not as uniformly or strikingly as in primary hpyophosphatemic rickets. Like patients with ordinary vitamin D deficiency, the children with vitamin D dependent rickets show a generalized renal amino-aciduria which is another differentiating point from primary hypophosphatemia in which amino-aciduria does not occur. Treatment of the increased requirement for vitamin D is by the administration of large amounts of vitamin D in doses which must be determined for the individual patient. Some patients have responded to 5,000 to 15,000 units of vitamin D whereas others have needed considerably larger amounts. When sufficient amounts of vitamin D are given the serum calcium and phosphate concentrations return to normal and the renal amino-aciduria disappears. The alkaline phosphatase activities are also restored to normal and radiographic healing occurs. It is important to continue vitamin D treatment at a level which will maintain the normal values since discontinuance of treatment will result in relapse, which is the basis of the term vitamin D dependent rickets. The metabolic defect of vitamin D metabolism or response is as yet unknown. Whether 25-hydroxycholecalciferol will be more effective in the treatment of these patients remains to be determined.

Hypophosphatemia of Renal Tubular Origin with Associated Rickets. Impairment of renal tubular reabsorption of phosphate due to intrinsic defects of renal tubular metabolism or to toxic injuries of renal tubule cells causes renal hypophosphatemia. The deficiency of inorganic phosphate in extracellular fluids then results in a reduced rate of deposition of bone mineral in matrix and consequent rickets. The forms of hypophosphatemic rickets not due to vitamin D deficiency may be classified under the heading of primary hypophosphatemia, acquired vitamin D resistant rickets, renal tubular acidosis, and the Fanconi syndrome.

Primary hypophosphatemia (familial vitamin D resistant rickets). This form of rickets is the result of a heredtary metabolic defect which involves the phosphate transport system of the renal tubules and possibly of the intestine so that severe hypophosphatemia results despite vitamin D therapy. A possible interference with calcium transport may also be present but this is responsive to large doses of vitamin D. This defect is usually inherited as a dominant characteristic, so that it may be traced through successive generations and also involve one or more siblings. In most families the inheritance is through a gene on the X chromosome so that the heterozygous females frequently have a milder disease than males with a single abnormal gene. The hereditary pattern may also be that characteristic of an autosomal recessive gene. In an unusual kindred in our clinic the genetic pattern is that of an autosomal dominant. Sporadic cases of a similar physiologic disturbance in infants and children without familial incidence have also been seen.

The severity of the physiologic and pathologic changes may be quite variable and the defect may not be recognized in some members of the family unless they are carefully studied. Hypophosphatemia and short stature may be the only findings. Biochemically the striking features are marked hypophosphatemia, relatively normal serum calcium concentrations, and moderate elevation of serum alkaline phosphatase activity in the rachitic children. Although hypocalcemia does not occur in these patients, a defect of calcium absorption is present, so that stool calcium is high and urine calcium excretion is low. If sufficiently large doses of vitamin D are given, increased efficiency of calcium and phosphate absorption from the intestine can be produced so that serum calcium levels and urine calcium excretion are increased, but the serum phosphorus levels remain abnormally low. This is in contrast to the response of the child with ordinary rickets to physiologic doses of vitamin D. In such children the serum phosphorus rises rapidly to normal levels following small doses of vitamin D, and, if a single large dose of 600,000 units of vitamin D is given, the serum phosphorus may rise to concentrations above the usual average values. Failure of the serum phosphorus concentrations to rise in response to vitamin D has suggested that the fundamental defect in resistant rickets is impairment of renal tubular reabsorption of phosphate. Studies of renal excretion of phosphate in such patients during periods of phosphate infusion do indicate that renal tubular reabsorption of phosphate is reduced. Renal aminoaciduria is not found in this variety of rickets. It has also been suggested that lack of response to vitamin D could be due to failure of 25-hydroxylation of vitamin D. This seems unlikely but it will be important to test the effect of 25-hydroxycholecalciferol.

The clinical picture is somewhat variable, depending upon the severity of the process. Retardation of growth precedes the appearance of obvious bony deformities of rickets but may not be seen until the child is between 6 and 18 months of age. Short stature and progressive skeletal changes of rickets after the first year of life in infants and children who have received some vitamin D or have been exposed to sunshine should suggest this syndrome. The roentgenographic changes are those of chronic rickets modified by the retardation of bone growth (Fig. 18).

If vitamin D alone is used in the treatment of this form of rickets extremely large doses of the vitamin, 50,000 to 250,000 units daily, may be needed. No apparent difference in response has been found with vitamin D_2 (ergocalciferol) or vitamin D_3 (cholecalciferol). Interestingly enough a related sterol, dihydrotachysterol, in amounts of 0.5 to 2 mg per day will also produce healing of familial vitamin D resistant rickets, although this compound has considerably less antirachitic potency in true vitamin D deficiency rickets than ergocalciferol or cholecalciferol. Frequently familial vitamin D resistant rickets can be treated successfully with large doses of vitamin D, but treatment is difficult and requires extremely close supervision of the patient, since the amounts of vitamin D given are close to the toxic range. The toxic quantity of vitamin D in these subjects is not necessarily greater than in normal individuals, despite their marked resistance to the physiologic effects of the vitamin. Inadequate dosage results in failure of complete healing and deformity but excessive dosage causes hypercalcemia and kidney injury which may be irreversible. Treatment is regulated by serum calcium and urine calcium determinations and bone radiographs. A dose of vitamin D which will produce complete radiographic healing without raising serum calcium levels above 11 mg per 100 ml or urine calcium excretion above 200 mg per day is considered optimal. The serum phosphate levels usually remain below normal with this treatment, and elevation of serum phosphate levels above 4 mg per 100 ml may be an indication of renal injury due to hypervitaminosis D. Because of the danger of hypervitaminosis D with vitamin D treatment alone, the addition of large amounts of phosphate to the diet is advised in an effort to increase serum phosphate concentration and hasten healing without increasing the dose of vitamin D to potentially toxic levels. For such treatment phosphate intake of 1.5 to 2.0 g daily in addition to ordinary diet is necessary. This amount of phosphate as a mixture of sodium and potassium phosphates is close to the limit of gastrointestinal tolerance and in some patients produces discomfort and diarrhea.

Following cessation of growth and fusion of epiphyses, the vitamin D dosage can be decreased. However, it is probably desirable to continue vitamin D in amounts of 25,000 to 50,000 units daily

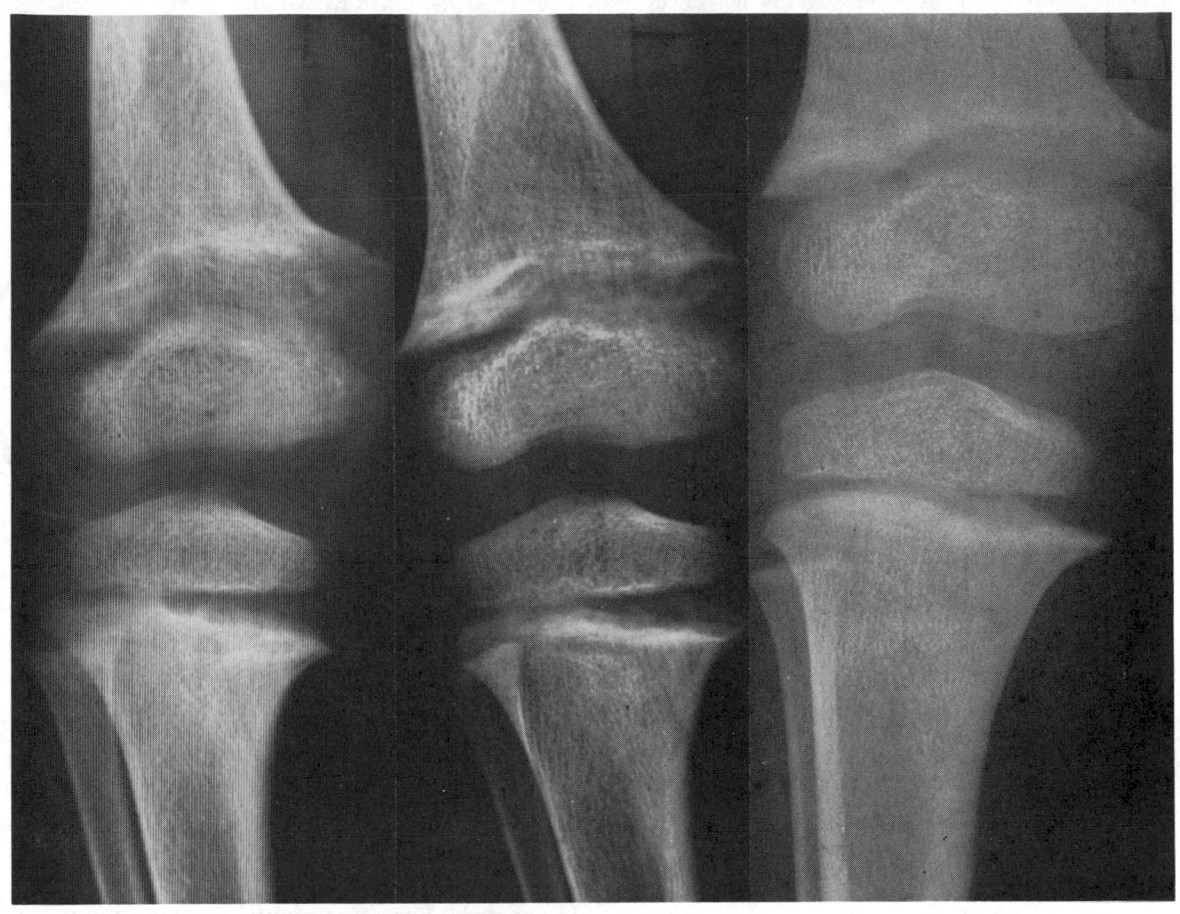

Fig. 18. Roentgenographic findings in 3-year-old patient with hereditary hypophosphatemia. A. Before treatment. B. Following four months of treatment. C. Following 10 months of treatment. The treatment in this case consisted of dihydrotachysterol without added phosphate. (Harrison and Harrison. *Clin. Orthoped.*, 33:147, 1964.)

to prevent the development of osteomalacic changes in late adult life, especially during pregnancy and lactation. Crystalline dihydrotachysterol is now available and can be used instead of vitamin D in the treatment of this disorder. Its major advantage is the lesser cumulative action of this sterol than of vitamin D. If hypercalcemia and hypercalciuria occur as a result of an excessive dose, they disappear much more rapidly if dihydrotachysterol has been given than if the treatment has been with vitamin D.

If the diagnosis is made early, and this may be facilitated by the familial story, adequate treatment with vitamin D and phosphate can usually prevent the deformities and the marked stunting of growth characteristic of the untreated child. Growth retardation is usually not completely overcome, however, despite good roentgenographic healing of rickets. If the diagnosis is not made until the second year of life or later, significant deformities may have developed and healing is so slow that these deformities may progress. Lateral and anterioposterior bow-

ing of the femora with genu valgum, and anterior bowing and medial torsion of the tibiae may cause serious disability. Supracondylar osteotomy may then be required to allow more normal gait as well as for cosmetic reason. Radiographic evidence of healing of the rickets should be obtained before osteotomies are done; if possible osteotomy should be postponed until growth has ceased. It is important to discontinue vitamin D for several weeks prior and subsequent to osteotomy, since if the large doses of vitamin D necessary to produce healing are continued during the period of immobilization, acute hypercalcemia and hypercalciuria are more likely to occur.

Hypophosphatemic vitamin D resistant rickets appearing at adolescence. Only a few instances of this rare entity have been described. In essence these patients show no metabolic defect during infancy and childhood, and growth and muscle power are normal. During adolescence or early adult life, bone and joint pains, swelling of joints, especially the ankles, and difficulty in walking develop. Severe muscle weakness may occur, and in several cases this has been marked enough to suggest a diagnosis of progressive muscular dystrophy. Generalized osteomalacia with Looser-Milkman zones and irregularity of the metaphyseal ends of the bones are seen on radiographic examination. The rachitic and the osteomalacic changes can result in extreme deformities of spine and extremities. Biochemically this syndrome is similar to hereditary hypophosphatemia in that the serum calcium concentrations are in the low normal range, 9 to 10 mg per 100 ml, while the serum phosphate levels are reduced often to less than 2 mg per 100 ml. Serum alkaline phosphatase activity is moderately elevated. Balance studies reveal poor intestinal absorption of calcium and reduced excretion of calcium in urine. Intestinal absorption of phosphate also is diminished, but renal clearances of phosphate are high despite the extremely low serum phosphate levels, indicating a defect in renal tubular reabsorption.

The treatment of these patients is similar to that of familial primary hypophosphatemic vitamin D resistant rickets, i.e., administration of large doses of vitamin D, 200,000 to 500,000 units per day, plus phosphate. Vitamin D_2 or D_3 may be used in equivalent dosage. The problem of vitamin D toxicity is important, since these patients may develop hypercalcemia, hypercalciuria, and renal injury on these dosages of vitamin D, even though the rickets and the osteomalacia may not be completely healed. The dose should be so regulated that the serum calcium is not increased above 11.5 mg per 100 ml and the urine calcium excretion does not exceed 400 mg per day. Striking improvement of symptoms and recalcification of bone can be achieved even though serum phosphorus levels remain below the normal range.

Renal tubular acidosis with rickets and osteomalacia. This syndrome is probably an inborn error of renal tubule cell metabolism. In the majority of the cases reported there has been no familial occurrence, but there have been several examples of siblings with this lesion, suggesting the possibility of inheritance as an autosomal dominant character. The primary biochemical disturbances are discussed elsewhere (Sec. 22.13). Treatment with alkalinizing solutions not only will correct the acidosis but will allow for healing of rickets without administration of large amounts of vitamin D.

If treatment has been started before the rachitic changes become severe, complete healing of the rickets without deformity can be attained. However, in some instances, such deformities as bowing of the femora and tibiae and genu valgum may become marked despite radiographic evidence of healing of the rachitic changes and osteotomy is required for correction of deformity.

The Fanconi syndrome. This name has been applied to a group of clinical states in which the common denominator is renal glycosuria, renal amino-aciduria, and hypophosphatemia with associated rickets and osteomalacia. In this syndrome is found the most obvious suggestion that hypophosphatemia is the result of impaired function of the proximal tubules, since the glycosuria and the amino-aciduria are evidences of proximal renal tubular dysfunction. The renal tubular injury may be the result of diverse agents, either congenital or acquired, so that actually there are a number of distinct forms of the Fanconi syndrome. These are discussed elsewhere (Sec. 22.13). Hypophosphatemia and rickets can be healed with administration of vitamin D, in doses of 25,000 to 50,000 units or more daily. Correction of acidosis is also important (Sec. 3.7).

Intrinsic Disorders of Bone Which Resemble Rickets

There are certain abnormalities of bone metabolism resulting in formation of bone and cartilage matrix in which bone mineral fails to deposit normally despite normal concentrations of calcium and phosphorus in serum. Two such diseases which may be confused with rickets because of similar skeletal deformities and roentgenographic changes are hypophosphatasia and metaphyseal dysostosis.

HYPOPHOSPHATASIA. This is a hereditary disease transmitted by a recessive gene. In the homozygote, tissue and serum alkaline phosphatase activities are markedly reduced. The serum phosphate levels are normal, and the serum calcium concentrations may be normal or irregularly elevated to levels as high as 12 to 15 mg per 100 ml. An interesting, unexplained biochemical marker of this condition is the appearance of large amounts of phosphoethanolamine in the urine. Roentgenograms show marked disorganization of mineralization at the ends of the shafts (Fig. 19). Abnormalities of dentition and of skull growth, with premature fusion of the cranial sutures, may complicate the picture. A severe infantile form exists in which there is failure of mineralization of most of the skeleton. Such infants die shortly after birth. Spontaneous improvement tends to occur in the less severe form as the child grows older. Cortisone therapy has been reported to be associated with improved calcification of the bones.

METAPHYSEAL DYSOSTOSIS. This is a rare disorder presumably of congenital origin. The affected children show progressive deformities of the long bones which mimic those of chronic progressive rickets. The roentgenograms resemble those of resistant rickets. Serum calcium, phosphate, and alkaline phosphatase concentrations are within normal limits, and vitamin D therapy is ineffective. The bony lesions are usually progressive and result in severe deformity although the severity of this disorder varies widely. Pathologically there is an excess of nonmineralized osteoid, but the underlying defect of the matrix is unknown. There is no known definitive treatment, but osteotomy is useful in correcting the deformities of the lower extremities.

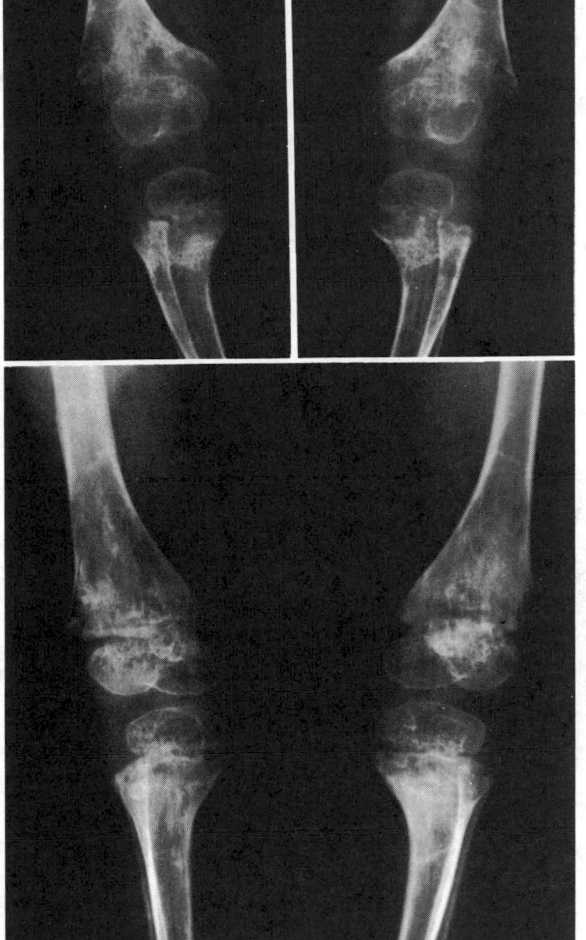

Fig. 19. Hypophosphatasia; roentgenograms of knees. Top, at age 2 years, 2 months. Bottom, at age 4 years, 10 months.

centrate, provided a suggestion from epidemiologic considerations that this disorder represents a form of vitamin D toxicity in infants who are particularly sensitive to amounts of vitamin D which would not be toxic to most infants. However, certain features of the disease, such as low birth weight, abnormalities of facial structure, and defects of the heart and great vessels, suggest that the disorder has its onset in intrauterine life. If vitamin D is the responsible agent, an unusual response of the fetus to the vitamin D levels of the pregnant woman must also be implicated.

The disease presents itself insidiously with "failure to thrive." Anorexia, irritability, vomiting, constipation, and growth failure start in the first months of life. Slow motor development and mental retardation are frequent findings. The facial appearance may be striking, the so-called *elfin facies*, with a depressed nasal bridge, prominent upper lip, receding mandible, high narrow palate, and low-set ears. In later childhood, dental malocclusion, hypoplasia, and caries are common. In the severe forms, renal calcinosis and kidney insufficiency develop with hypertension, proteinuria, and microscopic hematuria. Abnormalities of the great vessels, especially supravalvular aortic stenosis and peripheral pulmonary artery stenosis can also be an integral part of the syndrome. The major clinical manifestation of the aortic lesion is a loud systolic murmur in the first or second interspace to the right and sometimes also to the left of the sternum. There may be evidences of left ventricular hypertrophy. Skeletal roentgenograms reveal increased density of the base of the skull and of the metaphyseal ends of the long bones. There are no changes indicative of hyperparathyroidism. Submetaphyseal rarefaction similar to that seen in hypervitaminosis D has been reported. The serum calcium concentration is elevated whereas that of serum phosphate is usually normal, unless there is renal insufficiency. Elevated urea nitrogen and sometimes hyperchloremic acidosis are found in patients with renal injury. Hypercholesterolemia is also occasionally seen.

Idiopathic hypercalcemia can be differentiated from hyperparathyroidism by the absence of hypophosphatemia; the roentgenographic findings; the clinical picture, particularly the associated facies and cardiac lesions if present; and finally, if necessary, by the response to adrenocorticoids. In the former, the serum calcium concentrations return almost invariably to normal following 7 to 10 days of treatment with cortisol or prednisone whereas the hypercalcemia of hyperparathyroidism is usually refractory.

A puzzling problem is posed by the occasional patient with poor growth, mental retardation, suggestive facies, and the vascular lesions of supravalvular aortic stenosis and also peripheral pulmonic stenosis but with consistently normal serum calcium levels. The possibility that hypercalcemia was present in the early evolution of the disorder has been suggested and in some instances has been reinforced by evidences of renal calcinosis. In other cases, there are no findings to support hypercalcemia, however, and

Idiopathic Hypercalcemia

Idiopathic hypercalcemia of infancy is a mysterious entity in which hypercalcemia, defined by serum calcium concentrations of 12 mg/100 ml or greater, is present without evidence of exposure to known toxic quantities of vitamin D (greater than 2,000 U/kg day for several months), and is not the result of either hyperparathyroidism, tumors secreting parathyroid hormone-like material, metastatic tumor in bone, or sarcoidosis. The apparent increased incidence of this syndrome in England during and after World War II, associated with increased ingestion of vitamin D by infants in the form of a fortified milk product plus cod liver oil or other vitamin D con-the relationship of these cases to idiopathic hypercalcemia remains unsolved.

The treatment of idiopathic hypercalcemia is a diet very low in calcium and elimination of any vitamin D intake. Whether the latter measure should include avoidance of exposure to sunshine is probably only of theoretic importance since the hypercalcemia usually responds to reduction of calcium intake.

A suitable low-calcium feeding mixture for infants, can be made with strained meats as the source of protein with added carbohydrates and vegetable oil. All milk and foods prepared from or with milk are eliminated. High calcium vegetables such as kale, cabbage, and brussels sprouts are avoided, usually without difficulty, since these are not common items of the diet of infants and children. If the hypercalcemia does not respond within 2 weeks of dietary measures, or if severe manifestations of hypercalcemia such as anorexia, hypertension, vomiting, and convulsions are present, cortisol or prednisone in standard "suppressive" doses should be added. Adrenocorticoid therapy can be tapered rapidly after 4 to 6 weeks of full-dose therapy if the serum calcium concentration has decreased to normal and the low-calcium diet is continued. The patient can then be tested at intervals to see if the calcium intake can be increased. When addition of calcium to the food does not cause elevation of serum calcium concentrations the child can resume a standard diet. It is of interest that challenge with vitamins D after recovery from hypercalcemia does not produce an exacerbation. Hyperabsorption of calcium from the intestine is the major factor during the active process and this too eventually ceases since, as mentioned, these children can tolerate a normal calcium intake following recovery. The treatment of the cardiac lesions is discussed in the section on cardiology.

Since increased responsiveness to moderate doses of vitamin D is still the most likely mechanism for the production of idiopathic hypercalcemia it is important that vitamin D dosage in both the pregnant woman and the infant not be excessive. In both groups the daily dose of vitamin adequate to maintain normal vitamin D nutrition is not greater than 400 units. There is no need to exceed this dose except for the unusual patients with special vitamin D requirements, and there is every reason to insist that vitamin D intake for standard nutritional purposes be kept in the range of 400 units daily.

Diseases of the Parathyroid

PHYSIOLOGY. Potent extracts of the parathyroid gland have two major actions: mobilization of calcium and phosphate by dissolution of bone through the metabolic activity of osteoclasts and osteocytes, and enhancement of renal phosphate loss and reduction of serum phosphate levels by inhibition of net renal tubular reabsorption of phosphate. Another effect of parathyroid hormone upon renal tubular function, namely, increased reabsorption of calcium and magnesium has also been shown. Parathyroid hormone has been purified; it is a single polypeptide chain with a molecular weight close to 9,000 and the pure hormone has both calcium-mobilizing and phosphaturic effects. There is evidence that the action of parathyroid hormone is mediated through increased production of cyclic AMP in the target cells responsive to parathyroid hormone. Excessive parathyroid activity results in demineralization of bone and destruction of bone matrix with elevation of serum calcium and reduction of serum phosphate concentrations and increased output of both calcium and phosphate in the urine. Hypercalciuria results from the increased filtered load of calcium despite the action of the hormone on tubular reabsorption of calcium. In some patients with hyperparathyroidism, however, the tubular effect outweighs the increased filtered load and the urine calcium excretion is normal or actually low. Reduced parathyroid activity leads to hypocalcemia and hyperphosphatemia with usually little or no evidence of disturbance of bone salt deposition. Either demineralization of bone or increased bone density has been observed, however, in some instances of hypoparathyroidism; the reason for such differences is unknown. The activity of the parathyroids is controlled by the levels of calcium ion in the body fluids; a deficiency of calcium ion stimulates parathyroid cell hyperplasia and presumably increases hormone output whereas an elevation of calcium ion depresses parathyroid activity. Magnesium ion also participates along with calcium ion, in the control of parathyroid hormone production. In addition to parathyroid hormone another polypeptide hormone is concerned with calcium homeostasis; this is thyrocalcitonin, a hormone secreted by the thyroid. Thyrocalcitonin lowers the serum calcium concentration, apparently by inhibition of bone resorption. Its action therefore is antagonistic to that of parathyroid hormone and its secretion is stimulated by an increased calcium ion concentration.

PRIMARY HYPERPARATHYROIDISM. Primary hyperparathyroidism is rare in childhood but a few cases have been reported due either to a solitary parathyroid adenoma or to hypertrophy and hyperplasia of all of the parathyroids. In either instance the etiology is undetermined. A rare familial incidence of congenital hyperparathyroidism with diffuse hyperplasia of all the parathyroids has been reported, suggesting that this form of hyperparathyroidism may be due to a genetically determined defect of regulation of parathyroid activity. Hyperparathyroidism in association with other endocrinopathies has also been reported although the manifestations in these patients usually become apparent in later life. Neonatal hyperparathyroidism has been reported in infants born of mothers wth untreated hypoparathyroidism.

The clinical manifestations of hyperparathyroidism may be those of hypercalcemia, bone demineralization, or hypercalciuria. Hypercalcemia causes gastrointestinal disturbances, such as anorexia, nausea, vomiting, and abdominal pain. Failure of weight gain and muscular weakness are also seen. In infants, hyperparathyroidism can be another, albeit rare example of the myriad of diseases which present as "failure to thrive." Rapid elevation of serum calcium concentration to levels of 18 mg per 100 ml or more is associated with hypertension, stupor, and convulsions, and such crises may be precipitated in the hyperparathyroid subject by dehydration and oliguria secondary to vomiting or fluid deprivation. Hypercalcemia also impairs certain renal tubular functions, particularly concentrating mechanisms, which may result in polyuria. Prolonged hypercalcemia results in metastatic calcification of soft tissue most commonly in kidney, blood vessels, lung, myocardium, and subcutaneous tissues.

Pain in bones and joints, especially in the lower extremities, are manifestations of bone demineralization. Deformity of the long bones and vertebrae due to weakening of bone structure or to pathologic fracture occurs in the later stages. On radiographic examination, either diffuse demineralization or patchy cystic demineralization of bone may be seen. The most definitive lesion is subperiosteal erosion manifested by irregularity of the subperiosteal cortex particularly in the phalanges and tibias. The loss of the lamina dura surrounding the teeth is another example of subperiosteal demineralization. Demineralization of the distal portion of the clavicle may also be marked. In the infant and young child hyperparathyroidism may produce bone lesions resembling rickets. If the bone is examined histologically the characteristic lesion is osteitis fibrosa with disappearance of both bone mineral and matrix and replacement by fibroblastic proliferation. The degree of demineralization of bone varies with the calcium available to the body; this depends both on the amount of dietary calcium and the efficiency of its absorption. In adults, hyperparathyroidism without marked radiographic evidence of bone changes is not uncommon. These patients show mild hypercalcemia and hypercalcuria and the presenting manifestation may be renal calculi due to the increased concentrations of calcium and phosphate in urine; also renal injury due to calculi or to calcification of renal parenchyma is an important complication. The renal damage can progress to fatal renal insufficiency even though the hypercalcemia is corrected by parathyroidectomy. Diffuse renal disease with consequent phosphate retention reduces calcium ion concentration in extracellular fluid and stimulates secondary hyperplasia of the parathyroids. Thus, primary hyperparathyroidism and renal calcification may be followed, despite removal of a parathyroid adenoma, by the sequence of renal insufficiency, hyperphosphatemia, and secondary hyperparathyroidism. Secondary hyperparathyroidism can also be seen, of course, as a complication of other forms of progressive diffuse renal injury.

The diagnosis of primary hyperparathyroidism is suggested by the combination of hypercalcemia and hypophosphatemia. The hypercalcemia and associated hypercalciuria of hyperparathyroidism are not restored to normal by a low calcium diet. A variety of other causes of hypercalcemia in childhood must be considered in the differential diagnosis, including hypervitaminosis D, idiopathic hypercalcemia, sarcoidosis, leukemia, metastatic bone tumor, and immobilization hypercalcemia. In adults, certain tumors, particularly carcinoma of the lung, may cause a picture resembling hyperparathyroidism apparently by virtue of secretion of a protein resembling parathyroid hormone. Hypercalcemia has also been reported in children with congenital metabolic defects involving skeletal or renal metabolism, such as hypophosphatasia and renal tubular acidosis. Perhaps the most common cause of hypercalcemia in childhood is the excessive use of vitamin D in doses of 20,000 to 30,000 units or more daily over periods of several months. In hypervitaminosis D serum phosphate levels are usually somewhat increased rather than low as in uncomplicated hyperparathyroidism. Serum alkaline phosphatase levels are also low in the former and frequently increased in hyperparathyroidism. The striking radiographic change in most of the reported cases of hypervitaminosis D in children has been increased density of the calcified cartilage at the ends of the tubular bones with a broad zone of submetaphyseal rarefaction. Thickening of the subperiosteal bone is also seen.

The only pathognomonic test for hyperparathyroidism is increased concentration of parathyroid hormone in the plasma. The immunoreactive method for determination of plasma parathyroid hormone is not yet generally available, however. Hypercalcemia, hypophosphatemia, and diffuse demineralization of bone with or without osteitis fibrosa cystica strongly suggest the diagnosis. A bone biopsy may be of value if bony changes are marked. The use of an adrenal glucocorticoid or analog such as prednisone may be of help in differentiating hyperparathyroidism from other causes of hypercalcemia. In most instances, hypercalcemia of hypervitaminosis D, idiopathic hypercalcemia, sarcoidosis, or metastatic tumor returns to normal with suppressive doses of the steroids. In contrast, the hypercalcemia of hyperparathyroidism is relatively refractory to steroid treatment. This test employing a 10-day course of steroid therapy is usually, though not invariably, quite helpful. Surgical exploration for parathyroid adenoma or diffuse parathyroid hyperplasia is indicated if hypercalcemia is documented and no other cause can be found. Since parathyroid adenomata may be located in the mediastinum, the exploration must be thorough and extensive if an adenoma is not found in the usual anatomic position of the parathyroids in the neck. Hypocalcemia and tetany are observed frequently following parathyroidectomy in those patients in whom bone rarefaction is marked. During the postoperative period bone salt is rapidly deposited in the rarefied bone and intravenous injections of calcium gluconate along with oral administration of calcium salts in large amounts are necessary to prevent tetany.

SECONDARY HYPERPARATHYROIDISM OR RENAL RICKETS. As mentioned above, secondary parathyroid hyperplasia and hypersecretion are induced by elevation of serum phosphate and lowering of serum calcium ion concentrations. In renal insufficiency with marked reduction of glomerular filtration rate serum phosphate levels are elevated greatly beyond the normal. The serum calcium concentrations are reduced due to decreased intestinal absorption of calcium as well as to lessened solubility of calcium in the presence of phosphate excess. The resulting hyperfunction of the parathyroid does not necessarily restore normal levels of calcium ion or of phosphate in the presence of severe renal insufficiency, but it does produce osteitis fibrosa and bone demineralization. The frequent failure of maintenance of normal serum calcium concentration in renal insufficiency despite the excessive bone dissolution is in part due to calcium malabsorption. Patients with renal insufficiency show a resistance to the normal physiologic action of vitamin D on intestinal calcium absorption. The elevated serum phosphate concentrations are also responsible for reduction of serum calcium levels by the reprecipitation of calcium phosphate in soft tissues as well as bone. The bone lesions are more complex than those of primary hyperparathyroidism and histologic evidences of rickets and osteomalacia as well as osteitis fibrosa are seen. On radiographic examination the changes of rickets at the ends of the long bones and the subperiosteal erosions of hyperparathyroidism are both seen (Fig. 20). The rachitic changes have been variously ascribed to the chronic acidosis exhibited by these patients, to the low calcium ion concentrations, or to some hypothetical disturbance of bone matrix resulting in inhibition of calcificiability. Despite the hypocalcemia, metastatic calcification may be found in blood vessels and subcutaneous tissue in patients with marked hyperphosphatemia.

The clinical picture of secondary hyperparathyroidism is the result of the manifestations of chronic renal insufficiency and of the skeletal changes. The renal lesion may be due to hypoplasia of the kidneys, obstructive uropathy, chronic pyelonephritis, or chronic diffuse glomerulonephritis, but a probable necessary factor is slow progression of the lesion so that the skeletal changes become manifest before the metabolic disturbances of renal insufficiency are incompatible with growth. In the far-advanced stages dwarfism, anemia, and chronic acidosis are seen along with deformities of weight-bearing bones. Joint pain and interference with gait result from deformities of lower extremities.

Improvement of the skeletal lesions and lessening of disability may be obtained by the combination of a high-calcium, low-phosphate diet plus doses of vitamin D or dihydrotachysterol sufficient to increase the efficiency of intestinal absorption of calcium. It is usually necessary to reduce the absorption of dietary phosphate by an excess of calcium added as carbonate, lactate, or gluconate or by aluminum hydroxide suspension which precipitates phosphate in the intestinal lumen. The addition of 15 to 20 g of calcium lactate or of 6 to 8 g of calcium carbonate daily, supplying about 2.5 to 3.0 g of added calcium to a diet relatively low in phosphate, may suffice to lower serum phosphate levels without the use of aluminum hydroxide. In addition, a daily dose of 25,000 to 50,000 units of vitamin D or 0.1 to 0.5 mg of dihydrotachysterol is given to increase calcium absorption so that the serum calcium levels are increased and remineralization of bone with calcification of rachitic osteoid will occur. Excessive vitamin D or dihydrotachysterol will enhance metastatic calcification, however, so that treatment must be followed by careful monitoring of serum calcium levels and radiographic examinations of bones and soft tissues. The danger of metastatic calcification will be lessened if the absorption of phosphate is reduced.

The treatment outlined above should be started when the diagnosis of renal disease with severe reduction of glomerular filtration rate is made. The skeletal manifestations of secondary hyperparathyroidism may thus be prevented. Even when the skeletal changes are marked, as in Figure 20, they can often be reversed by treatment. In some patients, however, the hyperplasia of the parathyroids and resulting skeletal disease cannot be brought under control by efforts to increase calcium and reduce phosphate absorption. It has been suggested that the chronically stimulated hyperplastic parathyroids have become independent of control by the calcium ion concentration in the extracellular fluid and are behaving like primary hyperplastic glands. This concept is favored by the finding that the bone disease progresses even though the serum calcium is elevated above normal by activated sterol treatment, whether vitamin D or dihydrotachysterol. Under these circumstances, parathyroidectomy with removal of most of the hyperplastic tissue is the logical treatment. This has been done in a number of patients with successful results in terms of remineralization of bone and disappearance of the disability due to severe bone pain and deformity. An indication for parathyroidectomy is progression of skeletal lesions concomitant with metastatic calcification in soft tissues. The postparathyroidectomy hypocalcemia can be readily managed by adjustment of the vitamin D or dihydrotachysterol dosage and continued control of the serum phosphate levels by the calcium salt or aluminum hydroxide intake. If aluminum hydroxide is used it should not be the magnesium-containing preparation since hypermagnesemia can result from high magnesium intake.

IDIOPATHIC HYPOPARATHYROIDISM. Although one of the relatively uncommon endocrine disturbances of childhood, this is seen much more frequently than primary hyperparathyroidism. The etiology is still speculative. In some instances a congenital basis for parathyroid deficiency is suggested by the appearance of the initial manifestations in the neonatal period but more commonly the symptoms appear at a later age in a previously apparently well child. The con-

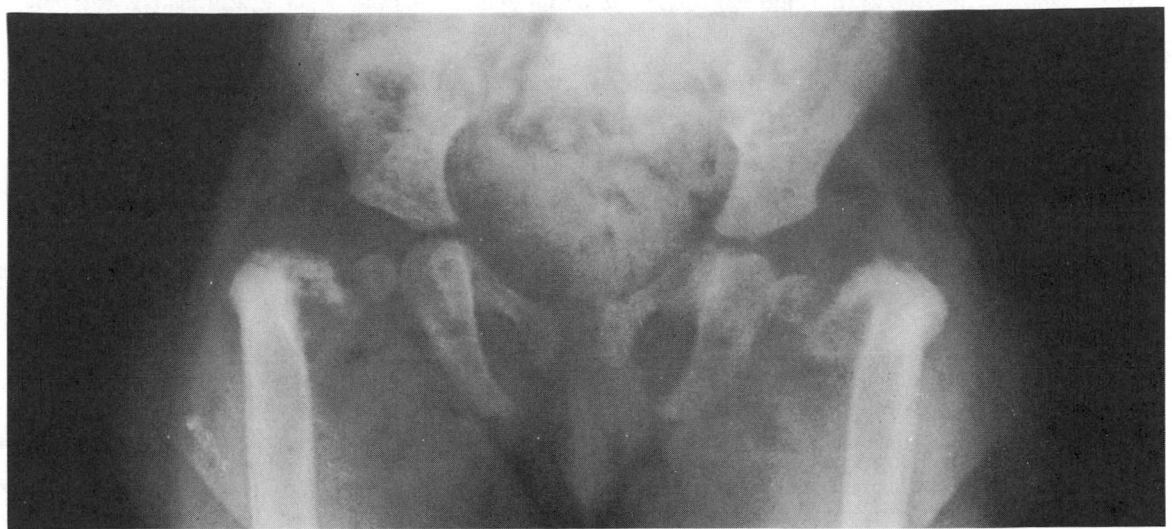

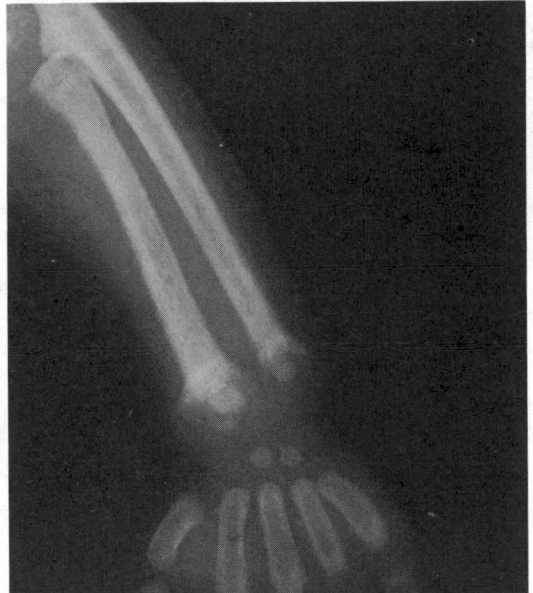 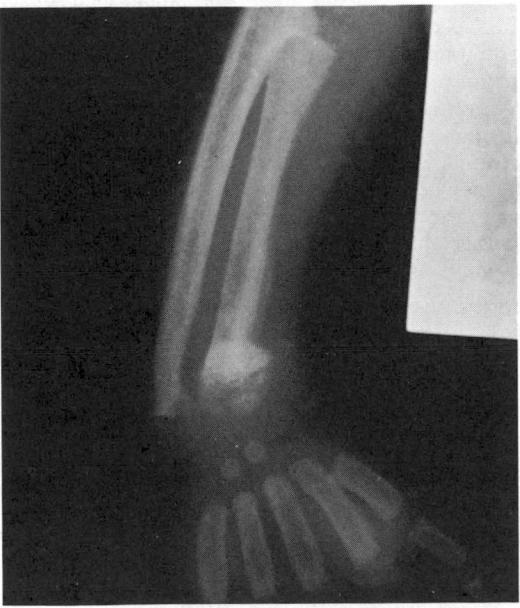

Fig. 20. Bone changes in secondary hyperparathyroidism. This child with congenital hypoplasia of both kidneys developed an extraordinary degree of secondary hyperparathyroidism with marked subperiosteal erosion and destruction of the femoral necks and the distal ends of the radius. These lesions healed with treatment with calcium salts and dihydrotachysterol as outlined in the text.

genital form is due to failure of development of the parathyroid gland and may be associated with thymic aplasia (DiGeorge's syndrome). A striking group of cases of familial hypoparathyroidism have been reported in children who also have severe moniliasis and, in a number of cases, adrenal insufficiency. The hematologic and central nervous system signs of pernicious anemia may also occur in association with hypoparathyroidism. The moniliasis is probably a complication of the ectodermal abnormalities of hypoparathyroidism. The pluriglandular syndrome of

hypoparathyroidism and adrenal insufficiency or in some instances pernicious anemia, has suggested the possibility of an autoimmune process causing atrophy of secreting cells analogous to the autoantibody theory of pathogenesis of Hashimoto's disease and acquired hypothyroidism.

Hypocalcemia in the newborn infant can be divided into early hypocalcemia, starting within the first 24 hours before feedings have been given, and hypocalcemia of somewhat later onset, usually after several days to several weeks of feeding. Early hypocalcemia is seen more commonly in infants born of diabetic mothers or after a difficult delivery. The mechanism is obscure but theoretically might result from stimulation of calcitonin output with inadequate parathyroid hormone response. The usual presenting manifestation is a convulsive seizure. Although the course is self-limited, symptomatic patients should be treated with 10 percent calcium gluconate; 5 ml may be given slowly intravenously to control symptoms and repeated if necessary or 10 to 20 ml may be given by continuous infusion over a 24-hour period.

Hypocalcemic tetany in the newborn after feedings have started may be viewed developmentally as a form of relative inadequacy of parathyroid function. Although capable of normal function the infant's parathyroids cannot respond adequately to the abnormal stimulus of the low serum calcium levels. In the young infant, serum phosphate levels are high because of the low glomerular filtration rate in relation to surface area with proportionately high tubular reabsorption of phosphate. The hyperphosphatemia is increased by the high phosphate load of cow's milk feedings. Reduction of serum calcium ion concentrations is probably secondary to the elevated serum phosphate levels and should stimulate parathyroid activity. If the parathyroid response is inadequate, hypocalcemia results. This type of hypocalcemia is the most common cause of convulsions in the newborn period. Other manifestations are vomiting, cyanotic spells, poor feeding and, in rare instances, heart block. The inadequate parathyroid response is self-limited and spontaneous return to normal of the homeostatic mechanisms for regulation of serum calcium and phosphorus levels usually occurs within a few weeks. The serum calcium of these infants can be increased within a few days by feeding a milk mixture with a high calcium to phosphorus ratio; 3 or 4 grams of calcium per gram of phosphorus. This is easily prepared by the addition of calcium lactate or gluconate to high-carbohydrate milk mixtures. For example: the addition of 25 g of carbohydrate and 11 g of calcium lactate to 500 ml of whole cow's milk provides 2,000 mg of total calcium and 500 mg of phosphorus. This treatment is effective mainly by the sequestration of phosphate in the intestine as unabsorbed calcium phosphate thus reducing the serum phosphate concentrations.

A few cases of persistent hypoparathyroidism have been seen in which the manifestations have appeared in the neonatal period. These infants have at first been thought to have tetany of the newborn, but in contrast to the infants with so-called physiologic hypoparathyroidism, they failed to respond completely to diets with a high calcium-to-phosphorus ratio and the hypocalcemia has persisted or recurred until more definitive treatment was given. A number of instances have been recorded of physiologic or congenital hypoparathyroidism in infants whose mothers were found to have hypercalcemia. Several of these mothers had proven hyperparathy-

roidism. It is desirable, therefore, to determine the serum calcium and phosphate concentrations of mothers of hypocalcemic infants. Maternal hyperparathyroidism could presumably suppress the development or function of the fetal parathyroids.

The entity of *pseudohypoparathyroidism* must also be differentiated. In this syndrome the parathyroids are anatomically normal despite evidence of parathyroid insufficiency. It has been proposed that there is no deficiency of parathyroid secretion in these individuals but rather a refractoriness of the end organs to the hormone. Recent studies have indicated that parathyroid hormone action is mediated through cyclic AMP production and this response to parathyroid hormone does not occur in patients with pseudohypoparathyroidism. Pseudohypoparathyroidism is congenital and multiple cases in one generation of a family have been seen. Associated disturbances of skeletal development are present which are not found in idiopathic hypoparathyroidism, particularly retardation of skeletal growth and marked shortening of the fingers and toes (brachydactyly). Mental retardation may also be an associated defect and metastatic calcification in subcutaneous tissues is more commonly seen than in hypoparathyroidism. The biochemical disturbances are indistinguishable from those of parathyroid insufficiency save for failure of response to parathyroid extract which is the differential diagnostic test.

Recurrent seizures are the most common presenting manifestation of hypoparathyroidism in childhood, either generalized convulsions or focal seizures. The classical symptoms and signs of hypocalcemic tetany, namely sensations of numbness and stiffness of hands and feet with brief contractures, carpopedal spasm, are less common as a presenting complaint. Laryngospasm with respiratory difficulty and high-pitched crow can occur in association with carpopedal spasm or with convulsive seizures. Other manifestations of hypoparathyroidism are lenticular opacities, hypoplasia of dental enamel, and other evidences of dysplasia of ectodermal structures such as thickening and irregularity of the nails and alopecia. In addition to cataracts, other eye manifestations which have been seen are severe blepharospasm and also unexplained papilledema. Symmetrical intracranial calcification in the region of the basal ganglia is also a striking finding in some cases of hypoparathyroidism. The electroencephalographic tracings of children with hypocalcemic convulsions show seizure discharges indistinguishable from those of idiopathic epilepsy and mistaken diagnoses have been made on this basis. All children with repeated, generalized convulsions should have determinations of serum calcium done before a diagnosis of epilepsy is made.

The diagnosis of hypoparathyroidism rests on the finding of hypocalcemia and hyperphosphatemia with normal renal function. Pseudohypoparathyroidism can be differentiated by the associated retardation of growth and the skeletal abnormalities as well as by testing the response of the patient to parathyroid extract. The Ellsworth-Howard test which has been used for this purpose measures the increase in urinary excretion of phosphate following intravenous injection of 2 ml (200 μ) parathyroid extract. Failure to show a severalfold increase of urine phosphate output has been considered evidence of refractoriness to parathyroid hormone. This test has given equivocal results, however, in patients who have subsequently shown a rise of serum calcium and a drop of serum phosphate when treated with larger amounts of parathyroid extract (5 to 10 ml/day) in divided doses intramuscularly over a period of 3 to 4 days. This latter procedure probably gives a more reliable indication of the total responsiveness to parathyroid hormone.

The hypocalcemia of hypoparathyroidism can be influenced by feeding calcium salts which increase intestinal absorption of calcium and reduce phosphate absorption. In children with congenital or idiopathic hypoparathyroidism this type of treatment is not adequate to maintain normal serum calcium concentrations. Hypoparathyroidism is usually therefore treated by oral administration of large amounts of activated sterols, either vitamin D_2 (ergocalciferol), vitamin D_3 (cholecalciferol), or dihydrotachysterol, which can restore normal calcium and phosphate homeostasis in the absence of parathyroid hormone. Dihydrotachysterol like vitamin D_2 is a product of irradiated ergosterol but is less effective as an antirachitic agent in the vitamin D-deficient subject. In hypoparathyroidism, however, dihydrotachysterol and vitamin D have essentially similar effects but dihydrotachysterol is several times more potent. Calciferol is the least expensive preparation and is available as the pure compound or as an accurately standardized preparation. Crystalline dihydrotachysterol is now available and has a major advantage of a shorter biologic half-life than calciferol. Hypercalcemia due to overdosage of dihydrotachysterol will disappear more rapidly when treatment is stopped than that due to overdosage of vitamin D. For this reason, crystalline dihydrotachysterol may be the treatment of choice in hypoparathyroidism. Dosage is variable and must be determined by the effect upon the serum calcium levels of the individual patient. In young infants doses of 0.5 to 1.25 mg (20,000 to 50,000 units) of vitamin D per day have been needed, whereas in the older patient the maintenance dosage ranges from 75,000 to 150,000 units per day. In children the dose of crystalline dihydrotachysterol in milligrams has been about 1/3 that of vitamin D_2. Occasional patients have required much larger amounts of activated sterol and in some instances patients have become refractory to one or more of the activated sterols but have responded when another sterol was substituted. In other instances refractoriness to all sterols has occurred in association with fat malabsorption which is one of the manifestations of hypoparathyroidism. In these patients a low fat intake or substitution of medium-chain triglycerides can be of value. Excessive doses of activated sterols produce hypercalcemia, hy-

percalcuria, and renal damage so that dosage must be guided by suitable laboratory tests. Urinary calcium determinations, either qualitative (Sulkowitch test) or quantitative measurements of 24-hour excretions, are of help as an index of excessive dosage but determinations of serum calcium also need to be made at intervals. Therapy must be continued indefinitely. Occasional patients with idiopathic hyperparathyroidism have shown periods of apparent remission for months after treatment was stopped because of hypercalcemia. After a number of months, however, the serum calcium has decreased again necessitating resumption of treatment.

The treatment of pseudohypoparathyroidism is similar to that of idiopathic hyperthyroidism. The serum calcium of these patients can be elevated by treatment with activated sterols even though parathyroid extract is ineffective.

Postoperative hypoparathyroidism resulting from removal or injury to parathyroids during thyroidectomy is similar to idiopathic hypoparathyroidism in its manifestations. These patients can often be controlled symptomatically by oral administration of high doses of calcium salts. If this does not suffice, treatment with activated sterols is employed as in idiopathic hypoparathyroidism.

REFERENCES

GENERAL

Fanconi, G. Physiology and pathology of calcium and phosphate metabolism. *In* Levine, S. Z., ed., Advances in Pediatrics. Chicago, Year Book Publishers, 1962, Vol. XII, p. 307.
Rubin, R. Dynamic Classification of Bone Dysplasias. Chicago, Year Book Publishers, 1964.

VITAMIN D DEFICIENCY

DeLuca, H. F. 25-hydroxycholecalciferol. The probable metabolically active form of vitamin D_3: Its identification and subcellular site of action. Arch. Int. Med., 124:442, 1969.
Harrison, H. E. Vitamin D and calcium and phosphate transport. Pediatrics, 25:531, 1961.
Follis, R. H., Jr. Deficiency Disease, Springfield, Ill., Charles C Thomas, 1958.
Glaser, K., Parmelee, H. H., and Hoffman, W. S. Comparative efficacy of vitamin D preparation in prophylactic treatment of premature infants. Amer. J. Dis. Child., 77:1, 1949.

NONVITAMIN D DEFICIENCY RICKETS

Albright, F., Burnett, C. H., Parson, W., Reifenstein, E. C., Jr., and Roos, A. Osteomalacia and late rickets: the various etiologies met in the United States with emphasis on that resulting from a special form of renal acidosis; the therapeutic indications for each etiological sub-group and the relationship between osteomalacia and Milkman's syndrome. Medicine, 25:399, 1946.
Dent, C. E., and Harris, H. Hereditary forms of rickets and osteomalacia. J. Bone Joint Surg., 38B:204, 1956.

Harrison, H. E., and Harrison, H. C. Hereditary metabolic bone diseases. Clin. Orthop., 33:147, 1964.

——— Harrison, H. C., Lifshitz, F., and Johnson, A. D. Growth disturbance in hereditary hypophosphatemia. Amer. J. Dis. Child., 112:290, 1966.

Prader, A., Illig, R., and Heierli, E. Eine besondere Form der primären Vitamin D resistenden Rachitis mit Hypocalcämie und autosomal-dominantem Erbgang: die hereditare Pseudo-mangel Rachitis. Helv. Paed. Acta., 16:452, 1961.

Tapia, J., Stearns, G., and Ponseti, I. V. Vitamin D resistant rickets—A long term clinical study of eleven patients. J. Bone Joint Surg., 46A:935, 1964.

Winters, R. W., Graham, J. B., William, T. F., McFalls, V. W., and Burnett, C. H. A genetic study of familial hypophosphatemia and vitamin D resistant rickets with a review of the literature. Medicine, 37:97, 1958.

IDIOPATHIC HYPERCALCEMIA

American Academy of Pediatrics Committee on Nutrition. The relation between infantile hypercalcemia and vitamin D—public health implications in North America. Pediatrics, 40:1050, 1967.

Bonham Carter, R. E., and Sutliffe, J. A syndrome of multiple arterial stenosis in association with the severe form of idiopathic hypercalcemia. Arch. Dis. Child., 39:418, 1964.

Garcia, R. G., Friedman, W. F., Kaback, M. M., and Rowe, R. D. Idiopathic hypercalcemia and supravalvular aortic stenosis. Documentation of a new syndrome. New Eng. J. Med., 271:117, 1964.

Lightwood, R., and Stapleton, T. Idiopathic hypercalcemia in infants. Lancet, 2:255, 1953.

PRIMARY HYPERPARATHYROIDISM

Albright, F., and Reifenstein, E. C., Jr. The Parathyroid Glands and Metabolic Bone Disease. Batlimore, The Williams and Wilkins Co., 1948.

Anderson, J., Harper, C., Dent, C. E., and Philpot, G. R. Effect of cortisone on calcium metabolism in sarcoidosis with hypercalcemia. Lancet, 2:720, 1954.

Committee Report. Hypercalcemia in infants and vitamin D. Brit. Med. J., 1:149, 1956.

Hillman, D. A., Scriver, C. R., Pedris, S., and Shragovitch, I. Neonatal familial primary hyperparathyroidism. New Eng. J. Med., 270:483, 1964.

Lowe, K. G., Henderson, J. L., Park, W. W., and McGreal, D. A. The idiopathic hypercalcemia syndromes of infancy. Lancet, 2:101, 1954.

Nolan, R. B., Hayles, A. B., and Woolner, L. B. Adenoma of parathyroid gland in children: report of case and brief review of literature. Amer. J. Dis. Child., 22:622, 1960.

Philips, R. N. Primary diffuse parathyroid hyperplasia in an infant of 4 months. Pediatrics, 2:428, 1948.

Pratt, E. L., Geren, B. B., and Neuhauser, E. B. D. Hypercalcemia and idiopathic hyperplasia of parathyroid glands in infant. J. Pediat., 30:388, 1947.

SECONDARY HYPERPARATHYROIDISM

Castleman, B., and Mallory, T. B. Parathyroid hyperplasia in chronic renal insufficiency. Amer. J. Path. 12:553, 1937.

Follis, R. H., Jr. Renal rickets and osteitis fibrosa in children and adolescents. Bull. Johns Hopkins Hosp., 87:593, 1950.

Gill, G., Pallotta, J., Kashgarian, M., Kessner, D., and Epstein, F. H. Physiologic studies in renal osteodystrophy treated by subtotal parathyroidectomy. Amer. J. Med., 46:930, 1960.

HYPOPARATHYROIDISM

Albright, F., Burnett, C. H., Smith, P. H., and Parson, W. Pseudohypoparathyroidism: An example of the "Seabright-Bantam Syndrome": Report of three cases. Endocrinology, 30:922, 1942.

Bakwin, H. Tetany in newborn infants. Amer. J. Dis. Child., 54:1211, 1937.

Dent, C. E., Morgans, M. E., Harper, C. M., Philpot, G. R., and Trotler, W. R. Insensitivity to vitamin D developing during the treatment of postoperative tetany. Its specificity as regards the form of vitamin D taken. Lancet, 2:687, 1955.

Gardner, L. I. Tetany and parathyroid hyperplasia in the newborn infant: Influence of dietary phosphate load. Pediatrics, 9:534, 1962.

Harrison, H. E. Idiopathic hypoparathyroidism. Pediatrics, 17:442, 1956.

——— Lifshitz, F., and Blizzard, R. M. Comparison between crystalline dihydrotachysterol and calciferol in patients requiring pharmacologic vitamin D therapy. New Eng. J. Med., 276:894, 1967.

Sutphin, W., Albright, F., and McCune, D. J. Five cases (three in siblings) of idiopathic hypoparathyroidism associated with moniliasis. J. Clin. Endocr., 3:625, 1943.

3.6

OBESITY IN CHILDREN AND ADOLESCENTS

ELSA P. PAULSEN

There are cogent reasons for those concerned with the present health and future well-being of children to be interested in the problem of obesity. Fat children suffer considerably from contemptuous attitudes of their peers, and frequently of their parents and other adults toward obesity. As a result, life-long feelings of inadequacy may be generated. Physical limitations imposed by their size and embarrassment over their appearance serve to deny them many pleasant and healthful activities of childhood. Furthermore, at least 80 percent of overweight boys and girls perpetuate their obesity into adult life, and make up about 50 percent of the grossly obese adult population. Epidemiologic studies of adult populations have shown a significant positive correlation between marked obesity and the morbidity and mortality attributed to diseases of the cardiovascular system.

Unfortunately, long-term success in the treatment of obesity in children, as in adults, has been a universal and dismal failure. If progress is to be made in lessening the prevalence of this disorder, increased emphasis must be placed upon prevention. In addition to the need for more understanding of psychologic determinants, greater effort is needed in a search for underlying biochemical abnormalities in the regulation of food intake and of the metabolic fate of foodstuffs.

DEFINITION.   Obesity, defined as a marked increase of body fat, is easily recognized by the clinician. It is more difficult to asses its severity, and especially to interpret lesser degrees of overweightness. An increase in lean body mass (LBM) rather than in fat may account for increased weight since the former may vary considerably among children of the same height. Also, data in weight tables drawn from selected ethnic and socioeconomic groups do not have universal applicability. Such weights are by definition normative and *not* necessarily desirable weights. The average or "normal" weights of adults in the United States over the past 30 years have increased significantly according to the authors of *Build and Blood Pressure Study 1959*. The correlation of the weight increases with decreased longevity prompted them to view moderate underweight as highly desirable. Hodges has noted a similar trend toward increased weight among children (Fig. 21). The weight increases over a 25-year period in Iowa children have been proportionately greater than height increases. Whether these increases in mean weight during the growing period will contribute to health problems in adult life poses an important question.

Even with their limitations, however, the height-weight tables remain at present adequate for estimating weight status. Weights greater than 8 to 10 percent above mean for the height and age of the child are generally indicative of overweight. Sudden weight increases from previously satisfactory levels may herald the onset of a weight problem. Weights greater than 20 percent above mean weight may be considered indicative of obesity.

PREVALENCE AND AGE OF ONSET.   There are no data from which the prevalence of obesity in preschool children can be estimated. The scanty data on grade school children suggest a prevalence rate of about 10 percent. Among high school students, surveys in various parts of the United States indicate rates ranging from 10 or 15 to as high as 30 percent. Differences in the cultural, social, and economic background of the children probably account for much of the variation.

Birth weights of obese and nonobese children do not differ, nor do the more obese have higher birth weights than the less obese. Heald and Hollander, however, noted a significantly greater mean weight at one year of age among 158 obese teen-age girls with a mean age 15 years than among 94 normal weight girls of the same age and social background. Mossberg cites evidence that there are two peaks for the onset of childhood obesity: 0 to 4 years, and 7 to 11 years.

Etiology

GENETIC FACTORS.   Good evidence from the studies of twins shows that genetic factors play some role in the development of obesity in children. Newman et al., studying a large number of identical and

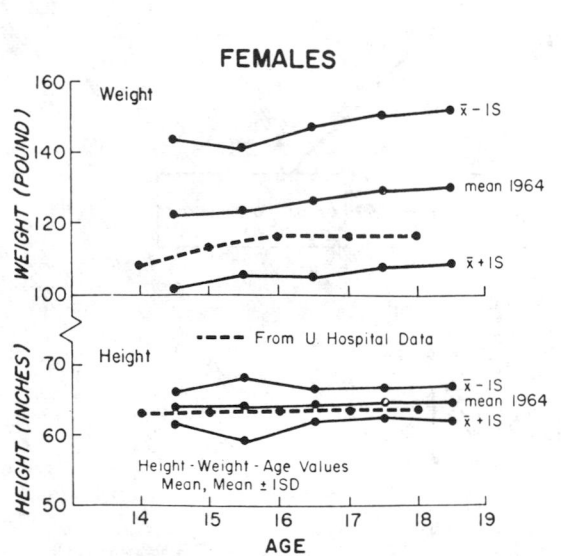
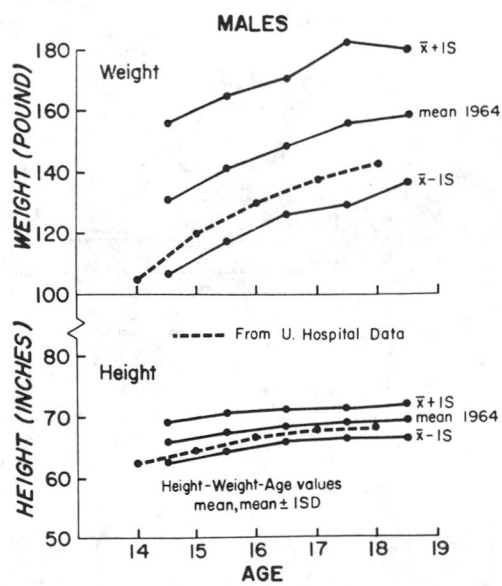

Fig. 21. Comparison of heights and weights of Iowa teenagers obtained in 1964 (solid line) with those published in 1943 (dashed line). From University Hospital Data and widely known as the "Iowa Norms." (From Hodges and Krehl. *Amer. J. Clin. Nutr.*, 17:200, 1965.)

fraternal twins and siblings of like sex, found an extremely high correlation for weight between identical twins but not between fraternal twins nor between siblings at comparable ages. The correlations retained significance even when twins were reared in different environments.

Seltzer and Mayer studying the somatotypes of obese adolescent girls found that obesity occurred significantly more often in endomorphic body types than in meso- or ectomorphic types. A large skeleton, large muscle mass, and absence of narrow elongated extremities characterize the obese girl. Such a correlation between obesity and body build would be further evidence of a genetic determinant in obesity, since the hereditary nature of body build seems securely documented.

Studies of the familial occurrence of obesity do not in themselves distinguish between hereditary and environmental factors since both may be operative. **ENERGY BALANCE.** Factors which control the balance between caloric intake and its expenditure and thus allow one either to maintain normal weight or to become obese remain only vaguely understood. It has been believed generally that humans metabolize food in a fairly uniform manner, and that excess calories, unless dissipated through physical activity, end up as stored fat. This simplistic view reduces obesity to overeating and/or lack of exercise. An alternate hypothesis which has some support from experimental studies is that the normal organism can within certain limits alter its metabolism to dispose of excess calories by such means as increasing radiant heat loss or increasing urinary excretion of calorie-rich organic molecules. Sims and co-workers found it exceedingly difficult to induce obesity in lean male volunteers, and indeed impossible in some.

Johnson and Stefanik found the caloric intake of obese adolescent boys and girls at camps and during the school year to be less than their nonobese controls. Observation of patterns of activity revealed that though the obese spent as much time at various activities they participated less actively. Quantitative data are lacking, however, to implicate the lessened energy output as the sole cause of their obesity or to show that the activity pattern preceded the obesity.

The hypothesis that organisms can alter their metabolism to dispose of caloric excesses, when viewed in the context of biochemical individuality, seems highly possible, and at least allows one to search for differences in efficiency of energy utilization. A difficulty arises in humans because individuals cannot be identified until they are already obese, a fact which obscures interpretation of data. In addition, only minor and perhaps presently undetectable increases in efficiency (1 to 2 percent) can, on a day-to-day basis, lead to obesity. Such differences, if they exist, could be genetic in origin, or they could be the result of adaptation to an unusual environment during fetal or subsequent development. White reported a significant incidence of adolescent-onset obesity and hyperglycemia among the offspring of diabetic mothers but not among those of diabetic fathers.

REGULATION OF APPETITE (FIG. 22). The higher centers of the brain are influenced in their regulation of food intake by conscious learning which in turn

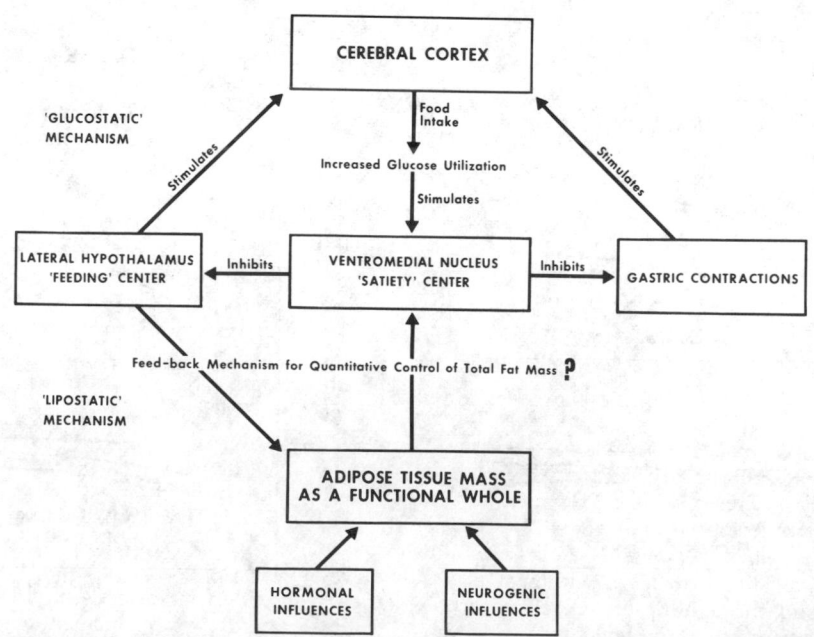

Fig. 22. Relationship between hypothalamic centers regulating appetite, and the cortex. Evidence for "Glucostatic" mechanism reviewed by Mayer (1966).

is based on the many environmental factors imping-ing on the growing child. Influences also emanate by subcortical activity from the hypothalamus. A "satiety" center in the ventromedial nucleus seems exquisitely sensitive to increases in glucose utiliza-tion within its own cells (specific glucoreceptor sites) and responds with increased electrical activity. This activity inhibits the lateral hypothalamus and gastric contractions. The lateral hypothalamus appears to be the site of the "feeding" center and inhibition of its activity lessens cerebral messages of hunger.

Kennedy introduced the concept that a metabo-lite of adipose tissue might be involved in a feedback mechanism between the adipose mass and the hypo-thalamus. The "lipostatic" theory lacks the experi-mental evidence which commends the "glucostatic" theory.

A preliminary report of hunger and satiety sen-sations in children and adults revealed that the obese experienced fewer or no hunger sensations, and were more occupied with thoughts of food before and after the meal than the normal control subjects. A marked difference between the groups was noted in the ability to stop eating. The obese required more will power to do so, and often continued to eat in spite of feelings of considerable discomfort.

Adipose Tissue

BODY COMPOSITION. The growth period imposes important changes in the absolute and relative amounts of adipose tissue, just as it produces the more obvious changes in height, weight, bone, and muscle mass. Two types of techniques are available for estimating body fat: (1) anthropometric evaluation which estimates subcutaneous fat either through skin-fold thicknesses, various body circum-ferences, or thickness of tissue from radiograms; and, (2) measurement of total body fat, either directly through estimation of specific gravity by underwater weighing or helium displacement, or indirectly by measuring LBM using deuterium to measure total body water, or by taking whole body counts of naturally occurring radioactive potassium (^{40}K). Subtracting LBM from body weight will thus ap-proximate body fat.

Normal development of fat stores in normal children has been studied. Maresh measured fat tissue widths from radiograms in children and young adults 2 months to 17 years of age. Forbes using ^{40}K measurements made observations in subjects from 8 years of age through the early twenties. Two periods of relative increase in body fat may be seen in his anthropometric data. One begins shortly after birth, becomes maximal between 6 and 18 months of age, and is similar in both sexes, although girls at this early age and throughout life have proportion-ately more fat than boys. In both sexes, there is then a regression of fat relative to the increases in bone and muscle. Around 8 years, the proportion of

body fat again begins to increase but obviously has a different course in the two sexes: boys have in-creases in LBM which exceed those in body fat with resultant decreases in the percentage of body fat; girls undergo both absolute and relative increases in body fat during adolescence.

Inspection of weight curves of four obese chil-dren revealed that the acceleration in weight gains resulting in overweight and eventual obesity *coin-cided with the normal periods of accelerated fat deposition.* Forbes has found by ^{40}K measurements that there is a group of obese children characterized by overweightness since birth, by a tendency to increased stature, advanced bone age, and who, in addition to markedly increased fat stores have in-creased LBM. He found a second obese group who had no increase in LBM, had normal bone ages and average heights. These children became obese during later childhood years. Bruch and Wolff reported that many obese children were tall and advanced in sexual maturation. Ultimate heights were not ex-ceptional, however, because of the earlier maturation.

THE ADIPOSE CELL. Recent studies have revealed that extreme obesity in adult humans is character-ized not only by increased amounts of lipid in the adipose cell but also by marked increases in the total number of cells. In addition, weight reduction did not lead to any significant change in cell number, but rather to a drastic reduction in cell size. In adult rats, procedures which increased fat stores such as overfeeding or hypothalamic lesions led to increases in cell size but not in cell number. Thus, these studies suggest that in man and in the rat, once the adult cell number is achieved, nutritional factors do not alter it. Hirsch et al. also examined fat cells of infants and children, and found increasing cell num-ber and size with age, but the exact age at which the adult cell number is attained has not yet been determined.

Knittle and co-workers have shown in rats, how-ever, that *early* in life nutritional factors can influ-ence adipose cell number. The caloric intake of weaning rats was altered by redistributing the pups of several litters to give some mothers litters of 4 and others of 22. After weaning, all had free access to food. Compared with those from the larger litters, the rats from the small litters were larger, fatter, both absolutely and relatively, and they had heavier epidiymal fat pads with significantly increased num-bers of adipose cells at maturity. Whether or not such cellular hyperplasia could be reversed or modified during the growing period is a question of funda-mental importance which at present remains un-answered.

METABOLISM. The body's major form of energy storage resides in the adipose tissue because of its mass and its high caloric density. However, rather than being inert, it undergoes constant changes. Its volume at any given moment depends upon the equilibrium between deposition and mobilization of triglyceride, the storage form of fat. Contrary to the prevalent notions of sluggish metabolism in the obese, recent studies utilizing radioactive-labeled compounds reveal that the metabolic activity of adipose tissue is greatly heightened in obese adults.

Triglycerides, which consist of three long-chain fatty acids per molecule of glycerol, are formed and deposited in the adipocyte as the result of two processes: (1) the incorporation of preformed lipids, both dietary and those synthesized in the liver, and (2) de novo synthesis from glucose within the cell. Preformed lipids are hydrolyzed at the cell wall by lipoprotein lipase and only the free fatty acids (FFA) enter the cell where, along with fatty acids formed in situ, they are esterified with α-glycerophosphate, the activated form of glycerol. Glycerol formed during lipolysis cannot be reutilized so that its active form must be synthesized from glucose within the cell. Therefore, since glucose cannot be derived through gluconeogenesis in adipose cells and glycogen stores are small, the rate of glucose uptake by the cell is one of the major regulators of triglyceride synthesis.

Triglyceride formation is also regulated by the rates of glucose utilization in the various metabolic pathways operative in the fat cell. In addition to entering the glycolytic pathway and serving as a source of α-glycerophosphate and of acetyl CoA for fatty acid synthesis, glucose enters the pentose or hexose monophosphate pathway. This metabolic path is very active in fat cells and is important as the source for nucleotides (TPNH, $NADH_2$) used as cofactors in the synthesis of triglycerides.

Tryglycerides are hydrolyzed by a "hormone-sensitive" lipase, distinct from lipoprotein lipase. The FFA can be reesterified or enter the circulation bound to albumin. They serve two functions: they are a primary source of the energy requirements of skeletal muscle, liver, and heart; and they serve as regulatory factors, primarily in the liver, but also in muscle and adipose cells. By influencing certain enzyme reactions, FFA in the liver can stimulate gluconeogenesis and increase ketone formation. In muscle, they interfere with glucose utilization. In the adipose cell, through a feedback mechanism they inhibit further free fatty acid release.

In obese subjects fasted ovenight, FFA are elevated well above normal. In such subjects one would anticipate an exaggeration of their metabolic influences. Indeed, Shreeve et al. have shown a twofold increase above normal of ^{14}C-glucose production from labeled pyruvate in obese adults fasted overnight. The utilization of the increased glucose entering the circulation is impaired in the muscle cells because of the high levels of FFA and is taken up by the adipose cells and stored as fat.

Obese subjects are reported to have impaired fat mobilization. This is based on the findings of lower than normal plasma FFA after prolonged fasting or exercise, decreased arteriovenous differences of plasma FFA after brief fast, and of resistance to the development of ketonemia after fasts of varying lengths. However, turnover studies using palmitate-1-^{14}C in obese subjects after 18 hours fasting cast doubt on this conclusion. Nestel, and Whyte found that turnover rates of plasma FFA when expressed in terms of body surface area were 25 percent greater in obse than in nonobese. For a given plasma FFA concentration the turnover rate was greater in the obese and was significantly correlated with plasma FFA level and with the fat mass of the subject. Obese subjects also had higher turnover rates of triglycerides than nonobese and these correlated with the elevated plasma triglyceride levels.

Thus there is evidence of heightened metabolic activity in adipose tissue of the obese rather than less: *increased* mobilization of free fatty acids countered by *increased* triglyceride formation. Also, in respect to lessened ketone levels observed in fasted obese subjects, the possibilities of increased turnover or alternate pathways of FFA utilization must be explored as explanations rather than decreased FFA mobilization.

REGULATORY AGENTS. *The Nervous System.* The hypothalamus is intimately involved through peripheral nerves in the release of some hormones affecting glucose and lipid metabolism. The sympathetic-adrenal medullary system is well known. Stimulation of the medial hypothalamus, or sympathetic area, in animals can elicit secretion of catecholamines. Not so well studied or documented is the hypothalamic "vago-insulin system" proposed by Gellhorn in 1941. Recent findings of increased pancreatic vein insulin levels in rabbits after stimulation of the parasympathetic area of the lateral hypothalamus or of the vagi nerves give credence to the hypothesis and should prompt further inquiry.

Endocrine Hormones. Insulin is the major regulator of body fat stores because it not only *stimulates synthesis* but *inhibits lipolysis* of triglycerides. It acts by enhancing glucose entry into the adipose cell as it does into muscle cells and FFA entry by maintaining the enzyme lipoprotein lipase; it appears to facilitate enzyme reactions of phosphorylated glucose leading to triglyceride synthesis within the cell; and it inhibits the "hormone-sensitive" lipase which hydrolyzes triglycerides.

It has been shown in rats that *estrogens* act synergistically with insulin in stimulating the synthesis of lipids from glucose. In in vivo studies, both female and male rats showed the effect at physiologic levels of estrogen. Such synergism, if present in humans, would explain the normally accelerated deposition of fat during adolescence and the heightened rate in obese youngsters at this age.

Lipolysis can be induced in man by numerous hormones but the physiologic role they play is not known in most instances. They include: catecholamines, growth hormone (GH), glucagon, cortisol, thyroxin, TSH, ACTH, and secretin. The lipolytic hormones are believed to act by enhancing formation of 3'5'-cyclic adenosine monophosphate (cyclic AMP) from ATP. Cyclic AMP catalyzes the conversion of inactive lipase to its active form. Abnormalities in plasma levels of the lipolytic hormones, growth hormone, cortisol, and glucagon have been found in both obese children and obese adults. Also, growth hormone levels are reduced in the fasting state, diurnal variation is suppressed, and responses to insulin-induced hypoglycemia, arginine, exercise, and prolonged fast are poor or absent. In experimental animals impaired growth hormone secretion is an early feature of obesity. In addition to its lipolytic activity, growth hormone can block fat synthesis in the adipose cell by inhibiting glucose oxidation and FFA synthesis.

There is no evidence of decreased thyroid function in uncomplicated obesity. Blood levels of protein-bound iodine are normal and studies with radioactively labeled thyroxin reveal no evidence of defective peripheral utilization. When, in addition to caloric restriction, dessicated thyroid was administered to obese subjects and to myxedematous patients, weight loss was observed in both groups. Densitometric studies revealed, however, that the loss was predominately from the lean body mass. Thyroid medication, therefore, as a therapeutic measure to stimulate weight loss in obesity is contraindicated.

Experimental Obesity

MAN. Sims and his colleagues have provided important insights into obesity by inducing weight increases of 15 to 30 percent in lean male volunteers by overfeeding them a normally constituted diet. They found obesity extremely hard to induce. Several volunteers, ingesting two to three times their normal caloric intake while following their usual daily routine for 3 to 5 months, were able to increase their weights by only 10 to 12 percent, and others failed to gain. Interestingly, as weight increased, they developed an aversion to breakfast but developed sensations of hunger between meals even though caloric intakes were as high as 10,000 cal/day. The metabolic and endocrine abnormalities seen in spontaneously obese subjects were induced in the volunteers who did become obese. This affords clearcut evidence that the endocrine abnormalities observed in spontaneously obese subjects are secondary to the obese state.

One interesting finding from experiments on obesity in mice is particularly relevant to observations in human obese subjects. When genetically obese mice were first reduced in weight by starvation and then fed ad libitum, they returned to their exact prestarvation weights. Such observations have been reported frequently in obese adults who achieved weight losses they were unable to sustain. There has been a suggestion from data collected by Maresh in two obese children that one can project a weight curve which the subjects follow when intake is not restricted and to which they return after periods of caloric restriction and weight loss.

Complications of Obesity

PSYCHOLOGIC. Investigators, such as Mayer, who concerned themselves for many years with obese children and adolescents believe there is scant objective evidence to support the concept that psychogenic factors alone play a primary etiologic role in these age groups. They are convinced, however, that the psychologic effects of obesity are very real and damaging, and tend to perpetuate the obesity. In projective tests given to obese adolescent girls, Monello and co-workers discovered that girls have intense feelings of discrimination, character traits of passivity, withdrawal, expectation of rejection by peers, and marked signs of self-rejection. Stunkard and Mendelson found that adults whose obesity began in the adolescent period often had poor self-images and tended to consider their obesity causally related to failures and disappointments. Other students of the problem of obesity, such as Bruch, have concluded that there may be primary psychogenic causes of obesity. The resolution of these viewpoints awaits further clarification.

MEDICAL. Obese subjects have decreased exercise tolerance because their increased mass requires more energy to perform a given task. The work of breathing is increased and lung volume is reduced. Exertion or respiratory infections may lead to severe distress. In extreme obesity, decreased ventilation with accumulation of carbon dioxide may lead to apneic spells, lethargy, and somnolence, a clinical state observed and immortalized by Charles Dickens and therefore sometimes referred to as the "Pickwickian syndrome."

Obese children often have itching, inflammation, and furuncles in moist skin folds and on the inner aspects of the thigh. Adolescent girls may develop menstrual irregularities. Obese children may have impaired glucose tolerance similar to adults. In one study, the incidence of significant impairment was 23 percent. In one of these children, reduction of weight to normal was accompanied by disappearance of the hyperglycemia and hyperinsulinism.

DIFFERENTIAL DIAGNOSIS. Lesions invading the hypothalamus such as craniopharyngiomas, tumors of the pituitary, or cysts (as in Froehlich's patient) can cause obesity. The sexual infantilism, growth retardation, and diabetes insipidus sometimes accompanying the obesity are due to invasion of the pituitary.

Prader and co-workers have described a syndrome of obesity, muscular hypotonia, hypogenitalism, hypogonadism, mental retardation, and, occasionally, asymptomatic hyperglycemia. Fasting hyperlipogenesis, a defect described in obese hyperglycemic mice, has also been observed in these patients. The Laurence-Moon-Biedl syndrome includes obesity.

The distinction between the rare case of Cushing's syndrome in children and uncomplicated obesity may be difficult. Several important differences are noteworthy. In Cushing's syndrome the distribution of fat is truncal, linear growth is impaired, and osteoporosis and hypertension are present. In uncomplicated obesity the distribution of fat is generalized, growth is normal or accelerated, and osteoporosis and hypertension are absent. (It is common to obtain falsely high blood pressure readings from a very obese arm. More accurate readings are obtained on the forearm.) The increased urinary 17-hydroxy corticoids (or 17-ketogenic steroids) frequently seen in the obese can be suppressed by amounts of dexamethasone which do not suppress the increases in Cushing's syndrome. Finally, in patients with Cushing's disease, but not in other obese patients, the diurnal variation in plasma cortisol concentration disappears.

Adolescent girls with generalized obesity, mild or moderate hirsutism, and amenorrhea or menstrual irregularities should be referred to an endocrinologist for evaluation. Several types of ovarian dysfunction, including the "Stein-Leventhal" syndrome, may present with this triad.

Treatment

PREVENTION.   Emphasis must be placed on prevention of obesity or its early detection, since treatment is so uniformly unsuccessful. There may be a need in the United States for a general reeducation of what and how much children should eat if the data of the Iowa study (Fig. 21) reflect a national trend. It appears that the childhood population (with certain well-known exceptions) as well as the adult population is being overfed. As already noted the increased weights in adults correlate significantly with an increased incidence of cardiovascular disease. The notion that fatness in a baby is desirable and a sign of health should, at the very least, be seriously questioned. Children should be trained from their very early years to stop eating when their normal needs are met and not be encouraged or forced to continue simply to "clean their plates." Since the potentially obese child cannot be identified at present, the family with obese members should be more attentive to following good habits of nutrition and exercise. Good pediatric care requires attention to weight and height gains in all children. Any doctrinaire point of view, however, would seem to be premature.

NUTRITION.   At the present time there is no evidence in humans that the composition of the diet or the eating schedule seriously enhances weight-losing. The pediatrician and the nutritionist should construct a diet which is varied and interesting, contains adequate nutriments for growth, and has a caloric content equal to or slightly below the child's requirement for his ideal weight. Greater caloric restriction in children is unrealistic unless the subject is in a supervised hospital setting. Total fasting or too low a caloric intake is contraindicated in the growing subject. Ideally, the first month of treatment should be carried out in a children's rehabilitation center. Here the child and his parents can learn and appreciate the results of the routine of diet and exercise that must be carried on at home if any success is expected.

EXERCISE.   Daily exercise in any form for at least an hour is desirable to establish a life style that will not encourage increasing obesity. The child should be encouraged in a variety of sports, especially those he can continue into adulthood. Members of the family should join with the youngster in these activities to encourage regularity of performance.

MEDICATIONS.   Thyroid treatment is not indicated in the absence of clinical and laboratory data clearly documenting a state of hypothyroidism. The use of anorexigenic drugs is not encouraged because, at best, they are effective for only brief periods of a few months. Also, drugs may interfere with meeting the problem of caloric balance squarely and realistically.

PSYCHOLOGIC SUPPORT.   The obese child under treatment needs to be seen often for encouragement and praise. The physician should elicit cooperation from the whole family. An obese parent, especially, should be encouraged to lose weight along with the child. A nagging battle between child and parent should be avoided as much as possible, and, although it is difficult for parents to do so, adolescents should be given major responsibility for their treatment program. Attention to the cosmetic features of obesity and its absence often provides motivation to adolescent girls.

In the majority of patients at present, little more than a holding operation can be effected; rarely a cure. However, even this is encouraging, and the patient should never be treated harshly or abandoned for failure to lose weight. Much evidence at present suggests that features of the problem are beyond the patient's control.

RESULTS.   While the struggle against established obesity often fails because the multiplicity of interrelated known and perhaps unknown factors, the occasional success and the support provided even without it makes the effort worthwhile. In the field of prevention and during the early development of obesity, the clinician may play a very important part in preserving later health.

REFERENCES

Bruch, H. Obesity in relation to puberty. J. Pediat., 19:365, 1941.

Build and Blood Pressure Study 1959. Chicago, Society of Actuaries, 1959.

Ellis, R. W. B., and Tallerman, K. H. Obesity in childhood—study of 50 cases. Lancet, 2:615, 1934.

Forbes, G. B. Growth of the lean body mass during childhood and adolescence. J. Pediat., 64:822, 1964a.

——— Lean body mass and fat in obese children. Pediatrics, 34:308, 1964b.

Garces, L. Y., Kerry, F. M., Drash, A., and Taylor, P. H. Cortisol secretion rate during fasting of obese adolescent subjects. J. Clin. Endocr., 28:1843, 1968.

Gellhorn, E., Cortell, R., and Feldman, J. The effect of emotion, shame, rage and hypothalmic stimulation on the vagoinsulin system. Amer. J. Physiol., 133:532, 1941.

Goodman, H. M. Growth hormone and the metabolism of carbohydrate and lipid in adipose tissue. Ann. N.Y. Acad. Sci., 148:419, 1968.

Grodsky, G. M., and Benoit, F. Effect of massive weight reduction on insulin secretion in obese subjects. 6th Congr. Int. Diabetes Fed., Symp., Stockholm, 1967.

Heald, F. P., and Hollander, R. J. The relationship between obesity in adolescence and early growth. J. Pediat., 67:35, 1965.

Hirsch, J., Knittle, J. L., and Salans, L. B. Cell lipid content and cell number in obese and nonobese human tissue. J. Clin. Invest., 45:1023, 1966.

Hodges, R. E., and Krehl, W. A. Nutritional status of teenagers in Iowa. Amer. J. Clin. Nutr., 17:200, 1965.

Johnson, M. L., Burke, B. S., and Mayer, J. Relative importance of inactivity and overeating in energy balance of obese high school girls. Amer. J. Clin. Nutr., 4:37, 1956.

Kennedy, G. C. The hypothalamic control of food intake in rats. Proc. Roy. Soc. Biol., 137:535, 1950.

Knittle, J., and Hirsch, J. Infantile nutrition as a determinant of adult adipose tissue metabolism and cellularity. Clin. Res., 15:323, 1967.

Maresh, M. Changes in tissue widths during growth. Roentgenograhpic measurements of bone, muscle, and fat widths from infancy through adolescence. Amer. J. Dis. Child., 111:142, 1966.

Mayer, J. Some aspects of the problem of regulation of food intake and obesity. New Eng. J. Med., 274:610, 662, 722, 1966.

Monello, L. F., Seltzer, C. C., and Mayer, J. Hunger and satiety sensations in men, women, boys, and girls: A preliminary report. Ann. N.Y. Acad. Sci., 131:593, 1965.

Mossberg, H. O. Obesity in children. Acta. Paediat. Scand., 35 (Suppl. 2), 1948.

Mullins, A. G. The prognosis in juvenile obesity. Arch. Dis. Child., 33:307, 1958.

Nestel, P. J., and Whyte, H. M. Plasma free fatty acid and triglyceride turnover in obesity. Metabolism, 17:1122, 1968.

Newman, H. H., Freeman, F. N., and Holzinger, K. J. Twins: A study of heredity and environment. Chicago, University of Chicago Press, 1937.

Opie, L. H., and Walfish, P. G. Plasma free fatty acid concentrations in obesity. New Eng. J. Med., 268:757, 1963.

Paulsen, E. P., Richenderfer, L., and Ginsberg-Fellner, F. Plasma glucose, free fatty acids, and immunoreactive insulin in 66 obese children. Diabetes, 17:261, 1968.

Prader, A., and Willi, H. Das Syndrom von Imbezillitat Adipositas, Muskelhypotonie, Hypogenitalismus, Hypogonadismus and Diabetes Mellitus mit "Myatonie"—Anamnese. Verhand. 2. int. Kong. psych. Entw.-Stör Kindes-Alt., Vienna, 1961, Part I, p. 353.

Seltzer, C. C., and Mayer, J. Body build and obesity—who are the obese? J.A.M.A., 189:677, 1964.

Shreeve, W. W., Hoshi, M., Oji, N., Shigeta, Y., and Abe, H. Insulin and the utilization of carbohydrates in obesity. Amer. J. Clin. Nutr., 21:1404, 1968.

Sims, E. A., Goldman, R. F., Gluck, C. M., Horton, E. S., Kelleher, P. C., and Rowe, D. W. Experimental obesity in man. Trans. Ass. Amer. Physicians, 81:153, 1968.

Stefanik, P. A., Heald, F. P., and Mayer, J. Caloric intake in relation to energy output of obese and nonobese adolescent boys. Amer. J. Clin. Nutr., 7:55, 1959.

Stunkard, A., and Mendelson, M. Disturbances in body image of some obese persons. J. Amer. Diet. Ass., 38:328, 1961.

White, P., Koshy, P., and Duckers, J. The management of pregnancy complicating diabetes and of children of diabetic mothers. Med. Clin. N. Amer., 37:1481, 1953.

Wolff, O. H. Obesity in childhood: a study of the birth weight, height and onset of puberty. Quart. J. Med., 24:109, 1955.

3.7
WATER AND ELECTROLYTE PHYSIOLOGY

LAURENCE FINBERG

Water, the major constituent of the body, comprising 70 percent of the fat-free mass, serves as the solvent for cell solids and as the transport medium between cells, tissues, and organs. Water also has the largest daily turnover of any body component and serves as the solvent for wastes; in addition, it plays a crucial role in body heat regulation.

In this section, normal and abnormal water physiology will be discussed in terms of body composition, obligatory expenditure and requirement of water, and finally, the pathogenesis of dehydration.

Body Water Composition

Part of the body water is within cells, and together with the dissolved solute, is termed intracellular fluid (ICF). Water outside of cells has a different solute composition and is termed extracellular fluid (ECF). These two compartments, representing the major anatomic and functional divisions of water in the body, undergo changes during early development. At birth, the ECF constitutes about 30 percent of the lean body mass, falling to about 25 percent at a few months of age, and to about 20 percent by the end of puberty. Conversely, the ICF increases from about 38 percent to 45 percent, and then to 50 percent of the lean body mass during these periods of development. The electrolyte composition may be shown best by diagrams such as those devised by Gamble, now called Gamblegrams (Fig. 23). These diagrams emphasize electroneutrality and indicate the usefulness of reporting concentrations in mEq/L. Since the major ionic constituents (Na^+, K^+, Cl^-, and HCO_3^-) are univalent, milliequivalence and milliosmolality are almost the same for the three fluids of greatest physiologic interest, the ICF, the ECF, and a subcompartment of the ECF, the blood plasma.

Water molecules and most ions diffuse freely across the cell membranes which separate the compartments. The distinctive composition of ICF and ECF result from an energy-dependent process which excludes Na+ from cells, at least relatively so from muscle cells, the most numerous in the body. The remaining differences are attributable to two factors: first, the impermeability of cell membranes to protein and some other large cellular anions; and secondly, the absence of osmotic concentration gradients owing to the rapid and free passage of water between compartments.

The ECF itself has several components; in addition to the interstitial water there are several specialized subcomponents, including tendon water, ocular, synovial, and cerebrospinal fluids, and, most importantly, the blood plasma, which accounts for about a quarter of the ECF or 6 percent of the body weight (Fig. 23). The plasma remains confined to the vascular space in spite of the free permeability of the capillary and the elevated hydrostatic pressure at the arterial end. Starling's analysis first made it clear that the hydrostatic pressure was offset by the relative impermeability of the plasma proteins, especially albumin, and that the plasma volume was dynamically preserved as the blood streams through the capillary bed.

Thus, plasma volume, as a fraction of the ECF, depends primarily on the amount of protein within the vascular space. Since the protein acts as an anion, a Gibbs-Donnan equilibrium applies to concentration differences of solutes between plasma and interstitial fluid. Since plasma volume has crucial significance to circulation, and preservation of circulation remains a prime consideration in problems of hydration, the chemical anatomy and the mechanism of partition of the ECF into plasma and interstitial fluid have major clinical relevance. Accordingly, the albumin content of plasma determines one of the most important aspects of water physiology.

Sodium and its accompanying anions do not diffuse into or out of the cerebrospinal fluid (CSF) and ocular fluid as rapidly as water. Hence, when sodium concentration in the ECF undergoes rapid change, a volume change occurs temporarily in the CSF until a new steady state develops some hours later. In this sense, whenever the osmolal concentration of ECF varies rapidly, the entire CNS may be thought of as analogous to a single large cell bathed in it. The water content of the CNS (ICF and ECF plus CSF) will either shrink with hypernatremia or expand with hyponatremia when either disturbance occurs rapidly. Thus, rapid infusion of 5 percent glucose in water will cause swelling of the brain, which, in some clinical circumstances, may be deleterious.

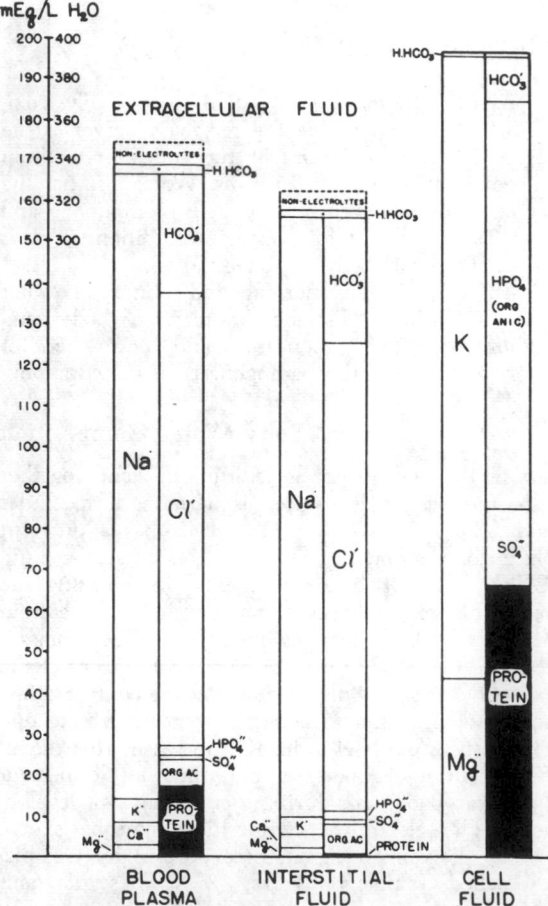

Fig. 23. The diagrams compare the composition of plasma, interstitial fluid, and ICF. While there are differences in total electrical charge owing to differing quantities of multivalent ions, the osmolal concentrations are obligatorily identical. (Reprinted by permission of the publishers from James L. Gamble. *Chemical Anatomy, Physiology, and Pathology of Extracellular Fluid.* Cambridge, Mass., Harvard University Press, Copyright 1942, by J. L. Gamble; 1947, 1954 by the President and Fellows of Harvard College.)

Chemical Homeostasis

In addition to diffusion, osmosis, and selective permeability or extrusion, there are other processes operating to maintain constancy of composition of body fluids. The most important of these is H+ ion metabolism, regulated principally by the lungs and kidneys. Despite the fact that H+ ion appears in minute concentration (nanomolar), a very narrow pH range must be maintained for life processes to proceed. Accordingly, acid-base homeostasis depends upon the presence of buffer systems, principally bicarbonate-carbonic acid, which afford maximum resistance to change at pH 7.4.

The mathematical statement of this buffering system may be summarized by the Henderson-Hasselbalch equation:

$$pH = pK + \log \frac{(HCO_3^-)}{(H_2CO_3)}$$

The value for the pK in biologic fluids is 6.1 and H_2CO_3 may be expressed as the partial pressure of CO_2 in mm of Hg multiplied by the solubility constant of 0.03. The equation then becomes:

$$pH = 6.1 + \log \frac{(HCO_3^-)}{P_{CO_2} \times 0.03}$$

At physiologic pH then:

$$7.4 = 6.1 + \log \frac{(HCO_3^-)}{P_{CO_2} \times 0.03}$$

$$\text{or } \log \frac{(HCO_3^-)}{P_{CO_2} \times 0.03} = 1.3$$

Antilog 1.3 = 20, so that a buffer ratio of 20:1 defines a normal pH. The chemical relationship among the reactants may be expressed:

$$H^+ + HCO_3^- \overset{\text{carbonic}}{\underset{\text{anhydrase}}{\rightleftharpoons}} H_2CO_3 \rightleftharpoons H_2O + CO_2 \uparrow$$

These interrelationships determine for the most part what happens to pH when there is an increased production of H^+, a loss of HCO_3^-, or when there is retention or excessive elimination of CO_2. Primary changes in H^+ or HCO_3^- are termed metabolic, whereas primary changes in CO_2 are respiratory. Any change in one of the reactants results in a change in the other two which affects the buffer ratio $(HCO_3^-)/CO_2$ in such a way as to minimize change in pH. When pH in blood goes below the normal range, an acidemia is said to be present. Conversely, a rise in pH is termed alkalemia. A change initiated by the addition of acid (H^+) or the loss of base (HCO_3^-) reduces the numerator of the buffer ratio. However, induced hyperventilation will then bring about a corresponding change in the denominator (CO_2). When the ratio is preserved with the reactants in lower absolute concentrations, the pH remains normal and the result is called acidosis; similarly, the opposite change is termed alkalosis. The terms metabolic and respiratory denote respective changes from metabolic or respiratory abnormalities, whether primary or compensatory. In this system of nomenclature only a change in pH receives the suffix -emia but a metabolic acidemia will usually be accompanied by a partially compensatory reduction in P_{CO_2} so that the disturbance has a respiratory component.

To assist in assessing the components separately, Sigaard-Anderson has introduced the term "base excess" to represent the metabolic component of a H^+ ion disturbance when the P_{CO_2} has been mathematically adjusted to a normal value of 40 mm of Hg. This quantity represents the amount per liter of strong acid (H^+) or strong base (OH^-) theoretically necessary to titrate the blood back to a normal pH. This number value, while not a biologic entity, provides a simple quantitative assessment of the metabolic side of a disturbance of the H^+ ion steady state.

The foregoing discussion ignores, for purposes of simplicity, the role of hemoglobin and other buffers which play lesser, but not insignificant roles, in acid-base adjustments. Ignored also are such factors as the effects of rate of change, the role of the skeleton, and many other contributing systems. For a more detailed discussion, the reader is referred to more specialized references. A consideration of the four types of disturbances follows. Each of them, when present, will almost always be accompanied by some degree of compensation.

METABOLIC ACIDOSIS. This condition may result from a primary increase in H^+ such as the accumulation of increased amounts of keto acids in diabetes, starvation, or salicylate intoxication, or from the primary loss of base (HCO_3^-) in the stool or urine. It also results when the kidney fails to excrete the normal amount of nonvolatile acid substances produced during metabolism of protein, chiefly acid sulfates and phosphates. Finally, tissue hypoxia leads to excess release of acid metabolites from anaerobic glycolysis or dying cells. The physiologic compensation for metabolic acidosis is hyperventilation, which by reducing the P_{CO_2}, maintains the buffer ratio closer to 20:1.

METABOLIC ALKALOSIS. This results from primary loss of H^+, for example, from loss of gastric secretion without pancreatic secretion, or from the administration of base. The vomiting of infantile pyloric stenosis is the classic example in pediatrics. Compensation for metabolic alkalosis is by hypoventilation which raises the P_{CO_2}; however, it is limited by the resulting hypoxia.

RESPIRATORY ACIDOSIS. This results from hypoventilation causing primary CO_2 retention. When the patient is breathing air, hypoxia necessarily also occurs, leading by way of disturbed metabolism to a metabolic acidosis as well. Partial compensation occurs through renal excretion of H^+ ion.

RESPIRATORY ALKALOSIS. This disturbance, a primary reduction in CO_2, results from hyperventilation and may be compensated by renal excretion of base as bicarbonate.

The preceding discussion outlines only the main elements of the whole complex problem of electrolyte and H^+ ion homeostasis. For most clinical problems, this knowledge will suffice, largely because several body organs function vigorously to maintain the status quo. These include the lungs, the kidneys, and the adrenal cortices. The lungs excrete CO_2 directly, which chemically includes an ion of acid (H^+) and of base (HCO_3^-), and thus they control directly the partial pressure of the gas (P_{CO_2}). As previously indicated, the kidney excretes the nonvolatile acid in the urine through a series of exquisitely adjusted mechanisms. The kidney also maintains ECF composition by excretion or retention of water, Na^+, K^+, Cl^-, HCO_3^- and divalent ions in addition to excreting organic substances. The adrenal and posterior pituitary add a fine regulatory control on the kidney for the excretion of water and electrolytes.

Maintenance Requirements

Water needs arise from ongoing expenditure of energy. This, in turn, occurs at a high rate in mammals, primarily to produce the necessary heat to maintain body temperature. Thus, water needs relate to caloric expenditure, which in turn depends in part on the relationship between mass and surface area. The two most commonly used reference points then are calories expended and surface area. Table 17 shows the relationship of both of these parameters to age and weight, the two measures which are most readily attainable. Basal values may be extrapolated when necessary by the rule of thumb that under ordinary ward conditions water needs are approximately 1½ × basal.

Physiologic water expenditures are as follows:

Skin and lungs	45 ml/100 cal metabolized
Urine (at 300 mOsm/L)	50 ml/100 cal metabolized
Stool	5 ml/100 cal metabolized
Total	100 ml/100 cal metabolized

The expenditure of 100 calories produces 12 ml of water so that the net requirement is 88 ml/100 cal. It should be emphasized that while deficits of water are usually estimated as a direct proportion of mass, maintenance requirements for water are related to energy expenditure which is not a linear function of mass.

Sodium requirements are very low but with intact renal function the range of tolerance is very broad. Potassium is less well conserved and must be provided more liberally; conversely, with renal insufficiency and oliguria, K^+ concentration in ECF may rise quickly to dangerous levels. Both of these cations may be safely administered for maintenance in amounts of 2 to 3 mEq/100 calories metabolized.

The Pathogenesis of Dehydration

Dehydration may be considered best clinically in terms of disturbances in the following five categories: volume, osmolality, H^+ ion status, ICF ion deficits, and ECF-skeleton steady state. Table 18 lists these factors with a brief outline of clinical and laboratory highlights. In the present discussion, physiologic principles will be stressed; in the following section these are applied to diarrheal disease of infancy.

VOLUME. In most dehydrated states, body water and solute are lost together in approximately physiologic proportion, the net loss being the total loss minus whatever intake has been maintained. The effect of such loss first becomes clinically manifest when plasma volume drops to the level where the circulation is impaired. Once this has occurred, the whole process becomes accelerated and danger becomes imminent. Although subjective evidence of dehydration occurs early, objective evidences such as tachycardia and dryness of skin and mucous membranes often do not appear until about 5 percent of the body weight has been lost over a very short time. When 10 percent weight loss has occurred rapidly without change in osmolality, circulation becomes significantly impaired and shock occurs. Slightly more loss, up to 15 percent of weight in a day, may be irreversible.

OSMOLALITY. The importance of osmolality derives from the division of the body water into compartments. The principal physiologic role of NaCl appears to be the partition of body water into its two main spaces, ECF and ICF. The body content of sodium (other than skeletal) and its accompanying anions, chiefly chloride, essentially determine the relative volume of water in the two compartments. For a given volume of body water, a higher sodium content will mean more ECF volume and correspondingly less ICF volume. Thus, high sodium content with volume loss produces cellular desiccation. Conversely, low sodium content with a deficit of water volume produces proportionately greater ECF loss. These two disturbances have been designated hypernatremic dehydration and hyponatremic dehydration, respectively.

Hypernatremic dehydration may be deceptive clinically because of the relatively greater preservation of the circulation. However, owing to several factors, the CNS shows disproportionate insult from hypernatremia. First, the nature of sodium and water transport into the CNS interstitium and CSF results

TABLE 17. *Approximate Basal Water Requirements in Relation to Age, Weight, and Surface Area* *

			Minimal Basal Water Requirement		
Age	Weight (kg)	Surface Area (m²)	ml/kg or cal/kg	ml/m²	ml/24 hr
Newborn	2.5-4	0.2-0.23	50	750	125-200
1 week-6 months	3.0-8	0.2-0.35	65-70	1000-1100	200-520
6 months-12 months	8.0-12	0.35-0.45	50-60	1000-1050	500-600
12 months-24 months	10-15	0.45-0.60	45-50	1000-1050	500-750

*From Finberg. *Pediatrics*, 45:1029, 1970.

TABLE 18. *Clinical Appraisal of Problems of Hydration*[*,†]

Point of Appraisal	Clinical Symptoms and Signs	Laboratory Determination of Greatest Value
1. Volume	Circulatory impairment Skin changes Eye and fontanelle changes Oliguria	Body weight Urea N in serum

2. Osmolality	For hypernatremia
	  CNS signs
	    disturbance of consciousness
	    hypertonicity of muscles
	    increased reflexes
	  Marked thirst
	  "Inapparent dehydration" with
	    good circulation for degree of
	    loss
	For hyponatremia
	  There occurs an exaggeration of
	    the signs listed under Volume
		Na^+ in serum

3. Hydrogen ion status	Hyperpnea in acidosis	CO_2 content (HCO_3^-) in serum or pH and Pco_2
4. Intracellular ion deficits	Abdominal distention Muscle weakness Diminished reflexes	K^+ in serum (limited use) EKG
5. Calcium homeostasis	Tetany Convulsions	Ca^{++} in serum (complex interpretation) EKG

*In this table, only the symptoms and signs of dehydration have been given. A companion group of signs for the corresponding disturbances of overhydration have been omitted for simplicity. The same points of appraisal and the same laboratory examinations may be advantageously used.
†From Finberg. *Pediatrics*, 45:1029, 1970.

in brain shrinkage and sometimes hemorrhage. The bleeding occurs secondary to capillary rupture after dilation owing to negative pressure when the shrinking brain pulls away from the rigid cranium. Thrombosis may in turn follow hemorrhage. Secondly, "idiogenic osmols" arise within body cells, including the brain, and this phenomenon may produce disturbances of neurologic function; at least the occurrence and the disturbances are associated. Finally, disturbances of calcium homeostasis with hypocalcemia occur during hypernatremic dehydration when potassium has been lost. Potassium losses are often large and replacement of this ion seems to facilitate ICF repair.

Experience has made clear that the twin dangers in treating hypernatremic dehydration are (1) too rapid infusion of dilute solution leading to brain swelling and convulsions, and (2) too much sodium in the repair solution enhancing CNS hemorrhage or resulting in generalized edema. Two important principles of management would appear to be gradual replacement of deficit when shock is absent, and generous provision of potassium when high urine output makes this safe.

Hyponatremic states may be symptomatic with diminished body water volume as in Addison's disease or following loss of gastrointestinal fluid with replacement of volume but not of electrolyte. On the other hand, in conditions such as K^+ deficiency or impairment of renal water excretion, the hyponatremia is more likely to be asymptomatic because the ECF volume is normal. Under these circumstances ICF volume is increased as is total body water.

In calculating requirements for therapeutic correction of symptomatic hyponatremic states, it must be realized that NaCl will be distributed osmotically throughout total body water, not the ECF alone, because water moves freely by osmosis to dilute administered solute. To avoid overhydration the salt should be administered as a hypertonic solution, 0.5 or 1 M, in amounts estimated from a space distribution equal to about 70 percent of the lean body mass. For example, the amount required to raise the Na^+ concentration 20 mEq/L in a 10 kg child would be $10 \times 0.7 \times 20 = 140$ mEq which is equal to 140 ml of 1M NaCl. For safety, only one-half the calculated amount should be given rapidly, the other half being given a few hours later after the patient's condition has been reassessed and electrolyte levels measured again, if possible.

HYDROGEN ION STATUS. Disturbances of H^+ steady state in dehydration are usually secondary to one or more of the following: circulatory failure with tissue hypoxia or diminished renal function, starvation with ketosis, or specific losses of acid or base. When volume and osmolality are adequately restored, the kidneys and lungs will usually adjust the H+ ion disturbances as long as neither renal nor pulmonary disease accompany the disorder. When indicated, base may be given as bicarbonate, lactate, or acetate. Similarly, H+ ion may be given as NH_4^+ salts, though this proves rarely necessary. In maintenance solutions the neutral chloride ion should account for about three-quarters of the anion, the remaining quarter being a base such as lactate.

The distribution space for administered bicarbonate requires a complex analysis beyond the scope of this discussion. For clinical purposes, one-third of the body weight can be taken as the immediate or short-term (a few hours) distribution space and about double this quantity for the long-term distribution. When an anion base such as bicarbonate or lactate is given, there must be an accompanying cation, usually Na^+. Care must be taken not to impose a sudden osmolal burden shifting body water suddenly from the brain to the ECF. Up to 3 mEq/kg of weight has been shown to be safe, whereas more than 9 mEq/kg in a 12-hour period produces risk of brain injury.

Administration of bicarbonate will not only increase the HCO_3^- but because of mass action the CO_2 (H_2CO_3) concentration will also rise. CO_2 diffuses more rapidly than HCO_3^- through body spaces. Hence, in the CSF, the CO_2 rise precedes the HCO_3^- rise, pH in CSF therefore falls while pH in plasma is rising. The effect is short-lived, and its clinical importance has not been demonstrated for changes produced by small bicarbonate infusions, but there is a suggestion that larger dosages, greater than 5 mEq/kg, may be dangerous.

INTRACELLULAR ION LOSSES (K+). In many clinical varieties of dehydration, potassium will be lost from the cellular water. Frequently this loss remains masked until ECF solute and volume have been restored. At this time, clinical evidences of K+ loss may appear, including muscle weakness, ileus, abdominal distention, and sometimes ECG changes. Because K+ replacement to cells must take place through the ECF, the rate must be carefully watched to obviate toxicity. A safe daily dosage when urine volume has become normal is 3 mEq/kg/24 hours. The concentration of potassium in intravenous solutions should not be higher than 40 mEq/L.

EXTRACELLULAR FLUID–SKELETON STEADY STATE. In a number of circumstances of dehydration, calcium levels in the ECF may fall. Renal impairment with Po_4 retention, rapid dilution of body fluids, and sudden change in pH may all encourage hypocalcemia and tetany. Hypernatremic dehydration particularly precipitates hypocalcemia by a mechanism distinct from those mentioned, but apparently only when there is a concomitant deficit of potassium. Any of these hypocalcemic states may be readily treated by 10 ml of 10 percent Ca gluconate per 500 ml of infused solution.

References

Darrow, D. C. The significance of body size. Amer. J. Dis. Child., 98:416, 1959.
——— A Guide to Learning Fluid Therapy. Springfield, Ill., Charles C Thomas, 1964.
Finberg, L. Hypernatremic dehydration. Advances Pediat., 16:325, 1969.
——— The management of the critically ill child with dehydration secondary to diarrhea. Pediatrics, 45:1029, 1970.
Harrison, H. E. Treatment of diarrhea in infancy. Pediat. Clin. N. Amer., 1:335, 1954.
Holliday, M., and Segar, W. E. Maintenance need for water in parenteral fluid therapy. Pediatrics, 19:823, 1957.
Sigaard-Anderson, O. Acid-Base Status of the Blood, 3rd ed. Baltimore, The Williams & Wilkins Co., 1965.
Welt, L. Clinical Disorder of Hydration and Acid-Base Equilibrium, 2nd ed. Boston, Little, Brown and Co., 1959.
Winters, R. W., Engel, K., and Dell, R. B. Acid-Base Physiology in Medicine. Westlake, Ohio, The London Co., 1967.

3.8
DIARRHEA IN INFANCY

ERWIN NETER and LAURENCE FINBERG

Diarrheal disease causes major morbidity and significant mortality in many countries. Although infection of the gastrointestinal tract represents but one of a number of causes of diarrhea, the discussion here will be limited to diarrheal disease caused by pathogenic microorganisms, including certain bacteria, viruses, protozoa, and fungi. Such infectious diarrhea may occur in otherwise healthy subjects or as a complication of underlying conditions, such as malnutrition and prematurity. It is particularly in the latter group that these enteric infections contribute to mortality.

Accurate information on the prevalence of diarrheal disease is not readily available even in countries with highly developed public health institutions. Among the reasons for this inadequacy are the following: (1) Diarrheal disease may be mild and self-limited and thus will not come to the attention of physicians. Unfortunately in some areas the same is true even when the disease is severe; (2) often, a clinical diagnosis is made, but the infectious nature of the disease is not ascertained, since microbiologic studies are not undertaken; (3) even when the etiologic agents are determined, all cases are not reported to public health authorities. Thus, in the United States only some 20,000 cases of salmonellosis a year are reported to the National

TABLE 19.   *Number of Deaths and Death Rates from Diarrheal Diseases (Exclusive of Diarrhea of the Newborn) 1965*

Countries	Number of Deaths	Death Rates Per 100,000 Population
Denmark	162	3.4
Canada	712	3.6
Australia	462	4.1
U.S.A.	7,899	4.1
Chile	5,062	59.0
Mexico	40,620	95.2
Colombia	19,834	109.4
Guatemala	10,775	242.8
South Africa (colored population)	6,455	368.6
United Arab Republic	133,628	—

Communicable Disease Center, whereas in all likelihood this infection occurs in some two million subjects. Therefore, the number of cases reported to Health Departments has to be considered as a minimal figure.

The scope of the problem of diarrheal diseases can be gleaned from reports of the World Health Organization. The number of deaths from enteritis, colitis, and gastritis, excluding diarrhea of the newborn, reported to the World Health Organization for the year 1965 exceeded 300,000. The number of deaths and death rates from diarrheal diseases from a few selected countries are presented in Table 19.

The fatality rates for enteric infections, including enteritis due to enteropathogenic *E. coli* and others, have decreased substantially over the past decades in the U.S.A. and certain other countries. This decrease can be attributed to several factors, including antiagents and nonspecific therapy, notably treatment of water and electrolyte disturbances. Also, better measures are now available to prevent or control outbreaks of diarrhea in nurseries. Finally, there appear to have been certain changes in host-parasite relationship that render current infections with enteropathogenic *E. coli* less severe than those seen two or three decades ago, and many patients are currently treated in outpatient departments or at home rather than being admitted for intensive care to hospitals. The factors responsible for this changing epidemiologic feature are not known.

ETIOLOGY. Infection of the gastrointestinal tract may be caused by bacteria, viruses, fungi, or protozoa. Certain microorganisms, such as *Salmonella, Shigella,* and enteropathogenic *E. coli* have been shown unequivocally to be causes of diarrheal disease. However, the role of other organisms, such as *Klebsiella, Proteus,* and certain viruses has not been as firmly established, since the presence of a suspected pathogen in the intestinal tract by itself does not provide unequivocal evidence of its etiologic role.

Among the 140-odd O groups of *E. coli* the following 10 are responsible for enteritis of infants: 026:B6 (60); 055:B5 (59); 086:B7 (61); 0111:B4 (58); 0119:B14 (69); 0124:B17 (72); 0125:B15 (70); 0126:B16 (71); 0127:B8 (63); 0128:B12 (67). Both designations of the surface K antigens are given here, e.g., B6 and 60. New serotypes of *Salmonella* are being described continuously and no fewer than 1,200 different types have been recognized thus far. Nonetheless, 10 of these serotypes accounted for 71 percent of all human isolates in 1967, according to the National Communicable Disease Center (Committee on *Salmonella*). Striking differences have been noted in the prevalence of *Shigella* around the world. *Shigella sonnei* has been particularly common in this country and in England whereas *Shiga bacillus* infections do not occur. In contrast, *Shigella flexneri* is more prevalent than *S. sonnei* in Japan, and *Shiga bacillus* dysentery is encountered in Asia. Staphylococci, probably through enterotoxin production, occasionally cause enterocolitis, notably as a superinfection accompanying antibiotic therapy. In addition, this microorganism is responsible for food poisoning (Sec. 14.15). Since newborn infants may harbor staphylococci in the intestinal tract in the absence of diarrheal disease, the isolation of this potential pathogen from the feces is not an indication for antibiotic prophylaxis. Cholera, caused by *Vibrio cholerae*, has become increasingly important in many countries of South Asia and the Western Pacific. Other potential pathogens, such as *Pseudomonas aeruginosa* and *Klebsiella*, are occasionally encountered, although the evidence for their etiologic role is incomplete. Among the protozoa, *Entamoeba histolytica* is responsible for dysentery in many parts of the world, particularly those with very hot climates. Two other protozoa, *Giardia lamblia* and *Balantidium coli*, also may cause diarrhea. Occasionally, *Candida albicans*, the etiologic agent of thrush, causes localized enteric infection, notably following antimicrobial therapy, although its presence in the feces is not always associated with overt illness.

Although detailed studies on the role of viruses in diarrheal disease have been carried out during the past two decades, surprisingly limited information on viral enteritis is available at this time. As early as 1943, Light and Hodes succeeded in transmitting to calves a filterable agent from newborns with diarrhea. Convincing evidence of the role of ECHO virus type 18 as cause of diarrhea in premature and older full-term infants was provided by Eichenwald and his associates. Other studies suggest that adenoviruses, too, may cause diarrheal disease in infants. Adenovirus type 3, responsible for respiratory disease, also may cause vomiting and mild diarrhea. This latter finding may explain the occurrence of this disease during winter months. Even when modern microbiologic techniques are employed, the etiology of diarrheal disease in many instances remains undetermined. In one such study by Moffet and co-workers, the proportion of patients in whom the cause remained unexplained ranged from 40 to 85 percent, depending upon age.

Usually, the diagnosis of the etiologic agent of diarrheal disease is based on isolation and identification of the microorganisms from fecal specimens. The blood culture is negative since in the vast majority of patients with enteritis neither enteropathogenic *E. coli, Salmonella,* nor *Shigella* invade the bloodstream. Although there is often an excellent correlation between the isolation of an enteric pathogen from the feces and the cause of the illness, isolation of an organ does not provide unequivocal evidence of the etiologic role of the isolate. Further support is provided if there is an increase in the titer of specific antibodies. The same considerations pertain to double or mixed infections. For example, when enteropathogenic *E. coli* is present together with *Salmonella* or *Shigella,* antibody titers increase against both microorganisms in some patients, suggesting double infection, whereas in others, antibodies against only one of the potential pathogens increase, suggesting a single infection in a carrier. Study of the immune response can also be of aid to diagnosis when a potentially pathogenic virus is present together with a bacterial pathogen.

All of the above mentioned microbial species may cause enteritis in older infants. Of the potential enteric pathogens, enteropathogenic *E. coli* has played the dominant role in outbreaks of diarrheal disease among newborn infants. Shigellosis is unexpectedly rare in the newborn, whereas salmonellosis occurs in all age groups.

TRANSMISSION. Diarrheal disease can be acquired from either carriers or patients with clinical illness; transmission may occur through personal contact or contaminated utensils, food, water, and occasionally flies or other insects. Certain enteric infections are largely restricted to man, including enteropathogenic *E. coli* enteritis and shigellosis. In contrast, salmonellae affect a large variety of animal species, and human infections may be acquired from infected animals, such as chicken, ducks, and eggs, and occasionally even from pets such as turtles. In countries where communal water supplies are adequately disinfected and milk and dairy products are pasteurized, transmission is usually from person-to-person, although accidental contamination of public water supplies is still a danger. For example, a waterborne outbreak of salmonellosis in California affected some 18,000 persons, representing more than 10 percent of all residents in the community. Safe water and dairy products remain a goal for the future in many countries of the world. Occasionally, enteric infection is transmitted from mother to infant during delivery. Acquisition by this route of enteropathogenic *E. coli,* salmonellae, and shigellae has been documented.

THERAPY. Enteric infection, particularly in older children, often is a self-limited disease and, even if available, specific therapy frequently is not required.

When indicated, selection of the chemotherapeutic agent or antibiotic should be based on the in vitro susceptibility of the etiologic agent, particularly since strains of a given species often differ in their sensitivities. Such information is particularly helpful when dealing with epidemics.

There is unequivocal evidence that certain antibiotics are effective in the treatment and prevention of enteropathogenic *E. coli* enteritis and of shigellosis. In striking contrast, none of the presently available antibiotics have been shown to be effective clinically either in the treatment of *Salmonella* gastroenteritis or in the elimination of the pathogen from the intestinal tract. In fact, recent evidence strongly indicates that the carrier state may be prolonged by ineffectual attempts at antibiotic therapy, and that unnecessary administration of antibiotics may lead to the emergence of increased numbers of antibiotic-resistant strains, in part through the process of transfer of genetic material, the R factors. Neither effective chemotherapeutic agents nor antibiotics are available for the treatment or prevention of viral enteritis.

Correction of the physiologic disturbances which accompany diarrhea and vomiting is of primary importance. Vomiting often represents an early manifestation of the response to either the infection or to abnormal water loss. Anorexia may be an even earlier symptom, and interference in intake hastens the appearance of serious functional disturbances involved in the pathogenesis of dehydration; these are loss of body water volume, changes in body fluid osmolality, disturbance of H^+ ion homeostasis, loss of intracellular ions, and a disturbance of calcium homeostasis. Each of these points of appraisal should be considered in evolving a therapeutic plan. In addition, clinical indications requiring supportive therapy require attention. Empirical observation has indicated that when diarrheal disease occurs in breast-fed infants, removal of the infant from the breast is rarely, if ever, necessary. There must be an early decision concerning the need for vigorous parenteral therapy requiring hospitalization. In North America and other areas where severe malnutrition has become rare and where the Shiga bacillus and cholera vibrio are not encountered, the need for such treatment is primarily in patients whose oral intake has been markedly reduced, usually by persistent vomiting. Consideration of the intake needed merely to offset normal ongoing water losses makes clear why, in the presence of abnormal water loss without replacement, the body weight may be reduced by 10 percent in only a few hours. Correction of dehydration requires an estimate of the degree of the physiologic disturbances which can be considered in five major categories.

Volume. First the volume of deficit already incurred must be estimated. A careful history will usually reveal gradual cessation of intake. The objective physical findings of dehydration first appear when about 5 percent of the body weight has been lost within a 24-hour period. Experience clearly justifies the useful clinical maxim that changes in body weight as great as 1 percent or more between two measurements within 24 hours may be considered to be loss or gain of water. At about 5 percent rapid weight loss, the clinical manifestations include dryness of mucous membranes and skin, mild tachycardia, and oliguria. When about 10 percent weight loss has occurred, the signs are more ominous and, except when hypernatremia is present, are predominantly circulatory since the losses are principally at the expense of the extracellular fluid (ECF). Tachycardia by this time has become pronounced, skin and membranes are very dry, and oliguria may be approaching anuria. The fontanelle, if open, will be palpably depressed, and the eyeballs will also be sunken into their sockets. The skin will show loss of elasticity and turgor. Owing to the nature of the subcutaneous tissue in the abdominal wall of infants, the abdominal skin remains in folds when gently pinched and the color (blood) returns slowly to the compressed skin. The extremities will show mottling and the distal portions will be cool to the touch. The infant frequently displays apathy and mild somnolence. When 15 percent of weight has been lost rapidly, a near moribund state of circulatory collapse will be present, frequently irreversible. Between each pair of landmarks, the clinician may reasonably interpolate the estimated percent of weight loss. The degree of accompanying undernutrition, when present, may modify the clinical picture.

Weight, the most important measurement, should be determined with precision since the admission weight will be the base line for gauging success during the critical period of management. The level of urea N in serum provides a rough guide to the accuracy of the estimated circulatory disturbance. Repair of total volume and the distribution of water between compartments are the two most important clinical determinants for successful therapy.

Osmolality. Measurement of sodium concentration in infants with diarrhea has shown that in about 65 to 75 percent the sodium concentration in serum is in the normal range, the infants being isonatremic; about 10 percent are hyponatremic, and from 15 to 25 percent hypernatremic. The importance of considering osmolality as reflected by the sodium concentration stems from its effect on the distribution of body water. In hypernatremic dehydrated states, partial preservation of ECF occurs at the expense of the intracellular fluid (ICF), and as a result, the circulation remains relatively intact.

Assessment of hypernatremia from the clinical history and physical findings alone cannot be accurate, but the experienced clinician will frequently suspect significant degrees of it. The clinical history almost always reveals an abrupt interruption in fluid intake, preceded occasionally by a high solute feeding. Skim milk with a high solute load per calorie, concentrated evaporated milk mixtures, or improperly made solutions of water, salt, and sugar have often been incriminated. Serious salt poisoning has resulted from unfortunate errors in mistaking salt for sugar. Anything which predisposes to excessive loss of water without proportionate solute loss may contribute to the background history. Persistent high fever, hyperventilation, and low humidity have all been contributory factors. Young infants whose surface area is large relative to their weight are especially susceptible.

The physical presentation of these infants will depend on the severity of the volume loss, the degree of hypernatremia, and the rate of occurrence of the dehydration. The earliest recognition of hypernatremia from physical findings usually occurs when an infant has lost about 10 percent of weight. Unlike the previous description, this infant will have a relatively intact circulation. The skin usually has a velvety sheen and the abdominal wall sometimes has a "doughy" consistency. High fever, often present, may be a result as well as a cause of the dehydration. Typically, these infants display a peculiar combination of lethargy when undisturbed and marked irritability when mildly stimulated. They will scream with a high-pitched cry and tremble only to slide back into somnolence when the stimulus is withdrawn. If the process is detected early, there may be evidence of avid thirst. The neurologic signs usually progress in roughly the following manner: hypertonicity of muscles in the extremities and mild nuchal rigidity, markedly active deep tendon reflexes, twitching of muscle groups, and generalized tremulousness; finally, either total obtundation of sensorium, or convulsions or both appear. The convulsions may be either focal or generalized.

Hyponatremia during dehydration occurs only when a high intake of water has been maintained without sufficient solutes. Giving large amounts of water or tea as the only oral intake or parenteral glucose water with insufficient sodium are the usual causes. In hyponatremic dehydration, there is a greater proportion of ECF depletion per degree of volume deficit. Thus circulatory embarrassment appears with a relatively small degree of deficit and quickly becomes profound, making evident the need for additional sodium in therapy.

Hydrogen Ion Homeostasis. In diarrheal diseases of infancy, a metabolic acidosis or acidemia usually develops as a result of three separate disturbances. First, stool losses usually contain more bicarbonate than body fluids, the source of the base being the digestive fluids. Since stool pH results in part from bacterial action in the gut in fermenting organic substrates, an acid stool may appear even though excess base is being lost from the body. Secondly, the partial starvation and dehydration that accompany diarrhea give rise to ketosis and increased lactic acid production, thus increasing the nonvolatile hydrogen load. Finally, disturbance in renal function, particularly reduced glomerular filtration rate, impairs the capacity of the kidney to excrete the nonvolatile acids. The last factor represents the limiting one in the interrelated processes. Consequently, whenever rates of glomerular filtration and urine flow can be reestablished quickly by proper adjustments of the vascular volume and the distribution of body water, the acidosis quickly recedes. If the process is very severe or lasting renal impairment exists, correction of acidemia may require administration of base.

The only reliable physical sign of acidosis is hyperpnea, which may be less apparent in young infants than in older children. The usual laboratory measurement for assessing acidosis has been the CO_2 content of the plasma which approximates the HCO_3^- concentration. In recent years, improved instrumentation has made it possible to measure arterial pH values and Pco_2 as well, and to evaluate the acid-base disturbance more completely. In most instances of diarrheal disease, correction of acidosis will be accomplished principally by the kidney.

Intracellular Losses. Careful studies of infants with diarrheal disease by Darrow, and later by Cooke and Darrow showed that potassium losses of 8 to 12 mEq/kg played an important part in the disability of these patients, particularly during the recovery period. Physical signs of potassium deficiency include abdominal distention, muscular weakness, and diminished reflexes. The ECG may show evidences of K^+ deficiency as well. Levels of K^+ in serum must be interpreted carefully since they may be normal or even high during periods of oliguria even in the presence of severe deficiency in total body potassium. Improving hydration and correcting the acidosis, if present, unmasks the K^+ deficiency both clinically and biochemically. At this point, CO_2 content tends to be high. Once urine output is assured, K^+ should be given routinely to infants with dehydration secondary to diarrhea.

Calcium Homeostasis. Disturbances in calcium homeostasis are not common. The problem is almost invariably hypocalcemia, which occurs more often in hypernatremic dehydration, although rarely to a level where tetany occurs. However, the presence of phosphate retention and the occurrence during therapy of rapid dilution and increasing pH may aggravate the situation and produce symptoms. Values for serum Ca^+ can be interpreted more fully if serum phosphate, protein, and pH determinations are also made.

IMPLEMENTATION OF FLUID THERAPY. The quantity and composition of the hydrating fluids should be selected on the basis of the needs of the individual patient. The volume of water to be administered in 24 hours should represent the volume of the estimated deficit, the estimated usual maintenance water, calculated as 1½ times the basal requirement, and additions for any ongoing abnormal losses. When hypernatremia is suspected or diagnosed, the volume to replace the deficit should be distributed over 48 hours rather than included in the first 24 hours of therapy.

If the usual isonatremic type of dehydration is present, the sodium content allocated to the deficit fraction should approximate ECF water or about 150 mEq/L. No sodium need be added to this figure on the first day. Thus, the maintenance fraction of the allocated water should contain glucose to combat starvation and ketosis, but no electrolytes. Potassium should be added after urine output is established. The anions for the Na^+ and K^+ should be Cl^- (75 percent) and base (25 percent) as bicarbonate, lactate, or acetate. In patients with very severe acidemia, some additional base should be given as bicarbonate. The infant who has lost 10 percent of his body mass will thus require 100 ml/kg of deficit water and 15 mEq/kg of deficit sodium (1/2 and 2/3 of this if he is hypernatremic), plus about an equal volume of maintenance water with glucose to which approximately 3 mEq/kg of K^+ will be added when safe to do so.

Although fluids may be given by other routes, continuous intravenous infusion should be used whenever possible in the early treatment of severe dehydration. The phases of treatment may be designated as emergency, repletion, early recovery, and resumption of nutrition. Unless near fatal undernutrition exists as a concomitant, there is no need to increase stool losses by oral administration of protein, fat, or even large amounts of glucose. Thus a brief period of 6 to 24 hours of fasting and thirsting, followed by a gradual buildup of nutrient, will be anticipated.

Emergency. The objectives during this phase, to restore circulation and renal function, are achieved through rapid intravenous infusion of sufficient solution to restore vascular volume. The amount depends on the choice of solution. Whole blood, single donor plasma, or 5 percent albumin, in doses of 20 ml per kg of body weight,* all have the advantage over noncolloid solutions of producing a more prolonged expansion of the vascular system. They may be followed by a similarly rapid infusion of 10 percent glucose in water which will hasten urine output and provide glucose to starving cells. Lack of immediate availability, expense, and fear of reactions or hepatitis constitute disadvantages to the use of blood or its derivatives. A solution of 10 percent glucose with 75 mEq/L of Na^+ (55 Cl^- and 20 HCO_3^-), in a dose of 40 ml/kg given in 15 to 30 minutes has been equally successful. This phase is omitted in infants with hypernatremia who are less likely to have circulatory impairment from volume depletion. However, if such a patient does present with even mild shock, either albumin or plasma should be given promptly since life processes must take priority over the slight risks of further increasing the sodium content.

Repletion. This phase follows the emergency treatment and generally lasts about 6 to 8 hours. The calculated amount of the remaining water and salt is given moderately rapidly by intravenous infusion. K^+ is withheld until urine formation has been observed. The volume given in this phase plus that already given will equal approximately the estimated deficit. However, the repletion will still be incom-

---

* The weight used for convenience may be the dehydrated weight. To offset this "error" the water of oxidation may be ignored.

plete owing to ongoing losses, normal and possibly abnormal.

Early Recovery. The third phase lasts until the end of the first 24 hours. The remainder of the calculated fluid is given, plus any additions for abnormal losses. In this phase fluids may be given by mouth, using if preferred, a glucose-electrolyte mixture. By the end of 24 hours, the patient should have gained 8 to 9 percent in weight. If the change in weight is significantly less or more, the situation should be reanalyzed.

Hypernatremic patients should be treated more slowly, omitting the rapid phase and expanding the total time for repletion to 48 hours. In addition, calcium gluconate, 10 ml of a 10 percent solution, should be added to each 500 ml of infusion, and the K^+ content of the fluid should be maximal (40 mEq/L) once urine output has been established. These measures enhance cellular hydration and protect against changes in CSF pressure.

Early Convalescence. Milk feedings should be resumed gradually, substituting about 20 percent of the day's volume with a glucose-electrolyte mixture. The glucose concentration should be about 5 percent and the sodium and potassium contents should provide 2 to 3 mEq of each ion per 100 ml of water. Too rapid resumption of calories increases stool osmolality which with impaired absorption, often causes normal stool water loss. Some infants have a transient intestinal lactase deficiency lasting up to a few months, making a lactase-free feeding desirable during this period. A protein hydrolysate with glucose as the carbohydrate has been used successfully in this circumstance. In some centers such a preparation is used routinely for a few weeks for sicker infants in the attempt to avoid a relapse.

DIFFERENTIAL DIAGNOSIS. There are several conditions which give rise to severe intractable diarrhea in infancy which are not infectious. Each of these is discussed elsewhere, but they should be mentioned here with the more usual diarrheal diseases. For example, diarrhea may be the predominant clinical manifestation of duodenal ulcer in infancy. Intracranial lesions in the diencephalon or subdural hematomas may present with severe diarrhea. Neural crest tumors which secrete amines may cause severe diarrhea as may some of the congenital immunologic deficiency states such as absent thymus (DiGeorge syndrome). Diarrhea may be a prominent manifestation of a number of inborn errors of metabolism such as hyperglycinemia, urea cycle deficiencies, and others. The congenital disaccharidase deficiencies also present as severe diarrheal disease.

SEQUELAE. The question of ultimate growth in infants who have had long-term diarrhea has been discussed in the section on malnutrition with which diarrhea, infectious and noninfectious, is so clearly related. Permanent neurologic damage, primarily following hypernatremic dehydration, represents an added hazard for those patients. One careful series indicated an 8 percent mortality and an 8 percent permanent cerebral sequelae rate. Precise data comparing hypernatremic dehydration with simple dehydration of diarrheal disease are not available from a prospective study, but it seems likely that the serious residual damage, presumably due to hemorrhage, is several fold higher in the hypernatremic group. Whether recognition and adjusted therapy improves this situation also remains unknown, but speculation from recent experience justifies hope that improvement will result.

REFERENCES

EPIDEMIOLOGY AND ETIOLOGY

Aserkoff, B., and Bennett, J. V. Effect of antibiotic therapy in acute salmonellosis on the fecal excretion of salmonellae. New Eng. J. Med., 281:636, 1969.

Benenson, A. S. Control of Communicable Diseases in Man, 11th ed. New York, The American Public Health Association, 1970.

Committee on Salmonella, National Research Council. An evaluation of the salmonella problem. Washington, National Academy of Sciences, 1969.

Despres, P., Herouin, Cl., Plainfosse, B., and Seringe, Ph. Discussion du role de *Klebsiella pneumoniae* dans les gastro-enterites infantiles. Presse Med. 77:463, 1969.

Duncan, I. B. R., and Hutchison, J. G. P. Type-3 adenovirus infection with gastrointestinal symptoms. Lancet, 1:530, 1961.

Eichenwald, H. F., Ababio, A., and Arky, A. M. Epidemic diarrhea in premature and older infants caused by ECHO virus type 18. J.A.M.A., 166:1563, 1958.

Elsea, W. R., Partridge, R. A., and Neter, E. Epidemiologic and microbiological study of a *Shigella flexneri* outbreak. Public Health Reports, 82:347, 1967.

Krugman, S., and Ward, R. Infectious Diseases of Children, 4th ed. St. Louis, C. V. Mosby Company, 1968.

Light, J. S., and Hodes, H. L. Studies on epidemic diarrhea of new-born: isolation of filtrable agent causing diarrhea in calves. Amer. J. Public Health, 33:1451, 1943.

Moffet, H. L., Shulenberger, H. K., and Burkholder, E. R. Epidemiology and etiology of severe infantile diarrhea. J. Pediat., 72:1, 1968.

Scrimshaw, N. S., Taylor, C. E., and Gordon, J. E. Interactions of nutrition and infection. Geneva, World Health Organization, 1968.

Top, F. H. Communicable and Infectious Diseases, 6th ed. St. Louis, C. V. Mosby Company, 1968.

Yow, M. D., Melnick, J. L., Blattner, R. J., and Rasmussen, L. E. Enteroviruses in infantile diarrhea. Amer. J. Hyg., 77:283, 1963.

TREATMENT OF DEHYDRATION

Cooke, R. E. Contributions of the laboratory to the practical management of disorders of body water and electrolytes. Pediatrics, 16:555, 1955.

Darrow, D. C., Pratt, E. L., Flett, J., Jr., Gamble, A. H., and Wiese, H. F. Disturbances of water and electrolytes in infantile diarrhea. Pediatrics, 3:129, 1949.

Govan, C. D., and Darrow, D. C. The use of potassium

chloride in the treatment of the dehydration of diarrhea in infants. J. Pediat., 28:541, 1946.

Finberg, L. Hypernatremic dehydration. Advances Pediat., 16:325, 1969.

Macauly, D., and Watson, M. Hypernatremia in infants as a cause of brain damage. Arch. Dis. Child., 42:485, 1967.

Powers, G. F. A comprehensive plan of treatment for the so-called intestinal intoxication of infants. Amer. J. Dis. Child., 32:232, 1926.

chapter 4

PHYSICAL GROWTH

FRANK FALKNER, Associate Editor

Introduction and Biometry

As a subject, growth is traditionally coupled with development. *Growth:* the multiplication of cells and size changes; *Development:* the maturation of structures and their functions. With increasing knowledge in the field, it is clear the two terms are intimately related, and in complex fashion. Thus, omission of one of the terms is for brevity and does not imply a neat separation of the subject matter of the two; hopefully, using the term growth to encompass both will break a tradition of questionable usefulness.

Biometry applies to biologic facts, mathematical analysis, and statistical methods. A very basic knowledge of biometry is useful for all students of human biology, but is mandatory for those specifically studying growth, because of the well-known, but not always remembered, very wide variability in parameters of growth found in normal infants, children, and adolescents. There appears to be, in all of us, an inherent attachment to the *average, standard,* or *norm.* This is encouraged by the large amount of normative data available and published. A norm indirectly *describes.* An individual child is weighed and noted to be heavy, light, or of average weight for his age. Many healthy normal children will have weights above and below the norm. The key question is: How far may they *deviate* from the norm and still cause no concern?

The *distribution curve* demonstrates how a set of measurements are distributed about the middle point or *central tendency.* The vertical axis shows the number of individuals; the horizontal axis is a scale of the units of measurement used. Figure 1 is an example of such a curve. Since exactly 100 babies were measured, the number of babies on the horizontal axis is also the percentage of the sample. *Class intervals* are regular convenient increases in measurement scale, and an individual's measurement is fitted into the appropriate "interval." The curve formed by the measurements on these 100 babies is roughly symmetric and is known as a *normal distribution* or *Gaussian curve.* Working from the middle point (central tendency), there are as many individuals below in measurement as above.

The *arithmetic mean* (the sum of individual measures divided by the number in the sample) is not quite the same as the *median* (the middle point where half the sample fall below, and half above), which it would be were the curve in Figure 1 to be exactly Gaussian.

We are interested in the mean, or the median, but what we really need to know is the *range* of

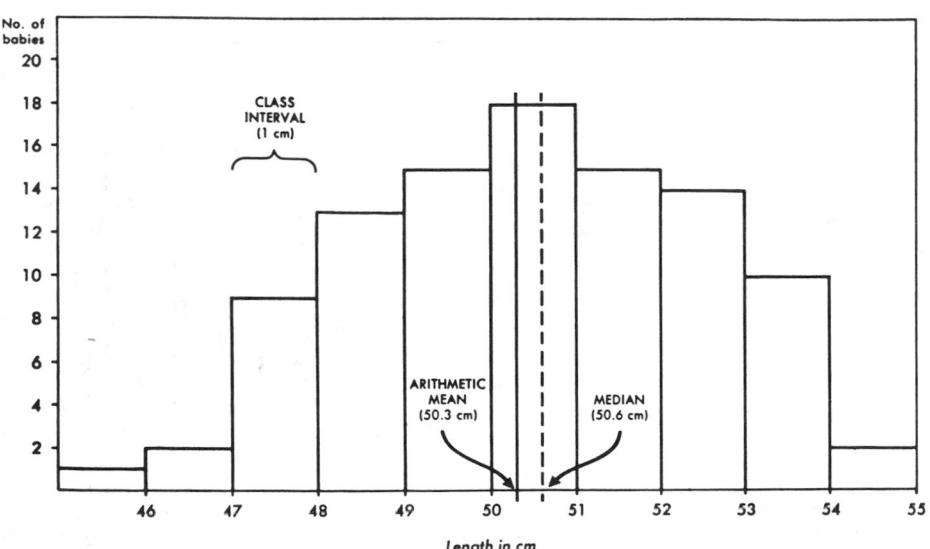

Fig. 1. A distribution curve of birth lengths of 100 male babies, class interval = 1.0 cm. (From Falkner. *Pediatrics,* 29:460, 1962.)

average measurements we may expect so that we can see whether an individual's specific measurement will fall inside it or not. These ranges are derived from distribution curves. We need, then, to know how any set of measurements in a sample is *dispersed* or *distributed* around the central point. For this we calculate and use *measures of dispersion*. By far the most practical for everyday usage is the *percentile*. The median is also the *fiftieth percentile*—50 percent of the sample above that measure, 50 percent below it. Clearly, it would be helpful to know at what point, say, only 5 percent of the sample fall below, and only 5 percent fall above. If we calculate the *5th* and *95th* percentile and place them in the distribution curve, we find the points shown in Figure 2. It will also give us, obviously, a *range* of measurements in which 90 percent of the whole sample fall; in this case between 47.2 cm and 53.8 cm. The 5th and 95th percentiles are often accepted as being a good "range of normality," but any combination (e.g., 10th and 90th) may be used depending upon the purpose.

Standard deviations (SD) are also used as measures of dispersion and tell how much a certain measure *deviates* about the mean point. As with the percentile, it can deviate to either side of the mean, smaller or larger; hence, there should always be a plus or a minus sign preceding the calculated standard deviation figure (which is in whatever unit of measurement is being used—centimeters in the sample here). If 1 SD is subtracted from the mean, and 1 SD added to it, we have a range of measures from -1 SD to $+1$ SD. In a Gaussian distribution, this will include some 67 percent of individuals. If we subtract, and add, 2 SD's to the mean (± 2 SD's), then this range will include a little more than 90

percent of individuals. This is clearly approximately the same range as given by the 5th and 95th percentiles, and indeed scientists commonly accept ± 2 SD's to indicate the outer limits of "normality." In the sample measured and shown in Figures 1 and 2, the SD was calculated to be ± 1.9 cm. So we could summarize the birth length information we have on a sample of 100 male babies as follows:

-2 SD's	46.5 cm
5th Percentile	47.2 cm
50th Percentile (median)	50.5 cm
Mean	50.3 cm
95th Percentile	53.8 cm
$+2$ SD's	54.1 cm

The use of percentiles as ranges is to be encouraged in clinical pediatrics and child health programs since they can be applied to either Gaussian or *skewed* distribution curves. Some measures used in growth study are distributed in skewed, or asymmetric, fashion. With very skewed curves, the standard deviation is not appropriate since it is a rigid numerical value which, in such cases, denotes something quite different on one side of the mean compared to the other when used as a range. Standard deviations are widely used when possible because further working of data and use of many statistical tests are based upon the calculation of SD. Fortunately, most of the measures we deal with in normal growth are not skewed to a degree to cause concern as regards everyday usage.

Collection of data used for presenting norms and ranges may be carried out in two basic ways. By far the commonest method is the *cross-sectional study*. Here, certain described individuals ("10-year-

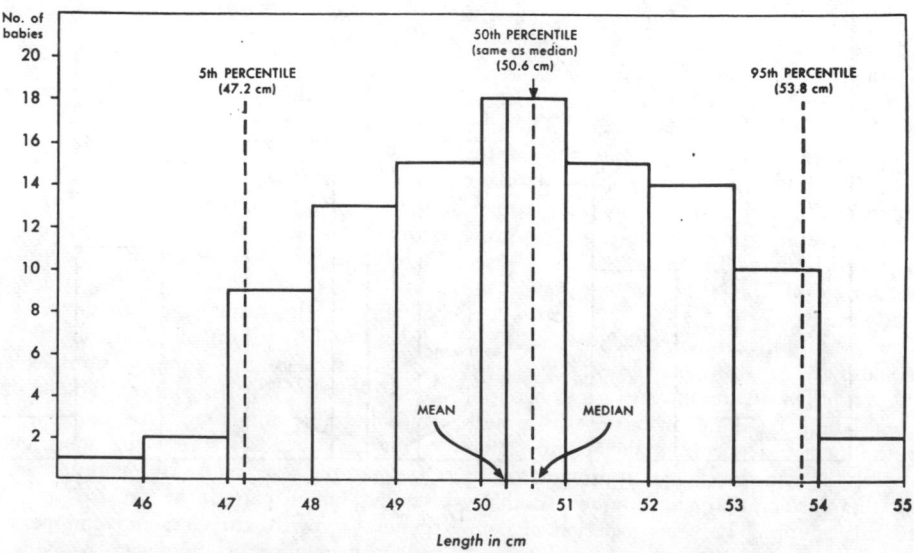

Fig. 2.   The same curve as in Figure 1 with 5th, 50th, and 95th percentiles added. (From Falkner. *Pediatrics*, 29:461, 1962.)

old Puerto Rican boys living in an urban U.S. environment") are measured once and resultant standards produced. This method produces data quickly and is basic to the formation of countless tables, charts, and grids, for various ages or age groups. Such studies are mainly productive of *distance* data. Thus, what point on an individual's total height growth curve has been reached at, say, age 8 years?

Since growth is a continuum from conception to adulthood, and then to death, we must also study change or *velocity* in growth and must then turn to the second basic method: the *longitudinal study*. Here the *same* individuals are measured at specific ages over a period of time, and these studies, while clearly more difficult to carry out, give us data concerning how much an individual has grown between, say 7 and 8 years—his *speed* of height growth, in fact.

The above examples of normative data describe an individual; however, we also need to *evaluate* the individual child, and this can be accomplished only if such data are related to a background of other parameters involving both normal and abnormal growth. It is here that the multidisciplinary approach to all growth problems must start.

Growth Patterns and Rate of Growth

The false conception that growth is steady throughout the seven ages of man is commonly held, and this is understandable because we think in terms of size achieved at various ages. But growth is not constant: both the velocity of many size indicators and the acceleration occurring in different organ systems vary widely at different ages and between different parameters of growth. It is very important, then, to consider velocity, or incremental growth.

Using the stable measurement of *stature* as an example, we can plot the curve of stature achieved at each age for one individual, and the resultant curve is shown in the top of Figure 3. If, from this curve, we calculate how much the boy grew in each preceding year, the lower curve in Figure 3 results. This curve shows, then, his growth rate for stature, and it will be noted that it demonstrates a dramatic difference in shape. Since stature and body weight follow this same overall growth pattern and indicate size, the incremental curve in Figure 3 can be used as a demonstration of the effect of age upon the human growth curve.

The newborn infant grows at a great pace, as every parent knows. As the early months pass, his growth is also rapidly *decelerating*. This concept is hard to grasp when thinking in terms of growth velocity for the first time; it is analogous to a fast motor car being braked hard. At approximately 3 years of age the deceleration stops rather suddenly and between this age and 10 years a period of comparatively steady growth occurs—in roughly equal annual increments. Often the slowest growth rate occurs just before the onset of puberty. The indi-

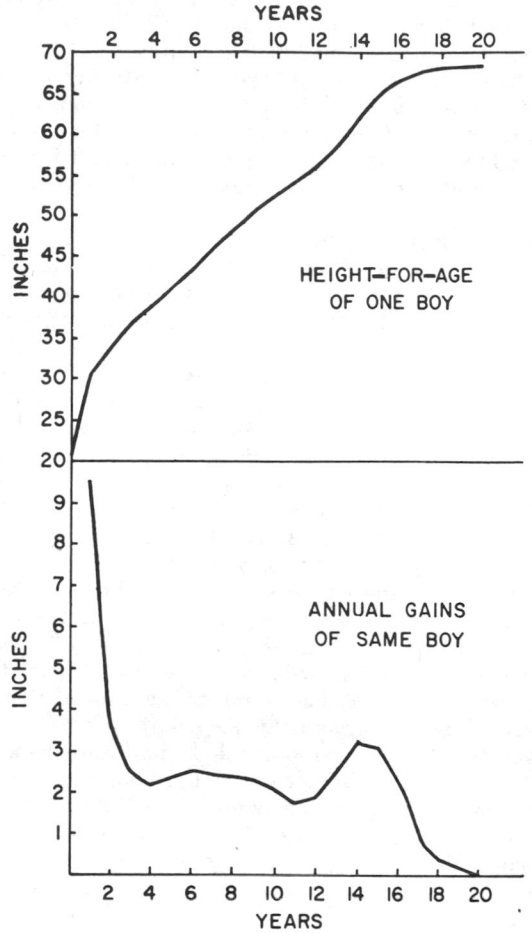

Fig. 3. *Top:* A distance curve showing the stature-for-age of one boy from birth to 20 years. *Bottom:* A velocity curve showing annual increments (gains) plotted from the upper curve. (From Falkner. *Pediatrics, 29:*450, 1962.)

vidual's puberty period then starts and the adolescent growth spurt begins. Marked *acceleration* occurs for, generally speaking, the only time in postnatal life. A sharp peak is reached (*peak velocity*), and then an equally rapid period of deceleration occurs. Finally, growth velocity becomes zero and adult status is reached. In any discussions of growth and related factors, it is important to keep the picture of the human growth curve in mind. Many tissues and major organs of the body follow the general human growth curve. Examples are respiratory and digestive organs, kidneys, spleen, blood volume, muscle mass, and bone mass.

Body weight, surely the most commonly used measurement of man, in overall terms follows the same general pattern of growth as stature, or the general growth curve. Some comment and caution in interpretation is, however, needed. *Birth weight* is considered to be within normal limits if it is between 5.5 and 13.0 pounds. A newborn baby weighing 8.0 pounds may double his birth weight at 6 months and weigh then 16.0 pounds; his first 6-month increment is thus 8.0 pounds. At 3 months of age, though, he may have lost suddenly, for some abnormal reason, say, 4.0 pounds, and after correction of the condition exhibited catch-up growth and thus reached 16.0 pounds at 6 months. Three things are illustrated by this example: body weight is itself an unstable measure and body weight decrements frequently occur; catch-up growth occurs; and when studying growth of an individual or in general (body weight especially), particularly in the early months of life, it is necessary that the incremental periods be short in order that the actual pattern of growth emerges and is not hidden.

During the early days of life there is a 5 to 10 percent body weight loss in healthy infants due largely to diminution of body water content. This normal phenomenon proceeds until the third or fourth day, when weight gain begins, and by the tenth day the birth weight has been regained. As very rough guides, body weight has usually doubled from birth weight by 4 to 5 months, and tripled by 1 year of age. The general course of growth is then followed. Interpretation of body weight patterns must always be based on the realization that a gain in weight may indicate fat growth, bone and muscle growth, a seasonal effect, catch-up growth, gain in total body water, increased caloric intake, and so forth. Body weight patterns, then, may hide important factors.

We must also recognize that important body components or systems may grow very differently and have their own particular growth curves. When a particular tissue or body complex is being considered, the particular growth pattern should be known in principle and taken into account. In health, *head circumference* is a reasonable indicator of *head and brain size*. Its velocity curve is very different from that of general growth. A period of rapid incremental growth occurs from birth, and then a marked deceleration until the age of approximately 10 years—the size of the skull having reached nearly 90 percent of its adult size by this age. Thereafter, the increments are minimal until adulthood. Put in lay terms, a 10-year-old's hat size will be not much different from that of his adult size. This measurement may also be used to give an example of the necessity to consider growth patterns within certain age groups or categories of babies and children. Patterns may occur which deviate from normal patterns yet are not, in themselves, indicative of pathologic processes. The onset of hydrocephalus is often unnecessarily feared in an *infant of low birth weight* (ILB). The increments of head circumference in these infants are much greater than those of full-term normal babies. Although the head size of an ILB is much smaller at birth than that of a full-term infant, at 3 months of age both groups of infants, on the average, have similar head circumferences. This is achieved by the greater velocity of head circumference growth in the ILB. Knowledge of this specific growth pattern is

helpful in evaluating the possibility of a developing hydrocephalus.

The growth rates of the *prostate, testis, ovary,* and *uterus,* are related to function; they have a slowly decelerating organ size-velocity curve in relation to percentage of adult size achieved, reaching zero by about 9 years. An intense period of acceleration starts when puberty begins, followed by deceleration until adult size is reached. *Lymphatic growth,* as manifested by lymph nodes, lymphoid tissues of the intestines, and the thymus, is peculiar: there is comparatively steady, quite rapid growth until maximum size is reached in the prepuberty period. At this point, the lymphoid body mass is nearly double that of the adult mass. Subsequently, the lymphoid tissue shrinks until adulthood is reached. This curious growth curve has important clinical application since the tonsils and lymph nodes are part of this system. The prepubertal child with very large tonsils may well be exhibiting a normal part of the lymphoid growth curve. If left alone and tonsillectomy is not performed, the tonsils will decrease in size as described.

Bone growth is obviously assessed by height measurement and thus follows the general growth curve. Individual bones in a child, however, may grow at widely different rates—an important factor influencing final body proportions. *Muscle growth* is closely similar to the overall pattern of bone growth, but of all the tissues, muscle is the one, especially in the male, which is laid down heavily during the adolescent growth spurt. The greater muscle mass growth in boys in this period is naturally reflected in the greater strength of the male. Since male strength is so much greater than female strength, another factor may be involved such as biochemical differences in the muscle cells themselves. As very approximate overall guides, it is estimated that 25 percent of total body weight is muscle mass at birth, the corresponding proportion at adulthood being 43 percent. *Body fat* has a complex growth pattern of its own. Fat increases steadily and quite rapidly for the first (approximately) 9 months of life. A plateau is then reached and increments will be zero. Soon thereafter, there is a true loss of fat until about 7 years. (Thus, any curve depicting fat growth must be able to record negative increments, or *decrements*.) At 7 years fat is gained once more. In many male children there follows an important clinical and social phenomenon. In such instances a growth spurt of fat occurs before the individual's general adolescent growth spurt. Such children seem suddenly to become obese, or to enter a "puppy-fat" phase. When the general body adolescent spurt begins (including muscle and bone mass), this external fat is stretched over the rapidly growing frame; and there is also an actual loss of fat, or return to decremental growth, during adolescence. Thus, the earlier preadolescent phase is replaced by the "string bean" phenomenon. The female child does not usually follow quite the same growth pattern of this tissue, and in early childhood her fat loss is less than the male's. Hence, the average female reaches adulthood with more total fat than the average male. Added to these normal patterns are such interrelated factors as hypercaloric food intake and true obesity. The complexity and importance of the fat growth are clearly apparent.

CELLULAR AND CHEMICAL GROWTH. The concept of human growth as a continuum from conception should be kept for all parameters of growth. We still hear and read today of the child being a miniature adult. This false notion is exposed at once when considering the body composition of fetus, newborn baby, older child, adolescent, adult, and the aged. All are markedly different. Immediately following fertilization of the human ova, cell multiplication proceeds at a prodigious rate, together with differentiation, followed by a diminution and then, towards the end of fetal life, a steady addition of cells with organ and systems growth. At birth, there is still some increase in cell numbers, but cell growth from then on occurs in the main by increases in cell size. Human cells fall into four groups: (1) Stable specialized cell groups that do not replace lost cells. Examples: striated muscle, smooth muscle, and neurons. (2) Constantly vigorous renewal cell groups. Examples: epithelial cells and hemopoietic cells. (3) Slowly increasing cell groups with very low but steady mitosis. Examples: thyroid, pancreas, and renal cells. (4) Diminishing cell groups where loss exceeds renewal or expansion. Examples: atrophy of genital tissue cells and involution of the thymus. DNA content of somatic cells is constant, and since DNA can be estimated quantitatively, important investigations can be carried out in this whole area. By such analysis, it is estimated that there are in the order of 1.3×10^{12} cells present in the full-term newborn baby. The content of DNA per unit of tissue weight decreases as the child grows, thus demonstrating the main tendency for cell size to increase rather than cell number. The comparable total cell estimate of an adult human is 100 times greater than at birth, or 1×10^{14}.

Total body water accounts for about 90 percent of early fetal weight, and at birth the proportion is 75 percent of body weight, dropping to 60 percent by 1 year of age, after which the proportion is more or less constant until adulthood. There are two components of body water—*extracellular* and *intracellular*. The drop of total body water percentage in the first year of life has more significance when the decrease is broken down into extracellular water drop of from 44 percent to 26 percent in this first year. This reflects the concomitant relative increase in muscle mass, the decreasing water content of fat tissue, and decreasing percentage of total body water. Intracellular water remains virtually the same after 1 year of age, at about 35 percent. Since *sodium* and *chloride* are the main mineral constituents of extracellular fluid, it follows that their growth patterns are similar to that of water. Conversely, *nitrogen* and *potassium* are mainly intracellular substances and increase, in

general, in quantity during growth. Potassium is a helpful indicator of changes in body composition because of this intracellular distribution unrelated to body fat. Potassium content increases after 1 year of age, reaching a plateau at about 9 years. At prepuberty and again at midpuberty, the male exhibits two peaks of rapid increases in body potassium, which then falls to adult levels. At puberty the female shows a steady decrease in body potassium over the puberty period until her adult level is reached—markedly less than that of the male. The difference in patterns between the sexes at adolescence is largely accounted for by the much greater muscle growth in the male, and the greater body fat growth in the female.

Growth patterns of water, protein, fat, minerals, and hence, bone and muscle, are, then, related and geared to amino-acid growth patterns. When the key constituents of body composition at various ages are examined and related to function, it at once becomes apparent that critical time periods in human growth occur. As Cheek has pointed out for some time, growth needs to be explored in terms of cell numbers, cell size, and body composition, especially in deviations from normal growth patterns. The importance of this area in nutritional growth factors is clear. One hormone may influence cell replication; another, cell size. If the remarkable complex interaction of all these factors go awry at certain critical points of growth, the extent of damage may be irreversible. Hence the need for particular attention and future study in these considerations.

CONTROL OF GROWTH AND CATCH-UP GROWTH. There is very little relationship between adult size and birth size. However, by 2 to 3 years of age the relationship of current size to adult size is quite good. Full-term newborn babies vary comparatively little in size; the size of the uterus, citing one of many factors, clearly limits this variation. How then, does the newborn baby destined to be a genetically tall adult get onto his own growth curve by 2 to 3 years of age? He exhibits *"catch-up" growth* and grows much faster than average, and especially so if he was a small baby at birth. He has made up most of the "deficit" by 6 months of age, and at this age ranges of body weights in different populations are not nearly as wide as at later ages. There certainly appears to be a *control of growth* mechanism at work here since by no means all small babies exhibit catch-up. Those that are destined to be healthy, genetically small adults do not; their growth is, as it were, aimed at their genetic target of smallness.

These control mechanisms work on a base of suitable environment. The newborn rat corresponds to the human fetus towards the end of gestation from the point of view of developmental periods. From two litters of newborn rats a small privileged group was created that fed exclusively from one mother, and compared with a much larger group of newborn rats who had to share another mother. In 21 days, as might be expected, the privileged group weighed up to three times as much as the large group and were significantly larger. After this all the baby rats were weaned and allowed unlimited food. The small, poorly nourished rats now grew at a faster rate than the privileged, well-nourished rats. This increased rate continued until the rate reached the average "normal" velocity curve which it then followed. The catch-up, however, was not sufficient to bring the originally poorly nourished rats up to the size of the well-fed rats. Studies of small-for-gestational-age "runt" pigs show that these newborn pigs remain small and never catch up. The role of maternal undernutrition in such phenomena is not clear and is probably very complex.

Reduced blood flow to the placenta and fetus and the concomitant transport of key nutrients to the developing fetus are clearly important factors. This subject stresses the need for intensive study and attention to *prenatal growth factors*. The studies mentioned indicate that if malnutrition (in the general sense) in fetal or very early childhood development is sufficiently severe, the organism may be irreversibly damaged. This damage may affect the grow-controlling mechanisms.

An interesting example of this area of growth is afforded in humans by monochorionic monozygous twins, who share the same placental mass. The pla-

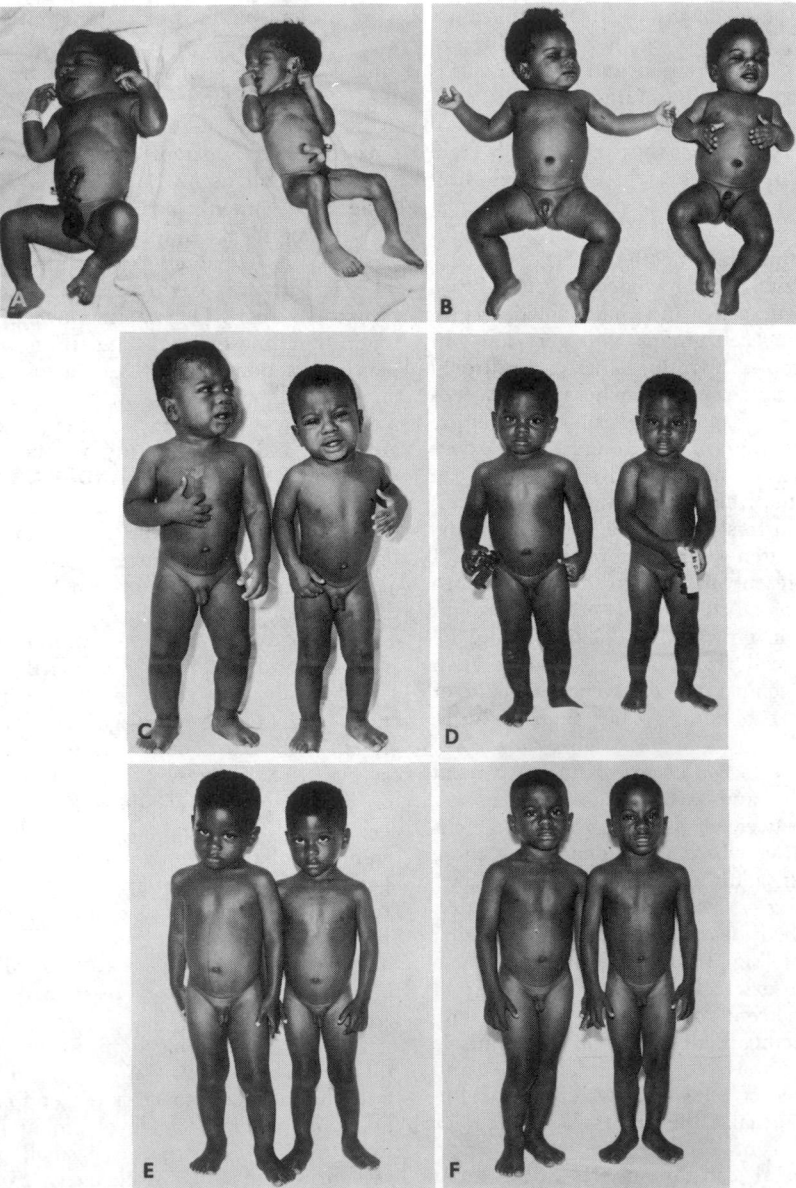

Fig. 4.   Monochorionic monozygous twins at birth, 9 months, 18 months, 2 years, 3 years, and 4 years of age. The low-birth-weight twin is on the right in each picture. (From Falkner. In *Human Development*. Courtesy of W. B. Saunders Co.)

cental transfusion syndrome is well known where one twin transfuses the other in utero via an arterio-venous shunt in the placental anastomoses of blood vessels. At birth the donor twin may be of very low birth weight, grossly anemic, and dehydrated. The recipient twin may be of much heavier birth weight, polycythemic, and hypervolemic. However, even in the absence of overt evidence of this syndrome, we still see identical twins grossly different in size at birth. In such cases it appears that the good relationship existing in average newborn babies between placental mass and newborn size, holds for twins who share the same placental mass, since this sharing may be very unequal. Figure 4 shows the growth of a full-term twin pair in which the birth weight of one was 2,806 g and the other 1,460 g. The corresponding dry weight of the placental part supplying the large twin was 85.90 g and that of the small twin, 37.40 g. There was a difference of 7 cm in their birth lengths, and in the first 6 months of life the smaller twin (who exemplifies the unsuitability of the term "premature" baby as defined by birth weight, for both were of course born at the same time and were full term) exhibited catch-up and lessened the 7-cm gap. Since that age, however, both twins grew at the same rate, and the smaller twin's catch-up has not been sufficient for him to reach his brother's size. At 4 years of age there was a 3.0 cm height and 2.3 kg body weight difference. Figure 5 illustrates the height velocity curves of the twins, who are, it should be remembered, genetically similar.

The corresponding notable difference in masses and dry weights of the twins' placental parts did not reveal any significant differences in *concentrations* of various key nutrients and minerals. However, a clear and possibly meaningful difference exists between the total *quantity* of such nutrients available. Total DNA and total nitrogen, for example, were markedly different in the above example. If the availability of placental nutrient factors falls below a certain needed level, deficiency could occur with resultant interference with growth and possible damage.

Current discussion centers upon whether there is, in fact, a centrally located *general control center* for growth in the human. A normal child is extraordinarily hard to deflect from his own target curve of growth. If he becomes seriously ill or malnourished, he may temporarily be deflected from his curve. Correction of the condition will in many cases elicit catch-up growth; he will accelerate at a fast rate, rise above his velocity curve, and then drop back into it. Presumably the control mechanism sees to it that his size is not affected ultimately by this phase, and also shuts off the compensatory phase when it has been successfuly completed. A hypopituitary dwarf treated with human growth hormone will usually increase his height velocity significantly; but the therapy does not stimulate maturation of the skeleton equally. Thus, the human pituitary gland alone does not appear to be such a general control center. Weiss and Kavanau have suggested that "antitemplates" control growth. These are postulated as circulating substances which *inhibit* growth. A monitoring system continually measures the organism's own size and growth rate by estimating the amount of substances circulating and produced by growing cells. This system signals when any overproduction occurs, and the antitemplate system immediately inhibits growth. Tanner (1963) postulated a single inhibitor substance emanating from a growth control brain center that also keeps a tally of developmental age, the tally being, in effect, the target growth curve. Growth velocity is continually adjusted so there is no mismatch between time tally and inhibitor concentration. These speculations surely involve genetic coding, and must also recognize the possibility, in the human, of a separate control mechanism for the dramatic adolescent growth spurt.

THE SECULAR TREND. The study of human biology reveals an interesting phenomenon: children from widely different populations have been maturing earlier and earlier and becoming larger and larger at each age—at least during the last century. The earlier maturation is largely responsible for the children being larger age for age; adult size has not increased nearly so dramatically as one might expect, since growth stops earlier. Therefore, it appears unlikely that a giant human race is in prospect. This secular trend is of a degree that cannot be simply related to improved socioenvironmental differences alone. Reliable records from many different countries and studies may be summarized as showing, since 1900, an average size increase of approximately 1 cm in height and 0.5 kg in weight for each decade in the preschool ages; about 2.5 cm and 2.5 kg for each decade during puberty; and 1 cm per decade for the adult. Social class differences have existed over this

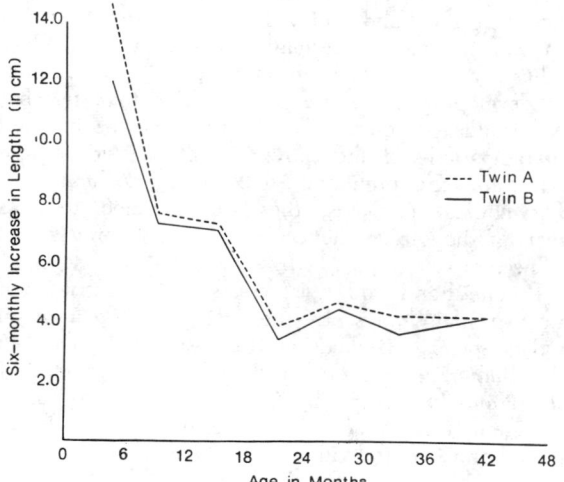

Fig. 5. Six-monthly increments of length in centimeters of monochorionic monozygous twins. Twin A was the smaller twin at birth. (From Falkner. In *Human Development*. Courtesy of W. B. Saunders Co.)

period and still do, yet the secular trend overrides them. The age of *menarche* is so conveniently clear-cut as an event in time that it serves as an excellent comparative maturity marker in widely different countries and samples. There is a remarkable similarity in patterns over more than a century. A summary reveals that the age of menarche has been decreasing approximately four months per decade since the 1840's. It is at present in the United States approximately an average of between 12.5 and 13 years.

It is certainly reasonable to attribute a major portion of factors involved in the secular trend to improved environmental conditions, particularly nutrition and socioeconomic conditions. Yet the trend is not only present in the underprivileged populations and samples, and it cannot be a question simply of caloric intake. Genetic influences have been altered by the tendency of genetic pools to be increasingly mixed as humans mate from wider and wider areas of the world. Possibly the genes concerned in tallness and larger size may be dominant. Mortality (particularly infant mortality) and morbidity rates have dropped continually and often sharply over the past century, and there may be a selection factor involved in the production of a healthier population of children and adults. The trend still continues, however, in countries where mortality and morbidity have plateaued in the last 15 years. Extrapolating the age of menarche into the past, it would seem this age was in the female's thirties in the Middle Ages. History does not confirm this conjecture. Extrapolation into the future produces the alarming picture of menarche before 10 years of age in very tall girls. In fact, we do not find such bizarre extrapolations accurate in human biology, and we therefore must consider seriously if the secular trend is an undulating curve over the centuries and that there is no simple all-embracing background to its causation or control. Interestingly, some successive groups of child patients and undergraduates from well-to-do families in North America followed over a 30-year period have plateaued and do not now exhibit the secular trend. Perhaps these groups represent optimal environment, care, and selection and it is possible that the secular trend levels off when such a crest, if it exists, is reached.

MATURITY. Particularly at times of rapid growth, chronologic age is apt to be unhelpful as a marker in describing an individual child. A "healthy 13-year-old boy" does not raise any set image before a human biologist because the boy may be smooth and round faced, of short stature, and tend to be obese from puppy-fat. Or he may be tall, thin, and with a notable mustache. The difference in the two healthy boys has very marked physiologic, morphologic, medical, social, and educational implications. The fact that there is such a very wide spread of age of onset of the adolescent spurt among healthy children indicates the need for a measure of age other than chronologic. *Maturational*, or *developmental*, *age* is therefore useful.

Maturation of the skeleton, or *skeletal maturity,* is probably the most acceptable and helpful indicator. Increase in length of the skeleton occurs by proliferation of cartilage cells in cartilaginous areas—a process which is continuous from early fetal life and which may be termed *chondroplasia.* As a sequential process, after vascular penetration of primary and secondary centers, the process of ossification of the cartilaginous areas starts by deposition of osteoid tissue. This may be termed *osteogenesis.* When ossification is complete, synonymous with epiphyseal closure or fusion, bone growth has ceased. The finality of this end point has vital importance in considering problems of growth.

In health the two processes are linked very closely and dissociation does not occur though the relative *rates* may differ. If dissociation does occur, the final size of the child will be affected. For example, if osteogenesis proceeds apace, while chondroplasia continues at a normal or less rapid rate than osteogenesis, the particular growth life of the skeleton would be diminished and stunting would occur. This does indeed occur in the adrenogenital syndrome in older children. Put another way, adult stature is determined by the speed of linear growth and by its duration, which is a function of skeletal maturity. The measurement of stature (height) is a good practical measure of linear growth (chondroplasia). The measurement of skeletal maturity (osteogenesis) is also clearly important.

Radiographic examination of the skeleton will reveal the stage of skeletal maturity (bone age). The maturity assessment can be made by comparing such radiographs with sets of standards, or counting, for example, the number of ossification centers present. Any part of the skeleton may be used, and standards exist for different parts. For practical clinical use, however, the hand and wrist serve best; the area is convenient, more information exists about it than other parts of the skeleton, and a variety and number of developing bones are present. The total number of secondary centers of ossification may be counted in radiographs of the extremities of one side of the body and the number also compared to standards. For clinical purposes, the latter method requires more radiography, hence x-irradiation, and seems unnecessary.

The hand and wrist assessment is carried out in two main ways. In the *atlas* method, a given radiograph is matched with the standard plates in the *Radiographic Atlas of Skeletal Development of the Hand and Wrist* by Greulich and Pyle. These represent various ages, and the plate most closely resembling the individual radiograph designates the age standard and hence the *bone age.* The Greulich-Pyle standards are based upon best average representation from a sample of healthy, well-to-do children in the U.S. Separate standards are needed for boys and girls since the female child is more maturationally advanced than the male. Ideally, as with height and weight for example, standards should be made for various different populations and races. A more recent method (*Tanner-Whitehouse*) provides a series of average standard appearances and stages through which each bone passes, which are then matched with each bone of the individual radiograph. Each stage has a numerical score assigned to it. These scores are added to give a skeletal maturity score for the whole hand and wrist area. Either percentile status of skeletal maturation (just as in height and weight) or a bone age may be determined by this method. Bone age is determined by the chronologic age at which the given score is at the 50th percentile (median). Only one set of stages is needed for both boys and girls, and the skeletal maturity score will simply be higher for girls than for boys.

Since, in health, all individuals reach ultimately 100 percent maturity of any maturational indicator, skeletal maturity provides a good common developmental scale and indicates the percentage maturity obtained at any stage of development. *Prediction* of growth, to some extent, may then be made by estimating the skeletal maturity status and relating it to the general growth curve. The concept then arose of the difference, in health, of *early, average,* and *late* maturing children, who ideally need their own three separate standards of growth. An individual compared with general standards may suddenly start to exhibit a new growth pattern, especially as his puberty approaches. He may, in fact, merely be maturing "early" or "late."

Children may be classified into six main groups according to their patterns of maturation.

1. Average children who will closely approximate the common mean curve for height and weight at stated ages.
2. Early maturing children who are tall in childhood solely because they are more mature than average children; their curves will fall above the mean curves of average children but not greatly so. They will not be unusually tall adults.
3. Early maturing children who are also genetically tall. They are taller than average from early childhood and continue to mature rapidly. These children will reach adult status early and will be tall adults. Their curves will always fall well above the mean.
4. and 5. These groups are the opposites of 2 and 3. They are late maturers, with or without genetic shortness, whose growth curves will fall below the average in the same way that those of groups 2 and 3 fall above them.
6. Finally, there is an indefinite group whose members often find their way into the "growth clinic." They are children who start puberty much earlier or much later than one would expect. The spurt may occur suddenly, before it is expected, or it may be a muted gradual process when it

is delayed. Since the child's "total growth life" is longer or shorter than the average, he may well become a much taller or shorter adult than would have been expected.

Other *indicators of maturity* include the *deciduous* and *permanent dentition,* and the execretion, for example, of the *17-ketosteroids.* For application in pediatrics, however, these examples are not truly practical and are not as easy to interpret as might be thought. Since it is the onset of puberty and the puberty period where so many of the growth problems found in pediatric practice occur, and where such normal ranges of growth patterns exist, the much neglected maturity indicators associated with the adolescent growth spurt are of invaluable help. The *secondary sexual characteristics* form the basis of these indicators.

The sequence of appearance of these indicators is not the same for all boys and girls, but it is much less variable than the age at which they occur. The comparative orderly and usual sequence makes for a practical, useful method of maturity assessment. *Pubic hair* stages are used in both boys and girls. Useful pictorial standards and descriptions for five stages (with Stage 1 being prepubertal) are found in the Appendix. Five stages of genital development are similarly described for boys (Appendix), and five stages of breast development for girls (Appendix). An individual child would thus have two ratings. For example, "12-year-old boy, bone age 14 years, puberty rating, genitals: 3, pubic hair: 4." —clearly an early maturer.

The first sign of puberty in the boy is usually increase in size of the *testes*—Stage 2. Some scant pubic hair growth may coincide, but usually starts later and coincides with the onset of the adolescent height growth spurt and *penis* growth in size. *Facial, axillary,* and other *body hair* growth starts about two years after pubic hair growth has started. The *male breast* undergoes change and marked enlargement, termed *gynecomastia,* occurring in midpuberty in at least 50 percent of boys (a recent study suggests that with careful palpation this would be found in 85 percent). True adolescent gynecomastia, when visible and commonly slightly tender, causes much distress among healthy male adolescents and its transient nature must be stressed. Subsidence is nearly always completed within 1½ years from the occurrence. *Breaking of the voice* is a gradual process, but the start occurs comparatively late in puberty. In girls, growth of the *breast* is usually the first sign of puberty—Stage 2. Pubic hair may, as in boys, appear at this time, but usually growth occurs later and coincides with the onset of the adolescent height growth spurt. *Menarche* is such an easy event in time to pinpoint that it is a valuable maturity marker in the female. The most important fact to know as regards sequence of events in female puberty is that menarche invariably occurs *after* the peak height growth velocity and thus towards the end of puberty. It does not usher in puberty as so many are led to believe. Here is an example of the need to assess all indicators of maturity; a genetically tall girl of, say, 11 years may frequently be labeled as not having started puberty because menarche has not occurred. Thus, the patient and her parents are alarmed at the possibility of her becoming a giant. However, the great majority of these children are early maturers whose breast stage assessment will often reveal that they are in a late stage of puberty and about to menstruate for the first time. They are well along the decelerating velocity height curve and will grow little more. Assessment of the bone age will usually further pinpoint the true stage of maturity and help to allay the anxiety of the child and parents.

Two things must be stressed: the age of onset of puberty varies very widely indeed in healthy children of both sexes. There is another important variation, too, among individual children: the average boy passes from genital Stage 2 to 4 in about

2 years. Exceptionally, this may take up to 5 years. So that while in many children linkages between the various maturity indicators are strong, in some they are loose; and not only does the rate of passage through puberty vary, but it is unrelated to early, average, or late maturation. A healthy girl may complete her puberty phase in 2 years; at the other extreme another may reach adult stages of breast and pubic hair growth and yet menarche may not have occurred. As very approximate guidelines, 95 percent of girls will exhibit the first sign of puberty between 8½ and 13 years; maximum (peak) height velocity on average at 12 years, with menarche on average at 13.2 years. Correspondingly, boys' first sign of puberty is between 9½ and 13½ years, and maximum (peak) height velocity is on the average at 14 years.

The female child is, on the average, more advanced than the male in nearly all maturation indicators at sometime or other: in skeletal maturity, probably from late fetal life onwards; in permanent dentition; in the onset of the adolescent growth spurt.

Particularly at the prepubertal and pubertal phase of growth it is helpful to assess the total maturity status picture of an individual child by using some of the preceding methods of assessment. Figure 6 diagrammatically summarizes guidelines in health for the aforementioned indicators of maturity. **GENERAL FACTORS INFLUENCING GROWTH.** It is difficult to think of any commonly found factor in all pediatric or child health practice and study which does not have some influence, direct or indirect, negative or positive, upon growth. Thus, in the following section only the broadest areas will be discussed, emphasizing the need to turn to specific chapters for detailed information and the need to consider the general subject of growth as a backdrop to the whole of pediatrics and child health. *Racial influence* is much interrelated with genetic influence, and it is difficult to assess when concomitant important environmental and nutritional factors are involved. Some examples follow: Japanese-born children when reared in California mature at a faster rate and reach a larger size than contemporary Japanese reared in Japan, though the body shape and proportions retain the Japanese characteristics. Menarche occurs at different average ages in different racial groups living in the same environment. When socioeconomic conditions are similar, the Negro newborn baby in the early months grows at a faster rate and is advanced in psychomotor development compared to the Caucasian baby. Indeed, this fact appears to hold even when the Negro newborn baby is reared in much more adverse socioeconomic conditions than the Caucasian baby. Finally, as a simple example, healthy Maori children are shorter and stockier than white New Zealanders at all ages from 5 to 20 years. *Environmental* and *hereditary* influences on growth are the two broad key factors. An influence upon growth can very rarely, however, be labeled as either environmental or ge-

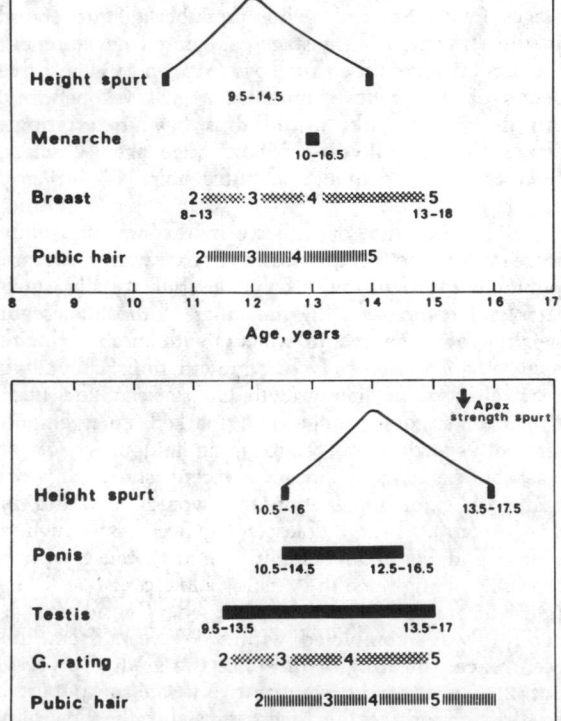

Fig. 6. Diagrammatic representation of the sequential occurrence maturational indicators from age 8 to 17 in an average healthy girl and boy in relation to age scales. The age range within which some of the changes occur is indicated by the figures below them. The breast, genital, and pubic hair ratings, or stages, refer to those mentioned in the text and which appear in the Appendix. (From Marshall and Tanner. *Arch. Dis. Child.*, 45:22, Fig. 8, 1970.)

netic, for to do so implies that these are two clear and distinct categories and that each factor belongs entirely in one or the other. Environment and heredity are inseparable; they interact constantly. It is thus important to assess the *weighting* of genetic or environmental influences in speaking of a certain factor. It is appropriate, then, to state that a certain influence on growth is largely one in which, for example, the genetic weighting is heavy. Again, if a certain growth pattern is unfolding, either normal or abnormal, we need to know whether the factor(s) causing this pattern is largely genetic, largely environmental, or a fair mixture of both.

Genetic factors on growth are very strong in the human. They have been estimated to account for as much as 80 percent of all influences. The study of genetics using the human child as a subject, and the study of genetic influence upon early growth, is difficult and reveals many gaps in our knowledge. Inquiry must start before conception, the human has few progeny, his gestation period is long, as is his life span; before data have been gathered on two generations, the investigator is aged. Yet specific studies on disease and healthy populations have shown, for example, that measuring the parents as well as the individual child greatly enhances the assessment of a child's growth status. Ideally we need growth standards and charts incorporating this parental factor. Experienced physicians always pay attention not only to *size* but also past maturation patterns of parents when evalualing the growth status of their offspring. Parental body build is a second parameter in need of consideration in assessing child growth. *Endocrine factors,* in very broad terms, act at certain different stages of growth and interact. There are basically four hormones involved: 1. *Thyroid* has a strong influence on later fetal growth and in the first year of life during those periods of rapid growth and maturation. 2. *Pituitary growth hormone* is the single most important hormone stimulating growth after the second year, but it does not appear to influence maturation. 3. *Androgens,* from the adrenal cortex, ovary, and testis, are a major influence in the onset of the adolescent growth spurt and concomitant maturation. 4. *Estrogens,* in both boys and girls, seem to be involved in maturational patterns, particularly skeletal maturation during adolescence. The action of hormones is synergistic and highly complex. Their influence on growth and responsibility for each morphologic change, coupled with specific feedbacks on each other, are not fully understood. It is at once apparent that the preceding brief section is a much oversimplified introduction.

Nutritional influences on growth are fundamental. Surprisingly, and no doubt due to the complexity of the subject, there are some large gaps in scientific knowledge. What is the true influence of maternal good nutrition, malnutrition, or overnutrition upon fetal growth and early childhood growth? Does overnutrition in children stimulate growth in stature and increase maturation or decrease longevity? These are some unanswered questions.

Malnutrition, speaking broadly, retards growth, and influences body weight much more than stature growth. If malnutrition is eliminated, catch-up growth occurs and stature growth proceeds at greater velocity than skeletal maturation. This gives a greater chance that predestined normal adult height can be achieved. If the period of malnutrition has been prolonged and/or severe, as in the rat study described earlier on p. 237, and occurs at certain critical growth periods, then human catch-up growth may also not be sufficient to eliminate the growth deficit and permanent stunting, and late maturation can occur (see also p. 238, concerning identical twins). It is pertinent to align this finding with similar indications as regards mental development and reveal deficit, and permanent stunting and late maturation in normal growth. A good example is afforded by a study showing that when malnourished young children were well fed, rapid brain and head circumference growth followed, which was presumably catch-up growth.

Illness, in general, is somewhat akin to malnutrition as an influence on growth. Frequent short illnesses do not result in permanent growth retardation, whereas prolonged severe illness may indeed do so. Again, the degree and force of catch-up growth is all important. Evidence is bearing out the long-held view that *emotional environment* is a factor influencing growth. Emotional starvation, as exemplified by studies of maternal deprivation of infants and young children, can retard growth. Catch-up growth occurs if adverse and emotional environment is corrected; but, again, the degree and duration are of importance, and stunting can occur. There is some evidence that hormonal influences may be interrelated with this factor. *Seasonal influence* on average growth curves is significant in many parameters, such as height, weight, and peak velocity. However, the effect of seasonal variations are usually not reflected in growth curves of individual children. The cause of seasonal effect is not known, but presumably variations in hormonal secretions are involved to some degree. On the average, body weight growth is greater in late summer and fall than in winter or spring; height growth, on average, is greatest in spring. There is some indication that seasonal influence on growth is stronger in children from poor socioeconomic background. *Climate,* long thought to be an important influence upon growth, appears to have but a minor effect upon growth patterns. This fact emerges when the climate factor is separated from other environmental and from racial ones. The menarche of well-to-do Nigerian girls occurs at the same average age as with Alaskan Eskimo girls; age of reaching puberty stages in Nigerian and English boys is similar. Careful studies reveal similar growth patterns within the same country and race, between children reared in different parts of their country with greatly differing climatic conditions.

Clinical Appraisal of Growth

Careful inspection of data on growth can be of value in pediatric care and child health considerations. The pediatrician and his ancillary colleagues may be alerted early to the possibility of an imminent important health problem. We may well be overwhelmed, however, by the quantity of data on growth that has appeared in recent times. General considerations are important and we can proceed to take stock. First, a brief and general word on growth assessment in the *perinatal period*. Since we cannot measure the fetus in utero, we have to concentrate on birth weight. If a baby is born, say, eight weeks before full term, whatever caused this may have affected his fetal growth. Birth weight within normal range in a baby born at 34 weeks will be unlikely to stimulate consideration of what the birth weight would have been had he remained in utero for the normal six remaining weeks. It would possibly have been abnormally high, or low. Obviously extrauterine growth standards are needed for babies born from 30 weeks of gestation and onwards.

An individual child assessed clinically for growth should ideally be compared to standards derived from a similar group of children. The original sample should be homogeneous and the individual child fitted into its characteristics. This can rarely be achieved in practice to an ideal degree. We are becoming involved more frequently in the care of children from other countries, and in other countries. For growth assessment in Nigeria, for example, is it best to use U.S.A. or British standards, standards made from a wide cross section of Nigerian children, or standards derived from a most privileged sample of Nigerian children? To most the latter would seem preferable, but it is unusual to find such standards. At least it is important to note the characteristics of the sample being used for comparison, and this sample should be homogeneous in age, sex, basic race, and socioeconomic background. Standards derived from a sample of 6-year-old Californian girls in which there was a considerable proportion of Southern Japanese girls would not be helpful. Nor should a Japanese girl be fitted into standards of Californian girls. The date of the study producing the standards should be noted, for as we have discussed, the secular trend should make us hesitate to use standards compiled some time ago. Thus, it is clearly necessary that the standards used in pediatrics and child health be renewed and polished constantly.

The great majority of standards used rely upon height and weight data. Two important points must be made: First, whenever standards are derived from a large sample of children for, say, height at certain ages, the curves of the averages, and ranges, presented will naturally absorb the individual pat-

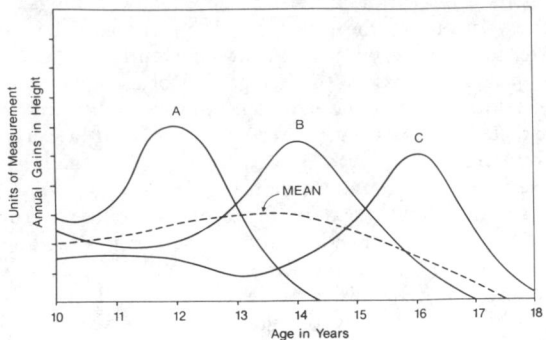

Fig. 7. Annual height gains of three individual boys, A, B, and C. The dotted line is the mean of these three boys' annual increments. (From Falkner. *Pediatrics*, 29:464, 1962.)

terns of each child measured. The result is a smooth curve with no peaks or irregular changes. An individual child will, however, usually exhibit such peaks and changes yet be growing perfectly normally on his own individual curve. This is particularly important in the immediate preadolescent and adolescent growth periods. An example is shown in Figure 7 of the mean curve derived from three boys who are an early, an average, and a late maturer in that they are reaching their own maximum velocity in height during their own adolescent growth spurts at different times. By the same token, an individual child plotted on typical distance curves for both height and weight achieved for age, may be following a regular channel perhaps above the mean curves. At 13 years of age, for example, he may rather suddenly drop below the means and at 14 and 15 cause concern because his size is not increasing as it should. It is in fact most probable that he is merely a late maturer and is growing normally on his own individual curve. Ideally, then, particularly at adolescence, we should use three separate standards—for early, late, and average maturers. These are exactly what Bayer and Bayley have produced and advocated.

The second and fundamental point is that there is no clear-cut place where abnormality starts and normality ends in any parameter of growth. The best way of illustrating this overlap is to return briefly to the discussion on distribution curves in the introduction to this chapter. If we consider an imaginary sample of dwarfed children, and another sample of normal healthy children at a certain age, two distribution curves can be made from data on their height for that age. Figure 8 shows the result. The hatched area is where the two curves overlap, and should an individual child fall in this area the question is at once raised, "Is he a very tall dwarf, or a very, very small normal individual?" It is indeed in such overlap areas, even though imaginary and exaggerated purposefully in this example, that a great number of "growth problems"

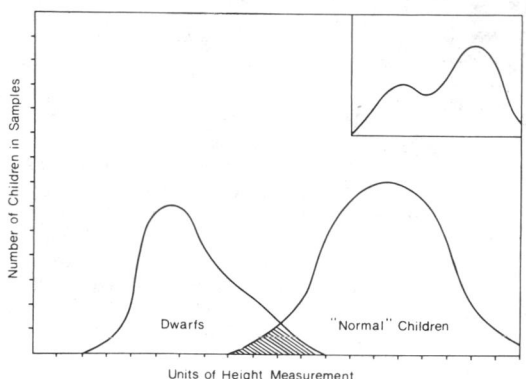

Fig. 8. Distribution curves of height of two samples of children at a certain age. The right-hand inset is the bimodal curve resulting from pooling of the data from both samples. (From Falkner. *Pediatrics,* 29:463, 1962.)

confronting the physician occur. A further point should be kept in mind in consideration of this example: If all children concerned in both curves had been grouped together, a *bimodal distribution curve* would result and is shown at the right-hand top of Figure 8. If any growth parameter produces such bimodal curves it is important to question whether there is a hidden separate abnormal or different sample involved that needs to be separated.

As already discussed, in practice we should expect a healthy child to fall between the 95th and 5th percentiles, or within ±2 standard deviations of the mean, of growth parameter standards used for screening or following growth. A child's measurement falling outside these average limits should cause suspicion and careful appraisal. We cannot go further than that. As many suitable parameters as possible, including the all-important maturity indicators, should be considered and take part in the total assessment. It is especially important to plot the sequential growth of the individual and to do so with the sensitive growth velocity concept constantly in mind. A child with normal weight achieved at a certain age may be found to be growing abnormally when his height velocity has been considered and plotted. Conversely, a child whose height is abnormal may be growing at a stable normal rate and therefore can usually be spared immediate extensive investigation. It is always helpful to pay attention to *parental size* when assessing the growth of their child. If a child is found to be at the 5th percentile point in average height at a certain age, and we ignore his parents' size, then we merely note that he is a very small child just within normal limits. If we do know and take in consideration the parents' height, and both fall at the adult average height standards' 50th percentile, then their child in fact drops to about the 1st percentile and at once causes concern. The above example is also illustrative of an important biometric point which was at first

thought surprising to those not thinking in such ways. A point can be made that standards of child size that ignore parental size are unrealistic. Ideally we need standards incorporating this parameter. In the absence of such standards, we must at least note parental size whenever possible, when assessing an individual child's pattern of growth.

The *growth standards* for *body weight, length, stature, head circumference,* and *surface area* presented in the appendix may be used as guidelines for recording and comparing growth patterns of children. It is mandatory that all aspects of any resulting interpretation of growth status of an individual child, or children, be considered in the light of the whole subject matter of this chapter.

TECHNIQUES OF MEASUREMENT. The pediatrician and his ancillary colleagues need not become proficient in techniques suitable for use primarily in research and growth studies. Babies and children, however, must be measured in a practical and reasonably accurate fashion. When the child's growth velocity is being assessed and gains or increments are being measured, the accuracy is doubly important mainly for the following two reasons: First, two different measures separated by a time interval are necessary to provide an increment. Thus there are two potential errors involved in place of a single one. Second, in contrast to a measure of height at a certain age, the incremental measurement will be considerably smaller in amount than that of total size achieved. At age 6, for example, the mean 5- to 6-year increment is 2.5 inches; 6-year median height is 45.9 inches.

Body weight must be obtained and recorded as nude weight. Clothing varies greatly from child to child, from season to season, from shoe to shoe. If it is not possible to weigh the nude child, his clothing should be weighed later and that weight subtracted; or much better, he is weighed in known-weight standard clothing (light robe; gym shorts) or in his underclothing, the weight of which is known by experience. Such clothing weights are then subtracted. In infancy, it is surprising what a large percentage of a weight reading is made up by an unremoved wet diaper. A very frightened or upset child may be weighed in his mother's arms. Both are weighed together and her clothed body weight determined and then subtracted from the weight of both. Many good *scales* are available, and two types are needed; baby scales, and scales for older children, ideally a platform beam-balance. Both kinds should be rugged and checked periodically. Surveys have shown alarming variations in accuracy for scales used in different settings, and in beam balances up to ±7 pounds. Recording of nude body weight to the nearest ounce in infancy, and to the nearest one-fourth pound in older children, is necessary.

Recumbent length and stature (standing height) are not the same and recumbent length is always greater. The amount can differ by as much as one inch. Recumbent length is used, ideally, for

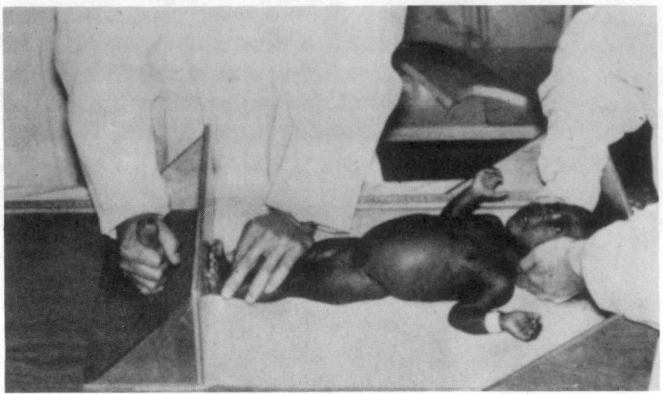

Fig. 9. A portable measuring board, and illustration of the technique of obtaining recumbent length. A wooden rule is fixed to one side of the board to which is attached a rigid headboard at right angles. A movable footboard, with hand holder, is made from two wooden rectangles fixed together at right angles. (From Falkner. *Pediat. Clin. N. Amer.*, 8:15, 1961.)

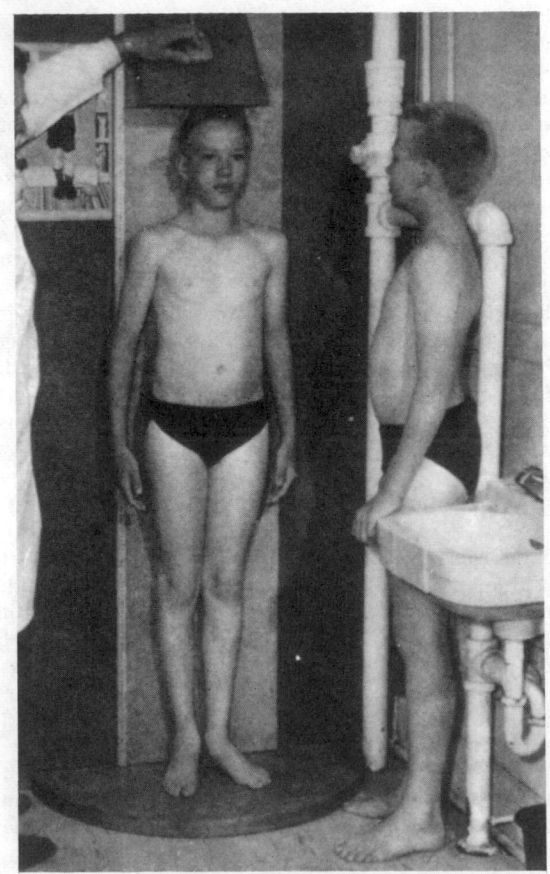

Fig. 10. A wall board and illustration of the technique of obtaining standing height. The same principles of construction as outlined in Figure 9 apply with the apparatus parts being naturally much larger. (From Falkner. *Pediat. Clin. N. Amer.*, 8:16, 1961.)

infants and young children up to 2 years of age. It is difficult sometimes to persuade a 2 to 3 year old to stand correctly, and this changeover point is not rigid. For recumbent length a *measuring table* or *portable board* is needed. There is no excuse for measuring an infant, however small, with a cloth tape measure as he lies on a mattress. Neither the table nor board need be elaborate or expensive. Figure 9 shows an example of one of the many acceptable designs. Two persons are required for the measurement. The baby is recumbent on the long axis of the board, and his mother, or any other second person, holds the crown of his head firmly up against the headboard. The baby should be maintained flat on his back as if looking straight up at the ceiling. The measurer brings the legs down onto the table with the lateral edge of one hand and brings the footboard up to the heels with the other. Should the mother notice the baby's head has moved away from the headboard, she gently but firmly stretches her baby and replaces it. This gentle stretching is ideally required to counteract the baby's common contraction of his frame. The measurement is read while the footboard is kept running alongside the raised rule, and the footboard's base on the board.

Stature, or *standing height,* is measured with exactly the same principles used with the measuring board, only the subject is fixed perpendicularly against a wall. Wobbly perpendicularly movable arms projecting from a central pole in wide use are to be eschewed. Figure 10 is illustrative of a simple suggested design. The child stands erect, with heels, buttocks, and shoulders against the wall board. Heels are together, and a comfortable stance encouraged with the feet angled at 45° to each other. The axis of vision must be horizontal and the child asked to look straight ahead. The child then "makes himself as tall as he can" but keeping his heels firmly on the ground. The head block is now brought down onto the crown of his head and stature recorded.

Should either *crown-rump* or *sitting height* measures be wanted, both measuring devices can be used with the appropriate position of the baby or child altered.

Head circumference is a particularly important measure in infancy, especially when following increases in size. The measuring tape must be *narrow* and preferably a flexible metal; at least it must not be stretchable. The tape crosses the frontal bone above the supraorbital ridges. It is passed round the head at the same level on each side and posteriorly at the level of the occiput, where it is moved to read the maximum circumference. The tape should be firmly drawn to the skull surface and/or with sufficient tension to crush the hair against the skull.

REFERENCES

Acheson, R. M. Maturation of the skeleton. In Falkner, F., ed. Human Development. Philadelphia, W. B. Saunders Co., 1966, Ch. 16, pp. 465-502.

Aherne, W. A weight relationship between the human foetus and placenta. Biol. Neonat., 10:113-118, 1966.

Bakwin, H. The secular change in growth and development. Acta. Pediat., 53:79-89, 1964.

——— and McLaughlin, S. M. Secular increments in height. Is the end in sight? Lancet, 2:1195-1196, 1964.

Barter, J., and Forbes, G. B. Correlations of K⁴⁰ data with anthropometric measurements. Ann. N.Y. Acad. Sci., 110:264-270, 1963.

Bayer, L. M., and Bayley, N. Growth Diagnosis. Chicago, University of Chicago Press, 1959.

Bayley, N., and Pinneau, S. R. Tables for predicting adult height from skeletal age. J. Pediat., 40:423, 1952.

Boyne, A. W. Secular changes in the stature of adults and the growth of children, with special reference to changes in intelligence of 11-year-old. In Symposia of the Society for the Study of Human Biology. Oxford, Pergamon Press, 1960, Vol. III.

Cheek, D. B., ed. The Physiology of Human Growth and Body Composition. Philadelphia, Lea and Febiger, 1967.

Falkner, F. Some physical measurements in the first three years of life. Arch. Dis. Child., 33:167, 1958.

——— ed. Child Development: An International Study. Modern Problems in Paediatrics. Basel and New York, S. Karger, 1960.

——— The problems of estimating the effect of severe illness on physical growth of children. Amer. J. Dis. Child., 100:587, 1960.

——— Office measurement of physical growth. Pediat. Clin. N. Amer., 8:13, 1961.

——— ed. Human Development. Philadelphia, W. B. Saunders Co., 1966.

——— Prenatal influences upon small-for-date infants. Pediat. Clin. N. Amer., 17:5-8, 1970.

——— Elementary Biometry. Basel, S. Karger, 1971.

——— Banik, N. D. D., and Westland, R. Intrauterine blood transfer between uni-ovular twins. Biol. Neonat., 4:52-60, 1962.

——— Steigman, A. J., and Cruise, M. D. The physical development of the premature infant. I. Some standards and certain relationships to caloric intake. J. Pediat., 60:895-906, 1962.

Forbes, G. B. Chemical growth in infancy and childhood. J. Pediat., 41:202, 1952.

Garn, S. M. Modern Problems in Paediatrics, Basel and New York, S. Karger, 7:50-55, 1961.

——— and Haskell, J. A. Fat thickness and developmental status in childhood and adolescence. Amer. J. Dis. Child., 99:746, 1960.

Geber, M., and Dean, R. F. A. Gesell tests on African children. Pediatrics, 20:1055-1065, 1957.

Greulich, W. W., and Pyle, S. I. Radiographic Atlas of Skeletal Development of the Hand and Wrist, 2nd ed. Palo Alto, Stanford University Press, 1959.

Harris, J. A., Jackson, C. M., Paterson, D. G., and Scammon, R. E. The Measurement of Man. Minneapolis, University of Minnesota Press, 1930.

Kassius, R. V. Size and growth of babies during first year of life. Milbank Mem. Fund Quart., 35:24, 1957.

Marshall, W. A., and Tanner, J. M. Variations in pattern of pubertal changes in girls. Arch. Dis. Child., 44:291-303, 1969.

——— and Tanner, J. M. Variations in the pattern of pubertal changes in boys. Arch. Dis. Child., 45:19-28, 1970.

McCance, R. A. Food, growth, and time. Lancet, 2:621, 1962.

——— and Widdowson, E. M. Nutrition and growth. Proc. Roy. Soc., 156:326, 1962.

Meredith, H. V. Stature and weight of children in the United States with reference to the influence of racial, regional, socioeconomic and secular factors. Amer. J. Dis. Child., 62:909-932, 1941.

——— and Knott, V. B. Illness history and physical growth. Amer. J. Dis. Child., 103:146, 1962.

Mills, C. A. Geographic and time variations in body growth and age at menarche. Hum. Biol., 9:43-56, 1937.

Oettle, A. G., and Higginson, J. The age of menarche in South African Bantu (Negro) girls. Hum. Biol., 33:181, 1961.

Patton, R. G., and Gardner, L. I. Growth Failure in Maternal Deprivation. Springfield, Ill., Charles C Thomas, 1963.

Prader, A., Tanner, J. M., and Von Harnack, G. S. Catch-up growth following illness or starvation; an example of developmental canalisation in man. J. Pediat., 62:646-659, 1963.

Roche, A. F., and Wettenhall, H. N. B. The prediction of adult stature in tall girls. Aust. Pediat. J., 5:13-22, 1969.

Scott, R. B., Ferguson, A. D., Jenkins, M. E., and Cutter, F. F. Growth and development of Negro infants. Pediatrics, 16:24-29, 1955.

Smith, D. W. Compendium on shortness of stature. J. Pediat., 70:463, 1967.

Sobel, E. H., and Falkner, F. Normal and abnormal growth patterns of the newlyborn and the pre-adolescent. In Gardner, L. I., ed. Endocrine and Genetic Diseases of Childhood. Philadelphia, W. B. Saunders Co., 1969.

Sontag, L. W., Snell, D., and Anderson, M. Rate of appearance of ossification centers from birth to the age of 5 years. Amer. J. Dis. Child., 58:949-956, 1939.

Stuart, H. C., and Reed, R. B. Longitudinal studies of child health and development. Pediatrics, Ser. 11 (Suppl.), 24:875, 1959.

Tanner, J. M. In Growth at Adolescence. Springfield, Ill., Charles C Thomas, 1962, p. 148.

——— Regulation of growth in size in mammals. Nature, 199:845-850, 1963.

——— Earlier maturation in man. Sci. Amer., 218:21, 1968.

——— Growth and endocrinology of the adolescent. *In* Gardner, L. I., ed. Endocrine and Genetic Diseases of Childhood. Philadelphia, W. B. Saunders Co., 1969.

——— Healy, M. J. R., Lockhart, R. D., Mackenzie, J. D., and Whitehouse, R. H. The prediction of adult body measurements from measurements taken each year from birth to 5 years. Arch. Dis. Child., 31:382-391, 1956.

——— Whitehouse, R. H., and Healy, M. J. R. A New System for Estimating the Maturity of the Hand and Wrist. Paris, International Children's Centre, 1962.

——— Whitehouse, R. H., and Takaishi, M. Standards from birth to maturity for height, weight, height velocity, and weight velocity in British children. Arch. Dis. Child., 41:454, 1966.

Thompson, A. *In* Hytten, F. E., and Leitch, I., eds. The Physiology of Human Pregnancy. Oxford, Blackwell Scientific Publications, 1964, pp. 308-309.

Vandenberg, S. G., and Falkner, F. Hereditary factors in human growth. Hum. Biol., 37:357-365, 1966.

Van Der Werff Ten Bosch, J. J., and Haak, A., eds. Somatic Growth of the Child. Leiden, H. E. Stenfert Kroese N.V., 1966.

Weiss, P., and Kavanau, J. L. A model of growth and growth control in mathematical terms. J. Gen. Physiol., 41:1-47, 1957.

Widdowson, E. M., and Kennedy, G. C. Rate of growth, mature weight and life-span. Proc. Roy. Soc. [Biol.], 156:96-108, 1962.

——— and McCance, R. A. Some effects of accelerating growth. I: General somatic development. Proc. Roy. Soc. [Biol.], 152:188-206, 1960.

Wilson, D. C., and Sutherland, I. Age at menarche. Brit. Med. J., 1:1267, 1950.

Winick, M., Coscia, A., and Noble, A. Cellular growth in human placenta. I: Normal placental growth. Pediatrics, 39:248-251, 1967.

Yerushalmy, J., Vandenberg, B. J., Erhardt, C. L., and Jacobziner, H. Birth weight and gestation as indices of "immaturity." Amer. J. Dis. Child., 109:43, 1965.

Abnormal Physical Growth

(See also Section 16.2)

The growth and development of infants and children may be influenced adversely by multiple factors, some of which undoubtedly are not yet recognized. There are, however, as indicated in Table 1, many factors known to be responsible for disturbances of growth, and they must be considered in assessing an infant or child with an abnormality of physical growth and development. The prenatal disturbances and most of the postnatal disturbances are considered in detail in other sections. The discussion here, therefore, is limited to consideration of some of the mechanisms involved in disturbances of growth, and attention is directed to certain abnormalities not discussed elsewhere.

Growth Retardation

Growth retardation seen during infancy or childhood often originates from defects in intrauterine growth. For example, virus infections such as rubella can cause, in utero, growth retardation involving many tissues including the brain. Interferences with the blood supply in utero can also cause retarded somatic growth, although Wigglesworth has shown that a rat's brain is not reduced in weight under these circumstances. Chemical toxins and radiation may also retard growth in utero.

Factors which inhibit cell multiplication in utero may well give rise to the so-called primordial dwarf (see below).

The most universal cause of growth retardation is *poor nutrition* (see Sec. 3.4). The effect of malnutrition on growth provides a model for understanding some of the mechanisms involved in growth retardation. For example, in the type of malnutrition associated with protein deprivation but with satisfactory caloric intake, as occurs in kwashiorkor, cell cytoplasm is sacrificed and cell size is grossly diminished, while the rate of multiplication of cells is not arrested. In contrast, with malnutrition due to restriction of calories without disproportionate reduction of protein, mitosis stops and the rate of multiplication of cells diminishes, but protein synthesis continues and in time the cells increase in size. Thus, disturbance of the balance between protein and caloric intake disturbs the balance in the distribution of energy between protein rebuilding and synthesis ("maintenance"), and mitosis ("growth").

Hypoxia has an effect similar to that of calorie deprivation, and failure to multiply muscle cells is one factor contributing to growth retardation in hypoxic children with congenital heart disease. Such children may also have a reduced caloric intake, and chemical analysis $\left(\dfrac{\text{Protein}}{\text{DNA}} \text{ ratio} \right)$ and histologic examination reveal that some of them have abnormally large muscle cells. On the other hand, some children with congenital heart disease have small muscle cells, suggesting poor protein synthesis. Cheek has demonstrated that some patients with congenital heart disease, without cardiac failure, have excess loss of albumin into the gastrointestinal tract and, presumably, have protein enteropathy. Finally, the fact that congenital heart disease in some children is associated with maternal rubella indicates that

TABLE 1. *Factors Responsible for Disturbances of Growth*

Retarded Growth

Prenatal Disturbances
1. Intrauterine growth disturbance influencing:
   (a) DNA (rubella, aminopterin, radiation, chromosomal defect)
   (b) Placental circulation (placental insufficiency, tobacco smoking)
   (c) Bone growth (tetracycline, thyroxin)

Postnatal Disturbances
1. Improper cell nutrition
   (a) Reduced dietary intake
   (b) Restricted intestinal absorption of nutrients (celiac disease, disaccharide deficiency, intestinal atresia)
   (c) Errors of carbohydrate, fat, amino acid, or nucleotide metabolism (diabetes mellitus, galactose intolerance, hyperglycinemia, hereditary oretic aciduria)
2. Altered mineral metabolism
   (a) Renal (chronic nephritis)
   (b) Adrenal (salt-losing syndromes)
   (c) Parathyroid (hypoparathyroidism)
3. Disturbance of bone metabolism or skeletal growth
   (a) Mineral metabolism
   (b) Bone matrix
4. Alteration in tissue oxygenation or carbon dioxide tension
   (a) Pulmonary (fibrocystic disease)
   (b) Cardiovascular (congenital heart disease)
   (c) Autonomic dysfunction (pheochromocytoma)
   (d) High-altitude living
5. Disturbances in central nervous system regulation
   (a) Prenatal (mongolism)
   (b) Perinatal (kernicterus)
   (c) Postnatal (meningitis)
   (d) Psychologic (maternal deprivation)
6. Hormonal dysfunction
   (a) Growth hormone (hypopituitarism, primordial dwarfism)
   (b) Thyroid hormone (hypothyroidism)
   (c) Sex hormone (gonadal dysgenesis)
   (d) Adrenocortical hormone (Cushing's syndrome)

Overgrowth

Prenatal Disturbances
1. Excess insulin production (infant born of diabetic mother)
2. Parabiotic twin
3. Hemihypertrophy

Postnatal Disturbances
1. Constitutional
2. Hormonal imbalance
   (a) Excess growth hormone (gigantism)
   (b) Excess thyroid hormone (thyrotoxicosis)
   (c) Excess androgenic hormone (congenital adrenal hyperplasia)
   (d) Removal of growth inhibitory hormones (cortisol)
3. Obesity and overnutrition

the relationships between congenital heart disease and growth retardation are highly complex. A similar complexity may be involved in other conditions associated with growth failure.

There is now convincing evidence that *maternal deprivation* may be a primary cause of growth retardation (see also Sec. 3.4). It appears that gentle physical contact, sounds of the human voice, and other adequate stimuli are all necessary for growth. Neglect and rejection of a child by the parents can result in decreased growth independent of restricted food intake. The mechanisms involved in these instances are not yet understood, but studies in rats suggest that interference with certain hypothalamic functions may prevent the sensitive regulation of endocrine function and energy exchange required for optimal growth. Moreover, emotional stimulation causes derangement with a release of adrenalin which, like cortisol, is a powerful inhibitor of cell multiplication.

A *dwarf* is a person conspicuously smaller than others of his kind. The height any individual attains depends upon both the rate at which growth occurs and the length of time it continues. The latter is determined by the age at which the epiphyses fuse with the shafts of the long bones.

The most common cause of short stature in children with delayed sexual development is *constitutional delayed growth*. The usual example is a 10-year-old boy whose bone age and height are equivalent to those of an 8-year-old; at 12 years his bone age and height are those of a 10-year-old. These relationships continue until the boy is 16 or 17 years, when he has an adolescent growth spurt and secondary sexual characteristics appear. Before this time, the physician who is unaware of the child's previous rate of growth may erroneously attribute the slow growth to disease. It is important in assessing such children to inquire about the growth pattern in the parents and siblings, since this type of growth is often familial. Reassurance about the probability of attaining normal ultimate height is especially important in these children.

Primordial dwarfism is a rare condition in which there is usually a history of the child having had a normal gestational age but low birth weight. Postnatally, linear growth is parallel to, but significantly below, three standard deviations from the mean. Some primordial dwarfs fall progressively behind in height from year to year. They may have the pinched faces and bird-headed appearance of the Cockayne-Neil syndrome. Their bone and dental maturation is normal, and the onset of puberty is at the usual age.

The best-known syndrome is that of *progeria*. These children appear normal at birth, but, within a few months or years, growth almost ceases and they develop a characteristic appearance—loss of scalp hair and subcutaneous fat, deformities of joints, and sometimes arteriosclerosis.

Primordial dwarfs have no detectable cause of dwarfing. They do not respond to growth hormone, suggesting a type of end-organ insensitivity. However, more than one mechanism may be responsible for the growth retardation in these patients. Two girls with primordial dwarfism were found to have large muscle cells for their body size and a gross reduction in the number of cells normal for their age. One of the two girls had intrauterine growth retardation, whereas prenatal growth in the other was normal.

Although pituitary dwarfism and hypothyroidism are discussed elsewhere, it should be pointed out here that, for their body size, most dwarfs have reduced caloric intake. Pituitary dwarfs with normal or slightly small muscle cells cannot multiply cells at a satisfactory rate. Presumably, human growth hormone affects the multiplication of cells, since this hormone increases cell number. Hypophysectomised rats actually lose muscle cells. Hypothyroid children have abnormally big muscle cells which decrease dramatically when thyroid hormone is given. At the same time, hypothyroid children also have fewer muscle cells, possibly as a result of secondary pituitary insufficiency. Finally, the hypopituitary patient has a reduced level of amino acids per cell while the hypothyroid child has increased levels. Thus, the transport of amino acid into muscle cells may be critical in the one instance, while its utilization within the cell may be important in the other.

For too long, studies of growth have been concerned solely with weight and height, and with the mathematical aspects of growth, neglecting the underlying mechanisms suggested here. For a more detailed discussion, including the role of the trace metals, copper, zinc, and manganese, see Cheek's monograph.

Overgrowth

The most frequent problem of overgrowth in children in the United States is *obesity,* which is discussed in Section 3.6. *Tallness* can be associated with obesity, but it is usually related to the genetic background and is described as *constitutional tall stature.*

Gigantism is a rare condition. Certain pituitary tumors secrete large amounts of growth hormone, and if they develop before puberty they cause excess linear growth. Such tumors developing after puberty and after epiphyseal fusion has occurred result in *acromegaly* with increased deposition of bone. Some acromegalic changes are also found in gigantism; the distinction between the two conditions is not clearly defined, especially in regard to bone changes.

In patients with gigantism there may be erosion of the sella turcica; bone age is not advanced and puberty is delayed. The concentration of growth hormone in the blood is greatly increased, and blood glucose and inorganic phosphate may also be elevated. Gigantism secondary to eosinophilic adenomas usually begins after infancy, an exception being the Alton Giant described by Behrens and Barr.

Sotos and associates have described a syndrome in infants and children who have excessively rapid growth unrelated to any known disorder; they also have acromegalic features and a nonprogressive cerebral disorder with mental retardation. At 4 years the height is equivalent to that expected at 6 or 7 years; subsequently the growth rate returns to normal. Such infants are usually above the 90th percentile in height at birth; they have a downslant to the eyes, advanced bone age, and early puberty. Early fusion of the epiphyses probably prevents gigantism in adult life. The condition appears to be due to a hypothalamic defect.

It is not uncommon to find slight differences between the two sides of the body during growth, so-called *hemihypertrophy.* It may be difficult to distinguish between *hemiatrophy* on one side and hemihypertrophy on the other. Hemiatrophy develops in some patients with cerebral disease, especially in disorders involving the parietal lobe. Hemihypertrophy is usually most readily apparent in the musculature, but it may also affect the cerebral cortex, spinal cord, kidney, adrenal gland, or spine, leading to scoliosis in the last. It has been suggested that the division of the ovum into two unequal parts may be responsible for some cases; in rare instances diploid-triploid chromosome mosaicism has been found. There are undoubtedly multiple causes of congenital asymmetry. Dermatoglyphic findings suggest that asymmetrical disturbances of growth may take place before the eighth week of fetal life, since, in some cases, the dermal patterns are abnormal.

One half of children with hemihypertrophy have hemangiomas, which suggests faulty development of the vasculature in utero. Other evidence of intrauterine growth abnormality is found in the occurrence of syndactylism or polydactylism with pigmentation or with abnormal nail growth; reduced birth weight for gestational age is also common. There may be hypospadias or cryptorchidism with elevated urinary gonadotropins.

Congenital arteriovenous aneurysm interference with lymphatic flow may give rise to localized hemihypertrophy.

REFERENCES

Bayer, L. M., and Bayley, N. Growth Diagnosis. Chicago, University of Chicago Press, 1959.

Behrens, L. H., and Barr, D. P. Hyperpituitarism beginning in infancy: The Alton giant. Endrocrinology, 16:120, 1932.

Birch, H. G., and Gussow, J. D. Disadvantaged Children: Health, Nutrition and School Failure. New York, Harcourt, Brace & World, Inc., 1970.

Cheek, D. B., ed. The Physiology of Human Growth and Body Composition. Philadelphia, Lea & Febiger, 1967.

———— and Cooke, R. E. Growth and growth retardation. Ann. Rev. Med., 15:357, 1964.

———— Brasel, J. A., Elliott, D. A., and Scott, R. E. Muscle cell size and number in normal children and in dwarfs (pituitary, cretins and primordial) before and after treatment (preliminary observations). Johns Hopkins Med. J., in press.

Goodman, H. G., Grumbach, M. M., and Kaplan, S. N. Growth and growth hormone. II. A comparison of isolated growth hormone deficiency and multiple pituitary hormone deficiencies in 35 patients with idiopathic hypopituitary dwarfism. New Eng. J. Med., 278:57-68, 1968.

Hubble, D. Endocrine control of growth and skeletal maturation. *In* Hubble, D., ed. Paediatric Endocrinology. Oxford, Blackwell Scientific Publications, 1969, pp. 1-33.

Jackson, C. M., and Stewart, C. A. The effects of inanition in the young upon the ultimate size of the body and of the various organs in the albino rat. J. Exp. Zool., 30:97-128, 1920.

Johnston, A. W., and Penrose, L. S. Congenital asymmetry. J. Med. Genet., 3:77, 1966.

Kaplan, S. A. Hypopituitarism. *In* Gardner, L. I., ed. Endocrine and Genetic Diseases of Childhood. Philadelphia, W. B. Saunders Company, 1969, pp. 98-115.

Patton, R. G., and Gardner, L. I. Short stature associated with maternal deprivation syndrome. *In* Gardner, L. I., ed. Endocrine and Genetic Diseases of Childhood. Philadelphia, W. B. Saunders Company, 1969, p. 77.

Powell, G. F., Brasel, J. A., Raiti, S., and Blizzard, R. M. Emotional deprivation and growth retardation simulating idiopathic hypopituitarism. New Eng. J. Med., 276:1279, 1967.

Prader, A., Tanner, J. M., and von Harnack, G. A. Catch-up growth following illness or starvation. J. Pediat., 62:646, 1963.

Rose, S. M. Failure of survival of slowly growing members of a population. Science, 129:1026, 1959.

Sobel, E. H. Growth problems. *In* Cooke, R. E., et al., eds. The Biologic Basis of Pediatric Practice. New York, McGraw-Hill Book Company, 1968, pp. 1564-1574.

—— Organic disorders interfering with somatic growth. *In* Gardner, L. I., ed. Endocrine and Genetic Diseases of Childhood. Philadelphia, W. B. Saunders Company, 1969, pp. 60-76.

—— and Falkner, F. Normal and abnormal growth patterns of the newly born and preadolescent. *In* Gardner, L. I., ed. Endocrine and Genetic Diseases of Childhood. Philadelphia, W. B. Saunders Company, 1969, pp. 6-19.

Sotos, J. F., Dodge, P. R., Muirhead, D., Crawford, J. D., and Talbot, N. B. Cerebral gigantism in childhood. New Eng. J. Med., 271:109, 1964.

Soyka, L. F., Bode, H. H., and Crawford, J. D. Effectiveness of long-term growth hormone therapy for short stature in children with growth hormone deficiency. J. Clin. Endocr., 30:1-14, 1970.

Talbot, N. B., and Sobel, E. H. Endocrine and other factors determining the growth of children. Advances Pediat., 2:238-297, 1947.

Tanner, J. M., Whitehouse, R. H., and Takaishi, M. Standards for height, weight, height velocity and weight velocity: British children, 1965. I and II. Arch Dis. Child., 41:454-471 and 613-635, 1965.

Widdowson, E. M. Harmony of growth. Lancet, 1:901-905, 1970.

Wigglesworth, J. S. Foetal growth retardation. Brit. Med. Bull., 22:13, 1966.

Wilkins, L. The Diagnosis and Treatment of Endocrine Disorders in Childhood and Adolescence, 3rd ed. Springfield, Ill., Charles C Thomas, Publisher, 1965.

Winick, M., and Noble, A. Cellular response in rats during malnutrition at various ages. J. Nutr., 89:300-306, 1960.

—— and Rosso, P. The effect of severe early malnutrition on cellular growth of human brain. Pediat. Res., 3:181-184, 1969.

chapter 5

NORMAL DEVELOPMENT: PERSONALITY AND BEHAVIOR

SIBYLLE ESCALONA, Associate Editor, with the collaboration of L. JOSEPH STONE

Introduction

Personality development is manifested in the organization of behavior. Age-typical behavior patterns reflect successive stages in psychologic growth much as changes in height, weight, and dentition reflect physical growth. In the field of child development, relevant behavioral facts are known, but no single theory of psychologic development has found general acceptance. This discussion, therefore, will focus on a summary of behavioral changes associated with chronologic age, with emphasis on the *patterns* of organization rather than on specific items of behavior. This choice was made because, except during infancy, the behavior of children differs widely with variations in socioeconomic and cultural factors, as well as with differences in the quality of interpersonal relationships that characterize individual families. From the large body of available data, selection of patterns of behavior organization was made by the following criteria: that they show invariant sequences, that they are especially useful for developmental diagnosis, and that they have direct implications for pediatric practice.

During the last several decades representative pediatric care has expanded in scope and now includes responsibility for the maintenance of mental as well as physical health. In this country, professional responsibility for safeguarding personality development, during the early years of childhood, rests primarily with pediatricians. For this reason, the section on infants and toddlers contains a relatively detailed account of developmental changes, and also provides behavior norms. Beginning with the preschool years, developmental diagnosis requires knowledge of behavioral aspects not manifested in the doctor's office and includes behaviors not directly relevant to physical health. Although firsthand observation of the child, combined with detailed reports from parents, enables the physician to detect developmental disturbance, a complete diagnosis of its nature is best delegated to specialists in child behavior. For later stages of childhood behavior, norms do exist with respect to important aspects of behavior, such as the development of intelligence, of perception, and of neuromuscular coordination. These norms can be found in the sources given in the bibliography. However, except in the hands of child development specialists, they are of limited use for developmental diagnosis and are not included in this text. Instead, condensed summaries of major developmental changes are presented.

Infancy and Toddlerhood

Behavioral Changes

In terms of "biologic time," that is, the degree of change over a chronologic time span, development during the first two and a half years of life is more extensive than at any later time. It also has been shown that experiences early in life tend to have more lasting effects upon subsequent developmental course than is true of experiences in later childhood. During the early stages of development, the organism functions in a relatively unitary manner. Up to the age of approximately two years, significant deviation from the norm in any one system, for instance neuromuscular coordination or vocalization, is frequently associated with aberrant functioning in other systems. Behavior norms are therefore useful for developmental diagnosis in the case of infants and very young children. However, caution is indicated in the clinical application of age norms. Some of the behaviors listed below may be seen as much as six weeks earlier than statistical norms indicate, in the absence of significant developmental acceleration. However if several or all behavior items are noted to occur four weeks or more beyond the upper limit of the normal range, a degree of behavioral retardation has occurred.

MOTOR DEVELOPMENT. The motoric behavior of the neonate is regulated chiefly by subcortical mechanisms. Certain of these reflexes, such as the rooting reflex, are specific and patterned, whereas others, such as crying and random movement, are diffuse. Changes in bodily coordination consist of a gradual loosening of reflex patterns, which increasingly permits voluntary directed movement, as well as more differentiated and articulated motions. Two of the important and representative sequences are shown in Table 1.

SENSORY DEVELOPMENT. Although all sensory modalities are intact at birth, major changes occur during the first few months of life. These concern the manner in which sensory stimulation is integrated with motor adaptation, and the relative importance of the

TABLE 1. *Development of Voluntary Movements*

Behavior	Age
Prehension and Hand-Eye Coordination	
Reflexive grasping (no thumb opposition) to palmar stimulation	At birth
Intentional reaching and grasping at sight of object	4 to 5½ months
Simple purposive manipulations (shaking rattle, banging)	6 to 7 months
Delicate pincer grasp, small pellet or string	9 to 10 months
Postural Control and Locomotion	
Sitting with support	3 to 4 months
Sitting alone one minute	7 to 8 months
Crawling, abdomen in contact with floor	6 to 7 months
Creeping, on hands and knees	8 to 9 months
Standing alone briefly	12 to 13 months
Taking several steps unaided	12 to 14 months

various sense modalities in regulating the infant's behavior. During the early months, the near receptors (tactile, kinethestic, thermal, and possibly olfactory) are the most important. Neonates and very young babies see and hear, but their behavior is rarely guided by sights and sounds in the environment. After binocular fixation has stabilized (usually during the fourth month), vision becomes increasingly important. Infants learn to recognize persons and things in the environment through multiple association of sight with movement, with touch, and with sound. It is thought that subsequent cognitive development, as well as many significant steps in emotional development, derive from these early sensorimotor integrations (Piaget).

SPEECH DEVELOPMENT. Vocalizations that precede speech follow an invariant sequential pattern (McCarthy). They are related to the acquisition of speech as such, and are important in mediating the infant's communication with other human beings long before he is able to recognize conventional words. The first vocalization other than crying consists of indistinct throaty sounds (3 to 5 weeks). These are followed by cooing, which consists of fairly clear vowel sounds (10 to 12 weeks), and next by the production of single and multiple syllables (babbling, 6 to 7 months). In most children this sequence is followed by a phase during which infants produce sounds closely resembling ordinary speech, but devoid of conventionally associated meaning. This so-called jargon phase (at 9 to 13 months) overlaps with the acquisition of the first conventional words.

The first several stages, up to and including multisyllabic babbling, appear with great regularity at the stated ages. They vary in amount, but not in kind. Later stages of speech development show marked individual differences. For instance, the first

conventional word appears at a *mean age* of 12 months, but the normal range extends from 8 to 15 months (Mussen et al.). During the second year and beyond, language development is so variable that it is of limited usefulness for diagnostic purposes. Accelerated speech development is often linked with high intelligence, but this association is not reliable. It has been shown that among exceptionally gifted individuals, speech development may also be delayed.

PERSONALITY DEVELOPMENT. Development during the first years of life lays the groundwork for later personality development and establishes patterns that remain significant for the remainder of the individual's life (Spitz). A large body of clinical data supports the assumption that the affectional tie between the infant and his mother (and/or other caretaking persons) plays a vital role in supporting developmental progress. Research has shown that infants and toddlers reared in institutions that do not provide individualized attention and close attachment to another human being show retardation and pathology in all areas of functioning: intelligence, motor development, speech, and even physical growth (Bowlby; Provence and Lipton; Spitz). Infants reared in families where the mother is unable to provide affectionate attention and care may also fail to thrive, though the disturbance is seldom, if ever, as severe as that observed in institutionalized infants.

It is useful to review the various stages of sensorimotor development as outlined above in the light of their significance for the growing personality, and in connection with typical changes in social behavior.

In the beginning, infants respond to stimulation from the environment but do not perceive objects and people in it at all clearly. There is no behavioral evidence to suggest that small infants interpret their experience. Beginning at about 3 months, toys, objects, and people are responded to and acted upon more consistently, mostly in terms of pleasurable or unpleasurable activities they generate. Mother, or any person who behaves appropriately, is greeted with smiles and motions of approach; the infant's own hands and suitable objects are brought to the mouth, looked at, shaken, banged, and otherwise manipulated. An increasing number of objects are "recognized" in that they are used in particular ways, and behavior in response to persons acquires features quite different from behavior in motor play or play with objects. Gradually, behavior reflects early forms of anticipation and memory, of intentionality and direction, and of more stable positive and negative feelings. Babies who up to then enjoyed visits to the pediatric office may, by 6 or 7 months, cry before any procedure has begun, and may specifically remember injections or other unpleasant events. This change from easy accommodation to seemingly unreasonable fearfulness should be regarded as developmental progress.

During the second half of the first year, babies

normally develop strong selective ties to the mother and to certain other people; strangers are not welcomed until the child has had a chance to adapt to them, and the mere absence of mother may bring distress. During the same time span, babies develop preferences and dislikes and communicate by sound and gesture. Toward the end of the first year they are oriented to the familiar environment, knowing which doors lead where, where the cookies are kept, and some of the forbidden areas such as electric outlets and hot stove.

Certain changes in social behavior occur nearly as regularly as those reflecting neuromuscular maturation. These are summarized in Table 2. It should be remembered that the *direction of change* is far more important than the exact age at which a new behavior emerges.

The behavior integrations summarized above, including changes in motility, in the response to objects, and in the adaptation to the social environment, are merely different facets of a single developmental course. In their totality, they constitute early steps in the development of cognition, affect, and social communication. Cognitive development is thought to be closely linked to the child's growing capacity to recognize and manipulate objects, and to the increasing orientation in space that results from locomotor activity. Early activities such as grasping, releasing, and manipulating toys, utensils, or any other thing, later activities such as creeping and then walking at will, learning how to open doors and drawers, how to climb furniture, and how to fill and empty containers, and innumerable other activi-

ties all serve to acquaint the baby with the attributes of the physical environment. On an action level, the child comprehends the nature of space, of means-ends relationships, of size, weight, and texture, and of simple physical causality. Beginning at about the age of 12 to 14 months, healthy children are spontaneously motivated to move about, to approach everything in sight (as mothers put it, to "get into everything"), and to push, pull, roll, throw, and, in all other ways, act upon objects. In developmental perspective, the exercise of this universal tendency is a necessary component of the basic early learning processes.

These explorations of the environment, in combination with constant interaction with adults and often with other children, serve to promote a growing comprehension of the social environment. In the course of daily routines, such as eating, being dressed and bathed, played with and scolded, helped and restrained, young children develop specific attitudes and expectations toward other people. In particular, the mother (or those who perform maternal functions) becomes the focus of intense feelings of pleasure, and simultaneously the baby becomes aware of helplessness and anxious discomfort when she is absent. Thus, the minute details of mother-child interaction influence the course of development in all areas, including basic attitudes such as a sense of trust and security and its opposite, a sense of threat and helplessness.

Diagnostic and Prophylactic Implications

The pediatrician is in an excellent position to observe the infant's developmental progress, to observe the developing mother-child relationship, and to support both by means of his continuous relationship with the mother.

Until the age of approximately 2 years, a child who thrives in most respects and who shows the expected changes in motor skills, speech, and social behavior may be presumed to have made normal psychologic progress. In the absence of physical illness, mental retardation, and other organic pathology, significant retardation in one or more of these behavior areas suggests the presence of developmental deviation of social and emotional origin. A systematic exploration of the baby's functioning in all important areas, and observation over a period of weeks or months, is necessary in order to determine whether one is dealing with a transient maladaptation, or with symptoms that require intervention. If failure to conform to normative standards in one area is found to be associated with deviation of behavior in other areas as well, referral to a specialist (such as a developmental neurologist, developmental psychologist, or a pediatrician with specialty training in developmental diagnosis) is indicated.

Pediatricians are also in a strategic position to support optimal conditions for the development of

TABLE 2. *Development of Social Behavior*

Behavior	Approximate Age
Occasional smiles, not regularly associated with specific stimulus	3 weeks to 3 months
Indiscriminate smiling at human face or at stimuli (such as masks) conforming to the general outline of human faces	3 to 6 months
Discriminate smiling, limited to familiar or well-liked faces. Physiognomic expression of partner affects response. Total strangers are smiled at with delay, or not at all	After 6 or 7 months
Approach by stranger causes distress varying from sober withdrawal to disconsolate crying. Behavior may last a few days or may intermittently persist into the second year	7 to 9 months
Separation from mother causes distress, even if stranger anxiety has disappeared	12 to 20 months

their quite normal patients. Developmental considerations will underlie much of his advice to parents on child rearing and, at times, will affect other aspects of medical care. A few examples are provided below. They are illustrative and by no means inclusive. Advice to parents will be guided by the physician's understanding of the infant's primary needs, combined with his knowledge of the particular family and its resources. These needs include the following:

1. A sufficient degree of stimulation and of freedom for bodily activity. In the case of young infants, advice may deal with appropriate clothing, selection of toys, the baby's daily program, and cautioning against the overuse of restraining devices such as highchairs and playpens. With babies over 18 months of age, advice may also concern itself with providing opportunities for play in larger and outdoor settings, and with cautioning parents against overly stringent restraint of the baby's tendency to freely approach all accessible parts of the environment.

2. Individualized care at all times; the continuous presence of mother or of a very few constant care-taking persons after the fifth or sixth month. Advice may concern appropriate arrangements in the case of working mothers, or in situations where mothers must plan on extended absences from home.

3. A stable and mutually comfortable relationship between mother (or mother substitute) and child. Helping mothers to achieve and maintain predominantly positive feelings and convictions in dealing with their babies is a complex and subtle process which has received increasing attention in the pediatric literature (Korsch, Levy). Some phases of infant and toddler care are likely to bring existing difficulties into the open, and thus provide an opportunity for prophylactic intervention. These include the timing and method of toilet training, techniques of accustoming the child to sleep through the night without protest, and weaning the child from breast or bottle. Clinical evidence suggests that marked difficulties in accomplishing these transitions are likely to be the result of some inadequacy in the mother-child relationship. Excepting the extremes of punitive severity and of total laxity, available evidence suggests that the precise technique or timing is less important than the qualities of feeling that develop as mothers struggle to impose the desired changes upon their children's behavior. The pediatrician's advice will be the more effective, the more it tends to relieve the mother's anxiety and tension, and the more it prevents her from applying techniques that invite certain failure. In general, mothers are able to maintain warmth and equanimity in dealing with their babies in proportion to the degree to which they can feel competent in the maternal role. Such a sense of basic adequacy derives from the mother's total adjustment as a human being, and many sources of maternal anxiety cannot be altered by the pediatrician. Since even good advice is rarely helpful if it runs counter to the mother's ingrained attitudes, it is useful for the pediatrician to select from the mother's demonstrated repertoire of child-rearing techniques those that seem relatively best adapted to the child's needs. By encouraging some among her current practices, it is often possible to discourage indirectly the use of alternative and less desirable ones.

Modifications of medical care are exemplified below:

1. Hospitalization of the infant is at times inevitable. Although hospitalization is always a major intervention, for optional procedures it is relatively safer if separation from the mother occurs before the age of 6 months or can be postponed to the later preschool age. If hospitalization during the crucial period (between 6 months and 2½ years) is necessary, prophylactic care includes plans to minimize the trauma of separation. Parents should be permitted and encouraged to visit frequently. In the case of prolonged hospitalization, it is sometimes possible to assign a nurse or aide to full-time care of the infant. At this age infants are able to develop a relationship to one new person who cares for them most of the time, but cannot do so when their care is shared by many persons. Such an arrangement will not eliminate the young patient's need for his mother, but it can be effective in preventing more severe reactions (listlessness and developmental regression) that otherwise are likely to occur.

2. Physical illness or trauma necessarily restricts both bodily activity and environmental stimulation. The retarding effects of such deprivation can be counteracted by providing sensorimotor stimulation in unaffected body systems. For instance, a baby with a cast on his leg may be encouraged to use his hands by having access to numerous small toys, and by being played with more than is usual. He may be given food to eat by hand, and in general can be encouraged to respond to people and things around him to compensate for the fact that his illness prevents him from generating these learning experiences spontaneously.

The Preschool Years

Behavioral Changes

MOTOR COORDINATION AND LOCOMOTION. Throughout the preschool years (2½ to 6 years), body motion in general, and locomotion in particular, are centrally important components of behavior. During the second and third year, walking becomes a means to an end (by contrast to the early toddler stage when it was a challenging activity in its own right). Gradually, children learn to run smoothly, to accelerate, decelerate, and come to a halt with precision. In walking stairs, the feet begin to alternate (usually by the third birthday); jumping is acquired first on both feet and finally on one foot.

Between the ages of about 2½ and 3½ or 4 years, children are highly motivated to climb, push, pull, ride cars, and, in general, to apply coordinated gross muscle activity whenever possible. Fine coordinations, requiring delicate precision, as in block building, bead stringing, or using pencil and crayon, may be partially mastered during the third year, but become important and are perfected to a significant degree between the ages of 3½ and 6 years.

More important than the learning of motor skills is the manner in which bodily activity expands the child's awareness of the environment and enhances a sense of the self as an independent action agent. Purposive movement in relation to objects enables children of 2 and 3 years to recognize that they can exercise choice. It teaches by experience that they have the power to make things happen, and to oppose the wishes of others, as well as to comply at will. For the younger preschool child, such motor activity also mediates cognitive development in continuity with the varieties of earlier sensorimotor learning. Through direct physical encounters with the environment, the child notices similarities and differences among objects and events, thereby acquiring his first concepts. The importance of motility at this age is further evidenced by the fact that affective states, such as triumph, impatience, joy, and anger, are typically experienced most intensely in the context of body activation. Two- and three-year-olds literally jump for joy and flail their limbs in rage, and the heightened awareness of the body self is closely linked to the child's growing recognition of his own emotional state. Thus, cognitive development, social development, and the development of a sense of self are closely related to motility.

Children above the age of 4 years continue to derive from body mastery a vital sense of an active self. Fine coordination, which requires motor inhibition, now becomes the primary challenge. Emphasis shifts from discovery of the body as a powerful tool, to the acquisition of the *power to control* movement impulses, in the interest of achieving a specific goal. Thus, during the later preschool years, children begin to perceive the body as differentiated to some extent from a purposive self that directs body movements.

LANGUAGE AND INTELLECTUAL DEVELOPMENT. Language and speech become a major mode of communication, and an important component of thought and of imaginative life, beginning in the third and fourth year of life. Development of language and of associated mental activities is dependent upon environmental stimulation to a very high degree. For instance, the average vocabulary of 2-year-old American *middle-class* children is estimated at about 300 words (Mussen et al.). In this same socioeconomic group, vocabulary usually trebles between the second and third birthday, doubles between the third and fourth birthday, and increases at a much reduced rate thereafter. Normative data for children of lower socioeconomic groups have not been systematically obtained, but vocabulary, sentence length, and all other verbal measures consistently reflect a significantly lower level of achievement in socially and culturally disadvantaged groups. Language development has been shown to be retarded and impoverished by institutionalization during the early years of life (Bowlby; Mussen et al.; Provence and Lipton; Spitz). Conversely, it has been shown that specific verbal stimulation and precept promote language development. For instance, in children of comparable socioeconomic background it was found that language competence was more advanced in children from homes where family meals with conversation were the rule, by comparison to homes where there was little opportunity for the child to participate in family talk (Mussen et al.).

The dependence of language development upon socioeconomic, cultural, and other environmental factors is of great importance because the development of concept formation, problem solving, and, in fact, the whole range of behaviors subsumed under the term "intelligence" is intertwined with the acquisition of verbal skills. Thinking operates by means of symbols, and words are among the earliest and most important symbols in human experience. Research has shown that many varieties of problem solving can emerge only in the presence of the appropriate vocabulary. In addition, verbal ability and general intelligence remain highly correlated. For instance, among the many items included in standard intelligence tests, vocabulary scores show the highest correlation with general intelligence (as expressed in the Intelligence Quotient based upon total performance on the test). Children who, for any reason, are deprived of adequate learning opportunities in the verbal sphere are thus at a serious disadvantage with respect to the subsequent development of most of the complex mental functions.

The discovery of language is equally significant for social development. It relates to the comprehension of the social environment much as motor activity relates to the comprehension of the physical environment. The preschool child's experiments with speech elicit verbal and attitudinal responses from other people. In this fashion, the child acquires a working knowledge of adult communication patterns. He also learns the rules of social conduct that prevail in his particular milieu. A simple but powerful idea of "good" and "bad" is acquired, at least as much by virtue of the adult's verbal encouragement and disparagement as by actual reward and punishment. Thus, no sooner does the young child learn to direct behavior in terms of his own choices and goals, than he encounters the limitations to free choice in the form of social taboos.

PERSONALITY DEVELOPMENT. It is generally held that enduring attitudes and dispositions are formed during the first five years of life. It is during the preschool years that children develop patterns of relationship with others which will play a role in determining the quality of all subsequent interpersonal relationships. In the experience of young children, the feelings associated with parents and other significant people determine also the growing perception of the self. Children who are made to feel that they are loved, that they fulfill their parents' expectations, and that they are a source of pleasure and pride, tend to conceive of themselves as essentially adequate and worthy of love. If the behavior of the surrounding adults communicates to children that they are unable to live up to what is expected, that they are a burden or a source of worry, or that they are unimportant, then they are likely to perceive of themselves as unworthy and inadequate. Both of these perceptions of the self are extremes and although they do occur, the majority of children experience both positive and negative evaluations from adults; they learn therefore to perceive the self as capable of "good" and lovable actions; yet they are also intermittently threatened by anxious insecurity. It is important to recognize that young children are egocentric, meaning that they respond to all experience chiefly as it affects themselves. On the basis of such age-typical egocentrism, it is possible for a child between 3 and 5 years of age to misinterpret the attitudes of others by assuming that he is the cause of observed harassment or pain in his elders, when these negative responses exist for totally different reasons, such as illness, poverty, or other factors beyond the child's comprehension.

In consequence of developmental advances during the preschool stages, children inevitably develop more intense emotions, both positive and negative. Especially during the third and fourth year, children are normally subject to conflicting needs and impulses. On the one hand, they are increasingly aware of their need for the parents' protective presence and the continued assurance of their love and interest. On the other hand, the inherent striving for independence gains ascendancy. For these reasons, paradoxical behavior is nearly universal among 2- and 3-year-olds (and often beyond). It is the age of demonstrative affection and of clinging behavior; yet it is also the age of stubborn resistance and of temper tantrums. These behavioral vacillations should be recognized as growth promoting and as a necessary stage in the achievement of lasting, but more flexible human relationships; in fact, a complete absence of conflict between child and parent during the early preschool years signifies a true developmental lag. However, it needs to be stressed that the duration, intensity, and particular mode of such contests of will are extraordinarily variable.

By 4 and 5 years, most children have achieved stable patterns of interaction with others. They know what they themselves are able to do, they know what they will be allowed to do, and they know what they can expect of others under many circumstances. However, in consequence of increasing intellectual capacities, and of a more highly developed imaginative life, a new set of complexities is introduced. Typically, children now develop feelings of loving possessiveness, especially towards the parent of the opposite sex. Typically, also, they attempt to emulate behavior observed in significant persons, especially in the parent of the same sex. To the previous feelings of straightforward affection or outright anger, a host of more subtle emotions are added. Older preschool children feel and verbalize such feelings as jealousy, disappointment, guilt, discouragement, ambition, and many more. These new and complex feelings arise in relation to family members, but they are likely to color the child's behavior in encounters with all others, pediatricians included.

If it was said that basic personality patterns are formed before the age of 6, it is because during those years children acquire ways of dealing with a wide range of emotions; ways of protecting themselves against disruptive anxieties, ways of tolerating or resolving inner conflicts, and ways of reconciling what they know to be inner wishes, fears, and fantasies, with what they recognize as real outer circumstances. These adaptations engender a degree of stress. For most children, an important behavior first developed during the third year becomes dominant at ages 4 and 5; namely, *imaginative play*. Whether "make believe" consists of verbal role play (prominent in middle-class children), of largely silent action with toys (more frequent in lower socioeconomic groups), or of passive but intense participation in TV programs (nearly universal in the United States), it provides a mechanism for the mastery of complex emotional experience by dint of repetitive and symbolic reenactment. A marked paucity of imaginative play at those ages constitutes a deviation from normal development, and may signify retardation in the integrative aspects of personality development.

Diagnostic and Prophylactic Implications

Ordinarily, pediatricians are aware of outright pathology and of significant mental retardation in their preschool patients, and rely on the services of specialists (child psychiatrists, child psychologists, neurologists, and others) to provide appropriate diagnosis and care. In addition, parents report more freely on aspects of their children's behavior which have caused them distress or concern than on behavior which they do not recognize as relevant to developmental progress. Difficulties in the areas of eating, sleeping, discipline, and emotional control may reflect normal and transient problems in the mutual adaptation between child and family. However, these and similar behavioral difficulties may also be symptoms of significant deviation in personality development. It is an essential pediatric function to assess the significance of fairly common behavior problems of this sort. Such assessment will be based primarily on an evaluation of the degree to which the symptom prevents the child from engaging in age-appropriate activities, and upon the degree to which the child's behavior in *other* areas (play, language, socialization, and so forth) deviates from what is normally expected.

Irregularities in psychologic development are overlooked more easily when they are manifested by behavior that causes no disruption in family life. Familiarity with behavior patterns common at the preschool ages enables the physician to evaluate the significance of both conspicuous and inconspicuous behavioral syndromes. Some of the age-characteristic behavioral tendencies are summarized in Table 3, as an aid to the pediatrician in assessing the developmental appropriateness of frequently occurring behavior constellations. The absence of one or several of these behavior patterns at the appropriate age does

not constitute sufficient evidence for the diagnosis of developmental deviation. However, such departure from usual and expected behavior merits further exploration.

In planning prophylactic or therapeutic intervention, it is of practical importance to localize the primary source of the difficulty. Developmental failure of identical nature may arise primarily on an endogenous basis, it may be the result of environmental deprivation or stress, or it may be attributable to a noxious combination of biologic and environmental factors. The specific characteristics of the behavioral symptom very rarely indicate its etiology. From the point of view of psychologic health, the consequences of maldevelopment are equally serious whether they are due to environmental circumstances or to intrinsic deficits. Especially in the case of economically disadvantaged families, therefore, pediatric intervention may involve the use of community resources such as day care centers, recreational agencies, and other social services.

TABLE 3. *Illustrative Behavior Patterns for the Preschool Age Period and the Developmental Relevance of Each*

Behavior	Developmental Relevance
In 2- and 3-year-old children:	
Child moves about a great deal, dislikes confinement in space, apt to endanger himself by heedless motor activity.	Pleasure in locomotion, exploration of space and literal testing of strength are means of acquiring sense of self, and mediate comprehension of the environment.
Child's behavior toward mother and other intimates markedly different from that towards strangers or mere acquaintances. Discomfort at separation from mother. Periods of negativistic behavior, temper outbursts or stubborn opposition.	These behaviors indicate the emergence of a highly selective, intense, dependent tie to mother, and the resulting conflict between desire for autonomy and desire for security. Absence of such behavior may be associated with emotional disturbance, or developmental lag.
Child comprehends speech, including references to objects and persons not immediately perceptible. Interested in learning what things are called, makes his wishes known by words and phrases.	Acquisition of words as symbols and participation in adult communication patterns are a prerequisite for comprehension of the social environment.
In 4- and 5-year-old children:	
Child engages in imaginative play of some sort; this may be solitary, using toys or merely words; it may be "make believe" in play with others. Nursery rhymes, picture books, TV programs are of interest and at times reflected in child's play.	The emergence of imaginative play signifies that more complex emotional and social experience has occurred. Adaptation to the new stresses is aided by such play, as is a more differentiated perception of self and environment.
Child correctly uses pronouns, as in "I want" (not Johnny wants).	Provided language ability is otherwise within normal limits, the correct use of pronouns reflects the cognitive recognition of the self as a reciprocal respondent to others. The failure to use pronouns flexibly is often associated with mental retardation or with serious psychopathology.
Child's activities with crayon, blocks, toys, and so forth, have representational character; that is, an arrangement of lines on paper or blocks in space is intended to represent a person, thing, or situation. In children who have little access to conventional toys, the same capacity can be shown in their activity with mud and stones or in playful manipulation of household furnishings.	The representation of an idea is a behavioral reflection of the intellectual capacity to deal with mental representations; that is, with symbols, images and thoughts. Absence or marked delay of this function indicates either retardation or significant impairment in the appropriate use of intellectual capacity.

Middle Childhood

Behavioral Changes

The behavior of school-age children is so diversified, and developmental changes occur in such a wide variety of contexts, that a review of major sequences in separate behavior spheres is not feasible within these pages. Development in middle childhood is dominated by some central sequences which find expression in every aspect of functioning, from body coordination to social behavior and emotional life. A summary of behavior trends typical for children of selected ages will be preceded by a condensed account of important features of personality development.

During the time span from 6 to 12 years, children attain a degree of detachment from family and home environment. School attendance brings the demand and opportunity for the learning of skills, but quite as important is the fact that the society of peers introduces a new perspective for all of the child's experience. Children now learn to see themselves as members of multiple and overlapping social groups; for instance, those defined by grade placement, place of residence, ethnic origin, and national identity. Depending upon the social setting, the nature of the child's exposure to the larger community will vary. In middle-class urban groups, public facilities such as playgrounds, movies, public transport, and libraries will be encountered. Urban slum children are apt to roam the streets and parks, to invade department stores or waiting rooms and ride the escalators, or to jump on the rear of trucks and buses to obtain free rides. Rural children learn to cover greater distances to reach their school, the movie, or the ball field, and to become adept at knowing where to find apples or berries, often in forbidden areas at a distance from home. All of these experiences have in common that they expose the child to adult-centered situations and to impersonal adult authority. Such expansion of social experience has developmental relevance. It counteracts the child's self-centered perspective and compels him to perceive himself as but a small unit in a large system to which he must adapt. Social regulations require punctuality, homework, observance of traffic laws, the exchange of money for service, and the like. Those demands are not addressed to the child as an individual, nor is compliance rewarded.

Simultaneously, the peer group exposes the child to different but equally rigid demands. It expects prowess at games and loyalty toward the group, even at the risk of opposing adult authority. And in both of these settings, the child is forced to recognize that he will be judged by performance, not by intention. A boy who is poor at athletics loses status; so does a girl who is too fat or unattractive; and so does a child who is slow to learn. In other social groups, a boy may be ridiculed for awkwardness in evading the police, or for being too small to carry his weight in a street fight. Girls can be made to suffer because they cannot join their friends except by bringing along a younger sibling in their care, or because they are not allowed to use lipstick as early as their friends.

Thus the child finds himself judged not only by actions over which he has control, but also by attributes for which he is not responsible—such as race, social status, or endowment. The development of realistic standards of achievement comes about through constant comparison with age mates. Whether it be academic grades, skill at games, or friendship patterns, the child finds himself in competition with other members of his group. While in the preschool years his self-evaluation was derived from how he was evaluated by his parents, in middle childhood self-evaluation is largely a function of achievement as compared to that of other children. The behavior patterns typical for this age, and many behavioral difficulties (normal as well as pathologic) can be understood in the light of the child's dread of inferiority and his driving need to establish a sense of competence.

In middle childhood the learning process becomes intentional; it is no longer only a by-product of experience and of play. Apparently the readiness for learning is a basic biopsychologic phenomenon for, throughout the centuries and in all cultures, it is at about this age that children have been exposed to formal teaching. From the point of view of developmental diagnosis, the primary consideration is that the child acquires knowledge and techniques in areas that go beyond the requirements of daily experience. School curricula are designed to channel learning capacities in constructive directions. For the great majority of children, reading, writing, and arithmetic are at the core of the learning process. However, in the absence of scholastic motivation, many children apply their learning capacities to other spheres, such as baseball history, the lives of movie stars, or gangster lore. Even in the face of academic failure, substantial learning of this kind bespeaks developmental progress, though it also bespeaks maladaptation in the social sphere. In dealing with children who fail to achieve in school, it is important to identify such misdirected but successful learning, as contrasted to the dominance of simple action learning, or the arrest of learning typically seen in mental retardation or in major psychopathology.

During middle childhood, children's awareness of their body undergoes significant change. Between the ages of about 6 and 9 years, a sense of competence is still dependent on a sense of bodily mastery. It is for this reason that children value games involving complex coordination (for instance, rope skipping in girls and ball games in boys). Sometime after the age of 9 or 10, most children regard the body as an attribute of the self, and no longer as its essence. The overriding need for competence typically leads to paradoxical behavior in relation to their own bodies. School-age children, and especially boys, tend to test their bodily skills to the limit, often to the point of recklessness. At the same time, the fear of bodily injury is universal, and slight injuries may elicit disproportionate reactions of distress and fear. School-age children are proud of their scratches and bruises, yet they also tend to exaggerate very minor body damage. It is helpful to recognize that both aspects of the paradox reflect the same developmental trend; namely, the concern with body mastery as a symbol of general adequacy, and the concern with bodily harm as a symbol of generalized vulnerability.

Diagnostic and Prophylactic Implications

By combining information obtained from the child and the parent, the pediatrician can obtain a diagnostic impression about the child's developmental progress in areas other than physical growth. As has been said for earlier age groups, significant retardation or deviation in a single behavior area merits detailed inquiry but does not necessarily denote a developmental disorder. This fact has practical importance with school-age patients because marked individual differences occur not only as a function of sociocultural factors, but also within similar social groups as a function of differential endowment and of personal behavioral style.

Parents are sometimes disturbed at their child's failure to conform to an expectation too narrowly conceived. For instance, a boy who functions well in school and who seems well adapted and content may avoid athletic games and may fail to share the dominant interests of his immediate peers. If the pediatrician finds that the child nonetheless finds opportunities to strive for achievement by standards set in terms of the performance of others, but does so through stamp collecting or through radio "ham" activities, he may assure the parents that the child's disposition makes these activities a suitable arena for social growth. Conversely, parents with high academic ambitions may fail to recognize that a child who spends his time in outdoor play may nonetheless be working at a vital developmental task.

When exploration reveals maladaptation or developmental immaturity, the pediatrician's most effective tool is knowledge of community resources. By virtue of their confidence in the physician, many parents are willing to accept professional help if it is presented in the context of a comprehensive health program. These same parents might otherwise refuse to seek appropriate help on behavior problems because of diffidence and fear of social stigma.

In middle childhood, the pediatrician can play an important supportive role by virtue of the fact that it is possible to maintain a direct doctor-patient relationship, in addition to the ongoing contact with the parents. Children between 6 and 12 years of age are often puzzled by growth changes observed in themselves, and tend to be apprehensive concerning the integrity of their bodies. Occasional private conversations with child patients, providing explanations for normal body feelings and for transient pains, can do much to prevent a buildup of anxiety. In addition, physical symptoms without medical basis, such as vomiting and headaches, are a common complaint among school-age children. Especially in patients up to the age of 10, physical symptoms of this sort are

---

TABLE 4. *Typical Behavior Patterns of Middle Childhood*

Behavior	Developmental Relevance
Involvement in association with other children in fairly stable gangs or cliques. Marked concern with popularity, excessive distress at even temporary rejection by other children.	Comparative sharing of experience, learning to subordinate own wishes to group, and security of group membership orient the child to his place in the social scheme and build a more mature sense of self.
Interest in structured games that have rules; such as, ball games, table games, and marbles.	Objective standards which are necessary for social functioning are voluntarily practiced in structured games. This aids acceptance and mastery much as imaginative play does at the preschool age.
Marked preferences for children of same sex with exclusive interest patterns. Dolls, domestic role play, dressing up, and so forth in girls. Sports, cops and robbers, and so forth in boys. Provocative disparagement of opposite sex. Typically, this attitude is professed, yet not consistently maintained.	Clarification of future social role includes sex role. Playful variations on anticipated modes of adult functioning serves to intensify appropriate expectations and to endow own sex role with positive values.
Open or covert criticism of adult behavior previously accepted. Comparing other children's parents with own, often favorably; verbal insistence on fairness, honesty, and so forth.	Generally applicable standards, once comprehended, are perceived as absolute. Greater objectivity and decreased self-centeredness lead to a rather unbending and concrete application to adults of whatever judgments the child feels are applied to him. Whether openly or otherwise, judging others as one is being judged is a step towards social participation on a level of mutual responsibility.

readily developed as the result of emotional stress. The pediatrician's response to the initial symptom can be crucial in determining the subsequent course. It is useful to convey to child and parent that subjectively the illness is real, and that blame or ridicule is therefore inappropriate. In many instances, the symptom will disappear spontaneously, provided the adults involved do not lend it too much importance. Occasionally, children given to mild hypochondria are found to function aberrantly in other less visible ways as well. In such instances, the physical complaint provides an entering wedge for referral to appropriate professional resources.

Some of the behavior patterns typical of middle childhood and directly relevant to central developmental changes are listed in Table 4.

Adolescence

Behavioral Changes

The onset of puberty and adolescence is biologically defined, but the term adolescence also designates the final stage of child development terminating with young adulthood. Physical maturation adheres to a "biologic timetable," but the corresponding psychologic developments are dependent upon environmental factors as well. In modern society, adolescence, judged by behavioral criteria, may end as early as age 17 and may last as long as to the age of 25 years. The prolongation of adolescence is characteristic of middle and upper socioeconomic groups. This is attributed to the fact that college and preparatory vocational training at advanced levels tend to prolong an actual state of dependency (upon parents for support and upon teachers for instruction).

The ambiguity of the adolescent state is reflected in pediatric practice. Many adolescent patients shift to adult types of medical care. Yet, in his capacity of family doctor, the pediatrician is consulted about adolescent behavior. In private practice it is not unusual for the pediatrician to care for teen-age patients until they move away from home. A summary of major developmental change is presented here in extremely condensed form.

Broadly conceived, the two major developmental steps accomplished during adolescence are: the final dissolution of the direct dependent tie to parents and home, and the achievement of what has been called a "sense of identity" (Erikson). By the latter term is meant that the young person now commits himself to a particular role in adult life. Whether his future be the result of choice or of necessity, the adolescent must come to terms with a restricted and defined set of expectations for his adult life.

Adolescent behavior is notoriously unstable. Among recurring behavioral trends, the following are outstanding: Open defiance of parental authority, either in the form of rebellion or of sullen indifference. A sharply critical attitude toward prevailing social values and customs, side by side with enthusiastic (if often transient) commitment to religious or social beliefs markedly different from those held by the family. Frequently, disillusionment with adult values and practices leads teen-agers to form strong attachments to adolescent groups. Such groups often share critical attitudes toward adults, and may pin their faith for the future on the greater sincerity of their own generation. It is on the basis of this developmental mechanism that students and other youth groups can play a significant role in social reform and in political life. Typical behaviors also include mood swings, from spurts of gaiety to periods of discouragement and apathy. Frequently, adolescence brings the development of new and intense interests. Such preoccupations may concern sports, religion, science, music, automobiles, or nearly any other thing —the characteristic feature being an exclusive interest so strong as to approach dedication. Adolescents are, of course, preoccupied with their developing relationships with young people of the opposite sex. It may safely be assumed that even the minority of teenage boys and girls who do not participate in the usual dates and dances are nonetheless deeply concerned not only with sexual matters, but quite as much with the emotional experiences associated with man-woman relationships. Lastly, it is characteristic of the adolescent state that the intense experiments with adult aspects of living go hand in hand with episodes of irresponsibility and with behavior that strikes adults as flighty and self-contradictory.

The vacillations of adolescent behavior are in large measure due to conflicting pressures from within, related to sexual maturation, and from without, in relation to changing social status. It is useful to recognize that in addition to developmental processes, social customs contribute to adolescent confusion. The family mores typical of modern industrial society expose young people to contradictory demands. Most boys and girls above the age of 15 years are expected to perform responsibly, yet they are not generally free to make decisions, and in many areas they must obey adult dictates. Adolescence has been described as a sort of no man's land; teen-agers must forego the benefits of childhood, yet they are not granted the advantages of adult status.

Diagnostic and Prophylactic Implications

Pediatricians can encourage and support normal developmental progress of their adolescent patients chiefly in two ways: firstly, through informed advice to parents, quite as is usual in behalf of younger patients; secondly, the doctor enjoys a privileged position by virtue of the fact that he is close to the family, yet able to preserve neutrality concerning family affairs. Most adolescents find it difficult to ask for information or advice from adults toward whom they entertain strong personal feelings (such as parents), or from adults toward whom they have obligations (such as teachers). In their struggle to affirm newly found maturity, adolescents can be helped by the mere fact that a respected adult will listen to their view of things and that what is said will remain confidential.

For the most part, adolescent problems differ from adult concerns primarily by their urgency and by the absolute manner in which they are posed, and only secondarily in contents.

In addition, and more specifically, most adolescents entertain doubts and curiosities concerning the physical aspects of sexuality. Most teen-agers are familiar with the facts of human reproduction. However, they are seldom informed concerning peripheral sexual phenomena. Needless anxiety is often experienced as adolescents carefully observe their own sensations, compare themselves with other youngsters of like sex, and contend with considerable misinformation supplied by peers. Among the topics that typically generate anxiety are the following: The observation that sexual maturation occurs at different chronologic ages, which is of concern especially to those who mature relatively late. The observation of changes in the appearance of the genitalia over time. The occurrence of sexual sensations in sleep and at other unexpected times. The question of whether bodily harm can result from masturbation or from erotic activity that has become almost conventionalized under the euphemistic term "petting." Adolescents are reluctant to discuss these concerns with adults, though such reticence does not characterize the conversations of teen-agers with one another. Information provided by the physician is often readily received and greatly reassuring because the doctor's expert knowledge is respected, and because he is likely to be the only adult who can discuss the matter without implying moral censure.

In the United States the use of psychedelic drugs by adolescents has become a significant social, psychologic, legal, and medical problem. Inevitably, pediatricians become involved not only with the medical aspects of the situation (see Chap. 13), but with the anxieties and conflicts that are always associated with the use of such drugs. In discussing the topic with young patients and with their families it is helpful to recognize that adolescent interest in psychedelic drugs is not necessarily pathologic, nor is it always prognostic of serious psychologic and social maladjustment. Indeed, at the present time, the critical and rebellious attitudes that have been typical of adolescents at all times, easily find expression through the use of drugs. The practice promises the opportunity for especially vivid and intense emotional experience; it defiantly opposes what some call "the establishment"; it creates a sense of unity and closeness with likeminded young people; and it dramatizes independence from the parent generation. Pediatricians have the opportunity to recognize the essentially normal and universal motivations that, in many instances, led to the interest in psychedelic drugs. At the same time, the attendant dangers (from impure drugs, addiction, interference with normal physiologic processes, and so forth) can be discussed objectively, and in the absence of moral censure.

REFERENCES

Bowlby, J. Maternal Care and Mental Health. World Health Organ. Monogr. Ser., 2, 1951.

Carmichael, L., ed. Manual of Child Psychology, 2nd ed. New York, John Wiley and Sons, 1954.

Erikson, E. H. Childhood and Society, 2nd ed. New York, W. W. Norton and Co., 1963.

Gesell, A., and Amatruda, C. Developmental Diagnosis. New York, 1947.

Hoffman, M. L., and Hoffman, L. W., eds. Review of Child Development Research. New York, Russell Sage Foundation, 1964.

Korsch, B. M. Practical techniques of observing, interviewing and advising parents in pediatric practice as demonstrated in an attitude study project. Pediatrics, 3:18, 1956.

Levy, D. M. Advice and reassurance. Amer. J. of Public Health, 44:1113-1118, 1954.

McCarthy, D. Language development in children. In Carmichael, L., ed., Manual of Child Psychology. New York, John Wiley and Sons, 1954.

Mussen, P. H., Conger, J. J., and Kagan, J. Child Development and Personality, 2nd ed. New York, Harper and Row, 1963.

Piaget, J. The Origins of Intelligence in Children. New York, International Universities Press, 1952.

Pratt, K. C. The neonate. In Carmichael, L., ed., Manual of Child Psychology, 2nd ed. New York, John Wiley and Sons, 1954.

Provence, S., and Lipton, R. Infants in Institutions. New York, International Universities Press, 1962.

Spitz, R. Hospitalism. The Psychoanalytic Study of the Child. New York, International Universities Press, Part I, Vol. 1:53-74, 1945. Part II, Vol. 11:113-117, 1946.

——— No and Yes. New York, International Universities Press, 1957.

Stone, L., and Church, T. Childhood and Adolescence, 2nd ed. New York, Random House, 1968.

chapter 6

ABNORMALITIES OF PSYCHOLOGIC GROWTH AND DEVELOPMENT

WILLIAM S. LANGFORD, Associate Editor

Over half of the children seen in urban pediatric practice present behavior and personality problems. About 10 percent are brought to the doctor because of these difficulties alone; in the remainder the difficulties may be discovered in the course of an examination for some somatic complaint. In addition to these specific disorders there are many situations in which the pediatrician needs to possess sound psychiatric knowledge in his routine care of children in health and disease. He is often consulted by parents in regard to the rearing of the child; the difficulties of the parents themselves may become his concern. The psychiatrically minded pediatrician should be able to deal with the great majority of these disorders himself; with a certain amount of diagnostic acumen he should be able to weed out from his clinical material those cases which require the additional time needed for a psychiatric approach, and among these he should be able to recognize the more complex and deep-seated disturbances which require the services of a trained psychiatrist.

It is well-nigh impossible to list either the causes or the manifestations of personality maladjustments. The manifestations may involve any system in the body; the causes are as complex as human personality itself. It is important to remember that similar underlying causes may give rise to different symptoms in different children, and the same symptom in different children may result from different causes. One should not conclude that a given symptom must have a single cause; it is more apt to be the result of many underlying factors. All difficulties cannot be explained by the intelligence quotient any more than they can be laid at the door of repressed sexuality or inferiority complex. If one is to deal successfully with this group of disorders he must evaluate all such factors and obtain a picture of the child as a whole—in action both past and present.

A careful history of the complaint is essential. It should cover the exact mode of onset, development up to the time of consultation, and all therapeutic attempts already made. In the personal history of the child attention should be paid to his birth, early feding, habit formation, developmental data, illnesses, operations or injuries, changes of residence and schools, scholastic attainments, and many other important events in the child's life. The way the child has responded to the various events and the attitudes and activities of those about him with reference to these happenings should be included.

One should find out about the child's general emotional reactivity to the various life situations. To what types of situations does he respond with fear, anger, jealousy, resentment, boistcrousness? Is he generally aggressive or timid, outgoing or seclusive, appreciative or dissatisfied? How does he respond to others, both inside and outside the family group? In addition, one should inquire into the environment, not only its physical aspects but also the personalities, attitudes, and examples set by those in the home, and their possible direct or indirect effect on the child.

Such information regarding the child and his environment is obtained through interviews with the parents and other adults with whom he comes in contact, as well as through observations of the home and its occupants in action. An interview with the child is essential, and it is best conducted with him alone. One should determine whether he is aware of his difficulties, and evaluate his attitudes toward them. His attitudes and feelings toward the members of his family, his teachers and playmates, his attitude toward authority, should be investigated. The child's fears, worries, preoccupations, interests, and aversions should be explored. A careful inquiry into his hatreds and resentments, his feelings of deprivation and difference, and attitudes toward his body and sex should not be neglected. A friendly, nonjudicial, and nondisciplinary role should be taken, and all semblance of a cross-examination should be avoided. The child should be induced to tell his story in his own way. It is unwise to "trap" him or to accuse him.

In addition to an exact knowledge of his physical state it is often important to have accurate knowledge of the child's intellectual functioning. Various objective criteria are available for this purpose. The Gesell, Merrill-Palmer, and Stanford-Binet tests and the Wechsler Intelligence Scale for Children (WISC) are the ones most frequently used. Some of these are especially adapted for use with young children; others are devised to evaluate the nonverbal aspects of intelligence. The most useful single test in the child of school age is the Stanford-Binet. Few physicians have sufficient familiarity in administering these tests to obtain valid determinations. Tests should be given by those experienced in their use. Many communities now have clinical psychologists available in the school setup with whom arrangements can be made for the administration of these tests. The competent clinical psychologist can also provide valuable information about the child's personality and its functioning from the Rorschach and Thematic Apperception tests. The physician should be familiar with the evaluation of these tests, the integration of the information obtained from them with other pertinent information about the child, and the interpretation of the test results to parents.

Having amassed such information regarding the child and his milieu one can form an opinion of what is wrong and what can be done about it. Constructive symptomatic treatment is often important; it is discussed with the different clinical manifestations. But it cannot be too strongly emphasized that unless the underlying difficulty is corrected, little permanent benefit is likely to follow treatment of the symptom alone. The symptom is the child's way of solving the underlying problem; the examination discloses what the problems are and how the child is solving them; the goal of treatment is to help the child to solve the problem in a more constructive manner or to remove or modify the problem. One should help him to adjust to the reasonable demands of a reasonable environment. This involves working with the child and with the environment.

In his work with the child the physician should attempt to establish a friendly relationship and encourage the child to talk about his problems; distorted ideas and ignorance can be corrected. A tolerant, noncritical attitude is of the greatest importance. Reassurance that other children have the same difficulties often gives a child a feeling of security and comfort. Creation in him of self-confidence and a spirit of collaboration in working to overcome his difficulties is important. If he is old enough, the plans made for his benefit should be explained to him. Correction of physical disorders should take place regardless of any relationship they may have to the personality difficulty. Several special methods have been developed for direct work with children. Among these is the psychoanalytic technique as adapted to children by Anna Freud and her co-workers and in a somewhat different manner by Melanie Klein. These methods have their enthusiastic advocates, but most workers in the field of child psychiatry believe that the greater number of children's personality and behavior disorders do not require such drastic therapy. Another special method is that of utilizing one of the methods of "play therapy"; the child who is unable or unwilling to verbalize is helped to express himself through the medium of play which is, after all, the natural language of childhood. These, as well as other specialized procedures developed for intensive direct psychotherapy with children, do not lend themselves to pediatric practice and are best left to the well-trained child psychiatrist.

In work with the family, unwholesome attitudes and methods of handling should be changed where possible. Suggestions should be given which recommend themselves to the parents as practical and reasonable. Destructive criticism, spanking by the parents, and argumentation are to be avoided. Complete correction of an emotionally unsatisfactory home atmosphere is often impossible, and the physician may have to content himself with ameliorative measures. His advice may not bring about an immediate change in the home situation, but not infrequently a friendly, noncritical attitude on his part will in time do much to help the parents in their management of the child. Sometimes the parents' own personality difficulties are such that referral to a psychiatrist becomes necessary. This is not easy to do, because they are frequently unaware of their own problems.

The difficulty with the home is not necessarily a noxious personality; it may be merely a lack of something which can be provided. A warmhearted nurse or a pet animal may help supply the needs of a child who craves more affection than he receives. Companions of his own age or new interests may be what is needed; boys' clubs and boy scout activities are often of value.

Placement away from the home should be thought of only when the parents' attitudes are unmodifiable and are injuring the child, or when the home is broken and does not provide suitable facilities for normal mental and emotional development. In urban apartment life the strain of a young child at close range may prove too great for the best-adjusted mother, and placement in a nursery school for part of the day is often helpful. Boarding schools and summer camps may provide a child with outlets which he needs and may serve to relieve emotional tension at home. Such placement should not be used indiscriminately as a cure-all for behavior and personality difficulties. One should be certain that the child will come under the supervision of someone who understands the problem and has both the ability and the time to handle it. As a rule children who are tense, shy, and fearful do not do well when thrust into a large group. Temporary removal from the home setting is likely to accomplish little that is permanent unless in the meantime some constructive changes have been made. Permanent placement away from home is sometimes necessary; it is a traumatic experience for the child and, unless the foster home is well selected, it may be a leap from the frying pan into the fire. If such a step is chosen, consultation with a child placement agency is important.

Such a study as outlined above takes time—more time than the busy physician may feel that he can spare. But the time needed by the observant pediatrician is apt to be less than would appear at first glance. Before he is consulted for a personality disorder he is often in possession of a great deal of the relevant information. He has followed the child from birth and knows the home—its standards and its occupants. If he has kept his eyes and ears open, he has watched the reaction of the child and parent in different situations, and knows their attitudes toward each other. He may be aware of marital discord. He has seen the way in which the mother accepts advice in the management of the child in sickness and health. He is on friendly terms with both child and parent, and his counsel will be the more acceptable since it is given with a knowledge of the personalities involved. A willingness to listen to the parents' story as they elaborate it spontaneously when giving the routine history will often give pertinent clues. The physician who is anxious to get the routine questioning over with, or who uses an outline form, will miss such remarks as the following:

"He was a delicate baby at birth and I always gave in to him until his brother came." "If I know he is physically fit then I can punish him." "He's got to move his bowels for me or he won't have room in his stomach for food." "I was happy (about the pregnancy) for my husband's sake." "His bones are weak; it's my fault; I didn't give him enough vitamins." "What do I do? Only housework." "She did everything late—walked at 1 year." "He feels inferior and has a mother complex." "I have to wash him but he would do it himself." "Do you think she will get too close to the window and fall out?" (The child was being watched by the clinic secretary.) Such remarks often fall on deaf ears. They are most valuable in giving insight into the parent-child relationship. Similarly, worries, questions, or statements made by the mother during the examination may reveal the source of the child's difficulties. During the physical examination of older children, which is best done in the parents' absence, much can be learned regarding the child's attitude toward his body, himself, and his companions. The knowledge so gained will prove useful in dealing not only with functional disorders but also with acute or chronic physical illnesses.

It frequently happens that the pediatrician becomes aware of various personality disorders when he is being consulted primarily about a physical illness. The mother is usually quite upset about the organic disease and finds it difficult enough to understand the treatment for that, and she will only be more confused if additional advice is given her regarding the personality difficulties. It would seem better to wait until the child is on the road to recovery before attempting to readjust the psychologic disorder. It is during routine health examinations that greatest opportunity exists for helping to correct these difficulties.

Pediatric practice offers many opportunities for preventive work in the field of personality dysfunction. The pediatrician is consulted by parents frequently during the early years of the child's life. During these consultations he can communicate to the parents sound advice and counsel; often he is able to bring about gradual changes in untoward attitudes in the parent and through anticipatory guidance can help them to meet new phases in the child's development constructively. The establishment of a good psychologic hygiene in feeding and weaning situations, the guidance of parents in psychologically and physiologically sound methods of toilet training, and help to them in other aspects of child training fall within the province of the pediatrician. Parents are often confused about general principles involved in helping the child to pattern his physiologic as well as his emotional behavior to conform to the ordinary standards of our society. They are apt to resort to harsh or coercive methods in their efforts to make the child conform; this is apt to result in long-lasting emotional disturbances in the child. The pediatrician may be of great help in aiding them to differentiate discipline, which is basically training and education, from punishment. Harsh punitive measures have little place in child rearing and are not helpful in establishing a good state of mental health in childhood. Mismanagement of a child who is reacting negativistically can be largely prevented by preparing the parents to expect this phase. Jealousy reactions are more easily prevented than cured.

Acute illness often brings up problems of management. At such times the child receives a good deal more concern, attention, and coddling than usual and may give these up with considerable reluctance. Many children become distinctly "babyish" during acute illness, and the reaction may persist beyond the convalescent period unless it is well handled. Bed-wetting may occur, in a child previously dry, during an acute illness and may cause much concern on the part of the parents. Feeding difficulties often begin following an acute illness; the decrease in appetite may result in forcing or coaxing or urging of food. Children are quick to realize the distinct gains from illness and make the most of them. In general, sickbed practices should be discontinued as soon as possible. Many children are apt to regard illness as punishment. They have been told that they will get colds if they disobey and go out without their rubbers; that heart trouble comes from running too much; or that diabetes comes from eating too much candy. Many children have been threatened with a visit to the doctor as a punishment.

The management of *chronic illness*, such as rheumatic heart disease or chronic nephritis, may tax the pediatrician's resourcefulness in order to instill and maintain a healthy attitude toward the disease in both the child and his parents. The patient may lapse into chronic invalidism, or may perhaps rebel against restrictions on his activities and lead a life which may cause further damage to his heart or kidneys. Self-blame on the part of the parents for not having been able to prevent illness is especially apt to occur when the disease is chronic or has sequelae; this feeling is apt to affect their attitudes toward the child. Parents show astoundingly little imagination in providing diversion for children who require prolonged bed rest. The child tires of the usual games after an hour or two, and reading bores him when it is all he has to do day after day. Construction games, as Erector or Meccano sets, soap-carving, weaving, knitting, and other devices with which the child can make something, are especially helpful. Brief, supervised visits by selected playmates are especially enjoyed. Orthopedic patients, it has been observed, are especially apt to masturbate after spending long periods in bed with insufficient amusement. Prolonged bed rest on a soft diet leads to constipation, which is usually treated by repeated enemas. Children finally get to rely on them, if not actually to enjoy them, unless the physician is aware of this possibility. Discussion of the child's illness either in his presence or just beyond his hearing is unwise. Stray words are misinterpreted and the child may be alarmed by the secrecy; his already existing fears may be increased.

Operations may precipitate much anxiety in a child's life. It is surprising how frequently children are tricked into operations or deceived as to the reason for coming to the hospital. One boy of our acquaintance, who had been told he was coming to the hospital only for an examination, when he awoke from the anesthetic after an appendectomy, said, "Daddy, you're a liar," and refused to speak to him up to the time he left the hospital two weeks later. It is well, on the other hand, not to announce an impending operation to a child too long in advance. Traumatically induced anesthesias are bad. A preliminary hypnotic is insurance against an anesthetist who is too rough-and-ready.

In dealing with personality and behavior aberrations, one must be familiar not only with the physical and mental growth of children but also with their emotional and social development. From a dependent outlook a child gradually expands his horizons from the home to the neighborhood school, and finally to the community at large. The question often arises: is he able to take the next step in increasing social horizons at the usual period, or is his dependence on others unduly prolonged? Paralleling this expansion of social horizons the child develops from a self-centered individual, thinking only in terms of himself and how things affect him, to a more social being able to relate himself to others. During the earlier part of this quite normal period of egocentricity the child is apt to respond with emotional outbursts to anything that interferes with his wishes. The child learns to regulate his emotional responses through a process of growth and sympathetically applied social pressures. This transition is a gradual one, and usually by the seventh or eighth year when the child has got over some of his egocentricity most parents will heave a sigh of relief.

Like the adult, the child has certain basic psychologic needs—a need for affection, for order in his universe, and a need for self-expression. Unless these needs are satisfied, evidences of maladjustment are apt to appear. They are present at all times, but at certain critical stages in his development one or another may become more acute. All children need mothering. Personality difficulties resulting from emotional deprivation are well known. In infants there is need for cuddling. It is a common observation in

children's hospitals that convalescent infants do better when they are sent home or are given considerable fondling and mothering by the nurses. We have seen many "hypertonic" infants with marked restlessness, irritability, and vomiting quiet down when a calm, soothing nurse could be substituted for an overwrought, tense, and agitated mother. The growing child's needs are more acute; he needs to "belong" to the home, regardless of whether he is good or bad. He likes to feel that he is wanted and loved. All too many parents attempt to bring affection into discipline, telling the child he will not be loved any more unless he conforms. Such withdrawal of affection may lead to vindictive behavior—a desire to hurt the parent. The oversolicitous, indulgent parent who smothers the child with affection may produce similar results.

Aside from the security which comes from personal affection the child likes to be reasonably secure in a consistent environment. He resents frequent changes of residence with the loss of old playmates and formation of new acquaintances. He needs to have the same restrictions placed on his activities, rather than being able to do a thing one time and not the next. It is somewhat differently expressed in the young child's desire to have a story told in exactly the same way time after time or to cover exactly the same route on his daily airings. He thrives better on reasonable restrictions of his activities; unbridled freedom is just as unsatisfactory to him as too many restrictions with "don'ts" barraging him from all angles.

Perhaps the most basic need, however, is the need to be accepted and treated as a unique individual who is to grow and develop at his own rate of speed and not according to some preconceived standards. It is the physician's job to prevent the application of rigid weight gain requirements, standardization of amounts of food to be eaten, sleeping and feeding schedules. Aldrich, Gesell, and Davis have pointed out the lack of inherent dangers in letting the infant determine his own schedules in feeding. The need to express his individuality often becomes more acute at certain periods in a child's development. At about the age of 2 one often encounters a period of resistance and negativism. The child who has hitherto been more or less submissive and dependent discovers his own ego. The demands of the daily routine are met with a succession of "no, no's" and the parents often feel that their child has had a profound change in personality. Unwise discipline may bring on resentment and hostility and may create anxieties in the child. On the other hand, submission may result in the child's tyrannizing the home. The situation requires insistence on matters of daily routine with gentle firmness, at the same time ignoring the more irrelevant "I won't" and "no" replies. Demands on the child should be reasonable. He needs the same sympathetic good-natured attitudes and encouragement that are needed in all contacts with children who are constantly learning new things and adapting themselves to new situations, to rules, and to regulations. This period of negativism is often a passing phase, but even when it persists a while longer need occasion no concern. Parents may be reassured with the thought that the resistive child is apt to be a more worthwhile individual in later life than his more complacent brother, although the latter will certainly cause them less inconvenience.

The physician can be helpful in watching for signs of maladjustment during the so-called critical periods of childhood such as weaning, the period of resistance, beginning of school, and the preadolescent and adolescent years. It is at these times that the child is in most need of sympathetic handling and encouragement; much can be done to improve his security and to relieve untoward pressure and tension. One should remember that the child's feelings of being slighted or deprived are just as real and important to him as if there were a factual basis for them.

Just as important as the knowledge of the child is an awareness of factors in the parents which affect the parent-child relationship. The oversolicitous mother is frequently found in pediatric practice. Her immunity to advice, reasoning, pleading, and exhortations is well known. Her condition is easy to identify, difficult to correct. The mother usually is aware of her difficulties but is unable to do anything about them. One must go into the factors which have produced this reaction, the causes of which are probably almost as numerous as there are mothers. It may go back to an earlier rejection of the child, frequently to attempts at aborting the pregnancy, or not wanting to become pregnant although submitting, the oversolicitude being then in the nature of "making up" to the child for the earlier rejection. Another mother may feel that she must prevent all colds in a child who once had otitis. Self-blame for a preventable illness is frequently the focus out of which overprotectiveness develops; this is often precipitated by a chance remark of the physician. Parents' attitudes toward their children may go back to their own early lives. One highly protective father, raised on a farm where he had to do daily chores, resolved that his son should never have to do anything about the house. The boy, living in a small city apartment, developed into an aggressive youngster who rode rough-shod over everyone. Parents' own early deprivations and conflicts may markedly influence their attitudes toward their children. One mother who had always tried to surpass her older sister continued this rivalry with her child. A competition between the sisters arose which took the form of going into debt buying things for their children. Concern about their own earlier masturbation or sex difficulties may lead to destructive handling in this sphere. The need to be a good parent is frequently seen. These parents will blindly follow rules laid down for them. Their relationship with their children loses its spontaneity and produces insecurity in the child. Confused by a maze of rules and regulations, some parents live in constant fear of inflicting psychic trauma on their child. They should be made to realize that a certain amount of psychic trauma is the inevitable lot of every child and adult, and that a youngster growing up without such experiences would probably be ill-prepared for adult life. The physician should be able to give them the needed emotional support which will enable them to use better what knowledge they have and to accept new knowledge.

Common Psychopathologic Symptoms and Syndromes

The more common psychopathologic symptoms and symptom complexes seen in childhood, and the situations out of which they most frequently arise, will now be discussed. Such suggestions for treatment as are given apply mostly to the constructive handling of the symptom. For the more general approach and for therapeutic measures the reader is referred to the foregoing paragraphs.

Alimentary Disorders

ANOREXIA. Anorexia from faulty feeding habits is common in children of all ages from infancy to adolescence. The practice of forcing food to make a child gain weight at some preconceived rate, or to compete with a neighbor's child, is all too frequent. Transitory periods of anorexia due to minor indispositions, fatigue, or emotional factors are common; by forcing food at such times an overzealous parent may precipitate chronic feeding difficulty. Sometimes a child, impressed by parental concern over food intake during acute illness, may keep up the poor feeding habits as a means of gaining attention. A spoiled child may dominate the home by his feeding behavior. Feeding problems are apt to arise during the so-called period of resistance or negativism in the third year, which often coincides with the time the child is losing his chubby infantile physique, a change that may be construed by the mother as malnutrition.

In addition to forcing food it should be appreciated that emotional states such as excitement, tension, and unhappiness markedly decrease the appetite; a search for their origin should be made. Punishment at mealtimes is unwise; children with unpleasant associations eat poorly. Imitation of adults may determine the feeding pattern. Dawdling with the food is often seen in daydreaming children. The opposite type of child, who is so active and interested in his environment that he does not have time to eat, also eats very little.

Many of these difficulties can be prevented by warning parents to expect variations in appetite. A jittery, uncertain nurse or mother is prone to accept the physician's word as law. When a new food is suggested she believes the baby has to have it and a forcing pattern may be started. Unskillful weaning from the breast or bottle may precipitate the difficulty. In recent years feeding problems have decreased in frequency in clinical practice. This seems to be associated with more relaxed methods of feeding geared to the infant's own needs and appetite.

The constructive management of the feeding problem itself is discussed elsewhere (Sec. 3.3). Environmental factors producing tension and anxiety in the child should be sought for and corrected. As a rule improper handling in the home will not be confined to feeding, and a broad program of readjustment must be instituted.

ANOREXIA NERVOSA. This syndrome, first described in adults by Gull a century ago, has been seen with greater frequency during the past two decades. Previously anorexia nervosa was seen primarily in late adolescence and early womanhood, the younger cases being in the 15-year-old age group. However, in the period since 1950, there have been more than 40 girls between 9 and 14 years admitted to the Babies Hospital with this syndrome, whereas only one was seen in the previous fifteen years. The reasons for the appearance at a younger age are not entirely clear, but would seem to be related to the earlier maturation of the human young.

This disorder is characterized by extreme emaciation, with weight losses up to 50 percent of body weight. Accompanying the weight loss there is increased body hair especially on the back and extremities; decreased body temperature to as low as 96° F., rectally; decreased pulse rate; lowered blood pressure; lowered leucocyte count; amenorrhea or delayed menses; and a marked degree of hyperactivity with excessive energy output. There is no loss of breast tissue or falling out of axillary or pubic hair as a result of the malnutrition. Plasma proteins in our outpatients were usually normal at the time of admission. The BUN tended to be elevated when starvation was severe. Edema often appeared when the patients began to eat after prolonged starvation. In 50 percent of our cases radiographs of the chest showed a microcardia.

Most writers agree that the disorder is psychologic in origin and that it is a syndrome rather than a disease entity, the clinical psychiatric diagnoses ranging from neurosis to psychosis. It would appear that when it occurs in males it is more often a manifestation of a psychotic process with a marked eating inhibition. Only one of 48 of our female patients could be diagnosed as psychotic whereas all 3 male patients were so regarded. The clinical psychiatric picture varies from case to case but elements of compulsion neurosis, conversion hysteria, and mild depression are seen along with moderate to severe withdrawal reactions.

Characteristically anorexia nervosa begins with a self-imposed diet which gradually leads to extreme restriction of food intake and to marked weight loss, a fear of eating, and a concomitant preoccupation with food and diet. The youngsters coerce and manipulate their environment with much bargaining and complaining about food, weight, and eating. There is a marked distrust and suspicion of others leading to secrecy about eating, bathroom activities, and exercises. Any inconsistency uncovered in their dealings with people serves only to confirm their belief that people cannot be trusted.

Initial attempts to diet are explained by children who develop anorexia nervosa as an effort to "reduce." Their concerns about overweight may not be realistic and in most cases are not borne out by photographs or weight records. Sooner or later it emerges that they believe weight loss would make them more popular and gain them friends and social acceptance. Ultimately, many of the girls described their feelings when confronted with food as extreme anger or a "ball of fear" in the abdomen. They describe being hungry but unable to eat. Despite their emaciated appearance, the patients deny the extreme "concentration camp look," maintaining stoutly that their abdomens protrude and that their pipe-stem extremities are too heavy.

The family setting in which this syndrome develops is characterized by an emotionally unavailable mother whom the child had handled earlier by a high degree of conforming behavior, and a warm close relationship with the father which at pubescence became increasingly intolerable for the youngster. In some cases, the father's relationship seemed to be at a conscious level of trying to make up for his spouse's affectional unavailability and in others seemed to be associated with considerable degree of personal psychopathology.

In contrast to the cases described in the earlier literature, the more recent patients did not present early feeding problems. On the contrary, they ate well which may be related to the better emotional hygiene of infant feeding methods initiated around 1940. One outstanding thing in the past history was the absence of well demarcated oppositional behavior in the preschool period. The emergence of this behavior with the feeding problem later is an outstanding feature of this syndrome.

Because of the severe nutritional problem and the tendency of some of these patients to develop circulatory collapse, it seems important that these children be treated, at least for a while, in the hospital. Circulatory collapse may be heralded by a resting systolic blood pressure reading below 50 mm Hg which does not rise later in the day. In addition to this danger, the continual battle in the home between child and parent, the child's mistrust of all adults, and the need to increase the food intake, dictated a separation from this home until the youngster could gain some trust in herself and others, and until work with the family could effect some changes in the family balance.

Hospital management should consist of kindly firmness, consistent demands, low pressure on eating, and great patience. The important measures of the patient's progress are a decrease in vomiting, in hiding of food, in constipation, and less stress placed on weight gain. A skilled psychotherapeutic approach with the child and contacts with the family are highly important. A Sustagen R formula providing 2 calories per ml and offered as a medication is sometimes helpful in decentering attention on food intake until an effective psychotherapeutic relationship can be established. With patient urging by the nurse, the patient will usually take this "medication," which, by insuring some caloric intake, also serves to decrease the concern of the hospital personnel. Forced feedings or intermittent tube feeding has no place in the management of these patients. If the situation becomes desperate, feedings can be given through an indwelling naso-gastric tube. On the rare occasion that we have had to resort to this, the patients have left them in place. In our experience the initial change in attitude appears to take place only after 5 or 6 weeks of hospitalization when the patients become more friendly and agreeable and eating gradually becomes less of a problem. It is important *not* to give a target weight for discharge but to give the patient and her family the understanding that many different factors enter into this decision. Furthermore, plans for continuing ambulatory treatment must be discussed long before discharge from the hospital. In general our patients have been ready for discharge and their families able to accept them home after an average of 15 weeks of hospitalization. Unfortunately, not all patients respond and the disease has a mortality rate of 10 to 15 percent.

Treatment of these children and their families is a long, tedious task calling for great forbearance, patience, and tolerance, not only of the patients and their parents, but also for the emotional reactions of one's colleagues to a truly difficult, annoying, and anxiety-creating patient. However, the rewards are great: the appearance of a happy, pretty face replacing the gaunt, harried, and angry physiognomy makes the effort of treatment thoroughly worthwhile. The psychiatrist who works with these patients can see concrete evidence of the fruits of his efforts to salvage a personality and, in some instances, save a life.

EXCESSIVE APPETITE. Some children with emotional disturbances develop an excessive appetite which leads to obesity. Emotional tension or parental food forcing in these children does not lead to anorexia. These situations have been discussed in the section on overnutrition (Sec. 3.6).

PICA. Many children between the second and fourth years eat everything they can pick up from the floor: dirt, sand, plaster, wood, or coal. They may pick the fuzz from blankets or chew the paint from toys or furniture. The cause is obscure; in most cases the craving does not seem to be related to a dietary deficiency, although we have seen it disappear in one child with a moderately severe secondary anemia due to poor diet, after iron medication was given. Pica is a common symptom of hookworm

anemia. Certainly all children during the latter half of the first year show a well-marked hand-to-mouth reaction. This is apt to be prolonged in mentally deficient children, but by no means are all of the patients with pica mentally defective. In some instances it is seen in children with symptoms of a personality disorder. A girl aged three and a half would eat ashes, dirt, and trash on the street but would not tolerate so much as a speck of dirt at the meal table. She also had a strong aversion to toilet odors and showed marked hostility to her father. Hair is sometimes eaten and produces a "hair-ball" tumor (trichobezoar) in the stomach or gives rise to digestive disturbances. We have observed this in several children who sucked one thumb and pulled out their hair as an accessory movement with the other hand, afterward eating the hair. Here, of course, the treatment should be directed at the causes of the sucking habit. Pica is sometimes practiced sporadically as an attention-getting device. Usually the habit is innocuous, but it may lead to serious consequences; eating of paint is a common cause of lead poisoning in children.

Treatment should be directed toward the underlying causes if any can be discovered. In many instances close observation and good supervision are all that is needed. Mechanical restraint is rarely effective beyond the immediate period of its use. Kanner states that the persistence of the symptom beyond the fourth year may be regarded as a bad prognostic omen in normally intelligent children, occurring only in those with grave personality disorders.*

PSYCHOGENIC VOMITING. This occurs at all ages, even in young infants. It may be a symptom of mild emotional maladjustment or one manifestation of a serious neurotic disorder. It is brought on by a variety of factors and situations. At times the vomiting seems to be a primitive, undifferentiated response to disgusting or distasteful experiences or thoughts. In some children it occurs only with acute excitement. Sudden separation from a parent may be a factor. It is frequently seen as a response to a tense, hostile parent; as a more or less disguised form of hostile expression it sometimes takes the place of temper outbursts, especially when the child is afraid to display anger for fear of losing affection. When better relations are established it disappears. In children of indulgent parents the vomiting often serves as a tool by which the child can tyrannize the family. A common form is that which occurs on school mornings and is associated with a dread of going to school. The difficulty may be sought in school or the schoolwork, but often the fear of going to school is related more closely to relationships in the home. The vomiting pattern as an expression of

* Some amazing accounts of perverted appetite in older subjects have been collected by Gould and Pyle in *Anomalies and Curiosities in Medicine.* Philadelphia, W. B. Saunders Co., 1901.

personality difficulties often goes back to early gastro-intestinal upsets, to regurgitation from air-swallowing or to forcing of food by an overzealous mother. Sometimes prolonged overfeeding by a parent is the immediate cause. One should ascertain why the mother wants to overfeed. In one of our cases the disturbance began after pneumonia. The maternal grandfather had developed tuberculosis after pneumonia, which had been treated by enforced rest and large quantities of food. The mother was anxious to prevent tuberculosis in her child.

In psychogenic vomiting the patient may throw up with ease, or with nausea or retching; and other evidences of emotional maladjustment are usually present. Most of the children of school age whose vomiting has an emotional basis have had feeding problems in infancy as well. The diagnosis may, however, be extremely difficult. Regardless of the presence of personality difficulties, a thorough physical examination must be made to rule out other causes of vomiting (Sec. 23.2). We have been impressed by a number of children whose vomiting was eventually shown to be caused by an expanding intracranial lesion, yet who for weeks had been assumed to be emotionally unstable largely because their symptoms appeared only in the morning. The discovery of physical disease, on the other hand, does not spell a causal relationship. Most difficult to evaluate are cases in which somatic and psychic factors both play a part; the treatment must deal with all factors.

Some of these children vomit only particular foods to which they have aversions or with which they have unpleasant associations; in such cases the question of food allergy must always be considered. As a rule, however, only extreme hypersensitiveness causes vomiting; foods which later may cause marked urticaria or angioneurotic edema are usually eaten with pleasure and retained.

Successful treatment of these children depends on discovery and solution of the problems underlying the vomiting. Symptomatic treatment plays a small part in therapy.

CAR SICKNESS. This ailment, like seasickness, is unquestionably caused by the abnormal motion. It may be very troublesome in traveling. Only recently has it been appreciated that psychic factors may play an important contributory part in these cases. Emotional difficulties, such as fears and anxieties pertaining to accidents, are often present. When these are properly handled the symptom frequently disappears. The stomach of an emotionally balanced child is more tolerant of motion than that of an unstable, worried child.

Disorders of Elimination

ENURESIS. This condition is discussed in Section 22.17. Functional enuresis may occur as a result of inadequate habit training on the part of indifferent or oversolicitous parents who seem to prefer to blame it on "weak kidneys" or inheritance. Unwise toilet training or too harsh methods may bring out latent resentment or hostility which is expressed through wetting. This is especially apt to occur if the habit training is begun during the period of resistance and is too assiduously pursued. Children who because of crowded living conditions must sleep with a sibling have been known to wet only when sleeping with a certain brother or sister and not with the others. Enuresis may occur as a manifestation of a general emotional immaturity, often associated with a "baby talk" speech difficulty and thumb-sucking. The immaturity may be lifelong or may result from pressures coming on after the dry habit had been previously established. The more general underlying factors must be dealt with in these cases. A common situation, out of which may develop enuresis and other more infantile habits, such as a desire to take milk from the bottle and to be fed, is the birth of a younger brother or sister. A similar reversion may take place after a serious or distressing physical illness. The enuresis may be continued as a means of securing attention previously given.

The symptom may be very poorly handled. Corporal punishments, shaming, and scolding serve to focus the child's attention on his symptom. He may develop a feeling of shame and of being different from other children, which leads him into an unhappy, seclusive existence. Self-confidence is apt to be lacking after the difficulty has persisted a while.

The child and his environment should be studied before treatment is begun. A careful inquiry into toilet training, especially the time begun and the methods used, is important. The toilet facilities should be gone into in detail. Rarely, enuresis occurs as an isolated symptom of personality disorder, in which case it should make one suspicious of some as yet undiscovered organic difficulty. A general, psychiatrically oriented study of the child and his environment is indispensable in treating the child who has enuresis. The treatment program will depend on the findings. In every case, however, steps should be taken to assure constructive handling of the symptom.

ENCOPRESIS. Encopresis is the persistence of fecal soiling beyond the age of 2 years in the absence of any organic lesion of the rectum or anus. It is common in children who are seriously retarded mentally, and is usually associated with enuresis. A similar association is seen in children poorly trained. Toilet training may have failed because of unwise methods or because of emotional maladjustments on the part of the child. The difficulty usually lies in the parent-child relationship; anxiety and fear of the toilet may be a factor. Older children who have previously been clean may begin to soil after some disrupting event. Kanner has called attention to the frequency of this condition in emotionally unstable and immature children in association with temper outbursts. Treatment, particularly in the last-mentioned group, is difficult. The methods employed with enuresis may be helpful, but as a rule the condition calls for competent psychiatric help.

CONSTIPATION. The causes and the management of constipation are discussed elsewhere. It may be pointed out here, however, that psychic factors may be at the root of the difficulty. Unwillingness of the mismanaged child to cooperate with the parents may take this form; fear of the toilet is at times an underlying factor. The precipitating cause is usually undue concern on the part of the parents about the necessity of a daily bowel movement, a state of mind fostered by laxative manufacturers, by tradition, and sometimes by the physician. This concern often provides a child with an opportunity for occupying the center of attention. Therapy consists in allaying parental anxieties on the absorption of toxins and in adopting measures designed to correct any personality difficulty. In the spastic case atropine may be of help.

Motor Disorders

GENERAL MOTOR RESTLESSNESS. This is frequently seen among children and is a source of annoyance to teachers and parents, who are apt to nag at the children to sit still. Parents complain of it in terms of "fidgetiness," "jitteriness," and "nervousness," or say that the child is "highstrung" or "hyperkinetic." The child is continually on the go and, if asked to sit still, wiggles, taps his feet, plays with his fingers, or pulls at his clothing. The movements may resemble tics but are not as constant and the restlessness is usually carried over into sleep. It may be so severe that it resembles chorea. Parents' and teachers' diagnoses of "St. Vitus" or "verge of chorea" are frequently inflicted on these youngsters, and their activity may be curtailed in consequence.

The differentiation from chorea may be quite difficult but is usually possible. The restlessness which these children exhibit should also be distinguished from the activity of a normal hyperactive child. The hyperactive child is usually doing something whereas the restless child fidgets without purpose. The difficulty with most of these children lies with the restrictions under which they live; many of them actually suffer from a lack of opportunity for normal motor activity in play. This is apt to occur in children who live in small apartments where efficient household management limits their play activity at home and they cannot go out of doors unless accompanied by an adult. Children of the preschool age are affected most commonly. Adequate outlets for play and motor activity are of importance. Nursery school is of great assistance. In many children, however, general motor restlessness occurs as a manifestation (in company with other symptoms) of some underlying anxiety. The cause for this should be investigated and handled on the general principles outlined above.

HEAD-BANGING. This disorder is occasionally seen in older infants and young children. The head is struck rhythmically against the mattress, side of the crib, wall, or any other convenient place. It may be kept up for two or three hours at a time. The child rarely hurts himself, although there may be a localized thickening of the skin and underlying tissues. The child will stop if a sharp object is placed at the site of the banging. Like other habits, head-banging is frequently contagious. The disorder is not to be confused with that seen in temper tantrums. It usually runs a benign course and is rarely seen during waking hours after the fourth year, although it may persist in sleep or in semisleeping states until a much later period. Although head-banging may occur in mentally defective children, it is seen frequently enough in those of normal mental development. It is rarely a symptom of organic brain disease. The cause is obscure, but it seems to satisfy some basic need for rhythm. It is not necessarily accompanied by any symptoms of underlying emotional disturbance. When seen in older children during waking hours there may be accompanying symptoms of emotional immaturity, and it may be regarded as a persistent infantile pleasure-seeking device. In such cases the causes of the immaturity should be attacked.

TICS. Tics or habit spasms are sudden, rapid, frequently repeated, involuntary movements of circumscribed groups of muscles. They occur frequently in childhood and usually involve the face, although almost any part of the body may be involved. Blinking, grimacing, clearing the throat, sniffling, and jerking the shoulder are among those most frequently seen. Several varieties may be present in the same child, occurring either simultaneously or in succession. According to Kanner they rarely occur before 6 years of age; the incidence reaches its peak in the early prepuberty period. They are usually found associated with other symptoms of an emotional disorder, most frequently in tense, restless, overactive, and easily fatigued youngsters. They occur in children of all degrees of intelligence.

Tics are to be differentiated from chorea, a distinction which is not always easy. Choreic movements have a larger range of excursion and are repeated irregularly, while the tics are repeated in the same fashion and seem to have a more purposeful nature. Both types disappear in sleep and are made worse by emotional tension and fatigue. The tic differs from manipulations of the body, such as thumb-sucking or nose-picking, in that it is more rapid, is involuntary, and cannot be interrupted. The general motor restlessness seen in anxious, jittery children is different in that the twitching is not consistently localized and does not follow a definite pattern.

The tic is to be studied not only for its immediate precipitating cause but also for the setting in which it arises. It may originate as a voluntary, purposeful act, such as a defensive movement against some constant irritation; a tight collar may evoke a twisting of the neck, or an uncomfortable sleeve a shrugging of the shoulders. Blinking may first begin with a conjunctivitis and persist after the disappearance of the exciting cause. Imitation of others may also play a role. In a setting of environmental and emotional stress, the movement becomes detached from the original purpose and persists although it is no longer useful.

Treatment must be directed at the underlying emotional difficulties rather than at the tic itself. The more the child is made aware of the tic through parental admonition, massage, exercises before a mirror, or electrotherapy, the more the condition is apt to be aggravated. It is important that those in the child's environment stop calling attention to the symptom. The child is usually old enough to discuss directly his personality problems and to participate in the plans for his better adjustment at home, in his recreational life, and, if necessary, at school. Treatment should be begun as early as possible; the tic is notoriously resistant to treatment, especially when it has persisted over a long period of time. One tic is apt to be replaced by another or, having disappeared, is apt to return at a later date during a period of increased environmental tension.

A 7-year-old adopted boy returned to school in the fall following a happy summer spent at the beach with his mother and father. Shortly afterward he developed many facial tics exactly similar to those of a boy in his class. They did not disappear with removal from school or increased rest. The mother, an artist, was away from the home much of the time working at her studio. He, knowing of his adoptive status, resented the separation keenly after the close contact during the summer, and felt for the first time that he was being neglected and not loved as much as if he had been a natural child. When the mother arranged her time so that she would be home at least a part of his waking hours, he felt reassured that he was wanted and loved, and the tics disappeared as did his general tension and unhappiness.

A 9-year-old boy of low average intelligence (IQ 85) developed eye-blinking and head-tossing tics in response to exaggerated parental ambitions as to schoolwork. He tried hard to please his mother with good report cards; but in spite of the fact that he gave up all his playtime to study, his marks, although passing, did not come up to his or his parents' expectations. After the mother had been helped to view the educational process in a slightly different manner and the boy resumed his recreational outlets, the tics disappeared. They returned again for a brief time a few years later, at the beginning of adolescence, when he went through the usual period of rebellion against parental authority.

Sleep Disturbances

RESTLESSNESS, DISTURBED SLEEP. Disturbed or restless sleep is a common complaint in infancy and childhood. In infancy it is usually a result of physical factors such as hunger, digestive troubles, a wet diaper, or excessive cold or heat. Discomfort from illness may be responsible at any age. In the absence of physical disorder and, at times, in its presence, and of equal or greater importance, psychologic factors are to be considered, particularly tension and anxiety. Obsessive trends and masturbation fantasies may produce insomnia. Restless sleep is often seen in children who are overactive and jumpy in the daytime. Treatment must be directed toward the factors which have produced the daytime hyperkinesis as well. Drugs should not be used except to insure adequate rest for the child in the presence of acute physical illness.

One of the most frequent problems in childhood is unwillingness to go to sleep. The indulged child of oversolicitous, inconsistent parents presents this difficulty as but a part of general resistiveness to all routines—feeding, elimination, and general management. The child may refuse to go to bed, bargain for a few extra minutes, or, once there, insist on someone's staying with him or coming back whenever he calls. In crowded metropolitan life parents are prone to give in so that the child's protests or tantrums will not "disturb the neighbors," who retaliate by pounding on the walls or calling the police. Treatment is to be directed at the cause of the personality difficulties along the general lines discussed elsewhere. The problem of going to bed can often be handled with a little imagination—by making a game of the process.

Insomnia due to organic disease is usually easy to recognize. Occasionally it occurs as a postencephalitic manifestation, often in company with other grave behavior disorders. Such a possibility, though relatively infrequent, should not be overlooked.

Talking in the sleep is exceedingly common and is not to be viewed with alarm. The fragmentary words which can be pieced together usually indicate that the child has been reliving his play of the preceding day.

An interesting and not infrequent form of sleep disturbance, consisting of rhythmic rolling of the head back and forth just before the child falls asleep and known as *jactatio capitis nocturna*, also occurs. At times the head is beaten up and down against the pillow or mattress. It starts toward the end of the first year and usually disappears by the fourth year. It occurs in children of all degrees of intelligence and is not necessarily associated with any other symptoms. Some of the children accompany the rolling with humming or singing. In half the cases we have observed, the onset followed an otitis media. The significance of this condition is unknown. It does not seem to indicate any emotional disturbance, although it is annoying to parents. It seems to satisfy some demand for rhythm in the child and is not harmful.

SLEEPWALKING. Sleepwalking is usually considered nothing more than an enacted dream. The condition is sometimes confused with night terrors, in which the child gets up and walks or runs about in a state of great fright. In sleepwalking there are no affective changes and the activity seems more purposeful. It is often, though not invariably, an indication of underlying tension. Parents are apt to be upset by its occurrence because of the danger of falling downstairs or out of a window or going out of doors. Treatment involves a general approach to sources of tension and difficulty in the child and his environment. Precautions may also have to be taken to prevent the child from hurting himself.

NIGHTMARES AND NIGHT TERRORS. The significance of these two disturbances is the same. In the nightmare the child wakes up after a dream, is frightened but recognizes his surroundings, and is able to relate his upsetting experience; he remembers it the next morning. Night terrors occur more often in younger children and are not followed by waking. The child sits up in bed or runs aimlessly about the room, the eyes wide with terror, clutching at people and shouting for help. The attack cannot be cut short by soothing or calming alone; it may last 15 or 20 minutes, after which the child goes back to calm sleep. In the morning he cannot remember the event; even if wakened immediately there may be no recollection of it. Such attacks may come on nightly or months apart. Nearly all children have isolated disturbances of this nature, but their frequent occurrence calls for careful study. Anxiety is the commonest cause of these attacks; it may not be apparent from the child's behavior when awake. A careful study may lead to the discovery of some upsetting event, as in one child who had attacks nightly for two years after witnessing his father's death from being struck by an automobile. Lurid bedtime stories may be responsible. In other cases the difficulty may be anxiety caused by internal conflicts, as in the case of a 7-year-old girl who was tremendously concerned with religious and racial differences between her parents, one of whom was Jewish and the other Irish Catholic. The night terrors cleared after she had verbalized these worries and had been reassured that the non-Catholic parent was not destined for eternal damnation.

Physical factors may play a part in these, as in all sleep disturbances. Sometimes the difficulty is an overlarge evening meal. Giving the chief meal at noon and substituting a light supper may be helpful. We have seen some patients benefited by the administration of 10 to 15 g of glucose just before bedtime. The possibility of organic disease should not be overlooked. Often mistaken for a nightmare is the "night-cry" which may be the first symptom of tuberculosis of the hip.

EXCESSIVE SLEEP, NARCOLEPSY. It is rare that either infants or children sleep an unnatural amount of the time unless one of two causes is present—organic brain disease, most frequently tuberculosis meningitis, or the use of drugs. In certain individuals, however, there is seen a tendency to fall asleep which does not depend on intercurrent disease of the brain or upon drugs. It is not progressive

and may continue for years, perhaps throughout life. This condition is known as "narcolepsy." There seems to be little doubt that it depends on some cerebral lesion, but its nature and location are not well known and are probably inconstant. In one case, seen in Baltimore, which was operated upon, a large aberrant cerebral vein was found. Ephedrine and benzedrine have been found useful in symptomatic therapy.

Manipulations of the Body

Finger-sucking is important because of the concern it occasions parents. Sucking of the thumb or other fingers occurs during the first year of life in practically every child, especially when hungry. In the normal hand-to-mouth reaction during the middle and latter months of the first year, sucking the fingers occurs as a result of the sucking reflex. In the well-fed, happy infant this should cause no alarm. In spite of an adequate feeding regimen some children will indulge in it. There is little to be gained by restraints even during the first two years; after this they are definitely contraindicated, since they turn the child's life into a power contest and center his attention on the difficulty, intensifying rather than ameliorating it.

Parents have been subjected to many scares regarding the damaging effect of thumb-sucking on the formation of the jaw and alignment of the teeth. Lewis, after having followed many children for several years, has come to the conclusion that if the sucking disappears by the time of eruption of the permanent teeth there is no danger of permanent deformity, and such deformity as has already been produced will disappear spontaneously. A relationship of finger-sucking to masturbation has been propounded, much to the parents' concern. Finger-sucking, to be sure, is pleasurable to the child but has nothing else in common with masturbation; it is not to be regarded as an omen of sexual indulgence in later life.

Between the second and fifth years finger-sucking is most frequently seen in connection with fatigue, boredom, illness, punishment, and frustrating situations, without its being a symptom of any marked personality disorder. It represents a return to a more infantile mode of satisfaction. Prohibition and restraint are contraindicated and do more to fix the habit. Treatment should be directed rather toward sources of emotional dissatisfaction and toward keeping the child reasonably well occupied. The symptom itself may be handled by diversion, sometimes by an appeal to the child's pride. The parent should be reassured of its harmlessness.

After the age of 5 or 6, thumb-sucking is to be viewed a little less casually. Here the damage to the dentition may be permanent. The symptom, being a part manifestation of a general emotional immaturity, is frequently found associated with other, more infantile symptoms, such as enuresis or a "baby talk" difficulty in articulation. These children call for careful study and an adequate program of personality and environmental readjustment.

Occasionally, habits of pulling the hair or ear, or picking at fuzzy clothing or blankets, which originated as an accessory movement to finger-sucking, persist after the sucking itself has stopped. As a rule these have the same psychologic significance to the child as the sucking and are to be similarly handled. They are less apt to occasion parental concern.

Nail-biting (onychophagia) is frequently met with in practice, although not often as a primary complaint. It is an expression of tenseness, being usually found in fidgety, overactive children. Anticipation of a school examination, or excitement of any sort, may increase tension and the nail-biting ensues. It is less marked or may disappear when the child is at ease and happily occupied. The habit tends to occur in many members of the same family, and imitation seems to be a factor in its genesis. Sometimes the toenails are bitten. Restraints, such as the application of bitter drugs to the nails, do little good. Some children grow to enjoy the taste of the drugs; others turn to biting other parts of the fingers. Treatment should be directed at the child to relieve the causes of his tension. These are not always discovered, but much can be done to build up his self-confidence and security; nagging and constantly calling the child's attention to his difficulty serve only to increase the existing tension. Nail-biting responds slowly to treatment; in a period of readjustment other symptoms may disappear long before the nail-biting.

Language Disorders

Functional speech disorders are to be differentiated from those of organic origin. The latter group is most benefited by direct attack on the speech defect itself, through educative methods or correction of the organic disability if possible. Local conditions affecting the peripheral speech organs (defects of the tongue, lips, nose, palate, uvula, teeth, and larynx) produce speech defects some of which are characteristic, as in cleft palate. We doubt that tongue-tie is ever a cause of speech defect, despite the fortunately waning popular idea. Hearing defects are frequently found as a cause of speech disorder; the child reproduces only the imperfectly heard word. All cases of speech defect should have the hearing carefully investigated. Disorders of the central and peripheral nervous system, and certain endocrine disorders may also produce defects. There is one group of speech defects which, though not having an organic basis, cannot be classified with those of emotional origin. This group occurs in children who are given poor speech at home to imitate.

The most common functional speech defects are delayed speech, mutism, faulty articulation, and stuttering. All forms are more common in boys than girls.

Delayed speech development is found in mentally defective children but may also occur in children who are otherwise normally developed. Certain children do not need to develop speech in order to get their wants; those about them anticipate their wishes, or they make their wants known by signs. With a different approach speech usually comes promptly. Children who are left alone and who do not hear speech may be delayed in developing it. We have observed delayed speech development in children who show difficulties in motor coordination. There may be a family history of delayed speech development or of other types of language disorders. In many children who do not develop speech at the usual time there is an associated delay in the selection of the preferred hand. Here as in all cases of speech disorder one should guard against interference with handedness. Many youngsters with retarded language development are overactive and restless physically. In general, if a child uses no words at two years or no two-word sentences at three years he should be watched carefully. In any event if the language development is not normal by the fourth birthday, the situation should be carefully investigated; and if the intellectual development and hearing are normal, steps should be taken to provide training in sound and verbal productions.

Onset of speech may also be retarded in the presence of developmental word deafness where, in spite of normal hearing, the child does not understand what is said. When speech does develop it is apt to be imperfect and accompanied by echolalia. The child may seem to have a language all his own. Treatment is largely educational. Idioglossia (idiolalia) may develop in children without word deafness who are unduly segregated. The parents can usually understand the child and are often surprisingly unobservant of the phenomenon. Treatment here is association with other children. Delayed speech development, peculiarities of speech development, or loss of or deterioration of speech may occur in young children with psychoses.

Mutism usually occurs as a result of congenital or early acquired deafness but may exist as a functional disorder. Grossly retarded intellectual development may be a cause. Mutism may also occur as a symptom in hysteria and in certain negativistic children; here it is apt to be transitory. We have seen two young children who refused to talk for some time after a particularly traumatic anesthesia and tonsillectomy. *Aphasia* is a term usually applied to the loss of ability to speak or to use words appropriately. Organic cerebral damage may be a cause; a discussion of the neurologic aspects of aphasia is beyond the scope of this book. Functional aphasias are not infrequently seen. Temporary loss of speech sometimes follows typhoid fever; we have seen the diagnosis suggested from this symptom alone. In severe chorea, loss of speech is not uncommon. The condition is usually transient, clearing as the chorea improves, but occasionally it lasts for months. We have seen a case at the Babies Hospital in which it lasted for 10 weeks; suddenly the patient was able to say "yes" and "no" and within 36 hours speech had returned altogether.

Faulty articulation may be due to organic reasons, poor training or example, or retarded mental development. Frequently it is due to emotional immaturity. Lisping and "baby talk" are the more common types; they are often associated with other infantile traits, such as thumb-sucking and enuresis. Treatment is to be directed at the underlying causes of the immaturity; when these are corrected, the difficulty disappears with no specific speech training.

Stuttering is a frequent form of speech disorder; there are estimated to be about a quarter of a million stuttering children in the United States. The symptoms are well known and will not be described in detail. Although seen in some well-adjusted children and adults, there are many cases in which it appears to be a manifestation of a more or less severe personality disorder; as with other psychiatric syndromes in children, there are usually many associated nervous symptoms. The symptom comes and goes; it is apt to be worse in some situations and absent in others. A child may stutter at home and not in school, or only in the presence of certain individuals. It is intensified by emotional stress. The severe stutterer may, however, be able to sing or recite from memory or to count with no difficulty whatsoever. Stuttering is especially apt to begin at emotionally critical periods of the child's life, as at the beginning of school and at puberty. A relatively benign type of stuttering is very common in young children during the third and fourth years when the child's capacity to express himself is inadequate to his needs. This is the so-called physiologic stuttering, which usually clears up quickly if met calmly and not handled destructively. Stuttering may develop in children where there have been forcible attempts to change the handedness (usually from left to right) and is said to clear up when the interference is stopped. Orton has found that it is more common in individuals who are neither definitely left- nor right-sided and suggests that stuttering results from a confusion of cerebral dominance. In most of the stutterers with "mixed laterality," emotional factors also seem to be of importance.

Any treatment of stuttering must concern itself with the underlying problems. Unless these are first taken into consideration direct attacks on the peripheral speech function are not usually successful and serve only to focus the child's attention on his inadequacies and to produce further emotional tension. This is especially true with relatively young patients and in cases where stuttering is a recent development. By studying the child's personality and environment and investigating the circumstances surrounding the onset and variations in the mode of stuttering, the pediatrician can do a great deal in alleviating parental anxiety, helping to ease environmental pressures, and building up the child's confidence and general security. A healthy attitude toward the symptom itself on the part of the child and the family should be fostered; no stigma should be associated with it and it should be taken as an accepted fact like the color of the child's hair. These measures will often produce a striking improvement. After this is done the question of special therapy may be considered. If the emotional disorder is severe it should be handled by a competent child psychiatrist. Psychiatric treatment, however, produces far from uniform results. Similarly, special speech training produces variable results, perhaps because of the selection of pupils, but at times skilled training in a school for speech defects will achieve striking results.

Specific reading disability and reading retardation are disorders of another aspect of the language function. Specific reading disability, also referred to as "congenital word blindness" and strephosymbolia (Orton), is a relatively frequent condition in school children. It has been estimated that about 10 percent show some degree of reading difficulty. The condition may vary from a very slight disability to a complete inability to recognize the printed or written word symbol and hence to learn to read. Reading is an important part of the school curriculum; the failure of these children to learn to read, in spite of good intelligence, causes them to be looked on as lazy or lacking in intelligence by the parents and teachers if they do not understand the situation. As a result of these attitudes and of his own reactions to the inability to learn to read, in spite of his abilities in other directions, the child may develop behavior or personality symptoms. He regards himself as "dumb" and gives up trying, or he may utilize his time in school to play and indulge in petty infractions of regulations. All sorts of symptoms may develop; there is no uniform association, although in our cases enuresis seems to be quite frequent. When the child has received adequate help for his specific disability, the personality and behavior symptoms frequently clear up.

The disability itself is not difficult to recognize if one is aware of the condition. It occurs more often in boys than in girls and is often associated with a history of enforced change in handedness or with mixed sidedness in the child. The child will often apparently read well enough in the first grade or two; this is because he memorizes the brief assigned passages. In these children there is a tendency to read and reproduce letters or words as if they were reversed. The most frequent confusions of letters are *b* and *d*, *p* and *q*, *u* and *n*, *g* and *d*, *h* and *y*, the latter being more properly an upside-down reversal than left to right. Words are read backwards, *no* for *on*, *saw* for *was*. Occasionally, letters or syllables are transposed within a word. The child will change the order of words in a sentence, omit words, or guess at others, at times changing the context considerably. These errors are not constant; *saw* will be read correctly at one time and reversed at another. The disability seems to be worse when the child is under tension or pressure. The disability is often associated with similar errors in writing and spelling, and with other dysfunctions in the language sphere. There is frequently a family history of a similar or other language difficulty. The degree of reading disability is determined by educational tests. Treatment is in the form of remedial training and should be carried out by someone with special experience in the field. In general it includes more phonetic training and "sounding out" than is used in current reading teaching methods.

A specific reading disability is to be differentiated from reading retardation due to limitations of intelligence. In the latter case there is a general educational retardation. However, reversals and transpositions can also occur in children with defective mental development. One type of reading retardation occurs in children who have missed a good deal of school during the first year or so because of illness and have been promoted without having a good understanding of fundamentals. In other children frequent changes of school with different teaching methods and the necessity of adjusting to many new situations seem to be the important factors in the reading difficulty. There is also a group of children who are unable to learn to read because of emotional disturbances which prevent them from learning in general or which affect the acquisition of reading in particular.

Various theories have been advanced as to the causation of specific reading disability. It does not appear to be due to organic cerebral damage. Defective vision does not seem to play a role. Correction of refractive errors makes little difference in the reversals; the inconstancy of the errors in reading, which is characteristic, speaks against the incrimination of the visual apparatus. Orton regards it as a developmental language disability, occurring as do the other types in individuals in whom there is a difficulty in cerebral dominance. Other writers disagree and point out the significance of emotional factors. In any event there does exist a large group of children who present the specific factors described above which can be split off from those children who present reading difficulties without such features. Orton's theories afford no explanation of why some children develop language disabilities and others do not. In many of our cases there seems to be an associated emotional disturbance, usually environmentally determined, which precedes or coincides with the development of the reading disability. We feel that the best treatment is one on a broad base which offers special remedial reading work and at the same time tries to get at whatever emotional or other factors seem to be at work in producing the child's difficulties.

Sex Disorders

Children are more preoccupied with ideas of sex differences and sex activities than is usually thought to be the case. Questions regarding the differences between the sexes and the origin of babies are apt to begin by the end of the third year, and most children of 4, if given a chance, will ask such questions. The normal daydreams of the adolescent frequently show a gross sexual content.

A healthy attitude toward sex depends on good example, on proper sex information, and on wise supervision of activities with other children and adults. Sex information should be given with tact, frankness, and common sense. The child's questions from the early beginnings should be answered naturally and honestly. The parents would seem the natural persons to do this. It is distinctly unwise to give the child more than he asks for or wants to know; too much sex information, poorly digested, is apt to be as bad as too little. Sometimes a question or two directed at a child to determine the extent of his knowledge or musings will serve to reorient the information he already has and answer his questions for him. If his first questions are met with evasion or disapproval he may stop asking and turn to his playmates or elsewhere in order to satisfy his natural curiosity. Such information is apt to be incorrect, distorted, or obscene. If his questions have been satisfactorily answered, the child will return with additional queries as time goes by. Before adolescence is well under way it is advisable to explain the significance of menstruation to girls and nocturnal emissions to boys. This should be done with the stress on the normal biologic nature of the event, emphasizing the constructive aspects. The parent may want the backing of some printed authority if he or she finds the job too difficult, or a book may be given to the older child to read.

Sex difficulties in children vary all the way from a mild exploratory curiosity to instances of heterosexual and homosexual experience. *Masturbation* in both sexes is the most common sex complaint for which the physician is consulted. It is not an infrequent occurrence in children and is seen even in infancy. Nearly every infant in exploring his body discovers and takes pleasure in handling the genitals; this pleasure is probably no different from other manipulations like finger-sucking or playing with the ear; it is not to be regarded as masturbation. The term implies stimulation of the sex organs with the production of a specific sensory response. Erections occur even in infancy, both spontaneous and induced, but only very exceptionally does orgasm occur before the age of puberty; we have, however, observed it in a child of 2 years.

Local causes may precipitate masturbation. Any local irritation may cause the child to rub the parts, and, a pleasurable sensation being excited, this action is repeated until a habit is formed. Older children may discover masturbation in the course of self-exploration or may be taught the habit by playmates or, in exceptional instances, by adults. Masturbation is very contagious and may spread rapidly throughout a group of playmates or an entire school. Such factors are usually operative for a short time only and in well-adjusted children give rise only to transitory periods of masturbation, which need be viewed with no alarm. Persistent masturbation, on the other hand, is a more serious matter; frequently it is the expression of a more or less profound personality disorder. The child who seeks solace from genital stimulation is usually not getting the needed satisfaction from other phases of his life. Obstinate masturbation may occur in mental defectives, whose environment is often uninspiring and who generally are lacking in self-control. The habit is not to be regarded as the cause of the mental condition. In exceptional instances endocrine anomalies may cause increased sex pressure.

In infants and very young children masturbation may be accomplished by thigh friction or by rubbing the body against some object, as well as by manual stimulation. Frequently the child will sit with thighs crossed and sway backward and forward; this may last for some minutes, being accompanied by flushing of the face and some appearance of excitement. This may be regarded as a "queer trick" of the child, its nature not being appreciated; we have seen such episodes diagnosed as convulsions. Quite as frequently masturbation is suspected when it does not exist. Many children like to rock backward and forward without any sexual component in the pleasure derived therefrom. We know of instances in which a spastic child with a scissors deformity of his legs was mistaken for a persistent masturbator.

In the management of masturbation the first step should be the elimination of any local cause. Tight clothing, pinworms, eczema of the labia, vulvovaginitis, or balanoposthitis may be responsible, and correction of such factors will frequently be followed by disappearance of the masturbation, particularly if the habit has lasted only a short time. Phimosis and preputial adhesions are not to be regarded as causes per se, and circumcision should not be performed except for the usual indications. As a psychotherapeutic procedure it is contraindicated.

Any persistent case deserves a careful study of the child's life, which should include an inquiry into his relationships with other individuals and into his sources of satisfaction and dissatisfaction. Often it is possible to make constructive adjustments which will remove much of the tension and dissatisfaction in a child's life. It is of the greatest importance to prevent destructive handling of the situation. Mechanical restraints are poorly borne and may cause resentment and negativism. One 4-year-old boy told his parents "I will do it no matter how you try to stop me," and he did. Much worry and anxiety about the act may be produced in the child by threats and punishments. Threats of imbecility, insanity, physical illness, or punishment by circumcision or amputation have no place, and only serve to increase existing tension. The term "self-abuse" is an unfortunate one. A child is often told that others can tell by looking into his eyes that he is a masturbator. It is surprising to what lengths parents will go in order to force a child to stop at once. There is no evidence that any physical harm comes from masturbation, no matter how frequently practiced. The harm lies in the worry and guilt which develop in the child and in the fact that he may withdraw from the more usual contacts and occupations of his age and become wrapped up in the practice and its accompanying fantasies.

The general orthopsychiatric approach has been discussed in detail elsewhere. If there has been unwise handling of the masturbation itself, this should be stopped at once. If threats have been made the parent should explain that he was mistaken. Punishments should stop. The child should be reassured as to any dire physical consequences from the act; it should be explained to him as a normal phenomenon, and he should be encouraged in the belief that it will be of transitory nature. Opportunities for indulging should be kept minimal by an unobtrusive supervision which avoids all semblance of spying. The daily routine may be planned so as to avoid periods of lying in bed before going to sleep or after awakening; long, unoccupied periods at home or in school, which leave the child free to indulge in his fantasies, should be guarded against. Adequate exercise and healthy sleeping arrangements are important. Hospitalized children, particularly orthopedic patients, offer peculiarly difficult problems, the chief remedy for which is adequate diversion.

The possibility that endocrine anomalies may be responsible for excessive sex pressure, although a rare one, should not be overlooked. In cases of precocious puberty, libido may be very marked. We have seen an instance in which testosterone given for another purpose produced marked genital hypertrophy and frequent masturbation, both of which disappeared spontaneously when the treatment was stopped. Endocrine factors may be of importance even in the absence of external signs of sexual precocity. One of our patients, a little girl of seven years, showed for a considerable time regular monthly periods in which masturbation was practiced openly; at such times all sense of modesty was lost, the patient becoming virtually nymphomaniac. Similar instances have been observed by others. We know of one adolescent boy with periodic episodes of extreme libido accompanied by granulocytopenia and the excretion of large amounts of estrogens in the urine. Such exceptional cases may prove very difficult to control. Little, too, can be accomplished in the case of mental defectives. On the other hand, it has been our experience that in the great majority of normal children masturbation can be readily controlled by the removal of physical causes of irritation and by management along the lines indicated, even if the habit is of long standing.

Antisocial Behavior

The more common forms of antisocial behavior are disobedience, lying, stealing, cruelty to other children and animals, running away from home, destructiveness, truancy, and markedly aggressive behavior toward others. As with other manifestations of childhood personality disorders, the child must be treated rather than the symptom. The physician must be on his guard lest he be pushed into assuming a judicial or disciplinary role; his function is to interpret behavior both from the point of view of organic disease and in its psychologic setting. Through his influence in the home management of a child, he may be able to prevent many of these difficulties. First offenses and isolated occurrences, wisely handled, will usually subside spontaneously; but if they are taken too seriously, much harm may be done. The young child, being self-centered, demands and attempts to extract satisfaction of his wishes regardless of others. As he grows older he learns to appreciate property rights, the difference between right and wrong, truth and untruth, and the rights and feelings of others. What we expect of him depends on his training and the examples set for him. We cannot condemn the child for stealing coal when the whole family makes forays on the coal yard to get their fuel. The parent who covers up the young child's stealing in the store by buying some more of the cookies he has taken does not help him develop a sense of property rights. The handling of the situation demands a study of the child and the environment.

Among the more persistent patterns of antisocial behavior are those in which the disturbance takes the form of rebellion against what may seem to the child, and to us, an unjust or intolerable situation. After a more or less prolonged period of stress, antisocial behavior may break out as a sort of protest reaction. The family may be imposing on the child by piling up chores, relegating to him the care of younger children, or in other ways interfering with the time needed for recreation, as by too many planned extra-school activities, music lessons, religious instruction, and the like. One boy of 12, who was expected to take care of two younger brothers aged 4 and 6 years, after school hours and on weekends, became disobedient, assaultive to his brothers, and would remain away from home until the late hours of the night instead of coming home. The underlying factor may be found in the school situation—a harsh and unsympathetic teacher, or the presence of an unrecognized visual or hearing defect, mental retardation, or specific educational disability which may interfere with his progress and school work. Once the intolerable situation has been uncovered and steps taken to correct it, the undesirable behavior usually clears up. A situation less easily solved is the emotionally deprived child of neglectful or hostile parents. Here aggressive, rebellious behavior may result from the anxiety due to the child's feeling of lack of love. The feeling of belonging to the home and of being loved by the parents is one of utmost importance in the general security of the child. The treatment of the parent is probably best left to the psychiatrist, but much can be done to provide more contact for the child with a nurse or woman relative with an understanding and sympathetic personality. A pet animal may be of help. Antisocial behavior should be handled in the light of the total setting. It is needless to say that before attempting to handle these problems one should have thorough, unbiased, and unprejudiced information about the personalities, the backgrounds, and the difficulties of the children.

It is important to remember that organic factors may be at the root of the difficulty. Unrecognized illness is not infrequently responsible, as in the case of one of our patients, a boy whose rebellious behavior was traced to fatigue and irritability resulting from a chronic sinus infection with low-grade fever. With bed rest and appropriate treatment the behavior difficulty disappeared. Organic disease of the nervous system is frequently at the root of intractable antisocial behavior; too often it is unrecognized. It is met with in the *mentally defective* child who is unable to keep out of trouble because of his inability to deal with everyday problems; his defect is not appreciated and too much is expected of him. In other instances the behavior may be an epileptic equivalent. A behavior problem may be the presenting symptom in patients with brain tumors or neurosyphilis. A *postencephalitic* cause of chronic asocial behavior occurs more often than is usually suspected. The acute phase of the illness is frequently unrecognized, and such children may show no neurologic residuals. These children show a type of behavior very similar to that seen in children following severe *head injury,* and the behavior disorders which are observed as a residual of these two causes will be considered together.

In both there are impulsiveness of behavior with marked push of activity, distractability, and inability to persevere at any activity for more than a brief time. These children show extreme emotional instability, temper outbursts, egocentricity, and assaultiveness. Cruelty to animals and other children, truancy, sexual offenses, and delinquency are observed. After an attack of encephalitis or following a head injury a previously well behaved child may show a profound personality change. Such children often regret their behavior and sincerely promise improvement; but any change is transitory, and they return to the same mode of reacting. They state that they "cannot help it," and seem to be victims of their own whims and impulses; their inhibitory mechanisms appear to have been destroyed by the disease. There is often a purposelessness in their behavior. Persons in their environment become exasperated and can see no rhyme or reason in their "badness." Without a good history the diagnosis is exceedingly difficult. Institutions offer the best opportunity for care of these patients and for such reconstructive training as is possible. In a controlled atmosphere something can be done to develop habits and inhibitions. Unfortunately, such institutions are not often available, and one must do the best one can with the home situation. Those who care for the child should be helped to develop a calm, sympathetic, and understanding attitude.

Similar in some aspects is the child who represents the end results of faulty training and who seems to lack moral and social sense. The cause may be neglect or death of the parents or such a profound rejection of the parents that the child is unable to take over from them any of the rules of civilized living. Although readily distinguishing between what should and should not be done, he apparently does not care what he does so long as he satisfies his immediate desires.

In most of the well-defined chronic aggressive antisocial behavior patterns the pediatrician will find the services of the trained child psychiatrist of great help. He will be of the greatest assistance in recognizing the organic and nonorganic factors, in referring the child to the appropriate authority, and in sparing him from undue harshness on the part of those who feel that he is deliberately "bad."

Emotional Reactions

ANGER. Resentment is expressed by children in different ways at different ages. In infants it may take the form of excessive crying, which the physician or parent soon learns to differentiate from that associated with hunger or discomfort. If the child is well fed and free from physical pain and is not harassed by an agitated, uncertain mother or nurse or receiving too little emotional security, it is best to let him cry it out. Some parents will frequently hold to the unfounded superstition that crying will cause a hernia.

Breath-holding spells are a much more dramatic form of expressing anger. Sometimes in the midst of violent crying the child will suddenly stop breathing for a half minute or so. At other times the attack is an immediate response to an emotional unheaval. The infant becomes generally cyanotic about the mouth and face. He may throw his arms about aimlessly; twitchings of the extremities occur, but rarely; convulsions on an anoxemic basis have been described in severely protracted episodes of breath holding. The body is usually stiff but may be limp. The head is often thrown back. The attacks usually begin at the end of the first year, but may occur as early as the sixth month. They usually disappear by the end of the fifth year. In the older group they are accompanied by other symptoms of maladjustment. The attacks invariably cause such consternation that the child soon learns to use them as a weapon. The best treatment is to ignore them. The individual attack will terminate spontaneously; it can do no harm and does not cause death. Reported fatalities are undoubtedly due to confusion with other causes, such as laryngospasm. It is important to distinguish these attacks from tetany; a crowing sound and clonic convulsion

are presumptive evidence of the latter condition, and other confirmatory signs should be sought.

As the child grows older he may express resentment by sullenness, irritability, or *temper tantrums*. These last usually begin in the early preschool period; most children have at least a few at this age. They may persist until early adolescence or even into adult life. Tantrums are emotional outbursts resulting from frustration. The precipitating factor may be failure of the child to get his own way, attempts to get him to do something he does not want to do, depriving him of some object or action he wants, or jealousy. The child often finds a pattern for them in some older members of the family. The attacks are usually found in children of overprotective and oversolicitous parents, who encourage them by giving in. The child begins to use the outbursts more or less deliberately to gain his own ends. One 9-year-old boy when asked about his tantrums said, "Well, a fellow has to get his own way somehow." He was asked if his parents could not see through him: his reply was, "Sure, they catch on sometimes; but then they forget." The children who display tantrums are usually not happy, despite their domination of the home. They seem to resent the submission of their parents and desire someone who can impose reasonable limits on their impulses. They usually display other evidences of emotional instability and immaturity, the history of maladjustment going back to earlier difficulties in feeding, toilet training, and acquiring self-dependence. Tantrums are apt to be associated with fears and with other evidences of anxiety and tension.

Treatment should aim at providing good physical health and sufficient rest; ill or tired children are notoriously irritable. Environmental disharmony and poor example should be corrected when possible. An environment which provides sufficient freedom from constant "don'ts" and "keep stills" is important. It is often difficult to provide this in a small apartment where the child cannot find sufficient space to play in. Nursery school placement may afford suitable outlets and aid the child in his general social development. If any patent jealousies are present they should be dealt with. The tantrum itself must be handled constructively. Avoidance of situations which are sure to produce the reaction will materially aid in bringing about its cessation. The parent should make full use of the child's easy distractability when a tantrum seems inevitable. "Reasoning" is futile; signs of alarm or a similar tantrum on the part of the parent serve only to intensify the reaction. Punishment rarely brings about cessation and frequently adds to the anxiety already present in the child. The tantrums should be met with calm firmness; indifference wins more success than any method that places the child in the center of attraction. Pointed ignoring usually has a rather hostile or at times martyrlike component which the child appreciates as evidence that he is at least getting under the parent's skin. Proper, sympathetic handling at the age of resistance is apt to prevent the appearance of tantrums.

FEAR REACTIONS.   Fears of young infants are based on loud noises, loss of support, and strangeness of people or situations, and are not abnormal. The well-trained older youngster has developed through example and education a realization of danger which results in a way of reacting that avoids harm or injury. The child who has learned the perils of traffic and the inherent dangers of fire is not a fearful child; this is constructive use of fear.

In children past the age of infancy there may develop fears of darkness, thunderstorms, policemen, doctors, fires, ghosts, and many other things. Mild fears which do not affect the child's daily life are not at all uncommon and may arise out of imitation of adult patterns (thunderstorms) and misinterpretation of phenomena which are not understood, as creaking boards in the house or poorly made-out shadows in the dark. If the parent tends to act as if these dangers were real, the child feels that his fears are justified. However, fears which concern the child a good deal and which preoccupy him so much that they interfere with his daily life are rarely on this basis alone. Almost invariably the child displays other symptoms as evidence of emotional disorder. While a great many of the milder fear reactions may occur in relatively well-adjusted children, coming out of anxieties during the critical periods in emotional and social growth and development, severe chronic fear reactions call for careful psychiatric help. It is well not to try to "break" the child of his fears by forcing him into situations about which he is fearful. His fears should be recognized but not unduly emphasized. If amelioration of what seem to be the more specific etiologic factors in the background is not feasible, much can be done to improve the child's general emotional security. A friendly, noncritical ear can do much to build up self-confidence in the child.

ANXIETY ATTACKS.   The anxiety attack is a state of fearfulness which may come on in waves lasting from a few seconds to an hour or so. These are not rare in children. They usually occur in the evening. Most frequently they are found in preadolescent girls. In the attack the child is filled with dread; she clings to her parents and seeks reassurance. There is tachycardia and palpitation, difficulty in breathing, sweating, and flushing. She may complain of paresthesias, urinary frequency, and an urge to defecate. There is sometimes an aimless burst of motor overactivity. When questioned as to her fears she usually states that something terrible is about to happen and that she may die or faint. There may be only a few attacks or they may be very frequent. Between attacks the child may be relatively normal, or may show constant anxiety. In the latter case she may withdraw from all social contacts, refuse to be left alone, and lose all interest in play and school. Worry about the attacks may accentuate the condition.

Anxiety attacks are apt to occur in a home atmosphere of worry and insecurity. The precipitating factor—an operation, death, or sudden shock—acts as a trigger and is not to be regarded as the cause. A 9-year-old girl, whose father suffered from progressive postencephalitic parkinsonism, had heard some time before that her father had only two more years to live. She was worried and felt that her mother, who had more than a passing interest in a boarder in the house, did not appreciate the true state of her father's health. During the summer the child had shown mild sleep disturbances and considerable emotional irritability. The anxiety attacks began suddenly one evening in the fall when she was having her hair washed. In the afternoon she had seen an upsetting movie in which a man whose physical appearance was similar to that of the father was drowned. Treatment depends on what specific factors are involved in the individual case. The anxiety attack itself is a symptom; the state may be relatively benign or symptomatic of a more serious type of personality disorder. Because of the frequent somatic complaints during the attack, parents and physicians are apt to interpret it in terms of an organic disorder. It is important to assure both the child and his parents of good physical health after a careful physical study. The condition may be confused with paroxysmal tachycardia, in which anxiety is frequently complained of at the beginning of an attack. We have seen several cases of chronic hypochondriacal reactions in children which seemed to be started off by mishandling of anxiety attacks.

An anxiety state may exist without any individual attacks of anxiety being manifest. The child may be generally apprehensive and constantly change the fear which he expresses, shifting from fires to kidnappers, to physical disease, or to preoccupation with the possible illness or death of a parent. He realizes the unjustifiable nature of his fears but can do little about them.

JEALOUSY.   Jealousy is a relatively normal reaction in the preschool child, but if exaggerated it may seriously interfere in the child's personal relationships by producing resentments, hostilities, and inferiority feelings. The resentment of an older child who has had his "nose put out of joint" by the arrival of a new baby is a common phenomenon. Many children have attempted to injure the younger sibling; a regression to infantile traits is not unusual in this situation. Taking the child into the plans for the coming of the baby, and letting him do some little thing for his care after the birth, is the best course in preparing him to share his parents' attention and affection. It is unreasonable to expect him to play second fiddle. The practice of unfavorably contrasting siblings is a source of much unhappiness to children and produces the jealousy which underlies the resultant hostilities and temper outbursts.

A 6-year-old girl who had always been unfavorably contrasted with her 15 months younger brother, who was the mother's favorite, went into a severe anxiety reaction following the sudden death of her brother. All of her hostile wishes had come true. She felt it was her fault, and refused to eat. A year or so later the mother again became pregnant, but the child, having had a previous unfortunate experience, could not be induced to take any interest in another threat to her security with her mother. Until the new pregnancy occurred she had improved and had lost most of her inferiority feeling and her distant attitude toward her mother. All of her difficulties began anew, and now took much time and effort to abolish. It was not until after the birth of the baby, and until it was then demonstrated to her that she would not have to give up her share of attention and affection, that she finally became a normal, happy, well-adjusted girl.

The practice of pairing off siblings of nearly the same age with respect to hours of bedtime, new clothes, or even to the extent of holding one child back so that both can start school together precipitates the same reactions. Sibling rivalries and jealousies are particularly common in twins. Prevention of jealousy reactions and the train of other symptoms of emotional disturbances that follow is of great importance, and can be accomplished in the physician's ordinary contacts with the mother. Treatment of such reactions is, as usual, directed at the underlying causes.

School Difficulties

Children are frequently brought to the pediatrician with the complaint of difficulties in school, usually behavior abnormalities or a failure to make satisfactory progress. The child may be restless and fidgety, rebellious, or shy and withdrawn, indulging in daydreams to the exclusion of doing his work. These difficulties may arise out of a number of pathogenetic situations; only the more common will be mentioned.

Physical disorders may play a part. Chronic mild illness which interferes with efficiency and produces easy fatigability is to be looked for. Unrecognized visual or hearing defects are more common than is usually realized and many seriously interfere with school adjustment.

Moderately or even severely mentally retarded children may have been placed in grades where the work is beyond their ability. Placement in a grade where the work is in keeping with his abilities or in a special class will often bring about marked changes in the child. On the other hand, bright children are sometimes found in classes where the work is so easy that the child finds little to stimulate his curiosity or intellect. Proper placement or at least provision for a suitable range of interests is important. It is to be remembered that some of these children do poorly if they are in a class with an older group of children who are physically, socially, and emotionally more mature. Specific educational disabilities should be looked for, the most common being a reading difficulty.

Emotional disturbances frequently interfere with the child's adjustment at school. A child who has difficulty in his relationships with his parents may project this upon his teacher. One of our patients, whose mother had withdrawn all display of affection from him at the age of 2, in addition to other emotional difficulties, was unable to learn anything at school until after the parent-child relationship had changed. At the end of two years in school he had made less progress than the usual child does in two months. After the mother had been helped through psychiatric treatment he was able to use his good intelligence (IQ 120) efficiently and made excellent progress. On the other hand, the teacher's personality may contribute to the child's difficulties. The teacher has a difficult job at best, and there is evidence to show that many have more or less serious emotional maladjustments of their own. Persecutions by other children in school are, unfortunately, frequent enough and may cause much anguish in the child and interfere with his successful adjustment. These difficulties arising out of the school itself can usually be successfully handled by tactfully approaching the proper school authority. Sometimes a change in school is the only way out. One should be careful not to stress too much to the child or parent the fault of the school if the child is to remain there.

Preoccupation on the part of the child with home difficulties (quarrels between parents, illnesses, financial worries) may take up so much of his time and thought that the school work suffers. Children whose recreational time is so filled with special lessons and practice hours or with, at times, physically arduous work do not as a rule make satisfactory school adjustments. A temporary falling off in the caliber of the school work often occurs at the onset of adolescence when the tendency of the child to day dream and brood becomes marked. The preoccupations at these times are usually sexual or about home difficulties.

Hypochondriacal Trends

Hypochondriacal trends in children should be considered on a broad basis. Occasional complaints of headache on school examination days or other transitory complaints which help the child to avoid difficult situations or to gain occasional attention should not be regarded as hypochondriasis. Hypochondriasis is the chronic complaint habit. Chronic invalidism may occur after it becomes well fixed. In children hypochondriacal complaints may arise from a variety of situations. The child who has been physically ill may prolong the attention and fussing received during the acute phases of the illness through numerous complaints. A generally unhappy child, no matter what the underlying cause, may seek the attention gained by his complaints. Insecurity, emotional rejection by a parent, or oversolicitude are frequently important underlying factors. The patterns may arise out of imitation of adults in the home or out of the child's own experiences. The source of the complaint is often seen to be in the parent, who centers all of his or her attention on the child's bodily functioning, the child frequently having no complaints at all or none when not in the presence of the parent. We recall one mother who had had many hypochondriacal complaints centered about the gastrointestinal tract prior to the birth of the child. She gave these up and seemed to use the child as her hypochondriacal organ. Medical mismanagement is frequently a factor in intensifying and prolonging the complaint habit. The "diagnoses" may be supplied by the parents or physicians. The all too often prescribed rest cure at times serves to fix the idea in the child's mind that he is sick. A careful physical examination is important. It should be remembered that hypochondriacal complaints can exist in the presence of definite physical disorder. One should also not forget that pains and discomforts may well arise from a physical cause which is not detected in routine examination. An understanding of the child's personality and environmental setting is important in making a functional diagnosis and therapeutic plans. The child and his parents should be given to understand that there is nothing organic to account for the complaints. The underlying difficulties leading to the disorder should be dealt with if possible. In any event, the existing tensions should be ameliorated and the obvious environmental difficulties altered. It is important to remember that the hypochondriacal pain is just as real to the child as if it had an organic basis. If the child is told it is "just imagination" his cooperation may be lost. The symptom should be minimized and relegated to its proper state of relative unimportance. The prevention of hypochondriacal trends through adequate handling of convalescence and management of acute physical disease is an important function of the pediatrician.

Hysteria

In hysteria, emotional conflicts are usually expressed through physical symptoms which may simulate organic illness. The term has been used by various writers to include about all the personality symptoms which may occur in childhood. The frequency with which this diagnosis is made depends on the diagnostic criteria set up. There is little to be gained by so labeling the child unless it is accompanied by an attempt to understand the child and his difficulties. Mere classification of the symptoms or looking for so-called stigmas will not suffice. Nonetheless, it seems important to give a brief résumé of the symptoms commonly found. These may be the only feature of the complaint or may be discovered incidentally during the course of the investigation. Symptoms may be found singly or in almost any conceivable combination. They may last a long time or display themselves briefly with abrupt onset and cessation. Symptoms may be largely somatic, or psychic symptoms may predominate. They include disorders of sensation of all sorts: visual disturbances, including amblyopia, diplopia (even with one eye), and scotomas; deafness, which may be complete or limited only to certain hours or to contacts with certain individuals; disturbances of cutaneous sensation, anesthesia, hyperesthesias, hypesthesias, having no relation to peripheral or segmental nerve distribution; motor disturbances, such as paralyses, limps, or inability to walk although the legs can be used for other purposes quite normally, and, at times, choreiform manifestations, ataxic features, etc.; speech disturbances, including aphonia, mutism, and stuttering. The visceral symptoms include such things as vomiting, diarrhea, constipation, cough, and dyspnea; they may involve any or several organ systems. Other manifestations involving the total individual are amnesia and convulsive, hysterical, delirious, and stuporous states. The outstanding characteristic of the hysterical symptom is its massiveness. The paralyzed limb cannot move at all; the child with hysterical anorexia refuses all food to the point of collapse. The differentiation from organic disease often is not easy; the difficulty may be increased because of the tendency of hysteria to occur as a complication of some organic or constitutional disease. Careful and repeated examination is indicated. Hysterical anesthesia is characterized by its distribution, which corresponds to the child's idea rather than to any anatomic nerve distribution. Paralyses are apt to correspond exactly to the anesthetic area. Pharyngeal anesthesia with loss of the gag reflex is a common finding. Usually the symptoms occur in such combination that no other diagnosis can be made. The personality of the child and his attitude toward his symptoms are usually helpful. He is apt not to be disturbed by the symptoms; at times he actually seems to enjoy them. It is characteristic that the child is usually unaware of any emotional conflict within himself. He seems contented and more or less happy; one is unable to elicit any anxieties or tensions from him. The hysterical symptoms seem to have banished the conflicts from his conscious thinking. The personality is characterized by immaturity, constant striving to occupy the center of the stage, a display of assumed poise, and a tendency to carry all emotional expressions to extremes. Sudden, unaccountable changes in disposition are frequent. These children are quick to form likes and dislikes and to make ready judgments. They are very suggestible, and imitation, an important factor in all children, plays a leading role. Previous illnesses actually experienced, witnessed, or heard discussed may provide the pattern for many of the symptoms which the child with hysteria displays.

The condition in females is by no means as frequent in childhood as in later life, although at puberty it is said to occur twice as often in girls as in boys. It is rarely seen before the sixth or seventh year. Heredity is said to be of importance; it would seem to occur more frequently in children of neurotic antecedents. Whether this means an inherited constitutional predisposition or is a result of the impact of such individuals on the developing personality of the child is not certain. The psychoanalytic school, which has done much toward developing an understanding of the condition through the concept of the conversion of the emotional conflict into physical symptoms, believes that in children the conflict is primarily one between the child's sexual urges and fear of punishment, the condition being most apt to develop when the emerging sexual feelings cause anxiety. The children who develop hysterical reactions often show difficulties going back into infancy, such as feeding difficulties. Poor relationships with one parent, possibly associated with overdependence on the other, are also found, often developing in a setting of parental disharmony.

Treatment which does not go beyond consideration of the isolated symptom is not to be considered satisfactory. Hysterical symptoms have a tendency to disappear when no longer needed or as a result of some sudden shock or surprise. They also have a tendency to recur in the same or other forms unless the underlying difficulties are dealt with. Suggestive treatment or, at times, ignoring the symptom may do away with it. This is often important, especially when the symptom is profoundly affecting the child's daily life or threatening his physical health. Every attempt should be made, however, to direct the therapeutic approach toward the total child and those with whom he lives. Unwholesome attitudes and improper methods of handling the child should be corrected. The child should be guided into new interests in an effort to provide different and equally satisfying experiences. If the home environment offers no hope of modification, long-term placement outside of the home may be advisable, particularly if no psychiatric help is available for the child. In its more pronounced forms associated not only with serious symptoms but with marked involvement of the whole personality, competent psychiatric care is strongly indicated.

S.B. was first seen at the age of 13 years when she was brought in with a story of five months' illness. There were varying complaints of abdominal pain, nausea, diarrhea, sore throats, and in general "feeling awful." Repeated examinations by her physician had shown no cause for these symptoms. Shortly after the onset a normal appendix was removed with no improvement; in fact, she became fearful that the surgeon had done something amiss. The onset being at the beginning of the autumn term, she had not returned to school. Despite her protests that she wanted to go back it was obvious that she did not. The symptoms would clear up when it was evident that the return to school was postponed, but when it became imminent they would reappear with new vigor. Any attempt to coerce her was met by protracted outbursts of uncontrollable weeping and protests of illness, when she would become depressed

and state that no one loved her. This was in marked contrast to her usual attitude of being "as happy as a lark" sitting in bed and being waited upon. At least one of her "sore throats" seemed to have been caused by scratching the larynx. Removal of all the more pleasant aspects of her illness produced no improvement.

Even before the onset of the more acute symptoms her adjustment had not been entirely satisfactory. She had sucked her thumb until the age of 7 years. Although she conformed to the accepted social patterns of behavior, in an effort to make a good impression, she had always wanted the center of the stage, acting a part with one eye on the audience. Emotional responses were rare but when present were in the form of unexplainable outbursts of affection or rage. She was usually very solicitous about her mother, trying to please her at times when the average child would have thought more of herself. There was marked rivalry with the older sister, who seemed to be the mother's favorite. This rivalry had been growing more intense during the previous year when the sister began to stay up later at night, go to dances, and wear more grown-up clothes. The sister had always received a good deal more attention because of her many severe illnesses which necessitated much nursing and convalescent care. S. had been her father's favorite up to the time of his death 18 months before from hepatic cirrhosis. He had been in the habit of going on periodic alcoholic sprees when the realities of life had been too much for him. The mother, a self-centered person, seemed fond of her children as long as they did not interfere too much with her way of life. The grandmother, an aggressive person who liked nothing better than to run other people's lives, had close contact with the patient during summer vacations. She was fond of telling S. how much more the mother liked the sister; these sessions had recently been followed by exacerbations of the symptoms.

At 10 years of age the patient had been the victim of indecent exposure by a man; she had had to go to court to identify him. Shortly after the father's death, which had upset her considerably, the nurse whom she had had for several years died. Three months before the onset of acute symptoms an uncle who had lived with the family died of heart disease. For some months prior to the onset she had particularly resented the grandmother's domination, and another uncle soon afterward was sent to a hospital with alcoholic neuritis. S.'s symptoms began without warning the day after school started.

On examination S. was found to be a rather placid girl, with an affected attitude of poise, who showed great interest in her own symptoms and in those of the other patients. She was convinced that she was sick but showed little concern about it. She smiled when she said that she felt terrible and showed no resentment of the fact that the other members of her family thought that she was "faking." She complained spontaneously of decreased vision in the left eye. Physical examination showed moderate development of secondary sex characteristics. The only unusual findings were a marked diminution of sensitivity to pain, temperature, and vibration over the entire left side of the body, beginning at the midline, and absent pharyngeal and corneal reflexes. Areas of hyperesthesia could be suggested at will. Psychologic studies showed superior intelligence (IQ 120); academic achievement was two to three years above grade placement. She enjoyed her hospitalization, but nothing noteworthy was obtained in interviews until just before the time to go home, when she had several self-induced nosebleeds. She then accepted the fact that she had nothing organically wrong and said that she did not want to return to school because of her "terrible feelings"—a desire to weep without knowing why. She returned to school a few days after she went home and was soon enjoying it. In subsequent interviews it was learned that the weeping was caused by "terrible thoughts," usually about her father. The exact nature of these she characteristically "forgot." She later spoke freely of her resentment of her father's alcoholism and death. She had been told that she was like her father and she had no desire to die young. Without being specific she said that some of her thoughts about her father were "wicked." At the same time she became more openly hostile to her sister and was no longer a model of social propriety. On the last visit two months after discharge from the hospital there were no longer any sensory changes and she had lost her indifferent placidity along with her affected speech. Her emotional reactions were normally spontaneous. Subsequent reports have been equally favorable.

Compulsions

Compulsions in mild form are quite common in children. They consist of such well-known things as stepping over cracks in the sidewalk and ritualistic games. These are usually of minor importance, especially when seen in well-adjusted children, and are found as a rule in children of school age, the pattern being common to a group of playmates. Handwashing compulsions and obsessive fear of germs are not uncommon in childhood. Compulsion in a more severe form may occur in an emotionally malfunctioning child.

One of our patients showed many compulsions. When telling his mother of his experiences he felt that he must repeat everything, and that he must not stop on the third repetition, nor on any multiple of three, the seventh, or the thirteenth repetition. Similarly he must repeat his prayers that something might not happen to his parents. Before going to bed he would have to look many times to see that the doors were locked, the windows fixed so that no one could climb in, and that the lights were out, the gas and water turned off. He could wear only certain combinations of clothing, and dressed and undressed in definite order. At times he did not feel that it was proper to move his bowels, and he had to shake himself in a peculiar manner while urinating. His rituals interfered with his schoolwork, as did the fact that he did not feel that he could write except with "big" pencils. In addition he "had to fight" with his mother and grandmother, even though it was most upsetting to him.

Compulsions are said to occur most frequently in overconscientious, shy, punctilious, and perfectionistic individuals. These children are apt to be tense and fearful, doing poorly in school because of obsessive daydreaming. The interference of the compulsive rituals may also be a factor in poor school work and in preventing satisfactory adjustments in other activities. Teasing and nagging about the unreasonableness and nonsensical nature of his compulsions serve only to aggravate the child's withdrawal from outside activities. He realizes the ridiculousness of his acts but can do nothing about them. The individual compulsive acts may tend to disappear from time to time, only to return in the same or in different form. The personality characteristics tend to remain constant; doubting and inability to make decisions or to throw off disturbing thoughts are common. This more severe reaction is rarely seen before adolescence and is said to occur slightly more often in girls. Untreated individuals with these outspoken symptoms do not "outgrow" them and may develop more or less severely crippled personalities. In some children the disorder seems to presage later psychotic behavior. The underlying difficulties are usually deep-seated and call, as a rule, for good psychiatric care. If this is not available, environmental sources of tension should be corrected. The child can be given a chance to talk about his difficulties without fear of ridicule or of being told he should stop them. Removal from the home is frequently helpful.

Psychoses

The true incidence of the major psychoses in childhood is difficult to determine from reported statistics. Some tabulations fail to delimit the age of childhood clearly and include patients up to 15 or over. Another reason stems from the variability of diagnostic standards. Some psychiatrists, too, believe that schizophrenia does not occur before puberty. Lutz (quoted by Bradley) in 1937 noted 60 cases of childhood schizophrenia in a critical review of the literature. Of these, 30 were below 10 years of age and in only 14 did he believe the diagnosis to be justified. In recent years more cases have been reported; the most extensive group, over 100 cases, was discussed by Bender in 1947. Manic-depressive psychoses are exceedingly rare in childhood according to most workers, although some French writers claim that they are not uncommon. Common clinical experience, however, suggests that they are rarer in childhood than are schizophrenic psychoses.

The clinical picture of psychoses in children is different from that in adults. The immature personality of the child, the stage of his development at the time of onset of the psychosis, and the effect of the disturbance on the subsequent personality growth and development, all contribute to the differences in the symptom picture. In early childhood, language mechanisms, being as yet poorly stabilized, are profoundly affected by a severe disturbance in the emotional or mental sphere. Motility is greater in young children and movements are less persistently and purposefully directed than in later life. Mood, too, is more labile in children. Symptoms produced in these spheres may be quite variable in different children.

Limitations of space preclude a detailed discussion of the manifestations of the schizophrenialike psychoses in children; likewise the diagnosis and treatment of these disorders do not fall within the province of the pediatrician. He should, however, be aware of the possibility and make every effort to get suspected cases itno competent psychiatric hands as soon as possible. Recent work suggests that, if these severe personality disorders are recognized early and appropriate treatment measures instituted, the generally poor prognosis may be favorably altered in some instances. For a detailed discussion of these disorders reference should be made to textbooks of child psychiatry.

For purposes of convenience a differentiation can be made between cases with acute and those with insidious onset. In the first group, usually, older children, who have previously been reasonably well adjusted, suddenly, with no evidence of organic illness, develop acute symptoms. At first there may be a falling off in schoolwork, difficulties in concentration, and complaints of vague physical discomfort. Soon, perhaps touched off by a minor acute physical illness, an operation, or a severe emotional upset, there develop severe anxiety, sleep disturbances, motor restlessness, speech disturbances, confusion, bizarre bodily sensations, and loss of contact with people in the environment, with, at times, hallucinations. There may be stupor, posturing, muscular rigidity, and catatonic attitudes. The two pictures may alternate. Frequently there will be a regression of sphincter control. This episode may taper off gradually and the child go into a remission and function on a simpler level than before the episode. Sometimes the patient never recovers from the initial episode, but quite often there is a succession of remissions and acute psychotic episodes, with gradual diminution of the patient's capacity to function effectively.

In cases with insidious onset there is a slow, progressive development of deviations so that it is almost impossible to date their onset. Beginning with a gradual withdrawal from emotional contact with people, the child displays a detachment from the group, a loss of interest in play, and a tendency to brood. Speech becomes concerned with his preoccupations and is used less and less for communication. The range of interests becomes quite narrowed to matters which affect the child alone. Preoccupation with dates, planets, combinations of numbers, and the like is not infrequent. In many of the children there is an excessive dependence on adults (usually mother figures) which is clinging and is not on the basis of a real emotional tie. The whole picture is complicated by outbursts of impulsive aggressiveness and destructiveness which are completely unpredictable.

There seems to be no absolute relationship between symptoms and age of the child. However, those children closest to adolescence resemble the adult schizophrenic patient more.

Mahler and her co-workers divide the cases according to age at onset. Group I, with onset during the first two years of life, includes the cases of early infantile autism described by Kanner. In Group II, with onset between the third and sixth years, there is a period of essentially normal development, which is followed by striking deterioration and proneness to fulminating exacerbation of acute psychotic episodes. Group III comprises a more benign group of psychotics, with onset of psychotic withdrawal as late as the tenth year. In these children the personality development had gone further before onset so that the child had acquired greater capacity for defending himself against the disorganizing and disintegrating psychosis. This grouping is a convenient clinical one and has some prognostic implications.

The cause of schizophrenialike conditions in children is not known. Their differentiation from some of the organic central nervous system disorders is difficult. Some workers stress the constitutional aspects of these disorders, some look on them as being in the nature of encephalopathies, and others regard them as having a completely psychologic pathogenesis. Regardless of the concept as to basic cause, the child reacts in the light of his own personality, his past experiences, and the stage of his personality development in the setting of his relationships to his parents and other members of his family.

The treatment of these disorders is still not settled. Psychiatric treatment does have its beneficial effects. Electroshock therapy is also advocated by some; its place in the overall treatment program is not yet settled. Competent psychiatric care should be obtained early for suspected cases.

REFERENCES

Aichhorn, A. Wayward Youth. New York, Viking Press, 1935.

Aldrich, C. A., and Aldrich, M. M. Babies are Human Beings. New York, The Macmillan Co., 1945.

———— and Aldrich, M. M. Feeding Our Old Fashioned Children. New York, The Macmillan Co., 1941.

Anastasi, A. Psychological Testing. New York, The Macmillan Co., 1954.

Anderson, F. N. The psychiatric aspects of enuresis. Amer. J. Dis. Child., 40:591, 818, 1930.

Anthony, J., and Scott, P. Manic depressive psychosis in childhood. J. Child Psychol. Psychiat., 1:53, 1960.

Bakwin, H., and Bakwin, R. M. Clinical Management of Behavior Disorders in Children, 2nd ed. Philadelphia, W. B. Saunders Co., 1960.

Balser, B. H., ed. Psychotherapy of the Adolescent. New York, International Universities Press, 1957.

Baruch, D. W. New Ways in Discipline: You and Your Child Today. New York, McGraw-Hill Book Co., 1949.

Bender, L. Organic brain conditions producing behavior disturbances. In Modern Trends in Child Psychiatry, Lewis, N. D. C., and Pacella, B. L., eds. New York, International Universities Press, 1945, pp. 155-192.

——— Childhood schizophrenia, clinical study of 100 schizophrenic children. Amer. J. Orthopsychiat., 17:40, 1947.

——— and Nichtern, S. Chemotherapy in child psychiatry. New York J. Med., 56:2791, 1956.

Berman, L. The obsessive-compulsive neurosis in children. J. Nerv. Ment. Dis., 95:26, 1942.

Blanton, S., and Blanton, M. G. For Stutterers. New York, D. Appleton-Century Co., 1936.

Blitzer, J. R., Rollins, N., and Blackwell, N. Children who starve themselves: Anorexia nervosa. Psychosom. Med., 23:369, 1961.

Blom, G. E. The reactions of hospitalized children to illness. Pediatrics, 22:590, 1958.

Bradley, C. Schizophrenia in Childhood. New York, The Macmillan Co., 1941.

Bridge, E. M., Livingston, S., and Tietze, C. Breath-holding spells: their relationship to syncope, convulsions, and other phenomena. J. Pediat., 23:539, 1943.

Bruch, H. The role of the parent in psychotherapy with children. Psychiatry, 11:169, 1948.

——— Don't Be Afraid of Your Child. New York, Farrar, Straus and Young, 1952.

Chess, S. An Introduction to Child Psychiatry. New York, Grune and Stratton, Inc., 1959.

Childers, A. T. Hyper-activity in children having behavior disorders. Amer. J. Orthopsychiat., 5:227, 1935.

Cobb, S., and Cole, E. M. Stuttering. Physiol. Rev., 19:49, 1939.

Coekin, M., and Gairdner, D. Faecal incontinence in children; the physical factor. Brit. Med. J., 2:1175, 1960.

Conn, J. H. A psychiatric study of car-sickness in children. Amer. J. Orthopsychiat., 8:130, 1938.

Daniels, L. E. Narcolepsy. Medicine, 13:1, 1934.

Davis, C. M. Self-selection of diet by newly weaned infants. Amer. J. Dis. Child., 36:651, 1928.

——— Self-selection of food by children. Amer. J. Nurs., 35:403, 1935.

Dennett, M. W. The Sex Side of Life. New York, M. W. Dennett, 1928.

De Schweinitz, K. Growing Up. New York, The Macmillan Co., 1930.

Despert, J. L. Anxiety, phobias, and fears in young children, with special reference to prenatal, natal and neonatal factors. Nervous Child., 5:8, 1946.

——— The early recognition of childhood schizophrenia. Med. Clin. N. Amer., 31:680, 1947.

Dickerson, R. E. Growing into Manhood. New York, Association Press, 1933.

Dunton, H. D., and Langford, W. S. A psychodynamic study of pubescent girls with anorexia nervosa. Bull. Ass. Psychosom. Med., 1:51, 1962.

Eisenberg, L. The course of childhood schizophrenia. Arch. Neurol. Psychiat., 78:69, 1957.

Eissler, K. R. Searchlights on Delinquency. New York, International Universities Press, 1949.

Ewing, A. W. G. Aphasia in Children. London, Oxford University Press, 1930.

Falstein, E. I., Feinstein, S. C., and Jordan, J. Anorexia in the male child. Amer. J. Orthopsychiat., 26:75, 1956.

Finch, S. M. Fundamentals of Child Psychiatry. New York, W. W. Norton and Co., 1960.

Frank, L. K. The fundamental needs of the child. Ment. Hyg., 22:353, 1938.

Freud, A. Introduction to the Technique of Child Analysis. Monograph Series #48. New York, Nervous and Mental Disease Publishing Co., 1928.

Gallagher, J. R., and Harris, H. E. Emotional Problems of Adolescence. New York, Oxford University Press, 1958.

Geleerd, E. R. Observations on temper tantrums in children. Amer. J. Orthopsychiat., 15:238, 1945.

Gerard, M. W. Enuresis: A study in etiology. Amer. J. Orthopsychiat., 9:48, 1939.

——— The psychogenic tic in ego development. Psychoanal. Stud. Child., 2:133, 1946.

Gesell, A., et al. The First Five Years of Life. New York, Harper Bros., 1940.

——— et al. Youth, the Years from Ten to Sixteen. New York, Harper Bros., 1956.

——— and Ilg, F. L. Feeding Behavior of Infants. Philadelphia, J. B. Lippincott Co., 1937.

——— and Ilg, F. L. The Child from Five to Ten. New York, Harper Bros., 1946.

Goodenough, F. L. Anger in Young Children. Minneapolis, University of Minnesota Press, 1940.

Group for Advancement of Psychiatry. The contribution of child psychiatry to pediatric training and practice. Quart. J. Child Behav., 4:178, 1952.

——— The Diagnostic Process in Child Psychiatry. Report No. 38, New York, Group for Advancement of Psychiatry, 1957.

Gruenberg, B. C. Parents and Sex Education, 3rd ed. New York, The Viking Press, Inc., 1932.

Hall, M. B. Obsessive-compulsive states in childhood and their treatment. Arch. Dis. Child., 10:49, 1935.

Hattendorf, K. W. A study of the questions of young children concerning sex: A phase of an experimental approach to parent education. J. Soc. Psychol., 3:37, 1932.

Hinman, A. Conversion hysteria in children. Amer. J. Dis. Child., 95:42, 1958.

Hirsch, K., De. Tests designed to discover potential reading difficulties at the six-year-old level. Amer. J. Orthopsychiat., 27:566, 1957.

Hirschberg, J. C., and Bryant, K. N. Problems in the differential diagnosis of childhood schizophrenia. Proc. Ass. Res. Nerv. Ment. Dis., 34:454, 1956.

Hoyt, C. S., and Steckler, C. B. A study of forty-four children with syndrome of recurrent (cyclic) vomiting. Pediatrics, 25:775, 1960.

Huschka, M. The incidence and character of masturbation threats in a group of problem children. Psychoanal. Quart., 7:338, 1938.

Isaacs, S. Temper tantrums in early childhood in their relation to internal objects. Int. J. Psychoanal., 21:280, 1940.

Jessner, L., and Abse, W. Regressive forces in anorexia nervosa. Brit. J. Med. Psychol., 33:301, 1960.

Johnson, A. M., and Szurek, S. A. Etiology of antisocial behavior in delinquents and psychopaths. J.A.M.A., 154:814, 1954.

———— Falstein, E. I., Szurek, S. A., and Svendsen, M. School phobia. Amer. J. Orthopsychiat., 11:702, 1941.

Kanner, L. The invalid reaction in children. J. Pediat., 11:341, 1937.

———— Play investigation and play treatment of children's behavior disorders. J. Pediat., 17:533, 1940.

———— Autistic disturbances of affective contact. Nervous Child., 2:217, 1942-1943.

———— Early infantile autism. J. Pediat., 25:211, 1944.

———— Child Psychiatry, 3rd ed. Springfield, Ill., Charles C Thomas Co., 1957.

Kasanin, J. Personality changes in children following cerebral trauma. J. Nerv. Ment. Dis., 69:385, 1929.

Kaufman, I. Conversion hysteria in latency. J. Amer. Acad. Child Psychiat., 1:385, 1962.

Kay, D. W. K., and Leigh, D. The natural history, treatment and prognosis of anorexia based on a study of 38 patients. J. Ment. Sci., 100:419, 1954.

Langford, W. S. Anxiety attacks in children. Amer. J. Orthopsychiat., 7:210, 1937.

———— Thumb and finger sucking in childhood. Amer. J. Dis. Child., 58:1290, 1939.

———— The child in the pediatric hospital: Adaptation to illness and hospitalization. Amer. J. Orthopsychiat., 31:667, 1961.

———— and Klingman, W. O. Behavior disorders associated with intracranial tumors in childhood: Report of a case. Amer. J. Dis. Child., 63:433, 1942.

———— and Olson, E. Clinical work with parents of child patients. Quart. J. Child Behav., 3:240, 1951.

———— and Wickman, K. M. The clinical aspects of parent-child relationships. Ment. Hyg., 32:80, 1948.

Lay, R. A. Q. Schizophrenia-like psychoses in young children. J. Ment. Sci., 84:105, 1938.

Lehman, E. Feeding problems of psychogenic origin. A survey of the literature. Psychoanal. Stud. Child., 3-4:461, 1949.

Levine, M. I., and Seligmann, J. H. The Wonder of Life. New York, Simon & Schuster, 1940.

Levy, D. M. Psychic trauma of operations in children and a note on combat neuroses. Amer. J. Dis. Child., 69:7, 1945.

———— Finger-sucking and accessory movements in early infancy; An etiological study. Amer. J. Psychiat., 7:881, 1928.

———— Body interest in children and hypochondriasis. Amer. J. Psychiat., 12:295, 1932.

———— Maternal Overprotection. New York, Columbia University Press, 1943.

———— On the problem of movement restraint: Tics, stereotyped movements, hyperactivity. Amer. J. Orthopsychiat., 14:644, 1944.

Lewis, S. J. Undesirable habits influencing the deciduous detention. J. Amer. Dent. Ass., 18:1766, 1931.

———— The effect of thumb and finger sucking on the primary teeth and dental arches. Child Develop., 8:93, 1937.

Lourie, R. S. The role of rhythmic patterns in childhood. Amer. J. Psychiat., 105:653, 1949.

Mahler, M. S. Tics and impulsions in children: A study of motility. Psychoanal. Quart., 13:430, 1944.

———— Ross, J. R., Jr., and DeFries, Z. Clinical studies in benign and malignant cases of childhood psychosis (schizophrenia-like). Amer. J. Orthopsychiat., 19:295, 1949.

Money, J., ed. Reading Disability—Progress and Reserve Needs in Dyslexia. Baltimore, The Johns Hopkins Press, 1962.

Orton, S. T. Specific reading disability—Strephosymbolia. J.A.M.A., 90:1095, 1928.

———— Reading, Writing and Speech Problems in Children. New York, W. W. Norton and Co., 1937.

Pearson, G. H. J. Survey of learning difficulties in children. Psychoanal. Stud. Child., 7:322, 1952.

———— Adolescence and the Conflict of Generations. New York, W. W. Norton and Co., 1958.

Proctor, J. T. Hysteria in childhood. Amer. J. Orthopsychiat., 28:394, 1958.

Prugh, D. G., et al. A study of the emotional reactions of children and families to hospitalization and illness. Amer. J. Orthopsychiat., 23:70, 1953.

Rabinovitch, R. D., Drew, A. L., DeJong, R. N., Ingram, W., and Withey, L. A research approach to reading retardation. In Res. Publ. Assn. Res. Nerv. Ment. Dis., Neurology and Psychiatry in Childhood, McIntosh, R., and Hare, C. C., eds. Baltimore, Williams & Wilkins Co., 1954, Vol. 34, p. 363.

Rachman, S., and Costello, C. G. The etiology and treatment of children's phobias: a review. Amer. J. Psychiat., 118:97, 1961.

Rice, T. B. The Story of Life (For Boys and Girls of Ten Years). Chicago, A.M.A., 1939.

———— In Training (For Boys of High School Age). Chicago, A.M.A., 1939.

———— How Life Goes On and On (For Girls of High School Age). Chicago, A.M.A., 1939.

Robinson, J. F. Affective deprivation and early institutional placement. In Res. Publ. Assn. Res. Nerv. Ment. Dis. Neurology and Psychiatry in Childhood, McIntosh, R., and Hare, C. C., eds. Baltimore, Williams & Wilkins Co., 1954, Vol. 34, p. 424.

Senn, M. J. E., and Newill, P. K. All About Feeding Children. New York, Doubleday, Doran, 1944.

Shirley, H. F. Encopresis in children. J. Pediat., 12:367, 1938.

———— Pediatric Psychiatry. Cambridge, Harvard University Press, 1963.

Spitz, R. A. Hospitalism: An inquiry into the genesis of psychiatric conditions in early childhood. Psychoanal. Stud. Child, 1:53, 1945.

———— Anaclitic depression: An inquiry into the genesis of psychiatric conditions in early childhood. Psychoanal. Stud. Child, 2:313, 1946.

———— The psychogenic diseases in infancy: An attempt at their etiological classification. Psychoanal. Stud. Child, 6:255, 1952.

Thom, D. A. Normal Youth and Its Everyday Problems. New York, D. Appleton-Century, Inc., 1932.

———— Everyday Problems of the Everyday Child. New York, D. Appleton-Century, Inc., 1936.

Waldfogel, S., Coolidge, J. C., and Hahn, P. B. The development, meaning and management of school phobia. Amer. J. Orthopsychiat., 27:754, 1957.

Weisner, W. M., and Reffel, P. A. Scrupulosity. Amer. J. Psychiat., 117:314, 1960.

Witmer, H. L., ed. Psychiatric Interviews with Children. New York, The Commonwealth Fund, 1946.

———— Pediatrics and the Emotional Needs of the Child. New York, The Commonwealth Fund, 1948.

———— and Kotinsky, R., eds. Personality in the Making. New York, Harper Bros., 1952.

Wolf, A. W. M. The Parents' Manual. New York, Simon & Schuster, 1941.

Worster-Drought, C., and Allen, I. M. Congenital auditory imperception (congenital word-deafness); and its relation to idioglossia and other speech defects. J. Neurol. Psychopath., 10:193, 1929-30.

Yarnell, H. Firesetting in children. Amer. J. Orthopsychiat., 10:272, 1940.

Yoss, R. E., and Daly, D. D. Narcolepsy in children. Pediatrics, 25:1025, 1960.

Suicide in Children and Adolescents

JOSEPH RICHMAN and MILTON ROSENBAUM

This discussion of suicide in children rests upon two basic foundations. The first is that such suicidal reactions represent a form of communication sounding a call for help. The second is that the act of suicide in children is to a great extent socially determined and situationally based; it expresses a problem not only in the child, but also in the family and society.

The implications of these principles are threefold. First, the entire fate of the child may hinge upon the response of the important persons in his life to the appeal component of the suicide attempt. If the cry is answered early and constructively, completion of the suicide can be prevented not only in the present but subsequently. Second, the most important life-saving agents are the family, the school, and the physician; the physician may play an especially important role by virtue of his unique position as a helping professional and the mediator between life and death. Third, suicide in children expresses problems in living rather than wishes for dying. These problems reside in the situational context, such as family quarrels, school pressures, and social failures. In fact, in our crisis intervention work with suicidal children, we treat the situation as the patient, and work primarily towards alleviating family tensions and school or peer conflicts. In this approach the pediatrician or family doctor must become the doctor for the entire family.

Although the problems which precipitate a suicidal act may differ at different ages, certain dynamic and motivational features of suicide are common throughout the life span. Our own observations of several hundred suicidal persons of all ages appeared most meaningful when considered within both a family and an analytic frame of reference. We see suicidal behavior as based upon efforts to solve the problems appropriate to a person's developmental age and position within the context of his family, social, and school experiences.

Demography

GENERAL CONSIDERATIONS. Although the suicide rate in children is relatively low compared with that of adults, there are compelling reasons to focus on the problem in the young. There are few happenings as poignant and sad as the self-inflicted death of a young person. Even if the rate is not as great as in the aged, suicide in the young is still a sizable problem. It is among the four major causes of death for individuals under fifteen, and there is some evidence that the rate is increasing. The underlying problems of suicide may be common to all ages, and anything that lowers suicide rate at one age or among one group may reduce it for all. Suicide at all ages is probably the culmination of a disturbance which had its origins in childhood, and whatever can decrease the suicidal potential of children will have a favorable effect on the problem in adults.

In contrast to *completed* suicide, *attempted* suicide is more common in children than in adults, especially the aged. The rate is sufficiently high to suggest a problem of major proportions. Jacobziner estimated that there were 100 attempts for every completed suicide in children and adolescents. In fact, clinical experience reveals that the majority of both normal and emotionally disturbed children acknowledge the presence of suicidal thoughts and feelings at some time in their lives.

AGE AND SEX. Throughout the world the suicide rate increases with age. In males the increase with age is constant, while in females the suicide rate reaches a peak in the age group of 40 to 60 and then declines.

In both children and adolescents the male-to-female ratio of completed suicides is approximately 3 to 1. Among latency-age children there are more recorded attempts at suicide by boys than girls, but in adolescents the figures are reversed, there being from 3 to 10 female attempts for every male.

RACE. Among races in the United States there are pronounced differences in the peak ages for suicide. For both white and nonwhite males, the completed suicide rate has been approximately the same up to age 35, after which it remains relatively constant and low for the nonwhites, while rising steadily for the whites. However, recent evidence indicates that the suicide rate in blacks is rising. For example, in 1969, Hendin reported that in New York City the suicide rate for black males under the age of 35 was twice that for whites. For nonwhite females the suicide rate is uniformly low throughout all ages.

The figures for attempted suicides differ with ethnic groups, the rates being high in minority groups such as blacks and Puerto Ricans. However, a qualification should be made. The statistics are derived largely from police files and from municipal and state hospital records, which include a higher proportion of poor people, especially Puerto Ricans and blacks. Suicides of whites and of individuals belonging to middle- and upper-class groups are less likely to be reported, or a different cause of death may be given.

The emotional turmoil surrounding a suicide attempt is often particularly evident in the minority groups. Trautman described a characteristically intense episode of suicidal acting-out in Puerto Ricans, which he called "the suicidal fit," while Gould observed a similar pattern which he referred to as the "Puerto Rican syndrome." The traits associated with these conditions tend to diminish with increasing acculturation.

It has been our observation, however, that impulsivity and dissociative trends are prominent in many individuals from all walks of life who attempt suicide. As our relationships with the people involved in a suicidal act became more intimate, the ethnic and social differences tended to be minimized or disappeared. Among the families of higher socioeconomic classes the violence is more attenuated; also, less gross sexual deviations and less family disorganization were usually displayed. However, these apparently different characteristics now appear to us to be rather superficial. A greater acquaintance with the situation revealed, almost invariably, outbursts of uncontrolled aggression and either incestuous acting-out or other forms of sexual deviation. In contrast to Hendin, who considers the dynamics of suicide to vary in different countries and ethnic groups, it is our clinical impression that there are no major racial, ethnic, or socioeconomic differences in the dynamics of the suicidal individual and his family.

RELIGION. In general, most studies of *completed* suicides report a lower rate among Catholics and Jews than among Protestants, while in most studies of *attempted* suicide there has been a tendency to disregard this variable. In our practice, however, there appeared to be a large percentage of Catholics among the young patients who had attempted suicide. One can speculate that more distress would be required to drive a Catholic child to such a culturally dystonic act, but further research into this area is needed to provide conclusive data.

METHOD. Boys use guns and hanging as the most frequent methods for completed suicide, while girls resort to pills. The choice of less violent methods with their greater opportunities for rescue has been postulated as one basis for the lower suicide rate in females. In suicide attempts the most popular method in children and adolescents of both sexes is drugs.

SEASON. Jacobziner reported among adolescents more attempts in the spring, but in general no clear or consistent trends have been noted. Apart from any seasonal variation, it appears to us that weekends, holidays, and sometimes important anniversary dates are the most trying times for suicidally inclined youngsters.

DIAGNOSIS. In the literature a small tempest rages around the diagnostic characteristics of suicidal children and adolescents. Some report schizophrenia as the major diagnostic entity, others depression, and still others neuroses and character disorders.

The bulk of our youthful suicidal population were depressed, and most were diagnosed as having character disorders. In general, however, the diagnosis of psychopathology in the adolescent or younger patient is of limited value. It usually tells little about the seriousness of the actual attempt or of the circumstances surrounding it. Furthermore, in focussing on the diagnostic characteristic, one tends to assign the reason for the act to the personality disorder. As a result, the environmental and situational factors and the role of other significant persons are obscured or relatively disregarded. The diagnosis should not be ignored, but its meaning can be understood only in the total context.

Motives and Precipitating Events

A *precipitating event* refers to the existing situation or stresses which are instrumental in producing a suicidal act. A *motive* refers to the reason, purpose, or function of the act. The two are most often intertwined and inseparable, and are therefore best considered together.

Many difficulties lie in the path of examining and understanding these aspects. For example, not many children can say what events or motives precipitated their suicidal behavior. It is most valuable, therefore, to interview as many relatives and other significant persons as possible, both individually and as families. The most helpful first step is to elicit the actual concrete circumstances surrounding the suicidal act. Typically, the motives and precipitants are more complex than they appear to be. Eleven major categories of motives for suicidal behavior in children and adolescents can be identified. These include: (1) separation and object loss, (2) reunion wishes and fantasies, (3) aggression, (4) atonement, (5) precocious sexual disturbances, (6) manipulation and blackmail, (7) an attempt to escape from an unbearable situation, (8) school difficulties, (9) the expression of a disintegration of the personality, (10) a cry for help, and (11) a developmental crisis.

Rather than attempting to discuss all of these, we shall focus upon the five motives and precipitants which would be most important for the pediatrician to understand.

SEPARATION AND LOSS. Suicide and the more serious suicidal attempts are often a reaction to the loss or threatened loss of a loved one. This motive is intimately related to the family dynamics discussed in greater detail below. Rejection by friends, parents, and relatives, and a general sense of alienation from the other members of society appear relevant to this theme. It forms the most personal counterpart of the breakdown of integration between the individual and society, which Durkheim called *anomie*.

AGGRESSION. Aggression in suicide appears in various forms. These include retaliation, thwarted or blocked hostility or anger, a need to punish the surroundings or others for deprivation of love, and autoaggression. The most frequent precipitating event for a suicidal act in children and adolescents is a family quarrel. Aggression poses a suicidal threat when other forms of aggressive outlets are not available, and when the person must endure not only his own aggression turned against himself, but the accumulated aggression toward others. Under these conditions suicide is simultaneously an act of aggression against the self *and* the significant other or others. Suicide really represents the last word in retaliation. The two-edged nature of aggression in suicide is often seen more clearly in the cases where homicide or assault is followed by completed or attempted suicide. Such cases are more common than is generally known and the problem of suicide can be properly understood only when viewed as one aspect of the general problem of violence in individuals and society.

MANIPULATION AND BLACKMAIL. These include attention-getting, forcing reactions from the environment, attempts to control, and efforts to obtain more love. The interpersonal and family aspects of suicide are particularly evident in this category. We have been most impressed by the transactional, two-way nature of the interaction and the efforts to maintain a pathologic status quo involved in the manipulation.

SCHOOL DIFFICULTIES. Assuming the role of a student and meeting the demands of school constitutes one of the primary tasks of growing up. For most children, school is the first major separation from home. Therefore, the family that cannot tolerate separation often is unable to make the required adjustment. School failure and tension about studies, together with parental demands and difficulties at home, are almost universal in suicidal children and adolescents. A pattern of strain and failure is found not only in children who still attend school, but in the past school history of the older suicidal person.

A DEVELOPMENTAL CRISIS. This broadly integrative concept covers the needs, strivings, and goals of the young person, and the social and instinctual tensions characteristic of his age. During latency, when the first signs of suicidal behavior may become noticeable, the developmental task is that of establishing peer relationships and demonstrating adequacy in school. In the adolescent, the developmental task is that of forming a clear identity rather than a diffusion of roles. The young suicidal person has invariably failed to meet expectations for his age-appropriate role at home, in school, and in his social life. His suicidal act expresses an admission of a failure to meet the identity crisis and a regression to the infant-mother symbiosis.

We conclude that an understanding of the motives and precipitants of a suicidal act in childhood involves consideration of four aspects. First, the nature of the individual's personality, the stresses he is undergoing, and the resources he has available to him must be explored. Second, the role of the social and family networks must be examined and understood. Most of the suicidal acts we studied became considerably more understandable in the light of the family patterns within which the behavior was embedded and in the light of the motives and stresses of the other significant persons. Third, the present, here-and-now context must be explored; and fourth, the historic background of the act must be studied. In all our cases we found that the motives and precipitants of suicide were repetitive and cumulative. These unfortunate, unsuccessful, and repetitive experiences were designed to maintain regressive and infantile ties to the original family pattern.

The Family in Suicidal Childhood and Adolescence

The family foundations of a suicidal act are more evident in younger than in older age groups. An impressive body of evidence has been accumulated documenting the prevalence of parental disturbances and family disorganization in the background of suicidal children and adolescents, stemming from the first year of life. Studies of these families reveal a high incidence of deprivating and rejecting parents, destructive and grossly disturbed parent-child relationships, neglect, broken homes, and parental loss. It is not the parental loss in itself that is significant but the loss of parenting, which can occur also in ostensibly intact families.

The sheer bulk of the evidence of disturbed and disorganized family backgrounds in suicidal children is incontestable. Although a disturbed family is characteristic of all children with emotional problems and is not the exclusive prerogative of suicidal children, its significance in suicidal behavior is not to be minimized. More studies are needed to understand the relationships of family structure and interactions to a suicidal resolution. Our studies form part of this endeavor. We have seen many features we consider characteristic of disturbed families in general, and some which are more specific to families in which suicidal actions occur. The latter include marked disturbances in communication patterns of the family, in role distributions, and in the patterns of aggressive discharge or blocking of discharge.

Regarding the outcome of the aggressive impulses, the self-destructive activity was often a reaction to the destructive wishes of an important person. It was also a projection upon the suicidal child of the bad self of the parents and the entire family, combined with a ubiquitous intolerance for separation. The relationship between the suicidal person and the family or other significant persons is a double-binding one in which they can neither separate nor remain together. The relatives communicate to the suicidal child that he is a burden. However, he is not only forbidden to leave the family, he is forbidden to establish relationships with others. The suicidal act occurs in a closed family system which excludes outsiders and within which the suicidal child is alienated and isolated, yet forbidden to move out.

Suicide is not necessarily the direct result of family and personal disturbances, be it a broken home, object loss, or occupational or school failure. All of these are found in persons who are not suicidal. What is central is the way in which the disturbance is handled. In many of our cases of suicidal children we found a symbiosis with a mother who was rejecting and unable to empathize. No one was assigned age, sex, or socially appropriate roles in the family. Depression and low self-esteem were family characteristics. It was often a home where the parents engaged in questionable behavior and the siblings were unreasonably aggressive, but only the patient was labeled as bad.

Our experiences indicate that the suicidal person was one who met with such difficulties in family relationships from the beginning, with both child and mother, and often the whole family, displaying intense infantile fixations. Lourie has pointed out that the developmental crises leading to early depressive and suicidal syndromes are based upon poor and distorted answers to the problems of earlier development. Suicidal behavior is then potentiated by events in the present.

The present, however, is much more than a mere trigger, since the suicidal act is based not only upon these early problems and fixations, but is a resultant of an entire network of present-day relationships in which each significant person plays his suicidogenic part. We hypothesize, therefore, that suicidal behavior in children is a pattern learned in the family, handed down from one generation to the next, and sustained by suicidogenic relationships in the present.

Recommendations and Conclusions

An attempted suicidal act of a child is not wholly a tragedy. It is also a challenge and an opportunity which contains many positive potentials. Our data has led us to some recommendations regarding the role of the family, the school, and the doctor in the treatment and prevention of suicide.

First, early recognition of the potentially suicidal youngster is vital. Special courses and training in the recognition of danger signs is desirable for physicians, teachers, guidance personnel, and all those who may be involved with the disturbed child. A program to detect the potentially suicidal child is needed. Pupils who tend to be loners or outcasts form the greatest suicidal risks. They need someone to talk to and someone to help them in becoming members of the social group.

Second, the school assumes a special role because it is the threshold of the larger society outside the home. For effective suicide prevention the school and home should work closely together. Therapy and counseling services should be available in all schools at all levels. In addition to remedial and personal counseling for troubled pupils, we believe that every school, beginning with elementary school, should have a family counseling service available.

Third, sexual difficulties are as prevalent in the genesis of suicide as in general problems with aggression. The proper sex education, therefore, may help to prevent suicide.

Fourth, suicide is fostered by a violent and frustration-producing society. A social emphasis upon nonviolent means of solving national and international conflicts may prevent suicide.

Fifth, the teacher is a key figure. None of the psychiatric and social services in the schools can substitute for the sensitivity of the individual teacher, his awareness of the pupil who is in trouble and who may need him, and his availability when needed. The teacher's attitude can often make the difference between suicide or growth.

Sixth, the physician is a key figure, for reasons which have been discussed. The insensitivity of some doctors and teachers may have contributed to a suicidal act. There have also been many teachers and physicians whose influence has prevented suicides and preserved lives. However, there can be no statistics on persons who might have but did not commit suicide. Hence, their influence must go unnoticed, except in the lives and hearts of those they have met and touched. It is because of such individuals that there is hope that the cry for help will be answered.

REFERENCES

Durkheim, E. Suicide. (Tr. by J. A. Spaulding and G. Simpson.) New York, The Free Press, 1951.

Gould, R. E. Suicide problems in children and adolescents. Amer. J. Psychother., 19:228-246, 1965.

Hendin, H. Black Suicide. New York, Basic Books, Inc., Publishers, 1969.

Jacobziner, H. Attempted suicides in adolescence. J.A.M.A., 191:101-105, 1965.

Lourie, R. S. Suicide and attempted suicide in children and adolescents. *In* Yochelson, L., ed., Symposium on Suicide. Washington, D.C., George Washington School of Medicine, 1967, pp. 93-105.

Richman, J. Family determinants of attempted suicide. *In* Farberow, N. L., ed., Proceedings of the Fourth International Conference for Suicide Prevention, Los Angeles, 1968, pp. 372-380.

——— and Rosenbaum, M. The family doctor and the suicidal family. Psychiat. in Med., 1:27-35, 1970.

Rosenbaum, M., and Richman, J. Suicide: The role of hostility and death wishes from the family and significant others. Amer. J. Psychiat., 126:1652-1655, 1970.

Seiden, R. H. Suicide Among Youth, Bulletin of Suicid-ology Supplement. Washington, D.C., U.S. Government Printing Office, December, 1969.

Shneidman, E. S., Farberow, N. L., and Litman, R. E. The Psychology of Suicide. New York, Science House, Inc., 1970.

Stengel, E. Suicide and Attempted Suicide. Baltimore, Penguin Books, Inc., 1964.

Trautman, E. C. The suicidal fit: A psychologic study in Puerto Rico immigrants. Arch. Gen. Psychiat. (Chicago), 5:76-83, 1961.

Yacoubian, J. H., and Lourie, R. S. Suicide and attempted suicide in children and adolescents. Clin. Proc. Child Hosp., Washington, D.C., 25:325-344, 1969.

chapter 7

GENETIC PRINCIPLES IN PEDIATRICS

HAROLD M. NITOWSKY, Associate Editor

7.1
INTRODUCTION

The existence and extent of human diversity is readily apparent to the pediatrician as he deals with children who normally differ in their physical, physiologic, and behavioral attributes, and in their rates of development of these characteristics. Such diversity is manifest not only in health but also in individual variation in susceptibility and reaction to disease. Clearly, some of these differences can be attributed, at least in part, to environmental circumstances. However, they also reflect inborn or genetic differences, for, with the exception of monozygotic twins, no two individuals are exactly alike in their genetic endowment.

The importance of genetics to medicine has come to be appreciated increasingly in recent years. The identification of individual differences or disease states in which genetic factors play a leading role has grown at an exponential rate. Advances in our knowledge of human genetic disease have been dependent upon developments in a number of areas, but principally in three related disciplines. One of these, *population genetics,* deals with the study of the distribution of specific genes in different populations and the impact that such genes have on maintenance of gene frequency, natural selection, and evolution. Another discipline, *cytogenetics,* is concerned with the location and organization of the genetic material on the chromosomes and the genetic aberrations associated with morphologic or numeric abnormalities of these structures. *Biochemical genetics* deals with the chemical identity of the gene and its product, and the mechanisms by which the information coded in the genes regulates cellular metabolism.

Although for many years man was regarded as an unsuitable subject for genetic study, recent contributions to the broad discipline from studies of human inborn metabolic disorders and chromosome abnormalities seem to emphasize that for some studies of genetic mechanism or gene action man is still a unique subject for genetic investigation. The following sections provide a brief summary of some of the basic concepts of genetics, together with a review of some of the important developments in the area of human genetics and their clinical application.

7.2
MOLECULAR GENETICS

HAROLD M. NITOWSKY

Three basic properties were ascribed to the gene in the development of the concept of the fundamental unit of heredity. The gene had to have a specific function in the cell and it had to be capable of exact self-replication in order to preserve this functional specificity from one generation to the next. Moreover, it had to be susceptible to sudden change or mutation at some finite frequency so that new genes differing in function could arise and thereby permit evolution of living forms.

Classical genetics has elucidated how genes are arrayed in a linear order on the chromosomes, how they are transmitted to an individual from his parents via the ovum and sperm so that they are present in pairs, and how, because of alterations arising from mutation, multiple forms of a gene, or alleles, can occupy a particular gene locus.

The major advances in molecular genetics during the past two decades have provided insight into the basis for these unique properties of the gene. The discovery that the chemical nature of the genetic material is deoxyribonucleic acid (DNA), and the elucidation of the molecular structure of this substance provided insight into the basis and mechanism for gene specificity, gene mutation, and gene replication. Moreover, insight into the mechanism of gene action came with the unraveling of the genetic code and the recognition that the primary biochemical role of DNA in the cell is to direct the synthesis of enzymes and other proteins.

The DNA molecule is made up of two very long polynucleotide chains, coiled round a common axis to form a double helix. The regular alternation of phosphate and sugar groups forms the backbone of the DNA chain. A nitrogenous base, consisting of a purine (adenine or guanine) or a pyrimidine (thymine or cytosine), is attached to each sugar group and projects inward from the chain. The two chains are held together by hydrogen bonding between the pairs of bases projecting at the same level from each chain. Because of their molecular structure there are certain restrictions in hydrogen bonding in the DNA chains, so that adenine pairs with thymine and guanine with cytosine.

A gene can be regarded as a segment of DNA containing several hundred or thousand base pairs. Since variations in the linear sequence of base pairs along the chain can occur, a great many different permutations are possible, each of which is structurally and therefore functionally unique.

Because of the restrictions in pairing, the sequence of bases in one chain fixes the sequence of bases in the other. Replication of the DNA can occur by the unwinding and separation of the chains and the re-formation on each chain of a DNA molecule with a complementary base sequence. Gene mutations can be envisaged as the consequence of an alteration of the base pair sequence of the particular gene, reflecting perhaps the change of only one base for another in the sequence. Other more drastic changes of the DNA, such as the deletion or duplication of base sequences, also can result in mutation.

The phenotype of the organism can be attributed, in the final analysis, to the distinctive activities and properties of a complex of different enzymes and other proteins synthesized in the cells. By their action, these proteins define and control the complex pattern of metabolic and developmental processes that characterize the individual. Proteins are composed of one or more polypeptide chains which are made up of long strings of amino acids linked by peptide bonds in a specific linear order. There are 20 different amino acids, so that with sequences of 100 to 500 amino acids, the number of possible structures is large. The folding of the polypeptide chain, which results in a three-dimensional structure with characteristic properties and functional activity, depends on the linear sequence of amino acids.

Studies with microorganisms and other systems have shown that the sequence of amino acids in the polypeptide chain is determined by the sequence of base pairs in a given gene, and that each amino acid is specified by a sequence of three consecutive, nonoverlapping bases. Studies of the genetic code, which appears to have universal biologic application, have shown that the four characteristic bases of the DNA chain can occur in 64 different triplet sequences, and each of 61 of these triplets specifies one of 20 amino acids (Table 1). The excess number of triplets in relation to the number of amino acids indicates the presence of degeneracy of the code, in that a particular amino acid may be coded by two or more different base triplets.

Several types of ribonucleic acid (RNA) molecules are involved in the translation of the base sequence in the DNA into the corresponding sequence of amino acids in a polypeptide chain. The first involves the formation of a RNA chain that is complementary in base sequence to one of the separate DNA chains. Similar base pairing restrictions apply, except for the substitution of uracil for thymine. This RNA strand, known as messenger RNA (mRNA), separates from the DNA and passes out of the cell nucleus to the ribosomes in the cytoplasm, which are the site of protein synthesis. Amino acids attached to another species of RNA molecule, known as transfer RNA (tRNA), are incorporated into a polypeptide chain in a sequence specified by the mRNA

TABLE 1. *The Genetic Code*

First nucleotide	Second Nucleotide: A or *U*		G or *C*		T or *A*		C or *G*		Third nucleotide
A or *U*	**AAA** *UUU*	Phe	**AGA** *UCU*	Ser	**ATA** *UAU*	Tyr	**ACA** *UGU*	Cys	A or *U*
	AAG *UUC*		**AGG** *UCC*		**ATG** *UAC*		**ACG** *UGC*		G or *C*
	AAT *UUA*	Leu	**AGT** *UCA*		**ATT** *UAA*	Stop	**ACT** *UGA*	Stop	T or *A*
	AAC *UUG*		**AGC** *UCG*		**ATC** *UAG*		**ACC** *UGG*	Trp	C or *G*
G or *C*	**GAA** *CUU*	Leu	**GGA** *CCU*	Pro	**GTA** *CAU*	His	**GCA** *CGU*	Arg	A or *U*
	GAG *CUC*		**GGG** *CCC*		**GTG** *CAC*		**GCG** *CGC*		G or *C*
	GAT *CUA*		**GGT** *CCA*		**GTT** *CAA*	Gln	**GCT** *CGA*		T or *A*
	GAC *CUG*		**GGC** *CCG*		**GTC** *CAG*		**GCC** *CGG*		C or *G*
T or *A*	**TAA** *AUU*	Ile	**TGA** *ACU*	Thr	**TTA** *AAU*	Asn	**TCA** *AGU*	Ser	A or *U*
	TAG *AUC*		**TGG** *ACC*		**TTG** *AAC*		**TCG** *AGC*		G or *C*
	TAT *AUA*		**TGT** *ACA*		**TTT** *AAA*	Lys	**TCT** *AGA*	Arg	T or *A*
	TAC *AUG*	Met	**TGC** *ACG*		**TTC** *AAG*		**TCC** *AGG*		C or *G*
C or *G*	**CAA** *GUU*	Val	**CGA** *GCU*	Ala	**CTA** *GAU*	Asp	**CCA** *GGU*	Gly	A or *U*
	CAG *GUC*		**CGG** *GCC*		**CTG** *GAC*		**CCG** *GGC*		G or *C*
	CAT *GUA*		**CGT** *GCA*		**CTT** *GAA*	Glu	**CCT** *GGA*		T or *A*
	CAC *GUG*		**CGC** *GCG*		**CTC** *GAG*		**CCC** *GGG*		C or *G*

The DNA codons appear in boldface type; the complementary RNA codons are in italics. A = adenine, C = cytosine, G = guanine, T = thymine, U = uridine. "Stop" represents nonsense triplets which appear to designate chain termination.

template. The tRNA molecules are relatively small and occur as a series of distinct forms, each specific for a particular amino acid by virtue of the presence in the polynucleotide sequence of a base triplet complementary to a base triplet in mRNA which codes for the amino acids. The polypeptide chain is made sequentially, one amino acid being added at a time, starting from the amino terminal end. Thus, the information coded in the genes serves as a blueprint for the structure of all the cellular enzymes and other proteins. In addition to specifying structure, genes appear to be concerned in regulating synthesis of proteins, although the mechanism for such regulation remains to be elucidated for multicellular organisms.

Mutation

Mutation, or change in the genetic material, can readily be understood in terms of alteration of the base sequence of the DNA. When the term is used without further specification, it usually refers to a "point mutation," or a change in a single base with substitution of one for another. Thus, a change in DNA from CTT to CAT (Table 1) causes a substitution of valine for glutamic acid in the polypeptide chain, an alteration which occurs in the beta chain of sickle hemoglobin (Sec. 17.3).

A second class of mutation is that which results from nonhomologous pairing and unequal crossing-over, as depicted schematically in Figure 1. During the meiotic process in gametogenesis, homologous chromosomes pair, but if the matching is not precise, unequal crossing-over occurs. The result is either duplication or deletion of genetic material. Gene duplication has been demonstrated as an important factor in evolution. The separate genes that specify the various polypeptide chains of hemoglobin (the beta chain of hemoglobin A, the delta chain of hemoglobin A_2, the gamma chain of hemoglobin F and the alpha chain of all these hemoglobins), as well as the single polypeptide chain of myoglobin, appear to have evolved from a primordial common ancestral gene through the process of gene duplication and subsequent independent mutation of the separate genes.

Nonhomologous pairing with unequal crossing-over also can cause deletion of part of a gene or part of two contiguous genes. Study of the amino acid sequence in some abnormal hemoglobins suggests that this was the type of mutation responsible for the altered protein. Hemoglobin Lepore (Sec. 17.3) is presumed to be an example of a mutation due to unequal crossing-over. The genes for the beta and delta chains of hemoglobin are probably contiguous. In a person with hemoglobin Lepore, the normal beta and delta chains are replaced by a polypeptide chain that has the structure of the delta chain at one end and of the beta chain at the other. As shown in Figure 1, a fusion gene specifying a hybrid polypeptide chain of this type could have arisen by unequal crossing-over.

A third class of mutation is that which results in gross chromosome abnormalities. This class includes (1) abnormalities of chromosome number as a result of errors in chromosome segregation during mitosis or meiosis and (2) abnormalities of chromosome structure, e.g., chromosomal deletions, translocations, or inversions, as a result of chromosome breakage.

In general, mutations that represent a change in the genetic material are likely to be deleterious in terms of selection and evolution. Reliable estimates of spontaneous mutation rates have been obtained with microorganisms. These rates can be increased by such factors as ionizing radiation, by certain chemicals, or by an increase in temperature. On the other hand, precise estimates of mutation rates in man are difficult to obtain. The figures of one to five mutations per 100,000 loci per generation are frequently cited, and have been derived, at least in part, from studies of dominantly inherited pathologic traits. It has been estimated that each person carries a "genetic load" of four or more mutant genes which would be lethal in the homozygous state. Increase in the number of undesirable recessive genes by mutation may persist for many generations before being expressed in a homozygote.

Only those mutations that occur in the genetic material of the gametes will lead to heritable changes. Mutations involving somatic cells will be transmitted to the descendants of that cell, but not to subsequent generations of individuals. However, to the extent that such alterations may be associated with some forms of neoplastic disease, they may be considered a form of "lethal" mutation.

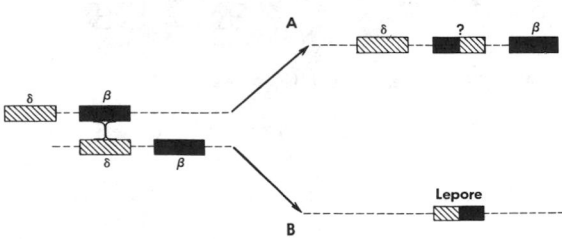

Fig. 1. Mutation as a result of nonhomologous pairing and unequal crossing-over. In *A*, gene duplication occurs from crossing-over between B and S genes. In *B*, a fusion gene occurs from crossing-over within a gene, a process presumed to have produced the gene for Lepore hemoglobin.

References

Synthesis and structure of macromolecules. Cold Spring Harbor Symp. Quant. Biol., 28, 1963.

Hurwitz, J., and August, J. T. The role of DNA in RNA Synthesis. *In* Davidson, J. N., and Colin, W. E., eds., Progress in Nucleic Acid Research. New York, Academic Press, 1963.

Peters, J. A. Classic Papers in Genetics. Englewood Cliffs, N.J., Prentice Hall, 1959.

Stahl, F. W. The Mechanics of Inheritance. Englewood Cliffs, N.J., Prentice Hall, 1964.

Vogel, H. J., Bryson, V., and Lampen, J., eds. Informational Macromolecules. New York, Academic Press, 1963.

Watson, J. D. Molecular Biology of the Gene. New York, W. A. Benjamin, 1965.

Watson, J. D., and Crick, F. H. C. Genetical implications of the structure of deoxyribonucleic acid. Nature, 171:964, 1963.

Ycas, M. The Biological Code. Amsterdam, North-Holland Publishing Co., 1969.

7.3

THE BEHAVIOR OF GENETIC DISEASE IN FAMILIES AND POPULATIONS

HELEN M. RANNEY

In the somatic cells of man and other diploid organisms, autosomes (all chromosomes except the sex chromosomes are autosomes) are found in pairs, one of each pair from each parent. Consequently, somatic cells contain two genes at each locus, which may in some examples be two base sequences responsible for the manufacture of autosomally controlled proteins. The term "locus" refers to any particular region on the chromosome that is occupied by a given gene. Alleles are alternate forms of genes which could occupy a given locus. Although two genes for each autosomal trait will be present in any individual, several alleles may be present in a group of individuals. For example, in the ABO blood group system, an individual may have any two genes—e.g., AA, or AO, or AB—but not, of course, three genes, although the allelic genes A, B, and O are present in a population. If the two genes are identical, i.e., AA, the individual is homozygous for that factor; if the two genes differ, e.g., AO or AB, the individual is heterozygous.

Studies of Families

Much of our knowledge of human heredity is derived from studies of the patterns of inheritance of certain characteristics or diseases. In these patterns, an example of which is illustrated in Figure 2, the proband (propositus, index case) is indicated by an arrow, males by circles.

AUTOSOMAL DOMINANT INHERITANCE. If the character or disease in question is manifest in the individual heterozygous for that gene, i.e., if a single

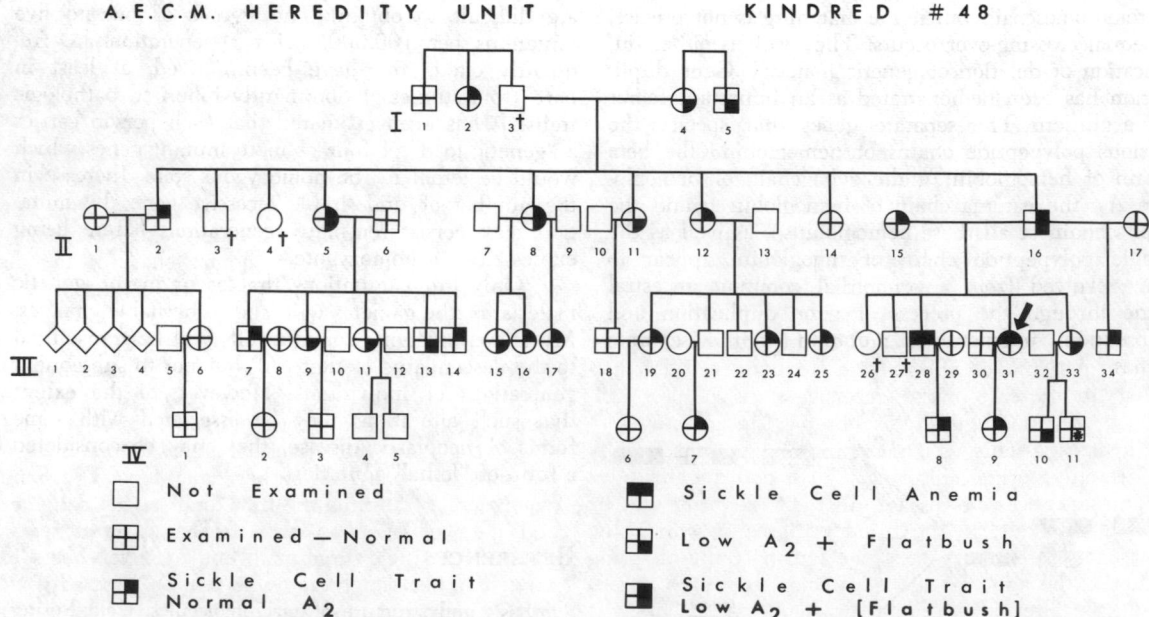

Fig. 2. Pedigree of a family in which three individuals (II-5, II-8, and II-16) were heterozygous for both a β-chain hemoglobin abnormality (Hb S) and a δ-chain variant (Hb Flatbush). (For technical reasons, presence of Hb Flatbush in the presence of Hb S had to be inferred from the accompanying depression of Hb A₂.) Note that the offspring of these three individuals had either Hb S or Hb Flatbush. Also from studies of generation I, the genes for S and Flatbush would be expected to be in repulsion in II-5, II-8, and II-16.

dose of the gene results in manifestations, then that character is *dominant,* and the gene itself is (more conveniently than correctly) referred to as dominant. In autosomal dominant inheritance, the trait will be found in one parent (of either sex) and in half the sons and half the daughters of an affected individual. This is the expected result of a mating in which a parent passes either the affected or the nonaffected chromosome to the offspring, and the corresponding chromosome derived from the other parent is normal. The offspring who have the abnormal chromosome would manifest the trait, and the remainder (one half) would be normal. The homozygous state for many diseases which exhibit a dominant mode of inheritance is not known; many are probably lethal before birth. When a disease is determined by a dominant gene, the disease is not usually encountered in offspring of unaffected individuals, and only occasionally is "skipping of generations" observed. In these circumstances, the apparently unaffected parent may have minimal or, indeed, undetectable evidence of the presence of the gene in question. When more sophisticated laboratory techniques are utilized, manifestations of the gene can frequently be detected in such phenotypically apparently normal parents. For example, when the apparently unaffected sibling of a patient with hereditary spherocytosis (HS) has a child with HS, the autohemolysis test may disclose a previously undetected erythrocyte defect in the parent.

AUTOSOMAL RECESSIVE INHERITANCE. Whereas in autosomal dominant inheritance, the trait or disorder is the result of a single abnormal gene, the designation *recessive* implies that both genes must be abnormal for the appearance of clinical manifestations. While the heterozygote is symptomatic in diseases which are determined by dominant genes, only the homozygote is symptomatic in the case of recessive genes. Since the heterozygous state for recessives does not generally result in readily detectable clinical manifestations, the patterns of inheritance of autosomal recessives have certain distinguishing features: (1) The parents, both usually heterozygous, are generally clinically normal. (2) The disease affects both sexes equally and sibships in which more than one child is affected are frequent. (3) Particularly in the case of rare recessive traits, a high incidence of consanguinity is observed in parents. (4) Affected patients who marry normal persons usually have only normal offspring. (5) If both parents have the same recessive disease, all their offspring will be affected. Thus, in the usual pedigree in which the parents are heterozygotes, one fourth of the offspring inherit the abnormal genetic factor from each parent and are affected; one half are heterozygotes like the parents; and one fourth are normal. In considering expected ratios, such as one half affected for the offspring of a parent with a dominant trait, or one fourth for offspring of matings of individuals heterozygous for a recessive trait, it should be emphasized that the ratios are theoretical and that families in which no individual has been affected will not be detected. In studies of small families which have been ascertained by the presence of an affected individual, inclusion of the probands will result in higher ratios than those predicted.

The distinction between dominant and recessive traits is useful but to some extent arbitrary. Heterozygous carriers of many recessive diseases can be recognized by appropriate tests, and are therefore distinguishable from normals. For example, the heterozygous state, sickle-cell trait, is readily recognized although serious manifestations generally occur only in homozygotes with sickle-cell anemia. The term "intermediate dominance" is sometimes applied to such diseases as sickling, and the concept of intermediate dominance could be extended to many diseases usually classified as recessive.

X-LINKED INHERITANCE. The differences in the sex chromosomes, XX for females and XY for males, provide the basis for characteristic patterns of inheritance for genes carried on the X chromosome. The traits determined by genes carried on the X chromosome may be either recessive or dominant in the female, but in the male, who has only one X chromosome, the trait will always be expressed. Alternatively stated, a female may be heterozygous or homozygous for an X-linked gene, but the male can only be hemizygous, and X-linked genes which are recessive in females will consequently have clinical manifestations in males. In large pedigrees, the pattern of inheritance may suggest X linkage, dominant or recessive, since the trait will *not* be transmitted from father to son. When the X-linked trait is a rare recessive, the affected individuals will be males who are related to each other through females. In pedigrees of serious X-linked recessive disorders such as hemophilia, the affected males may not survive to have children. The history of disease in maternal uncles and in the sisters' male children should be sought in possible X-linked disorders.

Recessive X-linked disorders are occasionally found in females who are homozygous for the disorder. Instances of homozygosity in females will, of course, be observed if the abnormal gene is common in the population, as in glucose-6-phosphate dehydrogenase deficiency in Negroes, or if consanguineous matings have occurred in the pedigree. The heterozygous female (carrier in the case of recessives) transmits the abnormal gene to one half of her sons and one half of her daughters. The hemizygous male transmits the trait to all of his daughters and none of his sons, and the homozygous female transmits a single abnormal gene to all of her sons, as well as her daughters (who will be affected if the trait is dominant, and will be carriers if the trait is recessive). An unaffected male in a family with an X-linked disorder will transmit the disorder to none of his children.

THE LYON HYPOTHESIS. Although many genes are known to be carried on the X chromosome, the X-linked gene products, such as antihemophilia factor (AHF) or glucose-6-phosphate dehydrogenase (G-6-PD), do not show significant quantitative differences between normal males (with one X) and females (with 2 X's). Furthermore there is a wide range of expression in the heterozygous female carriers for X-linked diseases: some carriers of hemophilia have no demonstrable deficiency of AHF, while others have intermediate levels. In 1961, Dr. Mary Lyon suggested that one X chromosome in each cell of the female is randomly inactivated in early embryogenesis, and that the descendants of each cell may carry the same pattern of inactivation. Thus each cell of the female would contain only one active X chromosome, and the levels of X-linked gene products would be the same in normal individuals of either sex. If random inactivation occurred when only a few cells were present, in some heterozygous carriers for AHF more normal than abnormal X chromosomes would be inactivated, and consequently decreased levels of AHF might be observed.

SEX INFLUENCE ON AUTOSOMALLY DETERMINED TRAITS. Certain traits are genetically determined by autosomal factors but have different manifestations in males and females. The most frequently cited example is pattern baldness, which is determined by an autosomal gene; it behaves as a dominant in men and as a recessive in women. Distinction between sex influence and X linkage may be difficult in small pedigrees which do not include significant numbers of father-son relationships. If a sex-influenced disorder results in infertility of affected males, the distinction between autosomal dominant and X-linked recessive inheritance may not be possible.

ALLELISM, INDEPENDENT ASSORTMENT, AND LINKAGE. While alleles appear to segregate as the chromosome number is reduced by half at meiosis, certain genes, as Mendel originally observed, assort independently. The most informative pedigrees concerning allelism vs. independent assortment of two genetic factors include two (or preferably more) offspring of a parent who is heterozygous for both traits under investigation and a parent who has neither trait; i.e., the parental mating is a testcross. Examples of the inheritance of human hemoglobins serve to illustrate the differences. Hemoglobins S and C, both β-chain abnormalities, behave as alleles and

segregate as indicated in Figure 3. Each child of a parent with sickle-cell–hemoglobin C disease will have either S trait or C trait, but no child will inherit both S and C or will inherit both normal hemoglobin genes.

Certain other abnormal hemoglobins are abnormal in the α polypeptide chain. Individuals with variants in both the α and β chains have been described (such individuals have four major hemoglobin components), and the composition of the hemoglobin of their offspring provides evidence for independent assortment (Fig. 4).

From examination of Figures 3 and 4, it is obvious that when the genes are allelic, only two types of offspring result from a testcross, but if the two genes assort independently, four types of offspring may occur.

In some recessive diseases, the demonstration of independent assortment may disclose that different genetic factors underlie what appears to be phenotypically the same disease. Thus, if two parents who appear to have the same recessive disorder (and would therefore be homozygous) have normal children, the inference that the parents do not have the same abnormal gene despite similar clinical manifestations is a good one. Ideas concerning allelism of certain genes determining proteins can be deduced from studies of protein structure. Alterations in a single polypeptide will probably be determined by alleles, as in the β polypeptide chain of hemoglobin. Nonallelic genes would be expected to control different polypeptides or proteins.

While in Figure 4, the α and β loci of hemoglobin are depicted on separate chromosome pairs, the available data would also be compatible with their presence on a single chromosome but separated by a considerable distance. In the latter circumstance the presence of parental genotypes (normal and double heterozygous) in the offspring would result from crossing-over. Each choromosome must carry many genes, and when two genes are very near each other on the chromosome, the likelihood of crossing-over is small. Thus by family studies of traits in humans it may not be possible to distinguish allelism from close linkage. (Differences in gene products may be used to favor linkage over allelism.) When genes are located farther apart on the same chromosome, the chances of crossing-over during meiosis increase; as a result of crossing-over the genes on opposite members of a chromosome pair in the parent will lie on the same chromosome in the gamete. (The importance of crossing-over for rearrangement of genes should be recalled: it results in the transmission of genes from either grandparent on the same chromosome.) If the genes lie sufficiently far apart on the same chromosome, crossing-over may be so frequent that pedigree data will suggest independent assortment. For demonstration of linkage, then, the loci must be at a distance sufficiently small that the recombinant types are encountered less frequently than in the 1:1:1:1 ratios which would result from independent assortment.

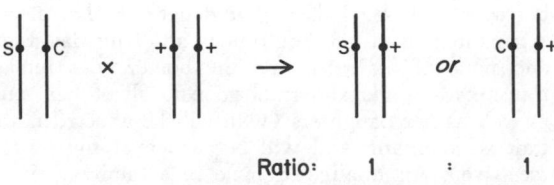

Ratio: 1   :   1

Fig. 3. Segregation of allelic genes for Hb S and Hb C. Vertical bars indicate portions of chromosome. Note that none of the offspring has either parental genotype. Studies of offspring of a testcross, i.e., marriage of heterozygote for two abnormal traits to a normal, is very useful for this type of analysis.

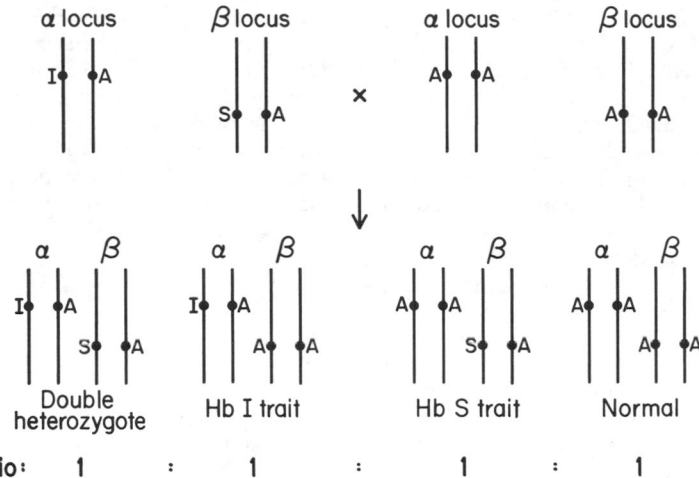

Fig. 4. Independent assortment of α- and β-chain loci appear in offspring. Note that four types of offspring may be observed from a testcross. Sufficient data are not available for choosing either independent assortment or linkage as the determining factor for the α and β Hb loci in humans.

As a result of crossing-over, genes which were originally in the *trans* position or linked in repulsion come to lie on the same chromosome, in the *cis* position or linked in coupling. The results of a testcross for two traits in the *cis* position will differ from the results if the genes are in the *trans* position. A theoretical example of studies of linkage in the *trans* position is depicted in Figure 5 (top): if two factors A and B (whose corresponding normal alleles are a and b) are observed to segregate in the offspring of the mating AaBb × aabb in the following ratios Aabb (40) + aaBb (40) + AaBb (10) + aabb (10), the genes for A and B are neither independent nor allelic. The less frequent types (AaBb and aabb) are the recombinants which resulted from crossing-over. Linkage and the relative distances between loci can be deduced from such pedigree data: the proportion of recombinants increases with the distance between loci. In the third type of offspring in the example of Figure 5 (top), genes A and B have come to lie on the same chromosome and are linked in coupling. Note in Figure 5 (bottom) that a testcross for linkage in coupling will result in predominantly parental types (AaBb or aabb) in the offspring. Whether linkage is in coupling or in repulsion can usually be established from studies of the parents of the double heterozygotes.

Data regarding autosomal linkage are difficult

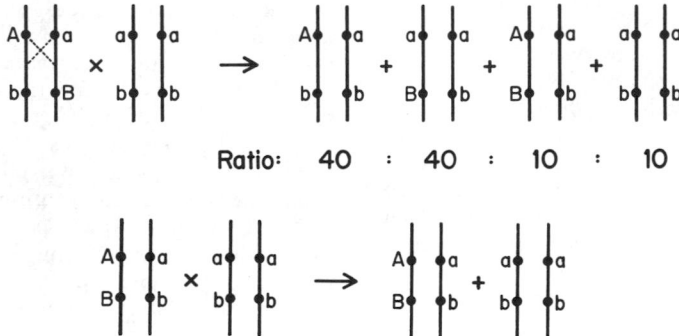

Fig. 5. *Top.* Linkage and crossing-over. Genes A and B are linked in repulsion. Testcross yields four classes of offspring of which the last two are recombinants resulting from crossing-over (indicated by dotted lines). Fewer of the offspring will be found in recombinant than in nonrecombinant classes. With linkage in repulsion, most of offspring receive either A or B and do not resemble parents. Chances for crossing-over increase as the chromosome segment separating the two genes becomes larger. *Bottom.* Offspring of testcross of individuals in third group of offspring in Figure 5A, in whom A and B are linked in coupling. Note that offspring have phenotypes like parents (AB/ab or ab/ab) in this case. Possible recombinant types are not given in this diagram.

to obtain, and only a few linkages are known. The ABO locus and the locus for the nail patella syndrome are linked; one type of hereditary elliptocytosis and the Rh locus are linked as are Lutheran blood groups and secretor. From Figure 2, it is clear that the δ chain of hemoglobin A$_2$ and the β chain of hemoglobin A are linked. The autosomes bearing linked genes have not been identified.

X LINKAGE. The mapping of the X chromosome is a great deal easier than the mapping of autosomes, since the fact that the genes are on the same chromosome is usually established from the pedigree. The occurrence of traits in the sons of mothers heterozygous for the two X-linked defects yields the necessary information; the father is irrelevant to the study since he transmits X-linked factors only to his daughters. To ascertain whether the X-linked traits were in repulsion or in coupling in the mother can be determined from studies of *her* father. Studies of X-linked genetic factors have been summarized by McKusick in a tentative map of the X chromosome: loci for Xg blood groups, G6PD, color blindness (deutan), and hemophilia appear to occur in that order.

ASSOCIATION OF BLOOD GROUPS WITH DISEASE. In recent years, the incidence of certain diseases has been noted to be greater in people with certain blood groups. For example, duodenal ulcer is more common in people with blood group O than in those with blood group A. Such association is not based upon genetic linkage; in large populations (as a result of crossing-over) genetic linkage is usually demonstrated for *loci* rather than for specific genes. The physiologic basis of association of disease with blood groups is not understood.

MULTIFACTORIAL TRAITS. While most of the traits that have been studied intensively from the biochemical standpoint are determined by single genes, numerous common traits are determined by several genes. Many of these multifactorial or quantitative traits, such as stature, skin color, or intelligence, are greatly influenced by environment. One of the outstanding features of multifactorial traits is the continuous distribution that is observed when the trait is measured in a large population. Such a continuous distribution contrasts with the discontinuous curves observed when unifactorial traits are studied, for in the latter case values may correspond closely to normal, homozygous, and in some cases heterozygous states. Statistical approaches to the evaluation of multifactorial traits are based on observation of resemblances among relatives.

Twin Studies

Studies of traits of monozygotic and dizygotic twins (Sec. 2.12) have long been used in distinguishing the effects of heredity and environment. Definitive interpretation of zygosity may not be easy. Determinations of genetic markers—e.g., blood groups, red cell and serum proteins, and enzymes—can establish dizygosity, but definitive proof of monozygosity rests upon tests for these markers and on acceptance of skin grafts between the two individuals or, when available, on studies of the fetal membranes. All monochorionic twins are monozygotic, but some monozygotic twins will have two chorions and even two placentas. Twin studies in which the concordance for a given trait of monozygotic twins is compared with that of dizygotic twins are valuable in analysis of some genetic problems.

Population Genetics

Some of the concepts of population genetics facilitate appreciation of the genetic aspects of disease. The loci available for a gene and its allele will, in a population of diploid organisms, be twice the number of individuals. In systems in which two or more different gene products can be detected, as in the MN blood groups or the hemoglobins, gene frequency can be determined by a simple count. For example, in a population of 10,000 which includes 1,400 individuals with sickle-cell trait, 50 individuals with sickle-cell anemia (homozygous for Hb S without other β chain abnormalities), and 8,550 individuals with normal hemoglobin, the gene frequency is as follows:

$$\text{Hb S} \ \frac{1,400 + (2 \times 50)}{20,000 \ (\text{total no. of genes})} = 0.075$$

$$\text{Hb A} \ \frac{1,400 + (2 \times 8,550)}{20,000} = 0.925$$

The Hardy-Weinberg principle indicates that the genetic structure of a large, stable, randomly mating population will be constant in successive generations. Observations on gene and genotype frequencies are useful in deciding about the equilibrium of a population. The gene frequency of a given trait is the proportion of the loci in a population occupied by that gene: hence the sum of the frequencies of all the alleles for a given locus will be unity. If p designates the frequency of Hb β^A and q of Hb β^S (p + q = 1), the observed value of either p or q may be used to calculate the chances that an individual will have two β^A genes (p^2), two β^S genes (q^2), or be heterozygous (2pq). In the example cited, gene frequency for Hb S and Hb A was determined by simple counting; calculation of expected genotype frequencies from values of p or q may indicate a significant departure from equilibrium, i.e., the observed frequency of one genotype may be quite different from that expected from gene frequency. For example, if nine (instead of 50) patients with sickle-cell anemia, 1,400 with sickle-cell trait, and 8,591 with normal hemoglobin had been observed in the population of 10,000, the value for q (Hb β^S) from counting would be 0.0709 and by calculation from q^2 $\frac{9}{10,000}$ would be 0.03. This population with frequencies of 14 percent sickle-cell trait and about 0.1 percent sickle-cell anemia would not be in equilibrium. Mutation, losses of homozygotes, immigration, and nonrandom mating will all obviously disturb the equilibrium, but in the absence of such factors, gene frequency will remain stable from generation to generation.

In addition to appraisal of the equilibrium of a population, calculations based upon the binomial or Hardy-Weinberg law find extensive use in studies of recessive diseases. If q^2 represents the incidence of a recessively determined disease, e.g., $1/10,000$, then q, the gene frequency, will be $\sqrt{1/10,000} = 1/100$. Since $p + q = 1$, the incidence of the remaining genotypes can be calculated: $p^2 = (99/100)^2 = 98.01\%$ (normals), $2\ pq = 2 \times 1/100 \times 99/100 = 1.98\%$ (heterozygotes). Such arithmetic demonstrates the strikingly high incidence of carriers for rare recessive disorders.

The unusual frequencies of certain traits (or diseases) in a population derived from a small ancestral group is explained by "genetic drift." McKusick has shown that in certain Pennsylvania Amish, descended from a few immigrants, the incidence of a very rare recessively determined disease, dwarfism-polydactyly, suggests a carrier (heterozygote) rate of about 13 percent in that population. One of the small group of original Amish emigres must have been a carrier for this gene, and its present high incidence represents the result of genetic drift. Genetic drift obviously will occur largely in small populations which for geographical or social reasons tend to marry within the group (isolates).

POLYMORPHISM. Traits that exist in a population in two or more discontinuous forms are said to be polymorphic. Sex as well as eye color are examples of polymorphism. When genes result in genetic death (i.e., failure of the individual to reproduce at the usual rate), as in sickle-cell anemia, a gradual loss of these genes from the population under study results. To maintain a polymorphism for deleterious genes, replacement of the genes lost by death of homozygotes is necessary. Obviously, different mechanisms might exist for such replenishment: (1) the mutation rate might be high enough to maintain the gene frequency, (2) families in which losses of homozygotes have occurred might deliberately have more children to make up for the losses, or (3) there might be some selective advantage of heterozygotes over normal homozygotes. The latter mechanism, called balanced polymorphism, has been invoked to explain the high incidence of sickle-cell trait in certain areas of Africa where homozygotes for hemoglobin S surely have a low reproduction rate. There is evidence to suggest that in these areas, children with sickle-cell trait are more resistant to fatal cerebral malaria than are children with normal hemoglobin. Thus, the genes for Hb S lost in patients with sickle-cell anemia are balanced by the loss of genes for Hb A in malaria, and a high incidence of Hb S trait is preserved. It seems probable that balanced polymorphism (or selective advantage of the heterozygote) explains the persistence of many genes that result in genetic death in affected homozygotes, but the specific advantage conferred by heterozygosity in areas with a variety of now disappearing endemic diseases may in many instances never be clarified.

CONSANGUINITY. The known increase in frequency of recessive diseases in the offspring of consanguineous marriages lends support to the notion that such marriages are not desirable. Each individual may be presumed to carry several deleterious recessive genes which will not be expressed in his offspring unless his marital partner carries the same genes. The chance that the offspring of two related parents will be homozygous for a given gene increases with the degree of relationship and is expressed as the coefficient of inbreeding (F). Values for F are $\frac{1}{8}$ for offspring of uncle-niece marriage and $\frac{1}{16}$ for children of first cousins. In families in which a rare recessive disease has been observed, the chances that a child will be affected are obviously greatly increased by consanguinity of the parents. However, despite the sound theoretic objection to consanguineous marriages, most of the offspring of first-cousin marriages in families lacking a history of recessive disease are healthy, a fact that may help alleviate the panic that sweeps some families when first-cousin marriages are announced.

REFERENCES

Baglioni, C. The fusion of two peptide chains in hemoglobin Lepore and its interpretation as a genetic deletion. Proc. Nat. Acad. Sci. U.S., 48:1880, 1962.

Carter, C. O. Human Heredity. Baltimore, Penguin Books, Inc., 1962.

Court Brown, W. M. Human Population Cytogenetics. Amsterdam, North-Holland Publishing Company, 1967.

Harris, H. Molecular basis of hereditary disease. Brit. Med. J., 1:135-141, 1968.

Kirkman, H. N., Riley, H. D., and Crowell, B. B. Different enzymic expressions of mutants of human glucose-6-phosphate dehydrogenase. Proc. Nat. Acad. Sci. U.S., 46:938, 1960.

Knudson, A. G., Jr. Genetics and Disease. New York, The Blakiston Division, McGraw-Hill Book Co., 1965.

Lyon, M. F. Gene action in the X-chromosome of the mouse (Mus musculus L). Nature, 190:372, 1961.

McKusick, V. A. Human Genetics, 2nd ed. Englewood Cliffs, N.J., Prentice-Hall, Inc., 1969.

——— Mendelian Inheritance in Man. Catalogs of Autosomal Dominant, Autosomal Recessive and X-Linked Phenotypes, 2nd ed. Baltimore, The Johns Hopkins Press, 1968.

Perutz, M. F., and Lehmann, H. Molecular pathology of human hemoglobin. Nature, 219:902-909, 1968.

Roberts, J. A. F. Introduction to Medical Genetics, 4th ed. London, Oxford University Press, Inc., 1967.

7.4

DEVELOPMENTAL GENETICS

S. GLUECKSOHN-WAELSCH

All biologic form and function, including processes of development, are under genetic control; the field that deals with the mechanisms by which genes act in development and differentiation is known as developmental genetics. Although its primary concern is with stages between fertilization and birth, in a broader sense developmental genetics covers problems of gene action throughout the lifetime of the organism. Until molecular studies revealed the concrete physicochemical nature of the genetic material, the concept of the gene had remained an abstraction defined primarily in operational terms. Since the material basis of the gene and the mechanisms of its primary action have been revealed, the domain of developmental genetics is frequently considered to be restricted to processes at the primary level of gene action, such as the transcription into mRNA of the genetic messages encoded in the nucleotide sequences of DNA, and their translation on the ribosomes into amino acid sequences. However, this summary will not deal with these aspects of gene action. Instead, attention will be focused on development and its genetic control after the synthesis of the immediate gene product has occurred, and the manifestation of the phenotype at the level of cells, tissues, and organs. Particular attention will be paid to the problem of congenital malformations.

Chromosomes and Development

It has been known since the turn of the century, as the result of the experimental studies of Boveri, that chromosomes, the carriers of genes, control development, and that normal development requires a full set of chromosomes.

More recent studies of specific congenital abnormalities associated with either deficiency or excess of chromosomes find their theoretic basis in the ingenious experiments and the inductive reasoning of Boveri.

The relevance of studies of developmental genetics to problems of pediatrics is readily apparent from the few examples discussed here. The role of genes during development extends from the control of protein and enzyme structure and synthesis to all phases of morphogenesis. Throughout development there appears to be a well-determined temporal and spatial pattern which underlies the sequential activation of different genes in differentiating cells, tissues, and organs. Moreover, the reaction of the developing organism to a variety of noxious agents is also under

genetic control, and susceptibility and resistance to teratogenic agents vary depending on the presence of different genes. Among the external agents causing chromosomal abnormalities are viruses, chemicals, and ionizing radiations. In view of the ever-increasing chance of exposure to these noxious agents which are part of our modern environment, the role of medical cytogenetics in its relation to developmental abnormalities continues to grow in significance. Quantitative estimates yield a figure of 0.5 percent as the overall incidence of chromosomal abnormalities responsible for congenital defects at birth in the general population. When anomalies of number and structure are included, the overall incidence of chromosomal abnormalities that are severe enough to cause prenatal death becomes considerably higher, and is estimated to be more than 5 percent.

Any attempt to understand or evaluate the role of genes during development must take into account the most characteristic property of any mammalian embryo, namely, the high degree of interdependence of its parts on all levels of development. The diversity of biochemical and metabolic processes, and the interaction of cells, tissues, and organs with each other, account for the fact that a mutational change of a single gene may lead to a multiplicity of manifestations. A better understanding of the mechanisms of the genetic control of all aspects of development is an important prerequisite for possible prevention and control of abnormalities of development.

Single Genes Affecting Development

A considerable proportion of single gene mutations, autosomal as well as sex-linked, produce effects clearly manifest at birth either in the form of morphologic or metabolic abnormalities. The analysis of mechanisms by which these gene-controlled disturbances arise falls within the domain of developmental genetics. The methods of analysis require observations of sequential stages of development and experimental procedures that are not applicable to humans. However, experimental material is available for study in the large variety of mutations in other mammals, particularly the laboratory mouse; studies of these mutants have revealed mechanisms of gene-controlled abnormal development which may apply to similar conditions in man.

Congenital renal agenesis and dysplasia may be caused by mutant genes in both man and mouse. The developmental mechanics resulting in these renal anomalies have been studied in detail in the mouse. It has been shown that inductive interaction between ureteric bud and metanephrogenic mesenchyme normally required for kidney morphogenesis fails to occur in mutant embryos. The reason for this failure to interact seems to lie in general growth retardation which affects the two primordia differentially. Therefore the ureteric bud, which is retarded in its growth, does not reach the metanephrogenic mesenchyme when the latter is ready to react to the inductive stimulus with further differentiation into secretory tubules. The effects of this mutation on temporal and integrative aspects of kidney differentiation clearly indicate that genes normally control these phases of differentiation.

Pleiotropic Effects

Developmental studies of mutant gene effects are particularly valuable when single mutations appear to cause multiple defects, a phenomenon referred to as *pleiotropy*. The mutations causing macrocytic anemia in the mouse are also responsible for abnormalities involving hair pigment and the gonads. The mutation causing kidney agenesis produces skeletal anomalies as well. Human congenital defects due to the action of pleiotropic genes include among many others, acrocephalosyndactyly with malformations of skull and extremities; osteogenesis imperfecta with brittle bones, blue sclerae, and otosclerosis; and Marfan's syndrome with anomalies of the eye, the skeleton, and the cardiovascular system. In the developmental analysis of pleiotropic effects caused by a single gene mutation, attempts are made to find the earliest and most immediate defect that could be responsible for all subsequent anomalies. As a result of such studies, a so-called pedigree of causes may be constructed where the original cause is the immediate effect of the mutant gene and all others arise from it secondarily. However, in the majority of cases it has not been possible to fit all pleiotropic effects into such "pedigrees" with ease. A good example is offered by the mutations that simultaneously cause abnormalities of erythropoiesis, of gonadal development, and of pigmentation. In spite of careful studies it has not been possible to establish a series of sequential effects connecting the three developmental systems so that the abnormality of one might be responsible for those affecting the others, as should be the case in a typical "pedigree of causes." It may be assumed that not one but three closely linked genes enclosed in a deletion are the cause of the abnormalities of the three systems. However, since one series of alleles at the W-locus, and another independent gene, *S1*, cause the same associated anomalies, this explanation of a deletion of three closely linked factors is unlikely. The observations of the pleiotropic effects indicate a close developmental relationship between the three systems, the nature of which remains to be demonstrated.

Previous developmental studies of gene-caused pleiotropic effects have revealed the existence of a variety of processes of developmental mechanics in mammals. In such investigations genes have been exploited as tools that cause defects of the type that can be produced experimentally in lower-vertebrate embryos. Retrograde studies of the consequences of such gene-caused defects have, in a number of instances, elucidated the chain of developmental processes leading to the final abnormality. Thus, the analysis of a series of mutations at the so-called T-locus in the mouse has revealed the existence of inductive interaction between notochord-mesoderm and the differentiating nervous system, as well as other mechanisms of early vertebrate development.

Penetrance and Expressivity

The genetic concepts of penetrance and expressivity have strong developmental implications. A dominant mutation with *reduced penetrance* is defined as one that manifests itself in only a certain proportion of heterozygotes. This reduced penetrance may be due to various causes, such as the protection which other genes or the maternal environment provides for at least a proportion of embryos to prevent the potential damage inflicted upon them by the mutant gene.

Expressivity refers to the degree of manifestation of a gene; the same gene may have slight and hardly noticeable effects or it may cause defects of considerable scope. Clinically, variable expressivity of a gene results in a disease state of greater or lesser severity. Mechanisms similar to those described for penetrance and operating during prenatal life may be responsible for the observed variations of gene expressivity.

A mutation in the mouse affecting kidney differentiation may serve as an example to illustrate developmental aspects of the concepts of penetrance and expressivity. This is a dominant mutation, and heterozygotes display a spectrum of phenotypes ranging from total absence of kidneys to normal appearance of these organs. In a study of 167 newborn heterozygotes, 6 percent were found to be perfectly normal and 13 percent had no kidneys at all. The remaining 81 percent showed kidney abnormalities of varying degrees. This dominant mutation, therefore, has a penetrance of about 94 percent, and an expressivity varying from reduction in size to total absence of kidneys. Developmental studies indicated that the varying degrees of expressivity could be traced back to different degrees of growth retardation of the budding ureter in early embryogeny. If the retardation was considerable, metanephrogenic mesenchyme failed to differentiate any kidney tubules; moderate retardation reduced the number of tubules and subsequently the size of the kidneys.

Prenatal Resistance and Susceptibility

Genes are involved in the control of resistance and susceptibility to a variety of agents during prenatal development. In mice, genetic analysis has revealed the genetic control of periods of susceptibility of embryos to several teratogens, such as those causing cleft palate. The different gene-controlled sensitive periods are responsible for the different effects of identical teratogens in genetically different animals. It is known that the palate of the mouth forms as the result of fusion of the palatal shelves. It has been shown that closure of the palate normally occurs at different times of development in different strains of mice. Those strains in which closure occurs early are less susceptible to the effects of teratogens than are those strains where closure occurs late. Gene-determined differences in the temporal pattern of a developmental process, therefore, may serve to explain differences in resistance and susceptibility to teratogens of different inbred strains of mice.

Lethal Genes

Genes causing prenatal or perinatal death in mammals are referred to as lethal genes. These have played a prominent role in the analysis of mammalian development and differentiation because of their particularly drastic and thus easily recognizable effects. A considerable proportion of prenatal and perinatal deaths in man is likely to be due to lethal genes which interfere with normal development and differentiation. Knowledge of possible mechanisms by which such lethal genes produce their effects has also been obtained from experimental material. A recessive mutation in the mouse has been described which produces a deficiency of all skeletal musculature and fetal death in homozygotes. In addition to the general and severe deficiency of all skeletal musculature, head abnormalities such as micrognathia and cleft palate were observed. Other skeletal abnormalities involved the cervical vertebrae, scapula, clavicle, and sternum. In contrast to the severe degeneration of voluntary muscles, the heart muscle appeared perfectly normal, and even nonviable homozygotes dissected immediately after birth showed a strong and regular heartbeat. Death of the homozygotes was ascribed to the muscular abnormality of thorax and diaphragm, and the subsequent inability to breathe.

The developmental study of this mutation revealed abnormalities of differentiation and subsequent degeneration of embryonic skeletal muscle cells, in contrast to perfectly normal differentiation of cardiac and smooth muscles. A striking additional abnormality was observed in the form of severe fetal edema. These abnormalities could be traced back to those stages of myogenesis when mononucleated myoblasts differentiate into myotubes with cross striations. All voluntary muscular components were affected regardless of gestational age. Thus, thoracic or limb musculature was found to differentiate abnormally three days sooner than tongue musculature, which eventually showed identical abnormalities. It may be concluded, therefore, that the mutation interferes specifically with skeletal muscle cell differentiation and is independent of time and stage of development.

This myopathy appears to differ from the known hereditary muscular dystrophies in man, where degeneration of fully differentiated muscle fibers is found rather than failure of initial differentiation. However, experimental studies of the muscular dysgenesis mutation have shown that under in vitro conditions the mutant myoblasts can differentiate considerably beyond the stage attained in vivo, and can form normal-appearing striated muscle fibers which, however, fail to undergo normal contractions. This mutation has been described in some detail because it may serve as a model system for the elucidation of similar but experimentally inaccessible developmental muscle abnormalities in man.

Phenocopies

The "phocomelia" mutation in the mouse is of particular significance because it produces a phenotype that bears a close resemblance to the abnormalities of limb development observed in so-called thalidomide babies. The similarity of a phenotype caused by environmental agents to one resulting from the effects of deleterious genes is implied in the term "phenocopy." Identical phenoytpes may owe their existence to a variety of causes, of both genetic and environmental nature. Cleft palate, for example, may be due to the effect of different genes and may also result from the exposure of the pregnant mother to teratogenic agents. Renal agenesis in the mouse may result from different mutant genes. Nervous system abnormalities, such as anencephaly, may arise from the action of dominant or recessive genes; they may also result from maternal exposure to radiation during gestation. Similarly, vitamin deficiencies of the mother during gestation period may lead to developmental defects indistinguishable from those caused by certain mutant genes. An important point in considering congenital defects is that the phenotype in itself does not reflect a specific genotype or a particular etiologic agent, and that different genotypes may produce similar or identical phenotypes. The developing mammalian embryo appears to be limited in the number of ways in which it may react to a variety of abnormal stimuli stemming from the action of genes or environmental factors.

Inborn Errors of Metabolism

Developmental genetics encompasses not only morphologic but also biochemical and metabolic aspects of development and their genetic control. A large proportion of genetically caused inborn errors of metabolism have their earliest effects during embryonic stages despite the homeostatic action of the maternal environment. An example of such a prenatal event is the recessive mutation in the mouse which causes absence of glucose-6-phosphatase activity. Homozygotes die within a few hours after birth as the result of severe hypoglycemia. However, breeding data reveal a significant deficiency of homozygotes even at birth, suggesting prenatal death of a proportion of such homozygotes. These deaths cannot be ascribed to prenatal hypoglycemia since fetal blood glucose levels were found to be normal, presumably because of the control exerted by the maternal organism. It is also a fact that, in the normal animal, enzyme activity does not appear until just before birth. It is conceivable that glucose-6-phosphatase which in the mature organism is involved in the conversion of glucose-6-phosphatase to glucose, may have functions other than that of releasing glucose to the circulation during embryonic development. The failure of such a function may be responsible for the observed prenatal death as well as the morphologic abnormalities found in a proportion of mutant homozygotes. There is little information about the possible intracellular effects on differentiation of enzymes known to be involved in metabolic processes. A genetically determined enzyme deficiency or abnormality may manifest itself in effects on differentiation even within a prenatally normal maternal environment.

A large number of congenital disorders in man with abnormal storage of glycogen produce the various glycogen storage diseases, each of which appears to be due to different mutant genes and different enzyme deficiencies. One of these, von Gierke's disease, which is due to a deficiency of glucose-6-phosphatase, is similar to the genetically caused glucose-6-phosphatase deficiency in the mouse. The latter offers a model system for further studies of the human disorder. In the mouse the mutation causing the enzyme deficiency behaves as a lethal gene, and homozygotes die within a few hours after birth. Death is most likely the result of severe hypoglycemia, since newborn homozygotes may be kept alive for a brief period by the subcutaneous injection of glucose. The interpretation of this mutation as a straightforward gene-enzyme defect encountered difficulties when the expected dosage effect could not be demonstrated in the heterozygous parents. In general, autosomal mutations affecting enzyme activity express themselves in heterozygotes with mean values for enzyme activity intermediate between those for normal and abnormal homozygotes. The failure to identify such a dosage effect in mice heterozygous for the glucose-6-phosphatase mutation raises the question whether this is indeed a mutation of the structural gene synthesizing the enzyme or one of a regulatory or controlling gene affecting a different facet of enzyme production. The additional pleiotropic effects of the glucose-6-phosphatase mutation in the mouse on ultrastructure of pigment granules raise the possibility that mutational effects on membrane structure of the endoplasmic reticulum leads to an abnormality of binding sites for the enzyme. It is possible that human inborn errors of metabolism also include those that reflect mutational changes of genes other than structural loci.

Genetic Control of Differentiation

Determination

Another aspect of developmental genetics is concerned with the role of genes not only in the synthesis of essential enzymes and proteins but also in the control and regulation of *differentiation*. The complexity of organization of the mammalian organism requires a large number of regulatory and controlling functions. These are carried out by corresponding genes, and also by genes involved in synthesis of enzymes and proteins. The great increase of DNA content in cells of higher organisms as compared with those of bacteria has been interpreted as reflecting possibly the need for controlling elements in complex processes of morphogenesis. Mechanisms of genetic regulation of morphogenetic processes are under study.

One of the most puzzling problems of differentiation is that of determination. At a certain stage of development, the multitude of developmental potentialities of a particular cell is narrowed down until the cell is channeled into one specific developmental pathway. Thus, the cell has become determined to differentiate into one type only, such as nerve, or cartilage, or muscle cell. This process of determination does not apparently involve a change in the cell's genetic make-up. Not much is known about the specific role of genes in determination; terms such as *derepression* or *repression* of genes are descriptive rather than analytical.

Among the questions to be answered is that of the reversibility of determination. Is a cell or a tissue that has been determined to give rise to a certain cell or tissue type, for example nervous tissue, capable, under the appropriate conditions, of differentiating into a totally different cell type, such as muscle? In transplantation experiments in Drosophila, Hadorn was able to demonstrate that determination may be reversed. He showed that, under certain experimental conditions, tissues already determined to form leg structures, for example, can be made to differentiate into head structures. This phenomenon has been called "transdetermination." Its discovery and interpretation for the role and state of genes in differentiation represent significant progress in modern developmental genetics.

Nuclear Transplantation

The question of gene activation and inactivation during development, and of the extent to which such inactivation is reversible, has been the subject of another important experimental approach, namely that of nuclear transplantation. These experiments have emphasized the effect of cytoplasmic factors on the pattern of gene activity in the nucleus. The mechanisms of differentiation and determination have been shown to involve significant nuclear-cytoplasmic interactions. Possible contributions to the elucidation of mechanisms of gene activation and inactivation during differentiation may come from further studies of the X-inactivation hypothesis of Lyon.

Development of Human Hemoglobins

One of the most intriguing areas of developmental genetics is that of the human hemoglobins. During the course of fetal life, the first hemoglobin is the Gower-1 type, a tetramer consisting of embryonic chains (ϵ) exclusively; it occurs in embryos of less than 8.5 cm. Subsequently α chains are synthesized and hemoglobin Gower-2 ($\alpha_2\epsilon_2$) is found before the twelfth week of intrauterine life. After the twelfth week, ϵ chains are no longer produced and γ-chain synthesis, which occurs at 9 weeks, takes over; these combine with the α chains to form hemoglobin F. Beta-chain production commences at about 13 weeks and continues throughout prenatal life on a low scale; it rises sharply at birth when γ-chain production starts to decline. Synthesis of the δ chain of the minor human hemoglobin commences during fetal development, and continues at a rate approximately 1/40 of that of β-chain synthesis. The developmental history of human hemoglobins reflects a sequential pattern of gene activation and inactivation. The question has been asked whether a specific organic site might be correlated with the synthesis of a specific hemoglobin type. In man this is not the case; the fetal spleen, liver, and bone marrow cells are all capable of synthesizing both adult and fetal hemoglobins. There also seems to be no way of correlating the development of specific hemoglobins at the molecular level with different sites of ontogenesis of erythrocytes. The remarkable stability of hemoglobin messenger RNA has been demonstrated in a variety of organisms, including rabbits and chickens. Evidence for such stability comes also from the persistence of hemoglobin synthesis in enucleated mammalian reticulocytes.

References

Averbach, R. Analysis of the developmental effects of a lethal mutation in the house mouse. J. Exp. Zool., 127:305, 1954.
Davidson, Eric H. Gene Activity in Early Development. New York, Academic Press, Inc., 1968.
Erickson, R. P., Gluecksohn-Waelsch, S., and Cori, C. F. Glucose-6-phosphatase deficiency caused by radiation-induced alleles at the albino locus in the mouse. Proc. Nat. Acad. Sci. U.S.A., 59:437, 1968.
Fraser, F. C. Some genetic aspects of teratology. In Wilson, J. G., and Warkany, J., eds., Teratology, Principles and Techniques. Chicago, The University of Chicago Press, 1965, pp. 21-38.
Gluecksohn-Waelsch, S. Lethal genes and analysis of differentiation. Science, 142:1269, 1963.
——— Genetic control of mammalian differentiation. In Geerts, S. J., ed., Genetics Today. New York, Pergamon Press, Inc., 1965, pp. 209-219.
——— and Erickson, R. P. The T-locus of the mouse: implications for mechanisms of development. In Moscona, A. A., and Monroy, A., eds., Current Topics in Developmental Biology, Vol. V. New York, Academic Press, Inc., 1970.
Hadorn, E. Dynamics of determination. In Locke, M., ed., Major Problems on Developmental Biology. New York, Academic Press, Inc., 1966, pp. 85-104.
Saxen, L., and Rapola, J. Congenital Defects. New York, Holt, Rinehart & Winston, Inc., 1969.

7.5
HUMAN CYTOGENETICS

HAROLD P. KLINGER

In 1956, the number of chromosomes in normal man was found to be, not 48 as thought earlier, but rather 46, including 22 pairs of autosomes plus the sex chromosomes, XX in females and XY in males.

Human chromosomes can be prepared for study in several ways. In the *direct method,* the dividing cells of a bone marrow aspirate are arrested in the metaphase stage of division by incubating them for a few hours in the presence of colchicine. Treatment with hypotonic solution results in swelling of the cells and separation of the chromosomes. The cells are fixed in this condition, spread on slides, and either dried quickly or squashed to disperse the chromosomes on one plane. In the *indirect methods,* peripheral blood leucocytes (stimulated to divide with phytohemagglutinin), skin, or other tissue cells are grown in vitro until active cell proliferation is obtained. Colchicine is used as before, and processing is essentially the same as for bone marrow. The slides can then be stained and the chromosomes counted and photographed at a magnification of about 1,000×.

The chromosomes at metaphase consist of two identical *chromatids* joined at the *centromere.* If the centromere connects the chromatids near their ends, the chromosome is called *acrocentric;* all other chromosomes are *metacentric.* The chromatid constriction at the centromere is called the *primary constriction.* Some chromosomes often show a *secondary constriction* at a specific site. The acrocentric chromosomes, with the exception of the Y, have such secondary constrictions on the short arms, leaving small chromatin knobs or satellites at their very ends.

The chromosomes are classified (Table 2) by first arranging morphologically homologous pairs (except

TABLE 2. *Description of Human Mitotic Chromosomes**

Group 1-3 (A)	Largest chromosomes with approximately median centromeres (metacentric), readily distinguished from each other by size and centromere position.
Group 4-5 (B)	Large chromosomes with submedian centromeres (submetacentric) that are difficult to distinguish from each other.
Group 6-12 and X (C)	Medium-sized chromosomes with submedian centromeres. The X chromosome resembles the longer chromosomes in this group, especially chromosome 6, from which it is difficult to distinguish. This group is the one that presents most difficulty in identification of individual chromosomes. Four of the C group autosomes are comparatively metacentric. They are usually numbered 6, 7, 8, and 11. The X chromosome belongs to this subgroup. Three chromosomes are submetacentric and are usually numbered 9, 10, and 12.
Group 13-15 (D)	Medium-sized chromosomes with nearly terminal centromeres (acrocentric) all of which have satellites which are variably detectable.
Group 16-18 (E)	Rather short chromosomes with an approximately median centromere in chromosome 16 and submedian centromeres in 17 and 18.
Group 19-20 (F)	Short chromosomes with approximately median centromeres.
Group 21-22 and Y (G)	Very short, acrocentric chromosomes with satellites variably present on 21 and 22. The Y chromosome is similar, but tends to have somewhat more parallel long arms, and is usually larger than 21 or 22.

*Adapted from Chicago Conference on Standardization in Human Cytogenetics, Birth Defects: Original Article Series, II:2, 1966. The National Foundation, New York.

the X and Y) according to length. The relative length of the arms and the position of the centromere are then used as further criteria with which to divide the human chromosomes into seven groups (A to G). The group to which a particular chromosome belongs can always be determined, but it is not always possible to decide which member of the group it represents. The X chromosome cannot be distinguished morphologically from the other large metacentric chromosomes of the C group (Nos. 6–12). The Y can often, but not always, be distinguished from the G group (Nos. 21 and 22). (Only the autosome pairs receive numbers.) Sex chromatin findings and

the study of DNA replication patterns with autoradiographic methods allow more precise identification of the X and Y as well as of some of the autosomes.

SEXUAL DIMORPHISM OF INTERPHASE NUCLEI. In the epithelial cells of buccal mucosa of females and in most other somatic cells except the oogonia, a chromatin mass, the sex chromatin or Barr body, can be demonstrated in the interphase nucleus. The Barr body is not found in male somatic cells. Studies of these sex chromatin bodies in the anomalies of sex development indicate that, in nuclei with a diploid autosome set, the number of Barr bodies in a nucleus is one less than the number of X chromosomes. Thus, in Turner's syndrome (XO) "chromatin negativity" is common, in Klinefelter's (XXY) a single Barr body is seen, and in XXX females, two Barr bodies occur. The presence of a Y chromosome, even together with two or more X chromosomes, is regularly associated with phenotypic males. Evidence obtained from cell cultures exposed to labeled thymidine indicates that the Barr body probably represents the positively heteropyknotic and inactivated X chromosome predicted by the Lyon hypothesis. While Barr bodies can be found in a variety of somatic cells, the use of buccal mucosa cells is probably the easiest technique.

A nuclear appendage of the polymorphonuclear leucocyte of females, the "drumstick," may be analogous to the sex chromatin and is also useful for detecting indirectly the probable X chromosome constitution of an individual.

CHROMOSOME ABNORMALITIES. Most chromosome abnormalities found in man may be put into four groups: (1) excess or loss of one or more chromosomes, resulting in aneuploidy; (2) breakage and loss of a piece of a chromosome (deletions); (3) breakage of two chromosomes with fusion of all or parts of the fragments onto each other (translocations); and (4) splitting of the centromere the wrong way at mitosis so that one arm is lost and the other duplicated to form a perfectly symmetrical chromosome with genetically identical arms (isochromosome formation).

Chromosome mosaicism refers to the existence in an individual of cells of at least two different chromosome complements; it probably arises from nondisjunction or anaphase lagging of one or more chromosomes in mitotic divisions after fertilization. If both types of cells are viable after nondisjunction, then some cells may contain 45 chromosomes and others 47.

Of the many different chromosome abnormalities found in man (Table 3), only a few of the more important examples will be mentioned here. Others are described in more detail in the following section, and further details can be found in the reviews listed at the end of this chapter.

Reference has been made to the XO and XXY chromosome composition of Turner's syndrome and Klinefelter's syndrome, respectively. Both of these

TABLE 3.　*Representative Karyotype Designations (According to Chicago Conference, 1966)*

Numerical Aberrations

45,X	45 chromosomes, one X chromosome.
47,XXY	47 chromosomes, XXY sex chromosomes.
45,XX,C−	45 chromosomes, XX sex chromosomes, a missing C group chromosome.
48,XXY,G+	48 chromosomes, XXY sex chromosomes, an additional G group chromosome.
46,XY,18+,21−	46 chromosomes, XY sex chromosomes, an extra No. 18 and missing a No. 21.
45,X/46,XY	A chromosome mosaic with two cell types, one with 45 chromosomes and a single X, the other with 46 chromosomes and XY sex chromosomes.

Structural Alterations

46,XY,t(Bp−;Dq+) or 46,XY,t(Bp+;Dq−)	A balanced reciprocal translocation between the short arm of a B and the long arm of a D group chromosome.
45,XX,D−,G−,t(DqGq.+	45 chromosomes, XX sex chromosomes, one chromosome missing from the D group and one from the G group, their long arms having united to form a D/G translocation chromosome.

anomalies arise as a result of nondisjunction in meiosis or in one of the early mitotic divisions after fertilization. In Klinefelter's syndrome three to four X's may be found in addition to one or more Y chromosomes (Fig. 6). Turner's syndrome may be associated with deleted X's or with isochromosomes for either the short or long arms of the X. In both syndromes chromosomal mosaicism of many types is often found and occasionally the sex chromosome abnormality is associated with an autosomal abnormality.

The first abnormality of the autosomes to be described was the "trisomy-21" associated with most cases of Down's syndrome. Nondisjunction appears to be the mechanism for the thrice-represented small chromosome. The nondisjunction may occur in the oocyte during meiosis or in an early cleavage stage of the zygote.

Translocation of chromosomes 15 and 21 accounts for other cases of Down's syndrome. These subjects have 46 chromosomes with two normal chromosomes 21, one normal chromosome 15, and an unpaired large chromosome presumed to include chromosomes 15 and 21. In this instance, as in the simple trisomy, the genetic material of chromosome 21 is represented in triple dosage. Studies of the parents (phenotypically normal) usually reveal that one of them has 45 chromosomes, with only one chromosome 15 and 21, but with a large translocation chromosome that probably includes most of the genetic material of chromosomes 15 and 21. Gametes from such a parent (Fig. 7) might be of several chromosome types with respect to 15 and 21; they may be (1) normal 15 and 21 producing a potentially normal zygote; (2) translocation chromosome only, resulting in a phenotypic normal carrier like the parent; (3) normal 21 plus "translocation chromosome," producing a potential mongoloid zygote; (4) chromosome 15 alone, producing a zygote monosomic for 21. This condition is generally lethal since only a few cases with monosomy for 21 have been found to date. Certain instances of Down's syndrome in families appear to be based upon 15–21 translocation. Translocation of 21 to other chromosomes, e.g., 22, has also been observed, as have patients with an isochromosome 21, i.e., a chromosome containing the long arms of 21 in duplicate.

Nondisjunction seems to occur more frequently in the oocytes of older women, since the relative frequency of some trisomic syndromes increases with maternal age. As expected, women carrying the translocation transmit this abnormality at any stage of their reproducing life.

The offspring of females with Down's syndrome and normal fathers have included both normal and affected offspring; at meiosis the ovum would be expected to receive either one or two chromosomes 21, and in the latter case Down's syndrome would be expected. Almost all monozygotic but few dizygotic twins are concordant for Down's syndrome.

A deletion of part of the long arms of a G chromosome has been found in association with chronic myelogenous leukemia. This structurally abnormal chromosome, called the Philadelphia chromosome (Ph[1]), is found only in the white cells of the bone marrow and peripheral blood of most subjects with the chronic form of the disease but not in other somatic cells or in individuals with acute or atypical leukemias.

INDICATIONS FOR HUMAN CYTOGENETIC STUDIES. A complete chromosome analysis is time-consuming and expensive. For this reason most cytogenetic laboratories must select the cases they can study.

Sex chromatin studies, which are relatively simple to perform, are often adequate for clarifying the following diagnoses: Turner's syndrome (XO or X plus deleted X) in women with idiopathic amenorrhea; triple-X or multiple-X syndromes in females who may have amenorrhea and may be sterile; testicular feminization syndrome in women who are likewise sterile and have amenorrhea as well as a mass (testes) in the inguinal canal. The latter are chromatin negative with an XY sex chromosome

A

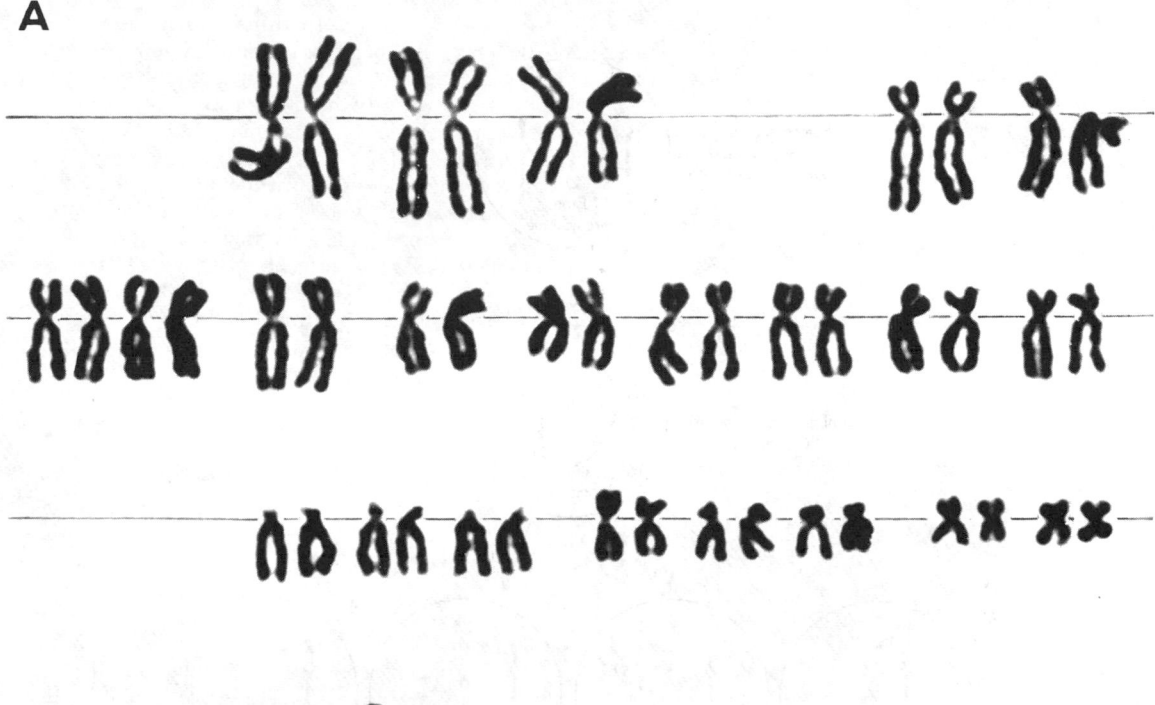

B

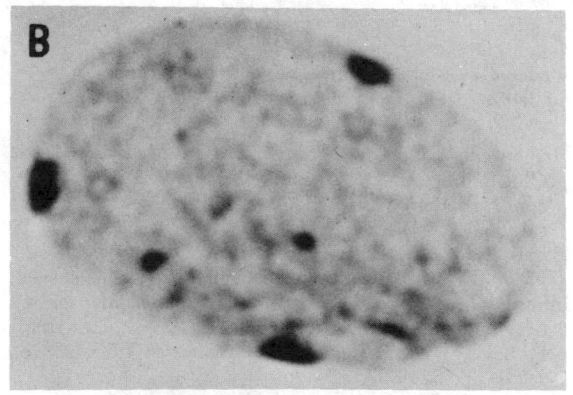

Fig. 6. A. Karyotype with 49 chromosomes (three extra X's) of a 12-year-old mentally deficient boy with undescended testes and skeletal and other anomalies. The four X chromosomes and the Y are at the left. B. Nucleus of the oral mucosa that contains three sex chromatin bodies, from the same patient.

complement. Further, Klinefelter's syndrome can be detected in males, even before puberty, because their cells contain one, two, or more sex chromatin bodies.

Much more time-consuming *chromosome analysis* is indicated in the following conditions: (1) in children born with major physical or mental defects of unknown cause and in those children without obvious defects who fail to grow for no known reason; (2) in parents of abnormal children in whom an inherited chromosomal abnormality such as translocation of 21 is suspected. This is particularly important if the parents are young and desire additional children; (3) in males or females with anomalies of the external genitalia or whose nuclear sex differs from the genital sex; (4) in females with primary or idiopathic amenorrhea who are sex chromatin positive. These may have an X isochromosome, a deleted X, or other structural aberration of the X chromosome or chromosomes; (5) in males with "idiopathic" aspermia or oligospermia; (6) in individuals where no cause for infertility can be determined; (7) in women who abort repeatedly; and (8) in families to which many congenitally abnormal children are born.

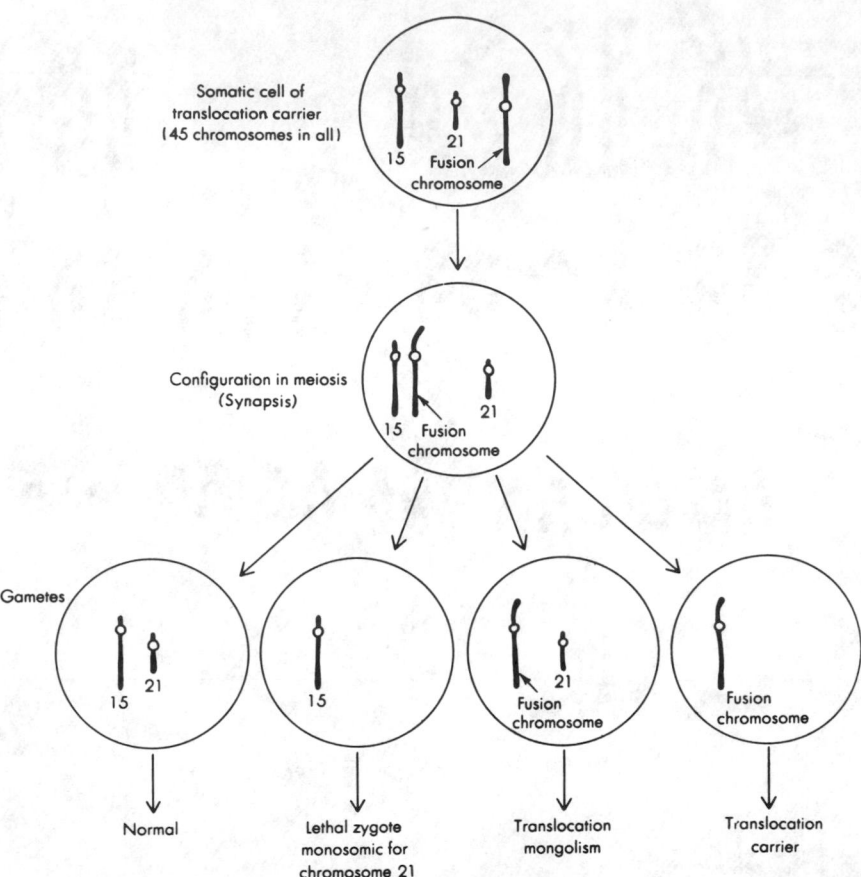

Fig. 7. Scheme of the chromosomal constitution of ova produced by a phenotypically normal woman carrying a 15-21 translocation. (Reproduced from McKusick; for further details see text.)

Karyotype Notation

The current nomenclature for designation of the human karyotype was adopted at a conference in 1966 at Chicago and represents a modification of previous recommendations (Denver, 1960; London, 1963). A description and recommended grouping of human mitotic chromosomes is summarized in Table 2. Several representative karyotype designations according to the new nomenclature are presented in Table 3.

References

Court Brown, W. M. Human Population Cytogenetics. New York, John Wiley & Sons, Inc., Interscience Publishers Division, 1967.

Gustavson, K. H. Down's Syndrome—A Clinical and Cytogenetical Investigation. Uppsala, Almqvist and Wiksells, 1964.

Hamerton, J. L., ed. Chromosomes in Medicine. Little Club Clinics in Developmental Medicine No. 5, London National Spastics Society and Heinemann Medical Books, 1962.

Harris, R. J. C., ed. Cytogenetics of Cells in Culture. New York and London, Academic Press, Inc., 1964.

Inhorn, S. L., and Opitz, J. M. Abnormalities of sex development. In Bloodworth, J. M. B., ed., Endocrine Pathology. Baltimore, The Williams & Wilkins Co., 1968, pp. 529-607.

Lindsten, J. The Nature and Origin of X Chromosome Aberrations in Turner's Syndrome. Stockholm, Almqvist and Wiksells, 1963.

Locke, M., ed. The Role of Chromosomes in Development. New York and London, Academic Press, Inc., 1964.

Lyon, M. F. Gene action in the X-chromosome of the mouse (Mus musculus L). Nature, 190:372, 1961.

McKusick, V. A. Human Genetics. Englewood Cliffs, N.J., Prentice-Hall, Inc., 1964.

Miller, O. J. The sex chromosome anomalies. Amer. J. Obstet. Gynec. U.S., 90:1078-1139, 1964.

Mittwoch, U. Sex Chromosomes. London and New York, Academic Press, Inc., 1967.

Moore, K. L., ed. The Sex Chromatin. Philadelphia and London, W. B. Saunders Co., 1966.

Ohno, S. Sex Chromosomes and Sex-Linked Genes. Berlin and New York, Springer-Verlag, 1967.

Overzier, C., ed. Intersexuality. New York and London, Academic Press, Inc., 1963.

Priest, J. H. Cytogenetics. Philadelphia, Lea and Febiger, 1969.

Turpin, R., and Lejeune, J. Les Chromosomes Humains. Paris, Gauthier-Villars, 1965.

Yunis, J. J., ed. Human Chromosome Methodology. New York and London, Academic Press, Inc., 1965.

7.6
DERMATOGLYPHIC ANALYSIS

HAROLD M. NITOWSKY

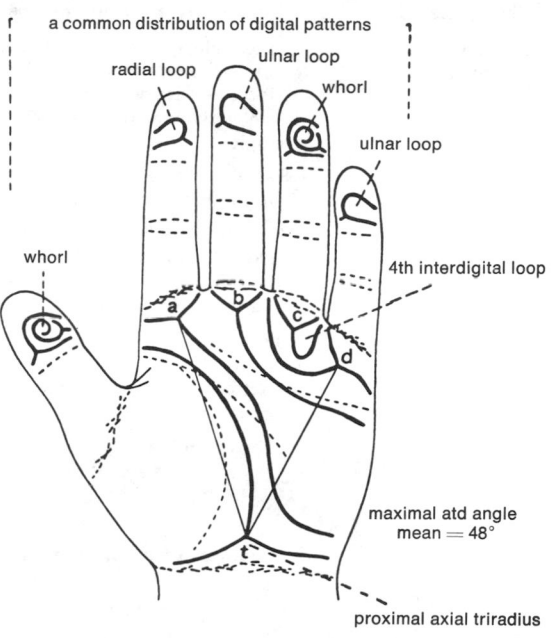

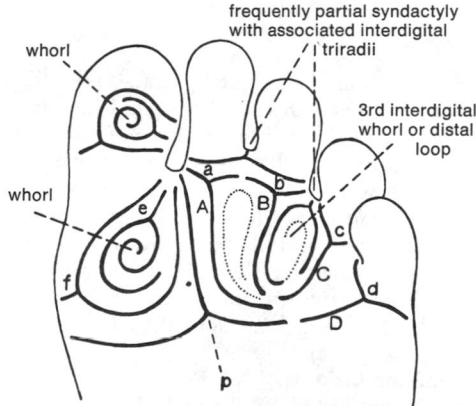

Fig. 8. Diagram of palm and sole showing pattern area, triradii, and finger pattern types. The solid lines and dotted lines denote the dermal ridge configurations, and the dashes within the palm represent the creases.

Epidermal ridges on the volar aspect of the hands and feet form a variety of pattern configurations termed *dermatoglyphics*. Although the ridge configurations are altered in characteristic ways in a variety of disorders, these alterations have seldom been pathognomonic for a particular condition. Rather, they simply provide additional data which, viewed in relation to the total pattern of malformation, may enhance the clinician's capacity to arrive at a specific overall diagnosis.

Ridges develop in relation to volar pads. The latter appear at about the sixth week of gestation and attain maximal size by the 12th to 13th week. At this time, patches of elevated ridges become evident and grow and coalesce as the volar pads regress. By the fourth month of fetal life the epidermal ridges are well developed. Palmar creases develop during the second and third months of intrauterine life. Once completed, the epidermal ridges and palmar creases remain unchanged, except in size, for life. Although genetic factors play an important role in determining ridge configurations, nongenetic factors may exert an influence as well. Variability of patterns is sufficiently great so that no two individuals have identical ridge patterns.

Dermatoglyphic patterns may be classified into various groups as follows:

A. Finger Patterns. These may be divided into arches, loops, and whorls, as illustrated diagrammatically in Figure 8. Triradii occur at the juncture of three sets of converging ridges. In the *arch* pattern, the ridges enter from one side and flow to the other side. The features that characterize a *loop* include a triradius, at least one recurring ridge, and a ridge count of at least one across a recurring ridge. If the ridges enter and leave from the ulnar side, an ulnar loop is formed; if from the radial side, a radial loop results. *Whorls* have at least two triradii, and

may consist of a spiral or ellipse pattern in the simple whorl or two interlocking loops in the double whorl.

B. Finger Ridge Count. A ridge count is obtained from the number of ridges crossed by a line from the triradius to the core of the pattern. The total finger ridge count averages 145 in males and 127 in females.

C. Palmar Patterns. The palmar areas is divided into various zones within which a pattern may or may not be present. These areas include the hypoth-

TABLE 4. *Dermatoglyphic Findings in Some Chromosomal Disorders*

Clinical Disorder	Dermatoglyphic Abnormalities
Down's Syndrome (Mongolism; 21 trisomy)	Excess ulnar loops; radial loops increased on 4th and 5th digit; increased atd angle; simian line; single flexion crease on 5th digit
E trisomy (18 trisomy)	Excess arches on digits—usually more than 6; single flexion crease on digits; simian line
D trisomy (13 trisomy)	Increased atd angle; simian line; arch fibular or arch fibular-S pattern on hallucal area
Turner's Syndrome (XO gonadal dysgenesis and cytologic variants)	Increased whorls on fingers; increased atd angle; s hypothenar pattern; increased a-b ridge count
Klinefelter's Syndrome (XXY and cytologic variants)	Loops with low ridge counts on digits; excess arches on fingers
Cri du chat (Bp—; short arm deletion of 5)	Increased atd angle; simian line

enar, thenar, and interdigital areas. Triradii are found normally beneath each finger and in the axial line of the palm. The distal triradii are called a, b, c, and d, from index to little finger, respectively. The axial triradius is called t, and is usually not more than 10 percent of the distance between the distal crease of the wrist and the proximal crease of the middle finger. However, the axial triradius may be displaced distally toward the ulnar or toward the radial border of the palm. More than one axial triradius may be present.

D. Palmar Creases. Normally, two deep transverse creases are found on the palm but occasionally only one is present. A single palmar crease, called a "simian line," and a single phalangeal flexion crease may be found in certain clinical disorders.

E. Foot Patterns. On the foot, the ridge patterns on the hallucal area and on the great toe are classified as arches, loops, and whorls. An open field in the hallucal area simply means a relative lack of complexity in patterning and thereby implies a low surface contour at the time ridges developed. The hallucal area of the sole usually has a loop or whorl pattern; a lack of such pattern is unusual in the normal. It is found in about half the patients with Down's syndrome and as an occasional feature in other disorders.

A summary of some aberrant patterns or unusual frequency or distribution of dermatoglyphic patterns in several chromosomal disorders is presented in Table 4.

7.7
GENETIC COUNSELING

HAROLD M. NITOWSKY

In the majority of instances, genetic counseling is concerned with advising patients on the risks of recurrence of hereditary disorders in future progeny. It is, therefore, indirectly involved with the prevention of these disorders. In addition to discussing recurrence risks, the genetic counselor must explain, as simply as possible, the nature of the disorder and the meaning of the term "genetic." Moreover, he has to dispel the feelings of guilt which parents often have after having a child with a genetic abnormality and provide appropriate advice and support as the occasion demands.

In considering human disease as part of a broad spectrum, one finds at one extreme, conditions that are entirely genetic in causation, and at the other end nutritional deficiencies and infectious diseases that are almost entirely due to environmental factors. Between the two extremes are many relatively common conditions, such as diabetes mellitus and certain congenital malformations, in which both genetic and environmental factors are involved. Disorders which are entirely genetic in etiology are either chromosomal abnormalities or are due to single gene mutations (unifactorial). The latter are individually rare, the mode of inheritance is simple (dominant, recessive, or X-linked), and the chances of recurrence are high (greater than 1 in 10).

Conditions which etiologically are partly genetic are generally due to the interaction between many genes and the environment (multifactorial). These disorders are common, the mode of inheritance is complex, and the chances of recurrence are usually low (less than 1 in 10).

Before providing genetic advice, it is essential to investigate the family pedigree which, as a minimum, should include information about the health of all first-degree relatives, i.e., parents, siblings, and children of the person seeking such advice.

If the disorder is not severe, it may be possible to trace it back through several generations. On the other hand, if the condition is severe, affected individuals may not survive to have children and to transmit the disease to subsequent generations. In such cases the affected individual is "sporadic," being the only person in the family with the defect, which is usually the result of a new mutation.

Single Gene Mutations

Autosomal dominant traits affect both males and females and often show great variation in expressivity (see p. 305). For example, in a patient with osteogenesis imperfecta the only manifestation of the disease may be blue sclerae, whereas other individuals, even in the same family, can be very severely affected with multiple fractures. Sometimes the gene may not express itself at all, in which case it is said to be nonpenetrant. This phenomenon may explain apparent "skipped" generations in certain pedigrees. On the other hand, careful examination often shows that the "skipped" individual has definite although mild manifestations, representing a forme fruste of the disorder. Careful clinical examination of both apparently healthy parents of a child with an autosomal dominant disorder is therefore essential before the possibility of a new mutation can be considered.

If an individual with an autosomal dominant anomaly marries a normal person, on the average, half their children will be affected. Some autosomal genes are expressed more frequently in one sex than the other. This is referred to as sex-influenced inheritance. For example, hemochromatosis is much more common in males than in females, who often do not develop symptoms until after the menopause.

Autosomal recessive traits also affect both sexes and since only homozygotes manifest the disorder, the heterozygous parents are unaffected. On the average, one in four offspring of two heterozygotes have the abnormal trait. Unlike an autosomal dominant trait, it is generally impossible to trace the disease through several generations. All the affected individuals in a family are usually in one sibship. The parents of a child with a rare recessive disorder are often related, since relatives are more likely to have inherited the same gene from a common ancestor. The rarer a disorder the higher the incidence of consanguinity. However, the fact that in a particular family the parents are not related does not preclude the condition from being recessively inherited. On average, one in four of the offspring of two heterozygotes is affected.

An X-linked recessive trait is one that is due to a mutant gene on the X chromosome. Hemizygous males (with the mutant gene on their single X chromosome) are affected but heterozygous females (carriers) are usually normal. Diseases inherited in this manner are transmitted by healthy female carriers and by affected males if the disorder is not severe or is treatable. All the daughters of an affected male will be carriers and all his sons will be normal. In severe X-linked disorders, such as Duchenne muscular dystrophy, affected males do not survive to have children and the disorder is transmitted by female carriers. In the case of a woman who is a carrier of Duchenne muscular dystrophy, half her sons will be affected and half her daughters will be carriers.

Quite often in serious X-linked conditions there is only one affected male in a family. Such a sporadic case may be the result of a new mutation in the X chromosome which is inherited from the mother. There is also the possibility, however, that the mother might be a carrier, the mutant gene by chance not having been transmitted to any of her male relatives but inherited only through the female line perhaps for several generations.

Multifactorial Inheritance

There are many fairly common conditions in which there is a definite familial tendency, the proportion of affected relatives being greater than in the general population. However, the proportion of affected relatives is often of the order of 5 percent and, therefore, much less than would be expected for single gene mutations. Although the low familial incidence in some of these conditions has been ascribed to genes being "incompletely penetrant," this explanation is rather unsatisfactory. It is much more likely that such conditions are caused by many genes and the effects of environment, or the so-called multifactorial inheritance.

In multifactorial inheritance, it may be assumed that there is some hypothetic underlying attribute that is related to the causation of the disease. This is referred to as the individual's liability, which includes not only his genetic predisposition but also the environmental circumstances which render him more or less likely to develop the disease in question. It may be assumed further that the curve of liability has a normal distribution in both the general population and in relatives, but the curve for the latter is shifted to the right. In the general population the proportion of individuals above the threshold for manifestation of the disorder constitutes the population incidence. Among relatives, the proportion above the threshold is the familial incidence. This model has been applied to measurable characters (such as stature and intelligence) and also to explain the familial incidence of such conditions as diabetes mellitus, congenital pyloric stenosis, cleft lip with and without cleft palate, anencephaly and spina bifida, club foot, and congenital dislocation of the hip.

In conditions in which the inheritance is believed to be multifactorial there are several consequences of the model depicted. The incidence will be greatest among the relatives of more severely affected individuals because presumably they are more extreme deviants along the curve of liability. By similar reasoning it would also be expected that the incidence among siblings born subsequent to the index case would be greater the more affected relatives there were in the family. In spina bifida, for example, after the birth of a single affected child the incidence among subsequent siblings is approximately 4 percent, but 10 percent after the birth of two affected children, and evidence suggests the risk is higher still if another close relative is also affected.

Determination of Recurrence Risks

Estimation of the risks of recurrence in the individual case depends upon a precise diagnosis and an established etiology. Before giving genetic counseling, a careful clinical examination and investigation of the affected individual is essential. In order to arrive at the correct diagnosis, it may be necessary to refer to death certificates and autopsy and biopsy reports. It may also be necessary to examine the parents or other relatives in certain situations. Without such information it may not be possible to give reliable genetic advice.

In establishing the etiology, the pedigree should include information on the health of at least all first-degree relatives, consanguinity, abortions, maternal exposure to radiation, drugs and infections during pregnancy, and details of any birth trauma. Finally, the possibility of genetic heterogeneity must always be considered. The literature should be searched for information on this point and on the relative frequencies of the various modes of inheritance. When the precise diagnosis is known and the mode of inheritance clearly established, genetic counseling is usually straightforward and based on expected Mendelian ratios. However, in the case of autosomal recessive conditions an individual, whether homozygous or heterozygous, is unlikely to have affected children unless married to someone who carries the same mutant gene, which is unlikely if the condition is rare.

In fairly common conditions in which genetic factors appear to play a part but where there is no simple mode of inheritance, the risks of recurrence are based on the observed frequencies of the conditions among relatives of affected individuals, so-called empiric risks. Many of these conditions are probably heterogeneous and include disorders of various causation. Empiric risk figures are therefore rather unsatisfactory as they merely represent an "average figure" for any one condition. A list of empiric risk figures for some common disorders is shown in Table 5. If a genetic etiology for a particular condition has not been established and yet the family history clearly suggests a particular mode of inheritance, then genetic counseling should be based on the fam-

ily history since this condition may represent a unique situation.

In general, trisomy-21 (Down's syndrome), trisomy-D, trisomy-E, and other chromosomal abnormalities are usually the result of errors in meiosis during gametogenesis and the chances of recurrence are small. If, however, one of the parents happens to be a mosaic or carries a balanced translocation the situation is different. If one of the parents is a mosaic it may be very difficult to give reliable genetic advice because it is impossible to estimate what proportion of the parental gonadal tissue is normal. If one of the parents carries a translocation, genetic counseling depends upon the cytogenetic findings and the sex of the carrier parent.

A common problem arises when healthy parents have a child with a particular disorder or abnormality and there is no history on either side of the family of anyone similarly affected. There are several possible explanations for such a situation. Firstly, the disorder may be a phenocopy, perhaps due to maternal exposure during pregnancy. Secondly, it may be due to a chromosome abnormality, but apart from Down's syndrome, most disorders associated with specific chromosome abnormalities are very rare and the chances of recurrence are small. A third possibility is that of a new autosomal dominant mutation, in which case there is little chance of recurrence in subsequent children. This is a distinct possibility if the condition is known to be inherited as an autosomal dominant, if it is always fully penetrant, and if on examination both parents are found to be unaffected. Fourthly, it might be an autosomal recessive disorder. Evidence in favor of this etiology would be parental consanguinity or the demonstration that both parents are heterozygotes by an appropriate biochemical or other type of test. Finally, it could represent an X-linked recessive disorder. It is important to recognize this possibility because an unaffected sister might then be a carrier. Clinical evidence might suggest this mode of inheritance. It might also be possible to demonstrate a biochemical or other ab-

TABLE 5.   *Empiric Risks for Some Common Disorders*
(Percent)

Disorder	Incidence	Sex Ratio M:F	Normal Parents Having a Second Affected Child	Affected Parent Having an Affected Child	Affected Parent Having a Second Affected Child
Anencephaly	0.20	1:2	2	—	—
Cleft palate only	0.04	2:3	2	7	15
Cleft lip ± cleft palate	0.10	3:2	4	4	12
Club foot	0.10	2:1	3	3	10
Congenital heart disease (all types)	0.60	—	1-4	1-4	—
Pyloric stenosis	0.30	5:1			
male index			2	4	13
female index			10	17	38
Spina bifida	0.30	2:3	4	—	—

normality in the mother but not in the father, which would suggest that the disorder was X-linked.

Genetic Advice

Factors that influence the parents' decision as to whether or not they will accept the risk of having an affected child include the severity of the abnormality, whether or not there is an effected treatment, the actual risk, their religious attitudes, socioeconomic status, and education. The genetic counselor usually does not try to influence the parents' decision, although when the risks involved are high, advice in regard to family limitation may be indicated.

Contraception is not the only course of action open to the parents faced with this problem. Other alternatives include sterilization or artificial insemination by donor (if the father is affected). With the liberalization of the abortion laws, if there is a substantial risk of a serious abnormality, termination is another possibility should the mother become pregnant. Recently, selective abortion has also become a possibility whereby a pregnancy need only be terminated when it is known that the fetus is abnormal. Abnormality in the fetus can be determined on a small amount of amniotic fluid obtained by transabdominal amniocentesis around the 14th to 16th weeks of gestation. Sex-chromatin, chromosome, or biochemical studies are done on cultures of amniotic fluid cells. A known carrier of an X-linked disorder that cannot yet be diagnosed in utero might choose selective abortion of a male fetus rather than the only other alternative of totally restricting her family. In certain disorders, antenatal diagnosis is now possible and fetuses known to be affected may be selectively aborted. Parents who have already had an affected child can thus be spared the possibility of a similar outcome in subsequent pregnancies.

There is ample evidence to suggest that a significant number of persons in the population are at high risk of having a child with a serious hereditary disorder, and are unaware of the fact. In the past the ascertainment of such individuals has often been a matter of chance depending largely on the awareness of their physician. There may be justification, therefore, to set up genetic registers in which families at high risk are recorded so that individuals in these families can be followed up and given appropriate counseling when they reach childbearing age.

In giving genetic advice it is not sufficient merely to quote risk figures but, as far as this is possible, the nature and cause of the disease should be explained to the parents. Feelings of guilt and misconceptions about etiology should be removed. Other problems may also have to be discussed including child adoption, abortion, sterilization, and perhaps even artificial insemination. Since the consequences of genetic counseling can be profound and far-reaching, such advice should never be given lightly. It involves not only familiarity with the medical and genetic aspects of hereditary disease but also an awareness of the serious personal problems that are often involved.

References

Carter, C. O. The inheritance of common congenital malformations. Progr. Med. Genet., 4:59-84, 1965.
——— Comments on genetic counseling. *In* Proceedings of the Third International Congress of Human Genetics. Baltimore, Johns Hopkins Press, 1967, p. 97.
Fraser, F. C. Genetic counseling and the physician. Canad. Med. Ass. J., 99:927, 1968.
McKusick, V. A. Mendelian Inheritance in Man, 2nd ed. Baltimore, Johns Hopkins Press, 1968.
Motulsky, A. G., and Hecht, F. Genetic prognosis and counseling. Amer. J. Obstet. Gynec., 90:1227, 1964.
Roberts, J. A. F. Genetic prognosis. Brit. Med. J., 1:587, 1962.

chapter 8

ANOMALIES OF METABOLISM

HAROLD M. NITOWSKY, Associate Editor

8.1
BIOCHEMICAL ASPECTS OF GENE ACTION

HAROLD M. NITOWSKY

The term *inborn error of metabolism*, introduced by Garrod at the turn of the century, has been applied to a group of genetically determined biochemical disorders due to specific congenital defects in the structure or function of protein molecules. Many of the inborn metabolic errors have significant clinical and pathologic consequences which are a direct result of the biochemical disorder. However, the importance of these disease entities goes beyond their immediate relevance to clinical medicine. Studies of specific inborn metabolic errors have been instrumental in elucidating normal biochemical pathways, in establishing the structure and function of various species of macromolecules, and in illuminating genetic concepts and mechanisms. Thus, the definition of the enzymatic defect in phenylketonuria, albinism, and alkaptonuria provided important information about the pathways of aromatic amino acid metabolism. Similarly, studies of hemoglobin variants provided insight into the structure and function of the normal hemoglobin molecule.

Since the primary amino acid sequence of proteins is dependent on the nucleotide sequence of the gene which codes for the polypeptide, variations in protein structure or function are the overt manifestations of gene mutation. Many mutations are easily detected by virtue of the chemical or clinical disturbance resulting from the altered protein. On the other hand, an even greater number of mutations may remain inapparent because the changes in the protein lead to no significant functional disturbance or, conversely, are lethal and therefore may never be observed.

Mutations not only affect the primary structure of the protein, but also influence the rate of synthesis of a protein and hence its concentration in the cell. In microorganisms, there is ample evidence for control or regulator genes which modulate the rate of synthesis of polypeptides by acting on the specific structural genes. Theoretically, mutations involving regulator gene loci may produce

See Appendix for tables of normal values.

effects which are indistinguishable from those involving structural gene loci by controlling the quantitative expression of structural genes and their products. Such mutations might be expected to yield a wide range of effects from complete cessation of synthesis of a specific protein to markedly exaggerated production. The change from production of fetal to adult type hemoglobin, the induction of enzymes in response to hormones or chemical agents, and the mechanisms inherent in cellular differentiation suggest that regulator genes exist in man and other higher organisms. However, there is inadequate evidence to support the contention that any of the inborn errors of metabolism result from mutations involving regulator rather than structural gene loci. In virtually every instance where such a mechanism has been postulated to account for diminished enzyme activity, isolation and purification of the enzyme has revealed a structural alteration leading to diminished substrate affinity, altered catabolic rate, or some other change accounting for loss of activity. Even increased enzyme activity, such as that of hepatic delta amino levulinic acid synthetase in acute intermittent porphyria, may reflect a structural rather than a regulator gene mutation. Such structural alterations may be associated with enhanced affinity or stability of the protein and therefore greater activity.

Although Garrod stressed enzymatic defects which produce a block in an anabolic or catabolic pathway, inborn errors have been described for all types of protein. Mutations have been described affecting function of cell membranes in the intestine, kidney, and other organs, which lead to a diminution in the transport of sugars, amino acids, phosphate, vitamins, cations, and water. These mutations may reflect alteration or absence of a specific membrane carrier protein or *permease,* or an abnormality in the membrane receptor sites for hormones or other mediators. Other mutations involve serum proteins, such as albumin or the immunoglobulins. As with all the inborn errors, such abnormalities may have important clinical consequences or none at all. Thus, the immunoglobulin deficiency syndromes may lead to considerable morbidity and early demise, whereas variation involving serum transferrins have no obvious deleterious effects.

The majority of the inborn errors are characterized by a decrease in or an absence of an intracellular enzyme activity. The loss of enzyme function in many of these disorders may be produced by complete cessation of enzyme synthesis or by the production of a mutant protein which has lost the ability to carry out its usual function. Although it is difficult to distinguish between these possibilities, immunochemical studies have been useful as a means of differentiating between lack of synthesis and formation of an antigenically similar but functionless cross-reacting material (CRM). An example of this phenomenon in man comes from studies of recessively inherited isolated growth hormone deficiency, in which some patients demonstrate a CRM-positive material that appears to be ineffective biologically.

Other inborn errors, as exemplified by citrullinemia, are characterized by only a partial loss of enzyme activity, reflecting a decreased affinity of the enzyme for its substrate. Similarly, in other inborn errors, such as cystathioninuria, the mutant enzyme binds necessary cofactors abnormally and thus shows decreased activity. In such instances, enzyme activity may be restored to nearly normal levels in vivo as well as in vitro in the presence of high coenzyme concentrations.

The mutant enzyme or protein may be unstable and show an accelerated rate of destruction in vivo. This mechanism accounts for diminished enzyme activity in some forms of G6PD deficiency. Still another mechanism of reduced enzyme activity may involve a change in subunit interaction or aggregation as a result of an alteration of one of the component polypeptide subunits.

Genetic Heterogeneity

A specific clinical or biochemical phenotype may be produced by more than a single genotype. The term genetic heterogeneity is used to describe this phenomenon. Recent studies have shown that genetic heterogeneity exists for many inborn errors of metabolism. Indeed, this is not surprising in view of the findings with the many hemoglobin variants. There is growing evidence that the single amino acid substitutions, deletions, duplications, and other alterations which have been described for the hemoglobin molecule also apply to other protein species, including enzymes and serum proteins. Genetic heterogeneity may result from allelic mutations (more than one mutation at a single locus) or nonallelic mutations (involving different loci). The presence of such heterogeneity may be demonstrated by genetic, clinical, and chemical investigations. Differences in the mode of inheritance per se have indicated heterogeneity in certain phenotypically similar disorders, as in the case of Hurler's and Hunter's syndromes. In other instances, variations in the manifestation of the defect in the heterozygote has revealed genetic heterogeneity. Such findings in studies of families with cystinuria have led to the conclusion that the disorder results from at least three different allelic

mutations. In other instances, discovery of separate specific biochemical steps in a complex metabolic pathway has led to evidence of genetic heterogeneity. For example, the elucidation of the separate pathways for glycogen synthesis and degradation led to the recognition of several different enzyme defects and distinguishable disorders which can result in the common end point of excessive glycogen accumulation in the liver. The identification of genetic heterogeneity has clinical as well as genetic significance. The recognition of transient elevation of blood phenylalanine in the newborn infant as an entity which is distinct and different from phenylketonuria has obvious therapeutic implications, as well as important ramifications for family planning and genetic counseling.

Consequences of Enzyme Defects

The effect of a given genetic alteration on cellular metabolism in the inborn errors will depend on the function of the mutant protein and the severity of the defect. It is possible, however, to make certain generalizations about the consequences of these defects in terms of a hypothetical metabolic process, as shown in Figure 1.

1. *Precursor deficiency (Fig. 1a).* If the specific transport system for substance A into the cell is defective, the intracellular concentration of A may be so low that enzyme AB will not be saturated with its substrate. This could slow the entire reac-

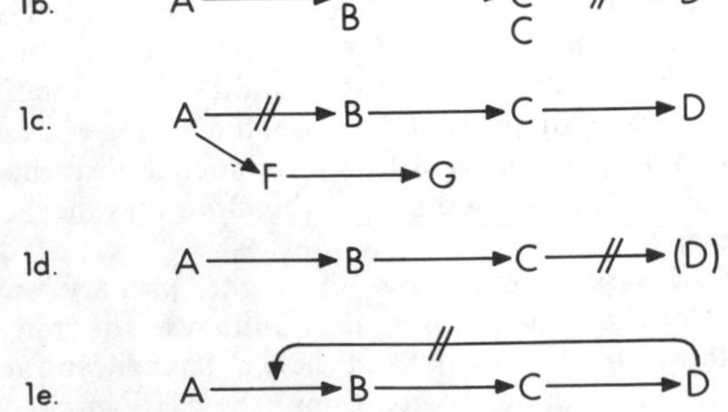

Fig. 1. Schematic representation of biochemical sequence, where A,B,C,D = substrate and products of major pathway; F,G = products of alternate pathway; E_{AB}, E_{BC}, E_{CD} = enzymes catalyzing conversion of A to B, B to C and C to D.

tion sequence and result in inadequate formation of B, C, and D. In Hartnup disease, intestinal transport of tryptophan is defective. Since tryptophan is an important precursor of intracellular nicotinamide, patients with this disorder may exhibit cerebellar ataxia, a characteristic dermatitis, and other signs of nicotinamide deficiency.

2. *Precursor accumulation (Fig. 1b)*. A defect in enzymes AB, BC, or CD might lead to intracellular accumulation of the immediate or remote precursor of the reaction. The marked increase in blood galactose levels in patients with a galactokinase deficiency is an example of such a disturbance. In homocystinuria, on the other hand, in addition to homocystine, the immediate precursor of the blocked reaction, methionine, a remote precursor, accumulates as well.

3. *Alternate pathway utilization (Fig. 1c)*. If conversion of substance A to substance B is impaired by a defect in enzyme AB, an accessory pathway to F and G may become prominent. Thus, in phenylketonuria, absence of phenylalanine hydroxylase activity leads to overproduction and excretion in the urine of phenylpyruvic, phenyllactic, and phenylacetic acids, compounds which are ordinarily not detected in the blood or urine.

4. *Product deficit (Fig. 1d)*. If product D is the physiologically active product of the reaction sequence, a block at any one of the steps prior to D may result in inadequate formation of D. Thus in albinism, melanin is not formed because of a lack of tyrosinase activity.

5. *Absence of feedback control (Fig. 1e)*. The end product of the reaction sequence, D, may regulate the activity of the first enzyme in the biosynthetic pathway, enzyme AB. This phenomenon of end product or feedback inhibition has been studied intensively in microbial systems. Several inborn errors of metabolism in man are associated with abnormalities in feedback regulation, although the biochemical events involved are not well understood. Thus, in the Lesch-Nyhan syndrome, a defect in hypoxanthine guanine phosphoribosyl transferase results in the failure to regulate de novo synthesis of uric acid and leads to marked overproduction of this end product.

Inborn errors of metabolism may have their important clinical effects in almost any body system, and many will be described in the sections of this book devoted to specific organ systems. Thus, the hemoglobinopathies (Chap. 17), disorders of the clotting mechanism (Chap. 17), disorders of pigment metabolism (Chap. 26), defects of hormone synthesis (Chap. 16), defects of vitamin metabolism (Chap. 3), defects of intestinal digestion (Chap. 23), and defects of mineral metabolism (Sec. 15.12) are discussed elsewhere. The following sections are devoted to metabolic and transport disturbances involving amino acids, purines and pyrimidines, carbohydrates, lipids, porphyrins, serum proteins, and enzymopathies involving the formed elements of the blood.

REFERENCES

Bondy, P. K., ed. Duncan's Diseases of Metabolism. Philadelphia, W. B. Saunders Co., 1969.

Harris, H. The Principles of Human Biochemical Genetics. Amsterdam, North-Holland Publishing Co., 1970.

Stanbury, J. B., Wyngaarden, J. B., and Frederickson, D. S., eds. The Metabolic Basis of Inherited Disease, 3rd ed. New York, McGraw-Hill Book Co., 1971.

Anomalies of Amino Acid, Purine, and Pyrimidine Metabolism

The disorders of the metabolism of purines and amino acids are among the classic inborn errors of metabolism. Gout has been known since Hippocrates, and it was with the study of disorders of amino acid metabolism that Garrod introduced the inborn errors of metabolism to the world and ushered in the field of human biochemical genetics. This area of genetic disease has also continued to disclose new or previously unrecognized diseases.

8.2
DISORDERS OF AMINO ACID METABOLISM

WILLIAM L. NYHAN

The diseases of amino acid metabolism present with a wide variety of clinical manifestations. These

TABLE 1.   *Inborn Errors of Amino Acid Metabolism**

Disorder	Enzyme Defect	Manifestations
Phenylketonuria	Phenylalanine hydroxylase	Blonde hair, blue eyes, eczema, $FeCl_3$, M.R.†
Tyrosinosis (Medes)		Urinary reducing substance
Tyrosinosis	p-Hydroxyphenyl pyruvic acid oxidase	Hepatic cirrhosis; renal Fanconi syndrome
Alkaptonuria	Homogentisic acid oxidase	Dark urine, reducing substance; ochronosis; arthritis
Albinism	Tyrosinase (melanocyte granules)	Lack of pigment, local or universal: skin, hair, and eyes
Histidinemia	Histidase	Speech retardation, $FeCl_3$, may have M.R.†
Imidazole amino-aciduria		Convulsions late, cerebromacular degeneration
Maple syrup urine disease	Branched-chain keto acid decarboxylase	Urinary odor, coma, flaccidity, opisthotonus, death‡, M.R.†
Hypervalinemia	Propionyl CoA carboxylase	Odor, convulsions, coma, M.R.† death‡
Isovaleric acidemia		
Ketotic hyperglycinemia		Recurrent vomiting and ketosis, thrombocytopenia, neutropenia, osteoporosis, death,‡ M.R.†
Methylmalonic acidemia	Methylmalonyl CoA isomerase	As in ketotic hyperglycinemia
Nonketotic hyperglycinemia		Convulsions, cerebral palsy, M.R.,† death‡
Oxalosis		Renal calculi, renal failure
Hyperprolinemia	Proline oxidase, Δ^1-pyrroline-5-carboxylic acid dehydrogenase	Nephropathy, deafness, M.R.†
Hyperhydroxyprolinemia	Hydroxyproline oxidase	Small kidneys, hematuria, M.R.†
Argininosuccinic aciduria	Argininosuccinase	Trichorrhexis nodosa, seizures, M.R.†
Citrullinemia	Argininosuccinate synthetase	M.R.†
Hyperammonemia	Carbamylphosphate synthetase, ornithine transcarbamylase	Episodic coma, M.R.†
Hyperlysinemia		Convulsions, hypotonia, growth retardation
Cystathionuria	Cystathionase	M.R.†
Homocystinuria	Cystathionine synthetase	Ectopia lentis, thromboembolism, failure to thrive, M.R.†

*In each instance it is recognized that there may be heterogeneity in which multiple forms of a defective enzyme may lead to different phenotypic manifestations. For instance, in the decarboxylation of the branched-chain keto acids a complete deficiency leads to classic maple syrup urine disease; a different level of defect leads to a milder disease known as branched-chain keto-aciduria. In this table only one form has been listed.

†Mental retardation.

‡The disorders designated as causing death are those which often have a rapidly fulminating course in early infancy.

disorders and some of their major manifestations have been summarized in Table 1. Many of these abnormalities interfere with the development of the central nervous system and thus lead to mental retardation. On the other hand, some defects are associated with no abnormality of intelligence, suggesting that other inborn errors of metabolism may occur in populations of children with normal mentality which have never been screened. Another population of children in which evidence of a metabolic disease should be sought is among ill infants in the newborn period. An increasing number of metabolic disorders is now known to produce severe illness and death very early in life. Obviously, this type of infant may die undiagnosed, and his disease may not be readily discovered if it is one that is rare or only recently

described. A listing of some of these diseases is given in Table 2. Diagnosis and early management are especially important, as not all of these diseases necessarily lead to mental retardation. Exchange transfusion or dialysis may be lifesaving at the time of initial diagnosis early in infancy.

The most common of the inborn errors of amino acid metabolism is phenylketonuria. All of the others appear to be relatively rare.

Phenylketonuria

Phenylketonuria is a genetically induced disorder of metabolism in which phenylalanine cannot be converted to tyrosine (Fig. 2), and phenylpyruvic

TABLE 2. Inborn Errors of Metabolism which May Lead to Overwhelming Illness or Death in Early Infancy

Disorder	Diagnostic Clues and Screening Procedures*
Isovaleric acidemia	Smell, thin-layer chromatography for isovalerylglycine
Ketotic hyperglycinemia	Ketonuria, serum or urine glycine
Maple syrup urine disease	Smell, paper chromatography of branched-chain amino acids, 2,4-dinitrophenylhydrazine test
Methylmalonic acidemia	Ketonuria, methylmalonic acid in urine
Nonketotic hyperglycinemia (Propionic acidemia)	Serum or urine glycine

*All of these procedures should be followed in the case of positive results by definitive quantitative assays.

acid is excreted in the urine. Since the advent of programs in which entire populations of neonatal infants are screened for the presence of phenylalanine in the blood in concentrations higher than 6 mg/100 ml, it has become evident that there are a variety of phenylalaninemias, or hyperphenylalaninemias, in addition to the classic form of phenylketonuria.

CLINICAL FINDINGS. In classical phenylketonuria, the most important clinical characteristic is mental retardation. Most untreated patients are among the lower grades of the mentally defective population, with intelligence quotients under 30. However, borderline intelligence has been documented in a few untreated phenylketonuric individuals.

Phenylketonuric infants appear normal at birth, but early symptoms occur in over half of them. Vomiting severe enough to lead to operation for pyloric stenosis, irritability, an eczematoid rash, or a peculiar odor may also be present in the early months. The characteristic smell of phenylketonuric patients has been described as mousey, wolflike, musty, or barny and has been correlated with the excretion of phenylacetic acid in the urine.

General physical development is usually nor-

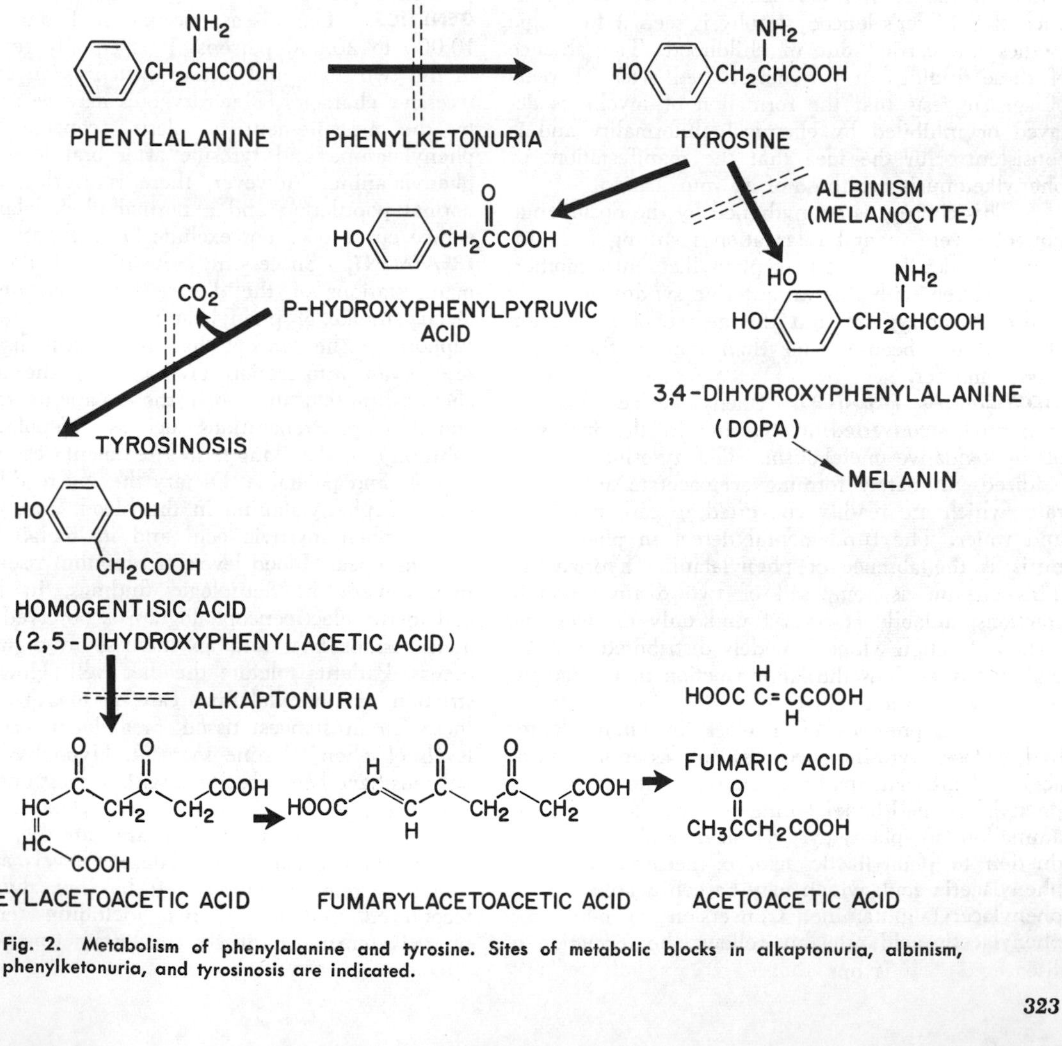

Fig. 2. Metabolism of phenylalanine and tyrosine. Sites of metabolic blocks in alkaptonuria, albinism, phenylketonuria, and tyrosinosis are indicated.

mal, and these are often good-looking children. They are fair-haired, fair-skinned, and blue-eyed in over 90 percent of the cases, but dark skin, hair, or irides do not exclude the diagnosis. Eczematoid dermatitis occurs in about a fourth of the patients. Widely spaced incisor teeth, pes planus, partial syndactyly, epicanthus, and microcephaly are less common manifestations.

Neurologic findings are not prominent; a third of the patients have none, while minimal signs, such as hyperactivity of the deep tendon reflexes or mildly hypertonic muscles, occur in another third. More severely involved patients may have full-blown manifestations of spastic cerebral palsy. Purposeless hand posturing, rhythmic rocking, and tremors of the hands may occur. Hyperkinetic activity, uncontrollable temper, and other behavior problems are common. Seizures occur in about a fourth of the patients, predominantly in those most severely retarded, but electroencephalographic abnormalities have been described in approximately 80 percent. The pneumoencephalogram may reveal cortical atrophy.

Autopsy reports are scarce, but lack of myelinization in the central nervous system or an appearance of Schilder's leucodystrophy is seen if histologic studies are carried out in childhood. The absence of these findings in patients studied after 21 years of age suggests that the formation of myelin is delayed or inhibited by chemical abnormality and is consistent with the idea that the manifestations of phenylketonuria are those of an intoxication.

This concept is strengthened by the documentation of severe mental retardation resulting from intrauterine development in a phenylketonuric mother. The children with this intrauterine syndrome are, of course, heterozygotes, but the degree of retardation observed has been greater than that of the homozygous mother.

BIOCHEMICAL FINDINGS. Phenylalanine (Fig. 2) is normally converted to tyrosine in the first step of its oxidative metabolism. The tyrosine is then oxidized, ultimately forming acetoacetate and fumarate, which are readily converted to carbon dioxide and water. The fundamental defect in phenylketonuria is the absence of phenylalanine hydroxylase. This enzyme is composed of two distinct protein fractions, a labile fraction found only in liver and a stable fraction which is widely distributed in mammalian tissues. It is the labile fraction that is lacking in phenylketonuria.

In the presence of a block in phenylalanine hydroxylase, tyrosine becomes an essential amino acid and alternate pathways are used to metabolize phenylalanine. Phenylalanine is converted by transamination to phenylpyruvic acid and further reduction to phenyllactic acid, or decarboxylation to phenylacetic acid, which may be conjugated to form phenylacetyl glutamine. Conversion to o-hydroxyphenylacetic acid probably follows the formation of o-tyrosine. In phenylketonuria, phenylalanine and these metabolic products accumulate in body fluids. These compounds are not abnormal metabolites, but normal metabolites in abnormal amounts. Plasma concentrations of phenylalanine range from 6 to 80 mg per 100 ml in patients with phenylketonuria, in contrast to values approximating 1 mg per 100 ml in controls. Most patients with classic phenylketonuria have concentrations well over 30 mg per 100 ml throughout infancy. There is a roughly linear relation between levels of phenylalanine in the blood and the urinary excretion of phenylpyruvic acid.

There are a number of secondary effects of the accumulation of phenylalanine and its metabolites. Decreased pigmentation has been related to the inhibition of tyrosinase by phenylalanine. Decreased levels of 5-hydroxytryptamine (serotonin) in phenylketonuric patients appear to follow the inhibition of 5-hydroxytryptophan decarboxylase by phenylpyruvic, phenyllactic, and phenylacetic acids. Similarly, these metabolites which accumulate in phenylketonuria inhibit the glutamic acid decarboxylase of brain and thus would be expected to inhibit the formation of γ-aminobutyric acid.

GENETICS. The disease occurs in 1 out of every 10,000 to 20,000 persons. It is equally represented in the two sexes and is transmitted as an autosomal recessive character. Heterozygotes may be recognized by the measurement of plasma concentrations of phenylalanine and tyrosine after oral loading with phenylalanine. However, there is overlap with the normal population and a normal phenylalanine tolerance curve does not exclude heterozygosity.

TREATMENT. Successful prevention of the clinical manifestations of the disease by restriction of the dietary intake of phenylalanine has provided strong support for the concept that the clinical disease represents an intoxication produced by the abnormal chemical milieu in which these patients must live and develop. Preparations such as Lofenolac (Mead Johnson) make long-term treatment economically feasible and palatable. Dietary therapy readily lowers levels of phenylalanine in the blood, and, concomitantly, phenylpyruvic acid and its metabolic products disappear. Blood levels of serotonin rise. Clinical improvement in neurologic findings, in behavior, and in the electroencephalogram is observed. Eczematoid lesions heal and an increase in pigmentation occurs. Patients tolerate the diet well. However, restriction of phenylalanine can be too great; under these circumstances tissue breakdown occurs and levels of phenylalanine increase. Hypoglycemic convulsions have been observed, with at least one fatality. These complications should not occur in patients receiving these diets if they are carefully observed and if their plasma phenylalanine levels are determined at regular intervals. It has not always been recognized that all infants, including those with phenylketonuria, require a certain amount of phenylalanine. These minimal essential quantities are known and should influence management.

The management of an infant on a low phenylalanine diet is not easy. It should certainly never be undertaken in a baby that does not have phenylketonuria. Phenylketonuric infants often vomit or refuse feedings. Infections may complicate their metabolic state. Whenever possible, management should be directed by someone with experience with these problems, and laboratory facilities for the routine determination of the serum concentration of phenylalanine are essential.

The major purpose of dietary treatment is to minimize mental retardation. A cooperative study on this subject is in progress in the United States. In general, diets are effective in preventing mental deficiency as well as neurologic abnormalities, if started in the first weeks of life. A loss of 5 IQ units for each 10 weeks that treatment is delayed has been calculated. This figure is admittedly only approximate but it provides a strong argument for early diagnosis and the early institution of dietary therapy. Treatment of patients for the first time after the age of 3 years is without effect on mental development. Therapy may be of use in the clinical management of older patients because of beneficial effects on eczema, seizures, or uncontrollable behavior even in the absence of effects on intelligence.

DIAGNOSTIC SCREENING. It has now become routine in the United States and some other countries to test all infants in the population in order to recognize all patients with phenylketonuria as early as possible. Urine tests are of limited value for this purpose, as phenylpyruvic acid is not detected until plasma phenylalanine levels exceed 15 to 20 mg per 100 ml and may be absent from the urine of phenylketonuric patients for 1 to 2 months. Current screening procedures employ an assay for the concentration of phenylalanine in a drop of blood spotted on a piece of filter paper. The most common is an inhibition assay which depends on the competitive inhibition of growth of *Bacillus subtilis* by the phenylalanine analogue, β-2-thienylalanine. If a blood sample contains more than a certain concentration of phenylalanine, inhibition is overcome and the organism grows. Accumulating experience indicates that this method is effective for detecting individuals with levels of phenylalanine over 6 mg per 100 ml, at which level the test is considered positive. There are variations in the rate at which levels of phenylalanine rise in phenylketonuric babies, particularly if there are inadequacies in early protein intake. It is also true that infants leave newborn nurseries very early. Screening programs should make provisions for additional determinations in the first weeks of life if all hyperphenylalaninemic infants are to be detected.

A positive screening test alone does not serve as a diagnosis. It is not yet possible to distinguish reliably among all the types of hyperphenylalaninemia. Furthermore, in a disease in which the defect in enzyme activity is restricted to the liver, ready assessment of the primary molecular expression of the abnormal gene is difficult; it may never be possible in day-to-day clinical practice. Nevertheless, a method is emerging for distinguishing those infants who do require dietary treatment from those who do not.

The first step in the diagnosis is the quantitative analysis of the concentrations of phenylalanine and tyrosine in the blood. Most infants identified by the screening programs simply have a delayed maturation of amino acid–metabolizing enzymes; their tyrosine concentrations are very high. These infants can then be excluded and followed expectantly. In classic phenylketonuria, serum phenylalanine on a normal diet generally rises very rapidly to levels well over 30 mg per 100 ml, while the concentration of tyrosine remains low. Regardless of absolute concentrations, it is preferable to hospitalize infants with elevated serum phenylalanine and low tyrosine levels. Serum phenylalanine concentrations can then be followed while the infants are receiving a known daily intake of this amino acid, and fresh urine can be examined for the excretion of the metabolites phenylpyruvic acid and *o*-hydroxyphenyl acetic acid. Dietary therapy is recommended in patients who excrete these metabolites and who have high concentrations of phenylalanine in the blood.

Tyrosinosis

Tyrosinemia is much more common than phenylalaninemia. Tyrosinemia resulting from delayed maturation of tyrosine-metabolizing enzymes is particularly common in premature infants; it also occurs in scurvy and many forms of liver disease. In addition, there are two disorders known as tyrosinosis.

Tyrosinosis, in the form first described, is an extremely rare metabolic disorder characterized by the excretion of *p*-hydroxyphenylpyruvic acid in the urine. There are probably no clinical manifestations of this metabolic abnormality although the patient initially described had myasthenia gravis. These patients have a reducing substance in the urine, which is due to the excretion of *p*-hydroxyphenylpyruvic acid. Patients with liver disease excrete abnormal quantities of this keto acid, but levels found in tyrosinosis are nearly 10 times the highest values observed in liver disease. The metabolic abnormality of tyrosinosis could result from a deficiency of *p*-hydroxyphenylpyruvic acid oxidase (Fig. 2). Administered exogenously, homogentisic acid is metabolized normally. The oxidation of *p*-hydroxyphenylpyruvic acid to homogentisic acid requires ascorbic acid. The increased excretion of tyrosine and *p*-hydroxyphenylpyruvate which occurs in scurvy and in prematurity can be reversed by the administration of vitamin C.

A much more common form of tyrosinosis is manifested by abnormalities in hepatic and renal function. Symptoms may begin early in infancy with an acute rapid course to demise, or may progress more chronically. Although the disease has been described in two forms, acute and chronic, both have occurred in the same family, indicating that a single disease is involved. Most patients have presented with failure to thrive and have been found to have hepatosplenomegaly and cirrhosis of the liver. Icterus, ascites, and hemorrhage often ensue. They also develop renal tubular acidosis of the Fanconi type, with glycosuria, hyperphosphaturia, and generalized aminoaciduria. Associated with systemic acidosis and hypophosphatemia they have clinical rickets and typical radiographic changes. Mental retardation has not been observed regularly. A few patients have been found to have hepatomas at autopsy.

BIOCHEMICAL FINDINGS. Biochemical alterations include elevated plasma concentrations of tyrosine, usually in the range of 3 to 12 mg per 100 ml (normal, 1-2 mg per 100 ml), and the excretion of tyrosyl compounds in the urine. Of these compounds p-hydroxyphenyllactic acid is the most prominent; p-hydroxyphenylpyruvic and p-hydroxyphenylacetic acids are also formed in appreciable quantities. Methionine concentrations in the plasma are also usually elevated. Hypoglycemia may occur with liver failure. Coagulation defects are common. Study of the enzymes of liver obtained at biopsy have indicated a deficiency of p-hydroxyphenylpyruvic acid oxidase, but it has not been established that this is the primary expression of the abnormal gene.

GENETICS. Genetic transmission appears to be that of an autosomal recessive. A particularly high frequency (0.67/1,000 births) has been observed in a French-Canadian isolate. Frequency data are not available for other populations.

TREATMENT. Treatment with diets low in both phenylalanine and tyrosine has, in some patients, improved both the clinical and chemical features of the disease. Other patients have not responded to dietary therapy.

Alkaptonuria

Alkaptonuria results from a defect in the enzyme homogentisic acid oxidase. It is characterized by a dark color in the urine.

In this disorder fresh urine appears normal, but, on standing and particularly after alkalinization, oxidation of homogentisic acid proceeds and a dark brown or black color develops in the urine. This feature should permit the condition to be recognized very early in life, but, interestingly, the diagnosis is usually first made in adult life after routine urinalysis or in the investigation of arthritis. The urine also gives a positive test for reducing substance and a positive ferric chloride test. Testing for glucose with glucose oxidase sticks is negative. Alkaptonuria may be demonstrated by exposed undeveloped photographic film, which is immediately blackened by the urine.

CLINICAL FINDINGS. Persons with this condition are usually asymptomatic in childhood. After the third decade, deposition of brownish or bluish pigment is seen, particularly in the ears and sclerae. The deposition of pigment, which may be extensive in fibrous tissues, is referred to as ochronosis. Ochronotic arthritis occurs later. Symptoms may resemble those of rheumatoid arthritis or osteoarthritis. Some degree of limitation of motion is usually seen, and complete ankylosis is common. Degeneration in the intervertebral disks may be striking. The condition is inherited as a mendelian recessive character.

BIOCHEMICAL FINDINGS. Homogentisic acid is a colorless compound which is readily transformed on standing to a black pigment. Although homogentisic acid is excreted in large quantities in the urine, the compound is not detectable in blood. Normal individuals given homogentisic acid metabolize it completely, but alkaptonuric persons excrete it nearly quantitatively. This disorder is a classic model for the so-called no-threshold metabolic disorders, in which, in spite of a metabolic block due to an absence of an enzyme, accumulation of metabolic intermediates behind the block is observable only on analysis of the urine.

The suggestion of Garrod that the disorder resulted from an absence of the enzyme in the liver which catalyzed the oxidation of homogentisic acid (Fig. 2) marked the birth of the one-gene-one-enzyme hypothesis and thus a frontier in biochemical genetics. This concept was confirmed by La Du and colleagues, who found the enzyme catalyzing the conversion of homogentisic acid to maleylacetoacetate to be absent in biopsied liver from an alkaptonuric patient.

Albinism

Albinism is an inherited metabolic anomaly in which the defect is confined to the pigment cell, the melanocyte, which cannot form melanin.

CLINICAL FINDINGS. Albinism occurs in fish, birds, and mammals, and in all races of man. Universal albinism, in which melanin is absent from the pigment cells of the skin, hair, and retina is readily recognized. A variety of localized forms occur in which the defect is confined to an area of skin, the eyes, or to a white forelock of hair. The skin in universal albinism is milk-white; the hair is white or yellow, and in Caucasians, very fine. The iris is generally blue. The pupil is red in children, but usually becomes black in adulthood. Photophobia is characteristic, as is horizontal nystagmus. Visual acuity is almost always decreased. The skin is sensitive to light, and these patients have a propensity to develop skin cancers. A few patients have been reported in whom universal albinism has been associated with prolonged bleeding time and peculiar pigmented reticuloendothelial cells in the marrow, lymph nodes, and liver.

BIOCHEMICAL FINDINGS. The relationship of the formation of melanin to the metabolism of phenylalanine and tyrosine is indicated in Figure 2. Melanin is a polymer which exists in nature in high molecular weight. It is a brown or black insoluble material contained in the melanin granules of the melanocytes, where the entire transformation from tyrosine takes place. These granules can be demonstrated with the electron microscope and have been shown to be present, but without melanin, in albinism. The enzyme tyrosinase is a copper-containing oxidase which catalyzes the first two steps in the conversion of tyrosine to melanin. The first step, the conversion of tyrosine to 3,4-dihydroxyphenylalanine, is the limiting step, for the second step and most of the rest of melanogenesis may proceed nonenzymatically. Tyrosinase has been demonstrated in tissues radioautographically, by a method in which ^{14}C-labeled tyrosine is converted to melanin, and has been shown to be absent in albinism.

GENETICS. Universal albinism is inherited as a mendelian recessive character although more than one mutant gene can produce the disorder. Normally pigmented children have occurred in a family in which both parents were albinos. Localized forms of albinism may be inherited as dominant, recessive, or, as in the case of ocular albinism, sex-linked characters.

Histidinemia

Histidinemia is a disorder of intermediary metabolism in which large amounts of histidine are found in blood and urine. The condition must be included in the differential diagnosis of phenylketonuria, for the urine is positive when examined with ferric chloride.

CLINICAL FINDINGS. The condition may occur without clinical manifestations, but more than half of the patients have had speech retardation. Mental retardation and growth retardation have also been observed in individual patients. Relatively fair hair and blue eyes have been common.

BIOCHEMICAL FINDINGS. Histidine (α-amino-β-imidazolylpropionic acid) is normally converted by histidase to urocanic acid, which is further metabolized to formiminoglutamic acid and ultimately to glutamic acid. In histidinemia elevated concentrations of histidine have been demonstrated in the plasma, urine, and cerebrospinal fluid. Imidazolepyruvic, imidazolelactic, and imidazoleacetic acids are excreted in the urine, and imidazolepyruvic acid is responsible for the positive ferric chloride test. Many patients also have elevations of alanine in the plasma.

A deficiency of histidase in this condition was indicated by the separate administration of histidine and urocanic acid. The absence of histidase has now been demonstrated by direct assay of the enzyme in skin. When histidine cannot be converted to urocanic acid, it is converted to imidazolepyruvic acid

and its derivatives, much as phenylalanine is metabolized in phenylketonuria.

Maple Syrup Urine Disease: Branched-Chain Keto-Aciduria

In this syndrome cerebral degeneration occurs very rapidly in the newborn period and there is an odor in the urine reminiscent of maple syrup. The branched-chain amino acids, leucine, isoleucine, and valine, are present in high concentration in the blood and urine, and the keto acid analogues are found in the urine.

CLINICAL FINDINGS. Infants with maple syrup urine disease appear well at birth. In the typical case, symptoms begin at 3 to 5 days of life and progress rapidly to death within 2 to 4 weeks. Early manifestations of the disease may be feeding difficulty, irregular respirations, or progressive loss of the Moro reflex. Characteristically, these patients develop convulsions, opisthotonos, and generalized muscular rigidity with or without intermittent flaccidity.

In most patients death occurs early in infancy following the appearance of a state of decerebrate rigidity. Severe hypoglycemia has occasionally been observed. Slight cortical atrophy has been seen on pneumoencephalography. In patients surviving past the first year, pathologic lesions of defective myelinization similar to those of phenylketonuria have been reported.

A few patients have been described in whom milder forms of the disease have occurred with characteristic biochemical abnormalities. This condition is known as *intermittent branched-chain amino-aciduria* and appears to represent a distinct alteration at the same locus as that of classical maple syrup urine disease. Ataxia and repeated episodes of lethargy progressing to coma have been seen without mental retardation. These episodes have been induced by infection and by surgery with anesthesia; they have responded to the removal of milk from the diet and the substitution of parenteral fluid therapy.

The finding which permits either form of keto-aciduria to be distinguished from other cerebral degenerative diseases of infancy is the characteristic odor of maple syrup, caramel, or an "oast house" to the urine, skin, or hair. The odor may become evident after 1 or 2 days of life and persist thereafter, but considerable variation in intensity has been observed, and in some specimens the odor cannot be detected. Freezing may intensify the odor. Keto acids may be recognized in the urine by means of 2,4-dinitrophenylhydrazine. The yellow precipitate may be extracted into ether and from it into sodium carbonate solution.

BIOCHEMICAL ABNORMALITIES. Maple syrup urine disease is an abnormality in the metabolism of the branched-chain amino acids. As stated above, increased quantities of leucine, isoleucine, and valine are found in the plasma and urine. Methionine concentrations were originally thought to be increased but the elevated chromatographic peak has now been separated from methionine and identified as allo-isoleucine.

The catabolism of the branched-chain amino acids is initiated by deamination to the keto acids, α-ketoisocaproic acid, and the corresponding derivatives of isoleucine and valine. This is followed by decarboxylation to coenzyme A derivatives, in similar fashion to the decarboxylation of α-ketoglutarate to succinyl coenzyme A. Subsequent steps correspond to steps in the oxidation of the straight-chain fatty acids.

The presence of the keto-acid derivatives of leucine, isoleucine, and valine in the urine and the absence of the decarboxylation products suggest that the block was in the oxidative decarboxylation of the keto acids. This can be demonstrated in leucocytes or fibroblasts in culture. Patients with the classic disease are unable to convert leucine-1-^{14}C to ^{14}CO$_2$, a conversion that is readily made in control infants. The oxidation of α-ketoisocaproic acid to CO$_2$ is similarly deficient. In patients with intermittent and branched-chain keto-aciduria there is a partial defect in this decarboxylation process.

GENETICS. The familial nature of these diseases has been documented. They appear to be transmitted as autosomal recessives.

TREATMENT. Success in the dietary therapy of phenylketonuria provided a model for the treatment of other metabolic disorders. Furthermore, the metabolites which accumulate in branched-chain keto-aciduria have been shown to inhibit the formation of α-aminobutyric acid in vitro. In maple syrup urine disease, experience has now been accumulated with the prolonged use of a synthetic diet made up of individual amino acids, in which the intake of leucine, isoleucine, and valine is closely controlled. Plasma concentrations of the branched-chain amino acids can in this way be maintained with normal limits. However, therapy is very difficult. It may require continuous hospitalization, and most patients have probably had permanent brain damage before treatment is started. Experience with siblings of previous cases, in whom very early diagnosis is possible, indicates that a normal IQ may be achieved. So far, results of treatment have usually fallen considerably short of this objective.

Hypervalinemia

Hypervalinemia has so far been observed in a single patient in Japan. The patient was retarded both mentally and physically, and was hyperkinetic. Vomiting and difficulty with feeding were prominent findings early in infancy. Treatment with a diet low in valine was associated with lowering of the plasma concentration of valine, improvement in weight gain, and reduction of vomiting and hyperactivity.

The plasma concentration was as high as 10 mg per 100 ml. There was an increase in the urinary excretion of valine but none in that of the other branched-chain amino acids, and no keto-aciduria. A defect in the transamination of valine has been observed in the leucocyte.

The Hyperglycinemias

A number of disorders of amino acid metabolism present with abnormal concentrations of glycine in the blood, urine, and cerebrospinal fluid. These include ketotic hyperglycinemia, nonketotic hyperglycinemia, and methylmalonic aciduria. Isovaleric acidemia may also present with hyperglycinemia. All of these disorders have devastating clinical manifestations in early infancy.

Ketotic Hyperglycinemia

Ketotic hyperglycinemia is characterized clinically by mental retardation, neutropenia, thrombocytopenia, and osteoporosis. Two pathologic fractures have been seen in the only patient to live beyond infancy.

CLINICAL FINDINGS. Most patients with recognized ketotic hyperglycinemia have died early in life. Recurrent episodes of metabolic acidosis and massive ketosis, similar to that observed in diabetic coma, have been among the most striking manifestations of the disease. This is one of the few conditions in which ketonuria is seen in the first days of life, another being glycogen storage disease. Symptoms have begun as early as 18 hours after birth with vomiting, acidosis, and ketonuria. The deaths have occurred in intractable acidosis, and it seems probable that other patients may have died unrecognized early in life. Thrombocytopenia and purpura have not been seen after the first 6 to 9 months of life. Neutropenia appears to be a function of glycine toxicity and can be reversed by measures designed to lower levels of glycine. Convulsive seizures and electroencephalographic abnormalities have been observed in the first 6 months of life but have disappeared thereafter.

BIOCHEMICAL FINDINGS. The diagnosis can be suspected clinically. It should be documented chemically by quantitative assay of the concentration of glycine in plasma. Examination of the urine by paper chromatography may be helpful, but large amounts of glycine are excreted in normal urine, and a prominent glycine spot is commonly encountered. It is, therefore, easy to miss hyperglycinuria with the methods commonly used in screening the urine for amino acids. In hyperglycinemia plasma glycine concentrations are often as high as 10 times those of controls. The oral administration of glycine is followed by prolonged elevation of plasma glycine. Demonstration of the abnormal tolerance test produces no clinical symptoms. This is the only method of challenge that would be recommended in the study of an infant with ketotic hyperglycinemia.

The concentrations of glycine in the blood and urine can be effectively lowered by the administration of benzoate. However, this does not prevent the production of typical metabolic acidosis by the intake of protein. Restriction of dietary protein reduces the frequency and severity of these attacks and neutropenia is readily reversed. Ketosis can regularly be produced by the administration of usual dietary amounts of leucine, isoleucine, threonine, valine, or methionine. Attacks also develop in association with infection, and elevated concentrations of leucine and valine have been observed in the plasma during such episodes. Tolerance tests with these amino acids are also abnormal. These observations were made by giving challenging doses of amino acids, proteins, and protein hydrolysate under carefully controlled conditions to a relatively old patient. An infant suspected of having hyperglycinemia should never be subjected to a challenge with these acids which may produce intractable acidosis.

The mechanisms involved in this unusual toxic response to such a variety of amino acids are not clear. However, a defect has now been found in the oxidation of propionic acid by the leucocytes of a patient with the disease. This fluid suggests a defect in the formation of methylmalonyl CoA from propionyl CoA and explains similarities between this disease and methylmalonic acidemia. It is consistent with clinical problems secondary to isoleucine, methionine, and threonine acidemia. However, it cannot account for leucine or valine toxicity. In these patients, we have also observed defective conversion of proprionate to CO_2 in vivo and in cultured fibroblasts, as well as defective conversion of glycine to CO_2 in vivo.

GENETICS. The disease is familial and is probably transmitted as an autosomal recessive.

TREATMENT. Diets in which very small amounts of protein (0.5 g/kg/day) are supplemented with the amino acids other than those listed above appear to be tolerated by patients with the disease. At least two infants have now been diagnosed early in infancy and raised on such diets. Both have reached the age of 6 years and appear normal mentally.

Methylmalonic Acidemia

At least three different disorders are now known to present as methylmalonic acidemia. They all appear to have identical clinical manifestations similar to those of ketotic hyperglycinemia.

CLINICAL FINDINGS. Episodes of ketoacidosis may begin very early in life. They may lead to coma and death. Neutropenia is a prominent manifestation and thrombocytopenia may also occur. These patients usually have osteoporosis. Mental retardation has been observed regularly in surviving patients. In-

fections, which occur commonly, may precipitate life-threatening ketoacidosis. Some patients have had chronic monilial infection. The red cells are normal and there is no megaloblastosis. Growth retardation is striking. Convulsions, as well as abnormalities of the electroencephalogram, have been observed.

BIOCHEMICAL FINDINGS. Methylmalonic acid is found in elevated concentrations in the plasma. Levels of about 10 mg per 100 ml are common. Urinary excretion of methylmalonic acid may exceed 500 mg per day. This compound is not normally detectable in blood or urine. In patients it has also been found in the cerebrospinal fluid and in tissues obtained at postmortem. Increased amounts of glycine are found in blood and urine, but, in contrast to methylmalonic acid, levels of glycine correlate poorly with the clinical status of the patient. Concentrations of vitamin B_{12} in the blood are normal.

Methylmalonic acid is normally formed from methylmalonyl CoA, which is a product of the propionyl CoA carboxylase reaction in which CO_2 is fixed to the propionic acid molecule. Methylmalonyl CoA occurs in two isomeric forms which are interconverted by a racemase. One of these is converted by methylmalonyl CoA isomerase (mutase) to succinyl CoA, leading to metabolism through the citric acid cycle. This pathway is a branch point in the metabolism of amino acids, fats, and carbohydrates. The amino acids isoleucine, valine, methionine, and threonine, which are all precursors of methylmalonic acid in man, are catabolized along this pathway.

A defect in methylmalonyl CoA isomerase has seemed likely from the appearance of methylmalonic acid in the urine. This isomerase has a B_{12} coenzyme. Furthermore, propionic acid oxidation is defective in vivo, in leucocytes, and in cultured fibroblasts. Methylmalonic acid oxidation is also impaired; succinate oxidation is normal.

TREATMENT. Treatment with diets low in threonine, isoleucine, valine, and methionine is under study and appears quite promising. Patients have been treated with vitamin B_{12} in large doses. Some have responded and some have not, thus possibly delineating two forms of the disease. In a third form of methylmalonic acidemia, increased quantities of homocystine and cystathionine were found in the urine. The patient with this form of the disease was found to have a defect in the activity of tetrahydrofolate methyltransferase, and the data indicate a defect in the accumulation of coenzymatically active derivatives of vitamin B_{12}.

Nonketotic Hyperglycinemia

All patients with nonketotic hyperglycinemia have had severe seizure disorders. One patient had almost continuous status epilepticus for much of his first year of life. This disease can also produce overwhelming illness in the neonatal period. Convulsions or lethargy have been observed in the first days of life. Death in the first year of life is common.

CLINICAL FINDINGS. Four patients with this defect have been described in detail; very severe mental retardation was present in each, accompanied by little functional cortical activity. Two had irritability and microcephaly. Hypertonicity alternating with hypotonicity has been present in the same patient; hyperreflexia was generally observed. Porencephaly and ventricular dilation have been seen on pneumoencephalography. The electroencephalogram was abnormal.

BIOCHEMICAL FINDINGS. Plasma concentrations of glycine are elevated, ranging approximately from 5 to 12 mg per 100 ml. The amounts of glycine in the urine and cerebrospinal fluid are also increased. This disorder was originally described as *hyperglycinemia with hypooxaluria*, but it is now apparent that hypooxaluria is not a regular component of this disease. Neutropenia has been observed in only one patient. None has had ketoacidosis. On the other hand, respiratory acidosis has been observed at times of extreme illness.

A defect has been found in vivo in the conversion of carbon 1 of glycine to CO_2 and of carbon 2 of glycine to carbon 3 of serine. This would be consistent with a defect in an enzyme catalyzing the conversion of glycine to CO_2 and hydroxymethyltetrahydrofolic acid.

Sarcosinemia

Sarcosine is the N-methyl derivative of glycine. It is formed generally from dimethylglycine, which may be a product of betaine or choline. Normally, sarcosine is not present in amounts sufficient to be detected in the blood or urine, although occasionally sarcosinuria is found after the ingestion of lobster or other foods.

Only two patients have been reported with sarcosinemia. Both had subnormal intelligence. Sarcosine concentrations in the blood ranged from 1.4 to 5.6 mg per 100 ml. Urinary sarcosine ranged from 77 to 168 mg over 24 hours in a patient less than 1 year of age and from 474 to 703 mg over 24 hours in a 6-year-old. A deficiency of hepatic sarcosine dehydrogenase has been postulated.

Hyperoxaluria and Oxalosis

Primary hyperoxaluria is a metabolic disorder in which large amounts of oxalate are excreted in the urine, leading to calcium oxalate lithiasis and nephrocalcinosis. When there are extrarenal deposits of calcium oxalate, the condition is known as oxalosis. In most of the 20 to 30 patients who have been reported, the diagnosis was not established during life.

CLINICAL FINDINGS. An early onset of symptoms of urolithiasis, hematuria, urinary tract infections, passage of calculi, and colic, as well as nephrocalci-

nosis and extrarenal deposits, are sufficiently characteristic to warrant investigation of oxalate metabolism. Renal failure is common; the mean age at death in 16 cases was 4 years. Attempts at treatment have not been effective.

BIOCHEMICAL FINDINGS. Oxalic acid (HOOC-COOH) is a dicarboxylic acid that produces a calcium salt of very low solubility. It may be formed from glyoxylic acid, which may be formed from glycine or glycolic acid. It may also be a metabolite of ascorbic acid. In hyperoxaluria, levels of oxalate excretion may approximate 30 times those of control subjects. It is clear that the oxalate found in the urine is of endogenous origin and that glycine is a precursor. Isotopically labeled glycine is rapidly converted to urinary oxalate, but the proportion of oxalate made from glycine is the same in patients and controls. In patients, the rate of conversion of injected glyoxylate-^{14}C to respiratory CO_2 was only 20 percent that of controls. This finding would appear to localize the site of the defect to the metabolism of glyoxylic acid. There is a carboligase which catalyzes the reaction of glyoxylate and α-ketoglutarate to α-hydroxy-β-ketoadipate. This enzyme is present in the soluble and mitochondrial portions of the cell. It has been reported that the soluble but not the mitochondrial enzyme is low in activity in the liver of oxaluric patients.

GENETICS. In most instances, the disease has been an isolated one, although it is probably a rare recessive character. Four affected siblings and one instance of affected identical twins have been reported.

TREATMENT. There has been a report of successful management of oxalosis by renal transplantation followed by treatment with calcium carbimide. The latter might be expected to inhibit glyoxylate formation by tying up glycoaldehyde. This approach is currently in dispute, but certainly renal transplant alone has been unsuccessful, as oxalate has been deposited in the transplanted kidney.

Hyperprolinemia and Hydroxyprolinemia

Hyperprolinemia was first recognized in a family in which cerebral dysfunction, renal anomalies, and deafness occurred in various members. The initial patient, a male infant, presented at 2 years with congenital renal hypoplasia, deafness, convulsions, and mental retardation. He was found to have hyperprolinemia, as were three female siblings who had electroencephalographic abnormalities. One of the siblings had renal hypoplasia, nerve deafness, hematuria, and electroencephalographic abnormality. Neither her proline levels nor those of the father were abnormal. Hematuria and deafness occurred frequently in the mother's family in a pattern suggesting dominant inheritance.

Plasma proline concentrations in affected persons were between 7.8 and 20.1 mg per 100 ml. Proline was not elevated in the cerebrospinal fluid. Urinary proline and hydroxyproline, which are not found normally after the neonatal period, were prominent, and in some instances glycine excretion was increased. The infusion of proline into normal adults produced hydroxyprolinuria and glycinuria as well as prolinuria, indicating that the urinary findings are secondary to a basic defect in the metabolism of proline.

Hydroxyprolinemia has been described in a mentally retarded girl who also had increased numbers of leucocytes and erythrocytes in the urine and radiographically small kidneys. Shortness of stature was also observed. Her mother was also mentally retarded, but had no hydroxyproline abnormality.

Thus both hyperprolinemia and hydroxyprolinemia have been associated with mental retardation and with nephropathy. Reports of additional families affected with these conditions increases the likelihood that the metabolic defects and clinical manifestations are related. On the other hand, in involved families, some members with the metabolic abnormality have had no clinical defect; the reverse has also been true. Therefore, it remains possible that these abnormalities of protein metabolism are simply biochemical phenotypes without clinical disease.

Free hydroxyproline was first observed on a routine paper chromatogram. Quantitative assay indicated markedly elevated quantities of hydroxyproline in the blood and urine. Interestingly, the amounts of glycine and proline in the urine were normal.

It is now known that there are two forms of hyperprolinemia; type I in which there is a deficiency of proline oxidase, and type II in which the next enzyme on the degradative pathway, Δ'-pyrroline-5-carboxylic acid dehydrogenase, is deficient. In prolinuria a defect in hydroxyproline oxidase has been observed.

Cystathioninuria

Cystathioninuria is a rare metabolic disorder first reported in two adults with mental deficiency. It has also been observed in patients with thrombocytopenia and endocrinopathy, as well as in individuals with no disease. It is possible that the biochemical defect is coincidental.

CLINICAL FINDINGS. The first patients were 64 and 44 years old when their disease was recognized. Developmental retardation was present from birth. One was otherwise normal except for talipes calcaneovalgus. The other had acromegaly, small ears, deafness, and facial clefts. Abnormal amino-aciduria has generally been found in the course of routine screening. Cystathioninuria also occurs in an acquired or secondary fashion in patients with neuroblastoma or, rarely, with hypothyroidism.

BIOCHEMICAL FINDINGS. Cystathionine is an intermediate in the formation of cysteine and homoserine from methionine and serine. Cystathionine is normally cleaved to form cysteine and ketobutyrate. The compound is not usually found in the urine, but, in the patients studied, as much as 500 to 1,300 mg was excreted each day. Cystathionine could not be detected in the blood in the first patient, but concentrations have ranged from 1 to 10 μmoles per 100 ml in the others. Administration of methionine led to an increase in cystathionine excretion, and pyridoxine (vitamin B_6) to a decrease. High doses of B_6 have been used, approximately 5 to 10 mg per kg per day to maintain blood and urine concentrations near zero. The enzyme cystathionase has been found to be defective in the liver, and the in vitro addition of large amounts of pyridoxine corrects the defect. Thus, the abnormality appears to be in the enzyme structure responsible for proper binding of the coenzyme.

In genetic studies, small but abnormal quantities of cystathionine may be found in the urine of heterozygotes. This may be increased by the oral administration of 100 mg per kg of methionine.

Homocystinuria

Homocystinuria is a disorder of the metabolism of the sulfur-containing amino acids, which appears to be relatively common. It has been reported in more patients than any other inborn error of amino acid metabolism except for phenylketonuria. Homocystinuria is especially prevalent in Ireland, where a frequency of 0.7 per 100,000 population has been estimated.

CLINICAL FINDINGS. Most patients have been mentally retarded. Many have had marked failure to thrive, have been thin and hypertonic, and have died before 1 year of age. Less severely affected patients have had mental retardation without systemic disease. Ectopia lentis is the most characteristic feature of the disease. Cataracts have also been seen, as well as glaucoma. The hair is usually fair and sparse, the complexion fair, and the eyes blue. A malar flush and livido reticularis are characteristic. Most patients have had skeletal abnormalities (genu valgum, pes cavus, pectus excavatum or carinatum) and osteoporosis. Thromboembolic phenomena, both arterial and venous, have been prominent, and have often been the cause of death in the disease. Occlusion of coronary, renal, or cerebral arteries or veins may lead to major complications such as hemiplegia or renal hypertension as well as death. Many patients have convulsions, and the EEG is usually abnormal. Classical tests of clotting function have been normal, but platelets from these patients have shown unusual adhesiveness. Furthermore, the addition of homocystine to normal blood causes the platelets to become sticky.

BIOCHEMICAL FINDINGS. Homocystine is not found in body fluids under normal conditions. It is an intermediate in the metabolism of methionine. After the conversion of methionine to S-adenosylmethionine, demethylation yields S-adenosylhomocysteine, which breaks down to homocysteine. The latter compound is normally combined with serine in the presence of cystathionine synthetase to form cystathionine. Free homocysteine condenses to homocystine, as cysteine does to cystine.

A spectrum of biochemical deviations from normal has been observed in patients with homocystinuria. The presence of homocystine in the urine may be the only readily detectable abnormality. The amounts of homocystine in the urine of these patients usually exceed 20 mg per day and can be increased by the oral administration of methionine. The mixed disulfide of cysteine and homocysteine is also present in the urine. Screening of urine for the presence of homocystine can be carried out by the addition of nitroprusside following treatment with cyanide. In some patients the compound has been detected in the blood; in others, plasma methionine levels were elevated, ranging from 5 to 100 times normal. Plasma cystine concentrations are usually decreased.

Liver biopsy indicate that the enzymatic defect is in the enzyme cystathionine synthetase. This is consistent with an absence of cystathionine in the brain, which has been found in this condition.

GENETICS. The disorder is transmitted as an autosomal recessive trait and heterozygotes have approximately half the normal level of activity of cystathionine synthetase in the liver. However, detection by loading tests has not proved to be reliable.

TREATMENT. Experience with treatment has provided evidence of genetic heterogeneity in homocystinuria. Some patients respond to the administration of large doses (100 to 500 mg per day) of pyridoxine and some do not. Some respond to vitamin B_{12}. The form of methylmalonic aciduria (see p. 329) in which homocystinuria and cystathioninuria are also part of the anomaly, provides further evidence of heterogeneity. It also indicates a relationship of the metabolic defect to B_{12}. Dietary treatment has been employed with some success using methionine restriction and cystine supplementation.

Hyperlysinemia

Seven patients with unusual lysinemia have been reported. Mental retardation was present in five. Three also had physical retardation. Synophrys, impaired sexual development, prognathous jaw, high maxilla, and slight webbing of the fingers have been seen in some patients. Others had convulsions, poor somatic growth, flabby ligaments, and hypochromic anemia, all symptoms reminiscent of those of animals on lysine-deficient diets. Hypotonia and electroencephalographic abnormalities were common.

Concentrations of lysine were elevated in the blood (with levels generally exceeding 6 mg per 100 ml), urine, and cerebrospinal fluid. Lysine tolerance tests were abnormal. Consanguinity has been observed in two families.

A different disorder has been described under the heading of lysine intolerance in which the subject had episodic ammonia intoxication and coma. Such a patient would be clinically indistinguishable from those described under hyperammonemia.

Beta-Alanine Abnormalities

HYPER-BETA-ALANINEMIA. *Hyper-beta-alaninemia* has been reported in a single infant who died very early in life. Symptoms were those of neonatal somnolence, hypotonia, and intermittent seizures, which could not be controlled with the usual anticonvulsant therapy. Deep tendon reflexes were depressed.

Beta-alanine was found to be elevated in the blood, urine, and cerebrospinal fluid. Large amounts of taurine and beta-aminoisobutyric acid were also found in the urine. Gamma-aminobutyric acid was present in the plasma, urine, and cerebrospinal fluid. The concentration of gamma-aminobutyric acid in brain tissue obtained at postmortem was markedly increased.

CARNOSINEMIA. *Carnosine* is the dipeptide of beta-alanine and histidine. It is normally present in high concentrations in muscle and thus is a common dietary constituent. It is not normally found in the blood. Two unrelated patients have been reported with carnosinemia. Both had progressive neurologic degeneration with onset early in infancy. Both also had grand mal and myoclonic seizures, with electroencephalographic abnormalities and severe mental retardation. Carnosinase activity, which is normally present in the serum, was absent in these patients.

Carnosinemia should be distinguished from normal dietary carnosinuria and from imidazole aminoaciduria. Patients with carnosinemia have persistent carnosinuria while receiving a diet free of carnosine. They do not have 1-methylhistidine in the urine. Anserine, β-alanyl-1-methylhistidine, is found in the urine without 1-methylhistidine following a load of anserine or a meal rich in this compound, such as white meat of chicken. Patients with imidazole amino-aciduria have had convulsions, late onset cerebromacular degeneration, and large amounts of carnosine, anserine, and 1-methylhistidine in the urine, but they have not had carnosinemia.

REFERENCES

PHENYLKETONURIA

Auerbach, V. H., DiGeorge, A. M., and Carpenter, G. C. Phenylalaninemia. *In* Nyhan, W. H., ed., Amino Acid Metabolism and Genetic Variation. New York, McGraw-Hill Book Co., 1967, p. 11.

Centerwall, W. R., and Centerwall, S. A. Phenylketonuria. Children's Bureau Publ. No. 388, 1961.

Fölling, A. Über Ausscheindung von Phenylbrenztraubensaure in den Harn als Stoffwechselanomalie in Verbindung mit Imbezillität. Hoppe-Seyler Ztschr. Physiol. Chem., 277:169, 1934.

Guthrie, R., and Susi, A. A simple phenylalanine method for detecting phenylketonuria in large populations of newborn infants. Pediatrics, 32:338, 1963.

Jervis, G. A. Phenylpyruvic oligophrenia deficiency of phenylalanine-oxidizing system. Proc. Soc. Exp. Biol. Med., 82:514, 1953.

Lyman, F. L., ed. Phenylketonuria. Springfield, Illinois, Charles C Thomas, Pub., 1963.

Mabry, C. C., Denniston, J. C., Nelson, T. L., and Son, C. D. Maternal phenylketonuria. New Eng. J. Med., 269:1404, 1963.

Paine, R. S. The variability in manifestations of untreated patients with phenylketonuria. Pediatrics, 20:290, 1957.

TYROSINOSIS

Hsia, D. Y., ed. Symposium on treatment of amino acid disorders. Amer. J. Dis. Child., 113:31, 1967.

Medes, G. A new error of tyrosine metabolism: Tyrosinosis. The intermediary metabolism of tyrosine and phenylalanine. Biochem. J., 26:917, 1932.

Scriver, G. R., Partington, M., and Sass-Kortsak, A. Editorial committee conference on hereditary tyrosinemia. Canad. Med. Assoc. J., 97:1045, 1967.

Shear, C. S., Nyhan, W. L., and Tocci, P. M. Tyrosinosis and tyrosinemia. In Nyhan, W. L., ed., Amino Acid Metabolism and Genetic Variation. New York, McGraw-Hill Book Co., 1967, p. 97.

ALKAPTONURIA

Garrod, A. E. The incidence of alkaptonuria: a study in chemical individuality. Lancet, 2:1616, 1902.

───── Inborn errors of metabolism. London, Oxford University Press, 1923.

La Du, B. N., Zannoni, V. A., Laster, L., and Seegmiller, J. E. The nature of the defect in tyrosine metabolism in alkaptonuria. J. Biol. Chem., 230:251, 1968.

ALBINISM

Fitzpatrick, T. B. Albinism. In Stanbury, J. B., Wyngaarden, J. B., and Frederickson, D. S., eds., The Metabolic Basis of Inherited Disease. New York, McGraw-Hill Book Co., 1960, p. 428.

Hermansky, F., and Pudlak, P. Albinism associated with hemorrhagic diathesis and unusual pigmented reticular cells in the bone marrow: Report of two cases with histochemical studies. Blood, 14:162, 1959.

Kukita, A., and Fitzpatrick, T. B. Demonstration of tyrosinase in melanocytes of the human hair matrix by autoradiography. Science, 121:893, 1955.

HISTIDINEMIA

Ghadimi, H., and Zischka, R. Histidinemia. In Nyhan, W. L., ed., Amino Acid Metabolism and Genetic Variation. New York, McGraw-Hill Book Co., 1967, p. 133.

La Du, B. N., Howell, R. R., Jacoby, G. A., Seegmiller, J. E., and Zannoni, V. G. The enzymatic defect in histidinemia. Biochem. Biophys. Res. Commun., 7:398, 1962.

Zannoni, V. G., and La Du, B. N. Determination of histidine deaminase in human stratum corneum and its absence in histidinemia. Biochem. J., 88:160, 1963.

MAPLE SYRUP DISEASE

Dancis, J., Hutzler, J., and Levitz, M. Metabolism of the white blood cells in maple syrup urine disease. Biochem. Biophys. Acta, 43:342, 1960.

───── Hutzler, J., and Rokkones, T. Intermittent branched chain ketoaciduria: variant of maple syrup urine disease. New Eng. J. Med., 276:84, 1967.

Goedde, H. W., and Keller, W. Metabolic pathways in maple syrup urine disease. In Nyhan, W. H., ed., Amino Acid Metabolism and Genetic Variation. New York, McGraw-Hill Book Co., 1967, p. 191.

Menkes, J. H., Hurst, P. L., and Craig, J. M. A new syndrome: Progressive familial infantile cerebral dysfunction associated with an unusual urinary substance. Pediatrics, 14:462, 1954.

Snyderman, S. E., Norton, P. M., Roitman, E., and Holt, L. E., Jr. Maple syrup urine disease with particular reference to diet therapy. Pediatrics, 34:454, 1964.

HYPERVALINEMIA

Dancis, J., Hutzler, J., Tada, K., Wada, Y., Morikawa, T., and Arakawa, T. Hypervalinemia: A defect in valine transamination. Pediatrics, 39:813, 1967.

HYPERGLYCINEMIA

Childs, B., Nyhan, W. L., Borden, M., Bard, L., and Cooke, R. E. Idiopathic hyper-lycinemia and hyperglycinuria, a new disorder of amino acid metabolism. I. Pediatrics, 27:522, 1961.

Hsia, Y. E., Scully, K. J., Rosenberg, L. E. Defective propionate carboxylation in ketotic hyperglycinemia. Lancet, 1:757, 1969.

Tada, K., Yoshida, T., Morikawa, T., Minakawa, A., Wada, Y., Ando, T., and Shimura, K. Idiopathic hyperglycinemia (the first case in Japan). Tohuku J. Exp. Med., 80:218, 1963.

METHYLMALONIC ACIDEMIA

Morrow, G., III, Barness, L. A., Auerbach, V. H., DiGeorge, A. M., Andot, T., and Nyhan, W. L. Observations on the coexistence of methylmalonic acidemia and glycinemia. J. Pediat., 74:680-690, 1969.

Mudd, S. H., Levy, H. L., and Abeles, R. H. A derangement in B_{12} metabolism leading to homocystinemia, cystathioninemia and methylmalonic aciduria. Biochem. Biophys. Res. Commun., 35:121, 1969.

Oberholzer, V. G., Levin, B., Burgess, E. A., and Young, W. F. Methylmalonic aciduria: an inborn error of metabolism leading to chronic metabolic acidosis. Arch. Dis. Child., 42:492, 1967.

Rosenberg, L. E., Lilljeqvist, A. C., and Hsia, Y. E. Methylmalonic aciduria. New Eng. J. Med., 278:1319, 1968.

Stokke, O., Eldjarn, L., Norum, K. R., Steen-Johnson, J., and Halvorsen, S. Methylmalonic acidemia: a new inborn error of metabolism which may cause fatal acidosis in the neonatal period. Scand. J. Clin. Lab. Invest., 20:313, 1967.

NONKETOTIC HYPERGLYCINEMIA

Ando, T., Nyhan, W. L., Gerritsen, T., Gong, L., Heiner, D. C., and Bray, P. F. Metabolism of glycine in the nonketotic form of hyperglycinemia. Pediat. Res., 2:254-63, 1968.

Gerritsen, T., Kaveggia, E., and Waisman, H. A. A new type of idiopathic hyperglycinemia with hypo-oxaluria. Pediatrics, 36:882-91, 1965.

Rampini, S., Vischer, D., Curticus, H. C., Anders, P. W., Tencredi, F., Frischknecht, W., and Prader, A. Hereditare hyperglycinamie: Klinische bild und bestimmung von glyoxylsaure und oxalsaure im urin bei je einem patienten mit der acidotischen und der nicht acidotischen form. Helv. Paediat. Acta, 22:135-9, 1967.

Ziter, F. A., Bray, P. F., Madsen, J. A., and Nyhan, W. L. The clinical findings in a patient with nonketotic hyperglycinemia. Pediat. Res., 2:250-3, 1968.

SARCOSINEMIA

Gerritsen, T., and Waisman, H. A. Hypersarcosinemia. An Inborn Error of Metabolism. New Eng. J. Med., 275:66, 1966.

Hagge, W., Brodehl, J., and Gellissen, K. Hypersarcosinemia. Pediat. Res., 1:409, 1967.

HYPEROXALURIA

Crawhall, J. C., Scowen, E. F., Watts, R. W. E. Conversion of glycine to oxalate in primary hyperoxaluria. Lancet, 2:806, 1959.

Elder, T. D., and Wyngaarden, J. B. The biosynthesis and turnover of oxalate in normal and hyperoxaluric subjects. J. Clin. Invest., 39:1337, 1960.

Smith, L. H., Jr., and Williams, H. E. Hyperoxaluria (glycolicaciduria). In Nyhan, W. L., ed., Amino Acid Metabolism and Genetic Variation. New York, McGraw-Hill Book Co., 1967, p. 239.

Solomons, C. C., Goodman, S. I., and Riley, C. M. Calcium carbimide in the treatment of primary hyperoxaluria. New Eng. J. Med., 276:207, 1967.

HYPERPROLINEMIA AND HYDROXYPROLINEMIA

Efron, M. L. Familial hyperprolinemia. Report of a second case associated with congenital renal malformations, hereditary hematuria and mild mental retardation, wtih demonstration of an enzyme defect. New Eng. J. Med., 272:1243, 1965.

——— Bixby, E. M., Palattao, L. G., and Pryles, C. V. Hydroxyprolinemia associated with mental deficiency. New Eng. J. Med., 267:1193, 1962.

——— Bixby, E. M., and Pryles, C. V. Hydroxyprolinemia. II. A rare metabolic disease due to a deficiency of the enzyme hydroxyproline oxidase. New Eng. J. Med., 272:1299, 1965.

Shafer, I. A., Scriver, C. R., and Efron, M. L. Familial hyperprolinemia, cerebral dysfunction and renal anomalies occurring in a family with hereditary nephropathy and deafness. New Eng. J. Med., 267:51, 1962.

CYSTATHIONINURIA

Frimpter, G. W. Cystathioninuria: Nature of the defect. Science, 149:1095, 1965.

——— Haymovitz, A., and Horwith, M. Cystathioninuria. New Eng. J. Med., 268:333, 1963.

Harris, H., Penrose, L. S., and Thomas, D. H. H. Cystathioninuria. Ann. Hum. Genet., 23:442, 1959.

HOMOCYSTINURIA

Barber, G. W., and Spaeth, G. E. The successful treatment of homocystinuria with pyridoxine. J. Pediat., 75:463, 1969.

Carson, N. A. J., Cusworth, D. C., Dent, C. E., Field, C. M. B., Neill, D. W., and Westall, R. G. Homocystinuria: a new inborn error of metabolism associated with mental deficiency. Arch. Dis. Child., 38:425, 1963.

Gerritsen, T., and Waisman, H. A. Homocystinuria, an error in the metabolism of methionine. Pediatrics, 33:413, 1964.

Mudd, S. H., Finkelstein, J. D., Irreverre, F., and Laster, L. Homocystinuria: An enzymatic defect. Science, 143:1443, 1964.

——— Levy, H. L., and Abeles, R. H. A derangement in B_{12} metabolism leading to homocystinemia, cystathioninemia, and methylmalonic aciduria. Biochem. Biophys. Res. Commun., 35:121, 1969.

HYPERLYSINEMIA

Colombo, J. P., Richterich, R., Donath, A., Spahr, A., and Rossi, E. Congenital lysine intolerance with periodic ammonia intoxication. Lancet, 1:1014, 1964.

Ghadimi, H., and Zischka, R. Hyperlysinemia and lysine metabolism. In Nyhan, W. L., ed., Amino Acid Metabolism and Genetic Variation. New York, McGraw-Hill Book Co., 1967, p. 227.

Woody, N. C., Ong, E. B., and Pupene, M. B. Paths of lysine degradation in patients with hyperlysinemia. Pediatrics, 40:986, 1967.

BETA-ALANINE ABNORMALITIES

Perry, T. L., Hansen, S., and Love, D. L. Serum carnosinase deficiency in carnosinaemia. Lancet, 1:1229, 1968.

Scriver, C. R., Pueschel, S., and Davies, E. Hyper-β-alanemia associated with β-aminoaciduria and γ-aminobutyric aciduria, somnolence and seizures. New Eng. J. Med., 274:636, 1966.

Disorders of the Urea Cycle

Argininosuccinic Aciduria

Argininosuccinic aciduria is one of a group of metabolic defects involving enzymes of the urea cycle.

CLINICAL FINDINGS. Twelve patients have been reported. All but one were severely mentally retarded; 7 had generalized seizures, 6 electroencephalographic abnormalities, 5 ataxia, and 3 hepatomegaly. Seven had short, brittle hair which seldom needed cutting and was diagnosed as trichorrhexis nodosa. The biochemical findings of the disease may be found in patients in whom mental retardation is only mild and there are no other abnormalities.

BIOCHEMICAL FINDINGS. Argininosuccinic acid is an intermediate formed from citrulline and aspartic acid, which is not normally found in body fluids. The disorder represents a failure in the cleavage of this compound to arginine and fumaric acid. Activity of argininosuccinase, the enzyme which catalyzes this reaction, was found to be essentially inactive in specimens of liver obtained from patients with this disorder.

Low concentrations of argininosuccinic acid in plasma and its very high rate of urinary excretion are consistent with very efficient renal clearance in this condition. For these reasons this condition and similar disorders have been called no-threshold aminoacidurias to distinguish them from disorders of transport, in which an amino acid occurs in the urine without elevation in plasma concentrations. High concentrations of argininosuccinic acid are found in the cerebrospinal fluid. Therefore, it has been suggested that the enzyme defect is present in the brain and that argininosuccinic acid produced in the brain may produce cerebral symptoms. Disruption in the urea cycle is indicated by the fact that these patients develop postprandial elevations of blood ammonia and signs of ammonia toxicity. Dietary protein restriction is indicated for these reasons.

Citrullinemia

Citrullinemia is another disorder of urea cycle metabolism. It was originally recognized through screening survey for amino acids of the urine of mentally retarded children.

CLINICAL FINDINGS. Citrullinemia has been studied in two unrelated patients. Both appeared normal for about the first half year of life. Thereafter, episodic vomiting ensued which could be related to a postabsorptive elevation in blood ammonia. Severe vomiting, coma, and seizures developed. Both have developed microcephaly and severe mental retardation with IQ values less than 40.

BIOCHEMICAL FINDINGS. The urinary excretion of citrulline in an 18-month-old patient has been as high as 2 to 3 g per day. Concentrations in plasma were elevated (20 to 35 mg/100 ml) and smaller elevations were found in the cerebrospinal fluid. As in the case of argininosuccinic aciduria, urea excretion was normal in one patient, but the other had a persistently low BUN. The metabolic block in this disease is in the formation of argininosuccinic acid from citrulline, and argininosuccinic acid synthetase has been found to be deficient in liver and in fibroblasts cultured from the skin.

GENETICS. The disorder is presumably transmitted as an autosomal recessive. The parents of the first patient were first cousins.

Hyperammonemia

Hyperammonemia is a generic term for a number of other disorders of the urea cycle. These include *carbamyl phosphate synthetase deficiency* and *ornithinemia* with ornithine transcarbamylase deficiency.

CLNICAL FINDINGS. Clinical manifestations have been those of ammonia intoxication, mental retardation, and recurrent episodes of vomiting followed by lethargy, stupor, and coma. Onset of these attacks has been as early as the first 6 weeks of life and as late as 9 years, with slurred speech, headaches, and screaming, followed by stupor. Microcephaly was also prominent.

BIOCHEMICAL FINDINGS. Ammonia concentrations in blood and cerebrospinal fluid were found to be markedly elevated. Concentrations over 500 and 300 μg per 100 ml respectively were seen. Assay of the enzyme ornithine transcarbamylase, which converts carbamyl phosphate and ornithine to citrulline, revealed a deficiency in liver obtained from one patient by biopsy. In an analogous syndrome with diminished activity of the hepatic enzyme carbamyl phosphate synthetase, there was some elevation of the plasma concentrations of glycine and diminished incorporation of ^{15}N-glycine or ammonia into urea.

REFERENCES

ARGININOSUCCINIC ACIDURIA

Allan, J. D., Cusworth, D. C., Dent, C. E., and Wilson, V. K. A disease, probably hereditary, characterized by severe mental deficiency and a constant gross abnormality of amino acid metabolism. Lancet, 1:182, 1958.

Miller, A. L., and McLean, P. Urea cycle enzymes in the liver of a patient with argininosuccinic aciduria. Clin. Sci., 32:385, 1967.

Westall, R. G. Argininosuccinic aciduria: identification and reactions of the abnormal metabolite in a newly described form of mental disease, with some preliminary metabolic studies. Biochem. J., 77:135, 1960.

CITRULLINEMIA

McMurray, W. C., Rathbun, J. C., Mohyuddin, F., and Koegler, S. J. Citrullinuria. Pediatrics, 32:347, 1963.

Morrow, G., III, Barness, L. A., and Efron, M. L. Citrullinemia with defective urea production. Pediatrics, 40:565, 1967.

Tedesco, T. A., and Mellman, W. J. Argininosuccinate synthetase activity and citrulline metabolism in cells cultured from a citrullinemic subject. Proc. Nat. Acad. Sci., 57:829, 1967.

HYPERAMMONEMIA

Efron, M. L. Disorders of the ornithine urea cycle. *In* Nyhan, W. L., ed., Amino Acid Metabolism and Genetic Variation. New York, McGraw-Hill Book Co., 1967, p. 219.

Freeman, J. M., Nicholson, J. F., Masland, W. S., Rowland, L. P., and Carter, S. Ammonia intoxication due to a congenital defect in urea synthesis. Proc. Amer. Pediat. Soc., 74:36, 1964.

Levin, B., Abraham, J. N., Oberholzer, V. G., and Burgess, E. A. Hyperammonaemia: A deficiency of liver ornithine transcarbamylase. Occurrence in mother and child. Arch. Dis. Child., 44:152, 1969.

Russell, A., Levin, B., Oberholzer, V. G., and Sinclair, L. Hyperammonaemia: A new instance of inborn enzymatic defect of the biosynthesis of urea. Lancet, 2:699, 1962.

8.3
DISORDERS OF AMINO ACID TRANSPORT

WILLIAM L. NYHAN

Hartnup Disease

Hartnup disease is an unusual disorder in which the transport of certain amino acids, including tryptophan, is abnormal in the intestine and in the renal tubule. It was named for the first family described, in which 4 of the 8 children of parents who were first cousins were affected. The constant feature of the disease is an amino-aciduria of characteristic pattern.

CLINICAL FINDINGS. Clinical characteristics are intermittent and variable. Affected siblings in the original family did not develop clinical manifestations until 6 to 8 years of age. Patients have appeared to develop pellagra, with a red scaly eruption on the exposed skin. Photosensitivity is present, and manifestations in the skin are related to exposure and dosage of ulraviolet. In addition, patients have cerebellar ataxia occurring in attacks of variable severity which nevertheless are completely reversible. Other patients have had attacks of collapsing or fainting, severe headache, or psychiatric abnormalities similar to those observed in pellagra. Mental retardation is common but not uniform, and deterioration has not been documented. Attacks have been precipitated by infection, sulfonamide therapy, and by dietary inadequacy. Cases have been reported very infrequently in North America, which may reflect a degree of protection against clinical symptoms by a generally very adequate diet.

BIOCHEMICAL FINDINGS. Even in the absence of symptomatology patients may be recognized by the amino-aciduria. It is renal in type, and plasma concentrations of amino acids are normal or somewhat decreased. The following amino acids are excreted in 5 to 10 times the usual amounts: threonine, serine, asparagine, glutamine, alanine, valine, isoloeucine, leucine, tyrosine, phenylalanine, histidine, and tryptophan. This is a large group of amino acids, but the pattern of excretion is striking. It differs from the commonly encountered generalized amino-aciduria in that the excretion of glycine, glutamic acid, and lysine are normal, and there is no free proline or hydroxyproline in the urine. The dibasic amino acids, arginine and ornithine, are excluded as well as lysine. The urine in this condition is also characterized by the presence of a number of indolic derivatives of tryptophan. Indican (indoxyl sulfate), indolylacetic acid, indolylacetylglutamine, and breakdown products of indolylpyruvic acid are readily recognized using paper chromatography. On the other hand, normal products of tryptophan metabolism such as kynurenine and nicotinic acid are found in reduced amounts. These patients respond to an oral load of tryptophan with abnormally increased excretion of indican and indolic acids. Tryptophan loading after sterilization of the intestinal flora with antibiotics results in a small increase in indole excretion in control subjects, while patients with Hartnup disease have virtually no increase in indole excretion and unabsorbed tryptophan accumulates in the feces. These observations indicate that there is a defect in the absorption of tryptophan in the cells of the intestine as well as in the kidney. The indoles found in the urine in this disease are secondary to the action of intestinal bacteria on unabsorbed tryptophan.

GENETICS. Genetic analysis suggests transmission as an autosomal recessive character.

TREATMENT. Most patients have been treated with nicotinamide. It is not certain that improvements observed in cutaneous and neurologic manifestations with treatment were not spontaneous, but treatment is recommended, as is good general protein nutrition.

Cystinuria

Cystinuria is an inherited defect in renal tubular function in which the reabsorption of cystine, lysine, arginine, and ornithine is impaired. The abnormality is of clinical significance because of the insolubility of cystine, which forms stones when present in the urine in high concentration. The excretion of the other three amino acids does not influence the health of the patient.

CLINICAL FINDINGS. Patients with cystinuria generally develop calculi some time before the age of 30 years. Some have large numbers of calculi requiring surgical removal for relief of colic or obstruction. Repeated infections of the urinary tract and renal failure are common. The stones represent aggregations of cystine varying from tiny sands of gravel to staghorn calculi filling the renal pelvis or huge calculi of the bladder. Pure cystine crystals are radiolucent, but variable contents of calcium provide opacity in many stones. These patients do not have symptoms other than those resulting from stone formation. Statistically, groups of patients with cystinuria are shorter in stature than others. They should be distinguished from patients with *cystinosis*, in whom the Lignac-deToni-Fanconi syndrome of glycosuria, generalized amino-aciduria, phosphaturia, and renal rickets is associated with deposits of cystine in tissues such as the kidney, cornea, and the bone marrow. Such patients do not have abnormal amounts of cystine in the urine.

BIOCHEMICAL FINDINGS. In cystinuria the concentrations of cystine and the other amino acids in the blood is not elevated. The clearances of cystine, lysine, arginine, and ornithine are markedly elevated. That of cystine approximates the glomerular filtration rate. These amino acids compete for a common tubular transport mechanism, and infusion of lysine in control individuals results in an increase in the excretion of the other three amino acids, while in cystinuric individuals lysine infusion does not alter the excretion of the other three, indicating that they are already being excreted maximally. Evidence has been obtained that, as in Hartnup disease, there is also a disorder of intestinal absorption in some patients with cystinuria which involves the amino acids cystine, lysine, arginine, and ornithine. Inefficiently absorbed lysine, arginine, and ornithine are converted by intestinal bacteria to the diamines, cadaverine and putrescine, which may be detected in the urine as well as in the feces.

GENETICS. Genetic studies indicate that there are at least three forms of cystinuria in which the homozygotes are clinically indistinguishable. They are now designated type I, II, and III. In type I the heterozygotes are detectable only by studies of intestinal transport of cystine or the dibasic amino acids. This is the most common form, accounting for almost two-thirds of all carriers. Type I homozygotes, of course, also have the intestinal transport defect. In types II and III the heterozygotes excrete increased amounts of cystine and lysine in the urine. Excretion of arginine and ornithine may also be increased. Type II differs from type III in that an oral load of cystine does not appear to be absorbed into the blood, and lysine transport is altered in intestinal cells in vitro. The three genes are allelic, and double heterozygotes have been observed who carry two different abnormal genes and thus have clinical manifestations of homozygous cystinuria.

Cystinuria is relatively common, occurring about once in every 20,000 live births. The condition can be screened for as in homocystinuria using the simple cyanide nitroprusside test. Confirmation of the diagnosis requires a quantitative assay of cystine content.

TREATMENT. Treatment of cystinuria is aimed at the prevention of urinary lithiasis. Stones are regularly seen when cystine concentrations are over 300 mg/L, which occurs with excretions of over 250 mg of cystine per gram of creatinine. Crystallization and stone formation can be minimized by increasing urine volumes or by increasing cystine solubility. However, very large amounts of oral fluids are required. Alkalinization can markedly promote the solubility of cystine, but this effect is small until the urine pH is over 7.6, which is not readily achieved physiologically. Systematic drinking of water through the night is essential for the maintenance of adequate urine volumes, but in practice very few adults and almost no children will drink enough to prevent stones. Penicillamine therapy has, therefore, brought about a real advance in the management of this disease. Penicillamine forms a mixed disulfide with cysteine which is considerably more soluble than cystine. The addition of this compound to readily crystallizing cystinuric urine prevents crystallization. Similarly, the oral administration of penicillamine to cystinuric patients is capable of reduction of cystine content in the urine to levels at which stones should not form.

This type of therapy requires careful quantitative monitoring of cystine excretion and its concentration in urine, if success is to be achieved.

Dibasic amino-aciduria and *hypercystinuria* are two conditions which relate to cystinuria. In dibasic amino-aciduria the dibasic amino acids, lysine, ornithine, and arginine, are excreted in large amounts because of a renal tubular absorptive defect, but cystine excretion is normal. Lysine transport in the intestine appears also to be abnormal. The trait is inherited as a dominant and appears to have no clinical manifestations. In hypercystinuria, cystine is excreted in the urine in increased amounts due to a specific tubular transport defect, while the excretion of the dibasic amino acids is normal. Clinical manifestations have not been observed, but the disorder has been reported in only one family. Anyone with large amounts of cystine in the urine is in danger of developing calculi.

Iminoglycinuria

Renal iminoglycinuria appears to be a benign chemical abnormality without clinical abnormality. Its occurrence has provided interesting information on human renal tubular transport. In this situation, there is selective impairment in the transport of proline, hydroxyproline, and glycine. Net renal tubular reabsorption of the imino acids is about 80 percent of normal and that of glycine is about 60 percent of normal. An intestinal transport defect for the same amino acids has been observed in some families but not in others.

In most heterozygotes there is impaired renal tubular transport of glycine. Thus, these individuals may present with tubular hyperglycinuria. It is thought that this accounts for patients with glycinuria who were reported by deVries as having a dominantly inherited condition. On the other hand, some heterozygotes may be "silent," that is may have no glycinuria. These observations and those on intestinal transport suggest that there is more than one allelic mutation responsible for iminoglycinuria.

REFERENCES

HARTNUP DISEASE

Baron, D. N., Dent, C. E., Harris, H., Hart, E. W., and Jepson, J. B. Hereditary pellagra-like skin rash with temporary cerebellar ataxia, constant renal amino-aciduria, and other bizarre biochemical features. Lancet, 2:421, 1956.

Milne, M. D., Crawford, M. C., Girao, C. B., and Loughridge, L. The metabolic abnormality of Hartnup disease. Biochem. J., 72:30P, 1959.

Scriver, C. R. Hartnup disease. A genetic modification of intestinal and renal transport of certain neutral alpha-amino acids. New Eng. J. Med., 273:530, 1965.

CYSTINURIA

Crawhall, J. C., Scowen, E. F., and Watts, R. W. E. Effect of penicillamine on cystinuria. Brit. Med. J., 1:588, 1963.

Harris, H., and Robson, E. B. Cystinuria. Amer. J. Med., 28:774, 1957.

Rosenberg, L. E. Genetic Heterogeneity in Cystinuria. In Nyhan, W. L., ed., Amino Acid Metabolism and Genetic Variation. New York, McGraw-Hill Book Co., 1967, p. 341.

IMINOGLYCINURIA

DeVries, A., Kochwa, S., Lazebnik, J., Frank, M., and Djaldetti, M. Glycinuria, a hereditary disorder associated with nephrolithiasis. Amer. J. Med., 23:408, 1957.

Rosenberg, L. F., Durant, J. L., and Elsas, L. J. Familial glycinuria. An inborn error of renal tubular transport. New Eng. J. Med., 278:1407, 1968.

Scriver, C. R. Renal tubular transport of proline, hydroxyproline and glycine: III. Genetic basis for more than one mode of uptake in human kidney. J. Clin. Invest., 47:823, 1968.

8.4
DISORDERS OF PURINE AND PYRIMIDINE METABOLISM

WILLIAM L. NYHAN

Gout

Primary gout, in which increased concentrations of uric acid are found in the blood, has been recognized since antiquity as a genetically determined disorder. It is now clear that populations of hyperuricemic patients are quite heterogeneous. The numbers and types of these disorders are just beginning to be defined.

Hyperuricemia may or may not be associated at any period of life with clinical manifestations such as acute gouty arthritis, tophaceous accumulations of uric acid in and around joints and elsewhere, urinary calculi or crystalluria, and progressive renal failure. It may be that primary gout is renal in etiology as well as metabolic (Table 3). In addition, secondary gout may occur in association with conditions in which large numbers of cells are being

TABLE 3.   Types of Hyperuricemia*

Primary:	1. Metabolic—Overproduction
	2. Renal—Diminished clearance
Secondary:	1. Cell Turnover—Leukemia, polycythemia vera, hemolytic anemia
	2. Renal—Glomerular insufficiency
	3. Pharmacologic—Block in urate secretion, chlorthiazide and other diuretics, hyperlactic acidemia

*Any condition which produces hyperuricemia may lead, if sufficiently prolonged, to all of the clinical manifestations of gout.

broken down, especially in leukemia and its treatment, and in conditions in which there is chronic glomerular insufficiency. Uric acid levels in the blood may also be secondarily raised by compounds which compete with uric acid for renal tubular secretion, such as chlorothiazide. Lactic acid accumulating endogenously in metabolic disease may also produce this effect. Elevations of uric acid in the blood have been found in glycogen storage disease due to glucose-6-phosphatase deficiency, and clinical gout has been reported in patients with this disease. Hyperuricemia has also been reported in diabetic ketoacidosis, pregnancy, obesity and its treatment with total starvation, hypercholesterolemia, hypoparathyroidism, and psoriasis. Concentrations of uric acid in mongolism may be somewhat higher than in control children. Since gout of any type is rare in childhood, even apparently clear examples of secondary gout in children should be investigated for the presence of a primary inherited disorder.

Primary gout is predominantly a disease of adult males, occurring in the female after the menopause. Hyperuricemia is found in approximately 25 percent of the relatives of gouty individuals. Among these individuals, it generally develops in the male after 16 years of age. Occurrence of gout in a teen-age male appears to represent the occasional early manifestation of a particularly severe case. In the earlier literature, only 17 patients less than 10 years of age with gout had been reported. In this group, male predominance was not as striking as in older individuals. There was no predilection for disease in the lower extremities and the great toe; the clinical symptoms started in the upper extremities. The early occurrence of tophi, deformities, and renal failure was striking and severe gout was a prominent feature in other members of the family. It is probable that all of these patients had had hyperuricemia on the basis of overproduction of uric acid, but only one was studied from this point of view. In this patient, in whose family severe early gout was common, excessive quantities of uric acid were excreted in the urine as early as 3 months of age, and he converted considerably more ^{15}N-labeled glycine to uric acid than did controls.

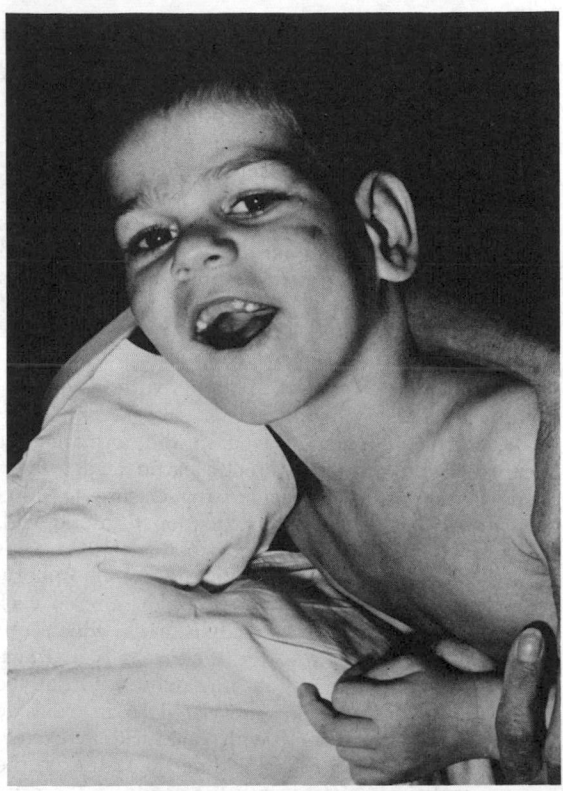

Fig. 3. G. W., a 5-year-old boy with hyperuricemia and complete deficiency of the enzyme hypoxanthine guanine phosphoribosyl transferase. He had mental retardation and athetoid cerebral palsy. Self-mutilation is evident in the bitten lower lip.

LESCH-NYHAN SYNDROME. Another type of hyperuricemia in childhood was defined in 1964 in association with a disorder of the central nervous system. This syndrome is relatively more common than other types of hyperuricemia in children. Although they have not all been reported, the author has obtained information on over 100 additional patients since 1964. As the pathogenesis of this problem has become clearer, other forms of hyperuricemia have been recognized in children, and certain subgroups of gout in adults have been defined.

The cardinal clinical features of this syndrome are mental retardation of major proportions, cerebral palsy, choreoathetosis, and self-destructive biting (Fig. 3). The biting is not associated with anesthesia. It can be inhibited only by firm physical restraint. Most of the patients have destroyed their lips and some have partially amputated fingers. Manifestations characteristic of adult-type gout have been observed, including hyperuricemia, acute arthritis, hematuria, urinary obstruction associated with crystalluria and calculi, and tophi.

BIOCHEMICAL FINDINGS. Adults with gout have have been subclassified on the basis of whether or

not they excrete increased amounts of uric acid in the urine. Patients excreting more than 600 mg of uric acid per day are termed hyperexcretors, while non-hyperexcretors with gout often excrete less uric acid than controls. Control children excrete approximately 10 mg/kg/day, while patients with the Lesch-Nyhan syndrome excrete over 40 mg/kg/day. Overproduction of uric acid occurs in those patients in whom hyperexcretion is seen. This has been most accurately studied by determining the conversion of isotopically labeled glycine to uric acid. Among adults with overproduction gout, approximately twice as much glycine is converted to uric acid as in controls. These patients were found to convert 20 times as much glycine to uric acid as controls, representing a rate of overproduction of uric acid from glycine greater than any previously recorded.

GENETICS. The Lesch-Nyhan syndrome is transmitted as an X-linked recessive character. The primary expression of the abnormal gene is in the activity of the enzyme hypoxanthine guanine phosphoribosyl transferase (HGPRT), which catalyzes the reaction of these purines with phosphoribosyl pyrophosphate (PRPP) to form their respective nucleotides, inosinic and guanylic acids. There is no detectable activity of the enzyme in the erythrocytes of these patients. The enzyme is apparently present normally in all tissues of the body. Thus, the defect can be detected in cultivated fibroblasts and in cells obtained at amniocentesis, permitting prenatal diagnosis. Female heterozygotes have been shown to have two cell populations, which is definitive confirmation of the Lyon hypothesis of X-inactivation. The female carrier can be detected by the examination of cultured fibroblasts.

The treatment of gout in the adult has depended on the use of uricosuric agents. However, since most hyperuricemic children have increased urinary urate, use of these agents is contraindicated and may lead to acute renal failure. Dietary therapy has little to recommend it.

TREATMENT. The treatment of acute gouty arthritis is with colchicine, which must nearly always be given in dosage sufficient to produce diarrhea in order to terminate an acute attack. The development of allopurinol for the treatment of hyperuricemia is a significant therapeutic advance. This agent, hydroxypyrazolopyrimidine, lowers uric acid concentrations in blood and urine by the inhibition of xanthine oxidase. Side effects are extremely rare and it is highly effective in treating those aspects of gout or hyperuricemia, such as arthritis, nephropathy, and tophi, which are caused by uric acid. Treatment with allopurinol has no effect on the cerebral manifestations of hyperuricemic children.

OTHER HYPERURICEMIAS. It is now apparent that there are a number of different X-linked defects in the enzyme HGPRT. Partial deficiencies account for a certain number of adults with overproduction gout. Patients have been observed in the pediatric age group in which partial defects in this enzyme have led to urolithiasis, but no abnormalities of the central nervous system have been seen.

Other types of hyperuricemia have begun to be recognized in childhood in which there is overproduction of purine de novo but no abnormality in activity of HGPRT. One of these patients also had mild mental retardation, failure to cry with tears, and behavior suggestive of autism.

Xanthinuria

Xanthinuria is a rarely encountered metabolic disorder in which large amounts of xanthine are excreted in the urine.

CLINICAL FINDINGS. It may occur without any clinical manifestations, although it was initially recognized in a 4-year-old girl with urinary xanthine calculi and attendant signs of hematuria, frequency, and nonopaque filling defects on pyelography. On the other hand, most individuals in whom xanthine stones are found do not have this disorder. Patients with xanthinuria do not have elevated concentrations of xanthine in the blood. The condition may be diagnosed by the presence of abnormally low concentrations of uric acid in the serum. The differential diagnosis of hypouricemia includes disorders such as Wilson's disease and the Fanconi syndrome, in which renal abnormalities result in inefficient renal tubular reabsorption. This is the defect in the Dalmatian dog where uric acid is cleared at the rate of glomerular filtration. A similar anomaly has been reported in a healthy young man.

BIOCHEMICAL FINDINGS. Xanthine is the immediate precursor of uric acid. It is formed normally from guanine through the action of guanase, and from hypoxanthine via xanthine oxidase. Xanthine oxidase is an enzyme of very general substrate specificity which is also responsible for the conversion of xanthine to uric acid. It is found in liver, milk, and intestinal mucosa. Studies carried out on biopsy material from a patient and controls indicated that this enzyme is deficient in xanthinuria.

TREATMENT. Treatment of xanthinuria involves the promotion of solution of xanthine in the urine by increasing fluid intake and by alkali therapy.

Orotic Aciduria

Orotic aciduria is an inherited disorder of pyrimidine metabolism. It has been studied in detail in a single patient who died of overwhelming varicella at two and a half years. However, extensive studies have been carried out on the family which serve to establish the autosomal recessive genetic transmission and to localize its metabolic defect. Furthermore, iatrogenic orotic aciduria has been observed to be a regular concomitant of cancer chemotherapy with 6-azauridine.

CLINICAL FINDINGS. Orotic aciduria is characterized clinically by megaloblastic anemia that is resistant to therapy with vitamin B_{12}, folic acid, or ascorbic acid. Leucopenia, retarded growth, and blue sclerae were also noted. A devastating response to what is ordinarily a mild infection is often seen in megaloblastic anemias of early life. The feature which led to the recognition of the condition was crystalluria. Crystals precipitated on standing at room temperature, and were particularly prominent at times of acute illness when the patient reduced his fluid intake. Urethral and ureteral obstruction have been observed as the result of precipitated crystals.

BIOCHEMICAL FINDINGS. The biosynthesis of pyrimidines begins with the reaction of carbamyl phosphate, the compound involved in the formation of citrulline from ornithine, and aspartic acid, which yields carbamyl aspartic acid. Ring closure to dihydroorotic acid is followed by oxidation to orotic acid. Orotic acid is converted to its ribonucleotide, orotidylic acid, via the enzyme orotidylic pyrophosphorylase. Orotidylic acid is converted in the presence of orotidylic decarboxylase to uridylic acid, which can then be incorporated into the nucleic acids or transformed to other pyrimidine nucleotides. Orotidylic acid is also readily dephosphorylated to its riboside orotidine. Patients treated with 6-azauridine excrete large amounts of both orotic acid and orotidine in the urine, which is consistent with the action of the drug as a competitive inhibitor of orotidylc decarboxylase. In congental orotic aciduria only orotic acid is found in excess in the urine. Enzymatic studies carried out on the parents of the first patient indicated reduced activities of both orotidylic acid decarboxylase and orotidylic pyrophosphorylase. These studies have been traced through four generations of this family, establishing an autosomal recessive mode of transmission. Erythrocytes and fibroblasts of homozygotes have now been shown to be deficient in the activity of both enzymes.

TREATMENT. Therapeutic approach to this condition has been successfully made by replacement of the missing nucleotide or its precursor. Excellent remission has been obtained with a mixture of the pyrimidine nucleotides cytidylic and uridylic acids. Hematologic response in the patient mentioned was accompanied by weight gain for the first time in 18 months and marked improvement in activity and development. Concomitantly, the amounts of orotic acid in the urine decreased, an effect which suggests a negative feedback effect of the nucleotides on earlier steps in pyrimidine biosynthesis. Preparations of nucleotides are not well tolerated by mouth. However, the response to oral uridine, which is readily tolerated, is equally good. Patients with the disease have now been successfully maintained on this therapy for long periods of time.

Beta-Aminoisobutyric Aciduria

The excretion of large amounts of beta-aminoiso-butyric acid in the urine appears not to be a disease but a laboratory curiosity and an example of human variation that may be under genetic control.

This compound is a breakdown product of the DNA pyrimidine, thymine; it may also be formed from valine. Since it reacts with ninhydrin it may be found in the urine in the course of analysis for amino acids. Beta-aminoisobutyric aciduria may be found as a genetic trait or in conditions such as leukemia, where its presence may reflect increased breakdown of cellular nucleic acids. The genetic trait is inherited as a recessive character. It occurs in about 10 percent of Caucasians, 20 percent of American Negroes, and as many as 40 percent of Orientals and American Indians.

REFERENCES

HYPERURICEMIA OF CHILDHOOD

Kogut, M. D., Donnell, G. N., Nyhan, W. L., and Sweet-man, L. Disorder of purine metabolism due to partial deficiency of hypoxanthine guanine phosphoribosyl-transferase. Amer. J. Med., 48:148-161, 1970.

Lesch, M., and Nyhan, W. L. A familial disorder of uric acid metabolism and central nervous system function. Amer. J. Med., 36:561, 1964.

Nyhan, W. L., James, J. A., Teberg, A. J., Sweetman, L., and Nelson, L. G. A new disorder of purine metabolism with behavioral manifestations. J. Pediat., 74:20-27, 1969.

Rosenthal, I. M., Gaballah, S., and Rafelson, M. D., Jr. Gout in infancy manifested by renal failure. Pediatrics, 33:251, 1964.

Seegmiller, J. E., Rosenbloom, F. M., and Kelley, W. N. Enzyme defect associated with a sex-linked human neurological disorder and excessive purine synthesis. Science, 155:1682, 1967.

XANTHINURIA

Watts, R. W. E., Engelman, K., Klincnbcrg, J. B., Sceg miller, J. E., and Sjoerdsma, A. Enzyme defect in a case of xanthinuria. Nature, 201:395, 1964.

OROTIC ACIDURIA

Fallon, H. J., Smith, L. H., Graham, J. B., and Burnett, C. H. A genetic study of hereditary ortoic aciduria. New Eng. J. Med., 270:878, 1964.

Huguley, C. M., Jr., Bain, J. A., Rivers, S. L., and Scoggins, R. B. Refractory megaloblastic anemia associated with excretion of orotic acid. Blood, 14:615, 1959.

Smith, L. H., Jr., Huguley, C. M., Jr., and Bain, J. A. Hereditary orotic aciduria. *In* Stanbury, J. B., Wyngaarden, J. B., and Frederickson, D. S., eds., The Metabolic Basis of Inherited Disease. New York, McGraw-Hill Book Co., 1966, p. 739.

Anomalies of Carbohydrate Metabolism

JAMES B. SIDBURY, JR.

A discussion of carbohydrate metabolism must consider dietary intake, transport, assimilation, storage, and mobilization of the sugars. In the liver, cells not only take glucose from the surrounding media but also return it for regulation of its concentration in the media (interstitial fluid and blood). The liver mobilizes glucose in response to specific hormones. The deposition of glucose into glycogen is affected by glucose concentration and certain hormones, such as insulin and hydrocortisone. Fatty acid metabolism is intimately related and in part regulated by carbohydrate metabolism. Similarly, certain amino acids are considered gluconeogenic because through transamination and a series of enzymatic steps they are able to form glucose and glycogen. Figure 4 shows the interrelationships among these intermediates. We are only just beginning to understand some of the controlling systems. They are complex and involve several different mechanisms, such as hormonal stimulation or inhibition, and feedback control, whereby one of the intermediates of a series of reactions inhibits an earlier step in the series when the latter reactant has reached a certain concentration. Each enzyme protein, hence enzyme activity, is under genetic control. Mutations can and do occur, resulting in an absence, decreased amount, or alteration of the activity of the affected enzyme protein, which may then give rise to an abnormal function and a recognizable alteration which we call a disease. More often than not the disease we recognize (phenotype) is not a direct reflection of the altered or absent protein function but rather due to other enzyme systems which have been secondarily altered by the primary event. The study of these genetic metabolic abnormalities can reveal considerable knowledge about normal metabolic interrelations.

The clinician is faced with many problems in

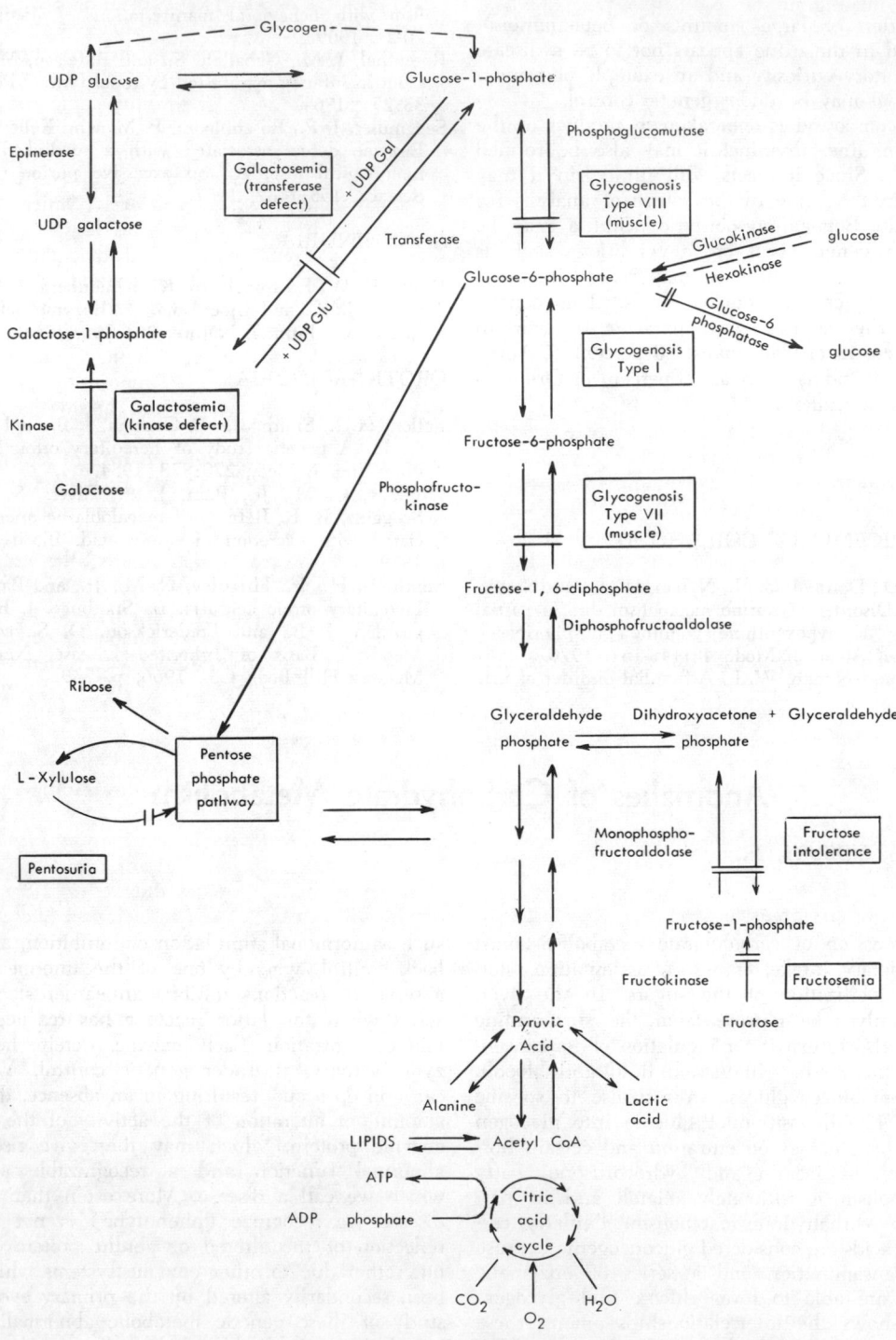

Fig. 4. Pathways of carbohydrate metabolism.

diagnosing and treating patients with these condi-tons. The proper tests must be performed to reveal the abnormality. The information is then used to supply the missing substance when possible, such as insulin in diabetes; to design a diet which bypasses the defective system, as with galactose in galactose-mia; or to provide an agent which will in some way overcome the failure of regulation, such as ACTH and cortisone in some patients with hypoglycemia.

8.5
DIABETES MELLITUS IN CHILDREN

WILLIAM B. WEIL, JR. and
ARTHUR F. KOHRMAN

Diabetes mellitus is a chronic disease, usually hereditary, in which the basic lesion is unknown. It is thought that the fundamental genetic abnor-mality is present from conception, despite the variable time of clinical onset in childhood or adult life. The disease, when clinically apparent, is seen initially as a complex disturbance in carbohydrate utilization; later, most patients show abnormalities of the vascu-lar system. The onset, extent, and sites of vascular damage are highly variable in different patients.

This disease has been recognized for thousands of years, the term *diabetes* presumably having been given to it by the Greeks because of the characteristic polyuria. The Latin term *mellitus* was apparently added by the Romans, who noted the honeylike quality of the urine. From the earliest time until 1914, the life expectancy of a child with diabetes mellitus was approximately one year after the onset of the clinical disease.

In 1914, an intensive starvation diet program was developed which, when followed assiduously, doubled the life expectancy of the juvenile patient with diabetes mellitus—an increase from one year to two years. With the discovery of insulin in 1921, the life expectancy of the juvenile diabetic was im-mediately increased manyfold. The initial insulin produced commercially had a relatively short dura-tion of action and repeated injections were required each day. The first of many modifications of insulin by combination with other materials in order to prolong the hypoglycemic effect was accomplished successfully in 1936 with the production of prota-mine zinc insulin.

The prevalence of diabetes mellitus in children under 15 years of age is estimated to be 40 cases per 100,000 population in the United States. The incidence of this disease in children is of the order of 10,000 new cases each year in the United States.

ETIOLOGY. The fundamental cause of diabetes mellitus remains unknown. The metabolic disturb-ances in childhood diabetes can be corrected by the administration of exogenous insulin; however, it is apparent that simple insulin deficiency does not ex-plain all the abnormalities seen in the natural history of the disease.

The development of sensitive radioimmunoassay techniques for insulin measurement has resulted in a large body of new information. The observation of elevated serum levels of insulin (or insulinlike substances) in preclinical and early clinical diabetes, in both children and adults, has led to speculation that the appearance of clinical diabetes may only mark the visible result of long-standing progressive chemical abnormalities. The fundamental lesion might reside in the peripheral (extrapancreatic) body tissues, in the pancreas, or in both. There are experi-mental observations which support a variety of in-terpretations and only general approaches can be discussed here.

A primary insensitivity to insulin action in the peripheral muscle and adipose tissue might initially force elevated insulin secretion for maintenence of normoglycemia, with ultimate exhaustion of pan-creatic secretory capacity. Similarly, the presence of serum antagonists to insulin, or of specific antibodies, might require augmented insulin production for ho-meostasis. The well-known diabetogenic action of growth hormone and adrenal corticosteroids might contribute to a peripheral demand for increased in-sulin secretion through stimulation of lipolysis and hepatic gluconeogenesis. Indeed, some investigators suggest a major role for growth hormone in the ini-tiation of the sequence of events leading to clinical diabetes.

There is evidence that thickening of small ves-sels, previously thought to result from long-standing diabetes, is evident before the onset of the clinical disease or even of glucose intolerance. Such vascular changes might serve to prevent circulating insulin from reaching the peripheral cells. Thus, several lines of research point to an important, if still undefined, role for extrapancreatic factors in the etiology of dia-betes.

Recent investigations into the synthesis of in-sulin have identified a precursor of insulin, called proinsulin, in the pancreatic islets. The insulin mole-cule is apparently formed initially with a polypep-tide bridge between the A and B chains, which is ordinarily cleaved from the molecule before the insu-lin is released into the circulation. However, in some circumstances the whole proinsulin molecule or vari-ous fragments of it are found in the blood. It is possi-ble that specific genetic defects in the biochemical processes of synthesis, cleavage, or release may be important in the etiology of diabetes. The demonstra-tion of circulating proinsulin and its fragments may provide an explanation for the inactive forms of insulin and insulinlike substances reported by many investigators.

Diabetes mellitus may also result from a variety of situations in which there is an extensive reduction or loss of pancreatic tissue mass, such as after pancreatitis, pancreatectomy, or following malignant replacement.

PATHOLOGY. Early in the course of juvenile diabetes, gross and microscopic examination of the pancreas may fail to reveal pathologic changes, and assays indicate the presence of detectable, and often normal, amounts of insulin. The beta cells in the islets of Langerhans, the presumed source of insulin, contain secretory granules which are believed to represent "packages" of insulin for transport to the circulation. These granules may be normal in quantity and staining characteristics in the first years of the diabetic state in children. After several years of clinical diabetes, the beta cells are diminished in number and lose their granulation; insulin is no longer detectable. Still later in the course of the disease the islets become hyalinized and atrophic.

In long-standing diabetes mellitus there is usually extensive disease of vessels of all sizes. Spasm, localized edema, and obliteration of the small vessels of the eye are responsible for the retinopathy which is seen in many protracted cases of diabetes. These changes, plus hyalinization, also occur in the vessels of the glomerulus; in some patients, the result is a characteristic diabetic glomerulosclerosis, with serious renal malfunction. Arteriosclerosis and obliteration of larger vessels result in the peripheral and cardiac vascular insufficiency seen in the older diabetic. However, none of these pathologic manifestations of diabetes is ordinarily a problem in the juvenile diabetic of recent onset and they rarely appear before middle life. The changes in vision sometimes reported by the young diabetic are most often related to alterations in contractility of the crystalline lens, presumably a result of osmotic changes secondary to fluctuation of blood glucose levels; changes in the refractive index of the aqueous humor are also implicated.

Of great interest are recent electron microscopic observations of thickening of the basement membrane of small vessels in peripheral muscle of prediabetic individuals who had neither hypoglycemia nor glucose intolerance. These observations raise the question that the terminal vascular phenomena heretofore considered to be complications of long-standing diabetes may actually be independent expressions of another more basic lesion. It is then pertinent to consider whether the degree of control of the abnormalities of carbohydrate metabolism in diabetes is necessarily related to the onset or progression of vascular complications.

PATHOPHYSIOLOGY. Whatever the basic abnormality in diabetes mellitus, the metabolic disturbances apparent clinically can be related to three general alterations: (1) reduced entry of glucose into the cell; leading to (2) unavailability of carbohydrate as a substrate for energy needs; and (3) utilization by the cell of alternate substrates, namely fatty acids derived from adipose stores and amino acids from body protein. Alterations in carbohydrate metabolism include accumulation of ingested carbohydrate in the blood, increased glycogenolysis, reduction of hepatic glycogen synthesis, and increased gluconeogenesis from amino acids.

Fat is the alternate substrate first utilized when carbohydrate is unavailable. The result of increased fatty acid oxidation is the increased production of acetyl CoA, and subsequent accumulation of the by-products of acetyl CoA metabolism: acetone, acetoacetic acid, and β-hydroxybutyric acid. This process is enhanced by the increased lipolysis seen in the absence of insulin. In the normal individual, the ketone substances can be used as sources of energy, primarily in muscle, but in the untreated diabetic they accumulate faster than they are utilized. The result is elevated ketone levels in the serum and urine. Since the ketone substances have a lower pK' than bicarbonate, the major extracellular buffer, bicarbonate is converted to carbonic acid and water, with elevation of H^+ in the body fluids; the ketones are excreted as sodium salts. These processes contribute to the excessive sodium losses in the urine and the large obligatory water loss resulting from osmotic diuresis due to hyperglycemia and glycosuria.

The result of these events is the picture of hyperglycemia, glycosuria, ketonemia, acidemia, and severe dehydration characteristically seen in the diabetic with untreated ketoacidosis.

Elevated serum cholesterol is another result of increased acetyl CoA production. Lipolysis is very active in the untreated diabetic, and serum triglyceride and free fatty acid levels are also high.

The utilization of protein to supply amino acids for gluconeogenesis is coupled with decreased rates of protein synthesis. These factors combine to produce the diminished rate of growth and cachexia frequently seen in the untreated juvenile diabetic patient.

Natural History of Juvenile Diabetes Mellitus

Although a diabetic state has been recognized in the immediate neonatal period, this appears to be a transitory and self-limited process without known cause. However, cases of permanent diabetes mellitus have been reported beginning in the first 6 months of life.

Marked differences exist in the manifestations of this disease in children and adults. These are summarized in Table 4. Because of these differences, the approach to diagnosis and treatment is altered in a way appropriate to the age group involved. It is well

TABLE 4.   *Comparison of Childhood and Adult Forms of Diabetes Mellitus*

Characteristic	Child	Adult
Onset	Rapid, obvious	Slow, insidious
Obesity	No role	Predisposing factor
Dietary treatment alone	Not adequate	Possible in 1/3 of cases
Use of oral hypoglycemic agents	Contraindicated	Helpful in 1/3 of cases
Need for insulin	Universal	Present in 1/3 of cases
Hypoglycemia and ketoacidosis	Common	Uncommon
Symptomatic degenerative vascular changes	Only after adolescence	May be present at time of diagnosis

recognized, however, that the childhood, juvenile, or labile form of the disease may occur at any age, but with much less frequency after the age of 30 years. Similarly, the adult or stable form is occasionally seen in adolescence but becomes much more common after 30 years of age.

The progression of the abnormalities in carbohydrate metabolism have been arbitrarily divided and classified in various ways by different authors. Most of these classifications have been devised for the description of the course of the disease in the adult population, in which the transition from one stage to the next is not easily recognized and tends to occur as a subtle and gradual process. However, it is possible to apply the same terminology to the natural course of the disease in children if one recognizes that the various stages may appear abruptly and be of relatively shorter duration.

PREDIABETES AND SUBCLINICAL DIABETES. *Prediabetes* refers to that period of life from birth until the first abnormalities in carbohydrate metabolism can be detected. During this period, there is evidence to suggest that, in some cases, biochemical abnormalities such as increased insulinlike activity in the serum may be demonstrable. It is at this stage that the earliest changes in the vascular system have been detected. By definition, the fasting blood sugar, glucose tolerance test, and cortisone-stressed glucose tolerance test are all normal in the prediabetic stage.

The second stage of this illness has been termed *subclinical diabetes*, and represents the period during which carbohydrate metabolism may be abnormal in the presence of infection or other stressful situations such as surgery or trauma. Similarly, the cortisone-stressed glucose tolerance test will be abnormal during this period, whereas the fasting sugar and glucose tolerance test in the absence of stress will remain normal. The child is otherwise asymptomatic and the presence of the disease is usually noted accidentally. A urinalysis performed during an acute illness or following trauma or surgery will be reported as indicating the presence of glucose in the urine. Immediate investigation with a glucose tolerance test will reveal an abnormality in carbohydrate metabolism. A short period later, the abnormality will revert to normal.

Current opinion favors the consideration of all such individuals who show transient glucose intolerance as potential diabetics or prediabetics.

The duration of the prediabetic and subclinical stages is unknown, and individuals may remain in one or the other of these stages throughout childhood. The glucosuria and mild hyperglycemia with trauma, acute illness, or surgical procedures may recur with stress in later years, although the natural course of these children's condition is not thoroughly established. It is conceivable that some individuals may live a full lifetime at this stage of diabetes without ever becoming clinically apparent diabetics.

The use of oral hypoglycemic agents has been advocated for children in this stage, in an attempt to postpone the onset of overt diabetes. One might argue that the use of such agents could actually hasten the appearance of the clinical state by accelerating the rate of insulin secretion. The use of these agents, therefore, will remain controversial until more is known concerning the etiology and natural history of the diabetic state.

LATENT DIABETES. The third stage in the progression of the diabetic state has been termed latent or chemical diabetes. This period is characterized by an abnormal glucose tolerance test but normal fasting blood sugars. There are elevated blood sugar levels following meals, and glucosuria results. From retrospective evaluation, it would appear that this stage of diabetes is relatively brief in children, lasting from several days to several months. Postprandial hypoglycemic episodes may occur periodically in this stage prior to the onset of overt diabetes. As a premonitory indication of overt diabetes, such episodes are much more common in adults than in children.

OVERT DIABETES. Overt clinical diabetes mellitus usually appears abruptly in children, and the transition from the latent to the overt stage is frequently precipitated by some stress such as infection or emotional upset.

The pattern of the age of onset of overt diabetes in children suggests several factors that may be important in precipitating the transition to this stage. Twenty to 25 percent of children with diabetes have their onset under 5 years of age. Thirty-five percent develop the disease between 5 and 10 years of age, and the remaining 40 percent of children develop diabetes between 10 and 15 years of age. In addition to the increased incidence with each 5-year age group, there are four peak years of incidence in childhood. The two most readily recognized peaks are at approximately 6 and 12 years of age. These correspond to the beginning of the school years and the beginning of adolescence. In some series there have been smaller peaks at approximately 3 and 9 years of age.

Diagnosis

Diagnosis of diabetes mellitus in young people is usually simple and straightforward. Characteristically, the transition from the latent to the overtly diabetic state occurs rapidly and dramatically. The classical symptoms of polyuria, polydipsia, and polyphagia are prominent and occur in at least three-fourths of the cases.

Polyuria is frequently manifest by nocturia or by some change in previously established patterns of urination such as the onset of enuresis. Constipation may result from dehydration associated with polyuria. Weight loss or failure to gain weight is the next most common complaint.

Another manifestation frequently encountered is fatigability and lethargy. On occasion the preliminary symptoms are so mild that they are relatively unnoticed by the family, and the presenting complaints may be abdominal pain and vomiting, characteristic of ketosis; increased respiratory effort, resulting from acidosis; or the decreasing state of consciousness of diabetic coma.

SEVERITY OF INITIAL ILLNESS.   The symptoms with which the child presents will be directly related to the severity of his diabetes at the time of admission. One can arbitrarily divide the degree of severity into four states. The first state, in which hyperglycemia and glucosuria are present, will be associated with symptoms such as polyuria, polydipsia, polyphagia, weight loss, and easy fatigability. The second state is that with hyperglycemia, glucosuria, ketonemia, and ketonuria; additional findings may include abdominal pain, anorexia, and vomiting. The third clinical state is characterized by the added element of acidosis, defined by a serum bicarbonate of less than 15 mEq/L and/or a venous pH of less than 7.3. Such patients will have hyperventilation, dyspnea, and fatigue as prominent complaints. At the fourth level of severity the children demonstrate hyperglycemia, ketosis, acidosis, and coma. In this situation, the decreasing state of consciousness may be the most important element.

The more advanced the diabetic state when first seen, the simpler it is to arrive at the proper diagnosis. There are few conditions other than diabetes which could produce the symptoms presented by the patient with hyperglycemia, glucosuria, ketonuria, and acidosis. In the less severe states, it becomes increasingly difficult to make the diagnosis with certainty. Abnormal elevation of blood sugar values are essential for the diagnosis of untreated diabetes mellitus, since glycosuria may also occur in the metabolic disturbances associated with alterations in the renal tubular handling of glucose.

In the presence of borderline or equivocal laboratory findings, and in the absence of ketonuria and lacking a classical history, definitive therapy should be withheld until the diagnosis becomes more obvious. The patient whose values are not clearly abnormal is likely to be in a subclinical or latent diabetic stage which has been exacerbated by a recent stressful situation. It is difficult to determine if or when such an individual is going to become frankly diabetic. Until more information is available about the natural course of these early stages of diabetes in children, it is well not to treat them with hypoglycemic agents. If such a child is going to become frankly diabetic, there is no known harm in waiting until more obvious findings are present. The difficulty with this course is in communication with the family. A thorough explanation of the implications inherent in a diagnosis of diabetes mellitus will usually convince the family that one should have a very clear picture of the diagnosis before proceeding with treatment.

Once a diagnosis of diabetes mellitus is suspected, the child should be hospitalized for confirmation of the diagnosis, for treatment, and to begin teaching the child and his parents about the disease. In the presence of acidosis or coma, the need of immediate hospitalization is obvious, but in the presence of glucosuria and ketonuria alone, hospitalization should be equally prompt. Unsuspected acidosis may already be present or acidosis may develop in a matter of hours in any child with glucosuria and ketonuria. The child with glucosuria alone but with a typical history should be hospitalized within 24 hours. Once symptoms are present, the course may become rapidly progressive at any time. For the same reasons, treatment should be begun as soon as the diagnosis is established.

LABORATORY DIAGNOSIS.   The actual level of blood glucose which can be considered abnormal will vary with age and with the technique of measurement. After the first week of life, during which normal blood glucose levels are about half the values seen thereafter, the normal values are relatively constant. Fasting blood glucose values above 120 mg/100 ml would be accepted by most laboratories as abnormal. In questionable diagnostic situations or where there is a possibility of extraneous factors influencing the result of the fasting values, a glucose tolerance test should be done. The most discriminatory glucose tolerance test is the intravenous test, since it bypasses the problem of gastric emptying and variations in absorption. It is performed as follows:

IV Glucose Tolerance Test

1. Dose: 0.5 g/kg: inject in 2 to 4 minutes

2. Blood glucose at 5, 10, 15, 20, 30, 45, 60 minutes

3. Plot on semilog paper:
   Ordinate—log glucose concentration
   Abscissa—time (minutes)

4. Determine (by inspection) time required for concentration to fall by 50% ($t_{1/2}$)

5. Disappearance constant = $\dfrac{0.693}{t_{1/2}} = K$

6. $K \times 100$ = percent fall per minute

To facilitate comparability of data, and to approach a true estimate of glucose tolerance, the preferred expression of the data is as a disappearance curve plotted on semilogarithmic paper. From this curve, a linear slope for the disappearance of glucose, and a "K_t" value for disappearance rate can be derived. Although there are limited data from which to establish diagnostic values in children, it appears that a K_t value greater than 1 percent per minute is normal; a value of less than 1 percent per minute indicates impaired glucose tolerance. If for some reason an intravenous test can not be done, a properly performed oral glucose tolerance test is reasonably useful.

In diabetic ketoacidosis, the laboratory values which prove useful include blood glucose and serum acetone, carbon dioxide content, pH, sodium, and potassium. Of interest, but not generally of immediate value, are the serum cholesterol, total lipids, blood urea nitrogen, creatinine, calcium, and phosphorus.

To a considerable extent, the serum sodium is inversely related to the elevation of the blood sugar. In general, an increase of 180 mg/100 ml in the blood glucose will be associated with a decrease of 5 mEq/L in the serum sodium. This relationship is based on osmotic equalities but may be modified by other physiologic variation.

In the presence of the lipemia often seen in untreated diabetes, the levels of all serum electrolytes may be falsely low, due to displacement of the aqueous phase by the lipids contained in the serum. Although children with diabetic ketoacidosis are usually potassium-depleted when first seen, initial serum potassium values may be low, normal, or elevated. The use of the electrocardiogram with the observation of T-wave changes is an effective way of monitoring changes in serum potassium levels.

Infection is often a precipitating agent in any abrupt change in the course of the diabetic state and procedures necessary to detect infection should always be considered. Leucocytosis itself does not indicate the presence of infection, since white blood cell counts of 20,000 to 30,000 are not uncommon in diabetic ketoacidosis without infection.

There have been several studies attempting to relate the outcome of diabetic coma to various signs, symptoms, and laboratory tests. Little correlation has been found between survival (or death) and the ordinary determinations which are part of the initial evaluation of ketoacidosis. However, *serum ketone levels*, measured as acetone, have been shown to correlate with survival. In addition, the serum acetone determination is especially useful in the initial hours of treatment of diabetic acidosis. This procedure can be easily carried out in any minimally equipped laboratory, literally at bedside, without special technical help or equipment. It is performed as follows:

Serum Acetone Determination

1. Draw blood; after clotting, separate serum (table-top centrifuge)

2. Add one drop serum to each of 4 to 10 small test tubes

3. Add water:
   1 drop to 1st tube (1:2)
   2 drops to 2nd tube (1:3)
   3 drops to 3rd tube (1:4)
   then serial dilutions from 1:4 tube to 1:8, 1:16, 1:32

4. Test each tube with Ketostix or Clinistix, or Acetest tablet

5. Record highest dilution which gives faintest purple color (i.e., 1:2, 1:3, 1:4, etc.)

Initial Management

The severity of the diabetic state at the time of admission will determine the approach to therapy. Appropriate treatment is given for infection or for shock if present.

Children with glucosuria alone are continued on oral feedings; insulin therapy, after an initial dose of 1 unit of regular insulin per kilogram of body weight, is then prescribed as indicated below for the second day of treatment in the more seriously affected children.

Children with glucosuria and ketonuria, with or without acidosis and coma, will ordinarily require larger amounts of insulin and intravenous fluids.

The treatment of diabetic ketoacidosis consists essentially of four substances: insulin, glucose, salts, and fluids. The course of the patient in response to adequate therapy is shown in Figure 5. Although the specifics of the treatment of diabetic acidosis are variously defined by different authors, a practical summation is indicated in the following approach.

INSULIN. The amount of regular insulin administered initially is based on the child's condition when he arrives at the hospital. Regular insulin is given in a dose of 1, 2, 3, or 4 units per kilogram of body weight (Table 5), corresponding to the four clinical states of severity described above. The first state, defined as the presence of glucosuria alone, requires 1 unit per kilogram; the second state, characterized by glucosuria plus ketonuria, 2 units per kilogram. For the third state, in which glucosuria and keto-

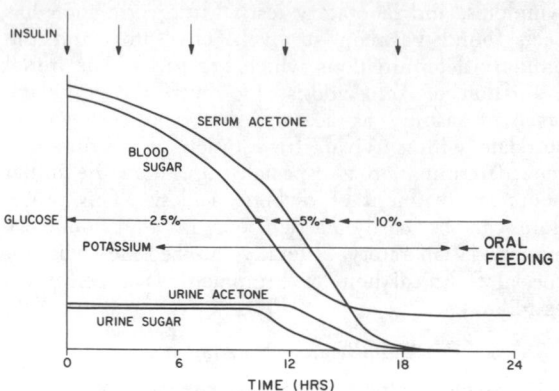

Fig. 5. Course of first day's treatment.

nuria are associated with acidosis, the patient receives initially 3 units per kilogram. Four units per kilogram are required in the presence of glucosuria, ketonuria, acidosis, and a decrease in the level of consciousness, which represent the combined features of the fourth state of severity. The entire amount of insulin is given subcutaneously unless there is evidence of actual or impending peripheral vascular collapse. In such a situation, one half of the initial dose of insulin is given intravenously.

The initial dose of insulin is followed in 2 to 4 hours with a second one. The amount of the second dose is based on the change in serum acetone. If the serum acetone has risen in the intervening 2 to 4 hours, the amount of insulin given is twice that of the initial amount. If the serum acetone is unchanged, the initial amount of insulin is repeated. If the serum acetone has fallen since its initial determination, one half of the initial dose of insulin is given at this time. The same schedule is used for the insulin dosage given 6 to 8 hours after the onset of therapy.

The fourth administration of insulin will be given at approximately 12 hours after the onset of therapy. At this time the serum acetone should be

TABLE 5. *Initial Treatment in Diabetes*

	Presenting Status	Initial Insulin Dosage*	IV Fluids
I	Glucosuria only	1 unit/kg	Usually not needed
II	Glucosuria Ketonuria	2 units/kg	Usually needed
III	Glucosuria Ketonuria Acidosis	3 units/kg	Yes
IV	Glucosuria Ketonuria Acidosis Coma	4 units/kg	Yes (possible shock)

*All insulin given subcutaneously except in shock.

considerably lower, and the blood glucose should have fallen to values approaching normal. The urinary glucose will also have decreased. At this time one can base the amount of this fourth dose of insulin and the subsequent one at 18 hours on the degree of glucosuria and ketonuria. An empirical rule which is usually satisfactory is to give 5 units of insulin for each "plus" of the urine sugar measured with Benedict's solution or with glucose oxidase tablets (Clinitest) or paper strips (Dextrostix strips), 5 additional units in the presence of detectable ketonuria, and 10 additional units if the ketonuria remains 4+. For children under 5 years of age, the amount of insulin for the fourth and fifth injections should be halved.

Children with previously treated diabetes mellitus will not often require the same vigorous approach to insulin therapy. No more than half the amount of insulin calculated as above should be given as the initial injection in the previously treated diabetic child. Only individual evaluation will be helpful in determining subsequent insulin dosage.

GLUCOSE. The amount of glucose to be administered during the initial hours of therapy has been a subject of considerable controversy. During the first few hours of treatment there is undoubtedly sufficient glucose in the body stores to meet most requirements, but it is unable to enter cells for utilization. Additional large amounts of carbohydrate given before cellular glucose uptake is restored may have deleterious effects. Serious hyperosmolarity may occur, with neurologic sequelae; in addition, the excess unusable glucose will accentuate osmotic diuresis, and add to fluid and electrolyte losses, especially of potassium.

Since some carbohydrate is required to maintain isotonicity of the intravenous fluids, 2.5 percent glucose can be given safely during the early hours of therapy.

As soon as the urine glucose begins to fall below 4+ or the blood glucose is approaching 200 mg/100 ml, it is necessary to supplement available carbohydrate by increasing the glucose in the infusion to 5 percent. Once the urine glucose becomes 1+ or negative, or the blood glucose is less than 180 mg/100 ml, it is preferable to increase the infused glucose to 10 percent. The added glucose will provide sufficient substrate so that additional insulin can be given to restore carbohydrate metabolism to normal, which, in turn, will promote the correction of the ketosis and acidosis. Usually, after 18 to 24 hours of treatment, clear oral fluids high in carbohydrate may be started. As the oral feedings become adequate, the intravenous fluids may be discontinued, usually 24 to 36 hour after the onset therapy.

FLUIDS. All fluids are given intravenously initially and nothing is given by mouth for 18 to 24 hours. The quantity of parenteral fluid required during the treatment of diabetic acidosis can be calculated in the same manner as in any situation requiring parenteral fluids.

It should be recognized that the fluid requirements will not be stable throughout the 24-hour period, since the hyperventilation and solute diuresis will have abated, usually within 12 hours. A useful and convenient initial fluid is half-strength lactated Ringer's in 2.5 percent glucose. Additional sodium bicarbonate is indicated in those situations where it is judged that the respiratory center may fail due to the excessive stimulation of an extreme degree of metabolic acidosis (e.g., venous pH below 6.95). If urinary output is adequate, initiation of potassium replacement can be started at once rather than waiting 4 hours as usually recommended.

In the patient with impending or actual shock and severe acidosis, the possibility of lactic acidosis should be considered, and initial fluids should probably contain all alkali as sodium bicarbonate, rather than lactate.

Therapy for ketoacidosis occurring in a child previously diagnosed and treated will be similar to that in the untreated diabetic. However, these children frequently have less hyperglycemia than those who have had no previous therapy. Therefore, insulin requirements are often somewhat less, as mentioned above, and glucose requirements are increased. **TREATMENT ON THE SECOND DAY.** During the second day of therapy, the child should be on oral feedings given at times corresponding with the general meal pattern. He should receive approximately four injections of regular crystalline insulin during the 24-hour period. The amount of insulin to be given before each meal and at approximately 10 P.M. can be judged much as the dosage has been established in the previous 12 hours: 5 units of regular insulin for each plus of urinary glucose, 5 units for slight acetone, and 10 units for 4+ acetone. These urines are obtained prior to each meal and prior to 10 P.M.

Occasionally during the period from 18 to 48 hours after the onset of treatment, hyperglycemia and glucosuria will not occur in spite of the infusion of hypertonic glucose. Under these circumstances, insulin should be withheld until hyperglycemia or glucosuria is again noted.

LATER TREATMENT. From the amount of insulin required during the second 24-hour period, one can judge relatively accurately the daily insulin requirement for the next few weeks. In general, this will be equivalent to 2 units/kg of body weight/day. An insulin mixture can be started on this basis on either the third or fourth day (see below).

The philosophy of management which one adopts after the first few days will, to a great extent, determine much of the therapy from this time on. At one end of a therapeutic scale, there is the concept that normoglycemia and no glucosuria are the ideal standards of control. In this concept, hyperglycemia is felt to have a profound influence on the

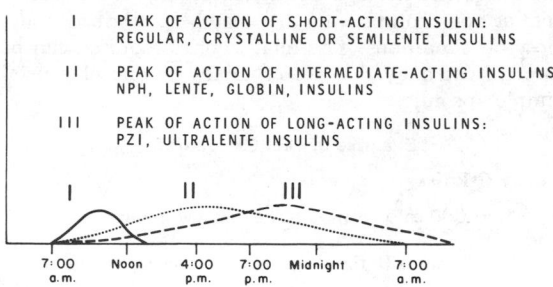

Fig. 6. Curves of activity of various forms of insulin.

subsequent development of the degenerative complications of this disease. Adherents to this concept believe that individuals with proper training and supervision can maintain a state of normoglycemia without undue difficulty and without the occurrence of hypoglycemic reactions.

At the other end of the therapeutic scale there are physicians who feel that the degree of glucosuria is of little consequence, and therapy should be constituted so that the patient is free of ketonuria and overt symptoms. This group believes that the control of carbohydrate metabolism will have essentially no effect on the ultimate vascular degenerative phenomena.

A middle course, adapted by the majority of physicians, sets as its goal the achievement of the least hyperglycemia and the least glucosuria compatible with both a relatively normal everyday life and the greatest freedom from hypoglycemic reactions. With this program it is usually possible to achieve reasonable control of carbohydrate metabolism with a single injection of insulin given prior to breakfast each day.

Three major types of insulin are now available: short-acting (regular, crystalline, and semilente); intermediate (NPH, lente, and globin); and long-acting (PZI and ultralente). The curve of activity of these insulins is shown in Figure 6.

Although there are occasional instances requiring unusual dosage forms and combinations, the physician is well advised to select one common mixture and to use this with the majority of patients. The most common insulin mixture is a combination of an intermediate insulin, such as NPH or lente, and regular insulin mixed in the same syringe. These are usually given in the ratio 4:1 (intermediate:regular), in keeping with their relative duration of action.

The choice between the two common strengths —40 units/ml (U40) and 80 units/ml (U80)—is a matter of ease of measurement versus volume of fluid given. With a total dose of more than 30 units per day, it is generally simpler to use U80 insulin and a U80 syringe.

DIET. During the period of hospitalization, regulation of dietary intake hastens the approximation of the daily insulin requirement. It is assumed that after discharge the average child will receive a reasonable diet at home, and such a diet may be prescribed under hospital conditions. The total calories required can be approximated by the use of tables or one of several simple formulas:

Example of Diet Calculation

Daily Calories

1. 1,000 calories plus 100 times age in years

or

2. 90 minus (3 times age in years) per kg per day

Example:

8-year-old child, weight 28 kg, total calories =

1. 1,000 + 8 (100) = 1,800 calories

or

2. 90 − 3 (8) = 66 cal/kg or 66 (28) = 1,848 calories

Approximate Distribution:

225 g carbohydrate (*1/2* of 1,800 = 900 calories)

67 g fat (*1/3* of 1,800 = 600 calories)

75 g protein (*1/6* of 1,800 = 300 calories)

The diet would be divided to give approximately ¼ of the calories at each meal, ⅛ at a mid-afternoon feeding, and ⅛ at a bedtime feeding.

Control of the diabetic state during this first week of therapy is judged on the patient's general condition and on the measurement of the amount of glucose in the urine. Urinary glucose, when measured quantitatively, is a reasonable integrated measure of the above-normal fluctuation in the blood glucose. Urine collections are divided into three portions: the first collection is made between 7 A.M. and 1 P.M., the second from 1 P.M. until 7 P.M., the third from 7 P.M. until 7 A.M. The first period corresponds to the duration of action of regular insulin; the second, to the hours covering the maximum action of intermediate insulin. The overnight collection reveals to some extent whether or not a second injection of intermediate-acting insulin is required prior to the evening meal. Control is considered adequate when the glucose in the urine amounts to 5 percent or less of the total ingested calories; control is excellent when this can be reduced to less than 2.5 percent.

Following the initial 7 to 10 days of therapy, edema of the lower extremities may occur abruptly. The pathophysiology is not clear, but it has been considered similar to that occasionally seen after the onset of refeeding starved individuals. No specific therapy is indicated as the process is self-limited.

Patient and Family Education

The educational program for the family is equal in importance to the medical management of the patient and should go hand in hand with the treatment and education of the child. Since adequate education of the family plays a major role in the ultimate success in the management of the child on an ambulatory basis, the instructional process will be discussed in some detail.

INITIAL EXPLANATION. During the first day of hospitalization, a preliminary discussion with the family is indicated. Confirmation of the diagnosis should be explained to the family and a general description given of what diabetes mellitus is. It is usually wise to state that the disease is hereditary and that a "carrier state" must have come from both sides of the family, regardless of the fact that no family history may be apparent in either or both parental lines at the time.

Parents often feel guilt that their child's diabetes is the result of errors in dietary supervision, discipline, or other child-rearing practices. Such parents should be clearly told that the presence of the disease was determined at conception, and that the onset of clinical diabetes is not known to be related to any extrinsic factors. The family should be reassured that the child's life can be a near normal one under proper medical management.

Later one can explain in a systematic way the various facets of carbohydrate metabolism and the management of diabetes that will enable the family to work intelligently with the physician. It is useful to schedule a series of daily one-hour conferences with the parents covering specific topics each day as well as allowing time for the family to raise questions. Each day it is wise to summarize the discussion of the previous day and to check the understanding of what has already been discussed.

EDUCATIONAL INFORMATION. The discussion with the family can be divided into four major topics:

1. Information about mechanisms which are responsible for *control of the blood sugar*. The family should receive detailed clarification about factors which tend to raise the blood sugar, which are primarily food, emotional tensions, and infections; and about those which lower the blood sugar, which are insulin and exercise.

In the discussion concerning food, an important point to raise is that the body has the ability to break foods down to small units and to rebuild these into any one of the major nutritional components (carbohydrates, proteins, or fat). Consequently, all foods have a tendency to raise the blood sugar. The simple carbohydrates such as glucose raise the blood sugar quickly because of their rapid entry into the body and direct utilization. Fruit sugar (fructose) raises the blood sugar somewhat more slowly, since several steps are necessary to convert fructose to glucose; and starches raise the blood sugar still more slowly, since additional enzymatic steps are required for its conversion to glucose. Proteins, because of the many reactions required, raise the blood sugar very slowly. This explanation of the handling of foods forms a good introduction for the discussion of *dietary management*.

Since it is impossible to regulate constantly all the variables involved in the control of blood sugar, it seems impractical to attempt to control rigidly more than the insulin administration. Day-to-day variations in the amount of exercise and in the emotional state of a child can be compensated for by the resultant variation in the child's natural inclination and needs for food. These natural drives control appetite so well in the normal child that growth in height and weight usually proceeds smoothly and proportionately. The same phenomena occur in the diabetic child receiving adequate insulin. With this reasoning, the child with diabetes is allowed to set his own level of caloric intake and to adjust this level with supervision from meal to meal and day to day. The only external control generally necessary is a moderate restriction in the intake of simple carbohydrates. The explanation given to the family for this limitation is that with the loss of the fine regulation of insulin release in diabetics, sudden loads of glucose are not utilized and are consequently wasted in the urine. It is also important to indicate the significance of sugar in the urine, as it reflects changes in the blood sugar, and to clarify the difference between instantaneous measurement of sugar in the blood and the summation of blood sugars as represented by sugar in the urine.

2. Information on the subject of *hypoglycemia*. The origin of the symptoms in hypoglycemia should be explained on the basis of the lack of glucose for brain metabolism. The signs and symptoms of hypoglycemia should be described in detail with their progression from hunger to irritability, jitteriness, somnolence, confusion, and staggering, to decreased awareness, and finally coma and convulsions. The relationship of the early signs to epinephrine secretion, and the somewhat self-limited aspect of the hypoglycemic convulsion, should be emphasized. The treatment of hypoglycemia with oral or parenteral glucose and the possible use of glucagon or epinephrine injections should be discussed. More importantly, stress should be placed on the prevention of hypoglycemia by knowledge of the periods when it is most likely to occur and recognition of its earliest symptomatology.

3. Information concerning *hyperglycemia, ketosis, acidosis,* and *coma.* The mechanism for the development of these events, their signs, symptoms, treatment, and prevention should be clarified, and particular attention should be called to the difference between hypoglycemia (rapid onset and relatively frequent occurrence) and hyperglycemia and ketosis (slower onset and the possibility of intervening therapy).

4. Information concerning *practicalities of management,* including discussion of the various kinds of insulins—e.g., the short-, intermediate-, and long-action insulins; the role of insulin mixtures; and the differences between U40 and U80 insulin. The storage of insulin and the maintenance of the insulin in current use at room temperature should be clarified. Injection techniques should be discussed in de-tail. The disposable needle and syringe can be recommended. Finally the role of the so-called self-regulated diet should be stressed. Whole family participation in the diet and the importance of midafternoon and prebedtime feedings and their composition should be emphasized.

It is also well to point out differences between the manifestations of diabetes in adults and in children and to indicate that the vascular complications of adults are not a problem during childhood. Foot care, infections, cuts, bruises, broken bones, and related phenomena are of no more consequence in the child with diabetes than they are in nondiabetic children.

As much of this information as possible should be shared with the child himself. If possible, a dietitian who understands the concept of a self-regulatory diet, a nurse, and a social worker should be included in the educational process, but the majority of it is best handled by the physician.

FAMILY REACTION. During the early discussions with the family and in their subsequent visits, it will be apparent that at least four stages exist in the family's acceptance of this disease. In the initial stage of *disbelief,* the family makes statements such as "It can't be true," "I'm sure the doctor will find that there's something else wrong," and so on. This stage usually lasts one or two days, but may on occasion be very prolonged, even though such a parent may appear to accept the doctor's statements. In the second stage of *acceptance* the family understands the problem intellectually but is not yet emotionally ready to accept the total picture. The duration of this intellectual acceptance may vary from a week to a year or more in some families. Eventually the family develops an *emotional acceptance* in which it can freely discuss the problems involved in this disease with the physician, the child, and other medical personnel. The fourth and final stage of *social acceptance* occurs when the family has accepted the disease not only intellectually and emotionally but on a social level as well. In this stage, the family is comfortable in discussing the problem with those individuals in the child's environment— such as the teacher, neighbors, and others who need to have some knowledge of the child's condition for proper supervision. The stage of total acceptance may appear as early as a month or two after diagnosis in some families, but may take as long as 5 to 10 years in other families.

PREPARATION FOR HOME CARE. By the time the child is regulated on an intermediate insulin or insulin mixture and the family is adequately educated for home care, the mother should have had the opportunity to give several insulin injections on her own, and she should feel relatively comfortable doing this. She should also have accurately tested a number of urine specimens for sugar and acetone. The urine sugar should be measured using Benedict's solution, Clinitest tablets, or Dextrostix paper strips.

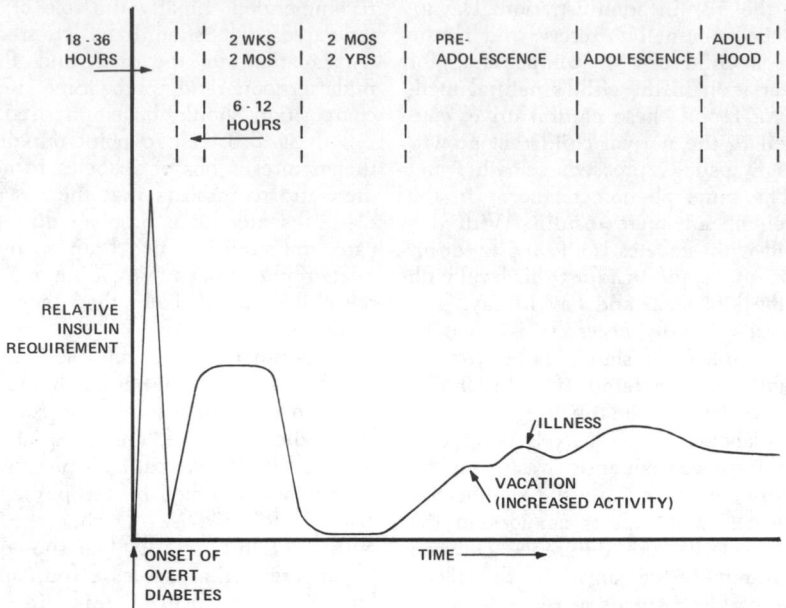

Fig. 7. Relative insulin requirements during typical natural course of juvenile diabetes mellitus.

With the older child, a number of these activities can be performed by the child. It is our belief, however, that most children should not be expected to give their own insulin injections prior to adolescence, although they might well be taught this technique for use in special situations.

Extended Care of Juvenile Diabetes

The care of children with diabetes mellitus can be handled extremely well in the office of any physician who is willing to accept the child's abnormality of carbohydrate metabolism as only one of a number of aspects of a total problem. Assessment of the overall management of these children must include consideration of social and emotional health as well as evaluation of carbohydrate metabolism.

INITIAL HOME CARE. Following discharge from the hospital, it is wise to have the mother call the physician for several mornings prior to giving the insulin injection in order to discuss the results of the previous day's urinalyses and the insulin dose for that day. In this way, final control of the insulin requirement can be achieved at home in the child's more natural surroundings.

CHANGING INSULIN REQUIREMENTS. The insulin dose will generally average approximately 2 units per kilogram initially. This insulin requirement will persist for a period of approximately 2 to 6 weeks following the initiation of therapy (Fig. 7). The child's urine and blood glucose will usually then *decrease,* and hypoglycemia may occur. The family should already be aware that the insulin requirement

may drop precipitously over a period of 2 to 5 days, and may actually go to zero at this time. On the average, the insulin requirement will fall to less than half a unit per kilogram. The child's condition will then remain relatively stable during a period varying from two months to two years. The number of hypoglycemic reactions and the tendency to ketosis and acidosis will greatly diminish. If the family has been adequately prepared, the apparent "improvement" will not promote any idea that the child is recovering from the disease or is likely to be permanently cured.

The inevitable increase in insulin requirement may be gradual or abrupt and may occur in association with a traumatic episode or infection. The final insulin dosage will approach a value of 1 unit per kilogram per day and will remain in that range throughout the remainder of the child's life. There is great individual variation, however, and the range is wide.

EVALUATION OF CARBOHYDRATE METABOLISM. The level of the blood glucose will be affected not only by the amount of insulin administered but by multiple variables which include food intake, the amount of physical activity, and the emotional state of the child. The result of these multiple factors is that blood glucose levels vary greatly during a 24-hour period, and this variation may often occur quite rapidly. As a consequence, single glucose determinations are of limited value in attempting to evaluate control of carbohydrate metabolism throughout the day. However, since most children have a relatively normal renal threshold for glucose, the amount of glucose in the urine is proportional to the time and degree of elevation of blood glucose above 180 mg/100 ml. Therefore, evaluation of carbohydrate metabolism on a ambulatory basis may be accomplished by a combination of occasional 24-hour urine glucose determinations and the daily testing of single specimens in the home. For most children, examination of the urine glucose prior to breakfast and prior to the evening meal will suffice for daily testing at home.

Two alternatives exist regarding the collection of daily urine specimens: The first voiding obtained may be examined, or the bladder may be emptied and a second specimen may be collected a few minutes later. The first urine voided upon arising reflects blood glucose variation during most of the night, whereas the sample obtained by a second voiding will reflect the blood glucose as it exists at that time. Similarly, in the afternoon, the first specimen obtained prior to the evening meal will reflect blood glucose levels during much of the afternoon, and a second specimen will reflect the blood glucose level for the few minutes prior to its being obtained. In general, one is more interested in the longer time period, so that the first specimen obtained in the morning and the first specimen obtained in the late afternoon are more useful for overall evaluation purposes.

Although urine analyses for glucose are valuable for assessment of control of carbohydrate metabolism, several difficulties occur. It is not uncommon to find glucose in the urine in the presence of hypoglycemia. This discrepancy occurs when insulin activity and exercise combine to lower the blood glucose relatively suddenly to hypoglycemic levels, while the bladder contains urine which was formed during previous periods of hyperglycemia or normoglycemia. In this circumstance, the glucose-free urine formed more recently dilutes only partially the older urine which contains glucose, and the overall specimen is positive for glucose. This sort of problem has led many physicians and families to abandon the urine sugar method because of presumed unreliability.

Another problem with single urine specimens is that without a knowledge of volume and without a precise determination of the percent glucose in the urine, the total carbohydrate balance during a 24-hour period is unknown. As a result, a 4+ urine glucose may mean good control in one child and extremely poor control in another. For any one child, however, the daily pattern of urine testing tends to reflect a relatively consistent pattern of control for that particular child. Therefore, a quantitative measure of 24-hour urinary carbohydrate compared with the findings of the daily urine tests provides a better evaluation of the daily changes.

It is easy to obtain a 24-hour urine specimen in the home, to preserve it with thymol crystals, to have the family measure and record the total volume, and to mail an aliquot to the physician for evaluation. If the 24-hour urinary carbohydrate is evaluated every 2 or 3 months, a reasonable estimate of carbohydrate control can be obtained, particularly when this is combined with daily urine testing by the child or a parent.

Reasonable control, which can be obtained with most preadolescent children, becomes more difficult during adolescence. If one does not require an arbitrary value for control but can be satisfied with something approaching this value, one can be comfortable with the management of the majority of children with diabetes mellitus. In essence, the aim in the regulation of carbohydrate metabolism is to achieve the minimum amount of carbohydrate in the urine (and the most nearly normal blood glucose), even to the point of total absence of glucosuria, provided that there are no hypoglycemic reactions and a maximum of normality in the child's daily life.

Problems of undernutrition and overnutrition in children with diabetes are generally managed as they are in nondiabetic children. An exception is the child who has had prolonged periods of inadequate amounts of insulin. This chronic insufficiency of insulin results in stunted growth due to the catabolic tendency of the untreated diabetic state and in the development of a massively enlarged liver with marked fatty infiltration. This complex has been termed the Mauriac syndrome and is treated by providing more adequate insulin therapy.

A more common problem is the child treated with excessive insulin who overeats in response to frequent hypoglycemia, and whose blood sugar frequently vacillates between hypoglycemia and hyperglycemia. In such patients, insulin dosage may be raised by the physician or family to very high levels in small increments, in an attempt to render the patient aglycosuric. The result is transient hypoglycemia followed by an increased intake of food, which produces, in turn, more glycosuria. The cycle is then repeated with an elevation of insulin dosage. In such a step-wise fashion, huge insulin doses can be reached, and fairly well tolerated. The clue to the diagnosis of this situation is the regular recurrence of hypoglycemia or aglycosuria in a patient who is usually spilling sugar and showing great fluctuations in blood sugar level, and who is receiving excessive doses of insulin. In such a child, reduction in insulin dosage results in less hypoglycemia, less hunger, lowered caloric intake, and then decreased hyperglycemia. However, such reduction may have to be done extremely slowly to avoid ketosis.

ACTIVITY. Since activity and insulin requirement vary inversely, the insulin requirement will tend to decrease with the onset of the increased activity of summer vacation, and the reverse will occur in the fall. On the other hand, it is impractical to attempt to adjust insulin daily on the basis of expected activity because of the vagaries in every child's day. This kind of daily fluctuation is best countered by allowing the child's appetite to coordinate activity and dietary intake.

INTERCURRENT ILLNESS. There is no way to predict whether the child's insulin requirement will rise or fall with an infection. With the increased rate of metabolism usually associated with infection and fever, there will be increased caloric utilization, and the insulin requirement will rise. However, with infections which are marked by severe anorexia or vomiting, the food intake may fall sharply and the insulin requirement may decrease somewhat.

A satisfactory approach during a period of illness is to revert to regular insulin, giving the child four injections a day, based on his usual requirements. The amount of each injection is modified during the course of the day in accordance with dietary intake and urine testing. One begins such a day by giving one-third of the total day's requirement as a single injection of regular insulin before breakfast. The child's course is assessed again at midday, and if he is eating but does not have excessive ketonuria and glycosuria, one-fourth of the total day's requirement is given at this time. However, if the child has eaten poorly and the urine sugar is negative, this dose of insulin is omitted. If, on the other hand, the child has eaten but the urine is positive for sugar and acetone, the noon dose of insulin may be increased to twice the estimated amount. This same evaluation is carried out in the evening, and the dose of insulin is prescribed in the same way. Before sleep the same routine is established, and the estimated dose at this time is one-sixth of the total daily dose.

The important adjunct to insulin during a period of illness is caloric intake. Since the child will utilize calories whether he eats or not, some insulin will always be required. It is reasonable in an ill child, if medically indicated, to restrict oral intake to clear fluids high in carbohydrate. With a flexible insulin program, any type of intake, or even lack of oral intake for a period of 6 to 12 hours, is entirely compatible with home care. The early use of such a flexible program in an illness will frequently prevent the complications of hypoglycemia and of acidosis which otherwise might appear.

FAMILY RELATIONSHIPS. The regulation of the carbohydrate metabolism of diabetic children requires relatively little of a physician's time. Considerably more time should be devoted to dealing with the child's anxieties and concerns about his illness and with the parents' attitudes and concerns about the child and about themselves.

Early in the illness, the physician works primarily with the mother or both parents who work more closely with the child than does the physician. Nevertheless, the relationships between the parents, between the child and both parents, and between the diabetic child and his brothers and sisters, all play a role in the overall success of the management of the patient.

The interaction between the disease and family relationships will also relate to the age of the diabetic child. Prior to adolescence, the child's dependence on his mother may be increased by the physical bonds necessitated by the care of the diabetic state plus the mother's tendency to be overprotective. In adolescence these same factors may increase the tension in the independence-dependence conflict which is characteristic of this age. This may result in an overly dependent preadolescent and an extremely rebellious adolescent.

The occurrence of diabetes in a child may also alter the relationship between the mother and the nondiabetic siblings. These well children may resent the diabetic child because of the real or imagined added attention he receives. The well children may also become hostile or overly solicitous because of guilt toward the child with diabetes. In addition, the well children may reject the mother, demand increased attention from her, or overact to the attention or lack of attention they receive from the mother.

There is no doubt, from the evaluation of difficult management problems, that each of the family interrelationships can at times provoke considerable instability in the attempt to establish relatively normal carbohydrate metabolism. But the majority of problems are centered around the mother-child relationship, and it is this area that needs to be examined first when difficulties in diabetic management are encountered. However, one will often have to examine *each* of the relationships and include the child's relationships with his peers and his school situation before entirely clarifying a problem. In these situations, the assistance of a social worker may be quite valuable.

With time, the physician-child relationship should become dominant so far as the care of the diabetic state is concerned. It is a mistake, however, to move too rapidly. The technical ability and intelligence of many children make it possible for them to give their own insulin and to assume the entire management of their care at a very early age. Because of this possibility, there has been a tendency for physicians to feel that this seeming independence is a sign of maturity which should be encouraged. However, the preadolescent child's personality is most often not equipped to handle these serious responsibilities, although his intellectual ability is sufficient. An overconcern with bodily needs engendered prior to adolescence can lead to problems of hypochondriasis and overconcern with bodily functions in the adult. Although the child may well wish to learn how to give his own insulin in order to spend the night with a friend, it should not be assumed, therefore, that he should routinely administer such a potentially dangerous medication.

ADOLESCENCE. The limitations imposed by this disease must be minimized in the adolescent with diabetes, who, like other adolescents, is basically in rebellion against most of the restraining persons, problems, and forces around him. This is not the time for the physician or family to emphasize the restrictive aspects of his illness, but the time in which the physician should be willing to accept the vagaries in diabetic management which occur, and to express an understanding of the influences which have led to these irregularities.

The tendency of this age group to eat irregularly, to consume large quantities of carbohydrate, and to keep irregular hours is well known and accepted for the nondiabetic child. The intense desire of the adolescent diabetic child to conform to this pattern should be taken into serious consideration in the management of such a child. A period of erratic and unpredictable behavior at this age does not indicate a pattern which will persist in adult life. The physician's role is to help the adolescent understand why he is trying to deny the idea that he has diabetes by omitting his insulin, by eating irregularly, or by refusing to test his urine. The physician should not encourage punitive measures to try to correct his behavior. To help the parents of the adolescent diabetic to understand and share in such an approach is also an important task of the physician.

Finally, it is important to anticipate that during adolescence it is likely that there will be another period of relatively rapid increase in insulin requirement. This requirement will often exceed the 1 unit per kilogram average that has been the pattern until this time. However, following the turmoil and rapid growth of adolescence, the insulin requirement will generally decrease and stabilize for the remaining years.

SUMMER CAMPS. Concern with emotional needs leads many families and physicians to the consideration of summer camps for diabetic children. These camps have a tendency to fall into two types.

One type of camp is intended as a medical facility in which to teach the diabetic child how to cope with his problem and how to live as an independent person. In such a camp, emphasis is placed on teaching the children to give their own insulin and to select their own diet. They also learn to understand the basic physiology of carbohydrate metabolism and the manifestations of hypoglycemia and ketoacidosis. A primary goal of such a camp is to increase the child's fund of knowledge about diabetes during the 2 to 4 weeks he is a camper. It is apparent that such activities are appropriate to children who are 14 years of age and older, and less so to younger children.

The philosophy of a second type of camp is to provide a summer recreational experience which will encourage the child's concept of himself as a near-normal individual who can partake in ordinary children's activities comfortably without fear. The care of the diabetic state is kept as unobtrusive an activity as possible, and the goal is to provide the child with a happy and educational experience in terms of play, sports, and group living. The fact that such a camp segregates diabetic children from other children tends to negate the concept of normality. However, in the first few years of overt diabetes, particularly during the period from age 7 to 10, the child with diabetes needs assurance that he can function in a camp situation without parental support, before he is ready to participate in regular camp activity with nondiabetic children. Such reassurance is occasionally necessary in older children as well.

It would seem reasonable to consider a camp experience for the younger child in which the emphasis is on group living and normal activity and not on teaching and training in diabetic techniques. The child who is 14 or 15 years of age might well benefit from an education program with emphasis on training for living with diabetes. Thus, there may well be need for both philosophies in summer camps for diabetics, but each of these philosophies is appropriate at different times.

The adolescent will have quite individual needs, and these will depend on the duration of his disease as well as his own level of adjustment. Many of these children will do better in a regular summer camp for several years.

ROLE OF OTHER DRUGS. Although it has been claimed that the oral hypooglycemic agents, particularly the biguanides such as phenformin, have a role in the treatment of juvenile diabetes, it would appear that this is probably not true. Although these compounds may appear to supplement or even completely replace insulin during the early periods of juvenile diabetes, the effect is transient, and these compounds offer no protection against ketoacidosis. Therefore, it would appear advisable to eliminate these compounds from management programs for the child with diabetes.

Recent evidence has indicated that the thiazide group of compounds have a hyperglycemic action. Although this is not a contraindication to their use in appropriate situations requiring a diuretic, one should be aware that they have a tendency to raise the blood glucose in some diabetic children.

The adrenal glucocorticoids are also diabetogenic, and their use in the child with diabetes mellitus will frequently lead to an increase in the insulin requirement. Much has been written about the problem of "steroid diabetes" and whether or not a permanent diabetic state can be induced with these compounds. It would appear that transient diabetes mellitus can be induced in some individuals with corticosteroids, and in a few of these permanent diabetes will result. However, it may be that this action occurs only in those who were in a subclinical or latent diabetic state prior to the onset of steroid therapy; the steroids may then act as a precipitating factor as described under the section on the natural course of the disease.

Glucagon, another hyperglycemic agent, has been proposed in the management of hypoglycemic reactions of diabetes mellitus. This compound is derived from the alpha cells of the islets of Langerhans and acts on the phosphorylase system to increase the conversion of glycogen to glucose. The advantage of glucagon over epinephrine for the treatment of hypoglycemia is the absence of the sympathomimetic activity with glucagon.

PROGNOSIS. Mortality from diabetes mellitus during childhood has become minimal. However, deaths do occur from massive overdosage of insulin or from ketoacidosis. The single clinical factor which correlates with mortality in ketoacidosis is the duration of this process. This fact emphasizes the need for prompt diagnosis and institution of therapy when ketoacidosis occurs.

The ultimate prognosis for the childhood diabetic remains obscure. For adults whose disease began 30 to 40 years ago, the prognosis has been poor, since up to 90 percent of these individuals have developed disabling and frequently fatal degenerative vascular complications. It is of interest, however, that in most long-term series at least 10 percent of affected children remain free of these complications well into adult life.

REFERENCES

Aagenase, O., and Moe, H. Light- and electron-microscopic study of skin capillaries of diabetes. Diabetes, 10:253, 1961.

Bennett, E. M., and Johannsen, D. E. Psychodynamics of the diabetic child. Psychol. Monogr., 68:1, 1954.

Danowski, T. S. Diabetes Mellitus in Children and Young Adults. Baltimore, Williams and Wilkins Co., 1957.

Joslin, E. P., Root, H. F., White, P., and Marble, A. The Treatment of Diabetes Mellitus, 9th ed. Philadelphia, Lea and Febiger, 1952, Ch. 26.

Kelley, H. G., Rao, P. T., and Jackson, R. L. Insulin requirements in children with diabetes mellitus maintained in good control. Amer. J. Dis. Child., 89:31, 1955.

Kety, S. S., Polis, B. D., Nadler, C. S., and Schmidt, C. F. The blood flow and oxygen consumption of the human brain in diabetic acidosis and coma. J. Clin. Invest., 27:500, 1948.

Larsson, Y., Sterky, G., and Christiansson, G. Long-term prognosis in juvenile diabetes mellitus. Acta Pediat., 51:Suppl. 130, 1962.

Leibel, B. S., and Wrenshall, G. A., eds. On the Nature and Treatment of Diabetes. Amsterdam, Excerpta Medica Foundation, 1965.

Reaven, G. M., and Farquhar, J. W. Steady state plasma insulin response to continuous glucose infusion in normal and diabetic subjects. Diabetes, 18:273, 1969.

Rosenbaum, P., Kattine, A. A., and Gottsegen, W. L. Diabetic and prediabetic nephropathy in childhood. Amer. J. Dis. Child., 196:83, 1963.

Siperstein, M. D., Unger, R. H., and Madison, L. L. Studies of muscle capillary basement membranes in normal subjects, diabetic, and prediabetic patients. J. Clin. Invest., 47:1973, 1968.

Steinberg, A. G. Heredity in diabetes mellitus. Diabetes, 10:269, 1961.

Steiner, D. F., et al. Proinsulin and the biosynthesis of insulin. In Recent Progress in Hormone Research. New York, Academic Press, Inc., 25:207, 1969.

Weil, W. B., Jr., Diabetes mellitus. In Green, M., and Haggerty, R. J., eds., Ambulatory Pediatrics, Philadelphia, W. B. Saunders Co., 1968.

Williams, R. H. The pancreas. In Williams, R. H., ed., Textbook of Endocrinology, 4th ed. Philadelphia, W. B. Saunders Co., 1968.

8.6
MELLITURIA

G. N. DONNELL and W. R. BERGREN

Mellituria is defined as the presence of a sugar in the urine; it may result from several causes, including increased ingestion, altered gastrointestinal absorption, altered metabolism of a particular sugar, or a defect in renal tubular transport. The existence of mellituria may be missed on routine examination because the glucose oxidase test, used commonly, detects only glucose. To avoid this error, a test based on copper reduction should also be employed.

In the newborn or premature infant small amounts of dietary sugars such as sucrose, lactose, galactose, or fructose may appear in the urine. Varying amounts of these sugars may also be found in the urine of some patients with sepsis, gastrointestinal diseases, or liver involvement. Normal individuals sometimes excrete lactose or sucrose following ingestion of large quantities of these sugars. Lactosuria is not uncommon during the last trimester of pregnancy and lactation.

Altered metabolism of sugars may lead to increased concentrations in blood and overflow into the urine, as in diabetes mellitus, galactosemia, and fructosuria. On the other hand, in disorders characterized by defective renal tubular transport, glycosuria without hyperglycemia is frequently observed. This occurs in renal glycosuria, in the disorders generally classified as the Fanconi syndrome, in Wilson's disease, and following poisoning with certain drugs and heavy metals. Primary renal glycosuria and the glycosurias associated with various renal tubular disorders are described elsewhere in this text. The present discussion is limited to melliturias resulting from disorders of sugar metabolism.

Galactose Metabolism

The term galactosemia implies the presence of abnormal amounts of galactose in the blood. Usually the term has been employed to describe the disorder resulting from deficiency in activity of the enzyme galactose-1-phosphate uridyl transferase (transferase). However, another genetic disorder, galactokinase deficiency, is also associated with elevation of blood galactose. It would be preferable, therefore, to identify galactosemia on the basis of the specific enzyme deficiency.

The principal dietary source of galactose is the disaccharide lactose, which is enzymatically hydrolyzed in the intestine to the monosaccharides glucose and galactose. The major pathway for the utilization of galactose involves its phosphorylation to galactose-1-phosphate, a reaction which is catalyzed by galactokinase. The next step, catalyzed by transferase, leads to the formation of the nucleotide sugar, uridine diphosphate galactose (UPDGal). Finally, UPDGal is transformed to UDPG by the action of the enzyme UDPGal-4-epimerase (epimerase).

A secondary metabolic pathway, in which galactitol is formed, is of interest because this sugar alcohol is thought to be responsible for the cataracts seen in classical galactosemia and in patients with the galactokinase defect.

The significance of other minor pathways for galactose utilization is not yet clear. Galactose-6-phosphate has been isolated from erythrocytes of patients with galactosemia, and it has been postulated that this intermediate can be oxidized by glucose-6-phosphate dehydrogenase. Direct oxidation of galactose by a dehydrogenase to form galactonic acid, with subsequent steps leading to the formation of carbon dioxide and of xylulose, has been described. Still another pathway involves the formation of UDPGal from Gal-1-P by a UDPGal pyrophosphorylase.

Galactose-1-Phosphate Uridyl Transferase Deficiency (Galactosemia)

CLINICAL MANIFESTATIONS. The infant with galactosemia usually appears normal at birth, and the clinical manifestations follow milk feeding. There is early evidence of liver involvement, with hepatomegaly as the most constant physical finding. Jaundice is often seen, and it persists in varying degrees until institution of diet therapy. Weight loss due to vomiting, and occasionally to diarrhea, is not uncommon. Lethargy and hypotonia are frequent. The clinical course of some infants is fulminant, and death may occur early from inanition, infection, or hepatic failure. A clinical diagnosis of overwhelming sepsis may often be suspected; severe infections complicate the disease and are frequently the cause of death.

Cataracts may be noted in some patients as early as a few days of age, but due to the difficulty in detecting small lenticular opacities in the young infant, they are generally not diagnosed until later.

Although clinical manifestations may vary in degree, the majority of infants have severe symptoms. Prompt treatment is urgent. Untreated children who survive beyond the first few weeks usually manifest signs of mental retardation. Specific neurologic abnormalities are often absent, although convulsions have been described occasionally. Nonspecific patterns have been observed in electroencephalograms.

In a small number of milder cases, the diagnosis may be overlooked for weeks or months. Vague digestive difficulties, retarded physical and mental development, cataracts, and perhaps intolerance to milk should suggest the diagnosis of galactosemia. This possibility is strengthened if mellituria and proteinuria are present.

PATHOPHYSIOLOGY. It is not known how the enzyme defect leads to changes in the liver or to mental retardation. No specific histologic alterations have been reported in the brain. In the untreated infant, changes in the liver vary with age and severity of the disease. The prominent feature in the young, severely ill infant is a marked fatty change of the liver, which may result in part from starvation and infection. In infants who remain untreated, the picture is that of cirrhosis. One pathologic feature commonly seen in the liver, particularly from patients from 3 weeks to 4 months of age, is a rosettelike arrangement of liver cells about dilated canaliculi, which are filled with bile pigment. This finding should suggest galactosemia, but it is not pathognomonic of this disease.

Galactitol and galactose-1-phosphate accumulate in tissues. Although the cataracts can be ascribed to the formation of galactitol in the lens, the relationship of the biochemical abnormalities to the other manifestations of galactosemia remains unclear. It has been postulated that one mechanism may involve the inhibition of a variety of enzyme systems by galactose-1-phosphate.

DIAGNOSIS. Although the diagnosis of galactosemia can be suspected on clinical grounds, laboratory confirmation is essential. The presence of galactose and protein in the urine of the symptomatic patient depends upon the continuing ingestion of galactose. However, the presence of galactosuria is not in itself diagnostic, and a more specific test is necessary. The most useful test is assay of galactose-1-phosphate uridyl transferase activity in erythrocytes. In the untreated patient, measurement of galactose-1-phosphate content of erythrocytes also has been employed. The galactose tolerance test is unnecessary, and, in fact, may be hazardous in the infant in that it may induce hypoglycemia and hypokalemia.

TREATMENT. The treatment of galactosemia involves the exclusion of galactose from the diet. Whenever a diagnosis of galactosemia is suspected, dietary treatment should be instituted pending enzyme studies for confirmation of the diagnosis. Additional treatment may be required for infection, hypoglycemia, hyperbilirubinemia, hypoprothrombinemia, or anemia. Avoidance of the most important sources of dietary galactose, namely milk and foods containing milk products, is the basis for the galactose-restricted diet. Casein hydrolysates, meat-based preparations, and soybean formulas may be employed as milk substitutes. Galactose-containing oligosaccharides are known to be present in some foods, especially legumes, but these compounds are not digested in the intestinal tract.

Problems in adherence to the diet can occur because of carelessness of the parent, actions of the child, or intake of foodstuffs not suspected of containing galactose. Education of the parent and of the child, together with careful interim dietary histories, are helpful in uncovering any problems. One source of galactose that is frequently overlooked is the lactose employed as a binder or sweetener in drug products.

PROGNOSIS. Dietary treatment of the infant with galactosemia can be lifesaving. Most of the clinical features are reversed. Jaundice disappears in a few days, and weight gain resumes within one or two weeks. The liver diminishes in size relatively quickly, but in some patients it does not return to normal for several months. Cataracts may improve, but residual lesions may persist indefinitely.

A normal growth pattern can be achieved on dietary therapy, but the long-term effects on intellectual status are difficult to assess. Children treated continuously from birth develop apparently in a normal fashion, while most untreated patients tend to develop mental retardation. It is generally accepted that the outcome is better with early treatment, but there are reports of apparently successful results with treatment starting as late as one year of age.

The question of the age at which diet therapy can be safely discontinued is unsettled. Increased tolerance to galactose with increasing age has not been demonstrated, even though a number of alternate pathways for the metabolism of galactose have been postulated. Because galactose constitutes a significant component of the diet of the infant, the potential for accumulation of harmful metabolites is much greater during infancy than in the older child or adult. An adult galactosemic might conceivably tolerate a regular diet, but the ability to do so would not constitute adaptation to galactose in the usual sense. Relaxation of dietary restrictions for all but milk and milk-containing foods might be a reasonable position to adopt for the school-age child.

GENETICS. Galactosemia is inherited as an autosomal recessive abnormality, with the carrier having half-normal erythrocyte transferase activity. Recently a genetic variant of transferase has been described as the Duarte variant in which the homozygote also has half-normal transferase activity. Individuals with the Duarte variant are asymptomatic. It is essential for genetic counselling to distinguish between the Duarte variant and the galactosemia heterozygote. This can be accomplished by starch gel electrophoresis.

Galactokinase Defect

Thus far only a small number of patients have been identified with reduced galactokinase activity. The first example of this disorder was recognized by Gitzelmann in 1965 in a patient described earlier as having "galactose diabetes" associated with neurofibromatosis. The important clinical feature of the galactokinase defect is nuclear cataracts. None of the other manifestations of galactosemia has been seen, although in one infant mild hepatosplenomegaly without more definite evidence of liver disease was noted. The liver decreased in size on a galactose-restricted diet.

The biochemical lesion has been identified as a deficiency in galactokinase activity. Erythrocyte transferase activity is normal. Galactose and galactitol are found in the urine on an unrestricted diet, but erythrocyte galactose-1-phosphate levels are not elevated. These laboratory findings, together with assays of erythrocyte galactokinase, provide the basis for diagnosis. Treatment consists of a galactose-restricted diet.

Inheritance of the disorder is thought to be of the autosomal recessive type. Reduced erythrocyte galactokinase activity has been found in the parents of all the recognized patients.

Fructose Metabolism

Fructose is an important source of dietary carbohydrate because it is a constituent of the disaccharide sucrose and also is present in fruits and vegetables as the free monosaccharide. Certain oligosaccharides, such as raffinose and stachyose, contain fructose, but these sugars do not play a role in human nutrition.

There are two principal routes by which fructose is metabolized in man. In the liver, fructose is phosphorylated to fructose-1-phosphate in the presence of ATP and the enzyme fructokinase. This enzyme also has been demonstrated in kidney and intestinal mucosa. In muscle and adipose tissue, fructose is phosphorylated by hexokinase to fructose-6-phosphate.

The principal disorders of fructose metabolism are essential fructosuria and hereditary fructose intolerance. In addition, a disturbance of fructose metabolism secondary to an abnormality of galactose metabolism has been described.

Essential Fructosuria

Essential fructosuria is a relatively rare genetic disorder which is apparently transmitted as an autosomal recessive abnormality. The incidence in the general population has been estimated to be approximately 1 in 130,000. Because recognition is difficult, the incidence is probably higher. Individuals with essential fructosuria are asymptomatic. The diagnosis is based upon the finding of a reducing sugar in the urine which can be identified as fructose by chromatography. The sugar is present only after ingestion of foods containing fructose or sucrose. When fructose loading tests are done, abnormally high levels of blood fructose are found in comparison with results in normal individuals. The enzyme defect involves a deficiency in the activity of liver fructokinase.

Hereditary Fructose Intolerance

CLINICAL FINDINGS. Individuals with hereditary fructose intolerance are asymptomatic if fructose is excluded from the diet. Ingestion of fructose-containing foods results in clinical manifestations of hypoglycemia, such as tremors, disorientation, vomiting, and, if severe, convulsions and coma. In the infant, if fructose-containing foods are continued, the symptoms may progress to death. Chronic ingestion in infants may also result in clinical findings similar to galactosemia, including failure to thrive, hepatomegaly, vomiting, jaundice, hyperbilirubinemia, albuminuria, and amino-aciduria. However, in contrast to the infant with galactosemia, the breast-fed infant with hereditary fructose intolerance remains symptom-free.

The symptoms of hereditary fructose intolerance are variable and depend upon age. Symptomatology tends to be severe in infants and milder in older individuals. In some patients, gastrointestinal symptoms are striking, while in others hypoglycemia predominates. In the older child, a strong aversion usually develops to sweets, fruits, and other products containing fructose. This may explain why patients with hereditary fructose intolerance have unusually good teeth with a minimum of caries.

PATHOPHYSIOLOGY. The primary enzymatic deficiency in hereditary fructose intolerance is a marked reduction of fructose-1-phosphate aldolase activity. How the resulting accumulation of fructose-1-phosphate is related to symptomatology is unknown. It has been postulated that there is inhibition of enzymes involved in glucose metabolism, which results in both reduced release of glucose from the liver and interference with gluconeogenesis. It has been shown that the fructose-induced hypoglycemia of hereditary fructose intolerance is not due to hyperinsulinism. Insulinlike activity and immunoreactive insulin levels remain unchanged or are even lowered during fructose-induced hypoglycemia.

In affected individuals, chronic fructose ingestion may cause hepatomegaly due in part to an accumulation of lipids. Serum enzyme levels (SGOT) may be increased. Histologic examination of the liver has revealed findings of early cirrhosis.

The diagnosis of hereditary fructose intolerance is often suggested by history, but requires confirmation by laboratory tests. The administration of fructose orally or intravenously results in characteristic findings. There is a precipitous and prolonged fall in blood glucose and in serum phosphorous. Serum potassium may fall, but this response is variable. Blood fructose levels remain high for an extended period, and fructose may be found in the urine. During the course of the test, severe hypoglycemia may be induced, and glucose administration may be required for therapy.

TREATMENT AND PROGNOSIS. Treatment consists of the immediate correction of hypoglycemia by intravenous administration of glucose-containing solutions. Long-term therapy of this condition involves the avoidance of fructose- and sucrose-containing foods. As a rule, the prognosis for treated patients is very good.

GENETICS. Hereditary fructose intolerance appears to be inherited as an autosomal recessive abnormality. However, a dominant pattern of inheritance also has been described, which raises the possibility that there are two genetic forms of the disorder. It is not possible at the present time to identify the presumed heterozygotes for the trait, and resolution of the mode of genetic transmission requires further study.

Familial Galactose and Fructose Intolerance

A form of fructose intolerance, distinct from hereditary fructose intolerance, has been described in two sisters. Both fructose and galactose induced severe hypoglycemia, and there was a fall of serum phosphorus after fructose administration. The activity of erythrocyte galactose-1-phosphate uridyl transferase was normal. Fasting values for immunoreactive insulin were elevated in both patients, but fell during fructose or galactose-induced hypoglycemia. Serum insulin rose to high levels after oral glucose administration, but the blood sugar curves were normal. The pathogenesis of this syndrome is not yet understood.

Pentose Metabolism

Small amounts of arabinose, xylose, and ribose may be found in the urine of normal individuals, and trace amounts of xylulose and ribulose also have been reported. Ribosuria (D-ribose) has been reported in patients with muscular dystrophy. The only condition in which there is a marked excretion of pentose is essential pentosuria.

Pentosuria

Essential pentosuria is a benign disorder, principally affecting Jewish people, which is inherited as an autosomal recessive character. The sugar found in the urine is L-xylulose, which is excreted in increased amounts due to a block in conversion of xyulose to xylitol. The condition usually is discovered as an accidental finding. No treatment is required. A number of drugs are known to increase the rate at which glucose enters the uronic acid pathway; aminopyrin

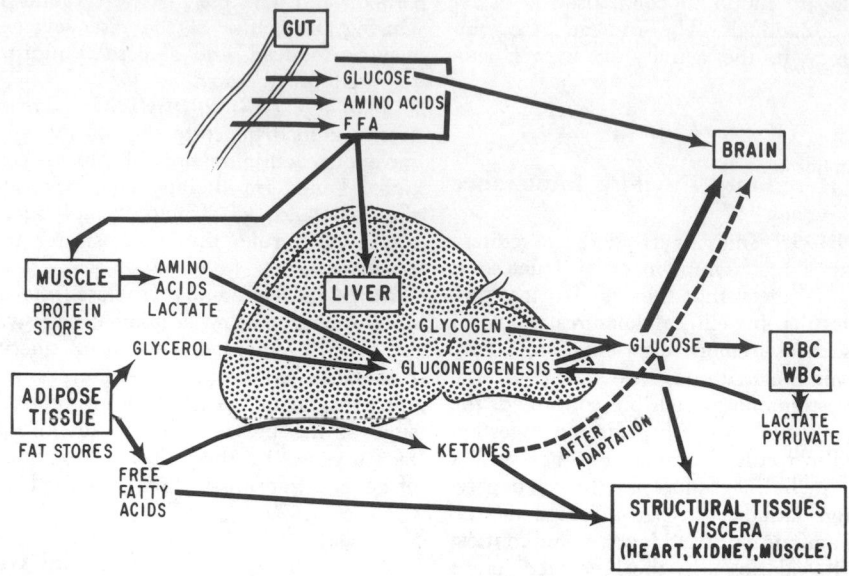

Fig. 8. Pathways of carbohydrate metabolism.

and antipyrin have been reported to increase the excretion of L-xylulose in pentosuric subjects. It has been stated that persons heterozygous for the defect in essential pentosuria can be recognized by use of a glucuronolactone loading test.

REFERENCES

Herman, R. H., and Zakin, D. Fructose metabolism. Amer. J. Clin. Nutr., 21:245, 315, 516, 693, and 778, 1968.

Hiatt, H. H. Pentosuria. In Stanbury, J. B., Wyngaarden, J. B., and Fredrickson, D. S., eds., The Metabolic Basis of Inherited Disease, 2nd ed. New York, McGraw-Hill Book Co., 1966.

Hsia, D. Y.-Y., ed. Galactosemia. Springfield, Ill., Charles C Thomas, Publ., 1968.

8.7

HYPOGLYCEMIA

LYNNE L. LEVITSKY and
MARVIN CORNBLATH

Hypoglycemia is not a disease entity but rather an indication that there is an imbalance among the multiple metabolic and endocrine controls that maintain carbohydrate homeostasis. In the normal individual, blood glucose is derived from exogenous sources and hepatic glycogen reserves, as well as from hepatic, and to a lesser extent, renal transfor-mation of amino acids, glycerol, and lactate. These sources are balanced against glucose utilization primarily by neural tissues, but also by structural tissues and visceral organs when glucose is in free supply (Fig. 8). Normoglycemia is maintained both by substrate control and by hormonal influences.

Hypoglycemia may be defined as that level of blood glucose which is significantly lower than the mean for a similar population under similar conditions. In practice, a true whole blood glucose below 40 mg/100 ml after the neonatal period, below 30 mg/100 ml in the normal newborn baby during the first 72 hours of life, and below 20 mg/100 ml in the low-birth-weight infant during the first month is considered significantly low. These hypoglycemic values are often associated with clinical manifestations.

Signs and Symptoms

Clinical manifestations of hypoglycemia are secondary to disordered neuronal function and may or may not be associated with evidence of sympathetic discharge. Not all patients with chemical hypoglycemia have clinical symptoms. The mechanism for cerebral adaptation to low blood glucose levels is not well understood but may involve utilization of other substrates such as ketone bodies to fulfill energy requirements.

Manifestations of hypoglycemia vary with age. In the newborn, nonspecific signs which suggest this abnormality are often noted. Apnea, cyanosis, irregular respirations, refusal to feed, limpness, tremors, twitching, weak or high-pitched cry, sweating, sub-

TABLE 6. *Classification of Childhood Hypoglycemia*

I. **Endocrine**
 A. Deficiency
  1. Growth hormone
  2. Thyroid
  3. Corticosteroid
   a. Congenital adrenal hyperplasia
   b. Addison's disease
  4. Epinephrine
  5. Glucagon
 B. Excess
  1. Insulin
   a. Infants of diabetic mothers
   b. Islet cell adenoma
   c. Islet cell hyperplasia
   d. Erythroblastosis fetalis
   e. Prediabetes mellitus

II. **Metabolic**
 A. Hereditary
  1. Glycogen storage disease affecting the liver
  2. Galactosemia
  3. Fructose intolerance
  4. Glycogen synthetase deficiency
  5. Cystinosis
  6. Maple syrup urine disease
  7. Tyrosinemia
 B. Acquired
  1. Fatty degeneration of the liver
  2. Hepatitis and cirrhosis
  3. Malnutrition
   a. Kwashiorkor
   b. Low phenylalanine diet
 C. Poisoning or toxic
  1. Alcohol
  2. Salicylate and acetaminophen
  3. Propranolol
  4. Oral hypoglycemic agents (e.g., tolbutamide)
  5. Insulin
  6. Hypoglycin (Jamaican vomiting sickness)
  7. TRIS Buffer

III. **Miscellaneous**
 A. Tumors
  1. Fibrosarcoma
  2. Wilms' tumor
  3. Hepatomas
  4. Undifferentiated carcinoma
 B. Central nervous system
  1. Tumors
  2. Thalamic lesions
  3. Hemorrhage
 C. Cold injury
 D. Renal glycosuria
 E. Severe diarrhea and malabsorption

IV. **Idiopathic**
 A. Neonatal transient
 B. Infant "giant"
 C. Beckwith's syndrome (visceromegaly, umbilical hernia, microcephaly, and hypoglycemia)
 D. Familial
 E. Ketotic
 F. Leucine sensitive
 G. Epinephrine unresponsive
 H. Unknown

normal temperature, coma, and convulsions have been associated with low blood sugar levels. The clustering of certain manifestations such as "jitteriness," tremors, and convulsions seems to be particularly significant in diagnosis. In the older child or infant, hypoglycemic attacks may be manifested by pallor, listlessness or irritability, staring, motor incoordination leading to ataxia and strabismus, limpness, and rarely, episodic abnormal behavior and inattention. If the episode is accompanied by sympathetic discharge, sweating and tachycardia may also be noted. The child may complain of headache, nausea, anxiety, hunger, and dissociative feelings. Symptoms may progress to coma and seizures if the episode is not rapidly terminated. A response to administration of glucose is important in all age groups to confirm the diagnosis.

Incidence

Hypoglycemia in the neonatal period has been estimated to occur in 2 to 3 per 1,000 live births. In low-birth-weight infants and infants who have had a complicated prenatal history, the incidence may be 20 times as high. Hypoglycemia is much less frequent after the neonatal period; data from published series suggest a prevalence rate of 2 per 1,000 pediatric hospital admissions. However, published reports from specialized centers are biased by selective referral and sampling, making the true prevalence difficult to estimate. Further, the delay in diagnosis often seen after onset of symptoms suggests that there may be many undiagnosed cases. Finally, mildly affected patients may recover with maturity and never undergo diagnostic evaluation.

Classification

A classification of childhood hypoglycemia based upon the site of disturbance in the carbohydrate homeostatic mechanism would be desirable. However, such a unifying classification is not possible with the present inadequate understanding of the basic mechanisms of most types of hypoglycemia. For this reason a classification which is useful therapeutically is offered (Table 6).

ENDOCRINE DEFICIENCY STATES. Isolated growth hormone deficiency and associated hypoglycemia have been described. Many hypopituitary patients are also markedly susceptible to insulin hypoglycemia, and they may have low fasting blood sugar values.

Hypoglycemia has been reported rarely with hypothyroidism. When present, it may reflect secondary unresponsiveness to growth hormone and corticosteroid release.

Adrenal insufficiency, whether due to an enzymatic defect as in congenital adrenal hyperplasia, or associated with actual destruction of adrenal tissue, may be associated with episodes of fasting hypoglycemia.

Epinephrine has a marked generalized glycogenolytic effect, stimulates gluconeogenesis, and inhibits insulin secretion and peripheral utilization of glucose. Decreased levels of urinary catecholamines have been described in spontaneous neonatal hypoglycemia and in children with idiopathic hypoglycemia. However, patients who have undergone total adrenalectomy do not seem to require epinephrine supplementation to maintain glucose homeostasis. Further, hypoglycemic children with deficient epinephrine release appear to regain their ability to secrete catecholamines if carefully fed and kept normoglycemic for a period of time. Therefore deficient catecholamine release observed in childhood hypoglycemia may be secondary to continued hypoglycemic stress rather than primary to the illness. This question is still not settled.

Glucagon stimulates hepatic glycogenolysis and gluconeogenesis; deficiency of this hormone has been postulated as a cause of hypoglycemia. A few hypoglycemic children have been discovered at pathologic examination to have a decreased number of glucagon-secreting pancreatic alpha cells. Now that a reliable immunoassay for glucagon exists, it should be possible to determine whether there is a specific hypoglycemic syndrome secondary to deficient glucagon release. In a small number of hypoglycemic children we have studied thus far, no glucagon deficiency has been observed.

ENDOCRINE EXCESS (INSULIN). In any situation where there is an excess amount of insulin-secreting tissue or an abnormal response of this tissue to provocative stimuli, hypoglycemia can result. Infants of diabetic mothers, and infants with erythroblastosis fetalis, as well as a certain number of children with persistent neonatal hypoglycemia of unknown etiology, have been shown to have hyperplasia of the pancreatic islet cells at postmortem examination. Raised insulin levels in response to various stimuli have been observed in these conditions.

Islet cell adenomas may produce severe hypoglycemic symptoms because of chronically increased insulin release. These tumors seem to occur more frequently in infants and children than previously recognized. Unfortunately, no specific diagnostic test for the islet cell adenoma exists in childhood, but recent evidence suggests that relatively elevated fasting plasma insulin levels are significant in diagnosis. Symptoms produced by these adenomas may often be severe enough to set them apart from more easily controlled types of hypoglycemia.

In prediabetes mellitus, hypoglycemia is occasionally seen both in the fasting state and postprandially. This is thought to be secondary to erratic responsiveness of the beta cells to normal insulinogenic stimuli. It is most often seen in the preadolescent and adolescent age group.

HEREDITARY METABOLIC DISEASES. Various inherited enzymatic defects have been implicated as causes of hypoglycemia. The glycogen storage diseases which affect the liver (types I, III, IV, and VI) are associated with hypoglycemia of greater or lesser degree. Deficiency of glycogen synthetase has also been associated with severe hypoglycemia (see p. 368) Infrequently, galactosemia may be associated with hypoglycemia.

Hereditary fructose intolerance secondary to fructose-1-phosphate aldolase deficiency is associated with severe hypoglycemia due to inhibition of hepatic glucose release. Children with hereditary fructose intolerance present in infancy with vomiting, drowsiness, and coma following fructose ingestion. In the older child, there is a history of avoidance of all sweet-tasting foods. Fructosuria, hypoglysemia, and fructosemia following fructose ingestion establish the diagnosis. Fructosuria itself may be a benign, asymptomatic condition secondary to fructokinase deficiency.

Several other inborn errors not involved directly in carbohydrate metabolism have also been associated with hypoglycemia. These include cystinosis, tyrosinosis, and maple syrup urine disease.

ACQUIRED METABOLIC DISEASES. Since the liver is the major site for glycogen storage and for gluconeogenesis, any illness which affects its functioning may lead to hypoglycemia. Hepatitis and cirrhosis as well as protein-calorie malnutrition can lead to disruption of hepatic architecture and function. The syndrome of fatty infiltration of the viscera and encephalopathy, first described by Reye, is also associated with hypoglycemia, probably secondary to liver damage.

A number of pharmacologic agents may produce hypoglycemic symptoms. Insulin, alcohol, salicylates, acetominophen, and the oral hypoglycemic agents such as tolbutamide are the most commonly implicated agents in this country. However, with increasing use, other drugs will probably be more often reported to have this potential. In particular, propranolol, a beta adrenergic blocking agent, and TRIS buffer have been found to produce hypoglycemia. In other areas of the world, local toxic agents are often important. For instance, the seeds of the unripe ackee fruit contain hypoglycin, the agent responsible for hypoglycemia in Jamaican vomiting sickness.

OTHER KNOWN CAUSES OF HYPOGLYCEMIA. Tumors have been shown to produce hypoglycemia either because of their enormous energy requirements when large or widespread or because of the production of material with insulinlike activity. Central nervous system damage secondary to tumor, direct trauma, hemorrhage, or severe electrolyte imbalance may be associated with abnormalities of carbohydrate metabolism. Any situation in which there is insufficient absorption of carbohydrate and glucose-producing substrate, as in severe diarrhea and malabsorption, or which is associated with excess loss of carbohydrate, as in renal glycosuria, may be accompanied by hypoglycemia.

IDIOPATHIC HYPOGLYCEMIA. *Neonatal.* As discussed earlier, hypoglycemia is relatively common in the newborn population. It occurs most frequently in low-birth-weight for gestation male infants with poor energy reserves, in the smallest of discordant twins, in polycythemic infants, and in infants of toxemic mothers. Fifteen percent of hypoglycemic infants have had concomitant central nervous system pathology. Usually the hypoglycemia is of a transient nature and responds readily to intravenous glucose and corticosteroids. It may be associated with hypocalcemia.

The nature of transient neonatal hypoglycemia has been studied in some detail and represents a syndrome with multiple pathogenetic tracts. In many infants reduced glycogen stores have been inferred because of poor hyperglycemic response to glucagon and epinephrine. Increased insulin responsiveness has been postulated as well, because of a rapid clearance rate (K_t) for intravenous glucose, high random serum insulin levels, and a greater hypoglycemic response to leucine and tolbutamide than in the normal infant. Further, some of these infants appear to have low cortisol production rates.

A few children with idiopathic neonatal hypoglycemia have a more persistent problem. The "infant giant" presents as a large infant, with the features of an infant of a diabetic mother and intractable hypoglycemia which often is not controlled even with pancreatectomy. Patients with this condition may be leucine sensitive and some have had hyperplasia of the beta cells of the pancreas. Most of these children have died in early infancy. Those who have survived longer and then died have had uniformly severe central nervous system damage.

Another group of large infants with less severe hypoglycemia has been described by Beckwith. They present with microcephaly, macroglossia, omphalocele, gigantism, visceromegaly, and often transient hypoglycemia. In these children it is also likely that beta cell hyperplasia plays a role in the hypoglycemic symptomatology. In addition, leucine sensitivity may first be identified in the neonatal period, and a certain number of children with familial hypoglycemia of unknown etiology have been described in this age group.

Older Children. In approximately 70 percent of older infants and children hospitalized with hypoglycemia, the disorder is found to be of the idiopathic type. Although a specific configuration of symptoms and signs may permit further therapeutic classification in these children, the etiology of the illness is not well understood.

Approximately one-half of the children with idiopathic hypoglycemia whom we have studied appear to suffer from ketotic hypoglycemia. In this condition, first well described by Colle and Ulstrom, a high fat, low caloric provocative diet rapidly produces ketosis and then hypoglycemia. Insulin levels remain low throughout the episode and there is,

indeed, some evidence that children with this condition have a general insulinopenia.

Children with ketotic hypoglycemia are usually male, underweight for height, with poor body fat stores, and may have a history of hypoglycemia or malnutrition in the neonatal period. They commonly present between the ages of 1 and 6 years with a history of symptoms following an overnight fast, often associated with illness or the ingestion of a high fat diet. Symptoms range from listlessness to coma and convulsions, and tend to recur at relatively infrequent intervals and to improve with age. These symptoms respond readily to food intake or intravenous glucose, but not to glucagon. There has been an absence of liver glycogen in the patients who have been studied with liver biopsy while hypoglycemic. The syndrome appears to be associated with a failure of gluconeogenesis but the mechanism is not understood.

In our experience approximately 10 percent of children with idiopathic hypoglycemia are leucine sensitive. In these children, the pancreatic islet cells appear to be hyperresponsive to leucine as well as to certain other branch-chain metabolites. Administration of such substances therefore produces a prompt fall in blood sugar secondary to insulin release. This seems to be an exaggeration of a normal response, for most individuals have some fall in blood sugar and an increase in insulin output when stimulated by leucine. High protein meals invariably provoke hypoglycemia and frequently central nervous system symptoms. The age of onset in leucine-sensitive hypoglycemia is almost always under 1 year and there may be a familial pattern. These patients, in contrast to those with ketotic hypoglycemia, are often severely symptomatic, and therefore suffer an extreme degree of hypoglycemic damage. Mental retardation is the rule rather than the exception. Leucine sensitivity developing after the age of 3 or 4 years may suggest an islet cell adenoma.

A significant number of children do not fit into any of the categories described on the basis of their clinical histories and the standard provocative tests. Some of these children appear to have a familial hypoglycemic syndrome, while others have spontaneous recurrent hypoglycemic episodes. Undoubtedly, as our knowledge of the control of gluconeogenesis and glucose release and utilization grows, more of these children will be reclassified etiologically.

Diagnosis

The yield of specific etiologic diagnoses in the study of children with hypoglycemia is low. However, the effect of specific therapy is beneficial enough to justify pertinent investigation.

Most of the specific hypoglycemic syndromes can be eliminated from consideration in the usual

TABLE 7. *Specific Tests in Hypoglycemia*

Three days of preparation on a high-carbohydrate diet are necessary
before each carbohydrate tolerance test

Test	Method	Interpretation
24- to 36-hour fast	Fast with water ad lib and blood samples for glucose, insulin, and free fatty acids every 2 to 6 hours. Terminate with 50% glucose in water intravenously if symptomatic, and continue intravenously until patient is feeding well.	This provocation should be used to verify the diagnosis of hypoglycemia. It is nonspecific. Elevated fasting plasma insulin levels may suggest islet cell adenoma.
Glucagon tolerance test	0.03 mg/kg (to 1.0 mg) is given intravenously or subcutaneously after a 4- to 12-hour fast. This is repeated several hours after a meal if no hyperglycemic response is noted initially. Samples at 0, 15, 30, 45, 60, 90, and 120 minutes for glucose, insulin, and free fatty acids.	A rise in blood glucose of 25 to 50 mg/100 ml is normally found within 15 to 45 minutes. A return to fasting levels takes 60 to 90 minutes. Unresponsiveness may be seen in severe hepatic depletion or hepatocellular disease, or glycogen storage disease. Patients with debrancher enzyme (type III) defect or glycogen synthetase deficiency may respond a few hours after meals. Patients with Von Gierke's disease remain unresponsive.
Ketogenic diet	1,200 calories/1.73 m² of body surface area, made up as 800 g whole milk, 285 g 20% cream, 17 g Casec, and 100 g water. This mixture provides approximately 1 cal/g. Given in 3 equal parts at 8 AM, 12 noon, and 5 PM after careful high-carbohydrate preparation and an overnight fast. Water ad lib. Check all urines for acetone. Blood samples for glucose and free fatty acids every 4 hours. Glucagon tolerance test should be done if the patient is symptomatic, or at the end of 24 hours. Intravenous glucose may be necessary to terminate symptoms.	Normally, acetonuria develops after 8 to 12 hours. A susceptible child becomes hypoglycemic 4 to 12 hours later. Unresponsiveness to glucagon at the termination of the test is typical in ketotic hypoglycemia.
Leucine tolerance test	150 mg/kg orally, dissolved in dilute alkaline solution or CO_2-free water, and given flavored or by nasogastric tube after an overnight fast, if possible. Samples at 0, 15, 30, 45, 60, 90, and 120 minutes for glucose and insulin.	A fall in blood sugar to at least 50% of the fasting value is diagnostic of leucine-sensitive hypoglycemia. Symptoms may occur in the first 45 minutes. Some drop in blood sugar is expected in most normals as well.
Oral glucose tolerance test	Age — Glucose dose: 0-18 mo, 2.5 g/kg; 1½-3 yr, 2 g/kg; 3-12 yr, 1.75 g/kg; 12 yr, 1.25 g/kg. Give in a chilled, flavored 25% solution after an overnight fast. Samples for glucose and insulin at 0, ½, 1, 1½, 2, 3, 4, and 5 hours.	In reactive hypoglycemia, a rapid rise and a fall of the blood glucose to hypoglycemic levels may be seen at 3 to 5 hours. With failure of absorption a flat glucose curve and minimal insulin response may be seen. Hepatic disease sometimes produces a diphasic curve, as may delayed absorption.
Intravenous glucose tolerance test	Age — Glucose dose: 2 yr, 1 g/kg; 2 yr, 0.5 g/kg (maximum 25 g). Give intravenously over 2 to 4 minutes in a 25% to 50% solution after an overnight fast. Samples for glucose and insulin at 0, 5, 10, 15, 20, 30, 45, 60, 75, 90, 120, 180, and 360 minutes from an indwelling scalp vein needle at a site other than that used for glucose administration.	A disappearance rate constant (K_t) is derived by the formula $K = \dfrac{0.693}{t_{1/2}}$, where $t_{1/2}$ is the time required for a 50% drop in blood glucose, as determined from a semilogarithmic plot of blood glucose against time. A marked fall in blood sugar and persistent hypoglycemia in the second hour may be seen in children with a rapid disappearance rate. A K_t of less than 1% is seen in diabetes or in the normal neonate. A K_t of greater than 3% implies rapid disappearance of blood glucose. The pathophysiologic significance of a rapid disappearance rate remains to be elucidated.
Arginine tolerance test	0.5 g/kg of *L*-arginine hydrochloride in a 5% solution is infused over 30 minutes. Samples at 0, 30, 45, 60, 90, and 120 minutes for glucose, growth hormone, insulin, and glucagon if possible.	Normally a rise in blood glucose of 10 to 20 mg% is seen after arginine infusion. This may be higher in diabetics. A variable insulin response is noted with a peak at 30 to 45 minutes, and a variable growth hormone response is also noted at 30 to 45 minutes. Glucagon response is noted at or before 30 minutes. This test may detect, therefore, decreased responsiveness to insulin, growth hormone, and glucagon release.

TABLE 7. (continued)

Tests	Method	Interpretation
Epinephrine tolerance test	0.03 mg/kg intramuscularly (maximum 0.3 mg). Samples as in glucagon tolerance test.	Interpretation as for glucagon tolerance test. Usually a glucagon tolerance test is substituted to avoid sympathomimetic side effects.
Tolbutamide tolerance test	20 mg/kg intravenously (maximum 1 g) after an overnight fast. Samples at 0, 5, 10, 20, 30, 45, 60, 90, and 120 minutes for glucose and insulin.	Normally, glucose falls by 20 to 40% of fasting levels in 20 to 30 minutes and returns to within 10% of the initial level by 90 to 120 minutes. Many hypoglycemic children have been reported to be quite sensitive to tolbutamide. This test has not been reported to be diagnostic for islet cell tumors in infancy, childhood, or adolescence.
Insulin tolerance test	0.1 unit/kg intravenously after an overnight fast. Samples at 0, 10, 20, 30, 45, 60, 90, and 120 minutes for glucose and growth hormone.	Should only be done in normoglycemic individuals. A fall of at least 50% in blood glucose by 30 to 45 minutes and a rise in growth hormone levels to over 10 ng/ml are usually seen. In growth hormone deficiency, profound, symptomatic hypoglycemia may be elicited.

patient simply by a careful history and physical examination. Where sufficient doubt exists (as in a child with short stature in whom growth hormone deficiency is suspected) the appropriate provocative tests should be performed (Table 7). Investigation of children with idiopathic hypoglycemia requires an understanding of the ages at which the various syndromes are known to occur (Fig. 9).

A reasonable approach to the evaluation of the child with hypoglycemia may be derived from this graphic representation.

First, all children should undergo routine laboratory examinations including hepatic function tests, tests for urinary glucose, reducing sugars and ketones, serum electrolytes, and serial blood glucose determinations.

In the immediate neonatal period, diagnosis is most important. Once the diagnosis has been made by *replicate* low blood sugar levels, therapy should be started. Further evaluation may be undertaken if the hypoglycemia proves to be persistent.

In the infant who is symptomatic before 6 months of age, one should be most suspicious of an inherited metabolic defect. A glucagon tolerance test after a 4- to 12-hour fast, depending upon the severity of the hypoglycemia, should be done to evaluate hepatic glycogen stores and the glycogenolytic mechanism. A leucine tolerance test should then be carried out in this age group. Further testing, such as tolbutamide and glucose tolerance tests, may be carried out. However, these tests are of questionable value in determining a therapeutic regimen.

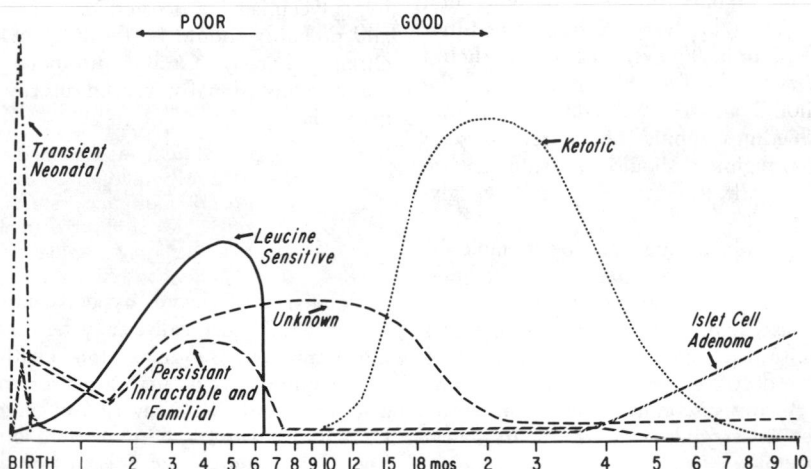

Fig. 9. Age distribution of the various types of idiopathic hypoglycemia. Incidence data is grossly estimated for graphic presentation. (Adapted from Cornblath and Schwartz. *Disorders of Carbohydrate Metabolism in Infancy*, W. B. Saunders Co., 1966.)

In the child over 18 months of age, ketotic hypoglycemia is the most likely diagnosis. Therefore, following a standard glucagon tolerance test, a high-fat, low-calorie ketogenic diet should be offered and a glucagon tolerance test should be repeated at the conclusion of the dietary stress. If these tests do not produce a diagnosis, a 24- to 36-hour fast may be necessary to delineate the nature of the hypoglycemia. Tolbutamide, leucine, and glucose tolerance tests may provide useful information if the previous tests are not informative.

It is important to note that evaluation of free fatty acids, growth hormone, insulin, catecholamine, and corticosteroid secretion, as well as blood glucose, during these procedures may add valuable insight into the pathogenesis of the hypoglycemia. Further advances in knowledge of pathogenesis will require studies of production and utilization of gluconeogenetic substrates, particularly glycerol, lactate, and amino acids.

Therapy

Therapy in the specific hypoglycemic syndromes should be directed at alleviation or amelioration of the causative factors.

In the neonatal period, hypoglycemia is often a temporary problem. Yet because of the severity of sequelae, immediate and adequate therapy is imperative. When hypoglycemia has been confirmed by replicate blood glucose determinations, administration of 1 to 2 ml per kg of 50 percent glucose in water intravenously should be followed by a constant infusion of 10 to 15 percent glucose in water, at a rate sufficient to supply the infant's fluid needs. If an infusion of glucose higher than 15 to 20 percent is required to maintain blood sugar at an adequate level, or if frequent monitoring is impossible, oral hydrocortisone (2.5 mg/kg every 12 hours) or intramuscular ACTH (2 units/kg every 12 hours) should be administered. After the first 48 hours of life, the infusion fluid should also contain adequate sodium (40 mEq/L). Feedings should be started as soon as possible. This regimen should be sufficient to control all infants with transient neonatal hypoglycemia.

When the child's blood sugar has been stable for 48 hours and he is taking adequate oral feedings, the concentration of glucose administered parenterally can be decreased slowly to 5 percent in water and then discontinued. Dosages of steroids and ACTH should be decreased carefully over a period of several days. Abrupt discontinuation of either intravenous glucose or steroids may result in severe reactive hypoglycemia.

In older children with excess insulin release either on an anatomic or functional basis, alteration of dietary habits will often be sufficient to control hypoglycemia. If inadequate, corticosteroid therapy may be required. In more severe cases, therapy with diazoxide, a potent inhibitor of insulin release, is often beneficial. The side effects of diazoxide, including neutropenia, edema, hypertrichosis, and hyperuricemia, preclude its routine use. In addition, sudden death has been seen in a newborn treated with this drug. In children with severe idiopathic hypoglycemia, as well as in those with tumors and hyperplasia of the islet cells, subtotal pancreatectomy (80 to 90 percent) has proved to be of benefit.

Dietary management has proved useful in the more common forms of idiopathic hypoglycemia. Children with ketotic hypoglycemia respond well to a low-fat, high-carbohydrate diet, with bedtime supplementation. If supplemental carbohydrate is offered when the patient becomes ketotic, nearly all attacks may be aborted. Therefore it is important in home management to check urinary ketones at least daily, and more frequently during times of illness or decreased appetite.

Leucine sensitivity may sometimes be managed with dietary restriction of protein, high-carbohydrate supplementation 20 to 30 minutes after a meal, and frequent feedings. Often, however, more potent therapy such as diazoxide is necessary to relieve the symptomatology.

When no specific pattern of hypoglycemic attacks can be determined and when no specific therapy is available, frequent high-carbohydrate feedings remain the most useful therapeutic regimen.

Glucagon and epinephrine have proved useful for immediate management of hypoglycemic symptoms, except when there is total depletion of glycogen reserves or failure of glycogenolysis as in ketotic hypoglycemia and certain of the metabolic defects. Long-acting preparations, such as zinc glucagon and epinephrine in suspension, have largely been replaced by diazoxide in the treatment of patients with severe hypoglycemia. Corticosteroids are still quite useful and probably should be the drug of choice for initial chronic therapy. Growth hormone supplementation has also occasionally proved useful in severe hypoglycemia.

Prognosis

Prolonged and severe hypoglycemic insults at any age and from any cause may be associated with lasting neurologic sequelae and death. The hypoglycemic syndromes occurring earlier in life are usually associated with more severe and more frequent symptoms and therefore with a more guarded prognosis. Sporadic hypoglycemic episodes of short duration occurring later in childhood often do not appear to affect intellectual or motor development.

TABLE 8.   *Types of Glycogen Storage Disease*

Type	Enzyme Defect	Defect Demonstrable in			
		Erythrocytes	Leucocytes	Liver	Muscle
0	UDPG-glycogen transferase	—	—	yes	yes
Ia	Glucose-6-phosphatase	no	no	yes	yes
Ib	Functional glucose-6-phosphatase deficiency	no	no	no*	no
IIa	Lysosomal α-1,4-glucosidase	no	inconstant	yes	yes
IIb	Lysosomal α-1,4-glucosidase	no	—	yes	yes
III a,b,c,d	Amylo-1,6-glucosidase and/or Oligo-1,4→1,4-glucantransferase	yes	yes	yes†	yes†
IV	Amylo-1,4→1,6-transglucosylase	yes	yes	yes	yes
V	Muscle phosphorylase	no	no	no	yes
VI	Liver phosphorylase	—	yes	yes	no
VII	Phosphofructokinase	yes	yes	—	yes
VIII	Phosphohexosisomerase (inhibitor?)	—	—	—	yes‡
IXa	Phosphorylase kinase	—	yes	yes	no
IXb	Phosphorylase kinase	—	yes	yes	no
X	Phosphorylase kinase	—	—	—	yes

*See text p. 369.
†See Table 9.
‡See text p. 372.

REFERENCES

Anderson, J. M., Milner, R. D. G., and Strich, S. J. Pathological changes in the nervous system in severe neonatal hypoglycemia. Lancet, 1:372, 1966.
Baker, L., Kaye, R., Root, A. W., and Prasad, A. L. N. Diazoxide treatment of idiopathic hypoglycemia of infancy. J. Pediat., 71:494, 1967.
Cochrane, W. A., Payne, W. W., Simpkiss, M. J., and Woolf, L. I. Familial hypoglycemia precipitated by amino acids. J. Clin. Invest., 35:411, 1956.
Colle, E., and Ulstrom, R. A. Ketotic hypoglycemia. J. Pediat., 64:632, 1964.
Cornblath, M., and Schwartz, R. Disorders of Carbohydrate Metabolism in Infancy. Philadelphia, W. B. Saunders Co., 1966.
Ehrlich, R. M., and Martin, J. M. M. Tolbutamide tolerance test and plasma-insulin response in children with idiopathic hypoglycemia. J. Pediat., 71:485, 1967.
Kenney, F. M., and Preeyasombat, C. Cortisol production rate. VI. Hypoglycemia in the neonatal and postneonatal period and in association with dwarfism. J. Pediat., 70:65, 1967.
Kogut, M. D., Blaskovics, M., and Donnell, G. N. Idiopathic hypoglycemia—A study of twenty-six children. J. Pediat., 74:853, 1969.
Mann, J. R., Rayner, H. W., and Gourevitch, O. Insulinoma in childhood. Arch. Dis. Child., 44:435, 1969.
Norman, M. G. Encephalopathy and fatty degeneration of the viscera in childhood: I. Review of cases at the Hospital for Sick Children, Toronto (1954-1966). Canad. Med. Assoc. J., 99:522, 1968.
Pildes, R., Forbes, A. E., O'Connor, S. M., and Cornblath, M. The incidence of neonatal hypoglycemia—a completed survey. J. Pediat., 70:76, 1967.

8.8
THE GLYCOGENOSES

JAMES B. SIDBURY, JR.

DEFINITION.   The glycogen storage diseases may be defined as heritable diseases associated with qualitatively or quantitatively abnormal glycogen distributed generally or in specific organs, and which cannot be explained by a physiologic mechanism or disease, such as Mauriac's syndrome, excessive insulin therapy in diabetes, or steroid therapy. Eleven different types of glycogen storage disease have been enzymatically defined. The first four types were classified by Cori, and subsequent types have been designated in the order of the chronology of their enzymatic definition, except type O which is designated to reflect the nature of that abnormality. Subtypes have been indicated to reflect differences in clinical manifestations, differences in tissue distribution of the altered enzyme, or alteration of in vivo activity without the ability to demonstrate an abnormal enzyme in vitro (Table 8). All of the glycogenoses appear to be autosomal recessive conditions except type IXa, which is X-linked. Clinically, the glycogenoses can be subdivided into those affecting primarily the liver (types O; I; Ia; IIIa, b, c, d; IV; VI; IXa, b) and those manifesting primarily muscular involvement (types IIa, b; V; VII; VIII; X).

Type O

CLINICAL MANIFESTATIONS. Affected infants may have a seizure or apneic spell shortly after birth or later, when four hourly feedings are reduced to three feedings a day. The hypoglycemic seizures are indistinguishable from those of any other etiology. Mental retardation may become apparent as the infant grows older.

GENETICS. Two families have been described and in neither was there consanguinity. There was a sibship cluster of cases and both males and females were affected. Biochemical evidence of heterozygosity has not been demonstrated but the disease would appear to be autosomal recessive.

LABORATORY FINDINGS. The primary clinical laboratory finding is fasting hypoglycemia. There is no rise of blood glucose in response to glucagon administration in the fasting state, but a rise is obtained 2 to 3 hours after a meal. Glycogen synthetase is markedly diminished in the liver obtained at biopsy.

PATHOPHYSIOLOGY. While fasting, the available glycogen becomes depleted because the rate of synthesis of glycogen is markedly decreased as a result of a deficiency of the enzyme primarily responsible for its synthesis. Thus an inadequate amount of glucose is produced by the liver to regulate blood glucose under fasting conditions. Transamination of amino acids and gluconeogenesis are not rapid enough or quantitatively sufficient to maintain the blood sugar alone in the infant, as judged by the findings in this condition and types III, VI, and IXa glycogenosis. The glucagon response in the fasting state reflects the lack of available glycogen, and that following a meal demonstrates that the enzyme is not completely absent, for sufficient glycogen is synthesized to obtain a positive glucose response to glucagon.

TREATMENT. Intravenous administration of glucose is indicated to correct severe hypoglycemia. Frequent feedings with relatively high sugar content is indicated for prevention. A high protein intake should also be helpful in maintaining gluconeogenesis maximally. ACTH was shown to be helpful in the initial study and may be of benefit in the induction of the enzymes involved in gluconeogenesis.

PROGNOSIS. The experience to date has been poor. In the originally described family one child is mentally retarded and in the second family the four affected children have died.

Type I

CLINICAL MANIFESTATIONS. The infant with absent hepatic and renal glucose-6-phosphatase may be symptomatic in the neonatal period and present with hepatomegaly and hypoglycemic convulsions. This is one of the few conditions associated with ketonuria in the neonatal period. The disease may be first noted in the later months of the first year on finding a very large liver during a routine examination. The infants are usually chubby but lag in linear growth. The skin is thin, the venules are prominent, and a prolonged bleeding time is demonstrable early. There is individual variability in the response to hypoglycemia. Some will have an almost undetectable blood glucose level after a 4- to 6-hour fast without symptoms of any kind; others will require frequent glucose feedings to prevent recurrent hypoglycemic convulsions after a similar fast.

From the end of the first year to about the fifth year of life is the most difficult period of management. The growth retardation, immense hepatomegaly, and characteristic general appearance (Fig. 10) persist. There is increased fatigability, and the activity of these children is subdued when compared with that of their peers. Infections, which these children do not handle well, may be associated with epistaxis, which can be severe. Mild upper respiratory infections are prolonged and often difficult to manage. Ketoacidosis, abetted by lacticacidosis, may become rapidly profound with infections. Hypoglycemia is also a problem during these periods. Removal of the tonsils and adenoids and dental extractions are usually associated with hemorrhage.

From the fifth year until puberty, which is often delayed, management is easier, since patients usually develop the ability to maintain a normal blood sugar during an overnight fast, even though there is a persistent absence of liver glucose-6-phosphatase.

The enlarged liver, diminished stature, and variably increased adipose deposition persist after puberty. Stamina improves but the patients are never hearty. Gout is a frequent problem in late adolescence, in the twenties, or later. Mental development is not affected.

GENETICS. The condition occurs in males and females equally, and in siblings of unaffected parents. The frequency of consanguinity in the parents is not as high as might be anticipated. Detection of heterozygosity has been reported; the parents were found to have reduced glucose-6-phosphatase levels in their intestinal mucosa. The evidence supports an autosomal recessive type of transmission. The incidence in Sweden is reported as 1 in 400,000 live births.

LABORATORY FINDINGS. The clinical biochemical findings can be very helpful in differential diagnosis.

is a rise in blood lactate in response to these agents. When galactose is given intravenously there is a rise in lactate, but characteristically no rise in blood glucose.

Study of biopsied tissue is diagnostic. The muscle shows no abnormality of glycogen content or enzyme activity. The liver has increased fat and glycogen; the latter may be only very modestly increased. Glucose-6-phosphatase activity is absent in the liver and the kidney. Histochemically the parenchymal cells of the liver are swollen and show an increase in fat and glycogen. The proximal tubular cells of the kidney are engorged with glycogen. Type Ib demonstrates all of the clinical, laboratory, and pathologic findings of type Ia, which is the more frequent prototype, except that no deficiency of glucose-6-phosphatase can be demonstrated in vitro in biopsied liver material.

PATHOPHYSIOLOGY. The fasting hypoglycemia results from the absence of the liver glucose-6-phosphatase activity and points up the central role of this enzyme in the regulation of blood glucose. The absence of this enzyme also prevents a rise in blood glucose after liver phosphorylase activation by epinephrine or glucagon. Similarly, the conversion of intravenous galactose to glucose-1-phosphate, then to glucose-6-phosphate and to glucose, does not take place in the absence of this enzyme. The high lactic acid results from glycogen breakdown during fasting and the inability to form free glucose; hence it leaves the liver as lactate. The phosphorylated sugars cannot be transported out of the cell. The fasting ketosis results from the lowered blood glucose, leading to epinephrine release, which in turn mobilizes fatty acids from adipose tissue. The excess fatty acids are incompletely oxidized; hence ketone bodies are formed. The increased fatty acids in the liver and the increased availability of the intermediates of the Embden-Myerhof pathway would make α-glycerol-phosphate more available for esterification with fatty acids, resulting in increased triglyceride synthesis. The increased cholesterol synthesis could result from the inadequate fatty acid oxidation, and cholesterol synthesis, like ketone synthesis, would be pushed by the excess of intermediates.

It is surmised that the high uric acid results from increased activity of the hexose monophosphate shunt pathway, which generates increased phosphoribosyl pyrophosphate, a building block for uric acid synthesis, and thereby fosters increased synthesis. On the other hand, the high blood uric acid is not accompanied by comparably elevated urine uric acid excretion. Both ketone bodies and lactate are competitive inhibitors of tubular excretion of urate, and this mechanism is felt to play a more important role than overproduction in the elevation of the serum uric acid.

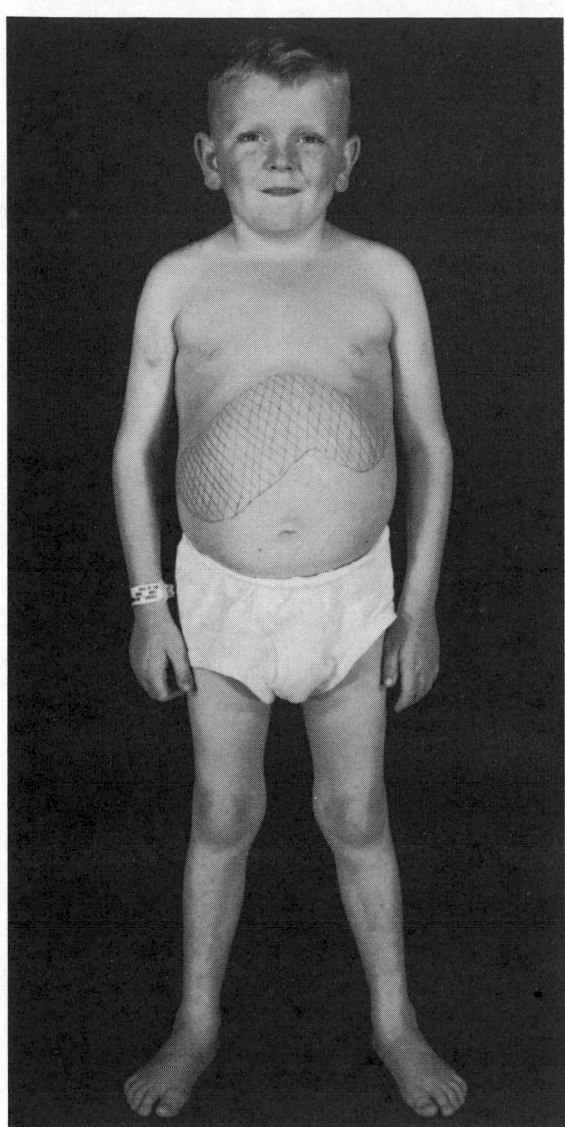

Fig. 10. A 9-year-old boy with type I glycogen storage disease who shows the characteristic general appearance.

These individuals show a fasting hypoglycemia, ketosis, hyperlactic acidemia, elevated nonesterified fatty acids, and lipidemia. All of these abnormal values improve or return to normal with glucose administration. Hyperuricemia is also found. There may be a normal or diabetic type glucose tolerance curve, the latter being more frequent in older children and adults. There is no rise in blood glucose in response to administered epinephrine or glucagon in infants and young children, but there may be a delayed response in older children and adults. There

TREATMENT. The basic approach to management is dietary. A normal diet with high-carbohydrate feedings between meals is the basic pattern. A high-protein diet can be defended on theoretical grounds in attempting to maintain a positive nitrogen balance, but it cannot be depended on to maintain blood glucose. Not infrequently carbohydrate feedings through the night are necessary in the first two years of life and even longer.

Infections should be treated promptly and vigorously. An alkalinizing agent, preferably sodium bicarbonate, should be administered throughout any illness. Because of an existing lactic acidemia, sodium lactate is not recommended for the correction of acidosis. Epistaxes are managed by conventional local measures. Symptomatic hypoglycemia is treated with oral glucose. The response to anabolic steroid therapy has been variable.

In the postadolescent period, gout becomes a major concern. 4-Hydroxypyrazolopyrimidine has been found effective in lowering the serum uric acid, but it is too early to give a final evaluation of its usefulness.

PROGNOSIS. It is difficult to give a categorical prognosis. The severity of the condition is variable. In the first two years of life, death usually results from rapidly evolving profound acidosis triggered by infection. Hepatomas have been demonstrated at necropsy. Gout occurs some time after adolescence, and death has been reported at 40 years of age with gouty nephritis. Some of the older patients have shown signs of early angina and coronary symptoms. These observations represent very small numbers, and a true evaluation of prognosis must await further observations.

Type II

CLINICAL MANIFESTATIONS. Type II glycogenosis is also known as generalized or cardiomegalic glycogenosis and as Pompe's disease (IIa). The affected infant may be weak and have a poor sucking response from birth, or the infant may show no symptoms during the neonatal period and progress normally for 2 or 3 months. After this period there is steady retrogression, increasing irritability, feeding difficulty due to exertional dyspnea, cyanosis, increasing weakness or flaccidity, pooling of saliva in the pharynx, loss of reflexes, and progressive cardiomegaly. A progressively abnormal EKG pattern evolves, characterized by a short P-R interval, very large QRS complexes, and deeply inverted T waves. Toward the end of the course of the disease the infant appears somewhat undernourished, spontaneous movements are weak and infrequent, and the tongue is often enlarged. The muscles are markedly weak although they are firm or even hard on palpation. The heart is very large with weak heart sounds, and often a gallop rhythm is present.

In type IIb the child is usually slow in motor development, and in particular walks later than normally. At 2 or 3 years of age, the child presents the picture of muscular dystrophy with apparent "pseudohypertropic" muscles. There is significant weakness, but no cardiac involvement either clinically or by EKG.

GENETICS. The condition appears to be transmitted as an autosomal recessive disorder. There is a disproportionate number of affected males. Heterozygosity has been demonstrated in cultured fibroblasts. Type IIb also appears to be an autosomal recessive disorder, but the incidence is significantly lower than type IIa, which has been estimated to occur once in 400,000 live births.

DIFFERENTIAL DIAGNOSIS. The differential diagnosis includes congenital heart disease, primarily aberrant coronary vessels, truncus arteriosus, or endocardial fibroelastosis, as well as the "floppy baby" syndrome and cretinism. The firm and distinctly palpable muscles distinguish this condition from other floppy babies, and the protein-bound iodine concentration and a roentgenologic bone age survey assist in ruling out cretinism. Muscle biopsy permits a more definitive and positive diagnosis. Type IIb must be distinguished from other myopathies, primarily Duchenne's muscular dystrophy.

DIAGNOSIS. The usual clinical biochemical parameters of carbohydrate metabolism are normal. There is a marked increase in normal glycogen in the heart and skeletal muscle, liver, and neuronal cells. An absence of lysosomal α-glucosidase has been demonstrated in the tissues of these patients. With electron microscopy, engorgement of the lysosomes with glycogen can be demonstrated, whereas the amount of cytoplasmic glycogen appears normal. The relationship of the defect to the symptoms is not clear.

TREATMENT. No effective treatment is known. A low-carbohydrate, high-fat, and high-protein diet has been tried but failed to alter the prognosis. Anabolic agents and adrenal steroids have been tried. Intravenous administration of an α-glucosidase of microbial origin and human α-amylase also have been tried. An agent which could transiently produce a leakiness of the lysosomes may be effective.

Type III

CLINICAL MANIFESTATIONS. Clinical manifestations of type III are very similar to those of type I. The liver may be equally large but there is usually less growth retardation. Although clinical manifestations may be so mild that only the enlarged liver is present, all symptoms noted for type I glycogen storage disease, including hypoglycemia, may be found. As far as appearance, the boy in Figure 10 could very well have had type III glycogen storage disease.

The clinical chemical findings in type III are distinguished from those of type I as follows: the

TABLE 9. *Enzymatic Defects in Type III Glycogenosis*

Sub-type	Amylo-1,6-glucosidase		Oligo-1,4→1,4-glucantransferase	
	Liver	Muscle	Liver	Muscle
a*	Deficient	Deficient	Deficient	Deficient
b	Deficient	Present	Deficient	Deficient
c	Present	Deficient	Present	Present
d	Present	Present	Deficient	Deficient

*Most common type.

fasting blood lactate values are normal; the lactate rise following glucagon or epinephrine is minimal; the lactate production from muscle with anoxic exercise is subnormal (see type V); the blood glucose response to glucagon or epinephrine two hours after a high-carbohydrate meal may be significantly improved over that in the fasting condition; the blood glucose rises following intravenous galactose administration; the serum uric acid concentration is normal or minimally elevated; and the red cell glycogen concentration is often significantly elevated. The fasting blood sugar, blood ketone concentration, and serum nonesterified fatty acid values are of no assistance in distinguishing the two types.

ENZYMATIC DEFECT. The enzymes involved in debranching glycogen are amylo-1,6-glucosidase and oligo-1,4 → 1,4-glucantransferase. Either or both of these enzymes may be absent in either liver, muscle, or both, on the basis of which four subtypes (a to d) are defined (Table 9). In each instance, the glycogen in affected tissues is abnormal in structure, being short-chain or limit-dextrin in type. Thus far the data appear to be compatible with an autosomal recessive mechanism of transmission.

TREATMENT. The treatment differs from that of type I glycogenosis in that a high-protein diet is helpful, utilizing gluconeogenesis to maintain the blood glucose. Many of these patients do not require any treatment.

PROGNOSIS. The prognosis for type III is considerably better than for type I, in both morbidity and mortality. These children are sometimes management problems during the first 4 or 5 years of life, but they spontaneously improve thereafter. Around the time of puberty, the hepatomegaly, lipemia, and fasting ketosis are minimal. The ultimate height is normal. Reproduction is normal. A myopathic syndrome has been observed in the third or fourth decade.

Type IV

There are now several patients reported with documented type IV glycogenosis. The patients presented at about 1 year of age with an enlarged, nodular liver and splenomegaly. The clinical picture was no different from cirrhosis of any other origin. One patient had grossly abnormal liver function tests; in another they were minimally deranged. Death usually results from portal hypertension, debilitation, and intercurrent infection. The glycogen isolated from a number of tissues of the body was shown to be abnormal, having the characteristics of amylopectin; hence the designation of amylopectinosis, or long-chain glycogen storage disease. The glycogen formed had fewer than normal numbers of the 1,6-glucosidic branch points. This glycogen is also considerably less soluble than normal glycogen. The glycogen content of the tissues was not excessive. Hence an awareness of the possibility, and specific investigations of brancher enzyme activity or glycogen structure are required to detect further cases. Treatment is symptomatic. The condition is transmitted as an autosomal recessive trait and heterozygosity has been detected biochemically.

Type V

Type V glycogenosis, also known as McArdle's disease, results from a complete absence of phosphorylase in the striated muscles. The liver phosphorylase activity is normal, demonstrating that genetic control of liver and muscle phosphorylases are different. Although the disease is generally considered to become clinically manifest in adult life, it may begin earlier, and three phases can be delineated: (1) easy fatigability during childhood and adolescence; (2) severe cramps on exertion, associated with transient myoglobinuria, developing between 20 and 40 years; and (3) subsequently increasingly severe weakness and wasting of individual muscle groups. This condition demonstrates the requirement for glucose during sustained muscular activity, although the mechanism involved is not understood.

There are relatively few patients reported with this condition. The genetic studies would tend to support an autosomal recessive means of transmission although the overwhelming preponderance of affected males is unexplained. The incidence of consanguinity is high.

Although muscle biopsy with enzymatic analysis of phosphorylase and glycogen content is necessary for definitive diagnosis, there is a rapid, easy screening procedure based on the fact that under anaerobic conditions glycolysis occurs with the production of lactate. If circulation to the arm is impeded with a blood pressure cuff and the fist is then exercised, the normal individual will show a marked, prompt rise in venous blood lactate. In constrast the patient with type V glycogenosis will show no rise. A similar response can be observed in fasting patients with type III glycogenosis involving the muscle, as well as with types VII, VIII, and X.

Glucose feedings and glucagon injections are reported to benefit exercise tolerance, but this has not been consistently observed. Vocational guidance is indicated.

Type VI

This type bears a strong clinical resemblance to types I and III. These forms can be distinguished in an individual patient only by tissue enzyme assay. An enlarged liver and growth retardation may be prominent. In general, this type tends to be clinically more benign than either type I or III, although variations in severity, particularly in type III, provide many exceptions.

The fasting blood sugar, lactate, ketone bodies, and lipids may be near normal. Uric acid is moderately elevated. The response of blood glucose to glucagon and epinephrine varies from normal to absent; it does rise following intravenous galactose. Liver phosphorylase activity is decreased but not absent. Leucocyte phosphorylase is decreased, whereas muscle phosphorylase is normal.

Management of these patients in general has not been a problem. On theoretical grounds it seems justified to recommend a high-protein diet. It would appear at this time that the prognosis is relatively benign.

Type VII

Recently, siblings of both sexes in a Japanese family, who were offspring of a consanguinous marriage were described with symptoms identical to those of type V glycogenosis. However, the defect in the muscle was shown to be a markedly lowered level of phosphofructokinase. The level in the erythrocyte was also lowered, but not to the degree found in muscle.

Type VIII

A myopathy with late onset in two Japanese brothers has been described whose symptoms were similar to those described for type V glycogenosis in that the symptoms are precipitated by exercise, occasionally associated with myoglobinuria, and there is a failure of a lactate rise in response to anoxic exercise. Administration of fructose before the anoxic exercise test resulted in a lactate response which was unexpected and was not demonstrable in normal individuals. All of the enzymes assayed in muscle were normal, but muscle homogenates failed to form lactate normally from glycogen, glucose-1-phosphate, or glucose-6-phosphate. In contrast normal lactate production was observed when fructose-6-phosphate or fructose diphosphate was used as substrate. It was concluded that an inhibitor to phosphohexosisomerase was present in the muscle of those individuals.

Type IXa and b

Type IXa is clinically similar to types I, III, and VI. Most prominent of the signs and symptoms is an enlarged abdomen with hepatomegaly. Affected individuals may show hypoglycemia, and growth and motor retardation in the early years. The laboratory data reveal occasional hypoglycemia, mild fasting elevation of blood lactate and uric acid, and usually a normal response to glucagon or epinephrine. The most distinctive feature of this disorder is that it appears to be X-linked, and thus occurs primarily in males. Laboratory studies to identify patients with the disorder have been carried out primarily with leucocyte enzyme assays.

Type IXb is very benign. The primary finding is hepatomegaly. The clinical laboratory findings are usually normal. The condition occurs in both males and females. The demonstration of deficient phosphorylase kinase has been carried out with liver biopsy specimens. In general, no therapy has been indicated.

Type X

The symptoms in this type of muscle glycogenosis are similar to type V, and just as with type V they begin earlier in life than with types VII and VIII. The identifications of the etiology of this type as a deficiency of phosphorylase kinase in muscle rests on histochemical methods. Standard biochemical methods have yet to be employed for demonstration of the enzyme deficiency.

Undefined and Mixed Types

There is a small but significant number of patients in whom tissue enzyme analyses do not show an abnormality in the usual enzymes studied.

There have been patients described who have evidence of two distinct enzymatic defects related to glycogen metabolism. Also there have been studies on siblings who have different types of glycogen storage disease. Care must be taken in the handling of tissues in order to avoid factitious enzyme defects.

REFERENCES

Cori, G. T. Glycogen structure and enzyme deficiencies in glycogen storage disease. Harvey Lect., 48:145, 1953.

Hers, H. G. Glycogen storage disease. In Levine, R., and Luft, R., eds. Advances in Metabolic Disorders. New York, Academic Press, Inc., 1964, pp. 1-44.

Huijing, F., and Fernandes, J. X-chromosomal inheritance of liver glycogenosis with phosphorylase kinase deficiency. Amer. J. Hum. Genet., 21:275, 1969.

Hug, G., Schubert, W. K., and Chuck, G. Deficient activity of dephosphorylase kinase and accumulation of glycogen in the liver. J. Clin. Invest., 48:704, 1969.

Lewis, G. M., Spencer-Peet, J., and Steward, F. M. Infantile hypoglycemia due to inherited deficiency of glycogen synthetase in the liver. Arch. Dis. Child., 38:40, 1963.

Satoyoshi, E., and Kowa, H. A myopathy due to glyco-

lytic abnormality. Arch. Neurol., 17:248, 1967.

Strugalsaka-Cynowska, M. Disturbances in the activity of phosphorylase kinase in a case of McArdle myopathy. Folia Histochem. Cytochem., 5:151, 1967.

Tauri, S., Okuno, G., Ikara, Y., Tanaka, T., Suda, M., and Nishikawa, M. Phosphofructokinase deficiency in skeletal muscle. A new type of glycogenosis. Biochem. Biophys. Res. Commun., 19:517, 1965.

Anomalies of Lipid Metabolism

8.9
PLASMA LIPIDS AND LIPOPROTEINS

HERBERT J. KAYDEN

Normal values for plasma lipids at various ages are shown in Table 10. Compared with children and adults, infants have somewhat lower cholesterol and phospholipid values. The total concentration of lipids may vary normally from 400 mg to 1,000 mg per 100 ml.

Normally, in the fasting subject, the largest fraction of plasma lipid is the *phospholipid*, 70 percent of which is lecithin (phosphatidyl choline) and 20 percent sphingomyelin, the remainder consisting of phosphatidyl ethanolamines, phosphatidyl serines, inositol phosphatides, and lysolecithin. Seventy to 75 percent of the *cholesterol* is normally esterified with long-chain unsaturated fatty acids, mainly linoleic (18:2) and oleic (18:1). The *triglyceride* fraction includes small amounts of monoglycerides and diglycerides. The plasma glycerides, even in the postabsorptive state, are a mixture of *exogenous* or

dietary triglycerides and *endogenous* triglycerides synthesized mainly by the liver from glucose or from free fatty acids transported from fat depots. The *free fatty acids* are sometimes referred to as unesterified fatty acids or nonesterified fatty acids; although they make up only a few percent of total plasma lipid, they are of particular metabolic importance; their turnover rate is measured in seconds or minutes. They represent lipid that can be burned for energy, and their concentration in plasma is distinctly related to the availability of other calorigenic foodstuff. Their concentrations and transport are lowest when glucose metabolism in adipose tissue is proceeding at a high level, but in the absence of glucose or insulin, free fatty acids are released by adipose tissue and become available to liver, muscle, and other tissues for oxidation. Many factors control this release, including the sympathetic nervous system, catecholamines, glucagon, anterior pituitary hormones, and other endocrine organs. The role of adenyl cyclase and cyclic AMP (3',5'adenylic acid monophosphate) as the final mediators of the release of free fatty acids from adipose tissue has been studied in recent years. Since levels of free fatty acids vary widely in normal subjects, they are of limited diagnostic value. No disease has been identified as being due solely to abnormalities in the metabolism of free fatty acids, but their central role in lipid metabolism cannot be overemphasized.

All the lipids of the plasma are present in association with peptides, the combination being referred to as *lipoproteins*. Free fatty acids are bound to albumin, mainly by ionic association. Binding of lipids to the other polypeptides, designated as alpha and beta according to the electrophoretic mobility of the lipoprotein, is through weaker hydrophobic forces and to a lesser extent by ionic binding. Quantitative lipoprotein measurements have been limited in the main to research laboratories, but their clinical usefulness is now becoming apparent with the discovery of genetically determined disorders characterized by abnormal lipoprotein patterns. Techniques for qualitative analysis of lipoprotein distribution patterns are widely available, particularly by electrophoretic separations on paper, cellulose acetate, agar, or agarose.

TABLE 10.   *Fasting Plasma Lipids (mg/100 ml)*

Age	Cholesterol	Phospholipid
Newborn (cord blood)	75 (50-100)	115 (85-145)
0-1	140 (100-180)	180 (130-230)
1-19	180 (115-240)	215 (155-265)
20-29	180 (125-240)	235 (175-300)

Other Lipids	Range, mg/100 ml
Triglycerides	25-150
Free Fatty Acids (FFA)	.3-.7 mEq/liter
Cerebrosides (expressed as hexoses)	3.5-5.7
Vitamin A	0.02-0.07
Vitamin E	0.6-1.2

TABLE 11.   *Lipoproteins of Blood Plasma*

	Density	Electro-phoretic Migration		S_f Classification (Svedberg flotation units)
		Starch	Paper	
High	1.063-1.21	α_1	α_1	
Low (LdL)	1.019-1.063	β	β	0-12
	1.006-1.019	β	β	12-20
VLdL	<1.006	pre-β	pre-β	20-400
Chylo-microns	<1.006	α_2	origin	400-10^5

	Approximate Concentration (%)			
	Protein	Trigly-ceride	Choles-terol	Phos-pholipid
High	48	4	21	27
Low	21	8	34	37
	7	41	39	13
VLdL	3	50	19	28
Chylo-microns	2	92	2	4

The patterns of lipoprotein distribution are shown in Table 11. The ultracentrifuge separates the lipoproteins into density classes measured by S_f (Svedberg) units. A second method of separating lipoproteins is by electrophoresis, which separates them into alpha (high density) and beta (low density and very low density) fractions. Chylomicrons are normally seen only during absorption of dietary fat.

Hyperlipemia (Hyperlipoproteinemia)

Hyperlipemias are classified by the fraction which is predominantly elevated, i.e., hyperglyceridemia (hypertriglyceridemia), hypercholesterolemia, and hyperphospholipidemia. An even more appropriate classification is one based on the specific liproprotein fraction which is elevated. The appearance of the plasma is particularly affected in the hyperglyceridemias. Although slight elevations in the plasma triglyceride level do not change its appearance, moderate elevations cause a change from normal opalescence toward lactescence, and marked elevations make the plasma appear milky or even creamy. These changes are due to the increase in the chylomicron or in the very low density lipoprotein fraction. If the plasma is turbid or lactescent or if a disorder of lipid metabolism is suspected, total plasma lipids, total cholesterol, phospholipid, and triglyceride fractions should be measured. A qualitative analysis of the lipoprotein distribution obtained by paper or gel electrophoresis is helpful. More detailed analysis of lipoproteins will require ultracentrifugal separation and quantitative measurements of the lipids in each lipoprotein fraction. The

exact classification of the disease may require measurements of plasma lipids during periods of dietary alterations. Such measurements, taken together with family studies and the clinical features, offer the best basis for classification.

The classification of the hyperlipidemias is under continual review, due mainly to recent developments in the techniques of discriminating between the various lipoprotein and lipid classes. There is general agreement on separating the hyperlipidemias into two major categories: (1) those classified as inborn errors of metabolism based on heredity or gene mutation and (2) those which are secondary to another disease. The latter group includes the nephrotic syndrome, uncontrolled diabetes mellitus, untreated hypothyroidism, certain phases of glycogen storage disease, and some types of pancreatitis. An extensive review of hyperlipidemic patients and their families, carried out by Fredrickson and co-workers, has led to a classification of these subjects into five types. Some of these groups encompass previously defined clinical syndromes, others are newly proposed. The limits for each type are not precise, and there are many patients who cannot be fitted into the proposed classification. The system, however, is widely used and represents an initial attempt at classification. As more subjects are studied, the boundaries for each group may be changed, and new types defined.

Two inherited diseases which result in a lowering of serum lipid and lipoprotein levels have been recognized. *Abetalipoproteinemia* is due to an inability to synthesize the apoprotein of the beta lipoproteins or to a defect in the synthesis of the complete beta lipoprotein molecule from available lipids and peptides. *Tangier disease,* characterized by a deficiency in alpha lipoprotein, is due to synthesis of an abnormal polypeptide of the alpha apoprotein.

FAMILIAL HYPERCHYLOMICRONEMIA (FAT-INDUCED HYPERLIPEMIA, BURGER-GRUTZ HYPERLIPEMIA, FREDRICKSON TYPE I HYPERLIPOPROTEINEMIA). This is a rare familial disorder; about 35 cases have been reported, the great majority being recognized before 10 years of age. The plasma is grossly lipemic, due to a massive chylomicronemia while the patient is on a normal diet. The lactescence of the plasma usually clears after a few days on a fat-free diet, although chemical analysis shows that triglyceride levels have not returned to normal. The striking increase in plasma lipids, with levels frequently exceeding 3 g and in some cases 10 g per 100 ml, is due almost entirely to an increase in triglyceride.

Although the disease may be discovered accidentally by examination of the plasma during routine blood studies, it is more often recognized by the discovery of hepatomegaly, splenomegaly, eruptive xanthomas, or an attack of abdominal pain associated with fever and peritoneal irritation, which may lead to laparotomy, with no surgical condition being found. The abdominal pain is episodic and may vary in pattern; it may be localized to the left upper quadrant with tenderness of the spleen, or the pain may be more generalized in the epigastrium, or midabdominal region, sometimes radiating to the back. General malaise and anorexia are common; nausea, vomiting, or collapse are rarely observed. Spasm, rigidity and rebound tenderness, leucocytosis, and fever may be present. In one of the first patients, a 12-year-old girl, with this disorder studied by Holt and associates, the febrile bouts with abdominal pain occurred when the hyperlipemia reached a high level. During each attack, the blood lipids cleared dramatically, with concomitant enlargement of the liver and spleen. The cause of the abdominal discomfort is not known. Although some attacks may be precipitated by an excessive intake of fat, they may also occur when the patient is on a fat-restricted diet and relatively little hyperlipemia is present. The diagnosis of acute pancreatitis has been made in some of these patients, but as a rule no pathology in the pancreas is found, and serum amylase and lipase values are normal. However, the possibility of genuine pancreatitis should not be overlooked; Klatskin and Gordon have shown that some of these patients may subsequently develop pancreatitis.

In the presence of marked hyperchylomicronemia, lipemia retinalis may be seen. There is a pale to white appearance of the retina, and both veins and arteries have a creamy appearance, making it difficult to distinguish between them. The presence of foam cells in biopsies of bone marrow, liver, and spleen from patients with hyperlipemia has been noted. The fat particles are thought to be phagocytized by reticuloendothelial cells and do not appear to represent increased synthesis of fat in situ.

Studies of carbohydrate metabolism in these patients have failed to reveal any abnormalities, either in the standard glucose tolerance test or by measurement of blood glucose levels or of plasma insulinlike activity following intravenous tolbutamide. Diabetes is not often found in the family histories of these patients. As far as it is known, the condition does not predispose to either vascular or ischemic heart disease.

The precise nature of the metabolic defect in familial fat-induced hyperlipemia remains unknown, but a number of studies implicate a disturbance in a removal mechanism for chylomicrons. In the normal subject, the administration of heparin is followed by the release of lipolytic activity in the plasma, which can be demonstrated in a number of ways: by clearing of alimentary lipemia, by release of fatty acids, and by a fall in plasma triglycerides. This activity has been called "clearing factor," "lipoprotein lipase," or "postheparin lipolytic activity" (PHLA), the latter being the preferred term. The assay is carried out under standardized conditions. In patients with familial lipemia of this type, measurements of PHLA are sometimes normal, but in most cases are reduced and in some instances almost completely absent.

Based on family studies it appears that patients with idiopathic familial fat-induced hyperlipemia are homozygous for a rare autosomal gene. Heterozygotes, however, are not readily demonstrated, since they rarely have any demonstrable degree of hyperchylomicronemia. The ultimate prognosis for these patients is not at all unfavorable. It is not a life-threatening disease and with maintenance of a low-fat diet (20 to 25 percent of calories) the painful abdominal attacks can usually be avoided.

FAMILIAL HYPERBETALIPOPROTEINEMIA (FAMILIAL HYPERCHOLESTEROLEMIA, FREDRICKSON TYPE II HYPERLIPOPROTEINEMIA). This disorder is perhaps the best known syndrome of altered lipid metabolism because of the presence of cutaneous and tendon xanthomas and the appearance of accelerated atheromatous disease of the coronary arteries. The major plasma abnormality is the elevation in the beta lipoprotein fraction of density class 1.019 to 1.063. The degree of elevation of plasma cholesterol is determined mainly by genetic factors, although diet and drugs may modify the increase to some extent. Extensive familial studies have shown that this disorder is transmitted as an autosomal dominant with nearly complete penetrance. Homozygotes have a severe form of the disease with striking elevation in serum cholesterol levels (even to 1,000 mg per 100 ml) and advanced atheromatous disease early in life. Heterozygotes will demonstrate the abnormal gene by elevated and increasing levels of beta lipoprotein, easily measured by the cholesterol level, and by xanthomas, corneal arcus, and vascular disease developing during the first three decades of life.

Several studies have shown that the diagnosis of this disorder can be established in infancy, even by examination of cord blood. It is obviously essential to study the parents in an attempt to establish whether the child is heterozygous or homozygous for the abnormal gene. In one study, based on lipid levels in cord blood, five affected infants had total cholesterols of $107 \pm$ (SD) 16 mg per 100 ml and beta cholesterol of 69 ± 15 in comparison with normal total cholesterol of 72 ± 14 mg per 100 ml and a beta cholesterol of 33 ± 7. In studies of 57 kindreds, the 233 children under 20 years of age with at least one affected parent could be divided into three phenotypes based on their serum cholesterol level: 10 homozygotes with mean total cholesterol of $678 \pm$ (SD) 170 mg per 100 ml; 103 heterozygotes with mean total cholesterol of 313 ± 69; and 120 unaffected sibs with mean total cholesterol of 178 ± 27.

The appearance of skin or tendon xanthoma is in part genetically determined; homozygotes usually demonstrate lesions in the first two decades, heterozygotes rarely until after age 20. The xanthomas are fixed to tendon, periosteum, or fascia, and to the skin as tuberous xanthomas. They are often conspicuous about the elbows, wrists, knees, and ankles, as well as on the hands and feet. The development of an arcus corneae (arcus juvenilis) and xanthelasma may occur before puberty in homozygotes, but rarely before early adult life in heterozygotes.

Atheromatous lesions are very frequent in this disease and appear not to have been altered by any of the various therapeutic regimens attempted so far. The coronaries are particularly affected, and involvement of the endocardium may lead to angina, myocardial infarction, and heart failure due to deformed and incompetent valves. Sudden death in childhood due to acute coronary occlusion may occur. The degree of arterial involvement increases with age, but the cerebral and peripheral vessels are seldom involved.

The nature of the metabolic defect in this disorder is unknown. Measurements of rates of synthesis and of degradation of cholesterol have not shown any significant deviations from normal, although the pool size of cholesterol is much increased. The nature of the increased beta lipoprotein appears to be normal, although no detailed study of its peptide composition has been carried out.

Treatment for this disorder should be instituted early in life. A diet restricted in cholesterol and fat with the major portion of the fat derived from polyunsaturated fatty acids seems most useful. A number of drugs including cholestyramine and clofibrate have been tried; the former may be effective and is a logical substitute for the surgical procedure of ileal bypass.

BROAD BETA HYPERLIPOPROTEINEMIA (FREDRICKSON TYPE III HYPERLIPOPROTEINEMIA).

This is a rare lipoprotein disorder that has not been described in subjects under the age of 25. The serum has elevated cholesterol and triglyceride levels, and increased amounts of beta lipoprotein which are of unusually low density flotation rate because of increased amounts of triglyceride. The term "broad beta" is derived from paper electrophoretic analysis of the serum lipoproteins, which demonstrates a broad beta region composed of both beta and prebeta bands which merge with each other. Xanthomas appear in adulthood; palmar xanthomas characterize this disorder as well as the more common tuberous and tendinous xanthoma. Accelerated vascular disease is common, but coronary atherosclerosis appears to be less frequent than major peripheral arterial disease.

FAMILIAL HYPERPREBETALIPOPROTEINEMIA (CARBOHYDRATE-INDUCED HYPERLIPEMIA; ESSENTIAL FAMILIAL HYPERLIPEMIA; ENDOGENOUS HYPERLIPEMIA; FREDRICKSON TYPE IV HYPERLIPOPROTEINEMIA).

This disorder of lipid metabolism has been frequently described in adults and only occasionally in children, although family studies are relatively limited. The distinguishing feature is the increased level of serum lipids on fat-restricted, carbohydrate-rich diets, and its reduction toward normal values when these relationships are reversed. The serum is lactescent, reflecting the increase in lipoproteins whose density is less than 1.006. Electrophoretic analysis shows an increased concentration of lipoproteins with "prebeta" mobility. It is generally accepted that these circulating very low density lipoproteins are synthesized by the liver from carbohydrate and that the rate of synthesis of glycerides exceeds the rate of removal of the glycerides by peripheral tissues. There is a wide variation in the concentration of serum lipids in these patients, and when the level of triglycerides is very high (5 to 10 g percent), they, too, may exhibit abdominal pain, eruptive xanthoma, and hepatosplenomegaly. In many of these patients, an impaired glucose tolerance can be easily demonstrated; in others, impaired carbohydrate tolerance occurs only after intravenous tolbutamide. There is suggestive evidence that this disorder is associated with a high incidence of atherosclerosis and coronary artery disease. The mode of genetic transmission of this disorder is not known. In the kindreds studied, all of the affected members have the same type of abnormality; however, the numbers studied are few. The most effective treatment appears to be moderate carbohydrate restriction with maintenance of optimal weight. Drug therapy, mainly with clofibrate, has been reported to be effective.

MIXED TYPE OF FAMILIAL HYPERCHYLOMICRONEMIA AND HYPERPREBETALIPOPROTEINEMIA (COMBINED FAT- AND CARBOHYDRATE-INDUCED HYPERLIPEMIA; FREDRICKSON TYPE V HYPERLIPOPROTEINEMIA).

Some patients appear to represent mixed types of hyperlipemia and may have both hypercholesterolemia and hyperglyceridemia. Features of both disorders are observed; namely, tuberous, plantar, and tendon xanthomas, and frequently ischemic heart disease. This group of patients appears to have both fat- and carbohydrate-induced lipemia. Low postheparin lipolytic activity is also apparent in some; others have abnormal glucose tolerance. Whether this is a separate group, genetically and biochemically distinct, remains to be established.

Abnormal plasma lipids and lipoprotein distributions are noted in association with a number of acquired conditions and diseases. Alimentary lipemia after a fat meal is a normal phenomenon. In unregulated diabetes and in several forms of glycogen storage disease, lipemia (hyperglyceridemia), sometimes very marked, may occur. The nephrotic syndrome is associated with an increase in certain plasma lipoprotein fractions, especially an increase in cholesterol and a lesser rise in phospholipid. Frank lactescence of the plasma with eruptive xanthomas is sometimes seen. Atheromatous plaques may be noted on autopsy. The degree of the cholesterol elevation bears an inverse relation to the plasma albumin level. Hyperlipemia may occur in severe hypothyroidism; the serum is usually clear and the abnormality is an increase predominantly in the beta lipoprotein fraction (measured most often by serum cholesterol), although there is also some elevation of the triglycerides.

Alterations in lipoprotein patterns occur in liver disease, particularly in biliary cirrhosis. Cohlan and Kayden reported a striking instance in a 20-month-old infant with biliary obstruction due to a large choledochal cyst who had a plasma cholesterol level of 1,500 mg per 100 ml and phospholipid concentration of 3,200 mg per 100 ml. High-density lipoprotein was almost entirely absent, and an unusual low-density lipoprotein class was the major lipid component of the plasma. Corrective surgery resulted in prompt correction of the abnormal plasma lipid pattern with disappearance of eruptive xanthoma.

Alpha Lipoprotein Deficiency
(*Tangier Disease*)

This rare familial anomaly, discovered on Tangier Island in the Chesapeake Bay, is characterized by absence of high-density or alpha lipoprotein. A distinctive color (grayish yellow) and enlargement of the tonsils due to deposition of cholesterol esters are clinical features of the disease. Such deposition occurs also in the cornea, intestinal mucosa, and at times elsewhere. There is an unusual lipid pattern in the plasma—low cholesterol and phospholipid together with normal or elevated triglyceride. The disease is inherited by means of double autosomal mutant alleles; the presence of a single pair of autosomal mutant alleles is reflected in a decrease in high-density plasma lipoprotein.

Beta Lipoprotein Deficiency

This rare disorder has been recognized since 1950 and 23 cases have been identified. Synonyms for this disease include Bassen-Kornzweig syndrome, acanthocytosis, referring to the spiny appearance of many of the erythrocytes, and abetalipoproteinemia (ABL), designating the absence from the plasma of low-density lipoproteins.

The clinical features form a characteristic triad of abnormal red blood cells, malabsorption of fat, and ataxia. The child is born of normal parents, appears normal at birth, but is slow to gain in weight and height. Steatorrhea and abdominal distension appear in the first year, and a diagnosis of celiac disease is often made. There is defective absorption of triglycerides, fatty acids, and vitamin A. The plasma levels of vitamin A are low, the triglyceride levels extremely low (less than 15 mg per 100 ml), and the cholesterol levels usually less than 50 mg per 100 ml. Alimentary lipemia is not found, and analysis reveals only very small, if any, rises in plasma lipids after a fat meal. It appears that exogenous lipid is normally hydrolyzed in the intestine of these patients, absorbed, and resynthesized into triglyceride, but the formation of chylomicrons and their delivery to the thoracic duct is impaired, presumably owing to the inability to synthesize their lipoprotein coating. Biliary and pancreatic secretions are not abnormal, which, together with normal concentrations of sodium and chloride in sweat, distinguishes beta lipoprotein deficiency from cystic fibrosis of the pancreas. The peroral biopsy shows no villous atrophy, but the mucosal cells contain many lipid vacuoles, especially at the villus tip. Electron micrographs reveal normal mitochondria and endoplasmic reticulum, with lipid droplets throughout the cytoplasm of the cell. The erythrocytes exhibit a characteristic anomaly with spiny excrescences, mistaken frequently for crenated cells. They are best demonstrated in Dacie's solution (buffered formalin). The lipid composition of the acanthocyte is different from that of normal cells in the distribution of phospholipids and fatty acids.

The neuromuscular system is also involved, and the diagnosis of Friedreich's ataxia is often made. Awkwardness is first noted, progressing gradually to frank ataxia in later childhood. It is more marked in the lower extremities. There is absence of the deep reflexes and loss of vibratory and position sense; diminished pain and temperature sense follows. Increasing ataxia is associated with pronounced adiadokokinesis, past pointing, and also abnormal plantar reflexes. Muscle weakness involving the lower extremities and pectoral girdle may lead to inability to stand without assistance in early adult life. Extraocular muscle imbalance is not uncommon, and nystagmus may also be seen. The development of retinitis pigmentosa occurs about the time of adolescence, manifested first as scotomas, and progressing to impairment of vision and ultimately blindness.

The erythrocytes in beta lipoprotein deficiency are unusually susceptible to autohemolysis. When sterile defibrinated blood is incubated at 37° C, from 15 to 90 percent of the cells will be hemolyzed in 48 hours as contrasted with less than 5 percent normally. This observation suggested a study of vitamin E metabolism in these patients. Kayden and Silber found that there was no determinable vitamin E in the plasma. Parenteral α-tocopherol raised vitamin E levels to about 10 to 20 percent of normal but without immediate symptomatic improvement other than correction of autohemolysis. Supplemental oral α-tocopherol therapy (in an aqueous preparation) in large doses is recommended to provide the antioxidant effect of vitamin E in the tissues.

No therapy for the disease has been found to be effective. Although medium-chain triglycerides have been reported to be useful in decreasing the steatorrhea and improving caloric balance, the patients do absorb a proportion of the dietary long-chain fatty acids. Evidence from animal models indicates that the route of absorption is via the portal venous system which is not usually an important pathway for long-chain fatty acids. Linoleic acid, the essential fatty acid, should be supplemented in the diet in the form of corn, safflower, or rapeseed oil. Adipose tissue biopsy with measurement of fatty acid composition by gas chromatography is an important guide to the metabolic balance of fatty acids. The genetic defect in this disorder requires that patients be homozygous for the rare mutant gene. Some degree of consanguinity has been recorded in 7 of the 14 affected families involving 19 patients. The basic defect or defects in this syndrome have not been established. Circulating beta lipoprotein cannot be detected by paper electrophoresis, ultracentrifugation, or immunologic testing. Whether this is due to an inability to synthesize the apoprotein portion of the betalipoprotein, or to an inability to form complete lipoprotein molecules from freely available lipid and peptide moieties, continues to be an area of study. There are reports of some families with low levels of serum beta lipoprotein but without steatorrhea. Abnormally shaped erythrocytes and neuromuscular disease may be present. The relation of these variants to abetalipoproteinemia remains to be established.

Progressive Lipodystrophy

This striking but rare condition is characterized by a gradual disappearance of the subcutaneous fat, usually limited to the upper half of the body. Girls are affected about twice as frequently as boys. The onset may occur as early as 2 years of age but is usually in later childhood, adolescence, or early adult life. The tendency for fat to disappear from the face, chest, and upper extremities and to remain at the waist and hips is common enough in elderly persons, in whom it cannot be regarded as pathologic; in lipodystrophy it is the extent of subcutaneous fat loss and its early onset which characterize the disease.

The condition develops insidiously without apparent cause. It begins in the face and is usually most marked in the cheeks, giving the patient a cadaverous appearance. Disappearance of the orbital fat may cause the eyes to be deep-set. As the condition progresses, the pectoral fat and that of the arms tends to vanish, and the muscle patterns stand out sharply. As a rule atrophy of fat does not extend below the iliac crest. The process is nearly always symmetric, but a few instances have been described in which it remains strictly unilateral; other atypical cases are recorded in which the entire body was affected, or in which only the lower half was involved. As a rule, no complicating disturbances are found, but in some instances irregularities of pigmentation and abnormalities of the hair and nails have been noted.

The cause of this condition is unknown. In a patient carefully studied by Harris and Reiser there was normal absorption of fat, deficient oxidation of fat as compared with controls, an abnormal increase in the serum fats after a fat meal, and exaggerated creatinuria; but the significance of these changes and their relation to the syndrome are not clear. The asymmetric distribution of the body fat is hardly compatible with a general metabolic error. The disease has been attributed to disturbances of sympathetic innervation. There can be no doubt that nervous stimuli to the fat depots are important in causing them to discharge; evidences of abnormal sympathetic activity—such as decreased or increased sweating and abnormal responses to sympathomimetic drugs—are, however, rarely encountered. A more probable cause is atrophy of the fat cells themselves; in a description of two autopsied cases the statement is made that both fat and fat cells were absent.

The diagnosis rarely causes difficulty. Some of these cases have been reported as instances of progeria. Lipodystrophy is not difficult to distinguish from genuine malnutrition in which the musculature as well as the subcutaneous fat are wasted with ensuing reduction in activity. A condition seen in late infancy and early childhood which may cause confusion is the infantile diencephalic syndrome usually caused by a cerebral neoplasm. In this condition there is disappearance of subcutaneous fat with preservation and prominence of the musculature; the patient remains alert and cheerful. A rotary nystagmus may be the only indication of brain disease.

Little can be accomplished in the way of therapy. Whether fat from a skin graft will grow in an affected area is not known. Attempts to overcome the patient's lean appearance by a high caloric diet will usually lead, particularly in females, to a condition of "steatopygia"—a great increase in fat deposition in the unaffected region about the hips and buttocks, which Parkes Weber has aptly termed the "ultra-Rubens Venus." The administration of cortisone fails to produce a "moon face" in these patients.

A congenital form of generalized lipodystrophy has been reported in 10 patients. There are similarities as well as differences between the congenital form and the late varieties. The congenital variety affects the two sexes equally, appears to be an autosomal recessive in mode of inheritance, and may demonstrate chromosome abnormalities. Endocrine abnormalities have been reported in some patients with the congenital form. Hypertriglyceridemia is frequently seen in this disorder.

Febrile Relapsing Panniculitis
(Weber-Christian Syndrome)

This syndrome of recurrent crops of painful subcutaneous nodules which occur during febrile periods was originally described by Weber in 1925 and by Christian in 1928. Though seen primarily in adults it has been described in children and infants from ages of 6 months to 11 years. Diagnosis is established by biopsy of subcutaneous nodules which reveal characteristic areas of fat atrophy with macrophages and lymphocytes as the inflammatory reaction. Polymorphonuclear leucocytes and suppuration are not present, leading to additional terms for diagnosis of febrile, relapsing, nonsuppurative, nodular panniculitis. The cause is not known and no specific therapy has been found; antibiotics, antihistamines, corticotropin, and corticosteroids have all been used without lasting effect. The disease is chronic and has only very rarely been considered to be a cause of death.

Abnormal Short-Chain Fatty Acid Metabolism ("*Odor-of-sweaty-feet Syndrome*")

An inborn error of short-chain fatty acid metabolism has been described in two families by Sidbury, Smith, and Harlan. The infants appear normal at birth, but shortly thereafter become lethargic, take feedings poorly, and have an unusual odor, similar to that of sweaty feet. The symptoms are progressive, and within a few days dehydration, acidosis, a high-pitched cry, and convulsions appear. The terminal episode, which occurs before the fourth week of life, is sepsis with a gram-negative organism associated with pancytopenia. The characteristic unpleasant odor is present in the exhaled air and in all body fluids; it is due to a high concentration of butyric and hexanoic acids. It is postulated that the defect in these infants is a deficiency or alteration of green acyl dehydrogenase, the specific dehydrogenase involved in β-oxidation of fatty acid esters of chain length C6 and C4. The disease is probably an autosomal recessive disorder. The term "odor-of-sweaty-feet syndrome" has been applied to this disease but a similar odor is noted in patents who have an abnormality in leucine metabolism, which results in the accumulation of a short-chain branched fatty acid, isovaleric acid. Children with isovaleric acidemia have mild mental retardation and periodic bouts of vomiting, acidosis, and lethargy or coma, usually precipitated by infection or marked protein ingestion. During these bouts the odor of sweaty feet is markedly intensified, and abnormal amounts of isovaleric acid are found in the blood.

Heredopathia Atactica Polyneuritiformis (*Refsum's Disease*)

A hereditary disorder of the nervous system was first described under the title of "heredopathia atactica polyneuritiformis" by Sigvald Refsum in 1946. The disorder is referred to as Refsum's disease, or HAP. It is characterized by retinitis pigmentosa, peripheral polyneuropathy, cerebellar ataxia, and elevated cerebrospinal fluid protein without pleocytosis. A large proportion of cases demonstrate cardiac conduction abnormalities, pupillary changes, nerve deafness, anosmia, ichthyosis, and bony abnormalities. An autosomal recessive pattern of inheritance is probable in this disorder. HAP has recently been classified as a disorder of lipid metabolism when it was shown that patients with this disease accumulate phytanic acid (3,7,11,15-tetramethylhexadecanoic acid) in their blood and tissues. The phytanic acid is not endogenously synthesized, but originates in the diet. Patients with HAP have a defect in the oxidative pathway for degradation of phytanic acid, namely the formation of α-hydroxyphytanic acid, which is presumably the first step in phytanic acid oxidation. This defect can be demonstrated in fibroblasts grown in tissue culture from skin biopsies of affected patients. The disease has been reported in many countries and has been recognized in children.

Familial Lecithin:Cholesterol Acyltransferase Deficiency

This genetic disorder was recently described in the adults of two Scandinavian families. The disease is characterized by corneal infiltration, anemia, proteinuria, and an abnormal plasma lipid distribution. The serum cholesterol is found to be almost entirely unesterified, whereas normally more than two-thirds of serum cholesterol is esterified with fatty acids. A striking deficiency in the plasma enzyme lecithin: cholesterol acyltransferase (LCAT) activity is present in all patients. It has been postulated that activity of the enzyme is responsible for the esterification of plasma cholesterol, and that the source of the fatty acids in esterified cholesterol is from plasma lecithin. The activity of this enzyme is also reduced in patients with liver disease, and this may explain the altered ratio of free and esterified cholesterol found in such patients. An accompanying biochemical feature is the low level of plasma lysolecithin. The erythrocytes in patients with this inborn error of metabolism are large, frequently target cell in appearance, and contain more cholesterol and phospholipid (lecithin) per cell than is normally present. Studies are being continued to determine the exact role of LCAT and to establish what the primary defect is in this disorder. It is presumed that the deficient enzyme activity is present at birth.

REFERENCES

PLASMA LIPIDS AND LIPOPROTEINS

Cohlan, S. Q., and Kayden, H. J. Reversible hyperlipemia and skin xanthomata in obstructive biliary disease due to choledochal cyst. Amer. J. Med., 32:989, 1962.

Fredrickson, D. S., and Lees, R. S. Familial Hyperlipoproteinemia. *In* Stanbury, J. B., Wyngaarden, J. B., and Fredrickson, D. S., eds., The Metabolic Basis of Inherited Disease, 2nd ed. New York, Mc-Graw-Hill Book Co., 1966.

——— Levy, R. I., and Lees, R. S. Fat transport in lipoproteins—an integrated approach to mechanism and disorders. New Eng. J. Med., 276:34-44, 94-103, 148-156, 215-225, 273-281, 1966.

——— Ono, K., and Davis, L. L. Lipolytic activity of post-heparin plasma in hyperglyceridemia. J. Lipid Res., 4:24, 1963.

Holt, L. E., Jr., Aylward, F. X., and Timbres, H. G. Idiopathic familiar lipemia. Bull. Hopkins Hosp., 64:279, 1939.

Jakovcic, S., Fuhrmann, W., and Hsia, D. Y. Essential familial hyperlipidemia in childhood. Pediatrics, 34:822, 1964.

Klatskin, G., and Gordon, M. Relationship between relapsing pancreatitis and essential hyperlipemia. Amer. J. Med., 12:3, 1952.

Knittle, J. L., and Ahrens, E. H., Jr. Carbohydrate metabolism in two forms of hyperglyceridemia. J. Clin. Invest., 43:485, 1964.

Lee, G. B., Culley, G. A., Lawson, M. L., Adcock, L. L., and Krivit, W. Type II hyperlipoproteinemia in mother and twins. Circ. Res., 39:183, 1969.

Lees, R. S., and Fredrickson, D. S. The use of paper electrophoresis in the diagnosis of hyperlipemia. J. Clin. Invest., 44:1968, 1965.

Levy, R. I., Lees, R. S., and Fredrickson, D. S. The nature of pre-beta lipoprotein. J. Clin. Invest., 45:63, 1966.

Lloyd, J. Disorders of the serum lipoproteins. 1. Lipoprotein deficiency states. Arch. Dis. Child., 43:393, 1968.

——— Disorders of the serum lipoproteins. 2. Hyperlipoproteinemic states. Arch. Dis. Child., 43:505, 1968.

Rausen, A. R., and Adlersberg, D. Idiopathic (hereditary) hyperlipemia and hypercholesterolemia in children. Pediatrics, 28:276, 1961.

ALPHA LIPOPROTEIN DEFICIENCY

Fredrickson, D. S. Familial High-Density Lipoprotein Deficiency: Tangier Disease. In Stanbury, J. B., Wyngaarden, J. B., and Fredrickson, D. S., eds., The Metabolic Basis of Inherited Disease, 2nd ed. New York, McGraw-Hill Book Co., 1966.

——— Inheritance of high density lipoprotein deficiency (Tangier disease). J. Clin. Invest., 43:228, 1964.

Kocen, R. S., Lloyd, J. K., Lascelles, P. T., Fasbrooke, A. S., and Williams, D. Familial α-lipoprotein deficiency (Tangier disease) with neurological abnormalities. Lancet, 1:1341, 1967.

BETA LIPOPROTEIN DEFICIENCY

Bassen, F. A., and Kornzweig, A. L. Malformation of the erythrocyte in a case of atypical retinitis pigmentosa. Blood, 5:381, 1950.

Farquhar, J. W., and Ways, P. Abetalipoproteinemia. In Stanbury, J. B., Wyngaarden, J. B., and Fredrickson, D. S., eds., The Metabolic Basis of Inherited Disease, 2nd ed. New York, McGraw-Hill Book Co., 1966.

Isselbacher, K. J., Scheig, R., Plotkin, G. R., and Caulfield, J. B. Congenital β-lipoprotein deficiency: an hereditary disorder involving a defect in the absorption and transport of lipids. Medicine, 43:347, 1964.

Kayden, H. J., and Silber, R. The role of vitamin E deficiency in the abnormal autohemolysis of acanthocytosis. Trans. Ass. Amer. Physicians, 78:334, 1965.

Lees, R. S. Immunologic evidence for the presence of β-protein (apoprotein of β-lipoprotein) in normal and abetalipoproteinemic plasma. J. Lipid Res., 8:396, 1967.

Simon, E. R., and Ways, P. Incubation hemolysis and red cell metabolism in acanthocytosis. J. Clin. Invest., 43:1311, 1964.

Ways, P. O., Parmentier, C. M., Kayden, H. J., Jones, J. W., Saunders, D. R., and Rubin, C. E. Studies on the absorptive defect for triglyceride in abetalipoproteinemia. J. Clin. Invest., 46:35, 1967.

PROGRESSIVE LIPODYSTROPHY

Braun, F. C., Jr., and Forney, W. R. Diencephalic syndrome of early infancy associated with brain tumor. Pediatrics, 24:609, 1959.

Fairney, A., Lewis, G., and Cotton, D. Total lipodystrophy. Arch. Dis. Child., 44:368, 1969.

Harris, J. S., and Reiser, R. Lipodystrophy; report of a case, with metabolic studies. Amer. J. Dis. Child., 59:143, 1940.

Seip, M., and Trygstad, O. Generalized lipodystrophy. Arch. Dis. Child., 38:447, 1963.

Weber, F. P. Lipodystrophia progressiva. Proc. Roy. Soc. Med. (Neur. Sect.), 6:127, 1913.

FEBRILE RELAPSING PANNICULITIS

Sanford, H. N., Eubank, D. F., and Stenn, F. Chronic panniculitis with leucopenia. Amer. J. Dis. Child., 83:156, 1952.

ABNORMAL SHORT-CHAIN FATTY ACID METABOLISM

Efron, M. L. Isovaleric acidemia. Amer. J. Dis. Child., 113:74, 1967.

Sidbury, J. B., Jr., Smith, E. K., and Harlan, W. J. An inborn error of short chain fatty acid. J. Pediat., 70:8, 1967.

HEREDOPATHIA ATACTICA POLYNEURITIFORMIS (REFSUM'S DISEASE)

Refsum, S. K. Heredopathia atactica polyneuritiformis. Acta Psychiat. Scand. (Suppl.) 38:9, 1946.

Steinberg, D., et al. Refsum's disease—a recently characterized lipidosis involving the nervous system. Ann. Intern. Med., 66:365, 1967.

Herndon, J. H., Jr., Steinberg, D., Uhlendorf, B. W., and Fales, H. M. Refsum's disease—characterization of the enzyme defect in cell culture. J. Clin. Invest., 48:1017, 1969.

FAMILIAL LECITHIN: CHOLESTEROL ACYLTRANSFERASE DEFICIENCY

Norum, K. R., and Gjone, E. Familial plasma lecithin: cholesterol acyltransferase deficiency. Biochemical study of a new inborn error of metabolism. Scand. J. Clin. Lab. Invest., 20:231, 1967.

Gjone, E., and Norum, K. R. Familial serum cholesterol ester deficiency. Clinical study of a patient with a new syndrome. Acta Med. Scand., 183:107, 1968.

Hamnström, B., Gjone, E., and Norum, K. R. Familial plasma lecithin:cholesterol acyltransferase deficiency. Brit. Med. J., 2:283, 1969.

8.10
LIPIDOSES

ROSCOE O. BRADY

Pediatricians are frequently confronted with infants whose primary difficulty is failure of development of motor and intellectual capabilities consistent with their age. The diagnosis of the disease process in these patients may be quite difficult. An attempt should be made to arrive at a correct solution because therapy is presently available for some of these patients, and effective treatment may be forthcoming for others in the future. Remarkable progress has been achieved in the past few years toward the elucidation of the biochemical abnormalities in heritable lipid storage diseases. Patients with these diseases present a wide variety of medical problems. Abnormalities of lipid metabolism should always be considered in infants whose mental development is slower than normal, especially if there is concomitant splenomegaly and hepatomegaly. The following section provides a brief review of the group of autosomal recessive inherited disorders of lipid metabolism known as the sphingolipidoses.

Tay-Sachs Disease

This condition is the most common heritable lipid disease. The gene frequency of this condition is 1 in 100 in persons of Ashkenazi Jewish ancestry, which means that 1 in 50 of these individuals is a heterozygous carrier of the trait. Somewhere between 100 and 200 infants are born each year in the United States with Tay-Sachs disease. The incidence is much less frequent in children of non-Jewish ancestry. The metabolic defect in Tay-Sachs disease has recently been identified as an absence of a N-acetylgalactosaminidase in affected tissues.

CLINICAL MANIFESTATIONS. The hallmark of Tay-Sachs disease is severe and progressive mental retardation. Patients with this disease appear relatively normal until 5 to 7 months of age, when evidence of impairment of maturation of the central nervous system becomes manifested by inability to learn and by arrested motor development. These patients show progressive mental deterioration accompanied by amaurosis. Towards the end of the second year or early third year of life, they become totally blind and die soon thereafter. There is usually a cherry-red spot in the macular region of the eyes of these patients. They have little or no organomegaly except for an increase of about 40 percent in head size compared with children of the same age.

PATHOPHYSIOLOGY. All of the lipids under consideration in this section have in common a portion of their molecule called ceramide, which consists of the amino alcohol sphingosine to which a long-chain acid is linked through an amide bond to the nitrogen atom on carbon 2 of sphingosine (Table 12). In patients with Tay-Sachs disease an acidic glycolipid called Tay-Sachs ganglioside accumulates in neuronal cells in the form of concentrically layered membranous cytoplasmic bodies. These intracellular inclusions consist of cholesterol, phospholipid, and protein in addition to Tay-Sachs ganglioside. However, the only striking abnormality detected on chemical analysis of brain tissue from patients with Tay-Sachs disease is a marked increase in Tay-Sachs ganglioside, which normally constitutes about 5 percent of the total brain gangliosides. Furthermore, the oligosaccharide backbone of Tay-Sachs ganglioside (glucose-galactose-N-acetylgalactosamine) is shorter than all of the major brain gangliosides, which have a tetrahexoside chain (glucose-galactose-N-acetylgalactosamine-galactose). The discovery of the absence of the terminal molecule of galactose prompted the speculation that the metabolic abnormality in Tay-Sachs disease might be a deficiency of a galactose-transferring enzyme required for the completion of the tetrahexoside portion of the molecule. However, this possibility has been ruled out by direct experimentation. It was considered more likely that the metabolic abnormality in Tay-Sachs disease was due to a deficiency of a catabolic enzyme. Since Tay-Sachs ganglioside is branched in the terminal portion of the molecule, there are two potential sites for an initial catabolic reaction in the enzymatic degradation of Tay-Sachs ganglioside. The first possibility is the hydrolysis of the terminal molecule of N-acetylgalactosamine; the second is the initial hydrolysis of the N-acetylneuraminic acid moiety. It has been shown that there is a complete absence of the N-acetylgalactosamine-cleaving enzyme in tissues of patients with Tay-Sachs disease while the N-acetylneuraminidase activity is within normal limits.

These results complement the data obtained in other studies using artificial substrates, which revealed that there are at least two enzymes in most human tissues which catalyze the hydrolysis of *p*-nitrophenyl-β-D-N-acetylgalactosaminide and 4-methylumbelliferyl-β-D-N-acetylgalactosaminide. These enzymes can be separated from each other by starch gel electrophoresis, and one of these enzymes, called component A, was completely absent in extracts of tissues from patients with Tay-Sachs disease. Together these studies provide good evidence that the metabolic defect in Tay-Sachs disease is the absence of an N-acetylgalactosamine-cleaving enzyme which participates in the catabolism of Tay-Sachs ganglioside. However, there are at the present time several points which still require clarification. For example, it is not yet clear whether N-acetylgalactosamine or N-acetylneuraminic acid is actually hydrolized first in the normal sequence of catabolic reactions. The resolution of these questions is essential for our complete understanding of the pathogenesis of Tay-Sachs disease.

TABLE 12.   *Structures of the Sphingolipids*

a. Sphingosine: $CH_3 \cdot (CH_2)_{12} \cdot CH = CH \cdot CH\,(OH) \cdot CH(NH_2) \cdot CH_2^*OH$

b. Ceramide: $CH_3 \cdot (CH_2)_{12} \cdot CH = CH \cdot CH\,(OH) \cdot CH \cdot CH_2OH$

$$\begin{array}{c} | \\ N\!-\!H \\ | \\ C\!=\!O \\ | \\ (CH_2)_n \\ | \\ CH_3 \end{array}$$

c. Tay-Sachs ganglioside: Ceramide-glucose-galactose-N-acetylgalactosamine
    |
    N-acetylneuraminic acid

d. Monosialoganglioside: Ceramide-glucose-galactose-N-acetylgalactosamine-galactose
    |
    N-acetylneuraminic acid

e. Galactocerebroside: Ceramide-galactose

f. Ceramidelactoside: Ceramide-glucose-galactose

g. Ceramidetrihexoside: Ceramide-glucose-galactose-galactose

h. Glucocerebroside: Ceramide-glucose

i. Hematoside: Ceramide-glucose-galactose-N-acetylneuraminic acid

j. Globoside: Ceramide-glucose-galactose-galactose-N-acetylgalactosamine

k. Sulfatide: Ceramide-galactose-3-sulfate

l. Sphingomyelin: Ceramide-phosphorylcholine

*Point of attachment of various components.

DIAGNOSIS. Tay-Sachs disease can generally be diagnosed on the basis of the clinical findings. It seems likely that at least two confirmatory laboratory tests will be useful. The first, and perhaps more definitive, procedure is based on the determination of hexosaminidase activity in tissue biopsy specimens using labeled Tay-Sachs ganglioside as substrate. Muscle tissue is a convenient source of enzyme for this assay. The disadvantage of this test lies in the difficulty and expense involved in the preparation of the substrate. For this reason, methods have been sought to simplify the diagnosis using artificial substrates and more easily accessible enzyme sources, such as washed leucocyte preparations or serum samples. It has been shown that tests such as these will permit the antenatal diagnosis of fetuses with Tay-Sachs disease either through direct assay on fetal cells which can be obtained by amniocentesis, or even enzyme activity in the amniotic fluid itself, or by growing cells in tissue culture for subsequent enzyme assays. The availability of tests for the identification of heterozygous carriers of Tay-Sachs disease will be helpful for accurate genetic counseling.

TREATMENT. At the present time, no therapy is available for this disorder. It is possible that therapeutic trials in the sphingolipidoses will be directed in the future towards enzyme replacement. This procedure is fraught with a number of potential complications, primary among which is the danger of sensitization to a foreign protein, especially if other than human sources are used; there is also the probability that the exogenously administered enzyme cannot pass through the blood barrier.

Another therapeutic possibility has recently appeared on the experimental horizon. Skin fibroblasts from patients with enzyme deficiencies which are grown in tissue culture may be partially restored to normal by the presence of cells from normal individuals or from patients with entirely different metabolic derangements. This phenomenon is called metabolic cooperativity, and at least in Hurler's syndrome, the factor which restores the deficient cells appears to be a protein, possibly an enzyme. If this restoration can be demonstrated in cultured cells from patients with Tay-Sachs disease, there is the possibility that such a factor may prove efficacious for the therapy of this disease.

Generalized Gangliosidosis

Generalized gangliosidosis is a very uncommon lipid storage disease which is characterized by psychomotor retardation, hepatomegaly, some degree of splenomegaly, and foam cells in the reticuloendothelial tissues. There is vacuolation of the lymphocytes, and skeletal abnormalities occur which involve the skull, trunk, vertebral bodies, and humerus. The neurons in the central nervous system are swollen and contain cytoplasmic inclusion bodies. The predominant material which accumulates in the brain and other tissues of these patients is monosialoganglioside. There is also some increase in keratosulfate in the tissues of these individuals.

The metabolic defect in patients with generalized gangliosidosis is a deficiency of a β'-galactosidase which catalyzes the hydrolysis of the terminal molecule of galactose of monosialoganglioside. There is only 7 percent of normal galactosidase activity in tissues from these patients judging by assays with p-nitrophenyl-β'-galactopyranoside as substrate. This finding might suggest that other naturally occurring substances with a terminal galactose molecule such as galactocerebroside, ceramidelactoside, or ceramidetrihexoside might also accumulate. However, direct examination of the catabolism of these substrates using authentic labeled glycolipids as substrates revealed quite the opposite. The enzymatic hydrolysis of galactocerebroside was within normal limits in extracts of brain tissue from patients with generalized gangliosidosis and the hydrolysis of ceramide lactoside and ceramidetrihexoside was actually increased 200 to 300 percent over that of age matched controls. These findings amply demonstrate the pitfalls which must be scrupulously avoided when attempting to elucidate a metabolic abnormality based solely on data obtained with artificial substrates.

Gaucher's Disease

Patients with Gaucher's disease have been classified as having infantile, juvenile, and adult forms of the disorder on the basis of the rapidity of progression of hepatosplenomegaly which exists in all of these patients and the presence or absence of central nervous system difficulties. Patients with the infantile form of the disease show very rapid organ enlargement and impairment of neuronal function. The patients with juvenile form are also characterized by rapidly progressing splenomegaly and hepatomegaly along with rarefaction of the long bones and pelvis; however, these children generally have no CNS derangement. Patients with the adult form of Gaucher's disease have slow enlargement of the spleen and liver, involvement of the long bones and pelvis, and are frequently seen in hematology clinics because of a mild hypochromic anemia and prolonged clotting time due to thrombocytopenia. In all three forms of this disease large lipid-laden "Gaucher cells" which stain for both fat and carbohydrates are seen in bone marrow smears. There is usually an increase in serum acid phosphatase which is not inhibited by tartrate.

PATHOPHYSIOLOGY. The enlarged systemic organs in patients with Gaucher's disease contain an increased amount of the sphingoglycolipid called glucocerebroside. The biochemical defect in this condition has been shown to be a deficiency of the β-glucosidase which catalyzes the hydrolysis of the glucose moiety of this compound. Tissues from patients with the infantile form of this disease are virtually devoid of glucocerebrosidase activity. Patients with the juvenile form have from 50 to 10 percent of normal glucocerebrosidase in their tissues. Patients with the adult form of Gaucher's disease have a rather wide range of activity of this enzyme in their tissues; it may be as much as 40 percent of the normal value. This scatter of cerebrosidase activity is clearly indicative of the genetic heterogeneity of Gaucher's disease. It is presumed that these differences are caused by alterations or deletions of the amino acid sequence in the enzyme, which of course is ultimately traceable to alterations of the DNA in the involved gene.

The major source of the glucocerebroside which accumulates in peripheral tissues of patients with Gaucher's disease is probably the glycolipids in senescent leucocytes of which ceramide lactoside and hematoside are the chief components. Some glucocerebroside also arises from erythrocyte stroma which contains hematoside and globoside as major constituents. The glucocerebroside in neuronal cells in the brain probably arises in the course of turnover of gangliosides. It is currently assumed that patients with the juvenile and adult forms of Gaucher's disease have sufficient residual glucocerebrosidase activity in brain to prevent accumulation of this substance during the period of active ganglioside metabolism and these patients are therefore spared difficulties of the nervous system.

DIAGNOSIS. The diagnosis of Gaucher's disease can usually be made on the basis of the organomegaly, the presence of "Gaucher cells" in marrow preparations, and increase in serum acid phosphatase. A test is now available for confirmation of the diagnosis which is based on measurement of glucocerebrosidase activity in washed leucocyte preparations. Sufficient cells can be obtained from a few millimeters of venous blood, and the assay is conveniently performed with ^{14}C-labeled glucocerebroside as substrate. Experiments are currently underway to try to devise analytic conditions which will permit accurate assays using artificial substrates such as p-nitrophenyl-β-D-glycopyranoside or 4-methylumbelliferyl-β-D-glucopyranoside as substrate.

The enzymatic defect in Gaucher's disease can also be demonstrated by assaying glucocerebrosidase acting in extracts of skin fibroblasts grown in tissue culture. We are attempting to adapt this test for the detection of heterozygous carriers of the Gaucher trait, which is not presently feasible, using solid tissues, leucocytes, or spermatozoa as source materials. In addition, it is now possible to diagnose Gaucher's disease in utero by assaying glucocerebrosidase activity in cultured fetal cells.

TREATMENT. Therapy for this disorder at the present time is symptomatic, including, importantly, genetic counseling. Most of the concepts outlined for the treatment of Tay-Sachs disease can generally be applied to considerations of the therapy of Gaucher's disease. Enzyme replacement trials may be a little nearer at hand in Gaucher's disease since the cerebrosidase has now been isolated from human and beef spleen in a pure state. Still other therapeutic approaches, including organ (spleen) transplantation, have been suggested.

Metachromatic Leucodystrophy

Patients with metachromatic leucodystrophy (MLD) present a number of signs of central nervous system derangement. The disease becomes evident in affected infants within the first 30 months of life and is manifested by weakness, speech and swallowing difficulties, ataxia, and paralysis. In addition, there is a decrease of the conduction velocity in peripheral nerves.

PATHOPHYSIOLOGY. An acidic glycolipid called sulfatide accumulates in brain, kidney, and bile ducts and stains metachromatically yellowish-brown when tissue sections are treated with cresyl violet dye. The accumulated sulfatide may cause some renal and hepatic dysfunction. The metabolic defect in MLD has been shown to be a deficiency of an enzyme which catalyzes the cleavage of sulfuric acid from sulfatide. There are at least three sulfatases in human tissues whose activity may be assayed with the artificial substrate, nitrocatechol sulfate. These enzymes are designated as arylsulfatases A, B, and C respectively. In classic cases of MLD, there is a consistent deficiency of arylsulfatase A. Sulfatide is considered to be the natural substrate of this enzyme. This information provided the background for the development of a convenient diagnostic procedure based on the differential determination of arylsulfatase activity in leucocytes. The mean level of arylsulfatase A activity in leucocyte preparations from patients with MLD was only 10 percent of that found in control leucocyte preparations. Arylsulfatase B activity was within normal limits. The facility and reliability of this test make it the diagnostic procedure of choice at the present time. The diagnosis of MLD previously depended on measurement of the amount of sediment-bound urinary sulfatide or sulfatidase activity in urine; both of these determinations may vary with the volume, cellular composition, and degree of bacterial contamination of the urine.

TREATMENT. There is no specific therapy. An unsuccessful attempt has been made to treat MLD by the intrathecal and intravenous administration of beef brain arylsulfatase A. The investigation was performed with care and included brain biopsy before and after administration of the enzyme; however, there was no histologic evidence of improvement. If urine does indeed contain significant sulfatidase activity, one might consider it as a potential alternative source for obtaining sphingolipid hydrolases.

Niemann-Pick Disease

Patients with Niemann-Pick disease are generally severely retarded, cachectic, and have hepatosplenomegaly. There is some involvement of the long bones, although of a lesser degree than in patients with Gaucher's disease. Some patients with Niemann-Pick disease have an olive-yellow coloration of the exposed areas of the skin, and about 30 percent of them have a cherry-red spot in the macula. A large, waxy cell which stains for both lipid and phosphorus is seen in marrow preparations. Most of these patients seen in pediatric clinics are of the classic infantile type with rapidly progressing symptomatology. More recently, as our diagnostic acumen has increased, Niemann-Pick patients have been detected with less rapid progression of their disease.

PATHOPHYSIOLOGY. The lipid which accumulates in various tissues of patients with Niemann-Pick disease is a phospholipid called sphingomyelin. The enzymatic defect in Niemann-Pick disease is now well established as a deficiency of the enzyme called sphingomyelinase which catalyzes the hydrolytic cleavage of the phosphorylcholine portion of this sphingolipid.

DIAGNOSIS. A reproducible assay for sphingomyelinase activity was developed using sonicated leucocyte preparations. The activity of this enzyme is markedly depressed in leucocytes obtained from patients with Niemann-Pick disease. This test again provides both diagnostic and prognostic information, since the rapidity of progression of the disease is inversely related to the amount of residual sphingomyelinase activity. Similar findings were obtained in sphingomyelinase assays in extracts of skin fibroblasts grown in tissue culture. Patients classified as Niemann-Pick Type D (Nova Scotia variant) have normal sphingomyelinase activity in their cultured fibroblasts. It may be that this disease has been incorrectly classified, and rightly belongs to the group of cholesterol storage diseases although it is manifested by an ancillary and lesser accumulation of sphingomyelin.

Fabry's Disease

SIGNS AND SYMPTOMS. Fabry's disease was long considered to be a dermatologic disorder because of the occurrence of small, dark reddish-purple macules and papules in the umbilical region, on the scrotum, and over the lateral iliac areas. The disease was called angiokeratoma corporis diffusum universale. It has been recognized subsequently that this condition is an X-linked inherited metabolic disorder in which hemizygous males are most severely affected. The outstanding manifestation of the disease in these patients is a severe, progressive impairment of kidney function which becomes increasingly difficult to manage in the third and fourth decade of life. Patients with Fabry's disease may also have electrocardiographic abnormalities and cardiac dysfunction. Ophthalmologic abnormalities, including cataracts, corneal opacities, and edema of the retina, are frequently present. There may also be bouts of fever, burning pains in the extremities, and disorders of the gastrointestinal system. Female carriers of the abnormal gene may be symptom-free or may have mild ocular and skin involvement.

BIOCHEMICAL LESION. A glycolipid called ceramide trihexoside accumulates in many tissues of patients with Fabry's disease. The high concentration of this material in kidney glomeruli is probably responsible for the impairment of function of this organ. The enzymatic defect in hemizygous males with Fabry's disease is a complete absence of the enzyme which catalyzes the hydrolysis of the terminal galactose moiety of ceramide trihexoside. Heterozygous female carriers of this disease exhibit an intermediate level of activity of this enzyme in their tissues.

The most likely source of the accumulating ceramide trihexoside seems to be globoside from senescent erythrocytes. Normally, a small quantity of ceramide trihexosidase is excreted in the urine. Increased levels of ceramide trihexoside have been detected in the serum and urine of males with Fabry's disease. This compound is only very slightly soluble in water and the increased quantities presented to the kidney in these patients may precipitate in the glomeruli.

DIAGNOSIS. The diagnosis of Fabry's disease may be established by determining the level of ceramide trihexosidase activity in biopsy specimens of intestinal mucosa. Sufficient tissue may be obtained by suction biopsy in the region of the ligament of Treitz. The enzymatic assay is again greatly facilitated by the use of appropriately labeled substrate. The activity of ceramide trihexosidase is quite stable in acetone powders of kidney tissue and can be shipped in this form without refrigeration for subsequent assay, a procedure recently employed for confirming the diagnosis of a patient with Fabry's disease.

TREATMENT. At the present time, a number of patients with Fabry's disease are being treated by hemodialysis to alleviate their renal insufficiency. Some consideration should therefore be given to the possibility of kidney transplantation in these patients. The extensive current research directed toward the solution of difficulties related to organ transplantation should eventually permit the development of new, safer procedures. Enzyme replacement therapy probably will be attempted in patients with Fabry's disease in the not too distant future.

Globoid Leucodystrophy
(*Krabbe's Disease*)

The etiology of Krabbe's disease is not securely established at the present time. Infants with this condition exhibit severe mental retardation, and "globoid bodies" are seen in histologic sections of brain tissue. These bodies are reported to contain cerebroside and sphingomyelin. Perhaps the most definitive chemical alteration in brain tissue of patients with Krabbe's disease is an increase in the ratio of cerebroside to sulfatide. Normally, there is about three times as much cerebroside as sulfatide in brain. In Krabbe's disease, this ratio may be as high as 12:1.

Intensive investigations have failed to reveal any abnormality of sphingolipid catabolism in patients with Krabbe's disease. These observations suggested that the metabolic defect in Krabbe's disease might be a deficiency of a sulfate-transferring enzyme. A decrease in enzymatic sulfation in extracts of brain tissue have been reported in patients with Krabbe's disease. However, other investigators have not been able to confirm this finding. More recent observations have implicated a deficiency of galactocerebroside β-galactosidase as the primary enzymatic defect in this disorder.

REFERENCES

Austin, J., Balasubramanian, A., Pattabiramam, T., Saraswathi, S., Basu, D., and Bachhawat, B. A controlled study of enzyme activities in three human disorders of glycolipid metabolism. J. Neurochem., 10:805, 1963.

Bachhawat, B. K., Austin, J., and Armstrong, D. A cerebrosidesulphotransferase deficiency in a human disorder of myelin. Biochem. J., 104:15C, 1967.

Brady, R. O. Cerebral lipidosis. Ann. Rev. Med., 21:317, 1970.

——— Genetics and the sphingolipidoses. Med. Clin. N. Amer., 53:827, 1969.

——— The sphingolipidoses. New Eng. J. Med., 275: 312, 1966.

——— Gal, A. E., Bradley, R. M., Martenson, E., Warshaw, A. L., and Laster, L. Enzymatic defect in Fabry's disease. Ceramidetrihexosidase deficiency. New Eng. J. Med., 276:1163, 1967.

——— Kanfer, J. N., Bradley, R. M., and Shapiro, D. Demonstration of a deficiency of glucocerebroside-cleaving enzymes in Gaucher's disease. J. Clin. Invest., 45: 1112, 1966.

——— Kanfer, J. N., Mock, M. B., and Fredrickson, D. S. The metabolism of sphingomyelin. II. Evidence of an enzymatic deficiency in Niemann-Pick disease. Proc. Nat. Acad. Sci. U.S.A., 55:366, 1966.

——— Kanfer, J., and Shapiro, D. Metabolism of glucocerebrosides. II. Evidence of an enzymatic deficiency in Gaucher's disease. Biochem. Biophys. Res. Commun., 18:221, 1965.

———— O'Brien, J. S., Bradley, R. M., and Gal, A. E. Sphingolipid hydrolases in brain tissue of patients with generalized gangliosidosis. Biochim. Biophys. Acta, 210: 193, 1970.

Fratantoni, J. C., Hall, C. W., and Neufeld, E. F. The defect in Hurler and Hunter syndromes. II. Deficiency of specific factors involved in mucopolysaccharide degradation. Proc. Nat. Acad. Sci. U.S.A., 64:360, 1969.

Greene, H. L., Hug, G., and Schubert, W. K. Metachromatic leukodystrophy. Treatment with arylsulfatase-A. Arch. Neurol., 20:147, 1969.

Johnson, W. G., Weinreb, N. J., and Brady, R. O. Unpublished data, 1970.

Kampine, J. P., Brady, R. O., Kanfer, J. N., Feld, M., and Shapiro, D. Diagnosis of Gaucher's disease and Niemann-Pick disease with small samples of venous blood. Science, 155:86, 1967.

Kattlove, H. E., Williams, J. C., Gaynor, E., Spivak, M., Bradley, R. M., and Brady, R. O. Gaucher cells in chronic myelocytic leukemia: an acquired abnormality. Blood, 33:379, 1969.

Kolodny, E. H., Brady, R. O., and Volk, B. S. Demonstration of an alteration of ganglioside metabolism in Tay-Sachs disease. Biochem. Biophys. Res. Commun., 37:526, 1969.

———— Uhlendorf, B. W., Quirk, J. M., Jacobson, C. B., and Brady, R. O. Gangliosides of cultured skin fibroblasts: Accumulation in Tay-Sachs disease. Abstracts, XIIIth Int. Conf. Biochem. Lipids, Athens, Sept. 1969, p. 39.

Mehl, E., and Jatkewitz, H. Evidence for a genetic block in metachromatic leukodystrophy. Biochem. Biophys. Res. Commun., 19:407, 1965.

Okada, S., and O'Brien, J. S. Generalized gangliosidosis: Beta-galactosidase deficiency. Science, 160:1002, 1968.

———— and O'Brien, J. S. Tay-Sachs disease: Generalized absence of a beta-D-N-acetylhexosaminidase component. Science, 165:698, 1969.

Percy, A. K., and Brady, R. O. Metachromatic leukodystrophy: Diagnosis with samples of venous blood. Science, 161:594, 1968.

Sandhof, K., Andreae, U., Jatkewitz, H. Deficient hexosaminidase activity in an exceptional case of Tay-Sachs disease with additional storage of kidney globoside in visceral organs. Life Sci., 7:283, 1968.

Sloan, M. R., Uhlendorf, B. W., Kanfer, J. N., Brady, R. O., and Fredrickson, D. S. Deficiency of sphingomyelin-cleaving enzyme activity in tissue cultures derived from patients with Niemann-Pick disease. Biochem. Biophys. Res. Commun., 34:582, 1969.

Anomalies of Protein Metabolism

8.11
SERUM AND METAL-BINDING PROTEINS

FRED S. ROSEN and
CHESTER A. ALPER

At least 60 different proteins have been identified in and isolated from human serum. They serve (1) to clot the blood; (2) to effect humoral defense mechanisms; (3) to transport fats, metals, vitamins, and hormones; (4) to maintain the oncotic pressure of the blood; and (5) to inhibit various proteolytic enzymes. Each serum protein has a characteristic catabolic or synthetic rate and ratio of distribution between the vascular and extravascular spaces. Although many serum proteins display genetic variation, such molecular differences are, in general, without clinical significance.

The Immunoglobulins
(See also Chap. 10)

The immunoglobulins constitute the most heterogeneous group of proteins in the serum. At the present time, five distinct classes of immunoglobulins are recognized: gamma G or IgG; gamma A or IgA; gamma M or IgM; gamma D or IgD; and gamma E or IgE. Furthermore, the gamma G globulins are divided into four distinct subclasses and gamma A globulins into two subclasses. Although antibody function is associated with immunoglobulins, no antibody function has as yet been shown to be associated with gamma D globulins. The concentration of gamma A globulin is relatively high in comparison to other immunoglobulins in almost all body secretions such as tears, saliva, colostrum, succus entericus, and respiratory tract secretions. Reaginic activity responsible for the Prausnitz-Kustner (PK) reaction is associated with the gamma E globulins.

The immunoglobulins are almost exclusively synthesized in the lymphoid tissues of the spleen, lymph nodes, intestinal tract, and tonsils. In man lymphoid cells are apparently derived from a bone marrow precursor cell, whose morphologic identity is as yet uncertain. Some of these cells emigrate to the thymus gland where they rapidly divide, undergo a maturation process, and become committed to the recognition of antigen and the mediation of cellular immunity. Although many, if not most, of these cells remain dormant or die in the thymus gland, a significant fraction of them enters into a traffic pattern in which they circulate through the periarteriolar spaces of the spleen and subcortical regions of lymph nodes and thence back to the bloodstream. A hormonal factor produced in the thymus gland has been postulated to explain the vital function of this gland in the expansion and maturation of the lymphoid cell population, but it has not been isolated. Furthermore, germinal center cells and plasma cells which are responsible for immunoglobulin synthesis appear to be controlled by another, as yet undefined, mechanism. In avian species, a lymphoepithelial organ associated with the gastrointestinal tract, called the bursa of Fabricius, fulfills this role, complementing the function of the thymus gland. No similar discrete organ has been identified in man.

X-Linked Agammaglobulinemia

DEFINITION. This is a hereditary defect in synthesis of all immunoglobulins. Impairment of antibody synthesis in affected males is associated with severe, recurrent pyogenic infection.

ETIOLOGY AND PATHOGENESIS. The failure of immunoglobulin synthesis is associated with an absence of plasma cells and germinal centers in all lymphoid tissue. However, "thymic-dependent" lymphocytes appear to be present in normal numbers, and cellular immunity of the tuberculin-type, cutaneous contact type, and allograft rejection type are intact. The thymus gland is normal.

SIGNS AND SYMPTOMS. Affected boys are usually well for the first 9 to 15 months of life due to passive protection afforded by transplacentally acquired maternal antibody. Thereafter, repeated otitis media, sinusitis, conjunctivitis, pneumonia, and furunculosis due to the common pyogenic pathogens are the most prominent clinical manifestations. The usual childhood viral infections are tolerated without untoward complications. Vaccination is benign.

Besides the physical findings associated with purulent infection, the paucity of tonsillar tissue in the oropharynx may be quite striking, particularly in the presence of overt or repeated infection. Lymph nodes are difficult to palpate in young boys with this defect.

COMPLICATIONS. Suppurative complications are numerous, and unrelentingly progressive bronchiectasis in the untreated child compromises pulmonary function and may ultimately become life-threatening. Nonsuppurative complications include arthritis of the rheumatoid type in about one-third or more of patients prior to replacement therapy. Other collagenlike diseases have been observed, particularly a dermatomyositislike syndrome which is fatal and characterized by a lymphoproliferative phenomenon reminiscent of lymphoma. Other lymphoreticular malignancies have been reported with greater than anticipated frequency.

LABORATORY FINDINGS. The serum concentration of *all* the immunoglobulins is less than 5 percent of normal. Specific antibodies are virtually undetectable after antigenic stimulation. This may be readily verified by attempting to measure serum isohemagglutinins or by demonstrating a positive Schick test despite recent toxoid inoculation. The diagnosis must be firmly established by obtaining a regional lymph node 5 to 10 days following stimulation with tetanus and diphtheria toxoids and/or typhoid vaccine. It is most convenient to obtain an ipsilateral inguinal node following inoculation into the thigh.

TREATMENT. Appropriate antibiotic therapy is indicated for acute suppurative infections. The response to intensive antibiotic therapy is usually quite satisfactory. Frequently, prolonged antibiotic therapy, together with replacement therapy, is indicated to resolve bronchiectasis, perforated tympani, or other structural damage which has resulted from recurrent or chronic infection.

Human gamma globulin is available as a 16 percent solution. It has been established that 100 mg/kg (0.6 ml/kg) injected intramuscularly at monthly intervals provides adequate prophylaxis against recurrent infection. Initially, a loading dose of 300 mg/kg (0.8 ml/kg) is given in several sites over a 48-hour period. The monthly maintenance dose is aimed at keeping the serum gamma globulin concentration above 150 mg per 100 ml.

Acquired Agammaglobulinemia

Agammaglobulinemia of late onset has no clear-cut genetic transmission although familial clustering of cases has been noted. Acquisition of agammaglobulinemia affects both sexes equally and may occur at any age. The signs, symptoms, complications, and treatment are the same as outlined above. Lymph node biopsy also reveals absence of plasma cells, but in contrast to the X-linked defect, germinal centers may be present as abiotropic remnants or exhibit an unusual exuberance. In older children and adults, steatorrhea and other symptoms of spruelike disease are common. Gluten, milk, or other dietary exclusion may prove helpful.

Dysgammaglobulinemia

Partial immunoglobulin defects of several varieties have been observed. About 0.7 percent of the normal population lacks gamma A globulins. The defect is usually benign but may be associated with celiac syndrome, recurrent respiratory infection, or collagen disease. On the other hand, absent or markedly decreased serum gamma G and gamma A associated with elevated gamma M levels represents a syndrome in which there is not only undue susceptibility to infection but also recurrent neutropenia, erythrocyte antibodies, and other autoimmune phenomena. The defect is transmitted as an X-linked recessive or may be acquired.

Transient Hypogammaglobulinemia of Infancy

Newborn infants synthesize gamma M and gamma A globulins. The former class of antibodies reaches normal adult levels by 6 months of age, whereas gamma A globulins slowly rise in concentration during the first decade of life. Infants sustain a period of physiologic hypogammaglobulinemia between 3 and 4 months of age, at which time rates of synthesis of gamma G globulin rise rapidly as peripheral lymphoid tissue matures. A prolongation of physiologic hypogammaglobulinemia up to 24 months of age may occur. Affected infants sustain recurrent bouts of otitis media and frequent respiratory infections with wheezing and other signs of infectious asthma. Multiple occurrences in families have been noted. Replacement therapy is indicated until the infant spontaneously attains normal serum gamma globulin concentrations.

Hereditary Thymic Dysplasia
(*Lymphopenic Agammaglobulinemia*)

DEFINITION. This is a hereditary disease characterized by a combined deficiency in cellular and humoral immunity.

ETIOLOGY AND PATHOGENESIS. This defect is known to be transmitted as an X-linked or autosomal recessive phenomenon. The phenotypic expression of the two genetic varieties is essentially the same. The thymus gland is vestigial, exhibiting no Hassall's corpuscles, and few, if any, lymphocytes. Primitive, embryonic spindle cells constitute a tiny thymus gland, usually weighing less than 1 g, which has failed in most instances to descend from the neck into its normal position in the anterior mediastinum. The thymic defect is probably secondary to the failure of normal stem cell migration into the gland during the twelfth week of embryonic life, which may exert a tropic or organizer effect on the normal embryogenesis of the thymus. Peripheral lymphoid tissue is completely devoid of formed lymphoid elements. Plasma cells are usually but not invariably absent, and one or more immunoglobulins may be detected in the serum in normal or near normal concentration.

SIGNS AND SYMPTOMS. Affected infants become ill during the first few months of life, and normal growth and development ceases by 6 to 12 months. Protracted monilial infection of the mouth and skin is the most common first sign of the disease. Intractable diarrhea also occurs very frequently, and *Shigella, Salmonella,* or enteropathic *Escherichia coli* can be cultured from the stool. Fatal pulmonary infection due to *Pseudomonas* or *Pneumocystis carinii* is also commonly encountered. Vaccination results in fatal progressive vaccinia. Measles results in fatal giant cell pneumonia. Chicken pox may also cause death in affected infants.

LABORATORY FINDINGS. Persistent lymphopenia (less than 3,000 lymphocytes/mm^2) and unresponsiveness of leucocytes in in vitro culture to phytohemagglutinin stimulation are found. It is impossible to elicit dermal hypersensitivity to common antigens, such as monilia or streptokinase, despite overt infections with the organisms which evoke such hypersensitivity. It is also not possible to provoke contact hypersensitivity to 5 percent dinitrofluorbenzene (DNFB). Lymph node biopsy, if possible, reveals absence of all lymphoid elements. Skin grafts from unrelated donors are accepted.

TREATMENT. Successful establishment of cellular chimerism has been achieved by transplants of bone marrow cells from histocompatible siblings. Transplants of incompatible bone marrow, or even blood transfusions, cause fatal graft versus host disease. This complication starts 5 to 10 days after administration of incompatible cells with fever, a macular rash starting on the face, hepatosplenomegaly, diarrhea, and finally bone marrow aplasia with anemia and thrombocytopenia. Death is usually caused by hemorrhage and infection.

Congenital Aplasia of the Thymus Gland
(DiGeorge Syndrome)

This is an uncommon congenital malformation resulting from a failure of embryogenesis of the organs derived from the third and fourth pharyngeal pouches, namely, the thymus and parathyroid glands. Affected infants have neonatal tetany. Malformations of the ear pinnae, nasal clefts, micrognathia, and cardiac malformations, particularly a right-sided aortic arch, are part of the syndrome. The defect is usually incomplete and some thymic and parathyroid tissue may be present in an ectopic position in the neck. Undue susceptibility to infection results from abnormal cellular immunity in these infants. The immune defect has been corrected by transplants of fetal thymus.

Wiskott-Aldrich Syndrome

This is an X-linked recessive condition. Affected boys have eczema, thrombocytopenia, usually elevated levels of gamma A globulins, recurrent respiratory tract infections, progressively decreasing cellular immune function, and failure to form antibody to polysaccharide antigens as manifest by low or absent isohemagglutinins. Death from lymphoreticular malignancy is common.

Hereditary Ataxia-Telangiectasia
(Louis-Bar Syndrome)

This is an autosomal recessive disease. Affected individuals have progressive cerebellar ataxia, usually starting in the second year of life, and they develop cutaneous and ocular telangiectasia during the first decade of life. In 70 percent of patients, serum gamma A globulins are absent. Cellular immune function is impaired. Progressive sinobronchopulmonary infection and lymphoreticular malignancy is common.

Cellular immunity is also depressed in sarcoidosis, Hodgkin's disease, in patients on high doses of steroids or lymphocytotoxic agents, in "autoimmune" lymphopenia, cartilage hair hypoplasia, intestinal lymphangiectasia, uremia, and lepromatous leprosy.

Serum Complement System

The serum complement system (see also Chap. 10) is composed of nine serum proteins, designated in sequential order of their interaction C1, C4, C2, C3, C5, C6, C7, C8, and C9. At least three inhibitors or inactivators are known to modify the rates of interaction between these components. Activation of the entire system by antigen-antibody interactions involves a series of limited proteolytic reactions, a "cascade" such as occurs in the activation of the coagulation system (Fig. 11). It is now apparent that the components of the inflammatory response are generated during complement activation so that chemotaxis, enhanced phagocytosis, and bacteriolysis or other cell death is mediated by this system. Certain peptide fragments which split off of the various components act to increase vascular permeability, release histamine, and contract smooth muscle.

Individuals genetically deficient in C2 have been described. Both heterozygous and homozygous deficients have been found. The defect is without clinical significance. Individuals who are heterozygous for C3 deficiency are also without clinical symptoms. The homozygous deficiency in man has not yet been found. The measurement of serum C3 (β_1C globulin) has useful clinical import, as its concentration is markedly diminished in systemic lupus erythematosus, acute glomerular nephritis, and certain children with nephrotic syndrome characterized by lobular, proliferative glomerulitis (so-called progressive or hypocomplementemic glomerulonephritis).

Recently a patient with undue susceptibility to infection has been found to have a very low serum C3 level due to rapid endogenous catabolism of this protein. In view of the importance of C3 in the enhancement of bacterial phagocytosis, his inability to utilize C3 in vivo results in extreme susceptibility to pyogenic infection. Two infants with inherited dysfunctional C5 also exhibit susceptibility to infection. The most clinically significant defect of the serum

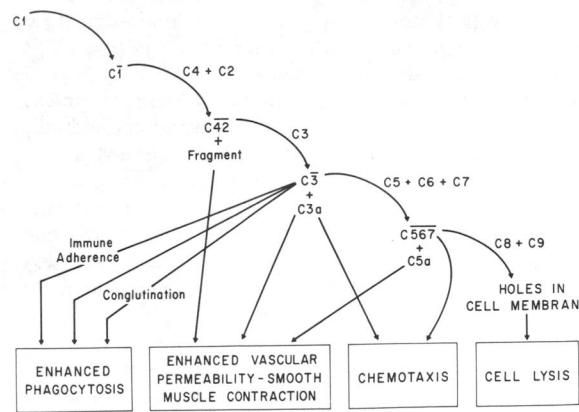

Fig. 11. A schematic representation of the pathophysiologic mechanisms mediated by complement. A bar indicates an activated component; e.g., C3. (Adapted from Cinader and Lepow. In Cinader, B., ed. *Antibodies to Biologically Active Molecules.* London, Pergamon Press, 1967, Vol. 1, p. 15.)

complement system occurs in individuals with hereditary angioneurotic edema (Osler-Quincke's disease). Such patients lack the serum inhibitor of activated C1 esterase, an acid labile alpha-2 globulin with a molecular weight of 140,000. This defect appears to be related to the pathogenesis of angioedema.

Hereditary Angioneurotic Edema
(*Osler-Quincke's Disease*)

DEFINITION. This is a hereditary disease characterized by recurrent episodes of circumscribed edema involving primarily the subcutaneous tissues, the oropharynx and larynx, and the gastrointestinal tract. **ETIOLOGY AND PATHOGENESIS.** Hereditary angioneurotic edema is transmitted as a Mendelian autosomal dominant phenomenon. The serum of affected individuals lacks C1 esterase inhibitory activity. In 85 percent of affected kindreds this alpha-2 globulin is markedly diminished in concentration in the serum of affected persons (average, 17.5 percent of normal); in the remaining 15 percent, a nonfunctional protein which cross-reacts completely with an antibody to normal C1 esterase is found in normal or elevated concentrations in the serum.

During attacks of angioneurotic edema, free C1 esterase is detectable in the plasma. As a result, the titers of C2 and C4, which are the natural substrates of C1 esterase, fall. Purified C1 esterase, when injected intradermally, provokes angioedema formation. Individuals with hereditary C2 deficiency, however, are unresponsive to C1 esterase. This fortuitous observation led to the conclusion that C1 esterase cleaves a vasoactive peptide from C2. A kininlike peptide has been generated in and isolated from the plasma of affected individuals. This peptide, as well as C1 esterase, provokes the formation of wide endothelial gaps in postcapillary venules, such as are seen in biopsy and autopsy tissues of angioedematous parts. Leakage of vascular fluid from these sites is presumed to cause angioedema.

SIGNS AND SYMPTOMS. The age of onset of attacks of angioedema varies widely in affected individuals, although in the majority of patients the first symptoms occur in the first decade of life. The disease characteristically becomes more severe at pubescence. Angioedema formation is clearly provoked by trauma. Anxiety, extremes of temperatures, menses, and excessive physical activity have also been noted to cause attacks. The swelling evolves rapidly to affect a circumscribed area of skin. The edema does not pit, does not itch, and does not become red or discolored. Although a sensation of pressure may be reported by the patient due to the extensive edema formation, the affected part looks remarkably undistinguished. The attacks last 48 to 72 hours and then rapidly subside during which phase the edema may pit. All patients with this defect have gastrointestinal symptoms which present as intestinal colic and bilious vomiting. If the colon is affected, profuse watery diarrhea may occur. Laryngeal edema is a common occurrence and has been fatal in about one third of patients. A peculiar mottling of the skin, reminiscent of erythema marginatum, occurs frequently in affected children and may herald the onset of an attack.

COMPLICATIONS. Fatal pulmonary edema as the result of laryngeal obstruction is the principal cause of death in affected individuals. Otherwise, the disease is benign. Unnecessary surgical procedures are frequently performed when an awareness of the relationship of the gastrointestinal symptoms to the disease process is lacking.

LABORATORY FINDINGS. Serum C1 esterase inhibitor activity is lacking in an assay system which measures the hydrolysis of N-acetyltyrosine ethyl ester by a known amount of C1 esterase. Immunochemical estimations of C1 esterase inhibitor are not completely reliable since, as previously mentioned, 15 percent of affected families have normal amounts of a nonfunctional protein. Assay of C2 or C4 titers is also useful in establishing the diagnosis.

TREATMENT. There is no specific treatment for angioedema. Patients with laryngeal edema should be observed in a recovery, operating, or emergency room prepared for imminent tracheostomy if required. About half of affected adults have a very satisfactory response to daily administration of a methyl testosterone linguet. Such therapy is generally not recommended for children.

Metal-Binding and Related Proteins

Properly speaking, *transferrin* is the only known serum metal-binding protein in the sense that a metal-binding protein serves to bind and thereby transport a metal. Transferrin is a beta globulin with a molecular weight of 85,000 and is capable of binding two atoms of ferric iron. Normally, transferrin is one-third saturated with iron; the total iron-binding capacity of serum is a direct measure of the transferrin concentration of serum. The transferrin concentration falls in the presence of tissue injury or necrosis and rises in iron-deficiency states. Serum transferrin may also be low due to gastrointestinal or urinary protein loss. Although at least 16 genetic variants of transferrin are known, none are of clinical significance. *Atransferrinemia* has been observed in only two children, both of whom had hepatosplenomegaly and severe iron-deficiency anemia.

Haptoglobin is an alpha-2 globulin which is highly polymorphic in man. It binds to hemoglobin via the globin chains. The haptoglobin-hemoglobin complex is rapidly removed from the circulation by reticuloendothelial cells, particularly those of the marrow. Since the rate of synthesis of haptoglobin is uninfluenced by its serum level, the serum haptoglobin concentration falls during in vivo hemolysis in proportion to hemoglobin release. Hemoglobinuria does not occur until the capacity of circulating haptoglobin to bind hemoglobin has been exceeded. *Hereditary anhaptoglobinemia*, which occurs in some Negroes, is without clinical consequences. The serum concentration of haptoglobin rises markedly during acute phase reactions and accounts for the elevation of alpha-2 globulins observed on serum electrophoretic patterns during any inflammatory process.

Another alpha-2 globulin, *ceruloplasmin*, whose name derives from its beautiful sky-blue color in the purified state, contains eight atoms of copper, but does not serve to transport this metal. It has a molecular weight of 160,000. Normal serum contains more than 25 mg percent of this protein. It also is an acute phase reactant and its concentration is increased during pregnancy or female hormone administration. This elevation may impart a green color to the plasma. Serum ceruloplasmin concentration is almost invariably below 25 mg percent in patients with Wilson's disease.

Wilson's Disease

DEFINITION. This is a hereditary disorder of copper metabolism of unknown pathogenesis which results in cirrhosis of the liver and degeneration of the basal ganglia due to excessive copper deposition.

ETIOLOGY AND PATHOGENESIS. Wilson's disease is inherited as an autosomal recessive disorder. Individuals who are heterozygous for the trait are clinically unaffected.

Affected individuals have increased total body stores of copper. This results from an increase in intestinal copper absorption and a failure of the normal hepatic conjugation and excretion of copper. The intermediate steps in these processes are not understood. The excessive accumulation of copper in the liver results in hepatocellular necrosis and eventually cirrhosis. Copper deposition may ultimately occur in the basal ganglia of the brain, resulting in cystic degeneration of those structures, and in the renal tubules, resulting in amino-aciduria. The diminished concentration of ceruloplasmin appears to be a secondary effect of the basic defect, which remains obscure.

SIGNS AND SYMPTOMS. Wilson's disease presents most frequently in children as cirrhosis of the liver, accompanied by ascites, splenomegaly, hypersplenism, and esophageal varices. The onset usually occurs after 7 years of age. All children with juvenile cirrhosis are prime suspects for this diagnosis.

The neurologic complications of Wilson's disease are rare in children and may present as behavior or convulsive disorders, in addition to the more classic symptoms of Parkinsonism associated with disease of the basal ganglia.

The characteristic deposition of yellow-green copper salts in the limbus of the cornea, known as the Kayser-Fleischer ring, is pathognomonic of Wilson's disease, but ordinarily it is not readily seen without the aid of a slit lamp.

DIAGNOSIS. The diagnosis of Wilson's disease is based upon: (1) the presence of a Kayser-Fleischer ring; (2) decreased serum ceruloplasmin; (3) increased urine copper excretion; and (4) increased liver copper content.

TREATMENT. The reversibility of the hepatic and central nervous system damage in patients with Wilson's disease by proper chelation therapy makes the treatment of this disease a very satisfactory experience for the physician. Furthermore, it appears at the present time that the disease can be prevented in affected siblings of propositi.

Between 1 and 1.5 g of penicillamine is given daily in equally divided doses. In addition, 20 mg of pyridoxine is taken to prevent vitamin B_6 deficiency. A low copper diet which excludes shellfish, nuts, chocolate products (including cola drinks), dried fruits, and certain green vegetables must be rigidly maintained.

Allergic reactions to penicillamine, including hives, eczema, and angioedema, and leucopenia with eosinophilia frequently occur within a month of the onset of therapy. Because chelation therapy is life saving in these patients, it should be continued in the face of such untoward reactions which can be controlled with antihistamines and prednisone.

British anti-Lewisite (BAL) is a useful adjunct in the treatment of the neurologic complications.

Alpha₁-Antitrypsin Deficiency

The major inhibitor of tryptic activity in serum is an alpha₁-glycoprotein with a molecular weight of 45,000; this globulin accounts for 90 percent of such inhibitory activity in serum. At least eight genetic variants are recognized, one of which is associated with very low levels of this protein in the serum. It was first noted that individuals homozygous for this deficiency state sustain panlobular progressive emphysema without preceding bronchitis which becomes manifest in the fourth or fifth decade of life. Recently several kindred have been described with alpha₁-antitrypsin deficiency in which affected infants have neonatal hepatitis. Following clinical resolution of the hepatitis, a period of well-being is followed by the advent of hepatic cirrhosis. There is no known therapy for this defect at present. The deficiency occurs in approximately one in 2000 births so that it is one of the most frequent genetic deficiencies known.

Analbuminemia is a very rare disorder which appears to be inherited as an autosomal recessive gene. It is without clinical significance except for a propensity toward mild pedal edema in affected individuals.

REFERENCES

Giblett, E. Genetic Markers in Human Blood. Oxford, Blackwell Scientific Publications, 1969.

Janeway, C. A., Rosen, F. S., Merler, E., and Alper, C. A. The Gamma Globulins. Boston, Little, Brown and Co., 1967.

Muller-Eberhard, H. J. Chemistry and reaction mechanisms of complement. *In* Dixon, F. J., Jr., and Kunkel, H. G., eds., Advances in Immunology. New York, Academic Press, Inc., 1968, Vol. 8.

Schultze, H. E., and Heremans, J. F. Molecular Biology of Human Proteins with Special Reference to Plasma Proteins. Amsterdam, Elsevier, 1966, Vol. I.

8.12
DEFICIENCIES OF ERYTHROCYTE AND LEUCOCYTE ENZYMES

ERNST R. JAFFE and SUSAN R. HARRIS

Enzymes of the Erythrocytes (See also Chap. 17)

Studies of hereditary hemolytic disorders have provided important information about the metabolic activity of human erythrocytes and about the inheritance of disease processes in man. Fourteen enzyme deficiencies have been reported to be associated with hemolytic disorders; seven are well defined, and seven are less well established. Despite the extensive data that have been accumulated, the precise mechanisms by which these enzyme deficiencies produce hemolysis are still unknown.

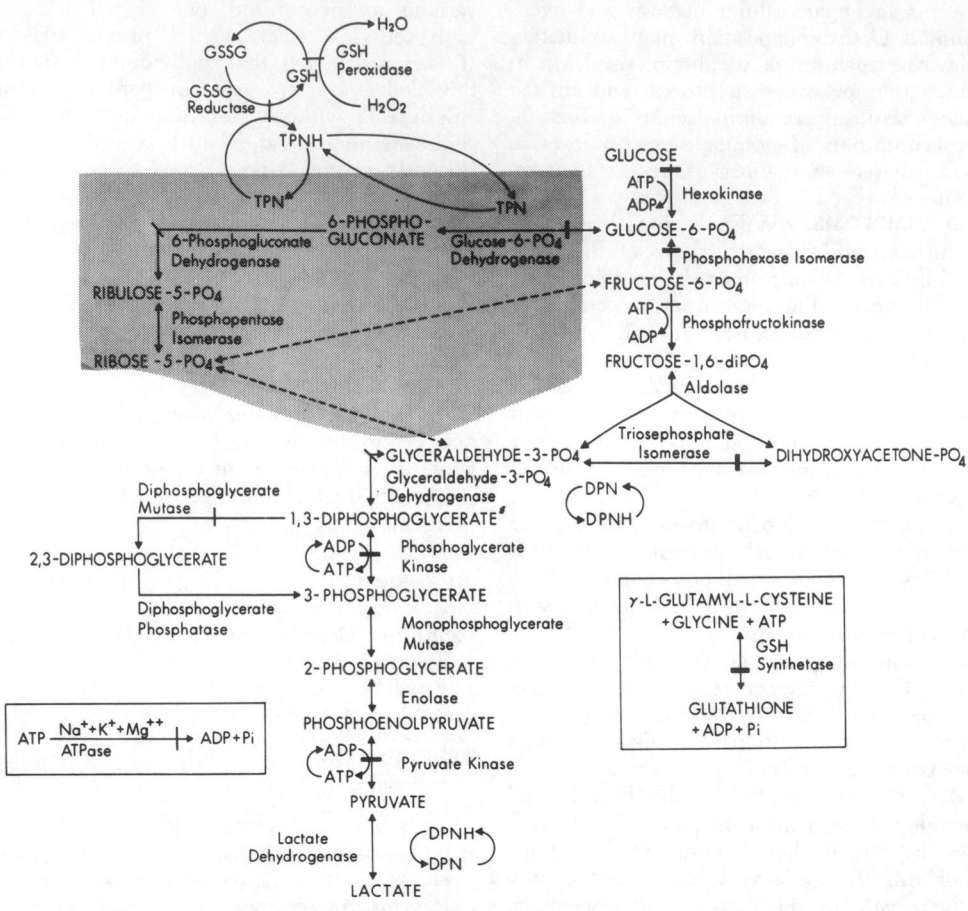

Fig. 12. Enzymatic reactions involved in the metabolism of glucose and reduced glutathione (GSH) in mature human erythrocytes. Reactions enclosed in the shaded area comprise the hexosemonophosphate (HMP) shunt pathway. Interrupted lines indicate omission of several reactions. Bold bars indicate enzymatic deficiencies whose association with hereditary hemolytic disorders is well established, while lighter bars indicate enzymatic deficiencies which have been reported to be associated with hemolytic disorders. (Modified from Jaffe, E. R. *Blood,* 35:116, 1970.)

To appreciate the hemolytic disorders associated with enzymatic deficiencies, it is necessary to consider the relationship between metabolic activity and the functions of the erythrocyte. The mature human erythrocyte is limited to glycolysis as the only significant source of the energy required for its functions (Fig. 12). For an expenditure of two molecules of adenosine triphosphate (ATP) per molecule of glucose used, the erythrocyte can generate four molecules of ATP, a potential net gain of two. This ATP can be used to maintain, by means of an ATPase system, the high intracellular potassium and low sodium contents characteristic of human erythrocytes against concentration gradients and passive leaks. ATP can also be utilized for the resynthesis of purine nucleotides and the synthesis of pyridine nucleotides, both essential cofactors for glycolysis. Maintenance of the lipids of the erythrocyte membrane also appears to require metabolic activity and ATP.

Metabolic activity is involved in maintaining hemoglobin in a state suitable for the reversible binding of oxygen, a process which requires that the iron of the heme moiety be in the ferrous state. Reduced diphosphopyridine nucleotide (DPNH) is required for the reduction of any formed methemoglobin (ferrihemoglobin) to ferrohemoglobin. A deficiency in this system results in hereditary methemoglobinemia (see below), but not in hemolysis. The binding of oxygen to hemoglobin can be influenced by organic phosphate esters, especially 2,3-diphosphoglycerate (2,3-DPG), which are generated by the cell's metabolic machinery. The Rapoport-Luebering or 2,3-DPG cycle provides the mechanism for the generation of 2,3-DPG, permits a bypass of an ATP-generating step, may serve to conserve DPNH for the reduction of methemoglobin, and may play a role as a regulator of glycolytic activity. Finally, metabolic activity, in an unknown fashion, appears to be required to maintain the organization, shape, and structure of erythrocytes.

In addition to the direct pathway from glucose to lactate (Embden-Meyerhof pathway), the erythrocyte has an active hexose monophosphate (HMP) shunt through which normally 5 to 10 percent of the glucose utilized passes before reentering the mainstream of glycolysis. This shunt is the only source for the generation of reduced triphosphopyridine nucleotide (TPNH), the preferred cofactor for the reduction of oxidized glutathione (GSSG) to reduced glutathione (GSH). Although its precise function is still unknown, the human erythrocyte contains about half as many molecules of GSH as hemoglobin. HMP shunt activity is required to maintain the intracellular concentration of GSH, which may be involved in protecting hemoglobin against irreversible oxidative denaturation, guarding membrane lipids against peroxidation, and shielding essential enzymes against inactivation.

In contrast to the mature erythrocyte, the immature cell or reticulocyte is capable of much more metabolic activity. Reticulocytes contain some ribonucleic acids, can make proteins, lipids, heme, and purine nucleotides, can perform oxidative phosphorylation with an intact cytochrome system and tricarboxylic acid cycle, and may be able to utilize amino acids and fatty acids as energy sources. The concentrations of ATP and, probably, other organic phosphate esters such as 2,3-DPG, are higher, and the activities of several, but not all, enzymes are considerably greater in these young cells.

The limited metabolic apparatus of the normal mature human erythrocyte is sufficient to support all of its essential functions for about 120 days. By mechanisms not yet clearly understood, the survival of cells significantly deficient in the activity of any one of the enzymes involved is jeopardized. In addition, the spleen, while not necessarily the only site for destruction of erythrocytes, may influence the circulating cell, its metabolic activity, and its lifespan. In patients with a glycolytic enzyme deficiency, the greater metabolic potential of the reticulocytes probably makes it possible for these young cells to survive and function at least long enough to prevent the patient's death.

The erythrocytes of newborn infants differ from those of older children and adults not only in the type of hemoglobin that they contain, but also in their metabolic activity. Although the consumption of glucose by these erythrocytes is increased, the activities of phosphofructokinase, DPNH-methemoglobin reductase, GSH peroxidase, and catalase are decreased and the stability of ATP upon incubation in vitro is reduced. These transient physiologic alterations may contribute to the increased susceptibility of newborn infants to toxic methemoglobinemia and drug-induced hemolysis, and may make the anemia associated with inherited deficiencies in enzymatic activities more severe.

Hereditary Nonspherocytic Hemolytic Anemias (See also Chap. 17)

Some of the hematologic characteristics and biochemical abnormalities which have been described in hemolytic disorders associated with deficiencies in the activities of enzymes are summarized in Table 13. Considerable variability in the severity of the hemolysis is obvious. Except for the great majority of patients with G6PD deficiency to be discussed later, most patients have been noted to have jaundice, splenomegaly, and mild to marked reticulocytosis. Increased need for blood transfusions has often been noted in association with infections. The hemolytic process is often apparent from birth, but not infrequently the illness is first detected in adult life. In keeping with the autosomal recessive mode of inheritance of most of these enzyme deficiencies, parent to child transmission is rare and has usually been explicable on the basis of a mating between heterozygous and homozygous subjects. G6PD deficiency and phosphoglycerate kinase deficiency are inherited as sex-linked characteristics and, therefore, are most manifest in males. While not as curative of the anemia as in hereditary spherocytosis, splenectomy appears to have ameliorated the anemia in many patients, especially those with pyruvate kinase deficiency.

Pyruvate kinase deficiency is probably the most common of the enzyme deficiencies associated with spontaneous nonspherocytic hemolytic anemia. Considerable heterogeneity in the clinical severity and in the biochemical abnormality has been described. The disorder is associated both with marked quantitative decreases in pyruvate kinase activity and with normally active enzyme that is catalytically inefficient at low concentrations of the substrate, phosphoenolpyruvate. Although pyruvate kinase deficiency is most common in people of Northern European origin, it has been found in Italians and Japanese, a Mexican child, an American Negro, and a Syrian girl.

Of particular interest are those enzyme deficiencies which are not limited to the erythrocytes. Deficiency in the activity of *triosephosphate isomerase* is associated with a severe, incapacitating, progressive neuromuscular disorder. The deficiency has been documented in the erythrocytes, leucocytes, skeletal muscle, serum, skin fibroblasts, and spinal fluid of affected subjects. The patients appear to develop normally, except for evidence of hemolysis, during the first 6 to 7 months of life and then suffer progressive neuromuscular impairment with initial generalized spasticity and subsequent weakness. These patients are also susceptible to frequent infections. All but one of the nine known cases have died before the age of 6 years. Intermediate levels of triosephosphate isomerase activity are demonstrable in

TABLE 13. *Hematologic and Biochemical Abnormalities Described in Hemolytic Anemias Associated with Deficiencies in Enzymes Related to the Glycolytic Pathways*

Enzyme	Severity of Anemia	Retic* %	Normal RBC* Activity %	Deficiency in WBC*	Mode of Inheri- tance*
A. Well-Established Deficiencies with Hemolysis					
Hexokinase	Moderate	4-24	14-50	No	AR
Phosphohexose Isomerase	Moderate	12-82	14-30	Yes	AR
Triosephosphate Isomerase	Severe	10-33	6-14	Yes	AR
Phosphoglycerate Kinase	Severe	6-25	<5	Yes	X
Pyruvate Kinase	Mild, Severe	5-80	5-20	No	AR
Glucose-6-Phosphate Dehydrogenase	None, Severe	1-40	0-26	No, Yes	X
GSH Synthetase	Mild, Moderate	2-15	~0	—	AR
B. Deficiencies Reported with Hemolysis					
Phosphofructokinase	Mild	3-10	30-60	No	AR, X?
Glyceraldehyde-3-Phos- phate Dehydrogenase	Mild	—	57-68	Yes	?
2,3-DPG Mutase	Moderate, Severe	2-7	12-39	—	AR, AD?
6-Phosphogluconate Dehydrogenase	None, Severe	1-25	3-80	Yes	AR
GSSG Reductase	None, Severe	1-33	0-74	No	AD?
GSH Peroxidase	Mild, Moderate	1-11	30-85	—	AR
ATPase	Moderate	1-4	44-63	No	AD?

*Retic = reticulocytes; RBC = erythrocytes; WBC = leucocytes; AR = autosomal recessive; AD = autosomal dominant; X = sex-linked.

the erythrocytes and leucocytes of clinically normal heterozygous parents of affected children.

A moderately severe hemolytic disorder associated with a deficiency in the activity of *phosphoglycerate kinase* in both erythrocytes and leucocytes has been demonstrated in two young males in a large Chinese kindred. These boys have, in addition to hemolysis, a neurologic disorder with abnormal behavior, emotional lability, and impaired speech. Despite deficient phosphoglycerate kinase activity in the leucocytes, recurrent infections have not been a significant problem. The mode of inheritance appears to be sex-linked. A glycogen storage disease (type VII) has been observed in patients with possible myoglobinuria and mild, well-compensated hemolysis with a severe deficiency in *phosphofructokinase* activity in the muscle and a 50 percent reduction in the activity of this enzyme in the erythrocytes. A systemic disorder has not been apparent in *phosphohexose isomerase* deficiency where the leucocytes share the defect with the erythrocytes.

Glucose-6-Phosphate Dehydrogenase Deficiency
(See also 17.3)

Over 80 different variants of G6PD have been established on the basis of altered electrophoretic mo-

bilities, kinetics, or physicochemical properties of the enzyme. Many of these variants are associated with no clinical effect and no significant decrease in activity, while others are associated with mild to moderately severe hemolytic anemia even in the absence of any known precipitating agent. The three most common variants, A−, Mediterranean, and Canton, are present in erythrocytes with normal or nearly normal life-spans, but are associated with drug-induced hemolytic anemia and, in the case of the latter two, with favism. G6PD deficiency has been held responsible for an increased incidence of neonatal jaundice in some population groups. Viral and bacterial infections, such as hepatitis and pneumonia, acidosis, and other intercurrent diseases have been incriminated in the precipitation of hemolysis in deficient subjects. Significantly decreased activity of G6PD has been documented in leucocytes and other tissues with variants other than A−, but no clinical findings clearly attributable to this deficiency in the tissues have been defined.

The biochemical abnormalities in G6PD deficient erythrocytes reflect the decreased ability of the hexose monophosphate shunt to respond to stimulation. The concentrations of GSH in deficient erythrocytes are only slightly reduced, but the GSH concentrations fall dramatically upon incubation of the cells with oxidant drugs, such as acetylphenylhydrazine. The decline in the concentration of GSH under

TABLE 14. *Compounds Reported to Have Induced Hemolysis of G6PD Deficient Erythrocytes**

Agents Producing Clinically Significant Hemolysis

    Acetanilid
    2-Amino-5-sulfanilylthiazole
    Diaphenylsulfon
    Fava beans
    Furazolidone
    Furmethonol
    N-Acetylsulfanilamide
    Naldixic acid?
    Naphthalene
    Neoarsphenamine
    Nitrofurantoin
    Nitrofurazone
    Pamaquine
    Pentaquine
    Phenylhydrazine
    Primaquine
    Quinocide
    Salicylazosulfapyridine
    Sulfamethoxypyridazine
    Sulfanilamide
    Sulfapyridine
    Toluidine blue

Agents Thought to Produce Hemolysis in Presence of Other Illness

    Acetophenetidin
    Acetylsalicylic acid
    Ascorbic acid
    Chloramphenicol?
    Chloroquine
    Dimercaprol
    Menadione
    Methylene blue
    Quinacrine
    Sulfisoxazole
    Sulfoxone

*Adapted from Beutler, E., *Seminars Hemat.*, 8: (in press), 1971.

instead of aspartic acid, distinguishes the two most common variants of G6PD, B and A+, both of which have normal catalytic activity. In the Hektoen variant, which is associated with increased enzyme activity and no hemolytic disorder, tyrosine had replaced a histidine of the normal B variant. Other substitutions can be expected to be found.

Deficiencies in the activities of other enzymes in the HMP shunt pathway and related reactions have been reported. A well-compensated hemolytic process is evident in patients whose erythrocytes contain very low concentrations of GSH with a deficiency in GSH synthetase activity. The mild hemolysis in this disorder, in contrast to the much more severe hemolysis which may occur in some Caucasian patients with G6PD deficiency and nearly normal concentrations of GSH in their erythrocytes, raises several fundamental questions about the role of GSH in erythrocytes and its place in the hemolysis associated with G6PD deficiency. Although extremely low levels of 6-phosphogluconate dehydrogenase activity have been reported in the erythrocytes and leucocytes of many individuals, only a very few have had evidence of hemolysis. Thus, the cause and effect relationship between deficient 6-phosphogluconate dehydrogenase activity and hemolysis must be questioned. Since environmental modifications can have profound effects on the metabolism of erythrocytes, these factors must also be considered in studies of enzyme deficiencies. For example, decreased activity of GSSG-reductase has been noted in the erythrocytes of many patients with diverse diseases. The decreased GSSG-reductase activity can be increased markedly by the administration of riboflavin in vivo or the addition of the enzyme's coenzyme, flavin adenine dinucleotide, to the hemolysate in vitro. Treatment with riboflavin, however, has not influenced the patients' clinical courses. The relationship between GSSG-reductase deficiency and the associated diseases must therefore be reevaluated.

these conditions, as well as during a hemolytic episode, is accompanied by the formation of Heinz bodies, which probably represent denatured hemoglobin precipitated within the cell. The hemolytic properties of certain drugs (Table 14) in G6PD deficiency have been attributed to their ability to generate hydrogen peroxide, peroxyhemoglobin, or free radicals within the cells. This hypothesis, however, does not adequately explain the chronic hemolytic process in deficient individuals who have hemolysis in the absence of any known precipitating factor. The hemolytic consequences of G6PD deficiency may involve a series of simultaneous, related, or unrelated events: oxidation of GSH, oxidative denaturation of hemoglobin (Heinz bodies), lipid peroxidation, and membrane destruction with removal of the damaged erythrocytes by the reticuloendothelial system.

A single amino acid substitution, asparagine

Hereditary Methemoglobinemia with DPNH-Methemoglobin Reductase Deficiency

Hereditary methemoglobinemia not associated with an abnormality in the structure of the hemoglobin (e.g., hemoglobin M) results most often from a severe deficiency in the activity of DPNH-methemoglobin reductase. Over 260 proved or presumed instances have been described. Methemoglobinemia as high as 40 or 50 percent and impressive cyanosis may be encountered in patients with this disorder, but there is no evidence of hemolysis. Data from family and biochemical studies are consistent with an autosomal recessive mode of inheritance. Marked deficiency in activity is seen in erythrocytes of affected homozygotes, while approximately half the normal activity is usually evident in cells from acyanotic, asymptomatic heterozygous subjects. These heterozygotes, however, may be more susceptible than normal subjects to the methemoglobin-producing drugs and chemicals incriminated in toxic methemoglobinemia. The erythrocytes obtained from cord blood also have intermediate levels of DPNH-methemoglobin reductase activity. This decreased ability to reduce methemoglobin may contribute to the increased frequency of toxic methemoglobinemia in newborn infants. DPNH-methemoglobin reductase deficiency has a worldwide distribution and is particularly prevalent in inbred populations. Recent studies have demonstrated at least six different electrophoretic variants of DPNH-methemoglobin reductase. One variant is associated with only a slight decrease in activity. Thus, as is true for hemoglobin and G6PD, multiple aberrations in the DPNH-methemoglobin reductase system apparently exist, some with and some without functional consequences.

The marked cyanosis often associated with hereditary methemoglobinemia is in striking contrast to the minimal symptoms. The resulting decrease in oxygen-carrying capacity is sometimes associated with a mild compensatory erythrocytosis. When present, this erythrocytosis is usually not as great as would be expected from the degree of methemoglobinemia and the loss of oxygen-carrying capacity. Systemic symptoms are not prominent in hereditary methemoglobinemia, but an unusually high incidence of severe mental retardation has been noted in children with proved or presumed DPNH-methemoglobin reductase deficiency (21 cases in 12 different families). Less severe mental impairment has been reported in 11 children and young adults from nine other families. No satisfactory hypothesis has been proposed to explain the occurrence of variable degrees of mental retardation in only about 12 percent of patients with DPNH-methemoglobin reductase deficiency. Absence of DPNH-diaphorase (DPNH-methemoglobin reductase) has been demonstrated in the leucocytes of one child with severe mental retardation and hereditary methemoglobinemia, but the activity has been normal in the leucocytes of other similar patients.

A deficiency in TPNH-dehydrogenase (TPNH-methemoglobin reductase) activity has also been reported, but is not associated with methemoglobinemia or hemolysis.

Enzyme Deficiencies without Apparent Deleterious Effects on the Erythrocytes

The ease of obtaining erythrocytes for careful study has resulted in the discovery of numerous enzyme deficiencies and polymorphisms without apparent functional consequences for these cells. Deficient activity of catalase can be demonstrated readily in erythrocytes of affected patients. Hemolysis, however, is not apparent in acatalasemic subjects. Deficiency of galactose-1-phosphate uridyl transferase can be demonstrated in the erythrocytes of patients with galactosemia, but, except perhaps in the early newborn period, this deficiency is not associated with hemolysis. The deficiencies of enzymes demonstrable in erythrocytes associated with nonhemolytic disorders are listed in Table 15A. The alterations not known to be associated with any specific disorder are presented in Table 15B.

Enzymes of the Leucocytes

Although the examination of leucocytes has permitted the definition of several enzymatic deficiencies, none of these appears to be associated with significantly impaired leucocyte function (Table 15 C). Chronic granulomatous disease (CGD), on the other hand, appears to be a heterogeneous, genetically determined disorder of leucocyte function. CGD is usually apparent in early life and the repeated, severe bacterial infections ultimately result in death. The disease is characterized by chronic granulomatous and septic lymphadenitis with accompanying hepatosplenomegaly, inflammatory skin lesions, and recurrent pulmonary infiltrates. Osteomyelitis, pericarditis, and liver abscesses have been observed. Evidence for primary granulomatous disease (tuberculosis, brucellosis, sarcoidosis, cat scratch fever) is lacking. Immunoglobulin levels are normal, usually with increased IgG secondary to repeated infections. Complement levels and skin-window studies have been normal.

Although the phagocytic cells of the peripheral blood of patients with CGD can ingest bacteria normally, they kill them at a slower rate. The leucocytes appear normal on light and electron microscopy, but decreased degranulation and vacuole formation during phagocytosis have been described. Subsequent studies, however, have shown normal degranulation and adequate amounts of lysosomal enzymes. Leucocytes from patients with CGD fail to show the increased oxygen consumption, HMP shunt activity, and hydrogen peroxide production normally seen during phagocytosis. These cells also fail to reduce nitroblue tetrazolium (NBT) dye to formazan. The quantitative NBT test has become a useful histochemical diagnostic test when combined with quantitative bactericidal studies. DPNH oxidase has been isolated from leucocytes of guinea pigs and is believed to be the enzyme responsible for the respiratory burst during phagocytosis. This enzyme appears to be deficient in the leucocytes of some children with CGD. This deficiency has been proposed to be the basis of the metabolic abnormalities and diminished bactericidal activity. Normal DPNH oxidase activity in the leucocytes of some patients, however, has also been reported. The enzyme is cyanide insensitive and produces hydrogen peroxide. Recently, leucocyte myeloperoxidase activity, hydrogen peroxide formation, and fixation of iodine have been

TABLE 15. *Alterations in Enzymes Demonstrable in Erythrocytes and/or Leucocytes, but not Associated with Hemolytic Disorders*

A. Deficiencies in Enzymatic Activity in *Erythrocytes* Associated with Nonhemolytic Disorders

Enzyme	Associated Clinical Disorder
DPNH-methemoglobin reductase*	Hereditary methemoglobinemia
Catalase*	Acatalasemia
Galactose-1-phosphate uridyl transferase*	Galactosemia
Galactokinase	Galactose diabetes
TPN-linked xylitol dehydrogenase	Pentosuria
2,3-DPG phosphatase (?)	Cerebral dysgenesis, muscle hypotonia
Argininosuccinase*	Argininosuccinic aciduria
Amylo-1,6-glucosidase*	Type III glycogen storage disease
Amylo-1,4→1,6-transglucosylase*	Type IV glycogen storage disease
Orotodylic pyrophosphorylase Orotodylic decarboxylase*	Orotic aciduria
Hypoxanthine-guanine phosphoribosyl transferase*	Lesch-Nyhan syndrome; some cases of gout

B. Alterations in Enzymatic Activity or Electrophoretic Mobility in *Erythrocytes* without Known Disease

TPNH-methemoglobin reductase†
Carbonic anhydrase*
Glyoxylase
Phosphoglucomutase*
Malic dehydrogenase*
Lactic dehydrogenase*
Adenine phosphoribosyl transferase
Adenylate kinase*‡
Diphosphopyridine nucleotidase
Acid phosphatase†
Nonspecific carboxylesterases
Acetylcholinesterase§

C. Deficiencies in Enzymatic Activity in *Leucocytes* Associated with Nonhematologic Disorders

Glucocerebroside-cleaving enzyme	Gaucher's disease
Sphingomyelin-cleaving enzyme	Niemann-Pick disease
N-Acetyl hexosaminidase A	Tay-Sachs disease
Branched-chain amino acid decarboxylase	Maple syrup urine disease
Ketoacid decarboxylase	Intermittent branched-chain ketonuria
Galactosidase (ceramide trihexosidase?)	Fabry's disease
Galactocerebroside-β-galactosidase	Krabbe's globoid cell leucodystrophy
Isovaleryl coenzyme A dehydrogenase	Isovaleric acidemia
Valine transaminase	Hypervalinemia
Methylmalonic coenzyme A isomerase	Methylmalonic aciduria (B_{12} refractory)
Methylmalonic coenzyme A mutase	Methylmalonic aciduria (B_{12} responsive)
Propionyl coenzyme A carboxylase	Ketotic hyperglycinemia
Glycerate dehydrogenase	Nephrolithiasis
Pyruvate decarboxylase	Intermittent ataxic syndrome
Lysosomal-α-glucosidase	Type II glycogen storage disease
Phosphorylase	Type VI glycogen storage disease
Alkaline phosphatase	Hypophosphatasia
Acid phosphatase	Acid phosphatase deficiency
Arylsulfatase A	Metachromatic leucodystrophy

*Abnormality may be demonstrable in leucocytes.
†Activity decreased in some erythrocytes also deficient in G6PD activity.
‡Severe deficiency may be associated with mild hemolysis.
§Activity decreased in erythrocytes in paroxysmal nocturnal hemoglobinuria.

linked with bactericidal activity. Lactobacilli which produce hydrogen peroxide are killed normally by CGD leucocytes. Fixation of iodine and bactericidal activity against *Serratia marcescens* are defective; this organism does not produce hydrogen peroxide in excess of its capacity to destroy the compound. Pa-

tients with CGD have not been troubled by infections with lactobacilli, pneumococci, or streptococci (hydrogen peroxide-formers), but low-grade pathogens, such as *Klebsiella-Aerobacter* and *Serratia*, have been isolated frequently from these patients.

Despite amelioration of the infections by the

vigorous use of antibiotics, there is no satisfactory treatment for this disorder.

Because the first 28 cases were males, CGD was felt to be a sex-linked, hereditary disorder. More recently, females with a similar clinical syndrome have been described, and the activity of GSH peroxidase in the leucocytes of two such patients was shown to be significantly diminished. Using radioautography, the mothers of male CGD patients were found to have two populations of leucocytes: one which fixed iodine and one which did not. This observation was consistent with earlier findings of two populations of cells with respect to NBT reduction. Leucocytes from the fathers, however, also had decreased ability to reduce NBT and impaired bactericidal activity. The variability in the abnormalities demonstrable in patients with CGD and in presumed carriers has indicated the probable genetic heterogeneity of this disorder. One type may be sex-linked, while another may be due to an autosomal recessive gene.

Leucocyte Alkaline Phosphatase
(See also 17.8)

Leucocyte alkaline phosphatase (LAP) activity is consistently reduced in patients with typical chronic myelogenous leukemia. In this disease, the Philadelphia chromosome (deletion of the small arm of chromosome 21) is present in all hematopoietic cells of the bone marrow but not in skin fibroblasts, findings consistent with the concept that the disorder is acquired. LAP activity often rises in the blastic crises seen terminally in chronic myelogenous leukemia, without disappearance of the abnormal Philadelphia chromosome. LAP activity is also elevated in active Hodgkin's disease and in Down's syndrome (trisomy 21)

where it has been correlated with accelerated turnover of leucocytes. No consistent chromosomal abnormalities, however, have been seen in the former disorder. Low LAP activities have been found in juvenile chronic myelogenous leukemia where the Philadelphia chromosome defect is absent. Thus, the relationship between the chromosomal abnormalities and the leucocyte enzyme activity is, at present, uncertain.

REFERENCES

Baehner, R. L., and Karnovsky, M. L. Deficiency of reduced nicotinamide-adenine dinucleotide oxidase in chronic granulomatous disease. Science, 162:1277, 1968.

Beutler, E., ed. Hereditary Disorders of Erythrocyte Metabolism. New York, Grune and Stratton, Inc., 1968.

Good, R. A., Quie, P. G., Windhorst, D. B., Page, A. R., Rodey, G. E., White, J., Wolfson, J. J., and Holmes, B. H. Fatal (chronic) granulomatous disease of childhood: a hereditary defect of leukocyte function. Seminars Hemat., 5:215, 1968.

Holmes, B., Park, B. H., Malawista, S. E., Quie, P. G., Nelson, D. L., and Good, R. A. Chronic granulomatous disease in females. A deficiency of leukocyte glutathione peroxidase. New Eng. J. Med., 283:217, 1970.

Hsia, D. Y.-Y. Use of white blood cells and cultured somatic cells in clinical genetic disorders. Clin. Genet., 1:5, 1970.

Jaffé, E. R. Hereditary hemolytic disorders and enzymatic deficiencies of human erythrocytes. Blood, 35:116, 1970.

―――― and Hsieh, H.-S. DPNH-methemoglobin reductase deficiency and hereditary methemoglobinemia. Seminars Hemat., 8:417, 1971.

Stanbury, J. B., Wyngaarden, J. B., and Fredrickson, D. S., eds. The Metabolic Basis of Inherited Disease, 3rd ed. New York, McGraw-Hill Book Co., 1971.

Yunis, J. J., ed. Biochemical Methods in Red Cell Genetics. New York, Academic Press, Inc., 1969.

Other Anomalies of Metabolism

8.13
MUCOPOLYSACCHARIDOSES

B. SHANNON DANES

Acid mucopolysaccharides are one of the primary constituents of the extracellular matrix synthesized by connective tissue cells. Disorders involving their synthesis or structure may lead to developmental changes recognized as an abnormal clinical phenotype known as a genetic mucopolysaccharidosis.

Chemistry

In 1884 Krukenberg isolated material from the extracellular matrix which he chemically identified as a polysaccharide and named chondroitic acid. Not until 1938 was the term mucopolysaccharide suggested by Meyer to describe "hexosamine-containing polysaccharides of animal origin occurring either in a pure state or conjugated with protein through a salt linkage." Several chemically different acid mucopolysaccharides are known to occur in specific con-

TABLE 16.   *Mucopolysaccharides of Connective Tissue*

Compound	Amino Sugar	Uronic Acid	Sulfate*	Tissue Occurrence
Hyaluronic acid	Glucosamine	Glucuronic acid	0	Vitreous humor, Wharton's jelly, synovial fluid
Chondroitin sulfate A	Galactosamine	Glucuronic acid	1	Cartilage
Chondroitin sulfate B (dermatan sulfate)	Galactosamine	Iduronic acid	1	Skin, blood vessels
Chondroitin sulfate C	Galactosamine	Glucuronic acid	1	Cartilage
Keratosulfate	Glucosamine	Galactose	1	Cartilage
Heparitin sulphate	Glucosamine	Glucuronic acid Iduronic acid	1	Aorta Liver

*Moles per disaccharide repeating unit.

nective tissues (Table 16). The exact macromolecular structure of the polysaccharide-protein complex is not known and probably shows considerable structural heterogeneity. The biosynthesis is thought to be a three-step process: (1) synthesis of the protein core on the ribosome; (2) a sequential addition of monosaccharide residues from appropriate sugar nucleotide precursors; and (3) sulfation via phosphoadenosine-5'-phosphosulfate. Steps two and three are presumed to occur in the membrane of the endoplasmic reticulum and Golgi apparatus.

Little is known about the catabolism of sulphated mucopolysaccharides although it is evident that lysosomes are involved. It appears from cell culture studies that two pools of mucopolysaccharides occur within a cell, a secretory one which is small and turns over rapidly, and a large separate storage pool which turns over slowly.

In 1952 Brante isolated from the liver of two patients with the Hurler syndrome a substance with the properties of dermatan sulfate (chondroitin sulfate B) and suggested that the Hurler syndrome is an inborn error of mucopolysaccharide metabolism. In 1957 Dorfman and Lorincz demonstrated that two mucopolysaccharides, dermatan sulfate and heparitin sulphate, were found in excess amounts in the urine of patients with the Hurler syndrome. Independently, Meyer and his colleagues found the same excessive mucopolysacchariduria.

CLINICAL FEATURES. Since the first definitive clinical description of this disorder by Hunter and Hurler, it has become apparent that several distinct disorders can be recognized, reflecting genetically transmitted disorders of acid mucopolysaccharide metabolism resulting in visceral storage of dermatan sulfate and heparitin sulphate. In the brain there is also excessive cerebral storage of gangliosides GM_1, GM_2, and GM_3.

The general clinical features (Figs. 13 and 14) of this group of disorders are dwarfism, skeletal deformities, restriction of joint movements, deafness, abdominal hernias, hepatosplenomegaly, cardiac abnormalities, and usually mental retardation. The amount of mucopolysaccharides excreted in the urine may be increased or in the normal range (3 to 24 mg/24 hr) depending on the type (Table 17). Metachromatic inclusions are seen in the white blood cells in the peripheral blood and bone marrow.

There is a wide variation of these and other physical and laboratory findings reflecting storage of mucopolysaccharides in specific organs.

Based on clinical, genetic, and biochemical studies, six distinct types have been delineated and a classification evolved by McKusick.

TYPE I (HURLER SYNDROME). This autosomal recessive disorder is associated with mental and physical deterioration in the newborn period. Diagnosis is usually made in the first year. Clinical features include gargoyle-like facies with coarse features, lumbar gibbus, hydrocephalus, stiff joints, claw hands, excessive body hair, chest deformities, early and progressive clouding of cornea, and mental retardation. Dermatan sulfate and heparitin sulphate are found in excessive amounts in the urine. Growth and development are markedly impaired, leading to death in childhood.

TYPE II (HUNTER SYNDROME). This X-linked recessive disorder is usually less severe than type I. As in type I the striking clinical features are stiff joints, dwarfing, hepatosplenomegaly, and gross facial appearance. Similarly, dermatan sulfate and heparitin sulphate are increased in the urine. Features which distinguish type II from I are absence of gibbus and clear corneas. Deafness and mental retardation are not as profound as in type I but are progressive. Affected males usually live into adulthood, dying of cardiopulmonary impairment.

TYPE III (SANFILIPPO SYNDROME). The clinical features of this autosomal recessive syndrome are central nervous system involvement including mental retardation with only moderate somatic changes. Heparitin sulphate is increased in the urine. Meyer and Hoffman found that heparitin sulphate is found normally in liver and not in bone and cartilage. This

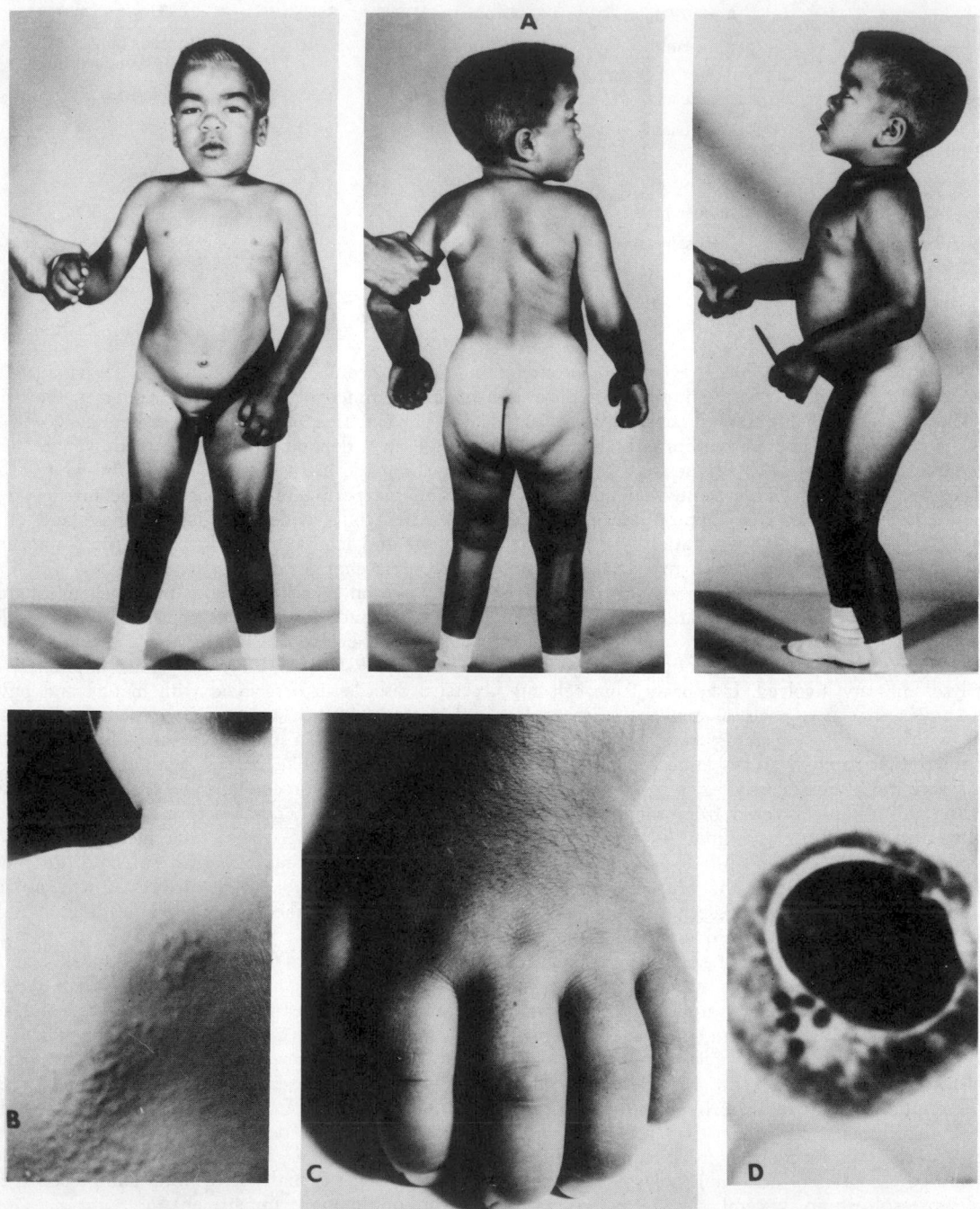

Fig. 13. Child with mucopolysaccharidosis type II (Hunter syndrome). *A.* General features. *B.* Nodular skin lesions on back thorax. *C.* Clawhands. *D.* White blood cell from peripheral blood showing metachromatic cytoplasmic inclusions.

may explain the minimal skeletal abnormalities in this type but raises the question of the role of heparitin sulphate in mental retardation. Because of minimal body impairment, patients live into adulthood. Severe mental retardation usually makes institutionalization necessary.

TYPE IV (MORQUIO SYNDROME). The Morquio syndrome has been recognized as a distinct clinical

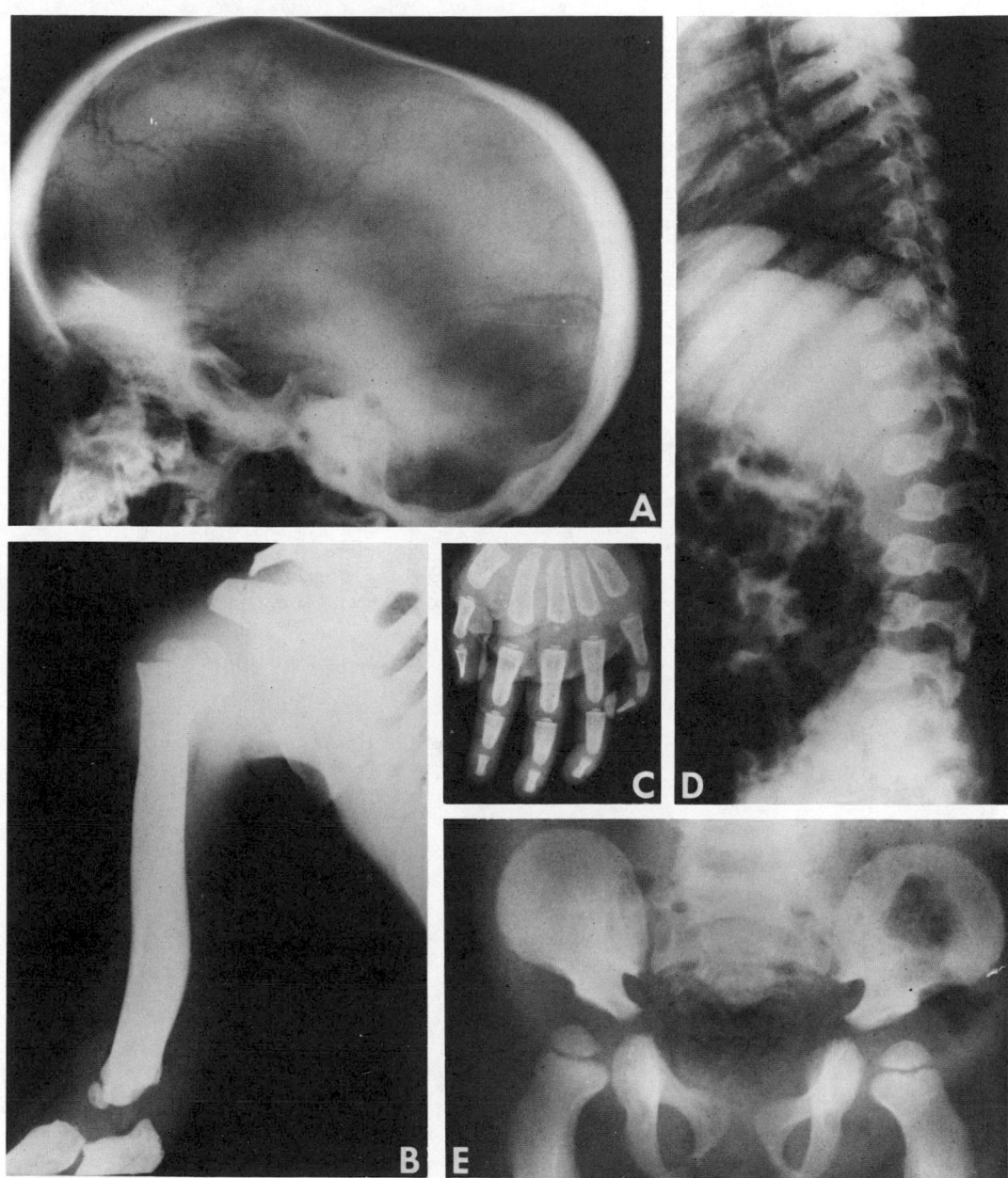

Fig. 14. Radiographic findings in the child shown in Figure 13, with mucopolysaccharidosis type II (Hunter syndrome). A. Skull. Lateral view is scaphocephalic (usually due to sagittal suture synostosis). The sella turcica is elongated as a result of deep erosion of the sphenoid bone. The frontal and occipital areas of the diploic space is thickened. B. Humerus. Varus configuration of the humeral neck, widening of the shaft, thick cortex, tapering of the distal shaft. C. Hands. The phalanges may be stubby and thick but the characteristic finding is the broad distal end of the metacarpals, which taper proximally. D. Lateral spine. Lumbar kyphos, beaking of lumbar vertebrae. Ribs are wide anteriorly. (On a frontal projection of the chest the ribs would be seen to taper posteriorly). E. Pelvis. Coxa valga at the proximal ends of the femurs is commonly seen. The acetabular cavities are usually shallow and the bases of the ilia are narrowed.

chondrodystrophy since Morquio's and Brailsford's descriptions in 1929. It was later considered to be a connective tissue disorder involving an inborn error of mucopolysaccharide metabolism, particularly keratosulphate.

Since the first description of the Morquio syn-

TABLE 17. *Characteristics of the Various Types of Mucopolysaccharidoses*

Type (McKusick)	Eponym	Clinical Features			Metachromasia in WBC	Mode of Inheritance	Urinary Mucopolysaccharides	Cell Culture		β-Galactosidase Activity
		Physical Involvement	Mental Retardation	Cloudy Cornea				Metachromasia	Uronic Acid	
I	Hurler	+++	+++	+++	Present	Autosomal Recessive	Dermatan sulphate Heparitin	Present	↑	→
II	Hunter	++	+	−	Present	X-linked Recessive	Dermatan sulfate Heparatin sulfate	Present	↑	→
III	Sanfilippo	+	+++	−	Present	Autosomal Recessive	Heparatin sulfate	Present	↑	→
IV	Morquio	+++	+/−	++	Rare	Autosomal Recessive	Keratosulphate	+/−	↑	
V	Scheie	+	+/−	+++	Rare	Autosomal Recessive	Dermatan sulfate	Present	↑	
VI	Maroteaux-Lamy	+++	−	+	Numerous	Autosomal Recessive	Dermatan sulfate	Absent	Normal	
(VII)	I cell disease	+++	+++	+++	Absent	Autosomal Recessive	−	Present	↑	→
(VIII)	Lipomucopoly-saccharidoses	+++	+++	+/−	Absent (vacuoles)	Autosomal Recessive	−	Present	↑	↑

Key to symbols: − absent, +/− mild or absent, + mild, ++ moderate, +++ severe, ↑ increased, ↓ decreased.

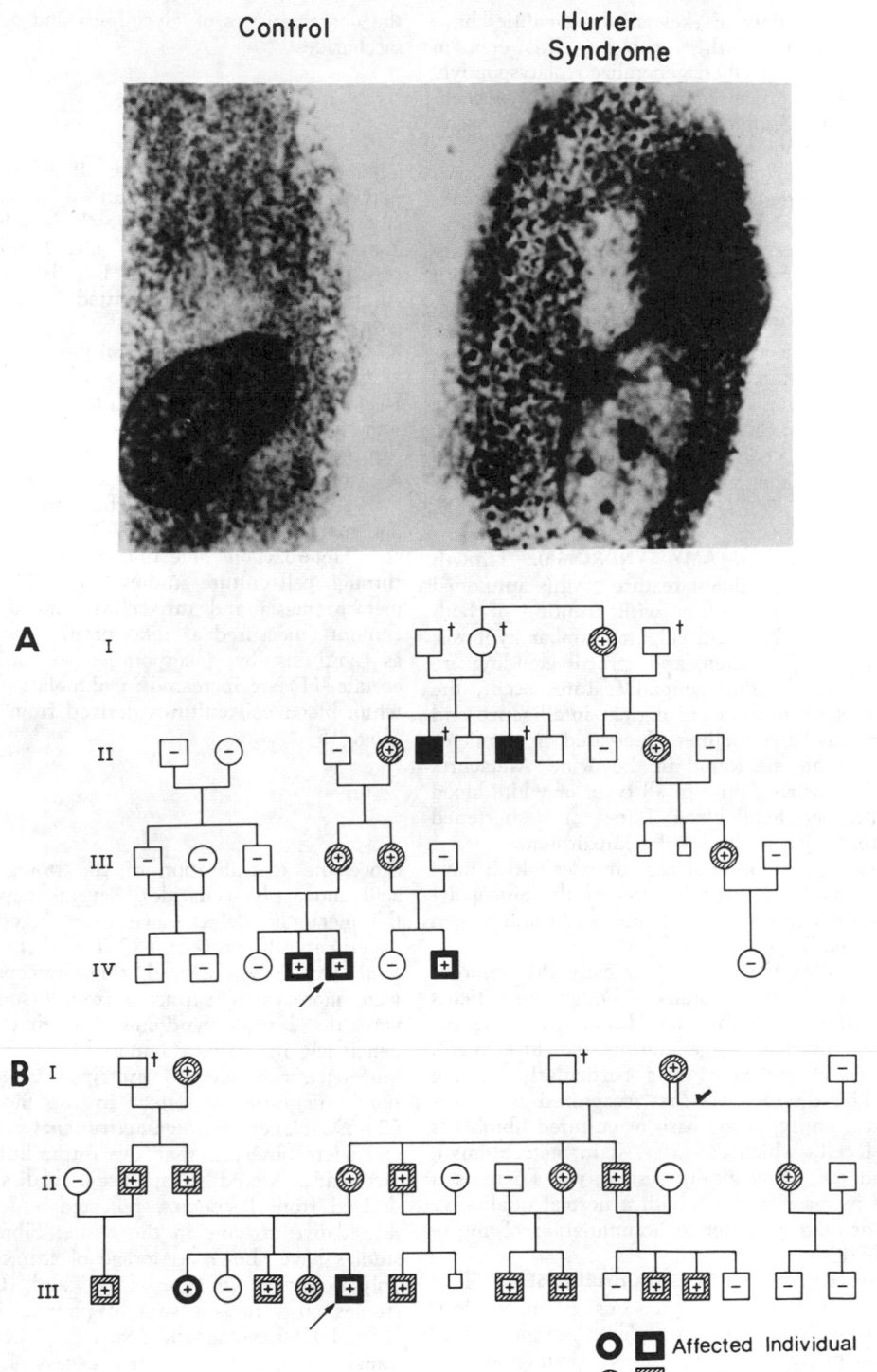

Fig. 15. Cultured skin fibroblasts stained for metachromasia (with toluidine blue O). Fibroblast from normal individual (normal) showed no metachromasia (stained blue); fibroblast from patient with the Hurler syndrome showed marked metachromasia (stained pink). Pedigrees of family A (Hunter syndrome) and family B (Hurler syndrome) based on studies on skin fibroblasts in cell culture. Homozygote and heterozygote status determined on metachromasia and uronic acid content of cells. (From Danes and Bearn. *Lancet*, 1:241, 1967.)

drome, a wide variety of skeletal abnormalities have been included under this eponym. This eponym should only be used when generalized platyspondyly associated with corneal opacities, dental abnormalities, aortic regurgitation, and usually urinary excretion of keratosulphate is present. These patients can be distinguished from the other mucopolysaccharidoses by the presence of distinct skeletal abnormalities and the absence of mental retardation, deafness, and gargoyle facies. Orthopedic and cardiopulmonary problems are the main clinical problems during adult life.

TYPE V (SCHEIE SYNDROME). This autosomal recessive syndrome has the least severe clinical manifestations. Stiff joints, coarse facies, cloudy cornea, and aortic regurgitation occur. The patients show the other general clinical stigmata to a minimal degree, with intelligence being usually normal. Increased amounts of dermatan sulfate are found in the urine. Decreased vision is the clinical problem in adults with this type.

TYPE VI (MAROTEAUX-LAMY SYNDROME). Growth retardation is the dominant feature of this autosomal recessive disorder. Dwarfism with stunting of both the trunk and limbs, genu valgum, lumbar kyphosis, anterior sternal protrusion, and corneal clouding are present. Although other general features occur, the distinctive characteristics are normal intelligence and severe osseous abnormalities. Increased amounts of dermatan sulfate are found in the urine. Metachromatic inclusions are found in all types of white blood cells of the peripheral blood. Life-span is shortened due to progressive cardiovascular impairment.

Recently, a group of storage diseases which have the clinical and radiologic features of the mucopolysaccharidoses without mucopolysacchariduria has been observed (see Types VII and VIII).

TYPE VII (I CELL DISEASE). Clinically this disorder resembles the Hurler syndrome although the patients are dwarfed at birth (in the Hurler syndrome patients are unusually large during the first year). Hyperplasia of the gums is a particularly striking feature. This disorder was first recognized as a separate clinical entity on the basis of cultured fibroblasts (named I cell) which are large, stain metachromatically, and are histologically distinctive. There is a threefold increase in lipids with a normal qualitative distribution and a moderate accumulation of mucopolysaccharides.

TYPE VIII (LIPOMUCOPOLYSACCHARIDOSES). This group, representing a heterogeneous group of disorders, has in common: gargoylelike dysmorphism, skeletal dysplasia, slowly progressive peripheral neuropathy with myelin degeneration, muscular weakness and incoordination, and moderate mental retardation. Laboratory findings include metachromatically staining material in the urinary sediment, vacuolization of lymphocytes with occasional metachromatic granules, coarsely vacuolated and granulated reticulohistiocytic cells in the bone marrow, and metachromatic myelin degeneration of peripheral nerves. Storage substances in mesenchymal and neural cells have the characteristics of glycolipids and acid mucopolysaccharides.

Genetics

The mode of inheritance for all the types of mucopolysaccharidoses so far described is autosomal recessive except for type II, which is inherited in an X-linked recessive fashion. The frequency for all types is very rare, less than 1 in 100,000 newborns. All types are widely distributed in all major ethnic groups.

Type II appears to be only one-fifth as frequent as type I. In the case of the X-linked recessive type II, one-third arise by new mutation in the X-chromosome which is transmitted to the affected son by his mother, and two-thirds from mutation of the X-chromosome occuring in earlier generations.

Analyses of karyotypes have shown that number and morphology are normal.

Heterozygote detection has been made possible through cell culture studies (Fig. 15). Both cellular metachromasia and intracellular mucopolysaccharide content (measured as total uronic acid content and as synthesis by incorporation of sulfate-^{35}S and acetate-^{3}H) are increased in fibroblast and peripheral white blood cell cultures derived from heterozygotes (Fig. 15).

Pathogenesis

Since the identification of the storage material as acid mucopolysaccharides, several explanations for the metabolic defect have been suggested but not experimentally proved: (1) *Defect in binding protein.* Dorfman observed that mucopolysaccharides were more easily extracted from tissues of patients with the Hurler syndrome and that there was a deficiency in serine (important in the linkage of mucopolysaccharides to proteins) in such preparations, suggesting a defect in the binding protein. (2) *Deficiency of degradative enzymes.* Van Hoof and Hers observed that the intracellular mucopolysaccharides stored in inclusion bodies, presumably derived from lysosomes, reflected a deficiency of a degradative enzyme in the tissue. Fibroblast culture studies have shown a storage of intracellular mucopolysaccharides in types I, II, and III. Enzymatic studies on various tissues of patients with types I, II, and III have shown a specific deficiency of lysosomal beta-galactosidase and excess of activity of a number of other lysosomal enzymes. The relationship of beta-galactosidase deficiency to the fundamental defect is obscure.

REFERENCES

Danes, B. S., and Bearn, A. G. Hurler's syndrome: A genetic study in cell culture. J. Exp. Med., 123:1, 1966.

Dorfman, A. Metabolism of the acid mucopolysaccharides. Biophys. J. (Suppl.), 4:155, 1964.

Fratantoni, J. C., Hall, C. W., and Neufeld, E. F. The defect in Hurler's and Hunter's syndromes: Faulty degradation of mucopolysaccharide. Proc. Nat. Acad. Sci. U.S.A., 60:699, 1968.

Ho, M. W., and O'Brien, J. S. Hurler's syndrome: Deficiency of a specific beta galactosidase isoenzyme. Science, 165:611, 1969.

Matalon, R., and Dorfman, A. Hurler's syndrome: Biosynthesis of acid mucopolysaccharides in tissue culture. Proc. Nat. Acad. Sci. U.S.A., 56:1310, 1966.

McKusick, V. A. Heritable Disorders of Connective Tissue, 3rd ed. St. Louis, C. V. Mosby Co., 1966, pp. 325-399.

8.14
THE PORPHYRIAS

NECHAMA S. KOSOWER

The porphyrias may be defined as a diverse group of disorders, for the most part hereditary, in which a significant increase in production, accumulation, and excretion of porphyrins and/or their precursors occurs, in association with specific, characteristic clinical entities. These conditions must be distinguished from a variety of disorders, such as liver diseases and anemias, in which some moderate accumulation and increased excretion of porphyrins can be found as a secondary manifestation which is of no apparent clinical significance.

Metabolism of Porphyrins

Porphyrins are cyclic tetrapyrrole compounds, which are widely distributed in nature as metal chelates with either iron, magnesium, or cobalt to give rise to hemes, chlorophylls, and cobalamines. Heme, in the form of hemoprotein complexes, plays an essential role in the transport of oxygen and in oxidative metabolism (e.g., hemoglobin, catalase, cytochromes).

The sequence of steps in the biosynthesis of porphyrins is shown in Figure 16. The first step is the condensation of glycine and succinyl CoA to form deltaaminolevulinic acid (ALA). The condensation is catalyzed by ALA synthetase, and requires pyridoxal phosphate as a cofactor. In a second step two molecules of ALA are condensed to form the monopyrrole porphobilinogen (PBG). This reaction is catalyzed by ALA dehydrase, an enzyme sensitive to thiol group inhibition.

PBG is polymerized to the cyclic tetrapyrrole uroporphyrinogen. Of the four possible uroporphyrinogen isomers, I and III are formed enzymatically in biologic systems. Only isomer III serves as a precursor for heme synthesis. For the formation of uroporphyrinogen III from PBG, two enzymes are required: uroporphyrinogen I synthetase and uroporphyrinogen III cosynthetase. In the presence of uroporphyrinogen I synthetase alone, only uroporphyrinogen I is formed. The formation of uroporphyrinogen III requires both enzymes, which can easily be distinguished by their susceptibility to heat inactivation. Successive decarboxylation of the four acetic acid side chains of uroporphyrinogen leads to the formation of coproporphyrinogen, apparently by a single enzyme. The colorless porphyrinogens can be oxidized to colored by-products, porphyrins, which are not intermediates for heme synthesis. Coproporphyrinogen III is converted by decarboxylation and oxidation to protoporphyrin IX, in reactions requiring molecular oxygen. The last step is the incorporation of iron into protoporphyrin IX by ferrochelatase, a sulfhydryl-sensitive enzyme. The first step and the last two steps in the pathway, i.e., ALA, protoporphyrin, and heme formation, are carried out in the mitochondria. The intermediate reactions are catalyzed by cytoplasmic enzymes.

ALA, PBG, and the porphyrinogens are colorless. The porphyrins are colored, absorb strongly at about 400 mμ, and when excited at this wavelength, fluoresce intensely around 620 mμ, emitting bright red light. ALA, PBG, and uroporphyrin are excreted in the urine (traces of uroporphyrin are excreted in feces). Coproporphyrin is excreted both in the urine and in the feces, and protoporphyrin only in the feces.

The capacity to synthesize heme is shared by all aerobic cells. The actual rates of synthesis and amounts of heme present, however, vary considerably. Most of the heme in the body is synthesized in erythroid cells for the formation of hemoglobin. Liver cells contain only a fraction of 1 percent of the amount of heme present in erythrocytes. Thus, mechanisms exist which regulate the synthesis of heme according to the function of the cell, in correlation with the rates of synthesis of the cellular apoproteins to which heme is bound. Under physiologic conditions, no appreciable accumulation of intermediates, nor overproduction of the end product, heme, occurs. The major rate-controlling step in heme biosynthesis appears to be the first reaction in the pathway, catalyzed by ALA synthetase. Two types of control mechanism have been shown to operate at this step: (1) inhibition of the enzymatic activity by the end product, heme, and (2) repression of synthesis of new enzyme molecules by heme, so that only low levels of ALA synthetase exist normally in most tissues. The formation of this enzyme can be increased by a variety of exogenous (i.e., drugs) and endogenous (i.e., some steroid metabolites) compounds. The induction of this enzyme might be of importance in some entities among the porphyrias.

Classification of the Porphyrias

The porphyrias are divided into two major categories: (1) Erythropoietic porphyrias, associated with dis-

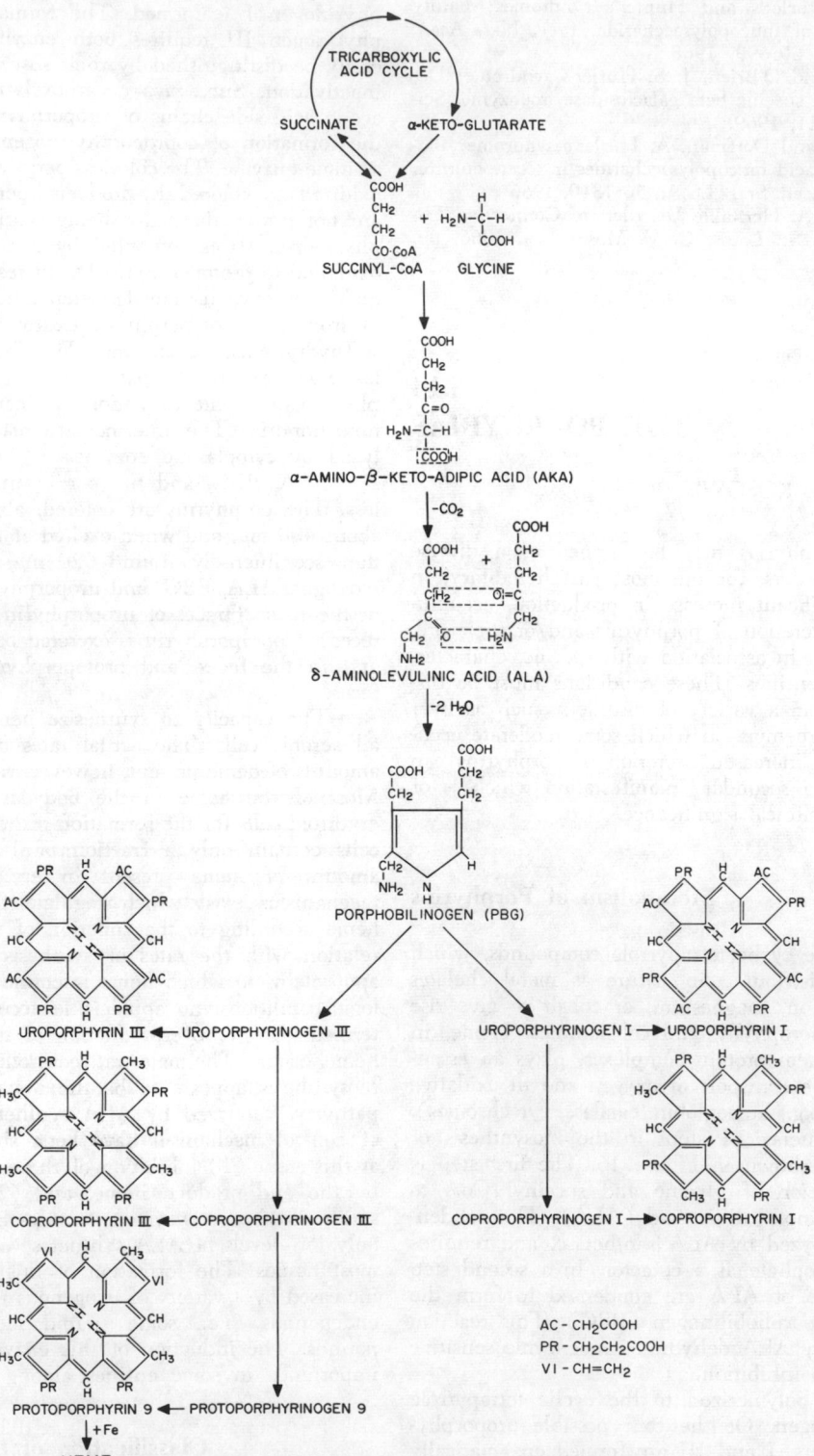

Fig. 16. Steps in the biosynthesis of porphyrins.

turbances of porphyrin metabolism mainly in the bone marrow; and (2) Hepatic porphyrias, disorders in which the liver appears to be the main site of altered porphyrin metabolism. This classification and the further division into entities are based upon clinical, biochemical, and genetic characteristics. It should be emphasized, however, that since the primary lesions and the mechanisms leading to the clinical manifestations are for the most part poorly understood, the following classification, accepted presently, may have to be changed with future knowledge.

I. Erythropoietic porphyrias
  A. Congenital erythropoietic porphyria (Günther's disease)
  B. Erythropoietic protoporphyria
  C. Erythropoietic coproporphyria

II. Hepatic porphyrias
  A. Acute intermittent porphyria (Swedish type)
  B. Mixed porphyria ("variegate," South African type)
  C. Hepatic hereditary coproporphyria
  D. Cutaneous porphyria (hereditary and acquired)

The main clinical and biochemical features of the porphyrias are summarized in Table 18.

Erythropoietic Porphyrias

Congenital Erythropoietic Porphyria (*Günther's Disease*)

This is a rare disease, which is characterized by cutaneous manifestations, splenomegaly, hemolytic anemia, and increased amounts of porphyrins in tissues, urine, and feces. Cutaneous lesions usually become apparent during infancy or early childhood, and consist of erythema, swelling, vesicles, and bullae which appear on the parts of the body exposed to sunlight either directly or through regular glass. The vesicles may contain porphyrins, the presence of which is demonstrated by the red fluorescence when inspected under Wood's ultraviolet light. The vesicles frequently become infected, with slow healing, resulting in marked scarring, pigmentation, and deformities. Eventual extensive mutilation of hands and face may result. Hypertrichosis is also found frequently. Teeth, which have a brown discoloration in ordinary light, show a red fluorescence when examined under Wood's light.

Splenomegaly and hemolytic anemia occur frequently. The anemia may fluctuate in severity in any patient, but is usually not marked. Hemolysis is reflected in elevated reticulocyte levels, erythroid hyperplasia of the bone marrow, and increased excretion of urobilinogen. There is a significant increase in the formation of "early labeled" bile pigment,

which may be derived from abnormal erythroid cells being destroyed either in the bone marrow or shortly after entering the circulation. Morphologic abnormalities in nuclear structure of some of the developing erythroid cells and increased porphyrin content of nuclei and cytoplasm of these cells (demonstrated by the red fluorescence of these cells when excited at $400 \text{ m}\mu$) have been demonstrated and might account for the accelerated destruction and the high amounts of porphyrins released into the circulation and tissues. The exact mechanisms for the hemolysis are, however, not known.

The first sign suggesting the presence of erythropoietic porphyria may be the excretion of red urine at birth or during the first year of life. The intensity of the color depends on the urinary concentration of porphyrins, which can vary from time to time. Porphyrins of the type I isomer, mainly uroporphyrin, are excreted in markedly increased amounts. Some increase in the excretion of type III isomer is also found. The excretion of ALA and PBG is normal.

GENETICS. Erythropoietic porphyria is inherited as an autosomal recessive trait. The disease is clinically manifested in homozygotes; individuals who are heterozygous exhibit neither clinical abnormalities nor increased porphyrin excretion. However, heterozygote detection might be possible in some cases; uroporphyrin I, normally absent in red cells, has been demonstrated in red cells of parents and some siblings of several patients. The abnormality seems to be overtly expressed only in the hematopoietic system and to involve overproduction of porphyrins of type I and type III, but with great preponderance of type I. A deficiency in uroporphyrinogen III cosynthetase activity, demonstrated under certain experimental conditions, has been proposed as the primary genetic lesion. However, such a lesion would not account for the increase found in isomers III. An alternate suggested possibility is an increase in uroporphyrinogen I synthetase activity, resulting from a primary lesion affecting a regulator gene. The actual primary genetic lesion is, thus, still unknown.

TREATMENT. Splenectomy has been of significant value in some patients and has been attended by arrest of the hemolytic process, diminshed erythroid hyperplasia, diminished synthesis and accumulation of porphyrin, and improvement in skin photosensitivity. In other patients, however, no significant improvement occurred. Treatment is otherwise limited to general supportive measures and protection from sunlight by means of clothing and skin ointments.

Erythropoietic Protoporphyria

This entity is more common than congenital erythropoietic porphyria, from which it differs markedly in clinical, biochemical, and genetic properties. Erythropoietic protoporphyria is characterized by photosensitivity with generally mild skin manifestations asso-

TABLE 18. *Manifestations of the Different Types of Porphyrias in Man*

Form	Inheritance	Clinical Manifestations	Biochemical Findings*
Congenital erythropoietic porphyria	Autosomal recessive	Photosensitivity, severe dermatitis, hemolytic anemia, splenomegaly, erythrodontia. Observed in early infancy and persistent through childhood and adult life.	Increased amounts of uroporphyrin and coproporphyrin, mainly type I, in bone marrow, erythrocytes, plasma, urine, and feces.
Erythropoietic protoporphyria	Autosomal dominant with variable expression	Photosensitivity, mild dermatitis. Usually first observed during childhood.	Increased amounts of protoporphyrin in bone marrow, erythrocytes, plasma, and feces.
Erythropoietic coproporphyria	Autosomal dominant with variable expression	Similar to erythropoietic protoporphyria.	Increased amounts of coproporphyrin in red cells and plasma. Increased amounts of protoporphyrin in feces.
Acute intermittent porphyria (Swedish type)	Autosomal dominant with variable expression	Acute attacks of abdominal colic, hypertension, nervous system involvement, no photosensitivity. Usually after puberty.	Increased urinary excretion of ALA and PBG during attacks and usually also during remission.
Mixed porphyria (South African type)	Autosomal dominant with variable expression	Photosensitivity and dermatitis, acute attacks of abdominal and neurologic manifestations. Usually after puberty.	Increased amounts of copro- and protoporphyrin in feces during attacks and remission; increased urinary excretion of ALA and PBG and porphyrins during acute attacks.
Hereditary hepatic coproporphyria	Autosomal dominant with variable expression	Photosensitivity (rare); gastrointestinal, neurologic, and psychiatric manifestations similar to those in AIP. Any age group.	Increased amounts of coproporphyrin III in feces and urine; excessive urinary excretion of ALA and PBG during acute attacks.
Cutaneous porphyria 1. Hereditary	Autosomal dominant with variable expression	Photosensitivity and dermatitis. Usually in adults.	Increased excretion of urinary uroporphyrin and coproporphyrin; fecal coproporphyrin and protoporphyrin normal or slightly increased.
2. Acquired	—	Photosensitivity and dermatitis. Children and adults affected.	

*Normal values (established for adults)

Urine µg/24 hr
ALA	<3,000
PBG	<1,500
Uroporphyrin	<40
Coproporphyrin	<300

Feces µg/g dry weight
| Coproporphyrin | <40 |
| Protoporphyrin | <50 |

Erythrocytes µg/100 ml
Uroporphyrin	0
Coproporphyrin	<2
Protoporphyrin	<60

Plasma µg/100 ml
| Total porphyrin | <1 |

ciated with increased accumulation and excretion of protoporphyrin. The photosensitivity usually becomes apparent in early childhood. The cutaneous manifestations may appear after a very short exposure to sunlight, and include pruritus, burning, erythema, and edema. A severe itching or burning sensation, lasting for hours or days, may be the only manifestation, but usually early erythema develops, followed by diffuse edema of the exposed parts. An urticaria may also occur. A vesicular eruption is sometimes seen, especially on the nose and cheeks, around the mouth, and on the dorsum of the hands. Chronic changes in the skin, such as thickening and mild scarring, may occur, but no deformities, hirsutism, erythrodontia, or marked pigmentary changes occur. Anemia and splenomegaly are absent.

A variable number of erythrocytes and the cytoplasm of nucleated cells in the bone marrow, exposed to ultraviolet light at about 400 mμ, exhibit red fluorescence which fades rapidly. Photohemolysis in vitro occurs after irradiation of red cells of these patients or of normal irradiated red cells suspended in protoporphyrin solution. The concentration of protoporphyrin in erythrocytes and in the plasma is elevated, and excretion of protoporphyrin (and less commonly coproporphyrin) in the feces is increased. Excretion of porphyrins in the urine is within normal limits, and no abnormal coloration of the urine is observed.

GENETICS.   Erythropoietic protoporphyria appears to be inherited as an autosomal dominant trait, with some family members manifesting the clinical disease and others presenting only the biochemical abnormalities. The primary biochemical lesion responsible for erythropoietic protoporphyria is not known. There is no impairment in the conversion of protoporphyrin to heme. The observed increase in protoporphyrin appears to be the result of overproduction of porphyrins in the bone marrow, though overproduction of hepatic protoporphyrin may also play a part.

TREATMENT.   Treatment consists in preventing undue exposure to sunlight with the aid of protective clothing and ointments.

ERYTHROPOIETIC COPROPORPHYRIA.   This is a very rare disorder, similar in clinical manifestations to erythropoietic protoporphyria, but with elevated concentrations of coproporphyrin in the red cells and increased fecal excretion mainly of protoporphyrin.

Hepatic Porphyrias

Acute Intermittent Porphyria (*AIP, Swedish Type*)

AIP occurs infrequently, but is not rare. It is characterized by gastrointestinal, neurologic, and psychiatric manifestations, often intermittent in nature. Photosensitivity is not a feature of the disease. Chemi-

cally, the most characteristic finding is the urinary excretion of large amounts of PBG and ALA.

The age of onset is usually after puberty, with the peak incidence in the third or fourth decade; in some patients, however, the onset has been described during childhood.

The various clinical manifestations are considered to be due to nervous system derangements. Abdominal pain, constipation, vomiting, hypertension, and tachycardia are manifestations of autonomic nervous system involvement. Peripheral neuropathy, bulbar paralysis, seizures, and psychiatric aberrations are manifestations of peripheral somatic and central nervous system involvement.

Abdominal pain, constipation, and vomiting are usually the initial complaints and can be so severe as to mimic bowel obstruction, renal or biliary colic, or pancreatitis, and lead to repeated exploratory laparotomies. However, usual signs of surgical abdomen are lacking; the abdomen is usually soft and rebound tenderness is lacking. Fever and leucocytosis are uncommon. Radiography may reveal intestinal distention proximal to areas of spasm. Tachycardia, hypertension, and oliguria are associated with severe attacks.

Peripheral neuropathy involves mainly the motor function and can range from weakness in some muscle groups to flaccid quadriplegia and paralysis of abdominal and respiratory muscles. Some sensory disturbances may occur, ranging from analgesia to hyperesthesia and pain. Upper motor neuron signs are infrequent findings. In addition, cranial nerves, the brain stem, or the cerebral cortex may be involved. Epileptiform seizures are not uncommon. Psychic aberrations are quite diverse and may consist of bizarre behavior or may mimic schizophrenia or manic-depressive states.

Some metabolic abnormalities related to hypothalamic functions have been described, especially inappropriate secretion of ADH.

The clinical course is extremely variable. Some affected individuals may be asymptomatic and show no more than an abnormally high urinary excretion of PBG and ALA; others may present with an acute explosive fatal episode, and still others may have intermittent attacks of varying severity. Death is usually due to bulbar palsy and respiratory failure. The patients who survive a severe acute attack usually recover, but restitution of physical and mental function may occur slowly over the course of months or years.

The characteristic finding in this disease is the persistent urinary excretion of abnormal amounts of ALA and PBG. During the active phase of the disease there is often greater excretion of these metabolites than during periods of remission, but this is not invariably so. A slight increase in excretion of coproporphyrins and uroporphyrins in the urine may occur. The freshly voided urine may be of red color or it may be colorless and darken upon standing in light to red or brown color. Fecal excretion of porphyrins is normal or only slightly increased. Other findings observed during some acute episodes include elevation of blood urea, hyponatremia, derangements of various liver functions, hypercholesterolemia and hyperbetalipoproteinemia, elevated protein-bound iodine in the serum, and mild leucocytosis.

Acute attacks may be precipitated or aggravated in individuals with this genetic disorder by the administration of various drugs, particularly barbiturates. Sulfonamides, griseofulvin, some steroids, dilantin, and other drugs have also been implicated. Other factors which appear to be associated with exacerbations of the disease are infections, menstruation, and the ingestion of alcohol.

GENETICS. The abnormality is inherited as an autosomal dominant trait, with variable expressivity. Some individuals may show abnormal urinary excretion of ALA and PBG and yet have no clinical manifestations. In some obligatory carriers, there may be no increase in the urinary excretion of ALA, PBG, or porphyrins. Repeated quantitative determinations of urinary ALA and PBG in children of known porphyric families is desirable; some of these children may not show increased excretion of ALA and PBG during early childhood but may later manifest clinical and biochemical abnormalities of porphyria. The genetic defect appears to result in overproduction of ALA in the liver, in which an increase in ALA synthetase activity has been demonstrated.

Among the porphyrias, neurologic manifestations seem to appear in situations where abnormal amounts of ALA (and PBG) are present, such as AIP, mixed porphyria, and hepatic coproporphyria (see below), as well as in lead poisoning. Excess ALA by itself is not sufficient, since it is also increased in AIP during remission. However, derivatives of ALA, such as pyridoxal-ALA imines, might be formed under some conditions and lead to derangements in pyridoxal-requiring neurologic functions. Some recent pathologic and biochemical findings have pointed to disturbances in pyridoxine metabolism in AIP. However, more work is required to determine the mechanisms responsible for the clinical manifestations as well as the primary genetic defect.

TREATMENT. No specific therapy is available. The gastrointestinal and psychiatric manifestations may be improved by chlorpromazine. Chloral hydrate is useful for sedation. Severe pain may necessitate the use of narcotics, but care must be exercised to avoid addiction. Paraldehyde is useful for the relief of convulsions. Tracheostomy for maintenance of a clear airway and the assistance of a mechanical respirator may be lifesaving. Above all, the patient and members of his family who may be genetic carriers should be instructed to avoid barbiturates and other drugs which have been shown to be harmful in this disease.

In some patients, the ingestion of very large amounts of glucose has been found to diminish the production of porphyrins and their precursors and to have some favorable clinical effects. Various other experimental therapeutic approaches, such as the suppression of ovulation in some female patients, are now under study. It should be emphasized that the administration of any drugs to patients with this disease should be carried out with great caution under carefully controlled conditions.

Mixed Porphyria
(South African Type)

Mixed porphyria (porphyria variegata) may be considered a separate entity among the known hereditary forms of porphyrias. It consists of cutaneous lesions and abdominal and neurologic manifestations occurring in various combinations in different members of affected families. The characteristic chemical finding is the persistent excretion of large amounts of coproporphyrin, protoporphyrin, and some uroporphyrin in the feces. In addition, certain porphyrin-peptide conjugates (porphyrin X), are present in the feces. Abnormal urinary excretion of ALA and PBG occurs only during acute attacks of abdominal pain and neurologic disturbances.

The cutaneous lesions are sometimes present during adolescence, but they are usually first noted during adult life. They are chronic and are usually limited to those parts of the body normally exposed to sunlight. They consist of photosensitivity and fragility of the skin, hyperpigmentation, and hypertrichosis. Trivial mechanical trauma may lead to abrasions and formation of bullae which heal with some scarring. Occasionally, acute photosensitivity with pruritus, erythema, and edema are observed after exposure to sunlight. The cutaneous manifestations may be the only clinical findings in some patients. In other patients, however, acute episodes of abdominal pain and of neurologic disturbances, indistinguishable from those of acute intermittent porphyria, occur. These acute attacks appear to be precipitated by various drugs, but especially by barbiturates and sulfonamides. Many patients are found to indulge heavily in alcohol.

A finding which distinguishes this disease from acute intermittent porphyria of the Swedish type is the persistent excretion of increased amounts of copro- and protoporphyrin in the feces. The urinary excretion of ALA and PBG is elevated during episodes of acute abdominal and neurologic manifestations; in contrast to the findings in acute intermittent porphyria of the Swedish type, these values usually return to normal when the acute attack subsides.

GENETICS. The disease is inherited as an autosomal dominant trait with variable clinical and biochemical expressivity. The primary genetic lesion is not known. As in AIP, liver ALA synthetase activity is increased, but the differences between the precursor excretion in AIP and the porphyrin excretion in mixed porphyria point to a different basic lesion.

Hereditary Hepatic Coproporphyria

This is a rare entity, similar in manifestations to mixed porphyria. Coproporphyrin III is the main porphyrin excreted both in feces and in urine. The genetic abnormality is transmitted as an autosomal dominant trait. Many of the affected individuals may show only increased fecal excretion of coproporphyrin III. Others manifest various symptoms which are similar to those of AIP and may be precipitated or aggravated by some drugs.

Excessive urinary ALA and PBG execretion is found during the acute attacks. Photosensitivity is not common, but may occur. The primary genetic abnormality is not known. The metabolic abnormality is considered to involve the metabolism of porphyrins in the liver.

Cutaneous Porphyria

A number of porphyria syndromes may be grouped together under the general heading of cutaneous porphyria. The clinical picture may consist of one or more findings of photosensitivity, abnormal skin fragility with bullous skin eruptions, hyperpigmentation, hypertrichosis, and scarring. The photosensitivity appears to be the result of reactions initially involving porphyrins, radiation at the wavelength at which porphyrins absorb strongly (at the 400 mμ region), and oxygen. The ensuing reactions may involve release and activation of chemical mediators (i.e., lysosomal enzymes, histamine), but the exact events leading to skin lesions in these entities as well as in the erythropoietic porphyrias are still poorly understood.

In many cases, functional and anatomic evidence of liver damage is present. In contrast to mixed porphyria, episodes of acute abdominal and neurologic manifestations are absent. Increased excretion of various porphyrins in the urine or feces has been described. The groups of cases, however, are diverse with respect to such variables as genetic factors, toxic or other environmental effects, manifestations of liver disease, age of onset, and patterns of porphyrin excretion in urine and feces. At present only some of these syndromes can be clearly distinguished by their known etiology or by their homogeneous clinical and biochemical pattern.

An outbreak of acquired cutaneous porphyria occurred some years ago in Turkey where thousands of cases, mainly in children, were discovered. Evidence of liver disease was present, in addition to the cutaneous lesions. Increased excretion of porphyrins in the urine and in the feces was found in all cases. The cause was found to be ingestion of wheat contaminated with the fungicide hexachlorobenzene.

Another variety of acquired cutaneous porphyria occurs among the Bantu population of South Africa. The exact etiology is not known, but the ingestion of alcohol or some other toxic substance is suspected to play a role. No familial pattern has been discovered. The urinary excretion of porphyrins is high with usually normal or only slightly elevated levels of fecal porphyrins.

Many other cases, some sporadic, some familial, have been described. Information about the possible primary lesion, genetic or acquired, is not sufficient at present to permit their classification.

Porphyria in Animals

A form of hereditary porphyria, very similar to human congenital erythropoietic porphyria, occurs in cattle. It has afforded the opportunity for detailed studies on many aspects of congenital erythropoietic porphyria.

There is no known naturally occurring disease among animals comparable to the human varieties of acute intermittent porphyria or of the cutaneous porphyrias. Abnormalities in porphyrin metabolism can, however, be produced in animals, in vivo or in tissue culture, by the use of a variety of chemical agents as mentioned earlier. Porphyria in animals and animal cells, whether hereditary or acquired, should help to clarify many aspects of normal porphyrin metabolism and of derangements in the human porphyrias.

REFERENCES

Miescher, P. A., and Jaffe, E. R., eds. Seminars Hemat., Vol. 4, no. 4, Oct. 1968.
Schmid, R. The porphyrias. *In* Stanbury, J. B., Wyngaarden, J. B., and Fredrickson, D. S., eds., The Metabolic Basis of Inherited Disease. New York, McGraw-Hill Book Co., 1966, pp. 813-870.

chapter 9

CYSTIC FIBROSIS OF THE PANCREAS

CHARLES U. LOWE, Associate Editor
with the collaboration of *ERIKA BRUCK and LUIS L. MOSOVICH*

DEFINITION AND HISTORY. Cystic fibrosis of the pancreas (CFP) was first identified as a specific clinical and pathologic entity in 1938 by Andersen and virtually simultaneously by Blackfan and May. However, case reports which clearly describe the same condition had previously been published by Fanconi and others in the European literature, as well as by Harper in Australia and Parmelee in the United States. Synonyms such as "mucoviscidosis" or "fibrocystic disease of the pancreas" were discarded in 1956 in favor of the term "cystic fibrosis of the pancreas," which has become official in English literature. However, none of these names adequately describes the generalized condition which profoundly affects many organ systems. The most serious manifestations are in the lungs and, secondarily, the circulation. Since the disease was first delineated in infants examined at autopsy, the concept of the illness has expanded and additional features of the affection have been recognized: (1) the illness is not always fatal in early childhood, and indeed many milder cases of the disease are not suspected or recognized until late childhood or even during early adult life; (2) the disease is familial and of genetic origin; (3) it is relatively common; and (4) the pancreas and the mucus-producing glands in the bronchi are neither the only glands involved, nor are they even invariably affected by the disease. Indeed, if there is one organ system which is almost invariably abnormal, it is probably the sweat glands. These produce a secretion with a content of sodium and chloride which is higher than normal. The abnormal electrolyte concentration in sweat was first described by Darling and co-workers in 1953; although this feature of the disease is not an important cause of serious disability, it has been extremely useful as a diagnostic test.

Abnormal function and structure may be detected in other organs such as the salivary glands, the liver, the male genitalia, and mucus-producing glands of the gastrointestinal tract. In patients with severe lung disease due to CFP, the heart and circulation may be affected secondarily, and growth is often severely impaired. Lesions of the bones, teeth, and eyes have been described; these may either be direct results of the disease present in the lungs or intestinal tract or be secondary to therapy.

The manifestations of the disease are protean. Several children in one family may be affected, not necessarily to the same extent, by all features of the disease. In its severe form, the disease places a great psychologic, social, and economic strain on family life.

INCIDENCE AND GENETICS. CFP occurs in all groups of the white race. It is rare among Negroes and Orientals and exceptional in Mongolians. There is no significant difference in the sex distribution of the disease.

Estimates of incidence in the white race vary from 1 in 4,000 to 1 in 2,000 live births, and the disease appears to be transmitted as a mendelian recessive trait. With this knowledge, one can calculate that about 2 percent of the population are carriers of the recessive gene. Since the affected homozygotes rarely reproduce, and since the incidence of the illness does not appear to be decreasing, one may assume either that there is a high mutation rate for the abnormal gene or that there is some genetic selection of the heterozygous carrier favoring survival over the noncarrier. Recent studies in California and in Australia have statistically documented an increased fertility in the generation of grandparents, and presumably preceding generations, of children with CFP. This might help to explain the present incidence of the disease.

PATHOGENESIS. Though the cause of the illness remains unknown, there is ample evidence that the elaboration of unusually viscid mucus is related to the basic lesion of exocrine structures. Although the mucus elaborated at various sites is usually abnormally sticky, it would be premature to assume that the defect is in the production of chemically abnormal mucus rather than an abnormality in some other mechanism involved in the elaboration of normal mucous. To date, no convincing evidence has appeared to implicate a mucus with specific structural abnormalities as the basic defect in the sense that hemoglobin S in sickle-cell disease is different from normal β chain hemoglobin. The factors contributing to the tenacity and increased viscosity of the mucous secretions are not clearly defined, although Dische found an abnormal relation between the amounts of fucose and sialic acid-containing mucoprotein fractions of the duodenal juice obtained from patients with CFP. The bradykinin-kallikrein system has been suspected of being involved in the production of abnormal secretions by glands, but studies done so far have failed to show any significant abnormality in this enzymatic system.

Johansen et al. have proposed a hypothesis which attempts to relate the defects in the pancreas, liver, and mucous and salivary glands to the electrolyte concentrating disturbance in the sweat glands. On the basis of their investigations of pancreatic secretion, they postulate as the basic biochemical abnormality an inhibition of the movement of water and electrolytes (principally bicarbonate, but chloride in the sweat gland, together wih sodium) from extra-cellular space into the secretory cell. The lack of water in the final secretion leads to an excessively high concentration of the macromolecular substances elaborated by the pancreas and other glands. The authors suggest that this inhibition of electrolyte and water transport is related to the structure or porosity of mucopolysaccharide-rich regions, either in the connective tissue or in a layer immediately adjacent to the cell plasma membrane.

Recent investigations which have demonstrated a considerably elevated concentration of acid muco-polysaccharides of normal composition in fibroblasts cultured from the skin of patients with CFP might give support to the hypothesis of Johansen et al. An apparently unique glycoprotein has been isolated from stool and tissue of affected patients. It has also been identified by immunofluorescent technics in tissue obtained by rectal mucosal biopsy. But it cannot be said at present that a basic genetic defect has been clearly defined and proved.

PATHOLOGY. The predominant gross and microscopic pathology may be related to obstruction of lumina by tenacious secretions.

Depending upon the organ studied, accumulation is observed in acini and ducts or within individual goblet cells. The extent of involvement of the salivary glands depends on the proportion of mucus-secreting elements they contain; therefore the sublingual glands are seriously affected while the parotid glands show only minimal changes. The mucosa of the stomach, small intestine, and colon is coated by a layer of tenacious mucus. The lumina of the glands and the mucus cells are distended. The salivary glands of the buccal mucosa present similar changes. Fibrosis is seldom observed in the salivary glands or in the mucus-secreting structures in the gastrointestinal tract.

The pancreas is smaller than normal, feels indurated, and has an irregular surface. Most of the ducts are atretic or obstructed by inspissated eosino-philic material. Early in life the lumina of acini and ductules are distended by eosinophilic material. The lesion is progressive; the lining epithelium becomes increasingly flattened, and the secretory cells undergo atrophy. The ducts and ductules distended by secretions have a cystic appearance, and around the cysts there may be considerable fibrosis (Fig. 1). Eventually the cystic structures as well as the eosino-philic material in the acini disappear. Though the islands of Langerhans are not intrinsically affected and the total number of β cells appears nearly normal, infiltration of the islets by fibrous tissue and distortion of their architecture have been observed.

Cirrhosis of the liver is present in about one-fourth of the cases examined at autopsy and in more than one-half of the cases coming to autopsy over the age of 3 years. The fibrotic lesions, which retract the capsule, are irregular and green in color. The biliary ductules are obstructed with secretions; in

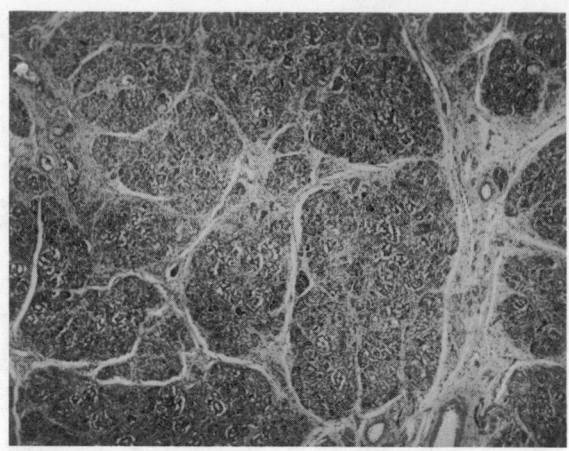

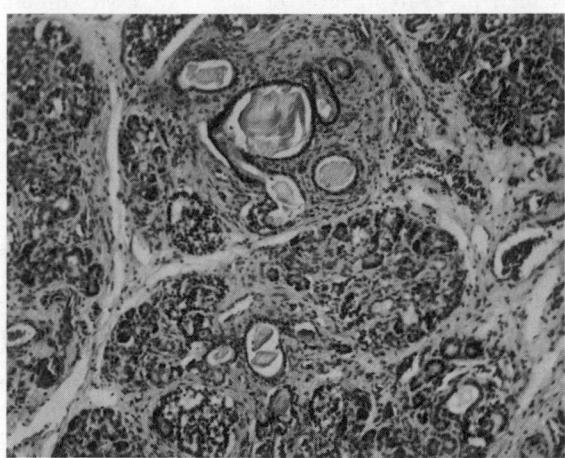

Fig. 1. Photomicrographs of pancreas in cystic fibrosis. *Top.* Early case. Low-power field. (Hematoxylin-eosin stain.) Note the distinct lobulation within the gland due to increase of the interlobular connective tissue, but no conspicuous dilation of glands and ducts. *Bottom.* Late case. Low-power field. (Hema-toxylin-eosin stain.) Note distinct dilation of several ducts and glands containing, in part, concentrically laminated secretions. Also distinct inter- and intralobular fibrosis. (We are indebted to Dr. Kornel Terplan of the Children's Hospital of Buffalo for providing the illustrations and interpretation of the pathologic material.)

the early stages prior to the appearance of fibrous tissue, there is ductule hyperplasia (Fig. 2). Later there is a marked fibroblastic reaction, and at this time when some ductules contain eosinophilic material, the epithelial lining of the ducts often disappears. One of the characteristics of the hepatic lesion is its focal distribution; areas of cirrhosis are adjacent to completely normal parenchyma.

The gallbladder often is small and may contain a colorless, opaque, viscid material; the cystic duct may be obstructed by secretions. The relationship, if any, between the parenchymal lesions in the liver and obstruction of the cystic duct is unknown.

The trachea, bronchi, and bronchioles are coated

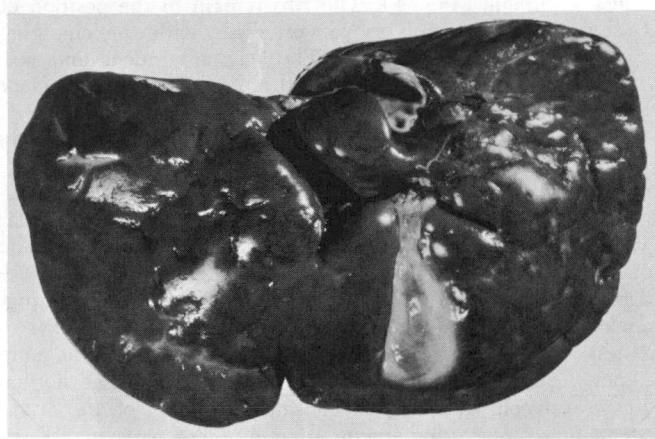

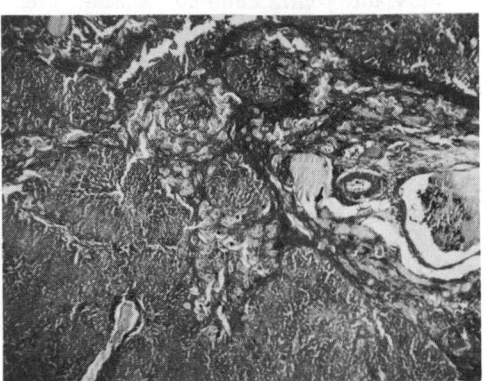

Fig. 2. *Left.* Gross photograph of the lower surface of the liver. Note the numerous, mostly shallow indentations of the capsular tissue, especially along the right liver lobe, and the collapsed gallbladder. *Right.* Low-power field. (Mallory's stain.) Note the marked increase of fibrous tissue in the large periportal field to the right, with numerous small bile ducts in the fibrotic periportal areas in the center of the photograph, and the distinct lobulation of the liver in the left half of the photograph due to perilobular fibrosis.

with tenacious secretions made up of mucus, leucocytes, and cell debris which may produce partial or total obstruction of the lumina with the consequent production of localized hyperinflation or atelectasis (Fig. 3). Peribronchitis, peribronchiolitis, and pneumonitis without tissue destruction are usually present, interspersed with areas of atelectasis, emphysema, and relatively normal parenchyma. Bronchiectasis, once thought to be rare in CFP, has been recognized to be present in most patients coming to autopsy after the age of 6 months and in some younger infants. Small bronchiectatic and peribronchial abscesses are frequently seen. The mucous membranes may show some degree of metaplasia. Around the bronchiectatic areas there is often highly vascular granulation tissue. Interstitial fibrosis is unusual, except in the oldest patients. Although ballooning of the lungs caused by airway obstruction is a common feature, destructive emphysema with loss of alveolar septa occurs to a significant extent only in patients over the age of 20 years and is usually confined to small portions of the lungs. The regional lymph nodes in the mediastinum are usually greatly enlarged and hyperemic.

Myocardial fibrosis has been reported. The mechanism of production of this lesion is not clear, although nutritional factors may be important. Hypertrophy of the right ventricle is frequently seen in patients with long-standing respiratory disease and is considered evidence of cor pulmonale.

The male genital tract is abnormal in all adults (only one exception has been reliably reported in a living man) and in the majority of children examined at autopsy. The most common abnormality is absence of the vas deferens; the spermatic cord consists of fibrous strands and a few smooth muscle fibers. In addition, the tail of the epididymis is usually atrophic, the ducts being absent or obstructed by inspissated granular eosinophilic material. The head of the epididymis may appear grossly normal or enlarged, but its ducts end blindly. The testes are normal in children; in some of the adults spermatogenesis is present but diminished in amount, and many abnormal forms have been observed. These

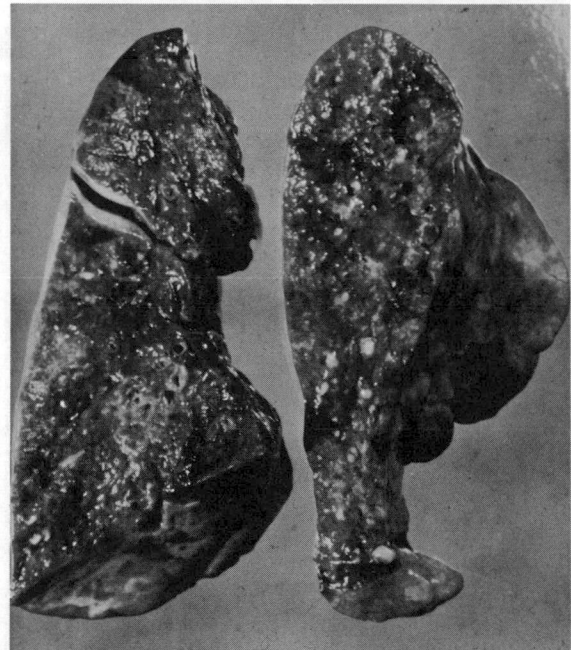

Fig. 3. Lung in cystic fibrosis. Gross photograph of cross sections of the left upper and the right upper and lower lobe. Note the uniform emphysema combined with only minimal atelectasis, due to masses of purulent exudate clearly seen in the lumina of the sectioned bronchi and bronchioli.

lesions of the genital tract are considered congenital developmental anomalies by some investigators; others, having observed normal genitalia in some of the infants and young children, consider them the consequence of progressive obstruction of the ducts, analogous to those in the pancreas, the liver, and the prenatal lesions leading to intestinal atresias.

Two types of lesions have been recognized in the retina, both ophthalmoscopically and pathologically: vascular engorgement and optic neuritis. The latter may lead to permanent impairment of vision and has been ascribed to chloramphenicol therapy.

In children older than 2 or 3 years, ceroid pigment deposits have been described in smooth muscles of the intestinal tract and, rarely, in striated muscles; this is presumably due to long-standing deficiency of vitamin E.

PATHOLOGIC PHYSIOLOGY.   *Respiratory System.*
The basic lesion in the lungs consists of the production of tenacious bronchial mucus which cannot be easily propelled by ciliary action. The accumulation of these secretions causes narrowing of the airways. This lesion may at first be spotty in distribution but in advanced cases becomes widespread. Obstruction of the airways constitutes a resistance to airflow, particularly in expiration, since the lumen of all bronchi are narrower during expiration than during inspiration. A check valve type of obstruction develops, leading to obstructive emphysema. When the obstruction is widespread, the volume of the entire lung may be considerably increased and lead to a deformity of the thorax with a striking increase in the anteroposterior diameter, as well as a low, flat diaphragm (Fig. 4). The ribs remain in the position of inspiration and move very little with the changing phases of respiration. The stagnant mucus and perhaps the composition of the secretions seem to favor the growth of bacteria, particularly staphylococci. A purulent bronchitis is superimposed on the obstruction caused by mucus and aggravates obstruction still further, causing impairment of alveolar ventilation. The ratio of dead space ventilation to alveolar ventilation may be increased above normal. The alveolar ventilation/perfusion ratio (V_A/Q) is reduced, to a different degree in each part of the lung. The blood returning from underventilated alveoli to the pulmonary vein will carry less oxygen and more carbon dioxide than blood which has perfused normal alveoli. As long as considerable parts of the lungs are intact, hyperventilation of these parts may serve to eliminate enough carbon dioxide so that the CO_2 content of the mixed blood in the left side of the heart and the systemic circulation will be normal. However, because of the shape of the dissociation curve of hemoglobin, local hyperventilation does not serve to increase the oxygen content in the pulmonary veins sufficiently to oxygenate the hemoglobin coming from the underventilated parts of the lung; even a small degree of local hypoventilation will therefore result in low oxygen tension in the blood of the pulmonary vein and of the systemic arteries. An increased alveolar-arterial nitrogen gradient confirms a low V_A/Q as the cause of low arterial blood oxygen tension. Low oxygen tension in arterial blood and an

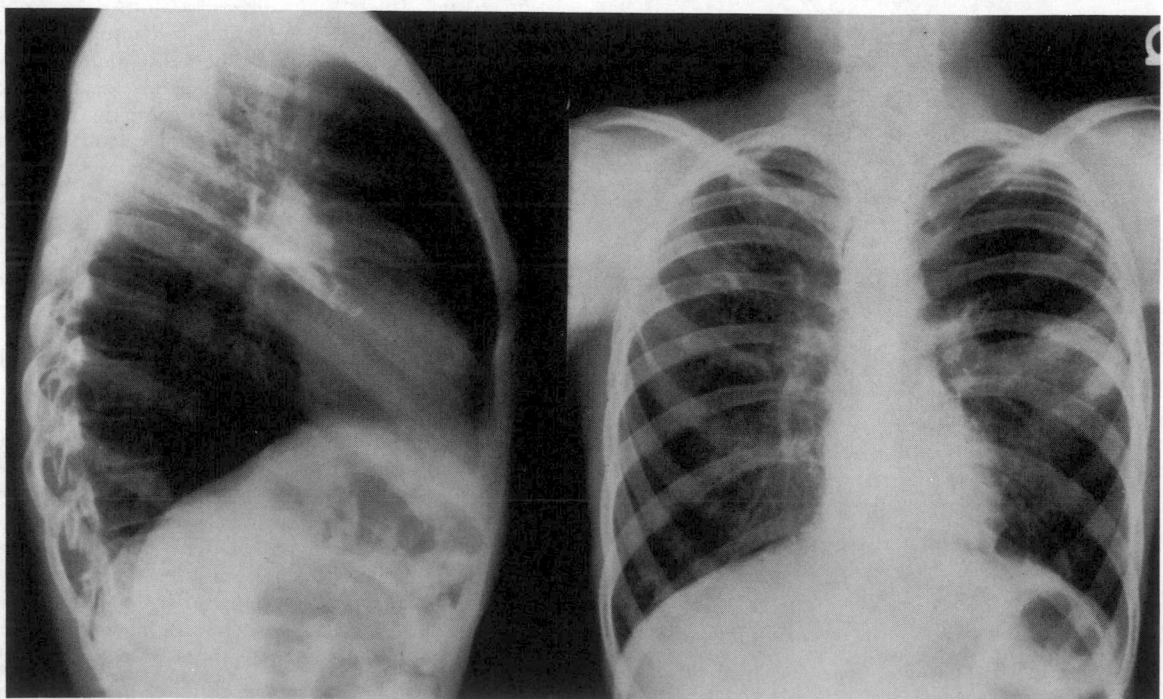

Fig. 4.   Roentgenogram of the chest of 12-year-old patient. Both the ventrodorsad diameter of the thorax and the radiolucency are increased. There are areas of infiltration in both lungs. The perihilar markings are very prominent.

increased alveolar-arterial oxygen gradient are often the first signs of abnormal lung function in children with CFP who both clinically and from other laboratory tests may appear quite well. When bronchial obstruction and alveolar hypoventilation become widespread, the carbon dioxide tension in the arterial blood will also rise and respiratory acidosis will develop. In severely ill children, metabolic alkalosis, caused chiefly by potassium deficiency, may be superimposed on this respiratory acidosis and lead to extremely high values for plasma bicarbonate concentration.

The obstructive emphysema which is associated with an increased volume of the lung, as well as with increased pressure in the alveoli, tends to raise the intrathoracic pressure. The gradient between the intrathoracic pressure and the atmospheric pressure will thus be diminished. Since during inspiration this gradient is responsible not only for the entry of air into the lungs but also for the entry of blood into the right atrium, both these vital functions are impaired in patients with obstructive emphysema. Hypoxemia, a characteristic of most patients with lung disease due to CFP, may be aggravated during periods of bronchopneumonia.

Cardiovascular System. Low alveolar oxygen tension causes an increase in the vascular resistance in the pulmonary *arteries* and is thought to be the main cause for the development of cor pulmonale; it is aggravated by association with respiratory acidosis. Congestive heart failure may occur gradually or acutely with severe hypoxia. Adaptive changes secondary to pulmonary hypertension result primarily in right ventricular hypertrophy, which is readily seen in postmortem specimens. Impaired venous return to the right atrium may contribute to the deterioration of cardiac function. Bronchial-pulmonary arterial anastomoses develop only late in the disease and probably contribute little to the pathogenesis of the heart failure.

Intestinal Tract. Patients with CFP fail to digest fat and protein to a normal extent and consequently absorb ingested food poorly. Normal adults and children beyond 1 year of age absorb 95 to 97 percent of the fat consumed in the diet. Children below 1 year of age may absorb less fat; during the neonatal period, especially among premature infants, absorption of dietary lipids may be only 70 to 80 percent. Because of the absence of pancreatic lipase, patients with CFP have steatorrhea, which is not evident when the patient is on a virtually fat-free diet. When they are given diets with normal fat content (35 to 50 percent of calories), the absorption varies, for reasons which are not entirely clear, from 50 to 75 percent of the intake. The variation is not only between patients, but occurs in an individual patient over time; it may be a function of dietary lipids. Absorption of any fat in the absence of pancreatic lipase has been explained by the production of small amounts of intestinal lipase and/or absorption through emulsification. In addition to steatorrhea, patients with CFP have azotorrhea and

excrete increased amounts of nitrogen in their stool as a consequence of the absence of trypsin. This is in contrast to patients with steatorrhea not caused by lipase deficiency (sprue, gluten enteropathy, etc.) in whom malabsorption reflects a mucosal lesion rather than incomplete digestion. While normal subjects absorb between 97 and 98 percent of dietary protein, patients with CFP may absorb only 40 to 80 percent. In spite of the absence of pancreatic amylase, carbohydrate digestion is not signficantly defective. Glucose absorption is normal although some older subjects have a flat oral glucose tolerance curve. This finding is construed as evidence of an acquired or intrinsic mucosal defect. Isolated lactase deficiency has been demonstrated in enzyme studies of intestinal mucosa in 25 percent of the patients examined; they also had characteristic clinical signs and laboratory tests. Wasting of fat and protein in stool is an obvious cause for poor weight gain unless the patient compensates by overeating. In fact, patients will often consume from 150 to 200 percent of the calculated normal caloric intake for subjects of comparable age, size, and weight. Absence of the pyloric reflex probably also contributes to the increased appetite. In normal subjects enterogastrone, released by the duodenal mucosa as soon as free fatty acids appear in the duodenum, enters the circulation and closes the pylorus through neuronal mediation. This sequence of events does not occur in patients with CFP, since in the absence of pancreatic lipase no free fatty acids will appear. Under these circumstances, meals, regardless of content of lipid, move continuously through the pylorus. Hence, the satiety which normally follows eating is rapidly dissipated in patients with achylia pancreatica, and these patients are prepared to eat again much sooner than a normal subject. In some patients, gastric emptying is so rapid that the patient is ravenously hungry within an hour of eating a large volume of food.

The incomplete digestion of fat and protein leads to a decrease in absorption of these dietary constituents; this in turn serves to enhance the bacterial flora in the lower portions of the intestinal tract. The mass of bacteria, together with the undigested food, causes the remarkable increase in bulk as well as the greasy appearance of the stool which is characteristic of this disease.

There is some evidence that the impaired absorption of lipids by patients with CFP is not only a reflection of incomplete lipolysis and emulsification, but may reflect a mucosal defect. The contribution of a mucosal defect to steatorrhea is, however, not entirely clear. Biopsy specimens of the intestinal mucosa in affected subjects appear to be microscopically normal.

Since the patients waste fat, their absorption of vitamins A, D, and E is impaired, and it is for this reason that increased amounts of these essential nutrients are usually offered to affected subjects.

Sweat Glands. The normal sweat gland produces an isotonic precursory secretion in the secretory coil which is modified by reabsorption of both water and electrolytes in the duct; sodium and chloride are always reabsorbed at a higher rate than water. In CFP the absorption of sodium and chloride is inhibited, so that final concentration of these cations is closer to that in plasma than it is in normal children. In normal children and adults, mineralocorticoids, such as DOCA, 9-α-fluorocortisol, or aldosterone, or a low-salt diet produce an increase in the reabsorption of sodium in the duct of the sweat glands, resulting in a reduction of the concentration of Na in the sweat by about 50 percent. In children with CFP, the reduction also occurs but is not more than 10 to 20 percent, so that the final concentration of Na remains abnormally high. Mangos and McSherry have demonstrated a substance in saliva and sweat of patients with CFP which inhibits sodium transport in glandular cells of animals, and in this respect resembles a group of basic polyelectrolytes such as polyornithine, protamine sulfate, and others. These basic polyelectrolytes influence sodium transport by interaction with the surface of the cell membrane at the lumen; their action can be inhibited by heparin. The identity of the substance present in saliva and sweat of patients with CFP and its relation, if any, to the basic defect in this disease have not yet been determined.

CLINICAL PICTURE. Although all patients with CFP are born with the disease, which represents a congenital metabolic abnormality, only a small number, perhaps 15 percent, of affected individuals will manifest symptoms in the newborn period in the form of the complication meconium ileus.

Typical Pattern of Development. A large proportion of children with CFP will have abnormal stool and eating patterns dating virtually from birth. The normal infant usually loses about 10 percent of his body weight following birth, and regains his birth weight within the next 10 days of life. Infants with CFP have a similar weight loss during the newborn period, but restoration may not occur for as long as 4 to 6 weeks. Failure to regain birth weight in the absence of any other cause may be considered a highly significant component of the history of the affected child.

The majority of patients with CFP have the disease at birth, and one may therefore assume that steatorrhea will be present at that time. It is possible that infants fed human milk will benefit from the lipase which it contains. In the absence of normal exocrine function of the pancreas, the total amount of stool passed per day is much larger than in a normal child of the same age; this bulk reflects malabsorption of both fat and protein. Few children with CFP have frank diarrhea, but if one does no more than weigh the stool output per unit time, it will be clear that the total weight is far greater than that found in any normal subject.

As a consequence of achylia pancreatica, appetite is significantly increased. In infants, this ravenous hunger predisposes to air swallowing, and unless careful feeding technique is used, the stomach may become distended with air and the patient may vomit. This sequence leads to reduction in feeding by the solicitous mother or the conservative physician and concomitant increase in hunger by the patient. Such a combination of events works to the disadvantage of the child, and may further retard weight gain and add to the wasted appearance of the infant. The solution to this problem is to interrupt feeding with frequent attempts to induce eructations. After several days with an improved pattern of eating, vomiting disappears. When substitution therapy with pancreatic enzymes is provided, the patient's appetite decreases and aerophagia is reduced. Whereas stools may be loose and weight gain poor for the first 2 or 3 months of life, subsequently many patients undergo amelioration of their intestinal symptoms as if some as yet unexplained adaptation to impaired digestion had occurred.

Although not all affected individuals give a history of coughing or wheezing during the neonatal period, this is an important finding when present. The cough may be dry and sufficiently paroxysmal as to suggest a diagnosis of pertussis. *Coughing and/or wheezing during the first 6 months of life is more likely to be due to CFP than to any other single cause.*

A typical patient with CFP presents sometime between 6 and 12 months of age because of a respiratory infection and poor weight gain. The roentgenographic picture of the chest may not be impressive, yet the patient coughs, and on auscultation some wheezing and rhonchi may be detected. In addition, the patient's appetite is ravenous, the weight is below what might be anticipated in relation to birth weight or food intake, and the stools are bulky and perhaps more frequent than normal. A bacterial culture of the nasopharynx usually reveals a flora of staphylococci which by phage typing are no different from those found in unaffected normal subjects. There may be some rhinorrhea or evidence of nasal obstruction, although this is not common. Unless the poor weight gain is outstanding and the stool pattern strikingly abnormal, the diagnosis may be missed at this time and the unsuspecting physician may assume that the patient has suffered a viral respiratory infection. Most infants will recover from this episode without much difficulty. However, episodes of respiratory abnormalities recur with increasing frequency, and eventually, through a combination of observation, careful history taking, and laboratory measurements, the diagnosis of CFP is established.

Another typical pattern of the illness is observed in youngsters in whom relevant complaints occur for the first time between 2 and 3 years of age. Cough is usually the first symptom, and even at this stage clubbing of the fingers may be present. While the cough may in some cases be productive, the volume of sputum is usually not great at this stage of the illness and cannot be estimated since young children usually swallow sputum instead of expectorating it. At this time the patient may show evidence of frank wasting or simply be pathologically small for age. The percussion note over the chest is usually hyperresonant. On auscultation, one may find scattered rales or rhonchi. Typically, rales are heard in the right upper lobe. At this time the roentgenogram of the chest becomes typical of that found in well-established cases of the disease (Fig. 4). The pattern has three components. There is almost invariably increased radiolucency of the thorax in the roentgenogram and an increase of the anteroposterior diameter of the chest. The diaphragm is often flat. In addition to emphysema, there are areas of segmental or disk atelectasis and infiltrations suggesting bronchopneumonia. The nasal mucosa may be red and boggy, not infrequently with polyp formation. The abdomen is not characteristically distended as in gluten enteropathy, but it may be larger than normal. The lumbar lordosis and thoracic kyphosis may reflect not only increased intestinal volume but also muscular weakness and the increased volume of the thorax. Treatment of the

respiratory infection will usually be followed by marked improvement in the patient's clinical state but rarely by disappearance of all evidence of the disease. The growth and weight gain of patients with CFP depend almost entirely on the severity of respiratory disease. Patients with no evidence of respiratory infection or impaired function may gain perfectly normally for many years in spite of the absence of pancreatic enzymes from their intestinal tract. By contrast, during periods of severe impairment of respiratory functions, both weight gain and longitudinal growth may be practically stagnant (Fig. 5).

In contrast to the typical patients, there are other youngsters with minimal evidence of disease who are detected only incidentally, rather than as a direct result of complaints, at ages beyond the third or fourth year of life. For example, a sibling may be born with meconium ileus, which alerts the physician to the existence of the genetic pattern in the family; and because of mild abnormalities such as stool frequency or increased appetite, or perhaps predilection to respiratory infections, an older child

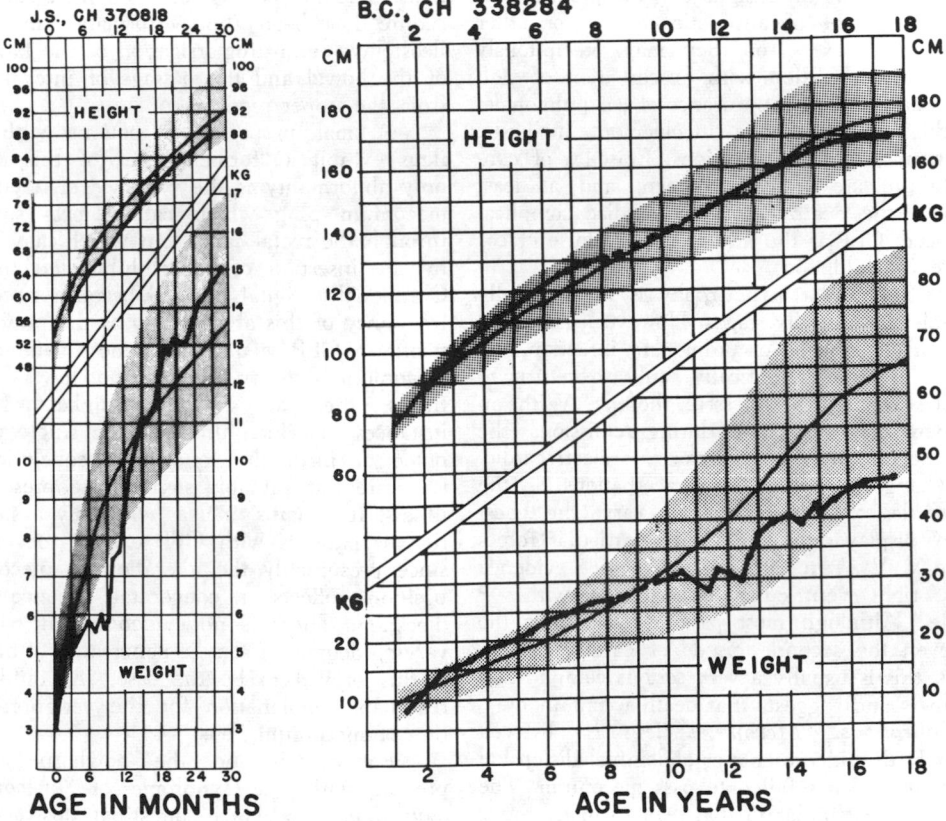

Fig. 5. Growth curves of two patients. The thin line indicates the mean, the shaded area ± 2 standard deviations of the mean. The heavy line is the patient's own record. J.S. had severe respiratory symptoms and signs between the ages of 3 and 9 months, then suddenly improved and was practically free of any respiratory signs during the second year of his life. He received no pancreatic extract at any time. B.C. had intestinal manifestations of cystic fibrosis in infancy but had no pulmonary involvement up to the age of 7. Between the ages of 10 and 12 years he developed moderately severe pulmonary insufficiency.

may be examined and found to have CFP. Some patients have only intestinal signs: large, bulky, foul-smelling stools which are associated with distention of the bowel and, in some cases, even an atonic megacolon and fecal incontinence. These patients often present with a complaint of abdominal pain.

Occasionally, a patient is first diagnosed as a case of CFP when he presents with an enlarged liver and spleen and is found to have cirrhosis of the liver. All of the diagnostic laboratory data may be present, and yet the child on physical examination may be found to be normal with respect to both development and chest findings. It is interesting that many of these patients show few or none of the typical abnormalities in the chest roentgenogram; nevertheless, some emphysema or increased peribronchial markings near the hilus may be noted. Despite the paucity of complaints and physical signs, however, the fingers are frequently clubbed, and careful respiratory studies indicate uneven ventilation and at times low oxygen tension in arterial blood. In rare instances the clubbing and low oxygen tension may be the result of severe liver cirrhosis rather than pulmonary disease. Patients may go for years without any increase in their signs and symptoms, even without the benefit of antibiotic therapy or other therapeutic maneuvers, or they may precipitously deteriorate in association with exacerbation of pulmonary disease and the appearance of cor pulmonale.

After infancy, cardiac involvement in cystic fibrosis assumes major proportions. Episodes of congestive failure are frequently seen, and at least one-third of the deaths are from cardiac complications. Indeed, CFP is the most common cause of cor pulmonale in childhood.

Right ventricular hypertrophy is not clinically recognizable in the early stages. However, with each severe recurrent episode of pulmonary infection, the heart may enlarge dramatically, only to return to normal size following successful therapy. With an improvement of oxygenation during remissions, the electrocardiogram may be normal; but electrocardiographic changes appear with exacerbations of the pulmonary lesion. These changes vary; the chest leads may display only late right ventricular forces (an R′ in V_1-V_{3R}) in early disease or give evidence of frank right ventricular hypertrophy with "P pulmonale." Although most patients rally after the first or even the second episode of cardiac decompensation, this is usually a very serious complication of the illness and suggests that death is imminent.

Complications. *Meconium ileus* is observed soon after birth and presents as abdominal distension in an infant who has failed to pass meconium. The clinical picture is similar to that seen in many forms of intestinal obstruction during the neonatal period. In some cases, it is possible to palpate a mass in the right lower quadrant which corresponds to the ileum distended by abnormal meconium. Perforation may occur; when this has happened in utero, meconium peritonitis with calcification follows and

may be seen radiographically. These intrauterine events may occasionally lead to atresia or stenosis of a bowel segment. Single or multiple ileal atresias in a newborn infant should arouse the suspicion of intrauterine meconium ileus due to CFP. The cause of the intestinal obstruction lies in the presence of abnormally viscid meconium which cannot be propelled by the bowel. In comparison with normal meconium which consists primarily of carbohydrates, this meconium has an unusual chemical composition, with increased protein content. The typical radiogram (Fig. 6) reveals distended loops of bowel; and in most cases, a curious reticulated pattern in certain segments of the small bowel suggests that the bowel is filled with sponge. The "spongy" radiographic picture represents air beaten into the sticky meconium by intestinal action. In many patients an apparent microcolon exists, the decreased caliber reflecting failure of meconium to pass beyond the ileocecal valve (Fig. 6, right). This colon will expand when the fecal stream reaches it, and must be distinguished from a true microcolon, which does not expand. Intestinal anomalies, other than ileal atresia, are rarely associated with meconium ileus. Therapy is surgical. The most successful procedure has been the performance of a Mikulicz ileostomy, permitting irrigation of the lower segment of the bowel and the passage of intestinal contents from the upper segment.

A small proportion of patients with meconium ileus exhibit a "forme fruste" of this illness. The only abnormality is the presence of a curious, hard meconium plug which cannot pass spontaneously through the rectal canal, but which may be removed by the insertion of a well-lubricated thermometer. Occasionally digital removal becomes necessary. The frequency of this abnormality as the presenting complaint in CFP is unknown; most patients with the meconium plug syndrome do not have CFP. Nevertheless, there are sufficient numbers of bona fide instances in which this was the single abnormality noted at birth that one must conclude that this is a rare but valuable sign of the presence of this illness. It remains unclear why only a small proportion of patients with CFP exhibit meconium ileus, since presumably the alteration in meconium composition reflects a congenital absence of tryptic digestion. There is no evidence that patients have varying degrees of achylia pancreatica at birth, though if this proved to be the case, it would provide a reasonable explanation for the variation in exhibition of meconium ileus.

Patients beyond the newborn period may present with the syndrome of *"meconium ileus equivalent,"* in which intestinal obstruction occurs owing to tenacious impacted stools. Rarely, a patient not previously known to have CFP may present at any age with this complaint. When enemas with proteolytic enzymes are unable to eliminate the obstruction, surgical correction is essential.

Atelectasis of a segment or of a lobe of the lung

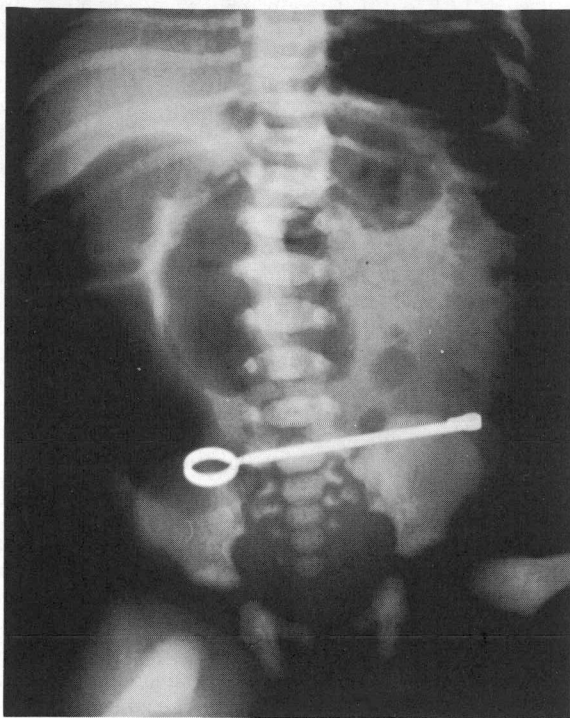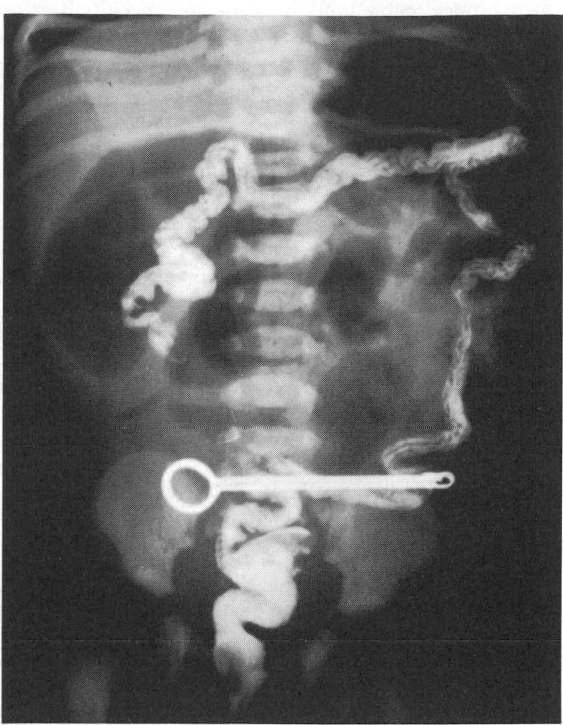

Fig. 6.   Roentenograms of the abdomen in a case of meconium ileus. *Left.* Distention of the loops of the small intestine is evident predominantly on the right side. *Right.* The barium enema reveals the apparent microcolon associated with this condition.

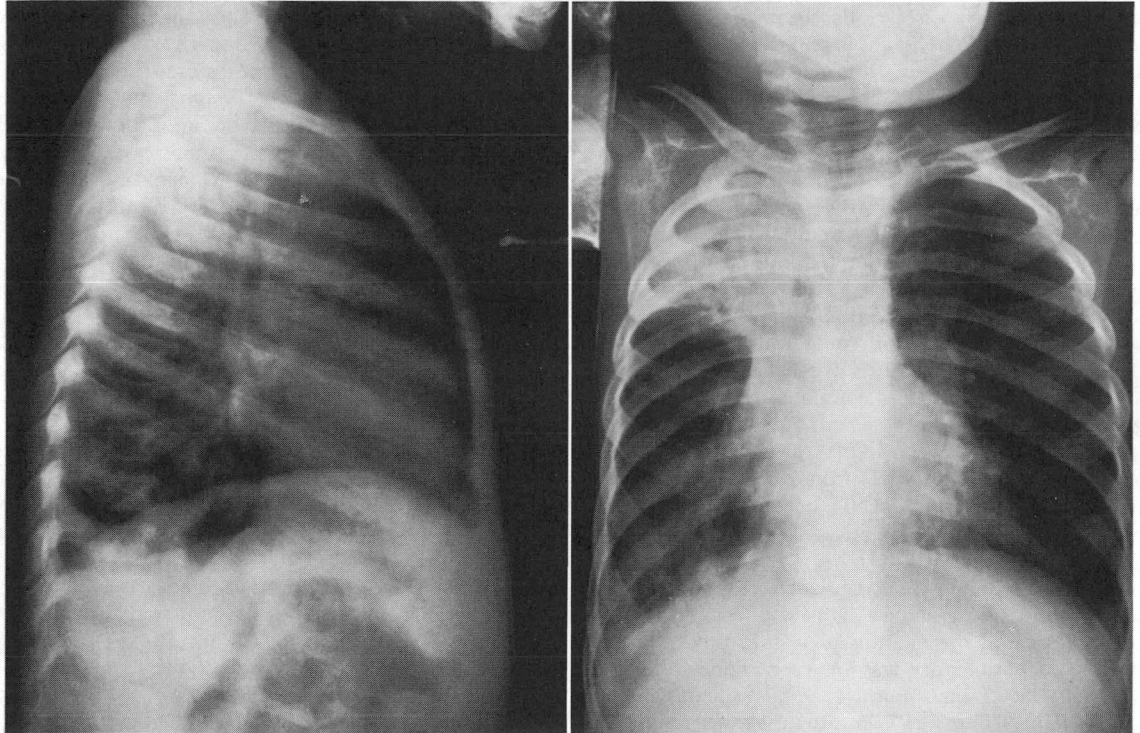

Fig. 7.   Roentgenogram of the chest of a 15-month-old patient in whom the primary manifestation of cystic fibrosis was atelectasis of the right upper lobe.

is not uncommon, and in some instances is the first manifestation of the disease (Fig. 7). Though the lobe may expand spontaneously, aspiration of the obstructing bronchial secretions under bronchoscopy is required in some cases. If the atelectasis persists and is refractory to treatment, resection may be indicated. One of the most common complications, which has been described in 33 percent of patients over the age of 2 years, is *mucoid impaction of the bronchi*. Some of the major bronchi are filled for long periods of time by solid casts consisting of thick secretions. The condition is recognized in the chest roentgenogram by the persistent presence of branching fingerlike or "cluster of grape" opacifications which are localized according to established bronchial segmental distribution. These lesions occur most frequently in the right upper and middle lobes. Their persistence for more than a month is likely to be followed by saccular bronchiectasis. Therapeutic measures short of bronchial lavage are usually unsuccessful in eliminating these impactions.

Hemoptysis is rare but may occur in older patients with bronchiectasis; the prognosis of this complication is usually poor since it indicates progressive destruction of lung tissue. *Pneumothorax* may occur spontaneously, usually in older children or adults, sometimes repeatedly in the same patient; closed drainage or rarely surgical repair of lung tissue is required for treatment. In contrast to staphylococcal pneumonia in otherwise normal children, empyema is exceptional in patients with CFP. Cor pulmonale, a common complication of protracted pulmonary disease, has been discussed above. *Clouding of the paranasal sinuses* is an almost constant radiographic finding, but suppurative sinusitis is very uncommon. The radiographic picture reflects the anatomic situation, since the paranasal sinuses are filled with rubbery, puttylike material. Nasal polyps are frequently seen and recur after surgical removal. The submaxillary *salivary glands* are frequently moderately *enlarged* in older patients. In rare cases, the parotid gland may also be affected.

Rectal prolapse is seen in some young patients, usually only in those with poor nutrition. The incidence of *duodenal ulcer* is higher in patients with CFP than in the general population of the same age group but is usually detected only at the time of postmortem examination. The reason duodenal ulcers occur more frequently is unknown but it may be related to agonal phenomena or to the presence of cirrhosis or achylia pancreatica.

Diabetes mellitus has been reported as a complication. Although the incidence of frank disease must be low, the glucose tolerance test is impaired in many cases and the amount of insulin produced during a glucose tolerance test has been found to be considerably lower than normal in all patients studied (about 100 patients in two different series).

Cirrhosis of the liver may be manifest by the increased consistency of the organ and by a nodular surface. Low serum levels of cholinesterase, elevation of ceruloplasmin and alkaline phosphatase in blood, and abnormal retention of BSP are confirmatory laboratory tests of this complication. Patients with cirrhosis may develop portal hypertension, hypersplenism, and bleeding from esophageal varices. The treatment is no different from that used for portal hypertension of other causes.

The *eyes* may present two types of abnormalities: one is related to hypoxia and consists of tortuosity of the veins, hemorrhage in the retina, and occasionally pseudopapilledema; the other is related to prolonged therapy with chloramphenicol and is characterized by optic neuritis and subsequent optic atrophy. The former frequently remits during amelioration of the hypoxemia, while in the latter case blindness supervenes unless treatment with the causative agent is promptly discontinued.

Pulmonary osteoarthropathy, with swelling of joints and occasional evidence of effusions in knees and ankle joints, is sometimes seen in older children with long-standing hypoxemia. These lesions are usually painless, although pain and tenderness have been reported in some patients.

Heat prostration due to excessive loss of NaCl in the sweat may occur during summer heat and in overheated homes in winter. The diagnosis is confirmed by finding severe hyponatremia. The clinical picture is that of circulatory collapse with hyperpyrexia, convulsions, and eventually death if proper treatment is not instituted. A similar syndrome may occur in a young infant subjected to thermal stimulation during performance of a sweat test. Therapy in either case is similar to that used for salt depletion due to other causes (see Chap. 3).

Anasarca and *hypoproteinemia* have been observed in infants with CFP who are either breast fed or given a soybean formula. Human milk does not provide enough protein to compensate for the azotorrhea; patients fed a soybean formula without pancreatic extract absorb only 10 to 35 percent of the total nitrogen intake. This protein deficiency may be fatal if not recognized early, but it is readily reversible with a high-protein diet.

Sepsis is very rare, as are complications such as pyelonephritis, peritonitis, or meningitis. Cerebral abscesses, common complications of chronic suppurative pulmonary disease from other causes, are virtually unknown. The exanthemas of childhood present no unusual danger; antibody levels in children with CFP indicate that many of them have acquired such antibodies without having had an apparent illness.

BACTERIOLOGY. In uncomplicated cases of CFP, urinalysis and most of the commonly performed hematologic and chemical laboratory tests give normal results. By contrast, bacteriologic studies show a characteristic, though not necessarily diagnostic, flora. In patients whose bacterial flora has not been modified by extensive antibiotic therapy, cultures of any part of the respiratory tract usually yield coagulase-positive staphylococcus aureus. These organisms have been the subject of extensive studies over many years, since their almost universal presence in the bronchi and the lack of invasion of bloodstream and tissues in patients with CFP are distinctly different from the natural course of staphylococcal infection in other human subjects. However, the staphylococci have been found to be identical in all respects to those causing common pyogenic infections, so that attention has turned to the host. Search is still in progress for a specific chemical component of sputum of CFP patients which might enhance the growth of staphylococci; however to date no positive or negative conclusions have been reached. Immunologic studies have revealed an unusual abundance of the secretory type of gamma globulin A (IgA with "secretory piece") both in the bronchial mucous membranes and in the bronchial lymph nodes of patients with CFP. One may speculate that this immunoglobulin is responsible for preventing invasion of tissues and bloodstream by the staphylococcus, although there is no evidence that in the bronchial lumen growth of the organisms is inhibited. The staphylococci are susceptible to antibiotic therapy and may eventually be eliminated from the respiratory tract. Usually they are replaced by gram-negative organisms, particularly *Pseudomonas aeruginosa*, which may prove much more resistant than the staphylococci to any kind of antimicrobial therapy. Even though *Ps. aeruginosa* is and remains sensitive in vitro to polymyxin B or colistin and sometimes to other broad-spectrum antibiotics, intensive therapy with these agents is usually unsuccessful in eradicating this organism from the respiratory tract. Indeed, it has been stated that once a patient with CFP has acquired this organism, it will stay with him until he dies. *Pseudomonas* often undergoes a metabolic alteration in patients with CFP and becomes "mucoid," i.e., the organism surrounds itself with a slimy coat which consists of polysaccharides resembling alginates. The capsular polysaccharide of the *Pseudomonas* apparently has toxic properties which enhance the virulence of the microorganism and perhaps other microorganisms as well; in addition, it forms very viscous gels, resistant to degradation, and would therefore contribute to the bronchial obstruction. Mucoid *Pseudomonas aeruginosa* has become the most common, in fact almost universal, organism cultured from the lungs of deceased patients. It may be present with or without staphylococci. Serotype-specific antibodies to *Pseudomonas aeruginosa* have been demonstrated in serum of patients whose sputum contained the organism. Other pathogenic micro-organisms, both gram-positive and gram-negative, may be encountered in patients with CFP. Among these, *Hemophilus influenzae* is relatively common and frequently associated with clinical manifestations of increased cough, bronchopneumonia, and elevated temperature. It is normally susceptible to broad-spectrum antibiotics and, unless sequestered

in completely obstructed parts of the lung, usually yields to intensive antibiotic therapy.

Failure of many attempts at antimicrobial therapy in patients with CFP may be due to the fact that most bacteria are luminal rather than within tissues, and to the difficulty of relieving obstruction and restoring normal pulmonary drainage. **DIAGNOSTIC TESTS.** The diagnosis of CFP should be considered established only when the composite picture, obtained from physical findings and diagnostic tests, is congruent. Although a variety of abnormalities has been described, including delayed pupillary response to light, histopathologic abnormality of buccal mucosa and secretory glands, increased viscosity of duodenal fluid, and increased sodium content of hair and nails, only three important laboratory tests need be considered.

Sweat Test. Patients with cystic fibrosis of the pancreas characteristically produce sweat with concentrations of sodium, chloride, and usually potassium well above those found in normal children. The rate of sweating is not increased. Normal values for concentration of sodium and chloride increase with the age of the patient (see Table 1); the dividing line between abnormal and normal values varies slightly from clinic to clinic and with the accuracy of the technical procedure.

TABLE 1. *Variations in Sodium Concentration of Sweat with Age (Normal Subjects)** *

| Age | Sex | Na (mEq/L) | |
		mean ± SD	range
1-12 months	male	10.7 ± 3.6	3.8-20.1
	female	11.4 ± 3.6	5.4-16.2
1-5 years	male	17.9 ± 8.7	7.1-13.0
	female	16.7 ± 8.7	6.1-37.9
6-10 years	male	16.5 ± 5.8	7.1-28.3
	female	20.6 ± 9.7	12.0-46.5
11-19 years	male	26.9 ± 13.3	5.3-52.2
	female	26.3 ± 13.1	7.4-61.3
20-60 years	male	51.9 ± 21.1	9.9-96.4
	female	36.5 ± 18.7	9.5-80.1

*From Lobeck and Huebner. *Pediatrics*, 30:172, 1962.

The techniques for inducing sweating as well as the condition of the patient may affect the absolute value. Most physicians consider values in children of Na or Cl above 60 mEq/L as abnormal, but during the first year of life, values as low as 45 to 50 mEq/L are suspicious since in normal infants the concentration is usually below 20 mEq/L. Sweat from the back, chest, forearm, or forehead may be produced by thermal or pharmacologic stimuli. Apocrine sweat should not be used. Pilocarpine iontophoresis is the most common form of pharmacologic stimulation; thermal stimuli may be general or local. Local heat may be applied by special aluminum discs or by moist, cloth-covered plastic pads heated to about 50° C. For general heat the patient is wrapped in blankets in a warm room for one-half to two hours. Whatever the stimulus, it is essential to wash the area of the skin used thoroughly with distilled water immediately before the actual collection of sweat to remove remnants of sweat previously produced. An ashless filter paper, which has previously been weighed in a covered weighing flask on an analytical balance, is placed on the washed area of the skin and covered with a larger, clean piece of plastic material, the edges of which are sealed with adhesive tape to prevent evaporation. After periods ranging from 10 minutes to 1 or 2 hours of sweat collection, depending upon the method and on the rate of sweating, the wet filter paper is taken off the skin and immediately placed back in the weighing flask. Evaporation of sweat and contamination from the fingers of the technician have to be avoided by handling the paper rapidly and only with instruments. A filter paper disk from the same batch is used for a blank analysis. The closed flask is then weighed again. Thereafter, the sweat is eluted with a solution of $LiNO_3$ or whatever fluid is used in the analysis for Na or Cl. Either sodium or chloride may be determined in the collected fluid, depending on the available laboratory facilities; the concentration of these two ions is usually almost identical.

Chloride electrodes have been devised in attempts to shorten and simplify the procedure. After thermal stimulation, this type of electrode may be applied directly to the skin for 10 to 15 seconds and chloride concentration may be read off a properly calibrated scale. Unfortunately, in addition to the rather poor precision (± 20 to 25 percent), numerous sources of error, particularly poor sweating, invalidate these instruments as means of making such an important diagnosis. It has now become clear that the concentration of sodium and chloride in sweat in normal adults is considerably higher and more variable than that found in children. One may distinguish between high levels of sodium in sweat occurring in some normal individuals and the high levels found in patients with CFP either by the administration of mineralocorticoids or the introduction of a diet low in sodium for several days, thus forcing the subject to conserve this cation at maximum levels. All normal adults with high levels of sodium in sweat, i.e., above 60 mEq/L, who are subjected to either regimen promptly lower the level of sodium. We have also seen a small number of children, 2 to 5 years old, who had sweat sodium levels above 70 mEq/L repeatedly when they were tested as outpatients. Because their clinical condition did not correspond to the diagnosis of CFP, they were tested on a sodium restricted diet and promptly responded with a low normal sodium concentration in sweat. These children had an unusually high salt intake in their diet over long periods. In contrast, subjects with cystic fibrosis of the pancreas will not significantly decrease the quantity of sodium in

sweat with salt restriction or mineralocorticoid medication. Levels of sodium in sweat above 60 mEq/L may be found in patients with adrenal insufficiency. Subjects who are poorly adapted to heat and subjected to a heat stress prior to adaptation, and persons with a variety of illnesses, such as liver glycogen disease, nephrogenic diabetes insipidus, and ectodermal dysplasia also have increased levels of sodium in sweat. In adults with CFP the sodium concentration in sweat is always above 90 and usually above 120 mEq/L.

Tests for Pancreatic Enzymes. In more than 95 percent of all subjects with CFP, activity of all pancreatic digestive enzymes is absent; of these, tryptic activity is the most convenient to measure in duodenal fluid. The sample for assay must be obtained through intubation. The tube is usually placed in the proper site under direct fluoroscopic visualization. It is important that the fluid be obtained over a relatively short period of time and delivered directly into a chilled receiver. Trypsin undergoes autodigestion, and a sample which is normal in tryptic activity will, upon standing at room temperature, rapidly lose proteolytic activity. It is useful to determine that the pH of the fluid is alkaline as an indication that the tube is in the proper place in the gastrointestinal tract. However, if, as frequently happens, the pylorus intermittently opens during collection, acid materials will be delivered to the duodenum, and the pH may suggest that the tube is in the stomach. The presence of bile in the sample will usually confirm proper position. The assay for trypsin is most easily conducted using the modified Fermi technique of gelatin liquefaction. It is well to control this test by incubation of duplicate samples, one of which contains soybean trypsin inhibitor. The inhibitor will prevent digestion of gelatin by pancreatic trypsin but not affect digestion by gelatinase produced by intestinal bacteria. If one of the two series of tubes shows inhibition, one can be reasonably certain that the test is in fact determining pancreatic trypsin. If the tubes containing soybean inhibitor show digestion comparable to that in the assay samples, one must assume that gelatin liquefaction is the result of action by bacterial ferments.

Feces are not suitable for assay of pancreatic enzymes; the test is not quantitative, and both false positive and false negative results are frequently encountered.

Vitamin A Absorption Test. The vitamin A absorption test provides indirect evidence for the presence or absence of pancreatic lipase activity. After an oral dose of 7,000 units of vitamin A per kilogram of body weight, the blood serum of a normal subject shows a peak level of vitamin A 5 to 7 hours later, which is 150 to 500 $\mu g/100$ ml above the fasting level. In sharp contrast, patients with CFP show virtually no elevation in the level of vitamin A in the blood after this test dose. It is important that the form of vitamin A used is one in which the vitamin is present as the ester of a long-chain fatty acid. If vitamin A alcohol or acetate, present in many so-called water-miscible products, is used as the test material, there will be no significant difference between the peak levels observed in normals and in patients with CFP.

The vitamin A absorption test will be abnormal in all forms of achylia pancreatica and also in patients with intestinal mucosal abnormalities, such as gluten enteropathy. In case of doubt, corroborative information may be obtained by repeating the test, using a water-miscible form of vitamin A. As pointed out, under these circumstances the level of vitamin A in blood of patients with CFP will rise normally; in contrast, patients with mucosal defects will show little or no improvement. It is worth remembering that the flat vitamin A absorption curve in CFP represents an abnormality in emulsification and, in all probability, digestion of the vitamin A, i.e., saponification of the vitamin A ester. In patients with mucosal abnormalities, the defect results from malabsorption and is independent of emulsification or lipolysis. In biliary tract obstruction, defective absorption may result from abnormalities in emulsification.

Various other tests of fat absorption have been proposed. Except for a complete fat balance over several days, which is too complicated for most hospitals, none of these methods is quantitative. The determination of vitamin A in serum is a relatively easy and reliable laboratory procedure; therefore this test is preferred. In persons who have a good intake of vegetables or other sources of carotene, a low level of carotene in serum is a good index of impaired fat absorption, but the level is normally very low in infants fed only milk and cereals.

Some patients may show reasonably normal activity of pancreatic trypsin early in life, only to have this function gradually disappear. The sweat test, as usually performed, is unreliable in infants below the age of 6 to 8 weeks because sweating per se is poorly established during the neonatal period. However, sweating can be invoked with pilocarpine within the first few days of life, and it has been demonstrated that the defect in salt conservation is present even at this early age. It appears that the basic defects are in most patients fully established at birth.

The diagnosis of CFP should not be made on the basis of the sweat test alone. However, if the sweat abnormality occurs in a patient in whom duodenal intubation and/or the vitamin A absorption test provide evidence of pancreatic abnormality and in whom there is a family history of CFP or typical lung disease, the diagnosis becomes fairly certain. Even if the diagnosis has been established by a sweat test and a typical picture of respiratory disease, it is of value in the individual patient to determine the presence or absence of involvement of the pancreas.

It cannot be stressed too strongly that the diagnosis of CFP should never be made nor ruled out on the basis of semiquantitative or otherwise presumptive tests with large margins of error. This is particularly true for screening tests and other tests on asymptomatic subjects. Even the well-established tests, like the quantitative sweat test, give occasional wrong results and, if not congruent with the clinical picture, should be repeated under strictly controlled conditions. Both a false positive and a false negative diagnosis may have catastrophic consequences for the mental health of the parents, if not the physical health of the child.

Diagnosis of Heterozygote Carrier of CFP. All the above-described usual diagnostic tests are normal in parents of children with CFP. This includes the concentration of sodium and chloride in sweat, as has been recognized since it became evident that most normal adults have higher values than normal children.

In the search for a genetic marker which might help to identify the heterozygote and, hopefully, also the basic inherited cause of the abnormalities observed in various organs, two encouraging discoveries have been made in the last few years. Spock, in 1967, described disorganization and inhibition of the normal rhythmic motion of the cilia in a tissue culture of rabbit tracheal mucosa by serum from patients with CFP. He identified the substance in the patient's serum responsible for this inhibition as a component of the euglobulin fraction and showed that it was present in known heterozygotes as well as in all homozygotes. Because of the extreme technical difficulty of this test, it has not had much practical application so far. In 1969, Bowman and her associates applied serum and saliva of patients with CFP and of heterozygotes to the cilia of live oysters, which are easier to obtain than tissue cultures of mammalian mucosa. She demonstrated inhibition of ciliary motion in less than 35 minutes with all of these sera and with only 2 of 64 sera of normal persons. The responsible factor in the serum was found to be nondializable, with a molecular weight of 75,000 to 180,000, and similar to the factor in saliva of patients which inhibits sodium transport, as described by Mangos.

In 1968, Danes and Bearn reported metachromatic granules in tissue cultures of fibroblasts of patients with CFP and also of their heterozygote parents. These granules were subsequently identified as mucopolysaccharides. It was hoped that the presence or absence of this metachromatic material could be used as a genetic marker. However, it soon became evident that metachromatic granules are present not only in mucopolysaccharidoses, which are rare and easily differentiated, but also in 15 to 25 percent of normal controls. Negative results in known cases of CFP have also been reported.

DIFFERENTIAL DIAGNOSIS. Since cystic fibrosis of the pancreas has become a well-known entity, many patients are suspected of having this disease who actually suffer from other conditions. Four different types of patients may require tests to rule out CFP. The first group of patients presents with intestinal obstruction. In the newborn period, atresia of the ileum not only can mimic the signs and symptoms of meconium ileus but in some cases may actually be produced by intrauterine meconium ileus. In older children with intestinal obstruction, "meconium ileus equivalent" should be considered in the differential diagnosis. Hirschsprung's disease in a newborn infant may present a picture very similar to the one of meconium ileus or the meconium plug syndrome.

Patients with steatorrhea or chronic diarrhea may suffer from gluten enteropathy rather than CFP. In the true celiac syndrome due to gluten sensitivity, symptoms characteristically do not start at birth but only after the child has received gluten-containing foods. Lung disease is not a part of this syndrome, although its absence does not rule out CFP. In addition, upper respiratory infections occur frequently in patients with the celiac syndrome and may cause confusion. The typical patient with celiac syndrome has anorexia, whereas patients with CFP have a voracious appetite, except during periods of severe infection. Tests for sweat electrolyte concentration and duodenal enzymes will decide the issue. The glucose tolerance test usually shows a flat curve in the celiac syndrome but is normal in patients with cystic fibrosis. The vitamin A absorption curve will be flat in both conditions, although usually less so in the celiac syndrome. However, when vitamin A alcohol is given, it will be absorbed normally in patients with cystic fibrosis, while the curve will still be flat in patients with the celiac syndrome. An annular pancreas or absence of specific enzymes may also cause steatorrhea or diarrhea, but such patients will have normal electrolyte concentration in the sweat and no lung pathology.

A third group of patients who present a problem in differential diagnosis are those with clubbing of the fingers or with respiratory symptoms such as chronic cough, wheezing, or repeated episodes of pneumonia. The importance of screening this group has become more evident since it has been established that children with CFP but without digestive complaints may present with respiratory signs and symptoms as late as the second decade of life. Chronic asthma is probably the most common of the conditions which may be mistaken for CFP. The reverse is also true. In infancy, bronchiolitis and pertussis present a clinical picture similar to that of pulmonary disease due to CFP. In older children, rare conditions such as bronchiectasis and various forms of pulmonary fibrosis may be mistaken for CFP, a far more common illness.

CFP must be included in the differential diagnosis of a large group of patients with failure to gain weight and to thrive for various reasons. Patients with most of these conditions, such as renal or heart disease and chronic infection, characteristically have anorexia and none of the stigmas of CFP.

Blizzard has reported a group of children in whom failure to grow and gain despite a very large food intake is related to severe parental deprivation. These children have a large abdomen and voracious but bizarre appetite, but no pulmonary disease. They resume weight gain and growth when their environment is improved. (See Chap. 4.)

TREATMENT. Specific therapy depends on the phase of the disease in the individual patient, the most intensive being required for obstructive and infectious lesions in the respiratory tract. Liquefaction and expectoration of the tenacious mucus in the bronchi is a primary aim of therapeutic efforts. Inhalation of a fog of fine water droplets which may penetrate into the distal branches of the bronchi has been the most effective means for the purpose of liquefaction, particularly since the availability of ultrasonic nebulizers which are capable of producing smaller (1 to 3 μ) and more uniform droplets than older types of machines. Addition of 10 or 5 percent propylene glycol to the water is less important for stabilization of droplets with ultrasonic than with jet-type nebulizers, but it is helpful in preventing spread of pathogenic bacteria with the aerosol. The exact fate of the droplets in the respiratory tract, their effect, and indications for therapy, either continuous in a tent or intermittent through a mouthpiece or face-mask, are still under debate. The only method by which a significant proportion of droplets reaches the lower respiratory tract may be the mouthpiece, which is the only effective way to give antibiotics or broncholytic or other drugs in exact dosage with the aerosol. Unfortunately mouthpieces are not tolerated by infants. N-Acetylcysteine and several proteolytic enzymes have been suggested, with varying degrees of enthusiasm, for the purpose of liquefying secretions. Of these, N-acetylcysteine (Mucomyst) is the most effective in reducing the consistency of thick sputum in vitro. A 20 percent solution has been given either by inhalation of an aerosol or by direct instillation through a tracheostomy or a bronchoscope. The results in vivo have been considerably less dramatic than in vitro, perhaps because not enough of the drug can be administered. In addition, few patients have been able to tolerate N-acetylcysteine for any length of time. Nausea, increased cough, irritation of mucous membranes after instillation, paralysis of cilia, bronchospasm and inactivation of antibiotics have been observed.

In the U.S. the preferred form of inhalation therapy is the use of a "mist tent" with ultrasonic nebulizer at night, with antibiotics or isoproterenol or other broncholytic drugs given as aerosol by mouthpiece when necessary. A specifically designed system of physiotherapy has proved to be of value in mechanically "shaking loose" the secretions. The method consists of clapping and vibrating a certain part of the chest of the patient manually while the patient is put in a position which allows drainage by gravity from the segment of the lung underlying this part of the chest. Lobe by lobe and segment by segment, the entire lung can thus be treated by a skilled physiotherapist or by the parents after appropriate instruction. This physiotherapy should be preceded by inhalation of a water mist. Postural drainage with clapping and vibration is considerably more efficient than uncontrolled cough in propelling sticky secretions toward the lower airways, since the high pressures produced with cough cause the bronchi to collapse. After physiotherapy has, presumably, loosened and displaced the secretions from one segment to the large bronchi or trachea, the patient should be encouraged to cough and expectorate. In severe cases, this kind of treatment may be required three or more times a day. Although some patients may spend as long as an hour at a time undergoing these manipulations, most children tire easily and effectiveness of the maneuvers rapidly diminishes. Breathing exercises designed to teach children slow, controlled exhalation should be used in those old enough to cooperate.

Antimicrobial agents play an important part in the therapy of the pulmonary lesion of CFP, though the prophylactic use of broad-spectrum antibiotics for months or years has been largely abandoned. The choice of agents should depend on the organism cultured from the individual patient at the time infection is manifest, and on its antibiotic sensitivity in vitro. Since *S. aureus* is by far the most common organism found in untreated patients, penicillin or oxycillin is frequently indicated. Infection with gram-negative organisms may require therapy with broad-spectrum antibiotics such as a tetracycline or chloramphenicol, and when *Ps. aeruginosa* or *Proteus vulgaris* is present, drugs like colistin or polymyxin B may be indicated. These antibiotics are given systemically by the oral, intravenous, or intramuscular route as well as in aerosols. Chloramphenicol palmitate is not suitable for either oral or aerosol administration since it has no antibacterial effect unless the palmitate is split off by lipase. A single agent may be given alone by one or several routes simultaneously (e.g., oral and aerosol) or in conjunction with other drugs. It must be recognized that by whatever route the antibiotic is administered, the nature of the lesion does not favor high concentrations of the antibiotic in the place where the microorganisms are concentrated, namely, in the depth of the bronchi. It is perhaps for this reason that high doses and prolonged therapy are usually required. Two weeks would be considered a minimum for treatment but frequently therapy has to be continued over many weeks.

Treatment with antimicrobial agents must be tailored to the individual patient, whose response will determine the duration of therapy. All signs and symptoms, including cough, fever, dyspnea, leucocytosis, and auscultatory and roentgen abnormalities in the chest, must be considered. When the condition of the patient improves and reaches a plateau, it has been our practice to continue therapy for an additional week. At that time, antibiotic therapy is discontinued and if the status quo is maintained, no further treatment is given until an exacerbation occurs; if it occurs within a few days after discontinuing therapy, the original program is resumed and continued for another 2 to 4 weeks. Chronic therapy may ultimately be essential. This empiric approach is based upon an experience of 20 years and an opportunity to observe and study the progress of the disease in hundreds of patients.

Because of the variety of organisms involved and also because of the secondary effects of antibiotic therapy, a culture of the sputum with sensitivity tests should be performed before and at intervals during the course of antibiotic therapy. In infants and young children who are not able to expectorate sputum, the nasopharynx may be cultured during a coughing spell.

During exacerbations, patients with severe pulmonary lesions frequently require hospitalization. Severe cyanosis and heart failure may require treatment with oxygen. Blood gases and pH should be monitored in these cases and oxygen concentration in the inspired air regulated judiciously. Patients with chronic respiratory acidosis may depend on hypoxia for the stimulation of respiration, and their respirations may be depressed if high concentrations of oxygen in the inspired air succeed in raising the oxygen tension in the arterial blood above the threshold of the chemoreceptors. Concentrations of oxygen between 30 and 40 percent, such as are obtained in the ordinary oxygen tent, do not usually raise blood oxygen to a dangerous level, but 100 percent oxygen should never be used, either by mask or in front of a tracheostomy tube, in these patients. For example, a child to whom the parents gave pure oxygen by mask after a coughing spell, became comatose and apneic within a few minutes and had to be revived with artificial respiration. During periods of severe hypoxemia, appetite may fall; food intake will improve if such children eat while in an oxygen tent.

Mucoid impaction or other signs of local obstruction may require aspiration of secretions and irrigation of the bronchi through a bronchoscope. Kylstra has devised a more radical and probably more effective method of bronchopulmonary lavage which has been used in some patients with CFP. The method, still in an experimental stage, consists of filling and irrigating one entire lung with saline through a bronchoscope with a triple-lumened tube, the third lumen being used to ventilate the other lung during the procedure. Because of the instrumentation required, only adults or children over the age of 15 years can be treated, and they have to have sufficient residual pulmonary function to tolerate elimination of half of this function during the lavage.

Debilitated patients with overwhelming amounts of secretions occasionally require tracheostomy to facilitate the removal of secretions by means of suction. Bronchoscopy should not be undertaken in such cases unless followed by tracheostomy, since the secretions invariably increase afterwards and frequent suction is essential. Such heroic measures usually constitute the last resort but have occasionally helped to tide a patient over an acute episode and restore him to a tolerable existence.

Treatment of *congestive failure* must be directed toward the correction of hypoxia. Results obtained with digitalis and diuretics are usually disappointing.

The therapy of the *digestive disturbances* usually presents a much smaller problem than that of the respiratory lesions. Although undigested fat and proteins as well as calcium and fat-soluble vitamins fail to be absorbed completely, the voracious appetite of these patients leads to a very large intake of food, so that absorption of as little as 50 percent of the ingested material may be adequate for satisfactory nutrition. An increased intake of a normal, well-balanced diet will satisfy the nutritional requirements of most patients even without replacement of pancreatic enzymes. Certain foods, usually with high fat content, are poorly tolerated by some children, with or without enzyme therapy; in these cases the diet should be individually regulated to avoid abdominal distress and diarrhea. For infants, the protein intake should be higher than that provided by human milk. It has been observed recently that soybean protein is absorbed much less completely than the protein in cow's milk in patients with CFP, and severe hypoproteinemia with edema has been observed in infants with this disease who were fed a soybean formula. CFP should be considered a contraindication for the feeding of soybean formulas unless pancreatic enzymes are administered simultaneously. Since medium-chain triglycerides (C8 to C12) can be digested by intracellular lipase in the mucosa of the intestine and therefore do not depend on pancreatic lipase, an attempt has been made to feed a medium-chain triglyceride formula to infants with predominant intestinal manifestations of CFP. The stools became less frequent, bulky, and offensive, but weight gain was not significantly improved. The expense and scarcity of this formula argue against the use of such preparation for babies with CFP whose nutrition can be accomplished more simply.

Intestinal complications may be prevented by the regular use of pancreatic enzymes. Bulky, foul-smelling stools, which may cause incontinence, abdominal pain, and social embarrassment, are a chief complaint of some of the patients and constitute an indication for the institution of enzyme therapy. A number of commercial preparations of pancreatic enzymes are available for replacement therapy (Viokase, Cotazyme, and Panteric granules in the United States). These are administered with meals and usually effect a partial correction of the deficit in digestion; they may be essential in infants. Complete correction is rarely achieved, regardless of the dose. The fat-soluble vitamins A, D, and E should be administered in a water-miscible and absorbable form to patients with pancreatic insufficiency. There is no evidence that the increased bulk or high fat content of the stools is deleterious. The calcium loss in stool is reduced by adequate vitamin D therapy.

Under ordinary circumstances, no specific therapy is required to compensate for the abnormal concentration of electrolytes in the sweat. However, in hot weather these children require the addition of sodium chloride to their diet to avoid the serious complications of dehydration and hypovolemia; the occurrence of such episodes led to the discovery of the sweat abnormality during the summer of 1953.

Occasionally patients with CFP require surgery for complications of the illness or for unrelated conditions such as appendicitis. They tolerate general anesthesia well, but the anesthetist should be aware of the diagnosis and choose an anesthetic which produces the least possible irritation of the bronchi. Because of the low ventilation-perfusion ratio in patients with pulmonary involvement of CFP, the "wash-out" and "wash-in" of foreign gases, i.e., the induction of anesthesia and recovery from it, are often prolonged, sometimes to two or three times the usual time. Secretions are usually increased and should be removed by frequent suctioning. Postural drainage should be resumed as soon after the operation as is compatible with minimal danger of bleeding.

Anabolic androgenic steroids have been used in desperation by some physicians in children with severe malnutrition and arrest of growth. No favorable effects on the basic condition or pulmonary function have been reliably documented, nor should they be expected, since these symptoms are usually indicative of terminal pulmonary insufficiency and infection. Because of the serious toxic effects of this treatment, it should be discouraged.

The general management of children with cystic fibrosis of the pancreas and their families has to take into account the serious impact on family life which is produced by the debility of the child, the ominous prognosis, the expense and time spent on treatment, and frequent hospitalizations. Particularly in families with more than one affected child, all these factors may seem overwhelming, and few families are able to cope with the problem without considerable support from physicians, social workers, physiotherapists, nurses, and teachers. In addition financial assistance from community resources is frequently necessary. An effort should be made to provide normal schooling and social life as long as possible; in severe cases, a home teacher will be required. The danger of exposure to respiratory infections and of physical fatigue of attending school has to be weighed against the psychologic effects of invalidism at home. A complete program of immunizations should be maintained, including pertussis, influenza, and measles. The welfare of the children depends to a large degree on the amount of education the parents are able to receive and to accept regarding the technical aspects of the therapy and interpretation of the symptoms, as well as an understanding of the child and his illness as a whole.

PROGNOSIS. The ultimate prognosis for patients with cystic fibrosis of the pancreas is grave. Nevertheless, it is difficult, if not impossible, to arrive at a prognosis in terms of time for a given patient who is either mildly or seriously affected by the disease.

It is well to remember that the initial descriptions of this illness indicated that all children were dead by the second year of life. Today there is an increasing number of patients in their teens and even some in early adult life. This improvement is both apparent and real. The availability of potent antibacterial agents used in conjunction with other therapeutic measures has helped to prolong the life of even those children affected at an early age. However, it is an oversimplification to assume that therapy alone is responsible for this change in life expectancy. This change reflects, in addition, an appreciation of the full spectrum of the illness at a time when improved diagnostic methods are available to assist in detecting the mild cases or even those with incomplete expression of the illness.

Those factors influencing the prognosis are at least in part beyond the control of the physician, for there is great variation in the expression of the illness in various patients and in each organ. The most that can be said is that severe pulmonary involvement early in life decreases life expectancy significantly. An episode of cardiac decompensation due to cor pulmonale is ominous. The digestive defect and the patient's response to it seem to have no influence on prognosis. The available therapy remains palliative; only when the basic defect is understood and corrected will there be a substantial change in the prognosis for these patients.

References

Andersen, D. H. Cystic fibrosis of the pancreas and its relation to celiac disease; clinical and pathologic study. Amer. J. Dis. Child., 56:344, 1938.
—— and Early, M. V. Method of assaying trypsin suitable for routine use in diagnosis of congenital pancreatic deficiency. Amer. J. Dis. Child., 63:891, 1942.
Antonowicz, I., Reddy, V., Khaw, K. T., and Schwachman, H. Lactase deficiency in patients with cystic fibrosis. Pediatrics, 42:492-500, 1968.
Blackfan, K. D., and May, C. D. Inspissation of secretions, dilatation of ducts and acini, atrophy and fibrosis of the pancreas in infants; clinical note. J. Pediat., 13:627, 1938.
Bodian, M., ed. Fibrocystic Disease of the Pancreas: A Congenital Disorder of Mucus Production—Mucosis. New York, Grune & Stratton, Inc., 1953.
Bowden, D. H., Fischer, V. W., and Wyatt, J. P. Cor pulmonale in cystic fibrosis. A morphometric analysis. Amer. J. Med., 38:226, 1965.

Bruce, G. M., Denning, C. R., and Spalter, H. F. Ocular findings in cystic fibrosis of the pancreas: a preliminary report. Arch. Ophthal. (Chicago), 63:391, 1960.
Clatworthy, H. W., Jr., Howard, W. H. R., and Lloyd, J. The meconium plug syndrome. Surgery, 39:131, 1956.
Cordonnier, J. K., and Izant, R. J., Jr. Meconium ileus equivalent. Surgery, 54:667, 1963.
Darling, R. C., diSant'Agnese, P. A., Perera, G. A., and Andersen, D. H. Electrolyte abnormalities of the sweat in fibrocystic disease of the pancreas. Amer. J. Med. Sci., 225:67, 1953.
diSant'Agnese, P. A. Bronchial obstruction with lobar atelectasis and emphysema in cystic fibrosis of the pancreas. Pediatrics, 12:178, 1953.
—— and Talamo, R. C. Pathogenesis and physiopathology of cystic fibrosis of the pancreas. Fibrocystic disease of the pancreas (mucoviscidosis). New Eng. J. Med., 277:1287-1295, 1343-1352, 1399-1408, 1967.
—— and Blanc, W. A. A distinctive type of biliary cirrhosis of the liver associated with cystic fibrosis of the pancreas. Recognition through signs of portal hypertension. Pediatrics, 18:387, 1956.
Dische, Z., diSant'Agnese, P., Pallavicini, C., and Youlos, J. Composition of mucoprotein fractions from duodenal fluid of patients with cystic fibrosis of the pancreas and from controls. Pediatrics, 24:74, 1959.
Esterly, J. R., and Oppenheimer, E. H. Observations in cystic fibrosis of the pancreas. III. Pulmonary lesions. Johns Hopkins Med. J., 122:94-101, 1968.
Fanconi, G., Uehlinger, E., and Knauer, C. Das Coeliakie-syndrom bei angeborener zystischer Pankreasfibromatose und Bronchiektasien. Wien. Med. Wschr., 86:753, 1936.
Farber, S. Pancreatic function and disease in early life; pathologic changes associated with pancreatic insufficiency in early life. Arch. Path., 37:238, 1944.
Fleischer, D. S., DiGeorge, A. M., Auerbach, V. H., Huang, N. N., and Barness, L. A. Protein metabolism in cystic fibrosis of the pancreas. J. Pediat., 64:349, 1964.
Gibson, L. E., and Cooke, R. E. A test for the concentration of electrolytes in sweat in cystic fibrosis of the pancreas utilizing pilocarpine by iontophoresis. Pediatrics, 23:545, 1959.
Goldring, R. M., Fishman, A. P., Turino, G. M., Cohen, H. I., Denning, C. R., and Andersen, D. H. Pulmonary hypertension and cor pulmonale in cystic fibrosis of the pancreas. J. Pediat., 65:501, 1964.
Grossman, H., Denning, C. R., and Baker, D. H. Hypertrophic osteoarthropathy in cystic fibrosis. Amer. J. Dis. Child., 107:1, 1964.
Handweger, S., Roth, J., Gorden, P., diSant'Agnese, P., Carpenter, D. F., and Peter, G. Glucose intolerance in cystic fibrosis. New Eng. J. Med., 281:451-461, 1969.
Johansen, P. G., Anderson, C. M., and Hadorn, B. Cystic fibrosis of the pancreas. A generalised disturbance of water and electrolyte movement in exocrine tissues. Lancet, 1:455-460, 1968.
Lobeck, C. C., and Huebner, D. Effect of age, sex and cystic fibrosis on the sodium and potassium of human sweat. Pediatrics, 30:172, 1962.
Lowe, C. U., Adler, W., Broberger, O., Walsh, J., and Neter, E. Isolation and study of a unique mucopoly-

saccharide from patients with cystic fibrosis of the pancreas. Science 153:3740, pp. 1124-1125, 1966.

—— May, C. D., and Reed, S. C. Fibrosis of the pancreas in infants and children; statistical study of clinical and hereditary features. Amer. J. Dis. Child., 78:349, 1949.

—— May, C. D., Stauffer, H. M., and Neuhauser, E. D. B. Fibrosis of the pancreas: enterogastrone and the "duodenal mechanism" in relation to increased appetite. Amer. J. Dis. Child., 79:91, 1950.

Mangos, J. A., and McSherry, N. R. Studies on the mechanism of inhibition of sodium transport in cystic fibrosis of the pancreas. Pediat. Res., 2:378-384, 1968.

Martinez-Tello, F. J., Braun, D. G., and Blanc, W. A. Immunoglobulin production in bronchial mucosa and bronchial lymph nodes, particularly in cystic fibrosis of the pancreas. J. Immunol., 101:989-1003, 1968.

Matthews, L. W., Doershuk, C. F., Wise, M., Eddy, G., Nudelman, H., and Spector, S. A therapeutic regimen for patients with cystic fibrosis. J. Pediat., 65:558, 1964.

May, C. D. Cystic Fibrosis of the Pancreas in Infants and Children. Springfield, Ill., Charles C Thomas, Publ., 1954.

—— and Lowe, C. U. The absorption of orally administered emulsified lipid in normal children and in children with steatorrhea. J. Clin. Invest., 27:226, 1948.

McGiven, A. R. Myocardial fibrosis in fibrocystic disease of the pancreas. Arch. Dis. Child., 37:656, 1962.

Mellins, R. B., Levine, O. R., Ingram, R. H., Jr., and Fishman, A. P. Obstructive disease of the airways in cystic fibrosis. Pediatrics, 41:560-573, 1968.

Schuster, S. R., Shwachman, H., Harris, G. B. C., and Khaw, K. T. Pulmonary surgery for cystic fibrosis. J. Thorac. Cardiovasc. Surg., 48:750, 1964.

Schwachman, H., Kulczycki, L. L., Mueller, H. L., and Flake, C. G. Nasal polyposis in patients with cystic fibrosis. Pediatrics, 30:389, 1962.

Spock, A., et al. In vitro study of ciliary motility to detect individuals with active cystic fibrosis and carriers of the disease. Bibl. Paediat., 86:200-206, 1967.

Trever, R. W., and Abrahams, I. W. Cystic fibrosis of the pancreas. Clinical features in adolescence and early adult life. Arch. Intern. Med., 106:253, 1960.

chapter 10

IMMUNOLOGIC MECHANISMS

JOHN B. ROBBINS, Associate Editor

The capacity of an individual to resist infection depends upon a number of separate factors which are maximally effective only when they act in concert. A deficiency or absence of a single factor may result in an overwhelming breach in the entire body defense. In other instances, deficiency or absence of any one of several different components of the immune response may predispose the host to the same or similar diseases. The integrity of each of these immune mechanisms is under separate genetic control. In human development, some components reach maximum activity later than others; consequently, the period between intrauterine life and early childhood is marked by changes in the immune capacity of the individual.

Acquired Mechanisms

To date a group of proteins, *immunoglobulins,* and a system of cells, *lymphocytes,* comprise the known acquired immunologic mechanisms. The biosynthesis of the components of these two systems is regulated mainly by foreign substances, termed immunogens. The specific reactivity of immunoglobulins and lymphocytes is referred to as antigenic specificity. That *immunogenicity* and *antigenicity* are separate properties may be illustrated by the immune reactions to the capsular substance of *Bacillus anthrax.* Infection or immunization with the whole bacillus induces the formation of antibodies to its capsular substance. The isolated and chemically purified capsular substance (polyglutamic acid) is antigenic, since it will react with these bacilli-induced antibodies. However, it will not stimulate their biosynthesis when injected and is therefore nonimmunogenic.

Development of Immunocompetent Cells

The genetic information that regulates the remarkable diversity of immunoglobulin structures and also the antigen-reactive sites of lymphocytes is presumed to be present in undifferentiated precursor cells. These cells are located in the bone marrow in adults and in the liver and bone marrow in the fetus. Although these precursor cells contain all the genetic information necessary for the expression of immunoglobulin structure and lymphocyte specificity, they will not react to the presence of a foreign substance. For both systems, antigen-reactive cells derived from these pre-cursors acquired this property during differentiation. The differentiation of lymphocytes follows the interaction of precursor cells with epithelial tissue of the thymus gland. The mechanism of maturation of the precursor cells to a lymphocyte is unknown, but there is some evidence to implicate a hormone-like substance secreted by the thymus gland. The bursa of Fabricius is a source of precursors of immunoglobulin-producing cells in avians, and Peyer's patches have been shown to contain precursors of immunoglobulin-producing cells in rabbits, but a comparable gland or source of cells has not been identified in man.

Differentiation of immunoglobulin-producing cells results in the restriction of genetic information regulating antibody synthesis to a single antigenic specificity and structure. Although not rigorously verified, it is likely that the genetic information of mature lymphocytes is similarly restricted to the expression of one antigen-reactive site. It is probable that only the "small" lymphocytes of the lymphoid tissue and body fluids comprise this system.

The process of differentiation of immunocompetent cells occurs at a very slow rate during the latter half of intrauterine existence and increases to a maximal level soon after birth. The regulatory role of the thymus during childhood and adult life is not known but some data from animal experimentation and the altered reactivity of humans with thymomas suggest a continuing function for this gland throughout extrauterine existence. No evidence exists for a continuing differentiation of immunoglobulin-producing cells in adult human life, suggesting that most of the acquired immunity in extrauterine life is due to the stimulation and multiplication of differentiated cells by immunogens.

Local exposure of differentiated cells of the lymphocyte system and immunoglobulin-producing cells to an immunogen results in mitosis and circulation of specific sensitized cells throughout the body. Infection or immunization with most agents will induce this "primary" immune response in both the immunoglobulin-producing and the lymphocyte system. However, the protective capacity toward various pathogens differs for the two systems. In general, immunoglobulins are highly protective against bacteria, viruses, toxins, and other foreign substances that invade the blood and extracellular body fluids. In contrast, lymphocytes are protective against intracellular parasites, such as mycobacteria, some viruses, and perhaps some malignancies.

In relation to the amount of total genetic information their precursor cells contain, differentiated immunocompetent cells are highly restricted in their capacity to synthesize such cell products as specific immunoglobulins. Studies using monospecific immunofluorescent reagents have shown that all immunoglobulins are synthesized in the plasma cell or lymphoid cell series. A single cell has been shown capable of synthesizing one immunoglobulin; i.e., only one structural characteristic, such as antigenic specificity, class, subclass, light chain type, and allotype, will be found within a single cell. Although not as well studied, it would seem that a mature lymphocyte has only one antigen-reactive site. Differentiation of immunocompetent cells would then appear to parallel or result from restriction in the total genetic information that can be expressed by the cell. The best explanation for the development of immunologic mechanisms, therefore, would be the acquisition by any individual of an increased number of differentiated cells. Unanswered are questions of whether differentiation is due to loss or repression of portions of the gene potential, or some modification of the cell membrane that restricts the interaction of immunocompetent cells to few substances.

Structure-Function Relationships of Immunoglobulin

The degradation of foreign substances is at least a two-step process involving a recognition mechanism and a catabolic process. The recognition mechanism is specific and serves to activate the catabolic process at the site of the foreign substance. The catabolism of the macromolecules into low-molecular-weight metabolites will result in elimination of the foreign substance without injuring the host's tissues. Immunoglobulins are one recognition system, and their structure is characterized by a common subunit composed of two different polypeptide chains designated as light and heavy. The recognition mechanism or antigen-binding capacity is located in the area of the molecule formed by the light polypeptide chain and that portion of the heavy polypeptide chain denoted Fd. In all immunoglobulin molecules, the portion having the same antigenic specificity seems to be identical and, thus, functions as the recognition unit of all antibodies. This unit may be prepared by the partial proteolysis of the immunoglobulin molecule (Fab fragment) free of the non-antigen-binding portion of the protein. Although such fragments retain all measurable antigen-binding activity of the parent molecule, such activities as phagocytosis and bactericidal reactions cannot be elicited. The biologic activity of the immunoglobulin molecule is contained in an inactive form within the structure of the heavy polypeptide chain denoted Fc. Following interaction of the Fab portion of the molecule with the antigen, a subtle alteration of the molecular configuration of the remainder of the immunoglobulin (Fc fragment) results in the formation of a biologically active site.

Extensive differences of the Fc fragments among immunoglobulin molecules have permitted a general classification separating them into classes which have been denoted IgM, IgA, IgG, IgD, and IgE. Further distinctions within these major classes involving smaller groups of amino acids in the heavy polypeptide chain have permitted subclass and allotypic designations. Each immunoglobulin class and subclass has distinct as well as shared biologic and protective activities. A summary of the general structure and biologic properties of these molecules is given in Table 1.

One explanation for the remarkable diversity of immunoglobulin structures with identical antigenic specificities is derived from the observations that various classes of immunoglobulins are restricted to certain body locations and that these molecules exhibit different secondary biologic activities following interaction with their antigens. As an example of this characteristic, it can be seen in Table 1 that the major component of the external secretory antibodies, IgA, does not activate or induce complement-dependent bactericidal reactions. Antibodies of the IgG class with identical specificity will activate the complement proteins. Another example of the highly specialized secondary biologic activities of immunoglobulins is the difference in the skin-sensitizing and complement-fixing properties of the subgroups of IgG globulins.

The antigenic composition of most infectious particles and other foreign substances is highly complex, and immunoglobulins are very diverse in terms of their wide range of specificities and secondary structural characteristics. In contrast, antibodies to some components of complex antigens such as polysaccharides are relatively homogeneous. For instance, most antibodies to the "I" public antigen of erythrocytes detected during infection with *Mycoplasma pneumoniae* are composed of immunoglobulins of one light chain type (kappa) and one heavy chain type (mu) IgM. Antibodies to several bacterial surface antigens consist almost entirely of the heavy chain IgG_2 subgroup and have type 1 light polypeptide chains. These findings have prompted investigation into the genetic control of immune response in much finer detail than was heretofore possible. They may provide a more thorough understanding of the differences between infection and disease in humans.

Investigation of the relationship between the structure and function of immunoglobulins has helped to explain the nature of the passive immunity acquired by the fetus during intrauterine life. Of all the immunoglobulins in the maternal circulation, only IgG passes through the placenta to the fetus. The concentration of IgG in the plasma of the normal human infant at birth is equal to or slightly greater than that found in the mother. Low levels of immunoglobulins other than IgG are present at birth since the normal fetus synthesizes relatively little immunoglobulin. The relative permeability of the placenta to IgG is highly selective; it is due to the structure of the Fc portion of the polypeptide

TABLE 1. *Biologic and Physicochemical Characteristics of the Classes of Immunoglobulins (Normal Adult Human)*

	IgM	IgA Serum	IgA Secretory (IgAsec)	IgG	IgD	IgE
Molecular weight	880,000	155,000	350,000	144,000	165,000	188,000
Plasma concentration (mg%)	50-150	75-400	Detectable but very low	900-1,900	0.5-50	$5\text{-}150 \times 10^{-3}$
Colostral concentrations (mg%)	40-50	None detected	200-500	90	None detected	None detected
Respiratory secretions (mg%)	0.1	Detectable but very low	4.0	Detectable but very low	None detected	$1\text{-}20 \times 10^{-3}$
Lacrimal secretions (mg%)	Detectable	Detectable but very low	0.6	Detectable but very low	None detected	Not done
Gastrointestinal secretions (mg%)	Detectable but very low	None detected	1.2	Detected	Not done	Not done
Degradation rate ($t_{1/2}$ in days)	5.1	5.8	Not done	23.0	2.8	2.3
Antigen combining sites	10	2	Presumed to be $\geqslant 9$	2	?	2
Complement fixation	4+ for one subclass	None	None	Detectable for 3 subclasses	None	None
Bactericidal reaction	4+ for one subclass	None	None	Detectable for 3 subclasses	None	Not done
Skin fixation	None	None	None	None	None	4+
Non-cytotoxic histamine release	None	None	None	None	None	4+
Antiviral activity	None detected	None	None	Present	None detected	None done
Anti gram-negative bacilli activity	4+	Present but ? positive value	Present but ? positive value	Present	None detected	None done
Anti-bacterial toxin activity	Little or none	Present	Not done	4+	None detected	None done
Placental transmission	Little or none	Little or none	None	4+	Little or none	Little or none
Body compartment	Predominantly intravascular	Predominantly intravascular	External exocrine secretions	Intravascular and E.C.F.	Predominantly intravascular	Intravascular and in external secretions
Site of biosynthesis	Much in spleen, other lymphoid tissue	Spleen, lymphoid tissue	Submucosa	All lymphoid tissue	Spleen, lymph nodes	Predominantly in submucosa
Carbohydrate concentration	7%	4%	4%	0-1%	4%	

Key: 4+ accounts for most or all of whole serum activity
1+ accounts for little of whole serum activity

chain and is not dependent upon the molecular size of this immunoglobulin, since many other proteins (albumin, growth hormone, and orosomucoid) with a much lower molecular weight than IgG do not readily traverse the placenta. Furthermore, preparation of the Fab and Fc fragments of the molecule by limited proteolytic digestion reveals that only the Fc fragment passes through the placenta. The placental transmission of IgG is not the same throughout intrauterine existence. The placental transmission of IgG is a developmental process in that the concentration of IgG has been shown to be related to the gestational age or birth weight of the newborn.

The timing of this process is such that premature infants may have very low levels of IgG at birth.

IgG GLOBULINS. The concentration of IgG found in children 6 years of age or older is the same as that reported in adults (approximately 900 to 1,900 mg/100 ml) (Table 2). IgG proteins account for over 75 percent of the total immunoglobulins in plasma; however, only 40 to 50 percent of IgG in body fluids is normally present in the plasma. The amount of IgG in interstitial fluid is equal to or greater than that in the plasma; however, since the volume of interstitial fluid is approximately four times the plasma volume, the average concentration

TABLE 2.   *Range of Plasma Immunoglobulin Concentrations During Normal Development*

Age	Immunoglobulin Concentrations (mg per 100 ml)				
	IgM	IgA	IgG	IgD	IgE ($\times 10^{-3}$)
Newborn	5-30	0-11	700-1,300	0.01	0
1-3 mo	15-70	6-50	280-750	Not done	
4-6 mo	10-90	8-90	200-1,200	Not done	Not established
7-12 mo	25-15	16-100	300-1,500	0.5-5	
13 mo-3 yr	30-120	20-230	400-1,300	0.5-5	
3-6 yr	22-100	50-150	600-1,500	0.5-5	
6 yr-adult	50-150	75-400	900-1,900	0.5-50	5-150

Because of the deficiency of a reference standard only the average ranges of values as determined by several laboratories are listed.

of IgG in the interstitial fluids is about one fourth of that in the plasma. About one half the IgG present in the plasma exchanges with that in the interstitial fluids daily. The rate of degradation of IgG in the older child or adult is approximately 28 mg/kg of body weight. In the normal child (2 years of age or older) the concentration of IgG in the plasma remains relatively steady, the amount degraded being replaced by an equal amount through synthesis. Therefore, the synthesis of IgG is approximately 28 mg/kg of body weight per day.

Although the normal fetus can synthesize IgG at 6 to 7 months' gestation, the synthesis of this immunoglobulin is so slight that at birth the rate of synthesis of IgG per kilogram of body weight is less than 1 percent of that observed in an adult. The IgG placentally transferred from the maternal circulation is degraded with a half-life of approximately 30 days. The lowest concentration of IgG is reached when the infant is between 1 and 3 months of age, and may fall as low as 300 to 600 mg/100 ml of plasma in the normal infant and to levels of less than 200 mg/100 ml in the premature infant. At about 4 months of age, the rate of synthesis by the infant equals the rate of degradation of maternally derived IgG. Most of the infant's IgG, which is the only immunoglobulin that the fetus normally has at birth, is derived from the mother. Consequently, the contribution of IgG to the immunologic system of the newborn is dependent upon the antibodies present in the mother's circulation during the last trimester of pregnancy. If the mother lacks certain IgG antibodies, such as anti-measles antibodies, the newborn will also lack such immunoglobulins. Antibodies transferred to the infant will be degraded, and the immunologic effectiveness of maternally transferred IgG depends then on two factors: (1) the concentration of specific antibodies in the maternal IgG, and (2) the sensitivity of the infecting organism to specific antibodies. In the case of measles virus, relatively small amounts of specific antibodies are highly effective in preventing

or modifying the disease; this is not the case for the varicella virus. If the concentration of IgG anti-measles antibodies at birth is 16 times the minimum amount necessary to prevent clinical measles, it would take more than 6 months for the levels of antibodies to fall below the minimal protecting concentration, since the half-life of such antibodies is about 1 month. If the level at birth were only twice the minimum amount of IgG anti-measles antibody needed, concentrations less than minimum would be reached after only 1 month of age.

As the newborn receives antigenic stimulation from the environment, antibodies are produced. This general level of biosynthesis is reflected in the change of immunoglobulins during development (Table 2). However, if specific maternal IgG antibodies, such as those against measles virus, fall to ineffective concentrations before the infant has synthesized his own specific antibodies, there will be a nonimmune period until such antibodies are synthesized. If, however, infection with a virus such as measles occurs in an infant partially protected with specific anti-measles antibodies maternally derived, active immunity can result. Thus, infection with measles during the first months of life in an infant partially protected with maternally derived IgG antibodies may actively induce anti-measles antibodies without clinical manifestations of disease. This situation accounts for the responsiveness of infants injected simultaneously with small amounts of gamma globulin containing anti-measles antibodies and live attenuated measles. In such instances, active immunity in the infant is first superimposed upon the gamma globulin and then replaces the passive immunity. However, the presence of these maternally derived IgG antibodies may interfere with the newborn's immune response to injection with conventional antigens designed to protect against disease. In the case of vaccination with certain live viruses, such as the attenuated strains of polio and measles, too high a concentration of maternal IgG antibodies in the infants may prevent subclinical infection and, consequently, adequate stimulation and synthesis of specific antiviral antibodies will not occur. Immunization of the neonate with substances such as diphtheria and tetanus toxoid may be inhibited completely by maternally derived IgG antibody. This specific immunosuppressive effect of passively acquired IgG antibodies has been utilized to prevent the isoimmunization induced in Rh-negative mothers by Rh-positive cells derived from the fetal circulation. Extensive efforts are also being made experimentally to use this property of IgG antibodies toward tissue antigens in an effort to prevent graft rejection. Because of these general properties, it has been postulated that IgG antibodies constitute one of the normal feedback mechanisms of all immunoglobulin synthesis.

The regulation of the synthesis of IgG antibodies by infection or immunization differs from that of other immunoglobulins. Following contact with an immunogen, a high rate of mitosis and protein synthesis occurs in the lymphocytes and plasma cells. Some of these new cells are released from the local lymph nodes and enter the circulation. As the level of immunogen is reduced by the catabolism induced by the newly formed antibodies, the synthetic activities of the remaining cells decline to a low rate but persist for the lifetime of the individual. Reexposure to the same immunogen results in an accelerated and more systemic response than that of the initial exposure. In man this "memory" phenomenon (anamnestic response) appears to be unique to IgG synthesizing cells and may be elicited for as long as 30 years following the initial stimulus; it is not a general property of all other immunoglobulins.

A variety of secondary biologic activities is found in the group of IgG globulins. IgG antibodies with neutralizing and protective activity have been detected against such diverse pathogens as bacterial surface antigens and toxins, viruses, and some protozoa such as plasmodia. Most immunoglobulin of commercially prepared gamma globulin is IgG protein.

IgM GLOBULINS. The plasma IgM concentration in older children is approximately 50 to 150 mg/100 ml and the plasma contains approximately 80 percent of the total body IgM. The half-life of this protein is about 3 to 4 days, indicating a more rapid rate of synthesis and degradation than for IgG molecules. Antibodies against somatic antigens of gram-negative bacteria, as detected by hemagglutination or the complement-dependent bactericidal assay, consist mostly of IgM proteins. Since the newborn receives virtually no maternal IgM it has been postulated that susceptibility to gram-negative infections observed at this age is related to the absence of passively acquired IgM antibodies. The so-called "natural" isohemagglutinins, rheumatoid factors, and cold agglutinins also consist mostly of IgM antibodies.

Serum IgM antibodies, detected first, appear to arise first in response to antigenic stimulation. As the immune response develops, these IgM antibodies are replaced in part or entirely by IgG antibodies. However, this sequential change in the class-specific antibodies that appear in the plasma following exposure to an immunogen can be attributed at all ages to the relative kinetics and specific secondary activities of the IgM and IgG immunoglobulins. In certain systems such as hemagglutination or hemolysis, IgM antibodies, mole for mole, may be several hundred times as effective as IgG antibodies. In terms of effectiveness of assay in such test systems, steady-state rates of synthesis will also favor the detection of IgM before IgG antibodies. The rate of IgM synthesis in relation to that of IgG is even greater in the infant than in the older child. Thus, this dissociation of immunoglobulin synthesis is exaggerated at the younger age when IgM antibodies may reach higher levels relative to IgG.

Any immunogenic stimulus during intrauterine life such as may occur with rubella, cytomegalovirus, toxoplasmosis, syphilis, or herpes simplex infection may result in the synthesis of IgM antibodies by the fetus. Similarly, if disseminated infection occurs in the neonatal period the normal pattern of IgM synthesis may be accelerated. Thus, examination of the plasma IgM concentration in cord serum or up to 2 weeks of life may aid in the diagnostic work-up of infants with unexplained disease. Unfortunately, elevated IgM levels in serum have not provided the subtle clue sought so eagerly in evaluating intrauterine or neonatal infection because IgM levels were normal in many infants with documented mild diseases caused by infectious agents. As with other assays, an elevated IgM level may be useful as a diagnostic tool, but a normal level does not rule out infection as a cause of unexplained symptoms.

IgD GLOBULINS. Specific antibody activity within the class of IgD immunoglobulins has been sought by many laboratories. One group of investigators has identified IgD anti-penicillin antibodies. As with other immune systems, the biosynthesis of IgD appears to parallel other immunoglobulins during development. Concentrations in plasma of 0.5 to 50 mg/100 ml have been reported in adults.

IgE GLOBULINS. Antiserum monospecific for the heavy polypeptide chain of this immunoglobulin was made available by the discovery of an IgE myeloma protein. This anti-IgE serum did not react with the other immunoglobulins and failed to precipitate with normal adult sera, indicating a very low concentration of this immunoglobulin relative to the other classes. To measure the concentration of this immunoglobulin in normal serum, a modification of antibody assays, using insoluble immunoabsorbents, was necessary. With this new assay, it was found that the concentration of IgE protein was approximately 5 to 150×10^{-3} mg/100 ml in normal adult sera. It can be seen that this concentration is several logarithms lower than other better-studied immunoglobulins. Of interest was the observation that the levels of this immunoglobulin, IgE, were significantly higher in patients whose history was compatible with the diagnosis of allergic asthma. Patients with intrinsic or constitutional asthma had levels of IgE that did not differ from the normal subjects. Direct analysis of IgE antiallergen antibodies showed that there was poor agreement with the skin test used to diagnose atopic allergy. This finding was consistent with the observation that there are many false positives when skin tests are used as an indicator of IgE-mediated allergy (atopic or reaginic). In contrast, when the provocation test was used (inhalation of the specific allergen) it was found that there was an extraordinarily high agreement (96 percent) between IgE antiallergen antibodies determined by the in vitro assay and the positive results from the provocation test. Evidence such as this, as well as physical-chemical characterizations of serum fractions purified from patients with atopic allergy by Ishizaka, has provided strong support to confirm the evidence that atopic allergy and immediate hypersensitivity are mediated by the IgE type of immunoglobulins.

Serum IgE levels in children with eczema and atopic dermatitis have been shown to be remarkably elevated. The quantification of IgE may, therefore, permit an accurate definition of eczema or other atopic or reagin-mediated diseases as well as a more accurate tool for the investigation of antigenic stimuli.

The protective value of an immunoglobulin whose biologic activity would seem to mediate disease has provoked a search for the role of this immunoglobulin in other diseases. An important observation was made when levels of immunoglobulins found in children in Sweden and those found in children in a nursery in Ethiopia were compared. It was reported that concentrations of immunoglobulins M, A, G, and D discovered in Ethiopian children were two to three times higher than those observed in Swedish children, presumably due to a higher incidence of chronic infectious disease in Africans. The levels of IgE in the sera of Ethiopian children, however, ranged from 10 to 20 times those found in Swedish children. It was also found that those Ethiopian children with active ascaris infections had the highest levels, ranging as high as $1,600 \times 10^{-3}$ mg/100 ml, compared with the mean level of 800×10^{-3} mg/100 ml in the children without obvious parasites. Similar findings were documented in individuals with larva migrans. This observation led to the speculation that IgE antibody molecules might be synthesized preferentially when an individual is exposed to macromolecular substances such as parasites and raised the possibility that IgE immunoglobulins have protective value against parasites that reside in the lumen of the gastrointestinal tract and perhaps in the lung. It has been known for many years that animals such as goats and sheep undergo a phenomenon known as self-cure which seems to be due to a noncytotoxic-mediated histamine release. In this model, newborn animals are heavily parasitized by roundworms during feedings and during their first spring season. A high mortality following the ingestion of these worms

occurs during the first feeding. Ultimately the parasites die during the summer and since the pastures are no longer infected, the surviving animals are no longer parasitized. The next spring, following ingestion of more parasites, the animals experience considerable peristalsis and diarrhea. The worms are then expunged and the second-year animals have a very high rate of survival. This process is repeated again and again into adult life so that the animals acquire a protection against intestinal roundworms. This self-cure seems to be mediated by IgE-like antibodies which result in histamine release following interaction with their antigen which is noncytotoxic. The cell that is concerned with the release of the histamine would seem to be the basophil. This self-cure process has been successfully established now in several laboratory animals.

The cellular localization of IgE resembles in many respects the submucous membrane localization of IgA-containing cells. However, in addition to being present in the spleen and lymph nodes, IgE-containing cells have been found in high concentrations in the submucous membranes of the respiratory and gastrointestinal tracts and in the tonsillar tissue. IgE has also been found in the serum and in external secretory fluid. However, the relation between these cellular sites and the symptoms of disease has not been established. In vitro studies, with anti-IgE reagents or specific allergens, have shown histamine release when these reagents interact with leucocytes (probably basophils). These in vitro assays can distinguish quantitative differences among individuals and may permit genetic studies of this unusual hypersensitivity phenomenon.

Immunologic Mechanisms of the External Secretory Tissue (IgA Globulins)

The external secretory tissue as an immunologic defense mechanism includes a discussion of IgA globulins. It was observed by many investigators that the general properties of antibodies of the external secretion, such as colostrum and milk, and the gastrointestinal fluid, differed from serum antibodies. In addition, many observations had indicated that the biosynthesis of antibodies of serum and external secretions occasionally were regulated independently. The structural and biologic basis for these observations was established by Tomasi and by Bellanti who showed that the major immunoglobulin component of external secretions was comprised of IgA immunoglobulins (IgA$_{sec}$) (Table 1) and that the regulation of synthesis for this group of external secretory immunoglobulins was separate from serum antibodies. Further studies have shown that there is little exchange between serum and external secretory immunoglobulins. Thus, transfusion of whole blood or plasma or injection of gamma globulin does not provide immunoglobulins for the external secretions in normal individuals.

All immunoglobulins have been detected in the external secretions (Table 1) but the ratios of their concentrations differ widely from those found in serum. In most secretions the predominant immunoglobulin is IgA, but the structure of this exocrine protein is different from the serum IgA. The basic structural unit of the secretory IgA consists of two light and two heavy polypeptide chains and a unique polypeptide which has been designated as the "T" chain. This protein is of unusual interest to physicians and biologists because the light and heavy polypeptide chains of IgA protein are synthesized in lymphoid and plasma cells of the external secretory submucosa, but the "T" polypeptide chain is synthesized in epithelial cells. This two-cell origin of secretory IgA synthesis is unique, but as yet no biologic function has been assigned to the "T" chain. Some investigators have indicated that the peptide affords an antiproteolytic property to the IgA molecule which prevents its rapid degradation by the gastrointestinal enzymes. The "T" chain synthesis has been shown to be independent of the regulation of the heavy polypeptide chain synthesis of IgA. Thus, free "T" chain can be detected in external secretions of patients with depressed synthesis of IgA, as occurs in X-linked hypogammaglobulinemia.

For many pathogens that interact with external secretory tissue first, the protective mechanism appears to be IgA; these pathogens include enteroviruses and bacterial pathogens in the gastrointestinal tract, and influenza and other respiratory tract viral pathogens. Synthesis of this group of antibodies occurs regularly after natural infection but may not be induced in all individuals by parenteral immunization with killed virus preparations, presumably because such material does not reach the external secretory tissue. In some cases, induction of serum immunity does not parallel immunity in the external secretory tissue and results in an abortive immune response to natural infection; this has been observed with rubeola and respiratory syncytial virus. Direct contact with the antigen, such as killed respiratory vaccines by aerosol inhalation, will induce local as well as systemic immunity and this technique of immunization has been advocated as a general biologic procedure.

Isolated *IgA deficiency* is one of the most common genetic differences yet observed in humans. To date, both serum and external secretory IgA deficiencies seem to be parallel, so that a serum analysis will be sufficient to diagnose this trait. The incidence of isolated IgA deficiency may be as high as 0.4 percent. In most situations or conditions, there is a compensatory increase in other external secretory immunoglobulins, notably in the IgM proteins, and this appears to confer a degree of protection comparable to normal individuals. However, in concurrence with other immunologic deficiencies such as ataxia-telangiectasia, hypogammaglobulinemia, and cellular immune deficiencies, IgA deficiency is associated with a high rate of therapeutic failure in preventing suppurative complications such as bronchiectasis and chronic gastrointestinal inflammation. Isolated IgA deficiency as detected by surveys of hospitalized patients has been correlated with a high rate of rheumatoid arthritis and other disease of a diverse nature, including a suspected high rate of malignancy.

Some critical areas of initial host-parasite interaction, such as the nasopharynx, derive their immunologic mechanisms from both the serum and external secretory tissue. Thus IgA is a major immunoglobulin component in the nasopharynx and it is derived from both the serum and the external secretory tissue. Although the mechanism of immunity conferred by lymphocytes in the external secretory tissue is less well documented than immunoglobulin synthesis, early reports indicate that the cellular-immune mechanisms of the external secretory tissue are regulated independently of the serum lymphocyte pool. Thus, local infection can result in sensitization of external secretory lymphocytes as well as serum lymphocytes, whereas immunization with a killed vaccine may result in sensitizing only the serum pool of lymphocytes. It should be emphasized that gastrointestinal inflammation and dysfunction as well as infection may be among the earliest symptoms of lymphocyte-mediated deficiency as well as immunoglobulin-deficiency syndromes.

Lymphocyte-Mediated Immunity (Thymic Dependent)

Specifically sensitized lymphocytes, circulating in the lymphatics and the external secretory tissues, constitute an important specific mechanism providing protection against bacterial and fungal pathogens, perhaps against foreign tissue such as viral-induced cellular antigens, and possibly against neoplasms. Although the development of this cell-mediated system is similar to the immunoglobulin system, it differs from it in several important respects. Specifically sensitized lymphocytes are not passively acquired in the newborn. The sensitization of lymphocytes can occur during intrauterine existence and during early infancy even in prematures, but this process seems to occur at a slower rate than in older children and adults. Specifically sensitized lymphocytes may interact with a variety of substances but do not participate directly in the catabolism of the immunogen. Rather, after interaction with the antigen they release several soluble substances, which are chemotactic for phagocytic cells, consisting predominantly of large macrophages and interferon. Thus, the antigen-reactive site is contained within the cell (lymphocyte) but the secondary biologic activity consequent to antigen interaction is due to the release of soluble substances.

The nature of the receptor substance on the lymphocyte responsible for the recognition of the antigen is unknown, but there has been partial characterization of biologically active substances released from the lymphocyte following interaction with the antigen. All of these lymphocyte-released substances seem to be low molecular proteins (molecular weight from 14,000 to 70,000). The released materials are stable under a variety of experimental conditions. These substances released from the lymphocytes attract and activate macrophages and increase the vascular permeability of the local area. Hence, lymphocyte-mediated immunity is also a two-component system with recognition and then a catabolic pathway.

The protective effect of this system of immunity seems to be directed toward cellular particles such as fungi (*Candida albicans*), intracellular parasites that alter the surface antigenicity of host cells (vaccinia and measles virus), and cells transformed by intracellular viruses or carcinogens. Of interest is that many years ago this system of immunity was postulated to be the protective moiety against *Mycobacteria tuberculosis* disease. That this conclusion was valid is illustrated by the altered reactivity of humans without lymphocyte-mediated immunity (thymic dysplasia). Such individuals have a unique susceptibility to systemic infection with the BCG attenuated strain of mycobacteria used for immunization and to moniliasis, and they have a high rate of lymphoid malignancies. Of biologic significance are the laboratory models established by neonatal thymectomy. These thymectomized laboratory animals have afforded the investigator the first opportunity to study lepromatous leprosy, another mycobacteria infection, heretofore confined to humans. Neonatal thymectomy has also provided experimental animals suitable for investigation of susceptibility to viral disease and carcinogen-induced tumors.

Tissue Transplantation Immunity

As with all foreign substances, antigens of mammalian cells induce all components of immune response when injected into a foreign host. Much experimental evidence supports the hypothesis that the *rejection* component of the immune response resides in the lymphocyte system. Under certain experimental and perhaps clinical conditions, serum antibody, actively induced or passively administered, may combine with cellular antigens and mask their immunogenicity for sensitization or interaction with the lymphocyte system. Thus, this "enhancement" effect may occur concomitantly with the cytotoxic effect of some antibodies, so that there is great difficulty in evaluating the effect of antibody-mediated cell injury and enhancement.

The antigens of tissues recognized within a single species have been called histocompatibility antigens, which serves to distinguish this type of antigenicity from the broad activity of cells of one species presented to another. One system of antigenic structures, the HLA system, has been compared with the well-studied system of H-2 antigens in mice and is thought to be responsible for most of the rejection phenomena observed in man. The structure of this histocompatibility antigen is regulated by two gene loci, similar to the phenotypic expression for the Rh system of erythrocyte antigens.

Sensitization toward histocompatibility antigens may occur during development. The source of this sensitization may be obvious, as in fetal-maternal immunization that occurs when fetal lymphocytes enter the maternal circulation during gestation or following the transfusion of whole blood. Sensitization toward mammalian histocompatibility antigens may also occur following infection with some bacteria such as group A beta-hemolytic streptococci which have been shown to contain cross-reacting antigens.

Classification of human histocompatibility antigens has been done using select sera taken from multiparturient women and individuals with lymphoid malignancies that synthesize unusual paraproteins containing antilymphocyte activity. Using a panel of such sera with a complement-fixation assay and with a known histocompatibility antigen as a marker, it has been possible to distinguish at least 11 major histocompatibility antigens in humans and identify on a semiquantitative basis some of the genetic disparities between individuals. A more precise evaluation of the histocompatibility between individuals is derived from analysis of the antigen-reactive cell induced by lymphocytes in vitro. In this assay, the antigen source is mitomycin-treated lymphocytes from one individual. These treated cells will not divide under the conditions of the assay. The degree of histocompatibility difference may be measured by the mitotic index or the DNA synthesis of the lymphoid cells from another donor. This assay will detect histocompatibility differences that are not discerned by serologic techniques.

The success of tissue transplantations, such as kidneys donated to patients with renal insufficiency and skin given to individuals with thermal injuries, has been related to the degree of histocompatibility between the donor and recipient. Tissue matching offers a method for assigning HLA identification to potential recipients so that a more accurate match can be developed when donor tissue becomes available. The success of such tissue banks serving the transplantation needs of several services within a community has been convincingly demonstrated.

Acquisition of "Natural" Immunity

Serum antibodies to various antigens of bacteria are detected following birth and are evident with increasing frequency during development. Figure 1 shows a relationship observed by Fothergill and Wright be-

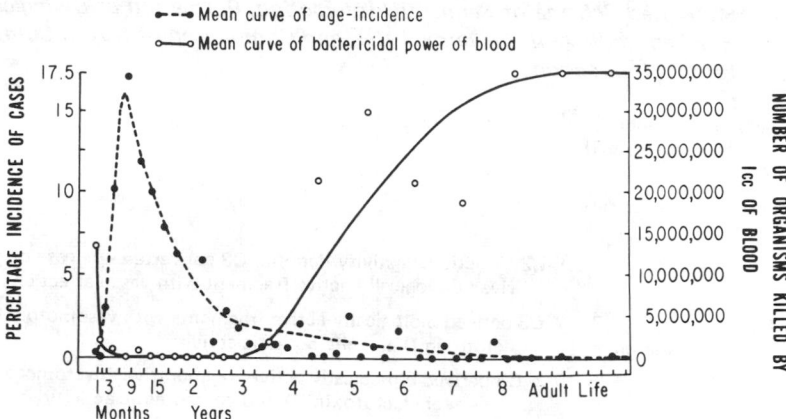

Fig. 1. Relationship between age incidence of *Hemophilus influenzae* meningitis and the presence of bactericidal antibodies against this organism in individuals of varying ages. (From Fothergill and Wright. *J. Immun.*, 24:273, 1933.)

tween the age incidence of *Hemophilus influenzae* meningitis and the presence of bactericidal antibodies against this organism in individuals of varying ages. Serum antibiodies, passively acquired during intra-uterine existence or synthesized during development, are the presumed immunologic mediators conferring protection. Since *H. influenzae* type b does not cause disease in most individuals, the immunogenic stimulus for these antibodies is not apparent. A similar relationship to that observed for *H. influenzae* meningitis has been established between the age incidence of meningococcal meningitis and "natural" antibodies to A, B, and C polysaccharides of these microorganisms. A similar development of other antibodies such as anti-blood group substance antibodies (isohemagglutinins) and anti-*E. coli* and *Pseudomonas* antibodies has been documented.

One alternate source of immunogens for antibodies to bacterial carbohydrate antigens may be the cross-reacting antigens of foodstuffs or of nonpathogenic bacteria. Extensive cross-reactivity between seemingly unrelated bacteria such as pneumococci, Klebsiella, Leuconostoc, and Rhizobium has been shown to be related to the same sugar moiety within these polysaccharides. Germ-free animals do not develop "natural" antibodies. The origin of anti-b isohemagglutinin in germ-free chickens was shown convincingly by Springer to be due to an *E. coli* following monocontamination with this bacteria. Anti-blood group substances, especially the B antigen, have been identified in many bacteria including *E. coli* and *Salmonellae*. Of interest to pediatricians is the occurrence of elevated isohemagglutinins that accompany infections with nonhuman ascaris larvae (visceral larva migrans). Another source of "natural" immunity may evolve from continuous contact with some plant substances such as phytohemagglutinin or bacterial products such as streptolysin S or staphylococcal exotoxins which are capable of inducing mito-

sis in many lymphoid cells. This mitosis is presumably due to interaction at other than the antigen-reaction site of these substances.

The acquisition of antibodies may be the source of protection against infection such as *Salmonella* and *Pseudomonas* which may cause different disease patterns in normal individuals at varying ages. For instance the invasive septicemic disease caused by *Salmonellae* other than *Salmonella typhosa* is almost exclusively seen in infants and children less than 8 months of age. In this case, the development of "natural" immunity in older individuals may have been due to infection with nonpathogenic bacteria with shared cross-reactivity of the somatic antigens of the more pathogenic *Salmonellae*. The presence of these cross-reacting antibodies induced by shared antigenic moieties may result in the accelerated synthesis of antipathogen antibodies and, thus, confer a high degree of protection. Although this cross-reactivity has been well documented for many bacterial antigens, virus-protein antigens do not seem to share extensive structural similarities.

Natural immunity has not been well studied in the lymphocyte-mediated system. It has been known that vaccination with BCG increases the resistance of experimental animals to a variety of infections with other organisms.

Many interactions between infectious agents and genetic characteristics of the host alter the susceptibility to infection. It has been known for many years that the resistance to lethal infection with falciparum malaria was heightened in individuals with homozygous or heterozygous sickle hemoglobin trait. However, the presence of this abnormal hemoglobin also increases the susceptibility of infected individuals to infection with pneumococci and salmonellae. In man and in animals the immune response is considerably altered following infection with a variety of viruses including measles. The initial

TABLE 3.   *Simplified Scheme of Sequential Interaction, Formation of Biologically and Biochemically Active Intermediates, and Completion of Serum Complement Protein Interaction*

1. Antigenic Site + Antibody   →   Active site for C1 q
                (IgM or IgG)

                        Ca++
2. C1, q, r, s   →   C1 esterase

                                    Mg++
3. C1 esterase + C4 + C2   →   C4,2 (functional activity denoted C3 convertase—release of C4-derived biologically active fragment with vascular activity)

4. C4,2 + C3   →   C4,2,3   + C3 derived biologically active fragments with vasomotor (Anaphylactotoxin I) and chemotactic activity
              (peptidase)

5. C4,2,3 + C5,6,7   →   C5,6,7 + C5 derived biologically active fragments with vasomotor (Anaphylactotoxin II) and chemotactic activity

6. C8 + C9   →   Cytolysis if antigenic site is a susceptible membrane structure

immune response, as well as the acquired immune response, may be depressed during infection with the wild type of attenuated strain of measles, and the affected host can show resistance to a variety of infections.

Nonspecific Factors

Complement

The activity of the factor known as complement is generated by plasma proteins that circulate in an inactive state and are activated in vivo by immunoglobulin molecules (IgG and IgM) following their combination with antigens. The action of complement follows the sequential activation of at least nine protein components that probably exert their effect on an enzymatic basis. The sequential fixation and activation leads to a final protein that is capable of inducing a distinct membrane defect in erythrocytes and other bacterial and viral cells. In the erythrocyte the lesion results in the loss of intracellular protein and metabolites and eventual lysis of the cell (hemolysis). This final step, however, is not the only activity of the complement proteins; in fact, many workers believe that other activities generated by the earlier components including chemotaxis, vascular permeability, and immune adherence are the significant protective activities of the complement system (Table 3). It should be noted that this nonspecific mediator of immunity is active toward many pathogens and is specifically initiated by the recognition molecule (immunoglobulin). The activated components quickly lose their function, perhaps by self-proteolysis as occurs with trypsin in the gastrointestinal tract, or by rapid denaturation of the components under physiologic conditions. To date it has been possible to measure several components of this system, C3, C4,

C5, and C1q, by conventional precipitation-diffusion analysis. The total activity of the complement system is measured by determining the hemolytic capacity of serum.

Recently, another series of protein inhibitors and activators, independent of the immunoglobulin system, has been shown to initiate the complement sequence commencing with C3. It has been proposed that this pathway may be important in the body reaction to rough or nonencapsulated bacteria. In this case, the complement protein sequence may be activated at C3 and completed to C5 which results in the generation of chemotactic factors and a receptor site on the microorganism for phagocytic cells.

Demonstration of complement proteins (C3 and C4) in the damaged glomerular structures in systemic lupus erythematosis has provided evidence that immunologic mechanisms may be injurious in such renal diseases as poststreptococcal glomerulonephritis (Chap. 22). The absence of the C3 component in some individuals provides the basis for increased susceptibility to infection; and the absence of serum inhibitor of C1, which has esterase activity, leads to the disease known as hereditary angioneurotic edema (Chap. 7).

Lysozyme

This protein of low molecular weight is found in most external secretions and intracellularly in many phagocytic cells. Lysozymes participate in the digestion of bacterial cell walls (muramic acid linkage) and may act synergistically with pathogens that have been partially catabolized by antibody-complement action. Lysozymal concentration in the urine may be increased several hundredfold in monocytic leukemia. This increase of lysozyme has been thought to be due to the secretion of this protein by the increased number of monocytes.

Phagocytic Cells

Phagocytic cells are ubiquitously distributed but appear under normal conditions to circulate in an inactive state. Following combination of antibody with a pathogen that results in activation of the complement system, or the combination of a specifically sensitized lymphocyte with its antigen, a variety of low-molecular-weight proteins are released that exert chemotactic and vascular permeability effects. (There is some evidence that the antibody-complement system and the activated lymphocytes release chemotactic factors for different groups of phagocytic cells.) Under these circumstances, phagocytic cells can penetrate venules and phagocytosis occurs. Intracellular catabolism of the pathogen is accomplished by release of catabolic membrane-bound enzymes such as cathepsins, proteases, ribonuclease, deoxyribonuclease, and lipase, contained in an inactive form within cytoplasmic structures known as lysosomes. Thus, a catabolic system may be activated at the site of a pathogen, consuming the invasive substance and finally itself.

REFERENCES

Amos, D. B. Human histocompatibility antigens. Fed. Proc., Immunology Society Symposium, 29:2010, 1970.

Bellanti, J. A., Artenstein, M. S., and Buescher, E. L. Characterization of virus. J. Immun., 94:344, 1965.

Berg, T., and Johannson, S. G. O. IgE concentrations in children with atopic diseases—A clinical study. Int. Arch. Allerg., 36:219, 1969.

Boyden, S. V. Natural antibodies and the immune response. In Dixon, F. J., and Humphrey, J. H., eds., Advances in Immunology. New York, Academic Press, 1966, Vol. 15, p. 1.

Cooper, M. D., Peterson, R. D. A., South, M. A., and Good, R. A. The functions of the thymus system and the bursa system in the chicken. J. Exp. Med., 123:75, 1966.

Crabbe, P. A., Carbonara, A. O., and Heremans, J. F. The normal human intestinal mucosa as a major source of plasma cells containing γA-immunoglobulin. Lab. Invest., 14:235, 1965.

Fothergill, L. D., and Wright, J. Influenzal meningitis— The relationship of age incidence to the bactericidal power of blood against the causal organism. J. Immun., 24:273, 1933.

Ishizaka, K., and Ishizaka, T. Identification of gamma-E antibodies as a carrier of reaginic activity. J. Immun., 99:1187, 1967.

LeClair, R. A. Pneumocystis carinii and interstitial plasma cell pneumonia: A review. Amer. Rev. Resp. Dis., 96:1131, 1967.

Muller-Eberhard, H. J. Complement. Ann. Rev. Biochem., 38:389, 1969.

Robbins, J. B., Kenny, K., and Suter, E. The isolation and biological activity of rabbit gamma-M and gamma-G anti-Salmonella typhimurium antibodies. J. Exp. Med., 122:385, 1965.

Rowe, D. S., Crabbe, P. A., and Turner, M. W. Immunoglobulin-D in serum, body fluids and lymphoid tissues. Clin. Exp. Immun., 3:477, 1968.

Springer, G. F., Williamson, P., and Brandes, W. C. Blood group activity of gram-negative bacteria. J. Exp. Med., 113:1077, 1961.

Tomasi, T. B., Jr., and Bienenstock, J. Secretory immunoglobulins. Advances Immun., 9:1, 1968.

Waldmann, T. A. Disorders of immunoglobulin metabolism. New Eng. J. Med., 281:1170, 1969.

chapter 11

ALLERGY

ELLIOT F. ELLIS, Associate Editor

11.1
PATHOPHYSIOLOGY OF ALLERGIC DISEASE

ELLIOT F. ELLIS

The term *allergy* was coined in 1906 by C. Von Pirquet, a pediatrician, to represent the changed reactivity that developed in an animal following contact with a foreign substance. Once the allergic state developed, subsequent contact with the same substance led either to a state of immunity, a condition favorable to the host, or to a state of hypersensitivity which was harmful. Von Pirquet was correct in his conclusion that immunity and hypersensitivity were closely related, and it is now known that both states are mediated by specialized cells of the lymphoid tissue (plasma cells and lymphocytes) and by their synthetic products (immunoglobulins). In recent years, the term "allergy" has been used in a more limited sense than that intended by Von Pirquet; it is generally applied to reactions of clinical hypersensitivity which cause disease in the host. Allergists as a group have tended to further restrict the scope of allergy by concerning themselves, for the most part,

with a particular segment of allergic conditions, designated as being "atopic" in nature. Modern usage of the term "atopy" (a neologism derived from Greek which in its literal sense means "out of place") would include diseases with the following characteristics: (1) spontaneous appearance in the absence of any known sensitizing event; (2) high familial incidence suggesting a genetic determination; and (3) presence in the blood of specific reaginic antibody (IgE) to a variety of environmental allergens. Diseases usually included in this category are hay fever, asthma, and atopic dermatitis. However, the concept of atopy is far from satisfactory since not infrequently the characteristics of atopy cannot be identified in patients with disorders clinically indistinguishable from those noted above. For example, in many cases of asthma no heredity factor can be identified and reaginic antibody is not demonstrable. Furthermore, the capacity to synthesize reagin is not limited to atopic individuals; many normal individuals can synthesize typical reaginic antibodies in the course of serum sickness, penicillin allergy, certain infectious diseases (pneumococcal pneumonia), and parasitic infestations (ascariasis). Nevertheless, hay fever, asthma, and atopic dermatitis are associated with each other so frequently that the concept of atopy remains a useful one.

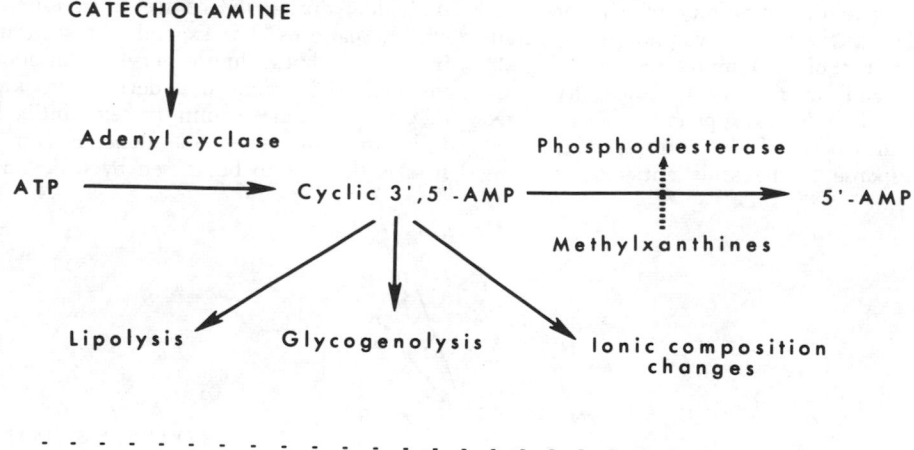

Fig. 1. Effects of catecholamines and methylxanthines on cyclic 3',5'-AMP. Catecholamines such as epinephrine or isoproterenol activate the membrane-bound enzyme adenyl cyclase which acts upon its substrate ATP to form the cyclic nucleotide cyclic 3',5'-AMP. Increase in intracellular concentration of cyclic AMP causes metabolic events indicated. Intracellular concentration of cyclic AMP is also regulated by the enzyme phosphodiesterase by which it is metabolized to inactive 5'-AMP. Methylxanthines, e.g., theophylline, inhibit action of phosphodiesterase and act to maintain intracellular cyclic AMP levels.

The nature of the defect in atopy has not been determined. It has been suggested that atopic individuals have a special propensity to synthesize reaginic antibody preferentially, especially when the antigen is introduced via a mucosal surface. This theory implies some sort of local or general defect in permeability of mucosal surfaces. Szentivanyi has postulated that the defect in asthma and probably in other atopic disorders is due to a partial "blockade" or to some other abnormality in structure or function of the beta adrenergic receptor, which has been identified as the membrane-bound enzyme, adenyl cyclase. This enzyme is part of the extremely important cyclic 3',5'-adenosine monophosphate (cyclic AMP) system which mediates the action of many different hormones and has profound influence on various cellular activities. The Szentivanyi theory is very attractive and explains the beneficial effects of catecholamines and methylxanthines in asthma, since both groups of compounds increase the intracellular level of cyclic AMP, leading to relaxation of smooth muscle (Fig. 1).

Heterogeneity of the Immune Response

The heterogeneity of the immune response is an extremely important concept in the understanding of allergic reactions. When antigen, such as diphtheria toxoid, penicillin, or ragweed pollen extract, is injected into a host, a large spectrum of humoral antibodies is formed in response to the antigenic stimulus. These antibodies all have specificities directed toward the injected antigen, but differ in immunoglobulin classes and subclasses and in important physiochemical and biologic properties. In addition, delayed hypersensitivity, or cellular immunity, which is mediated by specifically sensitized small lymphocytes, generally also develops as part of the immune response (Fig. 2). The clinical significance of the heterogeneity of the antibody response becomes apparent when it is recognized that antibodies of the same specificity, i.e., formed in response to the same antigenic stimulus,

TABLE 1.   Antibodies Differ in Biologic Activities

	IgG	IgA	IgM	IgD	IgE
Diphtheria toxin neutralization	Yes	Yes	No	?	?
Bacteriocidal activity	1	—	500-1000	—	—
Histamine release from leukocytes	No	No	No	—	Yes
Blocking activity	Yes	No	No	?	?
Placental transfer	Yes	No	No	No	No

manifest quite distinct biologic activities (Table 1). For example, IgG and IgA diphtheria antibodies neutralize diphtheria toxin, while IgM diphtheria antibodies have no toxin-neutralizing activity. On the other hand, IgM antibodies are many times more efficient in killing certain gram-negative organisms than are equimolar concentrations of IgG antibodies against the same organisms. Immunoglobulin E (IgE) is the only immunoglobulin thus far proved capable of sensitizing normal donor leucocytes for in vitro antigen-induced histamine release, while blocking antibody which develops in the course of hyposensitization therapy belongs to the IgG class of immunoglobulin. Human IgE is not actively transported across the placenta; therefore, a baby born of a mother reaginically sensitized to ragweed or other allergen will not be "born allergic" to the same allergen as a result of passive sensitization.

These differences in biologic activities of antibodies of different immunoglobulin classes directed against the same antigen may be expressed in an individual during the course of an illness as various clinical patterns. For example, as seen in Table 2, in serum sickness due to horse serum administration, the urticarial lesions that develop are known to be due to anti-horse serum protein antibodies of the IgE class. However, glomerulonephritis in serum sickness is thought to be caused by toxic immune com-

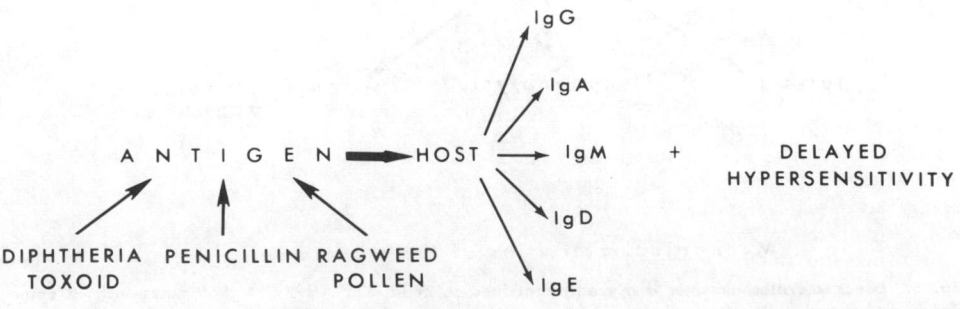

Fig. 2. Heterogeneity of the antibody response. See text for explanation.

TABLE 2. *Antibodies of Similar Specificities Mediate Different Reactions*

	Urticaria	Glomerulonephritis		
Serum sickness	IgE	IgG		

	Urticaria	Anaphylaxis	Exanthematous Reactions	Hemolytic Reactions
Penicillin allergy	IgE	IgE	IgG, IgM	IgG, IgM

	Nasal Symptoms	Protection from Systemic Reactions during Hyposensitization
Hay fever	IgE	IgG

plexes consisting of horse serum proteins and their specific IgG antibodies. In penicillin allergy, the immediate urticarial and anaphylactic reactions are mediated by IgE sensitivity to the minor haptenic determinants of penicillin, while the delayed exanthematous and hemolytic reactions are thought to be mediated by IgG and IgM antibodies. The nasal symptoms of ragweed hay fever are due to interaction of ragweed pollen with ragweed reaginic antibody of the IgE class. Blocking antibodies of the IgG class which develop during hyposensitization increase the patient's clinical tolerance to injected ragweed extract and allow the physician gradually to increase the dosage during the treatment period. Blocking antibody may also play a role in the improvement that occurs in individuals who benefit from immunotherapy.

Immunopathologic Mechanisms in Allergic Disease

The immunopathologic mechanisms by which the various classes of antibodies cause cellular and tissue injury have been elucidated by Gell and Coombs. Their classification of these mechanisms is illustrated in Figure 3.

In the Type I reaction, target cells, which have been identified as mast cells or their circulating counterparts the basophils, are passively sensitized by antibodies, which then subsequently interact with antigen on the cell surface. The reaction of cell-bound IgE antibody with specific allergen causes a conformational change in the antibody which triggers a chain of energy-dependent enzyme reactions. This results in the release of pharmacologically active substances, such as histamine and perhaps other vasoactive amines. These in turn are actually responsible for the reaction seen, e.g., the wheal and flare reaction in the case of the ragweed skin test, or the rhinorrhea and sneezing of the ragweed hay fever patient. Release of histamine requires that two reaginic antibody molecules fixed to the cell surface be bridged by an antigen with at least two determinants with specificities for the antibody molecules.

This requirement for bridging of reaginic antibodies by a multivalent antigen raises an interesting therapeutic possibility. It should be possible to prevent histamine release by injection of univalent, haptenic determinants derived from the antigen. These univalent haptens would bind to the reaginic antibodies

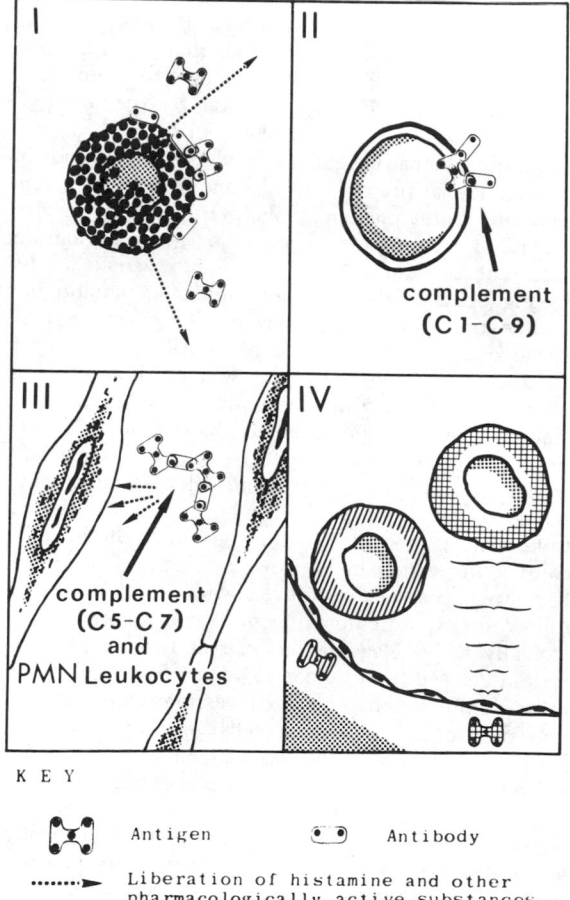

K E Y

Antigen   Antibody

········▶ Liberation of histamine and other pharmacologically active substances.

Fig. 3. Immunopathologic mechanism in allergic disease. Types of response. See text for explanation. (From Ellis. In *Advances in Pediatrics*, 1969, Vol. 16. Courtesy of Year Book Medical Publishers, Inc.)

fixed on the cell surface and prevent subsequent bridging by the multivalent antigen; however, the univalent haptens could not initiate histamine release in themselves. The antibody which passively sensitizes the mast cells in the Type I reaction has been variously designated anaphylactic, homocytotropic, reaginic, P-K (Prausnitz-Küstner), or skin-sensitizing antibody. While it is likely that the majority of reaginic antibodies belong to the IgE class, it is possible that reagins exist which belong to other immunoglobulin classes. Studies on the distribution of IgE-forming cells have shown that these cells are localized primarily in the respiratory and gastrointestinal tracts. This suggests that reaginic antibodies formed locally in these tissues may be responsible for disease occurring at these sites. It should be emphasized that antigen-reaginic antibody interaction is only one of the means by which mediator release may be effected. Since release of mediator is the final common pathway leading to the clinically recognizable action, e.g., the wheal and erythema in the skin test, other mechanisms leading to mediator release from target cells must be considered. It has been established that certain compounds, such as 48/80, and the drugs codeine and polymyxin cause histamine release by nonimmunologic or nonspecific mechanisms. Furthermore, aggregates of gamma G globulin, which are found in all commercial preparations of human immune serum globulin (human gamma globulin), can cause in vivo histamine release. For this reason, gamma globulin must not be administered by the intravenous route. As suggested by the above examples, one should not assume that clinical reactions resulting from release of vasoactive compounds are necessarily the result of an antigen-antibody reaction. While histamine has been established as the most important mediator in many Type I reactions, other pharmacologically active substances are known to be released as a result of antigen-antibody interaction. Slow-reacting substance of anaphylaxis (SRS-A), a lipid material of unknown composition with powerful bronchiole-constricting action in humans, is released from monkey lung passively sensitized with reaginic serum following exposure to antigen. Anaphylatoxins, biologically active cleavage products of the complement system derived from human C3 and C5, cause smooth muscle contraction, enhanced vascular permeability, and degranulation of mast cells with histamine release. These latter substances probably are not involved in Type I reactions since the interaction of reaginic antibody and antigen is not a complement-dependent reaction. Furthermore, pharmacologically active polypeptides, known as kinins, can produce many of the symptoms seen in anaphylactic Type I reactions. Kinins may be generated by immunologic mechanisms, particularly in abnormal immunologic systems. For example, antigen-antibody complexes of aggregated IgG and rheumatoid factor can initiate kinin production. Since pharmacologically active chemicals released as a consequence of immuno-logically caused injury are responsible for much of the tissue damage seen in atopic disease, a search for drugs that will either prevent mediator release (e.g., diethylcarbamazine, which prevents antigen-induced SRS-A release from rat leucocytes) or drugs which compete with mediators for tissue receptor sites (e.g., antihistamines) may well be fruitful.

In the Type II reaction, antibodies of at least two different immunoglobulin classes with similar specificities interact with antigenic determinants that are an integral part of the cell membrane or with antigens that have become attached to the cell membrane. Participation of the complement system is necessary in most reactions of this kind and, in contrast to the Type I reaction, the target cell is destroyed; hence the term "cytotoxic" or "cytolytic." A clinical example of this kind of reaction occurs when major group-incompatible red blood cells are transfused. The recipient's isohemagglutinins interact with the incompatible cells, the complement system is activated, and the sequential action of all nine components of complement results in lysis of the cells. In penicillin-induced hemolytic anemia, red blood cells on which penicillin determinants have been absorbed are lysed by antipenicillin antibodies and complement. In the glomerulonephritis of Goodpasture's syndrome, antiglomerular basement membrane antibodies react with glomerular basement membrane antigens in the presence of complement to cause the renal lesion.

In the Type III reaction (toxic complex reaction), injected antigen reacts with antibody to form soluble antigen-antibody complexes. Antigen-antibody complexes formed in moderate antigen excess (Ag_3Ab_2) are, for a number of reasons, "toxic," and are deposited in blood vessel walls in the glomeruli and elsewhere. Complement is fixed by the antigen-antibody complex; the C5 to C7 components are chemotactic for polymorphonuclear leucocytes, which are then attracted to the site of localization of the complexes. Liberation of cathepsins and other basic proteins from the polymorphonuclear leucocytes is actually responsible for the tissue damage seen. Antigen-antibody complexes have been implicated in the pathogenesis of certain forms of experimental and clinical renal disease, such as experimental serum sickness and the nephritis of lupus erythematosus.

The Type IV reaction is one of delayed hypersensitivity or cellular immunity. The pathogenesis of this kind of immune reaction is not well understood. While it is known that delayed hypersensitivity responses involve interaction of specifically sensitized mononuclear cells with antigen, the nature of the process by which the sensitized cells recognize antigen is not understood. Within limits of detection, humoral antibodies have not been implicated in the delayed type reaction. The small lymphocyte has been recognized as a cell of tremendous immunologic potential, and the interaction of sensitized lymphocytes and specific antigen has led to the production of a number of biologically active substances. One of these is a soluble factor that inhibits the in vitro migration of normal macrophages (called migration inhibition factor or MIF); another is a factor that causes aggregation of macrophages (called macrophage aggregation factor or MAF). Whether chemical mediators are involved in the immunopathologic damage that results from delayed hypersensitivity reaction is not known. Clinically, this kind of immune injury is seen most commonly as contact dermatitis caused by a large variety of unrelated chemicals which may be of quite simple structure.

Relevance of Immunologic Findings to Allergy Practice

It has been well established by passive transfer tests in vivo and by leucocyte histamine release in vitro that there is a reasonably good correlation between the titer of reaginic antibody to ragweed pollen and the likelihood of having symptoms on exposure to the pollen. Those individuals with the highest titers of reagin are the ones most likely to have symptoms on exposure to ragweed. The titer of ragweed reagin is affected both by seasonal exposure and by specific ragweed immunotherapy. Ragweed reagin titers rise during the pollen season and fall in the winter. During the early weeks of ragweed immunotherapy there is an increase of total serum IgE, presumably due to increase of specific ragweed reaginic antibody. Hyposensitization therapy, if continued, generally results in a gradual decline in reaginic antibody titers over the years of treatment. The likelihood of having a systemic reaction during a hyposensitization regimen

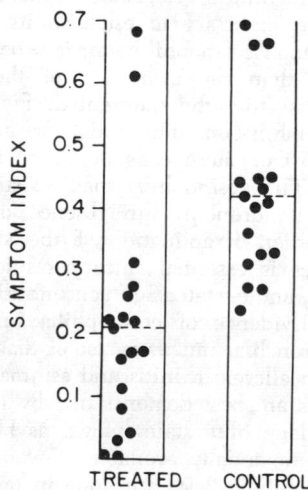

Fig. 4. Decrease in symptom index in children treated with ragweed extract compared to placebo treated controls. Symptom indexes were derived by recording presence and duration of nasal, eye, and bronchial symptoms plus number of antihistamine tablets taken in 18 treated and 17 control children. Median dose of whole ragweed extract in treated group was 22,000 protein nitrogen units. Thirteen of the 18 treated children had fewer symptoms than any of the controls. (From Sadan et al. *New Eng. J. Med.*, 280:623, 1969.)

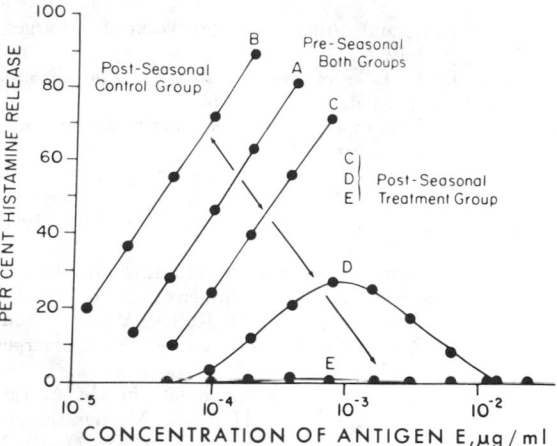

Fig. 5. Changes in cell sensitivity and cell reactivity observed with cells of treated and control children. In leucocyte histamine-release system, cell sensitivity is defined as quantity of antigen required for 50 percent histamine release. If cell sensitivity decreases, increased concentration of antigen is required for 50 percent histamine release. Decreased cell reactivity indicates that cells are unable to respond with maximal histamine release at any antigen concentration. Curve A represents initial cell sensitivity curve, both groups of patients. Curve B shows that cells of control group remained same or became more sensitive after pollen season. Curve C shows that cells of treated group either remained same or became less sensitive. Curves D and E show that in one-third of total treated children not only did cells become less sensitive to antigen but there was a change in their basic reactivity since they no longer released all of their histamine. This phenomenon was partial in three patients (curve D) and almost complete in three patients (curve E) whose cells released essentially no histamine at any antigen concentration. (From Sadan et al. *New Eng. J. Med.*, 280:623, 1969.)

appears to be related to both reaginic antibody titer and to blocking antibody production during hyposensitization. On the one hand, individuals with high reagin titers are those who most often develop systemic reactions in the course of immunotherapy, and on the other, those patients who develop good titers of blocking antibody are able to tolerate higher doses of ragweed extract in hyposensitization regimens. A most exciting finding in a recent study of children with ragweed hay fever was that a single course of hyposensitization with ragweed extract resulted not only in considerable clinical improvement (Fig. 4), but also in a striking decrease in the capacity of the subject's posttreatment leucocytes to release histamine on in vitro exposure to ragweed antigen E. In 3 of the 18 children in the study, there was a marked change in cell reactivity, since their cells released essentially no histamine at any antigen E concentration (Fig. 5). This finding places hyposensitization for ragweed pollenosis in children on a firm basis.

REFERENCES

Bloch, K. J. The antibody in anaphylaxis. *In* Movat, H. Z., ed., Cellular and Humoral Mechanisms in

Anaphylaxis and Allergy. New York, S. Karger, 1969, pp. 1-12.

Connell, J. T. Role of antibodies in allergic disease. New York J. Med., 69:551, 1969.

Ellis, E. F. Immunologic basis of atopic disease. Advances Pediat., 16:65, 1969.

Erdos, E. G. The Kallikrein-Kinin-Kininase system. In Movat, H. Z., ed., Cellular and Humoral Mechanisms in Anaphylaxis and Allergy. New York, S. Karger, 1969, pp. 233-236.

Frick, O. L. Immunopathologic mechanisms in the etiology of atopic disease. I. Antigens, antibodies, and antigen-antibody interaction. In Kelley, V., ed., Brennemann's Practice of Pediatrics. New York, Harper and Row, Publ., 1968, Vol. 2.

Giertz, H. Pharmacology of anaphylatoxin. In Movat, H. Z., ed., Cellular and Humoral Mechanisms in Anaphylaxis and Allergy. New York, S. Karger, 1969, pp. 253-259.

Ishizaka, K. Characterization of human reaginic antibodies and immunoglobulin E. In Movat, H. Z., ed., Cellular and Humoral Mechanisms in Anaphylaxis and Allergy. New York, S. Karger, 1969, pp. 63-89.

——— and Ishizaka, T. Biological function of γE antibodies and mechanisms of reaginic hypersensitivity. Clin. Exp. Immun., 6:25, 1970.

——— and Ishizaka, T. Human reaginic antibodies and immunoglobulin E. J. Allergy, 42:330, 1968.

Johansson, S. G. O., Bennich, H., Berg, T., and Hogman, C. Some factors influencing the serum IgE levels in atopic diseases. Clin. Exp. Immun., 6:43, 1970.

Lepow, I. H., Da Silva, W. D., and Patrick, R. A. Biologically active cleavage products of components of complement. In Movat, H. Z., ed., Cellular and Humoral Mechanisms in Anaphylaxis and Allergy. New York, S. Karger, 1969, pp. 237-252.

Lichtenstein, L. M. In vitro approach to problems in clinical allergy. New York J. Med., 68:2168, 1968.

——— and Norman, P. S. Human allergic reactions. Amer. J. Med., 46:163, 1969.

Melmon, K. L., Epstein, W., Tan, M., and Nies, A. A. Kinin generation caused by two immunologic systems (human IgG-rheumatoid factor complex and endotoxin-antibody-complement complex). In Movat, H. Z., ed., Cellular and Humoral Mechanisms in Anaphylaxis and Allergy. New York, S. Karger, 1969, pp. 224-225.

Osler, A. G. Immunology of reaginic allergy: in vitro studies. Clin. Exp. Immun., 6:13, 1970.

Pearlman, D. S. Immunologic mechanisms in the etiology of atopic diseases. II. Mediators of the allergic response. In Kelley, V., ed., Brennemann's Practice of Pediatrics. New York, Harper and Row, Publ., 1968, Vol. 2, pp. 17-28.

Robinson, G. A., Butcher, R. W., and Sutherland, E. W. Cyclic AMP. Ann. Rev. Biochem., 37:149, 1968.

Sadan, N., Rhyne, M. B., Mellits, E. D., Goldstein, E. A., David, A. L., and Lichtenstein, L. Immunotherapy of pollenosis in children. Investigation of the Immunologic Basis of Clinical Improvement. New Eng. J. Med., 280:623, 1969.

Stanworth, D. R. Immunochemical mechanisms of immediate-type hypersensitivity reactions. Clin. Exp. Immun., 6:1, 1970.

Szentivanyi, A. The beta adrenergic theory of the atopic abnormalities in bronchial asthma. J. Allergy, 42:203, 1968.

Vogt, W. Slow reacting substances. In Movat, H. Z., ed., Cellular and Humoral Mechanisms in Anaphylaxis and Allergy. New York, S. Karger, 1969, pp. 187-195.

Webster, M. E. The kinin system—a review. In Movat, H. Z., ed., Cellular and Humoral Mechanisms in Anaphylaxis and Allergy. New York, S. Karger, 1969, pp. 207-214.

11.2
DIAGNOSTIC METHODS IN ALLERGIC DISEASE

EDWIN A. BRONSKY and ELLIOT F. ELLIS

An etiologic diagnosis in allergic disease depends, as in any other disorder, upon correlating the information obtained from a carefully taken history with the findings on physical examination and the laboratory data. The initial work-up requires a prolonged follow-up observation period during which the effect of therapeutic measures on the patients' symptoms is evaluated.

HISTORY. The allergy history aims to obtain both general medical information about the child and also more specific information which may be helpful in determining the etiology.

LABORATORY STUDIES. A white blood count and differential may reveal eosinophilia. Although eosinophilia is often associated with allergic disease, it is not a constant finding. Repeated counts and differentials may be necessary to establish its existence or absence. A total eosinophil count is a better index of eosinophilia than the estimation of the percentage of these cells from the differential. Five percent or more eosinophils on differential or an eosinophil count of 250 or more cells per mm³ is considered significant. The eosinophilia may be strikingly high in allergic children in the absence of any other known disorder. Examination of the stools for ova and parasites is essential since parasitic infestation, eosinophilia, and elevated IgE concentrations are often associated. Evidence of eosinophilia in nasal secretions and bronchial mucus is also of diagnostic value, especially in allergic rhinitis and asthma. Eosinophils in secretions are best demonstrated by the use of an eosin-methylene blue stain known as Hansel's stain, which is commercially available.

SKIN TESTS. Skin tests are done in order to detect reaginic sensitization to pollen, mold, epidermal, household, and food allergens. A positive skin test indicates that reaginic antibody has become passively fixed to mast cells at the test site. It is inferred that reaginic antibodies are also fixed to mast cells in the shock organs, namely the nasal or bronchial mucosa. While this assumption is generally made, there is no definitive evidence that bears on this point. Positive skin tests must be correlated with the clinical history and do not necessarily indicate clinical sensitivity. A positive wheal and flare reaction can antedate the appearance of symptoms and, for unexplained reasons, can persist after the clinical sensitivity has disappeared, especially in the case of foods. Skin tests are done either by the cutaneous (scratch or puncture) or intracutaneous (intradermal) methods. In individuals with a high degree of sensitivity to the test allergen there is a real danger of precipitating a systemic reaction in the course of skin testing. For the nonspecialist, the cutaneous approach is the safest and should precede intracutaneous testing. In the hands of experienced individuals, the intracutaneous technique is quite safe. By measuring the size of the wheal and erythema the intensity of the reaction can be graded from 1+ to 4+, or described as "slight," "moderate," or "marked." Skin tests should not be done with allergens which, by history, have given an immediate reaction on exposure, especially with certain foods, such as peanuts, nuts, and other potent ingestants. The details of the skin testing technique have been presented by Crawford.

PASSIVE TRANSFER TESTS. The passive transfer method is used occasionally for detecting reaginic antibody in individuals in whom, for various reasons it is not possible to test directly. In this technique, serum from the suspected allergic individual is injected in 0.1 ml quantities into a number of sites in the back of a nonallergic recipient. After 24 to 48 hours, the injection sites are challenged with various suspected allergens. The tests are graded as in the direct testing method. The major drawback to passive transfer testing is the possibility of transferring serum hepatitis virus to the recipient.

MUCOUS MEMBRANE TESTS. In this procedure, suspected allergens are applied to the conjunctiva, nasal mucous membrane, or bronchial mucous membrane. Conjunctival tests are of limited practical value. Nasal challenge tests with pollen, in which changes in nasal airway resistance are measured, have been quite useful in experimental studies, but are not applicable to clinical practice. Bronchial challenge testing by inhalation of various concentrations of allergenic extracts provides useful information in asthmatic patients. It is especially valuable in individuals with multiple positive skin tests in whom it is difficult to determine which allergens are clinically significant. By including in the hyposensitization mixture only those allergens which give positive bronchial challenges one can eliminate other allergens that are clinically unimportant. The chief drawbacks to bronchial challenge testing are the time involved in doing the tests, and the possibility, although rare, of producing a severe episode of asthma. Details for performing bronchial challenge testing are described by Bronsky and Ellis.

SKIN WINDOW TESTS. In this technique, the skin is abraded with a sharp blade to the point of producing minute pinpoint areas of bleeding. Suspected allergens are then applied to the test site and covered with a clean plastic cover slip. The cover slip is kept in place with a small piece of cardboard

secured by adhesive tape, and is removed from 4 to 24 hours later. Control sites are also tested. In positive tests, increased numbers of eosinophils are found on the stained cover slip from the test site, and they are the predominant cell after 24 hours. There is a good correlation of positive skin window responses and pollen sensitivity. Conflicting results have been reported when the test has been used in the diagnosis of drug allergy.

OTHER IMMUNOLOGIC TESTS. Other tests, such as the leucocyte histamine release technique, lymphocyte transormation, sensitization of monkey ileum by human atopic serum (Schultz-Dale technique), and the quantification of total IgE levels and allergen-specific IgE, are useful in laboratory investigation of an individual who has atopic sensitivity.

TESTING FOR FOOD SENSITIVITY. The value of skin testing in the diagnosis of food allergy is controversial. The best correlation between positive food skin tests and clinical history seems to exist in those patients who develop immediate symptoms upon ingestion of the food and in whom the diagnosis of food allergy is already known. However, skin tests to a particular food are frequently positive in instances where the patient can eat large quantities of this food with impunity. The Rinkel provocation testing method, as well as its subsequent modifications, have been valueless in our experience.

Food allergy is best diagnosed by eliminating the suspected food from the diet, and, if improvement ensues, by reintroducing it. If the diagnosis is correct, untoward symptoms should reappear promptly. If elimination and provocation of symptoms can be documented on several attempts, the diagnosis of food allergy may be considered likely. However, since allergic disorders are characterized by remissions and exacerbations, great care must be taken in interpreting the results of food elimination and provocation trials. Furthermore, the patients' reactions become readily influenced by subjective emotional interpretations during allergy testing for food, and once the patient has the impression that he is allergic to a food substance, it is virtually impossible to test him objectively with any food substance without administering it in some disguised manner.

REFERENCES

Beers, Ray F., Jr. Skin tests. *In* Samter, M., ed. Immunological Diseases. Boston, Little, Brown and Co., 1965, Ch. 42.

Bronsky, E. A., and Ellis, E. F. Inhalation bronchial challenge testing in asthmatic children. Pediat. Clin. N. Amer., 16:85, 1969.

Crawford, L. V. Diagnostic procedures in atopic diseases. *In* Brenemann's Practice of Pediatrics. New York, Harper and Row Publ., 1968, Ch. 71.

Coombs, R. R. A., and Gell, P. G. H. Diagnostic and analytical methods. *In* Gell, P. G. H. and Coombs, R. R. A., eds., Clinical Aspects of Immunology. Philadelphia, F. A. Davis Co., 1968, Ch. 1.

Mathews, K. P. Other diagnostic procedures. *In* Samter,

M., ed. Immunological Diseases. Boston, Little, Brown and Co., 1965, Ch. 42.

Pepys, I. Skin tests in diagnosis. *In* Gell, P. G. H. and Coombs, R. R. A., eds., Clinical Aspects of Immunology. Philadelphia, F. A. Davis Co., 1968, Ch. 7.

11.3
PRINCIPLES OF TREATMENT OF ALLERGIC DISORDERS

DAVID S. PEARLMAN

Allergic reactions are extremely varied in nature and, because of the wide diversity of possible etiologic factors, often present highly individual problems. Specific therapy therefore depends upon the particular nature and severity of the disorder in question. However, general therapeutic considerations are substantially similar for all allergic disorders and fall mainly into three categories: (1) elimination or reduction of allergens and other stimuli responsible for the disorder; (2) induction of a state of increased clinical tolerance to these offending allergens ("hyposensitization"); and (3) modification of pathologic tissue processes by pharmacologic agents. The first two avenues of approach are sometimes referred to as "specific therapy" since they are concerned with preventing or altering the specific immuologic and nonimmunologic stimuli. Each of the therapeutic approaches listed may be sufficiently effective in its own right. For example, the mere avoidance of sulfonamides by an individual sensitive to sulfonamides would potentially eliminate completely the problem of sulfonamide allergy. It is frequently necessary, however, to utilize all three methods in order to achieve optimal control of an allergic disorder. Complete "cures" of allergic disorders are achieved rarely, if at all, but it is often possible to control symptoms to the point that they are virtually nonexistent for prolonged periods; in other circumstances, particularly in severe chronic asthma, therapy usually is only relatively successful. The participation of parents and the cooperation of the children themselves when old enough are of prime importance for a successful program of therapy, particularly when dealing with severe allergic disorders. The education of parents and children to the rationale of the therapeutic regimen, therefore, becomes an essential part of the proper management of allergic disorders.

Allergen Avoidance

Avoidance of offensive allergens constitutes potentially the most effective means for controlling allergic reactions. Unfortunately, it is often difficult to identify all the allergens responsible for allergic manifestations, and, even when they can be identified, it may be impossible to avoid them completely. Frequently, however, the exposure can be reduced to the point that contact with residual allergen evokes relatively mild symptoms if any at all. Drugs, chemicals, and, to a lesser extent, foods are the most easily controlled allergens. (See Sec. 11.2.) However, even extremely small amounts of these substances, often undetected, can produce profound symptoms in inordinately sensitive individuals.

Many inhalant allergens commonly found indoors including house dust, feathers, animal danders, kapok, and molds are very frequently offenders in atopic disorders. When substances such as these are proved or suspected allergens, an attempt should be made to minimize their concentration in the environment. The extent of the environmental manipulation recommended is based upon medical indications tempered by practical considerations. As a general rule, the severity of symptoms produced by allergens is in direct proportion to the intensity of exposure. If a child is sensitive to feather allergens, for instance, a feather pillow on which he sleeps is more likely to present a problem to him than a similar pillow located in a different bedroom. Consequently, the greatest efforts towards control of environmental allergens should be exerted upon those areas of the environment with which the child has the most intense contact. Because most small children ordinarily spend a large part of their daily lives in the bedroom, a significant reduction in exposure to common inhalant allergens can usually be accomplished simply by concentrating on that particular area of the home. In children with severe sensitivity to indoor inhalant allergens, it may be essential to attempt maximal control of the entire allergenic environment of the home, which often includes ridding the house entirely of pets. However, it is unusual that such strict control of the entire living area is needed or that such drastic measures as the elimination or large-scale replacement of furniture pieces or carpeting are required. Recommendations for controlling exposure to common allergens of the home environment are summarized in Table 3.

When the environment cannot be manipulated adequately to reduce allergen exposure to acceptable levels, temporary removal of the patient from the problem environment may be indicated. This may seem appropriate particularly when specific allergens are present for a limited time of the year (e.g., ragweed pollen), and the child can be sent to live for the duration of this period in an area free from such allergens. However, such a procedure is generally not practical for economic, emotional, and educational considerations, and should be recommended only after all other conventional forms of treatment have been found to be unsuccessful. A permanent change in residence is also rarely advisable except in a few well-defined situations; for instance, when a child with extreme animal sensitivity lives on a farm or ranch. Moreover, relief which results from

TABLE 3. *Directions for Environmental Control of Inhalant Allergens with Particular Emphasis on the Bedroom*

1. *All* pillows except those made of Dacron, and *all* mattresses and box-springs in the bedroom should be enclosed completely in an impermeable encasing*; zippers should be taped over to ensure a complete seal. Rubber pillows or mattresses are nonallergenic when new; however, they tend to absorb body moisture and harbor molds as they age, and, consequently, should also be enclosed. Mattress pads should be of synthetic material.

2. Bedsheets should be of smooth cotton or linen. Blankets and bedspreads should be made of synthetic material or other washable smooth fabric; quilts are allowed provided that they are stuffed only with synthetic material. (Chenille spreads, wool blankets, and other rough fabrics tend to act as dust traps.)

3. Stuffed furniture should be removed from the bedroom. (Furniture stuffed exclusively with foam rubber is permissible; however, much so-called foam rubber furniture contains other materials, such as horse hair, as well, and it is important to be certain that such products are not also present.)

4. Carpets or rugs should be made of synthetic material. Shaggy rugs are particularly difficult to keep clean and their use is discouraged. Carpet or rug underpads containing animal hairs should be removed; pads made of rubber can be substituted.

5. Window curtains should be of smooth fabric which is easily washed; synthetic material is preferred. Venetian blinds act as dust traps and should be removed; if necessary, window shades may be used in their place.

6. Forced air heating acts to stir up and recirculate dust and other allergens which settle out in the room, and may also be a source of allergens or irritants itself. Consequently, all forced air outlets in the bedroom should be closed and sealed off (aluminum foil or plastic wrap may be used). A portable room heater can be used if necessary to maintain adequate room temperature. Windows should be kept closed as much as possible. This is especially important in pollen-sensitive individuals during the offensive pollen season.

7. Toys stuffed with animal or plant products should be eliminated from the bedroom in particular, but preferably from the entire house. Washable toys stuffed with synthetic material are acceptable.

8. The bedroom closet should not be used as storage space for cleaning equipment or paraphernalia which might be a source of dust, mold, or other allergens (e.g., old books, fur coats). Similarly, dust mops, vacuum cleaners and the like should not be stored any place near the child's bedroom.

9. Plants tend to harbor molds and should not be kept in the bedroom. Aquariums also give rise to molds and are not allowed.

10. Flannel and silk bed clothes are undesirable, especially for the child with atopic dermatitis.

11. Atopic individuals tend to be sensitized very easily to feathery and hairy animals, and keeping of household pets should be discouraged when dealing with any child with an atopic disorder. Because of the emotional foothold often gained by pets once acquired, it is often very difficult to rid the environment of the animal, sometimes even when it is obvious that the animal is responsible for provoking severe symptoms. It is particularly important, therefore, to warn parents of atopic children against acquiring pets. When sensitivity to an animal present in the environment is known to exist, it is imperative to rid the animal from the child's environment completely. Although not generally recommended, under some circumstances it is possible to reach a satisfactory compromise by allowing the family to keep an animal such as a dog but house it outside the home, with the explicit provision that the animal is never allowed inside the home. Animal danders are notoriously difficult to eliminate from carpeting, and significant amounts of animal allergens may reside in the house many months after the animal itself has been removed from the environment.

12. The bedroom should be dusted daily and be given a thorough cleaning as often as is feasible, preferably each week. The child should not be present when the room is being cleaned.

13. Air filtration devices such as electrostatic precipitators may be employed, but are not recommended routinely. They are sometimes of great value, but at other times do not seem to make any difference to the patient's symptomatology. When used, it is recommended that they first be rented and employed on a trial basis for a month or two in order to determine their efficacy before a substantial amount of money is invested in their purchase. Air conditioners serve to filter outside air and are moderately effective in this regard. They are useful particularly during pollen season, but it should be remembered that their cooling effect may also aggravate symptoms in some individuals. In such circumstances, it may be of value to use the air conditioner as a filter but with the cooling component off.

14. Children should be discouraged from playing in areas likely to have high dust or mold concentrations, such as unfinished basements and attics.

15. Irritants such as tobacco smoke and strong odors (e.g., perfumes, paint) which frequently aggravate allergic disorders of the respiratory tract should be avoided as much as possible.

---

*Plastic encasings can be obtained inexpensively from local department stores. It is important to inspect them periodically for cracks or tears. More durable encasings can be obtained from: Allergy-Free Products for the Home, 1062 West Lynn Street, Springfield, Mo., or Allergen Proof Encasings, Inc., 4046 Superior Avenue, Cleveland, Ohio.

a change in residence is often temporary, and symptoms may recur within one or two years because of the development of sensitivity to new allergens in the area.

Institutionalization of children, particularly for severe asthma, is sometimes recommended in order to effect a change in the child's physical or emotional environment. Some children have been noted to improve markedly within a short time after being placed in an institutional environment. Providing the institution is adequately equipped and staffed, institutionalization may afford the additional opportunity for individualized observation or investigation of etiologic or contributory factors, and to assess the child's response to various therapeutic regimen.

Hyposensitization

In 1911, Leonard Noon observed that the repeated injection of a grass pollen extract into a pollen-sensitive patient resulted in reduced mucosal sensitivity to the pollen. Others soon reported that symptoms of hay fever could be relieved by this procedure and within a short time this "desensitization" procedure became widely used for treating hay fever and other atopic disorders. Only in the past few years, however, has the value of this form of therapy for hay fever and asthma been adequately substantiated by acceptable scientific criteria. The effectiveness of injection therapy appears to be allergen-specific and depends both upon proper antigen selection and the use of "high" doses of antigen. Injection therapy may produce remarkable relief of symptoms in some patients but is by no means always successful. Even when relief does result, it may be incomplete. Since clinical and skin reactivity to the allergen are seldom completely lost, even when profound relief ensues from the procedure, the term "hyposensitization" appears to be more appropriate than "desensitization."

The mechanism by which repeated injections of allergens increase the clinical tolerance to the same allergens is unknown. This procedure has been shown to induce neutralizing ("blocking") antibodies which presumably are able to block the critical reaction between allergen and skin-sensitizing antibody in the appropriate shock organs. The development of blocking antibodies has been suggested as the basis for the clinical improvement which may result from injection therapy, but the correlation between the amount of blocking antibody produced and the extent to which symptoms are ameliorated has been unconvincing. Blocking antibodies may play a role in increasing allergen tolerance, but cannot account entirely for the effectiveness of injection therapy. The production of antigen excess, the development of immunologic tolerance, and the partial depletion of mediator stores have also been offered as explanations for the success of injection therapy, but the extent to which any of these contributes to the mechanism of "hyposensitization" is at the mo-

ment purely conjectural. It has also been observed that the marked clinical relief experienced by many patients following hyposensitization may be accompanied by a striking reduction in the sensitivity of their peripheral leucocytes to the histamine-releasing effects of the allergen. The explanation for this alteration in cell sensitivity is not yet known. Whatever the mechanism(s) by which injection therapy leads to decreased clinical sensitivity to an allergen it appears to be related in some way to the antigenic properties of the allergen. Thus, the term "immunotherapy" has also been applied to this therapeutic procedure.

INDICATIONS FOR INJECTION THERAPY. Injection therapy is indicated when allergic symptoms cannot be controlled adequately by allergen avoidance or conventional drug therapy. As a general rule, it should be considered only for those allergens to which exposure cannot be reduced adequately by simple environmental manipulation. Although it has been claimed that injection therapy for pollen hay fever prevents the development of pollen asthma, this has not been well enough substantiated as yet to warrant the use of injection therapy on this basis alone.

PROCEDURES FOR INJECTION THERAPY. There are various forms of injection procedures, with specific variations to each. However, the general approach is essentially the same for each: a small amount of allergen extract, calculated to be clinically subreactive, is injected subcutaneously at frequent intervals and in progressive increments until a peak concentration is reached. Once this dose is reached, the patient may be maintained on similar doses given at less frequent intervals throughout the entire year ("perennial therapy"), or the inoculations may be discontinued and the procedure repeated each year before the problematic season ("preseasonal therapy"). In "coseasonal therapy," an alternate form of therapy less commonly used, treatment is instituted during the offensive pollen season and inoculations are given very frequently, as often as daily, using concentrations throughout the entire procedure ordinarily much smaller than the maximum doses employed in perennial or preseasonal therapy. Although coseasonal therapy has had a number of enthusiastic advocates, its effectiveness has not been clearly established and it is the least satisfactory form of injection therapy. There is little evidence to support the relative therapeutic merit of either preseasonal or perennial therapy over the other, and the choice of the procedure used is based largely on other considerations such as that of convenience (to the patient or to the doctor). Perennial therapy has the advantage of affording an opportunity for repeated observation and reevaluation of the patient over the entire year.

Selection of specific allergens is based upon their implication by history and the confirmation of the presence of skin-sensitizing antibodies to these allergens by skin testing. When feasible, provocative tests may also be helpful (see Sec. 11.2). In most patients it is considered safe to begin with an arbi-

TABLE 4.   *Approximate Equivalents of Allergen Concentration Using Various Terminology* *

> 1:100 dilution (weight by volume)
> 5,000 protein nitrogen units (PNU)
> 10,000 Noon units
> 10,000 pollen units
> 0.13 mg of total nitrogen
> 13,000 units of total nitrogen

*The equivalents listed represent the amount contained in 1 ml of material in which 1 g of pollen has been extracted with 100 ml of extracting fluid.

trary dose of 5 protein nitrogen units of an aqueous allergen extract (Table 4). In certain circumstances, however, a significantly smaller amount of allergen should be employed initially, particularly when clinical sensitivity to the allergen is known to be inordinately great, or when unusually large skin reactions to the allergen have been observed on skin testing. Smaller concentrations are also used when injection therapy is employed for insect hypersensitivity and in children who have had previous constitutional symptoms on low concentrations of extracts. The minimal concentration of allergen found by intracutaneous testing to evoke a wheal and erythema reaction also may be used as the starting dose for therapy. Dosage schedules are somewhat arbitrary, but successive increments of approximately 50 percent over the first dose until a maintenance dose is reached is more or less the general rule. It is important to be particularly cautious in increasing the dosage early in the course of therapy. At first, injections are usually administered once or twice weekly until the peak dose is reached. The peak or maintenance dose may be considered to be the highest concentration of extract tolerated by the patient (i.e., that which does not provoke constitutional reactions or severe local reactions) but is governed also by such practical considerations as the limiting concentration of allergen in extracts commonly available. In perennial therapy, this peak dosage is used as the maintenance dose and then is administered every three to four weeks throughout the year. During the seasons in which the offensive allergens are in the air, injections are sometimes increased to once per week using maintenance or half-maintenance dosage, with a reversion to longer intervals between injections after the pollen or mold season. Injections are given subcutaneously in the posterolateral aspect of the upper arm, alternating each time from one arm to the other. Great care is taken to insure that the injection is not given inadvertently into a vein. Mild local reactions consisting of less than 3 cm of swelling, some redness, and itching are common and are not usually cause for concern unless progressive, but severe local reactions require manipulation of dosage. Constitutional reactions varying from mild symptoms

of the disorder for which the injections are being given, to anaphylactic shock and death, are a potential hazard in all patients undergoing injection therapy. As a rule, the more severe the reaction, the earlier its onset. Most severe reactions can be expected to occur within 30 minutes after injection, and close observation of the patient during this time should be a routine part of the injection procedure. Aqueous epinephrine (1:1,000) and a tourniquet should always be readily available in case of emergency, and with any suggestion of a constitutional reaction, 0.2 to 0.5 ml of epinephrine should be administered intramuscularly without delay, using the opposite arm from that used for injection therapy. A tourniquet should be placed proximal to the area into which the allergen extract is injected in order to retard allergen absorption, and 0.1 to 0.2 ml of epinephrine can be given subcutaneously into the site of allergen injection in order to diminish the rate of allergen absorption. Further treatment of medical emergencies due to allergic reactions is discussed elsewhere in this section. The more common causes of reactions to injection therapy include the use of too large a starting dose, and increasing dosage too rapidly. Also, heavy natural exposure to an allergen may decrease the tolerance of a patient to a given amount of injected allergen, and natural allergen exposure must be taken into account when calculating dosages for injection therapy. Because injection therapy is a potentially dangerous procedure, it is essential that any physician employing such therapy fully familiarize himself with the proper protocol and problems which may be encountered. A more detailed discussion of these aspects of injection therapy may be found in standard textbooks of allergy.

The extent and duration of benefit from hyposensitization is variable and there are no hard and fast rules concerning the length of time injections should be continued. It is the usual practice to employ injection therapy for at least three years before it can be said that it has been given an adequate trial. Some allergists discontinue therapy when it has produced the desired relief for at least two consecutive years, while others prefer to continue it for a much longer or an indefinite period of time. The longer injection therapy is employed, the longer relief appears to be sustained after it has been discontinued. Although injection therapy may induce profound relief of symptoms, complete cures can rarely if ever be attributed to this procedure. Even in patients who have received dramatic relief from this form of treatment, discontinuation of therapy commonly leads to the redevelopment of symptoms within a few years.

Long-acting (depot) allergen preparations can be used in place of conventional aqueous extracts and have two main potential advantages: since the allergen is released more gradually in these preparations, it is often possible to inject a larger total amount of allergen at a given time; and fewer injections are needed at less frequent intervals than in therapy with aqueous extracts. The most commonly used is a pyridine-extracted alum precipitated preparation marketed as Allpyral. It is claimed that only half the number of injections ordinarily used with aqueous extracts are required using this preparation. There is some question, however, about the relative effectiveness of long-acting preparations compared to aqueous extracts. In addition, the use of long-acting preparation is sometimes associated with the development of cysts or sterile abscesses at the sites of injection. Treatment with aqueous extracts, therefore, is probably preferable in general to treatment with currently available long-acting preparations. In some circumstances, however, the considerations of convenience of fewer injections, and the possibility of administering larger amounts of allergen in patients who are unusually sensitive to aqueous allergen extracts, may outweigh the disadvantages.

Drug Therapy

A number of drugs have proved extremely effective in ameliorating allergic reactions, sometimes, in fact, alleviating the reaction completely. The improper use of these drugs, however, can serve instead to aggravate such reactions severely, and a thorough understanding of the actions of drugs used in the treatment of allergic disorders is essential. The principal groups of drugs commonly associated with therapy of allergic disorders include antihistamines, sympathomimetic amines, methylxanthines, and adrenal corticosteroids. Numerous other pharmacologic agents such as expectorants, antibiotics, sedatives, tranquilizers, oxygen, and bicarbonate sometimes used in the treatment of allergic disorders will also be considered here or under the specific disorders for which their use is appropriate.

ANTIHISTAMINES.   Antihistamines include a heterogenous group of compounds which share the ability to inhibit histamine activity by competing for the cellular receptors which it activates. For reasons which are poorly understood, these compounds are extremely effective antagonists of certain histamine actions but have relatively little or no effect on others. Antihistamines tend to be potent inhibitors of the increased capillary permeability and smooth muscle contraction (bronchial and gastrointestinal) induced by histamine, are able to antagonize some of the stimulatory effects of histamine on exocrine secretions, and can reduce histamine-induced pruritus. Their ability to interfere with the vasodilating activity of histamine, however, is less striking and they do not appear to alter the stimulatory effects of histamine on gastric secretion. Consequently, antihistamines have proved valuable in the treatment of urticaria, angioneurotic edema, and allergic rhinitis, and are useful in the treatment of anaphylaxis as a supplement to sympathomimetic drugs. They are also frequently helpful in relieving pruritus associated with allergic dermatoses, an effect probably related both to their histamine-antagonizing and potent local anesthetic properties. For obscure reasons, antihistamines are not generally helpful in asthma despite the fact that histamine is thought to be an important mediator in this disorder. They may actually be harmful, in fact, because of their potential drying effects on bronchial secretions. Thus, it is clear that antihistamines used in tolerable amounts are not effective therapeutic antagonists of all allergic phenomena. Because they act as competitive inhibitors, antihistamines also tend to be less effective antagonists of histamine-induced reactions than are physiologic antagonists such as epinephrine. For this reason and the fact that histamine may not be the only mediator involved, antihistamines are not the first drug of choice in medical emergencies due to allergic reactions.

Because of the striking similarity in structure between various biogenic amines (histamine, serotonin, catecholamines, acetylcholine), agents which competitively antagonize the actions of one amine have a tendency to exert a similar inhibitory effect on others. Thus, despite the specificity of action implied by the term "antihistamine," many compounds designated as such also possess significant antiadrenergic, antiserotonin, or anticholinergic activities. Some of the so-called side effects often encountered with the use of antihistamines can be attributed to this overlap in inhibitory activity against other amines. One such example is dryness of the mouth which may be experienced with the use of certain antihistamines, related to an atropinelike inhibition of salivary glandular secretion. Antihistamines have a particular propensity to induce drowsiness, an effect varying both with the specific compound used and individual responsiveness to the compound. Although frequently bothersome, this can sometimes be put to advantage when dealing with pruritic dermatoses, for instance, in which nocturnal itching and restlessness may be intense. Other side effects which may be encountered include fatigue, dizziness, tinnitus, incoordination, blurred vision, diplopia, euphoria, CNS excitation, anorexia, nausea, vomiting, constipation, diarrhea, urinary frequency, dysuria, palpitation, hypotension, headache, tightness of the chest, paresthesias, and impotence. Antihistamines can also induce hypersensitivity reactions and are especially prone to do so if applied topically to inflamed skin.

The type of side effects likely to be encountered varies to some extent with the specific structure of the antihistamine compound. Compounds with antihistaminic activity fall mainly into five structural groups listed in Table 5. Ethanolamines tend to be the most sedating as a group, but individual compounds from any group may exhibit this effect. (Of the compounds listed in Table 5, tripelennamine, diphenhydramine, doxylamine, and promethazine are most commonly associated with sedation.) Anticholinergic activity is particularly common amongst the ethanolamine group of compounds, but the incidence of gastrointestinal side effects in this group is low.

TABLE 5. *Major Groups of Antihistamines*

Group	Examples	
	Chemical Name	Brand Name
Ethylenediamines	tripelennamine	Pyribenzamine
	pyrilamine	Neo-Antergan
	thonzylamine	Neohetramine
	methapyrilene	Histadyl
Ethanolamines	diphenhydramine	Benadryl
	doxylamine	Decapryn
	diphenylpraline	Diafen, Hispril
	carbinoxamine	Clistin
Alkylamines	chlorpheniramine	Chlor-Trimeton
	brompheniramine	Dimetane
	triprolidine	Actidil
	pyrrobutamine	Pyronil
Piperazines	cyclizine*	Marezine
	meclizine*	Bonine
	hydroxyzine	Atarax, Vistaril
Phenothiazines	trimeprazine*	Temaril
	methdilazine*	Tacaryl
	promethazine	Phenergan

*Meclizine and cyclizine are used mainly as antinauseants, and in motion sickness. Trimeprazine and methdilazine are marketed largely as antipruritic agents.

Side effects involving the gastrointestinal system are most common in the ethylenediamine group, whereas undesirable CNS side effects are more likely to be encountered with a drug of the alkylamine group. In addition to the side effects listed for antihistamines in general, liver toxicity, photosensitization, and agranulocytosis have been associated with the use of phenothiazine compounds. Antihistamines with significant antiserotonin activity (e.g., cyproheptadine, Periactin) are also available and marketed as being of particular value in the treatment of allergic disorders, but these compounds appear to offer little advantage in general over other antihistaminic drugs. It is sometimes possible to diminish the undesirable side effects of a compound yet retain its therapeutic effect simply by lowering the dose of drug used. Alternatively, switching from one antihistamine to another may solve the problem. When this is done, it is generally advisable to select an antihistamine from a different structural group from the one previously used. When somnolence is the main problem, and when a decongestant effect is desirable, vasoconstrictor sympathomimetic amines with CNS stimulant activity, such as ephedrine, can be combined with antihistamines.

Antihistamines in general are readily absorbed when given orally or by a parenteral route. Oral administration ordinarily leads to a detectable therapeutic effect within 15 to 30 minutes. The duration of action of most antihistaminic compounds is usually short (3 to 6 hours) but a prolonged effect (8 to 12 hours) can be obtained from a number of commercially available sustained-release preparations. It is well to remember that, in addition to dosage, the timing of drug administration has an important bearing on its therapeutic effectiveness. For example, symptoms of hay fever which occur in the morning immediately upon arising may be relieved more effectively by a long-acting antihistamine taken 7 or 8 hours before, at bedtime, than by the same drug taken when symptoms are already beginning to occur. The onset of antihistaminic action may be accelerated by parenteral administration, but much caution should be exercised when giving antihistamines intravenously since rapid infusion can produce severe hypotension.

SYMPATHOMIMETIC AMINES. Allergic disorders, particularly of the atopic variety, are due in large part to the effects of vascular dilatation, increased capillary permeability, smooth muscle spasm, and mucus secretion induced by histamine and other chemical mediators of allergic reactions. The catecholamines, epinephrine and norepinephrine, act as the principal physiologic antagonists of these various responses. Sympathomimetic agents as a group exert many pharmacologic effects: they act as cardiac and CNS stimulants, exhibit various metabolic actions, are able to contract or relax smooth muscle, and can alter mucus secretion. The various activities possessed by these agents as a group, however, are not exhibited uniformly by each member of the group and these drugs, therefore, cannot all be used interchangeably to produce a given effect. Phenylephrine (Neo-Synephrine), for instance, is an effective vasoconstrictor without significant smooth muscle dilating action, whereas isoproterenol (Isuprel) is devoid of vasoconstrictor action but is a potent bronchodilator. Thus, phenylephrine is useful in controlling allergic rhinitis and urticaria, but not bronchospasm, whereas isoproterenol is potentially effective in asthma but is valueless in allergic rhinitis, urticaria, or angioneurotic edema. On the other hand, epinephrine is both a potent vasoconstrictor and bronchodilator and is useful in controlling angioneurotic edema, urticaria, asthma, and anaphylactic reactions. Because of this, and its rapid onset of action, epinephrine stands out as the first drug of choice in medical emergencies due to allergic reactions.

Sympathomimetic drugs are by no means free from undesirable effects and, moreover, are not always effective in a given disorder. Resistance to the therapeutic effects of epinephrine often occurs in severe asthma, for instance, and the continued use of this drug in the face of therapeutic unresponsiveness to it may actually intensify asthma by increasing agitation and promoting venous congestion and mucus plugging. Continued excessive use of epinephrine may also result in cardiovascular damage. Isoproterenol, particularly when used in inhalant form, may be effective in asthma even when resistance to epinephrine is apparent, and occupies a potentially valuable place in the treatment of acute and chronic asthma. The excessive use of isoproterenol aerosols, however, can also markedly aggravate asthma and such aerosols must be used cautiously and under proper supervision. It is imperative that their use be discontinued when resistance to their therapeutic effects is either apparent or suspected. Sympathomimetic agents should be used with particular caution in the face of severe hypoxemia with or without acidemia since these conditions may increase myocardial irritability to these drugs.

Norepinephrine and epinephrine are inactivated in the gastrointestinal tract and must be given parenterally. Epinephrine constricts cutaneous vessels but dilates skeletal muscle vessels and is therefore absorbed most rapidly when given intramuscularly. Epinephrine is ordinarily given subcutaneously, but intramuscular administration is advisable in anaphylaxis or other medical emergencies due to allergic reactions. The effects of aqueous epinephrine tend to be short-lived but can be prolonged by the use of special long-acting preparations such as Sus-phrine. In order to minimize the undesirable effects which may be evoked by this drug, long-acting epinephrine should be used only after therapeutic responsiveness to this drug has been demonstrated, using aqueous epinephrine. Norepinephrine (Levophed) finds its main use as a vasoconstrictor in shock; it is given by intravenous infusion. Various noncatecholamine sympathomimetic drugs such as ephedrine sulfate are effective when taken orally, and are useful when long-term employment of a sympathomimetic agent with vasoconstrictor and/or bronchodilator properties is desirable, such as in the treatment of chronic asthma or allergic rhinitis. The actions of oral sympathomimetic agents are significantly less potent than those of parenteral epinephrine and these drugs are an inadequate substitute for epinephrine in the treatment of anaphylaxis, severe paroxysms of asthma, or in any other severe allergic reaction.

METHYLXANTHINES. Theophylline, and its ethylenediamine derivative, aminophylline, are extremely effective smooth muscle dilators with a bronchodilating capacity which rivals that of the more effective sympathomimetic amines. They have proved especially valuable in the treatment of severe asthma and may be effective in the face of epinephrine resistance. These agents do not directly affect mucosal edema or mucus formation significantly, but may be associated with some degree of peripheral vasoconstriction mediated indirectly through an effect on the vasomotor center. They have also been shown to potentiate the therapeutic actions of sympathomimetic amines. There have been numerous reports of severe toxic reactions including death due to these drugs, which has resulted in some reluctance to use xanthines at all in the therapy of asthma. The toxic effects attributed to these compounds, however, are almost always the results of gross overdosage with these drugs and can be ascribed specifically to a lack of appreciation by those prescribing these drugs of the variability in their rate and extent of absorption with different routes of administration, or the failure to determine the amount of drug previously administered to the patient. Indications of drug toxicity include headache, insomnia, irritability, agitation, nausea, vomiting, hematemesis, palpitations, tachycardia, tachypnea, and excessive thirst; more severe reactions include convulsions, circulatory failure, and respiratory arrest. Abdominal discomfort is experienced by patients taking methylxanthines with some frequency and is not necessarily a reflection of drug toxicity. With proper precautions, the prolonged administration of these drugs is attended with few side effects.

Methylxanthines are relatively insoluble in water, and absorption from the gastrointestinal tract tends to be somewhat erratic. Nevertheless, effective drug levels can be achieved with the use of aqueous suspensions or tablets and the oral route is ordinarily preferred for chronic drug administration. The use of an alcohol base (e.g., Elixophyllin) significantly increases the solubility and efficiency of absorption. Rectal absorption by enema is relatively prompt, and is almost as efficient as intravenous administration. Absorption from rectal suppositories, on the other hand, is much slower and less predictable, and is the least desirable method of administration in general. Intravenous administration is usually accompanied by a prompt therapeutic response; infusion over a 15- to 20-minute period is generally recommended since it will ordinarily result in a rapid therapeutic effect which is often sustained for a few hours, and should obviate the potential problem of inducing profound hypotension which may occur when these drugs are injected too rapidly. Most methylxanthine preparations are extremely irritating when given intramuscularly and should not be administered by this route.

ADRENAL GLUCOCORTICOIDS. Adrenal glucocorticoids are capable of modifying almost all kinds of allergic reactions. Although their beneficial effects are usually attributed to their "anti-inflammatory" properties, the specific means by which these agents affect allergic reactions is unknown. Glucocorticoids are most useful in the treatment of disorders of delayed-type hypersensitivity such as contact dermatitis, and have proved to be invaluable in controlling severe asthma. They appear to be least effective in urticarial disorders. Because of the adverse side effects which accompany prolonged administration of these drugs (growth suppression, myopathy, "Cushingoid facies" and other abnormal fat deposition, electrolyte imbalance, hypertension, diabetes, and perhaps peptic ulcer), the use of systemic steroids is limited mainly to severe conditions which are refractory to other therapeutic measures. The main indications for the use of systemic steroids are severe acute asthma which may be life-threatening, and severe chronic allergic disorders, mainly asthma, which cannot be controlled adequately by other means of therapy. Short-term therapy with systemic steroids also has a place in the treatment of self-limiting allergic disorders such as serum sickness and severe contact dermatitis.

Adrenal glucocorticoids are effectively absorbed from the gastrointestinal tract, and are ordinarily

TABLE 6.   *Approximate Equivalents of Anti-inflammatory Activity of Various Glucocorticoids*

Hydrocortisone	20 mg
Prednisolone	5 mg
Methylprednisolone	4 mg
Triamcinalone	4 mg
Dexamethasone	0.75 mg

*These "equivalents" are only rough approximates, and should not be taken too literally. They represent, rather, a starting point for substituting steroid preparations.

given orally except in acute severe reactions, for which intravenous infusion is often preferred. It is important to realize, however, that the therapeutic action of these drugs is relatively slow even when administered intravenously (hours), and steroids are never the first drugs of choice in acute severe allergic reactions. When employed in the treatment of acute severe asthma or other serious reactions, it is generally advisable to use "high" steroid doses (e.g., 8 to 10 mg hydrocortisone/kg/24 hours in two to four doses; see Table 6) until the desired relief is obtained. In asthma, this frequently occurs in less than 24 hours and rarely takes longer than two or three days. Steroids may then be discontinued abruptly if used for such a short time; with daily steroid administration for more than a few days, it is best to discontinue their use more gradually by a regimen of tapering dosages. As a general rule, steroids should not be withheld in the treatment of severe allergic reactions in children who have been on prolonged steroid therapy of a few weeks or more within the preceding 18 months. The use of ACTH offers little advantage over the use of steroids and its effects are limited by the amounts of corticosteroids which can be liberated from the adrenal glands. Consequently, when a systemic steroid effect is considered necessary, the administration of steroids per se is generally preferred to the use of ACTH.

It has been suggested recently that a regimen of alternate-day prednisone therapy may be effective in controlling chronic asthma while reducing the degree of adrenal suppression and the incidence and severity of side effects frequently associated with long-term daily therapy. This effect may be confined only to certain adrenal glucocorticoid preparations, namely prednisone, prednisolone, hydrocortisone, and cortisone. Consequently, when chronic steroid administration is deemed necessary to provide adequate control of asthma or other allergic disorders, alternate-day therapy using one of the above steroids specifically should be considered. (Prednisone is significantly less expensive than most other steroids and is generally the steroid of choice whenever oral steroids are used.) It is a good procedure to achieve the desired therapeutic effect using daily steroid therapy first and to switch then to alternate-day therapy, beginning with twice the daily dose found necessary to control symptoms. The steroid may be taken as one dose, in the early morning on alternate days.

Adrenal steroids applied topically can be extremely effective in controlling a variety of allergic dermatoses. Many of the problems associated with the chronic use of systemic steroids are avoided ordinarily by topical therapy. It should be realized, however, that especially with the more potent fluorinated steroids extensive topical application can result in sufficient systemic absorption to produce adrenal suppression. This also holds true for steroid aerosols used to control severe allergic rhinitis and asthma.

EXPECTORANTS. Pharmacologic expectorants such as iodides and glyceral guaiacolate are employed mainly in bronchial asthma to liquefy the thick tenacious mucus characteristic of this disorder and, in doing so, facilitate expectoration. Iodides have been shown to have a definite therapeutic effect in a small proportion of individuals with asthma, but it is unclear whether their effectiveness in these cases can be attributed specifically to their expectorant actions. They are best used on a trial basis in individuals requiring constant medication, and can be discontinued if an obvious therapeutic effect is not observed within a few weeks. Despite its frequent use, the therapeutic effectiveness of glyceral guaiacolate has yet to be established. Iodides are relatively nontoxic but goiter, salivary gland inflammation, and gastric irritation may be associated with their prolonged use. Iodides frequently provoke acne in adolescents and for this reason are more usefully employed in the younger age groups. The chronic use of guaiacolate apparently is attended with few side effects. Hydration is an essential element to liquefaction of mucus, and although not ordinarily considered in the category of drugs, fluids taken in amounts sufficient to ensure adequate hydration are also extremely important in promoting expectoration of mucus.

SEDATIVES. Emotional factors play a role of variable importance in asthma and other allergic disorders. In some children, they are clearly responsible for precipitating or severely aggravating asthma, and many children will appear extremely anxious in the midst of an asthmatic attack. Often, however, this anxiety is an expression of the frequently underestimated severity of pulmonary obstruction rather than the main cause of it. Although the achievement of a sedative effect sometimes may be desirable, the use of barbiturates or other sedatives which have a depressant effect on the respiratory center are contraindicated in asthma. Tranquilizers have a potentially depressant effect on respiration and on bronchial reflexes, particularly in the presence of hypoxemia, and some also have a drying effect on mucus secretions. Their use, therefore, is discouraged as well. The phenothiazine group of tranquilizers presents an additional hazard since they may alter adversely the usual actions of sympathomimetic agents commonly used to treat asthma. Of particular concern is the fact that administration of epinephrine to a patient on phenothiazine drugs may preciptate severe hypotension. When sedation is desired, chloral hydrate (200 to 500 mg p.o. or by rectum) is considered to be the drug of choice. In allergic dermatoses in which itching is often a distressing problem, sedation, particularly at night, may be of value in relieving this distress. Sedative antihistamines such as diphenhydramine are particularly useful in this regard.

ANTIBIOTICS.   There are no special indications for the use of antibiotics in children with allergic disorders; they should be used on the same basis as in nonallergic children. The excessive use of antibiotics and chemotherapeutic agents in children with allergic disorders when no clear indication exists has been partly responsible for the frequent sensitization of these children to penicillin and other similar agents. Topical antibiotics tend to be especially sensitizing when applied to inflamed skin. Consequently, when indicated, antibiotics are probably best used systemically.

COMBINATION DRUGS.   It is often advisable to employ more than one drug in the treatment of a given allergic disorder. This is particularly true in the treatment of chronic asthma in which a combination of drugs with expectorant, bronchodilator, and decongestant properties are often employed. There are numerous commercially available preparations which combine various drugs (e.g., theophylline, ephedrine, and expectorants) for use in the treatment of asthma and many others which combine antihistamines and sympathomimetic vasoconstrictors for use in allergic rhinitis and other disorders. The advantage of such preparations lies mainly in simplicity and convenience of drug administration. The amount and proportions of the various drugs in these preparations, however, are not necessarily optimal for a given patient and their use should not be allowed to restrict the manipulation of individual drug dosages which may be appropriate for each patient.

OTHER THERAPEUTIC AGENTS.   A number of other agents including heparin and gamma globulin have been used in the treatment of asthma and other allergic disorders with sporadic claims of great effectiveness. There is little to substantiate these claims, however, and their place in the therapy of allergic disorders is highly questionable. A relatively new drug, disodium cromoglycate, currently under investigation, appears to offer some future promise in the therapy of asthma.

Prophylaxis of Atopic Disorders

In 1953, Glazer and Johnstone reported that the dietary restriction of cow's milk for the first few months of life from infants born in families with strong atopic histories significantly reduced the development of atopic dermatitis, allergic rhinitis, or asthma in these children. These findings, though extremely provocative, were severely criticized from the standpoint of the experimental design of the study. More recently, Johnstone and Dutton found that children with an immediate atopic family history from whom all cow products, chicken, egg, and wheat were restricted for the first nine months of life developed allergic rhinitis or asthma less frequently than did children on unrestricted diets. Although this last study is not entirely free from criticism, it can be said that there is at least strongly suggestive evidence that appropriate dietary control for the first few months of life may prevent the development of atopic disorders in some children.

REFERENCES

Deamer, W. C. Injection therapy in asthma and allergic rhinitis. Pediat. Clin. N. Amer., 16:243, 1969.
DiPalma, J. R., ed. Drill's Pharmacology in Medicine, 3rd ed. New York, McGraw-Hill Book Co., 1965.
Goodman, L. S., and Gilman, A., eds. The Pharmacological Basis of Therapeutics, 3rd ed. New York, The Macmillan Co., 1965.
Johnstone, D. E. Comparative value of hyposensitization and symptomatic therapy in pollenoses in children. New York J. Med., 60:1448, 1960.
——— and Dutton, A. M. Dietary prophylaxis of allergic diseases in children. New Eng. J. Med., 274:715, 1966.
——— and Dutton, A. M. The value of hyposensitization therapy for bronchial asthma in children—A 14 year study. Pediatrics, 42:793, 1968.
Michelsen, A. L., and Lowell, F. C. Antihistaminic drugs. New Eng. J. Med., 258:994, 1958.
Noon, L. Prophylactic inoculation against hay fever. Lancet, 1:1572, 1911.
Sadan, N., Rhyne, M. B., Mellits, E. D., Goldstein, E. O., Levy, D. A., and Lichtenstein, L. M. Immunotherapy of pollenosis in children. New Eng. J. Med., 280:623, 1969.
Sheldon, J. M., Lovell, R. G., and Mathews, K. P., eds. A Manual of Clinical Allergy. Philadelphia, W. B. Saunders Co., 1967.
Sherman, W. B. Hypersensitivity-Mechanisms and Management. Philadelphia, W. B. Saunders Co., 1968.
Siegel, S. C. Cortiocosteroids and ACTH in the Management of the Atopic Child. Pediat. Clin. N. Amer., 16:287, 1969.
Sly, R. M., and Heimlich, E. M. A review: Sympathetic and sympathomimetic action. Ann. Allerg., 24:259, 1966.
Speer, F., ed. The Allergic Child. New York, Harper and Row, Publ., 1963.
Wittig, H. J. Hyposensitization therapy in treatment of allergic disorders. Amer. J. Dis. Child., 120:578, 1970.

11.4
ALLERGIC RHINITIS AND SEROUS OTITIS MEDIA

SUMIO GO and DAVID S. PEARLMAN

Allergic Rhinitis

Allergic rhinitis is the most common clinical form of atopic disorder. Perennial and seasonal variants of allergic rhinitis are recognized clinically and simply reflect differences in the nature and duration of exposure to sensitizing allergens. Perennial allergic rhinitis, as the term implies, is characterized by year-round symptoms which frequently exacerbate during the winter months, and is usually the result of sensitization to various indoor inhalant allergens. Seasonal allergic rhinitis or "hay fever" refers to a more acute periodic disorder resulting from exposure to such seasonally produced allergens as tree, grass, and weed pollens. Both forms of rhinitis frequently coexist in the same individual.

INCIDENCE. Although allergic rhinitis has been reported to begin as early as the first few weeks of life, it usually does not develop until after the first or second year of age. The diagnosis of seasonal allegic rhinitis is made with increasing frequency during late childhood and adolescence but has its peak onset between 20 and 30 years of age. Both sexes are equally susceptible.

IMMUNOLOGIC MECHANISM. So-called skin-sensitizing or reaginic antibodies (now recognized to be of the IgE immunoglobulin class) have been implicated as being of primary importance in the pathogenesis of allergic rhinitis. Delayed-type hypersensitivity has been shown under experimental conditions to produce symptoms of allergic rhinitis, and although there is as yet no convincing clinical evidence to support its role in this disorder, it is possible that delayed-type hypersensitivity and other nonreagin-mediated immunologic mechanisms may play some part in the pathogenesis of allergic rhinitis. Reaginic antibody has been demonstrated in the allergic nasal mucosa where it presumably is bound to tissue mast cells. The reaction between airborne allergen absorbed by the nasal mucosa and reaginic antibody of the appropriate specificity results in release of pharmacologic mediators which ultimately give rise to the changes observed in the allergic nasal mucosa. Histamine appears to be the most important of these mediators in allergic rhinitis.

Clinical sensitivity to an allergen has been found to correlate well with the blood level of reaginic antibody specific for that allergen. For example, individuals with high ragweed reaginic antibody titers generally experience more severe symptoms on exposure to ragweed than those with low titers. Recently, clinical sensitivity has been shown to correlate even better with an in vitro test of the ability of an individual's peripheral blood leucocytes to release histamine. The interaction of allergen with reaginic antibody bound to tissue mast cells or to their circulating counterpart, the basophils, results in the release of histamine from its intracellular site into the surrounding medium. The higher the percentage of histamine release by an individual's leucocytes on in vitro exposure to an allergen, the more clinically sensitive he is likely to be to that allergen.

Intensive hyposensitization therapy (immunotherapy) recently has been shown to decrease the ability of the treated individual's leucocytes to release histamine on exposure to the appropriate allergen, suggesting the possibility that this "desensitization" of leucocytes demonstrable in vitro is directly related to the clinically beneficial effects of immunotherapy.

Although an immunologic reaction is the basis for symptoms in allergic rhinitis, nonimmunologic factors such as infection, alterations in ambient temperature and humidity, hormonal and psychic influences, and physical irritation may affect the severity and duration of the resulting symptoms.

CLINICAL FEATURES. Nasal itching with paroxysmal sneezing, sniffling due to a watery nasal discharge, nasal obstruction with or without accompanying itching of the eyes, and lacrimation are the most prominent features of acute allergic rhinitis in children. Symptoms may occur at any time of the day or night, but are often more intense in the early morning or late evening hours. Habitual rubbing of the tip of the nose upward with the palm of the hand is frequently observed in youngsters with allergic rhinitis and is appropriately termed the "allergic salute." Other symptoms encountered are itching of the palate, pharynx, face or ears, anosmia, epistaxis, headache due to pressure changes in the paranasal sinuses as a result of ostial obstruction, and easy fatiguability. In perennial allergic rhinitis, marked nasal stuffiness is frequently the outstanding symptom; sneezing, nasal itching, and eye symptoms are usually less marked than in acute seasonal rhinitis. In addition, the nasal discharge in perennial rhinitis tends to be thicker and more mucoid and may provoke cough and frequent throat clearing.

The edematous nasal mucosa is typically boggy and glistening in appearance, and varies from a blanched white to a bluish-grey in color; however, in milder cases, there may be only slight mucosal hyperemia. Severe blockage of the nasal passages, especially by swollen inferior turbinates, may be noted. The nasal discharge varies from a thin watery to a thick mucoid consistency and, unlike that associated with infectious rhinitis, rarely causes significant irritation of the external nares or upper lip. With extensive eye involvement, marked conjunctival edema and hyperemia, and distressingly severe tearing may be observed. The sunken, dark appearance of the infraorbital areas has been termed the "allergic shiner" and is attributed to venous stasis and malar edema due to impeded drainage of blood from these areas through a congested nasal mucosa. A transverse skin crease often marks the bridge of the nose which has been chronically subjected to the "allergic salute." A rather highly arched palate may be noted in the child who has had severe perennial rhinitis from an early age. Maldevelopment of the maxillary bone sometimes occurs and may result in an elongated facies and dental malocclusion.

COMPLICATIONS. Pronounced thickening of the mucosa of the paranasal sinuses is a common radiographic finding in the older allergic child. Although the usual symptoms of sinus disease occur in some of these children, the majority remains completely asymptomatic. The most common manifestation in symptomatic youngsters is pain over the involved sinuses, due to pressure changes resulting from obstruction of the ostia. A purulent nasal discharge may develop when the hypertrophied and edematous sinus mucosa becomes secondarily infected. Appropriate antibiotic therapy is indicated when bacterial infection of the paranasal sinuses supervenes. Treatment of the associated allergic rhinitis with environmental control measures, antihistamines and vascoconstrictor drugs, and hyposensitization therapy reduces the likelihood of symptoms due to obstruction of the sinus orifices. However, such therapy generally fails to cause significant reduction in the hypertrophy and edema of the sinus mucosa. Vigorous treatment of the asymptomatic child because of abnormal radiographic findings alone is unwarranted. Radical surgical measures should be avoided except in rare instances.

Although marked edematous swelling of the nasal mucosa may result in pseudopolyp formation, true nasal polyps are uncommon in children with uncomplicated seasonal or perennial allergic rhinitis. The incidence appears to be higher in perennial rhinitis, especially when infection has been a frequent complication, but is still much less than in adults. The well-described but poorly understood clinical triad of nasal polyps, aspirin hypersensitivity, and bronchial asthma sometimes has its onset during late childhood, and should be considered in the child with nasal polyps and severe asthma which appears to be unrelated to extrinsic allergens. Antiallergic measures aimed at relieving allergic rhinitis seldom cause complete regression of associated polyps. Polypectomy is sometimes necessary for relief of severe obstructive symptoms, but unfortunately the polyps frequently recur within a short time after the surgical procedure. The recurrence rate may be reduced by appropriate treatment of underlying allergic rhinitis.

DIAGNOSIS. The history and physical findings are of primary importance in the diagnosis of allergic rhinitis. In addition, nasal eosinophilia is so commonly found in allergic rhinitis that its presence is virtually pathognomonic of this disorder. Nasal mucus is best obtained by having the child blow his nose into a piece of waxed paper; a cotton-tipped applicator may be used to swab mucus from the very young or uncooperative child. The mucus is smeared onto a glass slide, stained with Wright's or Hansel's stain, and examined for eosinophils. The smear from an individual with allergic rhinitis characteristically shows large numbers of eosinophils. Repeated examinations are indicated when an initial smear is negative, since eosinophilia is not necessarily a constant finding. In evaluating nasal smears, it must be remembered that eosinophilia is common in normal infants during the first three months of life and that neutrophils may predominate when an infection complicates allergic rhinitis. Blood eosinophilia is frequently observed in allergic rhinitis but is not as helpful a sign as nasal eosinophilia.

Skin testing is of considerable value in the diagnostic work-up in demonstrating the presence or absence of reaginic antibodies to specific allergens. Negative skin tests to a wide sampling of commonly encountered allergens strongly suggests a nonallergic basis for the rhinitis, especially when other findings, such as a consistent absence of eosinophils in the nasal secretions, also point to this possibility. On the other hand, positive skin tests must be interpreted cautiously, with considerable reliance on supportive data obtained from a carefully taken history and other diagnostic studies. A positive skin test indicates that the allergen has stimulated production of reaginic antibody, but permits no conclusions per se regarding the role of that allergen in a given child's symptomatology. The many allergens accounting for positive skin test in the allergic child vary widely in their clinical importance, with some appearing to bear little if any responsibility for provoking symptoms. Furthermore, positive skin tests are sometimes elicited in completely asymptomatic children, where they also appear to be of no clinical significance. However, properly interpreted skin tests serve to implicate specific allergens in a child's allergic disease, and permit sound decisions regarding avoidance measures and the preparation of treatment extracts for hyposensitization therapy.

Symptoms of allergic rhinitis can be provoked by the application of an offending allergen to the nasal mucosa—a diagnostic procedure referred to as a provocative or direct mucosal challenge test. This technique is especially suitable for pollen allergens. Results of provocative testing can be expected to have greater relevance to the clinical problem than skin test results since the target tissue for the allergic reaction is being directly challenged. However, because mucosal challenge testing is an extremely time-consuming procedure, it is seldom used except as an investigational tool. Recent studies using this technique have yielded the interesting and clinically important observation that repeated exposure to a given pollen over the course of several days results in a heightened sensitivity to that allergen. The amount of pollen necessary to induce the same degree of nasal obstruction shows a dramatic and progressive reduction with successive challenges. This observation, termed the "priming phenomenon," presumably accounts for increasing reactivity of the nasal mucosa to naturally occurring pollen exposure as the season progresses. It has also been shown that an allergen to which reaginic antibody can be demonstrated, but which does not ordinarily provoke nasal symptoms, may do so after the nasal mucosa has been "primed" by an unrelated allergen.

DIFFERENTIAL DIAGNOSIS. It is sometimes difficult to distinguish perennial allergic rhinitis from rhinitis due to frequent viral infections. The child with the latter condition tends to be completely asymptomatic between the end of one infection and the beginning of another, while continuing low-grade symptoms are interspersed between periodic exacerbations in perennial allergic rhinitis. Furthermore, the nasal smear usually aids in differentiating the two conditions. Deviation of the nasal septum, polyposis, rebound mucosal congestion secondary to the topical use of vasoconstrictors, nasal obstruction due to hypertrophy of the adenoids, and the presence of a foreign body in the nose must be considered in the differential diagnosis. Vasomotor rhinitis is a condition clinically similar to perennial allergic rhinitis, for which an allergic mechanism has not been established. Differentiation between these two conditions rests primarily on the presence or absence of nasal eosinophilia and skin-sensitizing antibodies.

TREATMENT. As with all allergic disorders, the mainstay of therapy is to avoid or minimize contact with known or suspected allergens. Unfortunately, airborne pollen and mold allergens are difficult to avoid even with severe restrictions on outdoor activities. Moving to a geographic area free of the offending allergens may prove beneficial in some instances but more often provides only a brief respite from symptoms until sensitivity develops to allergens indigenous to that area. Furthermore, such a move often imposes serious socioeconomic hardships and should not be recommended lightly. Air cleaning devices of the electrostatic precipitator type, and to a lesser degree, the filtering systems of air conditioners, may be helpful in reducing the concentration of pollens, molds, and other inhalant allergens in the home. Environmental control measures aimed at reducing the amount and allergenicity of "house dust" in the home are especially helpful for the child with perennial allergic rhinitis. Important allergens in house dust include danders from household pets, molds, and various fibers from furniture, bedding, drapery, and rugs. Recently, a house-dust mite, *Dermatophagoides pteronyssinus,* has been implicated as a major allergen in house dust. Detailed instructions for making the allergic child's bedroom as free as possible of house dust and other commonly offensive indoor allergens can be found in Table 3 of Section 11.3.

Antihistamines are the drugs of choice in allergic rhinitis and are particularly effective in mild to moderate seasonal rhinitis. They are usually much less effective in perennial and severe seasonal allergic rhinitis. The numerous antihistamines have been classified on the basis of their chemical structure into a number of groups which display significant differences in pharmacologic activity. For this reason, a drug of a different group may prove beneficial to the patient who fails to obtain relief with an antihistamine from one group.

Sympathomimetic drugs with vasoconstrictor activity, such as ephedrine, phenylephrine, or phenylpropanolamine, may be given orally to complement the action of the antihistamines in patients whose symptoms are not adequately controlled with antihistamines alone. Nose drops containing a potent vasoconstrictor drug should never be used for more than a few days at a time since prolonged topical administration frequently results in a rebound congestion of the nasal mucosa, referred to as rhinitis medicamentosa. Vasoconstrictor-containing eye drops may be of value in controlling acute eye symptoms.

Corticosteroid therapy is sometimes necessary in the management of a patient with severe unremitting allergic rhinitis. In such instances, topical administration by means of an aerosol (such as the dexamethasone-containing Turbinaire unit) is generally preferable to the systemic route. Short-term oral corticosteroid therapy might be reasonably considered for the patient with debilitating seasonal rhinitis poorly responsive to other medications.

Hyposensitization therapy should be considered for children with allergic rhinitis which fails to respond satisfactorily to all other treatment measures. Such therapy of pollen-induced allergic rhinitis has been shown to be most effective when the offending pollen allergens have been accurately identified and high doses of appropriate treatment extracts are used. Less favorable results have been achieved with house-dust extracts, and evidence for the efficacy of bacterial vaccines remains unconvincing. Although hyposensitization therapy has been advocated by some for all cases of allergic rhinitis in order to prevent the subsequent development of asthma, there is as yet no good evidence for a causal relationship between the two conditions.

PROGNOSIS. Allergic rhinitis may get better, worse, or stay essentially the same for life. Although it is not common for allergic rhinitis to disappear completely, symptoms frequently diminish to the point where they present an extremely minor problem. Complete "cures" resulting from immunotherapy have been claimed, but this is not the usual experience. More often, symptoms are ameliorated while immunotherapy is being given, but return within a variable period of time after such therapy is discontinued.

Serous Otitis Media
(See also Chap. 31)

Serous otitis media is a middle-ear disorder characterized by the accumulation of sterile fluid of varying color, viscosity, and composition in the middle-ear cavity and mastoid spaces. Other terms which have been used to describe this condition include secretory otitis media, nonsuppurative otitis media, middle-ear effusion, catarrhal otitis media, hydrotympanum, tubal catarrh, hydrops ex vacuo, and "glue ears." A conductive hearing loss is usually associated with fluid accumulation in the middle ear, making prompt diagnosis and adequate treatment especially urgent.

INCIDENCE. In recent years there has been an apparent increase in the incidence of serous otitis media which is probably due in part to an increased awareness among physicians of this important clinical entity. However, undue reliance solely on antibiotic therapy in suppurative otitis media, especially when such therapy is grossly inadequate, is suspected to have given rise to a real increase in the incidence of this condition. Serous otitis media is of particular concern to the pediatrician since it occurs mainly in children under 10 years of age. The higher incidence in childhood has been attributed to anatomic characteristics of the eustachian tubes at this stage of development which predispose to obstruction and infection. A greater frequency of upper respiratory infections in children may also be a contributing factor.

ETIOLOGY. Eustachian tube obstruction or dysfunction appears to be of primary importance in the pathogenesis of serous otitis media. Obstruction or dysfunction may result from such diverse causes as adenoidal hypertrophy, nasopharyngeal or eustachian tube inflammation due to infection or allergy, neoplasms, surgical trauma of the eustachian tube orifice, faulty functioning of the tensor veli palatini, and dental malocclusion causing impaired temporomandibular joint function. Dysfunction of the eustachian tube rather than actual obstruction is a common finding in serous otitis media. This condition is characterized by a failure of the tube to open in the presence of negative intratympanic pressure; the normally functioning eustachian tube is closed at rest but opens with almost every swallow to allow equalization of either positive or negative intratympanic pressure with the ambient pressure. Sustained negative intratympanic pressure resulting from either obstruction or dysfunction of the eustachian tube causes transudation of fluid from blood vessels supplying the middle ear and is partially responsible for the fluid accumulation of serous otitis media. Fluid also results from active secretion by glands arising either through metaplastic change of the middle ear mucosa or by extension of secretory epithelium from the eustachian tube. Inflammation in the middle ear space, occurring as a primary pathologic process or as a consequence of eustachian tube obstruction, induces metaplastic changes in the mucosa, transforming the simple cuboidal epithelium to a columnar or squamous epithelium with an abundance of glands.

The middle ear fluid differs strikingly from case to case, ranging from a yellow serumlike fluid to a dark, mucoid, "gluelike" material. Transudation is probably responsible for the serous component of the fluid, while the mucous glands secrete the more viscid mucoid substance.

Role of Allergy. Serous otitis media has been reported in some studies to occur primarily on an allergic basis as a complication of allergic rhinitis. In other studies, allergy has been implicated only rarely as a cause of this condition. There is general agreement that swelling of the nasopharyngeal mucosa may occur in allergic rhinitis sufficient to cause eustachian tube obstruction and serous otitis media. However, controversy remains over the specific role of the mucous membranes of the eustachian tube and middle ear cavity in the pathogenesis of this condition. Although there has been speculation that these tissues may be capable of reacting to an allergenic stimulus, there has as yet been no convincing demonstration of such reactivity. Furthermore, most attempts to demonstrate eosinophils, cells which are characteristically associated with allergic disorders of the respiratory tract, in the resulting middle ear fluid have been unsuccessful. The case for an allergic etiology is especially hard to prove in a child who is free of other allergic respiratory manifestations such as allergic rhinitis.

CLINICAL FEATURES. Impairment of hearing is the most frequently encountered complaint in serous otitis media. The hearing loss is usually sudden in onset and frequently shows a fluctuating pattern. A history of recurrent earaches or a recent "cold" is not unusual. Older children sometimes describe their own voices as being abnormally loud or, in cases of unilateral disease, as seeming to echo into the affected ear. Some children experience a sensation of fluid moving in the ear with head motion, others complain of a feeling of fullness, heaviness, or pressure in the ears or head. "Popping" sounds in the ears and low-pitched tinnitus are also occasional complaints.

Speech comprehension is often significantly impaired despite retention of hearing sufficient for gross sounds. Serious learning and behavior problems may result from the unsuspected hearing impairment. Hearing loss is frequently overlooked in the child too young to be able to verbalize the appropriate complaints.

Examination of the ears usually reveals an abnormal-appearing tympanic membrane which may be relatively immobile. The normal landmarks are often obliterated by either retraction or ballooning of the membrane, which is frequently scarred, thickened, or opacified. The color of the tympanic membrane may be creamy white, amber, or even bluish-grey, reflecting that of the middle ear fluid. The malleus is sometimes quite prominent and may exhibit a chalky white appearance. The finding of a fluid level or air bubble behind the tympanic membrane is pathognomonic of serous otitis media but is observed in only a minority of cases. Undue reliance on this clinical sign will result in many missed diagnoses. In some cases, the tympanic membrane may appear normal, making diagnosis of this disorder especially difficult.

DIAGNOSIS. A history of recurrent ear infections, hearing difficulty, chronic obstructive nasal symptoms, or severe allergic rhinitis, coupled with any of the abnormal physical findings described above, should alert one to the possibility of this disorder. Additional observations are then indicated to confirm the diagnosis. Tests of hearing are described in Chapter 31. Examination with a pneumatic otoscope is essential for reliable evaluation of tympanic membrane motility; depending upon the viscosity of the fluid in the middle ear, the membrane moves poorly or not at all. Audiometric examination is mandatory when hearing impairment is suspected as a result of the preceding tests. It is not unusual to find a hearing loss of 10 to 40 decibels for all frequencies. Bone conduction is ordinarily normal, but in some cases the extreme viscosity of middle ear fluid impedes movement of the oval and round windows and causes decreased bone conduction as well as air conduction. Nerve deafness may be erroneously suspected in such instances. Finally, a diagnostic myringotomy or middle ear aspiration should be done in all cases of suspected serous otitis media. This is especially useful when a normal-appearing tympanic membrane is found in the presence of a conductive hearing loss. The thick "gluelike" material which fills the middle ear cavity is often impossible to remove by simple needle aspiration and may require evacuation through a generous myringotomy opening.

TREATMENT. All therapeutic efforts are aimed at keeping the middle ear cavity properly ventilated. At the time of the diagnostic myringotomy, an attempt should be made to aspirate all of the middle ear fluid. Any mechanical causes of eustachian tube obstruction, such as adenoidal hypertrophy, should be corrected. Antibiotic therapy is indicated if a smoldering nasopharyngeal or middle ear infection is implicated as the underlying cause of eustachian tube obstruction or dysfunction. Intensive antiallergic measures should be initiated when there is good evidence that an allergic mechanism is responsible for the middle ear disorder. Prolonged oral administration of an antihistamine-vasoconstrictor combination has been advocated in patients with significant nasal congestion. Although a good number of cases will respond to these therapeutic measures, the more difficult cases will continue to be plagued by reaccumulations of fluid. Repeated myringotomies may eventually resolve some of these cases. However, the more intractable problem cases will require continuous ventilation of the middle ear cavity by means of a small polyvinyl or polyethylene tube inserted through an incision in the tympanic membrane. Although some fluid may drain from the middle ear cavity by means of the tube, especially during the first few days after its insertion, its primary function is not to serve as a drain but as a substitute for the eustachian tube. It may be necessary to ventilate the middle ear cavity in this manner for at least several months before return of eustachian tube function. Unfortunately, serous otitis media frequently recurs after removal of the tube. In such instances, reinsertion of the plastic tube for an additional period of ventilation of the middle ear space may be necessary.

PROGNOSIS. With proper recognition and management, the prognosis in serous otitis media is generally favorable. Many cases will require only minimal therapy and some will undergo spontaneous resolution. Restoration of normal hearing and the prevention of progressive middle ear damage may be achieved even in difficult cases with aggressive therapeutic measures. However, in neglected cases, there is grave risk to permanent hearing loss as a result of extensive and irreversible changes within the middle ear cavity.

REFERENCES

ALLERGIC RHINITIS

Connell, J. T. Quantitative intranasal pollen challenges. J. Allerg., 43:33, 1969.

———— and Sherman, W. B. Skin sensitizing antibody. I. Relationship of the skin sensitizing antibody titer to the occurrence of symptoms in untreated persons with a positive ragweed skin test. J. Allerg., 34:409, 1963.

Johnstone, D. E. Comparative value of hyposensitization and symptomatic therapy in pollenosis in children. New York J. Med., 60:1448, 1961.

Rappaport, B. Z. Physiology of the nose and pathophysiology of allergic rhinitis. *In* Samter, M., ed., Immunological Diseases. Boston, Little, Brown and Co., 1965, pp. 562-568.

Sherman, W. B. Hypersensitivity—mechanisms and management. Philadelphia, W. B. Saunders Co., 1968, pp. 223-265.

SEROUS OTITIS MEDIA

Chan, J. C. M., Logan, G. B., and McBean, J. B. Serous otitis media and allergy. Amer. J. Dis. Child., 114:684, 1967.

Hoople, G. D. Otitis media with effusion—a challenge to otolaryngology. Laryngoscope, 60:315, 1950.

Kapur, Y. P. Serous otitis media in children. Arch. Otolaryng. (Chicago), 79:38, 1964.

Lecks, H. I. Allergic aspects of serous otitis media in childhood. New York J. Med., 61:2737, 1961.

McGovern, J. P., Haywood, T. J., and Fernandez, A. A. Allergy and secretory otitis media. J.A.M.A., 200:124, 1967.

Sade, J. Pathology and pathogenesis of serous otitis media. Arch. Otolaryng. (Chicago), 84:297, 1966.

Senturia, B. H., Gessert, C. F., Carr, C. D., and Baumann, E. S. Middle ear effusions: Causes and treatment. Trans. Amer. Acad. Ophthal. Otolaryng., 64:60, 1960.

Silverstein, H., Miller, G. F., Jr., and Lindeman, R. C. Eustachian tube dysfunction as a cause for chronic secretory otitis in children. Laryngoscope, 76:259, 1966.

Soboroff, B. J. Serous otitis media: A serious problem. Amer. J. Med. Sci., 253:493, 1967.

11.5
ASTHMA

ELLIOT F. ELLIS

Asthma is defined as a diffuse obstructive disease of the airways characterized by a high degree of reversibility. This definition purposely omits mention of etiologic factors, which differ from patient to patient, or are impossible to determine in many instances. The reversibility of asthma with treatment is an important feature of the illness and serves to differentiate it from emphysema, which by definition is irreversible. Asthma is the leading cause of chronic illness in children under 17 years of age and is responsible for 25 percent of days lost from school as a result of chronic illness. Because of its chronicity, it causes a great hardship to both the child and his parents. Contrary to older notions, a significant mortality rate threatens patients with this disease.

ETIOLOGY. Asthmatics may be divided into two broad groups: (1) those in whom, by history and allergy testing, the asthma can be identified as immunologic in nature and due to reaginic sensitization to pollens, molds, epidermals, house dust, and rarely, foods; and (2) those in whom no immunologic cause can be determined. This type of asthma occurs chiefly at both ends of the life spectrum, namely in infants and small children, and in adults whose asthma begins after 40 years of age. In the "nonimmunologic" group, infections of the respiratory tract are believed to play an important role. This hypothesis, however, is substantiated by clinical impressions only.

Role of Specific Etiologic Factors in Immunologic or Allergic Asthma. Inhalants are the major etiologic agents in allergic asthma. Seasonal asthma occurring in the spring, summer, or fall is usually due to sensitivity to the pollens of trees, grasses, or weeds, or a combination of these. Molds may be involved as either seasonal or perennial factors depending upon the section of the country. Asthma occurring primarily in the winter is likely to result from allergy to indoor inhalants, such as house dust or other household allergens. Multiple sensitivities are the rule in perennial asthma. However, in certain parts of the country, grass pollen, a seasonal allergen primarily, is present in the air nine months of the year and, therefore, may be responsible for perennial symptoms. Danders of dogs, cats, and various farm animals are especially potent allergens and must be considered as possible offenders in every case of asthma. The importance of foods as etiologic agents in allergic disease is a subject of considerable con-

troversy. Some allergists believe foods, including additives, to be a major cause of respiratory tract symptomatology, especially in infancy. In our experience, ingestants are rarely implicated in asthma at any age. In those cases in which asthma is shown to be food related, the food may be causing symptoms as an osmyl by the inhalant route rather than as an ingestant. It is important to remember that considerable harm can be done to a child's nutritional status by the erroneous diagnosis of food allergy and the injudicious introduction of unnecessary, restrictive elimination diets. Psychologic factors in asthma are discussed in Section 11.6.

PATHOPHYSIOLOGY. Asthma is primarily a disease of the small airways, 3 to 9 mm in diameter. Autopsy material from individuals who die *early* in the course of the disease is rarely available and comes from patients who died from a cause unrelated to asthma. In those few cases that have been studied, the paucity of pathologic findings is striking. As the disease progresses, there is an increase in the number of mucus-producing cells, increased prominence of the smooth muscle, and thickening and hyalinization of the basement membrane. In individuals dying in *status asthmaticus,* widespread obstruction is present in airways of all sizes by tenacious, stringy mucus infiltrated with eosinophils and other inflammatory cells. The acute symptoms of the asthmatic patient are produced by airway obstruction resulting from mucous membrane edema, increased secretions, and smooth muscle spasm. The relative contribution of each of these factors to the obstructive process is unknown, but it is likely that in the early stage of an acute attack of asthma, mucous membrane edema and smooth muscle spasm may be of prime importance. As the asthmatic attack progresses, secretions are increasingly responsible for the obstruction of the airways, a fact that has important therapeutic implications. The airways of patients with asthma are extraordinarily hyperreactive to a variety of so-called nonspecific stimuli such as cold air, irritating odors such as wet paint, and a number of other atmospheric irritants. The increased susceptibility of the asthmatic airway to the bronchoconstrictive action of acetylcholine and its congeners, and to histamine has been known for many years. A severe attack of asthma can be induced in the laboratory in an asthmatic individual by an inhalation of a dose of acetyl β-methacholine (Mecholyl), one thousandth of that necessary to cause even minor bronchoconstriction in a normal individual. The sensitivity to Mecholyl varies from patient to patient, but seems to be almost uniform in asthmatics. The airway obstruction in asthma results in various physiologic disturbances. These include abnormalities in mechanics of breathing, lung volumes, and in distribution of inspired air. The uneven ventilation of various segments of the lung in the asthmatic leads to a ventilation-perfusion imbalance, a major cause of the hypoxemia that occurs in the symptomatic asthmatic. Inadequate alveolar ventilation also results in CO_2 retention and leads ultimately, if ventilation is not improved, to respiratory acidosis.

CLINICAL MANIFESTATIONS. The symptoms in asthma are due to airway obstruction which leads to inadequate alveolar ventilation and maldistribution of inspired air. Wheezing, the cardinal sign of asthma, is a manifestation of partial airway obstruction; primarily expiratory, it may also be present during inspiration. There is a subjective feeling of tightness and the patient has difficulty both in inspiring and expelling air. The dyspnea is of variable intensity, and tachypnea is almost always present. In severe cases, the shoulder girdle is elevated, the chest hyperinflated, the accessory muscles of respiration are laboring, and the child frequently assumes a sitting position, hunching forward while supporting his body by extending his arms on the edge of a chair or bed. The degree of airway obstruction varies from patient to patient and at different times in the same patient. If severe, air exchange may be very poor and wheezing barely audible. Cyanosis may not be apparent during an attack, but there is always hypoxemia. The latter results from inadequate alveolar ventilation, combined with right to left shunting secondary to perfusion of underventilated areas of the lung. Accentuation of the second pulmonic sound may be produced by the pulmonary hypertension present during the acute attack. Between acute episodes, chronic hyperinflation may produce the barrel-chested appearance in a child affected by the disease to a significant degree. The shoulder girdle elevation may persist and result in a characteristic square-shouldered thoracic configuration. Clubbing of the fingers and toes is seen only rarely even in the most severe asthmatics, and when present, diseases other than asthma should be considered.

Status Asthmaticus. There is no unanimity of opinion concerning the definition of status asthmaticus. It is essentially a clinical judgment and is used here for severe asthma unresponsive to conventional therapy, including epinephrine, isoproterenol, and aminophylline. Status asthmaticus is a life-threatening situation since it leads to respiratory failure if not adequately treated. Experience has shown that the severity of status asthmaticus should not be assessed by clinical findings alone. Although the finding of poor air exchange on auscultation is ominous, analysis of arterial blood for Po_2, Pco_2, and pH is mandatory for the proper management of patients with status asthmaticus. Arteriolized capillary blood is less desirable for analysis than arterial blood, especially in the patient who has had repeated injections of epinephrine, which has a vasoconstrictive effect on the peripheral vascular bed.

LABORATORY FINDINGS. Children with asthma frequently show eosinophilia of the peripheral blood and respiratory tract secretions. The sputum is tenacious, almost rubbery in consistency, and loaded with eosinophils. In severe asthma with chronic hypoxemia, the hematocrit is commonly elevated. Blood gas and pH analysis during asymptomatic intervals are normal. Early in an acute attack of asthma mild hypoxemia may be present, the Pco_2 is usually reduced due to hyperventilation, and the pH is normal. As the attack progresses, hypoxemia worsens and the Pco_2 begins to rise, leading ultimately to respiratory acidosis and fall in pH.

Pulmonary function studies are of special value in asthma and should be part of the investigation of every asthmatic patient. Meaningful determinations can be made in children as young as 6 years of age. Asthmatics, even during periods of relative freedom from symptoms, may show abnormalities in: (1) *Lung volumes:* lower vital capacity (VC), higher residual volume (RV), higher functional residual capacity (FRC), and higher residual volume/lung capacity percentage (RV/TLC $\times$ 100); (2) *Mechanics of breathing:* lower maximum voluntary ventilation (MVV), lower forced expiratory volume at 1 second (FEV_1), lower maximum expiratory flow rate (MEFR); (3) *Distribution of inspired gas:* abnormal nitrogen and helium washout curves. These tests have greater diagnostic value when repeated before and after administration of a bronchodilator, in order to demonstrate the reversibility of the abnormal findings characteristic of asthma. It is preferable to follow the progress of a patient with asthma by simple tests repeated at frequent and regular intervals, rather than by complex and sophisticated tests done occasionally. Chest roentgenographic findings vary considerably. They can be entirely normal, or they can show marked degrees of hyperinflation with increased anteroposterior diameter, flattened diaphragms with minimal positional changes on inspiration and expiration, widening of the intercostal spaces, and increased lung markings. Roentgenographic evidence of atelectasis, involving usually the right middle lobe, is also frequent.

DIAGNOSIS. The typical case of asthma is readily recognized. In the average patient, the attacks of coughing and wheezing, their episodic nature, their rapid responsiveness to epinephrine or isoproterenol, and the relative freedom from symptoms between attacks, represent a clinical picture hard to confuse with any other respiratory disease. While it is true that "all that wheezes is not asthma," the majority of children who have recurrent cough and wheezing will, after appropriate testing, be found to have asthma. Moreover, the child with a chronic night cough, in whom wheezing is not observed by the parents, but who coughs and becomes unduly short of breath following exercise, can also frequently be shown to have the reversible airway obstruction of asthma. It is well to remember that wheezing audible to the naked ear may not be present until an encroachment of about 50 percent of the lumen of the airway exists. A trial on asthma therapy is warranted in all children with these symptoms.

The signs and symptoms of obstructive airway disease may present some diagnostic difficulties during the first two years of life. Many physicians are reluctant to make a diagnosis of asthma in a child under 2 years of age. Diagnoses such as asthmatic bronchitis, recurrent bronchiolitis, wheezy cold, wheezy bronchitis, bronchitis with wheezing, or capillary bronchitis may reflect inadequate appreciation by the physician of the natural history of asthma. Analysis of a large number of medical histories of children who ultimately develop typical asthma affords evidence of the occurrence of episodes of coughing and wheezing during the first year of life in a significant number of instances. Conversely, many infants and small children who have recurrent coughing and wheezing either without discernible cause, or associated with clinical evidence of respiratory infection, will be shown ultimately to have asthma.

In the differential diagnosis of wheezing, other causes of airway obstruction must always be considered. Respiratory syncytial virus can cause, in epidemic situations, an infectious bronchiolitis which produces in infants a clinical picture indistinguishable from asthma. Anomalies of the respiratory tract or great vessels causing either intrinsic or extrinsic narrowing of the airway, foreign bodies, and diseases such as cystic fibrosis of the pancreas can mimic the clinical manifestation of asthma in the infant or small child.

TREATMENT.   Effective treatment in asthma should be based primarily upon an attempt to identify etiologic factors. Elimination or minimization of exposure to the offendng allergens frequently produces good results. Directions for environmental control may be found in Table 3 (Sec. 11.3). Immunotherapy (hyposensitization) is indicated to allergens that cannot be avoided. Bacterial vaccines have been used empirically but are not recommended until convincing evidence of their efficacy has been obtained. Much can also be accomplished in the management of the child with asthma by the proper use of pharmacologic agents. A general discussion of drug therapy of allergic disorders is found in Section 11.3.

Treatment of Acute Attack.   An acute episode of asthma sufficiently severe to cause obvious distress can be effectively treated by subcutaneous injection of 0.05 to 0.2 ml of a 1:1,000 concentration of aqueous epinephrine hydrochloride (Adrenalin). The dose may be repeated twice at 20-minute intervals. It is not unusual for the patient to respond minimally to the first injection, but show significant improvement after the second dose is administered 20 minutes later. The undesirable side effects of epinephrine injection, such as pallor, tremor, and headache are minimized by using the smallest dose of epinephrine capable of producing a favorable clinical response. Sus-phrine (epinephrine 1:200 in a thioglycolate suspension) provides longer lasting relief than the aqueous solution. It is claimed that 25 percent of the epinephrine in this long-acting preparation is released rapidly and the remaining 75 percent released slowly over the next four to six hours. A pediatric dose of Sus-phrine ranges from 0.05 to 0.2 ml depending upon the size of the child. Isoproterenol (Isuprel) by inhalation gives a very rapid relief of symptoms if administered properly. This drug is aerosolized best and least expensively in a bulb type nebulizer to which five drops of isoproterenol and 1 ml of saline are added. Freon-propelled units that deliver a measured dose of 0.075 mg of isoproterenol per inhalation are available, but less desirable. Isoproterenol given by nebulization is of special value in the asthmatic child who awakens with a sudden attack of asthma in the middle of the night. Many parents have found that one or two inhalations will successfully abort the attack, allow the child to go back to sleep, and avoid midnight trips to the hospital emergency room or the physician's office. No more than two or three inhalations should be given every three to four hours. Progressively poorer and shorter lived responses to isoproterenol inhalation indicate that the patient's asthma is worsening and that medical attention is needed. Excessive use of aerosolized bronchodilators (especially the Freon-propelled units) has been implicated as a possible cause of sudden death in patients with asthma. For this reason, the Freon-propelled unit should remain under control of the parents, or the school nurse, and the child should not be allowed to have free use of the nebulizer. By restricting the nebulizer in this way, excessive use can be avoided and an unhealthy psychologic dependence on the nebulizing unit can be avoided. If response to the previously mentioned catecholamines is not satisfactory, some form of theophylline should be used. Aminophylline (85 percent theophylline and 15 percent ethylenediamine) is the most widely used theophylline preparation for oral and parenteral use. Theophylline is a common constituent of most combination bronchodilator preparations. However, its absorption from the upper gastrointestinal tract is unpredictable when given in the form of the usual tablet or suspension. Alcoholic solutions of theophylline such as Elixophylline, given by mouth, result in good theophylline blood concentrations and therapeutic responses. The use of Elixophylline in children is limited because the elixir is unpalatable and its alcohol content is 20 percent. Theophylline compounds can be administered successfully by the rectal route. The best and safest form of rectal theophylline is theophylline monoethanolamine (Fleet theophylline enema) which is packaged in a squeeze bottle unit that allows accurate administration of the desired dose. A dose of 7 mg/kg may be given every six to eight hours quite safely. The use of aminophylline suppositories is limited. Their absorption is unpredictable and they are generally available for pediatric use only in 125 and 250 mg strengths, which presents a problem in administration of an accurate dose to small children. The practice of cutting a suppository in half or longitudinally is undesirable and potentially dangerous because the drug may not be uniformly distributed in the suppository. In a hospital situation, parenteral administration of aminophylline by the intravenous route has proved safe and effective. The intravenous dose is 3 mg/kg body weight every six to eight hours. The drug is most conveniently given in 20 to 30 ml of isotonic fluid by slow intravenous infusion over a 15- to 20-minute period. This method of administration has been shown to provide more rapid relief of symptoms and higher plasma theophylline concentrations than when the same dose is infused more slowly over six to eight hours and in greater dilutions. Theophylline is a potent diuretic and additional fluids should be given to compensate for the increased renal water losses.

Treatment of Status Asthmaticus. Since hypoxemia is always present in this situation, oxygen should be administered, preferably by mask or intranasal catheter. Parenteral corticosteroids (methylprednisolone) should be injected in doses of 40 to 60 mg every six to eight hours, most conveniently into the tubing of the intravenous hydrating infusion, which is also an important part of the therapy. Blood gases and pH must be monitored constantly. The correction of metabolic acidosis is also essential. This requires the administration, as often as necessary, of sodium bicarbonate in doses calculated according to the formula: $mEq\ NaHCO_3 = base\ deficit \times body\ weight\ (kg) \times 0.3$. The use of sodium bicarbonate in respiratory acidosis in the absence of metabolic acidosis, is controversial. Respiratory acidosis is obviously best treated by improvement in ventilation. If blood gas analyses indicate that respiratory failure is present (roughly Po_2 less than 50 mm of mercury, and Pco_2 more than 50 mm of mercury), the patient requires highly specialized care in a well-equipped unit staffed by physicians and nurses thoroughly experienced in intensive care. Sedation of the patient with barbiturates is contraindicated. If sedation is absolutely necessary, chloral hydrate is the safest drug. Medical personnel who maintain a comfortingly calm attitude may often prove to be an excellent sedative for the anxious, hypoxic patient. Bronchoscopy in an ill asthmatic child is a hazardous procedure even in the hands of an expert endoscopist and is rarely indicated during an episode of status asthmaticus. A chest roentgenogram should be obtained in every patient in status asthmaticus in order to detect complications, such as mediastinal emphysema or pneumothorax. As the attack of status asthmaticus resolves, postural drainage will help mobilize the copious secretions frequently present. With the knowledge and technology available currently, mortality from status asthmaticus should be minimal.

DAY-TO-DAY MANAGEMENT OF THE ASTHMATIC CHILD.

In the child who has primarily a slight degree of wheezing most of the time, continuous treatment with an oral preparation containing a combination of noniodinated bronchodilators, such as Tedral or Verequad, given three or four times a day, gives better results than when these drugs are used for acute exacerbations only. Tachyphylaxis to the ephedrine in the compound does not seem to be a problem, and continuous administration of the compound does not seem to result in diminished effectiveness. Oral bronchodilators are available in suspension or tablet form. Small children are given

½ to 1 tsp. three to four times a day; older children can tolerate as much as 1 to 1½ tablets every 4 hours. The aminophylline in the mixture occasionally may cause nausea and vomiting. The ephedrine may produce jitteriness, "nervousness," and insomnia. These undesirable symptoms usually yield to an adjustment of dosage. The goitrogenic effects of iodides should preclude their use in children, despite their possible benefits as expectorants. Iodides also produce an acneiform eruption in adolescent patients. Antihistamines are generally not effective and may even have deleterious effects because of their atropinelike action which causes drying of secretions. A theophylline enema at bedtime to a child who awakens habitually with a nocturnal acute attack may result in a night of undisturbed sleep. In the patient with exercise-induced bronchoconstrictive episodes, the prophylactic inhalation of isoproterenol before engaging in activity may help to avoid the attack. Corticosteroid therapy in a nonhospitalized and asthmatic child should be considered carefully. Except in status asthmaticus, such therapy should not be initiated until all modalities of conventional treatment have failed and the child's life is severely restricted by his illness. Before steroids are instituted, the patient should have the benefit of an expert allergy work-up, environmental control measures, a home visit by the physician to verify implementation of the latter, and a trial on conventional drugs to maximum tolerance. Whenever corticosteroids are used, they should be given in adequate doses (1 to 2 mg/kg every 24 hours) and an attempt made to discontinue them as quickly as possible. A long weaning period is unnecessary following their short-term use in the treatment of an acute attack. In such instances return of normal hypothalamic-pituitary-adrenal function occurs more promptly when the drug is withdrawn abruptly. A four- to five-day course of therapy is often sufficient in a severe exacerbation. Prednisone, orally or methylprednisolone, parenterally, are the corticosteroids of choice. Suppression of linear growth is usually the most prominent undesirable effect of corticosteroid therapy. Alternate-day therapy with prednisone (a single dose equivalent to twice the daily dose or even more, given at 8 A.M. every 48 hours) appears to cause less growth suppression than daily therapy with equivalent dosage.

Postural drainage is useful especially in those asthmatics who have a significant amount of secretions. It is most effective when done on a regular basis, three times a day, and following inhalation of isoproterenol. Treatments with intermittent positive pressure breathing (IPPB) machines are of no significant therapeutic value. An aerosol is administered as effectively by a manual nebulizer as with a costly IPPB apparatus. Exercise and participation in competitive sports should be encouraged. Psychologic aspects of asthma are discussed separately (see p. 468). A number of asthmatic children continue to do very poorly despite optimal treatment. Referral of such children to one of the asthma residential treatment centers which specialize in the diagnosis and treatment of intractable asthma should be considered.

References

Ellis, E. F. Asthma. *In* Gellis, S. S., and Kagan, B. M., eds., Current Pediatric Therapy, Vol. 4. Philadelphia, W. B. Saunders Co., 1970, pp. 918-923.

Heimlich, E. M. Asthmatic Hyperresponsiveness. Pediat. Clin. N. Amer., 16:149, 1969.

Middleton, E., Jr. The anatomical and biochemical basis of bronchial obstruction in asthma. Ann. Intern. Med., 63:695, 1965.

11.6
PSYCHOLOGIC ASPECTS OF ASTHMA

JONATHAN H. WEISS

Attempts to "explain" asthma on the basis of any one of several single determinants have not only been unsuccessful, but may have been responsible for obstructing our understanding of its nature. Multideterminants have been demonstrated clearly in other disorders, especially the genetically determined inborn errors of metabolism (Chap. 8). Similarly, in patients with asthma a genetically determined constitutional factor may require for its expression the coexistence of one or more environmental factors, including not only a wide variety of allergens but also what might be considered psychologic equivalents of allergens. This view is supported by clinical experiences indicating that: (1) Asthma is affected by a variety of factors including allergens, infections, and emotions; (2) These factors may operate independently or in combination; and (3) The importance of any one factor varies both among individuals and in any one individual at different times.

The focus in this section will be on the individual patient. Diagnostic and therapeutic techniques will be described which should help the physician to include psychologic principles in his general care of the asthmatic child and his family. Finally, current investigative approaches concerned with underlying mechanisms will be presented.

Clinical Considerations

IDENTIFYING EMOTIONAL DETERMINANTS. Interpreting etiologic factors in asthmatic children is complicated by the fact that emotional stress can be both an effect as well as a cause of an attack. For example, attacks of asthma can, in some patients, be brought on by anxiety. In others, however, anxiety and panic seem to appear only after the onset of symptoms. Similarly, dependency and depression, regarded by some as contributing causes of asthma, may result also from the debilitating effects of chronic illness. Social withdrawal in asthmatics may be caused by self-consciousness about their symptoms, as well as by the limitations that the symptoms may impose on social and competitive behaviors. Aggressive acting out, sexual promiscuity, resistance to the medical regimen, all may stem from the need to deny disability and to gain compensatory social approval. In short, behavioral problems in asthmatic children cannot, without additional confirming data, be regarded solely as either causes or effects of asthma. Such confirming data can be sought in a number of ways.

The first is a structured "Precipitants Interview" (Purcell and Weiss) designed to elicit from the patient and/or his family a history of those things, including emotions, that have been observed to bring on asthma. Emphasis is placed on those precipitants that have been directly observed—not inferred suggested, or in any way hypothesized—to bring on attacks. Detailed information is obtained about each precipitant, including its frequency and relative importance, and the events that intervene between its occurrence and the onset of symptoms. Reports of significant emotional precipitants obtained in this way have been shown to predict respiratory responsiveness to a variety of psychologic manipulations, and have been useful for diagnostic purposes.

The second technique involves determining whether significant changes in the patient's life situation, especially separation from his family, appear to have had a beneficial effect. Prompt response to hospitalization without the use of potent medicines is an example of such an effect. Diminished severity of asthma when one or both parents are away is another example; however, most separations such as visits to relatives and hospitalizations involve simultaneous changes in both the physical (e.g., household allergens) and psychologic environment. Additional information is required, therefore, before the relative importance of different aspects of the change can be assessed. In other instances, however, such as improvement whenever the father is away, the evaluation is less ambiguous. Trial separations, where they can be arranged, may be considered for diagnostic purposes. The clinician, however, must be prepared to handle parental guilt and anxiety in response to what may be interpreted as a suggestion that the family is somehow "responsible" for the child's asthma. Finally, the stress-interview (Stevenson and Ripley) can be used for testing the precipitant effects of emotional stimuli. A "positive" (wheezing) response to the discussion of affectively charged material clearly points to the relevance of the subject; absence of response, on the other hand, is inconclusive.

TREATMENT TECHNIQUES. Although many questions concerning the role of emotions in asthma remain unanswered, and complete cures attributable to psychologic therapy are rare, significant relief can often be obtained by psychologic techniques, including the use of psychotherapy, institutionalization, and tranquilizing drugs.

Psychotherapy. In considering referral to the asthmatic child for psychotherapy, the attitudes of the family must be included. Feelings such as fear, shame, and resentment, and tendencies either to overindulge or to reject the patient, can have important effects on the child's adjustment, regardless of whether or not they have a significant effect on his asthma. For example:

A 7-year-old girl seen by the author had, in the preceding year, shown a marked deterioration in behavior. Irritability, demandingness, and social withdrawal had become prominent, and she had begun to express a growing pessimism that her asthma would ever be brought under control. Asked what he thought of this pattern, the patient's father expressed the belief that it was due to his daughter's growing up and becoming more realistic about the seriousness of her symptoms. Further probing, however, revealed that the father had been making a detailed study of asthma through consultation and correspondence with numerous investigators and physicians, and that he was becoming convinced that the outlook for his daughter was not good. Asthma, he believed, was neither well understood nor adequately treatable. When the striking resemblance of the father's and daughter's attitudes was pointed out, the father's response was a genuinely surprised, "I never thought of it that way."

A second consideration relating to the usefulness of psychotherapy has to do with the discrepancy that often exists between what patients report as relief following psychotherapy, and what is shown by objective indices of change, such as pulmonary function. Nevertheless, it appears that the "relief" given by psychotherapy is often accompanied by desirable behavioral changes such as return to work and lowered demands for medication. The use of psychotherapy, then, would appear to be warranted at least for rehabilitative purposes. The patient's physical condition must, of course, continue to be monitored, so that activities that remain beyond his capability, despite his newfound sense of well-being, will be avoided.

A final consideration concerns the psychotherapeutic role of the physician himself. What the patient and his family learn from the doctor can have important effects that may be neither anticipated nor intended. For example:

One family that had planned to spend a two-week golfing vacation at a resort 125 miles from home, wound up driving round trip daily from home to the resort after the first night when the patient had developed severe asthma. Asked why they would not chance a second night to see if the asthma recurred, the family replied that during the previous year they had sought treatment from a new allergist. After their first visit to him, the doctor had come to the patient's

home, "put on a pair of white gloves and went around tapping the walls and furniture for dust." The parents decided, "My God, if it's that serious, we aren't going to take any chances!"

A realistic explanation of asthma, its course, and treatment, given in an unhurried, sympathetic manner, can do much to provide psychologic support as well as useful information. Many parents, by the time they see the doctor, will have been exposed to various kinds of misinformation about asthma, and many will have adopted the idea that asthma is "our fault." Pointing out that asthma is affected by many things, and that the importance of any one, including emotions, would have to be determined for each case, can help to alleviate such guilt and foster more realistic and constructive attitudes. Parents must be helped to regard asthma in an appropriately objective manner that will permit them to avoid the pitfalls of overindulgence on the one hand, and rejection of the patient on the other.

Almost every variety of psychotherapy, including psychoanalysis, group therapy, environmental manipulation, behavior modification, and hypnosis, has been used for asthmatic children. Although some success has been reported for each of these, there is, as yet, no acceptable validation of the results. However, it does appear that in general, relatively mild asthma, of short duration, with a clearly defined emotional component, can be afforded some relief by psychotherapeutic means. At the very least, patients with what appear to be secondary behavioral difficulties can be helped to make a more satisfactory adjustment. In addition to focusing on relieving asthma, where this is possible, the patient's overall psychologic growth is a necessary and desirable consideration. Thus, the goals of psychotherapy must be broadly conceived and include improved attitudes of the family.

Institutionalization. In many instances institutionalization has provided a highly effective means of affording relief to asthmatic patients, especially those with a prominent emotional component. It should be considered, however, only when other therapeutic measures have been tried extensively and found to be relatively ineffective. There is some evidence to suggest that patients for whom emotions are particularly significant precipitants respond favorably to the effects of institutionalization because of the shift in the psychologic environment. It must be borne in mind, however, that simultaneous shifts in the physical environment must account for at least some of the noted improvement. It is important to remind parents of the multiplicity of factors that are relevant to asthma, and to communicate sympathetic understanding, rather than impatient condemnation, of any reluctance to separate from the child. Adequate preparation of the child is also extremely important, and he or she should be helped to understand that separation is not permanent and does not mean total loss of the family. Before separation occurs, it is crucial that both the parents and the child understand that the length of time he will be away from home will be determined by the institutional staff. If this point is not made clear, the child is left hoping that his parents will remove him at an early date, and our experience has been that he will probably not adjust well to institutional life, making premature removal more likely, especially if the parents are also uncertain concerning who makes the decision.

Tranquilizers. Since anxiety is often an important part of asthma, either as a cause, aggravant, or result of symptoms, tranquilizers have been considered useful for the following purposes: preventing the onset of attacks; reducing panic; reducing turmoil regardless of whether it affects the patient's specific clinical status; controlling the hyperstimulant effects of such drugs as ephedrine and theophylline; and finally, controlling anxiety during the initial period of institutionalization. Tranquilizing drugs must be used cautiously, however, for the following reasons: (1) Tranquilizers in sufficiently large doses may depress respiratory function; (2) The tranquilized patient may ignore important warning signs and delay seeking treatment; and (3) In cases of status asthmaticus, tranquilizers may impair the respiratory efforts of an already weakened patient. It is important, therefore, to try to help patients relax by conveying an attitude of confidence and optimism, before resorting to tranquilizers or sedatives. Finally, it must be emphasized that treatment of an asthmatic child and his family must comprehend all components of this complex disease. The belief that asthma which has a more prominent emotional component is somehow less real and less serious than asthma which is more directly related to exposure to inhalant allergens, is encountered not only in the parents of patients, but unfortunately in physicians as well. For example, one adolescent boy was referred to a psychologist for treatment in the early stages of status asthmaticus because, "It can't be serious, everybody knows that this patient's asthma is all 'psychic.'" This statement fails again to appreciate the fact that asthma has multideterminants. The analogy to bleeding ulcer is, in this connection, a useful one. Although chronic tension can be a significant antecedent to ulcer formation, the reality and seriousness of the lesion, and the need for medical management, is not questioned. Similarly, in asthma, the "lesion" is equally real, whatever the major environmental determinant. To focus excessively on the precipitant and ignore the symptom, then, can be dangerous. The treatment of any psychologic components must take place in the context of continuing medical supervision of the patient.

Research Considerations

The literature describing psychosomatic research in asthma has been grouped around four basic strategies designed to investigate the causal relevance of emotions to asthma. Attempts have been made to: (1) demonstrate an "asthmatic" personality (nuclear conflict, mother-child relations); (2) induce attacks of asthma or changes in the frequency and/or severity of asthma by psychologic means; (3) relate naturally occurring attacks or variability in asthma patterns to psychologic events in the patient and/or his environment; (4) "explain" asthma in terms of "established" psychologic principles (psychoanalytic concepts). Although many of the studies in each category have been methodologically and conceptually weak, the accumulated evidence no longer permits reasonable doubt that psychologic factors play a significant role in some if not all patients with asthma. What is needed now are more precise techniques for identifying the relevant psychologic factors, the patients for whom they operate, and the pathways through which they are mediated. At the same time more attention to treatment techniques derived from the newly developed family of behavior modification methods, including autonomic conditioning (see below) would be warranted.

ASTHMATIC PERSONALITY. Two major problems are associated with attempts to define an asthmatic personality. First, they often assume that asthmatics comprise a psychologically homogeneous population. Second, since they are usually retrospective studies on patients who have had asthma for a considerable time, there is always the possibility that a characteristic adjustment pattern, such as dependency, may be the result, rather than the cause, of the disease.

The assumption of homogeneity can be questioned from the results of a number of studies (Purcell; Block et al.) which have found considerable variability in the degree to which psychologic factors could be detected in different patients. Asthmatics appear to be decidedly heterogeneous with regard to psychologic components of their illness. "Specificity hypotheses" that relate asthma to specific personality profiles, attitudes, or relationshps have yet to be validated.

The weakness of retrospective studies was demonstrated by Neuhaus, who introduced a control group of chronic cardiac children in a study comparing asthmatics and normals. The two groups of children with chronic illnesses differed from the normal controls on measures such as maladjustment and anxiety, but did not differ from each other. There is a great need for further delineation of significant subgroups and for prospective, longitudinal studies beginning, ideally, with high-risk target groups who have not yet developed symptoms.

INDUCED CHANGES. Investigators of this category have attempted both to induce asthma by psychologic means such as stress interviews and suggestion, and to alleviate symptoms by psychotherapy, hypnosis, and the other techniques mentioned above. Although success has been reported in both types of studies, good objective measures of change have been largely lacking. Beneficial effects following experimental separation of the child and family have been carefully documented (Purcell et al., 1969), suggesting though not proving a psychotherapeutic effect. Studies designed to induce symptoms have shown relatively small increases in airway resistance accompanied by subjective distress (Luparello et al.); however, in the author's opinion, frank asthma has not been induced. More precise induction and treatment studies hold promise for greater understanding of the mechanism of onset of attacks and of the effectiveness of psychologic intervention. The use of subgroups in which emotional factors have been well defined would appear to be desirable in such studies.

PSYCHOLOGIC FACTORS AND SPONTANEOUS VARIATIONS IN ASTHMA. This approach, probably because of the great difficulties in making naturalistic observations, has had less attention than the others. As a result, little is known about the "natural history" of asthma either in terms of population norms, such as age of onset and age and rate of spontaneous remitters, or for individual patients. The only observations on natural variability known to the author relate to the supposed alternation of asthma and psychosis (Ross), and more recently, to the relationship between dream activity and onset of night attacks (Weiss). The former studies are generally inconclusive, with the more careful studies turning up less clear alternation patterns. The latter observations are as yet too new and too few to permit any definite conclusions.

An example of the interesting things that can emerge from "natural history" studies comes from a recent, as yet unpublished, epidemiologic test of the generality of the 2:1, male to female ratio in childhood asthma. The subgroups in which the greatest male to female discrepancy occurred—viz., middle-class, Protestant, small (two to five siblings) families—are known to be characterized by socialization practices which the authors hypothesize relate to emotional precipitation of asthma. A study of the behavioral events antecedent to the onset of spontaneously occurring attacks is being undertaken by us, using telemetry techniques and direct observations.

"EXPLANATION" OF ASTHMA BY PSYCHOLOGIC PRINCIPLES. Attempts in this category to understand underlying mechanisms in asthma have had a mixed history. Premature theorizing, and the application of principles that are themselves in need of confirmation, have been responsible for much unrewarded effort. For example, interpreting the symptoms of asthma in psychoanalytic symbolic terms has not advanced our understanding greatly, although it should be pointed out that the initiative for psychosomatic research in asthmatic children has often been taken by psychoanalytically oriented investigators.

More recently, operant conditioning principles derived from learning theory have been fruitfully applied to the study of autonomic activity in children with asthma. It has been convincingly demonstrated, for example, that autonomically controlled activities such as heart rate, blood pressure, and rate of intestinal contraction can be increased or decreased ("shaped") by operant conditioning techniques (Miller). As a result, there is speculation that psychosomatic illness may be the result of "shaping," and may be brought under control using conditioning techniques. These possibilities are of great interest and will undoubtedly receive much attention in the near future.

REFERENCES

Beecher, H. K. Measurement of Subjective Responses. London, Oxford University Press, 1959.

Block, J., Jennings, P. H., Harvey, E., and Simpson, E. Interactions between allergic potential and psychopathology in childhood asthma. Psychosom. Med., 26:307, 1964.

Freeman, E. H., Feingold, B. F., Schlesinger, K., and Grosman, F. J. Psychological variables in allergic disorders: a review. Psychosom. Med., 26:543, 1964.

Luparello, T., Lyons, H. A., Bleecker, E. R., and McFadden, E. R. Effect of suggestion on airway reactivity in asthmatic subjects. Psychosom. Med., 30:819, 1968.

Maurer, E. The asthmatic child. J. Asthma Res., 3:25, 1965.

Miller, N. E. Learning of visceral and glandular responses. Science, 163:434, 1969.

Moore, N. Behaviour therapy in bronchial asthma: a controlled study. J. Psychosom. Res., 9:257, 1965.

Neuhaus, E. C. Personality study of asthmatic and cardiac children. Psychosom. Med., 20:395, 1958.

Purcell, K. Distinctions between subgroups of asthmatic children: Children's perceptions of events associated with asthma. Pediatrics, 31:486, 1963.

——— Brady, K., Chai, H., Muser, J., Molk, L., Gordon, N., and Means, J. The effect on asthma in children of experimental separation from the family. Psychosom. Med., 31:144, 1969.

——— Weiss, J. H., and Hahn, W. Some psychosomatic disorders. In Wolman, B., ed., Handbook of Child Psychopathology. New York, McGraw-Hill Book Co., in press.

——— and Weiss, J. H. Emotions and asthma. In Costello, C. G., ed. Symptoms of Psychopathology. New York, John Wiley and Sons, Inc., 1970.

Ross, W. D. The association of certain vegetative disturbances with various psychoses. Psychosom. Med., 12:170, 1950.

Stevenson, I., and Ripley, H. S. Variations in respiration and in respiratory symptoms during changes in emotion. Psychosom. Med., 14:476, 1952.

Weiss, J. H. Birth order and asthma in children. J. Psychosom. Res., 12:137, 1968.

Weiss, J. V. Dreams and night asthma in children. Unpublished doctoral dissertation, University of Denver, 1969.

White, H. C. Hypnosis in bronchial asthma. J. Psychosom. Res., 5:272, 1961.

11.7
ATOPIC DERMATITIS
(See also Sec. 26.7)

ROBERT W. GOLTZ and ELLIOT F. ELLIS

DEFINITION. Atopic dermatitis (atopic eczema) is an inflammatory skin disease characterized by erythema, swelling, exudation, and crusting. It has a particular distribution, clinical course, and some genetic association with asthma and hay fever.

CLINICAL COURSE. Typically atopic eczema begins in infancy, usually during the first two to three months of life. However, its onset may be delayed until the first or second year. The eruption appears first as eczematous patches on the cheeks, then spreads to the rest of the face, the neck, the wrists and hands, and the cubital and popliteal fossae. In severe cases, the trunk may also be involved. The earliest symptom is actually pruritus followed by erythema. The typical exudative and scaly lesions of eczema may not appear if the child is prevented from producing them by scratching. Itching is intense, and affected children will use every available device to scratch their skin, often rubbing their faces incessantly on the sheets and against the sides of their crib. Because of the exudative nature of the lesions, secondary infection is a particular threat. In some cases lesions appear first at the time of introduction of cow's milk or the addition of wheat or egg to the diet. Opinions differ widely among pediatricians, dermatologists, and allergists about the relative etiologic importance of specific food sensitivity in atopic dermatitis. There are instances, however, in which the ingestion of certain foods seems to induce at least paroxysms of itching which lead to intense scratching.

Atopic eczema, once established, generally persists throughout infancy. Remissions usually begin at about 3 years of age; severe cases generally clear more slowly, milder ones earlier. The remission may then be followed by a period entirely free from eczema during childhood; or it may be incomplete, with persistence of moderate eczema in the cubital and popliteal fossae, on the wrists, face, and trunk throughout childhood. Characteristically an exacerbation tends to occur at puberty; the lesions persist through adolescence and early adulthood and then gradually disappear. In adults, lesions tend to be drier and secondary changes, such as hyperpigmentation of the skin, scaling, and lichenification are prominent. Lichenification consists of a papular thickening of the skin with accentuation of the normal surface lines. The areas involved remain, however, essentially the same as in childhood.

There are clinical variants which differ significantly from the typical form of eczema. In *nummular eczema,* round coinlike exudative patches, from one to several centimeters in diameter, appear in one or more localized areas. Such patches can occur anywhere, but characteristically in locations not typically affected by atopic eczema. Some patients have eczematous lesions in the usual sites and nummular spots scattered over the trunk and proximal extremities. Without involvement of typical areas, the diagnosis of the atopic state may be difficult to establish except by history. Nonetheless, many dermatologists consider nummular eczema to be basically an atopic state.

In some cases, persistent hand or foot eczema is also regarded by dermatologists and allergists as being based on an atopic diathesis. Such lesions may persist far into adult life, and thus differ not only in distribution, but also in course, from more typical atopic eruptions. The evidence in favor of the atopic nature of persistent hand eczema is based more on clinical impressions than on any other evidence. Similarly, *pityriasis alba,* the mild depigmentation and scaling of the cheeks seen in many children, is often thought to represent a mild form of atopic eczema. Proof in support of this assumption is again lacking. Observers have felt that the adult with atopic eczema presents a certain personality pattern, and that the exacerbations of the disease may be produced by such stimuli as nervous tension or fatigue. The exact role of psychic factors, however, remains to be clarified.

Certain environmental factors seem to lead to exacerbations of atopic eczema. In climates with sharp changes in season, the onset of cold weather may precipitate exacerbations. This occurrence may in part be related to the lower humidity of heated buildings, which may aggravate the generalized dryness of the skin characteristic of atopic individuals, thereby enhancing the pruritus.

There is no firm evidence that contact hypersensitivity is more frequent in atopic than in nonatopic individuals. However, it is a common observation that certain contactants, particularly wool, tend to exacerbate itching and so make eczema worse. It is thought that this effect is not immunologic but mechanical, the rough texture of the wool triggering pruritus, which leads to scratching, damage to the skin, and eczema. Other contactants, such as house dust and soaps, may produce the same sequence of events.

IMMUNOLOGIC AND PHYSIOLOGIC CONSIDERATIONS. The intimate association of atopic dermatitis with hay fever and asthma appears fairly well established on clinical grounds. The term dermal-respiratory syndrome was coined years ago following the observation that atopic dermatitis in the infant was the precursor of subsequent respiratory allergy. Prospective studies in infants with atopic dermatitis have confirmed that asthma develops in a high percentage of these affected infants. Among the atopic diseases, the highest mean levels of IgE (11 times higher than normals in one study) are found in individuals with atopic dermatitis. The reason for such an enormous increase in IgE is not readily apparent because atopic dermatitis has not been shown to be mediated by reaginic antibodies. In fact, classical atopic dermatitis has been observed in children with profound humoral antibody deficiencies. Moreover, the skin manifestation of antigen-reaginic antibody interaction is the wheal and not the eczematoid lesion, and whealing is not part of the clinical picture of atopic dermatitis at any time. It is also not possible to produce lesions of atopic dermatitis either by intracutaneous injection or by application to the skin of suspected allergens, such as foods. Individuals with atopic dermatitis show a number of abnormal cutaneous responses. Foremost among these is an exaggerated vasoconstrictor response manifested clinically by white dermographism. Light mechanical stroking of the skin produces within a minute a white line with a surrounding blanched area. This phenomenon is not under direct neural control and cannot be blocked by local anesthetics or peripheral nerve blocks. It is thought to be related to some intrinsic excessive reactivity of contractile elements of the small cutaneous blood vessels, which may also be responsible for a tendency in atopic dermatitis toward more rapid skin cooling and delayed warming. Abnormal responses to various pharmacologic agents have also been observed. Intradermal injection of histamine is not followed by a well-developed flare, while an intradermal injection of acetylcholine, a vasodilator agent, into an area of affected skin causes a "delayed blanch reaction" at the site of injection within two or three minutes. Such a reaction occurs only when injection is made into areas of skin involved with dermatitis. The phenomenon may be seen occasionally in other nonatopic dermatoses.

DIFFERENTIAL DIAGNOSIS. The course of the disease, the progression and distribution of the lesions, the pharmacologic and physiologic peculiarities of affected individuals, and the association with hay fever and asthma, are characteristic features of atopic eczema. However, not all cases are easily delineated even by these criteria. The eczematous skin reaction, characterized by erythema, swelling, exudation, scaling, and crusting, can be produced by a number of other mechanisms. The differential diagnosis includes diseases such as seborrheic dermatitis, contact dermatitis, infectious eczemas, and eczematous reactions occurring in the Wiskott-Aldrich syndrome and in phenylketonuria.

Seborrheic dermatitis begins generally on the scalp and extends to the external ear, the retroauricular spaces, the sides of the nose, and the eyelids. It may also involve the inguinal and axillary folds. The sites of predilection are thus quite different from those of atopic dermatitis, and the skin lesions consist usually of greasy, brownish scales contrasting with the weeping, crusted, or lichenified skin of the atopic individual.

Contact dermatitis (see p. 475) is generally limited to sites of exposure to the offending allergen, but may be widespread. However, even in extensive cases, the areas involved typically in atopic eczema, namely the flexural areas, are not selectively involved. Furthermore, atopic individuals are not immune from contact hypersensitivity. The two forms of dermatitis may occur concurrently, particularly where the contact reaction has been produced by injudicious treatment of the underlying atopic eruption with sensitizers such as neomycin, vioform, parabens, or lanolin. Similarly, atopic eczema may become secondarily infected with bacteria or fungi, resulting in a mixed infectious and atopic eruption.

The eruptions of the *Wiskott-Aldrich syndrome*

and *phenylketonuria* resemble atopic eczema but the sites of involvement are usually quite different. Lesions tend to be distributed widely, with no predilection for the cheeks, neck, hands, wrists, or cubital fossae. The course of the dermatitis also tends to be different in that the lesions appear earlier in life and do not wax and wane as they do in atopic eczema.

In adults or adolescents, characteristic secondary skin changes occur in atopic dermatitis which are helpful in making the diagnosis. Thickening of the skin with accentuation of the normal crosshatch markings causes the characteristic lichenification. Similarly there may be marked hyperpigmentation and extensive excoriation. Scarring, however, is not a prominent feature of atopic eczema. Individuals with this disease tend to have deep distinctive folds, "Morgan's lines," just beneath the lower eyelids, which persist even during periods of remission. Increased wrinkling of the palms is also present. The greater incidence of cataracts associated with atopic eczema appears only in patients beyond the pediatric age group.

COMPLICATIONS. Because of the exudative nature of the lesions, infection is a threat, especially during infancy and early childhood. The viruses of herpes simplex (Kaposi's varicelliform eruption) and vaccinia are especially dangerous. Infants and children with eczema should be protected from these infectious agents. They should not be vaccinated or even exposed to siblings or playmates who have been vaccinated. An attenuated virus vaccine has been developed which, in extensive trials, has been shown to be safe for primary vaccination of infants and children with atopic dermatitis.

MANAGEMENT OF ATOPIC ECZEMA. There is no rapid and complete cure for atopic eczema but a number of remedial measures are available which are most helpful. It is important to convey this notion to the parents of children with atopic eczema; such patients have often "shopped around" through many physicians' offices and clinics in a vain search for a simple and rapid cure. It must be established unequivocally that no miraculous cure is available anywhere, and that the treatment program will be directed toward relief of symptoms and improvement of the eruption, but without assurance of complete disappearance of lesions. Fortunately, in most children eczema is self-limited. The best available treatment amounts actually to the control of aggravating factors in the environment wherever possible.

CONTROL OF THE ENVIRONMENT. Atopic eczema tends to be exacerbated in cold, dry environments and to improve in warm, humid weather. Benefits derived occasionally from a total change in environment will most likely be of short duration only. A drastic change such as a move to a different part of the country would be ill-advised. It may be helpful, however, to start treatment of a severe exacerbation by hospitalizing the child for a few days.

A number of contactants which seem to aggravate eczema should be removed from the environment as much as possible. Exposure to wool, house dust, feathers, and animal danders should be eliminated or reduced to a minimum. Parents should be instructed not to purchase wool clothing, upholstery, blankets, or toys. It is advisable to implement environmental control measures described in Table 3 (Sec. 11.3). Soaps, detergents, and other defatting agents tend to aggravate atopic eczema, perhaps by augmenting the natural skin dryness associated with this condition. The water of the daily bath should be mostly tepid. After the bath, cutaneous applications of a lubricant may help seal the water absorbed by the skin. Bath oil, if used, should not be added until after the child has been in the tub for 20 minutes and the skin has become hydrated. Early addition of oil forms an effective seal and prevents hydration of the skin, which is the desired effect.

Diet. The importance of food allergy in the causation of atopic eczema is questioned. Numerous experimental attempts have failed to produce a flare-up of atopic dermatitis following administration of suspected foods. On occasion a child may develop, after ingestion of a food substance, diffuse flushing of the skin, with or without urticaria. This reaction induces itching and the subsequent scratching may initiate the itch-scratching-dermatitis cycle which leads to a flare-up of the eczema. When such children are subjected to food challenges and scratching is prevented in certain areas of the body, eczematoid lesions develop only where scratching occurs. It seems reasonable to eliminate certain foods where a history is obtained that they have repeatedly induced paroxysms of redness or itching. However, the role of food hypersensitivity should not be overrated. Skin tests are of little value in the diagnosis of food sensitivity. The high incidence of a positive intradermal skin test to egg white in infants with atopic dermatitis, even in those who give no history of having ever eaten eggs, is an unexplained observation. It is by far preferable to search for food sensitivity by controlled dietary eliminations and readministration, than by scratch or intradermal tests with food extracts. Since the disease is characterized by exacerbations and spontaneous remissions, the interpretation of the effects of feeding experiments is difficult.

Local Treatment. Benefits may be derived from a short period of hospitalization in the acute and weeping stages of infantile eczema. Wet compresses with cool Burow's solution, diluted 1:20, are antiinflammatory and anti-pruritic. As wet dressings they have the additional advantage of immobilizing and protecting the affected parts, thus preventing the child from scratching, a major aspect in the treatment of atopic dermatitis. Elbow restraints similar to those which are used on infants and small children following facial plastic surgery are very satisfactory. Ointments and creams containing corticosteroids are valuable in the management of exacerbations, both in the hospital and at home. The older and less expensive hydrocortisone has been largely replaced by more effective fluorinated compounds (Synalar, Fluonid, Cordran, Kenalog, and Aristocort creams). Percutaneous absorption of these corticosteroids with measurable adrenal-pituitary suppression is clinically insignificant in the average case. However, absorption through the skin is increased with widespread application to the damaged skin and the use of occlusive plastic dressings.

Secondary bacterial infection, when present, should be treated with appropriate, and preferably systemic, antibiotics. It should be remembered that neomycin and vioform, commonly added to topical corticosteroids for management of infection, are potent contact sensitizers, and may aggravate the eruption. Possible sensitization to other ingredients of topical therapy, such as parabens, ethylenediamine, mercurial preservatives, and lanolin derivatives, should be suspected whenever there is sudden worsening of the eruption, or even lack of rapid improvement.

The older remedies, crude coal tar and ichthyol, still have their place in the treatment of eczema. A salve containing 1 to 5 percent tar may be useful, especially in areas of skin which are lichenified. Coal tar is a photosensitizer and can also cause a sterile pustular folliculitis.

Systemic treatment with antihistamines, such as diphenhydramine (Benadryl) or promethazine (Phenergan), produces sedation and is helpful in controlling the itching. Small doses of aspirin may be useful. In our experience, barbiturates and other sedative drugs are to be avoided. They actually seem to increase itching, perhaps by selective depression of the cerebral cortex.

Systemic corticosteroids, useful in management of severe acute exacerbations of eczema, must be avoided as much as possible because of their side effects. As in other chronic diseases, patients tend to become dependent upon them. Because of the effectiveness of systemic steroids in atopic dermatitis, their use is often tempting. On the other hand, it may also be difficult to discontinue the steroids without producing a severe exacerbation. With appropriate local treatment and environmental control, plus acceptance by the patients of the fact that rapid and total clearing of the eczema is unlikely to occur, use of these potentially hazardous agents can often be avoided. Systemic corticosteroid therapy should be restricted only to the most severe of the acute exacerbations and should be discontinued as promptly as possible.

REFERENCES

Baer, R. L., ed. Atopic Dermatitis. Philadelphia, J. B. Lippincott Co., 1955.

Conference on infantile eczema. J. Pediat., 66:153, 1965.

Leider, M. Dermatoses based principally on allergic mechanisms. *In* Leider, M., ed., Practical Pediatric

Dermatology, 2nd ed. St. Louis, C. V. Mosby Co., 1961, pp. 201-245.

Lorincz, A. L. Atopic dermatitis. *In* Criep, L. H., ed., Dermatologic Allergy: Immunology, Diagnosis, Management. Philadelphia, W. B. Saunders Co., 1967, pp. 298-311.

Rostenberg, A., Jr., and Bogdonoff, D. R. Atopic dermatitis and infantile eczema. *In* Samter, M., ed., Immunological Diseases. Boston, Little, Brown and Co., 1965, pp. 635-645.

11.8
CONTACT DERMATITIS

ROBERT W. GOLTZ

DEFINITION. Contact dermatitis is an inflammatory skin reaction caused by contact of the skin with irritating or allergenic substances. In early stages the reaction is characterized by erythema and edema of the skin, leading to vesiculation and exudation, with crusting ("weeping dermatitis"). In more chronic cases, redness, melanosis, thickening of skin, and scaling supervene. Secondary changes such as bacterial infection, excoriation, and scarring may sometimes occur as complications.

MECHANISMS. Contact dermatitis may be caused either by substances which are primarily irritating to the skin, such as acids or alkalies, or by allergens which lead to this cutaneous expression of delayed hypersensitivity. With irritants, 100 percent of exposed individuals will develop dermatitis if exposed long enough to a sufficient concentration of the offending agent, while in the case of allergic contact sensitivity, only a certain percentage of exposed individuals will react even at very high dilutions of the contactant. The usual phenomena of delayed hypersensitivity, including recognizable incubation and reaction periods, can be defined. The percentage of individuals who will become sensitized to any given substance depends on its potency as an allergen, some substances producing contact hypersensitivity only rarely, others, such as dinitrochlorobenzene (DNBC) or poison ivy oleoresin, in almost 100 percent of normal individuals who are sufficiently exposed. Hypersensitivity may develop after the initial exposure, or only after repeated application to the skin. There is some evidence that single large applications of such sensitizers as DNCB produce higher levels of sensitivity than do repeated applications of small amounts. A rapidly induced sensitivity is generally more intense than a gradual one. Thus, allergic contact sensitivity is not an all-or-none process, but occurs in all degrees of intensity.

Affected individuals, once contact-sensitized, remain reactive indefinitely, although there may be a gradual diminution of the degree of reactivity, which may be rapidly increased again by reexposure. Paradoxically, however, unresponsiveness can be induced in experimental animals by repeated exposure to small amounts of topical sensitizers, a finding which may help to explain the phenomenon of "hardening" to a contact sensitizer sometimes seen in occupationally exposed industrial workers.

Contact dermatitis makes its first appearance on the part of the skin exposed to the causative agent. It often remains confined to such areas, and etiologic diagnosis can be made by a careful history and close examination to determine what substance has come in contact with the affected areas. In some cases, however, the dermatitis spreads beyond the initially exposed sites. This extension usually occurs by progressive involvement of contiguous areas, but transfer to distant sites may also occur, either through hand or fomite dissemination of the contactant, or even hematogenously. In some cases the dermatitis becomes generalized. Dissemination of the eruption may also result from application of therapeutic substances such as neomycin, vioform, or allergenic ointment bases, which produce a secondary or tertiary contact sensitivity. Bacterial infection may also play a role in dissemination of some cases of contact dermatitis. The concept of autoeczematization, resulting from production of secondary antigens due to skin destruction, is accepted by many dermatologists but disputed by others. Even in widely disseminated forms of contact dermatitis, however, the initially sensitized skin areas are usually the most severely affected, a finding which greatly helps etiologic diagnosis.

The management of contact dermatitis in children depends on finding and eliminating its cause, and on appropriate local and systemic therapy for the acute inflammation of the skin.

Elimination of the contactant depends on its identification, which can usually be accomplished by thorough history and close observation of the involved sites of the skin. Suspected substances can be applied to the skin in the form of patch tests, which are read in 48 hours. The concentration of the substance used on the skin in patch testing should be less than that which will produce primary irritation of the skin. Appropriate concentrations and vehicles for patch testing can be determined from tables in many textbooks of dermatologic allergy. Many dermatologists are hesitant to apply patch tests to individuals with acute contact dermatitis lest the patch itself induce dissemination of the eruption. However, others are willing to apply patch tests even in the face of acute dermatitis, feeling that identification of causative substances is worth whatever risk of dissemination may be incurred.

After elimination of the offending contactant, local therapy with wet dressings of Burow's solution, diluted 1:20, alternating with topical corticosteroid lotions or creams, is the treatment of choice. In acute phases the affected part should be elevated and immobilized to reduce edema. Among topical corticosteroids the fluorinated compounds (Synalar, Fluonid, Aristocort, Kenalog, or Cordran) are more efficacious than hydrocortisone.

Systemic therapy is less important than appropriate local therapy. Antihistamines may have some value in alleviating itching and producing sedation, but are not directly curative of contact dermatitis. Systemic corticosteroids, preferably prednisone, may be given in acute cases, but only for a short time. The dose to be given is initially large, followed by rapid tapering off. Systemic corticosteroid therapy should not be used as a substitute for proper etiologic investigation and elimination.

SPECIFIC FORMS OF CONTACT DERMATITIS IN CHILDREN.   Diaper dermatitis is probably the most common form of contact dermatitis in infants. It is apparently due to the irritating effect of ammonia, produced from urine in the diapers by bacterial action on urea. It occurs in areas of the skin most intimately in contact with the diaper, that is, the abdomen, thighs, and buttocks, while the inguinal folds and intergluteal cleft are spared. Ammoniacal diaper irritation is particularly severe during periods of teething. It can be prevented by frequent changing of diapers to avoid prolonged contact with urine, and by the use of disinfectant substances in laundering the diapers to suppress ammonia-producing bacteria. Another form of contact dermatitis in infants is that produced by the irritating substances (proteolytic enzymes) in feces. This usually occurs in the perianal area. Both of these forms of dermatitis are primarily irritant in nature and not due to allergic mechanisms.

Medications applied to the skin may be either primarily irritating or, more frequently, are sensitizers. We have already mentioned that such ointment ingredients as neomycin and vioform, and constituents of ointment bases, such as lanolin, parabens, ethylenediamine, and mercurial preservatives cause allergic contact sensitivity. Bithionol and salicylanilides, found in first-aid creams, lotions, and soaps, produce a photocontact sensitivity.

Allergic shoe dermatitis, frequently misdiagnosed as a fungus infection, is not uncommon in children. It occurs on the regions of the foot exposed most intimately to the offending part of the shoe. Causative substances include the chrome used in tanning leather, rubber cements, and antioxidants, dyes, nickel, and so on. Any child with recalcitrant dermatitis on the feet should be patch tested with substances known to cause shoe sensitivity.

Other articles of clothing may also cause contact dermatitis. Recently there has been an outbreak of dermatitis due to formalin and other chemicals used in synthetic fabrics, particularly in the popular stretch fabrics. This reaction occurs on the parts of the body exposed to the clothing, including the backs of the knees in the case of hosiery dermatitis, the outer portions of the axilla when dresses or shirts are the offenders, the bathing trunk area in the case of underclothing, and so on.

Perhaps the most frequent cause of allergic contact sensitivity in children is exposure to plants. In the United States the most important offenders are members of the genus *Rhus,* including poison ivy and poison oak. The ginkgo tree has also been reported to have caused an epidemic of *Rhus* sensitivity in an exposed school group. Poison ivy or poison oak dermatitis appears as an acute inflammation of the skin, often with very large blisters measuring up to 2 to 3 cm in diameter. Frequently these are linear in distribution because the plant parts strike the skin in that way. Dissemination of the eruption may occur through spread of the plant oleoresin to the face or genital areas by the hands. Exposure to *Rhus* oleoresin usually occurs by direct contact with the plant, but there are well-authenticated cases of individuals contracting poison ivy dermatitis in midwinter through wearing of clothing or boots still bearing oleoresin contacted months before, or by handling firewood which is contaminated with the plant oil. Similarly, pet dogs or cats may deliver the oleoresin to sensitized individuals on their fur. Dermatitis from exposure to the smoke of burning plants has also occurred. It should be remembered that the oleoresin is present in the berries and stems of the plants, as well as in the leaves, and exposure can occur even when the plant is no longer recognizable by its characteristic leaf structure.

Poison ivy dermatitis usually runs an acute course, lasting anywhere from one to three or four weeks, depending on the degree of hypersensitivity and the extent of exposure. Management consists of removal of the oleoresin from the skin as promptly as possible after exposure, although after a few hours even vigorous washing with soap and water is probably ineffective. Appropriate local therapy with wet dressings and corticosteroids is indicated. In severe cases a short course of systemic corticosteroid therapy is justifiable, and may result in considerable amelioration of discomfort as well as shortening of the course of the disease.

References

Baer, H., et al. Delayed contact sensitivity to catechols. II. Cutaneous toxicity of catechols chronically related to the active principles of poison ivy. J. Immunol., 99: 365, 1967.

———— et al. Delayed contact sensitivity to catechols. III. The relationship of side-chain length to sensitizing potency of catechols chemically related to the active principles of poison ivy. J. Immunol., 99:370, 1967.

Cronin, E. Shoe dermatitis. Brit. J. Derm., 78:617, 1967.

Epstein, E. Allergy to dermatologic agents. J.A.M.A., 198:517, 1966.

Fisher, A. A. Wearing apparel dermatitis. I. Cutis, 2:166, 1966.

———— Wearing apparel dermatitis. II. Cutis, 2:227, 1966.

———— Management of selected types of allergic contact dermatitis through use of proper substitutes. Cutis, 3:498, 1967.

———— Contact Dermatitis. Philadelphia, Lea and Febiger, 1967.

Lowney, E. D. Attenuation of contact sensitization in man. J. Invest. Derm., 50:244, 1968.

———— Immunologic unresponsiveness appearing after

topical application of contact sensitizers to the guinea pig. J. Immunol., 95:397, 1965.

Schwartz, L., Tulipan, L., and Birmingham, D. J. Occupational Diseases of the Skin, 3rd. ed. Philadelphia, Lea and Febiger, 1957.

11.9
URTICARIA AND ANGIOEDEMA

PHILIP FIREMAN

Urticaria (hives) is a common skin eruption characterized by discrete elevations of the skin, surrounded by erythema. The lesions may appear singly, in crops, or may coalesce; they are frequently pruritic, and generally short-lived, disappearing in minutes to hours and leaving no trace on the skin. Urticaria persisting longer than one to three months is arbitrarily defined as chronic urticaria. The term angioedema is applied to the more extensive lesions which frequently involve the eyes, lips, genitalia, and hands and feet, where the subcutaneous connective tissue is loosely bound. Angioedema of the larynx is a life-threatening situation and is frequently the cause of death in human anaphylaxis.

PATHOLOGY. The capillary is the target organ in urticaria; the major histopathologic change is edema. Small blood vessels in the upper part of the corium are involved in urticaria and the deeper vessels in angioedema.

ETIOLOGIC CLASSIFICATION. Urticaria is induced by many different stimuli. The etiologic factors may be classified on the basis of pathogenesis and clinical features into four major categories: (1) immunologic, (2) physical, (3) chemical, and (4) psychologic.

Immunologic Factors. The wheal and erythema reaction is the typical skin response produced by interaction of reaginic antibody and antigen. Thus, many cases of acute urticaria are thought to represent reagin-mediated hypersensitivity. Histamine, released from mast cells as a result of the allergic reaction, has been implicated as the chemical mediator responsible for the altered capillary permeability which results in hive formation. Other permeability factors are known to exist: kinins, certain components of the complement system, and a number of other poorly characterized compounds. The most common causes of immunologically induced urticaria are drug hypersensitivity, food allergy, infections, parasitic infestation, contact allergy, and inhalant allergy.

Drugs. In general, antibiotics, sedatives, analgesics, tranquilizers, insulin, and vaccines are the most common causes of urticaria due to drugs. Although virtually all drugs may be incriminated, penicillin and aspirin are especially frequent etiologic agents in children because of their widespread use. Establishing a specific diagnosis in patients taking more than one drug may be very difficult. The problems involved in the diagnosis of drug allergy are discussed in Section 11.10.

Foods. Foods are frequently suspected by both patient and physician as etiologic agents in acute urticaria. Seafoods, nuts, eggs, berries, chocolate, and various food additives are commonly implicated. The diagnosis of food allergy is discussed in Section 11.2.

Infections. Infections have been considered in the past as playing an important role in causation of both acute and chronic urticaria. While hives frequently occurs in the course of a viral illness, immunologic mechanisms are hard to demonstrate. Chronic focal infection in the tonsils, teeth, and elsewhere has been sought for vigorously, especially in patients with chronic urticaria, but even when found and treated, the urticaria has persisted in many cases. There are a few well-documented cases of urticaria due to cutaneous fungal infections. While infections must always be considered, it is not very often that their causative role in urticaria can be unequivocally established.

Parasitic infestations. Parasitic infestations are well known causes of urticaria. Parasites which have been implicated in cases of urticaria include *Ascaris,* hookworm, *Stronglyoides,* and amebae. Eosinophilia is frequently associated with parasitic infection, and skin testing with the appropriate worm antigen will frequently induce a wheal and erythema reaction.

Contactants. Contactants which are presumed to cause urticaria on an immunologic basis include animal hair or saliva, wool, metals, and pollen. Individuals with pollen hypersensitivity occasionally report that hives develops after physical contact with grass or weeds.

Inhalants. Inhalant allergy to pollens, danders, and various industrial dusts is a rare cause of urticaria.

Chemical factors. A wide variety of substances found in animal and plant tissues or synthesized chemically can induce histamine release on a nonimmunologic basis, thus causing urticaria. Proteolytic enzymes from animal and plant sources have been reported to act as nonspecific histamine releasers. Following enzymatic digestion, several foods are broken down to polypetides that are potent histamine liberators; this may explain the variability of the urticarial response from foods. Other substances which cause local histamine release include surfactants, such as bile salts, Tween 80, and lysolecithin; and drugs such as curare, polymyxin, codeine, dextran, polyvinylprolidone, and compound 48/80. Urticarial reactions occur after insect stings and bites, and are usually caused by the direct local action of the constituents in venom. This mechanism should not be confused with reaginic antibody-mediated urticarial or anaphylactic reactions following insect stings. The common pediatric clinical entity, papular urticaria, begins with a small hive which progresses to an erythematous papule. These lesions resulting from insect bites do not seem to be caused by immunologic mechanisms. Cholinergic urticaria is discussed in Section 11.13.

Physical Factors. Urticaria which develops after exposure to physical factors, such as cold, heat, light, and pressure, is a well-recognized clinical entity. This subject is discussed in detail in Section 11.13.

Psychogenic Factors. In poorly understood diseases such as chronic urticaria, psychic factors are suspected usually because all other etiologic agents have been excluded. Except in cholinergic urticaria, there is no good evidence that psychic factors play a primary role in causing urticaria.

Other Diseases. Other diseases, such as systemic lupus erythematosus, dermatomyositis, and other collagen-vascular diseases, may be associated with urticaria. Hodgkin's disease has on occasion been associated with urticaria, as have various malignant tumors. Systemic mastocytosis is a disease seen primarily in adults, in whom it produces symptoms of flushing and hypotension, bone lesions, and mast cell collections in the skin. These mast cell collections are pigmented and may become urticarial when stroked (Darier's sign). When the mastocytosis syndrome involves only the skin, it is referred to as *urticaria pigmentosa*. This variation of mastocytosis occurs in young children and subsides spontaneously before adolescence without systemic involvement. Hereditary angioedema is discussed in Chapter 8.

THERAPY. When the etiologic factors can be identified, elimination of them provides simple and adequate treatment for urticaria and angioedema. In many cases, even after the most careful investigation, the etiologic agents cannot be identified, and symptomatic treatment may be very useful. Aqueous epinephrine 1:1000, 0.1 to 0.3 ml administered subcutaneously induces prompt but temporary relief from the intense pruritus frequently associated with urticaria. Other sympathomimetics, e.g., ephedrine, may be useful and should be tried. All the antihistamines are generally useful in symptomatic treatment of urticaria; hydroxyrine (Atarax, Vistaril) and cyproheptadine (Periactin) may be of special value in those cases not responding to the usual antihistamines. The desired control of urticaria may necessitate increasing antihistamine dosage to a level at which side effects occur. However, corticosteroids are rarely indicated in the management of urticaria, and are not as effective as they are in other allergic disorders. Patients with angioedema of the mouth, pharynx, or larynx constitute a medical emergency and should be carefully watched for development of airway obstruction. Epinephrine is the drug of choice in these patients; parenteral antihistamines should be administered and equipment for intubation or tracheostomy should be readily available.

REFERENCES

Baughman, R. D., and Jillson, O. F. Seven specific types of urticaria with special reference to delayed dermographism. Ann. Allergy, 21:248, 1963.

Beall, G. N. Urticaria: A review of laboratory and clinical observations. Medicine, 43:136, 1964.
Calnan, C. D. Urticarial reactions. Brit. Med. J., 2:649, 1964.
Donaldson, V. H., and Rosen, F. S. Hereditary angioedema, a clinical survey. Pediatrics, 37:1017, 1966.
Fromer, J. L. Atopic urticaria: and angioneurotic edema. In Criep, L. H., ed., Dermatologic Allergy. Philadelphia, W. B. Saunders Co., 1967, Ch. 33.
Green, G. R., Koelsche, G. A., and Kierland, R. R. Etiology and pathogenesis of chronic urticaria. Ann. Allergy, 23:30, 1965.
Halpern, S. R. Chronic hives in children. Analyses of 75 cases. Ann. Allergy, 33:589, 1965.
Leider, M. Urticaria. Pediat. Clin. N. Amer., 6:823, 1959.
Miller, D. A., Freeman, G. L., and Akers, W. A. Chronic urticaria, a clinical study of fifty patients. Amer. J. Med., 44:68, 1968.
Mines, S. B., Levine, M. I., and Fireman, P. Serum immunoglobulin levels in acute and chronic urticaria. J. Allergy, 44:20, 1969.
Sheldon, J. M., Matthews, K. P., and Lovell, R. The vexing urticaria problem: present concepts of etiology and management. J. Allergy, 25:525, 1954.
——— Lovell, R. G., and Mathews, K. P. Dermatologic aspects of allergy practice. In A Manual of Clinical Allergy, 2nd ed. Philadelphia, W. B. Saunders Co., 1967, Ch. 11, pp. 226-267.
Siegel, S. C., and Bergson, J. C. Urticaria and angioedema in children and young adults. Ann. Allergy, 12:241, 1954.

11.10
DRUG ALLERGY

ELLIOT F. ELLIS

CLASSIFICATION OF DRUG REACTIONS. Allergic reactions to drugs represent only one mechanism by which an adverse effect can occur. The diagnosis of drug "allergy" is frequently made loosely, and for this reason, a classification of drug reactions is useful. The following classification is taken from Brown.

Overdosage. The toxic effects of the drug are directly related to concentration of the drug in the body. Overdosage may result either from excessive intake or from impaired metabolism or excretion of the drug. The toxicity of chloramphenicol in neonates occurs as a result of immaturity of the glucuronide-conjugating system, which allows toxic concentrations to accumulate. The renal and ototoxicity that occurs with kanamycin in the face of kidney impairment is due to interference with excretion of the drug.

Intolerance. The effects of the drug are qualitatively normal but quantitatively increased. Since drug dosages are based upon responses of an average population, it is not surprising that a significant number of individuals has an excessive pharmacologic response to an "average" dose of drug. The excessive somnolence observed in some individuals following administration of an average dose of barbiturate is an example of this kind of adverse reaction.

Side Effects. These are defined as undesirable but unavoidable pharmacologic effects of a drug. The designation of a particular action of a drug that exerts multiple pharmacologic effects as a side effect is quite arbitrary, and depends upon the reason for giving the drug. For example, if theophylline is being administered intravenously to a child in status asthmaticus for its bronchodilator property, its diuretic effect might be looked upon as an undesirable side effect since the diuresis produced may lead to dehydration of an already dehydrated patient. On the other hand, if theophylline is given to a cardiac patient for its diuretic effect, its central nervous system stimulating properties might be viewed as a side effect.

Secondary Effects. These are indirect effects of a drug unrelated to its primary pharmacologic action which may not occur in all patients. An example of a secondary effect is the disturbance in the bacterial flora of the gut as a consequence of antibiotic chemotherapy.

Idiosyncrasy. The reaction to the drug is qualitatively abnormal. Many reactions in this group are due to metabolic abnormalities in the patient. The hemolytic anemia observed in patients with a deficiency in glucose-6-phosphate dehydrogenase following injection of primaquine is considered to be an idiosyncratic reaction.

Hypersensitivity or Allergic Reactions. Hypersensitivity or allergic reactions are the result of sensitization to a drug by previous exposure either to the same drug or to a chemically related substance. These reactions are, by definition, mediated by antigen-antibody interaction. It should be emphasized that in a majority of drug reactions thought to be allergic in nature, the presence of an antibody to the drug itself cannot be demonstrated by either in vivo or in vitro methods. The following characteristics have been proposed as consistent with the diagnosis of drug allergy. It is important to emphasize that none of these findings excludes idiosyncrasy (Ackroyd and Rook).

1. The reaction observed does not resemble a known pharmacologic property of the drug.
2. On initial exposure, there is a latent interval before the reaction occurs. During this latent period, which may be of many years' duration, allergic sensitization has not yet occurred. However, once allergic sensitization occurs, the reaction, upon taking the drug, can be immediate and quite explosive.
3. Clinical reaction bears no relationship to the drug dosage. In anaphylactically sensitized individuals extraordinarily small amounts of drug have caused systemic reactions. This is especially true in the case of penicillin in which there are reports of anaphylaxis occurring from the minute amounts of the antibiotic contained in a vaccine used for immunization.
4. Similar reaction is produced by a chemically related drug. The phenomenon of cross sensitivity is seen in individuals allergic to one drug (streptomycin) who react to a chemically related drug (neomycin). The likelihood of cross sensitivity occurring between two drugs depends upon the degree to which antigenic determinants are shared. In the case of penicillin G sensitivity, the likelihood of allergic reactivity to ampicillin depends upon whether the sensitivity is due to antigenic determinants common to both drugs (in which case reactivity to ampicillin would occur).
5. Adverse reactions occur in only a small percentage of the population at risk.
6. Clinical picture is similar to that seen in typical allergic syndromes. This refers principally to drug reactions manifest as urticaria and contact dermatitis. Except in the case of aspirin-induced asthma (where the reaction is not thought to be antigen-antibody mediated) drug allergy rarely causes respiratory symptoms.

ROLE OF VARIOUS FACTORS IN DEVELOPMENT OF DRUG ALLERGY. Genetics. In experimental animals, strains have been bred which are either susceptible or resistant to cutaneous sensitization with picryl chloride. In contrast, genetic factors have not been identified in the human which predispose to the development of hypersensitivity.

Age. The incidence of drug allergy in children is considerably less than in adults. This observation is most likely a reflection of the fact that by virtue of age, children have not had the repeated exposure to drugs which leads to allergic sensitization.

Atopic State. It is alleged that individuals with atopic dermatitis, hay fever, and asthma are more prone to develop drug allergy than individuals without this history. The evidence for this is inconclusive. If it could be proved that the incidence of drug allergy were indeed higher in atopic individuals than normals, this would not necessarily indicate an increased predisposition to sensitization on the part of the former. It might be a reflection of the fact that individuals with atopic diseases, especially asthma, have a much greater exposure than normal individuals to all kinds of drugs and thus have a greater opportunity to become sensitized. Clinical experience indicates that the atopic individual may be more likely to manifest allergy to a drug such as penicillin by an urticarial or anaphylactic reaction mediated by reaginic antibody (IgE), while the nonatopic individual is more likely to develop disease mediated by non-IgE antibodies.

Route of Administration. As a general rule the oral route of administration of a drug is less likely to cause sensitivity than the parenteral route. The longer the course of therapy, the greater the probability of sensitization. Similarly, repeated courses of therapy increase the likelihood of inducing allergy to a drug. Topical application of a drug is associated with a high sensitization risk and should be avoided, especially on the inflamed skin.

Underlying Disease. Underlying disease appears to have a role in the likelihood of developing drug allergy. Patients who have impairment in cell-mediated immunity, as in sarcoidosis or Hodgkin's disease, seem to have reduced susceptibility to contact dermatitis. On the other hand, patients with hypogammaglobulinemia have a very low incidence of allergic reactions mediated by humoral antibodies. If their cellular immune mechanisms are intact, patients in the latter group are quite capable of developing disease mediated by delayed hypersensitivity mechanisms.

MECHANISMS OF DRUG ALLERGY. The majority of drugs that have been implicated in allergic reactions have molecular weights under 1,000. They represent haptens and are not immunogenic by the usual tests. As shown by Landsteiner, low-molecular-weight chemicals, such as drugs, become immunogenic only after forming covalent bonds with tissue proteins to form a drug-protein conjugate. A great deal of experimental evidence indicates that, as a general rule,

only drugs which react irreversibly with proteins, either in themselves or through a degradation or metabolic product, are capable of inducing hypersensitivity reactions. This is undoubtedly the reason why certain drugs are good sensitizers and others have a very low potential for causing allergic reactions. The studies of Levine and others in penicillin hypersensitivity have provided a model that has led to better understanding of mechanisms involved in drug allergy. According to this work, a number of protein-reactive compounds are formed from benzylpenicillin (penicillin G) under physiologic conditions, both in vitro and in vivo. One of these protein-reactive compounds, benzylpenicillinic acid (BPE) combines with tissue proteins to form the benzylpenicilloyl (BPO) haptenic group (Fig. 6). The BPO group has been designated the "major" haptenic determinant of penicillin hypersensitivity because approximately 95 percent of all the benzylpenicillin that reacts with tissue proteins in vivo forms BPO groups. In addition to the "major" determinant, there are several other haptenic determinants formed from benzylpenicillin. These are designated "minor" since only a small percentage of the benzylpenicillin that reacts with tissue protein goes to form the minor

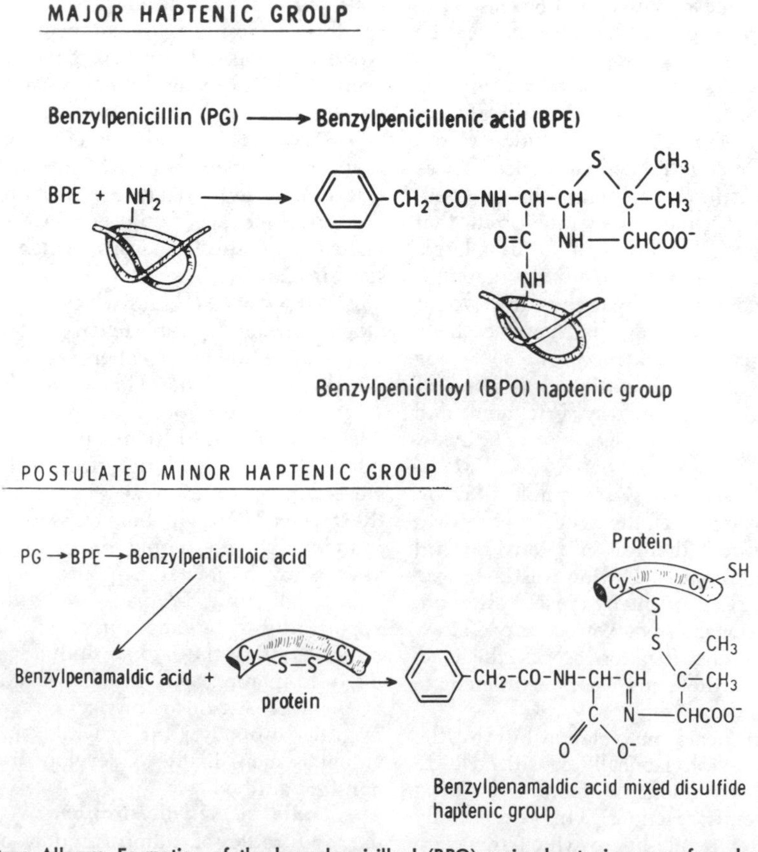

MAJOR HAPTENIC GROUP

POSTULATED MINOR HAPTENIC GROUP

Fig. 6. Drug Allergy. Formation of the benzylpenicilloyl (BPO) major haptenic group from benzylpenicillin through the chemically reactive intermediate benzylpenicillenic acid (BPE) and formation of the postulated minor haptenic group. (From Levine. In *Textbook of Immunopathology*, 1968, Vol. 1. Courtesy of Grune & Stratton, Inc.)

determinants. As has been emphasized by Levine, the minor determinants are minor in a quantitative sense only, since it appears that systemic anaphylaxis following penicillin administration is due to reaginic sensitivity to the minor determinants rather than to reaginic sensitivity to the BPO major haptenic determinant. The precise chemical nature of the minor haptenic determinants is not known, but one of them may be the benzylpenamaldic acid-mixed disulfide group (Fig. 6). The recognition of the chemical determinants responsible for penicillin hypersensitivity has led to the development of a group of skin test reagents used for predicting the likelihood of an anaphylactic reaction to penicillin (Table 7). Table 8 shows the relationship of immediate skin tests with the major determinant sensitivity skin test reagent (benzylpenicilloylpolylysine) and the minor determinant sensitivity skin test reagents (tested together as the minor determinant mixture) to the occurrence of immediate or accelerated allergic reactions to penicillin. It should be emphasized that the penicillin skin test reagents are predictive only of those reactions to penicillin that are mediated by reaginic sensitivity. Antibodies to penicillin of immunoglobulin classes other than IgE may be found in the serum of individuals who have received penicillin therapy. Furthermore, low titers of IgM penicillin antibodies may be detected in the serum of individuals with no history of ever having received penicillin. The stimulus for the formation of these antibodies is thought to be penicillin present in ingested food such as milk. Penicillin antibodies of the IgG and IgM class are thought to be responsible for certain of the late-occurring reactions following penicillin administration, such as hemolytic anemia, exanthematous skin eruptions, and arteritis and renal lesions occurring in "serum sickness-like" disease.

Skin testing for anaphylactic sensitivity to penicillin is a procedure that should be approached with great caution by the physician because of the possibility of inducing an anaphylactic reaction. If the patient has a good history of a previous immediate systemic or urticarial reaction following penicillin administration, neither skin testing nor test dosing should be undertaken. Nonetheless, when the penicillin skin test reagents become available their use should enable physicians to select those few individuals in the pediatric population who are anaphylactically sensitized to penicillin from a much larger group who have been labeled as allergic to penicillin on very tenuous grounds, and hence, have been denied use not only of this very effective antibiotic but

TABLE 7. *Skin Test Reagents for Penicillin Hypersensitivity*

Benzylpenicilloylpolylysine (BPL)	10^{-6}M
Potassium benzylpenicillin	10^{-2}M
Sodium benzylpenicilloate	10^{-2}M
Sodium benzylpenilloate	10^{-2}M
Sodium benzylpenicilloyl-amine	10^{-2}M

TABLE 8. *Relation of Immediate Skin Tests to the Occurrence of Immediate and Accelerated Allergic Reactions to Penicillin (Total Experience)**

Number of Patients with History of Penicillin Allergy	Skin Tests BPL	Skin Tests MDM	Immediate or Accelerated Reaction to Penicillin Therapy
185	Neg	Neg	1 had mild accelerated urticarial reaction†
8	Pos	Neg	5 of 8 had accelerated urticarial reactions
3	Neg	Pos	2 had accelerated reactions (urticarial or diffuse flush); 1 had an immediate urticarial reaction
9	Pos	Neg	Not treated with penicillins
4	Neg	Pos	Not treated with penicillins
8	Pos	Pos	Not treated with penicillins

*From Zolov and Levine. *J. Allergy*, 43:231, 1969.
†Six of the 185 developed exanthematic reactions.

also important chemically related antibiotics. Drugs are also capable of causing contact dermatitis, which is a form of delayed hypersensitivity. Contact dermatitis is considered in Section 11.8.

CLINICAL PATTERNS. Allergic reactions to drugs may involve virtually any organ in the body. Symptoms may be local or systemic. Cutaneous reactions are probably the most common manifestation of allergic drug reactions. Virtually any morphologic entity may be seen, but urticarial, exanthematous, and eczematoid reactions are the patterns most often seen. Exfoliative dermatitis, bullous dermatoses, including epidermal necrolysis, erythema multiforme, acneiform eruptions, lichenoid eruptions, and fixed eruptions are observed with varying degrees of frequency. Certain drugs are known to cause characteristic dermatoses. Photosensitivity reactions are considered on page 487. Fever either may be a manifestation of drug allergy alone or may occur in association with other reactions. The mechanism of drug fever is unknown. Serum sickness-like disease (see p. 485) is chiefly observed following the administration of certain drugs, especially penicillin. Systemic anaphylactic reactions are the most feared manifestation of drug hypersensitivity. In this regard, penicillin is the most common offender. Asthma alone is a rare manifestation of drug hypersensitivity. An unusual syndrome called triad asthma (asthma, nasal polyps, and aspirin sensitivity) is not uncommon in adults but is rare in children. The mechanism by which ingestion of aspirin causes asthma in these patients does not appear to have an immunologic basis. Since aspirin sensitivity usually develops in individuals who already have asthma, the use of aspirin probably should be avoided in asthmatic children. A number of drugs have been described as producing an illness closely resembling systemic lupus erythematosus. Hydralazine and procaine amide have been implicated especially in this regard. The disappearance of the disease following discontinuation of the drug in some patients and its reappearance following reinstitution of small amounts of the drug suggests, but does not prove, that the disease may have an allergic basis. It has been suggested that certain renal tubular lesions represent allergic reactions. However, in many of these instances hemolytic reactions were also present which made interpretation of the pathogenesis of the renal lesion difficult. In the case of tridione-induced nephrotic syndrome, which is reversible on stopping the drug, a hypersensitivity reaction is likely. A large number of drugs are known to produce jaundice on either an obstructive or hepatocellular basis or both. In certain cases the clinical course of the disease is suggestive of a hypersensitivity mechanism. Proof that immunologic mechanisms are indeed operative in adverse drug reactions has been most convincing in diseases involving the hematopoietic system. Thrombocytopenic purpura and certain cases of hemolytic anemia have been unequivocally shown by in vitro methods to be mediated by antigen-antibody interaction. The case for an immunologic basis for other blood dyscrasias such as agranulocytosis and aplastic anemia is less well established.

TREATMENT. The treatment of a drug-induced allergic reaction depends upon the clinical manifestations encountered. In most cases immediate discontinuation of the drug is indicated. In certain instances, especially in infants and small children who develop rashes while receiving an antibiotic, one can make a case for continuation of the drug until the etiology of the rash becomes clear. For example, an infant or small child receiving perhaps his first course of penicillin or other antibiotic during a febrile illness not uncommonly develops an exanthematous, nonurticarial rash. In this circumstance, it is much more likely that the rash is a manifestation of a viral illness rather than a cutaneous manifestation of drug allergy. It would seem wiser therefore to continue the drug for a few days more, while observing the course of the rash, than to label the child allergic to penicillin or other antibiotic for the rest of his life. The treatment of anaphylaxis, whether due to drug allergy or other cause, is essentially the same. It is important to be prepared for such an emergency, and all physicians who treat patients with injections of drugs, allergy extracts, or hormones are well advised to have immediately available the equipment and drugs listed in Table 9. In this situation which may provoke excessive anxiety, it is important for the physician to remain as calm as possible. If the drug has been given intramuscularly, epinephrine 1:1,000 in a dose of 0.3 to 0.5 ml should be given intramuscularly or subcutaneously into the opposite extremity. A tourniquet should be applied proximal to the injection site of the causative agent and 0.3 ml of epinephrine 1:1,000 injected subcutaneously into

TABLE 9. *Allergy Emergency Kit*

I. Drugs

   a. Epinephrine aqueous solution, 1:1000
   b. Injectable antihistamine (Benadryl)
   c. Injectable aminophylline
   d. Water-soluble corticosteroid esters (cortisol succinate, Solu-cortef)
   e. Injectable vasopressor (metaraminol bitartrate, Aramine; levarterenol bitartrate, Levophed)
   f. Parenteral fluids (5 percent dextrose in saline)
   g. Injectable anticonvulsant drug (Valium)
   h. Oxygen

II. Equipment

   a. Tourniquet
   b. Intravenous infusion tubing
   c. Assorted syringes and needles
   d. Airways
   e. Suction apparatus
   f. Surgical instruments for venesection
   g. Mechanical ventilator (Ambu bag)

the site. Both measures are designed to delay absorption of the causative agent into the circulation. Benadryl in doses of 15 to 30 mg should be given intramuscularly to counter the effect of further histamine release. If upper airway obstruction (glottic edema) develops, endotracheal intubation or tracheostomy must be done immediately. If there is evidence of peripheral vascular collapse, an intravenous infusion or cutdown should be done and the patient treated for hypovolemia with normal saline and then plasma or albumin as soon as available. Vasopressors may also be indicated, in which case metaraminol bitartrate (Aramine) is preferred. The drug is diluted in the intravenous fluid and run in fast enough to maintain a blood pressure in the 60- to 80-mm Hg range, which will insure renal perfusion. Cardiorespiratory arrest should be treated by external cardiac massage, and assisted ventilation with an Ambu bag and mask or mouth-to-mouth breathing. The outcome of an episode of anaphylaxis is usually determined within the first few minutes after it occurs. Generally, the rapidity with which the reaction occurs is directly related to its severity—those occurring immediately after drug injection are generally the most life-threatening. The cutaneous manifestations of drug allergy are generally self-limited and disappear when the drug is discontinued. Treatment is therefore symptomatic. Antihistamines are generally effective for urticarial lesions and pruritus. In severe cases, epinephrine 1:1,000 in doses of 0.1 to 0.3 ml are quite effective in providing short-term relief. More sustained relief may be obtained from injection of Sus-phrine in doses of 0.1 to 0.2 ml every six hours. Benadryl is the antihistamine of choice both for its antihistaminic and sedative properties. Ephedrine sulfate in a dose of 1 mg/kg every four to six hours may also be useful. Corticosteroids are reserved for those severe cases in which relief is not obtained from the foregoing measures. Prednisone, 2 mg/kg given as a single dose or in two divided doses, is the corticosteroid of choice.

DIAGNOSTIC PROCEDURES. In Vivo Tests. With the exception of penicillin, skin tests for reaginic sensitivity are of little value in drug allergy. The most likely explanation for this fact is that with most drugs it is a metabolic or degradation product, and not the drug itself, that combines with tissue proteins to form the immunogenic hapten-protein conjugate. The native drug would therefore not be expected to elicit wheal and flare reactivity. Since little is known about the degradation or metabolism of most drugs, suitable skin test reagents for demonstration of reaginic sensitivity are not available. For the same reason, the skin window technique (Rebuck) has not been useful in drug allergy diagnosis. On the other hand, skin testing for contact dermatitis by the patch test technique is a useful diagnostic procedure.

In Vitro Tests. The basophil degranulation test (Shelley) has not given satisfactory results in most investigators' hands. Similarly, despite enthusiasm on the part of some investigators, the lymphocyte transformation procedure has not been a practical tool for the diagnosis of drug allergy. A number of in vitro tests have been described for the diagnosis of certain drug-induced blood dyscrasias. The most useful of these have been (1) agglutination of platelets by the drug-serum mixture, (2) inhibition of clot retraction of patient's blood by drug, and (3) complement-fixation reaction with platelets, drug, and patient's serum. A description of the methods involved in performing these tests may be found in the reference by Ackroyd.

REFERENCES

Ackroyd, J. F. The diagnosis of disorders of the blood due to drug hypersensitivity caused by an immune mechanism. *In* Ackroyd, J. F., ed., Immunological Methods. Oxford, Blackwell, 1964.
—— and Rook, A. J. Allergic drug reactions. *In* Gell, P. G. H., and Coombs, R. R. A., eds., Clinical Aspects of Immunology. 2nd ed. Philadelphia, F. A. Davis Co., 1968.
Brown, E. A. Problems of drug allergy. J.A.M.A. 157:814, 1955.
Frick, O. L. Anaphylaxis. *In* Gellis, S. S., and Kagan, B. M., eds., Current Pediatric Therapy 4. Philadelphia, W. B. Saunders Co., 1970.
Levine, B. B. Immunochemical mechanisms of drug allergy. *In* Miescher, P. A., and Muller-Eberhard, H. J., eds., Textbook of Immunopathology, New York, Grune and Stratton, 1968, Vol. 1.
—— and Redmond, A. P. Minor haptenic determinant specific reagins of penicillin hypersensitivity in man. Int. Arch. Allergy, 35:445, 1969.
—— and Zolov, D. M. Prediction of penicillin allergy by immunological tests. J. Allergy, 43:231, 1969.
Meyler, L. Drug induced diseases. Excerpta Medica Found., Amsterdam, 1961, 1964, 1968, Vol. I-III.
—— Side Effects of Drugs. Excerpta Medica Found., Amsterdam, 1957, 1958, 1960, 1963, 1966, 1968, Vol. I-VI.
Parker, C. W. Drug reactions. *In* Samter, M., ed., Immunological Diseases. Boston, Little, Brown and Co., 1965.

11.11
INSECT ALLERGY

CLAUDE A. FRAZIER

Allergic reactions to insects occur in three different clinical forms: (1) immediate or delayed, local or systemic reactions to the stings of the Hymenoptera order of insects (bees, wasps, yellow jackets, hornets, fire ants); (2) inhalant allergy (rhinitis and asthma) to the pellicle fragments or other debris of insects; and (3) local cutaneous reactions caused by substances injected by biting insects. The first and second types of reactions will be discussed in this section. Cutaneous reactions caused by biting insects are covered in Chapter 26.

Allergy to Stinging Insects

Allergic reactions to the sting of one of the members of the Hymenoptera order are a problem of considerable magnitude in both adults and children. Each year in the United States more deaths are caused by insect sting hypersensitivity than by venomous snake bite.

IMMUNOLOGIC CONSIDERATIONS. The serious systemic reactions that follow a Hymenoptera sting appear to be due to anaphylactic sensitivity to venom antigens. The relatively few deaths which have been reported in individuals who have received multiple simultaneous stings are thought to be caused by the toxicity of highly reactive biologic agents, e.g., kinins, present in venom. Anaphylactic deaths have occurred in both "atopic" and "nonatopic" individuals, although there is some suggestive evidence that the individual with hay fever, asthma, or atopic dermatitis is especially predisposed to having a severe systemic reaction following a sting. Immunologic investigation of the venom and body antigens in the various members of the Hymenoptera order have shown both common and species-specific antigens. Furthermore, it appears that there are venom-specific antigens which are not found in the body of the insect. For this reason, some allergists have preferred to use venom sac material in hyposensitization programs in preference to whole-body extracts.

CLINICAL FINDINGS. The usual reaction to the bite of a stinging insect is one of intense pain followed by erythema and varying degrees of local edema. If the sting occurs in an area of loose connective tissue, such as around the eyes, the swelling may be considerable. Within 24 to 48 hours, the local reaction generally subsides. In some individuals the sting is followed very rapidly by a feeling of faintness which may progress to syncope and respiratory difficulty as a result of swelling of the glottis or obstruction of the lower airway. Generalized urticaria or angioedema may occur. The reaction described above is life-threatening and the patient must receive immediate attention if he is to have maximal opportunity to survive. In fatal cases, the symptoms have appeared with alarming rapidity, with death occurring in less than 10 minutes. While there is usually a history of previous stings, in a significant number of individuals experiencing anaphylaxis no such history can be elicited. Reactions of the late-onset type have been reported in which serum sickness-like disease, vasculitis, central and peripheral nervous system involvement, and recurrent angioedema have occurred.

TREATMENT. *Systemic Reactions.* Treatment of the individual experiencing a systemic reaction following an insect bite is essentially that instituted for anaphylaxis due to any cause (see p. 454). Epinephrine should be injected immediately at a site distant to the sting, and subcutaneously into the area of the sting to slow further adsorption. A tourniquet should be applied proximal to the sting if it has occurred in an extremity. If the stinging insect is a bee, the stinger and attached venom sac become embedded and continue to inject venom after the insect flies away. The stinger and venom sac should be flicked off or scraped off in order to prevent forcing more venom into the skin. The other members of the Hymenoptera order do not leave the stinging apparatus at the site of the sting. An injectable antihistamine should be administered to block the effect of further histamine release. Corticosteroids are not indicated in the treatment of the immediate systemic reaction. Isoproterenol is effective for the wheezing that may accompany an anaphylactic reaction but is not an effective pressor agent and does not restore blood pressure in the patient with peripheral vascular collapse. The drug is therefore a poor second choice to epinephrine.

Immunotherapy (Hyposensitization). Hyposensitization has been eminently successful in preventing the recurrence of serious systemic reactions. In a large collaborative study done under the auspices of the American Academy of Allergy, 90 percent of patients who had undergone hyposensitization reported a less severe reaction on re-sting. Most individuals who have had systemic reactions to stinging insects react on skin testing with insect extract with a wheal and erythema reaction typical of reagin-mediated allergy. Testing during the first few weeks after the reaction should be avoided, since a state of temporary anergy (nonreactivity) may result from the anaphylactic reaction. A significant number of patients who have had typical systemic reactions fail to exhibit positive skin tests regardless of when tested. The reason for this is unknown. Skin testing, however, is valuable for establishing the initial starting dose of the extract. For example, if the patient is tested with increasing concentrations of antigen and does not react with a positive skin test until a 1:10,000 dilution is used, then a 1:100,000 dilution of extract may be used very safely as the initial treatment concentration. A dose of 0.05 ml of the initial extract concentration may be increased safely by 50 percent at three- to seven-day intervals as tolerated. The highest dose recommended varies from 0.5 ml of a 1:100 dilution to 0.3 ml of a 1:10 dilution, injected monthly for a three-year period. Whether this period of treatment is adequate for conferring lifelong protection from subsequent stings has not been established. Since most people are unable to identify with certainty the type of insect that stings them, a polyvalent whole-body extract prepared from all members of the Hymenoptera order is usually employed in hyposensitization regimens. Venom sac material is preferred by some allergists who feel it unwise to inject insect body antigens not found in the venom. While theoretically sound, this idea is generally impractical because of the difficulty and cost of obtaining the venom sacs. Hyposensitization treatment is indicated in those individuals with a good history of systemic reactions, regardless of whether the skin test is positive or not. It is debatable whether a patient who has suffered a large local reaction (for example, swelling of an entire extremity) following a sting, should receive hyposensitization. Individuals who have had systemic reactions following bee stings must carry on their person at all times an "anaphylaxis kit" containing an epinephrine-loaded syringe, a tourniquet, and an ephedrine-antihistamine tablet. The patient must be instructed in the use of the kit and told to use it immediately should he be stung, because the rapidity of the reaction frequently precludes obtaining medical treatment in sufficient time.

PREVENTION. Patients should be instructed in the nesting habits of Hymenopterae and should avoid exposure to their habitat. Bright colors, perfumes, and the like are said to attract stinging insects and they should be avoided. An insecticide should be kept handy.

Inhalant Allergy to Insect Emanations

In certain parts of the United States, especially around the Great Lakes, inhalant allergy to the debris of the May fly and Caddis fly has been an important seasonal problem. A large variety of other insects, including moths, cockroaches, and house flies has been reported to cause symptoms of rhinitis and asthma in certain patients. Treatment is best accomplished by avoidance of the offending insects, but when this is impractical, good results may be obtained with hyposensitization treatment.

REFERENCES

Frazier, C. A. Insect Allergy. St. Louis, Warren H. Green, Inc., 1969.

Insect Allergy Committee of The American Academy of Allergy. Insect-sting allergy. Questionnaire Study of 2,606 Cases. J.A.M.A., 193:115, 1965.

McLean, J. A. Management of hypersensitivity to stinging insects. *In* Sheldon, J. M., Lovell, R. G., and Mathews, K. P., eds., A Manual of Clinical Allergy, 2nd ed. Philadelphia, W. B. Saunders Co., 1967, Ch. 15, pp. 300-325.

Report of the Committee on Insect Allergy of The American Academy of Allergy. J. Allergy, 35:181, 1964.

Sherman, W. B. Allergy to insects. *In* Sherman, W. B., ed., Hypersensitivity: Mechanisms and Management. Philadelphia, W. B. Saunders Co., 1968, Ch. 16, p. 200.

Shulman, S. Insect allergy: Biochemical and immunological analyses of the allergens. Progr. Allerg., 12:246, 1968.

11.12
SERUM SICKNESS

ROBERTO MASELLI and ELLIOT F. ELLIS

Serum sickness is a systemic reaction which follows the injection of foreign serum. Classic serum disease was seen chiefly from 1900 to 1940, when antisera produced in horses or rabbits were widely used in an attempt to confer passive immunity in a variety of diseases which have either become rare or no longer require such therapy. Since the advent of modern immunization programs and the availability of antimicrobial drugs, the incidence of classical serum sickness has greatly decreased. Treatment of patients for rattlesnake envenomation, botulism, other clostridial infections, diphtheria, rabies, and tetanus with antisera produced in animals is responsible for those cases of serum sickness that still occur. More common today is serum sickness-like disease which is usually a manifestation of drug allergy.

Classic serum disease occurs 8 to 12 days after the administration of foreign serum. Its cardinal features include fever (101° to 103° F), urticarial eruption, and lymphadenopathy, involving first the regional nodes and then becoming generalized. Splenomegaly is uncommon. Edema of the face is frequently present. Pain and swelling of one or more joints occurs in less than 5 percent of cases, and when present involves both small and large joints. Itching, which accompanies the urticaria, is the most distressing symptom of the illness. Occasionally, the rash is morbilliform, scarlatiniform, or multiform, but urticaria is by far more common. An accelerated form of the disease may be seen in individuals who have been previously sensitized to horse serum. The symptoms in these cases appear on the fourth to sixth day (or even earlier) following serum injection, and are more intense in terms of urticaria, edema, and fever. For reasons to be described below, the clinical illness may be diphasic or triphasic in character. The clinical course of serum sickness is usually benign and the disease rarely lasts more than a few days to a week. In rare cases, myocarditis, glomerulonephritis, encephalitis, Guillain-Barré syndrome, or peripheral neuritis may develop. All of these complications usually resolve completely except for the peripheral neuritis which may result in permanent disability.

Acute anaphylaxis is the most serious, albeit rare, manifestation of allergic sensitization to foreign serum proteins. The danger of anaphylaxis seems to be greatest in atopic individuals with a family or personal history of hay fever, asthma, or eczema, and in whom reinjection of foreign serum is made within 4 months of the original injection. Individuals at risk of anaphylaxis can be identified by skin testing (see below).

LABORATORY FINDINGS. Examination of the peripheral blood usually shows leucopenia primarily due to a decrease in polymorphonuclear leucocytes; occasionally, leucocytosis is seen. Eosinophilia is uncommon. The erythrocyte sedimentation rate is generally normal. An elevated titer of a Forsmann type heterophile antibody is frequently found. Adsorption of the serum with guinea pig kidney results in complete removal of sheep cell agglutinating activity. At the height of the illness the serum complement concentration may be low.

PATHOGENESIS. The likelihood of developing serum sickness after an injection of foreign serum is clearly related to the dose and route of serum administration. Injection of 10 ml of serum intramuscularly results in sensitization in about 10 percent of recipients. When large amounts of serum (100 to 200 ml) are given, a high proportion of the recipients develop serum sickness. Intravenous administration of serum is more likely to produce the disease than is intramuscular administration.

The immunologic mechanisms involved in serum sickness have been well studied in the rabbit. In the "one shot" serum sickness model, a single large dose of an isotopically labeled foreign protein is injected intravenously into the animal and the fate of the antigen is followed over a period of time following injection (Fig. 7). Initially, during a period of about three days, there is a sharp drop in antigen concentration as equilibrium is achieved with the extravascular plasma protein pool. A period of slower decline in antigen concentration follows as a consequence of nonimmune metabolism of the foreign antigen at a rate characteristic of the species of animal and the protein injected. During the third phase, immediately prior to the appearance of free circulating antibody, rapid immune elimination of the antigen occurs. As antibody synthesis is initiated, and while free antigen still remains in the circulation, antigen-antibody complexes are formed. The initial complexes formed in extreme antigen excess are small and fail to fix complement. As the concentration of antibody increases, progressively larger complexes are formed which,

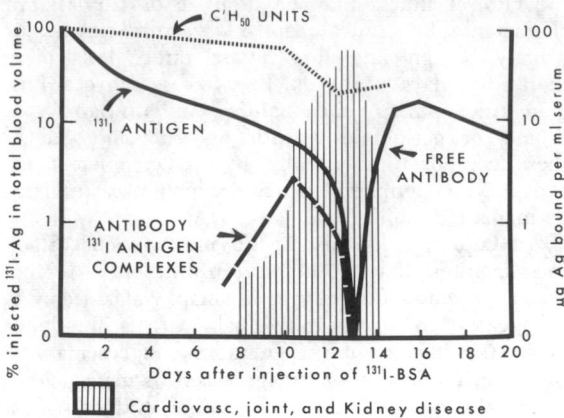

Fig. 7. Serum Sickness in the Rabbit. Changes in serum levels of free ^{131}I-labeled bovine serum albumin antigen, antigen-antibody complexes, free anti-BSA antibody and hemolytic complement activity (CH$_{50}$ units) following a large "one shot" dose of ^{131}I-labeled BSA. The presence of cardiovascular, joint, and kidney lesions is shown by the shaded area. (Modified from Cochrane and Dixon. *Calif. Med.,* 111:99, 1969.)

after a certain point, are rapidly removed from the circulation. Coincident with the appearance of complexes formed in moderate antigen excess, acute inflammatory lesions appear in the kidneys, arteries, heart, and joints. Serum complement level falls at the same time, presumably due to in vivo fixation of complement by antigen-antibody complexes. Immunofluorescent studies revealing the presence of antigen, complement components, and host immunoglobulin in the pathologic lesions suggest that antigen-antibody-complement complexes are instrumental in the formation of the lesions. The most effective complexes are those formed in moderate antigen excess (Ag$_3$Ab$_2$). Following elimination of the antigen-antibody complexes from the circulation free antibody appears and the inflammatory lesions rapidly regress. Further evidence for the pathogenetic role of antigen-antibody complexes in serum sickness is the observation that the disease does not develop in animals or humans who fail to marshal an antibody response to the injected protein. Horse serum is a complex mixture of at least 30-odd proteins, all of which may be immunogenic. The diphasic or triphasic illness seen in some individuals following a single injection of horse serum is representative of the fact that the timing of the disappearance of antigen, the appearance of antibody, and development of the tissue lesion differs with each foreign serum protein. The urticarial lesions of serum sickness are probably the result of reaginic (IgE) sensitization to the antigen. However, a possible role of antigen-antibody complexes in the pathogenesis of the urticaria has not been excluded. Reaginic sensitivity to horse serum proteins is also thought to be responsible for the rare cases of anaphylaxis that occur following horse serum injection. Because of the possibility of an anaphylactic reaction, skin testing for evidence of reaginic

sensitivity is mandatory before administration of a horse serum antitoxin. This is most safely accomplished by scratch or puncture testing with a 1:100 dilution of the horse serum product, followed by an intradermal test if the scratch test is negative. A conjunctival test with a 1:100 or 1:10 dilution of the serum provides confirmatory evidence of anaphylactic sensitivity or lack of it. If, despite a positive skin test, administration of the horse serum product is still indicated (as in rattlesnake envenomation), desensitization may be attempted. An intravenous infusion is started; epinephrine, injectable Benadryl, and a tourniquet are kept in readiness; and dilutions beginning at 1:1,000 of the horse serum are given subcutaneously in an extremity. One-tenth milliliter is given first, and if no reaction is observed, the dose is doubled every 20 minutes until full dose is given. The larger volumes are given intramuscularly. The desensitized state is transient only, and the patient may regain his anaphylactic sensitivity after a few months.

TREATMENT.   Treatment of serum sickness is symptomatic. The urticaria and pruritus usually are responsive to adequate doses of antihistamines. It may be necessary to increase the usual dose one and a half to two times to achieve the desired results. If the urticaria and pruritus are especially severe, epinephrine 1:1,000, 0.1 to 0.2 ml subcutaneously every two to three hours, may be tried. An epinephrine suspension (Sus-phrine) in a dose of 0.1 to 0.2 ml every four to six hours may provide more sustained relief. In unusually severe cases, a short course of corticosteroids, administered in the form of prednisone, 1 to 2 mg/kg every 24 hours in one dose or two divided doses, suppresses the symptoms while the disease runs its natural course. If such patients are known to be tuberculin positive they should also be started on INH, even without evidence of active tuberculous disease.

PREVENTION.   Serum sickness and serum sickness-like disease may be either prevented or the incidence greatly reduced by the following measures: (1) Adequate immunization of all children, especially to diphtheria and tetanus. In an individual who has had a primary immunization series with tetanus, administration of tetanus antitoxin is almost never necessary except under the most unusual circumstances where massive contamination of a wound has occurred. In the overwhelming majority of cases, since tetanus immunity is long-lived, a booster with fluid tetanus toxoid will insure adequate protection. (2) Use of hyperimmune antisera prepared in humans, for example tetanus hyperimmune globulin, when available, in preference to antisera prepared in animals. (3) Avoidance of the unnecessary use of antibiotics, especially penicillin, and the substitution of the oral route for the intramuscular route of administration when penicillin treatment is indicated.

REFERENCES

Arbesman, C. E., Rose, N. R., and Reisman, R. E. Immunologic studies of serum sickness. *In* Brown, E. A., ed., Allergology. New York, The Macmillan Co., 1962.

Cochrane, C. G., and Dixon, F. J. Cell and tissue damage through antigen-antibody complexes. Calif. Med., 111:99, 1969.

Siegel, S. C. Serum sickness. *In* Gellis, S. S., and Kagan, B. M., eds., Current Pediatric Therapy 4. Philadelphia, W. B. Saunders Co., 1970.

Smith, J. M., and Gell, P. G. H. Clinical aspects of immunology. *In* Gell, P. G. H., and Coombs, R. A., eds., Philadelphia, F. A. Davis Co., 1968.

Von Pirquet, C., and Schick, B. Die Serum Krankheit. 1905. English Trans.: Serum Sickness. Baltimore, Williams and Wilkins Co., 1951.

11.13
HYPERSENSITIVITY REACTIONS TO PHYSICAL FACTORS

ALAN A. WANDERER and
DAVID S. PEARLMAN

Hypersensitivity reactions to physical factors (cold, heat, light, pressure) are conventionally classified as physical allergies. This designation is misleading, since immunologic mechanisms have been demonstrated only in certain forms of light and cold hypersensitivity, while the pathophysiology of other "physical allergies" has yet to be elucidated. Hypersensitivity to physical factors may occur in patients with hereditary angioneurotic edema and various types of porphyrias. These entities are not included in this discussion since they are not primarily allergic disorders.

Hypersensitivity to Light

Various types of reactions provoked by light have been thought to be allergic in nature. In few instances, however, is there evidence to substantiate an allergic mechanism for these manifestations. "Allergic" skin reactions induced by light fall principally into two main categories: (1) urticarial manifestations occurring in patients with a constitutional sensitivity to light radiation ("solar urticaria"), and (2) photosensitivity reactions induced by drugs or chemical agents.

SOLAR URTICARIA. Solar urticaria occurs mainly in adults and older children and is characterized by an urticarial reaction following exposure to sunlight. Usually within a minute or two after such exposure, there is itching following rapidly by erythema and urticaria which is confined to uncovered areas. Ordinarily, signs and symptoms last only a few hours. With mild exposure, pruritus may be the only symptom; occasionally, with intensive and prolonged exposure, severe systemic manifestations, including shock, may occur. Solar urticaria will appear in individual patients at specific wavelengths of light, and in some patients a serum factor(s) is present which can transfer photoreactivity to a nonsensitive person. Photosensitizing serum factors seem to occur mainly in those patients in whom ultraviolet wavelengths, between 2,850 and 3,200 Å, activate the reaction. They are also produced in a few patients sensitive to wavelengths between 4,000 and 5,000 Å. These serum factors have been equated with antibody and it has been suggested that symptoms develop after reaction of this circulating antibody with substances in the skin which have been rendered appropriately antigenic by the energizing activity of specific wavelengths of light. However, it is still unclear if these serum factors are antibodies and whether an allergic mechanism actually underlies this form of light hypersensitivity.

Treatment of solar urticaria consists mainly in minimizing contact with sunlight, wearing protective clothing, or using sun screen preparations (e.g., Uval, Presun, A-fil). Antihistamines are sometimes useful. There is no good evidence that adrenal corticosteroids are of any value in this disorder.

PHOTOSENSITIVITY INDUCED BY DRUGS AND CHEMICALS. Numerous drugs and chemicals have been reported to sensitize the skin to the action of light radiation (Table 10). In some instances, the photosensitivity is thought to be immunologic in nature ("photoallergic reaction"); in others, the ordinary toxic effects of light radiation are in some way potentiated by the sensitizing substances ("phototoxic reaction").

Phototoxic reactions may occur after the first exposure to the sensitizing drug or chemical or may appear any time there is sufficient exposure to the photosensitizing material. Characteristically, these reactions are nonpruritic and are confined to the area of skin which has been exposed to the appropriate wavelengths of light. Reactions are most commonly erythematous, resembling an exaggerated sunburn;

TABLE 10. *Drugs and Chemicals Which Sensitize to Light Radiation*

Drugs

Sulfonamides, sulfonylureas, chlorothiazides, phenothiazines, demethylchlortetracycline, griseofulvin, barbiturates, antihistamines, oral contraceptives, aminosalicyclic acid

Coal Tar Ingredients

Dyes

Especially anthroquinones and anthracenes

Antibacterial Agents in Soaps, Cosmetics

Bithional, hexachlorophene, tetrachlorosalicylanilide

Furocoumarins (Psoralens)

In plants such as parsnip, dill, celery, carrot, lime, bergamot orange. Also, as ingredients of perfumes and lotions (oil of bergamot)

they frequently become hyperpigmented. Urticarial reactions and bullous dermatitis sometimes occur.

Photoallergic reactions require an induction period in which repeated contact with the photosensitizing substance must occur before symptoms develop. As a rule, they appear in only a small proportion of individuals exposed to the photosensitizing material. Photoallergic reactions can be of various types: erythematous, urticarial, or eczematous. They are not necessarily confined to the area of sun exposure. Pruritus is a common complaint and may be severe.

Photosensitivity induced by drugs or chemicals ordinarily disappears as the photosensitizing substance is eliminated from the body. This usually occurs within two to three weeks after discontinuation of the photosensitizing drugs. However, in some instances (e.g., phenothiazines), photosensitivity has been reported to persist for months and even years after the drug was last administered.

Treatment consists in immediate discontinuation of the suspected photosensitizing material, and avoidance of sunlight exposure for at least a few days thereafter. The patient should also be warned against the future use of substances which contain the photosensitizing material. Antihistamines are helpful in controlling urticaria and pruritus. Antimalarial drugs have been used successfully in some cases, but are not generally employed because of their toxicity.

Primary Cold Urticaria

Primary acquired cold urticaria is a disorder beginning usually between the ages of 10 and 60 years and characterized by the rapid development of urticaria after exposure to cold temperatures. Urtication is the outstanding sign of this clinical entity and is confined strictly to the areas of cold contact. Several case reports suggest that this form of cold hypersensitivity may be associated with systemic manifestations such as vomiting, dyspnea, or syncope. Some unusually sensitive individuals have drowned while swimming, presumably as a result of an anaphylactoid reaction precipitated by exposure to the cold water temperature. Except for such rare complications, primary acquired cold urticaria is basically a benign disorder which often disappears within one to three years after onset; in some instances it remains a lifelong problem.

The diagnosis of primary acquired cold urticaria depends in part on the exclusion of underlying disorders known to be associated with cold urticaria (Table 11). Cryoglobulinemias have occasionally been associated with cold urticaria and can be excluded by a simple laboratory screening technique. Cooling of cryoglobulin-containing serum to 4° C will cause gel or precipitate formation which will redissolve upon rewarming of the serum specimen. In addition, individuals with cryoglobulins and cold urticaria will often develop purpuric lesions, a useful differential diagnostic feature. A familial form of cold

TABLE 11. *Classification of Cold Urticaria*

1. Primary Cold Urticaria

  a. Acquired
    1. IgE mediated
    2. IgM mediated

  b. Familial

2. Secondary Cold Urticaria

  a. Cryoglobulinemia
    1. Primary
    2. Secondary (multiple myeloma, systemic lupus erythematosus, lymphoreticular neoplasms)

  b. Syphilis

  c. Cryofibrinoginemia

  d. Cold agglutinin syndrome

urticaria has been described which differs from the primary acquired form in that it begins in the first five years of life and urtication cannot be reproduced by a cold test.

The definitive diagnosis of cold urticaria depends on the development of a whealing response after application of a cold stimulus to the patient's skin. The cold test can be performed by holding a glass filled with ice water directly on the patient's forearm; a minimum of 5 minutes is suggested for the cold application and a longer exposure (up to 10 minutes) may be necessary in some patients. The initial cooling of the skin usually does not produce urtication, which characteristically occurs during the rewarming phase. The urtication is unique in that it is nonpruritic, is confined to the shape of the testing object, and is not associated with pseudopod formation.

Until recently there has been only circumstantial evidence that primary cold urticaria is an immunologic (allergic) disorder. It has been demonstrated that the sera of some patients possess a cold urticaria inducing factor which can be passively transferred to the skin of normal recipients. A serum transfer factor reportedly occurs in 25 to 50 percent of patients with primary acquired cold urticaria. At least two distinctly different types of serum factors have been found: (1) factors indistinguishable from immunoglobulin E (IgE); and (2) immunoglobulin M factors with physicochemical properties similar to cryoglobulins (i.e., proteins which precipitate maximally at low pH, low temperature, and low ionic strength). This latter observation suggests that some forms of primary acquired cold urticaria may be mediated by microprecipitation of cryoprotein-like serum factors, resulting in the release of pharmacologic agents capable of inducing the urticarial response. Various other mechanisms have also been considered to explain the pathophysiology of cold urticaria. In particular, autoimmune mechanisms involving cold-induced alteration of normal skin antigens have been proposed but, to date, there is no evidence to support this theory.

The treatment of cold urticaria has been empirical, since the mechanisms and pharmacologic mediators involved have not been completely elucidated. Avoidance of cold exposure, including the use of protective clothing, is a mainstay of therapy. Attempts to decrease cold sensitivity by graded exposures to cold temperatures have not proved effective in most patients. Corticosteroids and ACTH appear to be ineffective in the treatment of this disorder, and antihistamines have been used with mixed success. However, the authors have observed significant reduction of cold sensitivity in a limited number of patients treated with cyproheptidine. (Periactin). The medication should be given prophylactically four times a day by mouth in a dose according to age. The management of patients with cold urticaria should also include a careful explanation of possible systemic manifestations that might occur during exposure to cold environmental temperatures.

Hypersensitivity to Heat

Two forms of heat hypersensitivity have been recognized. There is a rare form in which an urticarial response is confined to the areas of skin directly in contact with heat. The more common form of heat hypersensitivity develops as a generalized urticarial response, occurring principally in adults and older children. The term "cholinergic urticaria" has been applied to this generalized form of heat hypersensitivity since acetylcholine in low concentrations induces whealing in patients with this disorder. Characteristically, cholinergic urticaria appears as large areas of erythema with minute (1 to 3 mm) wheals, often surrounded by smaller satellite wheals. The wheals may become larger as smaller wheals coalesce. The lesions are found predominantly over the upper trunk and upper extremities and are typically pruritic and short-lived, often disappearing in less than 30 minutes. Systemic symptoms occasionally occur and include abdominal cramps, diarrhea, salivation, angioneurotic edema, syncope, and shock. Cholinergic urticaria may be a relatively transient problem, disappearing in one or two years, but may last for the lifetime of the individual.

This form of urticaria can be induced by various forms of heat stress such as high ambient temperature, exercise, and fever. These heat stimuli appear to exert their effect by causing a general elevation in blood temperature. The thermoregulatory center is affected by the rise in blood temperature, resulting in stimulation of sweat glands via autonomic pathways. Although acetylcholine has been implicated as an important pharmacologic mediator of the reaction, there is reason to believe that histamine acts as the final pharmacologic mediator. Histamine is thought to be liberated by direct cholinergic stimulation or by histamine-releasing substances which are formed by the contact between sweat and certain skin products such as sebum. Psychic stimuli also may trigger cholinergic urticaria, possibly through the same final pathway as the heat stimuli.

A period of refractoriness to heat stress frequently follows a heat-induced reaction, and may last for as long as 24 hours. Because of this, a regimen of desensitization with frequent warm baths has been tried with some success. This is generally neither advisable nor necessary, since antihistamines and hydroxyzine (Atarax) have been frequently helpful in controlling symptoms.

Dermographism

The tendency to develop whealing and erythema after mild stroking of the skin has been referred to as dermographism or urticaria factitia. Approximately 5 percent of individuals, both atopic and nonatopic, will exhibit this phenomenon, although the incidence increases if stronger stroke pressures are applied. Clinically, the whealing usually conforms to the pattern of stroke pressure, and hence, self-inflicted scratches will produce linear eruptions. Urtication may also appear at sites of persistent pressure, as from constrictive garments. No systemic symptoms have been associated with dermographism. The disorder is acquired and apparently will remit and exacerbate unpredictably.

The diagnosis of dermographism can easily be made by applying a mild stroke pressure to the skin of the patient. An immediate whealing and flare response will develop which corresponds to the pattern of the stroke stimulus. Urticaria pigmentosa (mastocytosis) should be considered in the differential diagnosis of patients with marked pressure hypersensitivity.

The pathogenesis of dermographism is obscure. Early studies indicated that the sera of a small percentage of patients contained factors which could transfer pressure reactivity to the skin of normal individuals. This observation has not been confirmed in recent years. The chemical mediators which cause dermographism have not been identified, although histamine has been implicated because of the similar cutaneous reactions produced by dermal injections of this mediator. Very recently, dermal perfusion techniques have implicated vasoactive polypeptides, known as kinins, as possible mediators in this disorder.

Treatment consists in explaining to the patient the causal relationship between trauma or pressure and the development of urtication; the use of antihistamines is beneficial in some cases.

REFERENCES

Baer, R., and Harber, L. Reactions to light, heat, and trauma. *In* Samter, M., ed., Immunological Diseases. Boston, Little, Brown and Co., 1965, p. 704.

Costanzi, J. J., and Coltman, C. A., Jr. Kappa chain cold precipitable immunoglobulin G (IgG) associated with cold urticaria. Clin. Exp. Immunol., 2:167, 1967.

Daniels, F. Diseases caused or aggravated by sunlight, Med. Clin. N. Amer., 49:565, 1965.

Houser, D. D., Arbesman, C. E., Ito, K., and Wicher, K. Cold urticaria—immunological studies. Amer. J. Med., in press.

Kelly, F., and Wise, R. Observations on cold sensitivity. Amer. J. Med., 15:431, 1953.

Kirshbaum, B. A., and Beerman, H. Photosensitization due to drugs. Amer. J. Med. Sci., 248:445, 1964.

Moore, R. M., and Warin, R. P. Some clinical aspects of cholinergic urticaria. Brit. J. Derm., 80:794, 1968.

Sherman, W. B., and Seebohm, P. M. Passive transfer of cold urticaria. J. Allergy, 21:414, 1950.

Witherspoon, F. G., White, C. B., Bazemore, J. M., and Hailey, H. Familial urticaria due to cold. Arch. Derm. Syph., 58:52, 1948.

chapter 12

CONNECTIVE TISSUE DISEASES

GENE H. STOLLERMAN, Associate Editor

These inflammatory diseases of unknown cause or pathogenesis are often classified together because they have in common diffuse involvement of connective tissues. They are also referred to as "collagen diseases" because damage to collagen fibrils and to the ground substance of connective tissue is an anatomic characteristic of their pathology. The connective tissue diseases are of interest to rheumatologists because all may cause arthritis, and to immunologists because allergy, hypersensitivity, or "autoimmunity" is suspected to play a role in their pathogenesis.

Despite the similarities by which the connective tissue diseases are classified as a group, they represent distinct clinical entities and include rheumatic fever, rheumatoid arthritis, systemic lupus erythematosus, dermatomyositis, scleroderma, and polyarteritis nodosa. Although there is a certain amount of overlapping in symptoms, signs, and laboratory findings, each disease, when fully expressed, is readily distinguished from the others and has its own unique features. The etiologic agent of rheumatic fever has been identified as the Group A streptococcus, but because the pathogenic mechanism by which the organism produces the connective tissue lesion remains unknown, and because inflammation of the connective tissues and serous membranes is so characteristic of this disease, rheumatic fever retains its classification among the "collagen diseases."

Acute arthritis is often the presenting clinical picture of the connective tissue diseases; it should be regarded as a medical emergency for which a patient should be admitted to the hospital for careful study whenever possible. A suggested work-up of a patient with acute arthritis is presented in Section 12.7.

12.1
RHEUMATIC FEVER

Rheumatic fever is a delayed sequel to infection with Group A streptococci. It is an inflammatory disease which involves principally the heart, joints, central nervous system, and subcutaneous tissues. The usual manifestations in the acute form are migratory polyarthritis, fever, and carditis. Sydenham's chorea, subcutaneous nodules, and erythema marginatum may occur as other typical manifestations. No single symptom, sign, or laboratory test is pathognomonic of rheumatic fever, although several com-

binations of them are diagnostic. The various clinical manifestations are considered to be part of the same disease because they occur together with a frequency that far exceeds chance. They may occur singly, however, or in various combinations in any individual patient. Although the name "acute rheumatic fever" emphasizes involvement of the joints, rheumatic fever owes its importance to the involvement of the heart, which can be fatal during the acute stage of the disease or can lead to rheumatic heart disease, a chronic condition due to scarring and deformity of the heart valves. When overt evidence of the disease is present it is referred to as *acute rheumatic fever* or a manifestation of *rheumatic activity*. As the disease takes on a subacute or chronic form, especially in the absence of the more distinctive features, the patient is said to be in the *rheumatic state*. Because recurrent attacks of rheumatic fever occur so frequently, the individual once afflicted is regarded as a *rheumatic subject*.

ETIOLOGY. An imposing body of indirect evidence which supports the etiologic relationship of Group A streptococci to rheumatic fever can be summarized briefly, as follows: (1) Numerous clinical and epidemiologic studies have shown a close association of Group A streptococcal infections and rheumatic fever. (2) Antecedent streptococcal infection can almost always be demonstrated immunologically in the acute stage of rheumatic fever by increased titers of antibodies or streptococcal antigens. Moreover, in long-term prospective follow-up studies, rheumatic fever does not recur in the absence of intercurrent streptococcal infections. (3) Both primary and secondary attacks of the disease can be prevented by prompt treatment or prevention of streptococcal infections with antimicrobial therapy.

It is of interest that strains of Group A streptococci that infect the skin do not cause acute rheumatic fever although they can, and frequently do, cause acute glomerulonephritis. Furthermore, there are also some throat strains of Group A streptococci which cause acute glomerulonephritis but do not cause rheumatic fever. In fact, the simultaneous appearance of acute rheumatic fever and acute glomerulonephritis from the same antecedent streptococcal infection is virtually never seen. These observations suggest that there are rheumatogenic and nonrheumatogenic Group A streptococci and that the route of infection may also have some bearing on the pathogenesis of acute rheumatic fever.

The mechanism by which the Group A streptococcus initiates the disease process remains un-

TABLE 1. Convalescent Carriage of Group A Streptococci and Attack Rate of Rheumatic Fever*

3-5 Week Culture	No. of Patients	Rheumatic Fever	
		No.	%
Neg.	3,552	9	0.3
Pos.	1,141	32	2.8

*From Rammelkamp. Circulation, 17:842, 1958.

TABLE 2. Relation of Antistreptolysin O Rise to Attack Rate for Acute Rheumatic Fever*

Rise in ASO Titer (units/ml)	No. of Patients	No. of Patients with Acute R.F.	Attack Rate for Acute R.F. (percent)
0-120	856	7	0.8
121-250	553	19	3.6
Over 250	545	30	5.5
	1,954	56	2.8

*From Stetson. In McCarty, ed., Streptococcal Infections. Columbia Univ. Press, 1954.

known. A relatively small percentage of persons who suffer from streptococcal sore throats subsequently develops rheumatic fever. The organism is not demonstrable in the lesions when rheumatic fever appears several days or weeks after the acute streptococcal infection. For this reason, rheumatic fever, like glomerulonephritis, is often referred to as a "nonsuppurative complication" of streptococcal infection. No product of the streptococcus has been clearly incriminated as a cause of the lesions, either as a direct toxin or as an antigen inducing hypersensitivity. Gamma globulin has been demonstrated by fluorescent antibody methods to be deposited in the sarcolemma of the myocardial fibers of patients who have died of rheumatic carditis and in the biopsied auricular appendages of patients operated upon for mitral stenosis. Also, streptococcal antigens have been identified which cross-react immunologically with myocardial tissue. Furthermore, patients with rheumatic carditis or chronic rheumatic heart disease often have circulating antibodies to heart tissue. This finding has led to the suggestion that the myocardial lesions of rheumatic fever are the result of some form of autoimmunity induced by streptococcal antigens. However, the validity of this concept is not yet confirmed, since the immunologic phenomena might be secondary to cardiac tissue damage rather than a cause of it.

INCIDENCE AND EPIDEMIOLOGY. Although rheumatic fever may occur at any age, it is extremely rare in infancy; it appears most commonly between the ages of 5 and 15 years, when streptococcal infection is most frequent and intense. Similarly, the geographic distribution, incidence, and severity of rheumatic fever are, in general, a reflection of the frequency and severity of streptococcal disease. The attack rate of rheumatic fever following exudative streptococcal pharyngitis in epidemics averages approximately 3 percent. When streptococcal pharyngitis is sporadic and mild, the incidence of rheumatic fever may be very much lower. Two important variables of streptococcal infection which influence the attack rate of rheumatic fever have been emphasized: (1) the duration of throat carriage of Group A streptococci during convalescence from the pharyngeal infection and (2) the magnitude of the immune response to the antecedent streptococcal infection. Controlled studies have shown, for example, that rheumatic fever followed streptococcal pharyngitis in 3 percent of patients who carried the infecting strain for at least three weeks during convalescence, whereas the incidence in those who did not was only 0.3 percent (Table 1). Similarly, 5 percent of patients may develop rheumatic fever following a streptococcal infection which is associated with an increase in the antistreptolysin O titer of more than 250 units per ml, whereas less than 1 percent of patients with a small increase in antistreptolysin O titer (less than 100 units per ml) will develop this complication (Table 2). Although pharyngeal carriage of Group A streptococci is frequent in all populations, particularly in school children, the frequency with which rheumatic fever appears will depend upon the virulence and epidemicity of the strains encountered and upon the frequency with which infections are produced which are associated with prolonged survival of the organism in the host and with strong antigenic stimulation.

Environmental, bacterial, and host factors which appear to play a role in the development of rheumatic fever are important, therefore, primarily as they are related to the incidence and severity of preceding streptococcal infection. Thus, such factors as latitude, altitude, crowding, dampness, economic factors, and age all affect the incidence of rheumatic fever because they are related to the incidence of streptococcal infection in general.

The attack rate of rheumatic fever following streptococcal infections in patients who have had previous attacks of rheumatic fever is increased to as high as 5 to 50 percent and is also related to the intensity of the immune response to the reactivating infection. Furthermore, the frequency of rheumatic recurrences following streptococcal infection is consistently greater in those with rheumatic heart disease than in those who escape cardiac injury during the previous attacks (Table 3). The tendency to suffer recurrences of rheumatic fever following streptococcal

TABLE 3. *Ratio of Rheumatic Recurrences to Streptococcal Infections in Patients Stratified for Heart Disease and for ASO* Rise†*

ASO Rise, in Tube Dilutions	Heart Disease	No Heart Disease
0-1	3/24 (13%)	1/72 (1%)
2	10/36 (28%)	2/46 (4%)
3	6/16 (37%)	4/32 (13%)
4	9/14 (65%)	9/25 (36%)

*Antistreptolysin O.
†From Taranta. *Ann. Int. Med.*, Suppl. 5, 60:58, 1964.

infections declines with the passage of years since the preceding attack. It appears, therefore, that certain host variables, as well as differences in the severity of the antecedent infection, also influence the development of rheumatic fever. To what extent such variables are genetic or acquired has not been settled. It is common to obtain a family history of rheumatic fever as well as to encounter multiple cases among siblings of a single family. However, the concordance of rheumatic fever in identical twins is approximately 20 percent, which does not exceed that of poliomyelitis or tuberculosis, suggesting only a limited penetrance of genetic predisposition to rheumatic fever.

The mortality of acute rheumatic fever has been declining steadily for the past 30 years. However, it is still a major cause of death and disability in children and adolescents. Rheumatic fever is the most common cause of heart disease in patients below the age of 40, and is second only to hypertension and arteriosclerosis as a cause of heart disease in the older age groups. Accurate determination of the true incidence of rheumatic fever and rheumatic heart disease is impossible, since the disease has not been made reportable generally and its diagnosis is frequently indefinite. The best estimates of the current prevalence of rheumatic heart disease in elementary and high school children of large cities in the temperate zone of the United States is approximately 2 to 3 per 1,000. The occurrence of rheumatic fever is at least two to three times this frequency, because approximately 60 to 70 percent of patients with rheumatic fever recover without permanent stigmas of rheumatic heart disease. It is generally believed that the incidence of rheumatic fever, like that of streptococcal sore throat and scarlet fever, has been decreasing for several years in countries where housing and economic conditions have been improving steadily. The rate of decrease may have been accelerated by the wide use of antimicrobial therapy. Rheumatic fever remains, however, a worldwide disease having its greatest prevalence wherever poor economic conditions, overcrowding, and substandard housing are most common.

PATHOLOGY. The lesions of rheumatic fever are disseminated widely throughout the body, with special predilection for connective tissues. Focal inflammatory lesions occur particularly around the small blood vessels.

Cardiovascular Lesions. The heart is the site of the most characteristic and consequential involvement, and all of its layers, endocardium, myocardium, and pericardium, may be involved. This generalized involvement gives rise to the term *rheumatic pancarditis*. The detailed microscopic appearance of the inflammatory lesion varies with its location, the *myocarditis* of rheumatic fever being of particular interest. The most characteristic and specific pattern of rheumatic inflammation is found in the myocardial Aschoff body, a submiliary granuloma. This lesion, when present in its classic form, is generally considered to be pathognomonic of rheumatic fever. In many areas the inflammatory lesion is accompanied by swelling and fragmentation of the collagen fibers and alteration in the staining properties of the ground substances of the connective tissues. This change is described as "fibrinoid degeneration of collagen," but its chemical basis has not been established. Aschoff bodies with less exudative and more productive changes may persist for many years as the lingering traces of chronic rheumatic inflammation in patients with rheumatic heart disease, long after rheumatic fever has become clinically quiescent. Eventually the Aschoff body is converted into a spindle-shaped or triangular scar lying between the muscle bundles and surrounding blood vessels.

Rheumatic endocarditis produces the verrucous valvulitis of acute rheumatic fever which leads to the most serious permanent cardiac damage. It may heal with fibrous thickening and adhesion of the valve commissures and chordae tendineae, leading to variable degrees of valvular regurgitation and stenosis. Deformity resulting in functional impairment of the heart occurs most commonly in the mitral and aortic valves, less frequently in the tricuspid, and almost never in the pulmonic valves.

Extracardiac Lesions. Involvement of the *joints* is characterized by exudative rather than proliferative changes, and healing of these structures occurs without significant scarring or deformity. Edema and hyperemia of the synovial membranes occur with effusions into the joint cavities. The periarticular tissues are often also edematous, and focal necrosis may occur in the joint capsule. *Subcutaneous nodules*, seen during the acute phase of the disease, are composed of granulomas which resemble those of the Aschoff body, with localized areas of "fibrinoid" swelling of subcutaneous collagen bundles, and perivascular collections of large cells with pale nuclei and prominent nucleoli. Synovitis is usually mild and nonspecific. *Pulmonary* and *pleural* lesions are less definite and less characteristic. Fibrinous pleurisy and rheumatic pneumonitis may occur with exudative and proliferative lesions but without definite Aschoff bodies. Patients with active *chorea* rarely die. The pathologic findings which have been reported in the central nervous system are not consistent, and no characteristic lesion has been reported to explain this clinical manifestation. During active chorea the spinal fluid remains normal, being free of cells, with no increase in protein and no change in the relative concentration of various proteins. Similarly, there are no constant pathologic changes in the peritoneum to account for the frequent symptom of abdominal pain, although vascular lesions and focal peritonitis have been described in fatal cases.

CLINICAL FEATURES. The clinical manifestations of rheumatic fever vary from a low-grade intermittent fever to the classical features of polyarthritis, carditis, and chorea. The diagnosis cannot be definitely established on the basis of any single symptom, sign, or laboratory finding. When the major manifestations of carditis, polyarthritis, chorea, erythema marginatum, and subcutaneous nodules are readily apparent there is little question of the identity of the disease. The difficulty is that frequently these manifestations are not clearly expressed. It is necessary, therefore, to evaluate carefully the total clinical picture and laboratory findings before concluding that the patient is suffering from rheumatic fever.

Arthritis. The classic attack of rheumatic fever appears as an acute migratory polyarthritis accompanied by signs and symptoms of an acute febrile illness. The large joints of the extremities are most frequently affected, but no joint is impervious to the inflammatory process; one may find arthritis of the hands, feet, spine, or such joints as the sternoclavicular and temporomandibular. Joint effusions may occur but are not persistent. As pain and swelling subside in one joint, others tend to become involved. Although such "migratory" involvement is characteristic, it is not invariable, and several large joints may be inflamed at one time. To be acceptable as a criterion for the diagnosis of rheumatic fever, the polyarthritis should involve two or more joints, should be associated with at least two minor manifestations such as fever and elevation of sedimentation rate, and should be associated with a high titer of antistreptolysin O or some other streptococcal antibody. It is important to differentiate true polyarthritis from vague myalgias of the lower extremities, often referred to as "growing pains." The latter frequently come on at bedtime or during the night and tend to involve the calves, thighs, and popliteal regions rather than the joints. They do not involve the upper extremities.

Acute Rheumatic Carditis. Acute rheumatic carditis first manifests itself by the appearance of the heart murmurs of either mitral or aortic regurgitation, the former most frequently. Signs and symptoms of pericarditis and of congestive heart failure may super-

vene in more severe cases. Death may result from heart failure during the acute stage of the disease, or permanent cardiac damage may be sustained which results ultimately in serious disability. Carditis may vary from a fulminating, fatal course to a low-grade, inapparent inflammation. It is well to bear in mind that the vast majority of patients with carditis do not have symptoms referable to the heart. The latter occur only in more severe cases when heart failure or pericardial effusions produce the characteristic symptoms of cardiac insufficiency. For this reason, unless extracardiac manifestations, such as polyarthritis and chorea, are present, patients who have rheumatic fever manifested only by carditis are frequently not diagnosed and in later life may be discovered to have rheumatic heart disease without a definite history of rheumatic fever.

When carditis is manifest, there is usually tachycardia disproportionate to the degree of fever, gallop rhythms are often heard, and the heart sounds may become fetal or "tic-tac" in quality. Occasionally arrhythmias result. Prolongation of the conduction time may lead to dropped beats with varying degrees of heart block. Prolongation of the P-R interval and other changes in the electrocardiogram are very common, but these findings, in the absence of clinical manifestations of carditis, have a benign prognosis. Therefore, changes in the electrocardiogram alone, unassociated with significant murmurs or cardiac enlargement, do not by themselves constitute an acceptable criterion for the diagnosis of rheumatic carditis. Pericarditis may cause precordial pain, and a friction rub may be audible. Frequently, however, pericardial effusions are asymptomatic and are only detected by obtaining chest radiograms routinely at weekly intervals during the acute rheumatic attack. A sudden, striking increase in the apparent size of the heart may result from pericardial effusion and may be associated with respiratory embarrassment.

A definite clinical diagnosis of carditis can be made if one or more of the following can be demonstrated: (1) the appearance of, or change in the character of, organic heart murmurs; (2) definite increase in heart size demonstrated by radiogram or fluoroscopy; (3) pericardial friction rub or effusion; (4) signs of congestive heart failure. Rheumatic carditis is almost always associated with a significant murmur. Consequently, when other manifestations of carditis are not associated with a significant murmur, they should be labeled "rheumatic carditis" with caution. Murmurs indicating rheumatic carditis are:

1. Significant *apical systolic murmur* (mitral regurgitation). This is a long murmur, filling most of the systole. Its blowing quality and high pitch are its most important characteristics. It is heard best in the apical region and is transmitted toward the axilla. The intensity of the murmur is variable, particularly in the early stages of the illness, but is at least of grade 2 on a scale of 6. It does not change substantially with position or respiration. The mur-

mur of mitral regurgitation must be differentiated from functional (innocent) murmurs which frequently occur in normal individuals, especially in children. Functional murmurs usually occupy only a portion of systole. They may be quite loud, particularly in anxious or febrile patients, and are rather widely transmitted in thin-chested individuals. At times, functional murmurs are heard only intermittently and tend to vary with position and respiration. They are usually of two types: an ejection-type murmur heard best over the pulmonic area, and a low-pitched, vibratory "groaning" or musical murmur heard best along the lower left sternal border. The former is frequently transmitted to the neck and may be mistaken for aortic stenosis. The latter is frequently transmitted to the apex and is most likely to be confused with mitral regurgitation by those unfamiliar with its characteristic quality.

2. *Apical middiastolic murmur.* Mitral regurgitation and cardiac dilation accentuate the third heart sound. During tachycardia this may produce a proto-diastolic gallop rhythm. Frequently, however, in acute rheumatic fever with marked mitral regurgitation, the third heart sound is followed, or replaced, by a low-pitched diastolic rumble. This can be heard best with the patient in the left lateral recumbent position with the breath held in expiration. The same murmur may occur in other forms of acute carditis or in conditions causing rapid blood flow into the left ventricle, such as left-to-right shunts, hyperthyroidism, sickle-cell and other forms of severe anemia. It must be differentiated from the low-pitched, crescendo apical presystolic murmur followed by an accentuated mitral first heart sound, which is indicative of an established mitral stenosis rather than of acute carditis.

3. *Basal diastolic murmur.* This murmur of aortic regurgitation begins early in diastole; is high-pitched, blowing, decrescendo; and is heard best along the left sternal border after deep expiration with the patient leaning forward. It is of great diagnostic importance but may be difficult to hear and present only intermittently.

Subcutaneous Nodules. These are usually small, pea-sized, painless swellings over bony prominences and, therefore, also frequently go unnoticed by the patient. The skin moves freely over them. Characteristic locations are the extensor tendons of the hands and feet, the elbows, margins of the patellae, the scalp, over the scapulae, and over the spinous processes of the vertebrae. (See Fig. 1.) Nodules are frequently overlooked unless careful search for them is made. They tend to form in crops, and they persist for several days to several months before disappearing. They are more often present in severe cases in which other manifestations of rheumatic fever, particularly rheumatic carditis, are present. These lesions are very characteristic of acute rheumatic fever but may occur also in rheumatoid arthritis and even, although very rarely, in systemic lupus erythematosus.

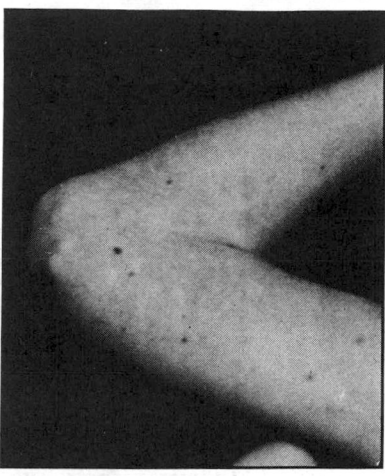

Fig. 1. Rheumatic nodules on the elbow of a patient 8 years of age.

Chorea (Sydenham's Chorea, Chorea Minor, St. Vitus' Dance).   This is a disorder of the central nervous system characterized by sudden, aimless, irregular movements, often accompanied by muscle weakness and emotional instability. Chorea is a delayed manifestation of rheumatic fever, and other manifestations may or may not still be present at the time it appears. Polyarthritis, when part of the same attack, always subsides before chorea appears. Carditis is often discovered for the first time when the presenting feature of rheumatic fever is chorea. Chorea may appear after a long latent period, up to several months, from the antecedent streptococcal infection and at a time when all other manifestations of rheumatic fever have abated. When no previous rheumatic manifestations are noted, such cases are called "pure chorea."

The clinical onset of chorea is often gradual. The child may be unusually nervous and fidgety, have difficulty in writing, drawing, and handiwork. He may stumble or fall, drop things, and grimace. As symptoms become more severe, spasmodic movements extend to all parts of the body, and muscular weakness may become so marked that the child cannot walk, talk, or sit up. Often the weakness is severe enough to simulate paralysis. The irregular, jerky, spasmodic movements may become so violent that the patient's crib or bed must be padded to prevent injury. Symptoms are exaggerated by excitement, effort, or fatigue but subside during sleep. Emotional instability is almost invariable in patients with chorea, and it is thought by some that emotional trauma may precipitate the disorder. All degrees of speech disturbance are seen.

Several characteristic signs may be elicited. An attempt to grip the hand forcefully results in spasmodic contraction which cannot be sustained. Extension of the arms with the hands and fingers outstretched may result in flexion of the wrist and hyperextension of the metacarpophalangeal joints, resulting in a "dishing" or "spooning" of the hands (choreic hand). Raising the arms above the head may result in pronation of the forearms, so that the backs of the hands come in contact (pronator sign). When asked to smile the choreic patient may grin broadly, then rapidly reassume a tearful or "poker-faced" expression. When the tongue is protruded it cannot be held quietly.

Erythema Marginatum. This evanescent pink rash is characteristic of rheumatic fever. The erythematous areas often have clear centers and round or seripiginous margins. They vary greatly in size and occur mainly on the trunk and proximal part of the extremities, never on the face. (See Fig. 2.) The erythema is transient, migratory, and may be brought out by the application of heat; it is nonpruritic, not indurated, and blanches on pressure.

Minor Clinical Criteria. These are clinical features which occur frequently in rheumatic fever. They also occur in many other diseases and therefore are of minor diagnostic value. Their usefulness consists in supporting the diagnosis of rheumatic fever when this diagnosis rests mainly on a single major manifestation.

Fever is perhaps the most common and yet the most variable minor clinical manifestation in rheumatic fever. In severe, acute cases the temperature may rise to 104° F (40° C) or higher and may persist for several weeks before gradually subsiding. It may then smolder in low-grade fashion for several weeks longer. The presence of fever cannot be regarded alone as a criterion of the activity of the rheumatic process. An unexplained low-grade fever in rheumatic subjects should, however, arouse suspicion of rheumatic activity.

Arthralgia is the occurrence of pain in one or more joints (not the muscles and other periarticular tissues) without evidence of inflammation, tenderness to touch, or limitation of motion. The presence of arthralgia in addition to polyarthritis does not make the latter any more strongly indicative of rheumatic fever, but in the presence of monoarticular arthritis, arthralgia in other joints strengthens the diagnosis of rheumatic fever. Other clinical features include abdominal pain, a rapid sleeping pulse rate (tachycardia out of proportion to fever), malaise, anemia, epistaxis, and precordial pain. *Rheumatic pneumonia* is a lesion encountered only when severe carditis is present and may be confused with pulmonary signs of congestive heart failure.

LABORATORY FINDINGS. There is no specific laboratory test to indicate the presence of rheumatic fever. The appraisal of rheumatic activity by laboratory findings is, however, of value, since various tests may indicate *continued* rheumatic inflammation when clinical features are not apparent.

Evidence of Preceding Streptococcal Infection: Streptococcal Antibody Test. The most reliable evidence of a specific infection capable of producing acute rheumatic fever is either an increased or, even better, a rising streptococcal antibody titer. These titers differentiate preceding streptococcal from other acute respiratory infections and are increased following asymptomatic as well as symptomatic streptococcal infections. These antibody levels are generally increased in the early stages of acute rheumatic fever. They may be declining, or low, if the interval between the acute streptococcal infection and the detection of rheumatic fever has been longer than 2 months, a situation which occurs most often in patients whose presenting rheumatic manifestation is *chorea.* (See Fig. 3.) However, patients whose only major manifestation is rheumatic carditis also may have low antibody titers when first seen. Their rheumatic attack may have been in progress several months before becoming symptomatic and thus recognized. Except in these two instances, *one should be reluctant to make the diagnosis of acute rheumatic fever in the absence of serologic evidence of a recent streptococcal infection. The antistreptolysin O test (ASO)* is the most widely used and best standardized streptococcal antibody test. In general, single titers of *at least* 250 Todd units in adults and *at least* 333 units in children over 5 years of age are considered

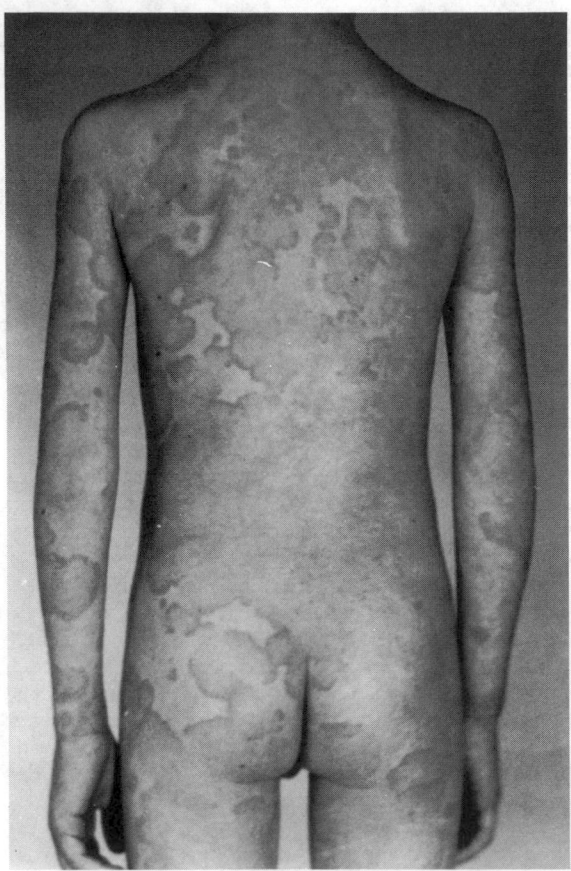

Fig. 2. Erythema marginatum.

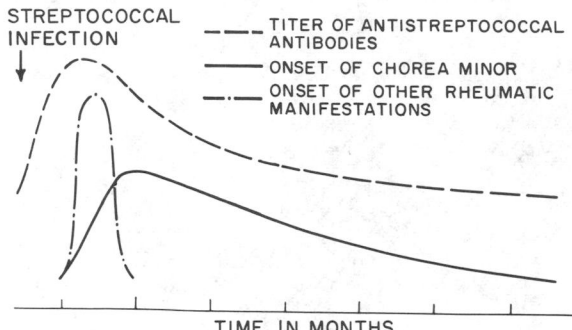

STREPTOCOCCAL
INFECTION

- - - - TITER OF ANTISTREPTOCOCCAL
ANTIBODIES
——— ONSET OF CHOREA MINOR
—·—·— ONSET OF OTHER RHEUMATIC
MANIFESTATIONS

TIME IN MONTHS

Fig. 3. Relationship among chorea minor, streptococcal infection, and other rheumatic manifestations. (From Taranta and Stollerman. *Amer. J. Med.,* 20:170, 1965.)

to be increased. Depending on the general prevalence of streptococcal infections, a varying percentage of the normal population may show titers of this magnitude.

About 20 percent of patients in the early stages of acute rheumatic fever, and most patients who present with chorea, have a low or borderline ASO titer. In these instances, it is advisable to obtain another streptococcal antibody test. Other streptococcal antibody tests that can be employed include the following: antihyaluronidase (AH), antideoxyribonucleotidase B (anti-DNase B), antinicotinamide adenine dinucleotidase (anti-NADase), and antistreptokinase (ASK). When two or more streptococcal antibody tests are performed it is possible to show an increased titer in almost all cases of acute rheumatic fever within the first 2 months after onset and in about half the cases presenting with chorea. (See Fig. 4.) Antibody determinations on serum samples obtained at 2-week intervals, preferably performed at the same time, are very useful in documenting a streptococcal infection, especially in patients with very low preinfection titers. A rise in titer of 2 dilution tubes or more can be demonstrated

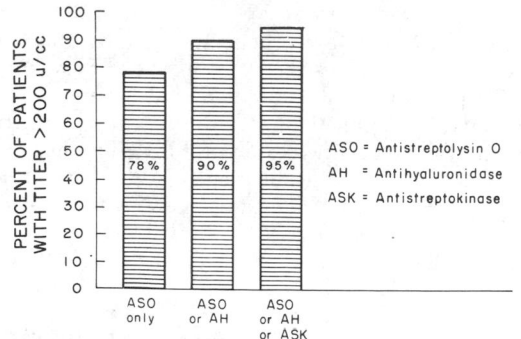

ASO = Antistreptolysin O
AH = Antihyaluronidase
ASK = Antistreptokinase

Fig. 4. Detection of recent streptococcal infection in 88 patients studied within 2 months of onset of rheumatic fever. (From Stollerman et al. *Amer. J. Med.,* 20:163, 1956.)

for at least one of the streptococcal antibodies in almost all recurrent as well as primary attacks of rheumatic fever. These streptococcal antibodies do not reflect rheumatic activity, and their rate of decline is independent of the course of the rheumatic attack.

Recently, antibody to Group A polysaccharide has been shown to persist longer in the sera of patients with rheumatic heart disease than in those who do not develop permanent cardiac lesions. The measurement of this antibody in human serum is difficult, however, and requires special methods not yet available to clinical laboratories.

Isolation of Group A Streptococci. Many patients continue to harbor Group A streptococci at the onset of acute rheumatic fever, but these organisms are usually present in small numbers and may be difficult to isolate by a single throat culture. Their demonstration may require special techniques. The administration of penicillin or other antibodies may also result in failure to isolate the infecting organism. In addition, a significant number of *normal* individuals, particularly children, may harbor Group A streptococci in the upper respiratory tract. For these reasons, throat cultures are less satisfactory than antibody tests as supporting evidence of recent streptococcal infection.

Acute Phase Reactants. These offer objective but nonspecific confirmation of the presence of an inflammatory process. *The erythrocyte sedimentation rate* and *C-reactive protein* tests are used most commonly. Unless the patient has received corticosteroids or salicylates, these tests are almost always abnormal in patients presenting with polyarthritis or acute carditis, whereas they are often normal in patients with chorea. The erythrocyte sedimentation rate (ESR) may be markedly increased by anemia and may be decreased in congestive heart failure. The test for C-reactive protein (CRP) in the blood is a sensitive indicator of inflammation and is negative in uncomplicated anemia. Heart failure, due to any cause, is often accompanied by a positive CRP test. Sera from normal individuals do not contain this protein, but relatively minor inflammatory stimuli may result in a positive reaction. Other laboratory findings which reflect inflammation, like the ESR and CRP, are quite nonspecific, including such reactions as leucocytosis, increase in serum complement, mucoproteins, alpha and gamma globulins, and fibrinogen. Prolongation of the P-R interval of the electrocardiogram, although neither specific for rheumatic fever nor diagnostic of serious cardiac involvement, is frequent in acute rheumatic fever (about 25 percent of all cases), and other nonspecific electrocardiographic changes are also common. Anemia, due to the suppression of erythropoiesis characteristic of inflammatory diseases or of chronic infections, is another feature of rheumatic activity.

COURSE AND PROGNOSIS. The course of rheumatic fever varies greatly and is impossible to predict at

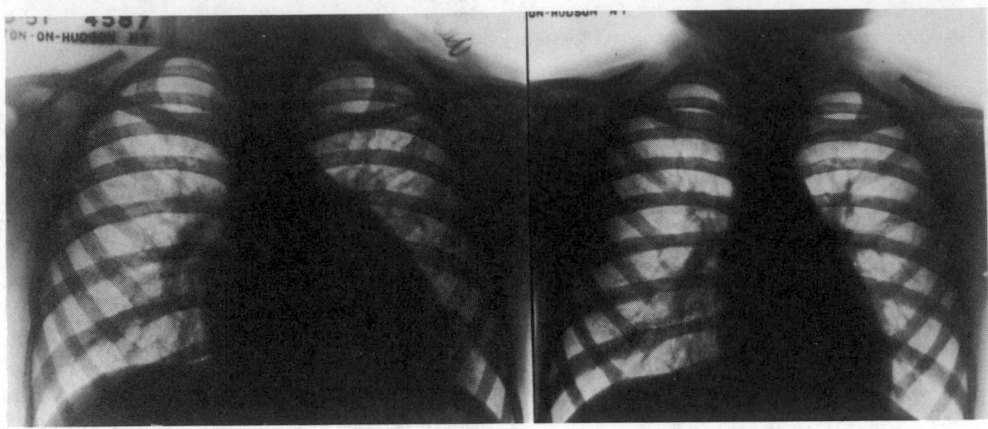

Fig. 5. Healing of acute rheumatic carditis in an 8-year-old girl during a period of 6 months of convalescence. Chest radiogram on left taken during acute rheumatic carditis with congestive heart failure. Chest radiogram on the right taken after complete recovery from the acute episode, 5 months later.

the onset of the disease. In general, however, approximately 75 percent of acute rheumatic attacks subside within 6 weeks, 90 percent within 12 weeks, and less than 5 percent persist more than 6 months. The latter usually consist of severe, intractable forms of rheumatic carditis or stubborn and persistent cases of Sydenham's chorea, both of which may persist for as long as several years. Once acute rheumatic fever has subsided and more than 2 months have elapsed after withdrawal of treatment with salicylates or adrenal corticosteroids, rheumatic fever does not recur in the absence of new streptococcal infections. Recurrences of rheumatic fever are most common within the first 5 years of the initial attack and tend to decline with increasing duration of freedom from rheumatic activity. The frequency of recurrences is dependent upon the frequency and severity of streptococcal infection, the presence or absence of rheumatic heart disease following an attack, and the duration of freedom from the last attack. Between 50 and 70 percent of patients may survive their initial attack of rheumatic fever without signs of heart disease. The murmurs of rheumatic heart disease usually appear during the first few weeks of the acute rheumatic attack. Approximately 70 percent of patients who develop carditis do so within the first week of the disease, 85 percent within the first 12 weeks of the disease, and almost all within 6 months from the onset of the acute attack. Thereafter, if significant murmurs have not appeared, the prognosis for a patient in whom recurrences are prevented is excellent. In several large studies it has been shown that about 95 percent of patients who escaped carditis during an acute rheumatic attack have normal hearts when examined 5 years later if recurrences have been prevented. Moreover, the prognosis differs markedly with the degree of cardiac involvement during acute rheumatic fever, as reflected by the intensity and the kind of murmurs heard and by the presence of congestive heart failure. The percentage of patients who,

5 years after the attack, will have stigmas and presumably permanent heart disease is approximately 20 percent in those whose attack of carditis was relatively mild and characterized only by a soft organic apical systolic murmur, 30 percent in those with louder organic apical systolic murmurs, 52 percent in patients with diastolic murmurs, and 70 percent in those with congestive heart failure of pericarditis. Thus, the healing rate of rheumatic carditis is quite high even in patients with severe attacks. (See Fig. 5.)

Recurrences of rheumatic fever tend to be "mimetic." Thus, patients who have Sydenham's chorea as the only manifestation of rheumatic fever frequently have repeated attacks of "pure" chorea. Those who have polyarthritis alone frequently have recurrences of this manifestation and develop acute carditis on subsequent attacks much less frequently than those in whom carditis was present in a previous attack. Recurrences are most damaging, therefore, in patients with rheumatic heart disease in whom the probability of reactivating carditis in a subsequent attack is greatest.

Chronic Rheumatic Carditis and the Course of Rheumatic Heart Disease. The remarkable variability in the course of rheumatic carditis and rheumatic valvular disease stems from several factors: (1) the variability in the duration and severity of the rheumatic inflammation; (2) the amount of scarring of the valves and myocardium following the abatement of the acute inflammation; (3) the location and severity of the hemodynamic lesion due to valvular insufficiency or stenosis; (4) the frequency of recurrent bouts of carditis; and (5) the progression of valvular calcification and sclerosis, which occurs as a secondary phenomenon in a deformed or injured valve without recurrent or persistent rheumatic inflammation (such as is seen in congenital valvular disease or following healed acute bacterial endocarditis). These factors, and possibly others not yet appreciated, produce striking variations in the clinical syndromes of rheumatic heart disease. The hemodynamic complications of long-standing inactive rheumatic valvular disease, as they present later in adult life (such as tight mitral or aortic stenosis or mitral, aortic, or tricuspid insufficiency) are described in detail in textbooks of adult cardiology. Two conditions are discussed below, however, which present particularly challenging problems in the diagnosis of rheumatic carditis.

Chronic rheumatic myocarditis. In this syndrome, the presenting picture is one of chronic heart failure in a patient with a markedly dilated heart with physical, roentgenographic, and electrocardiographic findings of mitral regurgitation. The differentiation of this syndrome from other forms of chronic myocarditis may be very difficult, if not impossible, when the associated extracardiac features of rheumatic fever (chorea, polyarthritis, and so forth) are not present. Although rheumatic fever does not produce *isolated* myocarditis but is almost invariably a *pancarditis,* the pericardial inflammation may not be clearly evident and the mitral valvulitis may not be distinguishable from mitral regurgitation due to dilatation of the mitral ring. In such cases one must search diligently for: an evanescent friction rub, evidence of pericardial effusion by special methods, the appearance of a soft aortic regurgitation murmur, rheumatic pneumonitis, and such extracardiac clues as fever responding promptly to salicylates, arthralgias, transient subcutaneous nodules, erythema marginatum, and so on. Disproportionate dilation of the left atrium, frequency of first or second degree heart block, and systemic reactions to the inflammatory process, such as normocytic-normochromic anemia, markedly increased ESR, increased alpha-2 and gamma globulins, all may contribute support for the clinical diagnosis of chronic rheumatic myocarditis.

Streptococcal antibodies may no longer be increased when the patient is observed with this syndrome, because the onset of the attack may have been insidious and several months may have elapsed before the patient received medical attention. The course of chronic rheumatic carditis may be intractable and end fatally after months or even several years. Often, however, the patient improves rather suddenly and even recovers cardiac reserve dramatically in association with the disappearance of systemic manifestations of the inflammatory process. The heart may remain large, it may decrease somewhat in size, or in occasional instances may return to almost normal size with varying degrees of residual valvular deformity. Such a course signals the termination of the "toxic" phase of the rheumatic process and thereafter the course of rheumatic heart disease depends on the variables in healing cited above.

Recurrent rheumatic carditis in patients with preexisting rheumatic heart disease. When rheumatic fever recurs in patients with rheumatic heart disease incurred in a previous attack, it may be difficult, and sometimes impossible, to determine whether or not the heart is inflamed again. In such patients, the following clinical findings confirm active carditis: (1) the appearance of a *new* murmur (such as aortic regurgitation in patients who previously had mitral disease only); (2) a pericardial friction rub; (3) sudden enlargement of the cardiac shadow due to pericardial effusion; and (4) *heart failure* in a patient who, prior to the recurrence, had good cardiac reserve despite his valvular deformities.

A particularly difficult problem to unravel is that of chronic congestive heart failure in a child or adolescent with long-standing rheumatic heart disease associated with severe aortic and/or mitral valvular lesions. In such patients *failure to respond to intensive therapy of congestive heart failure should always raise the issue of active rheumatic carditis.* Intractable heart failure due to hemodynamic factors alone is quite rare in young hearts, whose myocardial reserve usually can withstand even profound degrees of valvular insufficiency. Tight mitral or aortic stenosis is relatively rare in this age group. Increasingly aggressive cardiac surgery for severe rheumatic valvular deformity may tempt the clinician to permit open heart surgery for the insertion of a valvular prosthesis. Such procedures are usually disastrous when the cause of heart failure is active rheumatic myocarditis. In children or adolescents, the diagnosis of intractable heart failure due to the hemodynamic lesion of rheumatic valvular disease alone should be made only by the most experienced clinicians, and even then with considerable caution.

DIFFERENTIAL DIAGNOSIS. Early cases of rheumatic fever may be confused with other diseases which begin with acute polyarthritis. It is wise to exclude septicemia by blood cultures, particularly because such infections may be masked by penicillin given for presumed acute rheumatic fever. Polyarthritis due to subacute bacterial endocarditis in a patient with preexisting rheumatic heart disease may be considered to be a recurrence of acute rheumatic fever. If streptococcal antibodies are not increased, polyarthritis should be attributed to some cause other than rheumatic fever. At times, however, such antibodies may be increased coincidentally with the onset of some other rheumatic disease, such as rheumatoid arthritis, and observation of the course of the disease over several weeks or months will be necessary to clarify the situation. In rheumatoid arthritis, joint involvement may persist and characteristic joint deformities may appear. The latter are not seen in rheumatic fever. The rheumatoid factor so characteristic of rheumatoid arthritis is not usually present in rheumatic fever (less than 10 percent); its appearance when present is evanescent and in low titer. LE cells and antibodies against nuclear components are absent in rheumatic fever. Rheumatic pericarditis and myocarditis, associated with cardiac enlargement and heart failure, are both almost invariably associated with valvular lesions which produce significant murmurs.

Overdiagnosis of rheumatic fever should be avoided. Unless ill-defined febrile syndromes are clearly associated with a major manifestation of rheumatic fever (polyarthritis, carditis, erythema marginatum, subcutaneous nodules, or chorea), the diagnosis of rheumatic fever should not be made. A common error is the premature, vigorous administration of corticosteroids or salicylates before the signs and symptoms of rheumatic fever are unmistakable. This often leaves an ill-defined syndrome, only presumptively rheumatic fever; and the subsequent management of the patient, particularly the indications for long-term chemoprophylaxis, is in doubt. In the absence of a curative agent, one should not suppress the signs and symptoms of rheumatic fever until they are clearly expressed.

Particularly confusing in the differential diagnosis of rheumatic fever is the drug sensitivity with fever and polyarthritis which may occur after administration of penicillin for a previous pharyngitis. Urticaria or angioneurotic edema if present helps differentiate penicillin sensitivity in such cases. The abdominal pain of rheumatic fever may be mistaken for appendicitis, and the crisis of sickle-cell anemia may also be associated with joint pain, enlargement of the heart, and cardiac murmurs. The rapidity with which the arthritis symptoms of rheumatic fever are controlled with salicylates is characteristic of this disease. In other forms of arthritis, salicylates are usually much less effective. Dramatic response to salicylates does not in itself, however, establish a diagnosis of rheumatic fever.

In order to help clarify the diagnosis of rheumatic fever, the American Heart Association has accepted and modified criteria usually referred to as the "Jones Criteria." They are not to be used as a substitute for good medical judgment but are recommended as a guide for careful study of questionable cases. The criteria are presented in Table 4. The presence of two major criteria, or of one major and two minor criteria, indicates a high probability of the presence of rheumatic fever if supported by evidence of a preceding streptococcal infection. The absence of the latter should always make the diagnosis questionable, except in the situation in which rheumatic fever is first discovered after a long latent period from the antecedent infection (Sydenham's chorea or low-grade carditis). Because the prognosis may differ according to the major manifestations, for recording purposes the diagnosis of rheumatic fever should be followed by a list of the major manifestations present, e.g., rheumatic fever manifested by polyarthritis and carditis. An indication of the severity of carditis in terms of presence or absence of congestive heart failure and cardiomegaly is also advisable.

TREATMENT. There is no specific cure for rheumatic fever, and no known measures change the course of the attack. Good supportive therapy, however, can reduce the mortality and morbidity of the disease.

Chemotherapy. After rheumatic fever is first diagnosed, a course of penicillin should be given to

TABLE 4. *Jones Criteria (Revised) for Guidance in the Diagnosis of Rheumatic Fever*

Major Manifestations	Minor Manifestations
Carditis	Clinical
Polyarthritis	Previous rheumatic fever or
Chorea	rheumatic heart disease
Erythema	Arthralgia
marginatum	Fever
Subcutaneous	
nodules	Laboratory
	Acute phase reactants
	Erythrocyte sedimentation
	rate, C-reactive protein,
	leucocytosis
	Prolonged P-R interval

Plus

Supporting Evidence of Preceding Streptococcal Infection (increased ASO or other streptococcal antibodies; positive throat culture for Group A streptococcus; recent scarlet fever).

The presence of two major criteria, or of one major and two minor criteria, indicates a high probability of the presence of rheumatic fever if supported by evidence of a preceding streptococcal infection. The absence of this supporting evidence makes the diagnosis doubtful, except in situations in which rheumatic fever is first discovered after a long latent period from the antecedent infection (e.g., Sydenham's chorea, or low-grade carditis).

eliminate Group A streptococci. This is advisable even if bacteriologic examination yields throat cultures negative for streptococci, since the organisms may be present in areas inaccessible to swabs. It is preferable to administer penicillin parenterally. An effective course is either a single injection of 1.2 million units of benzathine penicillin intramuscularly or 600,000 units of procaine penicillin intramuscularly daily for 10 days. Attempts to reduce ultimate heart damage by administering penicillin early in the acute rheumatic attack in larger doses have not been successful to date. After completion of the therapeutic course of penicillin, continuous protection from reinfection with streptococci should be provided by instituting one of the prophylactic regimens described later.

Suppressive Therapy. Both corticosteroids and salicylates are of considerable value in controlling the toxic manifestations of rheumatic fever, in contributing to the comfort of the patient, and in combating anorexia, anemia, and constitutional symptoms. In severe rheumatic carditis associated with heart failure, such nonspecific anti-inflammatory effects may reduce the burden upon the laboring heart. Occasionally, they may tilt the balance in favor of survival of a critically ill patient. Corticosteroids are more potent than salicylates in suppressing acute exudative inflammation, and some patients in whom salicylates fail to control the disease respond quickly to relatively large doses of corticosteroids. Whether or not intensive corticosteroid therapy instituted early in the first rheumatic attack can reduce the degree of ultimate cardiac scarring is a point which is still somewhat at issue in patients with relatively mild cardiac involvement. Where carditis is more severe, all carefully controlled studies fail to reveal any clear superiority of corticosteroids over aspirin in terms of modifying the duration of the acute disease or residual heart damage after five years of follow-up. However, there is still considerable variation in the recommendations concerning the use of these agents.

Most authorities now use salicylates rather than corticosteroids to treat children with rheumatic fever but with no evidence of carditis, since the prognosis for recovery without permanent stigmas in such cases is greater than 95 percent. If signs and symptoms are not adequately suppressed by salicylates, corticosteroids are substituted. Patients with mild carditis are probably given corticosteroids in most instances, although it is in such cases that there is the greatest disagreement about their value. Patients with severe carditis are usually treated promptly with corticosteroids, particularly if heart failure is evident, in which case parenteral doses of mercurial diuretics are given and salt intake is restricted.

No arbitrary schedule of doses of corticosteroids or salicylates is recommended, although they should be adequate to achieve prompt symptomatic improvement. Salicylates are usually given as acetylsalicylic acid in a total daily dose initially of 0.15 g per kg (1 grain per pound) of body weight, up to a maximum daily dose of 10 g. Corticosteroids are usually started in doses comparable for different analogues to that of 10 to 15 mg of prednisone every 6 hours. The duration of treatment should be guided by the expected course of the disease and by the severity of the rheumatic process in the individual case. Because most rheumatic attacks last 6 weeks, treatment should be continuous at least for this period, with doses tapered during the last 2 weeks. Should clinical symptoms relapse (*rebound phenomenon*), an additional 4 to 6 weeks of treatment is advised. In stubborn attacks, such courses may have to be repeated several times. Weekly tests for C-reactive protein in the blood and for the erythrocyte sedimentation rate are useful in following the healing process, particularly when treatment with corticosteroids or salicylates is gradually withdrawn. With adequate suppressive doses, the C-reactive protein should disappear from the blood, and the erythrocyte sedimentation rate should decrease. Reappearance of C-reactive protein and an increase in the ESR upon withdrawal of treatment indicate continued rheumatic activity unless other causes of inflammation are present.

Salicylate *toxicity* is encountered frequently when large doses are administered. Some individuals develop toxic symptoms from relatively small amounts. Nausea, vomiting, headaches, tinnitus, blurred vision, and mental confusion are the most common symptoms. Delirium, mania, and hallucinations are more serious cerebral symptoms. Hyperpnea due to direct stimulation of the respiratory center may result in respiratory alkalosis; and in more severe cases ketosis, acidosis, and circulatory collapse may ensue. Salicylates tend to inhibit prothrombin synthesis and interfere with platelet adhesiveness and function. This can be severe enough to result in purpuric manifestations, ecchymosis, and other forms of hemorrhage.

The undesirable side effects of treatment with corticosteroids are described in Chapter 16.

Treatment of Heart Failure. Treatment of heart failure during acute rheumatic fever requires special consideration. Digitalis may fail to benefit the patient significantly in the presence of very severe myocarditis. In many instances, however, it may be used with success to relieve congestive heart failure, particularly if the mechanical factors of valvular insufficiency contribute to the problem. The rapidly excreted digitalis glycosides, such as digoxin, are useful during the stage of acute carditis because of the frequency with which digitalis toxicity may be encountered. Diuretics may help, particularly when treatment with steroids is complicated by fluid retention and an increase in the symptoms and signs of heart failure. Oxygen should be administered for severe heart failure and when cyanosis is present. Failure of the patient to respond to these supportive measures and to the antirheumatic agents is an ominous sign of overwhelming rheumatic carditis, and such cases frequently succumb.

Treatment of Chorea. The signs and symptoms of chorea usually do not respond well to treatment with antirheumatic agents. Because the patient with chorea is frequently emotionally unstable and because the manifestations of chorea may be exaggerated by emotional trauma, complete mental and physical rest is essential. Patients with chorea should be kept in a quiet room and cared for by sympathetic attendants. If the chorea is severe, large doses of phenobarbital rather than tranquilizers alone are usually necessary to control purposeless movements. Padded sideboards for the bed may be necessary to avoid injury to the patient. In the absence of other evidences of acute rheumatic disease, it is advisable to allow gradual resumption of physical activity when improvement is apparent rather than waiting for all choreiform movements to disappear, which may require many months.

Because of the great variability in the course of chorea it is difficult to evaluate the effectiveness of various therapeutic measures. It is well to remember that chorea is a self-limited disease which is usually not followed by significant neurologic sequelae and that good results are almost invariably obtained by patient, attentive nursing care and by conservative medical management.

PROPHYLAXIS. *Prevention of Recurrences of Rheumatic Fever.* The most efficient regimen for continuous prophylaxis against Group A streptococci is a monthly intramuscular injection of 1.2 million units of benzathine penicillin. The disadvantages and discomfort of this regimen have to be weighed against the individual patient's susceptibility to recurrences. Those with rheumatic heart disease, recent rheumatic fever, and exposure to an environment in which the incidence of streptococcal infection is frequent deserves the most effective protection. As a second choice, prophylaxis may be administered orally with either 1 g of sulfadiazine daily in a single dose or 200,000 units of penicillin given twice daily on an empty stomach. The duration of continuous prophylaxis cannot be fixed arbitrarily for all patients, although the safest generalization is that it be continued indefinitely. Certainly, those under the age of 18 years should receive a continuous prophylactic regimen. A minimum period of 5 years is recommended for patients who develop rheumatic fever without carditis over the age of 18. The decision to continue prophylaxis beyond this period should take into account a number of variables. Patients with rheumatic heart disease are more susceptible to reactivation of rheumatic fever if they contract a streptococcal infection. Moreover, patients who have had carditis in a previous attack are much more likely to suffer carditis again in a subsequent attack. Climate, age, occupation, household situation, cardiac status, and length of time since the previous attack are all significant variables which influence the risk of recurrence. The decline in recurrence rates with increasing age is due to (1) decreased rate of streptococcal infection and (2) decrease in the rate of rheumatic reactivation following streptococcal infection in older rheumatic subjects. Despite this decreased rate, however, the risk of rheumatic recurrence in adults remains relatively high when the streptococcal disease encountered is severe or epidemic.

Prevention of Initial Rheumatic Attacks. Early and adequate treatment of respiratory tract infection due to Group A streptococci will prevent initial attacks of rheumatic fever. If clinical streptococcal disease were properly detected by the use of throat cultures and adequately treated, the spread of infection in a given population would be prevented, the epidemiology of streptococcal disease would be modified markedly, and the incidence of rheumatic fever in the community would be diminished. In communities where Group A streptococcal disease has been diagnosed early and treated well and where socioeconomic standards are high, the Group A organisms cultured frequently from school children's throats may be of relatively low virulence and may cause rheumatic fever less frequently than in epidemics wherein virulent strains are prevalent.

Streptococcal pharyngitis is adequately treated by a single intramuscular injection of 600,000 units of benzathine penicillin in children less than 10 years of age or 1.2 million units in older children and adults. Any alternate plan of parenteral therapy or combined parenteral and oral therapy should provide for treatment over a period of 10 days. If oral penicillin is employed, at least 800,000 units per day in four divided doses must be given for no less than 10 days to achieve results comparable to a single injection of benzathine penicillin. Erythromycin in daily doses of 1 g for 10 days may be substituted in penicillin-sensitive individuals. Tetracycline is not recommended because some strains of Group A streptococci have acquired resistance to it. All Group A streptococci have so far remained extremely sensitive to penicillin.

REFERENCES

Ayoub, E. M., and Wannamaker, L. W. Evaluation of the streptococcal desoxyribonuclease B and diphosphopyridine nucleotidase antibody tests in acute rheumatic fever and acute glomerulonephritis. Pediatrics, 29:527, 1962.

Bland, E. F., and Jones, T. D. Rheumatic fever and rheumatic heart disease; a twenty year report on 1,000 patients followed since childhood. Circulation, 4:836, 1951.

Coburn, A. F., and Young, D. C. The epidemiology of hemolytic streptococcus during World War II in the United States Navy. Baltimore, Williams and Wilkins Co., 1949.

Combined Rheumatic Fever Study Group. A comparison of the effect of prednisone and acetylsalicylic acid on the incidence of residual rheumatic heart disease. New Eng. J. Med., 262:895, 1960.

Committee of the Council on Rheumatic Fever and Congenital Heart Disease. American Heart Association. Jones criteria (revised) for guidance in the diagnosis of rheumatic fever. Circulation, 32:664, 1965.

Committee on Prevention of Rheumatic Fever and Bacterial Endocarditis. American Heart Association. Prevention of rheumatic fever. Circulation, 31:948, 1965.

Denny, F. W., Wannamaker, L. W., Brink, W. R., Rammelkamp, C. H., Jr., and Custer, E. A. Prevention of rheumatic fever: Treatment of the preceding streptococcic infection. J.A.M.A., 143:151, 1950.

Dudding, B. A., and Ayoub, E. M. Persistence of streptococcal group A antibody in patients with rheumatic valvular disease. J. Exp. Med., 128:1081, 1968.

Irvington House Study. Rheumatic fever in children and adolescents: A long term epidemiologic study of subsequent prophylaxis, streptococcal infections, and clinical sequelae. Ann. Intern. Med. (Suppl. 5), 60:4, 1964.

Johnson, E. E., Stollerman, G. H., and Grossman, B. J. Rheumatic recurrences in patients not receiving continuous prophylaxis. J.A.M.A., 190:407, 1964.

Jones, T. D. The diagnosis of rheumatic fever. J.A.M.A., 126:481, 1944.

Kaplan, M. H., and Suchy, M. L. Immunologic relation of streptococcal and tissue antigens. II. Cross-reaction of antisera to mammalian heart tissue with a cell wall constituent of certain strains of group A streptococci. J. Exp. Med., 119:643, 1964.

Klemperer, P. The concept of collagen disease. Amer. J. Path., 26:505, 1950.

Markowitz, M., and Kuttner, A. G. Rheumatic Fever: Diagnosis, Management and Prevention. Philadelphia, W. B. Saunders Co., 1965.

McCarty, M., ed. Streptococcal Infections. New York, Columbia Univ. Press, 1954.

Rantz, L. A., Randall, E., and Ranta, H. H. Antistreptolysin "O." A study of this antibody in health and hemolytic streptococcus respiratory disease in man. Amer. J. Med., 5:3, 1948.

Siegel, A. C., Johnson, E. E., and Stollerman, G. H. Controlled studies of streptococcal pharyngitis in a pediatric population. I. Factors related to the attack rate of rheumatic fever. New Eng. J. Med., 265:559, 1961.

Stollerman, G. H. Factors determining the attack rate of rheumatic fever. J.A.M.A., 177:823, 1961.

—— Lewis, A. J., Schultz, I., and Taranta, A. Relationship of immune response to group A streptococci to the course of acute, chronic and recurrent rheumatic fever. Amer. J. Med., 20:163, 1956.

—— and Pearce, I. A. The changing epidemiology of rheumatic fever and acute glomerulonephritis. Advances Intern. Med., 14:201, 1968.

Taranta, A. Relation of isolated recurrences of Sydenham's chorea to preceding streptococcal infections. New Eng. J. Med., 260:1204, 1959.

Thomas, L., ed. Rheumatic Fever, A Symposium. Minneapolis, Univ. Minnesota Press, 1952.

Todd, E. W. Antihaemolysin titres in haemolytic streptococcal infections and their significance in rheumatic fever. Brit. J. Exp. Path., 13:248, 1932.

Wannamaker, L. W. Differences between streptococcal infections of the throat and of the skin. New Eng. J. Med., 282:23, 78, 1970.

—— and Ayoub, E. M. Antibody titers in acute rheumatic fever. Circulation, 21:598, 1960.

Uhr, M. W., ed. Streptococcus, Rheumatic Fever and Glomerulonephritis. Baltimore, Williams and Wilkins Co., 1964.

United Kingdom and United States Joint Report. The treatment of acute rheumatic fever in children: a cooperative clinical trial of ACTH, cortisone, and aspirin. Circulation, 11:343, 1955.

—— The evolution of rheumatic heart disease in children: five year report of a cooperative clinical trial of ACTH, cortisone, and aspirin. Circulation, 22:503, 1960.

Zabriskie, J. B., and Freimer, E. H. An immunological relationship between the group A streptococcus and mammalian muscle. J. Exp. Med., 124:661, 1966.

12.2
JUVENILE RHEUMATOID ARTHRITIS
(Chronic Polyarthritis; Still's Disease)

Rheumatoid arthritis is a systemic disease which not only involves the joints but produces extensive connective tissue and visceral lesions. Most investigators believe that rheumatoid arthritis in the child is the same clinical entity as that observed in the adult, but there are many differences between the childhood and adult form of this disease. The variety of names for rheumatoid arthritis in children has led to confusion. Juvenile rheumatoid arthritis describes the total disease entity and is the preferred designation, whereas the term "Still's disease" should be reserved for those cases exhibiting the classical triad of polyarthritis, lymphadenitis, and splenomegaly. The term "Wissler-Fanconi syndrome" (subsepsis allergica) refers to a clinical variety of juvenile rheumatoid arthritis in which preceding, during, or in the absence of polyarthritis, there is a septic course of high, usually intermittent fever, rash, and arthralgia with leucocytosis.

ETIOLOGY. The cause is unknown. Cultures from the joints and blood either have been sterile or have yielded organisms which may well be suspected as contaminants. Focal infections, capable of elaborating an arthropathic toxin, have been incriminated because infection of some degree is frequently demonstrable in the teeth, nasal sinuses, or other foci. Their surgical removal rarely produces significant benefit and usually has no effect whatever. Morever, there is no uniformity in the organisms recovered from such foci, and the symptoms of the disease have not responded to treatment with a variety of chemotherapeutic agents.

Unlike rheumatic fever, rheumatoid arthritis bears no relation to infections with Group A streptococci. In fact, the absence of an increase in specific streptococcal antibodies is useful in differentiating this condition from acute rheumatic fever. A positive agglutination reaction for streptococci, formerly thought to have some etiologic significance, is now regarded as a nonspecific phenomenon analogous to the agglutination of sensitized sheep cells, or gamma globulin-coated latex particles, by the rheumatoid factor in the serum of these patients (see below).

Girls are affected approximately two times as often as boys. Familial incidence is uncommon. Epidemiologic studies have so far provided no clues as to the effect of environmental factors.

PATHOLOGY. Fragmentary evidence suggests that the first recognizable lesion is a vasculitis. A sustained round cell inflammatory reaction follows, which may become granulomatous, end in scarring, or resolve. The main difference between the juvenile and the adult form of the disease lies in the effect of chronic inflammation on the rate of growth and maturation of the centers of ossification in the young patient.

The joint lesion involves the synovial membranes, joint capsule, and ligaments. The synovial membrane is thickened and rough and sometimes replaced by granulation tissue, which may project into the joint cavity in large villous processes (pannous formation). The joint fluid is only moderately increased in amount. In chronic cases erosion of the joint cartilages occurs when the synovial granulation tissue extends onto the cartilage. The bones become porotic periarticularly early in the course of the disease but as a rule show no other change even after months of disease activity. Fibrous or bony ankylosis may eventually occur. Ankylosis, flexion contractures, and localized growth disturbances are responsible for the deformities that are occasionally observed in patients who have recovered.

In some patients the spleen and lymph nodes are enlarged; histologically they show no characteristic anatomic alterations.

CLINICAL FEATURES. Although the disease commonly commences after the second year, it may make its appearance as early as the sixth month of life. There may be an acute febrile onset *with or without joint symptoms,* or a gradual progression of swelling, pain, and tenderness of one or more joints with little or no increase in body temperature. In some cases, the arthritis may begin with involvement of a single joint. In other cases, the original manifestations are so fulminating, and leucocytosis and fever so marked, that pyogenic infection, leukemia, or rheumatic fever is suspected. In still other patients, fever and general symptoms may be present for weeks or months before articular manifestations appear. The joints are usually attacked symmetrically, and many are affected—in most cases the shoulders, elbows, wrists, fingers, knees, ankles, and feet; less frequently, the joints of the cervical spine, jaw, and sternoclavicular articulation. Within a few weeks or months after onset, the appearance of the fingers becomes characteristic, the proximal interphalangeal joint being the one earliest and most severely affected, so that the digit tapers from a thick base to a fine tip, the so-called *spindle fingers* (Fig. 6). The articular involvement causes flexion of the joints to a greater or lesser extent, and this deformity increases with the progress of the disease. Attempts to bring the joints into their normal position by active or passive motion generally fail, both because of pain and because of the change in the periarticular structures. Often in patients with juvenile rheumatoid arthritis who do not complain of pain referable to their joints, the arthritis goes unrecognized. Fever is a special feature of juvenile rheumatoid arthritis in that it may be

the only presenting symptom, particularly in very young children, and the problem is often that of a fever of undetermined origin. Two common events usually clarify the diagnosis in such cases: the typical rheumatoid rash appears often at the height of the fever, or polyarthritis appears during the course of investigation of the cause of fever. Lymphadenopathy, which is usually generalized, occurs in about 20 percent of patients. The spleen is enlarged in about one-third of all cases, the liver somewhat less often. Ocular complications may be a striking feature of the disease. *Chronic iridocyclitis* is frequently severe and before the introduction of steroid therapy often caused blindness. Occasionally it occurs long before the onset of the arthritis and may produce serious damage before being recognized. *Uveitis* may also be insidious in onset and many of its effects are irreversible. It is important for physicians caring for patients with juvenile rheumatoid arthritis to be alert to these ocular complications. Prompt treatment with steroids will usually control these inflammatory lesions and prevent serious permanent ocular damage. However, *posterior subcapsular cataracts* may occur in patients who have received high doses of steroids for very long periods of time.

Subcutaneous nodules are relatively uncommon in juvenile rheumatoid compared with rheumatic fever. *Cutaneous manifestations* consist of a typical rheumatoid rash which is a blotchy, erythematous or violaceous, macular or maculopapular eruption, involving chiefly the trunk and also the volar aspects of the arms and the inner aspects of the thighs. The skin lesions may also be an early manifestation, even preceding the appearance of joint involvement. In some cases such eruptions appear and disappear from time to time throughout the course of the disease. Although *pericarditis* is frequently present below the threshold of clinical detection, it may appear as a clinical problem in about 5 percent of patients. The absence of myocardial and endocardial disturbances provides a striking contrast with acute rheumatic fever. Aortic valvular lesions have been described in juvenile rheumatoid arthritis, but these are quite rare.

Growth disturbances, particularly localized alterations in bone growth, are common. Local growth disturbances depend presumably on changes in blood supply to epiphyseal growth centers, which speed up both growth rate and fusion of epiphyses (Fig. 7). If the temporomandibular joint is involved, the accelerated rate of growth of the condylar center of ossification may eventually result in premature closure of the epiphysis, with cessation of further growth. The ramus of the mandible thus ends up shortened, producing a *micrognathous* effect, with overbite. These localized growth disturbances may occur in proximal or peripheral joints. A femoral head, for example, may become too big for its acetabulum. A digit may end up shorter than its normal counterpart because of premature closure of some of its epiphyses.

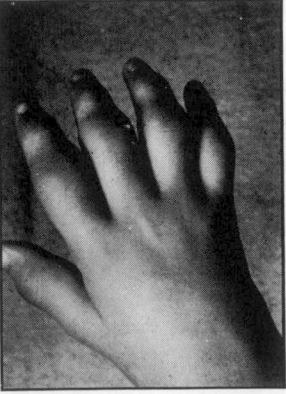

Fig. 6.   Fusiform swelling of fingers in rheumatoid arthritis.

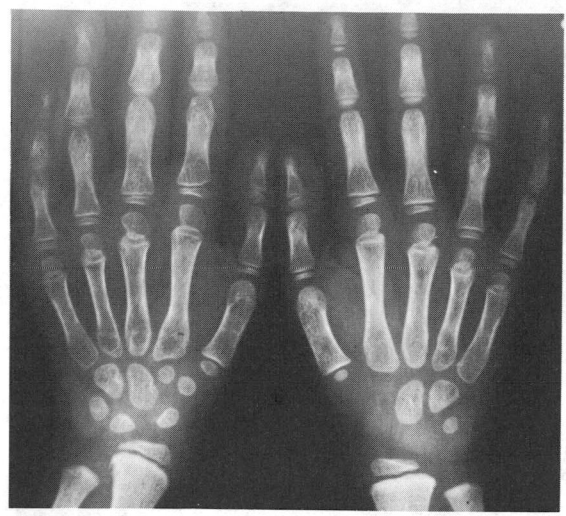

Fig. 7. Roentgenogram of hand in juvenile rheumatoid arthritis. Five-year-old girl with involvement of the left hand and wrist. There is soft tissue swelling about the proximal interphalangeal joints of the index and middle fingers, as well as the wrist. Periosteal accretion is present along the proximal phalanges of the involved digits, while at the same time the bones of the entire hand are porotic. Skeletal maturation in the carpal bones of the left wrist is accelerated to the 6-year-old level. The right wrist, for comparison, is normal.

LABORATORY FINDINGS. The most characteristic laboratory finding of rheumatoid arthritis is the presence in blood of an immunoglobulin M (IgM) which has been named *rheumatoid factor*. This substance has all of the features of antibody against immunoglobulin G (IgG) and is thus thought to be an autoantibody directed against conventional 7S antibodies. The mechanism of its production is unknown. It appears in other diseases, such as systemic lupus erythematosus, dermatomyositis, scleroderma, and subacute bacterial endocarditis, but less frequently and usually in lower titer than in rheumatoid arthritis. The usual serologic tests for rheumatoid factor, so reliable in adults, are positive in less than one-third of patients with juvenile rheumatoid arthritis, and then usually in low titer, leading some authorities to consider juvenile rheumatoid arthritis a different disease from the adult form. Others, however, have interpreted this as a diminished ability of the younger child to produce rheumatoid factor. The frequency with which rheumatoid factor has been identified varies greatly in different series, depending upon the nature of the tests used, the age range of the patients, and the number and frequency of the determinations; however there is general agreement that these tests are less useful diagnostically in children than in adults with this condition. In juvenile rheumatoid arthritis, the *erythrocyte sedimentation rate* may remain significantly elevated for months or even years despite therapy. A moderate degree of *normochromic, normocytic anemia* is usually present and is most marked during febrile periods. Mild *leucocytosis* often accompanies the fever; occasionally eosinophilia is present. In some cases, the concentration of globulin in serum is increased. *LE cells* are present less commonly than in adults with severe rheumatoid arthritis. Although also less common than in adults, *antinuclear antibodies* are present more frequently than LE cells.

A most helpful diagnostic finding is involvement of cervical intervertebral articulations (*zygapophysial arthritis*) (Fig. 8), which has not been observed thus far in either rheumatic fever or in systemic lupus erythematosus. Bony ankylosis of the posterior elements of the cervical spine may be considered virtually pathognomonic of juvenile rheumatoid arthritis. Sacroiliac abnormalities can occasionally be demonstrated radiographically; however, the classical adult rheumatoid spondylitis has no counterpart in infancy or childhood.

Joint fluid analysis is helpful but sometimes closed synovial biopsy or arthrotomy may be required. Synovial fluid analysis is similar to that of adults. The suppression of synovial complement activity, so characteristic of rheumatoid arthritis joint fluid in adults, may be less striking in the child. A suggested guide to the diagnostic features of synovianalysis is presented in tables 5 and 6 of Section 12.7.

DIAGNOSIS. The well-developed case of rheumatoid arthritis is easily recognized. It is at the onset of the disease that difficulty arises. *Acute rheumatic fever* poses the most common differential diagnostic problem. The absence of increased streptococcal antibodies points to rheumatoid arthritis. Persistence of polyarthritis for more than 3 months and the appearance of permanent changes in or around the joints, such as contractures, ankylosis, muscle wasting, and fusiform enlargement, rule out the diagnosis of rheumatic fever. The relative absence of pain in acutely involved joints should also raise a suspicion that an arthritic disease is juvenile rheumatoid arthritis rather than rheumatic fever. Similarly, the arthritis of rheumatic fever almost invariably responds to salicylates, whereas a significant percentage of patients with rheumatoid arthritis fail to show a satisfactory response to adequate doses of this drug.

Osteomyelitis and *suppurative arthritis* must frequently be considered, particularly when rheumatoid arthritis begins in one joint. In rheumatoid arthritis the disease rarely remains monoarticular more than a few months; but occasionally, when it does, *synovial biopsy* must be made to rule out *tuberculosis*. Less common conditions may cause confusion, including rat bite fever due to *Streptobacillus moniliformis*, allergic hydrarthrosis, systemic lupus erythematosus, ulcerative colitis or regional ileitis associated with arthritis, and leukemic bone pain. Although various criteria have been proposed for the diagnosis of juvenile rheumatoid arthritis, it is suggested that all of the following be met: (1) polyarthritis or monoarticular arthritis for a minimum period of 3 months,

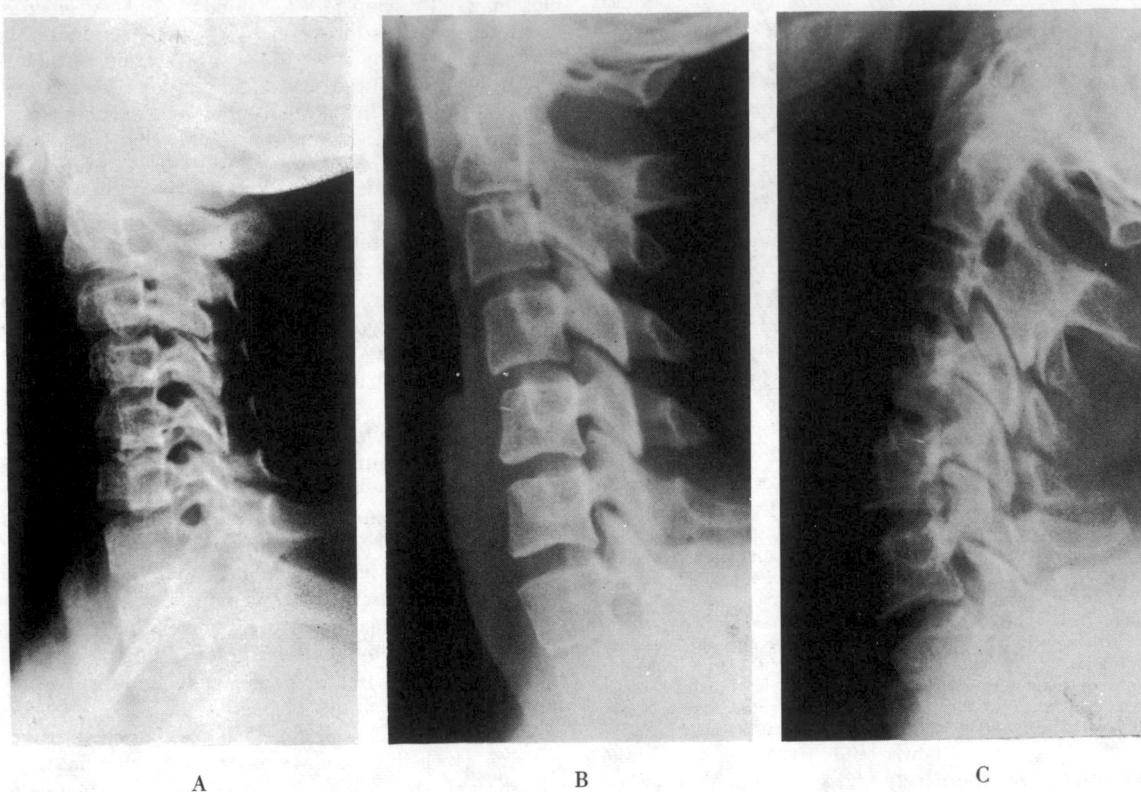

A   B   C

Fig. 8. Cervical spine in a patient with peripheral joint disease, pericarditis, subcutaneous nodules, and mandibular dysplasia. A. Age 9 years. There is loss of sharp margins of the articular facets of the C_2-C_3 zygapophysial joints and straightening of the cervical lordosis. B. Age 15 years. These joints are fused and the intervertebral disc is narrowed. C. Age 18 years. Resumption of normal cervical curvature in spite of bony fusion at the C_2-C_3 level.

or a period of less than 3 months if accompanied by at least one of the following: iritis, rash, flexion contractures, ankylosis, muscle wasting, anemia, white cell count of 20,000 or more without other explanation, complaints of cervical spine with or without radiographic changes in the cervical zygapophysial joints, polyarthritis with pericarditis in the absence of myocarditis and endocarditis, no symptomatic response to therapeutic levels of aspirin; (2) constitutional symptoms consisting of any combination of fever, weakness, and weight loss; (3) increased erythrocyte sedimentation rate; (4) exclusion of diagnosis of rheumatic fever, systemic lupus erythematosus, periarteritis nodosa, dermatomyositis, scleroderma, tuberculous synovitis, leukemia, or lymphoma.

TREATMENT. The objective of treatment of juvenile rheumatoid arthritis is to return the child to as nearly normal a life as possible with the least possible delay. Achievement of this goal involves the active participation not only of the patient but also of parents, who must understand the multiple facets of the disease, including its potential chronicity and the inability

to predict its course. Once the acute stage of the disease is controlled, the child should be home rather than in the hospital, activity should be encouraged as tolerated, attendance at school should be encouraged, and all means available should be used to prevent contractures and gross deformities.

Palliation of signs and symptoms of the disease requires the use of anti-inflammatory drugs. The drug of choice is acetylsalicylic acid in large doses, averaging initially 110 mg per kilogram of body weight per day in five or six divided doses.

Unlike the dramatic salicylate effect in rheumatic fever, the high fever of juvenile rheumatoid arthritis more often subsides gradually over 3 to 4 days and may require as long as 3 to 4 weeks. As severe systemic manifestations are controlled, attempts should be made to reduce aspirin to a minimum dose of 90 mg per kilogram per day in order to avoid acute salicylate intoxication. Early signs of salicylism, such as tinnitus, drowsiness, and hyperpnea, are easily overlooked in the very young child. Infants develop intense ketosis and acidosis rapidly following the earlier toxicity of respiratory alkalosis which results from hyperpnea.

Corticosteroids should be reserved for patients who do not respond to salicylates. Corticosteroids can bring about early and remarkable relief of symptoms and signs but should be used with caution. Their long-term effect on growth, endocrine balance, and resistance to infection is so apt to be harmful that it is wise to keep the dosage as low as feasible. Combined with salicylates, they also increase the chance of gastric irritation and resultant hemorrhage. Long-term use of corticosteroids also can increase osteoporosis, already marked from disuse, and lead to fracture or, more commonly, collapse of vertebrae or avascular necrosis of the femoral head. Given in high doses for long periods, corticosteroids can also lead to the formation of posterior subcapsular cataracts.

Other anti-inflammatory agents in children are of limited value because of dangerous toxic reactions. Gold therapy does not appear to be more toxic in children than adults but because of its obvious limitations its use should be reserved only for the most severe and rapidly progressive cases that can be controlled in no other way. Antimalarials (such as chloroquine) are of uncertain value. Reported instances of fatal cardiorespiratory arrest from as little as 1 g of chloroquine have made the use of this agent impractical in children despite its continued rather widespread use in adults. In children, phenylbutazone and oxyphenbutazone may produce severe toxic effects, such as hepatitis and pancytopenia. Indomethacin, used extensively in adults with rheumatoid arthritis, has been considered contraindicated in children because of reports of sudden death associated with its use in the younger age groups.

With the help of aspirin and judicious doses of corticosteroids, it is usually possible to keep patients sufficiently comfortable for them to want to engage in a normal amount of physical activity, which on the whole should be encouraged rather than restricted. An important aspect of management is the prevention of partial ankylosis and flexion contractures. During the phase of active arthralgia, the patient is inclined both to be totally quiet and to hold affected joints in a position of partial flexion for the relief of tension. Both of these tendencies may have harmful consequences if fully indulged. Inactivity hastens decalcification of bones and favors ankylosis. Maintenance of a joint in partial flexion tends to promote muscle shortening and renders the resumption of full range of motion more difficult after the period of discomfort has passed. Physiotherapy plays an important part in promoting relaxation and preserving muscle tone through light massage, and in preventing ankylosis by putting all joints through the full range of comfortable motion at least once daily. During rest it is better for the patient to lie flat on a fairly firm mattress rather than curl up on his side. Half-shell splints applied at night to the lower extremities may prove useful in preventing footdrop. Contractures and fixed positions of special importance, because of their relative frequency, are anteflexion of the neck, par-tial flexion of the elbow, pronation of the forearm, flexion of the wrist, metacarpophalangeal, or interphalangeal joints, flexion of the hip or knee, and footdrop. As soon as the stage of active discomfort shows signs of waning, whether through the influence of drugs or because of the unpredictable fluctuations of the disease, every encouragement should be given to the patient to resume all forms of muscular activity. Because of the unfortunate consequences of excessive inactivity, most authorities agree that activity should be encouraged even before fever has disappeared.

Although the long-term prognosis for life and for freedom from disability is good, the course of the disease is usually measured in years rather than months. Both the patients and the parents need repeated reassurance. Appreciating and lessening the patient's anxiety are of fundamental importance in helping him adjust to his disease, and a sustained and energetic effort should be made to minimize his pain and deformities until the process abates. The relatively good prognosis despite the chronicity of the disease should be emphasized: one-half recover without any joint deformity; one-third continue into adulthood and only one-sixth develop severe disability under medical management.

REFERENCES

Ansell, B. M., and Bywaters, E. G. L. Rheumatoid arthritis (Still's disease). Pediat. Clin. N. Amer., 10: 921, 1963.

Calabro, J. J., and Marchesano, J. M. The early natural history of juvenile rheumatoid arthritis: a ten year follow-up study of 100 cases. Med. Clin. N. Amer., 52:567, 1968.

Cohen, A. S. Synovial fluid. *In* A. S. Cohen, ed., Laboratory Diagnostic Procedures. Boston, Little, Brown and Co., 1967.

Grokoest, A. W., Snyder, A. L., and Schlaeger, R. Juvenile Rheumatoid Arthritis. Boston, Little, Brown and Co., 1961.

Grossman, B. J., Ozoa, N. F., and Arya, S. C. Problems in juvenile rheumatoid arthritis. Med. Clin. N. Amer., 49:33, 1965.

Lietmen, P. S., and Bywaters, E. G. L. Pericarditis in juvenile rheumatoid arthritis. Pediatrics, 32:855, 1963.

Martel, W., Holt, J. F., and Cassidy, J. T. Roentgenologic manifestations of juvenile rheumatoid arthritis. Amer. J. Roentgen., 88:400, 1962.

Schlesinger, B., et al. Observation on the clinical course and treatment of 100 cases of Still's disease. Arch. Dis. Child., 36:65, 1961.

Smiley, W. K., May, E., and Bywaters, E. G. L. Ocular presentations of Still's disease and their treatment. Ann. Rheum. Dis., 16:371, 1957.

Toumbis, A., Franklin, E. C., McEwen, C., and Kuttner, A. G. Clinical and serologic observations in patients with juvenile rheumatoid arthritis and their relatives. J. Pediat., 62:463, 1963.

12.3

SYSTEMIC LUPUS ERYTHEMATOSUS
(LUPUS ERYTHEMATOSUS DISSEMINATUS)

Systemic lupus erythematosus (SLE) is a diffuse inflammatory disease of connective tissues of unknown cause which occurs predominantly in females (approximately 8:1). The clinical manifestations, which vary greatly, include most often intermittent fever, arthritis or arthralgia, rash, and most characteristically nephritis, pleurisy, pericarditis, endocarditis, central nervous system lesions, and leucopenia. The blood of most patients contains an antibody capable of reacting with their own cell nuclear material. In children, SLE is considerably less frequent but has the same clinical and laboratory manifestations as in adults.

PATHOGENESIS. The cause of the disease is unknown. Recent investigations, however, point to the existence of an immunopathologic aberration giving rise to heightened reactivity to diverse antigenic stimuli. The evidence includes antibodies to a variety of human cellular components and other serologic abnormalities (see below); the emergence of lupus-like syndromes after the prolonged administration of certain drugs (trimethadione, diphenylhydantoin, sulfamethoxypyridazine, and paramethadione are most often incriminated in children); and the demonstration of complement and gamma globulin in the glomerular lesions of SLE. However, there is little direct evidence that these findings account for the tissue lesions, and they may represent secondary phenomena.

Genetic factors have also been implicated because the disease has been described in two or more family members, including identical twins, in more than one generation, and in families with hypergammaglobulinemia or agammaglobulinemia. Carefully controlled family studies, however, have failed to show an increased incidence of SLE among relatives. In highly inbred strains of mice, there is a disorder resembling SLE particularly with respect to the type of glomerular lesions and the demonstration of LE cells. However, among mice of several highly inbred strains a high incidence of antinuclear antibodies was found in one commercial breeding colony, whereas there was a very low incidence of such antibodies in an independent colony of the strain in a different part of the country. Such studies suggest an infectious etiology, at least for the antinuclear antibody phenomenon in mice. These animals provide an unusual opportunity for future investigations.

PATHOLOGY. Connective tissues in various organs may reveal nonspecific alterations such as fibrinoid change in collagen and cellular infiltration, either in the walls of small blood vessels or elsewhere. *Hematoxylin bodies,* found principally in the kidneys, spleen, lymph nodes, and heart, constitute the most specific and characteristic histopathologic finding. They are homogeneous purple-staining masses of altered nuclear material which have been shown to be morphologically and histochemically identical with the inclusion body of the LE cell. They are not found with great frequency despite the presence in fatal cases of an abundance of LE cells.

Alteration of collagen and subendothelial thickening of small blood vessels may obstruct the flow of blood. These changes may be widespread or sharply limited in distribution. In the kidney, "wire loop" glomerular lesions and thickening of the basement membrane of the glomerulus are typical, but not necessarily specific, changes. The same is true of the "onion skin" lesions of periarterial fibrosis in the spleen. The synovia of the joints may show changes in small vessels and connective tissue. A sterile, verrucous endocarditis (Libman-Sacks) is characteristic and not uncommon.

Recently inclusions have been observed by electron microscopy within the cytoplasm of endothelial cells of affected glomeruli and other lesions which resemble those seen in paramyxovirus infections. So far, however, attempts to isolate viral agents from such lesions have been unsuccessful and no consistent immunologic reaction with specific antisera to known viral agents has been found.

CLINICAL FEATURES. The clinical concept of SLE has changed in recent years because of wide application of diagnostic tests and consequent recognition of early, mild, and atypical cases. The disease has been detected in patients as young as 3 years of age. The initial symptoms may be either acute or insidious, and either mild or severe. High fever is usually present throughout the course of the malignant forms. Lupus nephritis is very frequent and usually runs a fatal course; statistically it is the most serious feature of SLE. Death may result from renal failure, less commonly from secondary infection or massive hemorrhage. Cases with a chronic course commonly exhibit low-grade fever, anorexia, and weight loss. Sometimes only one or two symptoms are present at the onset. In addition to fever, one of the following may be observed: arthralgia, arthritis, pleurisy, or renal involvement.

Skin lesions, seen in about three-fourths of the cases, take a variety of forms, most of them maculopapular patches or clusters. On the face, the so-called butterfly distribution may provide an important diagnostic lead; starting on the bridge of the nose, an erythematous rash slowly extends to the malar eminences. Similar lesions may be found in the episternal region and also on the fingers, toes, and palms of the hands. Not infrequently other skin lesions, such as vesicles, nodules, purpura, or a diffuse morbilliform rash may be found. Exposure to sunlight may aggravate the skin lesions. The hair often becomes dry and dull, and partial alopecia is not uncommon. In approximately half of the cases the mucous membranes are involved, with redness, thickening, and occasionally ulceration.

Arthralgia or arthritis is present during part of the course in most cases seen in children. Cardiac involvement occurs in about half of the patients, the manifestations varying from those of a simple tachycardia to the auscultatory, roentgenographic, and electrocardiographic signs of pericarditis, myocarditis, or endocarditis. Nephrotic edema and less frequently hypertension may be present as a consequence of kidney involvement. Pleural effusion is not infrequent, and the lungs may show radiographic lesions of the primary disease or of secondary pneumonia from the superimposed infection.

Splenomegaly and hepatomegaly are more common in children than in adults, and ascites may be found. Lymphadenopathy is infrequent and, if present, of slight degree. Except for anorexia there are usually no gastrointestinal symptoms attributable to SLE. Involvement of vessels may in rare instances be responsible for phlebitis or even for Raynaud's syndrome. The so-called cytoid bodies, often seen in the eyegrounds in adults, are seldom encountered in children, but papilledema has been described. A few patients experience convulsions or peripheral neuritis.

LABORATORY FINDINGS. Leucopenia, usually mild, is very common, and thrombocytopenia occurs in approximately one-third of patients. Anemia, found in 80 percent, is moderate, normocytic, and normochromic. The erythrocyte sedimentation rate is increased in almost all patients, and in one-half there is an increase in serum globulin concentration, usually in the gamma and alpha-2 fractions. Other evidences of plasma protein dysfunction include red blood cell autoagglutination, circulating anticoagulant, positive Coombs' test for absorbed gamma globulin on red blood cells, cryoglobulinemia, lowered serum complement levels (usually associated with glomerulonephritis), the presence of rheumatoid factor in approximately 20 percent of patients, and chronic biologic false-positive serologic tests for syphilis in up to 20 percent of cases.

The most specific serologic reaction is the *LE cell* phenomenon, which, if present, greatly strengthens the diagnosis. A typical LE cell is a polymorphonuclear leucocyte, filled with and distended by an inclusion body which is a globular mass of homogeneous material staining red-purple with Wright's stain (Fig. 9). The same material may lie extracellularly as an "LE body" or be surrounded by a ring of polymorphonuclear leucocytes, forming so-called *rosettes*. LE cells are formed when a gamma globulin from the lupus patient's serum, presumably an antibody to nuclear components of the cell, is allowed to act in vitro upon nuclei in the presence of active phagocytic cells. Such cells are not seen in peripheral blood freshly shed, and apparently the nuclei of live, intact cells are not affected by the LE cell-forming antibody. When clotted blood is allowed to in-

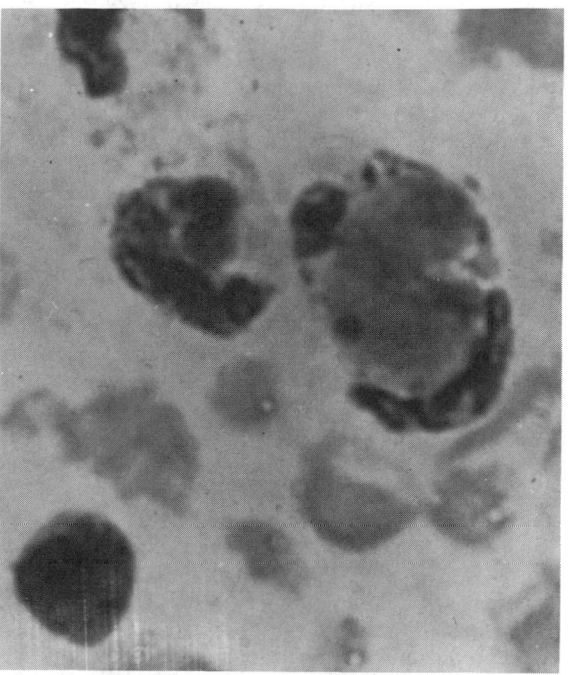

Fig. 9. LE cells. Polymorphonuclear leucocytes containing ingested homogeneous nuclear material.

cubate at 37° C, however, or when a preparation of phagocytic leucocytes containing some injured cells or dead cells interacts with the LE cell factor, the LE cell is formed.

In addition to the LE cell-forming antibody, the SLE patient almost always has antibodies to other nuclear components, such as DNA, histones, and isolated nucleoproteins. LE cells and other antinuclear antibodies are also found, though much less frequently and in lower titer, in rheumatoid arthritis, in patients under treatment with hydralazine or procaine amide, in Sjögren's syndrome, systemic sclerosis, subacute bacterial endocarditis, chronic hepatitis, and dermatomyositis. In SLE, however, approximately 90 percent of patients have positive LE cell tests, and antinuclear factors (ANF) may be demonstrated in an even larger proportion. The fluorescent antinuclear antibody test is, in fact, the most sensitive screening test for SLE. It is rarely negative in florid cases, is usually present even when LE cells cannot be demonstrated, and is usually present in much higher titer in SLE than in other diseases in which it also appears. Virtually all patients with lupus nephritis have demonstrable antinuclear antibodies in high titer by fluorescent antibody methods.

The findings on urinalysis are those of other forms of glomerulonephritis, consisting of varying degrees of proteinuria, cylindruria, and hematuria. A low serum complement level is very characteristic in this, as well as other, forms of acute glomerulonephritis.

DIAGNOSIS. In its initial phases SLE is often difficult to distinguish from a number of other diseases. Joint symptoms may be interpreted as due to rheumatoid arthrits or rheumatic fever. The rheumatoid factor is present, usually in low titer, in the serum of about 25 percent of adults with SLE, less frequently in children. The antistreptolysin O titer is usually normal in patients with SLE unless, of course, there has been recent, unrelated, streptococcal infection, an occurrence which, though fortuitous, may be confusing. The ANF test is quite useful because it is very rarely positive in acute rheumatic fever.

Other forms of glomerulonephritis may be difficult to distinguish from SLE, particularly when SLE presents with renal involvement alone. Renal biopsy also may provide some clue as to the severity and stage of the disease. Polyarteritis nodosa or other forms of diffuse arteritis involving multiple systems are often difficult to distinguish from lupus and frequently enter into the differential diagnosis.

Idiopathic thrombocytopenic purpura may be mistaken for SLE. If thrombocytopenic purpura is the first clinical symptom of SLE, it is usually accompanied by other diagnostic features, such as elevated sedimentation rate, splenomegaly, presence of antinuclear antibodies, or a positive LE cell test. Neoplastic disorders, such as lymphosarcoma and leukemia, may simulate SLE and must be excluded before the diagnosis is established. Subacute bacterial endocarditis and miliary tuberculosis must also be ruled out.

PROGNOSIS. SLE may have a benign course lasting for decades or may cause death in a few weeks. The usual pattern is intermediate. An important prognostic feature is the presence or absence of renal involvement. Lupus nephritis, usually appearing at or near the onset, has an ominous prognosis. Clinical manifestations of an arteritis are another unfavorable prognostic sign.

TREATMENT. Adrenal corticosteroids may produce dramatic improvement, but should be prescribed only during severe acute attacks or for significant involvement of a vital organ system. Such treatment is at times lifesaving. The decision to institute steroid therapy and its dosage must be individualized. The required amount is usually higher than that employed in the control of rheumatoid arthritis. Steroids should be withdrawn as the exacerbation subsides. Whether or not prolonged administration of prednisone (50 to 60 mg daily) is more effective than conventional doses in treating the nephropathy of lupus is not certain. In addition, the value of using immunosuppressive agents in combination with adrenal corticosteroids is still under investigation.

Between attacks or during exacerbations of modest severity, salicylates may reduce fever or joint pains.

Antimalarials have been used in combination with corticosteroids but their benefit is difficult to assess; the danger of chloroquine retinopathy and of cardiorespiratory arrest have virtually eliminated teatment with these agents in children, or at least restricted their usage to the most refractory cases only. Various general measures such as transfusions or digitalization are often helpful. Patients should be advised to avoid excessive exposure to the sun and to use drugs sparingly because of the frequency of adverse reactions.

References

Cook, C. D., Wedgwood, R. J. P., Craig, J. M., Hartmann, J. R., and Janeway, C. A. Systemic lupus erythematosus: description of 37 cases in children and a discussion of endocrine therapy in 32 of the cases. Pediatrics, 26:570, 1960.

Dubois, E. L. Lupus Erythematosus. New York, McGraw-Hill Book Co., 1966.

Harvey, A. M., Shulman, L. E., Tumulty, P. A., Conley, C. L., and Schoenrich, E. H. Systemic lupus erythematosus: review of the literature and clinical analysis of 138 cases. Medicine, 33:291, 1954.

Hanson, V., and Kornreich, H. Systemic rheumatic disorders in childhood: lupus erythematosus, anaphylactoid purpura, dermatomyositis, and scleroderma. Bull. Rheum. Dis., 17:435, 441, 1967.

Jacobs, J. C. Systemic lupus erythematosus in childhood. Pediatrics, 32:257, 1963.

Kornreich, H. K., Drexler, E., and Hanson, V. Antinuclear factors in childhood rheumatic diseases. J. Pediat., 69:1039, 1966.

Peterson, R. D., Vernier, R. L., and Good, R. A. Lupus erythematosus. Pediat. Clin. N. Amer., 10:941, 1963.

12.4
POLYMYOSITIS
(Dermatomyositis)

Polymyositis and dermatomyositis are clinical variants of the same disease process, in which the fundamental pathologic events are degeneration and inflammation within and about the skeletal muscle fiber. The principle clinical feature is weakness, involving especially the proximal limb and girdle musculature. Polymyositis indicates that the muscular disease component is widely distributed. Dermatomyositis is polymyositis with cutaneous manifestations.

ETIOLOGY. The cause is unknown. Approximately 15 to 20 percent of adult cases have an underlying neoplastic disease. Muscle symptoms may antedate the discovery of the neoplasm by as much as 2 years.

PATHOLOGY. Dermatomyositis in childhood has certain unique features which set the disease apart from the adult form. The prominence of vascular lesions which produce a systemic angiopathy involving the skin, muscle, gastrointestinal tract, adipose tissue, and the nervous system has not been characteristic of the pathologic findings in adults. Children are more apt to develop calcinosis than adults. The association with malignancy observed so often in adults, particularly older adults, is rare in children and when present is usually related to a lymphoma.

The pathologic changes in muscle observed with both the light and electron microscope are fundamentally the same, the difference between them being attributable to the varying degrees of muscle involvement due to the pathologic process. The light microscope reveals focal or extensive muscle fiber degeneration, vacuolation, hyalinization with loss of cross striation, and eosinophilic cytoplasm. In some fibers there is regeneration as evidenced by basophilia of the cytoplasm, large vesicular nuclei, and prominent nucleoli as well as phagocytosis of necrotic muscle fragments. Later in the course of the disease interstitial fibrosis becomes more prominent. The electron microscope reveals extensive disorganization of the sarcomeres in several fibers with fragmentation and disappearance of the "Z" line together with a decrease in filaments of actin and myosin. The most striking findings in the blood vessels of the connective tissue are thickening of the basement membrane of the capillaries and the abundant pinocytotic vesicles shown by the endothelial cells whose cytoplasm forms a thin layer superimposed upon the basement membrane.

CLINICAL FEATURES. The age of onset in childhood varies from infancy to adolescence. The onset is usually insidious but occasionally may be explosive. An acute onset and progressive course are most often seen in children with dermatomyositis or tumors. The most prominent clinical feature is *muscle weakness;* when this involves the proximal muscles of the shoulder and pelvic girdles, polymyositis must always be suspected. Typically, the patients become unable to comb their hair, reach for objects on high shelves, climb a high step, arise from a supine position or from a low chair, or maintain a steady gait. In severe cases, difficulty in swallowing occurs, and patients cannot sit up in bed or lift the head from the pillow. Muscle pain and tenderness usually occur more prominently in acute cases and may be absent or minimal in those with an insidious onset. Initially the muscles feel doughy and indurated, later firm; eventually they may become atrophic, and contractures of shoulders, elbows, hips, and knees may develop.

The skin lesions are present in about two-thirds of the reported series. The typical rash consists of swollen upper eyelids with "heliotrope" patches of color to the cheeks which cause a facies quite characteristic of dermatomyositis to the experienced observer. The rash may become confluent, particularly over the face and the V-area of the neck, and progress to scaling, telangiectasia, and fibrosis with depigmentation. Erythematous or violaceous patches are frequently present over the metacarpophalangeal joints, the interphalangeal joints, and also over the extensor surfaces of the elbows and knees. Subcutaneous, periarticular, and muscular calcifications are particularly common in children.

Joint involvement is usually mild and evanescent, ranging from vague polyarthralgia to diffuse, symmetric swelling of the small and large joints. This finding usually appears early in the course of the disease and rarely dominates the picture. The arthritis may occur before muscle symptoms and be confused, therefore, with other forms of polyarthritis. It heals without deformity and is not chronic. Visceral involvement in polymyositis is rare; such involvement should suggest other connective tissue disorders which may also involve the muscles (polyarteritis, systemic lupus erythematosus, rheumatoid arthritis) rather than primary polymyositis. Raynaud's phenomenon, as in other connective tissue disorders involving small blood vessels, is not uncommon in polymyositis. Myocardiopathy occurs rarely.

LABORATORY FINDINGS. Muscle necrosis in severe cases may cause liberation into the blood of muscle enzymes such as *creatine phosphokinase, aldolase, lactic dehydrogenase,* and *transaminases* (glutamic-oxaloacetic or glutamic-pyruvic), but their levels in serum do not always correlate with the intensity of the myositis. In low-grade chronic cases, however, they may not be increased, even with severe muscle weakness. *Creatinuria* is often increased, usually in proportion to the intensity of the process. The electromyogram should guide the selection of the site of muscle biopsy and usually reveals abnormal electrical activity in the affected muscle fibers. The presence of small potentials at rest and of polyphasic patterns on volitional activity are findings that strongly suggest polymyositis although they are not specific. Tests for rheumatoid factor, antinuclear antibodies, and LE cells are only rarely positive, usually in very severe cases, and acute phase reactants (C-reactive protein, increased erythrocyte sedimentation rate, and so forth) or hypergammaglobulinemia are present less often than in rheumatoid arthritis or SLE. Anemia is mild and leucocytosis occurs only in very acute and severe cases.

DIAGNOSIS. In addition to the clinical picture, the diagnosis is based on the muscle biopsy, which should be made, if possible, from the most acutely and severely involved muscles. Differentiation of polymyositis from muscular dystrophy may be exceedingly difficult and at times, particularly early in the course when weakness alone is the presenting symptom, impossible until further differentiating features appear. Myasthenia gravis or thyrotoxic myopathy can be excluded by specific tests. Vasculitis involving the muscles as part of other diseases is differentiated by visceral involvement or other features of the overlying disease, such as polyarteritis, SLE, and serum sickness. Polyneuritis may produce a strikingly similar acute picture with marked shoulder and pelvic girdle atrophy and involvement. Other causes of myositis which cause muscle weakness, pain, or tenderness must be excluded.

PROGNOSIS. The course of dermatomyositis in childhood is variable and difficult to predict. In those children who expire after one year of disease, death is attributed to infection, usually pneumonia, or results from heart failure. Those surviving the first year have a good prognosis for life and may have periods of prolonged remissions. In general, the prognosis is better in children, perhaps because fewer have associated neoplasms.

TREATMENT. Adrenal corticosteroids may increase muscle strength so dramatically that they provide a therapeutic test in obscure cases. In other cases, large doses may have to be continued several weeks before a favorable response is obtained, and some patients respond only partially. The symptomatic response is particularly poor in those with malignancies. Because the steroids tend to suppress or delay muscle wasting from disuse, early treatment permits more complete recovery. As in other chronic connective tissue diseases, the corticosteroids are palliative, and prolonged use of high doses is subject to the usual complications encountered with such therapy. Gastrointestinal perforation has been a particularly frequent complication of prolonged steroid therapy of childhood dermatomyositis. Judicious use of the steroids plus physiotherapy and encouragement may tide the patient over into periods of spontaneous remissions or complete recovery.

REFERENCES

Adams, R. D., Denny-Brown, D., and Pearson, C. M. Diseases of Muscle, 2nd ed. New York, Harper and Row, Publ., 1962, pp. 414-460.

Banker, B. Q., and Victor, M. Dermatomyositis (systemic angiopathy) of childhood. Medicine, 45:261, 1966.

Gonzalez-Angulo, A., Fraga, A., and Mintz, G. Submicroscopic alterations in capillaries of skeletal muscles in polymyositis. Amer. J. Med., 45:873, 1968.

Walton, J. N., and Adams, R. D. Polymyositis. Edinburgh and London, E. S. Livingston, Ltd., 1958.

Wedgwood, R. J. P., Cook, C. D., and Cohen, J. Dermatomyositis: report of 26 cases in children with a discussion of endocrine therapy in 13. Pediatrics, 12: 447, 1953.

12.5
PROGRESSIVE SYSTEMIC SCLEROSIS
(SCLERODERMA)

Progressive systemic sclerosis (PSS) is a diffuse disorder of connective tissues in which there are inflammatory, fibrotic, and degenerative changes in the skin (scleroderma), synovium, gastrointestinal tract, lungs, heart, and kidneys. It is a rare disease of childhood. The disease may make its appearance at any time in life, even in infancy, but is most common between 30 and 50 years of age, and two-thirds of the patients are women. Like other collagen or connective tissue disorders, the cause is unknown, although an immunologic disorder is suspected because of the prominence of hypergammaglobulinemia and rheumatoid and antinuclear factors. Although closely related in this respect to rheumatoid arthritis, SLE, and dermatomyositis, the intensive fibrosis of systemic sclerosis is its unique feature and is not well explained, so far, by conventional immunologic mechanisms known to produce tissue lesions.

PATHOLOGY. The most widely appreciated feature of PSS is that of a hyperplasia of collagen fibers in skin and viscera, but there are two other histologic reactions, namely, inflammation and vascular lesions, which appear to bear a close similarity to certain changes observed in rheumatoid arthritis and in systemic lupus erythematosus. The dermis gradually becomes thickened by coarse collagen bundles lying parallel to the epidermis. Skin appendages atrophy and dermal fibrosis extends into the subcutaneous fat. The same process takes place in the alimentary tract, most prominently in the esophagus, and in the lungs, myocardium, muscles, and serous membranes. Lesions of the small arterioles are found by careful study but florid arteritis is not a common feature. For example, small focal glomerular arterial lesions may be found at autopsy, but true glomerulonephritis is rare. Electron microscope studies in PSS have disclosed a striking decrease in the number of capillaries in striated muscles which are not clinically affected but reflect the capillary level of the basic vascular lesion. Furthermore, the endothelial cells of these capillaries reveal a very characteristic lamination of the basement membrane which is virtually pathognomonic of the disease.

CLINICAL FEATURES. The disease begins and progresses insidiously, the earliest symptoms usually being stiffness of fingers, Raynaud's phenomenon, or both. Actually, Raynaud's phenomenon and excessive sweating of the palms and soles may antedate other manifestations by years. Skin lesions appear first in the fingers and progress proximally up the forearms. The feet, face, neck, and upper anterior chest are next involved in that order. Early, the skin lesions may have nonpitting edema and a red-mottled discoloration, but eventually the skin becomes taut, waxy, and shiny and cannot be lifted from the subcutaneous tissues or wrinkled. The face becomes masklike, the jaw is opened with increasing difficulty, and pigmentation or vitiligo may appear. Fingers become immobilized in flexion; ulcers may develop and become infected, heal poorly, and become chronic. Diffuse subcutaneous and periarticular calcification occur, as in dermatomyositis. Low-grade arthritis appears in at least half the patients, It is usually symmetric and similar to rheumatoid arthritis in distribution, but permanent joint deformity per se is rare. Friction rubs are often audible or palpable owing to fibrinous tenosynovitis. Muscle weakness and atrophy accompany the progression of skin lesions.

Most patients develop some evidence of visceral involvement, most commonly dysphagia due to loss of esophageal peristalsis. Impaired motility of the stomach and duodenum lead to additional symptoms of dyspepsia, and intestinal malabsorption may occur. Some cases of malabsorption associated with Raynaud's phenomenon but without skin involvement ("scleroderma sine scleroderma") have been reported. The associated findings of calcinosis, Raynaud's phenomenon, sclerodactyly, and telangiectasis have been called the "SRST syndrome." Pulmonary symptoms occur owing to alveolar-capillary block, pulmonary hypertension secondary to pulmonary arterial disease, aspiration pneumonia due to dysphagia, and ventilatory restriction due to sclerodermatous encasement of the thorax or weakness of the diaphragm. Cardiac involvement leads to enlargement and heart failure, a major cause of death. Death due to renal failure from rapidly accelerated hypertension and "malignant" arteriolar disease occurs less often.

A localized or "focal" form of scleroderma occurs in which plaques of scleroderma appear sharply distinct from surrounding unaffected skin (morphea). This form may be also, but less commonly, associated with visceral involvement.

LABORATORY FINDINGS.   Increased erythrocyte sedimentation rate and hypergammaglobulinemia occur in some patients. Anemia and leucocytosis are not a feature, however, and the serologic acute phase reactions are less common than in the more exudative inflammatory diseases. Rheumatoid factor is found in one-fourth of patients, most of whom have joint involvement; LE cells are seen in less than 5 percent of cases, whereas antinuclear factors demonstrable by immunofluorescence tests are found more frequently. The frequency of this finding, however, may be lower in young children.

PROGNOSIS.   The usual course is prolonged and progressive over many years with occasional remissions or lack of progression for many months. Visceral lesions are unlikely to improve, and death, when due to the disease itself rather than to intercurrent conditions, results from heart failure, hypertension, uremia, pulmonary disease, or malnutrition.

TREATMENT.   Corticosteroids are of little value except in the early, edematous, erythematous stage of the disease, and then only to a limited degree. Treatment is supportive, depending upon the organ system involved. Physiotherapy may help to diminish deformity and preserve muscle strength.

REFERENCES

Coburn, R. F., and Schmid, F. R. Progressive systemic sclerosis. Quart. Bull., Northwest. Univ. Med. School, 34:49, 1960.

Kass, H., Hanson, V., and Patrick, J. Scleroderma in childhood. J. Pediat., 68:243, 1966.

Norton, W. I.., and Nardo, J. M. Vascular disease in progressive systemic sclerosis (scleroderma). Ann. Intern. Med., 73, 1970, in press.

Orabona, M. L., and Albano, O. Progressive systemic sclerosis: review of the literature. Acta Med. Scand. (Suppl.), 333:1, 1958.

Rodnan, G. P. Natural history of progressive systemic sclerosis. Bull. Rheum. Dis., 13:301, 1963.

Winterbauer, R. H. Multiple telangiectasia, Raynaud's phenomenon, sclerodactyly and subcutaneous calcinosis: a syndrome mimicking hereditary hemorrhagic telangiectasia. Bull. Hopkins Hosp., 114:361, 1964.

12.6
POLYARTERITIS NODOSA
(Periarteritis Nodosa, Polyarteritis)

A wide spectrum of clinical syndromes presenting as multiorgan or multisystem disease is associated with diffuse vasculitis or angiitis. The generic name "necrotizing angiitis" has been used to designate vascular lesions characterized by fibrinoid necrosis and inflammatory reactions involving all three coats of the vascular wall. The classification of these diseases as separate entitics, however, is sometimes difficult although their clinical "personalities" tend to separate them better than their histopathologic features. The distinction between polyarteritis nodosa and the group of diseases often lumped together as "hypersensitivity angiitis" can be made on the basis of the size of the arteries involved: the former affects medium-sized arteries and the latter involves small arteries, capillaries, and venules. Clinically, however, periarteritis nodosa is usually a progressive, fatal disease, whereas the diseases described as "acute diffuse angiitis" or "allergic angiitis" are usually explosive in onset, relatively brief in duration, and usually heal completely. They include such clinical entities as anaphylactoid purpura (Henoch-Schönlein's), serum sickness, drug hypersensitivity, and erythema multiforme. Each is discussed elsewhere in this volume.

ETIOLOGY.   The cause is unknown, but necrotizing arteritis of smaller vessels similar to human lesions can be produced in animals by sensitization to foreign proteins. Furthermore, death in patients with serum sickness or apparent hypersensitivity to such drugs as sulfonamides, arsenicals, iodines, and penicillin is sometimes due to a diffuse vasculitis indistinguishable from idiopathic polyarteritis. In the majority of cases, however, an inciting antigen or infectious agent is not apparent.

PATHOLOGY.   The arterial lesions are characterized by segmental necrosis, fibrinoid changes, and inflammation of all layers of the arterial wall and by acute inflammatory periarterial changes with polymorphonuclear leucocytes predominating and eosinophils prominent. Cellular response and fibrosis of the adventitia produce the characteristic nodules, and intimal occlusion leads to arterial thrombosis and infarction. Aneurysms may form and rupture, producing fatal bleeding or large hematomas. Most frequent localizations of the arterial lesions are the kidneys, peripheral nerves, brain, muscles, gastrointestinal tract, and heart.

CLINICAL FEATURES. The clinical features are protean, the onset is acute or insidious, and the course ranges from fulminating to chronic. Polyarteritis, therefore, simulates a great variety of diseases presenting clinical pictures of (1) fever of unknown origin with hyperglobulinemia and eosinophilia; (2) acute glomerulonephritis or malignant hypertension; (3) severe abdominal pain with melena or hematemesis; (4) acute carditis, pericarditis, pleurisy, bronchial asthma, or pneumonitis; (5) severe muscle pain with wasting and weight loss; (6) diffuse cerebral disease with encephalopathy; (7) peripheral neuritis, often focal with wristdrop or footdrop; (8) massive hepatic infarction.

LABORATORY FINDINGS. Leucocytosis, with a shift to the left, and eosinophilia occur frequently. Proteinuria, hematuria, and cylindruria indicate renal involvement. The erythrocyte sedimentation rate is increased, serum globulin levels are high, and other acute phase serologic responses correlate with the intensity of the inflammatory process. No laboratory finding is specific but, unlike rheumatoid arthritis, SLE, dermatomyositis, and systemic sclerosis, the rheumatoid factor is seldom seen and antinuclear antibodies are usually absent. Serologically, therefore, polyarteritis is more like rheumatic fever and serum sickness.

DIAGNOSIS. Biopsy constitutes the sole means of establishing the diagnosis, and even then the minority of muscle biopsies made for this purpose show lesions. Moreover, when some arteritic lesions are present, their interpretation may still be unclear. The diagnosis is made by the clinician rather than by the pathologist. A particular problem is the occurrence of a diffuse arteritis in other diseases. The polyarteritis of rheumatoid arthritis, for example, produces overlapping of the two diseases. They are distinguished only when the visceral lesions predominate in polyarteritis nodosa or the deforming arthritis predominates in rheumatoid arthritis. Other diseases in which chronic vasculitis may be a prominent feature include dermatomyositis, SLE, Wegener's granulomatosis (a necrotizing granuloma of the sinuses and upper respiratory tract associated with visceral lesions), and Weber-Christian's relapsing nodular panniculitis.

PROGNOSIS. Although the prognosis is generally poor, a fatal outcome occurring in weeks to months, occasional cases persist for 2 or more years and prolonged remissions have been reported. Death is most often due to renal failure, massive internal hemorrhage, or heart failure.

TREATMENT. There is no specific therapy. Unlike other connective tissue diseases, response to corticosteroids is usually very poor except when specific complications, such as hemolytic anemia, can be treated. Supportive measures depend upon the organ involved. Corticosteroids and immunosuppression are more apt to be effective in the diffuse angiitis serum sickness-like form of polyarteritis than in classical polyarteritis nodosa.

REFERENCES

Fager, D. B., Bigler, J. A., and Simonds, J. P. Polyarteritis nodosa in infancy and childhood. J. Pediat., 39:65, 1951.

Neale, A. V. Polyarteritis in childhood. Arch. Dis. Child., 24:224, 1949.

Rich, A. R., and Gregory, J. E. Experimental demonstration that periarteritis nodosa is a manifestation of hypersensitivity. Bull. Hopkins Hosp., 72:65, 1943.

Roberts, F. B., and Fetteman, G. H. Polyarteritis nodosa in infancy. J. Pediat., 63:519, 1963.

Rose, G. A., and Spencer, H. Polyarteritis nodosa. Quart. J. Med., 26:43, 1957.

Schmid, F. R. Arteritis in rheumatoid arthritis. Amer. J. Med., 30:56, 1961.

Zeek, P. M. Periarteritis nodosa and other forms of necrotizing angiitis. New Eng. J. Med., 248:764, 1953.

12.7
SUGGESTED WORK-UP OF ACUTE ARTHRITIS

Acute arthritis is a medical emergency, and patients with this complaint should be admitted to the hospital if possible. If an infectious agent is responsible for the arthritis, destruction of the involved joint may come within a matter of days. Also, complete bed rest is often indicated as a vital part of the appropriate therapy. In addition, an orderly and systematic work-up can be carried out much more easily with inpatients.

PRIMARY DIFFERENTIAL DIAGNOSIS OF ACUTE ARTHRITIS:

1. Rheumatic fever
2. Pyogenic arthritis (especially gonococcus)
3. Viral arthritis (especially rubella)
4. Acute gouty arthritis or pseudogout
5. Serum sickness
6. Traumatic arthritis
7. Rheumatoid arthritis
8. Systemic lupus erythematosus
9. Reiter's disease
10. Subacute bacterial endocarditis
11. Bursitis and calcific tendonitis
12. Palindromic rheumatism
13. Intermittent hydroarthrosis
14. Reflex sympathetic dystrophies
15. Erythema nodosum
16. Sarcoidosis
17. Hemophilic arthritis
18. Acute leukemia
19. Sickle-cell anemia

WORK-UP AND MANAGEMENT:

I. Historical and physical findings which may be helpful

   A. Pattern of onset

     1. Migratory nature: Moves from joint to joint leaving the previously involved joint markedly improved. This suggests infection, rheumatic fever, or serum sickness. Infections tend to localize in one jont.

     2. Progressive: Moves from joint to joint without marked improvement in the previously involved joint. The prototype is rheumatoid arthritis which may have an acute onset.

     3. Polycyclic: An acute onset with complete remission with periods in which the patient is completely symptom free. Prototypes are gout, palindromic rheumatism, and intermittent hydroarthrosis.

   B. Number of joints involved

     1. Acute gouty arthritis: Usually monoarticular at onset.

     2. Rheumatic fever: Multiple and migratory.

     3. Rheumatoid arthritis: Multiple and symmetrical.

   C. Distribution of joints involved

     1. Rheumatoid arthritis: Symmetrical, often affects smaller joints of hands and feet.

     2. Gout: Involves big toe in two thirds of attacks.

     3. Rheumatic fever: Usually involves larger joints.

     4. Systemic lupus erythematosus: Often involves tendon sheath.

     5. Gonococcal arthritis: Often produces tenosynovitis.

     6. Intermittent hydroarthrosis: Affects knees.

   D. Morning stiffness—most characteristic of rheumatoid arthritis.

   E. Deformity—often present from previous attacks of rheumatoid arthritis and chronic gouty arthritis. Rheumatic fever, serum sickness, palindromic rheumatism, and intermittent hydroarthrosis never lead to deformity.

   F. Severity of pain—when pain is severe, suspect gout, bursitis, or malignancy.

   G. Signs of inflammation—usually some in all diseases; however, gout tends to produce more intense cellulitis extending beyond the confines of the joint.

   H. Other signs and concomitant findings

     1. Signs of sympathetic overactivity in shoulder-hand syndrome and reflex sympathetic dystrophies.

     2. Serum sickness: Almost always associated with urticarial skin rash and history of exposure.

     3. Rheumatic fever: History of antecedent pharyngitis.

     4. Gonococcal arthritis: History of exposure, relation to menses, and physical findings of P.I.D.

II. Selection of procedures in acute arthritis without obvious etiology

   A. Cultures and stains mandatory to obtain before institution of any antibiotics

     1. Blood cultures

     2. Throat cultures

     3. Urethral and cervical cultures: Stain and culture on Thayer-Martin and chocolate agar media with incubation in a high CO_2 atmosphere

     4. Joint fluid cultures: Stain and culture aerobically and with CO_2 as above

   B. Antibodies to streptococcal enzymes

   C. Acute phase reactants: CRP, ESR

   D. Serum protein electrophoresis

   E. RA test

   F. LE prep and fluorescent antinuclear test

   G. Serum uric acid

   H. X-ray of affected joints

   I. Examination of joint fluid (Tables 5 and 6)
     Gram stain—AFB stain and culture
     WBC and differential
     Culture—aerobically and under CO_2 as above
     Sugar—simultaneous blood sugar
     Wet preparation microscopic exam for crystals, RA cells, and cartilage fibrils
     Mucin test
     Viscosity
     Color and turbidity

III. Therapeutic trial

   Select one mode of therapy based on preliminary findings. It is best to err on the side of using antibiotics alone rather than aspirin alone. Pain may be controlled with codeine or morphine without "masking" the course of arthritis. Infections may destroy joints within a few days if not promptly treated and a positive response to antibiotics is of diagnostic significance. If ASA alone has not achieved good therapeutic response within 36 hours, the addition of antibiotics should be considered. If proper antibiotics alone are used, there should be some defervescence and improvement in the joint disease within 36 hours if the etiology is infectious. Aspirin and antibiotics may be used together after the diagnosis is established and in the above circumstances. Failure to respond to adequate penicillin dosage is a useful exclusion of early gonococcal arthritis. The other anti-inflammatory agents may be required. Steroids may be life-saving in acute rheumatic carditis and systemic lupus erythematosus. Colchicine or indomethacin or

TABLE 5.   *Classification of Synovial Fluids According to Results of Various Tests*

	Normal	Group I (non-inflammatory)	Group II (inflammatory)	Group III (septic)	Group IV (hemorrhagic)
Volume (ml)	<2-3	>2-3	>2-3	>2-3	>2-3
Appearance	clear, colorless	clear, straw	turbid, yellow	turbid, yellow	bloody xanthochromic
Viscosity	high	high	low	low	variable
Fibrin clot	absent	usually absent	present	present	usually absent
Mucin clot	good	good	fair to poor	poor	variable
Nucleated cell count (mm^3)	<200	200-5,000	2,000-100,000	20,000-200,000	200-10,000
Polymorphonuclear leucocytes (%)	<25	<25	>50	>75	<50
Blood-Synovial fluid glucose difference (mg/100 ml)	<10	<10	>25	>50	<25
Culture	negative	negative	negative	often positive	negative

TABLE 6.   *Classification of Joint Diseases According to Synovial Fluid Changes*

Group I (noninflammatory)	Group II (inflammatory)	Group III (septic)	Group IV (hemorrhagic)
Traumatic arthritis	Rheumatoid disease	Infectious arthritis	Hemorrhagic diathesis
Degenerative joint disease	Rheumatic fever		Traumatic arthritis
Osteochondromatosis	Systemic lupus		Neuroarthropathy
Osteochondritis dissecans	erythematosus		Pigmented villonodular
Neuroarthropathy	Reiter's disease		synovitis
Hypertrophic pulmonary	Acute gouty arthritis		Neoplasms
osteoarthropathy	Acute chondrocalcinosis		
Pigmented villonodular	(pseudogout)		
synovitis			

phenylbutazone may be used in a therapeutic trial for acute gouty arthritis.

Recommended dosage in therapeutic trials:

A. Procaine penicillin: 600,000 units q 6 hours x 48 hours.

B. ASA: 4 to 8 g per day in divided doses. Salicylate level of 20 to 30 mg/100 ml should be attained.

C. Colchicine: 0.5 to 0.65 mg q 1 hour until symptomatic relief or significant G.I. disturbance. Patient may be premedicated with antiemetic and antidiarrheal drugs. The us-ual minimal dose before therapeutic success is 8 tablets.

D. Phenylbutazone: 400 mg stat, then 200 mg q 2 hours until therapeutic success, not to exceed 1,000 mg.

E. Indomethacin: 100 mg stat, then 50 mg q 2 hours until therapeutic success, not to exceed 30 mg.

Do not use corticosteroids until diagnostic procedures and more specific therapeutic trials are completed and it is determined that the course of the disease is chronic and requires symptomatic suppression of inflammation.

chapter 13

ACCIDENTS, POISONINGS, AND OTHER ENVIRONMENTAL HAZARDS IN CHILDHOOD

ARNOLD H. EINHORN

13.1
ACCIDENTS

ARNOLD H. EINHORN

Marked advances in medicine and public health have resulted in a significant decline in childhood deaths in the past 35 years. However, deaths from accidents did not decrease to the same degree. In 1969, accidents claimed the lives of more than 115,000 persons in the United States, and more than 15,000 of these fatalities were in children under 15 years of age. The number of accidental deaths in children from 1 through 14 years of age exceeds that of the combined fatalities from five leading diseases: pneumonia, meningitis, congenital malformations, rheumatic heart disease, and cancer. Mortality statistics, however, reflect only partly the magnitude of the problem, for they do not take into account the heavy toll of permanently disfigured and crippled children. Although comparatively few case studies of accidental morbidity are recorded, it is estimated that nonfatal injuries outnumber lethal accidents by a ratio greater than 200 to 1.

Accidents occur more frequently in boys than in girls, and the injury rates are highest in the summer, lowest in the winter. Low-income groups appear to be at a higher risk. The majority of injuries in children of all age groups are sustained in the home areas. However, motor vehicle accidents rank first among those which are fatal from birth to 14 years of age. Home accidents, including falls, fire, burns, poisonings, suffocation, and firearms claimed the lives of more than 4,000 children of less than five years of age in 1969. Suffocation from accidental aspiration of objects or foods into the respiratory passages, smothering by bedclothes or plastic materials, and mechanical strangulation were the most frequent type of fatal accidents in the first year of life. Deaths due to fire, burns, and explosion of combustibles ranged first among children aged 1 through 4 years, and second among infants less than 1 year of age. The predominance of such causes is obviously related to the fact that preschool children are apt to pull objects off stoves or play with matches when left unsupervised

in places where dangerous heating or other hazardous equipment is accessible. In children 1 through 4 years of age, the major causes of accidental deaths were the same for both boys and girls; beyond the age of 4 years, they were different in the two sexes. For children 5 through 14 years of age, drowning ranked first for boys and fourth for girls; motor vehicle traffic accidents to pedestrians was the leading cause of death in girls in this age group and the second ranking cause for boys. Four times as many accidental deaths occurred among teen-age boys as among girls of the same age. It is estimated that accidents result in the loss of nearly 10 million school days in children between ages 6 through 16, or 23 days per 100 children per year.

Developmental sequences through which children progress from infancy to maturity determine in part the types of accidents that are more apt to occur at specific ages. A small infant may roll over, or propel himself enough to fall from an open crib, a bed, or any unprotected elevated surface. At the age when the infant crawls or toddles, he has a natural tendency to take objects in his mouth, and the ingestion of poisonous substances or other dangerous objects or foreign bodies becomes a hazard from the second half of the first year of life through early childhood. With the acquisition of further mobility, the ability and urge to climb, the instinct to explore, to pull and grasp at objects, the accidents that take the most prominent place are falls, burns, scalds, electric shocks, and injuries from toppling furniture or colliding with heavy objects. Interest in moving and whirling objects is active long before caution has developed from painful experience. At a later age, the intense absorption of young children in play makes them reckless in street traffic, at water's edge, and in other dangerous settings. Throughout his growing years the child is in contact with an increasing variety of appliances, tools, or other objects which he may explore or use without proper guidance or supervision. This applies not merely to firearms, knives, and other sharp instruments, but also to matches, lamps, electrical equipment, kitchen utensils, tools, engines, and farm implements. As his social awareness grows, particularly in the school years, the child's temptation to accept a challenge becomes greater. He may try to demonstrate "maturity" by assuming prerogatives ordinarily reserved for adults.

Accident proneness or "repeatism" remains a subject of controversy and merits further study. While virtually all accidents that occur in children could have been prevented, it is nonetheless reasonable to regard all children as inherently susceptible to accidents. The variables elicited in the production of most accidents are multiple and complex, involving an interplay of host, etiologic agent, and environment. In the child, his inexperience, coupled with the exposure to the injurious agents and the unsafe environment, constitutes probably the major determinant. However, with regard to frequency of occurrence, individual differences seem to exist among children of comparable endowment exposed under similar circumstances to equally hazardous agents or environment. The pattern of behavior of a particular child, his attitude, his personal traits, and his adjustment to noxious situations also play an important role. Studies indicate that the child who gets involved frequently in accidents is overactive, restless, and impulsive, and has less feeling of security at home. Children in the nonaccident group have been said to be quiet, more timid, submissive, studious, and to come from more closely united family groups. It has been stated also that parents of repeaters were frequently involved in accidents.

Prevention of Accidents

Accidents are amenable to control, and the responsibilities of physicians and health agencies reside in the area of prevention. The same basic epidemiologic principles used to control communicable diseases can apply here and host, agent, and environment must be given consideration. It may not be possible to change the host readily, but the host can be safeguarded from hazards while both agent and environment are manipulated and made safer. Some examples are the use of seat belts, safety glass for doors, noninflammable material, safe toys, safe play areas, and supervised recreation.

Accident prevention requires protection, education, and legislation. Children must be shielded from hazards when they are too young to be taught how to cope with them. Description or even enumeration of all possible measures of protection is beyond the scope of this book; however, a few important principles are worth mentioning. The infant must not be left where he can fall or roll over; he must not be restrained by clothes that may choke him; he must not be given unsupervised access to places where he can drown, smother, scald, or burn himself; and he should not be given objects or toys with sharp edges or with detachable parts or tabs which might be pulled off and swallowed or aspirated. Even before the crawling stage, staircases should be guarded with proper gates and railings; low tables should be cleared of glass, pottery, lamps, and the corners of

tablecloths brought up out of reach. Particular attention must be devoted in the kitchen to keeping the toddler at a safe distance from the stove and keeping handles of pots on the stove out of reach. Small children should not be permitted to touch matches or table lighters. Unused accessible electric outlets should have plastic plugs. Care must also be taken with toys or household objects which by themselves may not be hazardous, yet may be responsible for accidents when they happen to come under foot; the classic example is the roller skate left on a stair.

The exploring toddler with his unsteady gait must be protected from falling from heights or from holding dangerous objects in his hands. As the child gets older and begins to accept responsibility, dependence on protection is lessened while greater emphasis is placed on educational experience and graduated exposure. However, an irreducible segment of accident risk will remain. The development of legislation incorporating effective control measures in the manufacturing of protection is an essential part of any accident prevention program. For example, paints used in coloring toys or cribs must be free from lead, arsenic, mercury, and other poisonous substances. Clothing must be made nonflammable.

The extent to which shielding and education are to be employed is a matter of judgment in which the characteristics of individual children and parents must be considered. Overprotection may have harmful results; the child who is too rigidly kept off the street or highway for fear of traffic accidents may, by escaping excessive supervision, become more susceptible to the unfamiliar hazard. Fear of injury should not interfere with gradual exposure to the normal environment. The family pediatrician may have the opportunity to judge if overexposure or overprotection from hazards exists. His advice may be helpful regarding the appropriate age to allow a child certain privileges or the use of potentially hazardous tools, instruments, or even toys, such as air rifles.

Parents can profit even more from education. While much can be accomplished through media of communication such as the press and radio, direct parental instruction by the physician at an early age of the child is of prime importance, along with repetition and even demonstration at the school level.

Accident prevention should be made into an integral part of well-child supervision. Families could be "immunized" against accidents through safety education together with other well-baby procedures. The pediatrician's knowledge of the child's developmental level and of the household should enable him to provide anticipatory guidance with regard to the type of accidents most likely to occur at specific stages of the child's development and in a given family. During home visits the physician should notice hazardous, unsafe conditions in the home and advise the family about corrective measures. In addition, every professional organization concerned with health and education, and every government agency involved in any aspect of public health and welfare, must be called to play a dominant role in safety educational programs. Education of the public by professional educators, physicians, and individuals in allied health disciplines must be intensive, and continuous, and should permeate every phase and activity of daily living. Finally, medical organizations can be actively instrumental in furthering introduction of appropriate legislation.

REFERENCES

Committee on Accident Prevention, American Academy of Pediatrics, Accidents in Children, American Academy of Pediatrics, Chicago, 1968.

Dickson, D. G., et al. Medically attended injuries among young children. Amer. J. Dis. Child., 107:618, 1964.

Haddon, W., Jr., Suchman, E. A., et al. Accident Research Methods and Approaches. New York, Harper and Row, 1964.

Jacobziner, H., Rich, H., et al. A study of non-fatal accidents, 1952-1959. Pediatrics, 26:414, 1960.

—— Prevention of childhood accidents. GP, 35:123, 1962.

King, B. G. Potentials of medical reseach in prevention of accidents. Southern Med. J., 57:406, 1964.

Langford, W. S., Gilder, R., Jr., et al. Pilot study of childhood accidents. Pediatrics, 26:414, 1960.

National Safety Council, Accident Facts. Annual Publication, Chicago, 1970.

U.S. Department of Health, Education, and Welfare, Office of the Assistant Secretary (for legislation). Accidents, Dec. 1964–Jan. 1965.

—— Public Health Service. Accidental Death and Injury Statistics. Washington, D.C., Oct. 1963.

Wheatley, G. M. Some approaches to research in childhood accidents. Pediatrics, 25:343, 1960.

13.2
BURNS IN CHILDHOOD

ARNOLD H. EINHORN

Burns merit special mention among the leading accidents in children because of their devastating effects. They also typify, par excellence, injuries that can be averted and yet occur with great frequency as a result of ignorance or carelessness. Severe burns constitute an extremely stressful experience for both the child and the family. Those who survive are not only maimed to variable degrees but they are likely to be affected by residual long-lasting psychologic trauma. Emotional disturbances exist in approximately 80 percent of the children who recover physically from severe burns and in 60 percent of the mothers. **INCIDENCE, EPIDEMIOLOGY, AND ETIOLOGY.** During infancy, childhood, and adolescence, burns outrank all other causes of deaths resulting from home accidents. More than 1,100 children from 1 to 4 years of age died from burns in the United States in

1969. In an analysis of 5,000 children under the age of 5 attending New York City Health Stations, burns totaled 22 percent of nonfatal accidents and the majority of these occurred in patients under 5 years of age. After 5, the incidence rate of burns drops precipitously.

The kitchen is a common place for burns from hot liquids. *Hot water* taps are frequently involved in scalding of toddlers left in tubs without supervision. *Flame burns* from open fires occur frequently in rural areas. In urban communities, indoor fires are hazards in teeming high-rise buildings, especially in crowded tenements. *Electrical burns* in infants and small children affect most commonly the hands and the mouth. Toddlers tend to explore electrical outlets at floor levels with their fingers. Irreparable damage to lips and tongue may occur in infants who suck the frayed ends of electric cords, or the live female extension cord connected to active outlets (Fig. 1). Electrical injuries produce severe tissue necrosis and eschar formation, which may lead to late vessel rupture and hemorrhage. Severe electrical burns combined with flame burns from ignited clothing may be sustained following contact with the "live" third rail by youngsters crossing railroad tracks or playing in unsupervised freight yards (Fig. 2). Extensive tissue damage can be produced in children by caustic alkali or acids, used mostly as household cleaning products. *Chemical burns* of the skin may also be caused by contact with gasoline, without ignition of the fuel.

Burns claim a greater number of victims in the nonwhite population, related probably to overcrowding and substandard housing. Many factors, such as lack of protective enclosures, defective heating devices, and excessive loads placed on inadequate electric wiring, contribute to the greater frequency of burns in families living in substandard housing.

In some episodes that appear to be purely "accidental" and to occur seemingly under circumstances beyond parental control, poor judgment and inexperience of the parent regarding child development may be contributing factors. A high incidence of psychopathology in the family unit antedating the burn incident has been reported by Long and Cope. Accidental burns associated with markedly disturbed family situations have been documented by Walter and Friedman. In some instances the parents were unable to cope with their children's preburn emotional problems, in others psychologic disturbances of the mothers resulted in lack of supervision of the children. These authors also emphasize the importance of considering the possibility of child abuse in all children with burns.

Smoke Inhalation and Burns of the Respiratory Tract. Respiratory tract injury from thermal burns is one of the major causes of mortality in burn patients. Respiratory tract involvement should be specifically suspected in patients with extensive facial burns, and in victims of fires that occurred indoors. Respiratory injury is often underestimated initially. In flame burns of the larynx and trachea rapid breath-

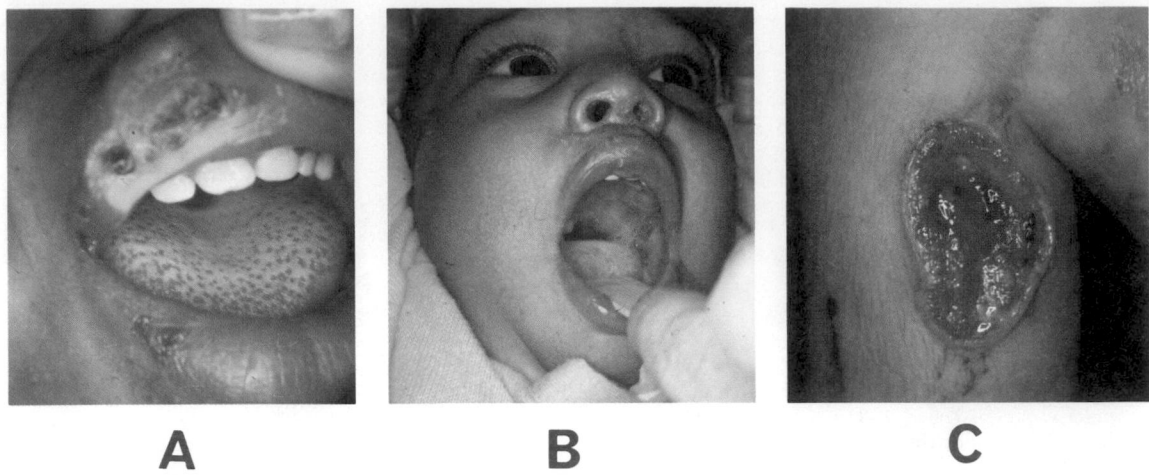

A   **B**   **C**

Fig. 1. *Electrical Burns.* A. Lesion of upper lip leaving disfiguring contracture. B. Intraoral and pharyngeal lesions. C. Necrotic area following eschar removal.

ing, dyspnea, and stridor are the manifestations of the upper airway obstruction resulting from the acute inflammation and edema of the glottis, vocal cords, and upper trachea.

In smoke inhalation there is frequently a deceptively mild initial phase during which the patient may have no symptoms or may manifest only mild bronchial obstruction and irritation. A latent period of 6 to 48 hours usually precedes the sudden onset of bronchiolitis, pulmonary edema, and severe airway obstruction resulting in diffuse bronchopneumonia and atelectasis. Low pulmonary compliance makes ventilation difficult, acute right ventricular decompensation may complicate the course, and eventual cardiopulmonary failure may develop. However, if victims of smoke inhalation can be managed through the acute phase of their illness they often make a complete recovery.

PREVENTION. Prevention is the most important aspect of the management of burns. The physician must, therefore, assume a dominant role not only in treatment and rehabilitation but also in prevention, chiefly through individual parental education, participation in community safety planning, and propagation of information on the common causes of burns.

Parents should be cautioned against the dangers created by defective heating or other electrical appliances, the overburdening of circuits, and inappropriate storage of electrical tools. Toddlers and small children must be kept away from fuels, lighters or matches, and electrical outlets. Parents must be instructed to keep hot containers and appliances out of the reach of children and to screen fireplaces. Children must be taught the dangers of playing with matches or firecrackers and must not be left in tubs or bathrooms without adult supervision. Likewise, the fear of accidental burns should be one of the chief reasons for discouraging the perilous practice of leaving children and infants alone in the house. Flammable clothing or bedding are potential hazards which can lead to disastrous fires. The Federal Flammable Fab-

rics Act and its Amendments of 1967, eliminating dangerous fabrics from the market, has helped reduce accidents and deaths from fires and burns caused by these dangerous materials.

TREATMENT OF BURNS. Minor burns constitute no threat to life. They can generally be managed in the homes and ultimately heal without disfigurement. Children with burns of 10 percent or over should be hospitalized and should receive parenteral therapy.

The extent and depth of a burn may be difficult to assess with accuracy. In general, there is a tendency to overestimate the extent and to underestimate the depth of burns. Evans' "rule of nine" or multiples of nine, commonly used to tabulate the extent of burns, has proved quite inexact when applied to smaller children. In infancy and early childhood the relative surface area size of different parts varies with age. The younger the child, the greater proportionally is the surface of the head and the lesser that of the legs. In smaller children modifications of Berkow's table which make allowances of this nature are perhaps more applicable for the calculation of burned body surface area (Figs. 3A and B).

The discussion in detail of the therapy of major burns is beyond the scope of this chapter. Severe burns should be viewed as "total body" injuries rather than complicated cutaneous injuries. In severe burns, involving 20 percent or more of body surface, general principles of management must be judiciously designed to maintain the circulation; prevent renal failure as well as water intoxication; prevent or treat infection; and aim toward early repair of the burn wounds. Survival will depend not only upon the immediacy and efficiency of the emergency care, but also on the prevention and control of complications that may develop weeks after the accident, such as septicemia, profound anemia and malnutrition, and gastrointestinal bleeding.

Fluid Therapy. Major thermal burns are followed almost immediately by a considerable outflow of fluid, protein, and electrolytes from the intravascu-

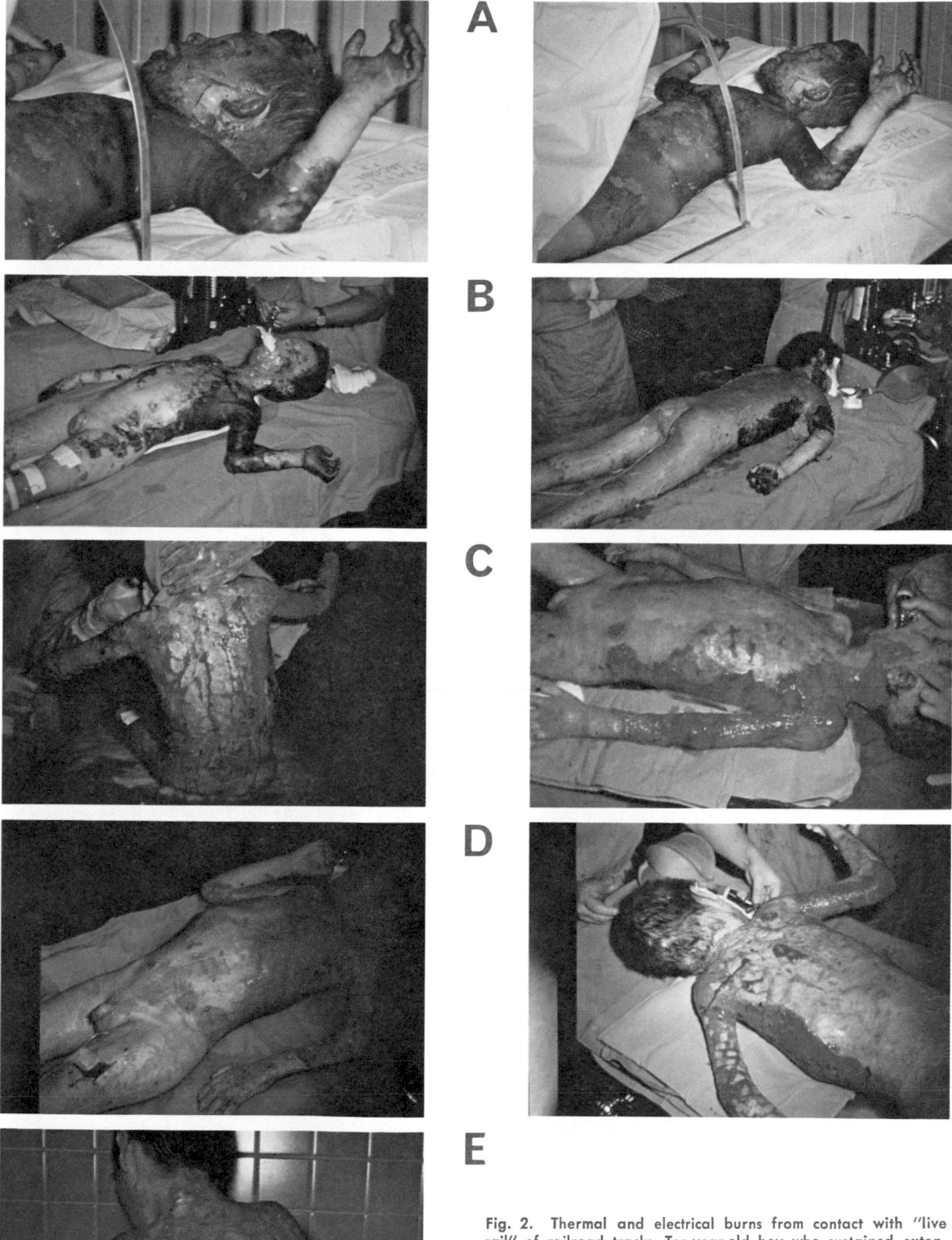

Fig. 2. Thermal and electrical burns from contact with "live rail" of railroad tracks. Ten-year-old boy who sustained extensive second and third degree burns exceeding 80 percent of total body surface. Figures show initial burn and subsequent course of lesions at various stages of repair. *A.* On day of accident. *B.* After two weeks. *C.* After one month. *D.* After six weeks. *E.* After five months.

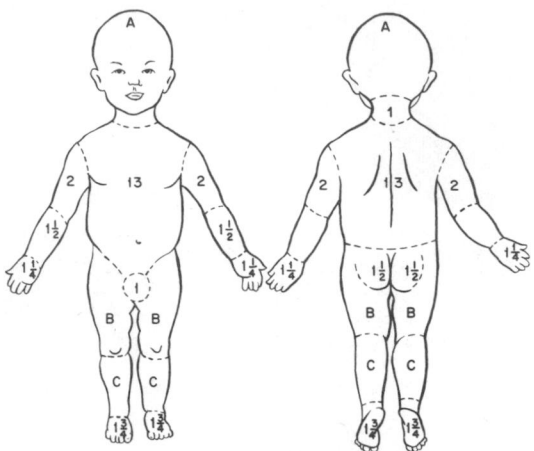

RELATIVE PERCENTAGES OF AREAS AFFECTED BY GROWTH

AREA	AGE 0	1	5
A = $\frac{1}{2}$ of Head	$9\frac{1}{2}$	$8\frac{1}{2}$	$6\frac{1}{2}$
B = $\frac{1}{2}$ of One Thigh	$2\frac{3}{4}$	$3\frac{1}{4}$	4
C = $\frac{1}{2}$ of One Leg	$2\frac{1}{2}$	$2\frac{1}{2}$	$2\frac{3}{4}$

% BURN BY AREAS

Fig. 3. A. Relative percentage of areas affected by growth (infants and young children). (Lund and Bowden's modification of Berkow's table.)

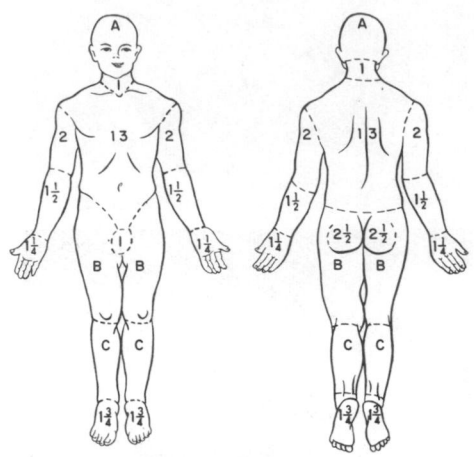

RELATIVE PERCENTAGES OF AREAS AFFECTED BY GROWTH

AREA	AGE 10	15	ADULT
A = $\frac{1}{2}$ of Head	$5\frac{1}{2}$	$4\frac{1}{2}$	$3\frac{1}{2}$
B = $\frac{1}{2}$ of One Thigh	$4\frac{1}{4}$	$4\frac{1}{2}$	$4\frac{3}{4}$
C = $\frac{1}{2}$ of One Leg	3	$3\frac{1}{4}$	$3\frac{1}{2}$

% BURNS BY AREA

Fig. 3. B. Relative percentage of areas affected by growth (children and young adults). (Lund and Bowden's modification of Berkow's table.)

lar compartment. An outpouring of fluid from the damaged capillaries occurs in the interstitial space creating the so-called abnormal "third space" or burn edema. Seepage from the burned surface results in additional losses, although to a lesser degree. Early hemolysis may further reduce the circulating blood volume. In severe burns 10 to 15 percent of the red cell mass may be destroyed. Within 48 hours hemoglobinemia and hemoglobinuria may be present. Compensatory shifts of intracellular water are usually adequate to maintain the circulation. Without replacement measures adequate in rate, volume, and composition, shock and renal failure threaten the patient's life.

In the first 48 hours after the burn, the primary objective of the therapy is to restore and maintain an adequate circulation. Corrective therapy should be based on the anticipated expansion of the extracellular fluid modified by the clinical appearance of the patient, the hourly urine output and specific gravity, hematocrit, plasma protein, and serum osmolarity. The intravenous administration of electrolytes, particularly sodium, water, and colloids in the form of blood and/or plasma must be started without delay, preferably via an indwelling polyethylene catheter in the vein. Parenteral potassium should not be given initially if there is oliguria.

A certain amount of controversy exists concerning the quantities and composition of fluids to be given intravenously. Various formulas have been proposed by which the initial needs may be calculated.

Any formula, however, is only an approximation of estimated requirements. Any scheduled fluid regimen should be constantly reevaluated and revised with great *flexibility* if during the subsequent course the patient's clinical appearance; the determination of hematocrit, plasma, proteins, and serum electrolytes; the variation in urine flow, urine specific gravity, and blood pressure indicate that the amounts are either excessive or inadequate. It is generally agreed that in burns over 50 percent of body surface, fluid replacement should be computed on the basis of a 50 percent burn.

A fluid replacement regimen broadly approximating the so-called Evans' rule appears as rational and satisfactory a guide to the fluid therapy of the burned child as any other proposed formula. We have found it most successful if applied with flexibility and if appropriate adjustments are made as indicated.

In the first 24 hours the patient is given:

1. Colloid solutions: 1 ml per kilogram of body weight per 1 percent of burn area as blood and plasma. Relatively little whole blood may be indicated in less extensive and superficial burns. In very extensive deep burns up to half the estimated colloid requirements may be given as whole blood.

2. Water and electrolytes: 1 ml per kilogram of body weight for each percent of burn area of a balanced solution—Ringer's lactate or a solution

consisting of two parts of 5 percent glucose in normal saline to one part of sixth-normal sodium lactate or bicarbonate.

3. One thousand ml of 10 percent glucose in water per square meter of *total* body surface (not burn surface) regardless of the surface of burn, to cover the daily requirements for insensible water loss and urine volume.

About half of these fluids should be given within the first eight hours and the remainder over the next sixteen hours. It is imperative that the rate and volume of the infusion be carefully and frequently verified and that the urine output be monitored at hourly intervals. The urine output and specific gravity are fairly reasonable indices of the adequacy of the fluid therapy.

An indwelling urinary catheter should be placed to facilitate accurate measurement of output. If the burn involves the external genitalia the catheter should be inserted before edema becomes significant and interferes with the procedure. The rate of urine flow varies naturally with the size of the child; 40 ml per hour per square meter of body surface is a satisfactory rate of urine flow. A low urine output usually means inadequate fluid but it may result from renal damage. An intravenous "water load" of 500 ml of 5 percent dextrose in water per square meter of body surface given rapidly in 45 to 60 minutes may resolve the problem. A prompt diuresis subsequent to the water load indicates that the amount of fluids given is inadequate; if no change in urine flow occurs, renal tubular damage should be suspected.

In the second 24 hours the amounts of colloid and electrolytes solutions should be reduced by half that given the first day, unless contraindicated by the urinary output and the blood chemistries. The same amount of nonelectrolyte solution should be continued.

At the end of 48 hours, resorption of the sequestered fluids occurs, followed usually by diuresis. The return to circulation of the edema fluid proceeds rapidly and may exceed the excretory capacity of the kidney—at this point unless the fluid output is carefully restricted, overhydration is likely to occur resulting in cardiac failure, pulmonary edema, and convulsions.

Other Measures.   In addition to fluid therapy other measures are of greatest importance in the management of burns. The susceptibility of burned patients to bacterial wound infections and to sepsis has been amply documented. The majority of fatal infections are those which are produced by *Clostridium tetani, beta hemolytic streptococcus, Staphylococcus aureus, Pseudomonas aeruginosa,* and other gram negative bacteria. The burn wound and the site of venous cannulation are the ones that are most prone to become infected. The successful control of infections in major thermal burns demands a series of rational measures including the administration of tetanus antitoxin or toxoid, the maintenance of strict aseptic technique by all personnel until the wound is healed, and the institution of vigorous and appropriate antibiotic therapy if there is evidence of bacterial infection. "Prophylactic" antibiotic therapy is probably unwise and may be responsible for the overgrowth of resistant organisms. The treatment of the suppurative thrombophlebitis of the venous cutdown is surgical, and requires excision of the entire length of the affected vein.

Pain is not a prominent feature of extensive deep burns. Morphine and barbiturates should be avoided, if possible, because their antidiuretic effect predisposes to water intoxication. If narcotics are prescribed they should not be given subcutaneously.

In smoke inhalation, or if there are burns about the face, the neck or the tracheobronchial tree, the patient may require tracheostomy. Prolonged intermittent positive pressure breathing with appropriate concentrations of oxygen, nebulized humidity, and elevation of the head to minimize edema of the head and neck are also essential in the management of patients with problems of a respiratory nature. Administration of antibiotics and steroids may also be indicated.

In severe burns it is best to withhold any oral intake during the first 48 hours, or to restrict it to occasional sips. In the initial post-burn period, a degree of ileus is generally present with acute gastric dilation and abdominal distention. The patient tends to vomit and may aspirate. The insertion of a nasogastric tube may relieve the gastrointestinal discomfort and may facilitate recognition of gastrointestinal hemorrhage from *Curling's ulcer,* a gastroduodenal ulceration encountered in approximately 10 to 25 percent of burned patients. This major complication has its peak incidence in the first 72 hours following the burn injury and has been documented in infants as early as eight months of age. The diagnosis should be suspected when blood or coffee-ground material appears in the gastric aspirate, coupled with a sudden drop of the hemoglobin.

Local Care.   The local care of the burn lesion depends on the extent and location of the burn. Both the *open* and the *closed methods* have their supporters and there are advantages and disadvantages to either method. Closed therapy is best used on small partial thickness burns treated at home on an outpatient basis, with the exception of burns on the face which should be left exposed. In hospitalized patients, the open method is generally preferred. Exposure maintains a dry surface, shows early formation of a protective eschar, and predisposes less to infection than moist and warm necrotic tissue beneath gauze dressings. It has been reported that exposure to a warm and dry environment affords the added advantages of raising significantly the rate of evaporation of water from the burned area; accelerating the drying of the burned surface; and reducing substantially the basal metabolic rate.

The more recent technique for the treatment of large burns using dressings continuously soaked with 0.5 percent silver nitrate solution has been encouraging. The septic phase of burns care appears to be favorably altered by this therapy and improved survival rates have been reported using this method in major thermal burns. It is postulated that these dressings provide a successful barrier to inordinate heat, diminish the water loss through burned skin, and provide a bacteriostatic effect on the wound. Deep wounds treated with 0.5 percent silver nitrate form eschars that separate bloodlessly and accept split thickness grafts readily. However, when this method is used substantial quantities of extracellular electrolytes are siphoned into the hypotonic dressing. Unless the patients receive large amounts of supplemental minerals, acute hyponatremia and severe hypokalemia may develop and may even result in fatalities. Methemoglobinemia has also been reported as a complication of the silver nitrate treatment when organisms cultured from the wounds are resistant to silver nitrate and capable of reducing nitrates to nitrites. *Bacillus subtilis, Pseudomonas aeruginosa, Aerobacter cloacae* are examples of nitrate-reducing bacteria. The appearance of cyanosis which does not respond to oxygen should suggest the possibility of methemoglobinemia. Methylene blue would not be sufficiently effective in the presence of a continuing source of nitrate; discontinuance of the silver nitrate treatment would be warranted, at least temporarily.

Physical Therapy. While in the severely burned child survival is understandably the immediate and foremost concern, function and appearance must also be major considerations in the total treatment of the patient. Cosmetic results will depend on the amount and depth of tissue destruction, on the control of local infections, and to a great extent on the surgery. Maintenance of function will depend on preservation of joint motion, primarily through the prevention of contractures, which in burns can ultimately involve skin, muscle, and joint capsule. Some degree of soft tissue contractures will be present in almost all patients with extremity burns, particularly in those whose burns extend over the joints. These contractures can be prevented by positioning, physical therapy, and splinting. The position of comfort for the burned patient favors contractures and once this position has been assumed it is painful for the patient to be moved from it. In the acute phase of the burn, or in the chronic phase after grafting, proper positioning is the most important measure for prevention of contractures. In general, the joints most affected should be held in full extension or nearly so. If the axillae are burned, shoulders should be at or near 90 degrees abduction; elbows, knees, and hips should be in extension; hips should be symmetrically abducted at or near 15 degrees; ankles should be in neutral position or at 90 degrees. Once contractures have become established, splinting, or skeletal traction are effective in correcting the contractures, alone or in conjunction with surgery. Early physical therapy is also very helpful in preventing deformities. Joints of both extremities can be moved easily if dressings are moist or if the extremity is immersed; motion is painful if dressings are dry.

REFERENCES

Cason, J. A., et al. Mortality and infection in extensively burned patients treated with silver-nitrate compresses. Lancet, 7544:651, 1968.

Evans, E. B., et al. Preservation and restoration of joint function in patients with severe burns. J.A.M.A., 204: 843, 1968.

Evans, E. I., et al. Fluid and electrolyte requirements in severe burns. Amer. J. Surg., 135:804, 1952.

Farmer, A. W. Management of burns in children. Pediatrics, 25:886, 1960.

Gifford, G. H., Jr., Marty, A. T., and McCollum, D. W. The management of electrical mouth burns in children. Pediatrics, 47:113, 1971.

Hendren, W. H. Treatment of the severely burned child. Pediat. Clin. N. Amer., 9:277, 1962.

Holter, J. C., and Friedman, S. B. Etiology and management of seriously burned children—psychosocial considerations. Am. J. Dis. Child., 118:680, 1969.

Lund, C. C., and Browder, N. C. Estimation of areas of burns. Surg. Gynec. Obstet., 79:352, 1944.

Metcoff, J., et al. Losses and physiologic requirements for water and electrolytes after extensive burns in children. New Eng. J. Med., 265:101, 1961.

Monafo, W. W., and Moyer, C. A. Effectiveness of dilute aqueous silver nitrate in the treatment of major burns. Arch. Surg., 91:200, 1965.

Oeconomopoulos, C. T. Electrical burns in infancy and childhood. Am. J. Dis. Child., 103:67, 1962.

O'Neill, J. A., et al. Surgical treatment of Curling's ulcer. Surg. Gynec. Obstet., 126:40, 1968.

Stone, H. H. Control of infections in major burns with special emphasis on pseudomonas infections. J. Pediat. Surg., 3:3, 1968.

Stone, N. H., and Boswick, J. A. Definitive initial care of burns. Modern Medicine, 37:226, 1969.

Ternberg, J. L., and Luce, E. Methemoglobinemia: A complication of the silver nitrate treatment of burns. Ped. Surg., 63:328, 1968.

Waller, J. A., and Manheiner, D. I. Non-fatal burns of children in a well-defined urban population. J. Pediat., 65:863, 1964.

Webster, J. R., et al. Recognition and management of smoke inhalation. J.A.M.A., 201:71, 1967.

13.3
DROWNING

ARNOLD H. EINHORN

Drowning accidents constitute a major threat to the lives of young children. Excluding deaths in floods and cataclysms, submersion ranks second as the leading cause of accidental deaths in children from 4 to 15 years of age. In 1969 fatalities from drowning exceeded 7,300 in the United States; of these about one third occurred in children under 15 years of age. Boys are distinctly more prone to such accidents than girls. This preponderance in males is more clear-cut in older children; from 5 to 14 years of age three fourths of the victims are boys; below the age of 5 the disproportion is less pronounced and the ratio is 2 to 1. Both fatalities and near-drownings have a year-round distribution. However, a seasonal peak is evident during the summer months, even in states where aquatic activities responsible for the majority of drowning accidents, such as boating, fishing, swimming, water skiing, skin diving, and scuba diving are possible throughout the year.

PATHOPHYSIOLOGY AND CLINICAL COURSE. In drowning, the events which lead to cardiorespiratory arrest and death succeed each other within a period of a few minutes after immersion. In general the sequence of morbid processes progresses more rapidly in freshwater drowning. Schematically, the aspiration of even small amounts of fluid into the airways causes laryngospasm. If the reflex closure of the glottis is severe and prolonged, movements of deglutition will appear and the victim often vomits. Asphyxia, if sufficiently pronounced and prolonged, will then produce relaxation of the glottis, with ensuing flooding of the lungs. Cardiac arrest may supervene very rapidly before, during, or after a phase of terminal apnea. In a small number of instances, relaxation of the glottis will not occur before death.

In the vast majority of fatal drownings, death is caused by asphyxia *with* fluid aspiration. Asphyxia without fluid aspiration occurs in less than 10 percent of deaths from immersion. In drowning with aspiration, fluid may enter the bloodstream via the lungs or may cause a shift of additional water from the circulation into the lungs. Resulting changes will depend upon the composition and volume of the aspirated fluid. In animal models, manifestations produced in freshwater drownings differ significantly from those elicited in seawater submersions.

Experimentally, in *freshwater drownings,* the aspirated water present in the lung floods the bloodstream producing rapid hemodilution, hypervolemia, fulminating pulmonary edema, and ventricular fibrillation. However, in man, ventricular fibrillation has not been documented in nonfatal submersions; hemodilution, if present at all, is generally mild to moderate and may affect all blood components, including electrolytes. Hyponatremia and hyperkalemia may be present. Arterial hypoxemia, hemolysis, severe pulmonary edema, central nervous system damage are the main features of freshwater submersion, in which the course tends generally to evolve more rapidly toward a fatal outcome than in seawater drowning.

Hemoglobinemia, "drowning hemoglobinuria," and oliguria with transient azotemia and proteinuria may develop in the survivors of freshwater near-drownings. A return to normal renal function, following several days of hyposthenuric diuresis is the usual course of this complication. Clotting defects and hemoconcentration can also be seen occasionally after freshwater submersions.

In *seawater drowning,* water is drained from the plasma into the lungs, producing pulmonary edema, hemoconcentration, hypovolemia, fall in blood pressure, and a variable degree of hemolysis. Passage of seawater solute into the blood may further increase the serum hyperosmolarity. Hypernatremia and elevation of the hematocrit are typical disturbances. The prognosis appears related to the degree of pulmonary edema, hemolysis, and the reversibility of hypoxic central nervous system damage and circulatory failure. In man, ventricular fibrillation has been reported in victims of saltwater submersion.

In both freshwater and seawater nonfatal submersions, if adequate ventilation and circulation are reestablished and maintained, alteration in blood volume and composition reverse themselves rapidly. Determinations of the following blood values should be made and repeated until normal: hematocrit, red blood cell and plasma hemoglobin, serum electrolytes, pH and blood gases, blood urea nitrogen, and clotting. Central venous pressure, urinalysis (including chemistry, cytology, concentration, and acidification), radiography of the chest, and electrocardiography are also essential.

TREATMENT. Although the apparent duration of submersion is often unrelated to the physiologic state of the victim, speed is of utmost importance in the management of nonfatal drowning. Irreversible central nervous system damage has been found to occur within three minutes after cardiovascular arrest, and from five to seven minutes after the beginning of total immersion.

The presence of breathing movements and coughing upon removal of the victim from the water, suggests that hypoxic damage and aspiration are probably slight. Hospitalization is nonetheless indicated for physical, roentgenologic, blood and urine examinations, and for observation. Consciousnes and absence of apnea are not synonymous of recovery in all patients. Sudden deaths have been reported after near-drownings, in victims who were conscious and breathing after first being rescued.

If the patient is not breathing spontaneously, artificial inflation of the lungs should be started immediately upon removing the victim from the water, or even, whenever possible, while the patient is still in the water. After clearing rapidly the patient's upper airways, the mouth-to-mouth technique should be used first. Subsequently, when oxygen, equipment, and adequate facilities become available, intermittent positive pressure breathing should be instituted. Postural drainage is of no value and should not be attempted.

If the carotid pulse cannot be felt, closed-chest cardiac massage must be performed concurrently, until the return of a palpable spontaneous pulse. In addition, restoration of normal circulation may require intracardiac injection of epinephrine, rapid intravenous infusion of fluids and elevation of the legs to increase venous return, intravenous administration of sodium bicarbonate for correction of the metabolic acidosis accumulated during the cardiac arrest, and external electrical defibrillation in case of ventricular fibrillation.

Maintenance of artificial respiration should not be restricted only to victims who are unable to breathe for themselves. In those patients who have been apneic, and in those who are, or were, cyanotic or unconscious, assisted intermittent positive pressure oxygen ventilation must be continued even after return of spontaneous breathing, as long as there is evidence of pulmonary edema, cardiovascular disturbances, hemolysis, hemodilution or hemoconcentration, electrolyte imbalance, and hypervolemia.

Tracheal intubation will facilitate prolonged positive pressure breathing and removal of secretions. Since vomiting is generally associated with drowning of significant severity, it is preferable to clean the tracheobronchial tree under direct laryngoscopic visualization before inserting the endotracheal catheter to begin assisted positive pressure ventilation. If artificial ventilation must be continued beyond 48 hours a tracheotomy should be performed. If aspiration into the lungs has been massive, systemic steroids may be useful. They may also contribute to relieve cerebral edema, if present. If evidence of pneumonitis exists, or if there are indications that the fluid aspirated may be heavily contaminated, therapy with appropriate antibiotics is recommended. Gastric evacuation and withholding of oral intake appear desirable in all patients with respiratory distress.

Fluids must be regulated to correct the electrolytes, to promote adequate urine output, and to treat the pulmonary edema. As long as there is evidence of cerebral or pulmonary edema, intravenous fluids should be restricted to 1,000 ml per m^2 per 24 hours or less, using fluctuations of weight, and urinary output and concentration as criteria for assessment and adjustments of fluid requirements. The recommended initial solution following *seawater submersion* is salt-poor plasma or albumin, 10 ml/kg; after *freshwater drowning*, potassium-poor plasma, albumin, or normal saline should be given. The solute composition of the subsequent solutions to be administered intravenously should vary in accordance with serum electrolyte values, acid-base status, and urine concentrations.

It may be necessary to use a hyperosmotic agent such as mannitol to reduce cerebral edema secondary to asphyxia and circulatory arrest. In case of severe hemolysis partial exchange transfusion has been recommended but seems rarely indicated.

In essence, treatment of a victim of submersion demands that no time be wasted before instituting respiratory and circulatory resuscitative procedures. It also requires continuing artificial ventilation until after correction of all systemic and pulmonary disturbances. However, as is the case in accidental episodes of any type or nature, adequate prevention may forestall in most instances the need for such measures, and may avoid the tragedy of loss of life or irreversible handicaps.

PREVENTION. Drownings result primarily from lack of supervision, absence of adequate protection, inexperience, overconfidence, ignorance, and poor judgment. A prerequisite for the application of adequate preventive measures is awareness of, and familiarity with, the circumstances which are conducive to such accidents.

Older children often drown while swimming, or while engaged in other aquatic activities without having the proper experience or supervision. Young children more commonly drown while left unattended in bathtubs or after a fall through the ice than while swimming. They are also found submersed in unprotected backyard ponds or swimming pools, or stray away unnoticed into water bodies while adults are engrossed in lively conversations or in other activities. The extremely dangerous practice of hyperventilating voluntarily for the purpose of lengthening the breathholding underwater time claims unnecessary victims among older children and adolescents, who may be good swimmers but received no adequate swimming safety instructions. In such cases sudden loss of consciousness may occur under water, secondary to the lowering of the carbon dioxide pressure, decrease of arterial oxygen tension, and cerebral ischemia.

Hazardous sites of potential exposure are burgeoning all over the country. Community or quasi-public swimming pools are more likely to employ lifeguards and attendants. However, this type of public recreational facility, once preponderant, is in the process of being outranked by the proliferation of private residential pools, often unsupervised and unprotected

The Committee on Accidents of the American Council of Pediatrics has made useful "waterproofing" recommendations which should be publicized by physicians and educators to help minimize the perils of water for children. It is imperative that children always be properly supervised by qualified adults in the vicinity of rivers, lakes, pools, ponds, and oceans. Young children must never be left unattended in bathtubs. Adequate enclosures must be provided for all pools and ponds. Children should be taught to swim or float as early as possible. Good swimming conduct should be encouraged at all times. All family members including the children should be instructed in water safety and in first-aid resuscitation techniques. Community action is equally important. Communities must have active water safety and public education programs. Appropriate regulations must be promulgated concerning construction, fencing, and supervision of all water sites where perilous exposure may occur.

REFERENCES

Committee on Accident Prevention, American Academy of Pediatrics. Perils of the Water: The Problems of Drowning and the Child. Committee Statement. Newsletter Supplement, 1968.

Giammona, S. T., and Modell, J. H. Drowning by total immersion. Effects on pulmonary surfactant of distilled water, isotonic saline, and sea water. Amer. J. Dis. Child., 114:612, 1967.

Modell, J. H., et al. Blood gas and electrolyte changes in human near-drowning victims. J.A.M.A., 203:99, 1968.

National Safety Council. Accident Facts, 1970 Edition, pp. 6-9.

Press, E., et al. An interstate drowning study. Amer. J. of Publ. Health, 58:2275, 1968.

Redding, J. R. Resuscitation and treatment following submersion. Pediatrics, 37:666, 1966.

13.4

POISONINGS IN CHILDHOOD— GENERAL

ARNOLD H. EINHORN

The ever-increasing number and variety of drugs and chemical household products found in or around every home constitute a dangerous source of potentially toxic substances. Accidental poisonings caused fundamentally by adult negligence victimizes primarily very young children. Perhaps nowhere is the need for adequate protection, education, and legislation as essential as in the field of poison prevention. **INCIDENCE, EPIDEMIOLOGY, AND ETIOLOGY.** Accidental poisoning has become a leading health problem, accounting for more than 3,000 deaths annually in the United States. The mortality is only part of the picture. The number of nonfatal poisonings is estimated to exceed one million a year, and many who survive the ingestion of poison are left with permanent disabilities. Some of these deficits may be subtle and are often overlooked. Intellectual impairment, for example, may result from chronic lead intoxication. It may, however, be secondary to poisoning by any product that affects primarily the central nervous system, producing convulsions or prolonged coma.

This type of handicap may only become apparent when the child enters school.

Children under 5 years of age constitute only 9 percent of the total population, yet approximately two-thirds of all poisonings reported in 1969 from 439 centers in 46 states occurred among youngsters of this age group (Table 1). The incidence was highest in the 2-year age group, the next highest in the 1-year-old group. Before 9 to 10 months of age, the infant is less exposed to the danger of poisoning because of his relative immobility and closer supervision.

Boys ingest poisons more frequently than girls, the ratio being roughly 3 to 2. A larger proportion of victims has been noted among children living in deprived social settings. In the United States, accidental poisoning is reported to be observed more frequently in nonwhite children, a reflection essentially of unfavorable economic conditions, with poor housing, overcrowding, larger families with inadequate supervision of children, unsatisfactory storage facilities, and lack of information on the subject.

Accidental poisonings also occur with greater frequency whenever there is a change, a disturbance or deviation from the ordinary routine—e.g, moving time, holiday rush, painting time, pre-vacation time, and during periods of stress, tension, illness, or death in the family. There are indications that episodes of poisonings tend to recur in the same child or within the same family among siblings. Whether this is related to accident proneness of the child or the family, or is the result of an accident-prone environment needs further study.

The degree of accessibility of the toxic agent, the phase of oral exploration, the mobility, the ever-

TABLE 1. *Accidental Ingestions Among Children Under 5 Years of Age—1969*

Type of Substance—Breakdown by Age and Comparison with Poisonings at all Ages.

	Total All Ages	Total Ages Under 5 Years	Under 1 Year	1st Year of Life	2nd Year of Life	3rd Year of Life	4th Year of Life
Medicines	67,427	40,651	865	7,106	17,170	11,511	3,999
*Internal	60,877	35,561	473	5,287	15,206	10,814	3,781
*Aspirin	17,658	14,494	106	1,479	5,941	5,272	1,696
*Other	43,219	21,067	367	3,808	9,265	5,542	2,085
*External	6,550	5,090	392	1,819	1,964	697	218
Cleaning and Polishing Agents	13,925	10,978	666	4,602	3,841	1,322	547
Petroleum Products	4,286	3,322	82	1,427	1,215	419	179
Cosmetics	5,754	5,109	188	1,790	2,376	596	159
Pesticides	5,747	3,952	276	1,523	1,278	598	277
Gases and Vapors	645	61	13	12	13	15	8
Plants	4,554	3,318	290	886	1,085	669	388
Turpentine, Paints, etc.	5,197	4,090	244	1,815	1,361	470	200
Miscellaneous	7,314	4,193	433	1,348	1,335	692	385
Unknown	1,452	481	22	137	173	97	52
Total	116,301	76,155	3,079	20,646	29,847	16,389	6,194

*These totals are included in medicines.

Source: Poison reports submitted to the National Clearinghouse for Poison Control Centers in 46 states.

Courtesy of U.S. Dept. of Health, Education, and Welfare, Public Health Service, Food and Drug Administration.

growing urge to reach, and the insatiable curiosity of the normal child are major determinants in the pathogenesis of accidental poisonings. As a result, both the incidence of poisoning and nature of poisons encountered are intimately related to the child's stages of growth and development. Thus, infants less than 1 year of age are more likely to be poisoned by household preparations such as bleaches, cleansing products, polishing fluids, or pesticides, which are generally stored at lower levels—on the floor, under the kitchen sink, or on the lower shelves. As the child becomes more mobile and able to reach higher places, often wrongly considered to be inaccessible to him, he is likely to ingest poisons stored in cupboards, medicine chests, and kitchen cabinets. These products are usually cosmetics and pharmaceutic products prescribed for adults. After 4 years of age, the child becomes more cautious as he gains knowledge and experience, and the incidence of poisonings declines sharply.

Highly deficient safety precautions in the homes, particularly with regard to storage, facilitate the accessibility of toxic agents. In virtually all instances of poisoning the substances involved are either improperly stored or carelessly placed within easy reach of children: on the floor, on low tables, in unlocked cabinets, or in women's handbags, which are often given to the youngster to play with. One study showed that only in 6 percent of cases were toxic agents stored in locked medicine cabinets.

Lack of awareness by parents of the potential toxicity of many familiar household chemicals used daily, cosmetics, and prescribed drugs is also an important contributory factor. Too often, parents fail to realize that the bad taste or flavor are no protection against poisoning and that common cleaning agents such as lye solution, gasoline, fuels, or kerosene may be ingested by a curious child who is looking for a drink or merely exploring.

Removal of a toxic substance from its original container increases the risk of accidental poisoning. Highly dangerous preparations such as carbon tetrachloride, oil of wintergreen, kerosene, benzene, turpentine, ammonia, furniture polish, and pesticides are frequently stored in drinking glasses, saucers, soda bottles, coffee cans, milk bottles, and fruit jars and mistaken by children for food or water. It is also not uncommon among certain cultural groups to buy large quantities of a product and redistribute it in unlabeled containers to friends and relatives. Errors of mistaken identity are often made when medications of different nature in bottles or jars similar in size, shape, and color are placed side by side in medicine cabinets or other locations.

The small collapsible cardboard container in which drugs are distributed are readily opened by children. Efficiency of different types of safety devices on medication packages varies greatly and may give parents a false sense of security. Package-opening abilities of children of "poison-prone" age tested by Jung and Done revealed that the snap-type "safety

cap" is almost as easily removed as an ordinary screw cap, and that the palm-and-turn cap, although more difficult to manipulate, can be opened by a significant percentage of children.

The practice prevailing in the United States of dispensing medications without naming the drug on the label, serves no legitimate purpose. It makes identification of any potentially harmful agent difficult, thus delaying prompt and appropriate treatment when required. Physicians or pharmacists who fail to warn parents explicitly about the inherent danger for children of any drug they may prescribe or dispense fail in their most basic of duties and responsibilities, contribute to the child's exposure to poisons, and enhance greatly the risk of accidental ingestions. In their homes, physicians, dentists, pharmaceutic salesmen, are notoriously negligent as regards poison prevention. Poisoning episodes occur relatively more frequently in their children and are attributable to the abundance of professional samples readily available in their homes.

TOXIC AGENTS.   Poisons can be ingested, inhaled, injected, or absorbed through the skin.

Inhalation.   In Table 2 are listed a representative sample of agents that may be responsible for poisoning by inhalation. Carbon monoxide fumes emanating from leaky furnaces or automobile exhausts cause severe tissue anoxia, nephrotoxicity, and neurotoxicity. The characteristic cherry red color of the skin, lips, and nails may not always be discernible. Survivors may be left with permanent brain damage. Inhalation of solvents, paint thinners, and the ingredients contained in insecticide sprays or powders can be damaging to various systems, and may cause convulsions; so does camphor, present in some moth repellents and in camphorated oil. Methylbromide may be emanated from a leaky refrigerator and produces CNS toxicity.

The inhalation of ethyl or isopropyl alcohol during spongebathing to reduce fever may result in alcohol intoxication and cause coma with or without hypoglycemia.

Glue Sniffing, the practice of youngsters and adolescents of inhaling deliberately a wide variety of organic solvents contained in glue, paint, thinners, nail polish removers, cleaning and lighter fluids has reached in recent years epidemic proportions. These various substances have in common a narcotic effect and induce states of inebriation and exhilaration. Ensuing EEG abnormalities, convulsions, and even fatalities have been documented (see also p. 567).

Skin Absorption.   Major poisons that may cause toxicity by absorption either through the broken or the intact skin are listed in Table 3. There is general agreement that boric acid is not only worthless as a medicinal agent but is potentially harmful, and that no valid reason exists to prescribe or dispense it. Yet instances of severe poisonings continue to occur in infants by misguided applications of boric acid or powders containing this agent to large areas of denuded skin on the diaper region, or for the treatment

TABLE 2. *Substances Apt to Produce Toxicity by Inhalation*

Carbon Monoxide	Camphor-Naphthalene Paradichlorobenzene
Methyl Alcohol	Chlorinated Hydrocarbons
Propyl Alcohol	(DDT, Dieldrin, Chlordane, Lindane)
Acetone	Pyrethrum
Carbon Tetrachloride	Methyl Chloride
Turpentine	Cyanide
Methyl Bromide (Refrigerant)	Parathion
Aniline	Fluoride
Mercury Vapors	Nicotine

Solvent Sniffing (Glue Sniffing)
(Toluene, Acetone, Hexane)

of eczema. Symptoms of boric acid toxicity are intense erythema, exfoliation of the skin, severe diarrhea and vomiting, and protracted convulsions. Neurologic symptoms may occur as late as one week after the poisoning. Boric acid poisoning is frequently fatal. Aniline dyes freshly stamped on diapers have been responsible for nursery outbreaks of methemoglobinemia, causing severe cyanosis, coma, or convulsions in small infants. Certain nose drop constituents, particularly sympathomimetic agents such as tetrahydrozoline (Tyzine), dextroamphetamine (Benzedrine), or ephedrine, may be absorbed through the nasal mucosa and produce central nervous stimulation.

Ingestion. The variety of harmful substances that can be ingested accidentally by a child is so great that it is impracticable to include in this section a listing of all such substances and the specific therapy for each product. For such information reference should be made to textbooks of clinical toxicology, and valuable help can often be obtained from the nearest Poison Control Center, the location of which should be known to every practicing physician. Over 1,000 products were found to be responsible for poisoning in an analysis of 116,301 poisonings from one control center. Table 4 and Figure 4 show the distribution of the various toxic agents accountable for approximately 350,000 poisonings in children under 5 years of age reported in over 40 states from 1965 through 1969. The most prominent members of each class are also identified. Drugs intended for internal medication caused approximately 48 percent of all poisonings. Aspirin, vitamins, antihistamines, tranquilizers, analgesics, and cough medicines were the chief offenders; household chemicals ranked second as the leading causes with soaps, cleaning agents, disinfectants, perfumes, and insecticides most frequently involved. Ingredients responsible for toxicity in common household products and in pesticides are listed in Tables 5 and 6 respectively.

It is not uncommon for children to chew berries, leaves, or other plant constituents. Ornamental plants, flowers, and shrubs (Table 7) found in the home, the garden, and along suburban and rural roads may be responsible for atropine-like, digitalis-like, or lysergic-

TABLE 3. *Substances Apt to Produce Toxicity by Skin or Mucous Membrane Absorption*

Skin	
Anilin	Chlorinated Hydrocarbons (Chlordane, Toxaphene, DDT, etc.)
Boric Acid	Mercury
Phenol	Nicotine
Topical Antihistamines	Organophosphates
Topical Anesthetics	Thallium

Mucous Membranes (Nose Drops)

Tetrahydrozoline HCl (Tyzine)
Dextroamphetamine (Benzedrine)
Ephedrine

TABLE 4.   *Accidental Ingestions Among Children Under 5 Years of Age*

Type of Substance by Year of Report
Reported by Poison Control Centers
1965-1969

Type of Substance	1969		1968		1967		1966		1965	
	No.	%	No.	%	No.	%	No.	%	No.	%
Medicines	40,651	53.4	38,354	53.6	38,360	52.8	34,670	53.6	34,483	54.4
Internal	35,561	46.7	33,758	47.2	34,081	46.9	31,213	48.3	30,870	48.7
Aspirin	14,494	19.0	15,523	21.7	16,887	23.2	16,076	24.9	16,328	25.8
Other	21,067	27.7	18,235	25.5	17,194	23.7	15,137	23.4	14,542	22.9
External	5,090	6.7	4,596	6.4	4,279	5.9	3,457	5.3	3,613	5.7
Cleaning and Polishing Agents	10,978	14.4	10,349	14.4	10,414	14.3	9,398	14.5	9,343	14.7
Petroleum Products	3,322	4.4	3,573	5.0	3,337	4.6	3,243	5.0	3,073	4.9
Cosmetics	5,109	6.7	4,286	6.0	4,639	6.4	3,785	5.9	3,271	5.2
Pesticides	3,952	5.2	3,965	5.5	4,087	5.6	3,715	5.8	3,856	6.1
Gases and Vapors	61	0.1	64	0.1	102	0.1	96	0.2	87	0.1
Plants	3,318	4.4	2,740	3.8	2,890	4.0	2,153	3.3	2,028	3.2
Turpentine, Paints, etc.	4,090	5.4	3,947	5.5	3,663	5.0	3,260	5.0	3,095	4.9
Miscellaneous	4,193	5.5	3,688	5.1	4,721	6.5	3,911	6.1	3,766	5.9
Not Specified	481	0.6	597	1.0	448	0.6	403	0.6	350	0.6
Total	76,155	100.0	71,563	100.0	72,661	100.0	64,634	100.0	63,352	100.0

Source: Individual reports submitted to the National Clearinghouse for Poison Control Centers. (1969—439 Centers, 46 states; 1968—420 centers, 43 states; 1967—395 centers, 43 states; 1966—356 centers, 41 states; 1965—341 centers, 40 states.

Courtesy of U.S. Dept. of Health, Education and Welfare, Public Health Service, Food and Drug Administration.

TABLE 5.   *Ingredients Responsible for Toxicity in Common Household Products*

Bleaches, Various Cleansing Agents, Detergents, Sanitizers, Disinfectants, Deodorants

Hypochlorites	Benzine
Na or K Hydroxide	Kerosene
Hydrochloric or Sulfuric Acid	Pine Oil
Ammonia	Turpentine
Oxalic Acid	Xylene
Formaldehyde	Carbon Tetrachloride
Methanol	Carbon Trichlorethane
Isopropanol	Naphthalene
Phenol	p-Dichlorobenzene
Cresol	Borates
Menthol	Quaternary Ammonium Compounds
Surfactants	

Cosmetics (perfumes, after shave lotions, nail polish removers, hair dyes)	Polishes, Solvents Paints, Waxes	Inks, Arts and Crafts Products
Essential Oils	Methanol	Glycol
Alcohols	Carbon Tetrachloride	Phenols
Acetone	Camphor	Cresols
Lead Acetate	Turpentine	Petroleum
Toluene	Formaldehyde	Distillates
Pyrogallol	Aromatic Hydrocarbons	Ketones
Borax	Mineral Spirits	Xylene
	Mineral Seal Oil	Oxalic Acid
	Naphtha	Lead Oxide
		Arsenic Oxide

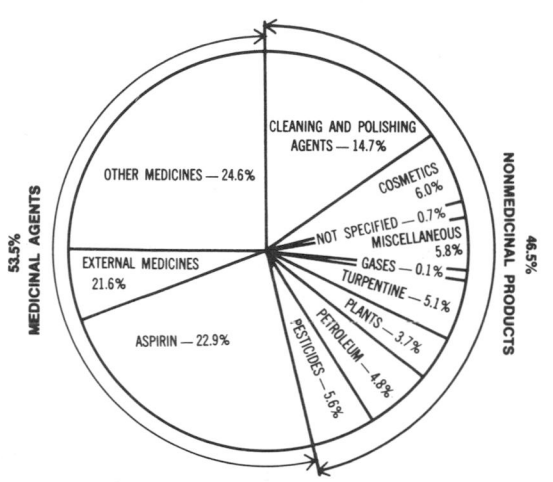

Fig. 4. Percentage distribution of 348,365 toxic agents responsible for poisonings in children under 5 years of age from 1965 through 1969. (Adapted from reports to the National Clearinghouse for Poison Control Centers, U.S. Dept. HEW, PHS, FDA.)

type poisonings. The leaves of rhubarb contain oxalic acid; their ingestion by children may cause caustic burns of the esophagus and severe hypocalcemic convulsions.

Even seemingly innocent edible foods may be a source of toxicity (Table 8). The exotoxin of *Clostridium botulinum* may contaminate home-canned foodstuffs. This neurotoxin produces generalized weakness with special predilection for the cranial nerves. Diplopia, strabismus, ptosis, difficulty in swallowing may be present, and respiratory paralysis may de-

TABLE 6. *Ingredients Responsible for Toxicity in Pesticides*

Chlorinated Hydrocarbons*
(DDT, Chlordane, Toxaphene, Dieldrin, Aldrin)
Pyrethrum
Nicotine
Camphor, Naphthalene, p-Dichlorobenzene
Strychnine
Cyanide
Arsenic, Copper, Antimony
Fluorides
Thallium
Phosphorous
Organophosphates
(Malathion, Parathion, TEPP, OMPA)
Warfarin

*Active ingredients often dissolved in:
  Aliphatic hydrocarbons (kerosene)
  Aromatic hydrocarbons (xylene)
which may also be responsible for toxic manifestations.

velop. Contamination of wheat and rye may cause ergotism and lathyrism. The former produces numbness of the extremities, striking circulatory changes which may lead to gangrene, skin changes, fixed miosis, central nervous stimulation or depression; the latter causes degeneration of the posterior and lateral columns of the spine. In the early 1960s, thousands of persons in Morocco and Turkey were the unfortunate victims of tri-ortho-cresyl phosphate poisoning after consuming cooking oil contaminated with this

TABLE 7. *Common Plants and Shrubs with Potential CNS Toxicity*

Plants	Toxic Part	Toxic Effect
Jimsonweed (Datura)		
Nightshade (Solanacea)	Berries	Atropine-like effect
Lantana		
Morning Glory	Seeds	LSD-like effect
Larkspur	Seeds	CNS excitatory symptoms
Oleander	Leaves	CNS depression, paralysis, miosis
Mountain Laurel, Yew, Rhododendron, Azalea	All parts	CNS depression
Foxglove	Leaves and Seeds	Digitalis-like effect
Vegetables		
Rhubarb	Leaves	Corrosive esophagitis Hypocalcemic convulsions (oxalic acid poisoning)
Potato	Leaves and sprouts	Depression with mental confusion
Mushrooms (*Amanita muscaria* and *A. phalloides*)	All parts	Parasympathomimetic effects

TABLE 8.   *Food and Toxicity*

Acute Ethylism
Botulism (Canned Food)
Ergotism (Wheat and Rye)
Lathyrism (Wheat)
Muscarinism (Mushroom)
Mussel Poisoning (Curare-like effect)

Chemical Contamination

"Ginger Paralysis"
Cooking Oil Paralysis   }   Tricresyl Phosphate Adulteration

chemical which affects selectively the peripheral nerves and causes severe polyneuritis.

DIAGNOSIS.   In the absence of either a definite history of ingestion or contact with a known poison, the diagnosis is often difficult and perplexing. Symptoms caused by poisons vary with the type of toxic agent and are generally nonspecific. The symptoms most frequently encountered in acute poisonings are burning in the mouth and throat, vomiting, nausea, abdominal pain, diarrhea, dyspnea, pallor, collapse, stupor, sudden loss of consciousness, or convulsions. These are nonspecific and can be produced by other childhood diseases. The physical examination seldom offers a definite clue to the nature of the poison. Consequently, a high index of suspicion must be maintained and the possibility of poisoning must be considered systematically in any sudden illness of unknown cause or in any puzzling situation where the differential diagnosis presents a difficult problem. Detailed and oriented questioning is often necessary in order to obtain a positive history. Since attempts at first-aid treatment prior to the physician's examination may mask the symptoms, inquiry should always be made as to the time of occurrence and the nature of the initial symptoms *prior* to treatment.

TABLE 9.   *Therapeutic Agents Causing Central Nervous Depression*

1. *Opiates* and Related *Synthetic Narcotics**
     (Meperidine, dextropropoxyphene)

2. *Barbiturates*, other *Sedatives* and *Hypnotics*
     (Chloral, paraldehyde, glutethimide)

3. *Antihistamines*
     Ethanolamines*   Ethylenediamine*
       (Benadryl)   (Chlor-trimeton)

     Alkylamines   Phenothiazine
       (Pyribenzamine)   (Phenergan)

4. *Tranquilizers*

     Phenothiazine Derivatives (Promazines and Piperazines)
     Meprobamate*
     Rauwolfia Alkaloids
     Benzodiazepine Compounds (Librium, Valium)
     Glutethimide* (Doriden)
     Dibenzepine Compounds (Tofranil)

*Acute toxicity may produce primary CNS excitation.

With some poisons certain characteristic features may help to establish the correct diagnosis and aid in the identification of the poison. A history of *pica* should call attention to the possibility of lead poisoning. The odor of vomitus or gastric contents may prove helpful in cases of poisoning with alcohol, benzene, kerosene, carbon tetrachloride, oil of wintergreen, phenol, ether, chloroform, or paraldehyde. The *odor of violets* in the vomitus or urine may suggest turpentine or eucalyptol poisoning; the *odor of bitter almonds*, cyanide poisoning; and a *garlic-like odor*, phosphorus or arsenic. Phosphorus poisoning produces *luminescence* of the urine and vomitus.

In cases of *somnolence, stupor*, or *coma*, poisoning with narcotics, hypnotics, sedatives, alcohols, tranquilizers, certain antihistaminics, and various depressant psychoactive drugs should be suspected including barbiturates, chloral hydrate, reserpine, opiates and analogues, glutethimide, impramine, benadryl, and phenothiazine derivatives (Table 9). A *cherry red color* of skin and nails associated with central nervous system depression is typical of carbon monoxide poisoning.

If *convulsions* are the presenting symptoms, the possibility of central nervous system stimulants should be entertained, such as strychnine, camphor, atropine, ephedrine, amphetamine, boric acid, parathion and other cholinesterase inhibitors, DDT and other chlorinated hydrocarbons, fluorides, oxalates, and fluoracetate. Convulsions may also be produced by toxic amounts of salicylates, dextropropoxyphene, glutethimide, meperidine, alcohols, benadryl, reserpine, diphenylhydantoin, and carbon monoxide.

Hyperexcitability, agitation, confusion, garrulousness, and delirium, associated characteristically with belladonna, alkaloids, cocaine, hallucinatory drugs, amphetamines, can also be seen as a result of barbiturate or carbon monoxide poisoning.

Dilated fixed pupils (mydriasis) and dryness of the skin and mucous membranes point to atropine or other belladonna derivatives, glutethimide, cocaine, amphetamine, and ephedrine (Table 10). *Pinpoint pupils (miosis)* may be the clue to poisoning with opiates, dextropropoxyphene, pilocarpine, nicotine, muscarine, ergot, or organic phosphoric esters. Absence of corneal reflex, with normal pupillary size and reactions, are features of meperidine poisoning.

Recurrent episodes of drowsiness and lethargy, *oculogyric crises*, retraction of the neck, sometimes with torticollis, opisthotonos, flexor rigidity, and hyperreflexia, are characteristic of phenothiazine poisoning.

Severe *cyanosis*, without respiratory depression and unaltered by oxygen administration, should alert to the possibility of methemoglobinemia secondary to poisoning with nitrates, nitrites, pyridium, potassium chlorate, aniline dyes, bismuth subnitrate, dinitrobenzene, phenacetin, sulfanilamide, toluidine, resorcinol, or xylidine.

Severe *acidosis* clinically apparent develops rapidly in salicylate, quinine, and methyl alcohol poisoning.

TABLE 10. *Specific Manifestations of Toxic Agents*

Extrapyramidal Syndrome (Dystonia, oculogyric crises)
Phenothiazine Derivatives, Reserpine

Cholinergic Syndrome (Miosis, bradycardia, sweating, salivation, lacrimation)
Organophosphates, Muscarin, Reserpine

Ataxia
Lead, Dilantin, Organophosphates, Antihistamines, Thallium, Reserpine, Dextropropoxyphene, Alcohol

Myoclonic Movements
Piperazine Derivatives, Reserpine

Ptosis
Botulism, Thallium, Dextropropoxyphene

Miosis
Morphine, Heroin, Dextropropoxyphene, Pilocarpine
Muscarine, Ergot, Cholinesterase Inhibitors

Mydriasis, and Dryness of Skin and Mouth
Belladona Alkaloids, Cocaine, Amphetamine, Glutethimide, Benadryl

Acidosis
Salicylates, Methanol, Quinine, Formaldehyde

Cyanosis due to Methemoglobinemia
Aniline Derivatives, Nitrites, Nitrates

Prominent *gastrointestinal manifestations* occur in poisoning with iron salts and other heavy metals, boric acid, cocaine, oxalates, fluoride, caustic agents, phosphorus, and cholinesterase inhibitors.

The toxic agent may sometimes be identified by its shape, size, and color. For some poisonings simple chemical tests may be available, such as the ferric chloride test for poisoning with salicylates or phenothiazine derivatives; the potassium ferricyanide test for ferrous sulfate; the copper wire screening test (Reinsch's Test) for arsenic, mercury, and thallium; or the semiquantitative test for urinary coproporphyrin in chronic lead intoxication. Albuminuria is a common finding in many heavy metal poisonings, such as lead, arsenic, or mercury. Whenever its existence is suspected spectroscopic examination of the blood permits the definite determination of the presence of methemoglobin.

TREATMENT. Every case of poisoning must be viewed and handled as an urgent emergency. Time is critical for removal of ingested toxins, since they may pass rapidly from the stomach into the intestinal tract. While every attempt should be made to identify the toxic agent, treatment should not be delayed until identification is definitely established. Overtreatment, however, must be avoided, since it may at times be more harmful than the poison itself. It is also unwise to waste time searching for nonexisting antidotes.

The primary objective in treating poisoned patients is to rid the patient of the toxic substance and to counter the damaging effect that may already have occurred. Treatment should be based on the following general principles of management: rapid evacuation of the poison; administration of a specific antidote if available or of a chemical neutralizer if indicated; institution of supportive and symptomatic therapy. Exclusive of those poisonings for which there are specific antidotes, speedy evacuation of the poison and supportive and symptomatic therapy are the mainstays of treatment and should be instituted immediately and concomitantly.

Antidotes (Table 11). Contrary to a widespread and erroneous belief there are, in fact, only very few effective specific antidotes. The narcotic antagonists nalorphine and levallorphan prevent and abolish promptly many of the effects of morphine, codeine, and those of morphine-like synthetic or semisynthetic compounds such as heroin, methadone, meperidine (Demerol), dextropropoxyphene (Darvon), and diphenoxylate (Lomotil). Among the chelating agents, effective in the treatment of heavy metal poisonings, desferroxiamine (Desferol) is specific for iron poisoning; dimercaprol (BAL) chelates lead, arsenic, and inorganic mercury; ethylenediamine-tetraacetic acid (EDTA) is a useful agent in lead and possibly in iron; *d*-penicillamine binds and promotes the rapid elimination of lead and copper. Vitamin K has been used effectively as an antidote for the treatment of *chronic* poisoning with rodenticides having anticoagulant properties. For the treatment of organic phosphate poisonings such as parathion, 2-PAM (2-pyridine aldoxime methiodide) has proved effective in conjunction with atropine. Amyl nitrate by inhalation, sodium nitrite and sodium thiosulfate intravenously may be lifesaving in cyanide poisoning, as may be methylene blue in methemoglobinemia.

Gastric Evacuation. Lacking specific antidotes, the most effective initial approach is to remove from the stomach as much of the toxic agent as possible before it is absorbed. In many instances this can be accomplished either by inducing emesis mechanically

TABLE 11.   *Antidotes*

Antidote	Poison	
1. **Atropine** (antagonizes muscarinic effect of acetylcholine) 0.2 to 2 mg (depending on age) 2. **2-PAM (Pralidoxime Chloride)** 25-50 mg/kg	1 *Amanita muscaria* 1 & 2 Organic Phosphate Esters (Parathion, DFP, TEPP, etc.)	
1. **BAL** (dimercaprol) inj. USP 3-5 mg/kg/qid 2. Ca Na$_2$ **EDTA** (Ca Na$_2$ Edetate) inj. (USP, 1-2% Sol.) 75 mg/kg/24 hr 3. **Penicillamine** (caps. 250 mg) po 100 mg/kg/day	**Heavy Metals**	
	Lead	1, 2 and 3
	Arsenic	1
	Mercury	1, (3)
	Copper	3
Desferroxiamine (15 mg/kg/hr X 6)	Iron	
Ethyl Alcohol (15-30 cc/q 4 hr)	Methyl Alcohol	
Methylene Blue (1% Sol.) 1 mg/kg (Tetramethyl-thionine Chloride)	Nitrites Nitrate Aniline Dyes	
Nalorphin Hcl (Nalline HCL) amp. 0.2 mg/ml, 0.1 mg/kg **Levallorphan** (Lorfan) amp. 0.05/ml, 0.02/mg/kg	Morphine, Other Opiates, Semi- and Synthetic Narcotics (Heroin, Meperidine, d-Propoxyphene, Methadone, Diphenoxylate)	
Nitrite, Amyl. Perles 0.3 ml; (Inhalation) **Nitrite, Sodium** (3% Sol., iv) 6-10 ml at 3-5 ml/min **Sodium Thiosulfate** (25% Sol., iv) 50 ml (12.5 g)	Cyanide	
Vitamin K	Warfarin	

or pharmacologically, or by prompt gastric lavage. However, such procedures are contraindicated for fear of aspiration in cases of poisoning with ammonia, kerosene and other petroleum products, and when the patient is comatose or convulsing. Gastric lavage and induced emesis are also contraindicated after ingestion of corrosive alkali or acids because of the risk of perforation of the esophagus, and in patients with strychnine, glutethimide, or antihistamine poisoning because of the danger of convulsions and laryngospasm.

Vomiting may be induced by gagging the child with the blunt edge of a spoon or with the finger, which should be protected to prevent injury from biting. This procedure is more effective if preceded by a few swallows of milk or warm water. Telephone instructions to the mother to induce vomiting when she first reports the poisoning could be lifesaving. It is essential to instruct the mother to hold the child on her lap in "spanking position," head down and facing the floor to prevent aspiration, and to save the vomitus for later examination.

Ipecac syrup USP * is the pharmacologic agent of choice to induce vomiting in cases of acute poisoning, except where vomiting is contraindicated. Because of their toxicity, apomorphine, copper sulphate, or tartar emetic are not recommended. Syrup of ipecac is relatively safe at the dose of 15 ml after one year of age. Since most poisonous ingestions occur in the home, it may be reasonable that this effective emetic be stored and readily accessible in all homes where toddlers live. Danger inherent in the presence of ipecac in the home medicine chest has been eliminated by limiting the amount of syrup available for over-the-counter sale to 30 ml. However, if emesis fails to occur following its administration, the ipecac will be absorbed and its own potentially toxic effects will be added to those of the poison for which it was given. Consequently, if the

---

* *Syrup of ipecac* should never be confused with the highly toxic fluid extract of ipecac, which has caused serious illness and death; the fluid extract should never be available in the home or the hospital emergency room.

poisoned child does not vomit within 20 minutes after the initial dose of syrup of ipecac, only one more dose may be given. If this second dose proves ineffective, the stomach should be evacuated by other means. Although experimentally ipecac-induced vomiting in dogs has been shown to be more effective in emptying contents of the stomach than gastric lavage, there is still considerable controversy regarding the relative merits of gastric lavage versus ipecac-induced emesis. The two modalities are probably not mutually exclusive and both can be used judiciously and advantageously. When emesis fails, gastric lavage may prove effective. Furthermore, since it may take 20 to 30 minutes for syrup of ipecac to induce emesis, the time element may preclude its use in severe poisonings, in which gastric lavage would appear to be the method of choice. Pharmacologically induced emesis is not recommended in phenothiazine poisoning, in patients who have taken an antiemetic or depressant drug, or when manifest toxic signs due to absorption of the poison have already appeared.

Chemical Neutralizers and Adsorbents.
Chemical neutralizing agents (milk, alkali, mild acids, nontoxic oxidizing or reducing substances) and nonspecific adsorbents such as activated charcoal, which decrease intestinal absorption of many poisons and demulcents, should be available in places where such emergencies are to be handled. Some chemical neutralizers (Table 12) modify the poison chemically into an inert or less toxic compound, decrease its systemic effects, and act as local antidotes.

Holt and Holz have strongly reemphasized the usefulness of activated charcoal in the treatment of ingested poisons. In their opinion, activated charcoal kept in a "black bottle to catch the eye" is probably the most effective single measure because of its broad spectrum of activity and its exceedingly rapid inactivation of the poison. Activated charcoal USP is treated to increase its adsorptive power. Other forms of charcoal are useless because they lack these properties. The value of activated charcoal as an emergency measure is confined to the first phase of therapy-inactivation of the poison before its absorption into the blood stream. It is effective against most poisons, except cyanide, and more potent and safer than the so-called universal antidote, which contains tannic acid as well as charcoal. Burnt toast, which is frequently recommended as a substitute for activated charcoal, possesses no adsorptive capacity and is of no practical value in the treatment of poisoning. Ipecac and charcoal should not be given concomitantly since the former would be absorbed, rendering both treatments ineffective.

Other First-Aid Measures.
Other measures may be advised by the physician before he arrives on the scene. If the poison was inhaled, as may be the case with carbon monoxide, the patient should be removed to another area which is well ventilated; artificial respiration may be required. If the toxic substance was spilled on the skin or eyes, copious washing of the contaminated parts with water should be advised.

Laxatives.
Saline cathartics, such as sodium or magnesium sulfate, may be used to speed the elimination of poisons which have already left the stomach or cannot be recovered by gastric evacuation.

Exchange Transfusion and Dialysis.
In severe poisoning with dialyzable and nephrotoxic substances, exchange transfusions, extracorporeal hemodialysis, or peritoneal dialysis may be lifesaving procedures.

Exchange transfusion is practical only in very small children. In addition to the technical difficulties which it involves, it carries also the risk of serum hepatitis. This procedure may be helpful, however, for certain dangerous poisonings in which metabolites accumulate and have serious late effects such as methanol, ethylene glycol, and possibly iron poisoning.

Dialysis removes effectively a variety of organic compounds from the blood such as barbiturates, salicylates, boric acid, carbon tetrachloride, anticonvulsants, and other materials. *Intermittent peritoneal dialysis* is safe and effective. It has a distinct advantage in that it can be instituted readily and requires a minimum of equipment. Improvements of equipment and technique have made this procedure increasingly useful. In this method a plastic catheter is introduced through a hollow trocar used for ordinary abdominal paracentesis. The availability of commercially prepared dialyzing fluids greatly facilitates its use. The addition of 2 to 5 percent albumin to the dialyzing fluid increases the rate of removal of poisons which are protein-bound, such as barbiturates and salicylates.

Hemodialysis is less applicable to young children. It is a formidable procedure which demands specialized centers and staffing. The indication for its use have been narrowed in recent years to a progressively more limited number of drugs.

TABLE 12. *Chemical Neutralizers with Some Local Antidote Effect*

Neutralizer	Poison
Calcium Gluconate or Lactate	Fluorides, Oxalic Acid, and DDT
Na Bicarbonate	Iron, Methanol
Starch	Iodide
Na (or K) Iodide	Thallium
Na Formaldehyde Sulfoxalate	Mercury
Ammonium Acetate	Formaldehyde

Prevention of Poisoning

Epidemiologic studies indicate that poisoning in children is preventable in over 90 percent of cases by applying ordinary safety precautions in the use, handling, packaging, and storage of drugs and household chemicals. Whereas prompt and appropriate treatment may be lifesaving when intoxications have occurred, prevention is an infinitely superior and indisputably more rewarding method of averting fatalities and other dreadful complications.

Physicians have a major responsibility in the field of prevention. They can and must make significant contributions to render homes safer and "poison-proof" for children. The physician must himself assume safe habits and attitudes, and scrupulously practice them at all times. He must display discipline and forethought, exercise the greatest care when prescribing drugs, order only the smallest amounts of medicine sufficient to meet immediate needs, and give explicit instructions to destroy, not merely discard, all "left-overs." Specific and detailed recommendations, verbal and written, must be left with adult members of the family about the dosage, time interval, and internal or external use.

Drugs must never be utilized if outdated, discolored, or in any way deteriorated. Degradation of paraldehyde to acetic acid has caused fatalities; several instances of Fanconi's syndrome have followed the use of degraded tetracycline. Pharmacologic interaction and synergistic effects are known to occur with multiple drug preparations. Hence drugs should always be dispensed singly and at the lowest effective therapeutic dosages.

Informing and educating the general public about the danger and prevention of poisoning, guiding and counseling individual families, and teaching of medical and paramedical hospital staff in training are part of a physician's responsibilities. His waiting room should contain educational material about the accidental poisoning problem and precautionary measures to be employed for its elimination.

As a leader in his community, the physician can motivate community groups to inaugurate safety programs. During home visits, he must observe or uncover possible existing poison hazards, prevail upon the families to eliminate them, provide education, and show the need for safe practices in the handling and safekeeping of drugs and other potentially dangerous substances. The importance of keeping medicines in their original containers and of storing all hazardous preparations out of the reach of children must be repeatedly and emphatically stressed. A safety list may profitably be distributed to parents. It is also of great importance that physicians be familiar with the location and functioning of the nearest Poison Control Center and to report all instances of poisonings, including side-reactions from drugs.

On a nationwide scale, the general public must be adequately protected. The marketing of potentially toxic products must be subjected to stringent regulations and, if possible, considerably curtailed. Distributions to the consumer of dangerous preparations must be prohibited unless sufficient protection is provided against the possible harmful effects by the use of safe packaging and danger warnings. Studies in Canada and in the United States have demonstrated that widespread public use of child-resistant containers to package solid prescription medications can reduce significantly the amount of accidental childhood poisoning.

The Federal Hazardous Substances Labeling Act applicable to common household preparations should prove very helpful if properly enforced. It is unwise, however, to place complete reliance on the label content, since many labels would not be understood by laymen. The Food and Drug Administration requires pharmaceutical companies to include brochures and package circulars to physicians on new drugs, therapeutic dose, level of toxicity, contraindications, types of side reactions encountered, and treatment of overdosage. This regulation constitutes an important step toward the prevention of many iatrogenic poisonings. For the prevention of accidental salicylate poisoning by children recommendations made by the F.D.A. were implemented voluntarily by the drug industry to limit the number of tablets in a retail container to 36; to print in a prominent position on each package a caution to keep out of reach of children; and to include on the package the warning: "In case of accidental overdose contact a physician immediately."

Since the thalidomide disaster, the Food and Drug Administration has initiated additional precautionary regulations with regard to testing and marketing new drugs. Although there is still need for improved quality control at the point of manufacture, these measures aim at ensuring the safety and potency of new drugs before they are released for general use. The drug-control bills voted by Congress will also protect public health and safety by establishing special controls for depressant and stimulant drugs (pep pills) and for counterfeit drugs.

Poisoning prevention merits wholehearted endorsement and support of all physicians. Many more lives could be saved and an untold number of poisonings prevented if the available knowledge gained wider and more immediate application.

References

Angle, C. R., et al. Neurologic sequelae in poisoning in children. J. Pediat., 73:531, 1968.

Arnold, F. J., Jr., et al. Evaluation of the efficacy of lavage and induced emesis in the treatment of salicylate poisoning. Pediatrics, 23:286, 1959.

Baltimore, C. L., and Meyer, R. J. A study of storage, child behavioral traits, and mother's knowledge of toxicology in 52 poisoned families and 52 comparison families. Pediatrics, 42:312, 1968.

Cushman, T. M., and Shirkey, K. C. Emergency management of poisoning. Pediat. Clin. N. Amer., 17: 525, Aug. 1970.

Done, A. K. Poisoning from common household products. Pediat. Clin. N. Amer., 17:569, Aug. 1970.

Gleason, M. N., Gosselin, R. E., and Hodge, H. C. Clinical Toxicology of Commercial Products, 3rd ed. Baltimore, Williams & Wilkins Co., 1969.

Holt, L. E., Jr., and Holz, P. H. The black bottle. J. Pediat., 63:306, 1963.

Jacobziner, H., and Raybin, H. W. Accidental poisonings in childhood and their prevention. J. Pediat., 49:592, 1956.

Lee, H. A., and Aimes, A. C. Hemodialysis in severe barbiturate poisonings. Brit. Med. J., 1:1217, 1965.

Lehr, E. L. Carbon monoxide poisoning. A preventable environmental hazard. J. Public Health, 60:289, 1970.

Moss, M. H. Alcohol-induced hypoglycemia and coma caused by alcohol sponging. Pediatrics, 46:445, 1970.

Reid, H. S. D. Treatment of the poisoned child. Arch. Dis. Child., 45:428, 1970.

Shirley, H. C. Ipecac syrup, its use as an emetic in poison control. J. Pediat., 69:139, 1966.

U. S. Department of Health, Education and Welfare, Public Health Service, Food and Drug Administration, Washington, D.C., National Clearinghouse for Poison Control Centers. Tabulations of 1968 Reports. Bulletin, Sept.–Oct. 1969. Products Most Frequently Ingested 1968. Bulletin, Nov.–Dec. 1969. Tabulations of 1969 Reports. Bulletin, Sept.–Oct. 1970.

Wehrle, P. F., et al. Epidemiology of accidental poisoning in an urban population—The repeater problem. Pediatrics, 27:614, 1961.

13.5
IRON POISONING

ARNOLD H. EINHORN

The widespread and sometimes indiscriminate use of medicinal iron preparations has resulted in a corresponding increase of cases of acute iron poisoning in children. Here, the careless adult is often the mother for whom iron therapy has been prescribed as part of prenatal care. Various oral preparations differ in their iron content. Ferrous sulfate is the product most commonly incriminated in poisoning.

Ferrous Sulfate USP—the hydrated salt, contains 20 percent elemental iron; the official tablets contain 300 mg of the salt (60 mg of iron); the syrup USP, 40 mg/ml of the salt (8 mg of iron); and the pediatric "drops" 125 mg/ml of the salt (25 mg of iron). *Ferrous gluconate,* also widely used, contains only 12 percent of metallic iron.

The exact mechanisms of the toxic effects of iron and the minimum fatal dose for a child are both still unknown. Although the mean lethal dose has been estimated at 300 mg/kg of elemental iron, as little as 1.0 g of ferrous sulfate (200 mg of iron) can cause death while recoveries have been reported from as much as 15 g. In children, the mortality rate

after ingestion of large doses of iron has been reported to be as high as 50 percent.

CLINICAL FEATURES. Symptoms of acute iron poisoning include vomiting, bloody diarrhea, pallor, and dehydration, followed by acidosis, shock, convulsions, and death. A characteristic clinical progression in three chronologic phases has been described by Aldrich in severe iron poisoning. The first phase begins within one half to one hour of ingestion with vomiting and bloody diarrhea. Acidosis and circulatory collapse may develop concurrently with these symptoms or may follow within 4 to 6 hours. In response to supportive therapy, a second phase of relative improvement may be observed lasting for 8 to 16 hours. Vomiting and diarrhea subside, acidosis and shock improve, and the child appears less ill or may actually be recovering. This period of improvement, however, is often misleading. About 24 to 48 hours after ingestion a critical, frequently fatal third phase supervenes with progressive collapse, coma, and convulsions. If this delayed third phase can be avoided or treated successfully, the child will make a complete recovery. Children who recover may develop within one to two months gastric scarring with ensuing pyloric stenosis or obstruction. Corrective surgery may be required to relieve the obstruction.

The pathogenesis of shock in acute iron poisoning has not been satisfactorily explained. It has been suggested that in iron intoxication, the product escapes into the circulation and produces shock by a vasodepressant effect. In fatal cases, postmortem examination may reveal, in addition to the corrosive gastritis, hemorrhagic necrosis of the liver, due to release of a vasodepressor material (VDM), identified as ferritin. Based on experimental findings a second mechanism has been postulated, which attributes the shock to capillary congestion and increased capillary permeability, resulting in a reduction of plasma volume and hemoconcentration. In a third hypothesis the shock is ascribed to loss of plasma protein by destruction, renal excretion, and depression of protein synthesis due to liver damage. Which of these three mechanisms is singly or predominantly responsible for shock is not known.

TREATMENT. Treatment consists in prompt gastric evacuation; prevention or correction of shock, dehydration, and acidosis; maintenance or restoration of renal function; and chelation with desferrioxamine in severe intoxications.

The stomach contents should be emptied by induced emesis and gastric lavage with sodium bicarbonate. Part of the lavage solution should be left in the stomach, where it may combine with any residual iron, and form a noncorrosive and insoluble precipitate, ferrous carbonate. Intravenous administration of plasma and/or blood to combat peripheral vascular collapse, and adequate fluids containing appropriate electrolytes to correct the acidosis and dehydration, are essential in all severe cases. Excretion of significant quantities of chelated iron will not take place without adequate correction of the hypovolemia and maintenance of a satisfactory urinary output. Exchange transfusions, hemodialysis, or intermittent peritoneal dialysis may also prove lifesaving especially if the child is in renal failure and excretion of chelated iron is thereby impaired.

The use of a highly effective iron-binding agent, desferrioxamine, has improved the outlook in the treatment of severe cases of iron intoxication. This chelating agent, specific for iron, is a siderochrome of microbial origin which had originally been used successfully in experimental iron intoxications in animals, and in hemosiderosis and hemochromatosis in man. In vitro its iron-binding capacity exceeds that of transferrin. The soluble hydrochloride salt binds 9.3 mg of trivalent iron per 100 mg of chelate.

Administered intravenously, desferrioxamine combines with iron to form ferrioxamine, which is largely excreted in the urine, though a small proportion is metabolized in the body. When given orally desferrioxamine does not prevent the absorption of iron from the injured, and even from the intact, gastrointestinal tract. As a result, excessive quantities of the iron-chelate complex, ferrioxamine, may enter the circulation, accumulate in the blood, and produce toxicity. Consequently oral therapy with this drug appears contraindicated. The results obtained with the parenteral use of this chelate-forming agent have been most encouraging. This treatment should, however, be restricted to children with severe iron intoxication. The intoxication should be regarded as severe if the amount of ingested iron is known to be large, and/or the serum iron concentration exceeds *within six hours of ingestion* 500 μg per 100 ml (serum iron ranges normally from 65 to 75 μg per 100 ml). Serum iron levels tend to decline six hours after ingestion regardless of the amount taken or the clinical condition.

The recommended dosage of desferrioxamine as used in the successful treatment of acute iron intoxication is 90 mg/kg given intravenously over a period of six hours, in 100 to 200 ml of 5 percent dextrose in water solution. The rate of infusion should not exceed 15 mg per hour. If the color of the urine becomes orange brown, an indication of the presence of ferrioxamine, additional desferrioxamine is administered continuously over the next 12 hours. If needed, the dose may repeated. The intramuscular route is also effective. Adverse reactions from the drug, such as hypotension, irritability, and convulsions have been reported, but may be minimized by proscribing both the oral therapy and the rapid infusion method, formerly recommended. If renal function is inadequate, peritoneal dialysis, hemodialysis, or exchange transfusion may be indicated as an additional means of removing chelated iron. Treatment with desferrioxamine also does not preclude the institution of vigorous supportive therapy which must be given concurrently.

REFERENCES

Aldrich, R. A. Acute Iron Toxicity. *In* Wallerstein, R. O., and Mettier, S. R., eds., Iron in Clinical Medicine. Berkeley, California, University of California Press, 1958.

Gevirtz, N. R., and Wasserman, L. R. The measurement of iron and iron-binding capacity in plasma containing desferrioxamine. J. Pediat., 68:802, 1966.

Goodman, L. S., and Gilman, A. The Pharmacological Basis of Therapeutics, Third Ed. New York, The Macmillan Co., 1967, pp. 1400-1402.

Henderson, F., Vietti, T. J., et al. Desferrioxamine in the treatment of acute toxic reaction to ferrous gluconate. J.A.M.A., 186:73, 1963.

Jacobs, J., et al. Acute iron intoxication. N. Eng. J. Med., 273:1124, 1965.

Leikin, S., et al. Chelation therapy in acute iron poisoning. J. Pediat., 71:425, 1967.

McEnery, J. T., and Greengaard, J. Treatment of acute iron ingestion with desferrioxamine in 20 children. J. Pediat., 68:773, 1966.

Movassaghi, N., et al. Comparison of exchange transfusion and desferrioxamine in the treatment of acute iron poisoning. J. Pediat., 75:604, 1969.

Santo, A. S., and Pisciotta, A. V. Acute iron intoxication. Amer. J. Dis. Child., 107:422, 1964.

Whitten, C. F., et al. Studies in acute iron poisoning. I. Desferrioxamine in the treatment of acute iron poisoning: Clinical observations, experimental studies and theoretical considerations. Pediatrics, 36:322, 1965.

—— Studies in acute iron poisoning. II. Further observations on desferrioxamine in the treatment of acute experimental iron poisoning. Pediatrics, 38:102, 1966.

Yun-Fei, Hwant, and Brown, E. B. Effect of desferrioxamine on iron absorption. Lancet, 1377:136, 1965.

13.6
KEROSENE POISONING

ARNOLD H. EINHORN

Kerosene and other petroleum distillates are derivatives of crude petroleum and mixtures of aliphatic and aromatic hydrocarbons. The accidental ingestion of products containing petroleum distillates caused the loss of 31 lives in the United States in 1967. In 1969, more than 6,000 cases were reported to the National Clearinghouse for Poison Control Centers in children under 5 years of age. The products most commonly available to infants and children in the homes include cigarette and charcoal lighter fluids; kerosene, fuel oil, benzine and naphtha; gasoline; solvents; mineral spirits, paint and lacquer thinners; furniture polishes and waxes containing primarily mineral seal oil; turpentine or pine products; insecticides in a petroleum distillate base; and oil paints, lacquers, and varnish; in this order.

The toxicity of petroleum distillates is related primarily to the danger of aspiration of the hydrocarbon product into the respiratory tract, where it produces intense local irritation. The development of pneumonitis, hemorrhagic bronchopneumonia, and/or pulmonary edema constitutes the greatest threat to the patient. Pneumatocele formation and pleural effusion may complicate the hydrocarbon pneumonitis. Pneumothorax may also occur after ingestion of kerosene. The pulmonary lesions may become rapidly very extensive, and a fulminating course may lead to a fatal outcome in 2 to 24 hours after ingestion.

The ingestion of kerosene and of other petroleum products, mainly benzine, gasoline, mineral seal oil, and lighter fluid can also cause systemic toxic effects. These consist essentially of central nervous system depression. Degenerative changes in the liver and kidneys and hypoplasia of the bone marrow have also been observed.

Aspiration hazards depend primarily on the viscosity, and possibly on the surface tension, of the hydrocarbon agent. Systemic toxicity is probably related to chemical composition, but the nature of this relation has not been adequately elucidated. Some materials which have low systemic toxicity may afford high aspiration hazards, because of their low viscosity, even in small amounts. Conversely, with some preparations, especially benzine or petroleum ether, toxicity is very serious, but risk of aspiration relatively minor. Some products, such as lighter fluids, gasoline, kerosene, and mineral seal oil-containing furniture polishes, which are very toxic systemically, are also readily aspirated because of their low viscosity. Viscous material, such as paint, glues, asphalt, rubber cement, represent insignificant aspiration hazards; fuel oil produces little systemic or pulmonary effects.

CLINICAL FEATURES. The clinical picture of hydrocarbon poisoning is strikingly similar in most patients; only the severity of the manifestation varies widely. The early symptoms usually produced by the ingestion or aspiration of petroleum products include a burning sensation in the mouth and throat, choking and gagging spells, cough, nausea, vomiting, hemoptysis, and pulmonary edema. Tachycardia, fever, and tachypnea often appear shortly after the ingestion. Typically, radiographic evidence of extensive pulmonary infiltration (Fig. 5) and emphysema may be demonstrated soon after the onset of symptoms, when physical signs are still minimal or even absent. In fact the time lag between the appearance of roentgenographic findings of pneumonitis and the appearance of clinical evidence of pulmonary disease may be considerable. Pneumothorax may occur secondary to kerosene ingestion (Fig. 6). Symptoms of central nervous system depression may also develop. The central nervous system involvement is manifested usually by generalized weakness, dizziness, lethargy, or unconsciousness. Sometimes irritability, mental confusion, and convulsions may constitute the clinical expression of the systemic toxicity of these compounds.

Both pulmonary and central nervous system complications occur more frequently in patients who vomit and when the ingested amounts exceed one ounce of petroleum distillate. The pulmonary complications are believed to be due primarily to the aspiration of the petroleum distillates into the lungs

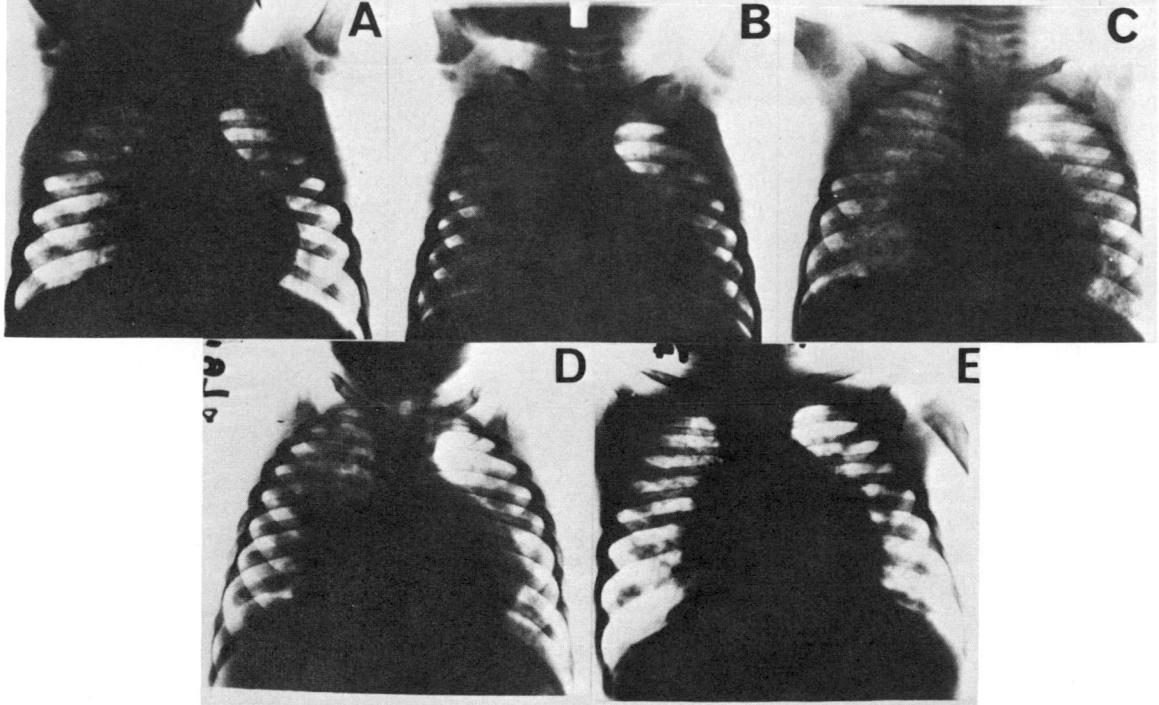

Fig. 5. Pulmonary infiltrations secondary to kerosene aspiration. A. Four hours after ingestion. B. Five days after ingestion. (Note cardiac silhouette enlargement.) C. Two weeks after ingestion. D. Three and a half months after ingestion. E. Five months after ingestion.

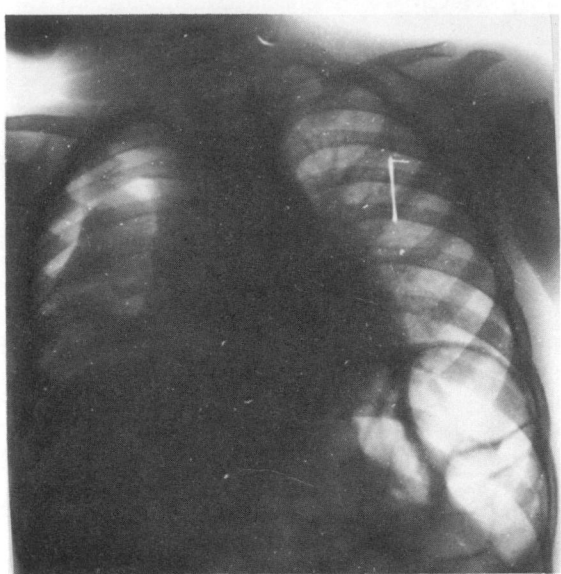

Fig. 6. Pneumothorax secondary to benzine ingestion.

rather than the absorption from the intestinal tract. However, patients have been known to develop pulmonary manifestations in the absence of both vomiting and gastric lavage. In addition, experimental data are available which suggest that gastrointestinal absorption without aspiration may also be responsible for toxic effects, provided large amounts of the products are ingested.

TREATMENT. Extreme caution must be exercised to prevent aspiration. Induced emesis is contraindicated. There is still considerable disagreement regarding the use of gastric lavage as a treatment for the accidental ingestion of petroleum products. Many experienced observers are convinced that gastric lavage promotes vomiting, thus increasing the risk of aspiration, and they strongly advise against its use. Others feel that prompt and cautious removal of the poisonous substance has beneficial effects. We have refrained from using this procedure except when the child is seen within one hour or less after the ingestion of the hydrocarbon and only when the quantity of product ingested is known to be large. In this particular instance we believe that the cumulative risk of spontaneous vomiting and gastrointestinal absorption outweighs the potential danger of a gastric lavage carried out with the utmost precautions to prevent aspiration.

Other symptomatic treatment such as oxygen administration, artificial respiration, humidity, and parenteral fluids should be instituted, if indicated. Antibiotics should be used only if there is evidence of superimosed bacterial infection. Corticosteroids may have a beneficial effect in the treatment and the prevention of the pulmonary complications of hy-

drocarbon aspiration. Their usefulness in this type of poisoning is currently under investigation.

REFERENCES

Ashkenazi, A. E. Experimental kerosene poisoning in rats. Use of C_{14}-labelled Hendecan as indicator of absorption. Pediatrics, 28:642, 1961.

Cooperative Kerosene Poisoning Study. Evaluation of gastric lavage and other factors in the treatment of accidental ingestion of petroleum distillate products. Pediatrics, 29:648, 1962.

Daeschner, W. C., Jr. Hydrocarbon pneumonitis. Pediat. Clin. N. Amer., 4:243, 1957.

Done, A. K. Poisoning from common household products. Pediat. Clin. N. Amer., 17:569, 1970.

Gleason, M. N., Gosselin, R. E., et al. Clinical Toxicology of Commercial Products, Third Ed. Baltimore, Williams and Wilkins Co., 1969, pp. 132-137.

Hardman, G., et al. Prednisone in management of kerosene pneumonia. Indian Pract., 8:615, 1960.

McNally, W. D. Study of kerosene poisoning in children. J. Pediat., 48:296, 1956.

National Clearinghouse for Poison Control Centers. Tabulations of 1969 reports. Bulletin, Sept.–Oct., 1970.

Talwatte, S. N. B., et al. Radiologic findings in poisoning from kerosene. Clin. Pediat., 9:422, 1970.

Wolfe, B. M., et al. The role of gastrointestinal absorption of kerosene in producing pneumonitis in dogs. J. Pediat., 76:867, 1970.

Wolfe, R. R., et al. Pneumatoceles complicating hydrocarbon pneumonitis. J. Pediat., 71:711, 1967.

13.7

LEAD POISONING

J. JULIAN CHISHOLM, JR.

Lead intoxication during childhood results mainly from the repetitive ingestion of toxic quantities of lead, most commonly in the form of tiny paint flakes that contain lead pigments. This disease is now recognized as a significant public health problem in the United States. In several of the larger cities, it is a reportable disease. Although the true incidence of plumbism is not known, it is most prevalent in children 12 to 36 months of age. Surveys show that 10 to 25 percent or more of children within this age range who reside in selected urban slum areas have evidence of increased lead absorption and, unexpectedly, that 2 to 5 percent have manifestations compatible with intoxication. Indeed, it seems likely that a large proportion of symptomatic cases completely escape clinical recognition. Lead intoxication may be an important etiologic consideration in mental retardation or severe behavior disorders in children of all ages. The chronic course of this intoxication is punctuated by recurrent acute symptomatic episodes. In children, the most serious clinical manifestation of plumbism is acute encephalopathy. Although chelation therapy together with appropriate supportive measures can apparently reduce mortality from acute encephalopathy to less than 5 percent, approximately 40 percent of the survivors sustain significant permanent brain damage. Furthermore, reports from Australia suggest that late lead nephropathy with secondary gout may be an important sequel of very protracted cases of childhood plumbism.

METABOLISM OF LEAD. Minute quantities of lead are found in all foodstuffs. Nevertheless, the normal dietary intake of lead rarely exceeds 1 mg/day and is usually much less. Ninety percent or more of all ingested lead passes out in the stool. For this reason, fecal lead content provides an excellent index of the amount ingested. Of the 10 percent or less absorbed from normal dietary sources most is excreted in urine or bile and only an inconsequential amount is retained in the tissues, mainly in bone. In healthy children urinary lead excretion rarely exceeds 80 μg Pb/day, in children with plumbism urinary lead excretion is quite variable but often is 150 μg Pb/day or greater. Normally, the quantity of lead inhaled is minute in comparison with alimentary intake. There is general agreement that continuous ingestion of lead in amounts greater than 1.5 mg/day results in net retention and ultimately in the accumulation of a toxic body burden of lead.

The initial response to excessive lead intake is an increase in urinary lead excretion. When excretory capacity is exceeded the concentration of lead in the tissues, including blood, begins to rise. If the excess quantity of lead absorbed each day is low, most is deposited in growing bone and blood lead concentration rises slowly. If the dose is high, a greater portion of the absorbed lead is accumulated in the soft tissues and blood lead rises more rapidly and to higher levels. The rate of absorption of inorganic lead salts depends both on the dose and the solubility of the lead salt ingested. Lead may be present as oxide, basic carbonate, or basic sulfate in putty and paint pigments which are the chief environmental hazards to children. These are poorly soluble salts. Daily fecal lead excretions ranging between 5 and 104 mg Pb/day have been found in children eating old paint chips. It requires apparently 3 to 6 months of such ingestion for accumulation of a potentially lethal body burden of lead. On the other hand, lead in illicit whiskey or lead leached by acidic foods and beverages from improperly lead-glazed ceramic food containers is ingested as the acetate, citrate, or malate. These are highly soluble salts of lead so that repetitive ingestion apparently results much more quickly in the absorption of toxic quantities.

The balance studies of Kehoe in human adult volunteers and clinical observations in children indicate that once excessive lead ingestion is terminated, it takes at least twice as long to excrete an excessive body lead burden as it did to accumulate the burden. Although metabolic evidence of toxicity usually abates after 6 to 12 months, it may, after protracted ingestion, be several years before blood lead levels return to normal. During this recovery phase most of the residual excess lead is stored in bone. Disorders which rapidly dissolve bone salts may also mobilize lead from bone into the soft tissues.

Serial measurements of lead in blood provide the best means for following these trends in children with lead intoxication. Table 13 shows the significance of various concentrations of lead in whole blood. Approximately 90 percent of the lead in blood is attached to the surface of red blood cells. Since the capacity of the blood to transport lead is limited by the mass of circulating erythrocytes available, whole blood lead values should be interpreted with due regard for the patient's hematocrit. Values should be corrected for any *marked* reduction in

TABLE 13. *Significance of Various Concentrations of Lead in Whole Blood* of Children*

Group	μg Lead/100 g Whole Blood	
	Median	Range
Normal Children		
Nonexposed, Urban	27	15-40 *
Exposed (Residing in Urban Slum Area), no ancillary evidence of increased lead absorption	43	14-71 †
Clinical Significance Uncertain		40-60 ‡
Increased Body Lead Burden (at least 2 values >60 μg Pb/100g whole blood)		
Metabolic Evidence of Toxicity often present: symptoms unusual		60-80 ‡
Metabolic Evidence of Toxicity universal: symptoms begin to occur		80-100 ‡
Metabolic Evidence of Toxicity universal: symptoms may be absent but risk of acute encephalopathy great, immediate, and unpredictable		>100 ‡

*Data from Robinson et al., Pediatrics, 21:793, 1958.
†Data from Bradley et al., J. Pediat., 49:1, 1956.
‡Data from Chisolm and Harrison, Pediatrics, 18:943, 1956.

See text for interpretation of blood lead values in presence of very low hematocrit. Specimens analyzed by atomic absorption technique tend to give lower values than specimens analyzed by the dithizon technique.

hematocrit before comparing them with the data in Table 13.

TOXIC EFFECTS OF LEAD. It is in the various soft tissues that lead exerts its serious toxic effects. Death from acute encephalopathy is the result of massive cerebral edema and softening which in turn stems from a diffuse vasculitis. Initially, there is an increase in capillary permeability with transudation of protein-containing fluid into the intervascular spaces of the brain. More severe lesions show necrosis of vessel walls with petechial hemorrhages. Neurons are destroyed, but it is the opinion of Blackman that neuronal injury is almost entirely limited to areas of vascular damage. Some of these lesions are irreversible and the resultant permanent brain damage is responsible for the convulsive disorders, behavior disturbances, perceptive deficits, and mental retardation which can follow the encephalopathy of early childhood.

Histologically, acute plumbism is characterized by distinctive eosinophilic intranuclear inclusion bodies in the liver, kidney, pancreas, and brain. In the kidney these lesions are most common in the proximal tubular epithelial cells. Functionally, this tubular injury can cause the Fanconi syndrome (hypophosphatemia, glycosuria, and aminoaciduria). This is usually seen either in very severe or very chronic cases, is associated with hypophosphatemic rickets, and is reversible. Albuminuria may also be present. Late lead nephropathy is characterized mainly by vascular injury resulting in scarred contracted kidneys and renal failure. The associated hyperuricemia and resultant gouty manifestations apparently reflect a selective decrease in the renal clearance of urate.

The metabolic pathway for the biosynthesis of heme is exquisitely sensitive to the toxic effects of lead. The enzymatic steps in this pathway inhibited by lead are shown in Figure 7 together with the intermediary metabolites accumulated and excreted. Coproporphyrin and δ-aminolevulinic acid can be consistently demonstrated in great excess in urine even in the absence of clinical symptoms. The coproporphyrinuria of lead poisoning is much greater than that associated with a variety of acute infections and is exceeded only by the coproporphyrinuria of severe acute hepatic injury and some of the inborn errors of porphyrin metabolism. A compensated hemolytic anemia is also present. Except for increase in reticulocytes the morphology of the peripheral blood in children resembles that of iron deficiency. At least two-thirds of erythrocytic cells in bone marrow show punctate basophilic stippling, but the number of basophilic stippled cells in the peripheral blood varies greatly in children because these abnormal cells are avidly removed by the reticuloendothelial system. The enzymes definitely inhibited by lead in the pathway for heme formation are sulfhydryl enzymes. In vitro studies show that lead inhibits many sulfhydryl enzymes and this is probably its principal toxic action in the body.

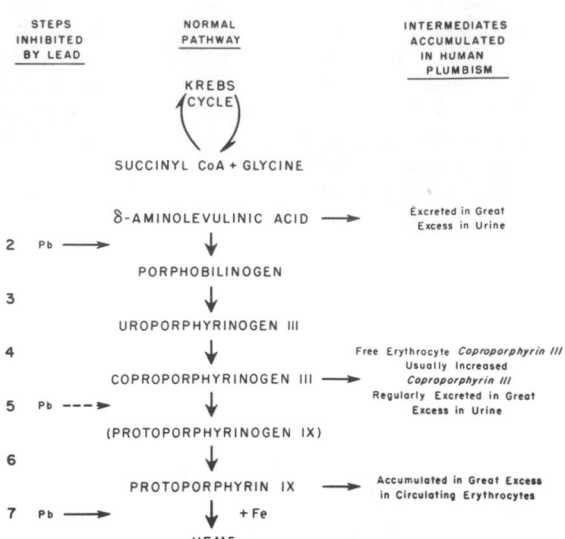

Fig. 7. Steps in biosynthesis of heme inhibited by lead. There is good evidence that lead partially inhibits the enzymes at Steps 2 and 7. The origin of the coproporphyrinuria is not entirely clear but may result from reduced ability of the liver to excrete coproporphyrin in the bile.

EPIDEMIOLOGY. The vast majority of cases occur in children 12 to 36 months of age who reside in dilapidated, urban slum houses. The causative factors in this, the most prevalent form of childhood plumbism in the United States today, are shown schematically in Table 14.

In virtually every case, pica is the behavioral factor that acts in concert with environmental exposure to cause intoxication. The word "pica" stems from the Latin word for magpie, a bird of omnivorous appetite. Today pica is the term applied to the habit of eating unnatural foods including dirt, string, ashes, clay, paper, plaster, putty, and paint flakes. Infants are apparently born with differing innate levels of oral activity. During the first year of life this takes the form of mouthing, but not ingesting, almost anything the infant can grasp. At about 12 months of age the orally oriented child may begin to ingest nonfood substances. This bent may be reinforced wittingly or unwittingly by the mother. According to Lourie and his associates, as many as 50 percent of both middle-class and poverty groups habitually and selectively ingest substances other than food. Lourie's group has stressed disturbed mother-child relationships as a cause of pica and, in particular, the substitution of oral gratification of the child's emotional needs for a more normal interpersonal relationship. In the mentally retarded or severely emotionally disturbed child such pica may persist throughout childhood. However, in the usual case the child tends to drop the habit between 3 and 5 years of age, particularly if he is able to indoctrinate a younger sibling into the same activity. It is

TABLE 14. *Etiologic Factors in Childhood Lead Poisoning in Urban Areas of the United States*

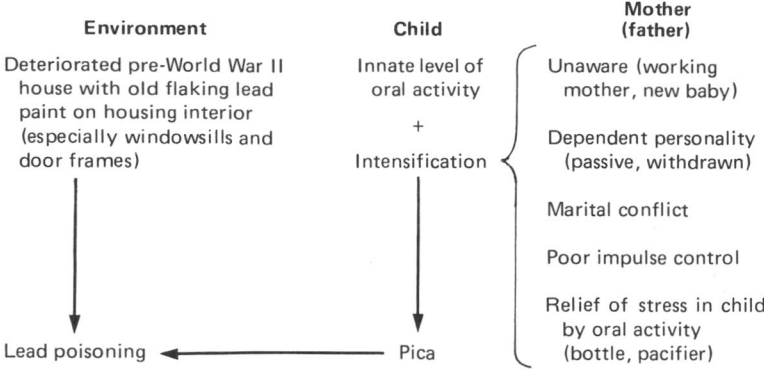

Environment	Child	Mother (father)
Deteriorated pre-World War II house with old flaking lead paint on housing interior (especially windowsills and door frames)	Innate level of oral activity + Intensification	Unaware (working mother, new baby) / Dependent personality (passive, withdrawn) / Marital conflict / Poor impulse control / Relief of stress in child by oral activity (bottle, pacifier)

Lead poisoning ← Pica

not surprising, then, that multiple cases of plumbism are often found in the same household. Since elimination of the child's pica is a vital part of therapy, its cause must be carefully sought in each case.

Although modern *interior* paints do not contain lead pigments, the interior woodwork, painted plaster, and wallpaper of houses built prior to 1940 may contain many layers of lead pigment paints which have never been removed. *Several tiny flakes of such paint may contain 100 milligrams of lead or more.* The daily ingestion of a few such flakes constitutes truly massive exposure. External paints containing lead pigments are still in use. A recent survey in Baltimore revealed that 50 to 70 percent of deteriorated housing in selected slum areas of the city contained dangerous quantities of lead on housing surfaces accessible to young children. The relationship between old housing and childhood plumbism is shown most clearly by the study of Griggs and co-workers. Young children who lived in both old and new housing but who were of comparable socioeconomic background were studied for evidences of plumbism by means of a door-to-door survey in Cleveland, Ohio. The concentrations of lead *and* coproporphyrin were abnormal in urine samples from 216 of 801 children residing in old houses but only 3 of 105 children residing in modern housing projects showed abnormal urines. Significant evidence of lead intoxication was discovered in 38 of the children from the old houses but was not found in any child living in the new housing project.

Cases of plumbism throughout the world are still traced to the consumption of acidic foods and beverages (fruit, fruit juice, tomatoes, tomato juice, wine, cider) which have been prepared or stored in improperly lead-glazed ceramic containers. Usually the offending dish, cup, or pitcher has been made by an amateur hobbyist or small inexpert manufacturer. Often most or all members of the family using the defective item will show evidences of plumbism. The following environmental sources of lead, while com-

mon in the past, are infrequent causes of childhood plumbism today: lead paint in children's toys and furniture, lead nipple shields, toys and baubles made of lead, soft well-water conveyed in lead pipes, and the burning of storage battery casings.

The characteristic seasonal distribution of symptomatic cases is shown in Figure 8. The sharply increased incidence during the summer months is not

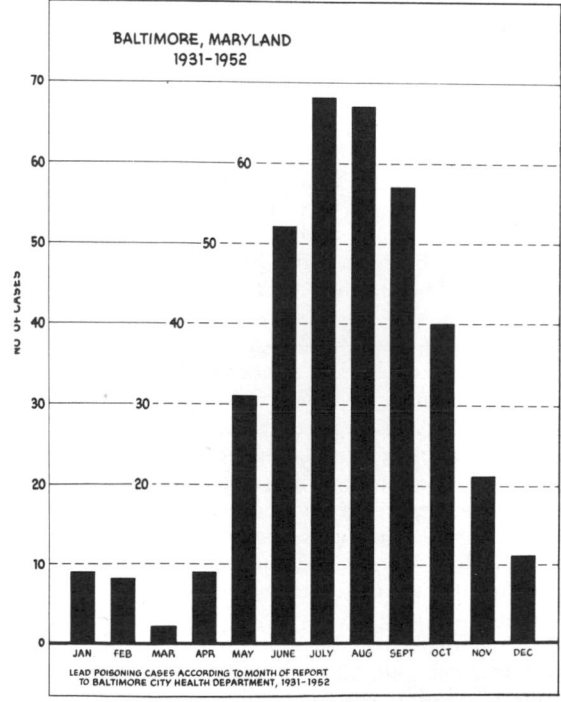

Fig. 8. Seasonal distribution of childhood plumbism. The increased incidence during the summer months shown above for Baltimore, Maryland, is typical for all large cities in the United States today.

adequately explained. There is no reason to doubt that the affected children ingest lead throughout the year. Studies in experimental animals show that absorption of lead from the gut is enhanced by the actinic rays of summer sunshine: they also show that mortality in lead-poisoned rodents can be increased by raising the environmental temperature. Clinical observation indicates that *prompt removal of children from environmental exposure to lead during the summer* and prior to the onset of symptoms can prevent serious acute episodes such as encephalopathy.

CLINICAL FEATURES.   Several clinical variants of plumbism are recognized in children. The following sequence of events is most common during the summer months in children under 3 and especially in those under 2 years of age who are actively ingesting lead. There is insidious onset of anorexia, apathy, anemia, hyperirritability, incoordination, subtle loss of newly learned skills, and sporadic vomiting. These complaints slowly intensify over a period of three to six weeks, after which acute encephalopathy can occur at any time. The onset of encephalopathy is heralded by the appearance of gross ataxia, persistent, forceful vomiting, periods of lethargy or stupor, and, finally, coma and intractable convulsions. The march of acute encephalopathy can also occur without the prodroma described above, but this is rare. On the other hand, symptoms may regress at any point in the above sequence, if abnormal lead ingestion temporarily abates. Thus, a child may suffer recurrent symptomatic episodes without ever having obvious encephalopathy. Since there are no abnormal physical findings specific for plumbism in the young child, these nonspecific complaints may at first suggest an emotional disturbance or seem to be adequately explained either by some minor intercurrent infection, gastrointestinal disturbance, or by the associated iron deficiency anemia which is almost invariably present. Nor is the history uniformly reliable, for pica may be denied even if the question is asked. Parents, seeing no direct cause and effect relationship, may attach little importance to their child's prolonged paint nibbling or they may not observe it at all. For these reasons, the diagnosis of plumbism can be missed if one relies entirely on history and physical examination.

As poisoning becomes more chronic, acute encephalopathic episodes tend to be both less frequent and less severe and other manifestations supervene. There may be progressive dementia suggestive of some degenerative cerebral disease. Chronic plumbism may also present as nonspecific mental retardation, behavior disturbance, convulsive disorder, or any combination thereof. Peripheral neuropathy when seen in childhood usually occurs during this chronic phase. Pain and tenderness in the affected limbs may be present initially, but examination usually reveals motor weakness with little objective sensory abnormality. Acute intercurrent infections can precipitate any of the above manifestations in a child with chronic lead poisoning. Lead lines on the gingiva may occasionally be seen in older children; otherwise,

there are still no specific abnormal physical findings. In the older child, it is difficult without appropriate laboratory tests to distinguish between clinical manifestations due to continuing lead ingestion and those due to the residual cerebral injury of previous acute episodes.

DIAGNOSIS.   Appropriate laboratory tests for lead intoxication should be included in the diagnostic evaluation of children with pica, convulsive disorders, severe behavior disturbances, and mental retardation particularly if the patient has resided in deteriorated housing. The physician must, of course, know the loci of endemic plumbism in his general area. An epidemiologic approach can facilitate early recognition which in turn can avert encephalopathy in a high proportion of cases. The following criteria are used in the author's clinic which serves a metropolitan pediatric population: Any infant or toddler who has been ambulatory for three months or longer, who lives in or visits an older section of the city, and who vomits during the summer or exhibits any of the other prodromal symptoms of plumbism receives *at the first clinic visit* the special laboratory tests necessary to establish or exclude the diagnosis of lead poisoning. Denial of pica is ignored. If any symptoms are present and any laboratory procedure gives evidence suggestive of plumbism, the patient is hospitalized forthwith to remove him from the toxic environment.

Fundamentally, the diagnosis of lead intoxication depends upon the demonstration of an increased body lead burden together with some metabolic evidence of the toxic effects of lead in the soft tissues. In children, body lead burden is best estimated by whole blood lead determinations (Table 13), although the 24-hour urine lead output may provide comparable information if quantitatively measured. Should these determinations yield equivocal results, as they may in very chronic or mild cases, the edathamil calcium disodium (CaEDTA) mobilization test for lead should be employed. Lead analyses are time-consuming so results may not be known for 24 to 48 hours. In many acutely ill patients treatment cannot be safely delayed even for 24 hours; in such cases provisional diagnosis and prompt institution of therapy rests upon metabolic evidence of toxicity and other ancillary tests.

These supportive laboratory tests include x-ray examination of abdomen and long bones (knees and wrists), hematology, and urinalysis. A flat plate of the abdomen may reveal radiopaque foreign material within the intestine. Such material may or may not contain lead; nevertheless, an abdominal x-ray can give positive evidence of pica in the face of a negative history. Storage of excess lead in bone produces characteristic radiologic changes at the metaphyses of long bones (Fig. 9). The intensity and breadth of these "lead lines" is a function of the duration of excessive lead absorption and the rapidity of bone growth but *is not related* to the severity of any symptoms that may also be present. These lines are usually most prominent in patients 2 to 5 years of age but are

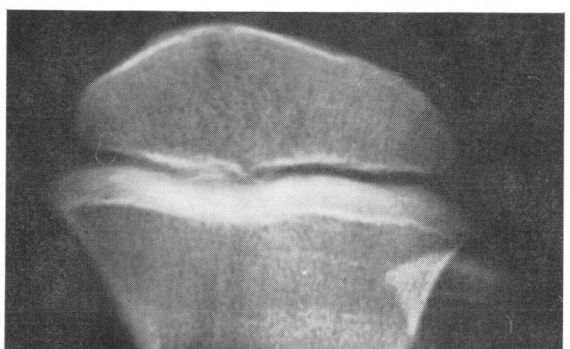

Fig. 9. Radiogram of proximal end of tibia of child with lead intoxication. Continuous broad band of increased density at metaphysis is characteristic of plumbism and reflects the densely packed, irregular trabecular structure of bone being formed in presence of excess lead. This continuous broad band is to be distinguished from the multiple but discrete growth-arrest lines seen by x-ray in growing bones following a variety of illnesses.

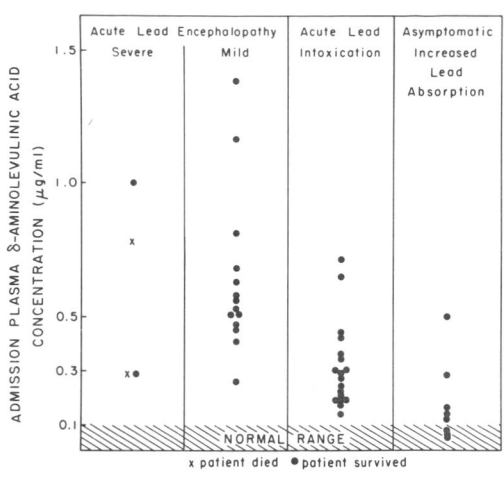

Fig. 10. Relationship between concentration of δ-aminolevulinic acid (ALA) and clinical symptoms in children with lead intoxication. Sample of plasma was drawn just prior to chelation therapy in each case. (From Chisolm. *J. Pediat.*, 73:1, 1968.)

often equivocal or absent in severely ill patients under 2 years of age.

Moderate anemia is usually found in symptomatic plumbism while severe anemia suggests that iron deficiency is also present. Basophilic stippling of erythrocytes is invariably found in bone marrow aspirates but is erratically found in peripheral blood smears. Serial complete hematologic studies are most useful in following chronic cases. Urinalysis may reveal albuminuria and the mild glycosuria associated with the Fanconi syndrome.

The concentration of δ-aminolevulinic acid (ALA) in plasma (or serum) and the output of δ-aminolevulinic acid and coproporphyrin in urine provide the most sensitive metabolic parameters of toxicity due to lead. Plasma δ-aminolevulinic acid levels tend to increase with increasing clinical severity of acute intoxication (Fig. 10). Values in excess of 0.2 μg ALA/ml plasma may be considered urgent indications for immediate chelation therapy. Increased 24-hour output of ALA constitutes metabolic evidence of intoxication. However, currently available data suggest that the estimation of the concentration of ALA in a single voided specimen may yield misleading information because of the wide variation in concentrations of ALA in random samples of urine. The single most useful rapid screening test for a presumptive diagnosis of plumbism is estimation of coproporphyrinuria. In moribund patients this test is occasionally negative. The technique of Benson and Chisolm is designed especially to detect patients in whom blood lead exceeds 100 μg Pb/100 g whole blood. This technique is briefly as follows:

Five milliliters of freshly voided urine is placed in a test tube or small separatory funnel and carefully acidified to pH 4.0 with glacial acetic acid (2 to 5 drops usually required). The pH is controlled with

pHydrion test paper Type D and the acidified urine is vigorously shaken to expel CO_2. Fifteen to twenty milliliters of fresh peroxide-free ether (anesthesia grade) is added down the side of the vessel to float off any bubbles. The tube is occluded with the thumb and shaken vigorously for 30 seconds to extract coproporphyrin into the ether. Pressure is maintained with the thumb until ether and urine layers separate. The ether layer is then transferred into a clean test tube containing 5 ml of 1.5 N hydrochloric acid; 0.25 ml of 0.1 percent alcoholic iodine solution is added to the ether-hydrochloric acid mixture. The tube is then occluded with the thumb and shaken well for 15 seconds to extract coproporphyrin into the hydrochloric acid (lower) layer. After the layers separate, thumb pressure is released and the hydrochloric acid layer is viewed in a totally darkened closet with a Wood's lamp for orange-red fluorescence. The lamp must be pointed away from the viewer. Orange-red fluorescence without bluish admixture is usually indicative of > 0.5 g coproporphyrin/ml urine which in turn is often associated with blood lead > 100 g Pb/100 g whole blood (Table 13) and is reason for immediate hospitalization. Faint orange fluorescence with bluish admixture in the hydrochloric acid under Wood's lamp illumination is consistent with less severe lead poisoning or with other diseases. The reader should consult the bibliography for greater detail.

The diagnosis of acute encephalopathy can usually be made on the basis of the clinical picture and positive laboratory evidence of intoxication but without resort to spinal fluid examination. Cerebral edema fluid can accumulate very rapidly in acute lead encephalopathy so that intracranial pressure is often dangerously high prior to the appearance of the obvious contraindications for lumbar puncture; namely, papilledema, retinal hemorrhages, bradycardia, bradypnea, and separation of sutures by skull x-ray. Indeed, these are often terminal signs. Lumbar puncture should be avoided unless essential for differential diagnosis, which includes tuberculous meningitis, various encephalitides, and other causes of increased intracranial pressure (e.g., tumor). If lumbar puncture is attempted, the least amount of cerebral spinal fluid should be collected dropwise and never allowed to spurt out. One ml is more than sufficient. In acute lead encephalopathy the fluid shows normal sugar content, mild pleocytosis, and moderate increase in protein content. Attempts to obtain fluid by ventricular tap are not warranted.

TREATMENT. The cornerstone of therapy is prompt identification and elimination of the environmental sources of lead. The urgent need for removal of environmental hazards stems from the fact that pica may be a persistent habit which cannot be easily or quickly terminated. Without elimination of abnormal lead exposure the incidence of permanent brain damage cannot be reduced despite the use of chelating agents to treat acute symptomatic episodes or to reduce soft tissue lead content. If the source of lead is a toy or crib, the problem is simple. More commonly, many areas of the home accessible to the child contain flaking lead paint. Proper removal requires that all of such paint be removed down to the bare wood and that painted plaster be entirely replaced or covered with new wallboard. Practical experience dictates that even the asymptomatic child should be placed in a convalescent home or temporary foster care until the lead sources in his own home are removed. Preferably, the family should be urged to move into better housing. While these corrective environmental changes are in progress, therapy for the social, behavioral, and nutritional factors which may have contributed to the child's pica should be instituted on a long-term basis. In children with minimally increased body lead burden (Table 13), who do not have metabolic evidence of toxicity, this may be all that is necessary. In an increasing number of cities lead poisoning is a reportable disease; in a few, local ordinances require removal of lead from housing surfaces.

Chelation therapy should be considered an adjunct to rigorous control of environmental hazards. The aim of chelation therapy is rapid, safe, and maximal reduction in tissue levels of lead. Coincident with this, there is often prompt improvement in symptoms. Although it is possible to reduce potentially lethal concentrations of lead in tissues very quickly, it is not yet possible to remove the entire excess body lead burden within a few days, weeks, or even months with available chelating agents. The oral use of chelating agents is hazardous if there is any possibility of concurrent excessive lead ingestion; under these conditions absorption of lead from the gut can be increased. Once abnormal lead absorption is halted, they can be used effectively to reduce tissue lead

content and to suppress metabolic toxicity more rapidly than can be achieved by the body's normal physiologic mechanism.

Edathamil calcium disodium (CaEDTA), 2,3-dimercapto-1-propanol (BAL), and d-penicillamine are the three chelating agents that are effective in plumbism. There is abundant experimental evidence to support the concept that successful chelation therapy requires the administration of a sufficient molar excess of chelating agent(s) over lead. If an insufficient amount of chelating agent is given, there may be a redistribution of heavy metal within the body and the toxic effect of the heavy metal may thereby be increased. Under this concept the highest dosage consistent with safety is required in children with the highest body lead burden. It is for this reason that combined BAL-CaEDTA therapy is indicated in patients with acute encephalopathy and in those with blood lead levels greater than 80 μg Pb/100 g whole blood: these are the patients in whom the highest tissue levels of lead are likely to be found. Since the toxicity, metabolism and excretion of BAL and CaEDTA differ greatly, both drugs may be used concurrently at the maximum safe dose for each drug (BAL = 4 mg/kg/dose q. 4 hours i.m. and CaEDTA = 12.5 mg/kg/dose q. 4 hours i.m. given at separate intramuscular sites). With this combination, blood lead concentration can be reduced much

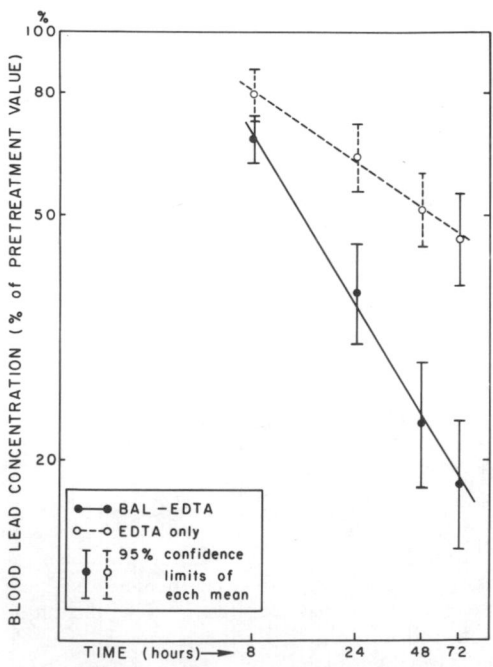

Fig. 11. Rate of decrease of blood lead concentration during first 72 hours of treatment with chelating agents: comparison between BAL-CaEDTA and CaEDTA only. Note that whole blood lead concentration is reduced to 50 percent of the pretreatment value in 15 hours in the BAL-CaEDTA group. Pretreatment values ranged between 100 and 798 μg Pb/100 g whole blood. (From Chisolm. *J. Pediat.*, 73:1, 1968.)

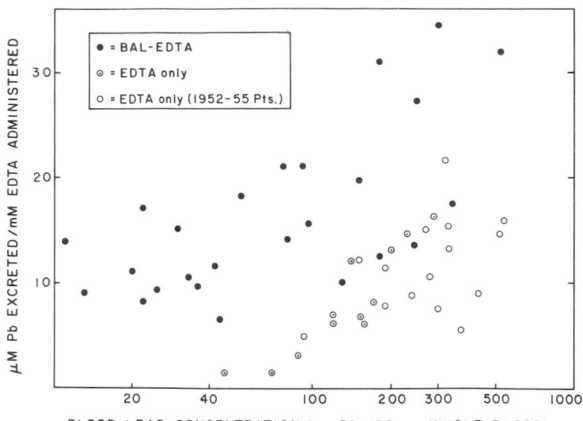

Fig. 12. Relation between urine lead excretion and blood lead concentration during initial 5-day course of therapy with chelating agents in patients with acute lead encephalopathy. The data indicate that, for any given concentration of lead in whole blood, urinary lead excretion when BAL and CaEDTA are administered simultaneously is approximately double that observed with administration of CaEDTA alone. Note that excretion of lead continues elevated during BAL and CaEDTA administration even in the presence of blood lead concentrations within the normal range during the latter part of the initial 5-day course of therapy. (From Chisolm. *J. Pediat.*, 73:1, 1968.)

more rapidly than with CaEDTA alone (Fig. 11) and urinary lead excretion is doubled (Fig. 12). BAL-CaEDTA therapy rapidly suppresses the toxic metabolic effects of lead, whereas CaEDTA administered alone in the face of very high tissue levels of lead may cause a transitory exacerbation of lead's toxic effects. Although nearly one half of the survivors of encephalopathy sustain permanent brain damage, combined BAL-CaEDTA therapy can apparently reduce the mortality of this complication of less than 5 percent. Medicinal iron must not be given concurrently with BAL. Patients must be monitored for the other important adverse side effects of these agents which occasionally preclude their use (see bibliography). When blood lead is less than 80 μg Pb/100 g whole blood and no symptoms are present, CaEDTA administered parenterally in a lesser dose (50 mg/kg of body weight/24 hours in divided doses) or *d*-penicillamine (100 mg/kg of body weight/day) given orally, 1½ hours before meals, suffice. *d*-Penicillamine should not be given orally for initial therapy if there is evidence of residual lead in the gut and the above dose should not be continued for more than five days. In the author's clinic initial therapy with BAL-CaEDTA, CaEDTA, or *d*-penicillamine is being immediately followed by *d*-penicillamine orally for 2 to 6 months for patients protected from further abnormal exposure. For long-term use the dose of *d*-penicillamine should not exceed 40 mg/kg of body weight per day.

In terms of the total clinical outcome, appropriate supportive therapy is just as vital to survival

and, perhaps, to the severity of residua as is the selection of chelating agents. In children with encephalopathy the critical determinants are (1) *prompt* institution of BAL-CaEDTA administration and (2) restriction of parenteral fluids to basal requirements and a minimal estimate of deficit replacement. Oliguria, in particular, presents a difficult therapeutic problem. It may result from dehydration secondary to protracted vomiting and, in severe cases, from concurrent renal injury due to lead. Nevertheless, adequate but not excessive urine flow must be established before CaEDTA can be given. The following regimen is used currently by the author in patients with acute encephalopathy: As soon as the patient is admitted, a continuous intravenous infusion of 10 percent dextrose in water (10 to 20 ml/kg body weight) is given over a period of 1 to 2 hours. Should this fail to initiate urination, mannitol (1 to 2 gm/kg body weight) is infused intravenously as a 20 percent solution at a rate of 1 ml/minute. As soon as urine flow is established, intravenous fluid therapy is restricted to basal water and electrolyte requirements and to a minimal estimate of the quantities required for replacement of deficits, convulsive activity, and fever. The adequacy of fluid administration is best monitored by measuring the rate of urine flow which usually requires indwelling catheterization of the bladder in comatose patients. The intravenous infusion is adjusted hourly until the rate of infusion is found that will maintain the rate of urine flow within basal metabolic limits (0.35 to 0.50 ml urine secreted/calorie metabolized/24 hours). This is equivalent to a urinary output of 350 to 500 ml/M²/24 hours. This technique is used to avoid excessive fluid administration which can further increase cerebral edema. Since some encephalopathic patients behave as though they have the syndrome of inappropriate secretion of antidiuretic hormone, serial measurements of serum and urine osmolarity may also be helpful in monitoring fluid therapy. Oral intake is prohibited until the patient is much improved. Convulsions are controlled with paraldehyde. (Diazepam will give quick but brief control.) Barbiturates are not given initially; instead, they are instituted on a long-term basis after several days. Body temperature is maintained at normal but not hypothermic levels. Oxygen is administered and cardiopulmonary function is artificially maintained if necessary. No time is wasted in attempts to evacuate residual lead from the bowel by enema. After urine flow has been established, a matter of two to three hours at most, chelation therapy is started. A single injection of BAL is given first. Beginning four hours later and every four hours thereafter for the next five to seven days, BAL and CaEDTA are injected simultaneously at separate intramuscular sites.

Surgical decompression and hypertonic solutions to relieve intracranial pressure and reduce the edema of acute encephalopathy are contraindicated, which is not surprising in view of the underlying pathology. The use of steroids for this purpose is controversial.

The judicious use of mannitol may in selected cases be helpful in ameliorating cerebral edema. Careful control of seizures is most important.

For the child with pica and increased body lead burden the almost ubiquitous hazard of dilapidated housing in our cities makes prolonged medical follow-up throughout the preschool years essential. The assistance of medical social workers is most valuable during this phase of therapy. At the least, periodic blood lead determinations are indicated for early detection of renewed exposure. The onset of seizures following encephalopathy may be delayed for some months. Recurrence of seizures usually indicates insufficient dosage of anticonvulsants, lapse of medication, or recurrent lead ingestion. For those who may have sustained permanent neurologic injury, the WISC and Bender-Gestalt tests, which are appropriate after 5 years of age, should be given to detect even the subtle cerebral deficits that can follow the severe plumbism of early childhood. This can be helpful in obtaining the special schooling facilities that the brain-damaged child needs. In general, it can be stated that aberrant behavior as well as convulsions tend to abate as puberty approaches but that intellectual deficits persist.

PREVENTION. The inadequacy of case-finding techniques and brief courses of chelation therapy *after* the onset of intoxication are all too clear. Large-scale screening in high-risk populations to identify those children with increased body lead burden *prior* to the onset of toxicity as well as screening of deteriorated housing seems the only sensible preventive approach. It is clear that any substantial reduction in mortality, morbidity, and permanent brain damage from this disease in the United States will require (a) widespread urban renewal to eliminate the substandard housing in which the disease is more prevalent, and (b) improvement in child guidance techniques and facilities in the population at risk.

REFERENCES

Benson, P. F., and Chisolm, J. J., Jr. A reliable qualitative urine coproporphyrin test for lead intoxication in young children. J. Pediat., 56:759, 1960.
Blackman, S. S., Jr. The lesions of lead encephalitis in children. Bull. Hopkins Hosp., 61:1, 1937.
Byers, R. K. Lead poisoning: review of the literature and report on 45 cases. Pediatrics, 23:585, 1959.
Chisolm, J. J., Jr. Aminoaciduria as a manifestation of renal tubular injury in lead intoxication and a comparison with patterns of aminoaciduria seen in other diseases. J. Pediat., 60:1, 1962.
—— Disturbances in the biosynthesis of heme in lead intoxication. J. Pediat., 64:174, 1964.
—— The use of chelating agents in the treatment of acute and chronic lead intoxication in childhood. J. Pediat., 73:1, 1968.
—— and Harrison, H. E. The exposure of children to lead. Pediatrics, 18:943, 1956.
—— and Kaplan, E. Lead poisoning in childhood—comprehensive management and prevention. J. Pediat., 73:942, 1968.
Emmerson, B. T. Chronic lead nephropathy: the diagnostic use of calcium EDTA and the association with gout. Aust. Ann. Med., 12:310, 1963.
Foreman, H. Toxic side effects of ethylenediaminetetraacetic acid. J. Chronic Dis., 16:319, 1963.
Griggs, R. C., Sunshine, I., Newell, V. A., Newton, B. W., Buchanan, S., and Rasch, C. A. Environmental factors in childhood lead poisoning. J.A.M.A., 187:703, 1964.
Kehoe, R. A. The metabolism of lead in man in health and disease (The Harben Lectures). J. Roy. Inst. Public Health, 24:81, 101, 129, 177, 1961.
Lin-Fu, J. S. Lead poisoning in children. U.S. Dept. of Health, Education and Welfare, Social and Rehabilitation Service, Children's Bureau publication number 452-1967 (U.S. Government Printing Office, Washington, D.C. 20402).
Millican, F. K., Layman, E. M., Lourie, R. S., and Takahashi, L. Y. Study of an oral fixation: Pica. J. Amer. Acad. Child Psychiat., 7:79, 1968.
Moncrieff, A. A., Koumides, O. P., Clayton, B. E., Patrick, A. D., Renwick, A. G. C., and Roberts, G. E. Lead poisoning in children. Arch. Dis. Child., 39:1, 1964.
Park, E. A., Jackson, D., and Kajdi, L. Shadows produced by lead in x-ray pictures of growing skeleton. Amer. J. Dis. Child., 41:485, 1931.
Perlstein, M. A., and Attala, R. Neurologic sequelae of plumbism in children. Clin. Pediat., 5:292, 1966.
Richet, G., Albahary, C., Ardaillou, R., Sultan, C., and Morel-Maroger, A. Le rein du saturnisme chronique. Rev. Franc. Etud. Clin. Biol., 9:188, 1964.
Schucker, G. W., Vail, E. H., Kelley, E. B., and Kaplan, E. Prevention of lead paint poisoning among Baltimore children. Public Health Rep. (Washington), 80:969, 1965.
Seto, D. S. Y., and Freeman, J. M. Lead neuropathy in childhood. Amer. J. Dis. Child., 107:337, 1964.
White, H. H., and Fowler, F. D. Chronic lead encephalopathy: a diagnostic consideration in mental retardation. Pediatrics, 25:309, 1960.

13.8

MERCURY POISONING

MITCHELL R. ZAVON

Mercury poisoning is uncommon among children in the United States. It is therefore less likely to be diagnosed than more common forms of poisoning. Compounds such as calomel used in clinical medicine in former years, modern antiseptic dyes, and diuretics may serve as a ready source of mercury. Mercurial compounds used in household products, in industry, and in agriculture represent additional hazards.

Mercury is a silvery heavy metallic liquid, one of the few metals whose vapor pressure is high enough to be clinically significant. Its very presence in an underventilated room can cause intoxication from inhalation of the vapor. Air saturated with mercury at 20° C contains about 15 mg of mercury per cubic meter. Contamination of laboratory floors and benches can result in significant vapor concentrations. In ordinary household use metallic mercury is found only in thermometers, though mercury salts, such as mercurous chloride (calomel), ammoniated mercury, and organic mercurials are apt to be found in the medicine cabinet.

Acute Intoxication

The most common source of acute mercury intoxication in children is mercuric chloride (mercury chloride) tablets. The fatal dose of mercuric salts without therapy is one gram in the adult and correspondingly less in the child. Ingested metallic mercury, as from a broken thermometer, is not absorbed. Compounds which are poorly absorbed, such as ammoniated mercury, thimerosal (Merthiolate), and mercury protoiodide, are less likely to cause acute poisoning. The fatal dose of these compounds is estimated to be three to five times greater than that of the more soluble salts. The mercurial diuretics, on the other hand, are almost as toxic as mercuric chloride when compared on the basis of mercury content.

Although mercury exposure may result only in a cutaneous hypersensitivity reaction, acute intoxication from absorption of mercury is a medical emergency. Systemic poisoning can also be caused by percutaneous absorption. Alimentary absorption is very rapid, and the course and prognosis will be determined within the first 15 minutes after ingestion. Mercuric chloride causes protein precipitation with marked necrosis of the mouth, throat, esophagus, and stomach. Within a few minutes of ingestion there are severe abdominal pain and vomiting, and when the mercury reaches the small intestine, severe bloody diarrhea develops. The patient may die within hours of ingestion of corrosive mercurial preparations from peripheral vascular collapse secondary to fluid and electrolyte losses. Acute renal failure, which can lead to uremia and death, may occur as early as 24 hours or as late as two weeks after ingestion.

If the patient survives this phase of the intoxication the primary gastroenteritis will subside within a few days. A second phase is ushered in in one to three days and includes stomatitis, colitis, and nephritis. These manifestations may occur irrespective of the route of entry or type of preparation and result from the slow but prolonged excretion of mercury by the salivary glands, intestinal mucosa, and the kidneys.

Though acute intoxication from inorganic mercurial compounds is more common, alkyl or aryl organic compounds can also cause acute poisoning. Gastrointestinal and renal symptoms are rarely seen with the organic mercurials. With these compounds nervous symptoms are predominant. They may appear after minimal exposure and manifest themselves after a long latent period. Ataxia, restriction of visual fields, paresis, and delirium are objective findings, but a much more vague syndrome may result with headache, diffuse paresthesias, and other vague dysfunctions.

TREATMENT. The objective of emergency treatment in acute intoxication is to precipitate the mercury in the stomach before removing it as rapidly as possible. Repeated gastric lavage, first with egg white or milk, then with a 5 percent solution of sodium formaldehyde sulfoxylate or a 2 to 5 percent solution of sodium bicarbonate, should be followed by the instillation of one-half to one ounce of sodium or magnesium sulfate in 6 to 8 ounces of water. Treatment with BAL (dimercaprol) within 3 hours after ingestion may prevent severe renal damage. A schedule for the administration of BAL is shown in Table 15. Maintenance of fluid and electrolyte balance is also essential.

Emesis should never be induced if corrosive salts have been ingested. BAL is not used in poisoning from alkyl mercury compounds, though it may be of some value in treating the sequelae of such poisoning.

Chronic Intoxication

The presence of large amounts of metallic mercury in any room may lead to contamination of the air with mercury vapor. Liquid mercury can get into cracks and persist for long periods of time, creating long-lasting potential hazards. Industrial hygiene agencies possess equipment for readily measuring air concentrations, and their assistance is suggested in such problems.

The type of chronic mercurialism described in industrial workers after prolonged exposure to excessive quantities of mercury vapor over a long period of time is virtually unknown among children.

ACRODYNIA ("PINK DISEASE"). This is the only important form of chronic mercury intoxication in

TABLE 15. *Schedule for Treatment with BAL in Mercury Intoxication*

	Severe Poisoning	Moderate Poisoning
1st day	3.0 mg/kg q 4 h × 6	2.5 mg/kg q 4 h × 6
2nd day	3.0 mg/kg q 4 h × 6	2.5 mg/kg q 6 h × 4
3rd day	3.0 mg/kg q 6 h × 4	2.5 mg/kg q 12 h × 2
Each succeeding day, to 10th day	3.0 mg/kg q 12 h × 2	2.5 mg/kg qd

children. Mercury-containing teething or soothing powders and calomel are the usual sources of mercury in children with acrodynia. In the United States, and other countries where these worthless powders are no longer used, acrodynia has virtually disappeared.

Some authors consider acrodynia to be solely a manifestation of sensitization to mercury. However, the fact that only a small percentage of infants receiving calomel develop the disease suggests that other determinants, unknown as yet, may play a contributory role. Part of the picture appears to involve sympathetic activity which has been shown to be potentiated by calomel in young rats. The mechanism here may be interference with the destruction of epinephrine in the body, which is dependent on methyl transferase, a sulfhydryl-dependent enzyme. The activity of the latter requires the substrate S-adenosyl methionine, which is inhibited by mercury.

The most common manifestations of acrodynia are irritability and restlessness alternating with periods of apathy, insomnia, hypotonia, anorexia, hypertension, and tachycardia. The clinical findings resemble those of pheochromocytoma. Salivation, stomatitis, and pink and cold extremities may occur if the disease is fully developed. Photophobia, alopecia, loss of teeth and nails, and variable skin rashes are other prominent findings. Frequent biting and rubbing of the hands and feet by the child are probably symptoms of paresthesias. Sweating is extreme, the volume sometimes exceeding urinary losses. Although the concentration of sodium and chloride is lower than normal, significant deficiencies of these electrolytes may occur. Hyperglycemia and glycosuria may also be present. Mercury is usually found in the urine in quantities exceeding 0.02 mg per liter but its absence in an occasional specimen does not rule out the diagnosis of acrodynia.

The course of the disease is variable. Although recovery occurs usually, intercurrent infections, especially gastroenteritis, and heat stress may lead to a fatal outcome. The metal mercury may remain in the body for a long time without causing symptoms, and can be tolerated after recovery from acrodynia.

Treatment of acrodynia must include detection and elimination of the source of mercury. The use of BAL in the dosage described in Table 15 for moderate metal poisoning has been recommended. The results reported to date are sufficiently encouraging to warrant a trial of BAL in cases of acrodynia where there are no other contraindications to its use. Antisympathetic drugs and replacement of sodium and chloride may be required.

Sensitivity reaction to mercury may occur without acrodynia. The involvement is usually cutaneous and may vary from a slight erythema affecting only the area of application of the topical medication, to a severe generalized cutaneous reaction. Treatment is similar to that of acrodynia.

OTHER SOURCES OF MERCURY. Mercury as a contaminant of water and thereby of fish has been widely reported. Deaths have occurred among Japanese children whose diet consisted largely of fish heavily contaminated with the organic mercurial compound, methyl mercury. There have been numerous reports of the presence of mercury in fish. However, it is doubtful from the evidence presently available that any demonstrable ill effects can result from the concentrations of mercury generally present in fish, which are only a fraction of the amount known to cause physiologic impairment or death.

LABORATORY ANALYSIS OF MERCURY. Confirmation of the presence of excessive quantities of mercury in urine or blood requires experienced laboratory personnel and the meticulous avoidance of mercury contamination of the specimen of body fluid. Concentrations of mercury in excess of 20 μg/L of urine can be considered abnormal but are not necessarily correlated with illness.

REFERENCES

Axelrod, J., and Tomchick, R. Enzymatic 0 methylation of epinephrine and other catechols. J. Biol. Chem., 233:702, 1958.

Browning, E. Toxicity of Industrial Metals. London, Thornton Butterworth, Ltd., 1961.

Cheek, D. B., and Wu, F. The effect of calomel on plasma epinephrine in the rat and the relationship to mechanisms in pink disease. Arch. Dis. Child., 35:501, 1959.

Friberg, L. Accumulation, metabolism and excretion of inorganic mercury (^{203}Hg) after prolonged subcutaneous administration to rats. Acta Pharmacol., 12:411, 1956.

Goodman, L. S., and Gilman, A. The Pharmacological Basis of Therapeutics, 2nd ed. New York, The Macmillan Company, 1965.

Warkany, J., and Hubbard, D. M. Mercury in the urine of children with acrodynia. Lancet, 1:829, 1948.

Zahorsky, J. Three cases of erythroedema (acrodynia) in infants. Med. Clin. N. Amer., 6:97, 1922.

13.9

ORGANIC PHOSPHATE ESTER POISONING

ARNOLD H. EINHORN

In the United States, fatalities from pesticides account for an average of about 10 percent of deaths from all solid and liquid toxic substances, the mortality rates being subject to some variations from year to year. Many of the insecticides available to the public, and responsible for an increasing number of accidental poisonings, are products containing alkyl esters of phosphoric acid. Included in this group are highly dangerous agents, such as parathion, tetraethyl pyrophosphate (TEPP), hexaethylphosphate, and octomethyl pyrophosphoramide (OMPA), in this order of increasing toxicity.

These organophosphate compounds, when ingested, inhaled, or absorbed through the skin or conjunctival mucosa, inactivate or inhibit the acetylcholinesterase enzyme at the site of cholinergic transmission, by combining with the active site of the enzyme. The enzyme inhibition results in excessive stimulation and overactivity of the parasympathetic nervous system. Acetylcholine, no longer opposed, accumulates and produces nicotinelike actions on the voluntary muscles, muscarinelike effects on the autonomic nervous system, and central nervous system manifestations from the accumulation in the brain and spinal cord. The alkylphosphorylation of acetylcholinesterase by agents such as parathion and TEPP is irreversible and the cholinergic effects may persist for several days.

Parathion, the class compound of this group, has to be converted in the body to an active metabolite, paraoxon, before effects occur. TEPP is direct-acting, considerably more potent and its toxic effects appear very shortly after exposure. Parathion is considered of "intermediary" toxicity. The mean lethal dose of parathion, when taken orally, is estimated at 200 to 300 mg (4 mg/kg). Yet, the ingestion of as little as 20 to 30 mg may be fatal in adults; children have died after swallowing only 2 mg, a dose of about 0.1 mg/kg; and death may result from a single drop of parathion in the eye. *Malathion,* the only organic phosphate insecticide approved for household use, is comparatively less toxic. Its anticholinesterase activity is relatively low, except on the erythrocyte cholinesterase which it depresses considerably. Although a safer product, with a toxicity of about one fortieth that of parathion, malathion is by no means without danger. There were nine deaths from malathion in Florida from 1959 through 1964; we have treated several children who arrived in near-fatal conditions following malathion ingestion; and others have reported similar instances. The lethal dose of malathion is approximately 1 to 2 g/kg.

CLINICAL COURSE. The time of onset, the nature of the initial symptoms, the intensity and sequence of the clinical manifestations, and the rapidity of the course depend on both the portal of entry and the size of the dose. In general, symptoms follow exposure without much delay; the time of death may range from less than 5 minutes to nearly 24 hours after a single, acute exposure. Toxic symptoms and signs are more severe and develop most rapidly after inhalation, often within a few minutes. The time interval is longer in gastrointestinal and cutaneous absorption, but shorter following ingestion than after skin absorption. After inhalation, ocular and respiratory effects appear generally first; gastrointestinal symptoms occur earliest after ingestion; and with dermal absorption, localized sweating and fasciculations of adjacent muscles are usually the initial manifestations.

Symptoms of organophosphate poisoning consist essentially of headaches; blurred vision and miosis; mental confusion, convulsions or coma; profuse sweating, lacrimation, and salivation; tightness of the chest; and excessive bronchial secretions. The physical findings include miosis (sometimes terminal mydriasis); muscle incoordination and fasciculations; areflexia; comatose or convulsive state; wheezing and diffuse crepitant rales of pulmonary edema; bradycardia; and mild to moderate hypertension. In most severe cases the outcome is fatal. The cause of death is primarily respiratory failure associated with circulatory collapse. The respiratory failure is secondary to severe pulmonary edema and respiratory paralysis of both central and peripheral origin. Laryngospasm, bronchoconstriction, and excessive tracheobronchial secretions are important contributing factors.

DIAGNOSIS. The diagnosis of organophosphate poisoning may be extremely difficult if the exposure is not known. The etiology should be suspected whenever sudden manifestations of central nervous system depression or stimulation and rapidly progressing respiratory distress are associated with excessive salivation and sweating, bradycardia, and constricted pupils. Mydriasis may, however, be present terminally and constitute a misleading feature. If time permits, the determination of cholinesterase activity in serum and blood, and the demonstration of p-nitrophenol in vomitus, gastric aspirate, or urine may be helpful in establishing the diagnosis. In parathion poisoning, the levels of both erythrocyte acetylcholinesterase and serum "pseudocholinesterase" are reduced to at least 50 percent of normal. Normal values for both red blood cell and plasma, or serum, cholinesterase range from 0.6 to 1.3 Δ pH Michel units per hour. If the addition of sodium hydroxide to a steam distillate of stomach contents or urine produces a yellow color the test is positive for p-nitrophenol. However, if the patient's condition is precarious and time is of essence, a therapeutic trial with atropine in appropriate dosage is warranted. An early and dramatic remission of signs and symptoms, and evidence of increased tolerance to atropine should be regarded as diagnostic. The disappearance of the excessive salivation, the relief of the respiratory distress, and the effect on the bradycardia are particularly useful criteria.

TREATMENT. Because of the rapidity of the clinical course, speed is of utmost importance. Combined therapy with atropine and/or a systemic cholinesterase reactivating oxime, PAM or Protopam chloride, which are both specific and highly effective, must be instituted without delay. Treatment should also include copious gastric lavage with 5 percent sodium bicarbonate solution, decontamination of the skin, removal of soiled clothing, maintenance of an adequate airway, oxygen administration, and artificial respiration, if indicated.

Atropine counteracts effectively the muscarinic actions and some of the central nervous effects of acetylcholine. It does not affect the peripheral neuromuscular paralysis. It should be given intravenously in dosages considerably larger (0.015 to 0.05/kg) than those used ordinarily: 0.2 mg to 0.5 mg for children under 2 years of age; from 2 to 10 years, 0.5 mg to

1.0 mg; and beyond the age of 10, 1.0 to 2.0 mg. The initial dose should be repeated every 15 to 20 minutes, until the acetylcholine effect subsides or signs of atropine toxicity appear. Tolerance of atropine is greatly increased in patients with organophosphate poisoning.

In children with severe intoxication, concomitantly with the atropine therapy, a cholinesterase reactivator PAM (2-pyridine aldoxime methiodide, pralidoxime iodide) or the chloride salt, Protopam chloride (pralidoxime chloride) in a dosage of 25 to 50 mg/kg, should be administered intravenously in 5 to 10 minutes, as a 5 percent solution in 0.5 normal saline in 5 percent dextrose, at a rate that should not exceed 200 mg per minute. If muscle weakness persists or recurs the dose may be repeated after one hour, and, if needed, may be given again periodically in severely intoxicated children, as the effects of the cholinesterase reactivator seem to subside.

Atropine and the oximes have different actions which do not interfere with each other. The oximes reactivate the acetylcholinesterase by freeing the active unit of the alkylphosphorylated enzyme. They have no effect on the excess of accumulated acetylcholine. The combination of PAM or Protopam chloride and atropine is more effective than either drug alone. Both should be used in severe poisoning; atropine alone is sufficient in moderate intoxications. PAM and Protopam decrease the tolerance of the patient to atropine, and great caution must be exercised monitoring the effects of atropine when the two drugs are used concurrently.

References

Cann, H. M. Pesticide poisoning accidents among young children. Amer. J. Public Health, 53:1418, 1963.

Eitzman, D. V., and Wolfson, S. L. Acute parathion poisoning in children. Amer. J. Dis. Child., 114:397, 1967.

Gleason, M., Gosselin, R., et al. Clinical Toxicology of Commercial Products, Third Ed. Baltimore, Williams and Wilkins Co., 1969, pp. 183-188.

Goldin, A. R, et al. Malathion poisoning with special reference to the effect of cholinesterase inhibition or erythrocyte survival. New Eng. J. Med., 271:1289, 1964.

Goodman, L. S., and Gilman, A. The Pharmacological Basis of Therapeutics, Third Ed. New York, The Macmillan Co., 1967, pp. 441-463.

Hayes, W. J., Jr. Epidemiology and general management of poisoning by pesticides. Pediat. Clin. N. Amer., 17:629, 1970.

Jacobziner, H., and Raybin, H. W. Parathion poisoning successfully treated with 2-PAM (Pralidoxime Chloride). New Eng. J. Med., 265:436, 1961.

Kopel, F. B., et al. Acute parathion poisoning, diagnosis and treatment. J. Pediat., 61:898, 1962.

Quimby, G. E. Further therapeutic experience with pralidoximes in organic phosphorus poisoning. J.A.M.A., 187:203, 1964.

Read, W. T., and Combes, M. A. A new specific antidote for organic phosphate ester poisoning. Pediatrics, 950, 1961.

Zavon, M. R. Diagnosis and treatment of pesticide poisoning. A.M.A. Arch. Environ. Health, 9:615, 1964.
—— Blood cholinesterase levels in organic phosphate intoxication. J.A.M.A., 192:137, 1965.

13.10
SALICYLATE INTOXICATION

ROBERT W. WINTERS

Salicylate intoxication is a frequent and often serious problem in children. There are several different situations in which salicylate intoxication may occur: (a) the accidental ingestion of acetyl salicylate (aspirin) or methyl salicylate (oil of wintergreen), usually by a toddler; (b) inadvertent therapeutic overdosage with aspirin, usually in an infant; or (c) suicidal attempt, usually in an adolescent. These different settings are of importance in determining the clinical picture, because of differences both in the age group involved in each and in the previous condition of the patient. Thus infants intoxicated from therapeutic overdosage are already ill from some other illness which has produced fever and therefore are likely not to be receiving a full fluid and caloric intake. Hence they are prone to develop a cumulative type of toxicity over a matter of several days and present a different picture from the previously healthy toddler who ingests a large amount of aspirin in a single dose. Patients poisoned with methyl salicylate are likely to have a more serious degree of salicylism than those who ingest aspirin, probably because oil of wintergreen has such a concentrated salicylate content.

SYMPTOMS AND SIGNS. Patients intoxicated from ingestion of a single large dose of aspirin or of methyl salicylate frequently show anorexia, vomiting, sweating, a flushed appearance, and fever. The most distinctive sign, however, is hyperventilation, in which both rate and especially depth of respiration are increased. There is usually a lag of several hours between the time of ingestion and the onset of clinically obvious hyperventilation. Serious degrees of salicylism may be accompanied by delirium, hallucinations, convulsions, coma, and acute pulmonary edema. Bleeding disturbances are not common in acute salicylism, being much more frequently encountered in chronic salicylism due to long-term high dosage with aspirin.

Salicylism due to therapeutic overdosage in an infant can be quite deceptive, since the infant is already ill with a febrile disease, usually an upper respiratory infection. In such cases the gradual development of salicylism with hyperpyrexia and hyperventilation may be interpreted as the development of pneumonia complicating the upper respiratory infection. If the intoxication has been present long enough, dehydration develops from vomiting, polyuria, sweating, and the increased losses of water through the lungs as the result of hyperventilation.

ABNORMALITIES IN BLOOD AND URINE. Several different types of disturbance in acid-base equilibrium occur in patients with salicylism. All except the very mildest cases show a reduction in the concentration of plasma bicarbonate and whole blood buffer base (i.e., a negative base excess), and all show a reduction in plasma Pco_2, reflecting the increase in alveolar ventilation. Blood pH, however, is alkaline in some patients, acid in others, and normal in still others. The pathogenesis of these acid-base abnormalities is discussed below. Plasma sodium concentration is usually normal, although in infants in whom large losses of water in excess of solute have occurred through the skin and lungs it is likely to be high. Plasma chloride concentration is usually somewhat elevated in relation to sodium. An increase in R fraction (see Sec. 3.7), computed as the difference between the sodium concentration and the sum of bicarbonate and chloride concentration, is fairly typical in infants and younger children, reflecting the increase in organic anions in the plasma of such patients (see below).

The urine will often show reducing substances, which in most cases represent salicylate metabolites, although hyperglycemia and glucosuria also occur. Ketonuria, detected by the nitroprusside test, is rather consistently present in infants and young children. Salicylate itself can be detected by the ferric chloride test following acidification and boiling to remove the ketone bodies.

PATHOPHYSIOLOGY AND ACID-BASE DISTURBANCES IN SALICYLISM. Figure 13 summarizes the known actions of toxic amounts of salicylate. First, salicylate acts directly upon the respiratory center or its central connections to produce a primary involuntary increase in alveolar ventilation. This effect occurs in all patients with any significant degree of intoxication, regardless of age. The *pure* effect of this action is to cause a fall in arterial plasma Pco_2.

Second, salicylate is a general metabolic stimulant apparently because it is capable of uncoupling oxidative phosphorylation. The result is a generalized increase in metabolic rate with attendant increases in oxygen consumption, carbon dioxide production, and heat production, evidenced in increased body temperature in salicylism. In terms of acid-base status the *pure* effect of an increase in CO_2 production would be an increase in arterial plasma Pco_2. In nearly all patients, the effect upon ventilation outstrips the effect on CO_2 production, and the final effect is a reduction of Pco_2. The interaction upon Pco_2, however, is the physiologic explanation for the hyperventilation which is so impressive clinically, since these patients are able to maintain low values for Pco_2 in the face of considerable increases in CO_2 production (see Sec. 3.7).

A third effect of toxic amounts of salicylate is an interference with the normal metabolism of carbohydrates and lipids such that ketone bodies and pos-

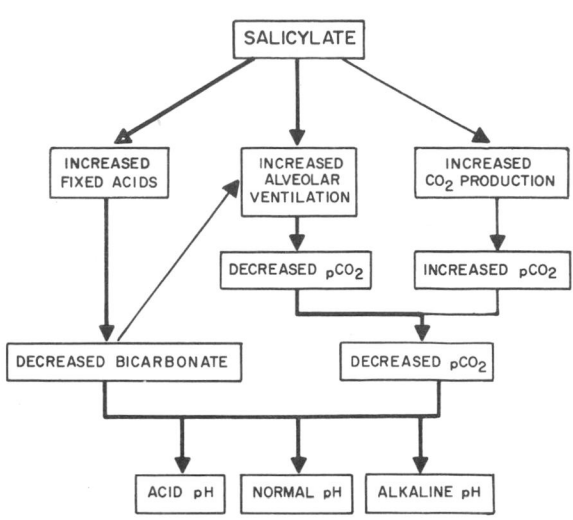

Fig. 13. Summary of pathogenesis of acid-base disturbances in salicylate intoxication. (From Winters et al. *Pediatrics,* 23: 260, 1959.)

sibly other organic acids accumulate in the blood. Unlike the other two effects, this effect seems to be much more marked in infants and young children than in adults. The *pure* effect of such a disturbance upon acid-base status is to reduce the concentration of bicarbonate and nonbicarbonate bases in blood as the strong acids are buffered.

The final acid-base disturbance any given patient develops represents the net result of the disturbance in the respiratory component, on the one hand, and the disturbance in the metabolic component, on the other. In adults and older children the picture is typically that of respiratory alkalosis with a low plasma Pco_2, a high blood pH, and a variable reduction in the metabolic component (i.e., plasma bicarbonate concentration and whole blood base excess) due to renal compensation. In infants and young children, however, the disturbance is characteristically a *mixed* respiratory alkalosis and metabolic acidosis, since both processes are proceeding simultaneously. Blood pH in such patients may therefore be normal, acidic, or alkaline depending upon the relative intensities of the respiratory and metabolic disorders.

DIAGNOSIS AND TREATMENT. In the presence of a history of salicylate ingestion and a compatible clinical picture, the diagnosis of salicylate intoxication is straightforward. In the absence of a history, however, the diagnosis can be readily confused with pneumonia, encephalitis, or diabetic acidosis. Salicylate intoxication may be readily differentiated from these by measurement of plasma salicylate concentration.

Any patient with a history suggestive of salicylate intoxication should be seen by a physician as soon as possible. Initial therapy should consist of attempts to rid the stomach of the drug. For this purposes induction of emesis by ipecac or by mechanical means is more satisfactory than gastric lavage. Even so, an appreciable fraction of the ingested dose may not be removed by emptying the stomach, and the patient should be observed for 12 to 24 hours before assurance can be given that salicylism will not develop.

Further therapy is dependent upon the clinical estimate of the severity of the intoxication. In general, patients with mild or moderately severe intoxication can be managed quite satisfactorily by a conservative regimen consisting of adequate rehydration and provision of liberal quantities of maintenance fluids. The specific quantities of such fluids can be formulated according to the principles discussed (Sec. 3.7). It should be remembered that in salicylism the metabolic rate is likely to be 25 to 75 percent higher than predicted from body weight, and this should be taken into account. Liberal quantities of carbohydrate should also be provided, particularly in a patient with ketosis.

In general, patients with mild or moderate degrees of salicylism do not require specific therapy of the acid-base disorder, since blood pH deviations are usually not wide, particularly in the mixed disturbance. In patients with alkaline blood pH values, all sodium given for repair of deficits and for maintenance is provided as the chloride. In patients with an acid or a normal blood pH, small quantities of bicarbonate may be included in the parenteral fluids. In general, it is our policy to use 1 mEq of bicarbonate for every 4 mEq of sodium in the fluids used for rehydration. In patients with respiratory alkalosis alone, the deviation in blood pH is rarely great enough to precipitate tetany unless bicarbonate has been administered on the mistaken assumption that the low total CO_2 content represents metabolic acidosis. Attempts to depress the respiratory center by narcotizing drugs are ill advised and potentially harmful, while any serious attempt to increase plasma P_{CO_2} by increasing the CO_2 concentration of the inspired air will almost certainly be accompanied by an intolerable dyspnea in the patient.

It is relatively easy to produce a considerable alkaline shift in blood pH in patients with salicylism by an abrupt elevation of plasma bicarbonate concentration through administration of exogenous bicarbonate, since the continuing presence of salicylate-induced respiratory stimulation keeps arterial plasma P_{CO_2} low. It is our opinion that such abrupt shifts in blood pH, usually undertaken to alkalinize the urine, are likely to be as potentially harmful as the relatively modest degree of acidemia which is present in most infants with mixed disturbance.

TREATMENT OF SERIOUSLY INTOXICATED PATIENTS.
While most patients with salicylism can be managed by conservative therapy, there is no doubt that a small group of seriously intoxicated patients require more vigorous therapeutic measures to accelerate the removal of salicylate. There are two general problems in such patients: (a) the criteria by which they

can be selected, and (b) which of the various means available to speed removal of the drug should be used. Selection of patients is essentially a matter of clinical judgment, although certain clinical findings and laboratory tests help in making this decision. Thus, hyperpyrexia (above 103° F), convulsions, coma, and acute pulmonary edema all suggest life-threatening salicylism. The concentration of salicylate in plasma per se does not correlate well with clinical estimates of severity. However, Done has suggested that plasma salicylate concentration, if corrected for decay, can be useful in assessing severity (Fig. 14). Thus the measured value for plasma salicylate is plotted as a function of the time after ingestion, and using an average slope for decay, it can be extrapolated back to zero time to obtain a virtual S_0 for plasma salicylate concentration at the time of ingestion. There is a reasonably good correlation between the value for S_0 and the clinical severity. The specific ranges are shown in Figure 14, and these are a useful additional guide to assessment of severity. The graph, however, can be used only for patients who have a single ingestion of salicylate at a known time, and the point used for the backward extrapolation must be at least six hours after ingestion in order to assure that a steady state of absorption and distribution has been achieved. In infants with cumulative toxicity, the graph cannot be used; such infants may have remarkably low values for plasma salicylate concentration and still be gravely ill with salicylism.

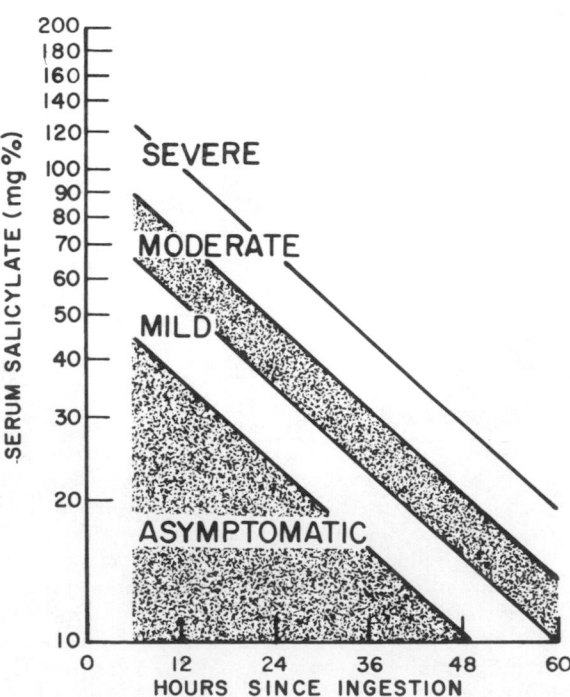

Fig. 14. Nomogram relating plasma salicylate concentration as a function of time following ingestion to severity of intoxication. (From Done. *Pediatrics,* 26:800, 1960.)

There are a variety of therapeutic measures available which will accelerate the rate of removal of salicylate from the body. These may be divided into two groups, depending upon whether they rely upon acceleration of renal excretion of the drug or upon extrarenal removal. The renal clearance of salicylate is markedly increased if the urine pH is alkaline; thus at a urine pH of 8.0 the clearance is about 20 times higher than if the urine pH is 6.0. The relationship is not linear, however, and to achieve a significant increase requires that urine pH be raised to above 7.5. This effect can be achieved through the administration of (a) exogenous sodium bicarbonate, (b) acetazolamide (Diamox), or (c) tris buffer or THAM. Large amounts of sodium bicarbonate (approximately 5 to 12 mEq/kg) are required to produce an alkaline urine; and as pointed out, this will likely shift blood pH to an alkaline value. In our opinion this alkalemia could be a serious threat in its own right, although this method of treatment has been recommended by others. Acetazolamide produces an alkaline urine through the inhibition of normal bicarbonate reabsorption from the glomerular filtrate. From the point of view of the acid-base status of blood, this effect will lower the plasma bicarbonate concentration, but the magnitude of this effect is relatively slight and can be readily overcome by exogenous administration of bicarbonate in quantities comparable to those being excreted. Acetazolamide has been shown to increase the rate of excretion of salicylate, and some authors recommend it. However, some caution may be indicated as the result of the observation that two severely poisoned children receiving acetazolamide developed serious neurologic complications in a manner suggesting that acetazolamide may have been etiologically important; one of these children died.

Alkalinization of the urine through administration of THAM occurs by virtue of the fact that this organic amine (abbreviated R-NH$_2$) raises the bicarbonate concentration through reaction with H$_2$CO$_3$:

$$R\text{-}NH_2 + H_2CO_3 \longrightarrow R\text{-}NH_3{}^+ + HCO_3{}^-$$

There is probably less of an alkaline shift in blood pH under these conditions, since THAM may also produce some degree of depression of respiration, raising P$_{CO_2}$ at the same time. A more complete evaluation of THAM in the treatment of salicylism is required before it can be recommended unequivocally.

Three types of measures which have been used to effect external removal of salicylate are (a) exchange transfusion, (b) peritoneal dialysis, and (c) hemodialysis. Exchange transfusion is applicable on a practical level only in young infants where a standard two-volume exchange can be carried out with reasonable quantities of blood over a reasonable time. Hemodialysis is unquestionably the most efficient means of removal of salicylate, and it is the treatment of choice in life-threatening salicylism in adults and older children. Intermittent peritoneal dialysis, particularly incorporating a final concentration of 5 percent human serum albumin in the dialysis fluid, is a useful and reasonably safe procedure for infants and young children. In salicylism, multiple cycles of dialysis are usually required, with the end point being dictated by clinical improvement of the patient, fall in plasma salicylate concentrate, and improvement of acid-base status.

REFERENCES

Done, A. K. Salicylate intoxication. Significance of measurement of salicylate in blood in cases of acute ingestion. Pediatrics, 26:800, 1960.

Etteldorf, J. N., Dobbins, W. T., Summitt, R. L., Rainwater, W. T., and Fischer, R. L. Intermittent peritoneal dialysis using 5 percent albumin in the treatment of salicylate intoxication in children. J. Pediat., 58:226, 1961.

Feuerstein, R. C., Finberg, L., and Fleishman, E. The use of acetazolamide in the therapy of salicylate poisoning. Pediatrics, 25:215, 1960.

Leiken, S. L., and Emmanouilides, G. C. The use of exchange transfusion in salicylate intoxication. J. Pediat., 57:715, 1960.

Oliver, T. K., Jr., and Dyer, M. E. The prompt treatment of salicylism with sodium bicarbonate. Amer. J. Dis. Child., 99:553, 1960.

Schwartz, R., Fellers, F. X., Knapp, J., and Yaffe, S. The renal response to administration of acetazolamide (Diamox) during salicylate intoxication. Pediatrics, 23:1103, 1959.

Whitten, C. F., Kesaree, N. M., and Goodwin, J. F. Managing salicylate poisoning in children. Amer. J. Dis. Child., 101:178, 1961.

Winters, R. W. Acid-Base Disturbances and the Treatment of Salicylate Intoxication. *In* Salicylates, Dixon, A. St. J., Martin, B. K., Smith, M. J. H., and Wood, P. H. N., eds. London, J. & A. Churchill, Ltd., 1963.

————— White, J. S., Hughes, M. C., and Ordway, N. K. Disturbances of acid-base equilibrium in salicylate intoxication. Pediatrics, 23:260, 1959.

13.11
POISONINGS DUE TO SNAKE BITES

ARNOLD H. EINHORN

A significant number of fatal and nonfatal reactions result from the bites of snakes, spiders, and lizards and from the stings of insects, bees, wasps, and scorpions. From 1950 to 1959, 460 deaths in the United States were due to the bites and stings of venomous animals. One fifth of all victims are children less than 5 years of age. Virtually all bites occur between April and October, during the season of greatest exposure.

It is estimated that in this country every year about 7,000 individuals are bitten by snakes. During 1950–1959, 138 persons died as a result of snakebites in the United States. An analysis of 1,538 snakebites treated in hospitals of ten selected states with high snakebite rates disclosed that the majority of the bites were inflicted by copperheads and rattlesnakes, and a small number by cottonmouth moccasins and by coral snakes.

SYMPTOMS AND SIGNS. A poisonous snakebite generally produces within a few minutes excruciating pain at the site of injury. A white wheal surrounds the site of puncture, soon followed by local redness and swelling which increases and extends rapidly (Fig. 15). The skin becomes dark and purplish and sanguineous fluid may ooze from the wound. In bites of the hand, the entire area may become swollen within one hour.

The patient may develop systemic ill effects such as generalized weakness, dizziness, profuse perspiration, nausea, and bloody vomiting. Subcutaneous and internal hemorrhages may occur with bleeding from the nose, the bladder, and the intestines. The pupils become dilated, the pulse weak, and respiration labored. Paralysis, loss of vision, convulsions, and coma may ensue.

TREATMENT. Treatment of a snakebite must be viewed as an emergency. The rapid administration of a specific snake antiserum is the treatment of choice. There is no unanimity of opinion with regard to the validity of using incision and suction or cryotherapy. The application of a tourniquet above the bite is also apparently of questionable value.

Incision and suction, largely a holdover from the past, may produce damage to tendons and nerves, hemorrhages, secondary infections, and scarring; they should only be used when no other form of treatment is possible. Cryotherapy may cause excessive tissue necrosis and gangrene. Snake venom antiserum specific for snakes of the region should be readily available in areas where snakebites are frequent. The patient should be rushed to the nearest source of antivenom. Tetanus antitoxin or toxoid antibiotics, and symptomatic treatment are also indicated. A polyvalent horse serum antivenin, commercially manu-

factured, is widely available in the United States. It is, however, of no value against coral snakebites.

The optimal dose of snake antivenin for children is not well established; it varies with the severity of the bite and accompanying symptoms. Cases with mild envenomation develop only moderate pain at the site of the fang wounds, less than five inches of surrounding edema, and no systemic involvement; these can be adequately treated with 10 ml of antivenin by intramuscular injection. In severe bites with intense focal signs and moderate to severe systemic manifestations, the administration of 30 to 60 ml of snake antivenin diluted in 1,000 ml of saline solution is recommended. Studies with radioisotopes have shown that antivenin accumulates rapidly at the site of the bite when the intravenous route is used. The injection of the antiserum into or near the area of the bite is of no particular value.

The administration of the antivenin carries with it the risk of anaphylaxis to horse serum. A skin test should be performed before the antivenin is used, and if necessary, the patient must be gradually desensitized throughout the administration. The use of glucocorticosteroid has also been recommended as an adjunct to other measures in the treatment of snakebites. It is most likely to be of value for the prevention or the treatment of the serum sickness secondary to the horse serum antivenin.

REFERENCES

Boys, F., and Smith, H. M. Poisonous Amphibians and Reptiles. Springfield, Ill., Charles C Thomas Co., 1959.

Parrish, H. M. Analysis of 460 fatalities from venomous animals in the United States. Amer. J. Med. Sci., 425:129, 1963.

——— Poisonous snake bites in North Carolina. N. Carolina Med. J., 25:87, 1964.

Russel, F. E. Treatment of rattlesnake bite. J.A.M.A., 207:159, 1969.

Snyder, R. Snake bites. Amer. J. Dis. Child., 103:117, 1962.

Wood, T. J., et al. Treatment of snake venom poisoning with ACTH and cortisone. Virginia Med. Monthly, 82:130, 1955.

13.12

INTENTIONAL ACCIDENTS
(MALTREATMENT OF CHILDREN)

ARNOLD H. EINHORN

Willful physical abuse by adults is a significant cause of disability or death in young children. Pediatricians, as well as social workers, remained unaware of this danger for many years after its existence had been recognized and reported by radiologists and medical examiners. Caffey was first to emphasize the

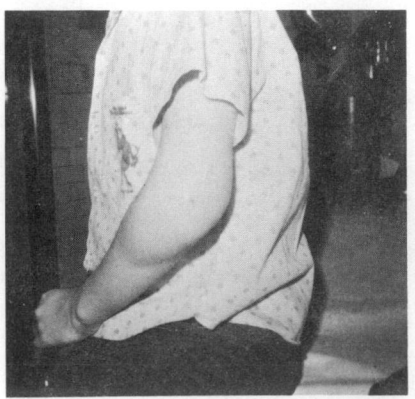

Fig. 15. Marked edema occurring within minutes after baby coral snake bite.

frequent association of chronic subdural hematoma in infants with multiple fractures of long bones. Woolley and Evans suggested intentional inflicted injury as possible cause of any unexplained skeletal lesions. In a cooperative study Kempe reported on several hundred victimized children hospitalized in one single year in various hospitals in the United States.

One wonders how many cases go unrecognized, unreported, and untreated. Most likely, many "accidental deaths" represent instances of deliberate injury inflicted on children by parents or substitute parents and made to simulate accidents. Many types of violence are on record as having been used to abuse or murder children, ranging from manual, pedal, or instrumental trauma to starvation, stabbing, shooting, drowning, strangulation, smothering, poisoning, and asphyxiation.

In rare instances, establishing the true cause presents no diagnostic difficulty when the character, circumstances, and the nature of the trauma or other type of assault are so obvious and extensive as to preclude anyone but an adult as the possible perpetrator. The abuse may occur in the presence of a witness, or even admission of direct or indirect guilt may be obtained. More often, however, history or evidence of maliciously inflicted injury will be lacking or concealed. Tracing the abuse by history may be exceedingly difficult. It is also not uncommon for the parents to seek medical attention for their mistreated child at different hospitals with each new episode of injury. Evasions, contradictions, and conflicting statements about circumstances of neglect and battering should arouse suspicion, especially if marked discrepancies between clinic findings and historical data are elicited.

There are clues which may be helpful to identify children who have been victimized. A high index of suspicion should be maintained in cases where children appear neglected, have poor hygiene, suffer from malnutrition, and present multiple soft tissue injuries, especially when there is clinical or radiographic evidence of trauma and yet a history of neglect and injury is denied. Parents who mishandle their children often claim the child has bruising tendencies and not uncommonly place the blame on a sibling whose strength would not be compatible with injuries of such magnitude. Examinations of a sibling for possible signs of abuse may sometimes prove to be of great confirmatory value.

A wide variety of findings can be observed in children who have been subjected to abusive handling by adults. Among other lesions commonly found are a variety of skin lesions, burns (Fig. 16), scars, abrasions (Fig. 17), ecchymoses or lacerations, soft tissue swellings, head injuries with fractures, intracranial bleeding, conjunctival hemorrhage, perforations of the intestines, splenic and renal ruptures, lesions of the genitalia, and fractures in various stages of healing. Roentgenographic bone changes may consist of metaphyseal fragmentation caused by twisting or pulling, periosteal hemorrhages followed by calcification, squaring of long bones secondary to new bone formation, or frank multiple fractures in various locations.

This complex problem of child abuse may be an index of social pathology. The reasons and motivations which produce the criminal actions against children are poorly understood. Parents of such children have been described as immature, antisocial, and unstable, often exhibiting uncontrollable, violent impulses which readily explode. Although by no means limited to them, child battering occurs more frequently in deprived groups where life conditions

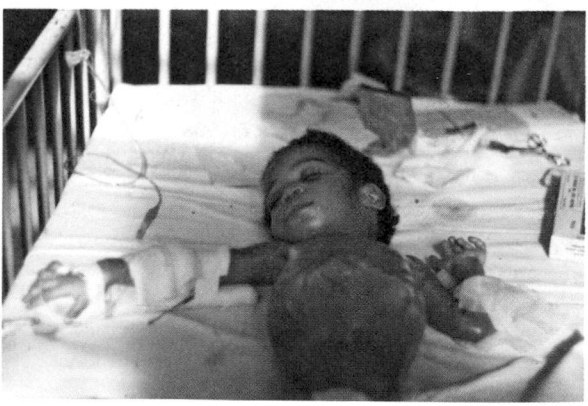
Fig. 16. Hungry infant placed in oven "because she was crying."

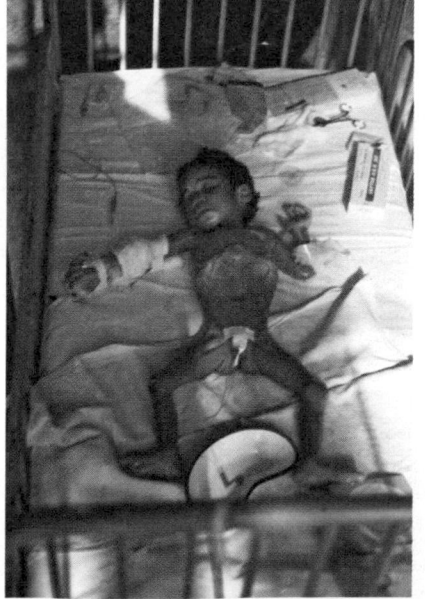

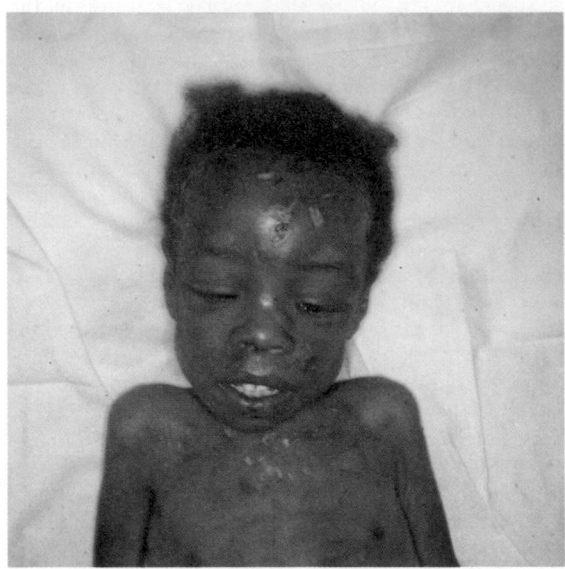

Fig. 17. Cigarette burns and belt buckle lesion from repeated strafings inflicted by parents.

References

Adelson, L. The slaughter of innocents. New Eng. J. Med., 264:345, 1962.
Caffey, J. Multiple fractures in the long bones of infants suffering from chronic subdural hematoma. Amer. J. Roentgen., 56:163, 1946.
Fontana, V. The Maltreated Child. Springfield, Ill., Charles C Thomas, 1964.
Helfer, R. E., and Kempe, C. H. The Battered Child. Chicago, The University of Chicago Press, 1968.
Holter, J. C., and Friedman, S. B. Child abuse: Early case finding in the emergency department. Pediatrics, 42:128, 1968.
Kempe, C. H., et al. Battered child syndrome. J.A.M.A., 181:17, 1962.
Paulsen, M. G. Legal protection against child abuse. Children, 13:43, 1966.
Silver, L. B., et al. Child abuse syndrome: The "gray areas" in establishing the diagnosis. Pediatrics, 44:594, 1969.
Silverman, F. N. Roentgen manifestations of unrecognized skeletal trauma in infants. Amer. J. Roentgen., 69:413, 1963.
Woolley, P. V., and Evans, W. A. Significance of skeletal lesions in infants resembling those of traumatic origin. J.A.M.A., 158:539, 1955.

are precarious, full of tensions, pressures, or aggravations. In many instances family ties are nonexistent, children are unwanted and often considered a burdensome handicap against whom frustrations are readily aired.

Once suspicion of willful injury has been aroused or confirmed, the method for dealing with the abused child are, unfortunately, random and inadequate. The help of social workers, psychiatrists, and agencies for the protection of the child may prove beneficial. Protective hospitalization, however, is mandatory to prevent possible repetition.

Returning the abused child to his home may be a threat to his health or life. Physical mistreatment of a child is legally a form of neglect. Juvenile courts have power over "neglected children" but criminal sanctions do little to help the child or to prevent recurrences of similar events. The major concern of the physician is the care and custody of abused children. In some states the law provides for protective services; in others, charters have been granted to voluntary agencies to carry out these protective services. Since legal or other protection can only be offered if instances of abuse or neglect are known, reporting of suspected cases has become mandatory. In an attempt to protect the children, the law requires physicians to report their suspicions to the police department or any special children's protective service operating in the community so that cases can be investigated and appropriate measures taken for the safety of the child. State laws protect physicians against liability for reporting.

13.13
DRUG ABUSE

MICHAEL COHEN and IRIS LITT

Drug abuse, which was an ancient and sporadic adult cultural phenomenon, has in recent years become a diffuse and major psychosocial, legal, environmental, and health hazard for our youth. Drug usage has broad implications for the young patient and the physician because of the potential for multisystem involvement at a time of accelerated physical and psychologic maturation. The adverse effects of drugs upon mood, temperament, and behavior have become a problem of major import with increasing medical and social significance. This section will be devoted to newly emerging drug-usage trends, coupled with an analysis of the physiology, psychopharmacology, and organ/system related complications of drug abuse in children and adolescents. The broader moral, social, and judicial aspects of the problem will not be discussed here. A lexicon of drug abuse terms is included (pp. 571–572).

Our observations are based on a three-and-one-half year experience with approximately 4,000 drug-using adolescents between the ages of 12 and 19 years. These teenagers represent poverty-level, low- and middle-income families within New York City and the surrounding suburbs. There was one female for every five males in this group. Medical appraisal of these teenagers was accomplished on an inpatient adolescent service and through several ambulatory care facilities for adolescents.

Heroin

Opiates were used for centuries for their ability to produce analgesia and euphoria. In the latter half of the 20th century these properties have been rediscovered and abused in epidemic proportions by adolescents, usually in the form of heroin.

IDENTIFICATION, ADMINISTRATION, AND DOSAGE.
Heroin is a semisynthetic derivative of the seed pods of *Papaver somniferum,* the opium poppy principally grown in Asia Minor. Acetylation of the parent morphine molecule to heroin renders it more potent as a respiratory depressant, analgesic, and euphoriant. In its pure form heroin is a white, crystalline powder which is bitter to taste. When obtained by the youthful consumer, it is usually a mixture of heroin and lactose. The lactose is added as a filler to dilute the opiate. A variety of other substances, such as quinine, procaine, or methylpyrilene, are additional adulterants used to disguise the sweet taste of the lactose. The final concentration of heroin after adulteration may range anywhere from 1 to 20 percent, or 1 to 30 mg. It is commonly sold in small glassine envelopes called "bags," costing in 1970 between two and five dollars. The content of individual envelopes varies widely and is limited only by the resourcefulness and lack of scruples of the seller.

The adolescent's first introduction to heroin is usually by the nasal route, called "snorting." In most cases, no more than one bag can be snorted in a six-hour interval without producing irritation and erythema of the nasal mucosa. This discomfort, combined with a half-hour interval between administration and desired psychopharmacologic effect, frequently leads to graduation to a subcutaneous route of administration, called "skin-popping." This has been a popular route for teenagers. The heroin is usually dissolved in heated water and then drawn up in a syringe or jagged-edged eyedropper referred to as the "works." We have found that the skin is rarely cleansed before it is punctured. Intravenous administration, or "mainlining," results in almost immediate psychologic and physical gratification. "Shooting up," or self-administration, is usually accomplished every six to eight hours by the addict. Constant use of the same blood vessel will result in typical scars, termed "needle tracks." The antecubital fossa is often avoided by the teenage users who know that it is the first place people look for tracks.

METABOLISM, PHYSIOLOGY, AND PSYCHOPHARMACOLOGY. Heroin is rapidly cleared from the blood and 90 percent is excreted within 24 hours after administration. It is rapidly hydrolized to 6-monoacetyl morphine and then to morphine. Detoxification proceeds by conjugation with glucuronic acid within the liver and then urinary excretion as free and conjugated morphine. Morphine can be detected in the urine by thin-layer chromatography up to 48 hours after administration. Quinine added to the heroin can be detected in urine up to 72 hours after the last dose.

Once heroin is converted to morphine, it may pass the placenta rapidly with a maximal effect observed in the fetus between one and six hours after administration to the mother. There is controversy as to whether heroin is excreted in human breast milk. Clinical observations support the contention that at high doses some heroin may be found in human milk.

In experiments at the cellular level, heroin as morphine enhances glucose uptake and phospholipid production, inhibits hydrolysis and release of acetylcholine, and also increases production of 5-hydroxytryptamine by rat brain slices.

People desire heroin because of its ability to produce euphoria and relieve pain. The frequent occurrence of drowsiness, nausea, and vomiting do not appear to be sufficient deterrents to its abuse. Lowering of body temperature associated with heroin use appears to be a direct effect on the hypothalamus. Increased rate of release of antidiuretic hormone contributes to the relative oliguria of the heroin abuser. Heroin also increases tone of the ureter and detrusor muscles. ACTH release is inhibited by chronic heroin use, and 17-hydroxy and 17-keto steroid levels are consequently lower. The electroencephalograph of the heroin user appears similar to that seen during normal sleep. Miosis caused by heroin appears to be a helpful clinical diagnostic sign of abuse because it does not disappear as tolerance develops. Dilation of a myotic pupil with 3 mg of Nalline is pathognomonic of opiate use.

Heroin has four times the effect of morphine as a respiratory depressant, primarily through reducing the medullary response to carbon dioxide. The rate, minute volume, and tidal exchange are equally depressed. The medullary cough center is similarly depressed and for this reason opiates have long been used as antitussives.

The physiologic effects of heroin on the gastrointestinal tract include increased tone of the antral portion of the stomach and first portion of the duodenum which results in delayed gastric emptying time. Hydrochloric acid production and biliary and pancreatic secretions are all decreased by heroin. The constipating effect of opiates in the form of paregoric is well known to pediatricians. Similarly, the action of heroin on the smooth muscle of the small and large intestine decreases propulsive contractions and augments anal sphincter tone, further contributing to the constipation which persists even as tolerance develops. Proliferation of hepatic smooth endoplasmic reticulum and focal areas of hepatocellular necrosis has been demonstrated in heroin users who have no evidence of clinical hepatitis, raising the possibility of a primary stimulatory and/or toxic effect of the drug on the liver.

The physiologic effects of heroin on the cardiovascular system are minimal. In normal subjects, morphine causes relaxation of the peripheral vascular bed without direct cardiac effects. In patients with aortic valvular disease, cardiac index, stroke index, and central venous pressure are increased after morphine administration.

MEDICAL COMPLICATIONS. Heroin became the leading cause of death among adolescents in New York City during 1969 and 1970. Because some complications of heroin abuse can be prevented, and most others treated if diagnosed early, it is imperative that physicians be able to recognize these medical complications.

Brain abscesses, secondary to septic emboli, were found in 18 percent of adult heroin addicts with bacterial endocarditis. Staphylococcus aureus is the usual etiologic agent. For undiscovered reasons, this complication appears less commonly in adolescent heroin users. Among the heroin-related neurologic diseases, disseminated intracranial micro abscesses, rather than a single large abscess, have been described as the more common lesion. Such micro abscesses may produce mild, nonfocal symptoms or go entirely unnoticed. Diagnostic appraisal may require lumbar puncture, electroencephalography, cerebral angiography, and cerebral air studies. Antistaphylococcal agents for periods of four to six weeks by the intravenous route form the basis of the usual therapy. Surgical drainage may be necessary after localization of the abscess.

Cerebral edema is found at autopsy in two thirds of heroin addicts who die suddenly from an "overdose" reaction. Basal ganglia necrosis and encephalomalacia have also been reported in some of these patients. Peripheral nerve injuries secondary to heroin injection are seen with increasing frequency in the teenage group.

The gastrointestinal tract is the organ system having the greatest number of complications resulting from heroin abuse. Approximately 10 percent of adult addicts described by Cherubin were found to have an active duodenal ulcer. One third of the 18 deaths due to peritonitis at the Lexington Rehabilitation Center were secondary to an ulcer. This observation may appear inconsistent with the decreased production of hydrochloric acid which results from heroin use. However, the delayed gastric emptying time, coupled with the ability of heroin to mask pain, may contribute to this complication. Misinterpretation of peptic ulcer symptoms as symptoms of acute opiate withdrawal was responsible for death from perforation in one series of four young addicts. Therapy in those teenagers with an ulcer diathesis but without perforation has included a relatively unrestricted diet with frequent antacid therapy but avoiding sedatives and anticholinergics.

Concealment of a heroin supply in a condom which is swallowed with the expectation of later recovery in the stool has led to intestinal obstruction in a small number of abusers. A still rarer cause of small bowel obstruction is the occasional practice of swallowing cotton pledgets through which heroin has been strained to remove particulate matter prior to injection.

Hepatitis is the single most common complication of heroin abuse in adolescents. Eighty percent of the teenage heroin users requiring hospitalization on our service had this diagnosis. Of these, seven patients developed hepatic encephalopathy resulting in four deaths over a two-year period. The two survivors showed persistent liver function abnormalities almost one year after onset of their illness and one, biopsied four months after recovery from coma, was found to have postnecrotic cirrhosis. The management of hepatic encephalopathy remains diversified, but in addition to the more standard approaches of intravenous replacement of fluid, electrolytes, and carbohydrate, parenteral antibiotics and intestinal bacterial sterilization, we have utilized corticosteroids and exchange transfusion. Twenty percent of 2,000 ambulatory, asymptomatic, heroin-using adolescents examined by our service had chemical evidence of hepatitis consisting of two or more abnormalities of liver function tests. Review of the literature indicates an apparent higher incidence of anicteric hepatitis in adult heroin users (60 to 80 percent), findings which may be due to differing criteria for the diagnosis, rather than a valid difference in incidence. Therapy for this ambulatory group consists of adequate and liberal diet, full activity, and gamma globulin prophylaxis to close contacts.

We have observed transient elevation of serum glutamic oxaloacetic transaminase associated with heroin withdrawal in the absence of other evidence of hepatic dysfunction. This may reflect mild striated muscle damage similar to that which has been documented by electromyography and creatinine phosphokinase determinations in acute barbiturate withdrawal.

Hepatitis is most commonly presumed to be viral in origin and related to the communal use of unsterilized needles. The observation of a few adolescents with hepatitis who had admitted only to having snorted heroin raises the possibility that heroin or one of its diluents may have a direct toxic effect on the liver. Support for this hypothesis is provided by the electron microscopic appearance of hypertrophied smooth endoplasmic reticulum and eosinophilic bodies in liver biopsies of some heroin addicts. Countervailing evidence of hepatic toxicity is found in human morphine addiction experiments which failed to demonstrate abnormalities of liver function. Approximately 500 heroin-using adolescents with hepatic dysfunction followed by us have had a prolonged clinical course marked by multiple exacerbations, quite different from the generally mild course seen with hepatitis in most children and adolescents not using drugs.

The heroin user, whether an addict or a dabbler, who is found by a physician to have fever of unknown origin should be suspected of having bacterial endocarditis. This may occur in a patient with or without a history of a preexisting cardiac lesion. In Louria's series, only one third of the patients had a history or physical findings compatible with underlying cardiac pathology. Sapira distinguishes two patterns of endocarditis, based on location of the affected valve. He believes right-sided endocarditis is usually caused by Staphylococcus aureus, affecting a previously normal tricuspid valve and may be associated with few, if any, clinical findings. One of our 15-year-old addicts suffered two bouts of Staphylococcus aureus endocarditis affecting the tricuspid valve and presented with findings of septic pulmonary emboli. Embolization to brain, spleen, and kidney, as well as to the lungs, has been documented with tricuspid valve involvement. The second pattern of bacterial endocarditis reported by Sapira presents the more characteristic manifestations of endocarditis; it affects the left side of the heart and may occur in a previously damaged, or intact, valve. In comparison with the staphylococcal involvement of the right-sided lesion, the left-sided lesions are more commonly caused by streptococcal or fungal agents, the latter particularly if previous valve damage exists. The appearance of septic emboli in the absence of pulmonary emboli is usually diagnostic of a left-sided lesion or a small intracardiac shunt. The initial diagnostic evaluation and therapeutic approach is similar to that of classical bacterial endocarditis seen in children with rheumatic heart disease. Antimicrobial therapy depends upon bacteriologic and fungal laboratory findings.

Angiothrombotic pulmonary hypertension is a rare complication of inadvertent intravenous injection of starch or other inert fillers used to dilute heroin; fibers of cotton used to strain heroin prior to injection may also play a role. Pulmonary granulomata may be caused in the same manner. While diagnosis must usually await post-mortem examination of lung tissue with a polarizing microscope, it may be suspected in the heroin user with evidence of decreased lung volume and diffusing capacity. The combination of depressed cough reflex and delayed gastric emptying time described previously is the most plausible explanation for the high incidence of aspiration pneumonia in adult addicts. For unknown reasons, pneumonia is uncommon in the adolescent heroin user.

Tuberculosis is found with greater frequency in adult heroin addicts than in the general population. However, in our experience the incidence of tuberculosis, based on routine tuberculin testing, is no higher in the heroin-using adolescent than in his non–heroin-using peers. Similarly, the increased prevalence (5 to 9 percent) of asthma reported in adult heroin addicts has not been documented in adolescents who use heroin.

Pulmonary edema is prominent only in association with heroin-overdose syndrome discussed below and which is usually fatal; it is radiographically evident even in the absence of clinical signs. Follow-up evaluation of a small number of patients with pulmonary edema who recovered suggests long-term sequelae, such as a reduced diffusing capacity. The pathogenesis of pulmonary edema in association with heroin abuse is unknown.

A variety of gynecologic disorders, including oligomenorrhea, amenorrhea, and menometrorrhagia have been described in adult heroin addicts. Amenorrhea appears with striking frequency in adolescent heroin users. The return of menses after cessation of heroin use varies inversely with the duration of drug utilization. We have postulated that gonadotrophin production or release is inhibited by heroin use, as has been demonstrated with ACTH release. The adolescent in whom a regular menstrual cycle has not yet been established appears more vulnerable to this effect than the adult heroin user.

Venereal disease occurs generally as a complication of heightened sexual promiscuity fostered by a frequent need to support heroin habituation through prostitution. Ironically, libido is actually decreased by heroin use. In addition to the increased incidence of venereal disease in adolescent heroin users, a high percentage of biologic false positive serology studies (VDRL) is found. The mechanism of this finding is not clear, but it does not apparently correlate with the presence of active liver disease which is also known to be associated with serologic false positive VDRL's. The finding of a VDRL that is weakly reactive over a period of two weeks is suggestive of a false positive reaction. Confirmatory tests, such as a Treponema Immobilization test, should be performed in such patients, although it is usually prudent to commence treatment on the basis of the screening test rather than risk failure of the patient to return for follow-up confirmatory test results.

In our experience the incidence of pregnancy in adolescent heroin users is no different from that in non–heroin-using girls. Assuming a probable greater opportunity for pregnancy associated with a higher rate of prostitution in the former group, this observation may be additional evidence of anovulation in the heroin users.

The complications of pregnancy in the teenage years, such as infants small for dates and a higher rate of spontaneous abortion and stillbirth, are the same as those seen in pregnancies of adult heroin users. The combination of adolescence and heroin use results in a still higher-risk pregnancy, with danger extending into the newborn period because of the frequent occurrence of the abstinence syndrome in the neonate (p. 573).

Abscesses are frequently observed as a complication of the use of an unsterilized needle for the subcutaneous or intravenous administration of heroin. Repeated use of the former route can also cause atrophy and subcutaneous fat necrosis, not unlike that found in patients with diabetes mellitus. The addition of sclerosing agents, such as mannite used as an adulterant in the heroin mixture to enhance its bitter quality, can result in necrotic skin ulcers. Hyperpigmentation of a vessel or lesions that resemble railroad tracks are indicative of intravenous use. Cigarette burns around the upper chest may result from the user falling asleep with a lighted cigarette in his or her mouth after injection or from a "street" method of attempting resuscitation of an overdose victim by stimulation with a lighted cigarette. Bullae have been described on the skin of overdose victims, similar to those found in association with carbon monoxide or barbiturate intoxication, and analysis of the fluid from such bullae may be diagnostic.

Tetanus is being observed with increasing frequency in heroin users. Currently, the group with the highest incidence is composed of older women addicts who have resorted to "skin popping" after their veins have sclerosed. The abscesses resulting from this method of administration provide excellent growth media for the clostridium organism. Among adolescents, in whom "skin popping" is often the preferred route of administration and in whom abscess formation is also common, tetanus is not as frequent a complication. Residual immunity in the adolescent years from childhood tetanus immunizations probably accounts for this difference. A booster of tetanus toxoid would seem indicated in all teenage drug users. Superficial skin infections are easily managed with improved hygiene and appropriate antibiotic therapy. Plastic surgery for cosmetic repair of these scars plays a specific and important role in the total rehabilitative effort of the teenage addict.

Significant eosinophilia without explanation has been observed in 25 percent of the 2000 adolescent heroin users we have examined. The possibility exists that this finding is related to a hypersensitivity state to heroin or one of its adulterants. This in turn may be related to the pathogenesis of the heroin "overdose" syndrome.

THE ABSTINENCE SYNDROME. Heroin withdrawal is characterized, physiologically, by a syndrome of progression from signs of yawning, lacrimation, restlessness, dilated pupils, insomnia, "goose flesh," muscle cramps, hyperactive bowel sounds, diarrhea, systolic hypertension, tachycardia, and, rarely, convulsions within 48 hours after discontinuation of heroin use. Only 25 percent of the heroin-addicted teenagers we observed manifested some or all of these findings. Evaluation of the withdrawal process was accomplished by use of an opiate withdrawal log (O.W.L.) score (Table 16). This score was designed to quantitate and objectively evaluate withdrawal. The occurrence of a seizure constitutes "severe" withdrawal even in the absence of other symptoms. It provides a means for following a patient systematically through a course of treatment.

Treatment of the abstinence syndrome or detoxification in adolescents is directed toward preventing the life-threatening sequelae of seizures and cardiovascular collapse. Chlorpromazine administration is undesirable in the case of the adolescent addict because of its potential for lowering the seizure threshold and for inducing hepatotoxicity and hypotension. Moreover, sudden death has been reported following its use in withdrawal. The inherent addiction potential of phenobarbital and its lack of superiority to other modalities makes it of little use in dealing with the adolescent. Methadone is effective in alleviating the symptoms of abstinence, but current treatment schedules require 8 to 11 days of hospitalization for this purpose.

A treatment regimen for adolescent heroin users utiziling diazepam has been effective in our experi-

TABLE 16. *Opiate Withdrawal Log (O.W.L.)*

Symptoms	Items Receiving No Points	Items Receiving One Point Each	Items Receiving Two Points Each
1. Yawning	Absent	Present	—
2. Dilated pupils (>8mm)	Absent	Present	—
3. Restlessness	—	Moderate	Severe
4. Lacrimation	Absent	Present	—
5. "Goose flesh"	Absent	Present	—
6. Muscle cramps	Absent	Present	—
7. Insomnia	Slept for 7 hr or more/24 hr	Slept 4-7 hr/24 hr	Slept less than 4 hr/24 hr
8. Hyperactive bowel sounds	Absent	Present after 48 hr from withdrawal of heroin	Present before 48 hr from withdrawal of heroin
9. Diarrhea	0-1 stools/12 hr	2-4 stools/12 hr	More than 4 stools/12 hr
10. Vital signs: Pulse Blood pressure	<72 <108/70	72-100 or 110-140/70	>100 or >140/70

The abstinence syndrome is clinically evaluated in each patient by scoring his symptom complex according to the above noted point system. An O.W.L. score of 1 to 5 points is considered "mild" withdrawal, 6 to 10 points is "moderate" withdrawal, and 11 to 15 points is "severe" withdrawal. (From Litt, Colli, and Cohen. J. Pediat., 1971).

ence in eliminating signs of withdrawal within 3 days and in preventing seizures and cardiovascular collapse. Treatment is based on evaluation by the O.W.L. score. Those who are scored as having "mild" withdrawal are treated with diazepam given orally in a dosage of 10 mg every 6 hours for 3 days. Patients in the "moderate" category are first given diazepam intramuscularly in two doses of 10 mg each separated by an interval of 4 hours; this treatment is followed by the oral regimen described above. In "severe" withdrawal, diazepam is given intramuscularly in doses of 10 mg every 4 hours for the first 24 hours, the same intramuscular dose every 6 hours for the next 24 hours, and 10 mg orally every 6 hours for the third day. All medication should be discontinued when the O.W.L. score falls below 2, usually within three days of onset of therapy. Occasionally, one dose of diphenoxylate hydrochloride 2.5 mg is necessary to control diarrhea. Insomnia will persist as long as a month after onset of abstinence symptoms, and is refractory to the usual sedatives. The patient should be made aware of this from the onset and warned of the danger of self-administration of other drugs in a search for sleep. Many barbiturate-using adolescents started using the drug after they felt they had successfully "kicked" their heroin habit and merely desired something to induce sleep. Because we have had no experience treating the heroin addict with a history of a seizure disorder with diazepam, we would not suggest depending on this drug alone in detoxifying such a patient.

ACUTE HEROIN TOXICITY.

Diagnosis. The adolescent who presents with lethargy or coma, constricted pupils, respiratory depression cyanosis, and/or rales should be considered to have a heroin "overdose" until proven otherwise.

Emergency Treatment. Treatment should be instituted immediately as follows:

1. Intubate the patient and administer oxygen by positive pressure.
2. Administer Nalline, 3 mg, subcutaneously unless the patient is in shock, in which case intravenous administration would be appropriate. Dilation of previously constricted pupils after Nalline provides evidence of opiate toxicity.
3. Start intravenous fluid therapy.
4. Obtain serum samples for morphine, barbiturate, and glutethimide levels.
5. Blood gas (CO_2 and O_2) studies should be performed.
6. Obtain urine for toxicologic analysis and carefully observe urinary output. A Foley catheter may be indicated.
7. Administer Nalline, 5 mg, intravenously if the Nalline test (#2 above) is positive. This may be repeated at 10-minute intervals until pulmonary ventilatory function improves. The total dose of Nalline should not exceed 30 mg.
8. A radiograph of the chest is often diagnostic of pulmonary edema. If present, the use of antibiotics in therapeutic doses is recommended.

It should be noted that the opiate overdose may be due to methadone, a situation seen with increasing frequency in children of adult addicts maintained on this drug who may keep it at home in orange juice. Treatment with Nalline should be continued at 4-hour intervals for 24 hours, as methadone is a longer-acting opiate than heroin.

Depressants

The recent increased use of depressants among teenagers appears to be related to the need for relief of insomnia associated with self-imposed heroin withdrawal. The ability of barbiturates to potentiate a heroin high and modify an amphetamine binge also contributes to extensive abuse.

IDENTIFICATION, ADMINISTRATION, AND DOSAGE. Synthetic central nervous system depressants are gaining in popularity among adolescents who abuse drugs. The more commonly used of this group are Tuinal (sodium amobarbital and sodium secobarbital), and Doriden (glutethimide or "CIBAS"). While these are prepared commercially for oral use, their abuse frequently involves intravenous administration following dissolution of pills or capsules in water. When barbiturates are appropriately prescribed for a seizure disorder, dosage falls in the range of 3 to 8 mg per kg per day. In the adolescent who has developed tolerance, self-administration may reach 3,500 mg per day. Tolerance does not develop to the lethal respiratory effect, however, and many accidental deaths have occurred by inadvertent overdose. The usual therapeutic dosage schedule for glutethimide is 0.125 to 0.5 g three times a day for sedation or hypnosis. We have encountered adolescents abusing up to 3.5 g daily, although in the nontolerant, 5 g will produce severe intoxication and 10 g may be fatal. Cross tolerance develops within this category of drugs, a fact utilized in detoxification and treatment of the complications of depressant withdrawal.

METABOLISM, PHYSIOLOGY, AND PSYCHOPHARMACOLOGY. Secobarbital and amobarbital, the most commonly abused barbiturates, are short-acting. They are well absorbed from the stomach or subcutaneous tissue, detoxified in the liver, and excreted in the urine. They pass the placental barrier and into breast milk. Glutethimide, on the other hand, is absorbed irregularly from the gastrointestinal tract. Because of its high lipid to water partition coefficient, it diffuses rapidly in vascular tissues. It is completely metabolized into the glucuronide and the glutaconimide which are excreted into the intestine by way of the biliary tract. Urinary excretion of the metabolites is slow.

Barbiturates have their major effect as depressants of the central nervous system as a result of their ability to raise the threshold of stimulation of neurons and prolong their time for recovery. For this reason they are used as anticonvulsants, hypnotics, anesthetics, and analgesics. Respiratory depression is a frequent complication of the effect of the drug on the medullary respiratory center.

Barbiturates decrease the tone of the gastrointestinal tract and delay gastric emptying time, a property used in the treatment of barbiturate overdose. Addiction and tolerance develop within one or two months of daily use of 200 mg or more of this sedative. The pharmacologic effects of glutethimide are very similar to those of secobarbital. However, glutethimide acts in addition as an anticholinergic to produce mydriasis, drying of the mouth, and decreased intestinal motility.

MEDICAL COMPLICATIONS. Complications of barbiturate or glutethimide abuse result from the method of administration, idiosyncratic reactions, and accidental overdoses. The use of an unsterilized needle for injection of sedatives is responsible for the same high incidence of hepatitis and abscesses in this group as found in the heroin addict. The practice of crushing and dissolving tablets and capsules for intravenous use has been implicated in the production of talc and starch granulomata and emboli in the lung, with resultant pulmonary hypertension. A variety of skin lesions, including a measles-like exanthem without Koplik's spots, a scarlatiniform rash, and sweat-gland necrosis with bullae have been described in association with barbiturate use. The fact that the lethal dose does not change in the presence of tolerance to the other effects makes overdose common. Slurred speech, short attention span, emotional lability, nystagmus, and ataxia are characteristic of the sedative addict, who thus may be mistaken for an alcohol inebriate. Definitive diagnosis is made by analysis of serum or urine for barbiturates or glutethimide.

THE ABSTINENCE SYNDROME. Symptoms of withdrawal generally appear between 12 and 16 hours after the last dose of a short-acting barbiturate or glutethimide. Anxiety, restlessness, and tremor are the first symptoms to appear followed in rapid succession by nausea, vomiting, and abdominal cramps. By 24 hours, the patient is weak with hyperactive reflexes and orthostatic hypotension and may experience a grand mal seizure within 72 hours after his last dose, if withdrawal is not appropriately treated. With the longer-acting barbiturates, seizures may not appear until one week after the last dose. Tachycardia and fever are also seen in glutethimide withdrawal.

The extremely high incidence of grand mal seizures following abrupt discontinuation of sedatives in an addict makes gradual withdrawal under close medical supervision imperative.

Whom to Detoxify.

1. Anyone using 200 mg or more per day of a barbiturate or glutethimide for more than a month.
2. Anyone using sedatives regularly, regardless of amount, with a history of a seizure disorder.

How to Detoxify.

1. Ascertain the usual total daily dose (termed X) and divide it into four equal doses. Therapeutically utilize phenobarbital on a gram-for-gram substitution for the abused agent. If there is doubt about the reliability of the patient, assume the true daily dose to be half that stated and proceed as below.
2. If the last dose was taken more than 12 hours before the patient was seen, or if he manifests signs of tremor, restlessness, or hypotension, administer the first dose intramuscularly; otherwise administer this and all subsequent doses by the oral route.
3. If the history is accurate, the first dose should cause signs of mild toxicity, such as nystagmus, dysarthria, or ataxia. If these signs do not appear within two hours of the first dose, recalculate the daily dose at $X+120$ mg. The next dose, given six hours after the first, should therefore be 30 mg more than the first. Continue to increase the dose until signs of mild toxicity appear.
4. Consider the dose at which signs of mild toxicity appear as the maintenance dose.
5. On the second day of treatment give maintenance dose divided in four equal doses.
6. On the third day reduce the total daily dose by 120 mg divided equally between the four doses.
7. Continue tapering until half of the maintenance dose is attained.
8. Give half the maintenance dose for two days.
9. Continue tapering. Stop tapering if restlessness, tremor, anxiety, or drop in blood pressure develops.
10. Chlorpromazine is contraindicated in detoxification of the depressant addict.

ACUTE SEDATIVE DRUG TOXICITY.

Diagnosis. Toxicity from barbiturates resembles that from opiates in that the patient is comatose, in respiratory distress, with constricted pupils unless hypoxia dilation has occurred, and manifests signs of shock. Bullae on the skin may be aspirated and their contents analyzed for the responsible drug if this is not known. Tonic muscular spasms, convulsions, hypotension, and paralytic ileus are seen commonly in glutethimide overdose in which, in contrast with barbiturates, the pupils are usually dilated.

Emergency Treatment.

1. With a barbiturate, perform gastric lavage and/or induce vomiting. Never induce emesis if glutethimide is ingested; it may precipitate apnea. Save the first 10 ml of gastric aspirate for toxicologic analysis.
2. Maintain an adequate airway. Use oxygen if

necessary but only by positive pressure. Keep the patient warm.

3. Start intravenous fluid therapy and monitor serum electrolytes, blood gases, and plasma barbiturate levels (3.5 mg per 100 ml is often a lethal dose for short-acting barbiturates, 8 mg per 100 ml for the long-acting variety).
4. Urinary bladder catheterization is frequently helpful. Alkalinizing the urine has no effect on the excretion of short-acting barbiturates, but may be helpful with long-acting barbiturates. A high urine output will also be helpful.
5. Analeptics have no place in the treatment of barbiturate poisoning.
6. Hemodialysis is effective in short- or long-acting barbiturates and glutethimide poisoning. However, dialysis is rarely indicated in a comatose patient solely for this purpose, since supportive measures alone will suffice.

Amphetamines

In the pursuit of a "high," the drug-using adolescent may discover oral amphetamines. However, once the user has been introduced to an intravenous injection of a sympathomimetic amine, slow stimulation is incidental to achieving the main objective of immediate and complete excitation.

IDENTIFICATION, ADMINISTRATION, AND DOSAGE. Discovered in the 1930s to have vasopressor action, by the 1940s amphetamines were abused by truck drivers and students alike for their ability to inhibit fatigue. In the 1950s they were abused by housewives and others for weight reduction and in the 1960s by teenagers for "kicks." Amphetamines are sympathomimetic amines which act by inhibiting amine oxidase. A survey of medical students in a western university in 1965 revealed almost half to have used amphetamines at least once. In 1968, 22 percent of 11th- and 12th-graders in a California high school had experimented with them. The problem is not restricted to the United States; seven percent of students in the 7th through 13th grades in Toronto had used stimulants according to one report, and Sweden is currently involved in an amphetamine crisis.

The drug's effects can be appreciated within one half hour of oral administration, or within five minutes of subcutaneous injection. Intravenous injection is "not recommended" by pharmacologists, a fact ignored by teenagers who prefer this route for the instantaneous effect described by Jeootes as a "total body orgasm."

Toxicologic analysis of a refrigerated casual specimen of urine or saliva will be diagnostic of amphetamine abuse.

METABOLISM, PHYSIOLOGY, AND PSYCHOPHARMACOLOGY. Amphetamines are well absorbed from the gastrointestinal tract. They are deaminated by the liver or excreted unchanged in the urine where they may be detected anywhere from three hours to three days after ingestion.

Their peripheral manifestations result from a direct effect on adrenergic receptors of muscles and glands. Amphetamines stimulate the medullary respiratory center and the cerebrospinal axis, and are utilized pharmacologically for their analeptic potential. In man, the psychic and psychomotor effects are dramatic. An initial oral dose of 10 mg results in mood elevation, wakefulness, self-confidence, greater concentration ability, increased strength, and appetite depression. Unfortunately, tolerance quickly develops to these effects and depression, confusion, paranoia, and headache are common in the chronic user.

In higher doses, the usual physiologic effect is systolic and diastolic hypertension. A concomitant decrease in cerebral blood flow has been demonstrated. The effect on the gastrointestinal tract is variable with the gastric emptying time at first increased and later delayed. Hydrochloric acid production is unaffected. The ability of amphetamines to contract the trigone and relax the detrusor muscles of the urinary bladder is responsible for their use in enuresis. It is thought that the beneficial effect of amphetamines in dysmenorrhea is related to the increased uterine tone and diminished amplitude of contractions they produce, although the effect on the central nervous system may also contribute to the beneficial results.

"Speed," the term used for intravenously injected amphetamine, produces an immediate chill, racing pulse, blurring of vision, dilation of the pupils, and elevated blood pressure. The user is consumed by a frenzy of activity directed at obtaining more drug to reproduce the alleged ecstasy of effect, the so-called Speed Binge. If unobtainable, a profound fatigue and depression sets in, called "crashing." The victim sleeps for days, paranoia is marked, and upon recovery he may act to kill before he is killed, hence the expression "Speed Kills." In fact, "speed" may kill the abuser as well.

MEDICAL COMPLICATIONS. The adolescent with dilated pupils, elevated blood pressure and pulse, blanched mucous membranes, weight loss, and paranoia is possibly an amphetamine user. Hepatitis may result from the use of unsterilized needles. As with barbiturates, pulmonary granulomata and emboli may be the consequence of intravenous injection of capsules and tablets containing talc or starch. Intravenous use has also been implicated in cerebrovascular accidents, although this complication is rarely seen.

ACUTE TOXICITY REACTIONS.

Diagnosis. Reactions consisting of vomiting, diarrhea, palpitation, arrhythmias, syncope, hyperpyrexia, and hyperreflexia, progressing to convulsion or coma, may result from as little as 30 mg, although there are reports of daily doses of 15,000 mg in chronic users.

Treatment of Acute Amphetamine Poisoning.

1. Lavage

2. Sedation with chlorpromazine
3. Acidification of urine with ammonium chloride
4. Hypothermia mattress, if indicated

Based on experiments on monkeys, the lethal dose for children is thought to be 5 mg per kg, and for adults 20 to 25 mg per kg. The lethal dose in mice is, however, influenced by environmental conditions. While the LD-50 for mice caged individually was 100 mg per kg, that for mice caged in groups was 25 mg per kg. At the lower dose the mice were observed to be excitable and aggressive while at higher doses they became too disorganized to attack. David Smith compares this group toxicity factor to the violence of speed users in a group setting. Tolerance definitely develops as does psychic dependence.

The treatment of the chronic user separated from his drug should consist of hospitalization with admission to a dark, quiet room. A professional in attendance to reassure the patient is helpful, and observation should extend for approximatey 47 to 72 hours. It is usually after the patient awakens that suicide or homicide are possibilities. Detoxification utilizing drug therapy is not necessary.

Marihuana

IDENTIFICATION, ADMINISTRATION, AND DOSAGE. Marihuana is produced from the resin in the inflorescence and highest leaves, as well as the recently fertilized ovary and unripened fruit, of the female plant *Cannabis sativa*. This plant, also a source of hemp fiber and seed oil, grows in temperate and hot, dry areas, particularly near human habitation. There is documentation that its hallucinogenic properties were known to man as early as 600 B.C. Analysis of cannabis resin reveals cannabinol, cannabidial, cannabidiolic acid, tetrahydrocannabinol-carboxylic acid, cannabirigeral, cannabichromine, and tetrahydrocannabinol. Cannabidiolic acid and cannabichromine have been found to have sedative properties. The hallucinogenic effects of marihuana appear to reside in the delta-1-tetrahydrocannabinol fraction which has recently been synthesized. The pure synthetic form is a potent hallucinogen, even more so than LSD. Marihuana is most commonly used in the form of "reefers" or "joints," which are made by rolling the crushed leaves and flowers in paper. Hashish, the preferred form, has about eight times the potency of marihuana; it is smoked in a pipe. Because there is no accurate method for toxicologic analysis of body fluids for marihuana, the extent of its use is difficult to ascertain. Based on various surveys, however, it must be concluded that at the present time marihuana is the most extensively abused substance among adolescents in the United States.

METABOLISM, PHYSIOLOGY, AND PSYCHOPHARMACOLOGY. The metabolic fate of the cannabinols in man is unknown. In rabbits, 20 percent of injected tritiated delta-1(6)tetrahydrocannabinol is excreted in the urine within four days in the form of the cannabinol. In the rat, 80 percent of injected delta-9-tetrahydrocannabinol is excreted in metabolized form in the feces, the remainder is eliminated in the urine. Half of the administered dose remained in the rat after one week, suggesting a slower excretory process than in the rabbit.

The pharmacologic effects of marihuana were first studied under controlled conditions by Weil, Zindberg, and Nelson in 1968, who described the maximal effect of smoking marihuana to be achieved at 15 minutes. At this time the heart rate is increased in both new and chronic users. Respiratory rate, on the other hand, is unchanged by marihuana in the new user; in the chronic user there is a small but statistically significant increase. Pupillary size is unaffected by marihuana.

The experiments of Weil et al. demonstrated that marihuana caused dose-related impairment of performance on simple intellectual and psychomotor tests, as well as interference with immediate memory. Comparison of the effects of marihuana with those of alcohol under controlled conditions in a setting of simulated driving performance was performed by other investigators. The marihuana-intoxicated group accumulated more speedometer errors than under drug-free conditions, with no significant differences in accelerator, brake, signal, steering, and total errors. The alcohol-intoxicated group, on the other hand, made more accelerator, brake, signal, speedometer, and total errors than under normal conditions.

MEDICAL COMPLICATIONS.   Adverse reactions to marihuana do occur; Weil et al. describe occasional depressive reactions, panic reactions, and toxic psychoses in the marihuana user without a history of hallucinogen abuse or previous mental illness. Of these, the panic reaction is the most common and treatment should consist of gentle, but authoritative reassurance that the patient is not psychotic and that the effects of the drug are only temporary. In those who have taken hallucinogens, marihuana use may cause "flashbacks" or recurrence of hallucinations. Derealization has been precipitated in schizophrenics who smoked marihuana. Adolescents who are chronic users of marihuana are prone to develop a syndrome of passivity and lack of goal direction.

Unresolved still are questions about potential permanent effects of marihuana, particularly on offspring of users. In lower animals, cannabis extract has been shown to be teratogenic in pregnant rats, hamsters, and rabbits when administered intraperitoneally. Subcutaneous injections of delta-9-tetrahydrocannabinol in hamsters reveals that placental uptake of the chemical is greater than in maternal blood or brain. In vitro experimentation with human leucocyte cultures have demonstrated no structural derangements or chromosomal breaks caused by delta-8- or delta-9-tetrahydrocannabinol. Whether marihuana by the route and in the doses commonly used in humans is indeed teratogenic awaits further investigation.

Marihuana has been condemned for its potential for later experimentation with heroin. While this may be true in some populations, we have found in a large inner-city ghetto population that for most heroin users the first contact was with glue sniffing rather than with marihuana.

Cocaine

Cocaine is abused for the euphoric stimulation it produces as well as for its ability to cause pleasant hallucinations.

IDENTIFICATION, ADMINISTRATION, AND DOSAGE. Cocaine is derived from the leaves of *Erythroxylon coca,* indigenous to Peru where the pre-Inca Indians discovered its stimulant properties. Cocaine is benzolmethylecgonine and is structurally similar to many local anesthetics with which it shares the ability to block nerve conduction. It is well absorbed from mucous membranes and until recently its abuse involved chewing or nasal inhalation. However, subcutaneous and intravenous administration are becoming increasingly more popular routes.

METABOLISM, PHYSIOLOGY, AND PSYCHOPHARMACOLOGY. Most of that which is absorbed is detoxified by the liver and excreted in the urine as benzoylecgonine. Approximately 9 percent is excreted unchanged. Both forms can be detected by gas liquid and thin layer chromatography of the urine.

The systemic effects of cocaine include initial central nervous system stimulation which manifests itself in restlessness, decreased fatigability, increased motor activity, increased respiratory rate, and emesis followed by eventual depression. The heart rate is increased as a result of central and peripheral sympathetic stimulation. This, in combination with centrally mediated vasoconstriction, produces hypertension initially. Vasoconstriction, direct action on the heat regulation centers, and the increased muscular activity it causes, combine to make cocaine pyrogenic. The sympathomimetic actions of the drug are thought to result from its ability to prevent destruction of epinephrine or by increasing cellular permeability to it.

Tolerance to these pharmacologic effects develops, and psychic dependence can be marked. The absence of characteristic withdrawal symptoms upon discontinuance of use in a chronic abuser suggests that physiologic addiction probably does not occur. Like the amphetamine abuser, the individual abusing cocaine is likely to develop paranoia. Formication, or the sensation of objects crawling on one's body, is another indication of mental deterioration.

MEDICAL COMPLICATIONS. Nausea, anorexia, emaciation, insomnia, tremors, and convulsions may occur in the chronic cocaine user. In addition, specific complications, related to the route of administration, occur. The most popular method of administration has been inhalation or sniffing. After prolonged use, this often results in perforation of the nasal septum.

Subcutaneous injection causes ischemia secondary to the vasoconstrictive properties of the drug. This, in combination with the lack of sterile technique, is responsible for the frequent occurrence of abscesses at injection sites and the potential for bacterial endocarditis and tetanus as described with heroin abuse. Intravenous injection of a large dose of cocaine may result in immediate death from cardiac failure due to a direct toxic action on the myocardium.

The high cost of cocaine today appears to be responsible for its use in combination with heroin, rather than alone. This combination is called a "speedball."

Since physiologic addiction does not occur there is no clinical abstinence syndrome to deal with. Poisonings require the immediate intravenous administration of short-acting barbiturates in conjunction with support of respiratory efforts. A tourniquet about the extremity used for administration of the cocaine may prove helpful. Most of the drug is detoxified within one hour of administration so that the prognosis is excellent if the patient can be adequately supported for a short period of time.

Glue Sniffing and Other Inhalant Abuse

Inhalants are used for their ability to produce exhilaration and euphoria. Solvent sniffing was first reported on the West Coast in the late 1950s and spread eastward a decade later as a phenomenon exclusively of children and adolescents. The plastic cement or glue used in making airplane models was the first agent so abused and continues to be the most popular in the young adolescent population of inner city ghettos. Experimentation with other inhalants such as cleaning fluids, hair sprays, and freezant aerosols has recently characterized middle-income suburban teenagers.

The ritual of vapor inhalation takes many forms. It ranges from that of saturating a rag with the desired substance, pouring or squeezing it into a paper or plastic bag from which it is inhaled, or placing it in a pan which is subsequently heated to promote rapid vaporization. Initial experimentation is usually a group phenomenon, while the habitué soon resorts to sniffing alone.

In the absence of routine toxicologic screening tests for the various substances abused by inhalation, the extent of such abuse is unknown. In the group of delinquent adolescents under our care, 10 percent admitted to glue sniffing. The mean age of onset of this practice was 13 years. Inhalation of cleaning fluid was responsible for admission of 5 percent of all drug-using teenagers from middle-income suburban families who required hospitalization. The mean age of this group was 15 years.

Plastic cement, or airplane glue, is a mixture of toluene and ethyl acetate. The popular cleaning fluid preparation most commonly used contains trichloro-ethylene and 1,1,1-trichloroethane.

Early uncontrolled studies have been cited to in-criminate glue sniffing as a cause of brain damage, leukemia, and liver damage. None of these allega-tions has been substantiated. Indeed, we performed studies of liver function on 450 glue sniffers and found no evidence of hepatic dysfunction.

On the other hand, cleaning fluid inhalation is, in our experience, a definite cause of hepatotoxicity and renal impairment. The sudden onset of vomiting, abdominal pain, and jaundice, in the absence of needle puncture marks, should alert the physician to the possibility of this form of abuse. Oliguria or anuria may be present. Recently, Bass described a syndrome of the sudden sniffing death (SSD), con-sisting of sniffing followed in rapid sequence by exer-cise or a stressful situation and then death. Autopsies on 110 such adolescent victims failed to elucidate the pathophysiology of the syndrome. He suggests that the myocardium may be sensitized by volatile hydro-carbons to the catecholamines released by the stress of the situation.

Death from suffocation resulting from the use of a plastic bag as the vehicle for delivery of the volatile substance is reported with regularity. Particularly in the ghetto, glue sniffing is frequently performed on apartment house roofs. It is not uncommon, under such circumstances, for the intoxicated teenager to misjudge distances or imagine he can fly and fall to his death.

Tolerance to the euphoric effects of glue de-velops, but there is no evidence of physiologic addic-tion. In the ghetto population, many heroin users report that glue sniffing provided their first contact with drugs. The vapor-inhaling teenager cannot be identified unless he is intoxicated at the time of examination and the odor detected, or if he suffers a complication of the inhalation. The toluene concen-tration can be determined in tissues at autopsy and the test should be performed in cases of suspicious deaths in teenagers.

Hallucinogens and Psychedelics

LYSERGIC ACID DIETHYLAMIDE (LSD). This com-pound was first synthesized in 1938 from ergot and five years later was found to have profound hallu-cinogenic properties. Its structure is similar to ergo-novine and both are oxytocics. LSD is thought to act on the central nervous system at the synaptic level, possibly by its effect on intracellular serotonin.

LSD is rapidly absorbed from the gastrointesti-nal tract and is widely distributed throughout the body, the greatest concentration being in the liver. There it is excreted as 2-oxy-LSD within 90 minutes of ingestion although its central nervous system ef-fects persist for days or longer. Radioactive LSD has been shown to pass the placenta in mice, but defini-tive evidence of its passage in humans is lacking. It is not yet known whether it can be transmitted to offspring through breast milk, but its wide diffusion throughout all body tissues makes this a likely pos-sibility.

In man, LSD in doses of 20 μg have produced both euphoria or dysphoria, visual or tactile distor-tions, or hallucinations and confusion. These effects may be relived without additional ingestion even months later in the so-called flashback phenomenon. Tolerance to these effects has been demonstrated and cross tolerance exists to other hallucinogenic agents such as mescaline. Regular users may ingest 500 μg per dose.

Dilated pupils, hyperthermia, pilo-erection, hy-perglycemia, and tachycardia are some of the sym-pathomimetic properties of the drug, which may help in distinguishing an LSD abuser from a psychotic. In this regard, it is helpful to recall that the latter frequently experiences auditory hallucinations which are rare in the LSD patient, whose hallucinations are usually visual.

The use of LSD by college students has re-portedly declined in recent years as information con-cerning reputed associated chromosomal damage be-came widely known. Data bearing on this subject appear contradictory upon closer scrutiny. Investiga-tion has proceeded from three approaches: the effect of LSD on human leucocytes in culture and in vivo; animal experimentation bearing on the impact of in-jected LSD on developing embryos; and observation of offspring born to known LSD users.

Cohen and his co-workers demonstrated that chromosomes of human leucocytes cultured in the presence of LSD had more breaks than controls. However, several subsequent studies of lymphocytes of LSD users failed to demonstrate chromosome dam-age. Alexander and co-workers showed that LSD ad-ministered to Wistar rats early in pregnancy resulted in a high incidence of stunted and stillborn offspring. Similar findings have been reported in mice and hamsters. However, Warkany and Takacs found no teratogenic effect of LSD in a different strain of rat. McGluthlin and co-workers report an increased inci-dence of spontaneous abortion in 27 human preg-nancies in which LSD was ingested.

A prospective study of 124 pregnancies in hu-man LSD users revealed that 5 of 59 live births in the series had severe congenital anomalies. Major central nervous system defects were found in four offspring while 4 of 14 abortuses studied had similar findings. The poor nutrition, high incidence of ill-ness, and multiple drug abuse patterns in the popu-lations studied necessarily make such observations difficult to evaluate. Nevertheless, evidence of adverse effects of LSD on human pregnancy appears tenable.

PEYOTE (MESCALINE). The decline in LSD abuse in suburban adolescents is paralleled by the ascendancy of peyote as the preferred hallucinogen. It is derived from the head or button of the cactus plant found in Texas and Mexico, which is dried and chewed or brewed into tea. First tried by the Aztecs, its hallucinogenic properties were realized by the Indians who in 1885 banded together to form the Native American Church based on its use.

The nine alkaloids thus far isolated from the peyote cactus are similar in structure to epinephrine; lophophorine, in the pure state, causes convulsion and death; pellotine causes drowsiness; anhalonidine stimulates the central nervous system; and mescaline induces hallucinations.

Less than half of the ingested mescaline is absorbed. Studies of radioactive mescaline indicate that it does not enter the neurones of the central nervous system and an indirect effect on serotonin has been postulated. Blockade of epinephrine receptors is an alternate mechanism of action.

Ingestion is followed by drying of lips, tongue, and skin which is first flushed and then pale, dilated pupils, bradycardia, hypoglycemia, nausea and vomiting, and, in severe cases, by diarrhea and body odor. Insomnia, chest pain, uterine contractions, headache, and numbness may occur.

Hallucinations produced by peyote are visual, olfactory, or auditory. These are reportedly pleasant although an occasional user experiences terror, tremor, or manic depressive psychosis.

Mescaline, like LSD, has been shown to be teratogenic in early pregnancy in hamsters.

NUTMEG. The seed of the apricot-like fruit of the tropical tree *Myristica fragrans,* has long been known to have hallucinogenic properties. The physiologic effects of nutmeg are tachycardia, dryness of mucous membranes, and often headache, nausea, dizziness, and shortness of breath. These undesirable effects occur at the usual dose of one teaspoon. The popularity of the drug is limited by the fact that this dose is necessary to achieve visual hallucinations, feelings of detachment, and distortion of time and space perception.

MORNING GLORY SEEDS. Hallucinogenic properties reside in the seeds of three species of the morning glory plant found in Mexico and the United States. These seeds, usually 15 at a time, are first soaked in water and then chewed to achieve the desired experience. An LSD derivative has been found in the seeds but with 1/20 of its potency.

SACRED MUSHROOM (TEONANACATI). The active ingredient of this plant, known since antiquity to produce hallucinations, has been identified as psilocybin. Psilocybin has approximately 1/200 the potency of LSD as a hallucinogen.

JIMSONWEED (STRAMONIUM). First used in the treatment of asthma, this Western American plant is now abused because of its hallucinogenic properties. Since it contains atropine, its popularity is limited by the side effects of that drug.

STP (2,5-DIMETHOXY-4-METHYL-AMPHETAMINE OR DOM). STP causes visual hallucinations and psychoses similar to those produced by LSD, but more potent in that they may last up to a week after a single dose. The respiratory paralysis and death reported with its use is most likely the result of contamination with atropine, rather than from the drug itself.

DMT (DIMETHYLTRYPTAMINE). This is a short-acting substance which produces hallucinations within one hour of smoking or injection.

THC (TETRAHYDROCANNABINOL). This, the active hallucinogenic principle of marihuana, has been synthesized and its abuse is now reported. A tablet of THC has five times the potency of a marihuana reefer.

Management of a "bad trip" or "bummer" whether from intoxication with a naturally occurring or synthetic hallucinogen requires a firm, authoritative, and reassuring approach. Repetitive defining of reality, e.g., "This is a book—feel the book," is essential. Admission to a quiet, nonthreatening room with dim lighting is often helpful. If one finds difficulty establishing verbal contact, tranquilizers are indicated. Chlorpromazine is contraindicated for those hallucinogens with anticholinergic properties or additives. Since it is often difficult to know with certainty if such a substance has been taken, it may be wise to avoid the use of phenothiazine derivatives. In such situations diazepam may be an effective alternative. The usual dose is 10 mg IM stat and then repeated in two and four hours if needed.

Alcohol

The current epidemic of drug abuse notwithstanding, alcohol remains the most commonly abused pharmacologic agent in our society. Experimentation with alcohol still represents the first intoxicating experience for the majority of youth in this country, surpassing even marihuana in frequency of abuse. Since alcohol abuse is currently more acceptable in the general society than abuse of drugs and since chronic alcoholism is rare among teenagers, and most of its medical complications eventuate only after years of abuse, the physician seldom encounters this particular drug abuse phenomenon in his professional relationships with teenage patients.

IDENTIFICATION, ADMINISTRATION, AND DOSAGE. Alcohol, or ethanol, is a clear liquid with the chemical formula C_2H_5OH. Alcoholic beverages (rye, bourbon, scotch) contain approximately 50 percent ethanol and are derived by fermentation of cereal grains, mash, and other additives. A 4-ounce glass of whiskey contains 44 grams of alcohol, which when it is consumed alone produces a blood level between 65 and 90 mg percent whereas the same amount ingested with a meal results in a level of 30 to 50 mg percent. Ingestion of beer containing 44 grams of alcohol (approximately 1250 milliliters) results in blood levels approximately half those produced by whiskey. The medicolegal definition of intoxication is a blood level of 200 mg percent or more, and a level over 500 mg percent may be incompatible with life. Tolerance to its effects and cross-tolerance with other central nervous system depressants has been documented.

METABOLISM, PHYSIOLOGY, AND PSYCHOPHARMACOLOGY. Alcohol is absorbed throughout the length of the gastrointestinal tract, within 2 to 6 hours after ingestion. Diffusion is uniform amongst all tissues, including the placenta. Almost 98 percent of alcohol is metabolized by hepatic oxidation to acetaldehyde in the presence of alcohol dehydrogenase. The acetaldehyde is then converted to acetyl coenzyme A. The concentration of unmetabolized alcohol in urine equals that in alveolar air and rarely exceeds 0.05 percent of the blood level.

The primary effect of ethanol is central nervous system depression mediated primarily by the reticular activating system. Disorganization of thought processes results from release of the cerebral cortex from this control system.

The analgesic effect of ethanol is appreciated by the laity and results from the ability of alcohol to raise the pain threshold by 30 to 40 percent, as well as its euphoriant potential. The vasodilation and hypothermia produced by ethanol are centrally mediated effects. The alcohol taboo in peptic ulcer disease has its basis in the fact that it stimulates gastric acid secretion and is irritating to the gastric mucosa. Oxidation of alcohol increases lipid production and accumulation of fat in liver and may be a factor in the production of the fatty liver of the chronic alcoholic. Alcohol has an inhibitory effect on the release of antidiuretic hormone by the posterior pituitary.

MEDICAL COMPLICATIONS. The complications of chronic alcoholism seen in adults, such as cirrhosis, polyneuritis, Wernicke's opthalmoplegia, and Korsakoff's psychosis, are the results of nutritional and vitamin deficiencies attendant on the life of the alcoholic and are not relevant to the teenage drinking problem. In our experience, the only complications of alcohol abuse in the adolescent have been acute pancreatitis, acute gastritis, severe central nervous system depression, and secondary trauma. All of these are dependent upon a rather large and acute ingestion.

THE ABSTINENCE SYNDROME. The withdrawal syndrome associated with alcohol addiction is a rare occurrence among teenagers but similar to that seen with other central nervous system depressants and may range in severity from tremulousness to hallucinations and delirium tremens. In contrast to the barbiturate withdrawal pattern, hyperthermia is more common and grand mal seizures are less frequent with alcohol withdrawal. While death may rarely eventuate, the untreated patient usually recovers within one week. Treatment of the abstinence syndrome involves stabilization with a drug exhibiting cross tolerance with alcohol. Pentobarbital, paraldehyde, and chlordiazepoxide have all been utilized successfully in a regimen of gradual withdrawal.

General Considerations About the Etiology and Management of Teenage Drug Abuse

The impact of the teenage drug abuse epidemic which began within the past five years has left its mark on all sectors of society and has taken on the proportions of a national health emergency. Parents, educators, clergy, corporate America, the armed services, judiciary, politicians and, not the least, the affected individuals themselves, caught up in the turmoil and concern, have responded mainly with facile rationalizations and lengthy polemics. The greatest, and most publicized, intellectual conflict exists between the adolescents and their parents. While the latter group attribute the indiscriminate use of drugs variously to rebellion, accession to peer pressure, an outlet for the scholastic underachiever, or emotional or psychiatric disturbance on the part of today's youth, adolescents, as might be expected, view it quite differently. To youths promiscuous with drugs, experimentation offers an opportunity to explore new sensate vistas, partake of a mystical and exciting experience, learn more about their own psychic function and attempt to achieve a goal of self-discovery. Many of the teenage nonparticipants, however, view illicit use of drugs as merely part of a life style they choose to ignore. To many adolescents, drug use represents a way of coping with a nonrelevant adult-oriented society. The true causes are obviously as varied as the individuals who use drugs and so also must be the approaches to therapy.

Surely, the adolescent drug abuser with underlying psychopathology may respond to intensive individual psychotherapy. For the academic underachiever, however, success will only follow a remedial teaching experience Likewise, the otherwise normal teenager who began to experiment with drugs because of peer pressure will probably do best in a group therapy or encounter-type program. Self-care programs for the youthful drug user are relatively new therapeutic vehicles and their long-term effectiveness have yet to be established. Similarly, alternative drug therapies, as espoused by the proponents of methadone or cyclazozine, have not had adequate trials among adolescent drug users. Such drug substitution programs may be an appropriate compromise when all other avenues have been explored and these agents have been shown to be nontoxic to the growing teenager. Civil commitment to closed rehabilitation facilities under state or federal auspices remains a last resort when all else fails.

The role of the physician in this complex medical-social-psychologic problem is varied. He is often called upon to be a resource person not only for his patient but for both the family and the community. His ability to recognize the stigma of drug use has implications for the physical and emotional health of his patients. His ability to detoxify a drug addict will often enable the latter to gain entrance into a suitable rehabilitation program, and thus provide the first opportunity to turn the tide. Until such time as his patient is desirous of accepting emotional rehabilitation, the physician can at least offer a much needed link to a health professional.

Lexicon of Drug Abuse Terms

ACID	Hallucinogen (LSD, LSD-25, LYSERGIC ACID DIETHYLAMIDE, CUBE, BLACK TABS, PURPLE FLATS, SUGAR, ACID, INSTANT ZEN, BLUE ACID, THE CHIEF, THE HAWK, BLUE DOTS, OWSLEYS, BIG D)
ACIDHEAD	Chronic LSD user (CUBEHEAD)
ADDICT	HOPHEAD, JUNKIE, DREAMER, SLEEPWALKER
ADDICTED	HOOKED, WIRED, VULTURE ON THE VEINS, MONKEY ON THE BACK
AMPHETAMINES	Stimulants (COPILOTS, BENNIES, CARTWHEELS, PEACHES, LID POPPERS, DEXIES, DOMINOES, FOOTBALLS, ROSES, ORANGES, HEARTS, JELLY BABIES, JOLLY BEANS, BROWNIES, BLACK BEAUTIES, DMA, DMDA, WHITES, WAKEUPS)
ARSENAL	Pusher's supply of drugs
ARTILLERY	Equipment employed in injecting drugs (WORKS, CANNON, FACTORY, G, GEAR, GUN, LAY-OUT, MACHINE, SPIKE)
BADHEAD	Emotionally confused from using drugs
BAG	Package of drugs (BUNDLE, FEED BAG)
BANG	To inject drugs
BARBITURATES	Depressants, sedatives (BARBS, GOOFBALLS, CANDY, DOUBLE TROUBLE, BLUEBIRDS, RED 88, NIMBY, PEANUTS, PINKS, RAINBOWS, RED DEVILS, YELLOW JACKETS, NEMMIES, BLUE DEVILS, BLUE HEAVENS, TOOIES, RED BIRDS, IDIOT PILLS, BLUE ANGELS, DOWNS)
BARBITURATE-AMPHETAMINE MIXTURE	GREENIES, FRENCH-BLUES, DOLLS
BLANK	Non-narcotic or low grade narcotic (DUMMY, TURKEY, LEMONADE)
BLOW	Inhale
BLUE-VELVETS	Injectable mixture of paregoric and an antihistamine
BOMBITA	Amphetamine injection (occasionally with heroin)
BUMMER	Bad experience with psychedelics
BUTTON	Head of peyote cactus (mescal cactus-mescaline)
CAP	Gelatin capsule
CHIPPING	Using small quantities of drugs on an irregular basis (DABBLING)
CIBA	Glutethimide, Doriden
COCAINE	Stimulant (COKE, C, CANDY, DUST, GOLD DUST, SNOW, SPEEDBALL, CHOLLY, CHARLIE, BERNICE, GIRL, GIN)
CODEINE	POP, SCHOOLBOY
COLD TURKEY	Narcotic withdrawal without medication
COMBINATIONS	Mixtures of two or more drugs, one of which is usually LSD (L.B.J. STAY AWAY, PEARL PILL, WHITE LIGHTNING, QUINT)
CRASHING	To end an amphetamine binge
DEALER	A pusher, seller, or supplier of drugs

DMT	A synthetic hallucinogen, variants are DET, DPT
DOM	A potent synthetic hallucinogen (STP, "Serenity-Tranquility-Peace")
DOWNS	Sedatives
DROP	To ingest a drug
FIX	An injection of drugs (JOLT, SHOT, CHARGE, WAKEUP)
FLASH	The immediate effect of injecting a drug, a "rush"
GLUE SNIFFING	Inhalation of volatile solvents (GASSING, HUFFING, FLASHING)
HEAD	A chronic drug user
HEROIN	HARRY, ANTI-FREEZE, BROWN, H, DOPE, BOY, HARD STUFF, DUGEE, WHITE STUFF, DOLLIES, HORSE, JUNK, SCAG, SMACK, SCAT
HOOKED	Addicted (STRUNG OUT)
KICK	To stop using drugs, to withdraw
MAINLINE	To inject drugs intravenously
MAO	Monoamine Oxidase Inhibitors
MARIHUANA	CONGO MATABY, DAGGA, DUBY, ACAPULCO GOLD, BOO, BU, GAGE, GAUGE, GANJA, GRASS, HASH, HASHISH, HEMP, HAY, MARYJANE, CANNABIS, KIEF, PANAMA RED, POT, ROPE, TEXAS TEA, WEED, MEZZ, MARY WARNER, MOTA, MUTA, MUD
MARIHUANA CIGARETTE	JOINT, STICK, REEFER, ROACH, ROCKET, PIN, TOKE
METHADONE	DOLLIES, DOLOPHINE
METHEDRINE	A potent amphetamine (MET, METH, METHAMPHETAMINE, SPEED, CRYSTALS, CHALK)
MORNING GLORY	A hallucinogen (WEDDING BELLS, HEAVENLY BLUE, FLYING SAUCERS, PEARLY GATES)
NOD	The stupor while on heroin
SCORE	To buy drugs
SHOOT UP	To inject drugs intravenously
SKIN POP	To inject drugs subcutaneously
SNIFFING	The inhalant route of drug abuse
SNORTING	The inhalant route for heroin abuse

Words and phrases in capital letters are synonyms.

References

GENERAL INFORMATION

Committee on Youth. American Academy of Pediatrics. Drug abuse in adolescence. Pediatrics, 44:131, 1969.

Goodman, L. S., and Gilman, A. The Pharmacological Basis of Therapeutics, 4th ed. New York, The Macmillan Co., 1970.

Litt, I. F., and Cohen, M. I. The drug-using adolescent as a pediatric patient. J. Pediat., 77:195, 1970.

Louria, D. B. Some aspects of the current drug scene with emphasis on drugs in use by adolescents. Pediatrics, 42:904, 1968.

HEROIN

Adelman, L. S., and Aronson, S. M. The neuropathologic complications of narcotics addiction. Bull. N.Y. Acad. Med., 45:225, 1969.

Cherubin, C. E. Epidemiology of tetanus in narcotic addicts. New York, J. Med., 70:267, 1970.

Gorodetzky, C. W., Sapira, J. D., Jasinski, D. R., and Martin, W. R. Liver disease in narcotic addicts. 1. The role of the drug. Clin. Pharmacol. Ther., 9:720, 1968.

Harris, W. D. M., and Andrei, J. Serologic tests for syphilis among narcotic addicts. New York, J. Med., 67:2967, 1967.

Holmes, A. W., Rosenblate, H., Eisenstein, R., and Baldwin, D. The liver disease of heroin addiction. Gastroenterology (abstract), 58:310, 1970.

Litt, I. F., Colli, A. S., and Cohen, M. I. Diazepam in the management of heroin withdrawal in adolescents: Preliminary report. J. Pediat., 78: 692, 1971.

Louria, D. B., Hensle, T., and Rose, J. The major medical complications of heroin addiction. Ann. Intern. Med., 67:1, 1967.

Marks, V., and Chapple, P. A. L. Hepatic dysfunction in heroin and cocaine users. Brit. J. Addict., 62:189, 1967.

Sapira, J. D. The narcotic addict as a medical patient. Amer. J. Med., 45:555, 1968.

——— Ball, J. C., and Penn, H. Causes of death among institutionalized narcotic addicts. J. Chronic Dis., 22: 733, 1970.

Steinberg, A. D., and Karliner, J. S. The clinical spectrum of heroin pulmonary edema. Arch. Intern. Med., 122:122, 1968.

Stoffer, S. S. A gynecologic study of drug addicts. Amer. J. Obstet. Gynec., 101:779, 1968.

DEPRESSANTS

Hadden, J., Johnson, K., Smith, S., Price, L., and Giardina, E. Acute barbiturate intoxication. J.A.M.A., 209:893, 1969.

Leavell, U. W. Sweat gland necrosis in barbiturate poisoning. Arch. Derm., 100:218, 1969.

AMPHETAMINES

Cox, C., and Smart, R. G. The nature and extent of speed use in North America. Canad. Med. Ass. J., 102:724, 1970.

MARIHUANA

Agurell, S., Nilsson, I. M., Ohlsson, A., and Sandberg, F. Elimination of tritium-labelled cannabinols in the rat with special reference to the development of tests for the identification of cannabis users. Biochem. Pharmacol., 18:1195, 1969.

Burstein, S. H., Menezes, F., and Williamson, E. Metabolism of $\Delta^{1(6)}$-Tetrahydrocannabinol, an active marihuana constituent. Nature, 225:87, 1970.

Crancer, A., Dille, J. M., Delay, J. C., Wallace, J. E., and Haykin, M. D. Comparison of the effects of marihuana and alcohol on simulated driving performance. Science, 164:851, 1969.

Idanpaan-Heikkila, J., Fritchie, G. E., Englert, L. F., Ho, B. T., and McIsaac, W. M. Placental transfer of tritiated-1-Δ^9-tetrahydrocannabinol. New Eng. J. Med., 281:330, 1969.

Neu, R. L., Powers, H. O., King, S., and Gardner, L. I. Δ^8- and Δ^9-Tetrahydrocannabinol: effects on cultured human leucocytes. J. Clin. Pharmacol., 10:228, 1970.

Persaud, T. V. N., and Ellington, A. C. Teratogenic activity of cannabis resin. Lancet, 2:406, 1968.

Pillard, R. C. Marihuana. New Eng. J. Med., 283:294, 1970.

Talbott, J. A., Teague, J. W. Marihuana psychosis. J.A.M.A., 210:299, 1969.

Waskow, I. E., Olsson, J. E., Salzman, C., and Katz, M. M. Psychological effects of tetrahydrocannabinol. Arch. Gen. Psychiat., 22:97, 1970.

Weil, A. T. Adverse reactions to marihuana. Classification and suggested treatment. New Eng. J. Med., 282:997, 1970.

——— Zinberg, N. E., and Nelsen, J. M. Clinical and psychological effects of marihuana in man. Science, 162:1234, 1968.

COCAINE

Fish, F., and Wilson, W. D. C. Excretion of cocaine and its metabolites in man. J. Pharm. Pharmacol., 21:135S, 1969.

GLUE SNIFFING AND OTHER INHALANTS

Bass, M. Sudden sniffing death. J.A.M.A., 212:2075, 1970.

Collom, W. D., and Winek, C. L. Detection of glue constituents in fatalities due to "glue sniffing." Clin. Toxicol., 3:125, 1970.

Kupperstein, L. R., and Susman, R. M. A bibliography on the inhalation of glue fumes and other toxic vapors—a substance abuse practice among adolescents. Internat. J. Addict., 3:177, 1968.

Litt, I., and Cohen, M. I. "Danger . . . vapor harmful": Spot remover sniffing. New Eng. J. Med., 281:543, 1969.

HALLUCINOGENS AND PSYCHEDELICS

Alexander, G. J., Gold, G. M., Miles, B. E., and Alexander, R. B. Lysergic acid diethylamide intake in pregnancy: fetal damage in rats. J. Pharmacol. Exp. Ther., 173:48, 1970.

Corey, M. J., Andrews, J. C., McLeod, M. J., MacLean, J. R., and Wilby, W. E. Chromosome studies on patients (in vivo) and cells (in vitro) treated with lysergic acid diethylamide. New Eng. J. Med., 282:939, 1970.

Houston, B. K. Review of the evidence and qualifications regarding the effects of hallucinogenic drugs on chromosomes and embryos. Am. J. Psychiat., 126:251, 1969.

McGlothlin, W. H., Sparkes, R. S., and Arnold, D. U. Effect of LSD on human pregnancy. J.A.M.A., 212:1483, 1970.

McLain, L. A. A study of peyote. Clin. Toxicol., 1:81, 1968.

Stenchever, M. A., and Jarvis, J. A. LSD. Effect on human chromosomes in vivo. Amer. J. Obstet. Gynec., 106:485, 1970.

Taylor, R. L., Maurer, J. I., and Tinklenberg, J. R. Management of "bad trips" in an evolving drug scene. J.A.M.A., 213:422, 1970.

13.14
NEONATAL NARCOTIC ADDICTION

ARNOLD H. EINHORN

In recent years narcotic addiction in this country has become a leading social scourge attaining devastatingly tragic proportions among adolescents and young adults. It is significantly more prevalent in the urban slums among the economically deprived, but is by no means confined to the underprivileged segment of the population. Many narcotic users are women of childbearing age. Maternal addiction during gestation may be associated with either increased fetal wastage or, in the liveborn offspring, an abstinence syndrome with symptoms similar to those found in the adult. In the newborn infant the syndrome is potentially life threatening.

Diacetyl morphine (heroin) is the agent predominantly incriminated in addiction, outranking by far morphine, the favorite drug of the past. Our observations are based on a 12-year experience with more than 200 newborn infants whose mothers were addicts; other drugs such as codeine, meperidine (Demerol), cocaine, and barbiturates (the latter often of medical origin) were only rarely involved. We have handled of late an increasing number of addicted newborns born to mothers participating in detoxification programs and receiving methadone to alleviate their abstinence syndrome. Some of these infants developed postnatally mild to moderate manifestations of withdrawal. Problems in the newborn have also been reported with methamphetamine, one of the sympathomimetic central nervous stimulants used by addicts especially in western states.

A newborn baby delivered of an active and habitual narcotic user is essentially a potential addict, whose addiction starts in utero. Morphine and heroin traverse the placenta and enter the fetal circulation freely, producing in the fetus the physiologic dependence and the tolerance that are the ingredients of addiction. Fetal restlessness and violent intrauterine jolts have been observed to occur prior to the time when the mother requires her "fix." These movements subside abruptly shortly after the injection of the drug. Delivery cuts off the supply of the drug to the baby who is then in danger of developing a characteristic narcotic withdrawal syndrome during the early neonatal period.

SIGNS AND SYMPTOMS. Some infants may remain entirely asymptomatic or exhibit only mild distress. In those who are symptomatic, the initial manifestations displayed most consistently are restlessness and tremulousness. In these infants the hyperactivity, hyperexcitability, sleeplessness, and coarse and flapping tremors are associated with incessant, prolonged, high-pitched crying. The heels, knees, knuckles, cheeks, nose, and chin of these unfortunate infants are often the site of skin abrasions as a result of the continuous writhing and squirming. Frequent yawning, sneezing, excessive lacrimation and salivation, nasal stuffiness, flushing of the skin, and sweating are also commonly observed. Despite a ravenous appetite, the infant generally experiences difficulty in feeding with ensuing failure to gain weight, which is a common feature of this condition. In a significant number of our infants some degree of tachypnea without other respiratory findings developed at the time of the onset of the hyperkinesia, or preceded it. In some, loose and frequent stools were associated with the onset of the other clinical manifestations.

If spontaneous improvement does not supervene, the untreated infant may become critically ill, developing hyperpyrexia, protracted vomiting and diarrhea, respiratory distress with severe tachypnea, labored breathing, cyanotic spells, apneic episodes, and convulsions. In the absence of treatment, death has been reported following severe dehydration and circulatory collapse. In our own series we had no mortality attributable directly to withdrawal distress. The only infant who died did not develop any abstinence syndrome; death did not appear related to the maternal addiction but to sepsis.

The time of appearance of the symptoms varies considerably. The first manifestations may occur as early as at birth, or as late as the fifth day of life; in the majority of infants they appear at the end of the first day or during the second day of life. It has been postulated that a direct relationship exists between the dose and timing of the maternal injection before delivery, and the time of appearance and severity of the infant's symptoms. This hypothesis has never been objectively documented and it is likely that other factors, yet to be elicited, may account for the individual variations.

DIAGNOSIS. Since symptoms subside in general quite rapidly after therapy has been instituted, and since, on the other hand, there is danger to the life of the untreated infants, recognition of this clinical entity is imperative. Consequently those responsible for the care of newborn infants should be familiar with the withdrawal symptom complex, and maintain a high index of suspicion, especially in high-risk localities where narcotic addiction is rampant. The correct diagnosis may be difficult. The agitation of the initial stage of the syndrome may be mistaken for neonatal hypoglycemia or hypocalcemia; intracranial disorders associated with brain injury, anoxia, cerebral hemorrhage, or meningitis; or neonatal thyrotoxicosis. The more advanced manifestations may be difficult to distinguish from sepsis, enteric infections or malformations of the digestive tract, respiratory disease, or adrenal insufficiency.

In most instances the addiction is known at the time of the infant's birth and a competent staff can handle the infant accordingly. Contrary to general belief, we rarely encountered on the part of the addicted mother reluctance to admit her habit. Such information was often volunteered, and the concern expressed by the mother about possible harmful effects on the infant and the fate of the baby appeared genuine. However, narcotic usage may be denied, or there may be no time to elicit from the mother any history. Narcotic addicts who give birth often received no prenatal care whatsoever, have no obstetrical records, and are often rushed to the delivery room in the latest stage of labor. In cases where no history is obtained or available, suspicion should be aroused by such clues as a compulsive urge on the part of the mother to leave the hospital against medical advice immediately after delivery; a history of hepatitis; an unusual resistance to the usual effective doses of analgesics during labor; a history or evidence of multiple skin infections or thrombophlebitides; or a history of changes of hospital with each past delivery. The finding of telltale puncture marks or scarring over venous trajectories should be looked for whenever the diagnosis is suspected.

Other than the manifestation of the abstinence syndrome, there are no specific helpful findings in the baby. The weights at birth were moderately low for gestational age in more than half of the infants which we observed; one half of these were preterm deliveries. The majority of the infants with low birth weights had clinical evidence of intrauterine malnutrition or dysmaturity. In addition, we have found clinical jaundice to be strikingly rare, and indirect bilirubin levels to be significantly lower than in other normal or even abnormal newborn infants of comparable weights and gestational ages. We have no valid explanation for this finding. There were no other demonstrable biochemical anomalies. Serial studies of blood gases; glucose; serum sodium, potassium, calcium, and phosphate, determined at birth on all our infants of addicted mothers, and repeated again on symptomatic babies at the onset of their distress, have been consistently normal.

Heroin, rapidly hydrolyzed in the body to morphine, is excreted in the urine where it can be elicited by chromatography. A rapid screening test based on such a determination represents a valuable diagnostic aid readily available.

TREATMENT.　Treatment should be instituted as soon as signs of restlessness appear. We recommend the use of paregoric USP, starting with three to six drops at each feeding and titrating thereafter the dose of the opiate solution according to the infant's response. Except in barbiturate withdrawal where phenobarbital is the drug of choice, we find paregoric most effective even in cocaine addiction. Other medications such as thorazine, phenobarbital, diazepam (Valium), or methadone have been advocated by others wtih varied claims of success. In our experience the infants' response to these drugs was more unpredictable and inconsistent, ranging from nil to moderately effective.

Duration of therapy depends upon the severity of the disease and should be considered adequate when the jitteriness is controlled enough to allow the infant to feed properly, sleep between feedings, gain weight, and maintain a normal temperature. Infants with severe symptoms may require several weeks of treatment. Mild cases can be weaned of the drug after a few days. Symptoms may recur if treatment is discontinued too soon and too abruptly. Gradual weaning generally seems to be less conducive to recurrences than sudden interruption of therapy. Loose stools may persist sometimes for weeks after therapy has been withdrawn; if this symptom remains isolated it does not constitute an indication to reinstitute treatment.

In severely affected infants, we have had exceptionally to resort to intramuscular morphine to control symptoms. Parenteral fluids may be necessary until the baby accepts oral feedings adequately, and a high caloric intake may be indicated to compensate for the increased expenditure due to excessive motor activity. A fatal outcome due to withdrawal distress symptoms was commonly observed in past years in untreated infants. However, mortality rate figures vary considerably, ranging from a high of 93 percent to a low of 17 percent in untreated infants, and in overall mortality rates, from 34 percent to 9 percent. We have had no mortality among our symptomatic infants who were all treated. We have no symptomatic controls in whom treatment was withheld deliberately or accidentally. After recovery physical growth, overall health, and developmental milestones have been normal on long-term follow-up of a significant number of our symptomatic infants and in those reported by others.

REFERENCES

Cobrinik, R. W., Hood, R. J., and Chusid, E. The effect of maternal narcotic addiction on the newborn infant. Pediatrics, 24:288, 1959.

Goodfriend, J., Shey, I. A., and Klein, M. D. The effect of maternal narcotic addiction on the newborn. Amer. J. Obstet. Gynec., 71:29, 1956.

Hill, R. M., and Desmond, M. M. Management of the narcotic withdrawal syndrome in the neonate. Pediat. Clin. N. Amer., 10:67, 1963.

Kahn, E. J., Newmann, L. L., and Polk, G. A. The course of the heroin withdrawal syndrome in newborn infants treated with phenobarbital or chlorpromazine. J. Pediat., 75:495, 1969.

Perlmutter, J. F. Drug addiction in pregnant women. Amer. J. Obstet. Gynec., 99:569, 1967.

Perlstein, M. Congenital morphinism. J.A.M.A., 135:633, 1947.

Schneck, H. Narcotic withdrawal symptoms in the newborn infant resulting from maternal addiction. J. Pediat., 52:584, 1958.

Sussman, S. Narcotic and methamphetamine use during pregnancy. Amer. J. Dis. Child., 106:125, 1963.

13.15
SUDDEN AND UNEXPECTED DEATH

JAY BERNSTEIN

An occurrence frequent enough to constitute a worldwide major public health problem is the unexpected and unexplained death of a young infant who had been apparently well or had suffered from only trifling signs of disease. The epidemiologic, clinical, and pathologic features of these cases follow a remarkably uniform pattern, constituting the syndrome of sudden unexpected death in infancy or so-called crib deaths. The incidence of this calamity has been estimated at approximately 3 per 1,000 live births, and it is believed that upwards of 25,000 deaths occur annually in the United States, accounting for approximately one fourth of infant deaths between the ages of 10 days and 2 years.

The victims are generally normally developed babies between 2 and 4 months of age. Such deaths are rare in the first two weeks of life and are relatively uncommon after six months. The infants are usually described as well nourished, although a careful comparison with normals shows that they may weigh slightly less than expected. Males predominate in most series, sometimes by as much as 2:1. Valdes-Dapena has pointed out that approximately one third had been born prematurely, and a disproportionately large number are one of twins. Recurrences in the same family are relatively common, an observation that often leads to speculation about possible hereditary predisposition. Most infants die in their sleep and are found dead in the early morning hours; relatively few collapse while someone is in attendance. Deaths also occur in hospitals among treated babies about to be sent home. A seasonal incidence, with a peak in the winter and cold spring months has been described. An interesting observation is that cases tend to cluster by days within a large geographic region, perhaps implicating unfavorable meteorologic factors such as cold. Smaller time-space clusters have been attributed to the combined effects of infectious agents and poor environmental conditions.

Families at all socioeconomic levels have been affected, but several studies point to an increased incidence in the lower social strata. Valdes-Dapena demonstrated that the geographic distribution of cases in Philadelphia has largely coincided with the distribution of dilapidated housing units, and she reported a fourfold increase among the nonwhite population. Similar findings have been reported by Adelson's group in Cleveland, who believe that the association of poverty and sudden unexpected death may explain the increased incidence in blacks. The British Ministry of Health investigation also showed that their cases tended to come from more crowded and poorer homes, and their observations were interpreted to indicate a lower standard of "mothering" than in matched controls.

Postmortem examination provides the cause of death in relatively few cases, the number varying with the significance attached to relatively minor respiratory tract lesions. The natural conditions that cause unexpected death in infancy include serious infections and congenital malformations. In most instances, however, perhaps in as many as eight or nine out of 10, the cause of death is not identified. The characteristic pathologic findings include petechiae in the thoracic organs, slight or moderate pulmonary congestion and edema, irregularly aerated and focally emphysematous lungs, and variable inflammatory lesions. Histologic examination often shows mucosal necrosis and ulceration in the larynx and minor degrees of inflammation in the tracheobronchial tree. Inflammatory changes in the lungs are usually negligible, consisting of slight septal thickening and hypercellularity, slight bronchiolitis and peribronchiolitis, and focal pneumonitis. The diagnosis of "interstitial pneumonia" to characterize these alterations remains, however, unconvincing and misleading. The thymus appears large, and lymph nodes throughout the body are numerous and prominent; these findings are no different from those seen in sudden death due to accidents, and they are generally regarded as normal. The lymphoid follicles may show evidence of an acute "toxic" reaction, a nonspecific finding commonly associated with infection. Minor degrees of meningitis and enteritis are encountered. Petechiae

are often seen in the meninges and brain, and there may be spinal epidural hemorrhage. Vomitus in the upper respiratory passages is currently regarded as agonal aspiration, rather than as a cause of fatal respiratory obstruction. In short, the findings are inadequate to explain the child's death.

Most laboratory studies have been unrewarding. Toxicologic investigations rarely uncover a case of poisoning. Bacteriologic cultures have occasionally been positive for pathogenic organisms. In this regard, the cause of death may reasonably be ascribed to certain fulminant bacteremias, such as meningococcemia, pneumococcemia, and streptococcemia. The finding of only mild meningitis in a fatal case of meningococcemia would suggest that the child died of overwhelming sepsis before an inflammatory reaction could be established, but this sort of reasoning has its limitations and will not apply to children with, for example, presumed infection and minimal pneumonitis. The isolation of bacterial pathogens from the lower respiratory tract of deceased infants and from members of their families has been cited as evidence that the infants die of fulminant infections of the respiratory tract. Virologic studies have produced widely divergent results, and several reports of viral isolations have not been confirmed by other studies intended to elucidate this point. The most promising report has come from Seattle, where a well-organized and coordinated prospective study has been in progress for several years. An aggressive search for viruses has yielded a 37.5 percent recovery rate of serotypes other than poliovirus in unexplained infant death as compared with 16.2 percent in controls. Viral isolations included most frequently adenovirus, ECHO virus, and rhinovirus.

Despite the lack of success in the search for a specific infectious agent, certain circumstantial evidence strengthens the concept of infectious etiology. A careful interview of the family will often elicit trivial or vague signs of prior illness in the infant. British and American studies have both shown a relatively high incidence of respiratory signs, particularly coryza, and some gastrointestinal complaints. A physician had frequently been called, but the disease seemed to be inconsequential and a fatal outcome was hardly anticipated. Other members of the family might also have had a cold or whatever ailment had been prevalent at the time. The observations suggest respiratory infection as the most common offender, in keeping with the postmortem findings of minor respiratory tract disease. At the present time, a virus remains the most attractive candidate, and considerable effort is being expended on its identification. Several organisms have been implicated, none conclusively, suggesting that either of several agents may initiate the same pathologic process. Nonetheless, a major question remains unanswered. What is the mechanism of death, considering the disparity between the anatomic findings and the outcome? The isolation of a virus from a specific site, such as the central nervous system, might be of significance, but most proponents of an infectious etiology prefer to believe that inflammation of the respiratory tract initiates a sequence of lethal events.

Other etiologic factors have been proposed, but their supporting evidence is more meager and less convincing. Certainly, there is no evidence to withstand critical examination that these infants are suffocated by bedclothes, and it is reprehensible to suggest to the already guilt-laden parents that their carelessness was responsible. Despite the superficial similarity of some anatomic findings to those in asphyxial death, even the smallest infant, as amply demonstrated years ago by Woolley, is capable of sufficient movement to avoid suffocation. Along the same lines, an infant may occasionally become entrapped inside a plastic bag, but the danger of his suffocating by being next to one has also been overrated. Cow's milk allergy has been suggested as a cause of fatal anaphylactic shock. Evidence of increased milk allergy in infants dying suddenly is, however, equivocal, and several workers have obtained contrary evidence. There is no evidence of impaired immunologic reactivity or of adrenal insufficiency, and the evidence for primary parathyroid hypoplasia and for primary spinal cord injury has been disputed. Abnormal or immature neural mechanisms and exaggerated reflexes form the basis of several theories that can be neither proved nor refuted. The possibility that respiratory inflammation may produce profound cardiopulmonary reflexes leading to cardiac arrest or may initiate laryngospasm and/or bronchospasm leading to respiratory arrest might have a basis in some peculiar physiologic or anatomic susceptibility of young infants.

It is, however, both truthful and challenging to admit the inadequacy of our present knowledge. An admission of our ignorance is not a reason for being nihilistic and overlooking thereby the admittedly relatively few cases of identifiable communicable disease or of infanticide. Approximately 5 percent of autopsies show some evidence of trauma, and it is not possible, despite investigation of the social environment, to estimate the incidence of undetected homicide.

Unexpected Death in Later Childhood

A small number of children are obvious victims of accidental or homicidal suffocation, poisoning, or anaphylactic shock. Others suffer cardiac arrest during anesthesia and even after simple needle puncture. However, an undetermined number of apparently healthy children expire suddenly and unexpectedly, usually because of overwhelming infection, laryngotracheal obstruction by a foreign body, or other unrecognized condition.

Serious infection, probably the most common cause of unexpected death in later childhood, includes fulminating septicemia, obstructive inflammation of the respiratory tract, and certain localized viral infections. Among the first group are meningococcemia, pneumococcemia, and streptococcemia, which may develop so rapidly that the usual signs and symptoms of disease are not apparent. Postmortem examination often discloses evidence of meningitis. Parenthetically, adrenal hemorrhage is not restricted to meningococcemia, being found in other types of sepsis, and it is doubtful that patients with this lesion do indeed die of acute adrenal insufficiency. Careful postmortem bacteriologic studies are indispensable to the proper diagnosis of these cases, and the pathologist must be guided by both experience and the histologic findings in judging the significance of positive cultures. Bacteria that ordinarily are of low or limited pathogenicity are probably of dubious significance.

Rapidly developing respiratory tract infection may, of course, lead to sudden, fatal obstruction of the airway. Retropharyngeal abscesses and diphtheritic tracheitis are now uncommon, but obstruction of the upper airway can result from laryngitis. Epiglottitis, often due to *H. influenzae*, unrecognized tracheobronchitis, bronchiolitis, bronchopneumonia, and pulmonary abscesses can also be severe enough to cause death very rapidly. Presumed viral lesions associated with unexpected death include encephalitis and especially myocarditis. Surprisingly severe myocardial inflammation, with widespread necrosis of muscle fibers, has been observed repeatedly in children who were barely sick before the moment of death. There is reason to believe that the myocardial infection is commonly caused by Coxsackie-virus and ECHO virus.

Congenital malformation accounts for many cases of unexpected death in childhood, congenital heart disease perhaps most commonly. Endocardial sclerosis and pulmonic stenosis are among the abnormalities frequently cited, and the list also includes aortic stenosis and anomalous origin of the left coronary artery. Many children will have had a brief period of distress prior to dying, but the onset is very acute and death is unexpected. Postmortem examination will sometimes show recent closure of the ductus arteriosus, a significant observation in cases of pulmonic stenosis. Vascular malformations, particularly in the brain, may underlie fatal hemorrhage, and exsanguination can also result from the rupture of hepatic hemangiomas. Among heritable disorders, sickle-cell anemia and cardiac glycogenosis are often mentioned. Fibrocystic disease has been unrecognized until a summer heat wave brought on increased sweating and fatal hyponatremia. Acquired diseases may also go unrecognized until the sudden terminal episode. Fatal intraspinal hemorrhage has been attributed to undiagnosed scurvy, and fatal intracerebral hemorrhage may be the initial manifestation of childhood leukemia. Sudden deaths caused by unsuspected foreign body obstruction of the larynx and trachea are more common than generally recognized.

Finally, a word must be said about unrecognized trauma. The story of the "battered" child is by now all too familiar. In cases of acute epidural hemorrhage without a history of head injury and in cases of ruptured viscera, the pathologist must maintain a high level of suspicion while carrying out a complete autopsy. Careful questioning of the family may elicit the all-important clue. Few deaths in older children need remain unexplained.

REFERENCES

Beckwith, J. B., and Bergman, A. B. The sudden death syndrome of infancy. Hospital Practice, Nov. 1967, pp. 44-52.

British Ministry of Health. Enquiry into sudden death in infancy. Reports on Public Health and Medical Subjects, No. 13. London, H.M.S.O., 1965.

Ray, C. G., Beckwith, J. B., Hebestreit, N. M., and Bergham, A. B. Studies of the sudden infant death syndrome in King County, Washington. I. The role of viruses. J.A.M.A., 211:619, 1970.

Steichen, F. M., Fellini, A., and Einhorn, A. H. Acute foreign body laryngo-tracheal obstruction: A cause for sudden and unexpected death in children. Pediatrics, 48:281, 1971.

Steele, R., Kraus, A. S., and Langworth, J. T. Sudden, unexpected death in infancy in Ontario. Part I: Methodology and findings related to the host. Canad. J. Public Health, 58:359, 1967.

Strimer, R., Adelson, L., and Oseasohn, R. Epidemiologic features of 1,134 sudden, unexpected infant deaths. A study in the Greater Cleveland area from 1956 to 1965. J.A.M.A., 209:1493, 1969.

Valdes-Dapena, M. A. Sudden and unexpected death in infancy: A review of the world literature 1954-1966. Pediatrics, 39:123, 1967.

Wedgewood, R. J., and Benditt, E. P., eds. Proceedings of the Conference on Causes of Sudden Death in Infants. Publication No. 1412. U.S. Dept. of Health, Education, and Welfare, Washington, D.C., U.S. Government Printing Office, 1966.

Woolley, P. V., Jr. Mechanical suffocation during infancy: comments on its relation to total problem of sudden death. J. Pediat., 26:572, 1945.

chapter 14

INFECTIOUS DISEASES

HORACE L. HODES and DAVID CARVER, Associate Editors

Bacterial Diseases

14.1
ANTIMICROBIAL THERAPY OF BACTERIAL DISEASES

PIERCE GARDNER and DAVID H. SMITH

It is estimated that more than 50 percent of a pediatrician's practice is comprised of patients with some type of infection. The initial problems of clinical differentiation and laboratory identification of the various infectious agents are beyond the scope of this discussion, which deals only with the antimicrobial therapy of bacterial diseases. Although controlled studies are few, a number of principles regarding the use of antimicrobial agents have gained general acceptance. A body of knowledge has developed concerning not only the interactions of drugs and bacteria, but also the host factors important in controlling infections. An understanding of the effect of antimicrobial agents on both sides of the host-parasite relationship is the basis for intelligent use of these important drugs. A discussion of drug therapy for tuberculosis may be found on page 684.

Principles of Antimicrobial Therapy

Before antibiotic therapy is initiated, cultures and, if feasible, smears of the infected lesions should be obtained. Single cultures suffice for most infections, but multiple cultures are required for certain infections, such as subacute endocarditis and tuberculosis, in which the cultured material may contain small numbers of bacteria. The responsibility of the attending physician also includes assuring prompt delivery of cultures to the diagnostic bacteriology laboratory and providing a summary of clinical information. The latter is important for optimal processing of specimens and may be crucial for identification of unusual or fastidious organisms. For example, anaerobic streptococci and bacterioides, which are common pathogens in brain abscesses, may not be recovered if the surgical specimen is not promptly delivered and cultured anaerobically.

Gram-stained smears of exudates often provide the first clue to the identity of the infecting agent, and are useful in evaluating the relative numbers of each type of organism in mixed infections. In patients who have received prior antibiotic therapy and in patients with rapidly progressive infections, such as myonecrosis due to *Clostridium perfringens,* the gram-stained smear is often the most important laboratory test on which therapeutic decisions are based. In the examination of purulent exudates, a technically acceptable preparation can be recognized by the pink (not blue) appearance of the polymorphonuclear leucocyte nuclei. The most common error in preparing gram-stained smears is inadequate decolorization. This error, due commonly to smears that are too thick, often results in misreading the precipitated gram stain as gram-positive cocci.

Specific therapy directed against the presumed or identified pathogen is preferable to broad-spectrum "shotgun" therapy. Treatment with a single antimicrobial agent is uscally adequate, although combinations of drugs may be preferable when synergistic antibacterial action can be expected against relatively resistant organisms or when mixed infections exist. The pharmacology and toxicology of the antibacterial agents must be considered in the physician's choice of drugs. Properties such as diffusion into the site of infection or route of excretion may be important determinants of the outcome of the drug program. Failure to develop an awareness of the common and serious side effects of drugs may result in needless deafness, renal failure, or other toxic effects. When organs important to drug excretion are functionally impaired, alteration of dosage may be necessary (see discussion under Special Situations, p. 591).

When the clinical situation dictates that antimicrobial therapy be started before the results of cultures are available, an effective choice of drugs can usually be made on the basis of (1) gram-stained smears of the infected materials; (2) the bacteria most likely to be involved in the disease process (see Table 2); (3) the probable sensitivity pattern of the suspected pathogens; and (4) pharmacologic properties of the drugs.

Once an appropriate antibiotic has been chosen, an adequate dose should be given by the correct route for an appropriate duration. For example, the primary goal of penicillin therapy for pharyngitis due to Group A streptococcus is the prevention of rheumatic fever. Therefore, therapy is continued for 10 days despite the usually prompt resolution of acute symptoms.

The choice of route of administration is often influenced by the clinical situation. A parenteral route is required if the patient is vomiting or if gastrointestinal absorption is impaired. Intravenous administration is recommended for patients in shock or when prompt high levels of an antibiotic are desired, as in bacterial meningitis.

Bactericidal antibiotics may have advantages over bacteriostatic drugs in patients with impaired host defenses, such as gamma globulin deficiencies, malignancies, patients receiving immunosuppressive agents or corticosteroids, and in infections such as bacterial endocarditis in which cellular and humoral defenses play a minor role.

Antagonistic effects of bactericidal-bacteriostatic drug combinations have been demonstrated in vitro and in animal studies, but have been difficult to document in clinical circumstances. Nevertheless, when alternatives are possible, a choice of drugs which do not exhibit in vitro antagonism is preferable.

Antimicrobial drugs are but one facet of the management of patients with infection. In severe infections careful attention to respiration, blood volume, and acid-base and electrolyte status may be lifesaving. Likewise, surgery has a primary role in the management of certain infections, such as abscesses and gas gangrene.

Evaluation of the efficacy of the selected therapy depends primarily on the response of the patient and only secondarily on the laboratory data. Laboratory data on resistance do not always correlate with clinical response. Therefore, if the patient is responding satisfactorily, therapy need not be changed because in vitro tests fail to demonstrate that the identified pathogen is sensitive to the drug being administered.

When carefully chosen antibiotic therapy fails to eliminate the infection for which it was prescribed, reassessment of the situation and intensification of diagnostic efforts are indicated. Common reasons for failures of therapy included misdiagnosis of viral infections and failure to take prescribed oral medications. Persistence of respiratory or urinary tract infections should lead to a search for structural abnormalities. Repeat cultures may indicate superinfection or alteration of the antibiotic sensitivity pattern of the original isolate. The role of L-forms in persistence of bacterial infections remains to be defined.

Prophylactic use of broad-spectrum antibiotics generally has been unsuccessful and carries the risks of superinfection, toxicity, and allergy. When specific therapy is directed against a specific organism, such as penicillin for Group A streptococci, prophylaxis is more likely to succeed (Table 4, p. 594).

The public health aspects of antimicrobial therapy should be considered by the prescribing physician. The indiscriminate use of antibiotics affects the bacterial ecology not only of the individual patient but also of his hospital or community environment. A selective force favoring the emergence of drug-resistant bacteria is created, thereby lessening the effectiveness of the antibiotic armamentarium for the treatment of future infections.

Mechanisms of Action of Antimicrobial Drugs

The clinical efficacy of an antimicrobial drug depends on its ability to inhibit bacteria at concentrations that are safe for mammalian cells. This selective toxicity is achieved by taking advantage of differences in the biochemistry of the parasite and the host. The rapid expansion of knowledge in the field of cell biology has defined certain of these differences and has resulted in a better understanding of the biochemical basis for the action of many antimicrobial drugs. A summary of the current understanding of the mechanisms of action of certain of the commonly used antimicrobial drugs is presented in order to illustrate certain principles for the proper clinical use of these agents.

Agents Affecting the Bacterial Wall

The bacterial wall gives the cell its characteristic shape, part of its pathogenicity, and its ability to resist osmotic and mechanical trauma. Since the osmotic pressure of bacterial cytoplasm exceeds atmospheric pressure, wall-deficient bacteria (L-forms) lyse in isotonic media. They can survive, however, in media of high tonicity.

All bacteria, including spirochetes and actinomycetes, contain in their walls a network of chains containing alternating N-acetylmuramic acid and N-acetylglucosamine connected by polypeptide cross-links. This polymer, which is called glycopeptide, is unique to bacteria. Disaccharide-polypeptide precursors of glycopeptide are synthesized in the cytoplasm and transported via a lipid carrier to a wall receptor outside the protoplasmic membrane, where the polypeptide side chains are polymerized by a transpeptidation reaction. The glycopepeptide layer is covered in most bacterial species by additional polymers whose macromolecules are exposed to the cell surface and which provide immunologic specificity. In gram-positive bacteria these surface polymers include teichoic acid, carbohydrates, such as the group-specific antigens of streptococci, and polypeptides, such as the M proteins of Group A streptococci. Gram-negative bacteria are covered by a lipopolysaccharide layer (LPS). The lipid is covalently attached to the polysaccharide, which consists of a "core," the composition of which is generally uniform for each major group of the Enterobacteriaciae, and side chains whose varying composition confer the surface (O) antigen specificity of the cell. Integrity of the glycopeptide layer is critical to the structure of the wall.

The outer layers are not structurally critical but they play a major role in the cell's pathogenicity, either by direct toxicity (LPS) or by protecting the bacterium from host defenses, such as phagocytosis (M protein) and immune lysis (LPS).

Penicillin was observed during early studies to lyse sensitive bacteria in isotonic medium and to produce protoplasts in hypertonic medium. These biologic observations are explained by recent studies that indicate that penicillin specifically inhibits the transpeptidation of glycopeptide and that treated sensitive bacteria produce defective walls. The semi-synthetic penicillins and the structurally related cephalosporins inhibit the same reaction. These findings and the specificity of glycopeptide for bacterial cells explain both the remarkable tolerance of man to penicillin and the wide spectrum of microorganisms inhibited by penicillin. Its effectiveness differs only quantitatively against gram-negative and gram-positive bacteria, spirochetes, and actinomycetes; however, it has no activity against bacterial protoplasts, mycoplasma, *Chlamydia,* fungi, rickettsia, protozoa, and viruses.

Bacitracin specifically inhibits glycopeptide synthesis by reducing the availability of the lipid carrier which transports the disaccharide pentapeptide subunits across the membrane. Vancomycin apparently blocks the wall acceptor of these subunits and thereby inhibits glycopeptide synthesis. Dormant bacteria do not produce glycopeptide and thus these antibiotics affect only actively growing bacteria.

Agents Affecting the Bacterial Membrane

The cytoplasmic membrane lies immediately beneath the bacterial wall. It retains required intracellular metabolites; it transports out waste products, wall subunits, and exoenzymes; and it excludes substances other than those carried into the cell by one of its transport systems. These systems, which are located in the membrane, promote active transport and have remarkable specificity. They therefore enable the cell to scavenge nutrients efficiently and to maintain a relatively constant intracellular ionic composition independent of extracellular concentrations. Bacteria do not possess mitochondria; their electron transport system is located in the membrane. Because of the importance of these functions, damage to the membrane is generally irreversible and lethal.

The bacterial membrane is composed of about 40 percent lipids, 60 percent proteins, and small amounts of carbohydrate. Membranes of different bacteria are antigenically distinct. The composition of the bacterial membrane differs notably from that of mammalian cells by the absence of sterols and the types of phosphatides in the lipids.

Polymyxin B and colistin (polymyxin E) contain methyl octanoic acid and a basic, cyclic polypeptide. These groups give these antibiotics the surface-active properties of a cationic detergent. The polymyxins distort the bacterial membrane, presumably by binding to its lipids, and rapidly kill resting and growing bacteria. The toxic effect of the drug on certain mammalian tissues, especially of the kidney and nervous system, may reflect the fact that the involved cells and the sensitive bacteria have the same membrane-binding sites for these drugs.

It should be noted that the lack of sterols in their membrane accounts for the resistance of all bacteria to the polyene antibiotics, nystatin and amphotericin B.

Agents Affecting Nucleic Acid Synthesis

Bacteria do not possess a nuclear membrane, but their single chromosome, a closed, circular molecule of DNA, is intimately related to the cytoplasmic membrane. The precursors of bacterial DNA and RNA are universal to all cells. It is not surprising, therefore, that few drugs which selectively inhibit bacterial nucleic acid synthesis have been discovered. Nalidixic acid selectively inhibits the polymerization of bacterial DNA, but its precise mechanism of action has not been defined. The recently discovered antibiotic, Rifamycin, selectively inhibits bacterial RNA synthesis by binding to the DNA-dependent RNA polymerase. These observations provide the most direct evidence that the RNA polymerase of bacteria differs significantly from that of mammalian cells.

Agents Affecting Protein Synthesis

Protein synthesis involves a series of complex, interrelated reactions. The nucleotide sequence (the genetic code) of the gene to be translated is encoded into mRNA, which complexes with several ribosomes to form a polysome. Amino acids make their way to the polysome following their enzymatic linkage to a specific member of the several species of tRNA. The specific recognition by the polysome mRNA of the tRNA portion of the amino acid-tRNA complex permits the binding of the complex to a specific anatomic site (A) on the ribosome. Operationally, this mRNA–tRNA interaction determines the sequence of the amino acids of the synthesized protein. In the presence of the required cofactors, the amino acid–tRNA complex is transferred from side A to an adjacent binding site (P). After another complex enters site A, the amino acid of the complex at P is transferred enzymatically to the amino acid of the complex at A, with the release of the tRNA bound to the first amino acid. This cycle is repeated until the polypeptide is completed and released from the ribosome (a matter of seconds in bacteria growing at 37° C).

The aminoglycoside antibiotics (streptomycin, neomycin, kanamycin, gentamicin) bind irreversibly to individual structural proteins of the 30S subunit of the ribosome, and in so doing, presumably distort binding site A. They therefore either stop protein synthesis or provoke errors in the interaction between the polysome mRNA and the tRNA of incoming complexes, which results in the incorporation of the "wrong" amino acid and the synthesis of "faulty" protein. All tetracycline drugs reversibly inhibit the binding of the amino acid–tRNA complex to the ribosome. Chloramphenicol binds to the 50S ribosomal subunit and reversibly inhibits protein synthesis either by inhibiting peptide bond formation or by some unknown step in the sequence. Erythromycin binds to the 50S subunit and reversibly inhibits protein synthesis, presumably by affecting the translocation reaction. These mechanisms account for the observations that (1) cross-resistance between these groups of drugs is uncommon; (2) the antibacterial effect of these groups of drugs is generally not additive or synergistic; and (3) L-forms are inhibited by these drugs.

The protein-synthetic schema described for bacteria is shared, at least in part, by many other types of cells; hence, certain of these drugs inhibit chlamydia, rickettsia, and mycoplasma. However, the protein-synthetic system of mammalian cells is relatively insensitive to all of these agents. Chloramphenicol does inhibit the protein synthesis and terminal respiration of isolated mitochondria. The biologic importance of these effects and their relation to the known effects of chloramphenicol on antibody formation and the hematologic system of man are not known. Similarly, it is not known if the toxic effects for man of streptomycin and tetracycline are due directly to their effects on the ribosome.

Agents Affecting Intermediary Metabolism

Intermediary metabolism includes those reactions that produce energy or macromolecular precursors. The discovery of the antibacterial activity of sulfonamides and the recognition that they compete with p-aminobenzoic acid (PABA) prompted the synthesis and testing of the antibacterial activity of thousands of analogs of essential metabolites. Unfortunately, only few agents have been found that possess the selective toxicity required of a clinically useful antimicrobial drug, and the sulfonamides remain as the best example of this class of drugs.

PABA is a constituent of folic acid, which is a cofactor in the transfer of 1-carbon fragments from serine to methionine, purines, and thymine. Because of their structural similarity to PABA, all sulfonamides competitively inhibit the enzyme that produces folic acid. They also compete as a substrate for the enzyme and are converted into a "faulty" product that further inhibits folate-dependent reactions.

The selectve toxicity of the sulfonamides depends on (1) the requirement of mammalian cells for exogenous folate; (2) the inability of all clinically important bacteria to utilize exogenous folate, presumably due to impermeability; and (3) a concentration of the products of 1-carbon metabolism in body fluids which is generally too low to reverse the effect of the concentrations of sulfonamide attainable during therapy.

The clinical uses of sulfonamides are affected by these molecular phenomena: (1) The drugs have a wide spectrum because almost all bacteria require exogenous folate; (2) all sulfonamides inhibit the same reaction, and therefore mutant bacteria whose affected enzyme is resistant to any given sulfonamide preparation are resistant to all others; (3) since the growth of treated, sensitive cells continues until the intracellular folate is depleted, sulfonamides do not act rapidly; (4) the high concentrations of products of 1-carbon metabolism, the noncompetitive antagonists of sulfonamides, which are present in sites of extensive tissue destruction, e.g., abscesses and burns, reduces the efficacy of the drugs; and (5) the toxicity of the sulfonamides for man cannot be related to their metabolic effects but is due to hypersensitivity or drug insolubility.

General Comments

Antimicrobial agents that produce an irreversible effect are defined as "bactericidal"; those whose inhibitory effect is reversed when the drug is removed are termed "bacteriostatic." Although these definitions appear to be absolute, the biologic importance between the two groups should not be overestimated. At minimally inhibitory concentrations, some bactericidal drugs are static or kill bacteria only after a long lag. Furthermore, bacteria do not always grow and divide after an indefinite period of stasis. Finally, the role of host defenses must always be included in considering the struggle between microbe and drug.

The oft-repeated cliché that multiple antibiotics need not be more effective than a single agent is supported by considerable experimentation and clinical experience. It has been noted earlier that a bacterium whose protein synthesis has been stopped at one step is generally not inhibited further by another drug inhibiting a subsequent reaction in the sequence. Similarly, the effect of two types of inhibitors of mucopeptide synthesis should be no more effective than one. For example, inhibiting protein synthesis with tetracycline or chloramphenicol prevents or stops the lethal action of inhibitors of mucopeptide synthesis and the aminoglycoside drugs, which kill only growing organisms. On the other hand, the penicillin-induced damage of the cell wall may facilitate the uptake of streptomycin. The lethal action of penicillins and aminoglycoside drugs in combinations is therefore often synergistic. The mechanisms of action of the antimicrobial drugs provide guidelines for decisions on the effectiveness of multiple drugs; however, each clinical situation must be evaluated individually.

Resistance to Antimicrobial Agents

Biochemical Basis of Drug Resistance

At least four mechanisms exist by which bacteria may be resistant to an antibiotic.

1. The "target" may be resistant to the drug. Only a subtle difference in the protein composition of the 30S ribosomal subunits distinguishes a strain resistant to several milligrams of streptomycin from one killed by a few micrograms.

2. The "target" may be sensitive but the cell envelope is impermeable to the drug. Most gram-negative bacilli, for example, are not affected by several thousand times the concentration of erythromycin that inhibits gram-positive bacteria. In contrast, the protoplasts of many "resistant" gram-negative bacilli are inhibited by one-thousandth the concentrations required to inhibit the parent strain.

3. The bacteria may produce an enzyme that inactivates the drug. The β-lactamase that cleaves the β-lactam ring of penicillin is the best known example of this mechanism. However, enzymes that specifically inactivate streptomycin, kanamycin, neomycin, or chloramphenicol by conjugating phosphate, adenylate, or acetate groups to the drugs ("natural detoxification") have been described.

4. Certain phenotypic or environmental phenomena may temporarily affect drug susceptibility. All drugs, with the exception of the polymyxins, affect only growing bacteria; thus, a deficiency of an essential nutrient in the milieu stops growth and makes the bacterium drug-resistant. Since streptomycin has little or no effect on bacteria growing anaerobically, "sensitive" (facultative anaerobic) bacteria are protected from the drug when shifted from an aerobic to an anaerobic environment. The activity of certain antibiotics is influenced by alteration of pH. For example, the increased activity of erythromycin and the aminoglycoside antibiotics at alkaline pH has clinical importance in the treatment of urinary tract infections.

The Genetic Basis of Drug Resistance

The bacterial chromosome contains several thousand genes, each of which mediates the synthesis of a single protein. A spontaneous alteration in the chemical composition of a gene, a "mutation," may prevent the synthesis of the gene product or alter its composition so that its function is affected. A mutation of the gene(s) mediating the synthesis of the macromolecular "target" of an antibiotic may render that bacterium drug-resistant. At cell division, the chromosome, including the mutant gene, is replicated and segregated into each of the two daughter bacteria. Although a spontaneous mutation occurs only once in every 10^6 to 10^8 cell divisions, treatment with the involved drug inhibits sensitive bacteria and permits those rare resistant bacteria to gain ascendancy. This mechanism of mutation and selection is the genetic basis for antibiotic resistance mediated by the bacterial chromosome.

Critical laboratory studies have indicated that spontaneous mutations affecting different genes occur independently of one another and at the same relative frequency. Thus, resistance via mutation to two drugs with different mechanisms of action occurs once in every 10^{12} to 10^{16} generations. Since this event is so rare, the use of two drugs to prevent the emergence of resistant strains has been successful in situations where resistance appears to be mediated only by mutation. Long-term therapy of tuberculosis provides such an example.

The prevalence in hospitals of resistant bacteria, particularly *S. aureus* and multiply resistant enteric bacilli, is much higher than one would expect from mutation alone. Furthermore, the observation that bacteria of different genera, such as *E. coli* and *Shigella*, with identical patterns of multiple drug resistance can be recovered from the stool of the same individual, cannot be explained easily by the theory of mutation and selection. Recent studies indicate that these findings are due, at least in part, to self-replicating, extrachromosomal genetic elements that may contain one or multiple genes mediating individual drug resistances. These factors, denoted variously as plasmids, episomes, or R (resistance) factors, are transmitted to daughter bacteria at cell division. They can be transmitted between bacteria, either by viruses (transduction), or by direct cell contact (conjugation), which occurs only in enteric bacteria. The plasmids of *S. aureus* cannot be transmitted to other genera of bacteria, whereas R factors of gram-negative bacilli can be transferred among all species of enteric bacteria. Transfer of R factors by transduction is relatively inefficient (1 bacteria in every 10^4 to 10^7 being affected) but transfer by conjugation may affect as many as 1 in every 10^2 to 10^3 bacteria under ideal circumstances. The interbacterial transfer of the R factor by either mechanism and the expression of its resistance genes is completed in less than one cell division.

A number of practical questions about R factors remain to be answered, but existing data indicate that they are widespread and commonly mediate the drug resistance of *S. aureus* and enteric bacilli isolated from clinical specimens.

Methods of Testing Drug Resistance

Antibiotic sensitivity tests attempt to predict the clinical effect of antimicrobial agents against infection caused by an isolated pathogen. The fact that no single method of testing antibiotic resistance is employed universally, indicates that all methods have deficiencies. The tube dilution method is the technique employed most commonly for obtaining quantitative data regarding antibiotic sensitivity. In this method, tubes of broth containing serial dilutions of drug are inoculated with a constant concentration of bacteria and are observed for the lowest drug concentration that (1) prevents growth, as manifested by turbidity (minimal inhibitory concentration), and (2) kills the bacteria, as determined by subculturing onto solid medium (minimal bactericidal concentration). The results obtained usually correlate well with the clinical efficacy of the tested drugs. Some laboratories spread bacteria on a series of plates of solid medium containing increasing drug concentrations and observe colony formation after incubation. These methods are not used routinely in most laboratories, however, because of the number of procedures and their cost.

In the method used most commonly, filter paper discs containing drugs are placed on a lawn of bacteria spread on the surface of nutrient agar. After an appropriate period of incubation, the area around the discs is observed for zones of inhibited growth and these are measured. This method is convenient, but for proper interpretation it requires rigid control of the quantity of bacteria plated and the concentration of drug in the disc, accurate measurement of the zone of inhibited growth, and comparison of this zone with those of bacteria whose drug susceptibility has been documented previously by the tube dilution method. When these standards are met, the results obtained with the disc technique correlate well with those obtained by the tube dilution method and with clinical experiences.

It should be emphasized that drug sensitivities need not be performed routinely on all bacterial isolates. For example, such tests are rarely, if ever, required for pneumococci and Group A streptococci, which show little variation of drug sensitivity patterns. For these organisms, tests should be performed on isolates from the urine, but only if a significant number of organisms is found in pure cultures. Drug sensitivity tests for anaerobic bacteria have not been as well standardized as those for aerobic bacteria, and therefore their relationship to clinical experiences is less well defined. Sensitivity tests should be performed routinely for other bacteria causing systemic disease, particularly S. aureus, Group D streptococci, Neisseria, and enteric bacteria. In cases of endocarditis or infection caused by an unusual bacterium, antibiotic sensitivities should be performed by the tube dilution assay, and the patient's serum should be assayed for antibacterial activity against the etiologic bacterium. In general, drug dosage should be adjusted to attain inhibitory activity in serum diluted 10-fold.

Antimicrobial Agents in Common Use

Antimicrobial Agents with a Narrow Antibacterial Spectrum

THE PENICILLINS. These antibiotics remain the drugs of choice for most infections due to gram-positive cocci, gram-positive bacilli, Neisseria, and spirochetes. In addition, they are effective against many anaerobic bacteria and some gram-negative rods. The wide variety of preparations allows the physician to tailor therapy to the clinical situation, but also requires that he be aware of pharmacologic differences such as absorption, peak blood levels, rate of renal clearance, and protein binding.

Oral Penicillins. Penicillin G (benzyl penicillin) is inexpensive and has been used successfully for many years; however it is acid-labile and is absorbed poorly when given with food. Penicillin V and Phenethicillin are relatively acid-resistant; they are absorbed from a full stomach, although higher blood levels are achieved when they are given 1 hour before or 2 hours after meals.

Parenteral Penicillin G. The various parenteral penicillin preparations result in widely differing peak blood levels and duration of antibiotic effects. To attain high blood levels rapidly, aqueous penicillin must be used. The rapid excretion of aqueous crystalline penicillin in patients with normal renal function requires that it be administered frequently, usually every 2 to 4 hours for optimal therapy. The interval should be extended to every 4 to 6 hours in newborn infants because of their lower rate of renal clearance of pencillin. Aqueous penicillin G is prepared as a potassium or sodium salt. One million units contains approximately 1.7 mEq of cation, which must be taken into consideration when large doses are administered to patients with poor renal function or electrolyte disorders.

Procaine penicillin is absorbed slowly, resulting in blood levels usually less than 1 unit per ml; it should be used, therefore, only in infections due to highly susceptible organisms such as the pneumococcus or Group A streptococcus. Benzathine penicillin produces blood levels of less than 0.5 units per ml for as long as 3 to 4 weeks. It is used primarily against Group A streptococci, prophylactically in patients with rheumatic heart disease or in certain epidemic situations, and therapeutically, when adherence to a program of oral penicillin seems improbable.

Beta-Lactamase–Resistant Penicillins. These semisynthetic penicillin analogs are used primarily in the treatment of infections due to Staphylococcus aureus resistant to penicillin G (beta-lactamase producers). They all are significantly less potent than benzyl penicillin against other microorganisms. The available preparations differ considerably in properties such as protein binding and in vitro effectiveness, but none is clearly superior to the others in clinical situations. The emergence of *S. aureus* isolates resistant to all these penicillins and also to the cephalosporins has been reported in Europe and parts of the United States.

Methicillin. Although it is relatively unstable in solution and compares unfavorably with the other beta-lactamase–resistant penicillins by in vitro testing, methicillin has the lowest protein-binding effect (20 percent) of the semisynthetic penicillins. It therefore may have theoretical advantages in certain infections in which protein binding may affect the concentration of the drug in the involved areas, such as the central nervous system. Due to its acid instability, no oral preparation is available.

Oxacillin. This drug can be given parenterally or orally. It is more active than methicillin against penicillin-resistant *S. aureus* in vitro, but it has higher protein binding (80 to 90 percent). Although oxacillin is acid-stable, blood levels following oral administration are markedly diminished by food in the stomach.

Nafcillin. Nafcillin may be given orally or parenterally, and shares with oxacillin the properties of marked activity against *S. aureus* in vitro and a high degree of protein binding. The drug is concentrated in the biliary tract. Although nafcillin is acid-stable, absorption from the gastrointestinal tract is not reliable.

Cloxacillin and Dicloxacillin. These drugs are available only as oral preparations. They are absorbed significantly better from the gastrointestinal tract than are the other beta-lactamase–resistant penicillins.

"Broad-Spectrum" Penicillins. *Ampicillin.* This penicillin analog shares the gram-positive spectrum of benzyl penicillin and, in addition, has greater activity against some gram-negative bacteria. Ampicillin has become one of the drugs most frequently used in the treatment of bacterial meningitis of unknown origin in a toddler-aged child, and is used in the treatment of infections caused by *Hemophilus influenzae*, *Shigella*, and enterococci. Since high concentrations are achieved in bile, ampicillin has been used in biliary tract infections caused by susceptible organisms, including *Salmonella*. Due to its limited gram-negative spectrum and its susceptibility to beta-lactamase, ampicillin should not be used alone in the treatment of sepsis of undefined etiology and should not be used to treat infections due to penicillin-resistant *S. aureus*.

Carbenicillin. Carbenicillin is a disodium penicillin analog with broad-spectrum antibacterial activity. However, it is less active against gram-positive organisms than other penicillins and is in-

effective against enterococci. The gram-negative spectrum of carbenicillin includes most of the common Enterobacteriaceae except *Klebsiella*. The primary use of carbenicillin has been the treatment of infections due to *Pseudomonas* and *Proteus*. Greatest efficacy has been reported in urinary tract infections. In general, results in other soft tissue infections have been favorable but more variable. Since carbenicillin and gentamycin are synergistic in their action against some *Pseudomonas* isolates, these two antibiotics are often used together in treating serious *Pseudomonas* infections.

Carbenicillin is inactivated by beta-lactamase and is poorly absorbed from the gastrointestinal tract. In the large doses required for parenteral therapy of *Pseudomonas* infections, sodium overload may occur due to the high sodium content of carbenicillin.

Adverse Reactions. Hypersensitivity to the penicillins is common to all preparations. Because all penicillins share the same basic chemical structure, patients with hypersensitivity to one preparation may react to any of the others. Immediate reactions include anaphylaxis, angioneurotic edema, and urticara. Therapeutic measures include prompt administration of epinephrine, maintenance of the airway, and support of the cardiovascular system. Delayed reactions include fever, eosinophilia, serum sickness, a variety of dermatologic conditions (ranging from a slight rash to exfoliative dermatitis) and occasional autoimmune phenomena such as vasculitis and Coombs'-positive hemolytic anemia. Intrathecal administration or large dosages in patients with reduced renal function may result in myoclonic jerks and convulsions. Although a variety of skin tests have been developed to detect penicillin allergy, a careful history of atopic reactions and previous experience with penicillins remains the single most important method of preventing hypersensitivity reactions.

ERYTHROMYCIN. The efficacy of erythromycin is restricted to gram-positive organisms, spirochetes, *Mycoplasma pneumoniae,* and some rickettsia. Most *S. aureus* currently isolated are sensitive to erythromycin, but resistance may develop during therapy. The drug diffuses well throughout most body fluids. Differences exist in the absorption and blood levels attained by the numerous erythromycin formulations currently available for oral administration, but clinical superiority of any one preparation has not been established. Among the oral preparations, erythromycin estolate yields the highest blood levels, but its use may be associated with cholestatic hepatitis, especially when administered for prolonged periods of time. Other adverse reactions are infrequent and are generally limited to mild gastrointestinal upset and rash. Parenteral preparations are available but are seldom used because large volumes must be administered to obtain adequate dosage by the intramuscular route and phlebitis frequently complicates intravenous use. Erythromycin is used most commonly in the treatment of *Mycoplasma* infections and as an alternative drug in patients allergic to penicillin.

LINCOMYCIN. Lincomycin is similar to erythromycin in absorption, distribution, and mechanism of action. Its antibacterial spectrum is also similar to that of erythromycin except that it is less potent against *Neisseria,* enterococci, and *Mycoplasma pneumonia.* Bacteria resistant to lincomycin frequently demonstrate cross-resistance to erythromycin. Lincomycin penetrates well into bone, and some studies suggest, but do not prove, its special effectiveness in the treatment of osteomyelitis. Oral administration of lincomycin is often accompanied by diarrhea and mild gastrointestinal complaints such as nausea. Higher blood levels and fewer gastrointestinal side effects have been reported for an orally administered chloride analog, clindamycin. Rare adverse reactions include cholestatic jaundice, neutropenia, and rash. Lincomycin is well tolerated by both the intramuscular and intravenous route.

VANCOMYCIN. Vancomycin is bactericidal for virtually all clinical isolates of gram-positive bacteria. It can only be given intravenously since it is not absorbed from the gastrointestinal tract and is too painful to use by the intramuscular route. Its use is further limited by its toxicity, which includes ototoxicity, nephrotoxicity, skin rashes, fever, and phlebitis. Because of its antibacterial effectiveness, vancomycin may reemerge as an agent useful against methicillin-resistant *S. aureus* and in severe infections caused by enterococci in patients allergic to penicillin. It has also been used successfully in the oral treatment of staphylococcal enterocolitis.

BACITRACIN. This polypeptide antibiotic is effective against almost all gram-positive bacteria. When used to treat systemic infections, the drug is given by the intramuscular route. Significant nephrotoxicity and hypersensitivity reactions have caused bacitracin to be largely supplanted by less toxic drugs in the systemic treatment of infections. Bacitracin is poorly absorbed when used topically or administered orally. Its primary use at present is in the topical treatment of localized infections due to *S. aureus.*

Agents with an Intermediate Antibacterial Spectrum

CEPHALOSPORINS. These agents are similar to penicillin in chemical structure and mechanism of action. Like the penicillins, they are effective against most gram-positive cocci including beta-lactamase producing *S. aureus,* but they appear to be less active against enterococci. In addition, the cephalosporins are bactericidal for most strains of *Klebsiella, Proteus mirabilis, E. coli, Salmonella,* and *Shigella* at concentrations that can be achieved in vivo.

Adverse reactions are similar to those manifested to penicillin. Although most patients with penicillin allergy tolerate cephalosporins well, a small, but definite risk of cross-sensitivity does exist. Commonly, patients receiving cephalosporin drugs develop a positive Coombs' test, but hemolytic anemia is rare. Cephalothin, which must be administered parenterally, is irritating, and phlebitis is commonly associated with its intravenous use. Cephaloridine, an intramuscular preparation, is well tolerated but in high doses is associated with renal toxicity. An oral preparation, cephaloglycin, has been reported to be effective in the treatment of urinary tract infections due to sensitive bacteria, although diarrhea is a common side effect.

The cephalosporins are used primarily to treat patients with infections caused by penicillin-resistant *S. aureus* or sensitive enteric bacilli. Since many gram-negative bacteria are resistant, these drugs cannot be expected to give broad-spectrum coverage in "gram-negative sepsis" due to an unknown organism.

SULFONAMIDES. Although sulfonamides show in vitro effectiveness against a wide variety of organisms including the common gram-positive cocci, many enteric bacilli, *H. influenzae, Nocardia,* and some *Chlamydia,* their clinical effectiveness is much more limited. Because certain products of tissue necrosis interfere with the action of sulfonamides (see p. 582), these drugs should be used primarily in infections with minimal suppuration.

Current major uses include treatment of urinary tract infections due to *E. coli;* prophylaxis against Group A streptococcal infections in patients with rheumatic heart disease; and, in combination with penicillin, in the treatment of otitis media. In established Group A streptococcal infections, sulfonamides cannot be relied upon to prevent postinfectious sequelae. Sulfonamides that are poorly absorbed from the gastrointestinal tract have been used primarily in patients undergoing bowel surgery or in patients with ulcerative colitis. Sulfonamides usually eradicate sensitive meningococci from the nasopharynx and have, therefore, been used for prophylaxis. However, types B and C meningococci, which are generally resistant to high levels of sulfonamides, have caused most of the infections in this country in recent years. The search for an effective alternative method of meningococcal prophylaxis therefore continues.

The use of sulfonamides has been associated with a wide variety of adverse drug reactions. Of these, mild hypersensitivity reactions (rash, fever) are the most common, although hepatitis, vasculitis, bone marrow depression, and Stevens-Johnson syndrome may occur. Sulfonamides are among the drugs that may produce hemolytic anemia in patients with glucose-6-phosphate dehydrogenase deficiency. Nephrotoxicity is now rare due to the use of more soluble sulfonamides such as sulfisoxazole and trisulfapyrimidines. Since sulfonamides interfere with bilirubin metabolism by competing for albumin-binding sites, the use of these drugs should be avoided in pregnant women at term and in neonates in order to avoid the risk of kernicterus.

STREPTOMYCIN. Streptomycin has variable effectiveness against the common enteric bacilli and *H.*

influenzae. Even when used against a bacterium which is sensitive to the drug by in vitro tests, streptomycin should not be used alone due to the rapid development of high-level resistance during therapy. The use of this drug to treat peritoneal soilage is questionable since both bacteroides, the most numerous organism in the bowel flora, and clostridia are streptomycin resistant. In vitro synergism with penicillin against enterococci has been demonstrated, and endocarditis due to enterococcus has generally been treated with this combination of antibiotics. Because the activity of streptomycin is greatly increased at alkaline pH, urine should be alkalinized for maximum effect in urinary tract infections. Streptomycin remains an effective first-line drug in the treatment of tuberculosis, but it should always be used with another antituberculous agent.

KANAMYCIN. Kanamycin is effective against all the commonly isolated Enterobacteriaciae. Pseudomonas and bacteroides are generally resistant. Kanamycin was introduced as an antistaphylococcal drug and remains an effective second-line drug against most strains of *S. aureus.* It also is active against *M. tuberculosis.* As with all the aminoglycoside antibiotics, it is poorly absorbed from the gastrointestinal tract and is administered preferentially by the intramuscular route.

Minor hypersensitivity reactions such as rash, eosinophilia, and fever may occur at any dose level. However, the serious adverse reactions, renal failure and irreversible deafness, are dose related. They are usually avoidable if the daily dose is limited to 15 mg per kg and the duration of therapy does not exceed 10 to 14 days in patients with normal renal function. These reactions are rare in young children. Renal function and auditory acuity, especially high frequency, should be monitored closely in patients receiving long courses of kanamycin. Rarely, neuromuscular block with respiratory paralysis has been reported when kanamycin has been administered to patients by the intraperitoneal or intravenous route. Neostigmine and calcium gluconate have been reported to reverse this complication. In situations in which toxic levels of kanamycin are present, prompt reduction of blood levels can be achieved by either peritoneal or hemodialysis.

NITROFURANTOIN. This oral agent affects most common gram-positive and gram-negative pathogens, with the exception of *Pseudomonas.* The prompt renal excretion of nitrofurantoin results in adequate urine levels but negligible blood levels. Therefore, it is used only in the treatment of infections confined to the urinary tract. Gastrointestinal upset and abdominal cramping are common side effects. A new preparation, nitrofurantoin macrocrystals, may cause less gastrointestinal upset and may result in greater tissue levels of the drug. Other adverse reactions include rashes, peripheral neuropathy, allergic pneumonitis, and hemolytic anemia in patients who are glucose-6-phosphate dehydrogenase deficient. Nitrofurantoin should not be administered to newborn infants because it competes with bilirubin for binding to albumin.

Nitrofurazone, another furan derivative, is widely used as a topical antibacterial agent.

NEOMYCIN AND PAROMOMYCIN. These drugs are similar to kanamycin in structure, action, and antibacterial spectrum, but they are rarely used parenterally due to a high incidence of nephrotoxicity and ototoxicity. Since they are poorly absorbed from the gastrointestinal tract, they have been used primarily for gastrointestinal conditions, such as infant diarrhea due to *E. coli,* and in suppression of bowel flora. Malabsorption and intercurrent staphylococcal entercolitis may complicate the oral use of these drugs. Increased absorption through inflamed bowel mucosa or from wounds irrigated with neomycin may result in toxic blood levels, particularly in patients with renal failure.

POLYMYXIN B AND SODIUM COLISTIMETHATE (POLYMYXIN E). In equivalent dosages, these two drugs are essentially interchangeable. They are effective against all *Pseudomonas* and common Enterobacteriaceae with the exception of *Proteus* and *Serratia.* *Bacteroides* species and the gram-positive bacteria are resistant. They are poorly absorbed from the gastrointestinal tract, penetrate tissues poorly, and do not enter the cerebrospinal fluid.

Sodium colistimethate contains dibucaine, an anesthetic which renders it less painful on intramuscular injection. Polymyxin B lacks an anesthetic and therefore, unlike sodium colistimethate, it can only be given intravenously or by the intrathecal route. Both drugs are excreted in the urine. They are used primarily to treat known *Pseudomonas* infections and "gram-negative sepsis" when *Pseudomonas* is suspected. Results in the treatment of soft-tissue infections outside the urinary tract have been variable. Nonabsorbed oral preparations of these drugs may be used in the treatment of gastroenteritis due to enteropathic *E. coli.*

Both polymyxin B and sodium colistimethate are nephrotoxic, and patients should be monitored closely for abnormalities of urine sediment or renal function while receiving these agents. Minor neurologic complaints such as circumoral paresthesias and mild ataxia are common. Rarely, high blood levels of these drugs may result in neuromuscular block with weakness and respiratory insufficiency.

GENTAMICIN. This aminoglycoside antibiotic is effective against *S. aureus* and most common gram-negative bacilli, including *Pseudomonas.* It is probably not effective against anaerobic organisms and enterococci. Like other aminoglycoside drugs, gentamicin is poorly absorbed from the intestinal tract, and is administered preferentially by the intramuscular route. The therapeutic role of gentamicin is not yet clearly defined, but success has been reported in a variety of severe infections due to *Pseudomonas, Serratia,* and "gram-negative sepsis" of unknown etiology. Where the drug has been used extensively the occurrence of gentamicin resistant *Pseudomonas* has been reported. Topical preparations are available for skin infections.

Adverse drug reactions are similar to those of other aminoglycosides. Ototoxicity, involving vestibular function more frequently than cochlear, as well as nephrotoxicity are dose-related and require that auditory and renal function be monitored closely during therapy.

NALADIXIC ACID. Naladixic acid is an oral agent which is bactericidal for most of the commonly isolated gram-negative bacilli except *Pseudomonas*. It is not effective against gram-positive organisms. It is absorbed well from the gastrointestinal tract but serum and tissue levels of the drug are variable. The drug is concentrated in the urine, and its use has been limited to treatment of urinary tract infections. Bacteria with high levels of resistance to naladixic acid are often isolated during therapy. Common adverse reactions to naladixic acid include gastrointestinal upset and allergic responses such as rash, fever, and eosinophilia. Occasionally, neurologic complaints including headache, dizziness, psychosis, and convulsions have been reported.

Antimicrobial Agents with Broad Antibacterial Spectrum

METHENAMINE. Methenamine has little native antibacterial activity but at a pH of less than 5.5 it hydrolyzes to produce formaldehyde and mandelic acid. Therefore, its use is limited to the treatment of infections of the urinary tract, where it acts as a surface antiseptic agent. In patients receiving methenamine, urine pH must be monitored, and acidifying agents such as ascorbic acid, methionine, ammonium chloride, or acid ash diet may be required to maintain acidity. If patients are unable to acidify their urine or if the infection is due to a urea-splitting organism, such as *Proteus,* the drug is ineffective. Adverse drug reactions are uncommon and consist of mild gastrointestinal upset, hematuria, and rarely ataxia. Metabolic acidosis due to the acidifying agents may occur in patients with impaired renal function.

CHLORAMPHENICOL. Chloramphenicol affects most common gram-negative bacilli, including *H. influenzae* and anaerobic bacilli, excepting *Pseudomonas,* and most gram-positive organisms, including *S. aureus*. It is also effective against many rickettsia, the *Chlamydia,* and *T. pallidum.* Chloramphenicol is well absorbed from the gastrointestinal tract and diffuses well into tissues and the cerebrospinal fluid. It can be administered orally or parenterally.

Restriction of chloramphenicol usage has been urged due to the rare but often fatal occurrence of aplastic anemia. Therefore, as alternative antibiotics have been developed, the indications for chloramphenicol have diminished. It still remains the drug of choice, however, in severe *Salmonella* infections; because of its ready diffusion into the brain and its effectiveness against anaerobic bacteria, it is also used preferentially by many physicians in the treatment of brain abscesses.

Other adverse reactions associated with chloramphenicol are reversible. They include interference, with iron metabolism, which is dose-related and manifested by increased serum iron and decreased iron-binding capacity, vacuolization of erythrocyte precursors in bone marrow, decreased circulating reticulocyte count, and anemia and depression of other marrow elements.

Chloramphenicol is conjugated in the liver with glucuronide and subsequently excreted in the urine. Because the glucuronide transferase system is not fully developed in premature infants, chloramphenicol may produce excessive blood levels and result in the "gray baby" syndrome. This shocklike symdrome may result in death unless the condition is recognized and drug therapy discontinued. Other rare reactions include optic neuritis and peripheral neuritis. Suppression of antibody responses by chloramphenicol has been reported.

TETRACYCLINES. The antibacterial spectrum of the tetracyclines is broad but patchy. Tetracyclines are moderately effective against the common Enterobacteriaciae (except *Proteus*) although increasing resistance, often mediated by R factors, has developed among *E. coli* and other previously sensitive enteric bacilli. Anaerobic organisms are generally sensitive. The tetracyclines also are effective against a wide spectrum of gram-positive organisms but resistance is common among stapyhlococcal and streptococcal isolates. While most isolates of *H. influenzae* and *Neisseria* are sensitive to tetracycline, other drugs are used preferentially.

A wide variety of adverse reactions has been associated with the tetracyclines, including gastrointestinal reactions, superinfection, dermatologic reactions, renal tubular acidosis (with outdated drugs), and pseudotumor cerebri. Permanent binding of tetracycline to calcium may produce a dose-related brownish stain of teeth when the drug is administered during the period of dental calcification extending from the fifth month of gestation to approximately 8 years of age.

There appears to be little difference in the clinical efficacy of the numerous tetracycline preparations which are available. The increasing prevalence of resistant strains of common pathogenic bacteria, the introduction of alternative antibiotics, and an increased awareness of the toxic side effects of the tetracyclines have caused them to be used less frequently than previously in pediatric infections.

Incompatibilities of Intravenous Drugs

Physical or chemical incompatibility of drugs mixed together in solutions for intravenous use may occur (Table 1). This may become apparent when inspec-

TABLE 1. *Incompatibilities of Commonly Used Antibiotics for Intravenous Administration**

Antibiotic	Incompatible Agents
Amphotericin B†	Potassium penicillin G, tetracyclines
Cephalothin	Calcium chloride or gluconate, erythromycin, polymyxin B, tetracyclines
Chloramphenicol	B-complex vitamin preparations, hydrocortisone, polymyxin B, tetracyclines, vancomycin
Methicillin‡	Tetracyclines
Nafcillin	B-complex vitamin preparations
Potassium penicillin G	Amphotericin B, metaraminol, phenylephrine, tetracyclines, vancomycin, ascorbic acid
Polymyxin B	Cephalothin, chloramphenicol, heparin, tetracyclines
Tetracyclines §	Amphotericin B, cephalothin, chloramphenicol, heparin, hydrocortisone, methicillin, potassium penicillin G, polymyxin B
Vancomycin	Chloramphenicol, heparin, hydrocortisone, potassium penicillin G

*Adapted from *Med. Lett. Drugs Ther.*, 9:17, 1967.

†Specific instructions for reconstitution are provided by the manufacturer; the agent should always be administered alone.

‡Physical stability or biologic potency may change after reconstitution; the agent should be administered alone soon after it is diluted.

§The agent should not be mixed with solutions which contain calcium. Ringer's solution may be used as a diluent because the pH of the solution is acid.

tion reveals color changes, gas formation, or precipitation in the bottle. More subtle changes of equal clinical importance, such as the effect of pH on the potency of certain drugs, may not be evident on inspection. For example, the addition of ascorbic acid may lower the pH and affect the stability and activity of pH-sensitive drugs such as penicillin. Since compatibility testing has only been carried out for a fraction of the possible combinations of intravenous drugs, in general it is preferable to mix each antibiotic in a separate bottle and administer each at the appropriate interval by a "piggy-back" arrangement, with flushing of the tubing between administration of different drugs.

Microorganisms Associated with Particular Infections

The choice of antibiotics in the initial therapy of severe infections and the choice of bacteriologic media and culturing techniques presupposes some knowledge of the bacterial pathogens most likely to cause certain types of infections. In some infections, such as erysipelas due to Group A streptococcus, the causative pathogen can be predicted with a high degree of accuracy on the basis of the clinical presentation. In other infections such as otitis media or pneumonia, the etiologic agent is much more difficult to predict on clinical grounds and the initial choice of therapy becomes an estimate of the probabilities based on the data available, especially the gram stain and clinical features, and knowledge of the common offending pathogens together with their antibiotic sensitivity

pattern. A list of common infections and the most frequently associated pathogens is presented in Table 2.

Choice of Antimicrobial Agents

Once a bacterial pathogen is known or suspected, the choice of antibiotics is dependent on a number of factors, including the antibiotic sensitivities of the pathogen; the absorption, distribution, and excretion of the drug; and the toxic effects of the drug. Therefore, the choice of drugs for a particular pathogen may be modified by the presence of hepatic or renal damage, a history of allergy, or the location of the infection. It is important to tabulate at regular intervals the antibiotic sensitivity patterns of common bacterial pathogens (particularly gram-negative bacilli and *S. aureus*) isolated in each hospital, since these patterns may vary widely from hospital to hospital or from one time to another. Rough guidelines regarding the antimicrobial agents usually effective against particular pathogens are offered in Table 3. These require modification to fit the clinical situation as indicated above.

Prophylactic Use of Antimicrobial Agents

The success of antimicrobial agents in therapy of bacterial infections led to optimism regarding prevention of bacterial diseases by prophylactic administration of these drugs to patients at high risk of developing infections; such patients included those exposed to a communicable disease, such as tuberculosis, or

TABLE 2.   *Microorganisms Most Likely to Cause Infection in Children**

Skin and Subcutaneous Tissues

Skin Infections
1. Dermatophytoses
2. *Staphylococcus aureus*
3. *Streptococcus pyogenes*
   (Group A)

Burns
1. *Staphylococcus aureus*
2. *Pseudomonas aeruginosa*
3. Proteus
4. *Streptococcus pyogenes*
   (Group A)

Decubitus Wound Infections
1. *Staphylococcus aureus*
2. *Escherichia coli* (or other
   gram-negative rods)
3. Anaerobic streptococci
4. *Streptococcus pyogenes*
   (Group A)
5. Clostridium

Traumatic and Surgical Wounds
1. *Staphylococcus aureus*
2. Gram-negative rods
3. Clostridium
4. Anaerobic streptococci

Eyes

Cornea and Conjunctiva
1. Viruses (herpes simplex and
   adenoviruses most common)
2. Chlamydia: trachoma, inclusion
   conjunctivitis
3. Pneumococcus
4. *Staphylococcus aureus*
5. *Hemophilus influenzae*
6. Coliform bacilli
7. Koch-Weeks bacillus
8. Gonnococcus (newborns)

Nasal Mucous Membrane

1. Viruses
2. *Staphylococcus aureus*

Sinuses

1. Pneumococcus
2. *Staphylococcus aureus*
3. *Hemophilus influenzae*
4. Klebsiella-Aerobacter
5. *Streptococcus pyogenes*
   (Group A)

Ear

Auditory Canal
1. *Staphylococcus aureus*
2. *Streptococcus pyogenes*
   (Group A)
3. *Pseudomonas aeruginosa*
   (chronic)

Middle Ear
1. Pneumococcus
2. *Hemophilus influenzae*
3. *Staphylococcus aureus*

4. *Streptococcus pyogenes*
   (Group A)
5. *Pseudomonas aeruginosa*
   (chronic)
6. Proteus (chronic)

Mouth

1. Herpes viruses
2. *Candida albicans*
3. Fusospirochetes (Vincent's
   infection)

Throat

1. Viruses
2. *Streptococcus pyogenes*
   (Group A)
3. Fusospirochetes (Vincent's
   infection)
4. *Candida albicans*
5. *Corynebacterium diphtheriae*

Trachea and Bronchi

1. Viruses
2. Pneumococcus
3. *Hemophilus influenzae*

Pleura

1. *Staphylococcus aureus*
2. Pneumococcus
3. *Hemophilus influenzae*
4. *Mycobacterium tuberculosis*
5. Anaerobic streptococci
6. *Streptococcus pyogenes*
   (Group A)

Lungs

Pneumonia
1. Viruses
2. Pneumococcus
3. *Mycoplasma pneumoniae*
4. *Hemophilus influenzae*
5. Klebsiella-Aerobacter
6. *Staphylococcus aureus*
7. *Mycobacterium tuberculosis*
8. *Streptococcus pyogenes*
   (Group A)

Abscess
1. *Staphylococcus aureus*
2. Pneumococcus
3. Bacteroides
4. Fusospirochetes (Vincent's
   infection)
5. Anaerobic streptococci
6. Klebsiella-Aerobacter

Enteric Tract

1. Viruses
2. *Staphylococcus aureus* (food
   poisoning)
3. *Escherichia coli* (especially in
   young children)
4. Salmonella
5. Shigella

6. *Staphylococcus aureus*
   (enterocolitis)
7. *Pseudomonas aeruginosa*
   (enterocolitis)

Liver and Biliary Tract

1. *Escherichia coli*
2. Klebsiella-Aerobacter
3. Proteus
4. Bacteroides
5. Salmonella

Urethra

1. Gonococcus
2. Mycoplasma
3. Mima
4. *Treponema pallidum*

Female Genital Tract

Vagina
1. Gonococcus
2. Herpes virus
3. *Candida albicans*
4. *Streptococcus pyogenes*
   (Group A)
5. *Treponema pallidum*

Bladder, Ureters, and Kidneys

1. *Escherichia coli* (or other gram-
   negative rods)
2. Enterococcus
3. *Staphylococcus aureus* (after
   surgery)

Central Nervous System

Meninges
1. Viruses
2. *Hemophilus influenzae*
3. Pneumococcus
4. Meningococcus
5. Coliform bacilli (enteric bacteria
   are the most frequent causes of
   meningeal infections during the
   perinatal period)
6. *Streptococcus pyogenes*
   (Group A)
7. *Staphylococcus aureus* (after
   surgery)
8. *Mycobacterium tuberculosis*
9. *Cryptococcus neoformans*
   (especially in newborns)
10. *Listeria monocytogenes*
11. *Coccidioides immitis* (in endemic
   areas)

Abscess
1. Bacteroides
2. Anaerobic streptococci
3. *Staphylococcus aureus*

Bones (Osteomyelitis)

1. *Staphylococcus aureus*
2. Salmonella (or other gram-
   negative rods)

TABLE 2. *Microorganisms Most Likely to Cause Infection in Children* (continued)

Bones (Osteomyelitis) (continued)

3. *Mycobacterium tuberculosis*
4. *Streptococcus pyogenes*
    (Group A)

Joints

1. *Staphylococcus aureus*
2. *Hemophilus influenzae*
3. *Streptococcus pyogenes*
    (Group A)
4. Gram-negative rods
5. Gonococcus

Blood (Septicemia)

Newborn Infants
1. *Escherichia coli* (or other
    coliform bacilli)
2. *Staphylococcus aureus*
3. *Streptococcus pyogenes*
    (Group A & B)

Children
1. *Hemophilus influenzae*
2. Meningococcus
3. *Staphylococcus aureus*
4. Pneumococcus
5. *Escherichia coli* (or other gram-
    negative rods)

Endocardium

1. *Streptococcus viridans*
2. *Staphylococcus aureus*
3. Anaerobic streptococci
4. Enterococcus
5. *Streptococcus pyogenes*
    (Group A)

Peritoneum

1. *Escherichia coli*
2. Enterococcus
3. Pneumococcus
4. Bacteroides (or other gram-
    negative rods)
5. Anaerobic streptococci
6. Clostridium

*Adapted from *Med. Lett. Drugs Ther.*, 8:15, 1966.

those with increased susceptibility to infection due to concurrent illness, debilitating disease, or major surgery. Unfortunately, attempts at prophylaxis against a broad spectrum of bacteria for prolonged periods generally have not been successful and carry the risks of adverse drug reactions, including allergy and toxicity, and superinfection.

Certain situations in which prophylactic administration of antimicrobial agents appear to be useful are listed in Table 4. In general, situations in which prophylaxis is successful are those in which a specific drug is directed against a specific organism. A number of other situations in which the role of prophylactic antimicrobial agents is less clear have been omitted from Table 4. These include premature rupture of membranes, prolonged labor, open heart surgery, prolonged neurosurgical or orthopedic operations, preoperative bowel flora "preps," and ulcerative colitis. While antimicrobial agents are commonly used in these situations, there are few controlled studies, and opinions concerning their efficacy vary widely.

Special Situations

Impaired Kidney Function

Since most antimicrobial agents or their metabolites are excreted by the kidneys, modification of dosage is frequently necessary in patients with impaired kidney function. Information on which to base recommendations is incomplete and the modifications suggested in Table 5 are intended as general guidelines only. Drugs which are nephrotoxic and excreted by the kidneys may result in a cycle of deteriorating kidney function and increasing blood levels of drug if close supervision is not maintained. All patients receiving nephrotoxic drugs should be monitored at frequent intervals for abnormalities of urine sediment and alteration of kidney function. Unfortunately, attempts to measure serum levels of antibiotics usually involve bioassays and usually are not feasible for general laboratories.

Until firmer guidelines can be established, it seems wisest to (1) avoid toxic drugs excreted by the kidney, when alternative choices exist; (2) use nephrotoxic drugs for as short a period as is consistent with good therapy; and (3) use short-acting preparations when the choice exists.

Impaired Liver Function

The liver and bile collecting system can affect antimicrobial agents in a variety of ways. Drugs may be concentrated in the gall bladder where levels may be several hundred times the serum concentration. Drugs may be modified or conjugated in the liver, often resulting in changes in physical properties such as solubility or biologic properties such as antimicrobial action or toxicity. Many drugs excreted by the liver are reabsorped in the small bowel (enterohepatic circulation) and subsequently excreted in the urine. The liver serves as the primary route of excretion or degradation for a small but important group of drugs (Table 5). Most of the toxicity studies have been done in animals and it is difficult to offer concrete guidelines for the management of these drugs in humans with impaired liver functions. Only minor amounts of cephalothin are excreted in the liver; therefore, alteration of dosage is necessary only in severe liver disease. Erythromycin and lincomycin are relatively nontoxic at high levels but since they are excreted primarily in bile, modification of dosage is advisable in patients with liver failure. Erythromycin estolate has been associated with cholestatic hepatitis and probably should be avoided in this setting. Chloramphenicol dosage should be reduced

TABLE 3.   *Choice of Antimicrobial Agents (Intended as* Rough Guidelines *Only)*

Organism	Infection	Drug	Dose/kg/day
I. Gram-Positive Cocci			
1. Group A Streptococcus*	Pharyngitis Cellulitis, Pneumonia Empyema, Bacteremia	Penicillin G (alt: erythromycin, cepha- lothin, lincomycin)	25,000 units 25,000-50,000 units 100,000 units
2. *Streptococcus viridans*	Subacute endocarditis (treat 4 weeks)	Penicillin G (alt: see 1)	250,000 units
3. Enterococcus	Subacute endocarditis (treat 4-6 weeks)	a. Penicillin and streptomycin b. Ampicillin (alt: erythromycin, vancomycin)	a. 250,000 units 15 mg b. 300 mg
	Urinary tract infection		a. 25,000 units 15 mg b. 50-100 mg
4. Pneumococcus	Pneumonia, Soft tissue (empyema) Meningitis	Penicillin G (alt: see 1)	25,000 units 100,000 units 250,000 units
5. *Staphylococcus aureus* (Penicillin-sensitive)	Abscess Pneumonia Endocarditis	Penicillin G	25,000 units 100,000 units 250,000 units
6. *Staphylococcus aureus* (Penicillin-resistant)	Mild infection Severe infection	β-Lactamase-resistant penicillin (alt: cephalothin, erythromy- cin, lincomycin, vancomycin)	25-50 mg (dicloxacillin) 300 mg (methicillin) 200-300 mg (oxacillin)
II. Gram-Positive Bacilli			
1. *Clostridium perfringens*	Gas gangrene†	Penicillin G (alt: tetracycline)	250,000 units
2. *Clostridium tetani*	Tetanus‡	Penicillin G (alt: tetracycline, erythromy- cin)	250,000 units
3. *Listeria monocytogenes*	Meningitis	a. Penicillin G b. Tetracycline (alt: erythromycin, ampicillin)	a. 250,000 units b. 50 mg
4. Corynebacterium	Diphtheria§	Penicillin G	25,000 units
III. Gram-Negative Cocci			
1. Meningococcus	Meningitis Meningococcemia	Penicillin G (alt: ampicillin, chloramsheni- col, erythromycin)	250,000 units 200,000 units
2. Gonococcus	Gonorrhea	Penicillin G (alt: tetracycline erythromy- cin, cephalothin)	2.4 million units (total dose) in males 4.8 million units (total dose) in females
IV. Gram-Negative Bacilli ‖			
1. *E. Coli*	Urinary tract infection	a. Sulfisoxazole (alt: trisulfapyrimidines) b. Ampicillin	a. 50-150 mg b. 50-100 mg
	Systemic infection	a. Ampicillin b. Cephalothin c. Kanamycin d. Sodium colistimethate e. Chloramphenicol	a. 200-300 mg b. up to 250 mg c. 15 mg d. 2-5 mg e. 100 mg
2. Klebsiella	Systemic infection	a. Cephalothin b. Kanamycin (alt: gentamicin, colistimeth- ate, chloramphenicol)	a. 250 mg b. 15 mg

TABLE 3.   *Choice of Antimicrobial Agents (Intended as* Rough Guidelines *only)* (continued)

Organism	Infection	Drug	Dose/kg/day
IV. Gram-Negative Bacilli‖ (continued)			

3. Enterobacter	Systemic infection	a. Chloramphenicol
		b. Tetracycline
		    (alt: streptomycin, gentamicin,
		    kanamycin, colistimethate)
			a. 100 mg
			b. 50 mg

4. *Proteus mirabilis*	Urinary tract infection	a. Penicillin G
		b. Ampicillin
		    (alt: cephalothin, kanamycin,
		    chloramphenicol)
			a. 250,000 units
			b. 50-100 mg

5. Proteus (indole positive)	Urinary tract infection	a. Kanamycin b. Chloramphenicol	a. 15 mg b. 100 mg
6. *Pseudomonas aerugenosa*	Systemic infection	a. Gentamycin b. Sodium colistimethate c. Polymyxin B d. Carbenicillin	a. 4-6 mg b. 2-5 mg c. up to 2.5 mg d. 400 mg
7. Salmonella#	Systemic infection	Chloramphenicol (alt: ampicillin)	100-250 mg
8. Shigella	Systemic infection	Ampicillin (alt: chloramphenicol)	100-250 mg

9. Bacteroides	Abscess	a. Penicillin G
		b. Tetracycline
		    (alt: chloramphenicol,
		    erythromycin)
			a. 150,000 units
			b. 50 mg

10. *Hemophilus influenzae*	Soft tissue infection
	Meningitis
		Ampicillin
		    (alt: sulfonamides, strepto-
		    mycin, tetracycline, chlor-
		    amphenicol)
			50-100 mg
			300 mg

*Always treat for 10 days to prevent postinfectious sequelae.
†Use of antitoxin (horse) in the absence of hemolysis.
‡Also use human antitoxin, 250 units.
§Also use horse antitoxin 20,000 to 80,000 units.
‖Specific sensitivities should be determined for most isolates.
#Treatment may prolong the carrier state.

TABLE 4.   *Situations in which Prophylactic Antimicrobial Drugs May be Useful*

Infection	Drug	Dose
1. Group A streptococcal infections; in patients with rheumatic heart disease	Penicillin (alt: sulfonamide, erythromycin)	a. 200,000 units penicillin G b.i.d., per os b. 600,000-900,000 units benzathine penicillin G im for 3-4 weeks
2. Meningococcal infection (no method uniformly effective)	a. Sulfonamides for sensitive strains b. Penicillin	a. 100 mg/kg/day for 3 days b. 25,000 μ/kg/day
3. Gonorrhea ophthalmia	a. Silver nitrate b. Penicillin	a. 1 drop 1% solution each eye b. Ophthalmic ointment 50,000 units/g
4. Prevention of bacterial endocarditis following manipulative procedures in patients with rheumatic heart disease a. *Streptococcus viridans* b. Enterococcus	 a. Penicillin b. Penicillin and streptomycin	 a. 25,000 μ/kg aqueous and 25,000 μ/kg of procaine penicillin 1 hour before; 25,000 μ/kg procaine penicillin for 2 days after dental extraction b. Same as above plus streptomycin 15 mg/kg 1 hour before, and b.i.d. for 2 days after urinary tract manipulation or pelvic procedure
5. Tuberculosis (any child with positive PPD reaction)	Isoniazid	10 mg/kg/day for at least 12 months
6. Urinary tract infection in patients with indwelling catheters	Neomycin (40 mg/L) plus polymyxin (20 mg/L) or 1/4% acetic acid irrigation	Constant bladder rinse via triple lumen catheter (1 liter/day maximum)
7. Enteropathic *E. coli* in newborn infants	Neomycin	50-100 mg/kg/day postoperative
8. Grossly contaminated injury including bites	a. Penicillin G b. Tetanus toxoid c. Soap and water	a. 50,000 units/kg/day b. 0.5 ml im (when indicated) c. Freely
9. Intravenous polyethylene catheter (avoid when possible)	Antibacterial ointment	Topical ointment to entry site

in patients with liver disease since the dose-related type of bone marrow toxicity is related to the serum levels of free (unconjugated) drug. Because of the small but definite hepatic toxicity of sulfonamides these drugs are best avoided in liver disease. All of the tetracycline preparations are concentrated in the liver and bile, although there is marked variation with regard to subsequent excretion in feces and urine. Chlortetracycline is the most dependent on hepatic excretion and should be avoided in liver disease. Other tetracyclines are excreted primarily in the urine but since severe dose-related hepatic toxicity may occur, tetracyclines should be used with caution and at low doses in patients with liver disease. Although variable amounts of isoniazid are acetylated in the liver, 40 to 90 percent of isoniazid is excreted by the kidneys and therefore no alteration of dosage is generally required unless concomitant renal failure exists.

Premature or Newborn Infants

In choosing antimicrobial agents for premature or newborn infants, it is important to recognize that, in the neonate, liver function and kidney function are not fully developed. Failure of infants to conjugate chloramphenicol with glucuronides may lead to accumulation of toxic serum levels and result in peripheral vascular collapse ("gray" baby syndrome). A number of drugs including sulfonamides and salicylates compete with bilirubin for albumin-binding sites and thereby increase the risk of kernicterus. Immaturity of renal tubular function in newborns prolongs the half-life of the penicillins and cephalosporins. Therefore, the dosage and frequency of administration should be reduced. High doses of

TABLE 5. *Modification of Antibiotic Dosage in Renal Failure*
(With some general rules of thumb based on fragmentary evidence)

Antimicrobial Agent	Major Excretory Route	Dosage Modification
I. Little or No Change		
A. Erythromycin	Liver	
B. Novobiocin	Liver	
C. Isoniazid*†	Liver	None
D. Oxacillin‡	Liver and kidney	
E. Penicillin (low dose)‡	Kidney	
II. Minor Alteration—Necessary only with severe renal impairment (creatinine clearance < 10 ml/min)		
A. Chloramphenicol §	Liver	
B. Cephalothin	Kidney and liver	In anuric patients give full dose on first day followed
C. Lincomycin	Kidney and liver	by half dose thereafter
D. Methicillin‡	Kidney	
E. Ampicillin‡	Kidney	
III. Moderate Alteration—Give full loading dose on first day		
A. Penicillin (high dose)	Kidney	With severe azotemia or anuria give 1/2 dose for 2-3
B. Tetracycline‡	Kidney	days
IV. Major Alteration—Give full loading dose on first day followed by:		
A. Cephaloridine†	Kidney	1. Normal or slightly reduced dose if creatinine clearance > 30 ml/min and blood urea nitrogen < 50
B. Kanamycin*†	Kidney	
C. Polymixin B*	Kidney	2. Half dose each day if creatinine clearance 10-30 ml/min and BUN > 50
D. Colistin*	Kidney	
E. Streptomycin†	Kidney	3. Half dose for 2-3 day if creatinine clearance < 10 ml/min or BUN > 80
F. Gentamicin†	Kidney	
V. Do Not Give		
A. Furadantin	Kidney	
B. Nalidixic acid	Kidney	
C. Sulfonamides	Kidney	
D. Methenamine	Kidney	

*Significant removal by peritoneal dialysis.
†Significant removal by hemodialysis: >25% arteriovenous difference.
‡Not appreciably removed by dialysis.
§Significant removal by hemodialysis: 15-25% arteriovenous difference.

penicillin in the newborn may result in central nervous system irritation with myoclonic jerks and convulsions.

Young children, in general, appear to be relatively free from the otoxic and nephrotoxic effects of the aminoglycoside antibiotics (streptomycin, kanamycin, and gentamicin); therefore, these drugs are used commonly in the treatment of gram-negative enteric bacilli, the predominant pathogens in newborn sepsis.

REFERENCES

Eichenwald, H. F. Some observations on dosage and toxicity of kanamycin in premature and full term infants. Ann. N.Y. Acad. Sci., 132:984, 1966.

Finegold, S. M., Davis, A., Ziment, I., and Jacobs, I. Chemotherapy guide. Calif. Med., III:362-387, 1969.

Gill, F. A., and Hook, E. W. Changing patterns of bacterial resistance to antimicrobial drugs. Amer. J. Med., 39:780-795, 1965.

Grossman, M. Antimicrobial therapy in the newborn infant. Pediat. Clin. N. Amer., 15:157-166, 1968.

Kunin, C. M. A guide to use of antibiotics in patients with renal disease. Ann. Intern. Med., 67:151-158, 1967.

Lynn, B. Antibacterial action of the penicillins. J. Pharm. Sci., 201:307-312, 341-344, 1968.

McCracken, G. H., Eichenwald, H. F., and Nelson, J. D. Antimicrobial therapy in theory and practice. I. Clinical pharmacology. J. Pediat., 75:742, 1969.

———— Eichenwald, H. F., and Nelson, J. D. Antimicrobial therapy in theory and practice. II. Clinical approach to antimicrobial therapy. J. Pediat., 75:923, 1969.

McDermott, W. Microbial persistence. Yale J. Biol. Med., 30:257, 1958.

Mortimer, E. A., Jr. Rational use of prophylactic antibiotics in children. Pediat. Clin. N. Amer., 15:261, 1968.

Novick, R. P. Penicillinase plasmids of Staphylococcus aureus. Fed. Proc., 27:29-38, 1967.

Petersdorf, R. G., and Sherris, J. C. Methods and significance of *in vitro* testing of bacterial sensitivity to drugs. Amer. J. Med., 39:766-779, 1965.

Smith, D. H. The current status of R factors. Ann. Intern. Med., 67:1337-1341, 1967.

Weinstein, L. Chemotherapy of microbial diseases. *In* Goodman, L. S., and Gilman, A., eds., The Pharmacological Basis of Therapeutics, 4th ed. New York, The Macmillan Co., 1970, Section XIV, pp. 1154-1343.

Weisblum, B., and Davies, J. Antibiotic inhibitors of the bacterial ribosome. Bact. Rev., 32:493-528, 1968.

14.2
SEPSIS NEONATORUM

HEINZ F. EICHENWALD and
GEORGE H. McCRACKEN, JR.

The term "sepsis neonatorum" refers to a bacterial disease of infants occurring during the first 30 days of life which involves primarily the bloodstream and frequently the meninges. Not included in this definition are simple bacteremias or septicemias following major diseases such as severe diarrhea, debilitating surgery, and massive pyoderma, or those found in infants with major congenital anomalies. Since the initial focus from which the bloodstream is invaded is not determinable in a majority of cases, the term "neonatal sepsis of obscure origin" is used interchangeably with "sepsis neonatorum."

INCIDENCE. There has been little change in the incidence of sepsis neonatorum since the introduction of antimicrobial therapy. The rate of occurrence differs among hospitals, depending, in part at least, on such factors as obstetric and nursery practices, prenatal care, the health and nutrition of the mother, and the incidence of prematurity. Furthermore, even in the same hospital, the incidence may vary greatly from year to year for reasons which are not usually apparent. Over a recent 10-year span, the average annual rate of sepsis neonatorum in a modern North American hospital was found to be approximately 1 in 1,000 live births, but the risk to premature infants increased to 1 case in 230 premature births.

Other predisposing factors include premature rupture of the amniotic membranes, particularly when associated with amnionitis; various obstetric complications such as maternal bleeding, toxemia, precipitous deliveries, and ceasarean sections; and postmaturity. The incidence of the disease is considerably higher in male infants.

ETIOLOGY. In recent decades there has been a steady and consistent increase in the proportion of neonatal sepsis due to gram-negative organisms. The distribution of etiologic agents varies from year to year and from institution to institution, but, in general, *E. coli* strains account for approximately half the cases with *Klebsiella*-enterobacter and *Pseudomo*-

nas forming the bulk of the remaining causative gram-negative bacteria. Occasionally, *Proteus* species, *Salmonella,* and *H. influenzae* are encountered.

Gram-positive bacteria associated with neonatal sepsis include *Staphylococcus aureus, Staphylococcus epidermis,* beta hemolytic streptococci (predominantely Group B), *Streptococcus fecalis,* and occasionally *D. pneumoniae.*

Among the bacteriologically less familiar organisms occasionally involved are *Vibrio fetus, mimea* species, *Listeria, Achromobacter,* and *Flavobacterium.*

PATHOGENESIS. An unknown but probably substantial proportion of cases of sepsis neonatorum originates in utero, following the so-called "amniotic infection syndrome," a relatively poorly understood pathologic entity. Infection may gain access to the amniotic sac before or after rupture of membranes; the fetus may then aspirate infected fluid, resulting in congenital pneumonia and sepsis. Alternatively, bacteria may reach the fetal circulation following invasion of the decidua from the amniotic cavity. Despite the obvious etiologic importance of amniotic infection, most infants born from mothers with proved amnionitis escape disease entirely. Nonetheless, attempts have been made to identify early cases of the "amniotic infection syndrome" by histologic or cytologic study of placental or cord sections and of whole amnion mounts, or by obtaining cultures from the external ear canal and gastric contents of newborn infants. In general, these methods have not proved useful in reliably selecting infants at risk.

Vibrio fetus and listeria are capable of transplacental passage; this route of infection is otherwise unusual.

After birth, bacteria may gain access to the baby's circulation from a variety of sites and in various ways. Infection may originate in the skin, the umbilical stump, the mucous membranes of the eye, nose, pharynx, ear, and in respiratory, urinary, and gastrointestinal tracts. However, it is usually impossible to identify the site of initial invasion because there may be little local inflammatory response. The only exception is found in infants developing sepsis after the first week of life; in this group, a fairly high incidence of urologic congenital malformations with associated urinary tract infection can be identified.

The organisms causing sepsis in the baby can be acquired originally from innumerable sources: the mother's vaginal tract; the infant's attendants; other infants via airborne spread; contaminated medicaments or ointments applied to the infant's skin, umbilicus, or mucous membranes; or, in the case of bacteria which commonly contaminate water reservoirs, from oxygen therapy and humidifying equipment, soap dispensers, and sink traps.

The factors which contribute to the increased incidence of sepsis during the newborn period, and specifically those which result in a predominance of gram-negative disease, are unknown. No single immunologic mechanism or defect appears responsible.

DIAGNOSIS. Onset may be as early as the first day, or at anytime thereafter. In general, infants with perinatal complications develop sepsis earlier than those without this history. The clinical picture of sepsis neonatorum is usually diffuse, nonspecific, and obscure, particularly among premature infants. The two most common manifestations are failure to thrive and nonspecific respiratory distress. Other patients may show one or several of the following signs and symptoms: pallor, apnea, cyanosis, hypothermia, fever, convulsions, bulging fontanel, anemia, jaundice, splenomegaly, hepatomegaly, vomiting, abdominal distension, and diarrhea. In babies maintained in incubators, fever or hypothermia may be manifested only by the requirement for frequent readjustment of incubator temperature after initial stabilization had been achieved. The so-called "classic triad" of neonatal sepsis (bleeding, splenomegaly, and sclerema) is now rarely observed and then only late in the course of illness. Thus, sepsis must be suspected not only in infants with some of these signs and symptoms, but more importantly, in others with obscure illnesses and those who are just not doing well.

A few microorganisms occasionally are associated with more distinctive clinical patterns. For example, *Pseudomonas* sepsis may produce necrotic purplish skin lesions with the appearance of a septic infarct. *Vibrio fetus* results in a fulminant meningoencephalitis. Listeria infection causes a generalized miliary granulomatosis often associated with bronchopneumonia and meningitis; granulomata may be present on the skin and mucous membranes. A peculiar erysypeloid indurated orange-red rash is characteristic of achromobacter.

LABORATORY DIAGNOSIS. Detection of bacteria in the blood or spinal fluid of the patient represents the only reliable criterion for diagnosis. Samples of spinal fluid should be stained and examined, and cultured whether or not white cells are seen; it is not uncommon in early illness for considerable numbers of bacteria to be present without a cellular reaction. However, blood or spinal fluid cultures are not uniformly positive in sepsis neonatorum; thus a considerable proportion of cases can only be considered "suspect." On the other hand, for a variety of technical reasons, the incidence of contaminated blood cultures is high during the newborn period, and this factor must also be evaluated during the diagnostic process. Additional sites and materials that should be cultured include the umbilical stump, skin lesions, mucous membranes, and urine (preferably obtained by suprapubic bladder puncture). In those instances where intrauterine infection is suspected and the pediatrician is present at the time of delivery, cultures of the external ear canal, skin of the infant, and cord blood obtained under sterile conditions may be useful in selecting therapy if the infant becomes ill.

Other laboratory aids are of relatively little help in the diagnosis of sepsis; the hemogram may be normal or show varying degrees of anemia, leucocytosis, or leucopenia. Leucopenia is frequently associated with high mortality. Platelet concentration may be decreased. Urine examination may or may not show albuminuria, cells, and/or casts. Direct hyperbilirubinemia is frequently seen in systemic infections of the newborn; however, elevation of the indirect fraction with or without direct hyperbilirubinemia occurs. Blood glucose levels may be severely depressed, occasionally elevated, or entirely normal.

DIFFERENTIAL DIAGNOSIS. The often vague and uncertain signs and symptoms of neonatal sepsis resemble those of a variety of infectious, hematologic, metabolic, or congenital conditions. Among these are congenital viral infections and toxoplasmosis, intracranial bleeding, idiopathic hypoglycemia of infancy, congenital heart disease, adrenal insufficiency, and hemolytic diseases of the newborn. Thus, since accurate clinical diagnosis is rarely possible, sepsis must be considered a possibility in any infant not doing well.

COMPLICATIONS. Since sepsis neonatorum is a generalized infection, many organs or systems may become involved. Meningitis is a common and frequently silent complication, with a prolonged clinical course and disastrous long-term effects on central nervous system function.

Pyarthrosis may involve any joint; in premature infants, septic infection localizes particularly frequently in the hip. The area of swelling is usually indurated but rarely inflamed and thus often mistaken for simple edema. Other organs affected may include the lungs, kidneys, bones, pericardium, myocardium, peritoneum, and parotids.

Shock is a common complication of sepsis. Since blood pressures are infrequently recorded in infants and other signs and symptoms are often subtle, this complication often remains unrecognized. Hypotension may also occur secondary to adrenal insufficiency.

THERAPY. Early diagnosis and prompt treatment of neonatal sepsis are essential. Because the etiologic agent is usually unknown at the time therapy is begun, proper selection of antimicrobial agents is based on knowledge of the pathogens most commonly encountered and their anticipated antimicrobial susceptibilities. In most areas of the United States, *E. coli* and *Klebsiella*-enterobacter species account for approximately 75 percent of cases of sepsis and/or meningitis in the newborn period. Group B and D streptococci and *Listeria monocytogenes* account for a significant portion of the remaining cases. Therefore, penicillin G and kanamycin are used as initial therapy. In those areas where a significant proportion of kanamycin-resistant, gram-negative organisms is encountered, gentamicin and penicillin G would provide logical therapy. However, the long-term toxicity of gentamicin in infants is not yet known; thus the drug should be used with some caution. Once the pathogen is identified and its drug susceptibilities are known, the most appropriate antimicrobial agent should be given parenterally for a minimum of 10 days. In those instances when antimicrobial agents are administered to high-risk infants with no objective evidence of bacterial disease, therapy need be administered for only 3 to 5 days.

Guidelines for determining duration of therapy are often lacking in the neonatal period since objective evidence of illness may be minimal. Culture of the blood and, if indicated, examination and culture of the spinal fluid should be repeated approximately 36 hours after initiation of therapy. If these cultures are positive, therapy should be altered. In the absence of deep tissue involvement or abscess formation, treatment is usually continued from 5 to 7 days after clinical improvement. When multiple organs are involved or clinical response is slow, it may be necessary to continue therapy for 2 or 3 weeks, rarely longer.

When epidemiologic or clinical signs suggest staphylococcal or pseudomonas infection, a different antibiotic regimen must be used. For staphylococcal infections, parenteral methicillin is administered until susceptibility studies have been completed. If the organism is susceptible to penicillin G, this agent is substituted. For suspected pseudomonas infection, intramuscular polymyxin B, colistinethate, or gentamicin is given; in occasional proved cases, carbenicillin is useful.

Once the etiologic agent has been identified, there is no advantage to the use of multiple antimicrobal agents, with the exception of penicillin with kanamycin for enterococcal infections. Specifically, nothing is gained by adding chloramphenicol, tetracycline, erythromycin, or other bacteriostatic agents to the various regimens outlined. Indeed, there is evidence to suggest that use of these agents may decrease the efficacy of the preferred bactericidal drugs, as well as expose the infant to additional hazards of drug toxicity.

SUPPORTIVE THERAPY. In general, it is desirable to observe newborns with septicemia in an incubator. This permits adequate observation and stabilizes the infant's temperature. Oxygen should be administered when the infant shows respiratory distress or cyanosis.

Maintenance of adequate fluid and electrolyte balance is accomplished by intravenous fluids during the early part of illness. As soon as possible, oral feedings should be resumed in order to provide necessary calories.

In infants with hypotension or shock, fresh whole blood or plasma is often necessary if there are no signs of disseminated intravascular clotting. An arterial catheter is useful to monitor blood pressure and to administer volume expanders. Sympathomimetic agents are usually not useful and corticosteroids have not been evaluated adequately enough in infants to be recommended, unless there are signs of adrenal insufficiency.

Hemoglobin concentration, blood urea nitrogen concentration, and urinalyses for cells and protein should be serially determined in every infant receiving kanamycin, the polymyxins, or the antistaphylococcal penicillins.

REFERENCES

Beutow, K. C., Klein, S. W., and Lane, R. B. Septicemia in premature infants. Amer. J. Dis. Child., 110:29-41, 1965.
Gluck, L., Wood, H. F. and Fousek, M. D. Septicemia of the newborn. Pediat. Clin. N. Amer., 13:1131-1148, 1966.
Gotoff, S. P., and Behrman, R. E. Neonatal septicemia. J. Pediat., 76:142-153, 1970.
McCracken, G. H., and Shinefield, H. R. Changes in the pattern of neonatal septicemia and meningitis. Amer. J. Dis. Child., 112:33-39, 1966.

14.3
BACTERIAL MENINGITIS

ARNOLD H. EINHORN

Inflammation of the meninges may follow the invasion of the spinal fluid by any one of a wide range of infectious agents. All varieties of bacterial meningitis occur more frequently in infants and children than in adults. Only bacterial infection due to pyogenic organisms will be dscussed here. Tuberculous meningitis will be described separately (p. 671). Although mortality rates have been altered dramatically as a result of the introduction of antibacterial therapy, pyogenic meningitides are still among the most serious infections encountered in pediatrics. Moreover, there are no effective measures available for their prevention.

The proportion of cases due to different organisms varies from year to year; there are also considerable geographic differences. In the absence of meningococcus epidemics, bacterial meningitis in infants and children is due predominantly to *Haemophilus influenzae*. Next in frequency are those caused by *Diplococcus pneumoniae* and *Neisseria meningitidis*. In the first month of life, gram-negative bacilli of enteric origin are more common; among the latter the colon bacillus holds first place. The unusual *Pseudomonas aeruginosa* (*pyocyaneus*) and *Proteus* meningitides follow, in general, diagnostic or surgical procedures, or spinal anesthesia. Staphylococcal meningitis is uncommon even in the newborn period. Sporadic cases or small outbreaks of *alpha* or *beta hemolytic streptococcus* meningitis occur, although very rarely, in the newborn nurseries. Isolated instances of meningitides due to *Listeria monocytogenes* have also been reported in the neonatal period; the morphologic similarity of these gram-positive, rod-shaped bacteria to nonpathogenic diphtheroids may constitute a difficulty in bacteriologic diagnosis. There has been an increasing number of reports of meningeal infections involving simultaneously two or more organisms. These *mixed bacterial meningitides* have their highest incidence in young infants. In approximately 15 to 20 percent of patients whose cerebrospinal findings indicate the presence of pyogenic meningitis, it is not possible to demonstrate any etiologic agent. Some of these may represent sympathetic meningitis; in others the organism had probably been suppressed by treatment administered earlier.

By and large, the clinical picture, pathologic lesions, and prognosis in pyogenic meningitis depend more upon the age of the patient, the duration of infection, and the kind of treatment the patient has received than upon the etiologic agent. Therefore, pyogenic meningitis will be discussed as a syndrome, the peculiar features of specific infections being pointed out where necessary.

PATHOLOGY. The typical pathologic picture in a patient who dies from pyogenic meningitis is seen today only in those who receive inadequate or late treatment. The reader is referred to pathologic texts for the great variety of lesions which may be found in the untreated disease.

The pathologic lesions which concern us here are those found early in the infection. It is important to recognize the clinical signs they produce and to define their cause while they are still reversible.

The common varieties of bacterial meningitis most often evolve from a metastatic lesion seeded during bacteremia, although they may result from an extension from a purulent regional focus such as otitis media, mastoiditis, or sinusitis. There is reason to believe that endothelial damage of cerebral vessels precedes meningitis caused by meningococcus or *H. influenzae,* and that the degree of vascular damage determines whether the patient will exhibit signs of encephalitis in addition to signs of meningitis. Thrombosis of small cerebral as well as meningeal vessels is found in some cases. In general, pneumococcal or *E. coli* meningitis of infants also appears to evolve from a metastatic lesion. However, staphylococcal meningitis is often secondary to a contiguous focus in all age groups. In the older child, as in the adult, meningitis caused by pneumococcus type III or beta hemolytic streptococcus is most frequently due to extension from a neighboring infection. Regardless of whether meningitis evolves from a metastatic lesion or from a neighboring focus, a respiratory infection nearly always initiates the process. In general, a febrile upper respiratory infection is followed by bacteremia of varying duration before invasion of the spinal fluid.

CLINICAL FEATURES. Since survival in pyogenic meningitis and residual sequelae depend not only on appropriate therapy but also on the early institution of treatment, the importance of early recognition of the meningeal infection cannot be overstressed.

In older children, headache and photophobia are often presenting complaints. Fever, vomiting, often projectile in type, and convulsions are common symptoms. In some instances persistent fever may be the only objective sign of illness. If the meningitis is not recognized and antibiotics or sulfonamides are given in doses inadequate for elimination of the infectious agent, most of the signs of meningeal inflammation and of increased intracranial pressure will be masked. These symptoms and signs are also frequently absent in children with fulminant disease.

In untreated patients older than 6 or 7 months, clinical signs of early meningeal inflammation are easily detected. These consist of hyperesthesia, pain and resistance on flexion of the neck, and positive Kernig and Brudzinski signs. Except for transient delirium, the sensorium is clear at the onset. In infants, nuchal rigidity is most often absent and the only specific feature of meningitis may be the increased tension or bulging of the anterior fontanel due to increased intracranial pressure.

The elevation of intracranial pressure in acute meningitis is partly due to impaired circulation of cerebrospinal fluid by purulent material, to cerebral edema, and probably to accrued cerebrospinal fluid production secondary to inflammation. In spite of the increased intracranial pressure, papilledema is rare early in the course of pyogenic meningitis. Blurring of the disk margins may be seen but without definite edema. Whenever papilledema is present early in the course of acute bacterial meningitis, the existence of an associated intracranial complication should be suspected, such as subdural empyema, brain abscess, or sinus thrombosis. Because of the heightened intracranial pressure, it is well to measure carefully the cerebrospinal fluid pressure when performing a lumbar puncture in meningitis, and to remove the fluid very slowly using a small gauge needle in order to minimize the danger of brain stem and temporal lobe herniation.

Petechial or purpuric lesions are most commonly present in meningococcal infection, but can be associated with sepsis and meningitis due to any other organisms. They have no particular characteristic distribution and are occasionally bullous or necrotic. In severe meningococcal infections with bacteremia, petechial lesions may appear and symptoms of shock (the Waterhouse-Friderichsen syndrome, p. 624) may develop with alarming rapidity before clinical signs of meningitis are detectable. There is reason to believe that these patients suffer from widespread effects of the bacterial endotoxins and of diffuse intravascular coagulation.

In the young infant less than 6 months of age, particularly in infants of 2 or 3 months or less, the clinical diagnosis of early meningitis may be a major problem. The clinical signs of meningeal irritation which are relied on in older subjects may not be found until the meningitis is well advanced, and different criteria must be used. In infants of *2 or 3 months or more,* fever is almost always present. Distention of the fontanel, if present, is a valuable sign. If the fontanel is too small or if dehydration prevents development of fullness of the fontanel, other manifestations should serve to arouse suspicion: unexplained fever, projectile vomiting, alternating drowsiness and irritability, a vacant stare, a high-pitched cry, and sometimes the presence of cranial bruits. In infants *less than* 2 or 3 months of age, fever is often absent. Hypothermia, cyanosis, jaundice, poor feeding, poor activity, irregular breathing, and unusual jitteriness or drowsiness are the signs which may point to meningitis. Sudden enlargement of the head over a 24-hour period may also constitute an important clue. Because the early recognition of meningitis in the young infant is so difficult, it is recommended that the spinal fluid be examined in all young infants with unexplained fever and in infants less than 3 months in the presence of any unusual symptom of illness.

The severity of the meningeal infection and of the accompanying cerebral involvement correlate fairly closely with the rapidity of progression of symptoms following onset. Convulsions, stupor, or coma appearing within the first 24 hours, often accompanied by high fever, indicate a serious infection. In view of the frequent association of convulsions with the onset of meningitis, a lumbar puncture should be performed in all patients with "febrile convulsions" occurring for the first time. The cerebrospinal fluid when first examined may show a very low sugar concentration of less than 15 mg per 100 ml and numerous organisms on direct smear (see below). Complete recovery may ensue if adequate therapy is applied immediately, even though the course during treatment may be alarming and marked by irritative phenomena or localized cerebral dysfunction such as hemiplegia or facial paralysis. In uncomplicated meningitis, early appearing focal cerebral signs and seizures can be related to cortical necrosis or occlusive phlebitis or arteritis. In most patients the sensorium clears markedly within 24 hours after institution of treatment, organisms are promptly eliminated from the spinal fluid, and the sugar concentration rises significantly.

Persistence of fever, stupor, and focal signs of cerebral irritation such as involuntary muscle movements and localized muscle weakness are not incompatible with eventual full recovery. In general, however, the longer such signs last, the more unfavorable the outlook. Prominent and persisting focal cerebral signs always raise the question of an associated focal process such as subdural effusion, subdural empyema, brain abscess, or a cerebral embolism produced by a bacterial endocarditis. Occasionally a patient with meningitis caused by *H. influenzae* progresses rapidly downhill despite early therapy, the cause of death remaining obscure even after autopsy.

ETIOLOGIC DIAGNOSIS. *Clinical Clues.* Bacteriologic identification of the organism causing meningitis is essential in order to select optimal therapy. It has been mentioned previously that the clinical signs depend more on the stage and severity of the meningitis, the child's age, and amount of treatment given, than on the type of infectious agent. However, certain clinical features may suggest the nature of the infectious agent.

H. influenzae type b meningitis is unusual in infants less than 2 months old. Its incidence is highest during the remainder of infancy and in early childhood; it declines to very low levels in the preschool and school-age child. In the United States *H. influenzae* is by far the commonest etiologic agent responsible for bacterial meningitis in children between 6 months and 3 years of age. In almost all cases the *H. influenzae* strains are type b. The majority of patients with *E. coli, Pseudomonas,* or *Salmonella* meningitis are less than 1 month of age. Enteric bacteria cause meningitis so rarely in older children that a congenital dermal sinus or immunologic defect should be suspected. Meningitis due to *Staphylococcus aureus,* a rare form of bacterial meningitis confined mostly to the neonatal period, may also be associated with communicating dermal sinuses or may follow neurosurgical procedures.

Most patients who develop *Diplococcus pneumoniae* meningitis are less than 6 months of age. The occasional older child, without sickle-cell disease or a

TABLE 6.   *Differential Diagnostic Features of Cerebrospinal Fluid in Meningitis*

Type of Meningitis	Cell Count	Predominant Cytology	Chemistry	
			Sugar	Protein
Sympathetic	low	Polymorphonuclear	Normal	+
Pyogenic	high	Polymorphonuclear	Low*	++++
Tuberculosis	moderate to high	Mononuclear	Low	+ to ++++
Lead Encephalitis	low	Mononuclear	Normal	++ to ++++
Viral Meningitis	low to moderate	Mononuclear†	Normal	+ to +++

*May be normal or only slightly reduced in early mild pyogenic meningitis.
†An early polymorphonuclear reaction is not uncommon.

history of head trauma, who develops pneumococcal (especially type III) or hemolytic streptococcal meningitis is usually found to have a purulent otitis media, mastoiditis, or lobar pneumonia. *D. pneumoniae* is the organism involved at any age in recurrent meningitides which result from basal skull fractures, particularly those with fractures of the cribriform plate of the ethmoid. There is also a higher incidence of pneumococcal meningitis in infants and children with sickle-cell anemia.

Petechial skin lesions suggest *Neisseria meningitidis,* although not all children with this variety of meningitis have petechiae; in a Baltimore epidemic only 25 percent of the infants and children showed this sign. The association of petechiae and purulent meningitis is by no means diagnostic of meningococcal disease only, for they can occur, although less commonly, with sepsis due to other organisms.

Swelling of one or several joints, particularly of the small joints of the hands or feet, may be associated early in the disease with the invasion of the bloodstream by *Neisseria meningitidis* or *H. influenzae.* In meningococcal meningitis a sterile effusion develops occasionally in a single large joint late in the course of the illness. However, purulent arthritides can occur, although rarely, as a septicemic complication of any form of bacterial meningitis.

Laboratory Findings. Only by examination of the cerebrospinal fluid can a definitive diagnosis of the meningitis be established and the etiologic agent identified. Cultures of blood and spinal fluid must also be obtained before antimicrobial therapy is instituted on any patient suspected of having meningitis. If petechiae are present, gram-stained smear of the scrapings from these lesions will frequently provide the bacteriologic diagnosis.

Specific differences in the type of spinal fluid cytology, in the number of cells, and in the concentration of sugar and protein characteristic of the various types of central nervous system infections are outlined in Table 6. A mononuclear cell response and normal concentration of sugar suggest a viral infection. In viral meningitides the spinal fluid cells are predominantly mononuclear within 24 to 48 hours after the onset of illness, although a transient polymorphonuclear preponderance is commonly seen at the early stage of the aseptic meningitis. In lead encephalitis, the findings are not unlike those seen in some viral infections. When the concentration of protein is normal or only slightly elevated, lead encephalitis is less likely. The decreased spinal fluid sugar of 40 mg per 100 ml, or less than one-half the blood sugar, distinguishes tuberculous meningitis from viral infections and lead encephalopathy. In any patient with a positive skin reaction to tuberculin who shows an increased number of cells with mononuclear predominance and an abnormally low concentration of sugar in the spinal fluid, treatment for tuberculous meningitis in indicated after collection of appropriate fluids for culture. In sympathetic meningitis, which is an inflammatory reaction produced by a contiguous infection such as mastoiditis or sinusitis without invasion of the spinal fluid, there may be a mild polymorphonuclear reaction, and a slight protein elevation, while the sugar remains normal and the fluid sterile. In mild pyogenic meningitis the findings may be identical except for the growth of bacteria on culture of spinal fluid and occasionally the documentation of bacteria on smear.

Every effort should be exerted toward an immediate bacteriologic identification whenever there is a predominance of polymorphonuclear cells and a decrease in the sugar concentration in the spinal fluid of a patient. Organisms may be sufficiently numerous to be seen on microscopic examination of a gram-stained smear of the spinal fluid, or in the sediment after centrifugation. The morphology of the bacteria on a direct smear with methylene blue and, if possible, by Gram's method, provides important clues. In the case of *H. influenzae,* meningococci, and pneumococci, immediate proof can be obtained by demonstration of capsular swelling on exposure of the organism to type-specific antibody. Thus in the presence of gram-negative pleomorphic rods which suggest *H. influenzae,* the capsular swelling test confirms this impression and immediately excludes other gram-negative bacilli, such as *E. coli, Salmonella,* and *Pseudomonas.*

The concentration of sugar in the spinal fluid *

---

* *Rapid semiquantitative screening tests for estimating the approximate concentration of spinal fluid sugar are valuable diagnostic aids in emergency situations. They are simple, quickly performed, and require only minute amounts of fluid.*

1. Screening test using Benedict's solution: One ml of qualitative Benedict's solution is placed in each of a series of 6 tubes of 75 x 12 mm size. The following volumes (ml) of spinal fluid are added to tubes 1 through 5: 0.05, 0.1, 0.15, 0.20, and 0.25. The sixth tube serves as control. The tubes are immersed in a boiling water bath for 10 minutes, after which the degree of reduction (presence of yellow pigment, varying from green to orange) is read in a bright light.

The sugar concentration may then be estimated as shown.

Tube Number	CSF Vol. (ml)	Reduction of Benedict's Solution				
1	0.05	+	0	0	0	0	0
2	0.1	+	+	0	0	0	0
3	0.15	+	+	+	0	0	0
4	0.2	+	+	+	+	0	0
5	0.25	+	+	+	+	+	0
6	0.00	0	0	0	0	0	0
Sugar concentration in mg/100 ml		>50	40-50	30-40	20-30	10-20	<15

2. Screening test using rapid enzyme-strips: This procedure developed by Cornblath and his group is a modification of the standard reagent strip (Dextrostix) technique.

With the aid of a microbulb, one drop of spinal fluid is applied to the reactive end of a reagent strip, allowed to stand for the three minutes, and then washed off with 5 N sodium hydroxide (NaOH) (20%). The orange color which develops is compared to a color chart prepared from plasma standards of known glucose concentrations. The color change produced is permanent and the reagent strip can be made part of the hospital record.

serves as a major guide in differentiating between bacterial and viral infection. It also offers a good index of severity of infection and its response to treatment; the lower the concentration, the more severe the infection. However, in mild pyogenic meningitis, spinal fluid sugar may be only slightly decreased or even normal. In overwhelming pneumococcal infection of the newborn, organisms may be present without cellular response or a decrease in glucose. On the other hand, low spinal fluid sugar has been reported in mumps meningoencephalitis.

In patients who respond to therapy, recovery from infection is accompanied by a prompt rise in the concentration of sugar to normal levels. However, in some young infants, the sugar may not respond in this fashion. Although the culture of the spinal fluid is found to be sterile within 24 hours after therapy is started, the sugar concentration continues below normal for several weeks or even longer. The blood sugar level is normal in these infants; and when the blood sugar is raised by intravenous injection of glucose, the spinal fluid sugar concentration measured at varying intervals thereafter shows some rise, but not to normal levels. These findings suggest that the infection has injured the transport mechanism.

The cause for the low spinal fluid sugar in bacterial meningitis was initially attributed to utilization of glucose by the bacteria. This explanation is no longer accepted. On the basis of experimental data, it has been postulated that the low spinal fluid sugar in bacterial meningitis results from a combination of increased cerebral glucose utilization secondary to increased glycolysis, and a defective glucose transport. **TREATMENT.** The application of the following principles will increase the probability of complete recovery in patients suffering from the common varieties of pyogenic meningitis:

1. Prompt identification of the infecting organism
2. Early intravenous administration of antibacterial therapy
3. Adoption of a therapeutic program designed for both rapid destruction of bacteria and suppression of emergence of resistant strains
4. Avoidance of toxic therapeutic agents
5. Recognition and treatment of hyponatremia

Dosage and route of administration must be planned to attain maximally effective concentrations in the spinal fluid as promptly as possible and to maintain these levels until viable organisms are eliminated. Antibiotics such as penicillin G, and the semisynthetic penicillins including ampicillin, and kanamycin diffuse poorly into the spinal fluid if the meninges are intact. Passage of most antibiotics with a *high* blood-brain barrier, i.e., which cross the brain barrier with difficulty, becomes significantly greater when the meninges are inflamed. In the case of penicillin and ampicillin, because of their relatively low toxicity, the limited diffusion can be overcome by using very large doses intravenously. These large doses are in the range of 6 to 12 million units daily for penicillin; for ampicillin 300 to 400 mg per kg per day. Under these circumstances, the concentration of the antimicrobial agent in the spinal fluid becomes bactericidal for organisms such as pneumococci, meningococci, hemolytic streptococci, and *H. influenzae.*

The therapeutic programs which may be used for the most frequently occurring varieties of pyogenic meningitis are outlined in Table 7. It is possible for a competent microbiologist to identify the etiologic agent by direct examination of the spinal fluid. However, this type of expert individual is rarely present or available at the time of the patients' admission, which makes a diagnosis from direct smear presumptive, at best. Consequently the initial therapeutic program in meningeal infections should be one which is as effective as possible against *all* the most common etiologic agents. Such a treatment regimen is outlined under the heading "Undetermined Etiology" in Table 7. Once the culture demonstrates the causative organism, the therapeutic program is adjusted accordingly. Otherwise the initial therapy is continued.

All patients with pyogenic meningitis are best treated with antibacterial agents by continued intravenous route for at least 10 days; longer if the patient remains febrile or even mildly symptomatic. Treatment of meningococcal meningitis can be discontinued earlier, usually after 7 days if the patient is clinically well, and the spinal fluid normal.

Therapeutic agents which are injurious to the patient should not be used when others which are safe are equally effective. Consequently there is virtually no indication for streptomycin in the treatment of pyogenic meningitis. With the increased emergence of resistant strains of meningococci, the use of sulfonamides in the treatment of meningococcal disease is contraindicated. Furthermore it is pointless to include sulfonamides in any combined therapy regimen for meningitis since this would expose the patient to the hazards of increased potential drug toxicity. The use of polymyxin should be limited to *Pseudomonas* meningitis; neomycin should be used only in proved *Proteus* meningitis. Because of its toxicity, chloramphenicol, which has been so effective in the treatment of *H. influenzae* meningitis, has been abandoned in favor of ampicillin as the first agent in the treatment of disease due to this organism. Chloramphenicol is still useful as an alternate in those cases where the patient is allergic to ampicillin.

The use of combined antibiotic therapy, when the etiologic agent is unknown, is no longer necessary except in the newborn. The degree of antimicrobial activity of antibiotic mixtures expected to exert a broad-spectrum effect is frequently unpredictable. It may be additive, reduced, or no greater than the most active drug in the combination. In some instances, the results of combining antibiotics are clearly inferior to those which follow the use of a single agent.

Ampicillin, presently the antibiotic of choice against *H. influenzae,* is also an excellent alternate

TABLE 7. *Recommended Treatment for Pyogenic Meningitis*

Organism	Drug	Initial Dose	Maintenance
Undetermined Etiology > 2 months of age	Ampicillin	Ampicillin: 150 mg/kg, iv in 30 minutes in saline solution, 3 ml/100 mg of drug	If organism remains unidentified: Ampicillin: 400 mg/kg in 6 divided doses, iv (dilute each 6-hour dose in 2 ml/kg solution and inject slowly) *Duration of Therapy:* 10 to 14 days
< 2 months	a. Ampicillin *and* b. Kanamycin* *or* Gentamicin†	a. Ampicillin: as above *and* b. Kanamycin: 7.5 mg/kg, im *or* Gentamicin: 2.5 mg/kg, im	a. Ampicillin: as above *and* b. Kanamycin: 15 mg/kg/day, in 2 divided doses, im *or* Gentamicin: 7.5 mg/kg/day in 4 divided doses, im‡ *Duration of therapy:* 14 days after spinal fluid is sterile If organism is identified, change to specific therapy outlined below:
Haemophilus influenzae	Ampicillin	Ampicillin: 150 mg/kg, iv in 30 minutes in saline solution, 3 ml/100 mg of drug	Ampicillin: 400 mg/kg in 6 divided doses, iv (dilute each 4-hour dose in 2 ml/kg solution and inject slowly) *Duration of therapy:* 10 to 14 days
Neisseria meningitidis	Penicillin	*Sodium* penicillin G: iv in 30 minutes in 50 ml/m² of saline < 1 yr: 100,000 U/kg 1-6 yr: 1,200,000 U 6-12 yr: 2,500,000 U	*Sodium* penicillin G: iv <1 yr: 250,000 U/kg/24 hr 1-5 yr: 2,500,000-5,000,000 U/24 hr 6-12 yr: 5,000,000-10,000,000 U/24 hr *Duration of therapy:* 7 days
Diplococcus pneumoniae or *Hemolytic streptococcus* (Group A)	Penicillin	*Sodium* penicillin G: iv in 30 minutes in 50 ml/m² of saline 1 yr: 100,000 U/kg 1-6 yr: 1,200,000 U 6-12 yr: 2,500,000 U	*Sodium* penicillin G: iv Dosage same as for *N. meningitidis* Duration: minimum 10 days after spinal fluid is sterile and patient clinically well

TABLE 7. *Recommended Treatment for Pyogenic Meningitis* (continued)

Organism	Drug	Initial Dose	Maintenance
Escherichia coli	Kanamycin*	Kanamycin: *im:* 7.5 mg/kg *Intrathecally:* 1.0 mg (in 0.85% NaCl solution) *or* Gentamicin: *im:* 2.5 mg/kg *Intrathecally:* (in 0.85% NaCl solution) < 2 yr: 1.0 mg > 2 yr: 2.0 mg	Kanamycin: *im:* 15 mg/kg/day in 2 divided doses *Intrathecally:* 1 mg once daily for 3 days (in 0.85% NaCl solution) *or* Gentamicin: *im:* 7.5 mg/kg/day in 4 divided doses‡ *Intrathecally:* (in 0.85% NaCl solution) < 2 yr: 1.0 mg/day > 2 yr: 2.0 mg/day *Duration of therapy:* at least 14 days after the child is well clinically, and spinal fluid is normal (except for moderate lymphocytosis)
	or Gentamicin		
Staphylococcus aureus	a. Methicillin	a. Methicillin: 150 mg/kg, iv in 3-4 ml/kg of saline over 30 minutes	a. Methicillin: *iv:* 400 mg/kg/day, in 6 divided doses for a minimum of 14 days after spinal fluid is sterile *po:* cloxacillin, 300 mg/kg in 4 divided doses for 14 days more *or*
	and b. Penicillin	*and* b. *Sodium* penicillin G: iv in 30 minutes in 50 ml/m² of saline < 1 yr: 100,000 U/kg 1-6 yr: 1,200,000 U 6-12 yr: 2,500,000 U	b. *Sodium* penicillin G (if organism sensitive to penicillin): *iv:* Dosage same as for *N. meningitidis* Duration: 14 days after spinal fluid is sterile; then if all clinical signs of disease have been absent for several days, change to: *po:* Penicillin V for 14 days more < 12 yr: 90,000 U/kg/24 hr, given in 6 divided doses > 12 yr: 6,000,000 U/24 hr, given in 6 divided doses *Duration of therapy:* minimum 28 days

TABLE 7. *Recommended Treatment for Pyogenic Meningitis* (continued)

Organism	Drug	Initial Dose	Maintenance

Salmonella	Chloramphenicol	Chloramphenicol succinate:
		iv:
		    <1 month: 25 mg/kg
		    >1 month: 50 mg/kg
		in 3-4 ml/kg of saline over 30 minutes
			Chloramphenicol succinate:
			iv:
			    <1 month: 50 mg/kg/day
			    >1 month: 100-150 mg/kg/day
			Duration of therapy: at least 14 days after spinal fluid is sterile; then after clinical improvement and spinal fluid has become normal (except for moderate lymphocytosis):
			po:
			    <1 month: 50/mg/kg/day
			    >1 month: 100/mg/kg/day for 7-10 days
			Duration of therapy: 20 days minimum

Pseudomonas aeruginosa (B. pyocyaneus)	Polymyxin B
	
	or
	
	Gentamicin
		Polymyxin B sulfate:
		iv: 1.0 mg/kg in saline solution (ratio: 1 mg/2ml)
		Intrathecally:
		(in 0.85% NaCl solution)
		    <2 yr: 1.0 mg
		    >2 yr: 2.0 mg
		or
		Gentamicin:
		im: 2.5 mg/kg
		Intrathecally:
		(in 0.85% NaCl solution)
		    <2 yr: 1.0 mg
		    >2 yr: 2.0 mg
			Polymyxin B sulfate:
			iv: 2.5 mg/kg/day in 3 divided doses into iv solution
			
			Intrathecally:
			(in 0.85% NaCl solution)
			    <2 yr: 1.0 mg/day
			    >2 yr: 2.0 mg/day
			or
			Gentamicin:
			im: 7.5 mg/kg/day in 4 divided doses‡
			Intrathecally:
			(in 0.85% NaCl solution)
			    <2 yr: 1.0 mg/day
			    >2 yr: 2.0 mg/day
			Duration of therapy: intravenous and/or intramuscular antibiotics are continued 14 days minimum *after* child is clinically well and spinal fluid normal (except for moderate lymphocytosis). *Intrathecal* therapy is given once daily for 3 days, then every other day until spinal fluid is normal.

*In some institutions *E. coli* has been reported to be resistant to Kanamycin, in which case Gentamicin should be used.

†Some authorities advocate intrathecal therapy as described under *E. coli* and Pseudomonas.

‡This dosage is higher than the generally accepted one of 5 mg/kg/day. It is recommended for severe infections on the basis of measured levels in serum, which should be determined together with close monitoring for renal and eighth nerve damage.

bactericidal agent against both the D. *pneumoniae* and *Neisseria meningococcus*. Consequently it is to be preferred as the single antimicrobial agent in older infants and children except in those who are hypersensitive to any of the penicillins, or if there is a strong possibility of an unusual causative organism. In the newborn and the very young infant the rationale for initial therapy with kanamycin and ampicillin is to ensure coverage against enteric bacteria, H. *influenzae,* and gram-positive and gram-negative cocci until the organism is identified.

The *intrathecal route* is seldom needed. The intravenous administration of appropriate antibiotics at dosages which are both safe and effective permits adequate concentrations to be attained within the cerebrospinal fluid within one hour after institution of therapy. Polymyxin B represents a notable exception in this respect. It diffuses poorly or not at all in the cerebrospinal fluid when given systemically in amounts which are reasonably safe. Consequently in meningitis due to pseudomonas, where polymyxin is used, the intrathecal route is indicated in addition to the intramuscular administration of this antimicrobial drug. Polymyxin E (colistimethate) should never be injected intrathecally.

Effectiveness of antimicrobial therapy will be reflected in the findings of the spinal fluid collected 24 hours following institution of therapy. With good response to treatment, the spinal fluid should be bacteriologically negative on direct stained smear and on culture, the glucose content increased, and the cytology show a marked shift from polymorphonuclear to mononuclear predominance. Total cell count and protein concentration may show an initial rise. A repeat lumbar puncture after 24 hours of therapy is desirable in all instances where the initial response to treatment is not satisfactorily dramatic. We strongly recommend that on every patient with pyogenic meningitis the spinal fluid be examined again on the day therapy is discontinued. Treatment should not be terminated unless the spinal fluid findings are negative except for the persistence of a lymphocyte count of less than 20.

Fluid Therapy; Prevention and Treatment of Hyponatremia. Severe hyponatremia accompanied by symptoms and signs of water intoxication may develop in the course of acute infections of the central nervous system. The hyponatremia of meningitis appears to be the result of inappropriate antidiuretic hormone secretion with ensuing water retention and to some extent losses of sodium in the urine. To prevent water intoxication, limitation of fluid intake during the acute phase of the illness is mandatory. Both the antibiotics and the daily requirements in electrolytes should be given in the smallest total amount of water possible. A total daily intake of approximately 1,000 to 1,200 ml per m² appears to be both safe and adequate. To achieve simultaneously the desired fluid restriction while providing the amount of sodium intake which is required, the antibiotics administered intravenously may be dissolved

in a mixture consisting of equal parts of 0.166 M sodium bicarbonate or lactate, normal saline, and 10 percent glucose. Subsequently the sodium content of the solution may be reduced by using 1 part of 0.166 M sodium lactate, 2 parts of normal saline, and 3 parts of 10 percent glucose. In the presence of severe symptoms of water intoxication, especially when convulsions occur, the patient requires treatment with hypertonic fluids: The administration of approximately 3 mEq of sodium chloride per kg, or .6 ml of 3 percent NaCl solution per kg, given over a period of 2 hours, appears to be both safe and effective.

Adrenal Corticosteroids; Treatment of Shock. Adrenal corticosteroids have been advocated as adjuncts to the antibacterial treatment of bacterial meningitis. Controlled trials with both small and large doses of corticosteroid failed to demonstrate any significant beneficial effect of steroid therapy. When shock is present, hydrocortisone in large doses should be given intravenously in combination with plasma. This recommendation is not based on the belief that meningococcemia and other severe bacterial infections cause a decrease in adrenal corticosteroid production. Available data indicate that, in fact, patients with severe and even fulminant meningococcemia, but without adrenal hemorrhage, may have normal or high levels of cortisol in the blood. Migeon has shown that fulminant meningococcemia with adrenal hemorrhage results in failure of adrenal function, concluding that such patients may require hormonal replacement therapy.

Shock due to bacterial endotoxins is due primarily to adverse effects on the circulation, with intravascular coagulation playing a role in some cases. These endotoxins produce at first prolonged vasoconstriction of arteries, arterioles, veins, venules, and capillaries. Vasodilation of arteries, arterioles, capillaries, and venules follows; the veins remain constricted. Blood pressure falls and blood flow to vital organs is diminished. Venous return to the heart is reduced, and cardiac output falls. Fluid goes from the capillaries into the tissues, decreasing the volume of circulating blood. When shock is severe or prolonged, it may become irreversible.

Results of experimental data in animals, and reports of beneficial effects in humans suggest that hydrocortisone in large doses of 25 to 50 mg per kg, given intravenously in a single injection, counteracts the vasoconstricting effects of the endotoxin and relieves effectively the shock. This therapy may be repeated in 1 or 2 hours, if indicated. Epinephrine and norepinephrine are contraindicated in the treatment of endotoxic shock since they only add to the vasoconstriction and decreased blood flow.

Additional Therapeutic Measures. Antipyretic medications are usually unnecessary. For marked hyperpyrexia, sponging with tepid water will help to reduce the body temperature. In the acutely ill patient, excessive temperature elevations may be forestalled by maintaining the patient in a cooled croupette tent.

The effect produced by intravenous urea, mannitol, or dexamethasone on the brain swelling of purulent meningitis is in general not as impressive as when the cerebral edema is associated with brain tumor, toxic encephalopathy, or cerebral trauma. However, dramatic improvement has occurred on occasion after administration of urea or mannitol in meningitis. Consequently their use is warranted in instances where the cerebral edema is progressing rapidly with signs of impending brain stem herniation, manifested by fixed pupils, disappearance of the "doll's eyes" phenomenon, decerebrate posturing or total flaccidity, and deteriorating respirations. Either osmotic agent is given intravenously over a 30-minute period: hypertonic urea as a 30 percent solution in 10 percent invert sugar, in a dosage of 0.5 to 1.0 g per kg; mannitol as a 10 to 15 percent solution at 1.0 to 2.0 g per kg of body weight. Less rebound occurs with the use of mannitol, which is therefore preferable to urea. If dexamethasone is used, the dosage is initially 0.2 to 0.4 mg per kg intravenously, followed by 0.1 to 0.2 mg per kg intramuscularly every 6 hours.

Heparin therapy has been recommended for the treatment of diffuse intravascular clotting associated with fulminant meningococcemia. Although the results have not been as encouraging as originally hoped, its use has not been abandoned pending further studies.

Convulsions, which frequently complicate the course of pyogenic meningitis, must be treated with appropriate anticonvulsant therapy (Sec. 15.9), and careful positioning of the patient to prevent aspiration. Phenobarbital alone or in combination with diphenylhydantoin, diphenylhydantoin alone, rectal paraldehyde, or Valium are usually effective in controlling the seizures. Once controlled, diphenylhydantoin should be continued by oral or intramuscular route throughout the entire illness.

In infants and children who appear seriously ill, we institute anticonvulsant therapy from the time of admission as a preventative measure. After an initial dose of phenobarbital combined with diphenylhydantoin, both at the dosage of 5 mg per kg, the patient is continued on maintenance therapy with diphenylhydantoin alone as during the acute phase of the illness. Whenever seizures appear during the course of the meningitis, water intoxication and subdural effusion should be suspected, and subdural taps are advisable, even on the first hospital day.

SUBDURAL EFFUSIONS COMPLICATING MENINGITIS. The frequency of this complication in the course of pyogenic meningitis was first pointed out by McKay and his associates. Subsequent investigators have confirmed the high incidence of this complication, approaching 50 percent in young infants in whom the subdural space is explored routinely. Recovery of 2 ml or more of xanthochromic fluid with a content of protein exceeding by 40 mg that of the spinal fluid is considered to indicate subdural effusion. The subdural fluid is either sterile and indistinguishable from that found in the later stages of a chronic subdural hematoma or may be purulent and yield on culture the same organism responsible for the meningitis.

Subdural effusions, extremely rare in meningococcal meningitis, most commonly accompany meningeal infections due to *H. influenzae* and *D. pneumoniae*. In several of our own patients with pyogenic meningitis, subdural empyema was present at the time, or within hours after the onset of symptoms. In all instances except one, the patients were infants less than 4 months of age; organisms involved were, in order of frequency: *D. pneumoniae, Salmonella,* and beta hemolytic streptococcus. Antibiotic levels determined by us on all fluids collected from the effusions consistently showed satisfactory levels.

The part played by subdural fluid collections in producing irreversible cerebral damage is a question which has stimulated great interest. Clinical signs of cortical injury can be found in children in whom no subdural fluid has been found. The majority of patients in whom an abnormal volume of subdural fluid is obtained have no clinical signs of cerebral damage. They may show only prolongation of the febrile state, irritability, and failure to take adequate food, especially fluids, and some are troubled by repeated vomiting. Because of unwillingness to perform a burr hole operation as a routine procedure, the incidence of subdural fluid collections in children older than one year is not well established.

Any of the following signs or symptoms occurring in a patient with purulent meningitis is an indication to perform a subdural tap for the presence of fluid in the subdural space: a marked bulging of the fontanel persisting after lumbar puncture; failure to show good clinical response despite 48 to 72 hours of adequate antimicrobial therapy; the presence of an area of erythema, edema, and local heat involving the region of the anterior fontanel, which may indicate a purulent subdural effusion; convulsions at any time in the course of meningitis; persistent vomiting recurring after initial clinical improvement; disturbances in auditory acuity; or changes in the optic discs. Transillumination of the skull, rapid increase of the head circumference on repeated measurements, the detection of persistent or recurrent intracranial bruits, echoencephalography, and electroencephalography are clinical and laboratory procedures which may be helpful in making the presumptive diagnosis.

Treatment consists of subdural taps through the coronal sutures, repeated on alternate days for 3 to 4 weeks. In the majority of cases, the fluid ceases to reaccumulate and no further treatment is necessary. If the fluid persists for a 3- to 4-week period despite repeated subdural paracentesis, surgical exploration is indicated for the possible removal of a membrane enclosing the subdural fluid.

PROGNOSIS. Prior to 1936 when the first sulfonamides became available, the most common varieties of meningeal infections were fatal, with the exception of meningococcal meningitis. The advances in antibacterial therapy made possible the survival and complete recovery of a large proportion of affected children. Overall case fatality rates range from 10 to

15 percent. Among the common types of purulent meningitides, *H. influenzae* infections in infants more than 1 year of age show the lowest fatality rate; mortality in influenzal meningitis occurs mainly in infants under 1 year of age. In pneumococcal meningitis the death rate exceeds 25 percent in infants under 1 year; it is lower in older infants and in children, but higher than in patients of a similar age group with *H. influenzae* meningitis. In meningococcal meningitis the highest mortality occurs in children with fulminant meningococcemia. The Waterhouse-Friderichsen syndrome is responsible for a 20 percent case fatality rate in meningococcus infections. Mortality rates and subequent disabilities are highest in the small infant; more than 65 percent of the infants of 1 month of life or less who develop pyogenic meningitis die. The higher proportion of deaths in those varieties of meningitides which are due to organisms other than *N. meningitidis*, *H. influenzae*, and *D. pneumoniae*, is in part a reflection of the high incidence of such infections in very young infants in whom the diagnosis has been delayed.

Accurate estimates of residual handicaps following pyogenic meningitis are not readily available, and the relative frequency with which these handicaps may be anticipated has not been well defined. At least 10 to 15 percent of the surviving patients show persistent neurologic sequelae including cerebral damage, hydrocephalus, motor deficits, spastic hemiplegia, visual or auditory impairment, vestibular damage, seizure states, mental retardation, hyperactivity, and inability to learn. Hydrocephalus, a dreaded complication due to inflammatory obstruction of the various pathways of cerebrospinal fluid circulation, is encountered primarily in young infants in whom the infection is detected late, at a far-advanced stage of infection. The majority of children with neurologic sequelae are left with significant intellectual impairment; sometimes manifestations of residual damage are subtle and may consist of mild cerebral dysfunction, specific learning disabilities, and behavior problems.

PROPHYLAXIS OF HOUSEHOLD CONTACTS AND NASAL CARRIERS. Prophylactic chemotherapy to contacts of meningitis due to *H. influenzae* or *D. pneumoniae* is not required. High carriage rates in household contacts of meningococcal meningitis, and frequent occurrence of secondary cases, warrant prophylactic treatment of all nasal carriers and of all intimate contacts without awaiting the results of the cultures. However, the emergence of sulfonamide-resistant strains of meningococci in the population has disqualified this formerly efficacious agent as the drug of choice in the prophylaxis of meningococcal infections. On the other hand, none of the antimicrobial agents which inhibit growth of *N. meningitidis* in vitro and are useful in the treatment of meningococcal infections has been uniformly effective in eradication of those microorganisms from carriers.

Results of reported trials with oxytetracycline, erythromycin, penicillin G, penicillin V, and ampicillin show clearly that none of these drugs has proved nearly as effective as was sulfadiazine, before the emergence of resistant strains. Phenoxymethyl penicillin (penicillin V), benzyl penicillin (penicillin G), and tetracyclines suppress the nasopharyngeal carriage of meningococci during treatment, but carrier rates revert to pretreatment levels when the drug is stopped. Secondary cases have developed in family contacts who received either phenoxymethyl or benzyl penicillin orally for 4 days.

Since none of the drugs tested appears superior to sulfonamides and since some strains of meningococci are still susceptible to sulfonamides, we recommend that contacts be treated with sulfonamides for 5 days, in doses of 1 g daily for children under 6 years of age, 2 g daily for children from 6 to 12 years of age, and 4 g daily for adults and children 12 years and older. The sulfonamides may be given either alone, or in combination with penicillin V, 1,600,000 units in four divided doses each day for four days.

A new antibacterial agent, Rifampin, with a high degree of activity against meningococcal growth in vitro was evaluated in a double blind-placebo study in known meningococcal carriers. Administration of Rifampin 600 mg daily for 4 days reduced the carrier rate by 93.3 percent, and this effect was sustained for 4 weeks. This agent was tolerated without difficulty during the prescribed course and produced no adverse effects except the appearance of bright red urine. Further studies on the use of this drug in the prophylaxis of carriers and contacts are needed.

REFERENCES

Alexander, H. E. Treatment of pyogenic meningitis, neurology and psychiatry in childhood. Res. Publ. Assoc. Nerv. Ment. Dis., 34:1, 1956.

Barrett, E., et al. Ampicillin in suppurative meningitis. J. Pediat., 69:343, 1966.

Berman, P. H., et al. Neonatal meningitis. Pediatrics, 38:6, 1966.

Dodge, P. R., and Swartz, M. N. Bacterial meningitis— A review of selected aspects: II. Special neurologic problems, postmeningitic complications and clinico-pathological correlations. New Eng. J. Med., 272:954-960, 1003-1010, 1965.

Eickhoff, T. C., et al. Changing susceptibility of meningococci to antimicrobial agents. New Eng. J. Med., 272:395, 1965.

Epstein, J. A., et al. Bilateral encapsulated subdural effusion complicating bacterial meningitis in infancy: Report of a case with review of literature. Arch. Neurol. Psychol., 69:242, 1953.

Fine, R. N., Kurtz, H. M., and Krieger, G. Hemophilus influenzae type a meningitis. J. Pediat., 70:962, 1967.

Gitlin, D. Pathogenesis of subdural collections of fluid. Pediatrics, 16:354, 1955.

Haggerty, R. J., and Ziai, M. Acute bacterial meningitis. Advances Pediat., 13:129, 1964.

Hitchcock, E., and Andreadis, A. Subdural empyema: A review of 29 cases. J. Neurol. Neurosurg. Psychiat., 27:422, 1964.

Lazarus, J. M., et al. Brief recordings: Meningitis due to the group B beta-hemolytic streptococcus. New Eng. J. Med., 272:146, 1965.

Leedom, J. M., et al. Importance of sulfadiazine resistance meningococcal disease in civilians. New Eng. J. Med., 272:1395, 1965.

Mace, J. W., et al. Cranial bruits in purulent meningitis in childhood. New Eng. J. Med., 278:1420-1422, 1968.

Mangos, J. A., et al. Sustained hyponatremia in nervous system infections. Pediatrics, 34:503, 1964.

McCrancken, G. H., et al. Changes in the pattern of neonatal septicemia and meningitis. Arch. Dis. Child., 112:13, 1966.

McKay, R. J., and Ingraham, F. D., et al. Subdural fluid complicating bacterial meningitis. J.A.M.A., 152:387, 1953.

Menkes, J. H. Causes for low spinal fluid sugar in bacterial meningitis: Another look. Pediatrics, 44:1-3, 1969.

Migeon, C. J., et al. Adrenal function in meningitis. Pediatrics, 40:163, 1967.

Overall, J. C. Neonatal bacterial meningitis. J. Pediat., 76:499-511, 1970.

Petersdorf, R. G. Why does the sugar disappear from C.S.F. in meningitis? Amer. J. Dis. Child., 100:307, 1960.

Robinson, M. G., et al. Pneumococcal meningitis in sickle-cell anemia. New Eng. J. Med., 274:1006-1008, 1966.

Smith, M. Acute bacterial meningitis. Pediatrics, 17:285, 1956.

Stiehm, E. R. Factors in the prognosis of meningococcal infections. J. Pediat., 68:457, 1966.

——— Neonatal meningococcal meningitis. J. Pediat., 68:654, 1966.

Swartz, M. N., and Dodge, P. R. Bacterial meningitis—A review of selected aspects. I. General clinical features, special problems and unusual meningeal reactions mimicking bacterial meningitis. New Eng. J. Med., 272:725-730, 779-787, 842-848, 898-902, 1965.

Wherle, P. F., et al. Critically ill child: Management of acute bacterial meningitis. Pediatrics, 44:991-998, 1969.

Whitecar, J. P. Recurrent pneumococcal meningitis. New Eng. J. Med., 274:1285, 1966.

Williams, R. D. B. Alterations in glucose transport mechanism in patients with complications of bacterial meningitis. Pediatrics, 34:491-502, 1964.

Winterbauer, R. H., et al. Neonatal meningitis. Pediatrics, 38:661, 1966.

14.4
BOTULISM

ALEX J. STEIGMAN

Botulism is the result of ingesting foods in which *Clostridium botulinum* has grown and produced a deadly neurotoxin. Although botulism is an intoxication rather than an infectious disease, outbreaks are the rule rather than the exception. Because prompt recognition of this uncommon disorder may be lifesaving, a high index of suspicion and constant awareness of the threat of botulism are mandatory. In the past several years botulism has caused more deaths than acute poliomyelitis in the United States.

THE ORGANISM AND ITS TOXIN. *C. botulinum* is an anaerobic or microaerophilic, gram-positive, spore-producing rod. Its worldwide natural habitat is soil, either inland or at the shores of bodies of fresh or salt water. Botulism rods can be classified into types a, b, c, d, e, and f, according to the immunologic specificities of the toxins each produces. Man is affected principally by types a, b, and e, and more rarely by type f.

The toxic effects arise at the myoneural junction, presumably by preventing the release of acetylcholine from the demyelinated ends of cholinergic nerves. Peripheral adrenergic nerves are not affected. There is no known pharmacologic antagonist. Type-specific or polyvalent therapeutic antitoxin is the only available direct antagonist for the toxins.

The spores can survive cold temperatures for some months and withstand boiling for several hours; they can be destroyed at 120° C in 30 minutes. When spores germinate they produce toxin over a wide range of temperatures, extending as low as 6° C. Optimimum production of toxin occurs at about 30° C. Fortunately, once toxin is formed it is relatively thermolabile and can be destroyed by boiling (100° C) for 10 minutes, or by heating at 80° C for 30 minutes.

A pentavalent toxoid can be prepared for active immunization of individuals at high risk, such as special laboratory workers engaged in "germ warfare" projects.

INCRIMINATED FOODS AND THEIR PREPARATION. Fruits, vegetables, meats, fresh and salt-water fish, and products derived from these foods, whether prepared at home or commercially, have all been involved. The foods may have been prepared as juices, soups, pickles, salads, or meat or fish pastes and spreads. They may have been smoked, salted, spiced, air dried, cured by hanging, or "vaccum packed" in cellophane bags. These foods needs not have been stored for long periods. Rapid toxin formation may occur in fresh fruits and gutted fish exposed to insufficient heat and provided with vacuum or anaerobic conditions. The spores may survive several hours at 100° C; there is some variation in strains. Generally speaking, outbreaks due to home prepared items are geographically restricted to the family and neighbors. Contaminated commercially prepared foods marketed on a large scale by modern distribution methods have scattered outbreaks, as has occurred with salmonella. The common source may go unrecognized for a time with tragic delay in the case of botulism in establishing treatment and control.

Unfortunately, the foods involved often have not undergone accompanying proteolytic changes. Consequently, the foods may have no offensive taste or odor to serve as a warning or as a clue when "mysterious illness" appears in a family or group. It is an understandable but regrettable fact that it often takes the second or third patient's illness in an outbreak to raise the suspicion of botulism.

CLINICAL OUTCOME. The clinical outcome in exposed persons depends upon several factors, including the amount of ingested toxin, the speed of onset of symptoms, the serotype of botulism involved, and the promptness of diagnosis and treatment. Not all persons react similarly to the ingestion of a given amount of toxin, which may be because of the amount of trypsin and the pH of the stomach at the time of ingestion. For example, in experimental animals the effects of type e toxin have been shown to be markedly potentiated in the presence of trypsin and a slightly acid pH. There may also be genetically determined biochemical differences among individuals in the effect of toxin on the myoneural junction.

THE CLINICAL PICTURE. Several hours to several days may elapse after ingestion of toxin before symptoms appear. Symptoms due to failure of acetylcholine release at the myoneural junctions include nausea, vomiting, blurred vision, lassitude, vertigo, diplopia, dry mouth, and abdominal fullness. With progression there is weakness and paralysis leading to dysphonia, dysphagia, urinary retention, and labored breathing.

On physical examination patients are usually afebrile and mentally alert, and deep tendon reflexes are preserved despite the weakness. The pupils are large and respond sluggishly. The mouth and tongue are dry; the abdomen is distended.

AIDS TO DIAGNOSIS. Blood counts, urinalyses, chemical examination of the blood and spinal fluid, and cultures of stools or gastric contents are not helpful in diagnosis. When suspected foods are still available, mouse inoculation under appropriate conditions may verify existence of the toxin and its specific type, and it may also be possible to culture the anaerobic *C. botulinum.*

The chief aid to diagnosis is awareness and suspicion of a suitable setting for botulism. In geographically confined outbreaks, a story of having attended weddings, parties, or picnics, together with knowledge of a similar "mysterious illness" in an index case help to sound the alarm. Poliomyelitis, small bowel obstruction, labyrinthitis, neuropsychiatric asthenia, behavior disturbances following a party or celebration, and many other mistaken diagnoses are understandably considered often in the first patient in an outbreak of botulism.

THERAPY. The chief purpose of therapy is to avoid respiratory insufficiency. Emergency facilities must be at hand for tracheostomy or tracheal intubation, together with mechanically assisted ventilation, which should be used before there are signs of advanced fatigue or exhaustion.

Because some toxin may remain unabsorbed in the bowel, cleaning enemas should be given. Antitoxin to be given intravenously should be obtained as rapidly as possible. Ideally, antitoxin specific for the toxin type involved should be given; however, the type is seldom known, especially with the initial patient in a small outbreak. For some time it was believed that only types a and b occurred with any degree of frequency in the U.S.A., but both types e and f have also been encountered.

Availability of Botulism Antitoxins in the U.S.A. (1) Bivalent (a and b) is prepared by Lederle Laboratories, whose regional distribution centers can expedite delivery. (2) Monovalent (e), prepared by Connaught Laboratories in Canada, is licensed for use in the U.S.A., and is available at all times by phoning the Communicable Disease Center in Atlanta, Georgia, or its field stations in Kansas City and San Francisco. (3) Polyvalent (abef) is prepared in Denmark by the State Serum Institute. Although not licensed for use in the U.S.A., a supply is on hand at the same three stations where type e antitoxin is kept.

As these antitoxins are of equine origin, preliminary skin tests for sensitivity are essential. Sensitive individuals must be desensitized prior to therapy. A single large intravenous dose is recommended rather than several daily doses. The dose for the bivalent and polyvalent antitoxins is 100,000 units or more; for the monovalent type e, 10,000 to 20,000 units.

There is no cross-protection among the several types. On recovery from botulism, patients are again fully susceptible to all types of the disease since botulism is an intoxication rather than an infection.

REFERENCES

National Communicable Disease Center, Atlanta, Georgia. Botulism in the United States, Review of Cases, 1899-1967.

United States Department of Health, Education and Welfare. Botulism. Public Health Service Publ. No. 999-FP-1.

14.5
BRUCELLOSIS
(UNDULANT FEVER)

ANGUS M. McBRYDE

This infection is occasionally encountered in children in all sections of the United States. It usually is caused by *Brucella abortus.* Infection with *Br. suis* is less common, and that due to *Br. melitensis* is rare. Young patients commonly acquire it by ingestion of raw milk, butter, or other milk products; in adults three-fourths of the cases result from contact with infected cattle. The incubation period cannot be determined accurately, but it has been known to vary from 6 days to 4 months.

Illness due to *Br. abortus* usually is less severe than with the other species. The organism produces clinical manifestations in only a small percentage of cases. In an institutional epidemic in which 48 children consumed infected milk, 9 developed agglutinins for the organism, and only 2 developed symptoms.

The clinical picture in acute brucellosis is inconstant. In most cases only constitutional symptoms are present, but there may be a variety of local symptoms. As a rule the onset is insidious, with fatigability, vague muscle pains, headache, difficulty in sleeping, excessive sweating, chilliness, or possibly fever alone. Nausea and anorexia are unusual. The constitutional symptoms vary in severity. In the majority of cases the fever is of the remitting type, rising from normal or subnormal in the morning to a late afternoon level of 101° to 102° F; it may follow this course for 2 or 3 weeks, with subsequent slow lysis, or there may be waves of septic fever for periods of days or weeks separated by remissions of indefinite length, the process generally wearing itself out over the course of several weeks or months. Characteristically patients experience a sense of well-being despite continued high fever. In chronic brucellosis the child usually has low-grade fever, tires easily, fails to gain weight, and is pale and irritable, the rectal temperature commonly being less than 101° F.

The physical findings in acute or chronic brucellosis are meager and variable. The spleen and liver may be enlarged. A mild leucopenia is the rule, with both relative and absolute increase of large lymphocytic cells. However, in acute brucellosis counts of 15,000 or more with a slight polymorphonuclear preponderance may occur.

Local symptoms have in our experience been rare. They are said to be more common with porcine and caprine infections. The most frequent local manifestations are those of the joints and lymph nodes. Arthritic pains may simulate rheumatic fever; an intermittent hydrarthrosis has been described. There may be generalized hyperplasia of lymph nodes or chronic changes in individual nodes or groups of nodes; these have been mistaken for tuberculosis. Among the rare manifestations are diarrhea, pleurisy, pericarditis, endocarditis, peritonitis, meningitis, encephalitis, and lesions of the bones and of the upper urinary tract. There may be purpuric skin lesions or chronic subcutaneous abscesses. Pathologically the lesion is an infectious granuloma, which may simulate tuberculosis.

Definitive diagnosis rests upon isolation of the organism from the blood, duodenal secretions, stool, or urine. The agglutination test is significant in titers of 1:160 or more; however, it may be negative in chronic brucellosis. Cross-agglutinations with *Pasteurella tularensis* may occur in low titer.

The opsonocytophagic test of Huddleson is an aid to diagnosis and, when positive, suggests an immune state rather than active infection. Only highly specialized laboratories can perform this test reliably.

Intradermal tests, using 0.05 to 0.1 ml of undiluted heat-killed *Br. abortus* vaccine containing two billion organisms per milliliter, are of value in diagnosis. They should be read at the end of 4 days and, if negative, again at the end of 7 days. In order to avoid necrosis in a sensitized individual a 1:100 dilution may be used first. Patients with ocular manifestations should not be tested. A positive skin test should be interpreted in the same manner as a positive tuberculin test. In childhood it has greater significance than in older age groups in suggesting recent and therefore active infection.

Brucellosis should be suspected in patients suffering from obscure fever of long duration. Such patients are often suspected of having tuberculosis, typhoid or paratyphoid fever, infectious mononucleosis, Hodgkin's disease, septicemia, rheumatic fever, malaria, or malignancy. Infection is best prevented in children by avoiding raw milk, butter, and cheese.

Even before specific antibiotics were available the prognosis was good, although exceptionally deaths occurred in children. Convalescence was usually slow, lasting 1 to 4 months, and was often characterized by loss of strength, fatigability, failure to gain weight, and secondary anemia.

The effect of therapy in acute brucellosis is difficult to determine, since in most cases recovery is spontaneous and chronic disease seldom follows the acute process. The treatment of chronic brucellosis is attended with little success. The tetracyclines constitute the treatment of choice. They should be continued for a minimum of 21 days in the acute disease, with oral dosage of 40 to 50 mg per kilogram daily divided into four doses. This regimen may be repeated within 6 weeks if a relapse occurs. In severe cases daily intramuscular injection of streptomycin in doses of 0.5 to 1 g may be administered simultaneously. In those rare children who are seriously ill, cortisone or its analogs can be given orally or parenterally and may result in marked improvement within 24 hours. They are not recommended for routine use.

Heat-killed brucella vaccines may be helpful in chronic brucellosis when given biweekly in gradually increasing desensitizing doses in conjunction with chemotherapy and antibiotics.

REFERENCES

Chavez Max, G. Tetracycline in the treatment of human brucellosis. Antibiot. Med., 1:216, 1955.

Glenchur, H., Zinneman, H. H., and Hall, W. H. The significance of the blocking antibody in experimental brucellosis. J. Immunol., 86:421-526, 1961.

Manthei, C. A. Current advances in brucellosis research. Pub. Health Rep., 79:1074, 1964.

Meyer, K. F. Trends in brucellosis control. Pub. Health Rep., 71:511, 1956.

Ruiz Sanchez, F., et al. Treatment of brucellosis with tetracycline. Antibiot. Med., 1:158, 1955.

Sharma, B. Treatment of brucellosis by nalidixic acid. Lancet, 1:1171, 1965.

Spink, W. W. Current status of therapy of brucellosis in human beings. J.A.M.A., 172:697, 1960.

——— McCullough, N. B., Hutchings, L. M., and Mingle, C. K. Diagnostic criteria for human brucellosis. J.A.M.A., 149:805, 1952.

Sprunt, D. H., and McBryde, A. Morbid anatomic changes in cases of brucella infection in man, with report of necropsy. Arch. Path., 21:217, 1936.

Wallis, H. R. E. Brucellosis in children. Brit. Med. J., 1:617, 1957.

Zinneman, H. H., Glenchur, H., and Hall, W. H. The nature of blocking antibodies in human brucellosis. J. Immunol., 83:206, 1959.

14.6
CHOLERA

CHARLES C. J. CARPENTER

Cholera is an acute infectious illness caused by an enterotoxin elaborated by *Vibrio cholerae* that have colonized the small bowel. In its most severe form, there is rapid loss of fluid and electrolytes from the gastrointestinal tract, resulting in hypovolemic shock, metabolic acidosis, and, if untreated, death.

ETIOLOGY. *V. cholerae* are short, curved, Gram-negative rods readily seen in Gram-stained smears of the watery excreta of patients with cholera. Rapid presumptive diagnosis can be made either by fluorescent microscopy using fluorescein-labeled type-specific antibody, or by a vibrio immobilization test employing dark field or phase microscopy and type-specific antisera. *V. cholerae* grow rapidly on a number of selective media, including bile-salt agar, glycerine-tellurite-taurocholate agar, and thiosulfate-citrate-bile-salt-sucrose (TCBS) agar. Of these culture media, TCBS agar has the distinct advantage of not requiring sterilization before use. On TCBS agar, vibrios can be distinguished from other enteric organisms by a characteristic opaque yellow colonial appearance. Distinction between the two major serotypes, Inaba and Ogawa, is made by slide agglutination with type-specific antisera.

Identification of the eltor biotype is important for epidemiologic purposes; it differs from the classical biotype in its resistance to polymyxin B, resistance to Mukerjee's choleraphage type IV, and its ability to lyse sheep erythrocytes.

EPIDEMIOLOGY. For the past two centuries, cholera has remained endemic in the Ganges Delta with annual epidemics in major population centers in West Bengal and East Pakistan. The disease has made periodic incursions into other portions of South and Southeast Asia and has given rise to six major pandemics since 1832. The sixth and most recent (1961-1970) pandemic, unlike the preceding ones, has thus far failed to reach Europe or the Western Hemisphere. Man is the only documented natural host and victim of *V. cholerae,* although a carrier state in other species remains a possibility. Several major epidemics have been waterborne, and water appears to play a major role in transmission of *V. cholerae* in endemic rural areas. During major epidemics, however, direct contamination of food with infected excreta may also be important. Individuals with mild or asymptomatic infections (contact carriers) probably play a major role in dissemination of epidemic disease. The gallbladder carrier state, which occasionally develops in adult convalescents, has never been observed in the pediatric age group. The role of such convalescent carriers in the transmission of the disease has not yet been clarified but is currently under intensive investigation. In the cholera-endemic areas of East Pakistan and West Bengal, cholera is predominantly a disease of children; attack rates are ten times greater in children below 10 years of age than in individuals over the age of 20.

PATHOGENESIS AND PATHOLOGY. All clinical manifestations and metabolic derangements in cholera result from the rapid loss of fluid and electrolytes from the gut. These losses are due to increased secretion of isotonic fluids by all segments of the small bowel. The increased electrolyte secretion is caused by a nondialyzable, heat-labile enterotoxin that is elaborated by pathogenic strains of *V. cholerae*. The enterotoxin exerts its characteristic effect on electrolyte secretion without causing detectable histologic damage to the gut mucosa. The only consistent pathologic alterations in the gut during cholera are slight edema of the lamina propria and moderate dilatation of capillaries and lymphatics in the tips of villi. Although the exact mechanism of action of the cholera enterotoxin has not been determined, current data suggest that it may act through cyclic adenosine 3′,5′-monophosphate to cause increased chloride secretion by the gut mucosal cells.

CLINICAL MANIFESTATIONS. The clinical onset of cholera consists generally of abrupt, painless, watery diarrhea. In severe cases, several liters of fluid may be lost within a few hours, leading rapidly to profound shock. At varying intervals after onset of diarrhea, vomiting may ensue; this is characteristically effortless and is not preceded by nausea. In the more severe cases, muscle cramps are almost invariably present and commonly involve the calves.

When first seen by the physician, the child who is severely ill with cholera is cyanotic, has sunken eyes and cheeks, a scaphoid abdomen, poor skin turgor, and thready or absent peripheral pulses. The voice is high-pitched or inaudible; the vital signs include tachycardia, tachypnea, and low or unobtainable blood pressure. There may be either low-grade fever or slight hypothermia. The heart sounds are distant, often inaudible, and bowel sounds are usually hypoactive. The patient usually remains oriented, although apathetic, even in the face of severe hypovolemic shock. In all epidemics there are large numbers of mild cases in which fluid loss from the gut is not severe enough to require hospitalization. There are even larger numbers of completely asymptomatic people who transiently excrete *V. cholerae*.

Loss of fluid and electrolytes continues for one to seven days, and subsequent manifestations depend upon the adequacy of replacement therapy. With prompt fluid and electrolyte repletion, physiologic recovery is remarkably rapid and uniform despite continuing voluminous diarrhea. If therapy is inadequate, the mortality rate in hospitalized cases may exceed 50 percent. The important causes of death are hypovolemic shock, uncompensated metabolic acidosis, and uremia. When renal failure occurs, the characteristic pathologic findings are those of acute tubular necrosis secondary to prolonged hypotension.

DIAGNOSIS. In endemic or epidemic areas, the working diagnosis of cholera should be made on the basis of the clinical picture; fluid and electrolyte replacement therapy should be instituted immediately. Choleralike illnesses may be caused by microorganisms other than *V. cholerae*. These diarrheal diseases produce similar physiologic and metabolic abnormalities and require identical intravenous and oral electrolyte therapy in all such cases.

Diagnostic culture techniques are relatively simple. A reliable and practical method consists of direct plating of feces on TCBS agar. Typical, opaque yellow colonies appear after 18 hours. Final identification requires agglutination with group- and type-specific antisera and demonstration of characteristic biochemical reactions. Immediate, tentative diagnosis may be made by direct observation by dark field microscopy of the characteristic rapid motility of the comma-shaped bacilli in fresh feces. Group- and type-specific antisera will immobilize homologous strains and clearly distinguish them from other vibrios.

PROGNOSIS. With adequate therapy the mortality rate approaches zero. Largely because of the mechanical problems inherent in the administration of large amounts of fluid to small children, a mortality rate of 1 to 2 percent still prevails in pediatric cases despite the best therapy currently available. It is not yet clear whether or not significant immunity to subsequent infection results from a single attack of cholera.

TREATMENT. The primary therapeutic principle is the prompt replacement of the fluid and electrolyte losses. In addition, since eradication of *V. cholerae* from the gut reduces fluid losses by 50 to 70 percent in the average cholera case, antimicrobial therapy (with tetracycline, chloramphenicol, or furazolidine) is also an important part of therapy.

Several solutions have been widely and successfully used for the initial rehydration and for maintenance of electrolyte balance in pediatric patients. Complications resulting from inappropriate hydration therapy, which will be discussed below, can be successfully prevented, *provided the treatment is closely supervised by trained medical and paramedical personnel.* The most effective single intravenous replacement solution is the NAMRU 2 solution, which contains the following concentrations of solutes: sodium, 90mEq/L; chloride, 64 mEq/L; potassium, 15 mEq/L; bicarbonate, 45 mEq/L (as acetate); calcium, 2 mEq/L; magnesium, 2 mEq/L; and glucose, 20 mg/L. This solution supplies adequate free water in addition to appropriate quantities of electrolytes. It also contains enough glucose to prevent the hypoglycemia which occasionally occurs in pediatric patients with cholera. Trials with this solution have demonstrated its effectiveness in maintaining electrolyte balance and blood sugar levels.

Determination of the appropriate volume and rate of fluid administration is at least as important as the electrolyte pattern of the fluid administered. As in adult patients, fluid requirements for pediatric patients may be estimated clinically and by using laboratory techniques. For clinical evaluation, the following guidelines are useful. *Mild dehydration* (slightly decreased skin turgor and tachycardia, but good peripheral pulse and normal sensorium) indicates an isotonic fluid deficit of about 5 percent of body weight. With *moderate dehydration* (marked decrease in skin turgor, tachycardia and hypotension, but normal sensorium), the fluid deficit is 6 to 10 percent of body weight. *Severe dehydration* (the above signs plus cyanosis, stupor or coma, absent peripheral pulses) is associated with a fluid deficit exceeding 10 percent of body weight. Plasma specific-gravity determinations are useful to estimate fluid deficit, and the same general principles as have been applied to adult patients may be followed for replacement therapy. However, because of the difference in ratio of extracellular to intracellular fluid volume in small children, a larger volume of fluid (6 ml/kg) must be given for each 0.001 unit elevation of plasma specific gravity. The initial estimated fluid deficit should be administered within 60 to 180 minutes after initiation of therapy. The rate of infusion must be closely monitored to prevent overhydration, for the survival of the child with cholera is dependent more upon continued close supervision than upon the precise composition of the intravenous fluid. Attention must be directed especially to *maintenance of adequate hydration* (whether judged by clinical or laboratory parameters), to *avoidance of overhydration* (determined by auscultation of lungs and inspection of neck venous filling), and to *providing free water,* as needed, by the oral route (generally the patient's own thirst mechanism is a good guide to oral water requirements).

Complications are both more common and more serious in pediatric than in adult cholera. The most serious include pulmonary edema (often with superimposed pneumonia), stupor, coma and convulsions, and cardiac arrhythmias occasionally leading to cardiac arrest.

Pulmonary edema may result from an over-rapid administration of the required intravenous fluids in the presence of severe metabolic acidosis, and/or from the administration of excessive quantities of intravenous fluids. Severe metabolic acidosis causes a shift of intravascular fluid from the systemic to the pulmonary circulation. The rapid administration of intravenous fluids, before the metabolic acidosis has been corrected, may cause pulmonary edema even in the absence of overt overhydration. Even after correction of acidosis, pulmonary edema occasionally occurs in children with cholera as the result of injudicious administration of too large a volume of intravenous fluids.

Exceedingly rare in adult cholera patients, stupor, coma, and convulsions may occur in up to 10 percent of small children. These central nervous system manifestations sometimes result from hypoglycemia and can readily be avoided by intravenous administration of glucose. They can also be due to electrolyte imbalance or to cerebral edema secondary to overhydration.

Available data suggest that the mean potassium concentration in the stools of children with cholera is higher than that of the adult. The physiologic consequences of potassium depletion are more serious in the pediatric than in the adult cholera patient. Serious arrhythmias, hypotension, and even cardiac arrest may occur in the pediatric cholera patient with degrees of potassium depletion (15 to 20 percent of total body potassium) which are generally tolerated by the adult. Since the potassium deficit is rarely severe at the time the pediatric cholera patient arrives at a treatment center, the hypokalemia can be avoided by intravenous administration of adequate quantities of potassium (4 mEq of KCl/100 ml of solution) as soon as urine output is satisfactory.

Alternate Routes of Fluid and Electrolyte Administration. While all moderately or severely dehydrated pediatric patients require intravenous fluids initially, the oral route has been successful for maintenance fluid and electrolyte therapy in children weighing 30 pounds or more. While oral glucose-electrolyte replacement solutions may ultimately prove as effective in pediatric as in adult cholera, it is currently recommended that oral glucose-electrolyte solutions be employed in pediatric patients *only* when adequate quantities of pyrogen-free intravenous fluids are not available.

PREVENTION. Immunization using the standard commercial vaccine (containing 10 billion killed *V. cholerae* per ml) provides significant protection for a period of 4 to 6 months. While immunization with toxoid affords significant protection in experimental animals, as yet there have been no trials in man. At present, careful hygiene represents the only sure protection against cholera.

REFERENCES

Griffith, L. S. C., Fresh, J. W., Watten, R. H., and Villaroman, M. P. Electrolyte replacement in pediatric cholera. Lancet, 1:1197-1202, 1967.
Gutman, R. A., Dratz, D. J., Whalen, G. E., and Watten, R. H. Double blind fluid therapy evaluation in pediatric cholera. Pediatrics, 44:922, 1969.
Hirschhorn, N., Lindenbaum, J., Greenough, W. B., and Alam, S. M. Hypoglycemia in children with acute diarrhea. Lancet, 2:128, 1966.
Lindenbaum, J., Akbar, R., Gordon, R. S., Greenough, W. B., Hirschhorn, N., and Islam, M. R. Cholera in children. Lancet, 1:1066, 1966.
Mahalanabis, D., Wallace, C. K., Kallen, R. J., Mondal, A., and Pierce, N. F. Water and electrolyte losses due to cholera in infants and small children. Pediatrics, 45:374, 1970.
Mosley, W. H. The role of immunity in cholera. A review of epidemiological and serological studies. Tex. Rep. Biol. Med., 27:227-241, 1969.
Pierce, N. F., Sack, R. B., Mitra, R. C., Banwell, J. G.,

Brigham, K. L., Fedson, D. S., and Mondal, A. Replacement of water and electrolyte losses in cholera by an oral glucose-electrolyte solution. Ann. Int. Med., 70:1173-1181, 1969.
Wallace, C. K., Anderson, P. N., Brown, T. C., Khanra, S. R., Lewis, G. W., Pierce, N. F., Sanyal, S. N., Segre, G. V., and Waldman, R. H. Optimal antibiotic therapy in cholera. Bull. World Health Organ., 39:239-245, 1968.

14.7
DIPHTHERIA

HORACE L. HODES

Diphtheria is a specific infectious disease caused by a toxin-producing organism, *Corynebacterium diphtheriae* (Klebs-Loeffler bacillus). It is characterized by membranous inflammation of the upper respiratory passages and degenerative changes in the viscera and nervous system, the latter caused by the toxin.

ETIOLOGY. The morphology and growth characteristics of *C. diphtheriae* are described in works on bacteriology. Only strains which produce the specific exotoxin are virulent and capable of producing the disease. It has been shown by Freeman that avirulent strains can be converted into virulent toxin producers when exposed to bacteriophages associated with toxin-producing strains.

EPIDEMIOLOGY. The disease is transmitted by direct contact with diseased persons or healthy carriers. Individuals with pharyngeal diphtheria are more of a menace than those with laryngeal disease.

The morbidity and mortality from diphtheria began to decline in the United States around 1900 following the introduction of diphtheria antitoxin. This decline was accelerated in the late 1920's with the introduction of programs of active immunization. In Baltimore, for example, the diphtheria rate was 260 per 100,000 in 1900, 124 per 100,000 in 1925, and 0.0 per 100,000 in 1960. Natural changes in bacteria-host relationships have probably contributed to this result.

PATHOLOGY. Pseudomembranous lesions are commonly found on the mucous membrane of the pharynx, tonsils, and uvula, less frequently in the nose, larynx, and lower respiratory tract. Occasionally the process extends to the middle ear or to the esophagus and stomach; it may also involve the skin or the mucosa of the genital organs. The pseudomembrane consists of necrotic epithelium embedded in inflammatory exudate which has coagulated on the surface. Inflammatory changes are found in the surviving underlying epithelium and may extend into the submucosa, where hemorrhagic manifestations may occur. The bacilli remain in these surface lesions; only exceptionally do they invade deeper structures and even more rarely cause bacteremia. Toxin, however, is absorbed from the local lesion, causing damage in distant organs and tissues.

Myocarditis is a common lesion, the changes being degenerative rather than inflammatory. They vary from simple cloudy swelling with loss of striations in the muscle fibers to well-defined foci of hyaline degeneration, often accompanied by fatty degeneration. Minute hemorrhages may be present, and in some cases there is an accompanying round cell infiltration. The conducting system is frequently involved.

The *liver* cells show degenerative changes at autopsy; there may be scattered areas of focal necrosis. Hepatic function may be impaired to some extent.

The *kidneys* commonly show cloudy swelling with swollen granular epithelial cells of the convoluted tubules. Exceptionally there is a well-marked interstitial nephritis with extensive accumulation of mononuclear cells between the tubules. Glomerular nephritis is almost unknown.

Lesions in the *adrenal cortex* similar to those present in meningococcemia are often found in fatal cases.

Degenerative changes in the *nervous system* occur in nearly all fatal cases. In the cord they are seen in the ganglion cells of the anterior horns and in the posterior root ganglia. The cranial nerves and their centers may be affected; the cortex, however, is spared.

Other lesions encountered are degenerative changes in the spleen and lymph nodes; there may be subcapsular hemorrhages. Subcutaneous hemorrhages are not infrequent. At times the hemorrhagic tendency may be attributed to thrombocytopenia, but in other cases the cause appears to be vascular.

SYMPTOMS. The incubation period of diphtheria is usually between 2 and 5 days. The onset is often insidious, with mild sore throat and only moderate fever. The throat, at first only red, soon exhibits a gray or white deposit upon the tonsils or the pillars. This patch may spread, or multiple patches may coalesce to form a membrane which may cover the tonsils, the soft palate, and the uvula. The grayish white membrane is adherent and cannot readily be removed by a swab; its borders are usually sharply defined. The cervical lymph nodes usually show some swelling.

The onset may be more abrupt, with higher fever and more marked constitutional symptoms, or a mild case may progress insidiously to a more severe one. The process may spread until it involves a large part of the pharyngeal surface, with extension into the nose or downward into the larynx. In other cases nasal or laryngeal diphtheria occurs without obvious involvement of the pharynx. Primary nasal diphtheria is seen particularly in infants and very young children; it may be very mild, the only sign being a bloody nasal discharge and excoriation about the nostrils. Laryngeal diphtheria at the onset is indistinguishable from other forms of acute laryngitis. A steady progression of symptoms, with increasing stridor, dyspnea, and cyanosis, indicates that the process is not a simple viral laryngitis.

In the average case of mild or moderate severity the process tends to subside spontaneously, usually by the fifth or sixth day. The membrane begins to loosen and separate; with its disappearance the local symptoms abate rapidly: the discharge ceases, the lymph nodes decrease in size, and deglutition and breathing become normal. With antitoxin, the process subsides more rapidly. Constitutional symptoms may outlast the local manifestations, and late complications may be seen even in a relatively mild case.

In some cases the disease runs a much more malignant course than that described, with a high fatality rate. The symptoms are severe from the outset. The membrane usually covers the entire pharynx, often extending to the nose and the middle ear, and occasionally spreading to the buccal cavity. There is great swelling of the tonsils and uvula, and it is often impossible to obtain a view of the pharynx. Sometimes the inflammation is of a necrotic character, and there may be extensive sloughing of the tonsils, the uvula, or the soft palate. The nasal discharge is generally abundant, and often offensive in odor. There is marked swelling of the cervical lymph nodes and frequently extensive infiltration of the cellular tissue of the neck, so that the head is thrown back to relieve pressure upon the larynx and trachea. The swelling sometimes forms a distinct collar, reaching from ear to ear and filling out the whole space beneath the jaw (bull-neck). Pressure upon the jugular veins leads to congestion of the face. The temperature is usually high; it follows no regular course, but generally fluctuates widely from 102° to 106° F. In some cases, however, it may never be above 101° F. The pulse is weak, rapid, and compressible. The peripheral circulation is poor, the extremities are often cold; there is striking muscular weakness, and both vomiting and diarrhea are frequent. There may be excitement, restlessness, and active delirium, or dullness, apathy, and stupor. The urine contains albumin and casts but rarely blood. Nervous symptoms are prominent in these cases. Death generally occurs while the local disease is at its height and may result from respiratory obstruction or from circulatory failure.

COMPLICATIONS. *Myocardial involvement* is demonstrable in about 50 percent of patients with diphtheria when frequent electrocardiographic records are made. It is more likely to occur in the severe forms, particularly those with bull-neck. It may develop as early as the second day or as late as 6 weeks after the onset. In fatal cases it usually develops early. A change in the quality of the first sound is the first physical sign. The sound becomes fainter, the muscular element is lost, the persistent valvular element giving rise to a "tic-tac" quality. The first heart sound may be replaced by a blowing murmur, and cardiac enlargement may be demonstrable. Nearly any form of arrhythmia may be noted—extrasystoles, dropped beats, and tachycardia. Abnormal electrocardiographic findings ordinarily have little clinical significance unless accompanied by clinical signs. This is particularly true of elevation of the S-T segment. On the other hand, prolongation of the P-R interval, ectopic beats, and heart block may be considered definitive indications of myocardial disease.

Cardiac failure may be heralded by a worsening of the quality of the heart sounds, by enlargement of the liver, or rales at the lung bases. There may be abdominal pain and vomiting. Venous pressure is elevated and circulation time prolonged. There may be evidences of peripheral circulatory collapse; the blood pressure falls abruptly, there is pallor and cold extremities, and death may follow quickly. In such patients Rich and Hodes observed severe degenerative changes in the adrenal cortex, changes which were not conspicuous in patients dying in cardiac failure without evidences of shock.

Some form of *paralysis* occurs in 10 to 20 percent of all patients with diphtheria. It may occur even after a mild attack, though it is more common in severe cases. The muscles of the palate are the first and often the only ones to suffer—less frequently the muscles of accommodation, the extraocular muscles, the pharynx, diaphragm, and the muscles of the extremities. The intercostals are sometimes affected. Palatal paralysis is revealed by a nasal quality to the voice and regurgitation of fluids through the nose. The more severe the attack and the longer antitoxin is delayed, the earlier and more widespread the paralysis is likely to be. In severe cases it develops by the fifth or sixth day. In other instances paralysis may develop as late as the sixth week, particularly paralysis of the extremities.

Disability from diphtheritic paralysis may be extreme. The patient may not be able to swallow or raise his head; he may require a respirator. Fortunately, it is rarely prolonged for more than 10 days even in the severest cases, and recovery is usually complete.

LABORATORY FINDINGS. The blood commonly shows a leucocytosis proportional to the severity of the attack, but in the most severe cases there is sometimes leucopenia. Immature granulocytes may be present. A moderate hypoplastic anemia is common, which may persist into convalescence. Thrombocytopenia occurs in some cases. Changes in the spinal fluid are found in a few instances of diphtheritic paralysis; there may be an elevated protein content and some increase in mononuclear cells.

DIAGNOSIS. Reliance cannot be placed upon a direct stained smear for identification of diphtheria bacilli. With proper media (Loeffler's, blood agar, or medium containing potassium tellurite) cultivation of diphtheria bacilli offers little difficulty early in the disease. Repeated cultures are, however, necessary in some cases. Microscopically, with fluorescent antibody technique the diagnosis can be made more rapidly and a higher percentage of positive cultures can be obtained. Cultures should always be made before antibiotics are given, for penicillin, tetracyclines, and erythromycin may interfere with the growth of *C. diphtheriae*. All positive cultures should be tested for virulence. The recovery of beta hemolytic streptococci from a culture does not rule out the diagnosis of diphtheria, for in our experience these are found in about 30 percent of cases of diphtheria.

There is nothing specific about the appearance of the throat in diphtheria, and several other conditions may give rise to pseudomembranous inflammations that may be clinically indistinguishable from it, including infectious mononucleosis, toxoplasmosis, streptococcal pharyngitis, moniliasis, and infection with Vincent's organisms. If serious doubt exists it is always safer to assume that diphtheria is present and to treat with antitoxin. A few points of clinical difference may, however, be mentioned. The membrane of diphtheria tends to be darker and grayer in color and more fibrous in appearance than in the other conditions mentioned; it tends to be more firmly attached to the underlying mucosa and when pulled away bleeding is more likely to occur. It usually begins on the tonsils, spreading toward the uvula.

Knowledge of the patient's immune status may be of help; a recent immunization or booster injection with diphtheria toxoid makes the diagnosis of diphtheria less likely.

Laryngeal and tracheobronchial diphtheria must be differentiated from other forms of croup (Sec. 19.4). Membrane is found on the tonsils or pharynx in about 85 percent of these cases; in its absence diagnosis may be difficult. Clinical differentiation cannot be definitely made between diphtheria and laryngotracheobronchitis caused by streptococci, *H. influenzae*, or viruses. The onset of laryngitis by *H. influenzae* is often extremely abrupt, and epiglottitis intense. However, again, when there is doubt about the diagnosis it is wise to assume that one is dealing with diphtheria.

TREATMENT. Diphtheria antitoxin should be administered as promptly as possible, following a skin or conjunctival test for sensitivity to horse serum. Antitoxin is capable of neutralizing only that toxin which is free in the circulation; it has no effect upon toxin which has become attached to cells, a process which takes place rapidly. It should be given in a single injection, the dose depending upon the severity of the case. In mild and moderately severe cases we inject 40,000 units intramuscularly, regardless of the age or weight of the patient. Patients with severe pharyngeal diphtheria or with laryngeal diphtheria receive 40,000 units intravenously in addition to 40,000 units intramuscularly. When given intravenously the antitoxin should be diluted 1:20 in 0.85 percent sodium chloride solution and administered at a rate not exceeding 1 ml per minute.

Some patients who recover from diphtheria after treatment with antitoxin are found to have a positive Schick reaction. For this reason many physicians give diphtheria toxoid as well as antitoxin to all patients with diphtheria. The first dose of toxoid may be injected at the end of the first week of illness, the second and third doses 1 and 2 months later.

Penicillin exerts a definite action against diphtheria bacilli, but antitoxin must always be given in addition. Penicillin is useful in two additional ways: It is effective against the streptococci which frequently are secondary invaders, and it decreases the number of persons who remain carriers after recovery. Aqueous procaine penicillin, 300,000 units, should be given intramuscularly daily to small children and twice this dose to larger children. Erythromycin in a dosage of 20 mg per kilogram per day may be used for children who are sensitive to penicillin, since this antibiotic acts in a similar manner against C. *diphtheriae* and streptococci. Antibiotics should be continued for 7 to 10 days. It should be reemphasized that antibiotics must never be used as a substitute for diphtheria antitoxin but in conjunction with it.

General Measures. All patients with diphtheria should be confined to bed and should remain there until it is certain that all danger of cardiac damage has disappeared. During the first 2 weeks of illness the patient should be kept flat in bed and all exertion avoided.

Patients suffering from diphtheria frequently have a low blood sugar level. For this reason the diet should be high in carbohydrate. During the acute stage of the disease a liquid diet containing fruit juices, sweetened cocoa, and milk is most satisfactory. Patients with bull-neck diphtheria, who are often unable to swallow, should receive intravenous injections of dextrose solutions in order to maintain a normal blood sugar concentration.

Treatment of Complications. With *laryngeal diphtheria* considerable benefit may be obtained from the use of a nebulizer or a steam tent in which oxygen as well as moisture is supplied. Experience and expert judgment are required in the matter of intervention to relieve an obstructed airway. One of the best indices is the patient's ability to rest quietly and to sleep. The degree of restlessness and distress, the amount of inspiratory retraction, and the presence of cyanosis are the criteria to be watched closely. Cyanosis demands immediate intervention. Tracheotomy is now the procedure generally employed; it should be performed under local anesthesia. It bypasses the laryngeal obstruction and permits removal of membrane from the trachea and bronchi.

Myocarditis requires absolute rest; the patient should not be permitted to move about in bed or feed himself. He should not sit up to use a bedpan or for any other reason. Digitalization is indicated for all patients who show clinical or electrocardiographic evidence of moderately severe myocarditis, even if compensated. With decompensation the treatment is similar to that described elsewhere for cardiac insufficiency (Sec. 20.13). Circulatory collapse requires the intravenous administration of plasma or blood and drugs to elevate the blood pressure; cortisone may be helpful.

There is no specific treatment for *paralysis*.

When this involves the muscles of deglutition gavage with a polyethylene tube is indicated.

TREATMENT OF CARRIERS. Some patients continue to harbor organisms for weeks or months after recovery. They should be given a course of penicillin—300,000 to 600,000 units of procaine penicillin daily for 10 days. If bacilli are still present in the nose or throat, erythromycin (20 mg per kilogram per day) should be given for 1 week. If this fails, tonsillectomy and adenoidectomy may be considered but should not be carried out until 3 months after the acute attack. Antitoxin is without value in the treatment of carriers.

PROGNOSIS. The outcome in a given case depends on several factors—the age of the patient, the location and extent of the membrane, the strain of the organism, and the promptness with which antitoxin is administered. The risk is greatest in younger children, particularly those with laryngeal involvement. Patients with extensive membrane and bull-neck appearance within 48 hours after onset have in our experience had a case fatality rate around 30 percent. With clear-cut myocarditis the fatality rate is equally high, and with shock the outcome is nearly always fatal. The importance of early antitoxin is shown by the figures in Table 8 from the Health Department in Chicago.

TABLE 8. *Influence of Time of Injection of Antitoxin on Mortality in Diphtheria*

Time Injection After Onset	Patients	Died	Case Fatality (Percent)
1st day	355	1	0.27
2nd day	1,018	17	1.67
3rd day	1,509	57	3.77
4th day	720	82	11.39
Later	469	119	25.37
Total	4,071	276	6.77

PROPHYLAXIS. Patients should be quarantined until two or three successive negative cultures are obtained one week after the discontinuance of antibiotics. All family and close contacts with a patient should have nose and throat cultures and, if positive, should be treated as described for carriers.

Exposed children, if unimmunized, should be given a 7-day course of penicillin (300,000 to 600,000 units of procaine penicillin by intramuscular injection daily) and active immunization should be started. Previously immunized children should be given a booster injection.

IMMUNITY. This may be measured by the *Schick* test or the *Moloney* test. The Schick test demonstrates the presence or absence of circulating antitoxin sufficient to neutralize a test dose of toxin injected into the skin. One-tenth of a milliliter of test material (containing 1/50 MLD toxin) is injected intradermally, and simultaneously a control injection is made using Schick test material heated to 60° C for 15 minutes to destroy the toxin. In the nonimmune individual a positive reaction (erythema 5 mm in diameter) develops at the test site within 48 hours. It reaches a peak in 4 to 7 days and then subsides, leaving a pigmented spot which may persist for weeks. No reaction ordinarily occurs at the control site. An occasional subject is sensitive to the peptone of the test injection and exhibits a false-positive test at the control area which usually appears within 24 hours and does not persist. A positive Schick test indicates susceptibility to diphtheria; conversely, a negative reactor may be regarded as immune.

The Moloney test consists of an intradermal injection of diphtheria toxoid (0.1 ml of a 1:100 dilution of fluid toxoid). A positive reaction (erythema developing in 18 to 24 hours) denotes allergy to products of the diphtheria bacillus and indicates immunity on a nonantitoxic basis. A positive reaction is rare in very young children but becomes more frequent with advancing age. A positive Moloney reaction may be regarded as evidence of immunity to diphtheria. Individuals with a positive Moloney test will react with constitutional symptoms following the usual injection of toxoid. Since older children are often Moloney positive, the Moloney test should be employed before giving toxoid to children more than 8 years of age.

Active Immunization. Although many infants are protected during the first few months of life by antitoxin received from the mother transplacentally, this is not necessarily the case, and it is currently recommended to start immunization at the age of 1½ to 2 months. Diphtheria toxoid (alum-precipitated or absorbed on aluminum phosphate or aluminum hydroxide) is the product of choice. It may be given alone or with pertussis vaccine and tetanus toxoid (DPT). An initial course of three injections of DPT a month apart, given in early infancy, is a commonly recommended procedure. An appreciable number of infants lose their immunity within a year as measured by the return of a positive Schick test. By the end of three years this number is large enough to be significant. For this reason a booster injection of DPT at 15 months of age is given. DPT is also given at 3 years of age. At 6 and 12 years, injections of combined diphtheria and tetanus toxoid of the "adult type" are recommended (Table 1, Sec. 32.3). "Adult type" toxoid is a specially purified material which gives little or no reaction, even when injected into patients who give a positive Moloney reaction.

References

Belsey, M. H., et al. Corynebacterium diphtheria skin infections in Alabama and Louisiana. Factors in epidemiology of diphtheria. New Eng. J. Med., 280:135, 1969.

v. Bókay, J. Die Diphtherie seit Bretonneau. Ergeb. Inn. Med. Kinderheilk., 42:453, 1932; 43:428, 1932.

Bretonneau, P. F., Trousseau, A., et al. Memoirs on Diphtheria. Selected and translated by Semple, R. H. London, New Sydenham Society, 1859.

Bundesen, H. N., Fishbein, W. I., and White, J. L. Diphtheria immunity in Chicago. J.A.M.A., 112:1919, 1939.

Freeman, V. J. Studies on virulence of bacteriophage-infected strains of C. diphtheriae. J. Bact., 61:675, 1951.

Frost, W. H. Papers of Wade Hampton Frost, M.D. In Maxey, K. F., ed. A Contribution to Epidemiological Method. London, The Commonwealth Fund, 1941.

Harding, M. E. The Circulatory Failure of Diphtheria. London, Univ. of London Press, 1920.

Hodes, H. L. Diphtheria. In Reimann, H. A., ed., Treatment in General Medicine. Philadelphia, F. A. Davis Co., 1947.

Pappenheimer, A. M., Jr. The Diphtheria Bacilli and the Diphtheroids. In Dubos, R. J., ed., Bacterial and Mycotic Infections of Man, 3rd ed. Philadelphia, J. P. Lippincott Co., 1958.

Report of the Committee on the Control of Infectious Diseases. Evanston, Ill., Amer. Acad. Pediat., 1961.

Rich, A. R. A peculiar type of adrenal cortical damage associated wtih acute infections, and its possible relation to circulatory collapse. Bull. Hopkins Hosp., 74:1, 1944.

Rolleston, J. D. Diphtheritic paralysis. Arch. Pediat., 30:335, 1913.

14.8
INFLUENZA BACILLUS INFECTIONS

HATTIE E. ALEXANDER

The influenza bacillus has played two major roles in human infections: as a secondary bacterial invader in epidemic influenza, attacking all age groups; and as a primary pyogenic agent responsible for a variety of clinical patterns, the severe infections affecting infants and children almost exclusively. The confusing name of this organism stems from its discovery by Pfeiffer during the influenza pandemic of 1893, when he believed it to be the cause of the disease. Even though its role in both epidemic and sporadic influenza has been clearly shown to be that of a secondary invader, the name *Haemophilus influenzae* has been retained.

In 1931 Pittman showed that the presence of a capsule and the elaboration of a specific soluble substance differentiate strains of *H. influenzae* which cause pyogenic infections from those which are found frequently in the healthy human nasopharynx. Six distinct types—a, b, c, d, e, and f—may be recognized by identification of the specific polysaccharide characteristic of the type, by either precipitin test, agglutination test, or demonstration of capsular swelling.

Gram-stained smears of biologic fluids infected with *H. influenzae* show a characteristic pleomorphism varying from coccobacilli in pairs or chains to rods of average size and long forms. Consequently, recognition of the organism on the basis of its morphology is difficult and frequently unreliable. Either the precipitin test or the capsular swelling test may be used to make an immediate diagnosis from infected spinal fluid when the organisms are sufficiently numerous to be seen on stained smear. Recognition of the organism and type may be made immediately by the capsular swelling test from nasopharyngeal mucus in patients with epiglottitis or pneumonia, from pleural fluid in empyema, and from joint fluid in arthritis. When these infections are mild the number of organisms is too small for immediate identification; cultivation of the organisms is then necessary for defining etiology. More than 90 percent of serious *H. influenzae* infections in infancy and childhood are due to type b organisms; only for this type has a therapeutic antiserum been developed. Occasionally severe infections are due to types a or f.

IMMUNITY AND AGE INCIDENCE. The pathogenic potentialities of *H. influenzae* as a primary agent are greatly conditioned by the age of the host. The severe pyogenic infections occur almost entirely in infants and children. The age incidence of meningitis was shown by Fothergill and Wright to be closely related to the bactericidal power of the blood. Most infants are passively immunized in utero; in consequence, the incidence of this variety of meningitis is very low under 2 months of age. As this protection is lost the disease becomes more frequent. In children aged 2 months to 3 years, the age range in which 80 percent of the cases of influenzal meningitis occur, the blood of subjects collected at random shows only a feeble bactericidal capacity toward this organism, whereas the sera of older persons and younger infants exhibit an appreciable lethal action. The increase with age in this protective power of blood is apparently the result of contact with the organism. Investigations carried out at Babies Hospital demonstrate the frequency of type b *H. influenzae* respiratory infections; mild infections are at least as common as severe ones and are overcome by the natural defense mechanisms of the host, without the need for specific therapy. The sources for dissemination of this infection are numerous. In hospital wards the spread of these organisms has been shown to be not unlike that of pneumococci. Siblings and often the mothers of children who develop meningitis harbor type b for long periods. In our experience children following recovery from meningitis harbor type b *H. influenzae* in the nasopharynx for many months, regardless of the treatment used.

Though the age incidence of severe *H. influenzae* infections other than meningitis has not been studied by immunologic procedures designed to evaluate the humoral immune status prior to infection, clinical experience suggests that with the exception of epiglottitis they follow a similar pattern. The latter syndrome is rarely seen before the age of 2 years.

SYMPTOMS. *Infections Due to Nonencapsulated H. influenzae.* It is seldom possible to assign a primary pathogenic role to this organism in any age group. In young infants it very occasionally causes meningitis or pneumonia accompanied by bacteremia. Epidemic conjunctivitis has been ascribed to the Koch-Weeks bacillus, an organism indistinguishable from *H. influenzae*. Subacute bacterial endocarditis is at times caused by *H. influenzae* in both children and adults.

This organism has been implicated in chronic lung infections and in some acute pulmonary infections when blood cultures are sterile and when no other bacterial pathogens are demonstrable in the nasopharynx. However, the role it plays in these infections is a controversial question which requires more evidence to answer.

The large reservoir of nontypable *H. influenzae* in the nasopharynx of normal children and adults has assumed greater significance since the demonstration that type specificity and therefore potential virulence can be induced in nontype-specific or R-forms of *H. influenzae* in vitro, by exposure to deoxyribonucleic acid isolated from type-specific *H. influenzae* cells. This raises the possibility that such a transformation may occur in the nasopharynx under appropriate stimuli.

Infections Caused by Encapsulated H. influenzae. Studies carried out at Babies Hospital indicate that encapsulated *H. influenzae* after entering the respiratory tract produces a nasopharyngitis in most children, usually with some fever. Many patients overcome the infection spontaneously; others develop sinusitis or otitis media. Any portion of the lower respiratory tract may be involved, from the epiglottis and surrounding structures to the pulmonary alveoli. From these foci in various parts of the respiratory tract invasion of the bloodstream may occur. The areas most commonly involved in metastatic infection are the meninges and joints. Rarely, pericarditis or subcutaneous abscess results. On one occasion we have seen *H. influenzae* cellulitis in the submental and in both anterior cervical regions; the patient exhibited a severe degree of toxemia, and meningitis followed. Periorbital and other facial forms of *H. influenzae* cellulitis are seen occasionally. Of the severe infections caused by these organisms, those found with greatest frequency are meningitis, obstructive infections of the respiratory tract, pneumonia and empyema, and pyarthrosis.

Meningitis. In this country, except during epidemics of meningococcal infections, *H. influenzae* is the commonest cause of meningitis in children. Influenzal meningitis is characteristically primary in that it develops following an unimpressive upper respiratory tract infection; there may be coincident paranasal sinusitis or purulent otitis media, but evidence for direct extension is lacking. Bacteremia is virtually always present in untreated patients.

There are no clinical manifestations which differentiate influenzal from other varieties of meningitis. The signs vary greatly from patient to patient, depending upon the age, stage of the disease, severity of the infection, and whether antibacterial treatment has been administered. The clinical picture is described on page 599.

Obstructive infections of the respiratory tract. When *H. influenzae* type b is responsible for obstructive laryngeal, laryngotracheal, or laryngotracheobronchial infections, the illness presents a characteristic history and the patient a characteristic appearance. The onset is sudden and the course fulminating. Dyspnea from laryngeal obstruction starts abruptly and increases rapidly, usually accompanied by high temperature. On examination of the pharynx there is diffuse erythema, often with evident edema, and when the tongue is pressed downward the enlarged, red, edematous, distorted epiglottis is easily seen. This syndrome is described in Section 19.4.

Pneumonia and Empyema with Bacteremia in Infants under 1 Year of Age. In older children type b *H. influenzae* may cause pneumonia which is clinically indistinguishable from the variety due to pneumococcus. In infants less than 1 year of age empyema and bacteremia are common concomitants, and the incidence of subsequent meningitis is high. Lumbar puncture is therefore advisable when empyema of this etiology is present in an infant, even if there are no decisive signs of meningitis. The causative agent of the pulmonary infection is strongly suspected when type b *H. influenzae* is found in nasopharyngeal mucus, either by direct typing or in cultures. Isolation of the same organism from empyema fluid or blood culture confirms the etiology.

Infections of bones and joints. Since the advent of effective antibacterial agents against *H. influenzae* infections, localization in the bones and joints has become not only a less frequent but a less ominous manifestation. Roentgenograms made at appropriate periods after onset of joint infection frequently show epiphysitis. Pyarthrosis, single or multiple, may be the only manifestation of *H. influenzae* infection; pyarthrosis may also be associated with meningitis, pneumonia, or rarely pericarditis. There are no clinical signs which distinguish influenzal pyarthrosis; immediate identification can usually be made by examination of the joint fluid.

PROGNOSIS. Before the days of specific therapy the case fatality rate in influenzal meningitis varied from 92 to 100 percent, depending upon the age of the patient; in infants it was virtually 100 percent. Since 1939 the proportion of survivors has greatly increased, so that now few patients die, although among survivors some increase has occurred in the incidence of neurologic and psychologic residua. Therapeutic failures can usually be ascribed to delayed diagnosis, both clinical and bacteriologic, or to suboptimal use of available therapeutic agents.

The prognosis in obstructive infections of the respiratory tract again depends mostly on treatment, but in this instance the provision of an airway is even more urgently needed than is control of the infection. Tracheotomy is frequently imperative within a few hours after onset of dyspnea. In other patients, when this procedure is not obviously urgent, exact criteria for intervention are controversial. Sudden complete obstruction, following manipulation within or outside the respiratory tract, is seen not infrequently. For this reason the Mosher "lifesaver" or some comparable simple device for establishing an airway is a necessary part of the equipment for handling these patients prior to tracheotomy. Since the probability of the need for tracheotomy is great and the risk of delaying too long is hazardous, early operation, while circumstances are still favorable, is conservative rather than radical therapy. In spite of almost uniform bacteremia in the first hours of the infection, distant metastases rarely give rise to late complications. With adequate pulmonary ventilation the infection can usually be brought rapidly under control, and prompt improvement is seen. As a rule the tracheotomy tube can be removed in 3 to 5 days. Late sequelae are unknown.

In cases with pyarthrosis our experience suggests that the degree of destruction present in the joint at the time treatment is started determines the prognosis of joint function, regardless of whether incision and drainage are carried out. We have seen complete recovery after antibacterial therapy without drainage and without injection of agents into the joint.

TREATMENT. A number of therapeutic agents have been effective in *H. influenzae* infections: specific rabbit antibody (for type b only), the sulfonamides, the tetracyclines, chloramphenicol, streptomycin, and ampicillin. Currently, ampicillin is considered the drug of choice for treatment of *H. influenzae* infections. Chloramphenicol is an alternate drug which is also effective.

For the treatment of patients with an obstructive infection of the respiratory tract, the measures used to relieve obstruction have been discussed under prognosis.

REFERENCES

Alexander, H. E. The Hemophilus Group. *In* Dubos, R. J., ed., Bacterial and Mycotic Infections of Man, 4th ed. Philadelphia, J. B. Lippincott Co., 1965, p. 724.

——— Advances in the treatment of bacterial meningitis. *In* Advances in Pediatrics. 5:13, Chicago, Year Book Publishers, 1952.

——— and Leidy, G. Mode of action of streptomycin on type b *H. influenzae;* nature of resistant variants. J. Exp. Med., 85:607, 1947.

——— and Leidy, G. Determination of inherited traits of *H. influenzae* by desoxyribonucleic acid fractions isolated from type-specific cells. J. Exp. Med., 93:345, 1951.

Barrett, F. F., et al. Ampicillin in the treatment of acute suppurative meningitis. J. Pediat., 69:345, 1966.

Fothergill, L. D., and Wright, J. Influenzal meningitis; the relation of age incidence to the bactericidal power of blood against causal organism. J. Immunol., 24:273, 1933.

Johnson, R. D., and Fousek, M. D. A study of the spread of *H. influenzae,* type b. J. Bact., 45:197, 1943.

McKay, R. J., Jr., Morissette, R. A., Ingraham, F. D., and Matson, D. D. Collections of subdural fluid complicating meningitis due to *Hemophilus influenzae* (type b); a preliminary report. New Eng. J. Med., 242:20, 1950.

Pittman, M. Variation and type specificity in bacterial species *Hemophilus influenzae.* J. Exp. Med., 53:471, 1931.

Rabe, E. F. Infectious croup. III. *Hemophilus influenzae* type b croup. Pediatrics, 2:559, 1948.

14.9
LEPTOSPIROSIS
(WEIL'S DISEASE)

HATTIE E. ALEXANDER

Leptospirosis, also known as Weil's disease, spirochetal fever, or spirochetal jaundice, is caused by leptospirae transmitted to man by the ingestion of water, food, or soil contaminated with the urine of animal carriers. Rodents, dogs, cats, pigs, horses, and cattle harbor leptospirae, the spirochetes persisting in foci in the tubules of the kidney. Surveys of rat populations in several cities indicate that 10 to 30 percent of adult animals may be carriers. Numerous serologic types of leptospira, each more or less specific for its particular animal host, have been identified.

In man infection occurs most frequently in individuals working where rats are numerous, such as sewer workers, miners, veterinarians, butchers, fishmongers, and poultry farmers. The usual portal of entry is a cut or abrasion of the skin. Infants rarely acquire this disease, but it does occur in older children contracted by playing with infected animals or by swimming or accidental immersion in polluted water. In cases due to immersion, infection probably enters through the conjunctivae or nasal mucous membranes. Leptospirae are rapidly destroyed in acid media, and entry by way of the gastrointestinal tract is therefore unlikely.

Leptospirosis is more common in Europe and Asia than in the United States, but the incidence in this country is increasing. Since 1939 sporadic cases, of both canine and murine origin, have been reported in children. In 1952 Beeson and Hankey found that in a series of 86 cases of aseptic meningitis 11 were caused by leptospirosis, 6 cases being due to *L. canicola* and 5 to *L. icterohemorrhagiae.*

SYMPTOMS. The severity of the symptoms varies to some extent with the type of leptospira. *L. cani-cola,* frequently contracted from dogs, produces a relatively mild infection. Icterus is rare, but conjunctival and meningeal symptoms are common. *L. icterohemorrhagiae* gives as a rule a more severe clinical picture, as described below.

The incubation period is usually 8 days but may be as short as 4 or as long as 19 days. Onset is characterized by chills and fever. The chief symptoms are toxemia, weakness, intense headache, and myalgia. Nausea, vomiting, and diarrhea may occur, and mental confusion early in the course of the illness is not uncommon. A tendency to hemorrhage may be present during the first week of illness, occasionally in the form of severe bleeding from the gastrointestinal tract. An exanthem simulating scarlet fever or rubella is not unusual. Congestion of the conjunctivae is a characteristic finding.

Fever of 102 to 104° F accompanied by polymorphonuclear leucocytosis continues as a rule for about 8 days and then falls by lysis, with parallel subsidence of other symptoms. Not infrequently the signs of infection subside for a day or two, only to recur with renewal of fever and other constitutional manifestations or even with meningitic signs.

The disease may present itself only as a benign aseptic meningitis. Regardless of whether meningeal involvement appears early or only after subsidence of an initial febrile phase, the spinal fluid shows a pleocytosis of 50 to 500 cells per cubic millimeter, lymphocytes usually predominating. The spinal fluid protein concentration is moderately elevated, the sugar normal as a rule. Leptospirae are not demonstrable in the spinal fluid.

Unfavorable signs accompany involvement of the liver or kidneys. Jaundice, when it appears, usually becomes manifest toward the end of the first week, at the time fever subsides; it is accompanied by hepatomegaly but not, as a rule, by enlargement of the spleen. Once present, jaundice may persist for a month or more. Although the intensity of icterus is not closely correlated with outcome, the case fatality rate in series of patients exhibiting jaundice may be as high as 30 percent. With renal involvement albuminuria of severe degree is an early sign; oliguria and anuria may lead to death in uremia. In the majority of instances, however, a sudden diuresis heralds recovery; and permanent renal damage is uncommon.

The appearance of conjunctivitis, jaundice, or marked albuminuria in a febrile patient, or the development of aseptic meningitis, should arouse suspicion of leptospirosis and lead to the instigation of specific diagnostic tests. During the early febrile stage leptospirae can be demonstrated in the blood by dark-field examination, by culture, or by inoculation into guinea pigs or hamsters. After the first few days of infection the bloodstream becomes free of organisms, even in cases with persistent or recurrent fever, but leptospirae appear in the urine and antibodies become demonstrable in the blood. The serum agglutinin titer reaches its peak 6 to 8 weeks following infection, after which it falls off slowly.

Direct microscopic examination of the blood by dark-field illumination is not a reliable method of excluding leptospiral infection because the organisms may be present in very small numbers and can therefore be easily overlooked. Errors in the opposite direction, false-positives, dependent on artifacts rather than on leptospirae, must also be guarded against. Intraperitoneal inoculation of patient's blood into guinea pigs or hamsters has been widely used for diagnostic confirmation, but is less satisfactory than culture methods because of the possibility of inapparent leptospiral infections in laboratory animals. Blood cultures when positive usually grow out in 14 days; samples should be held for 28 days before being discarded as negative. A positive culture should be forwarded immediately to a leptospiral typing center for definitive identification. Demonstration of a rising titer of agglutinins or complement fixing antibodies constitutes convincing evidence of recently acquired infection.

TREATMENT.   Chlortetracycline or oxytetracycline given within the first 4 days of illness and continued for 4 to 6 days shortens the duration of fever and usually prevents the secondary rise of temperature frequently observed in untreated cases.

REFERENCES

Ashe, W. F., Pratt-Thomas, H. R., and Kumpe, C. W. Weil's disease: a complete review of American literature and an abstract of the world literature; seven case reports. Medicine, 20:145, 1941.

Beeson, P. B., and Hankey, D. D. Leptospiral meningitis. Arch. Int. Med., 89:575, 1952.

Gordon, M. E. Canicola fever; report of first case in Connecticut and review of the literature. New Eng. J. Med., 247:708, 1952.

Martmer, E. E. Weil's disease; report of a case occurring in a child. J. Pediat., 14:48, 1939.

Symposium on the Leptospiroses. Medical Science Publication No. 1, Washington, D.C., Army Medical Service Graduate School, December 1952.

Woodward, T. E., Diaz Rivera, R. S., and Hightower, J. A. The variable clinical manifestations of leptospirosis. Bull. N.Y. Acad. Med., 29:642, 1953.

14.10
MENINGOCOCCAL
INFECTIONS

ELI GOLD

The recent realization that meningococci have become markedly more resistant to sulfonamides has provoked a great deal of interest in this organism and its behavior. Fortunately, there is no relationship between sulfonamide resistance and ability to produce disease or the severity of disease produced. Patients with illnesses caused by sulfa-resistant meningococci respond as well to penicillin therapy as those infected with sulfa-susceptible strains. The major new problem is the inability to eliminate the carriage of sulfa-resistant organisms; there appears to be no effective drug.

THE ORGANISM.   Meningococci (*Neisseria meningitidis*) are gram-negative, endotoxin-containing organisms which have some of the traits of gram-positive organisms. They inhabit the respiratory tract, from which they may be disseminated via the bloodstream, and have a spectrum of antibiotic sensitivity similar to that of pneumococci, streptococci, and some staphylococci.

N. meningitidis are extremely labile organisms and are rapidly inactivated outside the body by drying, heat, or contact with germicides. Smears of pus taken from infected sites characteristically contain large numbers of intracellular, gram-negative, biscuit-shaped diplococci. The organism has rather simple nutritional requirements but is susceptible to the toxic effect of amino acids and many other constituents of media. Growth of the organism is best on chocolate or Miller-Hinton agar (starch casein hydrolysate) in an atmosphere of 2 to 20 percent CO_2, using candle jar or CO_2 incubator. Typical colonies grown on transparent media are smooth glistening "tear drops" which contain cytochrome oxidase. Testing for this uncommon enzyme provides a rapid means for the presumptive identification of members of the *Neisseria* genus. Classical strains ferment dextrose and maltose, but many variants recently isolated from children ferment lactose. The meningococci have been divided into four groups—A, B, C, and D— by specific serologic reactions, but more and more nontypable strains are being isolated and additional groups called X and Y have been suggested.

EPIDEMIOLOGY.   The annual rate of meningococcal infection in the United States has ranged from 1.2 to 1.8 per 100,000 population, with epidemic peaks occurring at 8- to 10-year intervals. The incidence varies in different geographic portions of the country; highest rates have been in the Southeast and West. Most cases occur in late winter and early spring, with a decline in summer and early fall. Military cases have accounted for approximately 10 percent of the reported total. Age-specific attack rates are highest in infants less than 1 year of age, followed by a decline in rate throughout the childhood years. A secondary peak occurs in the 15- to 24-year-old age group, with a fall to insignificant levels thereafter.

Major epidemics of meningococcal disease prior to 1963 were caused by Group A strains; only sporadic or small foci of cases were the source of serotypes B or C. In the past several years, however, Group A organisms have accounted for less than 5 percent of meningococcal isolates submitted to the National Communicable Disease Center. Group B and, more recently, Group C organisms are the predominant serotypes associated with severe clinical disease. Concurrent with the observed change in distribution of serotypes has been the marked increase in prevalence of sulfa-resistant strains. Approximately 50 percent of Group B isolates and an increasingly larger proportion of Group C strains (approaching 90 percent) are resistant to 1.0 mg/100 ml or more of sulfadiazine (or related sulfonamide drugs). Although Group A organisms have been responsible for a relatively small number of illnesses, there is evidence that this serotype has also become resistant to the sulfonamides.

PATHOGENESIS. Meningococci are transmitted from person to person by droplet spread as are many other agents which inhabit the respiratory tract. Infection of a susceptible host is followed by a period during which meningococci multiply in the nasopharynx, but the development of disease is uncommon. Since the carrier rate for meningococci averages 10 percent, and the attack rate for meningococcal disease (meningococcemia and/or meningococcal meningitis) is approximately 1 in 100,000 population, it can be estimated that about 1 in 10,000 individuals who are infected by meningococci develop a significant illness. In these vulnerable few, the host is apparently unable to limit the growth and dissemination of the organism, and bacteremia with or without meningitis results.

Meningococcal infection is properly included among the large group of "childhood diseases" with which each individual eventually has contact. Transplacentally acquired antibody protects most infants during the first few months of life, after which there is a reciprocal relationship between presence of antibody and incidence of infection. Most infections are asymptomatic and result in the development of persistent, specific immunity. As the proportion of a specific age group without specific immunity decreases, the attack rates of meningococcal infection in that group diminishes.

The major clinical manifestations of generalized meningococcal infection are bleeding and shock produced by the action of endotoxin on the endothelium of small vessels.

CLINICAL DISEASE AND DIFFERENTIAL DIAGNOSIS. The symptoms and signs of meningococcal infection, similar to those which occur with other forms of bacteremia or meningitis, differ with the age of the patient. In approximately one-half of all patients, typical petechiae or larger purpuric lesions appear, usually most apparent on the chest, upper arms, and axilla. Older children typically have fever, headache, irritability, and lethargy, but hyperactivity, delirium, or the complaint of "aching all over" are not uncommon. Nuchal rigidity is a prominent sign except in young infants, where fever, poor feeding, vomiting, and lethargy are often the presenting complaints. A bulging fontanel may be the other major clue indicating infection of the central nervous system.

The usual history is that of rapid progression of the symptoms and signs over a period of hours, although the onset in some patients may be insidious. Suspicion of meningitis, especially if supported by evidence of meningeal irritation, is an indication for immediate lumbar puncture. Cerebrospinal fluid should be removed slowly, through a small needle, in sufficient quantity for smear, culture, cell count, sugar, and protein. Measurement of pressure is often also helpful. The typical cerebrospinal fluid findings are an increase in white blood cell count with a predominance of polymorphonuclear leucocytes (100 to several thousand cells); sugar of 40 mg/100 ml or less, or less than two-thirds of the blood sugar level; an elevated protein; and/or positive smear or culture. Rarely, a positive culture is obtained from a cerebrospinal fluid with few or no cells, but ordinarily the high cell count, low sugar, and elevated protein make it easy to distinguish bacterial meningitis from viral aseptic meningitis. If the diagnosis is confused by previous antibiotic treatment or atypical cerebrospinal fluid findings, it may be prudent to give the patient the benefit of antibiotic therapy, until the problem of etiology can be resolved.

The differential diagnosis of meningococcal meningitis may include other forms of central nervous system infection, bacterial and viral. Viral infections can usually be distinguished by the cerebrospinal fluid findings. The presence of petechial rash is more likely to occur with meningococcal infection than with *H. influenzae* or pneumococci, but if a definite bacteriologic diagnosis cannot be made from the cerebrospinal fluid smear, treatment with ampicillin or chloramphenicol combined with penicillin, which covers all three of these possibilities, should be begun; modifications of drug therapy can be made when culture results are available. A common problem in differential diagnosis is differentiating streptococcal infection with petechiae from meningococcemia, especially when sore throat and adenopathy are not present. In such cases, cultures are obtained and penicillin is administered until a specific diagnosis is made by the bacteriology laboratory.

TREATMENT. In the preantibiotic era, the mortality rate for meningococcal meningitis varied from 15 to 85 percent, depending on the particular outbreak and the age group affected. The death rate among young infants was 90 percent. The development of type-specific antiserum shortly after the turn of the century reduced the risk of death to about 30 percent; this figure fell to 12 to 15 percent with the advent of sulfonamides, but this is where it has remained. The availability of antibiotics, sophisticated fluid therapy, steroids, and other pharamacologic agents has not resulted in a further significant reduction in the mortality rate from meningococcal disease.

The diagnosis of meningococcemia with or without meningitis calls for the prompt administration of proper antimicrobial therapy. Penicillin is the drug of choice (ampicillin or erythromycin are alternates); ampicillin or chloramphenicol may be used in addition if the etiology of a bacterial meningitis is uncertain. Therapy should be given by the intravenous route (1,000,000 units every 4 hours) during the first 5 to 7 days.

Most patients with meningococcal infection whose illness is diagnosed promptly and who have the benefit of treatment with a proper antibiotic, recover and suffer no apparent residual effect. Those whose illness is not recognized or who do not receive adequate antibiotic therapy may have a prolonged course with thrombosis of cerebral vessels, infarction of brain, and permanent central nervous system damage. The major fear with meningococcal infection is shock, usually accompanied by extensive purpura, and followed by death (the Waterhouse-Friderichsen syndrome).

The precise mechanism of endotoxin shock in man is not clear; nor is it known whether fulminant shock and intravascular coagulation, which frequently occur together, are independent or related phenomena. Studies of endotoxin shock in different animals and by different workers provide conflicting ideas as to what happens in man and it is difficult to decide what specific therapeutic approaches are indicated in the human patient. There is no evidence at this time that the use of steroids, heparin, or vasodilators has altered the prognosis of endotoxic shock, but the total experience with the latter two forms of therapy is still small.

Patients with meningococcal infection should be treated with antibiotics and appropriate intravenous fluids. Vital signs, especially blood pressure, should be monitored and if hypotension develops, an immediate attempt should be made to maintain blood volume. Hydrocortisone in large doses (40 to 50 mg/kg) administered intravenously and repeated every 30 to 60 minutes for 3 to 4 doses has been advocated for such patients, mostly on the basis of theoretical indications; clinical experience with its use shows neither clear-cut benefit nor evidence of harm. Vasodilators such as isoproterenol or phenoxybenzamine have been shown to be of value in the management of shock in laboratory animals, but no one has had sufficient success in the treatment of meningococcal shock with these agents to recommend their general use. Intravascular coagulation with severe bleeding into skin and viscera, as frequently seen in fulminant shock, is associated with a decrease in components of the intravascular clotting reaction; platelets, factors V and VIII, prothrombin, and fibrinogen may all be low. This observation has been the basis for attempts to treat intravascular coagulation with heparin, but again, the results have been variable. It may be reasonable, in centers where adequate facilities are available, to measure clotting factors in patients with meningococcal shock and initiate treatment with heparin when there is evidence of intravascular coagulation and depletion of factors. Heparin may be given intravenously in a dose of 1 mg/kg every 4 hours as needed to maintain the clotting time at 20 to 30 minutes until coagulation factors return to normal levels.

Subdural effusions may occur following meningococcal meningitis and should be considered in any patient with an atypical course characterized by persistent fever, bulging fontanel, lethargy, vomiting, or neurologic signs. Increasing head size or translucent areas in the temporal areas visible by transillumination of the infant skull are presumptive signs of subdural effusions.

Recent postmortem studies have shown myocarditis with pulmonary edema and congestive failure occurring with relatively high frequency, especially in adults. Observation of patients with meningococcal infection for evidence of myocardial disease, and treatment of congestive heart failure when it occurs, may save some lives.

PROPHYLAXIS. The changes in the sulfonamide-sensitivity pattern of the meningococci have removed an effective tool for eliminating carriers or protecting contacts of cases. Penicillin and related drugs which are highly effective for treating systemic meningococcal infections do not eliminate the carrier state.

The probability of meningococcal disease occurring among close associates of a case is difficult to determine, but it is quite clearly greater than among the population as a whole. The choice of appropriate prophylaxis for close contacts of patients is at present controversial. Many physicians do not recommend any form of prophylaxis. Penicillin has been used by some with the thought that suppression of the meningococci may interfere with disease production even though the bacteria are not eliminated. There appears to be a trend to large doses of penicillin and the use of a parenteral route. Others use sulfonamide prophylaxis with the full understanding that the probability of the causative agent being resistant is greater than 50 percent. Close surveillance of all contacts is obviously required to identify any secondary cases promptly, regardless of what drugs may have been administered.

Vaccines prepared from purified meningococcal polysaccharides appear to be nontoxic, effective immunizing agents. The use of such preparations, especially in high-risk groups, may soon be feasible.

REFERENCES

Appelbaum, E., and Nelson, J. Sulfadiazine and its sodium compound in treatment of meningococcic meningitis and meningococcemia. Amer. J. Med. Sci., 207:492, 1944.

D'Agati, V. C., and Marangoni, B. A. The Waterhouse-Friderichsen syndrome. New Eng. J. Med., 232:1, 1945.

Gotschlich, E. C., Goldschneider, I., and Artenstein, M. S. Human immunity to the meningococcus. J. Exp. Med., 129:1385, 1969.

Haggerty, R., and Ziai, M. Acute bacterial meningitis. Advances Pediat., 13:129, 1964.

Hodes, H. L. Care of the critically ill child: Endotoxin shock. Pediatrics, 44:248, 1969.

——— Moloshok, R. E., and Markowitz, M. Fulminating meningococcemia treated with cortisone; use of blood eosinophil count as a guide to prognosis and treatment. Pediatrics, 10:138, 1952.

McGehee, W. G., Rapaport, S. I., and Hjort, P. F. Intravascular coagulation in fulminant meningococcemia. Ann. Intern. Med., 67:250, 1967.

Pascoe, D. J., and Lufkin, C. D. Meningococcal disease due to a sulfadiazine resistant strain. Pediatrics, 34:124, 1964.

Rich, A. R. A peculiar type of adrenal cortical damage associated with acute infections, and its possible relation to circulatory collapse. Bull. Hopkins Hosp., 74:1, 1944.

Swartz, M., and Dodge, P. Bacterial meningitis—a review of selected aspects. New Eng. J. Med., 272:725, 1965.

14.11
MYCOPLASMA INFECTIONS

WALTER L. HENLEY

Microorganisms of the genus *Mycoplasma*, originally known as pleuropneumonialike organisms (PPLO), are only 125 to 150 mμ in size. They are the smallest known microorganisms able to reproduce in a cell-free medium, and resemble L-forms of bacteria. Their evolution has been thought by some to be related to these forms, but they have not been known to revert. Mycoplasma are pleomorphic, lacking a rigid cell wall; they have a characteristic colonial morphology and require sterols and protein for growth.

Mycoplasma can be differentiated on an antigenic basis by the complement-fixing antibodies they elicit and by an indirect hemagglutination test using sensitized tanned red blood cells.

Mycoplasma pneumoniae is the most important member of the genus *Mycoplasma*. This organism is the cause of the kind of primary atypical pneumonia which is accompanied by the production of cold hemagglutinins; it was formerly known as Eaton's agent and is the only mycoplasma which is able to absorb and lyse certain types of erythrocytes within 24 to 48 hours. Other antigenically different mycoplasma have been isolated from the pharynx, urogenital tract, blood, and brain.

Mycoplasma hominis I has been recovered from the mouth, the urogenital tract, a pelvic abscess, and from the bone marrow of a patient with leukemia. In experimental infection with nasal inoculation it has produced exudative pharyngitis and tonsillitis in man.

Mycoplasma orale type I, *Mycoplasma salivarium,* and *Mycoplasma fermentans* are most often recovered from the mouth. Other strains known at present are *Mycoplasma orale* type II and *Mycoplasma pharynges,* which may be the same organism and which inhabit the oropharynx. *Mycoplasma hominis II* may not be of human origin, since it is antigenically indistinguishable from *Mycoplasma arthritidis,* indigenous to the rat.

Recovery of mycoplasma is not proof of an eti-ologic relationship in cases of urethritis, cervicitis, and vaginitis, since these organisms can be recovered from patients without disease. Similarly *Mycoplasma hominis* has been isolated in healthy patients as well as from patients with pneumonia. Mycoplasma have been isolated with greater frequency in patients with leukemia, which raises the possibility of latent infection. An antibody rise against some mycoplasma has also occurred when another diagnosis such as syphilis or trichomoniasis had been established.

Mycoplasma pneumoniae

With the discovery and widespread use of antibiotics, a group of patients with pneumonia was recognized who did not show the immediate favorable response to chemotherapy which is typical of patients with pneumococcal pneumonia. In many of these cases of atypical pneumonia a rise in cold hemagglutinins was noted. From such a case Eaton isolated an agent which measured 180 to 215 mμ. It could be propagated in eggs and tissue culture, and it could be visualized by immunofluorescence in animal lung studies.

Eaton's agent was thereafter most frequently isolated from atypical pneumonia patients who showed the rise in cold hemagglutinin antibodies. Because treatment with tetracycline and streptomycin was frequently successful in these patients, doubt arose that Eaton's agent was a virus. In 1962, Chanock and his co-workers successfully cultivated Eaton's agent on cell-free agar medium and identified it as a member of Mycoplasmataceae. They proposed the specific name *Mycoplasma pneumoniae,* which is now the accepted designation.

EPIDEMIOLOGY. *Mycoplasma pneumoniae* may cause pneumonia in any age group, but it most commonly affects adolescents and young adults. It may also cause upper respiratory disease and bronchitis, and it has been isolated from patients with otitis media. The prevalence of infection varies from year to year; the lowest incidence is usually found during the summer months. *Mycoplasma pneumoniae* spreads most readily on close contact with families and among military recruits and college students.

CLINICAL DISEASE. It is now known that atypical pneumonia may be caused by a number of microorganisms. These include adenoviruses, influenza viruses A and B, parainfluenza viruses, respiratory syncytial virus, members of the psittacosis/ornithosis group, and *Coxiella burnetti* of Q fever, as well as *Mycoplasma pneumoniae.* A rise in cold hemagglutinins and streptococcus MG agglutinins is associated with *Mycoplasma pneumoniae* infection. However, increases in cold hemagglutinins have been found in association with viral respiratory infections.

The incubation period ranges from 10 to 20 days, followed by rapid onset of fever, malaise, and persistent cough. Some children report anorexia and abdominal pain. Chills, headache, and conjunctivitis sometimes occur. Frequently there is little distress, especially in children. Roentgenologic evidence of pneumonia often is strikingly greater than is expected on the basis of the physical examination. In infants the disease may mimic bronchiolitis; in some cases the cough may be paroxysmal, as in pertussis.

PHYSICAL EXAMINATION. Physical examination may reveal rhinitis, pharyngeal erythema, and some enlargement of cervical lymph nodes. Rales or rhonchi may be heard. Dullness and decreased breath sounds are noted occasionally, but pleural friction rubs are uncommon. Respiratory and pulse rates are increased only slightly. Dyspnea and cyanosis are rare.

The child appears less ill than the fever might indicate. The cough is dry initially, but during the course of the disease sputum appears which contains pus and desquamated cells.

LABORATORY FINDINGS. There is usually no significant change in the leucocyte count, but a rise in the sedimentation rate is common. After approximately 2 weeks many patients show a rise in hemagglutinins against human group O erythrocytes, at 0° to 10° C (not at 37° C). Some patients develop streptococcus MG agglutinins.

Between 10 and 25 days after onset there is a rise in the complement-fixing and fluorescent antibody titers, and the former may remain elevated for 3 months. Complement fixation is the best serologic test for the diagnosis of *Mycoplasma pneumoniae* infection. Approximately one-half of the patients who show a rise in complement-fixing antibodies also have a rise in cold hemagglutinin antibodies.

RADIOLOGIC FINDINGS. Roentgenograms show infiltration that seems to fan from the hilum to the periphery. These findings are usually confined to one lobe. Occasionally more than one lobe is involved, or lesions resembling miliary granuloma are seen.

Increased bronchovascular markings due to peribronchial inflammation, bronchial and bronchiolar infiltration, and vascular engorgement can be seen, as well as areas of spotty atelectasis.

DIAGNOSIS AND DIFFERENTIAL DIAGNOSIS. The diagnosis is made by isolating the microorganism. It may be isolated from the nasopharynx more often in patients with pneumonia than in patients with upper respiratory tract infection. Prolonged infection occurs with isolation of the microorganism for more than 30 days.

Together with isolation of the organism an antibody rise should be demonstrated. *Mycoplasma pneumoniae* infection leads to elevation of complement-fixing and fluorescent antibody titers. Not every patient exhibiting a rise in the cold hemagglutinin antibody titer has *Mycoplasma pneumoniae* infection as shown by the complement-fixing antibody titer.

Other agents causing similar disease have been listed under Clinical Disease, and the determination of their presence also depends on isolation of the pathogenic microorganism and the demonstration of the corresponding antibody rise.

COURSE AND COMPLICATIONS. Usually the disease lasts from 1 to 2 weeks, but the x-ray findings may persist twice as long or longer.

Meningismus may be noted on physical examination, but meningoencephalitis is rare. Otitis media occurs occasionally. Pleurisy and pneumothorax are infrequent. Bronchiectasis, pericarditis, polyneuritis, and erythema nodosum have been reported.

TREATMENT. Tetracycline is useful in the treatment of *Mycoplasma pneumoniae* infections, but it is not invariably effective. Erythromycin is also effective in treating the disease and, as noted by Clyde and Denny, may be superior in children because of its narrow antimicrobial spectrum and lack of undesirable effects produced by the tetracyclines. The microorganism may not, however, be eradicated by the antibiotic. *Mycoplasma pneumoniae* is resistant to penicillin.

Humid air inhalation is the most important aid in avoiding accumulation of thick mucus and is the cornerstone of symptomatic treatment. Decongestant and expectorant medications are usually unnecessary. Dehydration should be prevented by oral intake of liquids. Intravenous fluids may be required in a dyspneic child; oxygen inhalation is needed only in rare patients with severe dyspnea and cyanosis.

Prolonged convalescent care may be necessary in a previously ill child.

PREVENTION. Patients with an elevated antibody titer resist reinfection. In one study 90 percent of volunteers with elevated antibody levels were protected against experimental infection, whereas 75 percent of control patients developed coryza or pneumonia. An experimental vaccine has proved effective, but no commercial vaccine is currently available nor is there a need, at present, for general vaccination of children.

REFERENCES

Balassanian, N., and Robbins, F. C. Mycoplasma pneumoniae infection in families. New Eng. J. Med., 277: 719-25, 1967.

Chanock, R. M. Mycoplasma infections of man. New Eng. J. Med., 273:1199, 1965.

Clyde, W. A., and Denny, F. W. Mycoplasma infections in childhood. Pediatrics, 40:669-84, 1967.

Cordero, L., Cuadrado, P., et al. Primary atypical pneumonia: An epidemic caused by Mycoplasma pneumoniae. J. Pediat., 71:1-12, 1967.

Grayston, J. T., Alexander, E. R., Kenny, G. E., Clarke, E. R., Fremont, J. C., and MacColl, W. A. *Mycoplasma pneumoniae* infections. J.A.M.A., 191:97, 1965.

Hayflick, L. The mycoplasma (PPLO) species of man. Trans. N.Y. Acad. Sci., 27:817, 1965.

Klein, J. O., Buckland, D., et al. Colonization of newborn infants by mycoplasmas. New Eng. J. Med., 280: 1025-30, 1969.

Rytel, M. W. Primary atypical pneumonia: current concepts. Amer. J. Med. Sci., 247:84, 1964.

14.12
PERTUSSIS AND
PARAPERTUSSIS

WILLIAM L. BRADFORD

Pertussis
(Whooping Cough)

Pertussis is an acute infection of the respiratory tract caused by *Bordetella pertussis*. It occurs endemically throughout the world and epidemically in many of the more thickly populated areas. The disease is essentially a progressive paroxysmal cough of varying intensity. It may last for several weeks and may be especially severe or even fatal in early infancy. Interstitial pneumonia and involvement of the central nervous system are important complications.

ETIOLOGY. The causative agent, known as the Bordet-Gengou bacillus, was first described in 1906. As a member of the genus *Haemophilus* it is generally called *Haemophilus pertussis*, but more recently it has been named *Bordetella pertussis* and placed in a separate genus (*Bordetella*) along with *H. parapertussis* and *Brucella bronchisepticus*.

Bord. pertussis is a small, gram-negative, nonmotile, coccoid bacillus approximately 0.5 μ in length. When first isolated, the organism is of uniform size; in older cultures it becomes pleomorphic. With appropriate staining methods capsules may be observed.

Among other organisms capable of producing infections of the respiratory tract resembling pertussis are *Haemophilus influenzae*, *Bord. bronchiseptica*, and *Bord. parapertussis*. The last two of these probably share common antigenic components with *Bord. pertussis* but do not convey cross-immunity.

INCIDENCE. Approximately 90 percent of cases occur under the age of 9 years, and 10 percent occur during the first year of life, when the mortality is greatest. Both incidence and mortality under one year of age are higher among Negro children.

Although pertussis is worldwide in distribution, the incidence varies in different regions of each country. In Massachusetts, where reporting is well established, the incidence has remained rather uniform for the past two decades among children 10 to 14 years of age but has markedly decreased among younger subjects since 1940, when pertussis vaccine came into general use (Fig. 1). A similar downward trend in the incidence of the disease throughout the United States is shown in Figure 2. In children over 10 years of age, the incidence is greater among females.

EPIDEMIOLOGY. In more thickly populated communities pertussis occurs sporadically throughout the

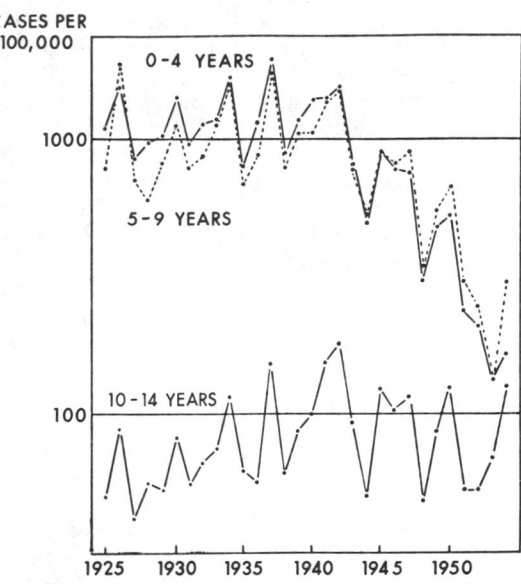

Fig. 1. Whooping cough trends in age-specific attack rates, Massachusetts, 1925–1954. (From Ipsen and Bowen. *Amer. J. Pub. Health.*, 45:312, 1955.)

year, with epidemic waves taking place every 2 to 4 years. The peaks of these epidemics may occur in any season. Outbreaks in the southern states generally reach their peaks in May; in the northern states, in January or February. Unlike the endemic occurrence in urban areas, the disease recurs in small rural communities in short epidemics, which fade rapidly and are followed by periods completely free of cases.

In family exposures the communicability rate is

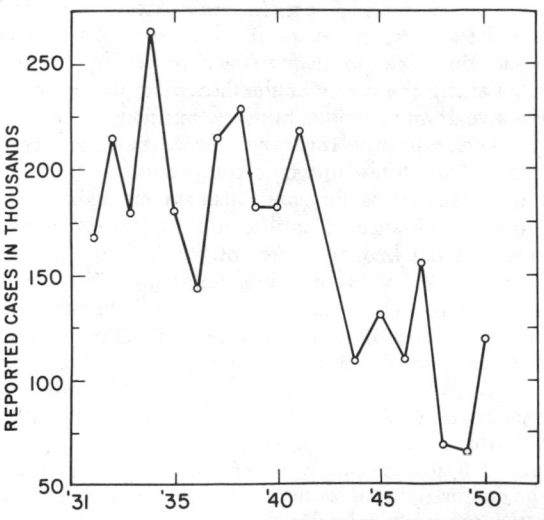

Fig. 2. Reported incidence of pertussis in the United States, 1931–1950. (From *Vital Statistics-Special Reports*, Vol. 37, June 15, 1953.)

high, resembling that of measles and varicella, with a secondary attack rate of from 80 to 90 percent among susceptibles. In schools and nurseries it is usually 20 to 50 percent. An out-of-doors exposure appears to involve less risk.

The carrier problem is unimportant since the organism is seldom found in individuals not suffering from the disease.

INFECTIVE PERIOD. Whooping cough is most communicable during the catarrhal period. The number of colonies recovered in cultures is usually highest during this period; they diminish rapidly during the spasmodic period and frequently disappear after the fourth week of the disease, although organisms may be recovered as late as the eighth week of the disease in rare instances. The first 3 weeks of the disease constitute the most infective period.

Paroxysms may persist for weeks and months after the patient has ceased to be contagious, and recurrence of cough, whooping, or vomiting is found with subsequent respiratory infections such as the common cold without evidence of a return of infectivity.

IMMUNITY. Individual susceptibility is great. In contrast to measles and diphtheria, both infrequent during the first 6 months of life as a result of immunity transferred from the mother, pertussis readily attacks infants of this age.

There is no reason to believe that any degree of immunity is conferred by age, although nonspecific factors may influence the degree of susceptibility. The apparent lower susceptibility observed in older children without a history of the disease is perhaps attributable to the protection conferred by unrecognized attacks. This fact should be considered in evaluating the effects of vaccine prophylaxis.

One attack of pertussis usually confers lasting immunity. Bacteriologically confirmed instances of second attacks are rare. We observed a case of average severity in a 3-year-old child whom we had treated for a rather severe attack at 6 weeks of age. In each instance the diagnosis was proved by culture.

During the course of the disease, or as the result of active immunization, humoral antibodies develop.

The causative organism, *Bord. pertussis,* contains at least three antigenic components: agglutinogen, heat-labile toxin, and heat-stable toxin. The relative importance of antibacterial and antitoxic immunity is not known at present.

PATHOLOGY. Catarrhal inflammation of the mucous membranes of the nose, pharynx, larynx, trachea, and bronchi is regularly present. According to Gallavan and Goodpasture, the essential lesion of pertussis consists of necrosis of the basilar and midzonal portions of the bronchial epithelium with infiltration of this area by polymorphonuclear leucocytes. Such a lesion is usually found immediately beneath a heavy distribution of the organisms, often in clumps, in the overlying epithelium.

Peribronchial infiltration, pulmonary emphysema, and patchy areas of atelectasis are often present. The cellular reaction around the bronchi often extends from the hilum along the bronchial rays to the middle or outer zones of the lungs. In the fully developed lesion, typical interstitial pneumonia results, characterized by thickening of the alveolar walls and infiltration by mononuclear cells. Edema and hemorrhages are early parenchymal lesions. Atelectasis frequently results from obstruction of a bronchus by a mucous plug. There is evidence that *Bord. pertussis* itself may be responsible to a considerable degree for the lung lesion, but the accumulation of mucus, pus, and cellular debris within the alveolar spaces is probably caused by infection with secondarily invading organisms.

The tracheal and peribronchial lymph nodes are enlarged. Bronchiectasis may supervene during the course of the disease or later. The brain is often found intensely congested, revealing scattered punctate hemorrhages or even large extravasations. Encephalitis, eosinophilic degeneration of the nerve cells, and lymphocytic plugs in the capillaries of the brain have been described, especially in patients who suffered from convulsions. In rare instances extensive degeneration of the cerebral cortex occurs.

INCUBATION PERIOD. The period between exposure and the earliest upper respiratory symptoms may vary considerably, but is usually 7 to 16 days. In a series of 1,123 cases, Lawson found the mean duration of the incubation period to be 13 days. It is often difficult to ascertain the exact time when the earliest manifestation of the disease occurs.

SYMPTOMS. The symptoms of pertussis are usually described as representing three stages—the catarrhal, the spasmodic or paroxysmal, and the stage of decline.

The Catarrhal Stage. This continues for about a week or 10 days. The onset may resemble a mild coryza indistinguishable from a common cold. There may be a slight elevation of temperature, and an ordinary attack of bronchitis may be suspected. Unless an exposure to pertussis is known, the disease is not suspected. After 5 or 6 days, however, the cough, instead of abating, gradually increases in severity and occurs in paroxysms. At first these are mild with only two or three daily, but they increase in frequency and severity, especially at night, until the typical whoop is heard which marks the beginning of the paroxysmal stage.

The Paroxysmal Stage. There now appear series of explosive coughs, from 10 to 15 in number, coming in such rapid succession that the child cannot get his breath between them. In a paroxysm the face becomes red, sometimes purple in color, the veins of the scalp and face are prominent, the eyes suffused and staring; then follows a long-drawn inspiration through the narrowed glottis, producing a crowing sound known as the *whoop;* then another series of rapid coughs follows, and another whoop is heard. In a single severe paroxysm, lasting several minutes, the child may whoop half a dozen times; with the final paroxysm a mass of tenacious mucus is usually brought up. In a young child vomiting is almost certain to follow if food has been recently taken. Physical exhaustion frequently follows a severe attack. There is profuse perspiration, and the child may be completely dazed. In infants the attack may result in asphyxia requiring artificial respiration. Older patients describe their sensations as those of impending suffocation. Children with pertussis tend to have slight edema of the face, with puffiness about the eyes attributed to increased venous pressure resulting from the paroxysms.

The number of paroxysms in 24 hours varies from half a dozen to 40 or 50. Severe paroxysms are always accompanied by many more of a milder form. Paroxysms are often excited by eating, by a cold drink, by exertion, a cold draft, tobacco smoke, or by imitation; they are usually more frequent during the night than the day, and in a closed room than when the patient is in the open air.

In less severe cases paroxysms of the type described may not occur, and even the typical whoop may not be heard throughout the attack. The diagnosis, however, is suggested by the paroxysmal nature of the cough which continues until the plug of mucus is expelled, the watery eyes, and the vomiting which follows a paroxysm. In young infants the whoop is frequently not present. The child sometimes coughs until he is asphyxiated, and yet no whoop occurs. The paroxysms can also be modified by intercurrent infections, especially by attacks of pneumonia or severe bronchitis. At such times they usually become less frequent and less typical and may be absent for several days, returning as the complication subsides. The literature contains a number of reports in which paroxysmal sneezing has been a conspicuous finding.

The site of the irritation which produces the cough is in the trachea and bronchi. Laryngoscopic examinations have shown catarrhal inflammation, occasionally with punctate hemorrhages in the larynx. More characteristic are the findings in the trachea, where there may be seen a plug of mucus before a cough attack, which is subsequently coughed up. There is little doubt that this collection of mucus is the exciting cause of the paroxysm, as it is a familiar clinical fact that the paroxysm continues until the plug is dislodged.

The average duration of the spasmodic stage is about one month. The spasms increase in intensity for the first two weeks, remain stationary for about a week, and then gradually diminish in severity. The course and duration of this stage are, however, subject to wide variations. In mild cases it may last only a week; in severe cases, especially in the winter season, it may continue for two or three months, at times almost subsiding, but flaring up again in all its previous severity with every superimposed respiratory infection.

The Stage of Decline. Gradually the severity of the paroxysms abates, the whoop ceases, and the cough resembles more and more that of ordinary bronchitis. This stage usually continues about three weeks, but may be prolonged indefinitely in the winter months. After it has entirely ceased the whoop may return with any superimposed respiratory infection and continue for weeks. This is not to be regarded as a true relapse of pertussis. The habit of the paroxysmal cough, once established, tends to recur with every slight bronchitis, often for months afterward.

Abortive Attacks. These are clinically indistinguishable from an ordinary bronchitis. They may be seen at any time but are prone to occur in children with a waning immunity, especially when the interval following the last previous injection of pertussis vaccine exceeds two years. Marked differences of opinion exist as to the true frequency of such episodes, and satisfactory data dealing with cases well studied bacteriologically are not available.

COMPLICATIONS. Hemorrhages. The hemorrhages of pertussis are mechanical and depend upon the intense venous congestion which accompanies the paroxysm. Epistaxis is the most frequent variety and occurs in severe cases, sometimes with almost every violent paroxysm, but it is rarely persistent enough to require local treatment. Hemorrhages from the mouth may have their origin in either the pharynx or the bronchi, the blood being brought up by coughing; such hemorrhages are usually small. Conjunctival hemorrhages are less frequent and are usually slight, although we have seen the entire sclera covered. Small extravasations into the cellular tissue around the eyes are occasionally seen, giving an appearance somewhat like an ordinary "black eye." Intracranial hemorrhages are not frequent, but they may be severe enough to produce death. They are usually meningeal; according to their extent and location they may produce various types of paralysis or convulsions, but rarely coma. The extravasations are often small, and the symptoms may disappear at the end of a few weeks. More extensive hemorrhages may cause permanent paralysis.

Respiratory System. Otitis media is a frequent complication in infants. The most serious complication of pertussis is interstitial bronchopneumonia, which develops most frequently at the height or toward the close of the spasmodic stage and causes by far the largest number of deaths. It is more common in winter and spring than in the summer months and is especially to be dreaded during infancy. The physical signs present no peculiarities; the cough changes somewhat in character during the pneumonia, and the whoop may not be heard. The prognosis of pneumonia in pertussis is serious because of the condition of the child at the time of its occurrence. Since there is always considerable emphysema, the rapidity of breathing is frequently out of proportion to the temperature, which often is only moderately elevated. If the child survives, chronic pneumonia with bronchiectasis may follow.

Pulmonary emphysema is invariably present in every case of pertussis which comes to autopsy. A certain amount of it undoubtedly occurs in every severe case, disappearing again with convalescence. In some cases rupture of alveoli may lead to pneumothorax or to interstitial emphysema; the air may find its way along the great vessels into the neck, and finally into the subcutaneous tissue of the entire body. Cases of general subcutaneous emphysema may terminate fatally, although this is exceptional.

Digestive System. Vomiting after coughing spells or after eating is almost a constant feature of pertussis. Gastric tetany may develop as a result of alkalosis caused by loss of the acid gastric secretions. Diarrhea, when complicating pertussis, adds to the hazard of the disease. The nutrition of a patient with whooping cough is often a serious matter. Dehydration or starvation may result in marked loss of weight. Such patients may become extremely emaciated and readily fall prey to some secondary infection, usually pneumonia.

Among the other complications of pertussis should be mentioned hernia, prolapsus ani, and ulcer of the frenum of the tongue caused by trauma from the lower teeth during coughing attacks.

Nervous System. Several factors may lead to nervous symptoms in pertussis. The possibility of tetany has already been mentioned. In other instances asphyxia from paroxysms may lead to convulsions. Punctate cerebral hemorrhages are frequently found in patients who have died following convulsions. Massive hemorrhage, which may cause monoplegia or hemiplegia, is rare. A low-grade serous meningitis, with lymphocytic reaction in the spinal fluid, usually going on to complete recovery, has been described more than once in the German literature. We have seen one such instance. A more serious but rare complication is widespread cortical degeneration—the so-called progressive cerebral sclerosis.

DIAGNOSIS. Little difficulty is encountered in the recognition of the typical case. In the catarrhal stage and in the atypical form of the disease diagnosis on clinical findings alone is often difficult. The history of definite exposure is helpful. Pertussis may be suspected when a cough not accompanied by fever or by physical signs becomes progressively more marked. When the cough becomes paroxysmal, accompanied by suffusion of the face and vomiting, there is little doubt even though the whoop does not occur. It should be remembered that small infants become cyanotic with choking spells and frequently do not whoop. When facilities for diagnostic culture are not available, it may be necessary to defer diagnosis until the development of more characteristic symptoms. Such a patient under observation should be isolated. Inquiry concerning previous active immunization should be made since a mild atypical form of the disease may result from partial immunity conferred by vaccine injection.

If the examiner wishes to elicit a paroxysm in order to judge its character, he can usually do so by depressing the tongue forcefully during inspection of the pharynx, by inserting an ear speculum into the external auditory canal, or by gently pressing the trachea.

Irritation from tuberculous tracheobronchial lymph nodes or from a foreign body in the air passages may give rise to a spasmodic cough indistinguishable from that of pertussis. Ordinary bronchitis may become confusing especially when it occurs in an allergic child. Severe spasmodic coughing may also result from the postnasal "drip," from infected adenoids or sinusitis. This type of cough often occurs at night or when the patient lies down. Infants suffering from the pulmonary lesion of cystic fibrosis of the pancreas sometimes exhibit pertussislike coughing episodes. The symptoms, and even the roentgenographic findings, in a case of nonbacterial pneumonia may closely resemble those of whooping cough.

Protracted spasmodic coughing may result from infection of the respiratory tract with *Bord. parapertussis, Bord. bronchiseptica,* or *H. influenzae.* Parapertussis closely resembles mild pertussis and can only be distinguished by culture. Infection with *H. influenzae* often gives rise to tracheitis in which the whoop is absent or only occasionally heard. Rarely pertussis begins as an obstructive laryngitis. The combination of tetany with acute respiratory infection in an infant may occasionally be mistaken for pertussis with convulsions. Infection by the adenoviruses or by the Eaton agent may closely resemble pertussis.

The blood examination is often helpful in diagnosis. During the latter part of the catarrhal period the total leucocyte count rises to a level of from 15,000 to 30,000 per mm³. In certain instances, particularly when pneumonia or convulsions exist, it may exceed 100,000. The lymphocytes account for the major part (70 to 90 percent) of the total increase in the number of leucocytes; the polymorphonuclear neutrophils remain unchanged in absolute number, or even decrease (Fig. 3). The leucocytosis of pertussis far exceeds that of any other afebrile disease of the respiratory tract except acute infectious lymphocytosis. The differentiation between these conditions may be made by cultural methods.

Demonstration of humoral antibodies, such as agglutinins, antihemagglutinins, complement-fixing and mouse-protective antibodies, and opsonocytophagic indices may be of some value in retrospective diagnosis. Since these antibodies usually appear in the third week of the disease and persist in significant degree for only a few months, they are of limited value in diagnosis.

The most valuable test is the isolation of the organism by culture from the respiratory tract. This may be accomplished by cough-plate or by nasopharyngeal swab methods. The technique of the nasal swab culture is simple. A small sterile cotton swab attached to a flexible copper wire is inserted into the nares until it touches the posterior pharyngeal wall and left in place for several seconds. The charged swab is then passed through a drop of penicillin (1,000 units per ml) previously placed on the surface of Bordet medium. The inoculum is streaked over the surface of the medium. After incubation at 37° C for 48 hours, typical colonies of *Bord. pertussis*

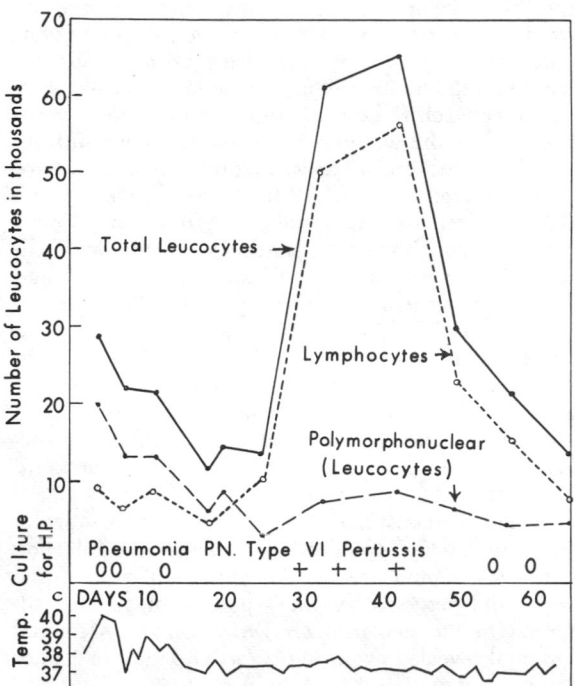

Fig. 3. Changes in the white blood count in an infant of 9 months who was incubating pertussis during the course of pneumococcal (type VI) pneumonia. Note the changes in the total lymphocyte and polymorphonuclear count. The cultures for *Bord. Pertussis* became positive as pertussis began.

TABLE 9. *Death Rates per 100,000 for Pertussis at Different Ages, All Races, Both Sexes**

Death Registration States, 1920-1967

Year	Total	Under 1 Year	1-4 Years	5-14 Years
1920	12.5	321.6	57.7	2.9
1930	4.8	163.5	23.4	0.9
1940	2.2	99.7	9.7	0.3
1950	0.7	23.7	2.5	0.2
1953	0.2	5.4	0.5	0.0
1957	0.1	3.2	0.3	0.1
1960	0.066	1.775	0.247	0.006
1967	0.019	0.819	0.038	0.002

*National Office of Vital Statistics.

may be observed, particularly in the zone where the growth of secondary invading organisms is inhibited by the penicillin. An important consideration is freshness of the media and prompt planting of the culture. The fluorescent antibody technique for identification of pertussis organisms in a smear is a promising development.

PROGNOSIS. The mortality of pertussis varies with age; the younger the patient, the higher the mortality. At one time (1940-1948) in the United States, pertussis caused almost four times as many deaths under one year of age as did measles, mumps, chickenpox, rubella, scarlet fever, diphtheria, and poliomyelitis combined; its general fatality rate is now less than 1 percent. From 1920 to 1957 the mortality rate fell from 12.5 to 0.1 per 100,000 population (Table 9), where it has remained. Although this decrease began before the introduction of effective active immunization and antibiotic therapy, there is little doubt that these factors now play important roles. Poverty, poor nutrition, and inadequate nursing care no doubt contribute to a bad outcome in certain cases.

PREVENTION. Isolation should be enforced for a period of 4 weeks. No special attention need be given to fomites. It is impractical to confine a child with the disease in a single room. Since the communicability rate is high in family exposures, it is desirable to re-

move susceptible infants from the house; and since pertussis may activate tuberculosis, the transfer to another environment of young children who react to tuberculin is advisable.

The nonvaccinated exposed infant should receive passive immunization although its efficacy has not been proved. It is accomplished by intramuscular injection of 1.25 ml of hyperimmune human serum (Hypertussis). The dose is repeated in 5 days, and one of the broad-spectrum antibiotics may also be given. After 2 weeks, if infection does not develop, active immunization should be instituted.

The actively immunized exposed subject should receive a booster injection of pertussis vaccine upon exposure.

Active immunization of all infants should be started between 6 and 12 weeks of age. This may be carried out by giving three or four monthly injections of vaccine totaling 12 antigenic units. This vaccine is combined with diphtheria and tetanus toxoids, and the injections are given intramuscularly into the thighs, preferably at different sites. Booster injections (2 or 3 antigenic units) are given 1, 3, and 5 years after the original course of vaccine.

Because encephalopathy has occasionally occurred following the injection of pertussis vaccine, caution should be observed in giving it to infants subject to seizures or to those who have had a general reaction to a previous injection. Such infants should receive smaller doses of the vaccine.

TREATMENT. The patient should be isolated for 4 weeks and protected from exposure to intercurrent infections. When paroxysms are severe or when the temperature is elevated bed rest is desirable. Normal room temperature is preferable. Excitement, dust, smoke, and even the cough of a nearby patient may stimulate paroxysms. When vomiting is excessive, frequent small feedings are advisable. When a meal is vomited, feeding may be repeated. A diet adequate in calories and vitamin content should be offered.

The severely ill patient, particularly an infant,

should be hospitalized. Oxygen should be used for patients with convulsions or dyspnea, with or without cyanosis. Asphyxia caused by accumulation of secretions may be relieved by gentle suction applied through a soft rubber catheter. There is no disease in which special nursing is more important.

Convulsions may be relieved by lumbar puncture, oxygen therapy, and the administration of sedatives. Magnesium sulfate (0.05 g per kg of body weight) may be injected intramuscularly. Codeine, paregoric, paraldehyde, and phenobarbital are useful sedatives, but excessive sedation is distinctly harmful.

In infants, intramuscular injection of gamma globulin prepared from hyperimmune human serum (Hypertussis), 1.25 to 2.5 ml, is usually recommended although, again, its efficacy is open to question. Chlortetracycline (aureomycin), oxytetracycline (Terramycin), and chloramphenicol (chloromycetin) appear to be of about equal value. Each of these drugs, when given in dosage of 50 mg per kg per 24 hours, may possibly exert a beneficial effect on the course of the disease. They are all effective in eliminating pertussis organisms from patients with the disease. Erythromycin appears to be even more effective in eliminating pertussis organisms, although as with the other drugs, its beneficial effect on the disease has not been established. There is no advantage to be gained by giving a combination of drugs. The possible therapeutic value of ampicillin (alpha-aminobenzyl penicillin) has recently been suggested.

Although a combination of immune gamma globulin with one of the broad-spectrum antibiotics is usually given, it must be remembered that a truly specific drug is not yet available.

In a previously immunized child, an injection of pertussis vaccine early in the catarrhal period is immunologically sound treatment, since an anamnestic response may be expected within 4 days.

Parapertussis

Parapertussis is an acute infection of the respiratory tract caused by *Bordetella parapertussis*. The disease so closely resembles that of mild whooping cough that differentiation can be made only by means of bacteriologic culture.

ETIOLOGY.   The causative agent was first described in 1937 by Eldering and Kendrick as a "group of cultures resembling both *B. pertussis* and *Br. bronchiseptica,* but identical with neither." In the same year it was recognized independently by Bradford and Slavin, who described it as "an organism resembling *Hemophilus pertussis* with special reference to color changes produced by its growth upon certain media." In 1938 Eldering and Kendrick named the organism *"Bacillus para-pertussis."* According to Miller, the organism may have been isolated in Copenhagen in 1933, though its clinical significance was not recognized at that time.

Bord. parapertussis is a short, ovoid, gram-negative, nonmotile bacillus, morphologically indistinguishable from *Bord. pertussis*. Under suitable conditions it produces a toxin which is neutralized by *Bord. pertussis* antitoxin. However, distinct differences between the two organisms exist in cultural, biochemical, and immunologic reactions. Cross-agglutination between *Bord. parapertussis* and *Bord. pertussis* is caused by the presence of a common minor antigen.

The true incidence is unknown, but cases have been observed in widely distant areas. Eldering and Kendrick reported bacteriologic findings in clinical whooping cough over the period 1935–1950 in Michigan. *Bord. pertussis* was isolated from 3,263, and *Bord. parapertussis* from 65 patients (2 percent). Lautrop studied 256 cases of spasmodic cough in Copenhagen between November, 1950, and March, 1952. *Bord. parapertussis* was found in 5 percent of all cultures examined, representing 16 percent of all positive cultures. In England the organism was isolated from 24 children compared to 482 with *Bord. pertussis.*

The demonstration of specific humoral agglutinins in random samples indicates that the infection is rather common, frequently overlooked, or confused with mild pertussis. About 7 percent of patients admitted to the pediatric service of Strong Memorial Hospital revealed agglutinin titers of 1:320 or higher for *Bord. parapertussis.*

Most of our cases have occurred during the summer or fall months. One small outbreak occurred among children attending a day camp.

IMMUNITY.   No instance of a second attack of parapertussis has been reported. There is no cross-immunity between parapertussis and pertussis. As in pertussis, specific agglutinins and mouse-protective antibodies appear in the serum of the recovered individual, but nonspecific *Bord. pertussis* antibodies do not appear. A few isolated observations indicate that the incubation period of parapertussis is from 7 to 14 days.

SYMPTOMS.   The onset of the disease resembles that of whooping cough. In some instances it is more abrupt, sometimes suggestive of acute tracheitis. The paroxysms are frequently shorter and are followed less frequently by whooping and vomiting than those of pertussis. The course of the disease often ends within 2 or 3 weeks. The total leucocyte count usually ranges between 12,000 and 25,000 cells per mm^3, with an increase in the absolute number of lymphocytes. Complications are rare. Zuelzer and Wheeler described two fatal cases in which *Bord. parapertussis* was isolated from the trachea at autopsy.

DIAGNOSIS.   The differential diagnosis of parapertussis is that of mild pertussis. The only method of recognition at the present time consists of isolation of *Bord. parapertussis* by cough plate or nasal swab culture. It is highly probable that certain suspected cases of second attacks of pertussis are in reality parapertussis. Moreover, the manner in which most instances of the disease have been discovered proves that even suspected primary attacks of pertussis are not infrequently parapertussis. We have observed nine children previously immunized with presumably adequate amounts of pertussis vaccine who subsequently developed suspected pertussis. In each instance nasal swab cultures yielded *Bord. parapertussis.*

TREATMENT. The patient should be isolated. Treatment is symptomatic. Mild cases require no specific therapy; the more severe cases should receive one of the broad-spectrum antibiotics. Ampicillin appears to be an effective therapeutic agent. From observations in our laboratory of in vitro and in vivo tests, the relative effectiveness of certain antibiotics against *Bord. parapertussis* and *Bord. pertussis* is illustrated in Table 10.

TABLE 10.   *Relative Effectiveness of Various Agents in Pertussis and Parapertussis Infections in Mice* *

	In Vitro†		In Vivo‡	
	Bord. para- pertussis	*Bord. pertussis*	*Bord. para- pertussis*	*Bord. pertussis*
Penicillin	266	0.91	—	—
Streptomycin	421	2.5	2.5	12.5
Aureomycin	3.1	0.64	5.1	12.5
Chloramphenicol	1.7	0.38	18.0	20.1
Terramycin	0.74	0.44	5.5	5.1
Polymyxin B	0.13	0.06	0.39	0.52

*By the time the disease is recognized clinically in children, there is considerable question as to whether or not antibodies favorably affect the clinical course.

†Concentration (mg/unit of medium) required to inhibit the growth of 50 percent of the cultures.

‡Mg per kg per day required to save 50 percent of the infected mice from death when injected daily for 5 days.

REFERENCES

PERTUSSIS

Ames, R. G., Cohen, S. M., Fischer, A. E., Kohn, J., McPherson, A. Z., Marlow, J., Rutzky, J., and Alexander, H. E. Comparison of the therapeutic efficacy of four agents in pertussis. Pediatrics, 11:323, 1953.

Bass, J. W., Klenk, E. L., Kotheimer, J. B., Lennemann, C. C., and Smith, M. H. D. Antimicrobial treatment of pertussis. J. Pediat., 75:768, 1969.

Bradford, W. L. The Pertussis Group. *In* Dubos, R. J., ed., Bacterial and Mycotic Infections of Man, 3rd ed. Philadelphia, J. B. Lippincott Co., 1958, p. 486.

———— Day, E., and Bery, G. P. Improvement of the nasopharyngeal swab method of diagnosis in pertussis by use of penicillin. Amer. J. Pub. Health, 36:468, 1946.

Byers, R. K., and Moll, F. C. Encephalopathies following prophylactic pertussis vaccine. Pediatrics, 1:437, 1948.

Gallavan, M., and Goodpasture, E. W. Infection of chick embryos with *H. pertussis* reproducing pulmonary lesions of whooping cough. Amer. J. Path., 13:927, 1937.

Lawson, G. M. Immunity studies in pertussis. Amer. J. Hyg., 29 Sect. B:119, 1939.

McGuinness, A. C., Bradford, W. L., and Armstrong, J. G. Production and use of hyperimmune human whooping cough serum. J. Pediat., 16:21, 1940.

Mortality Trends in the U.S., 1954-63. U.S. Dept. of Health, Education and Welfare, Washington, D.C., June 1966.

Nelson, J. D., Mattick, B. M., and McNabb, J. Susceptibility of *Bordetella pertussis* to ampicillin. J. Pediat., 68:222, 1966.

White, R., Fineberg, L., and Tramer, A. The modern morbidity of pertussis in infants. Pediatrics, 33:705, 1964.

Wiener, S. L., Tinker, M., and Bradford, W. L. Experimental meningoencephalomyelitis produced by *Hemophilus pertussis.* Arch. Path., 67:694, 1959.

PARAPERTUSSIS

Alexander, H. E., Leidy, G., and Redman, W. Comparison of the action of streptomycin, polymyxin and chloromycetin on *H. pertussis, H. parapertussis, H. influenzae,* and five enteric strains of gram-negative bacilli. J. Clin. Invest., 28:867, 1949.

Bradford, W. L. Parapertussis. Lancet, 75:232, 1955.

———— and Slavin, B. An organism resembling *Hemophilus pertussis*: with special reference to color changes produced by its growth upon certain media. Amer. J. Pub. Health, 27:1277, 1937.

Bruckner, I. E., and Evans, D. G. Toxin of *B. parapertussis* and relationship of this organism to *H. pertussis* and *Br. bronchiseptica.* J. Path. Bact., 49:563, 1939.

Day, E., and Bradford, W. L. Susceptibility of *Hemophilus parapertussis* to certain antibiotics. Pediatrics, 9:320, 1952.

Eldering, G., and Kendrick, P. *Bacillus parapertussis*: species resembling both *Bacillus pertussis* and *Bacillus bronchisepticus,* but identical with neither. J. Bact., 35:561, 1938.

———— and Kendrick, P. L. Incidence of parapertussis in Grand Rapids area as indicated by 16 years' experience with diagnostic cultures. Amer. J. Pub. Health, 42:27, 1952.

Lautrop, H. Parapertussis. Ugesk. Laeg., 116:421, 1954.

Medical Research Council Investigation. The prevention of whooping-cough by vaccination. Brit. Med. J., 1:1463, 1951.

Miller, J. J., Jr., Saito, T. M., and Silverberg, R. J. Parapertussis; clinical and serological observations. J. Pediat., 19:229, 1941.

Zuelzer, W. W., and Wheeler, W. E. Parapertussis pneumonia: report of 2 fatal cases. J. Pediat., 29:493, 1946.

14.13
RAT-BITE FEVER
(SODOKU; HAVERHILL FEVER)

WILLIAM L. BRADFORD

Two quite distinct infections may be conveyed by the bite of the rat, the symptomatology of which shows only minor differences. One of these diseases, caused by *Spirillum minus,* is known as sodoku. Although relatively common in Japan, it appears to be an infrequent cause of rat-bite fever in the United States. More common in this country are infections due to a pleomorphic fungus known as *Streptobacillus moniliformis.* The latter organism is occasionally acquired by means other than a rat bite, as in the milk-borne epidemic observed in Haverhill, Massachusetts, which was traced to a cow thought to have been bitten on the teat by a rat. Failure to differentiate between infections caused by these two agents has given rise to considerable confusion in the literature.

RAT-BITE FEVER DUE TO *SPIRILLUM MINUS.* A few well-authenticated cases have occurred in children in this country. The infection is characterized by a relatively long incubation period, 1 to 3 weeks, after which the wound, having healed, exhibits a return of erythema, induration, and tenderness; often there is evidence of lymphadenitis. As the infection becomes generalized, intermittent fever, chills, and a rash develop. The febrile periods are fairly regular, the temperature often reaching 104°F, lasting for a day or two, and then being followed by a period of several afebrile days. The rash is a generalized maculopapular one which tends to come out with the febrile periods and to disappear between them; the wound likewise flares up at these times. Muscle pain is common during the acute phase, but joint symptoms are exceptional.

The disease runs a relapsing course, the febrile episodes gradually becoming less severe and less frequent until eventually in the course of several weeks it subsides. Anemia develops in some cases, and a moderate leucocytosis is not uncommon. A false-positive Wassermann test is commonly obtained. The diagnosis can be established by growing the organisms in blood culture, by dark-field examination of lesions, and by animal inoculation. Guinea pigs or white mice, inoculated in the groin or genitals, will develop chancrelike lesions in which the organism can be identified; it can also be recovered from the blood and peritoneal fluid. It has characteristic morphologic features. Since laboratory mice and guinea pigs may harbor these organisms spontaneously, the animals inoculated should be studied first to make sure that their blood is free from organisms.

RAT-BITE FEVER DUE TO *STREPTOBACILLUS MONILIFORMIS.* Infections caused by this organism are characterized by a shorter incubation period, usually less than one week, by less evidence of reaction around the bite, and, as a rule, absence of lymphadenitis. Intermittent fever and rash are seen, the eruption being maculopapular or occasionally urticarial. The febrile periods are less regular than in the spirillar disease. Upper respiratory symptoms are sometimes present, and at times abscesses develop in one or another part of the body. The most constant difference is the development of arthritis in the majority of cases. The small joints of the extremities are often involved. The leucocyte count usually exceeds that seen in sodoku, often reaching 20,000 or even 30,000. A false-positive Wassermann reaction is occasionally encountered. Although fatalities have occurred, the disease tends to subside spontaneously in the great majority of cases even without specific treatment. Periarteritis nodosa has been observed as a rare complication.

Laboratory verification of the diagnosis depends on cultivation of the organism from the blood or joint fluid or on demonstration of agglutinins in the serum. Special culture media are required as well as familiarity with the characteristics of the organism, which may exist in two different forms: the typical streptobacillary form, consisting of long filaments which tend to fragment and which show peculiar nodular excrescences; and a more resistant vegetative form known as L, which consists of minute granules capable of passing a Berkefeld filter. This latter form is closely related to a group of organisms which cause pleuropneumonia in mice.

TREATMENT. The drug of choice for both varieties of rat-bite fever is penicillin. Moderate doses suffice for cure in cases of short duration, but in those that have run a prolonged course because of failure of recognition high dosage is required. In a few refractory cases addition of a tetracycline has eliminated the organisms.

REFERENCES

Adams, J. M., and Carpenter, C. M. Symposium on unusual infections in childhood; rat-bite fevers due to *Spirillum minus* and to *Streptobacillus moniliformis.* Pediat. Clin. N. Amer., 2:101, 1955.

Brown, T. M., and Nunemaker, J. C. Rat-bite fever; a review of the American cases with re-evaluation of etiology; report of cases. Bull. Hopkins Hosp., 70:201, 1942.

Place, E. H., and Sutton, L. E., Jr. Erythema arthriticum epidemicum (Haverhill fever). Arch. Intern. Med., 54:659, 1934.

Prouty, M., and Schafer, E. L. Periarteritis nodosa associated with rat-bite fever due to *Streptobacillus moniliformis* (erythema arthriticum epidemicum). J. Pediat., 36:605, 1950.

Schwartzman, G., Florman, A. L., Bass, M. H., Karelitz, S., and Richtberg, D. Repeated recovery of a spirillum by blood culture from two children with prolonged and recurrent fevers. Pediatrics, 8:227, 1951.

Watkins, C. G. Rat-bite fever. J. Pediat., 28:429, 1946.

14.14
SALMONELLA, SHIGELLA, AND ENTEROPATHOGENIC *E. COLI* INFECTIONS

ERWIN NETER

Salmonella *Infections*

Bacteria of the *Salmonella* group produce a variety of clinical symptoms ranging from the inapparent infection of a carrier, through mild gastroenteritis, food poisoning, suppurative lesions, and salmonella fever, to the clinical entity of typhoid fever.

The genus *Salmonella* is comprised of more than 1,300 serotypes. The group as a whole is characterized as follows: the organisms are gram-negative, motile bacteria, which produce acid or acid and gas from glucose and other substances but do not ferment sucrose, lactose, salicin, or raffinose; they do not produce urease, nor do they liquefy gelatin; they do decarboxylate lysine, arginine, and ornithine. Aberrant strains are only rarely encountered. The genus is subdivided largely on the basis of the antigenic structure of its members. It is the O antigen, a heat-stable lipopolysaccharide, which characterizes the serogroup (A, B, C, etc.), and the members of each group are further subdivided into serotypes on the basis of the heat-labile H or flagellar antigens. Most strains are biphasic and produce flagellar antigens of two kinds. According to the most recent classification, three species are recognized, namely S. *typhi* (or *typhosa*), S. *choleraesuis*, and S. *enteritidis*. The latter species includes all other serotypes. Since most of the pediatric literature has not employed this nomenclature, it is not used in this section. Certain strains contain yet another antigen, the Vi antigen. Although named virulence (Vi) antigen, its relationship to the pathogenesis of salmonellosis in man has not been elucidated. Bacteriophages are Vi-specific and can be used in differentiation of types. Infections with S. *typhosa*, S. *paratyphi* (para A), S. *schottmuelleri* (para B), and S. *hirschfeldii* (para C) are confined almost exclusively to man. A few other host-adapted serotypes, such as S. *pullorum* and S. *gallinarum*, cause disease in animals and only rarely in man. Most other salmonellae are harbored widely among rodents, hogs, and other mammals, as well as in birds; they may invade the eggs of ducks and hens and have been responsible for widespread infection in man through contaminated egg powder prepared for human consumption.

The more important serotypes in human disease, exclusive of S. *typhosa*, are S. *typhimurium*, S. *montevideo*, S. *newport*, S. *oranienburg*, S. *schottmuelleri*, S. *bareilly*, S. *enteritidis*, S. *choleraesuis*, and S. *derby*. Serotypes such as S. *paratyphi* A are only rarely encountered. The relative frequencies of certain serotypes differ in relation to the type of infection, such as gastroenteritis versus salmonella fever and septicemia. For example, in one large series (MacCready, et al.), S. *typhimurium* was responsible for approximately 79 percent of cases with gastroenteritis and only 4 percent with systemic infection; in contrast, the respective figures for S. *choleraesuis* were 26 percent and 56 percent. In addition, among all recognized cases of salmonellosis, the numbers and proportions caused by individual types vary in different localities and from one period to another. Nevertheless, S. *typhimurium* has been the most frequently isolated serotype in the past and in most parts of the world. Although the number of serotypes is increasing, it should be kept in mind that only a few account for the majority of human infections. Thus, based on the data from the National Communicable Disease Center, 50 serotypes accounted for approximately 91 percent of some 19,000 isolates from man. Typhoid fever is no longer as great a public health problem as are the other salmonelloses.

Salmonellosis

Strictly speaking, the term salmonellosis includes typhoid fever as well as infection by all other types of salmonellae. By custom, however, typhoid fever is discussed as a separate entity (p. 637). The term salmonellosis will be used here, as is conventionally done, to refer to infections caused by salmonellae other than S. *typhosa*.

EPIDEMIOLOGY. Infection is acquired by ingestion of the bacteria. These may be in food or water supplies which have become contaminated from the droppings of infected animals or by food handlers who are carriers. The disease also may be acquired more directly from a human carrier and from patients with mild or severe gastroenteritis by contact via hands or articles. Intensive family studies of children with clinical salmonellosis have brought to light the frequent occurrence of subclinical or mild intestinal infection of mothers and other children in the households, often preceding a more serious clinical infection in infants or younger siblings. Human-to-human (fecal-oral) infection is frequent in sporadic infections of young children. The meat of an infected animal may also contain the organisms, as may the eggs of infected fowl, notably hens and ducks. In 1952 a large number of cases were traced to egg powder contaminated with S. *montevideo*. An outbreak of S. *derby* infection among patients and employees of 53 hospitals in 13 states occurred in 1963 and probably was due to contaminated raw or undercooked eggs. Secondary infections arising from carriers and patients with mild infection played a significant role. A nursery epidemic has been described which was traced to contamination of the water in the trap of a resuscitating apparatus. More recently, a widespread, waterborne S. *typhimurium* outbreak, involving 18,000 out of 120,000 residents, occurred in California. The importance of human carriers in general is attested by the studies of Rubenstein and his co-workers, who showed that 54 percent of patients convalescent from salmonella infections excreted the organisms in the fourth week and 10 percent as late as the twelfth week, while 7 percent were still carriers after a year. Infants are more likely to remain carriers than are older children.

PATHOLOGY. Little is known of the pathologic anatomy of salmonella infections other than typhoid fever. In the rare fatal cases of enteric fever caused, for example, by S. *schottmuelleri* or S. *choleraesuis,* the lesions found in the intestine at postmortem resemble those seen in infection with S. *typhosa* except for being generally milder.

SYMPTOMS. Four general classes of clinical infection are encountered: (1) enteric fevers of protracted type resembling typhoid fever; (2) acute gastroenteritis or so-called food poisoning; (3) a localizing infection in which, following a bacteremic phase often unrecognized, foci of active disease become manifest in the form of meningitis, osteomyelitis, urinary tract infection, etc.; and (4) subclinical or inapparent infection.

Salmonella Fever. The symptoms of the septicemic infection caused by S. *paratyphi,* by S. *schottmuelleri,* and occasionally by other nontyphoid salmonellae clinically cannot be clearly differentiated from those of typhoid fever. The patient may have fever for several days without localizing signs or symptoms to suggest the diagnosis. At times rose spots appear, the spleen may become palpable, and leucopenia is present. Constipation is somewhat more common than diarrhea, and anorexia may be severe. The duration of the febrile stage tends to be shorter than in typhoid fever, lasting from 1 to 3 weeks, and the patient may at no time appear seriously ill. Relapse is exceedingly rare, and complications such as perforation of the gut almost unknown. Of all the clinical forms of infection produced by nontyphoid salmonellae, enteric fever is the most uncommon.

Gastroenteritic Type. In only a small percentage of infants and children with diarrheal disease from all causes is the illness due to salmonellae. Conversely, of all salmonella infections, gastroenteritis (including food poisoning) is by far the most common clinical entity. The incubation period may be as short as a few hours or as long as three days. The number of stools passed in 24 hours may be anywhere from 4 or 5 to 20 or more, and the degree of associated anorexia, nausea, vomiting, and abdominal pain is variable. In only a small proportion is blood or pus found in the fecal discharges, either grossly or on microscopic examination. Fever, when present,

is usually greatest at onset; at most it seldom persists more than a few days. Dehydration, acidosis, and a shocklike state may ensue unless appropriate measures are taken promptly to forestall water and electrolyte imbalance. The picture of toxemia with vasomotor collapse occasionally encountered has also been attributed to endotoxin, produced as a result of rapid multiplication of the organisms in the intestine. In the great majority of cases symptoms subside spontaneously within 2 to 4 days. Numerically the gastroenteritic type of salmonella infection predominates in early life, especially in infants, and the organism most frequently found responsible is S. *typhimurium.* Intestinal infection may occasionally lead to the development of appendicitis.

Localized Infections. Metastatic infection caused by salmonellae may follow the septicemia of the typhoidal form of the disease, may complicate a comparatively mild illness clinically indistinguishable from a digestive upset, or it may appear in the absence of any recognizable preceding symptoms. Among these distant localizations arthritis is the most common, but osteomyelitis, pyelonephritis, cystitis, meningitis, endocarditis, and soft tissue abscesses have also been reported.

Patients with sickle-cell disease seem to be particularly susceptible to salmonella osteomyelitis.

Inapparent Infections. There is reason to assume that subclinical infections with salmonellae are more common than is generally supposed. They are usually discovered in the course of epidemiologic surveys instituted following identification of an index case in a household, a hospital ward, or other relatively closed population group. Positive stool cultures or signficantly high serum agglutinin titers may be obtained in symptom-free subjects who had been exposed to an infected patient or who had consumed contaminated food. The duration of the carrier state bears little relation to the severity of symptoms at the time of the initial infection.

DIAGNOSIS. Salmonellosis should be considered in any obscure febrile disease and in every case of diarrhea, with or without vomiting. Among young subjects, isolated cases without any clue as to the source of infection are more frequent than those in which there is a history of a number of persons becoming sick after partaking of some common food.

The laboratory diagnosis rests on the recovery and proper identification of the pathogen from suitable materials. Salmonellae are isolated from rectal swabs or stool specimens in patients with gastroenteritis or food poisoning; the pathogen may be recovered also from the contaminated food in the latter instance. Depending upon the particular localized lesion, pus, spinal fluid, or urine is cultured. Salmonellae are identified on the basis of motility, biochemical activities, and antigenic structure. Serogroup determination by means of appropriate, commercially available group-specific antisera can be accomplished in most hospital laboratories. For final serotyping, the strains may have to be forwarded to special centers, such as state laboratories. In some patients, particularly with salmonella fever, a specific antibody response to the pathogen can be demonstrated, aiding in the etiologic diagnosis. Antibody studies on patients with gastroenteritis or food poisoning are not done on a routine basis.

PROGNOSIS. The prognosis of salmonellosis depends upon the localization of the infection, the age of the patient, and the presence or absence of underlying disease. In otherwise healthy infants and children, salmonella gastroenteritis has a favorable prognosis. The outlook is more guarded when infection occurs in premature infants or in subjects with underlying diseases, such as malignancy, or when the infection is systemic in nature. In a series of 2,625 cases analyzed by MacCready and others during a 16-year period, including patients of all ages, the overall case fatality rate was 1.4 percent. In *S. choleraesuis* infections the case fatality rate was 16.1 percent; for *S. enteritidis*, 4.8 percent. In contrast, the case fatality rate for typhoid fever in the same population was 8.0 percent. Meningitis, although a rare complication of salmonellosis, carries a serious risk to life. Clearly, fatality rates are substantially lower if special efforts are made to include subclinical and mild infections.

TREATMENT. In temperate climates the common varieties of salmonella infection in children are dealt with by the host defenses so effectively that by the time the etiologic agent is identified the patient is usually on the way to recovery. Chloramphenicol or ampicillin may be used for the treatment of salmonella fever, septicemia, and serious suppurative infections. The relative value of these and certain other drugs has not been definitively established. There is convincing evidence that antibiotics are not effective, either clinically or bacteriologically, in the treatment of salmonella gastroenteritis. In addition, recent studies have shown that, after antibiotic therapy, the carrier state is prolonged. For these reasons, antibiotics are not indicated for the therapy of salmonella gastroenteritis in otherwise healthy children; nor should chemotherapy be used for the treatment of carriers. These considerations do not apply to systemic salmonellosis.

PREVENTION. Measures for the control of salmonellosis of man include the following: appropriate water sanitation and food hygiene; control of such materials as fish meal; proper handling and cooking of potentially contaminated foods; isolation of patients with salmonellosis when admitted to hospitals; proper handling of contaminated discharges; strict enforcement of aseptic techniques; and continued education regarding fecal-oral spread of infection. Specific immunization against salmonella fever due to *S. paratyphi* A and B has been utilized for years, but there is no evidence of its efficacy. Furthermore, such immunization cannot provide significant protection against infection by many other salmonellae. The triple vac-

cine, containing also typhoid bacilli, is not recommended.

Typhoid Fever

Typhoid fever is caused by *S. typhosa,* a member of the genus *Salmonella.* This microorganism shares its O antigen with other members of group D, but the combination of O and flagellar antigens makes it antigenically unique. In addition, strains of *S. typhosa* may contain Vi antigen, whose presence renders the microorganisms inagglutinable or poorly agglutinable by the corresponding O antibodies. *S. typhosa* differs also from most other members of the *Salmonella* group in certain biochemical activities; characteristically only acid, and not gas, is produced from a variety of substrates, such as glucose, whereas the vast majority of other salmonellae produce both acid and gas. Antigenically homogeneous strains of *S. typhosa* can be divided into various phage types, depending upon susceptibility to standardized phages. Identification of phage type of isolated strains aids materially in epidemic investigations.

In the past, serious epidemics of typhoid fever occurred frequently. In developed countries typhoid fever has been strikingly controlled. Nonetheless, occasionally outbreaks do occur, such as the recent epidemics at Zermatt, Switzerland, and at Aberdeen, Scotland. Such unusual epidemics as the large-scale outbreaks of the past are due to contaminated water or food. The few sporadic cases seen in this country usually can be traced to a carrier.

It is important to keep in mind that bacteremia occurs early in typhoid fever; this initial bacteremic phase leads to localization of the pathogen in the intestine, skin, and elsewhere. For these reasons, the blood culture usually is negative during the third week, in spite of septic temperatures.

PATHOLOGY. In general, the lesions in a young patient resemble those of an adult except in severity. The ileum and upper colon often show only moderate congestion of the mucous membrane, with swelling of Peyer's patches, solitary lymphoid follicles, and mesenteric lymph nodes; ulcers, when present, are seldom large or deep. The spleen is usually enlarged. Lesions are rarely found in the heart, kidneys, and liver.

SYMPTOMS. In the older child, the history, physical signs, and courses are not significantly different from these features in the adult, but in general the disease is milder, its duration is shorter, and complications are infrequent. In infants the signs of illness are usually so nonspecific that the diagnosis of typhoid fever is seldom entertained; the first clue is usually provided by growth of the organisms in blood culture. The disease in infants is generally even milder than in children of school age. At all ages leucopenia and low red cell sedimentation rate are uniform features.

Pyogenic infection may in rare instances localize in the urinary tract, the central nervous system, bones and joints, or elsewhere.

DIAGNOSIS. The definitive diagnosis of typhoid fever is established by the isolation and identification of *S. typhosa* from the blood during the first week or 10 days of illness and/or from the feces after the first stage of the illness. In some patients the pathogen is present also in the urine and in respiratory secretions. Occasionally, it can be isolated from the rose spots. The diagnosis on immunologic grounds can be made by the demonstration of a specific antibody response (Widal test). A rise of the corresponding O and H antibodies, or high titers of these antibodies, provides strongly suggestive evidence of *S. typhosa* infection. It must be emphasized that increased H titers and normal O titers are seen in subjects after immunization with typhoid vaccine. Also, high O titers and normal *S. typhosa* H titers are encountered in patients with *Salmonella* group D infection other than *S. typhosa*. Carriers, excreting *S. typhosa* in the feces and not rarely harboring the pathogen in the biliary system, often have elevated titers of Vi antibodies.

TREATMENT. Therapy of *S. typhosa* infections in infants and children is governed by the same principles used in treating typhoid fever in adults. The problem of nutritional wasting, potentially severe, has been eliminated by liberal feeding early in the disease and by treatment of dehydration and electrolyte imbalance with parenteral injections.

Either ampicillin or chloramphenicol may be used for specific therapy. The former drug is preferred by some physicians, not because of superior effectiveness, but because of the rare though serious complication associated with the latter drug. Chloramphenicol is highly effective in daily dosage of 50 to 100 mg per kg of body weight, given intramuscularly in three divided and equally spaced doses, the total not exceeding 2 g daily, regardless of age. Even though bacteremia uniformly disappears within 12 hours after institution of this regimen, the patient seldom shows improvement for at least two days. In adults with marked toxemia, adrenocortical steroid therapy combined with chloramphenicol causes dramatic improvement within 24 hours. No evidence of harm from steroids has been encountered when they are given for only 4 or 5 days, by which time chloramphenicol has taken effect.

The duration of chloramphenicol therapy needed to prevent recrudescence is about 3 weeks, although many patients are cured after only 10 days. When the carrier state has developed, chloramphenicol alone will not eliminate organisms from the intestinal tract. Ampicillin (75 to 100 mg/kg/day) in three or four divided doses for 3 to 6 weeks is sometimes effective in the treatment of carriers.

Chloramphenicol has greatly reduced the fatality rate of typhoid fever, which in treated cases is now approximately 2 percent. In the recent Aberdeen typhoid outbreak, involving a total of 507 patients, including 86 children, not a single death occurred among the latter.

PROPHYLAXIS. The prevention of typhoid fever outbreaks requires proper water sanitation, food hygiene, and prevention of dissemination of the pathogen from carriers and patients. Every effort must be made to identify carriers. Such individuals must not be employed as food handlers, and the regulations in force regarding typhoid carriers must be carefully followed. Treatment of carriers by means of antibiotics has not yielded uniformly favorable results.

Personal protection against typhoid fever may be accomplished by active immunization. Although typhoid vaccine has been used for decades, only recently has its efficacy been established in controlled field studies. It has been shown that the phenol vaccine is superior to the alcohol vaccine, although both are substantially effective. More recent investigations suggest that the acetone vaccine may be even better. Routine vaccination against typhoid fever is not recommended for children living in countries where epidemics are rare. Travel to other countries, in which typhoid fever is still prevalent, can be accomplished by immunization with a potent vaccine according to the following schedule. For children older than 10 years, two subcutaneous injections of 0.5 ml, separated by 4 or more weeks, are recommended; for children between the ages of 6 months to 10 years, 0.25 ml should be used instead of 0.5 ml. If immunity has to be established more rapidly, three injections in the same doses at weekly intervals can be used. Under conditions of repeated or continued exposure, booster doses should be given at least every three years. Even if the interval is longer than three years after effective primary immunization, the single booster dose is probably adequate. Instead of subcutaneous injection of the booster dose, 0.1 ml of the vaccine may be given intradermally over the deltoid area.

Shigellosis
(Bacillary Dysentery)

Dysentery, an infectious disease involving largely the colon, may be caused by *Entamoeba histolytica* (amebic dysentery) or by members of the genus *Shigella* (bacillary dysentery). This section deals only with shigellosis. Only rarely are shigellae responsible for extraintestinal infections.

ETIOLOGY. Dysentery occurs with special frequency in summer and early autumn, but sporadic cases are seen at all seasons. The disease is more common in warm than in cold climates, and both the morbidity and mortality rates vary inversely with the standards of home hygiene of a given geographic area. Dysentery is apt to be prevalent in communities in which facilities for refrigeration of food are inadequate. Although shigellosis occurs in individuals of all ages, it is surprisingly rare, for unexplained reasons, in infants under the age of three months.

The genus *Shigella* is divided into four major groups: *S. dysenteriae, S. flexneri, S. boydii,* and *S. sonnei.* In turn, the *S. dysenteriae* group comprises 7 members, the *S. flexneri* group 12 members, and the *S. boydii* 7 members. The Shiga bacillus, belonging to the *S. dysenteriae* group, alone produces an exotoxin. In the past, the greater severity of Shiga bacillus infection had been ascribed to this toxin. In recent times, however, these infections have not differed substantially from those caused by other shigellae, and the role of this toxin in the pathogenesis of shigellosis remains obscure. In certain countries of the world, such as Japan, *S. flexneri* predominates; in other countries, such as England and the U.S. *S. sonnei* is the organism most frequently encountered. All shigellae may cause both sporadic and epidemic dysentery in man. The members of the *Alkalescens-Dispar* group, no longer included within the genus *Shigella,* generally do not cause dysentery and certainly are not responsible for epidemics. On the other hand, these organisms may produce extra-intestinal infections, such as those of the urinary tract. **EPIDEMIOLOGY.** The infection is believed to enter the body through the alimentary tract in all cases. Although dogs, particularly puppies, are susceptible to inoculation and sometimes exhibit the disease spontaneously, the important reservoir of the infection is man. Contamination of a food supply occasionally occurs on a large scale; a number of milkborne and some waterborne epidemics have been described, but these are rare. The house fly may play an important part in disseminating the disease, as was shown by the observations of Lyon in West Virginia. Most isolated cases are caused by carriers, often adults, who may never have manifested symptoms but who more often have suffered from a very mild, transient diarrhea that has attracted little attention. Between 2 and 3 percent of infected individuals carry the organism for more than 3 months. Subclinical infection occurs more frequently than is generally recognized. On rare occasions, shigellae may be transmitted from the mother to the newborn infant during delivery. The incubation period is usually 2 or 3 days, although it may vary from 12 hours to 8 days. **PATHOLOGY.** In fatal cases the disease involves chiefly the colon. The cecum and first portion of the ascending colon and the sigmoid are more commonly involved than the transverse portion. In less than half the cases the lower ileum is also affected, usually for a distance of about 50 cm, and the lesion here is always less advanced than in the colon.

There is at first a diffuse inflammation of the mucosa, which is swollen and reddened, without any tendency toward localization in the lymphoid structures. The vessels are dilated, and punctate hemorrhages are present. The secretion of mucus is increased. At this time microscopic sections show hyperemia and infiltration of the mucosa and submucosa with inflammatory cells, both polymorphonuclear leucocytes and mononuclear cells. The crypts often contain leucocytic exudate. The submucosa is usually slightly edematous.

As the process advances the more prominent portions of the mucosal folds are found to be more deeply reddened, and flecks of yellow opaque membrane appear to become confluent along the crests of the transverse folds. In a longitudinal direction the more flattened strips of mucosa produced by the taeniae are more conspicuously affected than the pouches between them. The formation of opaque, dry, yellowish membranes may extend to involve the whole mucosal surface in diffuse fashion, but usually it sloughs away in smaller or larger portions to produce irregular shallow ulcers. The whole intestinal wall is thickened and stiffened; swelling of the submucosa is obvious on cross-section. Microscopically the membrane is made up of fibrin, debris of cells of the exudate, and necrotic mucosa. It may involve only the superficial layers, leaving the deeper portions of the crypts intact, or may involve the whole mucosa. There are hemorrhages into the underlying tissues, which, though not yet necrotic, are infiltrated with inflammatory cells—polymorphonuclear leucocytes and mononuclear cells. The inflammatory reaction in the submucosa is now much more marked than in the early stages. Ulceration usually stops at the submucosa, but the muscularis mucosae may be destroyed, and sometimes the muscular layers are exposed. Perforation is very uncommon. Ulceration is usually not pronounced before the second to third week.

In more protracted cases the ulcers are lined by a pink, satinlike membrane, sometimes difficult to distinguish from mucosa, and in section this is found to be composed of a layer of granulation tissue densely infiltrated with mononuclear cells. Plasma cells are often quite conspicuous. New growth of epithelium can be seen at the margins of the ulcers. **SYMPTOMS.** Bacillary dysentery may be clinically indistinguishable from nonspecific diarrhea. The stools are loose for only a few days, fever is slight or absent, the appetite is scarcely affected, and the child hardly seems ill. In other cases the constitutional disturbance is equally mild, but the stools contain mucus with streaks of blood. Careful bacteriologic studies, applied to an entire community without regard to individual complaints, suggest that mild cases may actually outnumber those which are clinically more conspicuous.

In cases of moderate severity, in which clinical recognition is more likely, the onset is usually sudden, often with fever, vomiting, anorexia, and abdominal pain. Diarrhea promptly appears, and frequent thin green or yellow stools are passed which contain undigested food. Later the discharges contain blood and mucus and are often preceded by intestinal cramps and accompanied by tenesmus. With persistent anorexia the stools contain less and less food residue and consist mainly of bile-stained exudate; they may number 20 or 30 a day. The mucus may be clear and jellylike or may be mixed with pus and bile-stained flecks. Blood may be seen in almost every stool, usually streaking the mucus, but rarely in clots. These stools are almost odorless, having a faint musty rather than a fecal smell. Prolapse of the rectum is frequent and may occur with nearly every stool. For the first 24 hours the temperature is usually high, from 102° to 104° F, and thereafter it commonly ranges from 99° to 102° F. Vomiting is seldom troublesome after the first day, and abdominal distension is exceptional either at onset or later. The loss of water and electrolytes is often very great in the early stages and may lead to severe dehydration, with prostration, sunken eyes, dryness of mucous membranes, and sordes on the lips and teeth. Acidosis may develop rapidly. Indeed, the first few hours of an attack of dysentery may be most critical. Leucocytosis may be present, though it seldom exceeds 15,000. The duration of acute symptoms varies. The first sign of improvement is generally the disappearance of blood from the stools, which at the same time become less frequent, and the pain and tenesmus cease. Defervescence and recovery of appetite usually precede the return of entirely normal stools. Convalescence is often slow, and it may be weeks before the lost weight and strength are regained. In some cases the intestine remains hyperirritable for months after an attack, during which time minor dietary indiscretions may lead to a recurrence of diarrhea with mucus in the stools but without demonstrable dysentery organisms.

In the past, fatality rates from shigellosis were high, and in many underdeveloped countries this is so even today. Fatal dysentery is encountered only rarely in developed countries. Serious infection may develop in patients with underlying diseases. In the United States, fatal outcome of shigellosis is rare. In one epidemic, studied extensively in western New York, only one death occurred among more than 200 patients. The fatal case was that of a patient with leukemia under treatment with corticoid hormone who contracted a shigella infection.

COMPLICATIONS. Major complications are those of endotoxic shock with circulatory collapse. In children, convulsive seizures are not infrequent. Other complications have decreased in number and severity since sulfonamides and antibiotics came into general use. Invasion of the bloodstream and metastatic complications caused by dysentery bacilli themselves are very exceptional. There is no evidence available to indicate that shigellosis is related etiologically to ulcerative colitis.

DIAGNOSIS. Proctoscopic examination may disclose congestion and edema of the mucous membrane, indicating actual enteritis. The involved mucosa bleeds readily. In more severe cases fibrinous membrane may be found, or ulcers ranging in size from follicular to 1 or 2 cm in diameter. The absence of lesions in proctoscopic examination does not, of course, exclude bacillary dysentery.

Accurate diagnosis depends on bacteriologic evidence. In any case of diarrhea the stools should be carefully inspected for flecks of blood or streaks of pus, and suspicious material should be examined under the microscope. Appreciable numbers of polymorphonuclears are found in almost all cases of dysentery, as well as in salmonella enteritis. When both pus and blood are present there is strong probability that either shigella or salmonella infection is the cause, although amebic colitis cannot be excluded without additional evidence.

Bacteriologic examination of freshly passed feces or material obtained on rectal swabs usually results in the recovery of the shigellae. In some cases two or more cultures may be required. The pathogen is identified on the basis of morphologic characteristics, biochemical activities, and antigenic structure. Group-specific and type-specific *Shigella* antisera are available for identification. Since shigellae as a rule do not invade the bloodstream, blood cultures play no role in diagnosis. Diagnostic tests for the demonstration of the antibody response of the patients are not available for routine purposes, although they may be of considerable help in epidemiologic studies.

PROPHYLAXIS. In hospitals, patients with shigellosis should be under "enteric precautions" to prevent infection of other subjects. For the protection of household contacts the features to be stressed are the careful washing of hands, terminal sterilization of formulas for infants, adequate refrigeration of food, and protection from flies. Vaccines for active immunization are not available. Prevention of community outbreaks requires appropriate water sanitation, food hygiene, and other measures effective in prevention of dissemination of enteric pathogens.

TREATMENT. Proper control of dehydration, including restoration of lost electrolytes, is usually the most immediate concern in the treatment of dysentery. This has been discussed elsewhere (Sec. 3.8). A variety of antibacterial agents have been used in the treatment of shigellosis, including streptomycin, the tetracyclines, chloramphenicol, polymyxin B, colistin, furazolidone, and ampicillin. Ampicillin is the drug of choice of many physicians. Since the susceptibility of shigellae to these drugs differs substantially in various localities and at various times, it is strongly recommended, notably when shigellosis is prevalent in a community, to determine the in vitro susceptibility of the pathogens as a guide to clinical therapy. In view of the frequently mild course of shigellosis in children seen at the present time, clinical evaluation of the relative merits of various chemotherapeutic agents presents difficulties. Certain patients become carriers even after a course of chemotherapy. Only under unusual circumstances should further treatment be given in the attempt to eradicate the carrier state.

In considering diet for patients with shigella infections, the character of the stools should not be used to indicate the condition of the patient's digestion. His diarrhea may be only the result of the inflammatory process. The appetite is usually an excellent guide to follow. Residue should be avoided, but other dietary restrictions are not needed. Adsorbents, such as kaolin and pectin, have not impressed us with their usefulness. The same may be said of carob flour. Raw fruits have been widely recommended and except for citrus fruits are well tolerated, but they appear to have no specific virtue.

The appetite may totally fail in prolonged febrile cases and even after subsidence of the fever, in patients who are very weak. Transfusion may be of help. Since vitamin deficiencies, notably those of the B group, are likely to be seen in protracted cases, a supplement which provides for these factors as well as for vitamin C should always be given.

Opium may be of help when there is pain, tenesmus, and great frequency of stools. The dose should be regulated by the severity of these symptoms. The deodorized tincture (laudanum) and paregoric are, we believe, preferable to other preparations. Repeated small doses are better than a single large dose. Severe tenesmus, when associated with prolapse of the rectum, is sometimes effectively relieved by a suppository containing benzocaine.

Enteropathogenic E. coli *Enteritis*

ETIOLOGY. Epidemics of diarrhea occur from time to time in nurseries for newborn infants. At times, such outbreaks are characterized by rapid spread through the nursery and by a fulminating course. Epidemics have occurred at all seasons of the year and in many countries of the world. In several of the reported epidemics breast-fed infants have been as frequently stricken as those artificially fed, while in others the burden of illness has fallen chiefly on those receiving bottle feedings. At times, as much as half of the susceptible population in a nursery has been afflicted. Carefully studied individual epidemics have been shown to be caused by various enteropathogenic strains of *E. coli* (enteropathogenic *E. coli* or EEC), by certain strains of *Staphylococcus*, and by viruses such as ECHO virus 18. Among the 140-odd serogroups of *Escherichia coli*, the following have been associated with, and, in all likelihood, are responsible for, enteritis of infants and young children: O26:B6, O55:B5, O86:B7, O111:B4, O112:B11, O119:B14, O124:B17, O125:B15, O126:B16, O127:B8, and O128:B12. It is likely that a few additional serogroups of *E. coli* may eventually be proved to be enteropathogenic. For unexplained reasons *E. coli* O55:B5, O111:B4, and O127:B8 have been encountered more frequently in epidemics than have other serogroups, although all may cause sporadic infections.

Recent investigations have shed light on the mechanism of enteropathogenicity. Enteropathogenic strains from patients with this infection produce a characteristic lesion in the ligated small intestine of experimental animals, and this lesion is due to enterotoxin. It is likely that enterotoxin production is related to the presence of a transferable plasmid (genetic material in the cytoplasm). Thus, enteritis in susceptible infants develops, if the ingested strain multiplies in the small intestine and there produces the enterotoxin. It is of interest to note that serotypes of *E. coli* other than those found in infants are enteropathogenic in certain animal species by an essentially identical mechanism.

Epidemics clearly attributable to a filterable virus are now thought to be relatively rare. Information on viral enteritis is still scanty, and evidence suggests that various types of ECHO viruses (14 and 18), adenoviruses (3 and 7), and other viruses as well may produce enteritis in infants. The role of various serotypes of viruses as causes of epidemic diarrhea of the newborn is even less clear. Occasionally, outbreaks may be due to salmonellae or may be associated with organisms not ordinarily regarded as causing diarrhea but presumed to be pathogenic in very young infants. Examples of the latter class are the epidemic of *Pseudomonas aeruginosa* (*pyocyaneus*) infections reported by Ensign and Hunter, or those ascribed to *Klebsiella pneumoniae* (Friedländer's bacillus). Even with careful modern techniques the causative agent of some epidemics may remain unidentified, and it is not clear whether, and to what extent, microbial growth in milk may be responsible for diarrhea. Infection of infants with EEC from animals, notably cattle, through unpasteurized and unheated milk is a possibility, although the strains found in animals often differ in antigenic structure from human EEC.

EPIDEMIOLOGY. In the majority of epidemics studied in recent years the causative agent has been thought to be transferred from infant to infant for the most part by hands, linen, or equipment—in other words, by some error in nursery technique. It is important to keep in mind that infants with EEC enteritis frequently shed extraordinarily large numbers of pathogens in the feces. Occasionally, adults, including nurses, are fecal carriers of enteropathogenic *E. coli* or of other pathogens and thus may serve as a source of infection of newborn infants. Transmission of EEC, salmonellae, and shigellae from mother to child during delivery may result in infection of the newborn infant, who in turn may transmit the infection to others in the nursery. The importance of airborne transmission of the infection has not been satisfactorily evaluated, but it is currently believed to be minor.

PATHOLOGY. No specific pathologic changes are found. The intestinal mucosa is congested but shows no ulceration, and there may be evidences of parenchymatous degeneration or of secondary infection in other organs.

SYMPTOMS. The incubation period is usually short and may in some instances be a matter of only a few hours, diarrhea being the first symptom. Fever is not striking at the onset and may be absent in mild cases; in severe ones the temperature may rise rapidly as the condition progresses. Leucocytosis is not characteristic. The stools are watery; they contain neither blood nor pus and, as a rule, little mucus. The discharges may be very frequent, being passed with considerable force. The appetite is lost and often there is vomiting. Loss of weight may be precipitous, and serious dehydration may develop rapidly. The mucous membranes are dry and the pharynx and tongue often fiery red; the bacteriology of the respiratory tract, however, is not abnormal. Death may occur within a few days with acidosis and dehydration, or after some weeks of progressive nutritional failure. As a rule, however, symptoms abate gradually, and the infant eventually resumes his growth. The principal complications are secondary infections, chiefly of the respiratory or urinary tract, the meninges, or the skin. Unless effective chemotherapy is utilized, recurrence of EEC enteritis is not infrequent. Permanent residua are scarcely ever encountered.

PROGNOSIS. Case fatality rates in individual epidemics vary greatly but have tended in recent years to average less than 5 percent. Not for years has an epidemic been reported with as high a mortality as 50 percent in this country. In a widespread community outbreak of enteritis due to *E. coli* O111:B4, reported by Kessner et al., the fatality rate for neonates was 16 percent and for the entire population 5.9 percent.

DIAGNOSIS. Except during epidemics, an etiologic diagnosis in individual cases cannot be established on clinical grounds alone. Isolation and identification of the pathogen by appropriate laboratory methods, therefore, are essential. The fluorescent antibody technique makes possible rapid, presumptive identification of enteropathogenic *E. coli*.

PROPHYLAXIS. It is imperative to diagnose infectious enteritis of the newborn without delay and to take steps for the prevention and control of epidemics. Appropriate chemotherapy of infected infants, chemoprophylaxis of exposed individuals, and proper aseptic technique are required. It may be necessary to close the nursery to further admissions until the last infant has been discharged and the nursery has been disinfected. It is important that, should infectious enteritis develop in infants shortly after discharge from a nursery, the hospital be promptly notified. Attention should be called also to the appropriate reporting of cases to health departments, according to existing laws and regulations. The fact that several large hospital services have been entirely free from such epidemics over a period of several years may in all probability be ascribed to careful attention to routine procedures of nursing care and to the preparation and administration of feedings, in which terminal sterilization of formulas is believed to play a significant part. In addition, poorly understood changes in virulence of enteropathogenic strains may have played a significant role.

TREATMENT. A variety of antibacterial agents have been used for the oral treatment and prophylaxis of bacterial enteritis of the newborn (and of older infants), including neomycin, polymyxin B, colistin, ampicillin, and others. Chemotherapy is more often indicated in infections of the newborn than in those of older children. Since strains of EEC, and of other bacterial pathogens as well, not rarely are resistant to one or more antibacterial agents, in vitro susceptibility tests should be carried out, notably during epidemics, as a guide to clinical chemotherapy. An antigen has recently been prepared for possible use in the prophylaxis of this infection and is under clinical trial. The role of locally produced antibodies, notably IgA, in immunity remains to be explored.

Nonspecific treament differs in no essential way from that of diarrhea in infants (Sec. 3.8).

REFERENCES

SALMONELLA INFECTIONS

Abrams, I. F., Cochran, W. D., Holmes, L. B., Marsh, E. B., and Moore, J. W. A *Salmonella newport* outbreak in a premature nursery with a one-year follow-up. Effect of ampicillin following bacteriologic failure of response to kanamycin. Pediatrics, 37:616, 1966.

Aserkoff, B., and Bennett, J. V. Effect of antibiotic therapy in acute salmonellosis on the fecal excretion of salmonellae. New Eng. J. Med., 281:636, 1969.

Bate, J. G., and James, U. Salmonella typhimurium infection dust-borne in a children's ward. Lancet, 2:713, 1958.

Black, P. H., Kunz, L. J., and Swartz, M. N. Salmonellosis—a review of some unusual aspects. New Eng. J. Med., 262:811, 864, 921, 1960.

Cherubin, C. E., Fodor, T., Denmark, L. I., Master, C. S., Fuerst, H. T., and Winter, J. W. Symptoms, septicemia and death in salmonellosis. Amer. J. Epidemiol., 90:285, 1969.

Clyde, W. A., Jr. Salmonellosis in infants and children; a study of 100 cases. Pediatrics, 19:175, 1957.

Collins, R. N., Treger, M. D., Goldsby, J. B., Boring, J. R., Coohon, D. B., and Barr, R. N. Interstate outbreak of *Salmonella newbrunswick* infection traced to powdered milk. J.A.M.A., 203:838, 1968.

Committee on Salmonella. An evaluation of the Salmonella problem. Nat. Acad. Sci., Washington, D.C., 1969.

Eisenberg, G. M., Brodsky, L., Weiss, W., and Flippin, H. F. Clinical and microbiological aspects of salmonellosis. Amer. J. Med. Sci., 235:497, 1958.

Fuerst, H. T. The epidemiology of Salmonella infections in the City of New York. Bull. N.Y. Acad. Med., 40:948, 1964 (second series).

Galloway, H., Clark, N. S., and Blackhall, M. Paediatric aspects of the Aberdeen typhoid outbreak. Arch. Dis. Child., 41:63, 1966.

Han, T., Sokal, J. E., and Neter, E. Salmonellosis in disseminated malignant diseases. A seven-year review (1959-1965). New Eng. J. Med., 276:1045, 1967.

Hook, E. W. Salmonellosis: Certain factors influencing the interaction of Salmonella and the human host. Bull. N.Y. Acad. Med., 37:499, 1961 (second series).

——— Campbell, C. G., Weens, H. S., and Cooper, G. R. Salmonella osteomyelitis in patients with sickle-cell anemia. New Eng. J. Med., 257:403, 1957.

Hughes, J. G., and Carroll, D. S. Salmonella osteomyelitis complicating sickle-cell disease. Pediatrics, 19:184, 1957.

Kough, R. H., Scicchitano, D. C., and Smull, C. E.

Salmonellosis in a rural Pennsylvania hospital. Observations in 100 consecutive cases. Arch. Int. Med., 116:548, 1965.

MacCready, R. A., Reardon, J. P., and Saphra, I. Salmonellosis in Massachusetts; a sixteen-year experience. New Eng. J. Med., 256:1121, 1957.

Marx, M. B. The effect of interspecies contact upon diarrhea morbidity and salmonellosis in children. J. Infect. Dis., 120:202, 1969.

Medical Lett. Salmonella infections. 10:50, 1968.

Neter, E., Drislane, A. M., Harris, A. H., and Jansen, G. T. Diagnosis of clinical and subclinical salmonellosis by means of a serologic hemagglutination test. New Eng. J. Med., 261:1162, 1959.

Philbrook, F. R., MacCready, R. A., Van Roekel, H., Anderson, E. S., Smyser, C. F., Jr., Sanen, F. J., and Groton, W. M. Salmonellosis spread by a dietary supplement of avian source. New Eng. J. Med., 263:713, 1960.

Robertson, R. P., Wahab, M. F. A., and Raasch, F. O. Evaluation of chloramphenicol and ampicillin in salmonella enteric fever. New Eng. J. Med., 278:171, 1968.

Rosenstein, B. J. Salmonellosis in infants and children. Epidemiologic and therapeutic considerations. J. Pediat., 70:1, 1967.

—— Shigella and Salmonella enteritis in infants and children. Bull. Hopkins Hosp., 115:407, 1964.

Sanders, E., Sweeney, F. J., Jr., Friedman, E. A., Boring, J. R., Randall, E. L., and Polk, L. D. An outbreak of hospital-associated infections due to *Salmonella derby.* J.A.M.A., 186:984, 1963.

Schroeder, S. A., Aserkoff, B., and Brachman, P. S. Epidemic salmonellosis in hospitals and institutions. New Eng. J. Med., 279:674, 1968.

—— Terry, P. M., and Bennett, J. V. Antibiotic resistance and transfer factor in Salmonella, United States, 1967. J.A.M.A., 205:87, 1968.

Simon, H. J., and Miller, R. C. Ampicillin in the treatment of chronic typhoid carriers. Report on fifteen treated cases and a review of the literature. New Eng. J. Med., 274:807, 1966.

Szanton, V. L. Epidemic salmonellosis; a 30-month study of 80 cases of *Salmonella oranienburg* infection. Pediatrics, 20:794, 1957.

Watt, J., Wegman, M. E., Brown, O. W., Schliessmann, D. J., Maupin, E., and Hemphill, E. C. Salmonellosis in a premature nursery unaccompanied by a diarrheal disease. Pediatrics, 22:689, 1958.

Whitby, J. M. F. Ampicillin in treatment of *Salmonella typhi* carriers. Lancet, 2:71, 1964.

World Health Organization, Bull. W.H.O., 26:357, 1964.

SHIGELLOSIS

Bibile, S. W., Cooray, M. P. M., Balasubramaniam, K., and Gulasekaram, J. Comparative trial of drugs in bacillary dysentery. J. Trop. Med. Hyg., 64:300, 1961.

De La Torre, J. A., Olarte, J., and Joachin, A. Treatment of shigellosis with tetracycline in infants under 2 years of age. Pediatrics, 23:1136, 1959.

DuPont, H. L., Hornick, R. B., Dawkins, A. T., Snyder, M. J., and Formal, S. B. The response of man to virulent *Shigella flexneri* 2a. J. Infect. Dis., 119:296, 1969.

Eichner, E. R., Gangarosa, E. J., and Goldsby, J. B. The current status of shigellosis in the United States. Amer. J. Pub. Health, 58:753, 1968.

Fischler, E., and Wallis, K. Investigation of drug sensitivity in *Shigella* and its correlation with *in vivo* sensitivity. Ann. Paediat., 201:49, 1963.

Freitag, J. L. A water-borne outbreak of dysentery. Health News, 37:4, 1960.

Gerstmann, P. E., and LaVeck, G. D. Shigellosis: mass drug therapy in an institutional setting. Amer. J. Pub. Health, 53:266, 1963.

Gordon, J. E., Ascoli, W., Pierce, V., Guzman, M. A., and Mata, L. J. Studies of diarrheal disease in Central America. VI. An epidemic of diarrhea in a Guatemalan highland village, with a component due to *Shigella dysenteriae,* Type 1. Amer. J. Trop. Med. Hyg., 14:404, 1965.

Greenberg, M., Frant, S., and Shapiro, R. Bacillary dysentery acquired at birth. J. Pediat., 17:363, 1940.

Haltalin, K. C. Neonatal shigellosis. Report of 16 cases and review of the literature. Amer. J. Dis. Child., 114:603, 1967.

—— Nelson, J. D., Hinton, L. V., Kusmiesz, H. T., and Sladoje, M. Comparison of orally absorbable and nonabsorbable antibiotics in shigellosis. A double blind study with ampicillin and neomycin. J. Pediat., 72:708, 1968.

—— Nelson, J. D., Kusmiesz, H. T., and Hinton, L. V. Comparison of intramuscular and oral ampicillin therapy for shigellosis. J. Pediat., 73:617, 1968.

—— Nelson, J. D., Ring, R., Sladoje, M., and Hinton, L. V. Double-blind treatment study of shigellosis comparing ampicillin, sulfadiazine, and placebo. J. Pediat., 70:970, 1967.

—— and Nelson, J. D. *In vitro* susceptibility of shigellae to sodium sulfadiazine and to eight antibiotics. J.A.M.A., 193:81, 1965.

Jao, R. L., and Jackson, G. G. Asymptomatic urinary-tract infection with *Shigella sonnei* in a chronic fecal carrier. New Eng. J. Med., 268:1165, 1963.

Mata, L. J., Urrutia, J. J., Garcia, B., Fernandez, R., and Behar, M. *Shigella* infection in breast fed Guatemalan Indian neonates. Amer. J. Dis. Child., 117:142, 1969.

Medical Letter. Diarrhea caused by *Shigella.* 10:38, 1968.

Mitsuhashi, S. Review: The R factors. J. Infect. Dis., 119:89, 1969.

Moorhead, P. J., and Parry, H. E. Treatment of sonne dysentery. Brit. Med. J., 2:913, 1965.

Neter, E. *Shigella sonnei* infection at term and its transfer to newborn. Obstet. Gynec., 17:517, 1961.

—— Epidemiologic and immunologic studies of *Shigella sonnei* dysentery. Amer. J. Pub. Health, 52:61, 1962.

—— Harris, A. H., and Drislane, A. M. Comparative study of hemagglutination and agglutination tests for the determination of the antibody response of patients with *S. sonnei* dysentery. Amer. J. Clin. Pathol., 37:239, 1962.

Reller, L. B., Gangarosa, E. J., and Brachman, P. S. Shigellosis in the United States: Five-year review of nationwide surveillance, 1964-1968. Amer. J. Epidemiol., 91:161, 1970.

Salzman, T. C., Scher, C. D., and Moss, R. Shigellae with transferable drug resistance: Outbreak in a nursery for premature infants. J. Pediat., 71:21, 1967.

ENTEROPATHOGENIC E. COLI ENTERITIS

Baker, J. A., and Neter, E., eds. Epidemic and endemic diarrheal diseases of the infant. Ann. N.Y. Acad. Sci., 66:3, 1956.

Behbehani, A. M., and Wenner, H. A. Infantile diarrhea. A study of the etiologic role of viruses. Amer. J. Dis. Child., 111:623, 1966.

Danielsson, D., and Laurell, G. The fluorescent antibody technique in the diagnosis of enteropathogenic *Escherichia coli,* with special reference to sensitivity and specificity. Acta Path. Microbiol. Scand., 76:601, 1969.

Ewing, W. H. Sources of *Escherichia coli* cultures that belonged to O antigen groups associated with infantile diarrheal disease. J. Infect. Dis., 110:114, 1962.

Gordon, J. E. Acute diarrheal disease. Amer. J. Med. Sci., 248:345, 1964.

Hodes, H. L. The etiology of infantile diarrhea. *In* Advances in Pediatrics. Chicago, Year Book Publishers, 1956, Vol. 8, p. 13.

Kalser, M. H., Cohen, R., Arteaga, I., Yawn, E., Mayoral, L., Hoffert, W. R., and Frazier, D. Normal viral and bacterial flora of the human small and large intestine. New Eng. J. Med., 274:500, 558, 1966.

Kessner, D. M., Shaughnessy, H. J., Googins, J., Rasmussen, C. M., Rose, N. J., Marshall, A. L., Jr., Andelman, S. L., Hall, J. B., and Rosenbloom, P. J. An extensive community outbreak of diarrhea due to enteropathogenic *Escherichia coli* O111:B4. I. Epidemiologic studies. Amer. J. Hyg., 76:27, 1962.

Neter, E. Enteritis due to enteropathogenic *Escherichia coli.* J. Pediat., 55:223, 1959.

Ocklitz, H. W., Mochmann, H., Schmidt, E. F., and Hering, L. Oral immunization of mice with a soluble protective antigen obtained from enteropathogenic serotypes of *Escherichia coli.* Nature, 214:1053, 1967.

Olarte, J., Galindo, E., and Joachin, A. Sensitivity of Salmonella, Shigella, and enteropathogenic *Escherichia coli* species to cephalothin, ampicillin, chloramphenicol, and tetracycline. Antimicrob. Agents Chemother., p. 787, 1962.

—— Epidemic diarrhea in premature infants. Etiological significance of a newly recognized type of *Escherichia coli* (O142:K86(B):H6). Amer. J. Dis. Child., 109:436, 1965.

Schaffer, J., Lewis, V., Nelson, J., and Walcher, D. Antepartum survey for enteropathogenic *Escherichia coli.* Amer. J. Dis. Child., 106:84, 1963.

Smith, H. W., and Halls, S. Observations by the ligated intestinal segment and oral inoculation methods on *Escherichia coli* infections in pigs, calves, lambs and rabbits. J. Path. Bact., 93:499, 1967.

Stulberg, C. S., Zuelzer, W. W., Nolke, A. C., and Thompson, A. L. *Escherichia coli* 0127:B$_8$, a pathogenic strain causing infantile diarrhea. Amer. J. Dis. Child., 90:125, 1955.

—— Zuelzer, W. W., and Page, R. Epidemic of diarrhea of the newborn—nonassociation of cytopathogenic agents. Amer. J. Dis. Child., 95:30, 1958.

Yow, M. D. Antibiotic management of acute infectious gastroenteritis of infancy. Pediat. Clin. N. Amer., 10:163, 1963.

14.15
STAPHYLOCOCCAL COLONIZATION AND DISEASE

HENRY R. SHINEFIELD

Although staphylococcal disease occurs in all age groups, the most serious manifestations of illness caused by S. *aureus* are seen in the newborn baby or in infants and children with "altered host resistance."

DYNAMICS OF INFANT COLONIZATION. It is now clear that (1) the nares and umbilicus of the infant are colonized with S. *aureus* shortly after birth; (2) the major source of infection is the nursery personnel; (3) the attendants' hands are the most important source of infant contamination; and (4) fewer than 10 S. *aureus* cells will initiate umbilical colonization in 50 percent of newborns, while approximately 250 organisms will achieve a similar effect on the nasal mucosa.

Multiple factors in colonization of the newborn probably account for the fact that the colonization rate of 4- to 5-day-old infants in a given nursery may vary from 10 to 80 or 90 percent, despite no obvious changes in personnel, environment, or nursery techniques. The umbilicus is usually colonized before the nares, and the incidence of colonization is higher among males than females.

By the time the infant is 4 to 8 weeks old, the colonization rate of the umbilicus approaches zero, while nasal colonization after the first year of life is in the adult range of 20 to 40 percent.

CONTROL OF NURSERY INFECTION. The aim in all suggested programs for the control of staphylococcal disease in the newborn is to prevent colonization of the neonate with virulent strains of staphylococcus. General clinical experience as well as controlled investigations have proved that such protection cannot be achieved by strict asepsis on the part of nursery personnel, vigorous environmental control including the use of ultraviolet lights, or utilization of a "rooming-in" program for the newborn. As a last resort nurseries have been closed, but even this has not curtailed epidemics in all instances.

Washing with hexachlorophene soon after birth and daily thereafter has been suggested to control colonization. This technique has been associated with a diminution of staphylococcal skin colonization and skin lesions but has little or no effect on nasal colonization; also, it is not effective in controlling S. *aureus* colonization when it is initiated during the height of an epidemic. Hexachlorophene toxicity, observed experimentally, has not been demonstrated in man.

A method successfully employed by the author,

as well as others, to terminate premature and full-term infant colonization with virulent *S. aureus* during nursery epidemics utilizes the phenomenon of bacterial interference. Artificial colonization of the nares and umbilicus of newborn infants with a selected strain of *S. aureus* of low virulence within the first two hours after birth results in prompt termination of nursery outbreaks of infection and disease caused by hospital strains of *S. aureus*. Artificial colonization of newborns at present is indicated only during epidemics when both the staphylococcal colonization and disease rate of infants are high; routine colonization of all infants in nonepidemic periods is not recommended.

All individuals with staphylococcal lesions should be excluded from the nursery and obstetric area. The asymptomatic nasal carrier should also be removed from contact with the newborn infant when it is ascertained that the *S. aureus* strain carried is identical to the one causing trouble in newborns. Carriers of strains that are not contributory to infant disease need not be excluded from contact with the newborn. Many of the nursery attendants who are carriers of epidemic strains of *S. aureus* are transient carriers and lose their colonization when they are removed from the nursery or when the predominant nursery strain infecting infants is deliberately changed.

It is possible to eliminate nasal carriage from permanent carriers of *S. aureus* for short periods of time with the use of a variety of antibiotic regimens. Following the cessation of antibiotics the return of the resident strain may be prevented in about 60 to 80 percent of the cases by deliberate recolonization with a selected less virulent strain of *S. aureus*. If only antibiotics are used, the resident strain can be detected in the nares of 60 to 70 percent of the treated individuals within 2 to 4 weeks after therapy is stopped.

A surveillance program of periodic infant and attendant cultures in the nursery may be helpful in early detection of epidemics of *S. aureus*.

MANIFESTATIONS OF STAPHYLOCOCCAL DISEASE IN THE NEWBORN. Staphylococcal disease rates in the infant depend more on the strain of staphylococcus with which he is colonized than on the incidence of colonization. Colonization with "wild" or nonepidemic strains of *S. aureus* are associated with disease rates of about 5 percent, while colonization with virulent hospital strains, usually strains in phage Group 1, may result in disease rates approaching 70 percent. Epidemics of bullous impetigo (Ritter's disease) have been caused only by strains in phage Group 2. A specific toxin responsible for this manifestation of staphylococcal disease has been isolated from this group of staphylococci.

Although skin lesions may be seen while the baby is in the nursery, serious staphylococcal disease stemming from colonization of the newborn is most common when the infant is between 3 weeks and 6 months of age. Therefore, an accurate determination

of the incidence of nursery-acquired infection requires surveillance outside the hospital, which can be done by a telephone survey.

Aside from impetigo, illnesses in infants associated with *S. aureus* include septicemia, osteomyelitis, pneumonia, localized boils, meningitis, and mastitis. Staphylococcal disease also may be transmitted from the infant to the family in the form of maternal mastitis or furunculosis, which may then "ping-pong" through a family for periods as long as 6 or 7 years.

STAPHYLOCOCCAL DISEASE IN OLDER INFANTS AND CHILDREN. Aside from the newborn, infants and children usually afflicted with severe staphylococcal infection are those individuals who have deficiencies in host resistance, such as leukemia or other malignancies, cystic fibrosis, systemic collagen disease, or agammaglobulinemia. Included in this group with so-called "altered host states" are infants and children who have been subjected to cardiac or neurosurgical procedures, as well as those who have been treated for a long period of time with multiple or broad-spectrum antibiotic agents. Manifestations of staphylococcal disease in this group of individuals include septicemia with widespread metastatic lesions, staphylococcal pneumonia, endocarditis, enterocolitis, meningitis, and brain abscess. These syndromes are discussed in detail elsewhere.

An interesting feature of staphylococcal disease which follows cardiac or neurosurgical procedures (particularly those requiring rubber or plastic tubes) is the high proportion of strains of staphylococcus that are coagulase-negative; although these organisms are usually saprophytic, the ability of coagulase-negative strains of staphylococcus to produce disease in those circumstances as well as in the newborn is well documented.

In "otherwise healthy" children furunculosis, cellulitis, and osteomyelitis are the most common manifestations of staphylococcal disease.

TREATMENT. In general, therapy for staphylococcal disease should consist of a sound antimicrobial regimen coupled with surgery when indicated. Some staphylococcal infections, especially minor skin infections such as folliculitis, which occur occasionally require no treatment at all in most people. Established abscesses with localized collections of pus should be drained by methods ranging from incision and drainage of a skin abscess to closed underwater drainage of a pleural empyema cavity.

The selection of a drug and the route of administration in the therapy of staphylococcal disease are conditioned by the age of the patient, the severity of the illness, and the probable antibiotic resistance of the staphylococcus. Illness caused by *S. aureus* which develops in hospitalized patients and in infants recently discharged from the hospital or their contacts must be assumed to be disease caused by "hospital" strains of *S. aureus*, i.e., strains that produce penicillinase and are therefore resistant to penicillin.

Bactericidal drugs administered systemically should be used in the treatment of serious staphylococcal disease. When the organism is sensitive to benzyl penicillin (penicillin G), this is still the drug of choice. When the disease is associated with hospital strains of staphylococcus, the semisynthetic, penicillinase-resistant penicillins are the drugs of choice. If the patient is allergic to penicillin or one of its semisynthetic derivatives, cephalothin (Keflin) is used in the treatment of serious staphylococcal disease. However, it is becoming increasingly apparent that some of the patients allergic to penicillin are also allergic to cephalothin. A new agent, gentamycin, may also prove to be useful in treatment of patients allergic to penicillin. Oral administration of any antimicrobial agent in the treatment of serious staphylococcal disease is not recommended because of the unpredictable absorption, the care required to ensure administration on an empty stomach, and the necessity for monitoring serum levels.

In the treatment of moderate staphylococcal disease, oral medication may be used. Penicillin G or phenoxy penicillins are the drugs of choice if the organism is penicillin-sensitive. Erythromycin or lincomycin may be used if the patient is allergic to penicillin. If the organism is penicillin-resistant, the oral preparations of the semisynthetic penicillins (oxacillin, cloxacillin, or dicloxacillin) should be used.

Individuals and families with chronic recurrent furunculosis may be protected from lesions by artificial nasal colonization with a strain of S. aureus of low virulence (strain 502-A). This regimen includes a period of local and systemic antibiotic treatment prior to colonization.

Nonspecific agents used in the therapy of disease associated with S. aureus include various vaccines, toxoids, gamma globulin, and bacteriophage. In controlled observations there is no good evidence that any of these substances is of significant value in the treatment of staphylococcal disease.

REFERENCES

Boris, M., Shinefield, H. R., Romano, P., McCarthy, D. P., and Florman, A. L. Bacterial interference. Protection against recurrent intrafamilial Staphylococcal disease. Amer. J. Dis. Child., 115:521, 1968.

Gezon, H. M., Thompson, D. J., Rogers, K. D., Hatch, T. F., and Taylor, P. M. Hexachlorophene bathing in early infancy. Effect on staphylococcal disease and infection. New Eng. J. Med., 270:379, 1964.

Hurst, V. Colonization in the newborn. In Maibach, H. A., and Hildick-Smith, G. eds. Skin Bacteria and Their Role in Infection. New York, McGraw-Hill Book Co., 1965, pp. 127-141.

Light, I. J., Sutherland, J. M., and Schott, E. E. Control of a staphylococcal outbreak in a nursery, use of bacterial interference. J.A.M.A., 193:699, 1965.

Melish, M. E., and Glasgow, L. A. The staphylococcal scalded-skin syndrome. Development of an experimental model. New Eng. J. Med., 282:1114, 1970.

Schaffer, T. E., Baldwin, J. N., and Wheeler, W. E. Staphylococcal infections in nurseries. Advances Pediat., 10:243, 1958.

Shinefield, H. R., Ribble, J. C., Boris, M., and Sutherland, J. M. The Ohio epidemic. Amer. J. Dis. Child., 105:655, 1963.

———— Ribble, J. C., Eichenwald, H. F., Boris, M., and Sutherland, J. M. Bacterial inference. In Maibach, H. A., and Hildick-Smith, G., eds. Skin Bacteria and Their Role in Infection. New York, McGraw-Hill Book Co., 1965, p. 235.

———— and Ribble, J. C. Current aspects of infections and diseases related to staphylococcus aureus. Ann. Rev. Med., 16:263, 1965.

14.16 STAPHYLOCOCCAL ENTEROCOLITIS AND STAPHYLOCOCCAL FOOD POISONING

ALEX J. STEIGMAN

Staphylococcal Enterocolitis

Staphylococcal enterocolitis (pseudomembranous enterocolitis) is a serious condition which fortunately is rarely seen in children. Its most frequent occurrence is in adults being prepared for or convalescing from intestinal surgery. Multiple cleansing enemas and the use of antimicrobial agents especially orally may so reduce the content of gram-negative organisms that intestinal overgrowth with coagulase-positive *Staphylococcus aureus* occasionally results.

A distended, tender abdomen, fever, vomiting, diarrhea dehydration, and shock may occur very abruptly. Large shreds of small and large intestine appear in the stools. Treatment must be prompt and vigorous (as for cholera) with vast amounts of fluid and electrolyte replacement monitored closely by frequent laboratory assistance. Therapy for bacterial shock including corticosteroids is warranted. Vancomycin may be given orally since it inhibits staphylococci without reducing further the content of gram-negative bacteria.

The necrotizing enterocolitis of infancy such as may be seen in Hirschsprung's disease is also a severe condition but is quite a different disease. One might expect staphylococcal enterocolitis to develop in certain other children, such as those with cystic fibrosis taking oral antibiotics for extended periods; children with hepatic failure being treated with colonic irrigations and oral antibiotics; and infants and children undergoing extensive intestinal resections for various reasons. However, for the most part, children seem to be largely unaffected by this very serious condition.

Staphylococcal Food Poisoning

In the United States nearly 40 percent of all patients *reported* with acute food poisoning are of school age. Cases are most commonly due to the ingestion of preformed, thermostable, staphylococcal enterotoxins. When investigated properly the same phage type of coagulase-positive *S. aureus* is recovered from the responsible food(s) and from the nose and hands of persons who have been concerned with its preparation.

The clinical picture results from direct intoxication rather than infection and is due to enterotoxin A more often than enterotoxins B or D. Phage-types implicated include 6/47/53/54/75/83a; 53/83/85/86; 6/47/53/85; and 54/75/77.

School cafeterias, restaurants, picnics, and parties set the usual stage for outbreaks. Meats, poultry, fish, salads, and custards are the usual culprits when prepared in bulk and set aside to be cooled and reheated prior to serving. There is some individual personal variation in response to the same amount of tainted food ingested. From 25 to almost 100 percent of exposed persons may show symptoms. The responsible foods are not putrefied and have neither bad taste nor odor. Within an hour or up to about 7 hours, but usually after about 4 hours, symptoms appear as follows: increased salivation; nausea; vomiting and retching; midabdominal colicky pain *not* as a rule radiating to the right lower quadrant; sweating and prostration sometimes progressing to shock; muscle aching and headache. There is no fever and the accompanying diarrhea is relatively mild or in some patients absent.

Fatality is virtually unknown in staphylococcal food poisoning but the abrupt distress and prostration is very considerable, especially in school populations. Parenteral fluid administration may be necessary for the sickest children for 12 to 24 hours, rarely longer. Cathartics should *not* be given in the vain attempt to speed exit of the toxin. Patients may resume oral intake at their own discretion. There are no known sequelae; resistance to subsequent exposure does *not* result.

REFERENCES

Silverman, S. J., Knott, A. R., and Howard, M. Rapid sensitive assay for staphylococcal enterotoxin and a comparison of serological methods. Appl. Microbiol., 16:1019, 1968.

Terplan, K., and Paine, J., et al. Fulminating gastroenteritis caused by staphylococcus: Its apparent connection with antibiotic medication. Gastroenterology, 24:476, 1953.

14.17
STREPTOCOCCAL INFECTIONS

MILTON MARKOWITZ

General Considerations

Group A beta hemolytic streptococci are a frequent cause of illness in children. The more typical infections due to these bacteria include pharyngotonsillitis, scarlet fever, and the skin diseases impetigo and erysipelas. These infections are important in children both because of the morbidity associated with them and their suppurative complications as well as the potential seriousness of their nonsuppurative sequelae, rheumatic fever and acute glomerulonephritis. Many of the complications of streptococcal infections can be prevented by accurate diagnosis and adequate therapy.

Biology and Immunology of the Streptococcus. Streptococci are gram-positive organisms which tend to grow in chains. They are broadly classified by their reaction on mammalian blood cells. The clear zone of hemolysis surrounding colonies grown on mammalian blood agar distinguishes beta hemolytic streptococci from the alpha (green or partial hemolysis) and gamma (nonhemolytic) species.

Beta hemolytic streptococci can be divided into a number of groups based on a specific carbohydrate antigen (C carbohydrate substance) in the cell wall. Eighteen distinct serologic groups have been recognized and these groups have been designated by the letters A, B, C, etc. The serologic method of Lancefield is precise but not feasible as a rapid diagnostic test. Group A organisms can be identified more rapidly by using appropriate fluorescein-conjugated antiserum. Group A strains can also be distinguished from other groups by differences in sensitivity to bacitracin. A bacitracin disc containing 0.02 units placed on the primary blood agar plate will inhibit growth of most Group A strains, while non-Group A organisms are generally resistant to this antibiotic. This simple screening procedure is adaptable to use in routine laboratories and in office practice.

Human infections are caused chiefly by Group A organisms and it is the only group involved in initiating rheumatic fever and acute glomerulonephritis. Group B streptococci have been identified as a cause of neonatal sepsis and meningitis. Mild pharyngitis may sometimes be due to Groups C or G organisms. These groups are also frequently found in the pharynx of healthy carriers. Group D (enterococci) strains are associated with sepsis of the newborn, genitourinary infections, and bacterial endocarditis. The other groups may cause serious disease but they rarely occur in children.

The Group A streptococcal cell wall contains a protein layer made up of the M, T, and R proteins. Of these, the M protein is the most important constituent. It is an immunologically specific antigen, and with antisera containing specific M antibody, it is possible to subdivide Group A streptococci into more than 50 distinct types. The identification of M serotypes has provided a valuable tool for epidemiologic investigations. For example, studies of this nature have shown that certain types, notably type 12, are more frequently than others associated with outbreaks of glomerulonephritis (nephritogenic types).

Strains containing M protein resist phagocytosis by human leucocytes, and a relationship between streptococcal M protein content and virulence has been demonstrated. Antibodies to M protein form the basis for human streptococcal immunity. This antigen stimulates production of type-specific antibodies which protect against infection with an homologous type, but which confer no immunity against other M types. Thus, multiple streptococcal infections due to different types are the rule and immunity is acquired only over a period of many years.

The T protein is also an immunologically distinct antigen which can be used to type streptococci. Typing by T-agglutination is useful for identifying organisms not typable by the M protein precipitin method. In general, streptococci isolated from skin lesions can be typed only by the T-agglutination technique. Studies of streptococcal skin infections have shown that they are caused chiefly by a few special types.

Group A streptococci secrete a large variety of enzymes and toxins (extracellular substances). With the exception of erythrogenic toxin, the role of these substances in human disease is unknown. Erythrogenic toxin is responsible for the rash of scarlet fever. Streptococci vary in their ability to elaborate toxin, and it has been shown that streptococci infected with bacteriophage are good producers of erythrogenic toxin. Erythrogenic toxin stimulates the formation of antitoxin antibodies, which provide immunity against the scarlatiniform rash but not against streptococcal infections. However, since all toxins are not serologically identical, a second attack of scarlet fever may sometimes occur.

Many of the other extracellular substances are also antigenic and stimulate antibodies in man. Measurement of these antibodies is extremely useful as evidence of a recent streptococcal infection. The test for antibodies against streptolysin O (antistreptolysin O or ASO) is well standardized and is the most commonly performed streptococcal antibody determination. It is elevated in 70 to 80 percent of patients following an untreated streptococcal infection.

Epidemiology. Streptococcal infections occur during all seasons and in all climates. However, pharyngeal infections are most common in the northern regions of the United States during the winter and early spring months. On the other hand, skin infections occur more frequently during the summer months when abrasions and insect bites are likely to occur; streptococcal pyoderma is also prevalent in the southern parts of the country.

Streptococcal infections are uncommon under 2 years of age, although nursery epidemics have been described. The incidence is highest in young school-age children, chiefly because the school is an important locus for spread. Transmission usually occurs at school or in the home following direct contact with airborne droplets from the respiratory tract of symptomatic or asymptomatic individuals. The recently infected, untreated respiratory tract carrier is the most dangerous and most common source of spread. However, transmission may occur via other carrier sites including skin lesions, fingernails, and even the perianal region. These reservoirs may play an important role in disseminating streptococcal impetigo. Spread by contaminated food is an occasional cause of explosive outbreaks of pharyngitis.

Multiple cases in a family are common. The risk to child contacts in the same household varies from 20 to 50 percent, depending on the virulence of the organism, the degree of crowding, and other factors. Streptococci may spread through the family over a period of several weeks, but most of the acquisitions among contacts occur within a few days after the index case has been identified. While adults in the family are much less likely to acquire streptococci, studies have shown that as many as 15 percent of mothers may harbor the organism. For reasons which are not at all clear, some families appear particularly prone to streptococcal infections.

CLINICAL MANIFESTATIONS. *Pharyngitis.* The signs and symptoms of streptococcal pharyngitis vary greatly. The infection may go unrecognized because of the paucity of constitutional or localizing symptoms, or the patient may be extremely toxic. In the latter, there is a rapid onset of high fever accompanied by malaise, headache, sore throat, and severe pain on swallowing. Vomiting and abdominal pain may be prominent symptoms at the onset, suggesting a gastroenteritis. Coryza, hoarseness, cough, and diarrhea are uncommon. Examination of the pharynx and tonsils in the classical picture reveals one or more of the following findings: beefy redness of the pharyngeal tissues, edema of the uvula, flecks or confluent exudate on the tonsils, and petechiae on the soft palate. The anterior cervical glands are enlarged and tender. Skin petechiae are not uncommon and a frank scarlatiniform rash may be present.

The diagnosis of a streptococcal illness can be made with fair certainty on the basis of clinical findings alone only when a characteristic rash is present. In the absence of a rash, the diagnosis can be strongly suspected if the pharyngeal findings are typical, especially when exudate is present. The findings are generally less characteristic in patients without tonsils, and in a significant number of patients the pharynx shows a variable degree of redness without any of the other features noted above. Furthermore, pharyngeal exudate in children under 3 years of age is more often associated with viral than with streptococcal infections. Indeed, streptococcal illness in young children is usually atypical and is characterized by anorexia, low-grade fever, and purulent nasal discharge with excoriations around the nares.

It is apparent, therefore, that streptococcal respiratory disease can present with various clinical pictures and it is often difficult to distinguish between viral and streptococcal pharyngitis. An awareness of the current epidemiology of infections in the family or in the community can be helpful. However, the diagnosis can be made with assurance only by bacteriologic means. The throat culture is a simple and accurate method to confirm the diagnosis. Many communities have laboratories which process cultures sent in by mail. Some physicians have found it expedient to use a small office incubator and commercially available selective media (sheep's blood agar) which simplifies identification of beta hemolytic streptococci.

Scarlet Fever. Scarlet fever is a streptococcal illness associated with a characteristic rash. It is due to an infection with an erythrogenic toxin-producing Group A streptococcus in individuals who do not have antitoxin antibodies. It is now encountered less commonly than in the past but the incidence is cyclic, depending on the prevalence of toxin-producing strains and the immune status of the population. The modes of transmission, age distribution, and other epidemiologic features are otherwise similar to streptococcal pharyngitis.

Prior to 1940, scarlet fever often presented as a particularly virulent form of streptococcal disease with marked toxic manifestations and a high incidence of septicemia and suppurative complications. At the present time the disease is much milder, probably because antimicrobial agents abort the illness, although a change in virulence of the organisms may be playing a role.

The rash appears within 24 to 48 hours after onset of symptoms, although it may be present with the first signs of illness. It often begins around the neck and spreads over the trunk and extremities. It is a diffuse, finely papular, erythematous eruption producing a bright red discoloration of the skin which blanches on pressure. It is often more intense along the creases of the elbows, axillae, and groin. The skin has a goose-pimple appearance and feels rough to the touch. The face is usually spared and there may be a pallor around the mouth. After 3 to 4 days the rash begins to fade and is followed by a branny desquamation over the trunk and frank peeling of the skin around the fingertips.

In addition to the findings noted in streptococcal pharyngitis, there are punctate erythematous lesions on the palate and surrounding mucous membranes. The tongue is coated and the papillae are swollen. Following desquamation, the reddened papillae are prominent, giving the tongue a strawberry appearance.

The typical case of scarlet fever is not difficult to diagnose. However, the milder form with equivocal pharyngeal findings can be confused with rubella, exanthem subitum, and drug eruptions. Staphylococcal infections are occasionally associated with a scarlatiniform rash. A history of recent exposure to a streptococcal infection is helpful. Isolation of the beta hemolytic streptococci from the nasopharynx will confirm the diagnosis in doubtful cases. If the patient is seen several days after the onset, peeling around the fingers should arouse suspicion of a recent attack of scarlet fever.

Pyoderma. Streptococcal pyoderma or impetigo is a superficial infection of the skin which appears first as a discrete papulovesicular lesion surrounded by a localized area of redness. The vesicles rapidly become purulent and covered with a thick, confluent, amber-colored crust which gives the appearance of having been "stuck on" the skin. The lesions may occur anywhere but are more common on the face and extremities. If untreated, they run a chronic course spreading to other parts of the body. Regional lymphadenitis is common. The chronic form may involve the deeper layers of the skin, causing a condition known as ecthyma, but a concomitant deepseated cellulitis rarely occurs.

Streptococcal impetigo is generally not accompanied by fever or other systemic reactions. Impetiginized excoriations around the nares or the ear lobes are seen with active streptococcal infections of the nasopharynx or with purulent otitis media. However, impetigo is not usually associated with an overt streptococcal infection of the upper respiratory tract. Furthermore, streptococci can be isolated from the pharynx in only a minority of cases of streptococcal impetigo. For these reasons, the concept that the respiratory tract is the primary source of infection in streptococcal impetigo has been questioned and the evidence now suggests that infections can spread to other individuals directly from the skin lesions. Mutiple cases in the same family are common.

It may be difficult to distinguish clinically between streptococcal and staphylococcal impetigo. The latter are more often bullous, have a thinner crust, and occur more commonly in neonates and young infants. In older children, mixed infections are common. At times staphylococci overgrow the culture and obscure the presence of streptococci. However, careful bacteriologic studies have shown that streptococci are found with or without staphylococci in as many as 80 percent of children with impetigo. It would seem prudent, therefore, to treat impetigo in older children as a streptococcal infection.

Erysipelas. Erysipelas is an acute streptococcal infection involving the deeper layers of the skin and the underlying connective tissue. It is rarely seen in infants and children at the present time.

The skin over the affected area is swollen, red, and very tender. Superficial blebs may be present. The most characteristic finding is the sharply defined, slightly elevated border. At times, reddish streaks of lymphangitis project out from the margins of the lesion. A septic fever and other signs of infection are present. The characteristic skin lesion distinguishes this condition from other bacterial causes of cellulitis. Staphylococci, a common cause of cellulitis, produce a diffuse brawny inflammation without a sharply demarcated border. However, other bacteria may sometimes cause erysipelaslike lesions. Cultures obtained by needle puncture of the inflamed area will usually reveal the etiologic agent.

COMPLICATIONS. In the untreated or inadequately treated patient with streptococcal pharyngitis, the acute phase of the illness usually subsides within several days but the child may continue for some weeks to feel below par, with loss of appetite, pallor, fatigability, and low-grade fever. In such patients the pharynx and tonsils may show residual signs of infection along with slightly enlarged and tender anterior cervical lymph glands. The pharyngeal culture will usually demonstrate a moderately heavy growth of beta hemolytic streptococci. Antimicrobial therapy generally results in marked improvement.

Suppurative complications from the spread of streptococci to adjacent structures were very common before antibiotics became available and usually made their appearance within a week after onset of the pharyngitis. Cervical adenitis, otitis media, mastoiditis, and sinusitis still occur in children in whom the primary illness has gone unnoticed or when the treatment of the pharyngitis has been inadequate. Such patients are also vulnerable to serious metastatic infections involving the meninges, bones, or joints. The diagnosis is made by isolating beta hemolytic streptococci from the bloodstream or from the site of the localized abscess. Intensive antimicrobial therapy is indicated.

The nonsuppurative sequelae, rheumatic fever and acute glomerulonephritis, are well recognized complications of streptococcal infections, although the pathogenetic mechanisms are still poorly understood. The latent period between the infection and the onset of these complications varies from 1 to 2 weeks for glomerulonephritis and from 2 to 4 weeks for rheumatic fever. There is also a difference in the relationship of these sequelae to the site of the streptococcal infection. Glomerulonephritis can follow Group A streptococcal infections of either the pharynx or the skin, whereas rheumatic fever is a sequel of a pharyngeal infection and rarely if ever follows pyoderma. The attack rate of rheumatic fever following untreated streptococcal pharyngitis varies from 0.3 to 3 percent, the higher incidence occurring during selected epidemic outbreaks of streptococcal infections. There is no known relationship between the M serotype causing a streptococcal pharyngitis and the occurrence of rheumatic fever, although the possibility of "rheumatogenic" strains cannot be excluded. On the other hand, acute glomerulonephritis occurs more commonly after pharyngeal infections with certain M serotypes, particularly type 12 but also types 49, 1, and 4. Recent evidence also indicates that nephritis after pyoderma is more common following skin infections with a few serotypes. However, the types associated with pyoderma and nephritis (types 2, 55, and 57) differ from the nephritigenic types found in the upper respiratory tract. The incidence of acute glomerulonephritis varies with the prevalence of nephritigenic strains in the community. In outbreaks associated with nephritigenic strains in the pharynx or in skin lesions, the incidence of nephritis varies from 10 to 15 percent.

TREATMENT. Streptococcal infections should be treated with sufficient antibiotic therapy to eradicate the organisms. Treatment which accomplishes this goal will: (1) diminish the spread to family and school contacts; (2) virtually prevent all suppurative complications; and (3) minimize the chance of developing nonsuppurative complications, especially rheumatic fever.

The indications for treating patients with scarlet fever or with the classical features of streptococcal infections are usually straightforward and therapy is warranted prior to bacteriologic confirmation. In less typical cases, it is desirable to withhold treatment until the bacteriologic findings are known. This approach is feasible if the laboratory report can be made available within 24 to 48 hours. It may not always be possible to distinguish the true streptococcal infection from an intercurrent illness in a patient who happens to be carrying beta hemolytic streptococci in his pharynx. The number of colonies in the throat culture may be helpful since there are usually numerous colonies, and rarely fewer than 10, in patients with streptococcal infection. If the organisms are non-Group A streptococci, it is likely that the patient is a carrier. It has been suggested that certain Group A infections are relatively benign, rarely lead to complications, and therefore may not require vigorous therapy. There are no absolute criteria for selecting such cases and one should be aware that in at least a third of the patients with rheumatic fever the preceding streptococcal infection is subclinical in nature.

Group A streptococci are exquisitely sensitive to penicillin, and resistant strains have never been encountered. Penicillin is, therefore, the drug of choice for pharyngeal and skin infections as well as for the suppurative complications. The type of penicillin used and the route of administration are not nearly as important as the duration of treatment. A therapeutic level for a minimum period of 10 days is necessary to eradicate the organisms in most patients. Oral penicillin in doses of 800,000 to 1.2 million units daily for 10 days is a satisfactory form of treatment. If penicillin G is used, it must be administered either before or 2 hours after meals. Phenoxymethyl penicillin may be given without regard to food. The newer penicillins, dicloxacillin, nafcillin, and ampicillin, offer no advantage over the less expensive penicillins in therapy of streptococcal infections. The major problem with all forms of oral therapy is the risk that the drug will be discontinued before the 10-day course has been completed, chiefly because the child usually appears to have recovered in 3 or 4 days. Therefore, when oral treatment is prescribed, the necessity to complete a full course of therapy must be emphasized. If the parents seem unlikely to comply because of family disorganization, difficulties in comprehension, or for other reasons, parenteral therapy is indicated. A single intramuscular injection of 600,000 to 1.2 million units of benzathine penicillin G is the most efficacious, and often the most practical, method of treatment. Its only disadvantage is soreness around the site of injection which may last for several days. The local reaction is diminished when benzathine penicillin G is combined with procaine penicillin G. However, when this combination is used in a single injection, one must be certain that an adequate amount of benzathine penicillin G is administered.

From 10 to 15 percent of patients treated with a full course of penicillin continue to harbor beta hemolytic streptococci. The reasons for these bacteriologic failures are not clear. It has been suggested that penicillinase-producing staphylococci in the pharynx may interfere with the action of penicillin, but if this does occur, it is not the cause of most failures. Indeed, the use of penicillin active against both streptococci and staphylococci does not seem to reduce the incidence of bacteriologic relapses. Not infrequently, the pharyngeal culture following treatment shows beta hemolytic streptococci which prove to be non-Group A organisms and need be no cause for concern. However, if Group A streptococci do persist, a second course of penicillin, preferably with benzathine penicillin, should be given. There is some evidence to suggest that lincomycin may be more effective than penicillin for such patients, but this observation needs to be confirmed.

There are occasions when streptococci persist even after several courses of antibiotics. Organisms can be carried for months without any evidence of illness. Such individuals are not likely to develop complications. They are lightly colonized and are not dangerous to others. The carrier state may also aid in the development of type-specific immunity. When signs of illness do reappear, it is almost always due to an infection with a new serotype. Some individuals are especially prone to recurrent streptococcal infections, and in such patients the tonsils are often incriminated as a source of the difficulty. There is some evidence that tonsillectomy reduces the frequency of streptococcal infections, although this may be more apparent than real because it is easier to culture streptococci from patients with tonsils. While repeated proved streptococcal infections of the tonsils may be an indication for removal, the age of the child as well as other factors must be taken into consideration.

There is the additional problem of treating a patient who is allergic to penicillin. The sulfonamides should not be used since they suppress but do not eradicate the streptococcus. Since from 30 to 40 percent of Group A streptococci are resistant to tetracycline, this drug should also not be employed.

Erythromycin and lincomycin are satisfactory drugs for patients allergic to penicillin. Although resistant strains of Group A streptococci to both these drugs have been reported, the possibility of encountering such a strain is rare at the present time. The dosage for erythromycin or lincomycin is 25 mg per kg daily for 10 days.

Systemic penicillin therapy is indicated for streptococcal pyoderma. A possible exception is the patient seen early with very few lesions which clear rapidly following removal of the crusts and cleansing of the affected areas with hexachlorophene soap. If the lesions persist, spread, or recur, antibiotic therapy should be started. Ointments containing bacitracin or neomycin fail to eradicate the streptococci in a significant number of patients. Penicillin orally or an injection of benzathine penicillin G is effective for streptococcal pyoderma regardless of whether staphylococci are also present. The question of whether penicillin therapy reduces the incidence of nephritis following pyoderma cannot be answered at the present time.

Complete isolation of patients with streptococcal infections is not warranted. There is a rapid decrease in the number of organisms after 3 days of adequate treatment and children can usually return to school within 5 days. However, since it is necessary to maintain a therapeutic drug level for 10 days for maximum eradication of the organisms, if oral agents are used medication must be continued while the child attends school. As a matter of convenience the full daily requirement of oral penicillin can be given in two divided doses during the later stage of treatment. The use of a single injection of benzathine penicillin G obviates the need for maintaining treatment after the patient returns to school.

PREVENTION. The only specific indication for the long-term use of antibiotics to prevent streptococcal infections is for patients who have had an attack of acute rheumatic fever. Prevention can be accomplished by monthly injections of 1.2 million units of benzathine penicillin G, 200,000 units of oral penicillin twice a day or 0.5 to 1.0 g of sulfadiazine daily. While the latter drug should not be used for the treatment of streptococcal infection, it is an effective prophylactic agent.

The frequency with which streptococcal infections spread to other members of the family raises the question of prophylaxis for household contacts. The use of small prophylactic doses of penicillin or another antimicrobial agent is unwise since individuals already infected will be undertreated. An alternative method of treating the entire family with therapeutic doses for 10 days is expensive, and in families under good medical supervision is probably unwarranted. However, the incidence of positive cultures in members of families living in crowded quarters may be as high as 50 percent and since these families do not usually have easy access to medical care, treatment of the entire family at the time the index case is identified may be justified. A more desirable approach is to culture all members of the family within a few days after the first case is discovered and to treat the individuals with positive cultures as well as those who subsequently show evidence of clinical infection. This approach should always be used when a patient with acute glomerulonephritis is identified, since multiple cases in one family may occur.

Apart from rheumatic fever prophylaxis and the prevention of intrafamily spread, the ability to prevent streptococcal infections is very limited at the present time. Mass prophylaxis is generally not feasible except during epidemics in military populations and occasionally during large outbreaks in schools. The possibility of a streptococcal vaccine offers the promise of a more biologic and more easily applied method than is presently available. The M protein antigen involved in streptococcal immunity has been purified and has been shown to induce antibodies in human volunteers. The ideal vaccine would need to contain purified M antigens of more than 50 serotypes, a seemingly insurmountable problem. However, the majority of streptococcal infections is caused by a relatively small number of types, so that an effective vaccine against prevalent strains may be feasible. The question of complete safety has not been fully resolved and will not be until the relationship of streptococcal substances, such as M protein, to human disease has been elucidated. Until a better method for preventing streptococcal infections becomes available, the proper management of these infections is the surest way to minimize the incidence of complications.

REFERENCES

Breese, B. B. Beta hemolytic streptococcal infections in children. Pediat. Clin. N. Amer., 7:843, 1960.

Dillon, H. C. Group A Type 12 streptococcal infection in a newborn nursery. Amer. J. Dis. Child., 112:177, 1966.

Eickoff, T. C., et al. Neonatal sepsis and other infections due to Group B beta-hemolytic streptococci. New Eng. J. Med., 271:1221, 1964.

Lancefield, R. C. Current knowledge of type-specific M antigens of Group A streptococci. J. Immun., 89:307, 1962.

Maxted, W. R. The use of bacitracin for identifying Group A hemolytic streptococci. J. Clin. Path., 6:224, 1953.

McCarty, M. The hemolytic streptococci. In Dubos, R. J., and Hirsch, J. B., eds., Bacterial and Mycotic Infections of Man. Philadelphia, J. B. Lippincott Co., 1965.

Quie, P. G., Pierce, H. C., and Wannamaker, L. W. Influence of penicillin-producing staphylococci on the eradication of Group A streptococci from the upper respiratory tract by penicillin treatment. Pediatrics, 37:467, 1966.

Rammelkamp, C. H., Jr. Epidemiology of streptococcal infections. Harvey Lect., 51:113, 1957.

Rosenstein, B. J., et al. Factors involved in treatment failures following oral penicillin therapy of streptococcal pharyngitis. J. Pediat., 73:513, 1968.

Sanders, E., Foster, M. T., and Scott, D. Group A beta-hemolytic streptococci resistant to erythromycin and lincomycin. New Eng. J. Med., 278:1221, 1964.

Stollerman, G. H. Prospects for a vaccine against Group A streptococci: The problem of the immunology of M proteins. Arthritis Rheum., 10:245, 1967.

Wannamaker, L. W. Differences between streptococcal infections of the throat and of the skin. New Eng. J. Med., 282:23, 78, 1970.

14.18
SYPHILIS

LAURENCE FINBERG

Syphilis is an infectious disease with both acute and chronically relapsing phases. The causative organism becomes widely disseminated, and the resultant pathology may have a direct or indirect effect upon every organ and tissue of the body. Long clinically latent periods are common. In temperate climates with "developed" societies the principal mode of transmission of the disease is through sexual contact. In addition infants may be infected prior to birth, a form of the disease called prenatal or congenital syphilis. Although the term "congenital" is inaccurate, it is so widely accepted that it is used here interchangeably with "prenatal" as signifying syphilis acquired in utero or at birth.

The tropical diseases, yaws and pinta, and the condition known as endemic syphilis (sometimes given such local names as bejel in the Middle East and njovera or dichuchwa in parts of Africa) are closely related and probably represent clinical variants of syphilis. The variations probably result from environmental factors of climate and culture and, possibly also, genetic differences in parasite or host, or both. In these conditions, seen mostly in children, spread takes place through nonsexual direct bodily contact.

In the United States, the present reported incidence of syphilis exceeds 20,000 new infectious cases per year. The estimated actual incidence is 60,000. The occurrence of the disease, which had declined sharply following the introduction of penicillin from over 100,000 reported infectious cases in 1947 to a low of 6,250 in 1957, has thus shown a marked increase. Prenatal (congenital) syphilis, reported among infants under a year of age, has doubled in incidence during the past decade. Since the disease is both preventable and effectively treatable, the public health significance is apparent.

ETIOLOGY. Syphilis is caused by an anaerobic spirochetal organism, *Treponema pallidum*. The organism varies from 4 to 10 μ in length and usually consists of from 6 to 14 coils. The causative treponemes of yaws and pinta, although given different species names (*T. pertenue* and *T. carateum*), are morphologically and otherwise indistinguishable from

T. pallidum. Identification of the living organism is accomplished by dark-field microscopy of a preparation of the serous discharge from gently abraded lesions. A scraping of the moist umbilical cord of an infected infant provides a suitable preparation for finding the spirochetes. The presence of the organism in tissue is demonstrated by Levaditi (silver) stains. *T. pallidum* is destroyed by temperatures over 40° C and does not multiply at temperatures below 30° C. The organism cannot survive even for a few minutes without moisture; it is this characteristic, plus the anaerobic requirement, which makes transmission by fomites nearly impossible.

TRANSMISSION OF PRENATAL SYPHILIS. As already noted, syphilis is usually transmitted venereally. Since infection results in a bacteremia, the disease may also be transmitted via the bloodstream across the placenta from mother to fetus. Ample evidence strongly suggests that this event does not result in infection during the first half of pregnancy. From the fifth lunar month until termination of pregnancy, a mother may transmit the disease to her infant during periods of spirochetemia. Should the mother remain untreated she may continue to infect successive infants over a number of years and thus have two, three, or more infected babies. During early months of illness in the untreated mother the probability is about 95 percent that the infant will acquire the disease in utero. With the passage of years the probability diminishes. How many years a mother may remain infectious from the original illness cannot be stated with certainty because superinfection cannot be excluded in those instances when pregnancies separated by 20 years have produced syphilitic infants. Third-generation syphilis, which has undoubtedly occurred, must be subject to the same reservation. The phenomenon of diminution of severity of infection in succeeding pregnancies, Kassowitz's law, probably illustrates decreasing infective doses. The most severely infected fetus becomes a macerated stillborn with disseminated tissue damage; the least affected will be asymptomatic at birth; in between is the symptomatic syphilitic infant who has an increased chance of being born prematurely.

INFECTIOUSNESS OF THE ACUTE FORM. Any moist lesions on the maternal skin or mucous membrane may be infectious upon intimate contact, so that the birth process itself may be a time of acquisition of disease. Similarly, moist lesions, including nasal secretions, of an infected infant are infectious, but the contact must be rather intimate. Thus while care in handling infants with open lesions is needed, there is no airborne spread. The only caution required is for those whose hands might ordinarily touch the moist lesions or secretions to be alert either to avoid contact with open lesions or to wear protective gloves. Twenty-four hours after appropriate therapy with penicillin, patients are noninfectious.

PATHOGENESIS AND NATURAL COURSE. Syphilis in the early stages is a relapsing, intermittently infectious process. In the acquired form, there may be a primary, or chancre, stage with a lesion at the point of entry and in regional lymph nodes. This phase, often omitted even in older individuals, does not occur in the prenatal variety.

The early disease, characterized by intermittent hematogenous dissemination, causes symmetric and pervasive involvement of body tissues. As time goes on, the chronic lesions develop in localized foci in almost any tissue. Late lesions tend to be asymmetric, to involve marked tissue reaction, and to be noninfectious. Pathologic studies illustrate this distinction, showing primarily round cell infiltration and subacute inflammation in early disease and, in the late form, a granulomatous process with marked tissue necrosis and scarring.

The general types of pathology described may occur in any organ and tissue, making possible an extraordinarily large number of clinical variants. The disease occurring in infancy and early childhood has several pathologic features distinguishing it from disease acquired in later life. A severely affected fetus shows some unique features, including interstitial fibrosis of the liver, spleen, and sometimes other organs and a "pneumonia alba" consisting of increased connective tissue infiltrating the lung. Another difference is the rarity of cardiovascular involvement in the childhood disease contrasted with an incidence of 15 percent, most commonly aortitis, in adults. This difference, apparently attributable to developmental factors, seems to hold in children for both the congenital disease and that acquired prior to puberty.

Another major difference is the occurrence of the stigmas of congenital syphilis. These lesions are the result of precisely timed damage to developing tissue during the early phase of the disease with manifestations becoming visible only later in life. They are of three kinds: scarring of tissue affected early, such as the lips and nose; destructive lesions to tissues such as teeth which do not erupt until late childhood; and finally, tissue alteration leading to "allergic" type lesions such as interstitial keratitis. These stigmas, while characteristic of congenital syphilis, are in fact nonspecific and can be imitated, though rarely, by other disease processes.

The natural course of untreated syphilitic illness in the adult is well described in a very careful epidemiologic study carried out in Oslo over an extended period of time. Approximately 50 percent of patients, one-half of whom are seropositive, have no long-term ill effects. Roughly another quarter of the patients have late "benign" manifestations, such as gummas or liver involvement. The final 25 percent have one of the more severe late forms, cardiovascular syphilis or neurosyphilis. Most, but not all, of the late forms are seropositive.

No comparable data are available for childhood syphilis; moreover, many severely infected infants succumb or are stillborn, making the comparison more difficult. However, if one removes the cardiovascular complications and makes allowance for the early mortality in the infantile group, clinical experience suggests that the course of untreated syphilis in children is similar to that acquired in adults.

IMMUNOLOGY AND SERODIAGNOSIS. The antibody response to syphilitic infection has been widely studied but remains imperfectly understood. The infection confers good immunity against symptomatic reinfection if the original process is not treated during the first few years. During the early years of the disease while humoral antibody titers are high, living organisms persist and may be recovered. Even many years later organisms may be recovered, although the tissues appear altered in such a way that a new infection may not be acquired. Following adequate treatment early in the disease, reinfection occurs readily, the clinical course duplicating the original infection.

There are both nonspecific antibodies (reagin) and specific antibodies (treponema immobilizing) which appear in response to syphilitic infection. Both appear in the adult as IgM and IgG in size. The IgG may be transmitted by mother to fetus across the placenta, so that maternal antibody (reagin and specific) may appear in both the infected and noninfected newborn. The neonate is relatively incapable of manufacturing IgG, but he may make his own IgM antibody. Recently, Alford and co-workers demonstrated the presence of an IgM-fluorescent treponemal antibody in the serum of newborn infants. This test permits a specific serologic laboratory diagnosis to be made during the first days of life.

The nonspecific antibody is also found in response to other diseases, which may be divided into three categories useful in differential diagnosis. First, in other treponemal diseases, such as yaws and pinta, the titers are similar to those in syphilis, and indeed the significance is probably identical; for these conditions, the specific antibody response is also similar if not identical. Second, certain chronic diseases, especially leprosy, result in reagin production in moderately high titer; this point must be remembered in those areas where leprosy is prevalent. Finally, a large variety of infections and connective tissue diseases may produce a low titer of reagin, the "biologic false-positive." Those of special importance to the pediatrician are infectious mononucleosis, vaccinia, chickenpox, and lupus erythematosus. A number of mild viral infections may also result in an increased titer of reagin. For acute infections the phenomenon is transitory, and in all of these instances the titers are low and seldom exceed a dilution of 1:16.

Despite these limitations, reagin tests (serologic tests for syphilis or STS) remain a useful and valuable tool in the diagnosis of syphilis because of speed and ease of determination. The VDRL (Venereal Disease Research Laboratories) test and some of its modifications providing rapid usage give a high degree of sensitivity. The specificity requires interpretation by the clinician, occasionally reinforced by confirmatory use of the more cumbersome and expensive specific tests such as the treponema immobilization test (TPI). Thus far none of the specific tests has been adapted to a sensitive form that is at once technically rapid, reliable, and inexpensive, although because of its specificity the TPI has great value in resolving diagnostic problems.

The STS's commonly performed fall into two technical categories; those typified by the Wassermann and Kolmer, which use the technique of complement fixation; and those typified by the Kahn, Eagle, Mazzini, and VDRL, which measure flocculation. The flocculation technique is simpler and faster, hence more widely used for sera. Quantitative titration of these antibodies is possible and very useful both for diagnostic differentiation and for following patients, since in early disease the antibody disappears over a period of a few months following therapy. Measurement of antibody in cerebrospinal fluid requires a complement-fixation method.

When a flocculation test is performed on any serum which may have a high titer, it is important to run a high dilution specimen as well as the standard dilution during the initial screening process. Occasionally a high level of antibody may inhibit flocculation in the standard dilution and be interpreted as a negative test, the prozone phenomenon; this phenomenon is encountered commonly during early syphilis in infants.

The antibody transferred from mother to fetus transplacentally (7S) will produce a positive STS in the infant. The titer may be equal to but not higher than the mother's. The TPI antibody behaves similarly. Both disappear from the infant following a logarithmic curve, being unmeasurable in most infants at 8 weeks and in all at 12 weeks of age. Most infected infants have very little of their own (19S) antibody at birth (about one-third are seronegative, having neither passive nor active antibody), but invariably some is produced by 8 weeks of age. The two titer curves, one falling and one rising, merge to produce a single resultant with a variety of possible configurations. Using standard serologic procedures, interpretation of diagnostic significance may in some instances be made only after 8 or 12 weeks of age, though usually an earlier decision may be reached even without supporting clinical data. If adequate treatment is given early in the disease, the STS titer begins to fall within 4 weeks. From the foregoing facts the difficulties may be appreciated in interpreting, for clinical purposes, serologic data on an asymptomatic seropositive infant who has received penicillin.

CLINICAL FEATURES IN EARLY CONGENITAL (PRENATAL) SYPHILIS. As already indicated, the most severely infected infants are stillborn. Most liveborn syphilic infants have no visible lesions at birth. When lesions are present, they are most commonly on the skin and in the bones. In the first week of life, syphilis may produce a bullous lesion of the skin on the palms and soles. This almost pathognomonic lesion, though quite uncommon, has importance because no other syphilitic skin lesion at any age forms bullae or vesicles. The more usual pattern of skin involvement is a diffuse, symmetric, copper-colored, maculopapular rash most intense on face, palms, and soles. It is an infiltrative type of lesion which when gently scraped with a scalpel will yield serum teeming with treponemes. If left untreated, about 90 percent of syphilitic infants will eventually have some kind of skin lesion. Many varieties of papular skin rashes may occur and recur over the next months with a high predilection for mucocutaneous sites, oral and anal. Perioral lesions may result in scarring with fissures which persist. The recurrences become progressively less symmetric with time. The perianal condylomatous lesions (condyloma lata) so commonly seen in adults are also seen in infancy (Fig. 4).

A rather characteristic mucous membrane lesion of infants having no counterpart in the adult is the "snuffles," a rhinitis producing a serous discharge which frequently becomes secondarily infected. The lesion may extend to the nasal cartilage and cause sufficient damage to result in saddle nose deformity.

The disease produces widespread lesions in the skeleton, resulting in quite characteristic x-ray pictures revealing osteochondritis at metaphyseal plates, a generalized symmetric periosteal elevation, and symmetrically occurring osteomyelitic lesions (Fig. 5). The humeri are the most commonly involved bones, with the tibiae next. Indeed if other bones are involved, these two are almost sure to be also. Wimberger described a bilateral motheaten appearance of the medial aspects of the proximal tibiae that is highly characteristic of congenital syphilis. Over 90 percent of infants with manifest congenital syphilis show skeletal lesions similar to those just described. They have their onset typically between 1 and 3 months of age, and the process is usually self-limited, with healing occurring spontaneously over the next few months; the rate of healing is not noticeably affected by treatment. X-ray findings usually disappear by 5 months of age. Only rarely will these skeletal lesions remain active and cause permanent damage.

The bone lesions are often asymptomatic. Occasionally, perhaps because of secondary trauma, there

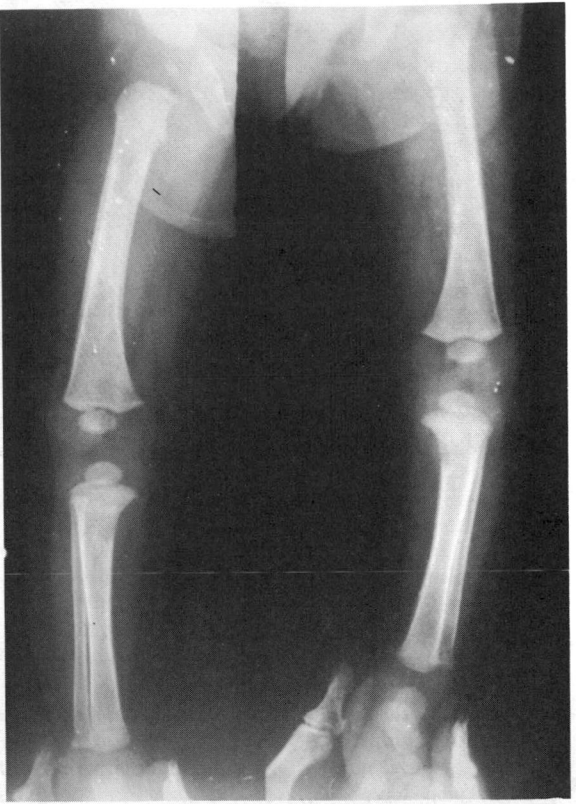

Fig. 5. Radiogram at 2 months of age showing periosteal elevation and bilateral tibial osteomyelitis.

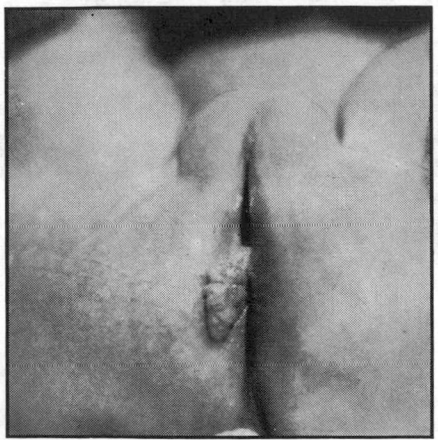

Fig. 4. Syphilitic condyloma in an infant of 9 months.

is pain, often manifested by a pseudoparalysis which may be unilateral, involving either an arm or a leg, as first described by Parrot. Later in infancy there may be recurring isolated bone lesions; dactylitis, frequently asymmetric, is a typical example.

Jaundice as a manifestation of syphilitic hepatitis sometimes appears early in congenital syphilis. This lesion does clear faster and more surely with treatment. Other viscera are involved less commonly. Splenomegaly and generalized lymphadenopathy are frequent manifestations of the early systemic illness. The epitrochlear nodes commonly enlarge as a part of this phenomenon. Palpation of these nodes therefore provides or heightens clinical suspicion of syphilis; this sign remains useful throughout early childhood.

Invasion of the central nervous system is common during early congenital syphilis, although it is usually asymptomatic. Examination of the cerebrospinal fluid will frequently reveal pleocytosis and an elevated protein content. This early invasion may be regarded as a part of the early disease, for which no additional treatment is needed. All patients treated for syphilis should have a spinal fluid examination 6 months to 2 years later, at which time any abnormality traceable to syphilis provides indication for retreatment.

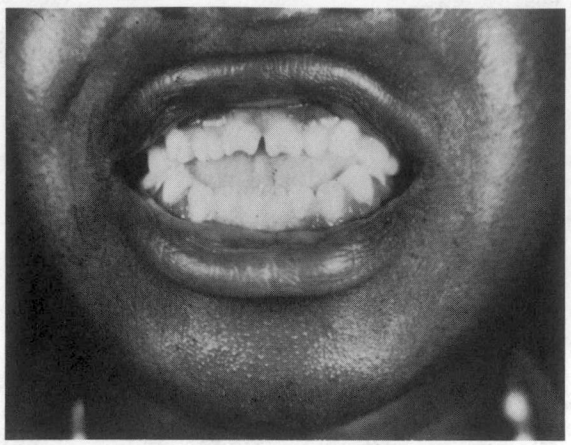 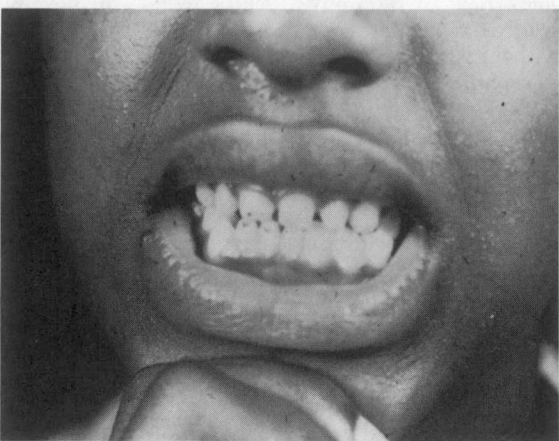

Fig. 6. Two common clinical variations of Hutchinson's teeth.

The serologic titer in all forms of congenital syphilis is high during the first 2 years and is reversible by treatment.

CLINICAL FEATURES IN LATE CONGENITAL SYPHILIS. The diagnosis of late congenital syphilis may be suspected from the stigmas, from the presence of continued active disease, or from a persistently positive STS in an asymptomatic child.

As already pointed out, the stigmas represent the end stage of an early lesion. The most common and most typical of the stigmas are Hutchinson's teeth. The lesion, the first of Hutchinson's triad, refers to the upper central incisors of the second dentition. Deciduous teeth often normally exhibit the characteristics caused by syphilis in the permanent teeth. Hutchinson's teeth are screwdriver- or peg-shaped and sometimes notched (Fig. 6). Frequently teeth other than the central incisors are also peg-shaped. Molars may have extra cusps which are poorly formed and crumble under normal use. All syphilitic teeth demonstrate deficient enamel and decay more readily than normal. The Hutchinson incisor is visible by x-ray in its preeruptive site from about one year of age. The scars of perioral lesions give rise to the fissuring called rhagades, another inactive end result of an early lesion (Fig. 7).

Examples of late congenital syphilis representing an active tissue response to earlier "sensitization" are interstitial keratitis, eighth nerve deafness, and Clutton's joints. The first two of these form the remaining members of Hutchinson's triad. However, since deafness is quite rare, the original triad itself is rare; Clutton's joints are a more common manifestation.

Interstitial keratitis has its onset between 3 and 20 years of age, most commonly between 6 and 14. It is an intense inflammatory vascular infiltration of the cornea accompanied by an iritis, which may be followed by a dense cicatricial scar producing blindness (Fig. 8). Although usually bilateral, it may

come in one eye before the other, and one side may be much more seriously affected. The lesion is not related to any other syphilitic activity; it is not prevented by treatment given after the first year of disease; it is not benefited by specific antiluetic therapy; patients may even be seronegative. The condition is a potential, and at one time was a common, cause

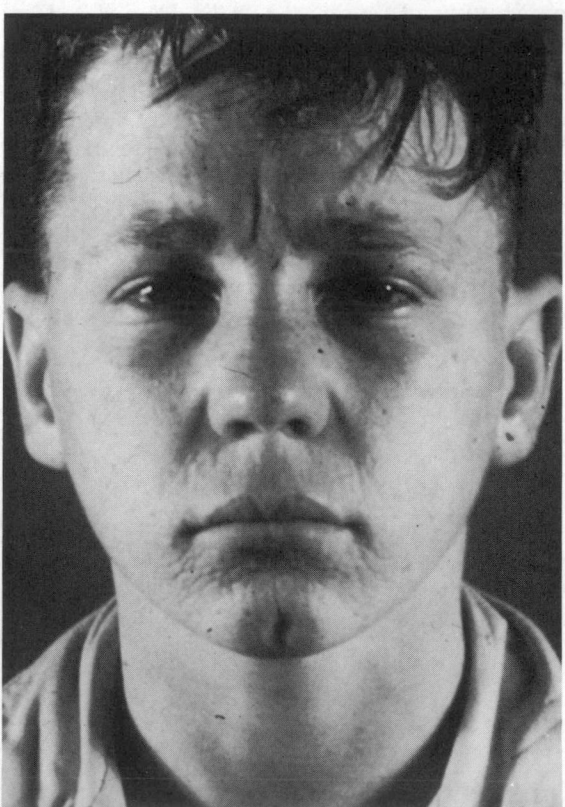

Fig. 7. Syphilitic facies showing rhagades.

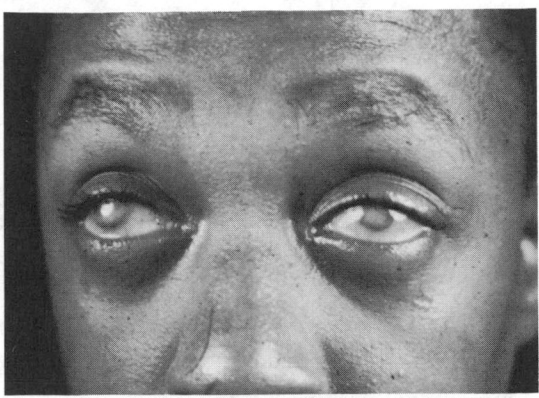

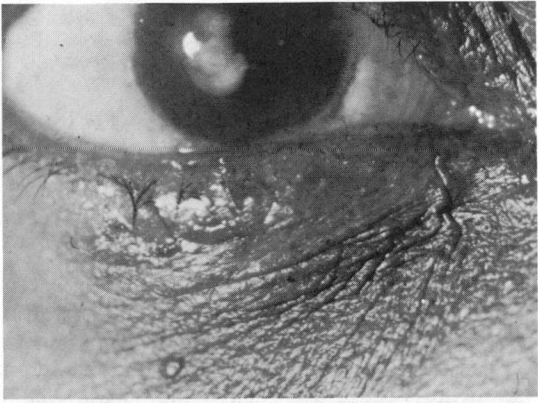

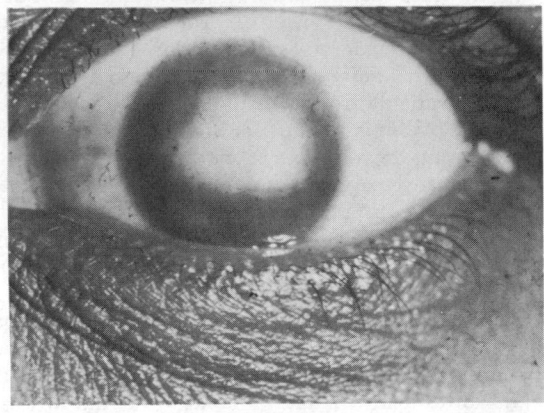

Fig. 8. Stages of interstitial keratitis. *Top.* Acute inflammation. *Center.* Early scarring. *Bottom.* Late cicatricial scar causing blindness.

of blindness. Early stages are characterized by marked photophobia, lacrimation, and a hazy appearance of the cornea. Later, as the acute inflammation subsides, scarring occurs.

Clutton's joints are symmetric synovial effusions, usually of the knees, sometimes painless but more often warm and painful. The process tends to be self-limited and benign. This manifestation, too, is unrelated to active syphilis and unresponsive to specific therapy.

Among active forms of late disease are gummas and osteitis, which are among the late "benign" syphilitic lesions. The palate and nasal septum are predilectional sites for destructive gummas, with saddle nose and perforated palatal deformities possible end results. Persistent periostitis gives rise to thickened clavicles and to a usually asymmetric "saber shin."

A more important form of active late syphilis is that involving the CNS, the most common type being meningovascular. Paresis, a more potentially dangerous form of CNS syphilis, occurs in juveniles and may be detected in a preparetic state by examination of the CSF. The examination shows complement-fixing antibody, pleocytosis, and elevation of protein concentration. If untreated, parenchymal involvement may be severe and eventually irreversible. Juvenile tabes rarely occurs.

Any form of late congenital syphilis may have become spontaneously seronegative by the time the disease is recognized. Paradoxically some patients become serofast, signifying an indefinitely high serologic titer unresponsive to treatment, even though therapy is otherwise successful. Paresis and active gummas are almost always found in seropositive patients with late congenital syphilis.

SYPHILIS ACQUIRED IN CHILDHOOD. The disease may be and has been acquired by sexual contact at any age after birth. The clinical and pathologic characteristics in children with acquired syphilis are similar to those of the disease in adults, except that children acquiring syphilis do not develop late cardiovascular lesions. Early skin lesions frequently take a serpiginous form, especially on darkly pigmented skin. Late skin lesions are often corymbiferous in distribution. Epitrochlear adenopathy is again a common clinical feature. When the disease is acquired after the early months of life, the stigmata, including interstitial keratitis, do not appear in later life.

TREATMENT. Syphilitic infection is exceptionally responsive to penicillin therapy. Thus far no naturally occurring resistant organisms have been described. Either a low continuous blood level or a high intermittent blood level for 7 to 10 days almost uniformly removes *T. pallidum* from the body.

The fetus may be successfully treated in utero via medication given to the mother. Here a high blood level in the mother is necessary to assure adequate transplacental levels in the fetus.

The neonate is successfully treated by a dose of 50,000 to 100,000 units of penicillin G per kilogram of weight. Either intermittent divided doses of aqueous penicillin or a single repository dose is satisfactory.

A troublesome pediatric problem is the proper management of a seropositive, asymptomatic newborn. Ideally one should not treat the baby until sufficient follow-up time has permitted distinction between passive transfer of antibody and manufacture of antibody. In practice, fear that follow-up will be unsuccessful, or an extremely precarious medical situation as in the small premature, has led to treatment by presumptive diagnosis. The use of penicillin treatment for a nonsyphilitic infection has sometimes made it necessary to assume that syphilis was also present without adequate proof. The important principle in any of these situations is to ensure adequacy of dosage and later follow-up.

Infants usually demonstrate a Herxheimer reaction which takes the form of a short, sharp febrile spike about 6 to 8 hours after the first dose of penicillin. This event is without danger and may even be helpful as a diagnostic aid when one decides to treat presumptively, since its occurrence indicates syphilitic infection.

For treatment given during the first few months of life, complete success is the rule. There is no lasting damage, nor are there sequelae of neurosyphilis and interstitial keratitis. The serologic titer as customarily measured gradually falls to zero. When treatment is delayed beyond a year or two, the stigmata, including interstitial keratitis, may occur. Late symptomatic neurosyphilis will not occur if treatment and retreatment are continued until the CSF is free of cells and the protein concentration falls to normal prior to the onset of symptoms. The clearing of the CSF of cells should occur within 3 months of treatment; failure constitutes indication for retreatment.

The treatment of late congenital syphilis should be undertaken if no prior treatment has been given or if evidence of activity is present. Herxheimer reactions occur about 25 percent of the time in active disease, and again are not deleterious. Previous comments about the use of spinal fluid cell counts as a measure of activity also apply here; neurosyphilis has not been observed subsequently in patients whose CSF was negative 5 years after therapy.

The allergic or hypersensitive manifestations of late congenital syphilis respond better to nonspecific therapy. In particular, interstitial keratitis is very responsive to topical corticosteroids instilled in the eye 4 to 6 times a day until symptoms disappear. The results are quite dramatic, and scarring with blindness appears to be preventable by this means. Clutton's joints are symptomatically relieved by systemic steroids, and eighth nerve deafness has been reported to have also benefited this way.

Serologic titer is not affected by treatment of late congenital syphilis but follows a natural course toward either seronegative or serofastness.

Although heavy metals traditionally, and antibiotics other than penicillin more recently, have known antisyphilitic properties, they are all so inferior to penicillin that their usage cannot be recommended.

REFERENCES

Alford, C. A., Jr., Polt, S. S., Cassady, G. E., Straumfjord, J. V., and Remington, J. S. ᵧM-Fluorescent treponemal antibody in the diagnosis of congenital syphilis. New Eng. J. Med., 280:1086, 1969.

Davis, B. D., Moore, D. H., Kabat, E. A., and Harris, A. Electrophoretic, ultracentrifugal, and immunochemical studies on Wassermann antibody. J. Immunol., 50:1, 1945.

Nelson, R. A., Jr., and Mayer, M. M. Immobilization of *Treponema pallidum* in vitro by antibody produced in syphilitic infection. J. Exp. Med., 89:369, 1949.

Rein, G. R., and Reyn, A. Serology of treponematoses. Bull. W.H.O., 14:193, 1956.

Stokes, J. H., Beerman, H., and Ingraham, N. R., Jr. Modern Clinical Syphilology, 3rd ed. Philadelphia, W. B. Saunders Co., 1944.

Syphilis and other venereal diseases. Med. Clin. N. Amer., 48:573-747, 1964.

Thomas, E. W. Syphilis: Its Course and Management. New York, The Macmillan Co., 1949.

14.19
TETANUS
(LOCKJAW)

EDWARD L. PRATT

Tetanus is an acute infection caused by *Clostridium tetani*, the tetanus bacillus, which was discovered by Nicolaier in 1884. The disease is characterized by stiffness of the skeletal muscles of any part of the body—particularly the muscles of the jaw—by tonic spasms and by convulsions. The symptoms are due to a powerful exotoxin which affects the neuromuscular end-plates and the motor nuclei of the central nervous system. Infection is acquired almost invariably from contamination of a wound.

ETIOLOGY. The tetanus bacillus is an anaerobic, sporebearing organism. It is widely distributed in the soil in many parts of the world. The bacillus is normally present in the intestines of horses, cattle, and other herbivora, and is found at times in man. From 2 to 30 percent of normal adults harbor this organism, the highest proportion being found in agricultural communities. The bacillus produces two soluble toxins, tetanolysin and tetanospasmin, the former an unstable hemolytic substance which apparently plays little part in the pathology of the disease. Tetanospasmin, the substance usually meant when tetanus toxin is spoken of, produces the convulsions and the stiffness of muscles. It has a peculiar affinity for nervous tissue. Unlike many other toxins it does not produce reddening of the skin. A number of subgroups of the bacilli have been identified, but the toxins they produce are identical.

IMMUNITY. All ages are susceptible to tetanus, presumably equally so. Protection is afforded only by active or passive immunization. Although some immunity appears to be conferred by an attack, this is very transient. Instances of relapse and second attacks, though rare, have been reported.

INCIDENCE. The incidence of tetanus reflects the geographic distribution of the organisms, the standards of cleanliness, and awareness of the risk from contaminated wounds. Although tetanus of the newborn has been practically eliminated from cities in this country, it is still common elsewhere due to the practice of applying animal excreta to the umbilical stump for hemostasis. The increasing use of prophylaxis in connection with wounds of all kinds and, in recent years, widespread use of active immunization have greatly reduced the incidence in children. Legislation restricting the sale of fireworks has eliminated that menace in many states. In many large pediatric hospitals scarcely one case a year is now seen.

PATHOGENESIS. Tetanus may occur when no portal of entry can be found; this was the case in 29 percent of a group of cases treated at the Children's Hospital in Boston. A wound which is apparently of little consequence often serves as a portal. The injuries most likely to lead to tetanus are puncture wounds, which provide ideal anaerobic conditions, and burns and crushing wounds which involve necrosis of tissue and which become contaminated with dirt. Blank cartridge wounds have been a common cause, the wadding carrying the organism. A considerable number of cases have been caused by infected vaccines, sera, or catgut. It is a mistake to suppose that tetanus bacilli are confined to the soil; the spores are readily spread by birds or insects. We know of an instance in which a splinter in the nose, acquired in the top of a tree, led to tetanus. It has followed the stings of bees and wasps.

The bacilli themselves are confined to the primary wound, where they proliferate and produce toxin. The manner in which the toxin is distributed through the body is still subject to some dispute. According to Abel and his collaborators, some of it diffuses from the nidus in the wound to the surrounding muscles, but the greater part is taken up in the circulation and is thus distributed to the tissues. Other investigators believe that tetanus toxin travels along axis cylinders to reach the spinal cord and medulla. Action of toxin at the myoneural junctions is responsible for the stiffness of muscles which forms a conspicuous feature of the symptomatology; the toxin's action in the central nervous system lowers the threshold of reflexes in which the lower motor neurons are involved and induces the susceptibility to reflex spasms and convulsions. Toxin combines firmly with nerve tissue and, when symptoms have once set in, it cannot be readily detached by antitoxin, however administered. On the other hand, toxin free in the circulating blood can be neutralized by antitoxin. If the patient survives, eventual recovery is complete.

Two clinical forms of tetanus are seen—generalized tetanus and local tetanus—the former representing the result of widespread distribution of toxin, and the latter caused by local distribution of toxin in the vicinity of the portal of entry. The two forms may be combined. In children local tetanus is distinctly rare, although the stiffness may make its first appearance in a single group of muscles, such as those of the jaw, the muscles of deglutition, or those in other parts of the body.

PATHOLOGY. There are no characteristic morphologic changes produced by tetanus. In some fatal cases cerebral edema has been found, and there may be various lesions secondary to the violent spasms, such as hemorrhage in muscles or even rupture of skeletal muscles, and compression fractures of vertebral bodies.

SYMPTOMS. These usually begin between the fifth and twelfth day after infection, although the incubation period may be considerably longer than this or, in the most serious cases, as short as a day or two. The local wound shows nothing peculiar, and the symptoms are essentially the same no matter where the wound is located. The onset is generally insidious, with gradually increasing stiffness of muscles, particularly those of the neck and jaw. Within 24 hours the disease is generally fully developed; the stiffness of the jaw and neck is then very marked, swallowing may be difficult, and other parts of the body musculature become involved. The spasms of tetanus are quite charactersitic. Cutaneous, auditory, or visual stimulation and attempts at voluntary motion initiate paroxysmal contractions of the muscles of the body as a whole which lasts for 5 or 10 seconds. During the spasm the body becomes as rigid as a board; the head is retracted, the back arched in opisthotonos, the legs and feet extended, the arms outstretched with fists clenched and thumbs adducted. The jaws are immobile, and the face assumes a peculiar, fixed expression known as the *risus sardonicus*. The eyebrows are raised, the palpebral fissures narrowed, the angles of the mouth drawn downward and outward, and the upper lip pressed firmly against the teeth. Consciousness is not lost; often the patient is very apprehensive.

At first these spasms are infrequent; there is complete relaxation between them, and they occasion little discomfort. As the disease progresses they become more numerous and prolonged, and may be painful; often they are initiated by the slightest stimulus. Relaxation between the seizures is then only partial, a considerable degree of rigidity persisting. The paroxysms may affect the respiratory muscles or those of the larynx with fatal results. The posture often gives little idea of the intensity of the contractions, for opposing muscle groups are equally involved. Partial or complete relaxation occurs during sleep or with anesthesia, and sedatives may afford some relief. Spasm of the sphincters with retention of urine is common. Sweating is sometimes very marked; fever is moderate or absent. The blood count and spinal fluid show no constant changes.

A number of our cases have not conformed to the typical picture just described. Trismus, although usually present sooner or later, was the first symptom in only 6 out of 22 cases. In others the symptoms were first noted in the neck, the back, the extremities, or the abdominal muscles. In some cases pain was severe from the outset; in others the only complaint was stiffness. The location of these initial symptoms bore no relation to that of the injury. In five instances the onset was with general convulsions.

The duration of tetanus in fatal cases is seldom more than 3 or 4 days; it may be less than 24 hours; on the other hand we have known a patient to die in convulsions as late as the twelfth day, at a time when recovery seemed well under way. Death usually results from respiratory failure, the temperature sometimes showing an abrupt terminal rise. Patients who recover seldom have much fever; after several days the paroxysms gradually decrease in frequency and the muscular rigidity diminishes, although several weeks may elapse before they disappear entirely. Trismus is often the last symptom to disappear.

DIAGNOSIS. There are few diseases with which tetanus is apt to be confused. The history of a wound, the onset with trismus, the facial expression, and the spasm accentuated by external stimuli are quite characteristic. In the neonatal period intracranial injuries or development defects of the brain may produce comparable symptoms, but after the first few weeks of life it is most unusual for convulsions to be excited by external stimuli, save in tetanus. Strychnine poisoning may simulate tetanus; trismus, however, is rare and persistent rigidity between paroxysms is not present, although the contraction resulting from external stimulation may last many seconds. Meningitis may be difficult to rule out without lumbar puncture. We have seen cases of serum sickness accompanied by arthralgia of the temporomandibular joint, in which for a while tetanus was suspected. The differentiation from rabies is discussed with that condition.

Apical abscesses of the molar teeth and peritonsillar or retropharyngeal abscesses may lead to trismus, but the generalized increase in muscle tone and risus sardonicus are not present. Ingestion of tranquilizers and antiemetics, particularly the phenothiazine derivatives, may lead to muscle spasms that are easily confused with tetanus. The history of availability or ingestion of such medicines, plus the lack of more or less symmetric increase in muscle tone and presence of a positive urine test for such drugs, should clarify the diagnosis.

Local tetanus should be thought of when stiffness of muscles and irritability to local mechanical stimuli develop in the neighborhood of a wound, particularly a compound fracture which has been put up in traction-suspension. Immobilization favors the development of local tetanus by slowing the lymph flow, and infected bone may harbor tetanus bacilli for a long time, permitting toxin to be formed many weeks after the original prophylactic injection of antitoxin.

PROPHYLAXIS. The ideal agent for *passive immunization* for children with "tetanus-prone" injuries who have not been actively immunized and have not had a tetanus booster within the past 10 years, or in whom the status of immunity against tetanus is unknown, is 250 units of human tetanus-immune globulin intramuscularly. Tetanus antitoxin from human serum eliminates the danger of foreign-serum reactions, provides protective levels of circulating antibodies for 3 or 4 weeks, and interferes less than antitoxin from animal serum with the immune response to fluid tetanus *toxoid*. In highly contaminated wounds with extensive tissue necrosis, twice the dose of human serum tetanus antitoxin should be given. If tetanus antitoxin from human serum cannot be obtained, the subcutaneous or intramuscular injection of 5,000 American units of antitoxin prepared in horses (or cows) may be given after all precautions, including scratch, intradermal, and ophthalmic tests for serum hypersensitivity, have been carried out. Every child given passive immunization should be started upon and followed through a complete course of basic active immunization against tetanus so that passive immunization becomes truly a once-in-a-lifetime procedure. An initial dose of fluid tetanus *toxoid* should be given at another site in another syringe at the same time the antitoxin is given.

Active immunization against tetanus is one of the most highly successful immunization procedures available. Every infant should receive three injections of DPT (combined tetanus toxoid, diphtheria toxoid, and pertussis vaccine), 0.5 ml each, at intervals of 4 to 6 weeks or more, starting at 2 to 4 months of age, followed by a booster at 15 to 18 months, and another booster at around 3 years of age (Ch. 32). From age 6 years on, boosters of tetanus-diphtheria toxoid, "adult type," should be given every 4 to 5 years throughout life.

All physicians should attempt to detect nonimmunized children and adults and urge active immunization plus a regular schedule of boosters. Ideal opportunities for doing this occur when patients appear for any injury, for checkups, requesting immunizations for travel, etc. Patients should have records of the status of their immunizations so confusion will not exist.

Recall injections even 15 years after a basic course of immunization or 15 years after the last booster will restore immunity to tetanus. Thus, for such individuals, a booster of fluid toxoid at the time of a mild or moderate tetanus-prone injury will be protective. Severe injuries, those heavily contaminated, or with large necrotic areas, or accompanied by extensive blood loss, may require both a booster of toxoid and 250 units of tetanus antitoxin from human serum in a different site from a different syringe, even though the patient was previously actively immunized.

TREATMENT. The management of tetanus should be governed by three basic considerations: (1) the prevention of additional toxin reaching the central nervous system; (2) control of life-endangering spasms while oxygenation and hydration are maintained; and (3) elimination of therapeutic risks. The expected worth of any measure must be balanced against any disturbance it may cause the patient.

Tetanus antitoxin in sufficient quantity will prevent toxin as yet unbound from reaching the central nervous system. The proof of this statement has been irrefutably demonstrated by the thousands of patients with contaminated wounds protected from tetanus by adequate passive immunization. The dose of antitoxin should be gauged by the severity of the disease and not by the size of the patient. Human antitoxin, if available, in doses of 3,000 to 6,000 units, always intramuscularly, is adequate according to the information available to date. If equine or bovine antitoxin must be used, clinical and immunologic data indicate that 20,000 to 60,000 American units are sufficient in clinical tetanus. Highly purified antitoxin and all precautions against sensitivity and thermal reactions should be employed. In mild cases the intramuscular route, being the safest, is preferred. In severe cases one third may be given intravenously and the rest intramuscularly. Intrathecal antitoxin can produce severe and at times fatal reactions, and the evidence that this route is more effective than the others has not been clearly demonstrated in patients.

It is essential that injuries receive proper surgical care, but mutilating operations undertaken merely because the lesion may be the site of elaboration of toxin are not indicated. Penicillin and other antibiotics used in the control of ordinary wound infection will not neutralize tetanus toxin.

The ideal agent for control of spasms without depression of vital functions or other toxic effects has not yet been discovered. In mild and moderately severe cases sedation with paraldehyde or secobarbital sodium may be satisfactory. In more severe cases meprobamate, in a dosage of 80 to 100 mg intramuscularly every 3 to 4 hours for neonates (up to 300 mg per dose for children), may be tried and, if necessary, supplemented by chlorpromazine, 0.5 mg per kilogram of body weight. Sedation, particularly the use of muscle relaxants (phenoxypropanediol, mephenesin, or methocarbamol), should be a joint, collaborative effort with a skilled anesthesiologist whenever possible. In severe cases, effective anticonvulsant sedation can be maintained only by continuous intravenous administration of 0.4 percent solution of pentobarbital (4 g of the powdered barbiturate added to a liter of 5 percent glucose in water). The rate of flow must be constantly supervised and is adjusted to maintain the patient at the level where he has no spasms when left undisturbed, and yet will respond with increased muscle tone if stimulated. Anesthesia should not be so light as to permit spasms to interfere with respirations nor so deep as to cause respiratory depression. A tracheotomy is essential. Theoretically curare and similar muscle relaxing agents should be ideal for controlling spasms, but their use in tetanus should be attempted only by skilled personnel and with the requisite equipment to combat respiratory depression or paralysis and to manage excessive secretions in the respiratory passages.

Isonipecaine (Demerol, meperidine) is the drug of choice for relief of pain.

Maintenance of oxygenation is of prime importance. One must prevent the accumulation of secre-tions in the pharynx and the tracheobronchial tree, control spasms of the pharynx and glottis or respiratory muscles, and avoid respiratory depression. Tracheostomy is the only adequate method of dealing with tracheobronchial obstruction and is essential for laryngeal or pharyngeal spasms. It should be performed early whenever indicated. In newborns, tracheostomies are unsatisfactory and dangerous. For these patients endotracheal tubes are preferred to tracheostomies to provide an adequate airway. A dependable apparatus for giving oxygen under controlled positive pressure should always be at the bedside. An efficient mechanical respirator should be available if possible.

Satisfactory hydration can be maintained by giving enough fluid intravenously to cover the expenditures from the lungs, skin, and kidneys. The concentration of glucose and of electrolytes in the hydrating fluid should be determined from estimates of requirements (Sec. 3.7). Small plastic tubes have lessened the irritation of tube feeding, but they should be used with special caution during the first week when severe spasms often follow any manipulation. Because of the risk of aspiration of food or gastric contents, resumption of oral feeding should not be hurried.

A darkened, noise-free environment, gentle skillful nursing, and clear accurate records of the amounts, frequency, and effects of the drugs administered are invaluable.

PROGNOSIS. Tetanus is relatively simple to prevent, but its treatment is still unsatisfactory. The overall mortality remains between 30 and 50 percent, in spite of all therapeutic measures. The most accurate indication of prognosis in an individual case may be judged by a composite of the following clinical features which, in order of their importance, are (1) the period of time from the onset of first symptoms recognized by the patient until generalized spasms occur; (2) the incubation period; (3) the severity of symptoms in the patient at the time of admission. When progression of symptoms has been longer than 60 hours and the incubation period over 8 to 10 days, appropriate management should lead to recovery. Most patients who survive 10 days of symptoms eventually recover completely. The disease leaves no sequelae.

Every patient with clinical tetanus should have, before discharge, films of the spine to detect crushing of the bodies of the thoracic or lumbar vertebrae, since these occur in a majority of the "severe" cases. Following recovery from clinical tetanus, the physician must accept the responsibility of seeing to it that the patient is actively immunized against tetanus, because tetanus is a nonimmunizing disease.

Instances have been reported of motor paralysis following antitoxin, given for either therapeutic or prophylactic purposes.

REFERENCES

American Academy of Pediatrics. Report of the Committee on the Control of Infectious Diseases, 15th ed. Evanston, Illinois, 1966.

Earle, A. M., and Mellon, W. L. Tetanus neonatorum: a report of thirty-two cases. Amer. J. Trop. Med. Hyg., 7:315, 1958.

Howard, F. H., and DeVere, W. Intramuscular meprobamate in the treatment of tetanus in infants and children. J. Pediat., 60:421, 1962.

Human antitoxin in prophylaxis and treatment of tetanus. Med. Lett. Drug Ther., 7:13, 1965.

Jenkins, M. T., and Luhn, N. R. Active management of tetanus, based on experiences of an anaesthesiology department. Anaesthesiology, 23:690, 1962.

Lafoere, F. M., Lowell, S. Y., and Bennett, J. V. Tetanus in the United States 1965-1966. New Eng. J. Med., 280:564, 1969.

Margileth, A. M., Shaul, J. F., and Love, J. The status of immunization in 1963. Med. Clin. N. Amer., 43:1393, 1963.

McComb, J. A. The prophylactic dose of homologous tetanus antitoxin. New Eng. J. Med., 270:175, 1964.

Peebles, J. C., et al. Tetanus. New Eng. J. Med., 280:575, 1969.

Pratt, E. L. Clinical tetanus; a study of 56 cases with special reference to methods of prevention and a plan for evaluating treatment. J.A.M.A., 129:1243, 1945.

Skudder, P. A., and McCarroll, J. R. Current status of tetanus control. Importance of human tetanus-immune globulin. J.A.M.A., 188:625, 1964.

14.20
TUBERCULOSIS

JOSÉ E. SIFONTES

Tuberculosis is a specific infection caused by the tubercle bacillus of Koch. It may involve almost any part of the body. The process may remain localized or become generalized; it may be either active or latent. According to some estimates, 50,000,000 of the world's population are afflicted, of whom 5,000,000 die annually. In the United States, about 50,000 new cases are discovered and about 9,000 die each year. About 35,000,000 persons in the United States are infected with the bacillus. The U.S. Public Health Service has estimated that at least three quarters of the new cases of tuberculosis in the future will come from persons who are infected at the present time.

Etiology

The tubercle bacillus belongs to the genus *Mycobacterium*. The mycobacteria constitute a genus of the family Mycobacteriaceae of the order Actinomycetales, usually spoken of as acid-fast bacilli because they do not stain readily and, once stained, resist decoloration by strong acids or by alcohol. The pathogenic mycobacteria include *Mycobacterium tuberculosis* var. *hominis*, *Mycobacterium bovis*, *Mycobacterium avium*, *Mycobacterium leprae* (Hansen's bacillus), *Mycobacterium paratuberculosis*, Johne's bacillus, *Mycobacterium ulcerans*, *Mycobacterium kansasii*, *Mycobacterium fortuitum*, Battey, and other unclassified species. All of these organisms produce lesions characterized by epithelioid cells and tubercles, but only the tubercle bacillus produces caseation necrosis.

THE BACILLUS. Tubercle bacilli usually occur in animal lesions as rod-shaped microorganisms; they vary in length from 1 to 4 μ and in diameter from 0.3 to 0.6 μ. They have no capsule and cannot be classified as gram-positive or gram-negative because of their peculiar staining characteristics. They grow best under aerobic conditions at pH 6 to 8, between 37° C and 41° C; they utilize carbon compounds for energy and ammonia or amino acids for nitrogen. Certain characteristics help to distinguish tubercle bacilli from other mycobacteria; these include virulence for guinea pigs, production of niacin, formation of serpentine cords, positive neutral red test, slow growth in the usual media (4 to 8 weeks), and failure to grow at 26° C. Most strains are susceptible to isoniazid, para-amino-salicylic acid (PAS), and streptomycin. In general, tubercle bacilli possess unusual resistance to antiseptics and toxic agents and can survive for long periods of time in the dried state in sputa and excreta. Disinfection of such material is accomplished by exposure to 5 percent phenol or 2 percent cresol for 12 hours, sunlight or ultraviolet rays, or a temperature of 60° C for 20 minutes.

The human and bovine types of tubercle bacilli are the principal agents of tuberculosis in man, bovine infection being now almost unknown in the United States. Human and bovine bacilli have a similar degree of pathogenicity for man. Progressive avian tuberculosis in man is rare.

Epidemiology

SOURCE OF INFECTION. The most frequent source of infection for infants and children is contact or close association with an adult suffering from the disease, usually a parent or some member of the household. The usual mode of infection is by inhalation of droplets of sputum sprayed by coughing, sneezing, or speaking. Dried sputum containing bacilli may become a part of the dust of the room and be inhaled or be introduced into the mouths of children by hands, toys, or other objects; this is an uncommon mode of infection. Bacilli may be conveyed by kissing. Instances are recorded in which the disease has been conveyed by injection, a human bite, mouth-to-mouth respiration, or ritual circumcision. The urine of patients with renal tuberculosis has been shown to be a potential source of infection. In congenital tuberculosis, which is very rare, infection is acquired through the placenta from a mother with disseminated tuberculosis. Infection through milk still occurs in certain countries where raw milk is sold and where destruction of tuberculous cattle is not compulsory.

PREVALENCE OF THE INFECTION. Untreated, persons infected with tubercle bacilli will probably harbor living organisms for life, but they will not transmit tuberculosis unless they develop active disease. Infection is measured by tuberculin testing of population samples and varies considerably in different countries and in different communities. In the United States the Public Health Service has estimated that there are 35,000,000 persons infected with tubercle bacilli and that 10 percent of these are less than 25 years old. Over the years, the prevalence of tuberculous infection has decreased progressively.

In the United States today the great majority of students entering college are tuberculin-negative. The principal factor tending to reduce infection in the population at large is early identification and segregation of the "open" case which serves as a source of spread of infection.

PREVALENCE OF TUBERCULOUS DISEASE. At the end of 1963 there were 320,000 cases in the tuberculosis registers of the United States; 105,000 of these were active cases. The Public Health Service has estimated that 1 active case infects a minimum of 3 other persons annually and that about 1 in 12 infections progresses to active disease during the first year. Thereafter on the average for all ages about 1.6 of every 1,000 infections progress to active disease each year. The younger the subject, the greater is the likelihood of activity. In the isoniazid prophylaxis trials conducted by the U.S. Public Health Service among children with primary infection, the risk of complication of untreated infants and children was highest in the first year of life. The rate of extrapulmonary complications during the first year of observation of infants less than one year old ranged from 16 per 1,000 for those with normal roentgenograms to 182 per 1,000 for those with parenchymal pulmonary lesions. Tuberculosis morbidity in infants and children has declined markedly wherever infected subjects are discovered early by routine tuberculin testing and treated promptly with isoniazid.

MORTALITY. Tuberculosis causes more deaths in the United States than all other infectious and parasitic diseases combined. In 1963 the number of deaths from tuberculosis was 9,311 (4.9 per 100,000 population). In 1963, two-fifths of all deaths from tuberculosis occurred in cities with a population of 100,000 or more. The average tuberculosis death rate for 128 of these cities was 7.6 per 100,000 residents as compared with 3.9 for the remainder of the country.

Since effective antimicrobial agents became available, deaths from tuberculosis among children have dropped sharply. In most instances death from tuberculosis in children in the United States results from disseminated tuberculosis or from tuberculous meningitis which was not recognized in time for therapy to be effective.

Immunity and Resistance

Acquired immunity to tuberculosis has been shown to occur in experimental animals as well as in human beings. When the first infection occurs, the bacillus may multiply freely, but later with acquired resistance, its multiplication becomes restricted and a delicate equilibrium is established between host and parasite which can shift either way during the course of the disease.

The exact *nature of immunity* against the tubercle bacillus is not known. It is possible that alterations in the phagocytes and mononuclears are responsible for the immune response. Another possibility is that the immunity is mediated in part at least by antibodies. A number of humoral antibodies develop in the course of tuberculous infection, but it has not yet been shown that they play a role in acquired immunity.

The course of infection in a given case will depend upon a number of factors, including the number and virulence of the infecting organisms, the state of hypersensitivity of the individual's tissues, and the resistance of the tissues to the survival and multiplication of the bacilli. Although the nature of this resistance is still a matter of uncertainty, there is evidence that many factors play a part. The tissue reaction tends to limit the spread of infection, but it may be quite ineffective because tuberculosis can advance through dense fibrous tissue and bone without difficulty.

Although the familial incidence of the disease is largely explained by contact, *genetic factors* may be of importance. Kallmann and Reisner have shown that when one of a pair of identical twins contracts tuberculous disease, the chance that the other will also become ill is considerably greater than is the case for nonidentical twins. Racial factors are thought to influence resistance to tuberculosis; the disease is more frequent among Negroes and American Indians, which may be due, however, to differences in living conditions. Among *environmental factors* the loss of resistance caused by inadequate diet seems to be clearly established, but the part played by deficiencies of individual foodstuffs is not well documented.

The influence of *age* upon resistance is shown by the greater susceptibility to tuberculosis during infancy and puberty. There are probably several factors which contribute to the higher susceptibility of the infant. He is usually infected by a parent or other immediate household contact and is therefore likely to receive large doses of bacilli at frequent intervals. However, it may be that, in addition, infants do not form antibodies against M. *tuberculosis* as well as do older children or adults. Factors responsible for the decreased resistance at puberty are not well understood. In a study of 1,000 children with primary tuberculosis followed to adult life by Lincoln, approximately 9 percent developed chronic pulmonary tuberculosis during the adolescent period. Factors believed to be important are the stresses imposed by growth and inadequate diet and rest. Johnston's observations on calcium and nitrogen metabolism in girls indicate that during puberty there are high retentions preceding the onset of menstruation while lower levels of retention are associated with the decelerating phase of growth. With inadequate diet there may be a negative balance coincident with the development of reinfection tuberculosis. It is possible also that endocrine factors at puberty exercise a direct adverse effect on resistance to tuberculosis.

Stress situations which give rise to stimulation of the adrenal cortex may serve to decrease resistance. It has been shown that the administration of ACTH or cortisone has this effect both in experimental animals and in man. The inflammatory tissue reactions of the disease may be inhibited while multiplication of organisms is accelerated.

The course of tuberculosis may be affected by *other diseases*. Certain acute infectious diseases, especially measles and pertussis, appear to have a deleterious effect. The incidence of tuberculosis is higher than normal in patients with diabetes, and it appears in more severe forms. Sickle-cell anemia has been observed more frequently than usual among Negroes with tuberculosis. An increased susceptibility to tuberculosis has been reported in patients with Hodgkin's disease and sarcoidosis. Trauma has been observed to precede activation of osseous, meningeal, and pulmonary tuberculous lesions. Such trauma may be psychic or physical, including accidents, surgical procedures, and excessive exposure to sunlight.

ALLERGY AND IMMUNITY. The allergic response to the proteins of the tubercle bacillus is typical of the delayed type of allergy (Sec. 11.1). It is mediated by a cellular rather than a humoral mechanism and can be passively transferred by washed leucocytes. An increase in the enzymes aminopeptidase and alkaline phosphatase has been noted in the infiltrating cells at the sites of positive tuberculin reactions. An exact relationship between allergy to tuberculin and immunity to tuberculosis has not been established.

Immunity to tuberculosis may persist in the absence of allergy to tuberculin. A few individuals lose allergy to tuberculin after they recover from tuberculosis; others develop a more intense reaction to tuberculin as they improve; in rare instances, patients with far advanced disease, miliary tuberculosis, or meningitis may become anergic to tuberculin. Allergy favors resistance under certain circumstances, since the inflammatory reaction adds to the cellular defenses. However, when necrosis results, the effect of allergy may be harmful and contribute to the spread of the infection. Although allergy to tuberculin is likely to confer a certain degree of protection against exogenous reinfection, the prevalence of tuberculosis among persons with positive tuberculin is five times higher in the United States than among tuberculin-negative persons.

Pathogenesis

The term "childhood type of tuberculosis" has been used to describe the *primary tuberculous infection;* however, with a larger proportion of the population reaching maturity without having acquired the disease, the primary infection occurs with increasing frequency in adults.

The common *path of infection* is inhalation; in exceptional circumstances the portal of entry may be the alimentary tract, skin, conjunctiva, genital tract, tonsils, middle ear, nose, parotid gland, or placenta.

The *incubation period* is the time between the first invasion of the tissues by the tubercle bacilli and the development of an altered tissue reaction. It can be measured by the tuberculin reaction, which usually becomes positive 3 to 5 weeks after exposure, although the range may be from 2 to 9 weeks.

When tubercle bacilli first gain a foothold in the body they set up a primary complex consisting of (1) the primary tuberculous focus at the site of invasion, (2) a tuberculous lymphangitis leading from this focus to the regional lymph nodes, and (3) lymphadenitis of one or more regional lymph nodes with extensive inflammation and a tendency to caseation. The primary complex may be located in any part of the lung or elsewhere in the body. In the majority of cases there is only one primary complex.

The primary tuberculous focus is usually not more than a few millimeters in diameter; however, with the development of allergy to tuberculin it may become surrounded by a perifocal reaction, which may be large enough to be visible in the roentgenogram of the chest. The original focus persists for months; usually it gradually decreases in size and heals completely, leaving a small scar which often contains calcium (Ghon focus). The *lymph nodes* show less tendency to heal completely and are often the site of caseation which may persist for years. Tracheobronchial compression produced by lymph node enlargement associated with the primary complex may occur. This is frequently associated with bronchial obstruction, *endobronchial lesions,* and obstructive emphysema. Most of the changes are the result of mechanical factors and need not be associated with actual progression of disease unless rupture into the bronchial lumen results in bronchogenic spread. Tuberculosis of the tracheobronchial lymph nodes may extend to other lymph nodes of the body via the lymphatic vessels and by hematogenous dissemination. Common sites of invasion are the *tonsils, cervical lymph nodes,* and *middle ear.*

Occasionally, especially in infants, the primary focus may progress locally, forming a caseous area which softens, excavates, and causes spread of the disease locally or by the bronchogenic route, creating the pathologic, clinical, and roentgenologic picture of locally *progressive primary pulmonary tuberculosis.*

Some degree of *bacillemia,* either directly from the primary focus or by way of the lymph nodes, probably takes place in every case, beginning during the incubation period and lasting for several days or even weeks. A phase of *occult hematogenous dissemination* occurs in a large proportion of primary infections, usually within 10 weeks. During the phase of occult hematogenous dissemination there may be no clinical findings. The bacilli entering the blood-stream may be destroyed, a few scattered tubercles may be established, or larger peripheral foci may be formed which may progress immediately to caseation, remain quiescent indefinitely, or be activated at a later time. Most complications of *primary tuberculosis* in children, such as tuberculous meningitis or tuberculosis of the skeletal system, can be explained best on the basis of hematogenous spread from the primary focus. Because of these postprimary manifestations the primary complex should not be considered a benign disease. *Hematogenous dissemination* may be massive, as in miliary tuberculosis. It may be intermittent and of varying dosage, producing recurrent prolonged unexplained fever, which characterizes protracted hematogenous tuberculosis.

Chronic tuberculosis of the "adult" or "reinfection" type, occurring in an individual already allergic to tuberculin, is sometimes seen in childhood; it is rare before the age of 10 years but becomes increasingly frequent after puberty. It may originate from endogenous or from exogenous sources. The endogenous type is believed to be the most common and occurs as a result of activation of a dormant focus in the pulmonary apices. It might be considered a distant complication of primary tuberculosis originating from seedings to the apices at the time of occult hematogenous dissemination. In certain cases this apical focus may be observed in the x-ray as a small apical calcification called a "Simon focus."

Clinical Forms

The following clinical pictures are grouped according to the location of the lesions. The order in which each type of lesion is presented follows, in most instances, the order of events in the evolution of the disease.

The *onset* of tuberculous infection is rarely observed except in the case of exposed children who are followed regularly. In many instances allergy to tuberculin is the only evidence that tuberculosis has gained a foothold. The patient may not be sick in any way; he may gain weight normally and is usually free from cough and other symptoms. Usually, however, there is an initial fever, which appears synchronously with the development of allergy. There is nothing characteristic about the temperature curve; it remains elevated for a few days, occasionally for as long as three weeks. Other constitutional symptoms are usually absent.

The development of allergy sometimes coincides with an attack of *erythema nodosum; phlyctenular conjunctivitis* may also occur at the height of the initial infection. Whether these two lesions represent a local response to circulating tuberculin or whether they represent sites where single organisms have lodged and perhaps succumbed, liberating tuberculin locally, is a matter of dispute.

During the phase of *occult hematogenous dissemination* there may be no clinical findings. In other cases its occurrence is revealed by careful examination of the patient, who may exhibit some enlargement of the spleen and superficial lymph nodes, a few papulonecrotic tuberculids, or a few red cells in the urine. The stage of occult dissemination may be present for a matter of a few days only, leaving no evidence of its occurrence.

The course of primary tuberculosis is benign in the great majority of cases. The primary lesion often disappears completely. In unfavorable cases the local process may advance and continue relentlessly to a fatal termination unless it is recognized and treated.

Congenital tuberculosis, in which the infection is acquired through the placenta, is a relatively rare event, although more than 100 proved cases and many more probable ones have been recorded. In most cases the mother developed miliary tuberculosis during the latter part of pregnancy. The child may be stillborn or may survive for 2 or 3 months. Until recently the condition was uniformly fatal. Two distinct types are found. In one, a blood vessel is eroded and the organisms reach the fetus by the umbilical circulation, producing extensive generalized tuberculosis. In the second type, ulceration occurs into the amniotic cavity, and as a result of fetal respiratory movements the infected fluid is inhaled. Extensive tuberculous lesions in the nasopharynx and bilateral tuberculous otitis media are usually found, in addition to widespread generalized tuberculosis. The diagnosis can be made at birth by the discovery of tuberculous lesions in the placenta. A positive tuberculin reaction demonstrable during the first month of life is presumptive evidence of congenital infection.

Pulmonary Tuberculosis

SIMPLE PRIMARY TUBERCULOSIS. During the incubation period following inhalation of viable organisms, the tuberculin test remains negative and nothing abnormal is detectable in the lungs either by physical or by roentgen examination. With the development of allergy to tuberculin, inflammatory changes occur in the pulmonary parenchyma immediately surrounding the primary focus and in the regional lymph nodes, the so-called perifocal reaction. Cough and expectoration are usually absent. If present, a cough is usually due to compression from lymph node enlargement rather than to direct pulmonary involvement. Except in progressive primary tuberculosis or in endobronchial tuberculosis, no signs of pulmonary involvement are detectable by physical examination. Roentgenologic changes are not found in every patient; at times they are absent even when constitutional symptoms are present. In many instances enlargement of tracheobronchial lymph nodes is the only finding. Conspicuous roentgen lesions may exist with no associated symptoms.

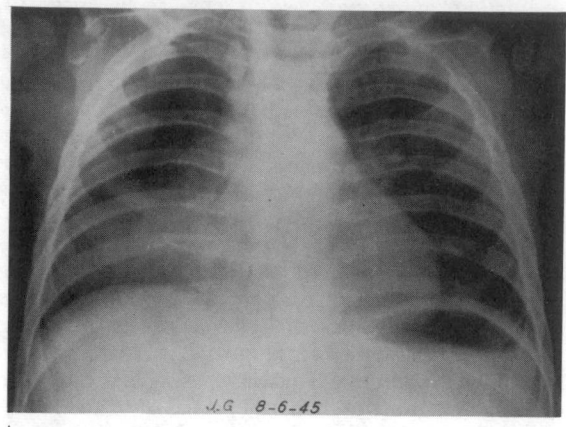

A

Fig. 9. Radiograms of patient with asymptomatic primary pulmonary tuberculosis showing evolution of Ghon complex from perifocal reaction to calcification. A. Patient J. G., 9 months of age. Clouding in right middle lobe, enlargement of right hilus and widening of mediastinum to the right. B. Eleven years later. Large area of calcification replacing clouding, and calcification of regional nodes in right hilar region. C. Localization of calcification in right middle lobe and in hilar lymph nodes.

B

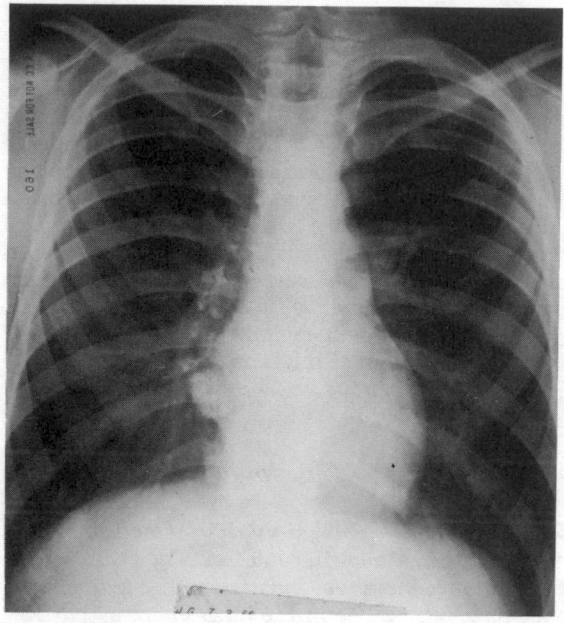

C

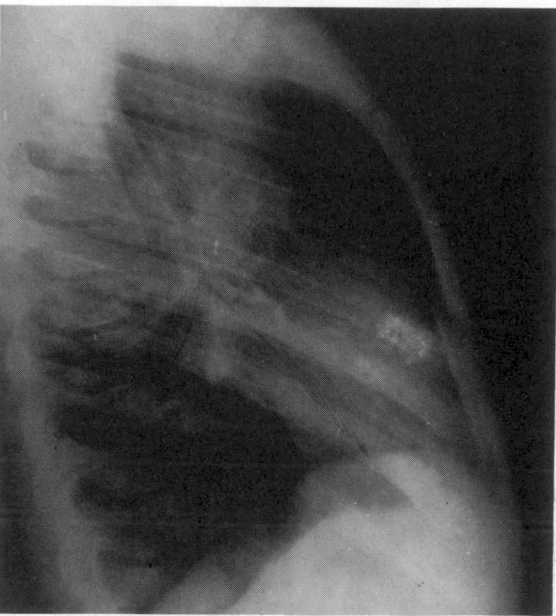

In serial roentgen films the perifocal reaction begins to contract appreciably in the course of months, and in a year or so it may disappear entirely, or it may undergo calcification and persist indefinitely as a so-called Ghon focus (Fig. 9). The enlarged lymph node shadows subside similarly, but they show a somewhat greater tendency to calcify during the healing process, as compared with the primary focus. Residual lymph node calcification is frequently multiple and may be bilateral when only a single primary focus is present. The apparent effect of isoniazid therapy upon the course of the pulmonary lesions is not dramatic, but it is highly effective in preventing local and extrapulmonary complications.

LOCALLY PROGRESSIVE PRIMARY TUBERCULOSIS. In sharp contrast to the cases just described, the pri-

mary parenchymal focus occasionally progresses locally to cavitation and may spread by way of the bronchi, producing tuberculous pneumonia. A similar clinical and roentgenologic picture may rarely be caused by bronchogenic dissemination arising from bronchial erosion by a regional node. Typical examples of progressive primary dissemination are illustrated in Figures 10 and 11.

Cavitation of the primary focus is seen more often in infants than in older children. The process of softening, once begun, tends to advance rapidly. Rarely, it may perforate the pleura, causing pneumothorax or pyopneumothorax. Small cavities are usually partially filled with caseous material and rarely communicate freely with a bronchus; hence, they do

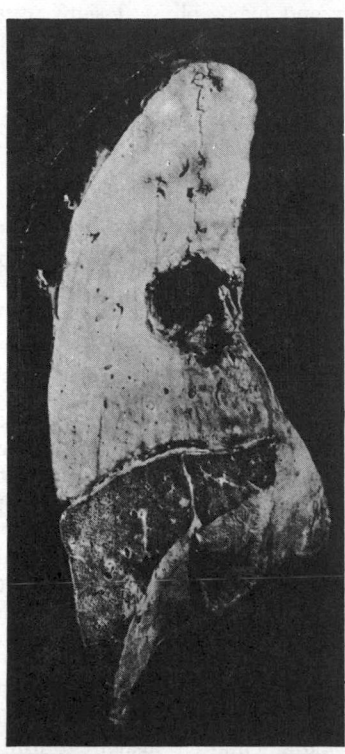

Fig. 10. Locally progressive primary tuberculosis. A vertical section through the middle of the right lung of a child 13 months old. The greater part of the upper lobe is uniformly caseous—a diffuse tuberculous pneumonia; near the center a cavity is seen. The part of the lower lobe shown is normal.

not, as a rule, give physical signs. Isoniazid therapy is highly effective in causing closure of cavities.

TUBERCULOSIS OF THE TRACHEOBRONCHIAL LYMPH NODES. The inflammatory reaction around tuberculous tracheobronchial nodes may involve adjacent structures and ultimately produce erosion and extension of the tuberculous process. Cases have been reported with erosion of the great vessels, causing sudden death. Encroachment on the superior vena cava may cause edema and cyanosis of the face. If ulceration takes place into the surrounding connective tissue, a mediastinal abscess may result, producing similar symptoms. Such an abscess may point in the suprasternal notch or at the xiphoid; it may burrow along the esophagus to the peritoneal cavity. Nodes adherent to the esophagus may cause dysphagia. These complications are rarely seen, but encroachment of tracheobronchial nodes on the bronchial walls is very common and produces the various clinical pictures of endobronchial tuberculosis.

ENDOBRONCHIAL TUBERCULOSIS. Bronchoscopic and bronchographic examinations have shown that bronchi are involved in a large proportion of children with primary tuberculosis. Immobilization of the bronchus is first noted; this is followed by edema and congestion of the bronchial mucosa adjacent to the adherent node, and then by the formation of granulation tissue. In some cases there is erosion of the wall and discharge of caseous material into the bronchial lumen. The rate at which the contents of the lymph node are expelled into the bronchus is usually slow and insidious; rarely it may be sudden

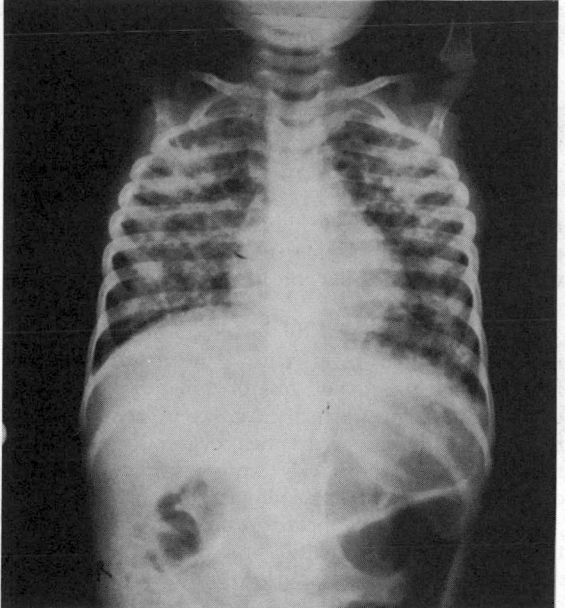

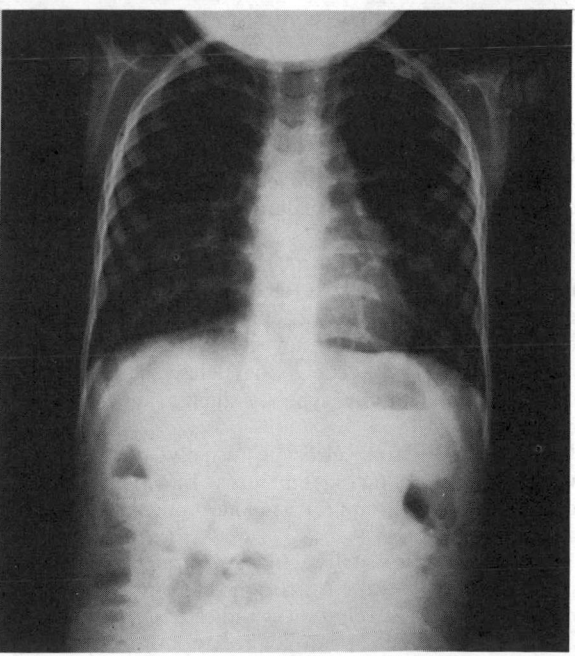

Fig. 11. Progressive primary tuberculosis in a 19-month-old infant (1954). A. Extensive bronchogenic dissemination in a very ill child with prominent physical signs of bronchopneumonia interpreted as spread from a cavity not visualized or from erosion of a caseous node into the trachea. B. Same child after one year of therapy with streptomycin, isoniazid, and PAS. Clearing of roentgen shadows was complete nine months after beginning of therapy.

and catastrophic. Pedunculated granulomas may develop which flap back and forth with each respiration; sometimes these become detached and are expelled. Bronchi of the right middle and right upper lobes are the most frequent sites of endobronchial tuberculosis.

Infants with endobronchial involvement frequently have symptoms, while older children are often entirely symptom-free. Cough, varying from high-pitched or brassy to paroxysmal, may be the only symptom. Wheezing is frequently present, and in severe cases the clinical picture closely resembles that of asthma, bronchiolitis, pulmonary migration of parasites, or aspiration of a foreign body. Dyspnea and cyanosis may be observed in severe cases. Symptoms are sometimes greatly relieved by a change to the prone position. The physical signs are those usually found with bronchial obstruction. Markedly diminished breath sounds alternating with loud rhonchi suggest intermittent obstruction by pedunculated granulation tissue. The response to antituberculosis therapy is slow, and corticosteroids may be needed to control severe respiratory distress.

CHRONIC PULMONARY TUBERCULOSIS (REINFECTION OR ADULT TYPE). Chronic pulmonary tuberculosis develops some years after the primary infection in individuals possessing some degree of acquired resistance. It is usually found in older children and during adolescence; it is more common in girls than in boys. The lesions may be found in any part of the lung, but they show a distinct preference for the apical and infraclavicular regions. Lymph nodes usually are not enlarged, and the infiltration does not involve the hilum. The clinical picture may resemble closely that of subacute nontuberculous pneumonia, or there may be no symptoms. Tubercle bacilli may be recovered if carefully searched for. Rapidly progressive disease may follow a minimal, almost asymptomatic lesion with little warning, especially in a girl near the menarche. Prolonged chemotherapy is indicated and offers an excellent chance of producing healing (Fig. 12).

The classical picture of chronic phthisis, with hectic fever, progressive emaciation, night sweats, etc., is rarely seen early in chronic pulmonary tuberculosis in childhood but may develop with advancing disease. Primary infections in adolescents may pass over into the chronic type by almost imperceptible changes.

PLEURISY. Pleural effusion usually takes place within a year following the initial infection. It may occur in any age group but is more common in school-age boys.

The onset is usually with fever, cough, and chest pain. Physical and roentgen signs of pleural fluid are readily obtained. Aspiration is indicated for diagnosis. The fluid is usually straw-colored to amber and contains 250 to 10,000 cells per mm³, most of which are lymphocytes. Tubercle bacilli may be cultivated in about one-fifth of the cases, and recovery of organisms is more likely if large amounts of fluid are cultured. The immediate prognosis is almost invariably good. Fever and major physical signs usually disappear in 3 to 4 weeks. The ultimate prognosis has improved with isoniazid therapy. Steroid therapy in conjunction with specific treatment will secure rapid defervescence and absorption of fluid and may prevent the formation of adhesions.

Hematogenous Dissemination of Tuberculosis

The occult hematogenous dissemination of organisms, believed to take place in the course of the initial infection, is usually of small degree and produces no symptoms. Later evidence of symptomatic hematogenous dissemination may be provided by the appearance of extrapulmonary lesions or of one or more calcified apical pulmonary lesions (Simon foci).

There are two forms of hematogenous dissemination which produce clinical symptoms; these are acute generalized miliary tuberculosis, which occurs when a large number of bacilli invade the bloodstream at one time, and protracted hematogenous tuberculosis, which results from repeated seedings of varying numbers of organisms.

ACUTE GENERALIZED MILIARY TUBERCULOSIS. Miliary tuberculosis occurs most frequently in infants and young children, usually during the first 6 months of the primary tuberculous infection. When a tuberculous focus discharges its contents directly into the bloodstream, fresh lesions of approximately uniform age are produced in various parts of the body to which the organisms have been carried. The disseminating focus may be a caseous lymph node or an intimal tubercle in an involved vessel.

Pathology. The widely scattered, numerous metastatic lesions are initially of uniform small size; the word "miliary" comes from the Latin *milium,* or millet seed, and implies a structure of less than 2 mm in diameter. Tubercles are distributed in the lungs and they may be found in any other organ, especially the spleen, liver, and kidneys. They may also be present in the skin. Tuberculous meningitis (p. 671) was a frequent complication before isoniazid therapy was introduced.

The onset is usually insidious; it is characterized by irregular fever with general symptoms of malaise, fretfulness, and loss of appetite. There may be gastrointestinal disturbances, as in any acute infection. There may be dyspnea, cyanosis, and a hacking cough, but respiratory embarrassment is seldom extreme. The respiratory rate is slightly accelerated, and fine rales may be heard in one or another part of the chest. As the disease progresses, rales become more constant and are usually found diffusely; physical signs of consolidation, however, are absent. The duration of the untreated disease varies from 3 to 8 weeks, rarely somewhat longer. Toward the end, wasting and prostration become more pronounced, and anemia usually develops.

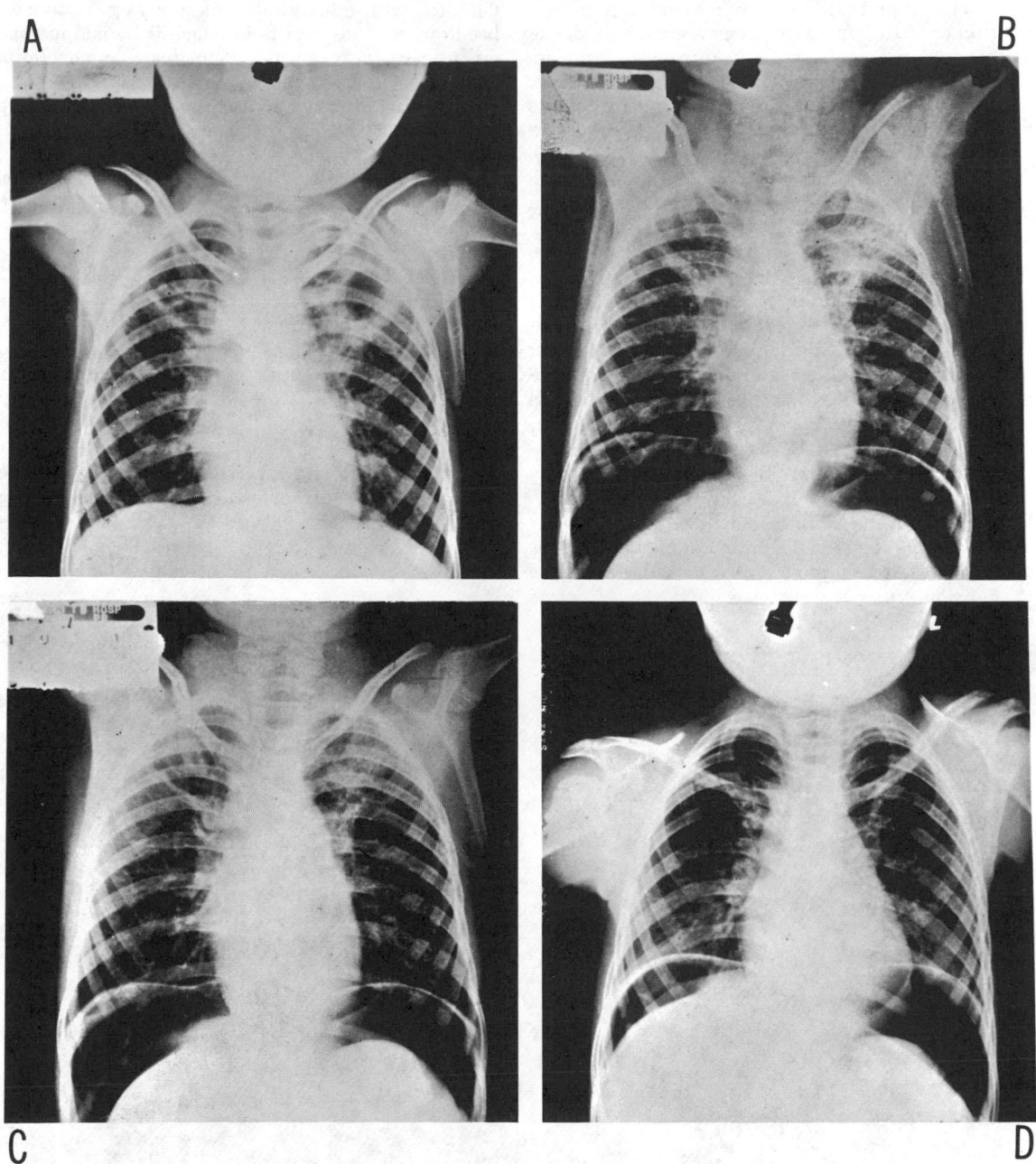

Fig. 12. Radiogram of the chest in chronic pulmonary tuberculosis of the reinfection or adult type, successfully treated. *A.* Ten-year-old girl with marked symptoms and physical signs. Radiogram shows bilateral infiltration of upper lobes with large cavity on left. Small cavities were also present on the right. *B.* Apparent closure of cavity after three months of therapy with pneumoperitoneum, streptomycin, and PAS. *C.* Further improvement after addition of isoniazid. *D.* Essentially normal lung picture 18 months after onset of therapy, confirmed by tomography. Treatment was stopped at this time and the patient remained well after follow-up of three years.

About half of the patients have enlargement of the spleen, liver, and superficial lymph nodes. In a small proportion of the cases there are cutaneous manifestations, the most common being papulone- crotic tuberculids, which may appear singly or in crops. A purpuric eruption, usually with small petechiae, occurs rarely. Tubercles can be found in the choroid in many cases.

The tuberculin reaction is of great assistance in diagnosis except in far advanced infection, when a dose of 100 to 250 TU may be required to elicit a positive test. In very early stages a roentgenogram of the chest may not reveal the presence of miliary tuberculosis. As miliary tubercles increase in size, they become visible in the roentgenogram as minute dots. In some cases with heavy seeding, these tubercles coalesce into larger "snowflake" masses (Fig. 13). A few other conditions will produce miliary opacities in the lung fields and must be considered in differential diagnosis, including histoplasmosis, coccidioidomycosis, histiocytosis, giant cell pneumonia, and inhalation of dusting powder.

Tubercle bacilli may be cultured from stomach washings, bone marrow, spinal fluid, blood, superficial lymph nodes, or urine. Bone marrow or liver biopsy may reveal miliary granulomas. There is usually leucocytosis (15,000 to 20,000) with an increase in the proportion of polymorphonuclear cells. Purpura may or may not be associated with thrombocytopenia. In the absence of specific therapy, miliary tuberculosis will almost invariably terminate fatally. Fatalities occurring with chemotherapy are usually due to delayed diagnosis or to coexistent tuberculous meningitis. Lumbar puncture with culture of the cerebrospinal fluid for *M. tuberculosis* should be performed as soon as miliary dissemination is recognized. Children with miliary tuberculosis may have tubercle bacilli in cerebrospinal fluid which is normal in every other way. In such cases there may be no clinical evidence of tuberculous meningitis.

Isoniazid therapy combined with PAS and streptomycin usually gives excellent results in miliary tuberculosis, symptoms often disappearing within 2 weeks. Roentgenologic evidence of miliary infection may be expected to disappear within as few as 10 to 14 weeks, but in some cases it persists for a longer period.

PROTRACTED HEMATOGENOUS TUBERCULOSIS. This form of generalized tuberculosis is caused by intermittent hematogenous dissemination of varying numbers of tubercle bacilli. In the course of weeks or months the local lesions progress and may become very extensive. Such cases often terminate fatally if untreated.

Symptoms of acute toxemia, fever, and leucocytosis may be present, especially in fulminating cases associated with tuberculosis of the skeletal system, massive enlargement of the superficial lymph nodes, and involvement of serous surfaces. The lesions in the lungs, when present, are usually of unequal size.

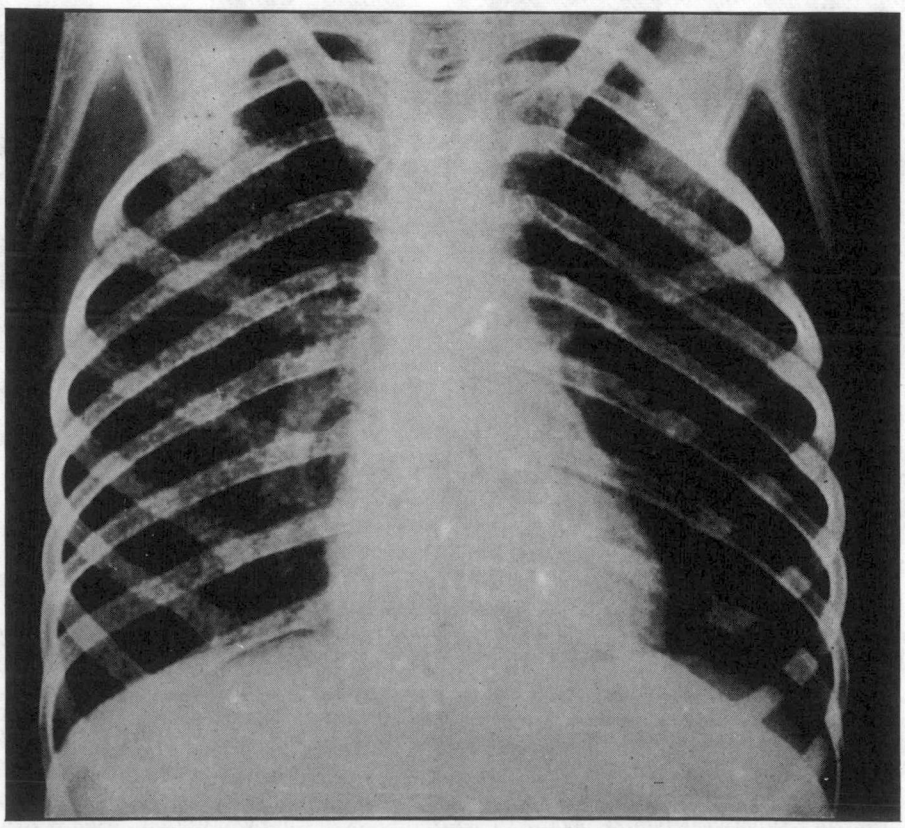

Fig. 13. Radiogram showing acute miliary tuberculosis. Hematogenous dissemination in the lungs of a girl 8 years of age.

Malnutrition may reach an advanced degree. There is poor appetite, great listlessness, and often marked anemia. Some of these patients present a more chronic picture, characterized by discharging sinuses from lymph nodes or bones, sometimes accompanied by chronic otitis. Untreated, these chronic generalized cases may go on for years, now better and now worse. A fatal outcome may be precipitated by the extension of a local process or by an intercurrent infection. Miliary tuberculosis or tuberculous meningitis may occur at any time.

In the acute phase these patients may present diagnostic difficulties; the only evidence of disease may be fever and leucocytosis, often suggesting leukemia or Hodgkin's disease. The diagnosis may be suggested by a positive tuberculin test and confirmed by favorable response to antituberculous chemotherapy. When specific therapy is begun even in a late stage the outlook is excellent.

Extrapulmonary Tuberculosis

Extrapulmonary lesions are almost always the result of hematogenous dissemination from the pulmonary focus. Many of these lesions occur early in the course of primary tuberculosis; meningitis, for example, usually appears within a year after onset of the disease. Other extrapulmonary seedings, such as those involving the skeletal system and lymph nodes, also usually occur within a year of the establishment of the primary focus. But such complications may arise months or years later with reactivation of foci which were laid down during the postprimary seeding. Gastrointestinal and renal tuberculosis usually occur late, often years after the initial infection.

Tuberculous Meningitis

Tuberculous meningitis is the most common cause of death from tuberculosis in infants and children. Without therapy the disease is uniformly fatal, usually within 3 weeks after its onset. Although it is seen in all age groups, most patients are under the age of 5 years, the peak incidence being soon after the end of the first year; it is relatively rare among infants under 6 months of age. It is frequently associated with generalized miliary tuberculosis.

PATHOLOGY. According to Rich and McCordock, meningitis is usually the result of the breaking down of a focus in the brain with dissemination of organisms in the spinal fluid. The exudate consists of a gelatinous inflammation, most extensive at the base of the brain. It usually extends into the fissure of Sylvius on each side. Fibrin, fluid, and mononuclear cells are the most conspicuous constituent elements. As the disease progresses, foci of ischemic necrosis are often present in the deeper layers, apparently the result of occlusion of vessels. Exudate may obstruct the basal cisterns, the foramina, or the aqueduct of Sylvius, causing dilation of the cerebral ventricles.

SYMPTOMS. In about two-thirds of the cases the onset is gradual; it may be preceded by a precipitating factor such as measles, trauma, or steroid therapy. Three stages are recognized. In the *first stage* the neurologic examination is normal. The most frequent early symptoms are disinclination to play, apathy, anorexia, fretfulness, irritability, and change in disposition. Sleep is disturbed. Children older than 4 years of age often complain of headache. At all ages, but particularly in infancy, early digestive symptoms are prominent. Vomiting occurs without apparent cause, and the child may be constipated. Usually there is also slight but continuous elevation of temperature. Indefinite symptoms may last for 4 or 5 days, or they may be spread over 2 or 3 weeks without perhaps being sufficiently severe to attract much notice.

In the *second stage* neurologic signs become apparent. In most cases the first pronounced cerebral symptom is persistent and increasing drowsiness; in infants it may be a generalized convulsion. The patient may suddenly scream out at night, often without waking. If undisturbed, the child may sleep a great part of the time, but he can be roused and may then appear quite rational. The neck may be stiff and the head drawn back. In infants, the anterior fontanel is tense and bulging. The pupils, which may be of normal size or dilated, respond slowly to light or not at all; they may be unequal. Occasionally strabismus, nystagmus, or ptosis is seen. Ophthalmoscopic examination usually shows papilledema, and tubercles may be found occasionally in the choroid. Often there is paresis of one side of the face, or of one arm or leg, or even hemiplegia. These neurologic signs may vary from day to day and even from hour to hour. Photophobia and hyperesthesia of the skin are sometimes observed. Marked dermatographia, the so-called *tache cérébrale*, is often present. Other vasomotor disturbances may be seen, such as flushing or irregular mottling of the skin. Tendon reflexes are variable. In the second stage of the disease they are usually increased; later they may be diminished or absent. Automatic movements of the extremities, particularly of the arms, are frequent. In some patients the picture may suggest encephalitis since there may be tremors, slurred speech, grimacing, chewing, and athetoid movement of the extremities.

In the *third stage* the patient becomes unresponsive; both arms are held stiffly close to the sides, elbows extended, forearms pronated, wrists partly flexed, and fists clenched. Opisthotonus is often marked and well-nigh constant. The pulse eventually becomes slow and irregular. Respirations are almost always irregular; a characteristic type consists in the excursions becoming deeper and deeper until there is a sigh, followed by complete arrest of respiration for several seconds; the phenomenon is then repeated. Untreated, the average duration from onset to death is around 20 days.

DIAGNOSIS. Changes in the spinal fluid are present early. As a rule pressure is elevated. The fluid is usually clear, occasionally slightly turbid with a ground-glass appearance. On standing, a delicate coagulum forms, usually adherent to the surface of the fluid. The usual cell count is from 100 to 250 per mm³, but it may be as low as 16 and as high as 3,000. Nearly all the cells, over 90 percent in most cases, are mononuclear. A predominance of polymorphonuclear cells is, however, occasionally observed. The protein is increased. A reduction in glucose concentration below 40 mg per 100 ml is usually present. If this reduction is not present on the initial examination it will almost invariably be found on serial examinations. Reliable interpretation of spinal fluid glucose values depends upon knowledge of blood glucose values, since the spinal fluid glucose is about 60 to 70 percent of the blood glucose in normal persons.

Tubercle bacilli may often be found by centrifuging the cerebrospinal fluid or by direct examination of the pelicle which develops on standing. However, a prolonged search is usually required. Culture or guinea pig inoculation of the cerebrospinal fluid is more likely to reveal tubercle bacilli.

A positive tuberculin test is usually present early in the disease and is of great diagnostic importance. In the late stage, allergy may wane, and negative results may be obtained with 5 TU of tuberculin. Roentgenologic evidence of pulmonary primary tuberculosis, even if calcified, is important in diagnosis. In the Bellevue series it was present in 89 percent of patients with tuberculous meningitis.

The differential diagnosis of tuberculous meningitis includes all the causes of the aseptic meningitis syndrome. In these conditions the cerebrospinal fluid glucose is not decreased. When the glucose is diminished, such possibilities as the following should be considered: partially treated purulent meningitis, mycotic meningitis, metastatic neoplasms, leukemic infiltration of the meninges, certain primary neoplasms that infiltrate the meninges, toxoplasmosis of the central nervous system, and luetic meningitis.

TREATMENT AND PROGNOSIS. In a patient suspected of having tuberculous meningitis, cultures for myobacteria should be promptly obtained, and therapy should be started at once; it should not be withheld pending the results of bacteriologic studies. The outcome in treated cases depends on the stage at which treatment is commenced, the likelihood of success being greatest with early treatment. Often little change for the better can be detected within 2 weeks, and as a rule the symptoms continue to advance for a week or 10 days. The first evidence of improvement is often seen in the laboratory findings—a rise in the spinal fluid sugar or a reduction in protein. Gradually it becomes apparent that the disease is not progressing. In successfully treated cases the return to normal often requires many months.

Obstruction of the subarachnoid space is an important complication. Spinal block is suspected when the pressure of the spinal fluid is low and the fluid shows protein values greater than 300 mg per 100 ml of cerebrospinal fluid. Spontaneous resolution of the spinal block may occur. Obstruction of the basal cisterns may be present when the patient is first seen and is evidenced by progressive increase in pressure of the cerebrospinal fluid. Steroids should always be used when a block is diagnosed and in severe cases may be given by both intravenous and intrathecal routes. Spinal, cisternal, or ventricular taps daily or twice a day are advisable in the presence of increased intracranial pressure until the pressure remains below 200 mm of water. With administration of steroids the intracranial pressure usually becomes normal after 48 to 72 hours of therapy. Intrathecal administration of streptodornase and streptokinase or tuberculin is not recommended.

General therapeutic measures must not be neglected in tuberculous meningitis. Maintenance of nutrition may require a prolonged period of feeding by gavage. Care is needed to avoid aspiration of vomitus. Bladder distension and fecal impaction may cause difficulty. With the associated electrolyte disturbances there is a tendency to increased loss of sodium and chloride through the kidney. Periodic electrolyte determinations of the blood serum should therefore be made. Too rapid or vigorous hydration often results in convulsions. Finally, during convalescence, rehabilitation procedures should receive attention to help the patient overcome residual physical handicaps.

The results of therapy have varied in different clinics. To some extent this may be attributed to the regimen, but mainly is due to differences in the age of the patients and time of onset of treatment. The fatality rate ranges from 0 to 15 percent in patients treated in the first stage, and from 80 to 90 percent in the third stage.

Residual mental or physical damage occurs most frequently in the younger infants and in those diagnosed late. Relapses are extremely rare provided isoniazid therapy is prolonged for at least 36 months. Sequelae may be obvious in patients treated later in the course of the disease, but in others they may not be detectable without pneumoencephalograms, electroencephalograms, and visual, audiometric, and psychometric examinations. Many patients have a mild degree of hydrocephalus which becomes arrested as the patient improves. Many develop a "silent" intracranial calcification during the healing stage. Behavior disturbances are common. Other important sequelae include convulsions, mental retardation, and blindness, which is often reversible. Deafness, which is permanent when it occurs, has become rare since intrathecal administration of streptomycin has been abandoned.

SEROUS TUBERCULOUS MENINGITIS. Under this term Lincoln described a group of cases which differ from classic tuberculous meningitis in their clinical characteristics and in their more favorable prognosis. They are believed to be patients in whom a cerebral focus close to the surface of the brain induces meningeal irritation but does not break into the subarachnoid space with discharge of large numbers of organisms. Symptoms are similar to those at the onset of typical tuberculous meningitis, but the steady progression to coma does not occur. Bacilli are seldom present in the spinal fluid, and the spinal fluid sugar does not decrease, although the number of cells may be increased. A number of instances of recovery were recorded before the days of chemotherapy. The distinction between classical and serous tuberculous meningitis is, however, not a sharp one. If they are not treated, some of these patients may develop true tuberculous meningitis at a later date; therefore all patients with serous tuberculous meningitis should receive chemotherapy for at least a year.

TUBERCULOMA OF THE BRAIN. Solitary tubercles in the brain substance occasionally give rise to focal neurologic syndromes and even at times to pressure symptoms independently of tuberculous meningitis. They are somewhat more common in the cerebellum than in the cerebrum. Clinically it is difficult to differentiate them from neoplasms.

The spinal fluid remains normal or shows only an alteration of pressure. Occasionally there may be a moderate increase in cells and protein. The diagnosis can rarely be made with certainty by clinical means alone but is sometimes suggested by the presence of associated tuberculous lesions. Conservative treatment is generally preferable to operative removal unless symptoms are progressive or the lesion is producing a neurologic deficit. Chemotherapy should be administered during surgery and for 24 to 36 months thereafter.

Tuberculosis of the Bones and Joints

Tuberculosis of the bones and joints is usually due to hematogenous spread from a primary focus, but the primary lesion is often healing or healed by the time the skeletal lesion is detected. As a rule bone lesions develop between the ages of 3 and 8 years. Trauma appears to play a part in some instances.

Although any bone may be affected, the vertebrae are the most common site of tuberculosis of the osseous system. The hip, knee, and small bones of the hands and feet are also frequently involved. About 10 percent of the patients with bone tuberculosis have more than one skeletal lesion, as well as other manifestations of extrapulmonary tuberculosis. Joint tuberculosis is secondary to disease of an epiphysial center. Disease of the hip starts in the femoral head; in the knee the process begins in one of the condyles of the femur; in the ankle, in the lower tibial epiphysis. In the long bones, the process begins near the epiphyseal line, but in the short bones it affects the central region. Caseation occurs early, and cold abscesses play a considerable part in the pathologic picture. Skeletal tuberculosis should be considered in the differential diagnosis of osteomyelitis, bone tumors, and skeletal lesions associated with the reticuloendothelioses.

TUBERCULOSIS OF THE SPINE (POTT'S DISEASE). The process usually begins in the center of a vertebral body and spreads to the periosteum, ligaments, intervertebral disks, and, in fact, to all contiguous structures. Secondarily it may involve the membranes of the cord, the roots of the spinal nerves, and even the cord itself. From two to five vertebrae are commonly involved. Any part of the vertebral column may be affected, but the disease is much more frequent in the thoracic region. Softening of the vertebral bodies may cause them to collapse, with the production of an angular kyphosis.

The onset is usually insidious. The most constant early symptoms are (1) pain caused by irritation of the nerve roots and referred to various parts of the body, following the distribution of the spinal nerves, (2) rigidity of the spine from muscle spasm due to an automatic attempt to prevent motion at the site of disease, and (3) the assumption of various postures calculated to relieve pressure upon the diseased vertebral bodies. In some cases the first symptoms are those of pressure paralysis; in others a localized abscess may be the first sign of tuberculous spondylitis. In addition to the local symptoms there is usually disturbed sleep and often night cries. Night sweats are frequently encountered.

In cervical Pott's disease pains are often felt above the point of disease, frequently in the form of occipital neuralgia; sometimes they are referred to the front or the side of the neck. Muscle spasm often takes the form of torticollis, sometimes of slight opisthotonos; at other times there is simply a fixation of the head and resistance to passive motion. The first thing to attract attention may be progressive weakness in the lower extremities, which may progress to paraplegia. Occasionally the presenting symptoms are those of retropharyngeal abscess.

Spinal deformity develops late. Usually the neck appears broadened or thickened in a nearly uniform way, and often the head seems to have settled downward upon the shoulders. In the lower cervical region kyphosis is not infrequent; but in the middle and upper regions there is more often an anterior prominence, which may be felt in the posterior wall of the pharynx.

With thoracic involvement the pain is referred below the site of disease and takes the form of intercostal neuralgia or pain in the epigastrium. There is a disposition to assume the prone position while sleeping. The child walks carefully, holding the spine erect and very stiff, and exhibits great caution in getting into or out of bed or in rising from a recumbent position. Kyphosis is found in the involved areas, and with it there is often a compensatory lordosis in the lumbar region.

Lumbar involvement is accompanied by pain and lameness, often referred to one leg, leading to the suspicion of hip disease. Pain may be felt in the groin, the buttocks, or the hypogastrium. The gait and attitude are very characteristic; throwing the shoulders well back, the patient walks stiffly, with short steps. Holding the spine with greatest care, he "walks with his legs but not with his back." In stoop-

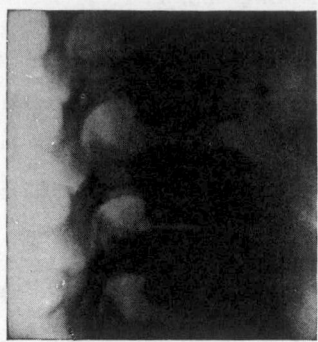

Fig. 14. Collapse of an intervertebral disk, the earliest radiographic sign of tuberculosis of the spine.

ing and rising, the same disinclination to bend the spine is seen. Deformity comes late and may be preceded by symptoms of psoas abscess: lameness, tilting of the pelvis with some lateral curvature, flexion of one thigh with resistance to full extension, and a palpable swelling deep in the iliac fossa or at the upper and inner aspect of the thigh.

The course is measured by months or years, marked by periods of remission and exacerbation. An exacerbation may follow trauma and may lead to paravertebral abscess.

The examination of a suspected patient must include a search for angulation which is not eradicated by suspending the child; the mobility of the spine must be tested; and, finally, one must search for secondary phenomena such as abscess or paralysis. Tenderness on pressure over the spinous process is rarely present, although pain may sometimes be produced by downward pressure upon the head or shoulders. Exaggerated tendon reflexes below the level of the kyphos are commonly found. With increasing deformity, paralysis may appear. Narrowing of the intervertebral disks (Fig. 14) may be seen in roentgenograms. In late cases the angular kyphos may be demonstrable, and the roentgenogram will show destruction of one or more vertebral bodies. A paravertebral abscess may be disclosed by roentgenogram at a relatively early stage, appearing as a fusiform shadow, usually symmetric.

Clinically, the spinal deformity resulting from Pott's disease may be confused with juvenile or adolescent kyphosis, trauma to the vertebral bodies, and curvatures depending upon muscle weakness. Lesions of the spine caused by the ordinary pyogenic organisms give more acute symptoms. Chronic spinal disease may, however, be caused at times by other organisms, such as in brucellosis and actinomycosis. Vertebral bodies are occasionally involved in eosinophilic granuloma. Narrowing of the intervertebral disks in the lumbar region may develop as a result of injury to the nucleus pulposus from lumbar puncture; this usually causes no symptoms.

TUBERCULOSIS OF THE HIP. The process usually begins in the femoral head, exceptionally in the acetabulum. The onset is usually gradual, with slight lameness; later there is pain, frequently referred to the knee or the inner aspect of the thigh, rarely to the hip itself. Starting pains at night—the "night cry" —are characteristic of tuberculosis of the hip. They are caused by sudden spasm of muscles which have become relaxed during sleep. The child often cries out without waking. Lameness, at first intermittent, becomes constant.

Deformity in the early stage is slight, but there is marked limitation of motion due to spasm. The hip tends to be fixed in partial adduction, external rotation, and flexion; extension, internal rotation, and abduction are resisted. Muscle atrophy appears early in the thigh and often affects the calf as well. In walking, the child protects the diseased side, throwing his weight as much as possible upon the sound limb and compensating for the flexion and limited excursion of the hip joint by an exaggerated lumbar lordosis and by excessive mobility of the lower spine. Fever and abscess formation are late features.

Early cases of tuberculosis of the hip may be confounded with the result of trauma, with rheumatic fever, poliomyelitis, osteochondrosis, nontuberculous epiphysitis, or caries of the lumbar spine.

Roentgenograms may show nothing at all for several weeks after the onset of the disease. The most important early signs are atrophy and areas of erosion in the epiphysis of the head of the femur or in the acetabular margin. This early erosion of bone is in contrast to the findings of Perthes' disease (osteochondrosis of the hip), in which erosion does not take place but there is molding, flattening, and fragmentation of the epiphyseal center of the femoral head. Sometimes, however, the x-ray does not enable one to distinguish immediately between the two conditions.

TUBERCULOSIS OF THE KNEE. Tuberculosis of the knee usually begins in one of the condyles of the femur or in the head of the tibia. The earliest symptoms are slight lameness and stiffness of the joint, which the child tends to keep partly flexed. At first these symptoms are noticed only occasionally; eventually, they become constant and are accompanied by pain in the knee or ankle. In some cases there are starting pains at night. Swelling is noticed early; at first it is limited to the bone originally involved, often the inner condyle. Later there is a general fusiform swelling, involving the entire joint and effacing all the normal outlines. Some tenderness upon pressure over the bone affected is present quite early, and there may be atrophy of the muscles of the thigh and calf. The knee resists extension and may even be held fixed at a right angle.

TUBERCULOUS DACTYLITIS (SPINA VENTOSA). This condition is seen most frequently before the age of 3 years. It usually begins as a painless enlargement of one of the phalanges or of the dorsum of the hand or foot from involvement of a metacarpal or

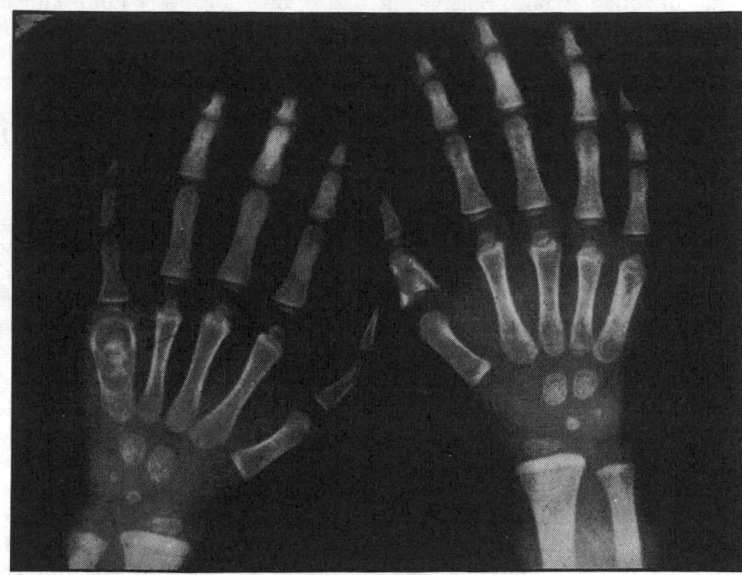

Fig. 15. Radiogram in tuberculous dactylitis.

metatarsal bone. Two or three months may elapse before the size of the swelling attracts much attention. Exceptionally the inflammation is more active and is accompanied by both pain and tenderness. When a finger is involved, the swelling is quite characteristic; it is smooth, hard, uniform, and generally spindle-shaped, extending beyond the involved phalanx. Later there is discoloration of the skin, and the process may go on to suppuration.

The condition is sometimes discovered by x-ray before it is clinically manifest (Fig. 15). A similar dactylitis may be seen in congenital syphilis; it does not, however, break down, and other evidences of the disease should make the diagnosis clear.

TUBERCULOSIS OF OTHER BONES. Tuberculosis may affect other bones including the skull, ribs, scapula, and bones of the foot. The skull lesions may have a punched-out appearance similar to that produced by the reticuloendothelioses. Tuberculosis sometimes involves the shafts of long bones. In cystic tuberculosis of bone, foci in the diaphysis of the humerus, tibia, ulna, or other long bones give rise to areas of localized expansion with thinning of the cortex. Such lesions may be single or multiple, but are seldom symmetric. Occasionally abscesses and sequestra are formed.

DIAGNOSIS AND TREATMENT OF SKELETAL TUBERCULOSIS. Skeletal tuberculosis should be suspected in patients with skeletal lesions characterized by insidious onset and persistent deformity. Abscess formation over the lesion, a positive tuberculin reaction, and evidence of healed or active pulmonary lesions are very suggestive. The roentgenographic appearance of the affected bone is one of bone destruction without bone formation until healing begins. Histopathologic studies support the diagnosis but do not establish it, since mycobacteria other than tuberculosis produce a similar picture. Recovery of *Mycobacterium*

tuberculosis from the lesion establishes the diagnosis.

The treatment of skeletal tuberculous lesions has changed considerably since isoniazid became available. It is now possible, without immobilization, bed rest, or major surgical procedures, to obtain excellent results in all forms of skeletal tuberculosis in patients who are treated. During the acute phase most children limit their activity spontaneously, and enforced immobilization is seldom necessary. An advantage of this policy is that osteoporosis is not seen in such patients. Surgical drainage of abscesses is still indicated, but fusion operations are now rarely necessary. During chemotherapy some skeletal lesions may appear to increase in size for a few months, and abscesses requiring drainage may develop. But healing is the rule without any change in type or dose of antimicrobial agents.

Tuberculosis of the Skin

Tuberculosis of the skin may result (1) from external inoculation, either primary or in individuals already infected; (2) from hematogenous dissemination; (3) from extension of a tuberculous lesion beneath the skin; or (4) from a hypersensitivity reaction as in erythema nodosum.

In *primary cutaneous infections* the lesion develops insidiously, sometimes engrafted on an apparently insignificant traumatic or pyogenic condition. In the course of a few weeks a discrete indurated granuloma or chronic ulcer marks the site of inoculation; the regional lymph nodes are invariably enlarged, and not infrequently break down. The primary lesion varies in size from a few millimeters to 1 or 2 cm; it is generally dry and sluggish and causes no pain. As a rule it is solitary, but occasionally two or more lesions are present.

If the infection is not primary, but occurs in a subject already tuberculous, the local lesion develops somewhat more rapidly; reaction in the regional nodes, on the other hand, is less conspicuous. A form of superinfection is *tuberculosis verruca cutis,* which used to be relatively common in pathologists. The lesion tends to occur in the exposed surfaces of arms and legs; it is usually single, large, raised, and covered with scaling epidermis.

More frequently seen in infants and children are the so-called *papulonecrotic tuberculids.* This lesion is a small red papule, 2 to 4 mm in size, which is soon surmounted by a vesicle. If the crust which presently forms is removed, a small pitlike depression remains, which heals quickly. Left alone, the lesion retrogresses and tends to become brownish, and the crust drops off. There finally remains a minute, shallow, pale depression surrounded by a pigmented zone. A tuberculid runs its course in 2 or 3 weeks. Anatomically it is a miliary tubercle, and bacilli have been demonstrated both in sections and in scrappings. Such lesions may appear in crops, and are not symmetrically distributed; sometimes they are very numerous, but more often only a few are present. They are more commonly found on the buttocks and posterior surfaces of arms and thighs but may be found in any part of the body.

Lichen scrofulosorum is a variety of tuberculid which is less conspicuous and more rare. The lesions usually appear in clusters and are generally found on the trunk, especially on the back or over the abdomen, and on the shoulder and thighs. In appearance and distribution they may resemble pityriasis rosea. A rare lesion that may accompany tuberculids is *erythema induratum* (Bazin's disease), which is characterized by large chronic indurated ulcers.

Scrofuloderma is a term applied to an indurated lesion with purplish discoloration which appears over tuberculous lymph nodes or bones. It may break down and discharge.

The term *lupus vulgaris* is applied to a circumscribed, indurated, reddish brown lesion which is exceedingly chronic and tends to heal in one area while spreading in another. By and large, lupus is a disease of adult life; its onset, however, is nearly always in childhood. The condition is usually found on the face, most frequently on the cheek, sometimes on the nose, ear, or eyebrow, but it may occur in any other part of the body.

Erythema nodosum is probably due to a local hypersensitivity reaction to tuberculin. It is characterized by fever and painful, reddish, subcutaneous nodules, 1 to 3 cm in diameter, usually located in the anterior tibial areas. These lesions seldom contain tubercle bacilli. Erythema nodosum is not pathognomonic of tuberculosis, since it may also occur in association with streptococcosis, sulfonamide therapy, histoplasmosis, coccidioidomycosis, sarcoidosis, lymphogranuloma venereum, and ulcerative colitis.

Most forms of tuberculosis of the skin show a satisfactory response to specific therapy. The rare cases of lupus vulgaris often require months and even years of antimicrobial therapy to effect a cure. Scar formation cannot always be prevented.

Tuberculosis of the Superficial Lymph Nodes

Tuberculosis of the superficial lymph nodes occurs in about 5 percent of all children with primary pulmonary tuberculosis. In most cases the process seems to be of hematogenous origin; in others it obviously results from lymphatic drainage from an active focus. Cervical nodes are more commonly affected than other superficial nodes. The process is rarely limited to a single node; it usually affects the deep chain which follows the carotid artery; the superficial nodes of the submaxillary and parotid groups may be involved later. Involvement is often bilateral. In exceptional instances cervical node involvement is part of the primary complex, the primary focus being in the tonsil or some other part of the pharynx.

The onset of cervical adenitis is insidious, without pain or constitutional symptoms. It can often be traced to an attack of tonsillitis or pharyngitis or may follow measles. Enlarged nodes generally appear in front of the sternomastoid muscle, sometimes behind it; at first they are freely movable and discrete, but later become fused in an irregular nodular mass which may adhere to the skin. As the process approaches the surface, spots of softening appear; the skin becomes discolored and finally gives way with the discharge of thick, curdy pus. When a node beneath the deep fascia breaks down, an abscess may form which gradually works its way to the surface. In untreated cases the sinus may continue to discharge for a long time or, if healed for a while, may reopen repeatedly. These sinus tracts may become secondarily infected.

It may be very difficult at times to differentiate between tuberculous nodes and acute pyogenic lymphadenitis, but a positive tuberculin test should arouse suspicion of tuberculosis. Diagnosis can be established by culture. Histopathologic appearance alone does not differentiate tuberculous lymphadenitis from that caused by other mycobacteria. Material for culture and histologic examination can be obtained by needle biopsy using a Menghini needle. Open biopsy is not desirable since it may leave unsightly scars. Calcification demonstrable by x-ray is very suggestive of tuberculosis. Malignancies, including leukemia and lymphosarcoma, and other infections such as toxoplasmosis, chronic pyogenic granulomas, tularemia, actinomycosis, and coccidioidomycosis should all be considered in the differential diagnosis.

Isoniazid therapy should be used in superficial adenitis. The response is slow, but eventually all nodes return to normal size and all sinuses heal, usually between 3 and 18 months after starting isoniazid therapy. Transient enlargement of nodes due to intercurrent infections should not cause alarm.

In cases which do not respond after prolonged therapy excision is indicated, but this is rarely necessary. Fluctuating nodes may be aspirated and drained through a No. 14 or 15 needle.

Tuberculosis of the Eyes, Ears, and Throat

TUBERCULOSIS OF THE EYES. Tuberculous involvement of the eye may occur as a *primary lesion* in the conjunctivae or rarely in the lacrimal apparatus with unilateral enlargement of the corresponding nodes. Tuberculosis of the *ciliary bodies* and *iris* and acute choroiditis are rare in children. *Choroidal tubercles* may be seen in patients with miliary tuberculosis, tuberculous meningitis, or hematogenous tuberculosis. The discovery of choroidal tubercles by a careful observer may sometimes be the clue to a diagnosis of tuberculosis in a patient with fever of unknown origin. They appear as oval areas of discoloration usually located at the periphery of the fundus and can easily be missed.

Phlyctenular conjunctivitis is probably due to a hypersensitivity reaction to tuberculin. Very rarely has it been possible to demonstrate organisms in these lesions, which are characterized by 1 to 2 mm gray nodules located on the limbus accompanied by injection of the blood vessels and marked photophobia. They occur in crops, may be bilateral, and in untreated cases may be recurrent. With isoniazid therapy they have become rare. Local corticosteroid therapy may help to relieve symptoms and is safe as long as it is given in conjunction with isoniazid.

TUBERCULOUS OTITIS MEDIA. This form of tuberculosis is not infrequently seen in patients with primary tuberculosis. It occurs as a result either of hematogenous spread or of direct extension from tuberculous adenoids. The main symptom is painless purulent otitis, which may become chronic and is often secondarily infected with pyogens such as proteus, *Ps. aeruginosa,* and staphylococci. Deafness occurs frequently. The management includes specific therapy for tuberculosis. The secondary invader must be isolated and sensitivity studies performed in order to determine the proper therapy. The mastoids should be investigated and surgery performed if indicated.

TUBERCULOSIS OF THE TONSILS. Primary tuberculosis of the tonsils is now rare. In most cases involvement of the tonsils is due to lymphatic and hematogenous spread from the pulmonary focus. Tuberculosis of the superficial cervical lymph nodes accompanies tuberculous tonsillitis. The response to isoniazid therapy is excellent. Tonsillectomy is seldom necessary.

LARYNGEAL TUBERCULOSIS. This is rare in young children but may be part of generalized tuberculosis. It is more frequently seen in adolescents with chronic cavitary pulmonary tuberculosis. In these cases the disease is highly contagious. Fortunately the response to therapy is excellent.

TUBERCULOUS RETROPHARYNGEAL ABSCESS. This condition is usually due to extension from a cervical Pott's disease. Occasionally it may be due to caseous retropharyngeal lymph nodes.

Abdominal Tuberculosis

The term "abdominal tuberculosis" refers to tuberculous involvement of mesenteric lymph nodes, gastrointestinal tract, and peritoneum. Contamination of milk by the bovine bacillus, a frequent cause in former days, is no longer a problem, but the same clinical picture may be caused by human strains. As these lesions are no longer common, the diagnosis is often missed and the disease discovered at the time of laparatomy or autopsy.

In a *primary infection of the intestine* the lesion at the portal of entry is seldom detected; the organisms pass to the mesenteric and, in some instances, the retroperitoneal nodes, which in early cases show a response quite similar to that seen in the tracheobronchial nodes; the process is usually unsuspected unless a roentgenogram, taken some time later, happens to reveal typical calcification (Fig. 16).

TUBERCULOSIS OF THE ABDOMINAL LYMPH NODES (TABES MESENTERICA). In primary infections the regional lymph nodes are the chief area of disease, whereas if the abdominal infection develops after there is some acquired resistance, the intestinal lesions are likely to be more conspicuous than those in the lymph nodes. The enlarged nodes in mild infections are usually small and as a rule produce no symptoms. At times, however, they may reach the size of a hen's egg or even larger. Pressure on the vena cava may lead to edema of the lower extremities; occasionally thrombosis of a large vein occurs. Compression of the portal vein may lead to portal hypertension, with ascites and dilation of the superficial abdominal veins; in rare instances pressure on the thoracic duct has caused chylous ascites.

As a rule, there is only slight and transitory constitutional disturbance or vague local symptoms. On examination, the enlarged, slightly tender masses may be found: retroperitoneal masses lie close to the spine and are not readily movable; the mesenteric nodes are more superficial and mobile.

A number of these patients, however, seek medical advice years later because of abdominal pains which recur at intervals. The symptoms continue long after calcification has occurred in the glands and are apparently produced either by traction from adhesions or by a flare-up of the old infection. It has been demonstrated that caseation, living tubercle bacilli, and calcification may coexist in such nodes for years.

TUBERCULOSIS OF THE GASTROINTESTINAL TRACT. In rare instances the esophagus may be involved through direct extension from tuberculous mediastinal nodes. The stomach is almost never affected by tuberculosis. The liver and the pancreas and spleen may be involved in miliary or protracted hematog-

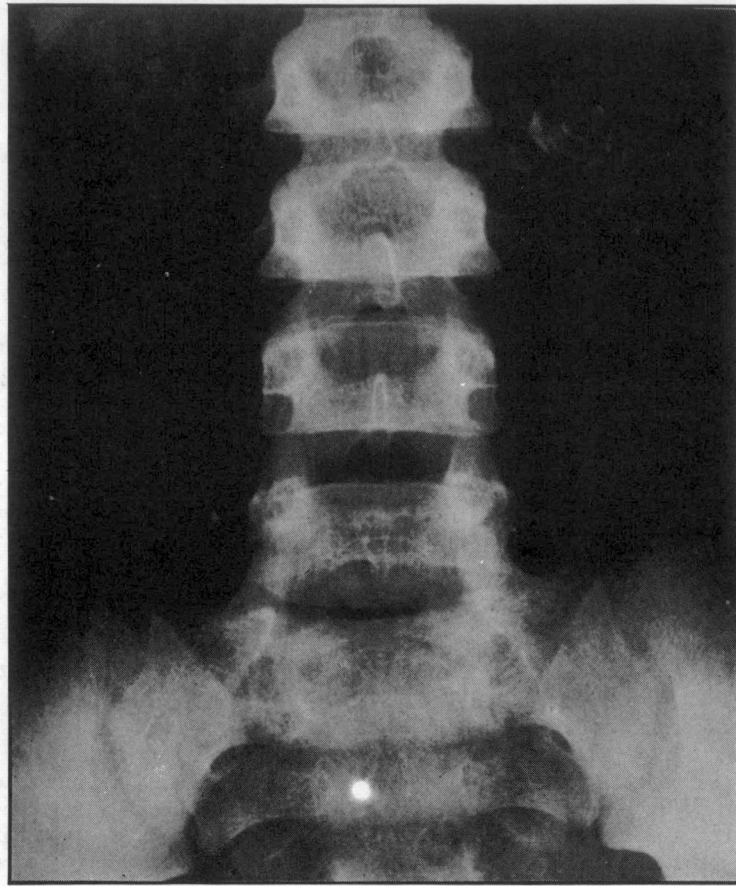

Fig. 16. Calcified abdominal lymph nodes in a child of 3 years.

enous tuberculosis. Tuberculous lesions of the small and large intestines are usually due to bacilli ingested as a result of far advanced pulmonary lesions. The most common sites of involvement are the lower half of the jejunum, the ileum, and the cecum. The intestinal mucosa and Peyer's patches are affected. Small tubercles are formed at first which break down, producing small ulcerations. In severe cases, stenosis of intestinal segments may occur, and occasionally a hyperplastic reaction of the connective tissues of the intestinal wall may result in masses which produce obstruction and simulate malignancies. With severe cases some degree of peritonitis is always found.

Symptoms are exceedingly variable. The small ulcers seen in young infants usually produce no symptoms. With more advanced lesions diarrhea is commonly present, associated with constitutional symptoms; the stools may suggest dysentery. Occult blood is a frequent finding. There may be localized abdominal pain, occasionally of a colicky nature, and tenderness. In advanced cases the symptoms may be combined with those of tuberculous peritonitis, and there are usually palpable lymph nodes as well.

Although tuberculous enteritis is rarely seen, it should be kept in mind when there is chronic diar-

rhea, intestinal hemorrhage, abdominal distension, or unexplained masses. The tuberculin test is usually positive. Roentgen examination in early cases may show hypermotility of the intestine; later, persistent spasm of a segment or stenosis of gut may be observed. The discovery of acid-fast bacilli in the stools is of no value in the identification of tuberculous lesions.

Tuberculosis of the anus and rectum is very rare in children; however, in all cases of fistula in ano the possibility of tuberculosis should be considered.

TUBERCULOUS PERITONITIS. Miliary tubercles in the peritoneum are usually present in acute generalized miliary tuberculosis, but they cause no local symptoms. Obvious peritonitis results from breakdown either of abdominal lymph nodes or of massive intestinal lesions. Two varieties, an ascitic and a plastic form, are generally described, but the distinction is not a sharp one. The ascitic variety is usually believed to result from rupture of a caseous lymph node into the peritoneal cavity; less frequently it arises from direct extension of an intestinal ulcer. The plastic form may follow the ascitic variety or may develop directly by extension from a lesion in any viscus, usually the intestine, or from a lymph node.

The onset may be insidious with a low-grade fever and indefinite general symptoms. Enlargement of the abdomen, developing slowly, is often the first symptom to be noted; pain and tenderness are unusual. Diarrhea may occur if there is associated enteritis. Vomiting is usually seen only in mixed forms with adhesions which cause partial obstruction. Aspiration reveals a turbid, straw-colored fluid containing numerous polymorphonuclear leucocytes; occasionally it is bloody. Organisms are seldom demonstrable in smears but are readily recovered by guinea pig inoculation and culture.

In the *plastic form* the viscera may become firmly matted together by adhesions. Caseous areas are found here and there, usually in the vicinity of the lymph nodes, and small collections of encapsulated exudate may be encountered. Nodular masses of various sizes and shapes may be felt anywhere in the abdomen, most frequently in the umbilical region and the right iliac fossa. Frequently palpation reveals a doughiness or peculiar loss of elasticity. Occasionally the process involves the abdominal wall, producing a cellulitis which may break down with fistula formation. Abdominal paracentesis in this form is contraindicated, for there is risk of perforating the intestine, which may be adherent to the abdominal wall.

All forms of abdominal tuberculosis respond favorably to therapy with isoniazid. Surgical therapy may be necessary in rare cases to remove masses of nodes or segments of intestine that produce symptoms due to obstruction.

Tuberculosis of the Urinary Tract

In generalized tuberculosis, miliary tubercles are frequently seeded on the surface of the kidney and in its substance. These usually give rise to no symptoms. Large areas of tuberculous involvement in the kidney are exceedingly rare in early life. In older children renal tuberculosis may exist as the only important lesion in the body. Nearly all such cases result from bloodstream dissemination of organisms; ascending infection is rare, and the bladder is involved late. As a rule, only one kidney is affected.

The process may begin in the cortex or in the pyramids, and in time is likely to spread and to form caseous abscesses involving practically the entire parenchyma, so that in advanced cases the kidney consists of a mere shell of renal tissue. Perinephric abscess sometimes coexists.

The symptoms are indefinite and usually of mild degree in comparison with the destruction present. There may be localized pain and tenderness in the region of the kidney, which may be palpable if there is pyonephrosis or perinephritis. Bladder symptoms, when present, may be almost as severe as in cases of calculus; urgency, frequency, dysuria, and tenesmus may occur singly or in various combinations. Hypertension is rare but may occur in advanced cases owing to renal artery sclerosis. Leucocytes usually appear in the urine as an early and constant feature, and blood is often present. The diagnosis is established by the urogram and the discovery of tubercle bacilli in the urine by culture or guinea pig inoculation.

Specific therapy has practically eliminated the need for surgery. Periodic excretory urograms are indicated about every 6 months initially and every 1 or 2 years for 10 years after therapy to rule out strictures of the ureters which may develop during healing. Regardless of what combination of antibiotics is used, isoniazid seems to be the major factor in the improved prognosis.

Tuberculosis of the Heart and Pericardium

In acute generalized miliary tuberculosis, tubercles are occasionally seeded in the myocardium. Miliary tubercles and minute caseous foci are, in rare instances, seen upon the mural endocardium, most frequently in the conus arteriosus of the right ventricle. Tuberculous valvulitis is rarely observed at postmortem examination associated with widespread miliary lesions in all the organs.

The pericardium is more frequently involved, but even this is an uncommon lesion in childhood. A diffuse serofibrinous pericarditis may result from the extension of a process in the mediastinal lymph nodes, and in these cases the visceral pericardium usually becomes thickened and rigid as fibrosis progresses. Recurrent attacks of cardiac distress and circulatory failure are associated with the tamponade effect of an effusion of serous or hemorrhagic pericardial fluid under pressure. Most of these cases are seen in children over 2 years of age, and in the past most of them have terminated fatally in spite of temporary relief from aspiration of the pericardial sac. Constrictive pericarditis may develop soon after the acute pericarditis or many years later. Most cases are now prevented by chemotherapy, and in those diagnosed and treated early, complete recovery is possible. Steroid therapy should be administered as part of the initial treatment of severe cases. In patients who have tamponade, pericardiotomy may be indicated. In patients who develop constrictive pericarditis, surgery may be necessary.

Diagnosis of Tuberculosis

Tuberculin tests included in routine annual physical examinations not infrequently lead to the recognition of primary tuberculosis. A history of contact with tuberculosis may be of invaluable aid in arousing suspicion of infection. Normal children who are known or thought to be in contact with tuberculosis should be tested immediately, and those who do not react should be retested 2 months later and every 6 months thereafter. All children admitted to a hospital or to an outpatient clinic should have a tuberculin test, and in any obscure clinical problem further investigations for tuberculosis should be carried out.

A child with a positive tuberculin test should have a complete history, physical examination, and a roentgenogram of the chest, even if he is afebrile and free from symptoms and physical signs. His family and other persons with whom he has been closely associated should also be tuberculin tested; those who react should have a complete physical examination and roentgenograms of the chest. Pulmonary or mediastinal shadows in an infant who reacts positively are usually tuberculous. A localized homogenous parenchymal shadow with enlarged hilar nodes is strongly suggestive of tuberculosis.

In gauging the activity of the disease, the recovery of organisms is the most reliable criterion. The presence of calcified foci, though it suggests healing, does not preclude an active process. Some help can be obtained from the presence of fever, constitutional symptoms, or an elevated sedimentation rate, but these must be interpreted in conjunction with the entire clinical picture. Failure to gain weight before therapy and rapid weight gain during the first two months of chemotherapy are very suggestive of active disease.

TUBERCULIN TESTS. Tuberculin consists of a mixture of proteins derived from the tubercle bacillus. These proteins elicit a delayed hypersensitivy reaction in individuals infected with the tubercle bacillus. The reaction is most intense at the site of contact of tuberculin with the tissues, whether it be skin, conjuctiva, pleura, or subarachnoid space. The tuberculin skin reaction is of enormous value in case finding and diagnosis of tuberculosis in children.

PRODUCTS. Two varieties of tuberculin are available for diagnostic use: purified protein derivative (PPD) and the old tuberculin of Koch (OT), a concentrated filtrate of a broth culture of tubercle bacilli (Table 11). Although old tuberculin has proved itself satisfactory for clinical use, purified protein derivative (PPD) possesses certain advantages, chief of which is its consistent potency compared to OT. PPD is prepared by precipitation of the proteins of tubercle bacilli grown in synthetic media. A highly refined product of PPD called PPD-S was adopted in 1952 by the World Health Organization as the international standard tuberculin. PPD is available commercially in tablet form which is then diluted with an appropriate amount of buffered diluent. OT is available as a concentrated fluid containing 1,000 mg/ml, which is diluted in a buffered diluent.

The potency of tuberculin is expressed in terms of tuberculin units (TU). One TU is approximately equivalent to 0.01 mg of OT and 0.00002 mg of PPD. It is best to use large amounts of dilutions, which are more likely to contain the specified concentration and less likely to lose potency through absorption of tuberculin by the glass. Vials containing 5 or more ml may be used for 6 months provided they are stored in a refrigerator and away from sunlight or ultraviolet rays.

The doses (per 0.1 ml) available and their rough equivalence to the first, intermediate, and second strength are given in Table 12.

The Seruminstitut of Copenhagen has manufactured a purified protein derivative, the PPD RT 23, for worldwide distribution in sufficient amounts to cover the global demand until 1972. It is being widely used by the WHO and by many health departments outside the United States. One TU (0.02 μg) of RT 23 corresponds to about 3 TU of the international standard PPD-S.

For mass tuberculin testing programs PPD is recommended in the 5 TU (0.0001 mg) dose. One TU (0.00002 mg) of PPD will detect about 95 percent of persons infected with tuberculosis, whereas 5 TU will detect about 99 percent.

TECHNIQUES. Two techniques are in more or less common use: the intracutaneous (Mantoux) and the multiple puncture tests (Heaf and Tine). The intracutaneous method is the most accurate and is the standard of reference in all quantitative work.

The syringe and needles used for tuberculin tests should be sterilized by autoclave. Since tuberculin adheres tenaciously to glass, a syringe used in tuberculin testing should be confined to that purpose alone, and a separate syringe kept for each dilution. Satisfactory disposable tuberculin needles and syringes are available commercially.

The test is most conveniently applied on the volar surface of the forearm. The skin is carefully washed with alcohol and allowed to dry. The needle, preferably three-eighths inch, No. 26 gauge, is inserted tangentially, and 0.1 ml of the diluted tuberculin is injected within and not beneath the skin, forming a raised wheal 7 to 8 mm in diameter.

Intracutaneous tuberculin tests should be read between 48 and 72 hours after the injection. The area of induration should be carefully palpated and measured with a millimeter rule and the maximum transverse diameter of the induration recorded.

As a rule, there is more or less associated erythema, but redness unaccompanied by induration may

TABLE 11. *Tuberculin Products for Diagnostic Use*

	First Strength		Intermediate Strength		Second Strength	
	Units	mg/0.1 ml	Units	mg/0.1 ml	Units	mg/0.1 ml
PPD	1 TU	0.00002	5 TU	0.0001	250 TU	0.005
OT	1 TU	0.01 (1:10,000)	10 TU	0.1 (1:1,000)	100 TU	1.0 (1:100)

TABLE 12.   *Summary of Therapy in Tuberculosis*

Drugs	Daily Dose/kg of Body Weight*	Mode of Administration
Isoniazid†	5-20 mg (maximum 400 mg)	Divided into 2 doses orally, iv, or im Give low dose once daily in A.M. for prophylaxis
Streptomycin	30-50 mg (maximum 1 g)	Once daily intramuscularly during acute phase
PAS	0.2-0.5 g (maximum 12 g)	Divided into 3 or 4 doses given t.i.d. or q.i.d., orally

Indication	Regimen
Progressive pulmonary tuberculosis, extrapulmonary tuberculosis; tuberculous meningitis, miliary tuberculosis, and *protracted hematogenous tuberculosis; tuberculosis of the superficial lymph nodes* and other progressive forms	Isoniazid combined with daily streptomycin. Streptomycin may be discontinued after 1 to 3 months if the course is favorable. Continue isoniazid for 24 to 36 months. PAS may be given when streptomycin is discontinued, if there are cavitary lesions, and discontinued after cavity closure
Asymptomatic primary tuberculosis, including children *under 5 years* of age with positive tuberculin reactions and roentgenograms within normal limits	Isoniazid alone; duration: one year or more
Recent tuberculin converters (within 18 months)	Isoniazid for one year
Positive tuberculin reactors 1. with "doubtful" pulmonary lesions 2. with silicosis 3. with diabetes	Isoniazid for one year
Positive tuberculin reactors or patients with *inactive tuberculosis* who have completed therapy 1. receiving steroids, antimetabolites, or alkylating agents 2. during measles, pertussis, or administration of live measles vaccine 3. undergoing surgery or extensive trauma	Isoniazid for 3 months. In the case of steroid therapy, continue for 3 months after steroids are discontinued

*Use high dose for critically ill patients, low dose for prophylaxis and long-term therapy after improvement, usually after 12 to 18 months of therapy.
†Pyridoxine is not necessary in children when these doses are used.

be disregarded. The delay of two days between application and interpretation of the test is highly important for the avoidance of false-positives. A reaction less than 5 mm in diameter is considered negative. A reaction 5 to 9 mm is considered doubtful and should be repeated. However, because of the known margin of error in the technique and interpretation of the test, it might be safer to repeat the test in all persons with reactions between 3 and 9 mm in diameter. A reaction 10 mm in diameter or greater is considered positive. When the reaction is severe, there is considerable local swelling and redness, occasionally with vesication or even ulceration at the site of injection; there may be local lymphangitis, enlargement of regional lymph nodes, and constitutional signs, including elevation of temperature. In these reactions local application of steroids is safe and helps to relieve the symptoms.

There are two *multiple puncture* tests now in use: the *Heaf test* and the *Tine test*. A special gun

and six-point cartridge * are used for the Heaf test. Fluid concentrated PPD is applied either to the cartridge or to the skin of the patient. Six punctures 1 mm deep are made through the layer of concentrated PPD containing 100,000 TU per milliliter. The reaction may be read between three and seven days later. Four papules or more is considered positive.

The Tine test is available from Lederle Laboratories as a sterile, disposable, dry device containing four points previously coated at the factory with old tuberculin. The points are driven into the skin and held for one second at a depth of about 2 mm, which is limited by the base of the device. The reaction is read 48 to 72 hours later. Any papule over 2 mm in diameter is considered positive. The Tine test appears to correlate with the 5 TU Mantoux test, and

---

* Available through the Panray Corporation as a kit containing a Stern Gun, cartridges, and Proto-derm (concentrated PPD).

the Heaf with the 100 TU. But any doubtful reactions should be checked with the 5 TU PPD by the Mantoux technique. The American Thoracic Society recommends that any reaction to these tests that does not consist of coalescent papules be considered doubtful. This is particularly true of papules under 2 mm in diameter which are frequently observed with the Tine test. The Heaf test is less likely to give false-negative reactions than the Tine test, but more likely to give an excess of adverse reactions and of false-positive reactions. The latter are more common in areas where the prevalence of infections with mycobacteria other than tuberculosis is high.

The use of the patch test (Vollmer) is not recommended.

SIGNIFICANCE OF THE TUBERCULIN REACTION. A positive reaction to tuberculin indicates the presence of allergy to tuberculin and the presence of tuberculous infection. Repeated tuberculin tests do not produce an allergic reaction in an individual not infected by tubercle bacilli. Repeated tests in the same sites in infected individuals are likely to result in reactions which appear progressively earlier, are more intense, and fade slightly sooner. Among BCG-vaccinated individuals a positive tuberculin test is expected and should not be interpreted as evidence of infection with virulent tubercle bacilli. A PPD prepared from BCG is under investigation as a possible means of differentiating allergy due to BCG from that resulting from natural infection. Allergy induced by BCG is claimed to be less intense by some workers but not by others. Most persons have strong reactions to tuberculin one year after vaccination; thereafter, allergy gradually fades so that most persons do not react by the tenth year after vaccination.

Allergy to tuberculin in persons infected with M. tuberculosis fluctuates under a variety of conditions and occasionally disappears entirely. Measles may cause a temporary anergy, usually for two to three weeks. Administration of live measles vaccine without gamma globulin has also been shown to produce a similar effect. Administration of other viral vaccines may depress the tuberculin reaction slightly. Varicella may produce anergy which is usually of less than 10 days' duration. Allergy may be reduced or abolished in some patients by the administration of steroid hormones. The inhibition reaches a peak during the sixth week of steroid therapy, at which time the mean size of the reaction decreases by 50 percent in tuberculous patients, so that in one-third the reactions become negative. Allergy returns within one week after steroids are discontinued. In moribund patients allergy tends to disappear. Occasionally in persons with minimal tuberculous infection, allergy may wane so that tuberculin tests with the usual dosage are negative. A negative test is obtained in a person so recently infected as to be in the incubation period. Subcutaneous, rather than intracutaneous, injection of tuberculin is occasionally responsible for a false-negative test. Patients under treatment with

isoniazid occasionally lose their reactivity to tuberculin.

The question of whether doses of tuberculin used for ordinary skin testing can cause exacerbation of a tuberculous focus has been raised. Lincoln has reported some observations suggesting that it may occur occasionally. This possibility suggests caution in the initial dosage when a high degree of allergy is suspected or in repeating tuberculin tests on a child who had a previous positive reaction.

Small reactions to 5 TU of tuberculin or any reaction to high doses of tuberculin (100 or more TU) may be of nontuberculous origin. Nonspecific reactions to tuberculin are more of a problem in certain geographic locations than in others. In the United States these reactions are common in the South and less frequently seen in the North. Cross-reactions due to infection with other mycobacteria are probable causes. Antigens prepared from various so-called atypical mycobacteria show cross-reactions with PPD; however, the reaction to the homologous antigen is usually larger and helps to identify the true source of allergy. The U.S. Public Health Service is investigating many antigens in the search for a "wide-spectrum" atypical mycobacteria antigen that will make it possible to differentiate, with a minimum number of tests, true allergy to M. tuberculosis from reactions due to other mycobacteria. At present PPD Gause and PPD Battey seem to be the most promising ones.

BACTERIOLOGIC EXAMINATION. Culture of material suspected of harboring tubercle bacilli is the most accurate method of diagnosing tuberculosis. Simultaneous culture and guinea pig inoculation do not increase significantly the positive yields, so that most institutions prefer to rely solely on cultures for recovery of the tubercle bacillus. Cultures must be obtained before antimicrobial therapy is initiated; otherwise it is very unlikely that tubercle bacilli will grow. Specimens which cannot be cultured immediately may be frozen until the bacteriologic examination can be performed. Direct examination of gastrict contents, stool, urine, sputum, tissue, and pus samples is not reliable, since acid-fast bacilli which are not M. tuberculosis may be observed.

Infants and children with primary tuberculosis usually cough little and, when they do, tend to swallow their expectorations, so that often it is possible to demonstrate the tubercle bacillus only by examination of the gastric contents. The patient must be examined in a fasting condition, preferably in the morning before he is fully awake. A Levin tube or a plastic gastric tube is passed in the usual way. With a glass syringe of 20 to 50 ml capacity, the gastric contents are withdrawn and placed in a sterile 250-ml container. The stomach is then washed with 30 to 50 ml of sterile water, and the gastric contents are again aspirated and added to the first aspiration.

In older children who expectorate, examinations of a single sputum specimen and a two- or three-day morning sample may be performed. For the latter examination the patient expectorates into the same container for two or three consecutive mornings, and the pooled material is examined. For children who do not produce sputum, an aerosol-induced specimen of respiratory tract secretions may be obtained.

Tubercle bacilli may be demonstrated in body fluids, such as pleural, pericardial, or peritoneal effusions, spinal fluid, and drainage from ears, cold abscesses, or sinuses. For urine cultures, an early morning sample is most satisfactory. In patients with hematogenous tuberculosis the bacilli may often be recovered from the bone marrow and less commonly from liver biopsy specimens.

BLOOD PICTURE IN TUBERCULOSIS. The morphology of blood usually shows little change in tuberculosis. Polymorphonuclear leucocytosis may be observed during acute exacerbations, particularly in hematogenous tuberculosis in which leukemoid reactions have been reported. The red blood count and hemoglobin may diminish, particularly in miliary tuberculosis. Some of these patients may have thrombocytopenia and purpuric manifestations. Fatal outcomes have been reported in patients with hematogenous tuberculosis in whom corticosteroid therapy has been administered for what was assumed to be a primary hematologic disorder. A high level of serum gamma globulin may be observed in children with primary tuberculosis. A low gamma globulin may occur in patients with tuberculous meningitis or miliary tuberculosis, and this persists in patients with poor prognosis. In patients with good prognosis the gamma globulin rises above normal values and, with recovery, returns to normal. The plasma albumin values may fall, and the alpha$_2$ globulins increase progressively with activity and extent of the disease. The sedimentation rate is usually elevated but does not serve as an accurate index of activity because of the many factors which affect it. C-reactive protein may be present or absent; its prognostic significance is still not certain.

Prevention of Tuberculosis

Prevention of tuberculous infection consists primarily in avoiding all possible exposure to persons or foods which might serve as sources of tubercle bacilli. Human sources are by far the most important. Persons with open lesions, either pulmonary or cutaneous, constitute the greatest menace. Experience has shown that individuals with adequately treated tuberculosis do not convey the disease. Infants and children with primary tuberculosis are seldom contagious even when *Mycobacterium tuberculosis* is recovered from their gastric contents. Raw milk should not be used for human consumption.

CHEMOPROPHYLAXIS. Small daily doses of isoniazid have been found to be effective in preventing the development of tuberculous disease in children with primary infection. Carefully controlled studies by the U.S. Public Health Service have demonstrated that isoniazid is highly effective, inexpensive, and nontoxic. In these studies the entire daily dose was administered at once in the morning and continued for a year, and it was demonstrated that this could be easily accomplished in most cases. Since the indications for this type of prophylaxis depend upon a positive tuberculin test, BCG vaccination would seriously impair it.

Isoniazid as a chemoprophylactic agent among contacts of tuberculosis cases has been extensively tested by the U.S. Public Health Service. The results indicate that about three-quarters of all forms of tuberculosis can be prevented during a year of isoniazid administration. Contacts with negative tuberculin as well as positive tuberculin were included in the study. Similar investigations in mental institutions and in villages in Alaska gave comparable results.

The success of contact prophylaxis is an important adjunct in breaking the chain of spread of tuberculosis from source case to contacts; however, the usual medical supervision of these contacts should be continued during and after isoniazid prophylaxis. Follow-up of participants of the U.S. Public Health Service Isoniazid Prophylaxis Trials for several years has demonstrated that tuberculosis can occur among those who took isoniazid, but the annual rates were around 50 percent lower than among those who received a placebo. The results of the U.S. Public Health Service studies also indicate that all persons with a positive tuberculin would benefit from a year of isoniazid in small daily doses, so that if it were possible to administer such therapy to all persons who react to tuberculin in a given community, it would be expected that the morbidity from tuberculosis in that community would drop by at least 50 percent within a year. Since most communities lack the resources to carry out such a program, it is recommended that only those persons at greatest risk be selected for isoniazid chemoprophylaxis. This group includes the recently infected (within 18 months) and others with positive reaction to tuberculin who (1) have doubtful lesions on x-ray, (2) are infants or children less than 5 years of age, (3) receive steroid therapy, (4) are immunized with live measles vaccine, (5) have measles or pertussis, (6) undergo major surgical procedures, (7) have silicosis, or (8) are on treatment with antimetabolites or alkylating agents.

Infants and children who must live in contact with an open case of tuberculosis should continue to take isoniazid until at least six months after the contact is broken. Previous BCG vaccination will not guarantee that these children will be protected; therefore BCG-vaccinated children under such circumstances should receive isoniazid as soon as their tuberculin reaction becomes positive following BCG take. Recommendations regarding drug therapy of these asymptomatic patients are given above.

VACCINATION. A number of procedures to vaccinate against tuberculosis have been employed; these appear to produce a partial immunity of variable degree and duration. These vaccines offer protection to those who have never been infected, but in creating protection cause tuberculin allergy and destroy the usefulness of tuberculin as a diagnostic tool. The ideal tuberculosis vaccine, not developed as yet, would be one that would confer adequate immunity without producing allergy to tuberculin. The best known and most widely used agent is BCG, an attenuated live bovine tubercle bacillus named for Calmette and Guérin. In the United States it is available from health departments or from the Research Foundation, Chicago, Illinois. Histologically, the lesion produced by BCG is typical of tuberculosis; it may progress to caseation and even calcification, but BCG infection differs from spontaneously acquired tuberculosis in the failure of the infection to become generalized and, as a rule, in the rapid retrogression and complete disappearance of the local lesions.

Vaccination with BCG is regarded as a safe procedure. Millions of children have been vaccinated uneventfully. Deaths resulting from dissemination of BCG are rare and, when they occur, are likely to be due to defects in the immune mechanism of the host. BCG should not be used in children with gamma globulin defects or with family history of such deficiency.

Indications for the use of BCG are still controversial. One important objection to its use is interference with the interpretation of the tuberculin test. The vaccine probably should be employed when contact with open cases of tuberculosis is unavoidable and chemoprophylaxis with isoniazid not feasible.

Immediately before inoculating a patient with BCG, unless the patient is a newborn, one should ascertain that he is tuberculin-negative and has a normal roentgenogram of the chest. Inoculation of a patient highly allergic to tuberculin may lead to local sloughing. Ideally the patient should be removed from contact with tuberculosis until his tuberculin becomes positive following vaccination. Vaccination may be carried out by oral administration, by subcutaneous injection, by multiple skin puncture, or by intradermal injection. The last-named procedure, introduced by Wallgreen, is now preferred. Vials containing the vaccine should be stored in the refrigerator and protected from sunlight or ultraviolet rays. The usual dose is 0.1 mg contained in 0.1 ml injected into the center of the deltoid region, using a No. 27 needle to form a wheal. A tuberculin test should be repeated 6 weeks later. If the skin test is negative after 9 or 10 weeks, revaccination may be carried out. The common reaction to intradermal vaccination consists of a papule which appears after 2 or 3 weeks, usually followed by a small sinus which heals spontaneously after some months. A tiny scar will usually remain. It is recommended that the successfully vaccinated individual be retested with tuberculin periodically and the diameter of induration recorded. This procedure will help to determine whether his allergy persists; it will also detect an increase in the size of the reaction which might be due to infection with *M. tuberculosis*. Possible reactions to the vaccine, especially when injected subcutaneously, include local ulceration or abscess formation, suppurative lymphadenitis, and the formation of nodules described as granulomas, lupus, or tuberculids. Calcification of a regional lymph node may occur. Hematogenous spread of BCG and disseminated disease have been rarely observed. All these complications respond favorably to therapy with isoniazid.

Treatment

The treatment of tuberculosis has been revolutionized by the advent of effective antimicrobial agents and by new surgical procedures which antimicrobial therapy has made feasible. General measures such as rest and adequate diet are still desirable, but they no longer occupy their former all-important place.

GENERAL MEASURES. Every child with tuberculosis, even asymptomatic primary tuberculosis, should have the best general care available. Rest in bed may be important during the early phases of the disease when the patient is toxic and febrile, and at this stage most children will rest spontaneously. After this phase, complete limitation of physical activity is neither necessary nor desirable. The child may go outdoors but should not be exposed to excessive sunlight.

In few patients is psychologic support more important than in the tuberculous child whose illness, often with minimum physical disability, provides great opportunities for worry and introspection. The use of masks and unnecessary isolation procedures should be avoided. The importance of recreational therapy and sympathetic guidance for these children cannot be overstressed; the child of school age should continue his studies. A child with primary tuberculosis who is afebrile and free from symptoms may return to school.

Sanatorium or hospital care is important for a seriously ill child and for one who is persistently contagious or whose home conditions are very poor, but in most instances the tuberculous child is best treated at home. Diet should be ample and nutritious. Forced eating should be avoided and is unnecessary, since after the second or third week of therapy most patients develop a voracious appetite. Supplementary vitamins may be given if indicated.

Protection from intercurrent infections is important. If a tuberculous child is exposed to measles, a preventive dose of gamma globulin should be given at once unless he has had measles or has received active immunization. If he has not been immunized against measles, he should receive live measles vaccine early during therapy.

ANTIMICROBIAL THERAPY. Antimicrobial therapy is indicated in all forms of active tuberculosis. Isoniazid is mainly responsible for the marked improvement in the prognosis of the tuberculous child. It is highly effective not only in saving life and in preventing complications which previously had a high mortality rate but also in shortening the course of the illness and preventing disability in less fatal forms. In endobronchial involvement, therapy does not apparently shorten the course but is useful in preventing and curing bronchogenic dissemination.

The antimicrobial agents used, the dosage, and the duration of therapy vary with the form of tuberculosis to be treated. In complications which formerly had a high fatality rate, the most potent drugs should be used in high dosage, and treatment must be prolonged to prevent relapse. The treatment should be most intensive in those complications such as tuberculous meningitis which may be rapidly fatal.

Several groups of antimicrobial agents have achieved an important place in the treatment of tuberculosis. The three most commonly used are (1) derivatives of isonicotinic acid, (2) streptomycin, and (3) para-aminosalicylic acid (PAS).

In severe forms and in cavitary lesions it is considered important to employ combinations of these antimicrobial agents rather than to use them singly. Not only are synergistic effects obtained, but the emergence of drug resistance is delayed or prevented under these circumstances. Any combination that includes isoniazid is desirable; at present isoniazid and daily streptomycin constitute the choice for beginning therapy in seriously ill children, such as those suffering from meningitis. After initial improvement, prolonged therapy can usually be continued with isoniazid alone.

Two *isonicotinic acid derivatives* are useful in the treatment of tuberculosis: isonicotinic acid hydrazide (isoniazid) and isonicotinic acid amide (pyrazinamide). These agents are highly specific for tuberculous infections; they are the most potent antimicrobial agents available against tuberculosis; they penetrate intracellularly and into all body fluids and act at all pH ranges; and they will reduce fever of tuberculous origin regularly after two to three weeks of therapy, providing some diagnostic value. Administered orally, they diffuse readily into the serous cavities, subarachnoid space, and cells. Isoniazid is the one in common use in children. It is rapidly absorbed, metabolized, and excreted within 12 hours. Certain individuals inactivate the drug much more rapidly and are called rapid inactivators. The proportion of these individuals is higher among certain peoples, such as the Japanese and Koreans. Although there is no evidence that rapid inactivation may affect adversely the outcome of therapy in children, it is suggested that for therapeutic purpose the daily dose of isoniazid be no less than 10 mg per kilogram. Toxic symptoms caused by isoniazid, described chiefly in aduts, are peripheral neuritis, hepatitis, psychosis, drowsiness in epileptics, increased reflexes, constipation, difficulty in starting micturition, positional hypotention, and dizziness; allergic reactions and mild gastrointestinal disturbances also have been described.

Significant neurotoxicity has not been encountered in children, and all other symptoms are rare. The doses and mode of administration appear in Table 12. In case of vomiting, the drug may be given intramuscularly in the same dosage. Isoniazid is tolerated well when given by the intrathecal route in doses of 25 mg daily, but this is seldom if ever necessary. Isoniazid is supplied in tablets of 50 or 100 mg or as a flavored syrup containing 10 mg per ml. The tablets can be crushed and mixed with any food or fluid. Preparations for parenteral or intrathecal use are available. The drug is stable at room temperature, and there are no known contraindications to its administration together with other medications. Pyrazinamide has strong antituberculous activity but is not recommended for general use because of hepatic toxicity. However, in critically ill patients with far advanced disease it may be helpful in addition to daily streptomycin in controlling progression of tuberculosis during the initial weeks of therapy.

Streptomycin, a compound derived from *Streptomyces griseus,* is highly active against the tubercle bacillus. Given intramuscularly it is readily absorbed into the bloodstream, diffusing into pleural and peritoneal fluids without difficulty, but not into thick-walled abscesses or empyema cavities. Passage from the blood into the cerebrospinal fluid is variable, increasing with the extent of meningeal inflammation. The drug is readily excreted in urine, 80 percent appearing within 24 hours; in the presence of renal impairment high blood levels may be encountered. Toxic manifestations consist of disturbances of vestibular function, eighth nerve deafness, paresthesias, local irritation, fever, vomiting, anaphylaxis, and a variety of skin eruptions, occasionally exfoliative dermatitis. Only streptomycin sulfate should be used, since dihydrostreptomycin is more likely to produce deafness. The drug should be given daily at the onset of therapy; its effectiveness when given twice a week has been questioned. Streptomycin should never be used alone in the therapy of tuberculosis.

Para-aminosalicylic acid (PAS) possesses bacteriostatic activity against the tubercle bacillus. It is valuable in preventing the emergence of drug resistance to streptomycin and isoniazid in cavitary tuberculosis.

The toxic manifestations caused by PAS are many. Some children tolerate it well, but many rebel because of gastrointestinal toxicity, especially after prolonged use. Other manifestations of toxicity include hepatic damage, rashes, anaphylaxis, hypoprothrombinemia, hypothyroidism, a picture similar to infectious mononucleosis, hemolytic anemia, and agranulocytosis. Patients sensitive to PAS may be desensitized by administering gradually increasing amounts until therapeutic doses are reached, but it is often better to discontinue the drug if intolerance is noted. This drug should not be used alone because of the development of bacterial resistance. It is supplied as a powder, granules, a syrup, or in 0.5 g tablets.

TABLE 13.   *Supplementary Steroid Therapy*

Indication	Drug	Dose	Duration
Severe endobronchial disease	Prednisone orally	Start prednisone with 3 mg/kg and decrease gradually to 1 mg/kg, begin tapering off to 0 at least 3 weeks before completion	8 weeks
Pleurisy with effusion with acute symptoms	Prednisone orally		4 to 6 weeks
Large pericardial effusions	Prednisone orally	Equivalent doses of other steroids may be used	4 to 6 weeks
Tuberculous meningitis:			
1. with neurologic signs	Prednisone orally		4 to 6 weeks
2. very ill, comatose or with severe block	Hydrocortisone iv or im to start steroid therapy or hydrocortisone by the intrathecal route	10 to 15 mg/kg 10 to 25 mg	Until initial improvement, then change to oral prednisone
3. critically ill, toxic patients with severe respiratory distress and extensive progressive pulmonary lesions or miliary tuberculosis	Prednisone orally or hydrocortisone iv, as above		6 to 8 weeks

A number of other antimicrobials have antituberculous activity and have been employed in cases resistant to streptomycin and isoniazid. Because of their toxicity, therapy with these antimicrobial agents should be attempted only in children with progressive disease due to bacilli resistant to isoniazid and streptomycin, as evidenced by in vitro tests and by clinical response. This situation is rare in pediatric practice and is likely to occur only in children with the adult type of cavitary pulmonary tuberculosis or in children who acquired their infection from an adult with resistant organisms. Three drugs are available for parenteral use which have an effectiveness that is comparable to that of streptomycin but greater toxicity: these are kanamycin, viomycin, and capreomycin. Each one of these three drugs can produce renal injury and eighth nerve damage. For use by the oral route in combination with one of the parenteral drugs, many other secondary drugs have been tested. Among these are ethioniamide, cycloserine (Oxamycin), pyrazinamide, TB-1, isoxyl, sulfisoxazole, and tetracyclines. Another drug, ethambutol, is now used commonly, in place of PAS with isoniazid. It appears to be equally effective and better tolerated. Its use requires periodic testing of visual acuity since loss of vision is an infrequent but serious toxic effect. Various combinations are being tested, using from two to four of these drugs in patients with bacilli resistant to isoniazid, streptomycin, and PAS. Favorite combinations have included kanamycin plus ethambutol or ethionamide and pyrazinamide or cycloserine. The use of these drugs requires detailed knowledge of their pharmacology, close observation of the patient, and adequate laboratory facilities. Although not yet approved for use in the United States, rifamycin has been widely used in other countries and appears to be a major antitubercous drug, comparable in activity to isoniazid.

Steroids and ACTH have been shown to diminish allergy to tuberculin and to cause striking temporary regression of some tuberculous lesions. In the absence of antimicrobial therapy, steroid hormones are definitely contraindicated in tuberculosis. However, they have been used as an adjuvant to antimicrobial therapy in meningitis, in endobronchial tuberculosis, in pleurisy with effusion, in cases of far advanced or miliary tuberculosis, and in tuberculous pericarditis. (See Table 13.) Under these circumstances the hormones have been well tolerated, and in some cases dramatically favorable results have been described.

The duration of antimicrobial therapy should not be less than one year. It should continue for at least 6 to 12 months after clinical stabilization has been established, as measured by failure to recover viable organisms and quiescence of roentgenologic and clinical findings. To prevent relapses in complicated primary lesions, long-term administration of isoniazid is probably more important than high daily dose. When unsatisfactory results are observed, particularly after a long course of therapy, a change to a different combination of drugs may be indicated and should be guided by bacteriologic examinations and susceptibility studies. This is rarely necessary in children, and most clinical manifestations interpreted as apparent worsening are due to nontuberculous disease, to the mechanical effect of endobronchial lesions, or to the need for drainage of enclosed abscesses. One should always hesitate to discontinue isoniazid in an apparently resistant case because, even when there is no obvious effect, isoniazid may be responsible for preventing dissemination. Such patients may not improve, but they do not become worse. In patients with cavitary lesions that persist after a year of therapy, surgical resection should be considered.

REFERENCES

ETIOLOGY

Dubos, R. J., and Hirsch, J. G. Bacterial and Mycotic Infections of Man, 4th ed. Philadelphia and Montreal, J. B. Lippincott Co., 1965.

Long, E. R. The Chemistry and Chemotherapy of Tuberculosis. Baltimore, The Williams and Wilkins Co., 1958.

EPIDEMIOLOGY

Beaven, P. W. Analysis of tuberculous infection from birth to old age; its relationship to clinical tuberculosis and deaths from tuberculosis. Dis. Chest., 17:280, 1950.

Davis, S., Finlay, S. C., and Hare, W. F. Congenital tuberculosis; report of a case. J. Pediat., 57:221, 1960.

Dearing, W. P., Olson, B. J., Self, L. R. W., and Bagget, M. W. Comparison of household attack rates in regions with high and low tuberculosis mortality. Nat. Tuberc. Ass. Trans., 37:316, 1941.

Doege, T. C. Tuberculosis mortality in the United States, 1900 to 1960. J.A.M.A., 102:103, 1965.

Heilman, K. M., and Muschenheim, C. Primary cutaneous tuberculosis resulting from mouth to mouth respiration. New Eng. J. Med., 273:1035, 1965.

Horwitz, O., and Palmer, C. E. Epidemiological basis of tuberculosis eradication. Dynamics of tuberculosis morbidity and mortality. Bull. W.H.O., 30:609, 1964.

Lincoln, E. M. Epidemics of tuberculosis. Advances Tuberc. Res., 14:157, 1965.

United States Department of Health, Education and Welfare, Public Health Service. The Future of Tuberculosis Control. Pub. No. 1119, Communicable Disease Center, Atlanta, Ga., 1963.

Wallgren, A. Le problème de la contagiosité de la tuberculose infantile. Rev. Franc. Pédiat., 12:717, 1936.

IMMUNITY AND RESISTANCE

Aisenberg, A. C. Immunologic aspects of Hodgkin's disease. Medicine, 43:189, 1964.

Boucot, K. R., Dillon, E. S., Cooper, D. A., Meier, P., and Richardson, R. Tuberculosis among diabetics; the Philadelphia survey. Amer. Rev. Tuberc., 65: No. 1 (Suppl.), 1952.

Dubos, R. J. Biochemical Determinants of Microbial Diseases. Cambridge, Mass., Harvard University Press, 1954.

Ferebee, S. H., and Palmer, C. E. The Epidemiologic Bonus. Editorial, Amer. Rev. Resp. Dis., 91:104, 1965.

Haroutunian, L. M., Fisher, A. M., and Smith, E. W. Tuberculosis and sarcoidosis. Bull. Johns Hopkins Hosp., 115:1, 1964.

Johnston, J. A. Nutritional Studies in Adolescent Girls and Their Relation to Tuberculosis. Springfield, Ill., Charles C Thomas, 1953.

Kallmann, F. J., and Reisner, D. Twin studies on genetic variations in resistance to tuberculosis. J. Hered., 34:269, 1943.

Lawrence, H. S. Some Biological and Immunological Properties of Transfer Factors. Ciba Foundation Symposium on Cellular Aspects of Immunity. Boston, Little, Brown & Co., 1960, p. 243.

Lincoln, E. M. The effect of antimicrobial therapy on the prognosis of primary tuberculosis in children. Amer. Rev. Tuberc., 69:682, 1954.

Lurie, M. B. Resistance to Tuberculosis. Experimental Studies in Native and Acquired Defensive Mechanisms. Cambridge, Mass., Harvard University Press, 1965.

Myers, J. A., Bearman, J. E., and Dixon, H. G. Natural history of tuberculosis in the human body. VIII. Prognosis among tuberculin reactor girls and boys of thirteen to seventeen years. Amer. Rev. Resp. Dis., 91:896, 1965.

Raffel, S. Immunity, 2nd ed. New York, Appleton-Century-Crofts, 1961.

Rich, A. R. The Pathogenesis of Tuberculosis, 2nd ed. Springfield, Ill., Charles C Thomas, 1951.

Sloan, R. D., Hanlon, C. R., and Scott, H. W., Jr. Tuberculosis and congenital cyanotic heart disease. Amer. J. Med., 16:528, 1954.

Strom, L. Vaccination against tuberculosis, clinical aspects. Amer. Rev. Tuberc., 74:No. 2 (Suppl.), p. 28, 1956.

Wallner, L., Thompson, J. R., and Lichtenstein, M. R. Clinical and histopathologic study of the effect of cortisone and corticotropin on tuberculosis. Amer. Rev. Tuberc., 66:161, 1952.

Weiss, W., and Stecher, W. Tuberculosis and sickle cell trait. Arch. Int. Med., 89:914, 1952.

PATHOGENESIS

Auerbach, O. Progressive primary complex. Amer. Rev. Tuberc., 37:346, 1938.

Canetti, G. Dynamic aspects of the pathology and bacteriology of tuberculous lesions. Amer. Rev. Tuberc., 74:No. 2 (Suppl.), 13, 1956.

Engel, S., and von Pirquet, C. Handbuch der Kindertuberkulose. Leipzig, G. Thieme, 1930.

Ghon, A. Primary complex in human tuberculosis and its significance. Amer. Rev. Tuberc., 7:314, 1923.

Lincoln, E. M., and Sewell, E. M. Tuberculosis in Children. New York, Toronto, London, McGraw-Hill Book Co., 1963.

Miller, F. J. W., Seal, R. M. E., and Taylor, M. D. Tuberculosis in Children. Boston, Little, Brown & Co., 1963.

Rich, A. R. The Pathogenesis of Tuberculosis, 2nd ed. Springfield, Ill., Charles C Thomas, 1951.

Wallgren, A. The time-table of tuberculosis. Tubercle, 29:245, 1948.

PULMONARY TUBERCULOSIS

Dressler, S. H., Anthony, E. M., Russell, W. F., Jr., Grow, J. B., Denst, J., Cohn, M. L., and Middlebrook, G. Ambulation of patients with pulmonary tuberculosis under protection of chemotherapy. Amer. Rev. Tuberc., 70:1030, 1954.

Gerbeaux, J., Baculard, A., and Couvreur, J. Primary tuberculosis in childhood. Amer. J. Dis. Child., 110:507, 1965.

Lincoln, E. M. Course and prognosis of tuberculosis in children. Amer. J. Med., 9:623, 1950.

—— and Adiao, A. C. Late discharge of tubercle bacilli in primary tuberculosis. Amer. Rev. Tuberc., 79: 31, 1959.

—— Davies, P. A., and Bovornkitti, S. Tuberculous pleurisy with effusion in children: a study of 202 children with particular reference to prognosis. Amer. Rev. Tuberc., 77:271, 1958.

—— Gilbert, L., and Morales, S. M. Chronic pulmonary tuberculosis in individuals with known previous primary tuberculosis. Dis. Chest., 38:473, 1960.

—— Harris, L. C., Bovornkitti, S., and Carretero, R. W. Endobronchial tuberculosis in children: a study of 156 patients. Amer. Rev. Tuberc., 77:39, 1958.

—— Sewell, E. M., and Anastasiades, A. A. The treatment of primary tuberculosis in children. Postgrad. Med., 16:422, 1954.

Lotte, A., Noufflard, H., Debré, R., and Brissaud, H. E. The treatment of primary tuberculosis in childhood. Pediatrics, 26:641, 1960.

Nestadt, A., and Harrison, I. Treatment of progressive primary tuberculosis with isoniazid alone. Lancet, 1: 1068, 1964.

Reisner, D. Incipiency and evolution of pulmonary tuberculosis. I. The initial manifestations of the disease. II. The behavior of the initial lesion and course of the disease during the observation period. Amer. Rev. Tuberc., 57:207, 229, 1948.

Sifontes, J. E., and Anastasiades, A. A. Primary tuberculosis in infants and young children; survey of a slum area in Puerto Rico. Amer. Rev. Tuberc., 76:388, 1957.

Wallgren, A. Primary pulmonary tuberculosis in childhood. Amer. J. Dis. Child., 49:1105, 1935.

HEMATOGENOUS DISSEMINATION

Debré, R., Brissaud, H. E., et al. Méningite Tuberculeuse et Tuberculose Miliaire de l'Enfant; Leur Traitement. Paris, Masson et Cie., 1953.

Heinle, E. W., Jr., Jensen, W. N., and Westerman, M. P. Diagnostic usefulness of marrow biopsy in disseminated tuberculosis. Amer. Rev. Resp. Dis., 91:701, 1965.

Leiner, C., and Spieler, F. Uber disseminierte Hauttuberkulosen im Kindesalter. Ergebn. Inn. Med. Kinderheilk., 7:59, 1911.

Lincoln, E. M. Hematogenous tuberculosis in children. Amer. J. Dis. Child., 50:84, 1935.

—— and Hould, F. Results of specific treatment of miliary tuberculosis in children; a follow-up study of 63 patients treated with antimicrobial agents. New Eng. J. Med., 261:113, 1959.

TUBERCULOUS MENINGITIS

Cheek, D. B. Further observations on electrolyte change in tuberculous meningitis; the ratio of the concentrations of bromide in serum and cerebrospinal fluid. Pediatrics, 18:218, 1956.

Lincoln, E. M. Tuberculous meningitis in children with special reference to serous meningitis. I. Tuberculous meningitis; II. Serous tuberculous meningitis. Amer. Rev. Tuberc., 56:75, 95, 1947.

—— and Sifontes, J. E. Tuberculous meningitis in children. Med. Clin. N. Amer., 37:345, 1953.

Lorber, J. The results of treatment of 549 cases of tuberculous meningitis. Amer. Rev. Tuberc., 69:13, 1954.

Sifontes, J. E., Sordillo, S. V. R., and Lincoln, E. M. Pneumoencephalography in tuberculous meningitis. J. Pediat., 50:695, 1957.

—— Williams, R. D., Lincoln, E. M., and Clemens, H. Observations on the effect of induced hyperglycemia on the glucose content of the cerebrospinal fluid in patients with tuberculous meningitis. Amer. Rev. Tuberc., 67:732, 1953.

Wasz-Hockert, O., Donner, M., Miettinen, P., Ranta, J., Pentti, R., Valanne, E., Kauthtio, J., and Heikel, P. Late prognosis in tuberculous meningitis. Acta Paediat., 51:Suppl. 141, 1962.

TUBERCULOSIS OF BONES AND JOINTS

Chofnas, I., Surrett, N. E., and Severn, H. D. Pott's disease treated without spinal fusion. Amer. Rev. Resp. Dis., 90:888, 1964.

Kaplan, C. J. Conservative therapy in skeletal tuberculosis; an appraisal based on experience in South Africa. Tubercle, 40:355, 1959.

Lack, C. H. Complications of skeletal tuberculosis and its treatment. Amer. Rev. Tuberc., 74:No. 2 (Suppl.), 124, 1956.

Milgram, L. Skeletal tuberculosis in children treated for primary and miliary tuberculosis. Amer. Rev. Tuberc., 75:897, 1957.

Sifontes, J. E., and Díaz de Garau, P. Skeletal tuberculosis in infants and children. Bol. Asoc. Méd. P. Rico, 57:392, 1965.

TUBERCULOSIS OF SKIN

Lincoln, E. M., Alterman, J., and Bakst, H. Erythema nodosum in children. J. Pediat., 25:311, 1944.

Miller, F. J. W., Seal, R. M. E., and Taylor, M. D. Tuberculosis in Children. Boston, Little, Brown & Co., 1963.

Platou, R. V., and Lennox, R. H. Tuberculous cutaneous complexes in children. Amer. Rev. Tuberc., 74:No. 2 (Suppl.), 160, 1956.

Valledor, T., et al. Tuberculosis primaria de la piel en la infancia. Rev. Cuba. Pediat., 26:147, 1954.

TUBERCULOSIS OF SUPERFICIAL LYMPH NODES

Anastasiades, A. A., Tsikoudas, E. C., Lincoln, E. M., and Daly, J. F. Tuberculosis of the superficial lymph nodes in children; a review with a report of experience of enzymatic debridement. Amer. Rev. Tuberc., 76: 588, 1957.

Davis, S. D., and Comstock, G. W. Mycobacterial cervical adenitis in children. J. Pediat., 58:771, 1961.

Harris, L. C. Generalized tuberculous adenitis in Bantu children in South Africa. Pediatrics, 23:935, 1959.

Lester, C. W., and Jones, J. M. Lymph node tuberculosis in neck, axilla and groin. Amer. Rev. Tuberc., 73:229, 1956.

TUBERCULOSIS OF EYES, EARS, AND THROAT

Long, E. R., Seibert, M. V., and González, L. M. Tuberculosis of the tonsils. Arch. Int. Med., 63:609, 1939.

Massaro, D., Katz, S., and Sachs, M. Choroidal tubercles. Ann. Int. Med., 60:231, 1964.

Philip, R. N., and Comstock, G. W. Phlyctenular keratoconjunctivitis among Eskimos in Southwestern Alaska. II. Isoniazid prophylaxis. Amer. Rev. Resp. Dis., 91: 188, 1965.

Wallner, L. J. Tuberculous otitis media. Laryngoscope, 63:1058, 1953.

ABDOMINAL TUBERCULOSIS

Alvarez-Pagán, M., and Sifontes, J. E. Abdominal tuberculosis in children. Bol. Asoc. Méd. P. Rico, 57:118, 1965.

Marina-Fiol, C. Aspectos actuales de la tuberculosis intestinal. Rev. Esp. Enferm. Apar. Dig., 19:12, 1960.

Okel, B. B., and McLean, R. L. Tuberculous peritonitis in the chemotherapy era. Southern Med. J., 55:156, 1962.

Wallis, H. R. E. Tuberculous mesenteric adenitis in children. Brit. Med. J., 1:128, 1955.

TUBERCULOSIS OF URINARY TRACT

American Thoracic Society, Committee on Therapy, Subcommitte on Surgery. The present status of genitourinary tuberculosis. Amer. Rev. Resp. Dis., 92:505, 1965.

Kaufman, J. J., and Goodwin, W. E. Renal hypertension secondary to renal tuberculosis. Report of cure in four patients treated by nephrectomy. Amer. J. Med., 38: 337, 1965.

Lattimer, J. K., and Boyes, T. Renal tuberculosis in children. Pediatrics, 22:1193, 1958.

Vázquez, G., and Lattimer, J. K. Danger to children of infection from exposure to urine containing tubercle bacilli. J.A.M.A., 171:29, 1959.

TUBERCULOSIS OF HEART AND PERICARDIUM

Boyd, G. L. Tuberculous pericarditis in children. Amer. J. Dis. Child., 86:293, 1953.

Hageman, J. H., D'Esopo, N. D., and Glenn, W. W. L. Tuberculosis of the pericardium. New Eng. J. Med., 270:327, 1964.

Platou, R. V. Clinically manifest tuberculous pericarditis; report of a case with observations on circulatory changes. Amer. J. Dis. Child., 57:1386, 1939.

DIAGNOSIS OF TUBERCULOSIS

Brody, J., Overfield, J., and Hammes, L. M. Depression of the tuberculin reaction by viral vaccines. New Eng. J. Med., 271:1294, 1964.

Committee on Epidemiology. The WHO Standard Tuberculin Test. Complementary Document I. Bull. Int. Un. Tuberc., 32:88, 1962.

Diagnostic Standards and Classification of Tuberculosis. National Tuberculosis Association, New York, 1961.

Edwards, P. Q., and Edwards, L. B. Story of the tuberculin test from an epidemiologic viewpoint. Amer. Rev. Resp. Dis., 81:No. 1 (Suppl.), 1960.

Handbook of Tuberculosis Laboratory Methods. Veterans Administration. Washington, D.C., 1962.

Lincoln, E. M., and Grethmann, W. The potential dangers of tuberculin tests. J. Pediat., 15:682, 1939.

Nagaya, H., and Sieker, H. O. Histochemical study of amino-peptidase and acid and alkaline phosphatase in the tuberculin reaction. Amer. Rev. Resp. Dis., 91:245, 1965.

Palmer, C. E., Edwards, L. B., Hopwood, L., and Edwards, P. Q. Experimental and epidemiologic basis for the interpretation of tuberculin sensitivity. J. Pediat., 55:413, 1959.

Robins, A. B., and Daly, J. N. Evaluation of the Heaf tuberculin test. New Eng. J. Med., 262:1008, 1960.

Seibert, F. B., and Dufour, E. H. Comparison between the international standard tuberculins, PPD-S and old tuberculin. Amer. Rev. Tuberc., 69:585, 1954.

Thorne, M. The tuberculin tine test compared to the Mantoux test with 5, 10 and 100 tuberculin units. Pediatrics, 36:385, 1965.

U.S. Department of Health, Education, and Welfare, Public Health Service. A Child Centered Program to Prevent Tuberculosis, P.H.S. Publ. No. 1280, Washington, D.C., U.S. Government Printing Office, 1965.

Wijsmuller, G. Naturally Acquired Tuberculin Sensitivity in New Guinea. Problems related to the interpretation of the Mantoux test in countries where more than one cause of tuberculin sensitivity prevails. Amsterdam, N. V. T. Koggeschip, 1963.

Zitrin, C. M. The C-reactive protein in childhood tuberculosis. Amer. Rev. Resp. Dis., 81:266, 1960.

———— Lincoln, E. M., Carretero, R., and Melly, E. Serum proteins in childhood tuberculosis. Amer. J. Dis. Child., 98:330, 1959.

PREVENTION OF TUBERCULOSIS

Blattner, R. J. Generalized BCG infection. Comments on current literature. J. Pediat., 65:311, 1964.

Comstock, G. W. Isoniazid prophylaxis in an undeveloped area. Amer. Rev. Resp. Dis., 86:810, 1962.

Ferebee, S. H., and Mount, F. W. Tuberculosis morbidity in a controlled trial of the prophylactic use of isoniazid among household contacts. Amer. Rev. Resp. Dis., 85:490, 1962.

Lincoln, E. M. Eradication of tuberculosis in children. Arch. Environ. Health, 3:444, 1961.

Mount, F. W., and Ferebee, S. H. Preventive effects of isoniazid in the treatment of primary tuberculosis in children. New Eng. J. Med., 265:713, 1961.

Palmer, C. E. BCG in the USA. Southern Med. J., 54: 52, 1966.

Rodríguez Pastor, J. Ambulatory treatment in tuberculosis control. The experience of Puerto Rico. Dis. Chest, 40:134, 1961.

Special Panel of Public Health and Tuberculosis Specialists. Public health service recommendations on the use of BCG vaccination in the United States. Communicable Disease Center Morbidity and Mortality Weekly Report, 15:350, 1966.

United States Public Health Service Cooperative Investigation. Prevalence of drug resistance in previously untreated patients. Amer. Rev. Resp. Dis., 89:327, 1964.

TREATMENT

American Thoracic Society. Preventive treatment in tuberculosis. A statement by the Committee on Therapy. Amer. Rev. Resp. Dis., 91:297, 1965.

———— Untoward reactions to drugs used in initial chemotherapy of cavitary tuberculosis. A statement by the Committee on Therapy. Amer. Rev. Resp. Dis., 91: 293, 1965.

Editorial. Rifamycin. New hope in the fight against tuberculosis. New Eng. J. Med., 283:655, 1970.

Lincoln, E. M., and Sewell, E. M. Tuberculosis in Children. New York, McGraw-Hill Book Co., 1963.

—— and Vera-Cruz, P. G. Progress in treatment of tuberculosis: results of antimicrobial therapy in a group of 420 children with tuberculosis. Pediatrics, 25: 1035, 1960.

Lorber, J. Isoniazid and streptomycin in tuberculous meningitis. Lancet, 1:1149, 1954.

McDermott, W. Antimicrobial therapy of pulmonary tuberculosis. Bull. W.H.O., 23:427, 1960.

Morales, S. M., and Lincoln, E. M. The effect of isoniazid therapy on pyridoxine metabolism in children. Amer. Rev. Tuberc., 75:594, 1957.

Munroe, W. D., Lawson, W., and Holcomb, T. M. Hemolytic anemia due to aminosalicylic acid. Amer. J. Dis. Child., 108:425, 1964.

Newman, R., Doster, B., Murray, F. J., and Ferebee, S. Rifamycin in initial treatment of pulmonary tuberculosis. Amer. Rev. Resp. Dis., 103:461, 1971.

Sifontes, J. E. The management of special problems in the chemotherapy of tuberculosis in infants and children. Amer. Rev. Tuberc., 74:No. 2 (Suppl.), 225, 1956.

Steiner, M., and Cosio, A. Primary tuberculosis in children. Incidence of primary drug-resistant disease in 332 children observed between the years 1961 and 1964 at the Kings County Medical Center of Brooklyn. New Eng. J. Med., 274:755, 1966.

14.21

DISEASES CAUSED BY OTHER MYCOBACTERIA

EMANUEL WOLINSKY

From 1 to 5 percent of cases of granulomatous disease, apparently tuberculous in origin, are caused by mycobacteria other than mammalian tubercle bacilli. In adults the commonest manifestation of such infections is chronic pulmonary disease, but in children they usually involve the cervical lymph nodes and the skin. Isolated instances of disseminated or pulmonary disease in children have been reported, but they are very rare.

BACTERIOLOGY. *Mycobacterium tuberculosis* and *M. bovis* are known as mammalian tubercle bacilli. The other mycobacteria associated with disease in man are:

M. leprae. The agent of leprosy.

M. avium (the avian tubercle bacillus). Very rarely causes diseases in man. There is only one report of avian tuberculosis in a child.

M. kansasii. These are slow-growing organisms that demonstrate a yellow pigment only after exposure to light. This species causes much of the adult human mycobacterial disease not due to mammalian tubercle bacilli throughout the world. It is not found commonly in the soil or water.

M. marinum (also known as *M. balnei*). Causes a tuberculosislike disease in fish and a chronic skin infection in man known as swimming pool granuloma. The organisms grow best at 30 to 33° C and are pigmented yellow only after light exposure.

M. ulcerans. The cause of severe ulceration of the skin so far limited to adults and children in Australia and Africa. The bacilli grow very slowly and only at 32 to 33° C.

M. intracellulare (Battery bacilli). These are slow-growing, essentially nonpigmented bacilli resembling *M. avium.* They are the major cause of nontuberculous mycobacterial disease of adults in the southeastern states, Australia, Japan, and other parts of the world, and are commonly found in the soil.

Scotochromogenic bacilli. These produce smooth, yellow-orange colonies and are commonly found in soil and water. They are very rarely associated with adult pulmonary disease but are the commonest agents of granulomatous adenitis in children. The organisms associated with disease are now called *M. scrofulaceum;* those found in nature but usually not associated with disease are called "saprophytic" or "tap-water" subgroup.

M. fortuitum. This is a fast-growing species, readily found in soil and dust, which rarely causes disease in man. It has been implicated in injection site abscesses, chronic pulmonary disease, and lymphadenitis.

CLINICAL CONSIDERATIONS. Lymphadenitis is the most common childhood disease associated with these mycobacteria. In most areas of the United States at the present time, granulomatous adenitis in a child is more likely to be due to infection with other mycobacteria than with *M. tuberculosis.* The involved nodes are usually submandibular and unilateral, although they may be seen in other locations such as the femoral, inguinal, epitrochlear, and mediastinal regions. Systemic indications of infection are usually lacking. The nodes tend to soften and break down more rapidly than tuberculous nodes, and once drainage starts it usually continues for many months despite chemotherapy. The disease has been described in children ranging in age from 10 months to 13 years, but it is most often seen in the preschool period.

There is usually no history of tuberculosis in the family and no evidence of the disease elsewhere in the body. The chest x-ray is negative. The tuberculin skin test is likely to be mildly positive because of cross-sensitivity, but the reaction to tuberculin derived from the homologous organism is usually greater than the reaction to standard tuberculin. The histologic appearance of the diseased tissue is the same as that seen in ordinary tuberculosis.

The etiologic agent in the majority of cases is a *M. scrofulaceum.* In certain areas, especially in Texas, *M. kansasii* may occasionally be cultured from the nodes. *M. intracellulare* or *M. fortuitum* may rarely be the cause.

The treatment of choice is complete excision. Should the node be too large and fluctuant when first seen, incision and drainage may be done until the lesion is small enough to be excised. Chemotherapy is of questionable benefit, since most of the strains are quite resistant to available drugs. Complete healing usually occurs, and relapse is rare.

According to our present knowledge the infection is not communicable, and these children do not need to be isolated or labeled as "tuberculous." It is important that childhood diseases associated with these mycobacteria be distinguished from ordinary tuberculosis so that the children are not subjected to unnecessary, prolonged courses of drugs and to the ostracism of self and family that accompanies the diagnosis of tuberculosis. Since the skin reaction to tuberculin may persist for many years even after excision of the involved nodes, this disease probably accounts for many of the false-positive skin reactions in patients who do not have tuberculosis. One should avoid the inclusion of these children in prophylactic chemotherapy programs as recent tuberculin converters or preschoolers with positive reactions.

The most definitive procedure for establishing the diagnosis is the recovery and identification of mycobacteria from cultures of material obtained by aspiration or drainage of the node. Guinea pig inoculation is not significant if negative because none of the strains is virulent for this animal. Results of comparative skin test reactions using several mycobacterial antigens are very helpful. Strong suspicion of the correct diagnosis should be stimulated by the unilateral submandibular location, lack of disease elsewhere, negative chest x-ray, lack of exposure to tuberculosis, lack of response to penicillin or to antituberculosis drugs, and weak skin test reaction to standard tuberculin.

Swimming pool granuloma is a benign self-limited skin disease consisting of ulcerating papules usually at the sites of minor abrasions received while swimming in contaminated pools. The causative organisms, *M. marinum* (also known as *M. balnei*), may be cultured from the skin and from the water in the pool. The lesions appear 2 to 3 weeks after infection and usually heal slowly after several months, leaving a scar. A large outbreak of this disease involving about 300 people, many of them children, occurred in Colorado in 1959. *M. marinum* is relatively resistant to isoniazid and aminosalicylic acid. The infection usually results in a long-lasting skin hypersensitivity to standard tuberculin.

A few cases of fatal disseminated mycobacterial disease in children have been reported; these infections were caused by Battey bacilli, scotochromogens, or *M. kansasii*. In addition, there have been a few reports of pulmonary disease in children in which *M. kansasii* seemed to be playing a role, but the significance of their isolation was not clear-cut.

For disseminated disease or severe disease other than accessible lymphadenitis, drug treatment may be attempted based on the identity of the infecting organism and its in vitro drug sensitivity pattern. *M. kansasii* will usually respond to an intensive triple-drug regimen of isoniazid, streptomycin, and either cycloserine or ethambutol, each administered daily. For the more drug-resistant mycobacteria, it may be necessary to resort to a four-drug regimen adding either ethionamide, kanamycin, or capreomycin.

REFERENCES

Bialkin, G., Pollak, A., and Weil, A. J. Pulmonary infection with *Mycobacterium kansasii*. Amer. J. Dis. Child., 101:739, 1961.

Black, B. G., and Chapman, J. S. Cervical adenitis in children due to human and unclassified mycobacteria. Pediatrics, 33:887, 1964.

Davis, S. D., and Comstock, G. W. Mycobacterial cervical adenitis in children. J. Pediat., 58:771, 1961.

Kendig, E. L., Jr. Unclassified mycobacteria in children. Amer. J. Dis. Child., 101:749, 1961.

Krieger, I., Hahne, O. H., and Whitten, C. F. Atypical mycobacteria as a probable cause of chronic bone disease. J. Pediat., 65:340, 1964.

Mollohan, C. S., and Romer, M. S. Public health significance of swimming pool granuloma. Amer. J. Pub. Health, 51:883, 1961.

Runyon, E. H. Advances in Tuberculosis Research. Basel, New York, Karger, 1965, Vol. 14, pp. 235-287.

Smith, D. H., Doherty, R. A., and DeLemos, R. A. Unclassified mycobacterial infection and disease in children residing in Massachusetts. J. Pediat., 67:759, 1965.

Yakovac, W. C., Baker, R., Sweigert, C., and Hope, J. W. Fatal disseminated osteomyelitis due to an anonymous mycobacterium. J. Pediat., 59:909, 1961.

14.22
TULAREMIA
(RABBIT FEVER; DEER FLY FEVER)

HATTIE E. ALEXANDER

Tularemia is an infectious disease caused by *Pasteurella tularensis* (*Bacterium tularense*). Primarily it is a septicemia of rodents, especially of wild rabbits and hares. Secondarily it is a disease of man, transmitted by handling infectious material or by the bite of an insect or infected animal. Direct transmission from man to man is not known. Although handling of wild rabbits is by far the most common source of infection, the disease has been acquired from many animals, including deer, foxes, coyotes, woodchucks, sheep, skunks, squirrels, opossums, and water rats, as well as from cats and dogs which have presumably preyed on infected wild animals. Many cases are caused by insect vectors, which include the deer fly, horse fly, wood tick, and bedbug, in addition to certain fleas and lice. Certain species of ticks are important reservoirs as well as vectors of tularemia in man, particularly the Rocky Mountain and Western wood ticks and the common Eastern dog tick. Transovarial transmission within these vectors is an efficient system for preservation of the parasite. A waterborne epidemic occurred in Russia from contamination of a brook by infected water rats. Tularemia is found in all parts of the United States, most frequently in those regions where it has been carefully searched for. It affects children less frequently than adults, for they have less opportunity of acquiring the disease, but it has been reported even in infants.

The organism is small, pleomorphic, gram-negative, nonmotile, and nonsporebearing, growing best at reduced oxygen tension. It seems able to penetrate the intact skin. Bacteremia is usually present in the first week after infection, seldom thereafter. Even from suppurating lesions, organisms cannot be readily stained or cultivated directly; they are recovered more easily after passage through a guinea pig. An attack conveys immunity.

Focal lesions are found usually in the lymph nodes draining the portal of entry, sometimes in the primary ulcer or as a chain of subcutaneous nodules connecting the primary focus with regional nodes. As a result of the initial bacteremia visceral lesions may occur in spleen, liver, lungs, bone marrow, and elsewhere. Histologically, the typical lesion is characterized by dense infiltration with mononuclear wandering cells, mainly macrophages; polymorphonuclear leucocytes are scarce. Foci of necrosis evoke a surrounding epithelioid reaction not unlike that seen in tuberculosis. Under experimental conditions *Past. tularensis* has been shown by Buddingh and Womack to multiply within body cells, an observation which may have important therapeutic implications.

The average incubation period is 3 to 4 days, but it may vary from 1 to 10 days. Five chief clinical types are recognized: the ulceroglandular, pharyngotonsillar, oculoglandular, glandular, and typhoid. In the first three the portal of entry is apparent. In most cases, particularly in severe ones, the onset is sudden with headache, bodily pains, vomiting, malaise, or prostration, chills, and fever. In the ulceroglandular and oculoglandular types there is local pain and tenderness with swelling of the regional lymph nodes, although at first nothing may be noticeable at the site of entry. A day or so later a papule may form at the portal of entry and undergo necrosis and ulceration. Redness and sometimes lymphatic injection appears over the glands, and in about half the cases suppuration ensues; in others there is a slow subsidence of swelling and induration over a period of two or three months. The ocular lesion is usually in the conjunctiva and seldom produces permanent damage to the eye. The pharyngotonsillar type at first resembles acute follicular tonsillitis in both its local and general aspects; later, a shaggy, necrotic exudate appears on the pharyngeal lesion, and the adjacent lymph nodes of the cervical chain may become greatly enlarged. In the glandular type the picture is the same except for the absence of evidence

of the portal of entry. The typhoid type shows only systemic symptoms, with no localizing signs whatever. The fever usually rises to a peak during the first two or three days and may be sustained or may be followed by a temporary remission of a day or two with a secondary rise. The usual course is two or three weeks, terminating by a slow lysis, but it may be somewhat longer; low-grade febrile recurrences may continue for several months. A maculopapular or pustular eruption may appear at any time after the first few days in some part of the body, not necessarily near the primary lesion, but is usually of brief duration. Sometimes there is a moderate leucocytosis. Convalescence is slow and is often accompanied by persistence of the glandular swelling or of discharges from broken-down nodes. It may be months before the process subsides entirely.

The manifestations of the disease are by no means confined to those described. The portal of entry may be anywhere on the surface of the body, even on the genitalia. Archer et al. found roentgenologic evidence of pulmonary involvement in the majority of cases, although relatively few showed symptoms. The disease may, however, produce chronic bronchitis, bronchopneumonia, and pleural effusion. Abdominal manifestations resembling those of tuberculous peritonitis are sometimes seen. Tularemic meningitis and encephalitis have been responsible for a number of deaths, and pericarditis has been reported. In general, the case fatality rate is low, between 3 and 5 percent, most of the deaths having been in adults. Ingestion of infectious material, however, is associated with a considerably higher risk, approximately 60 percent of the cases so far recorded having proved fatal; the deaths have generally occurred during the second or third week of the disease, and there has usually been extensive visceral involvement.

The diagnosis is not difficult if there is a history of contact with wild rabbits, but such information is not likely to be volunteered and is usually brought out only on questioning, after the disease is suspected. Tularemia should be considered in every case of obscure fever, particularly if there is glandular enlargement, and a history of contact with wild animals or evidence of insect bites should be sought. Such evidence is not always forthcoming. In one case seen in Baltimore the only contact that could be discovered was the family cat, which had been fondled by the patient and was known to have killed rabbits. Among diseases to be considered in differential diagnosis in the septicemic form are typhoid fever, undulant fever, rat-bite fever, and leptospirosis; primary tuberculous infection, rickettsialpox, and cat scratch disease in the ulceroglandular form; streptococcal pharyngitis, infectious mononucleosis, or diphtheria in the pharyngotonsillar form.

Tularemia can often be suspected on clinical grounds, but the diagnosis must be established by laboratory procedures, among which the agglutination reaction has the advantage of technical simplicity. During the second week of the disease agglutinins make their appearance in dilutions higher than 1:10, and the titer rises steadily, reaching a maximum between the fourth and seventh weeks, at which time it may be 1:1,000 or even higher. The titer gradually diminishes in the course of a year but usually persists in appreciable degree for many years after recovery. It is always desirable to test for brucella agglutinins as well as for those against *Past. tularensis* since there is considerable cross-reaction with either of these infections. The agglutinin titer is always higher toward the organism causing the infection.

Early in the course of the infection, before the agglutination test can yield diagnostic information, it is important to culture the blood in order to identify the infecting organism and thus permit effective treatment. Special media are required—for example, blood glucose cystine agar. Inoculation of guinea pigs is also of help.

Streptomycin, aureomycin, and chloramphenicol have all been shown to be effective in vitro against *Past. tularensis*. In experimental mouse tularemia, comparison of these three agents showed a clear superiority of streptomycin and aureomycin over chloramphenicol. These results, although not considered to provide a basis for valid therapeutic comparison in humans, delayed the clinical trial of chloramphenicol. Subsequent trial by Parker and others in a small group of patients has shown chloramphenicol to be equal in its efficacy to streptomycin and to aureomycin, each of which has been found highly effective in human infection. Selection of therapeutic agents will be influenced by the knowledge that the intracellular phase of the infection is an important one. Streptomycin, the most rapidly bactericidal agent of this group, is known not to enter cells in adequate concentration. Indirect evidence suggests that chloramphenicol does enter cells with greater ease. The combined action of streptomycin and chloramphenicol may prove to be the treatment of choice.

The following instance, observed in Baltimore, is of interest because three children in the same family were affected, each with a different type of the disease. A girl of 14 skinned and dressed a rabbit, and was probably assisted in this operation by a younger sister of 6 and brother of 4 who were present at the time. The three children slept in the same bed. The animal was cooked and eaten by the entire family. Two days later the eldest of the three developed headache, vomiting, and fever. Forty-eight hours later an "infected blister" was noted at the base of the thumb, and an axillary node on the same side became enlarged and tender. The blister was incised and pus obtained. The fever continued for 5½ weeks,

the local lesion healing slowly. The serum agglutinated *Past. tularensis* in a dilution of 1:1,280 on the twentieth day of the disease. An axillary node on the side of the lesion broke down during the sixth week.

The second patient, the younger brother of 4, was taken sick with fever and malaise 3 days after the rabbit skinning. He was later noted to have glandular enlargement and a palpable spleen, but no external lesions developed. His serum agglutinated *Past. tularensis* in a dilution of 1:320 on the eighteenth day. The fever was continuous for 3 weeks with irregular flare-ups for several weeks following. The patient remained ill for approximately 2 months. An x-ray of the chest taken 2½ months after the onset showed root infiltration and enlarged mediastinal glands; the tuberculin test at this time was negative to 1.0 mg.

The third patient, the sister of 6 years, was taken sick after an incubation period of 5 days with fever, malaise, and an inflamed eye with a watery discharge. The ocular inflammation reached its height in one week, subsiding gradually, but several small ulcers were still present on the lower lid at the end of 3 weeks. The submaxillary and preauricular nodes both suppurated, yielding sterile pus. A positive agglutination test was obtained in a dilution of 1:160 on the seventeenth day; during the sixth week the titer reached 1:640. The fever was continuous for 4½ weeks and intermittent for another 4 weeks.

REFERENCES

Archer, V. W., Blackford, S. D., and Wissler, J. E. Pulmonary manifestations in human tularemia; a roentgenologic study based on thirty-four unselected cases. J.A.M.A., 104:895, 1935.

Buddingh, G. J., and Womack, F. C., Jr. Observations on the infection of chick embryos with Bacterium tularense, Brucella, and Pasteurella pestis. J. Exp. Med., 74:213, 1941.

Daniel, W. A., Jr. Tularemia in infancy, with report of a case. J. Pediat., 24:326, 1944.

Francis, E. Tularemia. *In* Brennemann's Practice of Pediatrics. Hagerstown, Md., W. F. Prior Co., 1948, Vol. 2, Chap. 29.

Levy, H. B., Webb, C. H., and Wilkinson, J. D. Tularemia as a pediatric problem. Pediatrics, 6:113, 1950.

Parker, R. T., Lister, L. M., Bauer, R. E., Hall, H. E., and Woodward, T. E. Use of chloramphenicol (chloromycetin) in experimental and human tularemia. J.A.M.A., 143:7, 1950.

Waddell, W. W., Jr., and Birdsong, M. Tularemia with local lesions confined to the tonsils; a case report. J. Pediat., 20:368, 1942.

Young, L. S., et al. Tularemia Epidemic in Vermont 1968. New Eng. J. Med., 280:253, 1969.

Viral Diseases

14.23
SELECTIVE INHIBITION OF VIRAL REPLICATON

IGOR TAMM

While the last 25 years have seen great strides in the chemotherapy of diseases caused by bacteria, rickettsiae, and lymphogranuloma-psittacosis agents, relatively little progress has been made in the treatment of viral diseases. There are fundamental reasons for this. Microorganisms offer many more possibilities for selective inhibition of their multiplication than do viruses. For example, one of the distinguishing characteristics of many bacteria and related microorganisms is that they possess a muramic acid-containing cell wall. This structure, which is the site of action of a number of effective antimicrobial agents, is lacking in viruses. Also, certain microorganisms have a protein-synthesizing mechanism which is specifically sensitive to certain antibiotics. Viruses do not possess a protein-synthesizing mechanism of their own; instead they utilize the cellular machinery for protein synthesis, and any agent which stops viral protein synthesis by interfering with the synthesis of amino acids or with their incorporation in peptide chains will by the same action have a deleterious effect on the cell itself.

Viral Structure

Viruses are made up of the same small-molecular building blocks as the cells of their animal hosts, but the macromolecular components of viruses—their nucleic acids and proteins—possess a fine structure which is specific for the various viruses. The minimal chemical structure of a virus consists of nucleic acid (RNA or DNA) and a protein coat. The nucleic acid is usually present as a single large molecule, whereas the protein molecules are present in the form of repeating units. The complement of nucleic acid per viral particle varies from 2×10^6 molecular weight units (daltons) of RNA in poliovirus to 160×10^6 daltons of DNA in vaccinia virus. The estimated size of viral proteins ranges generally from 25,000 to 60,000 daltons. The specificity of viral nucleic acid and proteins resides in the sequence of the small-molecular building blocks, the nucleotides and the amino acids. The three-dimensional configuration of virus-specific macromolecules is fundamentally determined by the sequence of the small-molecular components, but metals, certain peptides, and other factors may also have a role.

One of the striking developments in virology has been the recognition that viruses fall into major groups on the basis of their fundamental physical and chemical properties. It is therefore not surprising that a number of the selective inhibitors of viral multiplication show group specificity in their action. Inhibitors whose effectiveness depends largely on biologic circumstances rather than on virus-specific features of the viral target may inhibit viruses in different major groups.

Targets for Selective Inhibitors

To infect a cell a virus needs to attach to the cell membrane, penetrate the cell, and release its nucleic acid into a proper compartment of the cell. Once released, the viral nucleic acid proceeds to express its potentialities of self-reduplication and of directing synthesis of new proteins. In the case of viruses with double-helical nucleic acid, there is first made a single-stranded messenger RNA which then acts as a template in viral protein synthesis. In viruses with a single-stranded RNA the viral RNA itself can act as a messenger in viral protein synthesis.

It is theoretically possible to visualize specific inhibition of viral replication at each of the several steps in the viral growth cycle if the assumption is made that there exist substances which can recognize and combine with specific reactive sites on virus-directed macromolecules. Virus-specific macromolecules fall into two categories, the viral structural components and the nonstructural virus-directed macromolecules, such as enzymes which catalyze the synthesis of viral nucleic acid.

Chemical knowledge is as yet insufficient to allow a deliberate and planned approach to the synthesis of selective inhibitors of viral multiplication. It is, however, encouraging that in recent years a number of selective inhibitors have been discovered. This has come about through research which has been essentially empirical though often guided by enlightened guesses. Studies of the mechanisms of action of these inhibitors have shown that the synthesis of virus-specific macromolecules can be inhibited without at the same time interfering with the synthesis of cellular macromolecules.

Inhibition of Virus Adsorption and Penetration

EFFECTS OF LARGE-MOLECULAR SUBSTANCES. Viral infectivity can be neutralized by several different kinds of large-molecular substances of biologic origin, which form specific complexes with the viral particle. The best known are the specific antibodies whose role in immunity to viruses is well established. Passively administered antibodies are capable of modifying certain viral infections if given sufficiently early in the infection. A number of mucoproteins present in serum and other biologic fluids are also capable of neutralizing some viruses, but their role in immunity is not clear, and there have been no reports of clinical successes in prevention or modification of viral diseases with such mucoproteins.

INHIBITION OF INFLUENZA VIRUSES BY 1-ADAMANTANAMINE. Recently a small-molecular chemical compound has been shown to inhibit an early step in the infection of cells with certain myxoviruses, such as influenza type A viruses. Myxoviruses are RNA-containing medium-sized viruses which possess a lipid-containing viral envelope covered with projections. The nucleic acid with its associated protein forms a single-stranded helical structure—the internal component of the virus. 1-Adamantanamine does not cause inactivation of myxovirus particles, and it does not interfere with the adsorption of virus to cells. The results so far reported indicate that 1-adamantanamine interferes with an early step in virus-cell interaction, but whether this step involves the penetration of the virus or uncoating of the viral particle is not clear. Not all myxoviruses are sensitive to 1-adamantanamine.

1-Adamantanamine has shown protective effects in experimental animals and in man infected with influenza A-2 virus. It represents an important approach to selective inhibition of viral multiplication.

Inhibition of Virus-Directed Biosynthesis

Certain benzimidazole derivatives and guanidine inhibit virus-directed biosynthesis in cells infected with the smallest RNA animal viruses, the picornaviruses. Isatin β-thiosemicarbazone and certain of its derivatives inhibit the synthesis of a number of virus-directed proteins in cells infected with the largest DNA animal viruses, the poxviruses. We have a clearer understanding of the mechanism of action of these chemical inhibitors of viral biosynthesis than of any of the other virus inhibitors.

INHIBITION OF PICORNAVIRUSES BY BENZIMIDAZOLE DERIVATIVES AND GUANIDINE. Picornaviruses are small lipid-free RNA-containing viruses. Over 100 immunologic types are known, which fall into two main subgroups, the enteroviruses and the rhinoviruses. The enteroviruses include polioviruses, Coxsackie viruses, and ECHO viruses. The rhinoviruses constitute a large subgroup of common cold viruses. In cells infected with picornaviruses there appears a new ribonucleic acid polymerase which catalyzes the synthesis of viral RNA. The formation of such a virus-directed enzyme in the infected cell clearly provides an approach to selective inhibition of viral replication. Even before the demonstration of the viral RNA polymerase in picornavirus-infected cells, it was discovered that 2-(α-hydroxybenzyl)-benzimidazole (HBB) and guanidine hydrochloride selectively inhibit the replication of many picornaviruses. The action of HBB and guanidine is selective in that the compounds lack significant effects on the multiplication of viruses in other major groups, such as reo, myxo, arbo, adeno, herpes, and poxvirus groups. Furthermore, cell metabolism and cellular growth rate are not affected by HBB and guanidine used at concentrations sufficient to inhibit the multiplication of drug-sensitive picornaviruses. The central feature of the mechanism of action of these virus inhibitors is that they stop the formation of the active viral RNA polymerase in cells infected with a sensitive virus. The synthesis of viral RNA is also inhibited in treated cells, and in the absence of production of new viral RNA little of the viral coat proteins is made.

Mutants of the drug-sensitive parent viruses have been obtained which either are resistant to the inhibitor or depend on the inhibitor for multiplication. The resistant mutants are able to synthesize viral RNA polymerase even in the presence of inhibitor, whereas the dependent ones actually require HBB or guanidine to make the enzyme which catalyzes the synthesis of viral RNA.

Resistant mutants emerge in cell cultures within a matter of days or weeks of infection with a sensitive enterovirus in the presence of HBB or guanidine. Given together, HBB and guanidine act synergistically, and also they show only partial cross-resistance. Thus, when a combination of the two inhibitors is used, the virus suppressive effect far exceeds the effect of either compound given alone. HBB and guanidine separately have shown slight protective effects in experimental poliovirus infections in the mouse, but no results of combined treatment have so far been reported.

INHIBITION OF POXVIRUSES BY ISATIN β-THIOSEMICARBAZONE AND DERIVATIVES. Poxviruses are large DNA-containing viruses which possess a complex structure. Of particular importance to man are the smallpox and vaccinia viruses.

Isatin β-thiosemicarbazone inhibits the multiplication of poxviruses in cell culture at concentrations at which no effects on cellular metabolism or growth rate are demonstrable. The drug does not interfere with the synthesis of viral DNA. It has in fact been shown by immunologic techniques that isatin β-thiosemicarbazone does not inhibit synthesis of new virus-specific antigens during the first one-third to one-half of the viral growth cycle. Among the early proteins are probably some enzymes which function in the synthesis of viral DNA. The drug does, however, prevent the synthesis of antigens which appear later. The late-appearing antigens may be required in the maturation of the viral particles, as production of complete infectious virus is blocked in the presence of isatin β-thiosemicarbazone. Electron micrographs of infected treated cells reveal abnormal poxvirus particles with the morphologic characteristics of immature precursor particles.

So far no drug-resistant or -dependent mutants of poxviruses have been obtained. Isatin β-thiosemicarbazone and its N-methyl derivative are prophylactically highly effective in experimental animals, and successful prevention of smallpox by the N-methyl derivative has been reported in smallpox contacts in a human population. However, these drugs have little or no effect once the smallpox infection has become established.

Inhibitory Effects of Structural Analogues of Deoxynucleosides

5-Iodo-2'-deoxyuridine (IUDR) inhibits the replication of many different DNA viruses, including, among others, herpes and vaccinia viruses. Detailed studies of the effects of IUDR on the multiplication of herpes and pseudorabies viruses in cell culture have shown that although the compound prevents the production of infective virus, it allows the synthesis of large amounts of viral DNA and protein, as revealed by acridine orange and fluorescent antibody staining of infected cells. Electron microscopic examination reveals the presence of structurally imperfect particles in the treated cell.

IUDR is sequentially phosphorylated by appropriate kinases in the cell to the corresponding monophosphate, diphosphate, and finally triphosphate. The triphosphate of IUDR serves as a precursor in DNA synthesis in place of the normal thymidine triphosphate, which is excluded in equimolar amounts. There is evidence that IUDR is incorporated into both cellular and viral DNA. A plausible hypothesis is that incorporation of IUDR into viral DNA leads to miscoding in the viral messenger RNA with resulting synthesis of faulty proteins. There may also be a number of other effects, such as inhibition of some of the enzymes in the DNA-synthetic pathway and interference with the regulation of the level of activity of the enzymes.

Since IUDR shows therapeutic effects in ocular herpes and vaccinia virus infections, the question arises as to the nature of its apparent selectivity. Concentrations of IUDR which have a marked effect on viral multiplication in cell culture also affect cell division. There is no evidence that the enzymatic mechanism of viral DNA synthesis is selectively affected by IUDR. It appears, in the light of these findings, that the chemotherapeutic effects of IUDR in the eye may be due to kinetic and quantitative rather than chemical and enzymologic differences between viral and cellular DNA synthesis. The commonly employed treatment regimen calls for intermittent administration of the drug, which may permit the survival of many of the cells. However, in larger

defects in the cornea IUDR apparently retards epithelial regeneration and wound healing.

Inhibition of Viral Replication by Microbial Constituents or Products

BACTERIAL CONSTITUENTS. The first substance known to show antiviral chemotherapeutic activity in an experimental animal was the capsular polysaccharide of *K. pneumoniae*. This substance is capable of protecting mice against death from pneumonia induced experimentally by pneumonia virus of mice (PVM). The polysaccharide also inhibits mumps virus multiplication in the embryonated chicken egg. The available evidence indicates that the polysaccharide inhibits a step in the intracellular replication of sensitive viruses.

Another example of a virus inhibitor obtained from a bacterial source is a substance from a *Corynebacterium*, which inhibits the multiplication of arboviruses but not of entero, vaccinia, herpes, or adenoviruses in cell culture. This selective activity is destroyed by trypsin but not by nucleases. The active factor does not appear to interfere with the adsorption or penetration steps in viral replication, but the precise mechanism of its action is not known.

Penicillium Mold Constituents or Products. Three substances with similar virus-inhibitory activities have been obtained from various penicillium molds. Helenine is obtained from *P. funiculosum,* and M-8450 and statolon from different strains of *P. stoloniferum.* These penicillium mold products inhibit the multiplication of viruses in a number of different major groups, such as picorna and arbovirus groups. So far no activity against influenza viruses has been reported, and studies with DNA viruses have given largely negative results.

Chemically helenine is a ribonucleoprotein, and statolon is a complex containing polysaccharide, protein, and RNA. An outstanding common characteristic of the action of helenine, M-8450, and statolon is that they require considerable time to exert their virus-inhibitory effect. The greatest degree of virus inhibition is obtained when cells are pretreated before inoculation of virus. In this respect the action of these penicillium mold products is similar to that of interferon. Of considerable interest are recent findings indicating that statolon and helenine induce the production of interferon in cells. Whether this effect entirely explains the virus-inhibitory activity of these mold products has yet to be determined.

A constituent of *P. cyclopium,* designated cyclopin, shows striking selectivity in that it inhibits the multiplication of arboviruses but not of enteroviruses. The action of cyclopin is in this regard strikingly different from that of the other penicillium mold products. Cyclopin is sensitive to trypsin. The mechanism of the virus-specific action of cyclopin is not clear.

Interferon

When cells are exposed to the action of any one of many different viruses they produce proteins which are capable of interfering with the multiplication of a wide variety of viruses. These proteins, called interferons, show host cell specificity: interferon produced in chicken cells shows no activity or little activity in rabbit cells, and vice versa. However, it does not matter which particular viral agent is used to elicit the production of interferon in cells; the product has in every case broad antiviral activity in the cell species in which it was produced. There is evidence that the production of interferon is under the control of the host's genetic apparatus. Besides viruses, other agents, including certain bacteria and macromolecular substances, are capable of inducing the production of interferonlike substances, which are, however, demonstrably different from virus-induced interferons in some of their physicochemical properties.

Interferons produced by viral action have a molecular weight in the range of 25,000. Interferon activity is sensitive to chymotrypsin, trypsin, pepsin, and papain. It is stable at acid and alkaline pH. A small fraction of a microgram of purified interferon has demonstrable antiviral activity in cell culture. However, to produce a milligram of interferon a very large number of cells is required. The mechanism whereby interferons inhibit the replication of viruses is not clear, although much effort has been directed toward this important question. Studies with RNA viruses have so far shown that interferon does not prevent virus adsorption or penetration but interferes with the synthesis of viral RNA.

Interferon has shown some therapeutic effects when used topically in vaccinia infections of the eye, but its effects after systemic administration to experimental animals have been slight. In recent years attention has been focused on the possible role of interferon in the recovery process in viral infections.

General Comments

The commonly used antimicrobial chemotherapeutic agents are without effect on viruses and on viral multiplication. Their only usefulness in viral infections lies in combating secondary bacterial invaders.

Selective inhibition of the multiplication of viruses is theoretically feasible and has been achieved in a number of experimental systems in the laboratory. In a few instances some clinical success has been obtained in the treatment or prevention of viral infections in the field. The outstanding problem in antiviral chemotherapy and prophylaxis lies in finding additional selective inhibitors for the diverse viruses which infect man. Further progress in the study of viral nucleic acids and proteins may be expected to open new approaches to the development of selective inhibitors of viral multiplication. Further empirical search should also continue to yield new inhibitors.

REFERENCES

Caspar, D. L. D. Design principles in virus particle construction. *In* Horsfall, F. L., and Tamm, I., eds. Viral and Rickettsial Infections of Man, 4th ed. Philadelphia, J. B. Lippincott Co., 1965.
DeClerq, E., and Merigan, T. C. Current concepts of interferon and interferon induction. Ann. Rev. Med., 21:17, 1970.
Eggers, H. J., and Tamm, I. Antiviral chemotherapy. Ann. Rev. Pharmacol., 6:231, 1966.
Green, M. Chemistry and structure of animal virus particles. Amer. J. Med., 38:651, 1965.
Hilleman, M. R. Immunologic, chemotherapeutic and interferon approaches to control of viral disease. Amer. J. Med., 38:751, 1965.
Smorodintsev, A. A., et al. The prospect of amantadine for prevention of influenza as in humans. Ann. N.Y. Acad. Sci., 173:44, 1970.
Tamm, I., and Eggers, H. J. Biochemistry of virus reproduction. Amer. J. Med., 38:678, 1965.
——— and Eggers, H. J. Selective Inhibition of Viral Reproduction. *In* Horsfall, F. L., and Tamm, I., eds. Viral and Rickettsial Infections of Man, 4th ed. Philadelphia, J. B. Lippincott Co., 1965, pp. 305-308.
Wagner, R. R. Interferon. Amer. J. Med., 38:726, 1965.

14.24
CAT SCRATCH DISEASE
(Benign Nonbacterial Lymphadenitis or Inoculation Lymphoreticulosis)

ANDREW M. MARGILETH

Cat scratch disease (CSD) is a nonfatal systemic illness characterized by tender regional lymphadenopathy frequently accompanied by a primary skin lesion and a history of cat contact or scratches or both. Persistence of an enlarged node for one to two months in a generally healthy child and gradual spontaneous resolution of the lymphadenopathy is the natural course of the disease.

EPIDEMIOLOGY. Over 1,000 patients have been reported since the first report of CSD by Debré in France in 1950. The majority (80 percent) have been less than 20 years of age. The disease is worldwide, occurring in all races; both sexes have been affected equally. In temperate zones most cases have occurred during the fall and winter. Several house and city epidemics have been recorded.

ETIOLOGY. The etiologic agent presumably is an organism of the psittacosis-lymphogranuloma group of Chlamydozoaceae, but has not been positively identified. In an unconfirmed study using pus from a lymph node, a hemagglutinating virus thought to be related to herpes simplex was detected. Recently, herpeslike virus particles have been found by Kalter et al. in the cell cytoplasm of biopsied lymph nodes. The mode of transmission is well known. The illness usually follows the scratch or lick from a kitten or cat (70 percent). Rarely, it has occurred following a dog or monkey bite, or a scratch from a thorn or codfish bone. Contact with cats occurs in about 90 percent of those afflicted. The disease has been transmitted only to man and monkeys. No cats studied have shown evidence of illness, and attempts to isolate virus from cat saliva or claws have been unsuccessful. Apparently the cat acts as a mechanical vector for the causative agent, since cats do not react to skin tests with CS antigen.

PATHOLOGY. Biopsied lymph nodes may show distinct yet nonspecific stages: reticulum cell hyperplasia followed by tuberclelike granulomata, then multiple microabscesses, and, ultimately, frank abscess formation. Consequently, a presumptive histopathologic diagnosis of tularemia, brucellosis, tuberculosis, or sarcoidosis might be considered.

CLINICAL MANIFESTATIONS. The patient generally does not appear to be ill in spite of the impressive size of lymphadenopathy; however, malaise, fever, and flulike symptoms may be present initially. From 3 to 10 days elapse from the scratch or contact until a primary skin papule or pustule forms; occasionally unilateral conjunctival granulomas occur. A primary lesion may be detected in 55 to 95 percent of patients, depending upon how carefully the child is examined and the time of the initial examination. Most primary lesions persist for 1 to 3 weeks; some for 7 weeks. Regional lymphadenopathy develops about 2 weeks (range 3 to 50 days) after the scratch. The enlarged node or nodes are invariably tender for the first one or two weeks and are commonly found in the head, neck, or axilla. Epitrochlear, inguinal, femoral, and popliteal areas are involved less frequently; multiple site involvement occurs in 10 percent of patients. In the majority of cases, the node size varies from 1 to 6 cm and the enlargement persists for 2 to 3 months. A few patients have lymphadenopathy for 6 to 24 months. Node suppuration occurs in about one-fourth of patients referred to hospitals but is seen less commonly (10 percent) in office practice.

No clinical signs other than lymphadenopathy are reported in one-third of the patients. About one-fourth have fever (101 to 106° F) lasting for 5 (1 to 17) days; 40 percent of patients have malaise or a flulike syndrome lasting about 4 (1 to 21) days. Exanthemata, which may be maculopapular or petechial, or which appears as erythema nodosum or multiforme, have been reported in 5 percent of affected patients. The rash usually lasts 3 to 5 days.

Unusual clinical manifestations have included: the oculoglandular syndrome of Parinaud (36 reported cases); encephalitis (31 cases); thrombocytopenic purpura (7 cases); osteomyelitis (4 cases); and primary atypical pneumonia (4 cases). Cat scratch disease should always be considered in any patient with an ocular lesion and parotid area swelling (Fig. 17A and B). The latter results from preauricular lymphadenopathy.

Children with central nervous system involvement may develop encephalopathy, meningitis, radic-

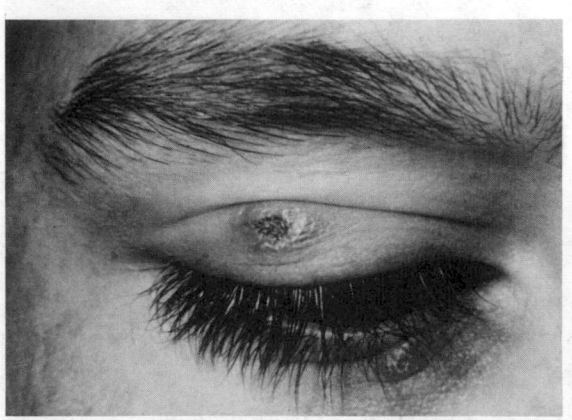
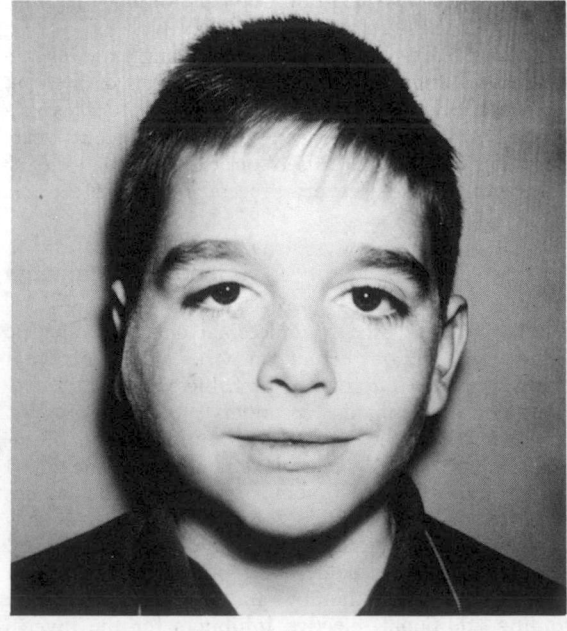

Fig. 17. Oculoglandular syndrome in a 12-year-old boy with crusted upper and lower eyelid pustules (A, Left) for two months and multiple preauricular lymph node involvement (B, Right) due to cat scratch disease. Lymphadenopathy persisted for seven months in spite of four aspirations of sterile pus.

ulitis, polyneuritis, or myelitis with paraplegia. Onset of neurologic symptoms is usually sudden, accompanied by fever, and occurs within 1 to 6 weeks of the onset of adenopathy. The frequency of major symptoms and signs involving the central nervous system found in 31 cases was: coma or convulsions in two-thirds, neurologic abnormalities in one-fourth, and lethargy, confusion, or both in one-sixth. In seven cases (22 percent) pleocytosis or elevated protein or both were detected. Electroencephalograms are abnormal in the majority of these patients. Severe manifestations have lasted for 1 to 2 weeks, with gradual recovery to normal status in 1 to 6 months in most patients. Recovery from thrombocytopenic purpura, osteomyelitis, pneumonitis, and Parinaud's syndrome has been complete.

LABORATORY DATA. Laboratory tests are not diagnostic, and few nonspecific abnormalities have been detected. Initially, the number of polymorphonuclear cells may be increased with a mild leucocytosis. The sedimentation rate is usually elevated during the first few weeks of lymphadenitis.

SKIN TESTS. A skin test using cat scratch antigen is positive in 94 percent of patients who are clinically suspected of having CSD and have had cat scratches. A negative skin test often occurs if the duration of illness is less than 3 or 4 weeks. The positive reaction consists of a wheal or papule with 5 mm or more of induration, with or without erythema, occurring 48 to 72 hours after intradermal inoculation of 0.1 ml of antigen. Induration may persist for 5 to 6 days. A positive test may be obtained for years after an episode of CSD. False-positive reactions have been reported in veterinarians, healthy persons, and family contacts; the overall incidence is only 5 percent. Thus, the limit of confidence for a positive reaction is about 95 percent. Repeated skin testing with CS antigen in the same patients has not produced positive reactions. Skin tests with atypical mycobacterium antigens have been negative in most patients with CSD.

ANTIGEN PREPARATION. Since CS antigen is not available commercially, all aspirated pus should be saved as a source of CS antigen. The pus is immediately diluted (1:4) with normal saline solution, cultured for fungi, bacteria, and mycobacteria, and heated for 24 hours at 60° C on each of three consecutive days to destroy possible hepatitis virus. After 8 to 10 weeks, if all cultures are negative, the material is ready for use in skin testing. No preservative is added; however, all antigens should be stored at temperatures below 0° C. Antigens prepared in this manner have been used for skin testing for 5 years without loss of activity.

DIAGNOSIS. Regional lymphadenopathy must be present during the course of the disease. Three of the four following manifestations would confirm the diagnosis in a typical case, whereas all four would be necessary in an atypical case: (1) a history of animal (usually a cat) contact, or presence of a scratch or a primary lesion; (2) aspiration of sterile pus from the node (a presumptive diagnostic test for CSD) or negative laboratory studies excluding other etiologic possibilities; (3) a positive skin test to cat scratch antigen (5 percent false-positives occur; use of only one antigen may give a false-negative result in 20 percent of patients); (4) node biopsy showing histopathology consistent with CSD.

If a negative skin test is found to one or two different cat scratch antigens applied simultaneously and again 4 weeks later, and if other studies are negative, a biopsy must be considered to rule out a benign tumor or lymphoma. The presence of tenderness favors cat scratch adenopathy rather than a tumor.

DIFFERENTIAL DIAGNOSIS. Cat scratch disease should be considered in all patients with persistent or chronic lymphadenopathy. Other causes are lymphogranuloma venereum, typical or atypical tuberculosis, bacterial adenitis, tularemia, brucellosis, histoplasmosis, coccidioidomycosis, toxoplasmosis, infectious mononucleosis, and benign or malignant tumors. In atypical forms of CSD, one must consider benign recurrent parotid lymphosialadenopathy, Parinaud's oculoglandular disease, encephalitis, pneumonia, thrombocytopenic purpura, erythema nodosum, and osteomyelitis, as well as fluctuant lymphadenopathy simulating cystic hygroma or a thyroglossal duct cyst.

TREATMENT. In the majority of patients no active therapy is needed. The best therapy is reassurance that the adenopathy is benign and in most cases will subside spontaneously within 1 to 2 months. Thus management consists of reassurance, analgesics for pain, and aspiration if suppuration occurs. Lack of response to antimicrobials is the rule, and a therapeutic trial of an antibiotic is not recommended. In the child whose node suppurates, needle aspiration is preferred to incision and drainage. Aspiration is best performed under local anesthesia. The needle (18 or 19 gauge) is inserted through normal skin at the base of the mass in order to avoid a chronic sinus tract in the event that a tuberculous lesion is present. Aspiration provides material for skin test antigen, relieves painful adenopathy, and allows the patient to become symptom-free within 24 to 48 hours. If fluid recurs, reaspiration may be necessary. Application of moist soaks to the primary lesion may effect drainage and shorten the duration of lymphadenopathy. The efficacy of steroid therapy in CSD is questionable and its use seems unjustified. Excisional biopsy of the node may be necessary in selected patients because of persistent pain or for diagnostic purposes.

PREVENTION. Because of increasing numbers of pets in the home (25 million cats in the U.S.), CSD will be difficult to prevent. Disposal of the suspect cat is not recommended since the cat involved is invariably well and less than 10 percent of family members scratched by the same cat develop CSD. The patient with CSD does not require isolation or quarantine, as there is no evidence of disease spread from man to man.

PROGNOSIS. The prognosis is excellent; lymphadenopathy usually regresses spontaneously in two months. One attack apparently confers lifelong immunity. Complications and sequelae are almost nonexistent and have not been reported in typical cases. In one patient with encephalopathy, death apparently occurred during treatment of continued seizures with hypothermia. A rare case has been reported to have had chronic adenopathy for 2 years. Only two patients have had a recurrence of the same adenopathy after a 3-year period of well-being.

REFERENCES

Carithers, H. A., Carithers, C. M., and Edwards, R. O. Cat-scratch disease. J.A.M.A., 207:312, 1969.

Kalter, S. S., Kim, C. S., and Heberling, R. L. Herpeslike virus particles associated with cat-scratch disease. Nature, 224:190, 1969.

Margileth, A. M. Cat-scratch disease: Nonbacterial regional lymphadenitis. Pediatrics, 42:803, 1968.

Pollen, R. H. Cat-scratch encephalitis. Neurology, 18:1031, 1968.

14.25
CHICKENPOX
(VARICELLA)

PHILIP A. BRUNELL and SAUL KRUGMAN

Chickenpox is a relatively benign acute contagious disease characterized by a generalized vesicular eruption and mild constitutional symptoms.

ETIOLOGY. Chickenpox is caused by varicellazoster (V-Z) virus. This virus is a member of the herpesvirus group, rather than the poxvirus group as the name chickenpox might imply. Varicella has been transmitted experimentally to man by inoculation of vesicular fluid obtained from patients with either zoster or varicella. V-Z virus can be isolated in cultures of human cells from young vesicles but not from respiratory secretions. Virus in vesicular fluid has been shown by electron microscopy to be spherical and to have two concentric outer membranes. It measures approximately 200 mμ in diameter.

Complement-fixing antibody can be demonstrated in sera obtained as early as seven days after onset of disease. Antigen for this test can be prepared from virus obtained from patients with zoster or with varicella.

EPIDEMIOLOGY. Varicella is predominantly a disease of childhood, with the highest incidence in the 2- to 8-year-old age group. It has occurred in all ages from the newborn period to the ninth decade of life. Both sexes and all races are equally susceptible. In temperate climates there is usually a higher incidence during the winter and spring months.

Chickenpox is highly contagious, comparable to measles in this respect. The primary attack rate following household exposure has been estimated to be 87 percent. Subclinical infection rarely if ever occurs.

Infection is spread chiefly by direct contact with patients who have varicella or zoster. Under hospital ward conditions the disease may be spread by indirect contact if adequate isolation technique is not practiced. Otherwise, it is only rarely contracted through the medium of a third person. Transmission via the airborne route is also possible and has received much emphasis in recent years. However, in our experience the airborne mode of transmission has played an insignificant role in the dissemination of infection.

The crusts, unlike those of smallpox, do not contain viable virus. The period of contagiousness probably extends from 1 day before to 5 days following the onset of rash. The incubation period ranges from 11 to 20 days but is usually about 14 days.

IMMUNITY. One attack of varicella usually confers a lifelong immunity to the disease; second attacks have been reported but are very rare. We have occasionally seen a relapse shortly after recovery from an attack. Although maternal varicella antibody is transplanted across the placenta when pregnant women get varicella, it is uncertain whether women who had varicella in childhood transfer their immunity to their fetuses. The rarity of the disease in the first three months of life suggests that the newborn infant possesses a transient immunity; on the other hand, infants born of mothers who have had varicella have developed the disease in the newborn period.

Chickenpox during the first 10 days of life may result in disseminated infection with a fatal outcome.

PATHOLOGY. The initial lesion is a macule which develops first into a papule and then into a vesicle occupying chiefly the prickle cell layer of the skin. The roof of the vesicle is formed by the stratum corneum and lucidum and the base by the deeper prickle cell layer. According to Unna, a reticulating liquefaction in a few prickle cells initiates the process of vesiculation. Ballooning degeneration takes place in the cells of the vesicle, forming giant cells which can be identified in scrapings of the base of the vesicle. The pathologic lesion is characterized by eosinophilic Cowdry, type A intranuclear inclusions.

Postmortem examination of infants who have died of varicella reveals characteristic cellular changes in the esophagus, pancreas, liver, renal pelves, ureters, bladder, and adrenal glands. The lesions, including the intranuclear inclusions, are similar to those seen in the skin. Autopsy reports of adults with primary varicella pneumonia described changes consistent with a viral pneumonia. The cellular exudate consists chiefly of large mononuclear cells, while polymorphonuclear cells and bacteria are scarce. Typical type A intranuclear inclusion bodies characteristic of chickenpox may be found in the alveolar septal cells.

SYMPTOMS. Symptoms prior to the appearance of the rash are mild or absent. A rash first appears on the scalp, face, or trunk. The majority of lesions progress rapidly from macule to papule to vesicle with a surrounding erythema. This red areola is most distinct at the time of the fully formed vesicle and fades as the latter dries. Occasional lesions are seen in which a vesicle is not surrounded by a red areola. The process of drying begins at the center; this causes a slight depression, giving the vesicle an umbilicated appearance. As the lesion dries and the areola fades, a crust forms which falls off in about 5 to 20 days, depending on the depth to which the skin has been involved.

The lesions appear in crops over a period of three to five days, involving the scalp, face, trunk, and extremities. The distribution of the lesions is predominantly centripetal, the greater concentration of the lesions being on the trunk rather than on the extremities. Vesicles also develop on the mucous membranes of the mouth, most commonly over the palate. They rupture rapidly so that the lesion presents as a shallow ulcer grossly indistinguishable from that of herpetic stomatitis. The palpebral conjunctiva, pharynx, larynx, and trachea may also be involved.

The most striking manifestation of the eruption is the presence of lesions in all stages in any one general area. Macules, papules, vesicles, and crusts are present in close proximity. The pocks are usually most abundant over the back and shoulders. In mild cases there may be little or no fever with only a few scattered lesions. In an average case the temperature ranges between 101° and 102° F. In severe cases the entire body is covered with innumerable lesions, and the patient is acutely ill with a temperature of 104° or 105° F. The fever gradually subsides as the crops of lesions cease to appear and the vesicles begin to dry and become crusted. There is no significant change in the number and type of blood cells.

Varicella, like many other viral infections, is much more severe in adults than in children. In our experience primary varicella pneumonia is not an uncommon manifestation of the disease in the older age group. The respiratory symptoms may be minimal or very marked with cough, severe dyspnea, cyanosis, hemoptysis, and varying degrees of prostration. These symptoms usually appear during the first week of the illness and are more apt to be associated with an extensive skin eruption. Physical examination of the chest reveals a paucity of signs. Roentgenograms show diffuse nodular infiltrations throughout both lung fields (Fig. 18), which clear slowly in the course of 2 to 6 weeks. During a 6-month period 10 out of 30 adults with varicella presented clinical and roentgenographic evidence of primary varicella pneumonia.

Recent prospective studies suggest that pneumonia may be less common in adults with varicella than our experience with hospitalized cases might indicate. Of 114 military personnel with varicella, it was found that only 4 percent had clinical signs and

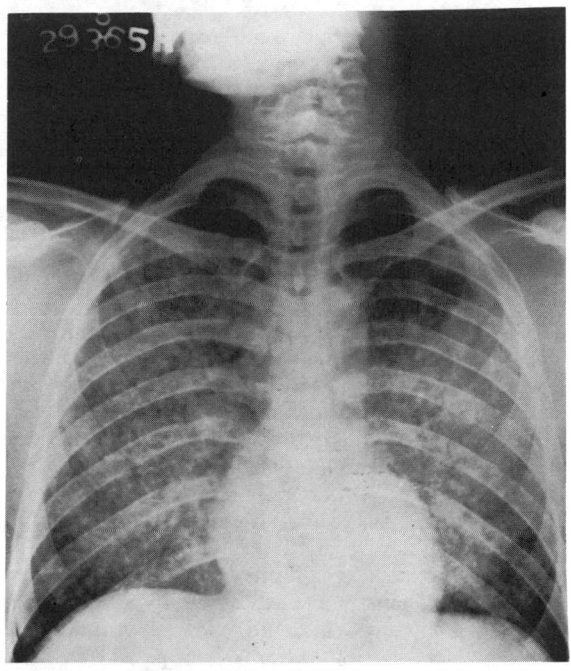

Fig. 18. Varicella pneumonia. Radiogram showing extensive diffuse nodular infiltration bilaterally.

16 percent had roentgenographic evidence of pulmonary involvement. Adults with varicella pneumonia may also have myocarditis, hepatitis, nephritis, and bleeding manifestations.

COMPLICATIONS. These are relatively uncommon in children. In one large series reported by Bullowa and Wishik, 5.2 percent of the cases presented some type of complication. Secondary infection of the local skin lesions with staphylococci may cause impetigo, furuncles, cellulitis, erysipelas, or conjunctivitis. Septicemia, suppurative arthritis, osteomyelitis, and acute glomerulonephritis may be sequelae to the local skin complications. Primary varicella pneumonia may be complicated by pleurisy with effusion and mediastinal emphysema.

Encephalitis, a rare complication of chickenpox, is similar to postmeasles and postvaccinal encephalitis, both pathologically and clinically, except for the frequent cerebellar signs seen with chickenpox enpehalitis. It is discussed in Section 15.11. Other nervous complications reported include transverse myelitis, peripheral neuritis, and optic neuritis.

An unusual and fatal course has been described by Haggerty and Eley in a scattered group of 12 children who contracted varicella while on cortisone therapy. The fulminating infection was usually hemorrhagic, ending in death within a few days. In these patients the daily dose of cortisone varied from 25 to 499 mg and had been given over periods ranging from a few days to two months before the development of varicella. The patients' ages ranged between

11 months and 8 years. Steroid therapy was being given for rheumatic fever, for various blood dyscrasias, or for asthma.

A report by Wright and associates calls attention to severe hypoglycemia as a complication of varicella. Three infants, 3 to 6 months of age, developed hypoglycemia with intractable seizures between the fourth and sixth posteruptive days and died within 24 hours. Spinal fluid sugar concentration in all three cases was below 11 mg per 100 milliliters.

Occasionally bullous or purpuric skin lesions may be seen in the course of varicella.

Varicella has been reported on a number of occasions in association with Reye's syndrome (Sec. 24.7).

DIAGNOSIS. Varicella usually poses no problem in diagnosis. One can usually elicit a history of contact about two weeks prior to the onset. The illness produces few systemic signs and often no prodromal symptoms. The primary skin lesion is a vesicle, but lesions in various stages of development—macules, papules, vesicles, and crusts—are present at the same time. The lesions are most numerous on the trunk and relatively sparse on the extremities.

The problem of differentiating varicella from smallpox occasionally arises. In smallpox the constitutional symptoms which precede the eruption are severe, whereas with varicella the patient is most acutely ill at the height of his rash. The lesions of smallpox are all of uniform age and size in any one general area; they take from 5 to 6 days to develop; they are deeper than the lesions of varicella and usually possess a central umbilication. The eruption of smallpox is usually centrifugal; that is, the concentration of lesions on the face, hands, and feet tends to be greater than on the trunk. The vesicular fluid of chickenpox does not produce lesions on a rabbit's cornea nor on the chorioallantoic membrane of a chick embryo. The vesicular fluid from smallpox lesions can also be used as antigen for a specific smallpox complement-fixation test. And finally, a smear prepared from the base of a vesicle and treated with Giemsa's stain reveals the presence of tremendously enlarged giant epithelial cells and intranuclear inclusions in varicella, herpes simplex, and herpes zoster, but not in smallpox. Modified smallpox may be clinically indistinguishable from varicella. Under these circumstances the diagnosis can be clarified by laboratory procedures.

Bullous impetigo may occasionally be difficult to differentiate from varicella. In rickettsialpox, vesicular lesions are superimposed on a firm papule. The eruption is usually preceded by a febrile illness with grippelike symptoms. An eschar is present at the site of the mite bite. Rickettsialpox and generalized herpes simplex can be differentiated from varicella by laboratory tests. Pemphigus, dermatitis herpetiformis, and drug eruptions may occasionally cause problems in differential diagnosis. Hemorrhagic chickenpox may be confused with meningococcemia or with hemorrhagic smallpox. Insect bites and papular urticaria may also be mistaken for the early stage of varicella.

TREATMENT. In general, isolation and quarantine in the home are unnecessary. Chickenpox is usually spread before it is clinically manifest; it is usually very benign and is one of those inevitable diseases of childhood. Even in institutions, quarantine is of questionable value.

Regular preparations of gamma globulin do not prevent the occurrence of chickenpox. However, Ross's data suggest that extremely large doses of gamma globulin used prophylactically may reduce the number of lesions and hence the general severity of varicella in family contacts.

A gamma globulin preparation obtained from the serum of patients convalescent from herpes zoster has been found to be effective in preventing chickenpox in household contacts. To be effective the preparation must be given within three days after exposure. The convalescent zoster globulin is not yet commercially available (April, 1972), but it should become so within the next year. Prophylaxis is recommended for children who are likely to experience severe disease. These include children under one month of age, those who are under treatment with steroids, and those with malignant diseases. The same is true for patients receiving immunosuppressive therapy. In the face of a known exposure or an epidemic, steroids should not be prescribed for susceptible individuals unless absolutely necessary in an emergency situation. If exposed to varicella, susceptible patients on long-term steroid therapy should have the steroid dosage lowered to a maintenance level.

Washing with soap will not spread the virus and may decrease the chances of bacterial infection. Bathing in a bath containing starch will provide temporary relief of itching. Calamine lotion is also used to relieve itching. Since scratching of lesions by children is inevitable, fingernails should be trimmed.

References

Almeida, J. D., Howatson, A. F., and Williams, M. G. Morphology of varicella (chickenpox) virus. Virology, 16:353, 355, 1962.

Blank, H., Burgoon, C. F., Baldridge, G. D., McCarthy, P. L., and Urbach, F. Cytologic smears in diagnosis of herpes simplex, herpes zoster, and varicella. J.A.M.A., 146:1410, 1951.

Brunell, P. A., and Casey, H. L. Crude tissue culture antigen for determination of varicella-zoster complement fixing antibody. Public Health Rep., 79:839, 1964.

——— et al. Prevention of varicella by Zoster immune globulin. New Eng. J. Med., 280:1191, 1969.

Bullowa, J. G. M., and Wishik, S. M. Complications of varicella: I. Their occurrence among 2,534 patients. Amer. J. Dis. Child., 49:923, 1935.

Charkes, N. D. Purpuric chickenpox: report of a case, review of the literature, and classification by clinical features. Ann. Intern. Med., 54:745, 1961.

Cheatham, W. J., Weller, T. H., Dolan, T. F., Jr., and Dower, J. C. Varicella: report of two fatal cases with necropsy, virus isolation, and serologic studies. Amer. J. Path., 32:1015, 1956.

Haggerty, R. J., and Eley, R. C. Varicella and cortisone. Pediatrics, 18:160, 1956.

Krugman, S., and Ward, R. Air sterilization in an infants' ward: effect of triethylene glycol vapor and dust-suppressive measures on the respiratory cross infection rate. J.A.M.A., 145:775, 1951.

Mitchell, A. G., and Fletcher, E. G. Studies on varicella: age and seasonal incidence, recurrences, complications and leukocyte counts. J.A.M.A., 89:279, 1927.

Nagler, F. P. O., and Rake, G. The use of the electron microscope in diagnosis of variola, vaccinia and varicella. J. Bact., 55:45, 1948.

Oppenheimer, E. H. Congenital chickenpox with disseminated visceral lesions. Bull. Johns Hopkins Hosp., 74: 240, 1944.

Ross, A. Modification of chickenpox in family contacts by administration of gamma globulin. New Eng. J. Med., 267:369, 1962.

Thomson, F. Contact infection with chickenpox. Lancet, 1:397, 1919.

Underwood, E. A. The neurological complications of varicella. Brit. J. Child. Dis., 32:83, 177, 241, 1935.

Weber, D. M., and Pellecchia, J. A. Varicella pneumonia: study of prevalence in adult men. J.A.M.A., 192:572, 1965.

Weller, T. H., and Coons, A. H. Fluorescent antibody studies with agents of varicella and herpes zoster propagated in vitro. Proc. Soc. Exp. Biol. Med., 86:789, 1954.

———— and Stoddard, M. B. Intranuclear inclusion bodies in cultures of human tissue inoculated with varicella vesicle fluid. J. Immunol., 68:311, 1952.

Wright, E. M., Lipson, M. J., and Mortimer, E. A., Jr. Varicella and severe hypoglycemia: a previously undescribed syndrome. Amer. J. Dis. Child., 92:512, 1956.

14.26
CYTOMEGALIC INCLUSION DISEASE

WALTER L. HENLEY

ETIOLOGY. Cytomegalic inclusion disease is caused by a cytomegalovirus, known originally as salivary gland virus because it was first isolated from such a gland by Smith. A similar virus was recovered by Weller and Hanshaw from children with clinical cytomegalic inclusion disease and by Rowe from adenoid tissue obtained at operation.

Minor antigenic variations indicate that several viruses belong to the human cytomegalic inclusion virus group. Among related viruses isolated from animals the serologic differences are greater than in the human group.

The virus has a DNA core and measures approximately 115 mμ. It resembles herpes simplex virus.

EPIDEMIOLOGY. The virus has been recovered in many parts of the world. It has been isolated at autopsy from salivary glands in 10 to 30 percent of persons dying from diverse causes.

The infant is born with a cytomegalovirus antibody titer corresponding to the mother's. Passive antibody levels fall, and acquired complement-fixing antibody can be detected in about 15 percent of children by the age of 2 years, in 30 percent of children by the age of 10, and in 80 percent of adults 35 or older. Antibody levels rise earlier with closer contact as encountered among siblings, in institutionalized children, and under crowded living conditions.

The virus is present in the saliva and urine, and therefore acquired infection requires relatively intimate contact. Congenital infection occurs through transplacental transmission of the virus. A mother may transmit the disease to her baby and continue to excrete the virus in her urine for some months after delivery. However, intrauterine infection of the infant does not occur during subsequent pregnancies. It remains to be shown whether this protection is related to specific antibody action.

In 20 to 40 percent of close contacts of infected patients, virus excretion, production of antibody, abnormal liver function tests, and hepatomegaly can be found.

CONGENITAL INFECTION. There is marked variation in the severity of the congenital infection. The disease may be so severe as to be fatal in the first few days of life; yet infection may be so mild that it remains undetected for several months after birth. The infant with severe disease shows involvement of the central nervous system, lungs, and liver. He may exhibit such symptoms as lethargy, convulsions, respiratory distress, jaundice, and purpura.

Physical examination may reveal microcephaly, chorioretinitis, hepatomegaly, splenomegaly, jaundice, petechiae and other hemorrhagic phenomena, pneumonitis, and occasionally gastroenteritis. The less severely affected infant may show some but not all of the above findings, the more frequent ones being jaundice, hepatomegaly, and ophthalmologic or central nervous system abnormalities.

Laboratory studies may show thrombocytopenia, abnormal liver function tests, and occasionally hemolytic anemia. Radiographic examination may reveal intracerebral calcifications and pulmonary infiltration, but these findings may be absent even in severe cases.

Patients who survive the neonatal stage of the disease may develop mental retardation, convulsions, motor disabilities, spasticity, and paralysis, as well as microphthalmia, blindness, and deafness. They may show evidence of chronic liver disease simulating hepatitis or biliary atresia.

ACQUIRED INFECTION. Patients may acquire the infection and present no clinical findings while excreting the virus. Others develop hepatosplenomegaly with or without clinical or laboratory evidence of hepatitis. Cytomegalovirus should be considered as an etiologic agent whenever hepatitis is encountered. However, it is noteworthy that mothers of infants with the congenital disease may have normal liver function tests.

Respiratory disease and pulmonary involvement become more frequent with increasing age, and the virus should be among those suspected in patients with unresponsive pneumonitis. Some respiratory illnesses diagnosed as colds or influenza during gestation may also represent cytomegalovirus infections. Ulcers of the gastrointestinal tract are often encountered. Necrosis of adrenal and kidney tissue and bone marrow depression occur in some patients.

Patients with a severe debilitating illness such as leukemia, those with "agammaglobulinemia," or those under therapy with immunosuppressive drugs may experience generalized cytomegalovirus disease. In such cases the virus has been isolated from the synovial fluid of an infected joint. The generalized infection may represent the patient's first experience with the virus or the dissemination of a latent infection.

Patients who receive large amounts of fresh blood by transfusion may acquire cytomegalovirus infection and exhibit signs of systemic illness. This is true of patients with leukemia, and those who receive large quantities of blood during open-heart surgery. The explanation for this is that the virus is present in the white blood cells contained in transfused blood. Apparently, storage of blood in the blood bank, which is accompanied by gradual destruction of leucocytes, decreases the risk of cytomegalovirus infection.

DIAGNOSIS AND DIFFERENTIAL DIAGNOSIS. Among the congenital infections which produce some or all of the manifestations of cytomegalic inclusion disease are toxoplasmosis, rubella, generalized herpes simplex infection or general bacterial sepsis, erythroblastosis fetalis, and congenital syphilis. Acquired cytomegalovirus has to be considered as a possible cause in any patient with hepatitis, unexplained hepatosplenomegaly, unexplained respiratory tract infections, or meningoencephalitis.

The best method of establishing the diagnosis of cytomegalic inclusion disease is isolation of cytomegalovirus from urine, saliva, or tissue biopsy. The virus can be grown in tissue culture of cells of human origin only. Fibroblastic or myometrial cells are satisfactory, and excellent results are achieved with tissue cultures made from skin and muscle obtained from newly aborted fetuses. Human cytomegalovirus does not withstand freezing well, so that specimens to be tested for virus should *not* be frozen, although they may be kept in an ordinary refrigerator. Best results are obtained when the specimen is inoculated in tissue culture with as little delay as possible.

When cytomegalovirus is recovered from a sick neonate the chances are very great that it is the cause of illness. Isolation of the virus from older infants or children, though most helpful, does not necessarily prove its etiologic significance. Viruria may persist for months after the onset of illness, and from 50 to 100 percent of patients with viruria have hepatomegaly or abnormal liver function tests, or both.

Mothers of infants with congenital cytomegalic inclusion disease have elevated antibody titers. With passive transmission the infant's titer is also high at birth, but it subsequently declines. Subsequent active infection may then be discerned by serial complement-fixation antibody titrations which show a new rise in antibody titer. A rise in the complement-fixation antibody titer accompanying virus isolation confirms the diagnosis of cytomegalic virus infection. The diagnosis can sometimes be made by demonstrating a rise in neutralizing antibody titer. The original strains isolated by Weller and Rowe are usually used.

Experienced examiners can recognize in fresh urine or gastric aspirate inclusion-bearing cells that are considered diagnostic, as well as typical histologic changes in tissue obtained by biopsy. However, inclusion-bearing cells cannot always be found. In addition, it should be noted that other viruses such as measles, rubella, varicella, mumps, herpangina, and attenuated poliovirus from oral live vaccine also cause the appearance of inclusion-bearing cells in the urine.

Calcification, particularly around the lateral ventricle, can be seen in x-ray of the skull in many patients with cytomegalic virus disease, but they are also found in toxoplasmosis. Diffuse bony sclerosis may be demonstrable on x-ray, but this may also occur in congenital rubella and syphilis.

PATHOLOGY. The disease is characterized by the finding of distinctly enlarged cells containing intranuclear and intracytoplasmic inclusions. They have been found in the salivary glands in 10 to 30 percent of routine autopsies and in almost every tissue examined at autopsy in patients with generalized disease. Cytomegalic inclusions are found in vascular endothelium and macrophages in the adult; in infants they occur mainly in epithelial cells.

The most frequently involved organs are the salivary glands, liver, spleen, lung, brain, kidney, and adrenal gland. The cytomegalic inclusion cell contains nuclear inclusions measuring about 10 μ. They stain reddish purple with hematoxylin and eosin. The cell itself measures about 30 μ and may have cytoplasmic inclusions which are granular and basophilic.

Changes in the placenta and fetal membranes are nonspecific and may resemble erythroblastosis fetalis. No cytomegalic inclusions have been found in the placenta.

Treatment. Although infected infants have been treated with corticosteroids and tetracycline, there is no evidence that these drugs have any value. Infants with microcephaly, cerebral calcification, blindness, or deafness have been irreversibly damaged in utero; they will almost certainly be mentally and physically retarded. General supportive therapy is the only treatment available at the present time. Exchange transfusion may be required in the newborn with hyperbilirubinemia.

In spite of the presence of specific antibody in the blood of a high percentage of the population, gamma globulin has not been effective in treatment of either congenital or acquired cytomegalic virus disease.

REFERENCES

Foster, K. M., and Jack, I. A prospective study of the role of cytomegalovirus in post-transfusion mononucleosis. New Eng. J. Med., 280:1311, 1969.

Hanshaw, J. B. Congenital and acquired cytomegalovirus infection. Pediat. Clin. N. Amer., 13:279, 1966.

——— Betts, R. F., Simon, G., and Boynton, R. C. Acquired cytomegalovirus infection. New Eng. J. Med., 272:602, 1965.

Kleinola, E., et al. Cytomegalo mononucleosis in previously healthy individuals. Ann. Int. Med., 71:11, 1969.

Long, D. J., and Hanshaw, J. B. Cytomegalo virus infection and the post perfusion syndrome. New Eng. J. Med., 280:386, 1969.

Medearis, D. N., Jr. Observations concerning human cytomegalovirus infection and disease. Bull. Hopkins Hosp., 114:181, 1964.

Starr, J. G., Bart, R. D., Jr., and Gold, E. Inapparent congenital cytomegalovirus infection—clinical and epidemiologic characteristics in early infancy. New Eng. J. Med., 282:1075, 1970.

Weller, T. H., and Hanshaw, J. B. Virologic and clinical observations on cytomegalic inclusion disease. New Eng. J. Med., 266:1234, 1962.

14.27
EXANTHEM SUBITUM
(ROSEOLA INFANTUM)

PHILIP A. BRUNELL and SAUL KRUGMAN

This disease was well described by Zahorsky in 1913 under the name of roseola infantum. Later it was given the name exanthem subitum by Veeder and Hempelmann. Although long ignored outside of North America or regarded as an atypical form of one of the other familiar eruptions, especially rubella, it has been reported from various parts of the world and now seems to be recognized with increasing frequency.

Circumstantial evidence indicates that the infection is caused by a filtrable virus. No organism is consistently recovered, and the course of the disease is uninfluenced by antibacterial therapy. Intramuscular injection of blood or serum taken from patients at the height of the fever has produced a similar illness in 3 of 14 recipients, with fever developing in six to nine days, an eruption appearing following defervescence on the ninth to twelfth day, and with associated neutropenia and relative lymphocytosis. Comparable transmission experiments suggest that the etiologic agent is also present in the patient's nasopharyngeal secretions. However, efforts to propagate it in tissue culture have thus far been unsuccessful. Consequently, many questions concerning the mode of spread of the contagion, both in the patient and in the community, remain unanswered.

About four-fifths of the recognized cases occur between the ages of 6 and 18 months, and perhaps 95 percent between 6 months and 3 years. There is no sex predilection. The disease may be found at any time of year, although peaks of incidence in May and October have been reported. The great majority of cases occur sporadically; even when no attempt is made to isolate the patient, transmission of the disease to siblings and other close contacts is decidedly rare, and institutional epidemics are almost unknown. Nevertheless, in urban life the probability that any individual infant will acquire the disease is relatively strong. In Rochester, N.Y., Breese found that about 16 percent of infants followed closely from the time of birth developed exanthem subitum by the age of 1 year. The rarity of cases after early childhood and the comparative lack of susceptibility of infants during their first six months of life suggest that virtually all adults have developed a lasting active immunity as a result of previous infection and that the mother transfers temporary immunity passively to her offspring. This hypothesis presupposes that a number of actual infections are subclinical or at least go unrecognized.

Nothing is known of the pathologic anatomy of exanthem subitum beyond its clinical manifestations.

The onset is acute, with fever which may reach 103° or even 105° F and occasionally with initial convulsions. Although irritability, drowsiness, anorexia, and often mild catarrhal symptoms are present, a striking feature of the disease is that the patient as a rule does not seem as ill as the height of his fever might lead one to expect. After two, three, or four days of fever the temperature falls by rapid lysis, and coincidentally with defervescence the rash makes its appearance. It is macular or maculopapular in type, looking not unlike that of rubella; it affects principally the trunk, neck, and retroauricular region, largely sparing the face and extremities. Itching, if present at all, is mild. After a few hours the eruption begins to fade, and within two or three days has usually disappeared, leaving neither pigmentation nor desquamation. Enlargement of lymph nodes, especially of the occipital and postauricular groups, is commonly present at the height of the rash. Mild leucocytosis may accompany the onset of fever, but characteristically the granulocyte count decreases promptly, leading to leucopenia with relative lymphocytosis by the second or third day. Systemic symptoms usually disappear with defervescence. In a small fraction of cases the eruption appears before the temperature has returned quite to normal. In others the febrile stage is prolonged to five or even six days.

Exanthem subitum is distinguished from rubella by the height and duration of fever preceding the appearance of the eruption. It is differentiated from measles by the absence of Koplik's spots, lacrimation, and coryza, as well as by the fact that the patient is afebrile or nearly so at the height of the rash. An eruption accompanying infectious mononucleosis or some of the enterovirus infections may cause difficulty until appropriate laboratory studies have been made. ECHO 16 virus and Coxsackie B5 virus may cause an illness accompanied by a rash which resembles roseola. Some patients ill with these viruses develop the rash after defervescence. In an infant or young child under treatment with a sulfonamide or penicillin, drug sensitivity may be wrongly inferred when a rash appears.

Treatment is purely symptomatic.

Complications are exceedingly rare, although the incidence of central nervous system involvement appears to be higher than can be accounted for simply by febrile convulsions. Stupor and coma have been described at the height of the febrile stage; some patients have shown prolonged or repeated seizures, stiff necks, increased intracranial pressure, and rarely a mononuclear pleocytosis in the cerebrospinal fluid, suggestive of encephalopathy. Many children showing these signs have recovered completely; others have been left with residua—hemiparesis, epilepsy, intellectual impairment, and sometimes cerebral atrophy demonstrable by pneumoencephalography. The pathogenesis of such complications is not well understood. Some may result from cerebral anoxia secondary to prolonged generalized convulsions at the height of the infection; others suggest direct invasion of the central nervous system, presumably by the virus which causes the disease. A guarded prognosis must be given when conspicuous nervous symptoms accompany the febrile stage.

REFERENCES

Berenberg, W., Wright, S., and Janeway, C. A. Roseola infantum (exanthem subitum). New Eng. J. Med., 241:253, 1949.
Breese, B. B., Jr. Roseola infantum (exanthem subitum). New York J. Med., 41:1854, 1941.
Burnstine, R. C., and Paine, R. S. Residual encephalopathy following roseola infantum. Amer. J. Dis. Child., 98:144, 1959.
Cherry, J. D., Lerner, A. M., Klein, J. O., and Finland, M. Coxsackie B5 infections with exanthems. Pediatrics, 31:455, 1963.
Clemens, H. H. Exanthem subitum (roseola infantum); report of eighty cases. J. Pediat., 26:66, 1945.
Hellström, B., and Vahlquist, B. Experimental inoculation of roseola infantum. Acta Paediat., 40:189, 1951.
Kempe, C. H., Shaw, E. B., Jackson, J. R., and Silver, H. K. Studies on the etiology of exanthema subitum (roseola infantum). J. Pediat., 37:561, 1950.
Letchner, A. Roseola infantum; a review of fifty cases. Lancet, 2:1163, 1955.
Veeder, B. S., and Hempelmann, T. C. A febrile exanthem occurring in childhood (exanthem subitum). J.A.M.A., 77:1787, 1921.
Zahorsky, J. Roseola infantum. J.A.M.A., 61:1446, 1913.

14.28
VIRAL HEPATITIS

JAMES W. MOSLEY

The term "viral hepatitis" is conveniently used for two etiologic entities, infectious and serum hepatitis. Although these diseases are separable on the basis of several characteristics, the illnesses are very similar. Unless the epidemiologic history provides adequate clues concerning specific diagnosis, the inclusive designation should be used. The labeling of all parenterally transmitted disease as "serum hepatitis," and all other cases as "infectious hepatitis," represents poor practice, although that assumption is usually correct for children.

Infectious and serum hepatitis are not the only forms of hepatic damage produced by viruses and viruslike agents. Yellow fever, for example, is one of the viral hepatitides; although nonindigenous in the United States since 1905, increased travel to enzootic areas creates the potential that imported cases will be seen. In addition, hepatic inflammation and jaundice can be caused rarely by viruses which are not usually hepatotropic. Such "hepatiticomimetic" infections should be remembered in differential diagnosis.

ETIOLOGIC AGENTS. Benign epidemic jaundice has been recognized for several hundred years. Throughout the earlier part of the twentieth century, attempts were made to implicate various bacterial agents as its cause, but no consistent association could be made. A viral etiology was sometimes suspected but could not be demonstrated with experimental animals. During World War II the disease became such a problem among military personnel that Japan, Germany, Great Britain, and the United States all carried out experiments with human volunteers. It was from these studies with volunteers that the existence of two etiologic agents with the characteristics of viruses was established (Table 14). Despite intensive efforts, there is not yet sufficient evidence to permit acceptance of any method for demonstrating multiplication of the agents in a tissue culture system or an experimental animal. Our knowledge of these agents has remained dependent upon volunteer studies and epidemiologic observations.

Infectious and serum hepatitis produce essentially the same clinical picture. It has been observed that the onset of the illness is more frequently insidious in serum hepatitis, with jaundice sometimes being the first symptom noticed. Fever is also infrequent in serum hepatitis, but common during infectious hepatitis. These distinctions are helpful, however, only on a statistical basis and are not reliable criteria for diagnosis in the individual patient.

TABLE 14.   *Characteristics Which Differentiate Infectious and Serum Hepatitis*

	Infectious Hepatitis	Serum Hepatitis
Prolonged viremia (for years)	Not described	Yes
Infection gives immunity to infectious hepatitis	Yes	No
Infection gives immunity to serum hepatitis	No	Yes
Hepatitis-associated antigen (Australia antigen) in serum	No	Yes
Person-to-person spread	Usual	Unusual or does not occur
Incubation period	15-45 days	50-180 days
Case fatality rate	Very low	Often high
Protection afforded by immune globulin	A small dose given once effective	Questionable, even with large and repeated doses
Disease in newborn due to transplacental transmission	Very rare	Occasionally occurs

In both infectious and serum hepatitis, viremia occurs during the incubation period and in the early phase of the acute illness. In addition, both agents produce infection on inoculation. Prolonged viremia in the asymptomatic individual, however, has been documented only for the agent of serum hepatitis, which appears to be responsible for parenterally transmitted disease much more often than the virus of infectious hepatitis. As long as the possibility of transmitting infectious hepatitis parenterally is kept in mind, "serum" hepatitis is a suitable designation for the second of these diseases.

The most important basis for distinguishing between infectious and serum hepatitis is evidence that they are immunologically distinct. As is true for many viral diseases, infection with the agent of either disease appears to confer immunity to that particular agent for the remainder of the individual's life. Infectious hepatitis does not, however, produce any resistance to serum hepatitis nor serum hepatitis to the infectious type. When volunteers who had been infected with one of these two agents were challenged with the other agent, they were as susceptible as those who gave no history of a previous episode of jaundice.

The immunologic differentiation of viral hepatitis into two etiologic entities has been reinforced by the recent demonstration of an antigen unique to serum hepatitis. Originally described as the Australia antigen in another context, its association with serum hepatitis has led to its redesignation as SH antigen or hepatitis-associated antigen (HAA). Antigenemia can be detected in the late incubation period in the majority of cases, persists into the acute illness in many, and becomes chronic in some. The relation of HAA to (or its identity with) the virus of serum hepatitis has not yet been established. Positive tests have been reported in a minority of cases labeled as infectious hepatitis, but epidemiologic documentation of that etiologic diagnosis has not been adequate.

The agent of infectious hepatitis is excreted in the feces and is infective when ingested. It is possible, therefore, for it to be transmitted from person to person, presumably by the fecal-oral route. The agent of serum hepatitis has not been demonstrated in the stool.

According to recent experiments in volunteers, serum containing the serum hepatitis virus is somewhat infective by mouth, but the implications of this observation with respect to spread by contact are not yet clear. Occasional instances of person-to-person transmission appear to occur, but present evidence still suggests they are unusual.

In volunteer studies and epidemiologic observations two distinct ranges of incubation period have been observed. In infectious hepatitis the interval from infection to onset of first symptoms is usually from 15 to 45 days, with an average of 28. This is true whether the infection is acquired orally or parenterally. In serum hepatitis the incubation period is usually much longer, ranging from 50 to 180 days. This distinction was so clear-cut in experimental studies that incubation period has been considered the most reliable way of differentiating these two diseases. Unfortunately, viral hepatitis following transfusion of whole blood, or unpooled derivatives, does not lend itself to etiologic categorization on this basis. Blood-associated cases have unimodally distributed incubation periods ranging from 15 to 180 days, with a peak in the 45 to 49 day interval. This phenomenon is not yet explained.

Infectious hepatitis is rarely fatal; if death occurs it is usually in an older adult. Serum hepatitis, on the other hand, carries a relatively high case fatality rate. Even among children, death occurs in 5 percent of cases which follow administration of blood and blood products. When serum hepatitis is transfusion-associated, the high case fatality rate may be related, at least in part, to debility caused by the disease for which the transfusion was given.

A difference of practical importance in these two diseases concerns the effectiveness of immune globulin. Whereas infectious hepatitis is easily modified with small doses in most persons having known exposure, there is considerable doubt that serum hepatitis can be modified by this material. If immune globulin is effective at all against serum hepatitis, large and repeated doses are required.

CLINICAL PICTURE. The onset of infectious hepatitis is usually abrupt in children. Typically, the child becomes sufficiently ill within a 12- to 24-hour period to curb his activities spontaneously. Less frequently, onset is gradual over a period of several days, with tiredness and appetite the only complaints. Other common symptoms during the preicteric phase of the illness include headache, vomiting, generalized aching, and right upper quadrant or upper abdominal pain. Constipation and diarrhea occur with equal frequency, and neither is found in more than 5 percent of cases. Mild nasal discharge or sore throat occurs in 10 to 20 percent of children; they are mild and patients seldom mention them spontaneously. Fever in the range of 100° to 101° F is frequent. It is occasionally accompanied by chilliness, although seldom by a frank, shaking chill. Some personality disturbances, such as fretfulness or irritability, also occur.

After 3 to 7 days of such symptoms, the urine becomes brown owing to the excretion of bilirubin. This finding is often the first clue to the diagnosis of infectious hepatitis in what has otherwise appeared to be a nonspecific febrile illness; it is followed in one to several days by detectable scleral, and then generalized, jaundice. In a large percentage of icteric cases, excretion of bilirubin into the gastrointestinal tract is sufficiently reduced to result in white or gray stools. The icteric phase of the illness may last from a few days to two weeks. It is seldom more prolonged in children.

It should be emphasized that infectious and serum hepatitis are generalized diseases. The nausea and vomiting may be related, at least in part, to the occurrence of gastritis and duodenitis. Various neurologic lesions may occur, most often prior to onset of jaundice. These have included peripheral neuritis, myelitis, and encephalitis. Hemolytic anemia and thrombocytopenia have been described; carditis also occurs. However, except for the gastrointestinal symptoms, these manifestations rarely cause clinical concern.

A number of children will experience anicteric hepatitis. Diagnosis is usually made when the illness follows exposure to a known source of infection, such as a jaundiced sibling. Symptoms of the preicteric phase in anicteric hepatitis have approximately the same frequency as in icteric cases, but the disease does not progress to detectable jaundice. In general, these symptoms are milder than those in icteric patients and of briefer duration. Icteric relapse is a very occasional event.

In addition to icteric and anicteric illnesses, the agents of infectious and serum hepatitis can produce asymptomatic infections. Such infections are detected from serial determinations of liver function when there is known exposure. The frequency with which abnormal results are found depends upon the particular test used and the frequency with which it is performed. Additional cases undoubtedly occur that are not detected by any test, but there is no reliable way at present to estimate their frequency.

LABORATORY DIAGNOSIS. Detection of HAA offers the first specific procedure for diagnosis in viral hepatitis. Antigenemia occurs in some 40 to 80 percent of cases presumptively diagnosed as serum hepatitis. The frequency with which it is detected depends upon how early in the illness and how often specimens are taken, and possibly upon the technique for testing. A positive test lends very strong support to a diagnosis of serum hepatitis, although it must be remembered that for a small percentage of individuals in the United States the result will be unrelated to the illness.

Otherwise, reliance is placed upon the so-called liver function tests. These could be more accurately described as "indices of hepatic dysfunction," because severe derangement of liver function is generally necessary to cause abnormal results. One must recognize also that all are to a greater or lesser extent nonspecific for any form of liver disease; none is specifically diagnostic of infectious or serum hepatitis. In general, these tests can be placed in one of three broad categories: (1) those in which release of enzymes by damaged hepatic cells results in an increased enzymatic activity in serum; (2) those in which there is decreased excretion into the bile of various substances, especially bilirubin and sulfobromophthalein; and (3) those that depend on an altered synthesis of protein, as indicated by a decreased serum level (albumin and prothrombin) or altered ratios of various components (flocculation tests).

For the usual patient seen in pediatric practice, laboratory tests are most helpful in the preicteric stage when the diagnosis is not clear. At that time the most useful are the serum transaminase (SGOT and SGPT) assay and a test for bilirubin in the urine. Of these two, the transaminase level is by far the more sensitive, but a qualitative test for bilirubinuria can be easily performed in the physician's office. If the latter is positive and the history is compatible, the child can usually be considered to have infectious hepatitis.

Once the diagnosis is established, laboratory tests are usually needed only in patients sufficiently ill to require hospitalization. To follow the course of the illness, the serum bilirubin or icteric index, serum albumin level, and prothrombin time provide the most useful indices of the tests commonly available. There is usually no point in determining sulfobromophthalein retention in a patient who is icteric or has an elevated serum bilirubin; either of the latter findings is already sufficient indication of decreased hepatic excretory capacity. The height of the serum transaminase activity does not necessarily indicate the severity of illness. Serum enzyme levels and thymol turbidity may remain elevated for varying periods in convalescence. Unless accompanied by other findings, they do not appear to indicate subclinical relapse.

DIFFERENTIAL DIAGNOSIS. Excluding newborns, infectious hepatitis is by far the most common cause of jaundice in children in the United States. There are other causes, however, which must be considered in every patient, even in an epidemic setting. Hepatitis is a frequent finding in infectious mononucleosis and occasionally jaundice is seen. The occurrence of pharyngitis sufficiently severe for the patient to complain of it spontaneously is suggestive of mononucleosis rather than infectious hepatitis. Pronounced lymphadenopathy and splenomegaly are also more suggestive of infectious mononucleosis. "Atypical" lymphocytes occur in both diseases, as well as in a number of other viral infections; finding more than 10 percent atypical lymphocytes suggests infectious mononucleosis. The heterophile titer is occasionally elevated in viral hepatitis, so appropriate absorption studies should be carried out if an abnormal result is obtained.

A history of exposure to a jaundiced dog is of concern in a jaundiced child only when the canine illness is produced by leptospirosis, especially that form due to *Leptospira icterohemorrhagiae*. Contact with urine from an infected dog can result in transmission to members of the family. Conjunctival suffusion, leucocytosis, proteinuria, pyuria, and frank meningitis are all suggestive of this diagnosis. Canine viral hepatitis is not responsible for clinically recognized human infections.

Other causes of jaundice in children include hemolytic anemia and cholelithiasis. The latter is most frequently seen in children with familial hemolytic disorders.

TREATMENT. There is no specific treatment for infectious or serum hepatitis. Several studies have shown that the important measures in promoting rapid convalescence are adequate rest and maintenance of a good caloric intake. These can be provided at home unless conditions there are unsatisfactory or the disease is of greater severity than usual.

During World War II, experience with adults suggested that absolute bed rest was requisite for reducing the frequency of chronic hepatitis and cirrhosis resulting from the infection. This concept has sometimes been applied stringently to children without regard to their clinical status. In general, parents should be encouraged to keep the patient in bed during the acute phase of the illness, especially as long as the child is willing to stay there. As he begins to recover and desires increased activity, quiet play may be allowed despite the persistence of jaundice. He should remain away from school until jaundice has disappeared.

The total caloric intake appears to be the most significant factor in promoting recovery. High-protein and low-fat diets are not necessary, especially in view of the difficulty of maintaining an adequate intake on a low-fat diet. The patient's appetite is often better in the morning than later in the day, and administration of a greater than usual share of the day's calories at breakfast is advisable.

Supplemental administration of the B vitamins is frequently recommended, although their value remains to be demonstrated. A decreased prothrombin time is usually not corrected by administration of vitamin K. The defect is in hepatic synthesis of prothrombin rather than absorption of vitamin K, unless the jaundice has been of long duration. Antibiotics are of no value in treatment, and routine administration of corticosteroids is to be strongly discouraged.

Progression to the more severe form of the disease occasionally occurs, indicated usually by deepening of jaundice and obtundation. Hepatic coma or precoma is a matter of serious concern and carries a very poor prognosis. Restriction of protein, administration of nonabsorbable antibiotics to reduce ammonia production by intestinal bacteria, and supplemental feeding with glucose intravenously, are employed as treatment. Administration of corticosteroids in large doses is traditional, and use of exchange transfusion is now frequent; benefit from either is doubtful.

EPIDEMIOLOGY AND PREVENTION. The epidemiologic history is of particular importance in viral hepatitis. There is no present prospect for development of vaccines, so that protection to a considerable extent depends upon recognizing modes of transmission which are preventable. In addition, passive immunization with immune globulin is effective when there is known or probable exposure to infectious hepatitis.

Infectious hepatitis appears to be most commonly transmitted from person to person, especially among children. A history of exposure to a jaundiced person from 15 to 45 days prior to onset of symptoms can be obtained in 20 to 40 percent of pediatric cases. However, even in a community-wide epidemic, prior exposure is not recognized by the majority of patients, and it is presumed that persons with anicteric illnesses and inapparent infections are the source of most such cases. If the patient lives in a part of the community in which infectious hepatitis is known to be occurring among other children, a diagnosis of infectious hepatitis must be suspected even when a history of definite exposure is not obtained.

The closer the contact, the greater the likelihood of person-to-person transmission, and as expected, individuals living in the household with a recognized case are at greatest risk. Among siblings of school age, the secondary attack rate has sometimes been as high as 40 percent. Most cases occurring in unprotected family members have their onset more than two weeks after that of the first case. This lag usually allows enough time for immune globulin to be administered to other family members before the end of the incubation period. The sooner immune globulin is administered, the more effective it appears to be. For persons with a known exposure, a single injection of 0.02 to 0.04 ml per kg of body weight (0.01 to 0.02 ml per lb) provides adequate protection. In practice, administration of 1 ml for children weighing less than 50 kg and 2 ml for all other persons is recommended.

It has been demonstrated that many household contacts to whom immune globulin has been administered have changes in liver function indicative of inapparent infection. It is probable, therefore, that immune globulin prevents clinical disease but not infection among exposed family members. There is no evidence that subsequent development of active immunity is impaired. Since a child can be spared a 1- to 3-week period of illness by giving him immune globulin, there appears to be no reason to withhold this material when household exposure occurs. It is also worthwhile to immunize passively adult members of the household regardless of their age, despite the fact that the secondary attack rate in adults is often much lower. When the disease does occur in adults, it is more severe.

It is probable that most of those who are susceptible are already infected by the time the nature of the illness is recognized. There is no point, therefore, in isolating ill persons from other members of the family, especially if immune globulin has been given.

Concern has often been expressed that administration of immune globulin to exposed individuals facilitates the spread of infectious hepatitis by permitting persons excreting the virus to remain ambulatory. In several situations it has been found that administration of immune globulin to half of the population was sufficient to curtail spread of the agent among those not receiving such protection. This suggests that persons experiencing inapparent infection as a result of having received immune globulin do not usually serve as a source for others. Accordingly, there is no reason to restrict activities of persons who have been exposed and received immune globulin as prophylaxis.

Infectious hepatitis transmitted from person to person is a cyclic disease with long-term rises and falls in incidence. Increases that amount to community-wide epidemics occur in most areas every 7 to 15 years. Sporadic cases usually occur between epidemics, especially in larger cities. During the course of the community-wide epidemic, the spread of the disease is slow, with cases building up over a period of several months. Although epidemic infectious hepatitis is usually most prevalent among children of school age, it is not necessarily true that the school itself is the major focus for interfamilial spread. Some children acquire infections at school, but more cases probably result from neighborhood play activity. Nevertheless, parents often demand immune globulin for their children whenever a case occurs in the school attended by their children. Because effective exposure seldom occurs as a result of school or even classroom contact, globulin administration is not needed and is probably not advisable.

In addition to transmission from person to person, infectious hepatitis may be spread through fecal contamination of water or food. It is, in fact, the only enteric virus for which transmission by common vehicle is well accepted. A common-source epidemic is most often recognized when a large number of cases occur in a 2- to 4-week period.

Waterborne disease most often results from private supplies with inadequate safeguards. Institutional, camp, and municipal supplies have become contaminated, however, and caused large-scale epidemics. When waterborne transmission occurs, cases among adults usually outnumber those among children. This is presumably due to a lower ratio of anicteric to icteric cases in adults. The average age of patients, however, would depend upon the nature of the population exposed to the contaminated supply. One would think that infectious hepatitis could be acquired by swimming or accidental immersion in contaminated water, but such transmission has not been documented.

Food can also serve as a vehicle for infection. The frequency with which epidemics traceable to food have been recognized has increased in recent years, presumably as a result of greater alertness. Most of the epidemics have taken place in school or other institutions in which a population eating in a particular cafeteria or other facility has remained together throughout the incubation period. Additional epidemics probably go unrecognized because the population is not so localized or questioning is not sufficiently detailed to point to exposure to a particular food. In some instances, a person assisting in food preparation has had a recognizable illness at an appropriate interval before the beginning of the epidemic; otherwise inapparent infection in a food handler is assumed. Contamination of a food at its source is known only with raw shellfish, although frozen strawberries have been suspected.

Careful questioning with regard to all exposures is worthwhile; the existence of common-vehicle epidemics has on a number of occasions been recognized first from the history of a particular exposure given by a few patients hospitalized at the same time. In addition, all cases should be reported, as routine investigation for potential vehicles is now practiced by many city and county health departments.

Any unit of whole blood has the potential for transmitting either infectious or serum hepatitis to its recipient, and there is no way at the present time to eliminate this hazard. The extent of the risk varies from hospital to hospital, depending at least in part upon the type of donor population utilized. The attack rate increases with the number of units given, and therefore the amount should be limited to the minimum which will accomplish the desired therapeutic end. Any of the available unpooled derivatives of whole blood have the same potential for hepatitis transmission as whole blood itself.

When plasma from individual donors is pooled for fractionation, a single donation from a carrier would contaminate all of the units derived from that pool. Although infectious hepatitis has not been shown to be transmitted by a pooled product, the risk of serum hepatitis is greatly enhanced. Blood fractions in present use with a high risk of icterogenicity are fibrinogen and concentrates of factors VIII and IX. Other components of plasma, however, can be rendered safe by heating at 60° C for 10 hours. Plasma protein fraction (plasmanate) and serum albumin are examples of such products. Pooled plasma itself is now largely withdrawn because of its hazard regardless of method of treatment.

Viral hepatitis transmitted by unsterile instruments is entirely preventable. Any instrument which breaks the skin of one person and then breaks the skin of another without being sterilized in the interval has the potential of transmitting either infectious or serum hepatitis. Syringes, needles, and other equipment which break the skin, therefore, should be sterilized by one of three means: (1) boiling for 30 minutes; (2) autoclaving at 15 pounds of pressure for 30 minutes; or (3) sterilization in dry heat at 160° C for 1 hour.

VIRAL HEPATITIS IN PREGNANCY. There is an increased risk to both the pregnant woman and the fetus when infectious or serum hepatitis occurs during pregnancy. Studies in both Israel and India have indicated that the attack rate and case fatality rate are higher for pregnant women, and that abortions, stillbirths, and premature deliveries occur with greatly increased frequency. In these situations, however, poor maternal nutritional status may have contributed significantly to the severity of illness.

Reports from the United States have been conflicting. In some series there appear to be higher frequencies of maternal and fetal deaths than would be expected. Nevertheless, it seems likely that viral hepatitis in pregnancy is not the serious disease that it is in areas where maternal nutrition is poor. Any increased risk in the United States appears to be greater for the fetus than for the mother. The occurrence of viral hepatitis during pregnancy is not an indication for interruption.

Data collected in Australia suggest a correlation between infectious hepatitis and mongolism. This correlation has not been apparent elsewhere. In addition, follow-up of children born to mothers who have experienced viral hepatitis at any time in pregnancy has not indicated an increased incidence of congenital abnormalities.

NEONATAL HEPATITIS. (See also Sec. 24.5.) Several viruses not ordinarily hepatotropic cause hepatitis as part of the clinical picture of infection during the neonatal period; these include several of the enteroviruses, cytomegalovirus, rubella virus, and *Herpesvirus hominis*. While an enlarged liver, jaundice, and parenchymal cell necrosis are easily recognized features of such infections, other systemic manifestations are usually obvious. Skin lesions, cardiac involvement, and central nervous system damage occur frequently and are clinically prominent. Similar findings are seen in many cases of congenital toxoplasmosis (p. 839). The specific diagnosis is derived from appropriate microbiologic and serologic studies.

The classification of hepatogenous jaundice unaccompanied by other evidences of generalized infection is uncertain. Biopsy in such cases reveals an unusual type of multinucleated giant parenchymal cell, with or without an inflammatory reaction. Whether this pathologic picture is etiologically specific is disputed; even those who feel that it represents a specific lesion differ concerning the responsible mechanism. Transplacentally transmitted serum hepatitis, infection by other viruses, toxic damage to the parenchymal cells, and biliary malformation are among the suggested causes.

The virus of serum hepatitis can be transplacentally transmitted and appears to be able to produce disease in the first few months of life. This statement is based on reports of cases in which the mother experienced an icteric illness during pregnancy and the infant developed jaundice after an interval compatible with the incubation period of serum hepatitis. In addition, in 5 to 15 percent of cases, other children of the same apparently healthy mother developed neonatal hepatitis following pregnancies separated by intervals ranging from one to several years. This finding is consistent with what is known about the prolonged carrier state in persons who have caused multiple cases of serum hepatitis among recipients of their blood donations over periods of up to 5 years in length. The most important support, however, is derived from study of a child with neonatal hepatitis and its mother, who in this instance had not had any icteric illness during her pregnancy. Their sera caused typical disease in adult volunteers 2 months or more after inoculation. From such observations and investigations, it seems probable that the virus of serum hepatitis is responsible for some cases of hepatitis in early infancy. The test for HAA should provide important new evidence.

It is generally held that the virus of infectious hepatitis does not cross the placental barrier and is not a cause of disease in the neonatal period. This opinion is based on the fact that few investigators have observed jaundice in an infant following the occurrence of infectious hepatitis in the mother, even when that disease occurred late in pregnancy. Some instances of apparent transmission have been reported, however, in which there was epidemiologic evidence to support the diagnosis of this type of hepatitis in the mother. It is not possible at the present time to say whether the apparent rarity or absence of transplacentally transmitted infectious hepatitis is due to failure of the agent to pass that barrier or failure of the infection to manifest itself clinically in this age group. Nevertheless, some authorities refrain from administering immune globulin at birth to infants of mothers who have had infectious hepatitis during the third trimester. Similarly, there appears to be no necessity to attempt passive protection of other infants in the same nursery; no instance of transmission under such circumstances has been reported.

In most cases of neonatal "hepatitis," parenchymal giant cell formation is not accompanied by necrosis or infiltration of inflammatory cells. A similar picture is seen in cases of extrahepatic bile duct atresia and ABO and Rh incompatibility. Nonspecificity of the parenchymal cell changes, therefore, seems likely. The absence of an inflammatory reaction or intracellular inclusions makes a viral causation for the majority of cases difficult to support. Until the etiology is established, the term "prolonged obstructive jaundice of uncertain cause" seems preferable to "hepatitis."

REFERENCES

Adams, R. H., and Combes, B. Viral hepatitis during pregnancy. J.A.M.A., 192:195, 1965.

Aterman, K. Neonatal hepatitis and its relation to viral hepatitis of mother. Amer. J. Dis. Child., 105:395, 1963.

Blumberg, B. S., Sutnick, A. I., London, W. T., and Millman, I. Australia antigen and hepatitis, New Eng. J. Med., 283:349, 1970.

Davis, D. J., and Hanlon, R. C. Epidemic infectious hepatitis in a small Iowa community. Amer. J. Hyg., 43:314, 1946.

Giles, J. P., McCollum, R. W., Berndtson, L. W., Jr., and Krugman, S. Viral hepatitis: Relation of Australia/SH antigen to the Willowbrook MS-2 strain. New Eng. J. Med., 281:119, 1969.

Harris, M. J., and Beveridge, J. Infectious hepatitis in children. Med. J. Aust., 2:594, 646, 1967.

Havens, W. P., Jr. Infectious hepatitis. Medicine, 27:279, 1948.

Kogan, A., Krenmal, R., and Peterson, D. R. The relationship between infectious hepatitis and Down's syndrome. Amer. J. Public Health, 58:305, 1968.

Krugman, S., and Giles, J. P. Viral hepatitis—new light on an old disease. J.A.M.A. 212:1019, 1970.

Mosley, J. W., and Galambos, J. T. Viral Hepatitis. In Schiff, L., ed., Diseases of the Liver. Philadelphia, J. B. Lippincott Co., 1969.

Motoshok, R. E., Karelitz, S., and Strauss, L. Homologous serum hepatitis in infants and children. Pediatrics, 3:651, 1949.

Reisler, D. M., Strong, W. D., and Mosley, J. W. Transaminase levels in the postconvalescent phase of infectious hepatitis. J.A.M.A., 202:131, 1967.

Schneider, A. J., and Mosley, J. W. Studies of variations of glutamic-oxalacetic transaminase in serum in infectious hepatitis. Pediatrics, 24:367, 1959.

Zuckerman, A. J. Viral hepatitis and the Australia-SH antigen. Nature, 223:569, 1969.

14.29
HERPESVIRUS HOMINIS
(HERPES SIMPLEX)
INFECTIONS

ALFRED L. FLORMAN

The skin manifestations of herpes were described in the time of Hippocrates. Indeed the word "herpes" is derived from the Greek word "herpo," meaning "I creep along."

When first isolated in 1912, the virus causing herpes was called herpes simplex; the current name *Herpesvirus hominis* serves to relate this virus to several others with somewhat similar properties. Included in the herpesvirus group are herpes B of monkeys, infectious laryngotrachitis virus of chickens, varicella-zoster, and cytomegalovirus of man. All are moderately large, ether-sensitive, DNA-containing viruses which under the electron microscope appear to have similar structure and shape.

It has been appreciated only relatively recently that *Herpesvirus hominis* infections in man are not restricted to the skin and mucous membranes and that the liver, adrenals, lungs, heart, and central nervous system may be seriously involved. The clinical forms in which they appear reflect the age and immune status of the patient.

Herpesvirus hominis can live in symbiosis with man and, as a successful parasite, regularly causes latent infections.

Virology

As a result of studies with the electron microscope, the complete viral particle or virion is known to consist of a roughly spherical central core which contains deoxyribonucleic acid (DNA) and measures 75 mμ in diameter. It is surrounded by a capsid which measures 100 mμ in diameter and has the symmetry of an icosohedron (20-sided figure). It is made up of 162 elongated capsomeres. Surrounding all this is an envelope derived from host cell membrane which measures 145 to 200 mμ in diameter. Incomplete forms in which core or envelope is missing have also been seen.

The viral particle consists of protein, lipid, DNA, and carbohydrate. On the average, for 1,000 parts protein there are 320 parts phospholipid, 100 parts DNA, and 25 parts carbohydrate. The virus is heat labile. It is destroyed by x-ray, ultraviolet light, ether, and a variety of detergents and proteolytic enzymes, but it resists glycerol. The natural host of the virus is man. However, it can be transmitted to a great many experimental animals including rabbits, guinea pigs, mice, hamsters, cotton rats, and embryonated hen's eggs. It also grows in tissue culture in several types of cells, rabbit kidney and Hela cells being used most frequently.

Although *Herpesvirus hominis* is a relatively homogeneous virus, strain differences can be demonstrated by preferential host selection, by the technique of neutralization kinetics, and by cytopathic effect in tissue culture cells. By these methods *Herpesvirus hominis* has been shown to exist in two types—type 1 and type 2.

Neutralizing antigens are in the viral particle. Complement-fixing (CF) antigens are in both the particulate and soluble fractions of the virus.

Following primary infection, the host responds regularly with CF and neutralizing antibodies. These appear between the fourth and sixth days and reach their peak by the fourteenth day. After primary infection in children, CF antibodies appear first and decline earlier than do neutralizing antibodies. Both antibodies are boosted by subsequent subclinical infections. In contrast, the CF and neutralizing antibody levels are stabilized in most adults and do not rise with the appearance of recurrent lesions.

Investigations of the class of immunoglobulins which appears after primary infection have shown that in adults IgM could be detected 7 days after infection, IgG after 14 days, and IgA after 21 days. Individuals with recurrent herpes infections were found to have lower IgA levels.

Herpesvirus has been shown to induce cellular production of interferon, but it does so poorly. It also stimulates a delayed type of skin hypersensitivity.

Epidemiology

Herpesvirus hominis is found throughout the world. It causes an endemic disease which may appear at any season. More than 90 percent of the infections are subclinical, and most adults, especially in urban areas, show serologic evidence of having been infected with the virus. There have been rare reports of outbreaks where, under very special conditions of close contact, in families and institutions, more than 50 percent of infections have resulted in clinical disease.

Primary infections occur in individuals who do not have circulating antibodies; in individuals with such antibodies, recurrent disease is seen.

Infants born of immune mothers are protected for the first 5 to 6 months of life, since most herpes antibodies are in the IgG class and cross the placenta. Neonatal herpes occurs only in infants born to nonimmune mothers. Although primary infections usually occur between the first and third years of life, they are occasionally seen in adults.

The incidence of infection is considerably higher among those in poorer socioeconomic areas, since spread is favored by overcrowding and close bodily contact. Trauma also helps to establish infection in a susceptible person.

The reservoir of infections is largely among subclinically infected carriers. Patients who have recovered from stomatitis may excrete virus in their saliva intermittently for as long as 7 weeks. Virus may also be recovered from the saliva and stool of asymptomatic adults.

The usual incubation period for primary infections is 6 or 7 days, although it varies from 2 to 12 days.

Recurrent disease results not from reinfection but rather from changes in either the external or internal environment which upset the symbiotic balance between the host and his latent herpes infection.

Exposure to ultraviolet rays, fever, menstruation, or stress is a common cause of such disturbances.

Pathogenesis and Pathology

In a primary infection, virus enters the body through the lips, mouth, skin, conjunctival sac, or genitals. Initial multiplication occurs at the site of entry, where a local lesion may develop. There may be a systemic reaction at this time. Virus then passes to regional lymph nodes, and from there it may invade the bloodstream and localize anywhere in the body.

The characteristic lesion is the skin vesicle. It is filled with fluid which contains exfoliated epithelial cells, syncytial giant cells, leucocytes, and fibrin. It forms as a result of ballooning degeneration of epithelial cells. Giant cells containing 2 to 15 or more nuclei, some with intranuclear inclusion bodies, are found in the floor of the vesicle. Similar inclusions may also be seen in epithelial cells at the edge of the lesion. These inclusion bodies represent areas in which virus has multiplied. An individual vesicle contains virus for only about 48 hours. Small giant cells result from changes in mitosis caused by infection, whereas large syncytial giant cells result from the attraction and fusion of neighboring uninfected cells to an infected cell. The surrounding skin shows capillary dilatation and inflammatory reaction. Necrosis in the skin is rare. The mucosal lesion resembles the skin lesion except that there is more fibrin and less fluid in the vesicle and the roof cells are more edematous. When the vesicle ruptures the characteristic ulcer is seen. The pathologic findings are indistinguishable in primary and recurrent lesions.

When visceral lesions develop as a result of viremia, necrosis is seen frequently with relatively little surrounding inflammatory reaction. Intranuclear inclusion bodies are found in small numbers at the edge of these lesions.

Clinical Observation

The clinical syndromes which result from infection in any one patient may involve more than one area and reflect the state of both his specific and nonspecific resistance. Indeed, recurrent herpes represents a relapse of one of the localized forms in the skin, mucosa, or cornea in an individual with circulating antibody. It is usually not associated with systemic illness but may be triggered by such an illness.

Superficial infections can often be recognized clinically. Previously, disseminated visceral or nervous system infections could be recognized only if they were accompanied by characteristic superficial lesions. Viral isolation now permits the diagnosis of herpesvirus infection even in the absence of such superficial lesions.

Diseases of the Skin

HERPES SIMPLEX. The names "cold sores," "fever blisters," and "herpes labialis" are all synonyms for this common recurrent disease. It usually involves the mucocutaneous junction of the lips and tends to reappear at the same site. A sensation of burning or itching may precede the appearance of red papules, which quickly become vesicular. The fully developed lesion consists of a group of thin-walled vesicles on an erythematous base, which dry with the formation of yellow superficial crusts and heal without a scar. Only very rarely do they become secondarily infected with bacteria.

PRIMARY HERPETIC DERMATITIS. In contrast to the grouped vesicles of the recurrent disease, scattered single vesicles are more usual in the primary illness. They may resemble the lesions of varicella, especially when they appear in crops and result in a generalized eruption. However, the individual lesions tend to be smaller. A primary infection is accompanied by systemic symptoms, including fever, malaise, and occasionally gastroenteritis. Stomatitis may or may not be present.

ECZEMA HERPETICUM (KAPOSI'S DISEASE). This is a severe form of this primary infection in a patient with eczema. The skin is the portal of entry. In patients under 1 year of age vesicles may continue to appear for as long as 9 days. Great areas of skin may be denuded, and large quantities of fluids, electrolytes, and protein may be lost. Fatalities may occur in untreated cases or in young infants, especially those born prematurely, in whom the disease is often associated with the visceral lesions of disseminated herpes. Recurrent attacks have been described, and despite the presence of circulating antibody the patient may again have a systemic reaction, which fortunately is usually milder than during the primary attack.

TRAUMATIC HERPES. This is a primary infection which follows a traumatic break in the skin of a susceptible individual. Vesicles appear about 2 to 3 days after the original trauma. They tend to follow lymphatic channels and may resemble herpes zoster in appearance. They may even be associated with vague, deep-seated pain. The regional lymph nodes become enlarged and tender, and the patient develops fever. The disease may last for 2 to 3 weeks. Following recovery, vesicles may recur at the site of the original injury. Several unusual forms of traumatic herpes have been described, including "herpetic whitlows," which are seen on the finger of susceptible nurses who handle infected secretions, and "herpes gladiatorium," which has been reported among wrestlers.

Diseases of the Mucous Membranes

ACUTE HERPETIC GINGIVOSTOMATITIS. This is the commonest manifestation of the primary infection. Its peak incidence is between 1 and 3 years, but it may occur at any age. There are fever, irritability, red swollen gums which often bleed, vesicles and ulcers on the oral mucosa, and local lymphadenopathy. The fever may be as high as 105° F. Because of pain the patients may refuse all feedings and become dehydrated. The lesions in the mouth vary in size and number. When they involve the tonsillar region the disease may have to be differentiated from bacterial tonsillitis and several other viral infections. This disease tends to last 1 to 2 weeks. Fortunately, pain disappears before the lesions are completely healed.

Although acute herpetic gingivostomatitis does not recur, occasionally recurrent attacks of labial herpes may be accompanied by local lesions of the gum and inner lip. Recurrent aphthae are not due to *Herpesvirus hominis.*

HERPETIC INFECTIONS OF THE GENITALIA. These occur more frequently in females than in males. Vesicles appear on the mucous membrane of the labia and lower vagina. As in the mouth, they quickly collapse and become covered with gray-yellow membranes. In primary infections there are associated fever and pain. Local lymphadenopathy develops, and vesicular lesions are occasionally found on the adjacent skin. When primary genital infections occur in a pregnant mother, they are an important cause of generalized disease in newborns. Similar genital lesions have been described in women with recurrent infections. However, these mothers usually have high levels of antibody which are passed to their infants in utero. Thus the risk of generalized disease is appreciably less in such infants.

In males, genital herpes causes urethritis with burning on urination and a watery or purulent discharge. Tiny vesicles may be present on the glans or prepuce. Recurrences are common and usually consist of clusters of eroded vesicles on the glans.

In children, type 1 and type 2 herpesvirus cause herpes of the genitalia with almost equal frequency. In contrast, in the adult, genital herpes is much more often due to the type 2 virus.

Diseases of the Eye

HERPETIC KERATOCONJUNCTIVITIS AND KERATITIS. Primary infections usually begin as a unilateral follicular conjunctivitis. Vesicles may be found on the lids, and regional preauricular nodes become enlarged. Fever and malaise are present, but pain is not a prominent complaint. Stomatitis may also be present. If only the conjunctiva is involved the disease lasts for only a few days; however, if it spreads to the cornea it may last for weeks. On the cornea small punctate or large ulcerlike erosions appear which progress into dendritic ulcers. Occasionally deeper structures may be involved, leading to a disciform keratitis, hypopyon keratitis, and iridocyclitis. Recurrent infections of the cornea are usually not associated with conjunctivitis.

Diseases of the Nervous System

PRIMARY HERPESVIRUS MENINGITIS. Clinically this is indistinguishable from other forms of viral meningitis. It occurs sporadically, and recovery is the rule. The virus can be isolated only rarely from the spinal fluid, which usually shows a lymphocytic pleocytosis. Herpesvirus was found to be the cause of 5 percent of 854 cases of aseptic meningitis studied in a United States Army laboratory.

PRIMARY ENCEPHALITIS. This is seen more frequently in older individuals than in children. Clinically there are fever, headache, occasional paralysis, mental confusion, stupor, coma, twitchings, and convulsions. The cerebrospinal fluid shows increased protein, mononuclear cells, and often red blood cells. The mortality is high, death occurring usually between the eighth and twelfth day. This condition is discussed in detail elsewhere (Chap. 15).

SECONDARY MENINGOENCEPHALITIS. This may occur as a part of a generalized infection in which the virus can be isolated from tissues besides the nervous system. It is most common in newborns.

Generalized Infections

IN NEWBORNS. The newborn of a mother without circulating antibodies is susceptible to *Herpesvirus hominis* infection. Such infection may be acquired transplacentally during the viremic stage of his mother's primary infection. It may also result from exposure to primary herpetic vulvovaginitis during his passage through the birth canal, or from exposure after birth to either a patient with disease or an asymptomatic person excreting virus in his saliva. Theoretically it is also possible for infection to occur in an infant who has received very little protective antibody from a mother with a low level of immunity. A few such cases have been reported. Similarly the explanation for the fact that infected premature infants usually do less well than infected infants born at term may be that the premature ordinarily receives less immune globulin from his mother. The mortality rate in the newborn period is very high.

When acquired at birth, the illness usually begins between the fourth and seventh day of life. If the illness is acquired in utero the infant may be born with vesicles. As with most infections in the newborn period the onset of illness is subtle. There may be only loss of appetite, lethargy, or low-grade fever. Sometimes, a few scattered vesicles may appear on the skin, or stomatitides may be noted. Then suddenly the baby becomes obviously ill. He may develop bleeding, purpura, jaundice, dyspnea, convulsions, and shock. Death occurs within hours or days. At autopsy the appearance of coagulation necrosis of the liver is very suggestive of *Herpesvirus hominis* infection. Inclusion bodies and virus can be found in almost all organs including the lungs, adrenals, liver, spleen, and brain. If the infant recovers, which is rare, he may have serious nervous system residua and chorioretinitis.

Less typically the illness does not go beyond the first stage of mild symptoms, and a few scattered vesicles may be the only sign of herpes infection.

IN OLDER INFANTS. Except in children with severe malnutrition or eczema, serious generalized disease is very uncommon. It may occur during an attack of severe gingivostomatitis with signs of liver disease, in which cases the mortality rate is also high.

Laboratory Diagnosis

The simplest diagnostic test is to examine scrapings from the base of a vesicle spread on a slide and stained with Giemsa, searching for multinucleated giant cells with intranuclear inclusions. These cells are found in lesions caused by herpesviruses (hominis and varicella-zoster) but not in those caused by vaccinia or variola viruses. The demonstration of characteristic intranuclear inclusion bodies in tissue obtained at biopsy or autopsy is also suggestive of herpesvirus infection.

A more definitive histologic technique is to treat smears of material from the base of a vesicle or sections of infected tissue with fluorescent herpes antibody to demonstrate viral antigen in the cells.

If viral isolation is attempted, material from vesicular fluids, scrapings, spinal fluids, or tissue suspension must be collected and if possible inoculated immediately into susceptible animals or tissue cultures. If specimens must be preserved they should be put in buffered glycerol or treated by rapid freezing in buffered protein-containing solutions. Inoculation of infected material onto the scarified cornea of the rabbit leads within 2 to 3 days to a keratoconjunctivitis which may be followed by encephalitis. If suckling mice are inoculated intracerebrally, they too will die with encephalitis. Embryonated chicken eggs are inoculated onto the chorioallantoic membrane where *Herpesvirus hominis* produces characteristic pocks. Inoculation of tissue cultures of rabbit kidney, human amnion, or Hela cells also produces typical cytopathic changes within a few days, consisting of giant cells and intranuclear inclusions. In contrast to these tests for *Herpesvirus hominis, Herpesvirus varicella-zoster* does not infect rabbits, suckling mice, or the chorioallantoic membrane. Even so, to prove that the effect produced in any of these test animals or tissue cultures is due to *Herpesvirus hominis* it is necessary to neutralize the effect with specific antiserum.

With special techniques of electron microscopy, it is sometimes possible to demonstrate the virus in vesicular fluid taken directly from the patient.

A serologic diagnosis of *Herpesvirus hominis* infection can be made with either the neutralization or complement-fixation tests. Both become positive early in convalescence. A rise in antibody titer can be regularly demonstrated only in primary infections. In recurrent disease a high titer of antibody is usually present in serum during the acute phase. Virus neutralization may be demonstrated by pock reduction on the chorioallantoic membrane, by protection of mice infected intracerebrally, or by prevention of cytopathic effects in tissue culture. For a serologic diagnosis, acute phase serum should be collected before the fifth day of illness. Convalescent phase serum is best collected 2 to 3 weeks after onset.

Treatment

Since most infections are self-limited, only supporting measures are needed, with special attention to fluid balance (Sec. 3.7). Sometimes the pain associated with lesions in the mouth is alleviated by local anesthetics, although care should be taken to avoid sensitizing preparations. Removal of skin crusts by soaks may be helpful. Secondary bacterial infections are infrequent. Occasionally they may become a problem in Kaposi's disease. In those instances appropriate systemic therapy based on results of cultures is indicated.

The early use of large doses of pooled gamma globulin to supply missing neutralizing antibody in severe primary infections has been suggested on the basis of both experimental evidence and theoretical considerations. Its possible use in human infections remains to be tested.

The metabolic antagonist 5-iodo-2'-deoxyuridine (IDU) is useful in the treatment of superficial herpetic infections of the eye (see Sec. 27.5). It must be applied locally in saturated solution (0.1 percent) at very frequent intervals, preferably hourly. It has been less effective in deep eye infections. Because of the possible serious consequences, all ocular lesions should be under the care of an ophthalmologist. Cauterization, scraping, and even keratoplasty may be required. The use of steroids in superficial eye lesions is contraindicated, though it may be necessary in deep infections together with IDU. The effectiveness of IDU in treating skin infections is unsettled.

A second metabolic antagonist, cytosine arabinoside (cytarabine), has also been effective in the treatment of superficial herpetic keratitis, giving approximately the same results as does IDU—that is, a cure rate ranging from 50 to 80 percent. Recently it was reported from Oxford by Juel-Jensen that cytosine arabinoside given intravenously had produced dramatic cure, within 24 hours, of a young adult male suffering from severe primary *Herpesvirus hominis* infection. He also reported prompt cure by cytosine arabinoside of severe herpes infection in two leukemic patients. The drug produced a similar result in a patient with severe eczema herpeticum and generalized herpes infection. Juel-Jensen also reported that cytosine arabinoside had brought about "a dramatic recovery" in a 26-year-old man suffering from simian herpesvirus encephalitis. The dose of cytarabine used to treat these patients was from 0.3 mg per kg of body weight to 2.0 mg per kg, given intravenously, once daily for 5 days. No deleterious effects of the drug were noted. The above data suggest that cytarabine may be useful in severe herpesvirus infections, but much more experience is required to determine whether this is actually the case.

Other uses of these antiviral agents are being investigated. IDU has been used intravenously in the treatment of herpes simplex encephalitis with some encouraging results. Cytosine arabinoside seems to produce healing of herpetic keratoconjunctivitis of rabbits even when applied after ulceration has begun.

Prevention

For the newborn or the infant with eczema exposed to a herpetic lesion, the administration of prophylactic gamma globulin in large doses (0.2 to 0.3 ml/kg) has been recommended to provide specific neutralizing antibodies which he may lack. There is no convincing evidence that this procedure has been successful in aborting serious disease, although it seems reasonable for these children who are at such high risk.

Nurses with herpetic lesions should not be permitted to work in nurseries with newborns. It has been suggested that if a mother has primary herpetic vulvovaginitis, the infant should be delivered by cesarian section to avoid contaminating it during passage through the birth canal.

A psychologic codeterminant is suggested by the experience that the frequency of recurrences appears to have been diminished by psychotherapy in some children.

Superficial x-rays and repeated smallpox vaccinations, to prevent recurrent disease, were recommended at one time. However, such measures are both ineffective and dangerous and are not recommended.

Both killed and live herpesvirus vaccines have been tried in patients with recurrent disease without consistently favorable results. Indeed both types of vaccine have induced new lesions.

Some new method of enhancing host resistance would be most valuable but has not yet been developed. Experimentally a number of nontoxic substances, such as one obtained from staphylococci, have been shown to enhance the resistance of mice to a subsequent challenge with *Herpesvirus hominis*.

REFERENCES

A.M.A. Council on Drugs. Evaluation of idoxuridine (IDU). J.A.M.A., 190:535, 1964.

Blank, H., and Rake, G. Viral and Rickettsial Diseases. Boston, Little, Brown & Co., 1955, Chap. 3, pp. 44-70.

Buddingh, G. J., Schrum, D. I., Lanier, J. C., and Guidry, D. J. Studies of the natural history of herpes simplex infections. Pediatrics, 11:595, 1953.

Florman, A. L. Viral diseases: unusual manifestations and simulations. Clin. Pediat., 2:3, 1963.

———— and Mindlin, R. L. Generalized herpes simplex in an 11 day old premature infant. Amer. J. Dis. Child., 83:481, 1952.

Hale, B. D., Rendtorff, R. C., Walker, L. C., and Roberts, A. N. Epidemic herpetic stomatitis in an orphanage nursery. J.A.M.A., 183:1068, 1963.

Juel-Jensen, B. E. Severe generalized primary herpes treated with cytarabine. Brit. Med. J., 2:154, 1970.

Miller, J. K., Hesser, F., and Tompkins, V. H. Herpes simplex encephalitis. Ann. Int. Med., 64:92, 1966.

Nahmias, A. J., et al. Typing of herpesvirus homines strains by direct immunofluorescent technique. Proc. Soc. Exp. Biol. Med., 132:1145, 1969.

Rhodes, A. J., and van Rooyen, C. E. Textbook of Virology, 4th ed. Baltimore, William & Wilkins Co., 1962, Chap. 12, pp. 136-144.

Scott, T. F., and Tokumaru, T. *Herpesvirus hominis* (virus of herpes simplex). Bact. Rev., 28:458, 1964.

———— and Tokumaru, T. The herpesvirus group. *In* Horsfall, F. L., Jr., and Tamm, I., eds., Viral and Rickettsial Infections of Man, 4th ed. Philadelphia, J. B. Lippincott Co., 1965.

Selling, B., and Kibrick, S. An outbreak of herpes simplex among wrestlers (*Herpes gladiatorum*). New Eng. J. Med., 270:979, 1964.

Slavin, H. G., and Ferguson, J. J., Jr. Zoster-like eruptions caused by virus of herpes simplex. Amer. J. Med., 8:456, 1950.

Stern, H., Elek, S. D., Millar, D. M., and Anderson, H. F. Herpetic whitlow. Lancet, 2:871, 1959.

Tokumaru, T. The role of gamma immunoglobulin in herpes simplex virus infection in man. Fed. Proc., 25:489, 1966.

Torphy, D. P., et al. Herpes simplex virus infection in infants: a spectrum of disease. J. Pediat., 76:405, 1970.

Ward, J. R., and Clark, L. Primary herpes simplex virus infection of the fingers. J.A.M.A., 176:226, 1961.

Wheeler, C. E., and Huffines, W. D. Primary disseminated herpes simplex of the newborn. J.A.M.A., 191:455, 1965.

Wilson, M. G., and Martini, M. Primary nondisseminated herpes-simplex infection in a newborn infant. New Eng. J. Med., 267:708, 1962.

Witzleben, C. L., and Driscoll, S. C. Possible transplacental transmission of herpes simplex infection. Pediatrics, 36:192, 1965.

Zuelzer, W. W., and Stulberg, C. S. Herpes simplex virus as the cause of fulminating visceral disease and hepatitis in infancy. Amer. J. Dis. Child., 83:421, 1952.

14.30
INFECTIOUS MONONUCLEOSIS
(GLANDULAR FEVER, PFEIFFER'S DISEASE)

SAUL KRUGMAN

Infectious mononucleosis is an acute infectious disease presumably of viral etiology. It is characterized clinically by fever, generalized lymphadenopathy, splenomegaly, sore throat, and other protean manifestations. The blood picture shows an absolute increase of atypical lymphocytes, and the serum usually has a high titer of agglutinins for sheep erythrocytes.

ETIOLOGY. The causative agent has not been identified. Transmission experiments made by Wising and by van den Berghe strongly suggest that the disease is caused by a virus. Bang and Julianelle, however, were unable to transmit the disease to either man or monkey; and Evans also failed to induce it in 21 human volunteers. Evidence from the Henles and their associates now indicates that the etiologic agent may be a herpeslike virus first detected in cell lines derived from Burkitt's East African malignant lymphoma. The regular appearance of antibody to this EB virus was demonstrated in patients with infectious mononucleosis. Furthermore, prospective studies by Evans, Niederman, and McCollum suggest that only persons who have no antibody against the EB virus are susceptible to infectious mononucleosis. However, some reservations have been raised by Glade and others against final acceptance of the EB virus as the cause of infectious mononucleosis. These include the fact that antibody against the virus appears during the course of a variety of unrelated lymphoreticular disorders, including Burkitt's lymphoma, carcinoma of the posterior nasal space, and sarcoidosis.

EPIDEMIOLOGY. The disease appears in both sporadic and epidemic forms. Epidemics have occurred in orphanages, schools, hospitals, and army installations. Experience with the sporadic form of the disease indicates that it is apparently not contagious. The portal of entry of the infective agent has been presumed to be the nasopharynx because of the frequency of pharyngitis and cervical adenitis. Children and young adults are most susceptible, but no age is immune. However, it occurs rarely during infancy.

PATHOLOGY. The pathology of infectious mononucleosis has been described by Custer and Smith, whose observations are based on nine autopsies and many biopsies. The gross changes are characterized by enlargement of the lymphoid tissues. In addition to the lymphadenopathy and splenomegaly, nasopharyngeal lymphoid hyperplasia is constant. Microscopically there are perivascular aggregates of normal and abnormal lymphocytes involving lymph nodes, spleen, tonsils, lungs, heart, liver, kidneys, adrenals, central nervous system, and skin. These pathologic findings indicate that infectious mononucleosis is a generalized infection with changes in almost every organ of the body.

SYMPTOMS. The incubation period has been estimated to range from 4 to 14 days. The onset, which may be acute or insidious, is usually ushered in with anorexia, general malaise, fever, lymphadenopathy, and sore throat. The temperature rises to 103° or 104°F and gradually falls by lysis over a variable period averaging 6 days. Lymph node enlargement is observed chiefly in the cervical group. However, any or all of the lymph nodes of the body may be involved. The tonsils may be slightly enlarged and reddened or may be completely covered by a membrane clinically indistinguishable from that in diphtheria. In approximately 50 percent of the cases a moderate enlargement of the spleen is detected. Less frequently the liver is also palpable. The patient may be jaundiced and may have symptoms similar to those seen in infectious hepatitis. A variety of skin rashes may be associated with the disease. The rash usually appears before the end of the first week as a scarlatiniform, morbilliform, vesicular, or discrete maculopapular eruption. Lassitude may persist for some weeks after the disappearance of other clinical signs.

The generalized nature of the disease accounts for its protean manifestations. Unilateral conjunctivitis, edema of the eyelids, or, occasionally, jaundice may be the presenting symptom. Central nervous system involvement has been noted with increasing frequency in recent years. It is discussed in detail elsewhere (Sec. 15.11). The picture may be that of benign aseptic meningitis or infectious polyneuritis (Guillain-Barré syndrome). The brain, meninges, spinal cord, cranial nerves, and peripheral nerves may be involved either separately or in any combination. The neurologic manifestations may precede, follow, or occur concomitantly with the onset of the disease.

LABORATORY FINDINGS. The characteristic finding in the blood during some stage of the disease is an absolute increase in the number of atypical lymphocytes. These cells vary markedly in size and shape. With Wright's stain the cytoplasm appears dark blue and vacuolated, presenting a foamy appearance. The nucleus is round, bean-shaped, or lobulated, with no nucleolus. Most commonly there is a lymphocytic leucocytosis. However, early in the course of the disease a polymorphonuclear leucocytosis may be present. At times leucopenia is observed during the first week of illness. Anemia is rare, and the platelet count is usually normal except for rare instances in which thrombocytopenia is noted. The serum transaminase level may be elevated in infectious mononucleosis. Therefore, this laboratory determination does not distinguish between infectious mononucleosis and infectious hepatitis.

Heterophil Antibodies. Paul and Bunnell demonstrated a high titer of sheep red cell agglutinins in the serum of patients with infectious mononucleosis. Titration of these heterophil antibodies constitutes a useful diagnostic tool. The test is usually positive 4 or 5 days after onset of the illness. Occasionally, however, the antibodies do not appear until after the fourth week of the disease. The high titer of antibody may disappear within two weeks, or it may persist for several months. Because of the marked variability in the time of appearance and disappearance of heterophil antibodies, it is important to obtain serial samples of blood serum in order to demonstrate a positive test. It should be emphasized that sheep cell agglutinins can develop during serum sickness and other disease entities; they can be demonstrated also in the serum of some normal individuals. In these latter conditions the antibodies exist in a lower titer and can be differentiated from those in infectious mononucleosis by absorption tests with guinea pig kidney and beef red cells as indicated in Table 15.

Peterson and his associates have described an ox cell hemolysin test which promises to be a valuable diagnostic aid in infectious mononucleosis. The titer of ox cell hemolysins is reported to rise during the first week of illness and to remain significantly elevated for a longer period of time than the titer of heterophil antibodies.

In some cases a false-positive Wassermann test may occur. This reaction usually reverts to negative by the third week. A positive cephalin flocculation test is found in about 90 percent of all cases, regardless of whether jaundice is also detectable.

In the cerebrospinal fluid a pleocytosis with predominance of mononuclear cells is present when there is central nervous system involvement. The concentration of sugar is normal and that of protein somewhat elevated. These findings have also been noted in some cases without clinical evidence of meningoencephalitis.

TABLE 15. *Absorption of Heterophil Antibodies in Differential Diagnosis*

Source	Titer after Absorption	
	Guinea Pig Kidney	Beef RBC
Infectious mononucleosis	Positive	Negative
Normal serum	Negative	Positive
Serum disease	Negative	Negative

DIAGNOSIS. The diagnosis is established by (1) a compatible clinical picture, (2) an absolute increase in atypical lymphocytes, and (3) a positive heterophil agglutination test. In view of the lack of specificity of the laboratory tests, the diagnosis rests on firmer ground if all three of the above criteria are fulfilled.

Atypical lymphocytes may be seen in a variety of clinical entities. These cells have been referred to as "virocytes." They have been demonstrated in infectious hepatitis, rubella, primary atypical pneumonia, and other diseases, although usually in small number—not more than 5 percent. In infectious mononucleosis there is characteristically an increase of these atypical lymphocytes to the extent of more than 10 percent of total leucocytes.

Heterophil antibodies have been detected in patients with infectious hepatitis, rubella, primary atypical pneumonia, tuberculosis, leukemia, and Hodgkin's disease. These agglutinins are usually present in low titer and are completely absorbed by guinea pig kidney. In contrast, in infectious mononucleosis the titer of antibodies after guinea pig absorption is usually of the order of 1:56 or more.

The lymphadenopathy and splenomegaly must be differentiated from sepsis, tuberculosis, and leukemia. The oropharyngeal manifestations of the disease are frequently confused with diphtheria, streptococcal sore throat, primary herpetic gingivostomatitis and pharyngitis, acute follicular tonsillitis, agranulocytosis, and leukemia. The jaundice usually suggests infectious hepatitis. In the presence of central nervous system involvement all of the lymphocytic meningoencephalitides must be considered. Most common among these are mumps meningoencephalitis, poliomyelitis, and Coxsackie and ECHO virus infections. The skin manifestations may suggest scarlet fever, rubella, secondary syphilis, typhoid fever, and the rickettsial diseases. Acute infectious lymphocytosis, pertussis, and leukemia may be confused with those cases that have a marked leucocytosis.

PROGNOSIS. In general the prognosis is excellent. However, there have been a few fatalities due to spontaneous rupture of the spleen. Associated central nervous system involvement may also be responsible for a rare death.

TREATMENT. Therapy is symptomatic. Antimicrobial agents do not affect the course of the disease. Vigorous palpation of the spleen should be avoided. If rupture does occur, immediate laparotomy is indicated.

REFERENCES

Bang, J. Experiments with the transmission of infectious mononucleosis to man. Acta Med. Scand., 113:304, 1943.

Custer, R. P., and Smith, E. B. The pathology of infectious mononucleosis. Blood, 3:830, 1948.

Davidsohn, I. Serologic diagnosis of infectious mononucleosis. J.A.M.A., 108:289, 1937.

Downey, H., and Stasney, J. Infectious mononucleosis: II. Hematologic studies. J.A.M.A., 105:764, 1935.

Evans, A. S. Experimental attempts to transmit infectious mononucleosis to man. Yale J. Biol. Med., 20:19, 1947-48.

——— et al. Seroendemiologic studies of infectious mononucleosis with E. B. virus. New Eng. J. Med., 279: 121, 1968.

Hunt, J. S. The pathogenesis of infectious mononucleosis. Amer. J. Med. Sci., 228:83, 1954.

Julianelle, L. A., Bierbaum, O. S., and Moore, C. V. Studies on infectious mononucleosis. Ann. Intern. Med., 20:281, 1944.

Niedermann, J. C., McCollum, R. W., Hanle, G., and Henle, W. Infectious mononucleosis. J.A.M.A., 203: 205, 1968.

Paul, J. R., and Bunnell, W. W. The presence of heterophile antibodies in infectious mononucleosis. Amer. J. Med. Sci., 183:90, 1932.

Peterson, E. T., Walford, R. L., Figueroa, W. G., and Chisholm, R. Ox cell hemolysis in infectious mononucleosis and in other diseases. Amer. J. Med., 21:193, 1956.

van den Berghe, L., and Liessens, P. Transmission de la mononucléose infectieuse humaine (fièvre ganglionnaire de Pfeiffer) au Macacus rhesus et passages succesifs d'un virus filtrant. Compt. Rend. Soc. Biol., 130:279, 1939.

Wising, P. J. A study of infectious mononucleosis (Pfeiffer's disease) from the etiological point of view. Acta Med. Scand., Suppl. 133:1, 1942.

14.31
INFLUENZA AND OTHER VIRAL INFECTIONS OF THE RESPIRATORY TRACT

ALFRED L. FLORMAN

The care of children with respiratory infections takes up a large portion of the practicing pediatrician's time. The majority of these infections are not influenced by antibiotics. It has been shown that about one half of respiratory infections in children are caused by viruses which can now be identified in the laboratory and that:

1. The respiratory tract can respond to infection in only a limited number of ways.
2. A single virus may provoke a variety of clinical syndromes, depending upon the specific and nonspecific resistance of the host.
3. Conversely a variety of viral agents may lead to a single clinical syndrome.
4. Although certain viruses may have a predilection for particular areas, in the individual patient these differences are often blurred.

Unfortunately the practicing pediatrician rarely has available facilities for rapid laboratory confirma-

TABLE 16.   *Relative Importance of Certain Viruses in Respiratory Diseases in Infants and Children**

Group†			Syndromes		
	URI‡	Croup	Bronchitis	Bronchiolitis	Pneumonia
Myxovirus					
Influenza	++	+	+	+	+
Parainfluenza	+++	++++	+++	++	++
Respiratory syncytial (RS)	+++	++	+++	++++	++++
Adenovirus	+++	+	+++	++	++++
Picornavirus					
Rhinovirus	++		+		
Enterovirus	+				+

*Modified from Chanock and Parrott. *Pediatrics*, 36:22, 1965.
†Relative importance graded on a scale of 0 to ++++.
‡URI = upper respiratory infections.

tion of his virologic diagnosis. Nevertheless, knowledge of the natural history of the viruses most frequently involved helps to sharpen his clinical acumen, permitting more rational therapy and a better understanding of the limitations of prophylactic immunization.

Among the recognized respiratory viral agents, the largest proportion are classified in three groups—the myxovirus, the adenovirus, and the picornavirus groups. The frequency of infection by each of these agents varies from year to year, season to season, and area to area. Table 16, modified from Chanock and Parrott, shows the relative importance of these viruses in a spectrum of five anatomically and clinically recognizable respiratory syndromes. "Upper respiratory infections" (Sec. 30.2) include rhinitis, pharyngitis, tonsillitis, and trachitis. "Croup" (Sec. 19.4) includes children with severe laryngitis as well as infants with hoarse cry, cough, and inspiratory stridor. The term "bronchitis" designates children with cough and scattered rhonchi, whereas "bronchiolitis" is used to describe young infants who have marked dyspnea and evidence of emphysema with or without fine rales. Children with "pneumonia" (Sec. 19.6) usually have less dyspnea but more striking rales or definite signs on x-ray. It is apparent from this table that the myxoviruses and adenoviruses have been associated wth the entire spectrum. Similarly it is seen that each one of the six viruses may be responsible for some upper respiratory infections. If one looks only at the most important associations, indicated as four plus, it is seen that croup has been associated most frequently with the parainfluenza viruses, bronchiolitis most often with the RS virus, and pneumonia with adenoviruses or RS virus.

Each of these respiratory viruses will be discussed separately. Comments will be made regarding what is known of their epidemiology, how they may be recognized clinically and in the laboratory, and our current approaches to prophylaxis.

The Myxovirus Group

In addition to the three respiratory viruses listed in Table 16 (influenza, parainfluenza, and RS), the myxovirus group includes the viruses of mumps, Newcastle disease, and probably measles. The prefix "myxo" is used to indicate that the prototypes have a strong affinity for mucoproteins found on the surface of erythrocytes and epithelial cells. They have a specific enzyme, neuraminidase, which is capable of removing neuraminic acid side chains from mucoproteins. The neuraminidase is distinct from the hemagglutinin.

The members of this group all have morphologic, chemical, and biologic similarities. Each has an RNA nucleoprotein core surrounded by an ether-sensitive lipoprotein outer envelope. The antigenicity is mainly in the envelope; the infectivity is in the core. Both are needed for a complete virion. Unlike the other myxoviruses, RS virus is not a hemagglutinator. However, it is placed in the myxovirus group because, under the electron microscope, it is morphologically similar to other members of this group.

Influenza Viral Respiratory Disease

The name "influenza" is derived from the Italian and goes back to the pandemic of 1743, which was thought to be under "celestial influences."
VIROLOGY.   The first influenza virus, called type A, was isolated in 1933 in ferrets by Smith, Andrewes, and Laidlaw. It was subsequently shown that mice, chick embryos, and tissue culture were more convenient laboratory tools than the ferret. Type A viruses have a tendency to develop many antigenic variants. The most striking appeared in 1946 and 1957 when the A prime and A2, or Asian, strains

were the cause of epidemics. Type B virus was first isolated by Francis in 1940. Although this type is less likely to develop strain variations, some changes were observed in 1945, 1954, 1959, and 1962. The type C virus, described by Taylor in 1949, is not an important cause of disease.

The soluble type-specific antigen is contained in the central core of the virus. Strain differences are associated with outer envelope antigens. The fully infectious virus can be shown by electron microscopy to be a spherical particle 80 to 120 mμ in diameter with a firmly packed central helix (9 to 10 mμ in diameter) and an outer envelope (7 to 10 mμ) which is studded with surface projections. These surface projections possess hemagglutinating activity. Incomplete forms of the virus are pleomorphic and even filamentous. They usually lack a central core.

The influenza virus gains entry into susceptible mucus-producing respiratory epithelial cells by enzymatic action. The enzyme, neuraminidase, is immunologically specific for each strain and is contained in the outer envelope of the virus. Its activity can be inhibited by specific viral antibody. Once inside the cell, the virus multiplies in the nucleus. However, it is not complete until it emerges at the cell surface, where it acquires its outer envelope.

Influenza virus was the first agent found to stimulate cells to produce interferon.

EPIDEMIOLOGY. Influenza type A is widely distributed in nature. It is recognized in swine, horses, ducks, and fowl as well as man. Influenza types B and C seem to be restricted to man.

Influenza A is most commonly encountered in large epidemics, which usually arise abruptly and spread rapidly but irregularly. Small focal outbreaks may occur anytime from early autumn to late spring. Type B epidemics are smaller. Type C appears infrequently and sporadically; it has not been found to cause epidemics.

Effective immunity to influenza is type-specific, and to a degree strain-specific. Its duration is relatively short, which may explain why epidemics in any one area appear to be explosive, to spread rapidly through susceptibles, to be over in a few weeks, and then to recur periodically. Pandemics, which are epidemics over a wide area, are characterized by the occurrence of secondary or even tertiary waves of disease. Although epidemic influenza has a low mortality rate, it is characterized by a high morbidity rate; 10 to 30 percent of a population may be infected at one time.

Because of the difficulties in accurately diagnosing and reporting this disease, statisticians have resorted to studying the excess mortality from respiratory disease in any one year as a base for charting epidemics of influenza and grading their severity.

All the factors responsible for the spread of influenza are not known. In a study at Fort Bragg in 1943 it was shown that the virus of influenza could be recovered from throat washings of patients most often on the first and second days of illness, and

never after the sixth day. It was also found that many soldiers had subclinical infections. They were asymptomatic but developed a good rise in antibody to the prevalent virus. Human contact and routes of travel have been carefully studied without accounting adequately for the frequent simultaneous appearance of peaks of incidence in widely separated areas of the world. One hypothesis is that following widespread seeding of the virus with few clinical cases, the sudden appearance of an epidemic reflects the introduction of some second factor not yet understood.

Although actual immunity from an attack of influenza is of short duration, serologic evidence of it usually persists for life and provides an interesting recapitulation of past infections. During his lifetime an individual may be exposed to many influenza viruses and so make many anti-influenzal antibodies; however, the dominant antibody remains that of the initial infection. This phenomenon has been called the "doctrine of original antigenic sin."

CLINICAL OBSERVATIONS AND PATHOLOGY. The classical clinical manifestations of influenza are well known. The incubation period is only 1 to 2 days. There is an abrupt onset of constitutional symptoms, chills, aches and pain, and fever of 101° to 104° F, with relatively minor respiratory symptoms. Conjunctival injection, nosebleeds, and a hacking persistent cough are not unusual. A biphasic temperature curve, rarely noted in adults, may be seen in children. If the temperature remains elevated for more than 4 days, pneumonitis should be suspected. Influenzal pneumonia leads to a rapid increase in alveolar fluid, a decrease in lung compliance, and an increase in pulmonary venous pressure. Consequently, individuals with preexisting poor pulmonary reserve are especially prone to the risk of pulmonary decompensation; children with mitral heart disease, cystic fibrosis, and chronic asthma are in this group.

Characteristic pathology is found in nasal respiratory epithelium. However, from the study of bronchial biopsies and autopsies it is known that the effects often extend to the lower respiratory tract. There is desquamation of ciliated epithelium with generative hyperplasia, hyperemia, increased secretions, and edema. Hyaline membranes and extensive edema are found in patients dying of influenzal pneumonia. The destructive reaction of the virus on cilia and epithelium and the outpouring of fluid are thought to predispose to secondary bacterial infections, although no bacteria are recovered in about 25 percent of deaths. Except in very young infants and in those with preexisting poor pulmonary reserve, the risk of death from influenza in the pediatric age group is low.

Routine laboratory studies are mostly negative. The white blood cell count is more often normal than leucopenic. If a secondary bacterial infection is superimposed or the disease process extends down into the lower respiratory tract, leucocytosis may be found.

SPECIFIC LABORATORY DIAGNOSIS. Specific diagnosis is made in the virology laboratory. The virus may be recovered from nasal or throat washings by inoculation into the amniotic sacs of 13- to 14-day-old chick embryos or into tissue cultures. The virus is readily identified by its hemagglutinating properties. Infection in man stimulates the appearance of a variety of specific antibodies within 5 to 7 days, although peak levels are usually not reached until 12 to 14 days. Complement-fixing (CF) tests indicate the type of influenza virus, and the particular strain is indicated by hemagglutination-inhibition (HI) or neutralization tests (NT). The CF test is less influenced by vaccination than the others and so is useful when dealing with a highly vaccinated population. Because most individuals have had previous exposure to influenza virus and possess some antibodies, a significant rise in titer must be demonstrated to make a serologic diagnosis of influenza. Serum must be collected for testing during the acute phase of illness and again during convalescence.

TREATMENT. Treatment is supportive. Antibiotics are indicated when bacterial pneumonitis is suspected. Since secondary invasion by staphylococci is frequent in children with influenzal pneumonia, the use of one of the pencillinase-resistant penicillins is recommended while awaiting the results of bacterial culture.

Although interferon appears to be effective in reducing viral multiplication in tissue culture, as yet it cannot be used in treating human infections.

PROPHYLAXIS. The appearance of specific antibodies and immunity following an attack of influenza suggested to early workers in the field possibilities of vaccination for prophylaxis. At present it is clear that killed influenza virus injected into patients will stimulate the production of specific antibodies and induce some degree of immunity. However, a number of practical difficulties have arisen. There is not a good correlation between the actual level of circulating antibody and the degree of immunity, although higher levels of antibody are generally associated with greater degrees of immunity. The significant level may be the antibody (IgA) in nasal secretions, which is not surprising in light of the pathogenesis of influenza and the unclear role of circulating antibody in a cellular disease not associated with a viremia.

Higher levels of antibody result when more antigen is injected, although the increase is not proportional since a 200-fold increase in amount of antigen may lead to only a 5-fold increase in antibody level. Even when given in the same dose, all strains are not equally good antigens. There is a practical limit to the amount of antigen that can be given. After a certain point there is a sharp rise in the incidence of systemic reactions with even small increments in virus. These reactions, which appear 6 to 8 hours after giving killed vaccine, are characterized by influenzalike symptoms. They have been related to the virus particles themselves, and not to an impurity in the vaccine. This type of reaction occurs more frequently in younger individuals. It is not entirely prevented by circulating antibody. Individuals who have had such reactions to first injections may also

get them to a lesser extent with subsequent ones. It has been suggested that these reactions may be the result of some primary pharmacologic toxic effect of the virus, or a sensitization to the protein of the virus. These reactions may occur in at least 10 percent of individuals inoculated with large doses. Consequently, limitations have to be placed on the amount of vaccine that can be given at any one time. It is interesting that there is no correlation between the severity of these reactions and the amount of antibody produced.

Since the vaccine is made from egg-grown virus, allergic reactions due to egg sensitivity have also been reported. These take place almost immediately, in contrast to toxic reactions. They are less frequent than toxic reactions, but the severity may be terrifying. Like other allergic reactions, they may occur after even very small amounts of vaccine are injected. Since the vaccine may be irritating when injected intradermally, it should not be used to test for egg sensitivity; the egg white scratch test material has been recommended for this purpose.

One of the greatest difficulties at present in the use of influenza vaccines is that in order to be effective they must contain the strain currently epidemic. Unfortunately these viruses, particularly type A, have a great tendency to develop shifts in antigenicity, necessitating frequent changes in the composition of the vaccine.

Vaccination against influenza is not recommended for routine use. It should be reserved for children with either chronic heart or pulmonary disease. The recommended dosage and schedule for immunizing children are as follows: Children 3 months to 6 years old are given 0.1 or 0.2 ml subcutaneously in three injections, the second being given 1 to 2 weeks and the third 2 months after the first dose. For children 6 to 12 years, 0.5 ml should be given subcutaneously in two doses with a 2-month interval between injections. Thereafter single yearly booster injections are given in amounts according to age.

Killed vaccines with adjuvants as well as vaccines with live attenuated strains have been tried in an attempt to obtain better protection. The experience with these vaccines in children is still too limited to be evaluated properly.

Amantadine, a synthetic compound which can be given orally, has been shown to be an effective agent in the prophylaxis of influenza A_2 disease. Preliminary reports indicate that it also may be effective in treatment.

Strains of influenza A, A_1, and A_2 have been shown to be sensitive to the action of amantadine in tissue culture, while other myxoviruses, including influenza B, mumps, Newcastle disease, and parainfluenza viruses, are resistant.

Parainfluenza Respiratory Disease

The parainfluenza viruses share many properties with the influenza viruses, but differ from them sufficiently so that in 1959 the name "parainfluenza" was suggested.

VIROLOGY. The parainfluenza viruses are slightly larger and more pleomorphic than influenza viruses. They also have an inner RNA helix, but it is less tightly coiled. Its outer lipoprotein envelope is studded with many spikelike projections, and although parainfluenza viruses agglutinate red blood cells, they do so less well than influenza viruses. They grow better in tissue culture than in chick embryos. Since infected tissue culture cells were early noted to absorb erythrocytes, parainfluenza viruses were originally called "hemadsorption viruses."

On the basis of serologic tests the parainfluenza viruses have been divided into four types. The specific antigens which are present on the envelope of the virus can be demonstrated with hemadsorption-inhibition or tissue culture neutralization tests. The complement-fixation antigens which are associated with the inner helix are also type-specific. There probably are additional antigens which the various parainfluenza viruses share with each other and with other myxoviruses, as suggested by the heterotypic serologic responses which often follow childhood infections. These occur in an unpredictable fashion but are seen most frequently after type 3 infections.

The first of the parainfluenza viruses to be associated with human disease was isolated in 1955 from infants with croup and was called the CA (croup-associated) virus. It is now classified as parainfluenza type 2. The Sendai virus in 1952 had been associated with pneumonitis in infants and was then classified as influenza type D. It has since been shown to be related to parainfluenza virus type 1. Parainfluenza type 1 was the original type 2 hemadsorption agent. The original hemadsorption type 1 agent is now known as parainfluenza virus type 3. Parainfluenza type 4 is the most recently identified and least studied. It is made up of two subgroups, A and B.

EPIDEMIOLOGY. Like the influenza A viruses, the parainfluenza viruses are widely distributed in nature. They have been found in monkeys, mice, pigs, and cows as well as man.

Parainfluenza infections are endemic. Although there are seasonal peaks and occasional epidemics during the colder months, these viruses can be recovered from children with respiratory tract illness throughout the year. By 2 years of age most children in the United States already have type 3 antibody. By the end of the tenth year a majority of children also have antibodies for types 1 and 2.

Although neutralizing antibody provides some protection against subsequent infections, this protection is not complete. Reinfections do occur. In one study of type 3 infections in a nursery, it was found that 17 percent of children who were infected during one outbreak were reinfected during subsequent outbreaks, even though the interval between outbreaks was less than 9 months. However, the illness during reinfection was less severe, corresponding to the experience that symptoms of reinfections are less severe

than those of children having primary parainfluenza infections.

CLINICAL OBSERVATIONS. The symptoms encountered most frequently are mild rhinitis, pharyngitis, and less often bronchiolitis. Fever lasting 2 to 3 days is usually associated with primary infections. Type 3 virus was found to produce fever in 78 percent of primarily infected children, type 2 in 66 percent, and type 1 in only 50 percent. Type 3 is responsible for an appreciable number of instances of severe bronchitis and bronchiolitis in children with primary infection. Although croup is the most serious illness produced by parainfluenza viruses, it occurs in only 2 to 3 percent of those infected. Type 1 is now the virus most frequently associated with croup. All of the parainfluenza viruses have been recovered from adults with upper respiratory tract disease. Experimentally, intranasal inoculation of adult volunteers has resulted in mild upper respiratory disease. Unfortunately, the clinical features of parainfluenza infections are not distinctive, and the diagnosis must be made by the virology laboratory.

SPECIFIC LABORATORY DIAGNOSIS. Specific diagnosis is made by recovery of virus from nasopharyngeal secretions in tissue culture. Primary monkey kidney cells are most sensitive. Best results are obtained if specimens are inoculated without freezing as soon as possible after collection. Infection is recognized when guinea pig red blood cells are added to the tissue cultures after 5 to 10 days and hemadsorption is observed. The specific virus is identified when this effect is neutralized or inhibited by an appropriately prepared antiserum. Type 2 parainfluenza virus sometimes also produces a characteristic syncytial cytopathic effect; other types do not.

Tissue culture neutralization and hemagglutination-inhibition tests are usually used for serologic diagnosis. The complement-fixation test is satisfactory only for types 2 and 3. The serologic responses to type 4 infection have not yet been adequately evaluated. Because of the tendency for heterotypic antibody responses with parainfluenza infections, virus isolation is the only certain means for identifying the type of infecting virus.

TREATMENT. Treatment is supportive and except in croup rarely presents a problem. Because of the life-threatening nature of this form of croup and the inability to differentiate clinically between those few instances due to bacteria, all patients should be treated with broad-spectrum antibiotics while awaiting the results of bacterial culture. The need for high humidity and careful observation of the patient with croup, who may require a tracheostomy, is well recognized.

PROPHYLAXIS. Prophylaxis with a polyvalent types 1, 2, and 3 formalin-inactivated vaccine is now being studied. Although preliminary reports suggest that neutralizing antibody can be elicited after two or three injections, this vaccine has not yet been tested in the field.

Respiratory Syncytial (RS) Viral Diseases

The name "respiratory syncytial virus" or "RS virus" was introduced in 1957. It indicates the association of this agent with respiratory disease and its effect on susceptible cells in tissue culture.

VIROLOGY. The RS virus under the electron microscope resembles influenza and parainfluenza viruses. It is of medium size. It has an inner coiled protein- and RNA-containing component and a spike-armed outer envelope, because of which it has been placed in the myxovirus group. However, unlike the other members of this group it does not hemagglutinate or hemadsorb. It is antigenically distinct, at least three diffusable antigens being found in RS infected cells. From neutralization tests in tissue culture with animal sera, there would seem to be at least two serotypes (CCA and Lang). However, such differences have not been demonstrated with human sera, and these serotypes share a common CF antigen. Although a number of species of animals can be experimentally infected with RS virus, only the chimpanzee and man develop signs of illness. Indeed this virus, first recovered from a chimpanzee with coryza, was originally called "chimpanzee coryza agent" (CCA). The present name was adopted after it was established that this virus was not a laboratory curiosity but a significant cause of human illness.

EPIDEMIOLOGY. The virus is widely distributed. In single geographic areas, outbreaks have occurred yearly. They are usually sharply circumscribed and appear only during the colder months. The virus spreads from person to person. It has been recovered from nasal secretions of patients from 3 days before onset of illness and for 4 days after. Both CF and neutralizing antibodies appear 14 to 18 days after onset of infection. However, neutralizing antibody does not protect completely. Reinfections are frequent and may even be associated with severe lower respiratory tract disease. In one study, about half of the occupants of a nursery who subsequently developed pneumonitis had antibody levels of 1:4 to 1:16 before the outbreak. In another study with adult volunteers the presence of high levels of circulating neutralizing antibody did not prevent experimental intranasal infection.

CLINICAL OBSERVATIONS AND PATHOLOGY. In infancy, infection with RS virus may result in bronchiolitis and pneumonia. In adults, RS virus usually produces only mild upper respiratory infections.

The onset of RS illness is associated with low-grade fever, coryza, sore throat, and cough. At this time it is indistinguishable from infection with other respiratory pathogens. However, 30 to 75 percent of infants then develop the dyspnea, wheezing, and emphysema of bronchiolitis, the higher frequencies occurring in infants with allergic diatheses. Infants with bronchiolitis look sicker than might have been expected from the height of the temperature. The leucocyte count varies between 5,000 and 20,000. The most worrisome phase of the disease is the first 48 to 72 hours after the appearance of dyspnea. The respirations then are rapid and shallow; as they become slower, fine rales and patchy pneumonic infiltrations may appear. Despite the precarious picture, death occurs in less than 5 percent of cases.

At postmortem the most prominent changes are extensive necrotizing and interstitial pneumonitis, atelectasis, and emphysema. There may also be necrosis of the tracheobronchial epithelium. Cytoplasmic inclusion bodies are sometimes found in these cells. In addition, increased numbers of eosinophils may be found in the areas of interstitial pneumonia.

SPECIFIC LABORATORY DIAGNOSIS. A specific diagnosis of RS infection can be made only in the virology laboratory by virus isolation and demonstration of a rise in antibody during convalescence.

The virus grows in a variety of primary diploid and heteroploid human cell cultures, such as Hela or Hep$_2$, as well as simian and bovine kidney cultures. Chances for isolation are best if nasopharyngeal swabs are inoculated directly without prior freezing. Characteristic syncytial cytoplasmic changes develop after 3 to 14 days. In some cultures intracytoplasmic eosinophilic inclusions can also be demonstrated. Isolates are identified by complement fixation using sera obtained from convalescent ferrets or guinea pigs. If serotyping is desired it must be done in tissue culture by neutralization with specific animal sera.

Both complement-fixing and neutralizing antibodies develop during convalescence, and so either may be used to demonstrate a rise in titer. However, since neutralizing antibodies may persist for long periods, if one suspects reinfection the test for complement-fixing antibodies is more desirable. Complement-fixing antibodies remain for only a relatively short time after an infection.

Young infants may not be good antibody producers, and so virus isolation may be necessary to prove etiology. Adams has suggested that an association with RS virus may be suspected if pharyngeal smears reveal large numbers of epithelial cells with cytoplasmic inclusion bodies.

TREATMENT. Treatment for milder cases is only symptomatic and supportive. However, the infant who has bronchiolitis needs full humidification and may require oxygen (Sec. 19.3). Dehydration and abdominal distension must be prevented, and parenteral fluids are often necessary. Because this syndrome is occasionally associated with bacteria, such as *H. influenzae,* ampicillin should be given until the reports of bacterial culture are available. For the severely ill infant, a short course of large doses of anti-inflammatory steroids has been advocated; however, a well-designed therapeutic trial conducted by Leer and his associates indicated that the corticosteroids used in the trial (betamethasone sodium phosphate) and perhaps corticosteroids in general offer little if any benefit in the general or routine treatment of acute bronchiolitis. Because of the location of this obstruction, tracheostomy is almost always contraindicated.

PROPHYLAXIS. Prophylaxis is not yet available. Because reinfections may occur even in the presence of high levels of neutralizing antibody, the problems of preparing a useful vaccine are formidable.

Adenovirus Group

The name "adenovirus" was proposed in 1956 as a group name for a family of respiratory tract viruses. The first members of this group were found when surgically removed tonsillar and adenoidal tissues were grown for prolonged periods in roller tube tissue culture. This unmasking procedure, which may have permitted the washing away of antibodies, led to the finding of a large number of transmissible agents that change and later destroy the growing tissue cells. Prior to 1956 a variety of initialed names had been used to designate certain members of this family. These included AD (adenoid degeneration), RI (respiratory illness), ARD (acute respiratory disease), and APC (adenoidal-pharyngeal-conjunctival) virus. There are now at least 45 immunologically distinct adenoviruses. Many are still "viruses in search of a disease." Nevertheless, at least eight have been frequently associated with human respiratory tract diseases.

Adenoviral Diseases

VIROLOGY. All members of the adenovirus group are similar in size, shape, and basic chemical composition. They are all related by sharing a major cross-reacting complement-fixing antigen. The viral particles as seen under the electron microscope are icosahedra (20 sided) and 70 to 80 mμ in diameter. They are composed of 252 hollow polygonal subunits called capsomeres arranged in cubic symmetry. Some also have a fiberlike structure. The fibers and capsomeres are surface structures and contain both group- and type-specific soluble antigens. Chemically the core of the adenovirus is classic double-stranded DNA. The shell consists of protein. All adenoviruses are ether-resistant, stable to temperature and pH change, and lack pathogenicity for common laboratory animals. However, they do multiply in nuclei of epithelial cells in tissue culture and produce characteristic cytopathic changes, including the appearance of intranuclear inclusion bodies.

Separation into specific types is based on tissue culture neutralization tests. However, since most adenoviruses are also hemagglutinators, they can also be divided into four subgroups on the basis of whether or not they agglutinate monkey and rat red blood cells.

Several types have been shown to be oncogenic for newborn hamsters and rats.

Adenoviruses, like herpes simplex, have the property of lying latent for long periods in infected cells, consistent with their discovery in supposedly normal tonsillar tissue.

EPIDEMIOLOGY. The adenoviruses are widely distributed in nature, about 28 different types having been recovered from man. Although infections are mostly endemic, types 3, 4, and 7 have often been associated with epidemic respiratory tract disease among military and summer camp populations. Types 4 and 7 produce a high rate of subclinical infections and so spread widely. Type 3 is more likely to produce overt disease, and since patients are then isolated, the virus does not spread widely. Neutralizing and complement-fixing antibodies appear after 7 days and reach their maximum titer in 2 to 3 weeks. The CF antibody level begins to decrease appreciably after 2 to 3 months. Neutralizing antibodies persist much longer. Only a two- to threefold decrease in neutralizing antibody titer has been reported after 1 to 2 years. There is a good correlation between specific neutralizing antibody and resistance to infection.

Serologic surveys in the United States indicate that antibodies to types 1 and 2 appear early and are present in the blood of the majority of young urban children. Antibodies to types 3, 4, 5, 6, and 7 are found more frequently in adult sera. Antibodies to the higher types are encountered only rarely. These antibodies are mostly in the IgG class and so may be passively transmitted from mother to newborn infant.

CLINICAL OBSERVATIONS AND PATHOLOGY. According to Chanock et al. there are at least six clinical syndromes which have been clearly associated with adenovirus. These are acute febrile pharyngitis, pharyngoconjunctival fever, acute respiratory disease, viral pneumonia, acute follicular conjunctivitis, and epidemic keratoconjunctivitis. The last two syndromes remind us that the virus may enter the patient by way of the conjunctival membranes as well as via the respiratory tract. Our concern here is with the first four syndromes, which reflect a spectrum of upper and lower respiratory tract diseases.

Pharyngoconjunctival fever was the first disease to be clearly associated with an adenovirus. It occurs chiefly in children who live and swim together in the summer. However, sporadic cases may occur in any season. Fever may reach 103° to 104° F and lasts for 1 to 10 days, subsiding by lysis. The sore throat is usually mild, as is conjunctivitis, which may persist for only a few days or as long as three weeks; conjunctivitis is follicular and frequently monocular. Headaches and listlessness are common complaints. Most outbreaks have been caused by a type 3 adenovirus. However, other types, especially 7 and 14, have also been found.

Acute respiratory disease (ARD) was recognized clinically during World War II to be a viral respiratory disease distinct from influenza and the common cold. It occurred in epidemic form chiefly among new recruits. Unlike influenza, it has a gradual onset; the chief signs and symptoms are fever of 100° to 104° F for 2 to 4 days, chills, headache, and malaise. Coryza, sore throat, and cough occur less frequently. Adenovirus types 4 and 7 are most frequently associated with the ARD clinical picture. However, like the other adenoviral syndromes, other types have occasionally also been found.

Pneumonia due to adenovirus in adults resembles the clinical picture of "primary atypical pneumonia." However, cold agglutinins and streptococcus MG agglutinins do not develop during convalescence as they do in mycoplasma pneumonia. Fever is almost always present. The pneumonitis may be unilateral or bilateral, but is most prominent at the bases. There are increased perihilar densities. Rales are frequently present, dullness rarely. Adenovirus types 4 and 7 are the types most frequently found.

Although this syndrome has been recognized chiefly in epidemics among young military recruits, it can occur among infants and young children. In one hospital outbreak, an adenovirus type 7 was incriminated in more than 20 cases, 8 of which were fatal. These children were all orphans living in an open and crowded ward. At autopsy an intranuclear inclusion body pneumonitis was found. The characteristic changes were in the epithelial cells of the bronchi and alveoli, where numerous cells were found in which the nuclei were enlarged and contained a central inclusion body surrounded by a clear zone. These changes are very similar in appearance to those described in tissue culture of cells infected with adenoviruses types 3, 4, 7, and 14.

Adenoviruses have also been associated with some instances of bronchiolitis. In one study an adenovirus was recovered from 14 of 42 patients. Ten of these were adenovirus type 2.

In addition to these clinical manifestations, adenoviral infections have occasionally been associated with a morbilliform rash and with gastrointestinal symptoms.

Experimentally adenoviral infection has been produced in susceptible human volunteers who do not have type-specific neutralizing antibody. A variety of routes have been successful—conjunctival, nasal, and intramuscular. The incubation period is about six days. Conjunctivitis, pharyngitis, and low-grade fevers have been produced as well as type-specific neutralizing antibodies.

SPECIFIC LABORATORY DIAGNOSIS. The specific virologic diagnosis may be made by recovering the virus and demonstrating a rise in type-specific neutralizing antibodies during convalescence. For recovery of virus, properly treated pharyngeal, lower respiratory tract, or ocular secretions are inoculated into tissue cultures of Hela or human amnion cells. Characteristic cytopathic changes are noted in 2 to 21 days. Cultures are then identified as adenovirus by a complement-fixation test. The agent is then classified into a hemagglutination subgroup by using monkey and rat red blood cells. The final specific typing is done with a hemagglutination-inhibition or tissue culture neutralization test. Since adenoviruses are ubiquitous, a rise in specific neutralizing antibody must also be demonstrated to establish the etiologic significance of the isolation of the virus.

A rise in complement-fixing antibody during convalescence provides presumptive evidence for a recent adenoviral infection but, unfortunately, gives no clue as to which adenovirus was involved, since all of the adenoviruses share a common complement-fixing antigen.

TREATMENT. Therapy is supportive. The diseases are self-limited, and secondary bacterial infections are rare.

PROPHYLAXIS. Prevention is chiefly a problem in military populations. There would seem to be little need for vaccinating children. The incidence of severe adenoviral infections in children is low. It has been estimated that use of a completely effective adenovirus vaccine would result in only a 6 percent reduction in the number of common respiratory illnesses experienced by an average child during the first 10 years of his life. Because of numerous difficulties, adenovirus vaccines prepared in monkey kidney infected with types 3, 4, and 7 have now been withdrawn from the market.

A new approach utilizes the observation that an asymptomatic intestinal adenovirus infection stimulates moderately high levels of neutralizing antibody. Adenovirus is grown in human diploid fibroblast tissue cultures to avoid simian virus contaminants, one of the difficulties encountered with the previous vaccine. It is administered live in enteric-coated capsules which do not release virus until they pass beyond the stomach. A preliminary report of a study with volunteers using such a vaccine with type 4 adenovirus indicates that it is apparently a safe and effective method of preventing severe acute respiratory tract disease caused by type 4 adenovirus.

The Picornavirus Group

The picornavirus group includes the enteroviruses (poliomyelitis, Coxsackie, and ECHO viruses) and the rhinoviruses. The laboratory characteristics of these agents and the diseases caused by the enteroviruses are discussed elsewhere (p. 740).

Rhinoviral Disease

The name "rhinovirus" or "nose virus" was adopted in 1962 for a group of agents formerly referred to as "common cold viruses," "Salisbury strains," or "coryzaviruses," which produce mainly upper respiratory tract infections.

VIROLOGY. Rhinoviruses differ from enteroviruses in being easily destroyed in acid (pH 3 to 5) and in growing better in tissue culture at 34° C than at

$37°$ C. There now are more than 60 distinct serotypes of rhinovirus, divided into two large subgroups, H and M. The H viruses multiply in roller tube tissue culture of human embryo kidney or human diploid fibroblast cells. The M strains multiply in monkey kidney cells as well as human cells. There are many more H than M strains.

EPIDEMIOLOGY. Epidemiologic studies are limited. It is often very difficult to differentiate among patients with colds, hay fever, perennial rhinitis, or vasomotor reactions to dust. During a 14-month period, from December 1960 to January 1962, a survey for rhinoviruses was carried out in the Camp Lejeune area of North Carolina. A total of 233 rhinoviruses were isolated from adults with mild upper respiratory illnesses. A different seasonal distribution pattern was observed for M and H types. M strains were isolated only during winter and spring months. H strains were more prevalent during summer and fall but were also found in each of the 14 months of the study. Among more than 1,500 infants and children who came to an outpatient service in the same area, 23 rhinoviruses were isolated during an 11-month period. The associated upper respiratory illnesses were not more severe in very young infants than in older children.

Rhinovirus infection is transferred from person to person by direct contact. Nevertheless, it has been estimated that there is only a one in five chance of a secondary case occurring in a family. Children appear to shed the virus more freely than adults. To account for simultaneous outbreaks of colds in widely scattered areas of the country, it has been suggested that there are many latent infections which are activated by stresses such as changes in weather. This assumption has not been proved.

Rhinoviruses have been recovered from nasal secretions and throats just prior to the onset of symptoms and for 1 to 6 days afterward. Unlike the adenoviruses, they have not been found in stools. The incubation period is 2 days.

Relatively little is known about immunity to rhinoviruses. From experiments with repeated challenge of volunteers, there is evidence for some incomplete specific immunity. Homologous neutralizing antibodies have been detected at least 4 years after an infection.

CLINICAL OBSERVATIONS. Because the symptoms of a common cold may be caused by so many different agents, it is of interest to quote from Andrewes and Tyrrell's description of what actually happened after they gave an M rhinovirus (strain HGP) intranasally to adult volunteers. About 40 percent of volunteers came down with clinical symptoms.

"In a mild cold the patient usually has a slight sore throat, particularly early, and nasal stuffiness, with perhaps sneezing and mild headache. He feels chilly and rather miserable. Nasal secretions rapidly increase and from 10 to 20 more paper handkerchiefs may be used each day. The nasal discharge is usually mucoid or mucopurulent and the nose may become completely blocked by swollen mucosa and sticky secretions. After increasing for a day the symptoms usually begin to subside and may be gone in 3 or 4 days. In a moderate cold there are definite constitutional signs such as malaise, headache and chills and in a severe cold the patient may be found to go to bed; anorexia and fever may occur, and the nasal symptoms may be more troublesome and prolonged. There may be cough; in the milder cases it may be due to the irritation of a postnasal discharge and in the more severe cases to a mild bronchitis due to infection of the lower respiratory tract. Following a cold there is quite often a period of nasal catarrh, especially if the illness was moderate or severe."

The experimental disease has not been induced in infants or children.

There is no conclusive evidence that rhinoviruses infect the lower respiratory tract. These agents seem to be exclusively upper respiratory tract pathogens.

SPECIFIC LABORATORY DIAGNOSIS. Rhinoviruses may be best recovered from nasopharyngeal secretions if immediately inoculated, without freezing, into roller tube tissue cultures of either human diploid fibroblasts such as WI-26 or monkey kidney cells. The cultures are maintained at $34°$ C and observed over a 21-day period for cytopathogenic effect, consisting of foci of small, highly refractile ovoid cells. The presence of a rhinovirus is confirmed by demonstrating its liability in acid. The specific serotype is identified by tissue culture neutralization tests with specific animal sera.

The serologic confirmation of rhinoviral infection is best made with neutralization tests. A rise in homologous neutralizing antibody titer can be demonstrated during convalescence. A complement-fixing antigen has been prepared from a viral concentrate of an M rhinovirus (HGP). Unfortunately the reactions of this antigen with human sera do not appear to be specific.

TREATMENT. Treatment is symptomatic. Antibiotics in so-called prophylactic doses are contraindicated (p. 589). However, when clinical signs of a secondary bacterial infection appear, such as a purulent rhinitis or otitis media, then cultures should be taken, and an appropriate anitbacterial agent should be given in full dosage.

PROPHYLAXIS. Prophylactic vaccination is not available; there are too many type-specific strains, and in the outbreaks that have been studied, more than one serotype has been found.

REFERENCES

Chanock, R. M., and Parrott, R. H. Acute respiratory disease in infancy and childhood: Present understanding and prospects for prevention. Pediatrics, 38:21, 1965.

Cramblatt, H. G. Viral respiratory illnesses of infants and children. Bact. Rev., 28:431, 1964.

MYXOVIRUS GROUP

Adams, J. M., Imagawa, D. T., and Zike, K. Epidemic bronchiolitis and pneumonitis related to respiratory syncytial virus. J.A.M.A., 176:1037, 1961.

Beem, M., Wright, F. H., Hamre, D., Egerer, R., and Oehme, M. Association of the chimpanzee coryza agent with acute respiratory disease in children. New Eng. J. Med., 263:523, 1960.

Canchola, J. G., Chanock, R. M., Jeffries, B. C., Christmas, E. E., Kim, H. W., Vargosko, A. J., and Parrott, R. H. Recovery and identification of human myxoviruses. Bact. Rev., 29:496, 1965.

Chanock, R. M., and Parrott, R. H. Parainfluenza viruses. In Horsfall, F. L., Jr., and Tamm, I., eds., Viral and Rickettsial Infections of Man, 4th ed. Philadelphia, J. B. Lippincott Co., 1965, Chap. 31.

———— and Parrott, R. H. Respiratory syncytial virus. In Horsfall, F. L., Jr., and Tamm, I., eds., Viral and Rickettsial Infections of Man, 4th ed. Philadelphia, J. B. Lippincott Co., 1965, Chap. 34.

Collins, S. D., and Lehman, J. L. Influenza epidemics during 1951-56 with a review of trends. Pub. Health Rep., 72:771, 1957.

Florman, A. L. Influenza—a critical review. J. Mt. Sinai Hosp. N.Y., 25:29, 1958.

Francis, T., Jr., and Maassab, H. F. Influenza viruses. In Horsfall, F. L., Jr., and Tamm, I., eds., Viral and Rickettsial Infections of Man, 4th ed. Philadelphia, J. B. Lippincott Co., 1965, Chap. 30.

Leer, J. A., et al. Corticosteroid treatment in bronchiolitis, Amer. J. Dis. Child., 117:495, 1969.

McGeorge, M. Severe obstruction bronchiolitis in infancy. Treatment with hydrocortisone. Clin. Pediat., 3:11, 1964.

Medearis, D. N., Jr., Neill, C. A., and Markowitz, M. Influenza and cardiopulmonary disease. Mod. Conc. Cardiov. Dis., 32:809, 1963.

Smorodintsev, A. A., et al. The prospect of amantadine for prevention of influenza as in humans. Ann. N.Y. Acad. Sci., 173:44, 1970.

Wright, F. H., and Beem, M. O. Management of acute viral bronchiolitis. Pediatrics, 35:334, 1965.

ADENOVIRUS GROUP

Chanock, R. M., Ludwig, W., Huebner, R. J., Cati, T. R., and Chu, L. Immunization by selective infection with type 4 adenovirus grown in human diploid tissue culture. I. Safety and lack of oncogenicity and tests for potency in volunteers. J.A.M.A., 195:445, 1966.

Edmondson, W. P., Purcell, R. H., Gundelfinger, B. F., Love, J. W. P., Ludwig, W., and Chanock, R. M. Immunization by selective infection with type 4 adenovirus grown in human diploid tissue culture. II. Specific protective effect against epidemic disease. J.A.M.A., 195:453, 1966.

Florman, A. L. The adenoviruses. Quart. Rev. Pediat., 14:7, 1959.

Ginsberg, H. S., and Dingle, J. H. The adenovirus group. In Horsfall, F. L., Jr., and Tamm, I., eds., Viral and Rickettsial Infections of Man, 4th ed. Philadelphiia, J. B. Lippincott Co., 1965, Chap. 40.

Varcosko, A. J., Kim, H. W., Parrott, R. H., Jeffries, B. C., Wong, D., and Chanock, R. M. Recovery and identification of adenovirus in infections of infants and children. Bact. Rev., 29:487, 1965.

RHINOVIRUSES

Andrewes, C. H. Viruses and common colds. Harvey Lect., 1961-62, Series 57, 1-15.

———— and Tyrrell, D. A. J. Rhinoviruses. In Horsfall, F. L., Jr., and Tamm, I., eds., Viral and Rickettsial Infections of Man, 4th ed. Philadelphia, J. B. Lippincott Co., 1965.

Bloom, H. H., Forsyth, B. R., Johnson, K. M., and Chanock, R. M. Relationship of rhinovirus infection to mild upper respiratory disease. J.A.M.A., 186:38, 1963.

Phillips, C. A., Riggs, S., Melnick, J. L., and Grim, C. A. Rhinoviruses associated with common colds in a student population. J.A.M.A., 192:277, 1965.

Portnoy, B., Eckert, H. L., and Salvatore, M. A. Rhinovirus infection in children with acute lower respiratory disease; evidence against etiological importance. Pediatrics, 35:899, 1965.

14.32
LYMPHOCYTIC CHORIOMENINGITIS

ALFRED L. FLORMAN

This disease, a form of benign lymphocytic meningitis, is caused by a specific virus which was first encountered by Armstrong and Lillie in 1933 while studying St. Louis encephalitis. Two years later Rivers and Scott proved that the virus is pathogenic for man, producing a meningitis or mild encephalitic syndrome, and soon afterward reports of cases in children began to appear. The name is derived from the marked involvement of the choroid plexus when monkeys are infected with this virus. Although accurate identification of the infection has been possible for several years, the number of recognized cases remains rather small and their distribution nearly confined to large cities. To some extent this is due to the fact that appropriate steps are not always taken for identification of the virus in suspected cases. Except for a single instance, reported by Komrower et al. from Manchester, England, in which the infection appeared to be transmitted from mother to fetus in utero, the disease seems not to be communicable from man to man. While a wide variety of animals are susceptible, the great reservoir of the infection is located in ordinary house mice; in five out of six attempts made, Armstrong and Lillie recovered the virus from mice trapped in the households of infected patients. Since a history of handling mice or of other direct contact is missing in the great majority of instances of proved infection, indirect transmission has been postulated, as by inhalation of desiccated mouse excreta or by some insect vector. The fact that the disease seldom occurs in midsummer would tend to exonerate mosquitoes and ordinary house flies.

In children meningitis is the most important manifestation of the infection. Some cases are limited to a grippelike illness without meningitic symptoms, and immunologic studies indicate that inapparent infection may occur in childhood as well as at older ages. However, pneumonic and bizarre neurologic syndromes, some of them fatal, such as are occasionally encountered among adults, have not been reported in children. The pathology of the disease, as it affects children, can therefore not be accurately described.

As a rule the onset of symptoms is abrupt, with fever, malaise, restlessness, loss of appetite, headache, occasionally with drowsiness or even stupor, vomiting, photophobia, and abdominal pain. The temperature is usually 101° to 102° F but may reach 105°. Neck rigidity and Kernig's and Brudzinski's signs are generally found, increasing the suspicion of bacterial meningitis and leading to diagnostic lumbar puncture. This procedure not infrequently makes the patient feel better, with less headache and general distress. Although the patient may seem quite ill for two or three days, improvement, once begun, progresses rapidly, and most children are afebrile and apparently well at the end of a week. Except for a few reported instances of pneumonia there are no complications and no residua.

The spinal fluid at the height of symptoms is under increased pressure and contains from 100 to 2,000 cells, which are almost all lymphocytes. Its protein concentration is usually somewhat increased, but sugar and chloride values are normal. Pleocytosis commonly outlasts the fever, but there may be a late increase in spinal fluid protein so that in convalescence its concentration may be out of proportion to the number of cells. False-positive serologic tests for syphilis have been reported in the spinal fluid of these patients. The sedimentation rate of the blood and the leucocyte count are usually unchanged.

Differentiation from bacterial meningitis is usually made quite readily from the findings in the spinal fluid. On the other hand, the conditions which may cause a mononuclear pleocytosis with normal concentration of sugar include mumps, poliomyelitis, Coxsackie virus and herpes virus infections, various specific and nonspecific forms of encephalitis, infectious mononucleosis, syphilis, leptospirosis, lymphogranuloma vererereum, lead poisoning, and even certain tumors. Every effort should be made to obtain satisfactory evidence of etiology. At the height of the disease the virus is present in the blood as well as in the cerebrospinal fluid; and even after defervescence, as long as pleocytosis remains, it may be recovered from the latter source by inoculation of susceptible animals, e.g., mice and guinea pigs. Retrospective identification of the infecting agent may be made by demonstrating a rise in the patient's serum titer of complement-fixing or neutralizing antibodies a few weeks after onset.

Treatment is symptomatic. Premature resumption of activity may result in prolongation of headache and malaise.

REFERENCES

Adair, C. V., Gould, R. L., and Smadel, J. E. Aseptic meningitis, a disease of diverse etiology; clinical and etiologic studies on 854 cases. Ann. Intern. Med., 39: 675, 1953.

Armstrong, C., and Lillie, R. D. Experimental lymphocytic choriomeningitis of monkeys and mice produced by a virus encountered in studies of the 1933 St. Louis encephalitis epidemic. Pub. Health Rep., 49:1019, 1934.

—— and Sweet, L. K. Lymphocytic choriomeningitis; report of two cases with recovery of virus from gray mice (Mus musculus) trapped in the two infected households. Pub. Health Rep., 54:673, 1939.

Farmer, G. M., and Janeway, C. A. Infections with the virus of lymphocytic choriomeningitis. Medicine, 21:1, 1942.

Green, W. R., Sweet, L. K., and Prichard, R. W. Acute lymphocytic choriomeningitis; a study of twenty-one cases. J. Pediat., 35:688, 1949.

Komrower, G. M., Williams, B. L., and Stones, P. B. Lymphocytic choriomeningitis in the newborn; probable transplacental infection. Lancet, 1:697, 1955.

Rivers, T. M., and Scott, T. F. McNair. Meningitis in man caused by a filterable virus. II. Identification of the etiological agent. J. Exp. Med., 63:415, 1936.

Scott, T. F. McNair, and Rivers, T. M. Meningitis in man caused by a filterable virus. I. Two cases and the method of obtaining a virus from their spinal fluids. J. Exp. Med., 63:397, 1936.

14.33
MEASLES
(RUBEOLA, MORBILLI, ROUGEOLE [FR.], SARAMPION [SP.], MASERN [GER.])

SAMUEL L. KATZ

Measles has been for centuries one of the commonest communicable diseases affecting children in all lands and, therefore, has been familiar to their parents and physicians. A marked reduction in the annual incidence of the disease has been evident in the United States ever since the licensure in 1963 of measles virus vaccines. Similar decreases in numbers of cases have occurred in other nations where these vaccines have been utilized. It remains clear that many years will pass before measles will be relegated to the list of rare infections, in this country or elsewhere, and its prevalence among less well-immunized populations will persist until systems for the delivery of health care reach all children. It is important, therefore, that physicians retain their familiarity with the disease and its complications. The cardinal manifestations have varied little since the earliest preserved description recorded 10 centuries ago by Rhazes, a Persian physician. Changes in environmental hygiene and sanitation as well as improved host nutrition have attenuated the overall clinical picture among many populations, but less fortunate people still undergo recurrent epidemics, with severity and complications often as marked as those described in 1670 by Sydenham in London. Alterations in the basic properties and behavior of the virus itself have not been substantiated.

Laboratory investigations conducted over the past 16 years have delineated most of the physical and biochemical characteristics of the virus, but previous clinical observations and experimental studies had already indicated many of its principal biologic properties. By scarification with blood obtained from acute measles patients, Home in 1758 had successfully transmitted measles and thereby also demonstrated the presence of viremia. Panum's classic report of the Faroe Islands outbreak of 1846 had documented respiratory droplet spread, the constant 2-week incubation period, close to 100 percent attack rates among exposed susceptibles, and "lifelong" immunity after a single attack as long as 65 years previously. Finally in 1911, Goldberger and Anderson, employing filtered respiratory tract secretions from measles patients, transmitted the disease to monkeys, proving both the "filterable" size of the agent and its presence in the nasopharynx.

THE VIRUS.   Measles is a paramyxovirus of the group which includes the mumps, parainfluenza, and Newcastle disease agents. It has many close similarities to canine distemper and rinderpest (cattle plague) viruses. Its internal component of ribonucleic acid (RNA) within a helical protein capsid is enclosed by an outer membrane of lipid and protein. Electron photomicrographs demonstrate virions which are roughly circular or oval and average 1,200 to 1,400 Å in diameter. In general, the virus is markedly heat-labile but remains very well preserved for long periods at low temperatures. It is rapidly inactivated by ultraviolet light and other forms of radiation, by proteolytic enzymes such as trypsin, and by chemical agents, including ether, acetone, and formalin. Measles virus propagates in a large variety of both primary cell cultures and stable lines, but the former generally are more sensitive in attempts to recover the agent from patients; successful propagation in the latter cultures usually requires a period of laboratory adaptation. Cells of human and simian origin seem most reliable for initial isolation of virus, but after varying numbers of serial passages, it then will multiply readily in cultures prepared from cells of other species. The growth rate in vitro is less rapid than that of many other agents; infective virus is released by budding slowly from intact cells until they lose their integrity, releasing the major portion of cell-associated virus.

The morphologic changes induced in cell cultures by measles virus are characterized by the formation of large, multinucleate giant cells or syncytia, and by the appearance of eosinophilic inclusions seen in both the nuclei and cytoplasm when infected cells are stained. A second cytopathic effect is the change of affected polygonal cells to a spindle or stellate form. Variation in the predominant cytopathology depends on the host cell system, virus population, and the constituents of the nutrient medium employed. Of particular note, however, is the marked similarity of these syncytia and inclusions induced in vitro to the multinucleate giant cells with inclusions observed in histologic specimens prepared from many tissues of patients with measles.

Following infection of man or experimental animals, antibodies appear in their serum after 12 to 15 days. They specifically neutralize viral infectivity, fix complement with viral antigen, and inhibit viral hemagglutination and hemolysis. The different antigenic components of the measles virion which induce the antibodies have been partially separated and identified by disruption of the viral particles. Measles strains isolated during the past 16 years by laboratories in widely separated nations have been carefully analyzed for possible antigenic variability, and no evidence has yet been found for the existence of strains possessing any significant variations. This homogeneity coincides well with the clinical and epidemiologic observations of the extreme rarity of second attacks of the disease. The sharing of some antigens and other properties with canine distemper and bovine rinderpest viruses remains principally of evolutionary interest. It has no significance in the protection of man against measles, but the reverse has been demonstrated—measles protects animals against infection with rinderpest and canine distemper viruses.

PATHOLOGY.   The cellular reaction, as with most viruses, is predominantly a monocytic one. Widespread lymphoid hyperplasia in adenoids, tonsils, thymus, spleen, Peyer's patches, appendix, and lymph nodes is characteristic, and within these reaction foci the large multinucleate giant cells are found. Inclusion-bearing cells also abound in the respiratory tract, trachea, bronchi, and bronchioles. With involvement of the mucosal lining of these passages, the affected epithelium is sloughed into the lumen along with macrophages, mucus, and cellular debris. Squamous metaplasia of bronchial mucosa characteristically follows. A pronounced peribronchial mononuclear exudate extends to varying degrees in an interstitial pattern, and macrophages appear in alveolar walls.

In the skin, an early hyaline necrosis of epidermal cells is followed by perivascular exudation of serum, proliferation of endothelial cells, and necrosis of epithelial elements. Destruction of hair follicles and sebaceous glands may occur in the affected areas, and a late perivascular lymphoid cuffing of small vessels has been reported. The buccal mucosal lesions (Koplik's spots) develop as a focal necrosis of the basal epithelium of the submucous glands with round cell collections and formation of vesicles.

Late in the course of the disease, as many as 70 percent of peripheral leucocytes may show chromosomal breakage for a short time. These breaks are indistinguishable morphologically from those observed in small numbers of cells from normal, control blood specimens, but they are striking in their abundance. Although their significance has not been determined, similar alterations of chromosomes have been found in the course of other viral infections.

When encephalomyelitis follows measles, a striking perivascular demyelination occurs predominantly in white matter but also in deeper cortical layers. Perivascular cuffing by microglial cells, lymphocytes, and plasma cells is apparent around small veins in which the endothelial cells are swollen. The neuropathologic findings of subacute sclerosing panencephalitis (SSPE) are described elsewhere (Sec. 15.11), but their hallmark is the presence of inclusion bodies in neuronal and glial cells.

PATHOGENESIS. Although all the events comprising the complete pathogenetic sequence are still not known, it is possible to construct a reliable outline by correlating presently available virologic and histologic data with clinical events. Infection is initiated when a susceptible individual receives, either directly by inhalation into his upper respiratory tract or perhaps indirectly via the conjunctival sac, virus-laden droplets discharged from the nasopharyngeal secretions of a measles patient. At the portal of entry, a short period of local viral multiplication and limited spread ensues, followed by a brief, low-titer, primary viremia which distributes the agent to distant sites, where virus replicates actively in lymphoid tissues. Subsequently a prolonged secondary viremia of higher titer occurs, associated with the onset of the clinical prodromata and the widespread dissemination of virus. From that time, about 9 or 10 days after the initial exposure, until the beginning of rash, virus can be regularly detected throughout the body, especially in the respiratory tract and in lymphoid tissues, and can be recovered with relative ease from nasophayngeal secretions, urine, and blood. The patient is most highly communicable to others during this 5- to 6-day period. With the onset of rash, about 14 days after initial infection, viral replication begins to diminish, and by the sixteenth day it is difficult to detect residual virus at any site other than in the urine, where it may persist for an additional several days. Also, coincident with the appearance of exanthem is the detection in serum of circulating measles antibodies found in nearly 100 percent of individuals by the second day of rash. A striking and continuing clinical improvement begins at this time, interrupted a few days later in a varying number of patients by secondary illness caused by bacteria which have migrated across the damaged respiratory tract lining. Sinusitis, otitis media, and bronchopneumonia develop more readily where edema and exudation as well as lymphoid hyperplasia have produced local obstruction and where the loss of ciliated epithelium has further compromised normal defense mechanisms.

Whether central nervous system (CNS) involvement is a direct result of viral invasion of the CNS during the secondary viremia is not known. As many as 10 percent of measles patients have been found to develop a significant cerebrospinal fluid (CSF) pleocytosis, and 50 percent of children with measles show electroencephalographic aberrations at the peak of clinical illness. Nevertheless, only 0.1 percent develop overt signs and symptoms of encephalomyelitis and it has not been possible, in the tissue culture era, to recover virus from CSF or CNS tissue of such patients. Typically, the CNS abnormalities appear several days after the acute illness, at a time when serum antibody is abundant and infectious virus is no longer detectable at the sites where it was plentiful earlier. These features have led to a popular hypothesis that the CNS involvement might represent some autoimmune-type disorder. The recent recoveries of measles virus from CNS tissues of SSPE patients, many months or years after primary measles infection, have emphasized the need for further clarification of the interactions of this virus and the CNS, in both acute and chronic conditions. Presently, this constitutes the most fascinating focus of current research on measles. SSPE may be a "slow measles encephalitis."

EPIDEMIOLOGY. In most countries measles has been a disease of early childhood, with its peak incidence among youngsters of preschool and early school age. The very high attack rate among exposed susceptibles results in a periodicity of epidemics at intervals of 2 or 3 years, when a new crop of susceptibles has arisen. In crowded urban areas, the 1- to 5-year-old group shows the highest incidence, while the age distribution is more apt to shift to the 5- to 10-year-olds in less congested or rural areas, where exposure may not occur until school attendance has begun. Late winter and early spring, in temperate zones, is the usual season for outbreaks.

Although nearly 100 percent of young adults have had measles or, in recent years, measles vaccine, a rare individual may escape the disease in childhood only to acquire it in the third decade or later, when exposed to infected children. The epidemiology in isolated island or other remote population groups is quite different. Under these circumstances, many years may elapse between outbreaks, allowing the accumulation of a large population of susceptibles of all ages. This group is then subject to an explosive and severe epidemic if the virus is inadvertently reintroduced into the community by a traveler who arrives while incubating measles.

The usual period of infectivity ranges from 6 or 7 days prior to the appearance of rash through the second or third day of the exanthem. This correlates well with the time of laboratory-detectable viral shedding noted above in the section on pathogenesis. Coughing and sneezing during the catarrhal period enhance the spread of droplet infection, which is the principal mode of contagion. The relative lability of the virus on exposure to light, drying, and heat limits its duration of infectivity and precludes transmission by an immune individual or by fomites. Man is the only known natural host, but other primates, especially Old World monkeys, are susceptible and may develop disease when intimately exposed to infected children or after deliberate infection with the virus in the laboratory. There are no known insect vectors.

IMMUNITY. A single attack of measles confers lifelong immunity which is not dependent upon repeated exposure to the virus. The immune individual whose serum antibody titer has diminished to low, or even undetectable, levels may occasionally show a rapid, anamnestic antibody rise after exposure or inoculation, but this occurs in the absence of any symptoms or signs of infection and without detectable virus shedding. Vaccination with live, attenuated measles vaccines confers comparable lasting immunity, whereas inactivated antigens have produced only a transient protective effect, persisting for 6 to 18 months.

When measles has been modified or aborted by the administration of immune gamma globulin early in the incubation period, the immunologic outcome is variable. In general, a durable immunity may follow the development of modified, but overt, disease. In contrast, the complete absence of any clinical manifestations coincides usually with a transient protective effect followed by a return to the fully susceptible state after the degradation (in the ensuing 6 to 8 weeks) of the passively-acquired antibody. However, a small but significant number of exceptions have been observed in which overt, modified disease was later followed by a return to full susceptibility; and, conversely, the complete prevention of detectable illness permitted subclinical infection and a permanent immunity. For any individual patient an absolute assessment of the immunologic results of globulin-altered infection can be obtained only by the determination of circulating measles-specific antibodies. Ideally, such an antibody test should be delayed until 6 to 8 weeks after globulin administration.

Since the virus-neutralizing antibodies are found among those immunoglobulins which cross the placenta readily, infants born to measles-immune mothers are protected against infection during their first 6 or 7 months of life. With the catabolism of maternal antibody, babies become increasingly susceptible in the second half of their first year and may, upon exposure, develop disease of varying severity. Those with modified or occult illnesses are thought to represent examples of partial protection by residual transplacentally-acquired antibody. The infant of the very rare mother who has never had either measles or vaccine is susceptible at birth and may, upon exposure, acquire the infection at any time postnatally.

Recent studies of secretory antibody in the IgA component of respiratory tract secretions have demonstrated the presence of measles-specific antibodies following natural infection or live, attenuated vaccine, but not after inactivated antigens.

CLINICAL PICTURE. In most cases the signs and symptoms of measles are highly reliable in their characteristic manifestations and in their time of appearance and sequence after infection. Approximately 10 days after exposure, fever and malaise first signal the onset of illness. Cough, coryza, and conjunctivitis —the three "C's"—begin by the next day. A gradual worsening of these catarrhal symptoms accompanies a steady rise in fever over the next 4 days. Two days prior to the appearance of exanthem, the classic enanthem (Koplik's spots) develops. With the onset of rash, 14 days after infection, the clinical picture attains its maximal severity, reaching a peak which coincides with involvement of the entire body by the eruption on its second to fourth day. A rapid defervescence then follows, with improvement of all symptoms except the cough. Constitutional symptoms throughout this 10-day period vary in their presence and extent, but headache, abdominal pains, vomiting, diarrhea, myalgia, and arthralgia are all frequent complaints. Fever reaching 105° or 106° F, often accompanied by chills, is not unusual when the rash is most florid. Febrile seizures may occur in children predisposed to them.

There is nothing unique about the coryza, which is characterized by nasal congestion, runny nose, and sneezing. The conjunctivitis causes edema of the lids, increased lacrimation, and frequently photophobia. Sharply demarcated, transverse, linear injection of the lower lid margins, Stimson's line, is present before the more generalized conjunctival inflammation obscures it. The hacking cough is especially distressing, with a progressive increase in its frequency and severity throughout the prodromal period. With the abrupt fall in temperature, after rash has covered the entire body, the catarrhal symptoms subside dramatically except for the cough, which persists for another 7 to 10 days.

Koplik's spots, pathognomonic of measles, appear 24 to 48 hours before the exanthem. They consist of a bluish white dot, about 1 mm in diameter, surrounded by a rose-red areola, and they tend to appear first on the buccal mucosa opposite the lower molars. Best seen in bright daylight, they are discrete and few in number initially, but within one day they increase rapidly and may spread to cover the entire buccal and some of the labial mucosa. At their peak, they are also seen on the lacrimal caruncle and have been described on the mucous membranes of the vagina and rectum. With the onset of rash they begin to fade and by the second day of the eruption have frequently disappeared. A nonspecific enanthem with red macular palatal lesions may precede the Koplik's spots and remain after the latter have faded.

The rash commences as discrete, irregular, erythematous macules behind the ears, on the neck, and along the hairline. As it progresses rapidly caudad over the ensuing 24 hours, to involve the face, trunk, and arms, careful palpation will reveal a papular component. Involvement of the legs and feet, by the end of the second or early in the third day, finds the lesions on the cheeks already coalescent; and in severe cases, confluent areas of rash also appear on trunk and extremities. The skin becomes edematous and the face swollen. Although the exanthem ordinarily blanches with pressure, a fine petechial component is often present but may not be appreciated until fading of the acute redness has left a faint brown discoloration to the skin. The exanthem fades slowly, in the same order of progression as its initial appearance, and this process usually begins by the third or fourth day after its onset. Subsidence of the florid eruption is followed by a fine, branny desquamation which is overlooked unless carefully sought. Among children with protein deficiency, the desquamation is far more extensive and may be complicated by multiple pyogenic skin abscesses. In some uncommon cases measles rash has a distinctly pruritic element.

The marked, generalized lymphadenopathy and splenomegaly which arise early in the course of the acute illness may persist for several weeks thereafter. The high fever at the peak of the illness may be accompanied in some children by marked irritability, somnolence, or even a state of delirium, but these are transient manifestations and resolve dramatically with the disappearance of the pyrexia. They do not correlate with the occurrence of subsequent central nervous system complications. "Black measles," a severe form of the disease with a generalized hemorrhagic rash, bleeding from the nose, mouth, and gastrointestinal tract, and marked systemic toxicity, is now rarely seen but was reported more frequently by authors in the past. Perhaps it included some features of disseminated intravascular coagulation.

DIAGNOSIS AND LABORATORY AIDS. The regular sequence of prodromal period, Koplik's spots, and generalized rash permit a clinical diagnosis of measles with a high degree of reliability. Except under unusual circumstances where definite confirmation is required, virus isolation in cell cultures or demonstration of an antibody rise is unnecessary. Of the available serologic tests, the measles hemagglutination-inhibition (HI) antibody determination is the most practical, combining ease and rapidity of performance with specificity and reliability of response. Within a day or two of the onset of rash, serum antibodies to the various measles antigens are detectable, and they increase rapidly thereafter to reach peak titers in the next 2 to 4 weeks. Complement-fixing antibodies may then gradually diminish over a period of years, while virus-neutralizing and HI antibodies persist indefinitely after an initial drop during the 2 to 6 months following their attainment of maximal titers.

Cytologic techniques for the demonstration of multinucleate giant cells in nasal secretions during the prodromal period and for the detection of inclusion-bearing cells in the urine, either at the time rash appears or soon after, have been helpful in a significant proportion of patients when examined in some laboratories. The material was stained best by the Papanicolaou technique, but Wright's stain has proved satisfactory for the nasal smears. A more reliable and specific test has been the examination of urinary sediments for cells containing measles antigen which can be labeled by fluorescent antibodies. Less specific laboratory support is found in the white blood cell count, which is low, with an absolute neutropenia and a marked lymphopenia, both in the prodromal period and during the rash.

The differential diagnosis includes rubella, infectious mononucleosis, roseola, scarlet fever, typhus, Rocky Mountain spotted fever, enterovirus or adenovirus exanthemata, and rashes due to drug sensitivity (especially barbiturates, hydantoins, penicillins, and sulfonamides). Koplik's spots are said to be pathognomonic of measles; when noted they are most helpful but must be distinguished from somewhat similar buccal mucosal lesions which may accompany some Coxsackie A9 infections. The latter occur without prodromata or exanthem. Rubella is a far milder illness, without cough and with distinctive lymphadenopathy usually of the posterior cervical, suboccipital, and postauricular nodes. Roseola (exanthema subitum) has an entirely different sequence, since the rash first appears after the fever has subsided. The peripheral blood picture in infectious mononucleosis contrasts strikingly with the leucopenia of measles.

COMPLICATIONS. A wide variety of complications may be observed beginning during the acute course of measles or arising shortly thereafter. The greatest number occur in the respiratory tract; other sites are also involved, though less commonly. Complications can be listed in different ways, but one method of consideration involves listing them under headings related to their etiology (Table 17). These are: those due to the primary viral process, those resulting from secondary bacterial invasion, and a third group whose cause remains uncertain.

Complications attributable to the initial measles virus infection include exaggerated or abnormal patterns of response. The widespread destruction of cells lining the respiratory tract and the accompanying reactive inflammation produce the usual catarrhal stage of measles. In the proper anatomic setting, and with only a moderate enhancement of these responses, severe laryngotracheobronchitis ("croup") or bronchiolitis may result. The former may cause sufficient airway obstruction to require relief by a tracheostomy, especially in children less than 3 years of age. Similarly, in infants only a moderate increase of local secretions and edema of the bronchiolar walls is necessary to produce a very acutely ill patient with wheezing, dyspnea, retractions, cyanosis, hyperresonance on percussion of the chest, and diffuse fine rales on auscultation. This latter picture does not differ from that of bronchiolitis due to respiratory syncytial (RS), parainfluenza, or other viruses.

An extremely rare, but almost uniformly fatal, interstitial pneumonia (giant-cell pneumonia) has

TABLE 17.   *Complications of Measles Virus Infection*

Viral	Bacterial	Etiology Uncertain
Laryngotracheobronchitis	Otitis media	Thrombocytopenic purpura
Bronchiolitis	Sinusitis	Effects on underlying disease
Pneumonitis	Mastoiditis	Tuberculosis
Keratoconjunctivitis	Pneumonia	Cystic fibrosis
Myocarditis	Noma	Malnutrition
Mesenteric adenitis-appendicitis	Furunculosis	Nephrotic syndrome
Interstitial (giant-cell) pneumonia		Encephalomyelitis and other acute CNS syndromes
Subacute sclerosing panencephalitis (slow measles encephalitis)		Depression of delayed cutaneous hypersensitivity

been noted in children who develop a progressive, persistent measles virus infection without the typical exanthem and with a unique failure to form measles-specific antibodies. To date, nearly all patients who have been studied with giant-cell pneumonia have had some severe underlying disorder, such as leukemia, Letterer-Siwe's disease, or the rare form of congenital agammaglobulinemia with lymphopenia and thymic dysplasia. The roentgen picture reveals a marked, interstitial pattern emanating from both hilar regions. Measles virus can be recovered repeatedly from sputum or nasopharyngeal swabs, and typical giant cells are seen when respiratory tract secretions are stained. Attempts to prevent this dire complication or to treat it with exceedingly large volumes of immune globulin or convalescent-measles plasma have rarely been successful.

A benign, asymptomatic keratoconjunctivitis accompanies measles but leaves no sequelae. It is of particular interest because of its persistence for periods as long as 4 months after the acute illness. The lesions can be visualized only by slit-lamp biomicroscopy but are said to be distinct from those caused by other agents. Myocarditis has been reported as a very rare complication but is of little clinical significance; transient electrocardiographic abnormalities occur commonly during measles. The diffuse lymphadenopathy which accompanies measles involves the mesenteric nodes and is thought to cause the abdominal pain, of varying severity, which commonly occurs during the acute illness. Symptoms and signs identical with those of acute appendicitis may result. Surgical intervention during the prodromal period has been resorted to sufficiently often to familiarize the pathologist with a picture of "measles appendicitis" characterized by some obliteration of the appendiceal lumen by the lymphoid hyperplasia and by the presence of typical giant cells in the mucosa.

Complications of bacterial origin result principally from the invasion by pyogenic organisms of areas whose lining cells have been damaged by the measles virus. Otitis media and bronchopneumonia are the commonest infections; they may be due to beta hemolytic streptococci, pneumococci, *H. influen-*

zae B, or staphylococci. The peribronchitis and interstitial pneumonitis present to some degree in nearly all measles patients are viral in etiology and resolve rapidly with the development of generalized rash and the subsidence of fever. A second fever spike, or failure of the initial one to drop after the eruption has reached its peak, suggests the presence of secondary bacterial infection. The appearance of a peripheral leucocytosis with a shift to the left is confirmatory. If physical findings are not sufficiently revealing, a chest film may disclose bronchopneumonia or a segmental or lobar involvement. Smears and cultures of sputum, tracheal aspirates, pleural fluid, blood, or other appropriate materials will assist immeasurably in establishing the etiology and will permit selection of a proper antimicrobial agent. Attempts at prevention of secondary bacterial complications by giving "prophylactic" antibiotics during the catarrhal stage of measles are injudicious and have been unsuccessful. Aside from failing to decrease the incidence of these infections, such indiscriminate use of antimicrobials tends to diminish those organisms which are susceptible to their effects, so that later complications result from invasion by more resistant bacteria or fungi which have flourished in the altered milieu. In areas where protein deficiency is a childhood problem, measles is accompanied by a higher rate of bacterial complications. In addition, manifestations such as noma and furunculosis, rarely seen in well-nourished children, may occur. Among these same unfortunate children who acquire measles in their early years and are often heavily parasitized by helminths and enteropathogenic bacteria, the vomiting and diarrhea that may normally accompany the illness are more virulent and may precipitate dehydration, acidosis, and frank marasmus or kwashiorkor. The amazingly high morbidity and mortality rates from measles which are reported by some nations in Latin America, West Africa, and Asia seem best explained by the patients' young age, these severe complications, and the unavailability of prompt therapy.

Of those syndromes which may follow measles, the most dreaded are the various CNS complications. By far the most common of these is encephalomyelitis (see Sec. 15.11), but toxic encephalopathy, retrobulbar neuritis, thrombophlebitis of cerebral veins, hemiplegias from vascular infarction, and ascending paralysis with polyneuropathy have all been reported. There is much speculation about their etiology; the hypothesis favored until recently invoked a hypersensitivity type of response similar to that found in experimental allergic encephalomyelitis. Against the possibility that encephalomyelitis is due to a direct invasion of the brain by the virus are the following factors: (1) failure to recover virus in cell cultures from either CSF or CNS tissue of patients; (2) the usual delay in the onset of symptoms until several days after appearance of circulating measles antibodies; and (3) an inability to reproduce the disease in susceptible monkeys inoculated with measles virus intracerebrally, intraspinally, and cisternally. However, the high incidence of abnormal electroencephalograms recorded in patients who have no CNS signs or symptoms during the acute stage, and the observation of rare giant cells in sections of CNS tissue from encephalitis patients, remain provocative. Coupled with the recent isolations of measles virus from brain of SSPE patients, these latter features call for a reinvestigation of the pathogenesis of all measles-CNS interactions.

With the exception of toxic encephalopathy, which appears with striking rapidity at the peak of fever and rash, the other more common CNS manifestations become apparent after the acute illness, following a period of improvement lasting two or more days. Seizures, altered state of consciousness, and sudden lapse into coma frequently mark the onset of encephalomyelitis. The patient's fever returns and there is a marked peripheral leucocytosis. The CSF findings and other laboratory determinations, as well as the subsequent clinical course, are indistinguishable from those of other postinfectious encephalitides. All patients show striking electroencephalographic changes. The incidence of overt encephalomyelitis appears to be about 0.1 percent. Mortality figures range from 10 to 25 percent, and significant sequelae in the motor, intellectual, sensory, or emotional spheres are said to occur in 20 to 50 percent of those who survive. The routine use of corticosteroid therapy has not altered these grim figures. Treatment consists of good nursing care with reduction of extreme pyrexia, control of seizures, maintenance of a clear airway, fluid and electrolyte replacement, and nutritional supplementation if the period of coma is prolonged.

During the early viremic phase of measles, there is a constant thrombocytopenia of insufficient magnitude to cause spontaneous bleeding, but it may reflect megakaryocytic damage by the virus. Another rarer, unexplained postinfectious complication, thrombocytopenic purpura, appears 4 to 14 days after the rash and may produce marked skin purpura, genitourinary and gastrointestinal bleeding, and epistaxis. In contrast to their lack of efficacy in the CNS syndromes, the corticosteroids produce prompt relief, with cessa-

tion of bleeding and steady return of platelet counts to normal. This response reinforces the concept that this complication may also be some form of "autoimmune" phenomenon.

The deterious effects which measles may exert on other underlying disorders are poorly understood. Reactivation or exacerbation of tuberculosis during measles has been repeatedly documented in outbreaks among populations with a high incidence of tuberculosis, and in hospitals where tuberculous children were residing. One provocative but unexplained feature is the loss of delayed cutaneous hypersensitivity to tuberculoprotein (and other antigens) which commonly occurs with measles and persists for many weeks thereafter, so that a previously positive reactor gives a negative skin test. The striking involvement of respiratory tract epithelium and interstitial tissues, coupled with the negative nitrogen balance occurring during acute measles, may partially explain the deterioration noted in some patients with cystic fibrosis who undergo unmodified measles. Infants with protein depletion may lapse into frank kwashiorkor during measles. This stems from a combination of events with decreased oral intake, increased gastrointestinal losses (due to vomiting and/or diarrhea), and the negative nitrogen balance of the infection. In contrast to these undesirable side effects, measles may induce a diuresis in children with refractory edema due to the nephrotic syndrome.

Since measles remains a disease of infancy and childhood among most populations, it is uncommon to encounter a susceptible woman who acquires the infection during pregnancy. Data collected from outbreaks among isolated communities involving susceptibles of all ages have shown that gestational measles frequently induces premature delivery, stillbirth, or abortion but is not associated with an increased incidence of congenital anomalies.

TREATMENT. Except for general supportive measures, there is no therapy for the patient with uncomplicated measles. Bed rest, avoidance of bright light if there is marked photophobia, encouragement of fluid intake, and the judicious use of antipyretics for high fever and of suppressants for distressing cough may be useful symptomatically. The provision of high humidity and, when indicated, increased oxygen concentrations offer some added relief to infants with severe croup or bronchiolitis. More specific measures, such as the use of proper antimicrobials, should be employed in the treatment of secondary bacterial complications.

PROPHYLAXIS. *Passive Immunization.* Human immune (gamma) globulin given soon after exposure can alter the clinical course and the antigenic effects of measles virus infection. The resultant immunity, after a modifying dose of globulin, is usually of lasting duration, while that which follows a preventive dose is most often transient, with return of susceptibility after 4 to 8 weeks. If exposed to measles, a susceptible child less than 3 years of age or an older child suffering from an underlying debilitating disease may promptly be given 0.25 ml per kg body weight to prevent measles. All others may receive 0.05 ml per kg to modify the illness and to reduce the rate of complications. The globulin must be administered intramuscularly and should be given as soon after exposure as possible. If more than 6 days have elapsed, one cannot rely upon globulin either to prevent or to modify the illness. Patients with globulin-modified measles display great variations in clinical course, with prolongation of the incubation period and varying expression of signs and symptoms, but they remain a source of potential contagion to their contacts. Because of its transitory nature, passive protection should always be followed in 8 weeks by the appropriate form of active immunization.

Dosages of globulin as large as 1.0 ml per kg or transfusions of correspondingly heroic volumes of convalescent plasma have been advocated for exposed, susceptible children with lymphoma, leukemia, disseminated malignancy, or other conditions characterized by depression of cell-mediated immunity because of their predisposition to develop giant-cell pneumonia. Unfortunately, the results of this seroprophylaxis have been unpredictable and variable.

Active Immunization. Subsequent to the licensure of attenuated measles virus vaccines in March, 1963, aggressive programs of immunization against measles were conducted in this country and elsewhere. The availability of safe, effective means for inducing active immunity, which appears comparable to that afforded by the natural, more virulent disease, has distinct advantages over passive methods. The attenuated vaccines provide an infection which is noncommunicable. Rather than depending upon capricious exposure to the natural disease, the optimal time and method for use of vaccine can be selected for any child. The secondary bacterial infections and neurologic complications which may accompany natural or modified measles do not follow attenuated vaccines. The prophylactic efficacy of live vaccines properly administered approaches 98 percent, whereas the long-term protection after modification or prevention with globulin is erratic.

Over the past 7 years more than 35 million children have received live measles vaccines in this country. Several types have been used (Table 18). With the original Edmonston B vaccines, globulin was used at the discretion of the physician to provide an even milder clinical response. If concomitant administration of globulin was desired, it was given intramuscularly at a different site and in a separate syringe to prevent any direct neutralization of the attenuated virus. The canine kidney cell product seemed to be the most reactogenic of all, and its use without globulin was inadvisable. The further attenuated vaccines evoke similar reactions to those noted after injection of chick cell Edmonston B with globulin. Continued surveillance of children who received live vaccines 8 to 10 years ago reveals the persistence of antibody and protective effect comparable to those

TABLE 18.   *Measles Virus Vaccines*

Inactivated antigens*
    Monkey kidney cell
    Chick embryo cell

Live attenuated virus
    Edmonston B†
        Chick embryo cell
        Dog kidney cell
    Further attenuated
        "Schwarz" }
        "Moraten" } Chick embryo cell

*Discontinued as of 1967-68.
†Usually accompanied by immune globulin.

which follow natural measles. The febrile responses which occur in 5 to 15 percent of children induce surprisingly little discomfort, toxicity, or disability. A modified exanthem of varying extent may occur after the fever, but it is observed in less than 5 percent of the inoculated children.

Among the initial disadvantages of inactivated vaccines were their requirement for three monthly injections to stimulate seroconversion and, later, the rapid disappearance of detectable antibody over the succeeding 6 to 18 months, with reemergence of susceptibility to measles. Because of those objections, their use was usually restricted to children for whom the live vaccine might carry some enhanced risk. Additionally, schedules were studied in which two or three monthly doses of killed vaccine were followed subsequently by an injection of the live, attenuated virus. The stated objective was to reduce to an absolute minimum any clinical reactivity of the live vaccine; this effect was achieved, but the procedure was cumbersome and costly, requiring a succession of visits to the physician or clinic. Another unfavorable feature of this schedule was the observation that as many as 25 to 50 percent of children immunized in this fashion developed fever and marked local reactions with pain, heat, erythema, and induration 2 to 5 days after the last injection. These adverse responses were self-limited and seemed to represent a form of delayed hypersensitivity reaction.

By 1967 a more serious syndrome had been observed in children exposed to natural measles, several years after immunization with killed vaccine alone. An atypical form of measles developed in these partially immune children. It was characterized by very high fevers, edema of the extremities, pneumonitis, and a hemorrhagic and/or urticarial rash most prominent on the extremities. The reports of such cases were sufficient to discourage any further use of inactivated measles antigens, and they are no longer available in this country. Some of the manifestations of the atypical illness strongly suggested a hypersensitivity phenomenon, the pathogenesis of which may have interesting relationships to other combinations of inactivated and live virus antigens (see Respiratory Syncytial Virus, p. 724) which have proved deleterious.

To insure the maximum 95 to 98 percent rate of seroconversion, live vaccines should not ordinarily be used for infants before age 12 months. However, they may be administered as early as 9 months of age if the likelihood of exposure is greater than usual. If given at an even earlier age, their immunogenicity is usually obviated by residual maternal antibody. In the rare instance of a baby born to a mother who is herself still susceptible to measles, successful use of attenuated virus is possible at any time but is inadvisable prior to age 3 months. Somewhat analogous to the effect of transplacental antibody, but less prolonged, is the interference with vaccination which will result from recent administration of immune (gamma) globulin or blood transfusion from an immune donor. Depending on the relative dosage administered, immunization should be postponed for 6 to 12 weeks to allow degradation of the exogenous antibody. Although it is possible to immunize safely and successfully with more than one live virus at the same time, this procedure is discouraged unless the pressure of time precludes completion of a normal schedule separating live vaccines by one month. If this case should arise, it is more advantageous and effective to give the live preparations simultaneously, rather than separating their administration by shortening the recommended interval. The latter, abbreviated schedule is more apt to result in failure of the subsequent attenuated infections because of circulating interferon elaborated in response to the initial live virus. A combined live measles-smallpox vaccine has been licensed, and it seems fair to predict that future combinations may include other live antigens, such as rubella.

Measles immunization has now taken its rightful place in the ideal preventive medicine program of every infant. For the unusual adult who has had neither measles nor immunization against it, live vaccine is safe, effective, and urgently indicated to prevent a disease which at this age is far more debilitating than in childhood. Continuing surveillance will be required to provide additional data on possible sequelae of vaccination and on the efficacy of national and international programs to achieve widespread protection against measles and its complications.

REFERENCES

Babbott, F. L., Jr., and Gordon, J. E. Modern measles. Amer. J. Med. Sci., 228:334, 1954.
Fulginiti, V. A., Eller, J. J., Downie, A. W., and Kempe, C. H. Altered reactivity to measles virus. J.A.M.A., 202:1075-1080, 1967.
Katz, S. L. Immunization with live attenuated measles virus vaccines: five years' experience. Arch. Ges. Virusforsch., 16:222, 1965.
Krugman, S., Constantinidis, P., Medovy, H., and Giles, J. P. Comparison of two further attenuated live measlesvirus vaccines. Amer. J. Dis. Child., 117:137-138, 1969.
——— Present status of measles and rubella immunization in the United States: A medical progress report. J. Pediat., 78:1, 1971.
Nader, P. R., Horwitz, M. S., and Rousseau, J. Atypical exanthem following exposure to natural measles: eleven cases in children previously inoculated with killed vaccine. J. Pediat., 72:22-28, 1968.
Panum, P. L. Observations made during the epidemic of measles on the Faroe Islands in the year 1846. *In* B. Roueche, ed., Curiosities of Medicine. New York, Berkley Publishing Corp., 1964, paperback.
Schaffner, W., Schlueederberg, A. E. S., and Byrne, E. B. Clinical epidemiology of measles in a highly immunized population. New Eng. J. Med., 279:783-789, 1968.
Scott, T. F. McN., and Bonanno, D. E. Reactions to live measles-virus vaccine in children previously inoculated with killed-virus vaccine. New Eng. J. Med., 277: 248-250, 1967.

14.34
MUMPS
(EPIDEMIC PAROTITIS)

SYDNEY S. GELLIS

Mumps is an acute contagious, generalized viral infection characterized by swelling and tenderness of the parotid and sometimes of the other salivary glands. Involvement of the testes in males who have reached puberty is frequent. Involvement of the central nervous system also occurs not infrequently, and either orchitis or meningoencephalitis may occur in the absence of salivary gland swelling.

ETIOLOGY. The contagious character of mumps was apparently first noted by Hippocrates in the fifth century B.C. Although a viral etiology had long been suspected, this was first established in 1918 by Wollstein, who transferred the disease to cats by injection of filtered saliva. In 1934 Johnson and Goodpasture transferred it to monkeys, and in 1945 Habel, and shortly afterward, Levens and Enders, successfully established the growth of the virus in chick embryos. Since then vaccines against the disease, skin tests employing attenuated virus, and complement-fixation and neutralization tests have been developed.

Communicability. Intimate contact is usually required to communicate the disease, spread occurring through droplets of saliva in which virus is carried. According to Enders a patient may become contagious about 48 hours before swelling of the parotid is noted. It is impossible to fix with certainty the duration of the communicable period; the virus has been demonstrated in the saliva of patients as late as the sixth day of parotitis. Most public health authorities require isolation until all swelling has disappeared and until complications, if any, have cleared.

It appears definitely established that patients with meningoencephalitis without parotitis may transmit the infection to contacts who subsequently develop parotitis. Mumps is endemic at all times; epidemics of the disease occur most frequently in the winter and spring months. The communicability of mumps is less than that of measles, chickenpox, or whooping cough, although the occurrence of mumps meningoencephalitis or orchitis without parotitis and the probable occurrence of subclinical parotitis suggest that the disease is more communicable than previously believed.

Incubation Period. The average incubation period is 18 days, but the range is said to extend from 8 to 37 days. The shortest interval observed by Enders has been 14 and the longest 25 days.

Immunity. The immunity following an attack of mumps is lifelong. Most cases of second and third attacks of so-called mumps have probably been confused with recurrent nonepidemic parotitis, which is frequently allergic in origin. The use of complement-fixation and neutralization tests will help distinguish this disease from mumps.

Susceptibility. Individuals of all ages are susceptible to mumps. The majority of cases occur in children between the ages of 5 and 15 years. Transplacental immunity probably accounts for the infrequency of mumps in the first half-year of life. The disease has, however, been observed in an infant one day old whose mother had mumps at the time of delivery. The oldest patient on record was a 99-year-old male.

PATHOLOGY. The most striking change in the salivary glands consists of edema. Minute hemorrhages may be found in the capsule, and there is intense hyperemia throughout the gland. The acinar cells show varying degrees of necrosis and infiltration with mononuclear cells; the walls of the salivary ducts are swollen, with resulting obstruction to the ducts. Subsequently the acinar cells regenerate; at no time is there any preponderance of polymorphonuclear cells, and fibrosis does not occur during healing.

SYMPTOMS. In the milder cases, the local symptoms are the first to attract attention; in more severe cases there are frequently prodromal symptoms of 12 to 48 hours' duration—anorexia, headache, vomiting, pains in the back and limbs, and fever. The initial temperature in a mild attack is 100 to 101° F; in more severe attacks the fever may range from 102 to 104° F.

Of the local symptoms, pain, which is referred to the posterior part of the jaw just below the ear, usually precedes the swelling of the salivary glands; it is increased by movement of the jaws and by pressure. Sour foods or liquids may increase the pain, though this finding is relatively infrequent in children and is not reliable as a diagnostic aid. The swelling may begin simultaneously in both parotids, but more frequently one side is involved a day or two in advance of the other. It usually reaches its maximum on the third day, remains stationary for two or three days, and then subsides gradually. The degree of swelling varies with the severity of the attack. When it is marked the patient may be so changed in appearance as to be almost unrecognizable. The swelling fills the lateral region of the neck between the jaw and the sternomastoid muscle and extends forward upon the face to the zygomatic arch, so that the center of the tumor is usually the lobe of the ear. Characteristically, the lobe of the ear is pushed upward and outward by the swelling. The other salivary glands may swell simultaneously with the parotids or several days later, even after the parotid tumor has disappeared. Occasionally, swelling of the submaxillary or sublingual glands occurs before that of the parotids, and in rare instances these may be the only glands affected. When the submaxillary gland is involved, the swelling also extends downward to include the neck. Involvement of the sublingual gland is accompanied by swelling below the tip of the chin and to one side or the other of the midline. The skin over the swollen glands retains a normal color but may become tense and shiny. In the large series of cases studied by McGuinness and Gall, 70 percent showed enlargement of both parotids.

The papilla at the mouth of Stensen's duct or Wharton's duct may be reddened and somewhat swollen. This is not a reliable sign since in many children the duct openings may normally have such an appearance. Since salivary secretion may be considerably diminished, dryness of the mouth may add to the patient's discomfort. Exceptionally, distressing salivation occurs.

The constitutional symptoms of mumps usually last from 3 to 5 days; the swelling continues about a week longer. In more severe cases swelling may continue for 10 to 14 days.

Meningoencephalitis. Since mumps is considered a generalized disease, meningoencephalitis cannot strictly be regarded as a complication. It is described in detail elsewhere (Sec. 15.11).

Other types of nervous system involvement which may occur in mumps consist of transverse myelitis, ascending paralysis, hemiplegia, optic neuritis, and eighth nerve deafness. Of these, deafness is the commonest; it is usually estimated that in 5 percent of the institutionalized deaf in this country the deafness was due to mumps.

Orchitis. Orchitis is rare in childhood; among 230 cases of mumps it was seen in only 10 boys, all of them over 12 years old. A report by Connolly suggesting that orchitis in infants and children is more common than generally thought requires confirmation. When orchitis occurs it is generally toward the end of the first or the beginning of the second week and is usually accompanied by fever, chills, and swelling of the testicle. The involvement is almost always unilateral. Just as meningoencephalitis may occur in the absence of apparent parotitis, so may orchitis make its appearance as the sole manifestation of mumps. The swelling and inflammation usually last from 4 to 7 days and may be followed by atrophy.

Involvement of Other Glands and Organs. Involvement of the ovaries in adult females is not uncommon, having been estimated to occur in 5 percent of cases. Inflammation of the thyroid gland, thymus, the breasts, lacrimal glands, and prostate has been reported but is quite uncommon. Pancreatitis may occur toward the end of the first week of mumps and is usually sudden in onset, with severe nausea and vomiting, epigastric pain, and tenderness. Pancreatitis occurs much less frequently in children than in adults. Recent studies of the possible relationship of mumps infection to endocardial fibroelastosis have given variable results, and the relationship cannot be said to be an established and acceptable one.

Myocarditis may result from mumps; electrocardiographic changes resembling those of rheumatic carditis have been reported. No symptoms are noted, but the sedimentation rate may be elevated for a considerable period. Rarely, hepatitis or nephritis may occur in the course of mumps. Pitting edema of the soft tissues overlying the sternum develops not infrequently, particularly if both parotids are greatly swollen or both submaxillary glands are involved.

LABORATORY TESTS. The white blood count in mumps parotitis is usually normal or slightly low, with a relative lymphocytosis. The count becomes higher with an increase in polymorphonuclear leucocytes in the presence of meningoencephalitis or orchitis.

The *complement-fixation test* developed by Enders and Kane has proved to be a reliable method for detecting antibody rise during convalescence from mumps. Henle has devised a special method of complement fixation using different antigen components from virus grown in chick embryos—the V (virus) antigen and the S (soluble) antigen, which is separable from the virus by ultracentrifugation. The S antibodies reach a high titer relatively quickly. The V antibodies develop later and will persist for years, whereas the S antibodies usually disappear in 6 to 12 months after the acute infection. Such tests have proved most helpful in diagnosis of mumps meningoencephalitis or orchitis in the absence of parotitis.

Skin tests employing virus grown in chick embryos and inactivated by heat, ultraviolet light, or formalin have been standardized by several different investigators. These tests are carried out in a manner similar to the tuberculin test and give rise to erythema and induration if antibody is present. The erythema or induration should be more than 10 mm in diameter at the end of 48 hours in order to be considered positive. However, the commercially available mumps skin test antigens give misleading results, and cannot be used to determine the state of immunity of exposed adults.

Virus neutralization tests involve the inoculation of chick embryos with virus-serum dilution mixtures after incubation, the harvest of chick embryo materials, and their subsequent testing for evidence of virus multiplication by complement fixation against a known positive mumps serum. The neutralization

tests have been employed less extensively than complement-fixation tests; neutralization antibody titer has been shown to be elevated early in the course of mumps. When low titers are found the likelihood of development of orchitis appears to be increased.

An elevation of *serum* or *urine amylase* is nearly always present in the first week of parotitis. This increase usually fades away by the end of the second week. There is some evidence that the increase is due only to inflammation of the parotid glands and that involvement of the other salivary glands or the testes has no effect on amylase levels. Therefore, a rise in amylase does not necessarily reflect pancreatitis, which may, however, occur.

PROPHYLAXIS. The relatively benign course of mumps in children as compared with that in adults argues for deliberate exposure to the disease during childhood. Active immunization against mumps is now feasible. An effective live attenuated mumps virus vaccine grown in chick embryo cell cultures is commercially available. After subcutaneous injection of the recommended dose (0.5 ml) of the vaccine, antibody against mumps virus appears in more than 95 percent of subjects. The vaccine has not caused fever or other clinical symptoms. The persistence of antibody following vaccination has not yet been determined, but excellent protection against contracting mumps has been demonstrated for over two years. Because of the uncertainty of the duration of the immunity afforded, and because mumps is not a serious disease in children before puberty, the Committee on Infectious Diseases of the American Academy of Pediatrics recommends that vaccine be given mainly to children approaching puberty, to adolescents and to adult males who have no knowledge of having had mumps. There is no known contraindication to vaccination of young children, except that revaccination before puberty may prove to be necessary.

It is recommended that children under 1 year of age should not be given mumps vaccine. Furthermore, it should not be given to children who are allergic to egg proteins, to any person suffering from an illness which alters resistance to infection, or to any person taking a drug which has the same effect.

There is no evidence that convalescent serum or hyperimmune serum globulin (human) is of value in protecting exposed susceptible persons. The same is true of inactivated mumps vaccines. The value of vaccination with live attenuated vaccine for protection of susceptible adults and pubescent and adolescent children who have been exposed to mumps is not known, but there is no contraindication to its use in this circumstance. The vaccination might protect against subsequent exposure if the exposure under consideration failed to cause infection.

TREATMENT. If the patient is only mildly ill, insistence on bed rest does not appear necessary; the severely ill patient will prefer to remain in bed. There is no evidence that continued activity by adults with the disease increases the danger of orchitis. Some patients obtain comfort from warm applications to the parotid areas, others prefer cold. Aspirin gives some relief, especially with regard to general malaise. Most young children with the disease continue on their regular diet with amazingly little discomfort. Diethylstilbestrol has been recommended for the prevention of orchitis in adults with mumps; it is of doubtful value.

There is no treatment for mumps meningoencephalitis. Repeated lumbar punctures may afford some patients considerable relief from headache, nausea, and vomiting.

REFERENCES

Bang, H. O., and Bang, J. Involvement of the central nervous system in mumps. Acta Med. Scand., 113:487, 1943.

Bashe, W. J., Jr., Gotlieb, F., Henle, G., and Henle, W. Studies on prevention of mumps. J. Immunol., 71:76, 1953.

Brunell, P. A., et al. Ineffectiveness of isolation of patients as a method of preventing the spread of mumps-failure of the mumps skin-test antigen to prevent immune status. New Eng. J. Med., 279:1357, 1968.

Buynak, E. B., et al. Combined live measles, mumps, and rubella vaccines. J.A.M.A., 207:2259, 1969.

Connolly, N. K. Mumps orchitis without parotitis in infants. Lancet, 1:69, 1953.

Eagles, A. Y. Analysis of a four year epidemic of mumps. Arch. Intern. Med., 80:374, 1947.

Eberlein, W. R., and Lynxweiler, C. P. The clinical picture of mumps meningoencephalitis and report of a case without parotitis. J. Pediat., 31:513, 1947.

Enders, J. F., Kane, L. W., Maris, E. P., and Stokes, J., Jr. Immunity in mumps. V. The correlation of the presence of dermal hypersensitivity and resistance to mumps. J. Exp. Med., 84:341, 1946.

Gellis, S. S., and Peters, M. Mumps with presternal edema. Bull. Hopkins Hosp., 75:241, 1944.

Habel, K. Cultivation of mumps virus in the developing chick embryo and its application to studies of immunity to mumps in man. Pub. Health Rep., 60:201, 1945.

——— Immunity response in mumps with complications. J. Lab. Clin. Med., 39:785, 1952.

Johnson, C. D., and Goodpasture, E. W. An investigation of the etiology of mumps. J. Exp. Med., 59:1, 1934.

Kane, L. W., and Enders, J. F. Immunity in mumps. III. The complement fixation test as an aid in the diagnosis of mumps meningoencephalitis. J. Exp. Med., 81:137, 1945.

Levens, J. H., and Enders, J. F. The hemoagglutinative properties of amniotic fluids from embryonated eggs infected with mumps virus. Science, 102:117, 1945.

McGuinness, A. C., and Gall, E. A. Mumps at army camps in 1943. War Med., 5:95, 1944.

Maris, E. P., Enders, J. F., Stokes, J., Jr., and Kane, L. W. Immunity in mumps. IV. The correlation of presence of complement-fixing antibody and resistance to mumps in human beings. J. Exp. Med., 84:323, 1946.

Meyer, M. B., Stifler, W. C., and Joseph, J. M. Evaluation of mumps vaccine given after exposure to mumps with special reference to the exposed adult. Pediatrics, 37:304, 1966.

Savran, J. Diethylstilbestrol in the prevention of orchitis following mumps. Rhode Island Med. J., 29:662, 1946.

Stokes, J., Jr., Enders, J. F., Maris, E. P., and Kane, L. W. Immunity in mumps. VI. Experiments on the vaccination of human beings with formolized mumps virus. J. Exp. Med., 84:407, 1946.

Thaggard, R., and Sutton, L. E. Mumps meningoencephalitis. Virginia Med. Monthly, 79:92, 1952.

Utz, J. P., et al. Clinical and laboratory studies of mumps. I. Laboratory diagnosis by tissue culture technics. New Eng. J. Med., 257:497, 1957.

Vosburgh, J. B., Diehl, A. M., Liu, C., Lauer, R. M., and Fabiyi, A. Relationship of mumps to endocardial fibroelastosis. Amer. J. Dis. Child., 109:69, 1965.

Wollstein, M. An experimental study of parotitis. J.A.M.A., 71:639, 1918.

——— A further study of experimental parotitis. J. Exp. Med., 29:377, 1919.

Wolman, I. J., Evans, B., Lasker, S., and Jaegge, K. Amylase levels during mumps; the findings in blood and saliva. Amer. J. Med. Sci., 213:477, 1947.

14.35
PICORNAVIRUSES, INCLUDING POLIOMYELITIS

EDWARD C. CURNEN, JR.

Picornavirus is a term introduced in 1962 by an international study group as a new name for a large family of viruses, with similar properties, which may have had a common phylogenetic origin. The word means small (pico), ribonucleic acid (RNA) virus. The picornaviruses include two major categories, those of human origin and those of lower animals:

A. *Picornaviruses of human origin*
   1. *Enteroviruses*
      a. *Polioviruses*
      b. *Coxsackie A viruses*
      c. *Coxsackie B viruses*
      d. *ECHO viruses*
   2. *Rhinoviruses*
   3. *Unclassified*
B. *Picornaviruses of lower animals*

Enteroviruses have their natural habitat in the alimentary tract. They include the polioviruses, the Coxsackie viruses, Groups A and B, and the ECHO (enteric cytopathogenic human orphan) viruses. Rhinoviruses (p. 726) are recovered mainly from the upper respiratory passages of man. Newly discovered strains of picornaviruses from human sources are designated as unclassified until further identification permits permanent assignment to an appropriate subgroup. Viruses with similar properties recovered from lower animals are also classified as picornaviruses.

Picornaviruses are relatively small, of the order

of 15 to 30 mμ in diameter; they have a ribonucleic acid (RNA) core and no lipid component, as indicated by resistance to inactivation by ether. The infective particles have been postulated to be constructed according to the principles of cubic symmetry, with an inner RNA core surrounded by a small number, perhaps 32, of regularly arranged protein subunits. Infection has been induced with RNA extracted from representative polio, Coxsackie A and B, and ECHO viruses. Viral activity is well preserved at $-70°$ and $-20°$ C. Thermostability varies under different conditions, but probably all picornaviruses are inactivated by heating at $60°$ to $65°$ C for 30 minutes. In contrast to enteroviruses, rhinoviruses are unstable at low pH in the range of 3 to 5.

Picornaviruses of human origin appear to be pathogenic in nature only for man, although many induce infection and disease when introduced experimentally into laboratory animals. Conversely, it has not been shown that picornaviruses of animals are significantly related to disaese in man. Enteroviruses are recovered from the oropharynx but more copiously and for longer periods from the feces. On the other hand, rhinoviruses are commonly recovered from the nose and throat and detected only rarely in the feces.

Picornaviruses of man, with the exception of a few Coxsackie A types, can be propagated in tissue cultures of various primate cells. Cultivation in cells of other animals has been less successful. Unlike enteroviruses, which multiply readily at $36°$ to $37°$ C, rhinoviruses grow best in rolled cultures at $33°$ C, a temperature which approximates that of the human nasopharynx. Growth of picornaviruses appears to occur exclusively in the cytoplasm and, with many but not all virus types, is associated with characteristic cellular damage or cytopathic effect (CPE). Interference has been noted between different enteroviruses as well as between members of this group and other viruses.

The antigenic properties of picornaviruses have been determined by a variety of techniques, but mainly by neutralization tests in experimental animals or tissue cultures and by complement-fixation tests. Although some cross-relationships have been noted within subgroups, identification of more than

TABLE 19. *Classification of Enteroviruses and Associated Illnesses*

Enteroviruses	
Poliomyelitis (3 types)	Paralytic poliomyelitis (mild to severe)
	Polioencephalitis
	Cerebellar ataxia
	Nonparalytic poliomyelitis
	"Abortive" poliomyelitis, pharyngitis, or undifferentiated febrile disorder
Coxsackie, Group A (23 types)	Aseptic meningitis (epidemic, types 7, 9; sporadic, many types)
	Paralysis (types 4, 7, 9)
	Encephalitis (types 2, 5, 6, 7, 9)
	Ataxia (types 4, 9)
	Guillain-Barré syndrome (types 2, 5, 6, 9)
	Herpangina (types 1-6, 8, 10, 22)
	Lymphonodular pharyngitis (type 10)
	Acute respiratory illness (types 9, 21, 24 in addition to herpanginal strains), pharyngitis or undifferentiated febrile disorder (many types)
	Exanthem (types 2, 4, 5, 9, 16)
	Hepatitis (types 4, 9, 10)
Coxsackie, Group B (6 types)	Aseptic meningitis (types 1-6)
	Paralysis (types 1-5)
	Encephalitis (types 1, 2, 3, 5)
	Epidemic myalgia (types 1-5)
	Encephalomyocarditis in early infancy (types 1-5)
	Myocarditis and/or pericarditis (types 1-5)
	Exanthem (types 1, 3, 4, 5)
	Orchitis (types 1-5)
	Hepatitis (type 5)
	Acute respiratory illness, pharyngitis, or undifferentiated febrile disorder (types 1-5)
ECHO (30 types)	Aseptic meningitis (types 1-7, 9, 11-23, 25, 30, 31)
	Paralysis (types 1, 2, 4, 6, 7, 9, 11, 16, 18, 30)
	Encephalitis (types 2, 3, 4, 6, 7, 9, 11, 14, 18, 19)
	Guillain-Barré syndrome (types 6, 22)
	Ataxia (type 9)
	Exanthem (types 1-7, 9, 11, 14, 16, 18, 19)
	Diarrhea (types 11, 14, 18)
	Acute respiratory illnesses, pharyngitis, or undifferentiated febrile disorder (types 1, 3, 6, 11, 19, 20, and others)

90 specific serotypes has been reliably established. Three types of poliovirus are recognized. The Coxsackie A viruses include 23 types, numbered 1 to 24, type 23 being identical with ECHO 9. There are 6 Coxsackie B viruses. The ECHO viruses number more than 30 types, although type 10 has been reclassified as a reovirus and type 28 as a rhinovirus. The rhinoviruses are represented by at least 30 well-established types, and evidence for the existence of more than twice that number has been reported.

Infection of man by a picornavirus usually is followed by the appearance of homologous antibody.

Characteristics of Enteroviruses

In addition to having the characteristic properties of all picornaviruses, enteroviruses have other features in common. Serologic surveys for detection of antibody in various population groups have indicated that experience with these agents is not only ubiquitous but also cumulative. In temperate zones enteroviruses and associated disorders occur mainly during summer and fall; in tropical areas, they may be encountered throughout the year. With the exception of Coxsackie A21 (Coe) virus, infection is more common among children than adults.

In low socioeconomic areas where hygienic conditions are poor, enteroviruses excreted in feces are distributed rapidly and at an early age. Although flies have been found to harbor enteroviruses in nature and experimentally, the importance of flies in transmission has not been determined. The extent to which respiratory secretions account for dissemination of infection by enteroviruses is also not known. As the oropharynx is a common portal for both alimentary and respiratory tracts, it is difficult to determine by which of these routes virus is seeded or to state whether pharyngitis and tonsillitis represent enteric or respiratory infections.

Enteroviruses have been associated with a varied and ever increasing number of clinical disorders. Current classification of the enteroviruses and the associated forms of human disease which appear to be induced by them are indicated in Table 19. It is evident that a single virus may have the capacity to induce more than one form of illness and that each clinical syndrome may be caused by any one of several different viruses.

Poliomyelitis
(Infantile Paralysis)

DOROTHY M. HORSTMANN

Poliomyelitis is an acute viral infection in which only a small percentage of those infected develop the characteristic clinical picture of fever, headache, vomiting, stiff neck and back, and sometimes flaccid paralysis of various muscle groups. More often it presents as a mild nonspecific febrile illness, or the infection remains completely asymptomatic. It is prone to appear in epidemic form, particularly in the summer. The disease has apparently been known since earliest times, but the first description appeared at the end of the eighteenth century in Michael Underwood's textbook of diseases of children. Not until the late nineteenth century did epidemics begin to appear. These increased in frequency and severity in certain parts of the world until the mid-1950's, when prophylactic immunization was introduced. In countries in which vaccination has been widely used, there has been a dramatic decline in incidence of the disease.

ETIOLOGY. The viral etiology of poliomyelitis was discovered by Landsteiner in 1908. At present the polioviruses are classified as members of the enterovirus family and share the physical and chemical characteristics of this subgroup of *picornaviruses* (p. 741). Three distinct serotypes are recognized, type I being the one most commonly associated with epidemics. There is some sharing of antigens, particularly between types II and I, and some degree of cross protection is indicated by both experimental and epidemiologic data.

HOST RANGE. The polioviruses induce paralytic disease in monkeys and chimpanzees, and some strains, particularly of type II, also infect mice. The discovery by Enders, Weller, and Robbins in 1949 that polioviruses will grow in tissue cultures of nonneural primate cells is a landmark of modern medicine and has had far-reaching implications for virology in general.

EPIDEMIOLOGY. The principles of the epidemiology of poliomyelitis were first worked out by the Swedish investigator Wickman, who published his monograph on the subject in 1908, the same year that isolation of the virus was reported by Landsteiner. Subsequent investigations proved that *infections* with polioviruses are common, but the *disease* is relatively rare except in epidemics, and even then the ratio of inapparent infections to clinical cases is probably more than 100 to 1 (Fig. 19). There is a marked seasonal incidence of the disease in temperate climates, with sharp increases in summer and fall; in tropical areas infection and cases tend to occur throughout the year.

Poliomyelitis has been both endemic and epidemic in all parts of the world. The age group attacked in endemic poliomyelitis and in early outbreaks is the youngest; 90 percent of paralytic cases are in children under 5 years of age. Once epidemics appear, they tend to recur, and after a few years an increasing proportion of cases occur in older children and young adults. This evolution of the epidemic disease has been correlated with changes in sanitary environment: in populations living under poor conditions of sanitation and hygiene the viruses are widely disseminated, infection (largely inapparent) and immunity are acquired in the first few years of

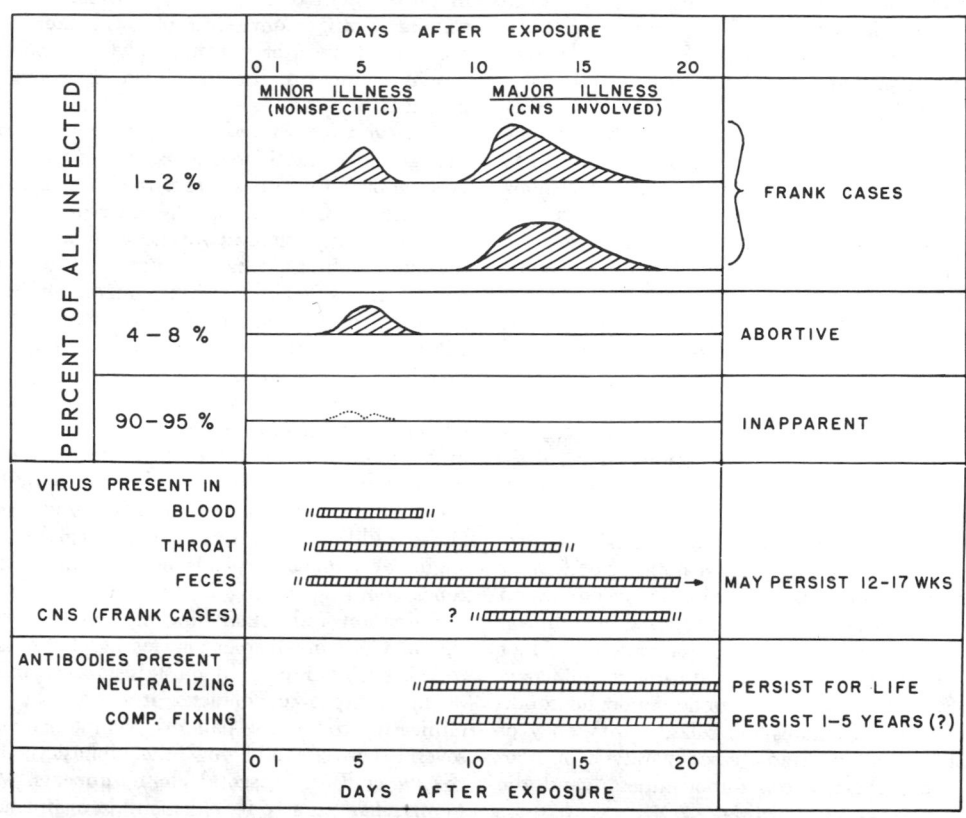

Fig. 19. Schematic diagram of the clinical and subclinical forms of poliomyelitis, showing presence of virus and antibodies in relation to development and subsidence of infection. (Redrawn from Paul, J. R. Reproduced from Bodian and Horstmann. In *Viral and Rickettsial Infections of Man*, 4th ed., Horsfall and Tamm, eds. Courtesy of J. B. Lippincott Co.)

life, there are no epidemics, and sporadic cases are confined to the infantile age group. With economic development and improved sanitation and hygiene, exposure and infection are delayed, the number of susceptibles builds up, and unless prophylactic vaccination is carried out, an epidemic may result when a virulent strain is introduced. The introduction of both inactivated and live attenuated oral vaccines has had a marked impact on the incidence of the disease in parts of the world where they have been used extensively. Virtual control of paralytic poliomyelitis has been achieved in large geographic areas, but in others, particularly tropical ones, first epidemics are still appearing.

Mode of Spread. Polioviruses are spread primarily by human association, and the healthy carrier is as infectious as the frank case. Young children form the bulk of susceptibles in any population and are the most effective spreaders of the virus. During active infection, virus is present in the throat and intestinal excreta; whether transmission is from the pharynx of one person to the oropharynx of another or whether the fecal-oropharyngeal circuit is the major one seems to depend upon the epidemiologic

circumstances. There is evidence that in populations with high standards of hygiene, pharyngeal spread is the more important, particularly during epidemics. In contrast, in populations living under conditions of poor sanitation, where fecal contamination is apt to be extensive, the fecal-oropharyngeal route is of greater importance and accounts for the high rate of poliovirus circulation among young children. In the family setting, both routes may be well traveled, particularly if there is a member under 2 years of age, who regardless of socioeconomic level can be regarded as creating a microclimate of poor sanitation.

PATHOGENESIS. Figure 19 correlates the pathogenesis of infection with the clinical course. Poliovirus enters the body by way of the oropharynx and is implanted in the walls of the pharynx and of the intestinal tract, where primary multiplication occurs, presumably in lymphatic tissue and/or mucosal epithelial cells. Three to five days after exposure, virus is present in the throat, blood, and feces. This may be accompanied by symptoms of the "minor illness," or the infection may be completely asymptomatic. In either event, the sites of viral multiplication at this stage appear to be the intestinal tract, the lymph nodes, and viscera such as liver and spleen. In the majority of infections this constitutes the entire course, and only in very few is there further progression and involvement of the CNS. The period of viremia which precedes CNS involvement lasts several days and disappears as antibodies develop. Invasion of the CNS is thought to be by way of the bloodstream, although experiments in monkeys and chimpanzees indicate that poliovirus can travel along neural pathways, and it is possible that this occurs in the natural infection under certain circumstances.

PATHOLOGY. The characteristic lesions of poliomyelitis are in the gray matter of the spinal cord, the medulla, the precentral gyrus of the cerebral cortex, and in the deep nuclei of the cerebellum. Neuronal necrosis, chromatolysis, neuronophagia, and "outfall" of cells occur. Focal and diffuse infiltration of leucocytes and perivascular cuffing are found in areas of neuronal damage. Besides CNS lesions, hyperplasia of lymph nodes is often observed and, in some cases, myocarditis is present.

CLINICAL MANIFESTATIONS. The clinical manifestations of poliomyelitis range from nonspecific "minor illness" to severe paralytic disease. The proportion of frank cases which can be diagnosed on clinical grounds alone is estimated to be not more than 1 or 2 percent of infections occurring during an epidemic, and may be considerably less under endemic conditions. Figure 19 illustrates the relative frequency of the several forms, the frank case (paralytic or nonparalytic), the abortive or "minor illness," and the completely inapparent infection.

Predisposing Factors. Factors which determine which expression the infection will take in a given individual are not completely understood: they include the nature of the infecting strain, whether highly virulent or not; age of the patient, older individuals being more likely to develop severe paralysis; and probably virus dosage. Other factors recognized as predisposing to the paralytic form are: (1) *Tonsillectomy.* If tonsillectomy is performed at a time when an individual has an inapparent infection and harbors poliovirus in his throat, bulbar poliomyelitis follows within 7 to 14 days in a considerable proportion of instances. There is also evidence that those whose tonsils have been removed at any time in the past are more susceptible to the bulbar form of the disease than are those with intact tonsils. (2) *Pregnancy.* Pregnant women have a higher incidence than do nonpregnant women of the same age, presumably due in part to hormonal factors but also to the generally greater exposure of pregnant women to young children. (3) *Recent inoculations.* Injections of diphtheria toxoid, pertussis vaccine, tetanus toxoid, or any combination of these three within one month (usually 8 to 17 days) prior to onset are associated with a higher incidence of paralysis. Following DPT immunization there is definite correlation between the site of injection and the site of paralysis. The extra risk of poliomyelitis from injections is apparently small, however, particularly

in children under 1 year of age, and is negligible in those under 6 months. (4) *Physical exertion and trauma.* Both trauma and physical exertion around the time of onset of the preparalytic phase have been shown to increase the likelihood of severe paralysis, particularly in adults.

Incubation Period. The range of the incubation period is considered to be 5 to 35 days, with an average of 7 to 10 days from the time of exposure to the onset of CNS signs. The interval between exposure, viral implantation in the alimentary tract, and the "minor illness" phase is considerably shorter, 2 to 3 days. Investigations with attenuated strains indicate that viral multiplication and excretion may occur in vaccinees within 24 hours, and contact infections may appear as soon as 3 days later.

Symptoms and Signs. Two basic patterns of clinical response are recognized, the *minor illness,* or abortive type, and the *major illness.* The *minor illness* (first phase), estimated to account for 80 to 90 percent of infections with any clinical signs, may be so mild as to be unnoticed. Usually there are slight fever, malaise, headache, sore throat, and sometimes vomiting, lasting 24 to 72 hours. The physical examination and spinal fluid are normal, and indication of CNS involvement is lacking. There is no more to the entire disease in most instances, and because of its nonspecific character it cannot be diagnosed clinically. In a few patients, symptoms recur after several days of well-being (the biphasic course), and the *major illness* (second phase) appears. More commonly, particularly in older children and adults, the major illness begins without a previous minor illness, with fever, headache, stiff neck, stiff back, muscle pain and tenderness, and sometimes hyperesthesias and parethesias. In paralytic cases, weakness of various muscles and loss of superficial and deep reflexes occur. The site of paralysis depends on the location of lesions in the spinal cord or medulla. In the bulbar form the cranial nerve nuclei are involved, with resulting paralysis of the pharyngeal, laryngeal, facial, and other muscles innervated by the cranial nerves. Difficulty in swallowing, nasal regurgitation, and nasal voice are early signs of bulbar poliomyelitis. Occasionally the clinical picture is dominated by encephalitic signs.

The influence of age on the clinical manifestations is marked. In the "childhood" type, the biphasic course is more common, the onset of symptoms of the major illness is sudden, fever is high, and the preparalytic phase is short, with paralysis often developing as the temperature falls and when the child begins to feel better. In the "adult" form of the disease, the onset is gradual, with a long prodromal period lasting up to a week, and with little fever; however, in contrast to the pattern in children, pain, either superficial or deep, is a prominent symptom. The type and severity of paralysis also vary in relation to age. Except for infants under 1 year, who tend to have predominantly spinal paralytic disease with high fatality rates, the disease is less severe in children than in young adults. This is evidenced by the greater frequency of quadriplegia, respiratory paralysis, and death in age groups over 15 years. Bulbar paralysis without spinal involvement is commonest in children, however. A difference in *sex incidence* of paralytic poliomyelitis is also related to age. Up to 15, males outnumber females approximately two to one, whereas in young adults there is a slight excess among females.

Physical Findings. The patient with the *minor illness syndrome* reveals no abnormalities except listlessness, fever, and some redness of the pharynx. In *nonparalytic poliomyelitis* the clinical findings are similar to those in aseptic meningitis associated with other enteroviruses, the severity of the illness tending to increase with the age of the patient. The temperature is elevated and there is neck and sometimes back stiffness, but the patient does not look as ill as one with bacterial meningitis.

In the preparalytic phase of *paralytic poliomyelitis,* the findings are similar to those in the nonparalytic case, but often the patient appears more acutely ill. His face is flushed even though the temperature is not high, and not infrequently he appears anxious, tremulous, and emotionally overwrought. Nuchal rigidity may be minimal and apparent only in the last degree of neck flexion. Stiffness of the back, tightness of the hamstrings, and stiffness, spasm, and tightness of other muscle groups may be present. The reflexes are normal and active early in the course; Kernig and Brudzinski signs are sometimes positive. A few hours before onset of paralysis there are often a loss or diminution of superficial abdominal and spinal reflexes, hyperactivity of the deep reflexes, and fasciculation of muscle groups. The site of the reflex changes and of fasciculation frequently heralds the site of paralysis. As weakness progresses, deep reflexes disappear, and with widespread paralysis all reflexes, superficial and deep, may be lost.

Types of Paralysis. In general, cases are defined as paralytic only if muscle weakness persists beyond 2 or 3 weeks. Localization and degree of paralysis depend on the site and concentration of neuronal lesions. A given number of destroyed nerve cells scattered over a wide area of the cord may produce no muscle weakness, while destruction of the same number concentrated in the anterior horn area supplying a given muscle may result in complete paralysis of that muscle. Cases are classified anatomically as *spinal,* if weakness is limited to muscles supplied by motor neurons in the cord, and *bulbar,* if the cranial nerve nuclei or medullary centers are involved. A combination of the two forms, *bulbospinal,* beginning with paralysis of the legs and ascending to involve abdominal and thoracic muscles of respiration, arms, and finally medullary centers and cranial nerve nuclei, occurs in the most severe cases, particularly in adults. Rarely, the clinical picture is predominantly one of encephalitis or of acute cerebellar ataxia.

In the *spinal paralytic form,* asymmetric involvement is characteristic. When the cervical cord is affected, weakness of the muscles of the shoulder girdle, arms, neck, intercostals, and diaphragm may appear. Lumbar cord involvement is reflected in paralysis of the abdominal muscles, back, and legs. The legs are more frequently affected than the arms, especially in young children. Paralysis of the bladder and urinary retention are seen in cases with weakness of the lower extremities, particularly in adults, and more commonly in men than in women.

In *bulbar poliomyelitis* the cranial nerve nuclei are the most commonly attacked, then the respiratory centers in the medulla, and least often medullary vasomotor centers. The tenth cranial nerve nuclei are involved most often, resulting in paralysis of the pharynx, the soft palate, and the vocal cords. Nasal voice, hoarseness, increased accumulation of secretions in the oropharynx, difficulty in swallowing, and regurgitation of fluids through the nose may develop. Paralysis of the facial nerve is also observed frequently. Less often, ocular palsies, pupillary disturbances, and weakness of muscles supplied by the fifth nerve are noted.

In *spinal poliomyelitis* respiratory failure results from weakness or paralysis of the intercostals, diaphragm, and abdominal muscles. One or both sides of the thorax and/or diaphragm may be affected, and accessory respiratory muscles in the neck and the alae nasi may come into action. Weakness of abdominal muscles results in difficulty in coughing and, consequently, difficulty in bringing up mucous secretions. As respiratory failure progresses, apprehension, changes in the sensorium, and cyanosis appear; respiration becomes more and more shallow, but a regular rhythm is maintained. In *bulbar poliomyelitis,* respiratory failure is a result of involvement of the respiratory center in the medulla or of paralysis of the pharyngeal muscles, with obstruction of the airway from pooled secretions; commonly a combination of these is present. Early signs of inadequate ventilation are irregularities in depth and rhythm of respirations, increased restlessness, anxiety, inability to sleep, rapid pulse rate, and a rising blood pressure; all of these signs may develop *before* cyanosis appears. At times respiratory failure occurs with alarming suddenness and progresses rapidly, with lengthening periods of apnea, Cheyne-Stokes respiration, mental confusion, and sometimes delirium. In addition there may be signs of circulatory collapse due to vasomotor center involvement. In this situation, the face has a dusky, flushed appearance, and the lips are cherry red. The pulse is rapid, 150 to 200 per minute, often irregular and difficult to palpate. The blood pressure is usually elevated, and the pulse pressure drops; shock and pulmonary edema add to the problems of respiratory failure in this highly fatal form of the disease. Circulatory disturbances arise frequently in the course of severe, life-threatening paralytic poliomyelitis and are associated with high mortality rates. Myocardial failure may be secondary to pulmonary complications, hypoxia, or electrolyte imbalance; in some cases signs of acute myocarditis develop, accompanied by typical ECG changes.

LABORATORY DIAGNOSIS. The *blood* shows no characteristic abnormalities. Moderate leucocytosis is not uncommon in the acute febrile stage. *Spinal fluid* findings are of considerable diagnostic aid in the major illness. An elevated cell count, above 8 to 10 cells, is characteristic; the usual range is 20 to 300, but occasionally as high as 1,000 or more. During the first few hours after onset of CNS signs, polymorphonuclear leucocytes predominate, but this is followed by a prompt shift so that approximately 90 percent of the cells are lymphocytes. In a small proportion of cases there is no increase in cells, and the CSF may remain normal even in the presence of severe paralysis. The CSF sugar content is not altered; the protein may be slightly elevated early in the course, rising gradually to moderate levels by the second and third weeks and returning to normal by the sixth week.

Virus isolation is the method of choice in confirming the diagnosis, and the earlier the specimens are taken, the greater is the chance of success. Tissue cultures of a variety of primate cells, either continuous line or primary outgrowth, are highly sensitive test systems. The virus is present in the throat during the acute phase of illness, and is shed in the feces for several weeks and occasionally for months (Fig. 19).

Neutralization and complement fixation are the commonly used *serologic tests* for the diagnosis of poliovirus infections. As shown in Figure 19, neutralizing and CF antibodies appear early in the course of the *disease,* which is relatively late in the course of the *infection.* As in other systems, a fourfold or greater rise in titer between the acute and convalescent specimens is diagnostic. Since a considerable number of patients already have high, even maximum, levels of antibody at the time of admission to the hospital, it is possible to demonstrate significant rises in not more than 50 percent of cases.

DIFFERENTIAL DIAGNOSIS. In the presence of an epidemic in which there are many paralytic cases, the *abortive form* and *nonparalytic poliomyelitis* can be suspected on the basis of epidemiologic evidence. However, an etiologic diagnosis can be made only in the laboratory, for these syndromes can be induced by a variety of other agents. The clinical findings in aseptic meningitis due to polioviruses do not differ significantly from those in aseptic meningitis associated with Coxsackie and ECHO viruses, mumps, herpesvirus, lymphocytic choriomeningitis, and leptospirosis. *Paralytic poliomyelitis* is usually not difficult to recognize, but it is increasingly evident that other enteroviruses are also capable of inducing a clinical pattern indistinguishable from poliomyelitis. However, polioviruses still account for the majority of cases of paralysis, particularly those with severe involvement, while transient mild weakness is more characteristic of infections associated with Coxsackie and ECHO viruses. Epidemic pleurodynia may resemble poliomyelitis very closely, especially when chest pain is accompanied by transient weakness of the diaphragm and involvement of the limbs. In geographic areas where arbovirus infections occur, diseases due to those agents must be considered. They are more apt to present predominantly an encephalitic picture, and limb paralysis, when it occurs, tends to be spastic rather than flaccid. Other diseases to be ruled out include meningoencephalitis due to mumps or herpes virus, postexanthematous encephalitis, shoulder girdle neuritis, Bell's palsy, infectious polyneuritis (Guillain-Barré syndrome), tuberculous meningitis, brain abscess, acute rheumatic fever, acute osteomyelitis, and, in some situations, hysteria.

TREATMENT. There is no specific treatment. The course of the disease is not altered by antimicrobial drugs, convalescent serum, or gamma globulin. Medical management consists of supportive therapy appropriate to any acute infection and anticipation and handling of complications.

General Measures. Patients with either the abortive or the mild nonparalytic form require no treatment other than bed rest at home for the duration of fever. In the more severely affected hospitalized case, mild analgesics are indicated for relief of headache and discomfort. Protection of the patient from undue activity in the early phase of the major illness is an important prophylactic measure. The treatment of *paralytic poliomyelitis* often requires the combined efforts of the pediatrician, orthopedist, and specialist in physical medicine. In the acute febrile stage, efforts are directed toward making the patient as comfortable as possible, maintaining his fluid and electrolyte balance, and protecting any weakened muscles. Pain and "spasm" of muscles may be relieved by intermittent application of moist hot packs for 20-minute periods several times daily.

As long as the fever persists there is likelihood of extension of paralysis, and close observation is necessary to detect complications demanding active measures. Problems which may arise include respiratory failure, circulatory disturbances, abdominal distension, urinary retention, and bacterial infection.

Respiratory Failure. The management of the acutely ill patient with respiratory failure poses a complex and often rapidly changing series of problems which severely tax the ingenuity and judgment of the physician even if he is experienced in handling such cases. If severe impairment of respiratory muscle function alone is present, the tank respirator is indicated. It should be used when signs of respiratory decompensation are progressive and the vital capacity reaches less than 50 percent of normal. For children, respiratory rates up to 30 with pressures of +3 to −12 or −15 are recommended, and for adults rates of 18 with pressures of +3 to −18, but these must be adjusted to the individual case, taking care to avoid underventilation or overventilation. Weaning from the tank respirator should begin within several days. The chest (cuirass) respirator and the rocking bed are useful adjuncts during the weaning period but are inadequate for handling the acute stage of respiratory failure.

In bulbar cases with central respiratory failure and obstruction due to pooling of bronchotracheal secretions, continuous O_2 inhalation, postural drainage, and removal of secretions with a suction apparatus generally suffice. If these measures fail to keep the airway clear, a high tracheostomy is indicated. This procedure is also necessary if abductor paralysis of the vocal cords develops, or if there are repeated bouts of pulmonary atelectasis requiring tracheal aspiration and bronchoscopy. Adequately humidified O_2 is given through the tracheostomy tube in concentrations of 40 to 60 percent, although emergencies may necessitate 100 percent for brief periods. Positive pressure respiration through a cuffed tracheostomy tube may be substituted for the tank respirator in patients requiring artificial respiration. The tank respirator is contraindicated in bulbar poliomyelitis unless a tracheostomy has been performed so that adequate suctioning of secretions can be carried out.

Bladder Paralysis. A parasympathetic drug such as urecholine is useful in inducing voiding. If the patient fails to respond, a second dose may be given before resorting to catheterization. Bladder paralysis usually lasts only a few days, and an indwelling catheter is rarely necessary.

Infection. Patients with respiratory problems, especially if tracheostomy has been performed, are particularly subject to pneumonia; urinary tract infections are not uncommon in those requiring repeated catheterization. The incidence of such infection is not reduced by prophylactic use of antimicrobials, and this practice is contraindicated, for it favors the emergence of drug-resistant organisms. Once infection develops, appropriate therapy should be given based on the nature and sensitivity of the infecting agent, as in other similar infections.

Convalescent Care. This is largely a matter of physical therapy and should begin soon after the acute phase has subsided, with gentle passive movements, progressing to active exercises as strength improves. Attention to the many emotional problems of the patient faced with some degree of disability is of major importance.

PROGNOSIS. Complete recovery is usual in nonparalytic poliomyelitis and in cases with slight muscle weakness. If paralysis is present, recovery of muscle function continues for a period of approximately 18 months to 2 years. However, 60 percent of the ultimate improvement is achieved by the end of 3 months, and 80 percent by the time 6 months have passed. The final result depends on the extent of nerve cell damage. Some muscles may show no recovery or never improve beyond 10 percent of normal function, while others recover normal strength.

Mortality. The death rate from paralytic poliomyelitis has been reduced in recent years due to improved techniques in handling respiratory failure, which is responsible for most of the deaths in both the bulbar and spinal paralytic forms of the disease. Overall mortality at present is estimated to be about 4 percent but is as high as 10 percent in severe epidemics involving older age groups.

PREVENTION. Poliomyelitis is now a preventable disease, and immunization is indicated for all children. Two types of vaccine are available, one a formalin-inactivated preparation (Salk) which is given by injection, and the other, a live attenuated virus vaccine (Sabin), administered orally. Passive immunization with gamma globulin is of uncertain value at best and is not recommended.

Inactivated Preparation. Following the introduction of inactivated poliovirus vaccine by Salk in 1955, the incidence of paralytic poliomyelitis declined sharply to less than 10 percent of former rates in countries where it was used extensively. The effectiveness of the vaccine depends upon the stimulation of antibodies which are capable of neutralizing the virus, presumably blocking it in blood and tissues, and thus preventing invasion of the CNS and paralytic disease. However, antibodies derived *only* from such vaccination do not significantly inhibit viral multiplication in the intestinal tract, although they have a suppressive effect on multiplication in the pharynx.

A basic course of immunization with inactivated vaccine requires four doses, the first three at monthly intervals and the fourth 6 to 12 months later. The vaccine is given in 1 ml amounts subcutaneously. For infants, the schedule is integrated with other immunizations (Sec. 32.3); quadruple vaccines (DPT and poliomyelitis) are available. For maintenance of adequate antibody levels, repeated yearly booster doses are recommended.

Inactivated vaccine has proved safe and effective; it is stable on storage in a refrigerator and causes remarkably few side effects. Sensitization to neither foreign protein nor penicillin has been significant. Yet in spite of its good record, certain problems remain which make it a less effective immunizing agent than the oral live attenuated virus vaccine. The problems include the rapid fall-off of antibody levels in infants and young children who have never experienced natural infection; the occurrence of epidemics in certain well-vaccinated areas, with 20 to 30 percent of the paralytic cases being in individuals who have received three or more doses; the difficulty of reaching a high percentage of young children with four or more doses of a vaccine that has to be injected; and the need for repeated booster injections over the years to maintain adequate antibody levels.

Live Attenuated Virus Vaccine (Sabin). Oral vaccine possesses certain advantages which make it the optimum form of immunization to protect the individual and the community from paralytic poliomyelitis. These are: (1) It simulates natural infection; in addition to antibody conversion, it induces a state of relative resistance of the intestinal tract to reinfection. In a well-immunized community this provides a potent barrier to invasion by wild polioviruses. (2) There are indications that antibodies induced by oral vaccine persist for years, thus obviating the need for repeated booster doses. (3) The vaccine induces infection and immunity rapidly, even in the youngest age groups. It is thus effective in stopping epidemics if given to a large enough segment of the susceptible population. (4) Ease of administration favors a high acceptance rate and is a particular advantage in community-wide programs. Some 350 million persons in various parts of the world have now been immunized, and the results attest to the safety and effectiveness of the vaccine. Since the vaccine induces an actual infection, there is a certain amount of contact spread, particularly among young children. This is limited, however, and there is no evidence that it results in harmful effects; some view it as an advantage, for it increases the number of persons immunized.

The vaccine is available in a trivalent form or as monovalent preparations of each of the three types. There is an increasing tendency to use the trivalent form because of its logistic advantages. Optimum use of the vaccine involves, first, a community-wide immunization program in which infants over two months of age, children, and young adults are covered; this is followed by a continuous program of immunization of infants and preschool children who enter the community. In all types of programs the main target is the preschool-age group, for such young children form the bulk of susceptibles in any population and are the chief spreaders of wild polioviruses.

Primary immunization of infants. Either monovalent or trivalent vaccines may be used. The first dose is generally given at approximately 2 months of age. If monovalent vaccines are used, they should be given in the order Type I, Type III, Type II, at 6- to 8-week intervals. If trivalent vaccine is given, *three doses* are recommended. Whether monovalent or trivalent is used in the primary course, a fourth dose, consisting of trivalent vaccine, should be given to infants at 12 to 15 months of age.

Primary immunization of other preschool children. The procedure may conform to that outlined for infants with the exception that the fourth dose may be omitted, or the primary course may consist of two doses at 6- to 8-week intervals followed by a third dose approximately 1 year later.

Primary immunization of all others. If monovalent vaccines are used, they should be given in the order Type I, Type III, and Type II. If trivalent vaccine is given, two doses 6 to 8 weeks apart are satisfactory.

Immunization of all children on entering school. A single dose of trivalent vaccine is regarded as desirable on entrance to school for all children who have previously been immunized with oral vaccine. This is designed to fill in any antibody gaps resulting from the occasional failure to achieve a vaccine take with one or another type during the primary course of immunization. If the child has never received oral vaccine, a full course using monovalent or trivalent vaccine should be given.

Procedure for partially immunized children. Oral vaccine may be ineffective if the complete series is not given. Persons who at some time have had a partial or complete series of injections of the inactivated vaccine (Salk) should receive a complete series of oral vaccine in either monovalent or trivalent form, as outlined above. After the full series of the oral form has been completed, no further injections of inactivated vaccine nor doses of oral vaccine need be given.

Immunization in the presence of an epidemic. The virus type responsible should be identified and the corresponding monovalent vaccine offered on a community-wide basis as quickly as possible. All age groups from 2 months up should be included.

The ultimate control of poliomyelitis in well-immunized populations has become a realizable goal since the introduction of oral vaccine. The marked decline in reported cases in the United States (59 in 1965) reflects the greatly reduced circulation of wild polioviruses. This in turn makes widespread vaccination of young children born into the community of greatest importance, since they are largely deprived of opportunities for acquiring natural immunizing infections. Failure to protect such children could result in the buildup of a susceptible population in which epidemics might reappear should a virulent poliovirus strain be introduced.

REFERENCES

Bodian, D., and Horstmann, D. M. Polioviruses. *In* Horsfall, F. L., Jr., and Tamm, I., eds., Viral and Rickettsial Infections of Man, 4th ed. Philadelphia, J. B. Lippincott Co., 1965, p. 430.

Hodes, H. L. Treatment of respiratory difficulty in poliomyelitis. *In* Poliomyelitis: Papers and Discussions Presented at the Third International Poliomyelitis Conference. Philadelphia, J. B. Lippincott Co., 1955, p. 91.

Horstmann, D. M. Enterovirus infections of the central nervous system. Med. Clin. N. Amer., 51:681, 1967.

Koprowski, H. Historical aspects of the development of live virus vaccine in poliomyelitis. Brit. Med. J., 2:85, 1960.

Magoffin, R. L., Lennette, E. H., Hollister, A. C., Jr., and Schmidt, N. J. An etiologic study of clinical paralytic poliomyelitis. J.A.M.A., 175:269, 1961.

Paul, J. R. Epidemiology of Poliomyelitis. Monograph Series No. 26, Geneva, World Health Organization, 1955, p. 9.

——— Status of vaccination against poliomyelitis with particular reference to oral vaccination. New Eng. J. Med., 264:651, 1961.

Russell, W. R. Poliomyelitis, 2nd ed. Great Britain, Butler and Tanner, Ltd., 1956.

Sabin, A. B. Prevention of poliomyelitis by vaccination.

In Levine, S. Z., ed., Advances in Pediatrics. Chicago, Year Book Publishers, Inc., 10:197, 1958.

Symposia on basic problems of respiratory distress and on the care of patients severely stricken with poliomyelitis. *In* Poliomyelitis: Papers and Discussions Presented at the Fourth International Poliomyelitis Conference. Philadelphia, J. B. Lippincott Co., 1958, pp. 421, 469.

Weinstein, L. Cardiovascular disturbances in poliomyelitis. Circulation, 15:735, 1957.

14.36
COXSACKIE VIRUSES

EDWARD C. CURNEN, JR.

ETIOLOGY. Coxsackie viruses have the capacity to induce fatal disease in suckling mice or hamsters. The term is derived from the town of Coxsackie in New York State, where strains were first encountered in 1947 by Dalldorf and Sickles.

Dalldorf classified Coxsackie viruses into two groups based on the histopathologic changes observed in suckling mice. In these animals Group A viruses induce flaccid paralysis and widespread necrosis of striated muscle without lesions elsewhere. Group B viruses cause spastic paralysis and disseminated disease characterized by focal myositis and, in addition, necrosis of fat, myocarditis, encephalomyelitis, hepatitis, and pancreatitis, the last produced by some strains in mature as well as in suckling mice.

Coxsackie viruses are among the smallest which affect man. Estimates based on filtration, centrifugation, and electron microscopy indicate that these viruses are spherical particles, approximately 28 mμ in diameter, and remarkably uniform in size.

Coxsackie viruses are unusually stable. Infected materials can be preserved for long periods in glycerin, or frozen at $-20°$ to $-70°$ C, and can be kept for many days at room temperature without significant loss of viral activity.

At present, 23 types of Group A, designated A 1 to 24, excluding A 23 (now classified as ECHO 9), and 6 types of Group B, designated B 1 to 6, are recognized. They can be identified and differentiated by neutralization and complement-fixation tests with specific immune sera prepared in animals, as well as by determinations of active immunity. Tests dependent on hemagglutination can also be carried out with the Coxsackie viruses which possess this property (A 7, 20, 21, and 24 and B 1, 3, and 5). Circulating antibodies can usually be detected in the human or animal host within two weeks of infection or the onset of symptoms.

Coxsackie viruses have been studied less extensively in laboratory animals other than the mouse. Strains of A 7, A 14, and Group B viruses have been found occasionally to induce poliomyelitislike lesions in monkeys. These and other Coxsackie viruses cause mild or clinically inapparent infections in monkeys and chimpanzees. Only two types, A 2 and A 8, have multiplied in chick embryos and two, A 2 and A 4, in cultures of chick cells. Strains of all six Group B viruses propagate readily in monkey kidney and various human cell cultures, and all but a few Group A types (1, 4, 5, 6, 19, and 22) have been grown in human amnion cells. Strains of Coxsackie B viruses have been observed to have an oncolytic effect after serial passage through Hela tumors in rats.

EPIDEMIOLOGY. Coxsackie viruses have been encountered in populated areas throughout the world. Like other enteroviruses they have been recovered most commonly from human feces and pharyngeal swabbings, and also from sewage and flies. Strains of all Group B serotypes and of many Group A viruses have been recovered from cerebrospinal fluid of patients with viral meningitis. Recovery of a Coxsackie virus during life from blood, urine, or other sources has not been common. Virus in relatively high titer has been found in the brain, myocardium, and other organs of newborn infants and rarely of older persons after death. Coxsackie viruses have been recovered from individuals of both sexes and different races, more frequently from children than from adults. No natural nonhuman reservoirs of infection have been found.

Some Coxsackie viruses cause epidemics of human disease at unpredictable intervals. At least nine Group A viruses may cause "herpangina," and Group B viruses types 1 to 5 have caused outbreaks of epidemic myalgia. All six Group B viruses can also induce meningoencephalitis, sometimes in association with epidemic myalgia; these agents are now recognized as important etiologic agents of the aseptic meningitis syndrome. Strains of Group B and A 7 and A 9 Coxsackie viruses have been associated with and are thought to be responsible for paralysis in individual patients. Group B viruses may also cause generalized infection with encephalitis, myocarditis, and hepatitis in newborn infants similar to that produced experimentally in suckling mice. Transmission may be from mother to fetus in utero or from mother to infant postpartum as well as from one infant to others in the nursery. Myocarditis and pericarditis in older children and adults have also been attributed to Group B Coxsackie viruses; in a few instances Group A viruses have been implicated on the basis of uncertain evidence. Hepatitis has also been reported in older patients infected with Coxsackie B 5 virus. Coxsackie A 10 virus has been recovered from the stools of hepatitis cases and contacts. Acute illnesses have been associated with exanthems in epidemics of infection with A 9 and A 16 Coxsackie viruses and in sporadic distribution with A 2, 4, and 5 and B 1, 3, 4, and 5 viruses.

The etiologic relation of Coxsackie viruses to other illnesses with which they have been found to be associated has not been so clearly established and in many instances has probably been fortuitous. This relationship is particularly likely for Group A viruses, which have been encountered much more frequently than Group B viruses in stools from healthy persons and from patients with poliomyelitis or other concurrent but apparently unrelated illnesses. Absence of reports of successive infections with strains of a single type of Coxsackie virus supports other indications that immunity to infection by a Coxsackie virus is type-specific and relatively enduring. The incubation period of infection by Coxsackie viruses may range from 1 to 14 days but is usually shorter, with a mean of 3 to 5 days. The spread of infection by Coxsackie viruses is similar to that by polioviruses, with communicability especially high in the home environment.

CLINICAL DISORDERS. *Aseptic Meningitis.* This syndrome can be induced by any one of a large number of viruses. All of the Group B and 16 different Group A Coxsackie viruses have been recovered from sporadic cases; Group B and A 7 and A 9 viruses have been associated with epidemics. All of the Group B viruses and at least 12 Group A types have been recovered from spinal fluid.

Clinical features of aseptic meningitis attributable to a Coxsackie virus are not distinctive. The onset may be sudden or gradual. Approximately half the cases exhibit a prodromal stage during which viremia has occasionally been detected. Anorexia, nausea, fever, headache, and abdominal pain are common complaints before the onset of meningeal signs. Later more severe headache, drowsiness, vomiting, and discomfort or stiffness of the neck or back appear. The temperature may rise to 104° F and usually subsides within 10 days. On examination hyperemia of the pharynx, occasionally with discrete ulcers of the mucous membrane, and resistance to nuchal flexion may be detected. Kernig and Brudzinski signs are likely to be demonstrable; tendon reflexes are usually normal.

The white blood count is generally normal. The leucocytes of the cerebrospinal fluid are increased in number, usually to about 500 but occasionally as high as 2,000. Although mononuclear cells are more numerous, initially the proportion of polymorphonuclear cells may be as high as 50 percent. The levels of sugar and protein in the fluid are normal.

Except in young infants with generalized infection the course is usually benign. Although rash, muscular weakness, or persistent myalgia may be present, they are not characteristic features.

Paralysis and Other Neurologic Disorders. Paralysis, encephalitis, and infectious neuronitis are relatively rare in association with Coxsackie viruses. Paralytic illnesses have been observed in patients infected with Coxsackie A viruses types 4, 7, and 9 and B viruses types 1 to 5. In most instances paralysis has been mild and transitory. Excluding newborns with generalized infection, encephalitis has been found in association only with Coxsackie A viruses types 2, 5, 6, 7, and 9 and B viruses types 1, 2, 3, and 5. Coxsackie A viruses types 4 and 9 have been recovered from fecal specimens of patients with ataxia, and types 2, 5, 6, and 9 have been encountered sporadically in patients with Guillain-Barré syndrome.

Epidemic Myalgia (Pleurodynia, Bornholm Disease). This entity was apparently first recognized by Finsen, who observed epidemics in 1856 and 1863 in Iceland. One name derives from the classical description by Sylvest, a Danish physician who studied an outbreak on the island of Bornholm. Group B Coxsackie viruses types 1 to 5 have been associated with epidemics of this disorder, and their role as etiologic agents is now generally recognized.

Epidemic myalgia has occurred in outbreaks throughout the world, with the highest incidence in the summer and fall. Several members of a family may be affected, each with somewhat different symptoms. The incubation period is commonly 2 to 4 days. Fever and pain usually develop suddenly, sometimes following vague prodromal symptoms. The characteristic feature is muscular pain, sometimes excruciatingly severe, typically located in the chest or upper abdomen, occasionally elsewhere. Pain in the lower abdomen may simulate that of an acute surgical condition. Tenderness or swelling may be detected at the site of pain. Headache is a frequently associated complaint, and occasionally stiffness of the neck is present. Splenomegaly is uncommon. Clinical laboratory findings are usually normal. The temperature often reaches 104° F and persists for a period ranging from 3 to 9 days. In approximately 25 percent of cases the course of symptoms and fever is diphasic. Meningitis, pleurisy, pericarditis, and, in mature males, orchitis are infrequent complications.

Encephalomyocarditis of the Newborn. Strains of Group B Coxsackie virus may cause acute, generalized, and sometimes fatal intrauterine or neonatal infection in newborn infants. Gear in South Africa first called attention to this association. Severe illness appears suddenly at any time during early infancy, sometimes a few hours or days after a brief episode of mild diarrhea. Cases have occurred when epidemic myalgia or aseptic meningitis attributable to the homologous Group B Coxsackie virus was present in the vicinity, and also following an acute febrile illness of the mother at about the time of delivery. In affected infants, hypothermia or fever, with elevations of temperature to 104° F, anorexia, tachycardia, cyanosis, icterus, pallor, cardiomegaly, hepatomegaly, electrocardiographic signs of myocarditis, and the development of circulatory collapse are characteristic features. Examination of the cerebrospinal fluid may reveal xanthochromia, pleocytosis, and an elevated level of protein. The course may be rapidly fatal or lead to complete recovery. In fatal cases virus has been recovered from the brain and spinal cord as well as from the myocardium and other organs. Postmortem examinations have revealed lesions in the brain, heart, liver, and other organs resembling those seen in experimentally infected newborn mice.

Acute Myocarditis or Pericarditis. The occurrence of myocarditis or pericarditis in older children and adults infected with a Coxsackie virus of Group B or less frequently of Group A has also been reported. In rare instances the virus has been recovered from pericardial fluid or, in fatal cases, from the myocardium. The etiologic role of these and other viruses in surviving patients with acute cardiac disorders has been difficult to establish.

Herpangina. Huebner and his associates first demonstrated the etiologic role of six different Group A Coxsackie viruses in relation to an acute self-limited febrile illness affecting mainly children during the summer months and characterized by distinctive faucial lesions. They pointed out that a similar clinical entity had been described in 1924 by Zahorsky and named by him "herpangina." This disorder has now been etiologically associated with nine Group A viruses (types 1 to 6, 8, 10, and 22).

Characteristically the illness is initiated by an abrupt elevation in temperature which ranges to 105° F and lasts from 1 to 4 days. Anorexia, dysphagia, and vomiting are frequently present, and patients over 2 years of age complain of sore throat. Headache and abdominal pain are also common symptoms. The pharynx is usually hyperemic, and frequently, although not invariably, one or more discrete grayish vesicles, averaging 1 to 2 mm in diameter, or at a later stage shallow ulcers surrounded by a red areola, may be seen. These are commonly located on the fauces, soft palate, and uvula, less frequently elsewhere in the oropharynx but not characteristically on the pharyngeal, gingival, or buccal mucosa. The lesions disappear within a few days after the temperature returns to normal. Recovery is usually uncomplicated, although associated esophagitis, genital ulceration, and parotitis have been reported. In typical cases the clinical laboratory findings are normal.

Acute Lymphonodular Pharyngitis. This is a self-limited febrile disorder similar to herpangina, observed in an epidemic associated with Coxsackie A virus type 10. Examination revealed small white or yellowish nodular lesions of the uvula, anterior pillars, and posterior pharynx which healed without ulceration. The acute course of illness resembled that of herpangina.

Fever with Lymphadenitis. Coxsackie A viruses types 5 and 6 were observed in Africa associated with a disorder resembling glandular fever. The illness was characterized by an abrupt onset with fever and tender swollen lymph nodes; stiffness of the neck and splenomegaly were noted in a few instances. The fever subsided in 4 to 10 days.

"Hand, Foot, and Mouth Disease." Coxsackie A viruses types 5 or 16 have been recovered mainly from infants and children with a syndrome called "hand, foot, and mouth disease" characterized by vesicular and ulcerative lesion in the mouth, and by a maculopapular rash and vesicles on the hands and feet. In some cases a transient erythematous rash has been seen on the buttocks as well as the extremities. The course is acute and usually self-limited, although four fatal cases in infants infected with Coxsackie A virus type 16 have been reported.

Exanthema. In addition to the maculopapular and vesicular skin lesions observed in some cases of infection with Coxsackie A viruses types 5 and 16, rashes have been reported in occasional association with other types of Coxsackie A and B viruses. These are generally maculopapular, although vesicles and urticaria or petechiae have been seen in some cases of infection with Coxsackie A virus type 9 and B viruses types 3 and 5.

Hepatitis. Evidence of hepatic disease in newborn infants with generalized infection by a Coxsackie virus of Group B is well documented. There is indication that other Coxsackie viruses may affect the liver in older subjects. Coxsackie A virus type 10 and B virus type 5 have been encountered in outbreaks of mild hepatic disorder, and Coxsackie A viruses types 4 and 9 have been recovered respectively from the blood and from the liver postmortem in individual patients with signs of hepatitis.

Acute Respiratory Illness and Other Undifferentiated Disorders. In addition to herpangina and other illnesses characterized by pharyngitis, Coxsackie A viruses have been found in association with acute respiratory illnesses including both undifferentiated and recognizable forms. A strain of type 24 virus (Pett) was recovered from the feces of children during an institutional outbreak of respiratory disease. Strains of A 21 virus (Coe) have been encountered repeatedly in outbreaks of acute respiratory infection, mainly among military recruits, and have been shown to cause "common colds" or mild febrile upper respiratory illness in human volunteers. In an outbreak of illness among infants and children attributed to infection with Coxsackie A 9 virus, three had pneumonia, and the virus was recovered from the liver and lung of one who died.

Infection with each one of the Coxsackie B viruses has produced a varied spectrum of clinical manifestations in the community and often within a single family. Sore throat or other respiratory symptoms may occur during the prodromal stage in patients with aseptic meningitis or pleurodynia and may be the only features of illness in other members of the household. Coxsackie B viruses of several serotypes have been encountered in outbreaks of febrile respiratory illness in families, camps, and institutions. Coxsackie B viruses types 3 and 5 were found in association with prevalent respiratory disease among infants and children during serial long-term studies in an orphanage. Coxsackie B viruses have also been recovered occasionally from patients with croup, bronchiolitis, vesicular pharyngitis, pneumonia, and pleurisy but are not considered to be major causes of these clinical entities. On the other hand, mild respiratory illnesses are probably frequently attributable to Coxsackie B viruses, especially during the summer and fall.

DIAGNOSIS. Diagnosis of infection by a Coxsackie virus may be suggested by the clinical and epidemiologic findings and can be verified in the laboratory by isolation of the virus and demonstration of a related increase in specific neutralizing antibodies. Tissue culture techniques have supplemented but not replaced the use of suckling mice for these purposes. Rises in titer of complement-fixing antibodies against heterologous as well as homologous Coxsackie viruses occur in human serum following infection by these agents; hence determinations by this technique are of limited diagnostic value. It should be emphasized that *infection* by a Coxsackie virus can be demonstrated by laboratory methods alone, but diagnosis of *disease* caused by one of these agents requires careful correlation of supporting clinical, epidemiologic, and laboratory evidence.

Differentiation of aseptic meningitis caused by a Coxsackie virus from bacterial meningitis, leptospyrosis, space-occupying lesions, or infections of the central nervous system caused by other viruses such as poliomyelitis, mumps, lymphocytic choriomeningitis, equine encephalitis, and ECHO or herpes simplex virus is often indicated by clinical and epidemiologic evidence and can usually be verified in the laboratory.

Recovery of a Coxsackie virus from cerebrospinal fluid collected during the acute stage of illness is positive diagnostic evidence. When both a Coxsackie virus and another viral agent, especially a poliomyelitis or ECHO virus, are isolated simultaneously from a patient, it may be difficult to determine the relative etiologic significance of each virus. Paralysis caused by an enterovirus other than a poliovirus has been encountered occasionally in individual patients but, with the possible exception of Coxsackie A virus type 7, not in epidemic distribution. On the basis of present knowledge, it seems reasonable for the clinician to attribute flaccid paralysis without associated loss of sensation occurring in the course of acute febrile illness to infection by a poliomyelitis virus unless supporting evidence is convincing that another agent is responsible.

Myalgia attributable to Group B Coxsackie viruses has to be differentiated from other causes of thoracic and abdominal pain. In epidemic myalgia the pain may suggest pleurisy or an abdominal emergency, but x-ray films of the chest rarely reveal pleural or pulmonary involvement. Consideration of epidemic myalgia, particularly during the season of prevalence or in the presence of a local outbreak, may avert unnecessary surgery. Orchitis complicating epidemic myalgia or aseptic meningitis must be differentiated from mumps.

Herpangina in the community is suggested by its occurrence in seasonal outbreaks and, in individual patients, by the presence of discrete vesicular or ulcerative lesions characteristically located on the anterior pillars of the tonsils, the soft palate, uvula, or tonsils. In this respect the lesions are usually distinctive and differ from those attributable to herpes simplex virus. The latter may occur in the faucial areas but are generally distributed more diffusely in the gingival and buccal mucosa on mucocutaneous borders and skin. Occasionally lesions similar to those of herpangina are seen in patients infected with Coxsackie B or ECHO viruses. The enanthems of other bacterial and viral diseases, moniliasis, infectious mononucleosis, blood dyscrasias, deficiency diseases, and heavy metal poisoning are unlikely to be confused.

Myocarditis in the newborn attributable to a Group B Coxsackie virus is suggested by tachycardia, signs of myocarditis, and circulatory collapse occurring during the neonatal period. The diagnosis is particularly likely if epidemic myalgia is prevalent in the vicinity or if the mother has an acute illness which could be attributable to infection by the same virus. This disorder must be differentiated from congenital heart disease and other neonatal anomalies or infections.

In older patients, carditis attributable to a Coxsackie virus may be difficult to distinguish from other forms of acute cardiac disease.

Knowledge of the clinical manifestations of infection by Coxsackie viruses is still incomplete. The possibility of infection by one of these agents should therefore be considered in any cases of unexplained illness occurring in characteristic epidemiologic circumstances.

PROGNOSIS.   Complete recovery from disease caused by Coxsackie viruses can usually be expected except in newborn infants, in whom infection with a Group B virus may prove fatal.

TREATMENT AND CONTROL MEASURES.   No form of therapy is known which acts directly on Coxsackie viruses. At present treatment is entirely supportive and symptomatic. Specific measures to control infection by these viruses are not available.

14.37
ECHO VIRUSES

EDWARD C. CURNEN, JR.

The development of tissue culture techniques for the recovery of viruses from the alimentary tract led to the discovery of a hitherto unrecognized group of viruses, some of which were promptly shown to cause human disease. These agents, referred to initially as "orphan" or human cytopathogenic enteric viruses, are now designated ECHO viruses.

ETIOLOGY.   The ECHO viruses characteristically induce cytopathic effects (CPE) in cultures of human and simian cells. When grown in susceptible cells under agar they produce areas of necrosis or "plaques," which have characteristics sufficiently distinctive to aid in identification. In general, ECHO viruses do not induce overt disease in monkeys or suckling mice. ECHO virus type 9, however, following passage in tissue culture, induces lesions in suckling mice similar to those resulting from infection by Coxsackie A viruses. Moreover, some ECHO viruses have been found experimentally to cause neuronal changes in monkeys; paralysis has been observed with types 7 and 14, and meningitis has been established in these animals with types 6 and 16. Chimpanzees, when infected with ECHO viruses types 4 and 6, excreted the homologous agent and developed antibodies against it without exhibiting clinical evidence of disease. Different cell systems in tissue culture and renal cells from different species of monkey vary in their susceptibility to ECHO viruses. Little is known concerning the histopathology resulting from infection by ECHO viruses in man, as few fatalities have been recorded. A virus later identified as ECHO virus type 2 was the only agent recovered by Steigman and his associates from the spinal cord of a child who died of a disease which clinically and pathologically resembled bulbar poliomyelitis.

Thirty different antigenic types of ECHO virus, numbered 1 to 33, have now been identified serologically, utilizing neutralization and complement-fixation techniques and, where possible, hemagglutination tests. Types 1 and 8 are now considered as type 1. Types 10 and 28 have been reclassified as reovirus and rhinovirus, respectively. Within certain types, especially types 4 and 6, striking differences between strains have been observed. Although slight antigenic relationships with other enteroviruses have been suggested, the ECHO viruses appear to be distinct entities within the family of enteroviruses and clearly distinguishable from other known viral agents which affect man. It is noteworthy, however, that viruses similar to ECHO viruses have been encountered, apparently as natural parasites, in monkeys, cattle, and swine.

ECHO viruses are relatively small particles, similar not only in size but also in other physical characteristics to Coxsackie and poliomyelitis viruses. Interference between ECHO viruses and active poliomyelitis vaccine viruses has been demonstrated in man. In the laboratory interference between ECHO viruses and other enteroviruses has been observed, providing, in the case of rubella virus, a technique for detection.

EPIDEMIOLOGY. ECHO viruses have been detected in many parts of the world both by recovery of virus and by demonstration of specific antibodies. Infection by these agents has occurred more commonly in warm seasons, in poorer socioeconomic conditions, and more frequently in children than in adults. Virus has been recovered more readily from feces than from the oropharynx or other sources, although in patients with meningeal involvement virus may also be found in the cerebrospinal fluid. At different times and in quite widely separate localities, epidemics of aseptic meningitis have been caused by ECHO viruses of types 4, 6, 9, 11, 16, and 30. In individual cases meningeal involvement has been attributed to a total of 24 types. Strains of at least 17 ECHO virus types have been recovered from cerebrospinal fluid. An exanthem has been encountered in association with infection by 13 types of ECHO viruses. Some patients infected with a type 9 or, infrequently, with type 4 virus had both aseptic meningitis and an ex-

anthem in the course of illness. Patients infected with type 16 virus have shown either rash or meningeal involvement, but to date both features have not been reported together in the same individual. Whenever aseptic meningitis attributable to one of these viruses has been epidemic, other instances of both less severe and inapparent infections by the same agent have also been found to be prevalent in the vicinity. The high attack rate and rapid dissemination of these viruses within families indicate both a high degree of communicability and a relatively short incubation period.

CLINICAL DISORDERS. *Aseptic Meningitis.* The onset is usually abrupt, with headache, often localized as retrobulbar, being the most frequent and severe symptom. Fever and stiffness of the neck or back are almost invariably present. Myalgia may be a complaint in more than 50 percent of the cases. In many patients with meningitis attributable to ECHO virus type 9 and occasionally in patients infected with a type 4 virus, a fine, sometimes morbilliform, maculopapular, erythematous exanthem appears during the acute phase of illness, distributed most commonly on the face and upper portion of the trunk. Lymphoid hyperplasia in the posterior pharynx and occasionally ulcerations of the oral mucosa resembling those of herpangina may be seen during infection with some of the ECHO viruses, including types 6 and 16. Cervical or generalized lymphadenopathy may be present. The course is usually benign, with fever lasting for about a week and malaise persisting sometimes for several weeks.

Patients wtih aseptic meningitis usually have total leucocyte counts of the cerebrospinal fluid below 500 cells per mm^3; in patients with type 9 infection, however, the counts frequently exceed 1,000. Polymorphonuclear forms are present in the cerebrospinal fluid early in the course of illness and, except with type 4 infections, may initially exceed 50 percent; eventually the cells are predominantly lymphocytic. The protein content of the fluid is normal or slightly elevated; the sugar content is characteristically normal. The white blood cell count is usually normal.

Most patients recover completely, but, in some, disability may be protracted for weeks or months and minor subjective or neuromuscular complaints may persist even longer.

Paralysis and Other Neurologic Disorders. Muscular weakness and paralysis associated with alteration of reflexes similar to those in poliomyelitis have been observed in patients with meningeal involvement infected with at least 10 types of ECHO virus, and fatal cases of infection with types 2, 6, 7, and 11 have been recorded. The findings indicate that some of these agents induce poliomyelitislike neuropathy in man.

Encephalitis has been reported in association with 10 types of ECHO virus, but the clinical pattern has been diverse and the evidence for an etiologic relationship has been inconsistent. Similarly, the etiologic significance of ECHO viruses types 6 and 22 in patients with Guillain-Barré syndrome remains uncertain. Cerebellar ataxia has been observed in patients infected with ECHO 9 virus.

Exanthem. Maculopapular exanthems have been recognized as a charactetristic feature of infection with types 4, 9, and 16 ECHO viruses. Rashes have been especially common in association with epidemics of type 9 infection both in patients with and in those without meningeal involvement. A rash (Boston exanthem) has also been a conspicuous feature in outbreaks of a mild febrile illness caused by strains of virus related to or identical with ECHO virus type 16.

Rashes have been observed in association with 10 other ECHO viruses; they appear to be more common in infants and children than in adults. Most frequently the exanthems have been maculopapular, but vesicles, urticaria, and petechiae have also been described.

Diarrhea. The association of certain ECHO viruses, particularly types 11, 14, and 18, with diarrheal disease in infants and children has been observed and an etiologic relationship suggested.

Acute Respiratory Illness. A number of ECHO viruses have been associated with acute respiratory illnesses. ECHO virus type 11 (U or Uppsala virus) was recovered in Sweden from children with nondiphtheritic croup; it was also found in children and adults with acute respiratory infections and induced brief febrile illnesses in experimentally infected human subjects. ECHO virus type 6 has been recovered from patients with mild illnesses during epidemics of meningitis attributable to this agent and from cases of pharyngitis and conjunctivitis among children and adults in Japan. Among infants in a Japanese institution, ECHO virus type 1 was reported to be associated with upper respiratory infection, diarrhea, and a rubellalike rash. A diagnosis of pneumonia was made in some cases during an epidemic of infection with ECHO virus type 9. ECHO virus type 19 has been encountered in infants and children with mild respiratory disease and has been recovered from a fatal case during an outbreak of severe respiratory disease in premature infants. ECHO virus type 20 was found in infants with minor respiratory disorders and diarrhea. Volunteers experimentally infected with this agent developed fever, pharyngitis, and, in two instances, coryza. ECHO viruses, however, do not appear to be of major importance in the causation of respiratory disease.

DIAGNOSIS. As with other enteroviruses, diagnosis of *infection* by an ECHO virus can be confirmed in the laboratory, but diagnosis of *disease* can be established only by careful correlation of associated clinical, epidemiologic, and laboratory evidence. All of the ECHO viruses are cytopathogenic and can be identified by neutralization tests with specific immune serum in cultures of renal cells from Rhesus monkeys. The presence of infection may be demonstrated by the detection of virus in the feces, oropharyngeal swabbings, or other specimens from the patient and by the demonstration of a related antibody response in the patient's serum of fourfold or greater magnitude. Because of considerable antigenic variation among strains of certain types, particularly 1, 3, 4, 5, 6, and 9, so-called prime strains and specific antisera may be required for serologic identification.

Aseptic meningitis caused by an ECHO virus must be distinguished from that attributable to a different virus, especially another enterovirus or mumps virus. In patients with a rash or lymphadenopathy, infectious mononucleosis, leptospirosis, and meningococcal or rickettsial infection may have to be considered. The cerebrospinal fluid findings are usually similar to those in other enteroviral infections. In patients infected with type 9, however, the leucocytes in the spinal fluid may exceed 1,000 per mm³ and be predominantly polymorphonuclear, suggesting a bacterial meningitis. Recovery of virus from the cerebrospinal fluid provides the most convincing confirmation of the diagnosis of meningitis attributable to an ECHO virus.

In patients with rash and without meningitis, rubella may be suspected. Exanthematous disorders associated with ECHO virus type 9 or type 16 (Boston exanthem) can be differentiated from rubella by the shorter incubation period of 3 to 8 days, absence of suboccipital adenopathy, and usually different seasonal incidence. Supporting evidence of infection with ECHO virus may be provided by the laboratory.

In patients with diarrhea and other minor illness the presence of associated infection with an ECHO virus may suggest a causal relationship, which is, however, difficult to establish.

PROGNOSIS. Infections with an ECHO virus are usually benign and self-limited. Patients with involvement of the central nervous system may occasionally develop paralysis or encephalitis, which in rare instances can be fatal.

TREATMENT AND CONTROL MEASURES. No therapy is known which directly affects any of the enteroviruses. Treatment is entirely supportive and symptomatic. Specific measures to control infection by ECHO viruses are not available.

References

Andrewes, C. H. Viruses and Noah's ark. Bact. Rev., 29:1, 1965.

Curnen, E. C. Immunology, epidemiology and clinical aspects of Coxsackie virus infections. *In* Poliomyelitis: Papers and Discussions presented at the Third International Poliomyelitis Congress. Philadelphia, J. B. Lippincott Co., 1952.

Dalldorf, Gilbert, and Melnick, J. L. Coxsackie viruses. *In* Horsfall, F. L., Jr., and Tamm, I., eds., Viral and Rickettsial Infections of Man, 4th ed. Philadelphia, J. B. Lippincott Co., 1965.

——— and Sickles, G. M. An unidentified filtrable agent isolated from the feces of children with paralysis. Science, 108:61, 1948.

Gear, J. Coxsackie virus infections in southern Africa. Yale J. Biol. Med., 34:289, 1961-62.

Huebner, R. J., et al. Herpangina; etiological studies of a specific infectious disease. J.A.M.A., 145:628, 1951.

International Enterovirus Study Group. Picornavirus group. Virology, 19:114, 1963.

Kibrick, S. Current status of Coxsackie and ECHO viruses in human disease. *In* Melnick, J. L., ed., Progress in Medical Virology. Houston, Hafner Publishing Co., 1964, Vol. 6.

———— and Benirschke, K. Severe generalized disease (encephalohepatomyocarditis) occurring in the newborn period and due to infection with Coxsackie virus group B: Evidence of intrauterine infection with this agent. Pediatrics, 22:857, 1958.

Lerner, A. M., Klein, J. O., Cherry, J. D., and Finland, M. New viral exanthems. New Eng. J. Med., 269:678, 736, 1963.

Melnick, J. L. Echovirus. *In* Horsfall, F. L., Jr., and Tamm, I., eds., Viral and Rickettsial Infections of Man, 4th ed. Philadelphia, J. B. Lippincott Co., 1965.

Sylvest, E. Epidemic Myalgia: Bornholm Disease. London, Oxford Univ. Press, 1934.

Wenner, H. A. The ECHO viruses. Ann. N.Y. Acad. Sci., 101:398, 1962.

Zahorsky, J. Herpangina, a special infectious disease. Arch. Pediat., 41:181, 1924.

14.38
RABIES

JAMES B. BRAYTON

DEFINITION. Rabies is an acute viral disease of the central nervous system characterized by encephalomyelitis. It is usually transmitted by bites of dogs, cats, bats, and wild animals. This disease is characterized by restlessness, excitation, and severe intermittent spasms of the larynx and pharynx, especially at the sight of food or water. The latter symptom accounts for the synonym "hydrophobia." Following the period of excitation, generalized paralysis occurs and death follows in a few days.

HISTORICAL BACKGROUND. Rabies has been prevalent since antiquity; it was described by Democritus in 500 B.C. and also by Aristotle in 322 B.C. Celsus recognized the association of a bite with the transmission of rabies and was the first to recommend cauterization of the bite wounds in A.D. 100. Galen in A.D. 200 advised surgical excision of the wound site. Transmission by saliva was reported in 1804 by Zinke. In 1881 Pasteur demonstrated that virus was present in the saliva and in the central nervous system of dogs. Pasteur in 1885 modified the pathogenicity of rabies virus and produced a vaccine from infected nerve tissue of rabbits. Fermi in 1908 discovered that by inactivating the virus-infected nerve tissue with phenol, he could produce an effective vaccine. Negri in 1903 demonstrated that inclusion bodies were present in this disease and this became a valuable diagnostic tool. Haupt in 1921 found that vampire bats could become symptomless carriers of rabies virus. Up to the present time various modifications of nerve tissue vaccines have occurred and now much of the postexposure prophylactic vaccine used in humans is made in duck embryo.

ETIOLOGY. Rabies fixed virus has been estimated by filtration to be from 100 to 150 mμ in diameter, and as with other large viruses it is not readily filterable. Electron microscopy shows that rabies virus looks like a bullet and has a symmetric structure somewhat like a beehive. Rabies is an RNA virus. It is resistant to phenol, antibiotics, and commonly used skin antiseptics with the exception of benzalkonium chloride and other quarternary ammonium compounds. Rabies virus is quickly destroyed by ultraviolet light, sunlight, strong acids, and alkalis. Aqueous suspensions of rabies virus are inactivated in 30 minutes at temperatures of 54° to 56° C. Infectivity may persist for years if the virus is desiccated and kept in a frozen state at 4° C.

EPIDEMIOLOGY. Rabies virus has an extensive host range infecting all warm-blooded animals experimentally. Virus can be recovered from the central nervous system, saliva, urine, milk, lymph, and blood. Natural reservoirs of rabies can be divided into two categories: the sylvatic, existing in wild animals; and the domestic, the domestic dog being the most important. Sylvatic rabies is well recognized among the badger, fox, skunk, wolf, mongoose, bat, and raccoon. The domestic category used to be the most important, with dogs, cats, and farm animals being primarily involved. During the last two decades the greatest incidence of rabies has shifted from the domestic category to the sylvatic form in the United States. Table 20 shows the incidence of rabies in the United States by type of animal during the period 1953 to 1969 as reported by the National Communicable Disease Center. In the United States and other developed countries, canine rabies has decreased in incidence due to the stringent control of dogs and widely used vaccination programs. The incidence of rabies in bats, including fruit-eating bats, in the United States has increased markedly in the last decade. During 1969, 38 states reported confirmed cases of rabies in bats. At times bats seem to tolerate infection with rabies virus more than other animals; they become asymptomatic carriers and remain infectious for indefinite lengths of time.

Rabies is enzootic in all continents except Australia and Antarctica. Some of the large islands, such as Britain, Hawaii, Cyprus, and New Zealand, are rabies free. Compared with many other diseases, on a global scale, human deaths and animal losses from rabies may not be striking but they are significant. Kaplan estimates that 700,000 to 1,000,000 people are subject annually to a vaccination regimen which sometimes causes serious side effects. Yearly human rabies deaths throughout the world are estimated in the thousands. Rabies occurs in any climate or season, and susceptibility does not seem to vary with age, sex, or race. The incidence of rabies infection is highest in children, probably because of their friendliness toward animals and their inability to defend themselves. The attack rate in persons bitten by rabid animals is difficult to estimate and depends on location of wound, depth of bite, presence of saliva

TABLE 20.   *Incidence of Rabies in the United States by Type of Animal, 1953 to 1969**

Year	Dogs	Cats	Farm Animals	Foxes	Skunks	Bats	Other Animals	Man	Total
1953	5,688	538	1,118	1,033	319	8	119	14	8,837
1954	4,083	462	1,032	1,028	547	4	118	8	7,282
1955	2,657	343	924	1,223	580	14	98	5	5,844
1956	2,592	371	794	1,281	631	41	126	10	5,846
1957	1,758	382	714	1,021	775	31	115	6	4,802
1958	1,643	353	737	845	1,005	68	157	6	4,814
1959	1,119	292	751	920	789	80	126	6	4,083
1960	697	277	645	915	725	88	108	2	3,457
1961	594	217	482	614	1,254	186	120	3	3,470
1962	565	232	614	594	1,449	157	114	2	3,727
1963	573	217	531	622	1,462	303	224	1	3,933
1964	409	220	594	1,061	1,909	352	238	1	4,784
1965	412	289	625	1,038	1,582	484	153	1	4,584
1966	412	252	587	864	1,522	377	183	1	4,198
1967	412	293	691	979	1,568	414	250	2	4,609
1968	296	157	457	801	1,400	291	210	1	3,613
1969	256	165	428	888	1,156	321	307	1	3,522

*Data prior to 1960 from USDA, ARS. Subsequent data from PHS, NDCD. From the National Communicable Disease Center, Zoonoses, Annual Rabies Surveillance Report, 1969, U.S. Dept. of Health, Education, and Welfare.

infected with virus, and protection afforded by clothing. Veeraraghavan reported that the comparative attack rates in persons bitten by proved rabid animals in India during 1946 to 1962 was 8.4 percent in those individuals who were given a complete course of nervous tissue antirabies vaccine, as compared to 50 percent in those persons who were not vaccinated.

PATHOGENESIS. Bite wounds usually introduce the virus in infective saliva. Occasionally licks may introduce the virus on abrasions but the virus will not be introduced through intact skin. The virus travels centripetally via the peripheral nerves at an estimated rate of 3 mm per hour towards the central nervous system. In the case of canine rabies, it should be noted that saliva is not infectious longer than five days prior to the onset of symptoms in the dog. The principal change of rabies infection is generally confined to the central nervous system and this consists of neuronal necrosis and nonsuppurative encephalitis. It is most pronounced in the thalamus, hypothalamus, substantia nigra, pons, and medulla. The spinal cord and sympathetic ganglia may also show similar changes. The most distinctive feature of rabies infection is the pathognomonic Negri bodies. These specific inclusion bodies are found in the cytoplasm of neurons and consist of acidophilic structures.

When the salivary glands are infected, degeneration of the acinar epithelial cells and a mononuclear infiltrate in the intersitital tissue may be seen. The lacrimal glands, the pancreas, and the tubular epithelium of the kidney may also show similar focal degeneration. The lymph nodes show a toxic degeneration. A specific diagnosis of rabies cannot be made, pathologically, unless Negri bodies are found in the neurons of the central nervous system, since the other pathologic findings are compatible with other viral encephalitides.

CLINICAL FEATURES.   The incubation period ranges from 8 days to 1 year; it is usually 1 to 2 months. It is likely to be short following severe lacerations of the head and neck.

Clinical cases may be divided into three progressive phases: (1) the prodromal phase, (2) the excitation phase, and (3) the terminal or paralytic phase. The prodromal phase may begin with pain and numbness at the site of the wound. Fever, irritability, headaches, restlessness, perspiration, and insomnia may follow.

The excitation phase appears rapidly and there is much apprehension and even terror. There is twitching, delirium, meningismus, and mild convulsive movements. One of the outstanding clinical features is related to swallowing. When attempting to swallow food or liquid, painful, violent spasms of the larynx and pharynx may occur. Later just the sound, smell, or sight of liquid may precipitate these violent spasms. During these periods cyanosis may be present. Choking and aspiration are quite common. The temperature is elevated to 103 to 105° F and generalized convulsions may occur. Maniacal behavior such as tearing of the clothes and bedding often occurs. However, biting and fighting is quite rare in human rabies. Intermittent periods of relative calm ensue and during these times the patient is often quite lucid.

The paralytic phase appears with progressive paralysis, cessation of spasms, and coma, with death following shortly. Occasionally progressive ascending paralysis may be the predominant symptom; this type of rabies is known as the "dumb" type of rabies. Human-to-human exposure must be considered and isolation procedures undertaken to protect hospital personnel caring for rabies cases. Ceseghino sites an instance in which 36 hospital employees, caring for a child with rabies, required duck embryo vaccination. Death in man usually ensues within a week after the onset of symptoms.

The white blood cell count ranges between 20,000 and 30,000 cells per mm³, with a polymorphonuclear leucocytosis predominating. The cerebral spinal fluid is usually clear, with normal or slightly increased pressure. Occasionally there is a mild pleocytosis of the cerebrospinal fluid consisting mostly of mononuclear cells ranging between 30 to 100 cells per mm³. The urine may show albumin, acetone, hyaline casts, and reducing substances.

DIAGNOSIS. When classic symptoms are present and there is a history of an animal bite the differential diagnosis is not difficult. Careful questioning should be carried out regarding animal bites and/or association with a rabid animal even months before symptoms appear. Tetanus as described elsewhere in this chapter should be considered. Symptoms of trismus and muscle spasms in tetanus are usually persistent, whereas they are intermittent in rabies. Other forms of viral encephalitides should be considered and often in these conditions convulsions occur early. Also the spinal fluid shows a marked pleocytosis. Strychnine and other poisons usually can be ruled out by a careful history. The paralytic form of rabies may be confused with poliomyelitis; this again often can be ruled out by taking a careful history. Viral isolation from the saliva, cerebral spinal fluid, lacrimal secretions, nasal secretions, and urine should be attempted, but negative results should not be considered since the virus is secreted intermittently from these sites. Occasionally, rising serum neutralization titers may be seen in patients with a prolonged clinical course.

After death, fluorescent antibody examination of brain tissue is fast, reliable, and accurate if carried out in a competent laboratory. Microscopic examination of brain tissue for Negri bodies is also reliable and accurate but takes several days. Mouse inoculations of brain tissue suspensions also require several days but allow isolation of the virus.

PROGNOSIS. The only known recovery from human rabies was reported in a recent case.

CONTROL. Measures for controlling canine rabies have been known for a long time. These include quarantine of susceptible dogs for the latency period of the disease, elimination of stray dogs, and the live virus vaccination of pets. Local and state regulations are necessary in order to have an effective uniform control program. Inernational cooperation is also necessary to prevent introduction of this disease into rabies-free areas.

Sylvatic rabies is harder to control, but poisoning, hunting, and trapping programs are of use in certain circumstances. Rabies in bats, throughout the world, still remains the most perplexing problem in overall control.

TREATMENT. Rational treatment can only be carried out when the following factors are considered as described by Krugman: (1) *Species of the biting animal.* Carnivorous animals, such as skunks, foxes, coyotes, wolves, raccoons, dogs, and cats, are most likely to be infectious. Farm animals, squirrels, opposums, weasels, muskrats, and mongoose may occasionally be infectious. Of course, bats should be highly suspected. Bites of rodents seldom require treatment. (2) *Circumstances of the biting incident.* An unprovoked attack is more likely to occur with a rabid animal, in contrast to a provoked attack such as those occurring when children tease or bother pets while they are feeding. (3) *Extent and location of the bite.* Severe exposures are multiple wounds, deep penetrating wounds, or any bite on the head, neck, hands, or fingers. Mild exposures are scratches, licks, and single lacerations on the body except the head, neck, hands, or feet. Open wounds or abrasions

TABLE 21.   *Vaccines Available for Rabies Immunization of Man and Animals**

Vaccine	Strain of Virus	Tissue Used for Preparation of Vaccine	For Use in:
Live virus:			
LEP†	Flury, 40-60 egg passage	Chick embryo	Dog
K†	Kelev, 60-70 egg passage	Chick embryo	Dog and cattle
HEP†	Flury, above 180th egg passage	Chick embryo	Cattle, cat, and dog
Nervous tissue	Fixed virus	Central nervous system	Man, dog, cattle, and other animals
Inactivated virus:			
Duck‡	Fixed virus	Duck embryo	Man
Nervous tissue	Fixed virus	Central nervous system	Man, dog, cattle, and other animals

*Modified from WHO Technical Report Series No. 321, Expert Committee on Rabies, Fifth Report, 1966.
†These vaccine strains should not be passaged in mice or other animals at any time.
‡In man, most commonly used vaccine in the U.S. at present.

can be contaminated with infected saliva by licking. (4) *Vaccination status of the biting animals.* Adult animals properly immunized have only a minimal chance of developing rabies and transmitting it. Table 21 describes vaccines presently available for immunizing man and animals. It should be noted that live virus vaccines should be given only to the recommended species. Other species of animals may be more susceptible and if they are given the wrong live vaccine they may develop a clinical case of rabies. (5) *Presence of rabies in the region.* Providing that adequate surveillance and laboratory facilities exist in the area, it is most important to know if rabies exists in that region and in what species. This type of information usually can be provided by local public health officials. (6) *Surveillance of biting animals.* Dogs and cats that bite humans should be confined and observed by a veterinarian for at least 5 days and preferably 7 to 10 days. Illness in the biting animal should be reported to the local health officials and the patient's physician immediately.

If the animal has to be killed to be captured, care should be taken not to traumatize the head. Likewise, if the animal dies the head should be shipped under refrigeration to a competent laboratory for diagnosis. In suspicious wild animals, the animal should be killed and its head submitted for laboratory examination.

Postexposure prophylaxis: (1) *Local treatment of the wound.* Immediately, the wound should be copiously flushed with water or soap and water. After removing all traces of soap, the wound should be flushed with a quarternary ammonium compound. One that is widely available is benzalkonium chloride (Zephiran). Soap will inactivate these compounds. Primary closure or suturing of the wounds is not recommended. Control of bacterial infections and tetanus prophylaxis should be carried out. (2) Table 22 presents a guide to specific postexposure treatment. If *passive immunization* is indicated, hyperimmune equine serum should be given as soon as possible, preferably within 24 hours after the biting

TABLE 22.   *Guide for Specific Postexposure Treatment of Rabies* *

Nature of Exposure	Biting Animal†		Recommended Treatment‡ (in Addition to Local Treatment)
	At Time of Exposure	During Observation Period of 10 Days	
No lesion; indirect contact	Rabid		None
Licks:			
1. Unabraded skin	Rabid		None
2. Abraded skin, scratches and unabraded or abraded mucosa	a. Healthy	Clinical signs of rabies or proven rabid (laboratory)	Start vaccine at first signs of rabies in the biting animal
	b. Signs suggestive of rabies	Healthy	Start vaccine immediately; stop treatment if animal is normal on 5th day after exposure
	c. Rabid, escaped, killed, or unknown		Start vaccine immediately
Bites:			
1. Mild exposure	a. Healthy	Clinical signs of rabies or proven rabid (laboratory)	Start vaccine at first signs of rabies in the biting animal
	b. Signs suggestive of rabies	Healthy	Start vaccine immediately; stop treatment if animal is normal on 5th day after exposure
	c. Rabid, escaped, killed, or unknown		Start vaccine immediately
	d. Wild (wolf, jackal, fox, bat, etc.)		Serum immediately, followed by a course of vaccine‡
2. Severe exposure (multiple, or face, head, finger, or neck bites)	a. Healthy	Clinical signs of rabies or proven rabid (laboratory)	Serum immediately; start vaccine‡ at first sign of rabies in the biting animal
	b. Signs suggestive of rabies	Healthy	Serum immediately; followed by vaccine; vaccine may be stopped if animal is normal on 5th day after exposure
	c. Rabid, escaped, killed, or unknown		Serum immediately followed by vaccine‡
	d. Wild (wolf, jackal, fox, bat, etc.)		

*Modified from WHO Technical Report Series No. 321, Expert Committee on Rabies, Fifth Report, 1966.

†This schedule applies equally whether or not the biting animal has been previously vaccinated.

‡Course of vaccine to be followed by supplemental doses of vaccine of nonnervous tissue if possible, 10 and 20 days after the last usual dose.

incident. A portion of the serum should be infiltrated around the wound site and the rest given intramuscularly. The recommended dose is 40 units per kg. Allergic reactions and serum sickness are common with this biologic preparation; thus, a careful history of previous allergy should be taken and skin or eye testing should be done for hypersensitivity. Hopefully, a rabies hyperimmune globulin of human origin will be developed for clinical use in the near future. In general, equine hyperimmune serum is recommended for severe exposures and all bites by wild animals and bats.

Active immunization in the United States is now done predominantly with the duck embryo vaccine (DEV). This is prepared by innoculating embryonated duck eggs with fixed virus, which is then inactivated with beta-propiolactone. Previously, nerve tissue vaccine (NTV) was used. This vaccine was prepared from infected rabbit brain tissue and inactivated with phenol or ultraviolet light. Both vaccines are comparatively effective as judged by the infrequency of treatment failures in the United States during the period from 1957 to 1967, as sited by Sikes. There was 1 treatment failure in 24,500 persons treated with DEV and 1 in 19,600 persons treated with NTV. DEV is used extensively, since it is relatively free of neurologic complications such as polyneuritis, ascending paralysis, and meningoencephalitis, which have been problems with the NTV.

The DEV is administered subcutaneously, giving daily 1 ml doses for 14 days and usually varying the injection site on the abdomen. In severe exposures or exposures involving wild animals two injections per day for the first 7 days and one daily injection for the next 7 days is recommended. Modification of the above regimens may be made if the biting animal is healthy 5 days after the exposure. At that time the vaccine may be discontinued. The daily dosage is the same for adults and children. If hyperimmune serum is given, the initial course should be followed at 10 and 20 days with booster doses of DEV.

Adverse reactions include local erythema, tenderness, and regional lymphadenopathy. Systemic hypersensitivity may be encountered and at times be related to previous immunizations with other avian vaccines. Cowdrey has reported an association with previous yellow-fever vaccination. Skin testing for hypersensitivity should be done before administering the first dose of vaccine. If anaphylaxis, dyspnea, or urticaria develop, epinephrine, antihistamines, oxygen, and steroids should be immediately available. Steroids should be used with caution; Burns has reported impairment of vaccine antibody responses with ACTH and cortisone in animals. If serious allergic reactions occur with DEV then the NTV should be used. If meningeal or paralytic reactions develop, vaccination should be discontinued.

PREEXPOSURE VACCINATION. Preexposure vaccination can be done with the DEV in high risk groups such as veterinarians, biologists, ecologists, and animal handlers. Two injections should be given subcutaneously in the deltoid region 1 month apart followed by a booster in 6 months. Boosters should be given every 2 to 3 years thereafter. After giving the first booster injection, serum neutralization antibody level should be determined. When an immunized person with previously demonstrated antibodies has a mild exposure, one booster dose of DEV should be given. If the exposure has been severe, five daily doses should be given, with a booster following in 20 days. If it is not known whether a previously immunized person had rabies antibodies then a complete DEV series should be given.

REFERENCES

Burns, K. F., Shelton, D. F., Lukeman, J. M., and Grogan, E. S. Cortisone and ACTH impairment of responses to rabies vaccine. Pub. Health Rep., 75:441, 1960.

Cereghino, J. J., Osterud, H. T., Pinnas, J. L., and Holmes, M. A. Rabies: A rare disease but a serious pediatric problem. Pediatrics, 45:839, 1970.

Cowdrey, S. C. Sensitization to duck-embryo rabies vaccine produced by prior yellow-fever vaccination. New Eng. J. Med., 274:1311, 1966.

Johnson, H. N. Rabies virus. *In* Horsfall, F. L., Jr., and Tamm, I., eds., Viral and Rickettsial Infections of Man, 4th ed. Philadelphia, J. B. Lippincott Co., 1965.

Kaplan, M. M. Epidemiology of rabies. Nature, 221:421, 1969.

Krugman, S., and Ward, R. Infectious Diseases of Children, 4th ed. St. Louis, C. V. Mosby Co., 1968, Chap. 16, pp. 210-220.

National Communicable Disease Center. Zoonoses, Annual Rabies Surveillance Report. 1969. U.S. Department of Health, Education and Welfare.

Sikes, R. K. Rabies vaccines. Arch. Environ. Health, 19: 862, 1969.

Veeraraghaven, N. I. Rabies. A. The value of 5% semple vaccine in human treatment—comparative mortality among the treated and untreated. Madras, India, Diocesan Press, Annual Report of the Director, 1962, and Scientific Report, 1963, The Pasteur Institute of Southern India, Coonoor, 1964, p. 33.

Weiss, T., et al. Recovery from rabies. Morbidity and Mortality Wkly. Rep., 19:479, 1970.

WHO Expert Committee on Rabies. Fifth Report, WHO Tech. Rep. Ser. No. 321. Geneva, World Health Organization, 1966.

14.39
RUBELLA

LOUIS Z. COOPER

Rubella (German measles, three-day measles) is the mildest of the common viral exanthems of childhood. It is an endemic and epidemic illness, apparently worldwide in distribution, which is characterized by a generalized maculopapular rash and postauricular and suboccipital lymphadenopathy. Fever and constitutional complaints are typically mild and complications are uncommon. Rubella is a disease of major significance because of the high incidence of congenital defects in children whose mothers are infected during early pregnancy. Typical anomalies caused by this congenital infection are known collectively as "the rubella syndrome." Deafness, congenital heart diseases, cataracts, and retardation are the most common of these defects.

HISTORY.   Rubella was first described in the English literature by W. G. Maton who in 1815 pointed out the features which distinguish it from scarlet fever and measles (rubeola). Henry Veale, in 1866, coined the "short and euphonious" name "rubella" as a substitute for Rotheln, a term then favored in Germany. J. Lewis Smith, the first Professor of Pediatrics at Bellevue Hospital, described an epidemic of this illness in New York City in 1874.

Rubella attracted little attention until 1941 when Norman Gregg, an Australian ophthalmologist, reported 68 cases of congenital cataract in infants whose mothers had had rubella during early pregnancy in the severe epidemic of 1940. He also pointed out that low birth weight, high incidence of congenital heart disease, and high mortality rate characterize the infant with severe congenital rubella. Many investigators subsequently confirmed and extended Gregg's pioneering observations.

The primary obstacle to diagnosis and control of rubella was overcome in 1962 when two independent groups, P. D. Parkman, E. L. Buescher, and M. S. Artenstein of the Walter Reed Army Medical Center, and T. H. Weller and F. A. Neva from the Harvard School of Public Health, simultaneously described the isolation of rubella virus in tissue culture and procedures for determination of specific rubella-neutralizing antibody in the serum. In 1964, the largest epidemic of rubella in at least 30 years swept across the United States. The magnitude of this epidemic, combined with the availability of specific diagnostic tools and the efforts of many investigators, produced an almost explosive expansion in our knowledge of rubella and the hazards of rubella acquired in utero and dramatized the need for adequate control measures. After extensive field trials, live, attenuated rubella virus vaccine was licensed in 1969, in time, hopefully, to prevent future epidemics and eventually to provide a solution to the rubella problem.

ETIOLOGY.   Rubella virus has been placed tentatively in the paramyxovirus subgroup, although it has certain features which suggest a relationship to the arbovirus group. Its pleomorphic appearance in electron micrographs has not been established with certainty. Initial estimates of particle size ranging between 100 and 300 mμ have been revised to 500 to 750 mμ by Best et al. The virus is thermolabile; inactivation is rapid at 37° C and at room temperature. However, it can be stored for short periods at −20° C and is relatively stable for months at −60°

C. Hemagglutination and complement fixation antigens have been prepared in several tissue culture cell systems and serve as the basis for practical serologic tests. The virus is destroyed by exposure to ether, chloroform, cesium chloride, and sodium deoxycholate, but replication is not prevented by 5-iodo-2-deoxyridine. Adamantine hydrochloride prevents growth in tissue culture but has no effect on rubella infection in man. Rubella appears to be both antigenically stable and distinct from all other known viruses.

EPIDEMIOLOGY.   Although rubella occurs in all areas of the world, variations in epidemiologic patterns have been described from country to country. In the past, these differences have been obscured by difficulty in clinical diagnosis and the significant, apparently variable incidence of subclinical infection. With the impetus provided by development of effective rubella vaccines and the availability of a practical serologic test (the rubella HI antibody test), recent studies have documented these differences. In most of the United States and Western Europe, rubella occurs primarily in children during the elementary school years (the first group experience) and during high school. Unfortunately a small but significant minority do not become infected until early adulthood. Rubella becomes a noticeable inconvenience when infection spreads through military recruit training centers and universities and creates its major problem among young women in early pregnancy.

Although rubella is an endemic illness in the United States, with a seasonal peak in the late winter and early spring, its greatest impact results from epidemics which occur at irregular intervals of approximately 6 to 9 years. During the most recent severe pandemic of 1964, the reported incidence of rubella in New York City increased tenfold over the mean for the 10 previous years. Fetal mortality, stillbirths, and infant morbidity and mortality, in association with congenital infection, were correspondingly high.

Serologic studies have demonstrated that approximately 75 to 90 percent of adult Americans have had rubella in the past. This immunity status is essentially the same in those with and without clinical histories of the disease. Susceptibility to rubella is much more common (approaching 50 percent) among young adults living in Puerto Rico and Hawaii. In contrast, on the island of Taiwan where pandemics occur at approximately 10-year intervals, rubella susceptibility among adults is a rarity. Protection of young infants by transplacentally acquired rubella-specific antibody occurs in direct proportion to the immunity status of women of childbearing age.

The immunity which persists after clinical or inapparent rubella is protective against another episode of the disease. Although heavy reexposure may provoke an anamnestic type of antibody response, there is no evidence at this time that reinfection can contribute to the chain of transmission or that fetal damage can occur if this event takes place during early pregnancy (See sections on Laboratory Study and Prevention and Therapy.)

COMMUNICABILITY. Infection is usually by airborne spread through infected droplets. Patients are most contagious for a few days before, during, and after the onset of rash, although virus may be present in pharyngeal secretions for as long as one week before and two weeks after the onset of rash. The patient with subclinical infection is also a source of rubella virus. Although shared eating utensils have been shown to transmit rubella, direct person-to-person contact appears to be the usual mode of spread, because of the relative instability of rubella virus. Persons who are immune to rubella have never been shown to carry the virus from an infected patient to a susceptible one. Infection acquired postnatally does not produce a chronic carrier state. In contrast, congenital rubella is characterized by chronic infection which may persist for months after birth. These infants are a particular hazard for hospital personnel. (See Congenital Rubella.)

Rubella is less highly contagious than measles. In both experimental and natural settings, relatively brief exposure of a group of susceptible children to a child with rubella produces variable results ranging from clinical and inapparent infection in some children to no infection in others. This unpredictability is one reason "rubella parties" for exposure of young girls in the past met with little general enthusiasm. The prevalence of rubella in a somewhat older age group than measles also has been interpreted as evidence that rubella is less contagious than measles.

CLINICAL MANIFESTATIONS. The clinical manifestations of rubella present a spectrum of disease ranging from totally inapparent infection to a characteristic pattern of adenopathy, rash, and low-grade fever. The incubation period is from 14 to 21 days. A typical clinical course begins with adenopathy, involving primarily the postauricular, occipital, and posterior cervical nodes, which may be slightly painful and moderately tender. Although these symptoms usually clear promptly as the rash fades, the nodes may remain palpable for several weeks. Adolescents and adults may complain of malaise, headache, a low-grade fever, sore throat, and mild coryza during a 1- to 5-day prodromal period which frequently accompanies the onset of adenopathy. In young children, the mild prodrome is usually overlooked.

The rubella rash is variable and has no feature which is indisputably diagnostic. It may be no more than a transient blush, but classically persists for 2 to 3 days in a pattern which has been called kaleidoscopic because of its changing appearance. Initially small, irregular, pink macules begin on the face and spread rapidly (usually within 24 hours) to the neck, trunk, arms, and ultimately to the legs. By the next day, these lesions may have coalesced, developed a maculopapular component, and become quite scarlatiniform. The face frequently is clearing by the time a full-blown rash is seen on the lower legs, where coalescence is uncommon. Branny desquamation is rare.

An exanthem (described by Forchheimer in 1898) consisting of punctate or slightly larger red spots on the soft palate may be present during the late prodrome and early rash phase. These lesions are not pathognomonic of rubella. Scarlet fever, infectious mononucleosis, measles, and other viral exanthems may be accompanied by similar palatal lesions.

Fever is uncommonly as high as 102° to 103° F, and may be absent in children. The illness is characteristically associated with little or no debility in children, and even in many young adults.

Polyarthralgia and polyarthritis are such common manifestations of rubella among women as to be considered a typical manifestation of the disease. Joint involvement is less common in men and is uncommon in children. Symptoms most typically appear with the rash or within several days after its onset, but rarely may precede the onset of rash by several days. Involvement, which is frequently symmetric, may range from subjective "morning stiffness" to full-blown arthritis characterized by swelling, redness, tenderness, and effusion. Objective signs and severe symptoms usually clear within several days to 2 weeks, but rarely may persist several months. The proximal interphalangeal joints are affected most frequently and, in decreasing order, the metacarpophalangeal joints, wrists, elbows, knees, ankles, feet, shoulders, and spine may be involved.

Paresthesia, most typically numbness and tingling or "pins and needles," often accompanies and may outlast the joint symptoms. This may be caused by compression of the median nerve in the carpal tunnel, presumably due to synovitis in the area under the volar carpal ligaments.

Although there are striking similarities between rubella arthritis and early, acute rheumatoid arthritis, the critical difference is in the course and subsequent outcome. Joint manifestations in rubella are transient and produce no deformity. There is no evidence that rubella causes or contributes to development of any form of chronic arthritis.

COMPLICATIONS. *Encephalitis.* Postinfectious encephalitis, clinically indistinguishable from that which may follow measles or varicella, is a serious but rare complication of rubella. It is less frequent (1 case per 5,000 is the highest estimate), however, than postmeasles encephalitis (1 case per 800 to 1,000). Symptoms and signs of central nervous system involvement usually develop 2 to 4 days after the onset of rash. Autopsies of fatal cases have revealed severe nonspecific neuronal degenerative changes without demyelinization and with minimal perivascular infiltration. In a subsequent report, no significant intellectual or neurologic impairment was noted among the three surviving children and three others with the same illness studied one year after the acute illness.

Rubella virus has never been isolated from cerebrospinal fluid or brain in cases of postinfectious encephalitis. The fact that the onset of symptoms coincides with the appearance of rubella antibody in the serum has encouraged speculation that this complication may have an immunologic component.

Thrombocytopenic Purpura. Many patients have slight but definite decreases in their platelet counts during the course of uncomplicated rubella. This thrombocytopenia, which usually occurs within one week after the onset of rash, is rarely severe and symptomatic. Presenting complaints usually include purpura, epistaxis, bleeding from the gums, hematuria, and gastrointestinal bleeding. Splenomegaly is not present. Abnormal capillary fragility also contributes to the problem of hemostasis. Megakaryocytes are present in normal numbers but platelet formation is rarely seen, a pattern similar to that commonly observed in idiopathic thrombocytopenic purpura. Prognosis is generally excellent but fatalities due to uncontrolled central nervous hemorrhage do occur rarely. Most patients become symptom-free within two weeks in association with return of platelet counts to normal levels. Rarely, patients are plagued by asymptomatic thrombocytopenia which persists for months. It is common practice to institute steroid therapy for symptomatic cases and to utilize platelet transfusion and fresh whole blood when necessary.

LABORATORY STUDY. ***Virology.*** Diagnosis of rubella can be confirmed only by virus isolation or demonstration of rising titers of rubella antibody in the serum. Although virus isolation is frequently impractical because of expense and the relative lability of rubella virus, serologic testing utilizing improved, standardized techniques should be available for rational diagnosis and management. Certain basic features of virus excretion and antibody response must be understood if these tools are to be used effectively:

1. Rubella virus may be cultured from the pharynx and serum as early as one week before the onset of rash. Virus is promptly cleared from the serum after the rash appears, but persists in pharyngeal secretions usually for several days after the rash and uncommonly for as long as two weeks (Fig. 20). Urine and stool are unreliable sources of rubella virus.

2. Rubella antibody may be measured in a variety of test systems based upon: neutralization, hemagglutination-inhibition (HI), complement fixation (CF), immunofluorescence (FA), and immunodiffusion and precipitation. Most of these techniques are appropriate only for research laboratories. However, the rubella HI antibody test standardized by the Center for Disease Control (CDC Standard Rubella HI Antibody Test) is a rapid, sensitive, economical, and reliable procedure well suited for general clinical use. In certain circumstances, the CF test can provide important additional information and serve as a useful back-up for the HI test.

The patterns of HI, CF, and neutralizing antibody responses during rubella are also illustrated in Figure 20. Absence of rubella HI or neutralizing antibody at the time of exposure indicates susceptibility to rubella. This is not necessarily true of CF antibody, which usually does not persist for years after infection. The presence of antibody at exposure confirms past rubella infection (or rubella vaccination); indicates protection from another episode of the disease; and in the pregnant woman, provides freedom from the fear of rubella-induced congenital malformation. The presence of low levels of these antibodies does not necessarily provide protection

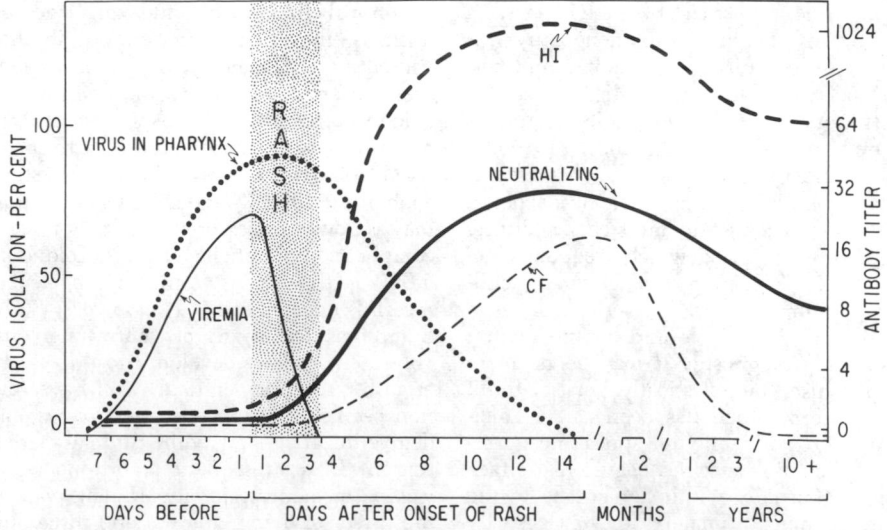

Fig. 20. Schematic illustration of the natural history of rubella demonstrating the pattern of viremia, virus excretion in the pharynx, and the development and persistence of HI, neutralizing, and complement-fixing (CF) antibody. (Modified from Cooper and Krugman. *Arch. Ophthal.*, 77:434, 1967.)

against subclinical "reinfection." Fortunately, the characteristics and implications of reinfection appear to be quite distinct from primary rubella, as will be detailed.

In patients with clinical rubella, HI and neutralizing antibodies are detectable within 24 to 48 hours after onset of the rash and peak titers are reached within 6 to 12 days. In most laboratories, rubella HI titers attain peak levels that are 10- to 100-fold greater than neutralizing antibody titers. In subclinical rubella (primary rubella without rash), HI and neutralizing antibody usually reaches detectable levels 14 to 21 days after exposure, a time which corresponds to the onset of rash in clinical disease. The initial immunoglobulin is rubella-specific IgM. However, this response is a transient one, and rubella IgG becomes the predominant antibody usually before peak titers are reached.

Following reexposure to rubella, a person with low level antibody (from past rubella or vaccination) may experience an anamnestic response. This "reinfection" phenomenon appears to be more common among persons with vaccine-induced immunity than with immunity as a consequence of unattenuated or natural rubella. There is no evidence at this time that the reinfected person is a significant source of contagion for others or that the fetus is at risk when this event occurs during early pregnancy.

The CF antibody response after rubella infection is slower than the HI response. Therefore, it is sometimes possible to demonstrate a diagnostic rise in CF antibody with paired sera which would not show such a rise in HI antibody. In spite of this delayed response, often it is not possible to confirm unequivocally the diagnosis of recent rubella when the first blood specimen is obtained more than one week after the rash.

The neutralizing, theta-precipitin, and FA antibody responses are similar to the HI, but titers are consistently lower. The iota-precipitin response, like CF antibody, is delayed and transient.

Other Laboratory Studies. The hemogram frequently is characterized by a mild leucopenia with a relative lymphocytosis which may include a few atypical cells. The platelet count frequently falls slightly, but severe thrombocytopenia is uncommon. Serologic tests for "rheumatoid factor" may be positive in patients with rubella arthritis. In general, the incidence of positive tests has paralleled the sensitivity of the test used and has been inversely proportional to its selectivity or discrimination.

DIFFERENTIAL DIAGNOSIS. Rubella should not be confused with measles. The typical measles prodrome, the prominent cough, conjunctivitis, Koplik's spots, and the general severity of the disease distinguish measles from rubella. Even mild scarlet fever is associated with more fever, pharyngitis, and anterior cervical adenopathy than is usually seen in rubella. (The characteristic scarlet fever rash is described elsewhere in this chapter.) A leucocytosis, positive culture of group A streptococcus, and rise in ASLO

titer help in diagnosing scarlet fever. In infectious mononucleosis, the pharyngitis, generalized adenopathy, and splenomegaly are more prominent than in rubella, and the rash is less prominent. A marked atypical lymphocytosis and positive heterophile and EB virus antibody titers support the diagnosis of infectious mononucleosis.

Exanthem subitum (roseola) occurs in younger children (6 months to 3 years). Characteristically, several days of high fever and defervescence precede the onset of a rash. No such clear-cut pattern exists for erythema infectiosum. The lacy appearance of the rash, prominence on the extremities more than the trunk, bright red raised rash on the face, and slightly more prolonged duration of this illness are said to distinguish it from rubella. Unfortunately, the etiologic agents responsible for these latter exanthems are still unidentified.

The greatest difficulty in diagnosis is produced by mild exanthematous illnesses occurring during interepidemic years. These may be caused by known agents, such as representatives of the enterovirus or adenovirus groups, or by agents as yet unknown. In the absence of epidemiologic clues, a typical clinical pattern, or virologic study, unequivocal diagnoses are impossible in these cases.

PREVENTION AND THERAPY. Control of rubella may be accomplished by widespread use of a safe, effective vaccine. In 1969, two strains of attenuated virus were licensed for use in the United States and Europe. These live attenuated rubella virus vaccines are prepared in duck embryo (HPV-77DE$_5$) and dog kidney (HPV-77DK$_{12}$) and rabbit kidney (Cendehill strain) cell cultures. The HPV-77 vaccine derivatives were attenuated during 77 passages in primary African green monkey kidney cell culture and the rabbit kidney vaccine was attenuated during 51 passages in primary rabbit kidney cells.

The strategy for use of rubella vaccine selected by the United States Public Health Service and endorsed by the American Academy of Pediatrics was based upon current knowledge of the characteristics of the vaccines and the epidemiology of rubella and recognition that the ultimate goal is prevention of congenital rubella.

The vaccines are highly immunogenic, producing seroconversion in more than 95 percent of susceptible vaccinees. They rarely produce rash or fever but do cause transient shedding of small quantities of vaccine virus from pharyngeal secretions. Nevertheless, for practical purposes, the vaccines are not contagious. It is not known whether inadvertent vaccination of women in early pregnancy is teratogenic.

There are some differences in frequency of reactions and immunogenicity among the three vaccines. For unknown reasons, although each of the rubella vaccines rarely causes other signs or symptoms of rubella, they are all capable of provoking arthralgia, arthritis, and paresthesias indistinguishable from natural rubella. As with natural (unattenuated) rubella, these complaints are common among women and relatively uncommon in children. The dog kidney preparation yields the highest antibody titers, but also is most likely to provoke these reactions. Until and unless a significant advantage can be demonstrated from the higher antibody levels obtained with this vaccine, many clinicians will prefer to use the other preparations to decrease the risk of these complaints.

Live, attenuated rubella virus vaccine is recommended for all boys and girls between the age of 1 year and puberty. Widespread use of vaccine in children should protect them, eliminate the reservoir responsible for epidemic rubella, and markedly decrease the likelihood of rubella exposure for susceptible women in early pregnancy. Postpubertal females should be vaccinated only after (1) determination of rubella susceptibility by HI antibody test and (2) assurance that they are not pregnant and that the risk of pregnancy is essentially nil for at least two months after vaccination. Pregnant women should not be immunized, but should be tested for rubella susceptibility. The immediate postpartum period is an excellent time to vaccinate susceptible women.

Careful studies of immunity to rubella following vaccination have demonstrated that following sufficient exposure, vaccinees may be reinfected. As with reinfection following natural rubella, this phenomenon is characterized by an anamnestic or booster type antibody response and transient, low-level pharyngeal shedding of virus. Viremia has not been detected. Additional studies will be required before current expectations can be confirmed that reinfection is not contagious and cannot lead to fetal infection.

The use of gamma globulin (commercially available human immunoglobulin) in prophylaxis of rubella during pregnancy is still a controversial issue. When administered in large quantities (0.15 to 0.25 ml per kg) before or shortly after exposure, the incidence of subclinical infection is increased and perhaps the rate of infection is decreased. However, gamma globulin does not prevent rubella or congenital rubella in a predictable or reliable fashion. (See Congenital Rubella). Recently, experimental lots of gamma globulin prepared from donors with high titers of rubella antibody (rubella immune globulin) have been shown to prevent detectable viremia, if not infection, when administered shortly after volunteers were challenged with rubella virus. Rubella immune globulin may eventually be useful in special circumstances, such as following exposure of those susceptible pregnant women for whom therapeutic abortion would be unacceptable.

There is no specific chemotherapy for rubella, and no symptomatic measures are necessary for this mild illness in most instances. Aspirin is of value in management of the constitutional complaints and arthritis more frequently seen among adults. It is the general consensus that corticosteroids are indicated for severe thrombocytopenic purpura. There is no evidence that the steroids are of benefit in rubella encephalitis.

Congenital Rubella

Rubella during early pregnancy frequently results in fetal infection, which may be chronic and may produce a spectrum of congenital illness known as the rubella syndrome.

PATHOGENESIS. The mechanisms responsible for the unique teratogenic potential of rubella are not known, although many steps in the sequence of maternal-fetal infection have been well documented.

Maternal viremia may persist for one week before the onset of rash and lead to placental infection. In early pregnancy, this infection does not persist in maternal placental tissue (the decidua), but does in the chorionic villi. Fetal viremia then may produce disseminated fetal infection. Timing is of great importance. Organogenesis occurs during the second through the sixth week after conception, so that infection is a maximum hazard to the heart and eyes at that time. During the second trimester of pregnancy, as the fetus develops increasing immunologic competence (e.g., the presence of plasma cells and ability to produce IgM), it no longer seems susceptible to the chronic infection which is characteristic of intrauterine rubella during the early weeks. In contrast to the situation which occurs with thalidomide or radiation, where a single exposure during early pregnancy exerts its effects at that time only, the available evidence suggests that chronic infection contributes to the acute illness seen in the newborn period (e.g., bone lesions, hepatitis, and purpura) and to the progressive psychomotor retardation observed occasionally during infancy.

Two mechanisms play important roles in rubella embryopathy. The most obvious is the ability of rubella virus to provoke an inflammatory response in certain organs. The more specialized mechanism has been elucidated in tissue culture studies and confirmed by clinical observation. Only a small number of cells (1 in 1,000 to 1 in 250,000) are infected in utero. Daughter cells from these clones are characterized by slower growth and limited doubling potential. At autopsy, infants with congenital rubella have hypoplasia or undergrowth of certain target organs; i.e., these organs have a subnormal number of cells. The key to the teratogenicity of rubella virus may ultimately be found in a molecular explanation of its ability to inhibit multiplication of human cells.

EPIDEMIOLOGY AND RISK. In urban areas of the United States, approximately 20 percent of women in the child-bearing age are susceptible to rubella (see Epidemiology). Prospective data from the Collaborative Perinatal Research Study indicate that 3.6 percent of pregnant women had rubella in the 1964 epidemic, in contrast to an infection rate of 0.1 to 0.2 percent in the interepidemic years. Although definitive information concerning the risk of serious malformations following maternal rubella is difficult to obtain, and experience has varied even in prospective studies, the hazard is clearly maximal during the first 8 weeks of pregnancy, when it probably exceeds 50 percent. Risk of serious abnormality appears to decrease progressively thereafter, with 20 percent a conservative estimate for the ninth through the sixteenth week. In our experience, the risk is minimal later in the second trimester and nil thereafter.

Spontaneous and therapeutic abortions contribute significantly to the mortality in congenital rubella. In a prospective study of the 1964 epidemic by Siegal, Fuerst, and Peress, fully 75 percent of 333 pregnancies complicated by rubella in the first trimester did not go to term. Specifically, 213 (64 percent) were terminated electively, and 38 (32 percent) of the remaining 120 aborted spontaneously.

CLINICAL MANIFESTATIONS. The consequences of rubella in utero are varied and unpredictable. Spontaneous abortion, stillbirth, live birth with anomalies, single or in combination, and normal infants are represented in this spectrum. Virtually every organ may be involved, either transiently, progressively, or permanently. It is beyond the scope of this text to describe in detail this wide range of rubella-associated disease, but because of their frequency, certain manifestations will be explored in greater depth.

Neonatal Manifestations. During the newborn period, congenital rubella may be manifested by a number of acute conditions which are self-limiting in those infants who survive. Neonatal thrombocytopenic purpura, characterized by a variable number

of red-purple macular "blueberry muffin" lesions, is the most common and striking of these manifestations (Fig. 21). It is usually associated with a high incidence of other transient lesions, such as radiolucencies in the metaphyseal portion of the long bones, hepatosplenomegaly, hepatitis, hemolytic anemia, and bulging anterior fontanel with or without pleocytosis in the cerebrospinal fluid. This clinical picture represents the most severe evidence of congenital infection. Low birth weight, congenital heart disease, cataracts, deafness, and retardation with and without microcephaly frequently accompany the transient lesions and contribute to a poor prognosis. The mortality rate in one group of 58 infants with purpura exceeded 35 percent in follow-up through the first year of life.

Cardiac Defects. Congenital heart disease may not be detected for days after birth. Patent ductus arteriosus, with or without stenosis of the pulmonary artery or its branches, and atrial and ventricular septal defects are the most common lesions, but more complex structural defects are not rare. Although many infants tolerate the cardiac defects well, others have developed congestive failure in the first months of life. The poor outcome in the group with congestive failure contributes significantly to the high mortality rate.

Hearing Loss. Deafness due to congenital rubella may be severe or mild, bilateral or unilateral. It is permanent and generally felt to be of the sensory type caused by damage to the organ of Corti, although defects in the middle ear structures have been reported. Mild or unilateral hearing loss fre-

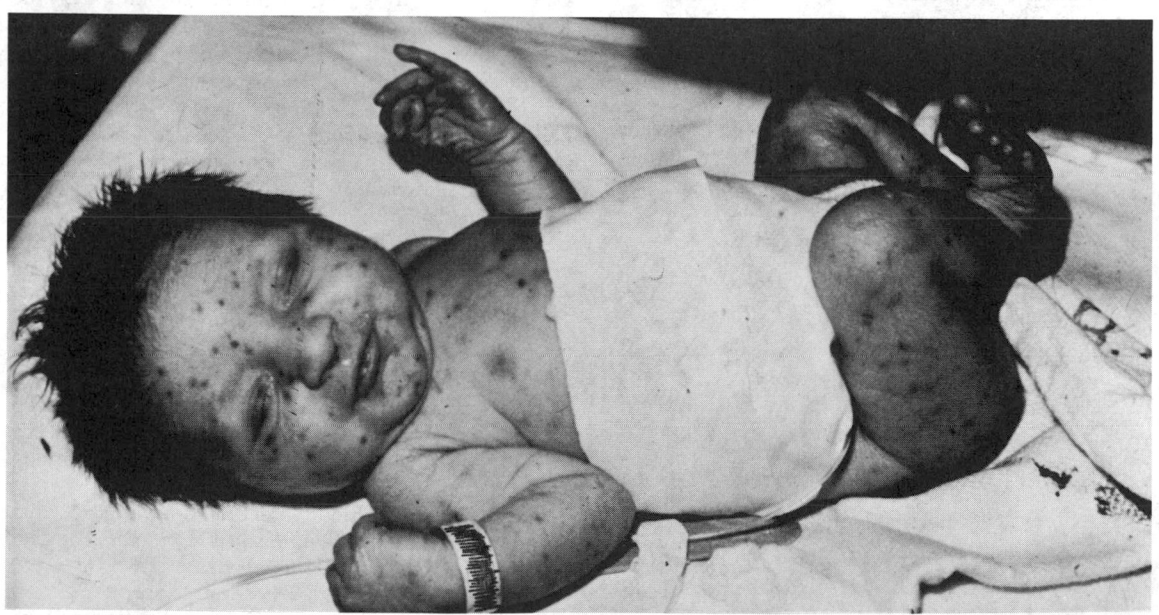

Fig. 21. "Blueberry muffin" lesion in infant with neonatal thrombocytopenic purpura due to congenital rubella.

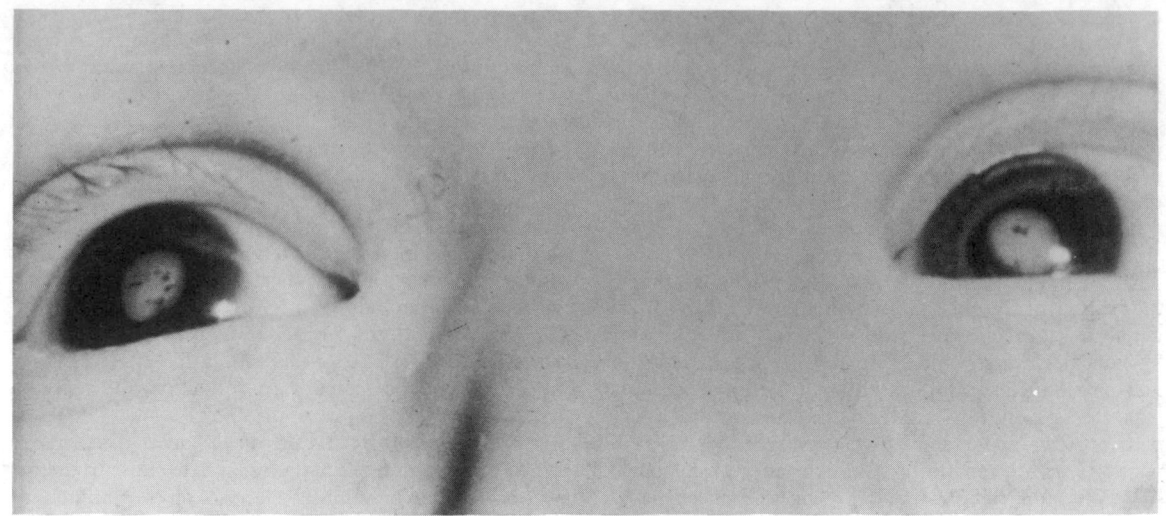

Fig. 22A.   Bilateral nuclear cataracts in patient with congenital rubella.

quently escapes detection unless children are studied longitudinally by audiometric testing. By the same token, it is clear that many children have communication disorders which are central in origin and which may be confused with sensorineural deafness. Deafness and communication disorders may be the only overt manifestions of congenital rubella, especially if maternal infection occurs after the first 8 weeks of pregnancy.

Eye Defects. The most characteristic ocular anomaly is a pearly nuclear cataract, which may be unilateral or bilateral; it is frequently associated with microphthalmia (Fig. 22A). The lesion may be absent at birth or so small that it may not be detected without careful ophthalmoscopic examination (using the +8 lens held 6 to 8 inches from the eye).

Congenital glaucoma, which may be present at birth or may develop during infancy, is clinically indistinguishable from hereditary infantile glaucoma.

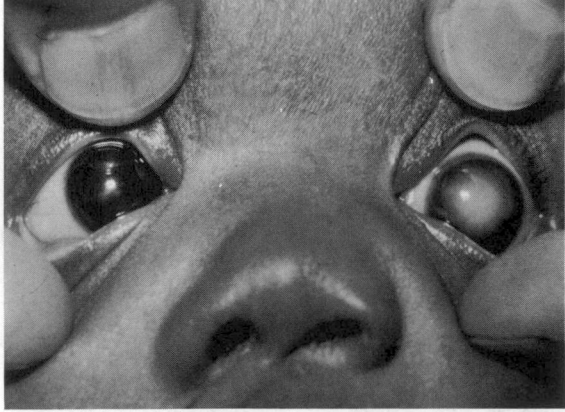

Fig. 22B.   Congenital glaucoma in patient with congenital rubella.

The cornea is enlarged and hazy, the anterior chamber is deep, and ocular tension, measured under anesthesia, is increased (Fig. 22B). Rubella glaucoma is a true phenocopy. It is important to distinguish this disease from corneal clouding, which is self-limited and is also seen during the newborn period in infants without congenital rubella. The glaucoma may require prompt surgical intervention; no therapy is necessary for transient corneal clouding.

Retinopathy, characterized by discrete, patchy, black pigmentation, quite variable in size and location, is probably the most common ocular manifestation of congenital rubella. There is no evidence that this anomaly of the pigment epithelium of the retina interferes with vision. However, recognition of this lesion is a valuable aid in the diagnosis of congenital rubella.

Developmental and Neurologic Defects. Rubella in utero frequently is pathogenic for the central nervous system. This neurovirulence of rubella virus has been confirmed by histopathologic and virus studies among autopsied infants, a high frequency of cerebrospinal fluid abnormalities including positive virus isolation among surviving infants, and a broad spectrum of developmental and neurologic defects.

Delayed psychomotor development during infancy is a hallmark of congenital rubella, even among many children who eventually do well. This severe, early lag corresponds temporally to the period of active clinical encephalitis well characterized by Desmond and her colleagues. The most common consequence of the permanent brain damage from this encephalitis is mental retardation, ranging from mild to profound. Behavioral disturbances and manifestations of minimal cerebral dysfunction are also common. Less common are severe spastic diplegia and autism. Communication disorders of central origin, masquerading as deafness, have been mentioned previously. The combination of cognitive and behavioral deficits with auditory and visual impairment frequently is severe enough to require residential placement. In our experience, seizure disorder has been rare among children with congenital rubella.

TEMPORAL RELATIONSHIP BETWEEN MATERNAL RUBELLA AND SPECIFIC CONGENITAL ANOMALIES. Cardiac defects, cataracts, and glaucoma occur predominantly after maternal rubella during the first two months of pregnancy. Hearing loss and neurologic manifestations may follow maternal infection any time during the first and, less commonly, through the second trimester. The transient manifestations of congenital rubella seen in newborn infants are most common after early maternal infection, but are observed occasionally after infection beginning in the third month.

LABORATORY STUDY. *Virus Isolation.* The infant with congenital rubella may remain chronically infected for months after birth. Virus has been cultured from pharyngeal secretions, urine, cerebrospinal fluid, and virtually every organ. Certain damaged organs may be more highly infected than those which are normal. The incidence of "virus shedding" decreases with advancing age, as seen in Figure 24. Isolation of virus from the blood is rare, and probably occurs only in infants who cannot produce antibodies. (See Immune Response, below.)

Immune Response. Newborn infants with congenital rubella have serum rubella antibody titers comparable to those observed in their mothers. Much of this antibody is transplacentally acquired IgG, but the presence of rubella-specific IgM reflects in utero antibody production by the fetus and, when present,

is diagnostic of congenital rubella. In all but rare infants, by the end of one year, IgG is usually the dominant rubella antibody. Detectable levels of HI or neutralizing antibody persist for years in most children. However, a minority, despite congenital infection, have declining titers of HI antibody, beginning during the second year of life. By age 5 years, approximately 20 percent of children with this disease have undetectable levels of antibody (Fig. 23). Loss of antibody cannot be correlated with severity of the clinical disease. For purposes of diagnosis, the presence of rubella antibody which persists in infancy beyond age 6 months without evidence of postnatal infection essentially confirms the diagnosis of congenital rubella. In our experience, the diagnosis may also be confirmed among children age 3 years and older whose HI antibody has declined to undetectable levels, by administration of rubella vaccine. In contrast to more than 95 percent of normal rubella seronegative children who develop good levels of antibody after vaccination, the seronegative child with congenital rubella rarely responds (e.g., only 2 of 21 such children had antibody boost to barely detectable levels).

Most infants with congenital rubella are no longer shedding virus and have a normal pattern of serum immunoglobulin at age 1 year. Rare infants, however, have persistent severe dysglobulinemia characterized by low levels of IgG with or without elevation of IgM. This may be associated with persistent infection and other evidence of altered immune response. Although evidence has been presented that lymphocytes from infants with congenital rubella failed to respond in vitro to the mitogenic stimula-

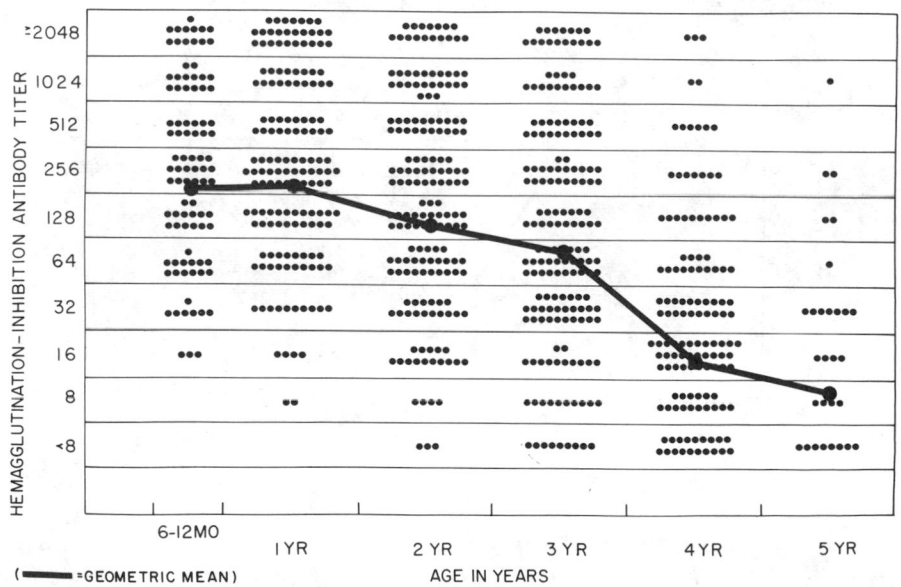

Fig. 23. Persistence of rubella HI antibody in 223 children with rubella syndrome. (From Cooper, Florman, Ziring, and Krugman. *Amer. J. Dis. Child.*, 122:397, 1971.

tion of phytohemagglutinin and had an increased number of chromosomal gaps and breaks, further studies have not confirmed these observations.

Other Laboratory Study. Since multisystem disease is common, many tests not involving the virus laboratory may be abnormal. A listing is beyond the scope of this text.

PROGNOSIS. In a large group of infants with neonatal thrombocytopenic purpura, the mortality exceeded 35 percent after the first year of follow-up; this was not usually due to bleeding but to sepsis, congestive heart failure, and general debility. Overall mortality in a group with various abnormalities due to rubella was approximately 10 percent. Mortality is greatest during the first 6 months of life. The long-term outlook for many infants with severe cardiovascular disease and severe growth and psychomotor retardation is guarded. However, a surprising number of children with multisystem involvement make excellent adjustments over the years. The prognosis for a "normal" life is excellent for children with only minor defects, and Menser, Dods, and Harley have emphasized that the developmental potential of many patients has been significantly underestimated during their preschool years.

DIFFERENTIAL DIAGNOSIS. Certain transient features of congenital rubella such as neonatal thrombocytopenic purpura, hepatosplenomegaly, hepatitis, and x-ray defects of the long bones are similar to those observed with other congenital infections such as cytomegalovirus, toxoplasmosis, and syphilis. Associa-

tion with other evidence of rubella teratology such as cataracts, glaucoma, and typical cardiac defects or a positive maternal history of rubella frequently simplifies the differential diagnosis. Confirmation depends on specific laboratory tests, which are becoming available in many areas.

MANAGEMENT OF CONGENITAL RUBELLA. *Isolation.* Infants with congenital rubella may be contagious as long as they are shedding this virus in their pharyngeal secretions. This problem is greatest during early infancy (Fig. 24). In general, infants who carry rubella for longer periods are the ones more severely damaged and retarded in growth and development, but in the absence of laboratory facilities one can only speculate about the probability that a given infant is contagious.

Specific Therapy. As in postnatal rubella, there is no specific therapy for congenital rubella. Since any organ system may be involved by this infection, consultation with other specialists should be sought when abnormalities are first suspected. A well-coordinated, aggressive effort to deliver early, comprehensive service to the infant with congenital rubella and his family can make an enormous difference in the ultimate lifestyle of the entire family constellation. The importance of early detection of auditory and visual impairment and incorporation of adequate educational therapy including parent education and counseling cannot be overemphasized. Referral to centers with particular interest in congenital rubella is advisable whenever practical.

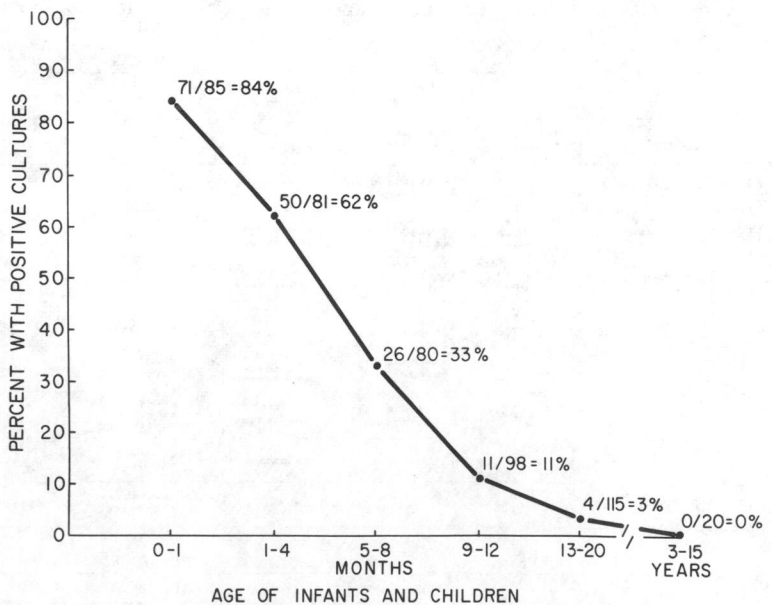

Fig. 24. Incidence of rubella virus isolation in infants with congenital rubella correlated with age at which cultures were obtained. The denominator indicates the number of infants with positive virus isolation. (From Cooper and Krugman. *Arch. Ophthal.,* 77:434, 1967.)

REFERENCES

Best, J. M., Banatvola, J. E., Almeida, J. D., and Waterson, A. P. Morphological characteristics of rubella virus. Lancet, 2:237, 1967.

Brody, J. A., Sever, J. L., and Schiff, G. M. Prevention of rubella by gamma globulin during an epidemic in Barrow, Alaska in 1964. New Eng. J. Med., 272:127-129, 1965.

Forcheimer, F. The Enanthem of German measles. Pediatrics, 6:4-7, 1898.

Green, R. H., Balsamo, M. R., Giles, J. P., Krugman, S., and Mirick, G. S. Studies of the natural history and prevention of rubella. Amer. J. Dis. Child., 110:348-365, 1965.

Gregg, N. Mc. Congenital cataract following German measles in the mother. Trans. Ophthal. Soc. Aust., 3:35-46, 1942.

Horstmann, D. M., Liebhaber, H., Le Bouvier, G. L., Rosenberg, D. A., and Halstead, S. B. Rubella: reinfection of vaccinated and naturally immune persons exposed in an epidemic. New Eng. J. Med., 283:771-778, 1970.

Kenny, F. M., Michaels, R. H., and Davis, C. Rubella encephalopathy. Amer. J. Dis. Child., 110:374-380, 1965.

Lundstrom, R. Rubella during pregnancy: A follow-up study of children born after an epidemic of rubella in Sweden, 1951, with additional investigations on prophylaxis and treatment of maternal rubella. Acta Paediat., 51(Suppl. 133):1-110, 1962.

Marine, W. M., Freeman, M. G., and McLennan, J. G. Localization of rubella virus in therapeutic abortions. Clin. Res. (abstr.), 14:59, 1966.

Maton, W. G. Some account of a rash liable to be mistaken for scarlatina. Trans. Med. Soc., London, 5:149-165, 1815.

Menser, M. A., Dods, L., and Harley, J. D. A twenty-five year follow-up of congenital rubella. Lancet, 2:1347, 1967.

Naeye, R. L., and Blanc, W. Pathogenesis of congenital rubella. J.A.M.A., 194:1277-1283, 1965.

Parkman, P. D., Buescher, E. L., and Artenstein, M. S. Recovery of rubella virus from army recruits. Proc. Soc. Exp. Biol. Med., 111:225-230, 1962.

——— Meyer, H. M., Jr., Kirschstein, R. L., and Hopps, H. E. Development of a live attenuated rubella virus. New Eng. J. Med., 275:569, 1966.

Plotkin, S. A., Boue, A. M., and Boue, J. G. The in vitro growth of rubella virus in human embryo cells. Amer. J. Epidem., 81:71-85, 1965.

Proceedings of the International Conference on Rubella Immunization, 1969. Amer. J. Dis. Child., 118:1-410, 1969.

Rawls, W. E., Desmyter, J., and Melnick, J. L. Serologic diagnosis and fetal involvement in maternal rubella. J.A.M.A., 203:627, 1968.

Rubella Symposium Issue. Amer. J. Dis. Child., 110:345-476, 1965.

Sever, J. L., Schiff, G. M., and Huebner, R. J. Frequency of rubella antibody among pregnant women and other human and animal populations. Obstet. Gynec., 23:153-159, 1964.

Siegal, M., Fuerst, H. T., and Peress, N. S. Fetal mortality in maternal rubella: results of a prospective study from 1957-1964. Amer. J. Obstet. Gynec., 96:247-253, 1966.

Smith, J. L. Rotheln. Arch. Dermatol., 1:1-13, 1875.

Stewart, G. L., Parkman, P. D., Hopps, H. E., Douglas, R. D., and Meyer, H. M., Jr. Development of a rubella virus hemagglutination inhibition test. New Eng. J. Med., 276:554, 1967.

Veal, H. History of an epidemic of rotheln with observations on its pathology. Edinb. Med. J., 12:404-441, 1866.

Weller, T. H., and Neva, F. A. Propagation in tissue culture of cytopathogenic agents from patients with rubella-like illness. Proc. Soc. Exp. Biol. Med., 111:215-225, 1962.

14.40
SMALLPOX
(Variola Major and Variola Minor)

C. HENRY KEMPE

Smallpox is an acute, highly contagious, exanthematous disease caused by a specific filterable virus and characterized by a three-day preeruptive febrile period which is followed by a generalized eruption.

It is a disease of great antiquity, known to have been endemic in Asia and Africa for many centuries before its introduction by the Saracens into Europe in the Middle Ages. Brought to North America by the Spanish conquerors, it soon devastated the native Indian population. During the seventeenth and eighteenth centuries smallpox was the most deadly epidemic disease of Europe and America; but with Jenner's demonstration in 1798 of the value of cowpox as a preventive of smallpox and the subsequent popularization of vaccination, variola major has become dramatically reduced in incidence. Outbreaks still occur sporadically through importation of cases from endemic centers in Southeast Asia, Central Africa, and Central and South America, the world's total incidence averaging about 400,000 cases annually.

In the twentieth century a milder type of smallpox (variola minor) appeared with the Brazil epidemic of 1910, to which the name *alastrim* was given. Smallpox occurring in a partially immune subject produces another mild form, often referred to as *varioloid*.

ETIOLOGY. Variola virus is comparatively large, having a diameter of about 200 mμ. When viewed through the light microscope its particles are barely discernible and appear spherical in shape, but studies with the electron microscope show single elements to be shaped like bricks, with central circular, denser areas. The central body, which contains deoxyribonucleic acid, has certain characteristics of a nucleus. Variola virus appears to be indistinguishable from vaccinia virus, both in appearance and in its chemical constituents. It withstands drying for many months, even when kept at room temperature. Anaerobic conditions favor survival.

Smallpox occurs more commonly in the colder months of the winter and spring than in summer. While susceptibility is universal, there being no natural immunity, the disease does not have the epidemic potential of either chickenpox or measles. The number of vaccinated individuals in the community seems to determine the spread of the virus in a given outbreak. During the incubation period exposed persons are not infectious; but with the onset of the fever which heralds viremia, the possibility of transmission of the disease by way of secretions of the nose and throat can be assumed. Virus has been demonstrated in the saliva on the first day of the skin rash. In cases of hemorrhagic smallpox, the patient may be infectious throughout the febrile period.

Infection probably spreads from the mouth and upper respiratory tract in the preeruptive stages; later, the skin lesions contribute the bulk of infectious particles to the patient's environment. Spread of infection is sometimes indirect; infected cotton or bed linen has been responsible for secondary cases not in direct contact with patients.

PATHOLOGY. The site of entry of the virus is believed to be the mucous membrane of the upper respiratory tract. The site of viral multiplication during the 12-day incubation period is not known, but the patient is not infectious. It is likely that primary multiplication of smallpox virus occurs early in the lymphoid tissue of the respiratory tract; a transient primary viremia then occurs, which results in infection of the cells of the reticuloendothelial system and further multiplication of the virus within these cells. The onset of the febrile illness occurs with the liberation of virus particles from the cells of the reticuloendothelial system, and heralds the secondary and more severe viremia. This secondary viremia is also short-lived because, while virus can sometimes be isolated from the patient's blood during the first 40 hours of the clinical illness, it is usually not found in the blood after the second day of fever except in patients who are destined to die. Lesions which later appear in the skin and mucous membranes undoubtedly result from dissemination of the virus at this time.

The earliest pathologic change seen on histologic examination is dilatation of the blood vessels in the corium and edema of the papillary body, followed by perivascular concentration of mononuclear cells. Epithelial cells of the malpighian layer swell and undergo degeneration. Fluid collects, and a loculated vesicle is formed. There now occurs a migration of mononuclear and polymorphonuclear cells from the engorged capillaries of the corium to the damaged epithelial layers to form a pustule. In cases of hemorrhagic smallpox there is extensive hemorrhage in the dermis, and the overlying epithelial cells may show necrosis. As the pustules dry, scabs form which consist of cellular exudate and necrotic epithelium, under which new epithelium grows in from the sides.

The peripheral blood shows an initial leucopenia with relative lymphocytosis. As secondary infection of pustules occurs, leucocytosis follows.

In patients who die during the early stages of the disease, the lungs frequently show pneumonic exudate, and hemorrhages are found in the alveoli. Hemorrhages may also be found in the submucosa of the intestinal tract, and focal areas of round cell infiltration may be seen in all other organs. In cases of hemorrhagic smallpox, extensive petechial hemorrhages may be seen in all organs.

Cytoplasmic inclusion bodies (Guarnieri bodies) are seen in the skin lesions of smallpox. These are generally eosinophilic, have a granular appearance with an irregular outline, and may be as large as the nucleus.

SYMPTOMS. The incubation period averages 12 days, with a range of 10 to 16 days. The onset of illness is abrupt and is characterized by high fever, to 104° F, accompanied by delirium, toxemia, headache, backache, and vomiting. The child is apprehensive and appears severely ill. The preeruptive febrile period generally lasts three days, the exanthem appearing toward the end of the third or the beginning of the fourth day, usually after appreciable symptomatic improvement. The eruption has a typical centrifugal distribution, being more marked on face, forearms, hands, legs, and feet than on the trunk. It quickly progresses through the papular and vesicular to the pustular stage. Characteristically, in each skin area affected, lesions tend to be at the same stage of development. Promptly after the appearance of the rash the child may feel better, and the temperature may drop slightly. Lesions are commonly seen on the mucous membranes of the mouth and throat, but these do not go on to pustulation. The pustular stage, occurring within a few hours of the vesicular eruption, usually begins on the fifth day of disease and is frequently accompanied by a secondary fever and a rise in leucocyte count. Pustules usually dry after 8 to 10 days and form scabs which drop off in the course of the next three weeks.

A direct relationship exists between the nature and extent of the rash and the the severity of the disease. Thus, a partially immune child may have a mild febrile illness which never progresses to eruption (*variola sine eruptione*). Modified cases of smallpox in vaccinated children, or in young infants who have acquired transplacental passive immunity, may have only a few discrete lesions. In other cases, the eruption may be profuse or even confluent. In hemorrhagic smallpox, lesions generally do not progress beyond the papular or vesicular stage, and extensive bleeding occurs into the lesions as well as elsewhere.

Infants with smallpox commonly experience febrile convulsions, vomiting, and diarrhea in the preeruptive phase. The fever generally remains high as the eruption appears, usually for two rather than for three days after the onset of the illness.

The preeruptive stage of variola minor (alastrim) may simulate that of variola major but is usually much less severe. It is presumably due to an attenuated strain of virus. The distribution and course of the eruption are the same, but the rash is generally much more mild and secondary fever is uncommon. The disease is indistinguishable from mild cases of variola major in well vaccinated children. The two types of disease are entirely distinct and an outbreak of variola minor (alastrim) never gives rise to cases of variola major. The two types may exist simultaneously as two spontaneous outbreaks, as in Detroit in 1924.

COMPLICATIONS.   Pyogenic infections of the skin and joints as well as osteomyelitis occur frequently unless antibacterial prophylaxis is employed. While accompanying pneumonitis is probably evidence of variola virus multiplication, secondary bacterial pneumonia can occur late in the pustular stage. Blindness may result from corneal lesions. A demyelinating encephalitis and peripheral neuritis may also occur.

DIAGNOSIS.   In the presence of an epidemic, smallpox may be diagnosed with relative ease in the preeruptive febrile stage, with accuracy by blood tests, and with strong probability on clinical evidence alone. At the very onset of an epidemic or in a sporadic case, a mistaken diagnosis of influenza or dengue is commonly entertained in older children, while in infants or small children any infectious disease may be suspected.

Occasionally a severe case of varicella causes difficulty, but a careful search will usually reveal lesions of different ages. Eczema vaccinatum may suggest smallpox if a history of vaccination or of contact with a successfully vaccinated person is not obtained.

When a typical eruption occurs in a subject whose disease has not been modified by active or passive immunity, the diagnosis of smallpox presents no great difficulty. In these circumstances the steps required to prevent spread of infection should be taken promptly without waiting for results of laboratory tests.

There are three main diagnostic tests available, each of which has special value, depending on the stage of disease and the type of specimen that can be obtained:

1. Smears on clean glass slides from scrapings of the *base* of smallpox lesions can be examined microscopically for *virus elementary bodies*. A positive answer may be obtained within one hour.
2. Complement-fixation tests can be used in two ways: (*a*) to detect the presence of free antigen (virus) in the patient's blood in the preeruptive febrile stage of the disease, or in the skin lesions from the earliest time of their appearance until the last scabs fall off; (*b*) to detect antibodies in the patient's serum. Results are available in 24 hours.
3. Virus isolation is relatively easy on the chorioallantoic membrane of the embryonated egg, utilizing the patient's blood in the first 2 or 3 days of illness (preeruptive phase) or material from skin lesions (eruptive or scabbing phase). Virus isolation is the most conclusive test, but results are not obtainable for 72 hours.

Collection of Specimens:

1. *Blood:* Collect 5 ml of venous blood. Allow to clot and separate the serum under sterile conditions. Freeze both serum and clot separately for shipment to the laboratory.
2. *Smears:* Scrape the base of several lesions with a sharp blade onto clean glass slides and allow to dry. Smears are of particular value in the papulovesicular phase of the eruption.
3. *Vesicle or pustule fluid:* Aspirate several vesicles or pustules, utilizing a tuberculin syringe with a small needle. After obtaining approximately 0.2 ml of fluid, place both the syringe and the needle, together with the contents, in a large tube. Seal securely, wrap, and forward, preferably refrigerated with solid carbon dioxide, to the laboratory.
4. All specimens must be careful labeled "Caution! Contains material from suspected smallpox patient. Vaccinate all persons in contact with this material."

PROGNOSIS.   Case fatality rates vary directly with the severity of illness. Hemorrhagic smallpox tends to be fatal in more than 98 percent of cases, confluent smallpox in 50 percent, discrete smallpox in less than 8 percent. While the average case fatality rate of variola major continues to be about 30 percent, that of variola minor is less than 1 percent.

TREATMENT.   There is no specific antibiotic therapy for smallpox. Penicillin and the broad-spectrum antibiotics are, however, highly effective in preventing secondary bacterial complications which frequently occur during and after the pustular phase of the disease. Procaine penicillin, 600,000 units per day intramuscularly, or one of the tetracyclines in doses ranging from 25 to 50 mg per kg per day intramuscularly, is indicated.

Hyperimmune vaccinal gamma globulin produced from the serum of recently vaccinated adults has been shown to be effective in the modification of smallpox in children known to have been exposed to the disease, provided it is given before the onset of fever. No observations are available on the use of hyperimmune vaccinal gamma globulin in the therapy of early smallpox.

N-Methylisatin-beta-thiosemicarbazone (Marboran) is now under trial as a therapeutic agent in the early stages of smallpox. Another thiosemicarbazone, 4-bromo-3-methyl-isothiozole-5-carboxaldehyde-thiosemicarbazone, is also being tested. There is some slight indication that the latter drug may decrease the mortality rate in severe smallpox in vaccinated patients.

In serious cases of smallpox in children, severe dehydration may result from the pain associated with swallowing. Intravenous fluid therapy may be difficult in the face of massive skin involvement. Increased fluid requirements are, of course, associated with any febrile illness, and fluid loss from skin lesions may be considerable. Oliguria and renal insufficiency may become irreversible. Early use of intensive parenteral fluid therapy or of gastric feeding through a polyethylene tube holds promise. Baths and local applications to the skin are to be discouraged. It is important, however, to attempt to clean the eyes with warm normal saline solution in order to prevent matting and to decrease the chance of permanent involvement of the cornea. In severe confluent smallpox and in hemorrhagic smallpox, shocklike states have been observed frequently; plasma, hydrocortisone, or prednisone may be of value in management of the most critical phase. Oxygen and, when indicated, digitalis are of considerable help.

PROPHYLAXIS. The general measures to be taken on the discovery of a case of smallpox include immediate vaccination of contacts, removal of the patient to an isolation hospital, and prompt revaccination of all hospital personnel. Some sanitary codes require that the patient's house be disinfected. All contacts of the patient during the infective period of the disease must be closely supervised for 16 days. Detailed inquiry into the source of infection may result in the discovery of a mild or atypical primary case and the subsequent discovery of other secondary cases. The immediate use of laboratory aids may be of value in identifying doubtful cases.

Active immunization of close contacts, by vaccination after exposure, generally will not protect from the disease; many fatal infections have occurred in individuals successfully vaccinated nine days before the onset of illness. However, vaccinia immune gamma globulin prepared from the serum of recently vaccinated adults, injected intramuscularly into household contacts of smallpox cases, may provide protection. Vaccinia immune gamma globulin administered soon after known exposure provides passive immunity some time prior to the viremia which signals the onset of clinical disease.

Vaccinia immune gamma globulin is given intramuscularly in a single dose of 0.12 to 0.24 ml per kg of body weight. The globulin is prepared and distributed with the financial cooperation of the American Red Cross. The vaccinia immune gamma globulin should be given 12 to 24 hours after the person exposed to smallpox is vaccinated.

N-Methylisatin-beta-thiosemicarbazone (Marboran) has been shown to greatly reduce the incidence of smallpox after exposure to the disease. This is true when the drug is used alone or in conjunction with vaccination. Among more than 1,100 household contacts who were given Marboran by mouth, only three mild cases of smallpox occurred. In a control group similar in number, age, and percentage vaccinated after the exposure to smallpox, there were 78 cases of smallpox and 12 deaths. The drug was shown to be effective even when given more than six days after the contact with a smallpox patient.

For prophylaxis, Marboran is given in doses of 1.5 to 3.0 g twice a day for four days. It very frequently causes vomiting, and an antiemetic should be used with it.

Immunity to smallpox is possible only in the presence of antibody, either acquired passively from the maternal circulation in infants less than 6 months of age or developed actively following smallpox vaccination or recovery from smallpox. In highly endemic areas, such successful vaccination confers solid immunity for approximately one year. Partial immunity may be conferred for many years, but in the presence of virulent smallpox yearly vaccination is required.

Vaccination Against Smallpox— Vaccinia

Smallpox vaccine commonly in use is prepared from the vaccinia lesions on the skin of inoculated calves or sheep or from the allantoic membranes of chick embryos. All currently used smallpox vaccine contains infective virus, and all successful vaccinations are deliberately induced mild viral infections. It is thought that within 1 year after primary vaccination the chance of an attack is reduced to one-thousandth of that in the unvaccinated, within 3 years to one-two-hundredth, within 10 years to one-eighth, within 20 years to one-half, and after 20 years there is little if any protection from clinical infections. However, the mortality in smallpox patients successfully vaccinated many years before is less than in the unvaccinated. There is no question that regular revaccination induces a high degree of immunity even to very massive exposure to the disease. Mass vaccination in the remaining endemic areas in Asia, Africa, and South America will, in time, reduce the susceptible population below that necessary to permit the survival of the pathogenic virus.

Recommended Program for Vaccinations in the United States

The United States Public Health Advisory Committee on Immunization Practices, supported by the Committee on Infectious Diseases of the American Academy of Pediatrics, has recently concluded that nonselective smallpox vaccination of the public is no longer justifiable and has recommended discontinuation of routine and compulsory smallpox vaccination in the United States.

"The policy of nonselective vaccination for protection against smallpox began when smallpox was widespread and uncontrolled. Under those conditions, it was a rational, necessary procedure, and legal regu-

lations were passed to ensure vaccination of the public.

Today, nonselective vaccination against smallpox unnecessarily exposes a large segment of the United States public to the risk of complications resulting from vaccination—a risk greater than the probability of their contracting the disease.

The probability of contracting smallpox in the United States today is extremely low and continues to decrease. There has not been a documented case of this disease in the United States since 1949, and importation is the only way in which smallpox could occur in this country. Importation is unlikely because worldwide eradication efforts have brought about a significant decrease in the number of cases of smallpox and in the number of smallpox-endemic areas. In this country, there is a national surveillance system to identify suspect cases. Upon confirmation of a suspect case, there are efficient emergency procedures for managing the case and contacts and preventing spread of the disease. For most people in the United States, the probability of contracting smallpox is so small that the risk of complications from vaccination outweighs the benefits derived from it. For this reason, nonselective vaccination of the public is no longer justifiable. Vaccination should routinely be required only of people at special risk: travelers to and from countries where smallpox is still endemic and health services personnel who come into contact with patients."

Contraindications to Vaccination

The recommendation to discontinue nonselective smallpox vaccination in the United States is so recent that in most states vaccination is still compulsory for children entering school. Moreover, vaccination is still indicated in some countries and in some instances in the United States. There continues to be a need, therefore, to emphasize and to observe scrupulously the contradictions in vaccination.

Primary routine vaccination is generally contraindicated in patients with failure to thrive, dysgammaglobulinemia, blood dyscrasias, eczema or other dermatitides, and radiation or other immunosuppressant therapy, as well as in those exposed to infectious diseases. Vaccination is also contraindicated in unvaccinated siblings of children with eczema. In the eczematous child, vaccination can safely be carried out with attenuated vaccine or under the cover of vaccinia immune gamma globulin during a period when the skin is relatively clear. If vaccination is carried out under these circumstances, it will spare the child the danger of acquiring accidental infection from a sibling or playmate at a time when he is not properly protected.

In adults, vaccination or revaccination is fraught with danger for patients with neoplastic diseases, including Hodgkin's disease, lymphomas, and other conditions involving the prolonged use of corticosteroids, nitrogen mustard, or radiation therapy.

In view of the new recommendations of the USPHS, travel to nonepidemic areas outside the United States by a person who has an absolute contraindication such as eczema or a neoplastic disease should no longer present a problem since smallpox vaccination would not be required on reentering the country. If such a person must travel to an endemic area, the use of vaccinia immune gamma globulin or chemoprophylaxis with N-methylisatin-beta-thiosemicarbazone should be considered so as to provide temporary protection and act as a substitute for the use of vaccination with live vaccinia virus.

Recommended Vaccination Techniques

To minimize the risk of unnecessary complications, the following practices are recommended:

AGE FOR PRIMARY VACCINATION. In nonendemic areas, primary vaccination is best carried out when the child is between 1 and 2 years of age. There is no conclusive data indicating the exact period when complication rates are minimal. Transplacental maternal immunity may modify early primary vaccination and, in endemic areas, make it desirable to vaccinate in the first month of life, provided the mother has been vaccinated. Vaccination of newborn infants has been carried out without complications. However, in such cases in endemic areas, revaccination should be carried out after an interval of six months. If primary vaccination is delayed for several months, children who are at increased risk, such as those suffering from the Swiss type of agammaglobulinemia, will have been readily identified by their clinical course and will, therefore, not become casualties of smallpox vaccination.

SITE FOR VACCINATION. Primary vaccination and revaccination are best performed on the outer aspects of the upper arm, over the insertion of the deltoid muscle, or behind the midline. Reactions are less likely to be severe on the upper arm than on the lower extremity or other parts of the body. With proper technique, resultant scars are small and unobtrusive.

PREPARATION OF THE VACCINATION SITE. With a clean skin, the best preparation is none at all. Chemical skin cleansers may leave a residue which contains virus-inactivating material, while vigorous physical cleansing of the site may create minute abrasions which then can become the site of secondary vaccinia eruptions, with resultant involvement of a comparatively large skin area.

VACCINATION TECHNIQUE. Regardless of age, routine primary vaccination should be carried out with no more than two or three pressures being made with the side of a needle. These pressure points should be in as close proximity as possible, and carried out only at one site. With the highly potent vaccines currently in use, more numerous pressures are not necessary and should not be utilized in a nonimmune individual. When children or adults are to be revaccinated after a lapse of more than five years, the same small number of pressures should be used. For revaccination within a five-year period, in individuals known to have had a major reaction, the full complement of 30 strokes can safely be used.

VACCINATION REACTION. The terminology for the reactions after vaccination or revaccination should follow that recommended by the Expert Committee on Smallpox of the World Health Organization. A successful primary vaccination is one which on examination after 7 to 10 days presents a typical Jennerian vesicle. If this is not present, vaccination must be repeated with fresh vaccine, applying a few more strokes of the needle. The successful revaccination is one which on examination one week (6 to 10 days) later shows a vesicular or pustular lesion, or an area of definite palpable induration and congestion surrounding a central lesion; this lesion may be a scab or an ulcer. These reactions are termed *major reactions*; all others should be called *equivocal reactions*. A major reaction indicates viral multiplication with consequent development of immunity. An equivocal reaction may merely represent an allergic response, which could be elicited by inactive vaccine or poor technique in someone who had been sensitized by earlier vaccination, or the equivocal reaction may result from sufficient immunity to prevent viral multiplication. Since the allergic response cannot be readily differentiated from the one due to true immunity, another vaccination should be performed using a different lot of vaccine if there is the possibility that it is of weak potency, and the procedure should be completed with an additional number of pressures. The site should be examined one week later, and if the result is again equivocal, revaccination should be repeated using a full 30 pressures as recommended by Leake. For the sake of expediency, an equivocal reaction to revaccination with a minimal insertion may be followed by vaccination at two sites, not less than two inches apart, using known potent vaccine. This method will make a third return unnecessary in almost all instances.

In summary, successful smallpox vaccination consists of the production of a major reaction. When potent vaccine and good technique are used, the repeated inability to produce a major reaction can be assumed to be due to solid immunity from previous immunization.

FREQUENCY OF VACCINATION. Revaccination is essential to reinforce the immunity conferred by previous vaccination. This not only maintains a high level of immunity against smallpox but minimizes the risk of complications on revaccination. To maintain adequate immunity against smallpox, revaccination should be carried out at approximately five-year intervals. Those at some increased risk, such as hospital personnel and public health personnel, members of the armed forces, and those working at port or airline offices, as well as shipping personnel, should be revaccinated at least once every three years. When exposure to smallpox is probable, by travel or residence in a smallpox endemic area, annual revaccination is desirable.

COMPLICATIONS OF VACCINATION. The true rate of complications in the United States is not known and is confused by the inclusion of more severe primary reactions among the complications. Complications are not reportable diseases through any of the usual state health department methods. Life-threatening complications of primary vaccination include eczema vaccinatum, postvaccinial encephalitis (Sec. 15.11), and vaccinia gangrenosa (progressive vaccinia). The prinicpal danger after revaccination is vaccinia gangrenosa, a condition in which the impairment of the patient's immune mechanism permits the continuing multiplication of the vaccinia virus. Vaccinia gangrenosa is seen in seemingly normal individuals as well as those suffering from dysgammaglobulinemia, Hodgkin's disease, leukemia, blood dyscrasias, and other conditions in which steroid therapy or ionized irradiation have been administered therapeutically. The presence of these conditions is an absolute contraindication to vaccination. Human vaccinial immune globulin (VIG), readily available on telephonic request from the American Red Cross, has frequently been shown to be effective in the prevention and treatment of eczema vaccinatum and has also been used extensively in the treatment of other complications, where it also produces a significant reduction in mortality. VIG reduces the incidence of postvaccinial encephalitis. Of 106,674 recruits of the Royal Netherlands Army, 53,630 received hyperimmune vaccinia immune gamma globulin while the remaining 53,044 received a placebo. In the gamma globulin treated group, 3 cases of postvaccinial encephalitis occurred as against 13 in the control group, with one fatality occurring in each group. Gamma globulin failed to have a major effect on the severity and duration of the encephalitis produced by the vaccination, and it was not effective in treatment. There is evidence that transplacental maternal immunity is also effective in modifying the course of primary vaccination; significant reactions are rarely reported in the very young infant whose mother has been vaccinated in the past. In cases of vaccinia gangrenosa, the simultaneous use of vaccinia immune globulin and N-methylisatin-beta-thiosemicarbazone appears to be of value. The therapeutic dose of the drug is 200 mg/kg orally initially, followed by 50 mg/kg every 6 hours for 3 days. After a rest of 3 days, another 3-day course may be required.

Adequate early treatment of the complications of smallpox vaccination can materially reduce the morbidity and mortality. Through the American Red Cross a group of experts is available for telephone consultation. When such consultation is used in conjunction with VIG and chemotherapeutic agents, effective diagnostic and therapeutic aids are available for all.

Conclusions

We in the United States are now in an interim period as regards smallpox prophylaxis. Whereas the areas of the globe where smallpox is endemic are gradually being diminished, there is an increased chance of exposure as a result of increasing travel to and from smallpox endemic regions. A number of changes in vaccination practice are indicated to avoid unnecessary complications. Reducing the risk of vaccinia complications by a more gentle vaccination technique and the recognition (and legal acceptance) of additional medical contraindications will help to eliminate many of the opportunities for complications to develop. It is likely that either modified live vaccinia virus or a killed product will soon be available for prevaccination in an effort to make possible safe immunization of those who require it.

REFERENCES

SMALLPOX

Bauer, D., St. Vincent, L., Kempe, C. H., and Downie, A. W. Smallpox prophylaxis. Lancet, 2:501, 1963.

Bedson, S. P., Downie, A. W., MacCallum, F. O., and Stuart-Harris, C. H. Virus and Rickettsial Diseases, 2nd ed. London, Edward Arnold, Ltd., 1955.

Downie, A. W. Infection and immunity in smallpox. Lancet, 1:419, 1951.

Goodpasture, E. W., Woodruff, A. M., and Buddingh, G. J. Vaccinal infection of chorio-allantoic membrane of chick embryo. Amer. J. Path., 8:271, 1932.

Kempe, C. H. Diagnostic Procedures for Virus and Rickettsial Diseases, 2nd ed. New York, American Public Health Association, 1956.

——— Berge, T. O., and England, B. Hyperimmune vaccinal gamma globulin; source, evaluation, and use in prophylaxis and therapy. Pediatrics, 18:177, 1956.

Stallybrass, C. O. The Principles of Epidemiology and the Process of Infection. New York, The Macmillan Co., 1931.

VACCINATION AGAINST SMALLPOX—VACCINIA

Bauer, D., St. Vincent, L., Kempe, C. H., and Downie, A. W. Prophylactic treatment of smallpox contacts with N-methylisatin-beta-thiosemicarbazone. Lancet, Vol. 2, 1964.

Kempe, C. H., and Benenson, A. S. Smallpox immunization in the United States. J.A.M.A., 194:2, 1965.

——— Benenson, A. S., and Jackson, J. R. Passive immunity to vaccinia in newborns: I. Placental transmission of antibodies. Yale J. Biol. Med., 24:328, 1952.

Krugman, S., and Katz, S. Smallpox vaccination. New Eng. J. Med., 281:1241, 1969.

Lane, J. M., and Millar, H. D. Routine childhood vaccination against smallpox reconsidered. New Eng. J. Med., 281:1220, 1969.

——— et al. Complications of smallpox vaccination. New Eng. J. Med., 281:1201, 1969.

Leake, J. P. Questions and answers on smallpox and vaccination. Pub. Health Rep., 60:221, 1946.

Public Health Service Recommendations on Smallpox Vaccination. Morbidity and Mortality, 20:339, 1971.

WHO Expert Committee on Smallpox: First Report. Publ. No. 283, World Health Organization Technical Report Series, Geneva, World Health Organization, 1964.

14.41
PSITTACOSIS-LYMPHOGRANULOMA-TRACHOMA AND INCLUSION CONJUNCTIVITIS AGENTS

The agents of this group should not be classified as viruses, but as Bedsoniae, which are more closely related to bacteria than to viruses. They are obligate intracellular parasites which have enzymes that can synthesize proteins and nucleic acids. Multiplication occurs by binary fission. In infected tissues, they produce intracytoplasmic aggregates or "elementary bodies," which are sometimes visible by light microscopy when stained with Giemsa or other basophilic dyes. Unlike most viruses, they are susceptible in vitro to sulfonamides, penicillin, tetracyclines, and other antibiotics, although the response of patients with clinical disease is not always dramatic. Infection can be transmitted to animals experimentally, and the Bedsoniae can be grown in the yolk sac of chick embryos.

Ornithosis

PSITTACOSIS. The infection was originally called psittacosis when its transmission to man from psittacine birds, chiefly parrots, parakeets, and lovebirds, was established. Subsequently the avian reservoir was found to be much larger, including pigeons, doves, chickens, turkeys, and pheasants. The bird which transmits the infection may be ill or may have an inapparent infection without recognizable symptoms. Close contact, as with a household pet, can often be established. Cases of ornithosis have been reported from all parts of the world, and all age groups are believed susceptible. Since the disease is not universally reportable, its exact incidence and distribution are not accurately known, but as many as 444 cases have been recorded in a single year from all parts of the United States. The disease, besides being an occupational hazard of commercial bird handlers, is also at times responsible for localized household epidemics.

Direct transmission of the infection from man to man appears to be possible. Serologic evidence strongly suggests that in some instances infection produces negligible symptoms.

In fatal cases the principal lesions are found in the lungs. There is patchy bronchopneumonia, sometimes with moderately large confluent areas of consolidation. Lymphocytes, histiocytes, and plasma cells predominate in the exudate, although polymorphonuclear cells may be found as well. Bacterial infection may be superimposed. Pleural effusion, splenic enlargement, and meningitis have been described.

The symptoms of ornithosis are those of a respiratory infection, with bothersome dry cough usually accompanied by weakness and anorexia out of proportion to the fever, which is often mild. Splenomegaly may be found. More rarely, jaundice, convulsions, meningitic signs, and abdominal pain have been described. The leucocyte count is either normal or low. Roentgenograms of the lungs frequently show faint and poorly localized shadows suggesting parenchymal involvement, less often a clear-cut picture of pneumonia or pleural effusion. The patient responds little if at all to antibacterial therapy. Active illness lasts from a few days to three or four weeks.

History of contact with a sick bird, perhaps a household pet or an unexpectedly friendly pigeon, provides an important diagnostic lead, though in many cases this information is lacking. Clear proof of the diagnosis during life may be obtained by recovery of the agent from the patient's blood after inoculation into the yolk sac of a chick embryo, or by demonstration of a rise in titer of complement-fixing antibody during an interval of 2 to 6 weeks. In some cases in which verification of the diagnosis is sought late in the course, after the organism is no longer in the blood, a high initial titer followed 6 months or so later by a fall may be taken as strongly suggestive of an attack of ornithosis. In fatal cases the agent is usually recoverable from pulmonary tissue.

Although the response to therapy may not be dramatic, treatment should include full dosage of one or more of the three types of drug known to protect against laboratory infection in experimental animals: a sulfonamide, penicillin, and a tetracycline. Experience with proved cases has been too meager to justify a more precise formulation of a therapeutic program.

Fatalities are rare in childhood. Convalescence is sometimes prolonged. Late residua have not been described.

Lymphogranuloma Venereum

LYMPHOGRANULOMA INGUINALE. This disease is occasionally seen in young children, who may acquire it by direct transmission from an infected adult. The primary lesion consists of a vesicle and subsequent ulcer, both of which are usually missed entirely, enlargement of lymph nodes being the first feature to attract attention. The nodes of the groin are commonly involved, although nodes in other areas, such as the neck, may be the only ones noticed to be enlarged. In some cases neither the initial ulcer nor lymphadenopathy is observed, residual scarring being responsible for the first symptoms; in these cases the most common syndrome is lower bowel obstruction from rectal stricture.

The lesion in biopsied material consists of a chronic inflammatory reaction in the involved lymph nodes and surrounding structures. There is conspicuous infiltration of cellular tissue with lymphocytes, histiocytes, and plasma cells; granulocytes, including eosinophils, and giant cells may also be found. Bacteria are absent, but basophilic cytoplasmic inclusions within macrophages may be seen, sometimes in the form of the fine granules, at other times as rounded masses as large as the nucleus or even larger.

Involved lymph nodes are sometimes painful as well as tender, and in the course of enlargement tend to adhere both to each other and to the overlying skin. Suppuration may occur, with discharge and sinus formation; as a rule, however, the nodes change but little in consistency, remaining firm and gradually becoming less tender. In the early stages there may be some fever and malaise, but in general the systemic symptoms are mild. Scarlatiniform eruptions and erythema nodosum have been described, and splenic enlargement and generalized lymphadenopathy may be observed. Meningitic symptoms are seen in some cases, but rarely is any change found in the cerebrospinal fluid. Banov described the case of a boy of 10 years whose presenting symptoms were abdominal pain, distension, and constipation due to constriction of the rectum caused by lymphogranuloma venereum; the boy denied sexual contact and had never been observed to have conspicuous lymphadenopathy. The organisms may be detected in the blood.

The virus may be recovered throughout most of the course of the infection. Almost equally strong proof of etiology is provided by demonstrating a fourfold or greater rise in titer of complement-fixing antibody between acute phase serum sample and convalescent phase sample. The antigen generally used is grown in chick embryo tissue culture. Demonstration of antibody at a level of 1:32 or greater, even without subsequent rise in titer, is almost equally significant. The Frei test, a skin test made originally with heat-killed material obtained from a bubo but now more commonly with tissue culture antigen, is carried out by intracutaneous injection and is read in much the same manner as a tuberculin test. When positive, it supports the clinical diagnosis of lymphogranuloma venereum. A negative test, however, may be obtained both early and late in the disease at a time when the complement-fixing antibody is readily demonstrable and even while organisms are in the blood, a circumstance which detracts greatly from the value of the Frei test. Adrenocortical steroids have been shown to suppress a positive test.

Differential diagnosis of chronic focal lymphadenopathy must include, in addition to lymphogranuloma venereum, chronic pyogenic bacterial infection, tuberculosis, tularemia, cat scratch disease, and lymphoma or other neoplasm. Lymphogranuloma must be considered in all cases of rectal stricture.

Treatment, as in ornithosis, consists in administration of full doses of a sulfonamide, penicillin, or a tetracycline or some combination of them. Excision of lymph nodes has been resorted to but should not be necessary. Rectal stricture may respond to carefully graduated dilation.

Trachoma and Inclusion Conjunctivitis

The trachoma and inclusion conjunctivitis (blennorrhea) agents are classified as members of the psittacosis group since they share morphologic and biologic characteristics, as well as the group antigen, with other members of the group. The TRIC (trachoma inclusion conjunctivitis) agents can be grown in the yolk sacs of embryonated eggs.

Trachoma infects many inhabitants of Africa and Asia. In the United States it is endemic in Indian reservations. Trachoma infection is limited to the eye. In endemic areas, agents shed from the eyes of active cases cause infection in early childhood which progresses slowly toward blindness. Initial manifestations include conjunctival hyperemia, follicular hypertrophy, lacrimation, and discharge from the eye. Inward curvature of the eyelids and lashes, conjunctival scarring, and corneal vascularization and opacification occur later. Either topical tetracycline therapy or systemic sulfonamides instituted early in the course of infection can cure trachoma infections and lead to complete healing. Conjunctival scarring and corneal vascularization and opacification are not reversible.

The inclusion conjunctivitis agent resides in the genital tract (cervix and urethra) of adults, and newborns are infected at the time of birth. The manifestations in newborns consist of an acute purulent conjunctivitis which occurs between the 5th and 17th day of life. Without therapy, the disease progresses for 1 to 2 weeks, and then gradually subsides over 3 to 6 months. The disease leaves no residual scarring, and corneal vascularization and opacification do not occur. The infection responds to topical therapy and tetracyclines. Adults can acquire a follicular nonpurulent conjunctivitis from swimming pools contaminated with genital secretions. Although the untreated infection can persist for months, it leaves without any residua. As in the newborn, topical tetracycline therapy quickly eliminates the infection.

REFERENCES

ORNITHOSIS (PSITTACOSIS)

Berman, S., et al. Ornithosis in infancy. Pediatrics, 15: 752, 1955.
Breton, A., Gaudier, B., and Ponté, C. L'ornithose-psittacose en pathologie infantile. Arch. Franç. Pediat., 17: 879, 1960.
Christensen, P. M. Ornithosis; a study of virus and antigen. Acta Path. Microbiol. Scand., Suppl. 118:1, 1957.
Strobel, W. Beitrag zum Krankheitsbild der Ornithose im Kindesalter. Deutsche Med. Wschr., 79:176, 1954.
Weiss, E. The nature of the psittacosis-lymphogranuloma group of microorganisms. Ann. Rev. Microbiol., 9:227, 1955.

LYMPHOGRANULOMA

Banov, L., Jr. Rectal lesions of lymphogranuloma venereum in children; review of the literature and report of a case in a ten-year-old boy with rectal stricture. Amer. J. Dis. Child., 83:660, 1952.
Favre, M., and Hellerström, S. The epidemiology, aetiology and prophylaxis of lymphogranuloma inguinale. Acta Dermatovener., 34:(Suppl. 30), 1, 1954.
Greaves, A. B., and Taggart, S. R. Serology, Frei reaction, and epidemiology of lymphogranuloma venereum. Amer. J. Syph., 37:273, 1953.
Levy, H. Lymphogranuloma venereum in children. J. Pediat., 11:812, 1937.
Roth, D., and Schulick, R. Isolated cervical lymphogranuloma venereum in a child. Pediatrics, 8:489, 1951.

14.42
HUMAN RICKETTSIOSES

HERBERT L. DuPONT and
THEODORE E. WOODWARD

Rickettsiae appear as pleomorphic coccobacilli and are either purple or pink with Giemsa or Macchiavello stains. Rickettsiae have the size and morphologic structure of bacteria and further resemble this group of microorganisms in that they divide by binary fission, contain RNA and DNA, and their growth in vivo is inhibited by broad-spectrum antibiotics. However, rickettsiae are so fastidious that growth requirements are met only by an intracellular milieu. Rickettsiae can be propagated by inoculation into susceptible animals such as the guinea pig, mouse, and chick embryo. However, cultivation in the laboratory is hazardous to exposed personnel because of the high infectivity of these organisms.

Human rickettsioses, with the exception of Q fever, are primarily arthropod-borne diseases characterized by high fever and generalized rash. They are spread by blood-sucking insects including lice, fleas, mites, and ticks. Rickettsial diseases are separated into four groups on the basis of epidemiologic, clinical, and serologic characteristics. Table 23 compares the various factors which characterize the important rickettsial diseases in man.

The pathologic lesion of the exanthematous arthropod-borne rickettsioses includes generalized small blood vessel involvement, observed especially in the skin, subcutaneous tissue, and central nervous system. The principal vascular changes consist of endothelial swelling and perivascular infiltration of mononuclear cells, plasma cells, and macrophages. In general, the symptomatology correlates with the degree and location of vascular involvement. Q fever differs in that the usual mode of spread is through inhalation of the causative agent. Cutaneous involve-

TABLE 23. *Human Rickettsioses*

		Group					
		Typhus		Spotted Fever		Tsutsugamushi Fever	Q Fever
	Disease	Epidemic typhus	Murine typhus	Rocky Mountain spotted fever	Rickettsialpox	Scrub typhus	Q fever
Epidemiology	Rickettsia	*R. prowazeki*	*R. mooseri*	*R. rickettsii*	*R. akari*	*R. tsutsugamushi*	*Coxiella burnetii*
	Arthropod vector	body louse	rat flea	tick	mouse mite	trombiculid mites	tick
	Animal reservoir	man	rat	tick, small animals	house mouse	small rodents	cattle, sheep, goats, ticks (?)
	Seasonal occurrence	Winter-Spring	Summer-Fall	Spring-Summer	Spring-Summer	Hot, rainy seasons (Summer)	Variable
Clinical	Incubation period	7-14 days	7-12 days	2-14 days	2-7 days	10-18 days	9-21 days
	Cutaneous manifestations	Spreads peripherally	Spreads peripherally	Spreads centrally, palms & soles	Initial lesion, generalized vesicles	Initial lesion, spreads peripherally	No rash
	Mortality Untreated	2-40% (depends on age)	2%	10-40%	0%	1-60% (depends on population)	< 1%
	Treated	< 1%	0%	1-10%	0%	< 1%	0%
Serology	Weil-Felix reaction	OX=19	OX=19	OX=19 OX=2	None	OX=K	None
	Complement fixation	Specific	Specific	Specific	Specific	None	Specific
Vaccine	Killed	Attenuates disease	Available, not adequately tested	Attenuates disease	None	Not available	Effective, high local reactivity
	Live	Promising	None	None	None	None	Promising

ment is not apparent and disease is generally confined to the lungs and liver. Ticks are infected naturally but are not important vectors.

In the early 1900's, Felix isolated a strain of *Proteus vulgaris* (OX-19) from the urine of a patient with typhus fever which was antigenically similar to *Rickettsiae prowazeki*. The patient studied had high titers of OX-19 agglutinins. Such OX-19 antibodies are found uniformly in patients with epidemic or endemic (murine) typhus and Rocky Mountain spotted fever. Other proteus strains have been antigenically related to the etiologic agents of scrub typhus (OX-K) and Rocky Mountain spotted fever (OX-2). Proteus agglutinins usually reach a peak after the second week of illness and fall to insignificant levels within three months following illness. Sera of patients with Q fever and rickettsialpox do not significantly agglutinate the proteus strains used in the Weil-Felix reaction. Specific serologic reactions using rickettsial antigens in complement-fixation, agglutination, or neutralization tests are more reliable than the Weil-Felix reaction since they specifically identify the rickettsial infection. Complement-fixing antibodies may persist in low titers for a decade or more after a rickettsial infection.

The tetracycline antibiotics and chloramphenicol are very effective in patients with rickettsial diseases. In scrub typhus, defervescence is dramatic in 24 hours; it is less rapid in patients with Rocky Mountain spotted fever and typhus fever. Relapses occur only if antibiotics are given very early in illness, prior to the fourth febrile day.

Tetracycline and chloramphenicol are rickettsiostatic drugs which suppress but do not destroy the organisms. It remains for the immune processes of the host to finally eradicate the infection. Also, these organisms may remain viable for years in various tissues. Viable pathogenic rickettsiae have been isolated from the lymph nodes of patients convalescent from scrub typhus, epidemic typhus, and Rocky Mountain spotted fever. In the case of louse-borne (epidemic) typhus, recrudescence can result decades following symptomatic infection (Brill-Zinsser disease).

A general discussion of differential diagnosis and treatment is given at the end of the sections dealing with specific rickettsial infections.

Typhus Fevers

The three major diseases in this group are louse-borne or epidemic typhus, murine or endemic typhus, and Brill-Zinsser disease. The diseases show similar clinical characteristics, which makes differentiation difficult in the individual case. Louse-borne typhus is the most serious of the diseases and differs from the others in overall severity, including frequency of complications and case fatality rate. The three illnesses are characterized by high fever, skin rash, and generalized vascular involvement. Except for the skin

lesion, no findings are typical. Lesions of small blood vessels occur in many organs of the body including the skin, brain, spinal cord, heart, liver, kidneys, and spleen. Invasion of vascular endothelium may result in formation of mural thrombi, and areas of skin necrosis over pressure points or symmetric gangrene of the extremities may rarely be seen. The etiologic agents of epidemic and endemic typhus are antigenically similar and cross-reaction occurs with proteus or rickettsial complement-fixation and agglutination tests. They may be distinguished by specific complement-fixation and agglutination tests and by the inability of the etiologic agent of epidemic typhus (*R. prowazeki*) to produce a scrotal reaction in guinea pigs (tunica vaginalis inflammation).

The most constant and outstanding clinical feature of rickettsial infection is an intense headache which usually is frontal or generalized and often is associated with retroorbital pain and photophobia. The differential diagnosis of typhus fever includes the other rickettsial diseases, meningococcemia, typhoid fever, measles, malaria, toxoplasmosis, and smallpox.

Epidemic Typhus

EPIDEMIOLOGY. The last recorded outbreak of epidemic or louse-borne typhus in the United States was in 1920 and 1921 among inhabitants of an Indian reservation in southwestern United States. While an occasional case of laboratory- or hospital-acquired infection may occur (usually as an airborne infection), the disease most commonly is transmitted to man by systemic introduction of infected louse feces through an abrasion in the skin. Unlike other rickettsial diseases, man is the reservoir of *R. prowazeki*. The body louse and occasionally the head louse are infected by feeding upon a person with rickettsemia. Rickettsiae multiply within cells lining the alimentary tract of the louse and are eliminated in feces. The cycle is continued by fecal contamination of a newly susceptible individual. Infected material may gain entrance into the body through abrasion or perforation of the skin. Other routes include the upper respiratory tract, by inhalation of dried infected louse excreta, and the conjunctival sac, through direct contamination. Infected lice usually die within a week of their infection. They are peculiarly adapted to humans and inhabit the linings and crevices of clothing. Sharing of lice with others occurs frequently in congested populations in close contact.

CLINICAL FEATURES. The incubation period of louse-borne typhus is 7 to 14 days and is shortened (as with other rickettsial diseases) by an increased infectious dose. The illness begins suddenly with initial symptoms of malaise, prostration, and chills, followed shortly thereafter by intense headache and high fever (103 to 105° F). The temperature, which invariably rises to 103° F or higher by the 48th hour of illness, persists for 12 to 18 days in untreated, uncomplicated cases. Several diseases, including epidemic typhus, are characterized by persistently elevated temperature. Others are murine typhus, Rocky Mountain spotted fever, malignant tertian malaria, leptospirosis, and lobar pneumonia.

Between the third and seventh day of disease, a faint rose-colored cutaneous eruption usually develops. Initially the skin lesions are macular and faintly papular, with variation in size (2 to 4 mm in diameter) and indefinite borders which fade with pressure. Within 24 to 48 hours, the lesions are macular, become dark red, and no longer blanch on pressure. The eruption first appears on the chest, flanks, inner arm surfaces, and then often spreads to the lower arms, buttocks, and thighs. The face, palms, and soles are rarely involved, in contrast to the distribution in patients with Rocky Mountain spotted fever. During the course of severe infection, the macules develop into petechiae and larger ecchymoses; others coalesce to form large hemorrhagic areas and necrotic lesions, particularly in those areas where there is pressure.

The mortality in untreated patients ranges from 2 to 40 percent, depending upon the age and underlying health of the infected individual. The illness is more difficult to recognize in children because of fewer constitutional symptoms and a sparse rash. Illness in children is less severe and produces fewer complications. Mortality rates increase with age. The severity of the infection relates to the degree of generalized vascular involvement. Hypotension, oliguria with azotemia, and stupor leading to coma may occur in a child with widespread, untreated infection. Superimposed bacterial complications which prolong morbidity and increase fatality include bronchopneumonia, parotitis, otitis media, and systemic abscesses.

Early in illness leucopenia with a relative lymphocytosis is common. Elevated leucocyte counts occur during the second or third weeks in untreated patients. Other common abnormalities are normocytic anemia, microscopic hematuria, hypochloremia, albuminuria, hypoalbuminemia, and azotemia in severely ill patients. The confirmatory laboratory findings are the demonstration of a significant rise in antibody titers for proteus OX-19 and specific rickettsial complement-fixation antigens. Rickettsial agglutinins or neutralizing antibodies and antibodies to an erythrocyte-sensitizing substance (ESS) are specialized serologic tests not ordinarily available.

CONTROL. The control of epidemic typhus includes destruction of lice through use of residual insecticides and disinfection of bedding and clothing laden with infected louse feces. Early identification and isolation of patients and institution of treatment with effective antibiotics plus vaccination of susceptible persons are important measures. The available vaccine is a killed, formalin-treated rickettsial suspension cultured in chick embryo yolk sacs. It confers limited, rather than absolute, immunity. It does significantly reduce mortality and morbidity. Of greater promise is a live vaccine prepared from the attenuated E strain of *R. prowazeki*, isolated initially in Madrid in 1941.

Results of a recent field trial conducted during an epidemic show this vaccine to be effective. Most convalescent patients are immune to subsequent attacks of either epidemic or murine typhus fever although there are relatively rare instances of recurrence (Brill-Zinsser disease).

Brill-Zinsser Disease

In 1910, Brill described patients in New York City whose disease clinically resembled classic typhus fever. After examination of epidemiologic and immunologic data, Zinsser postulated that the disease was a recrudescence of Old World typhus. Most patients had experienced attacks of typhus fever in endemic centers of Europe in early life. During the recurrent illness, which was less severe, the serologic response and characteristics of the rickettsia resembled louse-borne typhus. It was presumed that the rickettsiae persisted in the tissues of the host for years and under appropriate stress resulted in illness. Fever persists for 8 to 12 days, the rash is pink and macular, and death is unusual. Complement-fixing antibodies of the 7S type appear on about the third febrile day and reach high titers. The Weil-Felix titer is low or negative.

Murine (Endemic) Typhus

EPIDEMIOLOGY. Unlike louse-borne typhus, endemic or murine typhus occurs annually in the United States. The disease usually occurs in the southeastern costal states, with a high incidence in Texas. Port cities with heavy rat infestation are favored sites. Murine typhus, primarily an infection of rats, is caused by *R. mooseri*. Transmission occurs from rat to rat via the flea (*X. cheopis*) and by the rat louse. Neither the rodent nor flea succumbs to the infection, and rickettsiae remain viable and virulent in the rat flea for 5 or more weeks. There is no transovarian transmission of rickettsiae by fleas or lice. Man acquires endemic typhus when bitten by an infected rat flea, or possibly through inhalation of infected flea excreta. The infection may occur naturally in domestic cats with spread to humans by cat fleas.

CLINICAL FEATURES. The incubation period ranges from 7 to 12 days. Prodromal symptoms include headache, myalgia, arthralgia, and backache, followed by gradually increasing temperature which may reach 106°F in children and last two weeks if untreated. On the fifth to eighth day of illness, a cutaneous eruption occurs. As in epidemic typhus, the rash first appears on the trunk, spreads peripherally, and rarely involves the face, palms, or soles. Initially the skin lesion is a dull, red macular pattern with ill-defined margins, and it becomes slightly papular as it matures. In contrast to epidemic typhus the exanthem does not usually become purpuric and lasts only a few days in most cases. Twenty percent of children do not have a prominent rash. Central nervous system symptoms and peripheral vascular collapse are uncommon in this form of typhus fever except in the elderly. Murine typhus is usually mild to moderately severe with a mortality rate in the untreated of about 2 percent. Differentiation from epidemic typhus depends on the demonstration of specific complement-fixing antibodies or agglutinins using purified antigens. Proteus OX-19 agglutinins are elaborated in patients with murine or epidemic typhus.

CONTROL. Control of endemic typhus usually requires elimination of the rat reservoir, while insecticide spraying of rat burrows is effective in controlling the flea. A killed *R. mooseri* vaccine is protective in animals; there is no requirement for human use except in laboratory workers. Patients convalescent from murine typhus fever are solidly immune to epidemic typhus and vice versa.

Spotted Fever Group

At least eight antigenically related rickettsiae are included in the spotted fever group, of which five cause human disease. Rickettsiae are classified into subgroups according to the results of species-specific complement fixation testing in mice, cross-immunity studies in inoculated guinea pigs, and mouse toxin-neutralization tests.

Rocky Mountain spotted fever caused by *R. rickettsii* is identical with Sao Paulo typhus, which occurs in South America and particularly in Brazil. In the Mediterranean countries, fièvre boutonneuse or Marseille fever caused by *R. conori* differs in that a primary eschar or ulcer with adjacent adenitis often develops at the site of initial tick bite. The exanthem in such patients is characteristically reddish and papular. Immunologically related strains of rickettsiae cause tick-borne typhus in Africa, India, Russia, and in other countries. They are identified as Siberian tick typhus (*R. siberica*), South African tick-bite fever (*R. conori*), North Queensland tick typhus (*R. australis*), and rickettsialpox (*R. akari*).

Rocky Mountain Spotted Fever

EPIDEMIOLOGY. Infection usually results from a tick bite or occasionally through abrasions in the skin which become contaminated with infected tick feces or tissue juices. Infection may rarely result from autoinoculation or aerosolization of infectious inocula by laboratory personnel. Four species of ticks serve as human vectors of *R. rickettsii*. Ricketts demonstrated that adult female ticks harbor pathogenic rickettsiae throughout their life-span of several years. Rickettsiae may be found in all stages of the tick and can be transmitted during copulation or transovarially. Hence, they serve as vector and the major reservoir. Small animals, including squirrels, rabbits, puppies, chipmunks, rats, mice, and weasels, experience mild infections and are not important as agent reservoirs.

The most important vectors in the Midwest and Atlantic states are American dog ticks (*Dermacentor variabilis*) and the wood tick (*D. andersoni*) in the Rocky Mountain area. In some localities 3 percent of ticks are infected, although average incidence is less than 0.1 percent. Rickettsiae are introduced into human skin via infected salivary gland secretions or feces. Infected ticks which have hibernated during winter must ingest a blood meal and "reactivate" the virulence of rickettsiae before human infection occurs. Ticks are most active as disease vectors from April to September; they hibernate in the earth during winter.

The disease occurs generally throughout the United States with two major endemic regions, i.e., three Rocky Mountain states (Colorado, Montana, and Wyoming) and three south-Atlantic states (Maryland, Virginia, and North Carolina). Tick spotted fever was first identified in the Rocky Mountain area, yet more than half of the reported cases occur annually east of the Mississippi River.

Woodsmen and laborers who are exposed in rural endemic foci such as fields and forests are at risk of infection. Children become infected during picnics and occasionally when pet dogs harbor infected ticks.

CLINICAL FEATURES. Rocky Mountain spotted fever is a generalized infection of unusual severity occurring in scattered areas of the United States. Often the disease is not diagnosed due to its infrequency. A history of a tick bite is elicited in about 80 percent of patients. The incubation period ranges from 2 to 14 days, averaging about 7 days. Large infectious doses of rickettsiae are associated with short incubation periods and more serious infections.

Illness usually begins with nonspecific manifestations of headache, photophobia, chills, fever, myalgia, arthralgia, and anorexia. Fever usually appears abruptly and quickly reaches 103° to 105°F. Higher temperatures are characteristic of illness in children. A cutaneous eruption usually appears on the second to fourth day of illness. The initial lesions consist of pink, irregular macular areas of a few millimeters in diameter which first occur on ankles or feet, or on the flexor surfaces of the wrists, arms, or hands. The lesions blanch on pressure. It is possible to visualize the characteristic exanthem better by soaking the extremity with a warm water or alcohol compress, preferably in the afternoon, when the temperature is usually higher. Soon the lesions spread to the trunk and face. Within one to three days, the skin lesions assume a darker purpuric hue and fail to fade on pressure. If the disease is severe, the individual lesions may be macular and faintly papular. As the illness progresses, the lesions coalesce to form large areas of ecchymosis. Necrosis and gangrene of the extremities may occur, particularly in patients with vascular collapse. Mucous membranes of the oral cavity, pharynx, and genitalia may be involved. Pressure applied to an extremity with a tourniquet or sphygmomanometer may evoke petechiae (Rumpel-Leede phenomenon).

The exanthem is evidence of vasculitis involving small vessels. Rickettsiae invade and proliferate in endothelial cells, leading to swelling of the endothelium of capillaries, venules, and arterioles. Occasionally, large vessels are involved. *R. rickettsii* characteristically multiply in cell nuclei as well as in the cytoplasm. The media of vessels often show extensive changes and a surrounding mononuclear infiltrate is characteristic. Blood extravasates into the tissue immediately adjacent to involved vessels. Interference with arterial blood supply through thrombosis may lead to ischemic changes, especially in the skin, where necrosis and gangrene may result. Microinfarcts appear in severely ill patients throughout the central nervous system, heart, lungs, liver, kidneys, or other tissues. Central nervous system involvement is greater in patients with Rocky Mountain spotted fever than in other rickettsial diseases. It may simulate meningitis, encephalitis, or convulsive disorders. Headache is almost always present, the sensorium is clouded, and convulsions may occur. Deafness is common in severe cases and usually abates, as do the other neurologic manifestations, weeks later. Generally, those patients with an extensive widespread exanthem are more seriously ill than patients with a sparse rash. Electroencephalograms taken a year or more after infection have shown minor changes in spite of the absence of neurologic signs.

During the second week of illness in untreated patients, peripheral vascular collapse, azotemia, electrolyte disturbances, pneumonia, and pyogenic complications occur.

The acute stage of illness is associated with leucopenia (neutropenia) and occasionally coagulation defects with thrombocytopenia and depression of factors V and VIII. A true consumption coagulopathy may occur in more severely ill patients. Hepatomegaly and altered liver function occurs. The spleen is enlarged in about one-half of patients.

The cerebrospinal fluid pressure is often elevated, with occasional minimal pleocytosis of lymphocytes (10 to 200/mm^3) and elevated protein content.

The differential diagnosis of Rocky Mountain spotted fever once the rash has appeared includes typhus fever (epidemic and endemic), scrub typhus, meningococcemia, typhoid fever, measles, and enteroviral infection (with rash).

Rickettsemia extends into the middle of the second week of illness. Male guinea pigs may be infected by intraperitoneal injection of 4.0 ml of whole blood or emulsified blood clot. The animal develops fever and scrotal swelling with redness and hemorrhagic necrosis. Smears of the inflamed tunica vaginalis often show rickettsiae.

The Weil-Felix reaction with the proteus OX-19 strain is invariably positive; a titer of 1:160 or higher is diagnostic. Agglutinin titers for proteus OX-19 and OX-2 occur in patients with Rocky Mountain spotted fever; occasionally the OX-2 titer exceeds the OX-19. The complement-fixation test with rickettsial antigens is specifically diagnostic with serum titers of 1:16 or higher during the second and third febrile weeks. Such antibodies persist for at least 8 or more years in low titers; proteus agglutinins disappear within several months.

The mortality rate in untreated patients ranges from 10 to 40 percent, increasing significantly with age. In all rickettsioses, including Rocky Mountain spotted fever, children have a good prognosis. Yet, it is erroneous to infer that children suffer mild infections since mortality rates in children of 20 percent occur. Frequently, the illness is mistaken for measles until the pathophysiologic changes have progressed to a critical point. The available broad-spectrum antibiotics and use of measures to support the circulatory system could virtually eliminate fatality.

CONTROL. It is impractical to attempt eradication of *R. rickettsii* because of its established reservoir in ticks. Man acquires infection from the tick, which must be attached several hours before infection occurs. Children should be examined carefully after exposure in fields or wooded terrain. Ticks should be removed with forceps by gentle traction, and crushing of the arthropod should be avoided. Tick tissue juices and feces are laden with rickettsiae which are highly infectious. The site of tick attachment should be washed with soap and water and compressed with an alcohol sponge.

There are two types of vaccines. A phenol-formalin killed preparation obtained from infected tick tissues was developed in the early 1920's. The current commercially available vaccine is an inactivated suspension of rickettsiae cultivated in yolk sacs of embryonated eggs. Both vaccines produce immunity in guinea pigs. Field studies have been said to establish the protective value of the tick vaccine. Studies of Rocky Mountain spotted fever in volunteers have shown that neither vaccine affords a high order of protection against contracting the disease. Yet, the illness in vaccinated volunteers is milder and responds rapidly to specific antibiotic treatment.

Rickettsialpox

R. akari, the cause of rickettsialpox, is antigenically related to the etiologic agent of Rocky Mountain spotted fever. The disease was identified initially in 1946 during an outbreak among apartment tenants in New York City. The illness resembled adult "chickenpox"; isolation of a newly identified rickettsia characterized the illness.

EPIDEMIOLOGY. House mice harbor *R. akari*, which are transmitted to man by mites. The illness, which is always mild, occurs in persons who live in congested, large urban centers.

CLINICAL FEATURES. The incubation period ranges from 2 to 7 days following attachment of an infected mite. In 90 percent of cases, an initial lesion (site of mite bite) occurs as a firm red papule 0.5 to 2.0 cm in diameter. The center ulcerates, leaving a crusted eschar which may persist several weeks. The initial lesion is not painful nor does it itch. The illness is characterized by fever, chills, headache, and a sparse papulovesicular eruption. Within 1 to 3 days after the onset of fever, scattered erythematous macules and papules develop, showing no characteristic distribution. The skin lesions enlarge, become more papular, and then form vesicles. Within a week, the eruption disappears without scarring. The disease seldom lasts longer than 10 days. Complications and fatalities are rare. Rickettsialpox resembles varicella. The exanthem differs from varicella in that the lesions are deeply seated, randomly distributed, and are associated with an initial eschar. Several disorders which resemble rickettsialpox are: primary herpetic infection of the skin, generalized vaccinia, and mild smallpox.

CONTROL. Effective control measures include eradication of rodent reservoirs and use of miticidal chemicals. There is no vaccine.

Scrub Typhus

EPIDEMIOLOGY. Scrub typhus or tsutsugamushi fever is of significant military importance because soldiers are exposed in endemic rural and jungle areas. This is true in Asia and the Southwest Pacific theaters. The causative rickettsia, *R. tsutsugamushi* or *R. orientalis,* is transmitted to man by the larval or "chigger" stage of trombiculid mites. The reservoir includes the mite vector (infection can be transovarially acquired) as well as rats and other rodents. Scrub typhus occurs in persons whose occupation exposes them to infected mites.

CLINICAL FEATURES. The incubation period is usually 10 to 18 days. Initially a cutaneous lesion appears at the site of mite attachment, most commonly in the covered moist portions of the body such as the perineum, scrotum, buttocks, or axilla. The lesion begins as an asymptomatic pink papule and increases in size, with central necrosis forming a black scab 4 to 8 mm in diameter. The eschar may be noted at the onset of clinical signs, or 3 to 5 days prior to fever and other manifestations. The primary lesion is not painful and does not itch. Diffuse, tender adenopathy, more marked in the areas of the eschar, commonly occurs. Onset of illness is abrupt with chills, fever, headache, and prostration. By the end of the first febrile week, a maculopapular eruption develops on the chest and abdomen and gradually spreads to involve the entire body. The hands and face are usually spared. In severe cases, hematologic abnormalities or pulmonary or cardiac involvement may develop during the second week of illness and are associated with a poor prognosis.

During the second week of illness, the Weil-Felix reaction is often positive for the proteus OX-K strain, and is negative for proteus OX-19 and OX-2. The differential diagnosis includes typhoid fever, dengue, typhus fevers, malaria, and leptospirosis.

The mortality rate should be negligible in treated individuals. Twenty-four to 36 hours after institution of chloramphenicol or tetracycline toxic signs abate, the patient becomes afebrile, and rash and eschar regress. Patients with scrub typhus respond to antibiotic therapy more promptly than do those with the other rickettsial infections of man.

CONTROL. Infected mites are firmly implanted in endemic areas. Miticidal chemicals impregnated in clothing, insect repellents applied to exposed skin, and widespread use of insecticides are effective control measures for persons exposed. It is advisable to wear protective clothing when in endemic areas. In unusual situations it may be advisable to administer antibiotics prophylactically. Chloramphenicol has been given in 3-g single doses every 5 days for 7 doses and has prevented clinical infection. In these field studies there was no evidence of blood dyscrasia or bone marrow depression secondary to the chloramphenicol. Longer-acting antibiotics such as doxycycline are now being appraised.

Q Fever

Q fever is caused by inhalation of *Coxiella burnetii.* It is characterized by headache, fever, respiratory, and hepatic signs; unlike other rickettsioses, there is no rash.

EPIDEMIOLOGY. The agent resides in ticks which may serve as vectors in spreading infection to animals and rarely man. *C. burnetii* commonly produces asymptomatic infection in cows, goats, and sheep. Infected animals shed rickettsiae in their milk, and placentae may be heavily infected. The organism is hardy, withstands drying and wide temperature changes, and has been recovered from ambient air in the vicinity of infected animals. Human infection usually follows occupational exposure to infected livestock. A single organism may cause clinical infection, yet man-to-man transmission is surprisingly rare.

CLINICAL FEATURES. Nine to 21 days after exposure, illness occurs suddenly with chills, fever, malaise, and intense headache. Soon after the onset, a nonproductive cough commonly develops. Pulmonary rales are frequently audible and a chest roentgenogram reveals patchy consolidation. In patients with Q fever, respiratory manifestations usually predominate, but, in some individuals, hepatic involvement overshadows pulmonary findings, which may be absent. Such liver involvement suggests infectious hepatitis or an acute abdominal infection. Q fever may masquerade as "abacterial" endocarditis, pericarditis, myocarditis, aseptic meningitis, encephalitis, or obscure fever. Occasionally the illness mimics infectious mononucleosis.

Q fever should be suspected in a patient with "atypical pneumonia" or "infectious hepatitis." When the primary manifestations suggest pulmonary involvement, such illnesses are suggested as: primary atypical pneumonia, viral and bacterial pneumonia, psittacosis, influenza, and tularemia.

During the acute illness, there may be wide swings in temperature reaching 104 to 105°F with a gradual defervescence after 5 to 15 days. Severe complications are unusual and mortality rare. Pulmonary involvement consists of patchy interstitial pneumonitis containing fibrin and mononuclear exudate. The alveolar walls and ducts as well as terminal bronchioles are infiltrated by large mononuclear cells. Liver involvement, which is common if looked for, consists of focal necrosis with infiltration of round cells and eosinophils. Some patients may show widespread and severe liver cell necrosis with granulomata, and chronic changes possibly occur.

CONTROL. Most infections occur through direct or indirect contact with livestock. Since infection in livestock is of no consequence economically, eradication of this reservoir has not been undertaken. Whether long-term therapy with antibiotics placed in animal feed would be effective is unknown. Effective "killed" Q fever vaccine made from "phase I" antigen is available. This vaccine causes significant local reactivity and sterile abscesses particularly after booster doses. A live attenuated strain of *C. burnetii* is used in the Soviet Union and is under study in the United States.

Differential Diagnosis of Rickettsial Infections

Early in the infection before the rash has appeared, differentiation of rickettsial infection from other febrile illnesses is difficult. A history of a recent tick bite is helpful. The rash of meningococcemia resembles Rocky Mountain spotted fever, yet the lesions are tender and generally develop earlier in the infection. Gram-negative cocci can be identified upon staining of material from a petechial lesion in meningococcemia and the causative agent can be cultured from the site. The rash of rickettsioses occurs on about the fourth day of disease and gradually becomes petechial.

In the authors' experience, Rocky Mountain spotted fever is most often mistaken for measles. In measles, the prodromal period is characterized by fever, respiratory symptoms, and Koplik's spots. In measles, the rash begins on the face and neck and spreads to the trunk. Petechial lesions are uncommon. The rose spots of typhoid fever appear usually on the lower chest or abdomen and remain delicate, without hemorrhagic character. The rash of infectious mononucleosis is usually morbilliform on the trunk and rarely becomes petechial.

Murine typhus is usually a milder disease than louse-borne typhus or Rocky Mountain spotted fever; the rash is less extensive, nonpurpuric, and nonconfluent, and vascular complications are uncommon. Differentiation of rickettsial infections often must await results of specific serologic tests. The rash of Rocky Mountain spotted fever begins on the periphery of the body, while the rash of classical and endemic typhus is generally noted initially in the axillary folds and on the trunk, only later extending peripherally. Louse-borne typhus is not recognized in the United States except in the form of recurrent typhus fever (Brill-Zinsser disease). Rickettsialpox is differentiated from Rocky Mountain spotted fever by the initial lesion, the relative mildness of the illness, and by the early vesiculation of the rash. The Weil-Felix reaction is positive in Rocky Mountain spotted fever and in epidemic and murine typhus, but is negative in rickettsialpox and Q fever.

Treatment of Rickettsioses

All rickettsial infections respond to early therapy with either a tetracycline or chloramphenicol. The dose of either drug for children is 50 to 100 mg/day (orally in divided doses) for about 5 days. In each rickettsial disease, therapy can be discontinued once the temperature has returned to normal for 24 hours. Relapses generally occur only in those individuals treated during the first several days of fever. Such early treatment usually occurs in laboratory-acquired infections, when a diagnosis can be readily made. In instances when early therapy is instituted a short second course of antibiotic treatment might be utilized after an interval of 5 days without treatment. If a relapse occurs, another 5-day course of antibiotics should be given. There is no evidence that rickettsiae develop resistance to the drug.

Antibiotic therapy, while usually unnecessary, will shorten the duration of rickettsialpox. Q fever is readily controlled by specific therapy and relapses do not occur.

General and Ancillary Supportive Treatment

In spite of the dramatic specific therapeutic effects, there are certain limitations of modern regimens. The fever persists from 2 to 4 days following the initiation of antibiotic therapy. This is not particularly troublesome in most instances. Headache and other manifestations of toxemia may persist for variable periods after institution of treatment. In seriously ill patients, vascular collapse leading to shock, necrosis of skin and other tissues, and azotemia are serious considerations. The fundamental mechanism leading to tissue alteration and toxemia is unknown. In most instances, the use of antibiotics and application of measures directed to correct fluid, electrolytic, and nutritional deficiencies result in complete recovery. A general daily diet providing 3 to 5 g of protein per kg of normal body weight and adequate carbohydrate and fat will support the patient nutritionally. In uncooperative patients, hourly liquid feedings by gastric tube are indicated. At this critical stage—with associated hypoproteinemia, edema, and vascular weakness—blood transfusion, the parenteral administration of preformed-protein supplements, such as serum albumin, and the judicious use of a plasma expander may have a favorable effect on the impending circulatory collapse. With renal shutdown and uremia, overloading the circulation with protein supplements and fluids is to be avoided. Clinical judgment and frequent laboratory determinations of the hemoglobin, hematocrit, electrolytes, and plasma proteins will govern the tempo with which corrective measures are employed. The intravenous infusion of glucose and saline will correct electrolyte imbalance in most instances. The volume of fluid given should be based on the child's weight or surface area (see Sec. 3.7). Too rapid or copious administration of intravenous fluids may lead to additional tissue edema and increase greatly the load upon a weakened myocardium.

Adrenal cortical hormones may be utilized for their antitoxemic effects. The most striking clinical effects are alleviation of headache, earlier defervescence, dissipation of toxemia, and return of appetite. Hormone treatment exerts an ameliorating effect on toxemia in patients with Rocky Mountain spotted fever and typhus fever when used in conjunction with antibiotics. Steroids are unnecessary in the routine case, but are of practical value in patients first observed late in the course of illness when supplemental antitoxemia measures can be lifesaving.

There is evidence, with all rickettsial diseases, that following infection, in spite of antibiotic therapy, rickettsiae may persist in tissues and theoretically may reactivate following the use of corticosteroids or ionizing radiation, which lower host resistance. Perhaps there is a Brill-Zinsser form of recrudescence for each of the rickettsial diseases other than epidemic typhus fever.

REFERENCES

Harrell, G. T. Rocky mountain spotted fever. Medicine, 28:333, 1949.
Haynes, R. E., Sanders, D. Y., and Cramblett, H. G. Rocky mountain spotted fever in children. J. Pediat., 76:685-693, 1970.
Hazard, G. W., et al. Rocky mountain spotted fever in the Eastern United States. Thirteen cases from the Cape Cod area of Massachusetts. New Eng. J. Med., 280:57-62, 1969.
Ormsbee, R. A. Q fever rickettsia. In Horsfall, F. L., Jr., and Tamm, I., eds. Viral and Rickettsial Infections of Man. Philadelphia, J. B. Lippincott Co., 1965, p. 1144.
Smadel, J. E. Status of the rickettsioses in the United States. Ann. Intern. Med., 51:421, 1959.
—— and Elisberg, B. L. Scrub typhus rickettsia. In Horsfall, F. L., Jr., and Tamm, I., eds. Viral and Rickettsial Infections of Man. Philadelphia, J. B. Lippincott Co., 1965, p. 1130.
Snyder, J. C. Typhus fever rickettsiae. In Horsfall, F. L., Jr., and Tamm, I., eds. Viral and Rickettsial Infections of Man. Philadelphia, J. B. Lippincott Co., 1965, p. 1059.
Woodward, T. E., and Jackson, E. B. Spotted Fever Rickettsiae. In Horsfall, F. L., Jr., and Tamm, I., eds. Viral and Rickettsial Infections of Man. Philadelphia, J. B. Lippincott Co., 1965, p. 1095.

Mycotic Diseases

MURRAY WITTNER

14.43
ACTINOMYCOSIS

Human actinomycosis is caused by the ray fungus, *Actinomyces israelii,* producing an indolent granulomatous suppurative infection. *Actinomyces* is not infrequently found in buccal smears and tonsillar exudate from healthy individuals. Infection is thought to be caused by the traumatic introduction of the patient's own flora into his tissues.

A. israelii is encountered throughout the world and is a gram-positive, anaerobic, branching, filamentous actinomycete which has not been isolated from any source in nature other than mucous membranes, oral cavity, gastrointestinal tract, carious teeth, and tonsils of man.

There are three principal clinical forms: the oral or facial (cervicofacial), pulmonary, and abdominal. Each of these is slowly progressive, producing at times remarkably little local or systemic disability.

In the oral type, a hard swelling may form at the root of a carious tooth or around the site of a dental extraction. It causes little pain, but gradually enlarges, often producing marked deformity. The overlying skin becomes shiny and purple, and spontaneous discharge of thin exudate may occur either externally or within the buccal cavity, often persisting for weeks. This form carries the best prognosis of the three sites of infection.

Pulmonary involvement sometimes follows aspiration of a foreign body; at other times it develops insidiously. Pneumonia, at first acute, fails to resolve. Cough and mild fever persist, and the patient's condition gradually worsens. There may be little expectoration, and physical signs are those of a consolidated lung; the involved region may become secondarily infected, with production of foul sputum and clinical evidence of bronchiectasis. Septic fever often develops as the diseased area extends. Unless death supervenes, the thoracic wall is eventually eroded and characteristic pus containing "sulfur granules" is discharged or may be aspirated from a subcutaneous abscess.

Abdominal actinomycosis begins most frequently in the appendix, as a complication of a perforating gastrointestinal ulcer, or following penetration of the mucosa of the colon by a sharp object such as a knife, ingested bone, or gunshot wound. Differentiation from other types of appendicitis, salpingitis, cholecystitis, cystitis, or pyelonephritis is most difficult. A correct diagnosis is made only after exploratory laparotomy, unless some of the abscesses approach the surface of the body and rupture to produce a typical draining sinus from which the organisms can be recovered. The initial symptoms are insidious in onset and related to the organ involved. As the disease progresses, local granulomatous lesions form which may spread to involved associated tissue including bone, liver, gallbladder, or ovaries. The spine and ribs are rather frequently involved, apparently from metastatic hematogenous spread, though at times by direct extension from a pulmonary or abdominal focus. Areas of bone destruction seen in roentgenograms usually reveal a proliferative periosteal reaction as well. In time the infection tends to extend to the surface but not necessarily over the site of the deep lesion.

Actinomycosis may be suspected when an indolent inflammatory lesion is shown not to be caused by tuberculosis, which is far more common. Lesions about the jaw are usually mistaken, at least temporarily, for chronic pyogenic infection or tumor. All lesions resemble tuberculosis in x-rays, except that they tend to occupy unusual sites, such as the shaft of a rib or lamina of a vertebra. Exudate or aspirated material should be carefully searched for sulfur granules. These are yellowish gray masses about 2 mm in diameter, representing colonies of organisms. When pressed out on a slide they show the gram-positive mycelial filaments in characteristic radial arrangements at the margin of a central gram-negative zone.

These organisms are easily cultivated in thioglycolate semisolid medium, below the surface, provided the inoculum does not contain secondary invaders. To obtain pure cultures from contaminated sources, blood agar is seeded and incubated anaerobically. In the presence of active infection the blood may show agglutinins in high titer.

TREATMENT. The success of penicillin for the treatment of actinomycosis has greatly improved the once grave prognosis of this disease. Administration of antibiotics for 30 to 45 days is then followed by wide surgical excision of the lesions, with the surgical wound packed open for drainge. Following surgery, intramuscular penicillin is given in daily doses of from 2 to 5 million units for 12 to 18 months. In severe cases 12 million units of penicillin given daily intramuscularly or 10 to 20 million units given daily intravenously may be utilized.

In cases where treatment fails with penicillin, or this antibiotic cannot be tolerated, the use of antibiotics such as chloramphenicol, streptomycin, tetracycline, and sulfonamides may be used. Amphotericin B, nystatin, and griseofulvin do not inhibit *A. israelii* and are not useful for therapy.

REFERENCES

GENERAL

Douglas, J. B., and Healy, J. K. Nephrotoxic effects of amphotericin B, including renal tubular acidosis. Amer. J. Med., 46:154, 1969.

Drutz, D., Spickard, A., Rogers, D., and Koenig, M. G. Treatment of disseminated mycotic infections: A new approach to amphotericin B therapy. Amer. J. Med., 45:405, 1968.

Emmons, C. W., Binford, C. H., and Utz, J. P. Medical Mycology, 2nd ed. Philadelphia, Lea and Febiger, 1970.

Fetter, B. F., Klintworth, G., and Hendry, W. Mycoses of the Central Nervous System. Baltimore, William and Wilkins Co., p. 214, 1967.

Hildick-Smith, G., Blank, H., and Sarkany, I. Fungus Diseases and Their Treatment. Boston, Little, Brown and Co., 1964, p. 494.

Louria, D. B. Deep-seated mycotic infections, allergy to fungi and mycotoxins. N. Eng. J. Med., 277:1065 and 1126, 1967.

Wilson, J. W., and Plunkett, O. A. The Fungous Diseases of Man. Berkeley and Los Angeles, Univ. Calif. Press, 1965.

Wolstenholme, G. E. W., and Porter, R. Systemic Mycoses, Ciba Foundation Symposium. Boston, Little, Brown and Co., 1967.

ACTINOMYCOSIS

Dundon, S., and Byrnes, C. K. Pulmonary actinomycosis in childhood. J. Irish Med. Ass., 52:26, 1963.

Paul, F. M. Two cases of thoracic actinomycosis in children. Arch. Dis. Child., 37:276, 1963.

Peabody, J. W., Jr., and Seabury, J. H. Actinomycosis and nocardiosis: a review of basic differences in therapy. Amer. J. Med., 28:99, 1960.

Spilsbury, B. W., and Johnstone, F. R. The clinical course of actinomycotic infections: 14 cases. Canad. J. Surg., 5:33, 1962.

14.44
ASPERGILLOSIS

Aspergillosis is a mycotic disease caused by several species of *Aspergillus*. *A. fumigatus* has been implicated in most of the disseminated and pulmonary infections. On occasion, noninvading spherical colonies or "fungus balls" caused by *A. niger* have been isolated from bronchiectatic sacs.

Numerous species of *Aspergillus* flourish throughout the world, often growing as saprophytes on decaying vegetation. It is, therefore, reasonable to expect that human exposure to spores of potentially pathogenic species, especially *A. fumigatus*, is far more frequent than the relatively few clinical cases of disseminated and pulmonary aspergillosis.

Although primary aspergillosis has been reported occurring in the absence of underlying disease, or without prolonged antibiotic or corticosteroid therapy, this is so unusual that intensive clinical investigation of a patient for predisposing disease should be undertaken. Occupational exposure to large numbers of spores among bird fanciers, fur cleaners, and farmers, moreover, is usually associated with severe pulmonary hypersensitivity symptoms, termed "farmer's lung," rather than with deep-seated infection.

CLINICAL FEATURES. Pulmonary aspergillosis associated with underlying pulmonary disease such as tuberculosis, bronchiectasis, abscess, pneumonia, or carcinoma is the most frequent form of the disease. The infection may be highly virulent and unrelenting, spreading from the bronchi to the parenchyma as necrotizing pneumonia which may eventually cavitate. Fever, moderate to severe hemoptysis, and a productive cough with purulent sputum in which hyphae may be seen are frequent manifestations. Radiologic findings may be characteristic if fungus balls ("aspergilloma") are present.

Dissemination to the brain, heart, kidneys, bone, and skin may occur in a small number of cases. Aspergillosis is unusual in infants and children, most cases having been associated with prematurity, pneumonia, and antibiotic or steroid therapy.

PATHOLOGY. The hyphae may proliferate throughout the pulmonary tissues and, after invading blood vessels, result in widespread hematogenous dissemination. The fungus may proliferate on walls of tuberculous cavities or produce granulomatous lesions with radial proliferation of hyphae. In the areas of necrotizing pneumonia, hyphae can often be identified with hematoxylin and eosin. Occasionally, it may be necessary to resort to special stains in order to identify typical mycelial structure. In histopathologic sections the hyphae are 3 to 4 μ in diameter. They are septate and reveal dichotomous branching. The septa are readily identified in sections stained with Gridley (periodic acid-Schiff) technique.

In disseminated disease, lesions appear as acute pyogenic abscesses, and the symptoms depend upon the organs invaded. Brain, kidney, and myocardium are the most frequent sites of metastatic growth.

DIAGNOSIS. Direct examination of sputum for hyphal elements is often rewarding, but the significance of the positive examination must be viewed with caution. Even repeated positive preparations may only signify the presence of the fungus growing as a harmless saprophyte. Roentgenographic evidence along with the direct examination may provide stronger support for the diagnosis.

Sputum and bronchial aspirates should be cultured at room temperature with antibiotic on Sabouraud's medium.

THERAPY. Localized lesions or aspergillomas should be removed surgically since antibiotic therapy is usually ineffective. Intravenous amphotericin B has been used with encouraging results. (See p. 794).

REFERENCES

Blattner, R. J. Pulmonary aspergillosis in children. J. Pediat., 70:139, 1967.

Finegold, S. M., Drake, W., and Murray, J. F. Aspergillosis: a review and report of twelve cases. Amer. J. Med., 27:463, 1959.

Hughes, W. Generalized aspergillosis. Amer. J. Dis. Child., 112:262, 1966.

Luke, J., Bolande, L. R. P., and Gross, S. Generalized aspergillosis and aspergillus endocarditis in infancy. Pediatrics, 31:115, 1963.

Mahvi, T., Webb, H. M., Dixon, C. D., and Boone, J. A. Systemic aspergillosis caused by *Aspergillus niger* after open-heart surgery. J.A.M.A., 203:520, 1968.

Young, R. C., Vogel, C. L., and DeVita, V. T. *Aspergillus* lobar pneumonia. J.A.M.A., 208:1156, 1969.

Vedder, J. S., and Schorr, W. F. Primary disseminated pulmonary aspergillosis with metastatic skin nodules. J.A.M.A., 209:1191, 1969.

14.45
BLASTOMYCOSIS

North American blastomycosis, Gilchrist's disease, is caused by the fungus *Blastomyces dermatitidis*. It is confined to the North American continent, where the prevalence is greatest in the Mississippi Valley and the southeastern states. While cases usually occur sporadically and affect adults with outdoor occupations, a small epidemic was reported by Smith and others in 1955, in which 6 of the 11 cases were children, the youngest aged 6 months. Current evidence indicates there are close resemblances in the clinical patterns of blastomycosis and other deep mycoses, notably coccidioidomycosis and histoplasmosis.

It is now apparent that the lungs are frequently, if not invariably, the portal of entry for *B. dermatitidis*, resulting in a primary pulmonary form of the disease. At the present time little is known of so-called inapparent or subclinical cases of pulmonary blastomycosis such as are recognized in coccidioidomycosis. However, in the clinically apparent primary cases the resulting disease is insidious in onset, resembling a mild respiratory infection accompanied by low-grade fever, chest pain, and nonproductive cough. As the symptoms gradually increase in severity, night sweats, high spiking fevers, hemoptysis, weakness, anorexia, and weight loss are evident. Severe primary pulmonary blastomycosis is difficult to differentiate from active tuberculosis. Radiologic studies of the chest may show extensive involvement of mediastinal nodes. Occasionally there is evidence of extensive pulmonary miliary disease, and death may follow while the disease is still confined to the lungs, or the patient may recover slowly. More frequently, however, dissemination to extrapulmonary areas occurs.

Disseminated blastomycosis is the result of hematogenous spread of the infection from the lungs to other areas of the body. Most frequently the disease involves the cutaneous and subcutaneous tissues as well as bone, central nervous system, and urogenital tract. In contradistinction to South American blastomycosis, the gastrointestinal tract is usually spared. Granulomatous lesions of the liver and spleen are found in over 40 percent of disseminated cases. The kidneys, prostate, epididymis, bladder, and testes are often involved causing dysuria, pyuria, and hematuria.

Chronic cutaneous blastomycosis follows hematogenous spread from primary pulmonary infection. This is the most common form of North American blastomycosis, and is the initial presenting complaint of most patients. The skin lesions initially appear as benign, papulopustular nodules which enlarge peripherally to form elevated, ulcerating, and verrucous granulomas. As the lesion extends at its periphery, the central area heals leaving a soft atrophic scar. Primary cutaneous blastomycosis is an extremely rare form of the disease resulting from inoculation of *B. dermatitidis* into the skin. A papule forms at the inoculation site followed by an ascending lymphangitis and lymphadenopathy of the affected limbs, closely mimicking the clinical picture of sporotrichosis. In those cases that have been described, all patients recovered without developing the chronic cutaneous form or dissemination.

Clinical diagnosis must be confirmed by laboratory studies. These include microscopic examination of smears, scrapings, aspirates, sputum, and bronchoscopic washings for the presence of the characteristic yeastlike cells. This material should also be spread on the surface of Sabouraud's agar slants and incubated at room temperature or 30° C. The yeast phase may be obtained in culture by inoculating glucose blood agar medium and incubating at 37°C. Usually the blastomycin skin and complement-fixation tests are positive except in recently infected individuals. Since cross-reactions between North American blastomycosis and histoplasmosis are not uncommon, a single serologic examination must be interpreted with caution. However, serial serologic determinations obtained during acute, convalescent, and recovery phases are more specific. Most authorities regard a heightened intracutaneous test of the delayed hypersensitivity type and a low or absent titer in a complement-fixation test as indicative of a favorable prognosis, whereas a high complement-fixation titer has usually been correlated with extensive and often fatal disease.

The prognosis for life in chronic cutaneous blastomycosis is generally good; however, healing does not usually take place without appropriate therapy.

Untreated widely disseminated disease always has a poor prognosis. The aromatic diamidines, stilbamidine and hydroxystilbamidine, have been used with moderate success in many cutaneous cases, but they have not been useful in the serious disseminated form, especially when immunologic resistance is low. Excellent results have been obtained with the use of amphotericin B. Although internal lesions do not seem to respond as well, skin lesions heal promptly, obtaining up to 80 percent cures. It is notable that cases which failed to respond to previous therapy are now being successfully treated with amphotericin. (See p. 794.)

REFERENCES

Furcolow, M., Balows, A., Menges, R. W., Pickar, D., McClellan, J. T., and Sahba, A. Blastomycosis. J.A.M.A., 198:115, 1968.

Gephard, M. C., and Hanlon, T. J. Blastomycosis. Arch. Derm., 84:660, 1961.

Turner, D. J., and Wadlington, W. B. Blastomycosis in childhood: treatment with Amphotericin B and a review of the literature. J. Pediat., 75:708, 1969.

Utz, J. P., Bennett, J. E., Brandress, M. W., Butler, W. T., and Hill, G. J. Amphotericin B toxicity. Combined clinical staff conference at the National Institutes of Health. Ann. Intern. Med., 61:334, 1964.

14.46
COCCIDIOIDOMYCOSIS

Coccidioidomycosis, San Joaquin or Valley fever, is a mycotic infection caused by the fungus *Coccidioides immitis*. Several forms of the disease are recognized in man: an acute, subacute, or asymptomatic, nonfatal, self-limited primary infection usually of the respiratory tract; and a secondary, often fatal, granulomatous form of a chronic and progressive nature.

In the acute primary respiratory form, infection occurs almost exclusively by inhalation of airborne dust containing arthrospores of *C. immitis*. Coccidioidomycosis, therefore, is not contagious, and sources of infection are usually exogenous. It has been repeatedly demonstrated that soil is the natural habitat of *C. immitis*, and from such soil sources the fungus enters the lungs and causes primary pulmonary infection. As may be expected, the incidence increases sharply in the late, dry summer months, and measures which effectively diminish dust have been shown to reduce markedly the incidence of infection.

Even though the first case of coccidioidomycosis was reported in Argentina, practically all of the subsequent cases have been recorded in the United States. Endemic areas exist in the western states, particularly the southern half of California, southern Arizona, western and southern Texas, New Mexico, in the northern states of Mexico, and in the Gran

Chaco Region of South America. Occasional cases have been reported from Venezuela and Central America and possibly from Russia. In arid regions the peak incidence of acute infection occurs during the hot summer and autumn months when dusty field work is in progress. Infections have occurred in tourists simply passing through endemic areas during the hot, dry summer season. Cattle, sheep, dogs, and wild rodents in these areas are infected. The disease has been found in dogs in nonendemic areas, as in Iowa, Kansas, and the province of Quebec. In highly endemic areas 70 to 90 percent of long-time residents have been infected, and as many as 50 percent of susceptible individuals may become infected following 6 months' residence in an endemic area, with the highest incidence usually occurring in the dusty summer and fall months. In endemic areas of California, the incidence of positive coccidioidin skin tests increases from 17 percent in children residing in the area for 1 year or less to 77 percent for those who live in the area for 10 years or more. Thus, where the population is stable the disease is predominantly a childhood infection. As measured by skin tests, no sex difference is present for the acute form of the disease. However, because erythema nodosum is more common in females, particularly at puberty, the acute form with erythema nodosum tends to be seen more often in girls.

Age does not appear to be a factor in susceptibility to infection; a fatal pulmonary form in a 3-week-old infant has been reported. Primary pulmonary disease can occur at all ages, although extrapulmonary spread and pulmonary cavitation appear to be less common in children than in adults. Among patients with the granulomatous form of the disease, males predominate, although less strikingly in children than in adults. The progressive form occurs in about 1 percent of clinically manifest infections in white males and in a much higher proportion in Negroes and Filipinos. The primary infection, if it does not lead to dissemination, establishes a strong and lasting immunity.

Primary Coccidioidomycosis

In about 60 percent of cases no symptoms are present, and evidence of the existing infection is confined to the positive coccidioidin skin test. In the remaining 40 percent, symptoms of the acute primary infection occur from 10 days to 4 weeks (usually 10 to 14 days) following infection with arthrospores. Most of these cases are associated with mild symptoms resembling a cold or influenza. In a small minority of patients, however, the primary attack may be most severe, with fever, dry cough, malaise, muscular pains, backache, headache, sore throat, and marked anorexia. A nonproductive cough, occasionally blood-streaked sputum, or frank hemoptysis may occur, suggesting pulmonary cavitation. Pleuritic pains are present in about one-third of cases. During the initial

phase of the disease an erythematous rash may appear on the trunk, often extending over the entire body. When accompanied by sore throat and constitutional symptoms, the infection may be confused with scarlet fever or measles. Occasionally the rash may be vesicular and resemble varicella. Arthralgia, particularly of the knees and ankles, may be present. Conjunctivitis is commonly observed. The symptoms subside in about one week and in most cases without sequelae. In about 10 percent of clinically apparent cases, after about 3 to 18 days, the fever recurs and erythema nodosum develops. Raised erythematous, roughly circular, tender nodules appear on the anterior tibial surfaces and not infrequently on the lateral surfaces of the thighs, hips, and buttocks, as well as the extensor surfaces of the arms, forearms, and elbows. These later become purplish, then brown, disappearing in about one to three weeks. Patients manifesting erythema nodosum are not likely to experience the disseminated chronic form of the disease.

Physical examination of the lungs reveals little of significance. Occasionally a friction rub, a pleural effusion, or fine crackling rales can be demonstrated. Roentgenograms reveal soft patches of density extending out from the hilum, peribronchial thickening, peripheral or interlobar pleural effusions, and hilar adenopathy. Between 2 and 8 percent of the clinically apparent cases develop cavities, usually solitary (90 percent), either within or outside of the pneumonic patch. Cavities usually disappear a few weeks after the acute symptoms have subsided. Occasionally an unusually large cavity may persist and remain unchanged for months or even years in an otherwise symptomless patient. Persistence of a cavity is not in itself an expression of chronic disseminated form of the disease. Calcification occurs in healing primary pulmonic lesions as well as in hilar nodes. The roentgenographic changes are similar to, if not indistinguishable from, those of tuberculosis. Although a cutaneous lesion may be the first indication of infection, it usually indicates dissemination from a previously unrecognized primary pulmonary focus.

Disseminated or Progressive Coccidioidomycosis (Coccidioidal Granuloma)

This chronic form of the disease, fortunately rare, occurs more frequently in dark-skinned races. Dissemination of the infection usually takes place within 6 months after the acute illness, but may follow the acute illness without interval. After a year, dissemination is unlikely. Progressive invasive granulomatous lesions may occur in the lungs, lymph nodes, bones, joints, skin, or meninges. Pulmonary lesions consist of pneumonic areas, cavitation, pleurisy, or numerous discrete miliary lesions or abscesses. Bronchial adenopathy is present. Osteomyelitis, periostitis, and arthritis are common. The skin lesions usually begin as painless small nodules which gradually enlarge, suppurate, ulcerate, and then become encrusted. They occur most frequently in the scalp, on the forehead, nose, face, lips, supraclavicular region, thorax, hand and forearm, and leg and foot. In children from 1 month to 6 years of age, complaints referrable to the skeleton and soft tissues are more frequently encountered than are respiratory symptoms. In older children respiratory complaints predominate. Meningitis is more common in children, and unless early vigorous treatment is initiated, it is invariably fatal. The course of the granulomatous form of the disease is less prolonged in children.

DIAGNOSIS. While the clinical or epidemiologic history may arouse suspicion of the disease, a positive diagnosis of coccidioidomycosis may be made by the proper use of: (1) the coccidioidin skin test; (2) a precipitin test; (3) a specific complement-fixation test; (4) identification of *C. immitis* by culture or animal inoculation; and (5) histologic demonstration of characteristic double refractile spherules in biopsy material.

In positive reactors, 0.1 ml of a 1:100 dilution of coccidioidin injected intracutaneously produces induration greater than 5 mm in diameter when the test is read at 24 and 48 hours. An initial negative test during the acute illness followed by a positive reaction by the fourth week is diagnostic. A greater dilution should be used for patients with erythema nodosum, since they may be hyperreactive. A negative coccidioidin test in a patient with erythema nodosum usually eliminates the possibility of coccidioidomycosis. In disseminated or extrapulmonary granulomatous forms there may be no reaction to even undiluted coccidioidin. Injection of coccidioidin for skin testing does not stimulate antibody production and, therefore, does not interfere with subsequent dermal or serologic tests. Reactors to histoplasmin may also react slightly to high concentrations of coccidioidin, and tests must be interpreted with caution.

Diagnostic humoral antibodies develop more slowly than does skin reactivity in the uncomplicated acute respiratory form of the disease. Precipitins are present in 50 percent of the cases in the first week, 90 percent by the third week, frequently declining after the third week of the disease, and occasionally persisting for about four months. Complement-fixing antibodies appear after the first week of the disease and usually decline in the second month, but the complement-fixation reaction may persist for several years. Unusually high titers often correlate with the severity of the disease or with the presence of the disseminated progressive form. A rising complement-fixing serum titer is evidence of impending dissemination, a titer of 1 to 16 or higher being almost always indicative of disseminated disease. Negative serologic tests virtually rule out the chronic disseminated form of the disease. Generally, serologic tests are positive when the skin test is positive, and vice versa. The demonstration of antibodies against *C. immitis* is of particular diagnostic value in patients with clinical evidence of dissemination in whom the skin test is negative.

The organisms may be found in the sputum, in cultured gastric washings, in purulent exudates of lesions, and in centrifuged sediment obtained from cerebrospinal, peritoneal, or pleural fluid. Direct microscopic examination of a cover slip preparation is inaccurate. Suspicious cultures should always be confirmed by animal inoculation. Intraperitoneal inoculation of white mice or intratesticular inoculation of guinea pigs results in pure suspensions of the organisms for culture. The oganisms may be cultivated easily, but unusual care in the handling of infected material should be exercised, since the arthrospores are so light and easily broken away from the spore-bearing stalk that a mere puff of wind or breath can release a cloud of spores from a culture and carry them for considerable distances. All nonimmune persons are then in danger of becoming infected by inhaling the spores; infections have often occurred in this way, and on occasion have been fatal.

In tissue sections, the sporangium can be recognized as a double refractile spherical body which contains endospores and which shows no budding.

There is often a marked leucocytosis with a shift to the left. Occasionally a striking eosinophilia may be present, erroneously suggesting the presence of Löeffler's syndrome. The spinal fluid in 75 percent of the cases of meningitis contains complement-fixing antibodies. A "paretic" colloidal gold curve may be found.

TREATMENT. Primary coccidioidomycosis requires no therapy, since it is a self-limited disease. The disseminated form, however, had a fatality rate of about 50 percent despite all available therapy until amphotericin B was introduced. Oral and intramuscular administration of this antibiotic appear to be of little value. Intravenous administration of the drug should be employed in maximally tolerated doses daily or on alternate days until signs of the infection are eradicated. Such treatment is indicated in patients with disseminated infection or threatened dissemination, or with extending or exacerbating chronic pulmonary disease; it should also be given to individuals having persistent fever with malaise associated with pulmonary involvement and hilar adenopathy. Coccidioidal meningitis, which is usually fatal within a year if untreated, appears to be definitely improved by amphotericin B administration via combined intravenous and intrathecal routes. Dosage and length of therapy are discussed under cryptococcosis (p. 794).

REFERENCES

Ajello, L. Coccidioidomycosis, Symposium, 2nd ed. Tucson, Ariz., Univ. of Arizona Press, 1967.

Drips, W., Jr., and Smith, C. E. Epidemiology of coccidioidomycosis: a contemporary military experience. J.A.M.A., 190:1010, 1964.

Sarosi, G., Parker, J., and Tosh, F. Pulmonary coccidioidomycosis. New Eng. J. Med., 283:326, 1970.

Winn, W. A. Recent advances in the therapy of coccidioidomycosis. *In* Dalldorf, G., ed., Fungi and Fungous Diseases. Springfield, Ill., Charles C Thomas Co., 1962, p. 315.

———— Primary cutaneous coccidioidomycosis. Re-evaluation of its potentiality based on study of three new cases. Arch. Derm., 92:221, 1965.

Winter, B., Villaveces, J., and Spector, M. Coccidioidomycosis accompanied by acute tracheal obstruction in a child. J.A.M.A., 195:1001, 1966.

Ziering, W. H., and Rockas, H. R. Long-term treatment with amphotericin B of disseminated disease in a three-month-old baby. Amer. J. Dis. Child., 108:454, 1964.

14.47
HISTOPLASMOSIS

Histoplasmosis, or Darling's disease, is an intracellular infection caused by the dimorphic fungus *Histoplasma capsulatum*. The disease occurs throughout the world, affecting all age groups. The highest incidence of severe or fatal illness is in infancy and again in old age.

Histoplasmosis was first described by Darling in 1905, from three fatal cases in Panama. Almost four decades passed, however, before the notion was dispelled that histoplasmosis was usually a fatal infection. Epidemiologic studies demonstrated frequent positive dermal reaction to histoplasmin, an antigen prepared from cultures of *H. capsulatum*. The widespread incidence of positive reaction, especially in eastern central United States, provided important evidence of a widespread, benign, or inapparent, form of the disease. Subsequently, direct confirmatory evidence was obtained. It is erroneous to regard histoplasmosis as a disease of central United States, according to Emmons, since it is just as common on the East Coast of the United States as in the Mississippi Valley.

Histoplasma capsulatum has been isolated in soil many times, usually near old chicken coops, bat caves, and barnyards where the soil has been enriched with decayed manure of chickens, birds, or bats. Focal outbreaks of histoplasmosis are reported in families, children, or other individuals who have been playing in, or cleaning out, an old abandoned chicken house, or visiting caves inhabited by bats. *Histoplasma* can be isolated in soil under trees in which starlings and other birds roost, and this mechanism may be responsible for urban transmission.

In soil, or in the laboratory at room temperature employing Sabouraud's culture medium, *Histoplasma capsulatum* exhibits typical mycelial growth. Early aerial growth is white and cottony, later turning light tan to brown. Microscopic examination reveals branching septate hyphae bearing oval microcondia 2 to 4 μ in diameter. As the culture matures, round-ing macrocondia 8 to 14 μ are found; these are adorned with evenly spaced appendages that stain intensely for mucopolysaccharide. If inhaled or inoculated, spores promptly transform into typical yeast forms and reproduce intracellularly as oval budding yeasts, 2 to 4 μ in diameter, possessing a distinct capsule. The yeast phase can be reproduced in the laboratory if mycelial elements are transferred into enrichment medium and grown at 37° C.

PATHOGENESIS AND PATHOLOGY. There is considerable evidence to suggest that, in the vast majority of cases, the respiratory tract is the usual means of entering the body. Primary ulcerative lesions of the skin, mucous membranes of the mouth, nasopharynx, and intestinal mucosa have been described. Such lesions may disseminate or remain localized to the region involved. The organism is generally found within macrophages and other cells of the reticuloendothelial system. The primary pulmonary complex of histoplasmosis closely resembles that of tuberculosis, consisting of single or multiple small, subpleural lesions with lymphatic spread to regional hilar lymph nodes. Central caseous necrosis with epithelioid and Langhans type giant cells are often seen. These lesions frequently heal with calcification. In hematogenous dissemination, the lungs almost always show miliary "tubercles" as do the spleen, liver, lymph nodes, and bone marrow. All tissues and organs may be involved with the exception of cartilage and cortical bone.

CLINICAL ASPECTS. The clinical spectrum of histoplasma infection extends from inapparent or asymptomatic infection to fatal fulminant disease. Several clinical types have been suggested, and for purposes of discussion are as follows: (1) primary, acute form; (2) severe, disseminated form; and (3) chronic, cavitary form.

Primary, Acute Histoplasmosis. The disease as represented by this designation is usually a mild, or more often an asymptomatic, inapparent pulmonary infection in which the aspirated organisms stimulate the formation of one or more subpleural tubercles. As in primary pulmonary tuberculosis, macrophages laden with organisms travel along lymphatics to regional peribronchial and hilar nodes where secondary tubercles are formed. A significant proportion of these calcify and can be detected by chest x-ray. The histoplasmin skin test turns positive about 3 to 5 weeks after infection. Figure 25 illustrates the relationship of histoplasmin sensitivity to pulmonary calcifications and their frequency in an area of high endemic frequency. Occasionally, there may be large numbers of calcified scars. At times multiple lesions may be seen by x-ray throughout the lung fields, persisting for months or more before disappearing.

In symptomatic cases, demonstrated to be histoplasmosis by subsequent positive conversion of the histoplasmin skin in the absence of a positive tuberculin test, the most frequent pulmonary symptoms are nonproductive cough, shortness of breath, chest pain, hoarseness, and cyanosis. Fever, nightsweats, arthral-

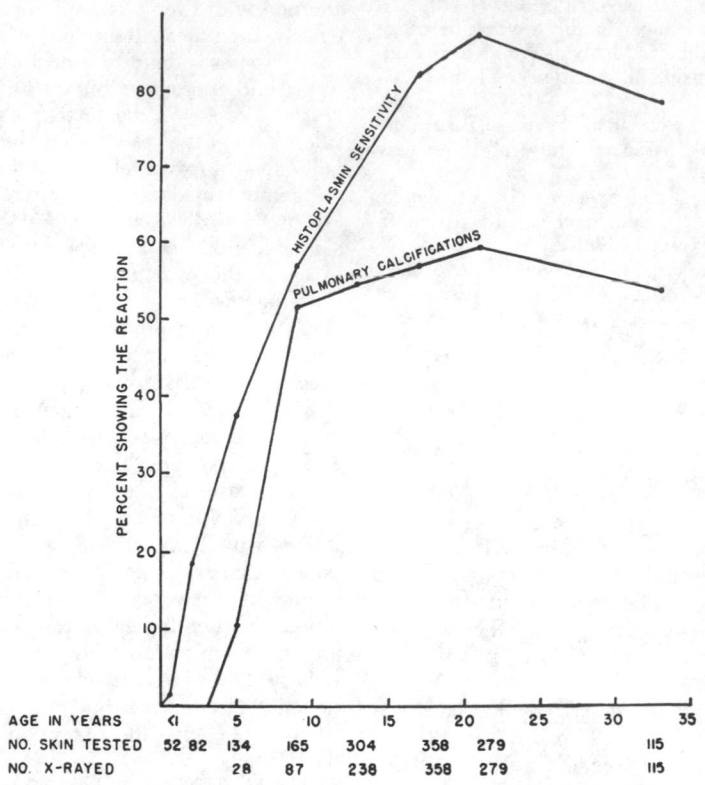

Fig. 25. The prevalence of histoplasmin sensitivity and pulmonary calcifications according to age in an area in which histoplasmosis is highly endemic.

gias, and weight loss are commonly seen. During this acute stage, erythema nodosum may be observed. Exposure to large numbers of organisms, as when children play in caves containing bat guano rich in *H. capsulatum*, may result in a severe and sometimes fatal pulmonary infection that may or may not have disseminated. Usually, however, these patients recover and the myriads of pulmonary tubercles eventually calcify (Fig. 26). The frequent finding of calcified splenic tubercles in individuals with no clinical history of histoplasmosis suggests that asymptomatic hematogenous dissemination frequently may occur. In mild, self-limited attacks no specific antifungal therapy is indicated.

Severe, Disseminated Form. This form of histoplasmosis occurs more frequently in infants, young children, and the elderly, debilitated patient. While pulmonary symptoms may be inconspicuous, fever, hepatosplenomegaly, anemia, leucopenia, weight loss, and generalized lymphadenopathy may dominate the picture. Signs and symptoms can be those of endocarditis, meningitis, or adrenal insufficiency; gastrointestinal involvement may be manifested by diarrhea. Pneumonitis is not infrequent. Lesions of the skin and mucous membranes of the mouth are frequent in young patients. Severe anemia, thrombocytopenia, leucopenia and, in the late or terminal stages, pur-

pura, ecchymosis, and gastrointestinal hemorrhage can occur.

Once the diagnosis of disseminated histoplasmosis is suspected, it should not be difficult to obtain cultural confirmation from blood, bone marrow aspiration, or biopsy of lymph node, liver, spleen, or ulcer. Cultures of blood and bone marrow will be positive in about half the cases. Histoplasmin skin test in disseminated disease may remain negative in about 50 percent of cases although the complement-fixation test usually, but not always, turns positive. Recent studies have pointed out that subsequent to a single positive histoplasmin skin test, complement-fixing antibody titers of up to 1:256 developed in 7 of 12 healthy persons. These titers persisted for months. Therefore, if complement fixation is to be done after skin testing, yeast phase antigens should be used. The value of the histoplasmin skin test is limited in disseminated disease. Conversion from negative to positive during acute illness is regarded as significant; a positive reaction in a young child is highly suggestive of active disease. In older individuals, however, it can only be interpreted as indicative of previous infection.

Chronic Cavitary Form. Chronic, cavitary pulmonary histoplasmosis is seen most frequently in adults. Radiologically and symptomatically it closely

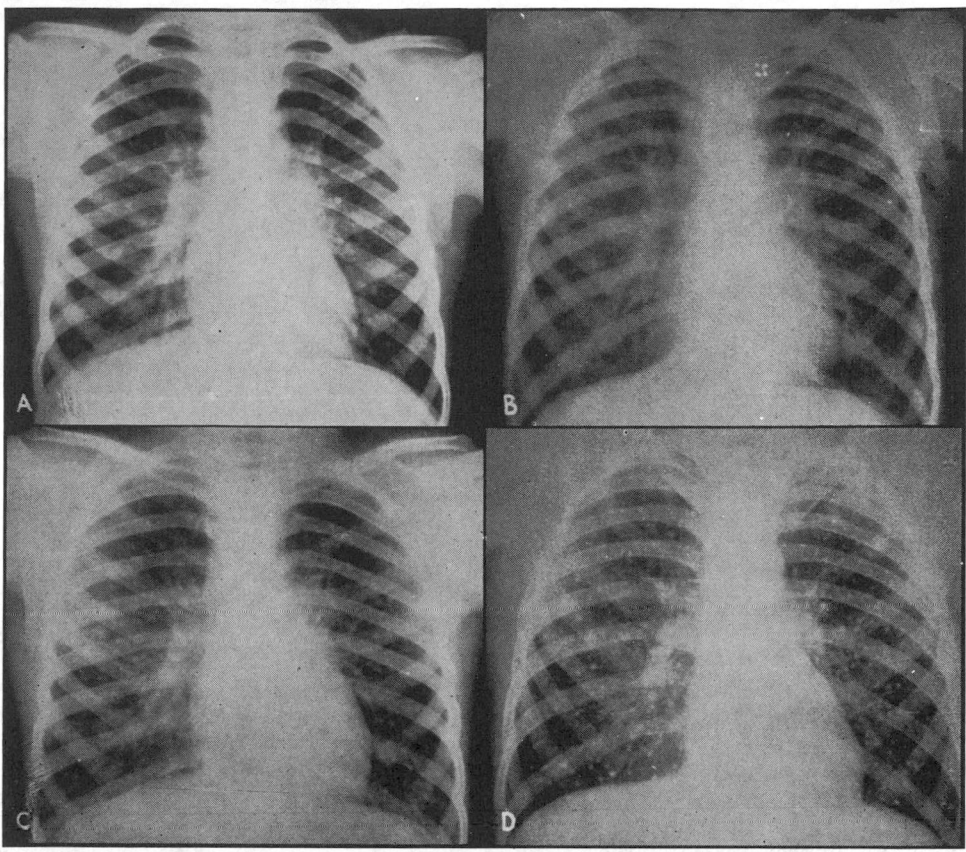

Fig. 26. The development of pulmonary calcification in a case of severe, nonprogressive histoplasmosis. *A.* January 1947; *B.* August 1949, at the time of the patient's hospital observation; *C.* November 1950; *D.* September 1961.

resembles cavitary tuberculosis. This type of histo-plasmosis represents disseminated disease and has a poor prognosis. These patients may demonstrate any of the severe manifestations of disseminated histoplasmosis and if untreated they usually die.

TREATMENT. Amphotericin B is the agent of choice for the treatment of disseminated histoplasmosis (see p. 794).

REFERENCES

Christie, A. Histoplasmosis and pulmonary calcification; geographic distribution. Amer. J. Trop. Med., 31:742, 1951.

———— and Peterson, J. C. Pulmonary calcification in negative reactors to tuberculin. Amer. J. Pub. Health, 35:1131, 1945.

———— and Peterson, J. C. Histoplasmin sensitivity. J. Pediat., 29:417, 1946.

Emmons, C. W. Histoplasmosis: animal reservoirs and other sources in nature of the pathogenic fungus, Histoplasma. Amer. J. Pub. Health, 40:436, 1950.

Friedman, J. L., Baum, G. L., and Schwarz, J. Primary pulmonary histoplasmosis: associated pericardial and mediastinal manifestations. Amer. J. Dis. Child., 109:298, 1965.

Furcolow, M. L., Mantz, H. L., and Lewis, I. The roentgenographic appearance of persistent pulmonary infiltrates associated with sensitivity to histoplasmin. Pub. Health Rep., 62:1711, 1947.

Palmer, C. E. Geographic differences in sensitivity to histoplasmin among student nurses. Pub. Health Rep., 61:475, 1946.

Parker, J., Sarosi, G., Doto, I., Bailey, R., and Tosh, F. Treatment of chronic pulmonary histoplasmosis. New Eng. J. Med., 283:225, 1970.

Tesh, R. B., Shacklette, M. H., Diercks, F. H., and Hirschl, D. Histoplasmosis in children. Pediatrics, 33:894, 1964.

Schwarz, J., and Baum, G. L. The history of histoplasmosis from 1906 to 1956. New Eng. J. Med., 256:253, 1957.

Vanek, J., and Schwartz, J. The gamut of histoplasmosis. Amer. J. Med., 50:89, 1971.

14.48
CRYPTOCOCCOSIS

Cryptococcosis (torulosis) is a cosmopolitan mycotic disease caused by a yeastlike fungus, *Cryptococ-*

cus neoformans. With few exceptions it is conceded by most workers that avian excrement, particularly pigeon feces, is the primary source of *C. neoformans,* and that occasional recovery from soil, which has been reported, depends upon previous contamination with avian feces.

Cryptococcus neoformans is a spherical cell that reproduces by budding and varies widely in size from 4 to 20 μ in diameter. It is surrounded by a mucopolysaccharide capsule that, depending upon the strain, varies in thickness from almost undetectable to nearly twice the diameter of the cell.

Cryptococcosis is seen most frequently in individuals with serious primary disease such as leukemia, lymphosarcoma, Hodgkin's disease, diabetes mellitus, or in those receiving long-term steroid or immunosuppressive therapy.

CLINICAL ASPECTS. Infection usually is acquired by inhalation of the organisms. Disease may remain localized to the pulmonary parenchyma, and subsequently hematogenous dissemination may occur to any organ of the body. Central nervous system involvement is particularly common, and cryptococcal meningitis is regarded as the most frequent cause of mycotic meningitis.

Pulmonary Cryptococcosis. Pulmonary infection may be clinically asymptomatic, and is discovered as a solitary nodule only by chance x-ray examination. However, pulmonary disease can be clinically apparent with cough, frequently productive of mucoid sputum, chest pain, fever, weight loss, occasionally hemoptysis, and night sweats. Single or multiple cavitary lesions, often bilateral, containing mucoid material may arise with or without symptoms. These lesions may persist for some time and subsequently heal spontaneously without drug therapy or dissemination to the central nervous system. Lesions, however, may be infiltrative and diffuse. Discovery of cryptococcus in sputum usually is regarded as clear-cut evidence of pulmonary cryptococcosis, although recently Reiss and Szilagyi have presented evidence that a carrier state may exist.

Cerebral Cryptococcosis. Dissemination to the central nervous system results in the signs and symptoms typical of meningitis, cerebral abscess, or tumor. These may include headache, nausea, vomiting, vertigo, low-grade fever, nuchal rigidity, positive Kernig's and Brudzinski's signs, papilledema, and increased spinal fluid pressure. Examination of the spinal fluid may reveal lymphocytosis, elevated protein, and reduced glucose. While untreated disease usually is fatal in 3 to 6 months, indolent cryptococcal meningitis may linger for years. Fulminant cases, fatal in a few weeks, also may occur.

DIAGNOSIS AND PREVENTION. The demonstration of budding organisms in India ink preparations of the spinal fluid is suitable to establish the diagnosis. *Cryptococcus neoformans* is readily cultured on Sabouraud's dextrose medium at 37° C but not at 44° C. Generally, serologic tests for diagnostic purposes have not been particularly useful. However, a complement-fixation test has recently been used and appears helpful in predicting relapse following amphotericin B therapy. The most effective measure for preventing cryptococcosis would be to reduce wild pigeon flocks. Handlers of pigeons can be protected by employing methods recommended by Walter and Coffee, whereby a solution of sodium hydroxide and lime are used in and around pigeon coops. This solution seems effectively to destroy *C. neoformans.*

TREATMENT. While treatment of focal pulmonary lesions is by surgical excision, cryptococcal meningitis is treated with amphotericin B. The relapse rate with amphotericin is about 25 to 30 percent; however, cryptococcal meningitis was almost always fatal prior to this drug.

Amphotericin B. Amphotericin B is the drug of choice for the treatment of cryptococcosis, as well as blastomycosis, disseminated coccidioidomycosis, disseminated histoplasmosis, and systemic candidiasis. It is not without a number of undesirable and sometimes imposing side effects. These include fever, chills, headache, nausea, vomiting, anorexia, phlebitis, anemia, hypokalemia, and azotemia. Amphotericin is poorly absorbed from the gastrointestinal tract and, therefore, is usually administered intravenously. Since it is excreted slowly by the kidneys it need not be administered more than once a day. Recent studies indicate, however, administration on alternate days provides suitable blood levels for therapeusis, and is tolerated far better by the patient. Therapy is initiated with a dose of 0.25 mg/kg and gradually increased while the patient is carefully observed for signs of drug toxicity. Renal function is monitored by blood urea nitrogen determination, serum creatinine, creatinine clearance, and the appearance in the urine of erythrocytes, leucocytes, albumin, or granular or cellular casts. As long as the patient tolerates the dose it is increased up to a daily maximum of 1 mg/kg, but in no instance greater than 1.5 mg/kg. Therapy usually spans a period of about 10 weeks or more with the total adult dose usually being between 2 to 4 g. If relapse should occur then treatment should be reinstituted. Thrombophlebitis at the intravenous site may be a serious technical impediment to prolonged intravenous therapy especially in children.

Renal toxicity caused by amphotericin B has been extensively studied. It has been shown that patients may develop a renal tubular acidosis syndrome, and that urinary excretion of potassium may result in serious hypokalemia. It is important, therefore, that patients receive potassium replacement. Similarly, citrate may be of value in order to reduce the likelihood of renal calcinosis, which is a frequent complication of amphotericin B therapy.

REFERENCES

Campbell, G. D. Primary pulmonary cryptococcosis. Amer. Rev. Resp. Dis., 94:236, 1966.

Littman, M. L., and Walter, J. E. Cryptococcosis: current status. Amer. J. Med., 45:922, 1968.

Randall, R. E., Jr., Stacy, W. K., Toone, E. C., Prout, G. R., Madge, G. E., Shadomy, H. J., Shadomy, S., and Utz, J. P. Cryptococcal pyelonephritis. New Eng. J. Med., 279:60, 1968.

Siewers, C. M. F., and Cramblett, H. G. Cryptococcosis (torulosis) in children. Pediatrics, 34:393, 1964.

14.49
PHYCOMYCOSIS

Phycomycosis (mucormycosis) is a collective term applied to mycotic infections most often caused by a species of *Absidia, Mucor, Rhizopus,* and *Basidiobolus.* These fungi are found normally throughout the world occurring as saprophytes in decaying vegetation, fruits, and feces of herbivores. Similarly, phycomycosis has been reported from all parts of the world, especially occurring in persons with uncontrolled diabetes mellitus, in those with debilitating and/or terminal disease, and as a complication of steroid or immunosuppressive therapy.

CLINICAL DISEASE. Increasing awareness of the clinical setting in which phycomycosis may occur probably accounts for part of the increased incidence and frequency of antemortem diagnoses. The triad of diabetic acidosis, facial or orbital cellulitis, and meningoencephalitis is well-documented. Pulmonary involvement is not uncommon. It may cause a severe necrotizing pneumonitis with multiple foci of pulmonary infarction. This is attributed to the characteristic invasion of blood vessels by hyphae resulting in vasculitis and thrombosis. Central nervous system involvement usually is by direct extension from orbital or paranasal sinus infection. Invasion of any portion of the gastrointestinal tract may occur. Signs and symptoms are variable and may include diarrhea, pain, melena, hematemesis, and peritonitis.

DIAGNOSIS. The diagnosis of phycomycosis should be entertained in debilitated patients in whom progressive, fulminating sinusitis, orbital cellulitis, or pneumonitis occurs. Histopathologic diagnosis is relatively clear-cut with the finding of very broad, rarely septate, haphazardly branched hyphae that deeply stain with ordinary hematoxylin. The hyphae are much broader than those seen in aspergilliasis.

TREATMENT. Amphotericin B is the drug of choice (p. 794). Further, every effort should be made to correct diabetic acidosis if it is present, since recent studies have suggested that diabetics and especially those in acidosis have impaired polymorphonuclear leucocyte mobilization.

References

Abramson, E., Wilson, D., and Arky, R. A. Rhinocerebral phycomycosis in association with diabetic ketoacidosis. Report of two cases and a review of clinical and experimental experience with amphotericin B therapy. Ann. Intern. Med., 66:735, 1967.

Straatsma, B. R., Zimmerman, L. E., and Gass, J. D. M. Phycomycosis: A clinicopathologic study of fifty-one cases. Lab. Invest., 11:1018, 1962.

14.50
CANDIDIASIS

Candidiasis is a fungus infection caused by yeastlike fungi of the genus *Candida.* Although *Candida albicans* has been implicated in the overwhelming number of cases, it is clear that other species of *Candida,* given the opportunity, may also cause severe illness. (Previously the causative organism was known as *Monilia* and, therefore, the disease was termed moniliasis.)

Candidas are frequently isolated from individuals in whom they do not seem to be causing disease. Typically, they can be found in sputum, feces, vaginal secretion, and mouth, but rarely in normal skin. Factors that predispose to production of superficial or deep-seated disease by *Candida* are not precisely known. It is recognized, however, that individuals with endocrine disorders such as diabetes mellitus, hypoparathyroidism, hypoadrenalism, and hypothyroidism, various blood dyscrasias such as leukemia and agranulocytosis, malignant states, malnutrition, and those receiving antibiotic, steroid, or immunosuppressive therapy are more frequently found with candidiasis than are individuals enjoying normal health. Occasionally, direct inoculation of organisms by drug addicts, who are otherwise healthy, has resulted in fatal candida endocarditis. Although disseminated candidiasis in the newborn period has been reported, it is far more common to encounter oral lesions, e.g., thrush (Sec. 28.5) together with lesions of the perianal and diaper areas (Sec. 2.10). Generally these children are otherwise healthy; some, however, may be premature.

Candida albicans found in skin, sputum, urine, and feces usually appears as rounded or oval budding cells, or blastospores, about 3 to 6 μ in diameter. These tend to elongate and form pseudohyphae. In deep-seated infections, pseudohyphae may be the form most easily recognized, although blastospores, if looked for, usually will be found.

Deep-Seated Candidiasis

There has been increased clinical awareness, as well as incidence, of deep-seated candidiasis. Moreover, it has become clear that other species of *Candida* besides *C. albicans* are opportunistic pathogenic organisms, and their recovery from patient material must not be dismissed routinely as a nonpathogenic contaminant. Other than *C. albicans,* the most frequently identified species have been *C. tropicalis, C. parapsilosis, C. guilliermondii,* and *C. krusei.*

Candidiasis of the alimentary canal may occur at any age, although it is more common in infancy and in the elderly, often following oral candidiasis.

Vomiting is the outstanding symptom of candida esophagitis and is often exacerbated by feeding. Diarrhea and dehydration are frequent accompaniments. The distal third of the esophagus is most often involved.

Intestinal candidiasis has been reported with increasing frequency, often related to antibiotic and steroid therapy. Enteritis is characterized by increasingly frequent loose bowel movements, abdominal discomfort, and rectal pain occasionally accompanied by mucosal bleeding. Sigmoidoscopic or macroscopic examination may reveal multiple gray-brown plaques that may be covered with friable membrane. Microscopic examination usually reveals both pseudohyphae and yeast forms. Granulocyte response is variable. The presence of mycelial elements in the bowel has been interpreted to mean mucosal invasion, whereas the predominance of yeasts or blastospores has been regarded as nonpathogenic or saprophytic existence.

Candidiasis of the urinary tract may cause cystitis or pyelonephritis, the latter being the result either of local spread from the bladder or of hematogenous seeding in disseminated candidiasis. While urinary tract disease can be particularly difficult to detect, in several recent studies the demonstration of candida by careful catheterization or suprapubic tap, taken together with elevated urinary protein and leucocytes, has been regarded as highly suggestive of invasive bladder and/or renal disease. Although present techniques for the diagnosis of upper urinary tract infection are inadequate, repeated isolation of the organism together with clinical and laboratory evidence of infection demands serious consideration of the etiologic role of candida.

Pulmonary candidiasis is quite rare despite the frequency in which the organism is isolated from sputum. Candida bronchitis, on the other hand, is relatively common, apparently occurring by direct spread from the oral cavity and oropharynx.

Systemic and disseminated candida infections have been increasing, most notably in individuals undergoing therapy for acute leukemia, although a few cases have been reported in otherwise seemingly normal individuals. The majority of these cases appear to be the result of direct inoculation into the bloodstream during long-term intravenous therapy. While spontaneous recovery from candidemia can occur upon removal of the source of infection, serious complications such as candidal meningitis, pyelonephritis, or endocarditis may intervene. Candida endocarditis resembles subacute bacterial endocarditis. Typically, large, bulky, friable vegetations occur that tend to embolize to large vessels of the extremities, head, and kidney. Blood cultures positive for candida are usually obtained. Despite therapy, the prognosis for this complication of candidiasis is almost uniformly poor.

DIAGNOSIS. Establishing a definitive diagnosis of candidiasis may be an extremely difficult exercise. Recognition of organisms isolated from human material is less troublesome than interpretation of their significance. Many workers regard the predominance of mycelial or M-forms as a reliable indication of a pathogenic infection with *C. albicans*. The trouble with this is that other species of *Candida* do not form pseudohyphae as readily or to the same degree as *C. albicans* and may still be pathogenic. Evidence has been obtained indicating increased invasiveness with transformation from yeast (Y-forms) to pseudohyphal growth. It is important, therefore, to collect and examine clinical material immediately, since the presence of protein often stimulates Y to M transformation and can lead to serious misinterpretation.

Intradermal or serologic tests generally are not helpful in determining invasive disease since many normal individuals will be positive reactors. Recent studies have shown that precipitating antibodies against cytoplasmic candidal antigens are a reasonably specific index of candidiasis. These tests are not yet generally available. It is important to reemphasize that one should *not* disregard recovery in blood cultures of "nonpathogenic yeasts" without careful patient evaluation and subsequent negative cultures. Demonstration of *Candida sp.* in biopsy material should be supported where possible, with cultural identification.

TREATMENT. Alimentary tract infection can be treated with 500,000 units of mycostatin administered orally four times daily for one week. If antibacterial therapy is implicated in the overgrowth of candida it should be withheld. Systemic or disseminated candidiasis is treated with amphotericin B (p. 794). Unfortunately, candidal endocarditis does not respond as well as other forms of systemic candidiasis to amphotericin therapy. It is believed the large, bulky vegetations preclude the drug's reaching and, therefore, inhibiting the organisms. Following surgical removal of valvular vegetations a clinical cure of candidal endocarditis has been reported. This may indicate the heroic measures that may be necessary to save life in candidal endocarditis.

PROGNOSIS. The outlook for recovery from alimentary tract infection is excellent if treatment is instituted promptly. The prognosis in systemic candidiasis is always guarded even with amphotericin therapy. Endocarditis has an ominous outlook, being almost uniformally fatal despite amphotericin or surgical therapy.

REFERENCES

Androile, V. T., Kravetz, H. M., Roberts, W. C., and Utz, J. P. Candida endocarditis, clinical and pathologic studies. Amer. J. Med., 32:251, 1962.

Kozinn, P., Taschdjian, C. L., Seelig, M. S., Caroline, L., and Teitler, A. Diagnosis and therapy of systemic candidiasis. Sabouraudia, 7:98, 1969.

Toala, P., Schroeder, S., Daly, A., and Finland, M. Candida at Boston City Hospital. Arch. Int. Med., 126:983, 1970.

Winner, H. I., and Hurley, R. Symposium on Candida Infections. Edinburgh and London, E. & S. Livingstone Ltd., 1966, p. 249.

——— Candida Albicans. Boston, Little, Brown & Co., 1964, 306 pp.

Parasitic Diseases

MURRAY WITTNER

Parasitic diseases are those caused by helminths, protozoans, and arthropods. The organisms included within this restricted definition afflict more than half the world's population, often resulting in chronic debilitating disease and death. Parasitic infections are more frequently encountered in tropical and subtropical areas, where they constitute the leading cause of serious infectious diseases. A warm and moist climate, poor sanitation, low socioeconomic status, and inadequate diet are among the important factors contributing to the prevalence of parasitic diseases in these areas. Many of the previously regarded "tropical diseases" are in reality cosmopolitan. The rise of immigration from tropical and subtropical areas and the advent of worldwide tourism have contributed to the increasing incidence of parasitism in temperate climates.

Children are infected with parasites more frequently than adults, owing for the most part to the infant's "oral" behavior and to his inability to ward off the bite of an arthropod vector. Furthermore, during the first decade of life there is greater morbidity and mortality from parasitic infection as a consequence of the lack of acquired humoral and tissue immunity in the young host. In southeast Asia, for example, malaria still remains a leading cause of infant mortality.

14.51
HELMINTHIC DISEASES

The word "helminth," derived from the Greek, means worm and is usually used to refer to five phyla: the roundworms (Phylum Nematoda), flukes and tapeworms (Phylum Platyhelminthes), the leeches (Class Hirudinea, Phylum Annelida), and two other phyla of little medical interest, the Acanthocephala and Nematomorpha. Diseases caused by helminths are summarized in Table 24.

Diseases Caused by Nematodes (Roundworms)

The nematodes are cylindrical, unsegmented, elongated white organisms. The parasitic species infecting man range from a fraction of a millimeter to well over a meter in length. The female is usually larger than the male, in some species by almost a thousandfold!

The nematode integument consists of a tough, resistant, relatively impermeable, noncellular, outer cuticle, secreted by an immediately underlying epithelial layer, the hypodermis. The cuticle may be smooth, striated, or adorned with spines. Suspended within the pseudocoelom, or body cavity, are a complete digestive tract, primitive excretory and nervous systems, and a highly developed reproductive system. The daily egg-laying capacity of some species may exceed a quarter of a million. It is understandable that these parasites have thrived so successfully throughout the moist warm areas of the world.

Nematodes have four larval stages, a molt separating each, and emerging from the final molt is a fifth stage, the immature adult. Depending upon the species, the initial molt may occur within the ovum (*Trichuris, Ascaris*), in the soil as free-living larvae (*Necator, Ancylostoma*), or in an intermediate host (*Wuchereria, Loa*). The final molts then occur in the definitive host.

The mode of entry into the final host may be by ingestion of infective ova (*Ascaris, Enterobius*), penetration of the skin by infective larvae (*Necator, Strongyloides*), or inoculation of the larvae by an insect bite (*Filaria*).

Ascariasis

Ascariasis is caused by infection with the giant intestinal roundworm, *Ascaris lumbricoides*. The ancient Greeks and Romans singled out this worm as the most common intestinal parasite, and it remains as the most frequently encountered and widely distributed helminth to this day. Stoll has estimated a world incidence of 644,400,000 with 3,000,000 infected in North America alone. It is the largest intestinal roundworm commonly infecting man; females measure 20 to 40 cm, males 15 to 30 cm. According to Brown and Cort, the female contains as many as 27,000,000 eggs at one time and may lay approximately 200,000 eggs a day. These broadly ovoid eggs are 45 to 75 μ in length and 35 to 50 μ wide (Fig. 27A and B). The fertilized egg consists of a remarkably impervious thin inner shell, a thick, transparent midlayer, and the characteristic, often bile-stained, mammillated outer shell. Unfertilized eggs are broader and longer (about 90 μ by 45 μ) and usually lack the albuminoid mammillated outer coat.

The eggs, which are passed in the feces, continue their development and become infective after the first-stage larva molts within the egg. The eggs are remarkably resistant to drying, low temperatures,

TABLE 24. *Human Parasitic Infections: Helminthes*

Disease	Parasite	Location in Man	Transmission	Typical Clinical Findings	Diagnosis	Treatment	Age-Incidence
NEMATODES Ascariasis	*Ascaris lumbricoides*	Adult: small intestine Larvae: lung	Ingestion of eggs from soil or food	Vague abdominal distress, nervousness, cough during lung stage	Eggs in feces	Piperazine	Most prevalent 2–14 years
Visceral larva migrans	*Toxocara canis, T. cati*	Liver, lung, kidneys, heart, brain, eye, striated muscle	Ingestion of eggs from soil	Hepatomegaly, eosinophilia, fever, hyperglobulinemia, geophagy	Clinical or biopsy	Thiabendazole (?)	2–15 years
Enterobiasis	*Enterobius vermicularis*	Ileocecal region	Ingestion of eggs	Perianal pruritis	Scotch tape swab	Piperazine, pyrvinium pamoate	Most prevalent 5–14 years; sharpest increase 2–5 years
Trichuriasis	*Trichuris trichura*	Ileocecal region	Ingestion of eggs from soil or food	Generally slight abdominal discomfort	Eggs in feces	Thiabendazole, hexylresorcinol, dichlorvos (?)	Most prevalent 5–10 years; heaviest infections 5 years of age
Hookworm disease	a. *Ancylostoma duodenale* b. *Necator americanus*	Small intestine	Larva penetrates skin	Abdominal pain and anemia	Eggs in feces	a. Bephenium hydroxynaphthoate b. Tetrachlorethylene	Infancy to peak incidence 16–30 years
Cutaneous larva migrans	*Ancylostoma braziliense, A. caninum*	Skin	Larva penetrates skin	Pruritus; inflammatory serpiginous skin lesions	Physical exam	Freezing Thiabendazole	Beyond infancy, sharpest increase 2–5 years with peak at 5–14 years
Strongyloidiasis	*Strongyloides stercoralis*	Small intestine	Larva penetrates skin	Diarrhea, abdominal discomfort	Larvae in feces	Thiabendazole	Children and adults, especially in children's institutions
Trichinosis	*Trichinella spiralis*	Early: small intestinal wall Late: striated muscle cysts	Ingestion of cysts in pork	Early: diarrhea, fever, eosinophilia, orbital edema Late: muscle pain	Skin test, biopsy	Cortisone; early: thiabendazole	All age groups, usually above 2 years
Bancroft's filariasis	*Wuchereria bancrofti*	Lymphatics, lymph nodes	Mosquito inoculation of larvae	Lymphangitis, fever, lymphedema	Microfilariae in blood (8:00 P.M.–2:00 A.M. in nocturnal forms), serologic tests	Diethylcarbamazine, surgery	Infection begins in infancy; disease seen in adolescents and adults
Malayan filariasis	*Brugia malayi*	Lymphatics, lymph nodes	Mosquito inoculation of larvae	Lymphangitis, lymphadenitis, lymphedema	Microfilariae in peripheral blood smear, serologic tests	Diethylcarbamazine, surgery	Infection begins in infancy; disease seen in adolescents and adults
Onchocerciasis	*Onchocerca volvulus*	Subcutaneous tissues	Inoculation of larvae by "black fly" (*Simulium*)	Subcutaneous nodules, blindness	Microfilariae in skin biopsy	Excision of nodules, diethylcarbamzine	In Central and S. America frequent in children less than 10 years. In Africa more often in children older than 10 years

Disease	Organism	Location	Mode of infection	Symptoms	Diagnosis	Treatment	Age groups
Loaiasis	*Loa loa*	Subcutaneous tissues	Inoculation of larvae by "deerflies" (*Chrysops*)	Fugitive swelling and inflammation	Microfilariae in peripheral blood smear in daytime	Excision of worm, diethylcarbamazine	Older children and adults
Dracontiasis	*Dracunculus medinensis*	Subcutaneous tissues	Ingestion of "water flea" (*Cyclops*)	Cutaneous ulcer, subcutaneous tunnels	Physical examination	Removal of worm, niridazole	Children after weaning (2-3 years)
TREMATODES							
Schistosomiasis	a. *Schistosoma mansoni*	Venules of large intestine	Cercariae penetrate skin	Early: fever, dysentery Late: hepatic insufficiency	Eggs in feces, rectal biopsy, liver biopsy	Stibophen, miracil D	Especially in children, 4 years of age and over
	b. *S. japonicum*	Venules of small intestine	Cercariae penetrate skin	Early: fever, GI complaints Late: hepatic insufficiency	Eggs in feces, liver biopsy, rectal biopsy	Tartar emetic, stibophen	
	c. *S. haematobium*	Venules of urinary bladder	Cercariae penetrate skin	Early: fever (esp. white child), urticaria, cough Late: urinary tract problems	Eggs in urine, cystoscopic examination	Stibophen, miracil D, tartar emetic	
Fascioliasis	*Fasciola hepatica*	Biliary ducts	Ingestion of metacercariae on vegetation	Biliary tract symptoms	Eggs in feces or duodenal aspirate	Emetine, bithionol	Older children, adolescents, and especially adults
Clonorchiasis	*Clonorchis sinensis*	Biliary ducts	Ingestion of metacercariae of freshwater fish	Biliary tract symptoms	Eggs in feces or duodenal aspirate	Chloroquine	Frequent reinfection beginning early childhood Disease in later adulthood
Fasciolopsiasis	*Fasciolopsis buski*	Small intestine	Ingestion of metacercariae on aquatic vegetation	Diarrhea, abdominal pain	Eggs in feces	Hexylresorcinol, tetrachlorethylene	Young children and adults In the first decade disease most severe
Paragonimiasis	*Paragonimus westermani*	Lung	Ingestion of metacercariae from crabs and crayfish	Rusty or blood-streaked sputum, fever	Eggs in sputum or feces	Bithionol, chloroquine	Infection often acquired during first decade
CESTODES							
Diphyllobothriasis	*Diphyllobothrium latum*	Small intestine	Ingestion of plerocercoid larva in fish	Usually asymptomatic; rarely, pernicious anemia or abdominal discomfort	Eggs in feces	Quinacrine, yomesan (niclosamide)	Occasional cases in childhood
Sparganosis	*Spirometra spp.*	Subcutaneous and muscle tissues	Ingestion of larvae or application of infected meat poultices	Fever, hypersensitivity reactions, pain and induration	Biopsy	Excision	All age groups

799

TABLE 24. (continued)

Disease	Parasite	Location in Man	Transmission	Typical Clinical Findings	Diagnosis	Treatment	Age-Incidence
Taeniasis solium	*Taenia solium*	Small intestine	Ingestion of cysticerci in pork	Usually asymptomatic; occasional abdominal discomfort	Eggs in feces and gravid proglottids with 7-13 uterine branches	Quinacrine, Yomesan	Gradual increase above the age of 2
Cysticercosis cellulosae	*Cysticercus cellulosae*	Muscle, central nervous system, eye	Ingestion of eggs in hog feces	Neurologic, visual symptoms	X-ray	Excision	Gradual increase above the age of 2
Taeniasis saginata	*Taenia saginata*	Small intestine	Ingestion of cysticerci in beef	Usually asymptomatic; occasional abdominal upset or toxic symptoms	Eggs in feces and gravid proglottids with more than 15 uterine branches	Quinacrine, Yomesan	Gradual increase above the age of 2
Hymenolepiasis nana	*Hymenolepis nana*	Small intestine	Ingestion of eggs from human feces	Abdominal discomfort	Eggs in feces	Quinacrine, Yomesan	Children 2-15 years
Hymenolepiasis diminuta	*Hymenolepis diminuta*	Small intestine	Accidental ingestion of insects infected with cysts	Usually asymptomatic	Eggs in feces	Quinacrine, Yomesan	Almost exclusively in children under 3 years
Hydatid disease	*Echinococcus granulosis*	Liver, lung, central nervous system	Ingestion of eggs from dog feces	Often asymptomatic, signs of intracranial pressure, cough, intraabdominal mass	Physical exam, x-ray, serologic	Surgical removal	Infection acquired in infancy, childhood
Dipylidiasis	*Dipylidium caninum*	Small intestine	Ingestion of cysticercoid in flea	Vague abdominal complaints	Eggs or proglottids in feces	Quinacrine, Yomesan	Almost exclusively in children and infants

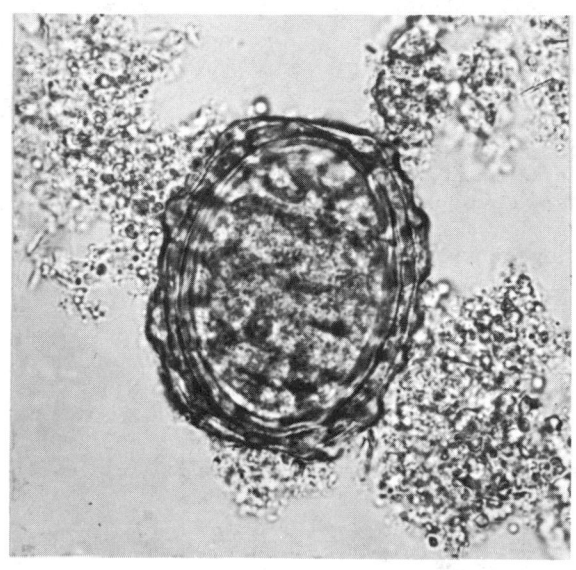

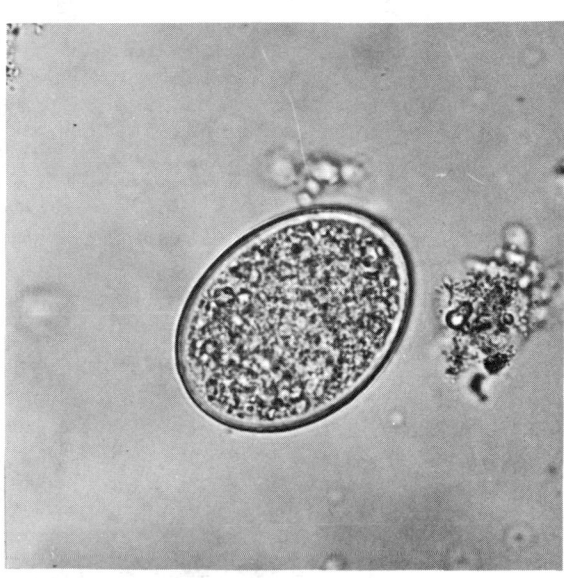

A   B

Fig. 27. *Ascaris lumbricoides.* A. Typical egg passed in fresh feces. B. Decorticate *ovum.* ×448.

and many chemicals. Development may be as rapid as several weeks, but in adverse situations can be delayed for extended periods, only to resume when suitable conditions return. Children often infect themselves and others by playing in the same areas where they eliminate their wastes. In regions where human wastes are used as fertilizer, as in the Orient, *Ascaris* infection is especially frequent.

Eggs containing the infective second-stage larvae never hatch in the soil; however, when ingested and stimulated by enzymes in the duodenum the larvae emerge actively from a small tear in the weakened egg shell. They quickly traverse the intestinal mucosa and enter the mesenteric lymphatics and venules. The larvae enter the portal circulation, reaching the pulmonary vascular bed, where they usually perforate the alveolar endothelium and epithelium to enter the alveolar space. They molt twice, and by the tenth day, fourth-stage larvae ascend the respiratory tree to the epiglottis and are swallowed (Fig. 28). The vast majority of ascarids finally settle in the jejunum. Following a fourth and final molt, copulation occurs, and mature females begin ovipositing in 2 to 2½ months.

PATHOLOGY. As with many of the helminthic diseases, the pathology found during the initial or larval migrating stages is quite distinct from that caused by adult worms. Intestinal penetration and migration through the liver are usually of little pathologic importance. Invasion of the respiratory system by migrating larvae, however, results in alveolar hemorrhages, and pulmonary damage can be extensive, especially if there are large numbers of larvae migrating. In young children *Ascaris* pneumonia (Löffler's

pneumonia) may be particularly serious, resulting in confluent bronchopneumonia, in which the alveoli are filled with red blood cells, eosinophils, fibrin, and polymorphonuclear leucocytes.

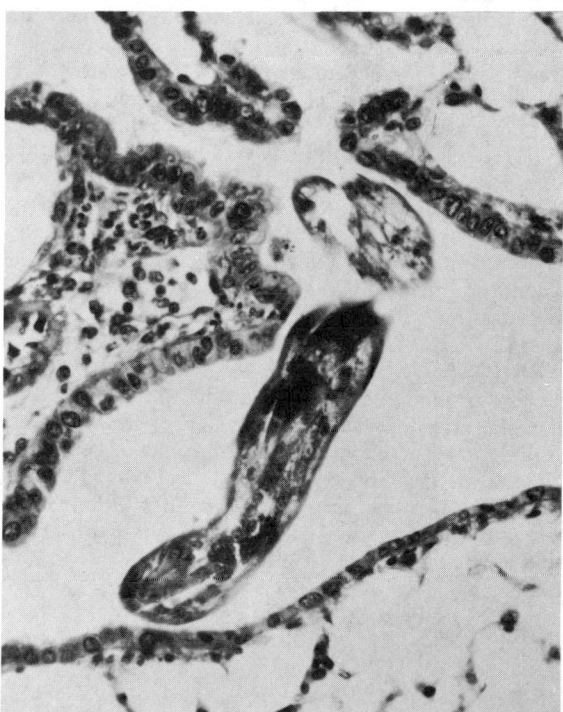

Fig. 28. *Ascaris* larvae in the lung of an experimental animal. ×320.

Occasionally, larvae may traverse the pulmonary circulation and produce serious lesions in the eye, central nervous system, and kidney. Thus, larval ascariasis can, on occasion, resemble visceral larva migrans (see below). There may be slight pathologic manifestations or none at all, with a small number of adult worms in the jejunum. Heavy infections, especially in children, may necessitate surgical intervention as a result of intestinal obstruction or occasionally of perforation. Rarely, ascarids may migrate into the biliary and pancreatic ducts causing jaundice or acute pancreatitis.

SYMPTOMS. During the period of larval invasion and migration, cough, dyspnea, fever of 103 to 105° F, bronchial rales, and dullness to percussion of the chest may be evident. Hemoptysis may occur, and larvae may be found in the sputum. Radiologic evidence of consolidation and widening of the pulmonary hilus may be seen, and a markedly elevated eosinophil count is often found (Löffler's syndrome). During this phase, other manifestations of hypersensitivity, such as urticaria, are frequently encountered in individuals who are repeatedly infected. In young children, pulmonary ascariasis may have a fatal termination in about 0.2 percent of cases.

Adult worms in the small intestine, unless they are numerous, are generally associated with few symptoms. They are presumed to subsist on semidigested food in the lumen, although there are occasional reports of erythrocyte digestion. The most frequently noted symptoms in children are vague epigastric pains, nausea, vomiting, and anorexia. At times, severe, intermittent, colicky abdominal pain may be the result of partial intestinal obstruction. The more serious problems encountered with *Ascaris* infection result from migration of adult worms into the bile and pancreatic ducts and complete intestinal obstruction. These complications may follow tetrachlorethylene therapy for concurrent hookworm disease or occur in debilitating illness when the environment becomes unsuitable for the worms' requirements. Worms may occasionally migrate cephalad, and emerge through the mouth or nose, or posteriorly and pass per rectum. These dramatic events cause a great deal of alarm in the patients and parents.

DIAGNOSIS. Generally, the diagnosis is established by finding and identifying eggs in the feces. Occasionally, an adult worm is passed or worms may be outlined with contrast medium during the course of a radiologic examination.

TREATMENT. The drug of choice for eliminating the adult worm is piperazine citrate (Antepar), available as a syrup or tablet. The dosage is:

DAILY DOSE OF PIPERAZINE CITRATE

Weight	Dose, grams
up to 30 lb	1.0
30–50	2.0
50–100	3.0
over 100	3.5

Therapy is given daily for two consecutive days. In severe cases it may be repeated after one week. Alternatively, thiabendazole may be used, 25 mg/kg twice a day for two days, but side effects are more commonly encountered and the overall cure rate is somewhat less. Larvae are not affected by any anthelmintics employed for therapy.

Intestinal obstruction often responds to medical management, consisting of duodenal suction, parenteral fluids, electrolyte correction, and the instillation of piperazine into the duodenal tube. If this fails, surgical intervention is required to remove the obstructing worms. No special effort should be made to remove all the worms in the intestinal tract.

PROGNOSIS. Individuals tolerate this infection quite well unless large numbers of larvae are migrating through the lungs or intestinal obstruction intervenes.

PREVENTION. Sanitary disposal of wastes, proper cooking of foods grown in night soil, and education, especially of children, would go a long way in decreasing the incidence of ascariasis.

Visceral Larva Migrans

Young children are frequently abnormal hosts of the dog ascarid, *Toxocara canis,* and occasionally of *Toxocara cati* of the cat. The worms are unable to complete their usual development in the human host, and provoke a severe tissue reaction causing considerable damage and, at times, acute disease.

Infected dogs seed the neighborhood with eggs, which proceed to develop into infective ova containing second-stage larvae. When ingested, the larvae hatch in the upper intestinal tract, penetrate the intestinal wall, gaining access to the mesenteric vessels, and usually migrate to the liver, less frequently to the lungs, kidneys, heart, brain, eye, and striated muscle.

Small children are most frequently infected, presumably as a result of their promiscuity with dirt as well as their close association with pets.

PATHOLOGY. Unlike human ascarid larvae, those of *Toxocara* are unable to complete their development in the human host, and provoke an intense inflammatory host reaction in the organs invaded. Lesions are necrotizing or granulomatous and heavily infiltrated with eosinophils. The larvae eventually are encapsulated by a dense fibrous wall and die. The liver is most frequently found to contain these tiny, gray-white granulomatous nodules. The retina and vitreous are occasionally invaded, sometimes leading to blindness.

SYMPTOMS. In mild infections the disease can be virtually asymptomatic, eosinophilia being the only clue. The most characteristic clinical picture, however, especially in a small child, is hepatomegaly, eosinophilia, fever, cough, and wheezing. On occasion, neurologic signs or impairment of vision may be the only manifestation of the infection. Pulmonary embarrassment can, at times, be severe. Hyperglobulinemia is often found. Geophagy is commonly reported in a large percentage of infected children.

DIAGNOSIS. Although diagnosis is usually made on clinical grounds, liver biopsy provides the best opportunity to make a definitive diagnosis. Serologic methods are not entirely reliable since cross-reactions with many nematodes may occur. Recent studies indicate, however, that the bentonite flocculation and/or indirect hemagglutination tests may be sufficiently specific, especially if differential absorption of *Ascaris* antibody is carried out prior to running the reaction with *Toxocara* antigen. As with several other helminthic infections, markedly elevated anti-A titers have been reported to be associated with visceral larva migrans infection.

PROGNOSIS. In most cases the prognosis is quite favorable. If the infection is heavy, however, or if larvae invade critical foci, the outcome can be serious or even fatal.

TREATMENT. Although thiabendazole has been advocated as specific therapy for this infection, it is uncertain whether this compound alters the course of the disease. Similarly, it is not yet clear if steroid therapy is helpful in severe cases.

PREVENTION. Periodic eradication of *Toxocara* infection in household pets by anthelmintics, and keeping children away from areas, such as sandboxes, in which dogs, and especially cats, defecate, may also be helpful.

Enterobiasis

Enterobiasis is caused by the pinworm, *Enterobius vermicularis*. Although pinworm infection is worldwide, it is more common in temperate climates, where children are more heavily clothed and in closer association with one another. Pinworms infect people in all socioeconomic levels, but residents of institutions or dormitories and family groups are more often affected; children are more susceptible than adults.

Adult worms are small, yellow-white, and elongated; typically they inhabit the appendix and nearby areas of ileum and ascending colon. Females are 8 to 13 mm and males 2 to 5 mm in length. The distended uterus may contain as many as 17,000 eggs, many of which are deposited on the perianal and perineal skin by the migrating gravid female. At room temperature, in humid conditions, the ova will survive 2 to 3 weeks, resisting destruction by usual household disinfectants. They are light and will float in air, especially when the bed linens or clothes are cast off, thereupon being ingested or inhaled and later swallowed.

Frequently the external migration of the gravid female is associated with intense perianal pruritus and scratching, so that anus-to-finger-to-mouth transmission is most common. Retroinfection may also occur when larvae of deposited eggs hatch and migrate back into the intestine, developing to maturity in 2 to 2½ weeks. Embryonated eggs, when deposited, usually require but a few hours to become infective, and, if swallowed, the larvae escape in the duodenum and develop to maturity in the cecal area within 2 to 6 weeks.

PATHOLOGY. The majority of infections are without significant pathologic lesions. The intense pruritus ani may provoke such severe scratching that local bleeding, secondary pyogenic infection, and lichenification may result.

Whether or not pinworms are a primary cause of appendicitis remains unsettled. Most pathologists consider their presence in an acutely inflamed appendix an unimportant incidental finding (Fig. 29).

In young females, the adult worms have been known to migrate into the vagina, uterus, and fallopian tubes, being encapsulated finally in the peritoneal cavity.

SYMPTOMS. Pruritus ani, most often intense at night, awakens the child or causes restless sleep. The child may become irritable and nervous. Perianal itching in young girls may lead to vaginitis and frequent masturbation. A significant eosinophilia seldom accompanies the infection.

PROGNOSIS. Usually prognosis is good, with few or no serious effects. Complete eradication of the infection is difficult, since reinfection occurs so readily.

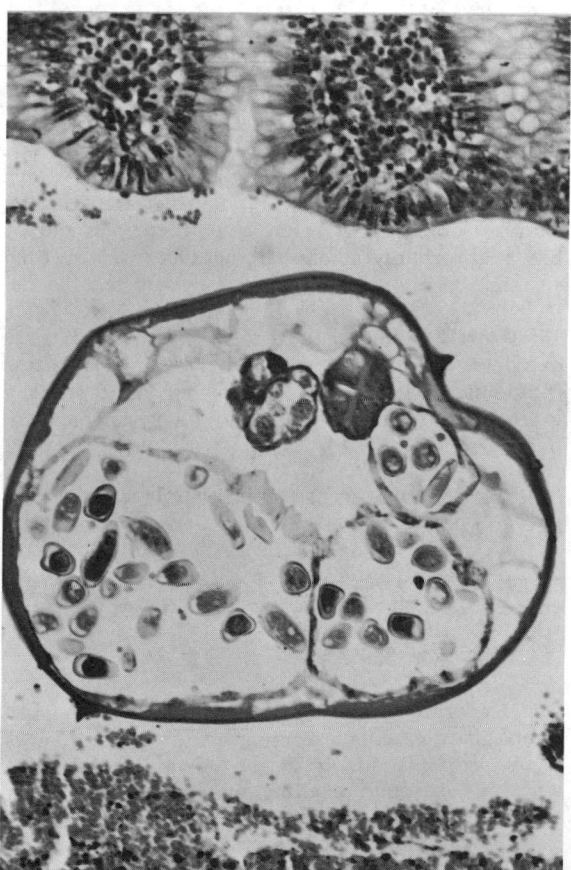

Fig. 29. Cross section of a female pinworm (*Enterobius vermicularis*) in the lumen of the appendix. ×140.

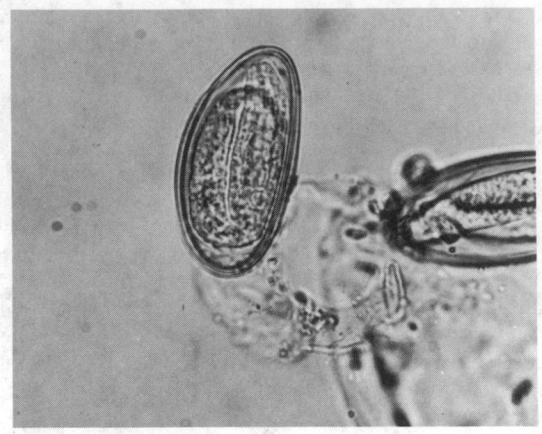

Fig. 30. Eggs of pinworm (*Enterobius vermicularis*) on Scotch Tape preparation. ×448.

DIAGNOSIS. Nocturnal perianal pruritus in children with mild eosinophilia strongly suggests pinworm infection. Small creamy-white worms often will be found if examination of the perianal region is made when the child is awakened by itching. Inasmuch as ova are seen infrequently in the stools, the Scotch tape swab technique (NIH swab) is the diagnostic method of choice. A 2.5-inch (6.0-cm) piece of Scotch tape is folded with its sticky side out over the end of a wooden tongue blade. It is firmly applied against either side of the perianal region. Next, the tape is placed sticky side down on a microscope slide and is examined directly for pinworm ova (Fig. 30). It is preferable to take the swabs in the morning immediately before the patient gets out of bed, and certainly before bathing. One swab on each of three consecutive days is usually sufficient to detect the eggs.

TREATMENT. There are several preparations that are excellent for treatment of enterobiasis. Piperazine compounds, which are highly effective, are best taken in the morning before breakfast for seven consecutive days.

DAILY DOSE OF PIPERAZINE CITRATE

Weight	Dose
up to 15 lb	250 mg
16–30	500 mg
31–60	1.0 g
over 60	2.0 g

Pyrvinium pamoate, which is a red cyanine dye, often gives excellent results with a single dose of 5 mg/kg body weight. Care should be exercised, since it will stain clothing and occasionally cause nausea and vomiting.

Since transmission and reinfection occur so readily, the physician often elects to treat the entire family simultaneously. Vigorous hygienic measures should also be instituted. Daily baths, frequent wash-ing of hands, laundering and boiling of bedsheets, underwear, and nightclothes, and vigorous vacuum cleaning all help to control reinfection. In the author's experience a second course of therapy three weeks after completion of the first has resulted in nearly 100 percent cure.

PREVENTION. Personal cleanliness is probably the most effective means of prevention. Fingernails should be cut short and hands washed frequently and vigorously. Infected children should sleep alone and wear tight-fitting pajamas. The bed clothes and linens should be boiled daily. It is nearly impossible, however, to control dust-borne infective eggs.

Trichuriasis

Trichuriasis is produced by the whipworm *Trichuris trichiura*. This nematode is most characteristic, having an attenuated whiplike anterior and a broader, fleshier posterior portion. The males are from 3 to 4.5 cm in length with a coiled posterior end; the females are from 3.5 to 5.0 cm with a blunt posterior end. The eggs are typically barrel-shaped, about 50 by 22 μ; they are usually bile-stained, the ends containing unstained polar plugs (Fig. 31). Adult worms live in the cecum with their anterior portions buried in the mucosa. Occasionally, the appendix and other portions of the large intestine are infected. The female lays large numbers of eggs daily which pass out in feces. After 2 to 4 weeks in warm, shady, moist soil an infective stage larva is present within the ovum. When ingested, the larva hatches in the upper small intestine, temporarily penetrates the crypts of Lieberkühn, where it feeds and develops, and then slowly makes its way to the cecal region, becoming a mature egg-laying adult in about 1 to 3 months.

Whipworm infection is cosmopolitan, but is far more common in warm, moist regions. The prevalence of infection is highest in children 5 to 15 years of age due to their relaxed hygienic habits. Con-

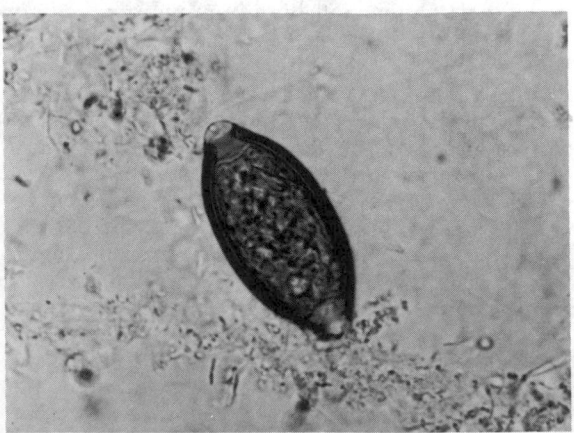

Fig. 31. Egg of the whipworm (*Trichuris trichiura*) in feces. ×280.

taminated food and water may be a source of infection as well.

PATHOLOGY. The worms produce a small inflammatory focus at the site of attachment to the intestinal mucosa, and ingest whole blood as a part of their diet. Heavy infections may be associated with superficial mucosal erosions, colitis, and, in young children, rectal prolapse. Individuals on marginal diets who have heavy whipworm infections may also develop a microcytic hypochromic anemia due to relentless chronic blood loss. Eosinophilia up to 25 percent can be found.

SYMPTOMS. Light infections are usually without clinical manifestations; occasionally, there may be complaints of anorexia, insomnia, or vague abdominal pain. In moderate, uncomplicated clinical infections, abdominal pain, often localized to the right lower quadrant, flatulence, fever of 99° to 101° F, nausea and vomiting, weight loss, and pruritus are the most frequent complaints. Heavy infections may be accompanied by diarrhea, tenesmus, blood-streaked stools, and rectal prolapse.

PROGNOSIS. In light infections, prognosis is excellent. Heavy infections, however, can lead to serious complications unless the worms are eliminated.

DIAGNOSIS. Without laboratory stool examinations, trichuriasis is difficult to differentiate from other intestinal nematode infections. Concentration techniques readily reveal the characteristic ova.

TREATMENT. Although thiabendazole, 25 mg per kg twice a day for 3 days, is advocated, this drug will only reduce the infection. In symptomatic, heavy infections, when worms are present on the rectal mucosa, thiabendazole is ineffectual and one must then resort to hexylrescorcinol enemas in order to rid the patient of these parasites. First, the bowel is cleansed with saline enemas. Next, the skin of the buttocks, thighs, and perineum are protected by liberally coating with petrolatum. A 0.2 percent aqueous hexylrescorcinal enema is administered and retained for 30 minutes, and then expelled. This procedure can be repeated 3 or 4 times at 96 hour intervals.

Recently, a new compound, dichlorvos, has been reported to be highly effective for the eradication of whipworm, ascarids, and hookworm. This compound, which is a cholinesterase inhibitor, has been shown to be relatively free of adverse side effects in the adult patient population studied, when administered as a single oral dose of 6 to 12 mg per kg body weight.

PREVENTION. Personal cleanliness, such as the washing of dirty hands, and sanitary waste disposal would essentially eliminate trichuriasis.

Hookworm Disease

Since ancient times, hookworm infection has been one of the major diseases of mankind. It currently infects an estimated one fourth of the world's population. *Necator americanus,* so-called American hook-

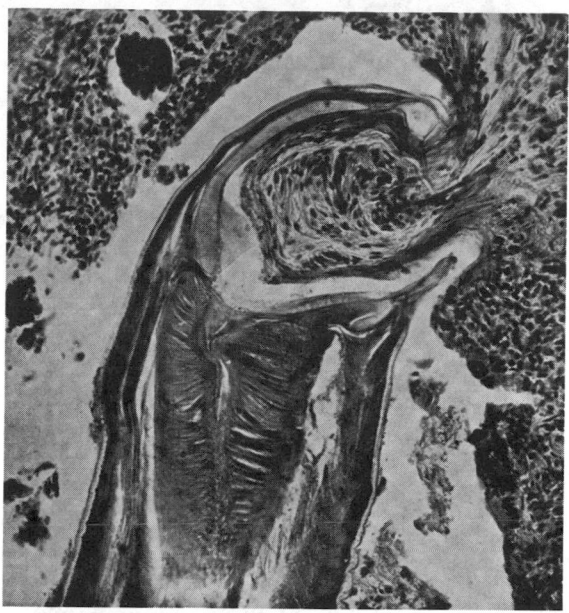

Fig. 32. Hookworm attached to intestinal wall. (From Hunter, Frye, and Swartzwelder. *Manual of Tropical Medicine,* 3rd ed. Courtesy of W. B. Saunders Co.)

worm, is the prevailing species in southern United States and most of the warm areas of the world. *Ancylostoma duodenale,* so-called Old World hookworm, is primarily a parasite of the Mediterranean basin, northern India, north China, Japan, and the west coast of South America. It accounts for approximately 15 percent of the world's hookworm infections.

Hookworms are about 1.0 cm long and 0.3 to 0.4 cm in greatest breadth, males being slightly smaller than females. They are creamy to gray-white and possess a distinctive oral or buccal capsule, containing cutting plates in *Necator* and two pairs of upper teeth in *Ancylostoma.* The posterior tip of the male forms a distinctive broad, transparent, umbrella-like copulatory bursa.

Adult hookworms reside in upper portions of the small intestine, attached to the mucosa by their buccal capsule (Fig. 32). A mature female lays thousands of eggs daily; the eggs are about 68 by 38 μ and of similar appearance in both species. Usually the eggs have reached the two- to eight-cell stage (Fig. 33A) when seen in the stool, although later stages may be found (Fig. 33B) if passage is delayed because of constipation.

If the eggs are deposited in warm, moist, sandy, shady soil they develop rapidly so that characteristic first-stage rhabditoid larvae hatch within 1 to 2 days. Growth is rapid, and a molt occurs after 3 days of feeding upon bacteria and fecal debris. The second-stage larvae continue to feed and grow, so that by the fifth to tenth day a second molt results in nonfeeding, filariform third-stage infective larvae.

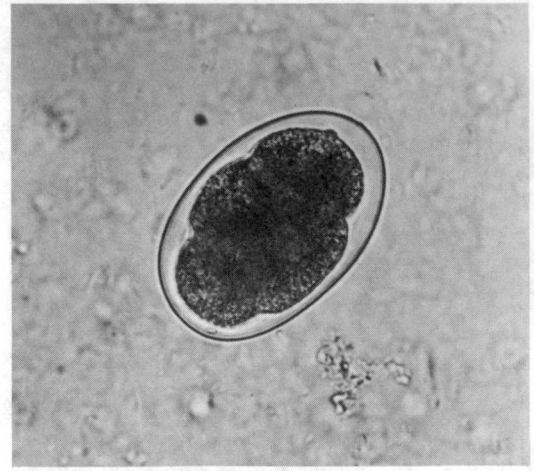 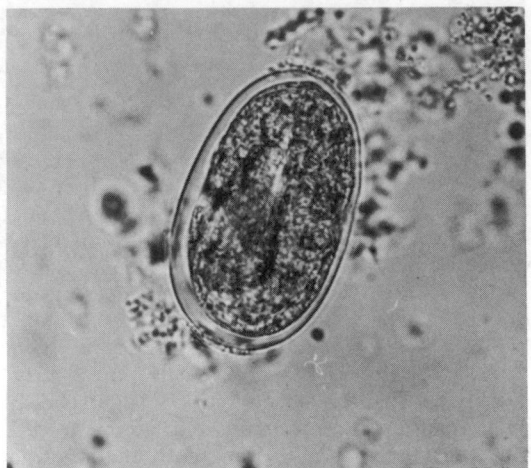

Fig. 33. Hookworm (*Necator americanus*) eggs recovered from feces. A. Typical 4-cell stage. B. Developing motile larva. ×448.

These are negatively geotropic and tend to rise to the top level of the moist soil, where they remain awaiting contact with human skin. They actively penetrate the skin, usually of the interdigital spaces of the bare feet, enter subcutaneous capillaries, and are carried to the lungs, where they penetrate the capillaries and enter the alveoli. The larvae next ascend the respiratory tree and are swallowed. During the latter period they undergo a third molt, forming a temporary buccal capsule by which they attach to the intestinal villi. After the fourth and final molt, they feed and grow to maturity, eggs appearing in the feces about 5 to 6 weeks after infection. While accidental ingestion of infective-stage larvae of *Ancylostoma duodenale* will result in direct development of mature adults, migration through the lungs by *Necator americanus* seems to be indispensable.

PATHOLOGY.   Larvae of *Necator* often produce extensive subcutaneous damage beneath the site of invasion, and they, together with pyogenic bacteria carried in with the invading larvae, may cause a papulovesicular lesion that later ulcerates and eventually clears in about 10 to 14 days.

Lobular pulmonary consolidation is distinctly uncommon during the lung phase. The important abnormality is a microcytic hypochromic anemia resulting from chronic continuous sucking of the host's blood. It has been estimated that each worm may take in, and partially utilize, about 0.5 ml of blood a day. Blood loss of this magnitude may be well compensated if the worm burden is small in an otherwise healthy, well-nourished individual.

SYMPTOMS.   "Ground itch" is associated with the initial larval skin invasion by *Necator*. During the course of the initial infection there may be cough, low-grade fever, acute abdominal disturbances, intermittent diarrhea, and a markedly elevated eosinophilia. As the disease becomes chronic, even with frequent reinfection, the symptoms depend primarily upon the individual's diet, state of health, and ac-

quired immunity. Therefore, patients with comparable worm burdens may be either symptomatic or relatively asymptomatic, the latter complaining only of vague abdominal discomfort. Similarly, anemia may be completely compensated by adequate diet, or the patient may complain of weakness, dizziness, and weight loss. As the worm burden increases there may be palpitations, tachycardia, and edema, associated with either hypoproteinemia and/or congestive heart failure. In children, physical and sexual development may be retarded. Picas such as geophagy ("dirt eaters") are often seen among infected children.

PROGNOSIS.   If poor nutrition is corrected, and specific anthelmintic therapy is provided, recovery is usual.

DIAGNOSIS.   Definitive diagnosis requires the identification of the eggs in the feces. Occasionally, rhabditoid larvae may be found in stools, and must be differentiated from rhabditoid larvae of *Strongyloides stercoralis*, which possess a much shorter buccal chamber. In tropical areas, of course, infection with both of these worms is frequently encountered. The ova of *Trichostrongylus orientalis* also must be differentiated from those of hookworm. The clinical picture of hookworm usually is not sufficiently distinctive to rely upon clinical impression alone.

TREATMENT.   Tetrachlorethylene remains the drug of choice for *Necator* infection and should be given in the morning on an empty stomach. Post-treatment purge is not desirable. The use of this compound in the presence of *Ascaris* infection is not recommended. There seems to be no reason, however, why *Ascaris* should not be eliminated first with piperazine (p. 802), after which hookworm therapy can be initiated safely. The usual pediatric dose of tetrachlorethylene is 0.06 ml per pound. The maximum dose is 5 ml. Treatment can be repeated after 2 weeks if necessary. Bephenium hydroxynaphthoate (Alcopara) is probably the drug of choice for the treatment of *Ancylostoma duodenale* infection. However, it is reported not to be as effective a therapy for *Necator americanus*. Treatment should be instituted on an empty stomach and food withheld for two hours after treatment. Alcopara is supplied in 5-g packets. The oral dose for older children and adults is 5 g taken twice a day for 2 days, with *Ancylostoma,* and for 3 days with *Necator* infections. Children weighing under 20 kg (44 lbs) receive 5 g once a day for 2 or 3 days. Since Alcopara has an unpleasant bitter taste, it can be administered in chocolate milk or a carbonated beverage. Nausea and/or vomiting may occasionally be encountered, but, in general, the drug is without serious side effects. It has been stated that if bephenium were to be absorbed in hypertensive individuals, it could result in a transient fall in blood pressure.

PREVENTION. The control of hookworm infection depends upon education of individuals in rural communities. Sanitary disposal of feces and wearing of shoes have had a marked effect in the reduction of infection in southern United States. Improvement in the nutritional status of infected individuals often will alleviate all clinical signs of infection.

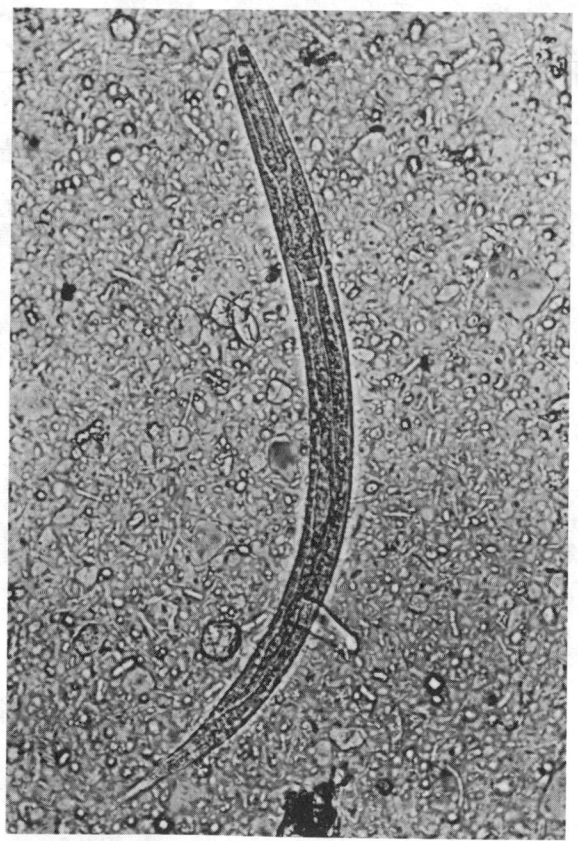

Fig. 34. Rhabditoid larva of *Strongyloides stercoralis* passed in feces. ×280.

Cutaneous Larva Migrans

Creeping eruption, or cutaneous larva migrans, is caused most frequently by infection with the filariform larvae of *Ancylostoma braziliense* which ordinarily infect dogs and cats, although other species of larval hookworms such as *A. caninum, Necator americanus,* and *Uncinaria stenocephala* have been incriminated. *Strongyloides stercoralis* (see below) occasionally causes a similar picture. In Southeast Asia the larvae of *Gnathostoma spinigerum* may cause creeping eruption, as will the fly larvae of the horse bot, *Gastrophilis.* These larvae migrate in the stratum germinativum, creating serpiginous dermal tunnels with marked erythema and pruritis. Secondary bacterial infection is common. The larvae may wander in the skin for several weeks to months, but they generally fail to gain access to the circulation.

Creeping eruption is frequently encountered in the southern United States, especially in the summer and fall months, in bathers, workmen, and children who have been exposed to moist, sandy soil contaminated with dog and cat feces. Generally, the infection is self-limited and requires no treatment. In persistent or severe infections, topical therapy by freezing with ethyl chloride has been used with varying success. Recent reports suggest thiabendazole, 25 mg per kg twice a day for 3 to 4 days, may be helpful. Topical application of a 10 percent aqueous suspension of thiabendazole has been advocated. Periodic anthelmintic therapy of dogs and cats should help reduce exposure to these worms.

Strongyloidiasis

Strongyloides stercoralis is the etiologic agent of strongyloidiasis. The disease is primarily one of warm areas, and is found sporadically in temperate climates. The parasitic female is an extremely small (2.2 by 0.04 mm), nearly transparent, thin worm, hence the name "threadworm." She resides buried in the mucosa of the upper small intestine, feeding and depositing eggs. Rhabditoid larvae hatch within the tissues and penetrate the mucosa to enter the lumen; these usually pass out with the feces (Fig. 34) After being deposited in the soil, the larvae may develop into infective-stage filariform larvae either directly, or indirectly, after one or more intervening free-living generations. In warm and very moist soil with organic debris, free-living generations develop within 24 to 36 hours into sexually mature males and females which mate and lay eggs. Rhabditoid larvae, which hatch in the soil, may repeat the free-living cycle indefinitely or may molt, producing filariform infective-stage larvae. Upon contact, they penetrate the skin, enter a subcutaneous capillary, and are carried to the lungs. Here they penetrate the capillary wall and enter alveoli, where they molt several times to become adolescent worms. They next ascend the respiratory tree, are swallowed, and invade the intestinal mucosa. It is not entirely clear where copulation occurs, or if parthenogenesis is the rule. Parasitic males have not been unequivocally identified in this species. If rhabditoid larvae molt in the intestinal lumen while passing down the bowel and become infective filariform larvae, auotinfection may occur. Filariform larvae may invade the mucosa of the ileum or large bowel, enter portal vessels to be carried to the lungs, and finally journey to the intestine to mature within the mucosa. Occasionally, they pass out in the stool and penetrate the perianal skin, causing autoinfection or "cutaneous larva migrans." It is entirely possible, therefore, that a relatively minor infection may become moderate to severe, and individuals may maintain their infection indefinitely without further outside reinfection.

The incidence of strongyloidiasis increases above 5 years of age, and is especially common in mental institutions, orphanages, and prisons.

PATHOLOGY.   Soon after the larvae penetrate the skin, pruritic erythematous blotches and papules appear. Giant urticarial lesions are seen in previously sensitized individuals. Serious pulmonary involvement is not often encountered, although there are occasional reports of transient patchy pneumonitis associated with marked eosinophilia (Löffler's syndrome). The principal lesion is found in the upper portions of the small intestine, where injury to the mucosa by both adults and migrating larvae may cause a severe duodenitis and jejunitis, with marked eosinophilic and mononuclear cell infiltration. In heavy infections, granulomatous inflammation and mucosal necrosis are extensive, leading to eventual fibrous scarring.

SYMPTOMS.   The initial larval invasion of the skin is accompanied by pruritus, and the pulmonary phase is often associated with a dry cough. Although mild infections may be entirely asymptomatic, a heavier worm burden is often accompanied by nausea, vomiting, epigastric pain, weakness, and mucous diarrhea, which may be exhausting and unrelenting. A sprue-like syndrome has been reported. Eosinophilia is nearly a constant finding with this infection, although it usually declines somewhat with chronicity.

PROGNOSIS.   Generally the prognosis is good, except in heavy, untreated cases. Absence of eosinophilia and presence of leucopenia are regarded as poor prognostic signs.

DIAGNOSIS.   The presence of rhabditoid larvae in the stool is diagnostic (Fig. 34). Care must be taken to distinguish the larvae of Strongyloides from those of hookworm, Trichostrongylus, and some other nonparasitic, fecal-inhabiting nematode larvae.

TREATMENT.   Thiabendazole (Mintezol), 25 mg per kg twice a day for 2 to 3 days, is the drug of choice. Side effects such as anorexia, dizziness, and nausea and/or vomiting are common. Diarrhea, pruritis, epigastric distress, and drowsiness may occasionally occur. Thiabendazole therapy has been associated

rarely with hyperglycemia, rash, leucopenia, hypotension, and bradycardia.

All individuals found to harbor this infection should receive therapy, inasmuch as fatal disseminated strongyloidiasis can occur in the elderly, the debilitated, and in individuals who may be undergoing therapy with steroids or other immunosuppressive agents.

PREVENTION.   Just as in hookworm infections, individuals should be cautioned against walking barefoot. Sanitary waste disposal together with education are most essential for control of this disease.

Trichinosis

Infection with Trichinella spiralis is found in most parts of the world in which raw or insufficiently cooked pork is consumed. Trichinosis, therefore, is comparatively common in the United States, Mexico, and Europe, and relatively unimportant in predominantly Moslem and Hindu countries.

When an individual ingests meat infected with Trichinella cysts, larvae excyst in the duodenum, invade the mucosa of the small intestine, and in from 5 to 7 days develop into tiny adults. After fertilization, the female continues to grow and may burrow deeply into the intestinal wall, where she begins to deposit larvae which invade the intestinal lymphatics and venules. About 1,000 to 1,500 larvae are discharged each day throughout the 1 to 4 months of life of the adult. By the second week, larvae are migrating throughout the body, and by the third week, encystment in striated muscle is in progress. Here the larvae may remain viable for years, but usually they succumb within 6 to 9 months, slowly calcifying.

Although human infection with these worms is a developmental blind alley, the disease is naturally perpetuated by cannibalistic rats. Pigs, bears, and other flesh-eating animals may be secondarily infected. Pigs fed unsterilized infected garbage are probably the main source of trichinous meat in eastern United States. From time to time, home-cooked sausage serves as the nidus of family, neighborhood, or church "epidemics." Ingestion of contaminated hamburger is another common source of infection. Generally, current meat-packing practices in the United States result in dispersing and diluting infected meat so that most infected individuals develop either mild or asymptomatic disease.

PATHOLOGY.   During the initial or intestinal stage of the disease there may be some petechiae and minor mucosal bleeding. The main lesions are found in striated muscle, where there is fiber hypertrophy, edema, and degeneration. An acute interstitial inflammatory exudate is commonly seen. Eventually the larvae become entombed in an ovoid cyst (Fig. 35). Although larvae do not encyst in the heart, their presence during migration often results in an acute myocarditis. Invasion of the central nervous system may provoke a nonsuppurative meningitis or

Fig. 35. Encysting larva of *Trichinella spiralis* in deltoid muscle. An acute inflammatory infiltrate is present about the fragmented muscle. ×448.

granulomatous inflammatory changes in the basal ganglia, medulla, and cerebellum. Eosinophilia may reach 90 percent during the height of larval invasion.

SYMPTOMS. Clinical symptoms depend primarily upon the number of worms ingested at any one time, as well as the number of larvae produced, and the sites of invasion. During the intestinal phase, invading larvae and adult worms often cause acute gastrointestinal symptoms, including nausea, vomiting, and diarrhea, as well as fever, diaphoresis, and urticaria. When larvae enter the general circulation, new symptoms may occur, so that edema of the eyelids and face, splinter hemorrhages of the nailbeds, fever, and cardiac and respiratory symptoms may become evident. Severe tenderness, pain, and spasm occur during the period of muscle invasion. Cardiac failure and death can occur at this time. Central nervous system symptoms include headache, stiff neck, and psychoses. Ocular involvement, especially periorbital edema and chemosis, is most typical and suggestive of the diagnosis. In patients surviving the period of muscular invasion, muscular tenderness is all that remains, gradually diminishing after about 12 to 18 months.

PROGNOSIS. Unless the infection is heavy, patients ordinarily do well.

DIAGNOSIS. Early diagnosis is difficult, unless one can elicit a history of eating raw or partially cooked pork. The presence of similar symptoms in members of the same family is often suggestive; however, other infections such as staphylococcal or salmonella food poisoning, shigellosis, and amebiasis must be considered. Eosinophilia, periorbital edema, and splinter nail hemorrhages are most characteristic. Later on, biopsy of the deltoid, biceps, or gastrocnemius muscles can provide the definitive diagnosis. The latex flocculation test becomes positive in 17 to 21 days and the complement-fixation tests, which become positive after 3 and 4 weeks, provide strong evidence for the diagnosis. In light infections muscle biopsy is often unrewarding, while serologic tests are diagnostic.

TREATMENT. Recent clinical trial suggests that thiabendazole, 25 mg per kg twice a day for 5 to 7 days, may be an effective remedy during the intestinal phase. It is not clear whether it is of benefit during the circulating or encysting stages. In human infections, administration of adrenocortical steroids during the period of larval invasion of the general circulation has been reported to reduce the febrile period and total duration of illness. In experimental studies, however, adrenocortical steroids cause a fourfold increase in invading larvae. They also suppressed immune reactions, favoring secondary infection.

PREVENTION. Since infection is primarily the result of eating raw or partially cooked pork and pork products, the disease can be prevented by thoroughly cooking the meat at 131 to 136° F for one hour. The thermal death point of the encysted larvae is from 143 to 162° F. Furthermore, larvae of *Trichinella* are killed by freezing for 36 hours at −27° C, 24 hours at −30° C, or 40 minutes at −35° C. The United States government does not inspect meat for infection by this worm; therefore, proper education in the preparation of pork and pork products is necessary. Boiling garbage before it is fed to hogs also will help to reduce the incidence of infection.

Dracontiasis

The guinea worm, *Dracunculus medinensis,* known since antiquity as the "fiery serpent," is found in Asia, Africa, and a few isolated regions in the western hemisphere. The female worm, which averages about 1,000 mm in length by 1 to 2 mm in diameter, usually lives in the subcutaneous tissues of the distal portions of the arms and legs. Here a papule, which forms near the anterior portion of the worm, vesiculates and ruptures, leaving an ulcer (Fig. 36). When the extremity is placed in water, a loop of the worm's uterus prolapses into the ulcer and freely discharges motile larvae into the water. This will recur each time the extremity is immersed, until the uterus is emptied and the adult worm dies, usually after several weeks. Thereafter, the larvae are ingested and mature in freshwater copepods of the genus *Cyclops.* When an individual drinks contaminated water, infective larvae are set free, penetrate the intestinal wall, and usually migrate to the retroperitoneal tissues, where they require about 8 to 12 months to mature. The female then migrates to the skin of an extremity in order to discharge her brood. The fate of the adult male worm is unknown.

In endemic areas infection begins in childhood, and individuals are reinfected repeatedly throughout life. Infection is uncommon before the age of 3, since young children and infants are breast-fed and seldom drink infected pond water.

PATHOLOGY AND SYMPTOMS. The presence of the worms in the deep tissues is usually without side

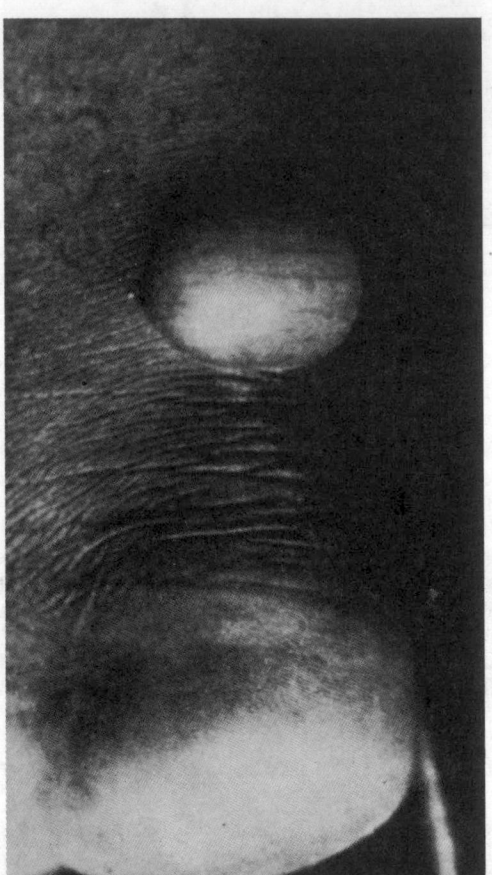

Fig. 36. Blister caused by the presence of the female guinea worm (*Dracunculus medinensis*) in the underlying skin. (From Basu. *Tropical Surgery*, 1965.)

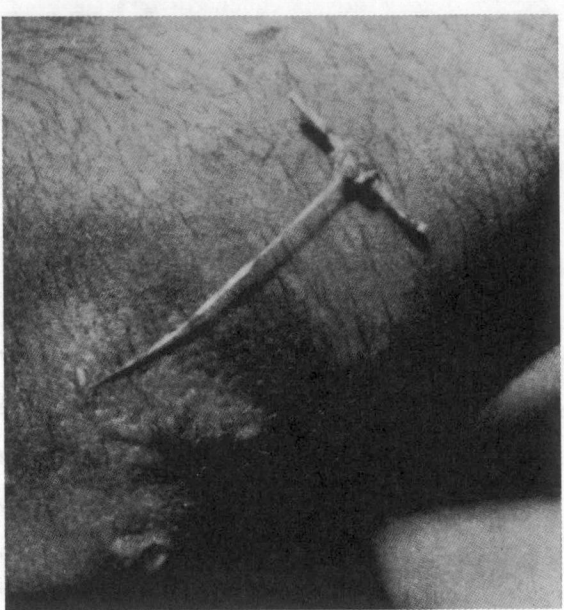

Fig. 37. The guinea worm is extricated from the elbow, several centimeters a day, by winding upon a stick. (From Basu. *Tropical Surgery*, 1965.)

advocated to prevent development of adult worms. Niridazole (Ambilhar) has been shown to be remarkably efficacious for the treatment of individuals infected with adult guinea worms. The recommended dosage is 25 mg per kg for 10 days.

Bancroft's Filariasis

effects. Migration to the skin is signaled by manifestations of severe hypersensitivity, such as urticaria, pruritus, erythema, and on occasion dyspnea and a shocklike state. The skin ulcer is seen most commonly on the ankle or between the metatarsal bones, although they have been described in almost all locations. A mild to moderate eosinophilia usually accompanies the infection. Secondary infection of the ulcer and worm tract may provoke fibroblastic proliferation that can result in contractures of the involved joint. **DIAGNOSIS AND TREATMENT.** Diagnosis can only be made at the time the skin ulcer appears or if the outline of the adult worm can be seen beneath the skin. Surgical removal of the worm is frequently advocated. The time-honored, native method of gradually rolling the worm upon a stick, a few centimeters a day, is as much used today as in ancient times (Fig. 37). Severe inflammation and necrosis usually follow if the worm is torn during removal. Therefore, the worm is killed by local infiltration with acriflavine or mercuric bichloride before removal is attempted.

Oral prophylactic diethylcarbamazine has been

Wuchereria bancrofti, the filarial worm responsible for Bancroft's filariasis, is a creamy-white, threadlike nematode. The adults invade and live coiled together in the lymphatics and lymph nodes, attaining considerable length; males reach 4.0 cm, females 8.0 to 10.0 cm. The gravid females discharge motile, sheathed embryos, i.e., microfilariae, that invade and circulate in the blood of their definitive host. If a suitable mosquito ingests microfilariae with a blood meal, larval development proceeds through a series of molts within the insect's thoracic muscles. After two weeks, infective third-stage filiform larvae have developed, migrate to the mouth parts of the mosquito, and enter the skin when the mosquito next bites. The larvae invade peripheral lymphatics, continue their development to adulthood, and copulate, microfilariae generally appearing in the peripheral blood in about a year.

Although man is the only known definitive host of Bancroft's filaria, there are many species of *Culex, Aedes,* and *Anopheles* mosquitoes that are natural vectors. The infection is found throughout all tropical and semitropical areas of the world. In endemic zones the incidence gradually increases with age, but infection begins early in childhood. In some Pacific islands, where a third of the population over 5 years of age may be infected, the disease may not be evident until many years have elapsed, and repeated infections have occurred.

PATHOLOGY. Living and dead adult worms provoke a severe lymphangitis wherever they lodge in the body. In the vicinity of the worm there occurs a perilymphangitic reaction composed of numerous eosinophils, plasma cells, macrophages, and foreign body giant cells, as well as an obliterative endolymphangitis due to reticuloendothelial cell proliferation. Lymphatic channels are eventually obliterated, being replaced by fibrous or hyalinized scar tissue. Sometimes worms calcify. Nevertheless, their presence acts as a persistent inflammatory focus, often called the focal point of O'Connor. Lymph flow improves between attacks as inflammation subsides. Repeated bouts of elevated lymphatic pressure with compensatory dilatation, varices, and collateralization finally lead to almost total obstruction as fibrosis becomes widespread. If obstruction occurs in areas of loose connective tissue, such as the retroperitoneum, spermatic cord, and mesentery, lymphatic varicosities result. If obstruction involves afferent lymphatics of more compact connective tissue, such as in the lower extremities, lymphedema and elephantiasis are seen.

SYMPTOMS. Acute symptoms are not usually observed in endemic areas, inasmuch as infection has usually been acquired repeatedly since infancy. Newcomers to these areas, however, may show the acute disease, which usually begins with fever and a painful, descending lymphangitis, funiculitis, or lymphadenitis. Other symptoms such as urticaria, erythema, fugitive swellings, and eosinophilia are frequently encountered. These attacks can recur for several months. The disease eventually passes to a chronic stage, indicated by lymphadenopathy, usually of the inguinal region. Lymphatic obstruction may finally lead to elephantiasis of various body members. Chyluria may occur if, as a result of retroperitoneal obstruction, distal lymphatic vessels rupture into the bladder, ureter, or kidneys.

PROGNOSIS. Generally, prognosis is good if repeated infection can be avoided.

DIAGNOSIS. Diagnosis is made by detecting microfilariae in the peripheral blood. Hematologic examination should be done between 8:00 P.M. and 2:00 A.M. in those areas where microfilarial nocturnal periodicity occurs. Serologic or intracutaneous tests employing *Dirofilaria immitis* antigen can be most helpful during the biologic incubation period, when microfilariae are not being produced. Lymph node biopsy may reveal the worms. If the worms are not found, the histologic features are often suggestive.

TREATMENT. Diethylcarbamazine (Hetrazan) quickly clears the blood of microfilariae. Evidence is not clear-cut as to whether this compound kills the adult worms or sterilizes the female. The dosage is 2 mg/kg three times a day, after meals, for at least 3 weeks.

During therapy, mild allergic manifestations are frequently encountered, such as fever, rash, and headache. Enlarged elephantoid limbs often respond to conservative management such as rest, elevation, and tight bandaging or stockings. Surgical intervention may be required in advanced disease. It is often necessary to treat recurrent bacterial cellulitis or lymphangitis with the appropriate antibiotics for mixed streptococcus-staphylococcus infections.

PREVENTION. The transmission of Bancroft's filariasis can be controlled by mosquito eradication. Since diethylcarbamazine prophylaxis reduces the number of microfilariae in the blood, the opportunity for transmission of the infection is greatly reduced.

Malayan Filariasis

Brugia (*Wuchereria*) *malayi* is an important filarial disease of man throughout southeast Asia, Ceylon, southern India, Korea, and China, producing lymphangitis, eosinophilia, and elephantiasis. Treatment is similar to that of *W. bancrofti.*

Onchocerciasis

Onchocerca volvulus is a filarial worm which causes "blinding filariasis." The adult worms are found coiled in subcutaneous nodules. Adult females shed microfilariae which "unsheath" immediately. These rarely enter the bloodstream, but usually migrate in subcutaneous and cutaneous tissue (Fig. 38), sometimes entering the conjunctiva. The blackfly, *Simulium sp.,* is the intermediate host in which larval development occurs. The fly transmits the infective stage upon taking its next meal.

Onchocerciasis is found extensively in west and central Africa and scattered in certain districts in Central and South America and southern Mexico. In Central America, onchocerciasis is limited to the highlands of Guatemala along fast-flowing river beds and streams, where black flies prevail. Although infection of children under 10 years of age is less common in Africa, children in western Africa are often found with tumors of the scalp and shoulders.

PATHOLOGY AND SYMPTOMS. A fibrous tumor forms about the developing adult worms. These tumors are quite common in the scalp and shoulders of Guatemalan children and about the pelvis in Africans. Ocular manifestations are associated with migrating microfilariae invading the cornea, orbit, and optic disk, resulting in photophobia, iridocyclitis, retinitis, and choroiditis. Vision, at first impaired, may be totally lost with invasion of the optic nerve. It is not entirely clear whether the ocular manifestations are a result of hypersensitivity to the microfilariae and their products or to direct injury by the invading worms.

PROGNOSIS. If ocular manifestations do not develop, prognosis is generally good.

DIAGNOSIS. Needle aspiration of a nodule and ex-

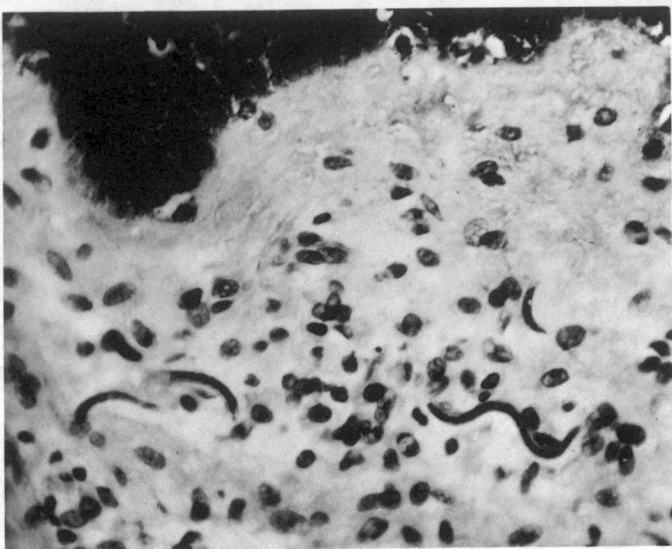

Fig. 38. Microfilariae of *Onchocerca volvulus* in subcutaneous tissues.

amination for microfilariae or biopsy of the top layer of epidermis can often provide absolute diagnosis.

TREATMENT. Excision of all nodules, followed by therapy with diethylcarbamazine, is probably the best procedure to prevent or minimize ocular and other allergic manifestations. The recommended dosage is 0.1 mg per kg daily for 2 to 3 weeks. Allergic symptoms can be controlled with antihistamines or steroids.

Suramin may also be employed in combination with diethylcarbamazine. A trial dose of 5 mg/kg should first be employed, followed by a dose of 20 mg/kg 5 days later. The same dose should be given every 5 to 7 days until a total of 10 doses have been administered.

PREVENTION. Elimination of the intermediate host and surgical excision of tumors as soon as they appear reduces the possibility of further transmission.

Loaiasis

Loaiasis is caused by the African eyeworm *Loa loa*. It is confined to an extensive area of the western and midcentral portions of Africa, where an estimated 13 million people are infected. The worm is transmitted with the bite of tabanid flies, members of the genus *Chrysops*.

The adult worms live and migrate through subcutaneous tissues, often causing a transient inflammatory reaction termed "fugitive swelling." It is not uncommon for the adults to wander under the conjunctiva, causing some consternation but little damage. Sheathed microfilariae are found in the peripheral blood during the day; i.e., there is diurnal periodicity. Allergic manifestations, such as giant urticaria, fever, and a markedly elevated eosinophilia of 50 to 80 percent, may occur. Surgcal removal of the adults from subcutaneous sites such as the back, breast,

groin, anterior chamber of the eye, or bridge of the nose effects a complete cure.

Although therapy with diethylcarbamazine is highly effective, it should not be undertaken without careful observation for serious allergic reactions. Antihistamines or steroid hormones may be used as an adjunct to specific drug therapy. The recommended dosage of diethylcarbamazine is 2 mg per kg of body weight three times a day for 19 days. It is not necessary to remove the dead worms; they will be absorbed in about 2 weeks.

Loaiasis can best be prevented by insect control measures and by treatment of existing infection, which diminishes the incidence of microfilariae.

Diseases Caused by Trematodes (Flukes)

The trematodes are exclusively parasitic flatworms that are leaflike, bilaterally symmetric, and lacking in a body cavity. All flukes that infect man have rather complex life histories during which there may be a succession of intermediate hosts in which multiplication takes place. Sexual reproduction occurs in the final host, man.

Adult flukes possess an outer, noncellular cuticle that may exhibit spines, tubercles, or hooks. They all possess a ventral sucker or acetabulum for holding their position, as well as an anterior muscular oral sucker that leads to a simple digestive tract. Whereas their excretory, nervous, and circulatory systems are rather primitive, they have highly specialized organs for reproduction. All the trematodes that infect man, other than the blood flukes (*Schistosoma*), are monoecious (hermaphrodites).

Trematode eggs shed in the final host pass to

the outside in either feces (*Schistosoma, Clonorchis, Fasciola*), urine (*Schistosoma haematobium*), or sputum (*Paragonimus*). A ciliated larva, the miracidium, emerges from the egg either before or after ingestion by a snail and usually becomes a saclike structure termed a first-generation sporocyst. The latter develops large numbers of reproductive cells that form either second-generation sporocysts (*Schistosoma*) or rediae (*Clonorchis, Fasciola, Paragonimus*), in which proliferate other germinal cells that develop into cercariae. These escape from the snail and by swimming or crawling make their way to another host. Most digenetic trematodes encyst in or on a second intermediate host, such as a fish (*Clonorchis*), crab or crayfish (*Paragonimus*), or vegetation (*Fasciola*), as metacercariae. The cercariae in the schistosomes actively penetrate their final host and develop to maturity, whereas metacercariae are consumed by the final host and excyst before maturing.

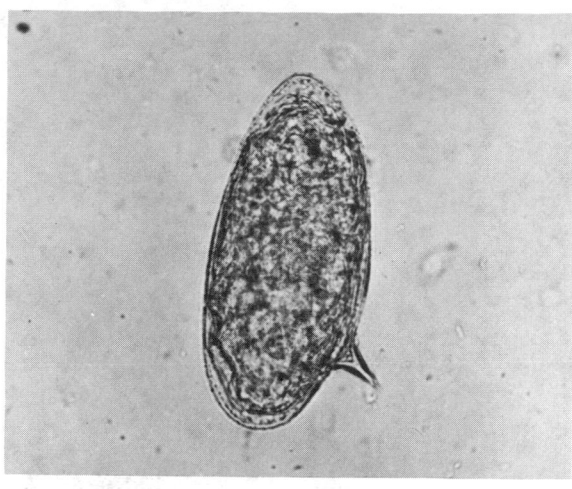

Fig. 39. *Schistosoma mansoni* egg recovered in feces. ×448.

Schistosomiasis

The blood flukes, *Schistosoma mansoni*, *S. japonicum*, and *S. haematobium*, have supplanted malaria as the chief world health problem. These worms are widely distributed, *S. mansoni* being found in Africa, Puerto Rico, Venezuela, Brazil, Surinam, many of the West Indian islands, Israel, and Arabia. *S. haematobium* is widespread in Africa, the Near East, Iran, Iraq, southern Portugal, and a small area of western India. *S. japonicum* is limited to China, several foci in Japan, the Celebese, Thailand, and the Philippine Islands.

The blood flukes are morphologically similar, but there are distinctive differences. The broader, robust males are characteristically found embracing the longer (10 to 26 mm) slender females within a gynecophoric canal during copulation and the ensuing oviposition. Typically, the sexually mature forms of *S. mansoni* are found in the mesenteric venules of the colon, those of *S. japonicum* in the venules of the small intestine, and adults of *S. haematobium* in the vesicle and pelvic venules. Consequently ova of *S. haematobium* are found predominantly in the urine, but ova of the other species are generally recovered in the feces. The eggs, which are fully mature when passed in feces or urine, are readily distinguished by their distinctive lateral or terminal spines (Fig. 39). Upon dilution of the excreta in water, a free-swimming ciliated miracidium hatches. It penetrates a snail, and rapidly undergoes metamorphosis and growth into a saclike first-generation sporocyst. The latter produces and liberates hundreds of second-generation sporocysts, each, in turn, producing myriads of fork-tailed cercariae that subsequently are shed into water. It is not unusual for a single miracidium to produce ultimately thousands of cercariae. Upon contact, cercariae quickly penetrate the skin of the bather, shed their tails, and enter the venous circulation. After a brief period in the pulmonary circulation, many schistosomules make their way to the intrahepatic portal vessels where they settle down, feeding on blood, growing to maturity, pairing, and mating. In several weeks they again take up their journey, leaving the intrahepatic veins, and migrate retrograde to their respective sites in intestinal or vesicle venules and begin ovipositing. Eggs first appear in feces in 6 to 8 weeks in *S. mansoni* infections; in 4 to 6 weeks in *S. japonicum*; and in urine in *S. haematobium* in 10 to 14 weeks.

PATHOLOGY. The important pathologic lesions are caused by deposition of eggs in the tissues. During the initial period there are always minute petechiae at the site of cercarial invasion. Small pulmonary infiltrates composed of eosinophils, neutrophils, and petechial hemorrhages may be found as the larvae (schistosomules) continue their migration. The deposition of eggs in the intestine provokes severe granulomatous inflammation, with pseudotubercle formation and fibroblastic proliferation. The affected intestinal wall may become thickened, fibrotic, and rigid. Eggs that are swept back into and lodge in the liver cause pseudotubercles and periportal fibrosis ("Symmer's pipestem cirrhosis," Fig. 40). Fibrocongestive splenomegaly, as a result of presinusoidal portal hypertension, is seen; collateral venous channels may become prominent, with the development of coronary and esophageal varices. Eggs may embolize to the lungs, causing endarteritis and periarteritis with formation of angiomatoid bodies and pseudotubercles. Although less frequently encountered, ova reaching the central nervous system cause granulomas and pseudotubercles.

Eggs deposited in the vesical venules pass into the urinary bladder, which may undergo mucosal hyperplasia and severe inflammation. Papillomas are commonly found; intramural fibrosis with calcification about the eggs often follows. As egg laying proceeds, the urethra and ureters are often involved in a proliferative fibrotic reaction, leading to elephantiasis of the penis and scrotum. Hydronephrosis and

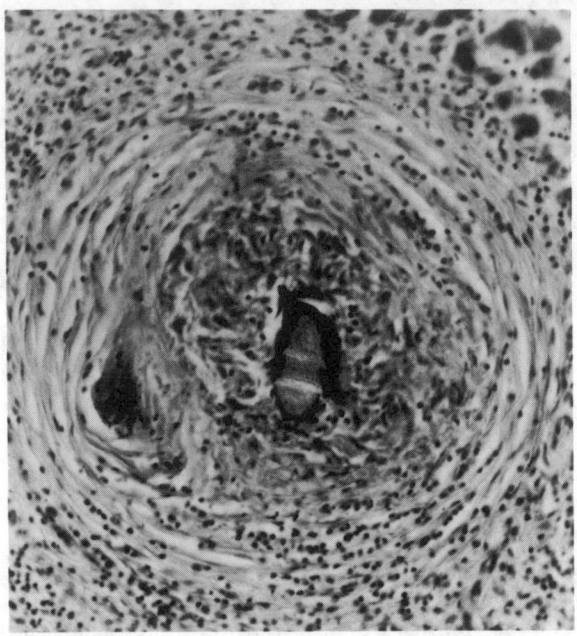

Fig. 40. Periportal fibrosis and pseudotubercle surrounding an ovum in Manson's schistosomiasis. Acid fast stain. ×140.

pyelonephritis are commonly seen. Although bladder carcinoma is frequently associated with schistosomal cystitis, direct proof of carcinogenesis is lacking. Intestinal carcinoma does not occur any more frequently than in the population at large.

SYMPTOMS. Cercarial penetration of the skin is often accompanied by intense itching ("kabure itch"), urticarial rash, and occasional vesiculation. Symptoms are usually absent until the parasites have reached the portal system. Children will occasionally have fever, eosinophilia, and an enlarged, tender liver and spleen. "Schistosomal fever" ("Katayama disease") or acute schistosomiasis may apear 4 to 10 weeks after exposure. It is characterized by intermittent bouts of chills, fever, and sweating, often misdiagnosed as malaria. Severe constitutional signs, epigastric pain, and "schistosomal dysentery," with blood and mucus in the feces, are virtually constant features of acute S. mansoni infection. Lymphadenopathy, splenomegaly, a tender and enlarged liver, arthralgia, urticaria, periorbital edema, and an eosinophilia of from 20 to 60 percent are frequent manifestations. Liver function tests are usually normal, although a positive cephalin flocculation test and some increase in bromsulphalein (BSP) retention may be recognized. Hypergammaglobulinemia is often pronounced. Despite the absence of eggs in stool or urine during this early stage, there is much evidence to suggest that these acute symptoms are a result of hypersensitivity to the ova and their miracidial secretions. The acute symptoms generally subside within a year to 18 months, but intermittent bouts of diarrhea and constipation can persist.

As a result of severe cicatrization of the bowel wall, intestinal obstruction may occur. Massive splenomegaly, portal hypertension, and venous collateralization may appear, but signs of hepatic failure are usually not evident until very late.

Pulmonary lesions are less frequent and rarely serious. In older children, dyspnea, cough, precordial pain, and occasionally hemoptysis and congestive failure are associated with pulmonary hypertension terminating in cor pulmonale. Since S. japonicum is a more prolific egg-layer than either of the other species, serious disease may occur with fewer worms, and the infection tends to be more severe, especially in children. Periportal fibrosis is an earlier manifestation. Initially, infection with S. haematobium may cause painless hematuria, but as cicatrization of the bladder wall proceeds, dysuria, frequency, and urgency are frequently present. Ureteral colic often accompanies ureteral fibrosis.

S. japonicum has been responsible for most of the cases involving the central nervous system, causing the sudden onset of severe headache, seizures, and sometimes coma. Eggs embolizing to the spinal cord may evoke symptoms of transverse myelitis.

PROGNOSIS. The outcome is most favorable in early or light infections with S. mansoni and S. japonicum, if treatment is provided. In heavy or late infections, with severe hepatic and intestinal disease, the outlook is serious; death may result from bleeding esophageal varices, hepatic failure, or intercurrent infection. Similarly, the prognosis is good in light and early infections with S. haematobium that are treated early. In advanced urogenital tract disease pyogenic infection is difficult to control, making the outlook very poor.

DIAGNOSIS. Identification of eggs that have been recovered in stool or urine, or obtained by rectal or bladder biopsy provides the specific diagnosis. According to many workers, direct examination of material biopsied from rectum or bladder and pressed between two glass microscope slides provides the best and swiftest means for making the diagnosis. Liver biopsy is often helpful in identifying ova.

Skin tests, useful in adults, have been less so in children. Cross-reactions with trichinosis must be excluded. The complement-fixation test becomes positive early in the infection, but the titer falls with chronicity. The circumoval precipitin test, which is specific, can be used as a guide in evaluating therapy; it becomes negative about 6 months after therapeutic cure.

TREATMENT. Specific drug therapy can be helpful if implemented before irreparable intestinal and hepatic damage have occurred. General supportive therapy, such as supplemental food and vitamins, should be provided. In advanced disease, toxicity of the usually chemotherapeutic agents may be life-threatening, especially when liver damage is already widespread.

In patients under 16 years of age, miracil D (Lucanthone) has been employed extensively for the treatment of S. mansoni and S. haematobium infections. The recommended dosage is 5 mg per kg, three times daily, for 7 consecutive days. Side effects, such as dizziness, nystagmus, nausea, and vomiting may occur. The skin may become yellow. Severe side effects, including mental aberration, confusion, and agitation, are seen in adults taking Lucanthone.

Niridazole (Ambilhar) has had extensive trials and has been shown to be effective against both *S. haematobium* and *S. mansoni*. Its toxicity, however, may limit its usefulness. At present stibophen (Fuadin) remains the drug of choice for *S. haematobium* and, in patients over 16 years of age, for *S. mansoni* infections. Stibophen is supplied in ampules containing 5 ml of a 6.3 percent solution or a total of 315 mg of drug (42.5 mg antimony). It is administered intramuscularly, 1.5 ml first day, 3.5 ml second day, 5.0 ml third day, and 5 ml every other day for 18 more injections (a total of 100 ml or 6.3 g Fuadin or 0.85 g antimony). Children weighing less than 50 kg usually receive two-thirds to three-quarters, and infants less than one year, one-half the above dosage. Therefore, treatment is started with 0.75 to 1.0 ml and increased to 4 ml. Treatment may be repeated after 4 months. Toxicity is not a frequent problem. Nausea, vomiting, diarrhea, and arthralgias may occur; if they are severe, the daily dosage should be reduced and the treatment period extended. Serious renal, hepatic, and/or cardiac disease may contraindicate stibophen therapy.

Sodium antimony dimercaptosuccinate (Astiban, TwSb) has been shown to be as effective as stibophen.

S. japonicum infection responds best to therapy with tartar emetic (potassium antimony tartrate).

Recent studies utilizing Hycanthone, a hydroxymethyl derivative of Lucanthone, have been most encouraging. It is not yet certain whether this drug effects a cure or just temporary cessation of ovipositing. Further studies with regard to serious toxicity and adverse patient reactions to this drug are necessary before its widespread use can be advocated.

PREVENTION. Although control of schistosomiasis seems possible on theoretical grounds, little progress has occurred. The infection has been increasing and spreading throughout the world. In some areas almost 100 percent of the population over 2 years of age is infected. Previously noninfected areas have recently become endemic, and the large migration of Puerto Ricans to the continental United States has placed schistosomiasis as a major disease in New York and several other large cities. In endemic areas children acquire the infection almost as soon as they can walk and wade in water in which they urinate and defecate. Presumably destruction of the molluscan host would prevent further development of the disease, but such control measures have been only temporarily effective. Mass chemotherapy has had only fair to moderate success, since there has been a high rate of reinfection.

Although improved sanitary waste disposal would help to control spread of schistosomiasis, education of the general population and the provision of controlled swimming facilities may ultimately lead to eradication of this disease.

Schistosomal Dermatitis

Swimmer's, clam digger's, or collector's itch is caused by cercariae of various species of avian and mammalian blood flukes. The infection is acquired by campers and bathers both in freshwater lakes and along the East and West Coasts of the United States.

The cercariae are liberated by snails and enter the skin. In a few moments, an intense pruritus is followed by an urticariform rash. These subside shortly, leaving a small macule, only to be followed in several hours by severe itching, edema, and papules which may persist for several weeks.

The initial exposure is relatively symptom-free, but with repeated exposure the reaction becomes more severe. Most of the cercariae are trapped and die in the upper portions of the dermis, many never getting beyond the prickle-cell layer of the epidermis.

The diagnosis is usually made by history and the presence of skin lesions. Bathing areas can be freed of this menace by destroying the snails or the food they require. Rubbing the skin dry with a towel or the application of rubbing alcohol immediately upon leaving the water may be effective in preventing infection.

Paragonimiasis

Paragonimus westermani, the Oriental lung fluke, is widespread throughout most of the Far East, parts of Africa, and South America. Adults usually live encapsulated in the lung and are about 1.0 cm long by 0.5 cm wide. The golden-brown oval eggs have an obvious cap (operculum) and measure about 100 by 55 μ. They are deposited in the lung, coughed up and expectorated, or swallowed and passed in the feces. After several weeks of development in water, a miracidium hatches and enters a snail. A few weeks later sporocysts and rediae are produced. Cercariae are soon released which invade crayfish or crabs, encysting in muscle and viscera. After a person ingests infected crayfish, the metacercariae excyst in the duodenum, penetrate the intestinal wall, and migrate in the peritoneal cavity, through the diaphragm, and into the pleural cavity and lungs. They develop to maturity in lung tissue, where their presence stimulates pronounced fibroblastic encapsulation. Their presence in extrapulmonary tissue, especially brain, may give rise to bizarre neurologic symptoms. In nature, there are many wild animals such as tigers, other cats, foxes, dogs, and pigs that may serve as definitive hosts for this trematode.

Infection usually is acquired by eating poorly cooked or pickled crab and crayfish. In some areas children are as frequently infected as are adults, and the incidence in females is far greater than in males.

An Oriental custom of treating measles, whooping cough, and diarrhea with the juice of freshly crushed crabs accounts for the large number of pediatric infections.

PATHOLOGY. The parasitized lung may possess small fibrotic nodules, which, in man, usually contain a single worm. The cysts are closer to the pleural surface than the hilum, and on cutting them a brown gelatinous material escapes. Following death of the worm, pulmonary cysts shrink and become densely fibrotic, occasionally calcifying.

Cerebral involvement is due to invasion by the adult or migrating metacercariae. A severe meningo-encephalitis or cerebral abscess may result. Parasites form nodules in other localities such as the omentum, pericardium, liver, spleen, and subcutaneous regions.

SYMPTOMS. Pulmonary symptoms first may be noted after about 3 months or longer, although the only evidence of infection may be persistent fever. Rusty-brown sputum is copiously produced. Frank hemoptysis, pain, and dyspnea are also commonly encountered. Since the pulmonary cysts are in open contact with bronchioles, sputum usually contains eggs. With central nervous system invasion, headache, seizures, hemiplegia, and visual impairment may occur. Eosinophilia is usual. Intestinal involvement may cause only vague abdominal symptoms, or at times, bloody diarrhea with mucus.

DIAGNOSIS. The clinical symptoms may require differentiation from tuberculosis, bronchiectasis, schistosomiasis, amebiasis, and brain tumor. The definitive diagnosis is made by finding the eggs in sputum or feces. In children, who usually swallow their sputum, it is more frequent to find ova in the feces.

PROGNOSIS. In light infection, or if the worms do not settle in some critical focus, the prognosis is good.

TREATMENT. Until recently there has been no satisfactory therapy for paragonimiasis. Emetine alone or combined with sulfonamides has been used with equivocal results. Early infections have been reported to respond satisfactorily to chloroquine. Bithionol (2,2'-thiobis [4,6-dichlorophenol]) taken orally in a dosage of 50 mg per kg of body weight every other day until 10 to 15 doses are administered has had excellent results with no relapses a year after treatment. Surgical excision of cerebral lesions is indicated.

PREVENTION. Avoiding the consumption of uncooked and pickled crabs and crayfish together with an intensive educational campaign is the best means of preventing this disease.

Clonorchiasis

The Chinese liver fluke, *Clonorchis sinensis,* is found throughout most of eastern Asia. It is a moderate-sized worm (10 to 25 mm by 3 to 5 mm) that lives in the biliary passages of man, although it occasion-ally invades the pancreatic duct. Its eggs (29 by 16 μ) are most distinctive, possessing a prominent operculum (cap). They are discharged into the bile ducts and passed out in the feces, hatching after ingestion by snails, in which sporocysts and rediae develop. Cercariae eventually escape from the snails and encyst under the scales or in the flesh of freshwater fish. If the uncooked, infected fish is eaten, the metacercariae excyst in the duodenum, enter the common bile duct, and migrate to the intrahepatic biliary radicals where they mature in about 3 to 5 weeks.

Infection with *Clonorchis* is common wherever uncooked fish is eaten. Although it is not unusual for young children to consume raw fish and acquire the infection, the disease is usually the result of cumulative infection during a lifetime of enjoying this delicacy. The incidence is quite low under 5 years of age, but it gradually increases with age. Metacercariae are quite resistant to refrigeration, brine, vinegar, and spices.

PATHOLOGY. The presence of the worms in the distal bile passages provokes ductal epithelial hyperplasia, fibroblastic proliferation of the wall, and periductal fibrosis with infiltration of neutrophils, eosinophils, lymphocytes, and plasma cells. In heavy infection, hepatic damage can be severe, leading to the development of extensive periportal fibrosis. Hepatomas are frequently encountered in severely diseased livers. Worms also seem to act as a nidus for stone formation.

SYMPTOMS. Depending upon the number of infecting worms, the disease may be asymptomatic or present as complete biliary obstruction. There may be an enlarged, tender liver, and recurrent bouts of chills and fever. In later years, signs of recurrent cholecystitis and biliary obstruction appear. It is not unusual for an infection with hundreds of worms to be active for 20 years or more with little or no serious side effects.

DIAGNOSIS. Recovery of eggs in the stools or duodenal aspirate will provide the definitive diagnosis.

PROGNOSIS. In light infections the outlook usually is good.

TREATMENT. Although no reliable therapy is available, chloroquine has been recommended. Patients often require several courses of therapy before a cure can be effected. The recommended dose is from 300 to 600 mg of chloroquine base a day until the patient has taken a total of about 15 g (base). Secondary suppurative cholangitis should be treated with appropriate antibiotics, and surgical intervention may be indicated for biliary obstruction.

PREVENTION. Avoiding raw fish is probably the best means of reducing infection. Since human feces are used to fertilize fish ponds in which carp are being raised, composting feces before use decreases the spread of clonorchiasis.

Fascioliasis

Fasciola hepatica, the sheep liver fluke, is found wherever sheep are raised. It is common in many areas of the United States, South and Central America, Europe, Cuba, Africa, and Hawaii. Children and adults are sporadically infected, although sheep and cattle are probably the natural definitive hosts.

Fasciola is a large (30 by 13 mm) leaflike worm that lives in the biliary passages. Immature, large (140 by 75 μ), bile-stained eggs are shed into the proximal biliary ducts and passed out with feces into water where they develop. A miracidium hatches and penetrates a snail. The sporocysts produce first-generation rediae. Second-generation rediae and then cercariae are formed. These emerge from the snail, and usually encyst on aquatic vegetation, such as watercress. If infected vegetation is consumed, the metacercariae excyst in the duodenum, penetrate the intestinal wall, and, migrating through the peritoneum, penetrate Glisson's capsule and hepatic parenchyma, settling and maturing in the biliary ducts.

PATHOLOGY. The presence of the flukes in the biliary passages stimulates ductal epithelial proliferation and periductal fibrosis with associated inflammatory cells. Eosinophilia may exceed 80 percent.

SYMPTOMS. Cases often present with right upper quadrant pain, fever, dyspnea, and hepatomegaly. In light infections, however, the initial period of invasion is often asymptomatic. After the flukes have settled in the biliary ducts, fever, hepatomegaly, urticaria, biliary colic, and occasionally jaundice, intermittent biliary diarrhea, weight loss, and generalized wasting occur. Eosinophilia is a constant finding. Children are more severely affected.

Ingestion of infected raw sheep and goat livers in countries of the Middle East may cause pharyngeal infection called *halzoun.* The young flukes migrate into the fossa of Rosenmüller and invade the eustachian tube, or cause fatal obstruction of the larynx and trachea.

DIAGNOSIS. Definitive diagnosis is made by recovering the eggs from the stool or duodenal aspirate.

PROGNOSIS. The outlook is serious in all but light infections.

TREATMENT. Early infections are apparently benefited by intramuscular emetine therapy, 1 mg per kg of body weight (maximum of 65 mg daily) for 10 to 12 days. Bithionol has also been used successfully at a daily dosage of 30 mg/kg for 20 days.

PREVENTION. Education of individuals living in endemic areas to avoid consuming uncooked green vegetables, especially watercress, would probably eradicate fascioliasis as a human disease.

Fasciolopsiasis

In Asia and the Southwest Pacific, *Fasciolopsis buski* is one of the more frequently encountered intestinal flukes of man and hogs. The worm is quite large (20 to 75 mm by 8 to 20 mm) and is found attached to the wall of the upper small intestine. Eggs are passed continuously in the feces and cannot be distinguished from those of *Fasciola hepatica.* Development is similar to *Fasciola,* cercariae encysting on the bulb of the water chestnut as well as other aquatic vegetation. Infection occurs by accidental ingestion of the metacercariae. Excystation occurs in the duodenum, where they attach to the wall and develop to maturity.

PATHOLOGY. The worms produce severe ulcerative lesions at their sites of mucosal attachment, and sometimes there is intestinal obstruction.

SYMPTOMS. In children the toxic and allergic manifestations of this infection are striking. Edema, mucous diarrhea, malabsorption, and generalized wasting occur. Heavy infections in childhood often reveal anasarca and ascites. Intoxication and severe prostration may end fatally if treatment is not initiated. Eosinophilia is always present.

DIAGNOSIS. Definitive diagnosis is made by finding the eggs in the stools and by clinical history. Fascioliasis must be excluded.

PROGNOSIS. Light infections that are treated have a good prognosis.

TREATMENT. Several anthelmintics are used for fasciolopsiasis. Hexylresorcinol in a dosage of 400 mg orally from 1 to 7 years of age and 1 g at 13 years of age and over yields relatively high cure rates. Tetrachlorethylene, 0.25 ml per year of age, can also be used. Hexylresorcinol is, however, less toxic and therefore preferred.

PREVENTION. Peeling or just immersion of vegetables in boiling water for a few seconds will prevent infection.

Diseases Caused by Cestodes (Tapeworms)

The cestodes are exclusively parasitic flatworms, generally referred to as tapeworms. The adult worms typically have a scolex or "head" which may possess suckers and/or hooklets and serves as an organ for attachment. The distal portion of the scolex is termed the "neck," which is the growth zone of the tapeworm so that "segments" or proglottids closest to the neck are most immature. Those further down the chain are mature, and the most distal group consists of gravid proglottids. Each mature proglottid possesses at least one complete, highly organized male and female reproductive tract. A digestive tract is usually absent, food being absorbed directly through the worm's integument. The nervous and excretory systems are poorly developed.

With the single exception of *Hymenolepis nana*, tapeworms that infect man require one or more intermediate hosts to complete their life cycles.

Adult cestode infections may persist for years, depriving the host of important nutriment. The larval infection, however, often produces the more serious and sometimes fatal disease.

Taeniasis

The pork tapeworm, *Taenia solium*, and the beef tapeworm, *T. saginata*, are the common tapeworms of man. The disease has been known since ancient times, and is found wherever insufficiently cooked pork or beef is consumed.

Infection with the pork tapeworm has become rather uncommon in the United States, although it remains an important disease in Mexico and parts of South America. Generally, beef tapeworm infection is more prevalent.

The adult worms live in the upper small intestine, *T. solium* measuring 2 to 8 m and *T. saginata*, 25 m or more. The scolex of the pork tapeworm, distinguished by the possession of a crown or rostellum that contains a double row of hooklets, is said to be "armed." The scolex of *T. saginata* is without hooks and, therefore, "unarmed." The gravid uterus holds tens of thousands of eggs, which contain a mature six-hooked (hexacanth) embryo, termed an oncosphere. The eggs are 30 to 40 μ in diameter and are similar in all members of the *Taenia* group. If the eggs are ingested by suitable intermediate host, such as hogs (*T. solium*) or cattle (*T. saginata*), the embryo is liberated. It penetrates the intestinal wall and enters the bloodstream. In the case of *T. solium* it may invade all the tissues of the body, where it develops into a cysticercus or "bladder worm." Cysticerci are ellipsoidal, white, translucent cysts into which the scolex is inverted. The cysticercus is dissolved when the infected pork is consumed. Next, the scolex evaginates, attaching to the intestinal wall, and it rapidly develops into an adult tapeworm. The cysticerci of *T. saginata* generally invade and develop in skeletal muscle; otherwise the life history is similar to that of *T. solium*.

PATHOLOGY. Infection with the adult worm seldom produces important lesions, although it may occasionally cause intestinal obstruction in children because of its huge size. If the eggs of *T. solium* are ingested by man, the larval stage may develop in every tissue of the body, a condition termed *cysticercosis cellulosae*. The consequence of this infection depends upon the organ that is invaded. The larvae generally cause an inflammatory infiltrate of eosinophils, plasma cells, neutrophils, and lymphocytes with eventual necrosis and fibrosis and calcification of the parasite. Human cysticercosis by *T. saginata* almost never occurs, only three authenticated cases having been reported in the world literature.

SYMPTOMS. The presence of adult *T. solium* usually causes little more than vague abdominal distress, perhaps alternating bouts of constipation and diarrhea. The symptoms in children, however, are often more pronounced. The huge adults of *T. saginata* are more likely to evoke severe hunger pains, weight loss, and epigastric pain, symptoms that may resemble peptic ulcer. It is not unusual for patients to report they can feel the worm moving. Eosinophilia may reach 55 percent. Neurologic complaints such as paresthesias, diplopia, and occasionally epileptiform seizures presumably result from absorption of neurotoxic material of helminthic origin.

The presence of cysticerci in muscle is generally of little consequence. Cerebral cysticercosis (Fig. 41), however, often provokes serious signs and symptoms which may mimic cerebral neoplasm. Headache, changes in behavioral pattern, and Jacksonian type seizures are common. Invasion of the orbit may cause pain and blurring, flashing, or loss of vision.

DIAGNOSIS. Since identification of the eggs is not specific, the definitive diagnosis is made by finding the proglottids in feces. Gravid segments of *T. solium* have 7 to 12 primary uterine lateral branches, whereas *T. saginata* have 15 or more. X-ray examination of

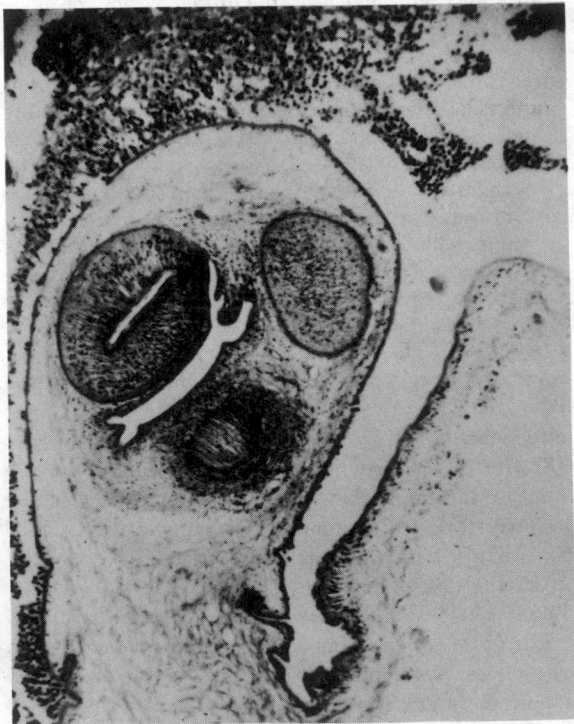

Fig. 41. Cysticercosis cellulosae of the brain discovered at autopsy.

muscle or brain may suggest the diagnosis if the cysticerci have calcified. Biopsy is required to diagnose cysticercosis.

PROGNOSIS. Intestinal infection has an excellent outlook, but cysticercosis can be most serious. In the brain or heart the prognosis is grave, although cerebral lesions have been successfully excised.

TREATMENT. Until recently quinacrine (Atabrine) was the drug of choice for the treatment of *T. solium.* The usual method of treatment is as follows:

1. Bland, liquid diet the day prior to treatment.
2. A sodium sulfate purge in the evening, and a cleansing enema in the morning prior to administration of the drug.
3. Quinacrine is given in the morning on an empty stomach, according to the following schedule:

Body Weight	Dosage
40-75 lb	400 mg total
76-100 lb	600 mg total
over 100 lb	600 mg total (adult dose)

In young children a 100 mg tablet is given every 5 minutes along with a 250 mg sodium bicarbonate tablet. In older children, two quinacrine tablets may be administered every 5 minutes until the total dose is given. Nausea and vomiting should be anticipated and avoided. Prochlorperazine (Compazine) can be administered an hour before drug therapy: 0.16 mg/kg orally or 0.08 mg/kg intramuscularly.

4. A saline purge is given several hours after therapy.

Recently, the aminoglycoside paromomycin (Humatin) has been shown to be effective in tapeworm infections. It is given to children with *Taenia* or *Diphyllobothrium* infections, as a single oral dose of 75 mg/kg of body weight, after a light morning meal. Patients with *T. solium* infections are sedated with prochlorperazine prior to therapy and then given a mild purgative (Fleet's phosphosoda) several hours after receiving paromomycin.

Several other simply administered drugs have been used in the treatment of taeniasis with excellent results. One of these, niclosamide (Yomesan), is recommended as the drug of choice for the treatment of *T. saginata, Diphyllobothrium latum,* and *Hymenolepis nana* infections. The following dosage schedules are suggested for *T. saginata* and *D. latum:*

1. Children weighing 25 to 75 lbs: 2 tablets (1.0 g) chewed thoroughly in a single dose.
2. Children weighing more than 75 lbs: 3 tablets (1.5 g) chewed thoroughly in a single dose.
3. Adults: 4 tablets (2 g) chewed thoroughly in a single dose.

No special dietary restrictions are necessary before or after treatment with Yomesan. The best time to take the drug is after a light meal with a few sips of water. Yomesan is not yet recommended for children under 2 years of age or pregnant women.

Treatment of cysticercosis is surgical removal whenever possible.

PREVENTION. Taeniasis can be prevented by thorough cooking of infected pork or beef. Refrigeration of beef at −10° C for 5 days and pork for 4 days, or heating at 72° C for 5 minutes will usually kill all cysticerci. Since cysticercosis may be acquired from contaminated food or water, sanitary waste disposal would eliminate this route of infection. Personal cleanliness by individuals harboring the adult worm would prevent hand to mouth infection. Care to avoid regurgitation of gravid proglottids and the subsequent release of eggs during therapy for the adult worm should prevent autoinfection.

Hymenolepiasis

The dwarf tapeworm, *Hymenolepis nana,* is found in most warm regions of the world. It is the most common tapeworm infection in southeastern United States and Latin America. The adult is only 0.5 cm in length and is attached to the mucosa of the ileum by a scolex that possesses four suckers and a retractable armed rostellum. The entire worm usually contains about 200 proglottids.

The gravid uterus holds about 100 to 200 mature eggs, 30 to 60 μ in diameter (Fig. 42). No intermediate host is required to complete the life cycle. The eggs are passed in the feces and ingested by a new or the same host (autoinfection). The embryo or oncosphere hatches and penetrates a villus, where it becomes a larva or cercocyst. The larva emerges from the tissue and attaches to the intestinal mucosa by its scolex. In 2 to 3 weeks the new worm is producing eggs. There is evidence that hyperinfection can occur when eggs liberated in the small intestine hatch and immediately penetrate a villus to undergo a new cycle. As a result of hyperinfection, children may harbor many hundreds or thousands of adult worms. Experimental evidence suggests that certain strains of *H. nana* undergo larval development in various fleas and mealworms. Subsequently, these larvae have developed to adults in mice. At the present time, human infection with murine strains is considered to be most unusual.

A closely related species, *H. diminuta,* which commonly parasitizes the rat and mouse, infrequently infects man. Most of the 200 reported human cases have been in children under 3 years of age. Development of this tapeworm requires an intermediate host. Presumably, infected rat fleas (*Nosopsyllus, Xenopsylla*) and mealworms (*Tenebrio*) are accidentally ingested, and the mature adults develop in about 3 weeks.

Since *H. nana* is usually transmitted directly, it is often found infecting entire families and institutions, children being most heavily infected.

PATHOLOGY AND SYMPTOMS. Little direct damage is done by the worms. In moderate to heavy infec-

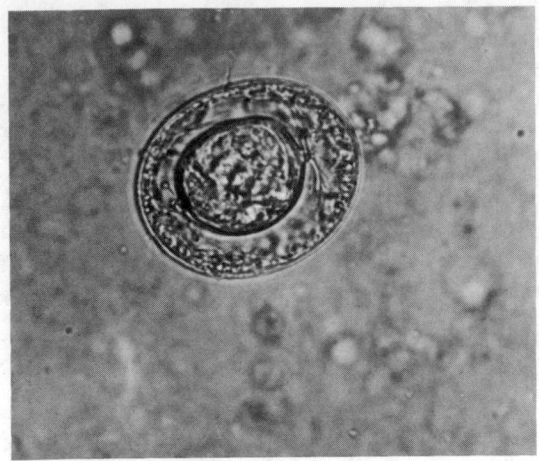
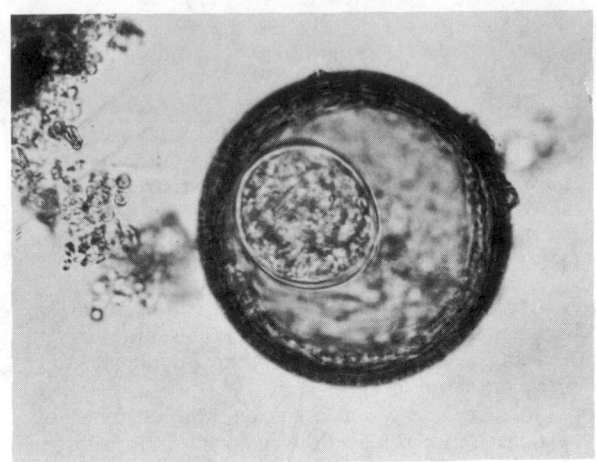

Fig. 42. A. (Left) *Hymenolepis nana* egg recovered from feces. Note polar filaments. ×448. B. (Right) *Hymenolepis diminuta* ovum. Polar filaments are absent and it is larger than *H. nana*. ×448.

tions, headache, dizziness, intermittent diarrhea, and abdominal cramps are sometimes noted. Slight eosinophilia is usual.

DIAGNOSIS. Definitive diagnosis is made by identifying characteristic eggs in the stool (Fig. 42).

TREATMENT. Niclosamide (Yomesan) therapy has been used with excellent results. The following schedule is recommended:

1. Children weighing 25 to 75 lbs: 2 tablets (1.0 g) chewed thoroughly on the first day, then 1 tablet (0.5 g) daily for the subsequent 5 to 7 days.
2. Children weighing more than 75 lbs: 3 tablets (1.5 g) chewed thoroughly on the first day, then 2 tablets (1.0 g) daily for the subsequent 5 to 7 days.
3. Adults: 4 tablets (2.0 g) chewed thoroughly in a single dose each day for 5 to 7 days.

Paromomycin therapy has been employed successfully by administering 45 mg/kg daily for 5 to 7 days. Mild diarrhea often accompanies this regime but stops once therapy is concluded.

Dipylidiasis

The dog tapeworm, *Dipylidium caninum*, is an occasional parasite in the small intestine of humans. The majority of human cases occur in children under 8 years, many in infants under 6 months. The ova of *Dipylidium* are ingested by the larval dog or cat flea, in which they become cysticercoid larvae. A child becomes infected by accidental ingestion of the infected flea.

PATHOLOGY AND SYMPTOMS. Infection is often asymptomatic, although some children experience vague intestinal disturbances. Allergic manifestations have been reported. Intestinal obstruction has been a rare complication.

TREATMENT AND PREVENTION. Treatment is the same as described under taeniasis (p. 819). Periodic

treatment of pets for tapeworm infection will control spread of this infection.

Diphyllobothriasis

Diphyllobothrium latum, the fish tapeworm, is a frequent human parasite in many of the lake regions of Europe, northern Minnesota, Michigan, and the adjacent regions of Canada. It is also found in Chile, Argentina, parts of China, and Africa. The Scandinavian custom of eating various delicacies made with raw fish and the practice of tasting raw fish when preparing gefüllte fish are some of the common means of infection.

The adult tapeworm lives in the small intestine, where it may attain a size of over 10 m; it consists of about 3,000 proglottids. The scolex possesses a pair of sucking grooves (bothria), by which it holds to the mucosa.

The gravid uterus expels its eggs in bursts through a uterine pore into the intestinal lumen, and the ova are evacuated in the feces. The operculate eggs, measuring about 66 by 44 μ (Fig. 43),

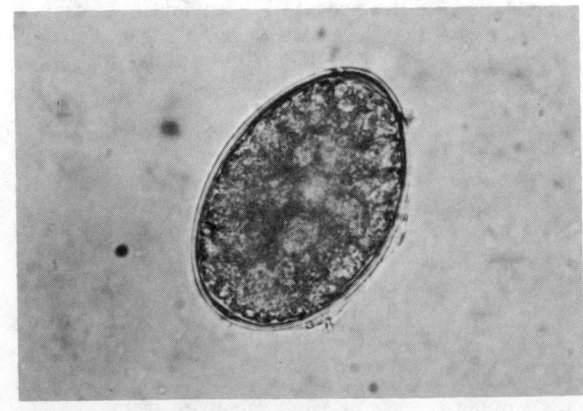

Fig. 43. Operculate egg of fish tapeworm (*Diphyllobothrium latum*) recovered in feces. ×448.

require about 2 weeks to develop in the water. A free-swimming ciliated embryo (coracidium) hatches and is ingested by a copepod (Class Crustacea, Phylum Arthropoda), in which it develops into a procercoid larva. When the infected copepod is eaten by a freshwater fish the procercoid larva invades the muscle, where it grows into a plerocercoid or sparganum larva. Usually the first fish is prey for larger fish, such as salmon, pike, perch, and trout, and the larva again invades the muscle of the second fish. If the fish is consumed raw or inadequately cooked, the plerocercoid larva develops into a mature adult in about 5 weeks.

PATHOLOGY. The presence of this parasite in the small intestine has frequently been cited as a cause of a profound macrocytic anemia resembling pernicious anemia. It has now been demonstrated convincingly that the worm deprives its host of vitamin B_{12}. Intestinal obstruction, as a result of infection with this huge worm, has been reported on several occasions.

SYMPTOMS. It is unusual for patients to have any serious complaints. Eosinophilia and leucocytosis are evident.

DIAGNOSIS. Discovery of the characteristic operculate eggs in the stool (Fig. 43) provides the specific diagnosis.

PROGNOSIS. In the absence of anemia, the prognosis is excellent. With elimination of the worm and treatment of the anemia with vitamin B_{12}, the outlook is similarly good.

TREATMENT. Treatment of fish tapeworm is the same as that described for taeniasis (p. 819).

PREVENTION. Careful cooking of freshwater fish would eliminate all possibility of human infection. Sanitary sewage disposal also would prevent viable eggs from reaching the intermediate host. Sale of fish originating in heavily infested lakes should be regulated. Freezing at $-10°$ C for 24 hours will kill the larvae.

On occasion, larvae of species closely related to *D. latum spirometra* have been found in human subcutaneous and muscle tissues. This condition is called sparganosis. The application of raw meat poultices to the eye as well as accidental ingestion of infected copepods is believed responsible for these infections. Ocular sparganosis may cause serious impairment of vision. Surgical removal of these worms is usually advocated.

Echinococcosis

Hydatid disease is the result of human infection with the larval stage of a dog tapeworm, *Echinococcus granulosus*. Similarly, the larval stage of *E. multilocularis*, a tapeworm of foxes and dogs and their relatives, may occasionally cause alveolar hydatid disease.

Sheep and cattle raising areas throughout the world are the most heavily parasitized regions. Most cases in the United States are found in immigrants

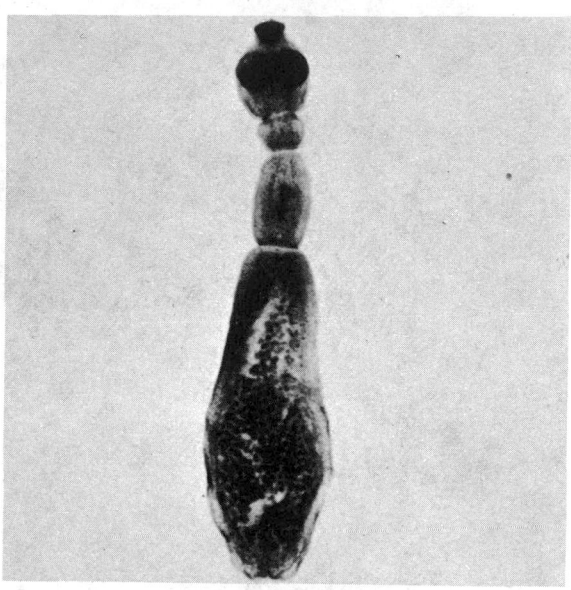

Fig. 44. *Echinococcus granulosus*, entire worm. ×28.

from endemic areas, such as Italy, Greece, and Syria. There have been, however, a number of autochthonous cases reported from various parts of the United States.

Most hydatid cyst infections are acquired in childhood and are attributed to close and unhygienic association with canine pets. The latter are the optimal definitive hosts, and humans serve as relatively uncommon but suitable intermediate hosts. Frequent natural reservoirs of hydatid cysts other than cattle and sheep include goats, camels, monkeys, reindeer, and moose.

The adult worm consists of a scolex and usually one immature, one mature, and one gravid proglottid (Fig. 44). They live attached to the villi of the dog's small intestine. The eggs or gravid proglottids are passed in the feces, and when swallowed, an embryo hatches in the duodenum, penetrates the intestinal wall, and enters the bloodstream. Most of the larvae lodge in the liver (48 to 70 percent), some settle in the lungs (15 to 29 percent), and a few make their way to various other foci throughout the body. Many larvae are destroyed by the host. The survivors, however, begin to develop into an expanding cyst which after 5 to 6 months is about 10 mm in diameter. The cyst wall is differentiated into an inner cellular germinal layer and outer noncellular friable laminated portion. Brood capsules, in which scolices may develop, bud off from the germinal layer. The brood capsule and its scolices are called hydatid sand (Fig. 45). When this unilocular hydatid cyst is consumed by a suitable definitive host, adult tapeworms develop in the small intestine.

The growth pattern of unilocular hydatid cyst in bone is quite different from that in liver or lung.

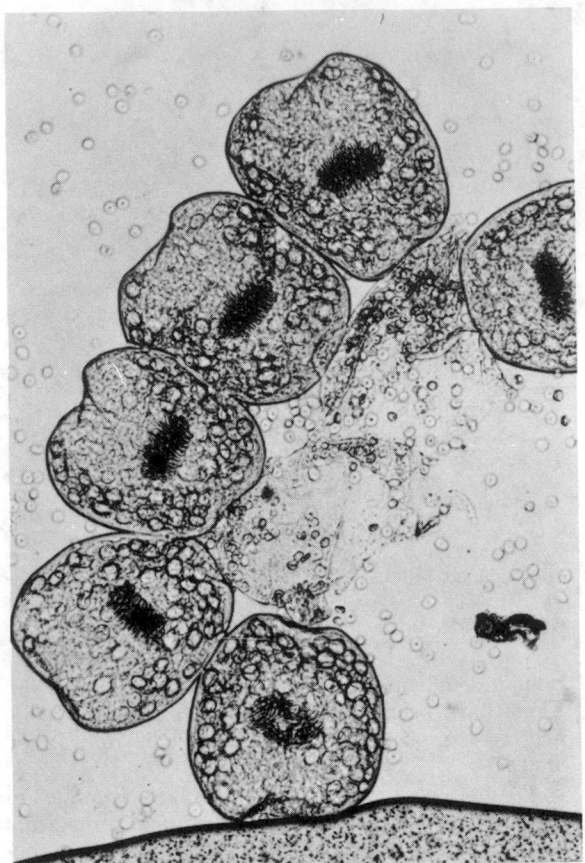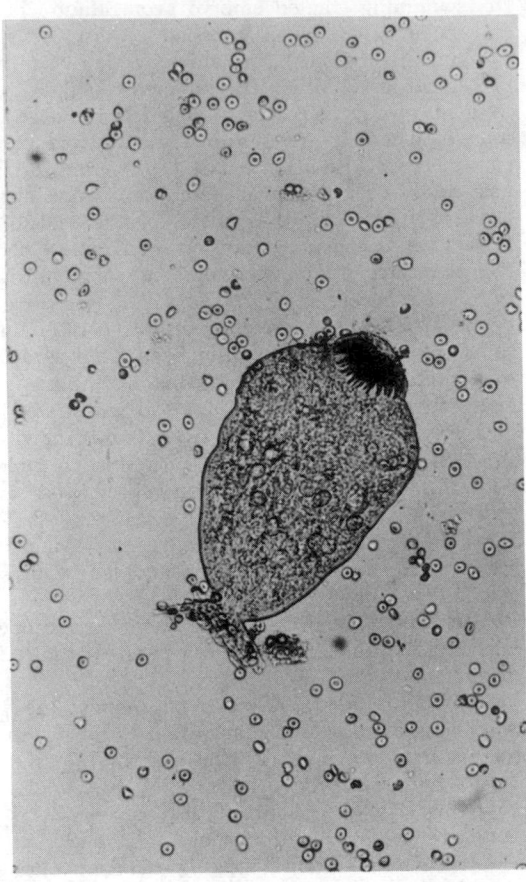

Fig. 45.   Hydatid sand. *Left.* **Scolices invaginated into cyst membrane.** ×140. *Right.* **Evaginated scolex with hooklets; stalk is present by which the scolex is continuous with the germinal epithelium.** ×140.

The hyaline outer wall is poorly developed, and the germinal membrane proliferates over the bony spicules, destroying bone tissue in its wake.

PATHOLOGY. The presence of the cyst in parenchymal tissue stimulates an encapsulating inflammatory and fibroblastic reaction. These expanding cysts may cause important destruction of hepatic and pulmonary tissues. The fluid within the friable cyst, moreover, may leak into surrounding tissue, causing a severe hypersensitivity reaction, sometimes culminating in fatal anaphylactic shock. At other times the leaking cyst may seed hydatid sand over the peritoneum or lung, resulting in the development of multiple cysts. A single unilocular cyst may grow to such huge proportions that it impairs hepatic function or obstructs major biliary ducts. Cerebral hydatid cysts usually destroy nervous tissue by slow expansion, while pulmonary cysts are usually well encapsulated, but may rupture and drain into the bronchi and be coughed up.

Osseous involvement results in progressive rarefaction of the bone and subsequent collapse. Calcified old hydatid cysts often are found by x-ray or as incidental autopsy findings.

SYMPTOMS. If the cysts develop in a particularly vital area, symptoms appear early. However, hepatic involvement is often without symptoms, and the cysts may become so huge as to be a physical burden. Pulmonary involvement may cause dyspnea, hemoptysis, and chest pain. It is not unusual for this disease to lie dormant 20 to 30 years before the onset of any symptoms. Hypergammaglobulinemia and eosinophilia are often present, and if leakage of hydatid fluid occurs, eosinophilia may rise dramatically.

DIAGNOSIS. Relatively specific serologic tests are currently available. The hemagglutination, bentonite-flocculation, and complement-fixation tests are all reliable. The Casoni skin test may be performed with some measure of confidence if proper controls are carried out. Finding the scolices, brood capsules, or daughter cysts in aspirated hydatid fluid obtained at surgery will provide the definitive laboratory diagnosis. Percutaneous aspiration of the cyst is dangerous and should not be attempted.

PROGNOSIS. If the cyst is not located in a vital position, patients will live for prolonged periods. If accessible to excision, the outlook is favorable.

TREATMENT. Surgical removal is advocated for all accessible cysts. The cyst wall is usually approached carefully, entered with a needle, and aspirated. The same volume of 10 percent formalin is returned to the cyst to sterilize its contents before enucleation is attempted. Recently, various hydatid antigens have been employed in an attempt to cure the infection. Although desensitization and general improvement may occur, they are not often curative. No chemotherapy is available currently.

PREVENTION. Dogs should be prevented from eating infected sheep carcasses, which should be buried or burned. Periodic anthelmintic treatment of dogs is advocated.

Multilocular Hydatid Disease

Alveolar hydatid infection caused by larval *E. multilocularis* in humans consists of irregular, usually empty cavities with wrinkled hyaline membranes, little fluid, and few if any scolices. The hyalinized walls are generally scanty, and the inner germinal membrane tends to proliferate. These irregular noncircumscribed growths are not usually operable; therefore, these infections always have a grave prognosis.

REFERENCES

GENERAL

Basu, A. K. Tropical Surgery. *In* Rab, C., and Smith, R., eds., Clinical Surgery (series). Washington, D.C., Butterworth, 1965, Part 8 of the series.

Belding, D. L. Textbook of Parasitology, 3rd ed. New York, Appleton-Century-Crofts, 1965.

Brown, H. W. Basic Clinical Parasitology, 3rd ed. New York, Appleton-Century-Crofts, 1969.

Faust, E. C. Human Helminthology, 3rd ed. Philadelphia, Lea and Febiger, 1949.

———— and Russell, P. C. Clinical Parasitology, 8th ed. Philadelphia, Lea and Febiger, 1970.

Garnham, P. C. C., Pierce, A. E., and Roitt, I. Immunity to Protozoa. A Symposium of the British Society for Immunology. Oxford, England, Blackwell Scientific Publications, 1963.

Goodman, L. S., and Gilman, A. The Pharmacological Basis of Therapeutics, 4th ed. New York, The Macmillan Co., 1970.

Hunter, G. W., Frye, W. W., and Swartzwelder, J. C. A Manual of Tropical Medicine, 4th ed. Philadelphia, W. B. Saunders Co., 1966.

Jelliffe, D. B. Child Health in the Tropics, A Practical Handbook for Medical and Para-medical Personnel, 2nd ed. London, Edward Arnold, Ltd., 1964.

Kagan, I. G. Evaluation of routine serologic testing for parasitic diseases. Amer. J. Pub. Health, 55:1820, 1965.

Kean, B. H., and Breslau, R. C. Parasites of the Human Heart. New York, Grune and Stratton, 1964.

Kudo, R. R. Protozoology, 5th ed. Springfield, Ill. Charles C Thomas, 1966.

Woodruff, A. W. Pathogenicity of intestinal helminthic infections. Trans. Roy. Soc. Trop. Med. Hyg., 59:585, 1965.

Van Der Hoeden, J., ed. Zoonoses. Amsterdam, London, New York, Elsevier Pub. Co., 1964.

Von Brand, T. Biochemistry of Parasites. New York, Academic Press, Inc., 1966.

NEMATODES

Anast, B. P., and Birch, C. L. Strongyloidiasis. *Strongyloides stercoralis*: report of 62 cases. J. Amer. Med. Wom. Ass., 18:623, 1963.

Babich, D. Strongyloidiasis. A report on twenty cases. Ethiopian Med. J., 4:57, 1965.

Bawa, Y. S., Chopra, J. S., and Sharma, T. D. Comparative study of bephenium hydroxynaphthoate and tetrachlorethylene in hookworm disease. Indian J. Med. Sci., 19:605, 1965.

Beaver, P. C., Snyder, C. H., Carrera, G. M., Dent, J. H., and Lafferty, J. W. Chronic eosinophilia due to visceral larva migrans. Pediatrics, 9:7, 1952.

Braun, R. C. Hookworm anaemia in a neonate. Ghana Med. J., 4:169, 1965.

Brown, R. E. Neurological manifestations associated with ascariasis. Trop. Geogr. Med., 17:121, 1965.

Choyce, D. P. Some observations on the ocular complications of onchocerciasis and their relationship to blindness. Trans. Roy. Soc. Trop. Med. Hyg., 52:112, 1958.

Danaraj, T. J., Pacheco, G., Shanmigaratnam, K., and Beaver, P. C. The etiology and pathology of eosinophilic lung (tropical eosinophilia). Amer. J. Trop. Med. Hyg., 15:183, 1966.

Duke, B. O. L. Studies on the chemoprophylaxis of loaiasis. II. Observations on diethylcarbamazine citrate (Banocide) as a prophylactic in man. Am. Trop. Med. Parasit., 57:82, 1963.

Edeson, J. F. B., and Wilson, T. The epidemiology of filariasis due to *Wuchereria bancrofti* and *Brugia malayi*. Ann. Rev. Entom., 9:245, 1964.

Foy, H., and Nelson, G. S. Helminths in the etiology of anemia in the tropics, with special reference to hookworms and schistosomes. Exp. Parasit., 14:240, 1963.

Gilbert, M. G., and Carbonnell, M. L. Pancreatitis in childhood associated with ascariasis. Pediatrics, 33:589, 1964.

Hawking, F. Advances in filariasis especially concerning periodicity of microfilariae. Trans. Roy. Soc. Trop. Med. Hyg., 59:9, 1965.

Hogan, M. J., Kimura, S. J., and Spencer, W. H. Visceral larva migrans and peripheral retinitis. J.A.M.A., 194:1345, 1965.

Huntley, C. E., Costas, M. C., and Lyerly, A. Visceral larva migrans syndrome: clinical characteristics and immunologic studies in 51 patients. Pediatrics, 36:523, 1965.

Jaggi, O. P. Pulmonary manifestations of intestinal ascariasis in children. J. Ass. Physicians India, 13:803, 1965.

Layrisse, M., and Roche, M. The relation between anemia and hookworm infection. Results of surveys of rural Venezuelan population. Amer. J. Hyg., 79:279, 1964.

Lee, D. L. The Physiology of Nematodes. London, Oliver and Boyd Ltd., 1965.

Mehrotra, M. P., and Malavuja, U. S. Single dose treatment of hookworm disease with bephenium hydroxynaphthoate. Indian J. Med. Sci., 17:930, 1963.

Most, H. Trichinellosis in the United States. Changing

epidemiology during past 25 years. J.A.M.A., 193:871, 1965.

Oduntan, J. O., Lucas, A. O., and Gilles, H. M. Treatment of dracontiasis with niridazole. Lancet II, 7506, 1967.

Richmond, H. G., and Guthrie, W. *Enterobius vermicularis* and the vermiform appendix. J. Path. Bact., 87: 415, 1964.

Rodger, F. C. Blindness in West Africa. London, H. K. Lewis and Co., Ltd., 1959.

——— A review of recent advances in scientific knowledge of the symptomatology, pathology and pathogenesis of onchocercal infection. Bull. W.H.O., 27:429, 1962.

Shrand, H. Visceral larva migrans *Toxocara canis* infection. Lancet, 1:1357, 1964.

Stone, O. J., Stone, C. T., and Mullins, J. F. Thiabendazole—Probable cure for trichinosis. Report of a case. J.A.M.A., 187:538, 1964.

Stone, O. J., and Mullins, J. F. Thiabendazole therapy for creeping eruption. Arch. Derm., 89:557, 1964.

Toussaint, D., and Davis, P. Retinopathy in generalized *Loa loa* filariasis. A clinicopathological study. Arch. Ophthal., 74:470, 1965.

Woodruff, A. W., and Thacker, C. K. Infection with animal helminths. Brit. Med. J., April 18, p. 1001, 1964.

TREMATODES

Aréan, V. M. Schistosomiasis. A clinicopathologic evaluation. *In* Sommers, S. C., ed., Pathology Annual, New York, Appleton-Century-Crofts, 1966, Vol. 1, pp. 68-126.

Cort, W. W. Studies on schistosome dermatitis. Amer. J. Hyg., 52:251, 1950.

Diaconita, G., and Goldis, G. Investigations on pathomorphology and pathogenesis of pulmonary paragonimiasis. Acta Tuberc. Scand., 44:51, 1964.

Dusek, J., Kubasta, M., Kodousek, R., and Kubastova, B. Needle biopsy of the liver in schistosomiasis mansoni: the value of histological examination. J. Trop. Med. Hyg., 68:189, 1965.

Einhorn, A. H., Futsch, A., Dwark, K. G., and Schookhoff, H. B. *Schistosoma mansoni* infection in children—Treatment with lucanthone hydrochloride (Nilodon). Amer. J. Dis. Child., 104:30-35, 1962.

Fripp, P. J. Bilharziasis and bladder cancer. Brit. J. Cancer, 19:292, 1965.

Gelfand, M. The frequency and bladder calcification in a sample of boys at St. Mary's Mission, Salisbury. Cent. Afr. J. Med., 11:14, 1965.

——— and Gilles, H. M. Filling defects of the bladder on intravenous pyelography in children passing schistosome ova in the urine. J. Trop. Med. Hyg., 69:4, 1966.

Gibson, J. B., and Sun, T. Chinese liver fluke—*Clonorchis sinensis*—its occurrence in Hong Kong. Bull. Int. Acad. Path., 60:94, 1965.

Hou, P. C., and Pang, L. S. C. *Clonorchis sinensis* infestation in man in Hong Kong. J. Path. Bact., 87: 245, 1964.

Kloetzel, K. Natural history and prognosis of splenomegaly in schistosomiasis mansoni. Amer. J. Trop. Med. Hyg., 13:541, 1964.

Lees, R. E. M. Lucanthone hydrochloride in the treatment of *Schistosoma mansoni* infection. Trans. Roy. Soc. Trop. Med. Hyg., 60:233, 1966.

Mous, A. H., Atta, A. A., El Rooby, A., El Garem, A., Wahab, M. F. Abdel, Raziky, S., and Hamed, A. Portal hypertension in hepatosplenic bilharziasis. J. Trop. Med. Hyg., 68:196, 1965.

Olivier, L. Schistosome dermatitis, a sensitization reaction. Amer. J. Hyg., 49:209, 1949.

Pantelouris, E. M. The Common Liver Fluke, *Fasciola hepatica* L. London, Pergamon Press, 1965.

Sadun, E., and Maiphoon, C. Studies on the epidemiology of the human intestinal fluke, *Fasciolopsis buski* (Lankester) in central Thailand. Amer. J. Trop. Med. Hyg., 2:1070, 1953.

Schacher, J. F., Khalel, G. M., and Salman, S. A field study of Halzoun (parasitic pharyngitis) in Lebanon. J. Trop. Med. Hyg., 68:226, 1965.

Stauber, L. A. Swimmer's itch in New Jersey. J. Parasit., 44:108, 1958.

Wang, C., Liu, J., Chang, T., and Miao, H. The clinical manifestations and bithionol therapy of paragonimiasis in Szechuan Province. Chin. Med. J. (Peking), 83: 163, 1964.

Wessel, H. U., Sommers, H. M., Cugell, D. W., and Paul, M. H. Variants of cardiopulmonary manifestations of Manson's schistosomiasis, Report of two cases. Ann. Intern. Med., 62:757, 1965.

World Health Organization. WHO Expert Committee on Bilharziasis. Third Report. Tech. Rep. Ser. No. 299, Geneva, 1965.

Yokogawa, S., Cort, W. W., and Yokogawa, M. Paragonimus and paragonimiasis. Exp. Parasit., 10:81-137, 139-205, 1960.

CESTODES

Bulletin of the World Health Organization on Echinococcosis. Vol. 39, #1, pp. 1-136, 1968.

Dixon, H. B. F., and Lipscomb, F. M. Cysticercosis—An analysis and follow-up of 450 cases. Privy Council, Med. Res. Spec. Rep. Ser. No. 299, London, 1961.

Heinz, H. J., and Klintworth, G. K. Cysticercosis in the aetiology of epilepsy. S. Afr. J. Med. Sci., 30:32, 1965.

LaFond, D. J., Thatcher, D. S., and Handeyside, R. G. Alveolar hydatid disease. J.A.M.A., 186:35, 1963.

Miller, M. J. Hydatid infection in Canada. Canad. Med. Ass. J., 68:423, 1953.

Seftel, H. C., and Heinz, H. J. Treatment of human tapeworm infections with Yomesan—single dose treatment in non-fasting subjects. S. Afr. Med. J., 38:263, 1964.

Swartzwelder, J. C., Beaver, P. C., and Hood, M. W. Sparganosis in southern United States. Amer. J. Trop. Hyg., 13:43, 1964.

Vachier, E., and Hillman, D. C. Solitary pulmonary hydatid cyst. Report of a case and discussion of its differential diagnosis. Pediatrics, 35:699, 1965.

Von Bonsdorff, B. *Diphyllobothrium latum* as a cause of pernicious anemia. Exp. Parasit., 5:207, 1956.

Wittner, M., and Tanowitz, H. Paromomycin therapy of human cestodiasis with special reference to hymenolepiasis. Amer. J. Trop. Med. Hyg., 20:433, 1971.

Yokogawa, M., and Yoshimura, H. Treatment of *Hymenolepsis nana* in children with cestocide Bayer 2353 (Yomesan). Jap. J. Parasit., 11:387, 1962.

14.52
PROTOZOAN DISEASES

MURRAY WITTNER

Representatives of each major group of the Phylum Protozoa cause serious human disease. As unicellular or "acellular" organisms, the Protozoa may be distinguished from all other phyla of the animal kingdom. Their diversity of size, shape, modes of reproduction, and environmental adaptation is without parallel. Many of the important protozoan diseases, summarized in Table 25, will be considered in this section.

Amebiasis

HOWARD B. SHOOKHOFF

Amebiasis is the condition caused by infection with *Entamoeba histolytica* or *Dientamoeba fragilis*. *E. histolytica*, as its name implies, is capable of penetrating and destroying tissues. Infection may extend to the liver and, occasionally, to other organs. *Dientamoeba fragilis* has not been proved to be invasive but does produce symptoms. Its effects are limited to the colon.

THE PARASITES. *Entamoeba histolytica* is a protozoan varying in size from about 10 to 35 μ in diameter. The infection is transmitted by resistant cysts, which vary in size from 5 to 20 μ. The nucleus typically shows a fine regular peripheral chromatin and a small, usually central, karyosome. The trophozoite is characterized by a progressive, flowing motility. The cyst is identified in its early stages by the presence of rod-shaped, refractile, chromatoid bars and, when mature, by the presence of two pairs of typical nuclei.

Dientamoeba fragilis has no known cyst form. The trophozoite is usually small, averaging 8 to 10 μ in diameter. Among the identifying characteristics is the presence of pointed or leaf-shaped pseudopods. Most of the organisms have two nuclei. This parasite is often overlooked because it can be found only in freshly passed stools examined promptly and with a consciousness on the part of the technician of its small size.

For further details concerning the identification of the pathogenic amebas and their differentiation from the nonpathogenic species found in the human intestinal tract, one should consult standard texts in the field of parasitology.

PATHOLOGY. The most frequent site of lesions is the cecum, in *E. histolytica* infections, but any or all parts of the colon, including the appendix, may be involved. Occasionally, the process involves the terminal portion of the ileum. The parasite evokes little cellular reaction when it invades the tissues of the colon. It causes lysis with edema, and this results in ulcers of varying size usually extending into the submucosa. The colon between the ulcers is usually normal, although in a few cases there is diffuse inflammation resembling that of nonspecific ulcerative colitis. In severe infections, the ulcers may extend to the peritoneal surface with perforation. Healing of ulcers rarely produces gross scarring.

Abscess of the liver due to *E. histolytica* may be single or multiple and most usually occurs in the right lobe. The process is one of liquefaction necrosis and the contents typically has a red-brown color. It is not true pus. As in the colon, *E. histolytica* evokes little cellular reaction. The parasites are found in the wall of the abscess; they are difficult to find in the necrotic contents.

Rarely, *E. histolytica* produces abscesses in the lung and brain, and granulomatous processes in the skin and colon.

The pathology of *D. fragilis* infections is not well known. There have been no fatalities. Since there is no tissue invasion, there are no ulcers and no metastatic complications.

TRANSMISSION AND PATHOGENESIS. Transmission of amebiasis due to *E. histolytica* results from the ingestion of cysts in food or fluids contaminated with human feces or on fingers or other objects directly contaminated with human feces. This last applies to persons in institutions who have lost control of their personal habits through severe psychiatric disturbance or mental retardation. It also applies to children brought up in environments devoid of sanitary facilities where the soil near dwellings is contaminated with dejecta. More normal persons living in environments which offer some degree of sanitary controls may be infected by ingestion of raw vegetables grown in fecally contaminated soil. Food and dishes may be contaminated by food handlers who are infected and fail to wash their hands effectively. Infection may also occur from improperly protected water supply or ice produced under unsanitary conditions.

After cysts are ingested, the wall is weakened by digestive enzymes. Trophozoites emerge from the cysts and attack the wall of the colon. The presence of intestinal bacteria is essential to production of lesions.

The mode of transmission of *D. fragilis*, which has no known cyst form, is unknown.

EPIDEMIOLOGY. Amebiasis is by no means a tropical disease. It occurs all over the world. In general, the prevalence of the infection varies inversely with the degree of sanitation. Where there is virtually no sanitary control of the environment, the rate of infection may exceed 70 percent. An example of this may be seen at times in institutions for the mentally retarded or regressed among patients that cannot be kept clean and exist in an environment of fecal contamination. Poor sanitation is not limited to warm areas of the earth. In areas with permafrost, satisfac-

TABLE 25. *Human Parasitic Infections: Protozoa*

Disease	Parasite	Location in Man	Transmission	Typical Clinical Findings	Diagnosis	Treatment	Age-Incidence
Malaria malignant tertian	*Plasmodium falciparum*	Intraerythrocytic	Sporozoites inoculated by female *Anopheles* mosquito	Fever, splenomegaly, anemia	Parasites in peripheral blood smear	Chloroquine, pyrimethamine, quinine	Peak incidence in first decade of life
benign tertian quartan oval	*P. vivax* *P. malariae* *P. ovale*					Chloroquine, primaquine	
Toxoplasmosis	*Toxoplasma gondii*	Central nervous system, lung, heart	Transplacental, insufficiently cooked meats (?)	Chorioretinitis, hydrocephalus, seizures	X-ray (cerebral calcification), serologic	Pyrimethamine, sulfonamides	Congenital and postnatal; incidence rises with age
Amebiasis	*Entamoeba histolytica*	Large intestine, liver	Ingestion of cysts in water and food	Diarrhea, abdominal distress, dysentery	Trophozoites or cysts in feces	Intestinal: Paramomycin, diiodohydroxyquin, Metronidazole Extraintestinal: Chloroquine, Metronidazole, emetine	Varies with sanitation, common in children's institutions
Dientamebiasis	*Dientamoeba fragilis*	Large intestine	Ingestion of trophozoites	Diarrhea	Trophozoites in feces	Diiodohydroxyquin, paramomycin	Higher incidence in institutions
Balantidiasis	*Balantidium coli*	Large intestine	Ingestion of cysts in water or food	Mild to severe diarrhea or dysentery	Trophozoites or cysts in feces	Tetracyclines, diiodohydroxyquin, paramomycin	Poor sanitation and close institutional contact
Giardiasis	*Giardia intestinalis*	Small intestine	Ingestion of cysts in water or food	Mucous diarrhea, abdominal distress, spruelike symptoms	Trophozoites and cysts in feces	Quinacrine, Metronidazole	Most common in children, especially in institutions
Trichomonas vaginitis	*Trichomonas vaginalis*	Vagina, urethra, prostate	Sexual contact; occasionally unsanitary bathing facilities	Vaginal discharge, pruritus, burning sensation	Trophozoites in vaginal or prostatic secretions	Metronidazole	Uncommon in preadolescent males or females

Disease	Organism	Location in host	Mode of infection	Symptoms	Diagnosis	Treatment	Epidemiology
Chagas' disease	Trypanosoma cruzi	Early: peripheral blood; Late: intracellular, heart	Trypanosomal forms enter skin or mucous membranes in feces of "kissing bug" (Triatoma)	Edema, myocarditis, neurologic symptoms, Romaña's sign, megaesophagus, megacolon	Early: trypanosomes in peripheral blood; Late: xenodiagnosis, serologic tests	Bayer 7602, levofur altadone (Altafur); None	Peak incidence in children 2-3 years
African sleeping sickness	T. gambiense T. rhodosiense	Blood, lymphatics, spinal fluid	Through skin by bite of "tsetse" fly (Glossina)	Fever, lymphadenopathy, meningoencephalitis	Trypanosomes in peripheral blood smear, lymph node aspirate, spinal fluid	Blood infection: suramin or pentamidine; CNS infection: tryparsamide, Mel B, Mel W	Usually in 20-30 year age group; more frequent in children during epidemics
Leishmaniasis kala-azar	Leishmania donovani	Within histiocytes and macrophages of spleen, liver, GI tract	Through skin, usually bite of "sandfly" (Phlebotomus)	Fever, hepatomegaly, malaise, bleeding diathesis	Bone marrow aspiration, liver biopsy	Ethylstibamine hydroxystilbamidine	Frequent in infants, adolescents
cutaneous oriental sore	L. tropica	Within histiocytes and macrophages in skin	Through skin, usually bite of "sandfly" (Phlebotomus)	Skin ulcer of exposed areas, ulceration of naso-oral mucosa, erosion of external ear	Smear and culture from ulcer scraping	Dry ice, stibophen (Fuadin), berberine sulfate	All ages and sexes; custom to give immunizing lesion
mucocutaneous	L. braziliensis	Within histiocytes and macrophages in skin and mucous membranes				Dry ice, stibophen, chloroquine, amphotericin B	Varies with region; in some more than 75% infection in children
Pneumocystis pneumonia	Pneumocystis carinii	Pulmonary alveolar cells and in alveolar exudate	?	Dyspnea, cough, fever	Sputum examination and open pleural biopsy	Isethianate pentamidine, hydroxystilbamidine	Especially in first 6 months of life; premature infants

tory drainage is difficult to establish, and amebiasis has been found prevalent in some Eskimo populations. The first case of amebic dysentery ever recognized occurred in Leningrad, in the colder fringe of the temperate zone.

Amebiasis is usually less common in children than in adults, but there is no inherent immunity. Amebic dysentery has been described during the first weeks of life. Such cases are rare, however, since many children are fairly well protected from peroral infection during their early months. Amebic infections, once acquired, tend to persist. The longer one lives, therefore, the more likely one is to be infected. In areas where sanitation is poor, there is a gradual increase in childhood infection during the first 15 years of life.

Epidemics of amebiasis occur occasionally and are usually related to some gross defect in the water supply system.

CLINICAL MANIFESTATIONS. Of all persons infected with pathogenic amebas, only a small proportion have severe symptoms at any one time. Many more have mild symptoms and probably half or more are asymptomatic. These are often called carriers but the term is misleading because they may develop mild or severe symptoms subsequently. Illness due to amebiasis usually has a subacute or chronic course. An acute onset is uncommon. The symptoms are frequently intermittent rather than continuous.

Severe cases are characterized by marked diarrhea, often with blood and mucus in the stools. Abdominal pain often accompanies the diarrhea but is not necessarily severe. Appetite is usually diminished and nausea may be present but vomiting occurs infrequently. Fever and leucocytosis are present in some cases but by no means all. If the febrile reaction is marked, it raises the suspicion that a liver abscess is also present. In these severe cases, sigmoidoscopy often shows abnormalities. Usually these consist of discrete ulcerations separated by a normal mucosa, but, occasionally, a diffusely inflamed, friable mucous membrane, indistinguishable from that of nonspecific ulcerative colitis, is found. Barium enema may be negative or there may be areas of spasm, especially in the cecum, which may be contracted and irregular. Occasionally, evidence of ulceration can be made out and, rarely, a localized, tumorlike process called ameboma is seen in the cecum or other portion of the colon.

The majority of patients with clinical disease have mild symptoms. In adults, these are of two types —gastrointestinal and constitutional. Aside from diarrhea, gastrointestinal symptoms are usually vague. Abdominal pain may occur but more often there is ill-defined distress or abdominal distention. Constitutional symptoms include fatigue, low-grade fever, and backache, or other ill-defined somatic aching. These symptoms are often not sufficiently severe to lead to medical consultation. Children are less likely to be articulate about such complaints. Abdominal pain seems to be the most common symptom but this is so frequent in children that it is difficult to evaluate.

A common clinical picture is recurrent mild diarrhea with poor appetite, pallor, sometimes mild fever, and some retardation of growth. Nausea may occur but vomiting is uncommon. The liver is often palpable and sensitive although actual abscess is relatively rare. There may be other, ill-defined abdominal tenderness.

In these relatively mild cases, sigmoidoscopy usually shows no abnormalities. Blood count, sedimentation rate of erythrocytes, and liver function tests are usually normal.

Amebiasis should be suspected in any child with vague persistent or recurrent ill health associated with gastrointestinal symptoms.

LABORATORY DIAGNOSIS. The clinical manifestations of intestinal amebiasis are not diagnostic. Even in those few cases with typical ulcerations seen through the sigmoidoscope, the diagnosis should be confirmed by the identification of the parasites in the stool, or in scrapings from the ulcers. Identification of amebas requires considerable experience, and errors are frequent unless the technician has received special training. Furthermore, specimens must be obtained under proper conditions. The most useful specimen is a freshly passed, diarrheal stool, which should be examined for trophozoites within 20 to 30 minutes in warm physiologic saline solution. If blood-streaked mucus is present, this is the most likely portion of the stool to show parasites.

If diarrhea is not present, it should be produced by the administration of a cathartic. For children over the age of 6 years, saline laxatives, such as the mixture of sodium phosphate and sodium acid phosphate marketed as Fleet's Phospho-Soda, can be used. The average dose is 25 ml of the solution and it is made more acceptable by administering a carbonated soft drink as a "chaser." In younger children, milk of magnesia given the night before the examination is usually more acceptable and more effective. The dose is from 10 to 20 ml depending on the size of the child. Any other laxative which is not oily and which can be expected to produce a partially liquid stool may be used.

If the specimen cannot be examined promptly, it may be preserved in a polyvinyl alcohol (PVA) mixture, and stained and examined at a later convenient time. This method is slightly less satisfactory than the fresh examination, since light infections may be missed. Cysts are not regularly preserved by this method.

Examination of nondiarrheal stools or of stools which are not fresh is by no means useless. In *E. histolytica* infections, if cysts are present, they persist for many hours or several days unless the specimen is allowed to dry out. If only a few cysts are present, they may be uncovered by concentration methods. Occasionally trophozoites can be found in formed stools if they are examined fresh.

The finding of amebic cysts or trophozoites by a reliable observer is definitive. A negative report on a formed specimen or a specimen which is diarrheal but not examined promptly cannot be considered to rule out the presence of such an infection. The yield of positive findings in a freshly passed, diarrheal stool is about four times that of a casual specimen in *E. histolytica* infections. With *D. fragilis*, the fresh specimen is mandatory. This parasite is often difficult to stain in preserved preparations.

The presence of cysts is often thought to indicate an inactive infection, a "carrier" state. This is incorrect. Either form of the parasite is diagnostic of infection. The clinical status of the patient is not indicated by the presence or absence of cyst forms.

Cultivation of the stool for amebas is generally much less successful than direct examination. It has some value as a supplementary method in cases in which the diagnostic characteristics of amebas found on direct examination are not definitive. Complement-fixation and hemagglutination tests on the blood serum, which must be performed in specialized laboratories, are frequently negative in intestinal amebiasis.

COMPLICATIONS. *Liver abscess* is the most frequent complication of amebiasis. Although the infection must gain entrance through the colon, it may occur in the absence of amebic colitis or a history suggestive of prior involvement of the colon. While less frequent in children than in adults, it is not extremely rare as was thought in earlier years. If the diagnosis is not made, the outcome is usually fatal.

The common clinical manifestations are fever, enlargement and tenderness of the liver, polymorphonuclear leucocytosis, and anemia. The liver enlargement is usually manifest to abdominal palpation and it is not infrequently possible to outline a distinct mass within the enlarged liver. Radiologic examination of the lungs may show upward displacement of the right leaf of the diaphragm. Occasionally this manifestation occurs in the absence of palpable enlargement and in such cases it is of great diagnostic importance. There may also be evidence of consolidation at the base of the right lung, or a right pleural effusion, or both. Children who are old enough to express themselves usually complain of upper abdominal pain. At times, pain is referred to the right shoulder or to the right lower quadrant of the abdomen.

Liver function tests are usually normal with the exception of the serum alkaline phosphatase, which is elevated in one-third of cases in adults. Such elevation may be difficult to interpret in children. Occasionally the leucocyte count is normal but marked elevation of the erythrocyte sedimentation rate is a constant finding.

The diagnosis of amebic liver abscess is supported by the finding of *E. histolytica* in the stools. However, in most reported series, this is stated to occur only in a minority of cases. One may suspect that the use of postcathartic specimens might well yield a higher proportion of positive results. Serologic tests are almost always positive but they are available only in a few specialized laboratories. If pus is aspirated from the liver, it may have the typical red-brown color, but just as often it is yellow or gray-green. Absence of bacteria on smear and culture is strongly suggestive of an amebic etiology of the ab-scess. Amebas are often not found on direct examination of aspirated pus, but may be found more easily if the pus is liquefied with a streptokinase-streptodornase mixture and the resulting sediment carefully examined. If surgical drainage has been performed, the pus escaping after the first day is very likely to show amebas, provided no specific therapy has been given, since it comes from the wall of the abscess.

Valuable indirect evidence of liver abscess may be obtained by scanning of the liver following administration of an appropriate radioactive substance. It must be emphasized that neither routine aspiration nor surgical drainage is recommended in most cases of suspected liver abscess. The safest procedure is to give specific therapy, usually emetine (see below), and observe the response. If the abscess is amebic, results are usually dramatic. If there is no response within 3 or 4 days, aspiration or surgical drainage is indicated. There may be a bacterial abscess, a secondarily infected amebic abscess, or a nonsuppurative lesion.

Amebic abscess may be complicated by rupture into the right pleural cavity, the right lung, the pericardium, the peritoneal cavity, the subphrenic space, or one of the hollow viscera of the abdomen. It may also perforate through the body wall. This last event and perforation into an adherent lung with spontaneous drainage through the bronchial tree may both actually have a favorable outcome. Otherwise, perforation is apt to have grave consequences.

Amebic abscess of the lung is usually secondary to abscess of the liver, although a few primary cases are reported.

Amebic abscess of the brain is extremely rare and usually secondary to liver abscess.

Amebic Granuloma. This may occur in the colon, where it produces the symptoms of a tumor. Granulomatous lesions of the skin usually occur where the skin is in continuity with an infected viscus, that is, at the anus, at the site of a drainage wound for a liver abscess, or at the site of a colostomy performed by mistake. They are usually painful.

TREATMENT. *Intestinal Amebiasis.* In children with asymptomatic infection, treatment with Diodoquin (diiodohydroxyquinoline) alone is usually sufficient. The dose is 0.325 g (½ tablet) three times a day for 20 days in children weighing less than 20 kg. From 20 to 39 kg, the dose should be 0.65 g twice a day, and for children 40 kg and over, 0.65 g three times a day.

When there are definite symptoms, such as recurrent diarrhea or abdominal pain, tetracycline in a dose of 0.25 g four times a day for 5 days should be given to children 20 kg or more in weight, preceding or simultaneously with the diodoquin. For children less than 20 kg, the dose of tetracycline should be 0.25 g three times a day.

In the case of severe dysenteric amebiasis, treatment should begin wtih emetine hydrochloride given by deep subcutaneous injection. The dose should be 1 mg per kg and should not exceed 60 mg, once a day for not more than 5 days. Often the dysentery will be controlled after two or three injections. At this point, they should be stopped and the tetracycline-diiodohydroxyquinoline treatment instituted. Emetine is potentially toxic to the myocardium, and daily observation of the heart and blood pressure is indicated during treatment. This drug may be lifesaving in severe infections and the clinician should not be dissuaded from using it because of its potential toxicity.

Liver Abscess. Most cases of amebic liver abscess will respond to chloroquine. The total dose of the phosphate should be 200 mg per kg with a maximum of 10 g. The usual daily dose is 5 mg per kg twice a day, the maximum individual dose being 250 mg. Many believe that chloroquine should be combined with emetine. The author feels that the best procedure is to give emetine as suggested for severe dysentery, and to discontinue it as soon as a clear clinical response has occurred. At this time, chloroquine treatment is instituted. In all cases, following the chloroquine, tetracycline and diiodohydroxyquinoline should be given. In a small minority of cases, aspiration or surgical drainage will be required. Incomplete resolution of the abscess is indicated by persistence or recurrence of fever, by persistence of leucocytosis, or by a persistently elevated erythrocyte sedimentation rate. The patient should not be dismissed from follow-up until temperature and leucocyte count have remained normal for at least two weeks after chloroquine has been finished and the sedimentation rate has shown progressive decrease toward normal range.

Granuloma of Skin. This requires emetine in the doses already indicated.

Determination of Cure. Warm stool examinations should be negative at approximately 1, 3, and 6 months after completion of all treatment before the child is discharged from observation.

Alternate Therapeutic Agents. For the treatment of liver abscess, metronidazole (Flagyl) in a dose of 750 mg three times a day for 10 days has been reported as highly effective. Further evaluation of this treatment and a determination of the correct dose for children is awaited.

If the treatment outlined above for intestinal amebiasis should fail, there are a number of other agents that can be substituted for diiodohydroxyquinoline. One of the most effective is paromomycin (Humatin). The dose should be 25 mg per kg per day, divided into two or three doses, for 5 days.

Primary Amebic Meningoencephalitis

MURRAY WITTNER

Culbertson's initial report in 1958 demonstrated that previously unsuspected free-living, soil-inhabiting amebae could invade the central nervous system and cause fatal meningoencephalitis. Within a few years, a number of reports appeared from various parts of the world essentially confirming this observation.

The organism isolated from pathologic lesions has been identified as *Naegleria gruberi*. Initial reports, however, described other species of free-living amebae, i.e., *Acanthamoeba sp.* and *Hartmanella sp.* At present, it is not entirely clear whether all these species may be implicated or just *Naegleria gruberi*. Unambiguous identification of these organisms is not routine and should be referred to a qualified protozoologist for confirmation.

Significantly, in almost every case of primary amebic meningoencephalitis a recent history of swimming in fresh or brackish water has been obtained. In one instance, however, recent extraction of two maxillary molars had occurred. It is believed the amebae gain access to the body through the nasal mucosa. Moreover, Culbertson has been able to produce the disease in mice by instilling *Naegleria* or *Acanthamoeba* into the nares of mice.

CLINICAL FEATURES. With a single exception, all cases have occurred in young, previously healthy individuals between the ages of 8 and 27 years. The onset of symptoms usually has been abrupt and has been fatal within 1 to 2 days. A fulminant course, marked by severe headache, nausea, vomiting, and rapidly deepening coma, has been reported. Cerebrospinal fluid examination may reveal large numbers of neutrophils, sugar may be low or normal, and the protein elevated. Erythrocytes may be found. Microscopic examination of fresh cerebrospinal fluid under high magnification on a warm stage may reveal motile amebae.

Most histopathologic studies have shown severe lytic necrosis and hemorrhage along the base of the brain in the regions of the olfactory bulbs and cerebellum; organisms, although difficult to discern, can be identified under high magnification with ordinary staining methods. Isolation of amebae from liver, spleen, and lung in one case, and the presence of myocarditis in several other cases, suggests that dissemination may occur. Presently, it is not entirely certain whether the portal of entry is always by way of the nasal mucosa, cribiform plate, and then into the neural tissue, since experimental infections may also result in severe hemorrhagic pneumonia.

THERAPY. At present no drug is available for the treatment of this fatal infection.

Malaria

Malaria is a disease of man, as well as other vertebrates, caused by sporozoa of genus *Plasmodium*. This disease has been known since antiquity. Hippocrates, who studied in Egypt, unmistakably described the various forms of malaria. Long before the etiology of malaria was discovered by Laveran at the end of the 19th century it was clear that malaria was related to the "emanations of the swamps," thus the name "malaria."

Presently there are four species of *Plasmodium* recognized as the usual etiologic agents of human malaria. These are *P. falciparum, P. vivax, P. malariae,* and *P. ovale.* Recently cases of naturally acquired simian malaria have been reported. It is not clear how widespread this may be. The discovery, however, was not unexpected, inasmuch as it is well known that other simian malarias could be successfully transmitted to man by artificial means.

Until recently, malaria was the most important parasitic disease of man (schistosomiasis now acquires this dubious honor); it infects an estimated 100,000,000 individuals throughout the world, and accounts for just under a million deaths annually. It is found, with few exceptions, throughout the tropical, subtropical, and parts of the temperate zones, wherever a suitable species of anopheline mosquito exists. Over the past two decades, however, extensive malaria-eradication programs have been responsible for eliminating, or reducing, this disease in many endemic areas of the world. Moreover, with widespread, low-priced travel becoming commonplace, it is essential to consider malaria in those individuals who have returned from malarious regions.

LIFE HISTORY. In order to complete successfully its life cycle, *Plasmodium* requires an alternation of a vertebrate host in whom schizogony occurs, with a female anopheline mosquito in whom sporogony takes place.

The studies by Fairly, during World War II, demonstrated that within one hour of an infective mosquito bite sporozoites disappear from the circulation. The mystery of their disappearance was finally solved when it was found that, upon leaving the circulation, the sporozoites invaded hepatic parenchymal cells, and underwent repeated nuclear divisions producing, as the end product of schizogony, many thousands of merozoites. The parasitized host cell next ruptures, releasing these merozoites, many of which are phagocytized by the host although others enter another hepatic cell to initiate schizogony anew. During this preerythrocytic cycle the patient's blood is free of parasites, and he cannot transmit the disease; i.e., this is a prepatent period. As this period ends, merozoites leave the liver and invade red blood cells, initiating the erythrocytic cycle. Within the parasitized erythrocytes, schizogony is repeated regularly, releasing new groups of merozoites into the bloodstream. After a period of time, some merozoites invade red cells, and rather than undergoing schizogony develop into macro- or microgametocytes. These subsequently must be ingested by a suitable mosquito in order to undergo further development. Merozoites formed as a result of the initial or primary preerythrocytic cycle in *P. falciparum* apparently differ from those of the other three species inasmuch as they do not reinvade liver cells, but enter the circulation and invade erythrocytes. Thus, unlike the other three species of human *Plasmodium, P. falciparum* does not maintain both exoerythrocytic and erythrocytic cycles simultaneously. This distinction is of the utmost importance with regard to therapy, and is probably the basis for relapse in vivax, malarial, and ovale infections.

Shortly after a suitable anopheline mosquito ingests gametocytes together with her blood meal, the male or microgametocyte forms 6 to 8 microgametes ("exflagellation"). Similarly, the female or macrogametocyte undergoes maturation to become a gamete, and fertilization takes place with fusion of the micro- and macrogamete. During the next 12 to 24 hours the resulting zygote elongates and becomes a motile ookinete which actively penetrates the epithelial cell brush border of the midgut and comes to rest on the inner aspect of the peritropic membrane of the mosquito's stomach. Here development proceeds as the zygote becomes a rounded, enlarged oocyst in which sporogony occurs resulting in thousands of sporozoites. Subsequently, the mature oocyst ruptures liberating huge numbers of sporozoites into the mosquito's hemocoel. These invade all the insect's tissues, many reaching the salivary glands. Thus, when the mosquito next feeds, infective sporozoites are inoculated into the human host; depending upon climatic conditions and other host factors, the mosquito cycle takes 7 to 20 days or longer.

PATHOLOGY. Other than destruction of a few liver cells there is little evidence to suggest that significant pathologic damage can be attributed to the pre- or exoerythrocytic stages. The fundamental lesion can be attributed to the cyclic destruction of erythrocytes with subsequent development of anemia of varying severity usually depending upon the plasmodial species involved. The observations of Kitchen suggest *P. vivax* invades reticulocytes, *P. malariae* prefers mature erythrocytes, and *P. falciparum* has no preference. This may, in part, account for the greater parasitemia often encountered in falciparum malaria. Erythrocyte destruction is enhanced by erythrophagocytosis of nonparasitized cells. Nevertheless, it is most unusual to obtain evidence of red cell sensitization by either direct or indirect Coombs' test. During acute episodes the hematocrit and hemoglobin determinations are reduced; reticulocytosis is usually present and bone marrow aspiration reveals erythroid hyperplasia. There may be moderate leucocytosis although leucopenia and thrombocytopenia are also frequently encountered early in the acute episode.

With increased destruction of erythrocytes, malarial pigment, termed hemazoin, as well as hemosiderin, cell debris, and merozoites, stimulate reticuloendothelial activity. The viscera, including the brain, may take on a slate-gray to black appearance as a result of sequestered malarial pigment.

The spleen may enlarge during an acute attack. At this time the capsule is thin, easily torn, and the pulp diffluent. After many years the capsule becomes thickened and the pulp fibrous. Splenomegaly is then irreversible. Splenic enlargement is so typical that palpation has been used for epidemiologic purposes to determine indices of prevalence, distribution, and intensity of malaria.

Hepatomegaly is also common. Kupffer cells are filled with brown to black hemazoin, and parenchymal cells with yellow hemosiderin. There may be centilobular necrosis which may be related to hypoxemia. Liver function usually is not seriously impaired although there may be increases in conjugated bilirubin, SGOT/SGPT, and BSP retention. Serum albumin may decrease, and there is almost always an absolute increase in serum globulins.

For many years it has been recognized that P. falciparum infected erythrocytes become sequestered in visceral capillaries where schizogony takes place. Recent experimental evidence has shown changes in the cell membrane of erythrocytes parasitized by late stage trophozoites and schizonts. It is believed these alterations are responsible for the tendency of these cells to clump and adhere to capillary endothelium. Thus capillary occlusion, or decreased flow, appears to be responsible for the hypoxemic lesions that may be found especially in the brain and gastrointestinal tract. Lesions resembling those of glomerulonephritis have been reported most frequently, although not exclusively, in children with P. malariae infection.

CLINICAL ASPECTS. Older children and adults may exhibit the typical clinical picture of malaria characterized by intermittent febrile episodes, anemia, and splenomegaly. The incubation period (interval from infectious mosquito bite to symptoms) in the nonimmune varies widely depending upon the species and strain of Plasmodium (P. falciparum, 9 to 14 days; P. ovale, 16 to 18 days; P. malariae, 18 to 40 days; P. vivax, 12 to 17 days). Certain strains of P. vivax, however, may have incubation periods of 6 to 12 months or more and, following the discontinuance of suppressant drugs, P. malariae and P. ovale can exhibit delayed primary attacks of several years.

The initial or primary attack often is heralded by a short prodromal period of several days to a week and consists of irregular fevers, anorexia, chilliness, arthralgias, abdominal discomfort, and mild diarrhea. This is followed by the primary attack, lasting several weeks, during which there are recurring intermittent paroxysms classically consisting of four more or less distinct stages: shaking chills, high fever, drenching sweats, and an apyrexial period. The paroxysms recur at approximately 48-hour intervals with P. vivax, P. ovale, and P. falciparum (tertian fevers); P. malariae recurs every 72 hours (quartan fever). Since the paroxysm coincides with rupture of infected erythrocytes and release of merozoites, pigment, and cell debris into the circulation, many workers have come to regard this as a cause and effect relationship. Acute splenic enlargement is often associated with left upper quadrant pain. Usually renal and hepatic function remain unimpaired. P. falciparum, or malignant tertian malaria, accounts for most of the severe or pernicious complications and nearly all the deaths. Almost any symptom referable to central nervous system involvement has been described and presumably is related to that area in which capillary occlusion and/or hypoxemia has occurred. The onset of cerebral malaria may appear unheralded and may occur when the parasitemia is low or high. Meningeal signs are especially common in children, but examination of the cerebrospinal fluid usually is normal. Alternatively, severe gastrointestinal, cardiovascular, respiratory, or urogenital symptoms can dominate the picture, and may have a fatal termination.

The natural history of malaria is such that clinical attacks or relapses become less frequent, and after a variable period the infection disappears. P. falciparum infection lasts about 9 months to a year, and P. vivax, 1 to 8 years; but P. malariae can persist for decades as a latent infection and relapses have recurred after 30 years.

While congenital malaria undoubtedly occurs in endemic areas, it is a rare event. In most instances the mother acquired the disease during pregnancy. This may result in fatal termination of the pregnancy, or the child may develop malaria early in the perinatal period.

During the first few years of life the acute disease may be unlike malaria as seen in adults. The child is restless, dull, irritable, with little or no appetite. Abdominal pain and vomiting are frequent. The liver and spleen are enlarged, temperature may range from 101° to 105° F and be continuous, remittent, or intermittent. Typical paroxysms seldom occur. If untreated the child's condition may worsen and he may die, or the acute symptoms may gradually abate, passing into a stage of chronic malaria. The spleen may become exceedingly large, extending into the pelvis, and is liable to spontaneous or traumatic rupture. Some children develop "malarial cachexia," which usually has a fatal outcome.

The development of immunity to malaria involves both humoral and cellular mechanisms. Increased phagocytic activity, hyperplasia of reticuloendothelial components, and the appearance of high titers of strain-specific protective antibodies in serum are important features of the immune response. In endemic or hyperendemic regions, infants are born with passive immunity to malaria as a result of placental transfer of protective antibodies. During the first few years of life repeated infection and active disease may result in acquired active immunity. Such immunity may keep individuals relatively free of clinical attack even in the presence of significant parasitemia. Serum gamma globulin levels become markedly increased with the development of immunity. Moreover, inoculation of hyperimmune globulin has been shown to prevent or diminish an acute malaria attack. Considerable evidence has been acquired indicating that individuals with abnormal hemoglobins, especially sickle-cell trait, have fewer parasites and milder disease than those with normal hemoglobin. Individuals with erythrocyte glucose-6-phosphate dehydrogenase deficiency are said to be similarly disposed.

DIAGNOSIS. The definitive diagnosis of malaria is made by microscopic identification of the organisms on stained thin and thick blood smears. It is important to examine thick films since they provide a higher concentration of parasites which is indispensable when parasitemia is low or thin films negative. Preferably, the blood smear should be stained with Giemsa's stain, although Wright's stain can be used. Since parasites are continuously present in peripheral red blood cells during schizogony, blood can be taken and examined at any time with *P. vivax, P. ovale,* and *P. malariae* infections. In *P. falciparum* infections, however, only rings may be present immediately after the fever peaks. If symptoms have been present for 7 to 9 days, usually gametocytes will be present in the peripheral blood and species identification can be readily made. Recently, the fluorescent antibody technique has been employed as a specific diagnostic test with excellent results; however, it is not yet generally available.

TREATMENT AND PROPHYLAXIS. The management of malaria not only demands prompt chemotherapy, but the patient must be given supportive care while being kept under careful observation.

Antimalarial chemotherapy is outlined in Table 26. Treatment of the acute attack is aimed at destroying erythrocytic stages of the parasite as rapidly as possible. For this purpose chloroquine is the drug of choice; it is a powerful schizonticidal 4-aminoquinoline that may be administered by the oral or, if necessary, by the intramuscular route. Clinical and parasitic response can usually be detected in 72 hours, although it may take another 72 hours for all signs and symptoms to subside. Gametocytes of *P. falciparum* will often be detected for several weeks thereafter.

Certain strains of *P. falciparum* from southeast Asia, and parts of South America, have been found resistant to therapeutic doses of chloroquine. Quinine should be employed when resistance is encountered. It is preferable to use oral quinine, but in serious situations, or if vomiting intervenes, it may be given by the intravenous route. Toxicity to quinine can develop rapidly if renal function is impaired. The use of quinine alone is often associated with a significant recrudescence rate which can be reduced appreciably by also giving pyrimethamine, 25 mg three times a day for 3 days.

Primaquine should be given for the eradication of persisting hepatic (exoerythrocytic) stages of *P. vivax, P. ovale,* and *P. malariae.* It is unnecessary, however, for *P. falciparum* malaria since secondary exoerythrocytic forms apparently are not formed. Similarly, it is unnecessary in the treatment of transfusion malaria since erythrocytic forms do not establish an exoerythrocytic cycle. Primaquine may cause hemolysis in individuals with glucose-6-phosphate dehydrogenase deficiency. In high doses it may cause hemolytic anemia, methemoglobinemia, and leucopenia. It should not be used concurrently with quinacrine (Atabrine), quinine, or sulfonamides.

Chemoprophylaxis with chloroquine is highly

TABLE 26. *Summary of the Clinical Use of Chloroquine, Quinine, and Primaquine in Malaria*

Clinical Situation	Drug and Usual Preparation	Route of Administration	Dose as Active Base or as Salt	Dosage and Schedule of Administration
Clinical attack	Chloroquine phosphate, USP XVII*	Oral	Base	0 hours, 10 mg/kg; 6 hours, 5 mg/kg; 24 hours, 5 mg/kg; 48 hours, 5 mg/kg
	Quinine sulfate USP XV†	Oral	Salt	20-30 mg/kg per day divided into 3 doses for 7-10 days
Emergency requirement for parenteral route	Chloroquine dihydrochloride‡	Intramuscular	Base	5 mg/kg, may be repeated once in 24-hour period
	Quinine hydrochloride, USP XV§	Intravenous	Salt	10 mg/kg well diluted in saline over 1-hour period, may be repeated twice in 24-hour period
Eradication, exoerythrocytic stage	Primaquine phosphate, USP XVII‖	Oral	Base	0.3 mg/kg once a day for 14 days
Personal prophylactic suppression	Chloroquine phosphate, USP XVII#	Oral	Base	5 mg/kg once a week

*Drug of choice; maximal initial dose 600 mg of the base.

†For use only in case of resistance to chloroquine and other antimalarials; maximal total daily dose 2 g.

‡Use oral route as soon as possible; maximal single dose 300 mg of the base.

§Use oral route as soon as possible; maximal single dose 650 mg.

‖Do not use concurrently with quinacrine or sulfonamides; discontinue if evidence of hemolysis; maximal single dose 15 mg of the base.

#Start 1 week before and continue 1 month after being in malarious area; maximal single dose 300 mg of the base.

effective, and will suppress all clinical activity of the disease except for resistant strains of *P. falciparum*. It is important to realize, however, that prophylaxis with chloroquine does *not* prevent infection, but only destroys erythrocytic stages. Hepatic or exo-erythrocytic stages remain unaffected, and clinical disease may become evident once prophylaxis is discontinued. Therefore, upon leaving a malarious area, it is essential to initiate primaquine therapy before suppression with chloroquine is stopped (see Table 26).

The transfusion of whole blood, or plasma, increasingly has become recognized as a means of acquiring malaria. Similarly, drug addiction, or the use of unclean hypodermic needles, has been implicated as a means of transmitting the disease. With this means of infection the incubation period is usually short, generally depending upon the number of parasites transmitted with the donor's blood. Malaria acquired as a result of blood transfusion can be an especially hazardous complication, in view of the perilous condition of the patient requiring a blood transfusion in the first place, as well as the difficulty in making the diagnosis of malaria by an unsuspecting physician—especially in nonmalarious areas.

African Trypanosomiasis

Two types of African trypanosomiasis are recognized: Gambian or Mid-African sleeping sickness, and Rhodesian or East African sleeping sickness. They are similar protozoan diseases caused by the hemoflagellates *Trypanosoma gambiense* and *T. rhodesiense*, and only occur in those areas of central, west, and east Africa in which various species of *Glossina*, the tse-tse fly, are found.

T. gambiense and *rhodesiense* are pleomorphic flagellates varying from 15 to 30 μ in length by 1.5 to 3.5 μ in breadth. In Giemsa-stained blood smears they may appear long and slender, with an undulating membrane and free anterior flagellum, or short and broad without a free flagellum. There are no intracellular forms, but at various stages of the disease they may be found in the peripheral blood, lymphatics, lymph nodes, cerebrospinal fluid, and neural tissue. The two species are morphologically indistinguishable, but maintain separate biologic characteristics in cross-inoculation experiments.

Outside of man there is no important reservoir host for *T. gambiense*, while *T. rhodesiense* is found naturally infecting wild game animals.

In the tse-tse fly, trypanosomes undergo cyclic development; multiplying in the mid- and hindgut and migrating anteriorly they occupy the salivary glands and ducts, becoming infective about 15 to 35 days after the infecting blood meal. Metacyclic infective forms are inoculated into the bite wound when the tse-tse fly next feeds.

Although all age groups are susceptible to infection, the factors that influence human prevalence rest more on occupational risk to suitable tse-tse flies, as well as their breeding and feeding habits. Thus, young adult males are found to be most frequently infected. During epidemics, when all age groups are infected, mechanical transmission may occur. Congenital transmission has been reported, but must be an unusual means of acquiring the disease.

PATHOLOGY AND SYMPTOMS. Within a few days an elevated firm erythematous nodule, that may subside in several weeks or go on to ulcerate, appears at the bite wound. At this time organisms may be found in the peripheral blood, and the initial symptoms of the acute disease may appear. These include: irregular spiking fever, rash, arthralgias, headache, and facial edema. These may persist for weeks or months, when lymphadenitis becomes apparent. The superficial nodes are especially evident, such as the posterior cervical chain (Winterbottom's sign). During the many months of lymphatic involvement, these tissues may become acellular and fibrotic. In about a year the disease enters a chronic stage with signs and symptoms of central nervous system involvement. Trypanosomes are found in cerebrospinal fluid, subarachnoid space, and brain substance. Meningoencephalitis and myelitis are evident. The meninges are thickened, and within the brain substance there is perivascular cuffing with lymphocytes and plasma cells. Foci of trypanosomes can be found in the brain tissue surrounded by microglial cells and macrophages. Neuronal degeneration and softening occurs in the late stages.

Neurologic symptoms become the most prominent features of the disease. The patient becomes listless, melancholic, and lethargic with slurring speech and tremors of the tongue and limbs. These finally merge into a deepening sleep from which it becomes ever more difficult to arouse the victim. Patients usually die either of malnutrition, malaria, dysentery, or other intercurrent infection.

The course of East African sleeping sickness can be fulminant, and, therefore, accelerated. If untreated, it usually terminates fatally in 8 to 12 months. Pathologic changes in the central nervous system are not as pronounced or extensive as those found in Mid-African sleeping sickness.

DIAGNOSIS. Definitive diagnosis is made by finding trypanosomes in blood and bone marrow smears, in lymph node aspirates in early or acute disease, and in cerebrospinal fluid in late or chronic disease. It is essential to employ both thick and thin blood smears, as well as to examine the buffy coat from 10 to 20 ml of citrated whole blood or the sediment from 5 ml of centrifuged cerebrospinal fluid. Culture and/or animal inoculation sometimes are the only successful means of obtaining a diagnosis. A recently developed fluorescent antibody test may prove useful.

TREATMENT. Early African trypanosomiasis yields far more readily to therapy than the late, chronic CNS stage. Prior to CNS disease, suramin (Naphuride, Antrypol) is the drug of choice. Although it is of low toxicity, it is excreted almost entirely by the kidneys, and may cause significant renal damage. Urinalysis should be done the day following administration of each dose of suramin to assure there is no evidence of renal damage. Therapy must be discontinued if albuminuria and/or granular casts appear. Suramin is given intravenously every 4 to 6 days. It is dissolved in 10 ml of sterile distilled water. The initial test dose is 300 to 500 mg; the subsequent adult dose is 1.0 g until a total of 10.0 g is administered. Even though suramin does not cross the blood-brain barrier, intrathecal administration should not be attempted.

Pentamidine is an effective alternative drug for the treatment of early African trypanosomiasis. It is given as an intramuscular injection of 4 mg/kg of the base daily or every other day for a total of 5 to 10 injections. Pentamidine is dissolved in no more than 3 ml of distilled water. The course may be repeated after one week. Patients should receive this drug while lying down since transient hypotensive episodes, palpitations, and vertigo are not uncommon. It is contraindicated in renal disease.

In chronic or late stage disease, tryparsamide (Fourneau 270), a pentavalent arsenical, is useful in Gambian but not Rhodesian trypanosomiasis. It is administered intravenously, freshly dissolved in 10 ml of sterile *distilled water* once each week. The dosage is 40 to 50 mg/kg of body weight. Ten to 15 injections should be given (the initial dose should be reduced and subsequent injections increased gradually up to the maximum of 40 to 50 mg/kg). A one-month rest period is necessary before repeating the course. Although acute toxicity is not a frequent problem, tryparsamide may cause optic atrophy, dermatitis, and any of the other well-known side effects of arsenicals. The onset of ophthalmologic disturbances demands immediate cessation of tryparsamide therapy.

Mel B (Melarsoprol, Arsobal) is a compound consisting of the trivalent arsenical melarsen oxide and BAL. It is considered more effective than tryparsamide for the treatment of CNS trypanosomiasis

and more effective against *T. rhodesiense*. It is administered in the hospital as a 5 percent solution in propylene glycol. The recommended dose is 3.6 mg/kg body weight intravenously on each of four consecutive days. The course of therapy is repeated after one week. Neither renal nor optic nerve toxicity is observed with this drug, but arsenic toxicity can be a problem.

PROGNOSIS. If therapy is initiated prior to significant central nervous system involvement, the outcome is usually favorable. Untreated infections often end fatally.

PREVENTION. With few exceptions control of the vector has proved to be a difficult, if not impossible task. Prevention of tse-tse fly bites and chemoprophylaxis may be the best means of eliminating the disease from an area. Both suramin and pentamidine have proved to be excellent in this regard.

American Trypanosomiasis

Chagas' disease is caused by the hemoflagellate, *Trypanosoma cruzi*, which was first discovered in 1911 in the blood of a seriously ill, wasted Brazilian child suffering from fever, lymphadenopathy, and anemia. The disease is limited to the Western Hemisphere, being prevalent in South and Central America and Mexico. There have been two autochthonous cases reported from the United States.

Trypanosoma cruzi is a pleomorphic spindle-shaped organism, 15 to 20 μ long, with a central nucleus, undulating membrane, and single flagellum (Fig. 46). In man or other mammals it has an intracellular phase in which the trypanosomal form undergoes profound morphologic changes to assume a leishmanial form, which is but 2 to 4 μ in diameter and is without a flagellum.

Other than man, various domesticated and wild animals serve as excellent reservoir hosts. Armadillos and opossums are most commonly infected throughout the endemic zones. In Maryland, Georgia, and Florida, many raccoons are naturally infected. Recent studies also have demonstrated naturally infected bugs in many parts of southwest United States and California.

Usually, infection is acquired when the organisms are deposited upon the skin along with the feces of biting reduviid bugs (*Rhodnius, Panstrongylus, Triatoma*). Depending upon the vector, the bite, which is commonly at the mucocutaneous junction of the lips or eyes, can be either extremely painful or painless, and the flagellates are introduced into the bite wound by rubbing or scratching, or they may traverse adjacent intact mucous membranes.

Chagas' disease is far more common in children than adults. Nearly 80 percent of patients are under 21 years of age, the disease being most frequent in infants between 2 months and 2 years.

PATHOLOGY. The primary or initial lesion (chagoma) is caused by invasion of histiocytes, fat cells,

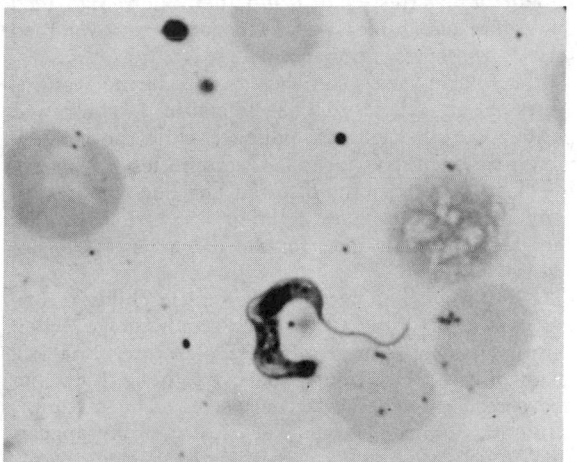

Fig. 46. *Trypanosoma cruzi* in the peripheral blood. ×1,277.

and other subcutaneous tissues of the bite area. The intracellular leishmanial forms proliferate rapidly, destroying host cells and quickly reinvading others. This pattern stimulates a marked inflammatory process that appears on the skin as a firm red nodule. As infection disseminates from the bite area, a gelatinous edema spreads along subcutaneous, fascial, and muscular planes. Lymphatic invasion with histiocytic proliferation and granulomatous lymphadenitis may cause regional lymphatic obstruction. Invasion and destruction of myocardial fibers is almost invariably found (Fig. 47) and is accompanied by a diffuse inflammatory exudate. Fibrinous pericarditis and pericardial effusion are nearly constant findings. Mild endocardial and subendocardial involvement is usually present. After many years, diffuse hypertrophy, focal fibrosis resembling ischemic changes, and scattered inflammatory infiltrates are found. Organisms may or may not be evident.

Gastrointestinal invasion, with destruction of muscle and ganglion cells, may cause megacolon and megaesophagus, although other tubular organs may also be affected. Central nervous system disease is characterized by invasion of neuroglial cells and by scattered glial nodules in the gray and white matter. Neuronal degeneration as well as perivascular and meningeal cellular infiltrates are commonly encountered.

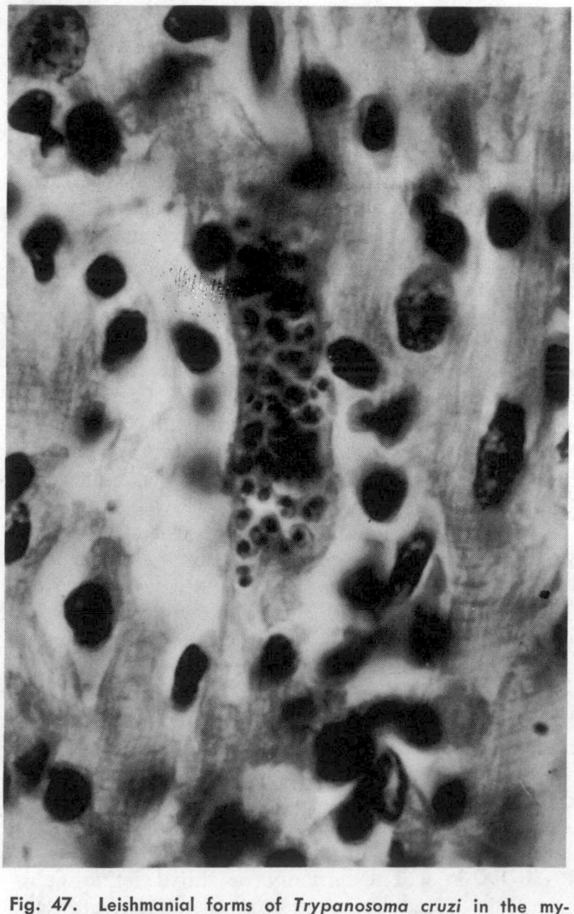

It is important to realize that trypanosomes ordinarily cannot be found in the peripheral blood beyond 30 or 40 days after the initial infection. Furthermore, it is evident that reproduction does not occur in the trypanosomal stage; most of the widespread manifestations of Chagas' disease must be attributed, therefore, to the leishmanial or intracellular stage of the infection.

SYMPTOMS. In children the onset of the disease is characterized by intermittent daily fever, followed by generalized nonpitting edema and unilateral palpebral edema (Romaña's sign). Lymphadenopathy, hepatosplenomegaly, urticaria, signs of meningeal irritation, various behavioral problems, and focal neurologic symptoms may be part of the clinical picture. Acute chagasic myocarditis may be accompanied by premature ventricular contractions, atrial fibrillation, partial or complete heart block, or progressive congestive failure. Usually, cardiac symptoms abate, leaving little early evidence of residual disease, although recent studies have suggested that myocardial infection may continue to smolder for many years and lead to severe heart disease in 20 to 30 years.

On clinical grounds, however, it is extremely difficult to differentiate coronary heart disease in older patients or rheumatic heart disease in younger patients from chagasic heart disease. Residual neurologic symptoms, such as focal or generalized seizures and behavioral disorders, may occur.

DIAGNOSIS. Definitive diagnosis depends upon the demonstration of the parasite in the blood or tissues. It must be emphasized that examination of the peripheral blood is of value only during the initial acute disease or during chronic exacerbation. Animal inoculation with patient's blood will often aid in the diagnosis. Liver biopsy, bone marrow aspiration, or splenic puncture will often provide the answer. At times, xenodiagnosis may be the only means by which organisms can be found. Laboratory-reared reduviid bugs are permitted to feed on the patient or his fresh blood and then allowed to feed on uninfected guinea pigs. The latter are examined for trypanosomes after about 45 days.

Serologic tests can be useful during various stages of the disease. The precipitin test may be positive during the acute episode, while the complement-fixation test (Machado-Guerreiro test) is useful for diagnosis of chronic disease. The fluorescent antibody and indirect hemagglution tests are becoming valuable diagnostic tools for the diagnosis of Chagas' disease.

PROGNOSIS. The outlook is serious in children during the acute illness. It is especially grave when neurologic symptoms dominate the picture. Chagasic heart disease is currently believed to be far more widespread than previously suspected. The prognosis is also grave once symptoms of cardiac failure appear.

TREATMENT. Supportive therapy is all that is currently available during the chronic stages of the disease. In the acute phase Bayer 7602, a 4-aminoquino-

Fig. 47. Leishmanial forms of *Trypanosoma cruzi* in the myocardium. ×1,277.

line compound, has been advocated, since it clears the blood of trypanosomal forms. It is, however, ineffective against the tissue stages. Recently, levofuraltadone (Altafur) has been used in oral doses of 30 mg per kg per day for 15 days, followed by 10 mg per kg per day for 3 months. This compound also appears to be active only against the trypanosomal forms.

PREVENTION. Residual spraying with DDT, dieldrin, or gamma benzene hexachloride (BHC) is an effective means of killing reduviid bugs. Education of individuals in the community in the habits of "kissing" bugs and their relationship to Chagas' disease is the most important facet of long-term control.

Leishmaniasis

There are three generally recognized species of *Leishmania* that infect man. Although morphologically indistinguishable, their serologic reactions, geographic distribution, and clinical manifestations are sufficiently distinctive to separate them. In some areas, however, overlapping characteristics are so prevalent that some workers, notably Adler, regard the three species as a complex with strain and racial intergrades.

Leishmanial organisms exist in mammalian tissues as small intracellular oval bodies 2 to 4 μ in diameter without a free flagellum. In the sandfly (*Phlebotomus sp.*) the oval body elongates (15 to 20 μ) and extends a single anterior flagellum (leptomonad form).

Kala-azar or visceral leishmaniasis is caused by *Leishmania donovani*, American or mucocutaneous leishmaniasis is due to *L. braziliensis*, and Oriental sore or cutaneous leishmaniasis is a result of infection with *L. tropica*. These organisms live and proliferate in the cytoplasm of reticuloendothelial cells, eventually destroying them. When sandflies bite an infected individual, the ingested leishmanial forms are transformed in the insect's intestine into leptomonad forms. From the midgut, enormous numbers of organisms, produced by longitudinal binary fission, migrate to the insect's buccal cavity to be inoculated during the next blood meal. Kala-azar is found in Asia, the Middle East, Africa, southern Europe (Mediterranean littoral), and South and Central America. The disease appears to exist in at least two epidemiologic forms:

1. A Mediterranean type, in which young children (1 to 4 years of age) and also dogs are usually infected. This type extends from the Mediterranean through central Asia into China; it is also present in parts of South America.
2. An Indian type, in which the disease predominates in children between 5 and 15 years of age; dogs are not important reservoir hosts. In east Africa the disease is in some ways similar to the Indian type.

PATHOLOGY. The principal pathologic lesions are a result of reticuloendothelial cell hyperplasia, especially in the spleen and liver. Later, the marrow and lymph nodes are filled with infected macrophages, and a concomitant leucopenia and anemia develop. Similarly, the kidneys may be filled with infected macrophages, and invasion of submucosal and mucosal macrophages in the intestine sometimes is associated with severe ulceration.

SYMPTOMS. Infantile kala-azar may begin either suddenly with high fever and vomiting, or insidiously with irregular daily fever, anorexia, weight loss, lassitude, and pallor. Purpura, cyanosis, severe anemia, diarrhea, and splenomegaly are also seen. A general bleeding diathesis often becomes evident shortly before death. After several months, patients usually die if the disease is untreated. In less fulminating cases the clinical course is more protracted, usually ending fatally after a year or two.

In older children the disease tends to assume a more chronic course with marked emaciation, edema, brittle hair, massive splenomegaly, and dusky slate-gray complexion (kala-azar is also called "black sickness"). Hyperglobulinemia, leucopenia, and anemia are typically found. As a result of the patient's general debility, death often results from such intercurrent infections as pneumonia, amebic or bacillary dysentery, and malaria.

Post–kala-azar dermal leishmanoid is a common complication of Indian and east African kala-azar. It is characterized by the appearance of hypopigmented, erythematous, or nodular lesions of the skin of the face, chest, neck, and buttocks. The lesions are believed to represent a hypersensitivity or allergic manifestation of visceral leishmaniasis, usually appearing either spontaneously or more commonly after inadequate therapy.

Cutaneous leishmaniasis, caused by *L. tropica*, differs from kala-azar by producing ulcers that usually heal spontaneously within several months to a year; visceral lesions are almost never found. Mucocutaneous leishmaniasis, caused by *L. braziliensis*, appears to have a number of clinical varieties, in which there may be extensive ulceration and mutilation of the mucous membrane of the mouth, hard and soft palate, pharynx, larynx, nose, and external ear. Secondary pyogenic infection often causes fatal termination in this disease.

DIAGNOSIS. Kala-azar is diagnosed by finding the organisms in stained smears of peripheral blood or bone marrow. Cultures of the blood or marrow are most useful. Splenic puncture and liver biopsy usually are the most rewarding procedures, but they are not without serious hazard in individuals with a bleeding diathesis. The Sia water test is usually positive, but is not specific, since it only indicates elevated serum globulin.

In the cutaneous forms of leishmaniasis, microscopic examination of tissue obtained from the edge of the ulcer or inoculation of some of the material into Novy, MacNeal, Nicolle (NNN) medium usually will confirm the diagnosis.

PROGNOSIS. Untreated kala-azar is fatal in 75 to 85 percent of infantile and 90 to 95 percent of adult cases. Properly treated, 85 to 95 percent of cases can be cured. Mucocutaneous leishmaniasis has an excellent outlook if treated before metastatic lesions to mucous membranes appear; otherwise the outlook is poor, since these lesions are often refractory to therapy. Uncomplicated *L. tropica* infections always respond well to therapy.

TREATMENT. Kala-azar usually responds to treatment with pentavalent antimonials. Ethylstibamine (Neostibosan) has been most effective. Children usually are given an initial intramuscular dose of 250 mg, followed by eight daily doses of 300 mg until a total of 2.65 g has been administered. Generally, the number of doses has to be increased for Chinese, Mediterranean, and African cases, since they are more resistant to therapy. In the antimony-resistant cases, stilbamidine or hydroxystilbamidine has been employed with excellent results. It is given very slowly intravenously on alternate days until the maximum dose of 10 injections of 3 mg/kg each has been given. Therapy is repeated two weeks later. The initial doses are usually reduced to test for sensitivity. Epinephrine should be available. Trigeminal neuropathy may folow stilbamidine therapy and can persist for years; however, hydroxystilbamidine therapy is reported to be free of this complication. Therapy for early mucocutaneous leishmaniasis is the same as for Oriental sore. If few ulcers are present they are treated by local infiltration with various antimonial compounds, such as stibophen (Fuadin); carbon dioxide snow or electrocoagulation can also be used. Systemic treatment is also instituted in order to prevent the development of secondary (metastatic) cutaneous or mucocutaneous lesions. The latter are often resistant to therapy and may require many courses of retreatment. Amphotericin B currently is being used for the treatment of mucocutaneous lesions (p. 794). Despite serious side effects, this drug seems to be effective in cases otherwise drug-resistant.

PREVENTION. There are many aspects to the control of leishmaniasis. Sandflies (*Phlebotomus*) can be readily eliminated by residual spraying with DDT. Since sandflies ordinarily do not fly very high, sleeping quarters should be above ground level. Animal reservoirs, such as infected dogs, should be destroyed. Early therapy will prevent family and neighborhood transmission.

Giardiasis

Giardia intestinalis (*G. lamblia*) is the most frequently diagnosed intestinal flagellate of man. It is found in most areas of the world, but is more prevalent in warmer regions.

Giardia lives in the duodenum and jejunum and has both trophic and cystic stages. The almost cartoonlike appearance of the trophozoite is well-known to every medical student. It is about 10 to 20 μ long by 5 to 15 μ wide and has four pairs of flagella and two nuclei. The trophozoite (motile stage) usually is found in liquid stools, whereas the cyst (8 to 10 μ by 7 to 10 μ) appears in formed feces.

Transmission is believed to be accomplished by ingestion of the cysts, probably following direct close contact as a pinworm disease (see p. 803), although contaminated food and water may also be a source of infection. Giardiasis is much more common in children, among inmates of institutions, and in orphanages. Occasional epidemics have been reported.

SYMPTOMS. In heavy infections it is not unusual for patients to have vague upper abdominal discomfort, mucous diarrhea, flatulence, and steatorrhea. In children the symptoms can be more pronounced, with celiac or spruelike symptoms.

DIAGNOSIS. Direct examination of the diarrheic stool will usually reveal motile trophozoites. Cysts can readily be found in formed stools by direct examination and concentration methods.

TREATMENT. The infection yields readily to quinacrine therapy. The recommended dosage is 2 mg/kg orally three times a day for 5 days with a maximum total daily dose of 300 mg. Giardiasis has also been treated successfully with metronidazole (Flagyl); it is given for 5 days in divided doses after meals:

Age	Metronidazole
under 2 years	125 mg (½ tab)
2 to 4	250 mg (1 tab)
5 to 8	375 mg (1½ tab)
9 and over	500 mg (2 tab)

Balantidiasis

Balantidium coli is the only common parasitic ciliate and the largest protozoan parasite of man. The motile or trophozoite form is from 50 to 200 μ long and 40 to 70 μ wide. Its surface is covered with cilia, and a prominent groove, the cytostome, is present anteriorly. When stained, a large bean-shaped macronucleus and smaller micronucleus are evident.

Although hogs and various primates are commonly infected with an organism morphologically indistinguishable from *B. coli*, it has been found extremely difficult to infect man with porcine or simian forms. It appears that the disease is transmitted from man to man by contact and poor sanitation. Therefore, it is not surprising to find an increased prevalence of this infection in mental institutions, prisons, and orphanages.

PATHOLOGY. The ciliates are found in the large intestine, where they usually invade the mucosa and produce ulcers similar to those caused by *Entamoeba histolytica*. Rarely, intestinal perforation or extraintestinal invasion occur.

SYMPTOMS AND TREATMENT. Although asymptomatic infection is common, it may be associated with mild to fulminant symptoms consisting of diarrhea or dysentery. The disease often resembles amebiasis, from which it must be differentiated. In asymptomatic cases spontaneous cure is not unusual. Treatment with carbarsone or diiodohydroxyquine has been successful. Recently oral tetracycline, 20 mg/kg three times a day (maximum of 2.0 g daily), has given satisfactory results.

Toxoplasmosis

Toxoplasma gondii is an obligate intracellular protozoan parasite that appears to have morphologic and taxonomic kinship with the class Sporozoa. Recent evidence has demonstrated close affinities of this parasite with the Coccidia, inasmuch as oocyst stages have been reported in cats. Although many species of *Toxoplasma* have been described since Nicolle and Manceaux established the genus for the organism they observed in the gondi, a North African rodent, all appear to be but a single species.

Jankü (1923) probably found the first human *Toxoplasma* infection (eye). However, 30 years elapsed before Wolfe, Cowan, and Paige isolated the organism from infants who had died of encephalitis. As more case reports appeared, it soon became evident that toxoplasmosis was widespread and could be acquired in utero as well as postnatally. Furthermore, as serologic methods were developed, it became clear that most human infection was inapparent or associated with only minor symptoms.

ETIOLOGY. Morphologic studies of *T. gondii* in peritoneal exudate or tissue culture have demonstrated that it is crescentic, 4 to 7 μ by 2 to 4 μ (Fig. 48) and appears to divide by a process termed "endodyogeny" rather than longitudinal binary fission. Masses of organisms may be seen within the cytoplasm of host cells, superficially resembling *Leishmania* or *Histoplasma*. Electron photomicrographs reveal rather elaborate, highly specialized organelles, clearly suggesting the sporozoan affinities of these organisms.

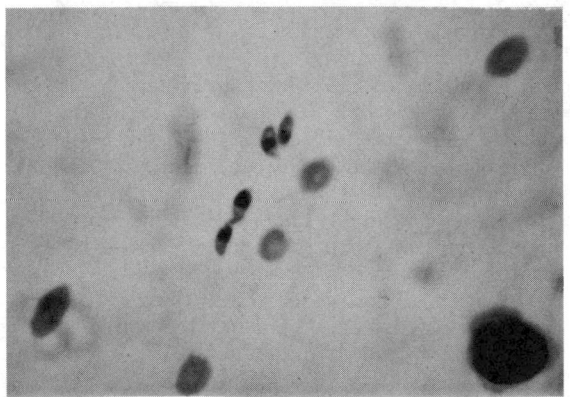

Fig. 48. Extracellular *Toxoplasma* in mouse peritoneal fluid stained by Wright's method.

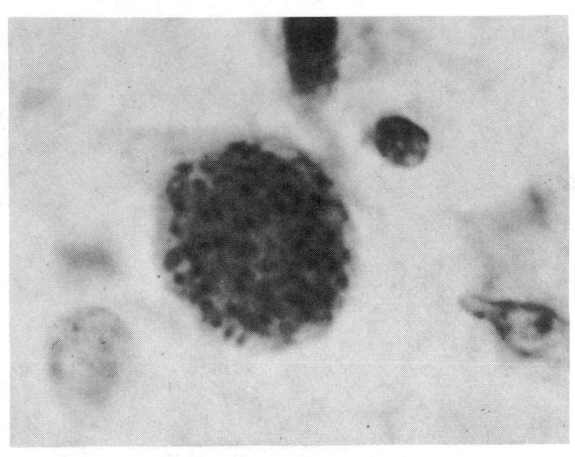

Fig. 49. Gyst containing large numbers of *Toxoplasma* in subcortical area of 9-month-old infant.

The intracellular proliferative forms can be found in almost every type of tissue cell other than erythrocytes. When an infected cell is overcrowded with parasites it ruptures, and the liberated parasites penetrate other cells. Groups of toxoplasmas surrounded by a limiting membrane are found in host tissue (Fig. 49). Previously, it was believed the membrane was primarily derived from the host, and, therefore, these structures were called "pseudocysts." Ultrastructural studies, however, have demonstrated that this membrane is derived primarily from the parasite; thus the structure is a true cyst.

Toxoplasma can be transmitted experimentally to numerous mammals and birds, and a large number of naturally infected animals have been found, including horses, dogs, rodents, chickens, pigeons, and ducks.

EPIDEMIOLOGY. Although congenital transmission of *Toxoplasma* has been clearly established, knowledge of the means by which postnatal or acquired toxoplasmosis is transmitted has been largely conjectural. Numerous experimental and clinical observations have indicated transmission could and did occur following ingestion of undercooked or raw infected meat. These observations, however, do not explain the equal rate of transmission noted in herbivores and vegetarians. The recent observations of Hutchinson that *Toxoplasma* could be transmitted by the eggs of the nematode *Toxocara cati* have been subsequently disproved by Jacobs as well as Frenkel. A dramatic report by Kean et al. of an epidemic of acute acquired toxoplasmosis in five medical students following ingestion of rare hamburger was recently reported. There are several examples of acquired toxoplasmosis in laboratory workers following accidental ingestion or inoculation. The presence of organisms in various body secretions and excretions allows the possibility of transmission by contact (oral, respiratory, or insect vector). There is no evidence, however, that this does occur.

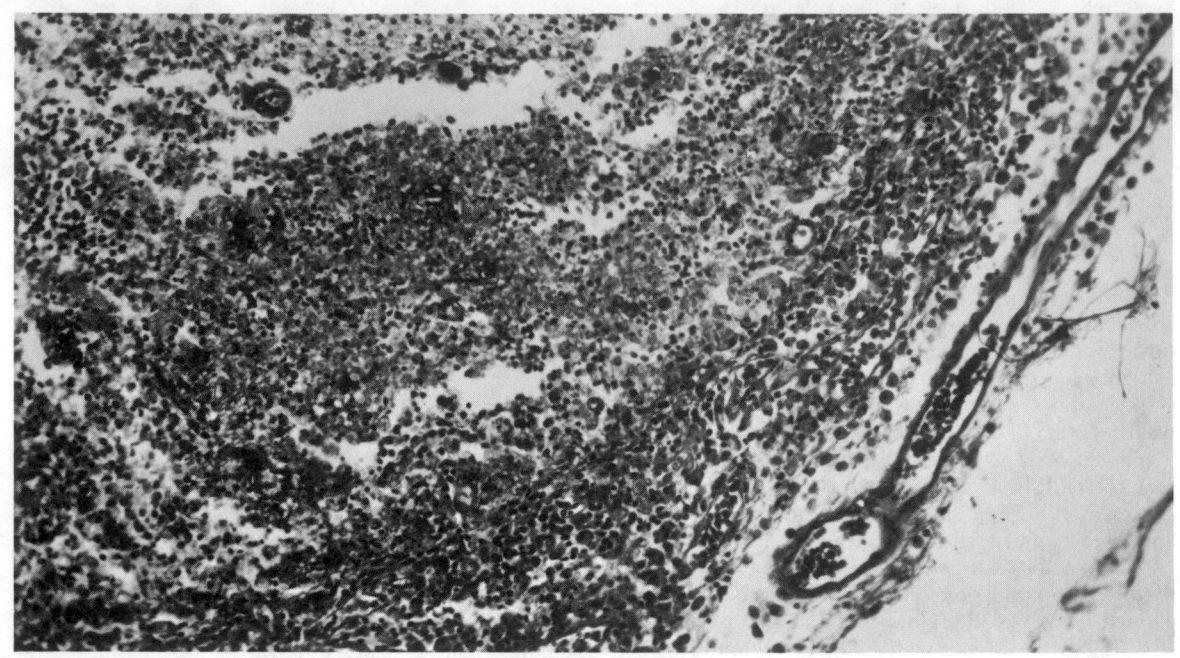

Fig. 50.   Active *Toxoplasma* lesion in the brainstem of a 3-day-old infant.

The incidence of human infection, based on skin and serologic testing, averages about 28 percent in the United States and western Europe. The incidence increases with age, however, so that by the fourth decade about 40 percent of the population has significant antibody levels.

PATHOLOGY. The pathologic lesions may be widespread, affecting many organs and tissues. In congenital disease, neurologic and ocular lesions are generally more common than in acquired disease.

In congenital toxoplasmosis, focal disseminated areas of necrosis and miliary granulomatous inflammation are found. The periventricular and aqueductal tissue of the brain may be particularly affected. Many yellow, soft areas are seen in the cortex, basal ganglia, medulla, and leptomeninges (Fig. 50).

Calcification, microcephalus, and hydrocephalus are all common sequelae. Toxoplasmic cysts (Fig. 50) may persist for years without provoking cellular reaction. Chorioretinal lesions are a result of necrosis and subsequent gliosis. The older, yellow-white lesions are fibrotic scars of the destroyed retina.

In extraneural sites, lymph node hyperplasia and focal necrosis are common. Pulmonary involvement usually consists of parasitized alveolar cells in areas of interstitial pneumonia. Proliferation of organisms in the myocardium, hepatic parenchyma, spleen, and adrenals is commonly associated with focal necrosis.

SYMPTOMS. The disease may present as a severe, fulminating, rapidly fatal infection, or there may be no symptoms whatsoever. The factors which determine this spectrum are only partially known but are believed to be related to host immunity, virulence of the infecting strain, and size of the inoculum.

In acute congenital toxoplasmosis the infant may be severely jaundiced, with a maculopapular rash, thrombocytopenic purpura, and hepatosplenomegaly. Seizures, opisthotonos, and chorioretinitis also occur. Spinal fluid may contain increased protein and cells. These children usually die in the first month of life. The majority of survivors have severe mental retardation, complete or partial blindness, and psychomotor disturbances.

Subacute congenital disease often is not observed until sometime after birth, when intracerebral calcification, chorioretinitis, hydrocephalus (sometimes progressive), and psychomotor disturbances are found (Fig. 51).

Acquired toxoplasmosis is usually asymptomatic. It is now clear, moreover, that there are at least three main clinical types. The incubation period of these varieties is unknown. The acute acquired form is a fulminating disease with an erythematous rash, fever, malaise, myositis, dyspnea, acute myocarditis, and encephalitis. Fatal outcome is common. A subacute glandular form is characterized by generalized lymphadenopathy, with or without fever. It is often mistaken for infectious mononucleosis, and the heterophil antibody test is negative. Recovery usually occurs solwly over a period of several months. Chronic toxoplasmosis may be asymptomatic except for chorioretinitis.

DIAGNOSIS. It is rather unusual to isolate the organisms from the blood or spinal fluid. Therefore, diagnosis usually rests upon serologic evidence. The

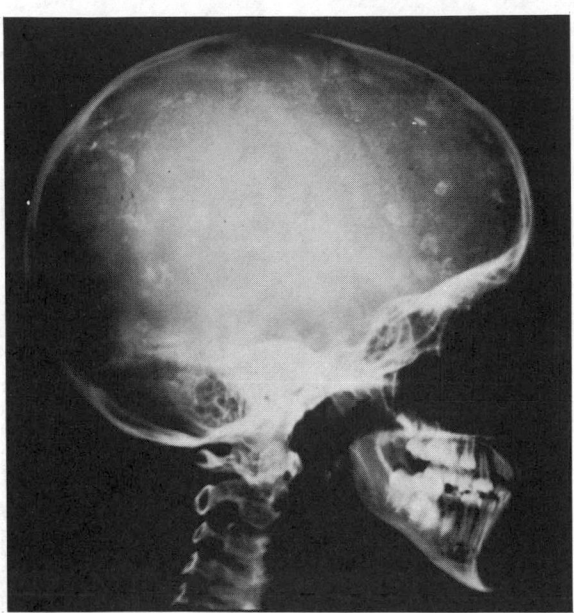

Fig. 51. Disseminated calcific deposits in the brain of a 6-year-old child with proven congenital toxoplasmosis.

Sabin-Feldman dye test depends upon the rationale that living *T. gondii* incubated with immune serum in the presence of fresh normal activator serum loses its ability to be stained with an alkaline solution of methylene blue. The test becomes positive 1 to 3 weeks after infection; the titer increases for many months, gradually declining over a period of 5 or more years. It may remain positive for life. The significance of low titers is not entirely clear. According to Feldman, while titers of 1:4 are probably significant, as well as reproducible, he usually considers titers of 1:8 or 1:16 positive in population studies. However, rising titers in serum specimens taken 2 weeks apart are indicative of recently acquired infection. Stable titers indicate only that the patient has had the infection.

The complement-fixation test is used as an adjunct to the dye test. It is useful to indicate active disease, a titer of 1:8 being significant. A toxoplasmin skin test is available, but is of questionable aid in a single situation. The hemagglutination test appears to be an excellent method that may supplant the more technically difficult dye test. The hemagglutination test becomes positive later than the dye test and usually correlates with it. Its main advantages are economy, speed, simplicity, and the use of a nonliving antigen. An indirect fluorescent antibody (IFA) test is now available and appears to closely parallel the Sabin-Feldman dye test. It is easily performed and appears quite reliable.

PROGNOSIS. Other than the relatively few severe neonatal cases, the disease is usually mild and has a favorable outlook. Rehabilitation of handicapped children may improve the prognosis in those in whom neurologic lesions remain.

Maternal infection, acquired before pregnancy has occurred, does not present a risk to fetus, provided the mother has dye-test antibodies. Infection acquired during pregnancy carries a high risk to the developing fetus. Future pregnancies, however, usually are assumed to be without risk.

TREATMENT. Chemotherapy is based on the experimental eidence in mice and tissue culture that pyrimethamine (Daraprim) and sulfonamides have marked synergistic activity against toxoplasma organisms.

Infants with active disease should be treated in the hope of arresting the process. Acquired cases should probably be treated; however, the benefit of therapy is difficult to assess since spontaneous remission is so frequent. Patients on immunosuppressive therapy having toxoplasmosis, those with toxoplasma meningitis, or patients with ocular manifestations when macular damage appears likely should also receive chemotherapy.

Recommendations for infants: sulfadiazine 100 mg/kg daily in divided doses and pyrimethamine, 1 mg/kg daily after a loading dose of 2 mg/kg daily for 3 days. Adults should receive sulfadiazine 3 g daily with 50 mg pyrimethamine daily for the first 3 days, then 25 mg thereafter (older children receive half this dose). Treatment should continue for 4 weeks. It is important to monitor the leucocyte and platelet counts twice weekly. Folic acid should be given during therapy.

PREVENTION. Detection and treatment of latent infection in pregnant women may prevent transmission to their offspring. No other practical measures are known for the prevention of toxoplasmosis.

Pneumocystis Pneumonia

Delanoe and Delanoe described cysts from the lungs of rats infected with *Trypanosoma lewisi* and in 1912 termed them *Pneumocystis carinii*. These organisms previously had been observed by Chagas in 1909 in guinea pigs infected with *T. cruzi* and by Carini in 1910 in rats also infected with *T. lewisi*. It was not until 1942, however, that human infection was described by van der Meer and Brug in two infants and an adult. The association of *Pneumocystis* with interstitial plasma cell pneumonia was first reported in premature infants by Vanek in 1951 in central Europe. Shortly thereafter, it became apparent that the disease was worldwide, often occurring in institutional epidemics. The taxonomic status of *Pneumocystis carinii* is not resolved; ultrastructural studies fail to support those who believe this organism is a protozoan with close sporozoan affinities. It resembles no other protozoan similarly studied. At present, the taxonomic position of this organism remains in doubt although some expert protozoologists now believe *Pneumocystis* is not a protozoan, but rather a fungus.

Although interstitial plasma cell pneumonia has

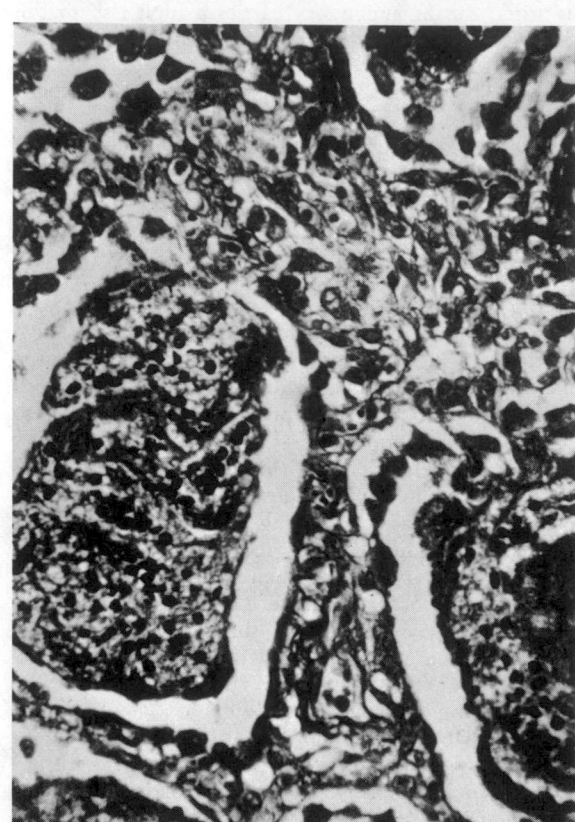 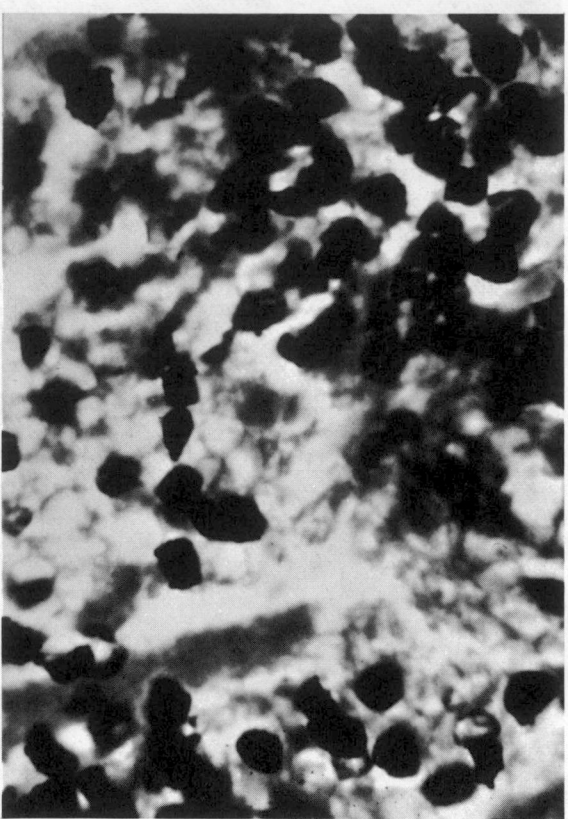

Fig. 52. *Pneumocystis carinii* pneumonia. A. Within the foamy alveolar exudate are small, intensely argyrophilic cysts demonstrated by the Gomori methenamine silver technique. ×280. B. Cysts of *Pneumocystis* under higher magnification from the same case as A. ×1,260.

been reported most often in premature or term infants during the first 4 months of life, sporadic cases are seen in older children and adults. Leukemia, lymphoma, hypogammaglobulinemia, and other severe debilitating diseases have often been associated with this infection. More recently, *Pneumocystis* pneumonia has been reported in a large group of patients receiving immunosuppressive therapy.

In smears of pulmonary exudate or in tissue sections, oval to round extracellular organisms which resemble cysts about 8 to 12 μ in diameter are found. These questionable cysts are intensely argyrophilic with Gomori's methenamine silver technique. Otherwise, in ordinary hematoxylin and eosin sections they are obscured by the characteristic foamy alveolar exudate (Fig. 52). Intracellular forms which may be schizonts are sometimes seen in alveolar lining cells.

PATHOLOGY. The lungs at postmortem are gray to pink, voluminous, firm, and airless. Alveoli are filled with a foamy eosinophilic material in which octonucleate cysts may be found. The alveolar septa are thickened and infiltrated with lymphocytes, monocytes, and sometimes plasma cells; neutrophils are notably absent.

SYMPTOMS. The onset of the disease may be slow and insidious. Cough, tachypnea, and cyanosis are often seen. Radiologic findings are not characteristic. In some instances marked respiratory distress does not appear until several days prior to death. In nonfatal illness, recovery may take many weeks.

Infant mortality is reported to vary from 10 to 50 percent with an average of about 40 percent. Since most cases in older children and adults have been associated with usually fatal underlying disease, prognosis is, of course, grave.

TREATMENT. Until recently, treatment of *Pneumocystis* pneumonia has been unsuccessful; however, several antiprotozoan compounds have been reported of benefit in a limited number of cases. Intramuscular pentamidine isethionate or intravenous hydroxystilbamide have given satisfactory results. The dosage of each is 4 mg/kg for 10 to 12 days. Gamma globulin is also administered if there is coexisting hypogammaglobulinemia. Megaloblastic bone marrow changes should be anticipated as a serious complication of drug therapy. Recently, nephrotoxicity has been reported to complicate therapy. Frequent sputum examinations and percutaneous or open lung biopsy have been advocated, since early diagnosis may be life-saving.

REFERENCES

AMEBIASIS

Adi, F. C. Clinical features of hepatic amoebiasis (a review of 120 cases). W. Afr. Med. J., 14(N.S.):181, 1965.

────── Amoebiasis. WHO Tech. Report Series No. 421, Geneva, 1969.

Dorrough, R. L. Amebic liver abscess. Southern Med. J., 60:305, 1967.

Gelfand, M., and Schnitzler, M. C. Amoebiasis in the African infant in Rhodesia. J. Trop. Med. Hyg., 69:144, 1966.

Healy, G. R. Use of and limitations to the indirect hemagglutination test in the diagnosis of intestinal amebiasis. Health Lab. Sci., 5:174, 1968.

Powell, S. J., McLeod, I., Wilmot, A. J., and Elsdon-Dew, R. Metronidazole in amoebic dysentery and amoebic liver abscess. Lancet, (Dec. 17):1329, 1966.

Scragg, J. N., and Powell, S. J. Emetine hydrochloride and chloroquine in the treatment of children with amoebic liver abscess. Arch. Dis. in Child., 41:549, 1966.

MALARIA

Barrett, E. L. Glucose-6-phosphate dehydrogenase deficiency: A brief review. Trans. Roy. Soc. Trop. Med. Hyg., 60:267, 1966.

Berberian, D. A. Recent advances in malariology. Amer. J. Med., 46:96, 1969.

Brooks, M. H., Kiel, F. W., Sheehy, T. W., and Barry, K. G. Acute pulmonary edema in *Falciparum* malaria. New Eng. J. Med., 279:732, 1968.

Bruce-Chwatt, L. J. Malaria and blackwater fever. *In* Diseases of Children in the Subtropics and Tropics. London, Edward Arnold, Ltd., 1958, Ch. 32.

Einhorn, N. H., and Tomlinson, W. J. Estivoautumnal (*P. falciparum*) malaria, a survey of 493 cases of infection with *P. falciparum* in children. Amer. J. Dis. Child., 72:137, 1946.

Immunology of Malaria. WHO Tech. Rep. Series No. 396, Geneva, 1968.

Powell, R. D. The chemotherapy of malaria. Clin. Pharmacol. Ther., 7:48, 1966.

Resistance of Malaria Parasites to Drugs. WHO Tech. Rep. Series No. 296, Geneva, 1965.

Russell, P. F., West, L. S., Manwell, R. D., and Macdonald, G. Practical Malariology, 2nd ed. London, Oxford Univ. Press, 1963.

Wilcox, A. Manual for the Microscopical Diagnosis of Malaria in Man, 1960 ed. USPHS, Washington, D.C., U.S. Government Printing Office, 1960.

Zuckerman, A. Current status of the immunology of malaria and of the antigenic analysis of plasmodia: a five-year review. Bull. WHO, 40:55, 1969.

GENERAL

Adler, S. Immunology of leishmaniasis. Israel J. Med. Sci., 1:9, 1965.

Allibone, E. C., Goldie, W., and Marmion, B. P. *Pneumocystis carinii* pneumonia and progressive vaccinia in siblings. Arch. Dis. Child., 39:26, 1964.

Beattie, C. P. Toxoplasmosis. Edinburgh, Royal College of Physicians, 1964.

Becroft, D. M. O., and Costello, J. M. *Pneumocystis carinii*. Pneumonia in siblings: diagnosis by lung aspiration. New Zeal. Med. J., 64:273, 1965.

Blattner, R. *Pneumocystis carinii* infection: treatment with pentamidine isothionate. J. Pediat., 67:332, 1965.

Comparative studies of American and African trypanosomiasis. W.H.O. Tech. Rep. Series No. 411, 1969.

Cortner, J. A. Giardiasis, a cause of celiac syndrome. Amer. J. Dis. Child., 98:311, 1959.

DeVita, V., Emmer, T., Levine, A., Jacobs, B., and Berard, C. *Pneumocystis carinii* pneumonia. Successful diagnosis and treatment of two patients with associated malignant processes. New Eng. J. Med., 280:287, 1969.

Duma, R. J., Ferrell, H. W., Nelson, E. C., and Jones, M. M. Primary amebic meningoencephalitis. New Eng. J. Med., 281:1315, 1969.

Esterly, J. A., and Warner, N. E. *Pneumocystis carinii* pneumonia. Twelve cases in patients with neoplastic lymphoreticular disease. Arch. Path., 80:433, 1965.

Feldman, H. A. Toxoplasmosis. New Eng. J. Med., 279:1370 and 1431, 1968.

Frenkel, J. K., Dubey, J. P., and Miller, N. L. *Toxoplasma gondii*: fecal forms separated from eggs of the Nematode *Toxocara cati*. Science, 164:432-433, 1969.

Glasser, L., and Delta, B. G. Congenital toxoplasmosis with placental infection in monozygotic twins. Pediatrics, 35:276, 1965.

Hawking, F. Recent work on *Trypanosoma cruzi* in Brazil and Central America. J. Trop. Med. Hyg., 67:211, 1964.

Hutchison, W. M. Nematode transmission of Toxoplasma gondii. Trans. Roy. Soc. Trop. Med. Hyg., 61:80-89, 1967.

Jacobs, L. *Toxoplasma* and toxoplasmosis. Ann. Rev. Microbiol., 17:429, 1963.

────── Toxoplasmosis. Advances Parasitol., 4:1, 1968.

Jones, T. C., Kean, B. H., and Kimball, A. C. Toxoplasmic lymphadenitis. J.A.M.A., 192:2, 1965.

Kean, B. H., Kimball, A. C., and Christenson, W. N. An epidemic of acute toxoplasmosis. J.A.M.A., 208:1002, 1969.

Lainson, R., and Strangeways-Dixon, J. The epidemiology of dermal leishmaniasis in British Honduras. I. The Human Disease. Trans. Roy. Soc. Trop. Med. Hyg., 57:242, 1963.

Livingstone, C. S. Pneumocystis pneumonia occurring in a family with agammaglobulinemia. Canad. Med. Ass. J., 90:1223, 1964.

Manson-Bahr, P. E. C. Variations in the clinical manifestations of leishmaniasis caused by *L. tropica*. J. Trop. Med. Hyg., 67:85, 1964.

────── and Southgate, B. A. Recent research in kala azar in East Africa. J. Trop. Med. Hyg., 67:79, 1964.

Marshall, W. C., Weston, H. G., and Bodian, M. *Pneumocystis carinii* pneumonia and congenital hypogammaglobulinemia. Arch. Dis. Child., 39:18, 1964.

Maumenee, A. E. Toxoplasmosis with special reference to uveitis. Survey Ophthal., 6:700, 1961.

Moore, G. T., Cross, W. M., McGuire, D., Mollohan, C. S., Gleason, N. N., Healy, G. R., and Newton, L. H. Epidemic giardiasis at a ski resort. New Eng. J. Med., 281-402, 1969.

Neal, R. A., Garnham, P. C. C., and Cohen, S. Immunization against protozoal diseases. Brit. Med. Bull., 25:194, 1969.

Perkins, E. S. Uveitis and Toxoplasmosis. London, J. & A. Churchill Ltd., 1961.

Remington, J. S. Toxoplasmosis and human abortion. Progr. Gynec., 4:303, 1963.

────── and Cavanaugh, E. N. Isolation of the encysted

form of *Toxoplasma gondii* from human skeletal muscle and brain. New Eng. J. Med., 273:1308, 1965.

—— Miller, M., and Brownlee, I. IgM antibodies in acute toxoplasmosis. I. Diagnostic significance in congenital cases and method for their rapid demonstration. Pediatrics, 41:1082, 1968.

Ryckman, R. E., Ryckman, A. E., Folkes, D. L., Robb, P. L., and Olsen, L. E. Epizootiology of *Trypanosoma cruzi* in southwestern North America. J. Med. Entom., 2:87, Parts I-VII, 1965.

Smith, E., and Gaspar, I. A. Pentamidine treatment of *Pneumocystis carinii* pneumonia. Amer. J. Med., 44:626, 1968.

Vaněk, J., and Jírovec, O. Parasitäre Pneumonie. "Interstitielle" Plasmazellen-pneumonie der Frühgeborenen, verursacht durch *Pneumocystis carinii*. Zbl. Bakt., 158 Abt I orig: 120, 1952.

Van Metre, T. E., Jr., Knox, D. L., and Maumenee, A. E. Specific ocular uveal lesions in patients with evidence of histoplasmosis and toxoplasmosis. Southern Med. J., 58:479, 1965.

Western, K., Perera, D., and Schultz, M. Pertainidine isethionate in the treatment of *Pneumocystis carinii* pneumonia. Ann. Int. Med., 73:695, 1970.

14.53
DISEASES CAUSED BY ARTHROPODS

MURRAY WITTNER

Arthropods (Phylum Arthropoda) are of medical importance as causal agents of disease in themselves, as obligatory intermediate hosts, or as mechanical vectors of innumerable disease-producing organisms. Included among the medically important arthropods are the true insects, centipedes, scorpions, spiders, ticks, mites, and various crustacea, including crabs, crayfish, and copepods.

As direct agents of disease or human annoyance, arthropods may cause:

1. *Serious envenomization,* which may be hemolytic, hemorrhagic, neurotoxic, or vesicating.
2. *Dermatitis,* which is the result of either bites or direct skin invasion.
3. *Myiasis,* which is due to invasion of organs or tissues by dipterous (true fly) larvae.
4. *Allergy or hypersensitivity,* which is often a result of certain insect stings or bites.
5. *Entomophobia* or psychoneurotic behavior in the presence of real or imaginary "bugs."

Hymenopterous Disease

The sting of a bee or wasp is accompanied by the introduction of venom, which, in nonsensitized individuals, usually causes pain, induration, and redness lasting several hours. The more important reactions in allergic individuals are discussed elsewhere (Sec. 11.11).

The sting of the fire ant (*Solenopsis*) results in an initial flare and wheal which later vesiculates. In several days to a week the pustule ruptures, encrusts, and forms a scar. Local application of ice or other soothing lotion to the area is all that is required.

The harvester ants, *Pogonomyronex,* readily attack man, and give a severe painful sting. Severe and fatal reactions in farm animals have been reported. Fortunately, this is quite rare in humans.

Arachnidism

The arachnids are a large group (class) of arthropods which includes the spiders, scorpions, mites, and ticks.

LACTRODECTISM.   Contrary to common belief, most spiders are harmless and shy. There are several spiders which, if provoked, can cause serious and sometimes fatal envenomization. Most notable is the bite of the female black widow spider, *Lactrodectus mactans,* which often is not felt and resembles a pinprick. At the point of the bite there may be slight swelling and two minute red spots. Immediately after the attack, lymphatic absorption of the toxin begins as the patient experiences local, sharp, throbbing pain that increases in intensity for several hours, by which time vascular spread has occurred. Symptoms are most severe and usually include leucocytosis, diaphoresis, nausea, vomiting, hypertension, and intense agonizing spasms, especially of the abdominal muscles. Spasticity of other muscle groups depends upon the area of the bite. Severely affected individuals develop profound shock, delirium, and coma, and death occurs in 4 to 5 percent of these. Usually, however, the symptoms regress, and the victim recovers.

The symptoms are generally more severe in children than in adults, and treatment should be initiated as soon as possible with 10 percent calcium gluconate or methocarbamol (Robaxin) as muscle relaxants. Antivenin should be given by intramuscular injection; it is usually effective within 30 minutes. If necessary, it may be repeated within an hour or two. Tourniquets or other procedures suggested for snakebites are ineffective.

The bite of the brown spider, *Loxosceles reclusus,* is discussed elsewhere.

SCORPIONS.   Scorpions possess a sting at the terminal portion of their abdomen, which they use to strike their victims swiftly and repeatedly. There are many dangerous species which accidentally sting humans, children being especially vulnerable. Most deaths are seen in children under 4 years of age. In Mexico, for example, where scorpions were responsible for 82 percent of 24,627 deaths from poisonous animals over a 10-year period, more than 80 percent of these fatalities occurred in children under 5 years of age and 94 percent in those under 10 years of age.

There are two types of scorpion venoms: a relatively harmless local cytotoxic material, and the often fatal neurotoxic venom which also has hemolytic and cytolytic properties. There is an immediate sharp pain as a result of the sting, which is often followed by numbness or drowsiness and peculiar itching sensations about the nose, mouth, and throat. There may be salivation, diaphoresis, nausea, vomiting, fever, spasm of muscles of mastication, and dyskinetic movements of the extremities. After a short while, salivation decreases, objects appear dim, strong light becomes painful, and strabismus is often pronounced. Pulmonary and gastrointestinal hemorrhage may occur, and generalized convulsions appear. These increase in severity, lasting several hours or until death. Generally, if the patient survives 3 hours, this is regarded as a good prognostic sign.

Treatment should be initiated as soon as possible, especially in youngsters. Specific antiscorpion serum is generally available in those areas in which these dangerous animals exist. A tourniquet should be applied above the wound, and an ice pack placed on the area to delay absorption. Morphine is contraindicated. Convulsions may be controlled with large doses of phenobarbital.

MITES AND TICKS.   The larvae of the North American chigger mite or red bug (*Entrombicula alfreddugesi*) may cause severe, almost intolerable itching followed by wheals and pustules. Children are especially sensitive. Treatment includes bathing the affected area with alcohol, and relief of itching can be obtained with topical anesthetics, such as the following mixture: 5 percent benzocaine, 2 percent methylsalicylate, 0.5 percent salicylic acid, 73 percent ethyl alcohol, and 19.5 percent water; Quotane ointment, a commercial preparation, is most useful. Diethyltoluamide is an excellent chigger repellant.

Scabies is caused by the itch mite, *Sarcoptes scabiei*, and is found in lower socioeconomic groups whose personal hygiene is often substandard. Most infestations are transmitted by personal contact in bed. The female mite enters the thin skin between the fingers, in the popliteal and antecubital fossae, and on the penis and breast. Initially, the infestation is undetected, but after a month or so, allergic manifestations appear as an intense vesiculopapular rash. In infants it may assume a more bullous appearance, especially on the face. The female mites may burrow several centimeters into the stratum corneum, and as a result of severe excoriation secondary pyogenic infection often complicates the disease.

Treatment is usually initiated with a prolonged warm bath or soaks in order to soften the skin and open the tunnels. A cream base containing 1 percent gamma benzene hexachloride (BHC) is applied over the entire body, and after 24 hours a cleansing bath is taken. This treatment kills both mites and eggs; therefore, a second application is usually unnecessary.

The bite of a tick can be extremely painful and associated with febrile symptoms. On occasion, the feeding female tick, especially in young children, causes a progressive, ascending, flaccid motor and sensory paralysis. Envenomization by the engorging tick is believed responsible. Prompt recovery usually follows removal of the offending organisms; however,

death by respiratory failure may occur if they are permitted to remain. Removal is best accomplished by gently pulling the tick off with the fingers. If sterile instruments are available they may be employed to apply gentle traction on the tick, after which the point of a needle or scalpel is slipped under the mouthparts. The tick will then come loose with a minimum of tissue. The area should be cleansed with antiseptic. Various repellents, such as dimethylphthalate or diethyltoluamide, are effective impregnated in clothing.

INSECTS.   The "bites" of many insects (Class Hexapoda) such as mosquitoes, bedbugs, fleas, and lice affect individuals differently. Some react with severe inflammatory manifestations; others seem completely oblivious. Contact with blister beetles may cause severe vesication. Many caterpillars (larvae of butterflies and moths) possess so-called urticarial hairs which cause severe dermatitis upon contact with the skin. The sting of certain caterpillars is often followed by severe pain, fever, nausea, vomiting, and, in young children, temporary paralysis which subsides as the local lesion heals. The female chigoe flea, *Tunga penetrans*, burrows into, and is almost completely enveloped by, the host's skin. Usually it penetrates between the toes or on the soles of the feet, creating nodular ulcerated swellings. Frequent washing with dilute Lysol or surgical removal and antiseptic dressings are necessary to obtain satisfactory healing.

Human infestation with lice usually is limited to three organisms: the head louse, *Pediculus humanus* var. *capitis;* the body louse, *P. humanus* var. *corporis;* and the crab louse, *Phthirus pubis.* Skin lesions caused by these insects are discussed elsewhere (Sec. 26.5). Pruritus, most intense at night, usually leads to loss of sleep, irritability, and general depression. Pediculosis is transmitted by personal contact under crowded and unsanitary conditions, often in cold climates. The head louse is especially prevalent in children, particularly young girls. It may become epidemic in girls' dormitories or institutions. Fortunately, the crab louse is not usually encountered in the pediatric age group.

Body lice can be readily eliminated by showering and by dusting with 10 percent DDT in pyrophyllite. About 2 ounces are used per person. All bedding and clothing are treated. If DDT-resistant lice are present, treatment with 1 percent gamma benzene hexachloride (BHC) in pyrophyllite will usually be successful. Head lice are also effectively destroyed by 10 percent DDT or 1 percent gamma BHC. The powder is left for one week, washed out, and the hair combed to remove nits.

CENTIPEDES.   Centipedes (Class Chilopoda) are provided with powerful poisonous claws, with which they attack and kill their prey. Although they are greatly feared, their bite is no more severe than the sting of a honeybee. The pain diminishes rapidly and usually requires no therapy. Remington has reported only a single death, in a 7-year-old child, from the bite of a centipede.

Myiasis

The invasion of organs and tissues by fly maggots (larvae of the Order Diptera) is termed myiasis. When maggot infestations are caused by species that usually are scavengers or saprophagous, the condition is termed *accidental myiasis*. If the maggot is of a necrophagous or facultative sarcophagous species it is called a semispecific myiasis; infestations caused by obligatory sarcophagous species are then termed obligate myiases.

Accidental myiasis is usually the result of ingestion of fly eggs in food or water. These infestations are transitory, larvae being passed in the stool without incident. On rare occasions, stubborn intestinal myiasis may result. Urinary myiasis has been reported, probably as the result of flies depositing their eggs about the external urethral orifice, especially in warm weather when individuals sleep without covers. The larvae presumably hatch and migrate into the urethra. Symptoms can be severe, with pain, blood, purulent discharge, dysuria, and frequency.

Various semiobligate myiases are caused by flesh flies (*Sarcophaga*) or blow flies (*Calliphora, Phaenicia*) when adults oviposit in or about open wounds. Severe damage can result from these infestations, which usually afflict helpless infants or the seriously injured. Cutaneous myiasis resembling furuncles may be caused by larvae of *Wohlfahrtia*.

Obligate myiasis, caused by the primary screwworms (*Callitroga*), may cause severe, sometimes fatal, suppurative nasopharyngeal and otic infestations. These flies are attracted to open wounds or nasal secretions in which they oviposit. *Hypoderma*, the eel fly, often attacks man, children being infested far more often than adults. The larvae actively penetrate the skin and wander for months (larva migrans) causing severe pain, cramps, and general malaise. The human bot fly, *Dematobia hominis*, however, deposits her eggs on the bodies of other blood-sucking flies, which, in turn, drop the eggs on the human skin. Larvae hatch and actively penetrate the skin, producing a large tumorous nodule in which they reside. After about 6 weeks, they leave the host, dropping to the ground, and enter the soil, where they pupate.

Children can be protected from myiasis by proper screening or netting. Dipterous infestations should be treated promptly by debridement or curetting, followed by topical antibiotic therapy with bacitracin, polymyxin, or neomycin and sterile dressing.

REFERENCES

Bettini, S. Epidemiology of latrodectism. Toxicon, 2:93, 1964.

Buxton, P. A. The Louse. London, Edward Arnold, Ltd., 1939.

Frazier, C. A. Allergic reactions to insect stings: a review of 180 cases. Southern Med. J., 57:1028, 1964.

Fuller, H. S. Medical and veterinary acarology. Ann. Rev. Entom., 1:347, 1956.

Herms, W. B., and James, M. T. Medical Entomology, 5th ed. New York, The Macmillan Co., 1961.

Horen, W. P. Arachnidism in the United States. J.A.M.A., 185:839, 1963.

Horsfall, W. R. Medical Entomology: Arthropods and Human Disease. New York, The Ronald Press, 1962.

Jung, R. C., Derbes, V. J., and Burch, A. D. Skin response to solenamine, a hemolytic component of fire-ant venom. Derm. Int., 2:241, 1963.

Keegan, H. L., and Macfarlane, W. V., eds. Poisonous Animals and Noxious Plants of the Pacific Region (A Collection of Papers based on a Symposium in the Public Health and Medical Science Division at the 10th Pacific Science Congress). London and New York, Pergamon Press, 1963.

Marinkelle, C. J., and Stalinke, H. L. Toxicological and clinical studies on *Centruroides margaritatus* (Vervais), a common scorpion in western Columbia. J. Med. Entom., 2:197, 1965.

McMillan, C. W., and Purcell, W. R. Hazards to health: the puss caterpillar, alias wooly slug. New Eng. J. Med., 271:147, 1964.

Miller, D. G. Massive Anaphylaxsis from Bee Stings. In Buckley, E., and Porges, N., eds., Venoms. Amer. Assoc. Adv. Sci. Publ. No. 44, pp. 117-121, Washington, D.C., 1959.

Mueller, H. L. Further experiences with severe allergic reactions to insect stings. New Eng. J. Med., 261:374, 1959.

Remington, C. L. The bite and habits of a giant centipede (*Scolopendra subspinipes*) in the Philippine Islands. Amer. J. Trop. Med., 30:453, 1950.

Rose, I. A review of tick paralysis. J. Canad. Med. Ass., 70:175, 1954.

Stalinke, H. L. Scorpions, revised ed. Tempe, Arizona, Poisonous Animals Research Laboratory, Arizona State Univ., 1956.

Symes, C. B., Muirhead-Thompson, R. C., and Busvine, J. R. Insect Control in Public Health. New York and Amsterdam, Elsevier Pub. Co., 1962.

Zinsser, H. Rats, Lice, and History. Boston, Little, Brown and Co., 1935.

Zumpt, F. Myiasis in Man and Animal in the Old World. A Textbook for Physicians, Veterinarians, and Zoologists. London, Butterworth and Co., 1965.

Unclassified Diseases

14.54
HEMORRHAGIC FEVERS

HEINZ F. EICHENWALD
VU VAN DZI

The terms "hemorrhagic," "virus hemorrhagic," and "epidemic hemorrhagic" fevers are used more or less interchangeably to describe a large number of separate entities occurring in many parts of the world, caused by a variety of related as well as unrelated etiologic agents. Many of these diseases have been studied incompletely clinically, virologically, or epidemiologically; little is known of some of them aside from their occurrence. Most are transmitted to man by arthropods (e.g., Southeast Asian hemorrhagic fever), others by arachnids such as ticks and mites (Omsk fever, Korean hemorrhagic fever), while others still may have no vector but are perhaps acquired from close contact with rodent reservoirs (Bolivian hemorrhagic fever). In general, the infections transmitted by arachnids are localized in occurrence and tend to affect adults more than children, while those acquired from mosquitoes are found over larger areas and usually cause more illness in the pediatric age group.

It is difficult to classify the different entities in any systematic or logical manner; thus it has become customary to identify each disease by its principal geographic location. From a strictly clinical standpoint, it is possible to divide the diseases loosely into those hemorrhagic fevers accompanied by a renal syndrome, and those with either slight or no kidney involvement.

Hemorrhagic Fevers with Renal Syndrome

The prototype for this group of disease is Korean hemorrhagic fever, more properly called Far Eastern hemorrhagic fever. Similar diseases occur in Siberia, European Russia, the Balkans, and Czechoslovakia. These illnesses are generally arachnidborne, but some are transmitted by mites, others by chiggers, and others perhaps by fleas. A variety of small rodents serve as reservoirs.

Far Eastern hemorrhagic fever is primarily a disease of adults; the few children that have been affected generally experienced a rather mild disease. **CLINICAL MANIFESTATIONS.** Illness begins abruptly with a febrile phase and chills, followed by lethargy and prostration. Generalized myalgias, headache, and abdominal pain occur commonly. A characteristic marked facial flush precedes the appearance of fine petechiae, which often occur initially on the soft palate and conjunctivae and later about the axilla and in skin areas subject to pressure or trauma. The febrile phase is further characterized by a rapid decline of blood platelet levels, associated with increased capillary fragility.

On the third to the fifth day, intense proteinuria occurs abruptly and the hematocrit rises. The patient complains of intense thirst but when fluids are administered his discomfort is increased and edema may result.

During the last day of the febrile phase (about 5 to 7 days after onset), hypotension or shock may occur, progressing on occasion to confusion and delirium. Massive proteinuria continues, blood urea nitrogen levels rise, and urine specific gravity falls. Toward the end of this phase, ecchymosis, hemoptysis, hematemesis, melena, and hematuria may occur.

As the patient's arterial pressure returns to normal, he enters an oliguric phase. Blood urea nitrogen levels now increase very rapidly and a variety of electrolyte disturbances are found. A peculiar hypervolemic syndrome occurs commonly, characterized by hypotension and distension of superficial veins, but without increased intravenous pressure or congestive heart failure. Further hemorrhagic manifestations often are noted at this time. The oliguric phase usually persists 3 to 5 days, and is followed by a diuretic phase lasting from a few days to several weeks and marked by fairly rapid improvement in renal function. A diuresis of from 3 to 8 liters a day may occur suddenly and the patient may again develop shock. Survivors then enter the convalescent phase which may last several weeks with gradual improvement in proteinuria and nitrogen retention.

PATHOLOGY. Histologically, the disease presents several distinctive features. Gelatinous, protein-rich, massive retroperitoneal edema is found in patients succumbing during the hypotensive phase. The kidneys are diffusely involved; lesions consist of areas of necrosis in the medullary pyramids. Microscopically, glomeruli and convoluted tubules are usually unaffected, but engorged vessels and extravasated blood are found around the loops of Henle and collecting tubules, with hemorrhage in the junctional zone. In addition, there is extensive necrosis of tubular epithelium and rupture of many tubules.

In other organs, there is similar evidence of widespread capillary damage manifested by dilation and rupture with extravasation of erythrocytes.

THERAPY. Treatment is supportive and symptomatic. No known drug favorably affects the course of the disease. Fluid intake should be restricted during the febrile phase; shock is treated in the usual manner. In severe cases of shock, the slow infusion of salt-poor albumin appears beneficial, and continuous administration of pressor drugs is perhaps helpful. During the oliguric and diuretic phases, water and electrolyte balance should be carefully maintained; during oliguria, therapy is that of acute renal failure.

PROGNOSIS. Patients treated by various techniques of modern medical care experience a mortality rate of about 5 percent; those cared for in their primitive villages by traditional methods die only slightly more frequently.

Hemorrhagic Fevers without Renal Syndrome

This group of diseases is generally caused by arboviruses; most are transmitted by mosquitoes, although a few are mite- or tickborne. The best studied and thus prototypic illness is Southeast Asian (Thai) hemorrhagic fever, which possesses an unusual epidemiology, and certain distinctive clinical features. **EPIDEMIOLOGY.** All four types of Dengue virus have been recovered from patients with this disease, although type 4 would appear to be uncommonly involved. Chikungunya virus also has been incriminated in the etiology of the disease; the frequency of occurrence of this type of arbovirus seems to vary from outbreak to outbreak. In any event, disease caused by the Dengue viruses or Chikungunya agent are clinically indistinguishable.

The disease characteristically occurs in sharp epidemics affecting large numbers of individuals over a period of relatively few weeks. Despite the high prevalence in many parts of the world of the causative viruses and their vectors, the occurrence of this type of hemorrhagic fever is limited to Southeast Asia. Furthermore, the disease is found only among certain groups of indigenous children, with Caucasians being affected very rarely, if at all, although the latter group frequently develops classical Dengue fever following infection. The age distribution is quite limited; few cases of hemorrhagic fever are found in patients older than 7 years of age. Furthermore, the disease occurs most commonly among urban dwellers and is rare in small rural villages, even though Dengue fever is highly prevalent in adults and children residing in these latter areas. Thus, certain local and host factors determine whether Dengue or Chikungunya virus infection produces Dengue fever or hemorrhagic disease.

The mosquito *Aedes aegypti* is the principal vector, transmitting the virus from human to human. No animal or avian reservoir has been identified. As a general rule, the disease is most prevalent during the rainy season when mosquitoes are abundant; in Thailand, for example, cases tend to cluster in the months from June to October.

CLINICAL MANIFESTATIONS. The onset of the illness is usually sudden with high fever, often accompanied by chills and nearly always by severe headache. Drowsiness and restlessness are common. The patient complains of severe aches in his joints and muscles, especially in those of the lower extremities, back, shoulder girdles, and retroorbital region. Gastrointestinal symptoms (nausea and vomiting in 70 percent; abdominal pain in 40 percent) are common. Respiratory symptoms and signs consisting of cough and pharyngitis occur in nearly half of the patients; radiologically, about two-thirds of these have evidence of diffuse interstitial pneumonia, with some developing a pleural effusion, usually consisting of varying quantities of slightly turbid, yellowish fluid.

By the third day of illness, hepatomegaly is apparent in the majority of patients.

In about 20 percent of children, a generalized maculopapular eruption appears during the first 2 to 3 days of illness, often fading rapidly, but may then be followed by a petechial rash. More commonly, petechiae may occur without any preceding skin manifestations. Purpura develops at some time during the course of the illness in nearly every patient, often associated with hematemesis, epistaxis, or melena. A peculiar shocklike state with hypotension and cold, cyanotic extremities but a warm, flushed body occurs during the third to fifth day in 30 to 40 percent of children. Convulsions during this stage signal a grave prognosis. After the fifth to the seventh day, the patient begins to improve, often with dramatic suddenness, and rapidly returns to his former state of health.

LABORATORY FINDINGS. A consistent finding is profound thrombocytopenia during the first 2 to 3 days of illness reaching its lowest levels at about the fifth day. Counts may remain low for 1 to 5 days, rarely longer, and will then return rapidly to normal. Occasionally, other hemostatic abnormalities are found, such as a moderate diminution of prothrombin and of factor V and VIII, but these changes are related to the degree of liver damage and appear to be of little clinical significance. No other consistent hematologic findings occur. Transient transaminase elevations are sometimes encountered and are probably also related to liver disease. Urine changes are limited to the occasional findings of albuminuria.

PATHOLOGY. Aside from scattered areas of hemorrhage, the only consistent pathologic findings are seen in the lungs, liver, and spleen.

The lungs show an interstitial pneumonia, with scattered histiocytes in the alveoli. The liver parenchyma is swollen with collections of fatty material in hepatic cells and occasional areas of lymphocytic infiltration. The malpighian corpuscles of the spleen reveal the most specific changes: granulomatous lesions with clumps of monocytoid cells, with abundant cytoplasm occasionally fused into a syncytium.

THERAPY. Therapy is symptomatic and supportive. The administration of oxygen is indicated in patients with extensive pulmonary involvement and dyspnea. Shock is treated in the usual manner with intravenous fluids and plasma or plasma expanders. While the use of glucocorticoids has been advocated, there is no evidence that these hormones favorably affect the course of the illness, reduce bleeding, or hasten the return of normal platelet levels.

PROGNOSIS. Mortality rates appear to vary somewhat from outbreak to outbreak, but the overall death rate is approximately 15 percent, higher in the infant under 1 year of age. With appropriate treatment of shock, a rate below 5 percent has been achieved. It has been noted repeatedly that children treated by practitioners of oriental medicine prior to hospitalization have unusually high death rates, possibly related to the use of a toxic herbal medication.

REFERENCES

Gajdusek, D. C. Virus hemorrhagic fever. J. Pediat., 60: 841, 1962.
Nelson, E. R. Hemorrhagic fever in children in Thailand. J. Pediat., 56:101, 1960.
Powell, G. M. Clinical manifestations of epidemic hemorrhagic fever. J.A.M.A., 151:1261, 1953.

chapter 15

THE NERVOUS SYSTEM

SIDNEY CARTER and ARNOLD P. GOLD, Associate Editors

15.1
DIAGNOSIS OF NEUROLOGIC DISEASE

Children with neurologic disorders comprise a significant portion of pediatric practice. It has been estimated that approximately 30 percent of all children admitted to an active teaching hospital either have primary neurologic disease or suffer from nervous system involvement secondary to other systemic conditions. Consequently, it is of great benefit to the pediatrician to have a thorough understanding of the fundamentals of good neurologic diagnosis.

Neurologic diagnosis is dependent on the evaluation of the history, the performance of a careful and detailed neurologic examination, and the utilization of appropriate ancillary procedures. Through evaluation of data compiled in this manner it is possible to localize a lesion to one or more areas of the nervous system. This localization is of primary importance in the establishment of a correct etiologic diagnosis because neurologic disorders have a predilection for specific areas of the nervous system. The astute clinician, then, attempts to answer two simple but very important questions: "Where?" and "What?" Ideally, an answer should also be found to a third question: "Why?"

Compilation and Evaluation of the History

A proper history is the initial guide to localization and differential diagnosis. The historical data must be documented by asking the proper questions of the persons most intimately involved, obtaining this information in a chronologic manner, and evaluating the symptoms and signs thus derived.

OBTAINING THE HISTORICAL DATA. Historical data are best obtained from both parents and, when possible, the child. It is of interest that even preschool children may supply invaluable diagnostic information. However, the initial history must be obtained in the absence of the child. Infants may be a source of distraction to both parents and physician, while older children may understand but often misinterpret historical facts and, as a result, suffer emotional trauma. Also, the cognizant child may, by his presence, limit the ability of the parents to relate a detailed and accurate history.

THE IMPORTANCE OF CHRONOLOGIC DOCUMENTATION. Chronologic presentation of the clinical manifestations will frequently suggest localization and etiology. Thus, in obtaining the history, it is essential to record the rate of onset and whether the signs and symptoms are progressive, regressive, or static in nature.

The rate of onset is important; diagnosis may be suggested by the rapidity with which the symptoms become evident. Thus, vascular disease may be a valid diagnosis when hemiplegia appears suddenly, while a subacute or insidious evolution of the hemiparesis is more characteristic of neoplasia.

Diagnosis of progressive lesions is largely dependent on the age of onset and the rate of evolution. For example, infantile amaurotic familial idiocy (Tay-Sachs disease) characteristically has its onset in early infancy and rapidly progresses to death in two or three years, while Friedreich's ataxia usually appears between the ages of 5 and 10 and slowly evolves for many years.

In static lesions of the nervous system, which account for two-thirds of the neurologic disorders of childhood, diagnosis must not be obscured by the fact that, despite the nonprogressive nature of such lesions, maturation of the nervous system may cause either improvement or worsening. As a consequence, in some cases of cerebral palsy, ataxia improves with age, while the hydrocephalus secondary to aqueductal stenosis becomes more marked, even though the disease itself is nonprogressive.

Evaluation of Symptoms and Signs

Certain manifestations by themselves suggest neurologic involvement, while others incriminate the nervous system only indirectly. The more important symptoms and signs and their relationship to localization and etiologic diagnosis are described here.

GASTROINTESTINAL COMPLAINTS. Children may exhibit abnormal feeding patterns following enteral or parenteral disturbances. Although the physician's attention is most often focused on possible local causes, it is most important, and at times lifesaving, to be aware of the multiple neurologic entities which may be the basis for altered function. Feeding problems, vomiting, and abdominal pain may be symptomatic of neurologic disorders.

TABLE 1.   *Normal Age for the Acquisition of Major Developmental Milestones*

Age	Motor	Language	Adaptive Behavior
4-6 wk	Head lifted from prone position and turned from side to side	Cries	Smiles
4 mo	No head lag when pulled to sitting from supine position Tries to grasp large objects	Sounds of pleasure	Smiles, laughs aloud, and shows pleasure to familiar objects or persons
5 mo	Voluntary grasp with both hands Plays with toes	Primitive sounds "ah goo"	Smiles at self in mirror
6 mo	Grasps with one hand Rolls prone to supine Sits with support	Range of sounds greater	Expresses displeasure and food preferences Holds arms out to be picked up
8 mo	Sits without support Transfers objects from hand to hand Rolls supine to prone	Combines syllables: "baba, dada, mama"	Responds to "No"
10 mo	Sits well Creeping Stands holding Finger-thumb opposition in picking up small objects		Waves "bye-bye," plays "patty cake" and "peek-a-boo"
12 mo	Stands holding Walks with support	Says 2 or 3 words with meaning	Understands names of objects Shows interest in pictures
15 mo	Walks alone	Several intelligible words	Requests by pointing Imitates
18 mo	Walks up and down stairs holding Removes clothes	Many intelligible words	Carries out simple commands
2 yr	Walks up and down stairs by self Runs	2- to 3-word phrases	Organized play Points to some parts of body

Feeding problems include difficulties with sucking and/or swallowing which result from brainstem (bulbar) dysfunction. Newborns, most commonly prematures, may exhibit these sucking and swallowing difficulties as a result of physiologic immaturity of the nervous system or because of maternal oversedation during delivery. However, lesions in the nervous system should always be suspected when these symptoms occur. If the child suffers diffuse involvement of the brain of the static type, as seen in the cerebral palsies, the earliest manifestation may be problems with sucking and swallowing. These symptoms frequently diminish and disappear with age. In all newborns with these problems, subdural hematoma and neonatal myasthenia gravis must be suspected and require prompt recognition. Difficulty with sucking and swallowing in the newborn is also symptomatic of congenital defects of the motor nuclei of the brainstem (Möbius' syndrome), familial dysautonomia, and myotonic dystrophy.

The appearance of sucking and swallowing problems in the older child usually implies a progressive disorder of the nervous system. In such cases consideration should be given to infectious processes such as bulbar poliomyelitis, brainstem tumors, and metabolic and/or degenerative disorders resulting from disorders of lipid and glycogen storage.

Vomiting in the form of minor rumination and regurgitation may be physiologic in nature. Pathologic vomiting, however, may be due to indirect or direct involvement of the vomiting center in the brainstem. Persistent vomiting in the absence of an overt cause should always raise the question of increased intracranial pressure. In the absence of increased pressure, tumors of the third and fourth ventricles, disease of the brainstem, seizure variants, and labyrinthitis should be suspected.

Abdominal pain which is acute and persistent may be the result of radicular involvement secondary to polyneuritis, spinal cord tumors, or a complication of a lumbar puncture, while chronic or recurrent abdominal pain, with or without vomiting, may be the sole manifestation of an epileptic state. Abdominal pain due to acute intermittent porphyria or to lead colic is very rarely observed in the pediatric age group.

DELAYED ACQUISITION OF DEVELOPMENTAL MILESTONES.   Developmental milestones represent the achievement of an expected physiologic function and include motor performance, language development, and adaptive behavior. Studies of large numbers of normal children have established age levels at which these various functions should be attained. Individual variations are common, and it should be noted that Table 1 is only an approximation of normal development.

While delay in the acquisition of a specific function may imply an impaired nervous system, there is a chance that such a delay is normal. However, multiple or global delay in achieving these milestones almost always signifies an underlying nervous system disorder, usually of the static type. This delay in the acquisition of many or all of the milestones usually indicates diffuse involvement of the brain and may be diagnosed as mental retardation or one of the more severe forms of cerebral palsy.

Specific delay in any one of the three areas of development is indicative of the following disorders: If *motor function* is delayed, cerebral dysfunction or disorders of muscle, spinal cord, or peripheral nerves may be the answer. If *speech* fails to develop, the causative factor may be either a brain disorder or peripheral hearing loss. Poor *adaptive behavior* usually implies a diffuse disturbance of the brain. In rare instances, of course, such behavior may be related to maternal deprivation or rejection.

ABNORMAL ENLARGEMENT OF THE HEAD. Every examination *must* include a measurement of head circumference. This has added value when it is compared with previous measurement and there is accelerated increase in size beyond the anticipated norm.

It is true, of course, that a head circumference greater than normal may be a physiologic manifestation of a familial trait. Pathologically, it is the result of alterations in any of the four cranial compartments: (1) the ventricles; (2) the brain; (3) the meninges; and (4) the skull and scalp. Accordingly, abnormal head enlargement may be due to any condition in which the cerebrospinal fluid flow is obstructed, since this causes enlarged ventricles with resultant hydrocephalus. The head may be large due to the presence of either too much or too little brain substance. An increase in brain substance is seen as a congenital abnormality in megalencephaly or in some metabolic and degenerative disorders. Decrease in brain substance is observed in hydranencephaly and porencephaly. In addition, an abnormally enlarged head may result from accumulation of fluid in the subdural space. Changes in the membranous bone of the skull, such as cleidocranial dysostosis or achondroplasia, as well as scalp involvement by cephalhematoma may result in an enlarged head.

MOTOR DISTURBANCES. Disturbances in motor function may be manifested as muscle weakness, ataxia, or abnormal involuntary movements. Symptoms of motor disturbance may be evidenced from early infancy by a delay in the development of the motor milestones. At a later age they may appear as a loss of, or a disturbance in, voluntary motor activity.

Muscle weakness may be the result of upper motor neuron disturbances. Lesions of the brain involving the motor cortex or its outflow will cause total or partial spastic paralysis of the extremities of the opposite side. Such lesions may be either congenital, fixed defects, or acquired disturbances due to tumors, vascular insults, or degenerative diseases. With fixed lesions the weakness does not increase and actually may improve by compensatory mechanisms. In acquired lesions, the sudden appearance of a hemiparesis suggests vascular disease, while a slowly developing weakness implies a tumor or degenerative disorder. Additional clinical features indicative of upper motor neuron disease are exaggerated deep tendon reflexes and the pathologic extensor plantar sign (Babinski reflex) on the involved side.

Lower motor neuron disturbances also may be responsible for muscle weakness. These disorders are characterized by a flaccid weakness, and result from involvement of either muscle, peripheral nerve, or anterior horn cells. In primary muscle disorders, such as muscular dystrophy, the weakness is greatest in the large girdle muscles. Symmetric involvement of the nerve trunks, as in polyneuritis, causes diffuse weakness; however, in this instance, the distal musculature of the hands and feet is more involved than the proximal girdle musculature. In anterior horn cell disease, weakness may be symmetric or asymmetric, involving isolated muscle groups. Lower motor neuron disease is further characterized by atrophy, hypoactive to absent deep tendon reflexes, and the presence of a normal plantar response.

Ataxia results from involvement of the cerebellum and its pathways. This unsteadiness of voluntary movements may be due to a congenital defect of the cerebellum (ataxic form of cerebral palsy), which is characterized by poor sitting and standing balance and the development of unsteady gait and hand function.

Acquired forms of ataxia may be either acute or insidious in onset. The ataxia which appears acutely may follow intoxications, the exanthems (particularly varicella), and nonspecific infections (acute cerebellar ataxia), or it may be episodic in nature, as in vertiginous epilepsy or vestibular neuronitis. Slowly developing ataxia may be observed with increased intracranial pressure, cerebellar and brainstem tumors, heredodegenerative disorders, as in ataxia-telangiectasia and Friedreich's ataxia, and some inborn errors of metabolism, such as Hartnup disease.

Abnormal involuntary movements may be either psychogenic in origin, as in tics, or the result of extrapyramidal dysfunction, as manifested by chorea, athetosis, dystonia, tremor, and ballismus.

Tics or habit spasms are the most common of the abnormal movements. They are characterized by isolated repetitive movements, such as winking, blinking, grimacing, twisting the neck, and shrugging the shoulders. More complex tic phenomena may have associated vocalizations, such as coughing, barking, and clearing the throat. When the vocal component is manifested by the use of obscenities, it is called the syndrome of Gilles de la Tourette.

Chorea is characterized by irregular, sudden, and jerky movements involving any group of skeletal muscles, including the face. Such movements may be indicative of rheumatic fever (Sydenham's chorea), encephalitis, hypoparathyroidism, and, less commonly, lupus erythematosus.

The movements of *athetosis* are slow and writhing, involving primarily the distal musculature. They may be accompanied by choreiform movements and are then described as choreoathetosis. Athetosis is a manifestation of kernicterus and congenital defects of the brain.

Dystonia is characterized by involuntary sustained muscle spasms of the neck, trunk, and extremities, resulting in abnormal posture. Dystonic movements may be a manifestation of dystonia musculorum deformans, some forms of encephalitis, and birth defects. They may be associated with rigidity in hepatolenticular degeneration (Wilson's disease). Children most commonly demonstrate dystonic phenomena as a complication arising from an idiosyncrasy to the phenothiazines.

Tremor of the basal ganglia origin occurs at rest, while the cerebellar form of tremor becomes evident in volitional movements. It is seen in its most benign form as familial or essential tremor and may be dramatic in the wing-beating tremor of Wilson's disease.

DISTURBANCES IN SENSATION. Pain, burning, tingling, and numbness are manifestations of sensory disorders. Episodic disturbances of this nature may be the only manifestations of a focal seizure or may be symptoms of hypoparathyroidism. Persistent sensory phenomena are seen in the polyneuropathies. Dysautonomic children, interestingly, have a raised pain threshold. There are also a small number of other children who have a congenital indifference to pain.

VISUAL LOSS. Sudden loss of vision is the manifestation of retrobulbar or optic neuritis, while transient impairment in visual function may be seen in seizure disorders or migraine. It is difficult to detect the onset of gradual visual loss, since children tend to be uncomplaining and parents unobservant; however, it does become evident when the child is observed holding books closer to his face, sitting nearer to the television set, or bumping into objects. It is difficult to detect a decrease in the field of vision in young children.

OCULAR DISORDERS. *Diplopia* follows rapid development of extraocular muscle paresis and is rarely, if ever, mentioned by children with long-standing eye muscle dysfunction. Nonparalytic *strabismus* is seen with extraocular muscle imbalance and often is a manifestation of nonprogressive lesions of the brain. Paralytic squint, on the other hand, is most commonly the result of involvement of the third and sixth cranial nerves. The turning in of one or both eyes may be the nonspecific result of increased intracranial pressure. Brainstem gliomas and myasthenia gravis also give rise to a variety of extraocular muscle palsies.

Nystagmus, exhibited as rhythmical, wiggling, jerky, or pendular oscillations of the eyeball, is associated with disorders of the eye, brainstem, and cerebellum. A searching type of nystagmic movement is seen in the blind. Pendular oscillations are most often ocular in origin, as in spasmus nutans and congenital forms of nystagmus. Vertical nystagmus is almost always a manifestation of brainstem dysfunction while the horizontal variety may indicate either brainstem or cerebellar pathology. Nystagmus in both vertical and horizontal directions of gaze is frequently the result of drug intoxication with barbiturates or hydantoins. Opsoclonus, a bizarre type of nystagmus, is characterized by coarse, irregular, nonrhythmic but conjugate eye movements in all directions of gaze. It often occurs in the syndrome of acute cerebellar ataxia with an occult neoplasm.

Ptosis may be permanent or intermittent and in some forms may be altered by the movements of the jaw (Marcus Gunn phenomenon). Permanent ptosis is seen congenitally and follows lesions of the third cranial nerve. The ptosis of myasthenia gravis is intermittent and is least evident on awakening; it increases with fatigue, and is most marked at the end of the day. When associated with miosis and enophthalmos (Horner's syndrome), ptosis is a manifestation of impaired sympathetic function.

Exophthalmos, when bilateral, usually signifies an endocrinopathy, while unilateral protrusions are most often secondary to retrobulbar tumors, optic nerve gliomas, or disease of the cavernous sinus.

HEARING LOSS. Defective hearing of peripheral origin may be secondary to kernicterus, trauma, exanthems (most commonly, mumps), tumors of the brainstem, drugs, or otologic disorders. Some children with intact peripheral pathways have apparent hearing loss. It is assumed that such children have impairment of the central connections of hearing (receptive aphasia). Often the first clue of an early hearing loss is the failure to develop normal speech patterns.

SPEECH DISORDERS. Defective speech may arise from impaired hearing or expressive difficulties. Delay in the acquisition and faulty development of speech patterns may be the first sign of fixed or progressive lesions of the brain, while loss of previously acquired speech is indicative of hearing disorders or degenerative disease of the brain.

POOR SCHOOL PERFORMANCE. Problems in learning are often related to visual or hearing defects. They may also be the result of unrecognized seizure states, particularly petit mal, or of progressive degenerative diseases. Specific learning disabilities, most commonly reading difficulties, are often seen in children with the syndrome of minimal cerebral dysfunction. Poor school performance may be the first indication of mild mental retardation.

PERSONALITY CHANGES. Personality changes often develop at some time during the course of neoplastic diseases, especially when the tumor involves the temporal lobe. The same is true of infectious, degenerative, or metabolic disorders. Hyperactivity and, less commonly, apathy are frequent manifestations of nonprogressive brain lesions.

HEAD TILT. Most commonly, this type of abnormal carriage of the head is related to tumors of the cerebellum or brainstem. Head tilt may also arise from local irritation of the cervical musculature, or it may be a manifestation of ocular and central nervous system pathology.

FACIAL WEAKNESS. Asymmetry of the face during crying or a complete lack of facial expression in a child is an indication of facial weakness. In the neonatal period this condition may be secondary to congenital anomalies, such as facial nuclear aplasia (Möbius' syndrome) and partial muscular hypoplasia (Hofnagel syndrome), or it may be acquired as the result of facial nerve compression. The older child, like adults, may demonstrate a peripheral facial weakness during the course of Bell's palsy, polyneuritis, brainstem gliomas, or mastoid disease. Rarely, there may be a progressive hemiatrophy of the face, which includes the facial muscles. Facial weakness limited to the lower half of the face (upper motor neuron paresis) may accompany a hemiparesis secondary to a brain lesion.

CONVULSIONS. In the newborn, convulsions may be due either to developmental or acquired lesions of the brain or to such metabolic disorders as hypoglycemia, hypocalcemia, hypomagnesemia, or pyridoxine dependency. Rarely, they may be a manifestation of maple syrup urine disease. Seizures taking place during this neonatal period may be confused with apneic or cyanotic spells of cardiac origin.

In children less than 2 years of age, seizures unassociated with fever are most often related to structural defects of the brain. Febrile convulsions, on the other hand, may be the only manifestation of meningitis or may be associated with extracranial infections. Breath-holding spells are common in this age group and, in some children, may be accompanied by convulsive phenomena. Focal motor seizures in children of this age group do not have the same significance as in adults. Often these focal spells will vary from side to side and, unless they persistently recur on one side, are usually not related to a specific brain lesion. Petit mal rarely occurs before 2 years of age.

HEADACHES. Headaches are relatively common in childhood. Undue irritability in young children may be an indication of recurrent or persistent headaches. Older children may have headaches which are related to increased intracranial pressure from any cause, or to migraine, tension, trauma, or systemic disease. These painful episodes may precede, follow, or be the only manifestation of convulsions.

VERTIGO. Evaluation of vertigo is very difficult and is dependent largely upon the ability of the child to describe this subjective phenomenon. Vestibular neuronitis results in paroxysmal episodes of vertigo, and seizures may be manifested only as vertiginous attacks. Vertigo may also be a symptom of Ménière's disease, which is rare in childhood.

COMA. Often a threat to life, coma in any age group is a perplexing problem. A careful history is invaluable in ascertaining the underlying pathology. Drug intoxication, trauma, and postictal states are common causes of coma. Less frequently, meningitis, encephalitis, cerebrovascular accidents, and metabolic disorders are accompanied by coma.

The Neurologic Examination

The neurologic examination is essential to the establishment both of nervous system involvement and of the site at which the pathologic process has occurred. Specific etiologic diagnosis may be possible when a detailed history is combined and evaluated with a thorough neurologic examination. For example, localization of a lesion to the brainstem is determined by the presence of multiple cranial nerve palsies, ataxia, and pyramidal tract signs. If the history shows slow progression, the lesion may be diagnosed as a probable tumor.

The *general pediatric examination* is of vital importance in providing data of significance in neurologic diagnosis. The head should be carefully measured and auscultated for intracranial bruits. Transillumination of the skull may indicate the presence of a subdural fluid collection, porencephaly, or hydranencephaly. Certain types of skin lesions are of significant value in neurologic diagnosis. For instance, depigmented nevi may be the initial cutaneous manifestation of tuberous sclerosis; later the child may develop the more classical adenoma sebaceum. Café-au-lait spots suggest neurofibromatosis, and port-wine facial hemangiomas often signify encephalotrigeminal angiomatosis (Sturge-Weber-Dimitri syndrome). Midline skin defects, patches of hair, or hemangioma may be associated with underlying defects of the spinal cord and brain.

In the *neurologic examination,* observation of the child is essential, since it may provide many clues to disturbed neurologic function. Successful observation depends upon the ingenuity of the examiner in obtaining the cooperation of the child. Ideally, the evaluation should be performed in a leisurely manner, and at all times a nonthreatening atmosphere should be carefully staged, perhaps with the child seated in his mother's lap. At some time during the examination the child must be completely undressed. Painful or difficult parts should be reserved until the end.

Examination of the newborn is difficult because the highly desired cooperation on the part of the patient is rarely available. In addition, it is difficult to determine whether the abnormal findings demonstrated in some newborns are a reflection of an immature nervous system or whether they represent transient or permanent defects.

The neonatal neurologic examination becomes significant when any of the following are demonstrated:

1. Alteration of the state of consciousness (lethargy, stupor, coma)
2. High-pitched, feeble, or absent cry
3. Manifestation of increased intracranial pressure
   a. Bulging fontanel
   b. Opisthotonus

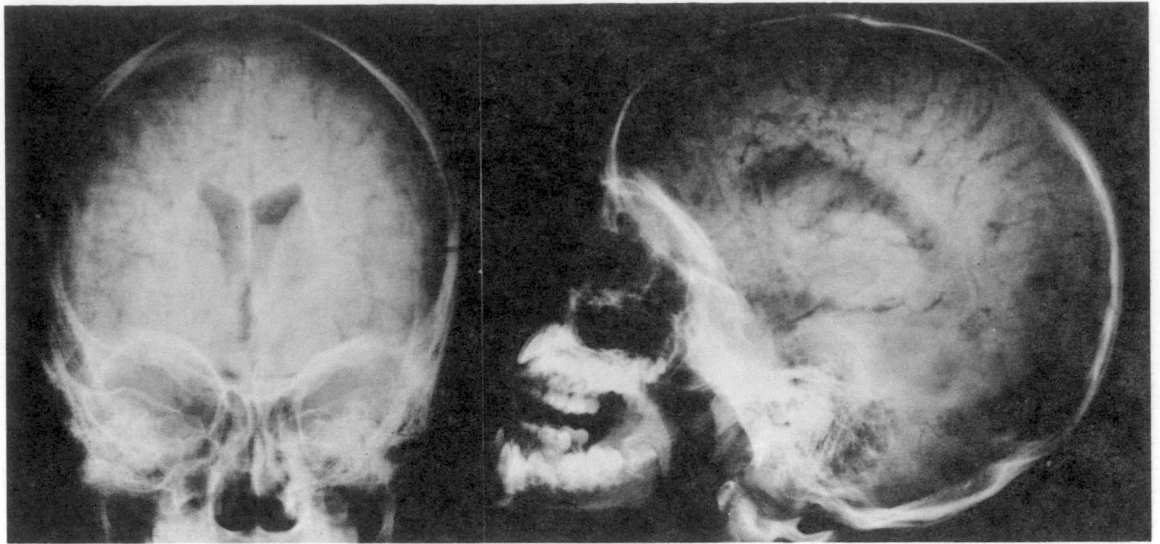

Fig. 1. Normal pneumoencephalogram in a girl 5 years of age.

c. Setting-sun sign of eyes
d. Dilated and unresponsive pupils
4. Abnormal or asymmetric positioning of extremities
5. Reduced spontaneous movements of extremity
6. Abnormalities in muscle tone (flaccid or spastic)
7. Abnormal reflex responses: Absent or delayed acquisition of neonatal reflexes
   a. Moro
   b. Root and suck
   c. Grasp
   d. Head control in vertical position
8. Abnormalities of the cranial nerves
   a. Failure to blink in response to light or sound
   b. Unequal or fixed pupils
   c. Facial asymmetry on crying
   d. Difficulties in sucking or swallowing
   e. Funduscopic abnormalities
9. Impaired response to pinprick, suggesting a spinal cord lesion

Evaluation of the older infant can be quite informative except that detailed sensory testing is usually not reliable. Neurologic examination of older children differs little from that of adults.

At the conclusion of the examination the physician should have evaluated the child's mental capacities, cranial nerve functioning, motor power, coordination, sensation and reflex phenomena. The findings of such an examination, plus the evaluation of the history, should lead to the performance of appropriate ancillary studies.

Ancillary Procedures

Additional diagnostic procedures must be carefully planned, and maximum information should be obtained from each study. Increasing knowledge in the field of electrophysiology, and improved radiologic techniques have made available a variety of new diagnostic aids. Many of these tests are highly specialized, and their value is dependent upon expert interpretation.

RADIOGRAPHIC STUDIES. *Skull.* Plain radiographs of the skull are indicated in all children with suspected intracranial disease and head trauma. Routine films include anteroposterior, posteroanterior, stereolateral, and base views. In special circumstances films of the optic foramina, mastoids, and laminograms may be necessary.

Significant findings on plain radiographs of the skull include evidence of increased intracranial pressure, premature closure of sutures, fractures, tumors of the skull, intracranial calcifications, and unilateral cerebral atrophy (Dyke-Davidoff-Masson syndrome).

Signs of increased intracranial pressure include suture diastasis, erosion of the posterior clinoids, and deepening of the sella turcica. The so-called beaten-silver appearance may be a normal finding and, by itself, is not evidence of increased intracranial pressure.

The presence of intracranial calcifications is usually abnormal and may be seen after infections with toxoplasmosis, cytomegalic inclusion disease, and chronic brain abscesses. Calcifications can also be found in association with tumors, vascular malformations, neuroectodermal dysplasias, and metabolic disorders. Calcification of the pineal gland is rare in childhood.

Spine. Radiographs of the spine are indicated following trauma and when there is a suggestion of an underlying congenital anomaly or a suspected tumor. They may also have diagnostic significance in certain metabolic disorders, such as Morquio's or Hurler's disease. Anteroposterior and lateral views should be taken routinely.

Contrast Studies. These radiographic procedures

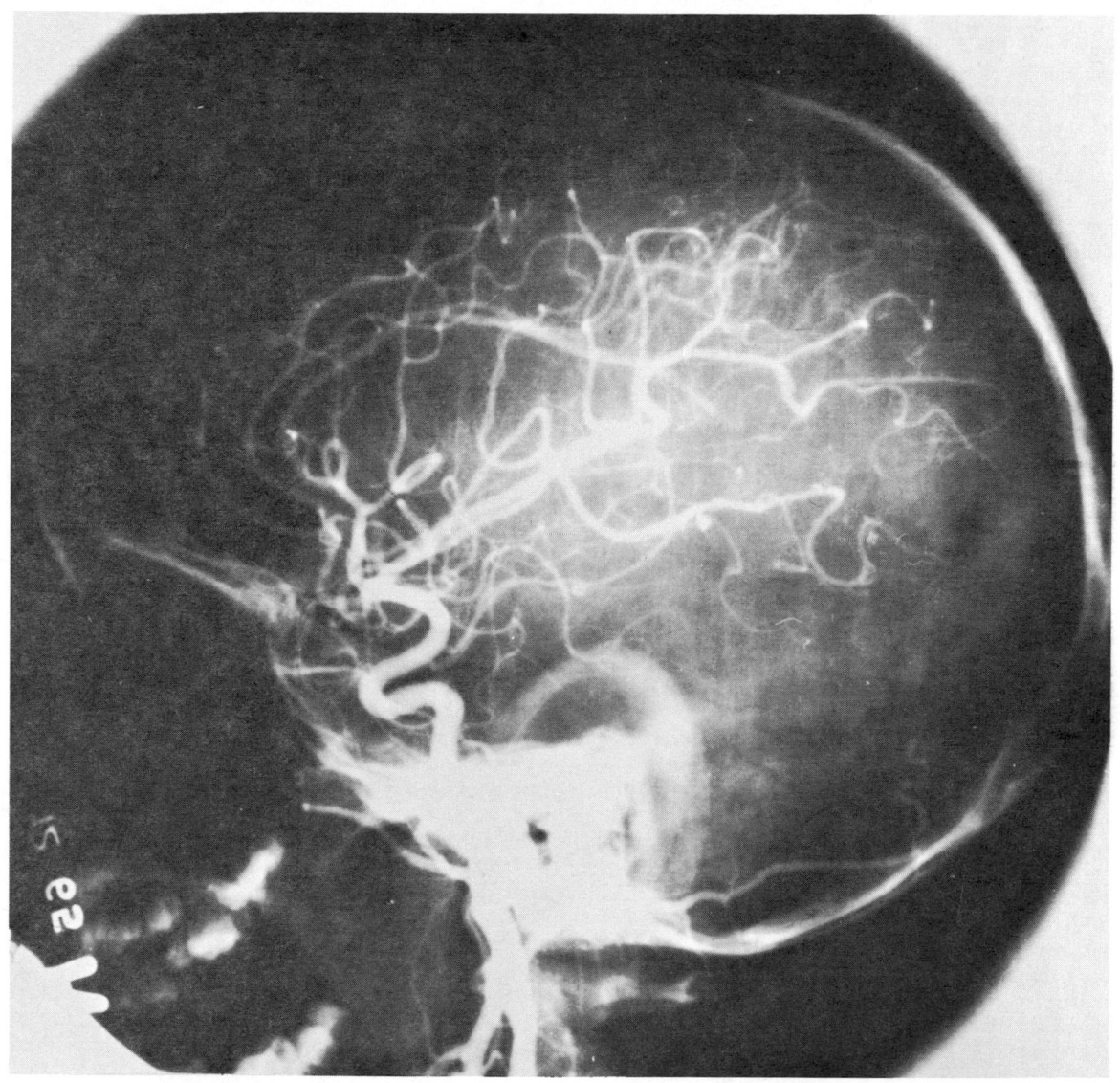

Fig. 2. Normal carotid arteriogram.

should only be performed in the presence of specific indications; their value is dependent upon proper performance and expert interpretation of the films. Contrast studies include air encephalography, cerebral arteriography, and myelography.

Air encephalography (Fig. 1) is primarily indicated in children with suspected mass lesions or with progressive neurologic disorders associated with increased intracranial pressure. Most epileptic children and those with nonprogressive conditions, including mental retardation, cerebral palsy, and abnormal behavior accompanied by learning disabilities, should not be subjected to this procedure. In the case of increased intracranial pressure, air is introduced directly into the ventricles (ventriculography). In most situations, however, air introduced via the lumbar subarachnoid space (pneumoencephalography) is adequate and is preferable for suspected brainstem and optic chiasm tumors.

Cerebral arteriography (Fig. 2) is a method of visualizing the vessels of the brain after injecting a major artery with a radiopaque substance; it is best utilized when there is evidence of a focal rather than a diffuse cerebral lesion. The primary indications for cerebral angiography include suspected vascular malformations, subdural hematoma, cerebral hemisphere tumors, and pseudotumor cerebri.

Myelography is a method of visualizing the spinal canal after the introduction of a radiopaque substance into the spinal subarachnoid space. The prime indication for this procedure is in cases of suspected intraspinal tumors.

LUMBAR PUNCTURE. Examination of the *cerebrospinal fluid* is the single most useful ancillary procedure in the evaluation of neurologic disease; it is mandatory in suspected infection of the central nervous system, and it may give considerable information in the evaluation of undiagnosed disease of the central nervous system. Lumbar puncture is also justified in all children with increased intracranial pressure when there is suggestive evidence of bacterial or viral infection of the central nervous system; it is contraindicated in the presence of increased intracranial pressure unrelated to infection, or when there is cutaneous infection at the site of the projected lumbar puncture.

Maximum information is obtained when the pressure of the cerebrospinal fluid is measured, the fluid is analyzed for its cellular, protein, and sugar contents, and a serologic examination is performed. Sedation and local anesthesia are important adjuncts, since reliable pressure measurements can be obtained only when the child is in a relaxed state and placed in a lateral recumbent position.

The pressure normally varies between 50 and 180 mm of water and is accurate only when measured with a water manometer. Rate of flow is a crude and often misleading method of estimating pressure. Jugular compression or formal cuff manometrics should be utilized when a spinal cord lesion is suspected.

Normal fluid is clear and colorless, but in the newborn, xanthochromic coloring is common. Hemorrhagic fluid may signify either a traumatic lumbar puncture or antecedent hemorrhage in the central nervous system. Differentiation is possible by the collection of fluid in three tubes and examination of the supernatant after centrifugation. Hemorrhagic fluid due to a traumatic lumbar puncture shows a progressive decrease in the number of red blood cells in the three consecutive tubes, and the supernatant is colorless; that due to antecedent hemorrhage shows no change in the three tubes, and the supernatant is xanthochromic.

The cell count of the fluid must be determined immediately; normally it does not exceed five white blood cells per cubic millimeter. If more than this number are present, a disorder in the central nervous system is suspected. Crenated red blood cells by themselves do not necessarily indicate previous hemorrhage.

Protein content has a normal range of from 10 to 15 mg per 100 ml in the lateral ventricles to a maximum of approximately 40 mg in the lumbar subarachnoid space. Newborns of both low and full birth weight have, normally, concentrations of protein in the range of 75 to 125 mg per 100 ml.

Sugar content is generally two-thirds of the blood sugar and its diagnostic value is enhanced when simultaneous determinations are performed. Significant decrease in glucose concentration is seen in hypoglycemic states, bacterial and fungal infec-

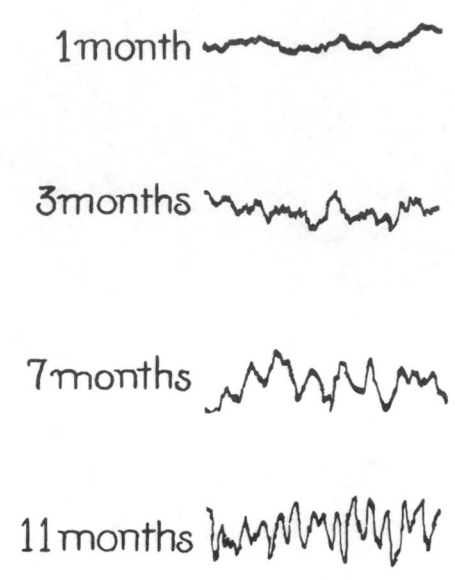

Fig. 3. Electroencephalogram in a normal infant at various ages, illustrating development of the fundamental rhythm. (From Lindsay. *J. Gen. Psychol.*, 19:285, 1938.)

tions of the central nervous system, and neoplastic meningeal infiltrations.

When indicated, the fluid can be analyzed for its gamma globulin or enzyme concentrations. Millipore techniques for obtaining and identifying cells may be invaluable in the identification of some intracranial tumors.

SUBDURAL PUNCTURE. This technique, an important diagnostic and occasionally therapeutic procedure, should be employed in all infants with suspected subdural hematoma or effusions and in those with unexplained macrocephaly; it is contraindicated in the presence of scalp infections. Cerebrospinal fluid may be inadvertently obtained at the time of the puncture and misinterpreted as a subdural fluid collection. True subdural fluid has either a xanthochromic discoloration or, when colorless, a protein content considerably higher than that of the lumbar subarachnoid fluid.

ELECTRODIAGNOSTIC PROCEDURES. *Electroencephalography* (EEG) is a relatively simple and innocuous method of obtaining additional information about the central nervous system. Pediatric electroencephalography requires familiarity with developmental changes in order to interpret properly deviations from the norm (Fig. 3). Electoencephalography has its greatest use as a diagnostic aid in seizure disorders and suspected space-occupying lesions. It is also useful in monitoring the progress of encephalitis and head injury.

Electromyography and nerve conduction studies are useful in determining the site of pathology in neuromuscular disorders. Electromyography aids in differentiating between primary muscle disease and disorders of neural origin. Nerve conduction studies may be of value in differentiating peripheral nerve from anterior horn cell disorders.

MISCELLANEOUS. *Echoencephalography* is a procedure in which high-frequency sound recordings are used to establish the shift of midline structures secondary to subdural hematomas and hemispheric mass lesions. More recently it has been useful in the determination of ventricular size (echoventriculography).

Radioisotope brain scans utilize iodinated albumin, mercury, or technetium radioisotopes in the localization of intracranial lesions, including neoplasms, abscesses, and vascular malformations.

Psychologic tests, when properly performed, can be of considerable diagnostic value in the documentation of organic brain dysfunction and in the delineation of intellectual potential. Projective tests may show evidence of personality disturbances. The results of these procedures are less reliable when repeated too frequently.

REFERENCES

André-Thomas, Chesni, Y., and Saint-Anne Dargassies, S. The neurological examination of the infant. Little Club Clinics in Developmental Medicine, No. 1. London, National Spastics Society, 1960.

Egan, D., Illingworth, R. S., and MacKeith, R. C. Developmental screening 0-5 years. Clinics in Developmental Medicine, No. 30. London, Spastics International Medical Publications, 1969.

Illingworth, R. S. An introduction to developmental assessment in the first year. Little Club Clinics in Developmental Medicine, No. 3. London, National Spastics Society, 1962.

Mayo Clinic. Clinical Examinations in Neurology. Philadelphia, W. B. Saunders Co., 1956.

Mealey, J., Jr. Brain scanning in childhood. J. Pediat., 69:399, 1966.

Paine, R. S. The immediate value of the neonatal neurological examination. Little Club Clinics in Developmental Medicine, No. 2, 62. London, National Spastics Society, 1960.

———— and Oppe, E. Neurological examination of children. Clinics in Developmental Medicine, No. 20, 21. London, National Spastics Society, 1966.

Prechtl, H., and Beintema, D. The neurological examination of the full term newborn infant. Little Club Clinics in Developmental Medicine, No. 12. London, National Spastics Society, 1964.

Schlagenhauff, R. E., Mazurowski, J., and Smith, B. H. Echoencephalography in neurologic diagnosis. New York J. Med., 67:1035, 1967.

15.2
PRENATAL AND DEVELOPMENTAL DEFECTS

WILLIAM E. DeMYER

Brain

Microcephaly and Megalocephaly

An abnormal head size warns of an abnormal brain. To evaluate head size, the maximum occipitofrontal circumference (OFC) should be measured. Any OFC ±2 standard deviations from the mean for the age raises strong suspicion of a brain disorder (Fig. 4A and B). Any OFC ±3 standard deviations almost certainly means an abnormal brain. A significantly small head is termed *microcephaly;* one that is too large, *megalocephaly (macrocephaly).* Microcephaly necessitates *micrencephaly,* a small brain. In megalocephaly, the brain actually may be very small, or it may be huge and heavy, a condition termed *megalencephaly.*

Early recognition of abnormal head size depends on serial OFC measurements of every infant from the time of birth. For accuracy, a thin, flexible steel tape is decidedly superior to cloth or paper tapes. Accurate serial measurements, plotted against the normal curve, show the rate of change of the OFC with time, providing clear evidence of a head that is going to be too large or too small. Since microcephaly and macrocephaly are statistical concepts, some neurologically normal subjects will be incorrectly stigmatized if the physician relies only on the OFC. The patient's weight at birth, his somatotype and chest circumference, and the somatotype and OFC of the parents and siblings must all be considered.

Once microcephaly or macrocephaly has been identified, therapy, prognosis, and family counseling must depend on diagnosing the *type* of cerebral lesion and its *cause.* First the history, genealogy, and physical examination must be evaluated for diagnostic clues to distinct entities such as Down's syndrome. Then diagnostic tests must be done in proper sequence, innocuous procedures being performed first. In the course of every infant's examination, the head should be transilluminated. In a completely dark closet, an ordinary flashlight equipped with a rubber adapter is placed against the infant's head. If the cerebrum is absent or greatly thinned, as from increased intracranial pressure, the entire cranium lights up (Fig. 5). Focal lesions such as subdural fluid accumulations, encephaloceles, porencephaly, or

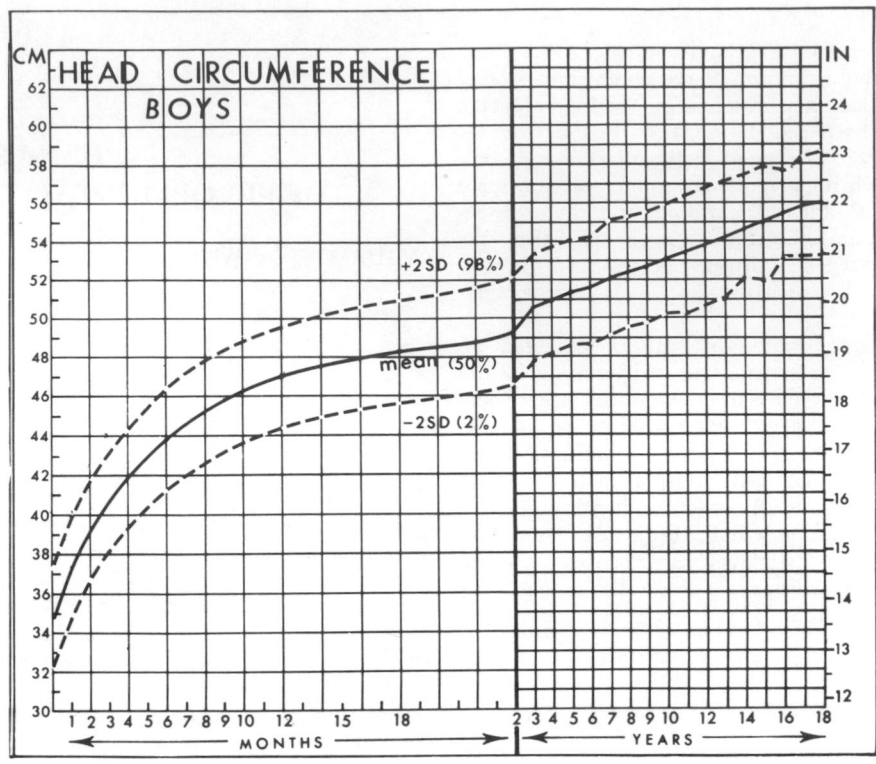

Fig. 4A. Graph of head circumference in boys from birth to 18 years of age. (From Nellhaus. *Pediatrics,* 41:106, 1968.)

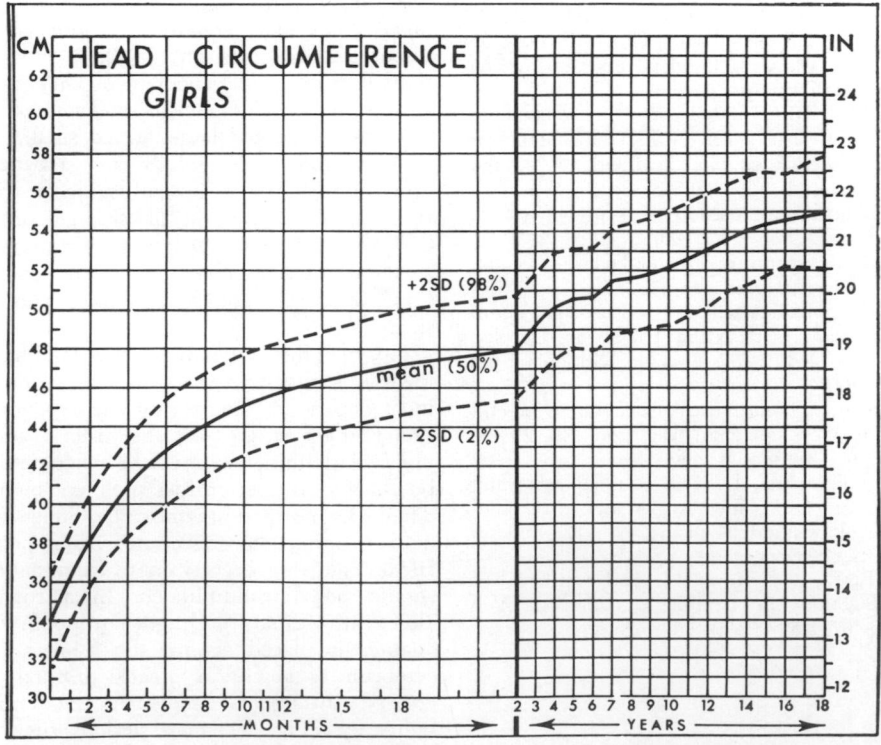

Fig. 4B. Graph of head circumference in girls from birth to 18 years of age. (From Nellhaus. *Pediatrics,* 41:106, 1968).

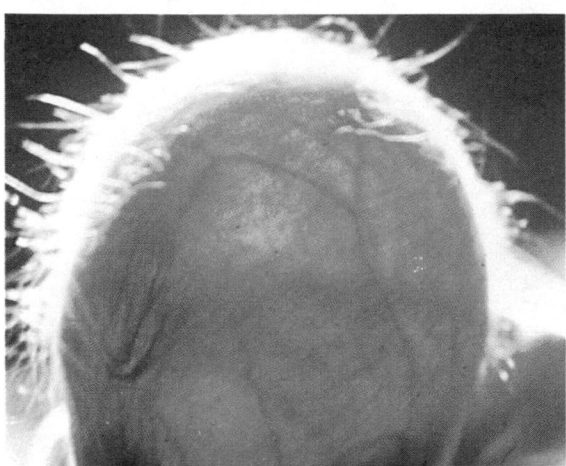

Fig. 5. Transillumination of skull in hydranencephaly.

atrophic defects in the cerebrum transilluminate more restrictedly.

Every infant with an abnormal OFC should next have skull radiographs and usually an electroencephalogram (EEG). Chromosome studies, nuclear sexing, and dermatoglyphic prints are useful if the patient has multiple somatic anomalies or if an intersex syndrome is suspected. If a degenerative, biochemical, or heredofamilial disorder is suspected, the chemistry of blood, urine, and cerebrospinal fluid should be examined. (See p. 856.)

Unless they have increased pressure and require ventriculography, most patients with an abnormal OFC should then have a lumbar puncture, the cerebrospinal fluid being examined for pressure, cell count, glucose, total protein, and protein electrophoresis. In some patients with microcephaly and in most with megalocephaly, air contrast studies, either pneumoencephalograms or ventriculograms, are necessary. In some instances cerebral angiograms are also required.

MICROCEPHALY. Aside from craniosynostosis, *microcephaly* is always secondary to micrencephaly. Any disorder which reduces brain size before maturation is complete may be responsible. A severe degree of micrencephaly implies a prenatal or early postnatal lesion. Common causes are malformations, prenatal or postnatal infections, hypoxia, and maternal disease. In experimental teratology, microcephaly may result from almost any teratogen, such as vitamin deficiency, drugs, or irradiation. Thus microcephaly, by itself, provides no clue as to its cause. The mother should be asked about the perinatal period, illnesses, and drug ingestion during the pregnancy. A history of infertility is common. Some cases are familial and follow a mendelian pattern.

In some microcephalics, the brain, although small, has a fairly normal internal and external configuration. Others may have malformation or destructive lesion, with symmetrically or asymmetrically dilated ventricles.

Microcephalics are usually mentally defective and may have cerebral palsy and seizures. In many instances, the combination of microcephaly with other clinical or laboratory findings permits a specific etiologic diagnosis.

Skull radiographs usually show a thickened calvarium and early closure of fontanels and sutures. Periventricular calcification suggests cytomegalic inclusion disease as the cause. Occasionally microcephaly is caused by craniosynostosis rather than primary micrencephaly. Although the sutures close prematurely in microcephaly, they usually are open at birth and in early infancy. In contrast, in craniosynostosis, the fontanels and sutures usually are obliterated at birth or during early infancy. Surgical opening of the sutures may be required in craniosynostosis but not in microcephaly.

MEGALOCEPHALY AND MEGALENCEPHALY. The most common cause of megalocephaly (an enlarged head) is increased intracranial pressure with hydrocephalus. The cerebral wall thins as the head enlarges. The brain weight, exclusive of intraventricular fluid, is normal or reduced. A much rarer cause of megalo*cephaly* is megal*encephaly*, an abnormally large and heavy brain.

Megalencephaly may be a primary malformation with huge gyri, often of simple pattern or with micropolygyria. It may be sporadic or associated with neurofibromatosis, tuberous sclerosis, myelomeningocele (Chiari malformation), and achondroplasia. The brain is large in pituitary gigantism but not in acromegaly; it is also large in the syndrome of "cerebral gigantism," in which no endocrine defects have been identified. Patients with primary megalencephaly are often mentally deficient and may have motor deficits and seizures.

In secondary megalencephaly, abnormal metabolic products accumulate in the brain. Included here are the infantile form of amaurotic idiocy, gargoylism, spongy degeneration of the white matter, and some of the leucodystrophies such as metachromatic leucodystrophy and Krabbe's disease. A large brain from cerebral edema or from neoplasms does not qualify as megalencephaly.

In hydrocephalus with increased pressure, the head enlarges rapidly, the fontanels bulge, the sutures split, and there may be papilledema. These features usually are absent in primary megalencephaly, but may occur in secondary megalencephaly. If the megalocephalic patient has none of the aforementioned features of increased pressure and no neurologic deficits, the most important step is to measure the OFC of siblings and parents. If other family members have enlarged heads without neurologic deficits, the patient, in all probability, has benign familial megalencephaly, and no further diagnostic procedures are necessary. If a simple familial large-headedness is excluded, the megalocephalic patient requires prompt, thorough investigation, including

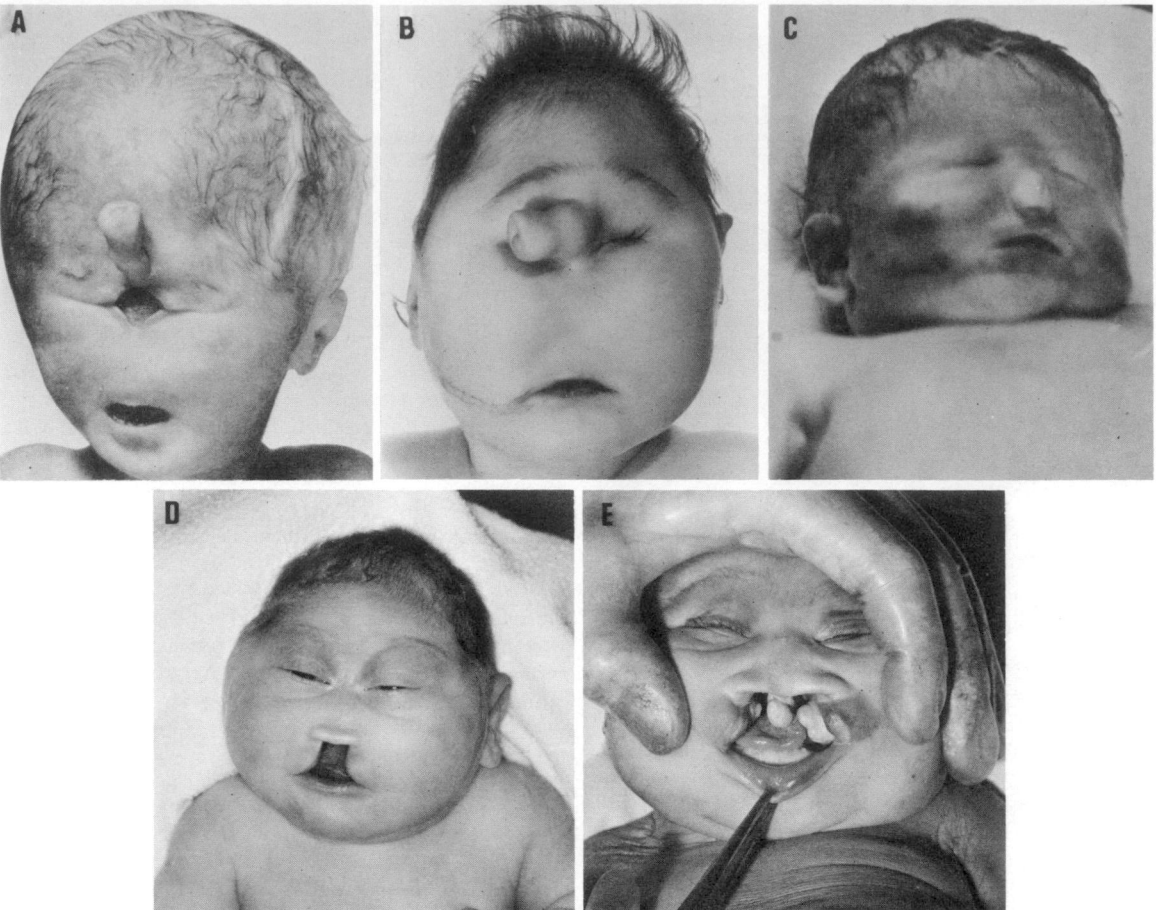

Fig. 6. Diagnostic facies of holoprosencephaly. A. Cyclopia. Notice the proboscis attached above the orbit. (From Potter. *Pathology of the Fetus and Newborn.* Courtesy of Year Book Medical Publishers, Inc.). B. Ethmocephaly. (Courtesy of Dr. P. Fluery.) The proboscis has migrated down between the orbits, which are separated but show hypotelorism, as do C, D, and E. C. Cebocephaly. The proboscis has migrated to the normal location for the nose. The single nostril leads into a cul-de-sac. D. With median cleft lip. Rudimentary nares and a nasal cavity are present. The nasal septum is lacking. E. With hypoplastic intermaxillary segment (philtrum-premaxillary anlage). A rudimentary nasal septum is present.

transillumination, skull radiography, and electroencephalography. Subdural taps for subdural hematomas or hygromas should be done in many cases. Air contrast studies are virtually mandatory. Pneumoencephalography is more informative than ventriculography, but ventriculography is often preferred when intracranial pressure is increased. Cerebrospinal fluid examination often should be deferred until it can be combined with the definitive air contrast procedure. Cerebral angiograms are less useful than air contrast studies in megalocephaly, but the "peeling away" of the cerebral vessels from the skull may disclose subdural fluid accumulations, particularly those missed by subdural taps.

Median Facial Defects and Holoprosencephaly (Arhinencephaly)

The holoprosencephalies are a teratologic series of graded severity, characterized by median malformations of the face and brain (Fig. 6). The unifying factor in this series is that the prosencephalon fails, in whole or in part, to undergo median cleavage into cerebral hemispheres or to form lobes. This holistic or *holo*-prosencephalon has a single-chambered ventricle and usually lacks olfactory bulbs and tracts.

Median facial anomalies consist of orbital hypotelorism in combination with a flat nose or proboscis, and oral deformities, such as a median cleft of the lip and palate. Some have trigonocephaly (a sharply pointed, keel-shaped forehead), and almost all are microcephalic. The crista galli, ethmoid, vomer, nasal, and premaxillary bones are absent or hypoplastic.

The unity of the median faciocerebral defects is explained by the role of prechordal mesoderm. This mesoderm normally gives rise to the median facial bones which are absent or hypoplastic in holoprosencephaly. Furthermore, by embryonic induction, this mesoderm determines not only the differentiation of the ectoderm as neural tissue but also its morphogenesis into lobated hemispheres.

According to the severity and pattern of median facial anomalies, at least five types of facies can be recognized which are pathognomonic of and predict the malformed brain. The facies are shown in Figure 6 arranged in order of decreasing severity. At the less severe end of the spectrum, when absence of the olfactory bulbs and tracts is the only brain abnormality, the face may have no obvious median defects; some of these subjects are eunuchoids.

The clinical diagnosis can be made from the pathognomonic facies, which are strikingly similar from patient to patient. Indispensable to the clinical diagnosis is orbital hypotelorism, as measured on posteroanterior skull radiographs, but one or more of the other median facial defects as detected clinically or radiographically must be present to distinguish the hypotelorism of holoprosencephaly from other conditions with *microcrania*. In categories A through D, the brain volume often is much smaller than the intracranial space, permitting transillumination of the head. The EEG records little or no electrical activity over the areas of transillumination but elsewhere shows repetitive seizure discharges.

The cause of holoprosencephaly is unknown. Most reported cases are regarded as sporadic, but familial cases occur. Some holoprosencephalics have 13/15 trisomy, others a 46-chromosome karyotype. The 13/15 trisomy patients usually have multiple extracephalic malformations, such as polydactyly, while the patients with 46 chromosomes usually have few or no extracephalic anomalies, although exceptions occur. The face predicts the malformed brain irrespective of karyotype or extracephalic anomalies.

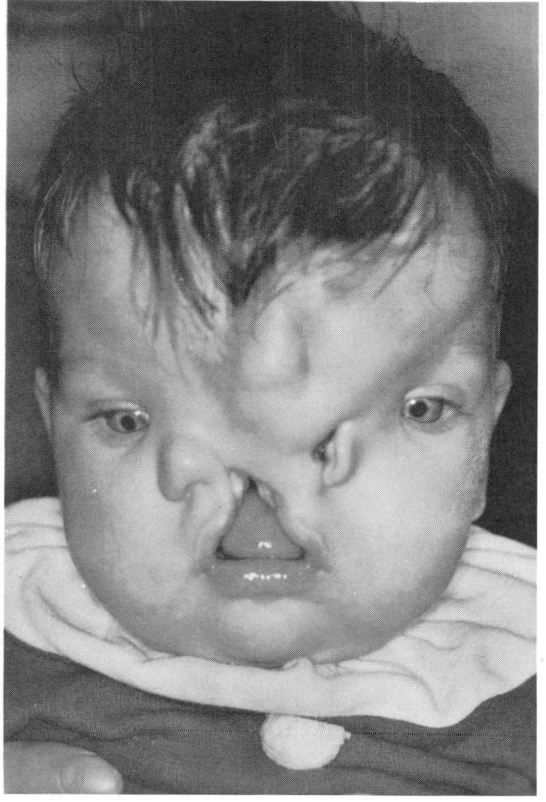

Fig. 7. Typical facies of median cleft face syndrome, consisting of median cleft lip, bifid nose, hypertelorism, and frontal encephalocele.

Median Cleft Face Syndrome: Hypertelorism, Median Cleft Lip, and Frontal Encephalocele

The stereotyped, stylized facies of holoprosencephaly should not be confused with another pattern of median facial defects consisting of frontal meningo-encephalocele, orbital *hyper*telorism, a bifid nose, and a median cleft of the lip (Fig. 7). In spite of the grotesque facies, these patients often are mentally normal or only mildly retarded. As in holoprosencephaly these patients also can be arranged into a teratologic series of graded severity. The least severe degree of this defect is a simple median notch in the nose or upper lip. As listed by Waardenburg, hypertelorism is associated with a number of other syndromes.

Hydranencephaly

In this congenital malformation, the cerebral hemispheres are missing or have huge, complete, symmetric defects in the cerebral wall because of either intrauterine destruction, malformation, or possibly severe increased intracranial pressure which has run its course before birth. The skull and scalp are well formed, distinguishing hydranencephaly from anencephaly, encephaloceles, and other dysraphic lesions. Most cases are sporadic.

In contrast to holoprosencephaly, most patients have no facial or extracephalic malformations pointing to the brain defect. The disorder may not be suspected in the young infant until he fails to show psychomotor progress, has seizures, or has spastic quadriplegia. Most patients die in infancy, but some survive for years.

The head may be small, normal, or, in some instances, may enlarge rapidly. In young infants, the head always transilluminates brightly, as in Figure 5. An air bubble placed through the anterior fontanel can be traced around the inner table of the skull on radiographs. Angiograms show attenuated vessels. In hydranencephaly the EEG shows little or no electrical activity, except over local remnants of cortex. In hydrocephalus with preserved cortex, where the head transilluminates brightly because of the extremely thin cerebral wall, the EEG shows generalized activity.

Agenesis of the Corpus Callosum

The corpus callosum is a large bundle of nerve fibers which connect the cortex of one cerebral hemisphere with the other. It is formed as the axons from cortical neurons of each cerebral hemisphere reach the midline, decussate, and grow to the opposite cerebral cortex. There the fibers synapse with the cortical areas which are a mirror image of their own area of origin. As these fibers accumulate at the midline, they form the corpus callosum. Agenesis or hypoplasia of the corpus callosum occurs if the fibers fail to grow out, are destroyed, or are prevented from crossing. When the fibers have reached the midline and fail to decussate, they pile up along the ventricular wall.

Although experimental studies show that the corpus callosum normally mediates interhemispheric transfer of information (and also may mediate interhemispheric propagation of some seizure discharges), there is no characteristic neurologic deficit or bedside test for agenesis. Air encephalography is the only way to make the diagnosis. If simple nondecussation of the corpus callosum fibers is the sole brain lesion, the individual may lead an apparently normal life. More commonly, agenesis of the corpus callosum is associated with other malformations, such as heterotopias, holoprosencephaly, or destructive lesions. In these patients, the neurologic deficits reflect the associated brain lesions.

Most cases of agenesis of the corpus callosum are discovered incidentally when air contrast procedures are done to elucidate a neurologic problem such as mental deficiency, epilepsy, or cerebral palsy. In the pure cases of agenesis of the corpus callosum, the ventricular shadows in posteroanterior pneumoencephalograms have a pathognomonic "bat-wing" outline. In other cases of agenesis or hypoplasia of the corpus callosum, the cerebrum may have only a single ventricle.

Hydrocephalus

ERNEST S. MATHEWS, JOSEPH RANSOHOFF, and FRED J. EPSTEIN

Hydrocephalus is a pathologic condition characterized by an increased volume of cerebrospinal fluid (CSF) which is or has been under increased pressure. Almost without exception the fluid accumulates in the ventricular system as a result of distal obstruction in the normal cerebrospinal fluid circulation. When the condition develops prior to fusion of the cranial sutures, it produces enlargement of the head which may reach extreme proportions.

Hydrocephalus attracted the attention of early physicians and was well described by Hippocrates. Although modern theories are based largely on the classical studies of Dandy and Blackfan, concepts of the physiology of the cerebrospinal fluid have undergone considerable modifications.

CEREBROSPINAL FLUID CIRCULATION. The anatomy of the CSF pathways can be divided into the ventricular system and the subarachnoid spaces. The paired lateral ventricles lie within each cerebral hemisphere and connect via the foramina of Monro to the midline third ventricle. This in turn connects via the aqueduct of Sylvius with the midline fourth ventricle of the posterior fossa. Along the floor of each lateral ventricle, in the roof of the third ventricle and in the roof and lateral recesses of the fourth ventricle, lies an outpouching of highly vascularized pia with a modified ependymal covering called the choroid plexus.

The subarachnoid space lies between the arachnoid membrane, which follows the inner surface of the dura mater, and the pial membrane, which hugs the contours of the brain and spinal cord surfaces. In certain areas, especially at the base of the brain, the subarachnoid space is enlarged into lakes or cisterns (cisterna magna, basalis, chiasmaticus). The ventricular system connects with the subarachnoid spaces via the medial foramen of Magendie at the outlet of the fourth ventricle and the lateral foramina of Luschka. Along the large venous sinuses in the dura, outpouchings of arachnoid villi form a unidirectional valvar system being composed of a labyrinth of small tubules which establish open connections between the subarachnoid spaces and the venous channels.

It is generally accepted that the CSF is formed mainly within the ventricular system, approximately 50 percent from the choroid plexus and 50 percent from the cerebral capillaries. The choroid plexus actively secretes a hypertonic sodium solution which is followed by a diffusion of water into the ventricles, maintaining a normal osmotic pressure. The equilibrium maintained for other electrolytes and solutes, however, involves active and passive transport systems at many sites throughout the entire central nervous system. Penetration across the blood-cerebrospinal fluid barrier is highly specific for the substance involved and in disease states may vary considerably from the normal.

In an overall sense, the circulation of CSF is a unidirectional flow from the ventricular system to the posterior fossa foramina into the cisterns and subarachnoid spaces. A significant percentage of the fluid is reabsorbed into the bloodstream via the arachnoid villi in the venous sinuses. The generating force for this flow is in part derived from the arterial pulsation of the choroid plexuses and perhaps that of other large arteries at the base of the brain. In addition, absorption is probably also dependent on the CSF pressure being greater than the intracranial venous pressure.

PATHOGENESIS. There are three possible mechanisms for the development of hydrocephalus. One is an obstruction of the cerebrospinal fluid pathways within the ventricular system (e.g., foramen of Monro or aqueduct of Sylvius) or in the subarachnoid pathways (e.g., tentorial incisura) with secondary dilation of the channels proximal to the site of obstruction. The second is defective absorption of the cerebrospinal fluid at the subarachnoid level, especially over the convexities of the brain at the level of the arachnoid villi. A third but rare contributing factor is the occurrence of a choroid plexus tumor which results in the overproduction of cerebrospinal fluid with secondary dilation of the ventricular system and all associated subarachnoid pathways.

When the block is within the ventricular system, the process has been designated as "obstructive hydrocephalus"; the term "communicating hydrocephalus" is applied to cases in which the site of blockage is in the subarachnoid pathways. Strictly speaking, however, all hydrocephalus is obstructive. It would seem preferable to discard the older terms in favor of more accurate descriptions of the site and nature of the obstruction, such as intraventricular or extraventricular.

ETIOLOGY. The three major causes of hydrocephalus are neoplasms, congenital malformations, and posttraumatic or postinflammatory lesions.

Neoplasms are seldom encountered in the neonatal period but may develop at any time thereafter. The most common sites of neoplasms of infancy and childhood which produce hydrocephalus are gliomas located in the third ventricle, in the periaqueductal region, or in the fourth ventricle and the cerebellum.

Developmental anomalies are present in a number of children with hydrocephalus. Spina bifida with meningomyelocele is often associated with Arnold-Chiari type II hindbrain malformation. In this type of malformation there are elongation of the lower brainstem and caudal displacement of the fourth ventricle into the upper cervical canal, and at the inferior tip of the fourth ventricle there is a small knuckle of medulla suggesting a buckling effect at this site. This impaction of the posterior fossa structures down through the foramen magnum with associated adhesive arachnoidal thickening and subsequent blockage of the cerebrospinal fluid pathways may finally result in ventricular dilation.

Stenosis of the aqueduct of Sylvius or "forking" of the aqueduct produces early, severe hydrocephalus (Fig. 8), resulting from the inability of this narrowed structure to carry the amount of cerebrospinal fluid which is normally produced. It can also appear secondary to progressive periaqueductal gliosis, with symptoms and signs occurring at any age during childhood, in adolescence, or even in adult life. These patients experience an overgrowth of fibrillary subependymal neurolgia which constricts or even occludes what apparently was once a normal aqueduct. Some cases follow obstruction of the aqueduct by a blood clot, with subsequent organization.

Occasionally described are congenital septa or membranes occluding the outlets of the fourth ventricle (Dandy-Walker syndrome). When these outlets of the fourth ventricle are obstructed, a huge cyst develops in the posterior fossa displacing the cerebellar hemispheres to either side and resulting in a dysgenesis of the cerebellar vermis and associated elevation of the tentorium. This condition may not be truly congenital but may be the result of inflammatory processes, as suggested by the fact that these patients often have obliterated basilar cisterns as well; hence, simple opening of this membranous cavity into the subarachnoid pathways of the spinal canal does not always relieve the hydrocephalus. However, opening of the septa which may occur at the rostral end of the fourth ventricle usually results in the relief of hydrocephalus.

Probably the most frequent cause of hydrocephalus is postinflammatory or posttraumatic obstruction of the basilar cisterns and associated subarachnoid pathways, particularly in the region of the tentorium. There may be intracranial bleeding at the time of birth or episodes of meningitis in the perinatal or neonatal period which go unrecognized. These processes lead to progressive fibrosis of the arachnoidal pathways at the base of the brain, which eventually obliterate the routes of the extraventricular circulation and absorption of the cerebrospinal fluid. Cysticercosis, toxoplasmosis, and other parasitic infections may produce ventricular or subarachnoid obstruction. Gradual arrest of the hydrocephalic picture theoretically results from the reopening of these channels when they have not been irreversibly obliterated.

Apart from the lesions responsible for the obstruction, there are secondary changes in the brain. Pressure from the distended ventricles leads to progressive thinning of the brain, the white matter suffering greater loss or demyelinization than the gray. The layer of brain surrounding the ventricles or the "cortical mantle" is sometimes no more than 5 or 6 mm in thickness and at times the ependyma of the ventricle and the pia are actually in contact. When the ventricular system has dilated to such as extent, there is often rupture of the septum pellucidum. This extensive ventricular enlargement resembles a large sac, and at times there are areas that have ruptured into the subarachnoid space forming external cerebrospinal fluid fistulas. Attenuation of the dural venous sinuses as well as atrophy of the choroid plexuses has been seen in these extensive pathologic states. In less marked cases there is only flattening of the convolutions. Atrophic changes in ganglion cells may be observed microscopically. With this degree of enlargement of the head, the bones are often thinned, the fontanels are enlarged, and the suture margins widely separated.

CLINICAL MANIFESTATIONS. In many cases of congenital hydrocephalus the infant dies in utero. In others the process may be so far advanced before birth that cesarean section or craniotomy may be necessary before delivery is possible. In the majority of cases nothing unusual is observed at birth, or the head is only slightly larger than the normal. In

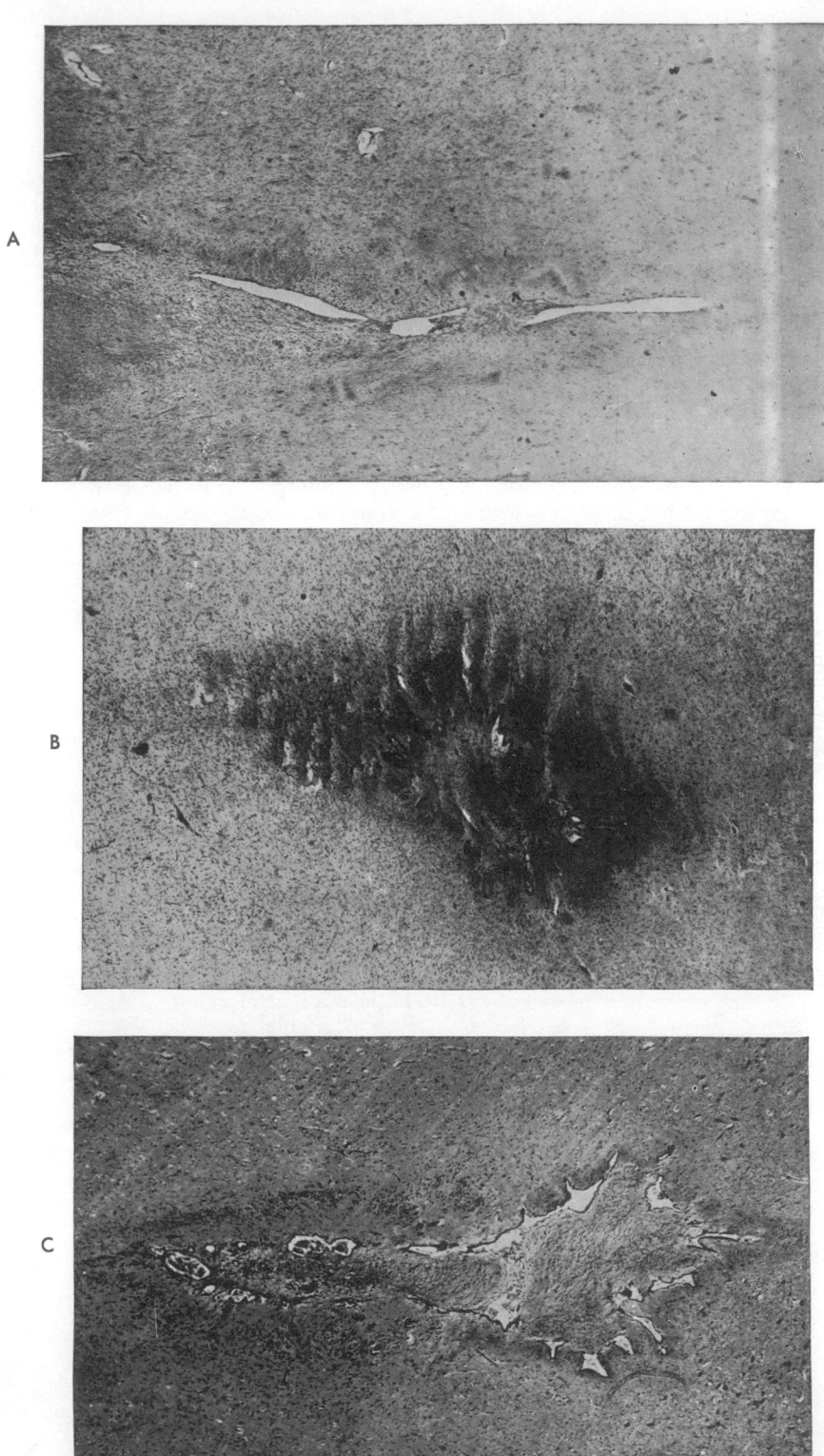

Fig. 8.   Lesions of the aqueduct causing hydrocephalus. *A.* Section of a congenitally malformed aqueduct showing "forking" with multiple interruptions of narrow slit. *B.* Section of a well-formed aqueduct plugged by inflammatory exudate in meningitis. *C.* Section of a well-formed aqueduct plugged by fibrous tissue probably representing organization of an old intraventricular blood clot. (Courtesy of Dr. F. R. Ford.)

the early weeks of life, it may be discovered that the head is increasing in size at an abnormal rate and the fontanels are enlarging. The eyes may assume a staring expression, with sclera visible above the cornea (sunset sign), and the infant may have difficulty in holding up his head. Scalp veins are prominent, and the forehead becomes overhanging in appearance. There is a disproportion in size between the large cranial vault and the normal face. As a rule the capacity of the head to expand with increased intracranial pressure protects the eyes. Although the orbits may be shallow and the globes depressed in relation to the slits, vision usually remains unimpaired, and the eyegrounds fail to show evidence of papilledema. In severe, chronic cases optic atrophy may be found. Strabismus when observed is secondary to sixth nerve paresis. Neurologic examination may show no abnormalities except for delayed ability to hold up the head and other developmental limitations which can be explained entirely by the abnormal weight of the cranium. In some children spasticity with confirmatory pyramidal tract signs may be observed while others may show ataxic phenomena.

In the child with decompensating hydrocephalus, signs of increased intracranial pressure may be observed, with vomiting, lethargy, and inability to gain weight.

DIAGNOSIS. In the classical case of far-advanced hydrocephalus, characterized by a large head, distended scalp veins, downward deviation of the eyes, and retarded motor milestones, one has no need for reference to charts of head circumference or other aids, for the diagnosis is obvious. In earlier cases, however, the diagnosis may be more difficult to establish.

Although the head size (occipitofrontal circumference) in comparison with the normal is of importance, repeated observations of the rate of head growth done carefully at the same level by a nonelastic steel tape are of paramount importance. Additional information can be obtained from measurements of the anterior fontanel, since active hydrocephalus does not occur in conjunction with a closing fontanel. On the other hand, if the fontanel is enlarging from month to month, additional investigations are warranted. Roentgenograms of the skull confirm the disproportion between the facial bones and the enlarged vault and may show thinning of the bone and widening of the cranial sutures.

Careful transillumination of the head carried out in a darkened room may be of value in disclosing the presence of porencephalic cysts, hydranencephaly, or elevation of the tentorium secondary to a posterior fossa cyst (Dandy-Walker syndrome). A large subdural effusion with an enlarging head must always be considered; it can be ruled out by careful subdural taps. Toxoplasmosis and rarely cytomegalic inclusion disease may result in hydrocephalus. Toxoplasma dye test on mother and child and a urine examination for cytomegalic inclusion disease should be performed routinely. The presence of bloody cerebrospinal fluid

may be indicative of a vascular malformation or a choroid plexus papilloma. Papilledema suggests a neoplastic cause for the hydrocephalus. Macrocephaly may result from conditions other than hydrocephalus (p. 851).

The final diagnosis of hydrocephalus rests on ventriculography or pneumoencephalography. These studies also give some indication as to the thickness of the cortical shell. If the ventricle is not tapped at a depth of 4 cm, hydrocephalus if present is not sufficiently advanced to require treatment. It is often helpful to inject neutral phenosulfonphthalein into the ventricles and check its appearance time in the lumbar subarachnoid space by spinal puncture. If no dye appears within 20 minutes, a block may be assumed to be present between the ventricles and the spinal subarachnoid space. This condition has been referred to usually as noncommunicating hydrocephalus.

Forty to 60 cm³ of air injected into one ventricle and subsequent "bubble" ventriculographic studies will demonstrate: (1) whether the ventricles communicate via the foramina of Monro, (2) the thickness of the cortical mantle, (3) whether there is an unsuspected midline neoplasm, and (4) whether communication exists between the ventricular system and the subarachnoid spaces (Figs. 9 and 10). At times, air injected via the lumbar route will be helpful in confirming a suspected aqueductal insufficiency. CSF obtained at the time of contrast study should be routinely examined for cells, protein, sugar, and serology.

TREATMENT. Evaluation of any medical or surgical therapy must be made against the background of the rate of spontaneous arrest and the physical and mental state of the survivors. Although some children with hydrocephalus do arrest spontaneously, with active and progressive hydrocephalus, surgery offers a better prognosis for survival and intellectual function. In the final analysis, therapeutic success would seem to depend on the careful individualized treatment of each hydrocephalic infant.

Surgical treatment for hydrocephalus is directed toward either reducing the amount of spinal fluid produced or rerouting fluid around an obstruction by a shunting procedure. Rerouting may conduct the fluid from one part of the central nervous system to another or to other body areas or cavities, where fluid is either reabsorbed or diverted to the ureter and excreted.

In 1918 Dandy proposed removal of the choroid plexus of the lateral ventricles, later modifying the operation to endoscopic electrocoagulation for the treatment of hydrocephalus. Both an open procedure, with direct exposure of the plexus through a transcortical incision, and endoscopic coagulation of the plexus are employed currently. Results with this treatment indicate an arrest in 65 to 70 percent, a case fatality rate of 10 percent, and a yield of normal children of about 25 to 30 percent. Choroid plexectomy when successful is the most satisfactory thera-

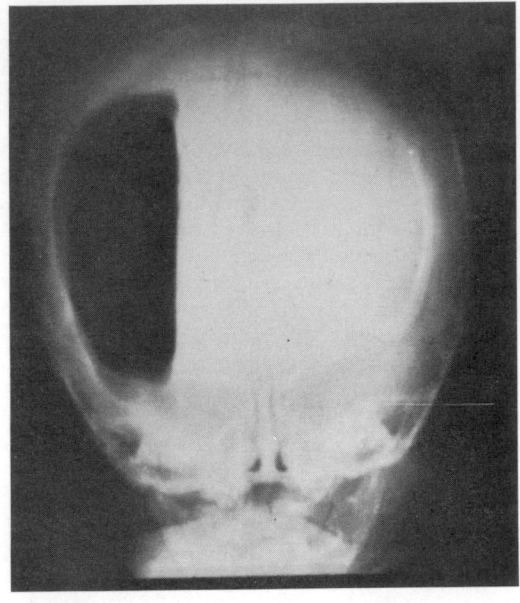
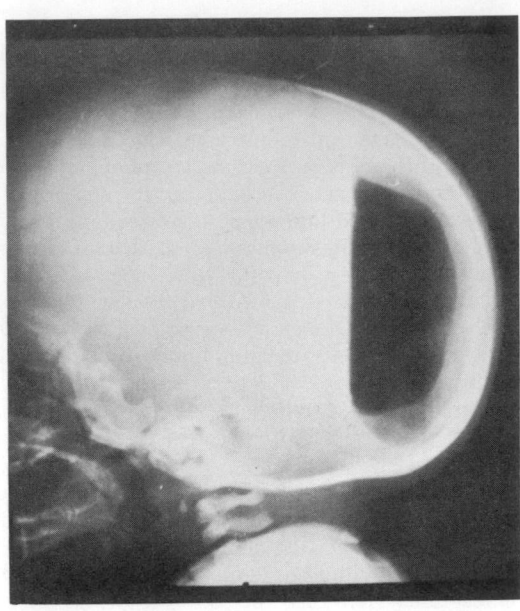

A   B

Fig. 9. Bubble ventriculogram demonstrating advanced hydrocephalus. A. Anteroposterior view with left side of head down, showing fluid level in dilated right ventricle. B. Lateral view with brow down, showing posterior extent of lateral ventricles.

peutic physiologic procedure; it avoids mechanical devices, such as tubes and valves, which are prone to block, slip out of place, or separate at joints, and also secondary infection, a frequent complication.

With the advent of antibiotics and the development of the inert plastics well tolerated by the body, shunting procedures have achieved great popularity. While no single shunt is invariably successful or applicable to all patients, satisfactory results are frequently obtained. The so-called universal shunting procedures drain the lateral ventricles and are applicable to all types of hydrocephalus; draining the lumbar subarachnoid space is helpful only when the ventricles communicate with the spinal subarachnoid space.

If the obstruction is in the third ventricle, aqueduct, or fourth ventricle, the procedure described by Torkildsen in 1939 is often employed. Depending upon the patency of the foramina of Monro, a catheter is carried from one or both lateral ventricles over the occiput into the cisterna magna. No large series of ventriculocisternostomies in infants or children is available for study. The theoretical objection has been offered that the surface subarachnoid spaces are not sufficiently opened or developed in the hydrocephalic infant and therefore the procedure merely changes a noncommunicating hydrocephalus to a communicating one. In addition it is technically difficult to institute such drainage in the infant's posterior fossa because of the extreme venous vascularization of the dura in this region.

As early as 1908, attempts were made to channel cerebrospinal fluid into the great veins and into the heart. Development of competent silicone valves allowing one-way flow has finally led to a successful bypass from the ventricle into the right atrium via the jugular vein. The valve is placed either along the course of the tube system or in the cardiac end. Experience shows that, in order to avoid thrombosis, the vascular end of the shunt must lie freely in the large moving pool of blood. Therefore in this type of shunt, periodic follow-up visualization of the cardiac end of the tubing must be carried out in the growing infant to prevent retraction of the shunt from the right atrium and thrombosis of the jugular vein. It may be reasonable to carry out elective revisions in hopes of maintaining function rather than to wait for signs of active hydrocephalus and then attempt revision. This type of shunt mechanism is not without complications. Infection seems to be the most frequent complication, and the bacterium that is often involved is *Staphylococcus albus*. It is of interest to note that there may be no evidence of infection in any other part of the body. Children who have chronically been infected with the *Staphylococcus albus* organism may also show associated hepatosplenomegaly and anemia. A low-grade fever is also not an uncommon finding and despite all methods of parental antibiotic therapy, including intrathecal injection, this bacteremia can almost never be cleared unless the entire shunt is removed and replaced with a new, sterile shunt mechanism. Pulmonary hypertension may also be encountered; it is believed that microemboli arising from the right atrium embolize to the pulmonary parenchyma and occlude the smaller ramifications of the major pulmonary arteries, resulting in this pathologic condition. When the silastic tubing breaks off into the vascular pathways, the

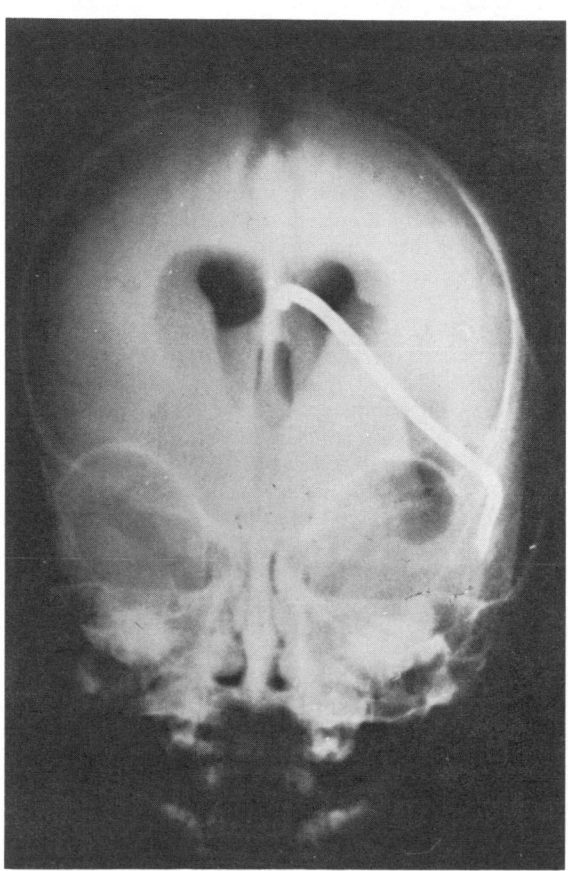

Fig. 10.   Ventriculogram four months following shunting operation. The patient is the same as the one illustrated in Figure 9. Note thickening of cortical mantle in response to decompression and growth.

fragments may lodge in the ventricular wall of the heart or pass into the parenchyma of the lung. The silastic tubing may also become disconnected and migrate into the cerebral ventricle. This is not a serious complication, and the "lost" tubing can remain intraventricularly without producing any neurologic deficit.

If a kidney is sacrificed, the ureter can be used to accept a plastic or silicone rubber tube to drain the cerebrospinal fluid from the ventricle or subarachnoid space, which is then excreted with the urine. As the fluid is lost to the body economy, salt depletion may become a problem; urinary infection may, of course, lead to secondary meningitis.

The peritoneal and pleural cavities have been used as sites into which cerebrospinal fluid may be shunted, both having the advantage of being relatively sterile areas from which the fluid can be absorbed into the general circulation. Difficulties have arisen because of occlusion of the tubing due to pleural or omental reaction or due to the inability of the cavity to absorb the fluid as rapidly as it accumulates. On the other hand, these procedures have been successfully employed in a large series of patients.

As a rule, a child who has an open myelomeningocele at birth and associated hydrocephalus is not shunted primarily into the vascular system in spite of negative cultures from his ventricular fluid. A peritoneal shunt is first employed; if necessary, this can be converted later in life to a vascular or pleural shunt.

Thus, many procedures are currently utilized in the treatment of hydrocephalus. The choice of operation depends on the site of obstruction to the flow of cerebrospinal fluid as well as the experience of the group undertaking therapy. No operation is foolproof, and all require meticulous follow-up care for the life of the child.

LOW-PRESSURE HYDROCEPHALUS.   In the past decade a series of reports has appeared defining a syndrome of occult or low-pressure hydrocephalus. The characteristic picture occurs in adults whose findings are those of disabling dementia with psychomotor retardation, often associated with ataxia and incontinence. This syndrome is rarely observed in children and is most frequently encountered as a complication of posterior fossa surgery. These chronically symptomatic patients have "a normal cerebrospinal fluid pressure" (180 mm or less). Pneumoencephalography reveals a communicating type of hydrocephalus without air being found over the convexities of the brain. Radioiodinated serum albumin (RISA) cisternography also confirms the diagnosis of an incisural block and probably is even more definitive in establishing the correct diagnosis. The underlying mechanism may be trauma, subarachnoid hemorrhage, or arachnoiditis secondary to infection. Shunting procedures utilizing low-pressure valves have often resulted in remarkable restoration of neurologic functions. This has also been the experience in most clinics, where the best results have been in patients in whom an episode of subarachnoid bleeding has occurred with secondary fibrosis of the subarachnoid space resulting in hydrocephalus.

Melanosis

In the normal state melanin-containing cells are present in most parts of the pia mater but are most numerous on the ventral aspect of the brain and upper cervical cord. In melanosis these cells undergo neoplastic changes and infiltrate the adjacent basal cisterna and cerebellum. Further extension may occur as a diffuse process with infiltration along the perivascular spaces of the brain and spinal cord, or rarely the melanoma cells cluster into tumor masses giving rise to localizing symptoms and signs.

CLINICAL MANIFESTATIONS.   With diffuse leptomeningeal involvement, cerebrospinal fluid pathways are blocked, producing signs and symptoms of increased intracranial pressure. Irritability, nausea, vomiting, headache, papilledema, or cranial nerve palsy may be present. The spinal canal extension may be accompanied by a myeloradiculopathy. Other clinical manifestations include those of progressive

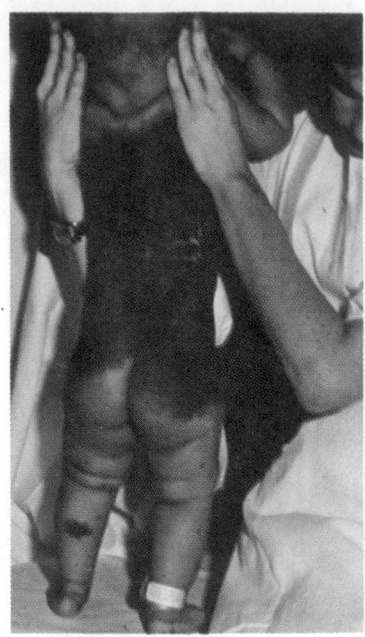

Fig. 11. Melanosis. The typical "bathing suit" nevus.

communicating hydrocephalus, posterior fossa tumor, or afebrile meningeal carcinomatous meningitis. This pathologic condition has been found in a hydrocephalic stillborn infant but may be present in any age group. Although commonly associated with giant hairy cutaneous nevi, melanosis should be regarded as a separate pathologic entity. On the other hand, when giant hairy nevi are seen in infancy, one should be alerted to the fact that the child may indeed be harboring melanosis of the leptomeninges (Fig. 11).

LABORATORY DATA. The lumbar puncture usually reveals xanthochromic spinal fluid with an elevated protein. There is an increase of white cells of various types, and in one single instance the spinal fluid was found to be "coal black" during myelography. It is not uncommon, when cytologic studies of the spinal fluid are done, to see clumps of large pleomorphic cells showing early mitosis and containing melanin.

DIAGNOSIS. The diagnosis should be suspected in the presence of the typical cutaneous nevi. Contrast air encephalography or ventriculography reveals an enlarged ventricular system secondary to a communicating hydrocephalus. When a posterior fossa tumor has been suspected and the posterior fossa explored, the typical involvement of the meninges by the process has been found.

The clinical course is usually rapid and progressive; the length of survival is greater when the spinal cord is primarily involved. The prognosis is poor, most therapy being unavailing. It is of interest that melanomas of the central nervous system, like other tumors of the central nervous system, rarely metastasize out of the confines of the cerebrospinal fluid axis, whereas malignant melanomas of the skin commonly metastasize to the brain.

Choroid Plexus Papilloma

This rare tumor has been found in the newborn but occurs most frequently in the first 2 years of life. It arises most commonly in the lateral ventricle, rarely in the third, but occasionally in the fourth ventricle with extension into the cerebellar pontine angle.

Its clinical course is insidious but may be sudden in onset, with intraventricular hemorrhage or with associated, sudden increase in intracranial pressure due to obstruction of one of the intraventricular foramina. The intraventricular location of this tumor results in the overproduction of cerebrospinal fluid with subsequent enlargement of the ventricular system as well as the subarachnoid pathways.

The tumor is histologically benign with a characteristic papillary architecture, its stroma being composed of vascularized connective tissue; it must be distinguished from the papillary ependymoma that also presents as an intraventricular tumor, but whose stroma is mainly composed of fibrillary neuroglia. It is rarely malignant but will invade local neural structures, losing the normal papillary architecture and showing obvious mitosis. The diagnosis is made from the clinical picture as well as by careful complete ventriculography in which all aspects of the ventricular system are well seen.

When the benign tumor is totally removed, the prognosis is excellent and the hydrocephalic condition arrested.

Defects of the Closure of the Neural Plate

KENNETH SHULMAN

Cranial Anomalies

ANENCEPHALY. The incidence of this catastrophic malformation ranges from 0.1 to 6.7 per thousand births, making it the most common central nervous system malformation incompatible with life. Female fetuses predominate, especially among prematures, with a ratio of between 3 and 7 to 1. The concordance rate in twins is low, identical twins approaching the incidence in fraternal twins. There is often an associated hydramnios in the mother, and the diagnosis of anencephaly can and should be made prepartum by x-ray of the hydramniotic abdomen. The fetus is either stillborn or dies a few minutes after birth, although rare instances of life lasting a few days are known.

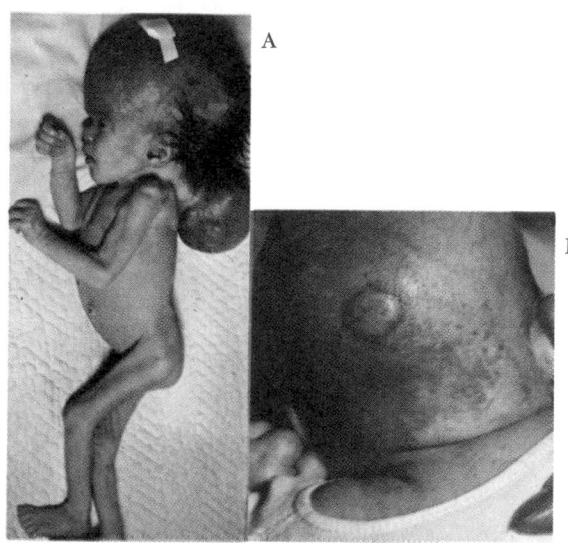

Fig. 12.   *A.* Large occipital encephalocele with associated hydrocephalus. *B.* Small occipital encephalocele with surrounding hemangioma.

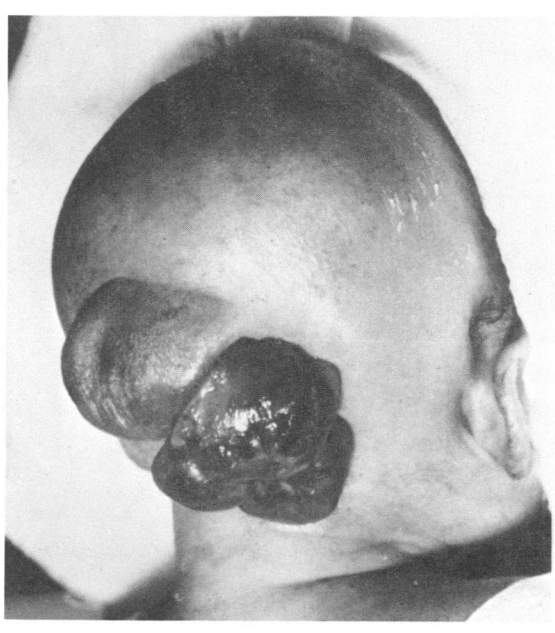

Fig. 13A.   Newborn in posterior for surgical repair of poorly covered encephalocele containing brain tissue.

The pathology ranges from complete absence of the central nervous system associated with open cranium and vertebral canal, all bones of the skull vault and vertebral lamina being unfused, to the less severe defect known as hemicrania, in which the bones of the posterior skull vault, the brainstem, and the cerebellum are present. The brain remnant is pervaded with a highly vascularized stroma and covered with a thin membrane, continuous with hair-bearing skin. Choroid plexus and ependyma are usually found in the brain remnant. With poor development of the central nervous tissue, the posterior lobe of the pituitary is also absent, as are the ganglion cells of the retina. The anterior pituitary may be present, but the adrenals are usually small. Other abnormalities commonly found with anencephalus are poorly lobated lungs, a large thymus, and a high arched palate.

That the brain vesicles may develop and undergo secondary infarction due to insufficient blood during the third to fifth week of fetal life is suggested by the findings that the major arteries do not penetrate the areas of the cerebral malformation but rather are replaced by a number of abnormal branches arising from the internal carotid arteries. Experimentally, the teratogenic agent must be applied early, shortly after gastrulation, to cause anencephaly in the mouse. The cephalic end of the neuropore remains open, but the cerebral hemispheres and striatum develop and then necrose before histogenesis of the cortex has occurred.

The management of the condition involves suspicion of the disease in the hydramniotic abdomen, so that destructive procedures can be carried out if birth is delayed. Usually, the anencephalic fetus is born prematurely and presents no obstetric difficul-

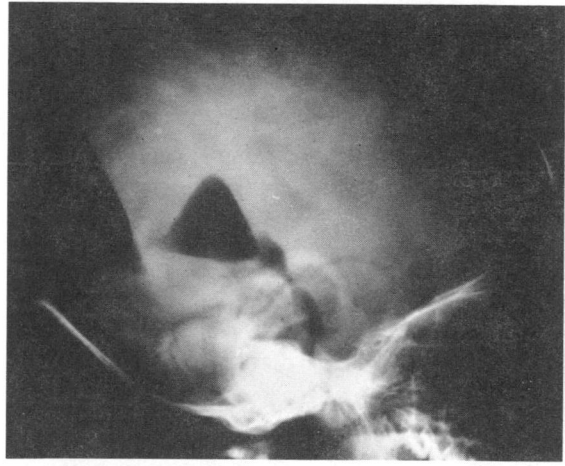

Fig. 13B.   Ventriculogram in same child at one week after repair of encephalocele showing marked ventricular dilatation.

ties. Neurosurgical treatment, of course, is not indicated.

CRANIUM BIFIDUM—ENCEPHALOCELE.   The term encephalocele has found wide neurosurgical usage in the description of all cystic masses associated with midline cranial closure defects (cranium bifidum); the term encompasses cranial meningocele and cranial meningoencephalocele. Whether or not brain is present within a cystic enlargement is not apparent before surgery, and more precise terminology is, therefore, not desirable. The occult form of closure defect, which is rare and not of major surgical interest, could

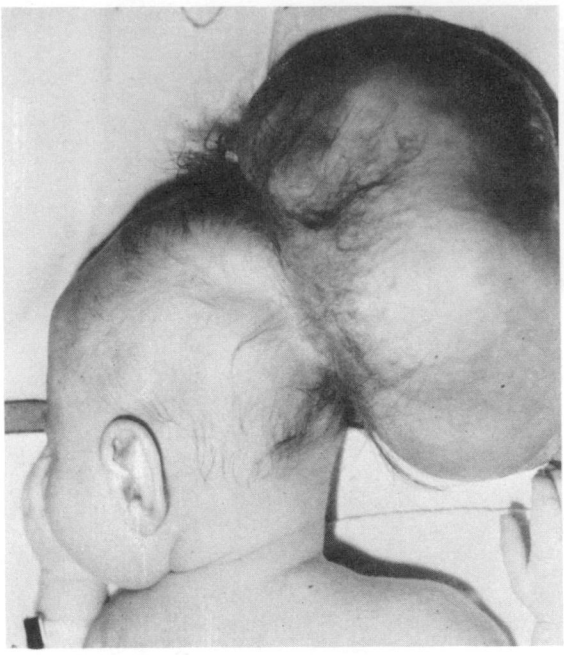

Fig. 14A. Large occipital encephalocele at 2 months of age. Because of size, surgery was inappropriately not done earlier, and contents of sac became infected with abscess formation.

be termed "cranium bifidum occulta." In the author's personal series of cases referred for neurosurgical care, encephaloceles have occurred with one-tenth the frequency of spina bifida cystica. The incidence of encephalocele has been estimated at one in every 3,000 to 10,000 live births. Occurring with greatest frequency in the occipital regions of the skull, the encephalocele is in the midline or slightly removed to one side. Those found at the anterior extreme of the skull present as nasal, nasopharyngeal, or naso-orbital masses.

Occipital Encephaloceles. Occipital encephaloceles vary in size from small pedunculated masses to those equal in size to the cranial cavity (Fig. 12). The base is usually small and well covered with non-hair-bearing skin. Those lesions with wider bases are more apt to contain significant amounts of brain tissue; and in the posterior encephaloceles there is a correlation between the amount of brain tissue within the sac and the associated anomalies of the brain residual in the cranial cavity, in a general way making overall prognosis less favorable. The most frequently associated secondary condition is hydrocephalus. Hence with sizable occipital encephaloceles one may perform a "bubble" ventriculogram prior to encephalocele repair, or before discharge after encephalocele repair, to assess the cerebrospinal fluid pathways (Fig. 13A and B). No exact relationship

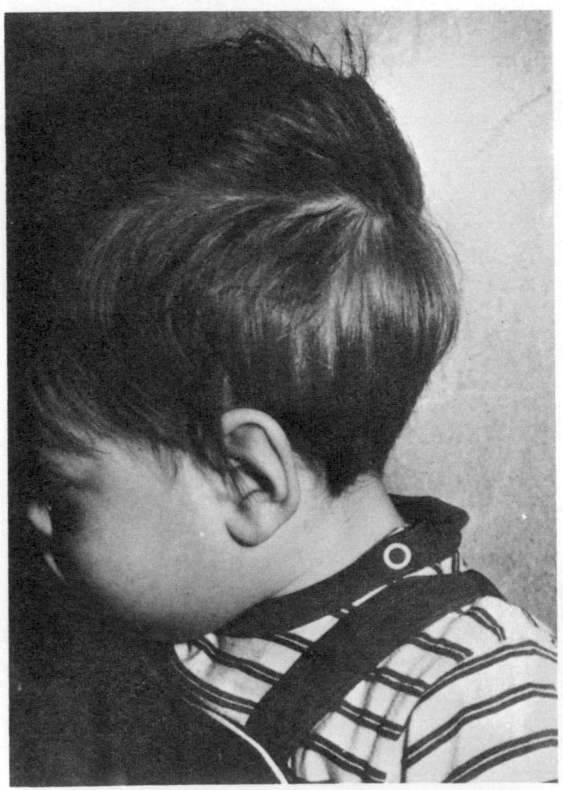

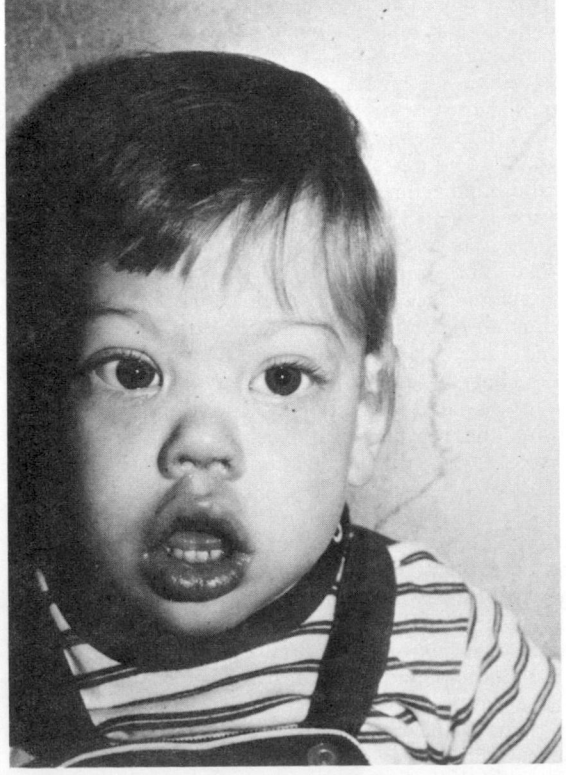

Fig. 14B and C. Same child at age 2 years. A ventriculo-atrial shunt is in place. Child has developed normally without neurologic deficit.

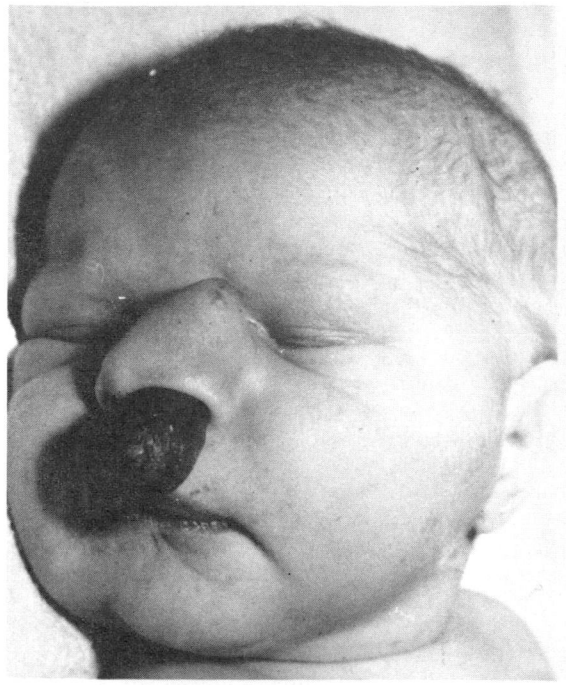

Fig. 15. Large nasal encephalocele in a newborn prior to repair by craniotomy plus nasal excision.

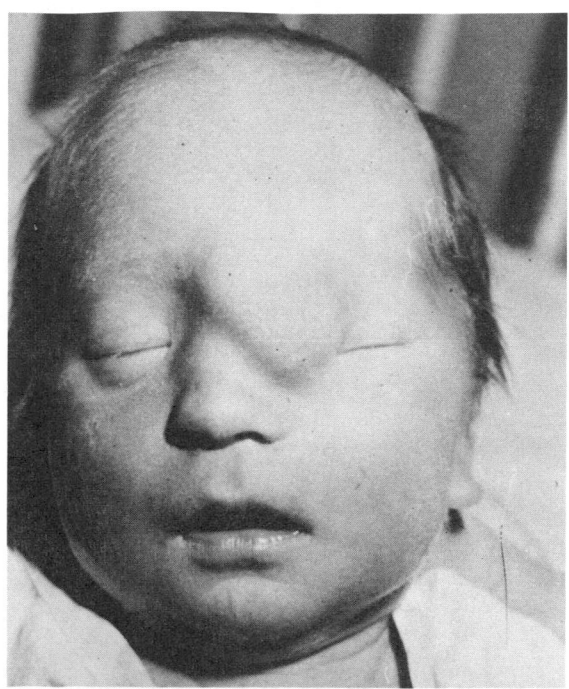

Fig. 16. Naso-orbital encephalocele in the newborn.

exists, however, between size of encephalocele and its contents. Adequate skin may cover the entire sac, or exposed brain or dura may occur at the tip of the lesion, making repair of the encephalocele an urgent matter.

Transillumination with a four-cell flashlight or a special electric lamp will often be useful in showing the contents of the sac. Skull x-rays will show the bone defect and its relation to cranial sutures and major intracranial venous sinuses.

Surgical repair of nearly all posterior encephaloceles in the newborn period is indicated in order to: (1) close over any communication through a skin defect with brain and meninges; (2) remove the mass so the child can be handled by nurses and the mother; (3) move the contents into more normal surroundings; and (4) prevent secondary skin breakdown over large encephaloceles, leading to infection and death. Surgery is well tolerated in the face-down position if care is taken to maintain the infant's temperature and replace proper amounts of blood during the procedure (Fig. 14, A, B, and C).

Because of the high incidence of hydrocephalus in infants with occipital encephaloceles, the child should be carefully observed for the signs of cerebrospinal fluid malabsorption and treated by shunting when this is diagnosed. The long-range care and prognosis will depend largely upon the success or failure in treating the hydrocephalus effectively. Moreover, a number of children will have more specific neurologic defects after encephalocele repair, especially those

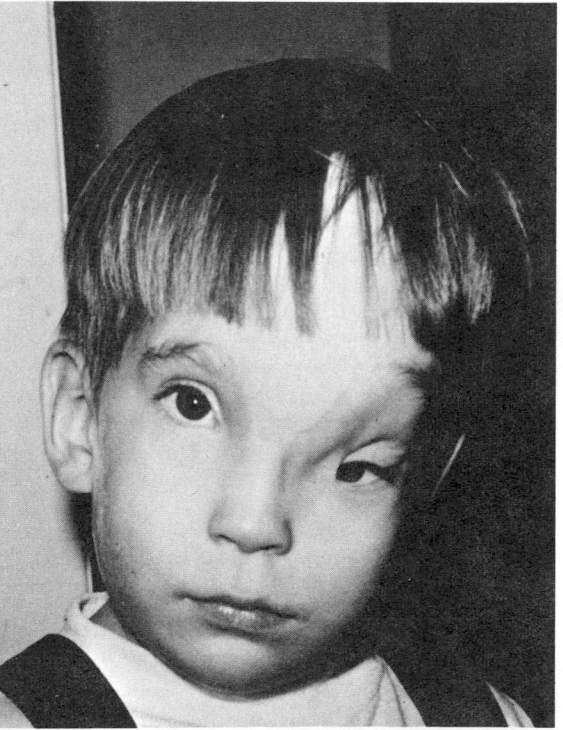

Fig. 17. Same child as in Figure 16 at 4 years of age after multiple surgical procedures with residual deformity. Left eye, however, is functional.

with a large amount of brain tissue within the sac. These deficits include blindness (occipital cortex) and incoordination (cerebellum).

Anterior Encephaloceles. Anterior encephaloceles are uncommon and comprise those that are nasofrontal, naso-orbital, or basal. The diagnosis is often quite difficult, particularly when the lesions extend into the nose and may be called polyps and biopsied, leading to catastrophic intracranial infection (Fig. 15). Encephaloceles at the nasal-orbital-cranial junction are obvious (Fig. 16) but their technical repair is often difficult. Compared with the occipital encephaloceles, the incidence of either hydrocephalus or significant associated brain anomalies is less with the anterior lesions.

Nasofrontal encephaloceles should be treated by frontal craniotomy with excision or replacement of intracranial contents, dural repair, and an attempt to fill the bony defect. Naso-orbital lesions, in which there is less risk of infection, should be repaired during the first year of life to obtain the best possible orbital alignment and cosmetic result (Fig. 17).

Spinal Anomalies

SPINA BIFIDA. Embryologically, the spinal cord develops from a thickening of the neural ectoderm, referred to as a medullary plate, in the midline of the embryo dorsally. With the proliferation of cells, the medullary plate invaginates to produce the medullary tube, which begins to close in the midline, first in the middorsal region, then at the anterior and posterior neuropores, with closure completed by the end of the fourth week. Segmentation of the medullary tube is accompanied by a separation into somites of the surrounding mesoderm, which comes to lie completely around the neural ectoderm and separates it from the ectoderm, which becomes the skin. The mesodermal segments give rise to the vertebral column, as well as the meninges and blood vessels of the spinal cord. In all forms of spina bifida, whether occulta or cystica, some part of the above process is deranged (Fig. 18). Spina bifida occulta is a condition which is fairly common and will be found in 10 percent of routine x-rays of the spine of children and adults. Although many names, such as myelodysplasia, myeloschisis, spinal dysraphism, meningocele, and meningomyelocele have been applied to the cystic form of spina bifida, it would seem that only the last two terms need be employed.

Spina Bifida Occulta. This form of spina bifida is rarely symptomatic. In a small number of children with the defect, neurologic difficulty will occur when the child is rapidly growing and the spinal cord is called upon to ascend. In such children there will be an underlying cord abnormality as the basis for the symptoms, such as dilation of the central canal (hydromyelia), a splitting of the cord (diastemato-

myelia, see below), or an associated congenital tumor, such as a lipoma or dermoid at the end of the cord, fixing it in the infantile position. A neurologic deficit resulting from such lesions will be noted as muscle weakness, leading to a gait disturbance, or sensory loss, resulting in trophic ulcers. Sphincter loss is not uncommon, and a child who was once toilet-trained may begin to become incontinent. Pain is usually not a feature. It is most important to investigate children who have progressive loss in these spheres by radiographs of the spine and myelography, if the former shows a defect. When progressive neurologic loss is demonstrated and a cause can be seen by the above studies, a good neurosurgical result may be expected if the lesion causing the loss can be explored and removed early or if the nerve roots of the cauda equina can be released from tension by section of the filum terminale. Aggressive preventive surgery in these lesions is usually not indicated, except when associated with a low spinal diastematomyelia.

Spina Bifida Cystica (Meningocele and Meningomyelocele). Like anencephaly, the geographic distribution and incidence varies widely in countries populated by Caucasians of similar backgrounds, with a reported incidence of 4.2 per thousand live births in Ireland, 2.8 per thousand in Buckinghamshire, and 1.5 per thousand in southeastern England. The lower socioeconomic groups seem to be more affected. Etiologic inquiries were made in 179 families and no evidence of any abnormal exogenous influence on pregnancy, such as infection, x-rays, drugs, or diet, could be elicited. It is possible, however, in all such studies that a prenatal insult sustained by the mother during her first month of gestation, and forgotten, could be of importance and not obtained by history. It has been shown in most series that the incidence of meningomyelocele in a second sib within the same family approaches 7.8 percent; and to this could be added the incidence of other congenital anomalies in siblings, a further 2.4 percent, making the risk taken by such a family in having another abnormal child considerable.

Meningocele. This is considered to be a cystic lesion in the midline of the back, containing only meninges or perhaps meninges and nerve roots, free of all central nervous tissue, well covered with skin, and unassociated with neurologic deficit. If this definition is subscribed to, meningocele comprises perhaps 10 percent of all cases of spina bifida cystica. This number may even be less, for if one excises such a lesion and examines the sac pathologically, a number that on clinical and gross pathologic examination were felt to be meningoceles will be found to contain nerve roots and spinal cord and would have to be classified as meningomyeloceles. The frequency of meningocele is about equal in the cervical, thoracic, and lumbar areas of the spine, although the incidence of spina bifida cystica is much higher in the lumbar region; thus, the chance of a lesion in the cervical or thoracic region being a meningocele is greater. As mentioned above, there may also be

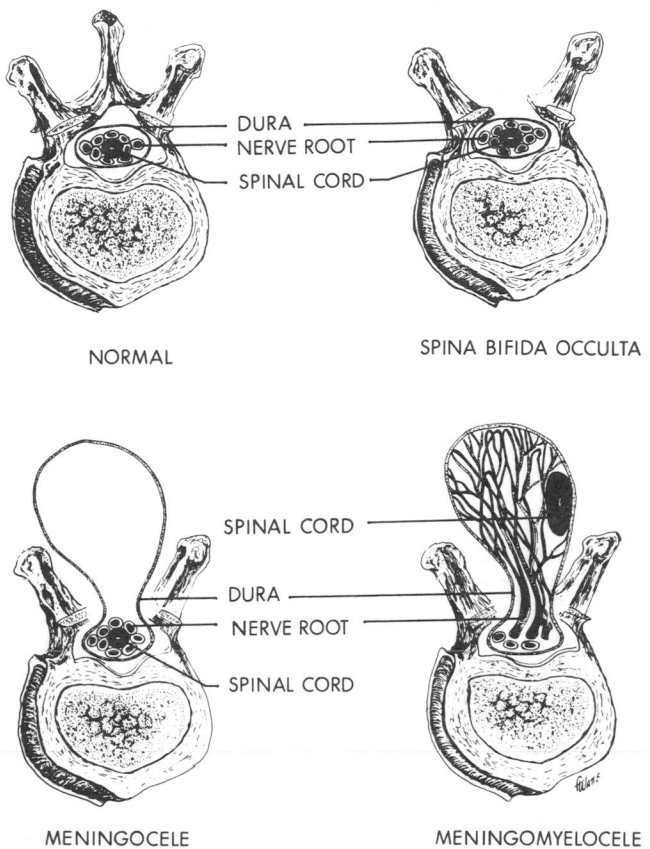

Fig. 18. The varieties of spina bifida.

associated cord abnormalities giving rise to neurologic deficit, but it is implied in the concept of meningocele that there will be no progressive neurologic symptomatology; therefore, it is advocated that the sac be closed sometime electively after the age of 3 months. By this time, a child who is destined to develop hydrocephalus will have done so, and it may be elected to treat the head enlargement prior to repair of the meningocele.

Meningomyelocele. In the meningomyelocele variety of spina bifida cystica, the neural ectoderm developing into the spinal cord and nerve roots appears to have failed to separate from the epithelium, leading to a sac containing cerebrospinal fluid, incompletely formed meninges, and malformed spinal cord. Most often, the neural plate which has failed to close is exposed in the center of the sac as a reddened, weeping area, the stroking of which may

Fig. 19. *A.* Meningomyelocele in lumbosacral region. Note paretic lower extremities and associated hydrocephalus. *B.* Same child. Detailed view of lesion.

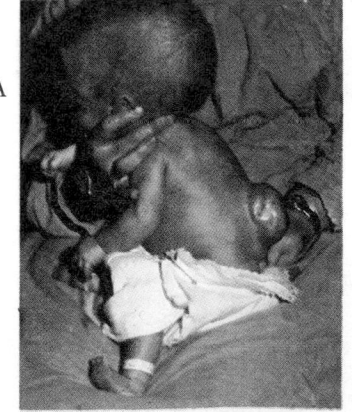

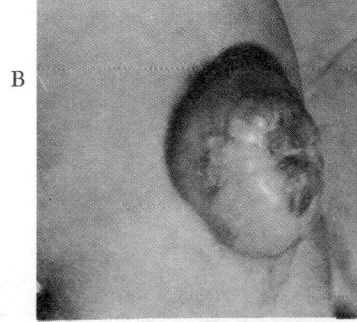

TABLE 2.   *Rehabilitation Potential of the Child with Spina Bifida According to the Neurologic Level of the Defect**

Segmental Level	Motor Power	Most Frequent Acquired Deformities Due to		Prognosis for Ambulation After Growth Period	
		Muscle Imbalance	Malposition	Minimum Function	Maximum Function
T_6	Upper extremities		Hip flexion	Wheelchair: dependent or bedridden	Wheelchair: partial use
			Hip adduction		
	Thorax (upper		Hip abduction		
to	trunk extensors)		Knee flexion		
			Scoliosis	Needs help for transfer	Transfers independently
T_{12}	Abdominals (trunk flexors)			Gait: none	Gait: swing to or drag to Elevation: limited to low steps
L_1	Hip flexion		Hip flexion Hip adduction	Wheelchair: dependent or bedridden	Wheelchair: not needed
L_2	Hip adduction	Early hip dislocation	Hip abduction Knee flexion	Needs help for transfer	Gait: four point and swing through
L_3	Knee extension		Scoliosis Lumbar lordosis	Gait: none	Elevation: standard steps
L_4	Knee flexion	Hip flexion	Lumbar lordosis	Wheelchair: dependent	Wheelchair: not needed
	Foot dorsiflexion	Hip adduction	Late hip dislocation	Gait: limited drag to or four point	Gait: four point and swing through
L_5	Ankle eversion	Ankle valgus		Elevation: none	Elevation: with handrail
S_1	Plantar flexion	Foot and ankle:	—	Wheelchair: not needed	Wheelchair: not needed
	Ankle inversion	varus		Gait: four points or alternate	Gait: independent walking
S_2	Hip extension	Equinus calcaneous		Elevation: independent with handrail	Elevation: independent
S_3 to S_5	Perineal musculature Sphincters			Independent	Independent

*Modified from Badell Ribera and Swinyard. 1964.

provoke involuntary movements of the legs. The sac often leaks in utero or ruptures at birth, so that cerebrospinal fluid drains freely; and it is distinctly unusual to have anything resembling normal skin covering the mass. The leakage of the cerebrospinal fluid with a threat of ascending meningitis makes immediate surgical closure of the defect the treatment of choice. Meningomyelocele is distinctly most common in the lumbosacral region (Fig. 19, A and B). In addition to the exposed, dysplastic neural plate, the spinal cord above often shows abnormalities, such as hydromyelia, diastematomyelia, or syrinx formation. Rarely, meningomyelocele may present ventral to the vertebra, as a pelvic mass which gives rise to symptoms of bowel obstruction.

By definition, some neurologic deficit will be present in the limbs and cutaneous areas below the mass. It is only in the sacral meningomyeloceles below the exit of the lumbosacral plexus that the lower extremities may be normal, with the loss being in the saddle area and in the sphincters. Such loss is detected in the newborn by dribbling of urine during crying and the inability to initiate a urinary stream in the male. A child with a lumbosacral meningomyelocele will most commonly present with reasonably good movements at the hips and knees with paralyzed ankles, the feet inverted and held in the position of equinovarus. Finally, if the mass is thoracolumbar, the legs may be flaccid, the lower abdominal musculature poorly developed so that the abdomen is protruberant, the hips will be congenitally dislocated, and there will be cutaneous and sphincter involvement.

The leaking meningomyelocele sac has certain

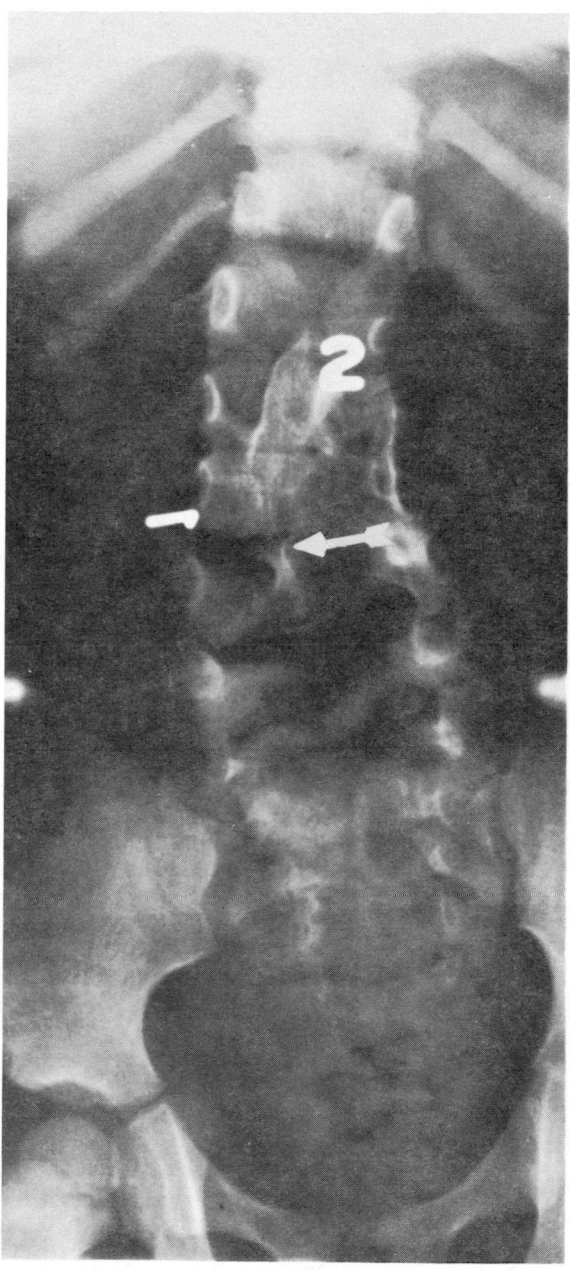

Fig. 20. Diastematomyelia. Plain radiograph showing bony spicule (arrow).

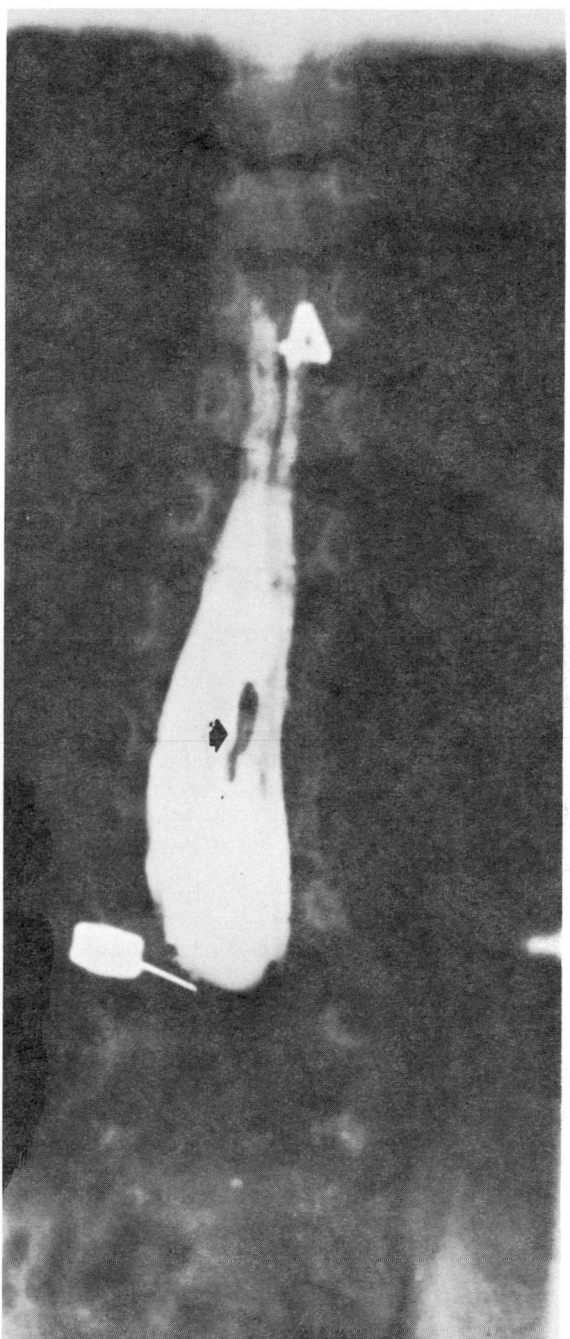

Fig. 21. Diastematomyelia. Myelogram (same child as in Figure 20) demonstrating level of spicule and splitting of cord.

powers of recovery and repair, stimulated partly, at least, by granulation tissue response to infection. This inflammatory fibrosis leads to scarring and permanent loss of neural function. This threat to function, plus the possibility of ascending infection if the sac is not closed, suggests that ideal treatment is closure as soon after birth as possible. If, indeed, it can be shown that neurologic function can be improved by such early closure, such surgery would be even more justified. This has recently been demonstrated in a series of children by Sharrard et al. Such return of neurologic function is probably due to the prevention of stretching of the neural plate by underlying accumulation of fluid or pus, or by the biochemical alterations associated with drying of the

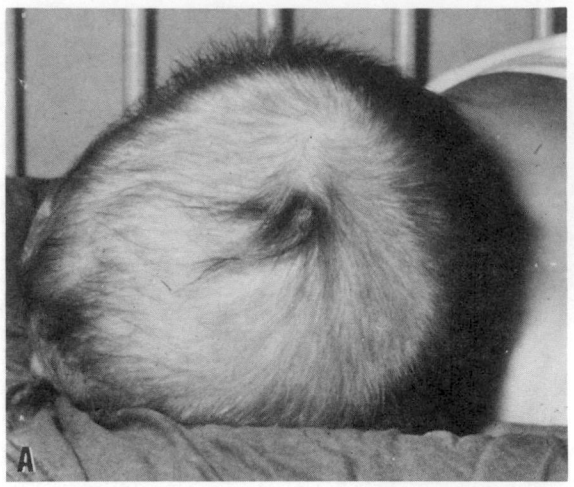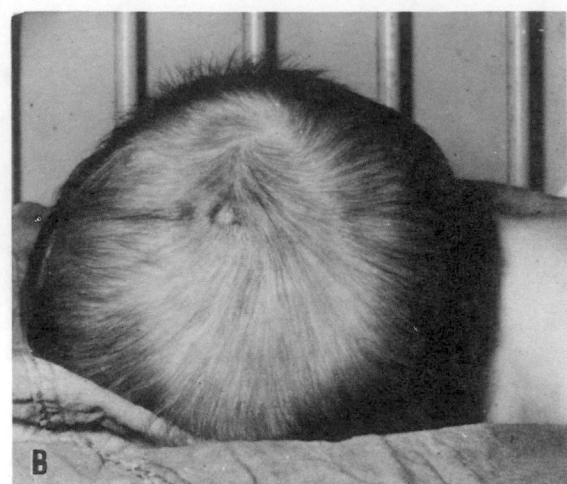

Fig. 22. Occipital dermal sinus. Child with recurrent meningitis. A. Head unshaven, sinus not readily apparent. B. Same child. Head shaven and sinus readily apparent.

neural plate. It may also be due, however, to a return of function residual in the neural plate, which has been lost upon birth because of trauma to the plate during delivery. In addition, early resolute surgical therapy seems justified in view of the natural history of children with meningomyelocele, which indicates that if the infant survives to 3 months of age, he has a 35 percent chance of living to the age of 12 years. Such children, if untreated, may well survive with neurologic loss which could have been prevented.

The paralysis secondary to meningomyelocele is part of the basic disease; the most serious complication of the disease is hydrocephalus. This occurs because of malformations within the brain, most commonly the Arnold-Chiari hindbrain malformation, and because of obliteration of the subarachnoid pathways by ascending infection secondary to an open cerebrospinal fluid fistula at the site of the meningomyelocele. Since better methods of treating the hydrocephalus are now available, many more normal children are being salvaged, and more rigorous therapy can be applied to the back defect.

It is the author's current philosophy, therefore, for the reasons stated above, that all meningomyeloceles be repaired as soon after birth as possible, regardless of the neurologic function of the child or the clinical indication of the hydrocephalus at this time, unless the child be afflicted with other congenital malformations which will limit life. Kidney and bladder function are evaluated radiographically, the legs placed in casts, if needed, and early ventriculography performed. Hydrocephalus is treated with a ventriculojugular shunt during the initial hospitalization. Patients are sent home on sulfisoxazole therapy and followed monthly by the neurosurgeon, orthopedist, urologist, and rehabilitation specialist at a birth defects center. The long-term rehabilitation potential of such children is shown in Table 2. With such a program, 80 percent of the children reach 3 years of age, and the developmental quotient is normal in 60 percent of the survivors.

DIASTEMATOMYELIA. In this condition, the spinal cord is divided into two halves, each of which may undergo modification of structure. It is most common in the lumbar and midthoracic areas. The two cords are separated by a fibrous or bony spicule, which can often be seen on x-ray (Fig. 20). Each half of the divided cord has its own pial investment, but the arachnoid and dura may be shared. Neurologic symptoms are produced in children because of the different rates of elongation of the spinal cord and vertebral column, with increasing pressure of the spur upon the ascending spinal cord with growth. Symptoms progressively develop, usually at about the age of 4 years or later. Therefore, diagnosis of diastematomyelia in the low thoracic or lumbar area is an indication for prophylactic surgery in a young child, to prevent the development of neurologic symptoms. Operations in older children with lesions at a higher level, where the ascent of the cord is not so great, are more questionable, unless progressive neurologic symptoms develop. Myelography (Fig. 21) is indicated prior to surgery. The operative results are generally good; and if there is a question, exploratory laminectomy is warranted, because of the low risk of harming the patient with careful surgery.

DERMAL SINUS. Dermal sinus tracts may occur at any place along the spinal axis but are most common in the lumbosacral area. They result developmentally from a failure of the neural ectoderm to separate from the skin ectoderm with a sinus tract covered by epithelial tissue, leading down to or through the dura. There may or may not be a spina bifida occulta on radiographs of the spine. Sinuses should be looked for in all children with recurrent, unexplained meningitis. If a sinus tract is found, it should be excised with preparations made for laminectomy and intradural exploration, if necessary. When possible, sinus tracts should be excised prior to infection, for once infection has taken place, the scarring around the intradural contents of the sinus is extreme and enhances the difficulty of the surgery.

In addition to spinal dermal sinuses, cranial dermal sinuses may occur at any place in the midline of the skull and scalp but are most common in the occipital region. The tracts, which appear as defects in the midline in the occipital bone, are directed obliquely and have hyperostosis around the bone edges (Fig. 22A and B). Prophylactic excision of such sinus tracts is indicated to prevent intracranial suppuration and abscess formation. It is advisable to study the child with pneumoencephalography prior to excision of the sac to determine whether there is intracranial extension, which should be surgically excised if it exists. A normal air study does not rule out intracranial extension, which can be explained by the fact that the brain and cyst are formed and developed over the same period of time, with the cerebral tissue not being displaced by the cyst, but merely failing to develop in the region.

REFERENCES

BRAIN

DeMyer, W. Technique of the Neurologic Examination: A Programmed Text. New York, McGraw-Hill Book Co., 1969.

Dodge, P., and Porter, P. Demonstration of intracranial pathology by transillumination. Arch. Neurol., 5:594, 1961.

Gorlin, R., and Pindborg, J. Syndromes of the Head and Neck. New York, McGraw-Hill Book Co., 1964.

Leiber, B., and Olbrich, G. Die Klinischen Syndrome. München/Berlin, Urban & Schwarzenberg, 1966.

Nellhaus, G. Head circumference from birth to eighteen years. Pediatrics, 41:106, 1968.

O'Neill, E. M. Normal head growth and the prediction of head size in infantile hydrocephalus. Arch. Dis. Child., 36:241, 1961.

——— Minimal rates of head growth in the first four months of life. Arch. Dis. Child., 37:415, 1962.

MICROCEPHALY

Book, J., Schut, J., and Reed, S. A clinical and genetical study of microcephaly. Amer. J. Ment. Defic., 57:637, 1952.

Bray, P., Shields, W., Wolcott, G., and Madsen, J. Occipitofrontal head circumference—an accurate measure of intracranial volume. J. Pediat., 75:303, 1969.

Davies, H., and Kirman, B. Microcephaly. Arch. Dis. Child., 37:623, 1962.

Greenfield, J. G., et al. Neuropathology. Baltimore, Williams & Wilkins Co., 1963.

Pryor, H., and Thelander, H. Abnormally small head size and intellect in children. J. Pediat., 73:593, 1968.

Winick, M., and Rosso, P. Head circumference and cellular growth of the brain in normal and marasmic children. J. Pediat., 74:774, 1969.

MEGALOCEPHALY AND MEGALENCEPHALY

Dennis, J., Rosenberg, H., and Alvord, E., Jr. Megalencephaly, internal hydrocephalus and other neurological aspects of achondroplasia. Brain, 84:427, 1961.

Ford, F. Diseases of the Nervous System in Infancy, Childhood and Adolescence, 5th ed. Springfield, Ill., Charles C Thomas Co., 1966.

Hook, E., and Reynolds, J. Cerebral gigantism: Endocrinological and clinical observations of six patients including a congenital giant, concordant monozygotic twins, and a child who achieved adult gigantic size. J. Pediat., 70:900, 1967.

Salmon, J., and Flanigan, S. Megalencephaly, a clinical study with chromosomal analysis. J. Neurosurg., 21:409, 1964.

MEDIAN FACIAL DEFECTS AND HOLOPROSENCEPHALY (ARHINENCEPHALY)

Currarino, G., and Silverman, F. Orbital hypotelorism, arhinencephaly, and trigonocephaly. Radiology, 74:206, 1960.

DeMyer, W., and White, P. EEG in holoprosencephaly (arhinencephaly). Arch. Neurol., 11:507, 1964.

——— Zeman, W., and Palmer, C. G. Familial alobar holoprosencephaly (arhinencephaly) with median cleft lip and palate. Report of a patient with 46 chromosomes. Neurology, 13:913, 1963.

——— Zeman, W., and Palmer, C. G. The face predicts the brain: diagnostic significance of median facial anomalies in holoprosencephaly (arhinencephaly). Pediatrics, 34:256, 1964.

Potter, E. Pathology of the Fetus and Newborn. Chicago, Year Book Publishers, 1952.

Yakovlev, P. Pathoarchitectonic studies of cerebral malformations. III. Arhinencephalies (holotelencephalies). J. Neuropath. Exp. Neurol., 18:22, 1959.

MEDIAN CLEFT FACE SYNDROME: HYPERTELORISM, MEDIAN CLEFT LIP, AND FRONTAL ENCEPHALOCELE

DeMyer, W. The median cleft face syndrome. Neurology, 17:961, 1967.

Waardenburg, P., Fanceschetti, A., and Klein, D. Genetics in Ophthalmology. Springfield, Ill., Charles C Thomas Publ., 1961, 1963, Vol. I, Vol. II.

HYDRANENCEPHALY

Farmer, T. W., ed. Pediatric Neurology. New York, Harper & Row, 1964.

Hamby, W. B., Krauss, R. F., and Beswick, W. F. Hydranencephaly: Clinical diagnosis. Presentation of seven cases. Pediatrics, 6:371, 1950.

Poser, C. M., Walsh, F. C., and Schneinberg, L. C. Hydranencephaly. Neurology, 5:284, 1955.

AGENESIS OF THE CORPUS CALLOSUM

Carpenter, M. B. Agenesis of the corpus callosum. A study of 18 cases diagnosed during life. Neurology, 4:200, 1954.

Koch, F., and Doyle, P. Agenesis of the corpus callosum. J. Pediat., 50:345, 1957.

Mountcastle, V., ed. Interhemispheric Relations and Cerebral Dominance. Baltimore, Johns Hopkins Press, 1962.

HYDROCEPHALUS

Adams, R. D., Fisher, C. M., Hakim, S., Ojemann, R. G., and Sweet, W. H. Symptomatic occult hydrocephalus with "normal" cerebrospinal fluid pressure. A treatable syndrome. New Eng. J. Med., 273:117, 1965.

Bering, E. A., Jr. Dynamics of cerebrospinal fluid. Clin. Neurosurg., 5:77, 1958.

——— Circulation of the cerebrospinal fluid, demonstration of the choroid plexuses as the generator of the force of flow of fluid and ventricular enlargement. J. Neurosurg., 19:405, 1962.

——— Hydrocephalus: changes in CSF in ventricles. J. Neurosurg., 20:1050, 1963.

Bouton, J. Primary melanoma of the leptomeninges. J. Clin. Path., 11:122, 1958.

Bowsher, D. A. A Possible Mechanism of Hydrocephalus. Ciba Foundation Symposium on the Cerebrospinal Fluid. Boston, Little, Brown and Co., 1958, p. 282.

Bruce, A. M., Lorber, J., Shedden, W. I. H., and Zachary, R. B. Persistent bacteraemia following ventriculo-caval shunt operations for hydrocephalus in infancy. Develop. Med. Child Neurol., 5:461, 1963.

Dandy, W. E., and Blackfan, K. D. Internal hydrocephalus, an experimental, clinical and pathological study. Amer. J. Dis. Child., 8:406, 1914.

Davson, H. Physiology of the Ocular and Cerebrospinal Fluids. Boston, Little, Brown and Co., 1956.

Farmer, T. W. Pediatric Neurology. New York, Paul B. Hoeber, Inc., 1964.

Fishman, R. A., and Greer, M. Experimental obstructive hydrocephalus. Arch. Neurol., 8:156, 1963.

Foltz, E. L., and Shurtleff, D. B. Five year comparative study of hydrocephalus in children with and without operation (113 cases). J. Neurosurg., 20:1064, 1963.

——— and Shurtleff, D. B. Conversion of communicating hydrocephalus to stenosis or occlusion of the aqueduct during ventricular shunt. J. Neurosurg., 24:520, 1966.

Friedman, S., Zita-Gozum, C., and Chatten, J. Pulmonary vascular changes complicating ventriculovascular shunting for hydrocephalus. J. Pediat., 64:305, 1964.

Gibson, J. B., Burnows, D., and Weir, W. P. Primary melanoma of the meninges. J. Path. Bact., 74:419, 1957.

Heisey, S. R., Held, D., and Pappenheimer, J. R. Bulk flow and diffusion in the cerebrospinal fluid system of the goat. Amer. J. Physiol., 203:775, 1962.

Hoffman, J. J., and Freeman, A. Primary malignant leptomeningeal melanoma in association with giant hairy nevi. Report of two cases. J. Neurosurg., Part I, 26:62, 1967.

Ingraham, F. D., and Matson, D. D. Neurosurgery of Infancy and Childhood. Springfield, Ill., Charles C Thomas, Publ., 1954.

Laurence, K. M. The natural history of hydrocephalus. Lancet, 2:1152, 1958.

Lin, J. P., Goodkin, R., Tong, E., Epstein, F. J., and Vinaguerra, E. Radioiodinated serum albumin (RISA) cisternography in the diagnosis of incisural block and occult hydrocephalus. Radiology, 90:36, 1968.

Matson, D. D. Clinical classification and evaluation of hydrocephalus. In Disorders of the Developing Nervous System. Springfield, Ill., Charles C Thomas, Publ., 1961.

——— Hydrocephalus. Clin. Neurosurg., 13:324, 1966.

——— Neurosurgery in Infancy and Childhood, 2nd ed. Springfield, Ill., Charles C Thomas, Publ., 1969.

Mathews, E. S., Sanchez, G., and Ransohoff, J. A preliminary report on a biological fluid transfer system for the treatment of hydrocephalus. Develop. Med. Child Neurol. (Suppl.), 13:103, 1967.

Ojemann, R. G., Fisher, C. M., Adams, R. D., Sweet, W. H., and New, P. F. J. Further experience with the syndrome of "normal" pressure hydrocephalus. J. Neurosurg., 31:279, 1969.

Pudenz, R. H., Russell, F. E., Hurd, A. H., and Shelden, C. H. Ventriculoauriculostomy: a technique for shunting cerebrospinal fluid into the right auricle. J. Neurosurg., 14:171, 1957.

Ransohoff, J. Ventriculopleural anastomosis. J. Neurosurg., 11:295, 1954.

——— and Hiatt, R. B. Ventriculo-peritoneal anastomosis in the treatment of hydrocephalus; utilization of the suprahepatic space. A preliminary report. Trans. Amer. Neurol. Ass., 77:147, 1952.

——— Shulman, K., and Fishman, R. A. Hydrocephalus, a review of etiology and treatment. J. Pediat., 56:399, 1960.

Rayport, M., Ransohoff, J., and Zimmerman, H. M., eds. Proceedings of the Rudolf Virchow Medical Society in the City of New York. Horn (Austria), Ferdinand Berger, 1967, p. 281.

Russell, D. S. Observations on the pathology of hydrocephalus. Medical Research Council, Special Report Series No. 265. London, Her Majesty's Stationery Office, 1949.

——— Rubinstein, L. J., and Lumsden, C. E. Pathology of Tumors of the Central Nervous System. Baltimore, Williams and Wilkins Co., 1963.

Scarff, J. E. Nonobstructive hydrocephalus treatment by endoscopic cauterization of the choroid plexus; long-term results. J. Neurosurg., 9:164, 1952.

——— Treatment of hydrocephalus: a historical and critical review of methods and results. J. Neurol. Neurosurg., Psychiat., 26:1, 1963.

Shick, R. W., and Matson, D. D. What is arrested hydrocephalus? J. Pediat., 58:791, 1961.

Selverstone, B. Studies of the Formation and Absorption of the Cerebrospinal Fluid Using Radioactive Isotopes. Ciba Foundation Symposium on the Cerebrospinal Fluid. Boston, Little, Brown and Co., 1958, p. 147.

Shulman, K., ed. Workshop in Hydrocephalus. Department of Neurosurgery, Univ. Pennsylvania School of Medicine and The Children's Hospital of Philadelphia, 1965, p. 157.

Strenger, L. Complications of ventriculovenous shunts. J. Neurosurg., 20:219, 1963.

Welch, K., and Friedman, V. The cerebrospinal fluid valves. Brain, 83:454, 1960.

Wislocki, J. B., and Ladman, A. J. The Fine Structure of the Mammalian Choroid Plexus. Ciba Foundation Symposium on the Cerebrospinal Fluid. Boston, Little, Brown and Co., 1958, p. 55.

Yashon, D. Prognosis in infantile hydrocephalus. J. Neurosurg., 20:105, 1963.

——— Jane, J. A., Cassell, S., Cameron, G., and Sugar, O. Cerebrospinal fluid diversion in infantile hydrocephalus. Arch. Neurol., 15:541, 1966.

DEFECTS OF THE CLOSURE
OF THE NEURAL PLATE

Alter, M. Anencephalus, hydrocephalus, and spina bifida. Arch. Neurol., 7:411, 1962.

Badell Ribera, A., and Swinyard, C. A. Rehabilitation of children with spina bifida cystica. Excerpta Medica Int. Congress Series No. 76, September, 1964, p. 180.

Cameron, A. H. The spinal cord lesion in spina bifida cystica. Lancet, 2:171, 1956.

Doran, P. A., and Guthkelch, N. Studies in spina bifida cystica (General survey and reassessment of the problem). J. Neurol. Neurosurg. Psychiat., 24:331, 1961.

Laurence, K. M. *In* Norman, A. P., ed., Congenital Abnormalities in Infancy. Philadelphia, F. A. Davis Co., 1963, pp. 21-81.

Lorber, J. The prognosis of occipital encephaloceles. Develop. Med. Child Neurol. (Suppl.), 13:75, 1966.
—— Results of treatment of myelomeningocele. Develop. Med. Child Neurol., 13:279, 1971.

Mealey, J., Jr., Dzennis, A. J., and Hockey, A. A. The prognosis of encephaloceles. J. Neurosurg., 32:209, 1970.

Schwiddle, J. T. Spina bifida. Survey of two hundred twenty-five encephaloceles, meningoceles, and myelomeningoceles. Amer. J. Dis. Child., 84:35, 1952.

Sharrard, W. J. W., Zachary, R. B., Lorber, J., and Bruce, A. M. A controlled trial of immediate and delayed closure of spina bifida cystica. Arch. Dis. Child., 38:18, 1963.

Shulman, K., and Ames, M. Results of intensive treatment of fifty consecutive children born with myelomeningocele. New York J. Med., 68:2656, 1968.

Smith, E. The pathogenesis and management of spinal myelomeningocele. Med. J. Aust., II:801, 1960.

Sugar, M., and Kennedy, C. E. The use of electrodiagnostic techniques in the evaluation of the neurological deficit in infants with myelomeningocele. Neurology, 15:787, 1965.

Till, K. *In* Wilkinson, A. W., ed., Recent Advances in Pediatric Surgery. Boston, Little, Brown and Co., 1963, pp. 240-259.

Vogel, F. S., and McClenahan, J. L. Anomalies of major cerebral arteries associated with congenital malformations of the brain. Amer. J. Path., 28:701, 1952.

15.3
THE STATIC ENCEPHALOPATHIES

SIDNEY CARTER and ARNOLD P. GOLD

Chronic and nonprogressive cerebral dysfunction results from varied causes and produces multiple clinical syndromes. The clinical picture is dependent on the site and extent of the lesion and the developmental age at time of occurrence. The developing nervous system is more susceptible to insults occurring during the first trimester than later in pregnancy. Cerebral palsy results from involvement of motor areas of the brain. Mental retardation usually follows diffuse cerebral involvement; however, small lesions occurring early in gestation may interfere with normal cerebral maturation and have as a consequence intellectual deficit. Impairment of the special senses, vision and hearing, follows involvement of select areas of the brain and their pathways. Convulsions most commonly result from cortical lesions. Speech disturbances may be a reflection of diffuse cerebral involvement or a focal lesion involving the speech area. Behavioral disorders and learning disabilities have a less well-defined anatomic localization. These syndromes may occur as isolated clinical phenomena or in any combination. Spastic diplegia may be the only manifestation of cerebral palsy; however, mental deficit, seizures, impairment of vision and/or hearing, or behavioral disturbances may accompany this motor deficit.

These defects of cerebral function may be the result of well-recognized anatomic or biochemical lesions, but in many impaired children the cause is not always apparent, may be unrecognized, or is yet to be defined. Prenatal factors affecting the developing nervous system are both endogenous and exogenous. The fetus may be affected by faulty implantation of the ovum, chromosomal anomalies, infections, trauma, radiation, and toxic substances. Later in pregnancy, maternal toxemia and diabetes may produce damage to the nervous system. Anoxia and trauma are the most commonly encountered causative factors in the natal period. Postnatally, infections, inborn errors of metabolism, trauma, toxins, and vascular disease are often incriminated.

Children with chronic nonprogressive lesions of the brain are being recognized with increasing frequency. More prevalence studies are needed, but available figures illustrate the magnitude of this common pediatric problem. It is estimated that 1 out of 1,000 live births will be severely retarded, 3 per 1,000 moderately retarded, and 25 per 1,000 mildly retarded. In the United States, 5,500,000 individuals have some degree of retardation. Cerebral palsy affects approximately 400,000 children. Approximately 5 percent of all children will have one or more seizures. Incidence of organically induced behavioral disturbances and/or specific learning disabilities is not available, but these conditions greatly outnumber any of the other clinical syndromes.

The Syndrome of Minimal Cerebral Dysfunction

Varied terminology has been applied to children with deviant behavior, specific learning disabilities, or both. These terms include Strauss syndrome, choreiform syndrome, minimal cerebral palsy, minimal cerebral damage, minimal cerebral dysfunction, the hyperkinetic child, organic reaction syndrome, brain-injured child, nonmotor brain damage, and chronic brain syndrome; they have a common feature in suggesting organicity as a basis for the observed clinical manifestations. The term minimal cerebral dysfunction appears to be satisfactory, in that it implies impaired cerebral function without implicating specific areas of the brain. This diagnosis is then used in describing children with normal or near normal intellect who demonstrate abnormal behavioral patterns, specific learning disabilities, or both.

CLINICAL MANIFESTATIONS. The clinical syndrome is variable, and the manifestations may change with age. Deviant behavior, learning disabilities, speech disorders, and poor coordination are the most common presenting complaints.

Behavioral patterns most frequently encountered are those relating to hyperactivity, but underactivity or even normal behavior can be seen. Hyperkinetic behavior is often evident in infancy with restlessness, irritability, and poor sleep patterns. Overactive behavior in the older child is without direction, is purposeless, and shifts from moment to moment. The hyperkinesis fluctuates; it is most marked when the child is confronted with new or stressful situations and is often diminished in familiar settings. Overactivity tends to diminish spontaneously at about 12 years of age and in most instances is significantly modified by 15 years. Less frequently, the behavior may be manifested by hypoactivity, in which the child is placid and retiring.

Behavioral changes closely related to the hyperactivity include a short attention span, irritability, low frustration threshold, impulsivity, distractibility, and social immaturity. Short attention span is characterized by difficulty in focusing and maintaining prolonged attention on a given task, with an inability to eliminate the distraction produced by minimal or trivial auditory, visual, or tactile stimuli. Impulsivity and distractibility are contributing factors. Shortened attention is variable and may be replaced by perseveration. During these periods, there is rigidity of behavior with an abnormal preoccupation for a single object or detail, and a resistance to change with failure to respond appropriately to changing stimuli. Emotional lability may be prominent, and the affective response inappropriately changes from one moment to another. Frustration threshold is often low, and insignificant conditions can provoke uncontrollable rage, unintentional aggressive outbursts, and temper tantrums. Social function is at a level below the chronologic or mental age. This social immaturity results in play with children of a younger age.

Specific learning problems unrelated to intellectual potential or deviant behavior are an additional feature of the minimal brain dysfunction syndrome. Impaired perceptual performance, above all for spatial relationships, results in academic difficulties primarily involving reading and number concepts. Specific reading disability, dyslexia, implies that the inability to read is unrelated to mental retardation, sensory impairment, inadequate schooling, poor motivation, or developmental lag. Reading is either not present or below age level and may be complicated by mirror reading. Some children also have an inability to write or to spell. They will often demonstrate mirror writing or letter reversals, and may be unable to discriminate p from q, b from d, n from u, and w from m. In some, there is inadequate ability to calculate. Many of these children are ambidextrous, which, with dyslexia, is attributed to failure to develop cerebral dominance.

Difficulties in abstract thinking are a common feature of the syndrome and are more evident with increasing age. During the early school years, learning is at a relatively concrete level, with little demand on abstract ideation. This disability may further complicate the difficulties in learning encountered by many of these children or may be the initial educational problem in some who have been previously successful at a concrete level with the use of rote memory.

Language difficulties are common. Some children remain nonverbal, but more commonly there is delay in the development of speech patterns. Once established, there are problems in the formation of phrases and sentences and a prominent tendency to preserve more immature modes of expression. Speech may be characterized by a paucity, misuse, and poor articulation of words. Flow of expressive language may be either slow, hesitant, or explosive.

Coordination is frequently impaired, and the children are often clumsy and awkward. Poor fine muscle coordination is initially demonstrated by difficulties with buttoning, zippering, or tying shoelaces. Subsequent manifestations are noted in the manipulation of scissors, coloring within a figure, drawing a straight line, and eventually poor handwriting. More gross incoordination is evident in the delay in learning to hop, skip, ride a bicycle, and catch a ball.

Social incompetence and environmental rejection result in secondary emotional symptoms characterized by aggression, destruction, withdrawal, and fantasy life.

Neurologic examination characteristically reveals a paucity of gross abnormalities. However, minimal subtle signs are usually present. Gait may be lumbering and awkward. After 7 years of age, there may be impaired tandem walking and difficulty in hopping and skipping. Examination of the motor system reveals impairment of rapid alternating movements, choreiform activity of extended fingers, and occasional tightness of various muscle groups, including hamstrings, posterior tibials, and pronators. Not uncommonly, there is a right-left confusion and a failure to establish handedness. The deep tendon reflexes may be asymmetric, but the plantar responses are usually physiologic. Eye muscle imbalance of the convergent or divergent types is commonly observed; it tends to diminish with age. Poor speech patterns are often associated with drooling and inability to perform rapid lateral tongue movements.

LABORATORY FINDINGS. There are no specific laboratory studies to confirm the clinical diagnosis. Urine test for phenylketonuria should be performed. Electroencephalograms are not in themselves diagnostic; they may be normal or show abnormalities

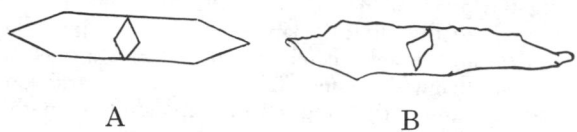

A   B

Fig. 23. Copying difficulties in a 9-year-old boy with brain damage. A. Sample. B. Copy.

of organization with voltage and frequency changes or even multispike and spike and wave activity. Plain radiographs of the skull are normal. Pneumoencephalography and cerebral arteriography are contraindicated.

Psychologic testing is the most helpful ancillary procedure in that it supplies further evidence to support the concept of impaired cerebral function and provides a guide of intellectual potential. Signs of organicity include discrepancies between a higher verbal and lower performance scale, which may be as great as 40 points, scatter on the subtests, and, above all, perceptual difficulties on the Bender Visual Motor Gestalt Test. Deviant perceptual performances (Fig. 23) are manifested by difficulty in copying forms and designs which are often correctly identified orally. There may be rotation or reorientation of the major axis of the figure. Difficulties with number concepts and abstract ideation may also be noted.

DIAGNOSIS. There is no isolated finding that is diagnostic of this clinical syndrome. Diagnosis can be accomplished only by combining the historical data with the results of the examinations. Differential diagnosis includes variants of the normal and psychiatric disturbances. Many normal children show hyperactivity which is more readily controlled and is unassociated with a short attention span, low frustration tolerance, or distractibility. Psychiatric disorders which may require differentiation include some neuroses, the character disorders, and certain psychoses. Not uncommonly, the child with minimal cerebral dysfunction may present with prominent emotional manifestations. These apparent functional phenomena usually result from frustrations produced by learning disabilities and the excessive demands made by the parents, peers, and school. Many physicians, including some psychiatrists, incorrectly interpret these secondary manifestations as primary emotional phenomena.

TREATMENT. A sound therapeutic program includes family counseling, a dynamic educational program, and medications to improve behavior.

Family counseling is of primary importance. Explanation of the physical nature of the disability not infrequently relieves parental anxiety and guilt. The family must be made to accept the handicap. Unnecessary pressures should be eliminated, realistic goals formulated, and a structured environment with consistent discipline and demands established. The family physician is often most effective in providing adequate parental guidance. A seriously disturbed

parent-child relationship may require psychiatric assistance.

Educational planning depends on the nature of the disability and the intellectual endowment. Adequate school placement is difficult to obtain even in the most sophisticated community. All too often, the neurologically impaired class is a heterogenous group with children of varied learning problems and intellectual abilities. Ideally the class should be small in size, limited to children of similar intellectual endowment and learning problems, and directed by a teacher trained in remedial education. Efforts should be made to minimize distraction and competition. Emphasis should be placed on individual performance and the use of concrete teaching aids. In some instances, residential placement may be desirable for both the child and family.

Drug therapy is unpredictable, and a particular agent may lose its effectiveness with time. Four groups of compounds have been particularly effective: amphetamines, methylphenidates, phenothiazines, and diphenylmethane derivatives.

Amphetamines. Dextroamphetamine sulfate (Dexedrine) is the most effective amphetamine. The apparent paradoxic effect of this drug is most frequently observed in youngsters demonstrating barbiturate-induced hyperactivity. Dexedrine is administered in daily doses of from 5 to 30 mg given after breakfast and lunch. Initially 5 mg is given, and this is gradually increased on succeeding days until the desired clinical effect is observed or serious toxic reactions become prominent. Undesirable side effects that usually necessitate discontinuance of this compound are either increased hyperactivity with irritability and emotional lability or, more rarely, marked lethargy. Prior to prescribing the drug, the parents should be alerted to the difficulty with sleep for the first three or four nights and anorexia that generally improves spontaneously in a few weeks. These findings are usually not sufficient to warrant discontinuation of the compound.

Amphetamine sulfate (Benzedrine) has a dosage and pharmacologic activity similar to Dexedrine. Occasionally a child will show a poor response with one compound while the other will be effective.

Methylphenidates. Methylphenidate hydrochloride (Ritalin) is often effective in children with hyperactivity. Response is similar to that observed with the amphetamine group and in therapeutic doses is less likely to result in sedation, lethargy, anorexia, and insomnia. After an initial trial with 5 mg orally, the school-age child requires 5 mg three times daily; if necessary, this is further increased to a total daily dose of 60 mg. Side effects are similar to those of the amphetamines and when present are managed in similar fashion.

Phenothiazines. Thioridazine (Mellaril) is the most effective and least toxic of the phenothiazine group of agents in managing the hyperkinetic behavioral syndrome. A preschool child generally requires 10 mg three to four times a day and the older child 25 mg two to four times a day. Toxic reactions are rarely seen but include extrapyramidal disorders, leucopenia, and agranulocytosis. These side effects are indications for prompt discontinuation of the drug. The specific treatment of extrapyramidal complications is discussed under basal ganglia diseases (p. 919).

Chlorpromazine (Thorazine) is often effective in controlling the acutely agitated child but has limited value in the long-term management of the hyperkinetic youngster. Thorazine is usually given in dosages of 20 to 80 mg/day, but up to 300 mg/day may be necessary to achieve the desired results. Extrapyramidal reactions or jaundice as complications of therapy are rarely observed in children. Drowsiness, nasal congestion, dryness of the buccal mucosa, and postural hypotension are infrequent side effects, but their presence is not an indication for discontinuing the drug. Increased sensitivity to light may be so marked in some children that the drug cannot be tolerated.

Other phenothiazines have limited usefulness in the hyperkinetic child because of relatively low therapeutic value or high incidence of toxic side effects. Specifically, prochlorperazine (Compazine) should not be prescribed in the pediatric age group because of the relatively high frequency of extrapyramidal involvement with this drug.

Diphenylmethane Derivatives. Diphenhydramine hydrochloride (Benadryl) is occasionally effective, especially in anxious children with repetitive motor activities such as tics, head banging, and body rocking. The preschool child generally requires 10 mg three to four times a day, and after 6 years of age, 25 mg three times daily may be necessary. Lethargy is a frequent minor side effect with this compound and, if disturbing, can be controlled by the addition of 2.5 to 5 mg of Dexedrine to the therapeutic regimen.

PROGNOSIS. The eventual outcome is dependent on the nature of the disability, the intellectual potential, the establishment of realistic goals, and the avoidance of secondary emotional features by a well-structured and accepting family and a sound educational experience. With this program, it is hoped that the individual will develop social competence and independence. The relatively recent definition of this entity precludes any definitive statement concerning long-term prognosis.

Cerebral Palsy

NIELS L. LOW

Cerebral palsy is the name given to a group of diverse nonprogressive syndromes affecting the brain and manifesting themselves by impairment in motor function. This term is usually limited to conditions which presumably had their onset before birth, during the perinatal period, or in the first few years of life. Since the clinical manifestations as well as the causes are variable, cerebral palsy is not a specific medical diagnosis; it may include mental retardation, learning disabilities, and seizures in addition to the motor deficit.

ETIOLOGY. Either genetic or acquired factors may be responsible for these syndromes. The acquired causes usually result in damage to the fetal central nervous system during the early gestational period. They may be related to faulty implantation of the ovum or to diseases of the mother. Extreme nutritional deficiencies, infections, injuries, toxins, and radiation can interfere with the developing fetal brain, leading to permanent motor defects.

During the perinatal period a rapid succession of events occurs which may damage the brain and result in cerebral palsy. Prematurity is one of the most common associated conditions and predisposes the neonate to asphyxia and cerebral hemorrhage. In certain instances prematurity may result from pre-existing abnormalities, and it may be difficult to determine whether the brain damage is the result or the cause of prematurity. Twenty to 25 percent of cerebral palsied children have birth weights less than 2,500 g. Pathologic studies indicate that the most common mechanism leading to brain injury is asphyxia. Multiple births are also frequently associated; these neonates are often of low birth weight and may have associated premature labor and expulsion. Asphyxia seems to be an important damaging factor, especially in the second-born twin. Another factor is the birth process, which can cause venous stasis. This primarily involves the deep-draining veins, with resultant hemorrhage from microscopic extravasation or actual rupture of these vessels. These vascular complications are often the result of asphyxia.

Kernicterus from neonatal hyperbilirubinemia has been recognized as one of the causes of the athetoid type of cerebral palsy. In such children nerve deafness, paresis of upward gaze, or mental retardation may occur.

In the postnatal period, there are many disease processes which are of etiologic significance. Infectious conditions, meningitis, or encephalitis may damage the brain. Marasmus and dehydration with subsequent venous thrombosis are occasional causative factors. Arterial occlusions occurring before or after birth which lead to infantile hemiplegia are not well understood.

PATHOLOGY. Gross malformations, regardless of basic origin, are found in about one-third of autopsied cerebral palsy children. In the other two-thirds the changes, often microscopic, may be primarily cortical or subcortical. The cortical lesions are characterized by laminar degeneration, fall-out of neurons, and cortical atrophy with narrowing of gyri and widening of sulci. The subcortical defects consist of atrophy of white matter, gliosis in the deep central structures, sometimes with cyst formation. Numerically, the cor-

TABLE 3.   *Clinical Classification of Cerebral Palsy*

Spastic cerebral palsy
  Spastic hemiplegia
  Spastic tetraplegia
  Diplegia
    1. Spastic
    2. Atonic
  Spastic paraplegia
  Monoplegias and triplegias

Dyskinetic cerebral palsy
  Athetosis
  Other forms

Ataxic cerebral palsy

Mixed syndromes

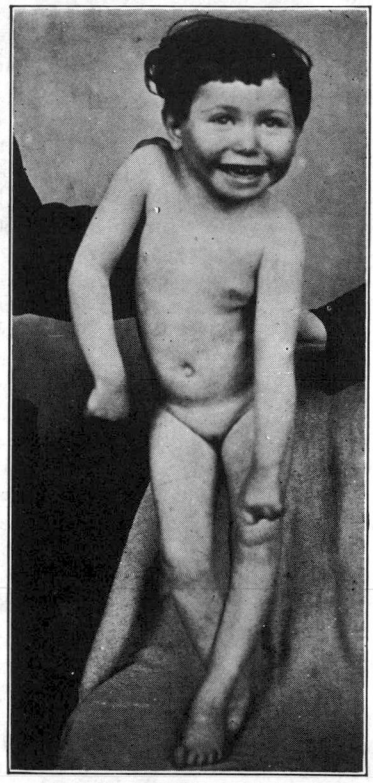

Fig. 24.   Child with spastic type of cerebral palsy.

tical changes are significantly more common in the postnatally acquired group, and the subcortical abnormalities are more frequently found in conjunction with perinatal complications. Athetosis, the aftereffect of kernicterus, show symmetric demyelination of the globus pallidus and the subthalamic nucleus.

CLINICAL CLASSIFICATION. The various syndromes are classified according to the predominant clinical manifestations. The classification given in Table 3 is descriptive and simple. The groups are defined as follows:

Spastic Cerebral Palsy. The spastic types of cerebral palsy are due to involvement of the upper motor neurons and are characterized by increased tone of the involved musculature, exaggeration of the deep tendon reflexes, clonus, abnormal reflexes (extensor plantar response), and a tendency to contractures (Fig. 24).

1. *Hemiplegia* implies that both extremities on the same side are involved; the upper extremity is usually more severely affected than the lower. In addition to increased deep tendon and periosteal reflexes in the involved arm and leg, there usually is some weakness of the peripheral muscles, especially dorsiflexors at the wrist and the ankle, and the forearm supinators. Because of this weakness and the tendency to contracture, the upper extremity tends to be kept flexed at the elbow, wrist, and fingers. In mildly affected children, the handicap may not be apparent while the patient rests in a sitting or standing position, but walking and especially running accentuate the abnormal position. In the mildest cases, the following maneuver is useful in eliciting spasticity: on supination of the previously outstretched pronated arm, there will be flexion of the elbow on the involved side.

The child with spastic hemiplegia characteristically walks more on the toes than on the heel, with a resultant circumduction of the affected leg in order to compensate for the apparent lengthening. Mildly affected children appear to have a normal gait; they walk well on tiptoes but are unable to walk on the affected heel with the toes elevated. This functional

asymmetry may be enhanced by running. Further evidence of a mild hemiplegia may be obtained from an examination of the child's shoes. The unaffected side shows normal heel wear, while the involved side demonstrates a scuffed toe and a relatively unworn heel. The signs of upper motor neuron involvement are often elicited in the paretic extremities. Characteristically, there is increased tone with tightness of the adductors of the thigh, the hamstrings, and the posterior calf muscles. This results in an inability to abduct fully the thigh, extend the leg at the knee, and dorsiflex the foot. The involved extremities, especially the upper, may be shorter in length and have a reduced muscle volume.

In addition to the weakness, the involved hand may show cortical sensory impairment with inability to discriminate objects (astereognosis). This is best demonstrated by having the child without the aid of vision identify familiar small objects placed in his hand. Useful function can rarely be attained in the presence of such a deficit.

There may be evidence of a central facial weakness and a homonymous hemianopsia.

2. The designation *tetraplegia* or *quadriplegia* is used when spasticity involves all four extremities to approximately the same degree. The clinical manifestations described above are present symmetrically, or nearly so, on both sides. Tightness of the hip

adductors and the hamstring muscles (knee flexors) is usually more marked in this condition than in hemiplegia. A few children with spasticity in all extremities have more involvement of the arms than the legs. Some clinics use the term "double hemiplegia" in these instances.

Such children with equal involvement of all four extremities usually manifest pseudobulbar palsy. Speech is unintelligible or dysarthric, swallowing is impaired, and lingual protrusion and palatal movement are restricted, but the gag reflex is usually present. These clinical manifestations are the result of bilateral involvement of the corticobulbar fibers and are considered an upper motor neuron lesion involving brainstem function.

3. *Spastic diplegia* is characterized by greater involvement of the lower than the upper limbs. The demarcation between tetraplegia and diplegia is not always clear and depends frequently on individual judgment regarding degree of involvement of the upper and lower extremities. The incidence of these two conditions in the literature varies because some clinics do not differentiate children with tetraplegia from those with diplegia. The child with typical spastic diplegia is frequently the result of a premature birth and is recognized by the clinical signs of spasticity in lower extremities while the abnormal findings in the upper limbs are relatively mild. In the young child the arms and hands may appear free of involvement, and only careful reexaminations may later demonstrate slight findings, such as weakness of dorsiflexors of the wrist or abnormal posturing when running.

Atonic diplegia is an unexplained variant of this form of cerebral palsy. It is characterized by marked delay in all motor milestones, decreased tone of the musculature of the lower extremities with increased range of passive movement, normal or increased deep tendon reflexes, and mental retardation. The presence of deep tendon reflexes differentiates atonic diplegia from anterior horn cell and peripheral nerve disease. A characteristic sign is flexion of the hips when the child is suspended upright under the arms (Foerster's sign). Atonic diplegia is a stage in the development of the affected child. As these children become older, hypertonicity usually supervenes and the hyperextensibility disappears. Because of this developmental change, this diagnosis usually can be made only in children between 6 months and 4 years of age.

4. *Spastic paraplegia* refers to the involvement of both legs with complete sparing of the upper extremities. Paraplegia is most often due to spinal cord pathology and only rarely results from brain disease. The differentiation between diplegia and paraplegia may be difficult, since hand involvement in diplegia may not be readily evident. Paraplegia, like spastic diplegia, is characterized by adduction spasm of thighs leading to a scissoring gait, tendency to flexion-contracture at the knees, and tightening of the heel cords (Achilles tendons) with resulting toe gait.

5. *Monoplegias* and *triplegias* are rare conditions. The terms are self-explanatory; they refer to involvement of only one or of three extremities. In triplegia, one arm is usually the limb that is spared.

Dyskinetic Cerebral Palsies. Dyskinesia implies an impairment of volitional activity by uncontrolled and purposeless movements which disappear during sleep. These movement disorders are often related to lesions of the basal ganglia. The most common type is athetosis, which is characterized by relatively slow, wormlike, writhing movements involving usually all four extremities, but also the face, the neck, and, to a lesser degree, the trunk. A child may display a similar pattern for years, but the clinical picture may vary somewhat with age. When the movements have a jerky component, they resemble chorea, and the term choreoathetosis is used. The abnormal movements are less apparent when the patient is relaxed, but increase under stress or tension. During various periods of the natural life cycle of this form of cerebral palsy, abnormal movements, rigidity, and dystonia may be seen. These variations do not justify a separate classification with arbitrary definitions and separations.

Athetosis is most commonly quite symmetric, but some degree of asymmetry may occur. Athetosis involving only one extremity or part of one is exceedingly rare. Because of the continuous movements of extremities and trunk, hypertrophy of some muscles is common, especially around the neck and in the paravertebral area. The athetosis due to kernicterus often has associated nerve deafness and paresis of upward gaze.

Lesch-Nyhan syndrome results from an inborn error of purine metabolism in which there is a deficiency of hypoxanthine-guanine phosphoribosyltransferase. The condition is characterized by choreoathetosis, mental retardation, self mutilation, and hyperuricemia.

Ataxic Cerebral Palsy. The ataxic variety of cerebral palsy is characterized by ataxic phenomena from early childhood and a lack of progression of the disease. It is related to a static lesion of the cerebellum or its pathways. Involved children have a wide-based gait, have difficulty in turning rapidly, perform fast repetitive movements poorly, and show decomposition on the finger-to-finger and finger-to-nose pointing test. Any evidence of progression, foot deformity, abnormal sensory findings, or familial history of ataxia would exclude the diagnosis of this form of cerebral palsy. The ataxic type has the best prognosis for functional improvement.

Mixed Forms. The clinical manifestations of more than one type of cerebral palsy may be present in some children. The combination of spasticity and athetosis is seen most frequently; ataxia and athetosis may be found. Although it may be difficult to separate the features of multiple involvement, the clinical phenomena in a child with a mixed form are characteristically the summation of the findings of both types involved.

ASSOCIATED CONDITIONS. Children who have motor disabilities which fall within the definition of cerebral palsy may have additional syndromes. The most common of these are seizure disorders and mental retardation.

The frequency of convulsions in children with cerebral palsy is difficult to assess, but approximately 25 to 35 percent of all cerebral palsied children have epilepsy. Seizures are more common in the postnatally acquired forms of cerebral palsy. They are present in over 40 percent of the children with hemiplegia and are less common in the other spastic varieties. Dyskinetic children have less than a 1 in 10 chance of developing convulsions, and ataxic patients less than 1 in 20.

Seizures may be evident in early infancy, but are more frequent in the 2 to 6 year age group. In some, the onset may be delayed until the second decade. The seizure type may in part be related to age of onset. Varied seizure patterns are seen. These include infantile spasms, grand mal, focal, multifocal, and psychomotor.

The prevalence of mental retardation is variously reported as being from 25 to 75 percent, but this figure is meaningless unless correlated with the type of cerebral palsy. The incidence is highest in the mixed group, less in the spastic type, still lower in athetosis, and least frequent in ataxia. Among the spastic children, retardation is found in decreasing frequency in the following types: severe tetraplegia, diplegia, paraplegia, hemiplegia, and monoplegia. Intelligence is statistically lower in cerebral palsy patients with seizures compared to those without epilepsy.

Aside from speech delay in mental retardation, cerebral palsy may be associated with a variety of speech disorders, including different degrees and expressions of aphasia, articulatory disturbances, apraxias, and abnormalities of rhythm.

Attention to visual handicaps is particularly important because of the high incidence of strabismus, refractive errors, and visual field defects. Visual-perceptual problems are commonly encountered in cerebral palsied children.

Deafness is uncommon except in children with athetosis due to kernicterus. Peripheral hearing loss (hypacusis) has to be differentiated from lack of response to speech and other auditory stimuli in children who are not deaf (central hearing loss or dysacusis).

INCIDENCE OF CEREBRAL PALSY. The difference among the various reported series is so great that no definitive frequency can be given. Most reports from the United States give a higher birth incidence than is found in the European literature. The most extensive survey throughout an entire country was made by Hansen in Denmark. He found a mean birth incidence (i.e., the number of cerebral palsied children per 1,000 births) of 1.3. This study also revealed that the birth incidence and the frequency of cerebral palsy in Denmark are on the increase.

Of all children with cerebral palsy, approximately 70 percent are spastic, 15 percent athetotic, 5 percent ataxic, and the remaining 10 percent have more than one type, usually spasticity with athetosis. In the Cerebral Palsy Clinic of the Columbia-Presbyterian Medical Center, the incidence of athetosis and ataxia has been decreasing over the last 10 years. Most spastics have either hemiplegia (40 to 45 percent) or diplegia (35 percent). Monoplegia and triplegia are rare forms.

LABORATORY DATA. The common laboratory tests, such as urinalysis, blood count, and sedimentation rate, are not contributory in the diagnosis and differential analysis of the cerebral palsies.

Plain roentgenograms of the skull are usually normal. Asymmetries may be seen in hemiplegic children, and relative microcephaly is not uncommon. Films of the skull should be a routine part of the work-up of cerebral palsied children.

Electroencephalography cannot be used as a diagnostic tool to differentiate cerebral palsy from other neuropathologic conditions, but clearly abnormal EEG's are common in all types of cerebral palsy, whether seizures are manifestly present or not. The most common EEG abnormality is spike seizure discharges. Asymmetries may occur with or without seizure discharges.

COURSE AND PROGNOSIS. By definition, cerebral palsy is the result of a static lesion of the brain which cannot be cured and does not progress; however, the clinical picture can change with time. Children with spasticity manifest a tendency to contracture, and without proper management the handicap may increase. Untreated spastics, who had walked earlier with or without aids, may become chairbound or bedridden. Frequent seizures may disable some children, and the associated repeated asphyxia may further reduce their intelligence. Apparent improvement may be seen in some nonretarded children with the athetotic or ataxic varieties of cerebral palsy.

While decreasing mortality among prematures and in children with meningitis increases the occurrence of cerebral palsy, the wide use of antibiotics and other improvements in medical care and socioeconomic conditions increases the life-span of these patients. The number of cerebral palsied adults is therefore likely to increase.

TREATMENT. The management of children with cerebral palsy varies with the child's age, the type and severity of involvement, presence or absence of seizures, and the degree of intellect. It is important that none of these aspects be regarded as isolated factors requiring treatment, but that the whole child and his family be properly cared for, including social and educational factors.

The motor aspects can be modified to a certain degree. Spastic children develop contractures, and this tendency can be counteracted by surgical and nonsurgical means. Tendons that are tight can be stretched by passive and active exercises. Stretching exercises can be made more effective with certain mechanical devices. Examples of such devices are short leg braces with an adjustable "stop" to prevent footdrop or toe-walking. This type of brace is sometimes used at night only to keep the foot dorsiflexed during sleeping hours. The Benesh Brace Boot (by Markell) prevents the patient's heel from slipping up within the shoe. Stretching of tight adductors of the thighs can be accomplished at night by a so-called "A" frame which separates the legs during resting hours. Various splints can be used to prevent contracture of wrist flexors, finger flexors, and thumb adductors. A variety of orthopedic procedures have been devised for the correction of contractures that do not respond to medical measures.

Athetosis and other forms of dyskinesia are affected only slightly, if at all, by exercises and appliances. In general, braces are contraindicated in athetosis.

Medications have been universally unsuccessful in reducing spasticity or influencing the abnormal movements of cerebral palsy. The management of seizures requires the daily use of anticonvulsants.

Significant mental retardation makes treatment a more difficult problem. Given two children with very similar physical handicap, one can expect better results in the child with normal or near-normal intelligence than in a retarded child. The best results can be obtained when parents and the child can actively cooperate in treatment.

Other ancillary methods of treatment can reduce the individual child's handicap. These include speech therapy for children with difficulties in verbal communication and early correction of visual handicaps. Psychotherapy may be of some value in occasional children; it is of more benefit in helping the family adjust to the handicapped child.

School placement has to be individualized just as are other forms of management. If the child is not retarded, and the physical handicap not severe, regular school placement is indicated. Special classes should be recommended only if the child is unable to perform adequately in a normal setting. Where available, classes for physically handicapped children of normal intellect or for the retarded should be recommended.

Institutional care may become advisable for severely retarded children who cannot be managed at home or who prove to be a significant social or emotional handicap to their siblings and parents.

REFERENCES

THE SYNDROME OF
MINIMAL CEREBRAL DYSFUNCTION

Association for the Aid of Crippled Children. The Child with Brain Damage. New York, 1959.
Bax, M., and MacKeith, R. Minimal cerebral dysfunction. Little Club Clinics and Developmental Medicine No. 10. National Spastics Society. London, Medical Education and Information Unit, 1963.

Birch, H. G., ed. Brain Damage in Children: The Biological and Social Aspects. Baltimore, Williams and Wilkins Co., 1964.
Bortner, M. Evaluation and Education of Children with Brain Damage. Springfield, Ill., Charles C Thomas, Publ., 1968.
Chalfant, J. C., and Scheffelin, M. A. Central processings dysfunctions in children. NINDS Monograph No. 9, Public Health Service Publication. Bethesda, Md., 1969.
Clements, S. D. Minimal brain dysfunction in children. NINDB Monograph No. 3, Public Health Serv. Pub. No. 1415. Washington, D.C., 1964.
Cruickshank, W. M. The brain-injured child in home, school, and community. Syracuse, Syracuse Univ. Press, 1967.
Eisenberg, L. The management of the hyperkinetic child. Develop. Med. Child Neurol., 8:593, 1966.
Graham, F. M., and Berman, P. W. Current states of behavior tests for brain damage in infants and pre-school children. Amer. J. Orthopsychiat., 31:713, 1961.
Haring, N. G. Minimal brain dysfunction in children. Public Health Service Publication No. 2015. Washington, D.C., 1969.
Kebanoff, S. G., Singer, J. L., and Wilensky, H. Psychological consequence of brain lesions and ablations. Psychol. Bull., 51:1, 1954.
Laufer, N. W., and Denhoff, E. Hyperkinetic behavior syndrome in children. J. Pediat., 50:463, 1957.
Mallison, R. Education as therapy. Seattle, Special Child Publications, 1968.
Money, J., ed. Reading Disability: Progress and Research Needs in Dyslexia. Baltimore, The Johns Hopkins Press, 1962.
Paine, R. S. Minimal chronic brain syndromes in children. Develop. Med. Child. Neurol., 4:21, 1962.
Passamanick, B., and Knobloch, H. Syndrome of minimal cerebral damage in infancy. J.A.M.A., 170:1384, 1959.
Siegel, E. Helping the Brain Injured Child. New York, Association for Brain-Injured Children, 1961.
Strauss, A. A., and Lehtinen, L. Psychopathology and Education of the Brain-Injured Child. New York, Grune and Stratton, Inc., 1947.
Tarnopal, L. Learning Disabilities. Springfield, Ill., Charles C Thomas, Publ., 1969.
Towbin, A. Organic causes of minimal brain dysfunction. J.A.M.A., 217:1207, 1971.

CEREBRAL PALSY

Andersen, B. Infantile Cerebral Palsy. Oslo, Oslo Univ. Press, 1957.
Christensen, E., and Melchior, J. Cerebral palsy—A clinical and neuropathological study. Clinics in Developmental Medicine No. 25. London, National Spastics Society, 1967.
Churchill, J. A. The relationship of Little's disease to premature birth. Amer. J. Dis. Child., 96:32, 1958.
Ellis, E. The physical management of developmental disorders. Clinics in Developmental Medicine No. 26. London, National Spastics Society, 1967.
Frost, P., Weinstein, G. D., and Nyhan, W. L. Diagnosis of Lesch-Nyhan syndrome by direct study of skin specimens. J.A.M.A., 212:316, 1970.
Gold, A. P., and Carter, S. Treatment of Cerebral Palsy. In Conn, H. F., ed., Current Therapy. Philadelphia, W. B. Saunders Co., 1969.

Hansen, E. Cerebral palsy in Denmark. Acta. Neurol. Scand., 35:(Suppl.)146, 1960.

Heimer, C. B., Cutler, R., and Freedman, A. M. Neurological sequelae of premature birth. Amer. J. Dis. Child., 108:122, 1964.

Kurland, L. T. Definitions of cerebral palsy and their role in epidemiologic research. Neurology, 7:641, 1957.

Lesch, M., and Nyhan, W. L. A familial disorder of uric acid metabolism and central nervous system function. Amer. J. Med., 36:561, 1964.

Malamud, N., Itabashi, H. H., Castor, J., and Messinger, H. B. An etiologic and diagnostic study of cerebral palsy. J. Pediat., 65:270, 1964.

Perlstein, M. A., Gibbs, E. L., and Gibbs, F. A. The electroencephalogram in infantile cerebral palsy. Amer. J. Phys. Med., 34:477, 1955.

—— and Hood, P. N. Infantile spastic hemiplegia. I. Incidence. Pediatrics, 14:436, 1954.

—— and Hood, P. N. Infantile spastic hemiplegia. III. Intelligence. Pediatrics, 15:676, 1955.

—— and Hood, P. N. Infantile spastic hemiplegia. Amer. J. Phys. Med., 34:391, 1955.

—— and Hood, P. N. Etiology of postnatally acquired cerebral palsy. J.A.M.A., 188:126, 1964.

Schachat, W. S., Wallace, H. M., Palmer, M., and Slater, B. Ophthalmologic findings in children with cerebral palsy. Pediatrics, 19:623, 1957.

Towbin, A. The Pathology of Cerebral Palsy. Springfield, Ill., Charles C Thomas, Publ., 1960.

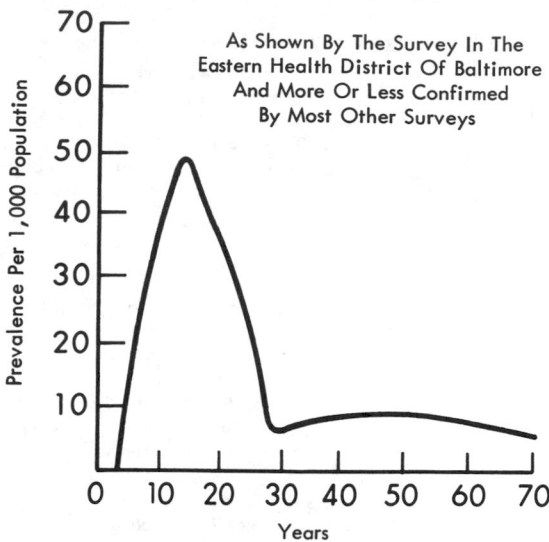

Fig. 25. Shape of curve for prevalence of mental deficiency.

Mental Retardation

LAWRENCE T. TAFT and HERBERT J. COHEN

Mental retardation is one of the most significant problems facing our society. The effects of this condition are often profound and devastating to both the child and his family.

DEFINITION AND DESCRIPTION. Mental retardation is a symptom associated with many syndromes and diseases. An individual is labeled as being mentally retarded if he performs two standard deviations below the mean on a standardized psychologic test. However, different psychologic tests measure different aspects of cognitive functioning and the tests are not "culture free." A low intelligence quotient may not always be a reliable "symptom" of intellectual incompetency. IQ scores, in certain cases, can be profoundly changed by a modification of the environment, test preparation, test familiarity, and improved motivation.

The primary concern for the individual who performs poorly on standard IQ tests is whether he is able to adapt and successfully compete in society. IQ tests that measure cognitive abilities do have some predictive value in determining future adaptation to society's demands. However, these demands are quite variable. A child with a low IQ may be considered handicapped in some settings and not in others. The child with a mild intellectual deficit may be unrecognized until he starts school, since at that time his behavior must accord to stricter standards and his intellectual competence in selected areas is first challenged. The same youngster, at the completion of school, may, once again, fade into the general population. He may then appear to function more competitively with his peers. Figure 25 illustrates the reported relative frequencies of mental retardation apparent at various ages. There is a decided drop in the frequency of identified cases after adolescence.

Adaptive difficulties can exist in individuals who function at any level on certain standardized psychologic tests. A child with an IQ score in the superior range may still have a reading disability and experience educational failure. It is unwise and incorrect to assume that the IQ tests used to delineate a specific population of "retardates" automatically absolve individuals who score slightly above this level from being functionally handicapped.

CLASSIFICATION AND ETIOLOGY. Degrees of mental retardation are defined by the terms mild, moderate, and severe. Mild retardation is equated with an IQ of 50 to 75, and indicates that the individual is both "educable and trainable." In general, most children in this category can reach a third to fifth grade level of academic achievement, and should be independent in activities of daily living. Prognostically, the majority of this group, especially those with an IQ greater than 65 and no severe emotional problems, can be expected to achieve an independent existence as an adult. They should be able to work as unskilled or semiskilled laborers, and be able to assume family responsibilities. Moderate mental retardation (IQ 25 to 50) implies that the individual will have no significant academic achievements but will be "trainable" and can go to school, primarily for training in self-care activities. The trainable individual may learn to read and write at a primer or

TABLE 4.   *Pathophysiologic Classification of Mental Retardation*

Prenatally Determined

Chromosomal (autosomal)
    A. Down's syndrome (trisomy 21; translocation 15/21, 21/22, 21/21; mosaicism)
    B. Trisomy 13
    C. Trisomy 18
    D. Partial deletion of long arm of 18
    E. Partial deletion of chromosome 4-5 (cri du chat syndrome)

Chromosomal (sex)
    Klinefelter's syndrome (XXY, XXXY, XXXXY)

Metabolic*
    Abnormalities of amino acid metabolism
        a. Hyperglycinemia
        b. Hyperlipemia
        c. Homocystinuria
        d. Oasthouse urine disease
        e. Congenital tryptophanuria
        f. Hydroxyprolinuria
        g. Cystathioninuria
        h. Hartnup disease
        i. Joseph's syndrome
        j. Lowe's syndrome (oculo-cerebro-renal dystrophy)
        k. Hypersarcosinuria
        l. Phenylketonuria
        m. Histidinemia
        n. Hyper-beta-alaninemia
        o. Hyperammonemia—type 2
        p. Albinism—oculocutaneous form
        q. Hypervalinemia
        r. Congenital lysine intolerance
        s. Methionine malabsorption
        t. Maple syrup urine disease
        u. Hydroxykynureninuria
        v. Hyperprolanemia
        w. Citrullinemia
        x. Arginosuccinic-aciduria
        y. Kwashiorkor
        z. Wilson's disease (hepato-lenticular degeneration)
    Abnormalities of lipid metabolism
        a. A-beta-lipoproteinemia
        b. Alexander's disease
        c. Cerebromacular degenerations (Bielchowski, Batten-Spielmeyer-Vogt, Kufs)
        d. Cerebroside lipidosis (infantile and childhood)
        e. Familial sudanophilic leucodystrophy
        f. Ganglioside lipidosis (Tay-Sachs)
        g. Globoid cell leucodystrophy (Krabbe)
        h. Isovaleric acidemia
        i. Kinky hair disease (Menke's disease)
        j. Lipogranulomatosis (Farber's)
        k. Pelizaeus-Merzbacher leucodystrophy
        l. Neurovisceral lipidosis
        m. Refsum's disease (heredopathia atactica polyneuritiformis)
        n. Sphingomyelin lipidosis (Niemann-Pick)
        o. Sulfatide lipidosis (metachromatic leucodystrophy)
        p. Sweaty socks syndrome
    Abnormalities of carbohydrate metabolism
        a. Galactosemia
        b. Mucopolysaccharidoses
            Hurler's Type
            Hunter's Type
            Sanfilippo's Type
            Morquio-Ullrich
    Abnormalities of purine metabolism
        a. Hyperuricemia
        b. Hereditary orotic aciduria

TABLE 4.   (continued)

Abnormalities of mineral metabolism
    a. Idiopathic hypercalcemia
    b. Pseudohypoparathyroidism
    c. Pseudo-pseudohypoparathyroidism

Syndromes† (classified as to prominent clinical findings)
  Skin abnormalities
    a. Linear sebaceous nevi—convulsions
    b. Congenital icthyosis with spastic paralysis (Sjögren-Larsson syndrome)
    c. Adenoma sebaceum (tuberous sclerosis)
    d. Café-au-lait spots (neurofibromatosis)
    e. Telangiectasia (ataxia-telangiectasia)
    f. Incontinentia pigmenti
    g. Facial port-wine nevus (Sturge-Weber-Dimitri)
  Cataracts
    Marinesco-Sjögren syndrome
  Emaciation
    Leprechaunism
  Obesity
    a. Laurence-Moon-Biedl
    b. Prader-Willi syndrome
  Cleft lip and cleft palate
    a. Oral-facial-digital syndrome
    b. Oto-palato-digital syndrome
  Facial anomalies prominent
    a. Cebocephalus
    b. Cerebro-hepato-renal syndrome
    c. de Lange's syndrome
    d. Dyscephalia mandibulo-oculo-facialis (Hallerman-Streiff syndrome)
    e. Leprechaunism
    f. Oculo-auriculo-vertebral dysplasia
    g. Rubinstein-Taybi syndrome (broad thumb and broad toe)
    h. Smith-Lemli-Opitz syndrome
  Digit abnormalities
    a. Rubinstein-Taybi syndrome
    b. Oral-facial-digital syndrome
    c. Oto-palato-digital syndrome
    d. Smith-Lemli-Opitz syndrome
  Tall stature
    Cerebral gigantism
  Dwarfism prominent
    a. Bird-headed dwarf (Virchow-Seckel dwarf)
    b. Silver's syndrome
  Cranial abnormalities
    a. Apert's (acrocephalosyndactyly)
    b. Craniofacial dysostosis (Crouzon's disease)
    c. Happy puppet syndrome
    d. Hydrancephaly
    e. Hydrocephalus
    f. Cloverleaf skull (Kleebattschadel syndrome)
    g. Familial microcephaly
    h. Kinky hair disease (Menke's syndrome)
  Muscle weakness
    a. Myotonic dystrophy
    b. Pseudohypertrophic muscular dystrophy

Fetal Teratogens
  Chemical
    a. Dietary inadequacies
    b. Vitamin deficiencies
    c. Drugs
  Physical
    a. Irradiation
    b. Trauma

TABLE 4.　(continued)

　　　　　Infectious agents
　　　　　　a. Cytomegalic inclusion disease
　　　　　　b. Influenza
　　　　　　c. Rubella
　　　　　　d. Toxoplasmosis
　　　　　　e. Syphilis
　　　　　Metabolic
　　　　　　a. Toxemia
　　　　　　b. Placental dysfunction
　　　　　　c. Diabetes mellitus

Perinatally Determined

　　　Birth anoxia
　　　Kernicterus
　　　Prematurity
　　　Birth trauma

Postnatally Determined

　　　Head trauma
　　　Poisonings
　　　　Lead
　　　　Carbon monoxide
　　　　Arsenic
　　　Infectious
　　　　Meningitis
　　　　Encephalitis
　　　Cerebrovascular accidents
　　　　Aneurysm
　　　　Arteriovenous malformation
　　　　Thrombosis
　　　Metabolic
　　　　Hyponatremia
　　　　Hypernatremia
　　　　Hypoglycemia
　　　Postimmunization encephalopathies
　　　　Rabies
　　　　Pertussis
　　　　Smallpox
　　　Cultural—familial
　　　Psychogenic

*The metabolic abnormalities are listed as being prenatally determined since they are genetic disorders. Some may not become manifest until a later age.

†These are not listed as being prenatally determined since they all appear to be due to abnormalities in morphogenesis.

first grade level. Vocational placement is usually limited to employment in a sheltered workshop, and supervised care is necessary. Severe retardates (IQ less than 25) acquire no academic skills; they are usually not trainable and require custodial care.

It is also useful to classify individuals with an intellectual handicap in two subgroups, defined as: (1) true mental defects (biologic); and (2) functional mental retardation. Retardation in those with true mental defects may be due to either structural or metabolic brain defects. Such individuals are not able to perform within the normal range on formal psychologic testing even when they are functioning at their highest level. In contrast, functional retardation implies that the affected individuals have the capacity to perform within the normal range but are unable to do so because of such factors as emotional disturbance, deprivation, cultural disadvantage, discrimination, or educational handicaps.

Anatomic and etiologic classifications for mental retardation are often inadequate since the pathogenesis and neuropathology have usually not been correlated with clinical manifestations. In addition, brain damage or maldevelopment (e.g., absence of the corpus callosum), may not be asociated with mental retardation. The classification in Table 4 lists most known determinants and/or diseases that have been associated with mental retardation. Many are described in detail elsewhere. In the vast majority of mild retardates, no single etiologic factor can be identified. A comprehensive evaluation, including physical and neurologic examinations, and biochemi-

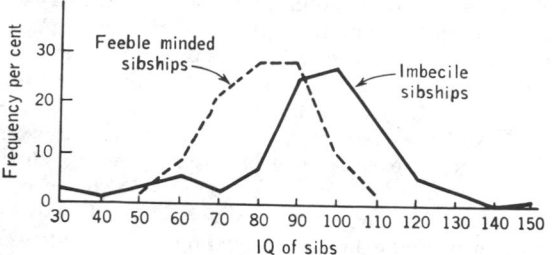

Fig. 26. Frequency distributions of the IQ's of sibs of feeble-minded and imbeciles with an IQ range of 30 to 68. (After Roberts. *Eugen. Rev., 44:*71, 1952.)

cal and cytogenetic studies, usually fails to prove the presence of clear-cut cerebral pathology.

INCIDENCE AND DISTRIBUTION. Based on the psychologic criteria noted above, mental retardation is found in approximately 3 percent of the population. Seventy-five percent of retardates are in the mild category, 20 percent in the moderate group, and only 5 percent are classified as severely retarded. However, there are marked variations in this distribution, associated with chronologic, cultural, and socioeconomic factors.

The prevalence of mild retardation is highest in low socioeconomic classes. In contrast, moderate and severe retardates are distributed more evenly from among all of the social classes. This finding has created considerable controversy as to whether biologic factors or social (experiential) factors play the major role in causing mild mental retardation. Severe deprivation, protein malnutrition, and environmental factors have all been demonstrated to cause a diminished rate and level of learning, and subsequent subnormal mental functioning. The high frequency of retardation in the lower classes has suggested that polygenic or multifactorial hereditary patterns are paramount. As shown in Figure 26, Roberts has demonstrated that mild retardates have siblings with lower IQ's than siblings of more severe retardates. Twin studies have generally supported the notion that heredity is of primary importance in determining eventual IQ results. However, the phenotypic expression of any genotype does depend to some extent on environmental factors. It is probable that there are certain biologic determinants of behavior and that external stimuli modify their expressivity and vary the degree or type of responsiveness. Many factors may operate in a relatively covert manner. The absence of clearly demonstrable CNS pathology in the mild retardate may simply reflect the lack of refinement of our clinical diagnostic tools, and many subtle abnormalities in function may go undetected.

PRESENTING SYMPTOMS. Suspicion of mental retardation may be aroused either by the recognition of a specific syndrome with its overt anomalies or by a developmental lag. Down's syndrome is a classic example of the former and is usually recognized at

TABLE 5. *High-Risk Factors Predisposing to Mental Retardation**

Family history

  1. Deafness, blindness, neurologic diseases, cerebral palsy, epilepsy
  2. Congenital malformations (including congenital dislocation of the hip)
  3. Mental disorder
  4. Elderly or very young mother

Prenatal

  1. Rubella (certainly) and other virus infections (possibly) contracted in early pregnancy
  2. Toxoplasmosis
  3. Hyperemesis
  4. Threatened abortion
  5. Severe illnesses in the early months necessitating chemotherapy or major surgery
  6. Exposure to radioactive substances during pregnancy
  7. Blood group incompatibilities
  8. Maternal diabetes mellitus
  9. Maternal thyrotoxicosis and toxemia
10. Uterine hemorrhage
11. Hydramnios
12. Multiple pregnancy

Perinatal

  1. Premature birth (39 weeks and earlier)
  2. Low weight at birth in relation to gestational age
  3. Postmature birth (42 weeks and later)
  4. Abnormal presentation
  5. Prolonged, precipitate, or instrumental labor
  6. Birth asphyxia
  7. Neonatal jaundice
  8. Presence of any congenital abnormality
  9. Induction of labor

Postnatal

  1. Difficulties in sucking and swallowing
  2. Convulsions
  3. Cerebral palsy
  4. Meningitis or encephalitis
  5. Any serious illness or infection in first few months of life

Symptomatic group

  1. Mother's suspicion that the child is blind, deaf, retarded, or otherwise abnormal
  2. Inattention to sound or to visual stimuli
  3. Delayed motor development
  4. Delayed development of vocalization and speech

*From Sheridan. *Monthly Bull. Minist. Health (London),* 21:238, 1962.

birth, as are most cases where multiple anomalies are present. Retarded children with delayed development only are diagnosed at a later age. Severe mental retardation is manifested in the first year of life by marked lags in motor and adaptive behavior. However, the diagnosis of mental retardation in a child with only motor retardation must be made with cau-

TABLE 6.   *Reasons for Early Diagnosis of Mental Retardation*

Early identification of treatable conditions
 1. Metabolic (e.g., PKU, cretinism, galactosemia)
 2. Surgical (e.g., subdural hematoma, hydrocephalus)

Genetic counseling for hereditable conditions
 e.g.—Tuberous Sclerosis

Prevent complications by:
 1. Parent counseling
 2. Appropriate schooling
 3. Behavioral management
 4. Recommendations regarding recreation

tion since such children may have cerebral palsy and normal intelligence. Moderate retardates are usually delayed in motor and adaptive behavior in early infancy but are not sufficiently deviant from the norms to arouse suspicion unless their speech development is significantly delayed. Mild retardates are often unrecognized until they are subjected to the more exacting demands of a school curriculum and are in direct competition with youngsters of normal mental capacity.

The mild retardate may be identified by developmental screening examinations. The presence of any "high-risk" factors (Table 5) should alert the physician that certain infants and children deserve a more careful developmental evaluation. Developmental tests such as the Denver Developmental Screening Examination, the Gesell Test, or modified versions of the latter, are useful in this regard. Although these tests cannot define a child's exact future IQ, they do have reasonable predictive value in identifying mental subnormality. For a preschool and kindergarten age child (aged 5 to 6 years), the Meeting Street School Test may be of value in identifying children at risk of educational failure.

ROLE OF THE PHYSICIAN.   The physician's primary responsibility, in the case of the retarded child, is to examine the patient and identify any specific etiologic and pathologic entities that are known to cause mental subnormality. A complete diagnostic evaluation should be performed on a child with symptoms of maldevelopment as soon as the problem is recognized. Though remediable conditions are not common, there are a few treatable conditions in which early institution of therapy can produce favorable results. Table 6 lists the important reasons for early diagnosis and early intervention.

PHYSICAL FINDINGS.   The presence of congenital stigmata enumerated in Table 7 may provide a clue that fetal maldevelopment has occurred. These findings may be due to chromosomal defects or to first trimester teratogenic influences on the fetus. A search for skin lesions such as adenoma sebaceum, vitiligo, and café-au-lait spots is important to help exclude a familial degenerative disease such as tuberous sclerosis. The presence of organomegaly should

lead to the suspicion of a lipid or carbohydrate storage disease. Careful eyeground examination can rule out optic atrophy, macular abnormalities, or pigmentary degeneration found in degenerative CNS diseases and chorioretinitis associated with congenital toxoplasmosis, cytomegalic inclusion disease, or rubella. Metabolic disorders, such as a cretinism or mucopolysaccharidosis, may be suspected if the child has coarse facial features. An unusual body or urinary odor may suggest an amino-aciduria. Constipation is a common finding in cretinism. Short stature is a frequent finding in both institutionalized and noninstitutionalized retardates. Not infrequently, complete investigations into known causes of short stature prove unrevealing. In these patients "brain damage" is assumed to be etiologically related to the dwarf stature, but the pathophysiologic mechanism is unknown. In nonbrain-damaged individuals short stature has been reported to be a consequence of emotional deprivation.

It is important to measure the head size at regular intervals. Appropriate graphs of normal values are available for premature as well as full-term infants and older children. A head circumference of three standard deviations or more from the mean should always be investigated. Head circumferences two standard deviations from the mean should be regarded with suspicion, especially if the circumference is out of proportion as compared with the child's percentiles for height and weight. In most cases of malnutrition, especially when this occurs after 1 year of age, the head size will grow at a relatively normal rate and will appear relatively large in comparison to body size. Microcephaly at birth suggests the possibility of: (1) prenatal rubella; (2) toxoplasmosis; (3) cytomegalic inclusion disease (CID); (4) Paine's sex-linked recessive microcephaly with amino-aciduria; (5) chromosomal aberration; or (6) fetal maldevelopment of unknown origin.

A head circumference that is normal at birth but subsequently has a slow rate of growth should arouse suspicion of: (1) perinatal brain damage; (2) a metabolic disorder (e.g., PKU); (3) a degenerative brain disease; or (4) rubella, CID, and toxoplasmosis acquired in utero.

LABORATORY STUDIES.   Investigations include screening test for amino-aciduria, serum electrophoresis to measure IgM, since it is occasionally elevated in the perinatal period in congenital infections, and confirmatory serologic tests for toxoplasmosis, CID, and rubella. Skull x-rays should be performed on microcephalic or retarded children, since identification of cerebral calcifications, though uncommon, may assist in detecting previously undiagnosed cases of CID, toxoplasmosis, or tuberous sclerosis. In most cases of mental retardation, an EEG is usually of little specific diagnostic help. However, abnormalities associated with subdural hematomas, infantile spasms, and petit mal status have occasionally been found, and

TABLE 7. *Physical Stigmata Often Associated with Mental Retardation*

Head

Dolicocephaly
Brachycephaly
Scaphocephaly
Asymmetry
Acrocephaly
Macrocephaly
Microcephaly
Frontal bossing
Flat or prominent occiput

Facial Appearance

Birdlike
Elfinlike
Expressionless
Coarse features
Odd shape
Odd general appearance

Hair

Low hairline anterior or posterior
Hirsutism
Alopecia
Kinkiness
Abnormal texture
Eyebrow hair meets in midline
White forelock
Short and blond
Abnormal pigmentation

Nose

Beaked
Broad or broad bridge
Flat
Clefted
Saddle-shaped
Thin
Upturned

Mouth

Micrognathia
Cleft lip
Cleft palate
Thin, thickened, or fissured lips
Thick alveolus or mandible
Hypoplastic mandible
Prominent maxilla
Open mouth
High arched palate
Prognathia
Large protruding tongue
Fissured or lobulated tongue
Cleft uvula

Chest

Shield-like
Deformed
Narrow
Pectus excavatum
Pigeon breast
Wide-spaced nipples

Abdomen

Protuberant
Large umbilical hernia

Skin

Pigmentary changes
Simian creases
Abnormal dermatoglyphics
Nevi
Hemangiomata
Acrocyanosis
Adenoma sebaceum
Depigmented
Petechiae
Blotching
Café-au-lait spots
Dryness
Increased elasticity
Fistulae
Nevus flammeus

Eyes

Abnormal shape
Slant—mongoloid or antimongoloid
Blue sclera
Coloboma
Brushfield spots
Epicanthal folds
Hypo- or hypertelorism
Cataracts
Corneal clouding
Long curly eyelashes
Heterochromia
Glaucoma
Abnormal corneal slope or size
Nystagmus
Ptosis

Philtrum

Short
Long

Teeth

Abnormal crown formation
Absent
Supernumerary
Enamel hypoplasia or aplasia
Enamel hypomaturation and hypocalcification
Intrinsic staining
Malposition
Delayed eruption

Neck

Short
Webbed

Genitalia

Enlarged
Small
Ambiguous
Hypospadias
Cryptorchidism
Bifid or small scrotum

Back

Gibbus
Marked kyphosis or lordosis

893

TABLE 7.   (continued)

Hands	Arms
Short metacarpals	Wide carrying angle
Broad	Enlarged wrists
Large or short	
Clawlike	**Feet**
Spadelike	
Polydactyly	Edema
Clinodactyly	Short metatarsals
Aplasia of digits	Rocker-bottom
Broad distal digits (thumbs)	Talipes equinovarus or valgus
Overlapping fingers	Syndactyly
Syndactyly	Dysplasia of toenail
Proximally placed thumbs	Overlapping toes
Simian creases	Short toes
	Broad big toe
	Increased distance between 1st and 2nd toe

these conditions require early and specific treatment. The deaf child may present with the clinical picture of pseudoretardation, and appropriate hearing tests should be made to exclude this possibility.

Routine cytogenetic studies are rarely abnormal in the great majority of retardates. Karyotypes should be selectively performed when there are physical stigmata or a family history to suggest a chromosomal disorder. Such studies can confirm the clinical diagnosis and prove of value for future family planning. **PSYCHOLOGIC TESTING AND SOCIAL BEHAVIORAL EVALUATION.** A comprehensive assessment of a suspected retarded child should always include a clinical psychologic evaluation. It is common practice to use patterns of functioning on standard psychologic tests to help differentiate the environmentally deprived, genetically determined, and organically impaired patient. Psychometric testing, performed in a one-to-one setting by an experienced psychologist, can be helpful in determining the extent to which emotional factors, sensory impairments, or perceptual problems are impairing learning capacity. This aids in defining the patterns of disability which will assist the clinician in prescribing appropriate remediation and treatment.

The results of psychologic tests are influenced by the child's attitude towards testing, familiarity with test situations, levels of anxiety in a strange and demanding situation, and the general environment in which he has developed.

Though the psychologist can competently evaluate some of these factors, a psychiatrist and social worker can be of great assistance in this regard. In the presence of suspected behavioral aberrations that may depress intellectual function, a psychiatric evaluation should be performed. Children with infantile autism or childhood psychosis may appear retarded but actually may have better intellectual potential. The child who is hallucinating and whose thinking is heavily involved with fantasy may not perform up to his intellectual potential. The same is true of the overanxious or inhibited child with subpar perform-

ance. A psychiatric examination is useful in determining the importance of emotional factors and their influence on intellectual functioning.

Evaluation of the family by a social worker is extremely helpful in clarifying the family's attitude towards the retarded or handicapped child. A study of family dynamics, siblings and extended family relationships, and the family's economic situation, are essential in assisting the physician in formulating appropriate recommendations. The family may confide important information to the social worker that they will not tell to the physician. In these situations, the social worker can communicate with the family more effectively than can the physician. Social service counseling for the families of retarded children is most useful after the completion of the diagnostic evaluation. The social worker may also be helpful to the family in establishing contacts between the family and appropriate community resources.

In many areas of the country, centers have been established to evaluate children with suspected mental retardation. These diagnostic centers are interdisciplinary and usually consist of a pediatrician or pediatric neurologist, psychiatrist, psychologist, social worker, educational consultant, and a nurse. Speech, occupational, and physical therapists are often included. The team approach is often useful in delineating all the factors affecting the function of the referred patient. This is especially helpful in cases that present complex diagnostic problems. However, the full-team approach appears unnecessary in the more straightforward cases where the diagnosis, treatment, and prognosis are more obvious. In such cases a physician with knowledge of community resources for retardates may well be able to handle the problem effectively, without referral to a major diagnostic and treatment center.

TREATMENT. *General Comments.* Since the causes of mental retardation are complex and multifactorial, there is no single therapeutic approach which is universally applicable to all individuals with this condition.

Cases of mental retardation due to apparently treatable metabolic disorders, e.g., PKU, are rare and are among the few currently known disorders where a relatively uncomplicated procedure, such as dietary changes, may produce a major change in the course of the disease. Conditions such as hydrocephalus that can cause mental retardation can be corrected by neurosurgical procedures. With early treatment, the results are generally favorable.

The need to identify curable conditions accurately and promptly is of obvious importance. But it is essential to stress that any therapeutic recommendations in the more complex multifactorial cases of mental subnormality must be based on a thorough understanding of the relative importance of the organic, psychologic, genetic, and social (environment) components in producing the intellectual deficiency. The child's parents must be given a practical and meaningful interpretation of the child's problems and behavior, along with an understanding of the anticipated changes in function and behavior that occur with maturation. Physicians dealing with parents of retarded children must be forthright in indicating when the prognosis is poor and, at the same time, admit when the prognosis is uncertain. The need for periodic reevaluation, in order to assess a child's progress, must be stressed. If the physician is candid with the family and conveys, with compassion and sympathy, his genuine concerns about the child to the family, then shopping for "other opinions" will be minimized.

Educational Programs. The major burden in the treatment of mental retardation usually falls on the shoulders of the educator. Many clinics that care for retarded and handicapped children include a psychoeducational consultant in the diagnostic team. Consultants of this type have been developing and applying increasingly sophisticated diagnostic techniques which go beyond the simple determination of IQ level. Tests such as the Illinois Test of Psycholinguistic Abilities (ITPA) have been increasingly applied in order to separate the various sensory modalities and integrative components from the conceptual and memory functions involved in learning. Use of Frostig tests have assisted in pinpointing perceptual problems, and the recent work of Birch and Lefford has demonstrated the significance of visual, kinesthetic, and haptic integrative defects in brain-damaged children. In addition, Birch and Belmont have devised a test of visual-auditory integration, a function which appears to be defective in some individuals with language disturbances and learning disabilities.

The above diagnostic procedures, by pinpointing areas of weakness and strength, can be useful in developing an educational prescription for the mildly retarded child with learning difficulties. It must be stressed that, whatever the remedial techniques that are applied, the success in a particular child is usually dependent on the child's basic abilities or disabilities plus: (1) the interest, attitude, and enthu-

siasm of the instructor; (2) the motivation and cooperation of the child; (3) the amount of time allotted for instruction, which may be related to class size; and (4) the degree of structuring in the program. The difficulty in accurately determining the relative importance of all of these variables has complicated the task of assessing the true worth of many of the special educational techniques that are currently being applied.

Types of classes or educational programs for the retarded vary in each community. Despite the division of retarded children into educable and trainable categories, the educational methods for teaching the two groups do tend to overlap. Higher- and lower-track classes in each category, if available, may provide a useful means of selecting children with better or improved functioning and using available resources more efficiently and effectively. The higher-track educable child should achieve a fourth to fifth grade level in reading and math, but have limited ability to reason abstractly. The lower-track educable child will struggle to acquire third grade skills. The higher-track trainable child may be "trained" in activities of daily living and learn first and second grade math, reading, writing, and spelling. The lower-track trainable usually acquires no formal academic skills.

Social and Recreational Needs. Of all areas of treatment for the retarded child, this is the most sensitive area to deal with appropriately. The retarded child is generally rejected by his chronologic peers, by society in general, and often by his siblings and even his family. Yet, like any other child, he has social and recreational needs. These are usually unmet. In school he is usually isolated with other children who show similar problems. Meaningful social relationship with healthy models are few and far between. Retarded children and adolescents desperately need after-school social and recreational programs and these are usually unavailable.

Behavioral Modification. *Operant conditioning.* Experimental techniques to modify retarded children's behavior by training or conditioning via a system of rewards and/or punishments, using positive and negative reinforcement, are currently being more widely applied. These methods, commonly called "operant conditioning," have produced some dramatic improvement in gross functioning, and in achieving independence in activities of daily living, in moderate to severely retarded and emotionally disturbed children. Similar techniques applied to more mildly retarded children appear to have produced some successful results in improving learning and behavior under experimental and controlled conditions. The suitability of these techniques, and the advisability of the application of these procedures on a more widespread basis, is rather uncertain.

Drugs. Drug treatment in mentally retarded children has essentially been confined to the application of appropriate medications to treat specific symptoms in selected patients. No specific medications have as yet been demonstrated to improve overall mental functioning in retarded children.

Certain drugs have been useful in treating mentally retarded children with concomitant medical problems. Retarded children with epilepsy should be given appropriate anticonvulsant medications. An occasional child with petit mal status may appear retarded and/or autistic. When this is diagnosed by EEG and effectively treated, it may result in a dramatic improvement in mental functioning. The same dramatic results have been reported in a few individuals with psychomotor seizures. A substantial number of children with "minimal brain damage" are very hyperactive and have a short attention span, and appear to function as mildly retarded children. In many of these patients, the hyperkinesis diminishes when they are placed on Dexedrine or Ritalin, which often has a paradoxical effect on brain-damaged children. In such cases, an improved attention span may result in better academic performance and, on retesting, improvement in IQ scores.

The retarded child with significant emotional problems may also benefit from drug treatment. A high anxiety level, stemming from feelings of frustration, recurrent failure, and a sense of rejection, all may have adverse effects on the academic performance of the brain-damaged child, whether or not he functions in the retarded range. A child of this type benefits from tranquilizers such as the phenothiazines, though the effective dosage level may be quite variable. With a decrease in the level of anxiety, concomitant improvement in intellectual functioning may occur. However, it should be pointed out that drug therapy in brain-damaged, hyperactive, anxious, or emotionally disturbed children merely permits the expression of the underlying intellectual potential and has no direct effect in improving intelligence per se.

Vocational training. The majority of mild retardates appear to fade into the general employed population. Academic failure does increase the probability of unemployment, but factors other than IQ level may have a significant determining role in this regard. In an increasingly complex technologic society, the labor market for unskilled workers is shrinking, and job openings for mildly mentally retarded individuals are becoming more scarce. Thus, vocational training of mild retardates for semiskilled or repetitive jobs, in which some retarded individuals show greater perseverance than nonretardates, is essential. Individuals must be selected who are emotionally stable, and they must be placed in situations where they are supervised and not required to make significant decisions involving abstract reasoning.

For the mild retardate, success as an adult in the community is more dependent on good social and emotional adjustments than on academic achievement. The mild retardate is more likely to be ostracized when he has a: (1) personality disorder; (2) speech defect; (3) motor problem; or (4) cosmetic defect. Motivational factors are also paramount in determining a young retardate's ultimate success. Failures experienced in early childhood often lead to loss of initiative and a fear of competing. Zigler has shown how important motivational reinforcement may be in helping a retardate achieve at a higher level.

It is difficult to provide employment for the moderate to severely disabled and retarded. Sheltered workshops, "half-way houses" (part-time residencies and part-time outside employment), and closely supervised restricted employment programs provide only a few of the answers to this complex and challenging problem.

Institutionalization. One of the most difficult problems facing the physician who cares for a retarded child is the role of institutional placement. Surveys of institutions that care for retarded children indicate that the majority of the resident children fall into the moderate to severely retarded range. In general, the most severely defective, and in particular, the more deformed or stigmatized the infant or child, the earlier the referral for residential care will be initiated.

When dealing with parents of a young infant with multiple deformities or Down's syndrome, where the prognosis is relatively clear, the pediatrician's or family physician's role as a counselor to the family is often compromised by what the obstetrician may already have told the parents. If the pediatrician is the first to inform the parents of the diagnosis, his approach may be more flexible. A complete exposition of diagnosis and all the prognostic implications during the first interview is usually too overwhelming for most young parents. The details of the problem are best elaborated in a series of visits and discussions with, if possible, *both* parents, so that genetic as well as prognostic implications can be explored. Social service and psychiatric assistance may be necessary to deal with feelings of guilt or severe depression in some of the cases.

The question of institutional placement almost always arises early in infants with Down's syndrome or with stigmata that are usually associated with mental retardation. Immediate residential placement is usually difficult to arrange even if the parents decide they wish to institutionalize the child rather than take the baby home with them from the hospital. The physician's responsibility in such cases is to inform the families of the facts and prognosis, and describe, without bias, the realities and/or rewards that result from living with and rearing a retarded and stigmatized child. The physician may offer advice in these matters, particularly if he is well acquainted with the family's social dynamics and finances. However, he should not make the final decision about institutional placement. The family is on firmest ground when the decision is made by them, and the physician acts only as an advisor.

The above principles generally apply to children who are diagnosed as being retarded at any age. In order for the parents to make an intelligent decision concerning home care versus institutional placement, the family must be aware of the child's diagnosis and prognosis, the available nonresidential educational, social, and community facilities for the child, as well as the nature of the residential facilities for the community. Visits to these residential centers and state schools should be encouraged prior to a submission of an application for admission. When the parents come to the physician for advice concerning this matter, he, too, should be aware of the nature of the facilities in his community. Parents' groups such as the National Association for the Help of Retarded Children or Association for the Aid of Crippled Children are often useful in supplying this information to the physician and the family. Finally, when the physician does advise the family on the question of residential placement, he should consider the total effect of the retarded child on this particular family. He should also provide the family with some needed insight and, as far as is possible, be supportive.

Institutionalization is considered most often when the affected children are at the chronologic extremes of the pediatrician's practice. The parent of the severely retarded or stigmatized infant has good reason for considering early placement. The parent of the mild to moderately retarded child usually maintains that child at home with the help of community programs. However, as adolescence approaches, behavior problems increase and become unmanageable. Vocational and recreational opportunities seem unavailable. There is fear of sexual abuse to naive female retardates or unwarranted concern about sexual aggressivity in male retardates. As a result, parents of retarded children reconsider or first consider the idea of residential placement. This is particularly true if the parents are advanced in age and concerned about "who will care for the child after they are gone."

There has been considerable controversy and discussion concerning the faults of most state institutions for the retarded in the United States and elsewhere. Archaic philosophies and limited allocation of funds have created many large overcrowded institutions with poorly trained staffs and limited therapeutic programs. However, it can be firmly stated that the tide is now turning. The problems of institutional care are being debated, new programs being created, and new funds being provided. No longer will children be "put away" in institutions but, for those who are able, they will be sent there for rehabilitation and training.

Chromosomal (Autosomal) Disorders Associated with Mental Retardation

TRISOMY 21 (DOWN'S SYNDROME). This disease entity was first described by Langdon Down in 1866.

It has more recently been demonstrated to be associated with a consistent cytologic anomaly, the presence of an excess of chromosomal material derived from all or part of chromosome number 21. Karyotypic analysis reveals that the majority of patients with Down's syndrome have 47 chromosomes with a trisomy of chromosome number 21 (Fig. 27). The underlying genetic mechanism for this event is nondisjunction.

A small percentage of individuals with Down's syndrome have a structural chromosomal abnormality called a translocation with a total chromosome number of 46. Translocations occur because of centric fusion of two chromosomes and most commonly involve chromosomes number 21 and 15. However, translocations involving chromosomes 21 and 25 have been reported.

There are individuals who have been found to be mildly or moderately affected whose cells karyotypically are mixtures of normal cells and cells trisomic for chromosome number 21. This condition is called mosaicism and results either from nondisjunction in early cell division of normal zygote or from the loss of a chromosome in a developing trisomic zygote.

There is a correlation with maternal age (Fig. 28). The trisomy 21 anomaly is encountered with increasing frequency with older mothers; while the rarer translocation anomaly is seen in younger mothers. However, the birth of a child with trisomy 21 may occur at any maternal age.

The etiology of the cytogenetic disturbance associated with Down's syndrome remains unknown. In addition to maternal age, autoantibodies (thyroid) and maternal radiation have both been implicated as possible etiologic factors.

Clinical Findings. Patients with Down's syndrome are usually recognized at birth and become more recognizable with advancing age (Fig. 29). No one symptom or combination of symptoms is diagnostic. Trisomy and translocation patients are clinically indistinguishable. However, mosaics have atypical signs, and normal intellect has been reported in some cases. The clinical features are listed in Table 8. The findings printed in italics are the most frequent ones reported.

Pathology. Extensive neuropathologic changes have been observed, but both the gross and microscopic abnormalities are variable and are not specific of Down's syndrome. Macro- and microgyria, delayed myelination of white matter, immature differentiation of ganglion cells, and abnormal embryonic cell piles are all fairly common findings. Thyroid, pituitary, adrenal, and thymus have been reported to show signs of maldevelopment and malfunction.

Intelligence. The intelligence of patients with Down's syndrome is variable and follows a bell-shaped curve, with a median IQ of 40 to 50 in home-reared children, and an overall range of 20 to 70. It has been reported that the rate of intellectual growth declines with passing years. This may

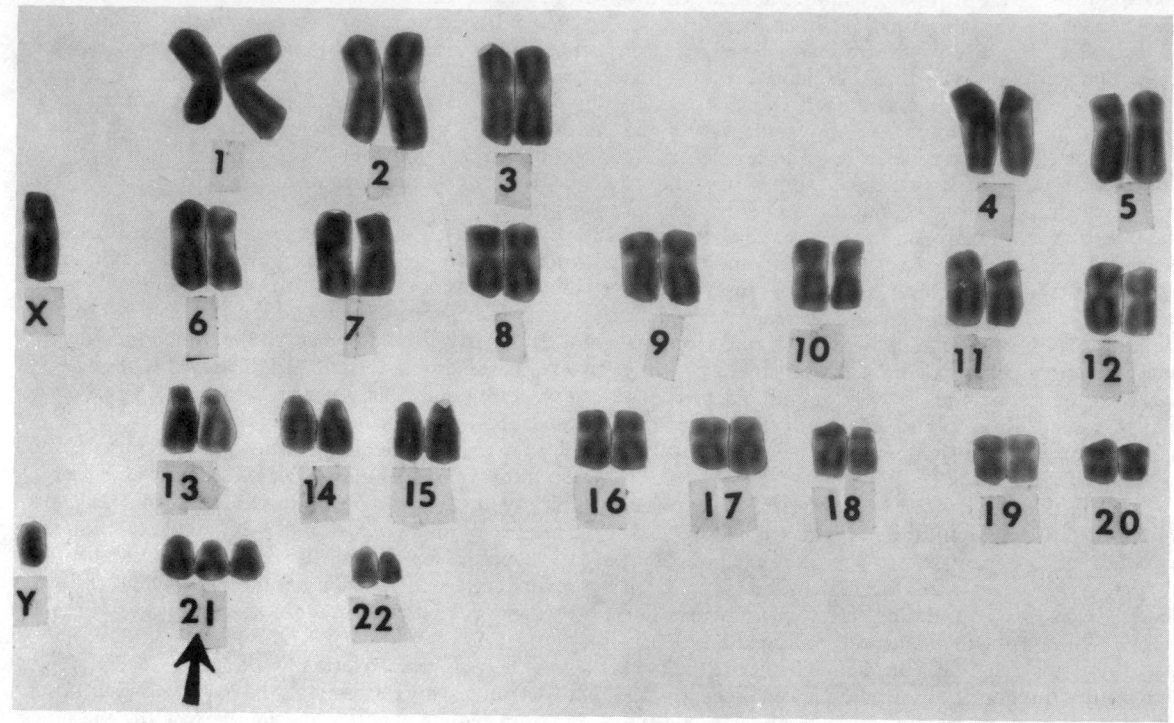

Fig. 27. Karyotype of child with Down's syndrome showing trisomy at chromosome 21 (arrow). (Courtesy of Drs. O. J. Miller and D. Warburton.)

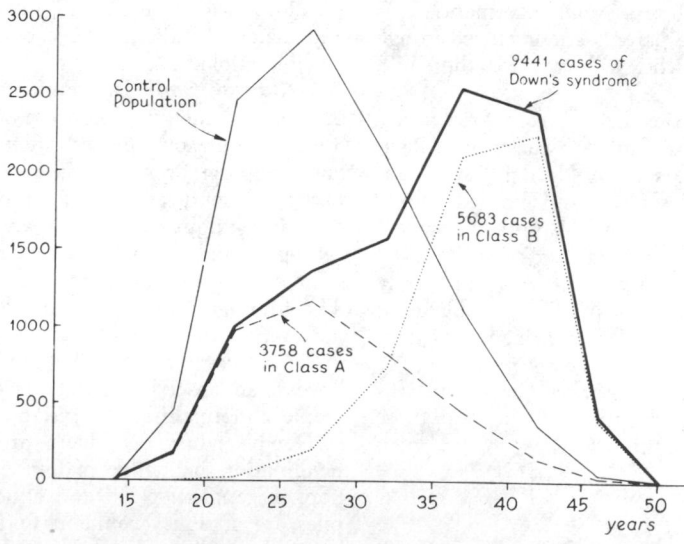

Fig. 28. Maternal age distribution of 9,441 cases of Down's syndrome with control population. (From Penrose and Smith. *Down's Anomaly.* Courtesy of J. & A. Churchill Ltd.)

reflect the possibility of CNS degeneration related to premature aging, or a possible arrest in psychologic and social capacities. It may be that since the tests have been standardized on normal individuals, they may not reflect "normal" maturation of children with Down's syndrome who have defective brains.

Development. Almost all uncomplicated Down's individuals ambulate by 3 to 4 years of age and over 90 percent develop simple language by 5 years of age. The aging process is more rapid. Cataracts

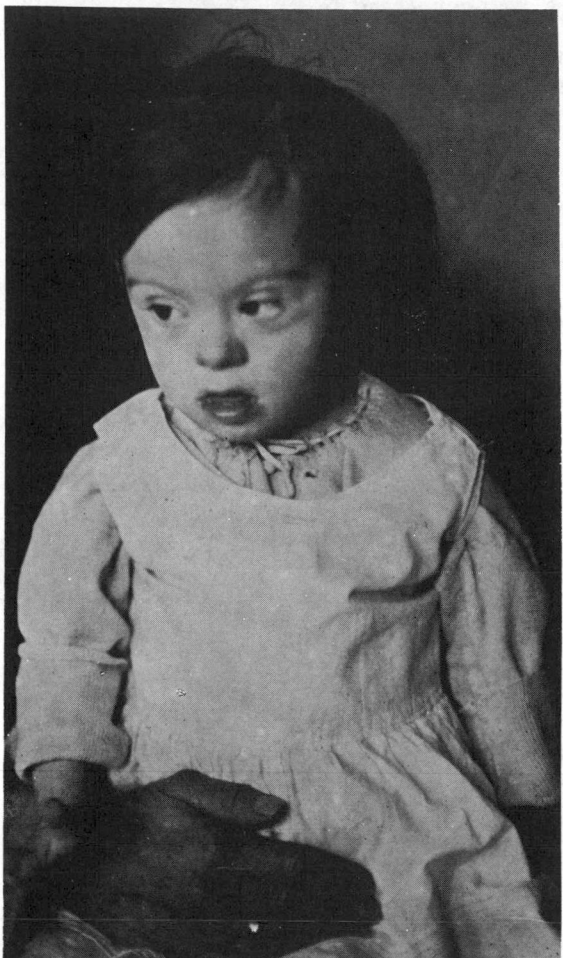

Fig. 29. Girl 4 years of age with Down's syndrome showing characteristic facies.

TABLE 8.   *Clinical Features in Down's Syndrome* *

Head	Microcephaly; *flat occiput;* brachycephaly
Eyes	*Inner and outer epicanthal folds slanted upwards and outwards;* bilateral speckling of iris (Brushfield's spots) around limbic area; strabismus; refractive error; cataracts in early adulthood
Ears	*Simple or aberrant helix formation;* low set
Nose	Usually small with flattened bridge
Mouth	Tongue large and fissured; *nasopharynx small* (causes mouth breathing); abnormal morphology and frequent absence of teeth
Neck	Short; occasional webbing
Hands	*Stubby, distal triradius; radial loop on digit IV and ulnar loops of all other digits;* digital loop between digits IV and V; *incurved short 5th fingers (clinodactyly) with single crease; single four finger breadth midpalmar crease (Simian line)* (usually bilateral)
Feet	Short and stubby; widespread 1st and 2nd toes; deep crease leading distally from angle of 1st and 2nd toes; distinctive dermatoglyphics
Abdomen	*Protruberant; umbilical hernia;* duodenal atresia; megacolon; microcolon
Skin	Dry; decreased elasticity
Heart	*Septal defects;* pulmonary stenosis; aortic stenosis
Genitalia	Male—testes undescended; small penis Female—labia minora underdeveloped; menopause early
Pelvis	Iliac wings large and flared; *iliac index measured on x-ray is decreased*
Neurologic	*Hypotonia,* normoreflexia; poor fine and gross coordination
Speech	Voice is usually low-pitched and "raucous"; speech has infantile omissions and substitutions

*The more common clinical features are italicized.

and arteriosclerosis are frequent complications in early adult life. A rapid metabolic turnover has been implicated as a possible cause for this phenomenon. For example, the life-span of polymorphonuclear leucocytes is shortened. This is illustrated by a decreased lobe count per cell.

Laboratory Findings. Laboratory investigations have yielded inconsistent findings, including the following reported abnormalities: serum serotonin is decreased; acid and alkaline phosphase of white blood cells are increased; and glucose-6-phosphate dehydrogenase of red blood cells is increased. Some variation and differences in these findings have been reported between the translocation and trisomic types.

Treatment. There is no specific medical treatment for this condition. Though many drugs have been tried in an attempt to improve this condition, treatments with vitamins, special diets, and thyroid medication have proved unsuccessful.

Prognosis. Individuals with Down's syndrome functioning within the mild to high moderate range

of mental retardation can be educated to early grade level accomplishments. Many of these can find employment in a sheltered workshop. Very few, if any, become independent in the community. Their cosmetic defect adds to their problem in being accepted, even if their IQ permits them to compete vocationally.

The average life-span of patients is shortened and one half die by the end of the third year, mostly as a result of respiratory infections and congenital heart disease. Most of the remaining patients succumb by 40 to 50 years of age for reasons believed to be related to rapid aging processes. Leukemia occurs three times more frequently than in normal children.

Genetic Counseling. If the mother is under 35 years of age, karyotypically normal, and has a trisomic

TABLE 9.   *Comparison of the Findings in Trisomy D and Trisomy E*

	Trisomy D (13/15)	Trisomy E (16/18)
Incidence	0.45 per 1,000 live births	0.23 per 1,000 live births
Sex ratio	F > M	F > M
Maternal age	30.8 years	34.4 years (control 28.5)
Birth weight	Average or low	Small for gestational age
Rate of growth	Normal	Slow
Mental retardation	Severe	Severe
Seizures	Minor motor; apneic episodes	Occasional
Tone	Hypertonic or normal	Hypertonic
Hearing	Impaired	Normal
Head	Microcephaly; sloping fore-head; abnormal calcification	Prominent occiput
Eyes	Microophthalmus; coloboma of iris; corneal opacities	Ptosis or lid abnormalities
Ears	Low set; abnormal helix	Low set
Mouth	Cleft palate; cleft lip	Small
Skin	Capillary hemangiomata Necrotic ulcers of scalp	Mottled; lanugolike hair
Hands	Polydactyly; flexed fingers, hyperconvex and narrow fingernails; retroflexible thumbs	Clenched fingers, index over third; syndactyly
Feet	Posterior prominence of heels, polydactyly	Big toe short and in hammer position; rocker-bottom feet
Heart	Dextrocardia; ventricular septal defect	Ventricular septal defect; patent ductus arteriosus
Kidney	Obstructive hydronephrosis	Double ureter
Hernia	Umbilical	Umbilical and inguinal
Genitalia	Abnormal scrotum; crypt-orchidism; bicornuate uterus	—
Skeletal	—	Short sternum, small pelvis, small mandible; delayed ossification
Other	Accessory spleen; enlarged gallbladder (stenosis of bile duct); incomplete rotation of colon	Eventration of diaphragm
Dermatoglyphics	Distal axial triradius; Simian crease; arch fibular pattern in the hallucal area of foot	Simple area pattern for nearly all digits; single flexion crease 5th finger; occasional Simian crease
Death	Early childhood	Early infancy

offspring, the risk of recurrence is low. In contrast, a mother over 35 years of age would have a six times greater risk of a recurrence.

If the propositus is found to have mosaicism or a translocation anomaly, chromosome studies should be performed on both parents, and on any siblings. A phenotypically normal individual may be a carrier of the translocation. Appropriate genetic counseling on recurrence risks can then be offered by the physician.

13/15 TRISOMY (D) (PATAU SYNDROME). The main clinical findings are listed in Table 9. These babies

A

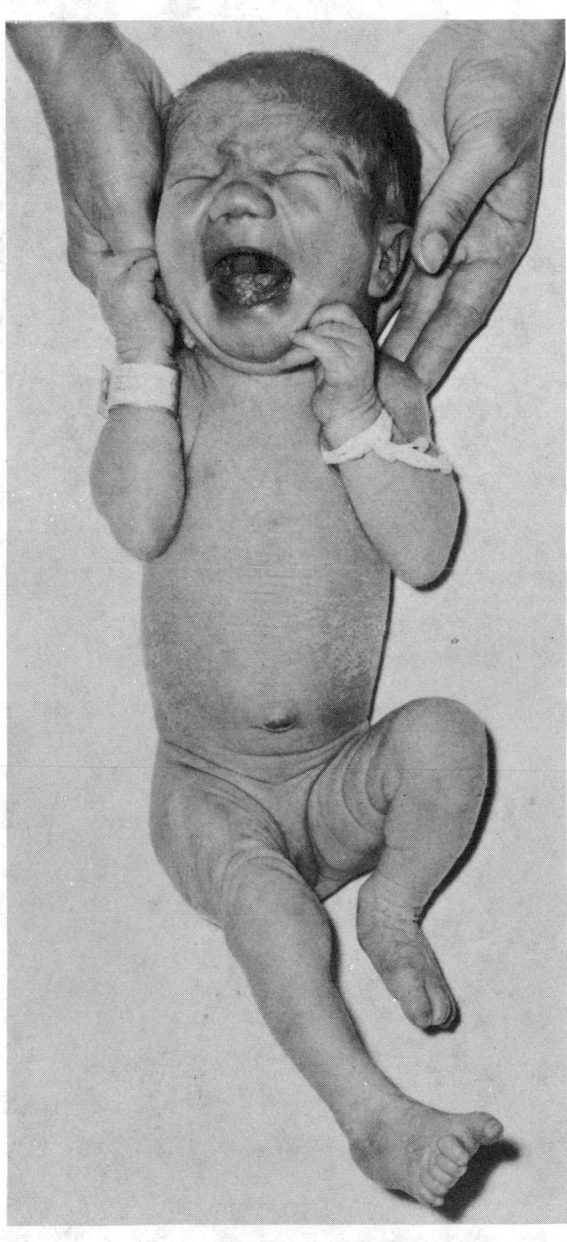

B

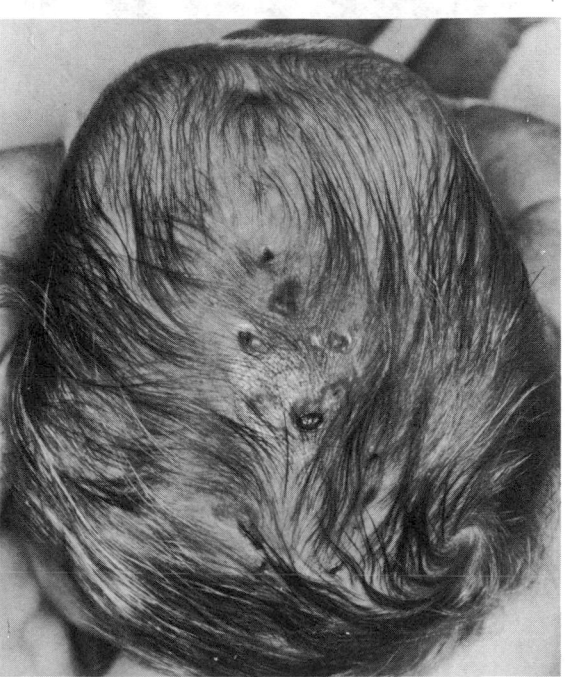

Fig. 30. Trisomy 13/15 (D) showing characteristic clinical features. **A.** (*Left*) Some of the anomalies associated with Trisomy 13: microphthalmia, cleft palate, and polydactyly. **B.** (*Above*) Typical necrotic ulcers seen in Trisomy 13. (Courtesy of Drs. J. Lindsten and P. Zetterquist.)

are usually easily recognized at birth since their deformities are quite vivid and distinctive (Fig. 30A and B). The majority have a cleft palate and lip, low-set malformed ears, microphthalmia, capillary hemangioma, polydactyly, and congenital heart disease. Familial D/D translocation has been described.

A shortened life expectancy is the rule, with death usually occurring in the first year of life.

TRISOMY E (18). The addition of an extra chromosome in the E group causes a distinct clinical syndrome (Fig. 31A, B, C, and D). Children with this chromosomal defect are of low birth weight and have numerous stigmata including a prominent occiput, micrognathia, low-set ears, overlapping of the second and third digits, multiple contractures (arthrogryposis), and rocker-bottom feet (Table 9). These infants fail to thrive, and usually die within the first few months of life. Congenital heart and renal anomalies are common postmortem findings. The few children who survive beyond the first few months of life have severe developmental retardation.

CRI DU CHAT SYNDROME (PARTIAL DELETION OF SHORT ARM OF CHROMOSOME 4 OR 5). Lejeune and his co-workers described this syndrome which is named after a characteristic cry of the infants so affected. Most observers have described the cry as resembling the mewing of a cat.

The clinical features (Fig. 32) are listed in Table 10. Findings such as an antimongoloid slant of the eyes, a moon facies, brachycephaly, epicanthi, and hypertelorism may suggest Down's syndrome. However, in this syndrome, increased maternal age is not common. Some familial translocations have been reported. Mental retardation is usually severe in cases of Cri du Chat, but despite this, the child's life-span is usually not significantly shortened.

MONOSOMY G (22/22 MONOSOMY, ANTIMONGOLISM). These patients are clinically almost the antithesis of the trisomy 21. Findings include antimongoloid slants of the eyes, hypertonia, and severe mental retardation. Only rare cases of monosomy G have been reported.

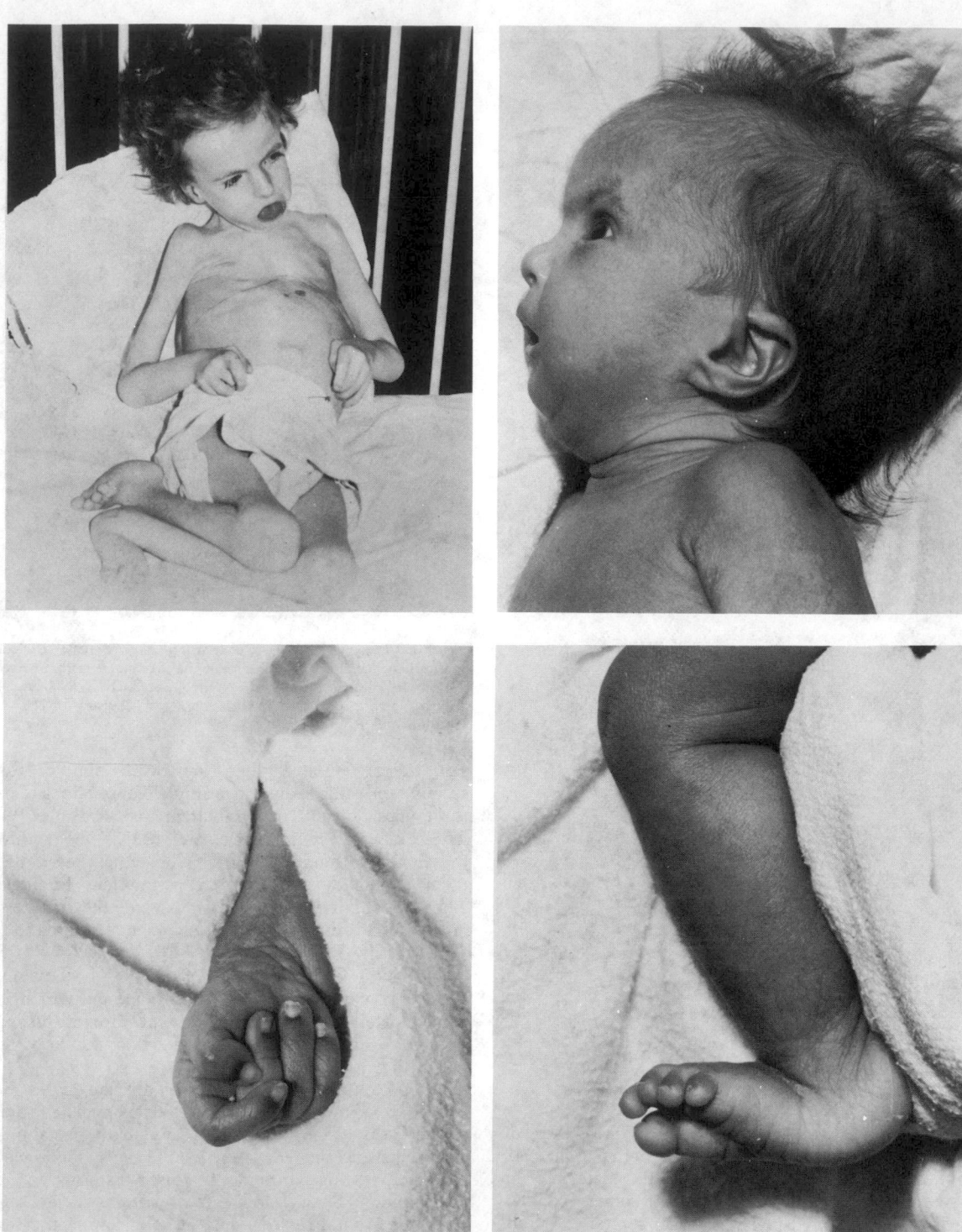

Fig. 31. Trisomy 18 (E) showing characteristic clinical features. A. Note emaciation, flexion contractures of extremities, abnormal positioning of fingers, and "rocker-bottom" feet. B. Profile of face demonstrating micrognathia and low-set ears. C. Abnormal positioning of index finger with deviation to ulnar side, crossing backward over the middle finger. D. "Rocker-bottom" foot with short big toe. (Courtesy of Drs. W. W. Weber, P. Mamunes, R. Day, and Phebe Miller.)

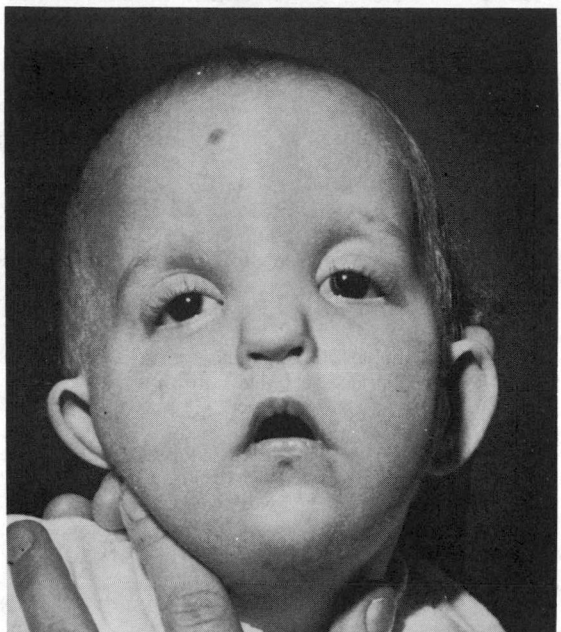

Fig. 32. Characteristic facies of Cat Cry syndrome (Cri du Chat). Note round moon face, hypertelorism, oblique palpebral fissures and low-set ears. (Courtesy of Drs. O. J. Miller and D. Warburton.)

TABLE 10. *Clinical Findings in Cri Du Chat Syndrome (Partial Deletion of Short Arm of Chromosome 4 or 5)*

Always present
    Abnormal cry
    Severe mental retardation
    Microcephaly
    Hypertelorism
    Epicanthus
    Abnormal dermatoglyphics

Frequently present
    Failure to thrive
    Brachycephaly
    Moon face
    Antimongoloid slant
    Low-set ears
    Micrognathia
    Hypotonia
    Strabismus

Occasionally Present
    Short neck
    Optic atrophy
    Congenital heart disease

RING CHROMOSOMES (A, 5, C, D, E, 16, 17, 18, AND X). Mental retardation is the one universal finding in the different ring chromosomal abnormalities. The clinical picture is variable. The findings are rarely distinctive enough to be identified as a single syndrome.

Sex Chromosome Abnormalities
(See also Sec. 16.11)

KLINEFELTER'S SYNDROME (XXY). The extra X chromosome causes a eunochoid appearance. On examination, arm span is noted to be greater than height, facial and body hair is sparse, and the patient's voice is high-pitched. Gynecomastia is usually present. Testes are small but the penis is of normal size. Compared with the general population there is an increase in the prevalence of asthma and diabetes mellitus. Many, but not all, are mildly retarded. Psychotic illness appears also to be more common and usually is diagnosed as a "severe anxiety neurosis."

Laboratory findings include an increased output of urinary pituitary gonadotropins. A decreased uptake of ^{131}I by the thyroid gland is occasionally noted. Klinefelter patients are usually infertile. Testicular biopsy reveals clumping of the Leydig cells and abnormalities of the seminiferous tubules. Life-span is not usually shortened.

TURNER'S SYNDROME (XO). Mild mental retardation is infrequently a feature of the syndrome.

"SUPERFEMALE" (XXX and XXXX SYNDROME). In the XXXX syndrome all have been retarded, while normal intelligence may occur with the XXX syndrome. Short stature is a common characteristic in these patients.

"DOUBLE MALE" SYNDROME (YY, XYY, XXYY, and XXXYY). XYY individuals have been reported to have a tendency toward aggressive, psychopathic, and antisocial behavior. Mild mental retardation is occasionally associated with these findings. It is uncertain to what extent the mental defect or the chromosomal anomaly influences or determines the behavioral traits observed in this syndrome.

Combined or Multiple Cytogenetic Abnormalities

Down's syndrome has been noted in association with Klinefelter's syndrome. XXY trisomy has been reported in 6.25 percent of males with Down's syndrome in a survey done soon after birth, and in only 0.35 percent of older males with Down's syndrome. The reported difference in relative frequencies may mean that the combination increases the patient's risk for a shortened life-span. Down's syndrome has also been reported in association with XXX, Turner's syndrome, and trisomy D. Of particular interest are the reports of Down's syndrome in patients with sibs who have another type of trisomy (XXY, trisomy E, XXX). This association may reflect a familial predisposition towards chromosomal errors, although they may be purely chance happenings.

References

Birch, H. G., and Lefford, A. Intersensory development in children. Monogr. Soc. Res. Child Develop., 28: Serial No. 89, 1, 1963.

—— and Lefford, A. Two strategies for studying perception in "brain-damaged" children. In Birch, H. G., ed., Brain Damage in Children: The Biological and Social Aspects. Baltimore, Williams and Wilkins Co., 1963.

—— and Belmont, L. Auditory-visual integration, intelligence and reading ability in school children. Percept. Motor Skills, 20:295, 1965.

—— Richardson, S. A., Baird, D., Horokin, G., and Illsley, R. Mental Subnormality in the Community. Baltimore, The Williams and Wilkins Co., 1970.

Chase, H. P., and Martin, H. P. Undernutrition and child development. New Eng. J. Med., 282:933, 1970.

Collman, R. D., and Stoller, A. A. Survey of mongolism and congenital anomalies of the central nervous system in Victoria, New Zealand. New Zeal. Med. J., 61:24, 1962.

Conen, P. E. The "D" syndrome. Amer. J. Dis. Child., 111:236, 1966.

Cravioto, J., DeLicardie, E. R., and Birch, H. G. Nutrition, growth and neurointegrative development: an experimental and ecologic study. Pediatrics, 38: (Suppl.)2:331, 1966.

D'Amato, G. Residential Treatment For Child Mental Health. Springfield, Ill., Charles C Thomas, Publ., 1969.

Denhoff, E., Siqueland, M., Komich, P., and Hainsworth, P. K. Developmental and predictive characteristics of items from the Meeting Street School Screening Test. Develop. Med. Child Neurol., 10:220, 1968.

Eisenberg, L. Behavioral manifestations of cerebral damage in children. In Birch, H. G., ed., Brain Damage in Children: The Biological and Social Aspects. Baltimore, Williams and Wilkins Co., 1963.

Frankenburg, W. K., and Dodds, J. B. The Denver Developmental Screening Test. J. Pediat., 71:181, 1967.

French, J. H., Graziani, L. J., and Scheinberg, L. C. Treatment of metabolic and endocrine causes of mental retardation. Mod. Treatm., 4:987, 1967.

Frostig, M., Lefever, D. A., and Whittlesey, R. B. A development test of visual perception for evaluating normal and neurologically handicapped children. Percept. Motor Skills, 12:383, 1961.

Gellis, S. S., and Feingold, M. Atlas of Mental Retardation Syndromes. Washington, D.C., U.S. Dept. of Health, Education and Welfare, 1968.

Gruenberg, E. M. Some epidemiological aspects of congenital brain damage. In Birch, H. G., ed., Brain Damage in Children: The Biological and Social Aspects. Baltimore, Williams and Wilkins Co., 1964.

Haeussermann, E. Estimating developmental potential for preschool children with brain lesions. Amer. J. Ment. Defic., 61:170, 1956.

Haggard, E. W. Social status and intelligence: an experimental study of certain cultural determinants of measured intelligence. Genet. Psychol. Monogr., 49:141, 1954.

Helm, A. W., and Wallace, T. G. The effects of repeatedly retesting the same group on the same intelligence tests: II. high grade mental defectives. Quart. J. Exp. Psychiat., 2:19, 1950.

Hsia, D. Y. Human Developmental Genetics. Chicago, Year Book Medical Publishers, 1968.

Illingworth, R. S. The predictive value of development tests in the first year with special reference to the diagnosis of mental subnormality. J. Child Psychol. Psychiat., 2:210, 1961.

Kirk, S. Early Education of the Mentally Retarded. Urbana, Univ. of Illinois Press, 1958.

—— and McCarthy, J. J. The Illinois Test of Psycholinguistic Abilities—an approach to differential diagnosis. Amer. J. Ment. Defic., 66:399, 1961.

Knobloch, H., and Pasamanick, B. An evaluation of the consistency and predictive value of the 40 week Gesell developmental schedules. Psychiat. Res. Rep., 13:10, 1960.

—— and Pasamanick, B. Predicting intellectual potential in infancy: some variables affecting the validity of developmental diagnosis. Amer. J. Dis. Child., 106:43, 1963.

Laufer, M. W., and Denhoff, E. Hyperkinetic behavior syndrome in children. J. Pediat., 50:463, 1957.

Lilienfeld, A. M., and Pasamanick, B. The association of maternal and fetal factors with the development of mental deficiency. Amer. J. Ment. Defic., 60:557, 1956.

Masland, R. L., Sarason, B., and Gladwin, T. Mental Subnormality. New York, Basic Books, Inc., Publ., 1958.

McCracken, J. S., and Gordon, R. R. Cri du Chat syndrome—a new clinical and cytogenetic entity. Lancet, 1:23, 1965.

Motulsky, A. G. Population genetics of mental retardation. In Jervis, G. A., ed., Expanding Concepts in Mental Retardation. Springfield, Ill., Charles C Thomas, Publ., 1968.

Parker, C. E. Mavalwala, J., Weise, P., Koch, R., Hatashita, A., and Cibilich, S. The 47, XYY syndrome in a boy with behavior problems and mental retardation. Amer. J. Ment. Defic., 74:660, 1970.

Penrose, L. S. A clinical and genetic study of 1280 cases of mental defect. Special Report Series No. 229, Medical Research Council, London, His Majesty's Stationery Office, 1938.

—— and Smith, G. F. Down's Anomaly. London, J. and A. Churchill Ltd., 1966.

Polani, P. E. Cytogenetics of Down's syndrome. In Jervis, G. A., ed., Expanding Concepts in Mental Retardation. Springfield, Ill., Charles C Thomas, Publ., 1968, Ch. 4.

Sheridan, M. D. Infants at risk of handicapping conditions. Monthly Bull. Minist. Health (London), 21: 238, 1962.

Sievers, D. J. Development and standardization of a test of psycholinguistic growth in preschool children. Unpublished Ph.D. Thesis, Univ. of Illinois, 1955.

Smith, D. W. The 18 trisomy and D trisomy syndromes. Pediat. Clin. of N. Amer., 10:389, 1963.

Stein, Z. A., and Susser, M. W. The social distribution of mental retardation. Amer. J. Ment. Defic., 67:811, 1963.

Taylor, A. I. Patau's, Edward's and Cri du chat syndrome. A tabulated summary of current findings. Develop. Med. Child Neurol., 9:78, 1967.

Telfer, M. A., Baker, D., Clark, G. R., and Richardson, C. E. Incidence of gross chromosomal errors among tall criminal American males. Science, 159:1249, 1968.

Tizard, J., and O'Connor, N. The employability of high

grade mental defectives: I. Amer. J. Ment. Defic., 54:563, 1950.

———— Psychological development of handicapped children. Brit. Med. J., 1:1041, 1960.

Uchide, I. A., and Soltan, H. C. Evaluation of dermatoglyphics in medical genetics. Pediat. Clin. N. Amer., 10:409, 1962.

Wertelecki, W., Schindler, A. M., and Gerald, P. S. Partial deletion of chromosome 18. Lancet, 2:641, 1960.

15.4
THE DEGENERATIVE AND DEMYELINATING DISEASES OF THE NERVOUS SYSTEM

ARTHUR L. DREW, JR.

The progressive, degenerative, and demyelinating diseases of the nervous system present themselves clinically with a wide diversity of symptoms according to primary anatomic sites involved (Table 11). They have a number of features in common. They are essentially hereditable and thus can be presumed to be the result of transmissible enzymatic defects most of which, at the present time, are not clearly defined. The basic mode of inheritance is that of a single autosomal recessive gene, although examples of sex linkage and dominant Medelian patterns are known. Recent transmission of Kuru and Creutzfeldt-Jakob disease from man to animal raises the possibility that some of the obscure degenerative diseases of infancy and childhood, for instance the spongiform encephalopathies, may be due to transmissible infective agents, "slow" or "temperate" viruses. Further, studies of subacute sclerosing panencephalitis reveal the presence of measles virus and suggest an atypical immune response as yet another pathogenic mechanism of progressive degenerative diseases of the nervous system.

Except for a few rare forms in which the degenerative processes are present at birth, this group of diseases is characterized by the insidious onset of progressive central nervous system degeneration in a previously normally functioning child. Thus, the history of developmental regression is of extreme diagnostic importance. Such a history should always be sought. There tends to be rather marked variability from case to case even within a given family. Numerous atypical, abortive, and transitional forms are encountered and described.

In none of this group of diseases is therapy satisfactory, although in the more chronic forms considerable symptomatic and supportive treatment can and should be offered. Genetic counseling is of great importance.

Although the genetic origin of many of these diseases is well established, details of pathogenesis are not clear. Nevertheless, it is possible to classify some general types. There is the group in which the evidence for the presence of an inborn error of metabolism has been established or strongly suspected. In this group, various amino-acidurias, hepatolenticular degeneration, cerebromacular degeneration, galactosemia, the mucopolysaccharidoses, and metachromatic leucodystrophy may be included. Another group consists of the diffuse cerebral scleroses and disseminated scleroses, in which the fundamental pathologic processes are primary demyelination. There are also a number of progressive degenerative syndromes involving the basal ganglia, spinal cord, cerebellum, and peripheral nerves to which the term "abiotrophy" has been applied. In these there is a slow, genetically predetermined, and systematic decay of neural elements. Disorders in which there are degenerative changes in the nervous system associated with skin lesions are classified as neurocutaneous or neuroectodermal syndromes.

The diagnosis of degenerative disease can be difficult, and the exact delineation of these progressive disorders presents a challenge to even the most sophisticated. They must be differentiated from the static nonprogressive entities such as cerebral palsy which often present with similar clinical manifestations. The importance of establishing a correct diagnosis has both prognostic and genetic significance.

Definition and classification has, in the past, been largely dependent, as indicated in Table 11, upon localization of the major site of the pathologic process. Involvement of the gray matter is suggested by the early appearance of seizures, especially the myoclonic variety, and progressive dementia. In white matter disease, the early manifestation may be a progressive spastic paralysis. Rapid advances in neuropathology and biochemistry are leading to a more precise definition of this group of diseases. More precise diagnostic methods are becoming available to the clinician. In an increasing number of cases, correct antemortem diagnosis is now possible. An awareness of the clinical features and the natural history of the disease, and the utilization of appropriate laboratory procedures all contribute towards establishing the correct diagnosis. The age of onset and rate of progression, ethnic origin, changes in head size, systemic and ophthalmologic abnormalities, and specific alterations in urine, blood, and spinal fluid, together with electroencephalographic, electromyographic, and nerve conduction studies, will provide invaluable clues in diagnosis. Good family histories and careful examinations of parents and sibs are mandatory in many of this large group of diseases. Cerebral biopsy, less frequently rectal biopsy, in carefully selected cases and where competent neuropathologic, histochemical, and electron microscopic studies are available, has proved to be of great value in the diagnosis and wider understanding of the degenerative diseases. Cerebral biopsies should not be done for the sole reason that a definitive diagnosis has not been made. They are justified when clinical and laboratory studies point to a

TABLE 11.   *Classification of Degenerative Diseases of the Nervous System*

Diseases of Cerebral Gray Matter

Cerebral Storage Diseases
    Cerebromacular degeneration—Amaurotic familial idiocy (AFI)

	Accumulated Material
Norman-Wood congenital AFI	GD_3 gangliosidosis
Tay-Sachs infantile AFI	GM_2 gangliosidosis
Tay-Sachs with visceral involvement	GM_2 gangliosidosis
Neurovisceral gangliosidosis	GM_1 gangliosidosis
Jansky-Bielchowsky late infantile AFI	
Batten-Mayou-Spielmeyer-Vogt juvenile AFI	lipofuscin
Kufs adult AFI	
Niemann-Pick disease	ceramide-P-choline
Progressive familial myoclonic epilepsy (Unverricht's disease)	Lafore bodies (mucopolysaccharides)
Gaucher's disease	ceramide-glucose
Fabry's disease	ceramide di- and trihexosidosis
Farber's disease	ceramide and gangliosidosis
Cerebral cholesterolosis	cholesterol
Heller's disease	
Mucopolysaccharidoses Types I-III	mucopolysaccharides
Krabbe's disease	ceramide-galactose
Glycogen storage disease Type VIII	glycogen

Nonstorage Cerebral Diseases
    Progressive degeneration of cerebral gray matter
    Alper's disease
    Necrotizing encephalopathy (Leigh's Disease)

Diseases of Cerebral White Matter

Leucodystrophies
    Pelizaeus-Merzbacher's disease
    Metachromatic leucodystrophy
    Globoid-cell leucodystrophy (Krabbe's disease)
    Spongy sclerosis (Canavan's disease)
    Sudanophilic (neutral fat, orthochromic) familial leucodystrophy
    Alexander's disease

Demyelinating Scleroses
    Acute disseminated encephalomyelitides
    Acute necrotizing hemorrhagic leucoencephalitis (Hurst)
    Multiple or disseminated sclerosis
    Neuromyelitis optica (Devic's disease)
    Balo's concentric sclerosis
    Schilder's disease (encephalitis periaxialis diffusa)

Degenerations of the Basal Ganglia (The Extrapyramidal Syndromes)

Juvenile parkinsonism
Huntington's chorea
Dystonia musculorum deformans
Hallervorden-Spatz disease
Hepatolenticular degeneration (Wilson's disease)
Status demyelinisatus
Dyssynergia cerebellaris myoclonica

Polymorphous Neuroabiotrophies

Cerebellar Degeneration
    Spinocerebellar degenerations
        Friedreich's ataxia
        Roussy-Levy syndrome
        Marinesco-Sjögren and Garland-Moorhouse syndrome
        Bassen-Kornzweig syndrome
        Ataxia-telangiectasia

TABLE 11. (continued)

Polymorphous Neuroabiotrophies (continued)

Brainstem and Spinal Cord Degenerations
    Progressive infantile spinal atrophy (Werdnig-Hoffman disease)
    Familial juvenile amyotrophic lateral sclerosis
    Fazio-Londes disease
    Familial amyotrophic dystonic paraplegia

Cranial and Peripheral Nerve Degenerations
    Leber's optic atrophy
    Peroneal muscular atrophy (neuromuscular atrophy, Charcot-Marie-Tooth disease)
    Hypertrophic interstitial neuritis (Dejerine-Sottas disease)
    Heredofamilial mononeuritis multiplex with brachial predilection
    Congenital indifference to pain
    Refsum's syndrome
    Hereditary sensory neuropathy associated with spinal cord disease
    Primary amyloidosis
    Alport's syndrome

Neurocutaneous Syndromes

Tuberous sclerosis
Neurofibromatosis
Encephalotrigeminal angiomatosis (Sturge-Weber-Dimitri syndrome)
Von Hippel-Lindau's disease
Neurocutaneous melanoses
Disseminated hemangiomatosis
Ataxia-telangiectasia
Hemangiectatic hypertrophy of a limb
Rud's syndrome
Sjögren-Larsson's syndrome
Darier's disease
Incontinentia pigmenti
Linear nevus sebaceus
Basal cell nevus syndrome

specific but unconfirmed diagnosis and where specific therapy or genetic counseling are demanding considerations. Some of these processes become evident in early infancy, while others appear in later childhood or early adolescence. Tables 12 A, B, and C outline the more common and better understood entities to be discussed in the sections dealing with degenerative diseases of cerebral gray and white matter.

Diseases of Cerebral Gray Matter

Cerebral Storage Disease

Progressive and excessive accumulation of cerebral lipids within the body of the nerve cell with variable degrees of secondary demyelination is the common pathology of this group. Accumulation is usually the result of defects in enzymatic degradation of lipid components (Table 13).

The major class of cerebral lipids involved in these diseases is the *sphingolipids*. These are fatty acid esters of N-acyl-sphingosine (ceramide) to which phosphoryl choline, hexose, hexoside, and sulfate are joined to form sphingomyelin, cerebroside, ganglioside, glycolipid, and sulfatide.

N-acyl-sphingosine—fatty acid $\longrightarrow$ *ceramide*
Ceramide—galactose—sulfate $\longrightarrow$ *sulfatide*
Ceramide—glucose $\longrightarrow$ *glucocerebroside*
Ceramide—galactose $\longrightarrow$ *galactocerebroside*
Ceramide—P-choline $\longrightarrow$ *sphingomyelin*
Ceramide—hexoside (S) $\longrightarrow$ *ganglioside*

N-acetyl-neuraminic acid (sialic acid)

Svennerhold has proposed what appears to be the best available nomenclature for the complex gangliosides:

G — *ganglioside*
M — *monosialic acid*
D — *disialic acid*
T — *trisialic acid*
1 — *tetrahexoside*
2 — *trihexoside*
3 — *dihexoside*

GM_2-ganglioside, the Tay-Sachs ganglioside, is thus a monosialicganglioside trihexoside.

The second major grouping of cerebral lipids consists of the *glycerophosphatides*. This complex group includes a variety of phosphatide compounds formerly denoted as cephalins and lecithins.

TABLE 12A.   *Differential Diagnosis of the Cerebral Degenerative Disorders of Infancy—Gray Matter*

	Tay-Sachs	Niemann-Pick	Gaucher's	Alper's	Subacute Necrotizing Encephalopathy
Age of onset	4-6 months	Under 6 months	Under 6 months	Under 1 year	Under 1 year, rarely late childhood
Rate of progression	Rapid Death 2-3 years	Rapid Death before 3 years	Very rapid Death before 2 years	Rapid Death before 3 years	Usually rapid Death before 3 years
Ethnic group	Almost all Jewish	50% Jewish	65% Jewish		
Genetic	Recessive	Recessive	Recessive Rarely, dominant		Recessive
Head size	Enlarges late	Normal	Normal	Reduces late	Normal
Skin and/or systemic	Normal	Hepatospleno- megaly Xanthoma of skin, rare	Hepatospleno- megaly	Normal	Normal
Eye	Cherry-red macula Optic atrophy	Cherry-red macula Optic atrophy	Normal	Normal	Optic atrophy
Seizures	Frequent, but late	Rare	Rare	Onset with seizures Myoclonus and other types	Seizures late and rare
Neurologic signs	Early: flaccid paresis Late: spastic paresis Dementia: early Hyperacusis	Spastic paresis Early: dementia	Early: retroflexion of head Strabismus Bulbar palsy Spastic paralysis Early: dementia	Spastic paresis Dementia Cortical blind- ness and deafness	Bulbar palsy Weak, infrequent cry Flaccid paresis with immobility
Blood	Absent fructose- 1-P-aldolase ↑ SGOT ↑ Vacuolated lymphocytes	Vacuolated lymphocytes ↑ Serum lipids ↑ SGOT	↑ Acid phosphatase	Normal	Normal
Urine	Normal	Normal	Normal	Normal	Normal
CSF	Normal	Normal		Normal	Normal
Biopsy	+Rectal	"Foam cells"— bone marrow	Gaucher cells— bone marrow		
X-ray		Diffuse pulmonary infiltrates Demineralization of bone			
Electroretino- gram	Normal				

The final major category of cerebral lipids is the *sterol group*, represented by cholesterol, which comprises about 20 percent of the lipid content of the cerebral white matter in unesterified form. The breakdown of myelin results in an increase in esterified fraction. The triglycerides, normally not present in the central nervous system, accumulate with the myelin breakdown and have been reported as elevated in plasma of patients with Heller's disease.

The specific enzymatic defects have not as yet been determined in all of the cerebral storage diseases (Table 13). The substrate, or storage material, has been fairly well documented in a number of the cerebral lipidoses. Infantile amaurotic idiocy (Tay-Sachs disease) Type I GM$_2$-gangliosidosis is the result of a deficiency in hexosaminidase A. Type II GM$_2$-gangliosidosis is a deficiency in hexosaminidase A and B and a juvenile Type III GM$_2$-gangliosidosis

TABLE 12B. *Differential Diagnosis of the Cerebral Degenerative Disorders of Infancy—White Matter*

	Krabbe's	Metachromatic Leucodystrophy	Spongy Sclerosis (Canavan)	Palizaeus-Merzbacher	Maple Syrup
Age of onset	3-6 months	1-2 years, rarely late childhood	0-4 months	6-24 months	1-2 weeks
Rate of progression	Rapid Death by 2 years	Slow Death by 3-5 years	Rapid Death by 3 years	Slow May survive to adult life	Rapid Death weeks to month
Sex or ethnic group			Most Jewish	Predominantly males	
Genetic	Recessive	Recessive	Recessive	Sex-linked recessive	Recessive (?)
Head size	Normal	Enlarges late	Enlarges early	Normal	Enlarges early
Skin or systemic	Normal	Normal	Normal	Normal	Normal
Eye	Late: optic atrophy	Late: optic atrophy	Optic atrophy blindness	Slow optic atrophy	Optic atrophy
Seizures		Rare	Uncommon	Late	Early, uncommon
Neurologic signs	Spastic paresis Nystagmus Head retraction Bulbar palsy Dementia	Changes in gait Ataxia Combined upper and lower motor neuron signs Bulbar palsy ⎫ Blindness ⎬ late Deafness ⎪ Dementia ⎭	Hypotonia ↓ Spastic diplegia ↓ Decerebrate rigidity	Pendular nystagmus Titubation of head ↓ Cerebellar signs in early childhood ↓ Spastic diplegia late childhood Slow dementia	Rigidity ↓ Decerebrate rigidity Opisthotonus
Miscellaneous		Reduced nerve conduction			+Paper chromatography
Blood	Normal	Normal	Normal	Normal	Hypoglycemia
Urine	Normal	Metachromatic bodies	Normal	Normal	Maple syrup odor +Dinitrophenyl-hydrazine
CSF	↑ Protein (150-300 mg%)	Normal or ↑ protein up to 200 mg%	↑ Pressure Protein normal or up to 200 mg%	Normal	
Biopsy	Brain	Sural nerve	Brain		
X-ray		Nonfilling of gallbladder	Suture separation		

has been reported with a partial deficiency in hexosaminidase A. In Gaucher's disease, glucocerebroside is the accumulated substance. The enzyme defect is a glycolipid-β-glucosidase. The accumulated material in Niemann-Pick's disease is sphingomyelin (ceramide-P-choline). In Fabry's disease, both dihexoside and trihexoside ceramides are stored as a result of a deficiency in trihexoside-β-galactosidase. Farber's disease is the result of ceramide and ganglioside storage. The enzymatic defect is not certain. Cerebral cholesterosis and Hand-Schüller-Christian disease are both characterized by cholesterol deposits. In metachromatic leucodystrophy, ceramide-galactose-sulfate (sulfatide) accumulates as a result of defective degradation, due to a deficiency of cerebroside sulfate sulfatase. A deficiency in thermolabile beta-galactosidase is believed responsible for the accumulation of mucopolysaccharide in Hurler's disease.

CEREBROMACULAR DEGENERATIONS. The traditional classification of these disorders has been based on the association of progressive gray matter degeneration with intracellular lipid storage, secondary white matter demyelination, and macular-retinal degenerative changes. Age of onset, ethnic grouping, and duration have been basic considerations in their nosology.

TABLE 12C.   *Differential Diagnosis of the Cerebral Degenerative Disorders of Childhood*

	Schilder's	Subacute Inclusion Body Encephalitis*	Progressive Familial Myoclonus Epilepsy	Cerebromacular Degeneration		
				Late Infantile	Juvenile	Adult
Age of onset	5-10 years	5-20 years	5-15 years	3-4 years	5-10 years	15-25 years
Rate of progression	Onset abrupt Death in months to 3 years	Variable Death in months to years	Slow Death in 3-10 years	Slow Death in 5-10 years	Slow Death in 10-15 years	Very slow
Genetic			Recessive	Recessive	Recessive	Recessive
Site of pathology	White matter	Predominantly gray matter	Gray matter	Gray matter	Gray matter	Gray matter
Eye	Early: optic neuritis Late: optic atrophy	Rarely chorioretinitis Late: optic atrophy	Normal	Pigmentary degeneration of macula Optic atrophy	Pigmentary degeneration of retina	Normal
Seizures	Early or late	Early: akinetic ↓ myoclonus	Early: grand mal ↓ myoclonus	Early	Relatively early	Early: myoclonus
Neurologic signs	Early: spastic parasis ↓ dementia Late: cortical blindness and deafness aphasia pseudobulbar palsy	Initial: impaired intellect emotional lability Early: dementia abnormal involuntary movements, ataxia, loss of speech Late: decerebrate rigidity	Progressive dementia Ataxia	Ataxia Spastic paresis Dementia Blindness	Blindness Dementia Parkinsonian syndrome Pseudobulbar palsy ↓ Total dementia Spastic quadriparesis	Dementia Ataxia
Laboratory	CSF—normal or ↑ protein ↑ gamma globulin	CSF Marked ↑ gamma globulin		Azurphilic granules in PMN leucocytes	Azurphilic granules in PMN leucocytes	
Electroretinogram				Abnormal	Abnormal	
EEG		"metronomic"				

*Etiologically related to a slow virus infection but clinical course is that of a degenerative disease process.

1. Congenital Amaurotic Familial Idiocy (Norman-Wood)
2. Infantile AFI (Tay-Sachs)
3. Late Infantile AFI (Bielchowsky-Jansky)
4. Juvenile AFI (Batten-Mayou-Spielmyer-Vogt)
5. Adolescent-Adult AFI (Kufs)

More recent neuropathologic and biochemical studies have led to more discrete biochemical characterization of this group of disorders. The following outline, based on recent work, begins to classify these lipid storage diseases at the molecular level as gangliosidoses.

THE GANGLIOSIDOSES.

1. Congenital form: GD_3-gangliosidosis
2. Classical Tay-Sachs disease: GM_2-gangliosidosis

with absence of anodal component of hexosaminidase (isoenzyme A)

3. Tay-Sachs disease with visceral globoside storage: GM_2-gangliosidosis with the absence of both anodal and cathodal components of beta-D-N-hexosaminidase
4. Neurovisceral gangliosidosis (Tay-Sachs with visceral involvement) (generalized gangliosidosis): GM_1-gangliosidosis with both fractions of beta-galactosidase absent.

Type 1: early infantile form with visceromegaly and skeletal changes

Type 2: onset 7 to 14 months without visceromegaly or skeletal changes

TABLE 13. *Metabolic Defects in Lipid Storage Diseases* *†

Constellation of metabolic diseases is characterized by inabilities to degrade sphingolipids

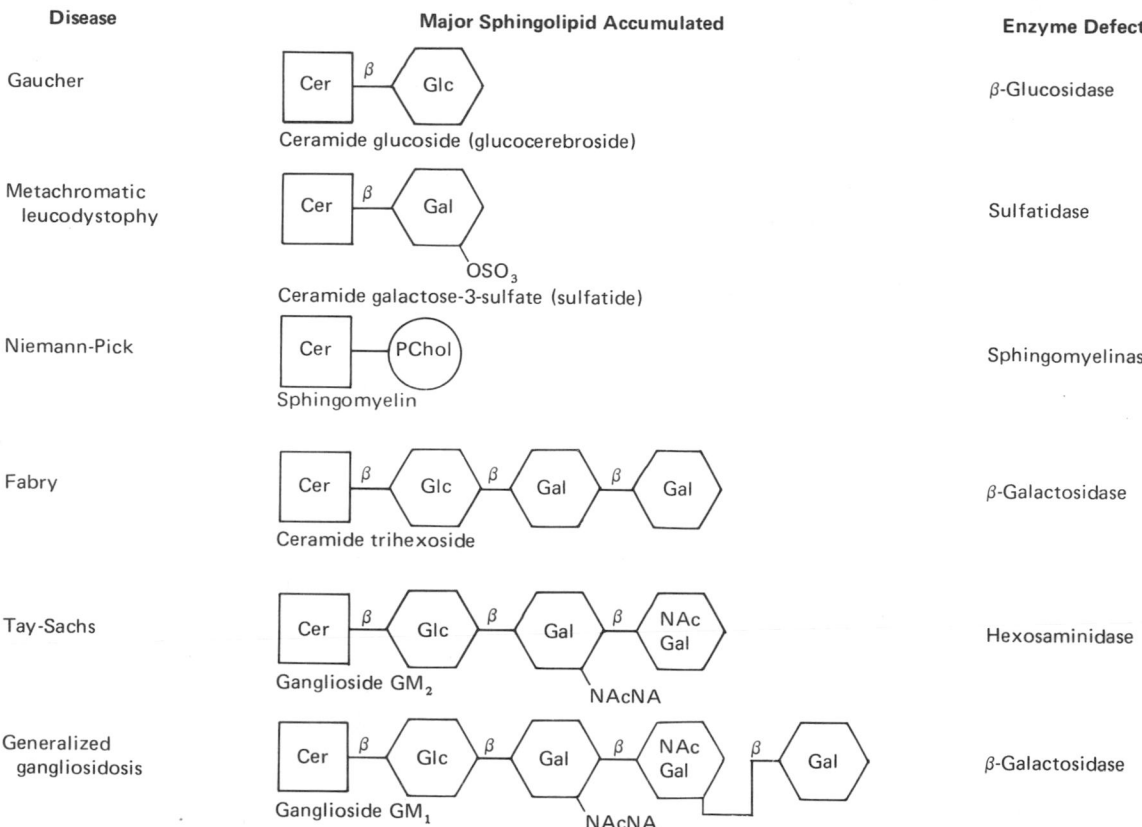

Disease	Major Sphingolipid Accumulated	Enzyme Defect
Gaucher	Ceramide glucoside (glucocerebroside)	β-Glucosidase
Metachromatic leucodystophy	Ceramide galactose-3-sulfate (sulfatide)	Sulfatidase
Niemann-Pick	Sphingomyelin	Sphingomyelinase
Fabry	Ceramide trihexoside	β-Galactosidase
Tay-Sachs	Ganglioside GM$_2$	Hexosaminidase
Generalized gangliosidosis	Ganglioside GM$_1$	β-Galactosidase

*From Brady. *Chemical Engineering News,* p. 61, Dec. 22, 1969.

†Cer = ceramide; Gal = galactose; Glc = glucose; PChol = phosphorylcholine; NacGal = N-acetylgalactosamine; NAcNA = N-acetylneuraminic acid.

A late infantile and juvenile form of GM$_2$-gangliosidosis has been described in which the anodal component of beta-galactosidase is absent.

OTHER SPHINGOLIPIDOSES.

1. Metachromatic leucodystrophy with the storage of ceramide-glucose-sulfate due to a defect in aryl-sulfatase
2. Nieman-Pick's disease—characterized by storage of sphingomyelin with a sphingomyelinase defect—several variants reported
3. Krabbe's disease—a defect in the metabolism of galactoceramide due to a deficiency in galactosyl ceramidase
4. Gaucher's disease—characterized by a defect in glycosyl ceramidase and the storage of glycosyl ceramide
5. Lactosyl ceramidosis—a partial defect in lactosyl ceramidase with the storage of galacto-glucose ceramide
6. Fabry's disease—a deficiency in hexosaminidase A and B with the storage of ceramide trihexoside

The presence or absence of vacuolated lymphocytes and azurophilic granules in the segmented white blood cells and the three architectural forms of storage material seen by electron microscopy are quite variable. The problem of determining the relation of genotype to phenotype in many of the gangliosidoses is as yet unsolved.

It has been demonstrated that, in a large percentage of the late infantile (Bielchowsky-Jansky) and juvenile (Batten-Mayou-Spielmyer-Vogt) forms of amaurotic family idiocy, lipofuscin is the abnormally deposited or stored material. The term ceroid

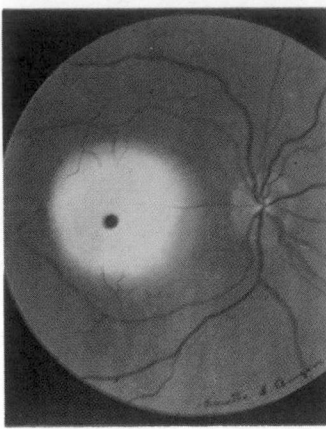

Fig. 33. Cherry-red spot in the fundus of a child with Tay-Sachs disease.

lipofuscinosis has been proposed, but as lipofuscin is an ubiquitous product of neuronal death it is far from certain that this finding represents the primary defect in the late forms of cerebromacular degenerations.

Despite the age of onset, all the cerebromacular degenerations share a progressive downhill course. Loss of vision, seizures of the myoclonic variety, dementia, ataxia, decerebration, and paralysis are the common clinical features. Abdominal distension, megalencephaly, hirsutism, thickening of facial features, and increased pigmentation of the skin are also noted in those surviving any length of time. Microcephaly is a feature of the Batten-Spielmyer-Vogt form.

Infantile Amaurotic Familial Idiocy (Tay Sachs Disease). The symptoms of the infantile form are first noted at 4 to 6 monthes of age, when it is observed that the infant's development, previously normal, appears to slow and then stop. Initially, there are apathy, muscular hypotonia, loss of previously acquired functions, and failure of vision with inability to follow or fixate. After a few months there are abnormal sensitivity to sound (hyperacusis) and progressive regression with increasing spasticity, blindness, and dementia. Seizures, usually myoclonic in type, may occur, and ultimately the head may enlarge. Examination of the fundi demonstrates optic atrophy and the pathognomonic "cherry-red spot" (Fig. 33), in which the perimacular areas show a grayish dystrophic change and the capillary elements of the choroid are seen as a bright red spot at the fovea. In contrast to the late infantile and juvenile forms where true tapetoretinal degeneration occurs, the electroretinogram (ERG) in Tay-Sachs disease is normal. The course is as a rule no longer than 18 to 24 months, although expert nursing care may lead to survival for several years.

Pathologically the neuronal cell bodies and some dendrites are grossly distended by fine lipid granules and are often vacuolated. These changes occur in cortex, cerebellum, basal ganglion, spinal cord, brainstem, and sympathetic ganglion. In cases surviving longer, secondary demyelination of fiber tracts and cystic softening of the brain with prominent gliosis are also seen. The stored lipid is a ganglioside containing neuraminic acid which, by electron microscopy, is found within the neuronal body as a membranous inclusion.

The clinical diagnosis can be supported by the demonstration of increased serum glutamic oxalacetic transaminase and an increased number of vacuolated lymphocytes in peripheral blood. The absence of the enzyme fructose-1-phosphate aldolase in the peripheral blood confirms the clinical diagnosis. Rectal biopsy and histochemical study of the ganglion cells in the sympathetic plexuses and cerebral biopsy can also confirm the clinical diagnosis. Cerebral biopsy is the most definitive method of diagnosis during life. The demonstration of a deficiency of either anodal or cathodal components of beta-D-N-hexosaminidase in the patient and/or fibroblast tissue cultures will be the most elegant definitive method of diagnosis.

Neurovisceral lipidosis (GM_1-gangliosidosis) (generalized gangliosidosis), a recessive disease with abnormal storage of GM_1-ganglioside in cerebral gray matter, spleen, liver, and renal glomerular epithelium, is usually fatal in the first 2 years of life. Radiographic changes resembling Hurler's disease are present. Beta-galactosidase deficiency leads to faulty degradation of the GM_1-ganglioside. Two forms of GM_1-gangliosidosis are described: an early infantile "pseudo-Hurler" form and a late infantile form without visceromegaly or skeletal changes.

Classical Tay-Sachs disease is inherited as a simple autosomal recessive trait having a high degree of penetrance and little variability in expression. Despite the markedly increased frequency in those of Jewish background, the disease has been reported among every ethnic group. The frequency among Jews originating from eastern Europe is higher than among Jews from other regions.

No favorable specific therapy is available. Supportive measures and parental genetic counseling should always be carried out.

LATER FORMS OF CEREBROMACULAR DEGENERATION. The other forms of cerebromacular degeneration are less typical clinically. The onset is somewhat later in life, varying from 3 years of age to adolescence. Mental deterioration, seizures, and progressive visual involvement are the earlier signs. Increasing evidence of pyramidal tract disease, ataxia, the onset of myoclonic seizures, and optic atrophy with pigmentary degeneration of the retina should lead to the suspicion of the diagnosis of late cerebromacular degeneration. The pigmentary degeneration is more marked in the macular and perimacular areas. Unlike the infantile form, there is no predilection for Jews. The genetic expressivity and penetrance are more variable. Progressive deterioration and the retinal changes should lead to clinical suspicion. The presence of vacuolated lymphocytes or azurophilic granules in the granulocytes of patient and heterozygous parents will be of some diagnostic significance. More specific enzymatic techniques are desirable and perhaps will be available in the very near future. Further diagnosis will depend upon cerebral biopsy or autopsy. The specific sphingolipid involved is as yet undetermined. However, the electron microscopy picture in the Batten-Spielmeyer-Vogt variety of the disease is totally different from that in Tay-Sachs. Presumably they are distinct biochemical entities. Pathologic findings are quite similar to the infantile form, but perhaps due to the longer course, secondary demyelination and gliosis are more prominent. Therapy is unknown; supportive measures for both patient and parents are all that can be offered at the present time. Batten-Spielmeyer-Vogt, Bielchowsky, and Kufs diseases are autosomal recessive genetic diseases.

GENERALIZED LIPIDOSES. There are a number of other diseases in which lipids accumulate in the cell bodies of the cerebral gray matter. These include Gaucher's disease, Niemann-Pick disease, Farber's disease, Fabry's disease, Heller's disease, cerebral cholesterosis, and the Hand-Schüller-Christian syndrome, as well as eosinophilic granulomas. These last two are granulomatoses of the reticuloendothelial system in which the central nervous system may become involved secondarily as a result of pressure effects of dural and skull granulomas or less commonly by actual involvement of the brain.

Niemann-Pick Disease (See also Sec. 8.10). This disease, in which ceramide-P-choline (sphingomyelin) is accumulated in foam cells, classically occurs in early infancy. The salient features are developmental arrest followed by progressive cerebral deterioration not unlike that seen in Tay-Sachs disease, hepatosplenomegaly, and blindness. Death usually occurs before the third year. The maculae show the "cherry-red" spot described in the infantile form of cerebromacular degeneration, although it is not reported in all cases. A few instances of later onset and more protracted course have been reported. In rare cases there is no evidence of cerebral involvement. Diagnosis can be established by demonstrating the characteristic "foam cells" in liver biopsy and bone marrow aspiration. Vacuolated lymphocytes in the peripheral blood have been reported. Pathologically there is ballooning of neuronal cells with secondary demyclination depending upon the duration of illness.

Gaucher's Disease. The infant with Gaucher's disease fails to thrive from birth. Enlargement of spleen and liver is found early. Strabismus, difficulty in swallowing, a feeble cry, and progressive decerebrate rigidity point to central nervous system involvement. Blindness and macular degeneration are not features of the cerebral forms of Gaucher's disease. Death usually occurs before the second year. Antemortem diagnosis can be made by bone marrow aspiration and demonstration of the characteristic

Gaucher's cells. Acid phosphatase levels are elevated. The storage cells contain increased amounts of ceramide glucose (glucocerebroside). In the nervous system some neuronal cytoplasmic accumulation of cerebrosides occurs, particularly in the brainstem nuclei. There are Gaucher's cell infiltrates in the cortex. In the juvenile and rare adult forms of cerebral Gaucher's disease, more definite cerebral neuronal cerebroside accumulation is found, possibly because of the slightly longer course of the disease.

Progressive Familial Myoclonic Epilepsy (Unverricht's Disease). This disease is a distinct clinical entity with a recessive pattern of inheritance. The disease usually has its onset with seizures in the first decade of life, with a later development of almost constant myoclonus of the stimulus-sensitive type. Ataxia and progressive mental deterioration subsequently appear. Terminally Parkinsonian features are evident, with death in early adulthood. Pathologically Unverricht's disease is a specific entity exhibiting Lafora bodies as both intracellular and extracellular inclusions. These bodies have the histochemical reactions of an acid mucopolysaccharide and resemble amyloid.

Similar clinical pictures, when examined pathologically, may be found to be late forms of cerebral lipidosis (Batten-Spielmeyer-Vogt). Others have proved to be one of a number of other progressive degenerative conditions such as dyssynergia cerebellaris myoclonica (Ramsey-Hunt), subacute sclerosing panencephalitis, Friedreich's ataxia, and hepatolenticular degeneration in which the site of major pathologic involvement is in the brainstem, dentate and olivary nuclei, and cerebellar peduncles. All give clinical manifestations very similar to those of the progressive familial myoclonic epilepsy. In the Lafora type of progressive familial myoclonus, pathologic changes are more generally distributed than in the other degenerative diseases exhibiting myoclonic syndromes.

Farber's Disease. Also called disseminated lipogranulomatosis, this disease produces central nervous system changes with ballooned-out nerve cells similar to those found in Tay-Sachs disease. The disease is familial. Lipogranulomas of the viscera are widespread, and there is severe joint involvement suggesting the periarticular changes of rheumatoid arthritis. The lipid involved appears to be a ceramide, probably sphingomyelin.

Fabry's Disease (See also Sec. 8.10). This disease is characterized by the selective storage of ceramide dihexoside and ceramide trihexoside in the nerve cells of the sympathetic nervous system, the myenteric plexuses, and subcortical nuclei of the central nervous system. Angiokeratoma corporis diffusum universalis, or Fabry's disease, has its onset in children as paroxysmal episodes of fever. Paresthesia and dysthesia of the extremities and proteinuria are early features. Skin lesions are highly characteristic of this disorder. At approximately 7 to 10 years of

TABLE 14.   *The Mucopolysaccharidoses*

	Hurler	Hunter	Sanfilippo
Genetic	Autosomal recessive	Sex-linked recessive	Autosomal recessive
Clinical	Dwarf, visceromegaly, gargoyle facies, corneal clouding, severe mental retardation, marked skeletal involvement	Less marked than Hurler, deafness, no corneal clouding	Childhood onset of severe mental retardation; minimal facial, skeletal, and visceral involvement
Urine	Chondroitin sulfate Heparitin sulfate	Chondroitin sulfate Heparitin sulfate	Heparitin sulfate

age, minute round bluish-red or black, blood-filled cavities are noted over the lower portion of the body and scrotum. The disease progresses into adult life with mild diabetes insipidus, elevated blood pressure, anhidrosis, and progressive renal failure. Fabry's disease is considered to be an inborn error of metabolism and represents a rare form of the lipid storage diseases.

Cerebral Cholesterosis.   This is a familial disease in which there is the marked accumulation of free cholesterol in the cerebellar and cerebral white matter. Extensive demyelination occurs. Clinically ataxia, mental deterioration, myoclonus, and bulbar paralysis occur. Xanthomas of the tendons are seen, and cataracts are frequent. In one variant form, accumulation of cholesterol is most marked in the basal ganglia and brainstem.

Heller's Disease.   Normal development through the first 2 years of life followed by gradual loss of speech during the fourth or fifth year, together with increasing motor restlessness and progressive dementia, should lead to a suspicion of Heller's disease. Few, if any, neurologic findings are seen in dementia infantilis. The abnormal EEG and early normal development aid in differentiating Heller's disease and childhood schizophrenia. Abnormal increases in plasma glycolipids and total lipids together with decrease in bound neuraminic acid in spinal fluid have been reported. Several biopsy reports link the condition with the cerebral lipidoses, although dementia infantilis may be a demyelinating disease. An important differential diagnostic consideration is subacute sclerosing panencephalitis (SSPE).

THE MUCOPOLYSACCHARIDOSES.   Six syndromes resulting from the abnormal storage of mucopolysaccharides have been described. The differentiating features of the three discussed below are indicated in Table 14.

Hurler's Disease (Gargoylism) (Type I).   This condition has been shown to be a mucopolysaccharide storage disease (see also Sec. 8.13). Not only is the central nervous system involved, but the skin, kidney, spleen, liver, heart, and skeletal system also contain excessive amounts of mucopolysaccharide glycolipids. The parenchymal cells of these organs and the cells of the reticuloendothelial system are distended and vacuolated. The nerve cells of the cere-

bral cortex are distended by a glycolipid substance akin to, and possibly identical with, the gangliosides. Similar changes, though less marked, are seen in the nerve cells of the spinal cord. A marked deficiency of a specific thermolabile beta-galactosidase has been reported in the liver of patients with Hurler's disease. Large amounts of compounds containing chondroitin sulfate-B and heparitin sulfate are excreted in the urine and can be detected by a urinary screening test (Fig. 34).

Clinically the Hurler's patient has macrocephaly and thick coarsened features, with the eyebrows joining in midline (Fig. 35). The tongue is thickened, tonsillar and adenoidal tissue are enlarged, and speech is thick and heavy. Relative dwarfism, kyphoscoliosis, thickening of the joints with progressive loss of mobility, protruding abdomen, umbilical hernia, hepatosplenomegaly, deafness, and corneal opacities make a typical case of Hurler's disease easily diagnosed. Radiographically there is thickening of the temporomandibular joint surfaces, an enlarged navicular-shaped sella turcica, and a curious characteristic beak-shaped formation of the lower thoracic and lumbar vertebrae. There is broadening of the metacarpals, and flat, broad ribs are seen. Large metachromatic granules are found within the polymorphonuclear elements of the peripheral blood and in fibroblasts cultured from the skin.

Mental retardation and physical incapacitation are progressive. Death usually occurs by age 10 to 12 and may be due to hydrocephaly but more often is due to cardiac failure.

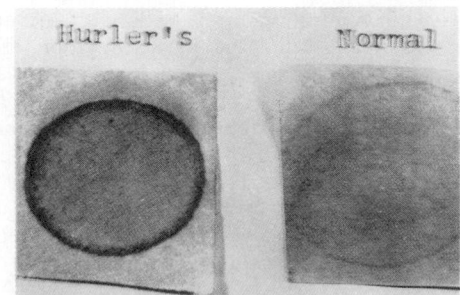

Fig. 34.   Berry spot test for detection of mucopolysaccharidoses.

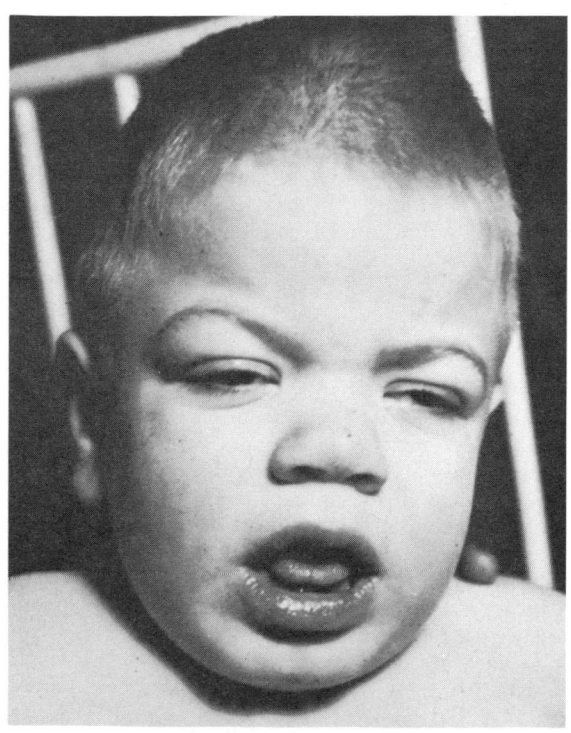

Fig. 35. Hurler's disease. Characteristic facies.

Hunter's Disease (Type II). This is the sex-linked recessive form and is less common than Hurler's disease. As a rule the clinical manifestations are less severe and more slowly progressive. Corneal clouding and deafness are not present. In both Hurler's and Hunter's diseases, true progressive megencephaly may lead to obstructive symptoms requiring a Holter valve or other shunting procedure. Fibroblast and leucocyte cultures from cases of both Hurler's and Hunter's continue to show abnormal accumulation of mucopolysaccharide as the result of inefficient degradation of the mucopolysaccharide. If fibroblast cultures of both Hunter's and Hurler's strains are mixed, the accumulation of mucopolysaccharide is corrected in about 10 days of mixed culture growth.

Sanfilippo's Disease (Type III). Only heparitin sulfate is excreted. Physical and radiographic manifestations are milder than in either type I or II, but mental retardation and severely disturbed behavior is progressive.

The remaining mucopolysaccharidoses have less neurologic interest and are discussed in Section 8.13. **GLYCOGEN STORAGE DISEASES.** *Type VIII.* This disease is characterized by slow speech and motor development with progressive spasticity and decerebration. Hepatomegaly is present early but disappears. Increased urinary catecholamines are found. Phosphorylase activity is reduced in the liver. This is inherited as a recessive trait.

Type II (Pompe's Disease). In this disorder an alpha-glucosidase deficiency results in generalized glycogen storage and may be associated with progressive and extensive neurologic involvement and progressive dementia.

Nonstorage Degeneration of Cerebral Gray Matter

The diseases of the cerebral gray matter which have been discussed can be grouped as "storage" diseases in which abnormal amounts of compounds are deposited within the neuronal cell body. There exist several other diseases involving the gray matter which cannot be strictly classified as "storage" diseases.

Progressive Degeneration of Cerebral Gray Matter (Poliodystrophy, Poliodysplasia). This condition is probably due to a variety of causes; it is not likely that the familial forms, the postencephalitic, postepileptic, and traumatic cases share a common etiology. The cases reported show a great diversity of signs and symptoms, and striking variability of duration and age of onset. Pathologically some cases show a diffuse degeneration of cerebral gray matter, and in others the pathologic findings are local or regional.

From the clinical point of view, progressive mental deterioration, seizures, myoclonic twitching followed by progressive spasticity, blindness, and often deafness should lead to the suspicion of progressive degeneration of the cerebral gray matter. Optic atrophy, abnormal involuntary movements, and ataxia occur. There are marked differences in clinical manifestations from case to case.

Alper's Disease. Diffuse cerebral degeneration in infancy has been reported as occurring in a familial distribution with quite uniform pathologic findings. There is an extensive neuronal loss and an increase in microglia, with gliosis of cerebral and cerebellar cortices, thalamus, and basal ganglia. The onset is with convulsions and myoclonus, followed by progressive mental and motor involvement, often associated with cortical blindness and deafness. The similarity of the clinical manifestations together with the uniform pathologic findings indicates that this form of poliodystrophy can be considered as a separate entity.

Necrotizing Encephalopathy (Leigh's Disease). This is characterized by the focal gray matter degeneration of the brainstem, basal ganglia, and subthalamic nuclei. There is extensive cranial nerve nuclear involvement. Pathologically the distinguishing features are spongy, necrotic areas of rarefaction with late cavitation. The onset usually occurs during the first year, often in the first or second month. The duration varies from several months to 2 or 3 years. Cases have been reported showing a later onset with survival from 10 to 12 years. Thus, it appears there is a chronic as well as a subacute form of infantile necrotizing encephalopathy.

Clinically the infant is quiet, cries infrequently, and has much difficulty in feeding due to bulbar cranial nerve palsy. Vocalization and speech deteriorate; spasticity and seizures occur later in the disease. Laboratory investigations are not rewarding. There is no therapy. Two adult forms of spongiform encephalopathy have now been shown to be "slow" virus diseases.

Diseases of the Cerebral White Matter

Recent advances in neurochemistry and electron microscopy have led to a number of classifications of white matter diseases. The term *dysmyelination* has been suggested for those diseases of white matter in which an inborn error of metabolism and enzymatic defect leads to faulty myelin formation, in contrast to the *demyelinating* or myelinoclastic group of diseases, in which there appears to be an abnormal myelin degeneration.

The myelinoclastic diseases are represented by multiple sclerosis, Devic's neuromyelitis optica, concentric sclerosis of Balo, and the diffuse sclerosis of Schilder. Acute necrotizing hemorrhagic leucoencephalitis and the acute disseminated encephalomyelitides secondary to infection and immunization procedures are also myelinoclastic diseases.

The second large grouping consists of the diseases of dysmyelination which are almost certain to be due to inborn errors of metabolism, with enzymatic defects which interfere with or prohibit the continuing normal processes of myelination. This group of diseases is made up of the leucodystrophies or diffuse scleroses. Demyelinating diseases are the result of exogenous agents, while the leucodystrophies are the result of endogenous defects.

Demyelinating diseases are of two general types. First, there are those in which are found multifocal perivenous lesions showing evidence of inflammation. Second, there are those with multifocal lesions but without evidence of inflammation. The first group is probably best thought of as an example of autoimmune disease; i.e., autosensitization to some component of myelin. The noninflammatory group is of even more uncertain cause and includes a number of conditions such as central pontine myelinolysis, progressive multifocal leucoencephalopathy, subacute combined degeneration, and the encephalopathies secondary to hypoxia and asphyxia.

Classification of the dysmyelinating leucodystrophies is subject to considerable debate. The principal source of confusion lies in the precise relationship of the leucodystrophies to the sphingolipidoses or cerebral storage diseases. One hypothesis is that the stored material in certain of the leucodystrophies represents the accumulation of myelin precursors or perhaps abnormal products of myelin formation which accumulate because of enzyme defects blocking nor-

mal myelin formation. The alternative is that the stored material represents products of myelin degeneration. As knowledge accrues, both hypotheses will probably be supported in one or more of the clinicopathologic entities to be discussed.

Krabbe's disease (globoid-cell leucodystrophy), metachromatic leucodystrophy, and Pelizaeus-Merzbacher's disease are the more common clinical types of true leucodystrophy. Krabbe's and metachromatic leucodystrophy can also be considered storage diseases.

Leucodystrophies

PELIZAEUS-MERZBACHER'S DISEASE.   This is a rare, sex-linked, recessive genetic disorder present from infancy. An autosomal dominant form of late onset has been described. The distinguishing feature is the presence of an arrhythmic dancing type of nystagmus noted shortly after birth. Other cerebellar signs are noted early in life. Progression is slow with remission lasting several years. In later childhood, spasticity, optic atrophy, dysarthria, and ataxia are seen. Intellectual deterioration is slow. Duration is variable, and sometimes death occurs before puberty, although patients living well into adult life are known. Pathologically, hypoplasia of axons and lack of stainability of myelin are the main features. There is little evidence of myelin breakdown. Chemically there is no evidence of the storage of sphingolipids nor any increase in cholesterol esters, which clearly distinguishes this disease as a separate entity from either the sphingolipidoses or the demyelinating diseases. There appears to be a basic defect in the process of myelination.

The normal or only slightly elevated spinal fluid protein helps to distinguish this disease from some of the other leucodystrophies. No specific treatment is available.

METACHROMATIC LEUCODYSTROPHY (SULFATIDE LIPIDOSIS).   This is an autosomal recessive disease due to a deficiency of the enzyme aryl sulfatase. The condition may become manifest anytime during childhood, most frequently about the age of 2 years. Late childhood and adult onset also occurs. Loss of ability to walk with hypotonia and areflexia are early manifestations and are subsequently replaced by spasticity and progressive paralysis. Optic atrophy, seizures, and myoclonus together with signs of progressive cerebellar involvement are noted. Atypical forms of this disorder have been described with isolated manifestations of abdominal distension, simulating intestinal obstruction, or progressive loss of speech. Decerebrate rigidity usually occurs within 2 or 3 years. A longer course may occur in those children with a later onset. An infantile form with onset at 1 to 2 years is distinguished from a juvenile form with onset age 4 to 10 years. The cerebrospinal fluid protein is characteristically elevated up to 200 mg percent. Nonfilling of the gallbladder is a common feature. Prolongation of peripheral nerve conduction time is usually found. Diagnosis may be made by sural or dental nerve biopsy with the demonstration of the accumulation of metachromatic-staining galactosphingosulfatides. Metachromatic sulfatides can be found in the urinary sediment or demonstrated chromatographically. The latter finding is highly suggestive but not pathognomonic. Urinary or leucocyte aryl sulfatase A deficiency is diagnostic of this disorder.

Pathologically there is widespread symmetric demyelination of the central nervous system and an accumulation of sulfatides and nonlipid hexosamine. Sulfatide deposits show marked metachromasis. Liver, kidney, and bile duct epithelia are also involved. Electron microscopy reveals the cerebroside sulfuric acid ester accumulations to be chiefly in the cytoplasm of the oligodendroglia, astrocytes, and large macroglial cells. By electron microscopy no inclusions are reported in the neuronal cells. By more conventional techniques intraneuronal deposits have been reported.

GLOBOID-CELL LEUCODYSTROPHY (KRABBE'S DISEASE). This is inherited as an autosomal recessive disease. At about 3 to 6 months of age, a previously normal infant develops stiffness of the lower extremities, spasms with head retraction, and extension of lower limbs. Flexion of the upper extremities occurs subsequently. Incessant crying is prominent. The disease finally terminates in decerebrate rigidity and death from bulbar paralysis. Rarely does the infant survive more than two years. The cerebrospinal fluid protein is usually elevated in the range of 150 to 300 mg percent, with a normal gamma globulin content and colloidal gold curve and a significant decrease in beta globulins. There is symmetric diffuse demyelination of the cerebral white matter. The characteristic globoid cells of mesodermal origin, possibly microglia or adventitial cells of vessels, are distended with a protein-bound glycolipid containing cerebrosides. These cells can be considered as large macrophages attempting to remove products of myelin catabolism. Defective synthesis of sulfatides and accumulation of ceramide-galactose due to an enzymatic defect in cerebroside sulfatransferase has been reported.

SPONGY SCLEROSIS (CANAVAN'S DISEASE, FAMILIAL SPONGY DEGENERATION OF THE NEURAXIS). This disease is probably an autosomal recessive trait with a higher frequency in those of Jewish ancestry. The onset is in the first months of life with arrest of psychomotor development, hypotonia, and seizures. The neck becomes flaccid, and a progressive spastic diplegia culminates in decerebrate rigidity. Optic atrophy ends in blindness. Macrocephaly occurs often with the separation of the sutures of the skull as a result of diffuse edema of both gray and white matter. Increased spinal fluid pressure may be observed, and the erroneous diagnosis of hydrocephalus may be considered. Protein content of the cerebrospinal fluid is usually normal. Death usually occurs prior

to the second year of life. Widespread demyelination, cerebral edema, and a characteristic spongy vacuolation are noted pathologically. As in Pelizaeus-Merzbacher's disease, there is evidence of a defect in normal myelination and some suggestion of demyelination. The relationship of this condition to subacute spongiform encephalopathy of adults is unknown.

SUDANOPHILIC (NEUTRAL FAT, ORTHOCHROMIC) FAMILIAL LEUCODYSTROPHY. This disease is pathologically characterized by the symmetric loss of myelin in cerebral and cerebellar white matter. Lipid-distended phagocytes are noted around the areas of demyelination. Clinically the onset occurs in late childhood with signs of progressive pyramidal tract and cerebellar involvement. Aphasia may occur. The loss of myelin and the increase in esterified cholesterol place this form of leucodystrophy closer to the demyelinating diffuse scleroses. However, its familial occurrence with a sex-linked inheritance and the symmetric nature of the lesions serve to warrant its retention in the group of dysmyelinative leucodystrophies. Addison's disease, often initially asymptomatic, is frequently associated with this disorder and may be the cause of coma and sudden death.

ALEXANDER'S DISEASE. This extremely rare and recently reported disorder, also known as dysmyelinogenic leucodystrophy, has been classified as both a storage disease and a leucodystrophy. The onset is in infancy with death usually occurring by the second year. All cases have been male, except one reported juvenile case. Clinically there is progressive dementia with spastic quadriplegia and enlargement of the head. Seizures are a common feature. Pathologically, eosinophilic staining material is deposited at all the interfaces of brain, brainstem, and spinal cord. Few deposits are noted in the cerebellum. In addition, there is widespread demyelination of cerebrum and cerebellum, with more severe involvement of the frontal lobes and less severe destruction in the occipital lobes. The eosinophilic material has histochemical properties suggestive of neurokeratin and appears to be located in the astrocytic footplates. The original case was reported as a fibrinoid degeneration of astrocytes, and another case was reported as megalencephaly with hyaline panneuropathy.

Demyelinating Scleroses

In contrast to the leucodystrophies, this group of diseases is myelinoclastic and pathologically multifocal, perivenous, and inflammatory. The absence of a familial distribution of cases further tends to distinguish these diseases from the familial leucodystrophies. Etiology is obscure, and several concepts of pathogenesis have been offered. The destructive action of some enzyme present in blood or cerebrospinal fluid, viral infection, capillary thrombosis, and autosensitization to some component of myelin have all been proposed as etiologically significant. At the present time, the autoimmune concept appears to be most tenable. Demyelinating diseases can be further separated into the diffuse and disseminated forms. Schilder's disease represents the diffuse demyelinating scleroses. The disseminated demyelinating scleroses include acute and chronic multiple sclerosis, acute necrotizing hemorrhagic leucoencephalitis, and the acute disseminated encephalomyelitides which follow infection and immunization procedures. Neuromyelitis optica and the concentric sclerosis of Balo are probably subtypes of the disseminated form of acute multiple sclerosis.

ACUTE DISSEMINATED ENCEPHALOMYELITIDES. These diseases occur following rubella, rubeola, variola, varicella, and occasionally the ill-defined "influenza" syndrome. Immunization against variola, rabies treatment, and rarely pertussis immunization may be followed by an acute episode of disseminated encephalomyelitis. Signs of an acute encephalitis with evidence of multiple sites of central nervous system involvement are associated with an elevation of spinal fluid protein and a lymphocytic pleocytosis in the spinal fluid. Fever, convulsions, stupor, ocular palsies, dysarthria, paraplegias, and cerebellar ataxia, together with urinary and fecal incontinence, may occur in various combinations. Severe forms of the disorder will leave permanent neurologic deficits. About 15 percent of all cases are fatal. There is no specific therapy. Unlike other forms of disseminated sclerosis, recurrences are rare.

Acute Necrotizing Hemorrhagic Leucoencephalitis (Hurst Disease). This is a fulminating and usually fatal disease following some minor upper respiratory infection. Pathologically one or more large hemorrhagic and necrotic foci of demyelination are found in brain, spinal cord, and brainstem. Presenting signs and symptoms depend upon the site of the lesion or lesions. Headache, fever, and signs of meningitis are present. Cerebrospinal fluid protein is elevated, and up to several hundred leucocytes may be present. These cells are predominantly neutrophilic, in contrast to the lymphocytic pleocytosis of the acute disseminated encephalomyelitides described above. No specific form of therapy is available.

Multiple or Disseminated Sclerosis. This disease is relatively rare in children. Although it has been observed in the first decade, the diagnosis should be made with extreme circumspection. The diagnosis is based upon the occurrence of multiple attacks and evidence of multiple sites of neurologic involvement. Preferential sites of involvement are segmental portions of the brainstem, spinal cord, and cerebellum. Cerebral symptoms are uncommon. In order of frequency, one encounters motor weakness of the extremities, retrobulbar neuritis, paresthesias, diplopia, disturbance of balance, and bladder difficulties. No characteristic laboratory features are present other than an occasional mild pleocytosis with some increase in spinal fluid protein. Gamma globulin may be elevated, and a first-zone colloidal gold curve elevation is a frequent finding. These cere-

brospinal fluid findings are not pathognomonic. The disease may be present in the absence of any abnormalities in the cerebrospinal fluid. Pathologically the findings consist of scattered areas of demyelination with little or no evidence of tissue reaction. The gray matter is usually spared. The disease occurs sporadically, and between attacks the symptoms may clear partially or even completely. Over a period of years, there is a tendency for slow, progressive neurologic disability.

Neuromyelitis Optica (Devic's Disease). Somewhat more common in children is neuromyelitis optica (Devic's disease). Although there are cogent neuropathologic reasons for believing that this is in every way identical with disseminated or multiple sclerosis, the clinical picture is sufficiently uniform to consider this as a special subclass of disseminated sclerosis. The disease is characterized by the association of a transverse myelitis and bilateral optic neuritis. These may develop simultaneously or one after the other. Visual loss is severe and is usually accompanied by ophthalmoscopic signs of inflammation of the nerve head itself. Involvement of the spinal cord, as a rule, produces a complete transverse myelitis. It may, however, be disseminated. On pathologic examination some cases presenting with this symptom complex show the classical lesions of multiple sclerosis. Others may show pathologic changes best classified as subacute or acute necrotizing hemorrhagic myelitis. In some cases of neuromyelitis optica, large confluent plaques of demyelination may occur within the cerebral hemispheres. In these cases there is invariably an elevation of cerebrospinal fluid protein and a mononuclear pleocytosis.

Recovery may be quite rapid and complete in several weeks. Some cases are associated with permanent residua, and those which fall in the classification of subacute necrotic myelopathy are usually fatal. No specific therapy is known, and management is entirely symptomatic.

Balo's Concentric Sclerosis. This condition has many of the histopathologic features of multiple sclerosis. However, in Balo's disease the lesions are primarily confined to the cerebral white matter. The distinguishing features are the occurrence of alternate concentric bands of destruction and preservation of myelin. Whether or not this form of the disease should be considered as a variant of diffuse cerebral sclerosis rather than disseminated sclerosis has not been determined.

SCHILDER'S DISEASE (ENCEPHALITIS PERIAXIALIS DIFFUSA). Schilder's disease shows an extensive demyelination of the cerebral white matter. The process is asymmetric and tends to originate occipitally, spreading forward to parietal, temporal, and frontal lobes. Histologically the lesions resemble those of disseminated or multiple sclerosis. The finding of increased esterified cholesterol and the decrease of myelin lipids further identifies Schilder's disease with the demyelinating diseases. The age of onset may be at any time past infancy, with a peak incidence between the ages of 5 and 10. The onset is acute, often with seizures, progressive visual loss, and gait disturbance. Progression is occasionally interrupted by short periods of quiescence. There is progressive dementia, frequent loss of hearing, aphasia, and paralysis. Spastic quadriplegia and decerebration are the final stages within a few months to several years after the onset. The frequent loss of vision is attributable to cerebral as well as optic nerve demyelination with a complex pleural picture of cortical blindness and optic neuritis. In contrast to the leucodystrophies, sensory and motor deficits tend to precede the dementia. Increased intracranial pressure may simulate brain tumor. Laboratory findings are nonspecific, although there may be some elevation of cerebrospinal fluid protein with an increased gamma globulin content and a first-zone colloidal gold curve. Prognosis is fatal and treatment is unknown. Antemortem diagnosis can be confirmed by cerebral biopsy.

SUBACUTE SCLEROSING PANENCEPHALITIS (SUBACUTE INCLUSION BODY ENCEPHALITIS [DAWSON], SUBACUTE SCLEROSING LEUCOENCEPHALITIS [VAN BOGAERT], AND PANENCEPHALITIS [PETTE AND DORING]) (SSLE;SSPE). Isolation of measles virus from brain biopsy material, the growth of measles virus from brain biopsy in tissue culture, and transfer of an unidentified encephalogenic agent from human brain biopsy to ferrets, strongly implicate the measles virus as the etiologic agent in SSPE. Clinically, intellectual deterioration and affective lability are often the early signs. This is followed by the appearance of myoclonic jerks and choreoathetosis. The age of onset is seldom before late childhood or adolescence, and the disease usually runs its course over months to years with eventual blindness, spastic quadriplegia, and virtual decortication. The electroencephalogram may be helpful in diagnosis when it exhibits slow high-voltage complexes appearing in a rhythmic metronomic fashion. This change is not pathognomonic. The presence of a markedly elevated gamma globulin or a strongly positive first-zone colloidal gold curve with increased immunoglobulin-G associated with M gradients serves to distinguish this condition from Schilder's disease and the other progressive degenerative cerebral disorders. Pathologically there is diffuse demyelination of hemispheric white matter and marked gliosis which is disproportionate to the myelin loss. Numerous eosinophilic-staining intranuclear bodies may be found in both nerve cells and the oligodendroglia. The entire central nervous system is involved, the changes being most pronounced in the cerebral hemispheres.

Degenerations of the Basal Ganglia
(The Extrapyramidal Syndromes)

A number of progressive degenerations involving the basal ganglia and its connections are seen in children. Clinically they are characterized by abnormal involuntary movements (hyperkinesia), paucity of spontaneous movement (bradykinesia), and rigidity. While athetosis, tremor, chorea, and dystonia may all be seen in other degenerative or acquired diseases of the central nervous system, those diseases in which these features are prominent are included in this group. The common pathologic features are degeneration and demyelination of the subcortical nuclear masses and their connections.

PARKINSONISM. A rare juvenile form of parkinsonism has been described as occurring either sporadically or occasionally in a familial distribution. The symptoms of resting tremor, paucity of spontaneous movement, and rigidity may become apparent in the early part of the second decade. The course is chronic, leading over a number of years to incapacity as a result of the rigidity and tremor. The pathology is essentially a progressive degeneration of the globus pallidus. Therapy is symptomatic and consists of the use of the belladonna group of alkaloids. Neurosurgical intervention probably has a place in the management of juvenile paralysis agitans. L-DOPA therapy may prove to be of therapeutic value as it has in adult parkinsonism.

HUNTINGTON'S CHOREA. Huntington's chorea has a mean age of onset of 44 years. There are confirmed reports of cases of Huntington's chorea which began at the age of 3 years; in less than 1 percent of patients with Huntington's chorea is the onset in the first decade. The disease is inherited as a dominant autosomal trait. The main pathologic lesions are found in the basal ganglia. Both caudate nucleus and putamen show a marked to complete loss of nerve cells. There is an astroglial reaction throughout these areas. Other extrapyramidal nuclei are invariably involved. The cerebral cortex is affected in all patients showing neuronal destruction and some glial hypertrophy. In some, a panatrophy of the cerebellar hemisphere is reported.

The clinical manifestations in childhood are rarely typical of those seen in the adult form of Huntington's chorea. The cases reported in childhood are essentially hypokinetic, in contrast to the characteristic choreatic movements seen in the adult forms. Bradykinesia, muscular rigidity, convulsive disorder, and progressive mental deterioration are the characteristic features in the childhood cases. However, the adult choreic clinical picture does occur in children and may lead to confusion with other hyperkinetic syndromes.

While it may be permissible on occasion to make a clinical diagnosis of Huntington's chorea in an adult in whom a family history is absent, it appears at the present time that because of the atypical features of the childhood form of the disease, the diagnosis should not be made in children unless there is a verified family pedigree of Huntington's chorea. No therapy is known. A variety of medications used for adult forms of extrapyramidal syndromes has been tried in a limited series of cases. No success can be reported. The disease is more

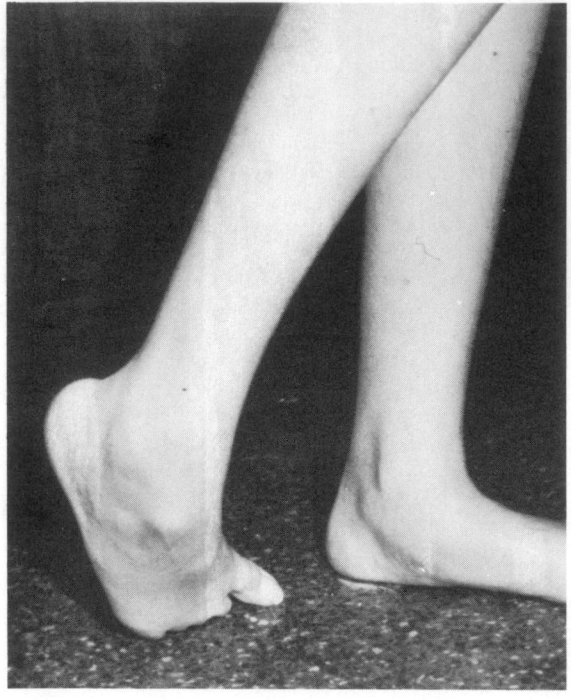

Fig. 36. Typical dystonic posturing of foot in early dystonia musculorum deformans.

rapidly fatal in children, lasting usually only three to five years after the first clinical manifestations. No specific metabolic error has been found in Huntington's chorea, although increases of dopamine have been reported in the urine.

DYSTONIA MUSCULORUM DEFORMANS. This disease has its onset about the fifth year with a slow, progressive course to complete incapacity in six to eight years. Some cases may show a less severe progression. The characteristic clinical manifestations of this inherited disease are slow, writhing dystonic movements involving neck, trunk, and extremities. The disease often has its onset with a bizarre gait disturbance that is frequently interpreted as a functional disorder (Fig. 36). Facial grimacing may also be present. In a typical case the eventual outcome is complete incapacity and the assumption of fixed dystonic postures. Pathologically, widespread but nonspecific degenerative changes are seen in the subcortical nuclear masses and cerebellum. Therapy has been entirely symptomatic. Some success in control of the movements may be achieved by thalamotomy. Since the disease is essentially a progressive one, unilateral thalamotomy may give relief for variable periods of time until the opposite side of the body becomes severely involved and a second operation may be indicated.

HALLERVORDEN-SPATZ DISEASE. This is a dominantly inherited, slowly progressive syndrome of dementia, spasticity, and a dyskinesia of the athetotic variety with some dystonic features. Emotional incontinence is common, and optic atrophy may be a late manifestation. Seizures and sensory impairment are not usually present. The disease usually has its onset in middle to late childhood, and death results within a period of 5 to 20 years. Pathologically, diffuse neuronal degeneration is found in cerebral and cerebellar white matter but particularly in the pallidum and the dentate nuclei. The cortical spinal tracts are severely degenerated. Neuroplasmic swellings in the gray matter are common. The characteristic pallidonigral hyperpigmentation is not always striking. The neuroplasmic swellings have led to the disease being described as a neuroaxonal dystrophy.

Increased iron is deposited in the globus pallidus and there is a delayed (about 10 days) "leakage" of radioactive iron into the area of the globus pallidus but no increased systemic uptake of iron. In one case in the author's experience, a significant increase of iron was found in the hair. Thus, there are a number of indications that this condition represents some type of abnormality of iron metabolism.

HEPATOLENTICULAR DEGENERATION (WILSON'S DISEASE). This is an autosomal, recessively inherited, progressive disease characterized by progressive degeneration of the basal ganglia and hepatic cirrhosis (see also Sec. 8.11). The disease is now identified as an inborn error of metabolism, the primary defect being the failure of proper formation of the copper-containing protein ceruloplasmin. The biochemical findings consist of a decreased level of plasma ceruloplasmin, an increase in the plasma nonceruloplasmin copper, and an increased urinary copper excretion.

Pathologic changes are seen throughout the central nervous system but are most marked in the basal ganglia. Increased amounts of tissue copper are found in the affected areas. A nodular cirrhosis of the liver is found, and it has been shown that the characteristic Kayser-Fleischer ring is due to deposition of copper within Descemet's membrane (Fig. 37).

The onset of disease is usually in the second decade. However, with the increasingly accurate methods of diagnosis provided by ceruloplasmin determinations, the diagnosis can be established earlier, often by the fourth or fifth year. Early symptoms may be unsteadiness of gait and trembling of the hands. Signs of increasing hepatic insufficiency may precede, accompany, or follow the neurologic involvement. Similarly, intellectual dulling or psychiatric symptoms, emotional lability, and anxiety states may occur with, before, or after the development of the neurologic picture. Neurologically Wilson's disease may mimic other progressive degenerations of the basal ganglia. Both bradykinetic and hyperkinetic forms are seen. The characteristic tremor is a posture-holding "wing-beating" type, but an atypical cerebellar intention tremor or the tremor at rest as in parkinsonism may be seen. Dysarthria, facial grimacing, excessive salivation, and progressive rigidity are other features of the disease. Many patients exhibit the typical Kayser-Fleischer circumcorneal

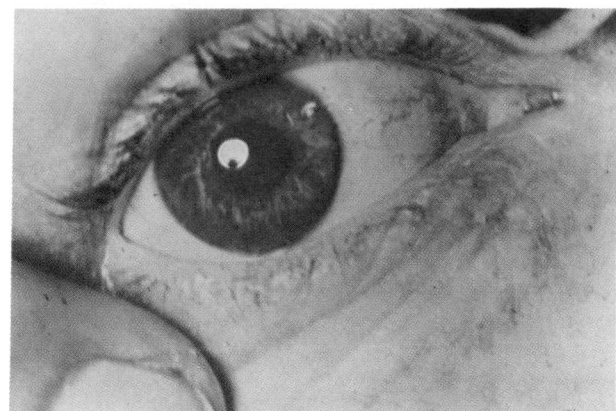

Fig. 37. Kayser-Fleischer ring. Note pigmentary change initially involves superior or inferior pole of Descemet's membrane.

greenish-yellow ring at the junction of cornea and sclera. At the present time, a diagnosis can be established by the demonstration of decreased ceruloplasmin content. However, some cases have been reported in which a normal ceruloplasmin is found.

Differential diagnosis includes all the progressive degenerations of the basal ganglia, and Wilson's disease must always be suspected in any child with juvenile cirrhosis.

Treatment is aimed at reducing dietary copper intake and removing copper from the tissues. The latter is accomplished by the use of dimercaprol or penicillamine. Without treatment, the disorder leads to death within five to six years. Therapy has been of considerable value in both adult and childhood cases.

ESSENTIAL OR FAMILIAL TREMOR. This condition is most apt to manifest itself in early adolescence but may appear in well developed form in childhood. There is a fine rhythmic tremor of the hands and fingers, accentuated by fatigue and emotional stress and little affected by movement or intention. It is best demonstrated with hands and arms extended and fingers spread. When benign tremor occurs as a sporadic case, Wilson's disease and other basal ganglia diseases must be ruled out. The condition most often appears as a dominant trait, and examination of other members of the family is most helpful. Considering the benign nature of the condition, treatment is rarely required. Rarely, thalamotomy may be effective in those severely involved.

STATUS DEMYELINISATUS. This disease has been described as a progressive degeneration of the lenticular nuclei. The onset is in infancy, and death occurs after variable periods of time up to the middle of the second decade. The condition has been reported as occurring on a familial basis. The symptoms are increasing rigidity, athetoid and dystonic movements, and progressive dementia.

DYSSYNERGIA CEREBELLARIS MYOCLONICA. Extremely rare, this disorder is familial. The exact mode of inheritance is uncertain, but in at least one case a dominant form of inheritance seemed most probable. The onset is with myoclonic muscular twitching involving the extremities as well as the face. Moderate to mild mental retardation is present. As the disease progresses, the myoclonic phenomenon tends to disappear, to be replaced by progressive cerebellar ataxia and severe intention tremor. Seizures may occur but are not as prominent a feature as they are in familial myoclonus epilepsy. Differential diagnosis from Wilson's disease should be made. The principal pathology appears to be in the dentate system. Familial paroxysmal choreoathetosis (Mount and Reback) may become of differential diagnostic interest in this and other diseases of the basal ganglia leading to hyperkinesia.

Polymorphous Neuroabiotrophies

A great variety of progressive degenerative disorders involving, in various combinations, cerebellum, brainstem, spinal cord, and peripheral nerves have been described in children. These diseases occur in familial distributions as recessive, dominant, and sex-linked traits. As syndromes they occur in many intermediate and transitional forms. Their exact interrelationships are unclear, and there are many pathologic similarities. One common feature is that cause is completely unknown, and therapy is unavailable. These disorders can best be classified in terms of the major clinical-pathologic symptomatology.

Cerebellar Degeneration

Pure, progressive degeneration of the cerebellum is rare in children. The more frequent age of onset is some time after 20 years. A familial history is present in a significant number of these cases. The first symptoms may be unsteady gait and dysarthria, followed by progressive cerebellar ataxia. Pathologically there is atrophy of the cerebellum with marked loss of Purkinje cells. Both pathologically and clinically these cases begin to merge with the spinocerebellar degenerations. There is often atrophy of the spinocerebellar tracts and the posterior columns, giving symptoms of position and vibratory sensory loss. Optic atrophy may occur, and other manifestations of brainstem and spinal cord involvement may be present.

Differential diagnosis from other forms of progressive cerebellar ataxias, cerebellar neoplasm, and in older cases multiple sclerosis must be made. One helpful diagnostic feature is the demonstration of significant cerebellar atrophy by pneumoencephalography.

Another form of progressive cerebellar atrophy occurring in children is that described by Louis-Bar under the term of ataxia-telangiectasia. This will be described in more detail in the neurocutaneous group of degenerative disorders (Sec. 8.11).

Olivocerebellar and olivopontocerebellar degenerations have been reported to occur on a familial basis. Rare cases are described in children, but for the most part, these are diseases affecting adults.

THE SPINOCEREBELLAR DEGENERATIONS. *Friedreich's ataxia* is the best known member of this group of disorders. It is genetically transmitted in both dominant and recessive modes. Sex distribution is equal. The age of onset is usually prior to 20 with the average being between 10 and 13 years. Cases have been reported earlier than this. Progression is steady, and ambulation becomes impossible within 5 to 8 years. The usual duration of disease is about 16 years, although considerably longer and shorter courses have been reported. The pathologic changes in the spinal cord consist primarily of degeneration in the dorsal columns and spinocerebellar and pyramidal tracts. However, peripheral nerves, medulla, pons, and cerebellum may also be involved. The spinal cord is usually smaller than normal, and the dorsal roots are atrophic.

Ataxia, dysarthria, nystagmus, posterior column sensory loss, reflex changes, and musculoskeletal deformities are the cardinal manifestations of this disorder. Ataxic gait is the earliest clinical sign. The ataxia begins in the lower extremities, but as the disease progresses, trunk, upper extremities, head, and neck become involved. Speech becomes dysarthric, and there may be impaired laughing, chewing, and breathing due to marked incoordination. A nodding head tremor is frequent, and nystagmus appears in over half the cases.

Sensory impairment characteristically involves the dorsal columns, with diminution of position and vibratory sensation.

Muscular weakness is a common feature of the disease, and prominent wasting as the result of disuse is seen late. However, in some families lower motor neuron atrophy is present early in the disease. The distribution of the atrophy is distal and similar to that seen in Charcot-Marie-Tooth disease.

Deep tendon reflexes are almost always absent in the lower extremities, and late in the disease those in the upper limbs may disappear. Abdominal reflexes are retained. A Babinski sign is almost a constant finding.

Optic atrophy is present in about 10 percent of the cases. Occasionally there may be involvement of other cranial nerves. Mental impairment progressing to dementia may be present in some cases.

Musculoskeletal deformities are common. Pes cavus and retraction and flexion of the toes with equinovarus tendency results in the typical "Friedreich's foot." Kyphoscoliosis is observed in the majority of children.

There are no distinctive laboratory features other than the frequent occurrence of electrocardiographic abnormalities suggesting progressive degeneration of the cardiac muscle. Terminal cardiac failure due to interstitial myocarditis is not infrequent. No treatment is available, and death usually occurs as a result of infection complicated by cardiac failure.

The Roussy-Levy syndrome, a variant of Freidreich's ataxia, is of principal importance because of its significantly better prognosis. This syndrome is either nonprogressive or excessively slow in its development. The salient features are pes cavus and areflexia of the lower extremities, often of the upper as well. The absence of ataxia, dysarthria, and nystagmus distinguishes it from the classical Friedreich's ataxia. Muscle wasting in the lower leg and hypothenar eminences occur in some families. A dominant genetic pattern is usual. Pathology is not well documented but is probably similar to that of Freidreich's ataxia with little or no spinocerebellar degeneration.

Other variants of spinocerebellar degeneration include cases of progressive ataxia occurring as hereditary syndromes associated with mental retardation, cataract, and pyramidal tract signs, together with poor growth and development. Another form of spinocerebellar degeneration is hereditary spastic ataxia with central retinal degeneration and vestibular impairment. In clinical practice, cases intermediate between Charcot-Marie-Tooth disease, familial spastic paraplegia, Roussy-Levy syndrome, progressive spinal atrophy, and the more typical form of Friedreich's ataxia are common.

Congenital spinocerebellar ataxia (Marinesco-Sjögren or Garland-Moorhouse) is recessively inherited and is associated with cataracts and mental retardation. Neurologically it is characterized by limb ataxia, dysarthria, areflexia, and pyramidal tract signs. Retarded somatic and mental maturation is a constant feature. Frequently, there is a dolichocephalic skull with epicanthic folds and strabismus.

Familial spastic paraplegia is a hereditary disorder characterized by the childhood onset of progressive spasticity of the lower extremities, with associated hyperreflexia, and the Babinski sign. The course is slowly progressive. Muscle atrophy is not part of this syndrome, and ataxia is not seen. Pathologically the degeneration is limited to the pyramidal tracts in the spinal cord.

There are two well recognized metabolic disorders in which there may be primary cerebellar involvement. *Hartnup disease* is manifested by cerebellar ataxia, a pellagroid skin rash, and moderate mental retardation. The disease is believed to be an inborn error of tryptophan metabolism with an associated amino-aciduria. The skin lesions and the cerebellar ataxia are inconstant and apparently reversible by administration of nicotinic acid. Ataxia may appear acutely and may be associated with acute delirium and hallucinations.

The Bassen-Kornzweig's syndrome is a recessively inherited disorder associated with a deficiency of beta-lipoprotein. In early childhood there is a prominent steatorrhea. Characteristic features are cerebellar and dorsal column signs together with retinal degeneration and retinitis pigmentosa. The red blood cells have many thorny projections from their surfaces. This acanthocytosis is a highly characteristic diagnostic feature.

Brainstem and Spinal Cord Degenerations

The feature that distinguishes this group of progressive neuroabiotrophies from the spinocerebellar degenerations is the fact that the predominant pathologic changes occur in the spinal cord and specifically in the pyramidal tracts or anterior horn cells. Again there are a number of combinations and intermediate forms.

These progressive degenerations of the spinal cord are characterized by the wasting of muscles and motor weakness. The cause is entirely unknown, but the strong familial tendency points to the operation of genetic factors. At present no treatment is known other than symptomatic relief.

The principal lesions are in the cord and brainstem, where the anterior horn cells and cells of the nuclei of the motor cranial nerves show a diminution of size and number. There are secondary degenerative changes in anterior roots and nerves and marked evidence of denervation atrophy in the voluntary muscle groups.

A number of clinical forms have been described, the chief distinctions being the age of onset and the rate of progression.

Progressive infantile spinal atrophy (Werdnig-Hoffman disease) is a uniformly fatal disease inherited as an autosomal recessive trait. The earliest signs can be noted at or shortly after birth, or the onset may be delayed until somewhat later in the first year. Progressive evidence of lower motor neuron weakness and atrophy appears in trunk, neck, pelvis, and shoulder girdles. The extremities are involved later, but the distal musculature of the hands and feet is frequently spared. Hypotonia and weakness progress to atrophy and paralysis. Areflexia is present. There is no evidence of sensory loss or cerebellar ataxia. Mentality is not disturbed. Facial musculature is often spared, but the tongue is frequently

atrophic and demonstrates prominent fasciculations. Some cases present with the clinical picture of arthrogryposis multiplex. Death almost always occurs in about two years as a result of intercostal paralysis and intercurrent respiratory infection.

There is an intermediate form of infantile progressive spinal atrophy in which the disease process is manifest at birth but progresses much less rapidly, sometimes appearing to have become stationary. Death usually occurs in the middle of the second decade.

Wohlfart, Kugelberg, and Welander have described a more slowly progressive variant of Werdnig-Hoffmann's disease. Since it is slowly progressive and primarily involves the girdle musculature, the *Kugelberg-Welander syndrome* has been descriptively called heredofamilial juvenile muscular atrophy simulating muscular dystrophy. Although of recessive inheritance, this condition may occur sporadically or be found in a family where the more usually fatal type is present. The course is slower and relatively favorable. The patient, having acquired normal gait patterns, gradually develops weakness in the lower extremities with subsequent involvement of the upper extremities. Paresis is maximal in the girdle musculature, and the deep tendon reflexes are lost. Fasciculations are characteristically absent.

The "floppy infant" or "limp child" syndromes can result from nonprogressive brain lesions as well as involvement of peripheral nerve and muscle. These disorders must be distinguished from Werdnig-Hoffmann's disease, which superficially has a similar clinical picture of hypotonia. Atonic diplegia and Down's syndrome, examples of nonprogressive brain lesions, have hypotonia with preservation of deep tendon reflexes and significant intellectual impairment. Polyneuritis can be distinguished by the occasional demonstration of sensory impairment, elevated cerebrospinal fluid protein content, and a decreased nerve conduction velocity time. Congenital myopathies (benign congenital myopathy, central core disease, nemaline myopathy) are differentiated by preservation of reflexes and muscle biopsy. Myasthenia gravis often presents with hypotonia and weakness, bulbar signs, and extraocular muscle impairment. These physical findings lessen or disappear with intravenous edrophonium (Tensilon). The term "benign congenital hypotonia" has been applied to children with hypotonia in early infancy who subsequently show improvement and ultimately may have little or no motor weakness.

Oppenheim's disease or amyotonia congenita is no longer considered a clinical entity and probably encompassed many disorders with hypotonia.

Closely related to the spinal atrophies is *familial juvenile amyotrophic lateral sclerosis*. This is a rare disorder and usually occurs later in the juvenile period. It is more closely allied to adult amyotrophic lateral sclerosis and to the familial form of that disease. In contrast to Werdnig-Hoffmann's disease, the onset is later in life and tends to manifest itself earlier by weakness and atrophy of the small muscles of the hands and feet with later involvement of the proximal musculature. A further important clinical differentiation is the presence of overactive reflexes and persistently pathologic plantar responses. The pathology is a combined degeneration of both upper and lower motor neurons.

Progressive bulbar paralysis of childhood (*Fazio-Londes disease*) is a rare familial form of progressive atrophy in which the cranial nerve motor nuclei are prominently involved.

Cranial and Peripheral Nerve Degenerations

Leber's optic atrophy represents a heredodegenerative disorder involving for the most part a single cranial nerve. This sex-linked recessive disorder may occasionally be transmitted as an autosomal recessive or dominant trait. Symptoms may begin as early as 5 years of age. Puberty appears to be the usual time of onset of progressive loss of central vision which is characteristic of the disease. Early, the optic discs may be slightly edematous. Finally, temporal pallor is marked, due to the severe involvement of the papillomacular bundle. In some cases spasticity, mental retardation, ataxia, and seizures have been described. Total blindness occurs rarely. No treatment is available.

Peroneal muscular atrophy (neuromuscular atrophy, Charcot-Marie-Tooth disease) has a strong familial tendency. All modes of inheritance have been reported in addition to sporadic nonfamilial cases. Males are somewhat more affected than females. The onset is almost always in childhood, shortly after the sixth year. The age of onset and rate of progression have a strong tendency to be constant in a given family. The rate of progression is usually very slow, and orthopedic management of the bilateral footdrop is frequently of great value.

Degenerative pathologic changes are found in both peripheral nerves and spinal cord. Anterior horn cells, anterior roots, dorsal roots and ganglia, pyramidal tracts, the dorsal columns, and Clark's column are degenerated. The muscles show severe atrophy secondary to denervation.

The outstanding clinical feature of this syndrome is the symmetrically distributed atrophy of the feet and lower legs which results in the virtually pathognomonic "stork-leg" appearance. Bilateral footdrop results in the typical high-stepping gait and the characteristic slapping sound as the foot flops to the floor unhindered by dorsal flexion. Later the muscles of the hands and forearms may become atrophic. The thigh, upper arms, and proximal muscle groups are usually spared. Paresthesias, cramps, and pain are occasionally reported. Diminished touch, pain, and temperature sensation may be noted, particularly in the distribution of the peroneal nerve. Achilles tendon reflex is absent, but other reflexes are often spared.

Signs and symptoms more characteristic of either Friedreich's ataxia or the progressive spinal atrophies may be observed in some cases and serve to reemphasize the close interrelationship of the entire group of spinal cord degenerations. *A hypertrophic neuropathic form of Charcot-Marie-Tooth disease* with "stork-leg" and high-arched feet with hammer toe is inherited as an autosomal dominant.

A number of other forms of heredodegenerative peripheral neuropathies are more rarely encountered in children. The *hypertrophic interstitial neuritis of Dejerine-Sottas* is characterized by a grossly palpable enlargement of the peripheral nerves. The peripheral nerve involvement is asymmetric and affects several single peripheral nerves such as the median nerve, resulting in a carpal tunnel syndrome together with a peroneal palsy causing a drop foot. This combination of multiple single nerves has been called "mononeuritis multiplex." One form of hypertrophic interstitial neuritis manifests itself during the first year of life with profound interference with learning to walk. A familial form of recurrent brachial neuritis has been reported and is occasionally seen in children. Hereditary neuropathy with interstitial neuritis and nerve deafness (*Alpert's syndrome*) is a rare condition first suspected bcause of deafness in childhood. Hereditary polyneuritis associated with retinitis pigmentosa and ataxia (*Refsum's syndrome*) and progressive hereditary sensory radicular neuropathy have also been reported in children.

Congenital indifference to pain may occur on a familial basis. All sensation is appreciated, but the patient is indifferent to pain. Severe and normally painful injuries are not painful to the child. Multiple fractures, neurotrophic joint changes, burns, and infections are common. Child rearing is hazardous and difficult.

Refsum's syndrome is an autosomal recessively inherited condition otherwise known as heredopathia atactica polyneuritiformis. A symmetric chronic polyneuritis and ataxia with other cerebellar signs are the principal neurologic findings. Retinitis pigmentosa is a common feature. Occasionally neurogenic hearing loss and anosmia are noted. Often electrocardiographic abnormalities are found. Epiphyseal dysplasia with pes cavus and shortening of the metacarpals and metatarsals may be seen. Ichthyosis of the skin is frequently present. Cerebrospinal fluid protein is increased without pleocytosis.

The onset is in childhood but may be delayed into the second or third decade. The course is essentially progressive with some tendency to relapses and remission. No therapy is available.

Pathologically an interstitial hypertrophic polyneuropathy is associated with posterior column degeneration and anterior horn cell degeneration. There is patchy demyelination of the brainstem and cell loss in the olivary, red, vestibular, cochlear, vagal, and dentate nuclei.

Biochemical studies by Klenk and by Kahlke have shown an accumulation of an unusual branched-chain fatty acid, 3,7,11,15,-tetramethyl hexadeca-noic acid (phytanic acid), in the fatty acids of phospholipid and cholesterol ester fractions of plasma and in liver and kidney. The accumulation of phytanic acid is the result of faulty alpha oxidation of phytanic acid to alpha-hydroxyphytanic acid. Dietary restriction of phytanic acid precursors has therapeutic promise.

Hereditary sensory neuropathy associated with spinal cord disease has been described as having its onset in adolescence. These cases are distinguished from hereditary sensory radicular neuropathy by virtue of the presence of spinal cord pathology. Familial lumbosacral syringomyelia may also occur and must be distinguished from the purely neuropathic syndromes. In the Anrade form of primary amyloidosis the neuropathy may strongly suggest lumbar syringomyelia.

The Neurocutaneous Syndromes

Since skin and nervous system have a common embryologic origin from the ectodermal layer, it is not surprising that there is a large number of neurologic conditions associated with cutaneous manifestations. Again the familial and hereditary nature of these disorders argues for a genetic origin and a basic enzymatic or metabolic defect as the primary pathogenic feature, although biochemical data are lacking.

Tuberous sclerosis (adenoma sebaceum, epiloia, Bourneville-Pringle's disease) is inherited as a dominant autosomal trait, the expression of which is dependent upon the presence or absence of a modifying gene. This accounts for the marked variability of expression noted in clinical practice (Table 15 and Fig. 38A, B, C, D, E, and F).

The full syndrome is characterized by seizures, mental deficiency, and adenoma sebaceum with foci of intracranial calcification, particularly in the peri-

TABLE 15. *Tuberous Sclerosis — Clinical and Pathologic Manifestations*

Skin	Depigmented nevi
	Adenoma sebaceum
	Shagreen patch
	Lipoma
	Subungual fibroma
Brain	Convulsions
	Retardation
	Intracranial calcifications
Eye	Retinal phakoma
Bone	Skull: areas of sclerosis
	Phalanges: areas of rarefaction; thickening of the cortex
Heart	Rhabdomyoma
Lung	"Honeycomb"
Kidney	Polycystic or angiomyolipoma

ventricular region, although they may be scattered throughout the hemispheres. The seizures are most often infantile spasms in the very young child and the grand mal type in the older child; any variant of convulsive disorder may be seen. In the full syndrome, mental deficiency is generally of a severe degree. However, cases of tuberous sclerosis with normal or near-normal intellectual capacity are seen. The characteristic skin lesions, fibroangiomatous nevi, have been mislabeled adenoma sebaceum. The sebaceous glands are only involved secondarily. Fibroangiomatous nevi may be present during the first year of life, but more commonly are not noted until about the age of 4 or 5. These lesions take the form of discrete pink or yellowish papules located principally on the face and in the so-called butterfly distribution on the bridge of the nose, the malar prominences, and along the nasal-labial folds. They may also occur on forehead, neck, and trunk. Individual lesions remain static, gradually growing redder and eventually becoming brownish. They do not itch nor do they suppurate; these features serve to distinguish them from acne vulgaris and seborrheic dermatitis. Other skin lesions consist of raised plaquelike flesh-colored lesions, which may be found anywhere on the body, and the "shagreen patches," which are slightly pigmented and raised and resemble coarse-grained leather. These are found principally on the trunk and lower extremities. Fibromas of the scalp are seen on occasion, as are areas of depigmentation. These latter may be one of the earliest ectodermal manifestations of tuberous sclerosis. If present, the subungual fibroma, a flesh-colored sessile growth emerging from the groove of the nailbed, is quite characteristic. Several types of retinal lesions may be observed. One is a small, flat, white or yellowish phakoma or spot on or close to the optic nerve head. These may be multiple. A second lesion seen in the fundus is a raised cluster of translucent white tissue. Systemic involvement may include multiple small fibroadenomas of the kidney, rhabdomyoma of the heart, and myomas of the uterus and vagina.

The brain contains many small firm sclerotic nodules (tubera) which are chiefly in the cortex but may be found in all parts of the central nervous system. They may project into the ventricle causing deformities which can be detected by pneumoencephalography (Fig. 38D). Hydrocephalus with increased intracranial pressure may develop as a result of one of these masses blocking the ventricular system. These nodules contain giant-sized haphazardly arranged cells, at times appearing to be astrocytic and at other times resembling ganglion cells. Adjacent to these collections of giant glial cells may be found degeneration of nerve cells and fibers and often cavity formation. Dense astrocytic gliosis is also seen.

The diagnosis can be established on the basis of the triad of seizures, mental deficiency, and adenoma sebaceum. In infancy, tuberous sclerosis should be suspected when infantile spasms coexist with depigmented skin lesions. In such children a careful evalu-

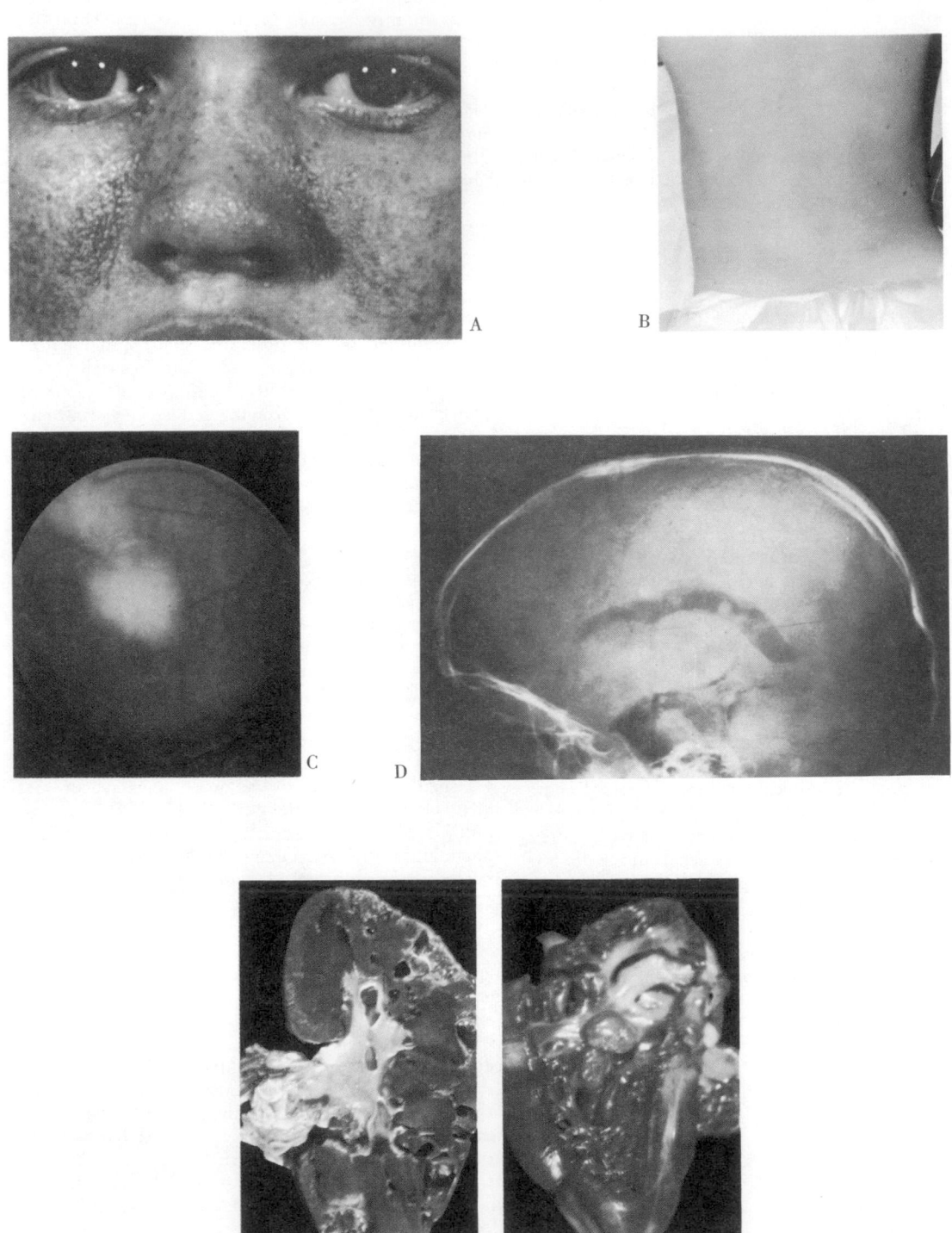

Fig. 38. Tuberous sclerosis. *A.* Adenoma sebaceum. *B.* Depigmented nevi. *C.* Retinal phakoma. *D.* Pneumonencephalogram demonstrating gliotic nodules projecting into ventricle ("candle dripping"). *E.* Polycystic kidney. *F.* Rhabdomyoma of heart.

TABLE 16. *Neurofibromatosis—Clinical and Pathologic Manifestations*

Soft Tissue	Café-au-lait nevus	
	Fibroma molluscum	
Neurologic	Peripheral nerve	Neurofibroma
		Plexiform neuroma
	Nerve roots	Intradural neurofibroma
	Spinal cord	Syringomyelia
		Tumors—ependymoma
	Cranial nerves	Optic nerve glioma
		Acoustic neuroma
	Brain	Convulsions
		Mental deficiency
		Brain tumors
Bone	Scoliosis	
	Congenital bowing and pseudarthrosis	
	Posterosuperior orbital wall defects. Unilateral pulsating exophthalmos	
	Disorders of bone growth	
	Macrocephaly	
Congenital anomalies	Spina bifida	
	Anomalies of vertebral segmentation	
	Pes cavus	
	Rib deformities	

ation of the family may reveal other cases of this disorder. X-rays of the skull often show intracranial calcifications. X-rays of the hands and feet may show small cystic lesions in the distal phalanges. Pneumoencephalography may outline the many glial nodules in the walls of the ventricles, giving what has been called "candle-guttering" with the effect of dripping wax.

Treatment is entirely symptomatic and is focused largely on the control of the convulsive disorder and management of the mentally defective child. Care should be taken in giving the prognosis in an infant or young child, since such great variation is seen in the neurologic as well as dermatologic aspects of this disorder.

Neurofibromatosis (von Recklinghausen's disease) is inherited as an autosomal dominant trait with marked variability of expression: while the characteristic pathology consists of neurofibromas of the peripheral, spinal, and cranial nerves, meningiomas and gliomas of the spinal cord and brain do occur. The condition includes the following manifestations (Table 16): multiple soft tumors beneath the skin (fibroma molluscum), multiple tumors situated along nerve trunks (neurofibromas), and pigmentation of the skin. Varying degrees of mental deficiency may occur. The peripheral neurofibromas are found along the course of nerve trunks, subcutaneous nerves, and cranial nerves. The auditory nerve is very frequently involved. The optic nerve is a frequent site of astrocytoma and less commonly meningioma. Within the spinal cord ependymomas, astrocytomas, and diffuse gliomas are seen. Pheochromocytomas are seen in the adult age group.

Clinically a common sequence is for excessive pigmentation to be noted during infancy; the charac-

teristic superficial skin lesions make their appearance in childhood or puberty; individual lesions grow slowly, with puberty and pregnancy apparently exercising an accelerating effect. Siblings, parents, and other members of the family will often show the typical skin lesions. These cutaneous manifestations may take two forms, "café-au-lait" spots and pigmented nevi (Fig. 39). The pigmented nevi appear at an earlier age and are in no way different from the common moles, save in their number. The "café-au-lait" lesions are fewer in number and tend to be distributed along the paths of the cutaneous nerves. They are roughly oval in outline, with the long axis parallel to the nerve.

The tumors may be confined to the subcutaneous tissues or may be predominantly within the bony confines of the central nervous system. The most common histologic lesion is the benign neurilemmoma. Fibromas are also present, and sarcomatous degeneration may occur in the adult. When the tu-

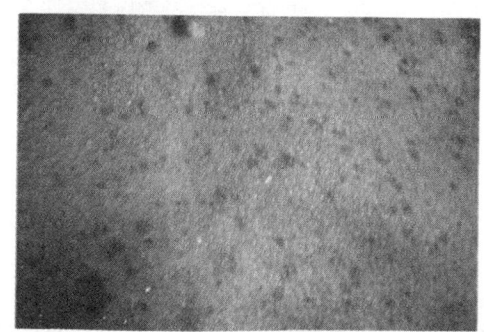

Fig. 39. **Neurofibromatosis. Café-au-lait nevus.**

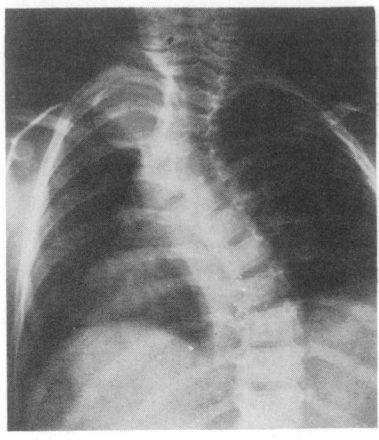

Fig. 40. Neurofibromatosis. Scoliosis and characteristic apical lesion.

TABLE 17. *Encephalotrigeminal   Angiomatosis (Sturge-Weber-Dimitri Disease)—Clinical and Laboratory Manifestations*

Skin	Port-wine facial nevus usually in trigeminal nerve distribution
Neurologic	Convulsions Hemiparesis Hemianopia Mental retardation
Ocular	Glaucoma
Laboratory	Skull x-ray: "trolley track" calcifications EEG: focal abnormalities Carotid arteriogram: vascular anomalies or thromboses

mors occupy bone they produce localized areas of rarefaction, or they may give rise to thickening or excessive linear growth of the long bone. The pendulous masses of fibrous tissue and skin are more characteristic of the adult form of neurofibromatosis and are rarely seen in children.

Neurofibromatosis must be differentiated from tuberous sclerosis. In the former, the lesions tend to involve the peripheral outflow of the central nervous system, whereas in the tuberous sclerotic patient, the central lesions are the primary pathology. Mental deficiency is much more frequent with tuberous sclerosis than it is with neurofibromatosis. Epilepsy may occur in both, but it is a very common complication in tuberous sclerosis and is relatively rare in neurofibromatosis. As in tuberous sclerosis, a parent may have a relatively benign form of the disease, whereas the child can be very severely involved from the neurologic point of view.

A great variety of signs and symptoms may occur in neurofibromatosis, depending upon the location of the lesions. Optic nerve tumors within the orbit may lead to progressive exophthalmos with optic atrophy. Astrocytomas of the third ventricle and hypothalamus may be associated with neurofibromatosis and result in the symptom complex of diabetes insipidus, adiposity, genital maldevelopment, or precocious puberty. The lesions may present themselves as intramedullary tumors of the spinal cord. In some families, bilateral acoustic nerve tumors may be the prominent feature with few skin manifestations.

The diagnosis is often aided by x-ray studies which may reveal large "scalloped" neural foramina in the spine, scoliosis (Fig. 40), or enlarged optic foramina if optic nerve tumors are present. With auditory nerve tumors, an enlarged internal auditory canal may be apparent on roentgenologic study. The diagnosis is best made on the basis of the nature of the cutaneous manifestations and evidence of multiple peripheral nerve lesions.

Therapy is surgical removal of the offending neurofibromas, but it must be recalled that no definitive cure can be expected owing to the multiple nature of the lesions. Surgery should only be carried out when a particular lesion becomes a major symptomatic problem for the patient. Definitive treatment is not possible. A conservative therapeutic policy seems advisable.

Polyostotic fibrous dysplasia (Allbright's syndrome) is important in the differential diagnosis of neurofibromatosis. In this condition large areas of tan or brown, irregularly outlined pigmentation appear on the skin and are associated with precocious puberty in the female.

Encephalotrigeminal angiomatosis (Sturge-Weber-Dimitri syndrome). This syndrome (Table 17) includes a port-wine vascular nevus often in the distribution of the first division of the trigeminal nerve (Fig. 41); convulsions, often focal and involving the contralateral side; contralateral hemipa-

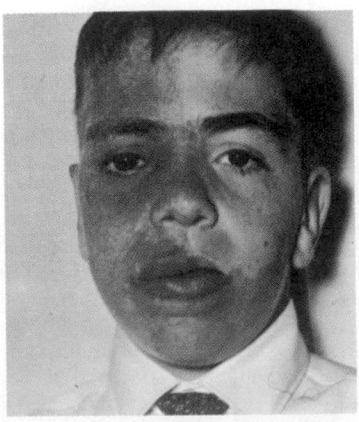

Fig. 41. Encephalotrigeminal angiomatosis. Characteristic port-wine facial nevus in distribution of trigeminal nerve. Note involvement of both sides of face.

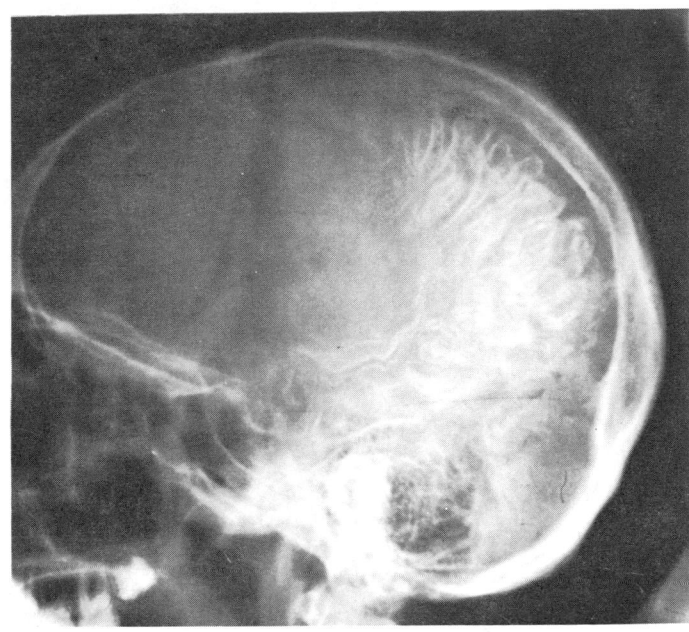

Fig. 42. Encephalotrigeminal angiomatosis. Skull x-ray showing characteristic intracranial calcification.

resis; and occasionally homonymous hemianopsia. Ipsilateral intracranial calcifications are found by x-ray. These calcifications are characteristically in paired lines, often called "trolley tracks" (Fig. 42). Additional symptomatology includes increased intraocular tension caused by angiomatous involvement of the uveal tract. This may give rise to enlargement of the involved globe. Approximately two-thirds of the children with this condition are mentally retarded, and somewhat more than 50 percent have convulsive disorders. A hemiparesis is less common.

There is great variability in the severity of the individual symptoms, and in some instances one or another may be missing entirely. Hemangiomas may be found in various parts of the body as well as on the face and rarely in the fundi.

The intracranial lesion is an angiomatous one which involves the meninges in the area supplied by the first division of the trigeminal nerve and sometimes also the superficial vessels occupying the sulci over the convexity, particularly in the occipital and parietal regions. This may cause atrophy of the underlying brain tissue, and the degenerative changes in cerebral tissue lying just below the gyral surface are frequently followed by the characteristic calcifications. The demonstration of intracranial calcifications limited to the convexity of the brain and showing the characteristic gyral pattern is almost pathognomonic. The diagnosis is usually made from the physical findings alone. Electroencephalography may show suppression of activity on the side which contains the nevus, and pneumoencephalography may reveal some cortical atrophy with dilation of the lateral ventricle on the involved side.

Therapy is entirely symptomatic, although early surgical intervention has been successful occasionally.

The differential diagnosis should include the Wyburn-Mason syndrome, in which telangiectasia or hypertrophic angiomas may appear on the face. However, in this condition there is the constant association of cirsoid angioma of the retina and mesencephalic aneurysmal angiomas. The syndrome of Van Bogaert-Divry is a combination of diffuse cortical meningeal angiomatosis in which dementia, severe convulsive disorder, pyramidal and extrapyramidal motor symptoms, and congenital poikiloderma with multiple telangiectasia are found.

Several other conditions must be mentioned in relation to the vascular malformations involving the central nervous system. *Von Hippel-Lindau's disease*, a disorder limited to adults, is characterized by hemangioblastomas of the cerebellum, liver, pancreas, and kidneys. Skin lesions are not seen in this condition, which is inherited as a dominant trait. *Neurocutaneous melanosis* consists of multiple pigmented nevi, often in the "bathing trunk" distribution (see Fig. 11), widely scattered over the surface of the skin. Intracranially, multiple pigmented and nonpigmented nevi are found in the meninges and in perivascular areas of brain and cerebellum. Multiple pia-arachnoid telangiectases are associated with the nevi. Progressive hydrocephalus is the clinical manifestation most often noted. *Disseminated hemangiomatosis* of the skin and multiple cerebral, pontine, and cerebellar hemangiomas have been reported to occur in familial distribution. Macrocephaly and pseudopapilledema may be associated with the multiple cutaneous strawberry hemangiomas.

Ataxia-telangiectasia (Louis-Bar) (Table 18) is a recessively inherited, progressive ataxia in which oculocutaneous telangiectasia is a diagnostic feature. Ataxia becomes evident when the child begins to

TABLE 18.   *Ataxia-Telangiectasia—Clinical and Laboratory Manifestations*

Inheritance	Autosomal recessive
Clinical	Onset 1½-3 years—Neurologic
	Progressive cerebellar ataxia and/or choreoathetosis
	Speech—slow and dysarthric
	Parkinsonian facies
	At 4-6 years of age—Telangiectasis
	Bulbar conjunctiva
	Butterfly area of face
	Elbows and knees
	At any age—Infections
	Primary sinopulmonary
Laboratory	Hypogammaglobulinemia

walk; intention tremor, dysarthric speech, and choreoathetosis develop later. About the age of 4 to 6 years, the telangiectatic lesions begin to appear. These are characteristically in the bulbar conjunctivae, the "butterfly" area of the face, and the external ear (Fig. 43). Later, the antecubital and popliteal fossae and creases of the neck also show the telangiectatic lesions. Frequent upper respiratory infections are another characteristic of the disease. These are believed to be due to a decreased serum gamma-1A globulin. The course is slowly progressive, and most children are incapacitated by the time they reach adolescence. The oldest surviving patient was 25 years of age.

Pathologically there is a primary and diffuse cortical cerebellar degeneration. The Purkinje cells are chiefly affected. The white matter is essentially spared. There are some changes in dentate and olivary nuclei, but the rest of the central nervous system appears to be relatively spared. The thymus has been reported as abnormally small and tonsils and adenoids virtually absent. Several patients have died of lymphoreticular malignancies. Excessive amino-aciduria with large amounts of a peptide containing proline and hydroxyproline has been reported.

Hemangiectatic hypertrophy of a limb (Klippel-Trenaunay syndrome) may be associated with ichthyosis, mental deficiency, and a convulsive disorder. Differential diagnosis from other forms of neurocutaneous syndromes and in particular neurofibromatosis should be made.

A variety of other dermatologic conditions are associated with central nervous system malfunction. Spastic paraparesis in cases of juvenile acanthosis nigricans has been reported. Ichthyosis, mental deficiency, and epilepsy are described in combination as *Rud's syndrome*. In some cases retinal degeneration and genital hypoplasia are noted. The combination of spastic diplegia, mental deficiency, and congenital ichthyosis is reported as an autosomal recessive trait under the term *Sjögren-Larsson's syndrome. Anhidrotic* or *hypohidrotic* ectodermal dysplasias may be associated with mild to moderate mental retardation. Follicular keratosis has been reported in association with mental deficiency (*Darier's disease*).

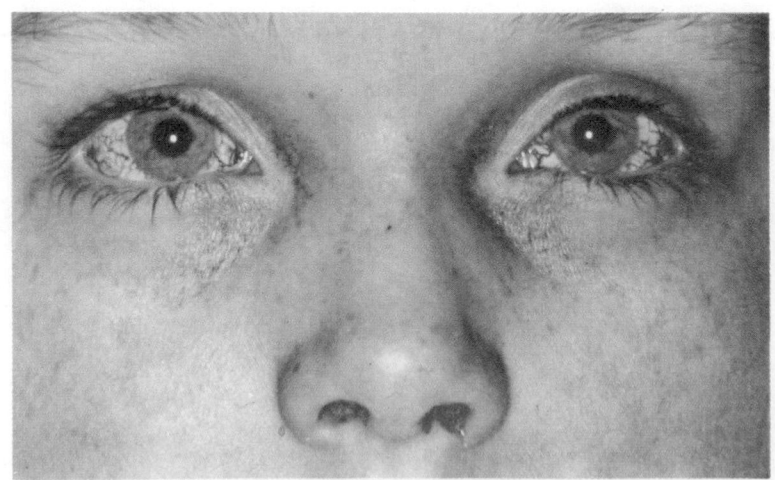

Fig. 43. Ataxia-telangiectasia. Typical bulbar conjunctival telangiectasia in 13-year-old boy. (Courtesy of Drs. E. Boder and R. P. Sedgwick.)

Incontinentia pigmenti (Bloch-Sulzberger's syndrome) has been reported as a familial disorder. Most cases are sporadic. There appears to be a definite prevalence in females. Typically during the neonatal period groups of vesicles occur in a linear distribution along the extremities. As these disappear, the linear verrucal skin lesions begin to show the characteristic gray-blue to brown pigmentation which is distributed in wavy lines, giving an appearance similar to the pattern of marble. In some cases the preliminary vesicular and verrucous lesions apparently do not occur. Alopecia and dental defects are also frequently seen. From a neurologic point of view, mental deficiency, spasticity, and hemiparesis occur. A convulsive disorder is frequent, and microcephaly is not uncommon. Pneumoencephalography usually shows ventricular dilation. In at least one case showing skin lesions almost exclusively confined to one side, the ipsilateral cerebral ventricle was more dilated than that on the side of the noninvolved skin. Congenital generalized melanoleucoderma (Naegeli's syndrome) may be confused with incontinenta pigmenti.

Linear nevus sebaceus is associated with a convulsive disorder and mental retardation. The skin lesion consists of very closely placed papules formed by thickening and hyperkeratosis of the epidermis with marked hyperplasia of the sebaceous glands. The lesion characteristically starts as an oval-shaped area in the center of the forehead extending as a fine line over the midline of the nose to the upper lip. Neurologic examination is normal, but the electroencephalogram shows focal discharges of high-voltage spikes in the parietal and occipital regions. Seizures and mental retardation are the prominent symptoms.

Ectodermal dysplasia (anhidrotic type) is a sex-linked recessive condition in which the brain damage, seizures, and mental retardation are probably due to repeated episodes of high temperatures. The features are aplasia of sweat, sebaceous, and mucous glands with hypotrichosis. Small, wide-spaced teeth with peg-shaped incisors are present.

The basal cell nevus syndrome, an autosomal dominant disorder, consists of brown, slightly raised, hard basal cell nevi appearing anywhere on the skin. These may appear in childhood and may later degenerate to basal cell carcinomas. Cysts of the jaw, hypertelorism, and lamellar calcification of the falx cerebri make up the complete syndrome. Mental deficiency, hydrocephalus, agenesis of the corpus callosum, and medulloblastomas have been reported with the disorder.

Supportive Therapy and Management of the Progressive Degenerative Diseases

Although no specific curative or definitive treatment can be offered in the diseases previously discussed, much can be accomplished by way of supportive therapy for both patient and family.

The problems of management can be divided into those pertaining to the patient and those which primarily concern the parents. Frank, sympathetic, and direct discussion with the parents should include a careful explanation of the definitive diagnosis, the course of the disease, the prognosis for life, and an offer of genetic counseling and supportive psychiatric assistance. Enlisting the aid of trained social workers and visiting nurses is often extremely helpful. In the less rapidly progressive disorders and where mental retardation, ataxia, spasticity, visual impairment, and seizures occur in a variety of combinations, the parents will need help in educational placement. School systems and teachers should be given adequate interpretations of the handicaps and instruction in their management.

The increasing incapacity of the child leads to serious problems in feeding, prevention of infection and decubiti, fluid and electrolyte balance, prevention of contractures, and bowel and bladder care. Gavage feedings almost always become necessary in the storage diseases and in the diffuse sclerosis. Too high a caloric intake is to be avoided in order to facilitate skin care and maintenance of good positioning. Passive exercise, footboards, and frequent scheduled turning are also indicated. Paralytic ileus is a common complication. Enemas and suppositories are often required. Urinary and fecal incontinence demand extra attention to skin care. In the terminal stages, machine aspiration will be needed. With careful instruction, most of these maintenance procedures can be carried out in a home environment and thus obviate the necessity for long and expensive hospitalization. In the terminal stages, hospitalization is essential.

In the spinocerebellar, spinal, and neuromuscular disorders where progression is slower, physical therapy, occupational therapy, and occasionally judicious orthopedic intervention may be helpful. However, parents, orthopedists, and patients should not be led to believe that such therapy is definitive and must come to understand the fundamentally progressive nature of the disorder.

Anticonvulsant therapy is often more difficult in the degenerative diseases than in other forms of symptomatic or idiopathic epilepsy, but the same basic principles apply as in all forms of seizure disorders. Myoclonic seizures are difficult to control, and exclusion of as many sensory stimuli as possible may be helpful, particularly in the "stimulus-sensitive" forms of myoclonus. Phenobarbital and Dilantin continue to be the most useful anticonvulsants. Paradione, Tridione, Zarontin, Valium, and occasionally the milder forms of tranquilizing drugs may be helpful in controlling the myoclonic activity.

In the phakomatous group of diseases a careful watch for the development of secondary glaucoma must be maintained. In many of the neurocutaneous syndromes the development of secondary malignancies and increased intracranial pressure should be a source of constant concern for the attending physician.

The treatment and management of the progressive degenerative diseases of the central nervous system represent a challenge for physicians as well as auxiliary personnel in nursing, physical therapy, occupational therapy, and psychologic and educational services. These patients and especially their parents present some of the most difficult physician-patient relationship problems to be faced in pediatric practice.

REFERENCES

Aita, J. A. Neurocutaneous Diseases. Springfield, Ill., Charles C Thomas, Publ., 1966.

Freeman, J. M., and McKhann, G. M. Degenerative diseases of the central nervous system. In Advances in Pediatrics. Chicago, Year Book Medical Publishers, 1969, Vol. 16.

Gellis, S. S., and Feingold, M. Atlas of Mental Retardation Syndromes. Washington, D.C., U.S. Govt. Printing Office, 1968.

Gibbs, C. J., Jr., and Gajdusek, D. C. Infection as the etiology of spongiform encephalopathy (Creutzfeldt-Jakob Disease). Science, 165:1023, 1969.

McKusick, V. A. Mendelian Inheritance in Man, 2nd ed. Baltimore, Johns Hopkins Press, 1968.

Stanbury, J. B., Wyngaarden, J. B., and Fredrickson, D. S., eds. The Metabolic Basis of Inherited Disease, 2nd ed. New York, McGraw-Hill Book Co., 1966.

CEREBROMACULAR DEGENERATION

Brady, R. O. Genetics and the sphingolipidoses. Med. Clin. N. Amer., 53:827, 1969.

Brown, N. J., Corner, D. B., and Dodgson, M. C. H. A sceond case in the same family of congenital familial cerebral lipoidosis resembling amaurotic family idiocy. Arch. Dis. Child., 29:48, 1954.

Derry, D. M., Fawcett, J. S., Anderman, F., and Wolfe, L. S. Late infantile systemic lipidosis. Neurology, 18: 340, 1968.

Donahue, S., Zeman, W., and Watanabe, I. Electron microscopic observations in Batten's disease. In Inborn Errors of Sphingolipid Metabolism. New York, Pergamon Press, Inc., 1966.

Hagberg, B., Hultquist, G., Ohman, R., and Svennerholm, L. Congenital amaurotic idiocy. Acta Paediat. (Uppsala), 54:116, 1965.

Harlem, O. K. Juvenile cerebroretinal degeneration (Spielmeyer-Vogt): Blood and EEG findings in a family of 10 members. Amer. J. Dis. Child., 100:918, 1960.

Jatzkewitz, H., and Sandhoff, K. On a biochemically special form of infantile amaurotic idiocy. Biochem. Biophys. Acta, 70:354, 1963.

Jervis, G. A. Juvenile amaurotic idiocy. Amer. J. Dis. Child., 97:663, 1959.

Kanof, A., Aronson, S. M., and Volk, B. W. Clinical progression of amaurotic family idiocy. Amer. J. Dis. Child., 97:656, 1959.

Kristensson, K., and Sourander, P. Occurrence of lipofuscin in inherited metabolic diseases affecting the nervous system. J. Neurol. Neurosurg. Psychiat., 29: 113, 1966.

Knudson, A. G., and Kaplan, W. D. Genetics of sphingolipidoses. In Aronson, S. M., and Volk, B. W., eds., The Sphingolipidoses. New York, Academic Press, Inc., 1962, pp. 395-411.

Korey, S. R., and Stein, A. Studies in Tay-Sachs disease. III. Biochemistry. B. Catabolism of gangliosides and related compounds. J. Neuropath. Exp. Neurol., 22: 67, 1963.

Landing, B. H., Silverman, F. N., Craig, J. M., Jacoby, M. E., Lahey, M. E., and Chadwick, D. L. Familial neurovisceral lipidosis. Amer. J. Dis. Child., 108:503, 1964.

Merritt, A. D., Smith, S. A., Strouth, J. C., and Zeman, W. Detection of heterozygotes in Batten's disease. Ann. N.Y. Acad. Sci., 155:860, 1968.

Norman, R. M., and Wood, N. Congenital form of amaurotic family idiocy. J. Neurol. Psychiat., 4:175, 1941.

Okada, S., and O'Brien, J. S. Generalized gangliosidosis: Beta-galactosidase deficiency. Science, 160:1002, 1968.

——— and O'Brien, J. S. Tay-Sachs disease: Generalized absence of a beta-D-N-hexosaminidase component. Science, 165:698, 1969.

Rayner, S. Juvenile Amaurotic Idiocy in Sweden. Uppsala Institute for Medical Genetics of the University of Sweden, 1962.

Suzuki, K. Cerebral GM_1-gangliosidosis: Chemical pathology of visceral organs. Science, 159:1471, 1968.

——— Suzuki, K., Rapin, I., Suzuki, Y., and Ishii, N. Juvenile GM_2-gangliosidosis. Neurology, 20:190, 1970.

——— Suzuki, K., and Kamoshita, S. Chemical pathology of GM_1-gangliosidosis (generalized gangliosidosis). J. Neuropath. Exp. Neurol., 28:25, 1969.

Svennerholm, L. Gangliosides. J. Lipid Res., 5:145, 1964.

——— The chemical structure of normal human brain and Tay-Sachs gangliosides. Biochem. Biophys. Res. Commun., 9:436, 1962.

Vogt, B. W., Aronson, S. M., and Saifer, A. Fructose-1-phosphate adolase deficiency in Tay-Sachs disease. Amer. J. Med., 36:481, 1964.

——— Schneck, L., Saifer, A., and Aronson, S. M. Tay-Sachs Disease. New York, Grune and Stratton, Inc., 1964.

——— et al. G_5 ganglioside variant of systemic late infantile lipidosis. Arch. Path., 87:393, 1969.

Wolfe, L. S., Callahan, J., Fawcett, M. S., Andermann, F., and Scriver, C. R. GM_1-gangliosidosis without chondrodystrophy or visceromegaly: Beta-galactosidase deficiency with gangliosidosis and the excessive excretion of a keratan sulfate. Neurology, 20:23, 1970.

Zeman, W., and Donahue, S. Fine structure of the lipid bodies in juvenile amaurotic idiocy. Acta Neuropath., 3:144, 1963.

NIEMANN-PICK DISEASE

Brady, R. O. The spingolipidoses. New Eng. J. Med., 275:312, 1966.

Crocker, A. C., and Farber, S. Niemann-Pick's disease: A review of 18 patients. Medicine, 37:1, 1958.

Forsythe, W. E., McKeown, E. F., and Neill, D. W. Three cases of Niemann-Pick's disease in children. Arch. Dis. Child., 34:406, 1959.

GAUCHER'S DISEASE

Banker, B. Q., Miller, J. Q., and Crocker, A. C. The cerebral pathology of infantile Gaucher's disease. In Aronson, S. M., and Volk, B. W., eds., Cerebral Sphingolipidoses. New York, Academic Press, Inc., 1962.

Kampine, J. P., Brady, R. O., Kanfer, J. N., Feld, M., and Shapiro, D. Diagnosis of Gaucher's disease and Niemann-Pick's disease with small samples of venous blood. Science, 155:86, 1967.

Maloney, A. F. J., and Cumings, J. N. A case of juvenile Gaucher's disease with intraneuronal lipid storage. J. Neurol. Neurosurg. Psychiat., 23:207, 1960.

Stein, M., and Gardner, L. I. Acute infantile Gaucher's disease. Pediatrics, 27:491, 1961.

PROGRESSIVE FAMILIAL MYOCLONIC EPILEPSY (UNVERRICHT'S DISEASE)

Aigner, B. R., and Mulder, D. W. Myoclonus. Arch. Neurol., 2:600, 1960.

Gilbert, G. J., McEntee, W. J., and Glaser, G. H. Familial myoclonus and ataxia; pathophysiologic implications. Neurology, 13:365, 1963.

Harriman, D. G. F., Millar, J. H. D., and Stevenson, A. C. Progressive familial myoclonic epilepsy in three families: its clinical features and pathological basis. Brain, 78:325, 1955.

Janeway, R., Ravens, J. R., Pearce, L. A., Odor, D. L., and Suzuki, K. Progressive myoclonus epilepsy with Lafora inclusion bodies: I. Clinical, genetic, histopathologic and biochemical aspects. Arch. Neurol., 16:565, 1967.

Odor, D. L., Janeway, R., Pearce, L. A., and Ravens, J. R. Progressive myoclonus epilepsy: II. Studies of ultrastructure. Arch. Neurol., 16:583, 1967.

Van Heycop Ten Ham, M. W., and DeJager, H. Progressive myoclonus epilepsy with Lafora bodies, clinical-pathological features. Epilepsia, 4:95, 1963.

FARBER'S DISEASE

Abul-Haj, S. K., Martz, D. G., Douglas, W. F., and Geppert, L. J. Pathogenesis of Farber's disease. J. Pediat., 61:221, 1962.

Farber, S. A lipid metabolic disorder—disseminated "lipogranulomatosis." Amer. J. Dis. Child., 84:499, 1952.

Prensky, A. L. et al. Ceramide and ganglioside accumulation in Farber's lipogranulomatosis. Proc. Soc. Exp. Biol. Med., 126:725, 1967.

FABRY'S DISEASE

Brady, R. O. et al. Enzymatic defect in Fabry's disease; ceramidetrihexosidase deficiency. New Eng. J. Med., 276:1163, 1967.

Kocen, R. S., and Thomas, P. K. Peripheral nerve involvement in Fabry's disease. Arch. Neurol., 22:81, 1970.

Low, H. O. C., and Reske-Nielsen, E. The central nervous system in Fabry's disease. Arch. Neurol., 25:351, 1971.

Matalon, R., Dorfman, A., Dawson, G., and Sweeley, C. C. Glycolipid and mucopolysaccharide abnormality in fibroblasts of Fabry's disease. Science, 164:1522, 1969.

Rahman, A. N., and Lindenberg, G. The neuropathology of hereditary dystopic lipidosis. Arch. Neurol., 9:373, 1963.

Wise, D. et al. Angiokeratoma corporis diffusum: Clinical study of eight affected families. Quart. J. Med., 31:177, 1961.

CEREBRAL CHOLINESTEROSIS

Jervis, G. A. Degenerative encephalopathy of childhood (cortical degeneration, cerebellar atrophy, cholesterinosis of basal ganglia). J. Neuropath. Exp. Neurol., 16:308, 1957.

Van Bogaert, L., Scherer, H. J., and Epstein, E. Une Forme Cerebrale de la Cholesterinose Generaliseé. Paris, Masson et Cie, 1937.

Wolman, M., Sterk, V. V., Gott, S., and Frenkel, M. Primary familial xanthomatosis with involvement and calcification of the adrenals. Pediatrics, 28:742, 1961.

HELLER'S DISEASE

Dietze, H. J. Dementia infantilis, Heller. Amer. J. Ment. Defic., 68:193, 1963.

Korey, S. R., and Winograd, H. Biochemical alterations in a case of Heller's disease. Amer. J. Dis. Child., 97:668, 1959.

HURLER'S DISEASE (GARGOYLISM)

Berry, H. K., and Spinanger, J. Paper spot test useful in study of Hurler's syndrome. J. Lab. Clin. Med., 55:136, 1960.

Foly, K. M., Danes, B. S., and Bearn, A. G. White blood cell culture in genetic studies on the human mucopolysaccharidoses. Science, 164:424, 1969.

Fratantoni, J. C., Hall, C. W., and Neufeld, E. F. Hurler and Hunter syndromes: Mutual correction of the defect in cultural fibroblasts. Science, 162:570, 1968.

——— et al. Intrauterine diagnosis of Hurler and Hunter syndromes. New Eng. J. Med., 280:686, 1969.

Hambrick, G. W., Jr. Skin changes in Hurler's syndrome. Arch. Derm., 85:455, 1962.

Ho, M. W., and O'Brien, J. S. Hurler's syndrome: Deficiency of a specific beta-galactosidase isoenzyme. Science, 165:611, 1969.

Lindsay, S., Reilly, W. A., Gotham, T. J., and Skahen, R. Gargoylism, study of pathologic lesions and clinical review of twelve cases. Amer. J. Dis. Child., 76:239, 1948.

McKusick, V. A. et al. The genetic mucopolysaccharidoses. Medicine, 44:6, 445, 1965.

Muir, H., Miltwoch, U., and Bitter, T. Diagnostic value of isolated urinary mucopolysaccharides and lymphocytic inclusions in gargoylism. Arch. Dis. Child., 38:358, 1963.

Renuart, A. W. Screening for inborn errors of metabolism associated with mental deficiency or neurologic disorders or both. New Eng. J. Med., 274:384, 1966.

Sanfilippo, S. J., Podosin, R., Langer, L., and Good, R. A. Mental retardation associated with acid mucopolysacchariduria (hepartin sulfate). J. Pediat., 63:837, 1963.

GLYCOGEN STORAGE DISEASE

Hug, G., Garancis, J. C., Schubert, W. K., and Kaplan, S. Glycogen storage disease types II, III, VIII, IX. A biochemical and electron microscopic analysis. Amer. J. Dis. Child., 111:457, 1966.

Smith, H. L. et al. Type II glycogenosis. Amer. J. Dis. Child., 3:475-481, 1966.

PROGRESSIVE DEGENERATION OF CEREBRAL GRAY MATTER

Alpers, B. J. Progressive cerebral degeneration of infancy. J. Nerv. Ment. Dis., 130:442, 1960.

Blackwood, W., Buxton, P. H., Cumings, J. N., Robertson, D. J., and Tucker, S. M. Diffuse cerebral degeneration in infancy (Alper's disease). Arch. Dis. Child., 38:193, 1963.

Dreifuss, F. E., and Netsky, M. G. Progressive poliodystrophy. The degenerations of cerebral gray matter. Amer. J. Dis. Child., 107:649, 1964.

Dunn, H. G., and Dolman, C. L. Necrotizing encephalomyelopathy. Neurology, 19:536, 1969.

Greenhouse, A. H., and Neuberger, K. T. The syndrome of progressive cerebral poliodystrophy. Arch. Neurol., 10:47, 1964.

Kamoshila, S., Aguilar, M. J., and Landing, B. H. Infantile subacute necrotizing encephalomyelopathy. Amer. J. Dis. Child., 116:120, 1968.

Leigh, D. Subacute necrotizing encephalomyelopathy in an infant. J. Neurol. Neurosurg. Psychiat., 12:216, 1951.

Richter, R. B. Infantile subacute necrotizing encephalopathy with predilection for the brain stem. J. Neuropath. Exp. Neurol., 16:281, 1957.

Robinson, F., Solitare, G. B., Lamarche, J. B., and Levy, L. L. Necrotizing encephalomyelopathy of childhood. Neurology, 17:472, 1967.

Tom, M. I., and Rencastle, N. B. Infantile subacute necrotizing encephalopathy. Neurology, 12:624, 1962.

DEMYELINATING DISEASES

Adams, R. D., and Richardson, E. P. The demyelinating diseases of the human nervous system. In Folch-Pi, J., ed., Chemical Pathology of the Nervous System. New York, Pergamon Press, Inc., 1961, pp. 162-191.

Korey, S. R. Glia, lipogenesis and formation of myelin. Arch. Neurol., 2:140, 1960.

Poser, C. M. Leukodystrophy and the concept of dysmyelination. Arch. Neurol., 4:323, 1961.

PELIZAEUS-MERZBACHER DISEASE

Gerstl, B., Malamud, N., Hayman, R. B., and Bond, P. R. Morphological and neurochemical study of Pelizaeus-Merzbacher disease. J. Neurol. Neurosurg. Psychiat., 28:540, 1965.

Zeman, W., DeMyer, W., and Falls, H. F. Pelizaeus-Merzbacher disease. J. Neuropath. Exp. Neurol., 23:334, 1964.

Zerbin-Rudin, E., and Peiffer, J. Eingenetischer Beitrag Zur Frage Der Spotform Der Pelizaeus-Merzbacherschen Krankheit. Humangenetik, 1:107, 1964.

METACHROMATIC LEUCODYSTROPHY

Abraham, K., and Lampert, R. Intraneuronal lipid deposits in metachromatic leukodystrophy. Neurology, 13:686, 1964.

Aurebeck, G., Osterberg, K., Blau, M., Chou, S., and Nelson, E. Electron microscope observations in metachromatic leukodystrophy. Arch. Neurol., 11:273, 1964.

Austin, J. H. et al. Metachromatic leukodystrophy. Arch. Neurol., 18:225, 1968.

—— et al. Metachromatic form of diffuse cerebral sclerosis. VI. A rapid test for the sulfatase A deficiency in metachromatic leukodystrophy (MLD) urine. Arch. Neurol., 14:259, 1966.

Bass, N. H., Witmer, E. J., and Dreifuss. F. E. A pedigree study of metachromatic leukodystrophy: Biochemical identification of the carrier state. Neurology, 20:52, 1970.

Hagberg, B., and Svennerholm, L. Metachromatic leukodystrophy. A generalized lipidosis. Acta Pediat. Scand., 49:690, 1960.

Mehl, E., and Jatzkervitz, H. Cerebroside 3 sulfate as a physiological substrate of arylsulfatase A. Biochem. biophys. Acta, 151:619, 1968.

Ogawa, K. Late infantile metachromatic leukodystrophy. The nature of the chromotope. Arch. Neurol., 4:418, 1961.

Schutta, H. S., Pratt, R. T. C., Metz, H., Evans, K. A., and Carter, C. D. A family study of the late infantile and juvenile forms of metachromatic leucodystrophy. J. Med. Genet., 3:86, 1966.

GLOBOID-CELL LEUCODYSTROPHY (KRABBE'S DISEASE)

Austin, J. Studies in globoid (Krabbe's) leukodystrophy. Arch. Neurol., 9:207, 1963.

—— et al. Defective sulfatide synthesis in Krabbe's disease (globoid leukodystrophy). Trans. Amer. Neurol. Ass., 92:175, 1967.

D'Agostina, A. M., Sayre, G. P., and Hayes, A. B. Krabbe's disease. Arch. Neurol., 8:82, 1963.

Hagberg, B., Sourander, P., and Svennerholm, L. Diagnosis of Krabbe's disease. Arch. Neurol., 8:82, 1963.

Norman, R. M., Oppenheimer, D. R., and Tingey, A. H. Histological and chemical findings in Krabbe's leukodystrophy. J. Neurol. Neurosurg. Psychiat., 24:223, 1961.

SPONGY SCLEROSIS (CANAVAN'S DISEASE)

Buchanan, D. S., and Davis, R. L. Spongy degeneration of the nervous system. Neurology, 15:207, 1965.

Hogan, G. R., and Richardson, E. P., Jr. Spongy degeneration of the nervous system (Canavan's disease). Pediatrics, 35:284, 1965.

Van Bogaert, L., and Bertrand, I. Spongy Degeneration of the Brain in Infancy. Amsterdam, North-Holland Publishing Co., 1967.

ZuRhein, G. M., Eichman, P. L., and Puletti, F. Familial idiocy with spongy degeneration of the central nervous system of van Bogaert-Bertrand. Neurology, 10:998, 1960.

SUDANOPHILIC (NEUTRAL FAT, ORTHOCHROMIC) FAMILIAL LEUCODYSTROPHY

Gerstl, B., Rubenstein, L. J., Eng, L. F., and Tavast-stjerna, M. Neurochemical study of a case of sudanophilic leucodystrophy. Arch. Neurol., 15:603, 1966.

Gordon, N., and Marsden, H. B. Diffuse cerebral sclerosis and adrenal atrophy. Develop. Med. Child Neurol., 8:719, 1966.

Van Bogaert, L., Edgar, G. W. F., and Karcher, D. Type orthochromotique (à substance soudanophile) diffus de la leucodystrophie familiale. Acta Neuropath. (Berlin), 1:289, 1961.

ALEXANDER'S DISEASE

Friede, R. L. Alexander's disease. Arch. Neurol., 11:414, 1964.

DEMYELINATING SCLEROSIS

Gall, J. C., Jr., Hayles, A. B., Siekert, R. G., and Keith, H. M. Multiple sclerosis in children. A clinical study of 40 cases with onset in childhood. Pediatrics, 21:703, 1958.

Greevic, N. Concentric lacunar leukoencephalopathy. Arch. Neurol., 2:266, 1960.

Kennedy, C., and Carter, S. Relation of optic neuritis to multiple sclerosis in childhood. Pediatrics, 28:377, 1961.

Low, N. L., and Carter, S. Multiple sclerosis in childhood. Pediatrics, 18:24, 1956.

McAlpine, D., Compston, N. D., and Lumsden, C. E. Multiple Sclerosis. Edinburgh, E. & S. Livingston, Ltd., 1955.

Multiple Sclerosis and the Demyelinating Diseases. Res. Publ. Ass. Res. Nerv. Ment. Dis., Baltimore, Williams and Wilkins Co., 1950, Vol. 28.

Stansbury, F. C. Neuromyelitis optica (Devic's disease); presentation of 5 cases with pathologic study, and review of the literature. Arch. Ophthal., 42:292, 1949.

SCHILDER'S DISEASE

Bowman, L. Diffuse Sclerosis (Encephalitis Periaxialis Diffusa). Baltimore, William Wood & Co. (a division of Williams and Wilkins Co.), 1934.

Poser, C. M., and Van Bogaert, L. Natural history and evolution of the concept of Schilder's diffuse sclerosis. Acta Psychiat. Scand., 31:285, 1956.

Zeman, W., and Whieldon, J. A. Clinical considerations in "Schilder's disease." Amer. J. Dis. Child., 104:635, 1962.

SUBACUTE SCLEROSING PANENCEPHALITIS (SSPE)

Chen, T. T. et al. Subacute sclerosing panencephalitis: Propagation of measles virus from brain biopsy in tissue culture. Science, 163:1193, 1969.

Gibbs, C. J., and Gajdusek, D. C. Infection as the etiology of spongiform encephalopathy (Creutzfeldt-Jakob disease). Science, 165:1023, 1969.

Jabbour, J. T. et al. Subacute sclerosing panencephalitis: a multidisciplinary study of eight cases. J.A.M.A., 207:2248, 1969.

Katz, M. et al. Transmission of an encephalitogenic agent from patients with SSPE to ferrets. Amer. Pediat. Soc. (Abstr.), May, 1968.

Lombroso, C. T. Remarks on the EEG and movement disorder in SSPE. Neurology, 18:69, 1968.

Metz, H., Gregorion, M., and Sandifer, P. Subacute sclerosing panencephalitis, a review of 17 cases with special reference to clinical diagnostic criteria. Arch. Dis. Child., 39:554, 1964.

Rustigan, R. Persistent infection of cells in culture by measles virus. J. Bact., 92:1792, 1966.

DEGENERATIONS OF THE BASAL GANGLIA

Bearn, A. G. Wilson's disease. *In* Wyngaarden, J. B., and Fredrickson, D. S., eds., The Metabolic Basis of Inherited Disease. New York, McGraw-Hill Book Co., 1966.

Byers, R. K., and Dodge, J. A. Huntington's chorea in children, report of four cases. Neurology, 17:587, 1967.

Cooper, I. S. Dystonia reversal by operation on basal ganglia. Arch. Neurol., 7:132, 1962.

DeMyer, W., Harter, D. H., and Zeman, W. Familial spasticity, hyperkinesia and dementia. Clinico-pathologic observations and comments on the nosology of Hallervorden-Spatz disease. Acta Neuropath. (Berlin), 4:28, 1964.

Denny-Brown, D. Diseases of the basal ganglia and subthalamic nuclei. *In* Christian, H. A., ed., Oxford Medicine. New York, Oxford Univ. Press, 1946.

——— Wilson's disease. New Eng. J. Med., 270:1149, 1964.

Goodman, R. M., Hall, C. L., Terango, L., Perrine, G. A., Jr., and Roberts, P. L. Huntington's chorea. Arch. Neurol., 15:345, 1966.

Hunt, J. R. Dyssynergia cerebellaris myoclonica, primary atrophy of the dentate system. Brain, 44:440, 1921.

Jervis, G. A. Huntington's chorea in childhood. Arch. Neurol., 9:50, 1963.

Johnson, W., Schwartz, G., and Barbeau, A. Studies on dystonia musculorum deformans. Arch. Neurol., 7:301, 1962.

Kerteaz, A. Paroxysmal kinesigenic choreoathetosis. Neurology, 17:680, 1967.

Mount, L. A., and Reback, S. Familial paroxysmal choreoathetosis. Arch. Neurol. Psychiat., 44:841, 1940.

Porter, H. Tissue copper proteins in Wilson's disease. Arch. Neurol., 11:341, 1964.

Pryles, C. V., Livingston, S., and Ford, F. R. Familial paroxysmal choreoathetosis of Mount and Reback. Pediatrics, 9:44, 1952.

Sternlieb, I., and Scheinberg, I. H. Diagnosis of Wilson's disease in asymptomatic patients. J.A.M.A., 183:747, 1963.

——— and Scheinberg, I. H. Penicillamine therapy for hepato-lenticular degeneration. J.A.M.A., 189:748, 1964.

Szanto, J., and Gallyas, F. A study of iron metabolism in neuropsychiatric patients (Hallervorden-Spatz disease). Arch. Neurol., 14:438, 1966.

Zeman, W., Koelbling, R., and Pasamanick, B. Idiopathic

dystonia musculorum deformans. II. The formes frustes. Neurology, 10:1068, 1960.

POLYMORPHOUS NEUROABIOTROPHIES

Dow, R. S., and Moruzzi, G. Physiology and Pathology of the Cerebellum. Minneapolis, Univ. Minnesota Press, 1958.

Greenfield, J. G. Spinocerebellar Degenerations. Springfield, Ill., Charles C Thomas, Publ., 1954.

Jervis, G. A. Early familial cerebellar degeneration. J. Nerv. Ment. Dis., 11:398, 1950.

Schut, J. W. The Hereditary Ataxias, Genetics and the Inheritance of Integrated Neurological and Psychiatric Patterns. Res. Publ. Ass. Res. Nerv. Ment. Dis., Vol. 33. Baltimore, Williams and Wilkins Co., 1954.

SPINOCEREBELLAR DEGENERATIONS

Alter, M., Talbert, O. R., and Croffead, G. Cerebellar ataxia, congenital cataracts, and retarded somatic and mental maturation. Report of cases of Marinesco-Sjögren syndrome. Neurology, 12:836, 1962.

Anderson, B. Marinesco-Sjögren syndrome. Develop. Med. Child. Neurol., 7:249, 1965.

Bergstedt, M., Johansson, S., and Miller, R. Hereditary spastic ataxia with central retinal degeneration and vestibular impairment. A clinical report on a family. Neurology, 12:124, 1962.

Mier, M., Schwartz, S. O., and Boshes, B. Acanthocytosis, pigmentary dysgenesis in three brothers. New Eng. J. Med., 271:593, 1964.

Thieffry, S., Arthuis, M., and Bargeton, E. Quarante cas de maladie de Werdnig-Hoffman avec onze examens anatomiques. Rev. Neurol., 93:621, 1955.

Walton, J. N. The "floppy" infant. Cereb. Palsy J., 2:10, 1960.

Wilson, S. A. K., and Bruce, A. N., eds., Neurology. Baltimore, Williams and Wilkins Co., 1955, Vol. 2, pp. 1126-1134, 1156-1167.

PERONEAL MUSCULAR ATROPHY

Austin, J. H. Observations on the syndrome of hypertrophic neuritis (the hypertrophic interstitial radiculoneuropathies). Medicine, 35:187, 1956.

Cammermeyer, J. Symposium on peripheral neuropathies. J. Neuropath. Exp. Neurol., 15:340, 1956.

Denny-Brown, D. Hereditary sensory radicular neuropathy. J. Neurol. Neurosurg. Psychiat., 14:237, 1951.

Dyck, P. J., Lambert, E. H., and Mulder, D. W. Charcot-Marie-Tooth disease: nerve conduction and clinical studies of a large kinship. Neurology, 13:1, 1963.

Gordon, N., and Hudson, R. E. Refsum's syndrome; heredopathia atactia polyneuritiformis; a report of three cases, including a study of the cardiac pathology. Brain, 82:41, 1959.

Jacob, J. C., Andermann, F., and Robb, J. P. Heredofamilial neuritis with brachial predilection. Neurology, 11:1025, 1961.

Khalifeh, R. R., and Zellweger, H. Hereditary sensory neuropathy with spinal cord disease. Neurology, 13:405, 1963.

Schwartz, G. A., and Liu, C. N. Hereditary (familial) spastic paraplegia; further clinical and pathological observations. Arch. Neurol. Psychiat., 75:144, 1956.

Schwartz, J. F., Rowland, L. P., Eder, H., Marks, P. A.,

Osserman, E. F., Hirschberg, E., and Anderson, H. Bassen-Kornzweig syndrome: Deficiency of serum β-lipoprotein. Arch. Neurol., 8:438, 1963.

Thilenius, O. G., and Grossman, B. J. Friedreich's ataxia with heart disease in children. Pediatrics, 27:246, 1961.

BRAINSTEM AND SPINAL CORD DEGENERATIONS

Brandt, S. Werdnig-Hoffmann's Infantile Progressive Muscular Atrophy. Copenhagen, E. Munksgaard, 1950.

Dubowitz, V. The Floppy Infant. Clinics in Developmental Medicine No. 31. London, Spastics International Medical Publications, 1969.

Gomez, M. R., Clermont, V., and Bernstein, J. Progressive bulbar paralysis in childhood (Fazio-Londes' disease). Arch. Neurol., 6:317, 1962.

Fenechel, G. M. The Spinal Muscular Atrophies in Motor Neuron Diseases. Norris, F. H. J., and Kurland, Lt., eds. New York, Grune & Stratton, 1969.

Green, J. B. Familial amyotrophic lateral sclerosis occurring in four generations. Neurology, 10:960, 1960.

Merritt, H. H. Hereditary optic atrophy (Lebei's disease). Arch. Neurol. Psychiat., 24:775, 1930.

Plott, D. M. Congenital laryngeal abductor paralysis due to nucleus ambiguus degeneration of the retina and ataxia neuropathy: A genetically determined syndrome with associated metabolic disorder. Blood, 16:1586, 1960.

Klenk, E., and Kahlke, W. Uber das Vorkommen der 3, 7, 11, 15-Tetramethylhexadecansaure (Phytan saure) in den Cholesterinestern and anderen Lipoidfraktionen der Organe bei einem Krankheitsfall unbekannter Genese (Verdacht auf Heredopathia atactica polyneuritiformia). Z. Physiol. Chem., 333:133, 1963.

Kugelberg. E., and Welander, L. Heredo familial juvenile muscular atrophy simulating muscular dystrophy. Arch. Neurol., 75:500, 1956.

Magee, K. R. Congenital indifference to pain. Arch. Neurol., 9:635, 1963.

Ogden, T. E., Robert, F., and Carmichael, E. A. Some sensory syndromes in children: indifference to pain and sensory neuropathy. J. Neurol. Neurosurg. Psychiat., 22:267, 1959.

Refsum, S. Heredopathia atactica polyneuritiformis reconsideracion. World Neurol., 1:334, 1960.

———— Salmonsen, L., and Skatvedt, M. Heredopathia atactica polyneuritiformis in children. J. Pediat., 35:335, 1949.

Richterich, R., van Mechelen, P., and Rossi, E. Refsum's disease (heredopathia atactica polyneuritiformis): An inborn error of lipid metabolism with storage of 3, 7, 11, 15-tetramethyl hexadecanoic acid. Amer. J. Med., 39:230, 1965.

Schwartz, A. R. Charcot-Marie-Tooth disease. Arch. Neurol., 9:623, 1963.

Steinberg, D., Mize, C., and Herndon, J. Phytanic acid in patients with Refsum's syndrome and response to dietary treatment. Arch. Intern. Med., 125:75, 1970.

Taylor, R. A. Heredofamilial mononeuritis multiplex with brachial predilection. Brain, 83:113, 1960.

NEUROCUTANEOUS SYNDROMES

Alexander, G. L., and Norman, R. M. The Sturge-Weber Syndrome. Bristol, John Wright & Sons, Ltd., 1960.

Blassingille, B., Sr. A rare form of ectodermal dysplasia. Mental retardation, congenital skin disorder and congenital spastic disorder. Neurology, 9:384, 1959.

Bowen, R. Hereditary ectodermal dysplasia of the anhidrotic type. Southern Med. J., 50:1018, 1957.

Burke, E. C., Winkelmann, R. K., and Strickland, M. K. Disseminated hemangiomatosis. Amer. J. Dis. Child., 108:418, 1964.

Chao, D. H. C. Congenital neurocutaneous syndromes in childhood. I. Neurofibromatosis. J. Pediat., 55:189, 1959.

———— Congenital neurocutaneous syndromes in childhood. II. Tuberous sclerosis. J. Pediat., 55:447, 1959.

———— Congenital neurocutaneous syndromes in childhood. III. Sturge-Weber disease. J. Pediat., 55:635, 1959.

Critchley, M., and Earl, C. J. C. Tuberous sclerosis and allied conditions. Brain, 55:311, 1932.

Crowe, F. W., Schull, W. J., and Neel, J. V. A Clinical, Pathological and Genetic Study of Multiple Neurofibromatosis. Springfield, Ill., Charles C Thomas, Publ., 1956.

Davidson. K. C. Cranial and intracranial lesions in neurofibromatosis. Amer. J. Roentgen., 98:550, 1966.

Feurstein, R. C., and Mims, L. C. Linear nevus sebaceus with convulsions and mental retardation. Amer. J. Dis. Child., 104:675, 1962.

Gold, A. P., and Freeman, J. M. Depigmented nevi: the earliest sign of tuberous sclerosis. Pediatrics, 35: 1003, 1965.

Gunther, M., and Penrose, L. S. Genetics of epiloia. J. Genet., 31:413, 1935.

Gutmann, L., and Lemli, L. Ataxia-telangiectasia associated with hypogammaglobulinemia. Arch. Neurol., 8:318, 1963.

Hartwell, S. W., Pickrell, K., and Quinn, G. Congenital anhidrotic ectodermal dysplasia. Clin. Pediat., 4:383, 1965.

Hilal, S. K., Solomon, G. E., Gold, A. P., and Carter, S. Primary cerebral arterial occlusive disease in children. Part II: Neurocutaneous syndromes. Radiology, 99:87, 1971.

Howell, J. B., Anderson, D. E., and McClendon, J. L. The basal cell nevus syndrome. J.A.M.A., 190:274, 1964.

Kofman, O., and Hyland, H. H. Tuberous sclerosis in adults with normal intelligence. Arch. Neurol. Psychiat., 81:43, 1959.

Kuster, F., and Olbing, H. Incontinentia pigmenti. Report on nine cases in one family and on one necropsy investigation. Ann. Paediat. (Basel), 202:92, 1964.

McPherson, A., and Auth, T. L. Bloch-Sulzberger syndrome (incontinentia pigmenti). Arch. Neurol., 8:332, 1963.

Meszaros, W. T., Guzzo, F., and Schorsch, H. Neurofibromatosis. Amer. J. Roentgen., 98:557, 1966.

Paine, R. S., and Efron, M. L. Atypical variants of the "ataxia telangiectasia" syndrome. Develop. Med. Child. Neurol., 5:14, 1963.

Paulson, G. W., and Lyle, C. B. Tuberous sclerosis. Develop. Med. Child. Neurol., 8:571, 1966.

Peterson, R. D. A., Kelley, W. D., and Good, R. A. Ataxia-telangiectasia, its association with a defective thymus, immunological deficiency disease and malignancy. Lancet, 1:1189, 1964.

Pollard, J. J., and New, P. F. J. Hereditary cutaneomandibular polyoncosis. A syndrome of myriad basal cell nevi of the skin, mandibular cysts, and inconstant skeletal anomalies. Radiology, 82:840, 1964.

Riley, H. D., Jr., and Smith, W. R. Macrocephaly, pseudopapilledema and multiple hemangiomata: previously undescribed heredo-familial syndrome. Pediatrics, 26:293, 1960.

Rosenthal, I. R., Markowitz, A. S., and Medenis, R. Immunologic incompetence in ataxia-telangiectasia. Amer. J. Dis. Child., 110:69, 1965.

Sedgwick, R. P., and Boder, E. Progressive ataxia in children with particular reference to ataxia telangiectasia. Neurology, 10:705, 1960.

Solitare, G. B., and Lopez, V. F. Louis-Bar's syndrome (ataxia-telangiectasia). Neurology, 17:23, 1967.

Thibault, J. W., and Manuelidis, E. E. Tuberous sclerosis in a premature infant: Report of a case and review of the literature. Neurology, 20:139, 1970.

Van Bogaert, L. Pathologie des angiomatoses. Acta Neurol. Psychiat. Belg., 50:526, 1950.

Warin, R. P., and Walske, M. M. Juvenile acanthosis nigricans in twins with neurological changes including spastic paraparesis. Proc. Roy. Soc. Med., 56:303, 1963.

Weber, F. P. Hemangiectatic hypertrophy of limbs, congenital plcbarteriectasis and so-called congenital varicose veins. Brit. J. Child. Dis., 25:13, 1918.

Wilcox, J. C. Melanomatosis of the skin and central nervous system in infants. A congenital neurocutaneous syndrome. Amer. J. Dis. Child., 57:391, 1939.

15.5
TUMORS OF THE CENTRAL NERVOUS SYSTEM

ABE M. CHUTORIAN

Brain Tumors

Brain tumors are surpassed in incidence only by leukemia as a cause of neoplasia in children. Exceedingly rare in the first year of life, the frequency of their occurrence remains fairly constant during each succeeding year. Some series indicate a significantly higher occurrence rate of medulloblastomas and ependymomas in boys than in girls, but otherwise there are no striking differences in sex incidence.

Important differences exist between children and adults as regards both the type and location of the tumors. Gliomas account for 75 percent of intracranial neoplasms in children, compared with 45 percent in adults. In children, 50 to 60 percent of brain tumors are infratentorial (cerebellar, fourth ventricular, and brainstem), whereas in adults they are chiefly supratentorial. Finally, 75 percent or more of brain tumors in children occur in the midline (third and fourth ventricle, optic chiasm, and brainstem). Many of the differences are accounted for by the high incidence of astrocytomas and medulloblastomas in children. The former arise predominantly, and the latter almost exclusively, in the posterior fossa. These differences are further accentuated by the fact that craniopharyngiomas and optic gliomas mostly affect children, whereas meningiomas, pituitary adenomas, acoustic neurinomas, and metastatic tumors occur chiefly in adults.

Many intracranial neoplasms in children can only be treated palliatively. It is also frequently impossible to differentiate on clinical grounds, or even following contrast radiographic studies, between those which can and those which cannot be totally extirpated. Furthermore, many relatively slowly growing neoplasms which cannot be totally removed may be associated with prolonged survival in the absence of severe neurologic deficit. For these reasons, specific diagnosis and appropriate treatment are eminently worthwhile.

CLINICAL MANIFESTATIONS. When a child presents with manifestations of increased intracranial pressure plus focal neurologic deficit, the possibility of brain tumor should be given serious consideration. In the following discussion of symptoms and signs an attempt is made to emphasize early factors that should alert the physician to suspect a cerebral neoplasm. Early diagnosis can often lead to effective therapy and a good prognosis.

Increased Intracranial Pressure. The classical symptoms and signs of increased intracranial pressure are headache, vomiting, diplopia, papilledema, enlarged cranium, and, late in the course, lethargy and somnolence.

Headache. Headache in children is rarely of localizing value, and furthermore there is frequently nothing to distinguish the character of the headache associated with brain tumor from that encountered in other illnesses. Perhaps the most important clinical feature is that the headache associated with tumor tends to remit and exacerbate. Presumably the remissions are associated with transient accommodation of increased intracranial pressure by ventricular dilation or spread of cranial sutures, with or without increased girth of the cranial vault. Thus at one or more points in the course of the illness, headache will be absent for variable and often considerable periods of time.

An intermittent headache, which recurs with increasing frequency and severity, which occurs after a prolonged period of recumbency, at night or on arising in the morning, and which is exacerbated by coughing or straining at stool, should arouse suspicion of increased intracranial pressure. Manifestations of these phenomena in younger or relatively inarticulate children may simply be marked irritability or even constipation due to reluctance to strain at stool.

With rare exceptions, headache tends to occur frontally or occipitally but is not of localizing value; it is seen with equal frequency in supratentorial and infratentorial tumors.

Cranial enlargement. When neoplasms arising in midline structures begin their growth early in life, obstructive hydrocephalus will occur; it cannot be readily differentiated from hydrocephalus due to other causes, such as aqueductal stenosis. Such midline tumors are usually in the posterior fossa.

Vomiting. Vomiting due to increased intracranial pressure is variable and intermittent in character and tends to occur on arising; it may or may not be associated with a headache. It may be an irritative phenomenon in the absence of increased intracranial pressure early in the course of posterior fossa neoplasms. In such instances it may be difficult to delineate the cause of the vomiting, but its recurrent nature should suggest an intracranial cause.

Diplopia and strabismus. Double vision is the result of a sixth nerve palsy. This is a nonspecific finding of increased intracranial pressure and does not have localizing value. Diplopia may not be apparent despite the presence of paralytic strabismus, the chief reason being the rapidity with which suppression of binocular vision occurs by central or peripheral mechanisms in children. Hence, it is more common for a parent to report a tendency on the part of the child to tilt the head to one side or to turn the head laterally to view objects near the central field of vision in compensation for some degree of abducens paresis and associated internal strabismus. Another mechanism of suppression of binocular vision involves partial closure of one eye, which may be interpreted as involuntary ptosis until each eye is examined separately while the other is covered.

Papilledema. Although choking of the discs may or may not be present with increased intracranial pressure, it may be the only sign that intracranial pressure is elevated. It is, therefore, especially important to obtain adequate visualization of the fundi in the presence of unexplained vomiting and headache. This examination is often difficult in uncooperative younger children, in whom sedation and dilation of the pupils will often be necessary.

It is unusual in children for optic atrophy to occur as a result of increased intracranial pressure early in the course of neoplasms arising distant from the optic chiasm. Optic atrophy may be the result of direct chiasmatic compression or infiltration (e.g., craniopharyngioma, chiasmal glioma) or the result of chronic increased intracranial pressure, where gliosis of the optic nerve prevents the development of edema.

The differentiation of papilledema from pseudopapilledema and papillitis (optic neuritis) is of diagnostic importance. In pseudopapilledema the blind spot may be normal in size, and it is usually possible to detect frank or buried drusen at some point along the disc margin. In papillitis, there is acute loss of vision and pain on ocular movement with central or paracentral scotomas on visual field plots.

Focal Neurologic Signs. Brain tumors may produce focal neurologic signs of localizing significance with or without manifestations of increased intracranial pressure.

Nystagmus. Nystagmus on fixation of gaze within the range of binocular vision is of particular importance in connection with intracranial neoplasms. However, its localizing value is limited, for either irritative or destructive lesions involving cerebellovestibular pathways in the same location may produce nystagmus whose quick and slow components are in the opposite direction. Furthermore, unilateral cerebellar hemisphere lesions may produce bilateral manifestations by virtue of compression across the midline, while lesions located entirely within the brainstem may produce nystagmus which is indistinguishable from that due to cerebellar lesions. If there are coarse movements on deviation of the eyes in one direction and fine rapid nystagmus, or none, on gaze in the opposite direction, the lesion is very apt to be on the side to which coarse nystagmus occurs.

Nystagmus may occur simply on the basis of increased intracranial pressure; it is also produced by many drugs, including phenobarbital and Dilantin. The presence of true vertigo in association with nystagmus indicates peripheral labyrinthine disturbance; in children it is rarely associated with neoplasia.

Pendular nystagmus on forward gaze with marked visual deficit occurs, as a rule, in the first two years of life and may be associated with peripheral or cortical blindness, congenital optic atrophy, or tumors in the chiasmatic region. It is also seen as a congenital phenomenon, in which case it may be unilateral or bilateral, without defective vision.

Vertical nystagmus implies intrinsic brainstem disease but may be produced by lesions causing brainstem compression. It may also occur as a drug-induced phenomenon.

A paretic ocular muscle may undergo nystagmoid movements when moving the globe in the direction of its major action.

Opticokinetic nystagmus is a normal phenomenon encountered in following a moving object such as a rotating drum. Diminution or absence of this phenomenon in one direction implies a lesion of the contralateral parietal lobe and hence is frequently, but not always, associated with hemianopia.

Impaired vision. The visual fields and acuity of young children are notoriously difficult to measure accurately. It is, therefore, mandatory for the physician to pursue vigorously the diagnostic evaluation of visual deficit in a child. Unless there is clearly full refractive correction of defective vision—and this is rarely documented in younger children—the possibility of a lesion within or in the neighborhood of the optic nerves, chiasm, tracts, or radiations must be kept in mind. For reasons that are not entirely clear, fully one-third of children with optic gliomas, and not infrequently children with craniopharyngiomas, have their visual deficit at least partially corrected with lenses for a variable period prior to diagnosis.

Visual field defects, generally bitemporal hemianopia, may be seen in optic atrophy without neoplasia but more often are a reflection of chiasmal compression by craniopharyngioma, chiasmal glioma, teratoma, or other tumors of the chiasmal area. Homonymous defects in the visual field may be seen

with any lesion involving the optic pathways behind the chiasm.

Cranial neuropathy. Cranial nerve involvement occurs as one of the first symptoms in 20 to 25 percent of children with brain tumor. Abducens paresis may be expected if intracranial pressure is increased; it is of no localizing value.

Supranuclear palsies are manifested chiefly by involvement of facial musculature, the tongue, or as pseudobulbar palsies. In a supranuclear facial paresis, the muscles of the forehead are spared, and orbicularis oculi muscles are *relatively* intact. Supranuclear lesions involving pathways to the hypoglossal nuclei result in weakness of the tongue with deviation to the contralateral side, but the atrophy and fasciculations characteristic of a nuclear lesion are absent. In pseudobulbar palsy, although swallowing and handling of secretions may be significantly impaired, the gag reflex and movements of the uvula are fully intact, differentiating this from bulbar palsy, where the reflex arc is impaired.

Nuclear palsies (e.g., bulbar palsy) occur as a result of brainstem tumors, in which case multiple cranial nerves are usually involved. Differentiation from intrinsic cranial neuropathies encountered in poliomyelitis, polyneuritis, meningitis, and other conditions such as myasthenia gravis and Möbius' syndrome does not, as a rule, present any difficulty. In brainstem gliomas, the pyramidal tracts and cerebellar outflow pathways are almost invariably involved, giving rise to a characteristic complex of symptoms and signs which will be discussed more fully in a later section (p. 944).

The cranial nerves may be involved in infranuclear palsy anywhere along their course within the brainstem or along the base of the brain to their respective destinations. Nasopharyngeal carcinomas, chondrosarcomas, rhabdomyosarcoma, lymphosarcomas, and chordomas are the neoplasms which characteristically involve multiple cranial nerves successively in their extramedullary course. They do not commonly have sufficient bulk early in their course to produce other signs and symptoms by compression of the base of the brain or brainstem.

Head tilt (Fig. 44). Abnormal posturing of the head is seen in association with extraocular muscle paresis, particularly of the superior oblique muscle, in which case it serves as a compensatory mechanism for the production of optimal binocular vision.

Lesions of the pathway from the flocculonodular lobe of the cerebellum to the vestibular nuclei are apt to produce head tilt, with the occiput tilted toward the side of the lesion. However, nuchal rigidity with some degree of head tilt occurs in association with posterior fossa neoplasms as a result of either traction upon the dura and lower cranial nerves or displacement of the cerebellar tonsils. In the latter instance, the head tilt is not of localizing value. It is well to remember that posterior fossa tumors abutting on the ventricular or subarachnoid spaces may produce cerebrospinal fluid pleocytosis and an elevated

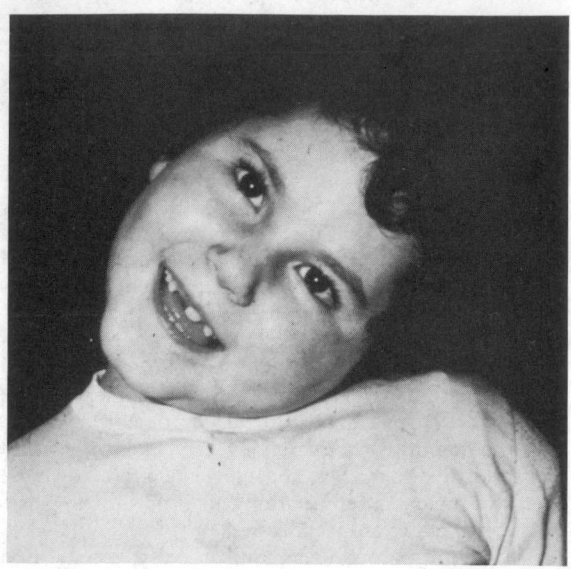

Fig. 44.   Extreme head tilt in a girl with a posterior fossa tumor.

protein content, which in association with nuchal rigidity may lead to a diagnosis of meningitis. The normal sugar and bacteriologic studies will militate against this diagnosis, but on occasion the difficulty of diagnosis is compounded by the presence of low-grade fever and, in the case of extensive subarachnoid seeding of a tumor, such as medulloblastoma, by a fall in the cerebrospinal fluid sugar.

Personality change.   Personality change is hardly to be considered specific to intracranial neoplasia. However, nonspecific changes such as irritability, apathy, emotional lability, pallor, and fatigue may be early symptoms of brain tumor in children. Their presence should alert the physician to the possibility of such a lesion.

Ataxia.   Incoordination of the axial musculature is frequently referred to as titubation. Ataxia caused by cerebellar neoplasm involves the axial musculature when the tumor is vermian or midline. Cerebellar hemisphere tumors produce ataxia in the ipsilateral extremities. False localization is not uncommon because of contrecoup effects or simultaneous involvement of the midline and hemispheral structures.

Ataxia is a common manifestation of brainstem gliomas due to involvement of the cerebellar pathways. The unsteadiness in such instances may be axial and/or of the extremities.

Ataxia by itself is not a valuable localizing sign. It may be seen in aqueductal insufficiency, presumably as a result of transmission of increased intracranial pressure to cerebellar pathways anywhere from the frontal lobes to the brainstem. Unilateral incoordination may result from a frontal lobe, thalamic, or cerebellar hemisphere neoplasm, and it may not be possible on clinical grounds to ascertain the source.

Ataxia may also be caused by proprioceptive defects produced by peripheral nerve, root, or posterior column lesions. In this instance, the ataxia is aggravated by eye closure.

Other causes of ataxia include degenerative, metabolic, and infectious or parainfectious central nervous system disorders. The latter include "acute cerebellar ataxia," characterized by its relatively acute onset, course, and absence of increased intracranial pressure (see p. 856).

Focal pyramidal deficit.   Upper motor neuron lesions of a slowly progressive type are usually first manifested in children by subtle changes of handedness, posture, and dexterity which are not a source of distress and therefore are often overlooked until the appearance of frank paralysis or marked spasticity. Examination usually reveals a combination of increased deep tendon reflexes, altered superficial reflexes, and Babinski or other pathologic reflexes, and some degree of spasticity. Frank weakness may or may not be manifest, but a tendency to disuse or abnormal postures of the suspected extremity often occur.

The chronicity of a lesion or its acute onset will help differentiate "congenital," vascular, traumatic, and toxic lesions from neoplastic causes. Since pyramidal deficit implies a cerebral, brainstem, or spinal cord lesion, the presence of parietal lobe phenomena is helpful in ascertaining the site of the lesion. If the child is old enough to cooperate, testing for corticosensory discriminations, visual field defects (hemianopia), and opticokinetic nystagmus may be helpful.

Although pyramidal tract deficit is rare in association with cerebellar tumors or neoplasms in the chiasmatic area, it is encountered occasionally when there is brainstem compression and/or infiltration.

Seizures.   Generalized, psychomotor, and focal motor or sensory seizures may be the initial symptom of cerebral hemisphere neoplasms in children. In some instances, the seizures persist for years before the diagnosis becomes evident. Seizures in the pediatric age group are more likely the result of static lesions or metabolic factors. For this reason selective criteria must be adopted to rule out or establish the presence of a cerebral neoplasm in an individual case.

Seizures are considered an unusual manifestation of posterior fossa tumors. Ictus infratentorialis refers to the intermittent decerebrate posture observed in some children with posterior fossa neoplasms or other lesions. It is perhaps not a true convulsive phenomenon, though its exact nature is not fully established. The best evidence currently is that such episodes are due to interruption of vermian or anterior lobe cerebellar stimuli to reticular nuclei. When the episodes are accompanied by cyanosis, respiratory irregularity, and alteration of consciousness, impending cerebellar herniation through the foramen magnum may be suspected. The occurrence of convulsions in children with medulloblastoma is most readily explained by the presence of cerebral hemisphere tumor implants.

At times the only explanation available is that cortical irritability is increased by the presence of increased intracranial pressure or cerebral edema.

Hypothalamic and Endocrine Dysfunction. Tumors giving rise to disturbances of hypothalamic and endocrine function include craniopharyngiomas, optic and other gliomas, anterior third ventricular dermoids, teratomas, and ectopic or "metastatic" pinealomas. Peculiarly, the manifestations differ very significantly among the different tumor types, despite the large bulk and apparently similar compressive effects of the different lesions. Thus, the occurrence of sexual and somatic infantilism is the rule in craniopharyngioma, whereas in chiasmal glioma, sexual change is uncommon. Any sexual abnormality in chiasmal glioma is apt to involve sexual precocity, the same being true also of pineal tumors and teratomas.

The diencephalic syndrome of infancy is characterized by emaciation and recurrent vomiting in a euphoric, alert baby. The lesion is usually an astrocytoma arising in the anterior third ventricle. The syndrome characteristically occurs before the tumor has produced macrocephaly or other manifestations of raised intracranial pressure.

All tumors occurring in the hypothalamic region share the propensity to produce early and progressive optic atrophy due to involvement of the optic chiasm.

DIAGNOSTIC PROCEDURES. Ancillary procedures of value in the diagnosis of brain tumors include:

1. Skull radiography
2. Electroencephalography
3. Echoencephalography
4. Radioisotopic brain scanning
5. Cerebrospinal fluid analysis
   a. Pressure, cells, protein, sugar
   b. Enzymes
   c. Millipore filtration for identification of tumor cells
6. Intracranial contrast radiography
   a. Pneumoencephalography
   b. Ventriculography
   c. Cerebral angiography

The various procedures will be discussed with specific reference to the diagnosis of different tumors.

TREATMENT. Specific therapy includes surgery, roentgen therapy, chemotherapy, and drugs employed to reduce increased intracranial pressure. Surgical and roentgen therapy are discussed separately for individual tumors.

Chemotherapy remains a palliative procedure of limited value in the treatment of intracranial tumors in children. Current experimentation with the use of intracarotid or intrathecal chemotherapy is not of sufficiently established value to be routinely recommended. However, various investigators have reported chemotherapeutic remissions of variable duration with the use of sequential intravenous vincristine therapy or intrathecal methotrexate. The chief indication for such treatment at the present time is clinical relapse following maximum permissible surgery and radiotherapy for glioblastoma, ependymoma, and medulloblastoma. The *prophylactic* potential of chemotherapy has not been reliably explored.

The use of adrenocortical steroids for the relief of increased intracranial pressure in children with brain tumor is recommended in selected cases. Dramatic results are sometimes obtained, and symptoms of increased intracranial pressure associated with cerebral edema are improved in the majority of patients. Variable but significant improvement of focal neurologic deficit has also been observed. The most frequent indication for the use of adrenocortical steroids is the occurrence of signs and symptoms of increased intracranial pressure during a course of roentgen therapy, when decompressive surgery either has already been performed or, for various reasons, is being avoided.

In older children, dexamethasone, 4 to 8 mg intravenously, may be given, followed with 2 mg intramuscularly four times daily for several days. Under ordinary circumstances, attempts to taper and discontinue the drug over a period of one to two weeks should be made. Corticosteroid therapy is of value postsurgically as well as preoperatively in selected cases. Patients who develop a *sterile* meningitis, often accompanied by a significant febrile reaction, following either posterior fossa surgery or the communication of a cystic lesion with the ventricular or subarachnoid space, may show striking remission of cerebrospinal fluid pleocytosis, hypoglycorrhea, fever, and meningeal signs after corticosteroid administration. Needless to say, bacterial infection should be ruled out prior to such therapy.

The value of steroid therapy in patients with neoplasms of the posterior fossa must be weighed against the increased risk of intestinal ulceration in these children.

In more acute situations demanding urgent treatment of increased intracranial pressure, parenteral urea or mannitol should be used and may be lifesaving. The combined use of dexamethasone and mannitol tends to prevent "rebound" of pressure which is characteristic following urea, and to a lesser extent mannitol.

Tumors of the Cerebellum

Astrocytoma

INCIDENCE. Approximately 25 percent of all brain tumors in children are cerebellar astrocytomas. The peak age incidence is 5 to 8 years, but no age group is excepted.

CLINICAL MANIFESTATIONS. Symptoms and signs in this group are not distinctive enough to differentiate them accurately from other posterior fossa neoplasms. They include:

1. Signs and symptoms of increased intracranial pressure, including headache, vomiting, abducens paresis, and papilledema
2. Ataxia, predominating in or confined to one side in the case of a cerebellar hemisphere astrocytoma
3. Nystagmus, sometimes of localizing value
4. Head tilt

Within this symptom complex there is considerable variation. Thus in some, a cystic astrocytoma confined to one hemisphere may produce ipsilateral intention tremor and ataxia before any other phenomena become evident, while in others it may result in signs of impending herniation of the cerebellar tonsils, with pyramidal deficit added as a result of brainstem compression, and possible impairment of vision due to chronic papilledema.

The course of cerebellar astrocytoma in children is insidious in onset, slow in progression, and relatively benign in outlook. The variation in duration of symptoms is, however, great enough to make this picture an unreliable criterion of the diagnosis. The majority have symptoms for two to seven months prior to diagnosis, some for as long as several years, contrasting sharply with medulloblastoma, where the majority are symptomatic less than two months prior to diagnosis.

DIAGNOSIS.   Papilledema and spread of the cranial sutures on radiograms of the skull are common findings. Tumor calcification is rare. Occasionally local occipital rarefaction of bone or enlargement of the opening which admits the occipital emissary vein will suggest the presence of a slowly growing cerebellar astrocytoma.

Ventriculography will establish more precisely the location of the tumor but not the precise tumor type, which is established at the time of suboccipital craniotomy.

Brachial and vertebral angiography, which provide information concerning the posterior fossa circulation, have assumed a limited, but growing, value in the diagnosis of posterior fossa mass lesions. These studies are most helpful in patients whose cerebellar deficit is so minimal that doubt exists in relation to the location of the neoplasm. The advantage provided by such study is the absence of disturbance of cerebrospinal fluid dynamics while diagnostic information is obtained. These studies are not routinely required.

Radioisotope brain scanning generally tends to be unreliable for the localization of posterior fossa tumors because of the high uptake of isotope by the occipitocervical musculature and the lateral sinuses.

THERAPY AND PROGNOSIS.   In approximately one-third of the cases, the tumor is located entirely within one cerebellar hemisphere. These tumors are apt to be cystic, the cysts being quite large in relation to the solid portion of the tumor, which may consist of a small mural nodule in the wall of the cyst. In other cases, solid tumor tissue surrounds a cyst. Surgical extirpation of these tumors is eminently successful, and many patients have been cured by total surgical removal of the tumor. In some instances in which the solid portion of the tumor predominates, "gross total" removal may be accomplished, but the fate of the patient may not be determined for many years because of the slowly growing character of these neoplasms.

The solid, midline astrocytomas tend to extend deeply toward cerebellar peduncles, aqueduct of Sylvius, and brainstem. The surgical results are, therefore, far less satisfactory than with the cystic tumors, but years of freedom from symptoms may follow decompression and partial extirpation of these more solid midline tumors. Partly because of their inherently slow growth and protracted course there is no proof that the growth of these tumors is altered by radiotherapy, which is therefore frequently withheld, especially following removal of a cystic cerebellar hemisphere astrocytoma. However, there is definite evidence that radiotherapy does affect astrocytomas of the brainstem and of the optic nerve and chiasm, which are similar histologically to many cerebellar astrocytomas. Furthermore, of 150 patients with cerebellar astrocytoma treated at Columbia-Presbyterian Medical Center, 93 had subtotal tumor excision and irradiation, with an average interval of seven years to the time of tumor recurrence. This compares favorably with other series, in which subtotal removal has not been followed by radiotherapy and the average interval to tumor recurrence is cited as three years. We therefore recommend radiotherapy for patients in whom it is believed tumor tissue has been left behind following surgery.

Postoperatively intravenous fluids are rarely required after 24 to 48 hours, but during this period it is best to use physiologic solutions to provide the usual maintenance requirements of water and electrolytes. Reduction of water and electrolytes postoperatively, as frequently advocated, is not believed necessary; in fact, it may prolong the postoperative recovery period.

Following removal of a cerebellar astrocytoma, the cerebellar deficit is characteristically aggravated, and ataxia and tremor are more pronounced. There is progressive improvement in these symptoms over weeks to months following surgery, and persistent symptoms are rarely disabling. The degree of residual deficit is variable; often it cannot be discerned without careful neurologic examination. Postoperative hydrocephalus secondary to aseptic inflammatory changes in the meninges is not infrequently encountered.

Medulloblastoma

INCIDENCE.   Of the posterior fossa tumors in children, medulloblastoma is the most frequent, comprising approximately 40 percent. There is a tendency for males to outnumber females in the ratio of about 3 to 2. The peak age incidence is approximately 3 to 5 years.

CLINICAL MANIFESTATIONS. The symptoms and signs of medulloblastoma are similar to those described for cerebellar astrocytoma. However, the onset is typically more acute, and despite the short history the complete picture of an advanced posterior fossa neoplasm is more apt to be encountered. The signs will be more characteristic of a midline cerebellar neoplasm (i.e., early obstructive hydrocephalus and prominent ataxia of axial musculature). Seizures are not common in medulloblastomas, their occurrence reflecting cerebral implantation of tumor. Similarly, in advanced cases with extensive seeding of a tumor along the subarachnoid space, the picture of a polyneuropathy may supervene, with loss of tendon reflexes, root pain, paresthesias, and cranial nerve involvement. The course is rapid and the outlook for long-term survival generally poor.

DIAGNOSIS. As in cerebellar astrocytoma, the majority of plain radiograms of the skull will show cranial suture spread or other x-ray evidence of increased intracranial pressure. Ventriculograms rarely admit air into the fourth ventricle because of frequent obstruction of the rostral end of this cavity, with the production of symmetrically dilated lateral and third ventricles. At times, air will enter a massively dilated fourth ventricle which is largely occupied by tumor.

The indications for angiography and the limitations of brain scanning are as described for the diagnosis of astrocytomas.

Medulloblastomas tend to shed their actively growing cells and seed them from their site of origin in the roof of the fourth ventricle throughout the subarachnoid space. Tumor implants become a source of further seeding. It is thus possible to make a diagnosis of recurrence or seeding of medulloblastoma in some cases by detecting tumor cells in millipore filtrates of cerebrospinal or ventricular fluid.

THERAPY AND PROGNOSIS. Since medulloblastoma cannot be differentiated with certainty from other cerebellar neoplasms without a tissue diagnosis, all of these patients should have a craniotomy. The tumor is characteristically bulky, and considerable portions must be removed in order to reestablish free flow of cerebrospinal fluid through the fourth ventricle. It is never possible to extirpate the tumor completely by surgical means.

The tumor is highly radiosensitive. Because of the strong proclivity of the neoplasm to seed tumor cells through the neuraxis, radiotherapy is initially routinely directed to the entire neuraxis. In general the outlook for long-term survival is poor. Seventy percent do not live more than three years. Newer techniques in radiation therapy are resulting in longer survivals.

Comments on chemotherapy have been made in the introductory section on treatment (p. 941).

Tumors of the Fourth Ventricle

Ependymoma

INCIDENCE. The third most frequent infratentorial neoplasm in children is the ependymoma. The tumor comprises approximately 10 percent of all posterior fossa tumors in children. Although the size of individual series of patients with ependymomas is not large, there does seem to be a tendency to male preponderance (2:1) and relatively early age of onset. Clinically these tumors resemble the picture of medulloblastoma more than that of astrocytoma. Choroid plexus papillomas and other lateral ventricle ependymomas are far less frequent.

The duration of symptoms is intermediate between that of medulloblastoma and astrocytoma, as is the ultimate outlook for survival. The average duration of symptoms prior to diagnosis is two to three months.

The point of attachment of the tumor is almost always the floor of the fourth ventricle, which is frequently filled with tumor, and early signs and symptoms of obstructive hydrocephalus are to be expected. However, the ependymoma is apt, more than other posterior fossa tumors, to be associated with repeated vomiting as the earliest manifestation, due to direct stimulation of emetic centers underlying the site of origin of the tumor. Apart from this tendency, the tumor on rare occasions arises in one of the lateral recesses of the fourth ventricle and grows out into cerebellopontine angle, producing combined ipsilateral selective cranial nerve involvement and cerebellar signs which in the adult would be more likely to signify the presence of an acoustic neurinoma or cerebellopontine angle meningioma.

The tumor otherwise produces the symptoms and signs described for the other posterior fossa neoplasms, including those associated with increased intracranial pressure, ataxia, nystagmus, and head tilt. On occasion, ependymomas extend intraspinally from the posterior fossa and may even seed to more distant sites in the subarachnoid space, but this tendency is far less marked than in medulloblastoma. Consequently, radiotherapy is not routinely directed to the entire neuraxis.

DIAGNOSIS. As is the case with medulloblastoma and astrocytoma, the majority of children with ependymomas show cranial suture separation and/or other signs of increased intracranial pressure.

Microscopically ependymomas show extensively distributed flecks of calcium, but this is only occasionally of sufficient extent to be of diagnostic help on plain radiograms of the skull.

The diagnosis is more apt to be confused with subacute meningitis than in the case of the other posterior fossa tumors, with the exception of the rare reticulum cell sarcoma, leptomeningeal carcinomatosis, and other similar neoplasms.

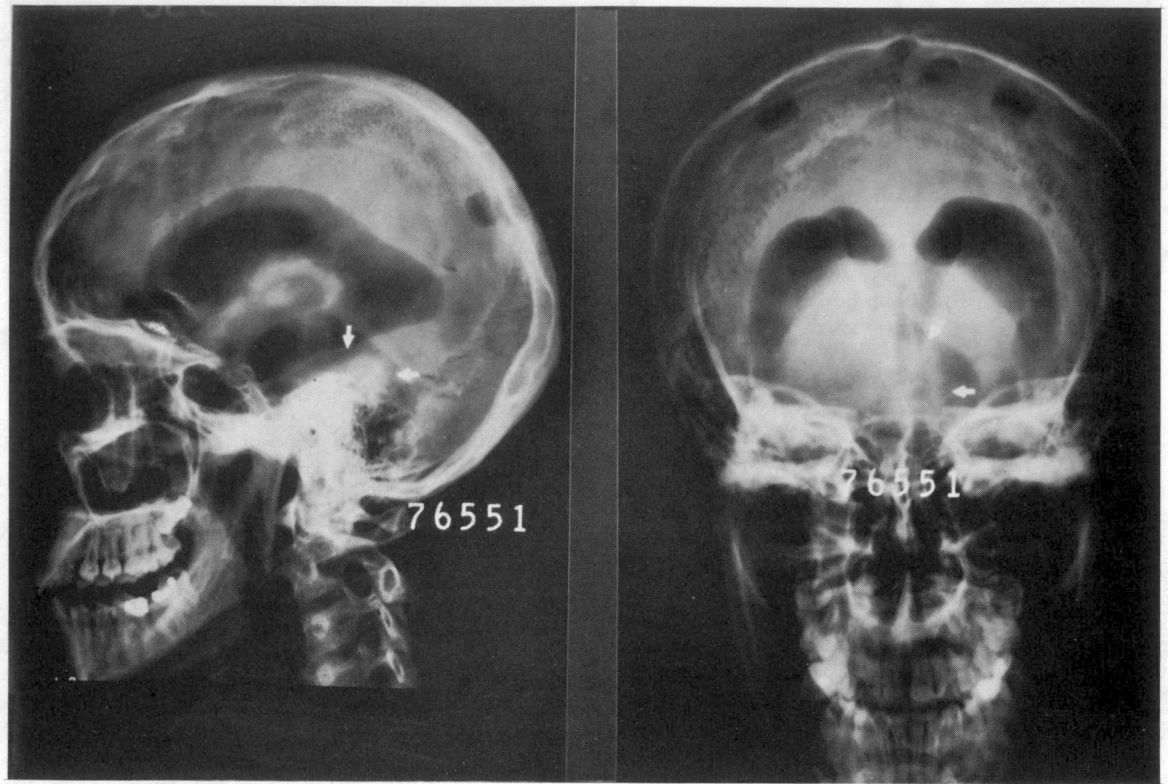

Fig. 45. Ventriculogram of a child outlining the ventricular system and demonstrating a large defect in the fourth ventricle (arrows). The defect and the displacement shown are due to the presence of an ependymoma.

The diagnosis ultimately depends upon the findings at craniotomy following ventriculography (Fig. 45). The indications for angiography and the limitations of brain scanning are as described for the diagnosis of astrocytomas.

THERAPY.   Ependymomas are inseparable from vital structures in the floor of the fourth ventricle. Surgery is, therefore, limited to the bulk of the tumor beyond the floor of the ventricle and is aimed chiefly at reestablishing free circulation of the cerebrospinal fluid.

X-ray therapy is directed to the posterior fossa after surgery. Comments on chemotherapy have been made in the introductory section under treatment (p. 941).

PROGNOSIS.   The immediate postoperative mortality is not high if the surgeon recognizes the inadvisability of excessive manipulation or extensive dissection because of the attachment of the tumor. In the rare cerebellopontine angle tumor, total excision is theoretically possible but even then is not ordinarily achieved.

Survival beyond the postoperative period is variable and is generally intermediate in duration between the rapidly advancing medulloblastoma and very slowly growing astrocytoma. Survival thus varies from several months to 10 years or longer, usually lasting several years.

Tumors of the Brainstem

Brainstem Gliomas

INCIDENCE.   Brainstem gliomas occur almost exclusively in children, though no age group is exempted; they constitute approximately 10 percent of all intracranial tumors in children. The average age of onset is approximately 6½ years. The duration of symptoms is typically 3 to 5 months but may be considerably longer or shorter.

CLINICAL MANIFESTATIONS.   This tumor, which presents with one of the most characteristic clinical pictures, is at the same time unfortunately one of the least amenable to effective therapy, except of a transient and palliative nature.

The onset of neurologic symptoms and signs is usually insidious, and increased intracranial pressure is infrequent, except as a late manifestation.

Because of their location, these tumors are apt to interfere early in the course of their growth with the function of cranial nerve nuclei, pyramidal tracts, and cerebellar pathways, giving rise to a characteristic triad of symptoms and signs.

1. Cranial Nerve Nuclei. Early in the clinical course there may be an isolated cranial nerve deficit; later multiple involvement is the rule. Although any cranial nerve nucleus may be affected, the most common are: VII, 90 percent; IX and X, 80 percent; V (sensory), 60 percent; and VI, 55 percent.

Since the tumor (astrocytoma or less often glioblastoma) is infiltrative in nature, "skip lesions" are common, and bilateral involvement of different cranial nerves is the rule.

Paresis of conjugate gaze, the most important sign localizing the lesion within the brainstem, occurs in more than half of the patients.

2. Pyramidal Tracts. Signs of pyramidal tract involvement occur in 80 to 90 percent of the children. Symptomatically, these may be masked by the more prominent ataxic manifestations or may present chiefly as subtle changes in gait, handedness, or posture of an extremity.

Hemiparesis is associated with reflex preponderance, and an extensor plantar response is the usual picture; frequently, however, bilateral reflex changes and rarely weakness of all extremities are seen.

3. Cerebellar Pathways. Both truncal and extremity ataxia are found in the majority of children, indicating involvement chiefly of corticopontocerebellar fibers coursing through the brainstem. Horizontal nystagmus is present in over half of the patients and vertical nystagmus in almost a third.

Other Signs. Occasionally nuchal rigidity and urinary retention occur and confuse the picture. Papilledema occurs at some time during the course in approximately a third of the patients. Sensory deficits occur uncommonly, and basal ganglia manifestations, such as tremor and choreoathetosis, are rare.

DIAGNOSIS. In keeping with the typical absence of symptoms and signs of increased intracranial pressure, the cerebrospinal fluid pressure is normal. Similarly, the cerebrospinal fluid cell count, protein, and sugar are normal. Rarely, growth of the tumor impinging on the leptomeninges will produce a low-grade pleocytosis and elevated cerebrospinal fluid protein.

Plain radiographs of the skull are usually unrewarding. In those instances, therefore, in which intracranial pressure is believed to be normal (the majority), pneumoencephalography is performed. The typical findings in brainstem tumor include posterior and upward displacement of the aqueduct of Sylvius and the fourth ventricle, best seen in the lateral view (Fig. 46). The pontine cistern is, characteristically, narrowed by the increased bulk of the tumor-bearing pons. Ventricular dilation of mild degree is often present but is rarely of striking proportion.

THERAPY. Craniotomy is seldom, if ever, indicated in patients with brainstem gliomas. The typical pneumoencephalographic findings, together with the clinical picture, are sufficiently diagnostic as a rule to justify radiotherapy. In our experience, one or more courses of radiotherapy are associated with an aver-

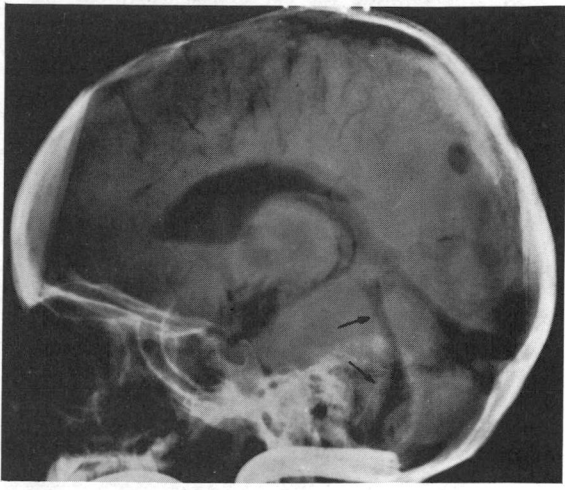

Fig. 46. Pneumoencephalogram of a child with a large tumor of the pons. Posterior displacement and bowing of the aqueduct and fourth ventricle is shown. The distance from the posterior portion of the pituitary fossa to the floor of the fourth ventricle is nearly twice the normal measurement.

age survival time of 12 months. Almost all the patients manifest significant improvement between 3 and 6 weeks after the onset of therapy, which currently consists of 4,000 r delivered as a single tumor dose over 28 days. Typically, there is incomplete clearing of cranial nerve palsies, pyramidal signs, and ataxic phenomena. In some instances, improvement is quite dramatic, in others only slight. Relapse may be expected in the majority within 6 months. In a very few instances, survival with useful function extends to several years or longer.

Tumors of the Third Ventricle

For the purpose of classification, tumors grouped in this area include pinealomas, colloid cysts, and hypothalamic gliomas. The latter produce the "diencephalic syndrome" of infancy. Suprasellar and chiasmatic tumors, which by virtue of their origin in the region of the anterior portion of the third ventricle may closely mimic signs and symptoms produced by tumors arising within the third ventricle, are discussed separately (p. 950).

Pinealomas

INCIDENCE. These rare tumors, which comprise less than 2 percent of all gliomas, occur chiefly (80 percent) in males; approximately one-third are in children under the age of 15 years. In this group, the average age of onset is 10 to 11 years.

CLINICAL MANIFESTATIONS. The most classical localizing sign of a pinealoma is paralysis of upward gaze (Parinaud syndrome), the first manifestation of which may be bilateral ptosis. This finding is indicative of pressure on the superior colliculi, above which the pineal gland protrudes. The inferior colliculi may also be involved, with the production of bilateral hearing loss. However, these signs have been produced by increased intracranial pressure in the absence of a tumor in the pineal area.

A further distinctive syndrome, produced uncommonly by pineal tumors, is that of macrogenitosomia praecox.

The other neurologic manifestations of pineal tumors are nonspecific. Increased intracranial pressure is produced by early obstruction of the aqueduct of Sylvius, which lies close beneath the colliculi. Ataxia, nystagmus, and nuchal rigidity occur in many of the patients, and pyramidal deficit results from pressure on the long tracts in the brainstem.

DIAGNOSIS. Calcification of the pineal gland, particularly if unusual in character or extensive, is sufficiently uncommon in children to suggest the diagnosis in the presence of the typical clinical picture.

Ventriculography is necessary to demonstrate the extent of the lesion and its effects. It may not be possible by this means to distinguish a pinealoma from tumors of the anterior lobe of the cerebellum or from the unusual vein of Galen malformations which occur in this area. The latter are associated with high-output cardiac failure in infancy, convulsions and psychomotor retardation in childhood, and hydrocephalus in the presence of an intracranial bruit. The diagnosis is established by arteriography.

TREATMENT. The infiltrative nature of pineal tumors precludes surgical removal. Shunting of cerebrospinal fluid, if possible by the Torkildsen procedure, is usually indicated, followed by deep roentgen therapy.

PROGNOSIS. Symptoms may be expected to abate following therapy, with freedom from recurrence averaging two to five years, after which time a second course of radiotherapy may be considered. Occasional patients enjoy many years of freedom from recurrence.

Colloid Cyst

These rare cysts arise, possibly from remnants of the paraphysis, in the anterior part of the third ventricle and produce symptoms by occluding the foramina of Monro. Although most of the patients have been diagnosed in adult life, approximately 50 percent have intermittent symptoms for as long as 10 years or more and have clearly had the onset of symptoms in childhood.

Since occlusion may be constant or intermittent, the symptoms may remit and exacerbate and at times are induced by flexion of the head and neck. Some patients present with unlocalized symptoms and signs of increased intracranial pressure, others have paroxysmal symptoms severe enough to lead to stupor or loss of consciousness, and a few undergo progressive dementia as a result of slowly progressive hydrocephalus.

The characteristic syndrome involves sudden severe headache, vomiting, and stupor, especially in association with changes in position which cause the tumor to occlude completely the foramina of Monro (head and neck flexion).

Endocrine symptoms have not been prominent. Several patients have shown transient glycosuria, especially during acute attacks. Scattered instances of obesity, weight loss, polyuria, polyphagia, and acromegaly have occurred.

Of 11 patients with colloid cysts surgically removed in the series of Cairns and Mosberg, 9 survivors were followed up to 15½ years; all were relieved of their preoperative headache and visual symptoms, with the exception of one with irreversible optic atrophy. Sudden death has occurred in about 20 percent of the patients. Occasionally an asymptomatic colloid cyst of the third ventricle is discovered at autopsy following death from unrelated cause.

Diencephalic Syndrome

The "diencephalic syndrome" is a rare symptoms complex described in young infants usually beginning at 2 to 5 months of age and associated with a glioma of the hypothalamus. The most striking features of the syndrome are the preservation of alertness and the presence of euphoria in the face of marked emaciation.

Emaciation is universal. Unusual alertness, wiry vigor, and hyperkinesias are common but are not necessarily striking in degree. Vomiting is usually present but is frequently of mild degree and does not as a rule account for the virtually total absence of subcutaneous fat. Optic atrophy and associated nystagmus, usually of the combined searching and oscillatory type, are common, as might be expected from the proximity of the tumor to the optic chiasm; these findings may, however, be absent despite advanced symptoms and signs.

Excessive diaphoresis, polyuria, and tremor are variable symptoms. Enlargement of the cranium has occurred but is not the rule. More often the head appears enlarged because of the wasted trunk and extremities. Acute peptic ulceration and gastric hemorrhage have occurred.

The occurrence of emaciation and excessive alertness in infants with hypothalamic tumor, rather than growth retardation, obesity, and other features more commonly associated with neoplasms of this region in older children, is unexplained. Marked emaciation does occur occasionally in older children with hypothalamic tumors and is not necessarily restricted to gliomas.

The diagnosis is confirmed by pneumoencephalography, which, because of the open fontanel, can be safely performed even in the presence of optic atrophy and the unusual instance of suspected hydrocephalus. Plain radiograms of the skull are not apt to be helpful, and the cerebrospinal fluid protein content is usually normal.

Because of the location of the neoplasm, surgical excision is impossible, and only roentgen therapy can be offered. The prognosis for long-term survival is poor, death usually occurring between 10 months and 2 years of age. Exceptional cases show a more striking response to radiotherapy and do well for many years.

Thalamic Tumors

Cerebral tumor is generally not considered in the differential diagnosis of extrapyramidal signs and symptoms in children. However, the existing literature has occasional reference to children with basal ganglia tumors and suggests that a Parkinsonlike syndrome may be produced by tumors involving one or both thalami. The actual frequency of tumors in this location in childhood is greater than the number of reported cases would suggest.

A rhythmic alternating tremor of one extremity is the common finding. Other manifestations include athetosis, torsion spasm, posturing, rigidity, and bradykinesia. More often, however, a thalamic tumor in a child is liable to masquerade as a tumor of either a cerebellar or cerebral hemisphere. Thus, a tremor indistinguishable from that produced by a cerebellar neoplasm or hemiparesis of varying degree may be the earliest or sole manifestation of a thalamic tumor in children. It is peculiar that despite the most profound hemiplegia associated with thalamic tumors in children, sensation may be completely intact even in older children, in whom it may be reliably tested. Signs and symptoms of increased intracranial pressure are frequently present, since the thalami form the major portion of the walls of the third ventricle.

These tumors are mainly astrocytomas and glioblastomas, and because of their inaccessible location the outlook is poor. In occasional instances, a cystic astrocytoma may be treated by partial excision and aspiration of the cyst, followed by radiotherapy, with a surprising number of years of remission.

Tumors of the Cerebral Hemispheres

INCIDENCE. It is generally stated that infratentorial tumors tend to predominate in children. However, experience in some large medical centers, including our own, indicates an approximately equal incidence of supatentorial and infratentorial neoplasms.

In general, approximately one-third of supratentorial tumors in children are gliomas of the cerebral hemispheres. There is no striking difference in the age or sex incidence. Half of the patients fall into the age group between 7 and 11 years.

CLINICAL MANIFESTATIONS. Personality change, a symptom difficult to document statistically with reliability, is probably the most common early manifestation of a cerebral hemisphere tumor in a child. In retrospect, intermittent irritability and/or listlessness virtually always antedate the more specific symptoms and signs which precipitate neurodiagnostic study.

Headache, vomiting, or both occur as early manifestations in 80 or 90 percent of the patients. However, headache without vomiting is much more common than in posterior fossa or midline supratentorial tumors (distal to midline channels of cerebrospinal fluid communication and to medullary vomiting centers). The diagnostic value of this symptom is, of course, related to the child's age and ability to verbalize.

Motor weakness occurs in over one-third of the patients. Focal pyramidal deficit is often demonstrated in the form of spasticity, hyperreflexia, and extensor plantar response in the absence of demonstrable weakness. Motor weakness may reveal itself in subtle fashion by change of handedness, reluctance to use an extremity, or unilateral abnormal posturing of the extremities on walking or performing other routine activities of daily living.

Convulsions are not present in the majority of patients with cerebral hemisphere tumors. Of 112 children with cerebral hemisphere tumors studied at the Columbia-Presbyterian Medical Center, 38 percent had seizures. Half of these children suffered from generalized convulsions. However, the seizures were frequently of mixed types with 80 percent having either focal or psychomotor attacks. Of considerable additional interest is the fact that one-third of this group of children with seizures and cerebral hemisphere tumors had convulsions for 3 to 10 years prior to diagnosis.

Papilledema of florid degree is not usually encountered but is present to some extent in the majority of patients at the time of diagnosis.

Aside from focal pyramidal deficit, other focal signs such as sensory deficit, visual field defects, and aphasic phenomena are rarely encountered, probably because of the large proportion of patients too young to cooperate reliably. The use of devices such as striped cloth or striped rotating drum to detect defects in opticokinetic nystagmus in children with parietal lobe tumors would increase the prevalence of this finding.

False localizing signs, particularly those ascribed to defects in cerebellar pathway function, have been discussed earlier. The findings on neurologic examination in children with cerebral hemisphere tumors are at times so sparse that a midline neoplasm or pseudotumor cerebri is suspected.

DIAGNOSIS. Ancillary studies are especially important for diagnosis in this group of patients because it is usually possible to localize the tumor precisely without resorting to ventriculography. The differential diagnosis includes space-occupying lesions of the hemisphere, such as subdural hematoma or hygroma, brain abscess, and, far less commonly

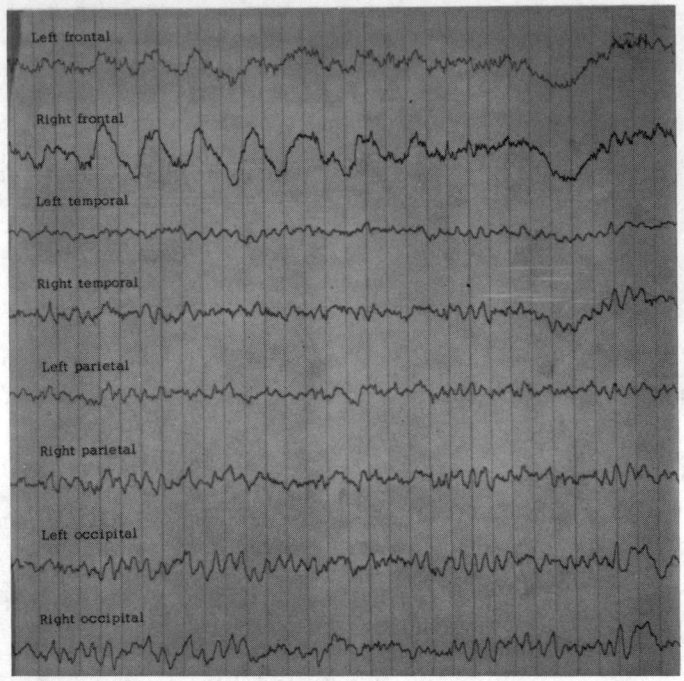

Fig. 47. Electroencephalogram showing a right frontal slow wave focus associated with an underlying astrocytoma.

in this country, parasitic or granulomatous lesions, such as hydatid cyst or tuberculoma. On occasion, an acute or subacute encephalitis, particularly herpes simplex encephalitis, will preferentially involve the temporal lobe to the extent of producing signs and symptoms of an expanding lesion within this structure. On rare occasions, a porencephalic cyst communicates with the subarachnoid space in ball-valve fashion so that a subarachnoid collection of fluid accumulates progressively and acts as a mass lesion.

In contradistinction to midline or posterior fossa neoplasms where the findings are nonspecific, consisting usually of generalized dysrhythmia which is maximal in the occipital regions, electroencephalography may be of definite localizing value in cerebral hemisphere tumors. The most consistent EEG abnormality is focal high amplitude slowing, though this is by no means diagnostic of a cerebral neoplasm (Fig. 47). The EEG is abnormal in over 90 percent of supratentorial tumors in children and is of localizing value in 75 percent. When the cerebral cortex is involved, localizing value approaches 90 percent.

Brain scanning for focal collection of radioisotope is of greatest value in the localization of cerebral hemisphere neoplasms. The diagnostic incidence approaches 90 percent in some large series as compared to approximately 60 percent for posterior fossa neoplasms. Evidence is accumulating to the effect that sequential scanning provides valuable information concerning tumor recurrence or extension following subtotal excision and/or radiotherapy. The use of technetium is currently favored for sequential scanning because of lower radiation exposure.

Plain radiograms of the skull are helpful in localizing cerebral hemisphere neoplasms when tumor calcification occurs (approximately 10 percent), or when local bony erosion is evident. The majority of patients show suture spread or other evidence of increased intracranial pressure, but somewhat less frequently and to a lesser extent than with posterior fossa neoplasms. Between one-fourth and one-third of plain radiograms of the skull are normal in children with cerebral hemisphere gliomas.

Echoencephalography (Fig. 48A and B) has been developed into a very useful tool for the detection of significant shifts of the midline cerebral structures created by any space-occupying lesion situated on one side of the midline. This diagnostic procedure is of particular value in children, since the pineal gland is rarely calcified in this age group. Ultrasound is deflected from normal midline structures in a characteristic manner, giving a prominent oscilloscopic deflection which can be photographed and measured in terms of distance from the right or left side of the cranial vault, after input of ultrasound from the appropriate side. Since structures in the vicinity of the third ventricle give rise to this deflection, lesions placed far anteriorly or posteriorly are less apt to give significant shifts, but the method has proved to be extremely useful as an initial screening procedure, entirely free of contraindications or complications. More than three-fourths of cerebral

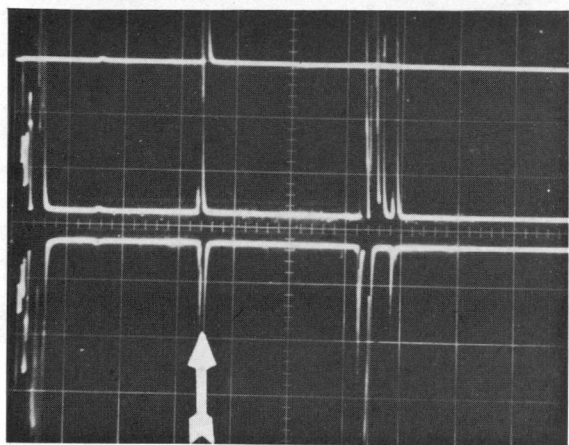

Fig. 48A. Normal echoencephalogram. Arrow indicates midline structures are in a normal position.

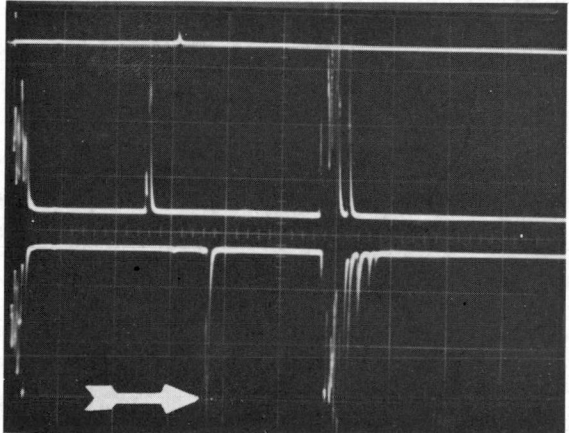

Fig. 48B. Abnormal echoencephalogram. Arrow indicates 10-mm shift of midline echoes from left to right. In this case due to a large left parietal lobe glioma in a 6-year-old boy.

hemisphere tumors are associated with a shift of the midline in excess of 2 mm, which is considered the upper limit of normal.

When signs of increased intracranial pressure are absent, lumbar puncture may be done and may reveal a moderate increase in cerebrospinal fluid pressure or in the protein content of the fluid. Cerebrospinal fluid enzymes may be elevated (e.g., transaminase, lactic dehydrogenase, phosphohexose isomerase). These findings are not specific and occur in other active lesions of the central nervous system.

Cerebral angiography is the contrast study of choice when focal findings or prior ancillary studies indicate the side of the lesion or when there is increased intracranial pressure without localizing signs. In experienced hands, percutaneous carotid angiography may be done under narcosis (combined seco-

TABLE 19. *Pathology of 104 Verified Cerebral Hemisphere Tumors*

Type of Tumor		Number
Astrocytoma (pure and mixed)		46
Solid	30	
Cystic	16	
Glioblastoma		13
Ependymoma		8
Meningioma		6
Sarcoma		5
Oligodendroglioma		4
Ganglioglioma		4
Malignant teratoma		2
Metastatic neuroblastoma		2
Choroid plexus papilloma		2
Miscellaneous		12
	Total	104

barbital, meperidine, and chlorpromazine), obviating the need for and the risks of anesthesia. The advantages of angiography include demonstration of the vascular supply and the extent of vascularity of a given neoplasm, information of considerable importance to the neurosurgeon in planning the surgical approach.

Air contrast studies may be indicated as a supplement to angiography in order to amplify equivocal findings or to provide critical information not obtained by angiography.

TREATMENT AND PROGNOSIS. Treatment and its outcome are in great part dependent on the histology of the tumor, though in general the results are disappointing. The histologic types encountered in 104 verified cerebral hemisphere tumors at the Columbia-Presbyterian Medical Center are outlined in Table 19. The different types will not be discussed separately.

Astrocytoma is the leading cerebral hemisphere tumor. It is far less commonly cystic than the cerebellar astrocytoma and only occasionally presents as a mural nodule in a large cyst. The tumor is so infiltrative in character that complete surgical excision is rarely, if ever, achieved, but many years of remission of symptoms can be achieved in a significant number of children. Obviously, the precise location of the tumor will dictate the extent of surgical excision possible. A tumor located within the motor and speech areas of the dominant cerebral hemisphere lends itself rather poorly to surgical intervention, whereas a tumor anteriorly placed in one frontal lobe can be attacked more radically.

Anticonvulsant medication is routinely recommended postoperatively for children with cerebral hemisphere neoplasms and is continued indefinitely when recurrence is expected, as it is in the majority. Otherwise, the indications for continuing anticonvulsant medication are the same as those employed in convulsions due to other causes.

TABLE 20.   *Symptoms and Signs in 56 Patients with Optic Nerve Glioma*

	Initial	Presenting	Subsequent
Diminished visual acuity	28	39	53
Exophthalmos	25	27	29
Nystagmus	8	8	14
Strabismus	6	11	17
Field cut	1	1	12
Disk change			
Pallor			36
Pallor and blurring			11
Blurring			8
Increased intracranial pressure	3	13	15
Enlarged head	1	1	4
Multiple café-au-lait spots		2	12
Paresis		3	4

Tumors of the Optic Nerve and Chiasm

INCIDENCE. Tumors of the optic nerve and chiasm consist almost entirely of gliomas (astrocytomas), of which over 95 percent occur in children. Meningiomas of the dural sheath of the optic nerve are exceedingly rare in children, occurring approximately 20 times less frequently than optic nerve gliomas. At the Columbia-Presbyterian Medical Center between the years 1940 and 1964, 5 percent of 1,124 intracranial tumors in children under 16 years were optic nerve gliomas. Surprisingly, almost one-third of the patients have their earliest symptom under the age of 2 years, and as many as 10 percent in the first 6 months of life. The diagnosis, however, is characteristically delayed for one to several years after onset.

CLINICAL MANIFESTATIONS. Table 20 indicates the various symptoms and signs at the time of onset and of diagnosis.

The difference between the number of children or parents complaining of diminished visual acuity and those showing visual defects on examination reflects the tendency for children to tolerate occult visual deficit. Exophthalmos is a particularly early and frequent (96 percent) sign when the tumor is confined to one optic nerve, though 20 percent of patients with chiasmal gliomas also have some degree of proptosis. Nystagmus is related chiefly to the presence of severe visual deficit prior to the age of 4 years, more particularly prior to 2 years of age. Increased intracranial pressure is present only when the chiasm is involved and a large tumor has occluded the foramina of Monro. Multiple café-au-lait spots, the most common manifestation of neurofibromatosis, are present in approximately 25 percent of the children. Strabismus, when encountered, is not paretic in type but relates to defective fixation of a poorly seeing eye. Optic atrophy is an invariable finding.

It may be confined to one optic nerve, despite early involvement of the chiasm.

DIAGNOSIS. The differential diagnosis in cases of optic nerve tumor includes other tumors of the orbit, particularly neurofibroma, and less frequently meningioma and retinoblastoma. The clinical and roentgenographic criteria outlined here make it clear that separation of these entities is possible in virtually every instance without resort to a tissue diagnosis. The most important differential point in regard to proptosis is that in optic glioma it is of mild degree, occurs in a straightforward axis with little lateral or vertical displacement of the globe, and is associated with a significant degree of optic atrophy and visual defect; other orbital tumors producing proptosis lead to more marked and bizarrely positioned protrusion of the globe, in the presence of remarkable preservation of vision, and usually absence of optic atrophy.

Chiasmal gliomas may be confused with other tumors arising in this area—craniopharyngioma, teratomas, dermoids, ectopic pinealomas, colloid cysts of the third ventricle, and hypothalamic gliomas. The characteristic features on plain radiograms of the skull are the most important means of differentiating chiasmal gliomas from other tumors in this region. They are indicated in Figures 49 and 50 and consist of enlarged optic foramina and typical deformity of the anterior clinoids. Helpful clinical features include multiple café-au-lait spots and the characteristic, though not invariable, absence of diabetes insipidus and growth retardation in children with chiasmal gliomas. Approximately 5 percent of children with chiasmal gliomas show endocrine changes which, if present, usually include precocious puberty.

Over 25 percent of children with optic gliomas are followed for one to three years after the onset of visual defects, strabismus, or nystagmus before the diagnosis is established. The optic disc pallor encountered is often ascribed to congenital optic atrophy. For unexplained reasons, the children may show some correction of visual acuity with appropriate refraction. Their age makes it impossible, in most instances, for

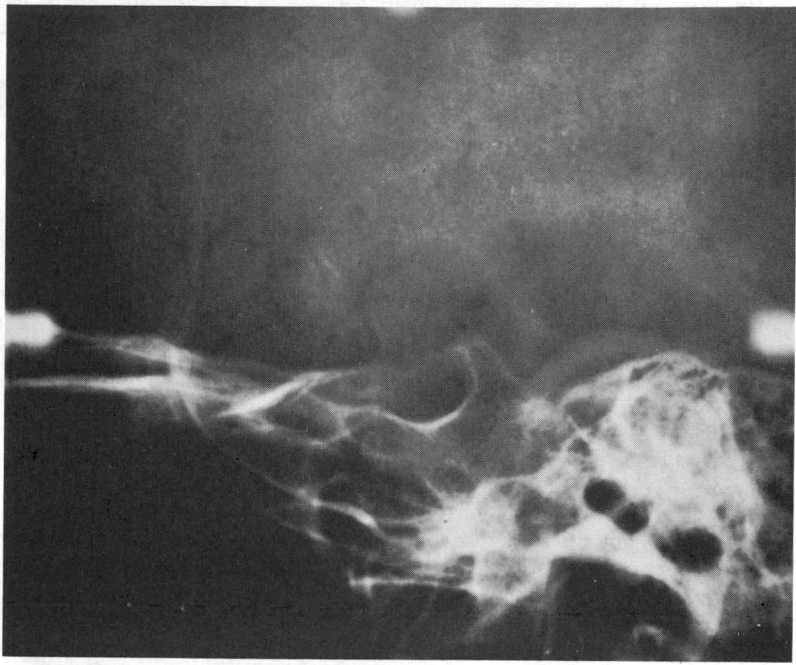

Fig. 49. J-shaped deformity of the sella in a 4-year-old boy with right optic nerve and chiasm glioma. A depression of the right lateral aspect of the chiasmatic sulcus with intact cortical margins is shown. The anterior clinoid process is thinned by the optic nerve tumor at the cranial porus of the right optic canal.

the ophthalmologist to be certain that full correction is achieved. It is, therefore, urged that when disc pallor of any degree is present, or visual defect is not fully corrected by refraction, the simple expedient of obtaining skull x-rays with adequate views of the optic foramina and sella turcica be considered.

The tools employed in the diagnosis or exclusion of optic nerve gliomas include, whenever possible, measurement of visual fields and acuity, careful examination of the fundi, x-rays of the skull, orbits, and optic foramina, and, in addition, intracranial

pneumography. In the presence of a chiasmal glioma, pneumoencephalography reveals a filling defect in the anterior portion of the third ventricle, which is invaginated by the optic chiasm. Intracranial involvement of a single optic nerve may also be detected by intracranial pneumography but may be missed by this study if the chiasm is not involved.

TREATMENT. If it is suspected that an optic nerve glioma is confined to a single optic nerve, a combined transcranial operation with unroofing of the orbit, preferably performed by a neurosurgeon and ophthal-

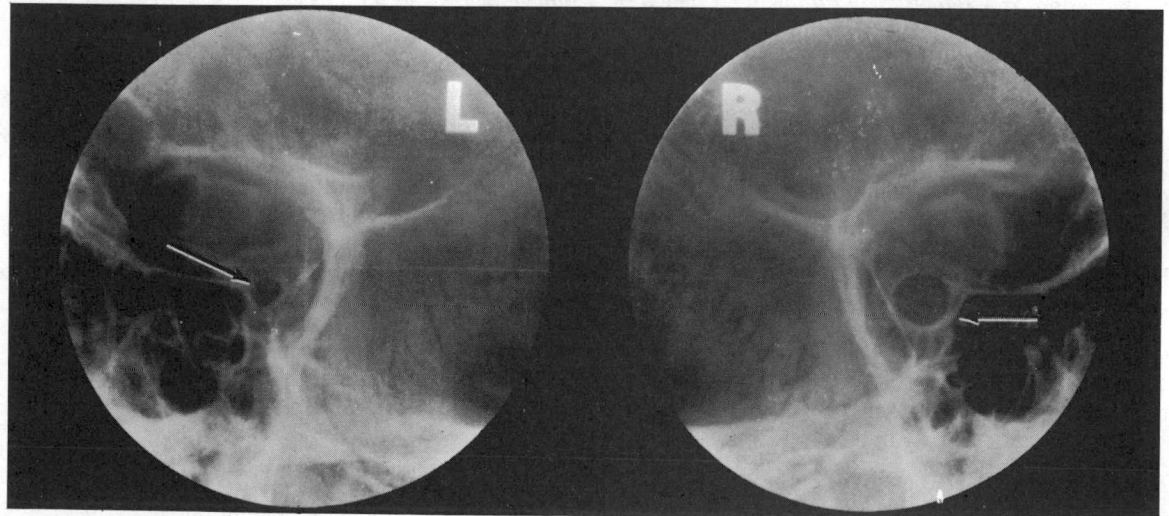

Fig. 50. Orbital and intracranial right optic nerve glioma in a 14-year-old boy. The normal left optic canal is oval and 5 mm in diameter. The right optic canal is enlarged to a circular lumen of 11 mm diameter with intact cortical margin.

mologist, is still indicated even if pneumography fails to reveal intracranial extension. In this manner, the tumor can be completely resected. It is almost always possible to preserve the globe, which subsequently serves as an excellent "natural prosthesis" and moves reflexly in conjugate fashion, directed by the eye with useful vision.

Chiasmal gliomas cannot be totally resected and are best treated by radiotherapy. It may be possible partially to resect a chiasmal glioma in order to reestablish cerebrospinal fluid communication when the foramina of Monro are obstructed, but more commonly ventricular shunting is indicated as an adjunct to radiotherapy. Transient diabetes insipidus may occur after surgery in this region and requires careful replacement therapy.

PROGNOSIS.   Patients with proptosis seem to do well, regardless of whether the chiasm is involved. Undoubtedly this is because proptosis reflects origin of a very slowly growing tumor in the optic nerve. Those with gliomas confined to the optic nerve can be offered a complete cure in virtually every instance.

For unexplained reasons, in some patients with chiasmal gliomas, whose tumors are identical histologically with those proved by biopsy in patients who do well, the course is rapid and they succumb to their disease within a year of diagnosis. More than 80 percent of these patients who do poorly have had increased intracranial pressure at the time of diagnosis. However, as many as one-third of patients with chiasmal gliomas who have shown long-term survival with useful vision also had increased intracranial pressure when diagnosed.

The majority with chiasmal gliomas treated with radiotherapy may be expected to survive with little or no neurologic deficit and with useful vision for many years. The longest follow-up of a patient known to us with a chiasmal glioma, following biopsy of the lesion and radiotherapy, without evidence of clinical relapse, is 30 years.

Craniopharyngioma

INCIDENCE.   The incidence of craniopharyngiomas is only slightly higher than that of all optic nerve gliomas but is severalfold that of chiasmal gliomas, with which they may occasionally, in atypical cases, be confused. Between 5 and 10 percent of all intracranial tumors in children are craniopharyngiomas. The majority of the children seen for the first time are between 7 and 12 years of age.

CLINICAL MANIFESTATIONS.   The cardinal signs and symptoms of craniopharyngioma are: (1) increased intracranial pressure; (2) visual defects; (3) endocrine dysfunction; and (4) hypothalamic dysfunction.

Increased Intracranial Pressure.   Increased intracranial pressure is due to upward extension of the tumor and obstruction of one or both foramina of Monro. The signs and symptoms of increased intra-

cranial pressure are not distinctive, but it must be remembered that occasionally optic atrophy prevents the occurrence of papilledema. Almost always, however, papilledema and disc pallor are both present at the time of initial diagnosis.

Visual Defects.   Visual acuity is usually diminished to a significant degree owing to chiasmatic compression and optic atrophy. Visual field defects are common and variable in type, though the typical finding, because of the midline position of the tumor, is bitemporal hemianopia. In very young, dull, or inarticulate children, it may be impossible to document the type or extent of visual deficit.

Endocrine Dysfunction.   The observed deficits in endocrine function are due to diminished pituitary activity; the principal manifestations are growth retardation and sexual infantilism. Preoperatively, clinical manifestations of hypothyroidism are not to be expected.

While these children tend to tire easily and may be hypotensive, obesity of the "female" type is more common than cachexia, and florid panhypopituitarism is distinctly rare.

Hypothalamic Dysfunction.   Diabetes insipidus is uncommon before surgical extirpation, but is encountered preoperatively in some patients.

Other signs and symptoms of hypothalamic involvement include growth retardation, somnolence, obesity, hypothermia or hyperthermia, hypertension or hypotension, inappropriate secretion of antidiuretic hormone, and alarming changes in vital signs. However, with the exception of somatic and sexual infantilism, these phenomena occur more often as postoperative complications than as part of the preoperative clinical picture.

DIAGNOSIS.   Approximately three-fourths of children with craniopharyngiomas show diffuse flecks of calcification in the sella or suprasellar region in plain radiograms of the skull (Fig. 51). Enlargement of the sella is present in half of the cases, and more than half show nonspecific signs of increased intracranial pressure, such as suture spread or demineralization of the vault or clinoid processes. When calcification is absent, it is wise to obtain films of the optic foramina and to study the anterior clinoids for evidence of a chiasmal glioma. Other tumors occurring less commonly in this region include teratomas, dermoids, colloid cysts, and hypothalamic gliomas. Calcification may occur in dermoid tumors and teratomas but is rare in the other tumors.

It is essential to document the extent of endocrine disturbance. The urine osmolality, serum electrolytes, and preoperative blood pressure require special attention so that optimal correction may be made preoperatively. Bone age is determined by radiograms of the hemiskeleton or of the hand and wrist. Other endocrine functions may be estimated by the various tests of anterior and posterior pituitary, thyroid, and adrenal function; and postoperative comparison can be made when the condition stabilizes so that optimal replacement endocrine therapy can be offered.

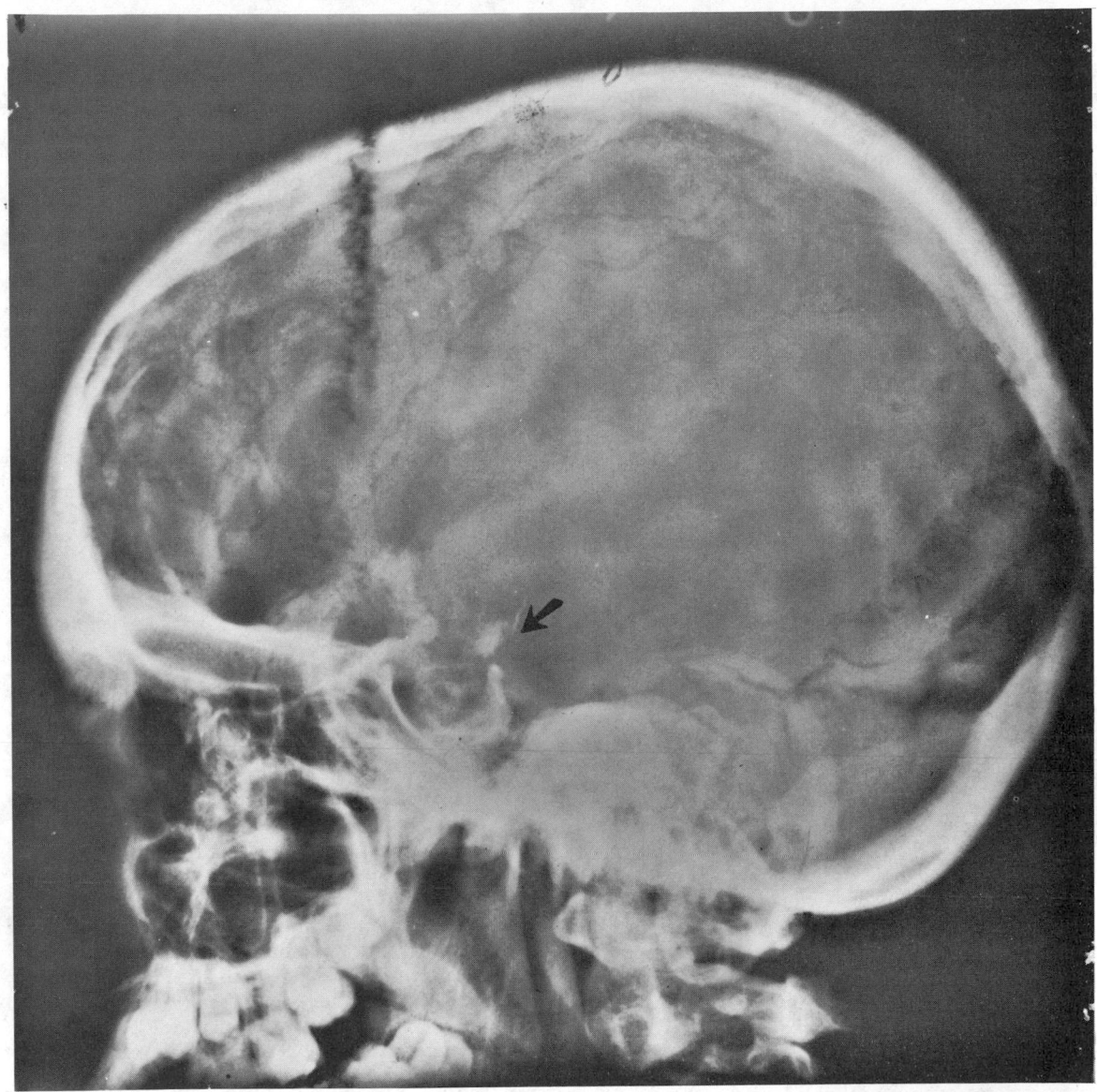

Fig. 51. Skull film of a child with craniopharyngioma showing sellar and suprasella calcifications (arrow), enlargement of the pituitary fossa, and separation of sutures.

The visual fields and acuity are carefully plotted, preoperatively and after stabilization, postoperatively, to permit comparison on subsequent examination for detection of recurrence.

The surgeon may or may not elect to perform ventriculography prior to surgical attack on the neoplasm. When the diagnosis seems secure, intracranial pneumography may be forgone. At times, cerebral angiography is performed so that optimal handling of stretched and distorted internal carotid and anterior cerebral vessels can be planned.

TREATMENT. Regardless of the results of endocrine study, cortisone should be given preoperatively and during surgery; its use has become the single largest factor in the marked increase in immediate postoperative survival and in the increase in the number of patients capable of having radical tumor removal. An average dose of cortisone is 50 mg on the evening prior to surgery and 50 mg on the morning of surgery. Approximately 100 mg of cortisone is given intravenously during surgery. On the first postoperative day, 100 mg of cortisone is administered, thereafter tapering the dose by 25 mg daily to a maintenance level of approximately 15 mg daily.

It is now believed possible for the experienced neurosurgeon to perform a gross total excision of the tumor in more than half of the patients. These tumors are encapsulated and almost always cystic to some extent. They may be located within the sella or entirely beyond the diaphragm of the sella in the pituitary stalk. The tumor capsule may adhere inseparably to the anterior cerebral or internal carotid vessels, the optic chiasm, or the hypothalamus. In such cases, only partial excision is possible and recurrence is invariable. However, dramatic remission of symptoms and restoration of vision may be achieved simply by aspiration of the "machinery-oil-like" fluid from a moderately sized or large cyst which has compressed surrounding structures.

The tumors, being squamous epitheliomas, are relatively radioresistant, but it is believed that radiotherapy may retard at least the rate of reaccumulation of cyst fluid.

In the immediate postoperative period, symptoms of diabetes insipidus may be severe, and careful attention to water and electrolyte balance is essential. For the first few days, replacement of water and electrolytes (Sec. 8.7) is generally advisable, without the use of vasopressin, because the immediate effects of surgery wane and diabetes insipidus is invariably lessened.

When the vasopressin is introduced, the aqueous parenteral preparation may be used, every 6 hours, if necessary. When the stable level of diabetes insipidus is determined, it is treated as described elsewhere (Sec. 16.12).

Cortisone and thyroid replacement are often necessary, particularly when a radical tumor excision has been performed. Details of treatment are described elsewhere (Sec. 16.2).

Accurate human growth hormone assays are now available, and human growth hormone can be secured in a limited amount. With this compound many children with previous growth retardation are showing reestablishment of normal growth curves. Normal pubescence may also be achieved by appropriate hormonal therapy, and even reproduction may be secured with the use of human chorionic gonadotropin.

The patient who has had excision of a craniopharyngioma must be followed with particular attention to visual fields and acuity and periodic skull x-rays for the detection of recurrence by extension of calcification or shift in the position clips placed at the time of surgery.

PROGNOSIS. Children treated prior to 1950 almost uniformly failed to survive. The long-term results of children treated more recently are being awaited but already are considerably more promising.

Even when total tumor excision is not possible, the interval from operation to recurrence may be many years, though occasionally it is less than a year. Repeated partial excision of solid tumor and capsule and cyst aspiration may keep such patients alive and functioning well for many years. Unfortunately, visual deficit often mounts with each insult, and the risk of postoperative morbidity and mortality is compounded.

Tumors of the Spinal Cord

Intraspinal tumors in infants and children are far less common than intracranial tumors, the ratio being approximately 1 to 5. Meningiomas and neurofibromas, relatively common in adults, are rarely encountered in children. Intraspinal lipomas, dermoid, and teratoid tumors, neuroblastomas, and intramedullary gliomas are the common intraspinal neoplasms in children. Approximately 20 percent of the tumors are of the dermoid and lipoma group, which are benign tumors of congenital origin. Gliomas and sarcomas each have a similar incidence, and together with the congenital group account for 60 percent of the total. Less common is the neuroblastoma which comprises 5 to 10 percent of intraspinal tumors in children.

Early diagnosis of intraspinal tumors in children is essential because of three considerations:

1. Irreversible neurologic deficit may occur when diagnosis is delayed, despite the otherwise favorable character of the neoplasm from the therapeutic point of view.
2. Intramedullary gliomas, contrary to popular belief, may at times either lend themselves to total surgical excision or respond dramatically to radiation therapy.
3. The lipoma, dermoid, and teratoid group of tumors, benign varieties of extramedullary tumors, may be associated, even after only partial excision, with prolonged relief of signs and symptoms.

CLINICAL MANIFESTATIONS. *Disturbance of Gait and Posture.* Disturbances of gait and posture are the most frequent symptoms of intraspinal tumors; in their presence an intraspinal neoplasm should always be considered. These changes may be due to weakness, spasticity, or compensatory posture to avoid pain. The most frequent disturbance of posture is a reluctance to flex the trunk; it may be present before frank neurologic deficit is detectable. There may be prominent paraspinal muscle spasm, a particularly important sign in the nonverbal or inarticulate child. The characteristic posture and gait of the child with a cervical intramedullary glioma are the flaillike drooping of the shoulders and reduced swing of the upper extremities due to segmental anterior horn cell involvement. Other abnormalities of gait depend upon the extremity involved and the degree to which changes of tone and power are pressed.

Pain. Pain is a common, but by no means universal, symptom of intraspinal tumor; it occurs as an initial complaint in approximately 50 percent of children. In the young child pain may be manifested by irritability and postural guarding. Older children frequently describe the pain as being accentuated by coughing, sneezing, or straining, as well as by flexion of the neck, trunk, or extension of the lower extremities.

Weakness. Approximately two-thirds of children with intraspinal tumors have some degree of weakness on initial evaluation. Functionally this may be evident only as a limp, easy fatigability, or reduced activity on one or more extremities. There is a flaccid paresis at the level of the lesion, below which the extremities are spastic. The weakness may be of the flaccid type below the level of the lesion when "spinal shock" occurs, as in rapidly evolving cord compression from neuroblastoma or other metastatic lesions.

Reflex Changes. Diminished deep tendon reflexes may be encountered within the limited segments occupied by tumor, due to encroachment on anterior horn cells, while hyperactive reflexes and extensor plantar responses are expected below the level of the lesion due to impairment of descending tracts. In "spinal shock," deep tendon reflexes are absent. Thus in intramedullary neoplasms of the cervical cord, diminished reflexes and loss of tone in the upper extremities are commonly associated with spasticity, hyperreflexia, and extensor plantar responses in the lower extremities. Absence or diminution of reflexes in the lower extremities is suggestive of a lesion of the cauda equina. An absent anal reflex is additional evidence of sacral cord or root involvement.

Impaired Bladder or Bowel Function. Bowel and bladder function may be impaired by involvement of descending tracts or by segmental loss of innervation in lumbosacral lesions. The result may be either a spastic, low-capacity bladder with frequency of urination, or a distended, atonic bladder with dribbling of urine. Laxity of the rectal sphincter and a diminished anal reflex with regressive bowel or bladder function are valuable objective signs in a child in whom the more subjective aspects of evaluation, such as sensory examination of the saddle area, are less reliable.

Sensory Impairment. In children the sensory examination is the most difficult and least reliable part of the neurologic examination. However, a careful examination may be rewarding even in an infant. Changes in facial expression or direction of attention may be helpful in fixing the level of a spinal cord lesion. Sensory deficits are ascertainable in one-third of children with intraspinal tumors, despite the fact that sensory complaints are rarely offered. There is often an absence or diminution of sweating below the level of the lesion, a valuable sign in this limited sensory examination in young children. The oft-cited tendency of intramedullary tumors to "spare" sacral sensation is particularly misleading in children.

Cutaneous and Skeletal Changes. Cutaneous or subcutaneous lesions may indicate an underlying neoplasm. Multiple café-au-lait spots in a child with spinal cord symptoms suggest the diagnosis of neurofibroma. In rare instances a single café-au-lait spot may mark the site of the tumor. A subcutaneous lipoma, nevus flammeus, dimple, sinus, or tuft of hair in the dorsal or lumbosacral region may be an innocent dermal anomaly; however, the presence of such a lesion in association with symptoms or signs of neurologic significance suggests the possibility of an underlying neoplasm of the lipomatous, dermoid, or teratoid type, with or without myelodysplasia and other anomalies.

Scoliosis may be a local manifestation of an intraspinal tumor or may be associated with neurofibromatosis even in the absence of any intraspinal tumor. However, an intraspinal tumor should be excluded in all patients with neurofibromatosis and scoliosis.

Miscellaneous Signs. Occasionally opsoclonus, with "polymyoclonia" or cerebellar ataxia, may be the only signs suggesting the possibility of an occult intraspinal ganglioneuroma or neuroblastoma.

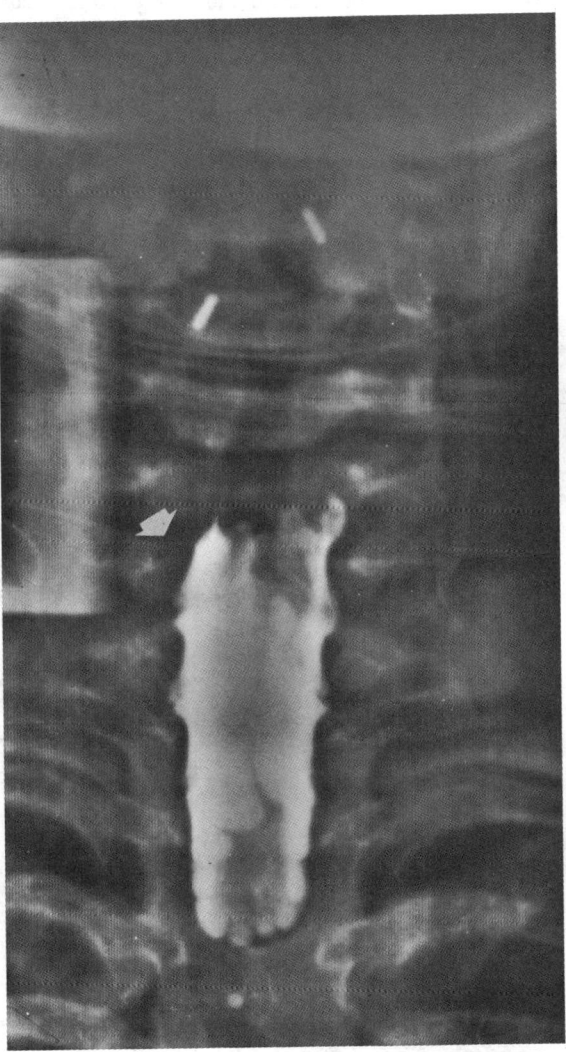

Fig. 52. Myelogram in a 4-year-old with complete spinal block due to an extradural compression. Neuroblastoma metastases to the cervical spine were demonstrated both radiographically and at surgery. The column of contrast material is seen to be displaced to the left (arrow) away from the pedicle of C-6. The cord is also seen to be displaced in the same direction. (Courtesy of Dr. Sadek Hilal.)

LABORATORY STUDIES. *Cerebrospinal Fluid.* Lumbar puncture is of considerable value in the diagnosis of spinal cord neoplasia. Radiographs of vertebral spines should always precede lumbar puncture. With suspected spinal cord lesions, careful manometric measurements should always be performed. The fluid may be slightly discolored or frankly xanthochromic. The cell count and sugar content are usually normal. In the presence of metastatic seeding (leptomeningeal sarcomatosis or carcinomatosis), there may be an increase in cells and a marked reduction in the sugar content. These findings, particularly when associated with nuchal rigidity, give rise to a picture that may be easily confused with bacterial meningitis. Cerebrospinal fluid protein is usually increased when a spinal cord tumor is present. In the presence of a complete subarachnoid block, the protein content is markedly elevated with an associated deep yellow discoloration (Froin syndrome).

Radiographic Studies. About two-thirds of children with intraspinal tumors have associated bony changes in the spine detectable on plain x-ray examination. Two significant findings suggesting an intraspinal tumor are widening of the interpedicular space and erosion of the pedicles. Myelography is the definitive diagnostic precedure and establishes the level of the lesion and its intramedullary or extramedullary location (Fig. 52).

DIFFERENTIAL DIAGNOSIS. The differential diagnosis of intraspinal tumors includes congenital defects (e.g., diastematomyelia), vascular malformations, tumors of the bony spine, and degenerative diseases. Diagnosis is often possible with a detailed history, careful neurologic examination, and the appropriate use of ancillary laboratory procedures.

TREATMENT. Therapy is largely dependent upon location of the tumor. Surgical extirpation is feasible for some extramedullary lesions; occasionally, partial removal and rarely total removal of an intramedullary tumor is possible. Decompressive laminectomy may give symptomatic relief.

Radiation therapy is utilized for inoperable tumors and as a supplement for radiosensitive mass lesions subtotally removed. Corticosteroid therapy may be of vital benefit in reducing cord edema associated with radiation therapy, or prior to surgical decompression.

REFERENCES

BRAIN TUMORS

Aron, B. S. Twenty years' experience with radiation therapy medulloblastoma. Amer. J. Roentgen, 105:37, 1969.

Bain, H. W., Darte, J. M. M., Keith, W. S., and Kruyff, E. The diencephalic syndrome of early infancy due to silent brain tumor: with special reference to treatment. Pediatrics, 38:473, 1966.

Bailey, P., Buchanan, D. N., and Bucy, P. C. Intra-cranial Tumors of Infancy and Childhood. Chicago, University of Chicago Press, 1939.

Bergstrand, C. G., Bergstedt, J., and Herrlin, M. M. Paediatric aspects of brain tumors in infancy and childhood. Acta Paediat. Scand., 47:688, 1958.

Bloom, H. J. G., Wallace, M. B., and Henk, J. M. The treatment and prognosis of medulloblastoma in children. Amer. J. Roetgen., 105:43, 1969.

Bouchard, J. J. Radiation Therapy of Tumors and Diseases of the Nervous System. Philadelphia, Lea and Febiger, 1966.

Bray, P. F., Carter, S., and Taveras, J. M. Brainstem tumors in children. Neurology, 8:1, 1958.

Cairns, H., and Mosberg, W. H., Jr. Colloid cyst of the third ventricle. Surg. Gynec. Obstet., 92:545, 1951.

Chang, C. H., Housepian, E. M., and Herbert, C., Jr. An operative staging system and a megavoltage radiotherapeutic technic for cerebellar medulloblastomas. Radiology, 93:1351, No. 6, 1969.

Cheek, W. R., and Taveras, J. M. Thalamic tumors. J. Neurosurg., 24:505, 1966.

Chutorian, A. M., Schwartz, J. F., Evans, R. A., and Carter, S. Optic gliomas in children. Neurology, 14:83, 1964.

Cuneo, H. M., and Rand, C. W. Brain Tumors of Childhood. Springfield, Ill., Charles C Thomas, Publ., 1952.

Davidoff, L. M. Some considerations in the therapy of pineal tumors. Bull. N.Y. Acad. Med., 43:537, 1967.

Dods, L. A diencephalic syndrome of early infancy. Med. J. Aust., 1:222, 1967.

Fokes, E. C., and Earle, K. M. Ependymomas: clinical and pathological aspects. J. Neurosurg., 30:585, 1969.

French, L. A. The use of steroids in the treatment of cerebral edema. Bull. N.Y. Acad. Med., 42:30, 1966.

—— and Galicich, J. H. The use of steroids for control of cerebral edema. Clin. Neurosurg., 10:212, 1964.

Gold, L. H. A., and Loken, M. K. Retrospective evaluation of isotope images of the brain in 852 patients. Radiology, 92:1473, 1969.

Hammill, J. F., and Carter, S. Brain Tumors in Childhood, Practice of Pediatrics. Hagerstown, Md., W. F. Prior Co., Inc., 1966.

Jackson, I. J., and Thompson, R. K. Pediatric Neurosurgery. Springfield, Ill., Charles C Thomas, Publ., 1959.

Lampkin, B. C., Mauer, A. M., and McBride, B. H. Response of medulloblastoma to vincristine sulfate: a case report. Pediatrics, 39:761, 1967.

Lassman, L. P., Pearce, G. W., and Gang, J. Effect of vincristine sulfate on the intracranial gliomata of childhood. Brit. J. Surg., 53:9, 1966.

Low, N. L., Correll, J. W., and Hammill, J. F. Tumors of the cerebral hemispheres in children. Arch. Neurol., 13:547, 1965.

Matson, D. D. Craniopharyngioma. Clin. Neurosurg., 10:116, 1964.

—— Neurosurgery of Infancy and Childhood, 2nd ed. Springfield, Ill., Charles C Thomas, Publ., 1969.

McFarland, D., Horwitz, H., and Saenger, E., Medulloblastoma—a review of prognosis and survival. Brit. J. Radiol., 42:198, 1969.

Mealey, J., Jr., and Mishkin, F. S. Brain Tumor Scanning in Children. In Bakay, L., and Klein, D. M., eds., Brain Tumor Scanning with Radioisotopes. Springfield, Ill., Charles C Thomas, Publ., 1969.

Millichap, J. G., Bickford, R. G., Miller, R. H., and Backus, R. E. The EEG in children with intracranial tumors and seizures. Neurology, 12:329, 1962.

Newton, W. A., Jr., Sayers, M. P., and Samuels, L. D. Intrathecal methotrexate therapy for brain tumors in children. Cancer Chemother. Rep., 52:257, 1968.

Odom, G. L., Davis, C. H., and Woodhall, B. Brain tumors in children: clinical analysis of 164 cases. Pediatrics, 18:856, 1956.

Panitch, H. S., and Berg, B. O. Brain stem tumors of childhood and adolescence. Amer. J. Dis. Child., 119:465, 1970.

Peirce, C. B. The efficacy of radiation therapy in the tretament of tumors of the brain and brain stem. Clin. Neurosurg., 10:195, 1964.

Planiol, T. Gamma-encephalography after ten years of utilization in neurosurgery. Progr. Neurol. Surg., 1:93, 1966.

Sassin, J. F., and Chutorian, A. M. Intracranial chordoma in children. Arch. Neurol., 17:89, 1967.

Tamaka, K., Ito, K., and Wagai, I. The localization of brain tumors by ultrasonic techniques (a clinical review of 111 cases). J. Neurosurg., 23:135, 1965.

White, P. T., and Ross, A. T. Inanition syndrome in infants with anterior hypothalamic neoplasms. Neurology, 13:974, 1963.

Zulch, K. J. Brain Tumors, Their Biology and Pathology. New York, Springer Publishing Co., Inc., 1957.

SPINAL CORD TUMORS

Coxe, W. S. Tumors of the spinal canal in children. Amer. Surg., 27:62, 1961.

Greenwood, J., Jr. Intramedullary tumors of the spinal cord; follow-up study after total surgical removal. J. Neurosurg., 20:665, 1963.

Haft, H., Ransohoff, J., and Carter, S. Spinal cord tumors in children. Pediatrics, 23:1152, 1959.

Hamby, W. B. Tumors in the spinal cord in childhood. J. Neuropath. Exp. Neurol., 3:397, 1944.

Matson, D. D., and Tachdjian, M. O. Intraspinal tumors in infants and children. Review of 115 cases. Postgrad. Med., 279, 1963.

Rand, R. W., and Rand, C. W. Intraspinal Tumors of Childhood. Springfield, Ill., Charles C Thomas, Publ., 1960.

Slooff, J. L., Kernahan, J. W., and MacCarty, C. S. Primary Intramedullary Tumors of the Spinal Cord and Filum Terminale. Philadelphia, W. B. Saunders Co., 1964.

Solomon, G. E., and Chutorian, A. M. Opsoclonus and occult neuroblastoma. New Eng. J. Med., 279:475, 1968.

Wood, E. H., Berne, A. S., and Taveras, J. M. The value of radiation therapy in the management of intrinsic tumors of the spinal cord. Radiology, 63:11, 1954.

Wyburn-Mason, R. The Vascular Abnormalities and Tumors of the Spinal Cord and Its Membranes. London, Henry Kimpton, 1944.

15.6
PSEUDOTUMOR CEREBRI

MELVIN GREER

Pseudotumor cerebri refers to the neurologic syndrome characterized by increased intracranial pressure unassociated with focal signs of neural impairment, convulsions, alteration in mentation, or cerebrospinal fluid (CSF) changes. The signs and symptoms may otherwise be identical with those of any intracranial mass or hydrocephalus. The course is benign and the prognosis is usually good. Impairment of visual acuity as a consequence of persistent intracranial hypertension is the major problem.

ETIOLOGY. Pseudotumor cerebri is a syndrome of multiple causes in which the pathogenesis of the intracranial hypertension is often not apparent. Brain edema cannot be proved as the causative mechanism, and the absence of convulsions in addition to the presence of a normal mental state argue against this impression. Radioactive iodinated serum albumin studies after intrathecal injections suggest that a defect in CSF absorption is the underlying factor. In any single patient, it is essential to consider first the common causes of increased pressure: neoplasm, infection, congenital malformation, hematoma, and degenerative and toxic states. On the other hand, the history may suggest the presence of a benign cause.

A common cause of pseudotumor cerebri in children is obstruction of the intracranial venous drainage, secondary often to chronic mastoiditis and occlusion of the major draining lateral sinus (otitic hydrocephalus). Less common causes of intracranial hypertension secondary to blockage of venous drainage include obstruction of the sagittal sinus following traumatic skull fracture, sinus invasion by metastatic neuroblastoma, and vena cava obstruction secondary to surgery or to an intrathoracic mass. Under these conditions CSF absorption is impaired, the intracranial venous system is dilated, and increased pressure is the result.

Hormonal aberrations have been implicated in children with pseudotumor cerebri following corticosteroid therapy, in girls entering menarche, and in obese adolescent females. Hypoparathyroidism and hypophosphatasia also have been considered hormonal causes of the syndrome; however, adequate documentation of intracranial hypertension in the latter disorder is unavailable.

Pseudotumor cerebri also has been recognized in the adolescent female during severe iron-deficiency anemia of menstruation and following chronic vitamin A intoxication. In infancy, the syndrome has been described following the acute ingestion of massive quantities of vitamin A as well as after pro-

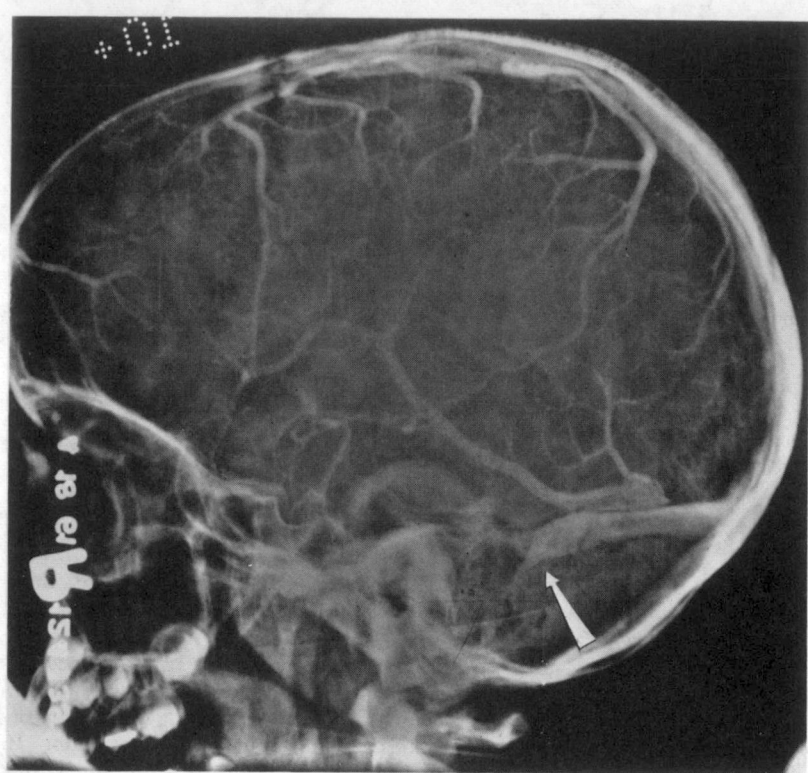

Fig. 53. Lateral sinus obstruction defined by venous phase of carotid arteriography in child with mastoiditis and pseudotumor cerebri. Arrow points to area of obstruction. (From Greer. *Neurology*, 12:472, 1962.)

longed vitamin A deficiency. However, signs such as fever, dehydration, diarrhea, irritability, and lethargy would indicate a toxic encephalopathy rather than a benign state as a result of deficiency or excess of vitamin A in infancy.

Nevertheless, it must be conceded that in some patients with intracranial hypertension, disturbance of mentation or seizures represent one end of the encephalopathy spectrum caused by an infectious, toxic, or metabolic process and, at the other end of the spectrum, the same underlying cause may be manifested by fewer overt signs of neural dysfunction and be considered a benign process.

A bulging fontanel accompanying fever in infancy has been termed meningism and is not unusual. Presumably it is related to an osmotic gradient between serum and CSF during fever which causes increased CSF volume. This may explain the intracranial hypertension described in roseola infantum. Afebrile infants who develop a bulging fontanel after being on tetracycline therapy for a few days and patients exhibiting intracranial hypertension after nalidixic acid therapy are two examples of iatrogenic causes of pseudotumor cerebri.

Other unexplained causes of pseudotumor cerebri in children include Sydenham's chorea, Aldrich's syndrome, and closed head trauma. Finally, there remain children with intracranial hypertension in whom no "etiology" can be found. This accounts for about one-third of all adequately studied children with pseudotumor cerebri.

CLINICAL MANIFESTATIONS. The presenting complaints include headache, nausea, vomiting, dizziness, blurred vision, and diplopia. The symptoms are intermittent and commonly exist for weeks. The examiner is struck by the child's well-being upon admission despite the florid papilledema and abducens nerve paresis which reflect the generalized increased pressure. There are no consistent signs of neurologic dysfunction, although mild unsteadiness of gait has often been described.

LABORATORY FINDINGS. Suture diastasis or erosion of the dorsum sella on skull roentgenography confirms the presence of intracranial hypertension. The electroencephalogram, echoencephalogram, and brain scan are normal, opposing the diagnosis of an encephalopathy or lateralized mass. Historical evidence suggesting mastoiditis or other extracranial diseases known to be related to intracranial hypertension calls for specific laboratory investigations such as mastoid x-rays, serum calcium, phosphorus, alkaline phosphatase, and vitamin A levels.

DIAGNOSIS. Carotid angiography (venous phase) may demonstrate intracranial venous sinus obstruction and, at the same time, exclude ventricular dilation (Fig. 53). If arteriography does not define sinus obstruction, a mass lesion, or ventricular dilation, pneumoencephalography may be performed. The air-filled

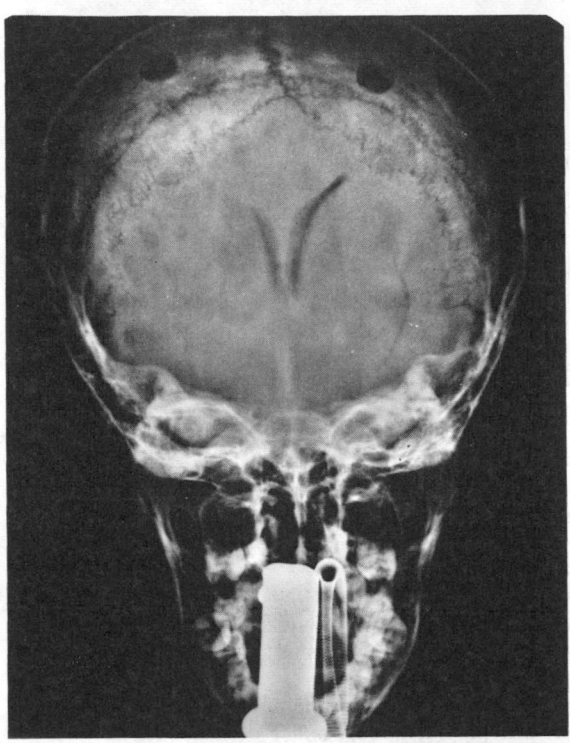

Fig. 54. Narrow lateral ventricles seen on ventriculogram (note burr holes) in child with pseudotumor cerebri in association with cessation of corticosteroid therapy for nephrosis.

ventricles commonly appear narrow (Fig. 54), and the CSF protein, sugar, and cell count are normal. Ventriculography has been commonly employed by the neurosurgeon as a diagnostic study of choice. In the presence of a mass lesion, of course, there exists a risk of cerebellar herniation and brainstem compression following pneumoencephalography; however, the more benign vascular study followed by air encephalography via the lumbar route lessens the trauma and risk attending ventricular puncture under general anesthesia in the child.

TREATMENT. Therapy is specific in the child whose intracranial hypertension is caused by lateral sinus obstruction (mastoidectomy, antibiotics), hypoparathyroidism (calcium, vitamin D), anemia of menstruation (iron, transfusion), drug intoxication (drug withdrawal), or possible adrenocortical insufficiency following cessation of corticosteroid therapy (reinstitution of corticosteroids).

In those children in whom no specific therapy for the increased pressure is available, the treatment is supportive. It is assumed that the illness in these instances is self-limiting. Indeed, in about one-half of the children in this group, the intracranial hypertension subsides spontaneously after air encephalography. The risk, however, of blindness because of persistent intracranial hypertension necessitates some treatment to reduce the pressure in those patients in

whom spontaneous recovery is not immediate. This can be accomplished by serial lumbar punctures. Corticosteroids and carbonic anhydrase inhibitors have also been employed to lower the increased intracranial pressure; however, the response to these drugs has been neither reliable nor proved.

In a small percentage of children, neither repeated spinal taps nor corticosteroids are effective in maintaining a normal intracranial pressure. It is always advisable to repeat neuroradiologic studies if the symptoms and signs persist for more than three months. If intracranial pressure is still elevated, surgical treatment may be warranted. Ventricular or spinal shunting is much preferred to the crude subtemporal decompression procedure, since the latter entails a postoperative risk of temporal lobe trauma and seizures.

REFERENCES

Bass, M. H. The relation of vitamin A intake to CSF pressure. Hospital, 24:713, 1957.

Beller, A. J. Benign post-traumatic intracranial hypertension. J. Neurol. Neurosurg. Psychiat., 27:149, 1964.

Chun, R. W. M., Smith, J., and Forster, F. M. Papilledema in Sydenham's chorea. Amer. J. Dis. Child., 101:641, 1961.

Collins-Williams, C. Idiopathic hypoparathyroidism with papilledema in a boy six years of age. Pediatrics, 5: 998, 1950.

Feldman, M. H., and Schlezinger, N. S. Benign intracranial hypertension associated with hypervitaminosis A. Arch. Neurol., 22:1, 1970.

Fields, J. P. Bulging fontanel: a complication of tetracycline therapy in infants. J. Pediat., 58:74, 1961.

Fraser, D., Yendt, E. R., and Christie, F. H. E. Metabolic abnormalities in hypophosphatasia. Lancet, 1: 286, 1955.

Greer, M. Benign intracranial hypertension. I. Mastoiditis and lateral sinus obstruction. Neurology, 12:472, 1962.

——— Benign intracranial hypertension. II. Following corticosteroid therapy. Neurology, 13:439, 1963.

——— Benign intracranial hypertension. IV. Menarche. Neurology, 14:569, 1964.

——— Benign intracranial hypertension. VI. Obesity. Neurology, 15:382, 1965.

——— Benign intracranial hypertension (pseudotumor cerebri). Pediat. Clin. N. Amer., 14:819, 1967.

——— Management of benign intracranial hypertension (pseudotumor cerebri). Clin. Neurosurg., 15:161, 1968.

——— Berk, M. S., and Williams, C. M. Dural metastasis, the cause of increased intracranial pressure in neuroblastoma. Amer. Pediat. Soc., 52, 1963 (Abstr.).

Hooper, R. Hydrocephalus and obstruction of the superior vena cava in infancy. Pediatrics, 28:792, 1961.

Marie, J., and See, G. Acute hypervitaminosis A of the infant. Amer. J. Dis. Child., 87:731, 1954.

Merritt, H. H., and Fremont-Smith, F. The Cerebrospinal Fluid. Philadelphia, W. B. Saunders Co., 1937.

Oliver, T. K., Jr. Chronic vitamin A intoxication: report of a case in an older child and review of the literature. Amer. J. Dis. Child., 95:57, 1958.

Oski, F. A. Roseola infantum. Amer. J. Dis. Child., 101:376, 1961.

Martin, J. P. Signs of obstruction of the superior longitudinal sinus following closed head injuries (traumatic hydrocephalus). Brit. Med. J., 2:467, 1955.

Rose, A., and Matson, D. D. Benign intracranial hypertension in children. Pediatrics, 39:227, 1967.

Schwaber, J. R., and Blumbert, A. G. Papilledema associated with blood loss anemia. Ann. Intern. Med., 55:1004, 1961.

15.7
CEREBROVASCULAR DISEASES

ARNOLD P. GOLD, JAMES F. HAMMILL, and SIDNEY CARTER

Cerebrovascular diseases include all morbid processes, primary or secondary, in which the blood vessels of the brain are involved. Although no available classification of the various conditions is fully satisfactory, Table 21 has been found clinically useful.

Cerebrovascular accidents are most frequent in the elderly. Although they are generally considered a clinical rarity in childhood, they are actually not infrequent. Cerebrovascular diseases account for about 5 percent of admissions to a pediatric neurology service and 10 percent of pediatric pathology material. Children with congenital heart disease not uncommonly have cerebrovascular complications. Ten percent of patients with tetralogy of Fallot have cerebrovascular accidents, and 25 percent of all autopsied cardiac cases have evidence of cerebrovascular occlusion. These figures of incidence would be more impressive if they included children with blood dyscrasias. Spontaneous cerebral hemorrhage secondary to a hematologic disorder is not uncommon and is found in 50 percent of leukemic patients at necropsy. In the pediatric age group, arteriovenous malformations are 10 times as common as intracranial aneurysms and are the most common cause of primary subarachnoid hemorrhage.

Occlusive Vascular Disease

Arterial or venous occlusion deprives the brain of oxygen with resultant necrosis (encephalomalacia) of the surrounding tissue. If death does not result from this lesion, a process of repair occurs over the subsequent months with the formation of an astrocytic or fibroblastic scar. The ischemic area, or infarct, is the nonspecific end result of any type of occlusion; however, the changes in the blood vessels or surrounding brain may be highly specific. Arteriosclerosis in progeria, vascular changes in granulomatous arteritis (Takayasu's disease), and the lesions produced by blood dyscrasias, all have characteristic anatomic changes.

Dural Sinus and Cerebral Venous Thrombosis

Obstruction of venous drainage may lead to cerebral edema and hemorrhagic infarction of the brain. In some cases, thrombosis of venous sinuses may occur without causing any gross cerebral lesion because anastomoses of the cerebral venous system are often effective in bypassing the obstruction, and the integrity of the venous circulation is maintained.

Venous occlusion occurs most commonly following pyogenic infections of the face, mouth, mastoids, or leptomeninges. Cerebral venous thromboses may also develop in association with dehydration, debilitating and cachectic states, traumas, sickle-cell disease, or polycythemia. Less frequently venous occlusion is observed in Sturge-Weber-Dimitri syndrome, lead encephalopathy, metastatic neoplasia, or thrombotic thrombocytopenia.

CLINICAL MANIFESTATIONS. The clinical picture of venous thromboses is related to extent of involvement, rapidity of occlusion, and the nature of the primary process.

Common manifestations include increased intracranial pressure, focal motor deficits, seizures, altered states of consciousness, and signs of circulatory stasis. Occlusion of a major lateral sinus may result in signs and symptoms of increased intracranial pressure without focal neurologic deficit. Those who develop focal signs may slowly recover or be left with a residual hemiparesis, seizures, or mental retardation. Superior sagittal sinus thrombosis is suggested by alternating hemiplegias and multifocal seizures. Signs of circulatory stasis may be pathognomonic for involvement of a specific vessel. Cavernous sinus thrombosis is characterized by exophthalmos of the homolateral eye, palpebral and conjunctival edema, and involvement of the third, fourth, fifth (first two branches), and sixth cranial nerves. Lateral sinus thrombosis may be accompanied by painful swelling in the mastoid region. Occlusion of the superior sagittal sinus results in venous distension over the scalp and eyelids.

LABORATORY FINDINGS. There is often a moderate polymorphonuclear leucocytosis and an elevated erythrocyte sedimentation rate. Changes in the cerebrospinal fluid vary according to the pathologic process. Unless there is an associated infection, the fluid, which may be under increased pressure, is usually clear and colorless with little or no pleocytosis. The Tobey-Ayer test, while not always reliable, may be of some value in the diagnosis of lateral sinus thrombosis. With this test, compression of the jugular vein on the affected side produces no rise in cerebrospinal fluid pressure, while compression of the normal side produces a prompt rise in pressure. The electroencephalogram may be normal, diffusely slow in the presence of increased intracranial pressure, or show marked abnormalities of a focal nature. Skull x-rays

TABLE 21. *Classification of Cerebrovascular Disease*

Occlusive Vascular Disease
    Dural sinus and cerebral venous thrombosis, associated with:
        Meningitis
        Infections of face, ears, or paranasal sinuses
        Dehydration
        Debilitating states (marantic)
        Metastatic neoplasms, e.g., neuroblastoma
        Congenital heart disease
        Lead encephalopathy
        Sturge-Weber-Dimitri syndrome (trigeminal encephaloangiomatosis)

    Arterial thrombosis
        Idiopathic or spontaneous, associated with:
            Dissecting cerebral aneurysm
            Arteriosclerosis (progeria)
            Cyanotic congenital heart disease
            Cerebral arteritis
                Acute infectious diseases
                Granulomatous (Takayasu's disease)
                Syphilis
            Collagen diseases
                Polyarteritis nodosa
                Lupus erythematosus
            Blood dyscrasias: sickle-cell disease, polycythemia, thrombotic thrombocytopenia
            Trauma to the carotid or cerebral arteries
            Complications of arteriography
            Extraarterial diseases
                Retropharyngeal abscess
                Mucomycosis
                Tumors of the base of the skull
                Craniometaphyseal dysplasia

    Cerebral embolism, associated with:
        Atrial fibrillation or other arrhythmias
            Rheumatic heart disease
            Congenital heart disease, right to left shunt
            Coronary thrombosis
        Acute or subacute bacterial endocarditis
        Infarcted necrotic placental tissue
        Air: complications of cardiac, neck, or thoracic surgery
        Septic: pneumonia or lung abscess
        Fat: complications of fractures of long bones
        Tumor

Intracranial Hemorrhage (includes intracerebral and subarachnoid)
    Arteriovenus malformation or angioma
    Intracranial aneurysm
    Trauma
        Cavernous sinus fistula
        Subdural hemorrhage
        Epidural hemorrhage
    Blood dyscrasias
        Leukemia
        Thrombocytopenic purpura
        Aplastic anemia
        Hemophilia
        Anaphylactoid purpura
    Hypertension
    Liver disease
    Complications of anticoagulant therapy
    Intracranial neoplasms
    Deficiency syndromes
        Vitamin B_1 deficiency (Wemicke encephalopathy)
        Vitamin C deficiency (scurvy)
        Vitamin K deficiency (hemorrhagic disease of the newborn)
    Toxic or infectious encephalopathy

may be normal or show signs of increased intracranial pressure and mastoid disease. The site and extent of the thrombosis can often be confirmed by evaluating the venous phase of a carotid arteriogram.

Arterial Thrombosis

Cerebral arterial thromboses produce a variable clinical picture depending upon the rapidity of occlusion, the collateral circulation, and the maintenance of systemic blood pressure. The arterial occlusion usually occurs in a previously healthy child, although in some instances it is a complication of certain systemic diseases (Table 21).

CLINICAL MANIFESTATIONS. Depending upon the cause, the child demonstrates clinical phenomena of the underlying disorder as well as the neurologic changes secondary to the vessel involved.

Acute infantile hemiplegia characteristically appears in the first year or two of life. Unexplained or idiopathic hemiplegia is uncommon after the preschool period. The previously well youngster may suddenly develop fever, have a series of convulsions, and be left with a hemiplegia which may partially clear. In addition to the hemiplegia, there may be a cortical hemisensory loss, hemianopia, and aphasia. Recurrent focal motor seizures, often resistant to anticonvulsants, may complicate the subsequent course.

If the child is seen years after the onset, the involved extremities may be short, atrophic, and spastic. Arterial thrombosis may result in either cerebral hemiatrophy with a small head circumference or cerebral porencephaly with resultant macrocephaly. Seizures at the onset of the hemiparesis are more common in children under the age of 2 years and herald a poor prognosis for future seizures, hemiplegia, intellect, and behavior.

LABORATORY FINDINGS. Cerebrospinal fluid analysis during the acute episode is usually normal, but a slight leucocytic pleocytosis may be found a few weeks later. Electroencephalograms, occasionally normal, are characterized by a slow wave focus over the involved area. Radiologic studies are frequently of diagnostic importance. Early plain skull x-rays are normal. After a period of time, the x-rays may show the effect of cerebral hemiatrophy or porencephaly. The characteristic features of atrophy include thickening of the cranial vault, overdevelopment of the frontal and ethmoid sinuses, and elevation of the petrous pyramid of the temporal bone on the involved side. Porencephaly is suggested by the bulging and thinning of the cranial vault on the affected side and cephalofacial disproportion. Arteriography may demonstrate the arterial occlusion, and air contrast studies may show cerebral atrophy or a porencephalic cavity or fistula.

Cerebral Embolism

In embolism, a cerebral artery is occluded by a fragment of an organized thrombus, by bacteria, air, fat, or tumor. The middle cerebral artery or one of its branches is the vessel most frequently occluded. Cerebral embolic phenomena in childhood are usually of cardiac origin. Cyanotic congenital heart and rheumatic valvar disease may be responsible for this complication. Atrial fibrillation and other arrhythmias favor the formation of mural thrombi, fragments of which may then become detached. Emboli may result from the vegetations of bacterial endocarditis or from neck and thoracic surgery. In the newborn period, cerebral emboli may originate from liberated infarcted placental tissue. Arterial air embolism has been encountered with greater frequency since the advent of newer techniques in thoracic surgery. Fat embolism is usually associated with fractures of long bones.

CLINICAL MANIFESTATIONS. Cerebral embolism is characterized by acute onset without significant prodromata. Occasionally, premonitory symptoms of headache, vomiting, and lassitude occur. The clinical picture may be complete within seconds to minutes and may appear at any time of the day, unrelated to physical activity. Convulsions, transient loss of consciousness, and headache may be initially observed. Focal neurologic findings depend upon the cerebral artery occluded. Transient blindness is the most characteristic manifestation of air embolism.

Fat embolism has a characteristic clinical picture. Twelve to 48 hours after a long bone fracture, fever and pulmonary signs and symptoms appear with respiratory distress and blood-tinged sputum. This is then followed in a few hours by neurologic manifestations, petechial hemorrhages in the skin, fat in the retinal vessels, and free fat droplets in the urine.

LABORATORY FINDINGS. A moderate polymorphonuclear leucocytosis is frequently observed. Cerebrospinal fluid analysis and skull x-rays are usually normal. Electroencephalograms most commonly show a slow wave focus over the involved areas which tends to be persistent.

Intracranial Hemorrhage

Intracranial hemorrhage is the result of a defect in the integrity of cerebral blood vessels with extravasation of blood into one or more of the following: brain, ventricles, and subarachnoid, epidural, and subdural spaces. Trauma is the most frequent cause of hemorrhage, but not infrequently it may result from rupture of a vascular malformation or aneurysm or may be associated with infectious, toxic, metabolic, or neoplastic conditions (Table 21).

Despite the varied causes, clinical manifestations of hemorrhage are similar, and etiologic delineation is further complicated by the nonspecific finding of blood in the cerebrospinal fluid. Proper management is largely dependent upon delineation of the specific cause, which is possible only with a complete clinical history and adequate laboratory facilities.

Subarachnoid hemorrhage is characterized by signs and symptoms of increased intracranial pressure and meningeal irritation. The onset is usually dramatic with severe headache, vomiting, loss of consciousness, and convulsions. Fever, often a misleading feature, may be prominent, and systemic hypertension is not uncommon. Evidence of meningeal irritation is an early clinical manifestation with nuchal rigidity and Brudzinski and Kernig signs. The child with intracerebral bleeding may have evidence of blood in the subarachnoid space, in which case there may be the symptoms and signs previously mentioned as well as focal neurologic deficit. Secondary hydrocephalus may be a complication in those children who survive subarachnoid bleeding due to partial obliteration of the subarachnoid space.

The neonate with intracranial bleeding shows a more nonspecific picture with apathy or restlessness, cyanosis or pallor, bulging of the fontanels, respiratory distress, convulsions, a high-pitched cry, vomiting, poor suck, and an exaggerated or absent Moro reflex.

Children with intracranial hemorrhage may show a polymorphonuclear leucocytosis greater than 20,000 per mm^3, a normal or moderately elevated erythrocyte sedimentation rate, and a transient hyperglycemia, albuminuria, and glycosuria. The electroencephalographic changes with subarachnoid hemorrhage are similar to those seen in closed head injury; the tracing is diffusely abnormal with generalized slow activity which disappears as the clinical state of the child improves. Blood in the cerebrospinal fluid is the most conclusive evidence of intracranial bleeding. This must be clearly differentiated from the hemorrhage due to a traumatic lumbar puncture. Failure of the fluid to clear in successive test tubes or a xanthochromic supernatant in a hemorrhage older than two hours is diagnostic of bleeding antedating the lumbar puncture. The fluid is usually under increased pressure, the protein content is elevated, and white cells are in proportion to red cells.

Vascular Malformations

Vascular anomalies are the most common cause of *primary* subarachnoid hemorrhage in children and are at least 10 times as common as intracranial aneurysms.

The vascular malformations are usually classified as traumatic, infectious, or congenital. Traumatic or infectious causes are rarely seen because anatomically the cerebral vessels are unique and the principal cerebral arteries and veins are not in juxtaposition. The sole exception is the internal carotid artery in the cavernous sinus.

Arteriovenous malformations occur most frequently in two areas: deep midline (the area drained by the great vein of Galen) and hemispheric (the area supplied by major branches of the internal carotid artery).

DEEP MIDLINE ARTERIOVENOUS MALFORMATION. The malformation involving the Galenic system is a direct anastomosis between major cerebral arteries, most commonly the posterior cerebral or the superior cerebellar artery and the great vein. There is marked enlargement of the vein, forming a midline aneurysm which not infrequently compresses and displaces the aqueduct, the third ventricle, and the quadrigeminal plate.

The clinical manifestations can be divided into three groups depending upon the size of the shunt and the corresponding age at which symptoms first appear.

1. The symptomatic newborn infant has a shunt of arterial blood into the venous circulation of such magnitude that it results in peripheral congestion and congestive heart failure.

2. In infancy there is less blood shunted, with a paucity of clinical cardiac manifestations; however, cardiomegaly may be present. In this group, hydrocephalus is the most prominent clinical feature as the markedly distended vein of Galen displaces and compresses the aqueduct of Sylvius. An important sign in this age group is an intracranial bruit.

3. The older child has a still smaller shunt, and dilation of the vein of Galen is only moderate. There is neither cardiovascular dysfunction nor hydrocephalus, but headaches and episodes of subarachnoid hemorrhage are common. Because of the small size of the shunt, an intracranial bruit is rarely present in this age group.

Laboratory findings are variable and depend upon the magnitude of the arteriovenous shunt. The electrocardiogram, especially in the younger child, may show an intermediate axis or left axis deviation, and in this age group cardiomegaly may be present on chest x-ray. The cerebrospinal fluid is usually under increased pressure and not infrequently shows evidence of recent or old hemorrhage. Increased oxygen tension in jugular venous blood is an important simple diagnostic test.

Radiographic findings are frequently of diagnostic importance. Plain skull films in the younger child may show evidence of increased intracranial pressure. Air contrast studies suggest a vein of Galen malformation by demonstrating a posterior midline mass displacing the aqueduct downward. Cerebral angiography is the definitive diagnostic tool and demonstrates a midline collection of contrast material outlining the vein of Galen (Fig. 55).

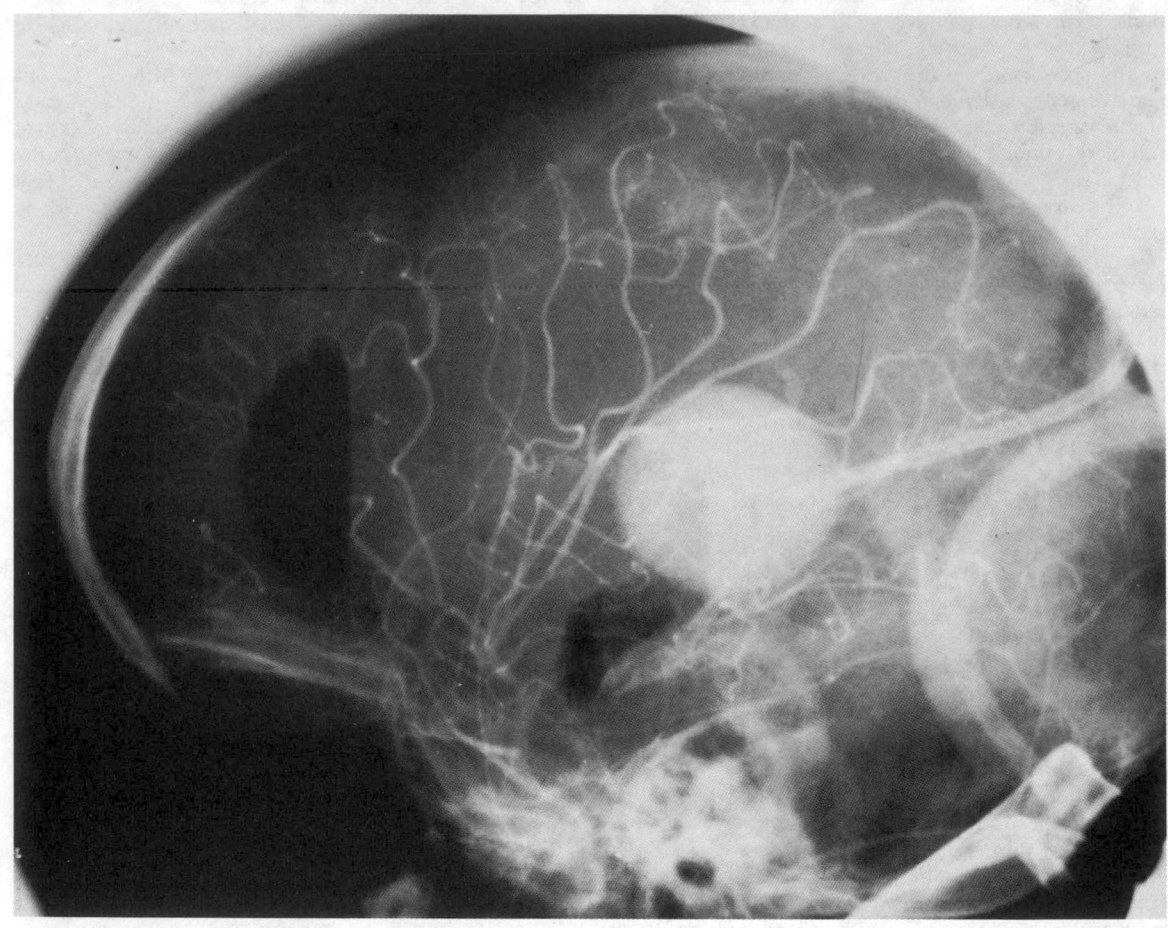

Fig. 55. Lateral view of carotid arteriogram demonstrates a markedly dilated vein of Galen. (Note air in dilated lateral ventricle from previous pneumoencephalogram.)

HEMISPHERIC MALFORMATION. This malformation involving branches of the internal carotid artery is most frequently found over the convexity of the brain in the territory of the middle cerebral artery. The lesion consists of an enlarged feeding artery and a mass of dilated, tortuous veins. The onset of clinical manifestations is most commonly in late childhood or in adolescence. The child may complain of periodic migrainoid headaches for many years, but diagnosis is frequently not made until the acute onset of subarachnoid hemorrhage. The child with a hemispheric malformation may complain of and localize a pulsatile sound in the head, and a pathologic bruit may be heard on auscultation. The cardinal clinical manifestations are related to the site of the malformation. Involvement of branches of the middle cerebral artery is characterized by clinical manifestations referable to the motor cortex with focal, motor or sensory, and generalized seizures followed by transient postictal paralysis which gradually becomes a permanent lateralizing sign. Parietal lobe involvement is suggested by contralateral sensory seizures and hemisensory deficit involving position, stereognosis, discrimination, and localization of tactile stimuli and body image. Posterior fossa malformations produce signs of cerebellar dysfunction and evidence of increased intracranial pressure.

Routine laboratory studies are often unrewarding, as skull x-rays, electroencephalogram, and cerebrospinal fluid analysis are often normal. Special studies are usually required. Visual fields may demonstrate a homonymous hemianopia. Radioactive isotope studies may show an abnormal uptake. The diagnosis can be confirmed only by cerebral angiography.

Traumatic Arteriovenous Fistula

This fistula can occur only in the region of the cavernous sinus where artery and vein are in juxtaposition. Following trauma there develops a highly characteristic clinical picture with pulsating exophthalmos, intracranial bruit, and involvement of the first two branches of the trigeminal nerve (facial sensory loss and diminished corneal reflex) and the oculomotor, trochlear, and abducens nerves (dilated and fixed pupil, diplopia, and extraocular muscle palsies).

Carotid angiogram is diagnostic, with demonstration of the cavernous sinus during the arterial phase.

Intracranial Aneurysm

Ruptured saccular aneurysms are a rare cause of subarachnoid hemorrhage in children. Many cases go unrecognized because the aneurysm commonly involves the bifurcation of the smaller peripherally placed arteries.

Clinical manifestations are due to direct pressure of the aneurysm on surrounding structures or to hemorrhage from rupture. The onset is often dramatic without warning, and death may result from massive bleeding. Hemorrhage into the subarachnoid space results in signs and symptoms of meningeal irritation and increased intracranial pressure. Intracortical hemorrhage may give rise to focal neurologic signs dependent on the areas involved. Unless the aneurysm is occluded by a thrombus, its presence can often be demonstrated by cerebral angiography. Early angiography is indicated except in the presence of coma with fluctuating vital signs.

Diagnosis of Cerebrovascular Diseases

Differential diagnosis must distinguish among the various types of cerebrovascular conditions and other conditions involving the central nervous system, such as brain tumors, abscess, trauma, epilepsy, and meningitis.

Treatment of Cerebrovascular Diseases

A rational therapeutic program must consist of a complete understanding of the pathologic process and its resultant alteration of function. For a given disease there are both nonspecific and specific therapeutic measures.

Nonspecific therapy consists of fluids to prevent dehydration and maintain circulation, antibiotics to combat infection, anticonvulsants to control seizures, and anticoagulants when indicated to prevent extension of the thrombus. Increased intracranial pressure secondary to cerebral edema may be managed by the introduction of light hypothermia and the use of corticosteroids and/or urea.

Venous and dural sinus thromboses are managed by strict control of fluids and electrolytes and,

when indicated, antibiotics and anticonvulsants. Mastoidectomy with decompression of the lateral sinus is indicated when this dural sinus is involved. Repeated and often daily lumbar punctures may be necessary to reduce the pressure, but if ineffective a lumboperitoneal shunt may be required to preserve vision.

Arterial thromboses are treated symptomatically. Anticoagulation is contraindicated. The only indication for vascular surgery is thrombosis of the extracranial portion of the internal carotid artery.

The management of arterial emboli is mainly symptomatic, including skillful nursing care. Anticoagulation may be used to prevent the formation of future emboli.

The treatment of arteriovenous malformations is both medical and surgical. Medical therapy includes treatment of cardiac decompensation, phlebotomy to control blood volume, and the careful management of fluids and electrolytes. Surgery is hazardous but offers the only possibility for a cure. It may be indicated if the vascular lesion is accessible and neither involves the dominant hemisphere nor supplies vital structures.

References

GENERAL

A classification and outline of cerebrovascular diseases. Neurology, 8:395, 1958.

Poser, C. M., and Taveras, J. M. Clinical aspects of cerebral angiography in children. Pediatrics, 16:73, 1955.

CEREBRAL VENOUS AND DURAL SINUS THROMBOSIS

Byers, R. K., and Hass, G. M. Thrombosis of the dural venous sinuses in infancy and in childhood. Amer. J. Dis. Child., 45:1161, 1933.

Greer, M., and Schotland, D. Abnormal hemoglobin as a cause of neurologic disease. Neurology, 12:114, 1962.

——— and Berk, M. S. Lateral sinus obstruction and mastoiditis. Pediatrics, 31:840, 1963.

Symonds, C. P. Otitic hydrocephalus. Neurology, 6:681, 1956.

CEREBRAL ARTERIAL THROMBOSIS

Banker, B. Q. Cerebral vascular disease in infancy and childhood: 1. Occlusive vascular diseases. J. Neuropath. Exp. Neurol., 20:127, 1961.

Bax, M., and Mitchell, R., eds. Acute Hemiplegia in Childhood. London, William Heineman, Ltd. (Little Club Clinics in Developmental Medicine, No. 6), 1962.

Bickerstaff, E. R. Aetiology of acute hemiplegia in childhood. Brit. Med. J., 2:82, 1964.

Byers, R. K., and McLean, W. T. Etiology and course of certain hemiplegias with aphasia in childhood. Pediatrics, 29:376, 1962.

Carter, S., and Gold, A. P. Acute hemiplegia in infancy and childhood. Pediat. Clin. N. Amer., 14:851, 1967.

Davie, J. C., and Coxe, W. Occlusive disease of the carotid artery in children. Arch. Neurol., 17:313, 1967.

Dyke, C. G., Davidoff, L. M., and Masson, C. B. Cerebral hemiatrophy with homolateral hypertrophy of the skull and sinuses. Surg. Gynec. Obstet., 57:588, 1933.

Freeman, J. M., and Gold, A. P. Porencephaly simulating subdural hematoma in childhood. Amer. J. Dis. Child., 107:327, 1964.

Gold, A. P., and Yahr, M. D. Childhood lupus erythematosus: a clinical and pathological study of the neurological manifestations. Trans. Amer. Neurol. Ass., 1960, p. 96.

Gross, R. E. Arterial embolism and thrombosis in infancy. Amer. J. Dis. Child., 70:61, 1945.

Hilal, S. K., Solomon, G. E., Gold, A. P., and Carter S. Primary cerebral arterial occlusive disease in children. Part I: Acute acquired hemiplegia. Radiology, 99:71, 1971.

—— Primary cerebral arterial occlusive disease in children. Part II: Neurocutaneous syndromes. Radiology, 99:87, 1971.

Ouvrier, R. A., and Hopkins, I. J. Occlusive disease of the vertebro-basilar arterial system in childhood. Develop. Med. Child. Neurol., 12:186, 1970.

Pitner, S. E. Carotid thrombosis due to intraoral trauma. New Eng. J. Med., 274:764, 1966.

Shillito, J., Jr. Carotid arteritis: a cause of hemiplegia in childhood. J. Neurosurg., 21:540, 1964.

Solomon, G. E., Hilal, S. K., Gold, A. P., and Carter, S. Natural history of acute hemiplegia of childhood. Brain, 93:107, 1970.

Tyler, H. R., and Clark, D. B. Incidence of neurological complications in congenital heart disease. A.M.A. Arch. Neurol. Psychiat., 77:17, 1957.

—— and Clark, D. B. Cerebrovascular accidents in patients with congenital heart disease. A.M.A. Arch. Neurol. Psychiat., 77:483, 1957.

Wisoff, H. S., and Rothballer, A. B. Cerebral arterial thrombosis in children: Review of literature and addition of two cases in apparently healthy children. Arch. Neurol., 4:258, 1961.

Wolman, L. Cerebral dissecting aneurysms. Brain, 82:276, 1959.

CEREBRAL EMBOLISM

Clark, R. M., and Linell, E. A. Case report: Prenatal occlusion of the internal carotid artery. J. Neurol. Neurosurg. Psychiat., 17:295, 1954.

Cohen, A. C. et al. Air embolism. Ann. Intern. Med., 35:779, 1952.

Schneider, R. C. Fat embolism: A problem in the differential diagnosis of craniocerebral trauma. J. Neurosurg., 9:1, 1952.

Wells, C. E. Cerebral embolism: The natural history, prognostic signs, and effects of anticoagulation. A.M.A. Arch. Neurol. Psychiat., 81:667, 1959.

INTRACRANIAL HEMORRHAGE

Chalgreen, W. S. Neurologic complications of the hemorrhagic diseases. Neurology, 3:126, 1953.

Gold, A. P., Ransohoff, J., and Carter, S. Vein of Galen malformation. Acta Neurol. Scand. (Suppl. I), p. 40, 1964.

Groch, S. N., Sayre, G. P., and Heck, F. J. Cerebral hemorrhage in leukemia. A.M.A. Arch. Neurol. Psychiat., 2:439, 1960.

Levine, O. R., Jameson, A. G., Nellhaus, G., and Gold, A. P. Cardiac complication of cerebral arteriovenous fistulas. Pediatrics, 30:563, 1962.

Lewis, I. C., and Philpott, M. G. Neurological complications of Schönlein-Henoch syndrome. Arch. Dis. Child., 31:369, 1956.

Silverstein, A. Intracranial bleeding in hemophilia. A.M.A. Arch. Neurol. Psychiat., 3:141, 1960.

Sullivan, M. P. Intracranial complications in leukemia in children. Pediatrics, 20:757, 1957.

15.8
TRAUMA TO THE NERVOUS SYSTEM

JAMES F. HAMMILL

Trauma results in the death of 15,000 children per year and 100,000 individuals of all ages. The number of deaths in this country due to trauma in the age group from birth to 14 years exceeds the combined fatalities from infectious disease, malignancy, and cardiovascular-renal syndromes.

Forty percent of all traumatic cases in childhood involve head injuries either alone or combined with other injuries. The peak age incidence is in the second year of life, with males outnumbering females 2:1. Peak seasonal incidence is in the spring and summer months during the late afternoon and early evening hours.

In spite of this magnitude of serious injury the mortality rate is in the range of only 0.5 percent, indicating three million childhood injuries per year with over 90 percent not requiring hospitalization.

Head injuries may affect the scalp, skull, or the nervous system; they may occur alone or in combination. Most injuries involving the nervous system represent simple concussion or mild contusion, and there is complete recovery without complications. Some, however, may be more serious or even life-threatening and require careful analysis and management.

Scalp Injuries
Lacerations

Scalp injury is most often due to blunt trauma; however, the resulting wound is usually a smooth linear cut due to the unyielding surface of the bone over which the blow occurs. Wounds of the skin layer are separated only minimally owing to fixation by the underlying fibrous tissue septa. When the galea is involved the wound will gape, particularly if it is in a transverse direction. Bleeding is quite marked because of the rich anastomatic blood supply of the

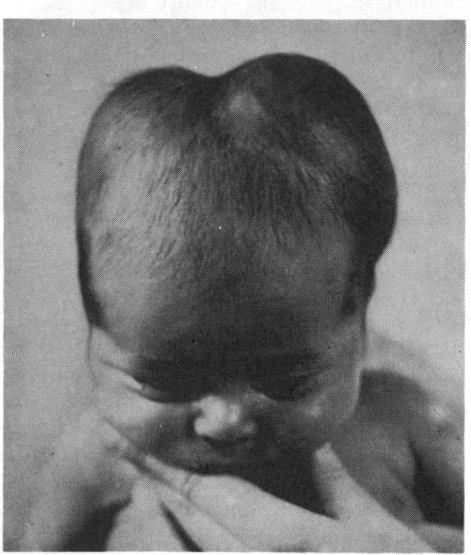

Fig. 56. Cephalohematoma involving both parietal bones in an infant 13 days old.

scalp and the limited contraction-retraction ability of the vessels firmly anchored in the dense connective tissue layer. Consequently, large lacerations heal quite well, and infection rarely occurs unless there is gross contamination or tissue destruction. However, the potential hazards of infection of the skull and intracranial contents are of considerable importance because of the magnitude of the problem when it does occur. Infectious complications are invariably the result of poor initial handling.

If the child's general condition prohibits immediate definitive wound care, and if hemorrhage is not excessive, a sterile pressure dressing may be applied. Where necessary, primary closure may be delayed for 8 to 12 hours without any significant increase in the incidence of infection. In the majority of cases the wound may be treated at once.

Hematoma and Cephalohematoma

Hematomas resulting from bleeding into an area of injury within the dense connective tissue layer of the scalp are common, but because of the density of the tissue they are generally not very large and absorb within two or three days. Galeal laceration permits bleeding from above to permeate the subgaleal loose connective tissue layer and may result in an extensive, rapidly appearing swelling that can assume enormous proportions, as there is no limiting membrane to prevent its spread.

Bleeding beneath the pericranium is most common in, but not restricted to, the incompletely ossified and highly vascular skull characteristic of the first two years of life. These collections are restricted by the pericranial suture line attachment,

occur most often in the parietal area, and are the swellings for which the term cephalohematoma is usually reserved (Fig. 56). Both subgaleal and subpericranial hematomas present findings on palpation that may be confused with an underlying depressed fracture. Subgaleal collections of partially clotted blood may develop a soft center surrounded by an indurated ring which may be mistaken for a rim of bone about an area of skull depression. The pericranial fibrous suture attachment demarcating cephalohematomas is also commonly confused with a depressed skull fracture. Fracture sites, depressed or linear, underlying hematomas require radiographic examination to clarify the diagnosis.

The larger hematomas are absorbed in 2 to 4 weeks. When cephalohematomas persist, pericranial proliferation occurs with the production of bony callus; ultimately a thin layer of bone may be formed in the involved area. Only rarely is there calcification of an entire nonabsorbed hemorrhagic area. Aspiration or open evacuation of hematomas is contraindicated as the partially clotted blood is difficult to aspirate and the risk of infection is great. In the infant, cephalohematomas may be of such size as to play a significant role in the development of anemia, and their breakdown products are commonly responsible for varied degrees of jaundice. A scalp swelling associated with an underlying linear fracture, meningeal tear, and leakage of cerebrospinal fluid into the subgaleal space may be noted. Collections of this type are termed subgaleal or subepicranial hydromas and are not uncommon over linear skull fractures in children. They are usually less extensive and softer than hematomas and have a less well-defined ring of induration. When the fluid is not mixed with blood, transillumination is greater than in the case of hematomas, and the mass may be noted to fluctuate with coughing and straining. These collections subside spontaneously with healing of the underlying dural tear. If they are large or if they persist beyond 4 to 7 days, the swelling may be reduced by lumbar puncture. This procedure may also be used as a differential diagnostic test to determine the type of fluid present. Pressure dressings do not hasten absorption of hematoma or hydroma and may contribute to skin breakdown and infection.

Craniocerebral Trauma

PATHOPHYSIOLOGY. The human head may withstand tremendous force and yet maintain both skull and cerebral integrity. The position of the head at impact, suture patency, and degree of movement at the craniospinal junction are important variables. Blood pressure may increase to 150 percent or more above normal to compensate for increased intracranial pressure in an attempt to maintain cerebral circulation.

Shock rarely occurs on a purely neural basis and is usually due to blood loss from associated extracerebral injuries. It may be noted terminally where it is an ominous prognostic sign correlated with extensive and irreversible cerebral damage. Adequate respiration and oxygenation are essential to blood pressure maintenance. Hypoxia may result in an increased blood pressure due to chemoreceptor effect in the absence of increased intracranial pressure but will soon result in hypotension due to cardiac hypoxia.

Experimental cerebral injury in the acute postconcussive phase shows marked circulatory slowing associated with the onset of cerebral edema. Within minutes brain volume may increase over 5 percent.

The mass movement of the intracranial contents following injury results in varied contusion patterns both at the point of impact and at a distance from it both ipsilaterally and contralaterally. Disruption of the blood-brain barrier results in laceration and subarachnoid and intracerebral bleeding. Marked movement may tear blood vessels between the brain and meninges and result in subdural collections. This vascular damage most commonly involves the cortical bridging veins entering the dural-encased superior longitudinal sinus, but may occur at any point. Disruption of extradural vessels, either venous or arterial, will result in extradural hematoma.

Transient unconsciousness after injury reflects a sudden physiologic block at the brainstem level. The brainstem reticular formation has an alerting function, mediating sensory input to higher centers. Following trauma, this formation may enter an absolutely refractory state, recovery from which directly correlates with return to consciousness. This mechanism is the commonest cause of the transient concussion picture and is due to increased cervicocranial mobility after impact permitting transmission of increased angular acceleration and shear strains to the entire brain but particularly the brainstem. Animals with the head relatively fixed can routinely sustain a head injury force double that usually resulting in concussion.

Skull Fractures

CLINICAL MANIFESTATION.   Skull fractures may involve the vault or base and may be of the simple linear type, diastatic (abnormal suture separation occurring at the time of impact), simple depressed, comminuted, or the ping-pong or pond variety. They may occur as an isolated manifestation of head trauma but more often are associated with underlying cerebral injury. Simple linear fractures and diastatic fractures resulting in suture separation are of little immediate significance other than to indicate the force of the blow and the point of maximal impact. Over 80 percent of all skull fractures are of the simple linear type and the parietal area is involved five times more commonly than other regions of the skull. Diastatic fractures have the same medicolegal significance as a fracture line and most often involve the lamboidal suture. A lamboidal suture separation

wider than 1.5 mm, particularly at several points in its course, is usually considered abnormal, as is a coronal suture spread of greater than 2 mm (Fig. 57).

Children less than one year of age have significantly less calcification of the vault than do older children, and there is greater elasticity of both its inner and outer tables. This explains the fact that fractures occur in the neonatal period, and occasionally later, in which both outer and inner skull tables are displaced inward but without an actual break in either. These have been termed ping-pong or pond fractures.

Fractures of the base of the skull may be indicated by bilateral orbital ecchymoses in anterior fossa lesions (Fig. 58) and by retroauricular ecchymosis (Battle's sign) with tympanic membrane discoloration in involvement of the petrous bone in the middle fossa (Fig. 59). Otorrhea and rhinorrhea imply basilar skull fracture and are potentially of more serious consideration because of the risk of infection. The posttraumatic collection of intracranial air in any of the meningeal spaces (aerocele) or the ventricular system (pneumoencephalocele) implies fractures through the paranasal sinuses.

LABORATORY DATA AND DIAGNOSIS.   Skull x-rays are the essential aid to diagnosis. There is seldom an indication for emergency films, as they rarely add to management of the immediate problem and are best delayed until the child's condition permits optimal radiographic study both of the skull and of all suspected areas of trauma. A skeletal survey to detect areas of multiple osseous injury is essential in infants and very young children; beyond these ages it becomes a matter of clinical judgment. Questionable drainage from the nose may be differentiated by collecting a specimen of the discharge and analyzing for glucose, which is present in negligible amounts in nasal secretions compared to cerebrospinal fluid. This may be done chemically or by the use of a glucose reacting test tape.

TREATMENT.   Simple linear fractures without underlying damage do not require treatment other than analgesics for headache and irritability. It is important to emphasize to the parents that a simple fracture of the skull is of itself little to be concerned about. Its mere demonstration in an otherwise intact child should not cause alarm, limit usual activities, or be considered ominous as regards prognosis. It is good practice to secure repeat skull films 3 months after the injury to demonstrate a uniting fracture line. In the absence of union, further films should be obtained at 2- to 4-month intervals to detect such complications as a leptomeningeal cyst. Fractures in children generally heal in 6 to 12 months.

Pond or ping-pong fractures of infancy usually do not require surgical elevation. In extremely rare instances an underlying defect of cerebral cortex may result in a lack of brain growth and failure of the skull depression to elevate; a 3-month period of ob-

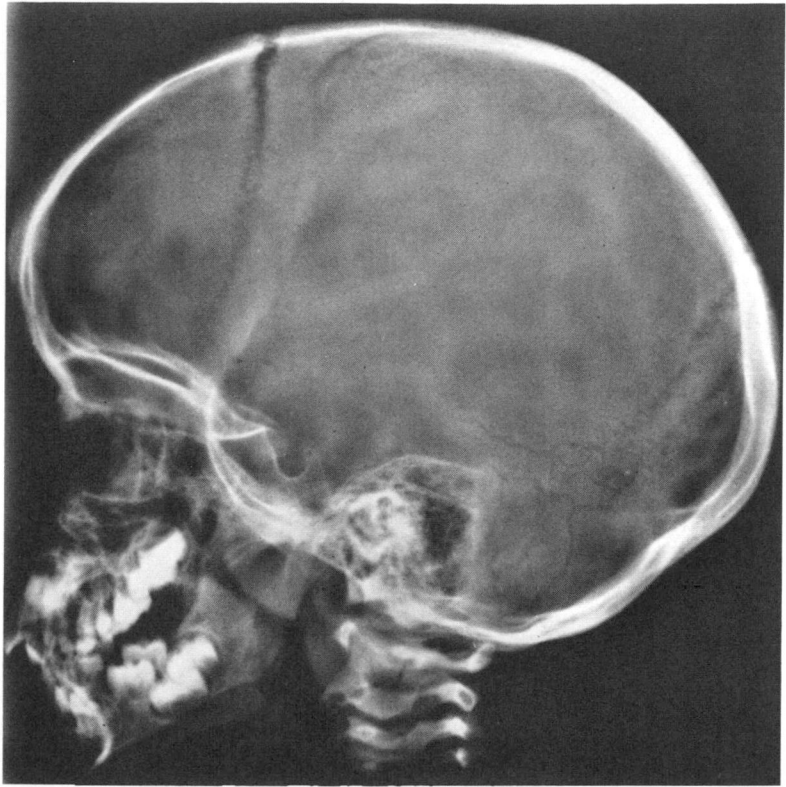

Fig. 57. Lateral skull film of a 4-year-old child with diastatic coronal suture separation.

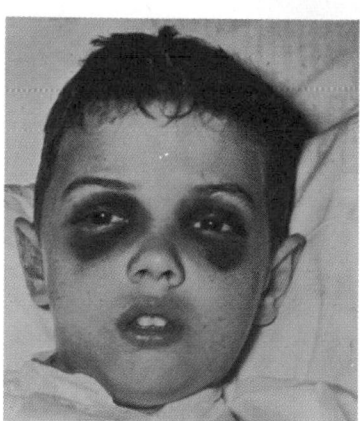

Fig. 58. Five-year-old child with bilateral orbital ecchymoses secondary to an anterior fossa basilar fracture.

servation will decide this. Early surgical intervention is rarely warranted regardless of the location or size of the depession (Fig. 60).

Fractures depressed more than 0.5 cm should be elevated to avoid the formation of undesirable cerebromeningeal cicatrices with the attendant danger of focal neurologic defect and seizures. Early surgery is indicated, as it is in all compound and comminuted skull fractures.

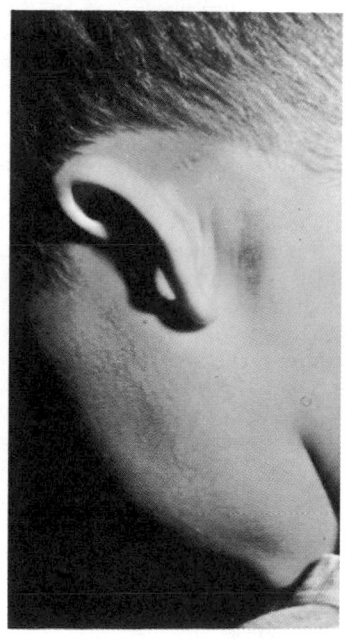

Fig. 59. Same child as Figure 58. Retroauricular ecchymosis (Battle's sign) due to fracture of the petrous bone in the middle fossa.

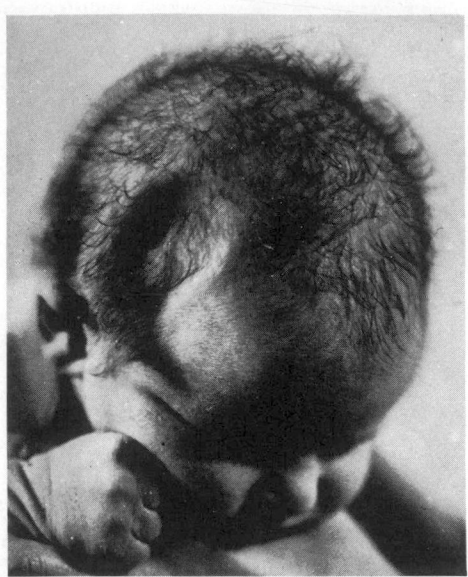

Fig. 60. Depressed fracture of skull from birth injury. Infant delivered by version and extraction with application of forceps to aftercoming head. Depressed fracture of right parietal bone, said to be related to abnormality of mother's pelvis. Difficulty in resuscitation and cyanosis during the first few hours. Right internal strabismus. No signs of increased intracranial pressure. Patient made a complete recovery without operation. Physically and mentally normal at age of 5½ years.

Basal skull fractures resulting in rhinorrhea or otorrhea require hospitalization. The child is maintained in a semiupright bed position, and plugging or irrigation of the involved orifices is contraindicated. The use of prophylactic antibiotics and chemotherapy is controversial; however, in the presence of a demonstrated cerebrospinal fluid leak, therapy is comparable to that for undiagnosed bacterial meningitis. Spontaneous cessation of cerebrospinal fluid drainage may occur. If flow persists beyond a week, surgical repair should be considered, as the danger of meningitis is overwhelming. This hazard remains as long as fistulous patency exists and may result in repeated infections, diffuse arachnoiditis, and secondary hydrocephalus.

Traumatic aerocele, if persistent, is also an indication for operative intervention. Intracranial air tends to be rapidly absorbed. If x-rays at 48- to 72-hour intervals show persistence of air or an increased collection, surgery should not be delayed.

In cases of rhinorrhea, coughing and sneezing may produce increased drainage and actually permit air to enter the intracranial cavity. Accentuation of headache under these circumstances may be the result of delayed intracranial air collection and be documented by repeat x-rays. Suppression of coughing and sneezing is indicated in all patients with posttraumatic otorrhea or rhinorrhea.

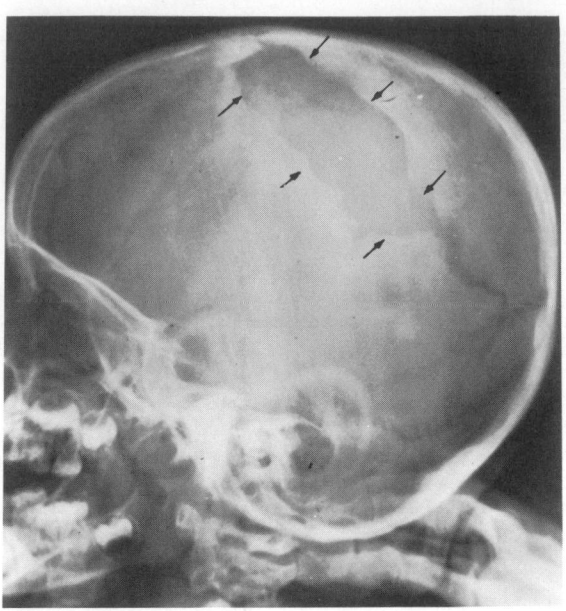

Fig. 61. Leptomeningeal cyst showing large area of parietal skull erosion eight months after a simple linear fracture.

A late sequela of a linear fracture in young children is a leptomeningeal cyst, or more accurately, a growing skull fracture. This results from dural laceration, projection of the arachnoid membrane into the fracture site and brain herniation producing bone erosion of the overlying skull over a period of months to years. The late onset of focal seizures, increased intracranial pressure, focal neurologic signs, and occasionally visible and palpable skull deformity should alert one to this posttraumatic complication. Skull x-rays are diagnostic (Fig. 61), revealing an area of erosion over a prior fracture site. Growing skull fractures are usually in the parietal area and should be suspected when the initial fracture line is wide or has been associated with a subepicranial hydroma.

Extradural Hematoma

Extradural hematoma refers to bleeding between the skull and dura usually from a tear in the middle meningeal artery due to a temporal bone fracture. Laceration of the dural sinuses or other branches of the extradural vascular complex may also result in hemorrhage into the extradural space. As the skull matures, vessels in this location are firmly imbedded in bony grooves and are more vulnerable to damage by fractures that involve these channels. Children less than 2 years of age rarely sustain extradural hemorrhage, as these vessels are less adherent to the calvarium. Because of the greater elasticity of the young skull, damage of this type may exist without any radiographic demonstration of fracture.

The typical clinical syndrome is apparent during the first 12 to 24 hours after initial injury. The child may be rendered briefly unconscious by the original trauma, regain awareness, and after a period of several hours lapse into coma with signs of increased intracranial pressure, hemiplegia, and at times focal seizures. An equal number present without a lucid interval; these children progressively merge from a moderate initial lethargy or stupor into a state of profound coma.

There is no mechanism for the absorption of an extradural hemorrhage, and its increasing mass rapidly raises intracranial pressure with a progressive rise in systolic blood pressure and slowing of the pulse. The eventual result is a decreased irregular respiratory rate with terminal hypotension and tachycardia. The relatively sudden elevation in intracranial pressure is responsible for subhyaloid retinal hemorrhages and early third nerve compression on the affected side, resulting in a fixed, dilated pupil. Subhyaloid hemorrhages are globular extravasations of blood onto the retina, rather than into it. They may change shape and position with head movement, being a mobile fluid collection between the retina and the subhyaloid membrane overlying it. In young children a fracture line may be absent, or not visible, suture diastasis may be the only evidence of trauma, and the lucid interval may be absent. The syndrome usually runs a course of 6 to 12 hours in adults but may extend from 24 to 96 hours in children because of the greater incidence of venous versus arterial bleeding. Either type is more commonly associated with anemia than in comparable adult injuries.

Extradural hemorrhage represents the most lethal complication of head injury, with a mortality rate in untreated cases of 100 percent and in operatively treated cases of almost 50 percent. It is one of the few medical emergencies requiring immediate operative intervention. Untreated cases seldom survive more than 2 to 3 days, although occasional instances with a course of 1 week or more have been noted.

Treatment demands immediate diagnosis via plain skull x-rays, echoencephalography, and arteriography, where feasible, followed by definitive surgery. Local conditions or the patient's status may preclude detailed evaluation and necessitate immediate surgery on clinical grounds. Prognosis for survival and neurologic integrity is directly proportional to the patient's preoperative status and duration of unconsciousness. Under optimal conditions complete recovery without residua may be expected.

Subdural Hematoma

In contrast to the infrequent occurrence of extradural hematomas in children and their relative rarity in patients less than 2 years of age, subdural hematomas are common, with approximately 85 percent occurring in children 1 year of age or less. The syndrome may present as an acute problem (within 3

TABLE 22. *Frequency of Signs and Symptoms of Subdural Hematomas*

	Percent
Anemia	70
Seizures	65
Vomiting	50
X-ray signs of increased pressure	50
Enlarged head	40
History of trauma	40
Retinal hemorrhages	40
Hyperirritability	35
Bulging fontanel	35
Focal neurologic defect	35
Slowed development	20
Skull fracture	20

days), subacutely (within 4 to 20 days), or chronically (greater than 20 days) as dated from the time of presumed trauma.

Hemorrhage in this instance is venous, the blood collecting in the potential space between dura and arachnoid. It arises from laceration veins bridging the area from the cortex to the superior longitudinal sinus or less often from venous bleeding associated with cerebral laceration or an actual venous sinus tear. Such collections in children are bilateral in 80 percent of the cases. These hemorrhages seldom absorb and tend to become encapsulated by dural proliferation.

In infancy the clinical picture differs from that in the older child and often consists of a gradually increasing intracranial pressure syndrome with an enlarging head, bulging fontanel, anemia, seizures, irritability, vomiting, and failure to thrive. The relative frequency of signs and symptoms is indicated in Table 22.

In young children the syndrome of subdural hematoma may be further delineated by subdural puncture through the lateral recess of a patent anterior fontanel. This must be performed bilaterally. When the diagnosis has been established, repeated daily aspirations of 50 ml or more of subdural fluid from alternate sides, within the limits of patient tolerance and ease of flow, may be made. This technique attempts to empty the subdural space and permit cortical reexpansion to obliterate it. If after 10 to 14 days this regimen has not been effective, it is unlikely that further attempts will be successful. Inability to tap the subdural space "dry" may be due to absolute enlargement of the cranial cavity by the hematoma to such a degree that the brain cannot reexpand to fill it, failure of expansion due to membrane formation about a chronic hematoma, secondary cerebral atrophy, a fistula from the subarachnoid into the subdural space, or continued bleeding. Surgical drainage, craniotomy with membrane removal, or a shunting procedure will be necessary. Careful attention must be directed to preventing or correcting

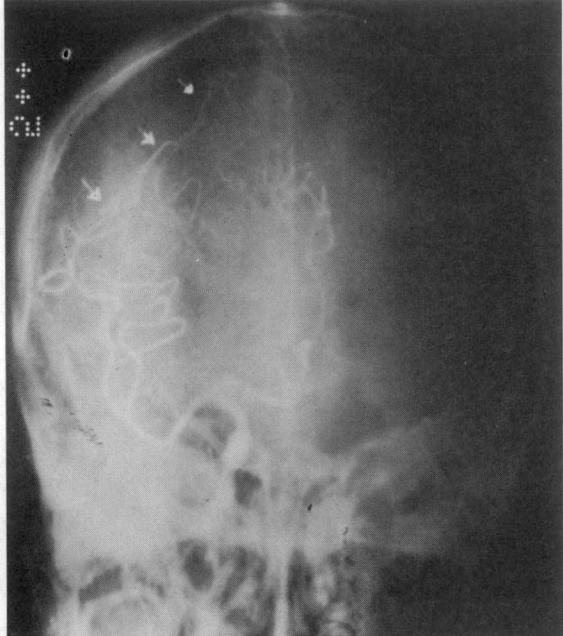

Fig. 62. Carotid arteriogram anteroposterior view, showing a subdural hematoma (arrows) displacing surface vessels and brain from the inner table of the skull.

anemia, hypoproteinemia, and electrolyte abnormalities during the period of therapy.

Subdural hematomas in older children require surgical drainage and seldom reaccumulate after operation.

Negative findings from subdural punctures do not absolutely rule out subdural collections. The exploring needle may not enter the fluid lake, or viscous, compartmented liquid may preclude withdrawal. Evidence of increasing intracranial pressure, focal seizures, and deterioration in general neurologic status and level of consciousness should alert one to the problem. Electroencephalography may reveal marked unilateral or bilateral cortical depression over subdural collections but is often normal or nonspecific. There is no absolute clinical picture that indicates the presence of a subdural hematoma. Cerebral angiography is the best diagnostic test to indicate the presence and extent of subdural collections and should be considered whenever the patient's course and findings are suggestive of this complication (Fig. 62).

Treatment is usually successful when the diagnosis is made early before cerebral atrophy and a fixed neurologic deficit have occurred.

Posttraumatic lacerations of the arachnoid membrane resulting in cerebrospinal fluid collections in the subdural space, termed subdural hygromas, present the same general clinical picture and problems as subdural hematomas.

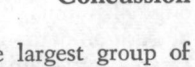

Concussion

Closed head injuries make up the largest group of cases of craniocerebral trauma. The term implies no injury to the underlying bone beyond that of a linear fracture.

The simplest type of head trauma is cerebral concussion. This refers to the situation following a sudden head blow in which transient loss of consciousness occurs but is followed by full recovery without sequelae. More prolonged unconsciousness often associated with some evidence of focal neurologic defect and varying degrees of amnesia implies a cerebral contusion or laceration.

Children with either category of injury often vomit and later are pale, apathetic, or quite irritable. Overwhelming cerebral stimuli of any type may result in convulsive phenomena. In young children this is particularly true following head injury, and such an episode, occurring usually within a matter of minutes after impact, does not necessarily imply a severe degree of trauma, an abnormality of seizure threshold, or significant increase in the possibility of future convulsive episodes.

The physician's problem is how extensively to evaluate the injury and how to manage the patient in the period immediately postinjury. In cases of simple concussion or mild contusion the child should be examined carefully with attention to gross evidence of skull fracture and associated damage to viscera and bones. Observation until full recovery of consciousness is mandatory, as is the recording of vital signs. In most cases the child will have partially recovered by the time he is seen and, other than pallor, irritability, and bruises, will have few signs on examination. These children are best managed at home, provided intelligent, not overly distraught parents can cooperate in noting the youngster's pupillary equality, level of responsiveness, and general motor power. Arousal of the patient every 2 hours to determine the level of awareness and other signs is advisable for 12 to 24 hours postinjury.

Cerebral Contusion and Laceration

Most severe degrees of head injury or prolonged unconsciousness require hospitalization with more detailed evaluation and management to delineate the extent of injury and the need for specific therapy. Immediate attention must first be given to airway maintenance, the treatment of shock, fractures, the alleviation of hemorrhage, the prevention of fat embolization, or the care of splenic rupture, lung perforation, aspiration, atelectasis, or other emergency.

Primary or subsequent evaluations of the head injury will require some details of history and time sequence of events related to the injury and an accurate record of the initial status and findings. Examination should include precise evaluation of the individual's level of consciousness with regard to lethargy, stupor, or coma and content of his verbalizations and performance. Is the child irritable, agitated, confused, disoriented, confabulatory, amnesic, or completely unresponsive? Is there a response to sound and pain stimuli? Is it appropriate or purposeless?

The reason for hospitalization is to assess the course of postinjury and intelligently anticipate and treat complications. All pertinent items must therefore be clearly recorded to afford any examiner or consultant the comparative analysis that is the essential feature in the management of head injury patients. Pupillary size and reaction, observed extraocular movements, findings from examination of the fundi, symmetry of facial movement (either spontaneous or with pain stimulus), corneal responses, gag reflex, spontaneous or induced limb movements, tonus, deep tendon reflexes, and response to plantar stimulation should be listed in addition to the vital signs, evidence of meningeal irritation, a description of the external discharge from ears or nose, and a careful examination of the scalp and skull.

Cerebrospinal fluid studies are of limited value in cases of head injury, and their routine use cannot be justified. On the other hand, when there is suspicion of concurrent meningitis, a lumbar puncture is clearly indicated. In the acute posttraumatic period a spinal tap has little differential value, since intracortical, subdural, or extradural hematomas may be characterized by either clear or bloody fluid. An elevated cerebrospinal fluid pressure is usual after any significant degree of cerebral contusion, whether or not there has been a posttraumatic subarachnoid hemorrhage. In the latter instance, headache and meningeal discomfort may be relieved by the withdrawal of cerebrospinal fluid after the patient's general condition has been stabilized for 72 hours or more.

The meningeal signs of subarachnoid hemorrhage are often delayed, not appearing until 8 to 24 hours after bleeding. Posttraumatic hemorrhage of this type is common. It is seldom a significant complicating factor other than in its production of discomfort and prolonging convalescence. Rarely, obstruction to the cerebrospinal fluid pathway may develop secondary to blood in the subarachnoid space by obstruction at the incisura. This situation is often temporary, but posttraumatic hydrocephalus on this basis, necessitating a shunting procedure, must be borne in mind. Depending on the degree of cerebral damage, the child may not regain full consciousness for a period of hours to several weeks. During this time supportive care may be complicated by problems involving nutrition and electrolyte balance, restlessness, seizures, respiration, fever, bladder care, and otorrhea or rhinorrhea.

Patients remaining unconscious for any signifi-

cant period of time may present a problem in fluid balance secondary to posttraumatic diabetes insipidus, paradoxic antidiuretic hormone excretion, and varied degrees of hyponatremia or hypernatremia. Fluid intake and urinary output should be recorded in conjunction with weight and serum electrolyte determinations until intake and output return to normal. Restlessness, increasing stupor, and seizures may result from gross electrolyte imbalance, usually on the basis of failing to recognize an increased thirst or by iatrogenic water intoxication. As soon as feasible, nutrition and fluid balance should progress from intravenous to nasogastric feedings and finally to normal oral feeding. Posttraumatic diabetes insipidus is usually transient but may require a period of Pitressin therapy, either by injection or as snuff. A number of children have a brief vasodepressor shocklike reaction to Pitressin tannate in oil and initially are best treated with an aqueous Pitressin preparation.

An agitated, lethargic-stuporous state characterizes many injured patients. Depressant drugs of the barbiturate or phenothiazine groups are best avoided in the acute period after injury. Valium, 2 to 4 mg intramuscularly or orally every 4 to 6 hours as needed, is safe as is paraldehyde 2 to 4 ml via the same routes. Bladder drainage, adequate hydration, loose restraints about wrist and ankles, boxing gloves for older children, and a well-padded crib or bed rails may be necessary to calm and protect the disturbed patient.

Convulsions, other than at the time of the initial impact episode, demand suppressant therapy. This usually implies an initial phenobarbital or paraldehyde regimen in conjunction with Dilantin therapy. Dosages, routes of administration, and the management of convulsive status are described in detail elsewhere (p. 995). The appearance of generalized or focal seizure phenomena may reflect the presence of a subdural or intracortical hematoma; however, convulsions are seldom the only manifestations in such cases and most often reflect underlying cortical contusion and laceration rather than a specific vascular complication.

Maintenance of a clear respiratory passage by proper positioning, suction, oropharyngeal airway, or tracheostomy is essential. Tracheostomy should be an elective procedure and preferably performed on a previously inserted endotracheal tube. In cases of severe brain damage with impaired gag and cough mechanisms, tracheostomy is an initial step in management to prevent aspiration, atelectasis, and pneumonia. In the young child requiring respiratory aid a properly positioned high tracheostomy with a tube of maximal caliber is essential.

Significant temperature elevations in the absence of infection occur after head injury. However, even in cases with posttraumatic subarachnoid hemorrhage, the temperature rarely exceeds 102° F unless there is severe cortical and brainstem involvement. The latter patient is usually in profound coma and may demonstrate marked temperature variations with elevations to 105° F or more. In these cases, if the patient is unresponsive to aspirin and sponging, the use of hypothermia may be considered with the temperature maintained at 92° to 96° F in an effort to decrease cerebral and general metabolic requirements in a situation of probable hypothalamic damage.

Urinary care may become a problem either because of continued soiling with skin irritation and breakdown or periodic retention. The usual diaper, urinary collection bag, or catheter techniques may be utilized. Should an indwelling catheter be necessary, prophylactic Gantrisin or similar drugs are not effective in preventing infection in the absence of scrupulous aseptic catheter technique and bladder irrigation.

Varying degrees of cerebral edema occur after head injury. It may be restricted to the contused, lacerated area or become generalized and present a picture not unlike that of acute lead encephalopathy with markedly increased intracranial pressure, focal neurologic signs, and seizures. Differentiation from hematoma formation or active intracranial bleeding is often impossible. The diagnosis is most frequently made retrospectively after clot or hemorrhage has been ruled out. General supportive care is all that is usually needed, but in critical situations efforts to decrease brain bulk and metabolism by intravenous urea and/or hypothermia may be of value. Osmotic loading substances, such as urea, produce a marked diuresis and decrease in cerebral bulk by dehydration. Rebound swelling does occur, and therapy may be needed over a period of days. Urea is given intravenously 1 g per kilogram of body weight each 8 to 12 hours with an indwelling bladder catheter in place and careful attention to electrolyte balance. Dosages of urea given in conjunction with hypothermia should be on a basis of 0.5 g per kilogram of body weight, as reduced elimination of urea occurs with lowered body temperature. Substances of this type always present danger when bleeding is present or a clot is developing. A more effective means of treating cerebral edema is with the use of steroids. Dexamethasone (Decadron) 4 to 16 mg daily for 3 days and gradually decreasing thereafter is the drug of choice in the treatment of cerebral edema. Therapy of this type is best accomplished in specialized treatment units where the necessary equipment and nursing personnel are available.

Intracortical hematomas are most often small; large solitary posttraumatic collections are uncommon. Surgically significant hematomas are usually clinically indistinguishable from extradural or subdural collections. Increasing intracranial pressure and progressive focal neurologic signs may result from an intracerebral clot in the absence of the more common hematomas. Diagnosis here reflects the same principles as in other intracranial collections, with detection being a function of ancillary studies. Many resolve without the need for surgical intervention; however, with increasing neurologic deficit and intracranial pressure and with angiographic and echo-encephalographic evidence of progressive displacement, surgery should be considered.

Sequelae of Craniocerebral Trauma

Combinations of fixed neurologic defects may exist after brain injury but are usually self-evident. The less predictable sequelae are seizures, organic mental changes, and the posttraumatic syndrome.

SEIZURES. Posttraumatic seizures are most often generalized rather than focal but may be of any type other than petit mal. The incidence of persistent convulsive phenomena after head injury is unknown and extremely difficult to determine. The severity of the injury, the duration of unconsciousness, the occurrence of early seizures other than at the time of impact, and serial electroencephalographic patterns are of some value in analyzing the problem.

Penetrating depressed fractures have a residual seizure incidence of 30 to 60 percent, particularly if associated with periods of unconsciousness greater than 24 hours and the presence of convulsions during the acute phase. Children surviving subdural, extradural, or intracortical hematomas have a similar late seizure potential. A normal electroencephalogram with absence of paroxysmal or focal abnormalities 3 months after injury tends to make posttraumatic epilepsy less likely than when such discharges exist. A progressively worsening tracing is quite suspect; however, a delay of months to a year or more in the development of any electrical abnormality may be seen in patients who have or will subsequently develop seizures. Gross irregularity of the electroencephalogram may be present after head trauma in a perfectly normal child, and at times the tracing may appear relatively normal in the presence of frank focal neurologic defect. Nevertheless, a tracing should be obtained after significant head trauma as a base line in cases with or without seizures concomitant with acute episode. Unfortunately, the electroencephalogram is often of little help, or actually misleading, in predicting the chances of epilepsy developing after any given injury.

In closed head injuries, late epilepsy occurs in less than 5 percent of cases. The seizures may present in 3 months to 4 or more years after injury, the peak incidence occurring between 6 to 18 months. Previously controlled seizure states in known epileptics may be exacerbated after head injury, although analysis of such groups has revealed no consistent pattern.

Convulsive phenomena during the acute episode will usually result in the patient being placed on anticonvulsant therapy, which should be maintained for at least a 2-year period of freedom from seizures before gradual withdrawal of the drug. The appearance of the electroencephalogram at this time bears little relationship to the occurrence of subsequent convulsions, either with or without medication. Some authorities feel a paroxysmal or focally abnormal electroencephalogram after injury is in itself an indication for prolonged anticonvulsant drug therapy. This remains a controversial point.

ORGANIC MENTAL SYNDROMES. Self-limited memory defects and minor personality changes may be noted after head injury. Persistent frank organic dementia is uncommon in children, as is intellectual defect, although with extremely severe and extensive injuries, particularly in infancy, psychomotor retardation is seen.

POSTTRAUMATIC SYNDROME. The problem of general sequelae following head injury, the posttraumatic syndrome, is less common in children than in adults; however, it does occur. The symptoms tend to vary somewhat from those in the adult (headache, irritability, and postural vertigo). They are more commonly in the realm of enuresis, disturbances of sleep pattern, episodically aggressive behavior, and decline in school performance. How much is due to organic rather than primarily psychologic factors is difficult to state. Symptomatic management with sedatives, tranquilizers, and sometimes psychotherapy may be needed. Investigation as to the presence of typical or fragmentary convulsive phenomena may be profitable, and improvement may be noted after the institution of anticonvulsant therapy.

A commonsense attitude toward general care during the acute phase is extremely important. Overhospitalization, unfounded gratuitous remarks about possible future brain damage, and prolonged litigation correlate highly with the incidence of posttraumatic behavioral dysfunction. The physician must maintain an attitude of expectancy for return to normal function both with the parents and with the child. The avoidance of oversolicitous, unnecessary limitation of school, play, and social activities will reduce a common factor in the etiology of the posttraumatic reaction syndrome.

Group statistical studies would tend to indicate that children with behavioral and mental defects are more prone to head injury and more prone to display sequelae than mentally stable individuals.

Injuries to the Spinal Cord

ETIOLOGY AND PATHOGENESIS. Trauma to the vertebral column and spinal cord constitutes less than 5 percent of childhood injuries. The enclosure of the spinal cord in a bony canal is of great protective value; however, the mobility of the cervical spine and enlargement of the spinal cord at this level make it the single most common area of spinal injury at all ages. Dislocation may occur without fracture and result in a neural defect well beyond what might be inferred from the seemingly minimal osseous-ligamentous disturbance. The additional support given the thoracic vertebrae by the trunk and the smaller size of the spinal cord in this area are further protective factors which can only be overcome by excessive force. The pelvis gives additional support to the lumbar spine; however, as the spinal cord ends at the second lumbar vertebra in the older child, there is somewhat less protection of the lower thoracic–upper lumbar area.

In infancy, birth injury is the commonest cause of spinal cord trauma. Forceful breech extraction with spinal hyperextension is the situation in which this is most likely to occur. Birth injuries of this type may also be seen with cephalic presentation or complications necessitating version maneuvers, cephalocervical angulation, and unusual traction. The majority of these injuries result in cord transection in the midcervical to upper thoracic area. Those resulting in high cervical lesions involve the cervicomedullary junction and are seldom compatible with life.

In older children, trauma may be indirect, as in whiplash injuries, where the spine is either hyperextended or flexed beyond its normal range. Direct trauma resulting in crush injuries to the spine and its contents is less common and most often due to impact secondary to falls from a considerable height. The general pathology of spinal cord injury varies from complete severance through contusion and compression.

DIAGNOSIS. Cord injuries in the newborn period may be suspected in any case of difficult extraction necessitating considerable force. Resuscitation may be difficult with intercostal paralysis, a retracted thorax, prominent abdomen, diaphragmatic respiration, and a weak cry. The child is noted to have flaccid, abducted, and motionless lower extremities. Sensory evaluation is difficult, but a level of decreased response may be detected compatible with the usual midcervical–upper thoracic area of pathology. Because of the site of injury, only upper extremity movements are noted, with shoulder and forearm motions but little else. In this areflexic spinal shock stage, respiratory, urinary, and skin infection is common and often fatal. Hyperreflexia may occur subsequently with mass reflex upon stimulation resulting in a total flexion in the involved areas that may be misinterpreted as functional return.

If there is survival, the late picture depends upon the site and severity of the spinal cord lesion. Whether or not the patient's paraplegia assumes a position of flexion, extension, flaccidity, or spasticity depends upon the completeness and extent of the spinal cord defect. A sharply demarcated level is uncommon, as the defect is more often of such longitudinal extent as to cover many segments and preclude the development of spasticity. Intercurrent infection, whether acute or chronic, will delay the development of spasticity or decrease its extent. Early bladder function tends to manifest itself as an overflow with constant dribbling, while later automatic function occurs with reflex emptying upon distension to a moderate volume.

Laboratory evaluation should include spinal x-rays, which are usually normal, although fracture or subluxation may be detected. A number of normal variations of the cervical spine in childhood (pseudo-dislocation, hypermobility, etc.) often make radiologic interpretation difficult and are causes of interpretive error. The cerebrospinal fluid is usually bloody and has an increased protein content.

The diagnosis is often self-evident but may at times be confused with neonatal asphyxia, intracranial injury, congenital defects, or progressive infantile spinal muscular atrophy.

MANAGEMENT. The newborn requires immediate airway attention, oxygenation, suction, and meticulous skin, bladder, and bowel care. Antibiotics may be of value if long-term catheterization is required and should be given early with evidence of any acute infection. Myelography and surgery are not indicated; they decrease survival potential and in no way enhance recovery.

Survivors are expected to have normal intelligence; they can use their upper extremities fairly well but rarely ambulate or even sit without support. Early in life urinary and rectal sphincter control may be adequate. However, as the child grows older, surgery may be required to maintain adequacy of function. Surgical procedures may also be indicated for the orthopedic problems.

Trauma to the spinal cord of older children presents many similar problems; however, immediate management tends to be more definitive, the initial goal being safe, rapid transportation of the patient to where he will receive definitive care. Injury in this group is more likely to be complicated by damage to the vertebral column. It is of paramount importance that the patient be handled so that additional injury to the cord is not produced by improper posture or undue mobility of the vertebrae at the level of injury. Other bodily injuries may also have occurred, and judgment must be exercised for their proper care in keeping with the demands of the spinal cord injury.

The patient must be so placed on the litter as to maintain the normal cervical and lumbar lordosis and to prevent movement which might cause additional injury. Intravenous fluids, intranasal oxygen, and catheterization are often invaluable adjuncts in the initial management of spinal cord injuries. During the early stages, the patient must not be given anything by mouth nor strong sedatives or any drugs which would mask neurologic changes.

Open injuries must be treated surgically. Closed cord injuries may require either surgical or nonsurgical treatment. Unwise surgery in patients with cervical injury may be fatal and indications for surgery must be appraised with great care.

The cervical spinal cord is typically injured by a fracture, a dislocation, or a fracture-dislocation of one or more vertebrae. Severe injury above the level of the fifth cervical cord segment is rarely compatible with life. The radiograms may show marked crushing of the bodies, fragmentation of the pedicles, laminae, and spines, and such dislocation that facets are locked entirely out of position. Under no condition whatsoever must the grave error be made of trying to reduce such dislocation anywhere in the cervical spine by closed manipulation. In most severe lesions of the vertebrae there will be a complete transverse physiologic loss of cord function, often at one or more segments above the uppermost visible vertebral injury. In other instances, the vertebral lesions demonstrated roentgenologically will be minimal in comparison with the marked neurologic loss. There are no means of knowing whether an early spinal cord injury is due to contusion, with physiologic interruption and anatomic preservation, or whether the lesion is one of frank anatomic discontinuity. Closed injuries to the cervical cord with evidence of vertebral dislocation are best treated by placing the patient on a firm mattress or special frame and applying continual traction to the slightly extended head. The vertebrae will in most instances relocate in almost normal alignment within 24 to 36 hours. Serial lateral bedside portable x-ray pictures will demonstrate progress of the restitution. Occasional spinal puncture may also be done to follow the manometric effect of the closed decompression. Traction is maintained for at least 6 weeks.

Immediate decompressive laminectomy for the injured cervical cord is attended by severe morbidity and high mortality, but there are two instances when it is proper to operate early: (1) if the state of the patient was initially one of incomplete loss of cord function and hours or days later increasing loss of function appears; and (2) if at any time after the injury, immediately or days later, good radiograms show clearly that a bone fragment rests upon the cord in such a way that traction could not or has not relieved its pressure. The possibility of a mass of centrally extruded intervertebral disk substance as a result of injury must not be overlooked.

The thoracic segments of the vertebral column form a relatively rigid mass. The thoracic vertebral canal is the narrowest of all parts of the canal, and the spinal cord throughout its thoracic extent has a somewhat less rich blood supply than at either the cervical or lumbar levels. Spinal cord injury at this level is usually the result of direct severe trauma and carries a poor prognosis. All these factors must be considered in the early care of closed injuries to this area. Cord compression will almost invariably reveal total block of the flow of cerebrospinal fluid. The value of surgical decompression is highly variable.

As with injury at the thoracic level, dislocation of one lumbar vertebral body under another, wedging of a body with kyphosis, or fracture of the posterior arches calls for immediate decompressive laminectomy. Injury of the conus medullaris (T_{12}-L_1 vertebral levels) is of grave significance. Below that level the delicate filaments of the cauda equina may be badly torn and attenuated, the injury being associated with considerable subarachnoid hemorrhage.

The long-term care and rehabilitation of patients with spinal injuries is a challenge that is often best met in a special center or unit geared to this type of care. Extensive efforts to reestablish bowel and bladder function will be needed as well as attention to skin integrity, to nutrition, and to late syndromes of pain, spasms, autonomic dysfunction, genitourinary complications, psychiatric problems, and programs of education and training.

Peripheral Nerve Injuries

Injuries to the peripheral nervous system are not common in childhood. Those seen early in life are usually due to damage of the brachial plexus or sciatic nerves.

The spinal roots of the fifth cervical through the first thoracic nerves form the brachial plexus. These roots are poorly stabilized at birth, and traction damage is rarely transmitted to the spinal cord. Injuries to infants result in almost pure root syndromes in comparison to the more distally involved and diffuse damage seen with injuries in older children and adults. Recovery is better in children than in adults as regards both spontaneous resolution and surgical results.

Etiologically any force changing the normal relationship of arm, shoulder, and neck may result in plexus injury. Birth trauma is the commonest cause. The plexus has points of fascial fixation to the first rib medially and the coracoid process of the scapula laterally. Abduction of the arm stretches the nerves under and against the coracoid, resulting in stretch, avulsion, or compression of the lower plexus. Lateral deviation of the head and shoulder depression stretch the nerves over and against the first ribs, resulting in similar damage to the upper plexus. Traction injuries of these types may occur with breech or cephalic deliveries.

Upper plexus root injuries, Erb-Duchenne type, are commonest. The shoulder sags, the arm hangs limp in internal rotation, and the wrist is pronated reflecting paralysis of spinati, deltoid, biceps, brachioradialis, and extensor carpi radialis muscles and often rhomboids, serratus, and levator scapulae as well. The deep tendon reflexes of the involved extremity are usually lost, but it is unusual to be able to demonstrate a sensory defect. Treatment requires the deformity be overcome to prevent posterior subluxation of the humeral head from the glenoid fossa. The arm is placed in abduction and external rotation by a brace or by pinning a towel over the wrist and fixing it to the mattress in the desired position. A full range of motion of the shoulder by passive exercises is performed daily. Well over 80 percent of these patients will have complete recovery in 3 months or less. Anomalous plexus configuration may include the fourth cervical root, or trauma may be transmitted to this level resulting in phrenic nerve damage and ipsilateral diaphragmatic paralysis, which is rarely a problem unless significant bilateral injury has occurred.

Lower plexus root injuries, Klumpke-Dejerine

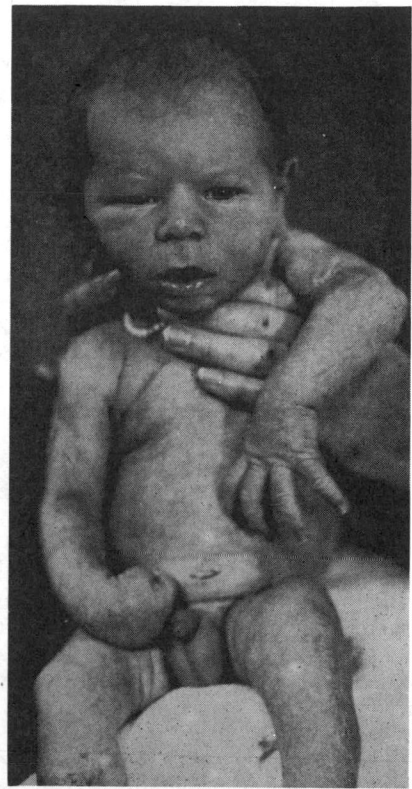

Fig. 63. Brachial plexus injury to an infant 12 days old. Involvement of the upper, middle, and lower trunks of the right brachial plexus, combined with right enophthalmos, a component of Horner's syndrome.

type, show more sensory and vasomotor involvement with paralysis of the flexors and extensors of the forearm and the intrinsic muscles of the hand. Marked involvement of the first thoracic root results in cervical sympathetic damage and a Horner's syndrome, often with delay of normal pigmentation of the ipsilateral iris. The deep tendon reflexes are usually intact, with a poor grasp response. Sensory changes involve the ulnar side of the hand and forearm. Dependent edema and cyanosis are common. Treatment involves splinting the forearm and wrist in a neutral position and passive range of motion exercises. The majority of cases completely recover within 3 to 6 months, although the overall prognosis is not as favorable as in the upper plexus lesions (Fig. 63).

Injuries to the brachial plexus in older children are usually of mixed upper and lower plexus types. If due to traction and hyperabduction, the prognosis may be good, although at this age the usual cause is severe trauma which often results in root avulsion or a degree of hemorrhage and scarring that precludes functional recovery.

Direct plexus surgery is consistently unprofitable. In cases with persistent defects, orthopedic procedures to stabilize joints in favorable positions and tendon transplantation, where feasible, are the only available treatments.

The peripheral nerves in the upper extremity may be involved alone or in varied combinations, due usually to direct laceration trauma or severe injuries with combined osseous-vascular-neural damage. Compression neuropathies are uncommon in childhood.

Serratus anterior palsy due to involvement of the long thoracic nerve (nerve of Bell) is usually a result of pressure on the shoulder or excessive forceful activity with the arms elevated. It is most frequently seen in prepuberal athletic boys in association with baseball pitching, weight-lifting, or carrying heavy loads. The scapula "wings" with horizontal forward pressure of the arms and there is weakness in lifting and arm elevation due to impaired scapula fixation. Treatment is expectant with full functional recovery anticipated, although some residual scapular winging may persist. Activities possibly associated with the lesion should be discontinued. During the first week the weight of the shoulder may be removed from the scapula by a simple arm sling, which is often not necessary unless the paralysis is total or there is considerable discomfort. Range of motion exercises, then more active shoulder strengthening maneuvers, are the only measures indicated.

The axillary or circumflex nerve that innervates the deltoid and teres minor muscles is usually injured only in association with anterior dislocations of the shoulder, particularly when associated with fractures of the greater tuberosity of the humerus. The axillary nerve winds around the surgical neck of the humerus and may be injured by fractures in this location. Injury to the nerve is detected by inability to abduct the arm to the horizontal position and a zone of hypesthesia of the lower posterior deltoid area. Therapy is that of the primary injury, and with rare exceptions full neural recovery can be anticipated.

Radial nerve injury is most commonly a result of fracture through the middle third of the humerus with neural stretch or contusion. The triceps muscle may not be involved, but there is marked weakness of the brachioradialis and the extensors of the wrist and fingers (wristdrop). Sensory loss in an area between index finger and thumb on the dorsum of the hand. In the acute state it is impossible to tell whether or not the nerve has been lacerated or severed. Therefore, where feasible, open reduction of the fracture and nerve repair are reasonable considerations. Later, electrical testing will give information as to whether or not there is anatomic continuity of the nerve. Where permanent residua exist in spite of all efforts, tendon transplantation gives quite effective wrist, finger, and thumb extension.

The ulnar nerve may be lacerated along its course in the forearm near the wrist or in conjunction with fractures as it passes behind the medial epicondyle of the humerus at the elbow. The epiphysis of the medial epicondyle does not fuse to the humerus until late adolescence and is particularly prone to avulsion. The ulnar nerve may be contused at the time of injury or compressed later by scar formation. Sensory loss involves the fifth digit and ulnar half of the fourth and extends along the medial side of the palm to the lower forearm. Weakness may involve the interossei, lumbricales, hypothenar muscles, adductor pollicis, the flexor carpi ulnaris, the deep flexor of the fourth and fifth digits, resulting in a defect in spreading the fingers, adducting the thumb, flexing the fourth and fifth digits at the distal interphalangeal joints, and poor opposition of the fifth finger.

Treatment is that of the primary injury. Surgical intervention depends upon the intactness of the nerve as determined by clinical and electrical studies and can consist of suturing or grafting the involved nerve.

The median nerve may be damaged similarly to the ulnar and is often injured with it. In addition to the more common laceration injury, there may be damage in anterior dislocation fractures at the elbow or wrist. Sensory loss is on the palmar surface of the hand and involves thumb, index, middle and radial half of the ring fingers, and the radial surface of the palm. Weakness of the pronators of the forearm, long flexors of the fingers, and short adductor and opponens of the thumb is the major motor defect. Therapeutic considerations are similar to cases of ulnar palsy.

Peripheral nerve injuries involving the lower extremities are almost exclusively of the sciatic nerve and its branches. It is the largest nerve in the body and at the knee divides into the tibial and common peroneal nerves. Iatrogenic trauma secondary to intramuscular injections is the leading cause of sciatic neuropathy in infancy. Lesions of this type are also seen in older children and adults. The "normal course" of the sciatic nerve in the hollow midway between the ischial tuberosity and the greater trochanter under cover of the gluteus maximus muscle varies greatly. This fact, taken together with the small size of the infant gluteal mass and the potential neurotoxicity of many antibiotics, makes it unwise to utilize this area for intramuscular injections. Intragluteal injections are contraindicated in infancy and should be used in older children with extreme caution. The anterolateral compartment of the thigh and deltoid areas is safer and always preferable.

Complete sciatic lesions produce total foot paralysis and loss of leg flexion. There is a flail footdrop, absent ankle jerk, and a sensory loss below the knee involving the entire leg except for its medial aspect.

The tragedy of nerve injury in infancy is accentuated by residua of short, small extremities due to lack of stimulation of muscular-tendon movement essential to bone growth. All cases of sciatic palsy must be carefully evaluated with a view toward surgery, although high lesions of this type rarely show complete recovery and are usually associated with a marked permanent disability.

The peroneal nerve is vulnerable to pressure neuropathy as well as other injury. It descends from the popliteal fossa to a superficial position on the lateral aspect of the leg passing posterior to the head of the fibula. Injury here results in sensory loss over the dorsum of the foot and anterolateral surface of the leg with weakness of the dorsiflexors and evertors of the foot and toes.

The tibial nerve descends deep in the calf, rounds the posterior aspect of the medial malleolus, and enters the foot. It innervates muscles controlling plantar flexion of the foot and toes and the intrinsic muscles of the foot. Sensory loss is usually confined to the sole.

Combined peroneal and tibial nerve injuries often occur. Treatment is similar to that described for ulnar nerve injuries.

Cranial Nerve Injuries

Trauma to the cranial nerves is seldom an isolated occurrence and usually reflects more diffuse craniocerebral injury.

The olfactory nerve is frequently torn as its filaments pass from the subfrontal area of the brain through the cribriform plate. The defect is rarely complete and usually asymptomatic. If severe anosmia persists, distortion of taste is the presenting complaint.

Trauma to the optic nerve occurs in association with orbital fracture but may be seen with cerebral contusion and hemorrhage into the nerve sheath. Injury to the chiasmal area is uncommon. The hypothalamus and brainstem usually receive the brunt of injury in this region with resulting fatality.

The commonest cranial nerve injuries are those involving the third, fourth, sixth, seventh, and eighth nerves.

Laceration of the carotid artery in its cavernous sinus position due to fractures or transmitted trauma may result in a carotid-cavernous fistula. Complications of this type are less common in children than in adults but may occur. Either immediately or within several days of injury the patient may become aware of a bruit. Subsequently third, fourth, and sixth cranial nerve paresis may occur with associated exophthalmos, periorbital engorgement, and diminished sensation in the first two divisions of the fifth cranial nerve. The bruit is strikingly prominent over the involved side and far more pronounced than the nonspecific cephalic bruits of childhood. It is obliterated or considerably reduced by ipsilateral carotid compression. Spontaneous occlusion of the fistula rarely occurs. Carotid ligation in the neck and often intracranially above the cavernous sinus is necessary.

Damage to the oculomotor nerves is more common, and permanent or transient dysfunction of the extraocular muscles occur more frequently in the pediatric age group than in the adult.

Fractures through the petrous portion of the temporal bone may damage the facial nerve. Paralysis may be immediate or delayed. Neonatal facial paralysis may follow forceps extraction or reflect unusual in utero positions. Immediate treatment is directed to corneal protection. Damage to the nerve distal to the geniculate ganglion may be associated with blood behind the tympanic membrane and a conductive hearing loss. Injury central to the ganglion tends to be associated with labyrinthine dysfunction and a pattern of sensorineural hearing loss, implying a level of injury that is not amenable to direct therapy. In all other instances evaluation and management are aimed at the functional state of the nerve. Electrodiagnostic tests to follow and determine the degree of degeneration and estimate anatomic continuity of the nerve are not infallible; however, when there is evidence of neural degeneration, careful evaluation and consideration should be given to operative intervention.

Surgical decompression and/or nerve graft, where feasible, give the best results. Hypoglossal facial anastomosis and plastic procedures to enhance facial symmetry are less satisfactory but are at times the only possible approach to the problem.

Fractures through the base of the skull, direct blows on or near the ear, or the extravasation of blood from subarachnoid hemorrhage may affect both vestibular and auditory components of the eighth cranial nerve as well as causing direct damage to the labyrinth, cochlea, or middle ear. Posttraumatic neural deafness has a relatively poor prognosis for full recovery. Labyrinthine dysfunction as evidenced by postural vertigo and increased sensitivity to motion is usually transient.

REFERENCES

Boshes, B. Trauma to the Spinal Cord. *In* Baker, A. B., ed., Clinical Neurology, 2nd ed. New York, Paul B. Hoeber, Inc., 1962, Vol. 3, Chap. 36, pp. 1639-1678.

Campbell, E. D. R., Hickey, R. P., Nixon, K. H., and Richardson, A. J. Value of nerve-excitability measurements in prognosis of facial palsy. Brit. Med. J., 2:7, 1962.

Caverness, W. E., and Walker, A. E., eds. Head Injury Conference Proceedings. Philadelphia, J. B. Lippincott Co., 1966.

Cloward, R. B. Single suture scalp closure. J. Neurosurg., 21:142, 1964.

Dillon, H., and Leopold, R. L. Children and the postconcussion syndrome. J.A.M.A., 172:86, 1961.

Drake, C. G., and Jory, T. A. Hypothermia in the treatment of critical head injury. Canad. Med. Ass. J., 87:887, 1962.

Epstein, J. A., Epstein, B. S., and Small, M. Subepicranial hydroma. J. Pediat., 59:562, 1961.

Gil, D. G. Physical abuse of children; findings and implications of a nationwide survey. Pediatrics, 44:857, 1969.

Gilles, F. H., and Shilli, T. O., Jr. Infantile hydrocephalus: retrocerebellar subdural hematoma. J. Pediat., 76:529, 1970.

Gurdjian, E. S., Lissner, J. R., and Patrick, L. M. Protection of the head and neck in sports. J.A.M.A., 182: 509, 1962.

Hanson, D. J. Intramuscular injection injuries and complications. Practitioner, 27:109, 1963.

Hawkes, C. O., and Ogle, W. S. Atypical features of epidural hematoma in infants, children and adolescents. J. Neurosurg., 19:971, 1962.

Haymaker, W., and Woodhall, B. Peripheral Nerve Injuries, 2nd ed. Philadelphia, W. B. Saunders Co., 1953.

Hjern, B., and Nylander, I. Acute head injuries in children. Acta Pediat. (Suppl.), 152, 1964.

Jacobziner, H., and Culbert, R. W. Non-fatal accidents in the school age child. Clin. Pediat., 2:484, 1963.

Jennett, W. B. Epilepsy After Blunt Head Injuries. Springfield, Ill., Charles C Thomas, Publ., 1962.

Kempe, C. H., Silverman, F. N., Steele, B. F., Droegemueller, W., and Silver, H. K. The battered child syndrome. J.A.M.A., 181:17, 1962.

Kozmin, P. J., Ritz, N. D., Moss, A. H., and Kaufman, A. Massive hemorrhage—Scalps of newborn infants. Amer. J. Dis. Child., 108:413, 1964.

Lende, R. A., and Erickson, T. C. Growing skull fractures of childhood. J. Neurosurg., 18:479, 1961.

Leventhal, H. R. Birth injuries to the spinal cord. J. Pediat., 56:447, 1960.

Lindsay, W. K., Walker, F. G., and Farmer, A. W. Traumatic peripheral nerve injuries in children: results of repair. Plast. Reconstr. Surg., 30:462, 1962.

Low, N. L., and Correll, J. W. Head pain due to leptomeningeal cysts. Brit. J. Surg., 53:971, 1966.

McLaughlin, H. L. Trauma. Philadelphia, W. B. Saunders Co., 1959.

McLaurin, R. L., King, L. R., Elam, E. B., and Budde, R. B. Metabolic responses to craniocerebral trauma. Surg. Gynec. Obstet., 110:282, 1960.

Mealey, J., Jr. Pediatric Head Injuries. Springfield, Ill., Charles C Thomas, Publ., 1968.

Monthly Vital Statistics Report. The U.S. Dept. Health, Education and Welfare, Vol. 19, No. 5, 1970.

Ommaya, A. K., Rockoff, S. D., and Baldwin, M. Experimental concussion—a first report. J. Neurosurg., 21: 249, 1964.

Rasmussen, J., and Gulati, D. R. Cortisone in the therapy of post-operative cerebral edema. J. Neurosurg., 19:535, 1962.

Rickham, P. P. Head injury in childhood. Helv. Chir. Acta, 28:560, 1961.

Selby, I. Skull fractures in infants. Acta Chir. Scand., 122:30, 1961.

Shulman, K., and Ransohoff, J. Subdural hematoma in children; the fate of children with retained membranes. J. Neurosurg., 18:175, 1961.

Tenner, M. S., and Stein, B. M. Cerebral herniation in the growing fracture of the skull. Radiology, 94:351, 1970.

Watkins, E. S., Stubbs, J. D., and Lewin, W. Urea in the management of head injuries. Lancet, 1:358, 1961.

Zimmerman, B. Effects of injury on electrolyte metabolism. J. Trauma, 3:141, 1963.

Zollinger, R. W., Creedon, P. J., and Sanguily, J., Jr. Trauma in children in a general hospital. Amer. J. Surg., 104:855, 1962.

15.9
PAROXYSMAL DISORDERS

DORA CHAO

Epilepsy

Epilepsy is as old as the human race. The early Greeks and then the Romans looked upon epilepsy as a sacred disease, a curse by some capricious gods. Although disputed by no less an authority than Hippocrates about 400 B.C., this misconception has persisted through the ages. Even today many epileptics and their families still suffer from social prejudices and feel the shame of a stigma. The period of scientific inquiry and social enlightenment began in the middle of the nineteenth century. The astute observations of Hughlings Jackson led him to theorize that fits were caused by occasional, excessive, and disorderly discharge in the cerebral gray matter. It was upon this fundamental premise that scientific studies have subsequently flourished in many directions, leading to the present-day understanding. The major advances have been:

1. The development of modern neurology, neuroanatomy, neuropathology, neuroradiology, especially knowledge of the functional anatomy of the brain.
2. The development of electroencephalography and its fruitful applications in clinical and experimental investigations.
3. The advance of drug therapy.
4. The development of surgical treatment of focal epilepsy and the knowledge gained therefrom.
5. The more recent development of neurochemistry, electron microscopy and electroneurophysiology have brought research on seizure mechanism to the cellular level.

While these developments opened up new vistas of knowledge, the clinician still has the age-old problem of adequate care and treatment of epileptic patients.

There is no accurate census of the incidence of epilepsy in the United States. One recent estimate places epilepsy at the head of a list of chronic disorders with 17 million active cases, or approximately 1 in every 100 individuals in the United States. In pediatric practice the problem of seizures is indeed a major one. About 5 in 100 children have had a seizure at one time or another in their lives, if only in association with fever; and the prevalence of bona fide epilepsy has been estimated to be 0.5 percent.

There is a brighter side of the picture, however. Overall, medical therapy of epilepsy with today's drugs and available service is about 50 to 60 percent effective. Increased understanding and acceptance by the public have also brought improvement in the social and economic outlook to the epileptic patient and his family. On this happy note the student of today may look forward to gratifying experiences in facing the challenge of the problems of the epileptic child.

DEFINITIONS. *Epilepsy.* The word *epilepsy* has its origin in Greek and means "to lay on" or "to seize." A *seizure* (an *attack*, a *fit*, a *spell*) is an episode of cerebral dysfunction produced by abnormal, excessive, neuronal discharge occurring in the brain which may be caused by a great variety of conditions. A seizure is therefore a symptom and not a disease. Its manifestations depend upon the location of the discharge and its spread. Thus, a seizure may manifest as a change in the state of consciousness, an abnormal sensory experience, disordered motor activities (tonic or clonic contractions), or disturbance of vegetative, intellectual, and behavioral functions. When seizures become recurrent, the condition is termed *epilepsy*.

Gibbs and Lennox defined epilepsy as a "paroxysmal cerebral dysrhythmia." They emphasized not only the abnormal rhythms but also their paroxysmal occurrence as the essential features of the epileptic dysfunction.

Convulsion. Convulsion implies generalized or widespread abnormal motor activity as a prominent component in an epileptic attack. Not all convulsions are epileptic in nature, and many types of epilepsy are without a convulsive element.

Prodrome. The prodrome consists of symptoms that appear hours or days before the onset of the actual seizure. For example, on the basis of past experience the family might recognize that the coming of a seizure is habitually heralded by the child becoming whiny, anorexic, and irritable.

Aura. Aura is the name given to the subjective sensations or experiences which habitually precede an epileptic attack and which are frequently recognized by the patient as immediate warning of an impending seizure. Physiologically, an aura is the beginning of the abnormal neuronal discharge and hence may be a helpful sign for localization of the epileptogenic focus.

Ictal. Ictus is derived from Latin and means a sudden attack. The adjective *ictal* means pertaining to an attack. *Preictal* and *postictal* refer to the time immediately before and shortly after a seizure; *interictal* refers to the interim period between attacks.

Classification

Until recently, four systems of classification were in general use: clinical, anatomic, electroencephalographic, and etiologic. This is inevitable because epilepsy is only a symptom of many disease conditions of diverse functional disturbances. It is recog-

TABLE 23. *Clinical Classification of Seizures*

Generalized convulsions (major motor)
  Tonic-clonic (grand mal)
  Tonic

Focal seizures
  Focal motor
  Focal sensory
  Frontal adversive
  Occipital
  Inhibitory
  Temporal lobe

Petit mal

Minor Motor
  Akinetic
  Myoclonic
  Infantile spasms

Psychomotor epilepsy

Autonomic epilepsy (convulsive equivalent seizures)

Miscellaneous

nized that by using them all in a given case, a broader understanding of the patient's ailment may be gained. Indeed, it was based upon this viewpoint that a new classification combining clinical seizure type, electroencephalographic expression, anatomic substrate, etiology, and age was proposed by the Vienna Congress, International League Against Epilepsy. The reader should consult the original publication for complete information; the reference is given in the bibliography.

1. CLINICAL CLASSIFICATION. This oldest and most widely used system is purely descriptive of the clinical features of the seizures. Some of the terms are apt because the pattern of attack is simple, for example, lapse or absence, akinetic or drop seizure, and massive myoclonic (jackknife) spasms. Some other terms are more ambiguous and require further definition because the seizure patterns are complex and cannot be characterized by a simple descriptive term or phrase; for example, minor motor seizure is a misnomer because the adjective "minor" gives a false implication in relation to the severity of the symptoms and the usually grave prognosis. These criticisms notwithstanding, classification by seizure pattern is meaningful and useful when used in correlation with other systems of classification. The major seizure types are listed in Table 23.

2. ANATOMIC CLASSIFICATION. Hughlings Jackson was the first epileptologist to attempt an anatomic classification when he used such terms as "uncinate fits" and "rhinencephalis seizures." This concept of focal origination of seizure discharge has led to extensive studies of functional anatomy of the brain. The advent of electroencephalography including cortical and depth electrography and the advancement of surgical treatment of focal epilepsies have extended such anatomic studies directly to the epileptogenic human brain in the modern operating theater. To the neurosurgeons it is not only logical and desirable but absolutely necessary to classify seizure symptoms on an anatomic basis. Inevitably the anatomic terms have become more or less identified with certain clinical epilepsies, for example:

Centrencephalic seizures: Grand mal epilepsy
                             Petit mal epilepsy
Diencephalic epilepsy   Convulsive equivalent
   (thalamic-   syndrome
   hypothalamic):   (autonomic epilepsy)
Focal cortical seizures
   Temporal lobe epilepsy: Psychomotor epilepsy
   Frontal lobe epilepsy: Adversive seizures,
                                Jacksonian epilepsy
   Parietal lobe epilepsy: Focal sensory seizures
   Occipital lobe epilepsy: Visual sensations

It should be noted that the anatomic system is still far from perfect or complete, and some anatomic designations, e.g., "temporal lobe," require additional definition (see psychomotor epilepsy). To the clinician the anatomic classification is an essential element in diagnosis.

3. ELECTROENCEPHALOGRAPHIC CLASSIFICATION.

The electroencephalogram provides a pictorial record of cerebral activity reflected at the cortex in electrical terms. In the course of its clinical application many specific patterns have been found to correlate with various clinical types of epilepsy with varying degrees of concordance. Some of the well-known examples of electroencephalographic patterns follow.

a. *Three per second spike and wave dysrhythmia* is the classic electroencephalographic abnormality found in genetic epilepsy of the pure lapse or petit mal attack. However, it also occurs in patients who may have grand mal attacks only, or both types of attack (Fig. 64).

b. *Paroxysmal polyspike and wave dysrhythmia* is closely correlated with myoclonic jerks (Fig. 65).

c. *Paroxysmal or continuous slow spike and slow wave dysrhythmia* is generally associated with diffuse encephalopathy of known or unknown etiology. The seizures are chiefly akinetic or myoclonic with or without generalized convulsion. The EEG pattern was referred to as "petit mal variant" by Lennox and the clinical picture has borne such names as minor motor seizures, atypical petit mal, myokinetic epilepsy, and the Lennox syndrome (Fig. 66).

d. *Hypsarhythmia* is a continuously abnormal electroencephalographic pattern characterized by high-voltage, poorly organized, slow and sharp wave activity mixed with bursts of irregular spikes and polyspikes and wave activity showing poor interhemispheric correlation. It is found in 90 percent of children with massive myoclonic spasms (Fig. 67).

e. *The 14 and 6 per second positive spike dysrhythmia* (Fig. 68) occurring in drowse or light sleep was believed to arise from diencephalic nuclei and/or limbic system, and is often found in children with seizure equivalent. More recently several investigators have observed it in 15 to 55 percent of apparently "normal school children" with a peak age incidence at 12 years. Although these observations appear to suggest an age and maturation dependence, and to have raised doubt regarding its pathologic significance, its frequent concordance (with or without other EEG abnormalities) with vegetative dysfunctions, posttraumatic, postbreath-holding, choreic and migraine syndromes remains an intriguing finding.

f. *Focal (or multifocal) discharges* may arise from epileptogenic focus (or foci) in the cerebral cortex or subcortical centers. The clinical seizure symptoms are dependent upon the functional attributes at the site of discharge and the manner of spread. Focal seizures may escalate into generalized convulsions. The so-called temporal lobe is the most common site of epileptogenic discharge (Fig. 69). Sometimes a primary lesion located elsewhere may remotely activate the temporal regions. The concordance between temporal lobe focus and psychomotor epilepsy is about 60 percent.

On the basis of correlative studies, certain electroencephalographic terms have frequently been used interchangeably with clinical terminology. This practice is not justified because the correlation is rarely perfect. For the clinician, the electroencephalogram is an invaluable tool in diagnosis, but it is unwise to dogmatically equate a certain electrographic pattern with a specific clinical seizure type.

4. ETIOLOGIC CLASSIFICATION.

The epilepsies may be divided into two general etiologic groups: genetic and symptomatic. The genetic epilepsies are characterized by the absence of a demonstrable structural lesion of the brain, the tendency to spontaneous cerebral dysrhythmia being genetically inherited. In contrast, the symptomatic epilepsies are associated with metabolic disorders or organic pathology of the brain acquired through developmental error, injury, or disease. In some cases symptomatic and genetic epilepsy may occur concomitantly.

a. Genetic Epilepsy. The etiologic role of heredity, first implicated by Hippocrates, has been established by extensive studies of epileptic families and relatives. Both Conrad and Lennox found that when epilepsy occurred in monozygous twins, both twins were affected in about 85 percent, whereas in dizygous twins, both were affected in only 3 percent and 15.9 percent of their cases, respectively. EEG studies of the epileptic families led Lennox and Gibbs to suggest that cerebral dysrhythmia underlying epileptic diathesis was inherited as a mendelian dominant factor. These observations were confirmed by the studies of Metrakos and Metrakos, who demonstrated further that the EEG trait and the clinical seizure of genetic epilepsy manifest themselves with greatest frequency between the ages of 5 and 12 years. The seizure manifestation is either generalized convulsion, pure petit mal, or a combination of the two, often with myoclonic components. In 4 to 8 percent of epileptics a hereditary factor seems involved. Even when there is no overt epilepsy, a low

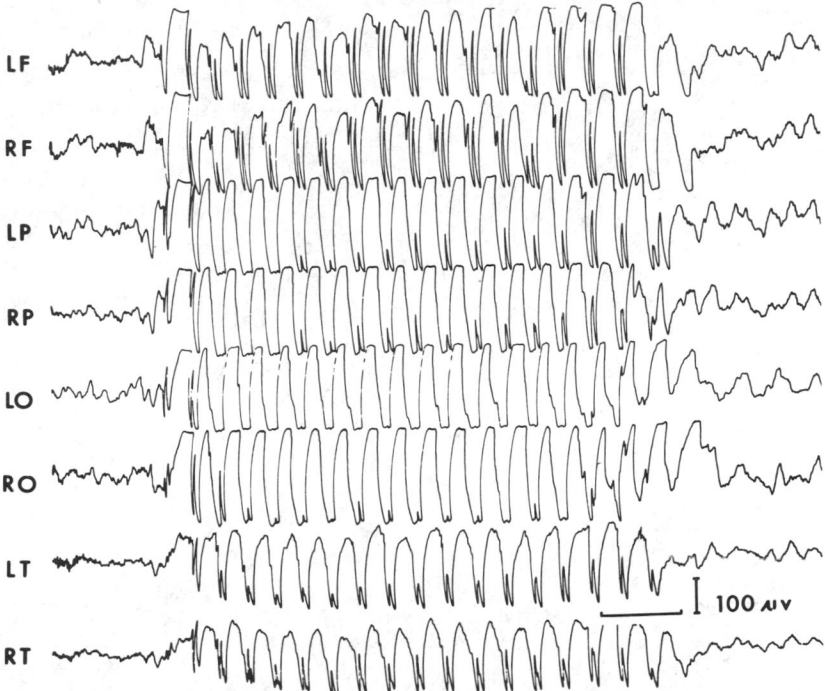

Fig. 64.   Three per second spike and wave dysrhythmia.

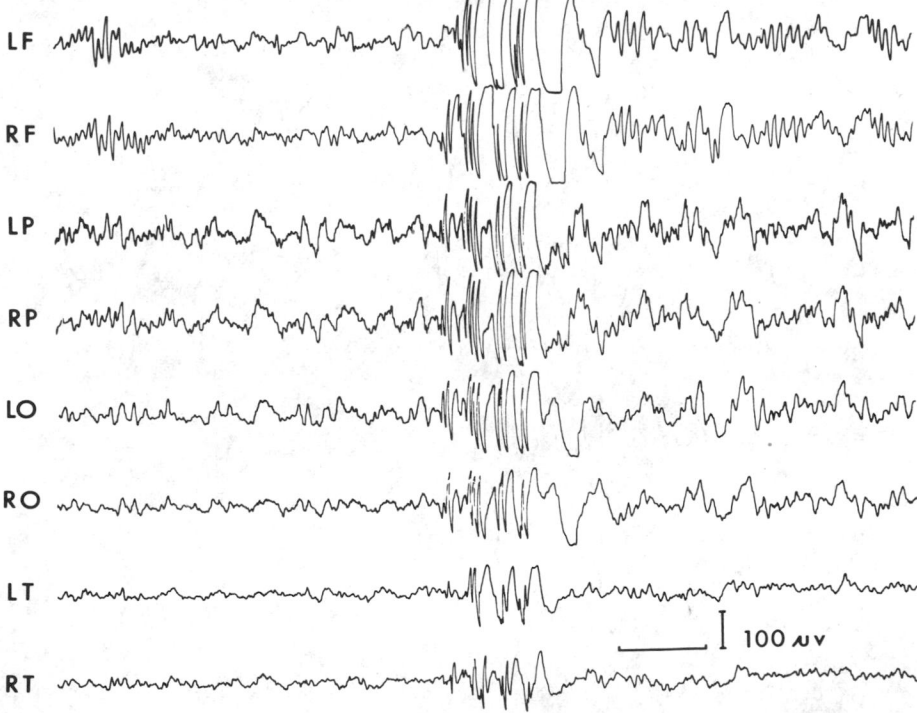

Fig. 65.   Paroxysmal polyspike and wave dysrhythmia.

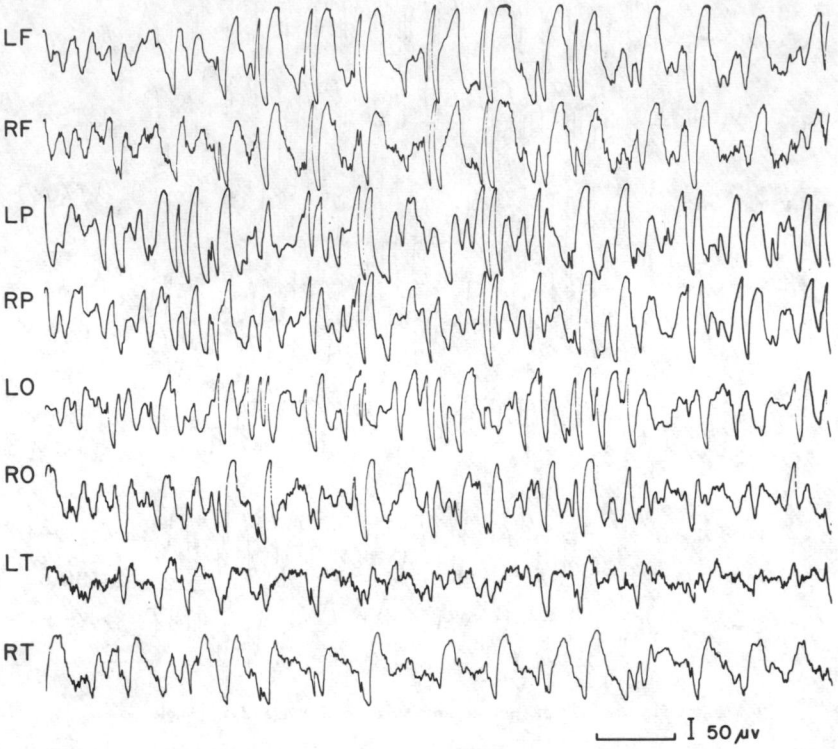

Fig. 66. Generalized slow spike and wave dysrhythmia.

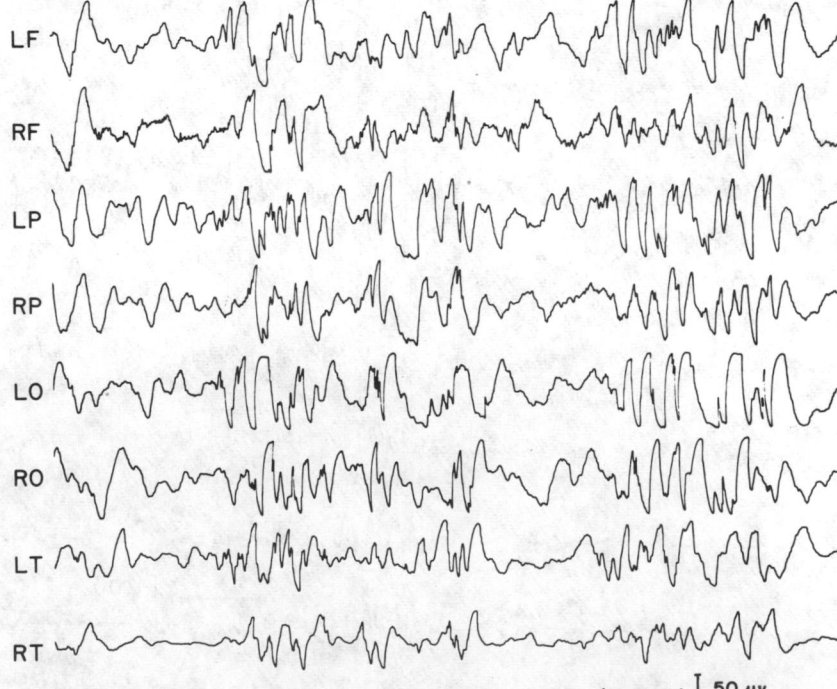

Fig. 67. Hypsarhythmia.

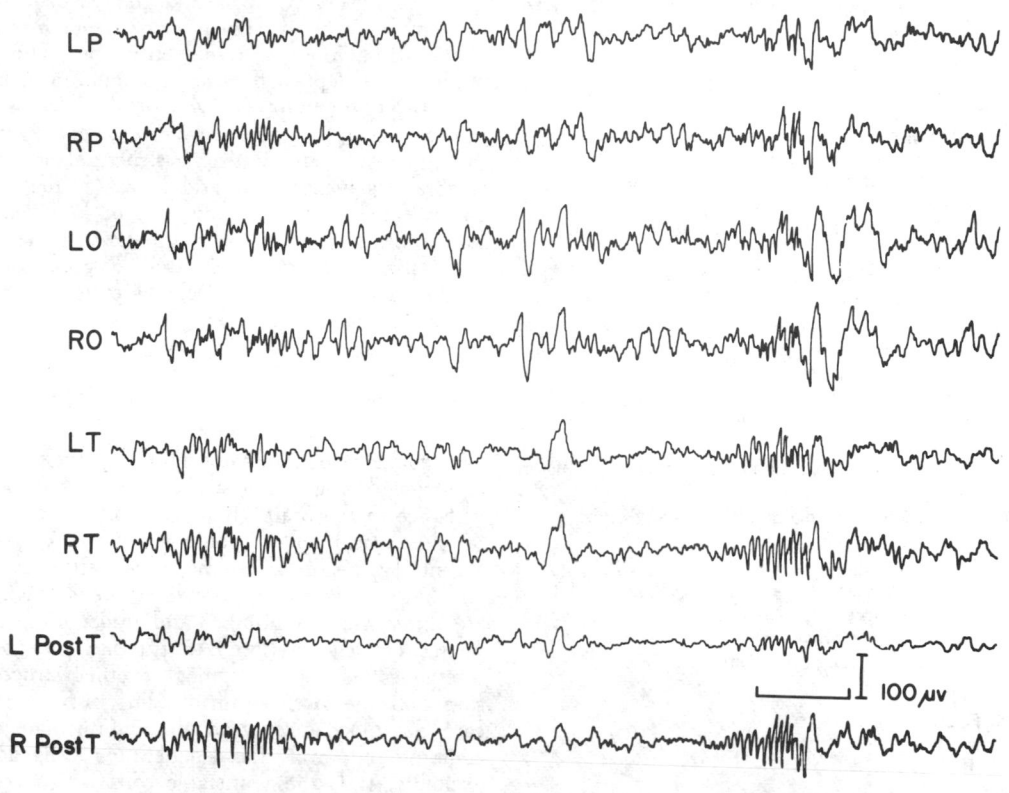

LP

RP

LO

RO

LT

RT

L Post T

100 μv

R Post T

Fig. 68. Fourteen and six per second positive spike dysrhythmia.

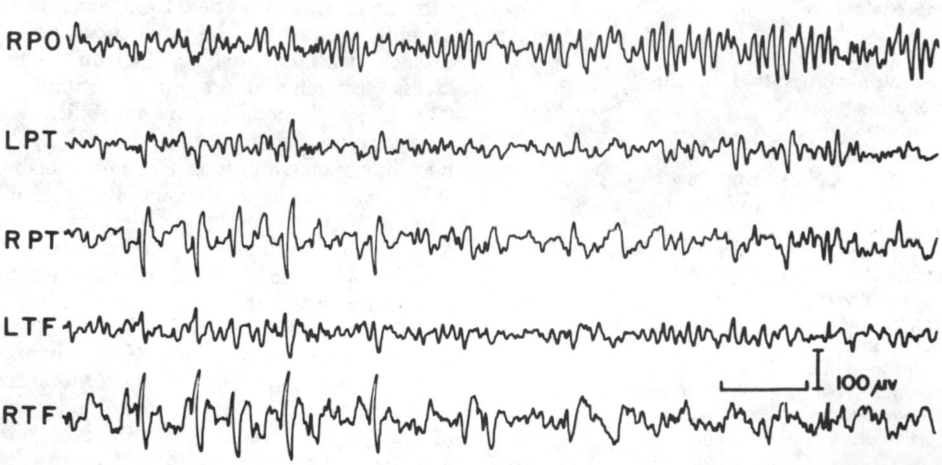

LFP

RFP

LPO

RPO

LPT

RPT

LTF

100 μv

RTF

Fig. 69. Temporal spike focus.

TABLE 24.   *Etiologic Factors Associated with Epilepsy*

Prenatal Factors
  Genetic
    Genetic epilepsy
    Inborn errors of metabolism
      Carbohydrate: glycogen storage disease, hypoglycemia
      Protein: phenylketonuria, maple syrup urine disease
      Fat: cerebral lipidoses, leucodystrophies
    Heredofamilial diseases: myoclonus epilepsy
  Congenital structural anomalies
    Porencephaly
    Vascular malformations
    Neurocutaneous syndrome
    Developmental defects of the brain
  Fetal infections
    Viral encephalopathy: rubella, cytomegalic inclusion disease
    Protozoan meningoencephalitis: toxoplasmosis
  Maternal diseases
    Toxemia of pregnancy
    Chronic renal disease
    Diabetes mellitus
    Radiation during pregnancy
    Drug usage and drug intoxication
    Trauma

Perinatal Factors
  Trauma
  Hypoxia
  Jaundice
  Infection
  Prematurity
  Drug withdrawal

Postnatal Factors
  Primary infection of central nervous system
  Infectious diseases of childhood with encephalopathy (e.g., measles, mumps)
  Head trauma
  Circulatory diseases
    Vascular anomalies
    Occlusive diseases: arterial, venous
    Hemorrhage
    Hypertensive encephalopathy
  Toxic encephalopathy
    Thallium
    Lead
    Convulsogenic drugs: INH, steroids
  Allergic encephalopathy
    Immunization reactions
    Drug reactions
  Physical and metabolic encephalopathies
    Fever and febrile convulsions
    Anoxia and hypoxia
    Prolonged convulsions with cyanosis
    Electrolyte disturbance
    Acute porphyria
    Hypoglycemia
    Hypocalcemia
    Hypomagnesemia
    Hypo- and hypernatremia and others
    Pyridoxin deficiency or dependency
  Degenerative diseases of the brain
  Tumors

seizure threshold may be evidenced by paroxysmal spike-and-waves or polyspike-and-waves occurring spontaneously or by activation of sleep, intermittent photic stimulation, or hyperventilation. The risk of producing epileptic offspring is about 2 to 4 percent.

b. Symptomatic or Acquired Epilepsy. The causes of symptomatic epilepsies are very diverse; but the end results are similar: a structural or metabolic cerebral lesion develops and serves as the focus of epileptogenesis. This process may be localized or diffuse, static or progressive, traumatic or inflammatory, neoplastic or degenerative, vascular or allergic. Some of the more common etiologic factors are listed in Table 24.

Pathogenesis

The common denominator in the pathology of epileptogenic diseases is a structural or a metabolic disturbance in the brain giving rise to seizure discharge.

A typical epileptogenic cortical scar consists of a central zone, in which no nerve cells survive, and an intermediate zone, in which the surviving cells are diminished in number and undergoing different phases of degeneration. An intermediate zone also intervenes between a tumor or other structural lesion and the normal surrounding tissue. In either case the blood supply to the intermediate zone is compromised, and the degenerating cells are more excitable. It is these unstable cells which constitute the epileptogenic focus.

Regardless of etiology and pathology of the cerebral lesions, the pathophysiology of seizure discharge may be identical. The basic mechanism appears to be prolonged depolarization with consequent hyperactive and hypersynchronous discharge from abnormal neurons. Such epileptic discharge may be circumscribed or may spread, and thus activate distant neurons, causing them to become secondarily or in some instances independently epileptogenic.

The biochemical basis of epileptic discharge remains incompletely understood. Experimental studies with epileptogenic cortex from animals and human patients suggest that the production and maintenance of such discharge involves (1) an accumulation of excess acetylcholine or other excitatory substance, (2) increased membrane permeability with increase in intracellular sodium ions, and (3) depletion of intracellular potassium ions. Systemic metabolic disturbances, such as hypoglycemia, hypocalcemia, anoxia, hypocapnia, and pyridoxin deficiency, are believed to exert their influence upon these basic factors and may become secondarily responsible for initiation of the epileptogenic discharge.

TRIGGERING MECHANISM. By and large epileptic attacks appear suddenly and fortuitously without any apparent immediate cause. On the other hand, many seizures do seem to occur under the influence of a triggering factor. The onset of these seizures may be cyclic and thus suggest a periodically recurring triggering mechanism, or provoked in an erratic manner. In the cyclic group the hormonal factors related to menstrual period, menarche, and menopause are conspicuous examples. In the induced seizures the provoking agents encompass a diversity of factors and mechanisms. These may be divided into nonsensory and sensory. Among the nonsensory group are hyperthermia, hyperventilation, metalobic disorders, physical stress, sleep deprivation, emotional disturbances, and so forth. The sensory triggers may be visual (e.g., photogenic, television, reading), auditory (musicogenic), vegetative, tactile, and proprioceptive; they may be spontaneous normal sensory stimuli of daily life or unexpected sensory experiences (startle reaction), and at times self-induced. Of the last group, the so-called startle epilepsy in brain-damaged children with or without cerebral palsy is an example. In these children hyperexcitable brainstem structures provide the pathologic substrate for escalation of normal startle reactions to epileptic seizures.

AGE FACTOR. Age and epilepsy are related in many ways. It is well known that epilepsy is much more common in children than in adults. In genetic epilepsy the appearance and disappearance of the clinical seizures and the electrical dysrhythmia are age dependent. Thus, pure petit mal attacks and the 3 per second EEG pattern have a peak incidence between 4 and 10 years and tend to disappear by the end of adolescence.

Seizures that occur before 2 years of age suggest a metabolic disorder or an underlying structural defect of the brain. Newborn infants are more likely to have poorly organized movements, such as twitching, trembling, or shaking, rather than a bona fide tonic-clonic convulsion. They often have apneic or blue spells, limp or stiff spells, vasomotor changes with flushing, pallor, and clamminess. Such seizure discharges probably originate mostly in subcortical structures; as the cortex develops, more differentiated types of seizure patterns become evident.

Seventy-five percent of structural growth of the brain occurs in the first 2 years of life. Generally speaking, the younger the child and the more immature the brain, the more susceptible it is to injury, and the more far-reaching the resultant functional disorganization.

Seizure Types

GENERALIZED CONVULSIONS. Generalized convulsions constitute the most common type of seizure in childhood. In the genetic type of epilepsy the seizure discharge is believed to originate in centrencephalic structures and to spread rapidly to both cerebral hemispheres with immediate loss of consciousness and generalized convulsions. As a rule, there is no aura preceding the onset and no localizing neurologic sign following the attack. In contrast, the symptomatic type may be associated with an aura and/or a postictal phenomenon that suggest a focal origin of the generalized seizure. With the rapid spread of the seizure discharge from the epileptogenic focus, the memory of the aura may be obscured. This is especially true in children.

The classical grand mal attack is usually precipitous in onset. Typically, the eyes roll up or to one side, the pupils dilate, and the face becomes flushed or pale. Consciousness is quickly lost, and the entire body is seized by a tonic spasm. There is often a sharp cry, and if standing, the child falls heavily to the ground. With the tonic spasm respiration is arrested and the child becomes cyanotic. After a period of 10 to 30 seconds, the tonic phase gives way to generalized clonic jerking lasting from 1 to 5 minutes or longer. Breathing is resumed but labored. There may be profuse perspiration and salivation, involuntary bladder and bowel evacuation, and the tongue may be bitten. Gradually the attack diminishes in severity; the muscle contractions become less violent and finally cease. If the duration of the attack is short, the child may recover his senses quickly and show little or no after effect. More commonly, however, he remains stuporous and sinks into postictal sleep lasting an hour or more. When he awakens, he may have headache, generalized fatigue, and restlessness for a variable duration. Postictally, transient neurologic deficits may be present, and these sometimes may be of significance in the diagnosis of a focal lesion.

Status Epilepticus. Grand mal seizures may occur in series without consciousness being regained between attacks. This condition is known as "status epilepticus." It may be induced by sudden withdrawal of anticonvulsant medication, incident to intercurrent infection, or without known cause. If not treated promptly and effectively, the status may persist for many hours or days with development of serious sequelae or even death. Transient postictal signs and symptoms include aphasia, ataxia, and mental sluggishness. Persistent symptoms and signs may develop indicating that irreversible brain damage has occurred as a result of prolonged cellular hypoxia. Status epilepticus should therefore be treated as a medical emergency.

Tonic Seizures. This is a type of seizure in which the patient's body stiffens, with increased tonicity of the entire musculature, and consciousness is lost. Such attacks arise when the midbrain is primarily involved in the seizure discharge.

FOCAL SEIZURES. When the initial event of a seizure consistently indicates a local origin in some part of the brain, it is focal epilepsy. The epileptic discharge may originate at any level of the nervous system. It may remain localized or spread across the midline to the opposite side and become generalized. Focal discharging lesions may be transient in young children. The significance of focal seizures in the young child is not the same as in older children or adults. Not infrequently the focal attack may vary from side to side, giving rise to multifocal epilepsy.

Focal Motor Seizures. These may manifest as involvement of one entire side of the body simultaneously (hemiconvulsion), or be limited to one extremity and/or the face. Jacksonian epilepsy is one which originates in one part of the motor cortex and spreads to involve the rest of the motor strip. The common points of onset are the thumb, the face, and the toe—structures having relatively large cortical representation. The orderly spread of the electrical discharge is reflected in the classical "march" which was described by Jackson 100 years ago. Jacksonian seizures frequently escalate into grand mal attacks. Following a seizure there may be transient paresis or paralysis lasting minutes or hours. This phenomenon, known as Todd's paralysis, is believed to result from a localized neuronal exhaustion. When Todd's paralysis becomes progressively longer in duration, or when the weakness persists during the interictal periods, one should suspect a progressive lesion. *Epilepsia partialis continua* refers to local convulsive movements of a continuous type, when a discharge maintains itself at a certain point continually.

Focal Sensory Seizures (somatic sensory seizures). Numbness and tingling are the usual sensations in seizures arising from the sensory cortex. The abnormal sensations may also proceed in a "march" and at times spread to the motor area with resultant motor seizures.

Focal Adversive Seizures. These attacks consist of turning of the head, eyes, and trunk away from the side of the cerebral lesion, with loss of consciousness. The seizure discharge is generally located in the prefrontal area, but other areas such as the occipital and temporal cortex may give rise to such attacks.

Occipital Seizures. Seizure discharges in the visual cortical areas produce simple visual impressions, such as dimness of vision, seeing shadows and clouds in front of the eyes, or a transient blindness.

Inhibitory Seizures (ictal paralysis). The epileptic discharge, even from the motor areas may produce inactivation or paralysis instead of excitation or motor activity. Such attacks are called inhibitory seizures.

Temporal Lobe (Psychomotor) Epilepsy and Diencephalic (Convulsive Equivalent) Epilepsy. These are the most common types of seizures of focal origin in childhood. They will be discussed separately.

PETIT MAL. In its "pure" form, absence or lapse attacks are characterized by episodes of abrupt, momentary loss of consciousness accompanied by cessation of voluntary activities. The child has a blank expression and stares into space (Fig. 70). The duration of each attack rarely exceeds 5 to 15 seconds. Just as abruptly, the child recovers his senses and resumes his activity as if no interruption had occurred. Typically, there is no aura and no postictal disturbance.

In 60 to 70 percent of patients, myoclonic jerks may occur. The common forms are slow rhythmic blinking of the eyes and rhythmic jerking of the

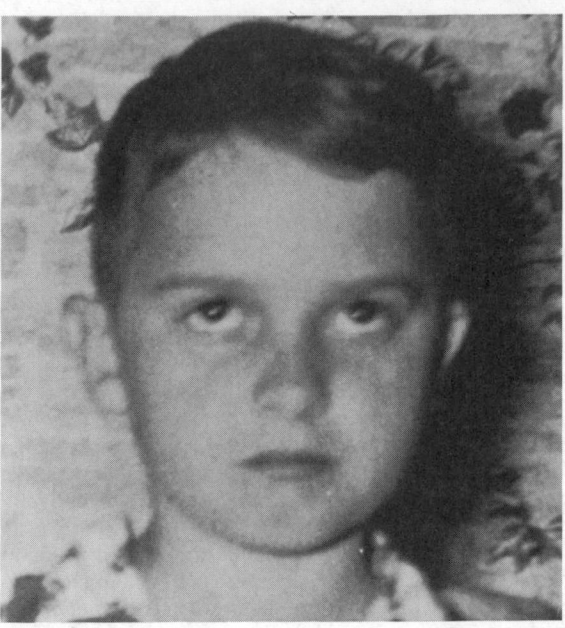

Fig. 70.   A 10-year-old having an absence attack.

head, arms, or trunk. The child rarely falls or loses bladder control. While having a petit mal attack, some children may perform semipurposeful motor acts such as snapping of the fingers, patting movement, or walking around or in circles. These have been termed *"petit mal automatism."*

The frequency of absence attacks varies widely, from occasional to hundreds a day. Attentiveness in work or play diminishes the number of attacks; idleness, fatigue, excessive hydration, emotional stress, menstruation, overventilation, and photic stimulation tend to increase the frequency.

When attacks occur in close succession for a prolonged period of time, mental function is continually impaired and the child remains dazed and confused. The sudden obtunding of mental function may lead to a false impression of degenerative or toxic encephalopathy. This is known as *"petit mal status"* (Fig. 71). It may be ushered in by a febrile illness, an emotional upset, menstrual period, or occur without obvious cause. The occurrence of petit mal status seldom affects the ultimate prognosis.

The age of onset of pure petit mal epilepsy is usually between 4 and 10 years. The incidence is slightly higher in girls than in boys (6:4). The child's physical and mental development is usually unaffected, and the neurologic findings are entirely normal. The attacks tend to decrease with time and approximately 50 percent completely disappear in the late teens; they may however, persist into adult life.

About one-third to one-half of patients with petit mal may develop grand mal seizures. In these, the petit mal seizures usually make their appearance first.

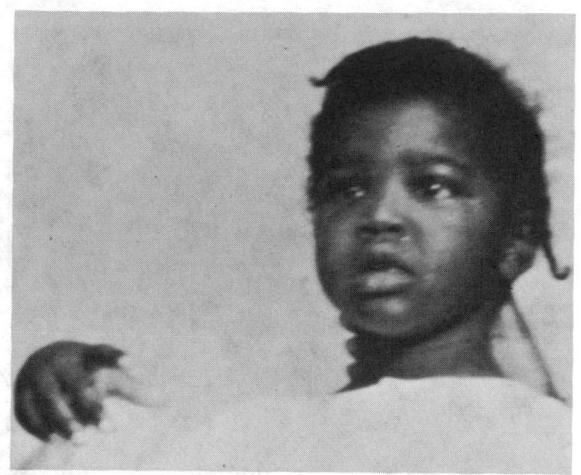

Fig. 71. A 4-year-old in petit mal status. Note obtund appearance and myoclonic jerk of hand.

The EEG abnormality of absence attacks is characteristic. Bursts of generalized bilaterally synchronous 3 per second spike and wave complexes appear, usually against a background of normal activity. Short bursts of such activity may not be accompanied by an overt clinical seizure, but may be associated with subtle impairment of mental efficiency. Bursts lasting longer than 5 seconds are often accompanied by clinical attacks.

MINOR MOTOR SEIZURES. *Akinetic Attacks.* Akinetic attacks are also known as drop fits. Postural tone is controlled by a balanced discharge of facilitatory and inhibitory impulses from the reticular formation in the upper brainstem. Drop seizures are believed to result from a sudden increase of inhibitory discharges which transiently overwhelms the influence of the facilitatory center and leads to sudden loss of postural tone.

The muscles involved may be limited to the neck, giving rise to head bobbing, or more generally resulting in collapse of the body. The attacks are so abrupt and unexpected that the patient and parents are caught unprepared, and significant injury may result.

Although akinetic attacks have been seen in genetic petit mal epilepsy, the majority of such attacks occur in patients with symptomatic epilepsy.

Akinetic attacks of symptomatic origin are by far the more common type. The children affected are much younger than the genetic group. The nodding seizures appear when the infant is able to assume sitting position, and the drop seizures occur when the child is able to get about. The frequency may be as high as several hundred seizures a day. Severe physical injuries are common, and there is a constant danger to life. The cause is frequently unknown; but in many cases the history may strongly implicate diffuse encephalopathy incident to past infections due to measles, other viral agents, immunization antigens, toxins, residua from tuberculous meningitis or tuberous sclerosis.

The EEG may show continuous runs of generalized slow spike and 1½ to 2 per second slow waves.

Various degrees of brain damage as evidenced by mental retardation and neurologic abnormalities —such as a Babinski sign, unequal deep tendon reflexes, abnormal muscle tone, apraxia, and incoordination—are frequently present.

As a rule the course is protracted, the seizures subsiding slowly and the EEG reverting gradually to a slow dysrhythmia. The child may become a slow learner or frankly retarded.

Myoclonic Epilepsies. Myoclonus is a phenomenon of clonic spasms of an isolated muscle or groups of muscles. Neither term necessarily implies epilepsy, although in some epileptic disorders myoclonus is a prominent symptom. Physiologically, myoclonus is believed to occur because of sudden release from inhibitory control of motor centers in the midbrain, the brainstem, or the spinal cord. The "uninhibited" discharge from these centers may spread to high structures, which may influence the myoclonus but are not essential in its occurrence. A variety of pathologic conditions may produce myoclonus, particularly those with diffuse involvement of the brain.

Clinically, *myoclonic seizures* may occur in genetic epilepsies in association with petit mal or grand mal attacks. More severe myoclonic seizures are not uncommon in symptomatic epilepsies incident to nonprogressive and progressive diffuse encephalopathies. That these myoclonic phenomena are epileptic in nature is attested to by the presence of cerebral dysrhythmia. The various types are:

1. *Myoclonic Seizures in Genetic Epilepsies.* Slow rhythmic jerks of the eyelids, the neck, or the arms are seen in 60 to 70 percent of children with absence attacks. These jerks do not alter the course or prognosis of the pure petit mal epilepsy. The EEG is that of the absence pattern.

Some patients with genetic epilepsy may have mixed seizures of myoclonic and grand mal attacks. The myoclonic seizures usually antedate the grand mal attacks by months or years. They tend to come on in the morning, causing the child to fall or to drop things without alteration of consciousness. Sometimes the parents may mistake these episodes for mere carelessness or teen-age clumsiness, only to realize their true nature when a long train of myoclonic jerks merges into grand mal attacks. The EEG may reveal paroxysmal multiple spike, slow wave, with normal background activity.

2. *Myoclonic Seizures in Nonprogressive Diffuse Encephalopathies.* The incidence in this group is highest between 2 and 6 years. Although the cause is often unknown, symptoms and signs of brain damage are almost always present, and a past history of undiagnosed infection or reaction to immunization may be obtained. Sometimes a history of childhood

infectious disease among the siblings may be a significant clue that the patient might have had a subclinical infection by the same etiologic agent. The myoclonus may occur alone or in association with akinetic attacks or grand mal seizures. In some cases the myoclonus may be no more than a shudder or quick jerks of the eyes, which may be unnoticed by the parents. In other cases the myoclonus may be more gross and more widespread. The jerks are usually arrhythmic. The EEG frequently shows generalized multiple spike and slow wave dysrhythmia. The course may be protracted with gradual improvement and subsidence of seizures in two or more years. Some degree of mental subnormality and residual neurologic deficit is quite common.

3. *Myoclonic Seizures in Progressive Diffuse Encephalopathies.* Severe or moderate myoclonus is a prominent feature in the middle stages of subacute sclerosing panencephalitis (inclusion body encephalitis, Dawson) and in neuronal storage diseases. The myoclonic attacks are usually diffuse in nature. The EEG may show periodic succession of high-voltage complexes which are synchronous in all leads with the myoclonic jerks. Treatment is ineffective. The underlying disease runs a protracted course with uniformly bad prognosis.

4. *Familial Myoclonus Epilepsy of Unverricht.* This is a relatively rare heredofamilial degenerative disease first described by Unverricht in 1891 and later by Lundborg. The onset occurs in childhood or at puberty and is marked by increasingly severe, arrhythmic myoclonic attacks involving chiefly the trunk and limb muscles. As the disease progresses, dementia, ataxia, and spasticity appear, and the myoclonus tends to diminish and disappear with the onset of generalized rigidity. Bulbar palsy and deepening stupor lead to death in 10 to 20 years. Pathologically, Lafora bodies having acid mucopolysaccharide reaction have been demonstrated in the ganglion cells of cerebellar and subcortical nuclei in many reported cases.

Massive Myoclonic Spasms. Massive myoclonic spasms (infantile spasms, massive spasms, lightning seizures, jackknife seizures) are types of seizures peculiar to infants and occur in diffuse encephalopathies of disparate causes. The seizures may first occur in apparently normal infants or in infants obviously defective since birth. The cause is unknown in about one-half of the cases. In the remainder, a history of cerebral insult occurring during gestation, birth, or infancy may be obtained. The nature of the cerebral insult may be a developmental anomaly, intrauterine factors of placental and maternal origin, birth trauma, anoxia, phenylketonuria, tuberous sclerosis, postnatal head injury, meningoencephalitis of bacterial or viral origin, and toxic or allergic encephalopathies. More recently there has been a growing belief that the basic disturbance responsible for epileptogenesis may be biochemical rather than structural, although its exact nature remains to be elucidated.

Massive myoclonic spasms are not an uncommon

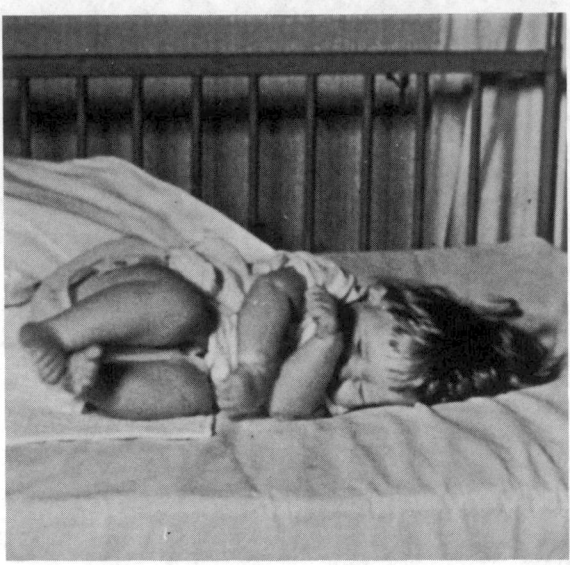

Fig. 72. A 6-month-old infant having a jackknife or flexor type of massive myoclonic spasms.

infantile epilepsy, second in incidence only to grand mal seizures. The peak incidence is between 3 and 6 months, although it has appeared as early as one day after birth; onset after the age of 2 years is uncommon. There is no significant difference in sex incidence.

The attacks may occur singly, but more often in series of successive episodes. Each attack is characterized by sudden, forceful myoclonic contractions involving the musculature of the trunk, the neck, and the extremities. In the flexor type, the patient adducts and flexes his limbs, drops his head, and doubles upon himself, much like closing a jackknife (Fig. 72). In the extensor type, the neck is extended, the arms spread out, and the body is bent backward in a manner aptly described as spreadeagle. A cry or grunt may accompany the more severe attacks. The infant may grimace or laugh, or appear fearful during or after the attack.

Individual attacks are momentary in duration, never exceeding one minute. The frequency varies from a few attacks to hundreds a day.

In 90 percent of the cases, the EEG shows a characteristic pattern known as hypsarhythmia; the severity of the electrical disturbance generally correlates with the severity of the clinical seizures.

The natural course of massive myoclonic spasms is protracted. After a period of months or years, the spasms may gradually diminish in frequency and severity and then cease. Occasionally they give way to focal seizures, grand mal seizures, or minor motor seizures. The sequelae of brain damage are permanent. With the onset of the seizures, development is arrested or regresses. As the attacks persist, mentality and motor functions continue to deteriorate. Ultimately 10 to 15 percent of the children succumb; of the surviving, more than 90 percent are mentally retarded.

PSYCHOMOTOR EPILEPSY. Psychomotor epilepsy is common in childhood; the incidence is highest between 3 and 6 years and becomes much lower after the age of 12 years. There is a slight preponderance of boys over girls. The seizure discharge usually originates in the "temporal lobe," which comprises the gray matter of the Sylvian fissure, the insula, the uncus, the amygdala, and the hippocampus, in addition to the three lateral temporal convultions. In the author's series of 250 cases, a temporal EEG focus was found in 60 percent in routine studies. Atrophic lesions due to birth injury, postnatal trauma, febrile convulsions in infancy, and thrombotic and infectious meningoencephalopathies are far more common than expanding lesions.

Prodromal symptoms of irritability or gastric upset may precede the onset of a seizure by hours or days. Sleep is a common precipitant. An aura of fear, gastric sensation, buzzing in the ear, or bad odor may usher in the attack. An infant who cannot express himself may hold up his hands to his ears or to the epigastrium with a facial expression of fear, pain, or alarm. The seizures are characteristically of brief duration, lasting from half a minute to 5 to 10 minutes. Consciousness is often impaired but rarely completely lost. The most common motor symptoms are drawing or jerking of the mouth and face, usually opposite to the side of the discharge. Aphasia or dysphasia may be present if the discharge originates from the dominant side. The eyes may stare in a searching manner. There may be tonic posturing or a desire to urinate. Coordinated but inappropriate movements may be performed repeatedly in a stereotyped manner (automatism), common examples being clutching, fumbling, kicking, walking or running in circles, swallowing, smacking, chewing, licking, and spitting. Pill-rolling, athetoid, or flinging movements are less common. Inhibitory seizures with loss of tone (limpness) or arrest of motion (freezing) may occur. Affective expressions such as laughing or crying are not unusual. Psychical symptoms such as forced thinking, rage, illusions, or hallucinations are rare in children. Chronic behavior disorder may be present. When the attack is over, there may or may not be postictal sluggishness or sleep. Amnesia of the attack is the rule.

AUTONOMIC EPILEPSY OR SEIZURE EQUIVALENT SYNDROME. This syndrome may be defined as an entity of epilepsy characterized by paroxysmal attacks of autonomic disturbances with or without associated seizures of other types and with or without disorders of other cerebral functions. The syndrome occurs in children of all ages with peak incidence at 6 to 7 years. Boys predominate by a 2:1 ratio. A history of birth injury, postnatal head trauma, encephalopathies, or prenatal injury, in the order named, may be elicited in 40 to 50 percent of the children. A family history of epilepsy is present in 20 to 30 percent of the patients.

The most common symptoms are headache and abdominal pain. The headache may be severe or mild, diffuse or ill-defined, and almost never hemicranial. The abdominal pain, which also varies in severity and may be accompanied by nausea, vomiting, and other visceral symptoms, has been diagnosed as an acute surgical emergency, leading to unnecessary laparotomy. Unexplained diarrhea may suddenly appear. Profuse salivation, thermal disturbances, and various vasomotor symptoms may be observed. Unexplained fits of rage or uncontrollable laughter have been reported. Syncopal episodes and sudden collapse with complete limpness may alarm the parents. The seizures generally last for minutes and rarely hours.

Not all of the above symptoms are observed in all the patients, but more than three symptoms should be present in recurrent attacks before such a diagnosis can be considered. Overexertion, anxiety, and sleep are the usual precipitants.

Nearly half of the children may have other types of epilepsy; psychomotor seizures, grand mal, and limp attacks are the commonest. Penfield described attacks of the above symptoms in a patient with a tumor in the third ventricle and suggested the term diencephalic autonomic epilepsy. Gibbs described the 14 and 6 per second positive spikes in sleep and suggested their thalamic-hypothalamic origin. It is probable that these seizure discharges originate in or near the hypothalamus. The correlation of convulsive equivalent with 14 and 6 EEG pattern is about 50 percent in our experience. Autonomic symptoms may also be produced by discharge from the insular and the orbitofrontal regions.

OTHER NONEPILEPTIC ICTAL PHENOMENA. The EEG may sometimes reveal abnormal activities in children with no overt seizures but with behavior or personality disorders. Besides focal abnormalities, generalized bilateral synchronous paroxysmal activity may be present. Similar findings may be recorded in children with aphasia, learning problems, and sleep disturbances. That an ictal discharge plays an important role in the mechanism of the disorder in such cases is supported by the fact that a good response to anticonvulsant therapy is sometimes obtained.

Diagnostic Evaluation

The first step in the study of a child who has a convulsion is to document its occurrence. Although anxious parents are, as a rule, poor witnesses, every effort should be made to obtain a description of the seizure, particularly premonitory symptoms, loss of consciousness, convulsive movements, duration of the attack, and the state of the patient following the attack. Breath-holding spells in infants may simulate convulsive seizures. In breath-holding spells there is always a precipitating factor, uusually a slight injury or some emotional disturbance which results in violent crying, ending suddenly in respiratory apnea.

The cyanosis in such attacks appears before loss of consciousness and convulsive movements.

The second step is to determine whether the seizure is associated with some organic lesion of the central nervous system or with some metabolic disturbance. Every child who has had a convulsion should be subjected to thorough study, including a complete history, general physical and neurologic examinations, x-rays of the skull, electroencephalogram, and contents of the blood.

HISTORY TAKING. Frequently a good history in itself provides the essential evidence for the diagnosis. Besides a description of the seizure per se, certain other details are of relevance: The *frequency* of attacks may increase with passage of time in untreated cases of petit mal, but remain stationary in psychomotor and convulsive equivalent seizures. The *duration* of the attack is pertinent. Absence attacks seldom exceed 30 seconds in duration, whereas psychomotor seizures often last for several minutes. Any prolonged convulsion accompanied by cyanosis may be detrimental to the brain. The *time* of occurrence may be of value in diagnosis. Early morning attacks or episodes recurring after a meal may suggest the possibility of hypoglycemia.

Factors tending to *precipitate* seizures, such as bright light, television, flickering light, loud noise, overbreathing, emotional disturbance, physical fatigue, hunger, menstruation, and fever, should be ascertained so that appropriate measures may be taken to diminish their influence.

Maternal history of illnesses, operations, medication during pregnancy, and miscarriage may be of importance. The events of *birth* must be recalled in detail. Precipitous delivery is as significant as prolonged labor. Induction of labor, instrumentation, operative procedures, and other obstetric complications are relevant. The condition of the *placenta,* if known to the mother or available in the hospital record, should be noted.

The *status* of the infant at birth and as a neonate is of utmost importance. His vitality, vigor, color, and activities (feeding, sleep, crying) are clues to future development.

In *infancy* and *childhood,* head injury, untoward reaction to immunizations, and infections are significant. Febrile convulsions are also important. The milestones in early childhood and school records are informative data of the patient's mental and motor development.

Headache, abdominal pain, restless sleep, and behavior disorders are frequent *"side"* symptoms, worthy of note. Their persistence after commencement of epilepsy treatment may indicate that medication is not sufficient. Symptoms referable to speech, vision, fine skills, and higher mental functions are also of relevance; their progressive deterioration is often a bad omen.

The type, dosage, duration of *previous medication,* and the patient's response are important data helpful in planning treatment.

FAMILY HISTORY. Inasmuch as epilepsy continues to be regarded as a stigma, a positive history of epilepsy in the family may not be obtained on the first round of inquiry. As it is of some importance in diagnosis, prognosis, classification, and epidemiology, renewed efforts should be made to conclusively establish the answer. A different approach in the inquiry or use of such terms as "fever spasms" or "fainting spells" in the place of epilepsy may sometimes be rewarding.

ORDER OF EXAMINATION. The examination begins with the interview. Much information may be gained by observing the child. His general behavior and affect, his response to the environment and to questions and commands constitute an impression and provide clues as to how he could best be examined later. He may be given a puzzle to work, pictures to color, or building blocks. His activities should tell something about his motor skills and his mental development. He may show subtle seizure activity that is not evident to the parents.

The sequence of examination should be flexible, and the most difficult parts, for instance, fundoscopy, should be reserved for the last. Often the parents may be asked to leave and the child be observed unobtrusively by the examiner alone.

NEUROLOGIC EXAMINATION. The head size should be measured. Before 2 years of age the head and chest circumference coincide. An abnormally large head may suggest congenital hydrocephalus, subdural hematoma, intracranial mass, cerebral neurofibromatosis, or Tay-Sachs disease. An abnormally small head may indicate brain damage with cerebral atrophy or congenital dysplasia. The fontanel and sutures should be noted for early closure or evidence of separation. Dilated venous channels on the scalp suggest increased intracranial pressure. Clusters of venous patches suggest arteriovenous malformation. Auscultation of the skull should be done with the child recumbent; a localized loud bruit suggests a vascular abnormality. Transillumination of the skull is useful in young infants. Asymmetry or other abnormality in the configuration of the skull must be explained. The spinal axis should be examined for dimples, sinus tracts, tufts of hair, or lipomatous deposits. Certain skin lesions are clues of cerebral anomalies, since the skin and nervous system have a common embryologic origin from ectoderm. Portwine nevus flammeus of trigeminal distribution is a clue for Sturge-Weber-Dimitri disease; adenoma sebaceum and cutaneous depigmentation suggest tuberous sclerosis; and café-au-lait spots and nodular masses over peripheral nerve distribution signify neurofibromatosis. All three conditions may be associated with epilepsy.

The retina, an extension of the brain, is a rewarding structure to examine carefully. In early infancy, choreoretinitis may be due to toxoplasmosis or cytomegalic inclusion disease. Cherry-red spot or pigmentary changes in the macular area point to cerebral lipidosis. Other retinal changes such as hemorrhage, exudate, papilledema, and optic atrophy also provide important clues to various other diagnoses which may be associated with the epilepsies. The eyes should be examined for cataracts; their presence suggests the possibility of prenatal viral infection or an inborn error of metabolism. Apart from the above, a complete neurologic examination as described elsewhere in this section should be followed. The presence of focal signs, however minimal, may contribute importantly to the total evaluation of the child. A brief psychologic evaluation should always be included, even though accurate psychometric tests may be left to the experts.

GENERAL PHYSICAL EXAMINATION. The findings of high blood pressure or evidence of congenital heart disease is of importance because hypertensive encephalopathy and cerebral anoxia may cause convulsions. The existence of multiple dysplastic features (e.g., hypertelorism, low-set ears, simian line, receding chin, yellow skin, silky skin) suggests the possibility of cerebral dysplasia being the cause of epilepsy. Hepatic and splenic enlargement may be indications of glycogen storage disease, Gaucher's disease, or Niemann-Pick disease.

If the history suggests petit mal absence seizures, hyperventilation for three minutes (approximately 100 deep breaths) may induce an attack and help confirm the diagnosis; a negative result should not be considered to rule out this possibility.

LABORATORY EXAMINATION. The diagnostic impression derived from the history and physical examination should determine the indication for laboratory studies and which tests should be performed.

Electroencephalography. Of the various labotory tests, the electroencephalogram is the most informative and least painful procedure. It frequently provides the only objective evidence of cerebral disorder in seizure patients. It is also helpful in differentiating diffuse encephalopathies from localized lesions. With serial studies, it may provide evidence as to whether the lesion is static or progressive. However, the electroencephalogram should not be considered as a means of obtaining a "penny in the slot" diagnosis. As has been discussed in the section on classification, although certain specific electroencephalographic patterns have been shown to correlate closely with certain seizures, it is not safe or wise to adopt without question a diagnosis suggested by the electroencephalogram contrary to that indicated by clinical evidence.

Electrocorticography and depth electrode recordings are highly specialized procedures to be carried out only when precise localization of an epileptogenic lesion is required prior to surgical exploration.

Radiographic Studies. Radiographic examination of the skull occasionally provides unique information. Asymmetry of the cranium with unilateral thickening of the vault, elevation of the sphenoid and petrous ridges, and increased development of the sinus cells are indicative of a cerebral hemiatrophy. Asymmetry associated with localized thinning and bulging of the vault may suggest an underlying expanding lesion such as porencephalic cyst. Increased intracranial pressure may be reflected by sellar changes and separation of sutures. Abnormal calcifications may help localize and provide a clue to the nature of the cerebral lesion.

More specific procedures such as cerebral angiography and air studies are indicated when there is a possibility of a vascular or neoplastic lesion. Ventriculography is the procedure of choice where there is evidence of increased intracranial pressure. Echoencephalography and brain scan may also be helpful.

Other Tests. Lumbar puncture and examination of the cerebrospinal fluid are of particular value when cerebral tumor or progressive degenerative or inflammatory disease is suspected.

A complete blood count and urinalysis should be routine tests; these data are useful as a base line for future reference, especially in case of drug toxicity. In a Negro child, a sickle-cell preparation should be done. The urinary amino acid screening test may be considered in epileptics whose etiologic factor is unknown. The urinary sediment should be examined for cytomegalic inclusion bodies and metachromatic bodies when indicated. The test for porphobilinogen in the urine is indicated in children with acute abdominal pain and convulsions and may result in the rare diagnosis of porphyria. A phenylpyruvic acid test of the urine should be routine, as 25 percent of PKU patients have epilepsy. Serum calcium and phosphorus determinations as well as a fasting blood sugar should be routinely performed to rule out a metabolic basis for the seizures.

Differential Diagnosis

The child with episodic disturbances in the state of consciousness may have a seizure disorder, syncope, migraine, or a functional disorder. In the epileptic patient it is essential to determine whether the attacks are associated with an underlying organic or metabolic disorder (symptomatic), are of undetermined cause (unknown), or are hereditary (genetic).

A. Diagnostic Criteria of Genetic Epilepsy:
  1. Age: grand mal—onset between 2 to 16 years
       petit mal—onset between 4 to 16 years
       mixed seizures—petit mal usually precedes grand mal
  2. Seizure pattern: absence, generalized tonic clonic, myoclonic, (rarely) akinetic seizures with no focal features
  3. Family history: family incidence of similar seizures or febrile convulsions
  4. Normal neurologic and physical findings. Usually normal intelligence
  5. Characteristic EEG pattern: bilaterally synchronous 3 per second spike wave or bilaterally synchronous paroxysmal slow dysrhythmia
B. Diagnosis of Symptomatic Epilepsy:

1. Space-occupying lesions should always be considered with focal seizures and focal EEG abnormalities. There is no need, however, to perform all kinds of investigations at the beginning. If the seizures are refractory to drug therapy or if the child develops progressive symptoms or signs, more definitive diagnostic studies may be necessary. Temporal lobe neoplastic lesions may be very slow growing and simulate genetic epilepsy.

2. Degenerative and infectious encephalopathies: Epilepsies are common in many types of chronic disease of the central nervous system. The presence of other manifestations of cerebral dysfunction is suggestive. These include regression of mentation and speech, change in personality or sleeping habits, visual complaints, headache, general or specific incoordination and clumsiness. Progressive EEG changes often accompany these manifestations. Subacute sclerosing panencephalitis, cerebral lipidosis, and some of the leucodystrophies are examples of this group.

Epilepsy must be distinguished from other paroxysmal phenomena including the following:

1. *Syncope.* These attacks are always provoked, not spontaneous. Careful history will reveal the precipitating factor. In infants, two types of syncope occur: the more common type is the breath-holding spell. Less frequently, fainting spells may follow trivial but unexpected trauma to the head; the infant may or may not cry before passing out. Older children may faint upon painful stimulation, fear, or strong emotional upset. In all these conditions, there is usually a positive family history of a similar disorder. In breath-holding attacks and syncope in older children, the mechanism is cardioinhibitory or Valsalva-like effect. In the infant who passes out following head trauma, a reflex mechanism involving the medullary centers appears responsible. In all types the tendency for this hyperparasympathetic activity is believed to be hereditary. In adolescents, particularly females, hyperventilation may precipitate a syncopal episode.

2. *Hysteria.* Older children from 6 to 16 years, may have episodes which stimulate epileptic attacks because of anxiety or other psychologic causes. Neurologic examination and EEG in such children show no evidence of abnormality.

3. *Migraine.* (p. 1002).

Course and Prognosis

Epilepsy is, by definition, a chronic disorder with recurrent paroxysmal symptoms. The course and prognosis vary with the nature and severity of the underlying disease. Medication is continued for 3 to 4 years after the attacks are arrested. In case of relapse, which is more frequent around puberty, drug therapy has to be reinitiated and a full course maintained for another 2 or 3 years.

The prognosis of genetic epilepsies is generally good. Pure petit mal attacks tend to diminish in frequency with age and by adolescence disappear in approximately 50 percent of patients. Favorable outcome is seen even in cases with petit mal status. Grand mal seizures of genetic type are often nocturnal and generally respond to medical therapy but they tend to disappear after age 20. Mixed grand mal and petit mal seizure pattern is more difficult to control.

Of the symptomatic epilepsies posttraumatic and focal epilepsies have a favorable prognosis. About one-half to one-third of psychomotor seizures are difficult to control. A time factor seems important in the treatment of psychomotor seizures. All efforts should be made to gain seizure control at the earliest possible time. Delay in initiating appropriate treatment may result in discrete EEG focus giving way to mirror foci and subsequently more diffuse abnormalities. In such cases the seizures may be more complex, protracted, and refractory to anticonvulsants. As a consequence the patient's intellect may be adversely affected. Other acquired epilepsies including massive myoclonic, minor motor, and mixed types are difficult to treat but the end result is not all unrewarding. In addition to the seizures, most children in this category may have other manifestations of brain dysfunction. In a small number of cases the physician would have to prepare the parents for the possibility of institutional care and help them in the painful process of making this decison.

Age factor is not as important as the pathologic nature of the cerebral lesion and the type of seizures produced. The *duration of seizure history,* however, is important. The prospect of successful treatment is diminished if symptoms are of long standing.

Serial EEG's are helpful as general guide in prognosis. The prognosis is better if EEG shows progressive improvement and finally normalizes. Generally the EEG reverts to normal before seizures arrest. In some cases the EEG abnormality persists for a long time but the child remains well. One should not attempt to "treat" the EEG. Progressive worsening of EEG calls for reevaluation.

Conditions which tend to *precipitate attacks* are important factors in prognosis; ways and means to eliminate or minimize these will be helpful. Sometimes surgical extirpation of a sensitized and accessible area of the brain may eliminate seizure build-up completely.

The *attitude of the family,* relatives, school authorities, and schoolmates may exert intangible but important influence upon the child's own reaction toward his illness. The physician can play an important role in obviating these influences by thoughtful counseling. The possibility of brain damage or even sudden death from seizures per se are common fears besetting the parents. Severe convulsions with prolonged anoxia may be fatal but this seldom occurs.

Convulsions with cyanosis lasting over 30 minutes may cause brain damage. The child who develops periodic bouts of status epilepticus generally has a poor prognosis.

Management

The management of the epileptic child should be considered in three aspects, namely, (1) the specific therapy of the seizure, (2) the overall management of the child as a person, and (3) the counseling of the parents. The emphasis may vary with individual patient and family; all should receive full attention of the physician.

PARENT COUNSELING. It must be realized that all parents need counseling and reassurance. They may be prejudiced about their child's "unspeakable affliction," have a sense of guilt or shame, and be worried, anxious, fearful, or even hostile. They may have "shopped around" without a clear idea of what the real trouble is or what the future holds for the child. The strain on their emotional and economic resources may threaten the welfare of the entire family. Clearly it is the obligation of the physician to enlighten, to reassure, to answer questions, and to help solve secondary problems. After a thorough work-up, in which the parents have participated in history taking, they should be apprised of the diagnosis, treatment plan, and prognosis as nearly as is known or presumed. The result is often surprising and gratifying. Most parents can become reconciled to even the worst diagnosis or the poorest prognosis if they are kept informed. As they learn to understand what it is and what to expect, they will be in a much better position to carry on the care of their child without unduly dislocating their family life. The importance of this to the total welfare of the epileptic child cannot be overestimated. Wisely carried out, parent counseling is a small investment in terms of time and effort on the part of the physician, with huge dividends to the family as their fears of uncertainty are allayed by understanding the definitive diagnosis and plans of treatment.

MANAGEMENT OF THE CHILD AS A PERSON. The epileptic child should be treated as a "person," not a "case." It should be reemphasized that epilepsy is only a symptom of an underlying disease which may exhibit other symptoms of equal or more serious import. The child may have emotional problems, either because of his seizures or because of poor schoolwork secondary to cerebral dysfunction. In addition, as the child grows into adolescence and young adulthood, educational, social, and economic problems arise and demand solution. The physician should provide suggestions and direction.

Generally speaking, the epileptic child should be encouraged to live as normal a life as is consistent with safety. If the seizures are under good control, such physical exercises as riding a bicycle, jumping rope, roller skating, and swimming (under supervision) may be permitted; and if the child is able, cer-

TABLE 25. *The Drugs of Choice for the Various Seizure Types (in order of preference)*

Generalized (major motor), focal, psychomotor, and convulsive-equivalent epilepsy
    Dilantin
    Phenobarbital or Mebaral
    Mysoline
    Mesantoin
    Celontin
    Phenurone
    Bromides

Petit mal
    Zarontin
    Tridione
    Valium
    Diamox
    Milontin
    Aralen

Minor Motor
    ACTH or adrenal corticosteroids
    Mogadon
    Ketogenic diet
    Zarontin, Tridione, Valium, and Celontin
    Dexedrine
    Meprobamate
    Gemonil

Status epilepticus
    Valium (iv)
    Sodium Nembutal (iv)
    Sodium phenobarbital (iv or im)
    Paraldehyde (iv, im, or rectal)
    Volatile anesthetics

tain competitive sports may be also allowed. Other than the ketogenic diet, dietary and fluid restrictions play no role in the management of epilepsy.

Although petit mal seldom affects the intellect, the same assurance may not be given for all genetic epilepsies expecially when the seizures are prolonged and numerous. Many types of symptomatic seizures are associated with brain damage. In addition to their seizures, these children usually have mental, motor, or speech deficits as well. These difficulties may in turn lead to secondary emotional disorders, and such children should receive special assistance to overcome their handicaps. They may need to attend special classes at school and require special vocational and social guidance.

DRUG THERAPY. Drugs are the principal weapons in the treatment of the epilepsies. With proper choice and dosage of drugs appropriate to the seizure type, about 60 percent of all epileptic attacks can be satisfactorily controlled.

Phenobarbital was introduced in 1912 and remains the best anticonvulsant among the barbiturates. The discovery of diphenylhydantoin (Dilantin) in 1936 marked the beginning of modern drug therapy for epilepsy. Eight years later, trimethadione (Tridione) was tested, and quickly proved its specific usefulness in the petit mal group. Since then a large number of new drugs have been added. Several barbituric acid derivatives with less sedative action have

TABLE 26. *Anticonvulsants for Childhood Epilepsy*

	Indications	Dosage				Toxicity
		0-1 Year	5 Years	12 Years and Up	mg/kg/day	
Aralen (chloroquine)	Petit mal*	60 mg, 1-2 times per day	200 mg per day	400 mg per day	15-20	Bleaching of hair, blurring vision
Bromides	Same as Dilantin	250-500 mg daily	500 mg, 2-3 times daily	500 mg, 4-6 times daily	50-100	Drowsiness, skin rash, mental dullness, toxic psychosis
Celontin (methsuximide)	Psychomotor* Minor motor†	75 mg, 2-3 times daily	150 mg, 3 times daily	300 mg, 2-3 times daily	15-20	Drowsiness, ataxia, skin rash, rare aplastic anemia
Dexedrine (dextroamphetamine)	Petit mal	1.25 mg, 2-3 times daily	5 mg, 2 times daily	10 mg, 2-3 times daily	0.25-0.75	Restlessness, irritability, sleeplessness
Diamox (acetazolamide)	Petit mal* All types†	125 mg, 3 times daily	250 mg, 3. times daily	250 mg, 4 times daily	15-30	Anorexia, paresthesia, drowsiness, polyuria, hyperpnea, headache
Dilantin (diphenyl- hydantoin)	Generalized Psychomotor Focal	20 mg, 3-4 times daily	50 mg, 3 times daily	100 mg, 3-4 times daily	3-8	Gum hypertrophy, ataxia, diplopia, nystagmus, rash, fever, nausea, vomiting, hirsutism
Gemonil (metharbital)	Minor motor*	25 mg, 4-6 times daily	50 mg, 4-6 times daily	100 mg, 3-4 times daily	5-15	Rare drowsiness
Librium (chlordiazepoxide)	Same as Phenobarbital	15 mg, 4-5 times daily	32 mg, 3-4 times daily	100 mg, 3-4 times daily	2-8	Drowsiness, irritability, rash
Mebaral (mephobarbital)	Minor motor	—	—	30-150 mg per day		Nausea, lethargy, dizziness
Meprobamate (Equanil, Miltown; methylpropyl pro- panediol dicarbamate)	Petit mal* Minor motor†	200 mg, 2-3 times daily	200 mg, 3-5 times daily	400 mg, 2-3 times daily	20-40	Drowsiness, hyperactivity

996

Drug	Indication		Dose		Blood level	Toxic effects
Mesantoin (methylphenylethyl hydantoin)	Same as Dilantin	25 mg, 3-4 times daily	50 mg, 3-4 times daily	100 mg, 4-6 times daily	4-10	Rash and fever, leucopenia and agranulocytosis, ataxia
Milontin (phensuximide)	Petit mal*, Minor motor†	50 mg, 4-5 times daily	250 mg, 3-4 times daily	500 mg, 3-6 times daily	20-40	Nephrotoxic (slightly)
Mogadon (nitrazepam)	Minor motor, Petit mal (not available in U.S.A.)	1 mg, 1-3 times daily	2 mg, 1-3 times daily	5 mg, 1-3 times daily		
Mysoline (primidone)	Same as Dilantin	50 mg, 3-4 times daily	125 mg, 2-3 times daily	250 mg, 4-6 times daily	12-25	Drowsiness, ataxia, skin rash
Paradione (paramethadione)	Same as Tridione					
Paraldehyde (paracetaldehyde)	Status epilepticus	1 ml, im or iv; 2 ml, rectally	3 ml, im or iv; 6 ml, rectally	3-6 ml, iv; 8 ml, im		Unpleasant odor, drowsiness
Peganone (ethyl phenyl hydantoin)	Same as Dilantin		500 mg, 2-4 times daily	1,000 mg, 3-4 times daily		Same as Dilantin except for hirsutism and gum hypertrophy
Phenobarbital (ethyl phenyl-barbituric acid)	Same as Dilantin*, Minor motor†	15 mg, 3-4 times daily	30 mg, 2-3 times daily	60 mg, 2-3 times daily	1-5	Drowsiness, skin rash, and fever, hyperirritability in infants
Phenurone (phenacemide)	Psychomotor	125 mg, 3-4 times daily	250 mg, 4-6 times daily	500 mg, 4 times daily	20-35	Hepatotoxic, leucopenia, agranulocytosis, rash, irritability, and mental derangement
Tridione (trimethadione)	Petit mal*, Minor motor†	25 mg, 4-6 times daily	150 mg, 4-6 times daily	300 mg, 4-6 times daily	20-50	Rash, leucopenia and agranulocytosis, nephrosis, photophobia, irritability
Valium (diazepam)	Status epilepticus*	1-2 mg, iv	5 mg, iv	10 mg, iv	Slow injection, 1-2 mg/minute	Drowsiness, ataxia
Zarontin (ethosuximide)	Petit mal*, Minor motor†	250 mg, 2-3 times daily	250 mg, 4-6 times daily	250 mg, 3-4 times daily	20-50	Drowsiness, skin rash, gastric upset, rare aplastic anemia

*Primary indication.
†Secondary indication.

become available: Mebaral (Mephobarbital), Gemonil (Metharbital), Mysoline (Primidone).

To the hydantoin family the following have been added: Mesatoin (methylphenylethyl hydantoin) and Pegonone (ethotoin) in the 1940's.

The suxinimides (Milontin, Celontin, Zarontin) have been found valuable in petit mal and psychomotor seizures. Meanwhile, a host of other drugs, not primarily anticonvulsant in action, have proved useful. Among these is acetazolamide (Diamox), whose effect is related to its inhibitory action on brain carbonic anhydrase.

Some tranquilizing agents have antiseizure properties: Librium is a weak antiepileptic agent but two of its analogs have been found more effective: Valium (diazepam) has become the drug of choice for all types of status epilepticus; Mogadon (nitrazepam) is widely used with success for minor motor seizures in Europe and South America but is not available in this country.

Tegretol (carbamazepine), chemically related to Tofranil (imipramine hydrochloride), a drug for trigeminal neuralgia, has been used in major motor and psychomotor epilepsies.

The amphetamines and the antimalarials also have their places in the antiepileptic armamentarium.

Finally, the adrenal steroids and ACTH preparations have produced some dramatic results in massive myoclonic and minor motor seizures.

For the indications, dosage, and toxic reactions, reference may be made to the drug tables (Tables 25 and 26).

General Principles of Drug Therapy. Of the large number of tested drugs, some are wide-spectrum (Dilantin, phenobarbital, Diamox) and others more specific (Tridione, Celontin, Zarontin) in their antiepileptic activity. The selection of the most effective drug or drugs for each individual patient requires judgment and experience. Some general guidelines are therefore of fundamental importance:

1. A prime factor in successful therapy lies in the choice of the most effective drug, which depends upon correct identification of the clinical seizure type and the associated EEG pattern of the epilepsy in question. Except for emergencies, therapy can be withheld until the clinical and laboratory studies have been completed and a diagnosis has been established.

2. Use one drug at a time. Give it a fair trial before discarding it as ineffective. Increase dosage to tolerance and give it for a reasonable period of time. A combination of two or more drugs may be required, especially for mixed seizures. Give each addition or deletion thoughtful consideration until a satisfactory regimen is found.

3. Give adequate dosage. Young children can tolerate comparatively large doses of anticonvulsants. They are also consistently outgrowing their dosage, requiring adjustment from time to time.

4. Duration of therapy should be prolonged; early termination of medication may be followed by relapse. A safe rule is to continue the medication for at least three or four years after the *last* attack.

5. Weaning from medication should always be gradual, with stepwise reduction of dosage and withdrawal of one drug at a time.

6. One hundred percent control of symptoms may not be achieved in every patient. It is better to have a functional child with satisfactory control than complete control at the expense of a drug-toxic child.

7. Sometimes a drug, or a combination of drugs, may activate instead of suppress the seizure activity. Be ready to review the problem and revise the treatment from a different approach.

8. Factors which trigger or aggravate seizures should be prevented or controlled; these include fever, constipation, allergic states, emotional upset, frustration, physical exhaustion, and premenstrual edema.

Specific Anticonvulsant Therapy. *Grand mal.* Most grand mal seizures, regardless of cause, respond well to Dilantin or phenobarbital, or both. It is wise to use only one drug at the beginning. Dilantin is the first choice because phenobarbital may cause hyperactivity and irritability in young children and sluggishness in children of school age. Mebaral (mephobarbital) is also an effective barbiturate and is usually well tolerated by children. Mebaral is metabolized to phenobarbital, and in equivalent doses its effect is half that of phenobarbital. The individual effective dose is therefore twice that of phenobarbital. Mesantoin (methylphenylethyl-hydantoin) may be used in place of Dilantin.

All these drugs may cause toxic symptoms from overdosage or idiosyncrasy. Fever, morbilliform rash, even exfoliative dermatitis may develop, and the drug should be discontinued. Sometimes, after the symptoms clear, another trial with smaller dosage may be tolerated. Other common toxic reactions from Dilantin overdosage are cerebellar signs (usually reversible), nausea, vomiting, and irritability (more common in infants). The more subtle symptoms of headache, dizziness, mental depression are often not recognized as idiosyncrasy or mild toxicity to Dilantin and may mislead to suspicion of disease of CNS, psychoneurosis, or even brain tumor. Most of these symptoms are reversible. More severe forms of idiosyncrasy to Dilantin may result in the development of Stevens-Johnson syndrome, lupus erythematosus, lymphadenopathy simulating lymphoma. These are urgent indications to stop Dilantin therapy immediately. Recent reports indicated that Dilantin, Mysoline, and phenobarbital, alone or combined, may cause subnormal serum folate values. Whether or not megaloblastic anemia reversible by folic acid therapy occurs in children and how prevalent needs further investigation. Gum hypertrophy occurs in about 50 percent of children on Dilantin therapy. This is not a contraindication to the use of Dilantin. Firm massage of the gums may alleviate this side effect. Excessive hair growth is also common in young children but this is generally reversible after the drug is discontinued. Mesantoin is more toxic than Dilantin and may produce neutropenia or aplastic anemia; periodic blood counts are indicated when this agent is used.

Mysoline (Primidone) is a satisfactory anticonvulsant drug. The desired dosage should be built up gradually, lest the child become oversedated. Mysoline may cause irritability, anorexia, and lethargy but is generally well tolerated by the majority of children.

Gemonil (Metharbital), a weaker anticonvulsant, is almost devoid of side effects and can be used as an adjunctive drug.

Individual Seizure Management. If the initial seizure, febrile or nonfebrile, is witnessed and found to be unduly prolonged (10 minutes or more), it should be controlled by the use of intravenous sodium phenobarbital. In such circumstances an infant under the age of 1 year may require 0.06 to 0.1 g; a child between the ages of 2 and 5, 0.12 to 0.2 g; and the older child, up to 0.3 g.

Status epilepticus. This condition is a medical emergency requiring immediate treatment. The mortality rate is 5 to 10 percent. The airway must be open, and oxygen is administered if cyanosis is present. The convulsions must be stopped and recurrence prevented by effective medication.

The specific anticonvulsants should always be given by the intravenous route and in amounts large enough to stop seizure activity quickly. A common error is the frequent use of small aliquots of anticonvulsants with resultant toxicity but continued status. In recent years diazepam (Valium) has superseded the barbiturates and paraldehyde as the drug of choice for the treatment of status epilepticus. The drug is given by slow intravenous injection at a rate of not exceeding 1 mg per minute. For infants the optimal single dose is 1 to 2 mg, for young children 2 to 5 mg, and for older children 5 to 10 mg. The response of the patient to intravenous therapy with diazepam may be monitored by EEG if available and the injection may be stopped promptly as electrical and clinical arrest of the seizure becomes evident. The majority of cases will respond favorably with prompt termination of seizure discharge and subsidence of clinical symptoms. In most instances one injection is sufficient. But if symptoms should recur, a second or even third injection may be required at 20 to 30 minute intervals. Diazepam has been found to be safe and less toxic than barbiturates or paraldehyde with respect to respiratory and cardiovascular depression. It should be borne in mind that Valium potentiates barbiturates. This form of therapy has also been used for petit mal status and epilepsy partialis continua. The focus of depressive action is believed to be in the brainstem reticular system. The next drug of choice is sodium nembutal administered intravenously because of its fast action. The dosage is 0.1 to 0.4 g depending on age. If respiration is depressed, it is preferable to use paraldehyde, another highly effective agent, to be given as a dilute solution of 4 ml in 100 ml of 0.25 N

saline in 5 percent glucose in water solution. Untoward side effects of paraldehyde are respiratory distress and acute cardiac failure. If used judiciously in a diluted solution, these complications are rarely seen. It can also be given rectally with a wide margin of safety. Volatile anesthetic agents including vinyl ether or chloroform may be useful in controlling status, especially when it is difficult to give medications by the intravenous route. Concomitant with the acute emergency therapy, long-acting drugs, preferably phenobarbital or Dilantin should be initiated by the intramuscular route.

Focal cortical epilepsy. Focal seizures respond favorably to the same drugs used in grand mal attacks. Multifocal seizures are less easy to conrtol.

Psychomotor seizures. Among focal cortical epilepsies, psychomotor epilepsy is the most common. Dilantin is the drug of choice and may be combined with phenobarbital. Celontin (methsuximide) is useful in some children, and its side effects include drowsiness, anorexia, skin rash, fever, and occasionally neutropenia. In some instances Celontin has proved to be more effective than Dilantin.

Because of the possible toxic action on the liver and bone marrow, Phenurone (phenacemide) has not attained popularity in the treatment of psychomotor epilepsy.

"Pure" petit mal absence. Zarontin (ethosuximide) is the drug of choice in the treatment of petit mal attacks. Untoward reactions include anorexia, abdominal pain, drowsiness, and occasional skin rash. Aplastic anemia has been rarely reported. Tridione (trimethadione) is also a relatively specific anti petit mal drug. A common cause of failure is timidity in dosage. Monthly blood count should forewarn the possibility of neutropenia. As the neutrophil count approaches the level of 1600/mm^3, reduction of dosage or change of medication should receive serious consideration. Skin rash with fever is an indication to stop the drug or decrease the dosage. Lupus erythematosus is an uncommon complication of both Tridione and Zarontin therapy. Other less important side effects are photophobia, drowsiness, and eosinophilia. Diamox (acetazolamide), either alone or combined with Tridione, is effective. In a rare patient in whom none of the foregoing drugs brings relief, an antimalarial agent, Aralen (chloroquine), has proved useful. The side effects are visual disturbances (lacrimation, blurred vision, ptosis, and strabismus), skin sensitivity, and occasional peripheral neuropathy. These symptoms are reversible except the retinopathy. Periodic examination of the visual field is mandatory since visual field defects precede the onset of retinitis and at this stage the eye lesions are still reversible.

Myoclonic epilepsy. This seizure type is more difficult to manage than pure petit mal attacks. The drug of choice is Celontin, whose effect may also be dramatic. Next choices are Valium, Tridione, Diamox, and Meprobamate. Corticosteroids or corticotropins may be effective in some resistant cases.

The myoclonic epilepsy seen in degenerative diseases is resistant to drugs.

Minor motor seizures. Akinetic Seizures. These seizures are almost always associated with organic brain disorders and are notoriously difficult to control. In a small percentage of patients beneficial results may be obtained from Valium, Celontin, Tridione, Zarontin, or Diamox. In some cases a trial of ACTH therapy is highly recommended (for dosage schedule, see massive spasms). With severe drop seizures, children often sustain bruises of face and eyes or even fractures of teeth or skull. Wearing a padded football helmet may prevent or minimize such injuries. The ketogenic diet may be the most effective form of treatment for this type of seizure but this requires the full cooperation of the child and the family.

Massive Myoclonic Spasms. This type of spasm is very resistant to the usual anticonvulsants. ACTH is the drug of choice. The efficacy of ACTH or steroid therapy appears to depend upon the underlying cause of the spasms and the promptness and intensity of the medication. The earlier and the more intensive the therapy, the better the response. In 50 percent of the cases the seizures may be controlled or improved. The attendant mental impairment, however, is much less affected by steroid or any type of therapy. The dosage and duration of treatment have varied at different clinics. The following schedule for Acthar gel by intramuscular injection in two divided doses is recommended:

> 1st week—40 IU/day
> 2nd week—40 IU/day
> 3rd week—30 IU/day
> 4th week—20 IU/day
> 5th week—20 IU for 3 days and
>   10 IU/day for 3 days

Proper precautions of steroid therapy should be closely followed. The sleeplessness and irritability which are often seen during the second or third week of therapy may be counteracted by oral or rectal chlorpromazine. Moon facies and acne are not uncommon. Significant electrolyte imbalance and hypertension are rarely observed.

Convulsive Equivalent (Autonomic Epilepsy). The majority of these patients can be successfully treated with anticonvulsant drugs. Dilantin, alone or in conjunction with Diamox, is most satisfactory. Diamox alone may sometimes be effective. Meprobamate, Mebaral, and Tridione may also be useful.

DIETARY TREATMENT. The value of starvation in the control of epileptic seizures has been recognized for centuries. However, it was not known that the effect was due to ketosis until shortly before the ketogenic diet was introduced as a form of antiepileptic treatment by Wilder in 1921. Since the advent of modern anticonvulsant drugs in ever increasing variety and effectiveness, the need of dietary therapy has become limited to selected patients in whom drugs have utterly failed or have to be discontinued because of intolerance or idiosyncrasy. The diet is most effective in patients with akinetic seizures.

The ketogenic diet is more expensive than ordinary meals, and its preparation requires intelligence and care. Rigid control must be enforced lest the effectiveness be diminished or lost. Therefore, it should be prescribed only for carefully selected children. The parents must have complete understanding and be willing to cooperate fully. The most suitable age of the child is between 2 to 5 years. Young infants may not tolerate the high fat content; older children may rebel and refuse to take the diet. Retarded or brain-damaged children may not cooperate in finishing their meals and may accept carbohydrate foods offered inadvertently.

Preferably the child should be hospitalized for the initiation of the dietary regime, which should be preceded by a period of total starvation (3 to 4 days) during which only water is given. If this is successful, the child is so hungry that he is ready and willing to eat what is served. The ketosis induced by the starvation is maintained as long as the dietary regime is not broken. Even minor infringement such as one cookie or a lump of sugar may diminish the effectiveness of the diet drastically. Like drug therapy, the diet should be continued for two to three years. In weaning from the diet, the proportion of fat should be decreased gradually over a period of weeks, lest sudden reversion of ketosis precipitate a convulsive attack.

The basic requirement of a ketogenic diet is to provide sufficient protein and calories for growth and maintenance with a fat to protein-carbohydrate ratio of 4:1 by weight. The procedure of calculation and a list of interchangeable dietary items have been described in detail by Livingston and Keith.

SURGICAL TREATMENT. With the advent of refined diagnostic techniques, the surgical treatment of certain types of focal epilepsy has become effective. This therapeutic approach requires a competent and experienced team which usually is available only in large medical centers. Indications for surgical therapy are clear in patients with progressive lesions of the brain (tumor, abscess, hematoma, and vascular malformation). For chronic epilepsy due to static or atrophic lesions, the primary treatment is medical, and surgery should be considered only when drug, dietary, and other therapeutic measures have failed after adequate trial.

The indication for surgery is limited further to cases in which clinical and laboratory studies clearly point to a well-localized lesion in a surgically accessible site in one cerebral hemisphere. Bilateral, diffuse, or subcortical lesions are contraindications for surgery, as are the genetic epilepsies.

The general status of the patient, his physical and mental deficits other than epilepsy, and the anticipated disability to surgical intervention should also be carefully evaluated before such treatment is recommended.

When surgery is indicated, exact cortical localization of the epileptogenic focus or foci must be accomplished through clinical and special radiographic and electrographic studies carried out preoperatively as well as during the operation.

A number of effective procedures have been developed: techniques for local excision, total lobectomy, and hemispherectomy have been perfected. The tendency has been toward wider excision of tissues surrounding the epileptogenic focus. In competent hands the surgical mortality is about 1 to 2 percent; complete control or marked improvement is obtained in more than 50 percent of properly selected cases.

Febrile Convulsions

Convulsive disorder can be divided into two major categories; the acute sporadic and the chronic paroxysmal. To the former belong the febrile convulsions of infancy and childhood. By definition, febrile convulsions are provoked by hyperthermia associated with an acute illness of extracranial origin. Acute convulsions associated with intracranial diseases of infectious, toxic, metabolic, vascular, and neoplastic origin are also classified in the first group but will not be considered here.

Although febrile convulsions are the most common seizure disorder in childhood its incidence is not accurately known but estimated to be around 5 percent. They commonly occur between 6 months to 3 years with the peak incidence at 18 months. The incidence in boys is slightly greater than in girls. There is a high familial incidence of febrile convulsions (around 30 percent) and of other epileptic disorders (around 15 percent) suggesting the importance of genetic predisposition.

DIAGNOSIS AND DIFFERENTIAL DIAGNOSIS. The most common cause of febrile convulsions is acute upper respiratory infection. A sudden sharp rise of temperature appears more important than the height of fever, as the threshold for convulsion differs in individual patients.

In an infant with fever and convulsions, the diagnosis of "benign febrile convulsion" must be differentiated from other acute convulsions. Of particular importance is the possibility of primary intracranial disease (e.g., meningitis) which demands immediate diagnosis and specific therapy.

When febrile convulsion is diagnosed with reasonable assurance, a second step must be taken to differentiate "benign" (or "typical") from "nonbenign" (or "atypical") febrile seizure. This is important in both management and prognosis.

Any child presenting a febrile convulsion deserves a careful work-up and planned follow-up. Laboratory studies should include examination of the cerebrospinal fluid; measurement of blood glucose, calcium, phosphorus, phosphatase, and urea nitrogen; radiographs of the skull; and an electroencephalogram.

Benign febrile convulsions most commonly occur in neurologically normal children within the age of 6 months to 3 years. In addition the following criteria are helpful in differentiating benign febrile convulsions from the nonbenign group:

1. Positive family history of febrile convulsions
2. An abrupt rise of temperature over 103° F inciting a generalized convulsion seldom longer than a few minutes in duration
3. No neurologic abnormality after the attack
4. Normal laboratory studies including electroencephalogram

In contrast children with *nonbenign* febrile convulsions often have a lowered seizure threshold which may be related to a preexisting but subclinical condition such as prematurity or birth trauma. In these cases fever acts as a trigger and the convulsive episodes are more prone to be repetitive with lowering degree of fever each time and finally with no fever at all. In this group we should also include those children who were neurologically normal but have sustained brain insult as a sequel to their first febrile convulsion. Helpful criteria in identifying the nonbenign group are:

1. Asymmetric or focal seizure with or without Todd's paralysis
2. Seizures longer than 30 minutes
3. Repeated seizures during one febrile illness
4. Presence of neurologic deficits before, during, or after the seizure
5. Persistent and significant EEG abnormalities
6. Onset of seizure before 6 months or after 3 years of age

Electroencephalogram. This test should not be used too soon following a seizure on in phase of fever. The optimum time for the test is a week following the initial attack; however, a single examination is of little assistance in prognosis. A serial study should be performed in children with recurrent febrile convulsions. Abnormal EEG's are found in about 25 percent of children with febrile convulsions and 10 percent have shown definite epileptiform activity.

PROGNOSIS. Febrile convulsions are not necessarily benign. The child may experience subsequent febrile seizures, develop afebrile seizures (epilepsy), or manifest signs of underlying brain dysfunction.

1. *Recurrent febrile seizures.* The risk of further febrile convulsions seems to increase with each additional attack: 35 percent recurrence after the first seizure; 47 percent after the second, and 60 percent after the third.
2. *Recurrent afebrile seizures or epilepsy.* From a 15- to 22-year longitudinal study, Livingston found the incidence of chronic epilepsy in the "benign" group was 2.9 percent and 97 percent in the "nonbenign" group. Psychomotor epilepsy has been found to occur more frequently

in children with a history of "benign" febrile convulsions.

3. *Brain dysfunction.* The nagging question regarding the possibility of brain damage and mental retardation as sequelae of febrile convulsions cannot be easily answered, as carefully planned, long-term follow-up studies are sadly lacking. Of the overall febrile convulsion group, the incidence of mental retardation has been reported as 6 to 8 percent and behavior disorder as 10 percent. It is unknown what proportion of these belong to the benign and nonbenign group of febrile convulsions.

In our experience, subtle changes of brain function are more common than straightforward mental retardation. These include behavior disturbance, speech disorder, learning deficits, and autonomic dysfunctions. The latter may manifest as sleep disturbance, and visceral, sensory, vasomotor, or other autonomic seizure equivalents. Fortunately, many of these symptoms are age-determined and tend to improve, even disappear with CNS maturation.

TREATMENT. The treatment of febrile convulsions should be directed at the control of the convulsions, the lowering of fever, the treatment of the underlying infection, and the use of maintenance anticonvulsants. There is a difference of opinion as to the value of long-term prophylactic anticonvulsant therapy. The difficulty in distinguishing the benign from the nonbenign febrile convulsion and identifying the complications that may result from a seizure has prompted us to recommend that all children be treated with daily anticonvulsant medication until at least 6 years of age after the initial febrile convulsion.

Migraine

Migraine is a paroxysmal disorder characterized by recurrent headaches, classically unilateral, often preceded by visual aura and followed by nausea and vomiting. A family history (sibling or parents) of headache described as migrainous is high. It is a common pediatric problem. From reliable longitudinal follow-up study it has been shown that in children with true migraine about 50 percent had hemicrania; 90 percent had nausea and vomiting; 60 to 70 percent had positive family history.

INCIDENCE. The diagnosis of migraine in infancy and early childhood is less certain because of incomplete clinical picture. Although classical hemicrania has been reported in a 2½-year-old, migraine is more competently diagnosed after the age of 5 years. The incidence in children is about 5 percent; it increases in older children to 10 percent. In the latter age group the symptomatology is closely similar to that of the adult patients.

It is interesting to note that the incidence in children is higher in boys than girls; but in adults it is higher in women than men.

ETIOLOGY AND PATHOGENESIS. The cause and mechanism of migraine are not completely understood. The consensus is that migraine is primarily a hereditary instability of the autonomic functions with secondary effects on cerebral and cranial circulation. The chain of events in the symptomatology is believed to arise under the influence of an active substance such as histamine or a neurohumor such as serotonin.

The paroxysmal attacks are often precipitated by emotional upsets, acute anxieties, traveling sickness, or physical exhaustion. Allergic disorders are common in migraine patients and their relatives. It has long been suspected that there might be a relationship between migraine and epilepsy. Although classic migraine and epilepsies are different clinically, the variants of these disorders are remarkably similar. A history of migraine is more common in the families of epileptic patients than normal population. According to Wolff, there are three phases in a migraine attack: (1) Vasoconstriction of intracranial arterioles resulting in cerebral ischemia. In the majority of cases, this occurs in the distribution of the common carotid system, thus evoking cortical and retinal phenomena as visual disturbances, paresthesias and visceral symptoms. In rare cases the basilar system is involved and the clinical picture in a child is that of "benign paroxysmal vertigo." (2) Vasodilatation of the extracranial vessels resulting in pressure upon sensitive nerve endings in the walls of the distended arterioles producing headaches of throbbing nature. (3) Exudation and tissue edema results in persisting head pain.

CLINICAL PICTURE. An aura or prodrome may or may not be present. The onset is usually sudden. Visual symptoms are seldom seen in young children. In older children, dimness or loss of vision and visual field defects are more common than circumscribed scotomas. Transient numbness and tingling of a limb or of the face, followed by clonic movements may precede the headache. Hemiplegia, ophthalmoplegia, and dysphasia lasting for varying periods are less common. Although hemicrania is characteristic of migraine, the headache in children may be bilateral or in the posterior aspect of the head and neck. Hemicrania, when present, is commonly preceded by pain behind the eye of the involved side. Closely following the onset of headache, nausea appears and vomiting is often distressing. After the vomiting, the headache may be instantly relieved; or if the patient falls asleep, he may awaken in an asymptomatic state. Attacks may be precipitated by mental tension, physical exertion, emotional stresses, and special sensory stimuli (bright lights, cinema and television, and loud noises). Attacks are often diminished in frequency and severity during vacation periods.

As a rule, between attacks, the physical and neurologic findings are normal and laboratory studies noncontributory.

ELECTROENCEPHALOGRAM. The EEG in children with migraine may be normal, but a significant number show various types of abnormalities, including focal and paroxysmal patterns. This fact often renders the EEG of little value in differentiating convulsive equivalent states from migraine headaches.

DIAGNOSIS. The diagnosis depends entirely upon the history. The most important features are the characteristic triad of symptoms, the chronic recurrent course, and the positive family history. At least two, preferably more, of these criteria should be satisfied before a diagnosis of migraine may be seriously considered.

DIFFERENTIAL DIAGNOSIS. While the diagnosis in cases of classical migraine offers no difficulty, atypical forms may be confused with convulsive equivalent syndrome or autonomic epilepsy. Headache and visceral symptoms are common features of both conditions. The incidence of convulsive equivalent epilepsy, however, is 10 or more times greater than migraine in the pediatric age group. A positive family history for migraine is helpful. Therapeutic response to antimigraine or anticonvulsant medication may clarify the diagnosis in difficult cases. In some instances it may be impossible to differentiate atypical migraine from atypical convulsive equivalent syndrome.

Headache is a common pediatric complaint, and its evaluation and diagnosis can be difficult. Consideration must be given to such conditions as intracranial mass lesions, vascular malformations, and functional disorders. Headache may also have its origin in multiple extracranial causes.

PROGNOSIS. The prognosis of childhood migraine is generally favorable but it is not uncommon for the headaches to persist into adult life.

PREVENTION AND TREATMENT OF ATTACK. The frequency and severity may be diminished if all factors known through experience to provoke attacks are avoided or minimized as much as possible. Premedication in anticipation of mental tension, physical or physiologic stress, or emotional excitement may be justified.

Ergotamine preparations have been widely used for the treatment of migraine. Cafergot, which is a mixture of 1 mg ergotamine tartrate and 100 mg caffeine in one tablet, may be given orally. One or two tablets are given as initial dose according to size of child. This can be repeated in 15 to 30 minutes for two or three times. Ergomar can be given sublingually and cafergot suppositories may be used rectally. These drugs must be given during the vasoconstriction phase. Once headache is established the attack runs its course and is little effected by ergot preparations.

For relief of well-developed migraine symptoms appropriate doses of salicylates and codeine, and induced sleep in a darkened quiet room are often followed by relief. In this writer's experience, the judicious use of Dilantin or Mebaral in adequate doses between migraine attacks has often led to long periods of remission.

Narcolepsy

Narcolepsy is a syndrome of paroxysmal episodes of irresistible sleep which may be associated with transient episodes of weakness or cataplexy.

ETIOLOGY. This condition is believed to result from disturbance of the sleep-wakefulness mechanism of the reticular activation system in the diencephalon. A primary and a secondary or symptomatic type are distinguished. In primary narcolepsy, a familial incidence has been estimated at around 10 percent. Inheritance is by autosomal transmission as a simple dominant factor. Secondary or symptomatic narcolepsy may be caused by diffuse or localized brain lesions, encephalitides being the most common. Head trauma, tumors in the region of the third ventricle, and the Pickwickian syndrome are among the less frequent causes.

INCIDENCE. This is a relatively rare condition, and no exact incidence is available. In Sours' series of 75 cases of primary narcolepsy, one-third were from 11 to 15 years of age at the time of onset. It predominates in males by a 3:2 ratio. Higher incidence in the Negro race has been observed by Ford.

CLINICAL MANIFESTATIONS. The onset is insidious and may coincide with major physiologic changes of life such as puberty. The somnolence has been described in an irresistible urge to sleep. The change from wakefulness to sleep is gradual. It usually occurs in hypnapagogic situations, although some patients may fall asleep while engaged in physical activities. Between episodes the patient may be alert but more often is drowsy.

Cataplexy may occur spontaneously, or more often is brought on by laughter, anger, or surprise. It is a sudden decrease or abrupt loss of muscle tone; the child sinks limply to the ground without loss of consciousness. The attack is usually brief and is followed by full recovery. Two other manifestations—namely, sleep paralysis and hypnapagogic hallucinations—are rare in children.

In the secondary type, the paroxysmal somnolence tends to last longer 'than in the primary type. Other symptoms of encephalopathy such as mental retardation, motor, speech, and behavior disorders may be present. The Pickwickians are characteristically obese and show cyanosis, hypercapnia, right heart hypertrophy, and congestive heart failure. The secondary narcoleptics do not exhibit cataplexy.

LABORATORY DATA. In primary narcolepsy, the EEG shows normal sleep activity during the narcoleptic attack, and the waking record is usually normal. When photic stimulation is used, two-thirds of the patients show poor following, considered indicative of lower reactivity of the nervous system. In the secondary narcolepsy, the EEG may be abnormal, depending upon the type of the underlying cerebral abnormality.

DIAGNOSIS. The diagnosis of narcolepsy suggests itself when the cardinal symptoms are present. The possibility of a hypothalamic neoplasm and other cerebral lesions should be excluded.

PROGNOSIS. In most cases the disorder does not interfere too much with the child's activities but is often responsible for poor schoolwork. Spontaneous remission occurs in many cases.

TREATMENT. The amphetamines, Dexedrine or Benzedrine sulfate, 10 mg, after breakfast and lunch, or Ritalin (methylphenidate hydrochloride) in the same dosage, are effective in alleviating the sleepiness and the cataplexy.

REFERENCES

EPILEPSY

General

Chao, D., Druckman, R., and Kellaway, P. Convulsive Disorders of Children. Philadelphia, W. B. Saunders Co., 1958.

Farmer, T. W., ed. Pediatric Neurology. New York, Paul B. Hoeber, Inc., 1964.

Ford, F. Diseases of the Nervous System in Childhood and Adolescence. Springfield, Ill., Charles C Thomas, Publ., 1966.

Gibbs, F. A., ed. Molecules and Mental Health. Philadelphia, J. B. Lippincott Co., 1959.

—— and Gibbs, E. L. Atlas of Electroencephalography, 2nd ed. Cambridge, Mass., Addison-Wesley Press, Inc., Vol. 2, 1952.

Jeavons, P. M., and Bower, B. D. Infantile Spasms: A review of the literature and a study of 112 cases. Clinics of Developmental Medicine, No. 15. Medical Education and Information Unit of the Spastic Society in Association with William Heinemann Medical Books, Ltd., London, 1964.

Lennox, W. G., and Lennox, M. A. Epilepsy and Related Disorders. Boston, Little, Brown and Co., 1960.

Livingston, S. The Diagnosis and Treatment of Convulsive Disorders in Children. Springfield, Ill., Charles C Thomas, Publ., 1954.

—— Living with Epileptic Seizures. Springfield, Ill., Charles C Thomas, Publ., 1963.

Millichap, J. G. Febrile Convulsions. New York, The Macmillan Co., 1968.

Penfield, W., and Jasper, H. H. Epilepsy and the Functional Anatomy of the Human Brain. Boston, Little, Brown and Co., 1954.

Robb, P. Epilepsy: A review of basic and clinical research. NINDB Monogr. No. 1, Public Health Service Pub. No. 1357, U.S. Dept. of Health, Education and Welfare, 1965.

Tower, D. B. Neurochemistry of Epilepsy. Springfield, Ill., Charles C Thomas, Publ., 1960.

Classification and Etiology

Burke, J. B. Significance of neonatal convulsions. Arch. Dis. Child., 29:342, 1954.

Caveness, W. F. Sequelae of cerebral concussion. New York J. Med., 61:1871, 1961.

Chao, D. Subacute inclusion body encephalitis. J. Pediat., 61:501, 1962.

Christensen, E., and Husby, J. Chronic subdural hematoma in infancy. Acta Neurol. Scand., 39:323, 1962.

Craig, W. S. Convulsive movements occurring in the first 10 days of life. Arch. Dis. Child., 35:336, 1960.

Edgar, G. W. F., and Post, P. J. J. Amaurotic idiocy and epilepsy. Epilepsia, 4:251, 1963.

Evans, J. H. Post-traumatic epilepsy. Neurology, 12:665, 1962.

Fowler, M. Brain damage after febrile convulsions. Arch. Dis. Child., 32:67, 1957.

Friedlander, W. J. Epilepsy. Amer. J. Psychiat., 120:674, 1964.

Gastaut, H. et al. A proposed international classification of epileptic seizures. Epilepsia, 5:297, 1964.

—— and Tassinari, C. A. Triggering mechanism in epilepsy, the electroclinical point of view. Epilepsia, 7:85, 1966.

Gerken, H., Doose, H., Volzke, E., Volz, C., and Hien-Volpel, K. F. Genetics of childhood epilepsy with photic sensitivity. Lancet, 1:1377, 1968.

Gibbs, F. A., and Gibbs, E. L. Age factor in epilepsy. New Eng. J. Med., 269:1230, 1963.

Lennox, W. G., Gibbs, E. L., and Gibbs, F. A. Inheritance of cerebral dysrhythmia and epilepsy. Arch. Neurol. Psychiat., 44:1155, 1940.

Low, M. L., Bosma, J. F., and Armstrong, M. D. Studies on phenylketonuria. VI. EEG studies in PKU. Arch. Neurol. Psychiat., 77:359, 1957.

Marson, C. A. A newly proposed classification of epileptic seizures: neurophysiological basis. Epilepsia, 6:275, 1965.

Metrakos, K., and Metrakos, J. D. Genetics of convulsive disorders: II. Genetic and electroencephalographic studies in centrencephalic epilepsy. Neurology, 11:474, 1961.

Rodin, E. A. Familial occurrence of the 14 and 6 positive spike phenomenon. Paper presented at the Eastern Association of EEG Meeting, New York City, 1963.

Schwartz, J. F. Photosensitivity in a family. Amer. J. Dis. Child., 103:90, 1962.

Sorel, L. The descendants of epileptic parents. Epilepsia, 10:91, 1969.

Symonds, C. Classificaiton of the epilepsies. Brit. Med. J., 1:1235, 1955.

Clinical

Aigner, B. R., and Mulder, D. W. Myoclonus, Arch. Neurol., 2:600, 1960.

Barslund, I., and Danielsen, J. Temporal epilepsy in monozygotic twins. Epilepsia, 4:138, 1963.

Bray, P. F. Temporal lobe epilepsy syndrome. Pediatrics, 29:612, 1962.

Chao, D. Seizures in infancy and early childhood. Med. Clin. N. Amer., p. 399, 1958.

—— Sexton, J. A., and Pardo, L. S. Temporal lobe epilepsy in children. J. Pediat., 60:686, 1962.

—— Taylor, F. M., and Druckman, R. Massive spasms in infancy and childhood. J. Pediat., 50:670, 1958.

Charlton, M. H., and Yahr, M. D. Long-term follow-up of patients with petit mal. Arch. Neurol., 16:595, 1967.

Currier, R. D., Kovi, K. A., and Saidman, L. J. Prognosis of "pure" petit mal. Neurology, 13:959, 1963.

Debiolley, D. Petit mal variant or Lennox syndrome. Electroenceph. Clin. Neurophysiol., 23:282, 1967.

Epstein, M. H., and O'Connor, J. S. Destructive effects

of prolonged status epilepticus. J. Neurol. Neurosurg. Psychiat., 29:251, 1966.

Frantzen, E., Lennox-Buchthal, M., and Nygaard, A. The electroencephalogram in children with febrile convulsions. Electroenceph. Clin. Neurophysiol., 23:389, 1967.

—— Lennox-Buchthal, M., and Nygaard, A. Longitudinal EEG and clinical study of children with febrile convulsions. Electroenceph. Clin. Neurophysiol., 24: 197, 1968.

Friderichsen, C., and Melchior, J. Febrile convulsions in children, their frequency and prognosis. Acta Paediat., Suppl. 100, 1954.

Gastaut, H. et al. Childhood epileptic encephalopathy with diffuse slow spike-waves (otherwise known as "petit mal variant") or Lennox syndrome. Epilepsia, 7:139, 1966.

—— Startle disease (pathological surprise reaction). Electroenceph. Clin. Neurophysiol., 23:494, 1967.

Gibberd, F. B. The prognosis of petit mal. Brain, 89: 531, 1966.

Hammill, J. F., and Carter, S. Febrile convulsions. New Eng. J. Med., 274:563, 1966.

Jaffe, R. J. Ictal behavior disturbance as the only manifestation of seizure disorder: a case report. J. Nerv. Ment. Dis., 134:470, 1962.

Lennox, W. G. Significance of febrile convulsions. Pediatrics, 11:341, 1953.

Livingston, S. Infantile febrile convulsions. Develop. Med. Child Neurol., 10:374, 1968.

Lombroso, C. T., and Lerman, P. Breathholding spells (cyanotic and pallid infantile syncope). Pediatrics, 39: 563, 1967.

Meyer, A., Beck, E., and Shepherd, M. Unusually severe lesions in the brain following status epilepticus. J. Neurol. Neurosurg. Psychiat., 18:24, 1955.

Niedermeyer, E. The Lennox-Gastaut syndrome: a severe type of childhood epilepsy. Electroenceph. Clin. Neurophysiol., 24:283, 1968.

Peterman, M. G. Febrile convulsions in children. J.A.M.A., 143:728, 1950.

Rogina, V., and Serafetinides, E. A. Epilepsy and behavior disorder in patients with generalized spike and wave complexes. Electroenceph. Clin. Neurophysiol., 14:376, 1962.

Samson, J. H., Apthorp, J., and Finley, A. Febrile seizures and purulent meningitis. J.A.M.A., 210:1918, 1969.

Steinschneider, A., Ginsberg, T., George, E. D., and Lipton, E. L. Febrile convulsions. Neurology, 14:362, 1964.

Swanson, P. D., Luttrell, C. N., and Magladery, J. W. Myoclonus. Medicine, 41:339, 1962.

Yanai, N. Febrile convulsions in children. Develop. Med. Child Neurol., 10:255, 1967.

Treatment

Bell, D. S. Dangers of treatment of status epilepticus with diazepam. Brit. Med. J., 1:159, 1969.

Carson, M. J. Treatment of minor motor seizures with nitrazepam. Develop. Med. Child Neurol., 10:772, 1968.

Carter, S., and Gold, A. P. Seizures in childhood. New Eng. J. Med., 278:315, 1968.

—— and Gold, A. P. Care of the critically ill child: management of status epilepticus. Pediatrics, 44:732, 1969.

Chao, D. Overall management of the epileptic child. Med. Clin. N. Amer., p. 461, 1958.

—— Drug therapy in paroxysmal disorders. Pediat. Clin. N. Amer., p. 3, 1963.

—— and Plumb, R. Diamox in epilepsy—a critical review of 178 cases. J. Pediat., 58:211, 1961.

Connelly, J. P. et al. Control of refractory epilepsy. Clin. Pediat., 2:624, 1961.

Gold, A. P., and Carter, S. Pediatric neurology. In Shirkey, H. C., ed., Pediatric Therapy. St. Louis, C. V. Mosby Co., 1968.

Gordon, N. Folic acid deficiency from anticonvulsant therapy. Develop. Med. Child Neurol., 10:497, 1968.

Hammill, J. F., and Carter, S. Febrile convulsions. New Eng. J. Med., 274:563, 1965.

Keith, H. M. Convulsive disorders in children with special reference to treatment with ketogenic diet. Boston, Little, Brown and Co., 1963.

Livingston, S., Villamater, C., Sakata, Y., and Pauli, L. L. Use of carbamazepine (Tegretol) in epilepsy. J.A.M.A., 200:116, 1967.

Nicol, C. F., Tutton, J. C., and Smith, B. H. Parenteral diazepam in status epilepticus. Neurology, 19:332, 1969.

Nygaard Jensen, O., and Vendeline Olesen, O. The clinical importance of folic acid in patients treated with anticonvulsant drugs. Excerpta Medica, Amsterdam, Int. Congr. Ser., 193:260, 1969.

Merritt, H. H. Medical treatment in epilepsy. Brit. Med. J., 1:666, 1958.

Penfield, W., and Paine, K. Results of surgical therapy of focal epileptic seizures. Canad. Med. Ass. J., 73: 515, 1955.

Peterson, W. G. Clinical study of Mogadon, a new anticonvulsant. Neurology, 17:878, 1967.

Prensky, A. L., Raff, M. C., Moore, M. J., and Schwab, R. S. Intravenous diazepam in the treatment of prolonged seizure activity. New Eng. J. Med., 276:779, 1967.

Rasmussen, T. Surgical aspects of focal epilepsy. Electroenceph. Clin. Neurophysiol., 15:1050, 1963.

Reynolds, E. H., Miller, C. G., and Matthews, D. M. Anticonvulsant therapy, folic acid and vitamin B_{12} metabolism and mental symptoms. Epilepsia, 7:261, 1966.

Sansoy, O. M., and Whorton, D. Chlordiazepoxide hydrochloride in treatment of convulsive disorders. Rocky Mount. Med. J., 63:56, 1966.

Scholl, M. L. Treatment of seizure disorders. New Eng. J. Med., 269:1424, 1962.

Walker, A. E. Surgical treatment of epilepsy. In Livingston, S., ed., Convulsive Disorders in Children. Springfield, Ill., Charles C Thomas, Publ., 1954, Chap. 14.

Wilder, R. M. The effect of ketonemia on the course of epilepsy. Mayo Clin. Proc., 2:307, 1921.

Wilson, P. J. E. Cerebral hemispherectomy for infantile hemiplegia. Brain, 93:147, 1970.

MIGRAINE

Berman, B. A. Migraine in children. Ann. Allerg., 21:91, 1963.

Bille, B. Migraine in children. Acta Paediat. Scand., 51: 614, 1962.

Bruyn, G. W., and Weenink, H. R. Migraine accompagnée. A critical evaluation. Headache, 6:1, 1966.

Chao, D. et al. The migraine syndrome. IV. Headache in children. Headache, 3:1, 1963.

Fenichel, G. M. Migraine as a cause of benign paroxysmal vertigo of childhood. J. Pediat., 71:114, 1967.

Gold, A. P., Chutorian, A. M., and Carter, S. Migraine and allied head pains in children. In Friedman, A. P., and Haims, E., eds., Headaches in Children. Springfield, Ill., Charles C Thomas, Publ., 1967.

Hinrichs, W. L., and Keith, H. M. Migraine in childhood: a follow-up report. Mayo Clin. Proc., 40:593, 1965.

Holguin, J., and Fenichel, G. Migraine. J. Pediat., 70:290, 1967.

Macoun, S. Migraine in school children. Develop. Med. Child Neurol., 5:62, 1963.

Mitchell, R. Migraine in childhood. Develop. Med. Child Neurol., 9:641, 1967.

Ohta, M., Araki, S., and Kuriowa, Y. Familial occurrence of migraine with a hemiplegic syndrome and cerebellar manifestations. Neurology, 17:813, 1967.

Vahlquist, B., and Hackzell, G. Migraine of early onset. A study of 31 cases in which disease first appeared between 1 and 4 years of age. Acta Paediat., 38:622, 1949.

Weil, A. A. EEG observation on "dysrhythmic" migraine. J. Nerv. Ment. Dis., 134:277, 1962.

Whitehouse, D., Pappas, J. A., Escala, P. H., and Livingston, S. Electroencephalographic changes in children with migraine. New Eng. J. Med., 276:23, 1967.

Wolff, H. G. Headache and Other Head Pains. New York, Oxford Univ. Press, 1948, p. 268.

NARCOLEPSY

Salfield, D. J. Narcolepsy in a child under 7 years old. Arch. Dis. Child., 35:538, 1959.

Sours, J. A. Narcolepsy and other disturbances in the sleep-waking rhythm: a study of 115 cases with review of the literature. J. Nerv. Ment. Dis., 137:525, 1963.

Spier, N., and Karelitz, S. The Pickwickian syndrome. Amer. J. Dis. Child., 99:822, 1960.

Yoss, R. E., and Daly, D. D. Criteria for the diagnosis of the narcoleptic syndrome. Mayo Clin. Proc., 32:320, 1957.

——— and Daly, D. D. Narcolepsy in children. Pediatrics, 25:1025, 1960.

15.10
THE PERIPHERAL
NEUROPATHIES

NIELS L. LOW

Polyneuritis

The peripheral nervous system may be affected by toxic agents, inflammatory diseases, and metabolic disorders of known and unknown causes. Diseases of peripheral nerves are classified as acute, chronic, and recurrent neuropathies. Single nerve involvement is termed mononeuritis; disease of multiple peripheral nerves, cranial nerves, or both is called polyneuritis.

Acute Polyneuritis

Synonyms for acute polyneuritis are polyneuropathy, polyradiculoneuropathy, infectious neuronitis, schwannitis, and Guillain-Barré syndrome.

ETIOLOGY. In the vast majority of patients, the cause is unknown. Since polyneuropathy of unknown origin is frequently preceded by an infection, it is commonly called postinfectious polyneuritis. However, etiologic delineation can be established in some cases, and it is above all of importance because of the possible therapeutic implications. Specific bacterial and viral agents known to produce this condition include diphtheria with its particular affinity for the ninth and tenth cranial nerves leading to impairment of gag, swallow, and phonation. Infectious mononucleosis, rubeola, rubella, Coxsackie, and other viral infections have been known to produce the clinical picture of polyneuritis. Metabolic and toxic states may likewise produce a neuropathy. Diabetes and lead, common in adults, are rarely observed in children. Mercury and other heavy metal toxins are also possible etiologic factors. Thallium toxicity is considered when the paresis is associated with alopecia and optic atrophy.

Tick paralysis is an uncommon form of very acute and overwhelming polyneuropathy that is apparently due to an unknown toxin released by the wood tick during a feeding on the human host. Tick paralysis causes respiratory muscle paralysis which can be fatal (Sec. 14.53). Removal of the tick results in prompt improvement and full recovery. The search for ticks, especially in the region of the head and neck in children, is imperative whenever tick exposure was possible.

PATHOLOGY. The earliest changes in the peripheral or cranial nerves are edema with early disintegration of myelin and axis cylinders. Phagocytosis and proliferation of Schwann cells occur later, while macrophages with myelin inclusion are seen only in those patients who die late in the disease. Marked involvement of the roots of cranial nerves and of the ventral roots along the spinal axis is common. Both the degree of elevation of CSF protein and the presence of meningeal signs are apparently related to the extent of root involvement, termed polyneuroradiculitis.

CLINICAL MANIFESTATIONS. The clinical picture of this syndrome is variable but is usually characterized by acute ascending motor paralysis, motor and sensory findings of peripheral nerve distribution, and cranial nerve involvement. A respiratory or gastrointestinal infection frequently precedes the disease by a few days to two weeks. Boys and girls are equally affected during the various age groups of childhood and adolescence.

Mode of Onset. Muscle weakness normally precedes sensory symptoms, but paresthesia in hands and feet may be the initial complaint. Weakness, usually first apparent in the lower extremities, may manifest itself from the onset as a quadriparesis.

Motor Manifestations. Paresis may remain mild or, more commonly, becomes profound. It is usually ascending, symmetric in distribution, and the distal parts of the extremities are more severely affected than the proximal muscle groups. With involvement of the intercostal nerves, respiratory paralysis will occur with varying degrees of reduction in vital capacity. Atrophy of the skeletal muscles in the affected areas tends to occur early, especially in the intrinsic muscles of the hands and in the calves. The muscle weakness is of the flaccid type.

Cranial Nerves. Any motor nerve from the third to the twelfth may be involved with resultant paresis in the corresponding muscles. Bilateral facial nerve paresis occurs in approximately one-third of the affected children; unilateral facial weakness is less common. Involvement of the ninth and tenth nerves has greater clinical significance because of the potential consequence of impaired gag, swallow, and cough. Other cranial nerves are rarely involved, but complete ophthalmoplegia may occur. Papilledema is occasionally observed; it is unrelated to cerebrospinal fluid pressure but is often associated with an elevated protein content of the fluid.

Autonomic System. Postural hypotension in some children is due to impairment of the preganglionic nerves in the ventral roots with subsequent reduction of vasoconstriction. Absent or reduced sweating in the involved areas is presumably due to a similar process. The mechanism leading to the arterial hypertension observed occasionally is unclear.

Sensation. A reliable sensory examination in young children may be difficult or impossible. Paresthesia, impaired sensation, or both are common findings but may be absent even in the older, more reliable child. Position sense is the most frequently impaired sensory modality, followed by vibration, pain, and touch in descending order of frequency.

Reflexes. The deep tendon reflexes are usually absent, but incomplete loss does occur. There is an approximate correlation between degree of weakness and loss of reflexes. Abdominal and cremasteric reflexes may also disappear during the early stages of the disease process.

Bladder and Bowel Dysfunction. Urinary incontinence or retention may occur transiently. Constipation is common; it is related to weakness of the abdominal muscles as well as the difficulty of defecating in the recumbent position. Fecal incontinence with absent anal reflex is uncommon.

Meningeal Signs. Slight nuchal pain and rigidity are commonly observed. Positive Kernig and Brudzinski signs are found in a moderate number of children.

LABORATORY FINDINGS. Most children with acute polyneuritis have a normal peripheral blood count, urinalysis, and sedimentation rate. The cerebrospinal fluid (CSF) should always be examined in a suspected case of polyneuropathy. The pressure of the fluid is usually normal, but a pleocytosis of 50 or even 200 to 300 white blood cells does not exclude the diagnosis of polyneuritis. Approximately three-fourths of these children show an elevated protein content in the CSF. This increase of protein may only be slight, but values occasionally exceed 400 mg per 100 ml. Most commonly, there is a slight rise of protein during the first one or two weeks of the disease, with a peak concentration at about four weeks, followed by a gradual decline over several more weeks. This frequent dissociation between a normal cell count and an elevated protein was described initially by Guillain, Barré, and Strohl, and polyneuritis is often called the Guillain-Barré syndrome. Because these laboratory findings are not present routinely and the dissociation does not signify a special or separate clinical entity, it is probably wise not to use that eponym. The CSF sugar should always be in the normal range. Electrical testing is a useful ancillary procedure. Electromyography may show fibrillation and positive potentials; and on contraction of the muscle abnormalities of the motor unit, the type characteristic of denervation may be evident. Conduction velocity of the motor nerve is usually decreased, and the chronaxie values are elevated.

DIAGNOSIS. When a child presents with muscle weakness associated with loss or reduction of tendon reflexes, acute polyneuritis should be suspected whether or not there are sensory changes. Electromyographic studies will reveal evidence of denervation, and conduction velocity of the nerve may be decreased. The flare reaction on the skin obtained by scratch or intradermal injection of histamine may be absent. Tests for diphtheria and infectious mononucleosis should be performed. Appropriate serologic tests for viral infections should be made. Diabetes should be excluded, and a detailed history should be taken for exposure to possible toxins such as mercury, lead, or thallium supported by laboratory tests as indicated. Primary disease of muscle and of the anterior horn cells of the spinal cord may give a clinical picture that simulates polyneuritis. Muscular dystrophy is differentiated by its slow development and tendency to involve proximal more than distal musculature. Polymyositis may be difficult to distinguish, but the deep tendon reflexes are usually retained. Electromyography is frequently of value in distinguishing muscle from peripheral nerve disease. Infantile spinal muscular atrophy (Werdnig-Hoffmann disease), characterized by muscle weakness secondary to anterior horn cell disease, is distinguished from polyneuropathy by its early age of onset, progressive course, tongue involvement, and absence of sensory findings.

COURSE AND OUTCOME. The clinical course is variable. The appearance of paresis may be very insidious but is usually progressive and tends to reach a peak within 7 to 10 days. Approximately one-half of the children show clinically recognizable improvement by the end of the second week of the illness. The period necessary for complete recovery varies from 2 to 18 months. Muscle strength returns much more rapidly than the tendon reflexes. Complete recovery without residua is the most common end result. With proper management and detailed attention to respiratory problems and complications, the mortality should be less than 5 percent.

MANAGEMENT. A therapeutic program recognizes the multiple etiologies and, when present, corrects or removes such factors. General supportive or symptomatic care may be lifesaving and is essential to achieve maximum rehabilitation. A supportive program should include complete bed rest, adequate hydration and nutrition, skillful nursing care, prevention of contractures and deformities, and the use of an indwelling catheter in the presence of urinary retention. Analgesics may be required for pain resulting from root involvement. Tracheostomy and/or a respirator may be lifesaving in the presence of respiratory difficulties. Physiotherapy is essential in all phases of the disease. Early in the course, it is limited to proper positioning and passive full range of motion; later, an active program of exercises, gait training, and bracing is employed.

Chronic and Recurrent Polyneuropathies

Occasionally, children are seen who develop polyneuropathy with a long, protracted chronic course. This neuropathic weakness leads to progressive atrophy and severe disability over a number of years. The cause of this form of chronic disease of the peripheral nervous system is unknown, and the mechanism is poorly understood.

Another group of children suffer from repeated attacks of apparently acute polyneuritis with incomplete recovery between attacks. The residua of these recurrences tend to increase with each exacerbation. It is not known whether the chronic and the recurrent types are two different forms of one disease or represent separate entities.

Some patients with "idiopathic" chronic or relapsing polyneuritis benefit from treatment with adrenocortical steroids. If an initial attempt over a period of a month of therapy results in improvement, the steroids may be required for months to years. In a 6-year-old child, prednisone is initially given in the dosage of 40 to 60 mg daily and, after the first 4 to 6 weeks, is gradually reduced to 20 mg a day.

Special Clinical Entities

Chronic hypertrophic polyneuropathy of Dejerine-Sottas is a familial disease of dominant inheritance characterized clinically by onset in childhood of slowly progressing weakness and sensory phenomena in the distal parts of the extremities. The disease is usually fatal by the second or third decade of life. The typical pathologic findings are axonal destruction and proliferation of Schwann cells leading to thickened palpable peripheral nerves. These changes may be diffuse along the entire length of nerves or may be of nodular or intermittent distribution.

Charcot-Marie-Tooth disease or peroneal muscular atrophy is also a familial disease with an autosomal mode of inheritance. It involves predominantly the lower parts of the legs and the small muscles of the hands. The clinical spectrum is variable; only the peripheral nerves may be affected, or the cord and probably even the muscles may also be involved. Peroneal atrophy progresses much slower than the previously mentioned hypertrophic neuritis. The differential diagnosis between Charcot-Marie-Tooth disease and the various hereditary forms of spinal degenerative disease may be very difficult, and at times impossible. One form may gradually change into the other in a given patient, and both forms may be seen in different members of a family. No specific therapy is available for this condition.

Progressive involvement of peripheral nerves is not uncommonly seen in periarteritis nodosa and less frequently in lupus erythematosus. *Chediak-Higashi syndrome* is a rare entity characterized by progressive neuropathic weakness and peroxidase-positive inclusions in leucocytes. *Acanthocytosis* (Bassen-Kornzweig disease), a recessively inherited disorder in the metabolism of beta-lipoproteins, is manifested by a celiac syndrome in early childhood, followed by polyneuropathy and deformity of erythrocytes. *Refsum syndrome* is a recessively inherited progressive form of polyneuritis with ataxia, retinitis pigmentosa, pupillary abnormalities, deafness, electrocardiographic changes, epiphyseal dysplasia, and ichthyosis. It is associated with an inborn error of metabolism with an inability to oxidize phytanic acid to dicarboxylic acid.

Acute attacks of the acute intermittent form of porphyria, rarely observed in children, are usually associated with polyneuritis. Abdominal pain is a prominent symptom in addition to marked irritability, convulsions, and sometimes psychosis. Increased urinary porphobilinogen is found during the acute episodes.

Heredofamilial neuritis with brachial predilection is characterized by recurrent neuropathy involving the shoulder and arms. The facial appearance of involved persons is conspicuously similar. The disease has a dominant inheritance and does not tend to progress to chronic disability.

Cranial Nerve Palsies

Cranial nerve palsies may occur with polyneuritis or may be manifestations of other disease states. Cranial nerves are characteristically involved in brainstem tumors and are frequently affected by acute poliomyelitis and some progressive degenerative diseases. Facial weakness may be due to primary muscle disease. Myasthenia gravis typically manifests itself in weakness of the extraocular muscles. Isolated impairment of one or both abducens nerves is usually secondary to increased intracranial pressure but occasionally its involvement is benign and unrelated to increased pressure. The third, fourth, fifth, and sixth cranial nerves may be involved in disease such as thrombosis, injury, or tumors in and around the cavernous sinus.

Isolated peripheral facial weakness may be present from birth or acquired. If congenital, it may be part of or the only manifestation of Möbius' syndrome. Acquired facial palsy may be present from birth and result from forceps pressure on the facial neve. In such patients full recovery can be expected. Isolated, acquired neuritis of the seventh cranial nerve is called *Bell's palsy*. The clinical signs of Bell's palsy are obliteration of the nasolabial fold on the affected side, a pulling of the corner of the mouth to the opposite (stronger) side, incomplete closure of the eyelid, and the inability to wrinkle the forehead on the same side. Retroauricular pain may be present, and taste may be impaired over the anterior two-thirds of the ipsilateral side of the tongue. The cause is unknown in most instances, but the palsy frequently follows mild respiratory infections. The association with purulent otitis media, acute mastoiditis, or parotitis is uncommon. Herpes zoster, syphilis, and sarcoidosis are rare causes. If there is no specific cause, recovery within a few weeks to several months can be expected in the vast majority of cases. It has not been established whether treatment with ACTH, adrenocortical steroids, or surgical decompression is helpful.

REFERENCES

POLYNEURITIS

Adler, K. Tick paralysis. Canad. Med. Ass. J., 94:550, 1966.
Appenzellar, O., and Marshall, J. Vasomotor disturbance in Landry-Guillain-Barré syndrome. Arch. Neurol., 9: 368, 1963.
Birchfield, R. I., and Shaw, C. M. Postural hypotension in the Guillain-Barré syndrome. Arch. Neurol., 10: 149, 1964.
Dunn, H. G., Buckler, W. St. J., Morrison, G. C. E., and Emory, A. W. Conduction velocity of motor nerves in infants and children. Pediatrics, 34:708, 1964.
Guillain, G., Barré, J. A., and Strohl, A. Sur un syndrome de radiculo-névrite avec hyperalbuminose du liquide céphalo-rachidien sans réaction cellulaire. Bull. Soc. Med. Hop. Paris, 40:1462, 1916.
Haymaker, W., and Kernohan, J. W. The Landry-Guillain-Barré syndrome. Medicine, 28:59, 1949.
Low, N. L., Schneider, J., and Carter, S. Polyneuritis in children. Pediatrics, 22:972, 1958.
Peterman, A. F., Daly, D. D., Dion, F. R., and Keith, H. M. Infectious neuronitis in children. Neurology, 9:533, 1959.
Seto, D. S. Y., and Freeman, J. M. Lead neuropathy in childhood. Amer. J. Dis. Child., 107:337, 1964.

CHRONIC AND RECURRENT POLYNEUROPATHIES

Austin, J. H. Observations on the syndrome of hypertrophic neuritis. Medicine, 35:187, 1956.
Dejerine, J., and Sottas, J. Sur la névrite interstitielle, hypertrophique et progressive de l'enfance. C. R. Soc. Biol., 5:63, 1893.
Donohue, W. L., and Bain, H. W. Chediak-Higashi syndrome: A lethal familial disease with anomalous inclusions in the leukocytes and constitutional stigmata: report of a case with necropsy. Pediatrics, 20: 416, 1957.
Haase, G. F., and Shy, M. Pathological changes in muscle biopsies from patients with peroneal muscular atrophy. Brain, 83:631, 1960.
Higashi, O. Congenital gigantism of peroxidase granules; the first case ever reported of qualitative abnormality of peroxidase. Tohoku J. Exp. Med., 59:315, 1954.
Jacob, J. C., Andermann, F., and Robb, J. P. Heredofamilial neuritis and brachial predilection. Neurology, 11:1025, 1961.
Refsum, S. Heredopathis atactica polyneuritiformis. Acta Psychiat. Neurol. Scand. (Suppl.), 38:308, 1946.
Richterich, R., van Mechelen, P., and Rosse, E. Refsum's disease (heredopathia atactica polyneuritiformis): An inborn error of lipid metabolism with storage of 3, 7, 11, 15-tetra-methyl hexadecanoic acid. Amer. J. Med., 39:230, 1965.
Schwartz, J. F., Rowland, L. P. et al. Bassen-Kornzweig syndrome: Deficiency of serum β-lipoprotein. Arch. Neurol., 8:438, 1963.
Taylor, R. A. Heredofamilial mononeuritis multiplex with brachial predilection. Brain, 83:113, 1960.

CRANIAL NERVE PALSIES

Boone, P. C. Bell's palsy. Acta Neurochir., 7:16, 1959.
Evans, P. R. Nuclear agenesis. Arch. Dis. Child., 30: 237, 1955.
Henderson, J. L. The congenital facial diplegia syndrome. Brain, 62:381, 1939.

15.11
INFECTIONS OF THE NERVOUS SYSTEM

DAVID B. CLARK

Bacterial meningitides are described under infections with specific organisms in Section 14.3. The discussion here is limited to craniospinal focal sepsis and certain encephalitides.

Craniospinal Focal Sepsis

Any portion of the brain, spinal cord, or meninges may be the site of abscess formation. Epidural abscess, usually small and often granulomatous, lies between skull and dura; in the vertebral column it is also called pachymeningitis spinalis. Subdural abscess or subdural empyema lies between dura and arachnoid. Brain abscess and intramedullary abscess are within the brain and spinal cord, respectively. Ventriculitis, an inflammation of the walls of the cerebral ventricles, may go on to filling of the ventricular system with pus, a pyocephalus. Subarachnoid loculations are circumscribed poolings of pus within the subarachnoid space; like ventriculitis and pyocephalus, they usually result from an inadequately treated meningitis. Meningitis circumscripta is the patch of localized meningitis often found above a brain abscess.

All of these conditions are secondary complications rather than primary illnesses. Craniospinal abscess is not a primary disease. It results from infection of the nervous system and its membranes by: (1) direct, penetrating trauma; (2) direct extension, by involvement of contiguous layers or along infected and thromboid veins, from paracranial and spinal foci in sinuses, mastoid air cells, scalp infections, spondylitis, or pleural or perirenal infections; and (3) hematogenous or metastatic spread from distant sites, usually in lung, heart, or bone, or cutaneous infections. Much more rarely, a primary pyogenic meningitis or infection via a congenital dermal sinus is responsible. Less than 10 percent of all craniospinal abscesses are without demonstrable primary sources. They are, in most cases, avoidable illnesses. They are always serious, their outcome if untreated or poorly treated being death or severe handicap. The physician has therefore the dual responsibility of preventing them where possible by prompt eradication or primary foci and, where this has failed, of recognizing abscess early and treating it vigorously.

EPIDEMIOLOGY. Incidence is very difficult to determine. For the antibiotic era, a figure between 1.5 and 3.0 per 10,000 hospital admissions is a fair approximation, at least for large general hospitals with active pediatric, neurosurgical, and neurologic services. There is no certain evidence that antibiotics have altered incidence materially. Modern therapy has not significantly affected routes of infection; metastatic abscess continues to outnumber abscess developing by extension by about 2:1.

Males outnumber females, but this is apparently an expression of greater vulnerability of the male to infections rather than of greater frequency of trauma. Race and socioeconomic factors are of importance only in that the better medical care available to some racial, cultural, or economic groups tends to remove potential primary sources early.

No age is spared, but craniospinal abscess is rare below 1 year and is predominantly a disease of the early decades of life. A third of all cases fall in the pediatric age group. The type and location of abscesses are to some degree age-dependent, expressing the age preference of the primary infection. Subdural empyema and pyocephalus, which often complicate meningitis, are, like meningitis itself, common in very young children, while brain abscess secondary to otitis media, sinusitis, and mastoiditis is more frequent in older children or adolescents.

BACTERIOLOGY. Almost any pyogen may be responsible: anaerobic or microaerophilic streptococci, pneumococci, staphylococci, and gram-negative bacilli are the most common. Fungi (actinomycetes, aspergillus, leptothrix, and nocardia) and even protozoa, particularly *Entamoeba histolytica*, are reported.

In many cases, more than one organism is present. Most abscesses, particularly brain abscess, will sterilize themselves in time, the hardier organisms persisting longer. Since sterilization is hastened by antibiotics, culturally negative abscesses are more and more frequently encountered, and great care must be taken to culture and to examine stained smears of pus if organisms are to be identified.

PATHOLOGY AND PATHOGENESIS. A fully formed brain abscess consists of a center of broken down leucocytes, tissue debris, and microorganisms, surrounded by a zone of granulation tissue and fat-laden phagocytes, and then a capsule of collagenous and glial fibers. Most peripherally there is a zone of edema, with inflammatory exudate about blood vessels, and some breakdown of white matter. Daughter abscesses may form in the capsule or surrounding edematous zone. Brain abscesses range in size from miliary foci to large structures containing 40 to 60 ml, the average being 15 to 30 ml. Walls of chronic abscesses may calcify.

Subdural empyema is initially an unencapsulated mass of pus, or infected meningitic effusion, which can flow freely in the subdural space, usually above the cerebral hemispheres or in the interhemispheric cleft; in time, it becomes encapsulated, principally from the dural side. Epidural abscess is usually much smaller, frequently a granulomatous mass with small droplets of pus rather than a single large abscess.

Both dead brain tissue and bacteria are required for the development of a brain abscess. Infective emboli provide these in metastatic abscess, septic thrombi in abscess by extension; in traumatic abscess, brain tissue is killed and infected by the same wound. Cranial epidural abscess usually occurs by direct extension from skull foci; subdural abscesses may also develop from direct extension or evolve from an infected effusion. Spinal epidural abscess is often metastatic.

All forms damage the nervous tissue by direct destruction of tissue, edema, compression, and vascular damage leading to tissue necrosis, and to some degree at least by toxemia.

Clinical Types

Cranial Epidural Abscess

This usually develops by direct extension from sinusitis, mastoiditis, or dental infections. The abscess is usually small and granulomatous. Symptoms, if not confused by those of the primary infection, are rather slight, consisting of headache, with pain and tenderness often localized at the site, fever rarely above 100° F, and a mild leucocytosis and elevated ESR. Physical signs are those of the primary illness, and frank neurologic signs are rare or absent.

The commonest and most important site of cranial epidural abscess is along the lateral and sigmoid sinuses. It develops as a complication of otitis or mastoiditis, and is a leading childhood cause of benign increased intracranial pressure, so-called pseudotumor cerebri. The sinus may be thrombosed or only compressed by granulation tissue. Frank otitis or mastoiditis need not be present, but scarred or perforated tympanic membranes and x-ray changes in the mastoid cells are constant. The symptoms and signs are those of increased intracranial pressure, including headache, vomiting, diplopia due to abducens palsy, and papilledema, often of startling degree, in a child who does not usually appear seriously ill.

In most cases of cranial epidural abscess, the skull x-rays are abnormal, demonstrating either the primary focus—such as mastoiditis, sinusitis, or osteomyelitis—or sutural separation, or both. The EEG is mildly abnormal, but seldom diagnostic. The cerebrospinal fluid may be normal or under increased pressure; infrequently it may show a mild increase in protein or a slight pleocytosis.

The important diagnostic distinction is from other forms of focal intracranial sepsis such as cortical thrombophlebitis, subdural empyema, and brain abscess and from brain tumor. Focal neurologic signs, other than the false localizing sixth nerve palsies or increased pressure, are rarely if ever present, seizures are unusual, the cerebrospinal fluid except for pressure is normal or near normal, and the EEG is not sharply localizing; the reverse of all these is true for the other septic forms. The presence of a primary focus and signs of infection, the absence of localized neurologic deficit, and the speed of evolution distinguish it from brain tumor. In many cases a contrast study such as arteriography or ventriculography is necessary.

Some cases will respond to antibiotics alone, although curettage of the granuloma may be necessary. Mastoid granulomas, with benign increased intracranial pressure, may require repeated lumbar punctures or even ventricular or spinal shunting, to protect vision, and a mastoidectomy is necessary. The prognosis is good.

Cranial Subdural Empyema

Subdural empyema occurs in the infant usually as a sequelae of a missed or poorly treated meningitis, with an infected effusion. The symptoms are usually submerged in those of the meningitis; the patients presenting as chronically ill infants with enlarging heads, intermittent fever, vomiting, and seizures. Some degree of hemiparesis is usually present, and there is a marked pleocytosis of the cerebrospinal fluid with increased protein. The diagnosis is established by subdural taps, but brain abscess must often be excluded by ventriculography or angiography.

In older children, the source is more commonly sinusitis, mastoiditis, or scalp furuncles, and the interval between the original infection and the onset of symptoms may be many weeks. Patients are usually quite ill, fevers of 102° or 103° F being common. Lethargy, confusion, or stupor are present, cranial tenderness is marked, and hemiparesis and seizures are common. The CSF is regularly abnormal; pressure and protein are increased, and a considerable pleocytosis, including polymorphonuclear cells is present. EEG's may show voltage suppression, spikes, and slowing. The most important distinction is from brain abscess and septic cerebritis, both of which may also be present, and contrast x-ray studies, preferably arteriography are usually necessary.

Treatment is surgical drainage, which in both infant and adult is best done through multiple trephine holes or osteoplastic craniotomies, since the tendency of the pus to migrate between the hemispheres and into subarachnoid cisternae makes drainage at best difficult. Prolonged massive antibiotic therapy and supportive measures, including fluids, are generally necessary. Older children may make a good recovery, but infants are generally left with serious neurologic residuals.

Brain Abscess

Abscess within the brain, like the other forms of craniospinal focal sepsis, can develop (1) as a metastatic abscess, by hematogenous spread from a distant source; (2) by direction extension from paracranial foci in sinuses, mastoids, dental alveoli, and scalp infections; (3) by direct contamination of the brain from without, through wounds and congenital dermal sinuses; and (4) rarely, as a sequel of pyogenic meningitis. The great majority fall in the first two categories, and of these, metastic abscess is about twice as common as abscess due to direct extension.

The common sites of origin of metastatic abscess are in the heart and lungs; osteomyelitis, dental alveolar sepsis, skin infections, renal and perirenal abscess less frequently constitute such sites. Of the cardiac sources, acute bacterial endocarditis is less common than subacute bacterial endocarditis, and both are more prone to cause multiple miliary lesions than large solitary abscesses.

A more frequent cardiac source is any congenital cardiac malformation capable of producing a right-to-left shunt; congenital pulmonary AV fistulas, with an intact heart, may equally predispose to abscess. The mode of infection of the brain here is not completely explained. Despite the frequency of bacterial endocarditis in congenital heart disease, very few children who develop brain abscess have convincing evidence for endocarditis; the abscesses themselves are usually single and massive, and only rarely have autopsied patients had signs of endocarditis. The most plausible explanation is that, due to polycythemia, the very cyanotic child suffers recurrent miliary cerebral infarcts and, because of this shunt, recurrent bacteremias. If the two coincide, the necrotic segment of brain becomes infected and an abscess evolves. Three or four percent of all patients with cyanotic congenital heart disease or pulmonary AV fistulas will, if their condition is not relieved, develop brain abscess.

Pulmonary sources of brain abscess are most commonly bronchiectasis, lung abscess, and empyema. Since all are relatively uncommon in childhood, abscess complicating them is comparatively unusual. Pyelitis, perinephric abscess, osteomyelitis, dental alveolar sepsis, and furuncles are all occasional causes.

Mastoiditis and, in the older child or adolescent, frontal sinusitis lead as sources of abscesses forming by direct extension. Because of the nature and evolution of the lesion, all of these are liable to cause associated epidural granulations or subdural empyema as well. Traumatic abscesses may follow craniotomy or accidental head trauma. The latter are known for the chronicity of their course, many weeks or months intervening between injury and onset of symptoms. An interesting variety is the frontal abscess which follows penetrating wounds through the orbit, such as pencils perforating the orbital roof after falls. A rare cause is infection along a congenital dermal sinus, usually leading from the occipital to the midline cerebellar region.

Solitary brain abscess resulting from meningitis is less frequent than might be expected. Smith and Landing found only 2 in 34 autopsied cases of *H. influenzae* meningitis, and Swartz and Dodge only 1 dubious instance in 207 clinical cases of various causes. It is not, however, unusual to have the headache, slight fever, stiff neck, and mild pleocytosis of a rapidly developing abscess mistaken for meningitis, the signs and symptoms of the abscess being mistakenly interpreted as its source.

Traumatic abscess, or abscess developing by extension, is adjacent to the primary focus and usually solitary, though daughter abscesses may develop about it. Frontal sinusitis leads to frontal lobe abscess; mastoiditis to temporal lobe or cerebellar abscess. Metastatic abscess of any sort is solitary and supratentorial in about four-fifths of all cases. Only in the miliary abscesses of bacterial endocarditis and with certain fungi such as nocardia are multiple abscesses really common.

SYMPTOMS AND SIGNS. Occasionally an initial stage of brain infection, with headache, fever, and perhaps even a little stiff neck, may be identified. More often, the onset is insidious or so mixed with the symptoms of the primary illness as to be indistinguishable. Except for some traumatic abscesses, the duration from onset to severe symptoms is not long,

two to six weeks at the most. The child is lethargic, eats poorly, and complains intermittently of headache. Fever due to the abscess itself is surprisingly slight, rarely over 100° or 101° F and often intermittent. A mild peripheral leucocytosis and anemia of infection may appear. Before long vomiting becomes evident, usually on arising and is seldom frequent or pernicious. Focal neurologic deficits and more obvious signs of increased intracranial pressure may develop progressively, or, more commonly, they are noted after the child has a seizure. These signs are, first, those appropriate to the region involved: hemiparesis, with sensory deficit in parietal lesions, visual field defects if temporal or occipital lobes become involved, and aphasias of varying degree, particularly with left-sided lesions. Posterior fossa or cerebellar abscesses produce ataxia and cranial nerve palsies and, especially if acute, skew deviations of the eyes. Second are the signs of increased intracranial pressure: papilledema, abducens palsies, and, in young children, sutural separation and Macewen's cracked-pot resonance. Third, and of great value, many patients describe or give evidence of localized percussion tenderness of the skull overlying the abscess.

DIAGNOSIS. The special diagnostic procedures of value, beyond physical examination and history, are: (1) blood count, ordinarily unrevealing except for moderate leucocytosis and perhaps anemia of infection; (2) elevated ESR; (3) x-rays, which may disclose a primary focus in sinuses, mastoids, and chest; x-rays of the skull usually are normal or show only separated sutures, although very old chronic abscesses sometimes are marked by curvilinear calcifications; and (4) EEG, which in 60 percent or more of the cases will demonstrate lateralized slowing, and finally a clear-cut focus of very slow (Fig. 73), usually high-voltage delta waves, due either to edema or probably to compression and disturbance of the reticular formation.

If abscess is seriously suspected, the CSF should ordinarily not be examined because of the danger of herniation. When done, the pressure is generally increased, and there is a mild to moderate increase in protein and cells, usually less than 50 and including a few polymorphonuclears. In the unruptured abscess the sugar content of the CSF is characteristically normal. Finding many cells is unusual, and cultures are regularly negative unless the abscess has begun to leak. This serious event causes sharp worsening of the clinical condition, high fever, marked sitff neck, and usually seizures and decerebration. Rupture is almost always into the ventricular system, rather than into the subarachnoid space.

If the story is clear-cut and the localization by symptoms, signs, EEG, and perhaps percussion tenderness is sharp, contrast studies may not be necessary but more commonly cerebral arteriography is the method of choice, except in very cyanotic cardiacs who may not tolerate it well and in abscesses placed far posteriorly in the occipital region where

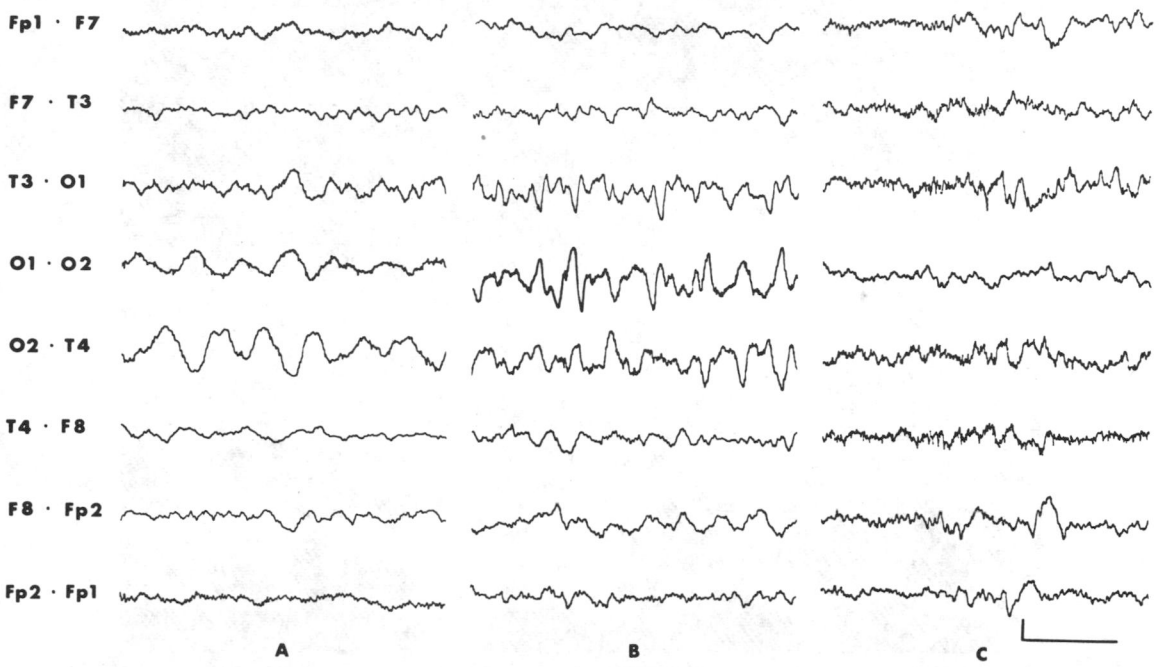

Fig. 73. EEG. Seven-year-old child with tetralogy of Fallot and right occipital lobe abscess. A. Before operation. B. One week after aspiration. C. Six months later. Note high-voltage slow focus, in leads 01-02 and 02-T4 disappearing on treatment.

localized deformity of the vessels may be difficult to define.

TREATMENT. The basis of treatment is surgical drainage. Some surgeons prefer trephination, tapping and drainage of the abscess, and instillation of a contrast material, usually Thorotrast, to label the abscess on successive skull films. The size of the abscess is then checked by x-rays at intervals (Fig. 74A and B), while the child is given antibiotics appropriate to the organisms cultured. If progressive shrinkage does not occur, the abscess is reaspirated until it does. Ordinarily two or three aspirations, over a period of a week to 10 days, are sufficient.

Total excision, preferred by other surgeons, requires that the abscess be well encapsulated, which is hastened by some days of antibiotic treatment before operation. In children with high intracranial pressure and advancing signs of intracranial decompensation, this time may not be available. Such preoperative antibiotic treatment also reduces edema and lessens the unavoidable destruction of brain tissue at the time of removal. It is also believed by some that total excision is attended by a lower incidence of seizures than is aspiration, though evidence for this is at best equivocal. Lastly, total excision avoids the possible delayed effects of retained thorium dioxide.

The author's preference is for aspiration, as a much shorter and simpler procedure with results which compare favorably with excision. In one in-

stance, the very cyanotic cardiac patient, it is certainly superior, since these patients tolerate prolonged anesthesia poorly, and the tremendous congestion of their brain makes excision much more hazardous. Each case, however, must be considered on its own merits.

Massive antibiotic therapy is, with one exception, always necessary. It is determined when possible by knowledge or strong suspicion of the nature of the organism involved. When in doubt, or when organisms can be seen on smear but not cultured, combinations of antibiotics should be used. Treatment is maintained for at least three weeks after the abscess is removed or drained and the child appears clinically well. The one exception is in the child, usually a cardiac patient, whose diagnosis is in doubt, in whom abscess is suspected but not proved, and the signs are not yet clear enough to warrant operation. Under such circumstances antibiotics can indefinitely prolong but never cure the illness; they also obscure its symptoms beyond the point of possible diagnosis, even by angiography or ventriculography. When this situation occurs it is often necessary to stop all antibiotics, to watch the child closely with daily neurologic examinations and EEG's every three or four days, and thus permit definite, localizing findings to appear.

During treatment of abscess, the primary focus should be identified and treated. Curettage of mastoiditis or frontal osteomyelitis and treatment of pul-

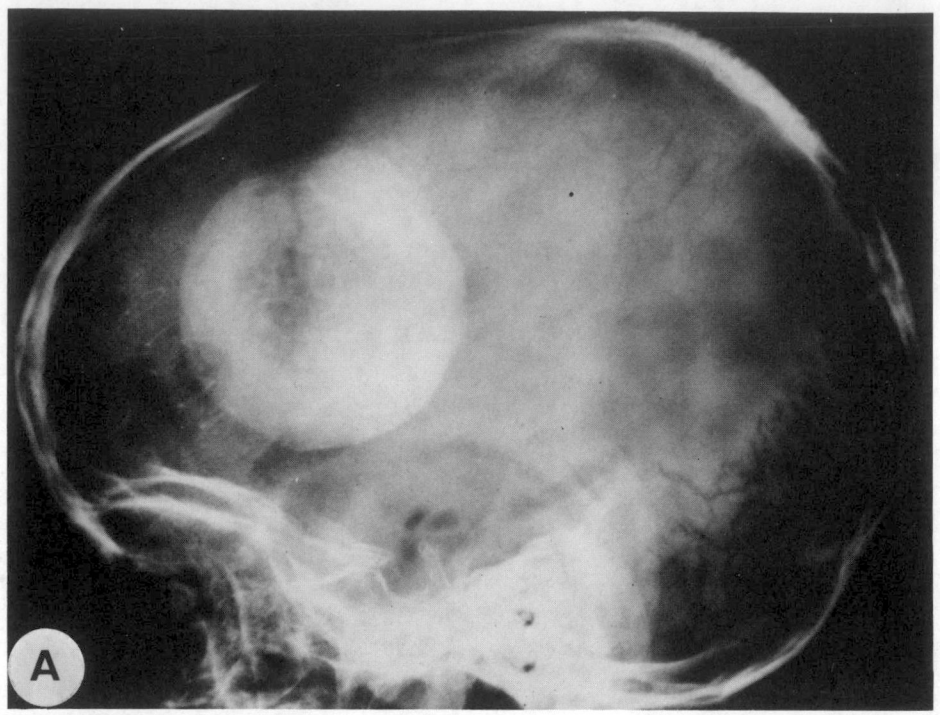

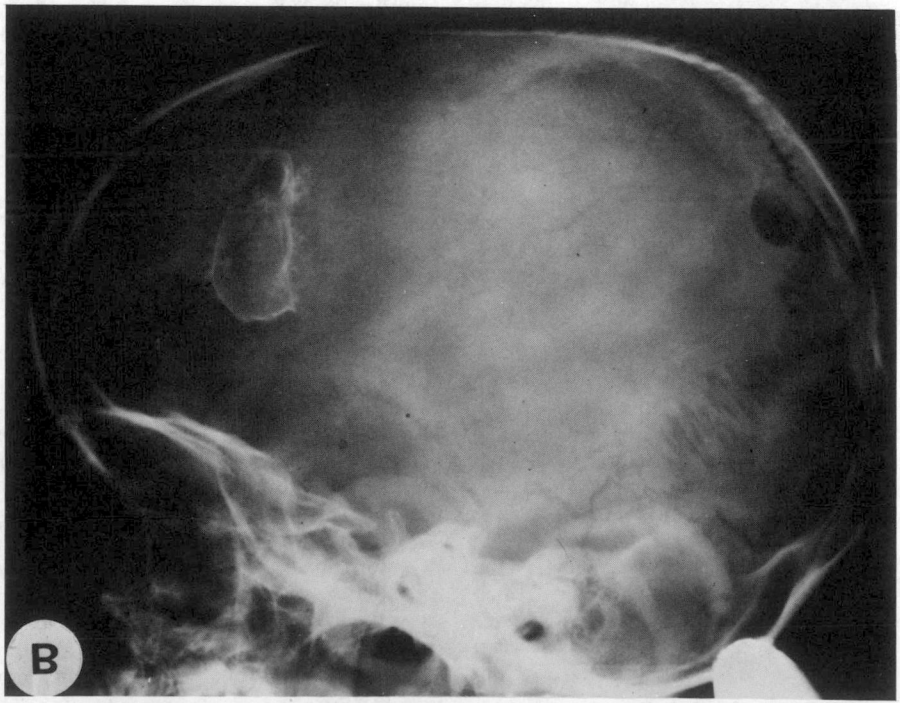

Fig. 74. *A.* Frontal abscess, aspirated and instilled with thorium dioxide. First day. *B.* After 10 days of antibiotic treatment and two additional aspirations.

monary infections should be pursued as rapidly as the patient's condition permits.

Lastly, it should not be forgotten that the incidence of seizures after brain abscess treated by any means is about 45 percent. Posterior fossa lesions and those restricted to the occipital and possibly the frontal poles are followed by seizures much less frequently than those in the central regions of the brain, but none is exempt. A good rule is to treat all patients with supratentorial lesions with anticonvulsants from time of operation for at least two years. Those who have seizures should be treated until seizure-free for three to five years.

PROGNOSIS. The mortality of brain abscess still exceeds 25 percent. With early recognition and prompt treatment, it can be brought well below this figure. It is always a serious life-threatening disease, and the neurologic residuals of hemiparesis, aphasic defects, seizures, learning impairment, and others are significant in one-half or more of the survivors.

Pyocephalus and Subarachnoid Loculations

Occasionally a young infant with severe or poorly treated meninigitis will develop a state in which the ventricles are filled with pus. A similar outcome may result from ascending infection in a meningomyelocele, the infection passing directly up the central canal and into the ventricles, without an intervening meningitis. There is always a severe ventriculitis and very extensive brain damage. The symptoms are persistent meningeal signs, enlarging head, "cerebral" cry, and signs of severe cerebral damage. Ventricular lavage and prolonged antibiotic therapy may in time clear the cerebrospinal fluid, but the end result is always bad and generally fatal.

Slowly resolving meningitis may also be accompanied by loculations of pus in subarachnoid cisterns, between the cerebral hemispheres, in the cavum septi pellucidi, or sometimes in the ventricles, usually in the temporal horns. These are usually small and generally respond in time to prolonged antibiotics. Their sudden rupture may account for brief exacerbation of meningeal signs, fever, and increase in cells in the CSF. Rarely, an intraventricular loculation may lead to localized enlargement of a part of the ventricular system, or a subarachnoid patch may be large enough to give local signs and permit surgical drainage.

Spinal Abscess

Abscesses involving the spinal cord are much rarer than intracranial abscess, the proportion being about 1 to 15. The causes, modes of development, and pathogenesis are, however, the same. Though any tissue or space may be involved, epidural abscess is the only one of practical importance. About half the cases are metastatic, the common sources being furuncles, bed sores, wound infections, or even infected acne. The other half develop by extension, from spondylitis or from pleural or perirental infections. Bacteriology is as variable as that of intracranial abscess, but staphylococci predominate because of the great frequency of primary cutaneous sources. The abscesses develop in the epidural space, posterior to the spinal cord and dura, and usually in mid or upper thoracic levels. Structurally, they may vary from frank, semifluid pus to thick granulations, with tiny droplets of enclosed pus. Acute forms begin with severe backache, local tenderness, fever of considerable degree, and leucocytosis. After two or three days to a week, sharp root or girdle pains appear. In another day or two, signs of spinal cord compression—stiffness and weakness of legs, heightened reflexes, and sphincter disorders—appear and are followed in hours to a day or two by complete paraplegia.

Epidural abscess developing from spondylitis may have a long phase of back pain and tenderness, but the time from root pains to complete paraplegia is often very short. In other instances, a slow, granulomatous infection may progress over weeks, months, or even years, simulating a spinal cord tumor.

The history of a previous infection, the back pain, worsened by flexion, local tenderness, and the evolution of signs of a spinal cord compression are generally present and highly suggestive. Plain x-rays will seldom do more than identify a primary focus, but lumbar puncture may either hit the abscess directly—and, unfortunately, be misinterpreted, since the pus is often so thick it will not flow through a needle—or demonstrate a low CSF pressure, with signs of spinal block, a very high protein, and increased cells, the Froin syndrome. Myelography is usually necessary to establish the lesion and its exact level.

Treatment is immediate surgical drainage and decompression, plus appropriate antibiotics. If decompression is done before paralysis or more than mild neurologic deficit has appeared, the results are excellent; if complete paraplegia has developed, complete recovery is less likely, and mortality may be high.

The important differential diagnostic possibilities include spinal cord tumor, metastatic tumor, and occasionally transverse myelitis due to viruses, spinal arteritis, or neuromyelitis optica. The importance of early decompression is so great that myelography should not be withheld if the least possibility of epidural abscess exists.

Intramedullary abscess is exceedingly rare, less than a dozen cases having been reported. It is diagnosed much as epidural abscess and, surprisingly, may respond well to midline myelotomy. Special note should also be taken of congenital dermal sinuses in the pilonidal area or thoracic region. The surface pore is often unimpressive, but the tract may lead to epidural space, to meninges, or into the cord itself. Recurrent meningitis or some form of spinal abscess almost always develops. The excision of such tracts, as soon as they are discovered, is very nearly an emergency procedure.

Encephalitis

HORACE L. HODES

Encephalitis may be caused by a variety of infectious agents including protozoa, fungi, bacteria, and viruses. The present discussion will be confined largely to this last group. Viral encephalitides are of two general types. In primary encephalitis there is direct invasion of the central nervous system by the virus, the pathologic changes being those of inflammation and neuronal injury. In secondary encephalitis the causative virus is not recoverable from the nervous system, some indirect mechanism apparently being responsible; the pathologic changes in this type are predominantly those of perivascular demyelination. A similar demyelinating process sometimes occurs in association with active immunization with viral antigens, notably after vaccination against smallpox and rabies.

Primary Viral Encephalitis

Viruses causing primary encephalitis in man include the following:

> Von Economo's disease (virus not isolated)
> Arthropod-borne encephalitides:
> > St. Louis encephalitis
> > Western equine encephalitis
> > Eastern equine encephalitis
> > Japanese encephalitis*
> > Russian spring-summer encephalitis
> > Murray Valley encephalitis
> > > (Australian X disease)
> Mumps
> Herpes simplex
> Infectious mononucleosis

Poliomyelitis, Coxsackie, and ECHO virus infections, rabies, and lymphocytic choriomeningitis belong in this group but are discussed elsewhere.

The pathologic picture in this group is in general similar for all the agents listed. Neuronal injury is apparent early in the disease, varying degrees of degeneration and necrosis of neurons and supporting cells being observed, followed by inflammatory changes. Neuronophagia, proliferation of glia, and perivascular infiltration with polymorphonuclear and mononuclear cells are seen. Areas of hemorrhage and necrosis in the ground substance of the gray and white matter are common, and cellular infiltration of the meninges is the rule.

---

* Originally designated Japanese B encephalitis.

Specific changes are seen in some of these infections such as the Negri bodies of rabies. Japanese encephalitis and Russian spring-summer viruses exhibit a particular tendency to attack the Purkinje cells of the cerebellum, whereas the related equine and St. Louis encephalitis viruses do not possess this property. For the most part it is, however, impossible to make an etiologic diagnosis from the pathologic changes.

The clinical picture is also nonspecific. The onset of symptoms may be gradual, following a prodromal illness resembling influenza. In other instances evidences of central nervous disorder appear with explosive suddenness. There may be fever, headache, and meningeal signs (stiff neck and Kernig and Brudzinski signs). Ataxia may be conspicuous. The sensorium is variably affected; there may be drowsiness and lethargy, followed by stupor and coma, or the patient may be excited, irritable, confused, or disoriented. Muscular twitchings, tremors, and convulsions may occur. Often there are bulbar symptoms —paralysis of the ocular or facial muscles or the muscles of deglutition. Respiration is commonly affected, becoming jerky or irregular. Profound variations in blood pressure and marked hyperthermia may occur. Involvement of the spinal cord may be revealed by paralytic and sensory disturbances or by loss of sphincter control. In infants, the onset is usually sudden and they are generally more severely affected than adults.

The blood commonly shows a moderate polymorphonuclear leucocytosis ranging between 10,000 and 15,000. The spinal fluid is under pressure and shows some elevation of protein and a pleocytosis (20 to 600 cells), mostly mononuclears; it may, however, be quite normal. The concentration of glucose is normal or slightly elevated and that of chloride is not affected. Electroencephalography shows widespread cerebral disturbance, irregular, slow, high-voltage complexes replacing the normal patterns.

Laboratory studies have shown that inapparent infections are common with all members of this group. The ratio of apparent to inapparent infections is highest with Eastern equine virus (1 in 18) and lowest with Japanese virus (1 in 500). In some inapparent cases it seems probable that infection gives rise to mild constitutional symptoms, but there is no evidence of invasion of the central nervous system.

The greater severity of the symptoms with Eastern equine encephalitis is notable; the fatality rate is higher, and permanent sequelae in the form of mental retardation, palsies, and convulsive disorders are more frequent. Such sequelae are also common in Japanese encephalitis in contrast to the Western equine and St. Louis virus infection. Clinical differentiation of the various types of encephalitis is, however, impossible; this must be made by recovery of virus or by antibody studies.

Primary encephalitis must be differentiated from a number of other conditions which affect the central nervous system. Helpful information may be revealed by a careful history. With a history of pica, lead poisoning is a strong possibility, and other evidences of this condition should be sought, particularly stippling of the red cells, lead lines in the bones, and the presence of an excess of lead in the plasma. The spinal fluid in lead encephalopathy is characterized by a relatively mild pleocytosis but a greatly increased concentration of protein. With a history of swimming in, or more particularly of falling into, stagnant water that may have been contaminated by animals, leptospirosis should be kept in mind. Tuberculous meningitis is readily confused with viral encephalitis. Evidence of tuberculosis elsewhere is important, particularly if the subject is an infant. A moderate decrease in glucose and in the chloride of the spinal fluid is characteristic of tuberculous meningitis as contrasted with viral encephalitis. Occasionally a low-grade bacterial meningitis will cause diagnostic difficulty, especially a mild meningococcal infection that may have been unrecognized. Such cases may present a predominantly lymphocytic reaction in the spinal fluid; the spinal fluid sugar is, however, likely to be reduced. Brain abscess may cause confusion at times; a history of preceding otitis media or of purulent meningitis may be helpful. Brain tumor may be a cause of difficulty, particularly when symptoms appear abruptly as may occur with pontine tumors. A pleocytosis of the spinal fluid may be observed with medulloblastoma; the mononuclear cells are not readily differentiated from lymphocytes unless a cell block is made.

The development of flaccid paralysis points to poliomyelitis as the cause of the disorder, though this has been observed in Coxsackie infections. Clinical evidence of mumps will also suggest the nature of the cerebral process, but by and large the identification of the agent rests with the virus laboratory. Recovery of virus from the blood is practical only in the case of Russian encephalitis, and from the spinal fluid in mumps and Coxsackie virus infections. A more practical procedure is the demonstration of a rising antibody titer in the blood or spinal fluid during convalescence; two specimens should be secured, one early in the disease and another two or three weeks later. Specific information can be obtained from neutralizing, hemagglutination-inhibiting, or complement-fixing antibodies, the last-named being the most useful.

Therapy for this group of infections is symptomatic. Sedation is often needed. When coma or bulbar symptoms are present, frequent aspiration may be needed to keep an open airway; tracheotomy may be necessary to remove secretions effectively. When tube feeding proves to be necessary, the danger of aspiration pneumonia must be borne in mind. Respiratory paralysis may require treatment in a tank respirator. Marked hyperthermia may be relieved by cold packs; it should be remembered that hyperthermia increases the need for water and electrolytes. Hypothermia has been employed in treating patients critically ill with viral encephalitis; its value

is difficult to establish because of the variable course of these infections. Anticonvulsants should be given if there are seizures. In some types, such as mumps encephalitis, complete and relatively rapid recovery is the rule. In other types a variable percentage of the cases exhibit residual damage.

The specific types of primary encephalitis will now be considered.

VON ECONOMO'S DISEASE (ENCEPHALITIS LETHARGICA: EPIDEMIC ENCEPHALITIS, TYPE A). This form of encphalitis is almost certainly caused by a virus, but a causative agent has never been isolated. It is possible that the sleeping sickness epidemic of 1712 was this disease. The first modern cases were observed in 1915 in Rumania and subsequently in France. In 1917 it was well described by Von Economo in Vienna. The disease appeared in the United States in 1918, and up to 1926 it was observed in many parts of the world, but no new cases have been observed since that time. Nothing is known about the spread of the infection. Most cases were observed in the winter and spring months. All ages were affected, most of the cases being in young adults.

The disease affects the central nervous system only. Lesions are most conspicuous in nuclear masses such as the cranial nerve nuclei, the substantia nigra, globus pallidus and subthalamic nuclei, the medulla and pons. The white matter is rarely affected.

Clinically the disease is usually characterized by fever, headache, oculomotor palsies, and frequently somnolence. A small percentage of the cases exhibit pleocytosis of the spinal fluid early in the disease. Sequelae are frequent and include parkinsonism, sleep reversal, and serious personality changes and mental abnormalities which may be so severe as to reduce the child to a state of idiocy. Lesions in the region of the pituitary and hypothalamus have been known to cause obesity, diabetes insipidus, or sexual precocity.

The immediate mortality is between 20 and 40 percent, the ultimate mortality being considerably greater because of the progressive nature of the disease. Not more than 25 percent are well after three years, and it appears that even fewer make a complete recovery.

The diagnosis is easy if typical symptoms are present and an epidemic is in progress, difficult if this is not the case. The progressive nature of the disease and the characteristic late symptoms are important features. Late cases may strongly resemble the posttraumatic syndrome. Unless a clear history of a previous acute episode is obtained the diagnosis cannot be made with confidence.

Treatment is purely symptomatic. If there is excitement or choreiform movements, sedatives are indicated. Residual behavioral disorders require special treatment (Chap. 6).

ARTHROPOD-BORNE VIRAL ENCEPHALITIDES (ARBOVIRUS ENCEPHALITIDES). These include St. Louis encephalitis, Western equine encephalitis, Eastern equine encephalitis, Japanese encephalitis, Russian spring-summer encephalitis, Murray Valley encephalitis. There are many common features. They all occur in epidemic as well as sporadic form, epidemics reaching their peak during the summer. In each instance, reservoirs of the virus exist among wild and domestic mammals and birds. Transmission of infection is accomplished by arthropod vectors, which usually become infected by feeding on the blood of birds, in which viremia is more prolonged than it is in mammals. The viruses in this group have a similar host range among laboratory animals; all produce fatal encephalomyelitis in mice. They are similar in size, and they produce similar pathologic changes in the central nervous system, primarily by direct invasion of neurons. Serologic tests indicate some degree of relationship between them. Outbreaks of St. Louis, and Western and Eastern equine encephalitis have occurred in many parts of the United States.

Epidemiology. St. Louis encephalitis was first observed in Illinois in 1932; larger epidemics occurred the following year in St. Louis and Kansas City. Since then the disease has been observed sporadically and in local outbreaks in western Canada and many parts of the United States, although not as yet in the northeastern area. Reservoirs of infection exist in animals and in domestic and wild birds. Cox demonstrated its presence in horses, but it appears that birds form the main reservoir. Two vectors are concerned in its transmission. It has been found that in chickens and in wild birds various mites transmit the infection from bird to bird, inducing a long-standing viremia without encephalitis. Mites can also transmit the infection to their own offspring; thus a large reservoir in birds is readily maintained. Bird mites do not, however, bite mammals, and transmission to the latter occurs by mosquitoes (particularly *Culex tarsalis* and *C. pipiens*). Prophylaxis consists in measures for mosquito control and protection from mosquitoes.

Western equine encephalitis is in most respects similar to the St. Louis type. The infection was first recognized in horses by Meyer in California in 1930, the first human cases being described in 1938. Outbreaks have been observed in California, Washington, Montana, Saskatchewan, Manitoba, the Dakotas, Nebraska, and Texas. The disease is observed among horses, but there appears to be a bird reservoir. The infection has been found in mites from chickens, blackbirds, and tropical birds; they appear to cause transmission from bird to bird, transmission from bird to mammal being caused by mosquitoes (chiefly *C. tarsalis*).

Eastern equine encephalitis was first discovered in horses by Ten Broeck in 1933, the first human cases being recognized in 1938 in Massachusetts. Both in horses and in man the disease is exceptionally severe, with a high mortality and a strong probability of residual damage among survivors. In the 1947 Louisiana epidemic, 3,700 horses and mules died of this infection. Ten human cases were observed, nine of them in children, of whom seven died. Outbreaks of the disease among horses have occurred in the East, South, and Middle West, in the Caribbean, Panama, and Brazil. In some of these epidemics the disease has developed in humans; in others antibodies to the virus have been found in man. The most recent epidemic occurred in New Jersey in 1959; 31 human cases were observed, of whom 21 died and only one of the survivors escaped permanent central nervous system damage. Recovery of virus from the mites and lice of chickens as well as from those of wild birds suggests that birds are the main reservoir for this virus; pheasants bred for the market seem to be particularly susceptible. Mosquitoes are apparently responsible for transmission from bird to mammal as well as from bird to bird. *Culex melanura* is regarded as the most important vector, although evidence from the New Jersey epidemic pointed toward *Aedes sollicitans*.

Prophylactic vaccines have been developed for Western and Eastern equine encephalitides which are recommended for horses and mules in infected areas and have been used in persons closely exposed to these viruses in the laboratory. They are not recommended for general use. Greater reliance may be placed on mosquito control.

Japanese encephalitis, though not as yet reported in this country, has been recognized in eastern Asia since the end of the nineteenth century. It is found in Japan, Taiwan, Korea, eastern China, and Indonesia, and outbreaks have been observed as far west as India and as far east as Guam. In the Okinawa epidemic of 1945 infection was demonstrated in horses; pigs and other domestic animals were also incriminated as reservoirs of virus. However, it is probable that nestling wild birds, especially of the heron family, are the most important source of infection for the mosquito vectors and the subsequent spread of the disease to man. Many species of mosquitoes have been shown capable of transmitting the infection.

Australian X disease, an epidemic form of encephalitis, was first recognized in Australia in 1917. More recently, this disease has been renamed Murray Valley encephalitis. The virus which causes this form of encephalitis, Murray Valley virus, is closely related to but distinct from that of Japanese encephalitis.

Russian spring-summer encephalitis is another arthropod-borne disease which is caused by a virus possessing properties similar to those of the viruses under discussion. This disease, which is transmitted by a wood tick, occurs in eastern Russia and Siberia. Domestic animals and rodents serve as reservoirs for the virus. Human cases occur chiefly among forest workers, and the great majority of patients give a history of having been bitten by ticks 8 to 15 days before onset of symptoms.

MUMPS MENINGOENCEPHALITIS. Mumps virus is probably the most common cause of encephalitis in the United States and Canada. Between 30 and 50 percent of mumps patients show pleocytosis of the spinal fluid, but only 5 to 10 percent show clinical evidence of meningoencephalitis (Sec. 14.34). Of importance is the fact that meningoencephalitis may be the only clinical manifestation of mumps; a large proportion of patients with so-called aseptic meningitis—acute nervous symptoms and a low-grade mononuclear pleocytosis in the spinal fluid—are infected by mumps virus.

In the great majority of cases the picture is that of a primary encephalitis; virus is present in the nervous system and can be recovered from the spinal fluid. The symptoms, though often marked, nearly always clear completely; they are largely meningeal, there being little evidence of brain involvement. The nervous manifestations tend to occur at the height of the parotitis. On rare occasions a secondary type of encephalitis develops after mumps. The pathologic changes resemble those of measles and other postinfectious encephalitides, the outstanding change being perivascular demyelination. In such cases the symptoms are encephalitic rather than meningeal. Paralysis, particularly of the cranial nerves, may develop and is sometimes permanent. Most of the rare fatalities occur in this type.

Symptoms of drowsiness, coma, or excitement, or the presence of paralytic manifestations do not in themselves indicate that the more serious type of encephalitis is present. Such cases often recover completely. Lennette has reported cases in which the muscles of the trunk and extremities were affected with flaccid weakness similar to mild paralytic poliomyelitis, most of which cleared up completely or almost completely in the course of months. By and large this is true of involvement of the cranial nerves. Deafness, however, when it develops is likely to be permanent, though in most instances it is unilateral.

The spinal fluid is generally under increased pressure and contains 50 to 500 cells, mostly lymphocytes. The protein is only moderately increased, and the sugar is normal or slightly elevated.

Diagnosis offers little difficulty when parotitis or orchitis is present. When these are absent it is often in doubt. A history of exposure to mumps is helpful. An important differential point between mumps and poliomyelitis is the character of the spinal fluid; early in poliomyelitis the cells in the spinal fluid may be predominantly polymorphonuclear, lymphocytes predominating at a later stage, whereas in mumps the cells are predominantly mononuclear from the start.

The laboratory diagnosis of mumps is considered elsewhere (Sec. 14.34), as is the prophylaxis of the disease. Convalescent gamma globulin from mumps patients has been employed in therapy, as have steroids. Evidence that they are of value is, however, unconvincing. General measures are adequate in the great majority of cases.

Herpes Simplex Encephalitis

The virus of herpes simplex is capable of producing encephalitis, which may occur at any age, sometimes in the newborn (Sec. 14.29). In most instances there have been perpetic vesicles in the skin and mucous membranes, but in some this has not been the case, evidence of central nervous system disease being the only clinical manifestation.

Lesions are found chiefly in the cortex but also in the hypothalamus, medulla, pons, and caudate nucleus. There is widespread evidence of neuronal injury, with necrotic changes particularly in the cortical gray matter. Perivascular accumulations of lymphocytes and mononuclear cells are found; proliferation of oligodendroglia may be present, and there may be petechial hemorrhages. Spherical or elongated acidophilic inclusion bodies similar to those seen in other tissues may be found in the nuclei of ganglion cells of the cortex. The meninges may be intensely infiltrated with lymphocytes and mononuclear cells.

The symptoms are both meningeal and encephalitic. Headache and fever are commonly present. There may be convulsions and delirium leading to stupor and coma and perhaps to fatal termination. Palsies of the cranial nerves may occur. A focal variant with unilateral temporal lobe predilection is also seen. In such patients, the clinical manifestations may mimic a neoplasm and ancillary laboratory studies confirm the presence of a "mass" lesion. The spinal fluid may be normal or show a mononuclear pleocytosis with counts ranging from 50 to 600 cells, an increase in protein, and no reduction of glucose.

In the absence of other manifestations of herpes the diagnosis can be made only by biopsy or laboratory criteria—the recovery of herpes virus from the spinal fluid or demonstration of a rise of complement-fixing antibody in convalescence. The mortality is high and the sequelae serious. Florman's patient, who became ill at 11 days, survived but was later observed to be spastic and severely retarded.

Dr. B. E. Juel-Jensen has reported very recently that the antimetabolitic cytosine arabinoside (cytarabine) had brought about a "dramatic recovery" in five patients with severe forms of generalized *herpesvirus hominis* infection, and that the same result had been obtained in the case of a man suffering from early simian herpesvirus encephalitis. The patients were given cytarabine intravenously once daily for 5 days in doses ranging from 0.3 to 2.0 mg/kg/per day. No toxic effects were noted in the patients treated. More experience with this drug in the treatment of herpesvirus infections of the central nervous system will certainly be reported soon.

Infectious Mononucleosis

Neurologic complications of this disease have been reported since 1931 in the English and American literature. The clinical picture may be that of the Guillain-Barré syndrome, or there may be a meningoencephalitis with mononuclear pleocytosis in the spinal fluid. Bulbar symptoms are often present. Recovery is the rule, but permanent damage may occur; a few fatalities have been reported. Diagnosis depends on the presence of nervous symptoms in association with other symptoms of infectious mononucleosis, a typical blood picture and a positive Paul-Bunnell test (Sec. 14.30). Specific laboratory procedures may serve to rule out other possibilities. Complement-fixation tests make possible the exclusion of mumps, herpes, and the anthropod-borne encephalitides. Coxsackie and ECHO viruses can be excluded by failure to recover them from spinal fluid or feces which have been inoculated into suckling mice or tissue cultures.

Postinfectious Encephalitis

Many acute infectious diseases, particularly those of viral origin, are followed by an acute encephalitis characterized by diffuse demyelination of the brain and spinal cord. Postinfectious encephalitis is also called secondary encephalitis, allergic encephalitis, and acute demyelinating encephalitis. It is seen most commonly following measles but may occur after chickenpox, rubella, smallpox, and vaccinia; some cases associated with mumps fall in this category. Similar involvement of the nervous system may occur after vaccination with antigens of various types. The incidence of such postvaccination encephalitis is higher after antirabies vaccination than with other commonly employed antigens.

The injury to the nervous system in these cases is not attributable to the presence of the infectious agent. Virus cannot be demonstrated in the nervous tissue when the disease is at its height; furthermore, the symptoms usually develop gradually during convalescence. Many theories have been advanced to explain this type of encephalitis. The most satisfactory one postulates a primary asymptomatic injury to the nervous system with the production of altered chemical substances which then act as antigens. Antibodies are then formed against these substances which react not only against this material but also with unaltered nerve cell constituents. The available evidence indicates that myelin may be involved in this reaction. Details of the experimental work supporting this view cannot be given here except to state that a disease very similar to postinfectious and postimmunization encephalitis has been produced in monkeys. Rivers and his co-workers accomplished this by repeated injections of homologous and heterologous nerve tissue. By the use of adjuvants with homologous nerve tissues the same result was achieved rapidly by Kabat et al. and by Morgan.

It should be noted that occasionally symptoms of central nervous system disease begin early in the course of a primary infection. In these cases the possibility cannot be excluded that encephalitis results from direct action of the virus on the central nervous system.

MEASLES ENCEPHALITIS. The incidence of measles encephalitis varies considerably from outbreak to outbreak. Published reports indicate an incidence as high as one case of encephalitis for each 600 cases of measles and as rare as one in 3,000. In our own experience the incidence has been approximately one case of encephalitis for every 1,200 of measles. Measles encephalitis is more likely to occur among children suffering from severe attacks of measles than among those with mild measles. Although no accurate statistical data are available, it appears that the incidence of encephalitis following modified measles is much lower than that following the natural disease.

Pathology. The brain is usually congested at postmortem, and a few petechial hemorrhages may be present over the cortex. On histologic examination the characteristic lession is seen to be perivascular demyelination with phagocytosis of lipid material by the microglia. The myelin sheaths of the nerve fibers in the affected areas are destroyed. In the center of each demyelinated area there is generally a small, distended vein which shows endothelial and adventitial thickening. In early cases the axis cylinders are usually not severely affected, but in cases of long standing, secondary degeneration of these structures may be present. Demyelinated areas are infiltrated with microglial cells which contain lipid material. Similar cells are found in the perivascular spaces, and lymphocytic infiltration of these spaces may be seen. About the margins of the demyelinated areas there is usually proliferation of the astrocytes and glial fibers. The gray matter is in general much less severely involved than the white matter, but evidences of neuronal degeneration may be found. The meninges show little change. The distribution of the lesions described is not uniform; they may be most common in the brain, the spinal cord, or the cerebellum.

Symptoms. In rare instances symptoms of encephalitis begin at the height of the measles eruption or even during the prodromal period. The onset may be delayed as long as two weeks after the appearance of the eruption. However, it usually develops on the fourth to sixth day after the appearance of the exanthem, when the fever has fallen and the rash has begun to fade. The temperature rises again and may rapidly reach a peak of 104° to 105° F. Headache, vomiting, and stiffness of the neck are common. In some severe cases convulsions are the initial symptoms; in others there is gradually deepening drowsiness, followed by stupor and coma. Evidences of bulbar involvement may be present, such as irregularities in the rhythm and rate of respiration and difficulty in swallowing. Death may occur within a few days after onset. In some instances consciousness returns gradually, in others quite suddenly. The period of coma may vary from 12 or 24 hours to more than three weeks. In neurologic examination after consciousness is regained the child is sometimes found to be entirely normal; in other cases monoplegia, paraplegia, or hemiplegia of the upper motor neuron type is noted. Mental confusion, disorientation, loss of memory, and speech disturbances may be present. Changes in personality are quite common. Nystagmus, ataxia, and loss of muscle tone pointing to involvement of the cerebellum are sometimes seen. In a relatively small proportion of cases the nervous symptoms are due entirely to changes in the spinal cord. These patients may show the picture of transverse myelitis or of ascending myelitis without involvement of the pons, medulla, or cerebrum. Paraplegia, loss of sphincter control, and changes in the reflexes are common findings.

Diagnosis. The symptoms of central nervous system disease appearing during convalescence from a typical case of measles usually makes the diagnosis of measles encephalitis apparent. Confusion arises chiefly in those cases, actually uncomplicated, in which nervous symptoms accompany the febrile rise which immediately precedes or coincides with the appearance of the measles eruption. These symptoms usually disappear promptly, in contrast to measles encephalitis in which they commonly persist for more than 24 hours. In case of doubt, lumbar puncture should be performed. In about 80 percent of cases of measles encephalitis, an increase in protein concentration in the spinal fluid and a mononuclear pleocytosis are found.

Treatment. There is no specific treatment for measles encephalitis. Convalescent serum and gamma globulin have been employed but without demonstrable benefit. Some authors have employed steroids with what they have considered favorable results. On the other hand, Karelitz and Eisenberg in a retrospective study of 42 patients with measles encephalitis published in 1961 concluded that cortisone had failed to afford any advantage. Hypothermia has been used by a number of pediatricians, including the author, with variable results, probably in keeping with the natural variability of measles encephalitis.

Good general care is essential. Particular attention should be paid to providing adequate calories, fluids, minerals, and vitamins when the patient is unable to swallow because of paralysis of the pharyngeal muscles or because he is comatose. In these instances intravenous administration of fluids and tube feeding are required. The danger of aspiration has been referred to in the treatment of primary encephalitis (p. 1016). The tank respirator should be employed to furnish artificial respiration when this is necessary. It should be emphasized that the course of measles encephalitis is strikingly unpredictable, and no child's condition should be regarded as hopeless so long as life exists.

Prognosis. Approximately 10 percent of the patients with measles encephalitis die in the acute phase of the disease. However, the general tendency is toward recovery. Many patients whose condition appears hopeless in the beginning recover completely. We have seen complete recovery in patients comatose for more than one month. Unfortunately, approximately 20 percent of the patients who survive the acute stage suffer permanent damage. The se-

quelae range from minor changes in personality to complete dementia and generalized paralysis. Weakness of one or more extremities, hemiplegia, and paraplegia may occur. Epilepsy may develop. Other sequelae include cerebellar ataxia, nerve deafness, and permanent injury to the optic nerves. Lesions in the region of the pituitary may lead to precocious puberty and other endocrine disturbances.

ENCEPHALITIS ASSOCIATED WITH VARICELLA, RUBELLA, AND SMALLPOX. Encephalomyelitis which in general resembles that following measles may occur in association with varicella (Sec. 14.25). The symptoms generally begin between two days and two weeks after the appearance of the rash, but in very rare instances the neurologic symptoms precede the eruption. The incidence of encephalitis is much lower than among patients with measles. We encountered only 14 cases of varicella encephalitis during a period of 12 years at the Sydenham Hospital in Baltimore, although this hospital treated practically all complicated case of varicella in a population of over one million. In general, chickenpox encephalitis resembles that of measles, but cerebellar symptoms are relatively more common. The course tends to be milder, and the prognosis is better. The mortality rate is low as compared with measles, and recovery is more likely to be complete. In some instances, however, mental defects, spastic paraplegia, and monoplegia have been noted.

Encephalitis is extremely rare in German measles (see Sec. 14.39). The symptoms begin some days after the acute phase. Complete recovery is the rule, but a few fatal cases have been reported.

Encephalitis associated with smallpox is similar to measles encephalitis. The incidence appears to vary from year to year. Marsden and Hurst reported 11 cases among 2,400 patients, but encephalitis did not occur among a series of 8,000 subsequent patients with smallpox. It is believed that the incidence of neurologic symptoms is not related to the severity of the smallpox. Four deaths occurred among Marsden and Hurst's 11 cases. The survivors usually recover completely or very nearly so. There is no specific treatment.

POSTVACCINAL ENCEPHALITIS. Encephalitis following vaccination against smallpox (Sec. 14.40) was first reported in 1907. This complication has been encountered most frequently in England, Germany, Austria, and The Netherlands, less frequently in the United States. During the spring of 1947 roughly four million people in New York City were vaccinated against smallpox. It was believed that approximately 45 cases of encephalitis could be attributed to vaccination, an incidence of about 1 per 100,000.

The pathologic features of postvaccinal encephalitis are similar to those which occur with measles and require no separate description. The incubation period is generally between 10 and 11 days after vaccination. Occasionally, the period has been as short as two days and as long as 25 days. The disease is very rare in children under 1 year of age and appears to be less common in persons who have been vaccinated previously. The onset is generally abrupt. Its clinical course and neurologic findings are similar to those of measles encephalitis, with the possible exception that involvement of the spinal cord occurs more frequently in postvaccinal encephalitis. Laboratory findings are like those of measles encephalitis.

ENCEPHALITIS FOLLOWING VACCINATION AGAINST RABIES.   The condition has been observed only with vaccines which contain mammalian brain or spinal cord. The newer killed virus grown in embryonated duck eggs is virtually free of nerve tissue, and experience with it to date encourages the belief that this complication has been avoided. Encephalitis, always rare, is somewhat more frequently seen with attenuated living Pasteur vaccine than with the killed Semple vaccine (Sec. 14.38). The clinical symptoms are similar to those of measles encephalitis except that cord symptoms are more frequent; sometimes only a transverse myelitis is seen. The onset usually occurs 10 to 20 days after vaccination is commenced; it may be abrupt or gradual. Paresthesia and pain in the extremities may be noted, followed by motor weakness, usually in the limbs; bladder function may be impaired. Bulbar symptoms may occur early; in other instances an ascending Landry type of paralysis has been observed. The spinal fluid is sometimes normal but may show a mild pleocytosis with excess of protein. Approximately 15 percent of the cases have been fatal, but recovered cases rarely show residual damage; only occasionally do paralytic phenomena persist.

PERTUSSIS ENCEPHALOPATHY.   The effects of pertussis upon the central nervous system warrant separate consideration here. The brain may be affected in several different ways (Sec. 14.12). In a few instances there are massive hemorrhages in the brain substance or in the meninges. Their cause is not clear, and they are variously explained as the result of damage to the vessels or of congestion due to paroxysms of coughing. Several writers have found inflammatory lesions in the cortex, but in the only case in which we found such lesions there was also bacterial endocarditis. A number of cases have been described in which there was extensive atrophy of the cerebral cortex due chiefly to loss of neurons. Whether this is to be regarded as a result of toxic encephalopathy or of disturbances of cerebral circulation, as some authors claim, is still uncertain. In our experience this process is rare.

The clinical manifestations of these lesions are not uniform. Convulsions are the commonest and usually the first symptoms of involvement of the brain. Exceptionally tetany has been observed. The convulsions may cease promptly and leave no sequelae, or the child may remain in a state of stupor and exhibit general muscular rigidity or hemiplegia. A great variety of neurologic syndromes are described, including tremors, loss of vision, mental defects, and paralysis. Meningeal symptoms may be encountered, usually with a lymphocytosis in the cerebrospinal fluid. The cases followed by generalized cerebral atrophy present a fairly typical picture. After a series of convulsions the child becomes comatose and remains unconscious for periods of weeks or months. There is progressive rigidity of all the muscles, which may reach extraordinary intensity. All cortical functions seem to be abolished. Death may be long deferred.

ENCEPHALOPATHY FOLLOWING PERTUSSIS PROPHYLAXIS.   We have described above the manner in which injections of vaccines containing viruses may bring about injury to the central nervous system. It should be noted that similar damage has been reported following the use of bacterial vaccines and antitoxins. The administration of typhoid vaccine or of tetanus antitoxin has on rare occasions been followed by lesions of the brain, cord, and peripheral nerves. A number of authors have observed similar results following vaccination against pertussis (Sec. 14.12). In 1948 Byers and Moll described 15 infants who had suffered convulsions and severe brain injury following such vaccination. The symptoms of involvement of the central nervous system began from 20 minutes to 72 hours after injection of the vaccine. Convulsions, irritability, drowsiness, and coma were observed. These explosive reactions occurred after the first as well as the second and third of the immunizing injections. Spinal fluid contained an increase concentration of protein in most of the cases in which it was examined, and a mononuclear pleocytosis was found in some. The eventual outcome was grave. Of 12 cases observed for a long period only one recovered completely. The remaining children suffered from various combinations of cerebral palsy, continuing convulsive seizures, cortical atrophy, and mental retardation.

The pathogenesis of the encephalopathy associated with pertussis vaccination is not clear. It is impossible to conceive of an allergic or hyperimmune antigen-antibody type of reaction occurring so abruptly after the first injection of vaccine. A number of observers have obtained toxic filtrates and endotoxins from *Haemophilus pertussis* which have produced fatal encephalopathy in animals. The reactions described here may have some such pathogenesis.

It should be stated that the incidence of pertussis vaccination encephalopathy is extremely low when the total number of vaccinations is considered. Certainly it is so low as to leave no doubt regarding the wisdom of continuing mass pertussis immunization programs. We should, however, interpret the data as indicating that pertussis immunization should not be continued if an injection of the vaccine is followed by very high fever, drowsiness, convulsions, or any other symptoms referable to the central nervous system.

Slow Viruses in Chronic and Subacute Encephalitides

ALEX J. STEIGMAN

It has recently been firmly established that the measles virus is an essential ingredient in the subacute progressive encephalitis which is variously called subacute sclerosing panencephalitis (SSPE), Dawson's inclusion encephalitis, and Van Bogaert's subacute sclerosing leukoencephalitis.

SSPE does not present as a concomitant or early sequel to measles. Many months or years may elapse between the occurrence of measles and the onset of SSPE. (For acute encephalitis in measles see p. 1020.) In 1933 Dawson hypothesized that SSPE might be due to a virus because intranuclear inclusion bodies were observed in the neurons in this disease. The recent sequential findings which lead to the conclusion that measles virus is associated with SSPE are: (1) electron microscopic demonstration of structures consistent with the nucleocapsids of a paramyxovirus such as measles; (2) the detection of measles-like antigen by immunofluoresence in SSPE brains; (3) the presence of unusually high levels of antibody to measles virus in the blood and spinal fluid of patients; and (4) the isolation of wholly infectious measles virus from brain tissue of patients with SSPE. This was accomplished by cocultivating the diseased brain cells in vitro with laboratory-established tissue culture cell lines. Such a strain of SSPE measles virus has been adapted to baby hamsters; the virus produces CNS disease in these animals.

SSPE generally evolves in three clinical stages. Initially one notes changes in personality, behavior, and intellectual ability sometimes accompanied by mild transient seizures. Then more ominous signs appear of loss of memory, apathy, myoclonic jerks, chorioathetoid and dystonic movements. Finally stupor, perceptual blindness, and decorticate spasticity occur.

The first human subacute "degenerative" CNS disease to be associated with a previously unrecognized virus was Kuru. This exotic condition is confined to a specific group of cannibalistic natives of the New Guinea highlands. The patients have a protracted afebrile grotesque neurologic course ending in death, the spinal fluid showing no increase in cells or protein. When Kuru was successfully transmitted in series to nonhuman primates following a long incubation period, great impetus was given to restudy the role of viruses in other subacute and chronic "degenerative" diseases of the central nervous system in man.

There is now some evidence and much speculation regarding other subacute and chronic disorders of the CNS of man in which a viruslike transmissible agent is involved. Most recently, brain suspensions from patients with Creutzfeldt-Jakob disease (spongiform encephalopathy) has produced a similar disease following a long incubation period in chimpanzees; and experimental transmission from chimpanzee to chimpanzees has been accomplished.

Viral investigation requiring long-term observation of experimental animals is now in progress for a number of obscure human neurologic disorders such as amyotrophic lateral sclerosis, multiple sclerosis, neuromyelitis optica, and Schilder's disease. It is recognized that factors other than those which occur in an acute episodic viral disease may well be involved in slow viruses affecting the human central nervous system. The suspicion that long-acting slow viruses might be associated in some fashion with chronic neurologic disease was first substantiated in *scrapie*. Briefly this is a slowly progressive neurologic degenerative disorder of certain genetic strains of sheep and goats. The disease can be reproduced by injecting suspensions of central nervous tissue of affected animals into healthy sheep and goats. The incubation period is one to five years; the protracted clinical course is afebrile and lasts for months. When infectious brain tissue is inoculated into mice the incubation period may be half a year or longer. The mysterious viral and immunologic characteristics of scrapie do not here concern us, nor do the growing number of naturally occurring chronic neurologic diseases of other animals now ascribed to slow viruses.

REFERENCES

CRANIOSPINAL FOCAL SEPSIS

Altrocchi, P. H. Acute spinal epidural abscess vs. acute transverse myelopathy: Plea for neurosurgical caution. Arch. Neurol., 9:17, 1963.

Dutton, J. E. M., and Alexander, G. L. Intramedullary spinal abscess. J. Neurol. Neurosurg. Psychiat., 17:303, 1954.

Evans, W. The pathology and etiology of brain abscess. Lancet, 1:1231, 1931.

Garfield, J. Management of supratentorial intracranial abscess: review of 200 cases. Brit. Med. J., 2:7, 1969.

Greer, M. Benign intracranial hypertension. I. Mastoiditis and lateral sinus obstruction. Neurology, 12:472, 1962.

Haymaker, W. Fatal infections of the CNS and meninges after tooth extractions. Amer. J. Orthodont. Oral Surg., 31:117, 1945.

Heusner, A. P. Non-tuberculous spinal epidural infections. New Eng. J. Med., 239:845, 1948.

Jenkins, R. B., Augustin, G. J., Putnam, L. E., and Horiwitz, N. H. Intracranial extradural and subdural empyemas. Report of a case and review of the literature. Med. Ann. D.C., 37:472, 1968.

Liske, E., and Weikers, N. J. Changing aspects of brain abscess. Neurology, 14:294, 1964.

Pine, I., Atoynaton, I. H., and Margolis, G. The EEG

findings in 18 patients with brain abscess. Case reports and a review of the literature. Electroenceph. Clin. Neurophysiol., 4:165, 1952.

Sanford, H. N. Abscess of the brain in infants under 12 months of age. Amer. J. Dis. Child., 35:256, 1928.

Smith, J. F., and Landing, B. H. Mechanism of brain damage in H. influenzae meningitis. J. Neuropath. Exp. Neurol., 18:248, 1960.

Swartz, M. N., and Dodge, P. R. Bacterial meningitis: A review of selected aspects. New Eng. J. Med., 272: 725, 1965.

Tyler, H. R., and Clark, D. B. Incidence of neurological complications in patients with congenital heart disease. Arch. Neurol., 77:17, 1957.

ENCEPHALITIS

Cramblett, H. G., Stegmiller, H., and Spencer, C. California encephalitis virus infections in children. Clinical and laboratory studies. J.A.M.A., 198:108, 1966.

Field, E. J., and Raine, C. S. Experimental allergic encephalomyelitis. An electron microscopic study. Amer. J. Path., 49:537, 1966.

Ford, F. R. Diseases of the Nervous System in Infancy, Childhood, and Adolescence, 4th ed. Springfield, Ill., Charles C Thomas, Publ., 1959.

Hodes, H. L. Common types of encephalitis in children. New York J. Med., 50:2277, 1950.

LaMotte, L. C., Jr., Crane, G. T., Shriner, R. B., and Kirk, L. J. Use of adult chickens as arbovirus sentinels. 1. Viremia and persistence of antibody in experimentally inoculated adult chickens. Amer. J. Trop. Med., 16:348, 1967.

Neal, J. B. et al. Epidemic Encephalitis: Etiology, Epidemiology and Treatment. Reports of the Matheson Commission. New York, Columbia University Press, 1929, 1932, 1939.

——— Encephalitis: A Clinical Study. New York, Grune and Stratton, Inc., 1942.

Pierce, N. F., Portnoy, B., Leeds, N. E., Morrison, R. L., and Wehrle, P. F. Encephalitis associated with herpes simplex infection presenting as a temporal lobe mass. Neurology, 14:708, 1964.

ARTHROPOD-BORNE VIRAL ENCEPHALITIS (ARBOVIRUS ENCEPHALITIDES)

Casals, J. Viruses: The versatile parasites; the arthropod-borne group of animal viruses. Trans. N.Y. Acad. Sci., Ser. 2, 19:219, 1957.

Clarke, D. H. Two nonfatal human infections with the virus of Eastern encephalitis. Amer. J. Trop. Med., 10:67, 1961.

Cox, H. R., and Fite, G. L. Serological distinctions between viruses of encephalitis in St. Louis, 1933, equine encephalomyelitis and vesicular stomatitis. Proc. Soc. Exp. Biol. Med., 31:499, 1934.

Goldfield, M., and Rowan, F. The 1959 Outbreak of Eastern Encephalitis in New Jersey. Paper presented at Conference of State Health Laboratory Directors. Washington, D.C., Nov. 2, 1960.

Hodes, H. L. Common types of encephalitis in children. New York J. Med., 50:2277, 1950.

Olitsky, P. K., and Casals, J. In Rivers, T. M., and Horsfall, F. L., eds., Viral and Rickettsial Infections of Man, 3rd ed. Philadelphia, J. B. Lippincott Co., 1959, p. 269.

Smorodintseff, A. A. The spring-summer tick-borne encephalitis. Arch. Ges. Virusforsch., 1:468, 1940.

Ten Broeck, C., and Merrill, M. H. Serological difference between Eastern and Western equine encephalomyelitis virus. Proc. Soc. Exp. Biol. Med., 31:217, 1933.

MUMPS MENINGOENCEPHALITIS

Donohue, W. L. The pathology of mumps encephalitis with report of a fatal case. J. Pediat., 19:42, 1941.

Lennette, E. H., Caplan, G. E., and Magoffin, R. L. Mumps virus infection simulating paralytic poliomyelitis; a report of 11 cases. Pediatrics, 25:788, 1960.

HERPES SIMPLEX ENCEPHALITIS

Florman, A. L., and Mindlin, R. L. Generalized herpes simplex in an eleven-day-old premature infant. Amer. J. Dis. Child., 83:481, 1952.

Gajdusek, D. C., Robbins, M. L., and Robbins, F. C. Diagnosis of herpes simplex infections by the complement fixation test. J.A.M.A., 149:235, 1952.

Haymaker, W. Herpes simplex encephalitis in man, with a report of 3 cases. J. Neuropath. Exp. Neurol., 8:132, 1949.

INFECTIOUS MONONUCLEOSIS

Epstein, S. H., and Dameshek, W. Involvement of the central nervous system in a case of glandular fever. New Eng. J. Med., 205:1238, 1931.

Thelander, H. E., and Shaw, E. B. Infectious mononucleosis with special reference to cerebral complications. Amer. J. Dis. Child., 61:1131, 1941.

POSTINFECTIOUS ENCEPHALITIS

Ferraro, A. Pathology of demyelinating diseases as an allergic reaction of the brain. Arch. Neurol. Psychiat., 52:443, 1944.

Hurst, E. W. A review of some recent observations on demyelination. Brain, 67:103, 1944.

Kabat, E. A., Wolf, A., and Bezer, A. E. Rapid production of acute disseminated encephalomyelitis in rhesus monkeys by injection of heterologous and homologous brain tissue with adjuvants. J. Exp. Med., 85:117, 1947.

Morgan, I. M. Allergic encephalomyelitis in monkeys in response to injection of normal monkey nervous tissue. J. Exp. Med., 85:131, 1947.

Rivers, T. M., and Schwentker, F. F. Encephalomyelitis accompanied by myelin destruction experimentally produced in monkeys. J. Exp. Med., 61:689, 1935.

MEASLES ENCEPHALITIS

Appelbaum, E., Dolgopol, V. B., and Dolgin, J. Measles encephalitis. Amer. J. Dis. Child., 77:25, 1949.

Ford, F. R. Diseases of the Nervous System in Infancy, Childhood, and Adolescence, 4th ed. Springfield, Ill., Charles C Thomas, Publ., 1959.

——— and Guild, H. Precocious puberty following measles encephalomyelitis and epidemic encephalitis. Bull. Hopkins Hosp., 60:192, 1937.

Hamilton, P. M., and Hanna, R. J. Encephalitis complicating measles; a report on 241 cases collected from the literature and on 44 additional cases. Amer. J. Dis. Child., 61:483, 1941.

Haymaker, W., and Smadel, J. The Pathology of the Viral Encephalitides. Washington, U.S. Army Med. Museum, 1943.

Hodes, H. L. Encephalitides and Postinfectious Encephalopathies. *In* McIntosh, R., and Hare, C. C., eds., Neurology and Psychiatry in Childhood. Res. Publ. Ass. Res. Nerv. Ment. Dis., Baltimore, Williams and Wilkins Co., 1954, Vol. 34.

—— Common types of encephalitis in children. New York J. Med., 50:2277, 1950.

Karelitz, S., and Eisenberg, M. Measles encephalitis; evaluation of treatment with ACTH and adrenal corticosteroids. Pediatrics, 27:811, 1961.

Litvak, A. M., Sands, I. J., and Gibel, H. Encephalitis complicating measles; report of 56 cases with follow-up studies in 32. Amer. J. Dis. Child., 65:265, 1943.

Shaffer, M. F., Rake, G., and Hodes, H. L. Isolation of virus from a patient with fatal encephalitis complicating measles. Amer. J. Dis. Child., 64:815, 1942.

Spragins, M., Shinners, B. M., and Rochester, B. Measles encephalitis; clinical and electroencephalographic study. Pediatrics, 5:599, 1950.

ENCEPHALITIS ASSOCIATED WITH VARICELLA, RUBELLA, AND SMALLPOX

Boughton, C. R. Varicella zoster in Sydney. II. Neurological complications of varicella. Med. J. Aust., 2:444, 1966.

Davison, C., and Friedfeld, L. Acute encephalomyelitis following German measles. Amer. J. Dis. Child., 55:496, 1938.

Margolis, F. J., Wilson, J. L., and Top, F. H. Postrubella encephalomyelitis; report of cases in Detroit and review of literature. J. Pediat., 23:158, 1943.

Marsden, J. P., and Hurst, E. W. Acute perivascular myelinoclasis ("acute disseminated encephalomyelitis") in smallpox. Brain, 55:181, 1932.

Wilson, R. E., and Ford, F. R. The nervous complications of variola, vaccinia and varicella, with a report of cases. Bull. Hopkins Hosp., 40:337, 1927.

Zimmerman, H. M., and Yannet, H. Nonsuppurative encephalomyelitis accompanying chickenpox. Arch. Neurol. Psychiat., 26:322, 1931.

POSTVACCINAL ENCEPHALITIS

Fatal viral encephalitis following 17D yellow fever vaccine inoculation. Report of a case in a 3-year-old child. J.A.M.A., 198:671, 1966. (A joint statement.)

Greenberg, M., and Appelbaum, E. Postvaccinal encephalitis: a report of 45 cases in New York City. Amer. J. Med. Sci., 216:565, 1948.

Ministry of Health (Great Britain). Vaccination, report of the committee on vaccination. London, H. M. Stationery Office, 1928.

PERTUSSIS ENCEPHALOPATHY

Byers, R. K., and Moll, F. C. Encephalopathies following prophylactic pertussis vaccine. Pediatrics, 1:437, 1948.

SLOW VIRUSES IN CHRONIC AND SUBACUTE ENCEPHALITIDES

Byington, D. P., Castro, A. E., and Burnstein, T. Adaptation to hamsters of neurotropic measles virus from subacute sclerosing panencephalitis. Nature, 225:554, Feb. 1970.

Chen, T. T., Watanabe, I. et al. Subacute sclerosing panencephalitis: propagation of measles virus from brain biopsy in tissue culture. Science, 163:1193, 1969.

Conference on measles virus and subacute sclerosing panencephalitis. Neurology, 18:1 (Part 2), 1968.

Gadjusek, D. E., Gibbs, C. J., Jr., and Alpers, M. Transmission and passage of experimental "Kuru" to chimpanzees. Science, 155:212, 1967.

Gibbs, C. J., and Gadjusek, D. C. Infection as the etiology of spongiform encephalopathy (Creutzfeldt-Jakob disease). Science, 165:1023, 1969.

Payne, E. E., Baublis, J. V., and Itabashi, H. H. Isolation of measles virus from cell cultures of brain from a patient with subacute sclerosing panencephalitis. New Eng. J. Med., 281:585, 1969.

15.12
DISEASES OF THE MUSCLES

J. GORDON MILLICHAP

Clinical disorders of muscle may involve primarily the muscle fiber or may be secondary to disease which occurs predominantly in organs other than muscle. In myopathies such as progressive muscular dystrophy and polymyositis the pathology is centered largely in the muscle, whereas in polyneuritis and progressive spinal muscular atrophy (Werdnig-Hoffmann disease), muscle dysfunction is secondary to lesions in the nerve and spinal cord. In both, hypotonia, weakness, atrophy, and contracture of muscles are the chief clinical manifestations.

The diagnosis of myopathy depends principally on the clinical features, but valuable additional information may be obtained from muscle biopsy, electromyography, nerve conduction velocities, radiographs of the soft tissues, and biochemical tests. Examples of the histologic and electrical changes characteristic of certain myopathies are shown in Figures 75 and 76. Muscle biopsy is most reliable when the specimen is taken in the early stages of disease and from muscle which is not completely atrophied. It may be helpful in the differentiation of polymyositis from muscular dystrophy, and in addition it reflects also the characteristic muscle changes due to lower motor neuron diseases. Electromyography is of particular value in the distinction of neuropathic from myopathic disorders. Decrease in nerve conduction velocity indicates peripheral nerve rather than anterior horn cell disease as a cause of neuropathic atrophy.

The interpretation of muscle histology and elec-

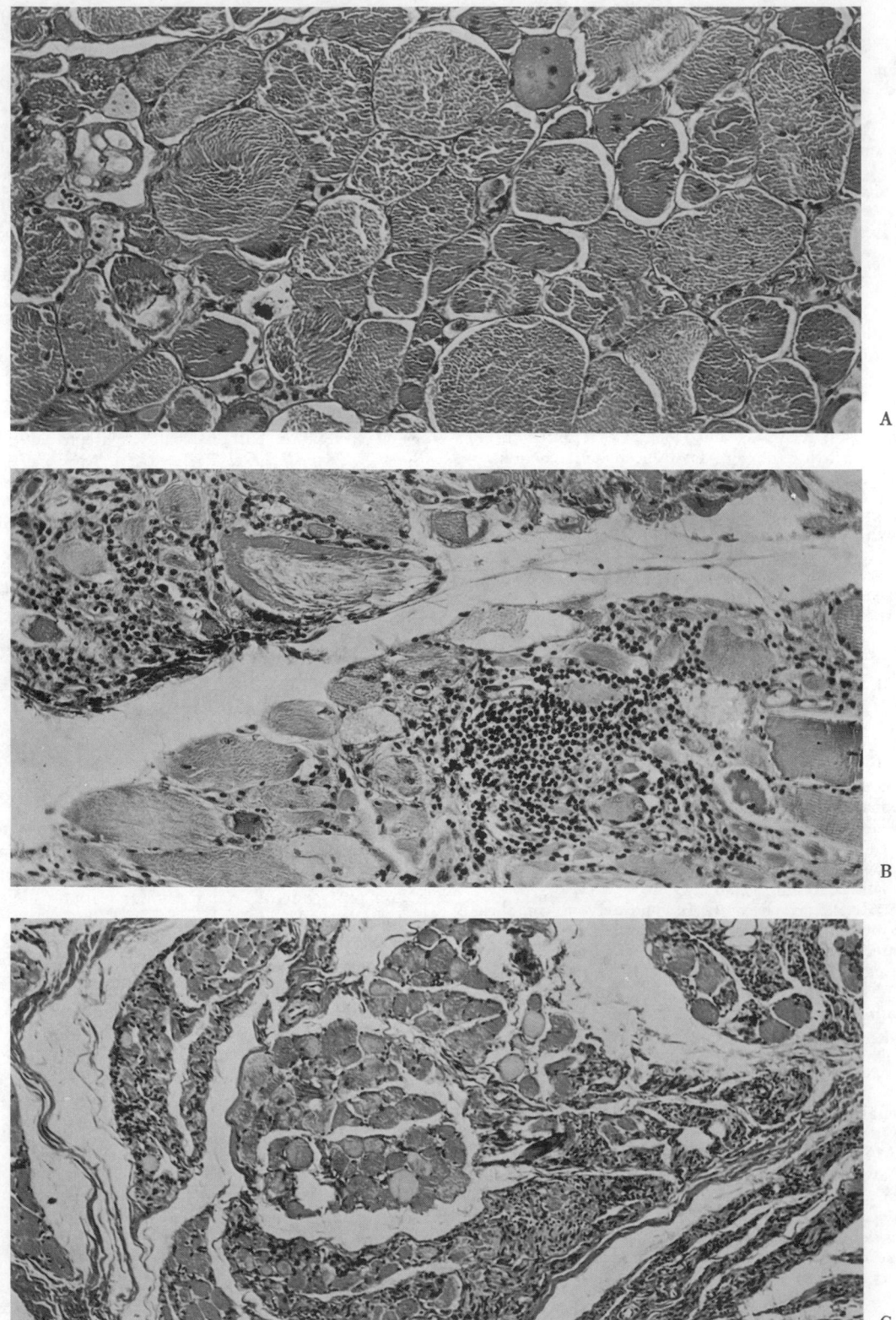

Fig. 75. A. Progressive muscular dystrophy. Section of muscle showing degeneration and variability of size of muscle fibers. B. Polymyositis. Section of muscle showing atrophy of fibers and infiltration with inflammatory cells. C. Infantile spinal muscular atrophy (Werdnig-Hoffman disease). Section of muscle showing groups of small atrophic fibers mixed with groups of normal fibers. (Courtesy of Raymond D. Adams, Boston.)

EMG in INFANTS and CHILDREN

NORMAL
Rest

Voluntary Contraction

INFANTILE MUSCULAR ATROPHY

PROG. MUSCULAR DYSTROPHY

DERMATOMYOSITIS

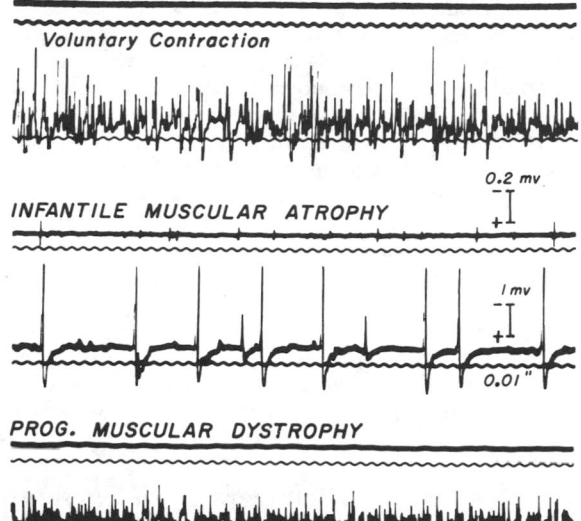

0.2 mv

1 mv

0.01"

Fig. 76. Electromyograms in neuromuscular disease. Electric activity of quadriceps femoris muscle detected with a needle electrode inserted into the muscle and recorded by photographing the trace of a doublebeam cathode-ray oscilloscope on moving film. The lower beam of the oscilloscope traced a timing signal of 100 cycles per second. On the upper beam, an upward deflection indicates a change of voltage in the negative direction at the tip of the needle electrode.

A pair of records is shown for each patient. The upper record of each pair was obtained from the resting muscle; the lower record of each pair was obtained during voluntary contraction of the muscle. Amplification of the signal in the upper record of each pair is 5 times the amplification of the signal in the lower record. Calibrations are in millivolts and are the same for each pair of records.

Normal Infant. Upper record, no electric activity in the resting muscle. Lower record, numerous motor-unit action potentials during voluntary contraction.

Infantile Spinal Muscular Atrophy. Upper record, fibrillation potentials in the resting muscle. Lower record, greatly reduced number of motor-unit action potentials. A large, single, motor-unit action potential recurs in the range of the needle electrode.

Progressive Muscular Dystrophy. Upper record, no electric activity in the resting muscle. Minimal electric activity may occasionally be observed. Lower record, numerous motor-unit action potentials during voluntary contraction. These are shorter in duration and lower in amplitude than normal.

Dermatomyositis. Upper record, fibrillation potentials in the resting muscle. This is a much more common occurrence in polymyositis than in progressive muscular dystrophy. Lower record, numerous motor-unit action potentials during voluntary contraction. These are shorter in duration and lower in amplitude than normal. (Courtesy of Dr. E. H. Lambert, Mayo Clinic, Rochester, Minnesota.)

tromyography without reference to the clinical findings is sometimes difficult, and the occasional limitations of these methods of investigation must be recognized when diagnosis and prognosis are assessed.

Limp Infant Syndrome

The limp infant (floppy child) syndrome is a term now used to describe all infants who have weak and hypotonic muscles, an increased range of joint movement or contracture, and various degrees of flaccid paralysis. In some infants hypotonia is marked and paresis slight, whereas in others muscular paralysis is profound. The symptoms may be obvious at birth or may present in late infancy. The prognosis is variable and dependent upon the underlying disease process. The disease may progress rapidly and death ensue early, but in some cases progression is slow, and in others the disease becomes arrested and recovery may be partial or even complete. This clinical picture may be produced by various diseases with primary lesions in the cerebrum, cerebellum, spinal cord, peripheral nerve, neuromuscular junction, or the muscle itself. Most commonly it is due to a degeneration or malformation of the anterior horn cells of the spinal cord (Werdnig-Hoffmann disease).

The differential diagnosis of the limp infant syndrome (Table 27) includes the following: infantile progressive spinal muscular atrophy of Werdnig and Hoffmann, congenital poliomyelitis, benign congenital hypotonia of Walton, congenital or early infantile muscular dystrophy of Batten and Turner, polymyositis, "central core" myopathy of Shy and Magee, glycogen storage myopathy, congenital universal muscular hypoplasia of Krabbe, congenital laxity of the ligaments, neonatal myasthenia gravis, infantile polyneuritis, hypotonic cerebral diplegia, cerebellar malformations, mongolism and others forms of mental deficiency, Lowe's syndrome, and various metabolic disorders, such as hypophosphatasia, rickets, and idiopathic hypercalcemia. In those cases described by Oppenheim which were characterized by improvement, the pathology was not recorded; the clinical picture and course correspond most closely to that of benign congenital hypotonia and universal musclar hypoplasia.

Benign congenital hypotonia is the term coined by Walton for a form of early amyotonia which characteristically improves with time and in which the muscle fibers occasionally may appear universally small for the age but usually show no structural abnormality. The infant is limp and hypotonic at birth, the deep tendon reflexes may be absent or depressed, but respiration is rarely affected. Sitting and walking are delayed, yet muscular wasting is not profound and the eventual development proves to be essentially normal.

Congenital universal muscular hypoplasia is a rare disorder described by Krabbe in which all skele-

TABLE 27.   *Differential Diagnosis of the Limp Child Syndrome**

Cerebral Diseases (Atonic Diplegia)
 Cerebral malformations
 Cerebral damage from hypoxia
 Cerebral birth injury
 Mongolism
 Metabolic (Lowe's syndrome, hypophosphatasia, rickets, hypercalcemia)
 Familial dysautonomia

Spinal Cord Diseases
 Infantile spinal muscular atrophy (Werdnig-Hoffmann)
 Poliomyelitis
 Spinal and birth injury

Peripheral Nerve Disease
 Polyneuritis

Neuromuscular Junction Disorders
 Developmental
  Congenital hypotonia?
 Metabolic
  Myasthenia gravis

Muscle Disorders
 Myopathies
  Infantile muscular dystrophy
  Arthrogryposis multiplex congenita
  "Central core" disease
  "Nemaline" myopathy
 Other conditions
  Glycogen storage disease of muscle
  Polymyositis

*Modified from Grinker, Bucy, and Sahs.

tal muscles are small and weak but otherwise normal. Deep tendon reflexes are normal or depressed. Changes of dystrophy or neurogenic atrophy of muscle are absent on histologic examination. The condition is nonprogressive.

Congenital or infantile muscular dystrophy is sometimes familial and is characterized by weakness which involves principally the proximal muscle groups, present at or soon after birth, and progresses at varying rates but in most cases slowly. The muscles are atrophied and hypotonic, but all movements may be performed, though feebly. The deep tendon reflexes are depressed or absent. Contractures of limb muscles tend to appear late, with equal involvement of the intercostals and diaphragm. The pharyngeal muscles are not involved and dysphagia is not a symptom of the disease. The diagnosis rests on the histologic appearance of the muscle (Fig. 75) and on the clinical course. Soft tissue radiographs may demonstrate severe wasting of muscles and thus aid in the differentiation of this disorder from benign congenital hypotonia.

"Central core" disease is a nonprogressive myopathy which is present at or shortly after birth, involves proximal muscle groups, and is said to have a distinctive histologic appearance of the muscle. Shy and Magee described five patients with this disorder

in three generations of a family. Sitting and walking were delayed, and although all patients were ambulatory, running and climbing stairs were never performed without difficulty. Deep tendon reflexes were active, and the muscles supplied by cranial nerves were spared. On biopsy examination of muscles, a central core of closely set myofibrils with an amorphous appearance and altered staining qualities was interpreted as a characteristic feature of the disease.

"Nemaline" myopathy is another rare, nonprogressive, congenital myopathy which may be distinguished only by muscle biopsy. Engel et al. have reported female patients, age 4 years and 16 years, with mild weakness and wasting of proximal muscles which, on histologic examination, show rod-shaped structures in the fibers.

Myotubular and mitochondrial myopathies are two of the more recently described congenital myopathies. They may present the classical features of the limp infant syndrome. Diagnosis is only possible by muscle biopsy.

Congenital Defects of Skeletal Muscles

Single muscles or groups of muscles occasionally fail to develop. Most frequently it is the pectoralis major, particularly the lower sternocostal portion, which is deficient. Congenital absence of muscles is clearly evident when the hands are pressed together while the elbows are abducted. Other muscles which may fail to develop include the trapezius, serratus anticus, and quadratus femoris.

Defects of skeletal muscles may occur together with other congenital abnormalities. Agenesis of the pectoral muscle is sometimes associated with malformation of a rib, a defect of the mammary gland, and scoliosis. Congenital absence of the abdominal muscles is most frequently seen in boys. There are concomitant genitourinary anomalies including enlargement of the bladder, dilation of the ureters, hydronephrosis, and cryptorchidism. The weakened abdominal wall is deeply furrowed, defecation and coughing are hampered, and death from pulmonary complications often results in early infancy.

Congenital Defects of Cranial Muscles

Congenital ptosis due to weakness of the levator palpebrae may occur as an isolated anomaly and without involvement of other muscles supplied by the oculomotor nerve. In some cases muscular dystrophy or myasthenia gravis has developed in later life, and a primary myopathy affecting the levator muscle has seemed a more likely explanation than a lesion involving the third cranial nerve of its nucleus. In the rare "jaw-winking phenomenon" of

Marcus Gunn, the ptosed eyelid is elevated when the mouth is opened or the jaw moved from side to side.

Congenital facial diplegia, or Möbius' syndrome, is characterized by bilateral weakness of the facial muscles and of the external rectus muscles of the eyes. It may occur alone or be associated with congenital malformations of the extremities. The condition is recognized soon after birth and has been explained by either a primary hypoplasia of cranial nerve nuclei or a primary deficiency of the muscles derived from the first two branchial arches. A dysgenesis of both neural and muscle tissue may occur concomitantly in some cases.

Congenital Clubfoot
(Talipes)

The abnormal posture of the foot and ankle in this relatively common deformity is usually plantar flexion (talipes equinus) and less frequently dorsiflexion (talipes calcaneus), inversion and adduction (talipes varus), or eversion and abduction (talipes valgus). Two-thirds of the children are males, and in a small percentage the condition is familial. The anterior tibial and peroneal muscles are atrophic and may be replaced by adipose tissue. The mechanism of the muscular atrophy and antenatal contracture is not definitely determined, but occasionally the amyoplasia is secondary to a developmental defect of the anterior horn cells of the spinal cord or peripheral nerves. The disorder is discussed from an orthopedic and therapeutic standpoint elsewhere (Sec. 25.2).

Congenital Torticollis
(Wryneck)

This deformity, associated with shortening and fibrosis of the sternomastoid muscle, is discussed elsewhere (Sec. 25.3).

Arthrogryposis Multiplex

Arthrogryposis multiplex congenita, also known as amyoplasia congenita or myodystrophia fetalis deformans, is characterized by deformity and rigidity of the extremities, the infant having the appearance of a wooden doll (Fig. 77). The limbs are fixed in almost any position, but most often the arms are rotated inward and extended at the elbows, with forearms pronated and hands flexed. Usually the lower extremities are flexed at the hips and externally rotated, the knees are either partly flexed or extended, and the feet are in equinovarus. The smallness of the limbs is contrasted with the unusually large and fusiform joints. The muscles are weak and

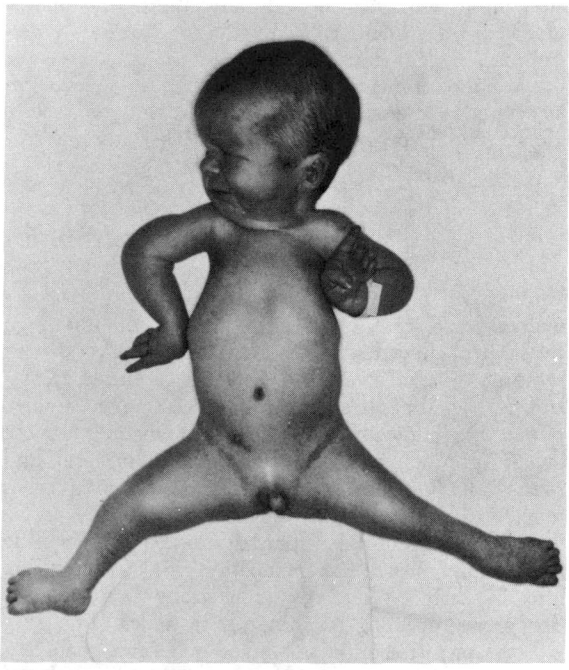

Fig. 77. Arthrogryposis multiplex congenita of the neuropathic type in an infant with unusual fixed postures.

hypotonic and the tendon reflexes are absent. The skin and subcutaneous tissues are thickened, wrinkled, and flabby. Other congenital abnormalities are sometimes associated.

Fixation of joints is the most distinctive and constant clinical feature of the syndrome, but the underlying pathology is varied and may involve the spinal cord, muscles, or joints. When the disorder is associated with congenital muscular dystrophy, a characteristic posture of flexion at the hips and knees and adduction of the legs has been observed. When contractures are due to a primary defect in the anterior horn cells of the spinal cord or nerve roots, an attitude of extension and abduction of the legs is more frequent. Orthopedic treatment may effect some improvement in posture, but little or no change in muscle power is to be expected.

Congenital Muscular Hypertrophy

This may result from varied causes. In the syndrome described by DeLange, there is generalized, symmetric muscular hypertrophy, hypertonia, and an increase in muscle power. The head is small or deformed and the neck is usually retracted. Infants affected are mentally deficient and survive for only a few months. A congenital lesion of the brain consisting of polygyria, microgyria, and multiple cystic cavities has been described in some cases. In the Debré-Semelaigne syndrome there is an associated thyroid deficiency (cretinism). In a third variety of congenital muscular hypertrophy there are macroglossia and cardiomegaly in addition to the hypertrophied skeletal musculature.

Some infants with omphaloceles may have an associated muscular hypertrophy as well as macroglossia and hypoglycemia (Beckwith's syndrome).

Muscular Dystrophies

Progressive muscular dystrophy is a primary degenerative disease of skeletal muscles of unknown causation, characterized by muscular weakness and wasting. The great majority of cases of muscular dystrophy can be classified into three major groups, which are clinically and genetically distinct. These are the pseudohypertrophic, facioscapulohumeral, and limb-girdle types. A number of less common types may be distinguished on clinical criteria.

The pseudohypertrophic dystrophy of Duchenne is a rapidly progressive myopathy which usually begins in early childhood, has a strong familial incidence, and occurs predominantly in males (Fig. 78). It is transmitted as a sex-linked recessive character. The commonest presenting symptoms are an abnormal gait, slowness and clumsiness in walking and running, and a tendency to fall frequently. Sitting, standing, and walking are delayed, and often there is difficulty in climbing stairs. Muscular weakness always begins in the muscles of the pelvic girdle and is responsible for the waddling gait. The method of rising from the floor by "climbing up the legs" (Gower's sign), although not a pathognomonic sign, is characteristic and results from weakness of the lumbar muscles and glutei (Fig. 79). The foot assumes a talipes equinovarus position, and the patient tends to walk on his toes, owing to weakness of the anterior tibial and peroneal muscles. Muscles of the shoulder girdle become involved after three to five years. The deep tendon reflexes usually are depressed or absent but, rarely, are hyperactive in the early stages of the disease. Positive Babinski signs and other evidence of an associated upper motor neuron lesion have been reported rarely. Pseudohypertrophy affects the calf muscles in 80 percent of cases, is uncommon in the hamstrings and glutei, and involves the deltoid and triceps rarely. Contracture and wasting of the muscles lead to atrophy and deformity of the skeleton, and obesity is a common complication of the resultant immobility. A moderate degree of mental retardation is not unusual. The essentially progressive nature of the disease is evident in the rarity of survival beyond the age of 20 years.

The Becker variant of pseudohypertrophic muscular dystrophy begins at a later age and has a slower rate of progression. Survival into late adult life is not uncommon with this form of muscular dystrophy.

The facioscapulohumeral dystrophy of Landouzy

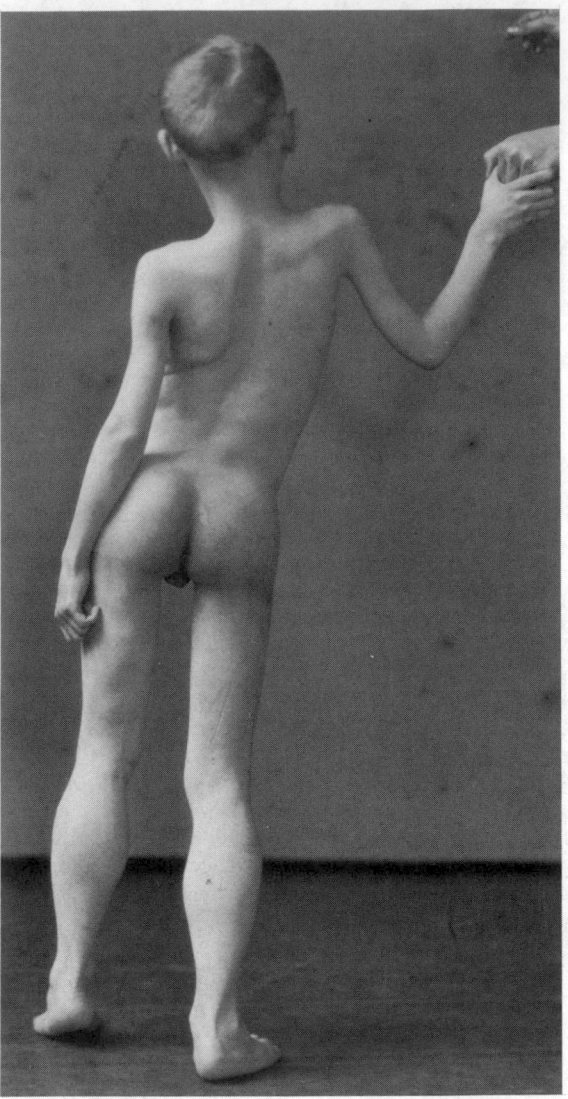

Fig. 78. Progressive muscular dystrophy: Duchenne type. A boy aged 10 years with weakness and atrophy of the proximal musculature, pseudohypertrophy of the calves and buttocks, scoliosis, lordosis of the lumbar spine, and a tendency to walk on the toes. (Courtesy of the Mayo Clinic, Rochester, Minnesota.)

and Dejerine is a slowly progressive myopathy which begins at any age from early childhood until adult life, is sometimes familial, and affects both male and female with equal frequency. It is usually transmitted by an autosomal dominant, rarely by an autosomal recessive gene. Inability to close the eyes completely may be noted from early childhood, and pouting of the lips and immobility of facial expression characterize the myopathic facies. The first symptoms usually include drooping of the shoulders with difficulty in raising the arms above the head and generally occur between 6 and 20 years of age. The deep ten-

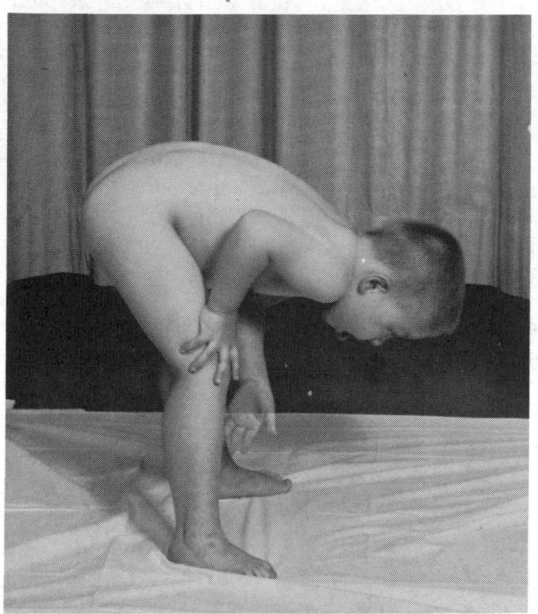

Fig. 79. Gower's sign in a boy with Duchenne pseudohypertrophic muscular dystrophy. The necessity to "climb up the legs" when rising from the floor.

don reflexes are depressed or absent in affected muscles. Weakness of the lower limbs is often delayed for 20 to 30 years, and pseudohypertrophy of muscles is uncommon. The disease may become arrested for prolonged periods, and most patients survive and remain active to a normal age. Contractures and skeletal deformities develop less frequently and constitute a less prominent clinical feature than in the Duchenne form of dystrophy.

Limb-girdle muscular dystrophy commences late in the first or in the second or third decade. It progresses more slowly than the Duchenne type but more rapidly than the facioscapulohumeral type of dystrophy. It is usually transmitted as an autosomal recessive, but occasionally by a dominant gene. Those cases which begin with muscular weakness in the shoulder girdle are classified traditionally as juvenile scapulohumeral muscular dystrophy of Erb. Those in which the pelvic girlde and thigh muscles are first affected are examples of the atrophic pelvifemoral dystrophy of Leyden and Möbius. The course of the disease, though relatively slow, nevertheless leads to severe disablement and death before the normal age. Pseudohypertrophy is rare, but prominence of the deltoid and gluteal musculature commonly occurs as a compensatory physiologic hypertrophy in the early stages of the disease.

Other less common forms of muscular dystrophy include Gower's type, in which the distal rather than the proximal limb muscles are affected first, and dystrophic ophthalmoplegia, which is very slowly progressive and is limited to the levators of the eyelids

and the external ocular muscles. In the ophthalmoplegic type, ptosis of the eyelids, the first symptom, presents at any age from infancy to adult life and is associated later with weakness of lateral and vertical movements of the eyes. A history of similar symptoms in the family is obtained in half the cases.

In about 10 percent of patients with progressive muscular dystrophy the electrocardiogram shows nonspecific abnormalities. Cardiomegaly is not uncommon, and cardiac failure due to dystrophic disease of heart muscle is sometimes the cause of sudden death.

Determination of certain serum enzymes may be a useful diagnostic aid. Elevated enzyme levels are observed only during the period when muscles are actively undergoing change. Late in the disease, these enzyme levels are often normal.

A marked increase of creatine kinase activity in the serum has been reported in patients with the Duchenne type of muscular dystrophy and in their female relatives (heterozygotes), and lesser degrees of abnormal activity occur in patients with other types of dystrophy. Also, elevations of glutamic oxalacetic transaminase and aldolase are observed. Reduction in the transformation of creatine to creatinine, the most constant biochemical abnormality, reflects only a decrease in total effective muscle mass and is not pathognomonic of dystrophy. Administration of vitamin E is followed by reduction in creatinuria but does not result in objective improvement of muscle function.

In treatment, physical rehabilitation may help to maintain residual function. Frequent but not violent activity is advisable, and all limb joints should be moved regularly both actively and passively through a full range to prevent contractures. Confinement to bed must be avoided. When possible, school attendance or occupation with tasks and hobbies should be encouraged. A cheerful and optimistic attitude of physician and parent is important in the psychologic management.

The Myotonias

Congenital Myotonia

Congenital myotonia (Thomsen's disease) is an anomaly of muscular contraction manifested by muscular spasms or cramps and hypertrophy. It presents during infancy, early childhood, or adolescence and is inherited as a Mendelian dominant or occasionally as a recessive factor. Muscular contraction is strong, but relaxation is delayed and normal motor function is impeded. The infant may be slow to stand and walk. The disease may affect most of the skeletal muscles but seldom involves the muscles of respiration or swallowing. Muscular hypertrophy, especially prominent in the lower limbs, may also affect the upper limbs and face. The child may have a Herculean appearance. Percussion of the surface of the muscle results in a sustained contraction and localized dimpling. Muscles of the thenar eminence, forearm, and tongue are especially susceptible. Tendon reflexes are normal or slightly exaggerated. On shaking hands the patient's grip is relaxed slowly and awkwardly in a manner pathognomic of myotonia; after tight closure the eyes are opened slowly. With repetition of muscular effort movement becomes more rapid, and relaxation following contraction is more prompt.

Symptoms of myotonia are relieved by quinine, calcium, and procaine amide; they are exacerbated by cold.

Dystrophia Myotonica

Dystrophia myotonica, or myotonic dystrophy, is a steadily progressive, familial disease in which a myopathy is complicated by myotonia. Cataracts, baldness, and testicular atrophy are frequently associated defects, and mental retardation is not uncommon. The disease is usually transmitted as a mendelian dominant character, and the phenomenon of anticipation is observed; the children are affected at an earlier age than the parent and are more likely to exhibit the fully developed syndrome.

Muscular weakness and wasting may begin at any age. The symptomatic infant has difficulty in sucking owing to bilateral facial weakness. Muscle weakness, hypotonia, and delay in attaining motor milestones are other manifestations during infancy. Rarely, pure myotonia may be the only feature of this disorder in early childhood. In contrast to most myopathies, the distal rather than proximal muscles of the limbs are affected primarily. The tendon reflexes are often depressed or lost. Ptosis of the eyelids and weakness and atrophy of the facial muscles may be early manifestations; in the older child, wasting of the sternomastoids and the development of a swanneck posture occur later. Weakness of laryngeal and pharyngeal muscles is apparent later in the monotonous and nasal character of the voice and the dysphagia. Myotonia, the most striking characteristic feature, does not involve all skeletal muscles but is particularly evident in the hands, face, and tongue. Electrocardiographic abnormalities point to involvement of the heart, and acrocyanosis is indicative of changes in peripheral blood vessels.

Electromyography is useful in confirming the diagnosis

Quinine and procaine amide control the myotonia to some extent, but otherwise treatment is of no avail.

Paramyotonia

This term is used to describe a syndrome of myotonia which usually is restricted to the tongue and which spreads to involve the muscles of the face and extremities only on exposure to cold. Unlike dystrophia myotonica, paramyotonia is nonprogressive and not complicated by muscular wasting; it differs from myotonia congenita in the lack of hypertrophy and the restricted involvement of muscles. The disorder is inherited by a single autosomal dominant gene and is not transmitted by unaffected members of the family. Originally described by Eulenberg, paramyotonia has been reviewed more recently by Drager and co-workers, who reported a family with 30 members affected. These patients complained of cramping of the muscles of the face in cold weather and slurred speech asociated with stiffness of the tongue after drinking cold liquids. Weakness of the extremities may occur in some attacks and may be associated with elevation of the serum potassium. The relation of paramyotonia to familial hyperkalemic paralysis is discussed elsewhere (p. 1034).

Myositis

Infectious Mysositis

Acute suppurative myositis may occur with bloodstream infection or in association with infectious arthritis. Staphylococci and streptococci are the most common causative organisms. Gas gangrene due to *Clostridium perfringens* develops only in traumatized or necrotic muscle. Tuberculous infection in striated muscle may be due to local extension from a neighboring joint or cold abscess or rarely may result from hematogenous dissemination.

Trichinosis is the most frequent parasitic infection of muscle in the Western Hemisphere; cysticerosis commonly involves muscle in infected patients in India and other Asiatic countries. Toxoplasma may invade muscle but causes no specific symptoms; the demonstration of the protozoan parasite in a biopsy of muscle is sometimes of value in the diagnosis of acquired toxoplasmosis.

Polymyositis

Polymyositis is an acute, subacute, or chronic disorder of muscle characterized by symmetric weakness predominant in the shoulder and pelvic girdles. Polymyositis is associated with cutaneous lesions in dermatomyositis (Sec. 25.2) and may also occur as a feature of scleroderma or rheumatoid arthritis.

Muscular pain, tenderness, atrophy, and depression of deep tendon reflexes are inconstant and appear late in the course of the disease. Dysphagia occurs in more than half the patients. The electromyographic and histologic abnormalities are characteristic but not pathognomonic of the disease. Nonspecific clinical features include fever, arthralgia, loss of weight, Raynaud's phenomenon, edema, and heliotrope erythema of the eyelids and face. The sedimentation and basal metabolic rates are frequently elevated, and examination of the blood may reveal

TABLE 28.   *The Clinical Differential Diagnosis of Polymyositis and Duchenne Muscular Dystrophy* *

Clinical Features	Polymyositis	Duchenne Muscular Dystrophy
Sex incidence	females > males	males only
Rate of progress	rapid	slow
Muscular weakness	symmetric and proximal	proximal
Dysphagia	common	unknown
Muscular atrophy	mild	marked
Pseudohypertrophy	rare	common
Muscle pain and tenderness	common	uncommon or rare
Deep tendon reflexes	absent, normal, or brisk	depressed or absent
Muscle biopsy	inflammatory cell infiltration	no inflammatory cells
Dermatomyositis, scleroderma, or rheumatoid arthritis	sometimes associated	not associated
Spontaneous remission	occasional	never
Response to cortisone	remission	none

*Modified from Walton and Adams. *Polymyositis*, London, E. & S. Livingstone, Ltd., 1958.

leucocytosis and eosinophilia. High levels of creatine phosphokinase and aldolase in the serum are indicative of persistent activity of the disease.

Most cases appear to be related etiologically to the collagen group of diseases, but some may result from unknown toxic and metabolic factors. In the absence of skin and joint involvement, the acute forms of the disease may bear a close clinical resemblance to idiopathic myoglobinuria while chronic forms may resemble progressive muscular dystrophy. The differentiation from muscular dystrophy (Table 28) is often difficult but is important in prognosis and therapy.

Some patients with polymyositis improve or recover spontaneously, but treatment with corticosteroids is advisable in those with evidence of progressive weakness.

Myositis Fibrosa

Generalized myositis fibrosa is a slowly progressive disease which begins in early life and is characterized by replacement of muscle with fibrous connective tissue. The muscles are firm and woody to palpation, their elasticity is lost, and in the final stages of the disease movement becomes impossible. The sternomastoids and muscles of the legs, neck, chest, and back are among those first affected. With the development of muscular contractures the joints become fixed in abnormal postures. Myositis fibrosa is sometimes classed as a chronic progressive form of dermatomyositis, since the histologic changes in the muscle may be similar to those of polymyositis. A therapeutic trial of corticosteroids may be considered.

Myositis Ossificans

Generalized progressive myositis ossificans is an uncommon disease of unknown cause which is charac-

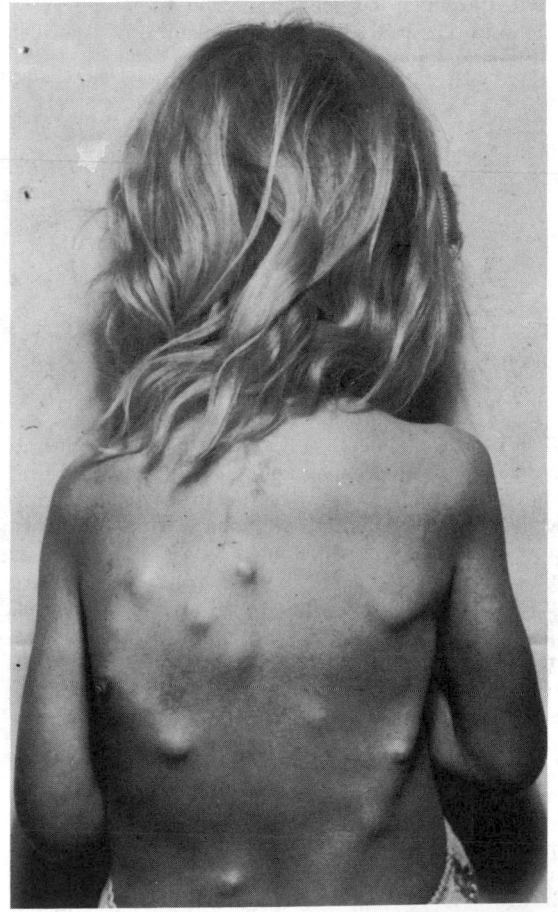

Fig. 80.   Generalized myositis ossificans in a young girl. The skeletal muscles were hard to palpation; movements of the shoulders, elbows, and wrists were limited; and the skin showed numerous hard swellings with occasional ulceration.

terized by the formation of soft, fluctuant, or hard swellings in the interstitial tissue of the muscle and related structures. The masses are of variable size and shape and consist at first of fibrous tissue, often with subsequent formation of bone; they sometimes shrink before ossification occurs. Usually they are painless, but the overlying skin is often reddened and occasionally ulcerated. The disease generally gegins before 10 years of age, and the muscles of the neck and back are affected first (Fig. 80). The swellings develop spontaneously or follow minimal trauma; they appear in succession over a period of months or years. The muscle fibers are not involved primarily but undergo atrophy and destruction secondary to pressure and inactivity as the result of disease in the interstitial tissue. Congenital anomalies, the most frequent of which is underdevelopment of the great toes or thumbs, are associated in about three-fourths of the cases.

The prognosis is grave, and survival beyond puberty is rare. Treatment is usually ineffectual, although it is claimed that remissions have been induced by corticosteroids.

Generalized myositis ossificans must be differentiated from a localized traumatic form and from calcinosis universalis, in which calcium is deposited in the subcutaneous tissues.

Metabolic Myopathies

Familial Periodic Paralysis

This hereditary and familial disease is characterized by intermittent attacks of flaccid paralysis with complete absence of deep tendon reflexes and electrical inexcitability of the muscles. The onset is usually before puberty, and attacks may recur for many years. The sexes are affected equally.

An attack generally begins with weakness in the muscles of the back and pelvic girdle, and flaccidity gradually spreads to involve the lower limbs, shoulder girdle, upper limbs, and neck. The respiratory muscles and muscles innervated by the cranial nerves are usually spared. Dysphagia may occur in severe attacks, and death, though rare, has been reported. Smooth muscle is not affected, but cardiac enlargement and a slow and irregular pulse are present in some cases. Attacks occur at any time but most commonly during sleep or inactivity. They may be preceded and accompanied by excessive perspiration and thirst and are precipitated by the ingestion of excess carbohydrate, exposure to cold, muscular exertion followed by inactivity, or the injection of insulin or epinephrine. Attacks are usually of two to three hours' duration but may last as long as seven days. Recovery is gradual and usually complete, though slight weakness may persist in some cases. The presence of vacuoles in muscle is characteristic.

The paralysis is associated with hypokalemia but is not related to the absolute concentration of serum potassium. The fall in the level of serum potassium is not reflected in an increased urinary excretion but may be related to a shift of potassium from the blood to the cells of the muscles and liver. An abnormal degree of binding of potassium by large protein molecules may occur.

In some cases, attacks have been preceded by an increase in the urinary excretion of aldosterone and retention of sodium. An abrupt fall in the level of potassium is serum and urine has been observed. As the attack subsides, there are diuresis of sodium, an increase in the urinary excretion of potassium, and a return to normal of the level of aldosterone in the urine. Attacks appear to be precipitated by retention of sodium; they may be prevented by restriction of dietary sodium. Potassium chloride is given for the treatment of acute attacks.

The prognosis is excellent, and the episodes become less frequent and less severe in adult life.

Hypokalemic Paralysis

The association of a low concentration of serum potassium and weakness or paralysis of skeletal muscles may occur in diabetic acidosis, in Addison's disease following the administration of excess desoxycorticosterone (DOCA), and in some cases of renal insufficiency. Complete paralysis as observed in familial periodic paralysis is rare. The more usual findings are diffuse muscular weakness and apathy, with delirium, coarse muscular twitching, and tetany. The electrocardiogram is of value in the differentiation of hypokalemic and hyperkalemic states.

Hyperkalemic Paralysis

Muscular weakness and elevated levels of serum potassium may be associated in patients with renal insufficiency, especially after the administration of potassium, in untreated Addison's disease, and in crush syndrome and hemolytic reactions. The onset and evolution of paresis are rapid, and the distribution resembles that of familial periodic paralysis. The legs, trunk, and arms are affected in an ascending sequence. The administration of 5 to 15 g of potassium by mouth to healthy individuals will often produce paresthesia, but muscular weakness is exceptional.

Hereditary Episodic Adynamia

As described by Gamstorp, this condition is characterized by attacks of spontaneously abating paralysis, affecting particularly the muscles of the extremities and the trunk and generally accompanied by an elevation of the serum potassium. The disease is inherited as a single, autosomal, dominant gene with complete or almost complete penetrance. The incidence is the same in both sexes.

The onset of episodic symptoms is usually before the age of 10 years. Attacks invariably occur during rest which follows exertion, and at least once a week; they last at most one hour. The extent and severity of the paresis vary from slight weakness of a single extremity to severe states in which the patient is unable to turn over or sit up. Respiration is seldom involved, and the muscles innervated by cranial nerves are affected only mildly. Deep tendon reflexes may be weak or absent, and Chvostek's sign is sometimes positive during attacks. Percussion myotonia may be elicited, and the disease is more troublesome in cold, damp weather. The clinical manifestations of adynamia episodica resemble those of paramyotonia. Nevertheless, Gamstorp maintains that the term adynamia episodica hereditaria should be retained for those patients who, in response to a small dose of potassium, have elevated serum levels and react with muscular weakness, regardless of the presence of myotonia.

As a general rule, paresis is accompanied by an increase in the level of serum potassium without change in the urinary excretion of potassium. Electrocardiographic changes are consistent with hyperkalemia. Attacks may be precipitated by oral administration of potassium in doses insufficient to produce symptoms in normal persons. Symptoms are prevented by glucose with or without insulin administered before, or simultaneously with, a provocative dose of potassium. Acetazolamide orally, calcium administered intravenously, the intake of food, especially bread, or gentle exercise may shorten the duration of attacks; but sooner or later the symptoms abate spontaneously. Improvement occurs, and attacks are less frequent after 30 years of age.

Other descriptions of a form of periodic familial paralysis resistant to or exacerbated by the administration of potassium have been given by Wyllie and Watkins.

Myohemoglobinuria

Myohemoglobin may appear in the urine spontaneously and without known cause or following crush injuries, extreme muscular activity, or the ingestion of eels or fish poisoned by resinous waste products of factories (Haff disease). In the cryptogenic cases (Meyer-Betz), paroxysmal attacks of myohemoglobinuria are associated with weakness or paralysis of skeletal muscles. The onset of illness is usually sudden and sometimes accompanied by nausea, fever, and vomiting. The affected muscles are swollen and painful. The disease may be familial, occur at any age, and vary greatly in severity. The patient may die from uremia or respiratory paralysis in the first attack or may recover and suffer repeated episodes of muscle weakness. Cardiac and smooth muscles are unaffected. The diagnosis of myohemoglobinuria is established by electrophoresis or spectroscopic examination; it may be suspected in a patient who shows no evidence of hemolytic anemia when the urine is dark and gives a positive reaction for occult blood in the absence of red blood cells. Serum enzymes are markedly elevated.

Glycogen Myopathies

Of five different types of glycogen storage disease described, two (Types II and V) have significantly increased amounts of glycogen in the skeletal muscle associated with weakness.

TYPE II: CARDIOMUSCULAR GLYCOGEN DISEASE (POMPE). This is the commonest variety of glycogen storage disease with generalized muscular weakness and hypotonia. Inherited as an autosomal recessive trait, it is associated with an absence of the enzyme α-1-4 glucosidase (acid maltase). Clinically it closely resembles Werdnig-Hoffmann disease in that the child often is asymptomatic at birth and manifests progressive hypotonia, areflexia, and muscle weakness at a few months of disease. Macroglossia and cardiomegaly are additional features. Diagnosis is based on the characteristic clinical findings, the presence of glycogen vacuoles in the muscle biopsy, and the absence of acid maltase activity upon enzymatic assay. The infant usually dies at 1 year of age from cardiac or respiratory failure. A late infantile variety, also associated with acid maltase deficiency, closely resembles Duchenne's pseudohypertrophic muscular dystrophy. It is manifested by either a delay in acquisition of motor milestones or by regression of previously acquired motor skills. Differentiation from Duchenne's muscular dystrophy may only be possible by electromyography, muscle biopsy, and appropriate biochemical studies.

TYPE V: McARDLE'S DISEASE. In this variety of glycogen myopathy, excessive amounts of muscle glycogen are associated with a total absence of muscle phosphorylase. The synthesis of glycogen is normal, but the degradation of glycogen to glucose-1-phosphate is deficient. The accumulation of pyruvic and lactic acids expected in the venous blood after exercise of ischemic muscle is lacking. The disease is familial and is transmitted by a recessive, rare, autosomal gene. Symptoms begin in childhood and occur only after moderately severe exercise. Muscular weakness, stiffness, and painful cramps develop with effort and disappear rapidly with rest. Between attacks, the physical examination, including deep tendon reflexes, is normal. The diagnosis is confirmed by the failure of venous lactate to rise after ischemic work and lack of phosphorylase activity in muscle. Symptoms may be prevented by limiting exercise.

TYPES I, III, AND IV. In Type I (Von Gierke's disease) skeletal muscle is not involved. Types III and IV, rare varieties, involve the liver mainly, and the myocardium and skeletal muscles to a lesser extent.

Endocrine Myopathies

Disorders of muscles may occur with a wide variety of diseases of the endocrine glands. In the majority of these myopathies, morphologic changes have been slight or absent, and a derangement of some enzyme system necessary for contraction of muscle has been invoked as a possible explanation for the muscle weakness.

Hyperthyroidism in association with a chronic form of myopathy has occasionally been reported, and an acute thyrotoxic myopathy which sometimes progresses to a form of bulbar paralysis may also occur. Treatment of the hyperthyroidism alleviates the muscle weakness. Thyrotoxicosis and myasthenia gravis may occur concomitantly, but the association of the two diseases is unexplained. About 5 percent of all patients with myasthenia gravis develop thyrotoxicosis at some time during their illness, and an inverse relation between the two diseases is occasionally observed. Symptoms of myasthenia may be aggravated by administration of antithyroid drugs and alleviated on their withdrawal. The frequency of abnormalities of the thymus gland and the occurrence of focal collections of small lymphocytes, or "lymphorrhages," in striated muscles in both myasthenia gravis and thyrotoxicosis point to some common factor of posisble significance in etiology.

Hypothyroidism may be complicated by true generalized hypertrophy of muscles. The Debré-Semelaigne syndrome, characterized by enlarged muscles, weakness, early fatigue, and slowness of movements, is one of the clinical manifestations of cretinism. The symptoms are relieved by thyroid medication.

In hyperparathyroidism, symmetric weakness, fatigability, and atrophy of limb muscles, with discomfort on muscular effort, are prominent symptoms which may be related to the disorder of calcium metabolism. Hypopituitarism is associated with muscle weakness and atrophy. Flexion contractures of the limbs observed in Addison's disease may be related to an excessive accumulation of sodium in the tendons and their consequent shortening. The deformities have been relieved following treatment with ACTH.

Myasthenia Gravis

Myasthenia gravis is characterized by undue weakness and fatigue following maintained contraction of voluntary muscles and a tendency to recovery with rest. Ocular movements, facial expression, mastication, deglutition, and speech are affected primarily. Muscles of the neck, trunk, and limbs may be involved, and respiratory embarrassment occurs in severe cases. Cardiac and smooth muscles are spared. The disease may develop at any age, but in children the first symptoms occur most commonly at or soon after birth or in relation to puberty. Three forms of myasthenia gravis of infancy and childhood are distinguished: (1) neonatal transient form; (2) neonatal persistent (or congenital) form; and (3) juvenile myasthenia gravis.

Myasthenic symptoms may occur with diseases other than myasthenia gravis, and a myasthenic syndrome has been described in association with muscular dystrophy, polymyositis, ocular myopathy, and thyrotoxicosis.

Neonatal transient myasthenia occurs in infants born to mothers with the disease. The majority of infants of myasthenic mothers are unaffected, symptoms developing in only 10 to 20 percent. There is no correlation between the severity of the infant's symptoms and the duration or severity of the mother's illness and her treatment during pregnancy.

At birth, or within a few hours thereafter, the infant becomes limp, his cry and movements are feeble, he is unable to suck, and swallowing and breathing are impaired. Muscular weakness and hypotonia are generalized and symmetric, and the Moro and deep tendon reflexes are absent or depressed. External ophthalmoplegia and ptosis occur relatively infrequently.

A newborn infant of a myasthenic mother whose previous pregnancy resulted in a neonatal death of undetermined cause should be carefully observed for signs of myasthenia. The diagnosis is established by the intramuscular or intravenous injection of edrophonium chloride (Tensilon) in a dose of 1 mg or neostigmine methylsulfate 0.1 to 0.2 mg. Symptoms should be relieved almost immediately (Fig. 81A and B). In moderate and severe cases and especially those with bulbar symptoms, a positive Tensilon test should be followed by continuous therapy with anticholinesterase drugs. In the milder forms of the disorder the infant may recover completely without specific therapy, but treatment must be instituted immediately should respiratory difficulty, choking, dysphagia, or inability to suck supervene.

Pyridostigmine bromide (Mestinon) and neostigmine bromide (Prostigmine) have a less rapid but more prolonged effect than Tensilon and may be effectively used in treatment. Mestinon is preferred because it is less toxic, having fewer muscarinic side effects. The required dosage differs in each patient and must be adjusted according to the individual response. The following have been found satisfactory as initial doses, to be given every four hours at the time of each feeding: oral doses, Mestinon bromide, 5 mg (5 drops of syrup of Mestinon, containing 60 mg per 4 ml); Prostigmine bromide, 1 mg. Parenteral preparations are approximately 30 times as potent as the oral: intramuscular doses, Prostigmine methylsulfate, 0.05 to 0.1 mg. When a dose level sufficient to relieve bulbar symptoms has been determined, further increments in dosage are unnecessary and may be hazardous.

Overdosage with anticholinesterase medication

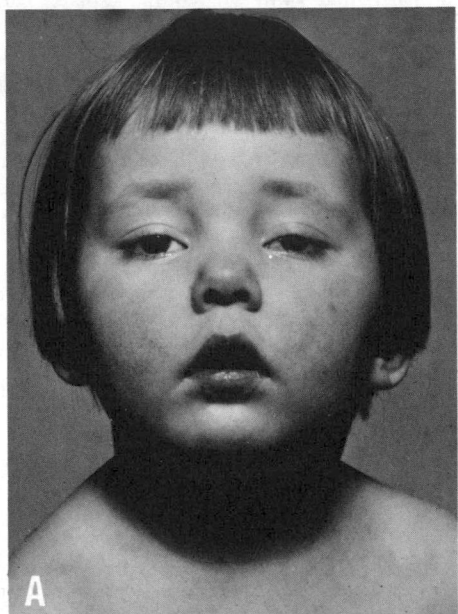 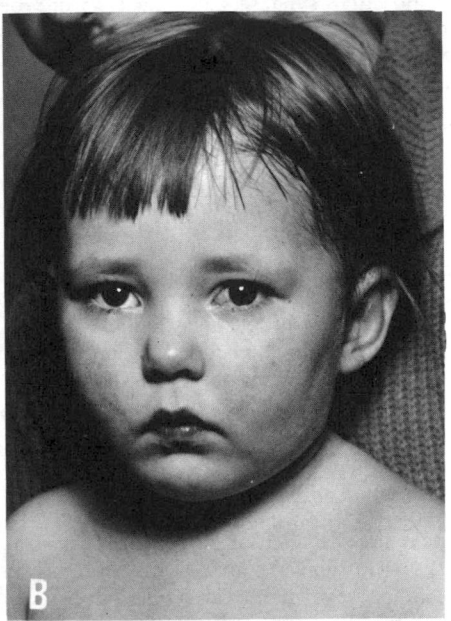

Fig. 81. A. A 3-year-old girl with myasthenia gravis. Ptosis, bilateral and asymmetric, was most marked at the end of the day and not apparent on waking. A right-sided exophoria was variable in degree. *B.* After Tensilon, 5 mg intravenously, the ptosis cleared within 30 seconds and the beneficial response lasted about 10 minutes. The patient was treated with regular doses of Mestinon, 7.5 mg three times a day.

(cholinergic crisis) is manifested by the following signs: increase in muscle weakness and worsening of respiratory difficulty and dysphagia after each dose of drug, muscular fasciculations, and prominent muscarinic side effects, which include excessive salivation, vomiting, diarrhea, pallor, sweating, and bradycardia. Tensilon, 0.05 ml (0.5 mg) given intravenously, will cause a mild and transient exacerbation of cholinergic weakness and may be used to differentiate the crisis due to excessive medication and that associated with a worsening of myasthenia. Atropine may be administered for anticholinesterase overdosage. The oronasopharyngeal secretions should be suctioned repeatedly and oxygen administered when indicated.

After the first week of treatment the gradual withdrawal of medication may be attempted. If symptoms increase, the original dosage is reinstituted, and the effects of withdrawal are observed again after two or three days. The duration of the illness is short, and the natural course is from a few hours to seven weeks. With efficient therapy recovery is complete.

Congenital myasthenia gravis occurs in infants born to mothers who are unaffected by the disease. In contrast to the transient neonatal type, involvement of bulbar musculature is unusual, and generalized muscle weakness is not severe. Ptosis relieved by sleep is the commonest presenting sign, and external ophthalmoplegia and diplopia occur frequently during childhood and later life. Other less common symptoms include weakness of the facial muscles and

limbs, a weak and nasal voice, and some difficulty in chewing and swallowing. A family history of myasthenia in brothers, sisters, and cousins is obtained occasionally.

In contrast to the late form, congenital myasthenia affects both sexes equally, is rarely complicated by acute myasthenic crises, and symptoms are only moderately severe but persistent. Ophthalmoplegia is largely resistant to anticholinesterase medication, and complete remission of the disease is rare.

In juvenile myasthenia gravis the onset may be in early childhood, but in the majority of cases symptoms begin after 10 years of age. The disease is occasionally familial; before puberty females are affected six times more frequently than males. The most common first symptom is intermittent and asymmetric ptosis which later becomes bilateral. Weakness of the legs which follows exertion as in swimming, generalized muscle weakness, and nasal voice also occur as frequent initial symptoms. Facial weakness, difficulty in chewing and swallowing, ophthalmoplegia, and diplopia are less common at the onset but frequently develop later. In young children, walking may be delayed, and the gait is awkward and interrupted by frequent stumbling. Older children are incapable of sustained activity, they tire easily, and their shoulders droop. As the disease progresses, muscles weakened by use take longer to recover, and some additional exertion or intercurrent infection may precipitate a paralytic failure of the respiratory musculature.

The primary lesion in myasthenia gravis is believed to involve defective transmission of impulses at the neuromuscular synapse, the exact nature of which is unknown. The motor nerve fibers conduct normally, and the response of skeletal muscle to direct stimulation is normal. The neuromuscular block and the symptoms of myasthenia are similar to those of curare poisoning, and an abnormal metabolite with a curarelike action has been postulated as a possible factor in etiology. Other popular theories of the mechanism of the neuromuscular block include a deficient synthesis of acetylcholine due to overactivity of the enzyme cholinesterase or an abnormal structure of the synapse.

The general character of myasthenia gravis is suggestive of an endocrine or metabolic disorder. The onset is often in relation to puberty, and remission or relapse is frequently associated with menstruation, pregnancy, or changes of thyroid function. At autopsy the central and peripheral nervous systems show no gross or microscopic abnormalities; focal collections of small lymphocytes, or "lymphorrhages" present in affected skeletal muscles cannot be considered causative. That the thymus may play a significant role in the mechanism of myasthenia is suggested by the coincidence of thymic hyperplasia in 50 percent of cases and the apparent beneficial effect of thymectomy in some patients. It has been suggested that myasthenia is an autoimmune disease in which the thymus reacts against protein antigens in the motor end-plate. Thyoma has been found in almost one-third of the reported cases in adults but is rare in childhood.

The differential diagnoses include bulbar poliomyelitis, diphtheritic paralysis, polyneuritis, intracranial tumor, and hyperthyroidism. The initial illness is commonly misdiagnosed as hysteria or laziness. Diagnosis is confirmed by the intravenous injection of Tensilon (Figs. 81A and B), which relieves the presenting symptoms within a few minutes. In children weighing up to 34 kg, the dose is 0.2 ml (2 mg); in those over 34 kg, 0.5 ml (5 mg) may be given. If Prostigmine is employed, the intramuscular dose is 0.25 to 1.0 mg of Prostigmine methylsulfate, dependent upon the weight or surface area of the child; the patient is examined for signs of improvement at 5- or 10-minute intervals for a period of 45 minutes, and Atropine may be required for the relief of muscarinic side effects.

Treatment with anticholinesterase drugs is instituted and controlled as outlined for neonatal myasthenia. Mestinon is given orally in initial trial doses of 5 to 10 mg at intervals of two to four hours, or Prostigmine in doses of 1 to 5 mg orally. Mytelase (ambenonium chloride) is prescribed occasionally; it causes less bronchial secretion than do other anticholinesterase drugs, and its use may be indicated in patients with respiratory paralysis. Five milligrams of Mytelase chloride are equivalent to 15 mg of Prostigmine bromide or 60 mg of Mestinon bromide.

Thymectomy may be followed by improvement and sometimes by complete remission. It is considered of particular value in young female patients who have had the disease for less than five years, and is indicated especially in patients with generalized muscle weakness and bulbar symptoms resistant to therapy.

The prognosis in children is variable but relatively good compared with adults. The case fatality rate is approximately 5 percent. The course is generally prolonged, and complete remission following drug therapy or thymectomy may be expected in less than 25 percent of cases up to six years from the onset; complete remission after this time is rare. Ptosis and ocular palsies are often refractory to treatment, and relapse and failure of response to medication are frequently related to systemic or upper respiratory infection and to menstruation.

REFERENCES

DISEASES OF THE MUSCLES

Adams, R. D., Denny-Brown, D., and Pearson, C. M. Diseases of Muscle. A Study in Pathology, 2nd ed. New York, Paul B. Hoeber, Inc., 1962.

Swaiman, K. F., and Wright, F. S., Neuromuscular Diseases of Infancy and Childhood. Springfield, Ill., Charles C Thomas, Publ., 1970.

Walton, J. N., ed. Disorders of Voluntary Muscle. Boston, Little, Brown and Co., 1964.

—— and Nattrass, F. J. On the classification, natural history and treatment of myopathies. Brain, 77:169, 1954.

LIMP INFANT SYNDROME

Banker, B. Q., Victor, M., and Adams, R. D. Arthrogryposis multiplex due to congenital muscular dystrophy. Brain, 80:319, 1957.

Batten, F. E. The myopathies or muscular dystrophies; critical review. Quart. J. Med., 3:313, 1910.

Bing, R. Ueber angeborene Muskeldefecte. Virchow Arch., 170:175, 1902.

Brandt, S. A case of arthrogryposis mulitplex congenita anatomically appearing as foetal spinal muscular atrophy. Acta Paediat. Scand., 34:365, 1947.

Debré, R., and Semelaigne, G. Syndrome of diffuse muscular hypertrophy in infants causing an athletic appearance. Its connection with congenital myxedema. Amer. J. Dis. Child., 50:1351, 1935.

DeLange, C. Congenital hypertrophy of the muscles, extrapyramidal motor disturbances and mental deficiency: A clinical entity. Amer. J. Dis. Child., 48:243, 1934.

Dodge, P. R. Congenital neuromuscular disorders. Res. Publ. Ass. Res. Nerv. Ment. Dis., 38:479, 1959.

Dubowitz, V. The Floppy Infant. Clinics in Developmental Medicine No. 31. London, National Spastics Society, 1969.

Engel, W. K., Wanko, T., and Fenichel, G. M. Nemaline myopathy. Arch. Neurol., 11:22, 1964.

Greenfield, J. G., Cornman, T., and Shy, G. M. The prognostic value of the muscle biopsy in the "floppy infant." Brain, 81:461, 1958.

Schreier, K., and Huperz, R. Über die hypoplasia musculorum generalisata congenita. Ann. Paediat., 186: 241, 1956.

Shy, G. M., and Magee, K. R. A new congenital nonprogressive myopathy. Brain, 79:610, 1956.

Tizzard, J. P. M. Neuromuscular disorder of infancy. In Walton, J. N., ed., Disorders of Voluntary Muscle. Boston, Little, Brown and Co., 1964, pp. 369-388.

Turner, J. W. A. Relationship between amyotonia congenita and congenital myopathy. Brain, 63:163, 1940.

Walton, J. N. The limp child. J. Neurol. Neurosurg. Psychiat., 20:144, 1957.

MUSCULAR DYSTROPHIES

Jackson, C. E., and Carey, J. H. Progressive muscular dystrophy; autosomal recessive type. Pediatrics, 28:77, 1961.

Mabry, C. C., Roeckel, L. E., Munich, R. L., and Robertson, D. X-linked pseudohypertrophic muscular dystrophy with a late onset and slow progression. New Eng. J. Med., 273:1062, 1965.

Milhorat, A. T. The diagnosis of muscular dystrophy. Proc. 3rd Med. Conf. Muscular Dystrophy Ass. Amer., Inc. Amer. J. Phys. Med., 35:103, 1955.

Murphy, E. G., and Charniak, M. M. Glutamic oxalacetic transaminase activity in the serum in muscular dystrophy and other neuromuscular disorders in childhood. Pediatrics, 22:1110, 1958.

Pearce, J. M. S., Pennington, R. J., and Walton, J. N. Serum enzyme studies in muscle disease. Part II. Serum creatine kinase activity in muscular dystrophy and in other myopathic and neuropathic disorders. J. Neurol. Neurosurg. Psychiat., 27:96, 1964.

Walton, J. N. Muscular dystrophy and its relation to the other myopathies. Res. Publ. Ass. Res. Nerv. Ment. Dis., 38:378, 1959.

Zellweger, H., and Hansen, J. W. Slowly progressive X-linked recessive muscular dystrophy (type IIIB). Arch. Intern. Med. (Chicago), 120:525, 1967.

THE MYOTONIAS

Adams, R. D., Denny-Brown, D., and Pearson, C. M. Diseases of Muscle, A Study in Pathology, 2nd ed. New York, Paul B. Hoeber, Inc., 1962.

Bastron, J. A. Myotonia and other abnormalities of muscular contraction arising from disorders of the motor unit. Res. Publ. Ass. Res. Nerv. Ment. Dis., 38:534, 1959.

Dodge, P. R., Gamstorp, I., Byers, R. K., and Russell, P. Myotonic dystrophy in infancy and childhood. Pediatrics, 35:3, 1965.

Drager, G. A., Hammill, J. F., and Shy, G. M. Paramyotonia congenita. Arch. Neurol. Psychiat., 80:1, 1958.

Hirsch, D. R., Dancis, J., and Ward, R. S. Myotonia congenita. J. Pediat., 35:760, 1949.

MYOSITIS

Adams, R. D., Denny-Brown, D., and Pearson, C. M. Diseases of Muscle, A Study in Pathology, 2nd ed. New York, Paul B. Hoeber, Inc., 1962.

Barwick, D. D., and Walton, J. N. Polymyositis. Amer. J. Med., 35:646, 1963.

Blau, A. Primary generalized myositis fibrosa; report of 2 cases with histopathology. J. Mount Sinai Hosp. N.Y., 5:432, 1938.

Eaton, L. M. The perspective of neurology in regard to polymyositis, study of 41 cases. Neurology, 4:245, 1954.

Pearson, C. M., and Rose, A. S. Myositis: the inflammatory disorders of muscle. Res. Publ. Ass. Res. Nerv. Ment. Dis., 38:422, 1959.

Riley, H. D., Jr., and Christie, A. Myositis ossificans progressiva. Pediatrics, 8:753, 1951.

Rowland, L. R. Muscular dystrophies, polymyositis and other myopathies. J. Chron. Dis., 8:510, 1958.

Walton, J. N., and Adams, R. D. Polymyositis. Baltimore, Williams and Wilkins Co., 1958.

METABOLIC MYOPATHIES

Buchanan, D., and Steiner, P. E. Myoglobinuria with paralysis (Meyer-Betz disease). Arch. Neurol. Psychiat., 66:107, 1951.

Conn, J. W., Fajans, S. S., Louis, L. H., Streeten, D. H. P., and Johnson, R. D. Intermittent aldosteronism in periodic paralysis. Lancet, 1:802, 1957.

Danowski, T. S., and Tarail, R. Potassium metabolism and dysfunction of the nervous system associated with hyper- and hypokalemia. Res. Publ. Ass. Res. Nerv. Ment. Dis., 32:372, 1953.

Debré, R., and Semelaigne, G. Syndrome of diffuse muscular hypertrophy in infants causing athletic appearance; its connection with congenital myxedema. Amer. J. Dis. Child., 50:1351, 1935.

Engel, W. K. Muscle biopsies in neuromuscular diseases. Pediat. Clin. N. Amer., Vol. 14, Nov. 1967.

Gamstorp, I. Adynamia episodica hereditaria. Acta Paediat. Scand., 45(Suppl.):108, 1956.

Gass, H., Cherkasky, M., and Savitsky, N. Potassium and periodic paralysis. Medicine, 27:105, 1948.

Hers, H. G. α-Glucosidae deficiency in generalized glycogen storage disease (Pompe's disease). Biochem. J., 86:11, 1963.

McArdle, B. Myopathy due to a defect in muscle glycogen breakdown. Clin. Sci., 10:13, 1951.

——— Metabolic myopathies. Amer. J. Med., 35:661, 1963.

Rowland, L. P., Fahn, S., Hirschberg, E., and Harter, D. H. Myoglobinuria. Arch. Neurol., 10:537, 1964.

Schmid, R., and Mahler, R. Chronic progressive myopathy with myoglobinuria. Demonstration of a glycogenolytic defect in muscle. J. Clin. Invest., 38:2044, 1959.

Shy, G. M. Some metabolic and endocrinological aspects of disorders of striated muscle. Res. Publ. Ass. Res. Nerv. Ment. Dis., 38:274, 1959.

Smith, H., Ameck, L. D., and Sielbury, J. Type II glycogenosis. Amer. J. Dis. Child., 111:475, 1966.

——— Zellweger, H., and Afifi, A. K. Muscular form of glycogemosis type II (Pompe): report of a case with unusual features. Neurology, 17:537, 1967.

Swaiman, K. F., Kennedy, W. R., and Sauls, H. S. Late infantile acid maltase deficiency. Arch. Neurol., 18:642, 1968.

Wyllie, W. G., and Watkins, A. G. Periodic familial paralysis. Proc. Roy. Soc. Med., 41:861, 1948.

MYASTHENIA GRAVIS

Keynes, G. The results of thymectomy in myasthenia gravis. Brit. Med. J., 2:611, 1949.

Kibrick, S. Myasthenia gravis in the newborn. Pediatrics, 14:365, 1954.

Millichap, J. G., and Dodge, P. R. Diagnosis and treatment of myasthenia gravis in infancy, childhood, and adolescence; a study of 51 patients. Neurology, 10: 1007, 1960.

Osserman, K. E. Myasthenia Gravis. New York, Grune and Stratton, Inc., 1958.

Rowland, L. P., Hoefer, P. F. A., and Aranow, H., Jr. Myasthenic syndromes. Res. Publ. Ass. Res. Nerv. Ment. Dis., 38:548, 1959.

Schwab, R. S., and Viets, H. R. Myasthenia gravis. Res. Publ. Ass. Res. Nerv. Ment. Dis., 38:624, 1959.

Simpson, J. A. An evaluation of thymectomy in myasthenia gravis. Brain, 81:112, 1958.

Strauss, A. J. L., Seegal, B. C., Hsu, K. C., Burkholder, P. M., Nastick, W. L., and Osserman, K. E. Immunofluorescence demonstration of a muscle-binding complement-fixing serum globulin fraction in myasthenia gravis. Proc. Soc. Exp. Biol. Med., 105:134, 1960.

Walker, R. P. Congenital myasthenia gravis. Amer. J. Dis. Child., 86:198, 1953.

Wyllie, W. G., Bodian, M., and Burrows, N. F. E. Myasthenia gravis in children. Arch. Dis. Child., 26: 457, 1951.

15.13
DISORDERS OF THE NERVOUS SYSTEM SPECIFIC TO CHILDREN

ARNOLD P. GOLD and SIDNEY CARTER

Spasmus nutans, familial dysautonomia, and acute cerebellar ataxia are disorders specific to patients of the pediatric age group. Though rare, they present with a typical clinical picture which distinguishes them from other neurologic entities.

Spasmus Nutans
(Head Nodding)

This disorder characteristically presents with a triad of signs; intermittent nystagmus, head nodding, and tilting of the head. The condition is self-limited, generally disappearing by 3 years of age.

The syndrome has its onset in infancy most often between the ages of 4 and 16 months. There is no particular sex incidence and it is more common in Negroes. The cause is unknown; there is no evidence to support vitamin deficiency and inadequate illumination as contributing factors. Spasmus nutans is seen more frequently during winter months.

Nystagmus may be the initial sign. It is often either unilateral or more marked in one eye and is characterized by rapid movements of a small amplitude in any direction. The abnormal eye movement disappears on covering the eyes and during sleep. The head nodding, which occurs in any direction, is typically slow and inconstant with a series of nods usually lasting but a few seconds. This movement is increased by placing the child in a vertical position and is abolished when supine. Head tilt is the least common finding and is often a compensatory posturing for the impaired vision secondary to the nystagmus.

Spasmus nutans must be differentiated from congenital nystagmus which tends to be familial, involves both eyes and fails to improve with time. Head movement when present is in the same direction as the nystagmus.

The condition is self-limited, and there is no specific therapy.

Familial Dysautonomia

RALPH E. MOLOSHOK

Familial dysautonomia, a congenital heritable syndrome, was first described in 1949 by Riley and coworkers. Although autonomic dysfunction is predominant, the striking features of this syndrome indicate the presence of a diffuse disturbance of function of the entire nervous system. The incidence in families is compatible with the hypothesis that it is transmitted by a recessive autosomal gene which is generally limited to persons of Jewish extraction.

Features which have been present in all cases are: reduced or absent tear production during crying, postural hypotension, coldness of the hands and feet, excessive perspiration, usually with transient blotching of the skin with excitement or during eating, relative indifference to pain, and emotional lability. Muscular coordination is impaired as manifested by difficulty in swallowing and chewing during infancy, prolonged drooling, dysarthria, and a delay in reaching the milestones of motor development. There is a general retardation of body growth, and pubescence is usually delayed. Scoliosis occurs in about half of the children who have survived past the age of 10 years. Deep tendon reflexes are either hypoactive or more frequently absent. Impairment of autonomic homeostatis is manifested by erratic regulation of body temperature with hypothermia, particularly during infancy, and periods of unexplained hyperpyrexia. Hypertension occurs with excitement or in association with febrile crises, while other patients are unable to maintain the upright position because of severe postural hypotension. Corneal anesthesia and defective lacrimation predispose to ulceration and scarring with impaired vision.

Severe life-threatening episodes are experienced in the course of the disease. Acute pulmonary crises occur as a result of bronchial hypersecretion, aspiration, and bronchopneumonia. Periodic bouts of intractable vomiting may be associated with bizarre self-destructive schizoid behavior. Severe hyperpyrexia may be accompanied by hypertension and diminished renal function or by a convulsive state. In a few instances sudden deaths have followed a shocklike state. Cardiac arrest and shock have been experienced during anesthesia.

The cause of this syndrome is unknown. No consistent anatomic findings have been seen at autopsy. It has been postulated that an inborn error of metabolism exists which affects the synthesis of a neurohumoral substance of importance to the transmission of nervous impulses. The studies of Smith, Dancis, and co-workers support this concept and have provided more precise means of diagnosis. Measurement of the urinary excretion of the metabolic products of the catecholamines has revealed that there was a uniform elevation of the ratio of homovanillic acid (a product of dopamine metabolism) to vanillyl mandelic acid (a product of epinephrine and norepinephrine metabolism).

A valuable diagnostic test is the response to the intradermal injection of 0.02 ml of a 1:10,000 dilution of histamine. The reaction of denervation is observed in patients with dysautonomia. Normally a wheal about 1 cm in diameter is produced and is surrounded by a red flare measuring 3 to 5 cm in diameter. The flare is dependent upon an axon reflex along sensory fibers; it has been uniformly absent in tests performed on patients with dysautonomia.

Hypersensitivity to the intravenous infusion of norepinephrine is another diagnostic feature in patients with dysautonomia, in whom a rise in blood pressure greater than 50 mm Hg is seen. While the normal pupil does not respond to the intraconjunctival instillation of a 2.5 percent solution of methacholine, in dysautonomia miosis occurs.

The absence of taste buds on the tongue, similarly a reaction of denervation, provides an objective anatomic diagnostic sign. Physiologic studies of respiration in dysautonomic children have revealed a relative insensitivity to hypoxia and to elevated carbon dioxide levels in the blood.

Prognosis for life must be guarded, as death has occurred in about 25 percent of the known cases, especially during the early years of life. These deaths have resulted from the acute crises described. The survivors have been handicapped by psychomotor difficulties although, with age, adaptation to stress appears to improve.

Treatment is strictly symptomatic. Guidance for the parents in the management of difficult behavior patterns in these children is most important. Vomiting attacks can often be controlled by the use of chlorpromazine in combination with phenobarbital. Inasmuch as these children adjust poorly to environmental change and stress, a stable routine of daily activity may prove helpful. The use of tranquilizing drugs has been of benefit to some children.

Acute Cerebellar Ataxia

STUART WEISS

Acute cerebellar ataxia, an unusual neurologic syndrome peculiar to the pediatric age group, is characterized by the sudden or subacute onset of ataxia of trunk, extremity, and ocular movement without other specific neurologic involvement or systemic symptoms. Complete recovery occurs within a few weeks to months in a high percentage of patients. Children between the ages of 1 and 4 years are most often affected; however, older children are occasionally seen with this syndrome. Sexes are equally susceptible.

ETIOLOGY AND PATHOLOGY. Frequently, a history of preceding nonspecific upper respiratory illness or gastrointestinal disturbance is obtained; however, most children develop ataxia without prior illness. Although some clinicians consider acute cerebellar ataxia as a transient sensitivity or inflammatory reaction in the cerebellum or cerebellar tracts to a nonspecific viral or systemic illness, others regard the syndrome as a viral cerebellitis, especially in the few severely involved patients.

Occasionally inborn errors of protein metabolism have been discovered in children with acute ataxia. Recurrent acute ataxia often precipitated by the stress of minor infections has been inherited in several families as a Mendelian dominant. No information as to the specific location or type of pathologic change is available to support any specific etiologic entity.

Recently, some children with acute cerebellar ataxia have been shown to have an associated often occult neuroblastoma.

CLINICAL MANIFESTATIONS. The major clinical feature of the syndrome is the rapid development of truncal ataxia with a lesser degree of extremity ataxia, which is less marked in the arms than in the legs. In the child more severely involved, there may be complete inability to support the body in a sitting position or to keep the head erect. Muscles of the trunk and extremities are hypotonic. Often an irregular, jerky tremor of the head and body is present.

Some children with severe ataxia may also develop jerky, irregular ocular activity with volitional eye movement (ocular dysmetria), others, involuntary darting multidirectional conjugate ocular movement (opsoclonus) and a few, a nystagmus with rhythmic fast-slow components. Isolated cranial nerve involvement, particularly the facial and less often the vagus, may occur in association with cerebellar ataxia. A specific viral infection (polio I) has been documented as the etiologic factor in the latter patients.

Vague systemic abnormalities such as lethargy, irritability, photophobia, and mild nuchal rigidity may accompany the neurologic deficit.

LABORATORY DATA. The patients who are usually afebrile at the time of hospitalization have normal peripheral blood counts, urinalysis, and serologic tests for syphilis. Erythrocyte sedimentation rates, heterophil agglutination, and total serum proteins are normal. Abnormalities of serum and urine amino acids by chromatographic analysis may be found in rare instances. Electroencephalographic abnormalities of major degree are uncommon. Lumbar puncture reveals a normal pressure, an occasional mononuclear pleocytosis to 50 cells, and normal protein, gamma globulin, and sugar values.

Viral cultures of throat, stool, and cerebrospinal fluid in a small number of children with acute ataxia have grown poliomyelitis virus type I and ECHO virus types 6 and 9. Confirmation of a specific viral infection with neutralizing and complement-fixing antibodies is desirable through acute and convalescent phase sera. Demonstrable acute changes in antibody titers and positive viral cultures are rare except in those cases of ataxia discovered during large-scale viral epidemics.

Roentgenograms of the chest and the vertebral spines as well as an intravenous pyelogram should be made to exclude an associated neuroblastoma.

DIAGNOSIS. A variety of diagnostic possibilities should be considered in a child with acute cerebellar ataxia. Posterior fossa tumors may produce ataxia abruptly. This ataxia is usually asymmetric in the degree of involvement of extremities and associated at the time of examination with evidence of increased intracranial pressure, cranial nerve palsies, head tilt, and nystagmus with preponderance in one direction. Active infection with poliomyelitis virus I, ECHO virus types 6 and 9, and influenza A virus has been demonstrated in occasional patients with acute ataxia. Classical acute ataxia in the course of varicella is of sufficiently frequent occurrence to be recognized. Infrequent association of acute ataxia without evidence of diffuse encephalitis has also been reported with rubella, rubeola, mumps, typhoid fever, and infectious mononucleosis.

Acute ataxia associated with myoclonic jerking and opsoclonus has been the initial manifestation of an occult neuroblastoma in several patients. These nonmetastatic neurologic abnormalities may antedate the discovery of the tumor by days to months. With removal of the tumor, the trunk and ocular ataxia may gradually improve.

Acute ataxia with a photosensitive pellagralike skin rash is the major clinical manifestation of Hartnup disease. Urinary screening for indican and indole acetic acid and characteristic blood and urinary chromatographic patterns of amino acids indicate this diagnosis in suspected patients.

Recently hyperpyruvic acidemia, hyperalanemia, and hyperalanuria have been discovered in one child with acute ataxia. Endogenous deficiencies of niacinamide and thiamin have been considered to be partly responsible for the above metabolic errors.

Certain exogenous toxins can produce a syndrome of acute ataxia. Excessive ingestion of drugs, such as diphenylhydantoins and barbiturates, or inhalation or ingestion of DDT (diphenyltrichloroethane), and lindane, causes ataxia as an early sign of toxicity. Lead ingestion and thallium poisoning produce acute ataxic syndromes which may not be readily reversible.

Demyelinating disease such as juvenile multiple sclerosis may be considered in the differential diagnosis if a previous history of neurologic deficit is present. The absence of a fluctuating course with successive exacerbations makes this diagnosis a rarity.

Acute labyrinthitis is characterized by positional vertigo, nausea, and vomiting in association with acute imbalance together with the absence of other distinguishing features of acute ataxia such as extremity incoordination and ocular dysmetria. Labyrinthine function is depressed on caloric stimulation.

PROGNOSIS. Most patients with acute cerebellar ataxia have a rapid recovery of extremity coordination and gait stability within periods of one week to six months following the onset of illness, emphasizing the benign prognosis with which this syndrome is identified. Some patients, as high as 33 percent in one series, have persistent neurologic deficit with ocular dysmetria, truncal and extremity ataxia, and lesser degrees of intellectual impairment. However, even in this group of patients gradual improvement has taken place over periods of several years.

Factors such as age of onset, sex, race, presence of prodromal symptoms, and specific laboratory data seem to have little significance in predicting the degree of recovery of the less fortunate children. There has been some correlation between the severity of the initial neurologic manifestations of the disease and a less favorable prognosis.

THERAPY. In the absence of a specific treatable cause of the syndrome, therapy of acute cerebellar ataxia is symptomatic, being directed toward maintenance of fluid and nutritional requirements, nursing supervision for general body care, and physical rehabilitation after the acute phase of illness is past.

The child should be kept at bed rest until the active progression of ataxia has ceased. Bed sides and rails should be protected with padding, as the children are often irritable and may strike their ataxic extremities against metal bed surfaces. Barbiturates or other sedatives should be used judiciously if the irritability or agitation is sufficiently severe to exhaust the child.

Nursing personnel and physicians should be careful to support the patient completely during care or treatment, as the ataxia may not allow normal muscular control of the head or trunk. Attempts at standing or walking the child should be withheld until the ataxia has sufficiently improved to avoid injurious falls. Similarly, excessively rapid attempts to achieve physical rehabilitation should be avoided lest the child become fearful and apprehensive because of inability to control the extremities or trunk during convalescence. In patients with unusually severe and persisting problems in balance, football helmets may be worn during rehabilitation.

Physical therapy to children over 3 years of age is aided by their ability to understand rehabilitation direction and to help themselves to develop functional balance in attempting ambulation.

Parental anxiety is best contained by guarded reassurance by the physician and a clear, simple explanation of the course and usual prognosis of the illness.

REFERENCES

SPASMUS NUTANS

Herrman, C. Head shaking with nystagmus in infants; a study of sixty-four cases. Amer. J. Dis. Child., 16: 180, 1918.

Norton, E. W. D., and Cogan, D. Ct. Spasmus nutans; a clinical study of twenty cases followed two years or more since onset. Arch. Ophthal., 52:442, 1954.

FAMILIAL DYSAUTONOMIA

Moloshok, R. E., and Moseley, J. Familial dysautonomia: pulmonary manifestations. Pediatrics, 17:327, 1956.

Moses, S. W., Rotem, Y., Jagjagoda, N., Talmor, N., Eichhorn, F., and Levin, S. Clinical, genetic and biochemical study of familial dysautonomia in Israel. Israel J. Med. Sci., 3:358, 1967.

Riley, C. M. Familial dysautonomia. Advances Pediat., 9:157, 1957.

———— and Moore, R. H. Familial dysautonomia differentiated from related disorders. Pediatrics, 37:435, 1966.

Smith, A. A., and Dancis, J. Physiologic studies in familial dysautonomia. J. Pediat., 63:838, 1963.

———— and Dancis, J. Response to intradermal histamine in familial dysautonomia; a diagnostic test. J. Pediat., 63:889, 1963.

ACUTE CEREBELLAR ATAXIA

Berglund, G., Mossberg, H. O., and Rydenstam, B. Acute cerebellar ataxia in children. Acta Paediat. Scand., 44:254, 1955.

Blaw, M. E., and Sheehan, J. C. Acute cerebellar syndrome of childhood. Neurology, 8:538, 1958.

Bray, P. F., Ziter, F. A., Lahey, M. E., and Myers, G. G. The coincidence of neuroblastoma and acute cerebellar encephalopathy. Trans. Amer. Neurol. Ass., 1969, p. 28.

Cottom, D. G. Acute cerebellar ataxia. Arch. Dis. Child., 32:163, 1957.

Curnen, E. C., and Chamberlain, H. R. Acute cerebellar ataxia associated with polio virus infection. Yale J. Biol. Med., 34:219, 1962.

Dyken, P., and Oldrich, K. Dancing eyes, dancing feet: infantile polymyoclonia. Brain, 91:305, 1968.

Goldston, A. S., Millichap, J. S., and Miller, R. H. Cerebellar ataxia with pre-eruptive varicella. Amer. J. Dis. Child., 106:197, 1963.

Goldwyn, A., and Waldman, A. M. Acute cerebellar ataxia in children, report of three cases. J. Pediat., 42:75, 1953.

Hill, W., and Sherman, H. Acute intermittent familial cerebellar ataxia. Arch. Neurol., 18:350, 1968.

James, T. Acute ataxia of cerebellar type in children. Report of a case with rapid and complete recovery. Glasgow Med. J., 33:455, 1952.

Keller, J. J., and Karelitz, S. Acute ataxia in a 20-month old female. Pediatrics, 1:754, 1948.

King, G., Schwartz, G. A., and Slade, H. W. Acute cerebellar ataxia. Pediatrics, 21:731, 1958.

Klingman, W. O., and Hodges, R. S. Acute ataxia of unknown origin in children. J. Pediat., 24:536, 1944.

Lasater, G. M., and Jabbour, J. T. Acute ataxia of childhood: A summary of fifteen cases. Amer. J. Dis. Child., 97:61, 1959.

Lonsdale, D., Faulkner, W. R., Price, W., and Smeby, R. R. Pyruvic acidemia with hyperalanemia: vitamin B dependency. J. Pediat., 74:827, 1969.

McAllister, R. M., Hummeler, K., and Coriel, L. L. Acute cerebellar ataxia. Case report with isolation of type 9 ECHO virus from cerebrospinal fluid. New Eng. J. Med., 261:1159, 1959.

Mendez-Cashion, D., Sanchez-Longo, L. P., Valcarcel, M., and Rosen, L. Acute cerebellar ataxia in children associated with infection by polio virus 1. Pediatrics, 29:808, 1962.

Shanks, R. A. Notes on cerebellar ataxia in childhood. Arch. Dis. Child., 25:389, 1950.

Solomon, G. E., and Chutorian, A. M. Opsoclonus and occult neuroblastoma. New Eng. J. Med., 279:475, 1969.

Walcher, D. N., and Ross, A. T. Acute cerebellar ataxia of undetermined origin in childhood. Amer. J. Dis. Child., 96:278, 1958.

Weiss, S., and Carter, S. Course and prognosis of acute cerebellar ataxia in children. Neurology, 9:711, 1959.

chapter 16

THE ENDOCRINE SYSTEM

MELVIN M. GRUMBACH, Associate Editor

16.1
NEURAL AND ENDOCRINE COMMUNICATIONS

RICHARD J. WURTMAN

Mammals have three kinds of cells that mediate communications between organs: neurons, neuroendocrine transducers, and glandular cells. Neurons receive and transmit information at the synapse, a specific anatomic locus with a characteristic appearance. Neuroendocrine transducers have a synaptic input but transmit their signals via the circulation. Glandular cells lack synapses and use the bloodstream as the source of their input and the medium for their secretions.

The transmission of signals across synapses is mediated by a well-described process: a specific neurotransmitter substance such as acetylcholine or norepinephrine, stored within a characteristic subcellular vesicle, is released into the synaptic cleft from the presynaptic cell. The neurotransmitter then diffuses across a short distance to reach a specialized receptor zone on the postsynaptic cell, where it alters the flux of specific ions. This causes a change in electrical potential within the postsynaptic neuron and alters the probability that an action potential will be generated and a nerve impulse propagated. Nearly all the compounds thought to function as neurotransmitters have similar chemical characteristics; they are low-molecular-weight, water-soluble amines and, possibly, amino acids. Moreover, they are rapidly inactivated by physical and chemical processes, such as enzymatic transformation or reuptake into their cells of origin. Their concentrations in the blood tend to be very low.

Hormonal signals, in contrast, are transmitted via the bloodstream. The array of chemicals used by the body as hormones is far broader than the current list of probable neurotransmitters; furthermore, the hormones seem to lack common chemical characteristics. Thus, insulin is water-soluble, while progesterone is highly nonpolar; thryroxine is a low-molecular-weight amino acid, while thyroid-stimulating hormone (TSH) appears to be a large glycoprotein; epinephrine is cleared rapidly from the circulation by enzymatic transformation or uptake into sympathetic nerve endings, whereas cortisol persists in the blood for rela-

tively long periods. The specific anatomic locus on or in the receptor cell at which a hormone acts has yet to be identified, but it almost certainly lacks the well-defined structural features of the postsynaptic membrane. Similarly, no characteristic electrical response seems to exist in hormone-responsive cells analogous to the ion fluxes and potential changes observed in the postsynaptic neuron. One can usually tell within seconds whether a given neuron has received and responded to a neurotransmitter; considerably more time is required to determine whether a thyroid cell has responded to circulating TSH.

Perhaps the most characteristic difference between the transmission of signals by neurotransmitters and by hormones lies in the techniques used by these communication systems to achieve "privacy." Nervous systems obtain privacy by anatomic means, a given neuron apparently transmitting signals only to the small number of cells with which it makes synapses, or to cells lying within a few hundred Angstroms of its terminal boutons. Thus, even though the particular chemical signal (e.g., acetylcholine) emitted when a specific neuron fires might be capable of stimulating billions of neurons within the brain, only hundreds actually respond, because only this number actually receives quanta of the neurotransmitter.

Communication systems that utilize the circulation to transmit signals attain privacy by biochemical means. A given signal may be distributed by the blood to every cell in the body; however, because the signal is coded, only the relatively small number of cells able to perform the decoding operation can obtain the information. The high degree of specificity attainable by hormonal communication systems is well illustrated by the physiologic regulation of the thyroid gland. TSH, the input to this organ, is carried by the circulation to every organ in the body; thyroxine, its output, is distributed in essentially the same volume. Only the thyroid gland, however, appears capable of responding to the information present in circulating TSH levels, while the heart, the liver, and most other organs show biochemical responses to circulating thyroxine.

Neuroendocrine Transducer Cells

The conversion of neural to hormonal signals is accomplished by neuroendocrine transducer cells. These cells are apparently stimulated by the same neuro-transmitter substances as neurons. Their output signals exhibit all the variety typical of hormones: epinephrine is water-soluble, while melatonin is relatively nonpolar; renin is a high-molecular-weight protein, while epinephrine and melatonin are low-molecular-weight derivatives of single amino acids. The output signals (the "releasing factors" or hypophysiotropic hormones) emitted by hypothalamic transducer cells, which mediate the neural control of the anterior pituitary, apparently act only on this single target organ. In contrast, oxytocin, a hormonal signal emitted by the paraventricular nucleus, carries instructions to both the uterus and the myoepithelium of the mammary glands.

The demonstration that a given cell functions as a neuroendocrine transducer requires two types of evidence. The cell must be shown by electron microscopy to receive a direct innervation, and it must be demonstrated that the cell's ability to secrete its hormone under appropriate physiologic conditions is impaired upon interruption of this innervation. With these criteria, at least five groups of cells have been shown to be neuroendocrine transducers:

1. The *chromaffin cells* of the adrenal medulla respond to a sympathetic cholinergic input by releasing the hormone epinephrine.
2. The *parenchymal cells* of the mammalian pineal organ respond to a sympathetic noradrenergic input by synthesizing and releasing the hormone melatonin.
3. The *cells of the supraoptic and paraventricular hypothalamic nuclei* respond to noradrenergic and/or cholinergic inputs by releasing the hormones vasopressin and oxytocin.
4. *Hypothalamic cells* that may reside within the arcuate nuclei appear to secrete "releasing factors" or hormones into the pituitary portal circulation, possibly in response to a noradrenergic or dopaminergic input.
5. The *juxtaglomerular cells* of the mammalian kidney respond to a sympathetic noradrenergic input by releasing renin into the bloodstream.

The list of neuroendocrine transducers will probably continue to expand. Whenever it can be demonstrated that the brain influences secretion of a hormone from a peripheral organ (e.g., insulin from the pancreas), a prima facie case is made for the participation of a neuroendocrine transducer in the secretory process.

REFERENCES

Wurtman, R. J. Neuroendocrine transducer cells in mammals. *In* Schmitt, F. O., editor-in-chief, The Neurosciences: Second Study Program. Rockefeller University Press, New York, 1970.

16.2
THE ANTERIOR PITUITARY

ROBERT M. BLIZZARD

The pituitary gland was initially termed "the master gland" and was considered to have physiologic importance out of proportion to its small size (500 to 600 mg in the adult). Its physiologic eminence has withstood the extension of medical knowledge, although it is now realized that this important structure does not function autonomously and that there are many influences exerted upon it by the nervous system and peripheral endocrine glands. Consequently, functions and diseases of the anterior pituitary must be considered in relation to the normal and abnormal physiology of other organs or organ systems.

Interrelations of Hypothalamus and Anterior Pituitary

The anterior pituitary (adenohypophysis) is derived from an out-pouching of the stomodeum (Rathke's pouch). The posterior pituitary (neurohypophysis) originates from the infundibular process of the diencephalon. When these two structures meet, the anterior wall of Rathke's pouch thickens to form the *pars distalis* of the anterior pituitary. The posterior wall forms the *pars intermedia* which is intermediate between the pars distalis of the anterior lobe and the posterior lobe (*pars nervosa*). The infundibular stem connects the hypothalamus and the pars nervosa. Paired extensions of the pars distalis form a cuff of tissue, the *pars tuberalis,* which surrounds the infundibular stalk. However, in Figure 1, for purposes of clarity, the pars tuberalis is drawn only on the anterior surface of the infundibular stem.

Occasionally the migratory tract of the adenohypophysis fails to obliterate completely and cysts are formed within the sella turcica. These may extend themselves by growth into the suprasellar area. Such cysts are called craniopharyngioma cysts. If the cysts are filled with tumor cells the tumors are called craniopharyngiomas.

As expected from the embryology, the *hypothalamus,* which is located directly above the pituitary, has no emitting neural fibers to the anterior pituitary, but several neural tracts traverse from centers in the hypothalamus through the neural stalk into the neurohypophysis or pars nervosa. The median eminence of the hypothalamus, a broadening at the cephalic end of the hypophyseal stalk, lies in close proximity above the pars tuberalis and probably plays

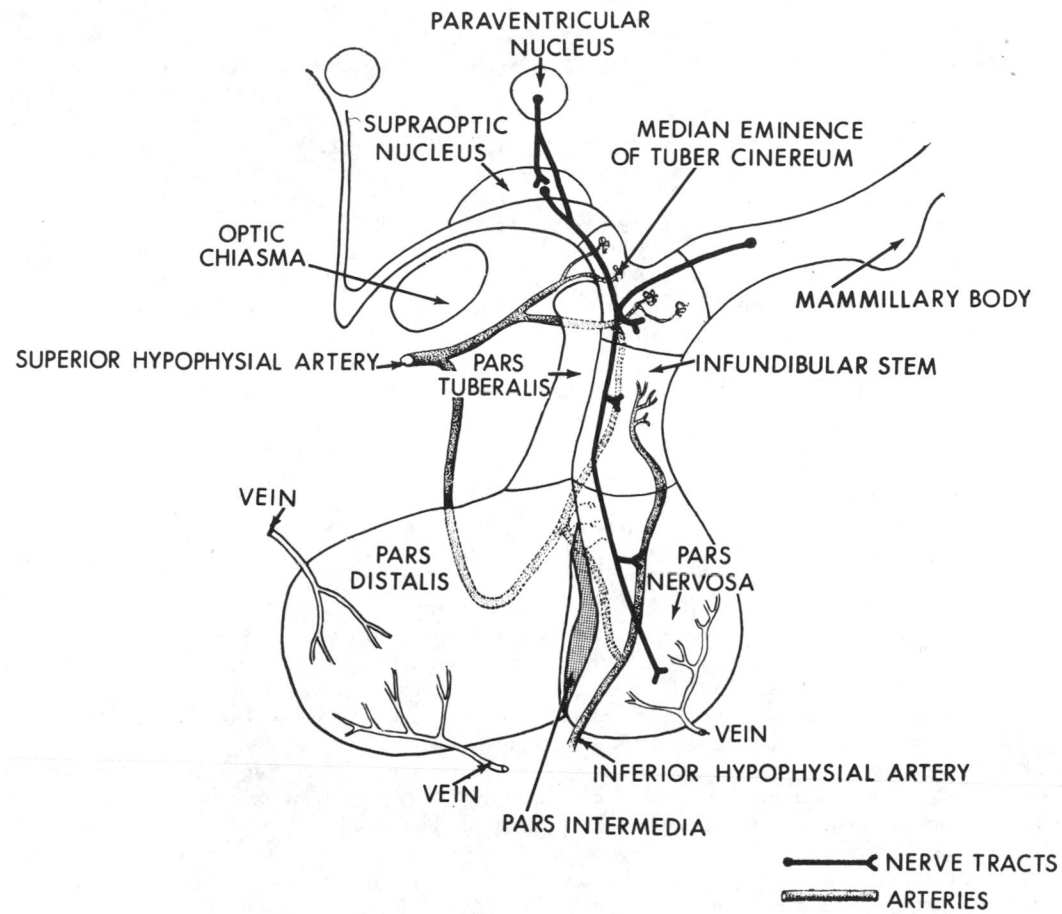

Fig. 1. Interrelations of hypothalamus and pituitary, including the arterial blood supply (which does not supply the anterior pituitary). The blood supply of the anterior pituitary (not shown) is completely venous in origin. The portal venous system originates in the median eminence and transports the neurohumoral secretions from the hypothalamus to the anterior pituitary. (Adapted from Crosby, Humphrey, and Luer. *In* Wilkins, ed., *The Diagnosis and Treatment of Endocrine Disorders in Childhood,* 3rd ed., 1965. Courtesy of Charles C Thomas, Publ.)

a direct role as intermediator between the hypothalamus and the anterior pituitary. Various neurohumoral substances produced in hypothalamic centers are absorbed by the portal veins in the median eminence and then conveyed to the anterior pituitary. There is evidence to support the thesis that there are hypothalamic releasing factors for most, if not all, of the hormones of anterior pituitary origin. Occasionally hypothalamic centers, such as appetite, thirst, and sleep centers, are involved in hypothalamic lesions and pituitary dysfunction, and symptoms related to disturbances of these centers may accompany the manifestations of pituitary dysfunction.

The optic chiasm lies directly anterior to the infundibular stalk, and visual disturbances, especially bilateral hemianopia, often result when there is a pituitary tumor extending out of the sella and compressing the chiasm.

The blood supply of the anterior pituitary is completely of venous origin, in contrast with that of the posterior pituitary, the median eminence of the hypothalamus, and the hypothalamus, all of which are supplied by the superior and inferior hypophyseal arteries. The portal veins of the anterior lobe originate in the median eminence and the upper and lower portions of the infundibular stem. Therefore, the origin of the blood supply is optimally located to receive *neurohumors* which are transmitted downstream to the anterior lobe. Since some of these vessels originate below the diaphragma sellae, a membranous diaphragm covering the sella through which the infundibular stem penetrates, stalk sections performed above the diaphragm may be only partially effective in producing decreased pituitary function. However, coagulation of the distal stalk usually produces complete necrosis and pituitary dysfunction.

Hormones of the Anterior Pituitary

There are many cell types in the adenohypophysis and each probably produces its own hormone. Initially the cell types were divided into chromophobes, eosinophils, and basophils; however, with refinement of staining techniques at least seven cell types are identifiable (Fig. 2). The eosinophils (acidophils) or alpha cells produce somatotropin (STH) and prolactin (LTH), which also is called mammotropic hormone. The basophils have been subcategorized as $beta_1$, $beta_2$, $delta_1$, and $delta_2$ cells. Melanocyte-stimulating hormone (MSH) and adrenocorticotropic (ACTH) are produced by $beta_1$ cells, while thyrotropic (TSH), luteinizing (LH), and follicle-stimulating hormone (FSH) are produced by the other three in that order (Fig. 2). Chromophobes have been subdivided into gamma cells ($beta_3$) and primordial cells (stem cells). Presumably, the $beta_3$ cells, like the $beta_1$ cells, produce ACTH.

The *homeostatic regulation* of the production or secretion of *pituitary hormones* is controlled by several factors: (1) circulating hormones of the peripheral endocrine glands; (2) stress; and in some instances, (3) circulating levels of nonhormonal substances—for example, blood sugar concentration, which affects STH release.

The secretion of many tropic hormones is controlled by feedback mechanisms, and the amount of tropic hormone is inversely related to the concentration of the circulating hormones produced by the peripheral endocrine glands. In primary hypothyroidism, for example, TSH is secreted in excess. Conversely, with exogenous administration of thyroxine or triiodothyronine in complete replacement dosages, the pituitary is put at rest via hypothalamic and pituitary suppression, and there is no further release of TSH. Similarly, with primary hypogonadism, the gonadotropins are excreted in excess, and exogenous administration of large amounts of estrogen or testosterone suppress the release of gonadotropins. Normally the levels of circulating cortisol and ACTH are inversely related in a similar manner.

Tropic hormones may be inhibited by excesses of certain peripheral hormones even though the tropic hormones are not directly responsible for the production of the latter; for example, excess hydrocortisone may inhibit growth hormone. Also, excessive production of certain tropic hormones may result from deficiencies of peripheral hormones for which they are not directly responsible; excessive prolactin and gonadotropin have resulted from a deficiency of thyroid hormone. These relationships have been termed "overflow stimulation."

Stress apparently functions independently of the feedback mechanisms. Surgical stress, for example, is associated with increased ACTH output even though circulating levels of hydrocortisone may be elevated. Similarly, stress induced by the intravenous administration of Piromen, a fever-producing bacterial endotoxin, results in increased secretion of cortisol and presumably ACTH.

Circulating blood sugar levels affect the circulating level of human growth hormone or somatotropin. The levels increase with hypoglycemia and decrease with hyperglycemia. Intracellular glucose levels may actually be the controlling agent, since exercise is also a stimulus to increasing the concentration of growth hormone in serum.

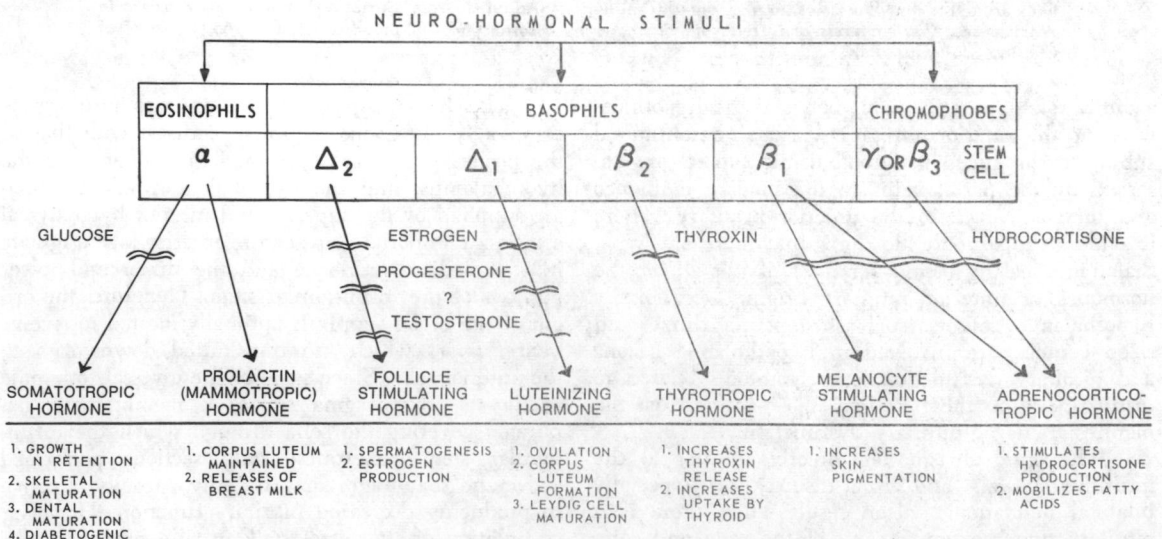

Fig. 2. Hormones produced by the anterior pituitary and their effects.

The *metabolic actions* of the pituitary hormones are multiple. Growth hormone, which has been isolated from human or simian pituitaries, is an unbranched polypeptide with a molecular weight of approximately 21,500 and is metabolically active in man and certain other mammals. Unfortunately growth hormone obtained from nonprimates is not metabolically active in the human because of structural variations. Pituitary glands of all ages contain growth hormone in a concentration varying from 4 to 10 percent of the dry weight.

The administration of growth hormone to hypopituitary dwarfs causes rapid growth of the skeletal system, usually without a proportionate increase in skeletal maturation. This relationship between linear growth and skeletal maturation contrasts markedly with the increase in linear growth occurring with testosterone treatment, which is accompanied by a proportionately greater rate of increase in skeletal maturation. In association with growth, nitrogen, potassium, and phosphorus are retained. Concentrations of serum urea and other nonprotein nitrogen falls, and free fatty acids are mobilized from fat for energy.

Growth hormone also has an action on carbohydrate metabolism. Individuals with growth hormone deficiency may have hypoglycemia, which improves when STH is given, despite an increase in insulin output in response to a glucose load. If increased insulin cannot be produced, as in a patient with diabetes mellitus, ketonemia and hyperglycemia occur.

Prolactin (mammotropic hormone) from human pituitaries has recently been chemically separated from growth hormone. Prolactin administered to hypophysectomized animals has some metabolic actions similar to STH. One preliminary report suggested that ovine prolactin administered to hypophysectomized animals has some metabolic actions similar to STH, and another suggested that ovine prolactin administered to growth hormone-deficient humans acted similarly in many respects to STH. Other actions are listed in Figure 2. There is no known action for prolactin in the male.

The gonadotropins, ACTH, and TSH act primarily upon their respective peripheral endocrine glands. In addition to the actions of ACTH listed, it also may play some role in mobilizing fat. Melanocyte-stimulating hormone is closely related chemically to ACTH. This hormone causes increased pigmentation and, as with ACTH, its production is inhibited by hydrocortisone or cortisone.

Laboratory Measurements of Pituitary Function

The development of immunoassay techniques in the past few years now permits the direct measurement of millimicrogram (nanogram) amounts of all the tropic hormones.

The easy availability of growth hormone immu-noassays in many hospital and commercial laboratories simplifies the evaluation of the short child who has suspected growth hormone deficiency (Table 1). Since STH concentrations are very variable during the day, specific stimuli are utilized to cause the release of growth hormone before serum is drawn for asessment of the STH concentration. The usual stimulatory tests are infusion of anginine monochloride over a 30-minute period, with serum specimens drawn at 0, 15, 30, 45, and 60 minutes, followed immediately with injection of 0.075 units/kg of insulin intravenously. Serum specimens are then drawn at 15, 30, 45, and 60 minutes. Absence of a significant (>6.0 mμg/ml) response either in the fasting or stimulated state is very suggestive of STH deficiency. Some normal individuals release STH only with one of these stimuli. Therefore, STH deficiency cannot be diagnosed unless there is failure to respond to both stimuli. Random sampling of serum specimens 3 to 4 hours postprandially, with exercise, or with deep sleep also may be utilized. A significant level in any of these specimens probably precludes growth hormone deficiency, but absence of STH in random specimens does not permit one to diagnose hypopituitarism.

Excessive STH production, such as occurs in acromegaly, also is determined by immunoassay. A glucose tolerance test (oral or intravenous) is performed and serum for STH is obtained at 15- or 20-minute intervals for 2 hours. Growth hormone will fall to insignificant values (0 to 3 mμg/ml) in the individual who is not producing excessive STH. With an eosinophilic adenoma of the pituitary, the values rarely fall below 6.0 mμg/ml.

In interpreting STH concentrations in adults, sex differences must be taken into account, as estrogens enhance the responses to the various stimuli. All children who are sexually infantile respond similarly; their responses to arginine infusion more closely simulate those of adult males than those of adult females.

Unfortunately STH is not excreted in significant quantities in urine, so that no measurements in urine are possible. For this reason and because the values in blood are inconstant during a 24-hour period, production or secretion rates to determine comparative amounts of growth hormone in various types of short stature are not obtainable. Hopefully, refinement of techniques in the near future will permit measurement of the total growth hormone produced in individuals instead of measurement of concentrations only.

The same types of immunoassay techniques now permit measurement of follicle-stimulating hormone (FSH) and luteinizing hormone (LH) in both serum and urine. The absolute values obtained vary in each laboratory, so that normal values must be determined for each laboratory. Urinary measurements can be carried out on acetone precipitates of an aliquot of a 24-hour urine specimen, or on kaolin extracts of the total 24-hour urine specimen. The values obtained for FSH are comparable by both methods, but

TABLE 1.   *Laboratory Determinations of Pituitary Hormones by Direct and Indirect Means*

Assays that can be used only to measure hormones in
pituitary extracts, and not in serum or urine, are not included.

	Blood		Urine		Reserve
	Direct	Indirect	Direct	Indirect	
Growth hormone	Immunoassay	Sulfation factor Insulin tolerance test			Immunochemical in blood with insulin and arginine stimulation
TSH	Immunoassay Bioassay	^{131}I uptake of thyroid gland Serum PBI and thyroxin and free thyroxine			
ACTH	Immunoassay Bioassay	Insulin tolerance test		17-OHCS excretion 17-KS excretion	Metyrapone stimulation
FSH	Immunoassay		Immunoassay Bioassay	Sperm count	Clomiphene stimulation
LH	Immunoassay		Immunoassay Bioassay	Testosterone	Clomiphene stimulation
LTH	Bioassay				

the values for LH are approximately four times higher when acetone precipitates are used. This discrepancy may represent loss of immunoreactive LH on the kaolin.

Direct measurement of gonadotropins also is possible by utilizing bioassays. Specific bioassays are available for determining FSH and LH specifically, but urinary gonadotropin determinations, as currently measured by most clinical laboratories, represent a summation effect of FSH and LH. Normal values for adults in the premenopausal age are 6 to 52 mouse units per 24 hours. Approximately 2 mouse units equals 1 rat unit.

Small amounts of gonadotropins are produced before adolescence and can be measured by immunoassay, but usually not by bioassay techniques since the quantities excreted are very small. Increased quantities occur normally at approximately age 10 years in both boys and girls, and increase with each stage of sexual development until adulthood. Then values in males and females are essentially similar, except in females during the ovulatory peak and postmenopausally, when values increase very significantly.

Unfortunately the direct measurement of pituitary gonadotropins is of limited value until adolescence. Children normally do not excrete sufficient gonadotropins prior to that time to differentiate hypopituitarism from constitutional delayed adolescence. These measurements become useful at the time of expected adolescence in a tall eunuchoid boy with sexual infantilism, when they assist in differentiating gonadotropic deficiency from primary testicular failure. In the former, the values will be preadolescent, and in the latter, either elevated or normal. This measurement also is of value in differentiating gonadal dysgenesis (Turner's syndrome) from hypo-

pituitarism in sexually immature females at adolescence. Patients with gonadal dysgenesis or primary ovarian failure will have an increase over preadolescent values, usually by the age of 10 to 11 years, while patients with hypopituitarism or constitutional delayed adolescence will have preadolescent values.

Administration of clomiphene citrate stimulates release of gonadotropins in sexually mature individuals, but not in preadolescent or early adolescent children. Therefore, its usefulness as a measure of gonadotropin reserve in children is limited.

Thyrotropic hormone also is measured by radioimmunoassay techniques. Normal values of < 2 to 7 μU are reported. The limit of sensitivity of the assay is usually 2 μU. Values increase with compensated or uncompensated hypothyroidism, in the first 24 hours of life, and with ingestion of certain goitrogenic agents over a prolonged period.

Thyrotropic hormone can be assayed biologically also. The number of methods developed in the past attest to the inadequacies of each, at least in the hands of others than those who developed the method. The method of Adams and Purves, which was modified subsequently by McKenzie, is probably the most satisfactory. This method measures the discharge of ^{131}I from the thyroid glands of appropriately treated mice by measuring the increase of radioactivity in the blood several hours after the injection of TSH. This method has the advantage of also measuring the long-acting thyroid stimulator (LATS) found in the serum of patients with Graves' disease. Long-acting thyroid stimulator is not TSH of pituitary origin. It is TSH-like, except that it has a different effective time relationship upon the discharge of ^{131}I from the thyroid gland of the assay animal. By several methods used by different workers, normal concentrations of TSH are approximately 0.2 milliunits (bovine units) per ml of serum.

A radioimmunoassay technique for measuring ACTH has been described recently. Possibly this assay will become available in the future for clinical investigation. Bioassays utilizing the concentration of 17-hydroxycorticosteroids or corticosterone in adrenal vein blood of hypophysectomized dogs or rats respectively, after injection of plasma, have been used as research techniques. Since these bioassay methods are tedious and not sufficiently sensitive to measure the hormone in the plasma of normal, nonstressed individuals, bioassays for ACTH probably will not become available for clinical use. However, extraction of plasma and testing by these methods has made it possible to determine that in the normal individual the concentration of ACTH varies from an average of 0.11 milliunits per 100 ml to an average of 0.25 milliunits. These values correlate with the diurnal variation of plasma 17-OH-corticosteroids.

Some clinics still must depend upon indirect measurements of pituitary function to determine if an abnormality exists. Indirect parameters usually are used when evaluating TSH production. Patients with hypopituitarism frequently have a low or low-normal protein-bound iodine (PBI), butanol-extractable (BEI), free thyroxine, and ^{131}I uptake even in the absence of clinical hypothyroidism. When these values are low, differentiation of primary thyroid disease from pituitary insufficiency is made by administering 5 to 10 units of TSH every day for 2 to 3 days and repeating the uptake and the chemical tests. A patient with primary hypothyroidism will not respond with increased values, whereas one with hypothyroidism secondary to hypopituitarism will have appreciable rises in all parameters. The normal responses to standard dosages must be determined for each laboratory; therefore, no specific normal values are given.

Evaluation of ACTH function also is usually measured by indirect techniques. The excretion of the cortisol metabolites, 17-hydroxycorticosteroids (17-OHCS) or 17-ketogenic steroids (17-KGS), may be of assistance, as patients deficient in ACTH often excrete subnormal values (normal values must be determined for each laboratory). However, some patients with partial hypopituitarism excrete normal amounts of 17-OHCS or 17-KGS, but cannot excrete increased ACTH in response to iatrogenically induced low serum concentrations of cortisol. Serum concentrations of cortisol can be reduced and ACTH reserve can be measured by giving metyrapone (SU-4885), an 11-hydroxylase steroid blocker. One then determines whether the urinary 17-OHCS or 17-KGS are appreciably increased. Normally these values double or triple as a result of an increased ACTH secretion. This occurs because of increased excretion of compound S (11-deoxy-17-hydroxycorticosterone), a cortisol precursor secreted when 11-hydroxylation of the steroid nucleus does not occur and which is measured also in the 17-OHCS or 17-KGS fractions. Failure

of the 17-OHCS or 17-KGS to rise normally, providing ACTH injection produces a significant increase of 17-OHCS or 17-KGS, rules out primary adrenal disease and is indicative of an abnormality in the hypothalamus or pituitary. Measurement of 17-ketosteroids (androgen metabolites) also can be used, but since androgens normally are not synthesized before puberty, these measurements are of little value in children unless one is looking for excessive excretion.

Tolerance tests related to carbohydrate metabolism may be used as indirect measurements of STH and ACTH production by the pituitary. Direct methods of evaluating pituitary function for STH, however, have decreased the usefulness of carbohydrate tolerance tests. The glucose tolerance test (GTT) frequently is diabetic in character when excessive STH or ACTH is present, assuming that ACTH-responsive adrenals are present. Hypoglycemic unresponsiveness at the 4th and 5th hour is frequently seen when there is deficient STH or ACTH. In children, glucose is administered on the basis of body weight. This test should be given prior to administering an insulin tolerance test, as it is safer. If hypoglycemic unresponsiveness is present with the GTT test, insulin is not usually given. If the test is normal and hypopituitarism is suspected, an intravenous insulin tolerance test, using 0.1 unit/kg, is given and normal saline is constantly infused over the next 60 minutes. This permits the immediate infusion of 50 percent glucose if the patient develops insulin shock. A positive test occurs if there is: (1) failure of the blood sugar to return to normal by 120 minutes; (2) a drop of the blood sugar by more than approximately 60 percent of the fasting level; or (3) the necessity to discontinue the test because of marked insulin sensitivity. Serum for growth hormone determinations should be obtained 5 times at 15-minute intervals if at all possible.

Growth hormone also can be measured indirectly, using the sulfation factor method which is a measure of STH-like activity. A normal test usually depends upon the individual producing or receiving STH prior to the time serum is obtained. This test is a measure of growth hormonelike substance, because addition of STH to serum from hypophysectomized individuals or animals is relatively ineffective, although serum drawn after injection of STH into a hypophysectomized animal reacts normally. In this test serum is incubated with radioactive sulfur and costal cartilages of immature hypophysectomized rats. In the presence of sulfation factor the sulfate is avidly taken up into the cartilage In the absence of somatotropin there is appreciably less sulfate incorporated.

Sulfation factor (SF) has been found to be normal in a few patients who have had surgical removal of tumors involving the hypothalamus and who were growing either normally or excessively but who had no measurable growth hormone by radioimmunoassay. The complete interrelationship between immunoreactive STH and bioassayable SF remains to be eluci-

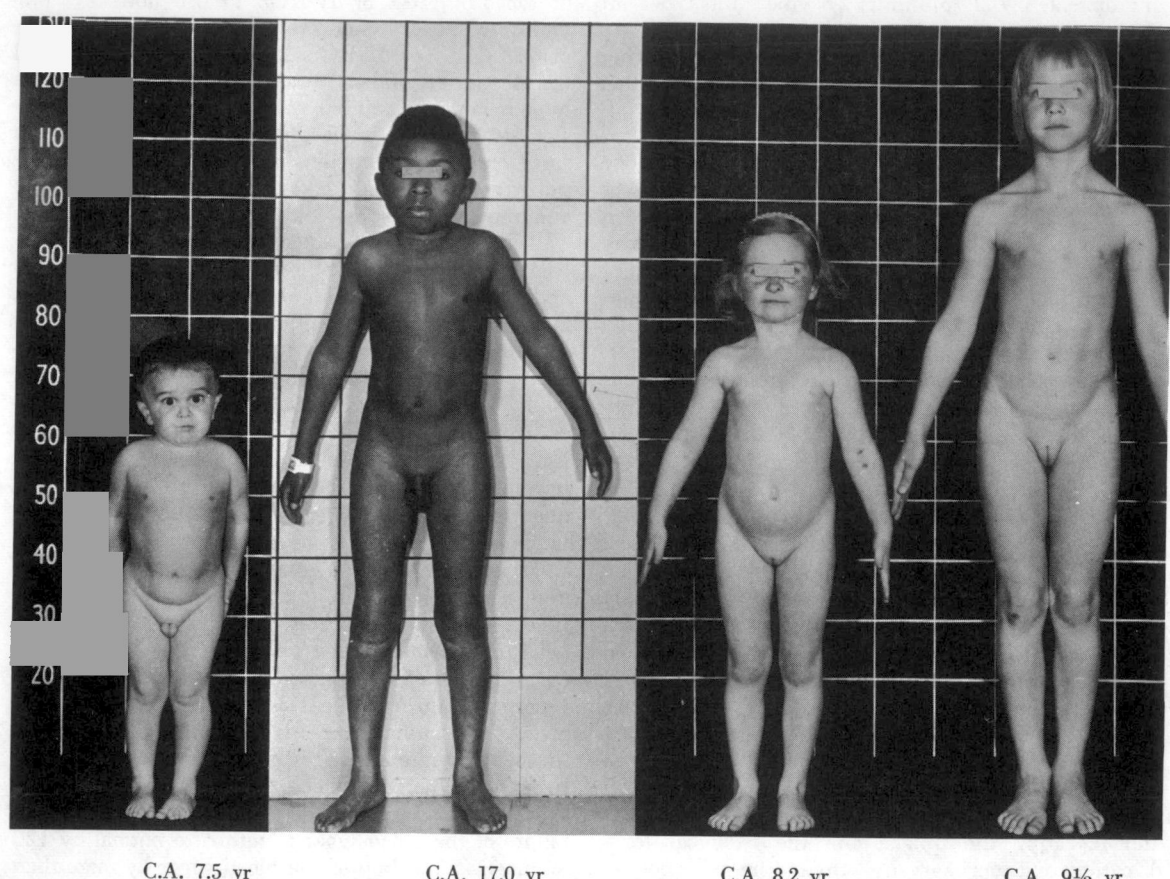

C.A. 7.5 yr	C.A. 17.0 yr	C.A. 8.2 yr	C.A. 9½ yr
H.A. 1.0 yr	H.A. 6.0 yr	H.A. 3.5 yr	H.A. 9½ yr
B.A. 5.5 yr	B.A. 7.0 yr	B.A. 5.0 yr	B.A. 9½ yr

Fig. 3. Variability of body contours in patients with idiopathic hypopituitarism. The patient in the center is normal. The other patients have hypopituitarism. The fifth and sixth patients from left have isolated growth hormone deficiency.

dated. This test has proved to be a valuable research technique but, unfortunately, is very expensive and too time-consuming for most laboratories to utilize.

Hypopituitarism

Hypopituitarism theoretically may arise (1) as an idiopathic entity with deficiency of either single or multiple tropic hormones, (2) from organic lesions in the hypothalamus or pituitary, (3) as a result of peripheral resistance to growth hormone, (4) from production of a tropic hormone that is biologically inactive, although measurable in the immunoassay, (5) secondary to an inhibition of tropic hormone release resulting from emotional disturbances, which is poorly understood, and (6) secondary to prolonged suppression of the pituitary by exogenously administered hormones (e.g., hydrocortisone). Each of these theoretical entities will be considered individually.

Idiopathic Hypopituitarism

This entity is probably more common than hypopituitarism of organic origin. Although all the tropic hormones may be deficient in any one patient, it is most common for somatotropin to be deficient alone, or in conjunction with another of the tropic hormones. Consequently, the presenting complaint of the pediatric patient with idiopathic hypopituitarism is nearly always short stature. Hypopituitarism should be suspected in any child growing less than 5.0 cm per year after 2 years of age, and in whom there is no explanation for the growth failure. Occasionally patients with isolated gonadotropin deficiency are observed, and these patients present at adolescence with sexual infantilism and normal stature. Isolated deficiencies of ACTH or TSH have only rarely been reported.

Growth retardation occurs before the age of 12 months in approximately 30 percent of patients with

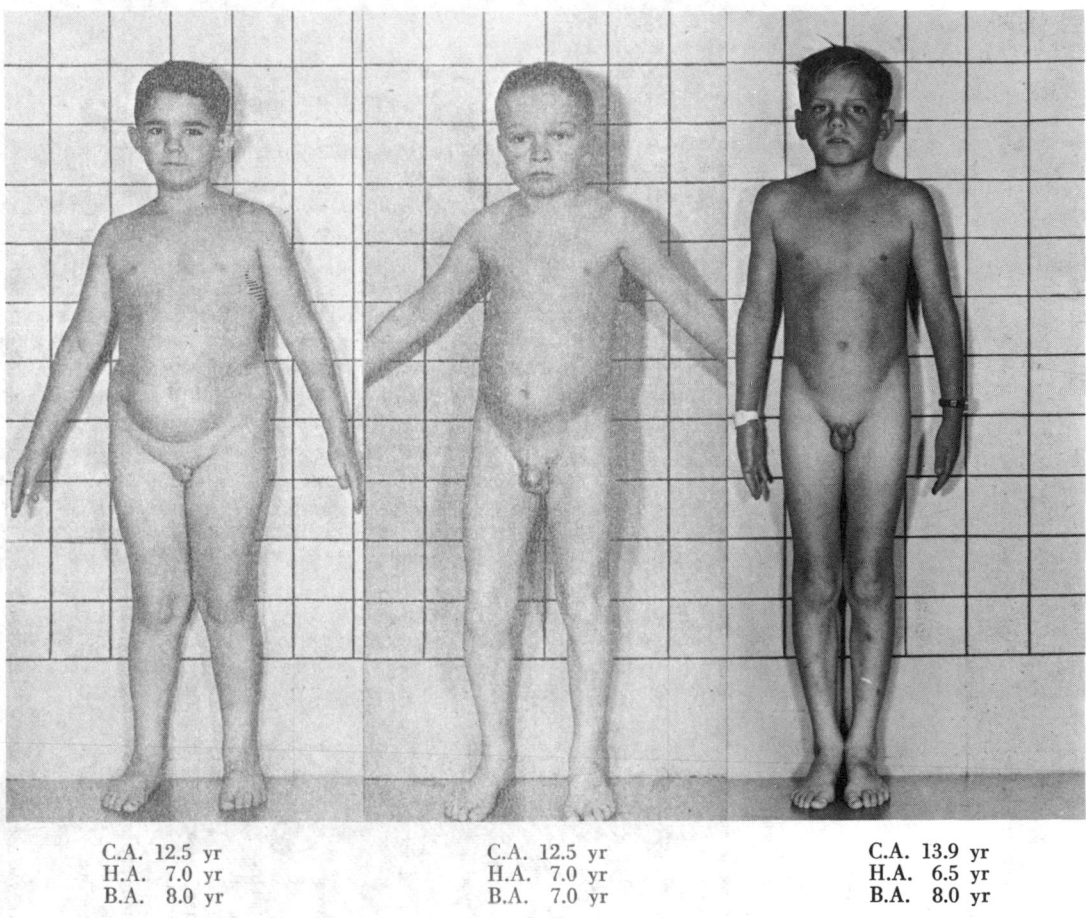

C.A. 12.5 yr	C.A. 12.5 yr	C.A. 13.9 yr
H.A. 7.0 yr	H.A. 7.0 yr	H.A. 6.5 yr
B.A. 8.0 yr	B.A. 7.0 yr	B.A. 8.0 yr

Fig. 3. (Cont.) See legend on facing page.

idiopathic hypopituitarism. The eruption of the primary dentition is often delayed, and even more frequently eruption of the secondary teeth occurs late. The body appearance is constant in that all the patients appear much younger than their stated age. However, the body contours are exceedingly variable (Fig. 3). Frequently, though not invariably, there is adiposity of the trunk with flabby musculature covered with "baby" fat. In other instances this is absent. Sexual infantilism often persists into adult life, although occasionally gonadotropins are produced in late adolescence and the individual develops secondary sexual characteristics. Diabetes insipidus does not occur in idiopathic hypopituitarism, and skull x-rays and visual fields are normal. Only one of approximately 75 patients initially diagnosed as having idiopathic hypopituitarism in our clinic subsequently developed a demonstrable organic lesion. However, this patient did not have a skull x-ray taken until central nervous system symptoms occurred, and he probably would have been diagnosed as having organic hypopituitarism initially if a skull x-ray had been obtained.

Diagnosis is made by utilizing the studies outlined in the preceding laboratory section of this chapter and those listed in Table 2. Skeletal age usually, but not always, is markedly delayed. There is less than 6.0 mμg/ml of growth hormone following arginine and insulin stimulation. The metyrapone test is abnormal in those with accompanying ACTH deficiency. The ^{131}I uptake and serum thyroxin determinations are low-normal or slightly low in some patients. Measurements of gonadotropins by bioassay are of little value in diagnosing this entity, as these are not usually measurable in the preadolescent by bioassay. Measurement of gonadotropins by immunoassay also is of little value, as normal children and hypopituitary children both have small amounts of immunoreactive gonadotropins in their serum and urine. The finding of gonadotropins by bioassay, or postadolescent values of FSH or LH by immunoassay in the serum or urine of a sexually infantile patient, eliminates this diagnosis.

Carbohydrate function studies are abnormal in approximately 65 percent of patients with STH deficiency. In our experience 40 percent of these patients tested with an oral glucose tolerance test have

TABLE 2. *Features in Differential Diagnosis of Children with Short Stature*

			Physical Features			
Family History	Hypothyroidism	Constitutional Delay	Hypopituitarism	Primordial Dwarfism	Gonadal Dysgenesis	Psychosocial Dwarfism
Family History	Occasionally	Often	Rarely	Occasionally	None	Occasionally
Birth Weight	Normal	Normal	Normal	Often low	Often low	Normal
Hypoglycemia	None	None	At times	Rarely	Normal	Normal
Dental eruption	Delayed	Minimally delayed	Delayed	Normal	Normal	Normal or delayed 1+
Facial features	Cretinoid or myxedematous	Slightly immature	Juvenile	Normal, progeroid, or pinched	Normal or peculiar†	Juvenile
Dwarfing	Minimal to marked	Minimal to moderate	Minimal to marked	Moderate to marked	Moderate	Minimal to marked
Sexual development	Infantile	Delayed	Infantile (½ of cases)	Normal	Infantile except sexual hair	Infantile
Body structure	Chubby	Normal	Normal	Subcutaneous tissue often decreased	Normal or peculiar†	Normal, chubby, or slender
Ratio of upper to lower segment	Immature	Slightly immature	Normal	Normal	Normal	Normal
Bone age	Delayed (1-4+)	Delayed (1-2+)	Delayed (2-4+)	Normal or delayed (1-2+)	Normal or delayed (1+)	Delayed (1-4+)
Water tolerance	Usually normal*	Normal	Often abnormal	Normal	Normal	Normal
Insulin sensitivity	Normal	Normal	Often	Normal	Normal	Often
Buccal smear	Normal	Normal	Normal	Normal	80% chromatin − 20% chromatin +	Normal
PBI or thyroxine	Usually low	Normal	Often low-normal or low	Normal	Normal	Often low-normal or low
^{131}I uptake	Usually low	Normal	Often low-normal or low	Normal	Normal	Often low-normal or low
Metyrapone	Normal	Normal	Often abnormal	Normal	Normal	Often abnormal
Growth hormone	Often abnormally low	Normal	Abnormal	Normal	Normal	Often abnormal

*Abnormality with severe chronic hypothyroidism.
†Patients with gonadal dysgenesis often have hypertelorism, receding mandibles, web necks, spicanthal folds, broad chests, inverted nipples, and lymphedema.

had chemical, reactive hypoglycemia at the 4th or 5th hour. Many have had a diabetic peak with a rapid drop to these levels. Sixty percent of patients studied with insulin have been insulin-sensitive by the criteria listed on page 1051.

An approach to the differential diagnosis of children with short stature is presented in Table 2. Excluded from this table are the more obvious causes of short stature, such as renal, cardiac, and skeletal disease; malabsorption; and other entities, discussed below, which either simulate, or have, growth hormone deficiency.

Idiopathic hypopituitarism usually is a sporadic disease; however, at least 63 families with 193 affected members have been observed. Approximately 50 percent of these families had (and 50 percent did not have) gonadotropin deficiency in association with growth hormone deficiency. Prognosis must be guarded regarding the incidence of this disease in subsequent offspring of parents who have sired a child with hypopituitarism.

Treatment consists of administering desiccated thyroid (1 to 2 grains per day) to those patients who have symptoms of thyroid deficiency, and cortisone (15–25 mg/m²/day in divided dose) to those who have hypoglycemia. Thyroid should never be administered without cortisone unless a normal metyrapone response has been obtained. At the age of 15 or 16 testosterone is given to males and estrogen plus testosterone to females. Testosterone in small doses is used in females to induce growth of sexual hair. Human growth hormone has been administered to a limited number of patients with growth hormone deficiency, and normal growth or supernormal growth rates usually have been obtained without toxicity, in contrast to the minimal response obtained when growth hormone in comparable amounts is given to patients with other types of dwarfism. However, between 5 and 10 percent of these patients develop antibodies to growth hormone, which are of a type that interferes with subsequent growth. This hormone will probably be more readily available in the future and should make it possible for hypopituitary patients to achieve normal heights. The hypoglycemia present in some patients is also controlled with growth hormone.

SPECIFIC GONADOTROPIN DEFICIENCY. Patients with specific gonadotropin deficiency must be differentiated from patients with primary hypogonadism, in whom the gonadotropin titer is positive at adolescence. Delayed release of gonadotropins in otherwise normal adolescent males may occur as late as 18 years of age; this entity can be differentiated from specific gonadotropin deficiency only by observations into adult life. Females very rarely have such prolonged delayed adolescence. Hyposmia or anosmia is a common associated defect. Treatment of males consists of replacement with testosterone or chorionic gonadotropin. Estrogen therapy is given to the fe-

males. Human menopausal gonadotropin is available to induce fertility.

ISOLATED ACTH AND TSH DEFICIENCY. Isolated ACTH and TSH deficiency are extremely rare. Differential diagnosis of ACTH deficiency from primary adrenal insufficiency can be made because the 17-hydroxycorticosteroid excretion of the former increases with ACTH administration, but not with adrenal insufficiency. Clinically, pigmentation and symptoms of salt loss usually are found in the adrenal-insufficient patient in contrast to the ACTH-deficient patient. The administration of TSH (p. 1051) followed by an increased ^{131}I uptake will differentiate the patient with TSH deficiency from the one with primary hypothyroidism.

Organic Hypopituitarism

Organic hypopituitarism arises from multiple causes, the most common of which is craniopharyngioma (see Sec. 16.1 for embryologic development). Fourteen of 19 patients in our clinic with organic hypopituitarism had craniopharyngiomas; of the remaining 5 patients, 1 had a *suprasellar undifferentiated carcinoma*, 1 an *aberrant pinealoma*, and 3 had *chromophobe adenomas*. Occasionally hypopituitarism arises from a basal *skull fracture* with interruption of the hypophyseal-venous portal system. Congenital malformations and other lesions of the hypothalamus also can result in the same disease. *Tuberous sclerosis, Hand-Schüller-Christian disease, encephalitis*, particularly of the von Economo type, *hamartomas*, and *von Recklinghausen's neurofibromatosis* have all been implicated; however, hamartomas are more prone to produce sexual precocity, and neurofibromatosis is more commonly associated with somatic overgrowth.

The presenting complaints of patients with organic hypopituitarism usually are those related to visual disturbances and central nervous system disease such as headache, rather than those related to growth disturbances or hypoglycemia, which are the usual presenting complaints of patients with idiopathic hypopituitarism. However, only 3 of 19 patients with organic hypopituitarism were of normal size, and the three with normal growth were the youngest patients in the group. The age of onset is variable, and signs and symptoms can occur as early as the first year of life.

The signs and symptoms are those of idiopathic hypopituitarism, accompanied often by visual disturbances, headache, vomiting, and/or diabetes insipidus. The latter occurs in 20 to 35 percent of the cases reported in various series; it may be obscured if there is associated ACTH and consequent cortisol deficiency. With administration of cortisone or related steroids the diabetes insipidus is uncovered, probably because of the enhancing effect of cortisol on the clearance of free water in the renal tubule.

With lesions involving the hypothalamus one may observe also dysfunction of the hypothalamus reflected as poikilothermia, hypersomnia, obesity, autonomic epilepsy, and uncinate fits.

Radiologic examination of the skull is of great assistance in differentiating organic from idiopathic hypopituitarism. Seventeen of the 18 patients observed in our clinic with this entity who had skull x-rays had gross abnormalities detectable; the other had an undifferentiated suprasellar carcinoma and a space-occupying lesion delineated by pneumoencephalography. The incidence of roentgen abnormalities has been high in other series. The most common pathology noted is calcification in the sella or suprasellar area, particularly with craniopharyngioma, since 80 percent of craniopharyngiomas have calcification. With a craniopharyngioma there frequently is destruction of the clinoid processes and flattening of the sella resulting from pressure exerted from above. In contrast, adenomas of the pituitary produce a large expanded sella. If calcification is not present and there are no sellar changes in a patient with hypopituitarism and central nervous system symptoms, one must suspect internal hydrocephalus or a glioma in the area of the chiasm or third ventricle, which also may produce the same symptoms.

The evaluation of endocrine function is as given on page 1051 and in the discussion of idiopathic hypopituitarism (p. 1053). Treatment must be directed toward hormonal replacement (as discussed under idiopathic hypopituitarism) and toward treatment of a space-occupying lesion if this is present. The latter is considered in the subsequent section of hyperpituitarism.

Peripheral Resistance to Growth Hormone

A group of patients with extreme short stature, high levels of growth hormone, and low sulfation factor, who fail to respond to injections of STH with significant increase in either nitrogen retention or sulfation factor, have been described in Israel and Lebanon. This condition exhibits autosomal recessive inheritance and may represent an entity with peripheral resistance to growth hormone. Possibly the pygmies also may fall into this category, as they have normal STH responses to arginine infusion and have insulinopenia, which occurs in many adult patients with idiopathic hypopituitarism. The blood urea nitrogen fails to fall and the free fatty acid concentrations fail to increase normally with growth hormone administration.

When initially described, the patients in Israel were thought possibly to have a biologically inactive, but immunologically active, growth hormone. Since these patients now are believed to have peripheral resistance to STH, the entity of biologically inactive, immunologically inactive hormone remains theoretical.

Psychologic Dwarfism Simulating Idiopathic Hypopituitarism

A group of patients with emotional deprivation simulating idiopathic hypopituitarism or psychosocial dwarfism has been described. These children are rejected emotionally by their parents, who are almost uniformly psychologically disturbed. The signs and symptoms include short stature, polyphagia, polydypsia, polyuria in spite of ability to concentrate their urine, encopresis, gorging and vomiting, shyness, and temper tantrums. The skeletal development usually is delayed to the same severe extent as the height age. The IQ has been less than 90 in a majority, but not all. Twenty-five proved cases have been observed in our clinic. Six of 11 tested with both arginine monochloride and insulin failed to respond with a significant increase in STH concentration. Low serum thyroxine levels or ^{131}I uptakes are uncommon. Fifteen have been more than 10 percent underweight for height, and caloric malnutrition may be a factor in some but not all patients.

This entity may be difficult to differentiate from idiopathic hypopituitarism by clinical and laboratory examination. The bizarre history is very helpful in this differentiation. However, the diagnosis can be proved only by removing the patient from the adverse environment and observing a rapid growth. The mean growth rate of the above-mentioned 25 patients was 6.6 inches per year during the first few months in a favorable environment.

Iatrogenic Hypopituitarism

Iatrogenic hypopituitarism refers to suppression of the pituitary and peripheral endocrine glands subsequent and secondary to the administration of exogenous hormones, particularly cortisol and similar steroids. Prolonged and continuous treatment with cortisol for periods greater than 2 to 4 weeks may be associated with an absent or diminished adrenal response to the administration of metyrapone. Since patients who have received cortisol or cortisol-like steroids for 30 days or longer may have circulatory collapse with surgical or infectious stress, cortisone (approximately 50 to 100 mg/m^2/day) should be given during such periods to all patients for one year following cessation of therapy.

Hyperpituitarism

Eosinophilic adenomas are the rarest of all pituitary tumors in childhood. A few patients have had gigantism during childhood with superimposed acromegaly in late childhood and adulthood. The children usually present as problems of overgrowth, and headaches occur commonly. Initially growth is symmetric, but with progression of the disease there is coarsening and thickening of the features and prognathism, kyphosis, and wide spacing of the teeth. The onset of sexual development is either at the usual time or late, but it progresses slowly and hypogonadism eventually occurs. Epiphyseal fusion occurs late. Muscular weakness and thyroid deficiency may also result.

Serum chemistries may be of some assistance. Hyperglycemia, a diabetic glucose tolerance test, and an elevated serum phosphorus level are all compatible with hypersomatotropism. Growth hormone is present in all serum samples and persists with glucose infusion, in contrast to the absence of growth hormone in the serum of normals receiving glucose. The visual fields are not usually affected; if affected, alterations occur late in the course of the disease. By skull x-ray a slightly enlarged sella is often, but not necessarily, observed. Tufting of the phalanges may be demonstrated by roentgenologic study. The bone age is only minimally, if at all, advanced. The differential diagnosis and treatment will be discussed subsequently in this section.

Both *chromophobe* and *basophilic* adenomas have been associated with Cushing's syndrome of the adrenal hyperplasia type. This is logical since both types of cells are believed to produce ACTH. The majority of such tumors have been found following subtotal or total adrenalectomy performed as treatment for the adrenal hyperplasia. However, in some reports the tumors were demonstrated in retrospect to have been present prior to adrenalectomy. Hyperpigmentation in association with Cushing's syndrome or after adrenalectomy is highly indicative of adenoma even in the absence of sellar enlargement visible by x-ray. Recent data suggest that nearly all cases of Cushing's syndrome of the adrenal hyperplasia type may be of pituitary origin and, therefore, possibly related to adenomas. In a few instances the pituitary lesion was a carcinoma instead of an adenoma, and metastases had occurred. Symptoms related to the central nervous system or visual tracts occur very late in patients with such tumors. X-rays of the sella frequently show no enlargement until late, and the visual fields also are not abnormal early. Exceptions do occur, particularly with some tumors which grow rapidly.

Treatment of pituitary tumors is usually directed toward relieving the central nervous system and visual problems which are created by an expanding lesion. However, the hyperfunction that sometimes occurs with eosinophilic, chromophobe, or basophilic adenomas may be the indication for treatment.

With tumors producing hypopituitarism, surgical treatment is undertaken when removal is required to prevent visual deterioration. Craniopharyngiomas and cystic chromophobe adenomas producing hypopituitarism are notoriously x-ray–resistant. Prior to surgery the patient must be given cortisone intramuscularly (100 mg/m²/day) for two or three days. Postoperatively, 25 mg/m²/day in divided doses should be given for several days, or continuously if the anterior pituitary is destroyed. Thyroid hormone may be required subsequently. Diabetes insipidus frequently results and requires treatment (p. 1151). Unfortunately, removal of cystic tumors very often is incomplete, and further observation is very important. Repeat surgery may be necessary.

Tumors associated with hyperfunction are less likely to damage the optic chiasm than those producing hypofunction, but also must be treated surgically when optic atrophy, papilledema, or limitation of visual fields is present. External irradiation frequently is beneficial with eosinophilic adenomas not affecting the optic tracts. The total irradiation given through multiple portals should not exceed 4,500 r, or cerebral necrosis and vascular damage may occur. Recently a technique for implanting radioactive gold or yttrium into the sella has been developed, and preliminary reports concerning adults treated in this manner suggest this may be a reasonably satisfactory form of treatment for eosinophilic adenoma. Treatment of such tumors with cyclotron irradiation or cryosurgery also has been effective in some cases. Further follow-up of patients treated with these modalities is necessary before their therapeutic advantages and disadvantages are fully appreciated.

The same forms of treatment have been utilized in treating pituitary tumors which produce Cushing's syndrome. External irradiation to the pituitary in the dosage stated above was used extensively in the past to control the symptoms of Cushing's syndrome with adrenal hyperplasia, but only with minimal success. For this reason subtotal or usually total adrenalectomy has been performed extensively. If hyperpigmentation subsequently occurs, in spite of adequate cortisone replacement, or if the sella is noted by periodic tomograms to be increasing, irradiation, surgery, or cryotherapy must be considered. Surgery is indicated if the visual fields are affected. Cryosurgery or irradiation is probably preferable; otherwise, pellet implantation with radioactive gold or yttrium or treatment with the cyclotron is superior to cobalt irradiation.

Functional Hyperpituitarism

Certain lesions or pathologic entities in some obscure way stimulate or simulate overactivity of the hypothalamic-pituitary axis, particularly in respect to their association with excessive growth. Gliomas of the optic tract, which may extend into the hypothalamus, are at times associated with somatic overgrowth, but without gross evidence of acromegaly or excessive production of TSH, ACTH, and so forth. Occasionally patients with neurofibromatosis also present with overgrowth. The bone age is normal in these patients, and they do not develop the tufting or other features

of the acromegalic patient. There also have been patients reported who have mental retardation of apparent congenital origin who have features simulating
those of the acromegalic and who grow excessively
during the first 4 or 5 years of childhood. After this
time the growth parallels the normal curve. These
patients with *"cerebral gigantism"* have an advanced
bone age and mature early, although they do not
have true sexual precocity as it is ordinarily defined.
With true sexual precocity the bone age continues
to advance rapidly out of proportion to linear growth,
and sexual maturation occurs early. In the entity under consideration the skeletal age advances proportionately to the acceleration in linear growth, and
sexual maturation occurs only one to two years before
the expected time. The mechanisms involved are
unknown.

Obesity has been considered to be associated with
functional hyperpituitarism since many obese children are overgrown, have a one- to two-year advancement of skeletal age, and frequently mature sexually
more rapidly than nonobese children.

Thyrotoxicosis and *Marfan's* syndrome are also
associated with overgrowth and must be differentiated
from acromegaly or true hyperpituitarism.

Occasionally one observes what is termed "overflow stimulation" of the pituitary. For example, in
some patients with chronic primary hypothyroidism of
long duration, the sella is enlarged. This is believed
to result from excessive TSH production and pituitary
hyperplasia which occurs because of thyroxine deficiency. At times sexual precocity and galactorrhea
also occur in such patients, and it has been postulated that excessive gonadotropins are produced in
addition to excessive TSH.

REFERENCES

Blizzard, R. M., Johanson, A., Guyda, H., Baghdassarian,
A., Raiti, S., and Migeon, C. J. Recent developments
in the study of gonadotropin secretion in adolescence.
In Heald, F. P., and Hung, W., eds., Endocrinology
of Adolescence. New York, Appleton-Century-Crofts,
1970.

Brasel, J. A., Wright, J. C., Wilkins, L., and Blizzard,
R. M. An evaluation of 75 patients with hypopituitarism beginning in childhood. Amer. J. Med., 38:
484, 1963.

Ciba Collection of Medical Illustrations. Embryologic
Development of the Pituitary. Boston, Little, Brown
and Co., 1965.

Daughaday, W. H. The adenohypophysis. *In* Williams,
R. H., ed., Textbook of Endocrinology, 4th ed. Philadelphia, W. B. Saunders Co., 1968, Chapt. 2.

Goodman, H. G., Grumbach, M. M., and Kaplan, S. L.
Growth and growth hormone. II. Comparison of isolated growth-hormone deficiency and multiple pituitary-
hormone deficiencies in 35 patients with idiopathic
hypopituitary dwarfism. New Eng. J. Med., 278:57,
1968.

Harris, G. T., and Donovan, B. T. The Pituitary Gland.

Berkeley and Los Angeles, University of California
Press, 1966, Vol. 1-3.

Herlant, M. Present state of knowledge concerning the
cytology of the anterior lobe of the hypophysis. Proc.
2nd Int. Congr. Endocr., Int. Congr. Ser. #83. London, Excerpta Medica Foundation, 1964, p. 468.

Powell, G. F., Brasel, J. A., and Blizzard, R. M. Emotional deprivation and growth retardation simulating
idiopathic hypopituitarism. I. Clinical evaluation of
the syndrome. New Eng. J. Med., 276:1271, 1967.

Raiti, S., and Blizzard, R. M. Human growth hormone:
Current knowledge regarding its role in normal and
abnormal metabolic states. Advances Pediat., 17:99,
1970.

Rasmussen, H. Organization and control of endocrine
systems. *In* Williams, R. H., ed., Textbook of Endocrinology, 4th ed. Philadelphia, W. B. Saunders Co.,
1968, p. 1.

Sotos, J. F., Dodge, P. R., Muirhead, D., Crawford, J. D.,
and Talbot, N. B. Cerebral gigantism in childhood.
A syndrome of excessively rapid growth with acromegalic features and a nonprogressive neurologic disorder. New Eng. J. Med., 271:109, 1964.

Wilkins, L. The Diagnosis and Treatment of Endocrine
Disorders in Childhood and Adolescence, 3rd ed.
Springfield, Ill., Charles C Thomas, Publ., 1965.

Youlton, R., Kaplan, S. L., and Grumbach, M. M.
Growth and growth hormone. IV. Limitations of the
growth hormone response to insulin and arginine and
of the immunoreactive insulin response to arginine in
the assessment of growth hormone deficiency in children. Pediatrics, 43:989, 1969.

16.3
THE THYROID

JUDSON J. VAN WYK

Thyroid disorders rank among the most common of the endocrine abnormalities encountered
during childhood. The incidence varies widely in
different parts of the world and is markedly influenced by the content of iodine in the diet and other
less well understood environmental factors. Most
forms of thyroid disease exhibit a sharp increase in
incidence with the approach of adolescence and
occur more frequently in females than in males. The
prevalence of certain thyroid diseases within families
reflects the importance of predisposing genetic factors.

The function of the thyroid gland is to concentrate iodide from the blood and return it to peripheral
tissues in a hormonally active form. Triiodothyronine
and thyroxine, the principal thyroid hormones, are
amino acids bearing, respectively, three and four
iodine atoms per molecule (Fig. 4).

The quantity of hormonal iodine available to
the tissues is highly critical, since this governs the
rate of tissue respiration and many other metabolic
processes, including those concerned with growth
and maturation. To maintain this level within permissible limits, the individual's body must husband iodine
in those vast areas of the earth where iodine is scarce

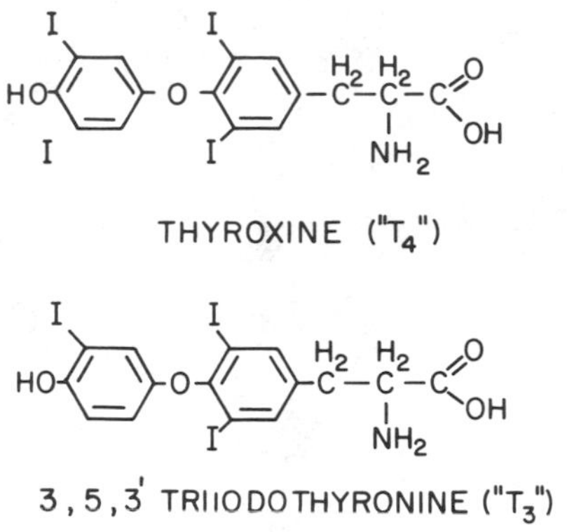

THYROXINE ("T$_4$")

3,5,3' TRIIODOTHYRONINE ("T$_3$")

Fig. 4.   Structure of thyroxine and triiodothyronine.

and protect against hormonal excess when iodine is in abundance. Normal thyroid function as well as many thyroid diseases can be understood best in terms of the thyroidal and extrathyroidal mechanisms which govern the economy of iodine.

The Physiology of Iodine Metabolism

Fate of Dietary Iodide

The distribution and fate of ingested iodine have been carefully documented with the use of ^{131}I tracers. Iodine is absorbed quantitatively from the upper gastrointestinal tract. After reaching the bloodstream, it is partitioned within minutes between two major compartments designated as the extrathyroidal iodide space and the thyroidal iodide space. The extrathyroidal iodide compartment has the approximate dimensions of the extracellular space. The thyroidal iodide space is expressed as that volume of plasma which contains the same quantity of iodide as that within the thyroid gland. The magnitude of the thyroidal iodide space is governed by the number of functioning thyroid cells and, more particularly, by the efficiency of the active transport mechanism in the basilar membrane of these cells, which confers upon the thyroid its unique ability to concentrate iodide to many times its concentration in plasma. This concentrating mechanism is often referred to as the "iodide pump."

As long as intrathyroidal iodide ions remain in reduced form, they are in reversible equilibrium with serum iodide and can flow back into the circulation as serum levels fall. Normally, however, once iodine has entered the thyroid gland it is very rapidly incorporated into organic compounds and is no longer in equilibrium with serum iodide.

Serum is being cleared constantly of inorganic iodide by two competitive processes: excretion by the kidneys and losses to the pool of organic iodinated compounds within the thyroid gland (Fig. 5). The proportion of administered ^{131}I finally accumulated by the thyroid in organic form is governed by the capacity of the iodide pump, the rate of conversion of iodide into organic compounds, and the rate of renal excretion. Iodide is excreted by the kidney primarily by glomerular filtration.

Although there is continuous secretion of iodide by the salivary and the digestive glands, normally all but a negligible proportion is reabsorbed, and there is no substantial fecal excretion of iodide. Fecal iodine is derived primarily from conjugated thyroid hormones secreted into the bile. These compounds are reabsorbed mostly in the enterohepatic circuit, however, and fecal losses of organic iodine normally account for only one-tenth of the daily excretion of this element, the rest occurring through the kidney. Fecal loss may be greatly increased, however, in patients who consume certain high-residue diets or who have intestinal malabsorption syndromes.

"Thyroidal Iodide Pump"

Routine studies of thyroidal ^{131}I uptake do not discriminate between radioactivity in the form of inorganic iodide and that which is bound organically. With special techniques, however, the rate at which plasma iodide is concentrated by the "iodide pump" and the rate of organification of intrathyroidal iodide can be calculated separately. The capacity of the "iodide pump," expressed as the thyroidal iodide space, is modified by many factors, including thyroidal size, stimulation by thyrotropic hormone, saturation of iodine stores, and competition by such other anions as thiocyanate and perchlorate.

Anions such as perchlorate and thiocyanate, which possess a molecular size similar to that of iodide, are likewise concentrated by thyroid cells, although much less efficiently than iodide itself. These substances do, however, have the capacity to compete with iodide for the intrathyroidal iodide space; thus, if a very large amount of one of these substances is administered within a few hours after a tracer dose of ^{131}I, all of the thyroidal ^{131}I remaining as ^{131}I is displaced rapidly back into the bloodstream. The decrease in thyroidal radioactivity reflects the proportion of thyroidal ^{131}I not yet organically bound when the competing anion is administered. This so-called "flush test" is usually performed 2 hours after the administration of the ^{131}I tracer. At this time, less than 10 percent of the thyroidal counts can be displaced normally by competing anions. A much greater fall is observed in patients with a selective impairment in their ability to oxidize iodide or in patients who have been exposed to certain goitrogenic agents which interfere with intrathyroidal oxidation (Fig. 6).

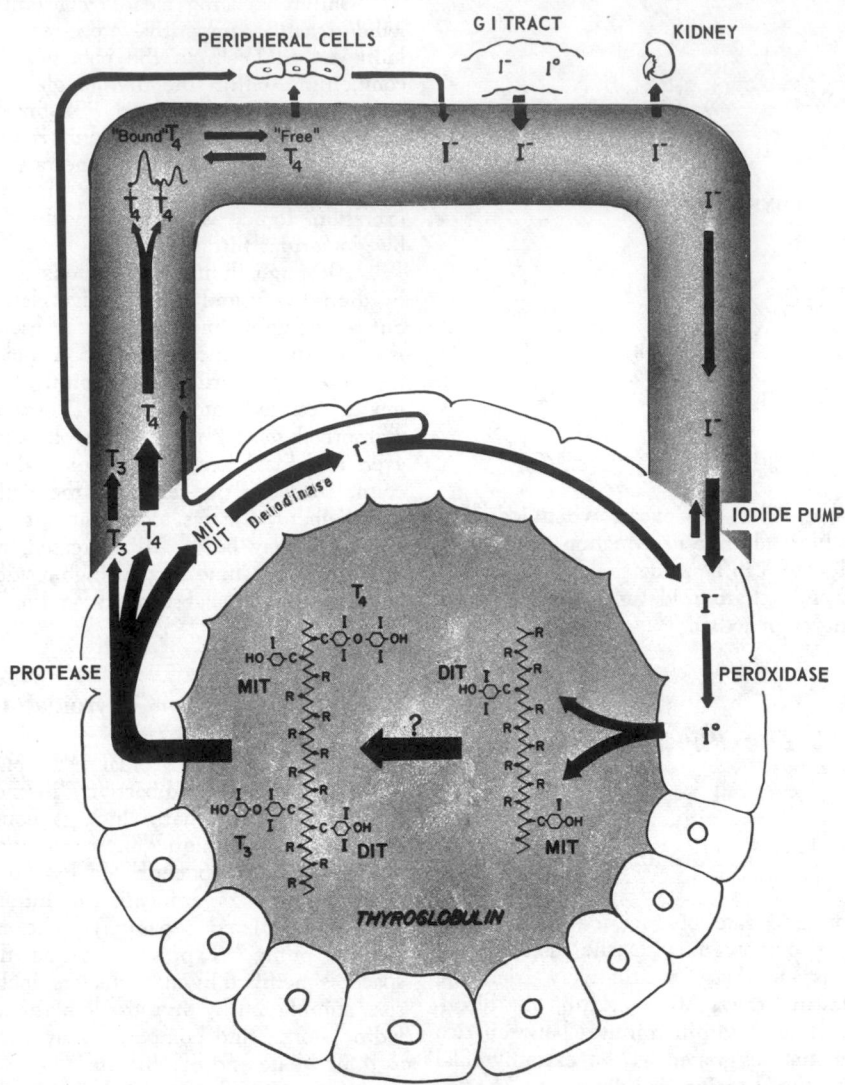

Fig. 5. The cycle of iodine metabolism. Tyrosine accounts for only 3 percent of the amino acid residues of thyroglobulin, and very little is known of the spatial relationships of the various iodinated compounds within the molecule. The schematic representation of thyroglobulin fragments within the follicle merely emphasizes that organic forms of iodine are made by iodination of tyrosyl residues in peptide linkage within preformed protein. It also indicates that synthesis of T_3 and T_4 occurs after that of MIT and DIT, although the mechanism is unknown.

Not shown in this diagram is the enterohepatic circulation of conjugated forms of thyroid hormone. Fecal losses of these organic forms of iodine normally account for less than 10 percent of the total iodine excretion. As shown in this diagram, the major excretory pathway for iodine is via the kidneys.

Organification of Iodide

Perhaps the most critical function performed by the thyroid gland is that of transforming inorganic iodide into an organic form. It accomplishes this by oxidizing iodide enzymatically into elemental iodine. Once in oxidized form, elemental iodine will spontaneously combine with any suitable organic substrate.

In biologic systems, the amino acid tyrosine is the only easily iodinated substrate available in significant quantities. The formation of organic iodine compounds within the thyroid is accomplished primarily by the iodination of tyrosine residues in preformed protein within the alveoli, rather than by de novo synthesis of thyroglobulin from preformed iodotyrosines.

The rate at which inorganic iodide is converted into the organic form is influenced markedly by thy-

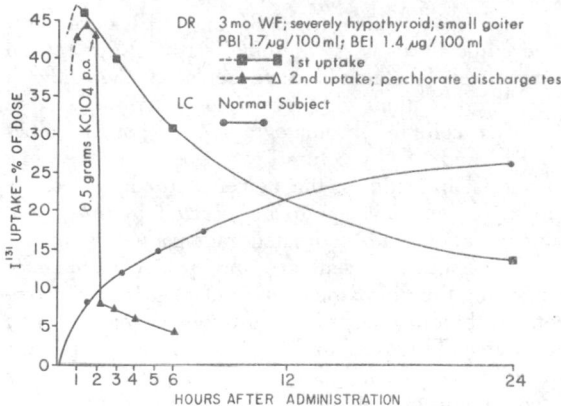

Fig. 6. Effect of peroxidase defect on kinetics of ^{131}I uptake in a 3-month-old cretin. Due to the hypothyroid state and resultant hypersecretion of TSH, the patient had developed a goiter and a greatly expanded thyroidal iodide space. This is shown by the very high early uptake. (Compare with normal subject.) Lack of organic binding is reflected by the subsequent logarithmic decrease of thyroidal ^{131}I. This fall parallels the decrease of plasma radioactivity due to renal excretion. The suspicion that the high early counts are mostly in the form of iodide was confirmed in a subsequent study by the administration of potassium perchlorate. This produced an abrupt discharge of thyroidal radioactivity.

rotropin stimulation, intrathyroidal iodine stores, and a variety of antithyroid drugs, many of which are reducing agents like propylthiouracil. The rate of organification is greatly increased by thyrotoxicosis and decreased in certain thyroid diseases which interfere with the functional competency of thyroid cells. Certain forms of cretinism and goiter are caused by congenital deficiency of the peroxidase enzymes. The metabolic lesion in such patients is similar to that in patients receiving propylthiouracil.

Whenever the ability to oxidize iodide is selectively impaired, the gland tends to undergo hyperplasia with expansion of the thyroidal iodide space. Following administration of ^{131}I to such patients, thyroidal radioactivity reaches an early peak followed by a fall due to diffusion of iodide back into the bloodstream (Fig. 5). If the block in oxidation is complete, thyroidal radioactivity falls at a rate which parallels the decrease in plasma radioactivity from renal excretion. When the block is less complete the uptake curve may not exhibit this reversing characteristic, and for this reason the "perchlorate flush" test is recommended as a more certain means of diagnosis.

Synthesis of Thyroid Hormones

Virtually any protein with accessible tyrosine residues can be iodinated in vitro if it is exposed to iodide in the presence of an oxidizing agent. Iodination occurs within seconds and requires no enzymatic mechanism. Subsequent analysis of such iodoproteins reveals that nearly all of the iodine is attached to tyrosine residues in the form of monoiodotyrosine (MIT) and diiodotyrosine (DIT). These substances are physiologically inactive.

The thyroid gland provides both an oxidizing system for activating iodine and a large quantity of physically accessible protein for receiving the iodine and storing it until required by body needs. Thyroglobulin is a large 19S glycoprotein with a molecular weight of about 660,000. It is composed of four subunits, with the monomer sedimenting as a 6S protein and the dimer as a 12S protein. Using isotopically labeled leucine as a marker, it has been demonstrated that thyroglobulin is synthesized as an uniodinated protein within the cytoplasm of acinar cells; it then migrates apically and is secreted into the lumen of the follicle as colloid. Mature colloid consists of thyroglobulin in various states of iodination. Only a small proportion of the tyrosine residues in thyroglobulin are iodinated normally.

The initial iodination of thyroidal proteins in vivo occurs in a manner similar to the nonspecific iodination of proteins in vitro. Iodide ions which enter the thyroid cell at the plasma membrane traverse the cell rapidly toward the apical membrane, where they are oxidized and readily iodinate the preformed thyroglobulin stored within the follicle. During the first several hours after in vivo iodination with radioactive iodine, all of the radioactive tracer attached to thyroglobulin can be identified as MIT and DIT, just as in the case of the nonspecific in vitro iodination of proteins. The thyroid gland is unique, however, in its capacity to convert MIT and DIT into the physiologically active hormones triiodothyronine (T_3) and thyroxine (T_4). Several days after the administration of ^{131}I, up to 35 percent of the labeled amino acids of thyroglobulin may be identified as thyroxine or triiodothyronine. Whether these more slowly formed iodothyronines are synthesized by coupling of neighboring molecules of MIT and DIT or by some other mechanism is not known. The mediation of a "coupling enzyme" has been postulated, but evidence for the existence of such an enzyme has not been forthcoming. It is clear, however, that whenever the thyroid gland is functioning inefficiently due to disease, iodine depletion, or exposure to certain goitrogens, there is a marked shift in the distribution of the iodoamino acids toward the less iodinated compounds, with a lower than normal percentage of iodothyronines compared with iodotyrosines, and a lower than normal ratio of diiodotyrosine to monoiodotyrosine.

Storage and Release of Thyroid Hormones

Since T_3 and T_4 are stored within the thyroid follicle as integral parts of the large thyroglobulin molecule, thyroglobulin must first be hydrolyzed into its constituent amino acids before the active hormones can be released. Although the details of this proteolytic process are poorly understood, the release of thyroid hormones into the bloodstream is markedly accelerated by pituitary thyroid-stimulating hormone (TSH) and inhibited by high intrathyroidal levels of iodine.

Normally, the only iodinated substances released into the circulation are T_3, T_4, and iodide. Since the iodotyrosines are considerably more abundant in thyroglobulin than are iodothyronines, large quantities of MIT and DIT would also be released into the circulation if it were not for the presence of a deiodinating enzyme which removes iodine from these specific compounds. The iodide released by this dehalogenating enzyme is made available for reentry into the thyroidal iodide pool, thus conserving iodine stores (Fig. 5). Dehalogenating enzymes are widely distributed in peripheral tissues as well as in the thyroid gland, but their normal function is not known.

Thyroid Hormones in Blood

The proper interpretation of the many available tests of thyroid function requires a detailed understanding of how T_3 and T_4 are transported in blood. Under normal conditions, T_4 and T_3 are released into the circulation in a ratio of approximately 85:15 and much of the T_4 is further degraded in the periphery to T_3. Since T_3 has about four times the metabolic activity as T_4, there is little doubt that T_3 plays as significant a role as T_4 in meeting the hormonal requirements of peripheral tissues.

The fate of these two hormones, however, is quite different. T_3 is bound only loosely to serum proteins and therefore disappears rapidly from the blood into tissue sites, whereas T_4 becomes attached more firmly to specific binding proteins in serum and has a much slower turnover rate. Thus, the plasma level of T_4 is normally around 30 times greater than that of T_3. Two specific thyroxine-binding proteins have been described: on electrophoresis, these may be differentiated as a thyroxine-binding prealbumin (TBPA) which migrates anodally to albumin, and a "thyroxin-binding globulin" (TBG) which migrates between alpha-1 and alpha-2 globulin. TBG binds T_4 much more strongly than T_3, and TBPA binds only T_4. Serum albumin has a much weaker binding affinity for thyroxine than TBG or TBPA; nevertheless it plays some role in thyroxine transport because of its high concentration in plasma.

PROTEIN-BOUND IODINE AND THYROXINE IODINE CONTENT OF PLASMA. The protein-bound iodine (PBI) content of plasma is usually measured by precipitating the serum proteins with trichloroacetic acid and determining the iodine content of the washed precipitate. Normally about 90 percent of PBI is in the form of thyroxine and is readily extractable with acid butanol (BEI). The remaining 10 percent which is not butanol-extractable consists of iodoproteins and iodopeptides in which iodinated amino acids,

mostly MIT and DIT, are incorporated in peptide linkage.

For many years the PBI and BEI have been used clinically to assess thyroidal status. Now, several commercial laboratories have replaced the difficult BEI determination with measurement of total serum T_4 after column chromatography. Although values for BEI and "T_4 by column" are essentially the same in normal individuals, the newer method is more reproducible and less apt to be affected by artifactual contamination with iodinated radiopaque dyes.

An exquisitely sensitive and specific method for measuring the thyroxine content of plasma is the competitive binding technique introduced by Murphy and Patee. Thyroxine and other iodinated compounds are extracted from plasma and incubated with a fixed amount of ^{131}I-labeled thyroxine in the presence of a standard pregnancy plasma, which possesses a high thyroxine-binding capacity. Since the thyroxine-binding sites of the standardized plasma do not distinguish between labeled and unlabeled thyroxine, the thyroxine in the sample which is being tested displaces labeled T_4 from the binding sites. After the equilibration is complete, the ^{131}I-thyroxine displaced from the protein receptors in the plasma is determined after separation on an anion exchange resin. The quantitative relationship between the thyroxine content of the unknown plasma and the radioactivity displaced is determined from a standard curve, established with known amounts of unlabeled thyroxine.

With specific methodologies available for measuring T_4 and T_3, a potential source of confusion is the growing practice of expressing results as µg of T_3 or T_4 instead of µg of T_3 or T_4 *iodine*. Since iodine comprises 65 percent by weight of the thyroxin molecule and 58 percent by weight of the triiodothyronine molecule, the values reported will be 1.5 times higher for T_4 concentrations and 1.7 higher for T_3 concentrations than their respective iodine equivalents.

In certain thyroid diseases, portions of the thyroglobulin molecule may enter the bloodstream without prior hydrolysis. Under such circumstances there will be an abnormally large discrepancy between the PBI and thyroxine iodine concentration, no matter how the latter is determined. Likewise, the PBI may be artifactually elevated due to iodination of serum albumin. This may occur following the intake of large quantities of iodine, or under conditions of thyroid hyperplasia when larger than normal quantities of serum proteins are exposed to the active form of iodine within the thyroid. An abnormally large discrepancy between the PBI and thyroxine iodine is characteristic of Hashimoto's struma, certain types of goitrous cretinism, and some cases of thyroid cancer. Discrepancies between the PBI and thyroxine iodine of greater than 2 µg/100 ml should be considered abnormal.

Certain iodinated radiopaque dyes, such as those used in intravenous pyelograms, artifactually elevate both the PBI and T_4 by column. Although the radiopaque media used in intravenous pyelography are usually all excreted within 5 to 7 days, those used in gallbladder studies, myelograms, and bronchograms may interfere with PBI and thyroxine iodine measurements for many years. Instances have been reported in which high PBI levels in babies were attributed to previous gallbladder studies in their mothers. Under such circumstances the competitive binding method for measuring plasma thyroxine levels provides the only reliable method of assessing the thyroidal status.

"FREE" THYROXINE. The total thyroxine concentration of serum is determined by the thyroidal secretory rate, by the rate of peripheral utilization, and by the capacity of the serum to bind thyroxine. Although clinical assessments of thyroidal status usually parallel the PBI or thyroxine level, it is important to recognize that it is not the protein-bound thyroxine per se which is immediately available to tissues but, rather, a minute fraction of this which is circulating in the form of "free" thyroxine. This moiety is in equilibrium between plasma-binding and tissue-binding sites. When an increase or decrease takes place in the number of thyroxine-binding sites in plasma, the PBI usually mirrors this change so that the same relative saturation of plasma-binding sites is maintained. Pregnancy or estrogen administration greatly increases the thyroxine-binding capacity and decreases the proportion of "free" thyroxine; however, since the PBI rises concomitantly, the absolute free thyroxine level does not change appreciably. Conversely, such drugs as Dilantin, salicylates, and methyltestosterone compete with thyroxine for serum-binding sites and, therefore, lower the PBI often to hypothyroid levels. However, the proportion of free to total thyroxine rises and there is little or no net alteration in the absolute level of free thyroxine. In nephrosis and other disorders associated with hypoproteinemia, the PBI may likewise be misleadingly low in otherwise euthyroid individuals. It is not uncommon to encounter families in which there is a hereditary increase or decrease in serum thyroxine-binding capacity. In such patients an erroneous diagnosis of hypothyroidism or hyperthyroidism may be made if reliance is placed exclusively on the serum PBI or thyroxine level.

Several dialysis techniques have been described for measuring the proportion of plasma thyroxine which is in the free state. By multiplying the total thyroxine content of plasma with this proportion, the absolute concentration of "free thyroxine" in plasma can be determined. Although free thyroxine measurements are theoretically superior to plasma thyroxine content in reflecting deviations from euthyroidism, technical problems and cost have limited wide acceptance of this method as a routine clinical tool.

INDIRECT RESIN UPTAKE TESTS. Several tests have been devised which reflect the *residual* thyroxine-binding capacity of serum. In these tests, labeled T_3 or T_4 is incubated with the patient's serum and either with red cells or an anion exchange resin. The final partition of the labeled hormone between serum and resin (or red cells) provides a measure of the residual binding capacity of the patient's serum. The uptake by resin is high either if the patient has a high thyroxine level, as in thyrotoxicosis, or if the thyroxine-binding capacity is diminished. Low values are characteristic of either hypothyroidism or such conditions as pregnancy in which the thyroxine-binding capacity is elevated. The resin tests are technically easy to perform and kits are available to carry them out in hospitals with limited laboratory facilities. Unfortunately, there is a large fluctuation in normal values from laboratory to laboratory and even in the same laboratory from day to day. For this reason, values obtained with unknown plasma samples should be compared with simultaneously analyzed control plasma samples representing the various thyroidal states.

PLASMA T_3 IODINE. All of the tests described in the preceding paragraphs are directed solely at assessing the free and total thyroxine concentration in plasma and ignore the contribution of triiodothyronine which, as pointed out above, probably accounts for over half the effective metabolic activity of the thyroidal secretions. The precise role of triiodothyronine in abnormal thyroid states is particularly elusive since this hormone is bound only weakly to serum proteins and is therefore rapidly taken up by peripheral tissues. The finding of a PBI or thyroxine iodine level in plasma in the range which usually characterizes the euthyroid, hypothyroid, and hyperthyroid states has clinical validity only if the ratio between T_4 and T_3 secreted by the thyroid remains within fixed limits. Should the proportion of T_3 rise, the same physiologic state will be maintained with a lower PBI. This principle is well demonstrated in hypothyroid children receiving replacement therapy. In these patients, the "normal" range of PBI will vary according to the nature of the substitution therapy. If triiodothyronine is used, the PBI will hardly be elevated above athyrotic levels, whereas if synthetic I-thyroxine is the sole form of treatment, euthyroidism can be achieved only if the PBI is maintained at higher than normal levels. In the case of desiccated thyroid, adequate therapy is usually accompanied by a PBI lower than that in normal children, who secret a mixture of T_3 and T_4.

Sterling has recently devised an ingenious method for direct measurement of plasma T_3 levels. This technique employs a combination of isotope dilution with ^{131}I-labeled T_3, several chromatographic steps, and a final competitive binding displacement technique with an anion exchange resin. With this technique the level of triiodothyronine (not T_3 iodine) was found to be 227 ± 27 ng/100 ml in euthyroid patients, 752 ± 282 ng/100 ml in thyrotoxicosis, and 98 ± 48 ng/100 ml in hypothyroid patients. More remarkably, several clinically thyrotoxic patients had high T_3 levels, but PBI and T_4 levels in the normal range. This condition quickly became dubbed

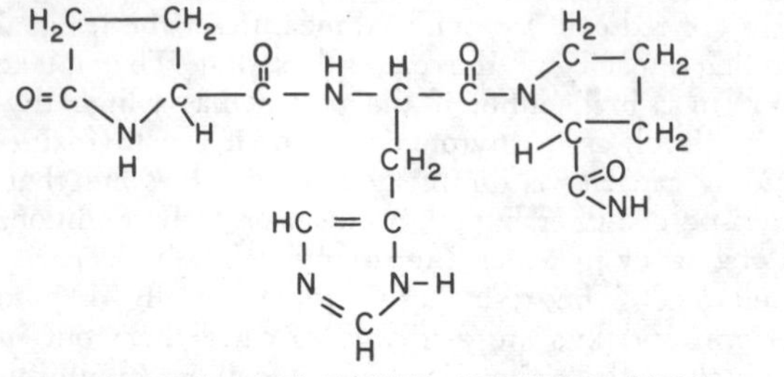

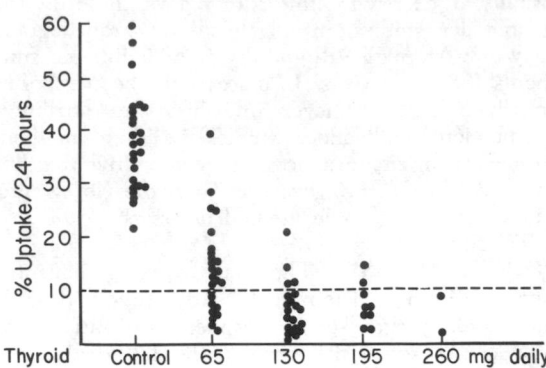

THYROTROPIN—RELEASING HORMONE (TRH)
L–(PYRO) GLUTAMIC ACID–L–HISTIDINE –L PROLINE AMIDE

Fig. 7. Structure of thyrotropin-releasing hormone.

"T_3 toxicosis." Of perhaps even broader implication was the finding that some patients with low thyroid reserve, such as after I^{131} therapy or subtotal thyroidectomy, preferentially secrete T_3 and are clinically euthyroid, although their PBI and T_4 levels are in the range usually ascribed to hypothyroidism.

Hypothalamic-Pituitary Control

The rate of thyroid hormone secretion is governed primarily by TSH from the pituitary. Under steady-state conditions, the release of thyroid hormones into the circulation exactly matches the rate of their degradation in the periphery. Should the peripheral level of thyroid hormone fall, the pituitary responds by releasing additional TSH. In the thyroid this is reflected by more rapid discharge of thyroid hormone, more rapid organification of iodide, and, if sustained for a prolonged period, by an increase in thyroidal size. The level of circulating TSH in plasma, as measured by the technique of radioimmunoassay, is exceedingly high in cases of primary hypothyroidism but unmeasurable when hypothyroidism is secondary to hypopituitarism.

The secretion of pituitary thyrotropin is at least partially controlled by a peptide hormone of hypothalamic origin called the thyrotropin-releasing factor (TRF). This neurohumoral substance reaches the anterior pituitary by way of the portal system of veins which course down the pituitary stalk from the median eminence of the hypothalamus. An elevation in the level of circulating thyroid hormone blocks the action of TRF on TSH secretion, whereas a decrease in circulating thyroid levels permits TRF to stimulate TSH secretion. In addition, there may be a direct feedback at the hypothalamic level between thyroid levels and the secretion of TRF. TRF is a tripeptide which consists of pyroglutamic acid, histidine, and proline amide (Fig. 7). The synthesis of this substance has now been accomplished and provides a powerful tool for testing the capacity of the pituitary to secrete TSH.

When a normal subject is given exogenous thyroid hormone, the endogenous secretion of TSH is

Fig. 8. The effect of graduated dosages of desiccated thyroid on the ^{131}I uptake of normal individuals. The dosages indicated on the abscissa were administered in each instance for a period of 8 days. The diminution of endogenous thyroid function is progressive with increasing dosage until maximum inhibition is reached at dosages which approximate the normal daily output of thyroid hormone. (From Greer. New Eng. J. Med., 244:385, 1951.)

diminished, thyroid hormone synthesis is curtailed, and the thyroid gland undergoes atrophy. For this reason, the administration of thyroid hormone to patients with normal thyroid function results in no net change in thyroidal status, unless dosages are used which exceed the normal daily output of thyroid hormone (Fig. 8). Therefore, the alleged benefit of thyroid hormone administration to children with sundry nonendocrine disorders has no rational basis.

Action of Thyroid Hormones

The oxygen consumption of most tissues falls markedly in hypothyroidism and rises above normal when thyroid hormone is present in excess. No doubt, most of the physiologic alterations in hypo- or hyperthyroid states are secondary consequences of this blunting or acceleration of tissue respiration.

IN VITRO EFFECTS. Attempts to identify the primary mechanism by which T_4 controls energy-producing processes have been only partially successful. Swelling of mitochondria can be observed when physiologic concentrations of T_4 are added to in vitro systems, whereas concentrations considerably greater than these are necessary to induce most of the other biochemical transformations which have been observed. There is, however, little doubt that T_4 plays an important role in protein synthesis, perhaps by enhancing the transfer of amino acids from soluble RNA to microsomal proteins. Some of these newly formed proteins are enzymes concerned with cellular respiration.

Many of the physiologic effects produced by thyroid hormone in the intact animal are slow to appear and require pretreatment for some period of time. Thus, it is difficult to segregate primary from secondary effects of T_4 administration. Attempts to extrapolate all of the physiologic actions of T_4 from in vitro observations have left many unexplained gaps in our knowledge.

INTERACTION WITH AUTONOMIC NERVOUS SYSTEM. One of the most persistently attractive hypotheses of thyroid hormone action is that these substances exert some of their effects by altering sympathetic nervous system activity. The striking similarity between adrenergic activity, on the one hand, and the signs of hyperthyroidism, on the other, have intrigued investigators for many decades, although the exact nature of this relationship remains elusive.

When compared with a euthyroid individual, the hyperthyroid patient is exquisitely sensitive to epinephrine and norepinephrine, whereas the hypothyroid subject is refractory. Brewster observed that sympathetic blockade by means of drugs or spinal anesthesia prevented the expected rise in oxygen consumption and pulse rate of animals treated with large quantities of thyroid hormone. Similarly, the administration of antisympathetic drugs, such as reserpine or guanethidine or the beta adrenergic blocking agent propranolol, diminishes tachycardia and some other symptoms in Graves' disease, without directly altering thyroid function. Hyperthyroid children excrete increased amounts of catecholamines, histamine, tryptamine, and tyramine. These findings might be explained by decreased degradation of these aromatic amines by the thyrotoxic patient, since both monoamine oxidase and catechol-o-methyl transferase activity are reduced in the thyrotoxic state. In the hypothyroid rat there is greatly accelerated synthesis of norepinephrine in the neurosecretory granules of the proximal neuron, although the total content of norepinephrine remains normal because of equally rapid degradation. These observations suggest that in hypothyroidism the postsynaptic receptor is refractory to neural transmission and that the defect is not in the metabolism of norepinephrine per se.

EFFECT ON NEURAL MATURATION. During infancy and childhood, the most conspicuous consequence of thyroid deficiency is inhibition of growth and maturation. Following the institution of adequate substitution therapy, a dramatic acceleration of linear growth and skeletal maturation takes place; a permanent loss of growth potential does not occur except in the more severe and long-standing forms of cretinism. Hypothyroidism during the period of rapid brain growth also inhibits neural maturation. However, these deficits are mostly irreversible, even when adequate substitution treatment is provided subsequently.

In the rat, the thyroxine-dependent period of brain maturation begins in intrauterine life and ceases at 20 days of age. In the nervous system of the human infant the period of thyroxin dependency is less clearly defined, but infants who are rendered hypothyroid after 6 months of age usually suffer no permanent mental impairment.

The dependency of the immature brain on thyroxine is particularly striking, since adult brain tissue differs from most other tissues by its singular unresponsivenes to thyroid hormone. The oxygen consumption by the brain of the fetus and neonate is markedly affected by the level of T_4, whereas this is not so in later life. A probable explanation lies in the fact that the adult brain uses glucose almost exclusively as its metabolic substrate, whereas the maturing brain and other tissues also metabolize fat and protein. Deficits in neural maturation which are incurred during the period of T_4 dependency are probably due to decreased tissue respiration and impaired synthesis of structural elements.

Thyroid Function in the Fetus

Ontogenesis of Fetal Thyroid Function

The thyroid requirements of the fetus are normally supplied by hormonal contributions from both the baby and its mother. It is still not possible to state quantitatively, however, how much thyroid hormone each member of this symbiotic pair contributes to the hormonal pool of the other or, more importantly, to what extent the mother or fetus can compensate for deficient hormone production in the other.

The fetal thyroid originates at the base of the tongue as a cluster of cells which migrate downward in front of the trachea, leaving the thyroglossal "duct" as an embryonic remnant. The placenta has an active transport mechanism for iodide which favors transport to the fetus. The ability of the thyroid to concentrate iodine is developed by the eleventh week of gestation and the production of T_4 begins soon thereafter. The synthesis of thyroglobulin has been demonstrated in human fetuses prior to the formation of iodinated proteins. During the latter part of gestation, the avidity of the fetal thyroid for iodine is so great that following the administration of ^{131}I to the mother, the radioactivity accumulated per gram of thyroid tissue is 10 times greater in the gland of the fetus than in that of the mother.

The capacity of the fetal thyroid to function effectively has been deduced primarily from observations following the administration of goitrogenic agents to animal mothers during pregnancy. Agents such as propylthiouracil readily cross the placental barrier and block hormone production in both the fetal and maternal thyroid glands. The fetus readily develops a goiter if the dosage is sufficiently large. Since these goiters develop only secondarily to TSH stimulation, and since maternal TSH fails to cross the placenta, it may be assumed that a fetal pituitary feedback must be in operation for these goiters to develop. The most cogent evidence for the existence of a functioning pituitary feedback regulatory mechanism in the fetus is the observation that hypophysectomy of the mother does not prevent the development of a thiouracil goiter in the fetus. More recently Fisher has extended these indirect observations by direct measurement of TSH and serum thyroxine levels in human fetuses of different ages. Fetal thyroxine levels rose steadily from the 11th week through term, but TSH levels were unmeasurable until the 20th week of gestation, when there was an abrupt rise in fetal TSH levels.

Concepts of the nature of the thyroid-pituitary feedback relationships of the mother and fetus respectively have been further complicated by the discovery by Hennen that chorionic tissue is rich in a material which behaves biologically and immunologically like pituitary TSH. This material is highest in maternal blood early in pregnancy and diminishes toward term. The physiologic role of placental TSH (human chorionic thyrotropin) is not yet known.

Many lines of evidence suggest that during a substantial portion of intrauterine existence the fetus is capable of regulating its own thyroid hormone production and taking care of at least a major portion of its own metabolic requirements. Normal children have been born to women who were myxedematous during pregnancy, and it has been observed that maternal hypothyroidism is partially alleviated during pregnancy.

Placental Transport of Thyroid Hormones

Studies of the placental transport of thyroid hormones from mother to fetus and from fetus to mother have been carried out in several animal species and at different gestational times. It is now clear that T_4 and T_3 move across the placental barrier in both directions but that equilibration takes place very slowly. Beierwaltes found that in pregnant beagles a much larger proportion of the fetal T_4 pool moved to the maternal side than in the opposite direction. There have been conflicting calculations on whether the net transfer of thyroid hormone is greater from fetus to mother or in the reverse direction. It is probable that the direction depends on the stage of gestation and the thyroidal status of each.

By administering ^{131}I-labeled T_4 to pregnant women at different times prior to delivery, and later measuring its concentration in cord blood and maternal serum, Grumbach and Werner demonstrated that the concentration in cord blood did not reach its maximum value until 18 hours had elapsed, and that even then its level was only one-third that in maternal blood. This slow transport is in marked contrast to amino acids which are not bound to proteins. Such amino acids equilibrate rapidly between the two circulations and reach a slightly higher concentration on the fetal side. The limitation in T_4 exchange across the placenta is probably due to the fact that most of the T_4 in serum is bound to proteins and only a small portion exists as the free amino acid. During pregnancy the thyroxine-binding capacity of

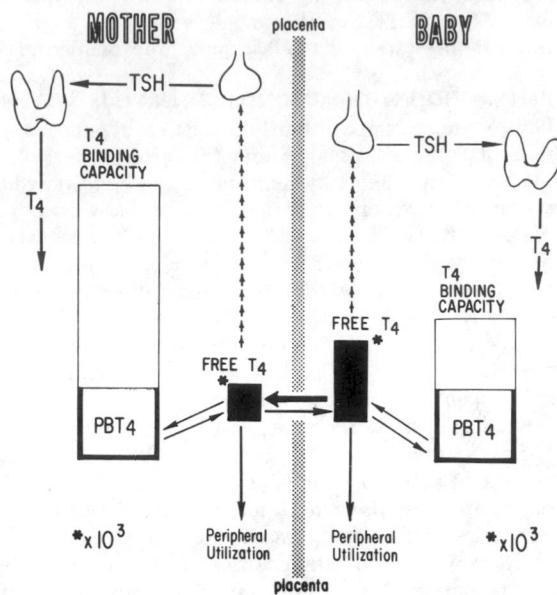

Fig. 9. Schematic diagram of the factors which influence the placental transport of thyroxine during normal pregnancy. The capacity of thyroxine-binding globulin to bind thyroxine (T_4-binding capacity) is represented by the clear bars, and the protein-bound thyroxine (PBT_4) is shown to occupy only a fraction of these total available binding sites. Note that the protein-bound thyroxine levels (PBT_4) of the mother and baby are about the same while the total T_4-binding capacity of the baby's serum is only half that of the mother's. Because the thyroxine-binding globulin of the baby is more saturated, his "free" thyroxine level is higher. It must be emphasized that "free" thyroxine is a relatively minute quantity in comparison with protein-bound thyroxine. In order to show graphically the different levels in fetal and maternal blood the solid black bars for "free" thyroxine have been drawn on a scale 1,000 times larger than the scale for T_4-binding capacity and PBT_4. The higher concentration of "free" thyroxine in fetal blood produces a gradient which favors transport from fetus to mother.

maternal plasma is increased approximately threefold, whereas the thyroxine-binding capacity of the fetus is only slightly above that of normal adults. Thus, although at term the total T_4 content is approximately the same in the two circulations, the proportion which is "free" is somewhat higher on the fetal side. This gradient favors greater movement of T_4 from baby to mother than in the reverse direction (Fig. 9).

Under conditions of fetal hypothyroidism, the lowered level of free T_4 on the fetal side would produce a gradient favoring the transport of larger quantities of maternal hormone to the fetus than normally occurs, although this compensation is usually not sufficient to completely prevent some degree of intrauterine hypothyroidism (Fig. 10). If means were available to diagnose fetal hypothyroidism before birth, it might be possible, by feeding exogenous hormone to the mother, to elevate her free T_4 levels sufficiently to fully compensate for the fetal deficiency. Beierwaltes found that this could be accom-

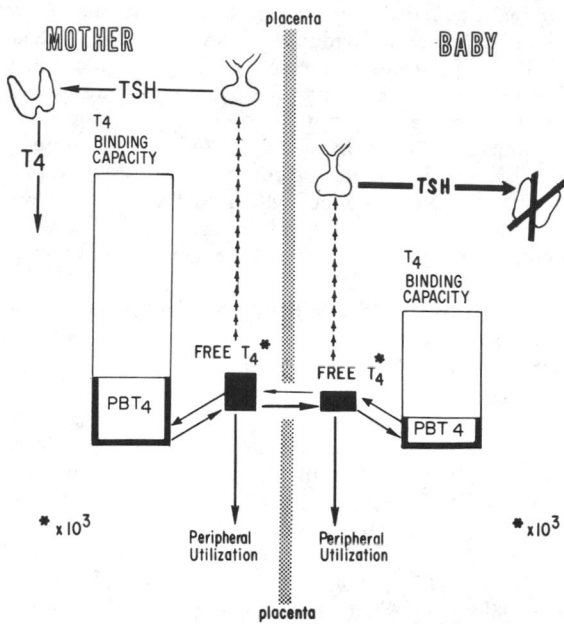

Fig. 10. This diagram is similar to Figure 9, but shows the relationship between a normal mother and a hypothyroid fetus. Note that "free" thyroxine is now relatively greater in maternal than in fetal blood, and this gradient now favors placental transport from mother to baby. There is, however, no absolute increase in maternal 'free' thyroxine and this remains a rate limiting factor in placental transport. If the mother is rendered hyperthyroid by exogenous medication, the resulting increase in her free thyroxine level will increase the net transport.

plished only by feeding the mother sufficiently large dosages of desiccated thyroid to render her thyrotoxic.

These formulations of fetal-maternal thyroid relationships are as yet incomplete, since they do not take into consideration the role of T_3 and the possibility of differential permeability of the placenta in either direction. Nonetheless, they are in agreement with available data and form a reasonable explanation for common clinical experiences. The only athyrotic cretin we have observed with completely unimpaired intelligence is one whose mother was hyperthyroid during most of her pregnancy. Conversely, devastating neurologic deficits have been found when both the infant *and mother* were hypothyroid during pregnancy. The observation that neural deficits are usually more severe in endemic cretins than in other types can probably be explained by the coexistence of a hypothyroid state in both mother and baby during pregnancy.

Hypothyroidism

Cretinism

CAUSES OF CRETINISM. "Cretinism" is an ancient term long used in Europe to describe a form of im-

TABLE 3. *Etiologic Classification of Cretinism*

Endemic cretinism

Embryonic errors in development (thyroid dysgenesis)
    Thyroid aplasia ("athyrotic cretinism")
    Thyroid dysplasia
        Ectopic remnant in pathway of descent
        Rudimentary thyroid in normal location

Inborn errors of hormone synthesis (goitrous cretinism, familial cretinism)
      Peroxidase defect (Pendred's syndrome)
      Failure to deiodinate iodotyrosines
      Failure to form iodothyronines
      Circulating iodoproteins
      Failure to concentrate iodine
      Peripheral resistance to thyroxine

becility and dwarfism which was common in areas of endemic goiter. Use of this term antedates knowledge of the condition it describes, but it has held fast throughout the unfolding of modern concepts of thyroid deficiency in children. The meanings of this term are vague, and the trend is to deemphasize the end result and apply this designation to any individual with a congenital deficiency in thyroid secretion dating from birth. An etiologic classification of cretinism is provided in Table 3.

ENDEMIC CRETINISM. On a worldwide basis, endemic cretinism is by far the most common variety of this disorder, although with the institution of iodine prophylaxis it is rapidly disappearing from developed countries. Endemic cretins often display deaf-mutism and more severe mental and physical retardation than is observed in other forms of cretinism. For this reason, it has often been suggested that factors other than iodine deficiency play etiologic roles. Data are not available to discount the possibility that associated genetic abnormalities due to inbreeding or additive environmental influences such as dietary goitrogens contribute to the pathogenesis of endemic cretinism. It is noteworthy, however, that endemic cretins are produced only after several generations of iodine deficiency.

EMBRYOLOGIC ERRORS IN DEVELOPMENT (THYROID DYSGENESIS). Errors of embryologic development may be responsible for either complete absence of thyroid tissue (thyroid aplasia) or anomalous differentiation of the gland (thyroid dysplasia). Athyrotic children have no detectable uptake of ^{131}I in the neck and develop severe clinical manifestations of hypothyroidism in early infancy.

With the advent of techniques to localize radioactive iodine, many patients who would have been classified previously as athyrotic have been found to have residual tissue capable of trapping iodine. In many instances the thyroid tissue is located ectopically in the pathway of descent from the base of the tongue. More rarely, aberrant tissue is located laterally. It is characteristic of these thyroid rests that they are small and incapable of responding to stimulation by TSH hormone. In addition, these glands often display defective peroxidase activity with positive perchlorate "flush" tests. The incidence of these thyroid rests in allegedly athyrotic cretins varies with the technique used to detect them and the age tested. In some cases, tissue which trapped radioactive iodine at birth could not be demonstrated at a later date when thyroid treatment was discontinued. In all probability, thyroid tissue capable of at least some degree of function is present at birth in most nongoitrous cretins.

Etiology of Embryologic Defects. Cretins are usually free of the multiple somatic anomalies which characterize mongolism and many other syndromes associated with mental retardation. The fact that thyroid deficiency and the consequences thereof are usually the only abnormalities present has led to a search for etiologic mechanisms which are organ specific. Although there is a slightly increased tendency for cretinism to recur in subsequent children born to mothers who have given birth to one such child, the distribution does not follow any Mendelian pattern of inheritance. A number of instances have been recorded in which identical twins were discordant for athyrotic cretinism. We have observed one mother who gave birth to two successive athyrotic cretins, although they were fathered by different men. Such observations give support to the belief that a maternal factor may play an etiologic role in some cases.

Blizzard has found antithyroid antibodies in 29 percent of a series of 121 mothers who had given birth to one or more cretins. These antibodies readily cross the placenta and remain in the blood of the baby for several months after birth. However, thyroid damage has not been demonstrated following the passive transfer of such antibodies, and active immunization of pregnant animals has not produced any thyroid disorder in the fetus, even when extensive damage was produced in the mother's gland. Although these antibodies are probably not themselves the cause of cretinism, they do suggest that an autoimmune process in the mother may be associated with arrested development of the fetal thyroid gland. One possibility is that lymphocytes of sensitized mothers traverse the placenta and produce a delayed hypersensitivity reaction in embryonic thyroid tissue.

INBORN ERRORS OF HORMONE SYNTHESIS. In 1950, Stanbury reported the first of a series of observations clearly demonstrating that cretinism may result from the inheritance of a metabolic error in the synthesis of thyroid hormones. Six distinct types of biochemical defects have been proposed, although in some of them the specificity of the findings is questionable. The characteristic findings in these defects are summarized in Table 4.

Where adequate data have been available for genetic analysis, the mode of inheritance has usually proved to be that of a simple autosomal recessive. In general, the clinical manifestations of cretinism due to a biochemical defect differ from those arising from an embryologic error in development only in the familial incidence of the former and in the propensity of the affected individuals to develop large goiters. The term "goitrous cretinism" has been applied to the former group of patients, but the term is misleading since thyroid enlargement is often not striking until a number of years have elapsed without treatment. Similar, but less severe, errors in synthesis may produce only simple goiters which first make their appearance in later childhood or adulthood. Such patients may remain euthyroid or develop only mild hypothyroidism.

Peroxidase Defect (Pendred's Syndrome). The first of the defects described by Stanbury was attributed to a deficiency of the peroxidase enzymes necessary to oxidize thyroidal iodide to iodine. Due to long-standing stimulation by TSH, radioactive iodide is concentrated at an accelerated rate in such a gland. Since the ^{131}I remains in reduced form, the thyroidal radioactivity falls at a rate which parallels the clearance of plasma ^{131}I by renal excretion. The administration of thiocyanate or perchlorate to such patients is followed by a precipitous fall in thyroid radioactivity (see Fig. 6). In a high percentage of cases this defect is associated with congenital nerve deafness.

The association between familial goiter and deaf mutism was first reported in 1896 by Pendred, an English country practitioner. In 1960, Fraser et al. reported 113 such cases in 72 families, with a distribution conforming to an autosomal recessive mode of inheritance. In these families, goiter was found to have an obligatory association with nerve deafness. A positive perchlorate discharge test was found in affected individuals. In most instances, affected individuals were euthyroid or only mildly hypothyroid, and the discharge of radioactivity following perchlorate was less complete than in cretins with this defect. Thus, the deafness could not be attributed to intrauterine hypothyroidism. The goiters tended to recur following partial thyroidectomy unless full replacement dosages of thyroid hormone were administered.

Failure to Deiodinate Iodotyrosines. Deficiency of iodotyrosine deiodinase is another hereditary defect which causes both cretinism and less severe forms of familial goiter. Since monoiodotyrosine and diiodotyrosine account for about two-thirds of thyroidal iodine stores, severe wastage of iodine would occur if these compounds were discharged into the bloodstream and excreted by the kidneys. The deiodinating enzyme which releases iodide from MIT and DIT is found both in the thyroid gland and peripheral tissues. Whereas cretins with this defect are severely deficient in both the thyroidal and peripheral enzymes, goitrous patients have been described in whom only the thyroidal enzyme was lacking. Mild deficiencies of the peripheral deiodinating mechanisms may occur as a nonspecific finding in myxedematous

TABLE 4. *Enzymatic Errors in Thyroid Hormone Synthesis*

	Normal	Peroxidase Defect	Failure to Deiodinate Iodotyrosines	Failure to Form Iodothyronines	Circulating Iodoproteins (abnormal thyroglobulin or defective proteolysis)	Failure to Concentrate Iodine	Peripheral Resistance to Thyroid Hormone
PBI	4.0-8.0 μg%	Low	Low or normal	Low	Normal or high	Low	High
BEI	3.5-7.5 μg%	Low	Low	Low	Low	Low	High
PBI-BEI difference	BEI 80% of PBI	Normal	Normal	Normal	Abnormal PBI-BEI discrepancy	Normal	High
^{131}I uptake	15-45%	Normal or high	Normal or high	Normal or high	Normal or high	Low	High
Perchlorate or thiocyanate dumping	<10%	>20%	<10%	<10%	<10%	<10%	<10%
Salivary plasma ^{131}I	>10%	Normal or high	Normal	Normal	Normal	Low	—
Urine after ^{131}I DIT	10% in first 4 hr as DIT; 90% as I⁻	Normal	High	Normal	Normal	Normal	Normal
Urine after ^{131}I	^{131}I	Normal	^{131}I DIT	Normal	Normal	Normal	Normal
Plasma after ^{131}I	Thyroxine	I⁻	^{131}I DIT, ^{131}I MIT	I⁻	^{131}I Thyroalbumin	I⁻	Thyroxine
Thyroid after ^{131}I	Thyroxine, 15-20%; MIT and DIT, 50-70%; I⁻, 10-20%	I⁻	I⁻ 80%, DIT and MIT 20%	DIT and MIT 80%, I⁻, 20%	DIT, MIT, Thyroalbumin	0	?

*Adapted with permission from Wilkins, L. *The Diagnosis and Treatment of Endocrine Disorders in Childhood and Adolescence,* 3rd ed. Springfield, Ill., Charles C. Thomas Publ., 1965.

subjects, but such abnormalities are corrected when the patient is rendered euthyroid.

The presence of this defect can be detected by direct enzymatic studies of thyroid tissue or by finding MIT or DIT in plasma or urine. The more usual test, which measures only the integrity of the peripheral deiodinase enzymes, is to administer ^{131}I-labeled diiodotyrosine and determine the chemical form of the radioactivity excreted in the urine. Whereas in the normal subject more than 90 percent of the urinary radioactivity is recovered in the form of iodide, patients with this defect excrete mostly unchanged ^{131}I-labeled diiodotyrosine.

Since the net result of this defect is a severe iodine deficiency, it is possible to treat such patients by administering massive amounts of iodine. However, it is simpler and more efficacious to treat these patients with thyroid hormone itself.

Failure to Form Iodothyronines. A third hereditary type of cretinism is associated with a rapid uptake of iodine and formation of thyroglobulin containing iodotyrosines but essentially no iodothyronines. It has been postulated that this defect is the result of a specific deficiency of a "coupling" enzyme. The biochemical significance of this defect remains unclear, however, since the exact mechanism by which T_3 and T_4 are formed is still unknown, and no enzymes have been described which perform this specific function.

Circulating Iodoproteins. Several cretins have been described with an excessive discrepancy between their PBI and BEI, suggesting that an abnormally large proportion of the circulating iodinated amino acids exists in peptide linkage. Such abnormal iodinated proteins may not represent a specific enzymatic defect, however, since they are encountered in a wide variety of thyroidal disorders, notably autoimmune thyroiditis, thyroid cancer, and after the administration of large amounts of inorganic iodine. Iodoproteins have been found in several patients with a primary peroxidase defect. Following hydrolysis of this protein only MIT and DIT are recovered. Immunologic studies suggest that in some instances the abnormal iodoprotein is produced by the iodination of serum albumin in its passage through a hyperplastic gland.

Although circulating iodoproteins may originate in several different ways, it is possible that in some instances they may be produced by a specific hereditary defect in thyroidal biosynthesis. Genetic abnormalities in the structure of thyroglobulin might render this protein resistant to proteolysis with the escape of incompletely hydrolyzed protein fragments into the circulation. Alternatively, the proteolytic mechanism might itself be defective. It is possible that cretins with circulating iodoproteins have a defect which is related to that in some patients with Hashimoto's struma. This condition also has a familial tendency and is characterized by the presence of circulating iodoproteins (see p. 1080).

Failure to Concentrate Iodine. Chapman, Stanbury, and others have described patients with hyperplastic thyroid glands, but no demonstrable uptake of radioactive iodide. It is notable that other iodine-concentrating tissues, such as salivary glands, likewise failed to concentrate iodine from the circulation. Whether the underlying abnormality is a specific defect in membrane transport or a circulating substance which blocks the uptake mechanism is not clear.

Peripheral Resistance to T_4. Another defect which has been suggested is a specific inability of peripheral cells to utilize T_4. Although a number of authors have reported patients who were alleged to require an unusually large dosage of thyroid hormone to correct hypothyroidism and restore a normal growth rate, most such reports have lacked sufficient documentation to prove a primary defect in peripheral utilization. Some of the patients who were allegedly resistant to desiccated thyroid may have received a preparation of low potency.

Refetoff, DeWind, and DeGroot have described a familial syndrome in which three siblings exhibited deaf mutism, stippled epiphyses, retarded skeletal age, goiter, and greatly elevated PBI and serum T_4 values. These patients grew normally and had a normal basal metabolic rate. Administration of 1,000 μg/day of T_4 or 375 μg/day of T_3 produced little or no metabolic effects. Thus, these patients must be considered to be relatively refractory to the metabolic effects of thyroid hormone even though clear evidence of hypothyroidism was lacking.

Familial Goiter Associated with Intrathyroidal Calcification. Murray and his colleagues have reported one unusual family in which goiter was known to occur in five generations. The goiters were unusually firm and heavily calcified. The goiters typically appeared during adolescence and were not associated with any demonstrable abnormality in thyroid hormone function.

DIAGNOSIS OF CRETINISM. Because of the partial protection which a fetus receives from its mother, a newly born cretin is not conspicuously short and rarely exhibits obvious clinical signs of myxedema. The complete picture of hypothyroidism does not emerge until this store of maternal hormone has dwindled. However, some degree of antenatal hypothyroidism must exist in most instances, since radiologic examination usually reveals that the skeletal development is retarded in comparison to that of a normal newborn.

Although many of the signs of hypothyroidism may be blunted in the newborn period, the diagnosis should be considered in those newborns who maintain a subnormal temperature, exhibit excessive circulatory mottling, or who fail to nurse properly and exhibit respiratory distress with feeding. The diagnosis should also be suspected in newborns who are inactive and cry infrequently, who are unduly constipated, or who have persistent unexplained jaundice. As the cretinoid infant grows older, the classical pic-

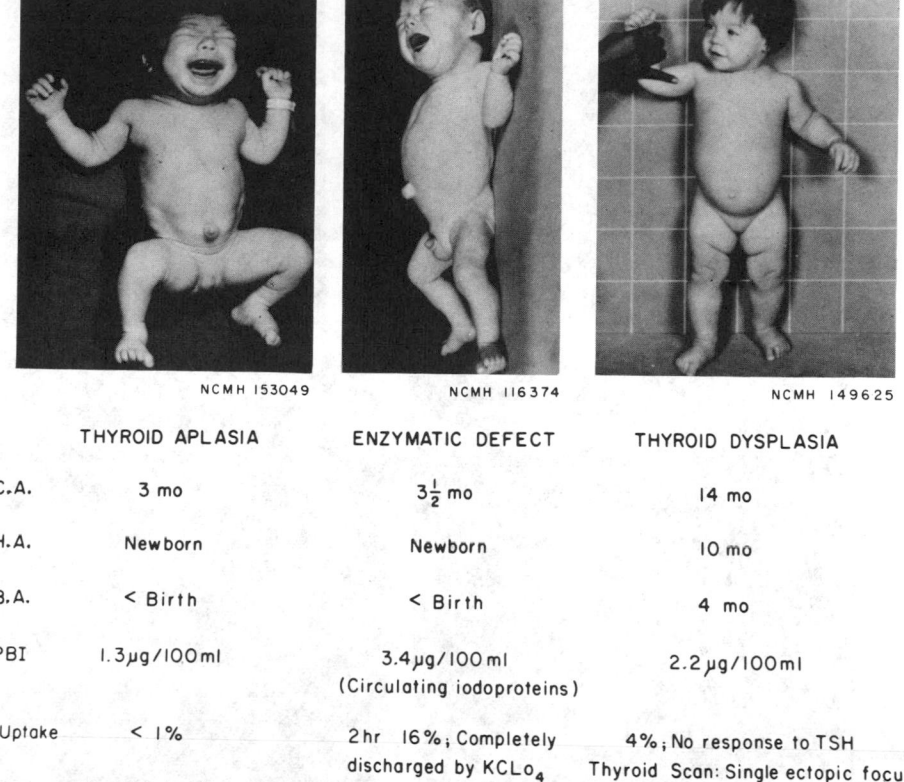

	THYROID APLASIA	ENZYMATIC DEFECT	THYROID DYSPLASIA
	NCMH 153049	NCMH 116374	NCMH 149625
C.A.	3 mo	$3\frac{1}{2}$ mo	14 mo
H.A.	Newborn	Newborn	10 mo
B.A.	< Birth	< Birth	4 mo
PBI	1.3 µg/100 ml	3.4 µg/100 ml (Circulating iodoproteins)	2.2 µg/100 ml
^{131}I Uptake	< 1%	2 hr 16%; Completely discharged by KCLo$_4$	4%; No response to TSH Thyroid Scan: Single ectopic focus

Fig. 11. The clinical picture in cretinism depends more on the severity of hypothyroidism than the etiologic mechanism. The first two infants both had severe peripheral mottling, muscular hypotonia, an umbilical hernia, and myxedema. The infant on the right has a functioning thyroid remnant that provided partial protection and obscured the diagnosis for over a year.

ture of untreated hypothyroidism becomes more apparent (Fig. 11). He fails to grow at a normal rate, and radiologic examination reveals retarded skeletal maturation and often a characteristic stippled appearance of the epiphyses (Fig. 12). The classical cretinoid facies is due to accumulation of myxedema in the subcutaneous tissues and tongue. The thickened tongue becomes protuberant, and the infant develops increasing difficulty in nursing and handling his salivary secretions. The cry is hoarse due to myxedema of the vocal cords.

The cretin is distinguished by marked muscular hypotonia and mental torpor. Constipation, umbilical hernia, and the characteristic "potbelly" are due to muscular hypotonia involving both the smooth muscles of the gut and striated muscle of the abdominal wall.

The deleterious effect of hypothyroidism on the heart and circulation constitutes one of the most constant features as well as the most immediate threat to life. There is usually a relative bradycardia and diminished pulse pressure. The cardiac silhouette may be enlarged due to myxedematous infiltration or pericardial effusion. The electrocardiogram may show low voltage and a prolonged conduction time. As a consequence of inadequate perfusion of peripheral tissues, the extremities are cool and may exhibit extreme pallor and circulatory mottling.

Hypothyroid infants exhibit numerous metabolic deficits. Insensible water loss is greatly diminished due to the lowered basal metabolic rate. The glomerular filtration rate is markedly impaired and inappropriate secretion of antidiuretic hormone has also been described. As a result of these changes, the administration of forced feedings or intravenous fluids may rapidly lead to water intoxication and hyponatremia. The conjugation and excretion of drugs are markedly impaired, thereby causing these patients to be exquisitely sensitive to small amounts of drugs such as barbiturates and narcotics. The conjugation of bilirubin is likewise impaired, thus accounting for prolonged neonatal jaundice. Carotenemia and hypercholesterolemia are further indications of the hypothyroid state, although in young untreated cretins the serum cholesterol is not strikingly elevated. Vitamin D intoxication has been encountered with dosages only moderately in excess of daily requirements. Most patients are moderately anemic and fail to respond to

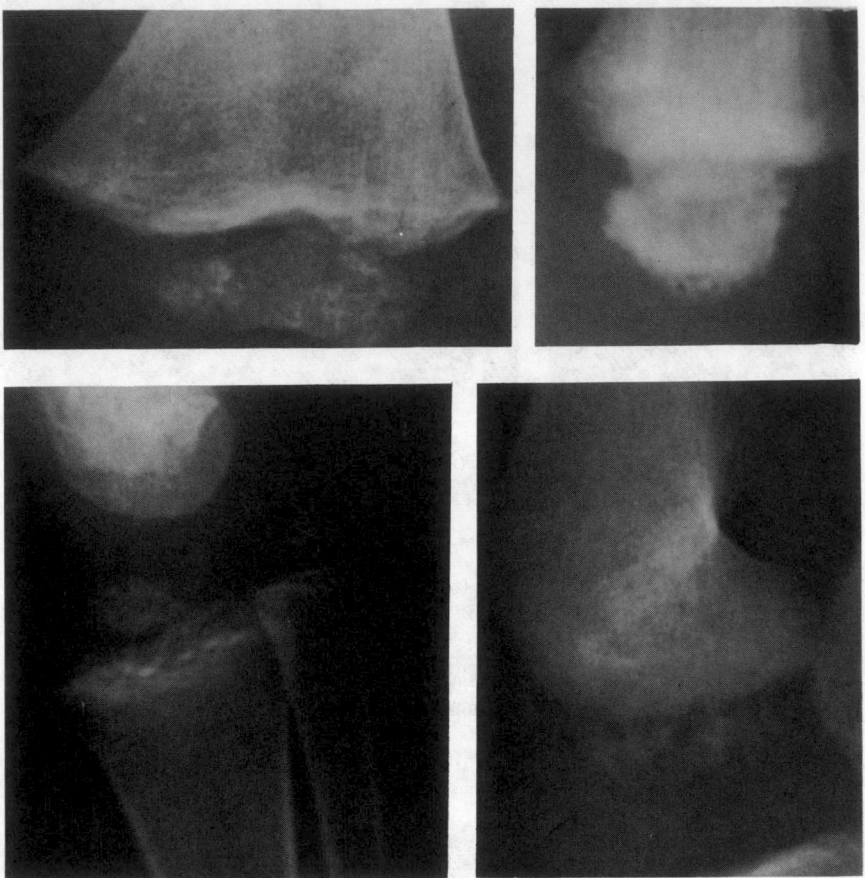

Fig. 12. Epiphyseal dysgenesis involving multiple centers in older untreated cretin. Such changes are frequently not seen until treatment is begun and rapid ossification has been initiated. By serial roentgenograms it has been demonstrated that dysgenesis may occur in any epiphysis which would normally have ossified during the span of life that thyroid deficiency existed.

iron. Reticulocytosis follows the institution of thyroid treatment.

Laboratory Diagnosis of Cretinism. Since there is every reason to believe that the prognosis for mental development worsens as treatment is delayed, it would be desirable to find some laboratory test which would reliably identify the hypothyroid infant in the newborn period. Unfortunately, tests which are useful in the diagnosis of hypothyroidism at a later age are difficult to interpret in the neonate, both because of the maternal contribution to the hormonal pool of the infant and because thyroid function tests in normal newborns fluctuate widely before stable values are achieved.

The changes in thyroid function which normally occur after birth reflect both a response to new environmental stimuli and a release from the hormonal influences of the mother. The thyroidal uptake of iodine, which is markedly elevated during the latter part of intrauterine life, remains elevated for the first 72 hours following birth with a fall to the generally accepted normal range by the fifth day. Van Middlesworth found the mean thyroidal uptake of ^{131}I to be 69 percent at 2 and 3 days of age. The serum PBI and BEI levels, which at birth are nearly identical to those of the mother, rise further from the third to the fifth day and then fall gradually to the levels characteristic of infancy (Fig. 13). The T_3 red cell or resin uptake test parallels the PBI and BEI, demonstrating that the hyperthyroxinemia is not due to an increase in binding proteins. Fisher has demonstrated that there is an abrupt discharge of TSH following birth which is probably due in part to rapid extrauterine cooling (Fig. 14). By 3 to 4 weeks of age, stable conditions of infancy are achieved. At this time, the thyroidal iodide space is approximately double that of adults and the serum thyroxine is also statistically above average adult levels. These values gradually decline during the first 2 years of life.

To complicate further the laboratory diagnosis of cretinism, most of the inborn errors of thyroidal

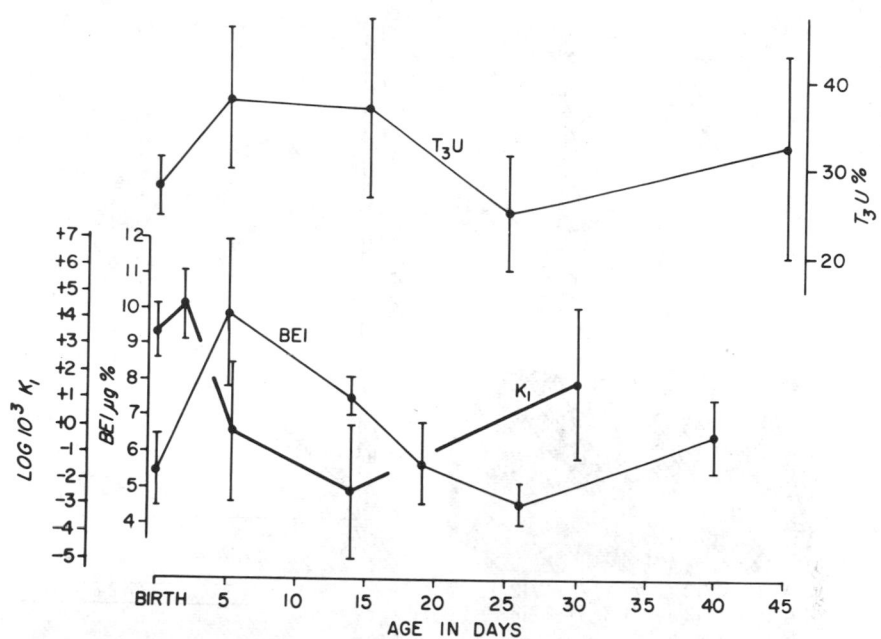

Fig. 13. Values for the BEI, T₃ resin uptake (T₃U), and fractional thyroidal clearance of ¹³¹I (K₁ is a measure of thyroidal iodine uptake) during the early weeks of life. The values shown are average values for normal newborns (±1 SD). (Data are from Fisher. *In* Sunderman and Sunderman, eds., *Clinical Pathology of Infancy.* Benson, Pickering, Kontaxis, and Fisher. *Obstet. Gynec.,* 14:11, 1959.)

biosynthesis are associated with a normal or elevated uptake of thyroidal ¹³¹I. In some of these patients circulating iodoproteins cause spurious elevations of the PBI. There is therefore no single finding which by itself will reliably discriminate the cretin from a normal newborn. The diagnosis of neonatal hypothyroidism should be based upon careful clinical observation of the infant, evaluation of epiphyseal maturation, measurement of the ¹³¹I uptake and *serial* measurements of the PBI or serum T₄ level. Where doubt still persists after these studies are completed, it is advisable to place the infant on full maintenance doses of thyroid hormone therapy for a full year and then temporarily withdraw therapy to confirm the diagnosis.

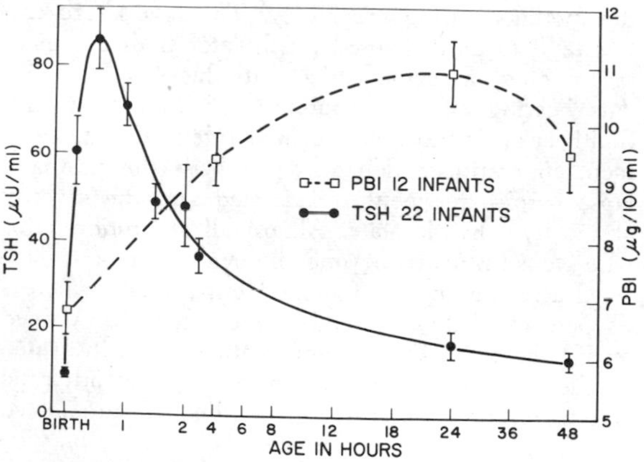

TREATMENT OF HYPOTHYROIDISM. Preparations available for the treatment of hypothyroidism are desiccated thyroid (USP), purified thyroglobulin (Proloid), 1-triiodothyronine (Cytomel), and 1-thyroxine (Synthroid). Satisfactory results can be achieved with any of these preparations providing the physician is fully acquainted with the characteristics of each. Since none of these preparations contains T₃ and T₄ in the precise ratio in which they are normally secreted, the effect on the PBI cannot be used to determine adequacy of treatment (see p. 1062). This judgment must rest on clinical observation. Recently, several manufacturers have marketed mixtures of T₃ and T₄ in supposedly physiologic proportions (Euthroid, Thyrolar). No therapeutic advantages have been demonstrated for these combinations other than providing more "normal" PBI levels during treatment.

For markedly hypothyroid infants the usual starting dose is 16 mg of desiccated thyroid daily, 25 μg of triiodothyronine, or 50 μg of 1-thyroxine. Ten days

Fig. 14. Serum PBI and TSH concentrations during the first 48 hours of extrauterine life. Note the change in time scale on the abscissa. (From Fisher and Odell. *J. Clin. Invest.,* 48:1670, 1969.)

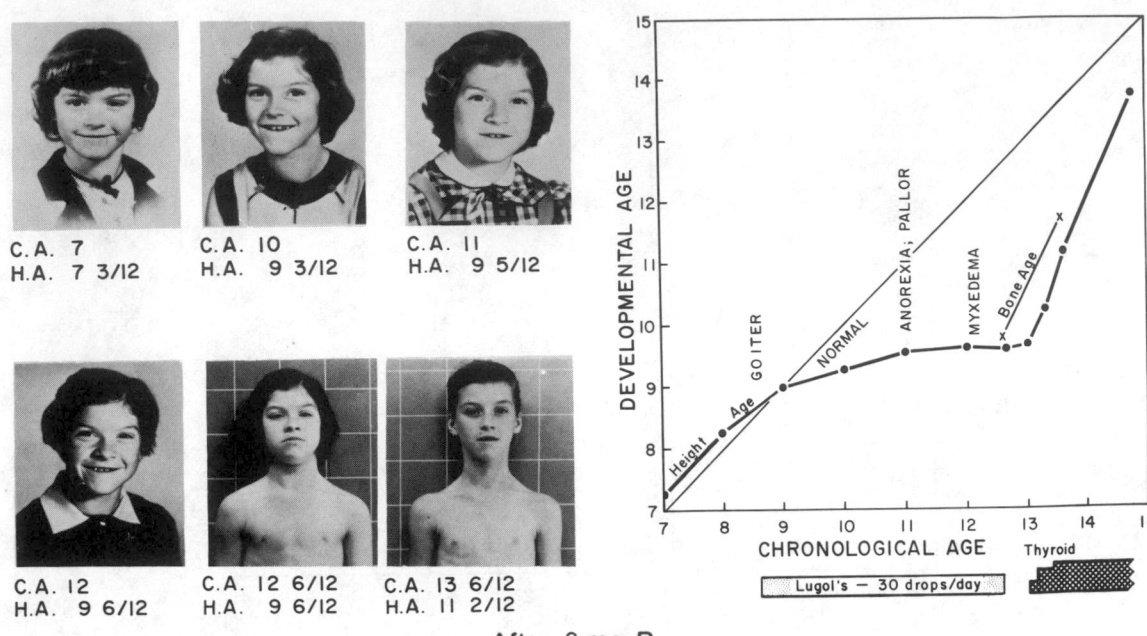

C.A. 7
H.A. 7 3/12

C.A. 10
H.A. 9 3/12

C.A. 11
H.A. 9 5/12

C.A. 12
H.A. 9 6/12

C.A. 12 6/12
H.A. 9 6/12

C.A. 13 6/12
H.A. 11 2/12

After 6 mo R$_x$

Fig. 15. Patient with familial goiter who developed hypothyroidism shortly after the institution of treatment with Lugol's solution. This patient is discussed in the text on page 1075.

to two weeks are usually required to observe the maximal effects from a constant dosage. In severely hypothyroid infants, the initial treatment should be instituted cautiously, since sudden deaths have occasionally occurred during this period. Some of these deaths have been attributed to the development of cardiac arrhythmias.

Adequate dosage in the first year of life ordinarily ranges between 45 and 60 mg of desiccated thyroid, 50 and 75 μg of T$_3$, and 75 to 100 μg of l-thyroxine. Persistence of bradycardia, circulatoy mottling, inactivity, hoarse cry, constipation, or delay in the relaxation phase of deep tendon reflexes may be taken as an indication for increasing the dosage. The enlarged tongue may not disappear for many months in the presence of otherwise adequate therapy.

The growth rate should be markedly accelerated after initiation of therapy and the growth deficit restored in 9 to 24 months, depending on the age and degree of dwarfism existing at the beginning of treatment. Supplemental vitamins should be prescribed to meet the increased requirements during the period of "catch-up" growth. The bone age is the most sensitive index of thyroid deficiency and may reveal inadequate dosage of thyroid hormone when other signs of hypothyroidism have been obliterated.

Overtreatment produces pathologic signs such as tachycardia, excessive nervousness, disturbed sleep patterns, and other findings suggesting thyrotoxicosis.

Excessive dosages over a longer period of time produce osteoporosis and undue advancement of bone age. Rapid shedding of lanugo and devitalized scalp hair is a normal consequence of treatment and does not indicate a need to reduce the dosage.

PROGNOSIS IN CRETINISM. Much confusion has arisen regarding the role of substitution therapy in preventing or ameliorating the mental deficit in cretinism. This is not surprising in view of the heterogeneity of causes, variations in degree of thyroid deprivation, and variations in the thyroidal status of the mothers during pregnancy. The less severe cretins tend to be diagnosed much later than the more severe ones, a factor which introduces a bias into data bearing on the importance of early treatment. Smith et al. found that the final intellectual achievement in cretinism depended on both the postnatal lapse before treatment was started and the severity of the hypothyroid state. Almost all athyrotic cretins who went untreated beyond the age of 6 months suffered a severe degree of mental impairment, whereas 45 percent of those treated before 6 months attained an IQ above 90. Even when treatment was instituted in the early weeks of life, however, few athyrotic cretins reached the level of intelligence anticipated from a consideration of their family background. Cretins with some residual thyroid function suffered lesser degrees of mental retardation even when treatment was delayed for many years.

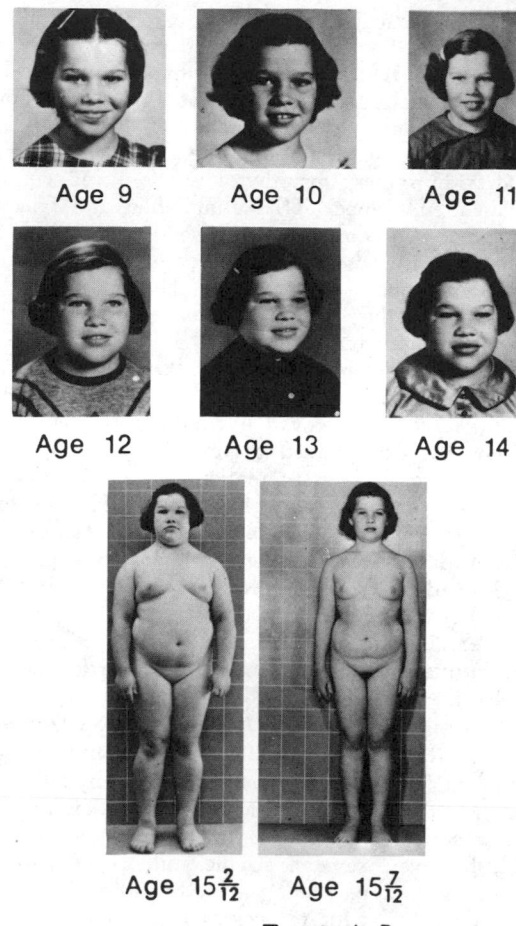

Age 9   Age 10   Age 11

Age 12   Age 13   Age 14

Age 15$\frac{2}{12}$ Age 15$\frac{7}{12}$

Treated 5 mo

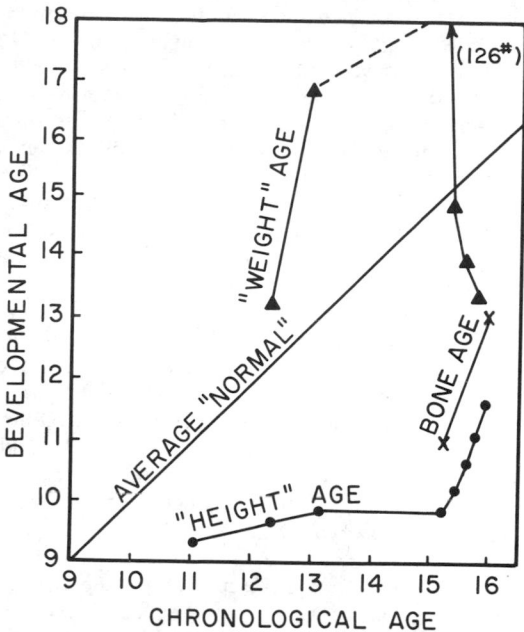

Fig. 16. The evolution of hypothyroidism in this 15-year-old girl is illustrated by these serial photographs and growth measurements which were obtained from school records. The height record suggests that thyroid function began to fall between 9 and 10 years, but the full clinical picture of myxedema required several years to emerge.

Acquired Juvenile Hypothyroidism

ETIOLOGY. Hypothyroidism may develop at any age in previously normal individuals and is more common in females than in males. In most cases the gland simply undergoes idiopathic atrophy. The onset is usually insidious and no precipitating cause can be identified. A high proportion of such individuals has been found to have circulating antithyroid antibodies, and it is probable that the hypothyroidism in these cases is the end result of an autoimmune process. In a minority of instances, acquired juvenile hypothyroidism may be attributed to some goitrogenic agent or may occur as a late manifestation of an inborn error of thyroidal biosynthesis.

The complex interaction of genetic factors, sexual predisposition, and environmental goitrogens is demonstrated by the 13-year-old girl illustrated in Figure 15. A small asymptomatic goiter had been found at age 8, and she was placed on 30 drops of Lugol's solution daily. The immediate slowing of her growth curve which followed the institution of this therapy clearly dated the onset of hypothyroidism to this point, although overt signs of myxedema developed insidiously and were not recognized until an additional four years had elapsed. Genetic studies of this child's family revealed a marked predisposition to goiter, which was apparently inherited as an autosomal dominant trait with greater expression in the female. A distinctive biochemical abnormality in this family was the presence of circulating iodopeptides. Some of these individuals were also found to be excessively sensitive to iodine and developed myxedema rapidly when moderate dosages were administered. A number of close relatives of the proband had been subjected to multiple thyroidectomies. Circulating antithyroid antibodies were found in these patients, and the histologic picture in their thyroid glands resembled that of Hashimoto's thyroiditis.

DIAGNOSIS OF HYPOTHYROIDISM IN CHILDHOOD. The most useful aid in the recognition of hypothyroidism in childhood is a serial record of growth performance. Usually a number of years elapse between the onset of hypothyroidism and the emergence of classical signs of myxedema. If growth records are available, however, the onset of hypothyroidism can be documented readily by the progressive downward deviation from a previously normal growth channel. The weight tends to increase, and in most instances the "weight age" exceeds the "height age" (Fig. 16).

The possibility of thyroid deficiency should be considered in any child who is not growing normally. A dwarfed child who is underweight for his stature is less likely to be hypothyroid than in the reverse circumstance. The retardation of bone age in hypothyroidism almost always equals or exceeds the retardation in linear growth. This finding is present, however, in other forms of dwarfism and is by no means pathognomonic of hypothyroidism.

Hypothyroidism is frequently suspected in obese, sluggish individuals. It should be emphasized, however, that the stature of most obese children is above the 50th percentile for age, and the skeletal maturation is likewise advanced. In contrast to this, children with untreated hypothyroidism are retarded in both height and bone age, unless the thyroid deficiency is of very recent onset. Thyroid function studies are not usually indicated in obese children with advanced stature.

The effects of hypothyroidism on the cardiovascular system produce some of the most useful clues to the diagnosis. The precordium is unusually quiet and the pulse pressure diminished. Circulatory mottling, pallor, and cool extremities are often striking. Although the skin and hair are dry, these alterations are often subtle and of little diagnostic value. The thyroid-deficient patient usually exhibits slowing of the deep tendon reflexes with a markedly delayed relaxation phase. These changes can be observed best by percussion of the Achilles tendon with the child kneeling on a chair. The responses are usually sufficiently characteristic for appreciation without the aid of recording devices. Simple electronic instruments, suitable for office use, are now available to record accurately the kinetic behavior of tendon reflexes. Since the speed of reflexes is modified by the "autonomic tone" at the time of the test, anxiety, drugs, and other extrathyroidal influences may render the results invalid as a test of thyroid function.

Hypothyroidism is usually a lifelong disease, and the diagnosis should always be fully supported with tests of thyroid function before treatment is instituted. With adequate treatment the child will be restored to full physical normality and the original diagnosis inevitably challenged. Minimal documentation should consist of determining the PBI and/or thyroxine iodine concentration, serum cholesterol, ^{131}I uptake, and bone age. None of these tests, however, invariably reflects the true thyroid status of the patient, and may provide misleading information, particularly in the presence of biosynthetic errors or after exposure to iodine-containing substances. In such cases a therapeutic trial is warranted if the child fulfills other clinical criteria for the diagnosis.

It is particularly important before undertaking treatment to discriminate between primary hypothyroidism and that secondary to hypopituitarism. A potentially helpful test to separate these conditions is the ^{131}I uptake test before and after the administration of thyrotropic hormone. The thyroid gland of a child with primary hypothyroidism is already under maximal endogenous TSH stimulation and fails to respond to the administration of additional TSH. In hypopituitarism the administration of TSH usually results in a marked increase of the ^{131}I uptake. A common procedure is to administer two intramuscular injections of bovine thyrotropin, 5 USP units each, 48 hours and 24 hours before the second iodine uptake test. Unfortunately about a third of the children in our clinic with proved hypopituitarism have, for unknown reasons, failed to respond to TSH, even after more prolonged stimulation. A more direct test is the radioimmunoassay of plasma TSH, but this procedure is not yet available widely. In practice, the clinical differences between children with primary and secondary hypothyroidism are usually sufficiently clear that detailed tests of pituitary function are not required. In rare instances a full battery of thyroid and pituitary function tests must be carried out to resolve the issue.

SYNDROME OF PRECOCIOUS SEXUAL DEVELOPMENT ASSOCIATED WITH JUVENILE HYPOTHYROIDISM. The sexual development of most hypothyroid children is retarded to the same extent as their retardation in skeletal maturation. This is not invariably the case, however, since a sizable number of patients with long-standing primary hypothyroidism have now been described with precocious menstruation, breast development, and galactorrhea. In the male, this syndrome is associated with excessive enlargement of the penis and testes. Most of these patients lack sexual hair, and the bone age is retarded in keeping with their hypothyroid state. The sella turcica in many has been enlarged. When the hypothyroid state is alleviated, the manifestations of sexual precocity regress and a normal puberty ensues later when the general level of maturity has progressed appropriately. In some instances the sella turcica has become smaller in size.

It was postulated by Van Wyk and Grumbach that the apparently inappropriate sexual development in such patients is due to an overlapping secretion of gonadotropins and prolactin along with the expected hypersecretion of TSH. It has subsequently been demonstrated that bovine thyrotropic hormone and bovine luteinizing hormone have a peptide subunit which is common to both molecules. This suggests that there is a common precursor for the biosynthesis of both molecules and that hypersecretion of one of them might be expected to cause overproduction of the other. Enlargement of the pituitary and sella turcica in long-standing myxedema was recognized over a century ago and has been confirmed many times since. The fact that the endocrine abnormalities and enlargement of the pituitary fossa are reversed following the administration of thyroid hormone suggests that these pathologic findings are secondary to compensatory hyperplasia of the pituitary rather than to a primary pituitary adenoma.

TREATMENT OF ACQUIRED HYPOTHYROIDISM. Substitution therapy in older children with hypothyroidism should follow the same guidelines outlined for the treatment of cretinism. The response of the hypothyroid child to even a small amount of hormone is so dramatic that full dosages may not have to be given. Parents are frequently alarmed by an initial rapid weight loss, excessive shedding of hair, and the increased assertiveness of previously passive children. These complaints are usually not supported by objective evidence of thyrotoxicity and disappear with continued treatment.

Goiter

Goiter and Transient Hypothyroidism of the Newborn

ETIOLOGY. The presence of a goiter at birth is usually caused by the ingestion of goitrogenic substances by the mother. Infants with cretinism due to an inborn error of metabolism may have a palpable thyroid gland, but only rarely is this sufficiently enlarged to be visible or threaten respiration. Infants with severe peroxidase deficiencies are more prone to have large neonatal goiters than infants with the other hereditary defects. In areas of the world where endemic goiter is common, congenital goiter is a frequent cause of neonatal death by asphyxiation.

In this country the most frequent and serious cause of neonatal goiter is the ingestion by the mother of large dosages of iodides during pregnancy (Fig. 17). In most instances the iodides have been prescribed as an expectorant in asthma or for the treatment of maternal thyrotoxicosis. There is convincing evidence that iodides potentiate those goiterogenic substances which act by inhibiting peroxidase enzymes. Many drugs given to patients with asthma are complex formulations which contain a variety of substances which might potentially influence thyroid function. In any event, the mothers of these children have often taken iodide for many years without developing large goiters themselves and were euthyroid during their pregnancies. The unusual sensitivity of the fetus to iodides is probably due to the great capacity of the fetal gland to concentrate this element during the latter portions of pregnancy. However, since many women take comparable dosages of iodides during pregnancy without apparent harm to their babies, it is suspected that the severely affected infants may have some additional predisposing abnormality.

Other goitrogens which have caused neonatal goiter are the thioureas, sulfonamides, and hematinic preparations containing cobalt. The thyroid gland of such babies usually exhibits extreme hyperplasia. Neonatal goiters due to propylthiouracil are rare unless exceptionally large dosages are given to the mother. The dosage of the drug appears to be a more critical factor than the mother's thyroidal status per se.

TREATMENT. Neonatal goiters due to maternal ingestion of goitrogenic substances are usually of short duration and disappear spontaneously. It may be necessary to interrupt breast feeding, as the thiourea drugs and iodides are secreted in breast milk.

If hypothyroidism is present or if the goiter is sufficiently large to cause dyspnea, it is advisable to provide full substitution therapy with thyroid hormone to achieve immediate euthyroidism and more rapid shrinkage of the gland. For this purpose T_3 may be the drug of choice because of its more rapid onset of action. Iodides are contraindicated since they make the gland more firm and may aggravate tracheal compression. If respiratory obstruction is severe, tracheal decompression must be carried out by surgical resection of the thyroid isthmus. Tracheostomy alone in these babies is hazardous, and an attempt to carry out this procedure usually ends fatally. Infants with large goiters at birth are often hypothyroid during intrauterine life as well as transitorily following birth. In such babies, permanent mental damage may have been inflicted even though a euthyroid state is quickly achieved in the newborn period.

Goiter in Childhood and Adolescence

ETIOLOGY OF SIMPLE GOITER. Simple thyroid enlargement is usually a response to compensatory stimulation by pituitary thyrotropic hormone. TSH is secreted whenever a fall occurs in the level of circulating thyroid hormone, regardless of cause.

IODINE DEFICIENCY AND ENDEMIC GOITER. When considered on a worldwide basis, the most common cause of thyroidal enlargement is endemic goiter. Although it has been demonstrated beyond reasonable doubt that iodine deficiency is the principal cause, there is no simple linear relationship between the iodine content of the soil and water and the incidence of thyroid enlargement. In some areas, particularly those which are more severely isolated, there is reason to believe that the pattern of the endemic goiter is modified by genetic abnormalities due to inbreeding or by goitrogenic agents in the water or diet. The concept suggested in the early part of this century, that pollution of water supplies might be an important etiologic factor in endemic goiter, has again been revived.

Simple goiter remains a common occurrence even in those regions of the world where iodine is plentiful or where the diet has been fortified by iodized salt. The possibility that a relative degree of

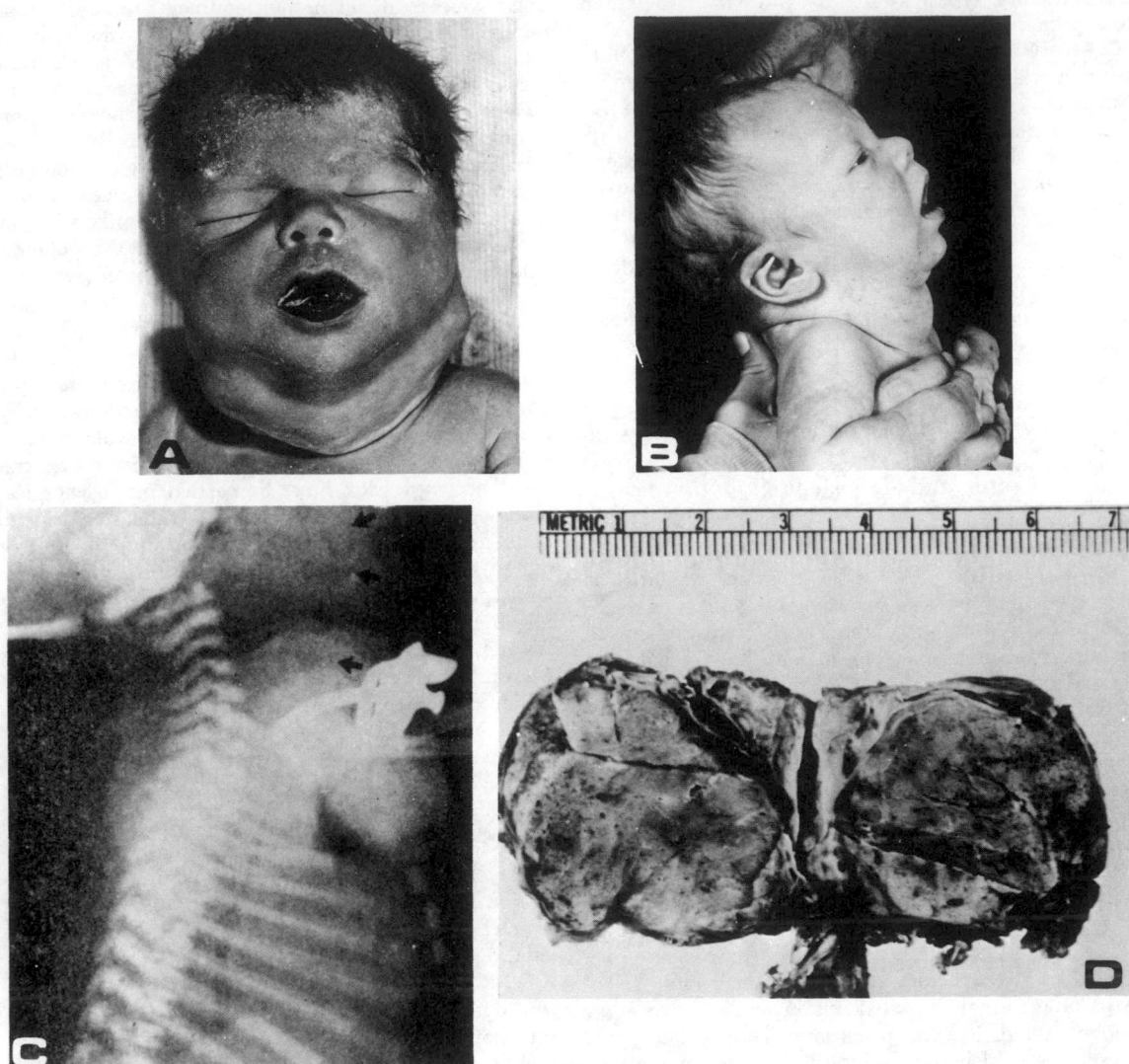

Fig. 17.   Iodide goiters in the newborn. The mothers of all 4 infants suffered from asthma and received medication containing iodides during their pregnancies. A. Full-term infant who died of asphyxiation 18 minutes after birth. B. One-month-old infant who survived, but may have incurred mild brain damage. At one month of age the PBI was 18 μg/100 ml and BEI 4.6 μg/100 ml. C. Roentgenogram of infant who expired 40 hours after birth. Marked tracheal compression extends far below the lower end of the tracheostomy tube. D. Pathologic specimen from infant who died 4 hours after birth. (Figures A and C from Galina, Avnet, and Einhorn. *New Eng. J. Med.,* 267:1124, 1962.)

iodine deficiency is responsible for some instances of goiter in nonendemic regions is difficult to exclude, since the requirement for iodine is moderately increased during adolescence and pregnancy and greatly increased in patients with certain types of errors in thyroidal biosynthesis. The presence of iodine deficiency should be suspected in any euthyroid goitrous individual with an abnormally high thyroidal uptake of [131]I. Indeed, iodine kinetic studies in iodine deficiency closely resemble those in hyperthyroidism.

If iodine deficiency is suspected, it can be corrected by the provision of iodized salt. The time-honored practice of administering Lugol's solution for the treatment of goiter is irrational and frequently harmful. Each drop of Lugol's solution contains approximately 8,000 μg of elemental iodine, an amount which is more than 50 times the daily requirement. Such massive dosages have an inhibitory effect on thyroidal biosynthesis and may provoke hypothyroidism in susceptible patients.

TABLE 5.   *Partial List of Goitrogenic Agents*

Anions
       Iodine (in large amounts)
       Perchlorate
       Thiocyanate

Cations
       Cobalt (in certain hematinic preparations)
       Arsenic salts
       Lithium salts

Drugs
       Propylthiouracil
       Methimazole
       p-Amino-salicylic acid
       Amino-glutethimide
       Phenylbutazone

Naturally occurring substances
       Goitrin (1-5 vinyl-2-thiooxazolidone) (present in cabbage and other members of the genus *Brassica*)
       Soybeans (not soybean milk as presently prepared)

As judged by ^{131}I kinetic studies, iodine deficiency is a rare cause of goiter along the Eastern seaboard. This is probably also true in many other parts of the U.S. Studies of urinary iodine excretion have revealed average values as high as 325 μg/day in some parts of the U.S., as contrasted with values in the range of 100 μg/day in Western Europe and values below 50 μg/day in most regions of endemic goiter. Since the accumulation of a tracer dose of ^{131}I is reciprocally related to the daily inorganic iodine consumption, regional differences in iodine intake are also reflected in the "normal" ^{131}I uptake values. The 24-hour ^{131}I uptake in apparently healthy children on the Eastern seaboard is frequently in the range of 10 to 20 percent, whereas in Europe uptakes of 30 to 50 percent are more characteristic. In iodine-deficient areas of South America, uptakes of 80 percent are common in euthyroid nongoitrous subjects.

Pittman demonstrated that, in Alabama, between 1959 and 1968, average normal values of ^{131}I uptake decreased from 28.6 to 15.4 percent. This was attributed to a tripling of the average daily consumption of inorganic iodides, primarily as a consequence of adding iodates to the manufacturing process for white bread.

EXPOSURE TO GOITROGENIC AGENTS.   Any food or drug which interferes with thyroid hormone synthesis is a potential cause of goiter. A partial list of such agents is given in Table 5. In only a small proportion of the patients presenting with simple goiter, however, is it possible to identify a known goitrogen. Dietary goitrogens are particularly difficult to identify since they may reach the subject through a devious route. Clements demonstrated a great increase in the incidence of goiter in Tasmanian school children after the introduction of a new forage crop of the genus *Brassica*. He was able to relate this increase to the presence of a goitrogenic agent in the milk of cows fed on this crop.

It is our impression that excessive intake of iodine is becoming an increasingly common cause of goiter. In some instances the source of this iodine has been traced to chronic medication with cold remedies and antiasthmatic drugs, but more commonly the source of exposure cannot be found. High levels of inorganic iodide inhibit thyroid function in the same manner as thiourea goitrogens. Peroxidase is inhibited and there is a shift to the left in the intrathyroidal iodoamino acids with an increase in the ratio of both iodotyrosines to iodothyronines and of MIT to DIT. Furthermore, high levels of iodides potentiate the effect of other drugs which by themselves are only weakly goitrogenic.

HASHIMOTO'S STRUMA (CHRONIC THYROIDITIS, LYMPHADENOID GOITER, AUTOIMMUNE THYROIDITIS).   In 1921, Hashimoto described four patients with goiters which on biopsy were characterized by diffuse infiltrations of plasma cells and lymphocytes, fibrosis, parenchymal atrophy, and eosinophilic degeneration in some of the acini. The disease has a marked predilection for females. Although it was once thought to occur only rarely before adolescence, it is diagnosed increasingly in younger children. The onset is usually insidious with no history of painful enlargement or fever. Occasional patients, particularly those in adolescence, transiently experience tachycardia, nervousness, and other signs suggestive of thyrotoxicosis, but exophthalmos is not present. The thyroid gland is usually irregularly enlarged and firm, with accentuation of the normal lobular architecture. Lymph nodes along the cervical chain may be unusually prominent.

The course of Hashimoto's struma, if left untreated, is highly variable. The gland usually undergoes slowly progressive enlargement, but at any state it may undergo atrophy with the emergence of myxedema. Satellite lymph nodes are often enlarged, especially the Delphian node above the isthmus. Not infrequently the goiter gives rise to the sensation of local pressure and difficulty in swallowing.

Although the exact mechanism remains unresolved, it is likely that the histologic picture in the thyroid gland of patients with Hashimoto's struma is due to an autoimmune reaction of the delayed hypersensitivity type. Similar lesions have been produced experimentally by immunizing animals with thyroid extracts from the same or different species or by infusing lymphocytes from previously sensitized animals. More than 95 percent of patients with Hashimoto's struma have circulating antithyroid antibodies. These antibodies may be of two distinct types: (1) the antithyroglobulin antibodies which are measured by either the precipitin reaction or tanned red cell hemagglutination test; and (2) antibodies to an intracellular microsomal antigen which are detected either by a complement-fixation reaction or by a cytotoxic effect on thyroid cells grown in tissue culture.

It is not yet certain whether autoimmune thyroiditis is a discrete disease entity or whether it may occur as the response to a variety of predisposing causes. Leboeuf and Bongiovanni have correlated the development of Hashimoto's thyroiditis with a preceding viral infection and have suggested that nonspecific inflammation of the thyroid gland may lead to cellular destruction with release of sensitizing components into the serum.

Hall found that the prevalence of autoimmune antibodies was very high in close relatives of affected individuals and concluded that the disease is due to a basic genetic defect in either the thyroid gland itself or the immune mechanism. Many patients with Hashimoto's struma have elevated levels of gamma globulin, and it has been reported that the coexistence of other autoimmune diseases such as rheumatoid arthritis, lupus erythematosus, and pernicious anemia is greater than might be expected by chance. The possibility that Hashimoto's struma occurs secondarily to some genetic abnormality in the thyroid gland itself is supported by the frequent familial association of this lesion with other types of thyroid disease. Autoimmune thyroiditis could be produced by incompetency of the follicular basement membrane with leakage of unhydrolyzed thyroid protein, which would then serve as an antigenic stimulus. The discharge of incompletely hydrolyzed thyroglobulin into the circulation might be enhanced by a primary genetic defect either in the proteolytic mechanism or in the structure of thyroglobulin itself. Doniach, however, has convincingly demonstrated that small amounts of unhydrolyzed thyroglobulin are found regularly in the plasma of apparently healthy individuals. Increasingly, therefore, the weight of evidence is lending support to the concept that Hashimoto's struma is due to some primary abnormality of the immune mechanism.

Although Hashimoto's struma has been defined in terms of a specific histologic picture, the presence of this disorder may be suspected on the basis of characteristic thyroid function tests. The most common finding is an abnormally large discrepancy between the PBI and thyroxine iodine concentration due to excessive quantities of iodinated protein in the circulation. The uptake of ^{131}I is exceedingly variable. In some patients defective oxidation of iodide within the thyroid can be demonstrated by an abnormal discharge of radioactivity following the administration of perchlorate.

One of the characteristics of this disorder is unusual sensitivity to iodides. This can be demonstrated by the iodide suppression test. In normal patients and in those with goiter from other causes, 2 mg of stable iodide reduces the 24-hour ^{131}I uptake by less than 50 percent. In one study of patients with Hashimoto's thyroiditis the average suppression was 77 percent (range 46 to 95 percent).

The abnormal sensitivity of patients with Hashimoto's thyroiditis to iodides has raised substantial questions whether excessive iodine intake may play some etiologic role. Thyroid enlargement with a histologic picture similar to that of Hashimoto's struma has been experimentally produced in dogs by feeding them chow with a high iodine content. Hashimoto's struma is rare in iodine-deficient areas with endemic goiter, whereas in many parts of the country the incidence of Hashimoto's struma has risen sharply and has paralleled the greatly increased intake of iodine already mentioned. While such observations are highly provocative, excess iodide ingestion fails to explain the familial pattern and immunologic abnormalities which are characteristic of the human disease. It can no longer be doubted, however, that iodide therapy is contraindicated in the treatment of patients with this disorder.

"ADOLESCENT" GOITER. The term "adolescent" goiter has no etiologic meaning, since the incidence of all types of goiter rises abruptly in the years preceding the onset of puberty. The increased incidence is more striking in girls than in boys. The reasons for the increased incidence at this time are not known, although the initiation of gonadal and pituitary hormone secretions may be ultimately responsible. Estrogens are known to affect thyroid function by increasing the T_4-binding capacity of plasma, and in other ways which are less well understood. The vague concept that more thyroid hormone is required to meet "the increased metabolic needs of adolescence" is probably without foundation since, expressed either on a weight or surface area basis, the caloric expenditure is greater in boys than in girls and in both sexes decreases during adolescence. An increased glomerular filtration rate of iodide has been shown to occur during adolescence, and this would increase susceptibility to iodine deficiency unless balanced by a proportionate increase in the rate of thyroidal uptake.

FAMILIAL GOITER. The most common finding in goitrous children has, in our experience, been a family history of goiter. Most of the biosynthetic abnormalities which have been identified in patients with goitrous cretinism have also been associated with less severe forms of goiter which develop in postnatal life. Pendred's syndrome and deiodinase deficiencies of milder degree have followed an autosomal recessive mode of inheritance. It has been suggested that predisposition to the development of Hashimoto's struma follows an autosomal dominant mode of inheritance.

In many children with a strong family history of thyroid disease, detailed tests of thyroid function fail to reveal identifiable defects. The genetic pattern in such families is suggestive of an autosomal dominant mode of transmission with greater expression in the female. In these families, Hashimoto's struma is a common finding. It is possible that the same basic lesion responsible for Hashimoto's struma may, in some individuals, cause only simple goiter without demonstrable antibodies of the usual type.

TREATMENT OF SIMPLE GOITER. Simple enlargement of the thyroid gland, particularly if it is mild in

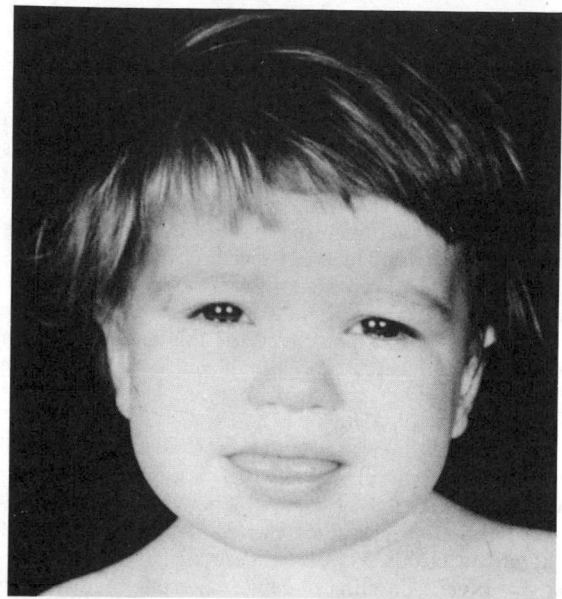

Fig. 18. Nineteen-month-old infant who became severely hypothyroid after a midline nodule, diagnosed as a "thyroglossal duct cyst," was removed at 12 months of age. Note the puffy face, pallor, and large tongue. (From Strickland, Macfie, Van Wyk, and French. J.A.M.A., 208:307, 1969.)

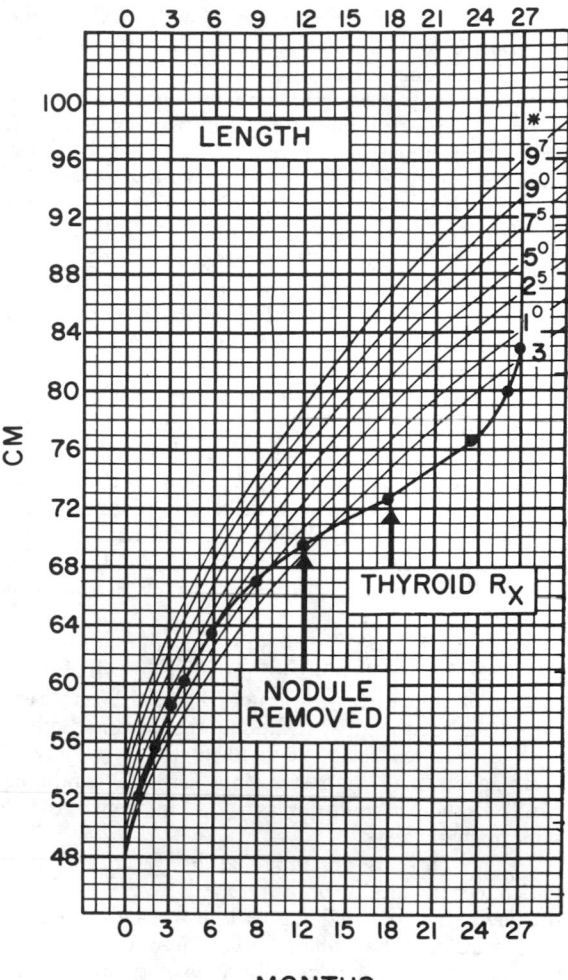

Fig. 19. Growth curve of infant shown in Figure 18. Note that the growth slowed prior to removal of her ectopic thyroid gland, suggesting that compensatory enlargement of the nodule was secondary to failing function. (From Strickland, Van Wyk, and French. J.A.M.A., 208:307, 1969.)

degree, often remains asymptomatic for many years or may regress spontaneously even if no therapy is prescribed. On the other hand, a high percentage of patients who develop nodular goiters in the third, fourth, and fifth decades of life give a history of mild diffuse thyroid enlargement during childhood or adolescence. It seems likely that nodular goiters in such patients have developed from recurring episodes of hyperplasia and involution. This suspicion provides the rationale for treating some patients in whom pressure symptoms or cosmetic considerations provide insufficient grounds for undertaking long-term therapy.

Appropriate treatment for most types of goiter consists of providing full substitution therapy with desiccated thyroid, l-thyroxine, or l-triiodothyronine. The dosages employed are 90 to 180 mg of desiccated thyroid, 75 to 150 μg of triiodothyronine, or 150 to 300 μg of l-thyroxine. After several years have elapsed, the need for continuing treatment should be reevaluated by withdrawing the medication for a period of several months.

In those patients whose glands mainly exhibit hyperplasia, regression to normal size is often dramatic following the institution of adequate replacement therapy. In Hashimoto's struma, however, there may be little visible response to treatment, particularly if there is much fibrosis and scarring. Even in these patients, however, full substitution should be continued indefinitely to inhibit further TSH stimulation. Iodides are contraindicated in most forms of simple goiter.

LINGUAL GOITER AND THYROGLOSSAL DUCT "CYSTS." (See also Sec. 28.4, p. 1850.) A number of children with ectopic thyroid glands first come to attention because of an enlarging mass at the base of their tongue or along the course of the thyroglossal duct. Surgical excision of a lingual thyroid is often undertaken because of progressive enlargement with attendant dysphagia and irritation from trauma. The enlargement may occur at any age but commonly is accelerated shortly before adolescence. In most, if not all, cases, the lingual thyroid is the only functional thyroid tissue present, and its enlargement represents a compensatory phenomenon for impending hypothyroidism. Provision of complete substitution treatment usually causes the goiter to shrink sufficiently so that surgery can be avoided. Full substitution must be continued for life.

Severe hypothyroidism occasionally follows the surgical removal of what has been presumed to be a thyroglossal duct cyst (Figs. 18 and 19). As with lingual thyroids, masses high in the neck often prove to be the only functional thyroid tissue present. In some cases, enlargement of the mass is correlated with failing thyroid function prior to surgery. Patients such as this may be considered to have mild forms of thyroid dysgenesis. In these cases the ectopic thyroid remnant has sufficient capacity to enlarge and function for the patient to be maintained in a euthyroid state for some time after birth, and cretinism does not occur. We have seen six children in whom such "thyroglossal cysts" proved to be the sole functioning thyroid tissue. In five of them the error was not recognized until growth had slowed and symptoms of hypothyroidism had appeared. For this reason it is prudent to perform a ^{131}I uptake study with scan prior to the surgical removal of midline masses in the neck of young children. If the mass accumulates iodine, surgery usually can be avoided by placing the child on full substitution doses of thyroid hormone.

SUBACUTE THYROIDITIS. Subacute thyroiditis is a self-limited inflammation of the thyroid which usually follows an upper respiratory illness. A few cases have been identified with the mumps virus and others with cat scratch fever. It is likely that a variety of viral agents may be responsible for this condition. Unlike other thyroid disease, the incidence is the same in both sexes.

The onset is accompanied by fever and pain which occurs locally or is referred to the angles of the jaws. The thyroid gland is exquisitely sensitive to palpation. The inflammation may persist for a number of weeks, but usually resolves spontaneously.

Symptoms usually can be controlled by large doses of acetylsalicylic acid, or, in severe cases, corticosteroids. The provision of suppressive dosages of thyroid hormone may also give symptomatic relief. The PBI may occasionally become elevated and mild symptoms of thyrotoxicosis may develop during the acute phase. Most patients do not develop antithyroid antibodies and recover normally with no residual defect in thyroid function.

Thyrotoxicosis

Juvenile Thyrotoxicosis (*Graves' Disease*)

Thyrotoxicosis in childhood and adolescence occurs almost exclusively as the consequence of diffuse thyroid hyperplasia rather than hyperfunctioning nodules. Girls are afflicted approximately six times as frequently as boys. Although the disease is not uncommon in preschool children and rarely may begin in infancy, there is a sharp increase in incidence with the approach of adolescence.

ETIOLOGY.   This disease no doubt has some genetic basis, since a high proportion of patients have come from families in whom thyrotoxicosis has occurred in a parent, grandparent, uncle, or aunt. Based on his pedigree analyses in Denmark, Bartels suggested that the predisposition to Graves' disease is inherited as a simple autosomal recessive trait with greater penetrance in the female. An exceedingly high gene frequency would be required for this mode of inheritance to explain satisfactorily the occurrence in successive generations, but a precedent for this genetic pattern is found in diabetes. A dominant mode of inheritance with variable penetrance cannot be excluded on the basis of available data.

Graves' disease is frequently cited as an instance of psychosomatic illness in which a hyperthyroid state is precipitated by some type of psychic trauma. Detailed psychiatric studies carried out on a group of thyrotoxic children were undertaken at the University of North Carolina to explore possible predisposing factors. In the majority of instances, it was not possible to identify acute precipitating stress, although in a few patients such an association was striking. Likewise, it was not possible to state with certainty that the psychologic pattern in families with thyrotoxic children differed significantly from that of other families, although all observers were impressed that these families contained more than their share of individuals with dominant and colorful personalities. Similar conclusions were reached by Hermann in a detailed study of 24 adult thyrotoxic patients. It was proposed at one time that central nervous system factors trigger the onset of thyrotoxicosis by stimulating the pituitary to release excessive quantities of thyrotropic hormone. This seems unlikely, however, since studies employing a direct immunologic assay of TSH have shown that plasma levels of thyrotropin are diminished in Graves' disease.

Evidence that Graves' disease arises from an intrinsic abnormality within the thyroid gland itself is based on certain peculiarities of iodine metabolism which are characteristic of this disorder. Werner has shown that in thyrotoxicosis the uptake of ^{131}I by the thyroid gland is not suppressed by the administration of T_3, whereas the administration of similar doses to normal individuals results in a fall of greater than 40 percent. Administration of stable iodide to patients with Graves' disease produces a greater than normal inhibition of both ^{131}I uptake and hormonal release from the gland.

Substantial progress toward the understanding of Graves' disease has come from the demonstration by Purves and Adams, by McKenzie, and by Kriss that the plasma of many patients with Graves' disease contains a substance with thyroid-stimulating properties which differs from normal thyrotropin. When injected into mice, this material, known as long-acting thyroid stimulator (LATS), has a much more prolonged action than normal thyrotropic hormone. LATS has now been isolated in relatively pure form from the blood of thyrotoxic patients and has been identified as a 7S gamma globulin. The origin of this presumed antibody is in lymphoid tissue, and in vitro cultures of lymphocytes from thyrotoxic patients yield substantial quantities of the LATS. When incubated with ^{14}C amino acids added to such lymphocyte cultures the radioactive label is incorporated into the 7S globulin with LATS activity. This material has been shown to bind to cytoplasmic microsomes in thyroid cells but not to cells from other organs. LATS stimulates adenyl cyclase in thyroid cell membranes in a manner similar to TSH. In other biochemical parameters as well LATS mimics the action of TSH. Papain digestion of LATS liberates a shorter chain which has a much briefer action on the thyroid, more nearly like that of pituitary TSH.

The long-acting thyroid stimulator is present in particularly high concentration in patients with pretibial myxedema. Total removal of the thyroid gland leads to improvement in this condition coincidentally with a fall in the circulating titer of LATS. Although cogent reasons have been advanced to consider LATS the causative agent in thyrotoxicosis, the correlation between LATS titers and clinical severity has been imperfect. Perhaps the strongest evidence so far is the demonstration of LATS in the serum from thyrotoxic infants of hyperthyroid mothers (see p. 1087).

CLINICAL FEATURES OF GRAVES' DISEASE. The onset of thyrotoxicosis usually is insidious, with a period of increasing nervousness, palpitation, and increased appetite. Extreme weight loss occurs in some patients, but not infrequently this is prevented by the development of a voracious appetite. Rarely, children, especially adolescents, actually develop a weight increase with the onset of this disease. There is a tendency for thyrotoxic children to be in the upper percentile channels for height. Except for exophthalmos and other eye signs, the symptoms of thyrotoxicosis are nonspecific and, for a prolonged period, may be mistaken for some other condition. Behavioral abnormalities, declining school performance, and nervous instability frequently dominate the clinical picture, and the patient is initially referred to a guidance clinic or psychiatrist. In other patients, cardiovascular signs are more prominent, and attention is focused on a cardiac murmur or decreased exercise tolerance.

Most of the signs and symptoms of Graves' disease are identical with those produced by a hyperactive sympathetic nervous system, and therefore can be fully simulated by anxiety, fright, or acute illness. Even in patients in whom tachycardia is not impressive, the pulse pressure is widened and the precordium overactive. Underlying heart disease is difficult to exclude in the presence of cardiomegaly, ejection murmurs, precordial thrill, and gallop rhythms. Other **signs** of sympathetic overactivity are tremor, increased

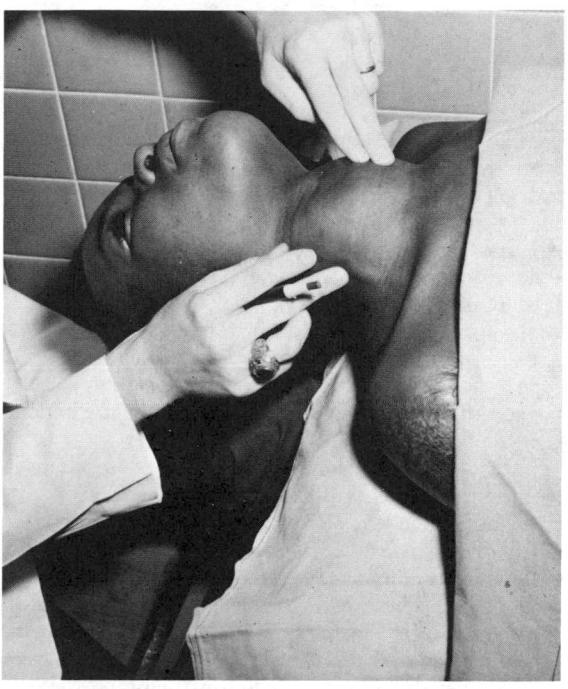

Fig. 20. A preferred method of palpating the thyroid gland. The neck is hyperextended over the end of an examining table. The lobular outline and consistency is then easily determined by bimanual palpation. The gland is outlined by skin pencil and transcribed on transparent paper. Serial records of thyroidal size and consistency provide one of the best methods for following the progress of the disease.

skin temperature, excessive perspiration, rapid tendon reflexes, and emotional lability. Even the increased basal metabolic rate may be mediated through a hyperactive sympathetic nervous system. It is sufficient only to recall that the highest metabolic rates encountered clinically are not in thyrotoxic patients but in those harboring a pheochromocytoma.

The size of the thyroid gland is highly variable, and the development of a goiter may escape notice in a patient whose gland is only slightly enlarged. A better appreciation of thyroidal size and consistency can be gained if the patient is examined in the supine position with the neck thrust forward by hyperextension (Fig. 20). Bimanual palpation during swallowing and during digital displacement of each lobe delineates the thyroid from other structures. Tracings of the two-dimensional projection of the gland as outlined by skin pencil provide a valuable method of recording serial changes.

The characteristics of the thyroid to be noted on physical examination are size, uniformity, and consistency. The presence or absence of a bruit or thrill provides some indication of the degree of hyperplasia, but otherwise these signs have no specific diagnostic value. During phases of active hyperplasia the thyroid typically has a resilient "bulging" characteristic which is lost as recovery takes place.

Eye Signs in Graves' Disease. Severe ophthalmopathy is much less common in children with Graves' disease than in older individuals, and malignant exophthalmos is virtually unknown. The eye findings in this disease may be grouped conveniently as those due to sympathetic hyperactivity and those due to specific pathologic changes in the orbit. Those due to sympathetic hyperactivity give the appearance of a stare, owing to retraction of the upper lid and a wide palpebral aperture. There is also a lag in the descent of the upper lid on downward gaze, infrequent blinking, and absence of forehead wrinkling on upward gaze. The eyes frequently present a glazed appearance. These findings to a large extent parallel the severity of the disease and disappear as the patient is rendered euthyroid.

In addition to these findings, there are changes in the orbit which are more specific for Graves' disease and which are accounted for by infiltrations of mucopolysaccharides, lymphocytes, and edema fluid within the ocular muscles, lacrimal glands, and retro-orbital fat. These changes lead to exophthalmos, ophthalmoplegia, chemosis of the conjunctivae, pain, swelling, and irritation. Although the inflammatory changes usually improve with treatment of the hyperthyroid state, some degree of exophthalmos tends to remain after recovery from the disease.

Unusual Findings in Hyperthyroidism. Accumulations of mucopolysaccharides in skeletal muscles and pretibial myxedema are findings which are particularly likely to occur in patients with severe exophthalmos and in individuals with dependent edema or previous trauma to their legs. Pretibial myxedema is rare in children.

Occasionally a patient with severe untreated hyperthyroidism first comes to the physician's attention because of profound muscular weakness and a history of collapse occurring suddenly with the attempt to walk or get out of bed. Severe muscular wasting is present in some, but not all, of these patients. It is likely that this degree of myopathy is not due to the thyrotoxicosis itself but is a secondary consequence. It has been demonstrated that patients with severe long-standing thyrotoxicosis become depleted of vitamins belonging to the B complex. Pyridoxine deficiency has been demonstrated in such patients by the finding that they respond to a tryptophan load by excreting abnormally large quantities of xanthurenic acid. This abnormality is completely corrected by administering pyridoxine. These and other unusual features, which are sporadically present in thyrotoxicosis, are probably secondary consequences of a long-standing hypermetabolic state rather than a direct result of increased thyroxine levels.

LABORATORY DIAGNOSIS OF HYPERTHYROIDISM. The diagnosis of hyperthyroidism usually can be made on clinical grounds, and laboratory confirmation can be limited to the determination of the PBI,

plasma thyroxine content, and uptake of radioactive iodine. Determinations of the plasma T_3 concentration and "free T_4" level may be helpful in occasional patients. The uptake of radioactive iodine at 1, 3, or 6 hours discriminates more reliably between hyperthyroid and euthyroid patients than the 24-hour uptake.

The T_3 suppression test may be of great help in diagnosing those patients whose chief findings are goiter and nervousness, but who lack eye findings and other clear signs of hyperthyroidism. T_3 is given for 8 days in a dosage of 100 μg daily, and the ^{131}I uptake is determined both before and at the completion of this treatment. In normal individuals and in those patients with simple goiter, the second iodine uptake should fall by at least 50 percent, whereas in Graves' disease the suppression is less marked.

Relationship of Graves' Disease to Hashimoto's Struma. Children with Graves' disease are more likely than adults to have circulating autoimmune antithyroid antibodies of the type found in Hashimoto's thyroiditis. Heavy lymphocytic infiltrates are a usual finding in the thyroid glands of children with classical Graves' disease.

Many instances have been reported of Graves' disease and Hashimoto's struma coexisting within a sibship. Reports that the incidence of Hashimoto's struma is rising whereas that of Graves' disease is declining suggest further that the two disorders may have some common etiologic basis with different expressions, dependent on other environmental factors and in particular the intake of iodides (see p. 1080).

Occasionally, patients are encountered with histologic and laboratory findings characteristic of Hashimoto's struma but who exhibit mild to severe thyrotoxicosis and resistance to thyroidal suppression by T_3. As in uncomplicated Graves' disease, the iodine suppression test is positive. The somewhat whimsical terms "Hashitoxicosis" or "Toximoto's Disease" have been applied to these patients. Perhaps these terms may serve a useful purpose in underscoring the points of similarity between the two disorders and stimulate further search for fundamental mechanisms common to both. Combined treatment with propylthiouracil and thyroid hormone, as outlined in the following section, is probably the preferable form of management of this group of patients.

TREATMENT OF THYROTOXICOSIS. Treatment of thyrotoxicosis must be directed toward reducing the secretory rate of thyroid hormones and, if possible, blunting the toxic effects produced by high circulating levels. Three principal methods are available for reducing thyroid secretions: (1) blocking thyroid hormone biosynthesis by means of drugs; (2) subtotal thyroidectomy; and (3) subtotal ablation with radioactive iodine.

Treatment with Radioactive Iodine. In terms of ease, cost, efficacy, and short-term safety, there is no doubt that treatment with ^{131}I is superior to either surgical thyroidectomy or the administration of antithyroid drugs. The potential hazards of radioactive iodine are the induction of permanent hypothyroidism, thyroid cancer, leukemia, and genetic damage. The magnitude of these risks in childhood is unknown, and estimations extrapolated from data in adults and from other species have varied widely. Until very recently, the prevailing practice in most centers has been to use ^{131}I only in rare cases where other forms of therapy cannot be utilized or carry an increased risk. With the passage of years since the introduction of radioactive iodine, however, there has been a perceptible lessening of fears concerning harmful late side effects. For this reason many clinics are now using ^{131}I more liberally in the treatment of thyrotoxicosis in childhood. The basis for taking a more cautious approach is summarized in the following paragraphs.

The late development of primary hypothyroidism after ^{131}I therapy has occurred in every series of patients studied, regardless of the dosage employed. The extent of this complication is only now being recognized, since hypothyroidism often does not develop until some years have elapsed. It is estimated that 50 percent of all patients treated with ^{131}I will be hypothyroid within 10 years of the time of therapy and a large majority within 20 years. Thus, a prolonged medical follow-up and possibly the requirement for lifelong medication cannot be avoided with this mode of treatment.

Radioactive iodine has now been used therapeutically *in adults* for a sufficient length of time that fears of inducing thyroid carcinoma have been largely alleviated. This is not the case in children. It has been well demonstrated that thyroid glands of young animals are much more susceptible to the induction of thyroid carcinoma than those of older animals. Radiation to the neck in infancy has been incriminated as the principal cause of thyroid cancer in children, whereas this has not been the case in adults. Lastly, several children treated with ^{131}I have been reported with the late development of thyroid nodules; and in at least one instance, the histologic diagnosis was that of carcinoma.

Following the administration of therapeutic doses of ^{131}I, gross abnormalities have been described in the chromosomes of white blood cells; the implications of this finding are uncertain. The development of leukemia *in adults* following ^{131}I treatment of thyrotoxicosis has occurred no more frequently than in the population at large. Since the number of children treated with therapeutic dosages of ^{131}I is relatively small, it is impossible to be certain that children will not develop leukemia more frequently than adults. In all probability, the risk of leukemia is sufficiently low that it would not by itself constitute a contraindication.

Available reports provide no evidence that fetal malformations occur more frequently in the offspring of women previously treated with ^{131}I than in infants of other women. An increased number of mutant genes of the recessive variety could be determined in a statistical sense, however, only after several generations had elapsed. The risk of genetic damage to those individuals whose entire reproductive life still lies ahead, therefore, cannot be ascertained directly. However, if the bladder is emptied frequently after therapeutic dosages of ^{131}I, the gonadal radiation dose should not exceed that resulting from many routine radiographic techniques.

It has been the practice at the University of North Carolina to reserve the use of ^{131}I for treating thyrotoxicosis in older adolescents who fail to follow a medical regimen and who cannot be adequately prepared for surgical thyroidectomy. However, it is this very group of patients who would prove unreliable in taking thyroid substitution therapy should they become hypothyroid. Several such patients have indeed become myxedematous and have failed to return to the clinic for follow-up supervision.

Subtotal Surgical Thyroidectomy. With proper preparation of the patient for surgical thyroidectomy, the immediate operative mortality has been all but eliminated. With proper surgical management most patients achieve a satisfactory remission, and the requirements for intensive medical follow-up are less rigorous than in those patients treated exclusively by pharmacologic agents. The incidence of hypoparathyroidism following subtotal thyroidectomy is still appreciable, however, and this serious complication may require lifelong treatment. Unless an adequate amount of thyroid tissue is removed, a satisfactory remission may not be achieved, or there may be a late recurrence. In the large Mayo Clinic series reported by Hayles et al., recurrences were encountered in 28 percent of 196 surgically treated patients. The average interval between surgery and relapse was 8 years, and in 3 patients relapses occurred more than 25 years later. When hyperthyroidism recurs in a surgical remnant, secondary operations are fraught with an increased hazard of injuring the recurrent laryngeal nerves or removing the parathyroid glands. If, on the other hand, sufficient thyroid tissue is removed to guarantee against such recurrences, the incidence of postoperative hypothyroidism is greatly increased. In some series, the incidence of permanent hypothyroidism after subtotal thyroidectomy has approached 50 percent.

Medical Management. Definitive medical management with antithyroid drugs is inefficient, since a prolonged period is required to render the patient euthyroid and close supervision by the physician is necessary for a period of years. Even in those patients successfully treated, a permanent remission is sustained in not more than 60 to 70 percent of patients. Although the surgical complications are avoided, a small percentage of patients are hypersensitive to propylthiouracil or methimazole and develop either skin rashes or a sufficient degree of leucopenia to require the discontinuation of the drug. Fortunately, these reactions are usually mild and disappear when the drug is withdrawn. Rare patients develop a lupus-like syndrome.

The choice of therapy in thyrotoxicosis must be individualized, taking into consideration any coexisting illnesses, the quality of thyroid surgery available, and the socioeconomic factors which play such a large role in determining the success of a prolonged medical regimen. The choice between subtotal thyroidectomy or definitive long-term medical therapy is usually best deferred for several months, since the initial management is the same, and, in any event, surgery is contraindicated until after the patient has been rendered euthyroid.

In severely toxic patients, reserpine by the intramuscular or oral route or propranolol is of great immediate value in initially alleviating the hyperexcitable state and tachycardia until such time as antithyroid drugs have sufficiently suppressed secretion of thyroid hormone. Reserpine depletes the stores of norepinephrine in nerve endings and produces sympathetic blockade but has no direct effect on thyroid function. The beta adrenergic blocking agent, propranolol, has been reported to be even more effective than reserpine, although we have had no personal experience with this drug.

In the U.S., propylthiouracil and methimazole are the most commonly used antithyroid drugs. Both are reducing agents which act in the thyroid by inhibiting the oxidation of iodide and thereby blocking the synthesis of thyroid hormones. They do not block the release of thyroid hormones into the circulation nor the effect of TSH on the "iodide pump." There is always a lag between the institution of antithyroid therapy and the achievement of a euthyroid state, since the biosynthetic block is not complete and the stores of preformed hormone must first be discharged. The rapidity of response to therapy correlates best with the initial size of the thyroid gland, rather than with the degree of thyrotoxicity. Those patients with a small gland and rapid thyroidal turnover usually exhibit marked improvement in several weeks, whereas in those patients with very large glands a satisfactory euthyroid state may not be achieved for many months.

The initial dosage of propylthiouracil varies between 300 and 600 mg daily in dosages spaced at 6 or 8 hour intervals. The dosage of methimazole is about one-tenth that of propylthiouracil. If these dosages are continued after the patient becomes euthyroid, the gland will enlarge further owing to added stimulation by pituitary thyrotropic hormone. This compensatory enlargement can be averted by titrating the dosage of antithyroid drug downward. Since this manipulation of dosage requires careful supervision of the patient at frequent intervals, it is the practice of some clinics to continue dosages of propylthiouracil as high as 300 to 400 mg daily for the duration of the illness and prevent the development of hypothyroidism and thyroid enlargement by adding thyroid hormone to the regimen as soon as the patient becomes euthyroid. Triiodothyronine is particularly useful for this purpose since it does not itself contribute to the PBI or thyroxine iodine concentration.

With dosages of 50 to 100 μg daily the PBI in adequately controlled patients on this combined regimen ranges between 1.5 and 2.8 μg/100 ml. Should the patient develop renewed symptoms of thyrotoxicosis with a low PBI, the dosage of T_3 can be lowered safely; however, renewed thyrotoxicosis in the face of a higher PBI suggests that the antithyroid drugs are either not being taken regularly or are being prescribed in too low a dosage.

Serious toxic reactions to propylthiouracil are rare, but may occur at any time in the course of therapy. Drug-induced leucopenia is often difficult to assess, since even without therapy patients with Graves' disease are prone to exhibit leucopenia and a relative lymphocytosis. It is less important to obtain blood counts at frequent intervals than to insure that the patient has a prompt hematologic investigation with every infection or unexplained fever. In those rare instances where severe granulocytopenia is attributable to the medication, corticosteroids often induce a prompt improvement in the blood picture. Although in some instances treatment can be resumed with methimazole, cross reactions are common. In such patients, surgery should be carried out after obtaining as complete a remission as possible with Lugol's solution. Sodium perchlorate in a dosage of 500 mg every 6 hours may be used as an alternative to Lugol's solution, but several fatal cases of aplastic anemia have occurred with this drug.

Skin rashes occur in about 5 percent of patients treated with propylthiouracil or methimazole. These usually occur early in the course of therapy and disappear when the drug is withheld. Often these rashes are mild and can be controlled with antihistamine drugs. As the patient becomes euthyroid the propensity toward allergic phenomena becomes less marked. Patients who are markedly hypersensitive to propylthiouracil and/or methimazole should receive alternative forms of therapy, as indicated above.

After all signs of thyrotoxicosis have disappeared, the best prognostic guide in judging when to discontinue therapy has been a marked diminution in the size of the thyroid and a loss of the resilient "bulging" quality which characterizes the hyperplastic gland. It is our policy not to discontinue therapy in less than two years. In many instances, treatment has been continued for three or four years before the gland has lost its hyperplastic character.

Although it is not known whether the definite management of thyrotoxicosis with antithyroid drugs has any influence on the fundamental disease process, it does permit the patient to remain euthyroid and in good health until such time as the disease has spontaneously run its course. When it is judged safe to discontinue therapy, propylthiouracil and T_3 are reduced in stepwise fashion over a period of 4 to 6 months. Although a mild rebound in thyrotoxic symptoms often occurs after discontinuing therapy, most patients settle down spontaneously and remain euthyroid without the need for reinstituting treatment.

Prior to the introduction of thiourea goitrogens in the treatment of thyrotoxicosis, it was customary to prepare patients for surgery by administering Lugol's solution. Large dosages of inorganic iodine not only block hormone biosynthesis but also inhibit the release of preformed hormone and render the gland less vascular. The effect on thyroidal status is more prompt than that of the thiourea goitrogens. Unfortunately, an iodine blockade can be maintained for only a limited period of time before escape occurs, and a fully euthyroid state is often not achieved. The use of inorganic iodine is therefore now reserved for severely toxic patients with impending thyroid storm and for the immediate preoperative preparation of patients who are to undergo subtotal thyroidectomy. In other patients, iodides may complicate long-term medical management by interfering with the involution of the gland.

Thyrotoxicosis of the Newborn

A rare form of thyrotoxicosis is that which occurs in infants born to mothers with Graves' disease. Uniformly, such infants have exhibited exophthalmos. The disorder is self-limited and disappears spontaneously after a period of approximately 3 months. LATS activity has been found in the plasma of these infants, and the disappearance of the activity has coincided with their recovery. It is significant that 7S gamma globulin traverses the placenta, whereas normal thyrotropin does not.

Infants with neonatal thyrotoxicosis are threatened by asphyxiation by tracheal compression as well as by the thyrotoxic state itself. We have observed one infant with permanent distortion of her orbits and another who died in thyroid storm 48 hours after birth. Although the disease is self-limited, the treatment should be based on the same principles governing the management of other forms of Graves' disease and guided by the urgency of the problem. In severe cases propylthiouracil, iodides, reserpine, propranolol, and vigorous supportive measures are indicated.

Thyroid Neoplasms in Childhood

Thyroid neoplasms should be suspected whenever a child is found to have a solitary mass with a consistency differing from the rest of the thyroid gland. A classification of thyroid neoplasms is found in Table 6.

In a review of 364 cases of thyroid cancer in children under 15 years of age, Winship found 72 percent to be predominantly of the papillary variety, 19 percent follicular adenocarcinomas, and 9 percent undifferentiated. These figures tend to be misleading, however, since many tumors were of mixed histologic types and with the passage of time there is frequently progression from one type of tumor into another.

TABLE 6. *Classification of Thyroid Neoplasms*

Benign adenomas
    Fetal or embryonal
    Follicular
    Papillary

Malignant tumors
    Differentiated carcinoma
        Papillary adenocarcinoma
        Follicular adenocarcinoma
        Hürthle cell carcinoma

Undifferentiated carcinoma
    Small cell
    Giant cell

Infiltrations by lymphomas and other tumors arising elsewhere

The ratio of females to males in children with thyroid cancer is only 2:1, in contrast to the much higher preponderance of females with thyroid enlargement from other causes. Nodular enlargement in the male is somewhat more likely to be cancerous than in the female. In either sex, however, a solitary nodule during the early decades of life has a much greater chance of being malignant than in older age groups. Estimates of the incidence of cancer in children with thyroid nodules have varied between 20 and 52 percent. About three-fourths of all cancers have spread to regional lymph nodes by the time that the initial diagnosis is made.

ETIOLOGY. In experimental animals, thyroid neoplasia can be induced by ionizing radiation or by any influence that leads to prolonged stimulation by thyrotropic hormone. These factors are often synergistic, since in the presence of TSH stimulation a smaller dosage of radiation will induce neoplasia than would otherwise be required. Thyroid tumors can be induced far more readily in young animals than in older ones.

It is now clear that the most important predisposing cause for the development of thyroid cancer in children and young adults is irradiation of the thyroid gland during infancy and childhood. In Winship's series of children with thyroid cancer, 80 percent had a history of prior x-ray treatment. In most instances this had been administered during early infancy to the upper mediastinum and neck for control of an "enlarged" thymus gland. Cancer also occurred following the irradiation of hypertrophied tonsils or adenoids in older children and adolescents. The average time which elapsed between the irradiation and the recognition of the tumor was 10.9 years. Adults who receive similar types of irradiation have not been shown to have an increased incidence of thyroid tumors.

DIAGNOSIS. Children with Hashimoto's struma frequently have a firm irregular gland with marked accentuation of the normal lobular pattern. The characteristic picture associated with this clinical condition, however, is such that the differentiation from a neoplasm is not difficult for a physician experienced in thyroid palpation. Resection of such a gland can often be avoided by confirming the clinical impression with a simple needle biopsy or small open biopsy.

A scan of the neck following the administration of ^{131}I is rarely decisive, since a solitary thyroid mass in any case requires pathologic examination. It is true, however, that a gland containing an isolated "cold nodule" in a scan is more likely to harbor a neoplasm than if the radioactivity is more uniformly distributed. **TREATMENT.** Since solitary nodules occur rarely in childhood, and because a high percentage prove to be malignant, it is recommended that every child with such enlargement be submitted to simple removal of the affected lobe. No further surgery is necessary if the mass is not a malignant tumor. Since papillary and/or follicular cancers are prone to involve multifocal sites in the thyroid gland, total lobectomy should be carried out on the side of origin and as much of the contralateral lobe excised as is compatible with preservation of the parathyroid glands and recurrent laryngeal nerves. Although accessible regional nodes should be removed, a mutilating neck dissection is rarely, if ever, warranted. It is important that following surgery the patient be maintained on full substitution dosages of exogenous thyroid hormone to protect the gland from any further stimulation by thyrotropic hormone. In those instances where metastases have already occurred, therapeutic dosages of ^{131}I should be administered following surgical removal of the local lesions in the neck. Frequently, metastatic lesions may be induced temporarily to take up radioactive iodine more avidly by the administration of exogenous TSH or propylthiouracil. Some thyroid surgeons no longer feel that it is necessary to remove all of the neoplastic tissue surgically and prefer to treat the patient with full substitution doses of exogenous thyroid indefinitely. In those patients with more aggressive forms of thyroid cancer, however, intensive radiation therapy, both externally and with ^{131}I, is employed.

PROGNOSIS. The prognosis in those children with proved thyroid cancer is far better than in most other types of childhood cancer. The course is usually an indolent one, with long periods in which there is little progression. In most instances, spread is confined to regional lymph nodes with little tendency to metastasize via the blood. This is particularly true of papillary carcinomas, which constitute the largest group occurring in chldhood. Cases of follicular adenocarcinoma, particularly of the Hürthle cell variety, however, tend to metastasize early to the lungs and bone.

References

General

Means, J. H., DeGroot, L. J., and Stanbury, J. B. The Thyroid and Its Diseases, 3rd ed. New York, McGraw-Hill Book Co., 1963.

Werner, S. C. The Thyroid: A Fundamental and Clinical Text, 2nd ed. New York, Harper and Row, Publ., 1962.

Wilkins, L. The Diagnosis and Treatment of Endocrine Diseases in Childhood and Adolescence, 3rd ed. Springfield, Ill., Charles C Thomas, Publ., 1965.

Physiology of Iodine Metabolism

Braverman, L., Ingbar, S., and Sterling, K. Conversion of thyroxine (T_4) to triiodothyronine (T_3) in athyreotic human subjects. J. Clin. Invest., 49:855, 1970.

Brown-Grant, K. The hypothalamus and the thyroid gland. Brit. Med. Bull., 16:165, 1960.

Danowski, T. S., Johnston, S. Y., Price, W. C., McKelvy, M., Stevenson, S. S., and McCluskey, E. R. Protein-bound iodine in infants from birth to one year of age. Pediatrics, 7:240, 1951.

Einhorn, J., and Larsson, L. Studies on the effect of thyrotropin on human thyroid function. J. Clin. Endocr., 19:28, 1959.

Fisher, D. A., Oddie, T. H., and Wait, J. C. Thyroid function tests: Findings in Arkansas children and young adults. Amer. J. Dis. Child., 107:282, 1964.

Greer, M. A. The effect on endogenous thyroid activity of feeding desiccated thyroid to normal human subjects. New Eng. J. Med., 244:385, 1951.

Harrison, T. S. Adrenal medullary and thyroid relationships. Physiol. Rev., 44:161, 1964.

Hennen, G., Pierce, J. G., and Freychet, P. Human chorionic thyrotropin: Further characterization and study of its secretion during pregnancy. J. Clin. Endocr., 29:581, 1969.

Ingbar, S. H. Simultaneous measurement of the iodide concentrating and protein binding capacities of the normal and hyperfunctioning thyroid gland. J. Clin. Endocr., 15:238, 1955.

—— Braverman, L. E., Dawber, N. A., and Lee, G. Y. A new method for measuring the free hormone in human serum and an analysis of the factors that influence its concentration. J. Clin. Invest., 44:1679, 1965.

—— and Freinkel, N. Regulation of the peripheral metabolism of the thyroid hormones. Recent Progr. Hormone Res., 16:353, 1960.

Klee, C. B., and Sokoloff, L. Mitochondrial differences in mature and immature brain; Influence on rate of amino acid incorporation into protein and responses to thyroxine. J. Neurochem., 11:709, 1964.

Mitchell, M. L., Harden, A. B., and O'Rourke, M. E. The in vitro resin sponge uptake of triiodothyronine I^{131} from serum in thyroid disease and in pregnancy. J. Clin. Endocr., 20:1474, 1960.

Murphy, B. E. P., and Pattee, C. J. Determination of thyroxine utilizing the property of protein-binding. J. Clin. Endocr., 24:187, 1964.

Oddie, T. H., and Fisher, D. A. Protein-bound iodine level during childhood and adolescence. J. Clin. Endocr., 27:89, 1967.

Odell, W. D., Wilber, J. F., and Utiger, R. D. Studies of thyrotropin physiology by means of radioimmunoassay. Recent Progr. Hormone Res., 23:47, 1967.

Pittman, J. A., Dailey, G. E., and Beschi, R. J. Changing normal values for thyroidal radioiodine uptake. New Eng. J. Med., 280:1431, 1969.

Reiss, J. M., Reiss, M., and Wyatt, A. Action of thyroid hormones on brain metabolism of newborn rats. Proc. Soc. Exp. Biol. Med., 93:19, 1956.

Sterling, K., Bellebarba, D., Newman, E. S., and Brenner, M. A. Determination of triiodothyronine concentration in human serum. J. Clin. Invest., 48:1150, 1969.

Wolff, E. C., and Wolff, J. The mechanism of action of thyroid hormones. In Pitt-Rivers, R., and Trotter, W. R., eds., The Thyroid Gland. Washington, Butterworths, 1964, Vol. 1.

THYROID FUNCTION IN THE FETUS AND NEONATE

Carr, E. A., Beierwaltes, W. H., Raman, G., Dodson, V. N., Tanton, J., Betts, J. S., and Stambaugh, R. A. The effect of maternal thyroid function on fetal thyroid function and development. J. Clin. Endocr., 19: 1, 1959.

DeNayer, Ph., Malvaux, P., Van Den Schrieck, H. G., Beckers, C., and DeVisscher, M. Free thyroxine in maternal and cord blood. J. Clin. Endocr., 26:233, 1966.

Dussault, J., Row, V. V., Lickrish, G., and Volpe, R. Studies of serum triiodothyronine concentration in maternal and cord blood: Transfer of triiodothyronine across the human placenta. J. Clin. Endocr., 29:595, 1969.

Fisher, D. A., Lehman, H., and Lackey, C. Placental transport of thyroxine. J. Clin. Endocr., 24:393, 1964.

―――― and Odell, W. D. Acute release of thyrotropin in the newborn. J. Clin. Invest., 48:1670, 1969.

―――― Odell, W. D., Hobel, C. J., and Garza, R. Thyroid function in the term fetus. Pediatrics, 44:526, 1969.

Freiesleben, E., and Kjerulf-Jensen, K. Effect of thiouracil derivatives on fetuses and infants. J. Clin. Endocr., 7:47, 1947.

French, F. S., and Van Wyk, J. J. Fetal hypothyroidism. J. Pediat., 64:589, 1964.

Grumbach, M. M., and Werner, S. C. Transfer of thyroid hormone across the human placenta at term. J. Clin. Endocr., 16:1392, 1956.

Marks, J. F., Hamlin, M., and Zack, P. Neonatal thyroid function: II. Free thyroxine in infancy. J. Pediatrics, 68:559, 1966.

Michener, W. M., Tauxe, N., and Hayles, A. B. Capacity of thyroxine binding globulin to bind triiodothyronine and thyroxine in maternal and cord blood. Pediatrics, 29:369, 1962.

Parkin, G., and Greene, J. A. Pregnancy occurring in cretinism and in juvenile and adult myxedema. J. Clin. Endocr., 3:466, 1943.

Raiti, S., Holzman, G. B., Scott, R. L., and Blizzard, R. M. Evidence for the placental transfer of triiodothyronine in human beings. New Eng. J. Med., 277: 456, 1967.

Robin, N. I., Refetoff, S., Fang, F., and Selenkow, H. A. Parameters of thyroid function in maternal and cord serum at term pregnancy. J. Clin. Endocr., 29:1276, 1969.

Schultz, M. A., Forsander, J. B., Chez, R. A., and Hutchinson, D. L. The bidirectional placental transfer of ^{131}I 3:5:3′ triiodothyronine in the Rhesus monkey. Pediatrics, 35:743, 1965.

Shepard, T. H. Onset of function in the human fetal thyroid: Biochemical and radioautographic studies from organ culture. J. Clin. Endocr., 27:945, 1967.

―――― Andersen, H. J., and Andersen, H. The human fetal thyroid: I. Its weight in relation to body weight, crown rump length, foot length and estimated gestation age. Anat. Rec., 148:123, 1964.

HYPOTHYROIDISM AND GOITER

Andersen, H. J. Studies of hypothyroidism in children. Acta Paediat., 50 (Suppl. 125), 1961.

Blizzard, R. M., and Chandler, R. W. The history and present concepts of autoimmunization in thyroid disease. J. Pediat., 57:399, 1960.

Boyle, J. A., Thompson, J. A., Murray, P. C., Fulton, S., Nicol, J., and McGirr, E. M. Phenomenon of iodide inhibition in various states of thyroid function with observations on one mechanism of its occurrence. J. Clin. Endocr., 25:1255, 1965.

Chamberlain, J. L. Thyroid enlargement probably induced by cobalt: A report of three cases. J. Pediat., 59:81, 1961.

Choufoer, J. C., van Rijn, M. H., and Querido, A. Endemic goiter in Western New Guinea. II. Clinical picture incidence and pathogenesis of endemic cretinism. J. Clin. Endocr., 25:385, 1965.

DeGroot, L. J., and Stanbury, J. B. The syndrome of congenital goiter with butanol insoluble serum iodine. Amer. J. Med., 27:586, 1959.

Falliers, C. J. Goiter and thyroid dysfunction following the use of iodides in asthmatic children. Amer. J. Dis. Child., 99:428, 1960.

Florsheim, W. H., Dowling, J. T., Meister, L., and Bodfish, R. E. Familial elevation of serum thyroxine-binding capacity. J. Clin. Endocr., 22:735, 1962.

Fraser, G. R., Morgans, W. E., and Trotter, W. The syndrome of sporadic goiter and congenital deafness. Quart. J. Med., 29:279, 1960.

French, F. S., and Van Wyk, J. J. Etiology and pathophysiology of congenital hypothyroidism. In Crispel, K. R., ed., Current Concepts in Hypothyroidism. Oxford, Pergamon Press, 1963, p. 17.

Galina, M. P., Avnet, N. L., and Einhorn, A. Iodides during pregnancy, An apparent cause of neonatal death. New Eng. J. Med., 267:1124, 1962.

Kusakabe, T., and Miyake, T. Defective deiodination of I^{131} labeled 1-diiodotyrosine in patients with simple goiter. J. Clin. Endocr., 23:132, 1963.

―――― and Miyake, T. Thyroidal deiodination defect in three sisters with simple goiter. J. Clin. Endocr., 24: 456, 1964.

LeBoeuf, G., Bongiovanni, A. M., Steiker, D. D., and Eberlein, W. R. Immunologic and thyroid function studies in euthyroid children with goiter. J. Pediat., 58:477, 1961.

Lissitzky, S., Codaccioni, J-L., Bismuth, J., and Depieds, R. Congenital goiter with hypothyroidism and iodo-serum albumin replacing thyroglobulin. J. Clin. Endocr., 27:185, 1967.

Little, B., Meador, C. K., Cunningham, R., and Pittman, J. A. "Cryptothyroidism," the major cause of sporadic "athyreotic" cretinism. J. Clin. Endocr., 25:1529, 1965.

Marshall, J. S., Levy, R. P., and Steinberg, A. G. Human thyroxine-binding globulin deficiency. A genetic study. New Eng. J. Med., 274:1469, 1966.

McGirr, E. M., and Hutchinson, J. H. Dysgenesis of the thyroid gland as a cause of cretinism and juvenile myxedema. J. Clin. Endocr., 15:668, 1955.

Murray, I. P. C., McGirr, E. M., Thomson, J. A., and Hutchison, J. H. The role of thyroid dysgenesis in non-goitrous cretinism and juvenile myxedema. Med. J. Aust., 2:6, 1966.

———— Thomson, J. A., McGirr, E. M., Macdonald, E. M., Kennedy, J. S., and McLennan, I. Unusual familial goiter associated with intrathyroidal calcification. J. Clin. Endocr., 26:1039, 1966.

Rallison, M. L., Kumagai, L. F., and Tyler, F. H. Goitrous hypothyroidism induced by amino-glutethimide, anticonvulsant drug. J. Clin. Endocr., 27:265, 1967.

Refetoff, S., DeWind, L. T., and DeGroot, L. J. Familial syndrome combining deaf-mutism, stippled epiphyses, goiter and abnormally high PBI: Possible target organ refractoriness to thyroid hormone. J. Clin. Endocr., 27:279, 1967.

Sedvall, G., Jönsson, B., and Petterson, V. Evidence of an altered thyroid function in man during treatment with lithium carbonate. Acta Psychiat. Scand. (Suppl.), 207:59-66, 1969.

Stanbury, J. B. Familial goiter. In Stanbury, J. B., Wyngaarden, J. B., and Fredrickson, D. S., eds., The Metabolic Basis of Inherited Disease, 2nd ed. New York, McGraw-Hill Book Co., 1966, pp. 215-257.

———— and Chapman, E. M. Congenital hypothyroidism with goiter: Absence of an iodide concentrating mechanism. Lancet, 1:1162, 1960.

Stewart, R. D. H., and Murray, I. P. C. An evaluation of the perchlorate discharge test. J. Clin. Endocr., 26:1050, 1966.

Strickland, A. L., Macfie, J. A., Van Wyk, J. J., and French, F. S. Ectopic thyroid glands simulating thyroglossal duct cysts. J.A.M.A., 208:307, 1969.

Van Wyk, J. J., and Grumbach, M. M. Syndrome of precocious menstruation and galactorrhea in juvenile hypothyroidism: An example of hormonal overlap in pituitary feedback. J. Pediat., 57:416, 1960.

———— Wynn, J. O., Deiss, W. P., Arnold, M. B., and Graham, J. B. Genetic studies in a family with "simple" goiter. J. Clin. Endocr., 22:399, 1962.

Volpé, R., Row, V. V., Webster, B. R., Johnston, M. W., and Ezrin, C. Studies of iodine metabolism in Hashimoto's thyroiditis. J. Clin. Endocr., 25:593, 1965.

Vought, R. L., London, W. T., and Stebbing, G. E. T. Endemic goiter in northern Virginia. J. Clin. Endocr., 27:1381, 1967.

Weaver, D. K., Batsakis, J. G., and Nishiyama, R. H. Relationship of iodine to "lymphocytic goiters." Arch. Surg., 98:183, 1969.

Wolff, J., Thompson, R. H., and Robbins, J. Congenital goitrous cretinism due to the absence of iodide-concentrating ability. J. Clin. Endocr., 24:699, 1964.

HYPERTHYROIDISM

Buchanan, W. W., Alexander, W. D., Crooks, J., Koutras, D. A., Wayne, E. J., Anderson, J. R., and Goudie, R. B. Association of thyrotoxicosis and autoimmune thyroiditis. Brit. Med. J., 1:843, 1961.

Elsas, L. J., Whittemore, R., and Burrow, G. N. Maternal and neonatal Graves' disease. J.A.M.A., 200:250, 1967.

Hayles, A. B., Kennedy, R. L., Beahrs, O. H., and Woolner, L. B. Exophthalmic goiter in children. J. Clin. Endocr., 19:138, 1959.

Hermann, H. T., and Quarton, G. C. Physiological changes and psychogenesis in thyroid hormone disorders. J. Clin. Endocr., 25:327, 1965.

Hung, W., Wilkins, L., and Blizzard, R. Medical therapy of thyrotoxicosis in children. Pediatrics, 30:17, 1962.

Kriss, J. P., Pleshakov, V., and Chien, J. R. Isolation and identification of the long-acting thyroid stimulator and its relation to hyperthyroidism and circumscribed pretibial myxedema. J. Clin. Endocr., 24:1005, 1964.

Lipman, L. M., Green, D. E., Snyder, N. J., Nelson, J. C., and Solomon, D. H. Relationship of long-acting thyroid stimulator to the clinical features and course of Graves' disease. Amer. J. Med., 43:486, 1967.

McKenzie, J. M. Neonatal Graves' disease. J. Clin. Endocr., 24:660, 1964.

———— Review: Pathogenesis of Graves' disease: Role of the long-acting thyroid stimulator. J. Clin. Endocr., 25:424, 1965.

Saxena, K. M., Crawford, J. D., and Talbot, N. B. Childhood thyrotoxicosis: A long term perspective. Brit. Med. J., 2:1153, 1964.

Sheline, G. E., Lindsay, S., and Bell, H. G. Occurrence of thyroid nodules in children following therapy with radioiodine for hyperthyroidism. J. Clin. Endocr., 19:127, 1959.

Sunshine, P., Kusumoto, H., and Kriss, J. P. Survival time of circulating long-acting thyroid stimulator in neonatal thyrotoxicosis: Implications for diagnosis and therapy of the disorders. Pediatrics, 36:869, 1965.

Thomson, J. A., and Riley, I. D. Neonatal thyrotoxicosis associated with maternal hypothyroidism. Lancet, 1:635, 1966.

Vinik, A. I., Pimstone, B. L., and Hoffenberg, R. Sympathetic nervous system blocking in hyperthyroidism. J. Clin. Endocr., 28:725, 1968.

Werner, S. C., and Spooner, M. A new and simple test for hyperthyroidism employing l-triiodothyronine and the twenty-four hour I^{131} uptake method. Bull. N.Y. Acad. Med., 31:137, 1955.

THYROID NEOPLASMS

Raventos, A., and Winship, T. The latent interval for thyroid cancer following irradiation. Radiology, 83:501, 1964.

Thomas, C. G., and Jenkins, S. G. Hormonal and isotope measures in thyroid carcinoma. Ann. Surg., 157:960, 1963.

Winship, T., and Rosvoll, R. V. Childhood thyroid carcinoma. Cancer, 14:734, 1961.

16.4

ADRENAL CORTEX

WALTER R. EBERLEIN

Structure

The adrenal gland in man consists of two endocrine organs which exist as separate structures in lower species: an outer cortex of mesodermal origin and an inner medulla derived, like all chromaffin tissue, from ectoderm. While treated here as separate glands of internal secretion, they are known to be mutually involved in endocrine homeostasis, each conditioning the cellular response to the hormone secreted by the other. This relationship may even extend to an effect

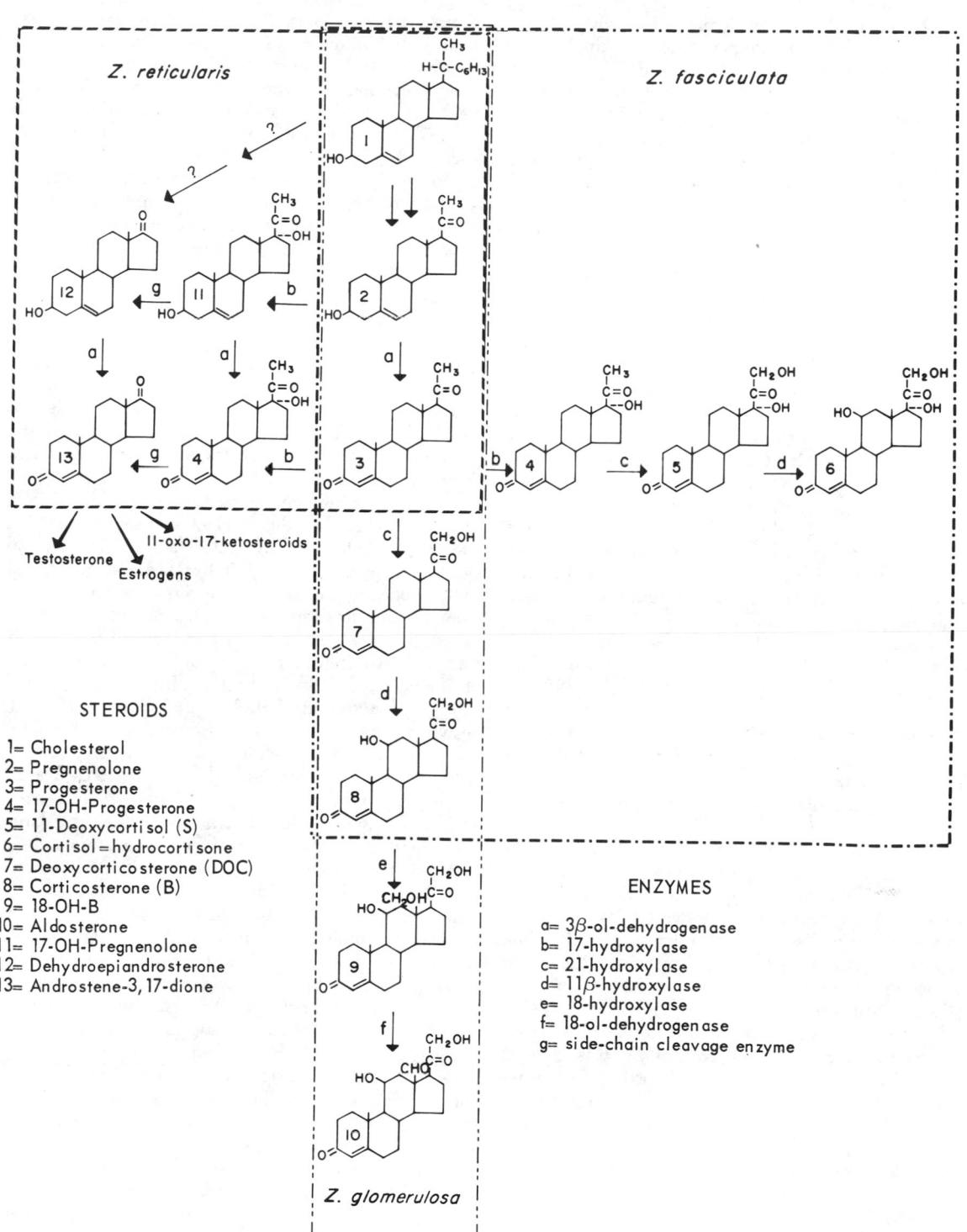

STEROIDS

1= Cholesterol
2= Pregnenolone
3= Progesterone
4= 17-OH-Progesterone
5= 11-Deoxycortisol (S)
6= Cortisol = hydrocortisone
7= Deoxycorticosterone (DOC)
8= Corticosterone (B)
9= 18-OH-B
10= Aldosterone
11= 17-OH-Pregnenolone
12= Dehydroepiandrosterone
13= Androstene-3,17-dione

ENZYMES

a= 3β-ol-dehydrogenase
b= 17-hydroxylase
c= 21-hydroxylase
d= 11β-hydroxylase
e= 18-hydroxylase
f= 18-ol-dehydrogenase
g= side-chain cleavage enzyme

Fig. 21. Secretions of the adrenal cortex.

upon the concentration or activity of enzymes within the adrenal itself.

During fetal life and at birth, in man and certain other primates, the adrenal differs strikingly from the adult gland in size, structure, and apparently in function. The adrenal at birth is about 10 to 20 times the size of the adult gland. More than 75 percent of its bulk is contributed by a broad layer of densely packed, histologically active cells which constitute the fetal zone. This zone is surrounded by a thin rim of cells which form the neocortex, while the innermost adrenal medullary tissue is scant. Within the first few days after birth, the enormous fetal zone begins to involute. This process of cell necrosis and phagocytosis accelerates rapidly during the second week of life, leading to virtual disappearance of the fetal zone usually by the fifth or sixth week after birth, although in some infants remnants persist until 1 year of age. As the fetal zone involutes, the neocortex extends by a process of downgrowth and differentiation to form the permanent structure of the adult adrenal cortex. The latter consists of a peripheral zona glomerulosa, an inner zona fasciculata, and, adjacent to a now enlarged medulla, the innermost zona reticularis. These histologic distinctions are known to reflect underlying biochemical differences among the three cortical zones, which in turn are dependent upon the concentration of specific enzymes regulating the synthesis of steroids in each.

Secretory Function

The zona glomerulosa is believed to elaborate aldosterone by the biosynthetic sequence illustrated in Figure 21. The rate of aldosterone secretion by the zona is apparently controlled via renin-angiotensin release from the kidney (Sec. 21.6).

The zona fasciculata in man, primarily concerned with cortisol (hydrocortisone) synthesis, is plentifully supplied with 17α-hydroxylase, in addition to the 21-hydroxylase and 11β-hydroxylase found in the zona glomerulosa. It is of interest that the zona fasciculata synthesizes both corticosterone (the major adrenocortical steroid in certain species) and 18-hydroxydesoxycorticosterone, but lacks an 18-dehydrogenase and does not form aldosterone. As far as is known, the secretion of cortisol by this zone is regulated via the level of unbound cortisol circulating in the blood. The amount controls the output from the hypothalamus of a peptide, corticotropin-releasing factor, which, acting upon the anterior pituitary, causes increased synthesis and discharge of ACTH.

Much less is known about the function of the zona reticularis. Its main secretory product appears to be dehydroepiandrosterone sulfate, implying that either this zone is rich in a side-chain cleavage enzyme or that an alternate biosynthetic pathway to this steroid exists. Testosterone, as well as estrogens, can be synthesized from dehydroepiandrosterone in

the adrenal. Possibly the altered function of the adrenal at adolescence, which leads to the production of androgenic steroids, the so-called adrenarche, may involve the induction of enzymes in the adrenal or elsewhere in the body which favor the conversion of dehydroepiandrosterone to testosterone. The tropic hormone, indeed the homeostatic mechanism, which regulates the secretory function of this zone, remains undefined (Fig. 21).

Very little is yet known about the secretory function of the adrenal cortex in intrauterine life. It has long been recognized that the fetal zone of the adrenal cortex fails to develop in the anencephalic monster who lacks an intact hypothalamic-pituitary axis. Recently, it has been reported that the adrenal atrophy characteristic of this state can be overcome by the administration of zinc ACTH after birth. While these two observations as well as others strongly suggest that the intrauterine development of the fetal zone is dependent upon the secretion of ACTH by the fetal pituitary, they do not exclude the possibility that some other tropic factor is operative during fetal life.

The measurement of steroids in umbilical vein blood indicates that the level of cortisol-like steroids (corticoids) is lower on the fetal than on the maternal side of the placenta, and it has been demonstrated that isotopically labeled cortisol can cross the placenta from mother to fetus. This indication of apparently lowered cortisol secretion by the fetal adrenal cortex stands in striking contrast not only to the large size of the adrenal at this age but also to the elevated levels of ketosteroids found in umbilical cord blood. In vitro experiments have suggested that the fetal adrenal is relatively deficient in steroid 3β-hydroxydehydrogenase activity, and this has been confirmed by histochemical staining techniques. It has been shown also that umbilical cord blood contains a large assortment of unusual steroids which are apparently secreted as a result of lowered steroid 3β-hydroxydehydrogenase activity in the fetal zone of the adrenal. Present evidence suggests that the placenta may metabolize some of these steroids to form progesterone, and especially estrogens, which are excreted in large amount by the gravid female as well as by the newborn infant during the first few days of life.

Such observations do not establish either the underlying cause of the 3β-hydroxysteroid dehydrogenase deficiency characteristic of the fetal zone of the adrenal cortex or the biologic action of the hormones consequently secreted by it. Although involution of the fetal zone during the first weeks of life leads to no evident disturbance in the newborn, it may not follow that the steroids produced by it play an unimportant role in fetal metabolic processes. The recent demonstration of the function of the thymus during fetal life, postnatally an expendable organ, emphasizes the need for much greater study of the effect of intrauterine endocrine gland function upon postnatal health and disease.

Action and Metabolism of Adrenocortical Hormones
(See also Sec. 16.5)

Hypoadrenalism

Addison's Disease

ALFRED M. BONGIOVANNI

The term *mineralocorticoid* is applied to such steroids as aldosterone and desoxycorticosterone which act upon the renal tubule and the sweat and salivary glands to produce sodium retention and potassium exchange, thus playing an important role in the regulation of salt and water balance. *Glucocorticoids,* among them hydrocortisone and cortisone, act to inhibit amino acid incorporation into protein and thus stimulate gluconeogenesis, which has been termed either an antianabolic or catabolic effect. Other observable effects are growth inhibition, osteoporosis, bone marrow stimulation (neutrophilia), and thymic involution. In larger doses these steroids suppress all phases of the inflammatory response of body tissues, which has led to their widespread pharmacologic use. Although the protein anabolic effects produced by potent *androgens,* such as testosterone, have been well studied, the biologic action of dehydroepiandrosterone, one of the main secretory products of the adrenal cortex, is largely obscure. It is known that adrenal androgens are responsible in part for the development of pubic hair in the female at adolescence and of axillary hair in both sexes.

The steroid hormones secreted by the adrenal cortex circulate in the blood attached to carrier proteins to reach their site of action—in effect, all tissues of the body. The steroids are metabolized in the same basic manner in the body, primarily by the liver. Degradation consists of saturation of double bonds, which usually causes loss of all biologic activity, the reduction of ketones to hydroxyl groups, and finally conjugation with either sulfuric or glucuronic acid. The salts of the esters formed, which are more water-soluble than the parent compounds, are conveyed in the blood to the kidney for excretion. Recent evidence indicates that certain steroids, notably dehydroepiandrosterone, are secreted by the adrenal already conjugated with sulfuric acid, a biologic fact of unknown significance in postnatal life.

The output of steroid hormones by the adrenal cortex is regulated by variable tropic hormone stimulation of the adrenal, which is in turn dependent upon the extent of steroid protein binding in the blood and by the rapidity of hepatic inactivation. Hence, abnormal secretory activity of the adrenal cortex may reflect a disturbance of an extraadrenal controlling mechanism, rather than primary adrenocortical disease. It has been calculated that the adrenal secretes 15 to 20 mg of cortisol/m² and 20 to 150 μg of aldosterone/m² daily.

Chronic adrenal insufficiency is a relatively rare disease in childhood, with insidious onset and of uncertain cause. Formerly it was attributable to generalized tuberculosis or, more rarely, histoplasmosis or blastomycosis, which destroyed the entire gland and produced symptoms indicative of a lack of all three types of hormones secreted by the adrenal cortex. With the decline in morbidity from tuberculosis, the sporadic cases of acquired adrenal insufficiency encountered are usually due to what has been considered primary adrenal atrophy. Most probably the histologic picture represents the end result of a preceding inflammatory or autoimmune disorder. Some subjects have had an influenzalike disease weeks or months before the gradual onset of the symptoms and signs suggestive of primary adrenocortical insufficiency. In many, antibodies to adrenal antigens can be detected in the blood.

Early in the disease few symptoms can be elicited. In more severe cases there may be complaints of weakness, fatigability, anorexia, and recurrent bouts of nausea and vomiting, which are serious symptoms of impending crisis. These may alternate with symptoms of hypoglycemia (hunger). Frequently, there is no history of salt craving. However, this bland state of affairs may change suddenly even under the minor stress of an infection or injury into acute adrenocortical insufficiency. An adrenal crisis is characterized by shock, stupor or coma, profound hypotension, cold clammy skin, feeble pulse, anuria, and occasionally diarrhea. Hyperpyrexia and convulsions due to hypoglycemia can occur and may suggest encephalitis.

In children, as in adults, the least variable early sign of this disease is increased pigmentation of the skin, especially marked on the extensor surfaces of the hands, elbows, and knees. This pigmentation often resembles a dirty skin rather than tanning from exposure to sunlight and is associated with dark freckles, with buccal or gingival pigmentation, and not infrequently with areas of vitiligo elsewhere on the body. The skin pigmentation is apparently due to the melanophore-stimulating hormonelike effect of the excessive ACTH secretion by the pituitary, as the result of decreased cortisol production by the adrenal as well as increased secretion of MSH (melanocyte-stimulating hormone). In addition to pigmentation there may be systemic and postural hypotension of variable degree. Weight loss is common, but gross malnutrition is rare except in the late stages of the untreated disease. The heart size is usually not remarkable in children, in contrast to the characteristic thin cardiac silhouette seen in adult subjects.

At the time of initial diagnosis the patient should be examined carefully for evidence of tuberculosis. The coexistence of hypoparathyroidism should be sought for, especially if the patient has moniliasis or alopecia. Addison's disease has also been found in association with diabetes mellitus, hypothyroidism, chronic lymphocytic thyroiditis, and, extremely rarely in childhood, pernicious anemia.

In the chronic stage of the disease in children the laboratory findings characteristic of severe adrenal insufficiency are often lacking: lowering of the serum sodium and elevation of the serum potassium levels, acidosis, hypoglycemia, either fasting or following a glucose tolerance test, and elevation of the blood urea nitrogen level. In some patients, the serum calcium level may be elevated. With the exception of the sodium-potassium alteration, none of these changes is pathognomonic of Addison's disease. The diagnosis rests upon the demonstration of an impaired ability of the adrenal to respond to ACTH stimulation or to salt restriction. A failure of the blood cortisol level to rise or of the urinary excretion of corticoids to increase in response to intravenous or intramuscular administration of ACTH is strong evidence of deficient adrenal reserve. A low urinary cortisol excretion is not by itself diagnostic of primary adrenal insufficiency. The excretion of 17-ketosteroids by the preadolescent child is normally minimal, and assay for these is of little diagnostic help.

The assessment of mineralocorticoid secretion by the adrenal is technically much more difficult. Gross deficiency of aldosterone production can be demonstrated by the failure of the patient to maintain a normal serum sodium level after three or four days on a diet containing 10 mEq or less of sodium, but lesser degrees of insufficiency can only be determined by demonstrating a failure of the urinary aldosterone excretion, or aldosterone production rate, to rise on salt restriction. The failure of the Addisonian to excrete a water load promptly is an abnormal response due to cortisol rather than aldosterone deficiency. The formerly much used Cutler-Power-Wilder test is rarely employed at present, because of both its relative nonspecificity and potential danger.

Fortunately, most children with this disease are restored to seeming health on oral glucocorticoid medication alone. All should be encouraged to use table salt liberally, especially during the summer months. An occasional patient who demonstrates a persistently low serum sodium or elevated potassium level, salt craving, or postural hypotension may require a change to mineralocorticoid *and* cortisol substitution therapy. The most convenient glucocorticoid to use is oral hydrocortisone or cortisone acetate, the dose varying from 15 to 25 mg daily depending on body size, given preferably at about 8- to 12-hour intervals. The newer cortisol analogs, designed to cause less salt retention or even to promote sodium excretion, should be avoided. The most potent therapeutic min-

eralocorticoid available at present is 9α-fluoro-hydrocortisone, a dose of 0.05 to 0.1 mg orally daily being sufficient at all ages.

Because of the ease with which this disease may escape control and the rapidity of development of the Addisonian crisis, all patients should be treated promptly for even mild infections with appropriate antibiotics. Intramuscular cortisone acetate as well as antibiotics should be given prior to dental extractions and elective surgery.

The treatment of acute adrenal insufficiency requires both intravenous and intramuscular administration of hydrocortisone (50 to 100 mg daily), intramuscular desoxycorticosterone acetate (DOCA) (1 to 2 mg daily), intravenous normal saline or saline solutions containing glucose, antibiotics, and other indicated supportive measures. Response to therapy is measured by following the serum electrolytes and blood glucose levels, as well as the state of consciousness. Too zealous salt and mineralocorticoid therapy may cause death from edema, hypertension, and cardiac failure. The amount of salt given should be reduced promptly with the earliest evidence of the development of presacral or pedal edema or of pulmonary rales.

Other Types of Adrenal Insufficiency

Adrenal insufficiency is rarely evident in children with primary hypopituitarism but can occur in such subjects upon treatment with desiccated thyroid or during severe stress. Acute adrenal insufficiency during the course of fulminant septicemias—most commonly meningococcemia, the so-called Waterhouse-Friderichsen syndrome—has been suspected frequently and treated, but relatively rarely documented as the primary cause of the peripheral vascular collapse and death in these subjects. While the value of steroid treatment remains debatable and has been held by some even to be injurious, it would appear safe to treat patients in whom the diagnosis is strongly suspected with at least moderate doses of hydrocortisone, such as 20 to 50 mg of cortisol phosphate, intravenously.

Adrenal insufficiency develops during the first weeks of life in infants due to bilateral congenital adrenal *hypo*plasia. In certain reported cases the pituitary has also been found to be atrophic, suggesting a lack of ACTH stimulation of the adrenal cortex during intrauterine or early postnatal life. In others apparently only the adrenal is abnormal, the gland weighing one-tenth or less the normal amount. Histologic examination discloses a rudimentary cortex consisting of irregularly arranged large cells, which resemble the cells of the fetal zone. A form of isolated cortisol deficiency apparently due to end-organ unresponsiveness of the zona fasciculata to ACTH has been described. Both X-linked recessive and autosomal recessive forms of inheritance are known. The infant is characteristically darkly pigmented from birth. Although some infants develop seizures during the first week of life, due to hypoglycemia, in others the clinical picture is one of poor weight gain, recurrent vomiting, which may be projectile and suggest pyloric stenosis, pallor, sweating, cyanosis, and eventually loss of consciousness and shock. The condition can be distinguished from congenital adrenal hyperplasia by means of urinary or plasma steroid assays. In congenital adrenal hypoplasia the serum electrolytes are characteristically normal during the first weeks of life.

In addition to those forms of congenital adrenal *hyper*plasia which are associated with adrenal insufficiency due to deficient secretion of cortisol and aldosterone (see below), two isolated defects of aldosterone biosynthesis have been described (familial hypoaldosteronism). In one there is deficient 18-hydroxylation of corticosterone and, in the other, defective dehydrogenation of 18-hydroxycorticosterone. Both result in a salt-losing syndrome and are transmitted as an autosomal recessive trait.

Undoubtedly, the most common type of acute adrenal insufficiency seen at present is in children who have received long-term steroid therapy for nephrosis, rheumatic carditis, rheumatoid arthritis, or bronchial asthma. On exposure to adequate stress, signs of adrenal insufficiency, owing to adrenal atrophy, may develop during the reduction of steroid dosage below the physiologic replacement level or as long as 9 to 12 months following cessation of treatment. The extent and duration of prior steroid treatment determine the rapidity of recovery from this acquired adrenal atrophy. Atrophy rarely occurs in less than 10 to 14 days of steroid treatment. The rate of recovery, however, appears to vary considerably among individuals, and since one cannot determine rapidly or predict accurately whether a given subject will be able to respond to stress normally, it is advisable, during the first six months following cessation of pharmacologic steroid treatment, to treat such children prophylactically with steroids prior to surgery and to give them oral or parenteral hydrocortisone at other times of evident stress. Usually, glucocorticoids need to be given for only two or three days, and treatment can be stopped abruptly. Since prior glucocorticoid administration does not cause atrophy of the zona glomerulosa and thus inhibit aldosterone secretion, treatment with DOCA is rarely necessary, but any evident sodium deficit should be corrected with intravenous salt solutions.

Hyperadrenalism

Hyperactivity of the adrenal cortex, a normal response to stress, occurs abnormally due to congenital or, rarely, acquired adrenal hyperplasia or to cortical neoplasms. The clinical picture which develops depends upon whether the type of steroid produced in excess is an androgen, glucocorticoid, mineralocorticoid, or a combination of them. In a given subject there may be evident dyscorticism, excessive production of one adrenocortical hormone and deficient secretion of another. The latter circumstance is characteristic of the most common form of adrenocortical disease to occur in childhood, congenital adrenal hyperplasia.

Virilizing Syndromes

CONGENITAL ADRENAL HYPERPLASIA. Congenital adrenal hyperplasia results from an inherited lack or deficiency of an enzyme required for cortisol synthesis. Theoretically one might expect to find an inherited disease due to the lack of any of the enzymes indicated in Figure 21. However, to date, only three separate forms of this disease have been associated certainly with a specific enzyme deficiency in the adrenal cortex: congenital adrenal hyperplasia due to deficiency of 21-hydroxylase, 11β-hydroxylase, and 3β-hydroxy-dehydrogenase (Fig. 22). Since the heterozygote state of the disease cannot as yet be detected, the presumption that each enzyme defect is transmitted as an autosomal recessive is based solely upon the greater than average frequency of consanguinity in the parents, the familial occurrence of the disease in the expected ratio of one affected to three nonaffected siblings, and the fact that in a sibship all affected children have the same type of enzyme lack although the severity may differ from one individual to the next. The combined frequency of all types of this disease is not accurately known but has been estimated variously to be between 1:5,000 and 1:50,000 livebirths. Among the Eskimos in Southwest Alaska the incidence of the salt-losing form is 1:500 livebirths.

In all types of congenital adrenal hyperplasia, interference with cortisol synthesis leads during the third and fourth months of fetal life to compensatory adrenal stimulation, the accumulation of steroid intermediates within the gland, and the release into the bloodstream of a variety of these products, which act peripherally as androgens. The adrenal androgens differ from those normally produced by the fetal testis, in both type and time of secretion. They do not alter the genetically determined development of the Wolffian-Müllerian duct system in the female but rather exert their action upon the final development of the urogenital sinus and external genitalia. Thus, the ovaries, fallopian tubes, and uterus of the female pseudohermaphrodite develop normally but the clitoris enlarges, the urethra rarely may become incorporated into the clitoris, and the labia fuse posteriorly to resemble a cleft scrotum (p. 1135). The most characteristic result of this virilizing process in the female fetus is the development or persistence of a urogenital sinus, the common opening into the perineum of the genital and urinary systems. Occa-

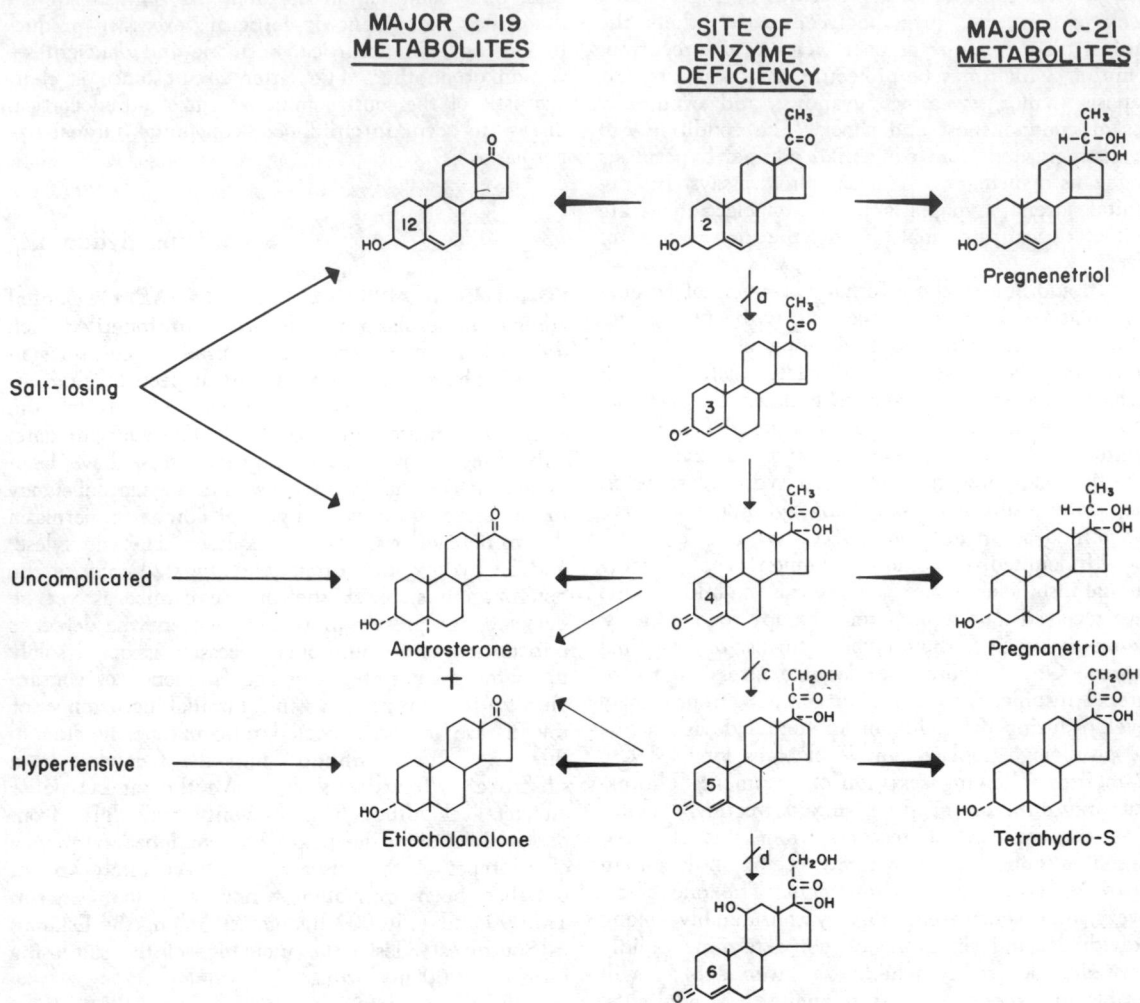

Fig. 22. Forms of congenital adrenal hyperplasia associated with specific enzyme deficiencies.

sionally, there may be an associated vaginal atresia. This ambiguous appearance of the external genitalia causes the female infant to resemble, at birth, a cryptorchid male with hypospadias; as a result some have been mistakenly reared as males. The genitalia of the male fetus, except as noted below, are not significantly affected by excessive adrenal androgen secretion, so that at birth there may be, at the most, penile enlargement and pigmentation, and stippling of the scrotum.

The virilizing process which begins in utero continues postnatally. In both sexes, this is accompanied at first by rapid linear growth. However, even more rapid epiphyseal maturation leads to early epiphyseal fusion and premature arrest of growth. Tall as a child, the untreated individual becomes a short adult. There is increased development of muscle mass, often at the expense of fat, to produce a lean, wiry body configuration. The genitalia become progressively masculinized. At 2 to 4 years of age, pubic hair appears, followed by axillary hair, acne, and, in the older untreated subject, even temporal recession of the hairline. The excessive secretion of steroid intermediates inhibits gonadotropin release from the pituitary and results, in the female at adolescence, in failure of appearance of such secondary sexual characteristics as breast development, as well as uterine infantilism and amenorrhea. In the older male, the absence of testicular stimulation is obscured by excessive adrenal androgen secretion, but the testes remain small and spermatogenesis fails to occur. Rarely, adrenal cortical rest tissue associated with one or both testes enlarges, and the mass may simulate a Leydig cell tumor. Laboratory study has demonstrated that this disease process, the "uncomplicated" form of congenital adrenal insufficiency, is due to a partial or compensated deficiency of the enzyme 21-hydroxylase (Fig. 22).

The clinical picture of intrauterine and postnatal virilization, common to all forms of the disease, is modified in the two clinical variations encountered. In some 30 percent of affected infants, evidence of adrenocortical insufficiency develops, usually at the end of the first week of life. The infant fails to regain birth weight, sucks poorly, vomits occasionally in projectile fashion, and may develop loose stools and become progressively dehydrated. Lethargy proceeds to somnolence and coma. The infant is often admitted to the hospital in circulatory collapse or is found suddenly dead in bed. The characteristic electrolyte disturbance of the Addisonian crisis is observed: lowered serum sodium and elevated serum potassium levels, lowered CO_2 content of the blood, and acidosis.

Infantile adrenal insufficiency associated with virilization has come to be called the "salt-losing form" of congenital adrenal hyperplasia. In most instances, it is due to a virtually complete lack of 21-hydroxylase, thus apparently differing from the compensated form of the disease only in severity; in the "salt-losing form" the enzyme deficiency severely interferes with both cortisol and aldosterone synthesis. In other infants, the primary defect appears to be a lack of the enzyme 3β-hydroxysteroid dehydrogenase (Fig 22). The clinical result of this different enzyme deficiency in the female is mild intrauterine virilization and postnatal deficient glucocorticoid and mineralocorticoid production. In the male, however, lack of the same dehydrogenase in the testis leads to incomplete masculinization of the fetus, producing cryptorchidism and variable degrees of hypospadias. Lack of an enzyme in the cholesterol desmolase system is associated with an exceedingly rare form of *non*virilizing adrenal hyperplasia (congenital lipoid adrenal hyperplasia) and severe cortisol and aldosterone deficiency. There is impaired conversion of cholesterol to pregnenolone, large lipid-packed adrenal glands, severe adrenal insufficiency, normal female genitalia in affected females, and, because the enzyme deficiency involves the testes as well, lack of male differentiation of the external genitalia in affected males. Plasma and urinary corticoids and 17-ketosteroids are low or unmeasurable.

In a small number of affected children of either sex, systemic hypertension is noted during the second or third year of life, along with the virilizing process. The hypertension is sustained rather than paroxysmal and is unrelated to evident cardiovascular or renal disease. Although usually only of moderate severity, it may progress to cause intracranial hemorrhage. In contrast to all other types of hypertension, the elevated blood pressure gradually returns to normal after institution of treatment with hydrocortisone. This "hypertensive form" of congenital adrenal hyperplasia is known to be due to a lack or deficiency of an enzyme required for cortisol synthesis, 11β-hydroxylase (Fig. 22). In such cases, there is additional interference with corticosterone synthesis, which leads to the accumulation of the direct precursor of this steroid, desoxycorticosterone, and the hypertension is believed to be due to the secretion of this biologically active steroid intermediate.

Recently a second form of congenital nonvirilizing adrenal hyperplasia has been defined which is due to a lack of 17-hydroxylase. The defect leads to deficient synthesis of cortisol, androgens, and estrogens, the latter two in both the adrenals and gonads. The increased secretion of desoxycorticosterone and corticosterone provide adequate glucocorticoids but result in hypertension and hypokalemic alkalosis. Affected females remain sexually infantile and at puberty secrete excessive amounts of FSH and LH. The affected male has a female phenotype or ambiguous external genitalia. The excretion of DOC and B metabolites are increased but urinary 17-ketosteroids are low.

Congenital virilizing adrenal hyperplasia in the female needs to be distinguished from other types of intersexuality (Sec. 16.11): true hermaphroditism, which is rare, and nonadrenal female pseudohermaphroditism. The latter is at present most commonly the result of the administration of certain synthetic progestational agents to the mother during early pregnancy. In the male, lacking an evident anomaly of the genitalia, congenital adrenal hyperplasia must be distinguished from such types of acquired virilization as adrenocortical adenoma or carcinoma, idiopathic sexual precocity, or, extremely rarely, interstitial cell tumor of the testis. In the two latter circumstances the testicles enlarge, whereas in congenital adrenal hyperplasia they remain disproportionately small for the advanced degree of secondary sexual development. However, an occasional inadequately treated child with congenital adrenal hyperplasia may develop testicular enlargement due to hyperplasia of adrenal rest tissue situated in the testis.

Diagnosis of congenital adrenal hyperplasia is established by steroid assays of urine or blood (Fig. 22). Although in all subjects there is deficient cortisol synthesis, measurement of cortisol in the blood or of cortisol metabolites in urine is of little specific diagnostic value. In all patients, urinary excretion of 17-ketosteroids is increased (except in the rare patient with a defect in the conversion of cholesterol to pregnenolone). In instances of 21-hydroxylase deficiency there is, in addition, increased excretion of metabolites derived from 17-hydroxyprogesterone, principally pregnane-3α,17α,20α-triol, which is also measurable in blood. In the hypertensive form of the disease the predominant corticosteroid metabolites derive from 11-desoxycortisol (Compound S). In the infant with 3β-ol dehydrogenase deficiency, the major urinary metabolites possess the Δ^5-3β-hydroxysteroid configuration. But it is to be noted that any of these products may also derive from steroids secreted by adrenocortical neoplasms. It is therefore mandatory to demonstrate that the elevated steroid levels found in the blood or urine fall to normal when cortisol replacement therapy is given. Since the diagnosis of this disease signifies the need for lifelong steroid replacement treatment, it should be positively established at the outset.

Treatment of congenital adrenal hyperplasia is both specific and supportive. Subjects with either the uncomplicated (21-hydroxylase deficiency) or hypertensive (11β-hydroxylase deficiency) forms of this disease require only cortisol replacement. A convenient form to use in the young infant is a liquid preparation, such as hydrocortisone cyclopentylpropionate, in a total dose of 15 to 25 mg daily, divided preferably into three roughly equal amounts given at 8-hour intervals. After earliest infancy oral hydrocortisone tablets may be used instead, the dose being slowly raised with advancing age to between 30 and 40 mg daily. The same amount of cortisone acetate intramuscularly need be administered only every third day, if preferred. For either type of patient, the newer cortisol analogs may be used in equivalent amount with equal success.

The treatment of the "salt-losing form" of this disease, due to lack of either 21-hydroxylase or 3β-ol dehydrogenase or a defect in the cholesterol desmolase system, requires initial correction of the electrolyte distrubance by means of intravenous saline solutions and intramuscular desoxycorticosterone acetate (DOCA), in a dosage of 1 or 2 mg daily. During the period of rehydration, complete 24-hour collections of urine should be obtained for the necessary steroid diagnostic studies. Only then should oral cortisol or intramuscular cortisone acetate treatment be begun. After the serum electrolytes return to normal, the infant may be maintained on oral sodium chloride, 1 to 4 g daily in 4 to 6 divided doses, the salt being added to the first 1 to 2 ounces of the formula. Mineralocorticoid therapy must then be continued, but in some patients after 6 to 9 months of age, electrolyte regulation is perfectly maintained with cortisol and salt substitution alone. For this reason, it is convenient in practice to implant in the young infant one, maximally two, 75 mg DOCA pellets subcutaneously, which exert a salt-retaining effect for 4 to 6 months. A second pellet may be inserted at the end of this period if needed. In certain infants, who show mineralocorticoid deficiency after the first or second year of life, the oral administration of 9α-fluorohydrocortisone, 0.1 mg daily, is preferable. The synthetic cortisol analogs should be used with caution, since they are designed to minimize salt retention.

On replacement therapy, the infant or child with congenital adrenal hyperplasia reverts to a normal rate of linear growth and epiphyseal maturation, both of which serve as long-term guides to therapy. Progressive virilization ceases, and with time the enlarged clitoris shrinks to some degree, the labia majora lose their rugated appearance and grow normally, partially or completely concealing the clitoris; however, the urogenital sinus persists. Correction of the latter abnormality requires plastic surgery, which may be performed once the patient is adequately controlled. If the diagnosis of congenital adrenal hyperplasia has been delayed and treatment not started until a later age, at which time epiphyseal maturation has advanced to the 13- or 14-year level, hydrocortisone treatment may, by causing a rapid release of gonadotropins which are no longer inhibited by the adrenal secretions, bring about development of ovarian or testicular function. Thus, the pseudoprecocity due to adrenal disease is converted into true sexual precocity, which, however, should be viewed as physiologic under these circumstances. Unfortunately, when treatment is not begun before the age of 7 or 8 years, a normal adult stature is rarely attained.

Hydrocortisone dosage, in these subjects whose adrenals are suppressed, must be raised to meet the needs of the body during periods of stress of any type. It is usually adequate to increase the dose of hydrocortisone to one and a half times the maintenance level for two to three days. Particularly in the salt-loser, with the most severe form of this disease, intramuscular cortisone acetate must be administered if the infant or child is unable to take hydrocortisone by mouth at such times. In addition, parenteral saline and DOCA treatment may be necessary. Since these infants are prone to infections, they should be given antibiotics on less indication than is usual in the case with the normal child. Unfortunately, the mortality rate among "salt-losers" remains as high as 20 to 30 percent in some reported series.

ACQUIRED ADRENAL HYPERPLASIA. Acquired adrenal hyperplasia producing only virilization is rare at any age and is extremely rare in childhood. Most commonly, one is dealing instead with an adrenocortical tumor or, in the male, sexual precocity. An occasional patient with a mild form of congenital adrenal hyperplasia is thought to have acquired adrenal disease, due to the gradual development of clitoral hypertrophy or the late appearance of sexual hair. Examination of the genitalia of the female may reveal mild fusion of the labia majora, indicative of intrauterine virilization. In both sexes the demonstration of elevated pregnane-3α,17α,20α-triol excretion and a prompt fall of the level upon treatment with hydrocortisone establish the diagnosis of congenital rather than acquired adrenal disease.

ADRENOCORTICAL TUMORS. Adrenal adenoma or carcinoma is not an uncommon cause of virilization in childhood. Such tumors apparently do not form or function during the first four months of fetal life and, thus, do not produce pseudohermaphroditism in the female. They may produce evident virilization in early infancy, however. The effect of the adrenal androgen is, as noted above, to increase muscle mass, hasten growth, advance epiphyseal maturation, as well as cause masculinization of the genitalia. The early signs of the latter in girls are clitoral hypertrophy and rugation of the labia majora. In the male, the phallus enlarges, the scrotum becomes stippled and pigmented, but the testes remain small. Erections may occur in both sexes, labial or pubic hair develops, axillary hair follows, and acne and seborrhea may become prominent. Characteristically, there are no symptoms suggestive of systemic disease, even in advanced cases. The child is usually considered healthy and is evidently more muscular than the average.

Virilization due to an adrenocortical tumor must be distinguished in the male from sexual precocity or interstitial cell tumor of the testis; in both sexes it must be differentiated from congenital adrenal hyperplasia and from precocious pubarche or adrenarche, the early appearance of pubic and axillary hair without other evidence of virilization. The diagnosis of adrenal tumor is suggested by the finding of a greatly increased excretion of urinary 17-ketosteroids, which is present in most cases. Usually, but not invariably, pregnane-$3\alpha,17\alpha,20\alpha$-triol excretion is low or absent. In most instances of tumor, the predominant steroids excreted are $\Delta^5 3\beta$-hydroxysteroids (Fig. 22), including dehydroepiandrosterone. The pattern is not unlike that found in congenital adrenal hyperplasia due to 3β-hydroxysteroid dehydrogenase deficiency; however, there is no salt-losing tendency, and the elevated urinary steroid levels do not fall significantly upon giving hydrocortisone. A greatly increased excretion of 17-ketosteroids may also be found in patients with interstitial cell tumor of the testis, but dehydroepiandrosterone is not the predominant 17-ketosteroid excreted, and usually the unilateral testicular tumor is easily palpable. The excretion of 17-ketosteroids in males with sexual precocity is at the normal adolescent level and is normal for age in the case of precocious pubarche.

It is usually not possible to distinguish between an adrenocortical adenoma and carcinoma on the basis of steroid assays. In some children, however, there are features of Cushing's syndrome associated with virilization; the presence of carcinoma should be suspected in these children. Certain patients with virilizing adrenal tumors may demonstrate an increased excretion of the metabolites of 11-desoxycortisol, as in the hypertensive form of congenital adrenal hyperplasia; in such instances the tumor is usually a carcinoma. Congenital malformations, especially hemihypertrophy, occur with increased frequency in children with adrenocortical tumors which produce virilization or Cushing's syndrome.

Most adrenocortical tumors in children are situated in the expected suprarenal area and, hence, are demonstrable by means of intravenous pyelography. Occasionally, air must be injected retroperitoneally to locate the mass. In rare instances, the tumor may occupy an extraadrenal site, such as along the spermatic vein or in the liver, and may not be revealed by x-ray unless calcification occurs.

The treatment is, of course, surgical extirpation of the tumor. In perhaps 70 to 80 percent of cases, the tumor appears to be benign, encapsulated, and unilateral; in the remainder, evidence of metastases to the regional lymph nodes is found at time of surgery. In roughly 10 percent of cases, the tumor is bilateral. Formerly considered hopeless, this situation can now be managed by total adrenalectomy and lifelong hydrocortisone and mineralocorticoid substitution therapy. Even though the adrenal tumor may appear grossly and histologically benign, it may recur locally or at a distant site. Conversely, histologic malignancy does not necessarily imply that the tumor has metastasized. The most serious prognostic omen is the demonstration of metastases in the lungs preoperatively or of extension to the regional lymph nodes at the time of surgery. Metastatic adrenocortical carcinoma in some patients regresses completely or partially upon continuous administration of the experimental drug o,p^1-DDD [2(2-chlorophenyl)-2-(4-chlorophenyl)-1,1-dichloroethane], in the amount of 3 to 8 g daily. The permanent value of such treatment, however, remains to be established. X-ray therapy and a variety of cytotoxic drugs either have been used without success or have proved to be too toxic.

Cushing's Syndrome

Chronically increased cortisol secretion by the adrenal cortex is associated with acquired adrenal hyperplasia or is due to a cortical neoplasm, either an adenoma or carcinoma of the zona fasciculata. Bilateral adrenal hyperplasia occurs more frequently than an adrenal tumor after the age of 9 years. It is considerably more common in females than in males. The cause of cortical hyperplasia is uncertain, although it is probably the result of a primary hypothalamic disturbance which leads to stimulation of the basophilic cells in the anterior pituitary and thus causes increased ACTH secretion or basophilic adenoma of the pituitary. Although Cushing's syndrome in adults may be associated with a variety of extraadrenal ACTH-producing tumors, such as carcinoma of the lung, pancreatic islets, or thymus, this is rarely the case in children. All types of the disease are rare at this age, but probably the most common form is a mixed picture of virilization and excess glucocorticoid production due to adrenocortical carcinoma.

The metabolic changes which characterize Cushing's syndrome are primarily the result of the antianabolic or catabolic effect of the excess cortisol secreted by the adrenal gland. The steroid favors deamination of amino acids in the liver, causing increased urea production and nitrogen excretion in the urine. The deaminated residues are incorporated into carbohydrate, leading to glycogen deposition and fat synthesis. The overall effect of this metabolic shift is the accumulation of fat (obesity) and protein wasting. Although the patient with advanced Cushing's syndrome is grossly obese, early in the disease fat tends to accumulate in certain sites such as in the cheeks, over the shoulder girdle to produce a "buffalo hump," and about the hips. The protein wasting which accompanies this process leads, in children, to growth impairment or arrest, delayed epiphyseal maturation, demineralization of bone which may cause pathologic fractures, and the development of the characteristic violaceous striae wherever the skin is stretched by deposited fat. The facies are florid. There is a variable systemic hypertension. If, as is not infrequent in childhood, the tumorous adrenal cortex also secretes androgens, the latter may partially counteract the effect of excess cortisol production on growth and bone. The resultant clinical picture is one of combined obesity and virilization.

Aside from obesity and impaired growth, there are few symptoms associated with Cushing's syndrome early in the course of the disease, but untreated it leads to progressive muscle weakness and debility. Hypertension usually progresses and may cause symptoms of cardiac insufficiency. Untreated, the disease slowly leads to debilitation and death over a period of several years, or the patient, because of cortisol suppression of the normal immune mechanism, may die suddenly of a bacterial or viral infection.

Since hydrocortisone has an anti-insulin effect, these subjects may have hyperglycemia and glycosuria or a diabetic-type response to a glucose tolerance test despite an augmented response of plasma insulin. Characteristically, they do not develop ketosis. Some patients demonstrate, instead, a hypochloremic, hypokalemic alkalosis due to the potassium-wasting effect of excess cortisol secretion. Bone demineralization is usually evident by x-ray; especially prominent is a thinning of the inner table of the skull and osteoporosis of the vertebral bodies. The total white cell count may be elevated, owing to an absolute increase of polymorphonuclear leucocytes associated with a relative decrease of lymphocytes and marked lowering of the eosinophil count.

In instances of "pure" glucocorticoid excess, Cushing's syndrome must be distinguished primarily from regulatory obesity in both adults and children. The latter condition is, of course, much more common at all ages. The distinction is usually relatively easy to make in children, due to the fact that regulatory obesity leads to an increased rate of linear growth and epiphyseal maturation, whereas excess cortisol, produced endogenously or administered exogenously, *inhibits* both growth and bone maturation. The obese girl of 9 or 10 not infrequently begins to show early adolescent development; in addition to true breast tissue, there is the appearance of labial or pubic hair. This seeming virilization, however, is not associated with clitoral hypertrophy or rugation of the labia majora such as may be produced by adrenocortical tumors. In the grossly obese child, fat is distributed widely and is not restricted to a few sites. The striae found in simple obesity do not assume the deep purple hue seen in Cushing's syndrome, which signifies

weakness of the capillary walls. Finally, osteoporosis is a characteristic finding in Cushing's syndrome and is extremely rare in regulatory obesity.

The diagnosis of Cushing's syndrome is established by steroid assays carried out on blood or urine. It is not adequate merely to demonstrate increased excretion of cortisol and cortisol metabolites in the urine or an elevated fasting level of cortisol in the blood, since either may result from the acute and transient stimulus of a variety of stresses, such as anxiety, physical pain, or other noxious stimuli invariably accompanying hospitalization. It is characteristic of the hyperplastic but not tumorous adrenal cortex in this disease that it overreacts to ACTH. The demonstration of overresponsiveness to intravenous or intramuscular ACTH is of diagnostic value in distinguishing Cushing's syndrome due to bilateral adrenocortical hyperplasia from cortisol-secreting adrenal neoplasms and from regulatory obesity. It is also usually possible to distinguish hyperplasia from tumors by means of the dexamethasone suppression test. This steroid, in a dose of 2.0 mg daily, shuts off cortisol secretion by the normal, but usually not by the abnormal, adrenal cortex. A dose of 8.0 mg daily usually completely suppresses cortisol secretion by the hyperplastic but not by the neoplastic gland. If the diagnosis of adrenocortical tumor is suggested by the above studies, the location of the tumor should be sought by means of intravenous pyelography followed, if necessary, by retroperitoneal air injection or aortography.

The treatment of all types of Cushing's syndrome is, at present, surgical. The solitary tumor, whether it is an adenoma or carcinoma, is removed. The contralateral adrenal cortex is usually atrophic due to the tumor's suppression of pituitary ACTH secretion. This suppression requires preoperative and postoperative administration of hydrocortisone to prevent the development of adrenocortical insufficiency. The dose of steroid is gradually tapered to stimulate endogenous ACTH release. The treatment of severe Cushing's syndrome due to bilateral adrenocortical hyperplasia requires removal of both adrenals. Bilateral total adrenalectomy with lifelong substitution therapy is preferable because of the considerable likelihood of regrowth of the adrenal remnant and recurrence of the disease if subtotal adrenalectomy is performed. In either case, the primary cause of the disease remains. In certain adult and adolescent subjects, massive basophilic hyperplasia of the pituitary may follow partial adrenalectomy, or a basophilic adenoma may develop which requires neurosurgical intervention. Attempts to treat Cushing's syndrome with pituitary x-ray irradiation alone are only occasionally successful, but this technique is worthy of trial when the disease is not at an advanced stage. Recently, cryosurgery and heavy particle irradiation of the pituitary gland have been utilized with success.

Hyperaldosteronism
(*Conn's Syndrome*)

Chronic excessive aldosterone secretion by the adrenal may be due to primary adrenal disease or may be secondary to renal, hepatic, or cardiac disease associated with edema formation. Primary hyperaldosteronism may be congenital or acquired. The latter form, not uncommon in adults but exceedingly rare in childhood, may be due to a benign adenoma or to bilateral adrenal hyperplasia. The rare cases of Conn's syndrome reported in children are almost invariably the result of congenital bilateral adrenal hyperplasia. This form of the disease differs from the acquired type in that there is malignant rather than benign hypertension and often papilledema. Polyuria, paresthesia, periodic paralysis, and tetany are common symptoms. Untreated, the childhood form progresses to chronic renal failure or to coronary artery disease in young adult life.

The diagnosis of this disease should be entertained in the hypertensive child who has hypokalemia, sometimes associated with hypernatremia and metabolic alkalosis. The hypokalemia is unaffected by potassium supplementation but responds to sodium restriction or to the administration of the aldosterone antagonist, spironolactone, which is of diagnostic value. Prior salt restriction may raise the serum potassium level and thus obscure the diagnosis. At present, the diagnosis can be established with certainty only by demonstrating an increased aldosterone excretion in the urine while the subject is on a high sodium intake or, isotopically, by demonstrating an elevated aldosterone secretory rate. Neither hyperplasia nor tumor can be demonstrated by x-ray.

In children this rare syndrome must be distinguished from the much more common forms of hypertension due to chronic glomerulonephritis or to renal vascular abnormalities (Sec. 21.6). Roentgenographic demonstration of small kidney shadows or needle biopsy of the kidney may be helpful. The rare syndrome of potassium-losing nephritis due to a congenital renal tubular defect, and often familial, needs to be excluded. Hypertension due to pheochromocytoma is rarely associated with hypokalemia. Hypokalemia may also result from the administration of diuretics, such as chlorothiazide.

The treatment of hyperaldosteronism is at present primarily surgical, the use of spironolactone being reserved for correction of the hypokalemia prior to surgery. In the congenital form of the disease, the only successful surgical treatment is bilateral, total adrenalectomy and lifelong glucocorticoid and mineralocorticoid substitution therapy. The prognosis for life accordingly remains guarded. The hypertension disappears in probably half the patients but persists in those who have sustained irreversible renal damage from the long duration of the disease prior to operation.

REFERENCES

Bierich, J. R. Nebennierenrinden-tumoren mit Wirkung auf die Sexualsphäre. Minerva Pediat., 17:725, 1965.

Biglieri, E. G., Herron, M. A., and Brust, N. 17-Hydroxylation deficiency in man. J. Clin. Invest., 45:1946, 1966.

Blizzard, R. M., and Kyle, M. Studies of the adrenal antigens and antibodies in Addison's disease. J. Clin. Invest., 42:1653, 1963.

Bondy, P. K. The adrenal cortex. In Bondy, P. K., ed., Duncan's Diseases of Metabolism, 6th ed. Philadelphia, W. B. Saunders Co., 1969, p. 827.

Bongiovanni, A. M., Eberlein, W. R., Goldman, A. S., and New, M. Disorders of adrenal steroid biogenesis. Recent Progr. Hormone Res., 23:375, 1967.

Childs, B., Grumbach, M. M., and van Wyk, J. J. Virilizing adrenal hyperplasia: a genetic and hormonal study. J. Clin. Invest., 35:213, 1956.

Forsham, P. H. The adrenals. In Williams, R. H., ed., Textbook of Endocrinology, 4th ed. Philadelphia, W. B. Saunders Co., 1968, Chap. 5.

Fraumeni, J. F., and Miller, R. W. Adrenocortical neoplasms with hemihypertrophy, brain tumors, and other disorders. J. Pediat., 70:129, 1967.

Gardner, L. I. Endocrine and Genetic Diseases of Childhood. Philadelphia, W. B. Saunders Co., 1969.

Gilbert, M. G., and Cleveland, W. W. Cushing's syndrome in infancy. Pediatrics, 46:217, 1970.

Hill, A. E., and Williams, J. A. Massive adrenal haemorrhage in the newborn. Arch. Dis. Child., 34:178, 1959.

Hubble, D. D., ed. Paediatric Endocrinology. Oxford and Edinburgh, Blackwell Scientific Publications, 1969.

Hutter, A. M., and Kayhoe, D. E. Adrenal cortical carcinoma, results of treatment with o,p¹ DDD in 138 patients. Amer. J. Med., 41:581, 1966.

Johannisson, E. The foetal adrenal cortex in the human. Its ultrastructure at different stages of development and in different functional states. Acta Endocr. (Suppl.), 130:1968.

Kenny, F. M., Hashida, Y., Askar, A., Sieber, W. H., and Fetterman, G. F. Virilizing tumors of the adrenal cortex. Amer. J. Dis. Child., 115:445, 1968.

Liddle, G. Cushing's syndrome. In Eisenstein, A. B., ed., The Adrenal Cortex. Boston, Little, Brown and Co., 1967, p. 523.

Loras, B., Baour, F., and Bertrand, J. Exchangeable sodium and aldosterone secretion in children with congenital adrenal hyperplasia due to 21-hydroxylase deficiency. Pediat. Res., 4:145, 1970.

Margaretten, W., and McAdams, A. J. An appraisal of fulminant meningococcemia with reference to the Shwartzman phenomenon. Amer. J. Med., 25:868, 1958.

Meador, C. K., Bowdoin, B., Owen, W. C., Jr., and Farmer, T. A., Jr. Primary adrenocortical nodular dysplasia: a rare cause of Cushing's syndrome. J. Clin. Endocr., 27:1255, 1967.

Migeon, C. J., Kenny, F. M., Kowarski, A., Snipes, C. A., Spaulding, J. S., Finkelstein, J. W., and Blizzard, R. M. Syndrome of congenital adrenocortical unresponsiveness to ACTH. Report of six cases. Pediat. Res., 2:501, 1968.

New, M., and Peterson, R. E. Aldosterone in childhood. Advances Pediat., 15:111, 1968.

Russell, A., Levin, B., Sinclair, L., and Oberholzer, V. G. A reversible salt-wasting syndrome of the newborn and infant. Possible infantile hypoaldosteronism. Arch. Dis. Child., 38:313, 1963.

Stempfel, R. S., and Tompkins, G. M. Congenital virilizing adrenogenital hyperplasia (the adrenogenital syndrome). In Stanbury, S. B., Wyngaarden, J. B., and Fredrickson, D. S., eds., Metabolic Basis of Inherited Disease, 2nd ed. New York, McGraw-Hill Book Co., 1966, Chap. 30, p. 635.

Van Wyk, J. J., and Grumbach, M. M. Disorders of sex differentiation. In Williams, R. H., ed., Textbook of Endocrinology, 4th ed. Philadelphia, W. B. Saunders Co., 1968, Chap. 8, p. 537.

Visser, H. K. A. The adrenal cortex in childhood. 1. Physiological aspects; 2. Pathological aspects. Arch. Dis. Child., 41:2; 113, 1966.

Wilkins, L. W. Diagnosis and Treatment of Endocrine Disorders in Childhood and Adolescence, 3rd ed. Springfield, Ill., Charles C Thomas, Publ., 1965.

16.5
ADRENAL CORTICAL HORMONES

ALFRED M. BONGIOVANNI

With the isolation, characterization, and synthesis of the natural adrenal steroids there came great therapeutic advances in the management of adrenocortical insufficiency. The ordinary physiologic requirements of these hormones were soon superseded by certain therapeutic actions of large pharmacologic doses. Currently steroids are used most extensively in amounts far exceeding the usual secretion rate of the adrenal gland under any circumstances and for conditions other than primary insufficiency. These therapeutic objectives are often associated with the recognized anti-inflammatory action of excessive amounts of the hormones.

Cortisol (compound F, hydrocortisone) may be regarded as the principal secretory product of the adrenal cortex for a variety of reasons. Of the several types of steroids, cortisol administered alone is able to satisfy most of the requirements for survival in the face of adrenal insufficiency. It is the major compound of the various adrenocortical products for controlling the pituitary-adrenal homeostatic regulation. The mechanisms which regulate the secretion and release of adrenocorticotropin (ACTH) are sensitive to the quantities of circulating cortisol and do not seem to respond to the mineralocorticoids, androgens, or estrogens of adrenal origin. Finally it is cortisol,

and its many natural and synthetic analogs, which possesses the anti-inflammatory and related pharmacologic properties which have found such extensive application in pediatric practice.

Normally the adrenal cortex secretes approximately 20 mg of cortisol per square meter of body surface per day. This quantity indicates the replacement dose of exogenous cortisol required for normal maintenance in the absence of adrenocortical function; for its pharmacologic actions the administration of a far greater amount is required.

The beneficial response of many disorders to the use of pharmacologic amounts of corticosteroids may be related to the anti-inflammatory action of these hormones, although in most instances the rationale is not clear. Thus the use of steroids is to be regarded as empirical, since the basic causes of diseases which respond are not removed or altered. Rather it is the clinical manifestations, themselves disabling or fatal, which may be controlled despite the persistence of often obscure etiologic elements. With treatment it is hoped that the inciting factor will become exhausted and that in due course steroid therapy can be discontinued without return of clinical disease. This felicitous outcome is not common. Thus the quest for the basic cause of disease and the application of specific therapy, when available, remains paramount. In some instances, the etiologic agent is recognized and steroids are used to prevent certain undesirable consequences in conjunction with specific therapy. Thus, in tuberculous meningitis, steroids may be given concurrently with antituberculous drugs to minimize damage to the central nervous system resulting from inflammation.

The number and the variety of diseases of childhood which respond favorably to steroids are large; however steroids should not represent the first choice of therapy in all conditions known to respond; e.g., in hypoglycemia steroid treatment is being supplanted by diazoxide. Table 7 lists some conditions in childhood for which steroids have been used with temporary or lasting success, and in which experience indicates that they are sometimes agents of choice.

ACTIONS. The glucocorticoids, i.e., compounds resembling cortisol with a Δ^4-ketone group, 17β-side chain, and 17α- and 11β-hydroxyl group, increase the rate of synthesis of hepatic enzymes involved in carbohydrate and amino acid metabolism. These effects are most notable after administration of glucocorticoids in vivo. Among the enzymes of carbohydrate metabolism which are increased are: glucose-6-phosphatase, fructose-1,6-diphosphatase, phosphoenolpyruvate carboxykinase, and pyruvate carboxylase. The enzymes concerned with amino acid metabolism which increase are tryptophan pyrrolase and various transaminases including tyrosine, alanine transaminase, glutamate-pyruvate transaminase, threonine dehydrase, and serine dehydrase. Certain of the latter enzymes, by causing diversion of the amino acid pool from other peripheral tissues, may account in part for

TABLE 7. *Some Disorders Which Respond to Pharmacologic Actions of Steroids*

Rheumatic fever with carditis
Rheumatoid arthritis
Lupus erythematosus
Serum sickness
Acute anaphylaxis
Status asthmaticus
Nephrotic syndrome
Ulcerative colitis
Idiopathic hypoglycemia
Cerebral edema
Iridocyclitis

Uveitis
Keratitis
Severe dermatitis (contact, drug)
Aregenerative anemia
Thrombocytopenic purpura
Pemphigus vulgaris
Boeck's sarcoid
Leukemia
Specific infections
 (e.g., meningococcemia,
  tuberculosis, brucellosis)*

*Under special circumstances and always with antibiotics.

the so-called "catabolic" effects in muscle and bone. In addition, they produce increased alkaline phosphatase in human leucocytes and HeLa cells in tissue culture. The glucocorticoids also induce precocious development of intestinal alkaline phosphatase and invertase and of retinal glutamine synthetase in embryos of several species. Most of these effects appear to be related to the regulation of the synthesis of messenger RNA through the operator-repressor gene system. However, it is difficult at present to correlate any of these actions with the various therapeutic effects of these hormones.

The glucocorticoids also stabilize lysosomes against the actions of various labilizing agents including vitamin A and ultraviolet irradiation, possibly through a physical interaction between steroid and membrane lipid which produces an orientation unfavorable to the penetration of some labilizing agents. These properties have been invoked by Weissmann as an explanation for the beneficial response of some "autoimmune" collagen diseases; he postulates a basic lysosomal fragility with release of degradative enzymes and denaturation of native constituents of cells. Bogden and Gray find a dose-responsive elevation of serum α-2-glycoprotein in response to glucocorticoids, which correlates well with anti-inflamma-

TABLE 8. *Effects of Large Doses of Adrenocortical Steroids*

Basic Action	Clinical Effects
↑ Gluconeogenesis and insulin insensitivity	"Diabetes"
↓ Protein synthesis	Growth failure, osteoporosis, muscle wasting, aseptic necrosis of joints
↓ Growth hormone release in some patients (?)	Growth failure
Variable sodium retention	Hypernatermia, hypertension
↑ Epinephrine response	Hypertension
Variable potassium loss	Hypokalemia, muscle weakness
↓ Ca absorption and ↑ loss	Osteomalacia
Fat redistribution	Buffalo obesity
↓ Vascular permeability, ↓ white cell migration, ↓ fibroblastic proliferation, ↓ antibody formation	Inhibits inflammatory reaction; impairs resistance to infection, ↑ resistance to petechial formation
↑ Gastric HCl and pepsin, ↓ mucus	Peptic ulcer
ACTH Suppression	Adrenal insufficiency
Central nervous system	Euphoria, psychoses, benign intracranial hypertension
↑ Urinary uric acid, creatine, amino acids	Growth failure
↑ Clotting	↓ Bleeding tendency, thromboembolism
↓ Eosinophils and lymphocytes	
↑ Neutrophils	
↑ Hepatic gluconeogenic enzymes and transaminases	Deprives peripheral tissues of amino acids
↑ Lysosomal stability	Presents autolysis and autoimmune reaction (?)

TABLE 9.   *Relative Potency of Steroid Hormones**

Compound	Anti-inflammatory	Sodium Retaining Activity	Forms
Cortisol (hydrocortisone)	1	1	Oral: 5, 10, 20 mg tablets; 10 mg/ml suspension im: 5 mg/ml, 50 mg/ml Local: 1, 2.5% ointment im: 25 and 50 mg/ml (acetate) iv: phosphate and hemisuccinate
Cortisone, acetate	0.8	0.8	Oral: 5, 25 mg tablets im: 25, 50 mg/ml
Prednisone and prednisolone (Δ^1-cortisone, Δ^1-cortisol)	3.5-4.0	0.8	Oral: 1, 2.5, 5.0 mg tablets im: 25 mg/ml (prednisolone acetate) iv: prednisolone phosphate Local: several forms
Triamcinolone (9α-fluoro-16α-hydroxyprednisolone)	5.0	0	Oral: 1, 2, 4, 16 mg tablets; syrup (diacetate) 5 mg/ml im: 25 mg/ml (diacetate)
Dexamethasone (9α-fluoro-16α-methyl-prednisolone)	25	0	Oral: 0.5, 0.75 mg tablets; 0.5 mg/5 ml elixir im: 4 mg/ml (also for iv) Local: various
9α-fluorocortisol	15	125	Potent salt retainer, not generally used systemically Local: various

*As compared to cortisol.

tory activity, although the basis for this relation is not known.

Some of the basic actions of steroids are listed in Table 8 together with the related clinical effects of each. Certain fundamental mechanisms produce the anti-inflammatory and other desirable results; however, many of the consequences are unwelcome. Although some of the newer synthetic steroids mitigate certain of these unwanted effects, it has not been possible to eliminate toxic effects completely. Salt and water retention is less marked and indeed reversed with some synthetic compounds, but even with cortisol this activity has not been very marked or consistent. Thus, under some circumstances, as in nephrosis, cortisol or cortisone produce diuresis despite some mineralocorticoid activity. The diminished incorporation of amino acids into protein (except in the liver) and the possible occasional suppression of growth hormone lead to virtual growth arrest in the child throughout the period of intensive treatment with large doses. Gluconeogenesis, as well as diminished peripheral utilization of glucose, produces variable degrees of hyperglycemia and glycosuria. Sometimes this may represent the expression of latent diabetes. The diminished inflammatory reactions, desirable for the control of many diseases, represent at the same time a disadvantage, since intercurrent in-

fections may overwhelm the child, if unrecognized or not susceptible to available antibiotics. Peptic ulcer, an uncommon complication of steroid treatment in childhood, may not be recognized.

DRUGS AND DOSAGE. Several steroids with anti-inflammatory and gluconeogenic activity are currently available for treatment; these activities are generally parallel. Table 9 lists some of the commonly used compounds and their relative potencies. While 20 mg of cortisol per square meter of body surface per day represents the physiologic quantity, some 10-fold greater amounts are necessary for initiation of treatment in most disorders. Within a short period of time the dosage is reduced to the minimal effective quantity. Dosages vary with the disease, its severity, and the individual response; e.g., in status asthmaticus, it may be possible to achieve improvement with large doses for short periods of time (two or three days), under which circumstances abrupt cessation of treatment is tolerated. Specific recommendations for dosage are to be found in discussions of specific diseases. To some extent, treatment is a matter of trial and error.

Adrenocorticotropin (ACTH) is now rarely used for those diseases which respond to adrenocortical steroids. This polypeptide hormone works by stimulating the adrenal cortex to produce a variety of steroids and has side effects. It is indicated only rarely in situations where steroids seem to have little effect, as in occasional cases of idiopathic hypoglycemia. Its main usefulness today is diagnostic, for the assessment of adrenocortical function.

ROUTE OF ADMINISTRATION. The absorption of the steroids after oral administration is rapid, with a peak blood level occurring within 30 minutes and a rapid fall to low levels after 4 to 5 hours. Following intramuscular administration, the rate of absorption is very slow and variable, but blood levels are sustained for 2 or 3 days depending upon the form of the steroid and the dosage. Because oral administration leads to inactivation of some portion of the dose by the liver, and because of the rapid absorption and excretion, oral doses are larger than parenteral doses. The intramuscular route has been favored by those who believe that sustained, moderately elevated levels are more effective than the variable high peaks which occur with oral treatment. However, recent evidence indicates that sporadic high levels are equally effective and attended by fewer side effects. At the present time there is a tendency to administer the daily dosage by mouth only once a day on alternate days, or even every three days. Under these circumstances, the dosage must be determined by trial and error. The amount necessary is generally not less than a single day's full dose; if given on alternate days, more than this amount may be necessary. Significant adrenocortical suppression does not seem to occur under these conditions. Intravenous preparations of steroids are required for acute emergencies only, and are used only temporarily. Depending upon the dose, the blood level after intravenous administration may remain significantly elevated for as long as 8 hours. If the indications for steroid administration are clear, it is well to administer the calculated dose intramuscularly as well as intravenously. In this manner the steroid level remains sustained following depletion of the intravenous drug.

PRECAUTIONS. The clinical consequences of the steroid hormones administered in large quantities are listed in Table 8. Certain of these are unavoidable, such as the redistribution of fat which produces the buffalo type of obesity and the moon face (Fig. 23). Indeed, in assessing the effects of treatment in patients with diseases which require pharmacologic doses, the absence of some manifestations of Cushing's syndrome would suggest inadequate treatment. However, even these signs may be minimized by intermittent treatment. The action on water and mineral metabolism, rarely marked even with cortisol, is now virtually absent with the newer steroids (Table 9). It is unnecessary to restrict sodium during treatment, especially in the presence of disease accompanied by anorexia, since it is difficult enough to feed the child without reducing the palatability of the diet. Hypertension rarely occurs unless the disease itself is associated with an elevated blood pressure, in which

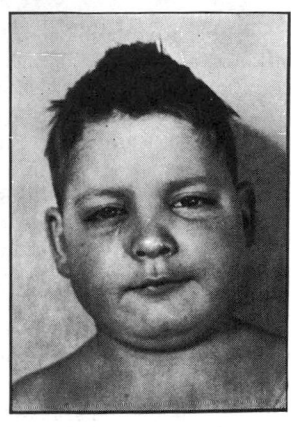

Fig. 23. Moonface following treatment of rheumatic fever with ACTH.

case it may rise further. Additional potassium is rarely required, particularly when the appetite is good and the intake of food adequate.

The risk of disguised infection at the start of therapy or acquired infection thereafter cannot be exaggerated. In areas where tuberculosis is prevalent or in children from groups known to be susceptible to tuberculosis, it is advisable to rule out its presence by the tuberculin test and/or chest x-ray. The presence of infection does not contraindicate the use of steroids where the basic disease is serious and known to respond, provided that appropriate and adequate antimicrobial therapy is administered simultaneously. Intercurrent infections are often masked, and a high index of suspicion must be maintained at all times. Although the routine use of broad-spectrum antibiotics is not advised throughout the period of steroid therapy, suitable antibiotics should be given upon the smallest provocation. Exposure to some infectious diseases for which there are no effective antibiotics, e.g., chickenpox, is cause for concern. Then, it is a good rule to reduce the dosage of steroids to approximately three times the physiologic replacement dose. This amount is adequate for the stress of possible superimposed infection and more than enough to prevent adrenal crisis, yet not so great as to arrest the natural defenses. After the infection has subsided, higher doses may be resumed if indicated. Glycosuria or moderate hyperglycemia do not necessarily denote true diabetes mellitus, and are not occasions to discontinue therapy. In true diabetes mellitus there is a retarded elevation in serum pyruvate and lactate following glucose ingestion, which is corrected by insulin. This is not the case in "normal" subjects treated with glucocorticoids, although blood levels of citrate and α-ketoglutarate remain unchanged and suggest an inhibition of pyruvate utilization. If the basis for steroid therapy is sound, treatment should be continued; if true diabetes mellitus is present, adequate doses of insulin should be added to the regimen.

The most troublesome problem in the chronic treatment of children with steroid hormones is growth arrest. Upon cessation, after continuous treatment for up to two years, there will be resumption of growth at a rapid pace to compensate for the temporary arrest. If treatment has to be continued for many years, the growth failure as well as arrest of osseous maturation will become relatively severe. There is evidence that large doses of human growth hormone administered throughout the period of treatment will overcome the growth retardation, but this hormone is not available in sufficient supply to meet this need. The concomitant administration of anabolic-androgenic hormones may restore growth and maturation, but further investigation into this matter is required before definite recommendations can be made. The use of anabolic steroids would also prevent osteoporosis and cessation of osseous maturational advancement. As noted, the intermittent administration of steroids seems to produce less growth arrest.

Among the other complications of steroid therapy with large doses are: proximal muscle wasting, euphoria, ocular hypertension with glaucoma, posterior subcapsular cataracts, osteoporosis, aseptic bone necrosis due to fat emboli, diminished radioactive iodine uptake by the thyroid, diminished PBI and thyroxine-binding globulin, increased renal excretion of iodine, pancreatitis, and nodular panniculitis (after discontinuation or dose reduction). It is curious that benign intracranial hypertension is sometimes a complication of treatment, especially in childhood, whereas such therapy under other circumstances is thought to reduce cerebral edema after trauma or surgery.

CONTRAINDICATIONS. Contraindications are few in life-threatening or crippling diseases which are known to respond to steroid therapy. Concurrent diseases, such as infection or peptic ulcer, will require direct treatment but will not necessarily contraindicate the use of steroid hormones; under such circumstances, however, steroid therapy may be deferred. The complications of steroid therapy previously outlined prohibit their use in trivial disorders or in conditions shown to respond to other more innocuous measures. Furthermore, their use in serious illness, in which they are known to be ineffective, is a temptation which must be resisted.

WITHDRAWAL. The continuous administration of steroid hormones in amounts equivalent to or greater than the normal production rate leads to suppression of ACTH secretion and to temporary adrenal hypoplasia and unresponsiveness. Recovery of adrenal function is gradual and is somewhat related to the duration of steroid therapy. When used only for several days, steroid therapy, even in large doses, does not lead to significant suppression of adrenocortical function except under most unusual circumstances. Abrupt withdrawal following short courses of treatment is usually without consequence. If treatment with large doses has been continued for more than two weeks, it must be assumed that there is some risk of adrenocortical insufficiency upon abrupt withdrawal; therefore, the steroids should be reduced gradually in order to permit restoration of adrenocortical function. Recovery of adrenocortical function may not begin until the dosage falls below the physiologic level. Therefore, the initial withdrawal can proceed by large (25 percent) reductions in dosage every 5 to 6 days until the physiologic quantity is reached. At this point, it is well to substitute cortisol or cortisone in equivalent dosage if more potent steroids were employed at the start. It is easier to reduce dosage by small gradations with these compounds and, since they are natural substances, they will be more effective in preventing adrenal insufficiency at this stage. Thereafter, reduction should be continued by 25 percent each week until the steroid is completely withdrawn. More rapid withdrawal is permissible if the child is in the hospital and under constant surveillance. The use of ACTH to restore adrenocortical function during withdrawal is not of proved value and is not recommended.

During withdrawal of steroids, the patient must be watched for the usual signs of adrenocortical insufficiency and for possible signs of recurrence of the disease for which they were given. In rare instances, disturbances resembling or identical with collagen diseases may occur even though the initial disturbance was not in this category. Lupuslike states and arteritis have been described; muscle pain and weakness are also common. It is sometimes difficult to distinguish the effects of withdrawal from those of the original condition. If either of these becomes prominent, it may be necessary to raise the dosage moderately and proceed with reduction at a slower pace.

References

Bogden, A. E., and Gray, J. H. Glycoprotein synthesis and steroids. II. α-2-GP synthesis—another parameter for study of glucocorticoids. Endocrinology, 82:1085, 1968.

Deane, H. W., ed. The Adrenocortical Hormones. Their Origin, Chemistry, Physiology and Pharmacology. (Handbuch der experimentallen Pharmakologie XIV/1). Berlin, Springer Verlag, 1962.

Janoski, A. H., Shaver, J. C., Christy, N. P., and Rosner, W. On the pharmacologic action of 21-carbon hormonal steroids ("glucocorticoids") of the adrenal cortex in mammals. In Deane, H. W., and Rubin, B. L., eds., Handbook of Experimental Pharmacology. New York, Springer Verlag, 1968, Vol. XIV, Chap. 12, pp. 256-338.

Weissmann, G. Lysosomes, autoimmune phenomena, and diseases of connective tissue. Lancet, II:1373, 1964.

16.6
ADRENAL MEDULLA AND SYMPATHETIC NERVOUS TISSUE

MARY L. VOORHESS

Histology and Biochemistry

The adrenal medulla and the sympathetic nerves and ganglia are derived from primitive neural crest ectoderm. These primordial pluripotential cells, called sympathogonia, differentiate into neuroblasts and thence to sympathetic ganglion cells, or into pheochromoblasts and mature chromaffin cells. Aggregations of ganglion cells form the sympathetic ganglia while chromaffin cells migrate primarily to the anlage of the adrenal cortex, penetrate its substance, and form the adrenal medulla. Other chromaffin cells form the paraganglia along the aorta. Ectopic rests of neural crest tissue have also been described in numerous sites in the chest and abdomen.

Sympathetic nerve endings, chromaffin cells, and brain are capable of synthesizing the catecholamines, dopamine, norepinephrine, and epinephrine. The main pathway for formation of these compounds is shown in Figure 24. The conversion of tyrosine to dopa is a rate-limiting step, and inhibition of the enzyme tyrosine hydroxylase results in decreased synthesis of the catecholamines. Synthesis of dopamine from dopa occurs in the cytoplasm of the adrenergic cell, where large amounts of dopa decarboxylase are found. Norepinephrine formation takes place in cytoplasmic granules, which are found in the adrenal medulla and in sympathetic nerve endings. Some of these granules contain phenylethanolamine-N-methyl transferase, the enzyme necessary for formation of epinephrine from norepinephrine. In sympathetic nervous tissue about 50 percent of the catecholamine content is dopamine and the other half is norepinephrine. Insignificant amounts of epinephrine are present because the methyl transferase enzyme is present in very small quantities. On the other hand, epinephrine accounts for 60 to 80 percent of the catecholamines of the adrenal medulla, the remainder being norepinephrine. In fetal and neonatal life the predominant catecholamine is norepinephrine.

The cytoplasmic granules in sympathetic nervous tissue and in the adrenal medulla are not only important in synthesis of the catecholamines but also in storage and biologic inactivation. When norepinephrine and epinephrine are bound to adenosine triphosphatase and stored within the granules they are inactive, but when they are released into the cyto-plasm by chemical or nervous stimuli they are active and can exert their physiologic and pharmacologic effects. Catecholamines that are free in the cytoplasm are subject to metabolism by monoamine oxidase, while catechol-o-methyl transferase is primarily responsible for degradation of circulating norepinephrine and epinephrine.

Figure 25 demonstrates the major pathways for the metabolism of norepinephrine and epinephrine. Studies in man, using intravenous isotope-labeled epinephrine, have shown that the main route of metabolic inactivation of circulating epinephrine is o-methylation followed by deamination. Approximately 90 percent of the infused radioisotope is excreted in the urine within 48 hours. Of a given intravenous dose about 5 percent of the epinephrine is excreted unchanged, 35 to 40 percent as free or conjugated metanephrine, and 35 to 40 percent as 3-methoxy-4-hydroxymandelic acid (VMA).

The concentration of free norepinephrine and epinephrine in plasma is extremely small (less than 1 to 2 μg per liter) and quantitative analysis is very difficult. However, the urinary excretion of the catecholamines and their metabolites can be determined easily. There is a gradual increase in daily output of these compounds from birth through childhood. In addition, there is diurnal variation in catecholamine excretion, the output decreasing during sleeping hours. The 24-hour urinary excretion of dopamine, norepinephrine, epinephrine, and VMA of healthy children of various ages is shown in Table 10. Because the methods of analysis used in clinical laboratories differ in specificity, the normal range of values will also vary in different laboratories. The physician must be cognizant of this fact.

Physiology and Pharmacology

The major source of circulating norepinephrine is the sympathetic nerve ending which constantly releases neurohormone to maintain sympathetic tone throughout the body; much smaller amounts come from the adrenal medulla. Sympathetic nerve stimulation, endogenous hormones such as histamine, and a variety of drugs cause norepinephrine release. This catecholamine primarily stimulates alpha receptors and causes generalized constriction of arterioles and venules, with rise in systolic and diastolic blood pressure and reflex bradycardia.

Epinephrine is released by the adrenal medulla in response to sympathetic stimulation, and it affects both alpha and beta adrenergic responses. It increases heart rate, cardiac conduction rate, and ventricular contractility, and relaxes bronchial musculature. It promotes glycogenolysis in liver and muscle, with subsequent increase in blood sugar and lactate. It also increases free fatty acid levels. Nevertheless, the adrenal medulla is not necessary for life; total adre-

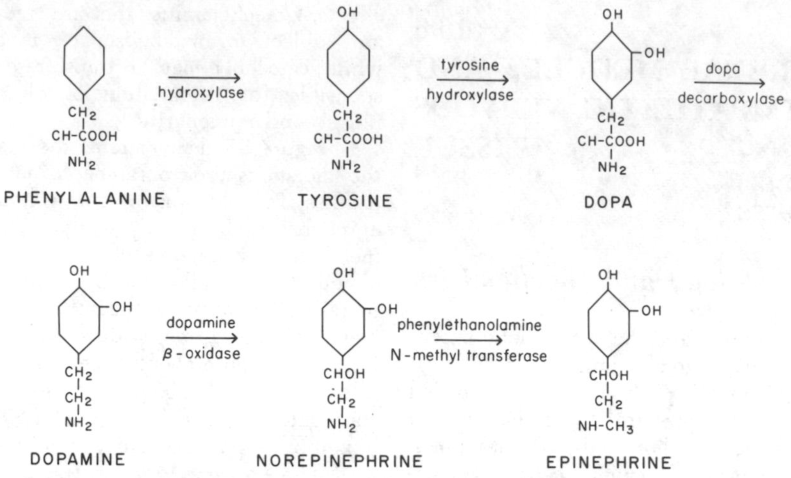

Fig. 24. The primary pathway for catecholamine synthesis.

nalectomy in man is followed by a marked drop in epinephrine excretion while norepinephrine remains unchanged.

Sympathetic nervous tissue produces dopamine, which causes dilation of systemic arteries and increase in cardiac output and renal blood flow. It apparently has no metabolic effects.

Pathology

The most commonly described abnormalities of the adrenal medulla and sympathetic nervous tissue in the pediatric age group are neoplasms, i.e., pheo-

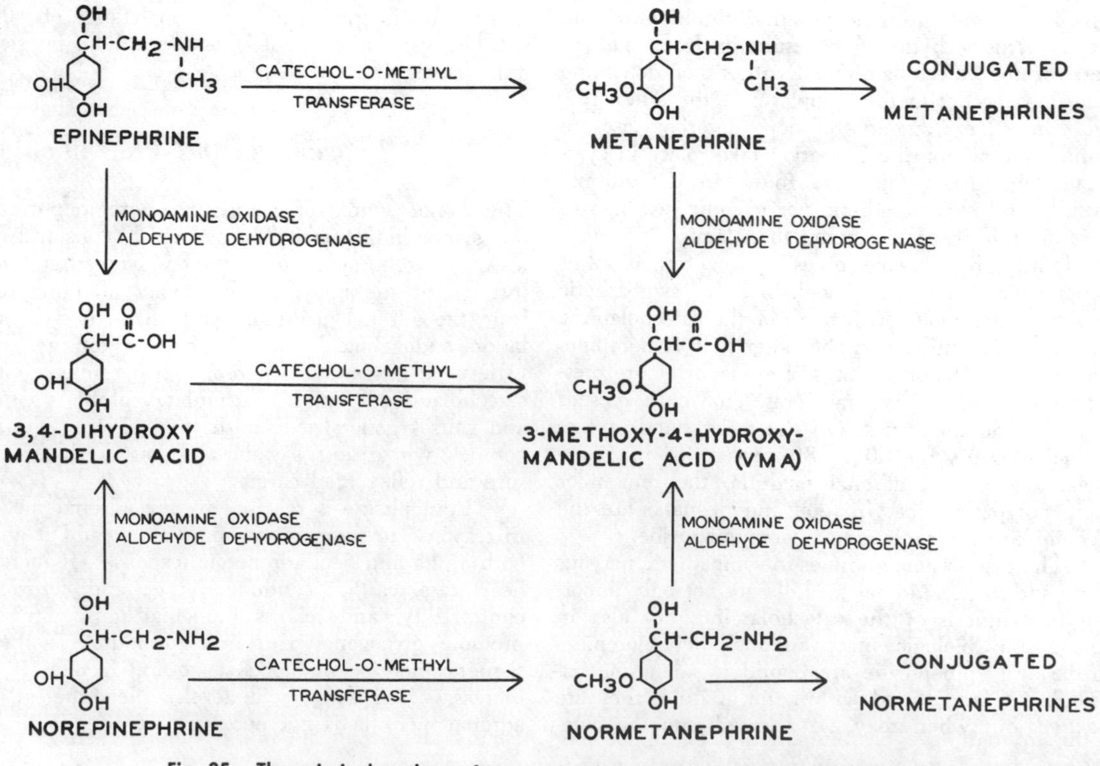

Fig. 25. The principal pathway for norepinephrine and epinephrine metabolism.

TABLE 10. *Normal Values for Daily Urinary Excretion of Catecholamines and VMA (Vanillylmandelic Acid)* *

Age		Dopamine	Norepinephrine	Epinephrine	VMA
			μg per 24 hours		
Birth to one year	Range	17.7-99	5.4-15.9	0.1-4.3	169-1350
	Mean	60.9	10.6	1.3	569
	1 SD	±24.3	±3.4	±1.2	±309
1-5 years	Range	48.3-217.2	8.1-30.8	0.8-9.1	465-2200
	Mean	124.1	18.8	3.2	1348
	1 SD	±40.7	±7.0	±2.7	±443
6-15 years	Range	79.9-364.7	19.0-71.1	1.3-10.5	1050-3740
	Mean	169.3	37.4	4.8	2373
	1 SD	±72.6	±16.6	±2.4	±698
Over 15 years	Range	170.9-377.0	34.4-87.0	3.5-13.2	2050-4250
	Mean	249.1	50.7	7.1	3192
	1 SD	±74.9	±15.7	±3.3	±669

*From Voorhess et al. *Pediatrics*, 39:252, 1967.

chromocytoma, neuroblastoma, or ganglioneuroma. These tumors generally are associated with increased urinary excretion of catecholamines and/or their metabolites. These findings are important aids both in diagnosis and in follow-up care of children with neoplasms of neural crest origin. Abnormalities of catecholamine excretion have also been found in such disorders as familial autonomic dysfunction, idiopathic hypoglycemia, and malignant melanoma.

Pheochromocytoma

CHARACTERISTICS. The pheochromocytoma most commonly arises from chromaffin cells of the adrenal medulla but may be found wherever chromaffin tissue is located throughout the body. In both children and adults the tumor involves the right adrenal medulla more often than the left, but many more tumors in children are bilateral or multiple. They may vary in size from tiny nodules to large lemons. It is difficult to determine by histologic criteria whether pheochromocytomas are malignant or benign; the cells of benign tumors often look malignant and invade veins. Most tumors are benign, however.

There is a 3:2 preponderance of reported cases in the male. The familial occurrence of pheochromocytomas has been reported many times; usually it is inherited as an autosomal dominant trait. The onset of symptoms may begin as early as a few weeks of age but most cases in children have been diagnosed between the ages of 6 and 14 years. The tumor may be present in association with such neurocutaneous syndromes as neurofibromatosis and von Hippel-Lindau's disease. Recently, several sporadic and familial cases of pheochromocytoma and medullary carcinoma of the thyroid have been reported. The tumor has also been found in patients with Cushing's syndrome.

SYMPTOMS AND SIGNS. The symptoms are caused by the large amounts of circulating norepinephrine and epinephrine produced by the tumor. Hypertension is present in all cases of functioning pheochromocytoma and in children is more often sustained than paroxysmal. The systolic blood pressure may reach levels over 250 mm Hg, with corresponding increase in diastolic pressure. Cardiac enlargement and hypertensive retinopathy may be found in long-standing cases. Headache, tachycardia, profuse sweating, nausea, vomiting, and visual disturbances occur frequently. The child often has an anxious expression, appears pale and weak, and complains of palpitations and abdominal pain. Sometimes these findings occur in paroxysmal attacks which take place at varying intervals, from several times daily to once every month or so. Rarely, abdominal massage over the periadrenal area will provoke an attack by causing liberation of catecholamines from the tumor. Polydypsia and polyuria occur more commonly in children than adults. Weight gain may be poor and sometimes there is pronounced growth failure. The extremities may be cool. A peculiar reddish-blue discoloration and edema of the tip of the nose and fingers has been described. Severe constipation is sometimes seen.

DIAGNOSIS. The most specific aid to diagnosis of pheochromocytoma is the finding of abnormally high levels of norepinephrine, epinephrine and/or normetanephrine, metanephrine, and VMA in urine. Very rarely does one find normal excretion of the catecholamines and their metabolites in the presence of a functioning tumor. The pattern of excretion varies from patient to patient, depending on the size of the tumor and the rate of synthesis and turnover of catecholamines. However, when a pheochromocytoma is present, the total catecholamine excretion is usually more than 300 μg/24 hours, even in young children.

Catecholamine excretion may be measured while a patient is being treated with reserpine, thiazides, guanethidine, and ganglionic blocking agents. Quinidine, tetracyclines, bilirubin, and alpha methyl dopa are among the compounds that interfere with fluorometric determination of the catecholamines. Vanilla-containing foods and fruits may cause falsely high levels of VMA.

The use of pharmacologic tests to establish the diagnosis of pheochromocytoma has been largely replaced by measurement of catecholamines. False-positive or false-negative results may occur with the phentolamine (Regitine) test, the tyrosine test, the glucagon test, and the histamine test. Likewise, intravenous histamine may provoke a serious hypertensive episode by causing the discharge of large amounts of norepinephrine and epinephrine from storage sites. Pharmacologic testing of children should probably be reserved for those cases where repeated measurements of catecholamines and metabolites are normal but suspicion of a pheochromocytoma is high.

Albuminuria, glucosuria, hyperglycemia, increased metabolic rate, and abnormal adrenal cortical function have been reported in some children with pheochromocytoma, but tests for these are of little value in establishing the diagnosis.

LOCALIZATION. Preoperative localization of the tumor is difficult. Chest x-rays may reveal a paravertebral or posterior mediastinal mass. Tumors arising from the adrenal medulla often are defined by intravenous pyelography and tomography. Presacral injection of carbon dioxide or oxygen and aortography are helpful in selected cases but such procedures are not recommended as routine tests. Often, the site of the tumor is not found before surgical exploration is carried out. It is important to remember that more than one pheochromocytoma may be present.

TREATMENT. Excision of the tumor should be carried out as soon as the child has been prepared adequately for surgery. Hypertension must be controlled preoperatively. This is usually accomplished by use of an alpha adrenergic blocking agent such as phentolamine (Regitine) or phenoxybenzamine hydrochloride (Dibenzyline). If symptoms of catecholamine excess persist, the addition of beta blocking agents to the therapy may be beneficial. Some patients with pheochromocytoma have a reduction in blood volume and total red cell mass. Identification and correction of hypovolemia should be carried out preoperatively and during surgery. Otherwise, shock may develop following removal of tumor because of the sudden drop in pressor amines and profound vasodilatation.

Careful observation for hypertensive crises is necessary during induction of anesthesia and manipulation of the tumor. Intravenous phentolamine is a suitable agent for controlling marked blood pressure elevation at these times. Beta blocking agents, such as propranolol, are useful in controlling cardiac arrhythmias.

A transabdominal approach is preferred when operating on a child with pheochromocytoma because of the high incidence of bilateral adrenal or multiple tumors. Rarely, an intravenous infusion of norepinephrine is needed to support blood pressure for 24 to 36 hours following surgery; in some patients, the blood pressure may remain elevated for several days after removal of tumor. When bilateral adrenal pheochromocytomas are excised, hydrocortisone must be available for treatment of adrenocortical insufficiency.

Several days after removal of tumor the 24-hour urinary excretion of catecholamines and metabolites should be measured to be certain that all functioning tumor has been removed. In those cases where surgical excision is impossible, or where malignant pheochromocytoma with metastases is present, the tyrosine hydroxylase inhibitor, alpha methyl tyrosine, may be effective in controlling symptoms of excessive pressor amine production.

Neuroblastoma

CHARACTERISTICS. The neuroblastoma is one of the most common malignancies of infancy and childhood. It arises from the immature and undifferentiated neuroblasts of neural crest ectoderm and may be found throughout the body wherever sympathetic nervous tissue is located. Most commonly it arises in the retroperitoneal area of the left or right adrenal gland or along the sympathetic chain in the abdomen or chest. The tumor metastasizes early to bone marrow, skeleton, lymph nodes, liver, and brain and may become widespread throughout the body. Sometimes retroorbital, skull, or skeletal metastases will herald the presence of neuroblastoma before a primary lesion is evident. In infants, the liver may be replaced largely by tumor with no other evidence of metastases.

Grossly, the neuroblastoma has a smooth, rounded shape, or it may be nodular. If extensive hemorrhage and necrosis have taken place it has a cystic appearance and its color is red to violet. The tumor is generally soft and friable. Although it is encapsulated early it soon invades surrounding tissue, and metastases may be so extensive that the primary site cannot be identified. Microscopically, the neuroblastoma is composed of sheets of small cells with deeply staining nuclei and sparse cytoplasm. The cells contain many mitotic figures, and blood vessel invasion is frequent. In some areas the cells are arranged in rosette formation.

Neuroblastoma occurs in both sexes, with a slight preponderance in males. Familial neuroblastoma has been reported in several kindreds but the pattern of inheritance is not clear. Some of the tumors may result from dominant lethal mutations. Miller has described a variety of malformations in association with neuroblastomas but there has been no special pattern to these occurrences.

The tumor occurs in early life, from birth to 6 years, with the peak incidence before age 3 years. It has been found in the fetus at autopsy, but initial diagnosis in late childhood is rare. Neuroblastomas appear to have the highest rate of spontaneous regression of any malignancy in man. Recent studies suggest that lethal immune reactions may occur between the lymphocytes and plasma of children with neuroblastoma and neuroblastoma cells.

SYMPTOMS AND SIGNS. The most frequent presenting complaint is an abdominal mass, which often is found on routine examination. Occasionally, unilateral periorbital swelling and ecchymosis with proptosis, a cervical mass, or a subcutaneous nodule is the first evidence of neuroblastoma. Early, the patient has little systemic evidence of disease but in advanced cases irritability, anorexia, weight loss, fever, bone pain, and anemia are prominent features. The tumor may grow so large as to fill the abdominal cavity; sudden enlargement of the mass may occur if there is extensive hemorrhage into the tumor. Weakness of the lower extremities or paraplegia may be found when the tumor invades the spinal canal. Some patients have hypertension and, rarely, a child will have paroxysmal attacks of flushing or pallor, tachycardia, perspiration, and so forth, similar to patients with pheochromocytoma. Opsoclonia and polymyoclonia also have been reported in association with neuroblastoma.

DIAGNOSIS. The most specific aid to preoperative diagnosis of neuroblastoma is measurement of the urinary excretion of the catecholamines and their metabolites. Abnormally high levels of dopamine, homovanillic acid (HVA), norepinephrine, the metanephrines, VMA, and other metabolites are found in most patients with neuroblastoma. However, the pattern of catecholamine excretion varies. About 12 to 15 percent of the children will have high catecholamine and HVA excretion with normal output of metanephrines and VMA. Very rarely, catecholamine levels are normal while excretion of metabolites is high. Thus it is advantageous to measure the output of either the catecholamines and VMA, or HVA and VMA of each patient. When neuroblastoma arises from dorsal root ganglia, abnormally high urinary excretion of the various compounds may be absent because these cells lack hydroxylase enzyme, which is necessary for the tyrosine to dopa step in catecholamine synthesis.

When neuroblastoma arises from the adrenal medulla the intravenous pyelogram shows lateral and downward displacement of the ipsilateral kidney with preservation of a normal calyceal pattern (Fig. 26); tumor originating from the paravertebral sympathetic ganglia often displaces the ureter laterally. Chest x-rays will reveal extension of disease along the paravertebral spaces into the thorax or the presence of tumor in the posterior mediastinum. Sometimes flecks of calcium are visible within the lesion. It is impor-

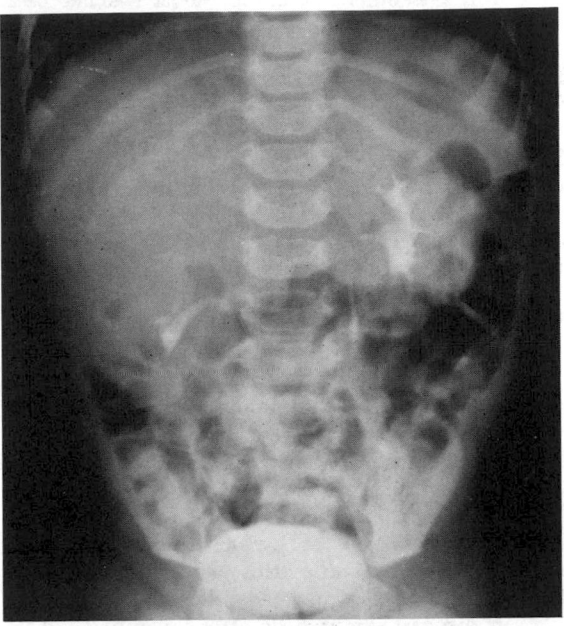

Fig. 26. Intravenous pyelogram showing downward displacement of the kidney by a neuroblastoma arising from the right adrenal medulla.

tant to look for neoplastic cells in the bone marrow when no evidence of osseous metastases is demonstrated on skeletal survey. Occasionally an inferior venacavogram, aortography, or lymphangiography will be helpful in delineating the extent of disease.

Wilms' tumor, Ewing's tumor, lymphomas, and sarcomas may mimic neuroblastoma but none of them is associated with abnormal catecholamine metabolism. Even though pheochromocytoma and neuroblastoma are both functioning endocrine neoplasms, the clinical manifestations of these two disorders permit the physician to differentiate one from the other.

TREATMENT. This should be vigorous and individualized for each patient. The surgeon, radiotherapist, and chemotherapist should all be involved in care of the patient from the start. Total surgical excision is undoubtedly the treatment of choice, but most often diagnosis is established too late for complete extirpation to be accomplished. If such is the case, it is advisable to remove as much of the tumor as possible without jeopardizing the life of the patient and then begin treatment with radiotherapy and/or chemotherapy. When distant metastases are present, most therapists advocate irradiation of the primary site followed by chemotherapy. The tumor is very radiosensitive, and dramatic reduction in tumor size and palliation from pain can be achieved even in far advanced cases. Cobalt 60 is preferred for irradiation and curative doses usually are in the range of 2,500 to 3,500 rads over a period of 3 to 4 weeks.

Because a specific chemotherapeutic agent for control of disseminated neuroblastoma has not been found, the recommended treatment will change as more effective drugs become available. It is important for the physician to review current literature before initiating therapy. At the present time cyclophosphamide (Cytoxan) and vincristine sulfate (Oncovin) in combination are the drugs of choice. The regimen of James is effective and consists of vincristine sulfate intravenously in a dose of 1.5 mg/m² the first day and every 2 weeks thereafter, and cyclophosphamide intravenously on day 8 and every 2 weeks thereafter in doses of 300 mg/m². Some therapists prefer to give cyclophosphamide orally in doses of 2.5 to 5.0 mg/kg/day and vincristine sulfate intravenously every 2 weeks in doses of 1.5 mg/m². Such combination therapy may be given continuously for months. Since these two drugs are both beneficial in treating neuroblastoma but have different mechanisms of action and different toxic manifestations, an additive effect can be obtained without increasing the risks of therapy. The primary toxicity of cyclophosphamide is bone marrow depression and cystitis, while vincristine sulfate causes neuromuscular side effects.

In the past, massive doses of vitamin B_{12} were reported to be effective in treatment of neuroblastoma. However, an evaluation of the experience of American investigators has indicated that there was no increase in the remission rate of neuroblastoma when vitamin B_{12} was used alone or in conjunction with irradiation or other chemotherapeutic agents in patients with advanced disease.

PROGNOSIS AND FOLLOW-UP CARE. Spontaneous cures have been reported in neuroblastoma but these are extremely rare, and hope should not replace vigorous treatment. The younger the patient the more favorable the outlook, the expectation of cure being best in patients less than 1 year of age who have no bony metastases. About 65 percent of such infants are cured of neuroblastoma. Survival of children who are more than 5 years old at diagnosis is practically nil. Metastases to bone, demonstrable either by x-ray or bone marrow aspiration, suggest a fatal outcome at any age although a few long-term survivors have been reported following combined drug therapy. In infants, neuroblastoma with metastases only to liver is curable in most cases. The survival rate with tumors arising from the neck, mediastinum, and sacrum is definitely better than the rate with those originating in the retroperitoneal area. The child who has no evidence of disease two years after treatment has been completed usually can be regarded as cured. Unfortunately, some patients have late recurrence after an interval of 8 to 10 years. The overall survival rate in most series is about 35 percent.

Serial determinations of the urinary excretion of catecholamines and their metabolites are helpful aids in following the response of the patient to therapy and should be an integral part of care. Urinary catecholamines are a more sensitive indicator of tumor

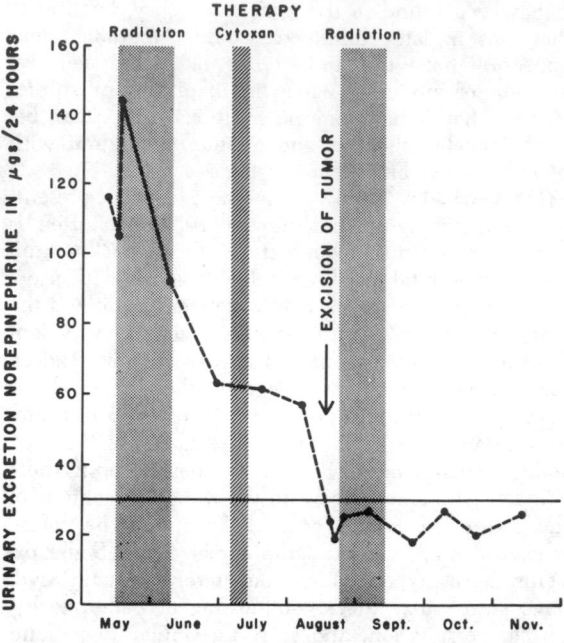

Fig. 27. Urinary norepinephrine excretion of a 4-year-old girl who had a retroperitoneal neuroblastoma which could not be surgically excised initially. Following radiation and cyclophosphamide therapy she appeared healthy, but elevation of norepinephrine output indicated the presence of persistent tumor. After excision of the residual neuroblastoma, the excretion returned to normal. Measurements below the line are normal. (From Voorhess et al. *Pediatrics,* 30:241, 1962.)

activity than VMA output and thus are the more valuable measurements. Response to therapy is accompanied by a decrease in catecholamine excretion to normal, while persistence of residual tumor or occurrence of metastases is indicated by high catecholamine excretion (Fig. 27). Many times, increased catecholamine output may signify the presence of functioning tumor when it is not otherwise evident.

Complications of long-term radiation therapy may develop in patients who survive. Radiation nephritis, bone growth abnormalities, and secondary bone tumors may become manifest many years later.

Ganglioneuroblastoma

Ganglioneuroblastoma is a histologic term used to refer to a tumor of neural crest origin which contains an abundance of mature ganglion cells as well as undifferentiated neuroblasts. It is much less malignant than the neuroblastoma but cannot be differentiated from neuroblastoma by biochemical studies. Both tumors are associated with increased output of catecholamines and their metabolites. Surgical excision followed by radiation therapy and/or chemotherapy is the treatment of choice.

Ganglioneuroma

The ganglioneuroma is a benign tumor which is comprised of mature ganglion cells and is generally found along the sympathetic chain in the posterior mediastinum or abdomen. It is not clear whether the tumor arises de novo from ganglion cells or represents a neuroblastoma which has completely differentiated into a mature lesion. The author has not seen a "pure" ganglioneuroma associated with abnormal catecholamine excretion except when accompanied by the syndrome of chronic diarrhea. Surgical excision is the treatment of choice. Careful serial sections of each tumor should be made by the pathologist to exclude the presence of undifferentiated neuroblasts.

Syndrome of Diarrhea and Neural Tumor

Chronic diarrhea with failure to thrive, malar flush, skin rash, persistent cough, abdominal distention, and hypokalemia may occur in association with tumors of neural crest origin. Bowel movements are generally foul-smelling, frequent, watery, and do not respond to medical therapy. Symptoms usually begin at 8 to 24 months of age and continue relentlessly until the tumor is surgically removed; then the diarrhea ceases. Ganglioneuroblastoma and ganglioneuroma are much more commonly associated with this syndrome than neuroblastoma. The output of catecholamines and metabolites is abnormally high before the tumor is removed and then falls to normal with successful therapy. The etiology of the diarrhea is not known, but there is a definite relationship between watery stools and tumor. Of interest is the observation that the diarrhea does not always reappear with recurrence of tumor. Adrenocorticosteroid therapy has been effective in controlling diarrhea when total excision of the tumor is not possible.

REFERENCES

Bill, A. H. The implications of immune reactions to neuroblastoma. Surgery, 66:415, 1969.

Chatten, J., and Voorhess, M. L. Familial neuroblastoma. Report of a kindred with multiple disorders, including neuroblastomas in four siblings. New Eng. J. Med., 277:1230, 1967.

deLorimier, A. A., Bragg, K. U., and Linden, G. Neuroblastoma in childhood. Amer. J. Dis. Child., 118:441, 1969.

Engelman, K. Principles in the diagnosis of pheochromocytoma. Bull. N.Y. Acad. Med., 45:851, 1969.

Fortner, J., Nicastri, A., and Murphy, M. L. Neuroblastoma: Natural history and results of treating 133 cases. Ann. Surg., 167:132, 1968.

Hume, D. Pheochromocytoma in the adult and in the child. Amer. J. Surg., 99:458, 1960.

James, D. H., Jr., Hustu, O., Wrenn, E. L., Jr., and Pinkel, D. Combination chemotherapy of childhood neuroblastoma. J.A.M.A., 194:234, 1965.

Miller, R. W., Fraumeni, J. F., and Hill, J. A. Neuroblastoma: Epidemiologic approach to its origin. Amer. J. Dis. Child., 115:253, 1968.

Priebe, C. J., and Clatworthy, H. W., Jr. Neuroblastoma. Evaluation of the treatment of 90 children. Arch. Surg., 95:538, 1967.

Rosenstein, B. J., and Engelman, K. Diarrhea in a child with a catecholamine-secreting ganglioneuroma. Case report and review of literature. J. Pediat., 63:217, 1963.

Sawitsky, A., and Desposito, F. A survey of American experience with Vitamin B_{12} therapy of neuroblastoma. J. Pediat., 67:99, 1965.

Solomon, G. E., and Chutorian, A. M. Opsoclonus and occult neuroblastoma. New Eng. J. Med., 279:475, 1968.

Steiner, A. L., Goodman, A. D., and Powers, S. A. Study of a kindred with pheochromocytoma, medullary thyroid carcinoma, hyperparathyroidism and Cushing's Disease: Multiple endocrine neoplasia, Type 2. Medicine, 47:371, 1968.

Voorhess, M. L., Pickett, L. K., and Gardner, L. I. Functioning tumors of neural crest origin in childhood: Followup report. Amer. J. Surg., 106:33, 1963.

16.7
THE PINEAL ORGAN

RICHARD J. WURTMAN

The mammalian pineal organ is a *neuroendocrine transducer*. Like the adrenal medulla, the supraoptic nucleus of the hypothalamus, the "releasing factor" cells in the median eminence, and the juxtaglomerular apparatus, the pineal converts an input of neuronal signals to a hormonal output. Pineal parenchymal cells receive nerve impulses from sympathetic neurons whose cell bodies lie outside the cranial cavity, in the superior cervical ganglia. They respond to these impulses by synthesizing and secreting a family of hormones, the methoxyindoles, of which the prototype is melatonin (5-methoxy-N-acetyltryptamine). Melatonin synthesis is controlled by environmental lighting, which acts via the retina. In rats, exposure to darkness stimulates melatonin synthesis while light suppresses it. Melatonin is secreted into the blood or cerebrospinal fluid and apparently acts on the brain to influence several physiologic processes that share a tendency toward time-dependence (i.e., they vary cyclicly or with age); these include the onset of puberty, ovulation, and sleep. Considerable information is available about the factors that control pineal function; much less is known about the uses to which the body puts melatonin and other pineal secretions.

EVOLUTION OF MAMMALIAN PINEAL. The mammalian pineal is a vastly different organ from the pineals (or epiphyses) of such lower vertebrates as the frog. The frog pineal is a true "third eye." It responds directly to light waves by generating nerve impulses, which it transmits to the brain via pineal nerves. The mammalian organ has lost any direct photosensitivity and neither generates impulses for transmission to the brain nor receives them from the brain. The biochemical activity of the mammalian pineal continues to be influenced by environmental lighting, but now via an indirect route. Light impinging upon the retina generates nerve impulses that travel along the optic nerves to the optic chiasm. Just behind the chiasm, a small bundle of accessory optic fibers leaves the main optic tract to run in the medial forebrain bundle of the lateral hypothalamus. These fibers feed into a multisynaptic pathway which extends through the brainstem and down the spinal cord, ultimately reaching the cell bodies of neurons that send presynaptic fibers to the superior cervical ganglia. Postsynaptic fibers from these ganglia enter the pineal and transmit signals directly to the pineal parenchymal cells. The points at which their terminal boutons impinge upon pinealocytes satisfy many of the morphologic criteria for synapses. In the rat, a nocturnal species, a shining light on the retina *decreases* the number of sympathetic nerve impulses reaching the pineal. The effects of light on the neural input to the pineal may be opposite in diurnally active animals.

Another important difference between frog and mammalian pineals concerns the uniqueness of the ability to synthesize melatonin. In mammals, only pineal cells contain the enzyme hydroxyindole-o-methyl transferase (HIOMT), which catalyzes melatonin biosynthesis. In frogs, this enzyme is widely distributed throughout neural structures. One can conclude that, with evolution, the pineal has changed from an organ that converts an input of environmental lighting into an output of neurotransmitter substances (released at synapses within the brain), to one whose input is a sympathetic neurotransmitter and whose output is a circulating hormone. The particular neurotransmitter released by the sympathetic nerves in the pineal is norepinephrine. The mechanism by which this substance enhances melatonin synthesis involves a "second messenger," cyclic adenosine monophosphate.

LIGHT, PINEAL FUNCTIONS, AND BIOLOGIC RHYTHMS. If rats are kept in a lighted environment, the activity of HIOMT, the enzyme that synthesizes melatonin, declines markedly, and melatonin synthesis and secretion probably show parallel declines. An environment of darkness causes HIOMT activity to increase manyfold. Because the environment in which most mammals live is characterized by a light and a dark period during each 24-hour day, melatonin synthesis is also rhythmic, and the pineal provides the rest of the body with a circulating "time signal." In rats, melatonin synthesis is least towards the end of the daily light period and rises sharply with the onset of darkness.

The discoveries that melatonin is *the* or, at least, *a* pineal output and that the synthesis of this compound normally varies within a 24-hour rhythm, have given physiologists new and relatively fruitful ways of examining pineal function. The question "What do pineal hormones do?" can now be rephrased as, "What other organs in the body respond to changes in melatonin secretion?" The answer to this question has been sought in two ways. One group of scientists has examined the effects of administered melatonin on neuroendocrine functions, while another has tried to determine which light-dependent and time-dependent phenomena in the body are altered when the source of melatonin, the pineal, is removed.

If melatonin is administered chronically to young rats, they experience a delay in gonadal growth and a subsequent disturbance in the ovulatory cycle, as indicated by changes in the vaginal estrous cycle. Melatonin implants in certain brain regions such as the median eminence and the midbrain block the rise in pituitary levels of luteinizing hormone (LH) that follow castration; hence, the pineal hormone might produce part of its gonadal effects by interfering with gonadotropin secretion from the pituitary. 5-Methoxytryptophol, another compound produced uniquely in the pineal through the action of HIOMT, also influences pituitary gonadotropin levels when implanted in the brain. Unlike melatonin, this compound acts primarily on follicle-stimulating hormone (FSH) secretion. It is possible that the mammalian pineal produces a family of hormones which influence gonadal function and which are chemically unique in that they are methoxyindoles, synthesized through the action of HIOMT.

Since HIOMT acts to convert hydroxyindoles, which enter the brain with some difficulty, to methoxyindoles, which have free access to the brain, and since melatonin implants in the brain modify pituitary gonadal function, it is generally held that the locus at which melatonin acts in producing its neuroendocrine effects resides within the brain. This hypothesis is supported by recent evidence that melatonin injections alter the levels of serotonin, believed to be a neurotransmitter substance, in the hypothalamus and midbrain, and that the pineal hormone can induce changes in the electroencephalogram and in behavior which resemble sleep.

When most birds and mammals are blinded, or exposed to continuous light or darkness, marked changes are observed in the timing of gonadal maturation and in subsequent ovulatory cycles. Blind humans exhibit a significant acceleration of menarche; blind rats show the opposite response. Hamsters kept in continuous darkness show a pronounced atrophy of the gonads; this effect is blocked by pinealectomy, suggesting that it is mediated by dark-induced changes in the secretion of melatonin or some other pineal hormone. Gonadal maturation is accelerated in most avian species by exposure to artificial "long days" (i.e., days in which light is presented for at least

14 hours). The stimulatory effect of light on the Japanese quail is blocked by removing the pineal; hence, in this species the pineal must normally *stimulate* gonadal maturation. Exposing a rat to continuous light or removing its pineal produces comparable increases in ovarian weight. The effects of the two procedures are not additive, suggesting that both operate by depressing the amount of an inhibitory pineal substance (melatonin) which acts on the neuroendocrine axis.

Very little information is available about the role of the pineal in producing the 24-hour rhythms observed in glandular secretion and other functions (e.g., body temperature, urine production). The pineal could provide the rhythmic signal that generates rhythms in functions such as adrenocortical secretion. More likely, it might serve to modify the phasing of an intrinsic rhythm.

THE HUMAN PINEAL AND DISEASE. Nine decades ago, Heubner, a German pathologist, first noted that certain pineal tumors were associated with precocious puberty in young boys. Heubner postulated that the pineal normally secreted a hormone that suppressed the onset of sexual maturation; that tumors which destroyed the pineal removed this "brake," and that precocious puberty soon followed. Pineal tumors composed of cells that resemble true pinealocytes might be expected to cause a delay in sexual maturation or an inhibition of gonadal function. This correlation has, in fact, been observed in a small number of patients.

It has still not been possible to prove or disprove Heubner's formulation, inasmuch as no pineal substance that inhibits gonad function has been shown to be present in the body fluids of normal prepubertal children or absent in children with precocious puberty induced by destructive pineal tumors. Melatonin or a related methoxyindole appears to be a good candidate for Heubner's inhibitory hormone. No assays are currently available, however, for measuring melatonin or its chief metabolites in clinical material, so that this hypothesis has not yet been tested. It should be noted that diencephalic tumors unrelated to the pineal can also lead to precocious puberty; thus it is possible that some, if not all, of the gonadal sequelae of pineal tumors result not from changes in the secretion of pineal hormones but from pressure exerted by the tumor on other brain areas. This "pressure hypothesis" fails to explain the correlation between the endocrine effects of a given tumor and its histologic appearance. Most cases of pineal tumors associated, in the male, with precocious puberty have involved pineal teratomas which secrete an LH-like hormone, while true pinealomas composed of cells that resemble pinealocytes have more commonly caused a delay in sexual maturation. Tissue samples from two children with parenchymal pinealomas and delayed pubescence were found to synthesize large amounts of melatonin in vitro. Progress in evaluating the role of the human pineal in health and disease must await the development of good assays for pineal secretions in blood and urine.

Human pineal organs typically show radiologically observable calcification by the end of the second decade of life. Microscopically identifiable calcification may be noted soon after birth. The etiology and the physiologic significance of pineal calcification remain obscure. Pineal calcification does not alter the activity of any pineal enzyme yet examined and probably has no effect on the ability of the pineal to synthesize its characteristic indolic hormones.

REFERENCE

Wurtman, R. J., Axelrod, J., and Kelly, D. E. The Pineal. New York, Academic Press, Inc., 1968.

16.8
THE OVARIES

PAUL C. MacDONALD

Menstrual Dysfunction in Adolescence

Ovarian dysfunction in the adolescent girl may be clinically evident on the basis of menstrual abnormalities characterized by (1) excessive uterine bleeding or (2) failure of menarche, i.e., primary amenorrhea. Excessive uterine bleeding must be controlled, irrespective of age, at the time of onset of hemorrhage. It is difficult to assign a maximum age for normal menarche. While 16 or 17 years could be arbitrarily selected as the time for initiating diagnostic studies in girls who have not yet experienced menarche, this could delay needlessly the investigation of patients with readily identifiable etiologic factors for the failure of sexual maturation. In addition, there are often severe social and emotional pressures on the sexually immature child whose peers are more advanced in pubertal development. For these reasons, early investigation of patients with complaints of primary amenorrhea or sexual immaturity is urged.

Excessive Uterine Bleeding

Following the onset of estrogen secretion by the adolescent ovary, maturation of secondary sexual characteristics becomes apparent, and vaginal bleeding ultimately occurs as the result of the estrogen stimulation of the endometrium. The nature of the bleeding episodes which initiate menstrual life, as in the mature woman, may be the result of four different hormonal environments and can be categorized as (1) *estrogen withdrawal* bleeding, characterized by a discrete episode of painless bleeding, usually of moderate amount; (2) *estrogen breakthrough* bleeding, which is unpredictable, irregular, and varies from scanty episodes of spotting to heavy or massive bleeding for prolonged periods of time; (3) *progesterone withdrawal* bleeding, a result of normal cyclic ovarian function following progesterone secretion from the corpus luteum—characteristic of normal menstruation and commonly associated with some degree of lower pelvic discomfort; (4) *progesterone breakthrough* bleeding, which occurs with continued uninterrupted endometrial stimulation by both estrogen and progesterone and is characterized by unpredictability in duration and amount of flow.

The first few bleeding episodes during adolescence are most commonly of the estrogen breakthrough or withdrawal type, since the early maturation of ovarian function is associated with the secretion of estrogen by an ovary in which ovulatory episodes are not yet occurring. Estrogen breakthrough bleeding may result in extremely heavy and prolonged uterine hemorrhage, sometimes of sufficient magnitude to induce profound anemia and, occasionally, overt hypovolemia. This sequence of events is the most common cause of menstrual excess in the adolescent girl; endometrial, uterine, or cervical tumors are extremely rare causes.

Excessive anovulatory bleeding in the adolescent can generally be managed by bed rest and substitute hormonal therapy, by correcting the anemia, and by measures to prevent recurrence of excessive bleeding until anemia is corrected. Most patients do not require blood transfusion or operative management. In acute, severe uterine bleeding due to anovulation, the parenteral administration of a combination of estrogen and progestogen will result in a marked decrease in uterine bleeding in the first few hours of treatment. Complete subsidence of bleeding can be anticipated in 24 to 36 hours. Following the initial treatment, hormonal therapy must be continued to ensure that no further bleeding results from withdrawal of the administered hormones. Parenteral estrogen plus progestogen should be continued at weekly intervals until anemia is corrected. At this time stopping parenteral hormone therapy will result in withdrawal bleeding of a predictable nature and usually of moderate amount. Thereafter, the cyclic administration of oral hormones for a period of three to six months will control the menstrual cycle, after which time the exogenous hormones should be withdrawn to determine if cyclic ovarian function has begun.

Primary Amenorrhea

A convenient approach to the differential diagnosis of primary amenorrhea is to subdivide the patients into four clinical categories: (1) no evidence of present or previous endogenous estrogen production, (2) clinical evidence of present or previous endogenous estrogen production, (3) an associated sexual anomaly, irrespective of endogenous estrogen production, and (4) signs of acquired masculinization, regardless of the state of endogenous estrogen production.

SEXUAL INFANTILISM—PHENOTYPIC FEMALES. In this category are those patients with primary amenorrhea associated with failure of development of secondary sex characteristics (breast, external genitalia, feminine habitus, and sexual hair), who may also be considered as patients with failure of estrogen secretion. They have a deficiency in ovarian function which may be due either to the inability of the ovaries to produce estrogen or to inadequate ovarian stimulation by pituitary gonadotropin. Accordingly, the differentiation resides largely in determining whether or not the failure of endogenous estrogen secretion is due to abnormal ovaries or to inadequate stimulation of normal ovaries.

The initial differentiation of these patients (Fig. 28) is conveniently started by determining the presence or absence of sex chromatin in the nuclei of exfoliated cells. Those phenotypic females with sexual infantilism and no sex chromatin material in exfoliated cells have deficient ovarian function due to gonadal dysgenesis (see Sec. 16.11).

The differentiation among the causes of estrogen deficiency in chromatin-positive patients is best accomplished by evaluating urinary gonadotropins. If the ovaries fail to function after the time that puberty should have occurred, there will be a marked elevation in urinary gonadotropins. Certain types of gonadal dysgenesis with positive sex chromatin fulfill these criteria. In addition, failure of ovarian development or ovarian ablation prior to puberty, for reasons other than demonstrable chromosomal defects, is also associated with estrogen deficiency and elevated urinary gonadotropins.

In those patients whose urinary gonadotropins are diminished or absent, the cause of the failure of appropriate secretion of gonadotropin must be sought. Examination of the fundi and visual fields and x-ray examination of the sella turcica are helpful in determining if the lack of ovarian stimulation is related to a pituitary or suprasellar neoplasm. Pituitary tumors as well as suprasellar tumors, e.g., craniopharyngiomas, are associated with a defective release of gonadotropin. In the absence of a demonstrable sellar or suprasellar neoplasm, consideration must be given to the failure of release of gonadotropin as a consequence of derangements in the pituitary, or as a result of hypothalamic or other central nervous system defects in the elaboration of FSH- and LH-releasing factors. Since many etiologically unrelated entities may result in gonadotropin deficiency, a convenient approach to this specific problem is the separation of patients with inadequate ovarian stimulation and sexual infantilism according to their somatic growth and development.

For example, those children suffering from pituitary dwarfism or profound hypothyroidism will ex-

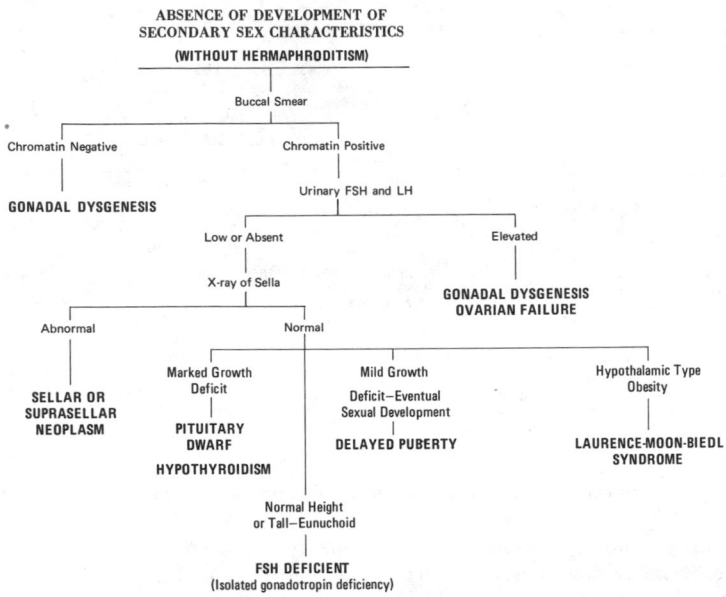

Fig. 28. Schematic diagram of differential diagnosis in sexual infantilism.

hibit impaired growth in addition to the sexual infantilism resulting from deficits in gonadotropin. Other individuals who exhibit modest or no deficit in growth, but with deficiency in sexual development without other associated abnormalities, may be considered to have an isolated deficiency of gonadotropin. If this deficiency is transient and sexual development occurs spontaneously, the problem is merely one of delayed puberty. However, other patients are occasionally observed who are identical in all other respects except for continued lifelong gonadotropin deficiency. These patients may be of normal height or extremely tall, with eunuchoid proportions—the female counterpart of the hypogonadotropic hypogonadism manifested in the male. Isolated gonadotropin deficiency is frequently associated with anosmia. A familial form has been described which is transmitted as an autosomal recessive trait.

Failure of gonadotropin release is seen occasionally in adolescents with the genetically determined Laurence-Moon-Biedl syndrome.

ISOSEXUAL FEMININE MATURATION—PHENOTYPIC FEMALES. This category consists of patients with primary amenorrhea who exhibit evidence of present or previous estrogen production with development of female secondary sexual characteristics, as evidenced by some degree of breast development, feminine habitus, and maturation of the external genitalia. The differential diagnosis of these patients is considered schematically in Figure 29. The key to the differentiation of this group resides in the distinction of four principal subgroups: (1) failure of menstruation due to abnormalities of the genital tract,

(2) estrogen production of insufficient duration to result in complete puberty with the establishment of menarche, (3) continuing estrogen production but amenorrhea due to anovulation, and (4) normal ovarian function but with a uterine defect.

Certain vaginal abnormalities may result in actual mechanical obstruction to the outflow of menstrual blood, the most common of which is an imperforate hymen, with accumulation of menstrual blood above the level of vaginal obstruction. Congenital absence of the vagina, with or without associated congenital absence of the uterus, is a cause of primary amenorrhea in an otherwise sexually mature woman. Other causes of vaginal obstruction include congenital transverse vaginal septa and agglutination of the labia secondary to vaginal infection, usually gonococcal vaginitis or a granulomatous process often initiated by reaction to a foreign body in the vagina.

Two diagnoses must be considered in patients with primary amenorrhea, normal development of female secondary sex characteristics, and congenital absence of the uterus: (1) congenital absence of the uterus due to agenesis of the upper Müllerian duct, and (2) the syndrome of feminizing testes. These two entities are easily distinguished, since, unlike the first, the buccal smear from those with testicular feminization is sex chromatin negative.

A distinction must be made between those who were previously, but are not presently, producing estrogen (subgroup 3, Fig. 29) and those who are continuing to produce estrogen and whose primary amenorrhea is due to anovulation (subgroup 2). This

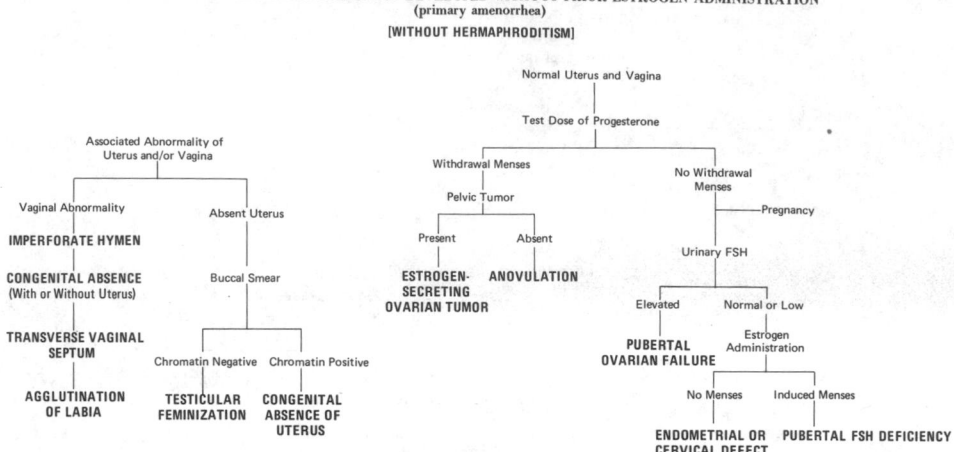

Fig. 29. Schematic diagram of differentiation of isosexual feminine maturation with primary amenorrhea.

distinction is made easily from the response to the administration of a test dose of progesterone. If withdrawal menses occurs following its administration, it is evident that the patient is continuing to produce estrogen in sufficient amounts to maintain adequate endometrial growth for progesterone withdrawal menses to occur. The failure of spontaneous initiation of menarche in this group is due to anovulation—specifically, adequate estrogen production without the associated cycles normally induced by corpora lutea function. This may be observed, rarely, with an estrogen-secreting ovarian tumor or, much more commonly, with persistent anovulation without tumor formation. The most common cause of chronic anovulation at the early stage of sexual maturation is the acyclic release of pituitary gonadotropins, the persistence of which results in the "sclerocystic ovary" syndrome. These events may also be associated with the development of hirsutism (see category 4).

If no withdrawal menses occur following the administration of a test dose of progesterone to a patient with evidence of previous or present estrogen production, then the following categories must be considered: (1) existing estrogen deficiency with physical evidence of previous estrogen production (subgroup 3, Fig. 29) and (2) failure of endometrial response despite continued estrogen production (subgroup 4). In this second category even the diagnosis of pregnancy must be considered, although its occurrence is extremely unusual in the first few menstrual cycles (because they are frequently anovulatory). Nevertheless, conception has been observed in girls prior to menarche, presumably with the first ovulatory episode and without previous menses. Generally, of course, the diagnosis of pregnancy can be safely excluded.

Serum or urinary gonadotropin levels are helpful in ascertaining whether the failure of withdrawal menses to occur after progesterone administration is due to ovarian failure, in which case marked elevations of gonadotropins will be found. The essential criterion is evidence of previous estrogen secretion of sufficient amount to result in some degree of feminization, but of insufficient amount or duration to result in menarche due to ovarian failure. This represents the extreme of premature menopause or premature ovarian failure. It has been reported with and without demonstrable chromosomal abnormalities—specifically those associated with gonadal dysgenesis.

In the individual with previous or existing endogenous estrogen production who fails to have progesterone withdrawal menses and whose urinary gonadotropins are normal, low, or absent, it is necessary to differentiate estrogen deficiency due to inadequate ovarian stimulation from primary amenorrhea with normal estrogen production and failure to have withdrawal menses following progesterone administration. Pubertal gonadotropin deficiency may result from pituitary or suprasellar tumors. More commonly, these deficiencies arise as the result of acute, severe psychic disturbances and are probably related to abnormal hypothalamic function.

Menarchal failure because of endometrial or cervical disease is an exceedingly rare cause of primary amenorrhea although reports of patients with "unresponsive endometrium" have appeared sporadically in the world literature. Equally rare are patients with primary amenorrhea due to obstruction in the uterine cervix to the outflow of menstrual blood.

INTERSEXUALITY—WITH OR WITHOUT FEMININE MATURATION. (See Sec. 16.11., p. 1146.) In this category there are two general types: those who (1) as female fetuses, were exposed to excessive amounts of androgen in utero and those who (2) as genetic male fetuses, produced inadequate quantities of testicular androgen in utero to promote normal

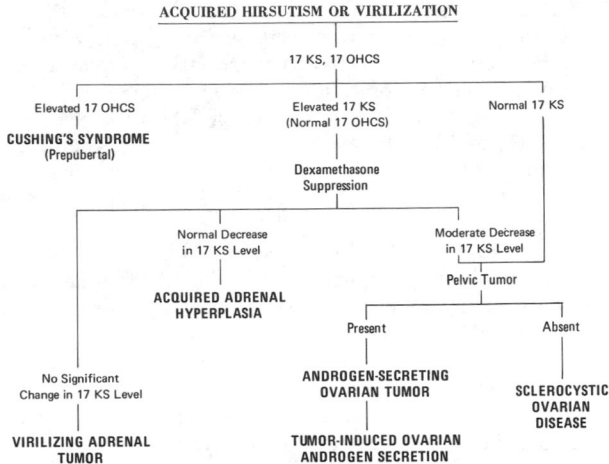

Fig. 30. Schematic illustration of the differentiation of adrenal from ovarian androgen excess.

masculinization of the external genitalia, or who responded inadequately to normal testicular androgen production. The differential diagnosis is described on page 1146.

ACQUIRED MASCULINIZATION—WITH OR WITHOUT ENDOGENOUS ESTROGEN. This final category includes those with acquired hirsutism or virilization: specifically, that group of patients in whom excessive secretion of androgen either by the adrenal cortex or ovary arises after birth. The differentiation between patients with acquired hirsutism or virilization and primary amenorrhea is identical with that of virilized patients with secondary amenorrhea, except for the timing of the onset of the excessive androgen production.

A convenient approach to this problem is the differentiation of adrenal from ovarian androgen excess. (See Fig. 30.) Excessive production of androgen of adrenal origin may be associated with Cushing's syndrome. The precise effect of adrenal hyperfunction on sexual maturation in the female is dependent upon the time of onset of Cushing's syndrome.

Virilizing adrenal tumors are commonly associated with massive elevations of urinary 17-ketosteroids. These function autonomously, as evidenced by the fact that the administration of potent glucocorticoids to diminish ACTH secretion will not decrease the urinary 17-ketosteroids to normal levels for the patient's age. (See Sec. 16.4.)

In patients with normal or only modestly elevated urinary 17-ketosteroids, the most likely diagnosis is androgen excess arising in the ovary. The administration of a potent glucocorticoid to these patients will result in a moderate or incomplete decrease in urinary 17-ketosteroids, because suppression of normal adrenal androgen secretions occurs through the inhibition of ACTH release, but glucocorticoids fail to inhibit ovarian androgen production.

Excessive ovarian androgen secretion may arise from androgen-secreting ovarian tumors, such as the arrhenoblastoma or hilar cell tumors, which are unusual in childhood and adolescence and occur more commonly in the fifth and sixth decades of life. Excessive ovarian androgen production may also be associated with a nonsecreting ovarian tumor, such as the pseudomucinous cystadenoma. The excessive androgen secretion in these rare cases apparently arises from induced hyperplasia of the normal interstitial cells of the ovary adjacent to the tumor, and not from the cells of the cystadenoma.

Patients in the category of primary amenorrhea with associated hirsutism usually have no evidence of Cushing's syndrome, normal or only slightly elevated urinary 17-ketosteroids, and no detectable ovarian tumor; they fulfill the criteria for the diagnosis of "sclerocystic ovarian disease."

The treatment of primary amenorrhea must be formulated for each patient on the basis of the specific etiologic factors involved, and a therapeutic regimen designed which will initiate orderly pubertal development while considering the prospects for fertility in later life.

Patients with estrogen deficiency resulting from inadequate ovarian development or premature ovarian failure can be treated only with supplemental estrogen. Those with estrogen deficiency resulting from inadequate stimulation of the ovary by gonadotropin may also require supplemental estrogen therapy, although great care should be exercised in determining the specific cause of gonadotropin deficiency. Correction of intrinsic disease, which may be associated with failure of gonadotropin release, is frequently accompanied by the onset of gonadotropin production. If this correction is not possible, due to tumor or pituitary defects, estrogen replacement will result in feminization. In this group there is hope for fertility.

With the recent development of techniques for harvesting human gonadotropin from menopausal urine, an agent is available for substitution therapy. This therapy should be reserved, however, for diagnostic confirmation of gonadotropin deficiency and/or induction of ovulatory episodes for the purpose of conception.

The treatment of "sclerocystic ovarian disease" associated with primary amenorrhea must take into account the age of the patient as well as her particular desires with respect to fertility. In a young girl, whose principal concern is amenorrhea and/or hirsutism, the therapeutic regimen should be designed to correct ovarian androgen excess and amenorrhea, not to induce ovulation. The cyclic administration of estrogen plus progestogen will result in cyclic menses and significant decrease in the secretion of ovarian androgen. Therapy designed to induce ovulation should be reserved until the patient wishes to become pregnant.

REFERENCES

Kase, N. G. The ovary. *In* Bondy, P. K., ed., Duncan's Diseases of Metabolism, 6th ed. Philadelphia, W. B. Saunders Co., 1969, p. 1191.

Lloyd, C. The ovaries. *In* Williams, R. H., ed., Textbook of Endocrinology, 4th ed. Philadelphia, W. B. Saunders Co., 1968, p. 459.

Ross, G. T., Cargille, C. M., Lipsett, M. B., Rayford, P. L., Marshall, J. R., Strott, C. A., and Rodbard, D. Pituitary and gonadal hormones in women during spontaneous and induced ovulatory cycles. Recent Progr. Hormone Res., 26:1, 1970.

Wilkins, L. W. Diagnosis and Treatment of Endocrine Disorders in Childhood and Adolescence, 3rd ed. Springfield, Ill., Charles C Thomas, Publ., 1965.

16.9
ENDOCRINE CHANGES AT PUBERTY

HOWARD E. KULIN

Adrenal androgen production increases at puberty (probably due to increased gonadotropin levels), but the primary events associated with sexual maturation in man occur in the hypothalamic-pituitary-gonadal axis. An understanding of these changes necessitates a brief review of the adult reproductive processes. The major advances made in this area in recent years have been due primarily to the development of methods which allow measurement of the small amounts of pituitary and gonadal hormones which are present in biologic fluids.

The hormonal events associated with the female menstrual cycle are illustrated in Figure 31. By utilizing 17-hydroxyprogesterone as an indicator of estrogen production, Ross and co-workers have shown that during the second half of the proliferative phase of the cycle, follicle-stimulating hormone (FSH) decreases and luteinizing hormone (LH) rises as the concentration of plasma estrogen increases. Maximum levels of estrogen coincide with the sharp, midcycle peak of LH associated with the process of ovulation. Thus, the neural centers which regulate LH-release in women appear to respond to an ovarian trigger (positive feedback) and may not have an inherent "clock mechanism" to cause the periodic midcycle rise in LH.

The transformation of the ruptured follicle into a functioning corpus luteum is marked by the increase in progesterone which immediately follows the midcycle LH peak. If conception does not take place, levels of estrogen and progesterone gradually decline during the second half of the cycle (luteal phase), and menses then follows approximately 14 days after ovulation. Toward the end of the cycle and just preceding menstruation, FSH begins to rise again and presumably stimulates the follicle which will rupture during the next ovulation.

Less is known about the apparently simple situation in the adult male. Testosterone from the Leydig cells of the testes and LH interact in the known negative-feedback relationship; however, scanty data are available on FSH control in the male. FSH is necessary for the production of adequate numbers of normal sperm, but presumably other factors, such as local testicular androgen, must also be present. In fact, whether the male neural centers are different from those in the female is also not known; on the other hand, data in the rodent indicate definite sexual differentiation of the hypothalamus, i.e., that ovarian cyclicity is an inherent trait of the female brain.

Hypothalamic-pituitary-gonadal interactions exist prior to puberty; the system is by no means quiescent. Recent studies indicate a large number of similarities with the adult. The prepubertal gonad not only actively secretes low levels of hormones, but both testes and ovary increase steroid production following the appropriate stimulus. After human chorionic gonadotropin (HCG) stimulation, prepubertal testosterone measurements quickly reach adult levels.

The prepubertal pituitary gland is also functional, for both FSH and LH biologic and immunoreactive activity have been detected in the urine of immature children. Interestingly, LH excretion appears to increase approximately tenfold at the time of adolescence, with lesser changes in FSH. Individual gonadotropins have also been measured in the plasma of prepubertal children, but the LH values indicate a smaller difference in pre- versus postpubertal subjects compared with urinary data. The prepubertal pituitary gland can also be stimulated to increase its output of gonadotropin. By administering purified LH-releasing factor prepared from the hypothalamus of pigs and sheep, a prompt rise in plasma LH was demonstrated in sexually immature children.

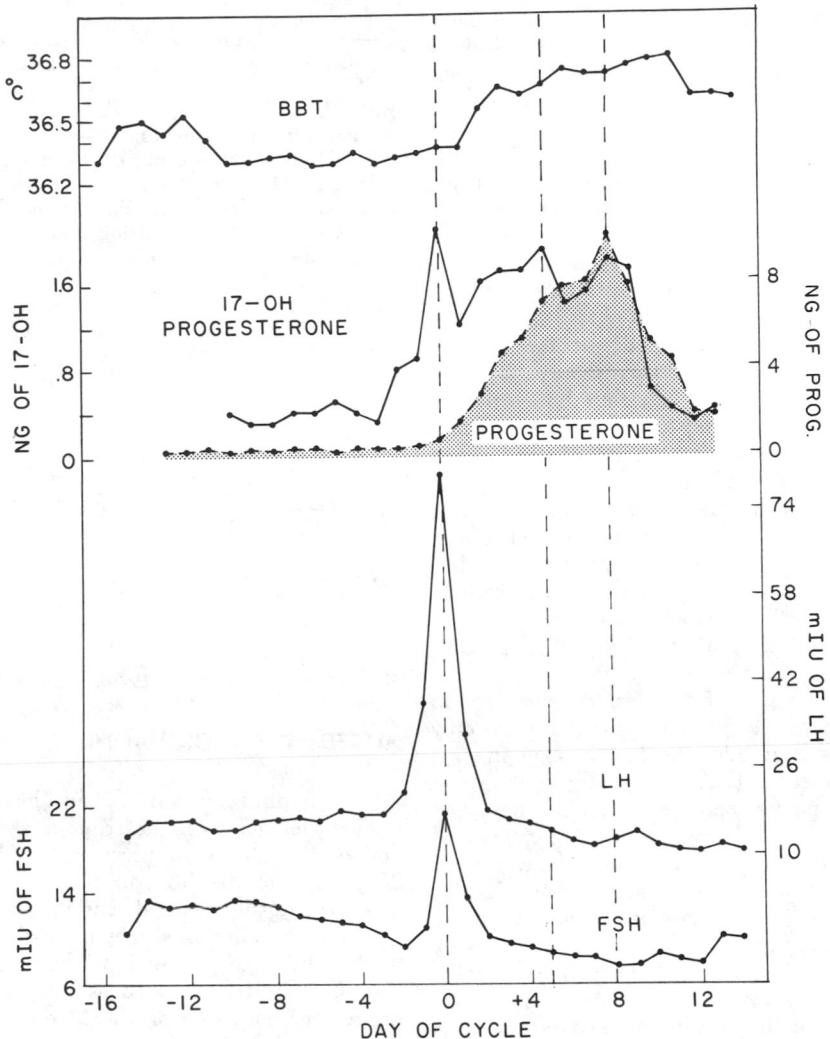

Fig. 31. Mean daily basal body temperature (BBT), daily plasma 17-hydroxyprogesterone and progesterone concentrations (ng/ml), and mean daily plasma LH and FSH concentrations (mIU/ml) during 16 presumptively ovulatory cycles synchronized around the day of the LH midcycle peak. (From Ross et al. *Recent Progr. Hormone Res.*, 26:1, 1970.)

Now that the functional capabilities of the prepubertal gonad and gonadotropin-secreting cells of the hypophysis are established, how are the two glands related to one another in the preadolescent? Negative feedback appears to exist, for a weakly estrogenic substance (clomiphene citrate) can suppress urinary FSH when administered to prepubertal children. Additionally, compensatory testicular enlargement is present in unilateral cryptorchid boys before the time of sexual maturation. Thus, the prepubertal decrease in hormonal secretions from one testis has presumably caused an increase in gonadotropins and subsequent stimulation of the remaining gonad.

Prepubertal hypothalamic-pituitary-gonadal inter-

relationships appear to be a miniaturization of those found in the adult, with regard to levels of gonadal steroid and gonadotropic hormones and negative feedback. The fundamental question of what initiates the rise in levels of these hormones at this time remains unanswered. Only insignificant changes occur during the first several years of childhood, but a rise does take place during puberty.

Though the precise stimulus which initiates puberty is not known, a well-recognized correlate of pubertal onset is bone age. Only when the neural centers have reached the expected maturational age of puberty does the process begin.

An important finding in association with the onset of puberty in man and lower animals is a change in the sensitivity of the negative-feedback system to gonadal steroids; the low levels of steroid which previously maintained low levels of gonadotropin no longer suffice. The hypothalamic-pituitary axis becomes relatively resistant to gonadal hormone feedback, and consequently gonadotropins slowly begin to rise. This rise in FSH and LH stimulates the gonad which, in turn, increases its output of androgen or estrogen. This process continues until the adult type "set-point" is reached and a new equilibrium is established. This new control level is probably not attained until mid- or late puberty, since a relative increase in sensitivity to steroid hormone feedback persists in the early pubertal child.

A further step in pubertal development is the ability, at least in the female, to produce the mid-cycle peak in LH secretion necessary for ovulation. This ability, which is related to the positive-feedback or stimulatory action of estrogen upon LH release, may not be achieved until midpuberty.

Thus, sexual maturation in man is not a sudden, abrupt process, but a series of interrelated events which take place over several years. Such a time course is consistent, too, with the changes in secondary sexual characteristics which occur during adolescence. Recent studies by Marshall and Tanner have carefully recorded these outward events.

The very first sign of pubertal development in boys (enlargement of testicular size) occurs only about 6 months later than the first change in girls (breast development). Thus, the timing of the onset of the pubertal process may be similar for boys and girls, in contrast to the progressive development of secondary sexual characteristics. Pubic hair, for instance, appears about 1½ years later in boys than in girls, and peak height velocity is reached almost 2 years later in boys than in girls. Peak height velocity in girls occurs before menarche which, in turn, takes place approximately 2½ years after the first signs of breast development. It takes approximately 4½ years for both boys and girls to reach adult configuration from the first signs of puberty.

References

Abrams, C. A. L., Grumbach, M. M., Dyrenfurth, I., and Vande Wiele, R. L. Ovarian stimulation with human menopausal and chorionic gonadotropins in a prepubertal hypophysectomized female. J. Clin. Endocr., 27:467, 1967.

Kulin, H. E., Grumbach, M. M., and Kaplan, S. L. Changing sensitivity of the pubertal gonadal hypothalamic feedback mechanism in man. Science, 166:1012, 1969.

——— Grumbach, M. M., and Kaplan, S. L. Gonadal-hypothalamic-interaction in prepubertal and pubertal men: Effect of clomiphene citrate on urinary FSH and LH and plasma testosterone. Pediat. Res., 1971 (in press).

Laron, Z., and Zilka, E. Compensatory hypertrophy of testicle in unilateral cryptorchidism. J. Clin. Endocr., 29:1409, 1969.

Marshall, W. A., and Tanner, J. M. Variations in pattern of pubertal changes in girls. Arch. Dis. Child., 44:291, 1969.

——— and Tanner, J. M. Variations in the pattern of pubertal changes in boys. Arch. Dis. Child., 45:13, 1970.

Rifkind, A. B., Kulin, H. E., and Ross, G. T. Follicle stimulating hormone (FSH) and luteinizing hormone (LH) in the urine of prepubertal children. J. Clin. Invest., 12:1925, 1967.

Root, A. W., Smith, G. P., Dhariwall, A. B. S., and McCann, S. M. Luteinizing hormone releasing activity of crude ovine hypothalamic extract in man. Nature, 22:570, 1969.

Ross, G. T., Cargille, C. M., Lipsett, M. B., Rayford, P. L., Marshall, J. R., Strott, C. A., and Rodbard, D. Pituitary and gonadal hormones in women during spontaneous and induced ovulatory cycles. Recent Progr. Hormone Res., 26:1, 1970.

Saez, J. M., and Bertrand, J. Studies on testicular function in children: Plasma concentrations of testosterone, dehydroepiandrosterone and its sulfate before and after stimulation with human chorionic gonadotropin. Steroids, 12:749, 1968.

16.10
SEXUAL PRECOCITY

ALFRED M. BONGIOVANNI

Man, unlike most other lower mammalian species, is characterized by a deferral of sexual maturation and of the ability to procreate until approximately 20 percent of the lifespan has been spent in what may be broadly termed childhood. The onset of sexual maturation is somewhat variable, particularly in the United States with its heterogeneous population. Certain groups, such as those originating from the regions bordering on the Mediterranean, undergo sexual development at a somewhat earlier age than the Nordic types. In the United States sexual development is evident generally at about 12 years in the female and 13 years in the male. There has been a tendency, due to unknown factors, for sexual maturation to occur somewhat earlier in the current generation of human subjects. A variation of two or three years in either direction must be considered as being within the normal limits. Obvious sexual development before 8 years in the female and before 9 years in the male may be arbitrarily regarded as sexual precocity.

Normal sexual maturation involves hypothalamic, anterior pituitary, and gonadal elements. The importance of the central nervous system has long been recognized in some lower species, where certain environmental stimuli are known to act through the nervous system in regulating reproductive rhythms. There is now ample evidence that the hypothalamus exerts control over the anterior pituitary, mediated by a family of neurohypophyseal polypeptides which are

TABLE 11. *Sexual Precocity—Classification*

I. Complete precocious puberty
   Activation of all levels, usually idiopathic or organic CNS lesion

II. Incomplete precocious puberty
   Sexual hair (precocious adrenarche)
   Breast development (precocious thelarche)

III. Feminization of males
   Gynecomastia with:
       True precocious puberty
       Feminizing adrenal tumor
       Feminizing testicular tumor
       Seminiferous tubule disease (Klinefelter's syndrome)
       Exogenous estrogens

IV. Masculinization of females
   Adrenal tumor or hyperplasia (in males or females)
   Arrhenoblastoma
   Exogenous androgens
   Constitutional (?)

TABLE 12. *Lesions in Isosexual Precocity*

I. Central nervous system
   a. Organic
       Neoplasms (pineal, hypothalamus, other)
       Postencephalitic scarring
       McCune-Albright syndrome
       Hamartoma of the tuber cinereum
   b. Idiopathic
       No definitive lesion (most common form in females)
       Familial (only males affected in most pedigrees)

II. Gonadal tumors
   Ovarian: granulosa cell, thecoma, other
   Testicular: interstitial cell

III. Gonadotropin-producing lesion
   Chorionepithelioma
   Teratoma
   Hepatoma (in males)

IV. Adrenal (in males)
   Tumor or hyperplasia

V. Exogenous hormones

released into the special portal system of the pituitary. The hypothalamic factor responsible for luteinizing hormone release from the anterior pituitary is well established and recent evidence indicates that it also has follicle-stimulating hormone releasing activity. The deferment of sexual maturation, certain analogies drawn from some diseases in man associated with delayed puberty, and experimental evidence suggest that the hypothalamus may also exert inhibitory effects over the pituitary. However, a factor which inhibits the release of pituitary gonadotropins has not yet been extracted from hypothalamic tissue. It is possible that melatonin from the pineal gland exerts an inhibitory effect on sexual maturation, as shown in some animal experiments. In man it appears that nonparenchymatous tumors of the pineal gland lead to sexual precocity in young males. On the other hand, parenchymatous tumors are associated with delayed sexual development and this may be the result of excessive melatonin secretion. It is also reported that an 18-year-old female with a secreting ectopic pinealoma exhibited hypogonadism, a clinical analogy of certain experiments in rodents wherein melatonin inhibits estrus. (See Sec. 16.7.)

It has been possible to measure serum FSH and LH by radioimmunoassay. Low levels of both hormones have been detected in prepubertal children. It has been suggested that the levels, although detectable, remain low because of a hypersensitivity of the hypothalamus to minute quantities of gonadal hormone through a negative feedback, which diminishes at the time of puberty and leads to the release of larger quantities of gonadotropins. (See Sec. 16.9.)

Genetic factors probably play some role in determining the age at which activation of this entire system will occur. There appears to be a relationship between the degree of epiphyseal maturation and the time at which such activation will occur. It is well to obtain a complete family history, especially with regard to the age of sexual maturation in the parents of the child with sexual precocity. In addition to the hypothalamic-pituitary-gonadal axis it seems that adrenocortical activation plays a complementary role in human sexual development. Especially in the female, certain normal androgenic manifestations of sexual development, e.g., sexual hair and clitoral enlargement, have been attributed to adrenal androgens.

A classification of sexual precocity in man by clinical criteria is presented in Table 11 and by cause in Table 12. In the category termed "complete precocious puberty" the entire hypothalamic-pituitary-gonadal axis is called into play. In the other types, various disturbances which represent single levels of this axis are responsible for the sexual precocity and, at times, the clinical manifestations differ accordingly.

Normal Development

By routine physical examination, the physician will become familiar with the usual and sometimes subtle sequence of events in the course of human sexual maturation. In the male, there is usually slight growth of the small testes of infancy until the 10th or 11th year, at which age the gonads usually enlarge more rapidly. The prostate then becomes more readily palpable as a unilobular, and later as a bilobular, mass on rectal examination. About the 12th year, hair appears in the pubic and axillary regions, at which time (but more often earlier) the male demonstrates widening of the areolae and nipples with increased pigmentation and tubercle formation. By the 15th year, hair as well as some degree of acne generally appear on the face, and by the 16th year, there is ejaculation with mature spermatozoa.

TABLE 13.   *Normal Urinary Hormonal Metabolites*

Age (yr)	17-keto-steroids (mg/day)	Estrogens as Estriol (µg/day)	Gonadotropins (mouse units/day)
1-5	1-3	0-5	0-5
6-10	2-6	2-8	0-5
11-16			
Male	5-15	2-8	0-10
Female	5-12	5-20	0-15
> 17			
Male	9-20	5-15	5-60
Female	6-15	10-25	5-60

These representations are average and vary widely among normal boys.

In girls, by the 11th year there is growth of the pelvis and some early budding of the nipples at the same time. Shortly thereafter, early breast development is noted by the appearance of palpable true glandular tissue which gradually increases in size and often begins unilaterally. Between the 11th and the 12th year, pubic and axillary hair appear, with some enlargement of the clitoris, and alterations in the vaginal mucosa which, on gross visible inspection, changes from a pink to a white shiny aspect. The uterus gradually enlarges, as may be appreciated by bimanual examination with a finger in the rectum. On the average, menses begins at 12½ years in the United States with a normal range of 9 to 17 years.

Values for normal urinary hormonal metabolites at different ages are shown in Table 13.

Complete Precocious Puberty

Approximately 85 percent of cases of sexual precocity in females and 35 percent in males can be explained only by an unusually early activation of the entire normal axis. Thorough study fails to reveal any peculiar lesion or disturbance in a display of what would be regarded as a natural course of events at a somewhat later age. Both the affected female and male exhibit the usual progressive manifestations of normal sexual development in all of its aspects. Thus, the female will show breast development, sexual hair, development of the labia minora and majora and, in due course, periodic menstruation. Ovulation undoubtedly occurs in some very young girls with sexual precocity. A number of pregnancies have been reported in such instances, usually attributable to the depravity of an adult male in the environment and not to the inclination of the child. The male will display the increase in pubic and axillary hair, facial hair, acne of variable degree, testicular as well as phallic enlargement, and emissions. There have been several reports of familial male precocious puberty occurring at an unusually early age through several generations. Isolated sexual precocity occurs predominantly in females whereas its familial incidence has been reported exclusively in males, except for the somewhat earlier age of development in both sexes characteristic of some racial groups. Small amounts of biologically active gonadotropins may be detectable in the urine of children with idiopathic precocious puberty (Table 14). In females the urinary estrogens are clearly elevated, usually within the range of normal adult females, and the vaginal smear and urocytogram demonstrate cornification. In males, the 17-ketosteroids are only slightly elevated, a matter sometimes causing confusion, but this may be attributed to the major androgenic substance, testosterone, which is elevated in affected boys and is poorly reflected in the measurement of urinary 17-ketosteroids. Thorough investigation reveals no clear evidence of central nervous system disorder, and the hormonal studies, while advanced for the age, are not beyond the limits of a somewhat older individual and under no circumstances surpass those of the normal adult. It is sometimes difficult to demonstrate the presence of gonadotropins in the urine during the early stages of sexual precocity with the commonly employed bioassay techniques, so that their apparent absence is of little diagnostic significance. Many such children have been followed for many years and seem to live normal lives in every respect without later manifestation of what might have been latent disease as described below. In recent years there has been some tendency to seek out abnormalities and there are reports of abnormal electroencephalograms, but there are no other manifestations of disease of the central nervous system.

In idiopathic precocious puberty the circulating FSH and LH are elevated in almost all instances, well above prepubertal levels although often they do not reach adult levels. Testosterone production rate is also elevated in males. In girls with idiopathic precocity the gonadotropins are also elevated. There have been no direct studies concerning the absolute quantities of estrogens produced, but the clinical manifestations, including cornification of the vaginal mucosa, attest to the indubitable elevation of estrogen secretion in response to the elevated gonadotropins.

There is no ideal treatment for idiopathic precocious puberty, although some drugs have recently

TABLE 14. *Sexual Precocity*

	Bone Age	Height Age	Gonado-tropins	17-Keto-steroids	Estrogens	Comment
Idiopathic precocious puberty	++	++	0 to +	+	+	Females > Males
Chorionepithelioma	++	++	++++	++	+++	Extragonadal
CNS lesion	as for idiopathic					CNS changes
Ovarian tumor	++	++	0 to +	+	+ to ++++	Often palpable
Adrenal hyperplasia	+++	+++	0	+++	++	Progressive virilization; suppressible
Adrenal tumor (virilizing)	+++	++	0	++++	0 to +	Not suppressible
Adrenal tumor (feminizing)	+++	++	0	++	++++	

been employed in an attempt to suppress the release of pituitary gonadotropins. Progestational agents in particular have been used and, in the female, they can arrest the menses and increase breast development. In general, the use of these agents is not advisable unless the psychologic trauma is great, especially for the very young female with menstrual bleeding, or when the situation is intolerable to the family, the school, or the community. There is less of a problem with boys and treatment for them is not ordinarily necessary.

A progestational agent, medroxyprogesterone acetate, has been employed in order to suppress gonadotropins. In doses of 200 to 300 mg every 2 weeks this usually successfully arrests the progression of sexual development, often with diminution of breast size, cessation of menses, and reversion of the vaginal mucosal cornification. On such treatment, the circulating LH and FSH are suppressed in some children but by no means in all of them. In some cases, the unduly rapid rate of growth with the undesirable premature epiphyseal fusion are also reported to be arrested by such treatment. Both the plasma testosterone and the testosterone production rates, usually elevated in boys with this condition, are frequently but not always suppressed. Although there is increasing evidence of a favorable effect on the abnormal growth pattern, this remains to be further clarified. But it is probably inadvisable to use such treatment, except in unusual instances and for psychologic reasons. Suppression of ACTH release and diminished cortisol secretion owing to the glucocorticoid properties of this steroid have been reported. There is a considerable body of evidence in lower mammals that this drug may lead to prolonged and even permanent hypogonadotropism. This has also been reported in a few adult females. The risk of producing hypogonadotropism and sterility in children who use this drug has not been adequately assessed, and for the present such treatment should not be given routinely. The

deceleration of the rapid growth rate on such treatment is probably due to the suppression of the secretion of gonadal hormones. Children with sexual precocity have been found to have higher growth hormone responses to provocative stimuli than prepubertal children, and these may be suppressed by this progestational agent.

The most important aspect of treatment obliges the physician to counsel the parents carefully in the management of the sexually precocious child. Dress should be appropriate to protect the child from sensationalism, the cooperation of the teacher should be sought, and the child must also be protected from the possibility of an encounter with a pervert. It should be emphasized that the physically precocious child is not generally given to heterosexual interest and activity beyond its chronologic years. The parents must be taught to accept the normal caresses and other overt manifestations of affection appropriate for the chronologic age, and must not shun these attentions in the mistaken belief that they represent indications of the overt libidinous attitudes of older individuals.

Certain lesions of the central nervous system may activate the hypothalamic centers prematurely, leading to the release of hypophyseal gonadotropins and thence of androgens by the gonads, with the consequent manifestation of sexual development. Various brain tumors, malignant and benign, may impinge upon the critical hypothalamic areas. A hypothalamic tumor, which is for the most part benign and which has long been associated with sexual precocity, is hamartoma of the tuber cinereum. In one such case, anatomic evidence has been adduced to indicate a specific effect on the anterior pituitary and the release of gonadotropins. These tumors rarely damage the hypothalamus itself and are generally not complicated by any secondary effect upon other parts of the brain. It is believed that they are usually asymptomatic. The question has been raised that such a tumor may be present in many children who are regarded as having idiopathic precocious puberty—one such instance was demonstrated by pneumoencephalography. It is doubtful that heroic diagnostic techniques are warranted to detect such a lesion in healthy children with idiopathic precocity. Congenital lesions of the brain, often associated with the clinical manifestations of ill-defined brain damage, are accompanied by sexual precocity. In this category, some would include the McCune-Albright syndrome, although a well-defined lesion of the central nervous system or endocrine glands has never been described. This disorder, more common in females, is associated with polyostotic dysplasia and prominent areas of skin pigmentation which are unilateral and generally on the same side as the bone lesions. Sexual precocity has also followed various inflammatory disorders of the central nervous system including meningitis, encephalitis and toxoplasmosis. Sexual precocity has been observed following recovery from measles encephalitis and tuberculous meningitis since the advent of successful therapy and prolongation of life. Inflammation and scarring may occur in certain critical areas of the hypothalamus, leading to irritation and premature discharge of impulses to the anterior pituitary. In these forms, the clinical picture and the laboratory findings will conform to those of idiopathic precocious puberty. Many of the cerebral lesions will, of course, manifest themselves by neurologic signs and symptoms, and certain tumors which are progressive and perhaps malignant will become evident sooner or later.

Pseudosexual Precocious Puberty

Certain forms of sexual precocity arise from disturbances below the level of the hypothalamus and are sometimes attended by unique manifestations or laboratory findings which serve to clarify the cause.

Disorders in the production of gonadotropins are a rare cause of sexual precocity. Lesions within the pituitary itself, and especially gonadotropin-producing tumors of this gland, are unknown as causes of sexual precocity in childhood. The classical gonadotropin-producing tumor is the chorionepithelioma, an exceedingly rare tumor in childhood. It may occur in any part of the body and has been found even within the cranial cavity. It is generally highly malignant. The manifestations of sexual precocity are usually difficult to differentiate from the preceding types and, in many respects, resemble complete puberty. However, it is always possible to demonstrate exceedingly high levels of chorionic gonadotropin (HCG) in the urine (and blood), which far exceed even the highest encountered normally at any age during life. These extraordinarily high titers are virtually diagnostic. More recently, hepatoblastoma has been recognized as a cause of sexual precocity in boys. There is evidence that this tumor may secrete an LH-like hormone

which, in turn, stimulates the testes and so produces sexual development. In boys testicular biopsy shows Leydig cell hyperplasia. The liver is apt to be enlarged, but there may be no evidence of gross hepatic functional disturbance. Teratomas, which may occur in the gonads, may be retroperitoneal, or can arise anywhere along the median or paramedian line from the base of the skull to the sacrococcygeal area, are often benign and sometimes contain trophoblastic elements which may secrete chorionic gonadotropin. Careful physical examination and serial x-rays may reveal the possible cause. Unfortunately, laboratory tests are not very helpful in hepatoma or teratoma since the gonadotropins may be only slightly elevated and hence similar to those in idiopathic precocious puberty. Several cases of hypothyroidism in childhood have been associated with sexual precocity, and in some females with galactorrhea. This is a rare occurrence and has been attributed to an inappropriate excessive release of pituitary gonadotropins in the face of deficiency of the thyroid hormone. Treatment with thyroid hormone is generally effective in arresting progressive sexual development. In other tumors producing gonadotropic hormones, surgical removal represents the only successful treatment. Finally, this form of sexual precocity may follow the administration of crude anterior pituitary extracts or various preparations of gonadotropins, including human chorionic gonadotropin. These compounds have been used from time to time for vague and unjustified reasons, including obesity, mental retardation, and so forth. As would be expected, the administration of HCG stimulates the testes which, in turn, secrete testosterone and thereby produce sexual precocity.

Sexual development as a consequence of gonadotropic stimulation, whether secondary to hypothalamic impulses or tumors which produce gonadotropin, always leads to those signs of sexual development appropriate to the sex. This is so because the ovaries in the female or the testes in the male are stimulated to produce their normal hormonal secretion; this type of precocity has been termed *isosexual*. Thus, it would be most unusual for extreme virilization to occur in the female or feminization in the male in the types described above. Other lesions, wherein the primary impetus lies in the autonomous production of gonadal hormones, may occasionally produce heterosexual sexual precocity. Thus androgen-producing tumors in the female or estrogen-producing tumors in the male bring about changes inappropriate to the basic sex of the child.

The bone age in the above forms of sexual precocity is generally moderately advanced, and the rapid epiphyseal maturation is progressive from the time of onset of sexual development. Thus, the eventual stature of these children is compromised due to early epiphyseal fusion, and the degree of limitation of final height is somewhat related to the onset of sexual precocity. During the early years, there is rapid physical growth and development probably primarily as the result of gonadal hormones which are secreted in response to higher stimuli. Hence, for a time the psychologic disadvantage in the disorder (aside from the early sexual development itself) resides in the large body size and the expectations imposed upon the child who appears older than his chronologic age. The development of muscular coordination also is not generally advanced so that a degree of clumsiness is present and the milieu unwittingly expects a better degree of physical and intellectual performance. Although the bone age is advanced, the mental and dental ages are generally not ahead of the chronologic age. These factors should be emphasized to parents, teachers, and other adults in the environment.

Androgenic Origin

Certain disturbances leading to sexual precocity of the male type, which may occur in either sex, arise from the autonomous production of androgens from one of several sources. Interstitial cell tumors of the testes constitute a relatively rare entity in boys. Although many of these tumors have been benign, metastases have been reported years after the removal of a primary tumor. Precocious muscular and skeletal development occurs, in addition to macrogenitosomia, acne, sexual hair, and deepening of the voice. Most such tumors are unilateral and are readily palpated on physical examination. Most cases in childhood have their onset before 6 years of age. The urinary 17-ketosteroids are generally elevated to the upper normal range for male adults or at times considerably above this. The urinary gonadotropins are not elevated. Increased levels of urinary and plasma testosterone have been reported. Detailed studies of the individual urinary 17-ketosteroids generally have revealed metabolites of testosterone, a factor allowing differentiation from adrenal lesions. The bone and height ages are advanced, with early epiphyseal fusion and eventual compromise of stature. The treatment is surgical. These testicular tumors must be differentiated from certain adrenal rests which may occur in the region of the testes, most often in conjunction with adrenal hyperplasia. In this latter situation the treatment is primarily medical, as for congenital virilizing adrenal hyperplasia.

Arrhenoblastoma of the ovary, a rare lesion in girls, leads to virilization in the young female and hence heterosexual precocity. The laboratory findings resemble those seen in interstitial cell tumors of the testes.

The most common lesions of childhood which lead to the production of large quantities of androgens reside within the adrenal cortex. Congenital adrenal hyperplasia may occur in either sex. In the female it is almost always associated with variable degrees of genital malformations present at birth. In the male, except in the case of the salt-losers, the diagnosis is often not apparent for months or years. In both sexes, the disease is progressive and is accompanied by a continuous hypersecretion of androgenic substances from the adrenal cortex. Thus, from earliest life the urinary 17-ketosteroids are always considerably elevated for the age of the child. Without treatment, these would exceed even the normal adult male levels by 4 or 5 years. Early muscular development, acne, rapid statural growth, advanced bone age, sexual hair, phallic enlargement, and deepening of the voice would occur in both sexes. In the female without treatment, appropriate feminine development would not occur at the usual age but unremitting virilization would continue. In addition to the elevated 17-ketosteroids, urinary pregnanetriol is also generally elevated. The disorder is genetic in origin, as is discussed in Sections 16.4 and 16.11. The most characteristic single diagnostic feature which distinguishes this disorder from adrenal tumor is the rapid return of the abnormal urinary steroids to normal levels for age within a few days of the administration of relatively small doses of cortisone or its analogs.

Adrenocortical tumors can occur at any time in life and may be associated principally with the secretion of excessive quantities of androgens. Such tumors have not been reported in earliest infancy, so that this disorder would not be associated with genital malformation in the female. However, the appearance of early virilization in either sex, with the characteristic clinical display resulting from the excess of androgens similar to that in adrenal hyperplasia, is characteristic. The urinary 17-ketosteroids are usually extremely elevated and almost always well above the normal adult range, sometimes reaching levels in excess of 50 mg per day. With adrenal tumors there is little, if any, suppression of the urinary steroids upon the administration of cortisone or similar suppressive steroids. This, together with the characteristic urinary pattern of 17-ketosteroids (comprised in large measure of dehydroepiandrosterone—usually in excess of 50 percent of the total), permits the diagnosis by chemical study.

An important clinical feature of adrenal hyperplasia or tumor as a cause of early virilization in the male is the extremely small size of the testes, an important differential sign from complete precocious puberty or from those forms which develop as a result of other lesions which produce gonadotropins. The adrenal lesion may be a well-encapsulated adenoma or adrenal carcinoma. The tumor is almost always unilateral and, in most instances, can be localized by a carefully performed intravenous pyelogram. If this is not successful, radiologic study by air insufflation or angiography may reveal the site. Treatment is primarily surgical and, on occasion, the contralateral adrenal gland may be atrophic. If complete unilateral adrenalectomy is performed, adequate preparation should be made for the possibility of acute adrenal insufficiency. However, in the pure virilizing types of adrenal tumor the contralateral gland is generally normal. The prognosis with adenomata is excellent, whereas in carcinoma early death is the rule. Following surgery, the course of the child may be monitored by periodic examination of the urinary 17-ketosteroids, which generally return to normal following removal of the tumor but rise again in the event of recurrence.

Early virilization may come as a result of the administration of androgenic hormones during childhood. As a rule this is iatrogenic, since the androgens are not so ubiquitous as estrogens and surreptitious exposure to such hormones would be most unusual. A number of so-called anabolic steroids are widely used in medicine. It should be noted that virtually more of them is free of androgenic action. Some degree of virilization would thus be expected in either sex, with the typical manifestations—including the advancement of bone age—which occur in the aforementioned disorders associated with excessive androgen production.

Occasionally, young females develop moderate generalized hirsutism without other evidence of an endocrine disorder. This is often constitutional and familial, but is distressing in our American culture. Usually, the urinary levels of 17-ketosteroids are only slightly elevated. Treatment is not indicated. Reassurance and advice for the early use of depilatories or electrolysis for facial hair is all that may be required. It is uncertain whether a few such girls may represent the early stage of one of the disorders within the category of the mild ovarian virilizing syndromes generally termed "Stein-Leventhal." However, most girls do not subsequently manifest the other components of this syndrome.

Estrogenic Origin

Certain autonomous lesions of the gonads or the adrenal cortex produce large quantities of estrogenic hormone and lead to early feminization in either sex.

Tumors of the ovary in the young female are an uncommon cause of feminization in early life. Most ovarion tumors which cause sexual precocity are of the granulosa cell variety, but it cannot be overemphasized that among all girls with sexual precocity this is an unusual cause. Too often, idiopathic precocious puberty in the female is falsely attributed to an ovarian tumor. Normal follicular cysts, revealed on exploration of the patient, have been misdiagnosed as ovarian tumors and one or both ovaries removed unnecessarily. Follicular cysts of the normal type are seen at almost any age, but especially during early infancy and the sexually productive years. Granulosa cell tumors are usually unilateral, smooth, firm, and encapsulated. The tumor generally grows rapidly, so that in most instances it is readily palpated by bimanual palpation with one finger in the rectum. It has been stated that most of these tumors in childhood are benign and that only approximately 30 percent are malignant, but accurate statistics on this are not available. The young girl often displays early breast development, usually advanced height and bone age, some sexual hair, and irregular vaginal bleeding. Ascites is sometimes present as well. Classical teaching is that the urinary excretion of estrogens, measured by any one of several methods, is considerably increased above the normal adult level and that urinary gonadotropins are absent. This is often true and would be in accord with the logical homeostatic regulatory mechanism, but it is not always so. On occasion, the urinary estrogens are only slightly elevated despite the precocious feminization. This has been attributed to necrosis of large portions of the tumor at the time the studies are performed. Detectable levels of urinary gonadotropins have also been reported. Hence, the laboratory investigations are not always reliable in this condition. Treatment is primarily surgical and usually involves unilateral oophorectomy.

Rarely, a luteinized follicular cyst of one ovary, which generally replaces most of the normal ovarian tissue, may be associated with sexual precocity. While some authorities have felt that such a cyst represents an ovarian manifestation of idiopathic precocity, on rare occasions the removal of such a lesion leads to regression of the symptoms and signs. When most of the ovary has been replaced by the cyst, oophorectomy is generally performed. On occasion, such cysts have been punctured and "unroofed" with good clinical results. This particular lesion must be regarded as extremely unusual in comparison with the occurrence of smaller secondary follicular cysts of the ovary in idiopathic precocious puberty, in which surgery should be avoided.

The adrenal cortex is known normally to secrete small quantities of estrogens. A most peculiar and unusual tumor of the adrenal cortex secretes large quantities of estrogens and leads to feminization in early life. Several cases of feminization of young boys have been associated with such adrenal tumors which may in fact be ectopic: one was an adrenocortical tumor embedded in the liver.

The widespread use of estrogens in human medicine and their incorporation into some skin creams has been responsible for the occasional and frequently unsuspected cause of feminization in the young boy or girl. A very careful history must be taken to rule out this possibility; when there is no other obvious explanation this question must be raised again and again. Children have been known to ingest estrogens which were present in the household and intended for the use of some other family member, or they have been exposed to cosmetics, which they have either ingested or applied to themselves repeatedly over broad areas of the body. The accidental chronic ingestion of estrogens in childhood has been related to poor control in manufacturing processes, so that certain vitamin capsules were found to be contaminated with sufficient estrogen to produce clinical effects. A helpful clinical sign is the presence of extremely darkly pigmented nipples, a notorious side effect of stilbestrol, which is one of the most widely used estrogens in human medicine. From time to time other curious and surprising exogenous sources of estrogens have been uncovered. Thorough and repeated inquiry into this matter is essential.

Partial Precocity

In some instances only a single manifestation of sexual development becomes apparent at an early age, whereas the other usual manifestations are deferred until the usual time. Premature thelarche represents the condition wherein true breast development occurs in early life; this is to be distinguished from neonatal hyperplasia of the breasts, which is probably the result of large quantities of estrogens transferred from the mother. Neonatal hyperplasia generally subsides spontaneously within a few weeks or months, and no specific treatment is recommended. Apart from this, between the ages of 2 and 8 years a girl may develop noticeable and progressive enlargement of the breasts with true glandular tissue, but without sexual hair or the early onset of menstruation. The exact cause of this condition is unknown except that it is benign and not susceptible to any known form of treatment. This type of breast development is apt to begin on one side before the other and frequently leads to concern about the possibility of malignancy. Malignancy of the breast in childhood is extremely rare. The author has seen girls who have been almost deprived of their entire breast anlage as a result of ill-advised biopsy in this condition. The second breast will eventually also show development, whereas other signs of complete sexual precocity do not make their appearance until considerably later. It is often difficult to ascertain whether early breast enlargement will not be accompanied shortly by all of the signs of complete precocity. These children should be followed two to three times a year.

There is generally very little in the way of unusual laboratory or x-ray findings. The bone age may be advanced slightly but it does not progress at the rapid rate seen in complete precocity. The vaginal smear is usually lacking in any estrogenic effect although on occasion a mild estrogenic effect may be noted. The serum LH and FSH are reported to be slightly elevated, but not so much as in complete precocity. Urinary steroids are usually within normal limits, although with highly sensitive techniques slight rises in urinary estrogens are sometimes demonstrable; these are not so high as they are in complete idiopathic precocious puberty. The condition does not always progress and often after a few months —for reasons which are not clear—may come to a halt or regress.

Occasionally, gynecomastia develops in the young boy, usually around the time of puberty. This condition does not merit further consideration except to emphasize the fact that it should be regarded as a normal phenomenon in many boys. The overall prevalence of gynecomastia in young boys is approximately 40 percent, with a peak prevalence of 65 percent at 14 years of age. Therefore, in most instances this is not a fundamentally abnormal condition. In the majority of boys entering puberty, such gynecomastia subsides within two to three years. Uncommonly, it may be progressive and mastectomy is then advisable for psychologic and cosmetic reasons. Androgenic therapy is without beneficial effect and at times has caused aggravation of the enlargement. In boys with progressive breast enlargement and somewhat small testes of abnormally firm consistency, the possibility of Klinefelter's syndrome (seminiferous tubule dysgenesis) must be entertained. However, most boys with moderate gynecomastia at the time of puberty have no basic endocrine or genetic disorder.

Another isolated phenomenon which occasionally occurs in young children, especially girls, is the development of sexual hair without other signs of sexual maturation. Talbot has termed this premature adrenarche based on the assumption that there may be early activation of the adrenal cortex without involvement of the gonads. Thus, the adrenal androgens, which normally rise slightly at the time of puberty, increase early in life and lead to the production of sexual hair but little else. There is very slight phallic enlargement in either sex and all other signs of sexual development are generally absent and do not appear until a later and more normal age. The urinary 17-ketosteroids are generally slightly elevated but barely reach normal adult levels in premature adrenarche. In girls, the serum LH and FSH are normal. No specific treatment is recommended for this condition, although if the hair is extremely troublesome it may be removed from time to time by use of any of the many cosmetic depilatories. This condition must be differentiated from adrenocortical tumors in particular; in the latter, the urinary 17-ketosteroids are usually extremely high. Bone age in premature adrenarche is generally slightly advanced but does not progress rapidly as in idiopathic precocious puberty or in disease of the adrenal cortex. Reassurance and watchful waiting represent the best therapy.

REFERENCES

Beas, F., Zurbrugg, R. P., Leibow, S. G., Patton, R. G., and Gardner, L. I. Familial male sexual precocity: Report of the eleventh kindred found, with observations on blood group linkage and urinary C_{19}-steroid excretion. J. Clin. Endocr., 22:1095, 1962.
Case Records. Massachusetts General Hospital, Case 43461: Luteinized follicle cyst with precocity. New Eng. J. Med., 257:987, 1957.
Hertz, R. Accidental ingestion of estrogens by children. Pediatrics, 21:203, 1958.
Jolly, H. Sexual Precocity. Springfield, Ill., Charles C Thomas, Publ., 1955.
Kenny, F. M., Midgley, A. R., Jaffe, R. B., Garces, L. Y., Vasquez, A., and Taylor, F. H. Radioimmunoassayable serum LH and FSH in girls with sexual pre-

cocity, premature thelarche and adrenarche. J. Clin. Endocr., 29:1272, 1969.

Liu, N., Grumbach, M. M., de Napoli, R. A., and Morishima, A. Prevalence of electroencephalographic abnormalities in idiopathic precocious puberty and premature pubarche: bearing on pathogenesis and neuroendocrine regulation of puberty. J. Clin. Endocr., 25: 1296, 1965.

Loop, J. W. Precocious puberty. Pneumoencephalography demonstrating a hamartoma in the absence of cerebral symptoms. New Eng. J. Med., 271:409, 1964.

Marshall, W. A., and Tanner, J. M. Variations in pattern of pubertal changes in girls. Arch. Dis. Child., 44:291, 1969.

——— and Tanner, J. M. Variations in the pattern of pubertal changes in boys. Arch. Dis. Child., 45:13, 1970.

Nydick, M., Bustos, J., Dale, J. H., Jr., and Rawson, R. W. Gynecomastia in adolescent boys. J.A.M.A., 178:449, 1961.

Odell, W. D., Ross, G. T., and Rayford, P. L. Radioimmunoassay for luteinizing hormone in human plasma or serum: physiological studies. J. Clin. Invest., 46: 248, 1967.

Rifkind, A. B., Kulin, H. E., Cargille, C. M., Rayford, P. C., and Ross, G. T. Suppression of urinary excretion of luteinizing hormone (LH) and follicle stimulating hormone (FSH) by medroxyprogesterone acetate. J. Clin. Endocr., 29:506, 1969.

Rivarola, M. G., Camacho, A. M., and Migeon, C. J. Effect of treatment with medroxyprogesterone acetate (Provera) on testicular function. J. Clin. Endocr., 28: 679, 1968.

Schally, A. V., Bowers, C. Y., and Locke, W. Neurohumoral functions of the hypothalamus. Amer. J. Med. Sci., 248:79, 1964.

Seckel, H. P. G., Scott, W. W., and Benditt, E. P. Six examples of precocious sexual development. I. Studies in diagnosis and pathogenesis. Amer. J. Dis. Child., 78:484, 1949.

Thamdrup, E. Precocious Sexual Development. Springfield, Ill., Charles C Thomas, Publ., 1961.

Van Wyk, J. J., and Grumbach, M. M. Syndrome of precocious menstruation and galactorrhea in juvenile hypothyroidism: an example of hormonal overlap in pituitary feedback. J. Pediat., 57:416, 1960.

Wilkins, L. Diagnosis and Treatment of Endocrine Disorders in Childhood and Adolescence, 3rd ed. Springfield, Ill., Charles C Thomas, Publ., 1965.

Wurtman, R. J., and Kammer, H. Melatonin synthesis by an ectopic pinealoma. New Eng. J. Med., 274: 1233, 1966.

16.11
ABNORMALITIES OF SEX DIFFERENTIATION

MELVIN M. GRUMBACH

The term "hermaphrodism" or "intersexuality" is generally applied to individuals with gonads of one or both sexes and some degree of ambisexual differentiation of the accessory sexual structures. Depending on the morphology of the gonad, patients with these congenital abnormalities have been described as male pseudohermaphrodites (when testes are present), female pseudohermaphrodites (when ovaries are present), or true hermaphrodites (when both testicular and ovarian tissue can be identified). This definition does not include postnatal virilization or feminization, or such psychiatric disorders as homosexuality and transvestism. An important group of human sexual anomalies is characterized by absent or defective gonads and, in many instances, a discrepancy between the nuclear sex chromatin pattern and somatic sexual development. Examples of the latter are to be found in the syndrome of gonadal dysgenesis (Turner's syndrome) and in a congenital testicular disorder, seminiferous tubule dysgenesis (Klinefelter's syndrome). Chromosomal aberrations are found in this interesting group of gonadal anomalies. Abnormalities of sex differentiation are not exceedingly rare; estimates of incidence, where available, are discussed with the specific disorders.

HUMAN SEX DIFFERENTIATION. The human embryo is potentially a bisexual organism equipped with gonadal and genital primordia capable of differentiating in either a masculine or a feminine direction. It is now well accepted that the sex of the zygote at fertilization is established by a chromosomal mechanism which results in an unequal balance of sex-determining genes. Evidence adduced from the detection of abnormal sex chromosome constitutions in man indicates that the Y chromosome has potent male determiners and induces testicular differentiation of the primordial bipotential gonad whereas, with rare exceptions, two X chromosomes are required for the differentiation of ovaries. The embryonic gonad is the first structure to emerge from the indifferent stage, and ultimately either its medullary (testicular) or cortical (ovarian) component becomes dominant. The bipotential primordial germ cells—progenitors of oogonia and spermatogonia—arise from an extragonadal site, migrate to the urogenital ridge, and implant themselves in the cortex and medulla. This earliest sex differentiation is followed by the sex-specific development of the genital ducts and, subsequently, of the urogenital sinus and external genitalia. Although the embryo possesses a male and a female set of duct primordia, normally only the homologous pair develops completely, whereas the opposite set retrogresses and persists as vestigial structures. In the male, the Wolffian ducts form the vas deferens, epididymis, and seminal vesicles; in the female, the Müllerian ducts differentiate into the fallopian tubes, the uterus, and the upper portion of the vagina. The urogenital sinus and the anlage of the external genitalia are neutral primordia which give rise to homologous structures in the male and the female. These homologous structures include the clitoris and penis, the labia majora and scrotum, the labia minora and corpus spongiosum which encloses the penile urethra, and the paraurethral glands and prostate.

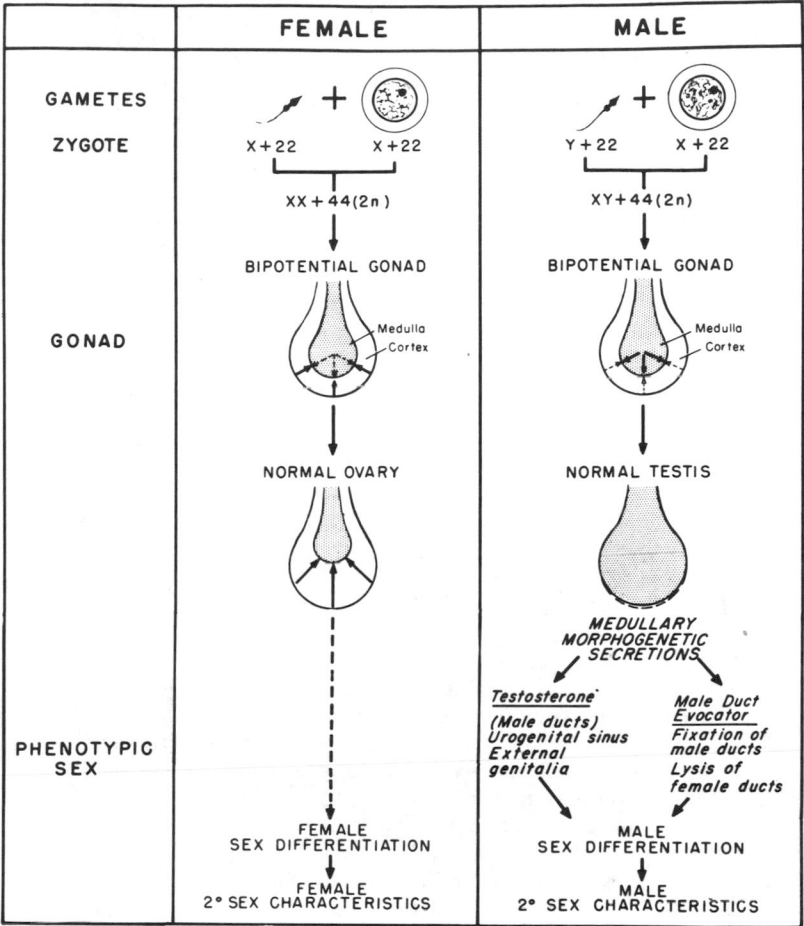

	FEMALE	MALE

Fig. 32. A diagrammatic scheme of human sex determination and differentiation. (Modified from Grumbach. *In* Astwood, ed., *Clinical Endocrinology I.* Courtesy of Grune & Stratton, Inc., 1960.)

The role of the gonad in embryogenesis of the accessory sex structures has been clarified by the fetal castration experiments of Jost and other embryologists and by analysis of abnormalities of sex differentiation in man. These studies support the concept of an inherent tendency of the fetus to develop along female lines irrespective of chromosomal sex, in the absence of fetal testes and their morphogenetic hormones. The fetal testicular morphogenetic hormones seem essential for the differentiation of male sex structures and for retrogression of the female ducts. The testicular secretions seem to be of two types: (1) a nonandrogenic duct-organizing secretion which leads to regression of the Müllerian (female) ducts and stimulates differentiation of the Wolffian duct; and (2) testosterone, secreted by the fetal Leydig cells, which induces male development of the urogenital sinus and external genitalia and stimulates growth of the Wolffian (male) ducts. Whereas a functioning fetal gonad is not a prerequisite for the development of a female genital system, exposure of the female fetus to androgenic hormones can arrest female differentiation of the urogenital sinus and external genitalia and induce masculinization of the lower genital tract.

A schematic representation of the present concept of sex determination and differentiation is shown in Figure 32. Intrinsic or extrinsic factors which adversely affect any stage of these mechanisms may lead to anomalies of sexual structure. These factors include (1) a sex chromosome abnormality arising in the ovum or sperm of the parent or in the zygote following fertilization, which affects gonadogenesis—as in the syndrome of gonadal dysgenesis or Turner's syndrome and seminiferous tubule dysgenesis or Klinefelter's syndrome; (2) a mutant gene—as in the feminizing testis form of male pseudohermaphrodism which leads to end-organ resistance to testosterone and other androgens in fetal and postnatal life; (3) translocation of sex-determining genes involving too minute an amount of chromosomal material to be visible by light microscopy, e.g., between a Y chromosome and an X or an autosome, which may be a cause of true hermaphrodism; (4) exposure of the fetus at a critical stage to inappropriate sex hormones which modify the sex-specific differentiation of the derivatives of the urogenital sinus and the primordia of the external genitalia—as in the form of female pseudohermaphrodism caused by congenital virilizing adrenal hyperplasia; and (5) undefined genetic or environmentally determined abnormalities in the differentiation of the primordial genital tract.

SEX CHROMATIN PATTERN—BARR BODY AND FLUORESCENT Y.   The discovery by Barr and his associates of a sexual dimorphism in nuclear structure provided a relatively simple method for indirectly assessing chromosomal sex. In the female a proportion of somatic interphase nuclei contain a focal mass of chromatin now known as the "sex chromatin." The sex chromatin is usually a planoconvex, not infrequently bipartite, mass which measures about 1 μ in diameter and is typically located against the inner surface of the nuclear membrane. In specimens from male subjects it is rare to find more than a few percent of nuclei which contain a mass of chromatin simulating the sex chromatin. Reliable techniques have been developed for detecting the sex chromatin pattern using such accessible tissues as skin, buccal, or vaginal mucosa and leucocytes. The oral smear method is preferred by many workers because of its simplicity and reliability. Preparations of good technical quality are essential to avoid errors of interpretation. In buccal smears from normal females, the proportion of chromatin-positive cells in well-preserved nuclei is not less than 25 percent in our experience. However, some workers have observed a decreased frequency of chromatin-positive nuclei in buccal smears of newborn females in the first 2 days of life.

The sex chromatin mass seen in somatic cells of normal females arises from a large part of one of the two X chromosomes in each cell. The two X chromosomes in female diploid somatic cells exhibit striking morphologic and functional differences. One X chromosome is in a highly condensed (heteropyknotic) state in interphase visible as sex chromatin, it completes DNA synthesis later than any other chromosome in the complement, and the action of genes located on the precociously condensed segments is suppressed. The other X chromosome, the single X chromosome in male somatic cells, is in a highly extended (isopyknotic) state during interphase, completes DNA replication with most of the complement, and is genetically active. This discordant behavior of the two homologous X chromosomes in female somatic cells serves as a mechanism of dosage compensation. The inactivation of much of the genic activity of all but one X chromosome in individuals with X polysomy minimizes the phenotypic expression of the extra X chromosome(s) in somatic cells. In X chromosome polysomy, more than one sex chromatin body is visible. With rare exceptions, the maximum number of sex chromatin bodies found in a diploid somatic nucleus is one less than the number of X chromosomes in the sex chromosome complex (Fig. 33). The size of the sex chromatin body is altered by certain structural abnormalities of the X chromosome. An abnormally large sex chromatin body has been associated with a large X chromosome, an X isochromosome composed of two long arms of the X but lacking a short arm.

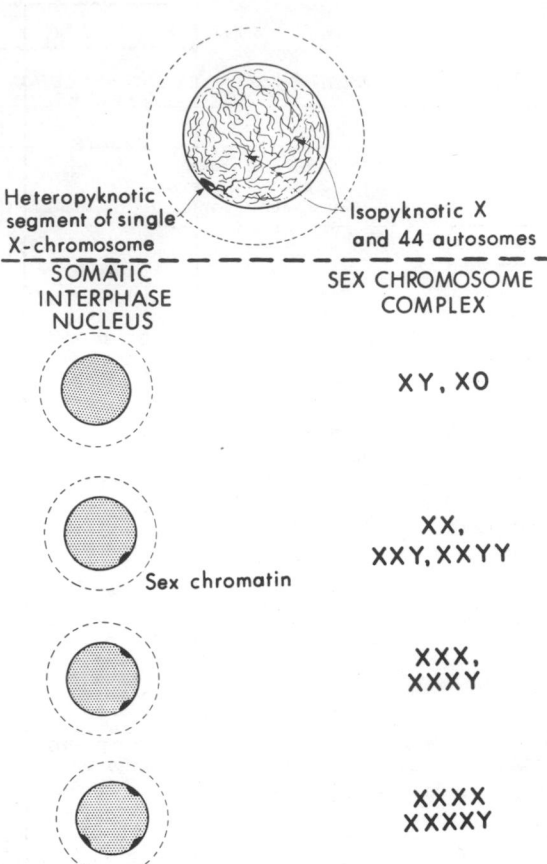

Fig. 33. Relation of sex chromosomes to sex chromatin. The upper portion of the diagram illustrates the heteropyknotic X-chromosome which forms the sex chromatin body in a female interphase nucleus. The other X-chromosome and the autosomes are largely in an extended (isopyknotic) state and give rise to the particulate chromatin. The lower diagram shows the correlation between the maximum number of sex chromatin bodies in diploid interphase nuclei and the number of X chromosomes in the sex chromosome complement, the number of sex chromatin bodies being one less than the number of X-chromosomes. In the presence of certain sex chromosome mosaicism of the XO/XX type, for example, the XO cell line often leads to a lowering of chromatin-positive cells below the normal range for female. (From Grumbach and Morishima. *Proc. Nat. Acad. Sci.,* 49:581, 1963.)

Small sex chromatin bodies may be found in individuals who have a deletion of the short or long arm of an X chromosome or a ring X chromosome. When there is a structurally abnormal X chromosome, the sex chromatin body is formed by the anomalous X chromosome and not the normal X.

Recently, a staining method for identification of the human Y chromosome has been reported. Quinacrine hydrochloride, an acridine derivative, produces intense fluorescent staining of the distal part of the long arm of the Y chromosome in metaphase preparations, in interphase nuclei including cells from

TABLE 15. *Abnormalities of Sex Differentiation*

Type	Sex Chromatin	Sex Chromosomes	Gonads	External Genitalia		Genital Ducts	Secondary Sexual Characteristics
				Phallus	Labioscrotal Fusion*		
Female pseudo-hermaphrodism							
With adrenal hyperplasia	Positive	XX	Ovaries	Medium to large	0-3+	Female	Precocious male
Without adrenal hyperplasia	Positive	XX	Ovaries	Medium to large	0-3+	Female	Female
Male pseudo-hermaphrodism							Female Primary amenorrhea ± Absent or sparse sexual hair Male
Simulant female (syndrome of feminizing testes)	Negative	XY	Testes†	Small	0-1+	Variable	
External genitalia ambiguous or with large phallus	Negative	XY (XO/XY)	Testes†	Hypoplastic‡ to large	1+ to 3+	Primarily male	Male: ± Eunuchoid; Female
						Primarily female	Usually male; ± Eunuchoid
True hermaphrodism	Positive Negative	XX> XY XX/XY	Ovotestis(es) or ovary and testis	Variable		Variable	Male or female
Syndrome of gonadal dysgenesis (Turner's syndrome)	80% Negative Positive	XO XO/XX §	Vestigial streak‖	Female (rarely) slight clitoral enlargement		Female	Infantile
Seminiferous tubule dysgenesis Tubular fibrosis (Klinefelter's syndrome)	Positive Negative	XXY# XY (rare)	Small testes	Male		Male	Male ± Eunuchoidism ± Gynecomastia ± Mental deficiency

*Degree of fusion: Absent = 0 to Extreme = 3+.

†Testes intraabdominal, inguinal, or labioscrotal.

‡Usually hypospadiac penis; occasionally penile urethra, urogenital sinus, separate vaginal orifice.

§Other sex chromosome abnormalities have been described in gonadal dysgenesis such as Xx, XO/XY, XO/XXX, XO/XX/XXX, X-isochromosome X, X deleted Y.

‖Characteristically only mesonephric vestiges; occasionally varying degrees of cortical and medullary rudiments.

#Other sex chromosome abnormalities which may be encountered in seminiferous tubule dysgenesis include XXYY, XXXY, XXXXY, XX/XXY, XXXY/XXXXY.

the buccal mucosa, and in Y-bearing sperm. Diploid nuclei which contain two Y chromosomes (e.g., XYY and other double Y karyotypes) have two fluorescent Y chromosomes.

CLASSIFICATION. The problem of classification of hermaphrodism has not been entirely resolved. Table 15 contains a classification which is convenient for clinical use based on gonadal sex and on the sex chromatin pattern. It is important to emphasize that such terms as "female pseudohermaphrodism" and "male pseudohermaphrodism" describe a heterogeneous group of disorders which have in common certain morphologic characteristics.

Female Pseudohermaphrodism

Individuals with this syndrome have ovaries, female ducts, and varying degrees of masculine differentiation of the urogenital sinus and external genitalia. The sex chromatin pattern is positive (female). The syndrome illustrates well the complexity of pathogenetic factors which may result in similar malformations. Table 16 contains a classification according to etiology.

The most common cause is congenital virilizing adrenal hyperplasia in the female. This disorder, described on page 1095, is caused by an inborn error of adrenocortical biosynthesis which results in a relative deficiency of hydrocortisone production and a relative excess of androgenic hormones and other steroids. The mode of inheritance is probably that of an autosomal recessive gene. The minimum incidence has been estimated at 1 in 53,000 live white births. At birth the external genitalia are, as a rule, conspicuously abnormal. The degree of masculinization can be judged by the size of the clitoris and the completeness of labioscrotal fusion, which determines the size of the urogenital sinus (Fig. 34). The phallus is invariably enlarged, often approximating the size of a penis (Fig. 35 and 36). It is generally bound in chordee, behind which a perineal hypospadias is situated. In rare cases the urethra extends to the tip of the phallus (Fig. 37). Commonly, the labia majora have the appearance of a bifid scrotum. Within the perineal opening of the urogenital sinus lie the orifices of the vagina and the urethra. Greater or lesser degrees of fusion of the labioscrotal folds result in a perineal opening which varies in size from that of a small urethralike opening to a relatively normal female introitus with a separate urethra and vagina (Fig. 34).

The appearance of the external genitalia is not specific, and the genital abnormality may be indistinguishable from that found in other forms of hermaphrodism with bilateral cryptorchidism. The feature which sets this disorder apart from all other varieties of hermaphrodism is the secretion of excessive quantities of adrenal androgen. The urine contains 17-ketosteroids and pregnanetriol in greater amounts than found in any of the other forms of abnormal sex differentiation. (In normal infants the excretion of 17-ketosteroids during the first 2 weeks of life may be as high as 2.5 mg per day, later diminishing to less than 1 mg per day.) In older children signs of virilization, rapid growth, and accelerated skeletal development are present (Fig. 37). Three main forms of congenital virilizing adrenal hyperplasia have been

TABLE 16.   *Classification of Female Pseudohermaphrodism*

Androgen-Induced
   Fetal source
      Congenital virilizing adrenal hyperplasia
         Virilism only (defective adrenal 21-hydroxylation—compensated)
         Virilism with hypertension (defective adrenal 11-hydroxylation)
         Virilism with salt-losing syndrome (defective adrenal 21-hydroxylation—uncompensated)

   Maternal source
      Virilizing ovarian tumor
      Iatrogenic
         Testosterone and related steroids
         Certain synthetic oral progestins and rarely stilbestrol

   Undetermined source

Other Teratogenic Factors
   Nonhormonal disturbances in the differentiation of urogenital structures

defined, each of which may be associated with female pseudohermaphrodism (Table 16); other forms of congenital adrenal hyperplasia not accompanied by virilization of the fetus have been described (see p. 1097, Sec. 16.4). With rare exceptions, affected pedigrees have exhibited only one form of the disorder.

Less frequent are forms of androgen-induced female pseudohermaphrodism caused by the placental transfer of androgens from the mother. In two instances a virilizing ovarian tumor existing in the mother during pregnancy resulted in partial masculinization of the external genitalia of the female fetus. More frequently the maternal source has been therapeutic: the administration of steroids with androgenic activity during pregnancy. In several instances testosterone or a testosterone analog had been administered during pregnancy. Comparable cases have been associated with the administration of certain oral semisynthetic progestins, such as 17 α-ethynyltestosterone (Lutocylol, Pranone, Nugestoral), 17 α-ethynyl-19-nortestosterone (Norlutin), and norethynodrel (Enovid), to pregnant women in an effort to control habitual or threatened abortion. Fusion of the labioscrotal folds and formation of a urogenital sinus occur when androgen has been administered before the thirteenth week of gestation, but enlargement of the clitoris may follow androgen treatment of the mother at any time during pregnancy. In rare cases diethylstilbestrol, an estrogen, has been suggested as a possible fetal masculinizing agent.

Another distinct and rare type of female pseudohermaphrodism is not caused by androgen excess. Associated developmental anomalies of the urinary tract and cloaca may be present, as well as absence of a fallopian tube or an ovary and a poorly developed uterus. There may be atresia of the rectum or recto-

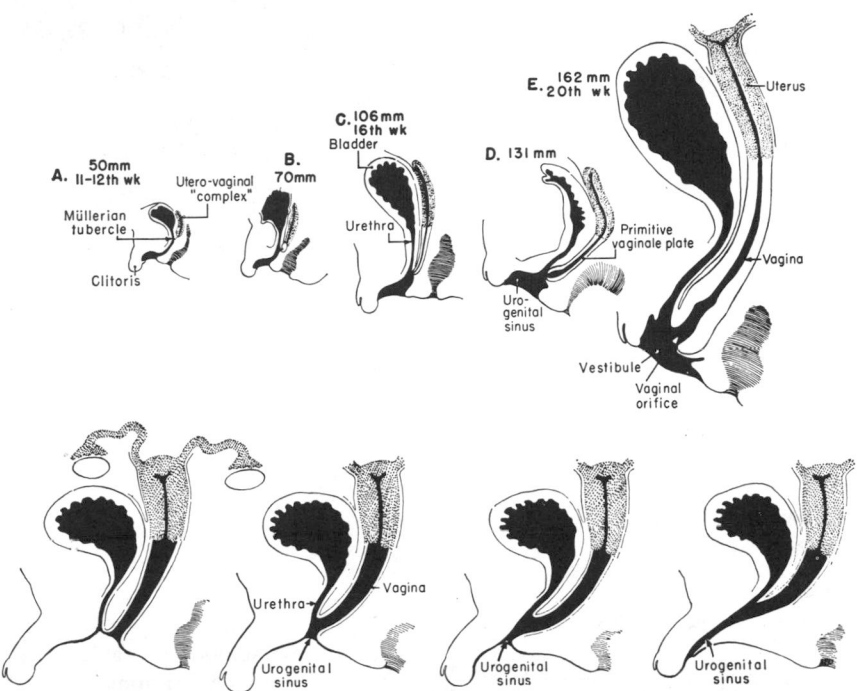

Fig. 34. Development of female pseudohermaphrodism. Upper diagrams show the sequence of differentiation of the female accessory sex structures. Note the gradual descent of the utero-vaginal complex (adapted from Koff). To modify the differentiation of the urogenital sinus, especially the urethral groove, it seems that androgens must act on the female fetus before the thirteenth week of gestation, although enlargement of the clitoris can be induced at later stages. The lower schematic diagram illustrates variations in the degree of masculinization of the urogenital sinus and external genitalia in androgen-induced female pseudohermaphrodism. (From Grumbach and Ducharme. *Fertil. Steril.*, 11:157, 1960.)

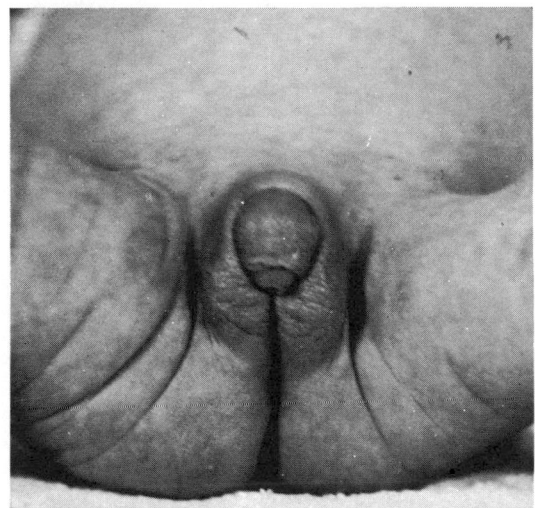

Fig. 35. The external genitalia in a 2-week-old female pseudohermaphrodite with congenital adrenal hyperplasia. The enlarged phallus, bound in chordee, overlies the funnel-shaped orifice of the urogenital sinus. The labioscrotal folds have the appearance of a bifid scrotum.

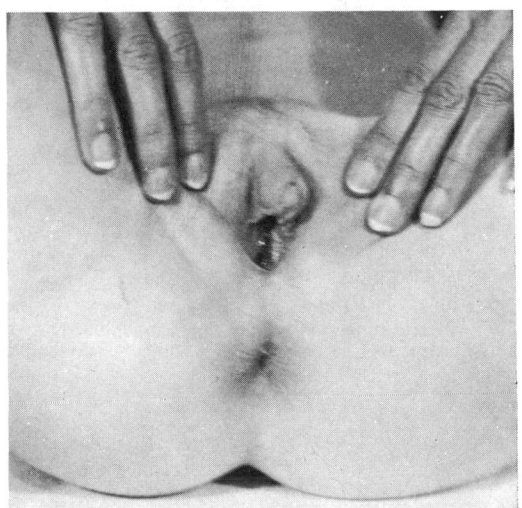

Fig. 36. Enlargement of the clitoris without fusion of the labioscrotal folds in a 4-year-old female with congenital adrenal hyperplasia. Hypertrophy of the clitoris was noted at birth. Separate vaginal and urethral orifices were identified by inspection. Note also the sparce pubic hair.

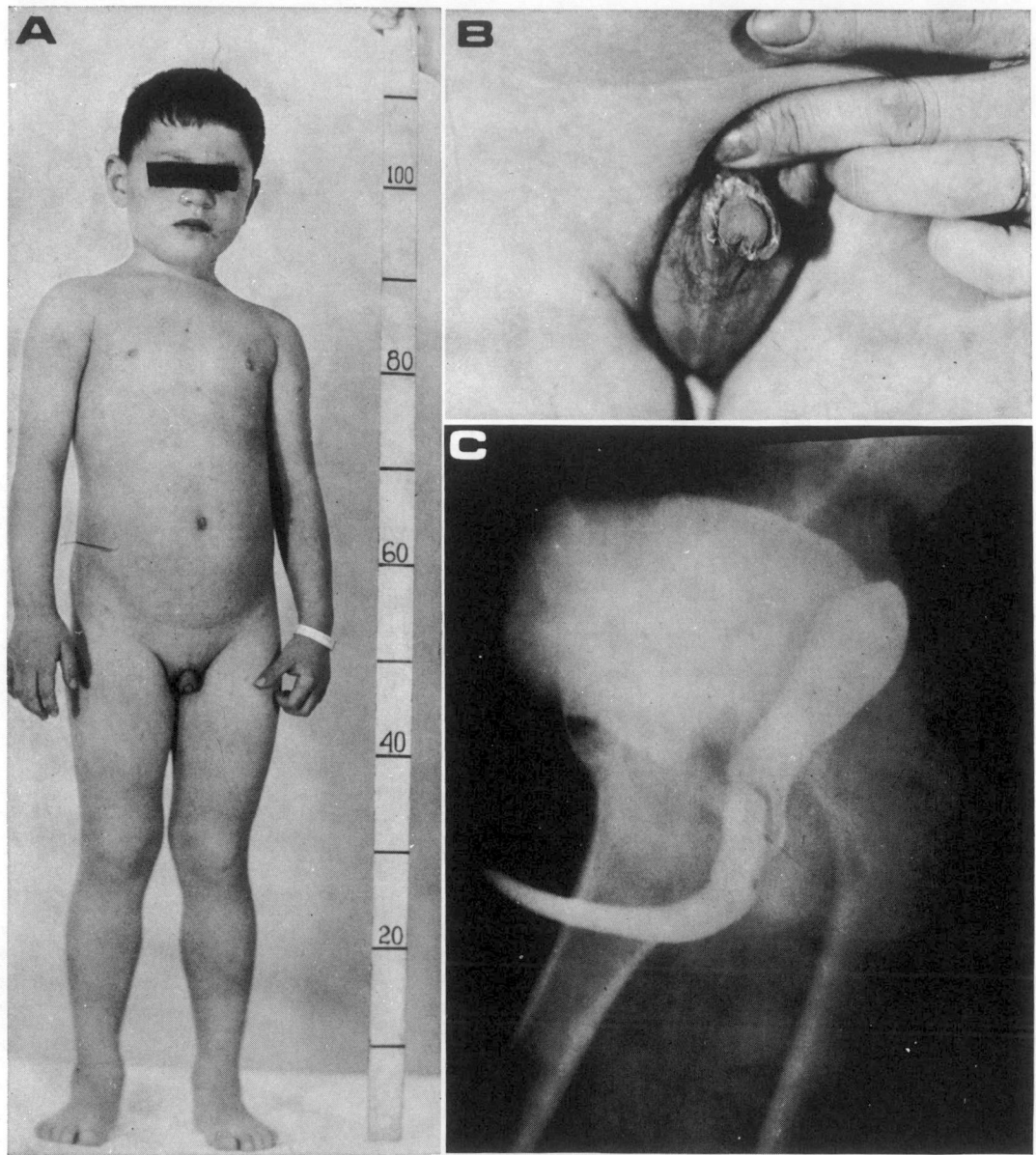

Fig. 37. A. A 45-month-old female pseudohermaphrodite, with congenital adrenal hyperplasia and a penile urethra, reared as a male. Height 112 cm (+2.5 SD), bone age 8 years, urinary 17-ketosteroids 11.5 to 13.8 mg per day, and pregnanetriol 3 to 4 mg per day. The sex chromatin pattern was positive. B. Appearance of the external genitalia. C. Urethrogram shows the urogenital sinus and distended vagina. Some of the contrast medium also entered the bladder. (From Grumbach and Ducharme. *Fertil. Steril.*, 11:157, 1960.)

vaginal fistula. Stenosis of the urethra may cause urinary retention in early infancy.

In individuals with nonadrenal female pseudohermaphrodism mistaken for cryptorchid males, the correct sex diagnosis may not be appreciated until gynecomastia and recurrent "hematuria" due to menstruation appear at adolescence. No sexual development occurs before puberty, at which time female secondary sexual characteristics appear.

Male Pseudohermaphrodism

Individuals in this group have testes, a variable degree of ambisexual development of either the genital ducts or the urogenital sinus and external genitalia, or both, and chromatin-negative nuclei (Fig. 38).

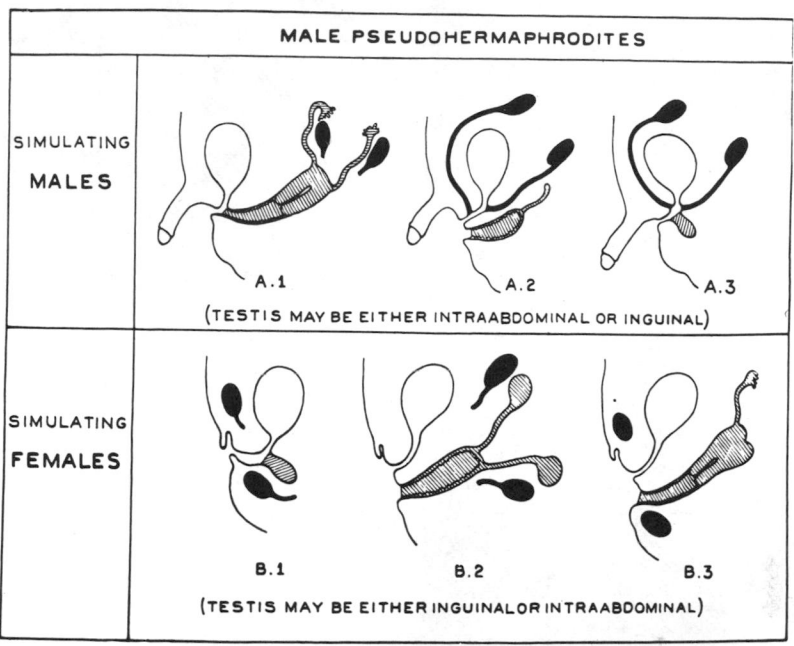

Fig. 38. Common anatomic findings in male pseudohermaphrodites. The black structures are testes and derivatives of the Wolffian ducts. The cross-hatched areas include derivatives of the Müllerian ducts and female urogenital structures. (From Wilkins et al. *Pediatrics*, 16:287, 1956.)

The morphology of the seminiferous tubules is usually abnormal, but frequently Leydig cells appear at the age of puberty. The appearance of the external genitalia varies from that of a normal female to that of a male, with a penile urethra and either bilateral or unilateral cryptorchidism. Commonly, there is perineal hypospadias. The testes may be located inside the abdomen, sometimes in the position of ovaries, in the inguinal region, or in the labioscrotal folds.

Male pseudohermaphrodism occurs in a heterogeneous group of disorders which have in common the failure of the fetal testis to bring about complete masculinization of the somatic sex structures. Since knowledge of etiologic factors is still fragmentary, current classification is based largely on morphologic characteristics. The form of male pseudohermaphrodism associated with the syndrome of feminizing testes results from a mutant gene which leads to end-organ unresponsiveness to androgen. In one instance an environmental factor, the administration of large amounts of stilbestrol early in pregnancy, was implicated. In the forms of male pseudohermaphrodism which represent variants of the syndrome of gonadal dysgenesis, a sex chromosome aberration such as XO/XY or XO/XY/XYY mosaicism, or a deletion of the Y chromosome, leads to dysgenetic differentiation of the testes.

Male pseudohermaphrodites can be conveniently divided into two types according to the anatomy of the external genitalia: (1) simulant females with feminizing testes and (2) those in whom the external genitalia are ambiguous or resemble those of the male (Fig. 38).

SYNDROME OF FEMINIZING TESTES (SIMULANT FEMALES). This syndrome is a relatively common and well-defined form of male pseudohermaphrodism; more than 100 cases have been reported. These patients are genetic males; their sex chromosome constitution is XY. They have testes, which are usually located in the inguinal canal or in the labial folds. Because these patients present a normal female appearance, the diagnosis is often not suspected. The occurrence of multiple cases within a family is frequent, and family pedigrees suggest that the condition is transmitted by either a sex-linked recessive or sex-limited autosomal dominant gene. The external genitalia are female in configuration; occasionally the clitoris is slightly enlarged and the labioscrotal folds are partially fused. Characteristically, there is a blind vaginal pouch. The development of the genital ducts is variable but the uterus is absent or rudimentary. At puberty estrogenic steroids secreted by the testes bring about feminization of body habitus, development of the breasts, and estrinization of the vaginal mucosa, but menstruation fails to occur. The testes also secrete testosterone, and at puberty the concentration of plasma testosterone is usually within the normal range for males. However, there is lack of response of the appropriate end-organs, both genital and somatic, to androgens in the fetus and at puberty, which leads to the female differentiation of the urogenital sinus and external genitalia and to the femini-

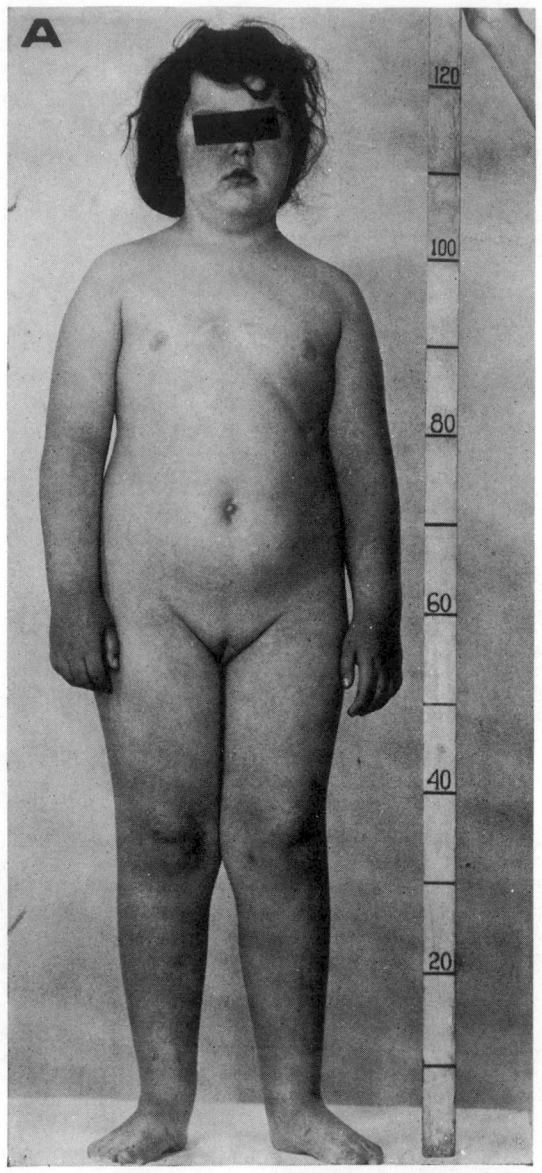

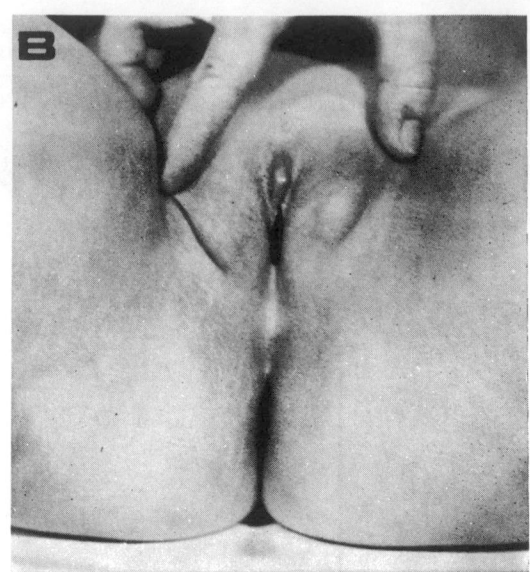

Fig. 39. A 5-year-old patient with male pseudohermaphrodism and feminizing testes. A. General appearance. B. Female external genitalia, showing bilateral labial masses which at operation proved to be testes. (From Grumbach and Barr. *Recent Progr. Hormone Res.*, 14:255, 1958.)

zation at puberty. Castration leads to a fall in urinary estrogens and testosterone, a rise in gonadotropins, and menopausal symptoms. In the majority of cases, pubic and axillary hair is absent or sparse, a manifestation of the impaired response to androgen of the hair follicles which give rise to sexual hair. In the classic form of the syndrome, the administration of large amounts of testosterone does not induce either masculinization or an appropriate degree of protein anabolism.

During childhood the discovery of a testis in an inguinal or labial hernia is usually the only clue to the diagnosis in the absence of a familial history (Fig. 39). The diagnosis should be considered in an adolescent girl with primary amenorrhea in the pres-

ence of otherwise female secondary sexual characteristics, especially when associated with absence of sexual hair and unilateral or bilateral hernial masses.

MALE PSEUDOHERMAPHRODISM AS A VARIANT OF THE SYNDROME OF GONADAL DYSGENESIS. A highly diverse phenotype has been described in patients with XO/XY mosaicism or a structural abnormality of the Y chromosome. The appearance has ranged from that of a sexually infantile phenotypic female, with or without somatic anomalies of Turner's syndrome and with bilateral streak gonads, through patients with a variable degree of masculine differentiation of the external genitalia, urogenital sinus, and genital ducts, to those who have virtually normal male differentiation of the genital tract. In some patients, a dysgenetic testis is present on one side and a streak gonad on the other. Short stature and the somatic anomalies of Turner's syndrome are inconstant features.

MALE PSEUDOHERMAPHRODISM WITH AMBIGUOUS EXTERNAL GENITALIA OR WITH A WELL-DEVELOPED PHALLUS. A diversity of malformations of the external and internal genital structures occur in this group. Commonly, the hypospadiac phallus is hypoplastic and bound in chordee by a long fibrous frenulum. In some cases there is a urogenital sinus; in others a vaginal pouch communicates with the urethra. A separate vaginal orifice is sometimes located between the labioscrotal folds. The anatomic findings may resemble those seen in female pseudohermaphrodites with the exception that testes and not ovaries are found in the mesosalpinx. The rare cases with a penile urethra are usually associated with female development of the internal reproductive organs. In many instances the derivatives of the genital ducts are rudimentary.

The development of secondary sexual characteristics at puberty also varies. Frequently, male characteristics appear, especially in male pseudohermaphrodites with fallopian tubes and a uterus and predominantly masculine external genitalia in whom the morphology of the testes is well preserved. However, adolescent sexual development may be impaired, with resulting eunuchoidism, sometimes associated with gynecomastia. In these cases urinary gonadotropin is often increased. In some patients the gynecomastia and feminine body habitus suggest primarily female development.

MALE PSEUDOHERMAPHRODISM WITH CONGENITAL NONVIRILIZING ADRENAL HYPERPLASIA (See p. 1097, Sec. 16.4). An exceedingly rare form of male pseudohermaphrodism is associated with clinical and biochemical evidence of adrenal insufficiency, a peculiar form of adrenal hyperplasia characterized by large adrenocortical cells distended with lipid material (congenital lipoid adrenal hyperplasia), and death in early infancy. The genital structures simulate the anatomic findings in the group with feminizing testes: female external genitalia, a short blind vaginal pouch, and testes. This familial disorder is due to a genetically determined enzymatic defect in the conversion of cholesterol to pregnenolone by the adrenal glands and testes; plasma and urinary 17-ketosteroids, androgens, and corticoids, including aldosterone, are exceedingly low.

A deficiency of 3β-hydroxydehydrogenase in the adrenal cortex and testes is associated with incomplete masculinization of the external genitalia in affected males, relatively minor degrees of masculinization of the external genitalia in the female, and often adrenal insufficiency owing to cortisol and aldosterone deficiency. The excretion of urinary 17-ketosteroids is elevated, and large amounts of steroids with a 3β-hydroxy configuration are found in the plasma and urine.

Defective adrenal and gonadal 17-hydroxylation leads to female differentiation of the external genitalia in affected males, a female phenotype in affected females, sexual infantilism at puberty, and hypertension and hypokalemic alkalosis. The secretion of corticosterone and deoxycorticosterone is increased; urinary 17-ketosteroids and 17-hydroxycorticosteroids are low.

True Hermaphrodism

This group of intersexes is composed of individuals who have both an ovary and a testis or, more commonly, in whom one or both gonads are ovo-testes. Although this disorder is rare, more than 100 cases have been reported, including two affected sibships. The sex chromatin pattern may be negative or positive; a preponderance of chromatin-positive cases has been observed. Development of the accessory sexual structures is highly variable. Predominantly masculine or feminine maturation occurs at puberty. A sex chromosome abnormality has not been demonstrated in most patients with true hermaphrodism. Usually an XX sex chromosome constitution has been found, although mosaicism is not readily excluded as a possibility. In a few instances sex chromosome abnormalities have been detected, such as XX/XY chimerism, thought to arise by double fertilization of a binucleate ovum or by fusion of two independently fertilized zygotes, and XX/XXY mosaicism. The occurrence of this syndrome in patients with an XX or XY karyotype suggests an environmental factor which disrupts gonadogenesis, or the translocation of sex-determining genes during spermatogenesis in the father, e.g., translocation of male-determining genes from the Y chromosome to the X or an autosome. Some of these patients are potentially fertile, and when possible, after deciding on the sex of rearing, an attempt should be made to preserve the appropriate gonad or gonadal segment, especially if an ovary is present in the mesosalpinx or a testis attached to its exocrine ducts in the scrotum.

Gonadal Dysgenesis—Turner's Syndrome (*Gonadal Dysplasia, Ovarian Agenesis, Bonnevie-Ullrich Syndrome*)

The typical form of the syndrome, first delineated by Turner in 1938, is characterized by a female phenotype, short stature, sexual infantilism, streak gonads, and a diversity of associated somatic anomalies (Fig. 40); these features are a consequence of the X chromosome monosomy (XO karyotype) of these individuals. The most common associated congenital malformations include atypical facies, broad shield-like chest, low hairline over the nape of the neck, webbed neck (in about 40 percent), congenital lymph-

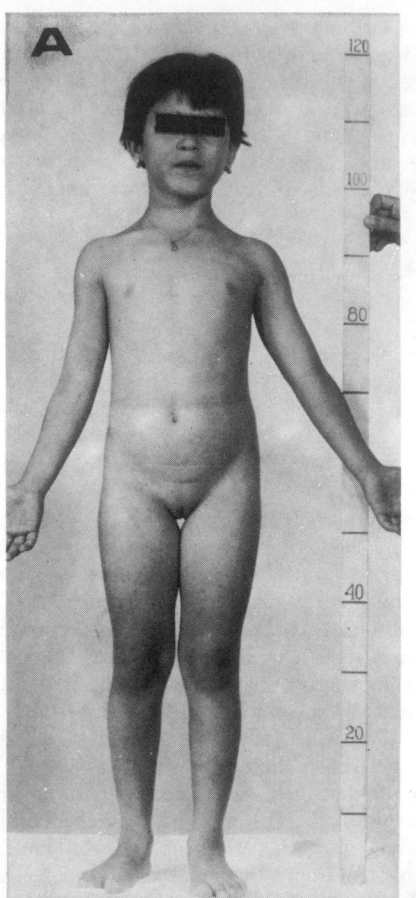
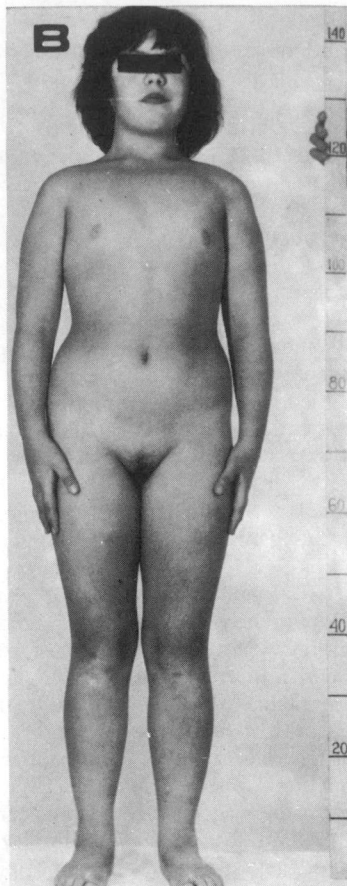
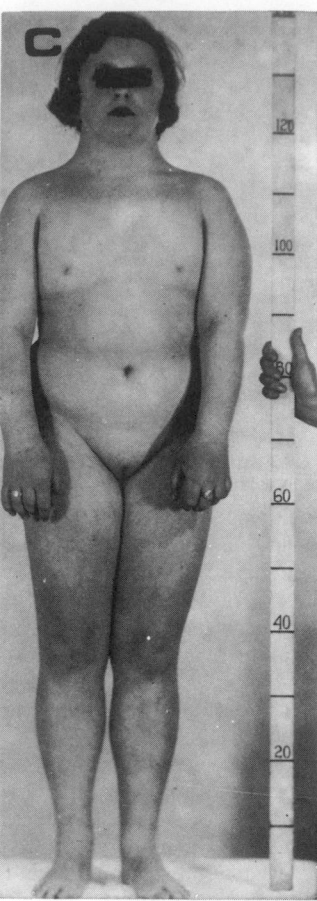
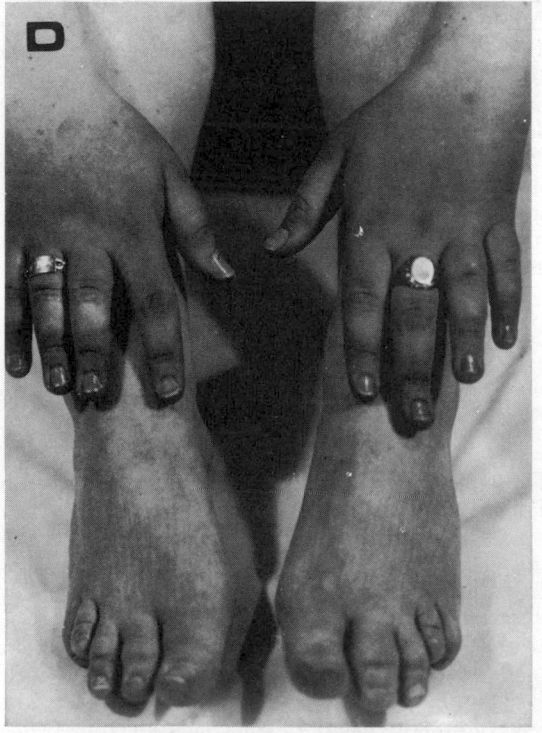

Fig. 40. Three patients with the syndrome of gonadal dysgenesis and chromatin-negative somatic nuclei. A. Age 9 years, 11 months. Short stature was the complaint. B. Age 15 years, 4 months. Typical habitus without webbing of the neck. Pubic hair is present, but estrogen-induced gonadotropin excretion was greater than 100 mouse units per day. C. Age 15½ years. Classical aspect of Turner's syndrome. D. The hands and feet of patient shown at top right, illustrating the useful clinical signs of conspicuous shortening of the fourth digits due to underdevelopment of metacarpals and metatarsals, puffiness over the dorsum of the digits between the interphalangeal joints, convexity of the nails, and the prominence of the pulp of the finger beyond the tip of the fingernail.

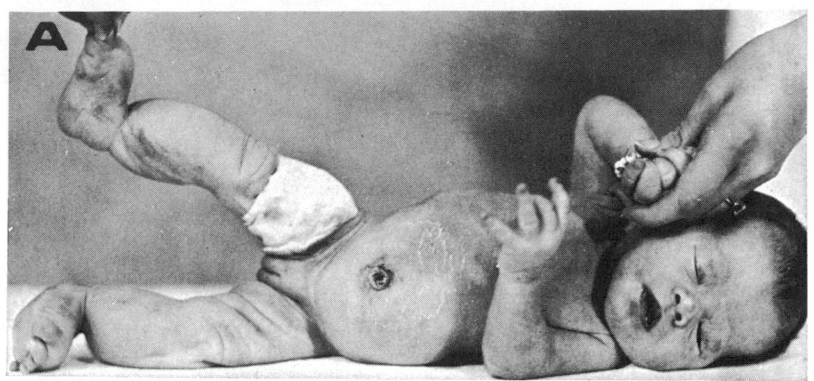

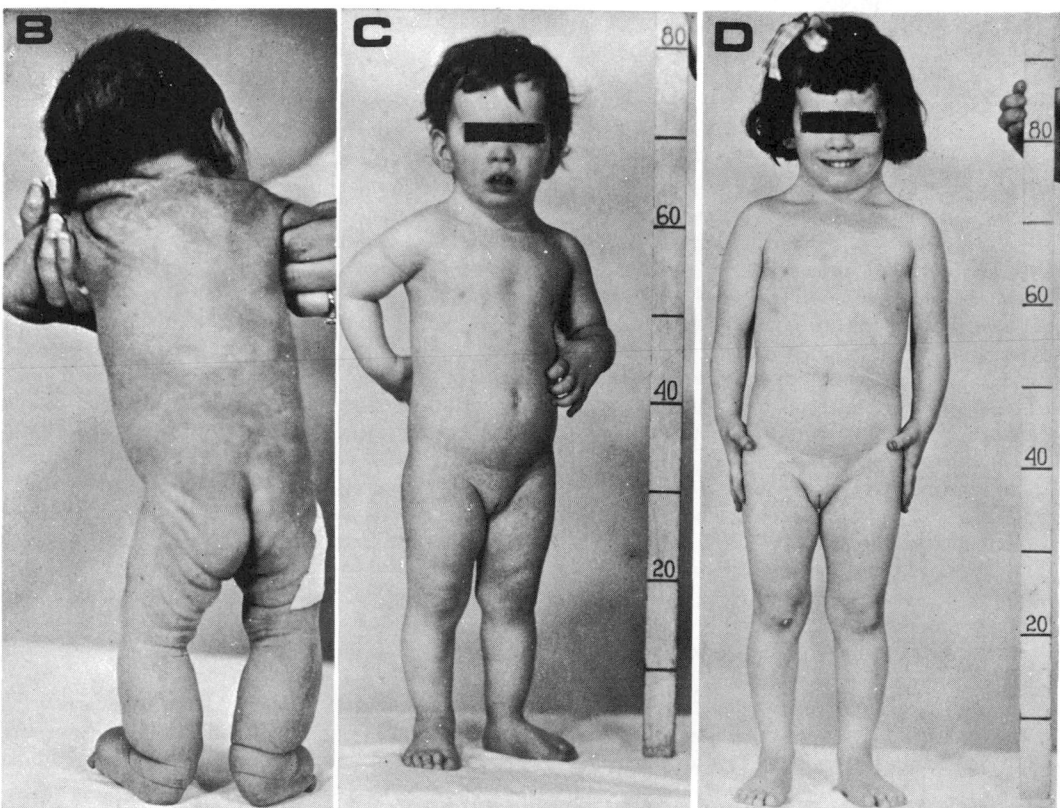

Fig. 41. A patient with the syndrome of gonadal dysgenesis, features of the Bonnevie-Ullrich syndrome, and negative sex chromatin pattern. *A* and *B.* Appearance at age seven days. Note the massive edema of the distal parts of the lower extremities, the puffiness of the hands, and the loose folds of skin over the nape of the neck. A dressing covers the site of a skin biopsy. *C.* At age 24 months, the neck is webbed, and only residual swelling of the feet is present. *D.* Age 4 years. Note the broad chest and microthelia. Urinary gonadotropin was not detectable at 5 mouse units per day. (From Grumbach and Barr. *Recent Progr. Hormone Res.,* 14:255, 1958.)

edema of the extremities, especially the hands and feet (in 30 percent of cases), coarctation of the aorta (in 20 percent), cubitus valgus, short fourth metacarpal (50 percent), high arched palate, a variety of skeletal anomalies, hypoplastic nails, microthelia, and cutaneous (pigmented nevi and predisposition to keloid formation), ocular, otitic (tendency for recurrent otitis media, perceptive hearing loss), and renal (most commonly horseshoe kidney) abnormalities (in about 50 percent of cases). A small proportion of patients are mentally defective; deficits of space-form recognition and directional sense are common despite a normal intelligence quotient. Skeletal maturation is normal or mildly delayed before puberty. Diminished mineralization of the hands, feet, and elbows is common.

The habitus is usually typical and consists of a short, stocky build, broad chest, short neck, and a small mandible. An increased number of pigmented nevi is frequently found. No true gonad is present; in each mesosalpinx there is a ridge of connective tissue devoid of any germinal elements. These individuals develop none of the secondary sexual characteristics caused by secretion of estrogen at puberty, but in contrast to hypopituitary dwarfs, sexual hair does appear. Very rarely some degree of feminization occurs at puberty, and in one instance fertility has been described. During adolescence the excretion of urinary gonadotropin rises to castrate levels; occasionally, elevated titers have been detected in childhood. Chromatin-negative nuclei have been found in about 80 percent of the cases. This latter finding, in association with the characteristic features of the syndrome, especially lymphedema and loose folds of skin about the nape of the neck (Bonnevie-Ullrich syndrome), provides a method for establishing the diagnosis as early as the neonatal period (Fig. 41). Pleural effusion may occur in the newborn.

Intrauterine growth retardation is common. There is an increased prevalence of twinning, but familial cases are exceedingly rare. About 5 percent of spontaneous abortions are estimated to have an XO karyotype. It is estimated that about 1 percent of all zygotes are XO but less than 5 percent survive to term. The mortality rate is increased in infancy.

The prevalence of chromatin-negative phenotypic females in surveys of newborn nurseries is 0.37/1,000; in comparison, the frequency of XXX newborn females is 1.2/1,000 and of newborn chromatin-positive phenotypic males 2.07/1,000.

The typical sex chromosome abnormality in chromatin-negative cases, first described by Ford et al., is an XO sex chromosome constitution with a diploid chromosome number of 45. The monosomic X sex chromosome complement may arise as a consequence of meiotic nondisjunction during gametogenesis in one parent or from loss of a sex chromosome (either the X or Y) during an early cleavage division of the zygote.

Other sex chromosome abnormalities have been described, all of which represent a less than complete absence of a second sex chromosome. The variable deficiency of the sex chromosomes is associated with a highly diverse modification of the classic XO phenotype. These clinical variants of the syndrome of gonadal dysgenesis are found in patients with sex chromosome mosaicism involving an XO cell line (such as XO/XX, XO/XX/XXX, and XO/XY mosaicism) or a structural abnormality of an X or Y chromosome such as an isochromosome-X (XX^I), an X or Y chromosome deletion (XX^D or XY^D), or a ring X or Y chromosome. Structural abnormalities of the sex chromosomes are commonly associated with XO mosaicism owing to loss of the heteromorphic chromosome from some cells (e.g., XO/XX^I, XO/X ring X).

Sex chromosome mosaicism involving an XO cell line and structural abnormalities of the X or Y chromosome usually modify the phenotypic expression of the classic form of the syndrome of gonadal dysgenesis associated with an XO karyotype. The modifications of the typical Turner phenotype in the variant forms of the syndrome are toward a more normal phenotype and usually involve all or any of the following aspects of the disorder: gonadal differentiation and function, stature, and the associated somatic stigmata. In the chromatin-positive variants associated with XO/XX or XO/XX/XXX mosaicism, normal stature may be achieved, a variable degree of ovarian function—including ovulation—may be found, and the associated somatic anomalies may be absent or minimal. In other cases with the same type of mosaicism, the phenotype is indistinguishable from the XO individual. In these forms of sex chromosome mosaicism the sex chromatin pattern is positive, but a diminished proportion of chromatin-positive cells is often found. When a diploid cell line containing more than two X chromosomes is present, multiple sex chromatin bodies are usually found in some of the chromatin-positive cells. The X isochromosome-X individuals have a positive sex chromatin pattern with larger Barr bodies, and the phenotype does not depart from the typical form, even though such somatic anomalies as lymphedema of the extremities, webbed neck, and coarctation of the aorta are rare in these individuals. In patients with a deletion of the short arm of the X (XX^D), short stature and typical stigmata are found. However, such a patient studied by the author exhibited well-developed female secondary sex characteristics and had dysfunctional menstrual bleeding. Patients with an XO/X ring-X karyotype usually have short stature and associated somatic anomalies but may menstruate.

XO/XY mosaicism is associated with a diverse phenotype (see male pseudohermaphrodism). The karyotype may be associated with a variable degree of testicular differentiation leading, in some cases, to ambisexual development of the external genitalia and, in others, to a virtually normal male phenotype.

Therapy is directed toward the correction of remediable congenital anomalies and sexual infantilism. In phenotypic females with elevated urinary gonadotropin, treatment with estrogen should be initiated at about 13 years of age, continuously for two to four months and then cyclically for three out of four weeks, to bring about the development of feminine secondary sexual characteristics and estrogen withdrawal bleeding. Gonadectomy is recommended in XO/XY and related forms of mosaicism because of the increased risk of gonadal neoplasm.

PURE OR XY GONADAL DYSGENESIS. This term has been applied to phenotypic females who have an XY karyotype, streak gonads, sexual infantilism, normal or tall stature, and lack the somatic stigmata of

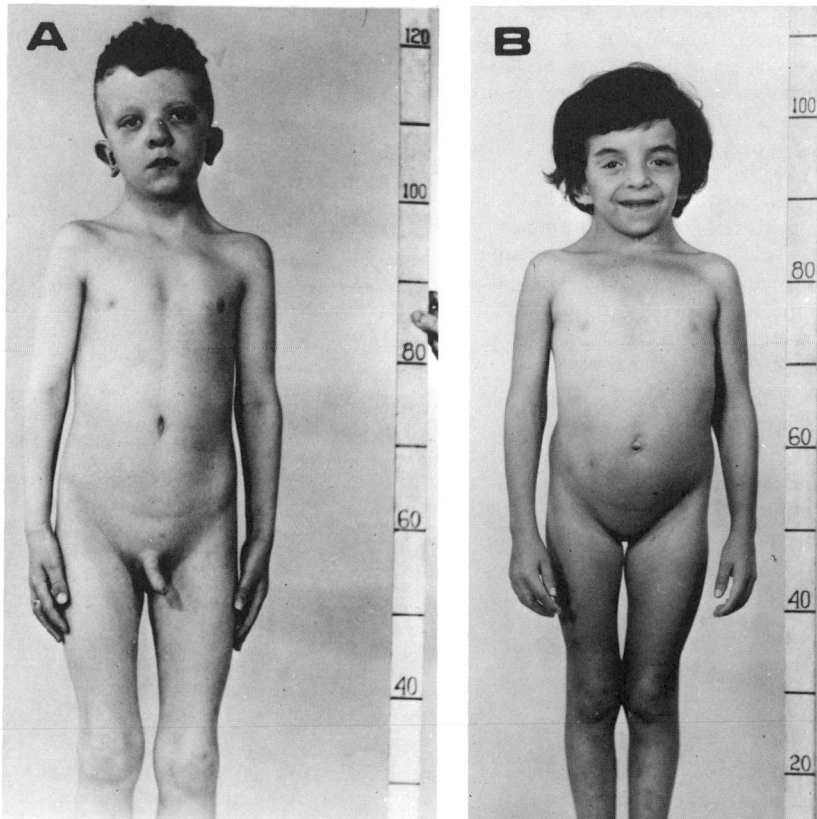

Fig. 42. A phenotypic male and female with the syndrome of webbed neck, ptosis, congenital heart disease, short stature, and hypogonadism. A. A boy of 9 years 7 months who exhibits the characteristic abnormalities: triangular facies, prominent brow, hypertelorism, ptosis, antimongoloid slant of palpebral fissures, broad apex nasi, low-set ears, webbed neck, pectus excavatum, pulmonic stenosis and atrial septal defect, short stature (−3.5 SD), bilateral undescended testes, and high-grade mental retardation. At 18 years of age, he was 154.0 cm in height (height age: 12 years 5 months); Leydig cell hypofunction was present. Biopsy of the testes showed germinal aplasia. XY/46 chromosome constitution with a normal karyotype. B. An 8-year-old girl with similar features. Height 106.2 cm (height age 4 years 4 months). Pulmonic stenosis was present. XX/46 karyotype. (From Grumbach and Barr. *Recent Progr. Hormone Res.*, 14:255, 1958.)

Turner's syndrome. The prevalence of gonadal neoplasms such as seminoma and gonadoblastoma is significantly increased. Familial occurrence is common and in some sibships an affected sibling has had male pseudohermaphrodism with dysgenetic testes and ambiguous external genitalia. The reported pedigrees suggest X-linked recessive or sex-linked autosomal dominant inheritance.

SO-CALLED MALE TURNER'S SYNDROME. Phenotypic males have been described who have short stature, webbed neck, and certain other somatic anomalies which occur in Turner's syndrome, and hypoplastic and frequently undescended testes. The similar appearance of these males to phenotypic females with the syndrome of gonadal dysgenesis had suggested that the origin of Turner's syndrome in both males and females was similar. However, with few exceptions, this is not so.

A few phenotypic males with this syndrome have a sex chromosome abnormality, such as XO/XY or XO/XYY, and represent a variant of the typical form of gonadal dysgenesis; in almost all other cases, the karyotype has been XY. These XY cases form a heterogeneous group, quite likely of diverse origin, and ought not to be considered the female counterpart of XO gonadal dysgenesis. Many of the cases previously considered as "male Turner's syndrome" are examples of the syndrome which is described next.

A SYNDROME OF WEBBED NECK, PTOSIS, AND HYPOGONADISM USUALLY ASSOCIATED WITH CONGENITAL HEART DISEASE AND SHORT STATURE. Among the group of phenotypic males with features of male Turner's syndrome, a distinctive entity has been described which has led to the recognition of its counterpart in the female and its differentiation from the syndrome of gonadal dysgenesis. These patients often have a characteristic facies—with ptosis, an antimongoloid palpebral slant, a broad flat nose, webbed neck, short stature, high arched palate, and malformed ears (Fig. 42). Congenital heart disease—most commonly atrial septal defect and/or pulmonic stenosis, but not coarctation of the aorta—is a cardinal but not invariable feature. Pectus excavatum, cubitus valgus, and impaired mental development are frequent associated findings. In males, one or both testes may be undescended. Germinal cell aplasia or hypoplasia of the testis is common, and usually there is evidence of androgen deficiency. Functioning ovaries are present in affected females. In both sexes, the karyotype is normal and gonadal differentiation is consistent with the chromosomal and phenotypic sex. Familial cases were not observed in the 16 cases we have studied, but there has been a preponderance of females. The origin of this disorder is unknown; it has been suggested that the syndrome may be related to an undetected deletion of a sex chromosome or autosome, or to a mutant gene.

Seminiferous Tubule Dysgenesis (*Klinefelter's Syndrome*)

The most common human sex chromosomal aberration, an XXY karyotype, is associated with the sex chromatin-positive form of seminiferous tubule dysgenesis or Klinefelter's syndrome. This disorder, a common cause of primary hypogonadism in the male, is characterized by a male phenotype, small, firm, defective testes (measuring less than 3.0 cm in length), and, in affected adults, azoospermia and sterility. During or after puberty the variable features, gynecomastia and androgen deficiency with signs of eunuchoidism, are present in about one-half of the cases. The excretion of urinary gonadotropin is elevated. Cryptorchidism is infrequent. These patients tend to grow tall, the characteristic feature being the disproportionately long legs which may be detected before puberty. Epiphyseal fusion is usually not delayed, and osseous development follows the male pattern. The diagnosis should be suspected in a long-legged adolescent boy with small, firm testes, gynecomastia, and poorly developed male secondary sex characteristics. The incidence of subnormal intelligence is increased; about 0.8 percent of males in institutions for the mentally defective are chromatin-positive. Behavioral disorders, mental disease, mongolism, and, in adults, chronic pulmonary disease, varicose veins, and mild diabetes mellitus also occur with increased frequency in this disorder.

INCIDENCE. In surveys of newborn infants, 30 of 14,526 male infants were found to be chromatin-positive, or approximately 1 in 500 males. Among 18 chromatin-positive male infants in whom karyotype analyses were reported by Maclean et al., 12 showed an XXY sex chromosome constitution, 1 had an XXYY sex chromosome complex, and 5 were

XY/XXY mosaics. Since the XY cell line may have a beneficial effect, some of the XY/XXY mosaics are potentially fertile.

The histopathology of the testis is variable. In one chromatin-positive premature infant the testicular morphology was normal. The prepubertal testis shows a diminished number of germ cells. With the onset of puberty and associated with the action of pituitary gonadotropins, the characteristic testicular defect is evident—hyalinization and atrophy of seminiferous tubules, absence of peritubular elastic tissue, aggregation and pseudoadenomatous groupings of Leydig cells, and occasional tubules lined by Sertoli cells. Rarely, spermatogenesis is seen in isolated tubules.

The typical sex chromosome aberration, first described by Jacobs and Strong and by Ford et al., is an XXY sex chromosome constitution and a diploid chromosome number of 47. The XXY karyotype can arise from meiotic nondisjunction of the sex chromosomes during parental gametogenesis, or from mitotic nondisjunction in an early division of the fertilized zygote. Evidence for both of these mechanisms exists. The mean maternal age is increased in chromatin-positive seminiferous tubule dysgenesis (but not as advanced as in mothers of infants with mongolism). This observation is consistent with a meiotic error occurring during oogenesis, giving rise to an XX ovum in some cases. The maternal age effect in chromosome errors appears to be a consequence of the long dormant diplotene stage (late prophase) of human ova from birth to ovulation. Studies of X-linked genetic markers (such as color blindness, the Xg^a blood group antigen, and glucose-6-phosphate dehydrogenase activity) in informative pedigrees indicate a maternal origin of both X chromosomes in some XXY patients. This may be a consequence of meiotic nondisjunction during oogenesis or mitotic nondisjunction in the zygote. In others, the nondisjunction occurs during spermatogenesis, probably at the first meiotic division, and the Y and one of the two X chromosomes is of paternal origin. The extra X chromosome is estimated to arise from the father in 40 percent of cases.

Other sex chromosome anomalies are less commonly found in this disorder. These include XX/XXY and XY/XXY mosaicism, an XX karyotype, and an XXXY sex chromosome complex; in this latter form radioulnar synostosis is a useful clinical sign. As mentioned previously, the XY cell line may have an ameliorating effect, and some patients with this form of mosaicism have been fertile.

OTHER VARIANT FORMS. Additional clinical features have been characteristic of certain variants of the XXY karyotype.

XXYY individuals, as a group, are taller and more long-legged than XXY patients, and quite consistent dermatoglyphic patterns have been described. Most of the cases are severely retarded mentally. Xg^a blood analyses indicate that the XXYY male is the result of successive errors in the first and second meiotic divisions in spermatogenesis and fertilization of an X-ovum by an XYY-bearing sperm.

In addition to severe mental retardation, the XXXXY cases studied have had a variety of associated malformations. The typical phenotypic features, while not pathognomonic, include (1) a variety of skeletal abnormalities (six out of nine had radio-ulnar synostosis, and short in-curved fifth digits); (2) hypoplastic external genitalia and very small and commonly undescended testes, exhibiting prepubertal testicular dysgenesis; (3) in many, a typical facies—including prognathism, epicanthal folds, hypertelorism, strabismus, a broad flat nose, and malformed ears; and (4) severe mental deficiency. A variety of other anomalies, including congenital heart disease, cleft palate, and microcephaly, may be present. The extra X chromosomes in XXXXY males are of maternal origin. The finding of three sex chromatin bodies in the buccal smear is strong evidence in support of the diagnosis. In a few instances, sex chromosome mosaicism has been found.

TREATMENT. The testicular lesion is irreversible. If androgen deficiency is present at adolescence, treatment with male sex hormone is effective. The gynecomastia is not affected by hormonal treatment, and mastectomy may be necessary in some patients for cosmetic reasons.

XYY SYNDROME. This sex chromosome anomaly occurs in about 1 in 500 male births. A large unselected group of XYY males has not yet been studied and our present knowledge is limited to surveys in selected populations such as prison inmates, and to isolated case reports. The phenotype is male; a small number of patients with undescended testes and less often hypogonadism has been described. Tall stature and severe acne are common characteristics of the XYY individuals detected in prison surveys. Impulsiveness and criminal and psychopathic behavior are associated with this syndrome, but the frequency of aberrant behavior among XYY males is not known. Some XYY males have a normal physique and exhibit normal behavior. Two fluorescent Y-chromatin masses are present in a high proportion of nuclei in quinacrine-stained buccal smears.

Diagnosis of Abnormalities of Sex Differentiation

In infants with ambisexual development it is of greatest importance to establish a diagnosis as soon after birth as possible, not only for psychologic and social reasons but also because of the dangers inherent in failure to recognize the salt-losing form of congenital adrenal hyperplasia (Sec. 16.4).

Table 17 lists the conditions which should alert the physician to consider an anomaly of sex.

Ambiguous or incomplete masculinization of the external genitalia is a cardinal feature of intersexuality, and this diagnosis should be excluded before such

TABLE 17.   *Features Suggesting an Anomaly of Sex*

Ambiguous appearance of the external genitalia
Phenotypic males with cryptorchidism, especially if the phallus is small
Phenotypic females with a mass in the groin or labium majus
An affected sibling with a sexual anomaly
Phenotypic females with prominent edema of the distal parts of the extremities and loose folds of skin over the nape of the neck

After Infancy

Short girls with features of gonadal dysgenesis
Adolescent boys with small testes, especially if associated with gynecomastia
Primary amenorrhea in an adolescent girl associated with breast development and sparse or absent pubic and axillary hair

an infant is regarded as a cryptorchid, hypospadic male. The appearance of the external genitalia may be highly variable; in some instances the phallus resembles a large clitoris. Usually, however, there is some fusion of the labioscrotal folds and only a single perineal orifice. The presence of a palpable gonad in a labioscrotal fold or in the groin is a strong point against the diagnosis of female pseudohermaphrodism. As indicated in Table 15, the appearance of the external genitalia in some forms of intersexuality is not ambiguous. In male pseudohermaphrodites with the feminizing testes syndrome the external genital structures are female (Fig. 39), whereas female pseudohermaphrodites in whom the orifice of the urogenital sinus is located at or close to the tip of the phallus (Fig. 37) have the appearance of cryptorchid males. Seminiferous tubule dysgenesis and the typical form of the syndrome of gonadal dysgenesis are not associated with anomalous development of the external genitalia. The diagnosis of the syndrome of feminizing testes should be suspected in phenotypic females with a firm mass in the inguinal region or labium majus. In instances in which a previous sibling or a relative has an abnormality of sex differentiation, the external genitalia of a newborn infant should be examined with special care and additional tests performed even if the external genitalia are normal, depending upon the nature of the disorder in the affected individual. Phenotypic female infants with prominent edema of the hands and feet and loose folds of skin over the nape of the neck may have the syndrome of gonadal dysgenesis (Bonnevie-Ullrich syndrome).

Table 18 summarizes the diagnostic procedures of value to the physician in the differential diagnosis of an infant with ambiguous external genitalia or in whom for other reasons an abnormality of sex is suspected.

Female pseudohermaphodism must be distinguished from other forms of intersexuality in which

TABLE 18.   *Steps in the Diagnosis of Intersexuality in Infancy*

History: family history, pregnancy (hormones), "crises," virilization
Inspection
Palpation of inguinal region and labioscrotal folds and rectal examination
Oral mucosal smear—sex chromatin pattern; karyotype—sex chromosome constitution
Excretion of 17-ketosteroids and pregnanetriol
Provisional diagnosis

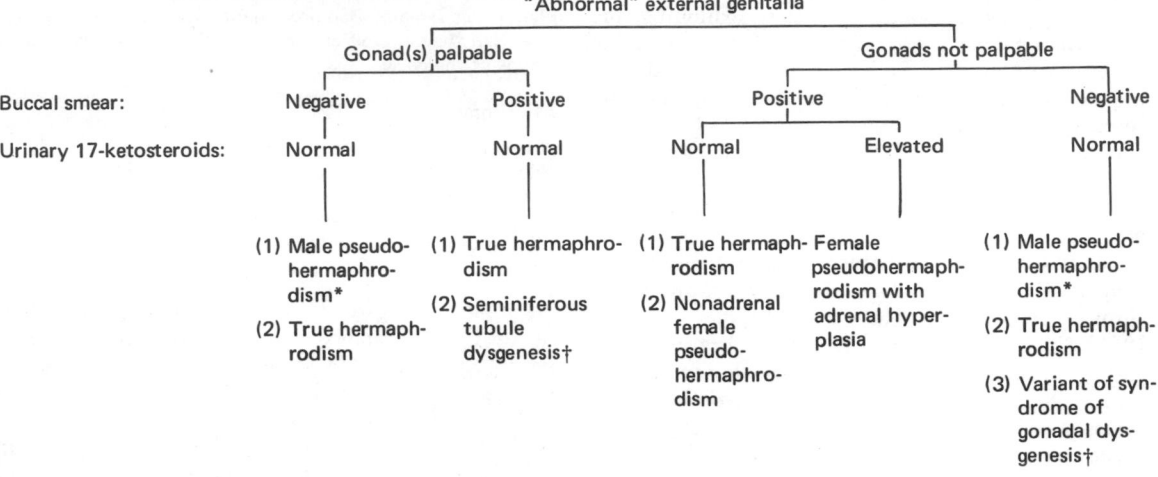

"Abnormal" external genitalia

	Gonad(s) palpable		Gonads not palpable	
Buccal smear:	Negative	Positive	Positive	Negative
Urinary 17-ketosteroids:	Normal	Normal	Normal / Elevated	Normal
	(1) Male pseudo-hermaphrodism* (2) True hermaphrodism	(1) True hermaphrodism (2) Seminiferous tubule dysgenesis†	(1) True hermaphrodism (2) Nonadrenal female pseudohermaphrodism / Female pseudohermaphrodism with adrenal hyperplasia	(1) Male pseudo-hermaphrodism* (2) True hermaphrodism (3) Variant of syndrome of gonadal dysgenesis†

"Vaginogram" (urogenital sinus): selected cases
Endoscopy, laparotomy, gonadal biopsy: restricted to suspected male pseudohermaphrodites, true hermaphrodites, and selected instances of nonadrenal female pseudohermaphrodism

*Excretion of 17-ketosteroids is increased in male pseudohermaphrodites who have congenital adrenal hyperplasia due to a defect in 3β-hydroxy dehydrogenase.
†In variants of the syndrome of gonadal dysgenesis the appearance of the external genitalia may be normal.

there is bilateral cryptorchidism. The configuration of the external genitalia is not a distinctive feature. The history may reveal other siblings affected with congenital virilizing adrenal hyperplasia, signs of progressive virilization, or evidence of dehydration, vomiting, and collapse suggestive of an Addisonianlike electrolyte disorder. The mother and the obstetrician should be queried concerning hormones administered during pregnancy.

The detection of chromatin-positive nuclei quickly limits the diagnostic possibilities to some form of female pseudohermaphrodism or to true hermaphrodism with undescended gonads. Twenty-four-hour specimens of urine should be examined for total 17-ketosteroids and, when possible, for pregnanetriol and 17-ketogenic steroids. In virilizing adrenal hyperplasia these steroids are excreted in increased amounts but not always in the first weeks of life. Laparotomy is a superfluous diagnostic procedure in this disorder. Serum electrolyte concentrations should be measured in any infant in whom adrenal hyperplasia is suspected.

Chromatin-positive patients who have normal values for urinary steroids may be either true hermaphrodites or nonadrenal female pseudohermaphrodites, a distinction which can be made after laparotomy and gonadal biopsy. However, those patients are no longer subjected to surgical exploration whose mothers were treated during pregnancy with hormones implicated as potential fetal masculinizing agents. It is sometimes advisable to inject a radiopaque contrast medium into the single perineal orifice to outline the urogenital sinus under fluoroscopic examination when a separate urethral and vaginal orifice cannot be identified by inspection. An intravenous pyelogram is of value for the detection of anomalies of the urinary tract in the nonandrogen-induced forms of female pseudohermaphrodism.

Chromatin-negative individuals with abnormal external genitalia may be either male pseudohermaphrodites (including a variant of the syndrome of gonadal dysgenesis) or true hermaphrodites. Exploratory laparotomy and bilateral gonadal biopsy are necessary for a definitive diagnosis. Prior to operation the anatomic findings should be defined by fluoroscopic and radiographic studies after the injection of radiopaque material into the hypospadiac orifice, and by urethroscopic examination.

Management

The responsibility of the physician lies in the recognition of ambisexual development, especially in the infant. Early diagnosis and skillful management obviate many of the serious psychologic and social problems of the patient and his parents, as well as the difficult decisions which may face the physician when the diagnosis is incorrect or the selection of sex is indecisive or delayed until childhood. It is during the period before the child has established a gender role that a carefully considered decision must be made of the sex most suitable for the subject with a disorder of sex differentiation and, if indicated, the assigned sex changed accordingly. The following discussion concerns the classic forms of intersexuality; ambisexual differentiation of the genital tract does not occur in the typical forms of gonadal dysgenesis and seminiferous tubule dysgenesis.

If the diagnosis proves to be female pseudohermaphrodism, the infant should be reared as a female irrespective of the appearance of the external genitalia. In female pseudohermaphrodism associated with congenital adrenal hyperplasia, corticosteroid therapy should be administered to prevent virilization and accelerated development (p. 1098). The genital defect is readily corrected by appropriate surgical procedures, which should be performed during the first 12 months of life. Since female pseudohermaphrodites have ovaries, fallopian tubes, and a uterus, they are potentially fertile.

In male pseudohermaphrodites the basis for deciding upon the sex of rearing is largely determined by the morphology of the external genitalia and the facility with which these structures can be surgically adapted to those of either a male or a female. It is desirable, whenever possible, to assign the sex of rearing in accordance with gonadal and chromosomal sex; however, these latter two variables are not absolute guides. In some male pseudohermaphrodites, for example, with an exceedingly hypoplastic phallus or with predominantly female external genital structures, as in the syndrome of feminizing testes, the genitalia cannot possibly be reconstructed to function as male organs. In most instances it is preferable to recommend that individuals with inadequate male external genitalia be reared as females. The studies of Wilkins et al. and of Money and the Hampsons indicate the feasibility and importance of assigning such patients to the sex which conforms to the genital morphology, although this may be contrary to gonadal and chromosomal sex. The decision once made should be firmly adhered to. Since many of these individuals are sterile, it is difficult to justify assignment of sex or change of sex in later childhood solely on the basis

of potential fertility. Alteration of assigned sex is even less justifiable if this potentiality cannot be realized because of anatomic factors or serious psychologic difficulties.

The assignment of sex in true hermaphrodism is based upon the morphology of the external genitalia and gonads. If the external genitalia are inadequate for a functional male, the individual should be raised as a female and testicular tissue removed. In instances in which the ambiguity of the genital structures is such that the individual could be reared, following plastic surgical procedures, as a male or a female, weight in the selection of sex should be given to whether the ovarian or testicular elements are better developed and to the potential for fertility; the gonad contrary to the selected sex should be removed.

The age at which gender role and sexual orientation become firmly established in childhood is uncertain. From their studies, Money et al. suggest that this generally occurs between 1½ and 2½ years of age. Contrary to former beliefs, psychosexual orientation does not appear to be instinctive and automatic, based on chromosomal sex, gonadal sex, or hormonal sex, but is a result of growing up and of all the experiences which this implies. An important aspect of management is the physician's role in relieving parental apprehension and misconceptions and in providing them with practical guidance. The parents should have a part in the decision after they have been provided with an explanation of the findings in terms of the bipotential character of the fetal genital tract and of the incomplete development of the sexual organs in their child. It is especially important to reassure the parents that their child is not "half boy and half girl" and that the anomalous development does not lead to homosexuality or transvestism. Serious psychologic disturbances may result from attempts to change the sex of rearing during childhood, once a gender role has been established. In general, such alterations should not be recommended in childhood after the age of 18 to 36 months. The rare exceptions in which, after careful consideration, it is decided to change the sex of rearing (e.g., instances in which the child feels uncertain about his or her gender role) require the concurrence and assistance of a psychiatrist and provisions for extended counseling of the patient and the parents.

The question of gonadectomy is a difficult one. The decision to remove the gonads should be based on the type of secondary sexual development to be expected at puberty, bearing in mind the form of male pseudohermaphrodism with feminizing testes and the risk of malignant changes in later life. The latter consideration is not of importance in childhood or adolescence; however, in rare instances a malignant tumor of the gonad has been found before the age of puberty in patients with intersexuality. When gonadectomy is performed, it is important that the parents be advised of the need for appropriate hormonal therapy at the age of puberty.

REFERENCES

Barr, M. L., and Carr, D. H. Correlations between sex chromatin and sex chromosomes. Acta Cytol., 6:34, 1962.

Carpentier, P. J., and Potter, E. L. Nuclear sex and genital malformation in 48 cases of renal agenesis, with especial reference to nonspecific female pseudohermaphroditism. Amer. J. Obstet. Gynec., 78:235, 1959.

Court Brown, W. M., Harnden, D. G., Jacobs, P. A., Maclean, N., and Mantle, D. J. Abnormalities of the sex chromosomes complement in man. Med. Res. Council Special Rep., 305, London, 1964.

——— Males with an XYY sex chromosome complement. J. Med. Genet., 5:341, 1968.

Federman, D. Abnormal Sexual Development—A Genetic and Endocrine Approach to Differential Diagnosis. Philadelphia, W. B. Saunders Co., 1967.

Ferguson-Smith, M. A. Karyotype-phenotype correlations in gonadal dysgenesis and their bearing on the pathogenesis of malformations. J. Med. Genet., 2:142, 1965.

French, F. S., van Wyk, J. J., Baggett, B., Easterling, W. E., Talbert, L. M., and Johnston, F. R. Further evidence of a target organ defect in the syndrome of testicular feminization. J. Clin. Endocr., 26:493, 1966.

Grumbach, M. M., and Barr, M. L. Cytologic tests of chromosomal sex in relation to sexual anomalies in man. Recent Progr. Hormone Res., 14:255, 1958.

——— and Ducharme, J. R. The effects of androgens on fetal development: Androgen-induced female pseudohermaphrodism. Fertil. Steril., 11:157, 1960.

——— Ducharme, J. R., and Moloshok, R. E. On the fetal masculinizing action of certain oral progestins. J. Clin. Endocr., 19:1369, 1959.

——— Morishima, A., and Liu, N. A distinctive clinical entity simulating Turner's syndrome in boys and girls associated with congenital heart disease, appropriate gonadal differentiation, and a normal sex chromosome constitution. J. Pediat., 67:966, 1965.

——— Morishima, A., and Taylor, J. H. Human sex chromosome abnormalities in relation to DNA replication and heterochromatinization. Proc. Nat. Acad. Sci. U.S.A., 49:581, 1963.

Jones, H. W., Jr., and Scott, W. W. Hermaphroditism, Genital Anomalies and Related Endocrine Disorders. Baltimore, Williams and Wilkins Co., 1958.

Jost, A. Problems of fetal endocrinology: The gonadal and hypophyseal hormones. Recent Progr. Hormone Res., 8:379, 1953.

Klinger, H. P., and Ludwig, K. S. A universal stain for the sex chromatin body. Stain Techn., 32:235, 1957.

Lewis, V. G., Ehrhardt, A. A., and Money, J. Genital operations in girls with the adrenogenital syndrome. Subsequent psychologic development. Obstet. Gynec., 36:11, 1970.

Lyon, M. F. Sex chromatin and gene action in the mammalian X-chromosome. Amer. J. Hum. Genet., 14:135, 1962.

Maclean, N., Harnden, D. G., Court Brown, W. M., Bond, J., and Mantle, D. J. Sex-chromosome abnormalities in newborn babies. Lancet, 1:286, 1964.

——— Mitchell, J. M., Harnden, D. G., Williams, J., Jacobs, P. A., Buckton, K. A., Baikie, A. G., Court

Brown, W. M., McBridge, J. A., Strong, J. A., Close, H. G., and Jones, D. C. A survey of sex chromosome abnormalities among 4514 mental defectives. Lancet, 1:293, 1962.

McKusick, V. A. On the X-Chromosome of Man. Amer. Inst. Biol. Sci., 1964.

Money, J., Hampson, J. G., and Hampson, J. L. Hermaphroditism: Recommendations concerning assignment of sex, change of sex and psychologic management. Bull. Hopkins Hosp., 97:284, 1955.

——— Hampson, J. G., and Hampson, J. L. Sexual incongruities and psychopathology: The evidence of human hermaphroditism. Bull. Hopkins Hosp., 98:43, 1956.

——— Psychologic evaluation of the child with intersex problems. Pediatrics, 36:51, 1965.

Moore, K. L., ed. The Sex Chromatin. Philadelphia, W. B. Saunders Co., 1966.

Morishima, A., and Grumbach, M. M. The interrelationship of sex chromosome constitution and phenotype in the syndrome of gonadal dysgenesis and its variants. Ann. N.Y. Acad. Sci., 155:695, 1968.

Overzier, C. Intersexuality. London, New York, Academic Press, Inc., 1963.

Paulsen, C. A., Gordon, D. L., Carpenter, R. W., Gandy, H. M., and Drucker, W. D. Klinefelter's syndrome and its variants: A hormonal and chromosomal study. Recent Progr. Hormone Res., 24:321, 1968.

Pearson, P. L., Borrow, M., and Vosa, C. G. Technique for identifying Y chromosomes in human interphase nuclei. Nature, 226:78, 1970.

Van Wyk, J. J., and Grumbach, M. M. Disorders of sex differentiation. In Williams, R. H., ed., Textbook of Endocrinology, 4th ed. Philadelphia, W. B. Saunders Co., 1968, p. 537.

Wilkins, L. Masculinization of female fetus due to use of orally given progestins. J.A.M.A., 172:1028, 1960.

——— The Diagnosis and Treatment of Endocrine Disorders in Childhood and Adolescence, 3rd ed. Springfield, Ill., Charles C Thomas, Publ., 1965.

16.12

PRIMARY DISTURBANCES OF WATER HOMEOSTASIS

WILLIAM E. SEGAR

PHYSIOLOGY OF WATER HOMEOSTASIS. Both the volume and the tonicity of the body fluids are maintained within remarkably narrow limits by a variety of highly sensitive mechanisms. If body water homeostasis is to be maintained, daily renal water excretion must equal water intake less extrarenal water losses. Water intake is regulated by thirst. Renal water loss is determined, primarily, by intrarenal mechanisms and by the action of antidiuretic hormone (ADH) on the renal concentrating system.

ADH, an octapeptide, is synthesized in the supraoptic and paraventricular nuclei of the hypothalamus. It is then transported within axons, in an inactive form bound to neurohypophyseal proteins called "neurophysins," from the cell bodies to the posterior lobe of the pituitary gland where it is stored until released into the blood.

In the absence of ADH, maximal water diuresis develops, urine osmolality usually being less than 100 mOsm/kg, and in the adult 10 liters or more of urine may be excreted daily. When ADH levels are high, urine osmolality may exceed 1,200 mOsm/kg and the normal daily urine solute load may be excreted in less than 500 ml of urine by an adult. Thus, the mechanisms that regulate ADH release from the posterior pituitary are important for the maintenance of body water homeostasis. The release of ADH is governed primarily by the effective intravascular fluid volume and by the osmolality of the extracellular fluid. However, pain, stress, emotional factors, and certain drugs also may stimulate the release of ADH from the hypothalamoneurohypophyseal system. During periods of hypotension, baroreceptors located in the aorta, carotid sinus, and carotid bodies also participate in the regulation of ADH release.

The experiments of Verney provided the initial convincing evidence that the release of ADH is controlled by the concentration in plasma of solutes, to which cells of hypothalamus are either partially or completely impermeable. His studies documenting the inhibition of water diuresis in dogs after intracarotid infusion of hypertonic saline, as well as those of Arndt and Gauer demonstrating induction of water diuresis after intracarotid infusion of water in the unanesthetized dog, provided evidence of an "osmoreceptive area" in the distribution of the carotid artery, probably the anterior hypothalamus. Several years before Verney's studies, Peters proposed the concept that the fullness of the intravascular space is "sensed" by the organism and that the contraction of this space leads to antidiuresis, whereas expansion results in diuresis. Gauer and Henry concluded that the "volume receptor" is located within the capacitance vessels of the thorax; the work of several investigators suggests that the left atrium is the likely site. Johnson and co-workers demonstrated that, in the anesthetized dog, physiologic changes in left atrial pressure are inversely related to blood ADH levels in the absence of alterations in renal hemodynamics or plasma osmolality. Segar and Moore demonstrated that the blood ADH level changes rapidly with change in position or environmental temperature, procedures which alter the distribution of blood within the vascular compartment despite constancy of the plasma osmolality. The rapidity of change in blood ADH concentration in these circumstances indicates a great sensitivity and a prime functional role for the "volume receptor" in the regulation of ADH release. On the other hand, the "osmoreceptor" may be functionally significant only during periods of overhydration and water diuresis.

When the concentration of ADH in the blood is less than 1 μU/ml, dilute urine is elaborated; with a blood concentration of 4 μU/ml or more, urine is

maximally concentrated. During periods of shock, anesthesia, or dehydration, the blood ADH concentration may increase to 10 μU/ml or more. The blood ADH concentration can be considered normal or abnormal only in reference to the state of hydration and the body fluid tonicity of the patient. A value of 0 μU/ml is normal in the hydrated prone subject but not normal if the subject is dehydrated, hypertonic, or standing. A value of 4 μU/ml is normal in the dehydrated or hypertonic patient but abnormal (or inappropriate) if the patient is overhydrated or hypotonic.

The half-life of ADH in man is approximately 7 minutes. During periods of prolonged antidiuresis, nearly continuous release of ADH must occur. Once released from storage in the posterior pituitary, ADH is carried to the kidney, where it exerts its only significant physiologic effect. While in the blood, ADH is dialyzable and ultrafilterable from plasma, indicating an absence of protein binding.

Urine formation begins with the passage of the ultrafiltrate of plasma through the glomerular membrane. This filtrate is isosmotic and most of it, perhaps 60 to 70 percent, is reabsorbed passively, accompanying the active reabsorption of sodium as the filtrate passes through the proximal tubule. As the filtrate moves through the loop of Henle, it first becomes more concentrated as water moves from the lumen into the hypertonic medullary interstitium near the tip of the loop; it is then diluted, as sodium is extruded and water is retained, as the fluid moves up the ascending limb. Therefore the fluid entering the distal convolution is hypotonic. Thus far the mechanisms for diuresis and antidiuresis are the same.

During water diuresis, little water is reabsorbed as the filtrate passes through the distal convolution and collecting duct but, because sodium reabsorption continues, a dilute urine results. During antidiuresis, the presence of ADH produces a marked increase in the permeability of the tubular epithelium to water, so that equilibrium of the filtrate with interstitial fluid occurs. Because the collecting ducts pass through the zone of marked interstitial fluid hypertonicity in the inner medulla and papillae, the fluid entering the renal pelvis becomes highly concentrated. In man, urine concentrations of 1,200 to 1,400 mOsm/kg may be reached. Higher concentrations are achieved by other mammals.

The action of ADH on cellular permeability has been studied experimentally on the toad bladder, a membrane with characteristics similar to those of the renal tubular epithelium, and has been shown to increase cellular permeability by making the membrane responsive to bulk flow. The nature of these membrane changes and the means by which they are induced remains unclear.

THIRST. Although thirst is a physiologic function of obvious importance, it has received relatively little critical study, and the factors regulating thirst in man remain poorly understood. However, it is known that local factors, such as dryness of the oral mucous membranes or fullness of the stomach, affect thirst. Systemic factors also contribute to the regulation of thirst because isotonic expansion of the body fluid inhibits it while hypertonicity produces thirst. Certain drugs alter thirst, and psychologic factors profoundly affect it. Several areas of the hypothalamus play a significant role in the regulation of thirst, and certain anatomic lesions alter it. Ablative lesions of the preoptic nucleus, ventromedial nucleus, anterior hypothalamus, and subcommissural organ cause adipsia, while similar lesions in the basal tuberal region cause polydipsia. Polydipsia can also be produced by stimulation of several of the hypothalamic nuclei with a weak electric current or by certain drugs.

Although a variety of stimuli induce a person with an intact central nervous system and no psychologic abnormalities to increase water intake above that usually consumed, there seems to be no physiologic mechanism available to man to signal him to reduce fluid intake below "normal." This is significant in the pathogenesis of several hyponatremic states.

Diabetes Insipidus and Primary Polydipsia

Diabetes insipidus is an uncommon disease characterized clinically by polyuria and polydipsia. Two forms of diabetes insipidus are encountered in children: (1) true antidiuretic hormone deficiency and (2) a familial sex-linked form in which blood ADH levels are increased. The former responds satisfactorily to the administration of exogenous ADH; the latter is refractory to this therapy.

CLINICAL MANIFESTATIONS.   Polyuria and polydipsia are the main clinical manifestations of diabetes insipidus. Urine volume may exceed 10 liters per day in the adult or 300 to 400 ml per kilogram of body weight per day in the infant. The onset of symptoms is frequently abrupt. In the alert, conscious adult or older child, these symptoms may be little more than an inconvenience. In the younger child, disturbances in sleep and activities are more serious. If the patient is able to meet his increased water requirement by increasing his water intake, no additional symptoms are noted. However, if the patient is very young, incapacitated, or unconscious, dehydration will develop rapidly. Hyperpyrexia occurs and, because the urine is hypotonic, hypernatremia develops. Either hyperpyrexia or hypernatremia, or both, may cause severe or fatal injury to the central nervous system.

The osmolality of the urine of the patient with diabetes insipidus is usually less than 150 mOsm/kg; specific gravity is 1.001 to 1.005. The urine may become isotonic, or, rarely, hypertonic during periods of dehydration if, as a result of hypovolemia, the glomerular filtration rate is decreased markedly. The serum sodium concentration and osmolality are usu-

ally normal or slightly increased in children with uncomplicated diabetes insipidus. During dehydration, both may increase to pathologic concentrations.

CLASSIFICATION.   *Antidiuretic Hormone-Deficient Diabetes Insipidus.*   This form of diabetes insipidus may be classified as primary or secondary, depending on the absence or presence of underlying disease. A specific cause for ADH deficiency cannot be found in approximately one-third of all patients. Of these patients, more commonly infants and children than adults, the majority must be classified as having an idiopathic form. A familial form of primary diabetes insipidus, which follows a Mendelian dominant pattern of inheritance, is quite rare. Unfortunately, the cause of diabetes insipidus may be difficult to ascertain. Unless the family history is diagnostic, the diagnosis of primary or idiopathic diabetes insipidus must remain suspect until careful observations for 5 to 10 years fail to demonstrate evidence of a neoplasm or histiocytosis.

Secondary diabetes insipidus may result from any lesion that damages the neurohypophyseal system. Trauma, either accidental or neurosurgical, is a major cause. Infections, tumors (particularly craniopharyngiomas, pituitary adenomas, and pinealomas), Hand-Schüller-Christian disease and, rarely, metastatic neoplasms or degenerative diseases of the central nervous system also can be causes. When secondary diabetes insipidus is produced as a result of trauma or a neurosurgical procedure, a triphasic clinical course often follows. Initially, there is a period of diuresis and, presumably, of ADH deficiency. After a few days, antidiuresis ensues. Severe hyponatremia may occur if water intake is not curtailed during this so-called interphase period. This phenomenon is thought to be due to the uncontrolled release of ADH from damaged neurohypophyseal tracts. Finally, persistent diabetes insipidus follows a few days later, once the ADH stores are exhausted.

Antidiuretic Hormone-Resistant (Nephrogenic) Diabetes Insipidus.   This is a genetically determined disorder which is clinically similar to diabetes insipidus. The renal tubular cells of these patients apparently are insensitive to ADH, and a hypotonic urine is excreted despite normal or high blood ADH levels. Polyuria and polydipsia result. The disease may be present from birth. These infants require very large daily water intakes (300 to 500 ml/kg of body weight per day). Dehydration may develop with extreme rapidity. Hyperpyrexia and failure to thrive are common complications. The renal mechanisms involved in this disorder are discussed elsewhere (Sec. 23.13).

Primary polydipsia is the ingestion of water in excess of that required to maintain normal water balance. Polydipsia is the result of a physiologic or psychologic thirst-drive. Traditionally, it has been assumed that primary polydipsia is a psychogenic entity, and it has been called "compulsive water drinking." Although primary polydipsia may occur as the result of a serious behavioral disturbance and thus be classified as psychogenic polydipsia, it is recognized now that pathologic lesions of the hypothalamus also may cause excessive thirst and produce the syndrome termed "neurogenic polydipsia." Because the hypothalamic regions regulating thirst and those concerned with ADH production are contiguous, diabetes insipidus may coexist with primary polydipsia. Primary (neurogenic) polydipsia also may mimic diabetes insipidus in a patient with known hypothalamic lesion. Each patient with polydipsia must have a comprehensive neurologic examination, and often a psychologic examination, before the condition can be classified as neurogenic or psychogenic.

DIFFERENTIAL DIAGNOSIS. Because polyuria and polydipsia can result from true diabetes insipidus, from hypothalamic damage that alters thirst but not ADH release (neurogenic polydipsia), from nephrogenic diabetes insipidus, or from psychogenic polydipsia (see below), various diagnostic procedures are needed to determine the cause of these symptoms. The urine osmolality will be low (<270 mOsm/kg) in each instance. The serum osmolality may be normal (275 to 290 mOsm/kg) or slightly increased in patients with diabetes insipidus or nephrogenic diabetes insipidus, but it will be normal or slightly low in those with primary polydipsia.

A water-deprivation test will often differentiate diabetes insipidus from primary polydipsia. Fluid should be withheld until the patient has lost 3 to 5 percent of his body weight. The patient with diabetes insipidus will suffer a rapid weight loss, and his urine will remain hypotonic. The patient with primary polydipsia will lose weight more slowly, and his urine osmolality will increase as dehydration occurs. Constant surveillance of the patient during the period of water deprivation is essential to avoid the effects of severe dehydration and to prevent surreptitious water intake. A patient with diabetes insipidus can produce a hypertonic urine (>300 mOsm/kg), despite the lack of ADH, if the glomerular filtration rate is decreased significantly as a result of severe dehydration. Chronic overhydration will result in a diminished capacity to concentrate urine due to "washout" of solute from the renal medullary interstitium, so that a patient with primary polydipsia may not demonstrate an increase in urine osmolality of the magnitude expected in response to water deprivation. Furthermore, because such a patient may be significantly overhydrated initially, a weight loss of 5 percent may be insufficient to produce underhydration. Physical examination will indicate if the water-deprivation test should be continued until a weight loss of more than 5 percent is achieved. The response of the kidney to water deprivation may be impaired by diseases such as interstitial nephritis, pyelonephritis, hypercalcemia, and chronic potassium deficiency. However, a slightly hypertonic urine is usually produced in all of these states.

Once it has been determined that the patient cannot produce a hypertonic urine despite dehydration, his response to exogenous ADH (vasopressin) should be tested. A patient with nephrogenic diabetes insipidus will exhibit no response, while one with diabetes insipidus will show an increase in urine osmolality. Either aqueous or long-acting vasopressin tannate in oil can be used. Aqueous vasopressin can be administered for one hour by slow intravenous infusion (5 μU/minute), or vasopressin tannate in oil can be given intramuscularly (5 U). Prompt diminution in urine minute volume and increase in urine osmolality can be expected in the former test; in the latter, the overnight urine specimen and the following three urine specimens should be examined for increased osmolality. The use of long-acting vasopressin tannate in oil is potentially hazardous. Should the patient have primary polydipsia and continue to drink excessively, hyponatremia and central nervous system symptoms may be produced following vasopressin administration. This complication may also arise when a child with previously untreated diabetes insipidus is first given vasopressin. The patient, "conditioned" to a large fluid intake, may not decrease his fluid intake despite his diminished need for water and, indeed, despite his inability to excrete the water load. If the patient's urine volume decreases after vasopressin administration, his fluid intake should be monitored until the test is completed.

An occasional patient will show a modest increase in urine osmolality with dehydration and a similar response to vasopressin administration, but a normal response (urine osmolality >600 mOsm/kg) to neither. De Wardener has suggested that if the response to dehydration is greater than that to vasopressin administration, the patient has primary polydipsia; if the urine osmolality, even though relatively low, is higher after vasopressin administration than after dehydration, the patient has diabetes insipidus.

TREATMENT. Reduction of the solute load by restricting the protein and salt content of the diet will ameliorate polyuria in either true or nephrogenic diabetes insipidus. This is usually necessary only for patients with nephrogenic diabetes insipidus, and one then must be certain the diet provides the calories and essential nutrients needed for normal growth. An adequate supply of water must always be available for the child with either form of the disease. Diuretics, particularly chlorothiazide, were first shown by Crawford to produce a slight but significant increase in urine solute concentration in children with nephrogenic diabetes insipidus. The mode of action of these drugs is uncertain, but if urine osmolality is increased from 100 to 200 mOsm/kg, the urine volume is decreased to half.

Commercial preparations are available for the effective treatment of diabetes insipidus. The short half-life of aqueous vasopressin precludes its use therapeutically. However, the suspension of vasopressin tannate in peanut oil (5 U/ml) is a satisfactory drug;

0.5 to 1.0 ml given intramuscularly will provide relief of symptoms for 24 to 72 hours. The injection should be repeated when symptoms recur. The ampule must be warmed and vigorously shaken before use.

A lysine vasopressin nasal spray is available, as is vasopressin powder snuff. Both of these preparations have the disadvantages of short duration of action, ineffectiveness with upper respiratory infections, and, with the snuff, frequent occurrence of chronic inflammation of the nasal mucous membranes.

Diabetes insipidus is difficult to manage in comatose patients, in patients who are recovering from neurosurgical procedures, and in other circumstances in which the patient's thirst drive is not available to aid in the regulation of water intake. These patients can be managed most easily by the daily injection of 5 U or more of vasopressin tannate in oil and, if hydration is satisfactory, by the administration of about 80 percent of the normal maintenance fluid intake. Body weight, urine volume, and serum sodium or osmolality should be monitored daily. More vasopressin is needed if body weight decreases, serum sodium increases, and urine volume is large. If weight increases, serum sodium decreases, and urine volume is small, too much water is being given. The patient is receiving an inadequate fluid intake if serum sodium increases as the weight decreases, despite a small urine volume.

In addition to appropriate medical or surgical therapy, patients with neurogenic polydipsia must be taught to restrict their fluid intake. Psychogenic polydipsia is evidence of a complex emotional disturbance and psychiatric therapy is usually necessary.

Excessive Antidiuretic Hormone Release

THE SYNDROME OF "INAPPROPRIATE ADH SECRETION." A variety of disease states, including malignant tumors (particularly bronchogenic carcinomas), acute and chronic pulmonary disease (such as tuberculosis and bronchopneumonia), hypothyroidism, and disorders of the central nervous system (such as meningitis, head injuries, encephalitis, Guillain-Barré syndrome, acute intermittent porphyria, and brain tumors) may be accompanied by hyponatremia and the production of hypertonic urine despite lack of evidence of hypovolemia. Efforts to treat the hyponatremia by sodium administration are usually futile; water restriction, on the other hand, results in correction of the disturbance in serum sodium concentration. Blood ADH levels are increased, resulting in an inability of the patient to elaborate other than a hypertonic urine. This and the persistently high blood ADH levels coupled with a "normal" fluid intake lead to water retention and dilutional hyponatremia.

In most cases the cause for the increased blood ADH level, and therefore for the hyponatremia, can be determined. Certain malignant tumors apparently synthesize a peptide similar or identical to ADH because, in these cases, high ADH levels are found. Analysis of the tumor reveals an extremely high content of ADH or ADH-like substances. ADH levels return to normal after effective treatment of the malignancy. Patients who have bronchopneumonia, asthma, or emphysema or who are receiving positive-pressure ventilatory assistance may exhibit hyponatremia and increased blood ADH levels. In these cases, the decreased filling of the left atrium, due to increased resistance to blood flow through the pulmonary bed, is the apparent cause. The blood ADH level decreases promptly and diuresis ensues, if ventilatory assistance is discontinued or if the underlying pulmonary disease is treated adequately. The low serum sodium concentration returns to normal as the excess water is excreted in the course of the diuresis.

CEREBRAL SALT-WASTING. Hyponatremia occasionally may occur with central nervous system lesions if the hypothalamic regions concerned with ADH production are stimulated by the pathologic process. A different pathogenesis for this syndrome of "cerebral salt-wasting" is more frequent, however. Patients with severe central nervous system disease or with conditions characterized by paralysis, such as the Guillain-Barré syndrome, lie motionless in bed. The blood pools in the dependent portions of the vascular compartment if periodic muscular contractions do not aid its return to the chest. Left atrial filling decreases, ADH release occurs, and the persistently increased blood ADH level combined with a normal fluid intake produces hyponatremia. If the legs of the patient are wrapped with an elastic bandage or if the foot of the bed is raised, blood return to the chest is enhanced, increased filling of the left atrium results in inhibition of ADH release, and a prompt diuresis ensues. Occasionally, the cause of the increased ADH production cannot be determined or, if known, cannot be corrected. Hyponatremia must then be treated by water restriction.

OTHER CONDITIONS. Increased blood ADH levels occur in all hypovolemic states. The blood ADH level is high in shock, in the nephrotic syndrome, and in other diseases characterized by hypoproteinemia and edema.

Pain and anesthesia cause ADH release, and high blood ADH levels are observed postoperatively. The blood ADH level may remain increased for 7 to 10 days after cardiac surgery and, because a dilute urine cannot be elaborated during this period, hyponatremia will develop unless water intake is decreased to 50 to 70 percent of maintenance level. Since physicians now are aware of this phenomenon, postoperative intravenous fluid administration is restricted routinely. However, once oral feedings are begun, these restrictions may be relaxed. Hyponatremia can then develop if, unaware of his inability to dilute the urine and experiencing no diminution of thirst, the patient resumes his "normal" fluid intake.

Hypodipsia is an uncommon condition characterized by chronic hypernatremia and hyperosmolality; it occurs in patients in whom the sensation of thirst is diminished or absent. Destructive lesions of the hypothalamus are the usual cause of this syndrome, although hypodipsia with serum hyperosmolality may occur in children with occult hydrocephalus or microcephaly. Hypodipsia has been produced experimentally in animals by ablative lesions of the hypothalamus. Rarely, destructive hypothalamic lesions cause both diabetes insipidus and hypodipsia. All patients with hypodipsia should be given a complete neurologic examination. Treatment consists of appropriate measures to ensure that the patient consumes an adequate amount of water daily.

REFERENCES

Andersson, B., Cale, C. C., and Sundsten, J. W. Thirst. *In* Wayner, M. J., ed., Thirst in the Regulation of Body Water. Proc. 1st Int. Symp. New York, Pergamon Press, Inc., 1964.

Arndt, J. O., and Gauer, O. H. Diuresis induced by water infusion into the carotid loop of unanesthetized dogs. Pflueger Arch. Ges. Physiol., 282:301, 1965.

Barlow, E. D., and De Wardener, H. E. Compulsive water drinking. Quart. J. Med., 28:235, 1959.

Bartter, F. C., and Schwartz, W. B. The syndrome of inappropriate secretion of antidiuretic hormone. Amer. J. Med., 42:790, 1967.

Berliner, R. W., and Bennett, C. M. Concentration of urine in the mammalian kidney. Amer. J. Med., 42: 777, 1967.

Bode, H. H., and Crawford, J. D. Nephrogenic diabetes insipidus in North America—the Hopewell hypothesis. New Eng. J. Med., 280:750, 1969.

Bower, B. F., Mason, D. M., and Forsham, P. H. Bronchogenic carcinoma with inappropriate antidiuretic activity in plasma and tumor. New Eng. J. Med., 271: 934, 1964.

Cannon, J. F. Diabetes insipidus: Clinical and experimental studies with consideration of genetic relationships. Arch. Intern. Med. (Chicago), 96:215, 1956.

Crawford, J. D., Kennedy, G. C., and Hill, L. E. Clinical results of treatment of diabetes insipidus with drugs of the chlorothiazide series. New Eng. J. Med., 262: 737, 1960.

Dashe, A. M., Cramm, R. E., Crist, C. A., Habener, J. F., and Solomon, D. H. A water deprivation test for the differential diagnosis of polyuria. J.A.M.A., 185:699, 1963.

De Wardener, H. E. Polyuria. J. Chronic Dis., 11:199, 1960.

Gauer, O. H., and Henry, J. P. Circulatory basis of fluid volume control. Physiol. Rev., 43:423, 1963.

Fitzsimons, J. T. The hypothalamus and drinking. Brit. Med. Bull., 22:232, 1966.

Johnson, J. A., Moore, W. W., and Segar, W. E. Small changes in left atrial pressure and plasma antidiuretic hormone titers in dogs. Amer. J. Physiol., 217:210, 1969.

Leaf, A. Membrane effects of antidiuretic hormone. Amer. J. Med., 42:745, 1967.

Peters, J. P. Body Water: The Exchange of Fluids in Man. Springfield, Ill., Charles C Thomas, Publ., 1935.

Randall, R. V., Clark, E. C., and Bahn, R. C. Classification of the causes of diabetes insipidus. Mayo Clin. Proc., 34:299, 1959.

Sawyer, W. H. Neurohypophysial hormones. Pharmacol. Rev., 13:225, 1961.

Schwartz, W. B., Bennett, W., Curelop, S., and Bartter, F. C. A syndrome of renal sodium loss and hyponatremia probably resulting from inappropriate secretion of antidiuretic hormone. Amer. J. Med., 23:529, 1957.

Segar, W. E., and Moore, W. W. The regulation of antidiuretic hormone release in man. 1. Effects of change in position and ambient temperature on blood ADH levels. J. Clin. Invest., 47:2143, 1968.

Share, L. Vasopressin, its bioassay and the physiological control of its release. Amer. J. Med., 42:701, 1967.

Smith, H. W. Salt and water volume receptors: An exercise in physiologic apologetics. Amer. J. Med., 23: 623, 1957.

Stevko, R. M., Balsley, M., and Segar, W. E. Primary polydipsia—compulsive water drinking: Report of two cases. J. Pediat., 73:845, 1968.

Thomas, W. C., Jr. Diabetes insipidus. J. Clin. Endocr., 17:565, 1957.

Verney, E. B. The antidiuretic hormone and the factors which determine its release. Proc. Roy. Soc. London (Series B), 135:25, 1947.

Wolf, A. V. Thirst, Physiology of the Urge to Drink and Problems of Water Lack. Springfield, Ill., Charles C Thomas, Publ., 1958.

chapter 17

THE BLOOD AND BLOOD-FORMING ORGANS

IRVING SCHULMAN, Associate Editor

17.1
FETAL AND NEONATAL ERYTHROPOIESIS

IRVING SCHULMAN

The Blood in Fetal Life

Blood formation in the embryo occurs first in the yolk sac. At approximately six weeks of gestation, erythropoiesis appears in the liver and reaches a peak in that organ by about the fourth month. Hepatic blood formation thereafter declines steadily throughout the remainder of gestation. Blood formation begins in the marrow at about the fifth month of gestation and increases rapidly, so that at the time of delivery the marrow is the only significant organ of hematopoiesis for all cellular elements found in the blood.

Figure 1 demonstrates changes in hemoglobin concentration during fetal life as determined from studies on human embryos. By 12 weeks of gestation a hemoglobin concentration of 9 to 10 g per 100 ml is already present. This rises to 14 to 15 g per 100 ml by 24 weeks. The rate of rise during the last trimester is slower than during earlier months, and at term a mean cord hemoglobin concentration of 16.6 g per 100 ml has been found. However, an extremely wide range of cord hemoglobin concentration (12 to 22 g per 10 ml) may be observed in apparently nor-

mal infants. Changes in erythrocyte counts and hematocrit follow the same general trends as those for hemoglobin concentration, and wide ranges at term are likewise seen (Fig. 2).

The red cells themselves undergo striking changes during gestation, again most marked during the first two trimesters. The mean corpuscular volume falls from approximately 200 cubic microns at the end of the first trimester to about 110 cubic microns at term; the mean corpuscular hemoglobin from 60 to 35 micromicrograms; and the mean cell diameter from 10.5 to 8.0 microns. The mean corpuscular hemoglobin concentration, however, remains virtually unchanged at 33 percent throughout gestation (Fig. 3).

Fetal life is characterized by the presence of a biochemically distinct hemoglobin. Fetal hemoglobin (FH) differs from the hemoglobin of later life (adult hemoglobin) in two of the four polypeptide chains of the globin moiety, fetal hemoglobin being composed of two alpha and two gamma chains as compared with two alpha and two beta chains in adult hemoglobin. Beta and gamma chains differ from each other in the amino acid sequence. During the first trimester, 100 percent of the hemoglobin in the embryo is of the fetal variety. The adult hemoglobin appears early in the second trimester but seems to remain below 10 to 15 percent of the total until about the thirty-fourth week, when a fall in the proportion of fetal hemoglobin begins which continues

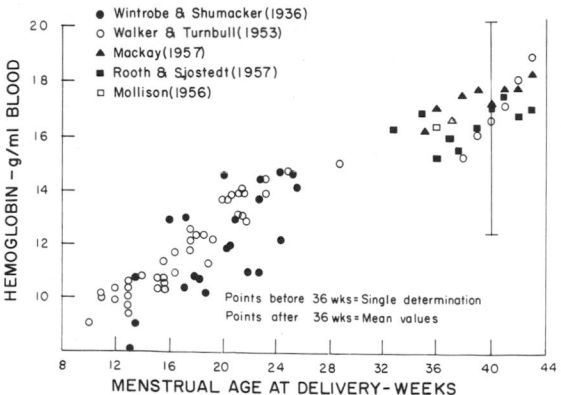

Fig. 1. Changes in hemoglobin concentration during fetal life.

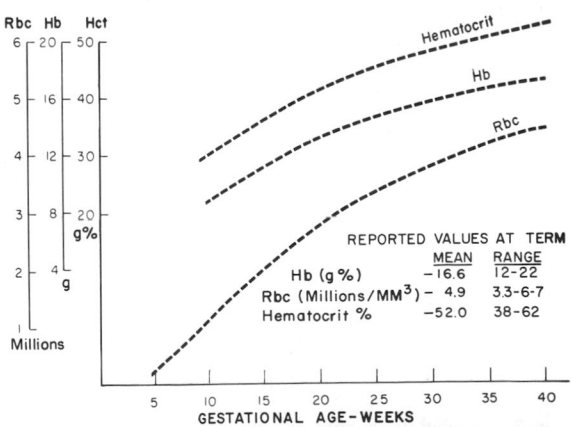

Fig. 2. Changes in hemoglobin concentration, red blood cell count, and hematocrit during fetal life.

TABLE 1. *Normal Blood Values at Various Ages**

Age	Hemoglobin (g/100 ml) Mean	SD	Red Count (in million RBC/mm³) Mean	SD	Hematocrit (volume of packed cells/ 100 ml) Mean	SD	Mean Diameter of RBC (in microns) Average	Mean Corpuscular Volume (in cubic microns) Mean	SD
Birth (Cord)	17.1	1.5	4.9	0.4	53	5	8.0	109	5
3 days to 2 mo	14.6	2.9	4.2	0.7	43	9	7.7	103	10
2 to 4 mo	11.1	1.0	3.9	0.4	34	3	7.3	87	5
4 to 8 mo	12.3	0.9	4.2	0.3	37	3		88	6
8 to 12 mo	11.8	0.7	4.3	0.2	37	1	7.2	86	4
1 to 1½ yr	11.7	0.8	4.3	0.2	36	2		85	3
1½ to 2 yr	12.7	1.0	4.3	0.2	38	2		89	4
2 to 3 yr	12.7	0.8	4.4	0.2	39	2		88	4
3 to 4 yr	13.2	0.8	4.4	0.3	40	3		89	5
4 to 5 yr	13.4	1.0	4.4	0.2	40	2	7.2	91	3
5 to 6 yr	13.3	0.7	4.4	0.2	40	2		91	4
6 to 7 yr	13.3	0.8	4.4	0.2	40	2		90	4
7 to 8 yr	13.3	0.7	4.4	0.2	40	2		91	5
8 to 9 yr	13.6	0.7	4.4	0.2	41	2		92	4
9 to 10 yr	13.9	0.7	4.5	0.2	41	2		92	4
10 to 11 yr	14.0	0.9	4.5	0.3	42	2		92	4
11 to 12 yr	14.2	0.8	4.6	0.2	42	2		92	3
12 to 13 yr	14.5	0.9	4.7	0.2	43	2		93	4
Adult men	16.5	0.8	5.4	0.3	48	2	7.5	89	4
Adult women	14.5	0.7	4.6	0.2	43	2	7.5	93	4

*Compiled from a number of sources, especially Merritt and Davidson (*Amer. J. Dis. Child.*, 46:990, 1933), Mugrage and Andresen (*Amer. J. Dis. Child.*, 51:775, 1936), Guest, Brown, and Wing (*Amer. J. Dis. Child.*, 56:529, 1938), and observations of Josephs. Care has been used in selecting healthy subjects. SD signifies standard deviation; the mean ±1 SD can be expected to include two-thirds of the observations in the population studied. Where the variation in the values measured is

steadily with advancing fetal age (Fig. 4). Together with the fall in mean percentage of FH there appears an ever widening range of values. Recent studies have shown that, contrary to long-held views, fetal hemoglobin possesses increased affinity for oxygen as compared with adult hemoglobin. This results from a lesser interaction of HbF than of HbA with 2,3-diphosphoglycerate (2,3-DPG), an intracellular compound which decreases oxygen affinity. Thus, the well-known observation that the oxygen dissociation curve of fetal blood is displaced to the left of that of adult blood can be explained on the basis of the distinct chemical structure of the fetal hemoglobin.

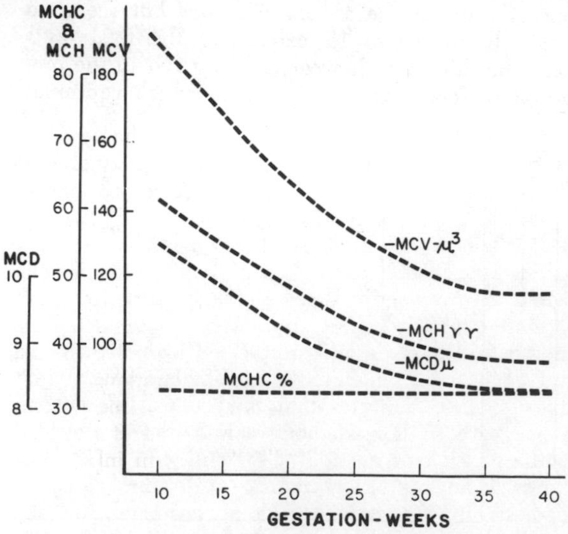

Fig. 3. Volumetric changes in red cells in fetal life. (MCV = mean corpuscular volume; MCH = mean corpuscular hemoglobin; MCD = mean corpuscular diameter; MCHC = mean corpuscular hemoglobin concentration.)

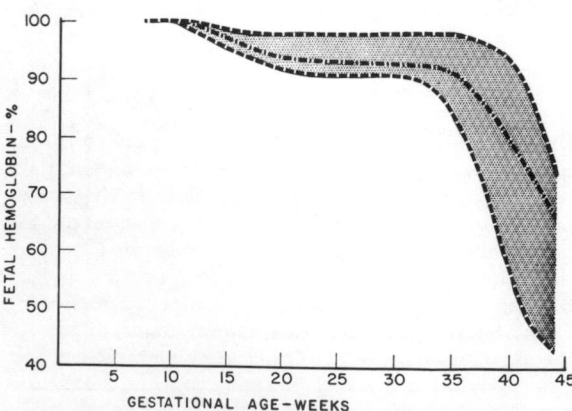

Fig. 4. Changes in concentration of fetal hemoglobin during fetal life.

Mean Corpuscular Hemoglobin (in micromicrograms)		Mean Corpuscular Hemoglobin Concentration (in g/100 ml of packed RBC)		Reticulocytes (per 100 RBC)	White Cells (per mm^3)	Granulocytes (percent)	Lymphocytes (percent)	Monocytes (percent)	Platelets (per mm^3)
Mean	SD	Mean	SD	Average	Average	Average	Average	Average	Average
35	2	32	1	3.0	20,000	70	20	10	350,000
34	3	34	1	0.3	12,000	31	63	6	300,000
29	2	33	1	1.5					
29	2	33	1	0.5	12,000	31	63	6	300,000
28	2	32	1	0.5	12,000	36	58	6	
28	2	32	1	0.5	11,000	40	54	6	
29	2	33	1	0.5	10,000	45	49	6	
28	1	33	1	0.5					
30	1	33	1	0.5					
30	2	33	1	0.5	8,000	60	34	6	300,000
30	1	33	1						
30	1	33	1						
31	2	33	1	0.5	8,000	62	32	6	
31	1	33	1						
31	1	34	1						
31	1	34	1						
31	1	34	1	0.5	8,000	65	29	6	300,000
31	2	34	1						
31	1	34	1	0.5	7,000	65	29	6	300,000
31	2	33	1	0.5	7,000	65	29	6	300,000

normally great, as in the white cell count at a given age or in the diameter of erythrocytes in an individual preparation, or where differences in technique account for divergent results, as in platelet counts, only the average or arithmetic mean is included in the tables.

The fact that fetal hemoglobin is relatively resistant to denaturation by alkaline solutions provides the basis for methods of measurement.

The erythrocytes of the full-term newborn infant appear to have the same life-span as adult red cells, 120 days. Those of the prematurely born infant have been reported to have a somewhat decreased longevity.

The total blood volume of the full-term infant averages 85 ml/kg. Higher values have been found in prematures. In both groups the blood volume at birth is influenced by the amount of blood transferred from placenta to infant during labor and delivery.

Postnatal Changes

Blood values obtained from capillary samples in the neonatal period tend to be significantly higher than those obtained from venous samples drawn simultaneously. Several studies have revealed that the hemoglobin concentration in blood obtained by heel puncture will average 2.5 to 3.5 g/100 ml higher than that in blood obtained by venipuncture.

The hemoglobin concentration tends to rise in the first few days after birth and then begins to fall steadily with a parallel fall in red cell count and hematocrit. In the full-term infant blood values reach a minimum level at approximately three months of life (Table 1). In prematurely born infants the rate

of fall is more precipitous, and the low point occurs earlier than in the full-term baby (six to eight weeks). The fall in blood values which occurs in the first two to three months of postnatal life in all normal infants leads to the so-called physiologic anemia in the term infant and to the early anemia of prematurity. In both groups the primary cause is the marked reduction in blood formation which begins shortly after birth. This decrease leads to progressive diminution in circulating hemoglobin, which, of course, leads to anemia. The degree of anemia is compounded by the rapid expansion in blood volume due to growth. The exaggerated changes characteristic of prematurity result from the more rapid rate of growth coupled with the somewhat decreased longevity of the erythrocytes in this group.

It is now well established that control of erythropoiesis is mediated through a humoral erythropoietic factor, erythropoietin. Release of this factor from one or more centers (kidney, pituitary) is stimulated by anemia and hypoxia and suppressed by polycythemia and exposure to high oxygen concentrations. Available evidence indicates that this control mechanism is operative in the newborn period and is involved in the physiologic anemia of the full-term infant and the early anemia of prematurity. Cessation of hematopoiesis in the early weeks of postnatal life appears to result from a reduction in the erythropoietin level secondary to the high hemoglobin concentration characteristic of the newborn. Resumption of active erythropoiesis follows release of erythropoietin as a consequence of the development of anemia. It would follow from these considerations that the infant whose hemoglobin concentration falls most rapidly would demonstrate a return of erythropoietic activity earlier than the infant whose hemoglobin concentration falls more slowly. The apparently paradoxical situation wherein the premature infant recovers erythropoietic activity earlier than the term infant, and wherein the smaller infant demonstrates active regeneration sooner than the larger baby, has been amply documented. It also follows that both physiologic anemia and the anemia of prematurity are normal events which are self-limited, and that in the majority of infants spontaneous improvement is to be anticipated. Despite the return of active hematopoiesis, the hemoglobin concentration rises only very gradually owing to the continuing rapid growth. The hemoglobin synthesized postnatally is almost entirely of the adult variety, and after the first year of life fetal hemoglobin is virtually completely replaced, with only 1 to 2 percent remaining in later life under normal circumstances.

Iron Metabolism

The sequence of hematologic events in fetal and neonatal life relates to the questions of iron needs in infancy and to the pathogenesis of iron-deficiency anemia.

Iron in the newborn infant is distributed in three main compartments, as shown in Table 2: (1) parenchymal iron in myoglobin and in certain enzymes, (2) storage iron primarily in liver and spleen, as ferritin and hemosiderin, and (3) iron in circulating hemoglobin.

Parenchymal iron content is estimated at 7 mg per kilogram, a figure derived from determination of muscle mass and its myoglobin content. This iron constitutes an irreducible minimum and also a basic and preferential need which must be satisfied throughout the entire growth period. Storage iron values are derived from liver and spleen analyses by Widdowson and Spray and by Lintzel and his co-workers, who observed a wide range, averaging 10 mg per kilogram. Values for hemoglobin iron may be derived from data on hemoglobin concentration and blood volume at birth. Almost 75 percent of the total body iron of the newborn infant is found in the circulating hemoglobin, and thus the wide range of hemoglobin concentration in neonates exerts considerable influence on the iron requirement in subsequent months.

When hematopoiesis ceases in the neonatal period the erythrocytes present in the circulation undergo the normal rate of destruction. For every gram of hemoglobin destroyed, 3.4 mg of iron are released. Since no adequate mechanism exists for iron excretion, the liberated iron is stored, primarily in the liver. The "physiologic" anemia of the first few months of life thus occurs in the face of iron excess and is not benefited by iron.

When blood formation resumes, the stored iron is again utilized for hemoglobin synthesis. In the normal term infant who is born with a normal hemoglobin concentration, the available iron reserves are sufficient to maintain both blood formation and growth until age 6 months, when stores become exhausted. In the absence of an exogenous source of iron a second fall in hemoglobin mass occurs as demands for tissue iron continue with growth. The anemia which may appear after 6 months of life is a true iron-deficiency anemia. The changes in a typical term infant are depicted in Figure 5.

The term infant born with a lower than normal hemoglobin concentration and the premature infant begin life with a smaller amount of total circulating hemoglobin and, therefore, with a smaller amount of total body iron (see Table 3). Such infants demand an exogenous source of iron at an earlier age than does the average term infant. The early anemia of prematurity, like the physiologic anemia of the term infant, is not due to iron deficiency. However, if exogenous iron is not provided to the premature by 2 to 3 months of age, a true iron-deficiency state will supervene (Fig. 6).

Fetal Hemorrhage

It has been demonstrated that the passage of fetal cells into the maternal circulation occurs very commonly throughout gestation. This has been docu-

TABLE 2.   *Distribution of Iron at Birth* *

	Average (mg/kg)	Range (mg/kg)
Parenchymal	7	—
Stores in liver and spleen	10	2-15
Hemoglobin	57	46-74

*After Widdowson and Spray (1951) and Lintzel et al. *Z. Ges. Exp. Med.*, 113:591, 1957.

TABLE 3.   *Distribution of Iron at Birth*

	Hb Conc. (g/100 ml)	Hb Mass (g)	Hb Iron (mg)	Storage Iron (mg)	Tissue Iron (mg)	Total Iron (mg)
Term 3.3 kg	17.0	55	185	34	23	242
Premature 1.5 kg	19.0	30	97	15	10	122

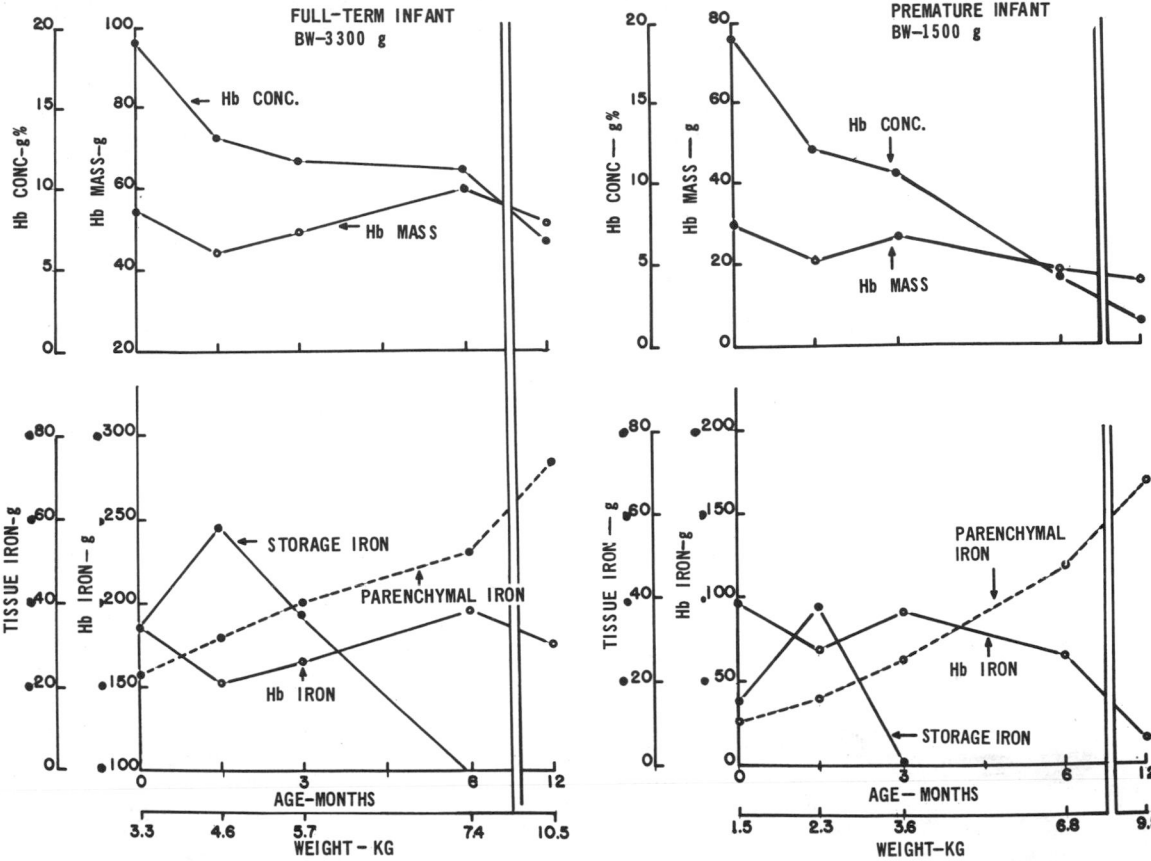

Fig. 5. Changes in hemoglobin concentration, hemoglobin mass, and body iron compartments in a full-term infant.

Fig. 6. Changes in hemoglobin concentration, hemoglobin mass, and body iron compartments in a premature infant.

mented by the finding of fetal hemoglobin containing erythrocytes in the blood of the mother. Usually only small amounts of fetal blood (0.1 to 0.2 ml) pass into the maternal circulation, but occasionally large amounts (50 ml or more) may cross the placenta and lead to significant anemia in the newborn.

In addition to the above, frank hemorrhage from the fetal surface of the placenta may occur during labor and delivery. This bleeding is usually associated with abnormalities of placental attachment such as placenta previa, premature separation of the placenta, or velamentous insertion of the cord. Occasionally the cord itself may rupture. Hemorrhage from a tear in the fetal vessels may lead rapidly to exsanguinating hemorrhage. Stillbirth may occur or the infants may be born with extreme pallor, profound shock, and failure of spontaneous respiration. These infants represent a critical emergency, and transfusion should be administered without delay. There is usually inadequate time for typing and cross matching, and group O, Rh-negative blood should be employed. If possible, sedimented or packed erythrocytes should be administered via the umbilical cord in a dose of 20 ml/kg of body weight initially. Establishment of an adequate airway and administration of oxygen should also be done. It should be emphasized that

if the hemorrhage has occurred shortly before delivery, the hemoglobin concentration may be normal, owing to the lack of time for hemodilution. Marked pallor and shock are indications for transfusion irrespective of the hemoglobin concentration.

REFERENCES

Dacie, J. R. The Haemolytic Anaemias, Congenital and Acquired. Part I. The Congenital Anemias. New York, Grune & Stratton, Inc., 1960.
—— Part II. The Auto-Immune Haemolytic Anaemias. New York, Grune & Stratton, Inc., 1962.
Harris, J. W. The Red Cell; Production, Metabolism, Destruction; Normal and Abnormal. Cambridge, Mass., Commonwealth Fund, Harvard Univ. Press, 1963.
Oski, F., and Vaisman, J. L. Hematologic Problems in the Newborn. Philadelphia, W. B. Saunders Co., 1966.
Smith, C. H. Blood Diseases of Infancy and Childhood, 2nd ed. St. Louis, C. V. Mosby Co., 1966.
Wintrobe, M. M. Clinical Hematology. Philadelphia, Lea & Febiger, 1961.

FETAL AND NEONATAL ERYTHROPOIESIS

Chown, B. Anaemia in a newborn due to the fetus bleeding into the mother's circulation; proof of the bleeding. Lancet, 1:1213, 1954.

Durkin, C. M., and Finn, R. Foetal haemorrhage into the maternal circulation. Lancet, 2:100, 1961.

Fraser, I. D., and Raper, A. B. Observations on the change from foetal to adult erythropoiesis. Arch. Dis. Child., 32:289, 1962.

Gunson, H. H. Neonatal anemia due to fetal hemorrhage into the maternal circulation. Pediatrics, 20:3, 1957.

Jacobson, L. O., and Doyle, M. Erythropoiesis. New York, Grune & Stratton, Inc., 1962.

Lintzel, W., Rechenberger, J., and Schairer, E. Ueber den Eisenstoffwechsel des Neugeborenen und Sauglings. Z. Ges. Exp. Med., 113:591, 1944.

Maurer, H. S., Behrman, R. E., and Honig, G. R. Dependence of the oxygen affinity of blood on the presence of foetal or adult haemoglobin. Nature, 227:388, 1970.

Rhinesmith, H. S., Schroeder, W. A., and Pauling, L. A quantitative study of hydrolysis of human DNP-globulin; the number and kind of polypeptide chains in hemoglobin A. J. Amer. Chem. Soc., 79:4682, 1957.

Schulman, I. Characteristics of the blood in Foetal life; in Oxygen Supply to the Human Foetus. Oxford, Blackwell Scientific Publications, 1959, p. 43.

——— The anemia of prematurity. J. Pediat., 54:663, 1959.

——— Iron requirements in infancy. J.A.M.A., 175: 118, 1961.

——— and Smith, C. H. Studies on the anemia of prematurity. III. The mechanism of the anemia. Amer. J. Dis. Child., 88:572, 1954.

Shiller, J. G. Shock in the newborn caused by transplacental hemorrhage from fetus to mother. Pediatrics, 20:7, 1957.

Widdowson, E. M., and Spray, C. M. Chemical development in utero. Arch. Dis. Child., 26:206, 1951.

The Anemias

GEORGE R. HONIG and IRVING SCHULMAN

An anemia may be said to exist when the hemoglobin concentration and hematocrit are below the normal range for the age of the child. In most circumstances the red cell count is also reduced, but in some hypochromic anemias this may not be the case.

ETIOLOGIC CLASSIFICATION OF ANEMIAS

I. *Impaired Production of Red Cells and Hemoglobin*

   A. *Deficiency of substances required for hemoglobin synthesis and erythropoiesis*
   1. *Iron deficiency*
   2. *Megaloblastic anemias*

   B. *Hypoplastic and aplastic anemias*
   1. *Congenital*
   2. *Acquired*

   C. *Bone marrow replacement*

   D. *Chronic infections, uremia, malignancy*

II. *Accelerated Destruction of Red Cells*

   A. *Intracorpuscular defects*
   1. *Abnormalities of the red cell membrane: Hereditary spherocytosis, elliptocytosis, stomatocytosis*
   2. *Red cell enzyme abnormalities*
   3. *Abnormalities of hemoglobin structure and synthesis: the hemoglobinopathies and thalassemia syndromes*

   B. *Extracorpuscular defects*
   1. *Autoimmune acquired hemolytic anemia*
   2. *Drug-induced hemolytic anemias*
   3. *Hypersplenism*
   4. *Accelerated hemolysis due to intravascular red cell destruction*
   5. *Other causes: uremia, liver disease, rheumatoid arthritis, burns, infantile pyknocytosis, vitamin E deficiency*
   6. *Erythroblastosis fetalis (Hemolytic disease of the newborn)*

III. *Blood Loss*

17.2
ANEMIAS DUE TO IMPAIRED PRODUCTION OF RED CELLS AND HEMOGLOBIN

GEORGE R. HONIG and
IRVING SCHULMAN

Deficiency of Substances Required for Hemoglobin Synthesis and Erythropoiesis

Iron-Deficiency Anemia

Pathogenesis. Deficiency of iron occurs most commonly during the age period of 6 months to 2 years and is the most frequent cause of anemia in infancy. As described in the previous chapter, the iron reserves of the normal, full-term infant are usually adequate to prevent anemia for the first 4 to 6 months of life even in the absence of significant amounts of exogenous dietary iron. After the age of 6 months, however, the diet must supply from 0.9 to 1.5 mg/kg of iron per day if anemia is to be prevented. Infants whose supply of iron at birth is decreased as a result of prematurity, multiple births, fetal hemorrhage, or external blood loss in the postnatal period will require a source of exogenous iron at an earlier age.

A diet consisting almost exclusively of milk provides grossly inadequate amounts of iron and most frequently forms the basis for the development of iron-deficiency anemia. Cow's milk provides only about 0.5 mg per liter and breast milk about 1.0 mg per liter. Iron-enriched cereals provide the major source of iron in the typical infant diet. Egg yolk, strained meats, and vegetables, which make up the remainder of foods usually given in early infancy, contain relatively little iron as is shown in the following table:

IRON CONTENT OF TYPICAL FOODS

Food	mg of Iron
Fortified cereals	2.5–5.0
Green and yellow vegetables	0.05–0.28
Strained meats	0.23–0.56 ⎬ per tablespoon
Fruits	0.10–0.32
Egg yolk	1.0 per egg
Milk	0.5 per liter

Healthy, full-term infants on a varied diet can derive adequate iron from food alone and do not require iron supplementation. Most cases of iron deficiency occur in infants who are not offered or refuse to eat cereals and other solid foods, and who ingest large quantities of milk. If one of the predisposing factors has been present, however, even an optimal diet cannot supply the needed quantity of iron, and additional exogenous iron must be given to prevent the development of anemia.

Iron-deficiency anemia occurs commonly in association with multiparity and low socioeconomic status, reflecting a greater frequency of low birth weight as well as inadequate postnatal intake of iron. Poor iron intake in lower socioeconomic groups is often ascribed to dietary inadequacy resulting from financial limitation or insufficient knowledge on the part of parents concerning proper infant feeding. Observations by Pollock and Richmond, however, have suggested that social, economic, and emotional factors may create disturbances in the parent-child relationship which are reflected as feeding problems, and may be of major significance in the development of iron deficiency.

While inadequate intake is the most common etiologic basis for iron-deficiency anemia during the first 2 years of life, it is a very infrequent cause thereafter. In later years blood loss becomes the most common cause and should always be looked for whenever iron-deficiency anemia occurs in later childhood and adolescence. Chronic blood loss may result from repeated epistaxis; from lesions in the gastrointestinal tract, such as polyps, ulcerative colitis, regional ileitis, or Meckel's diverticulum; from chronic parasitism as with hookworm infestation; or from hemorrhagic disease. Protein-losing enteropathy, either idiopathic or secondary to a variety of gastrointestinal diseases or abnormalities, is frequently associated with iron-deficiency anemia due to loss of blood and loss of iron bound to the iron-binding protein transferrin. The recognition that protein-losing enteropathy may occur as a transient, self-limited event raises the possibility that some cases of iron-deficiency anemia previously attributed to nutritional deprivation may in fact be due to iron loss.

Interpretation of the etiologic significance of blood loss is made more difficult by the fact that about 50 percent of infants with apparently clear-cut evidence of a nutritional basis for iron-deficiency anemia have also been found to have guaiac-positive stools. Recent investigations have demonstrated that iron deficiency is apparently capable of inducing a form of enteropathy with evidence of intestinal malabsorption. Duodenal biopsies in these children showed evidence of chronic inflammatory changes and mucosal atrophy. Following treatment with iron most of these abnormalities reverted to normal, and gastrointestinal blood loss ceased. A syndrome of chronic blood loss into the gastrointestinal tract resulting from intolerance to whole cow's milk has also been described and may further complicate gastrointestinal blood loss in patients with iron deficiency.

Clinical manifestations. Iron-deficiency anemia in infancy develops slowly and insidiously. As a result, the waxy pallor which may be readily apparent to others may go unnoticed by the parent even in extreme cases. The slow development of anemia allows physiologic adjustment by the infant, and hemoglobin concentrations even as low as 3 g/100 ml may be tolerated without significant interference with ordinary activity. The major symptoms are irritability and anorexia, with the infant refusing to take foods while accepting or even demanding copious amounts of milk. Careful history will frequently reveal that the child may drink a full bottle of milk every few hours. With the development of protracted anemia of a severe degree, physical activity eventually becomes diminished, and the child may become quite listless. This apathy is particularly evident in the presence of infection.

The marked pallor imparts an almost translucent appearance to the skin, particularly about the ears. The mucous membranes are also very pale and may be a more reliable clue to the diagnosis in dark-skinned children. Slight enlargement of the spleen may be found in about 10 percent of infants with iron-deficiency anemia, but the organ is usually rather soft. A soft blowing precordial systolic murmur is commonly found, but significant cardiac enlargement is rare.

Laboratory findings. The lack of iron interferes primarily with hemoglobin synthesis, and early in the course the red cell count may be entirely normal. As the hemoglobin concentration falls to low levels and as anemia persists, erythropoiesis may also be affected and the red cell count may fall to 3.0 million per mm³ or less. The hemoglobin level is always affected to a greater degree than the red cell count, and *hypochromia* and *microcytosis* of the red cells are characteristic findings. The red cells are small and demonstrate marked variation in size and shape. Central pallor of the red cells is increased, and the hemoglobin may be limited to a thin rim at the periphery of the cell. Red cell ghosts and fragments are commonly seen. The hematocrit is always low, and calculation of red cell indices reveals a reduction in mean corpuscular volume and mean corpuscular hemoglobin concentration. Reticulocytes are normal or low in number. The white cell count is variable, but moderate leucopenia with relative lymphocytosis is not uncommon. With moderately severe degrees of anemia (hemoglobin concentrations of 6 to 8 g/100 ml), elevation of the platelet count may be found. With severe degrees of anemia, thrombocytopenia may occur; it is corrected with treatment of the anemia.

Iron-deficiency anemia is characterized by a low serum iron (usually below 50 μg/100 ml) and

(1 mg iron per drop); elixir of ferrous sulfate 30 mg/4 ml (tsp); ferrous sulfate tablets 60 mg/0.3 g tablet. The recommended therapeutic dose for infants is 1.5 to 2.0 mg of elemental iron per kilogram body weight three times daily (total dose 60 to 90 mg/day). Although the recommendation is often made that iron be administered between meals to avoid formation of insoluble iron phosphates, our own experience has not demonstrated any interference with response when medication is given with meals, and the incidence of gastrointestinal disturbances appears to be less. During treatment the stools are usually black, and with the use of liquid iron the teeth may become temporarily discolored.

Routine use of intramuscular iron is not indicated, but certain circumstances may arise in which it is of value. These include: (1) the occasional patient in whom oral iron is not tolerated; (2) the rare individual who is unable to absorb iron; (3) the severely anemic infant in whom the use of intramuscular iron may obviate transfusion; and (4) the child who cannot be expected to receive adequate oral iron due to lack of parental cooperation. Intramuscular iron is available as an iron-dextran combination containing 50 mg of elemental iron per ml. It must be given deeply intramuscularly but is well tolerated and predictably effective. The dose of intramuscular iron may be calculated from the formula:

$$\frac{Normal\ Hb\ conc. - Initial\ Hb\ conc. \times 80 \times 3.4 \times 1.5 \times wt\ in\ kg}{100} = mg\ iron\ needed$$

Where 80 = *average blood volume in ml per kg*
3.4 = *mg of iron/gram of hemoglobin*
1.5 = *50% extra margin for iron stores*

an elevated iron-binding capacity (usually above 400 μg/100 ml), a pattern which occurs in no other anemia. The marrow reveals hypercellularity due to erythroid hyperplasia. Special stains demonstrate the absence of iron in the marrow.

In those cases in which protein loss into the gastrointestinal tract accompanies iron-deficiency anemia, as either cause or effect, analysis of the plasma proteins will disclose low levels of total serum proteins. Hypoalbuminemia may be severe enough to cause edema. In these cases low serum copper concentrations, resulting from decreased levels of ceruloplasmin, accompany the low serum iron. Because the loss of protein can also involve transferrin, the iron-binding capacity may not be elevated or may even be low.

Treatment. The therapy of iron-deficiency anemia in childhood is usually simple and gratifying inasmuch as the majority of patients respond readily to oral administration of iron. Although numerous preparations of iron are available, ferrous sulfate remains the treatment of choice; it may be given as drops for infants, elixir for young children, or tablets for older children. The content of elemental iron in these various forms of ferrous sulfate is as follows: concentrated ferrous sulfate used as drops, 25 mg/ml

The use of the following dosage, based on age, is probably equally effective: 100 mg for infants under 6 months; 200 mg, 6 to 12 months; 300 mg, 12 to 24 months; 400 mg, over 24 months. The first injection should consist of 1 ml (50 mg), with subsequent daily injections of 2 ml (100 mg) until the total dose is given. With oral iron, peak reticulocyte rise should occur in 5 to 7 days; with intramuscular iron slightly sooner. The degree of reticulocytosis and the subsequent rate of rise of hemoglobin concentration are inversely proportional to the degree of anemia. After reticulocytosis occurs, the hemoglobin rise averages 1 to 2 g per 100 ml per week.

Because of the high degree of tolerance of infants to rather severe degrees of anemia, blood transfusions are rarely needed in the management of iron-deficiency anemia. On rare occasions when an infant presents with profound anemia, particularly when accompanied by infection, transfusion may be required; it must be done with extreme caution to avoid sudden expansion of the blood volume and the induction of congestive heart failure. Packed red cells are preferred, and the initial transfusion should be limited to 5 to 10 ml/kg of body weight. If this is tolerated, the hemoglobin concentration may be elevated further by additional transfusion of 20 ml/kg of packed cells. It is usually not necessary to raise the hemoglobin concentration to normal levels by transfusion. An increase which is sufficient to remove the child from immediate danger is followed by iron medication. The routine use of digitalis prior to transfusion of the severely anemic child has not been proved of value, except in the infant with evidence of preexisting heart failure.

Megaloblastic Anemias

Megaloblastic changes in hematopoietic bone marrow cells result from any of a number of factors which produce a selective impairment of DNA synthesis. Nuclear maturation and cellular division are delayed, but cytoplasmic maturation remains relatively unaffected, resulting in the formation of macrocytic cells having overabundant cytoplasm. This defective maturational pattern closely resembles the phenomenon of thymineless death which occurs with thymine starvation of bacterial auxotrophs.

Megaloblastic anemia most often results from a deficiency of vitamin B_{12} or folic acid, both of which are required for DNA synthesis of hematopoietic cells. In rare instances these vitamins may be available in normal amounts but not utilized, as in liver disease; they also may be inhibited by certain drugs.

Vitamin B_{12} functions as the extrinsic factor and requires the presence of the intrinsic factor of the gastric mucosa in order to be absorbed. This absorption occurs primarily in the ileum. Folic acid, which is found in leafy vegetables as well as in animal tissues, is absorbed to a large extent in the jejunum. Megaloblastic anemias due to B_{12} deficiency usually result from lack of intrinsic factor, while those resulting from folic acid deficiency stem from dietary lack, failure of absorption, impaired utilization, or specific metabolic antagonism.

Hematologic findings. In the peripheral blood the characteristic red cells are macrocytic, and the anemia is associated with a high mean corpuscular volume, a high mean corpuscular hemoglobin, and a normal mean corpuscular hemoglobin concentration. The red cells show marked variation in size and shape, and occasionally nucleated erythrocytes may appear in the peripheral blood.

Although the megaloblastic anemias manifest primarily impaired erythropoiesis, maturation of the white cells and platelets is also affected. Leucopenia is common, and polymorphonuclear leucocytes are frequently abnormally large and contain hypersegmented nuclei. Thrombocytopenia is also commonly seen and may be severe enough to produce purpura. The diagnostic features are best seen in the marrow, which is hyperplastic and reveals megaloblastic erythropoiesis at all stages of red cell maturation. Involvement of the myeloid series produces giant metamyelocytes and band forms, which may appear before the characteristic megaloblasts develop.

VITAMIN B_{12} DEFICIENCY STATES. *Dietary Deficiency.* Vitamin B_{12} is primarily supplied by foods of animal origin; it is present in cow's milk and human breast milk in sufficient quantities to provide usual requirements during infancy. Megaloblastic anemia due to dietary lack of vitamin B_{12} has been reported, however, in a breast-fed infant of a mother who had untreated pernicious anemia. Negligible amounts of vitamin B_{12} were present in the mother's breast milk, and the anemia in the infant responded promptly to administration of the vitamin.

Juvenile Pernicious Anemia. Etiology. Pernicious anemia, the result of impaired absorption of vitamin B_{12} due to deficiency of intrinsic factor, is rare in childhood but has been recognized with increasing frequency in recent years. The disease as it occurs in childhood frequently differs from the typical Addisonian pernicious anemia of adults in that achlorhydria and gastric mucosal changes are rarely found, and serum antibodies to intrinsic factor or gastric parietal cells are usually not demonstrable.

Several studies have shown a deficiency of intrinsic factor and defective vitamin B_{12} absorption to be present in parents and siblings of patients with juvenile pernicious anemia. These findings have suggested that these cases of juvenile pernicious anemia may represent a homozygous form of a genetic deficiency of intrinsic factor secretion by gastric mucosa. The adult form of the disease is postulated to represent a heterozygous state in which protracted deficiency of vitamin B_{12} eventually leads to atrophy of the gastric mucosa and the development of anemia.

A number of cases have been reported in which juvenile pernicious anemia was present together with one or more endocrinopathies, including hypoparathyroidism, hypothyroidism, and Addison's disease. Available evidence indicates that these syndromes probably have an immunologic basis. Antibody to intrinsic factor, achlorhydria, and atrophy of gastric mucosa have been demonstrated in a majority of these patients.

Clinical manifestations. In most reported cases of juvenile pernicious anemia, symptoms have appeared during the first 2 years of life. Manifestations develop slowly, with pallor, anorexia, irritability, and diarrhea being most prominent. The tongue is typically smooth, shiny, and beefy-red due to papillary atrophy. Lymphadenopathy and hepatosplenomegaly are absent. Neurologic findings are infrequent in juvenile pernicious anemia, but can be precipitated by improper administration of large doses of folic acid. The most common neurologic manifestations include ataxia, impaired vibratory sense, hyporeflexia, paresthesias, and positive Babinski reflexes.

Laboratory findings. The anemia may be moderate to very severe, with the red cell count characteristically being more depressed than the hemoglobin concentration. The peripheral blood and bone marrow demonstrate the typical findings of megaloblastosis as described previously. Because of a rapid rate of hematopoietic cell destruction within the bone marrow in this disorder, a number of intracellular enzymes can be detected in the serum of these patients. Lactate dehydrogenase (LDH) is typically elevated, often to an extreme degree.

Diagnosis. Since megaloblastic anemia may occur in conditions other than pernicious anemia, and because the latter disorder requires lifelong treatment with vitamin B_{12}, it is imperative to establish a precise diagnosis. This may be accomplished by demonstrating low serum levels of vitamin B_{12} and by documenting both failure of gastrointestinal absorption of the vitamin and correction of it by concomitant administration of intrinsic factor. The diagnosis can be most readily established by use of the Schilling test, in which radioactive vitamin B_{12} is administered by mouth following injection of a large flushing dose of nonradioactive B_{12}. Normal individuals will excrete more than 15 percent of the administered radioactivity into the urine in the next 24 hours; patients with pernicious anemia will excrete less than 3 percent. With addition of intrinsic factor to the oral dose, a significant increase in urinary excretion occurs. In some patients a transient malabsorption of B_{12} has also been present, which disappears following parenteral therapy with the vitamin. In these instances administration of intrinsic factor produces minimal improvement in the Schilling test until the malabsorption improved.

An apparently familial variant of pernicious anemia has also been described in which a selective failure of vitamin B_{12} absorption is present, but production of intrinsic factor is normal. In addition to B_{12} deficiency, these patients also exhibit persistent proteinuria. Although the anemia responds promptly to vitamin B_{12}, the proteinuria remains unaffected.

Treatment. The parenteral administration of a large dose of vitamin B_{12} (usually 1 mg) as part of the Schilling test procedure provides at the same time adequate initial therapy. In most instances complete hematologic remission ensues in 2 to 4 weeks. Reversion of the bone marrow from megaloblastic to normoblastic erythropoiesis occurs at an extraordinary rate, so that megaloblasts may be completely absent after 3 days of treatment. Reticulocytosis is seen within 3 or 4 days after administration of vitamin B_{12}. Hematologic normality may be maintained by regular intramuscular injections of B_{12} in a dose of 30 to 50 μg per month. Although remissions have been maintained with very large oral doses of B_{12}, such therapy is unpredictable and expensive, and parenteral maintenance is recommended. Folic acid may also produce and maintain hematologic remission, but it has no effect in preventing or treating neurologic complications and should not be used in established pernicious anemia. Since vitamin B_{12} requirements are very small and hepatic storage is very efficient, relapses may not occur for weeks to months after cessation of treatment. Such relapses will eventually appear, however, and treatment is required for the life of the patient.

Other Causes of Vitamin B_{12} Deficiency. Intestinal absorption of vitamin B_{12} occurs almost exclusively in the distal portion of the ileum. Surgical resection of this segment of the small bowel results in B_{12} deficiency after a variable period of time, requiring parenteral administration of the vitamin. Impairment of vitamin B_{12} absorption has also been described in association with regional ileitis.

Intestinal infestation with the fish tapeworm (*Diphyllobothrium latum*) can produce a megaloblastic anemia with decreased serum levels of vitamin B_{12} as a result of utilization of a major portion of the dietary B_{12} by the parasite.

FOLIC ACID DEFICIENCY STATES. *Megaloblastic Anemia of Infancy.* Folic acid deficiency occurs frequently in combination with a deficiency of ascorbic acid, which is believed to be necessary for the reduction of folate to tetrahydrofolate. The disease is far less common than it was in the past, primarily because of widespread enrichment of infant foods with ascorbic acid. This disorder now tends to occur in infants with poor nutrition and repeated infections, especially diarrhea. Megaloblastic anemia has also occurred frequently in infants fed goat's milk, since this type of milk is a particularly poor source of folic acid.

The disease is most common between 6 and 12 months of age, and progressive pallor is the usual presenting manifestation. The disease responds rapidly, dramatically, and permanently to treatment with folic acid, which may be given orally or intramuscularly in a dose of 15 to 30 mg daily. Once hematologic recovery takes place, usually in 2 to 4 weeks, folic acid therapy may be discontinued. In some cases in which megaloblastic anemia occurs in the course of general malnutrition, folic acid treatment may lead to rapid rise in red cell count while the hemoglobin concentration lags behind, because of a coexisting iron-deficiency state. Treatment with iron will induce a second reticulocytosis and lead to complete correction of the anemia. In instances of very severe anemia, initial blood transfusion may be indicated.

Drug-Induced Megaloblastic Anemia. Methotrexate and related drugs which are employed in the therapy of leukemia function as antagonists of folic acid, and megaloblastic changes are regularly observed in patients receiving these drugs. These changes occur less frequently with 6-mercaptopurine, vincristine, and other agents which affect the synthesis of DNA.

Megaloblastic anemia is a rare complication of anticonvulsant drug therapy, and has been observed in patients receiving diphenylhydantoin, phenobarbital, and primidone. Serum folate levels are significantly decreased in affected individuals, and the anemia responds well to folic acid even if administration of the anticonvulsant drug is continued.

Folic Acid Deficiency Due to Intestinal Malabsorption. Deficiency of folic acid can accompany generalized intestinal malabsorption due to any cause. A severe megaloblastic anemia is commonly present in tropical sprue, but macrocytic anemia without megaloblastic changes in the bone marrow is more frequent in nontropical sprue. Folic acid deficiency occurs occasionally in celiac disease, but this disorder is more frequently accompanied by a hypochromic, microcytic anemia due to iron deficiency.

OTHER CAUSES OF MEGALOBLASTIC ANEMIA.

Hereditary Orotic Aciduria. Orotic aciduria is a rare familial disorder characterized by severe megaloblastic anemia and excretion of large amounts of orotic acid in the urine. Because of the limited solubility of orotic acid it appears as crystals in the urine. The anemia appears within the first year of life and is unresponsive to folic acid or vitamin B_{12}. Affected individuals are deficient in a pair of enzymes which catalyze the conversion of orotic acid to uridylic acid. Administration of uridine has resulted in hematologic remission.

Thiamine-Responsive Megaloblastic Anemia. A single example of this disorder has been reported in a child who developed severe megaloblastic anemia at age 11. Diabetes mellitus, bilateral sensorineural deafness, and amino-aciduria were also present. The anemia was unresponsive to vitamin B_{12}, folic acid, and a number of other vitamins, but a prompt remission occurred when thiamine was given. The child showed no evidence of thiamine deficiency, and normal levels of the vitamin were present, suggesting that greater than normal levels of thiamine were required for control of the anemia.

Hypoplastic and Aplastic Anemias

CHARLES F. ABILDGAARD

The hypoplastic and aplastic anemias are a diverse group of hematologic disorders which result from depression of hematopoietic activity in the bone marrow. The marrow hypoplasia may involve only erythropoietic elements to produce anemia, or, more commonly, all of the blood cell precursors may be decreased resulting in pancytopenia of the peripheral blood. The majority of cases are correctly designated as hypoplastic states, with the term aplasia referring to complete absence of recognizable hematopoietic elements in the bone marrow. The recognition of aplastic-hypoplastic syndromes most commonly results from clinical signs or symptoms related to anemia, granulocytopenia, or thrombocytopenia. A variety of condition has been implicated in the etiology of hematopoietic hypoplasia, and some forms occur as congenital familial disorders.

Congenital Aplastic Anemia

The familial type of aplastic anemia is most commonly represented by the Fanconi syndrome, in which the hematologic disorder is associated with a variety of congenital anomalies. These may include patchy pigmentation of the skin, understature, skeletal abnormalities (especially involving the thumb, radius, and long bones), hypogenitalism, microcephaly, microphthalmia, and renal abnormalities. The hematologic defect is characterized by quantitative bone marrow failure resulting in pancytopenia. Both sporadic and familial cases have been described, and the Fanconi syndrome appears to be transmitted as an autosomal recessive trait with variable penetrance. Chromosome studies in these patients have revealed a variety of breakages and structural abnormalities. Siblings of children with pancytopenia may have multiple congenital abnormalities without hematologic involvement.

Although the disorder is congenital, peripheral blood and bone marrow findings are most often normal during infancy and early childhood. Clinical manifestations due to bone marrow failure and pancytopenia do not usually occur until between 4 and 12 years of age, even in those patients who have associated congenital anomalies. The reason for the delay in onset of hematologic symptoms is unknown. Bone marrow examination may reveal nests of active hematopoiesis but hypocellularity is usually apparent. Elevated fetal hemoglobin levels are frequent and may precede clinical hematologic involvement.

Prior to the use of combined steroid therapy with adrenocortical steroids and testosterone, anemia was uniformly progressive, with a fatal outcome usually due to infection or bleeding. With the combined treatment the majority of patients improve. Most, however, require indefinite maintenance therapy. Responsive patients often may be maintained on moderate doses of testosterone and prednisone.

Congenital Red Cell Hypoplasia. This rare disorder is characterized by failure of erythropoiesis and results in progressive anemia without depression of leucocytes or platelets. Approximately 100 cases have been described under a variety of descriptive titles including pure red cell anemia, Blackfan-Diamond syndrome, chronic congenital aregenerative anemia, and erythrogenesis imperfecta. The etiology of this disorder is unknown, but available evidence suggests a possible immunologic basis.

The anemia is usually evident in the first 3 months of life and is nearly always apparent within the first year. Affected infants may exhibit pallor at the time of birth or may gradually develop irritability, listlessness, and loss of appetite with progressive development of anemia. The physical examination is usually normal, but some cases are associated with low birth weight and growth retardation.

The anemia is normocytic and normochromic, and there is marked reticulocytopenia. The diagnosis is confirmed by examination of the bone marrow which reveals absence or severe depression of erythroid elements with normal myeloid cells and megarkaryocytes.

Treatment with corticosteroids is effective in most patients if instituted early. As soon as the diagnosis has been established prednisone should be started at a dose of 1 to 2 mg/kg/day. Transfusions are indicated only if the anemia is severe, and should be given as packed red cells (10 to 20 ml/kg) to attain a hemoglobin level of 8 to 10 g per 100 ml. Prednisone is continued in full dose until reticulocytosis occurs, or for at least 4 weeks. A reticulocyte response may appear after the first week of treatment, but may not reach a peak until 2 to 3 weeks. Once a normal hemoglobin level is achieved, the dose of prednisone may be gradually reduced to the lowest amount capable of maintaining erythropoiesis. Effective maintenance therapy may be possible with doses as low as 5 mg prednisone two or three times a week. Most children will require indefinite maintenance therapy. Occasionally spontaneous remission of the anemia may occur, usually at the time of puberty.

Acquired Aplastic Anemia

Acquired aplastic anemia is an uncommon condition in childhood; it is characterized by peripheral pancytopenia and by decreased or absent hematopoietic elements in the bone marrow. Approximately one-half of the cases are associated with exposure to drugs, chemicals, irradiation, or other agents known to be capable of causing bone marrow damage. A large variety of agents have been implicated as causative factors in aplastic anemia, including chloramphenicol, sulfonamides, hydantoins, phenothiazides, insecticides, benzene, gold, quinine, and many others. In recent years chloramphenicol has accounted for approximately 75 percent of cases of aplastic anemia related to drug or chemical exposure. The mechanism of bone marrow damage by such agents remains unknown.

Several cases of aplastic anemia following viral hepatitis have also been described. Cases without history of toxic exposure are usually designated as idiopathic acquired aplastic anemia. Since the clinical manifestations, diagnosis, and treatment of acquired aplastic anemia do not differ for secondary or idiopathic cases, these will be considered together.

Clinical manifestations. The onset of acquired aplastic anemia is usually gradual, the symptoms being related to the progressive pancytopenia. Unless recognized early, severe anemia may develop with associated pallor, easy fatigability, weakness, and loss of appetite. The accompanying thrombocytopenia may lead to petechiae, easy bruising, and a variety of bleeding manifestations, with severe nosebleeds and gastrointestinal bleeding often being the most troublesome. As a result of leucopenia there may be an increased susceptibility to infections, which are frequently severe and may respond poorly to antibiotic therapy. Physical examination is usually unrevealing except for pallor and evidence of bleeding. Hepatosplenomegaly does not occur, and when found in association with bleeding and pallor should suggest the possibility of other diseases, particularly leukemia.

Laboratory findings. Examination of the peripheral blood reveals varying degrees of pancytopenia depending on the duration and severity of the disease. Severe depression of all blood cell types may be present. On differential white cell count there is usually a relative lymphocytosis. The diagnosis is established by examination of the bone marrow, which shows marked depression or absence of hematopoietic cells and replacement by fatty tissue. The absence of blasts (stem cells) is of special importance in differentiating aplastic anemia from the unusual case of leukemia in which the marrow may be initially hypocellular. Occasionally islands of hematopoietic tissue may be seen, and a repeat marrow sample from another site or a bone marrow biopsy may help clarify the diagnosis. Slight to moderate elevation of fetal hemoglobin may be present in aplastic anemia and appears to be of prognostic value in this disease. Patients having greater than 0.4 g/100 ml of fetal hemoglobin have usually recovered, while those with lower concentrations have generally had an unfavorable course.

Treatment. The aim of initial therapy is to correct the anemia and to provide necessary supportive measures for complications related to neutropenia and thrombocytopenia. Transfusion with packed red cells is required in nearly all cases of aplastic anemia, at the onset and at intervals as required to prevent excessive anemia. It has been recommended that red cell replacement be limited to maintaining a hemoglobin level of 8 to 10 g/100 ml in order to avoid suppression of erythropoietin production. Bleeding manifestations related to thrombocytopenia are frequently life-threatening; they are optimally treated with transfusions of platelet concentrates or with fresh whole blood. Administration of 1 unit of platelet concentrate for each 5 kg of body weight will usually control hemorrhage resulting from thrombocytopenia; the platelet transfusions may need to be repeated in 1 to 2 days if bleeding persists. Granulocytopenia poses a constant risk of infection; in the presence of recognized or suspected infection cultures should be obtained and antibiotic therapy started promptly. Whenever possible, bacteriocidal agents should be used. Prophylactic antibiotic therapy is not indicated. In the absence of adequate numbers of normal granulocytes, antibiotic therapy is often ineffective and septicemia is a frequent cause of death. Transfusion of fresh leucocyte concentrates prepared from blood of donors with leucocytosis may be a valuable adjunct therapy for severe infection.

Even with optimal supportive therapy, the mortality rate in children with aplastic anemia has been about 50 percent. However a significant improvement in the rate of recovery has occurred since the introduction of combined corticosteroid and testosterone therapy. The regimen employed most frequently has been Prednisone (10 to 20 mg per day in divided doses) and testosterone propionate (1 mg per kg daily, preferably given sublingually). In younger patients who are unable to take testosterone in the sublingual form, the drug is given orally in a dose of 2 mg per kg daily. Evidence of a return of bone marrow function frequently is not detectable until therapy has been given for a period of 2 to 3 months, and most patients will require treatment with these agents for 12 months or longer before the drugs can be discontinued. Premature cessation of therapy will often result in relapse.

Recently oxymetholone, a synthetic derivative of testosterone, has been shown to be more effective than other forms of testosterone in inducing hematologic remission in patients with aplastic anemia. Oxymetholone is given in place of the testosterone propionate in a dosage of 2 to 6 mg per kg per day. However, a high frequency of cholestatic jaundice has been observed in patients receiving this drug. This complication usually requires discontinuation of the medication, but if hematologic remission has been achieved with oxymetholone, less toxic forms of testosterone can often be substituted with satisfactory maintenance of marrow function.

Children who receive the combined steroid regimen often develop marked side effects of the drugs, including Cushingoid changes, marked weight gain, hirsutism, acne, masculinization, deepening of the voice, hypertension, and occasional glucosuria. Although these side effects are unpleasant, most are reversible if the child recovers and drugs are discontinued. Parents should be forewarned of the consequences of combined therapy since even gross changes may occur gradually and remain unrecognized. Excessive weight gain may be minimized by early dietary recommendations limiting salt and caloric intake. Other precautions recommended in the use of long-term, high-dose corticosteroid therapy (adequate potassium intake, regular blood pressure determination, frequent urinalysis) are also advisable.

Response to therapy is usually recognized by a decreasing requirement for transfusions. Once an adequate stable hemoglobin level is maintained without transfusions, it may be possible to reduce the prednisone dose or to give the full dose once every 48 hours without apparently reducing therapeutic effectiveness. Such a change in therapy is often followed by a marked decrease in the undesirable side effects.

Hospitalization of these patients should be minimized because of the hazards of resistant organisms present in the hospital environment. Although activities should be restricted to avoid trauma while thrombocytopenia is present, many children are able to attend school. If the affected child escapes fatal hemorrhage or infection and survives for the first 6 months of disease, the prognosis for complete recovery is greatly increased. Thrombocytopenia may persist for months to years despite recovery of red and white cell elements; it is not an indication for continued drug therapy. Patients with persistence of thrombocytopenia after recovery of erythropoiesis

rarely have serious bleeding manifestations. In those cases of acquired aplastic anemia suspected of being related to drugs or chemicals, reexposure to the offending agent should be carefully avoided.

Aplastic Crises. Transient episodes of erythroid aplasia are encountered in patients having a variety of chronic hemolytic states. These include hereditary spherocytosis, sickle-cell anemia, red cell enzyme deficiencies, and other conditions in which erythrocyte survival is shortened. The etiology of these aplastic crises is not known, but because of simultaneous occurrences in several members of families, an infectious basis appears likely. Early in the course of the aplastic episode erythroid elements are found to be entirely absent or greatly reduced in the bone marrow, while megakarycocytes and leucocyte precursors are present in normal numbers. Reticulocyte counts are low, and severe progressive anemia may develop requiring close observation and transfusions of packed red cells until marrow erythroid activity is resumed. The aplasia usually lasts for only a few days, and recovery is complete.

Anemia Due to Bone Marrow Replacement

GEORGE R. HONIG and
IRVING SCHULMAN

Leukemia and other malignancies, particularly lymphosarcoma and neuroblastoma, may cause severe pancytopenia due to replacement of normal marrow tissue by malignant cells. These conditions may also be associated with depression of bone marrow function in varying degrees including severe aplasia. The mechanism of this depression is poorly understood.

Osteopetrosis (Albers-Schöneberg disease), a rare disorder characterized by cortical thickening and density of bone, is often associated with progressive anemia and thrombocytopenia. The hematologic changes have largely been attributed to obliteration of the marrow cavities, but enhanced destruction of red cells may also be an important factor in the etiology of the anemia. After splenectomy the anemia is sometimes improved.

Systemic Inflammatory Diseases, Uremia, Malignancy

Anemia of Chronic Renal Disease. Severe renal disease with uremia is frequently associated with chronic anemia and at times with pancytopenia due to depression of all marrow elements. Failure of red cell production in such cases may be related in part to a decrease of erythropoietin, which is made primarily in the kidney. Transfusions may be required to relieve symptoms of the anemia of chronic renal disease and should be given as packed red cells in small amounts (5 to 10 ml/kg) because these patients are susceptible to congestive heart failure as a result of circulatory overloading.

Anemia of Systemic Inflammatory Disease. A variety of systemic diseases, including severe or chronic infections, rheumatic fever, and rheumatoid arthritis, may be associated with varying degrees of bone marrow dysfunction. The anemia is normocytic and normochromic but when long-standing may be microcytic and hypochromic. The reticulocyte count is normal or reduced. Typically, serum iron levels and the iron-binding capacity are both decreased. In some cases red cell survival may also be shortened, which contributes further to the severity of the anemia.

Refractory Hypochromic Anemias (Sideroachrestic Anemias). These disorders are a heterogenous group of anemias characterized by the presence of red cell hypochromia and microcytosis in the presence of large iron stores and increased levels of serum iron. The anemia and hyperferremia, in most cases, are believed to represent a disturbance in heme synthesis which results in decreased hemoglobin production and anemia. Bone marrow smears exhibit abundant stainable iron deposits, and erythroblasts containing iron inclusions (sideroblasts) are a frequent finding. The hematologic and clinical features of the refractory hypochromic anemias may closely resemble those of some of the thalassemias; quantitative measurements of hemoglobin A_2 and fetal hemoglobin, both in the patient and in other family members, may be necessary to distinguish between these disorders.

In a sex-linked variety of refractory anemia, affected males demonstrate a moderate to severe degree of anemia with hypochromia and microcytosis. Female carriers of this disorder exhibit two populations of red cells in peripheral blood smears; one population appears normal, and the other is hypochromic and microcytic. It is presumed that each of these red cell populations is linked to one of the X chromosomes, one of which is normal and one of which carries the abnormal trait. The anemia in males is often mild during childhood but becomes more severe during adult life. Transfusions are indicated if anemia becomes severe.

Hypochromic, sideroblastic anemia occurs rarely in vitamin B_6 (pyridoxine) deficiency. A number of cases has been reported, however, in which pyridoxine intake was adequate, but a moderate to severe degree of anemia was present which responded to large doses of the vitamin. This condition is believed to represent a B_6-dependency state, and if administration of the vitamin to these individuals is discontinued the anemia recurs. A trial of pyridoxine appears to be indicated in any patient having a hypochromic, sideroblastic anemia which is not due to thalassemia.

REFERENCES

IRON-DEFICIENCY ANEMIA

Beal, C. A. On the acceptance of solid foods and other food patterns in infants and children. Pediatrics, 20: 448, 1957.

Hoag, M., Wallerstein, R., and Polycove, M. Occult blood loss in iron-deficiency anemia of infancy. Pediatrics, 27:199, 1961.

Lowe, C. U., et al. Iron balance and requirements in infancy. Pediatrics, 43:134, 1969.

Naiman, J. L., Oski, F. A., Diamond, L. K., Vawter, G. F., and Shwachman, H. The gastrointestinal effects of iron deficiency anemia. Pediatrics, 33:83, 1964.

Pollock, G. H., and Richmond, J. B. Nutritional anemia in children: importance of emotional, social and economic factors. Psychosom. Med., 15:477, 1953.

Schulman, I. Iron requirements in infancy. J.A.M.A., 175:118, 1961.

——— and Abildgaard, C. F. Treatment of anemias of childhood. Mod. Treatm., 1:616, 1964.

Smith, N. J., and Rosello, S. Iron deficiency in infancy and childhood. J. Clin. Nutr., 1:275, 1953.

Wilson, J. F., Aeiner, D. C., and Lahey, M. E. Studies on iron metabolism: I. Evidence of gastrointestinal and dysfunction in infants with iron deficiency anemia: a preliminary report. J. Pediat., 60:787, 1962.

MEGALOBLASTIC ANEMIAS

Dallman, P. R., and Diamond, L. K. Vitamin B_{12} deficiency associated with disease of the small intestine. J. Pediat., 57:689, 1960.

Flexner, J. M., and Hartmann, R. C. Megaloblastic anemia associated with anticonvulsant drugs. Amer. J. Med., 28:386, 1960.

Huguley, C. M., Jr., Bain, J. A., Rivers, S. L., and Scoggins, R. B. Refractory Megaloblastic anemia associated with excretion of orotic acid. Blood, 14:615, 1959.

Lampkin, B. C., Shore, N. A., and Chadwick, D. Megaloblastic anemia of infancy secondary to maternal pernicious anemia. New Eng. J. Med., 274:1168, 1966.

Leikin, S. L. Pernicious anemia in childhood. Pediatrics, 25:91, 1960.

Luhby, A. L. Megaloblastic anemia in infancy; clinical considerations and analysis. J. Pediat., 54:617, 1959.

May, C. D., Nelson, E. N., Lowe, C. U., and Salmon, R. J. Pathogenesis of megaloblastic anemia in infancy. Amer. J. Dis. Child., 80:191, 1950.

Quinto, M. G., Leikin, S. L., and Hung, W. Pernicious anemia in a young girl associated with idiopathic hypoparathyroidism, familial Addison's disease, and moniliasis. J. Pediat., 64:241, 1964.

Rogers, L. E., Porter, F. S., and Sidbury, J. B. Thiamine-responsive megaloblastic anemia. J. Pediat., 74:494, 1969.

Spurling, C. L., Sacks, M. S., and Jiji, R. M. Juvenile pernicious anemia. New Eng. J. Med., 271:995, 1964.

HYPOPLASTIC AND APLASTIC ANEMIAS

Allen, D. M., Fine, M. H., Necheles, T. F., and Dameshek, W. Oxymetholone therapy in aplastic anemia. Blood, 32:83, 1968.

Bloom, G. E., and Diamond, L. K. Prognostic value of fetal hemoglobin levels in acquired aplastic anemia. New Eng. J. Med., 278:304, 1968.

—— Warner, S., Gerald, P. S., and Diamond, L. K. Chromosome abnormalities in constitutional aplastic anemia. New Eng. J. Med., 274:8, 1966.

Diamond, L. K., Allen, D. M., and Magill, F. B. Congenital (erythroid) hypoplastic anemia; a 25 year study. Amer. J. Dis. Child., 102:403, 1961.

Erslev, A. Hematopoietic depression induced by chloromycetin. Blood, 8:170, 1953.

Lee, G. R., MacDiarmid, W. D., Cartwright, G. E., and Wintrobe, M. M. Hereditary, X-linked, sideroachrestic anemia. Blood, 32:59, 1968.

Levy, R. N., Sawitsky, A., Florman, A. L., and Rubin, E. Fatal aplastic anemia after hepatitis. Report of five cases. New Eng. J. Med., 273:1118, 1965.

Pearson, H. A., and Cone, T. E., Jr. Congenital hypoplastic anemia. Pediatrics, 19:192, 1957.

Raab, S. O., Haut, A., Cartwright, G. E., and Wintrobe, M. M. Pyridoxine-responsive anemia. Blood, 18:285, 1961.

Reinhold, J. D. L., Neumark, E., Lightwood, R., and Carter, C. O. Familial hypoplastic anemia with congenital abnormalities (Fanconi syndrome). Blood, 7:915, 1952.

Report of the Forty-eighth Conference on Pediatric Research. Aplastic Anemia. Columbus, Ohio, Ross Laboratories, 1965.

Roberts, F. D., Hagedorn, A. B., Slocumb, C. H., and Owen, C. A. Evaluation of the anemia of rheumatoid arthritis. Blood, 21:470, 1963.

Shahidi, N. T., and Diamond, L. K. Testosterone-induced remission in aplastic anemia of both acquired and congenital types; further observations in 24 cases. New Eng. J. Med., 264:953, 1961.

Sjölin, S. Studies on osteopetrosis. II. Investigations concerning the nature of the anaemia. Acta Paediat., 48:529, 1959.

17.3
ANEMIAS DUE TO ACCELERATED DESTRUCTION OF RED CELLS
(HEMOLYTIC ANEMIAS)

GEORGE R. HONIG and
IRVING SCHULMAN

The hemolytic anemias result from an accelerated rate of destruction of red cells. Survival of the erythrocytes in these disorders is shortened in comparison with the normal red cell survival of approximately 120 days. For purposes of classification the hemolytic anemias are divided into two major groups, designated intracorpuscular and extracorpuscular disorders.

The *intracorpuscular hemolytic disorders* result from intrinsic abnormalities of the red cells which render the cells susceptible to premature destruction. These defects are genetically transmitted, and include abnormalities of the red cell membrane, cellular metabolic defects, and hemoglobin abnormalities. Because the red cell itself is defective in this group of disorders, an excessive rate of cell destruction will occur not only in the circulation of affected patients but also in the circulation of normal individuals who receive transfusions of these cells.

Extracorpuscular hemolytic disorders result from a variety of factors which exert a damaging effect on otherwise normal red cells, to produce an accelerated rate of cell destruction. The longevity of erythrocytes from these patients is normal when the cells are transfused into a normal recipient. The extracorpuscular disorders all represent acquired abnormalities.

Hemolytic anemias present a number of distinctive clinical and hematologic features as a result of the accelerated red cell destruction. There is an increase in the production of the indirect reacting bilirubin. The elevation of serum bilirubin level, however, is quite variable and is not an accurate guide to the degree of hemolysis because it is determined to a large degree by the functional capacity of the liver. Similarly, clinical jaundice may be striking or may be minimal. The output of urobilinogen in the stools and urine is increased, and in cases of massive intravascular hemolysis, hemoglobinuria may also occur. An increase in the reticulocyte count in the peripheral blood is characteristic, and when anemia is severe normoblasts may also appear. Erythroid hyperplasia of the marrow indicates the compensatory regeneration which is common to all hemolytic states except when aplastic episodes occur. The serum iron level is increased, as is the percent saturation of the iron-binding protein. Many of the hemolytic anemias are associated with striking morphologic abnormalities of the red cells, and in several of the diseases the diagnosis may be made by examination of the peripheral blood smear. Splenomegaly is characteristic of all hemolytic anemias, and changes in the bones due to marrow hyperplasia may be noted radiographically if the process is of long standing.

The degree of anemia produced by a hemolytic disorder will depend not only on the rate of red cell destruction, but also on the regenerative capacity of the marrow. It has been estimated that the human marrow can produce erythrocytes at six to eight times the normal rate in compensation for hemolysis. Thus it is possible for a hemolytic state to exist without demonstrable anemia. In most hemolytic disorders, however, the rate of red cell destruction exceeds the maximum compensating capacity of marrow, and anemia results. Nevertheless, a balance between destruction and production is reached in the majority of hemolytic anemias, and a steady state, at an anemic level, is characteristic. This balance may be upset by either an increase in rate of destruction or a decrease in the rate of production and under either circumstance the degree of anemia worsens.

Intracorpuscular Defects

Inborn Abnormalities of the Red Cell Membrane

HEREDITARY SPHEROCYTOSIS. This familial disorder transmitted as a mendelian dominant, is characterized by the production of small, spheroidal erythrocytes, chronic hemolysis, jaundice, and splenomegaly. Equally frequent in both sexes, it occurs primarily in Caucasians, but documented cases have been found in Negroes. Although the mode of genetic transmission is well established, the disorder may not be detected in either parent in as many as 30 percent of cases. In some of these apparently unaffected parents, however, abnormal red cell membrane permeability has been found, despite the absence of demonstrable spherocytes in their blood smears. These instances may represent incomplete expression of the abnormal gene.

Pathogenesis. The distinctive feature of hereditary spherocytosis is the production of red cells which, when mature, are small, thick, spheroidal, and have a small surface area and high mean corpuscular hemoglobin concentration. Recent findings by Jacob and Jandl suggest that hereditary spherocytosis is a disease of the red cell membrane in which the basic defect is an abnormal permeability to the influx of sodium into the cell. Normal intracellular concentrations of sodium can be maintained in these cells, however, by increased activity of the ATP-linked "sodium pump" mechanism. Production of ATP for this compensatory process depends upon glycolysis by the red cells. As long as adequate glycolysis continues, red cell cation concentrations and cell survival will be normal. When glucose metabolism is impaired, however, sodium and water accumulate in the cell, which then becomes more spheroidal and is ultimately destroyed. In hereditary spherocytosis circulation of the red cells through the spleen imposes the metabolic stress which impairs the energy production and leads to hemolysis. It is believed that the spherocyte, by virtue of its shape, is impeded in its passage through the splenic pulp and that during this period of cellular stasis glucose concentrations within the sinusoids of the spleen fall to levels which limit glycolytic activity of the red cells. The decreased synthesis of ATP which

then occurs leads to the development of osmotic swelling and premature destruction, both in the spleen and in general circulation. The critical role of the spleen in the production of hemolysis is demonstrated by the fact that splenectomy results in normal red cell life-span and cure of the anemia even though production of spherocytes persists. That the spleen itself is not abnormal is indicated by the finding that cells of a patient with hereditary spherocytosis are destroyed at an equally rapid rate when transfused into a normal recipient.

Because of the requirement for accelerated rates of glycolysis for adequate red cell sodium transport, incubation of these cells in vitro without added glucose results in cation imbalance and cell lysis. This phenomenon forms the basis of the autohemolysis test, in which sterile blood is incubated for 48 hours at 37° C, after which the degree of hemolysis is determined. The typical finding in hereditary spherocytosis is an abnormal degree of hemolysis after incubation of unsupplemented whole blood, but a nearly normal value for blood to which glucose has been added. The decreased ability of the red cells in this disorder to withstand lysis during incubation in hypotonic media (osmotic fragility test) is also accentuated when the test is done after incubation of the blood. This finding reflects unfavorable osmotic changes which result from uncompensated sodium influx.

Clinical manifestations. The initial appearance of symptoms calling attention to the presence of hereditary spherocytosis may occur on the first day of life or may be delayed until late in adulthood. It has not been uncommon to discover the disorder in a parent for the first time only after studies have been undertaken because of demonstrable disease in a child. The marked degree of variability in the symptoms and in their time of appearance appears to depend upon the intensity of the hemolytic component, the regenerative capacity of the marrow, and the occurrence of factors upsetting the stable state of the compensated hemolytic anemia.

When hereditary spherocytosis appears in the neonatal period it may mimic erythroblastosis fetalis, and the presence of spherocytes may suggest ABO incompatibility. Jaundice due to elevated bilirubin of the indirect variety may be pronounced and may require exchange transfusion for prevention of kernicterus. In late childhood, pallor is the most common manifestation, while icterus is grossly evident only rarely. In older children and in adults, scleral icterus is more common. Because of the splenomegaly the parents' attention may be drawn to an enlarging abdomen.

Not infrequently, the first manifestation of hereditary spherocytosis is the occurrence of an aplastic crisis (p. 1167). This event frequently follows a mild upper respiratory infection and is characterized by high fever, nausea, vomiting, pain in the abdomen, extremities, and back, and very marked pallor. With the absence of marrow regeneration and the persistence of hemolysis, the hemoglobin concentration and red cell count fall precipitously. However, as the circulating red cell volume decreases, the amount of bilirubin produced becomes progressively less and jaundice tends to disappear as the pallor worsens. The absence of reticulocytes and the removal of spherocytes from the peripheral blood may make the diagnosis very difficult at this point in the absence of a previous history in the patient or his family.

Splenomegaly may be detected in almost all patients, but the degree of enlargement is variable. In general, organ enlargement is slight in infancy and becomes more prominent with advancing age.

As a result of continuing hemolysis, gallstones are a frequent and important complication of hereditary spherocytosis. These stones, primarily of the pigment variety, are rare in children under 10 years of age, but have been reported in children as young as 3 years. After adolescence the incidence of gallstones increases steadily, and in adults an incidence as high as 85 percent has been reported. Quite commonly the presence of underlying spherocytosis is identified only after a patient comes under treatment for cholelithiasis.

Hemic cardiac murmurs are common and vary with the intensity of the anemia. Significant cardiac enlargement is infrequent. Chronic leg ulcers are extremely uncommon during childhood but may occur later. Growth and development are usually unimpaired.

Laboratory findings. As indicated earlier, the degree of anemia encountered in hereditary spherocytosis is quite variable. Except during periods of aplastic crisis, hemoglobin concentrations below 7 to 8 g/100 ml are unusual. Affected individuals with hemoglobin levels close to normal are, however, not uncommon. In these patients a moderate hemolytic defect coupled with efficient marrow response permits a high hemoglobin level to be maintained. In some of these patients a relatively small plasma volume contributes to the high hemoglobin concentration while the circulating red cell mass may be, in fact, reduced. This serves to explain symptoms of anemia even though the peripheral hemoglobin concentration and red cell count seem to be too high to be causing significant clinical manifestations.

Evidence of red cell regeneration is constantly found in the peripheral blood and, in cases where the anemia is slight, is a very important clue to the diagnosis. Reticulocytes are increased and tend to vary with the degree of anemia, the range being usually from 5 to 25 percent of the red cells. During aplastic crisis, reticulocytes may fall to zero, while during recovery from an aplastic crisis they may reach 90 percent of the total erythrocytes. Other evidences of regeneration are polychromasia of erythrocytes, normoblastosis, and erythroid hyperplasia in the marrow.

Spherocytes are small, round, dense, and darkly stained with absent central pallor. The number of spherocytes seen in the peripheral blood tends to vary directly with the degree of anemia. The white count and platelet count are usually normal but may be elevated in cases with brisk hemolysis. Osmotic fragility is increased over normal in all instances and may be accentuated in mild cases by incubation of the blood for 24 hours at 37° C. The Coombs' test is negative. The serum bilirubin is usually elevated only slightly and may be entirely normal.

Diagnosis. In the newborn period differential diagnosis from erythroblastosis fetalis is necessary. A positive Coombs' test, together with appropriate blood group findings in infant and mother, will serve to identify most cases of erythroblastosis fetalis. However, in instances where the infant is of blood group A or B and the mother is of blood group O, the distinction between hereditary spherocytosis and ABO incompatibility may be impossible, since not all of the latter patients have positive Coombs' tests and since spherocytes are found in both conditions. Detection of spherocytosis in the family and persistence of spherocytes and evidence of hemolysis past the neonatal period usually serve to indicate the correct diagnosis.

Since spherocytes can occur in conditions other than hereditary spherocytosis, most notably in the autoimmune hemolytic anemias, a search for other causes should always be undertaken when a family pattern is not evident. A positive Coombs' test will identify most cases of autoimmune acquired hemolytic anemia. Hemoglobin electrophoresis, which is entirely normal in hereditary spherocytosis, will serve to differentiate the hemoglobinopathies.

Treatment. Splenectomy is almost invariably followed by complete and permanent cure, with elimination of all manifestations of anemia and susceptibility to crisis. Because of evidence that splenectomy in young infants is followed by an increased susceptibility to bacterial sepsis and meningitis, however, the operation should be deferred wherever possible until after the age of 2 years. Because gallstones have been reported in young children, it is usually recommended that splenectomy be carried out at about the age of 3 to 5 years. Because of the high incidence of cholelithiasis and because of the constant jeopardy of aplastic crisis, splenectomy should be undertaken in all cases, even those with only mild degrees of anemia. Typically, the postoperative rise in red cell count is immediate and rapid, and striking leucocytosis and thrombocytosis become evident. The platelet count reaches a peak 8 to 10 days postoperatively and may reach levels of 1 million/mm³. However, postoperative thrombotic complications are extremely rare in children, and routine heparin therapy for elevated platelet counts is not recommended. Platelet and white cell counts tend to return to normal levels 3 to 4 weeks after surgery, but mild to moderate elevations may persist.

Transfusions are seldom indicated except during periods of crisis. Rarely a very young infant with severe anemia may require periodic transfusions until the age is reached when splenectomy may be undertaken safely.

HEREDITARY ELLIPTOCYTOSIS. This abnormality, which has been estimated to occur in 0.04 percent of the population, is characterized by the production of oval or elliptical erythrocytes which may constitute 50 to 90 percent of the total red cells. The defect is transmitted as a Mendelian dominant and in most instances produces no anemia and no evidence of illness. In about 12 percent of cases, however, the morphologic abnormality is associated with a chronic, congenital hemolytic anemia which may range from mild to quite severe and which is associated with jaundice, splenomegaly, evidences of marrow regeneration, and a tendency to aplastic crisis. In the symptomatic form the oval cells are accompanied in the peripheral blood by fragmented red cells, some spherocytes, and irregularly contracted erythrocytes. During the early months of life infants with the hemolytic form may show chronic anemia and jaundice, with very few elliptocytes evident until 3 or 4 months of age. In such infants the diagnosis may remain obscure until the typical red cells appear in sufficient number to indicate the basic problem. In the varieties of elliptocytosis associated with accelerated hemolysis the cells exhibit many of the features seen with the erythrocytes in hereditary spherocytosis patients. Osmotic fragility of the red cells is increased, particularly after incubation, and autohemolysis is greater than normal when sterile blood is incubated without added glucose. With glucose supplementation, however, the degree of autohemolysis is often reduced to normal. Transport to sodium by the red cells has been shown to be increased.

Individuals with asymptomatic elliptocytosis generally require no treatment. Those with active hemolytic disease are usually benefited by splenectomy.

CONGENITAL STOMATOCYTOSIS. This morphologic abnormality of the red cells occurs in association with a variety of hemolytic disorders which differ widely in the degree of their clinical severity. In stained blood smears the erythrocytes exhibit linear slitlike areas of central pallor, rather than the normal circular area of pallor, to produce a mouthlike appearance.

A familial pattern suggesting a dominant mode of inheritance has been present in several reported examples. Red cell survival in most cases has been severely decreased, and anemia, jaundice, splenomegaly, and rapid red cell regeneration have been present in the affected individuals. Osmotic fragility of the red cells is increased, and autohemolysis is abnormal, with improvement occurring when additional glucose is present. Studies of red cell cations have indicated abnormal degrees of permeability of the red cell membrane, and in some cases gross changes in the intracellular concentrations of sodium and potassium have been observed.

Splenectomy has sometimes resulted in clinical improvement, but the degree of abnormal hemolysis has not usually been affected.

Inborn Enzyme Abnormalities of the Erythrocyte
(See also Sec. 8.13)

METABOLIC PATHWAYS OF THE ERYTHROCYTE. In the maturation of red cells from the reticulocyte stage to that of the mature erythrocyte a number of metabolic pathways become inactivated, including the tricarboxylic acid cycle, the cytochrome-dependent pathway of electron transport, and the capacity for biosynthesis of lipids, protein, and heme. In the mature red cell energy for cellular functions is derived entirely from the metabolism of glucose. The Embden-Myerhof pathway, leading to the formation of lactate, is the major route of glucose catabolism; the hexose monophosphate shunt functions as a quantitatively less significant alternative pathway. (See Fig. 7.) Generation of ATP occurs in the Embden-Myerhof pathway and serves as the energy source for active cation transport across the red cell membrane and for cellular biosynthetic processes. Formation of 2,3-diphosphoglycerate by an accessory reaction to the glycolytic pathway provides a cellular reservoir of potential metabolic energy. Diversion of phosphorylated intermediate compounds into this reaction also serves to increase the intracellular pool of NADH, which is the major cofactor for the enzymatic reduction of methemoglobin in the erythrocyte. Although a relatively minor fraction of glucose metabolized by the red cell normally enters the hexose monophosphate shunt, the shunt pathway is of importance in that it is the only operative pathway in the mature red cell which results in the generation of NADPH. The latter performs an essential function as a hydrogen donor for the reduction of oxidized glutathione. This compound, a sulfhydryl-containing tripeptide, appears to be required to maintain a number of intracellular components in a state of reduction. In addition, reduced glutathione functions as the cofactor of glutathione peroxidase, an enzyme which catalyzes the breakdown of hydrogen peroxide. Peroxide formation can occur in the red cell by the interaction of a number of oxidative agents with oxyhemoglobin.

Because of the limited number of alternative metabolic pathways in the red cell, an enzymatic defect in any of the pathways of glucose catabolism can result in serious metabolic deficiencies leading to impairment of cellular function and shortening of the cell life-span.

ENZYMATIC ABNORMALITIES AFFECTING THE EMBDEN-MYERHOF PATHWAY. In general, defective enzymatic activity within the Embden-Myerhof pathway results in cell disturbances related to inadequate

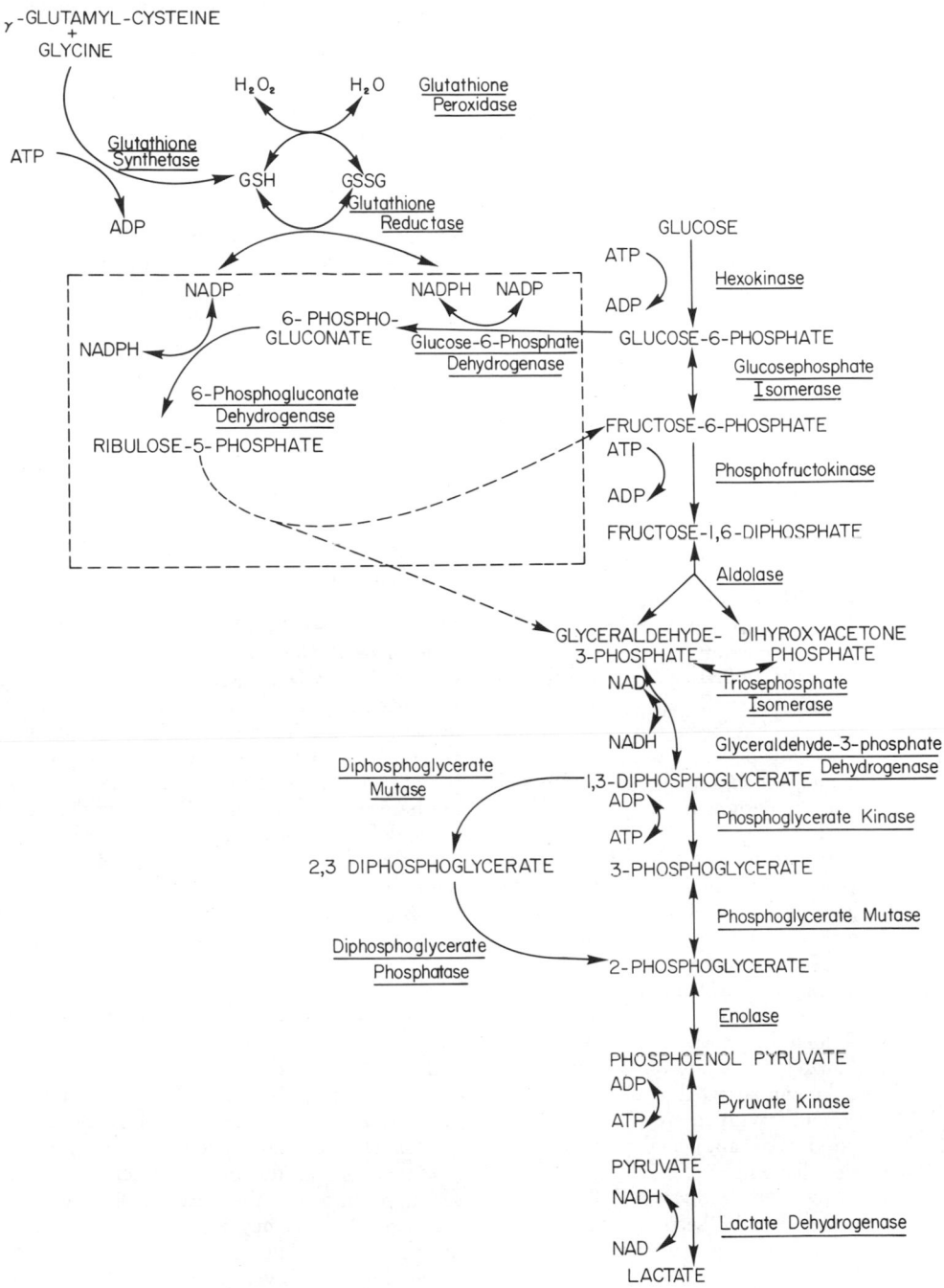

Fig. 7. Glycolytic metabolism and related pathways of the mature erythrocyte. The hexose monophosphate shunt pathway is represented by the enclosed rectangular area.

production of ATP. As metabolic energy becomes insufficient to maintain an adequate rate of ion transport across the cell membrane, entry of sodium and water into the cell occurs to produce cell swelling and premature lysis. When ATP production becomes severely impaired as a result of an enzymatic defi-

ciency in the glycolytic pathway, the life-span of mature red cells may be greatly shortened, but in many cases anemia can be compensated by the presence of large numbers of reticulocytes. The latter, because they retain the tricarboxylic acid cycle and other mitochondrial functions, are able to carry out energy-yielding metabolic reactions by alternative pathways.

Abnormalities of a variety of red cell enzymes related to glucose catabolism have been identified and it appears likely that others will be discovered in the future. The term "nonspherocytic hemolytic anemia" has been applied in the past to this entire group of disorders. Clinical and laboratory findings are those which characterize the intracorpuscular hemolytic anemias, with variable degrees of severity depending upon the nature and degree of the enzymatic defect. Although splenectomy is not curative in any of the known forms of these disorders, significant improvement in red cell survival may result, particularly in some forms of pyruvate kinase deficiency. Precise diagnosis for any of these disorders depends upon specific enzymatic analysis of red cell lysates.

Hexokinase Deficiency. This is a rare disorder associated with a moderate to severe degree of hemolytic anemia. It appears to be inherited as an autosomal recessive trait.

Glucosephosphate Isomerase Deficiency. The red cell enzyme deficiency state in affected individuals is associated with hemolytic anemia and striking degrees of reticulocytosis. It appears to follow autosomal recessive transmission.

Phosphofructokinase Deficiency. A mild hemolytic state with moderately reduced activity of red cell phosphofructokinase has been found in association with a metabolic myopathy in which activity of the corresponding enzyme in muscle was decreased. This disorder has been designated Type VII glycogen-storage disease.

Triosephosphate Isomerase Deficiency. The enzymatic deficiency in this condition is not limited to the red cell, and has also been found in the leucocytes and in skeletal muscle, serum, and spinal fluid. In the reported cases severe hemolytic anemia was recognized during the early months of life. Beginning at about 1 year of age severe neurologic changes developed, including spasticity, weakness progressing to generalized flaccidity, and retardation. Nearly all of the known affected children died by 5 years of age, frequently with severe infections. The disorder is transmitted as an autosomal recessive trait. Heterozygous carriers have been clinically normal.

2,3-Diphosphoglycerate Mutase Deficiency. This abnormality has usually been associated with a moderate degree of hemolytic anemia. It is probably inherited as an autosomal recessive trait.

Phosphoglycerate Kinase Deficiency. Reduced activity of this enzyme has been demonstrated in both red cells and leucocytes of affected individuals. A hemolytic anemia of moderate severity has been typically found. In a large family in which this disorder was present in several members, all of those affected were males, and a sex-linked mode of inheritance appeared likely.

Pyruvate Kinase Deficiency. Deficiency of pyruvate kinase is the most commonly encountered red cell enzyme abnormality within the Embden-Myerhof pathway. The severity of the anemia can vary widely, ranging from a mild compensated hemolytic state to profound anemia with marked shortening of red cell survival, requiring repeated transfusions. In the newborn period, pyruvate kinase deficiency can be a cause of neonatal jaundice, and exchange transfusions are sometimes necessary to prevent kernicterus.

At least two types of enzyme abnormality can be present in red cell pyruvate kinase deficiency. In the more common form decreased enzyme activity appears to be present. In the other type the enzyme exhibits lowered affinity for one of its substrates, phosphoenolpyruvate, resulting in lowered enzyme activity within the red cell. The latter abnormality can be missed by the usual assay procedures which employ an excess of the substrates, and can obscure the abnormality; the defect can be readily detected by a modified assay method.

All of the known forms of this disorder are inherited by an autosomal recessive mode. In severe forms of pyruvate kinase deficiency, splenectomy has been found to produce significant improvement in the degree of anemia and in the life-span of the red cells.

ENZYMATIC ABNORMALITIES AFFECTING THE HEXOSE MONOPHOSPHATE SHUNT AND METABOLISM OF GLUTATHIONE.

Red cell enzyme deficiencies of the hexose monophosphate shunt, or the pathway leading to the production of reduced glutathione, can cause premature destruction of erythrocytes, presumably from impairment of intracellular reductive mechanisms within the cell. Lesser degrees of enzymatic deficiency of these pathways are often associated with a mild or inapparent degree of hemolysis under normal conditions. When the metabolic requirements for these reaction sequences are increased, however, as by the action of oxidant drugs or chemicals which lead to formation of hydrogen peroxide, a severe hemolytic episode may occur.

Glucose-6-Phosphate Dehydrogenase (G6PD) Deficiency. Deficiency of erythrocytic G6PD occurs with worldwide distribution with highest frequencies in Negroes, Sephardic Jews, Mediterranean populations, and in the Orient. More than 50 variants of this enzyme have been identified, and there is a wide range in the degree of enzymatic deficiency which accompanies the different variant forms.

G6PD deficiency is transmitted as a sex-linked recessive trait. The disorder is common; in population surveys it was found to be present in 10 to 14 percent of American Negro males. Because of the high gene frequency of G6PD deficiency in the Negro population, homozygous females are also occasionally encountered. In heterozygous females intermediate levels of G6PD activity are often found, but the levels can vary considerably ranging from levels as low as those of affected males to entirely within the normal range. This variability of expression has been explained by the Lyon hypothesis of X chromosome inactivation. This theory suggests that in the female one of the two X chromosomes in each cell is inactivated. Thus some of the cells will have an active, maternally derived X chromosome, while others an active, paternally derived X chromosome, with the proportion of each cell type randomly distributed.

Three clinical forms of G6PD deficiency can be distinguished, based in part upon the severity of the enzyme deficiency in the erythrocytes:

Congenital nonspherocytic hemolytic anemia. This clinical expression of G6PD deficiency accompanies severely reduced degrees of enzymatic activity. Affected individuals have lifelong, ongoing hemolysis with anemia, splenomegaly, icterus, and aplastic crises. Neonatal hyperbilirubinemia is a frequent complication. All of the hemolytic manifestations in these individuals are greatly accentuated by oxidant drugs and chemicals.

Favism. Certain individuals having G6PD deficiency manifest acute hemolytic episodes when they are exposed to fava beans. The mechanism of this response is unclear. Fava bean sensitivity is an acquired characteristic in affected individuals and may be mediated by an antigen-antibody interaction with the erythrocytes.

Drug-induced hemolysis. With milder forms of G6PD deficiency, including the type which is commonly found in Negroes, the affected individuals are hematologically normal until exposed to a variety of drugs which act as oxidants, and then develop an acute hemolytic anemia. A list of drugs known to have produced hemolysis in G6PD-deficient individuals is given in Table 14, Section 8.12, page 395. Deficient individuals given one of the oxidant drugs usually show no change for the first one or two days. Hemolysis then becomes evident and the blood count falls over the next four or five days, depending upon the type and dose of the offending agent. The degree of anemia may be mild or extremely severe, accompanied by fever, back pain, jaundice, and sometimes hemoglobinuria. The hemolytic episodes are self-limited even if the drug is continued. This is explained by the fact that the young, newly regenerated red cells have higher enzyme levels than the older cells and are, therefore, resistant to drug action. Severe hemolytic anemia in the neonatal period has been observed in infants with G6PD deficiency whose mothers ingested oxidant drugs during pregnancy. Severe infections also appear capable of inducing hemolysis in G6PD-deficient individuals.

G6PD deficiency may be identified by quantitative enzyme assays. Rapid screening tests are also available. During a hemolytic episode, however, enzyme levels may be nearly normal, and a definite diagnosis may be available only after recovery.

Since drug-related hemolytic episodes are self-limited, blood transfusions are required only in the presence of severe anemia. No other type of treatment is of value.

Glutathione Synthetase Deficiency. This abnormality appears to be transmitted as an autosomal recessive trait. In affected individuals the concentration of glutathione in erythrocytes is markedly re-

duced and hemolysis with mild to moderate anemia is present. Exposure to oxidant drugs leads to an increased rate of hemolysis. Favism has also been reported in these individuals.

Glutathione Reductase Deficiency. In this disorder reduced enzyme activity occurs in platelets and leucocytes as well as in the erythrocytes. A variable degree of hemolytic anemia together with hepatosplenomegaly have usually been present. In some cases the hematologic abnormalities have been accompanied by neurologic disturbances including spasticity, retardation, and electroencelphalographic changes. An autosomal dominant inheritance appears likely. As with other abnormalities in this group, a variety of drugs and chemicals produce accelerated hemolysis.

Glutathione Peroxidase Deficiency. Deficiency of this enzyme in erythrocytes has been accompanied by mild compensated hemolysis in an individual in whom homozygous absence of the enzyme was demonstrated. Hemolysis following drug exposure has occurred in heterozygous individuals, and this disorder may predispose to hyperbilirubinemia in the newborn period. Inheritance is by an autosomal recessive mode.

Abnormalities of Hemoglobin Structure and Synthesis

Normal human hemoglobin is comprised of three different molecular species. In fetal life and in early infancy *fetal hemoglobin (hemoglobin F)* is the principal type of hemoglobin present in the red cells. Beyond the first few months of life the fetal hemoglobin becomes replaced by *adult hemoglobin (hemoglobin A)*, which remains thereafter as the predominant type. A minor component, *hemoglobin A$_2$*, which comprises only 2 to 3 percent of the total, is produced together with hemoglobin A and is not present in significant amounts during the fetal and newborn periods. The hemoglobin molecules are made up of four subunits, each of which consists of a globin protein moiety to which a heme group is attached. Amino acid differences in the globin chains confer the specificity upon the individual hemoglobin types. Each of the normal human hemoglobins contains a pair of identical alpha chains and a pair of specific chains characteristic of the particular hemoglobin molecule. In fetal hemoglobin a pair of gamma chains are present; in adult hemoglobin the gamma chains are replaced by a pair of beta chains, and in hemoglobin A$_2$ the nonalpha chains are designated delta chains.

Congenital disorders which primarily involve the hemoglobin molecule have been broadly classified into two major groups: (1) those in which the hemoglobin molecules are structurally abnormal as a result of changes in the amino acid sequence of the globin chains (hemoglobinopathies); and (2) those in which normal globin chains are produced, but to an abnormally reduced extent (thalassemias). Any of these types of disorders may result in anemia by a variety of mechanisms to be described subsequently.

Each of the component globin chains which make up the normal hemoglobins can be involved in a hemoglobinopathy or thalassemia; the resulting disorders are classified on the basis of the globin chain which is involved, e.g., the designations beta thalassemia or an alpha-chain hemoglobinopathy. Each of the globin chains of hemoglobin is genetically determined by a pair of alleles, with the exception of the gamma chains for which multiple pairs of alleles appear to be present. One-half of each allelic gene pair is inherited from each parent. Because of this genetic pattern, hemoglobinopathies or thalassemias can occur in a homozygous state, in which both of the allelic genes are abnormal, or in a heterozygous state, in which one of the allelic genes is normal and the other abnormal. In addition, each member of the gene pair may determine a different hemoglobinopathy or thalassemia abnormality, resulting in a double hemoglobinopathy or a hemoglobinopathy together with a thalassemia. When an alpha-chain gene is affected by either of these types of abnormalities, the effect of the disorder will often be manifested in fetal life and in early infancy because of the presence of alpha chains in fetal hemoglobin ($a_2\gamma_2$). In the case of beta-chain abnormalities, however, the normal fetal hemoglobin serves to protect the infant until 3 to 6 months of age, when the switchover from production of fetal hemoglobin to that of hemoglobin A ($a_2\beta_2$) occurs, at which time the beta-chain abnormality becomes apparent.

DISORDERS DUE TO ABNORMAL HEMOGLOBIN STRUCTURE (HEMOGLOBINOPATHIES). *Sickle-Cell Anemia.* *Pathogenesis.* Sickle-cell anemia results from the production of abnormal hemoglobin beta chains. The abnormality consists of a substitution of valine for glutamate in the sixth amino acid position, and this hemoglobin is designated hemoglobin S ($a_2\beta_2$ 6 glu→val). The amino acid substitution confers a change in the isoelectric point of the molecule to produce an altered electrophoretic mobility, thereby facilitating its identification. The abnormal molecule also exhibits physicochemical changes from which stem the peculiar reactions of hemoglobin S, to produce the clinical manifestations of the disease.

In the heterozygous individual one beta-chain gene locus is normal and the other carries the beta[s] mutation. In the homozygote both genes at the locus are abnormal, one beta[s] gene having been inherited from each parent. Despite the genetic equivalence of the normal and abnormal beta genes, the heterozygous individual produces only 25 to 45 percent hemoglobin S, the remainder being hemoglobin A. The homozygous individual is unable to synthesize any normal beta chains, and produces 80 to 100 percent hemoglobin S, the non-S component being fetal hemoglobin. Sickle-cell disease occurs almost exclusively in Negroes; the heterozygous state (sickle-cell trait) occurs in 8 to 10 percent of American Negro individuals. This high gene frequency has been attributed to a selective advantage due to a protective effect of sickle-cell trait against malarial infection: It has been demonstrated that entry of malarial parasites into an erythrocyte of an S-trait individual is followed promptly by sickling of the red cell and rapid sequestration of the cell by the reticuloendothelial system, which may represent the mechanism for this protective effect.

In the deoxygenated state, molecules of hemoglobin S align themselves into a series of parallel, equidistant particles which stretch the red cell membrane into the typical crescent-shaped sickle cell. The sickled erythrocytes are rigid and have markedly increased mechanical fragility. A critical fact in the pathogenesis of sickle-cell disease is that the red cells of individuals who are homozygous for hemoglobin S begin to sickle when the oxygen saturation of the hemoglobin is 60 to 70 percent; at 40 percent saturation, 75 percent or more of the cells will sickle. By contrast, the cells of individuals with sickle-cell trait will begin to sickle only at 30 to 50 percent oxygen saturation, and not until 20 percent saturation occurs will 75 percent of the cells sickle. From these data it is apparent that cells from homozygote will sickle at physiologic oxygen tensions to produce ongoing cell destruction and chronic hemolytic disease. The cells of individuals with sickle-cell trait, on the other hand, will sickle in vivo under only very unusual circumstances in which extremely low oxygen tensions develop in the tissues.

Any circumstance which will lead to a decrease in the blood oxygen saturation can accentuate the degree of red cell sickling. These conditions include acidosis, increased CO_2 tension, dehydration, stasis, and fever. As sickle changes occur, viscosity of the blood increases markedly and sets the stage for a self-perpetuating cycle in which hyperviscosity leads to further sludging and stasis of the blood, to produce increased hypoxia and acidemia, which in turn accentuate the sickling process. Based on the foregoing mechanisms, individuals with sickle-cell disease demonstrate two major phenomena: (1) chronic hemolysis due to the constant presence of irreversibly sickled cells and (2) intercurrent episodes involving vascular occlusions by masses of sickle cells in various organs and tissues.

Clinical manifestations. Symptoms of sickle-cell disease rarely appear before the fourth to sixth month of postnatal life, by which time hemoglobin S has replaced fetal hemoglobin and has become the predominating hemoglobin in the erythrocytes. In the young infant the initial manifestations may be unexplained fever and anemia, and it is axiomatic that any anemic Negro child should have the benefit of a test for sickling. Swelling of the hands and feet, termed the hand-foot syndrome, occurs in young infants with sickle-cell disease and may be the presenting manifestation. The syndrome is believed to result from aseptic infarction of the tubular bones in the hands and feet. Periosteal elevation and subsequent subperiosteal new bone formation are common, and after 1 to 2 weeks resorption of the infarcted bone results in multiple areas of rarefaction in the affected bones.

The usual course of a child with sickle-cell disease is that of a chronic hemolytic anemia producing few manifestations, punctuated by acute episodes termed crises. As indicated earlier, most of the acute manifestations of sickle-cell anemia appear to result from occlusion of blood vessels by masses of sickled cells, leading to tissue hypoxia. Because this phenomenon may occur in any organ of the body, sickle-cell disease is capable of producing an extraordinary variety of symptoms and may mimic many other diseases of childhood. The most typical and most common clinical event is the so-called painful crisis. This may follow infection, exercise, or high environmental temperature, but very often no precipitating factor can be identified. The predominant symptoms are fever, and pain in the abdomen, extremities, and back. The abdominal pain may be severe, cramping, and may be associated with vomiting, tenderness, rigidity of the wall, and diminished bowel sounds, thus simulating a surgical condition. Pains in the legs may be of muscular or osseous origin and commonly involve the joints, which may be warm and swollen. At the onset of a painful crisis the patient rarely exhibits an increase in the degree of anemia and very often shows a slight rise in hemoglobin concentration. This is thought to result from shrinkage of the plasma volume. During the recovery phase, which usually occurs after 2 to 3 days, the hemoglobin concentration may fall moderately and icterus may be accentuated. There is little evidence that the typical painful crisis involves accelerated hemolysis.

Other clinical manifestations depend upon the anatomic sites involved in the vascular occlusion characteristic of sickle-cell disease. Liver involvement may produce intense jaundice with both direct and indirect bilirubinemia and hepatic enlargement, thus suggesting hepatitis. Central nervous system involvement is fairly common and can include electroencephalographic abnormalities, convulsions, coma, and frank cerebral vascular accidents leading to permanent hemiplegia or other neurologic defects. Involvement of the lungs may produce pulmonary infarction, and because patients with sickle-cell anemia have increased susceptibility to pneumonia, differentiation between the two conditions may be difficult. Cardiac enlargement and heart murmurs are very common. The murmurs tend to be harsh and may be not only systolic but diastolic as well. These findings, together with the frequently associated fever and joint pains frequently suggest a diagnosis of rheumatic fever, and the differential diagnosis between a sickle crisis with joint pains and an attack of acute rheumatic fever is a common problem. Involvement of bone may produce aseptic necrosis of the head of the femur or humerus. Patients with sickle-cell disease are peculiarly susceptible to *Salmonella* osteomyelitis, and this complication must always be considered in episodes of protracted, and particularly localized,

bone pain. Renal involvement may produce flank pain and gross hematuria. Inability to concentrate urine, leading to a fixed specific gravity, is a constant characteristic of sickle-cell anemia and is found in virtually all patients after the first few years of life. Proteinuria, accompanied by the characteristic findings of the nephrotic syndrome, occasionally develops.

Sudden death may occur in the course of sickle-cell anemia, particularly in infants and young children, and has been attributed to massive sequestration of blood in the abdominal vasculature, or massive trapping of blood in the spleen, leading to hypovolemic shock. Chronic leg ulcers, usually in the area of the medial malleoli, tend to occur in adolescents and in adults.

Children with sickle-cell disease tend to be slight in appearance, with long, thin extremities and a protruding abdomen. Small stature and hypogonadism in adulthood are common. Some degree of scleral icterus is usually apparent, with intensification during crises and episodes of liver involvement. Splenomegaly is common during infancy and early childhood but is rare after 10 years of age, the shrinkage apparently being due to fibrosis from repeated infarcts. Some degree of hepatomegaly is usually detectable.

Laboratory findings. Between crises the hemoglobin concentration of patients with sickle-cell anemia remains fairly constant at levels from 6 to 9 g/100 ml. The red cell count is reduced proportionately. Reticulocytes are elevated except during aplastic episodes and range from 5 to 30 percent. The white cell count is usually elevated to levels ranging from 10,000 to 25,000/mm^3. Platelets are normal in number.

The blood smear reveals marked *anisocytosis* and *poikilocytosis*. Characteristic are the dense, thin, elongated sickle cells and increased number of target cells. (See Fig. 8.) *Polychromasia*, indicative of red cell regeneration, is prominent (in contrast, the blood smear of individuals with sickle-cell trait is usually normal). The marrow reveals striking erythroid hyperplasia. Serum bilirubin levels are moderately elevated (1 to 4 mg/100 ml) with predominance of the indirect fraction except in instances of hepatitis, liver infarction, or gallstones. Radiograms of the bones disclose widening of medullary spaces, thinning of the cortices, and generalized *osteoporosis*. In the skull, widening of the diploic spaces, thinning of the outer table, and radial alignment of the trabeculae produce a *"hair-on-end" appearance*. Infarction of bones produces increased bony density and later rarefaction; similarity to osteomyelitis may pose a diagnostic problem. Compression of osteoporotic vertebrae may occur.

Although sickle cells frequently may be found on ordinary blood smears, specific tests to demonstrate sickling should be done routinely. These tests most often depend upon desaturation of the hemoglobin in vitro. Although a variety of techniques are available, this is most effectively accomplished

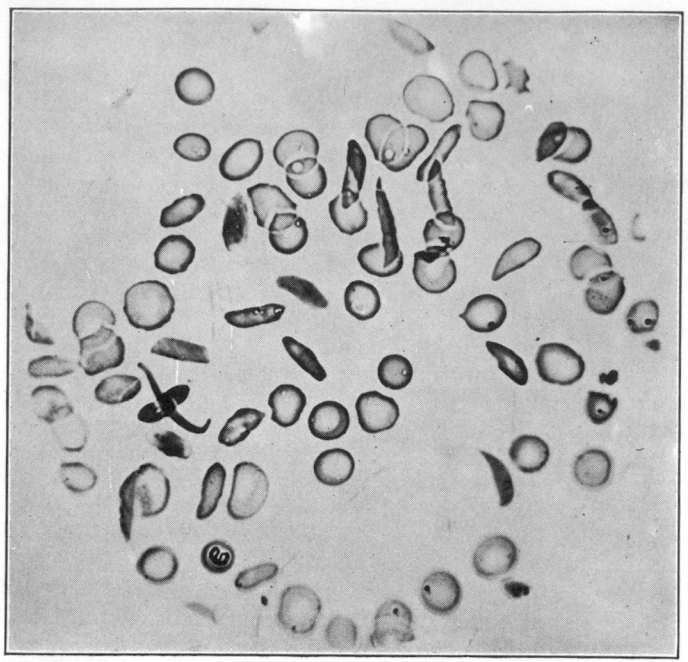

Fig. 8.   Blood in sickle-cell anemia.

by mixing blood with a reducing agent such as sodium metabisulfite and observing the development of sickling microscopically. It should be emphasized that all cells containing hemoglobin S will sickle under these circumstances, and thus a positive sickle-cell preparation will occur in both sickle-cell anemia and sickle-cell trait. Hemoglobin electrophoresis will demonstrate a single band of hemoglobin S with decreased mobility in sickle-cell anemia, and two bands representing hemoglobins A and S in sickle-cell trait. Rare instances have also been reported of hemoglobins other than hemoglobin S which demonstrate the sickling phenomenon (e.g., C_{Harlem} and $C_{Georgetown}$). These hemoglobinopathies are detected by their electrophoretic characteristics. Hyposthenuria is typically present in sickle-cell anemia as a result of impaired renal concentrating function, and the specific gravity of the urine usually ranges between 1.007 and 1.018, even after water deprivation.

Treatment.   Between crises children with sickle-cell anemia adjust well to the sustained chronic anemia, and no therapy is indicated. In painful crises bed rest, maintenance of hydration, and analgesics are indicated. Bone pain may be very severe, and narcotics may be required. Oral hydration is usually adequate, but with crises associated with severe abdominal pain and vomiting, parenteral fluids may be needed. With protracted crises transfusion with packed red cells may terminate the episode. *Oxygen* is of no value in relieving pain but is indicated with pulmonary complications and heart failure. Administration of oxygen over long periods of time may inhibit marrow function and thereby increase the degree of anemia. A large variety of treatments have been employed in attempts to prevent and terminate painful crises. These have been directed at increas-

ing the plasma volume (dextran, plasma), promoting vasodilation (Priscoline), preventing thrombosis (anticoagulation), altering pH (sodium bicarbonate), and reducing inflammation (ACTH and cortisone). None has proved effective.

Repeated transfusions suppress blood formation in sickle-cell anemia and may temporarily replace the patient's cells with normal cells so that crises do not occur. This procedure may be undertaken in preparing patients for surgery or during severe complicating illnesses. Studies on the effects of long-term regular transfusion therapy are in progress in several centers.

Occasionally secondary *hypersplenism* may develop in patients with sickle-cell disease, thus adding an extracorpuscular defect to the basic disease. This complication may be suspected clinically by a progressive fall in hemoglobin concentration, in the absence of crisis, in a patient previously well-compensated. It may be demonstrated more exactly by documenting decreased survival of tagged normal erythrocytes in the patient's circulation. In such instances splenectomy will remove the extracorpuscular defect and permit return of the earlier level of compensation. The basic disease, however, is not benefited by splenectomy, and the operation should be undertaken only when specifically indicated.

Hemoglobin C Disease.   Hemoglobin C is another abnormal hemoglobin resulting from a genetically determined synthesis of abnormal beta chains. In this hemoglobin, *lysine* replaces the glutamate residue present in the corresponding position in the beta chain of hemoglobin A ($a_2\beta_2$ 6 glu→lys). Hemoglobin C occurs primarily but not exclusively in Negroes, and the mode of genetic transmission is identical with that described for sickle-cell disease. Individuals homozygous for hemoglobin C have a congenital, chronic hemolytic anemia, usually of mild degree, accompanied by splenomegaly, but not by the painful crises characteristic of sickle-cell anemia. The striking feature of the blood smear is the large number of *target cells,* which, together with variable numbers of *microspherocytes,* may range from 40 to 90 percent of the erythrocytes. Reticulocytosis is usually slight and bilirubinemia is minimal. The abnormal hemoglobin may be demonstrated electrophoreetically. Transfusions are rarely required and the prognosis is excellent.

The heterozygote for hemoglobin C is generally asymptomatic. Target cells are increased in the peripheral blood smear, and electrophoresis demonstrates bands of hemoglobins A and C.

Sickle-Cell–Hemoglobin C Disease.
Inheritance of the gene for HbS from one parent and for HbC from the other produces sickle-cell—Hemoglobin C disease. The resultant disorder tends to be somewhat milder than classical sickle-cell anemia, but usually is more severe than homozygous HbC disease. The symptoms are largely those produced by the presence of the HbS, and the variation in severity of disease among different patients is dependent to a large degree upon the proportion of HbS, which may range from 35 to 65 percent of the total hemoglobin. The blood smear reveals striking target cell formation, and typical sickle cells may be found. The sickle-cell preparation is positive, and electrophoresis reveals the two bands corresponding to hemoglobins S and C.

Hemoglobin M Disease.
A variety of structural abnormalities of the hemoglobin molecule have been described in which amino acid substitutions are located in regions of the globin chains near the site of attachment of the heme groups. Due to the altered protein-heme interactions which result, the affected heme groups remain in the oxidized state and are unable to accept oxygen. The oxygen-binding abnormality of these hemoglobins is confined to the individual alpha or beta chains in which the amino acid substitution is present. These abnormalities have been found only in the heterozygous state.

Affected individuals manifest lifelong *cyanosis* beginning in infancy, but are asymptomatic. This condition requires differentiation from cyanosis due to cardiopulmonary disease, acquired methemoglobinemia, and methemoglobinemia resulting from a congenital deficiency of NADH-dependent methemoglobin reductase. The abnormal hemoglobins are identified by electrophoresis and spectrophotometric analysis.

Abnormal Hemoglobins Having Altered Oxygen Affinity.
A number of hemoglobinopathies have been identified in recent years in which amino acid substitutions in the globin chains produce changes in the protein configuration of the molecule, which in turn affect the interaction between the hemoglobin and oxygen. Some of these abnormal hemoglobins (e.g., HbG_{Kansas}) have shown a lower than

normal oxygen affinity, and have been associated with a mild degree of anemia. Other hemoglobin variants have exhibited an increased affinity for oxygen, together with impaired ability for oxygen release to the tissues (e.g., $HbG_{Chesapeake}$, HbG_{Yakima}, HbG_{Ranier}). The tissue hypoxia which occurs stimulates erythropoietin production, leading to a significant increase in erythropoiesis, and higher than normal levels of blood hemoglobin. Affected individuals exhibit a ruddy appearance but usually are asymptomatic. The hemoglobin abnormalities are identified in most cases by electrophoresis.

Unstable hemoglobins. A group of abnormal hemoglobins, particularly those having amino acid substitutions involving the hydrophobic inner core of the molecule, are characteristically unstable and undergo intracellular precipitation with the formation of red cell inclusion bodies. With some of these hemoglobin abnormalities, particularly notable in the case of Hemoglobin Zürich, protein instability and intraerythrocytic precipitation are greatly accentuated by the presence of oxidant drugs and chemicals which produce acute hemolytic episodes resembling those seen in patients with glucose-6-phosphate dehydrogenase deficiency. Chronic hemolytic anemia of variable severity is characteristic in all of the unstable hemoglobin disorders, and is accompanied by jaundice, splenomegaly, and red cell inclusion bodies ("Heinz bodies") demonstrable by incubation of the cells with supravital stains. The abnormal hemoglobins are identified by hemoglobin electrophoresis or by evidence of abnormal protein precipitation in a hemoglobin heat-stability test. Splenectomy has been of value in some of these patients.

Hereditary persistence of fetal hemoglobin. A familial abnormality characterized by continued synthesis of hemoglobin F in adult life has been described in Greeks and in Negroes. The latter type has been observed in the homozygous form in several asymptomatic individuals in whom fetal hemoglobin comprised 100 percent of their hemoglobin. In the heterozygous state affected individuals show 17 to 33 percent fetal hemoglobin, with the lower values being characteristic of the Greek type. A variety of doubly heterozygous states have also been described in which hereditary persistence of fetal hemoglobin coexists with a hemoglobinopathy or thalassemia. When this abnormality is present together with sickle-cell trait, the affected individuals exhibit no evidence of disease even though hemoglobin S may constitute as much as 70 percent of the total. This is believed to be due to the fact that the fetal hemoglobin is uniformly distributed in all of the red cells of these individuals, and because of the lack of molecular interaction between the two hemoglobin types sickling is also suppressed.

Hemoglobin Lepore disease. A number of abnormal hemoglobins are classed as Lepore-type hemoglobins and all of them appear to consist of a pair of normal alpha chain subunits and a pair of globin chains which represent a hybrid consisting of part of the normal beta and part of the normal delta chains. It is hypothesized that this abnormality may have arisen as a result of an anomalous chromosomal crossover, to produce deletion of part of each of the beta and delta structural genes and the formation of a hybrid gene.

Rare homozygous individuals have been found; hemoglobins A and A_2 were both absent from their red cells. Severe anemia was present and the percentage of fetal hemoglobin was greatly increased. Heterozygous individuals exhibit a mild hypochromic microcytic anemia. Heterozygosity together with heterozygous thalassemia or a hemoglobinopathy has also been reported.

Other Abnormal Hemoglobins. In addition to the hemoglobin abnormalities classified in the foregoing sections, a number of variants have been identified which produce little or no clinically adverse effects. Many of these abnormal hemoglobins have been detected in asymptomatic individuals as a result of population survey studies. Hemoglobin E is commonly found in areas of Southeast Asia and results in minimal disability even in the homozygous state. Hemoglobin D exists in high frequency in populations of Pakistan and Northwest India, and affected individuals are generally asymptomatic.

THE THALASSEMIA SYNDROMES.   *Beta Thalassemia.*
This disorder represents a group of congenital anemias in which the underlying defect consists of quantitative impairment in the synthesis of the beta globin chains of hemoglobin A. These entities were first recognized in Mediterranean area populations, but it has become apparent that they are worldwide in their distribution. In addition to a high incidence in Southern Europe, beta thalassemia has been found among Negroes, Cantonese Chinese, in much of Southeast Asia, in India, and in the Middle East.

Although the biochemical defect in all of these disorders is unknown it is apparent that a number of genetically different abnormalities are included in this classification. The quantitative degree of impairment of beta-chain synthesis is also variable, resulting in a spectrum of diseases of differing severity ranging from mild, inapparent anemia in the homozygous state to the most severe degrees of anemia found in any of the known congenital syndromes.

Because of the diminution of beta-chain synthesis, overall hemoglobin production is decreased, resulting in red cell hypochromia. The underhemoglobinization of the erythrocytes constitutes a major element in the pathogenesis of the anemia. A hemolytic component is also present, however: although beta-chain synthesis is decreased, the erythropoietic cells continue to produce normal quantities of alpha chains. The latter are unstable when uncombined with beta chains, and precipitate within the erythrocytes to form inclusion bodies, leading to premature red cell destruction.

Thalassemia Minor. This abnormality represents the coexistence of a beta thalassemia gene and a gene for normal beta-chain production. In a majority of instances the normal gene activity is sufficient to provide a nearly normal rate of hemoglobin synthesis, and these individuals are usually asymptomatic apart from mild pallor. Red cell counts are often normal but the hemoglobin concentration is slightly reduced. Blood smears reveal mild to moderate hypochromia and microcytosis. Occasional oval cells, target cells, and stippled cells are seen, and the reticulocyte count is usually normal. This syndrome is often designated "thalassemia minor." In some instances heterozygous individuals may exhibit more severe manifestations including anemia (hemoglobin concentration of 7 to 9 mg/100 ml), mild jaundice, splenomegaly, and slight to moderate elevation of the reticulocyte count: this has been termed "thalassemia intermedia." This designation, however, has also been applied to certain homozygous individuals with a relatively mild clinical disorder, and is a descriptive term rather than one having genetic implications.

In most cases of heterozygous beta thalassemia, the percentage of hemoglobin A_2 is elevated above the normal maximum of about 3 percent. In a less common genetic variant of beta thalassemia, which has been designated beta-delta thalassemia or high F-thalassemia, heterozygous individuals exhibit normal or slightly reduced levels of hemoglobin A_2, but hemoglobin F is elevated comprising 5 to 15 percent of the total. Rarely, both hemoglobins A_2 and F are elevated. Recently, it has been shown that some individuals may be heterozygous for beta thalassemia while demonstrating none of the foregoing features of the disease. In these instances the diagnosis was established by family genetic studies and specialized biochemical techniques. Red cell osmotic fragility is decreased in nearly all of the forms of beta thalassemia.

The heterozygous individual usually requires no therapy and life expectancy is normal. The anemia is not improved by hematinic agents and administration of iron should be avoided in the absence of a specific indication.

Homozygous Beta Thalassemia (Cooley's Anemia, Mediterranean Anemia).   Clinical manifestations. The clinical features of severe homozygous beta thalassemia ("thalassemia major") result from the effects of severe, chronic anemia, marked marrow hyperactivity, excessive tissue iron deposition, and striking splenomegaly and hepatomegaly. Because of the presence of large amounts of fetal hemoglobin at birth, the impaired synthesis of hemoglobin A does not become apparent during the first few months of life. During the second half of the first year of life, however, the infant begins to demonstrate pallor, irritability, anorexia, fever, and often an enlarging abdomen. The need for transfusion develops in early infancy and persists in most cases throughout life. As the child grows older, the effects on bone of the intense marrow hyperplasia produce characteristic changes in the facies. Involvement of the cranial bones leads to enlargement of the head due to frontal and parietal bossing; enlargement of the maxilla causes protrusion of the upper frontal teeth and forward and upward deviation of the upper lip, and marked malocclusion is common. The malar eminences are prominent, the bridge of the nose is broad and depressed, the eyes have a mongoloid slant, and an epicanthic fold is frequently present.

In the absence of transfusions, pallor is striking with advancing age, and with prolonged transfusion therapy the skin becomes darkly pigmented owing to deposition of both melanin and hemosiderin in the dermis. The pigmentation may be very intense in some children and is associated with even darker freckling. Some degree of scleral icterus is usually evident. Abdominal enlargement becomes evident early, and with continued hemolysis and transfusion the spleen may become enormous, producing lumbar lordosis and abdominal discomfort, anorexia, and occasionally vomiting due to pressure. Hepatomegaly develops somewhat more slowly, but the liver also reaches a very large size. Epistaxis is common in thalassemia major and is not attributable to demonstrated changes in the hemostatic mechanism. Painful crises do not occur as in sickle-cell anemia, but pain in the bones, apparently due to marrow hyperplasia, may occur when the hemoglobin concentration is allowed to fall to low levels. This type of bone pain is readily relieved by transfusions. Pathologic fractures of the femur and vertebral compression occur occasionally.

With transfusions given at sufficiently frequent intervals to maintain the hemoglobin concentration above 7 to 8 g/100 ml, children with thalassemia adapt surprisingly well and maintain a level of function which permits attendance at school and participation in most childhood activities. Lower hemoglobin concentrations result usually in symptoms of irritability, fatigability, listlessness, and anorexia; the parent and often the child can usually determine when transfusions are required. Children receiving transfusions at required intervals may show fairly normal growth in height and weight during the first 8 to 10 years of life. Thereafter, retardation of growth becomes very evident and the patients' final height is strikingly subnormal. The growth failure results primarily from failure of skeletal maturation, with retarded bone age noted through the adolescent years. Sexual maturation is delayed and hypogonadism is common in boys and girls.

Cardiac dilation and hemic murmurs are commonly heard throughout childhood. With judicious use of transfusions, cardiac failure in the early years of life can be avoided in most instances. As adolescence approaches and thereafter, the incidence of heart failure increases. The cardiac insufficiency is usually rather refractory to treatment and is often associated with bizarre atrial and ventricular arrhythmias, and is the most common cause of death from the disease.

The continued hemolysis and large number of transfusions required during the course of thalassemia major result in widespread deposition of iron in the tissues and visceral fibrosis. The increased absorption of iron, characteristic of hemolytic anemias, also contributes to the iron overload. Hepatic cirrhosis may develop, as well as pancreatic fibrosis and diabetes. Myocardial hemosiderosis may contribute to the cardiac complications of disease. When advanced and particularly when associated with cirrhosis and diabetes, the condition may be indistinguishable from hemochromatosis.

Crises due to sudden acceleration of hemolysis probably do not occur; aplastic crises, however, are a feature of this disorder as described previously.

Laboratory findings. Hemolysis and impaired hemoglobin synthesis combine to produce in thalassemia major the severest degree of anemia found in any of the congenital hemoglobin syndromes. In the absence of transfusion, hemoglobin levels fall to 5 g/100 ml or less before stabilization occurs. The anemia is severely hypochromic and the red cell count is, therefore, lowered to a somewhat lesser degree than is the hemoglobin concentration, ranging from 2.5 to 3.5 million/mm³. The blood smear (Fig. 9) reveals striking *hypochromia* with thin red cells in which the hemoglobin may be limited to a narrow rim at the periphery of the cells. There is marked variation in size and shape of the erythrocytes, ranging from small microcytes to large pale macrocytes. *Polychromasia*, representing regeneration, and *basophilic stippling* of red cells, indicating hemoglobin denaturation, are readily seen. Target cells are present but not to the same extent as in hemoglobin C disease or sickle-cell anemia. Normoblasts are plentiful in the peripheral blood, and their presence led to the name "erythroblastic anemia." The normoblasts usually exceed the reticulocytes, which range from 2 to 10 percent. The white cell count is usually elevated and the platelet count normal, except when complicating hypersplenism causes lowering of both.

Repeated transfusions, by suppressing blood formation, may modify the peripheral blood findings considerably. The bone marrow reveals intense erythroid hyperplasia extending to the very early erythroblasts. The osmotic fragility of the red cells is decreased. The serum bilirubin is usually elevated above normal, but only slightly. The serum iron is elevated and the iron-binding capacity is fully saturated, due to hemolysis and impaired iron incorporation into hemoglobin. Fetal hemoglobin concentrations may range from 40 to nearly 100 percent.

Radiographic examination of the bones demonstrates striking changes. The long bones are osteoporotic with prominence of the trabeculae. The cortices are thin, the medullary cavities are widened, and transverse lines are generally conspicuous. In the metacarpals and phalanges the expansion of the medullary cavity may produce an almost rectangular contour (Fig. 10). In the skull the space between the tables is widened, while the outer table is some-

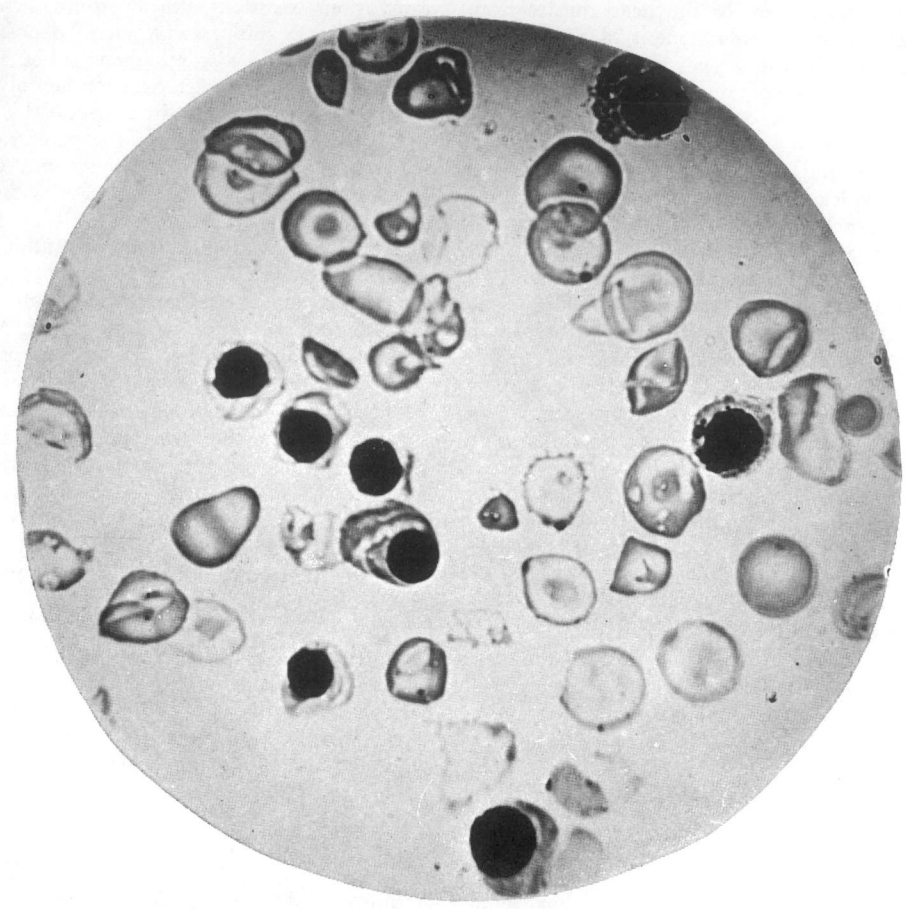

Fig. 9. Blood in thalassemia major.

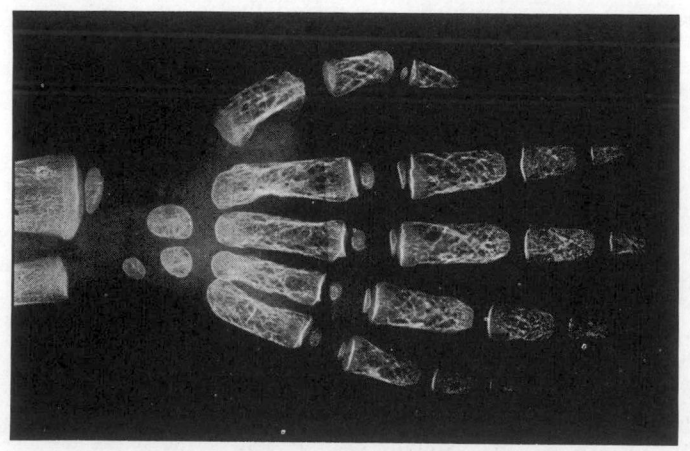

Fig. 10. Roentgenogram of hand of a 3-year-old patient with thalassemia major showing rectangular contour of bones.

times reduced to such thinness as not to be visible in the roentgenogram. The trabeculae connecting the inner and outer tables then give the appearance of *hair standing on end* (Fig. 11). Overgrowth of the marrow in the upper maxilla obliterates or greatly reduces the volume of the maxillary sinuses, their small size persisting into adult life. The earliest roentgen finding in the skeleton is usually in the base of the nasal process and consists of widening of the diploic space. Bone changes are reduced greatly by regular transfusions and tend to regress with cessation of growth.

Treatment. Blood transfusions remain the mainstay of therapy in thalassemia major, and the use of packed red cells is recommended. It has been shown that periodic transfusions (at 2- to 4-week

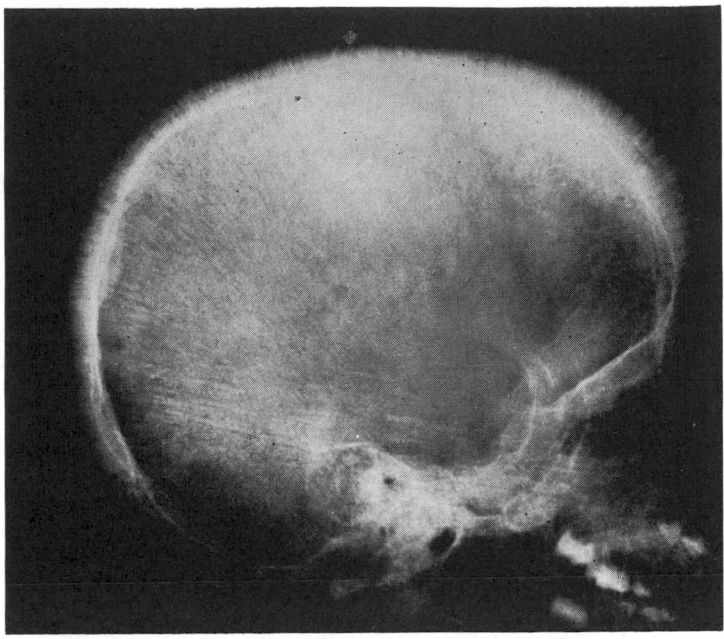

Fig. 11. Roentgenogram of skull of a 3-year-old patient with thalassemia major showing radial arrangement of bone spicules in calvarium.

intervals), in amounts calculated to keep the hemoglobin concentration between 6 and 9 g/100 ml, permit a reasonable level of activity, regular attendance at school, alleviation of severe symptoms of anemia, and relatively normal growth and development during early childhood. This mode of management, however, does not prevent development of cardiac failure in late childhood and adolescence. While the large amounts of iron administered in a regimen of regular transfusions offer the potential hazard of hemosiderosis, there seems little question that such patients fare better than those from whom transfusions have been withheld until extremely low hemoglobin concentrations developed. At present, studies are in progress to evaluate the effect of long-term transfusion therapy aimed at maintaining hemoglobin concentrations at close to the normal level (between 10 and 15 g/100 ml). Children who are transfused in this manner exhibit few of the clinical manifestations of the disease, but growth retardation may be an undesirable side effect.

Attempts to ameliorate the effects of iron overload by use of iron chelating agents (e.g., deferoxamine) have generally been unsuccessful. Splenectomy often becomes necessary in the course of thalassemia major. The most frequent indication is the development of secondary hypersplenism, as evidenced by increasing need for transfusion in order to maintain adequate hemoglobin concentration and by the demonstration of shortened survival of tagged normal donor cells. Splenectomy in such instances usually results in a decrease in transfusion requirement, but the basic disease is not altered. Occasionally the massive splenomegaly is, in itself, an indication for splenectomy, in order to alleviate abdominal discomfort. Because of the high incidence of septicemia and meningitis in thalassemic patients who have undergone splenectomy, the operation should be performed only when specifically indicated.

Prognosis. The availability of antibiotics and advances in blood banking and transfusion techniques have improved the longevity of children with thalassemia major. Nevertheless, the overall prognosis is still poor, and few patients survive past early adulthood, death occurring usually from cardiac failure.

Alpha Thalassemia. Two genetic forms of alpha thalassemia have been distinguished, based on the degree of suppression of alpha-chain synthesis. Individuals who are heterozygous for the more severe form (alpha thalassemia$_1$) exhibit mild to moderate anemia with red cell hypochromia and microcytosis. Although the cellular morphology is quite similar to that of beta thalassemia minor, neither hemoglobin A$_2$ nor hemoglobin F concentrations are elevated. Heterozygotes with the milder form (alpha thalassemia$_2$) are hematologically normal.

Homozygous alpha thalassemia$_1$ has been observed only in Chinese and Southeast Asian populations. Affected infants produce little or no alpha chains and nearly all of the hemoglobin present in the red cells consists of tetramer molecules containing only normal gamma chains (γ_4, "Hemoglobin Barts"). This abnormal hemoglobin has a high affinity for oxygen and fails to release oxygen adequately to the tissues. The infants are anemic, with edema, jaundice, normoblastemia, and hepatosplenomegaly. The syndrome resembles that of severe isoimmune hemolytic disease (erythroblastosis fetalis) but the direct Coombs' test is negative. In every reported case the infant died in utero or soon after birth.

Individuals doubly heterozygous with genes for both alpha thalassemia$_1$ and alpha thalassemia$_2$ ("Hemoglobin H disease") exhibit a moderately severe hemolytic anemia with jaundice, hepatosplenomegaly, skeletal changes, and inclusion bodies in the erythrocytes. Hemoglobin gamma$_4$ (Barts) is present together with fetal hemoglobin at birth, and as the fetal hemoglobin is replaced by hemoglobin A, hemoglobin molecules made up only of beta-chain subunits (β_4 "Hemoglobin H") begin to appear. Transfusions may be required in some cases and splenectomy may offer some benefit.

Sickle-Cell Beta Thalassemia Disease. This disorder results from inheritance of a hemoglobin S gene from one parent and a beta-thalassemia gene from the other. Because of suppression of the synthesis of hemoglobin A by the thalassemia gene, hemoglobin S predominates and comprises 65 to 90 percent of the total hemoglobin. Sickle-cell beta thalassemia is responsible for the majority of cases of sickle-cell disease in Greeks and Italians, but also occurs in Negroes. The disorder is associated with a chronic, moderately severe hemolytic anemia, frequently accompanied by splenomegaly. The clinical features are frequently indistinguishable from those seen in sickle-cell anemia, but in most cases painful crises are milder and less frequent. This combination should be suspected when one of the parents of a child with sickle-cell disease demonstrates a negative sickle-cell preparation.

Hemoglobin C-Beta Thalassemia Disease. As with sickle-cell beta thalassemia, a preponderance of the abnormal hemoglobin (hemoglobin C) is present in this condition. A mild to moderate hemolytic anemia may occur, but most affected individuals are asymptomatic. The clinical features are similar to those of homozygous hemoglobin C disease.

Extracorpuscular Defects

Autoimmune Acquired Hemolytic Anemia

This term is applied to an acquired form of hemolytic anemia in which antibodies directed against the patients' red cells may be demonstrated. The characteristic laboratory finding serving to distinguish this form of hemolytic anemia from the various types due to intracorpuscular defects is a positive antiglobulin (Coombs') test.

Pathogenesis. The disorder may occur at all ages in childhood and has been described in an infant as young as 6 weeks of age. While the majority of cases in both adults and children cannot be attributed to a specific cause and are therefore classified as "idiopathic," the disorder does occur in association with a number of other disorders including (1) malignancies, particularly lymphomas; (2) other so-called autoimmune or collagen diseases such as lupus erythematosus, rheumatoid arthritis, and ulcerative colitis; and (3) infections, particularly viral pneumonia. With many of these children an antecedent history of an upper respiratory infection may be elicited, and cases of autoimmune acquired hemolytic anemia have been described following Coxsackie, herpes, measles, and varicella infections.

The available evidence indicates that this disease involves production of antibodies against the patient's own cells. In most instances these antibodies are of the 7S gamma globulin variety with a thermal optimum at 37° C (*warm* antibodies). In a small percentage of cases, notably following viral pneumonia, the antibodies are most active at 4° C (*cold* antibodies) and may be 19S macroglobulins. Two major theories have been proposed to explain the synthesis of autoantibodies. The first postulates that red cell damage causes the cell to become antigenic for its own host (altered antigenicity). The second suggests that there is an aberration in antibody formation by the host so that antibodies against his own tissues are formed, and that this tendency to form abnormal antibodies may be genetically determined. Burnet has proposed that somatic mutations, occurring spontaneously or in response to infections, drugs, radiation, and so forth lead to the appearance of clusters of immunologically competent cells giving rise to antibodies which accidentally react with the host's own tissues (clonal selection theory). The interpretation that an abnormality in antibody formation is basically involved gains support from the fact that autoimmune hemolytic anemia is found in association with generalized "autoimmune" diseases such as lupus erythematosis. In addition to the theories discussed, the possibility also exists that the red cells may be involved as "innocent bystanders." In this mechanism antigen-antibody complexes of various types may become attached to the surface of the red cell where they fix complement and thus induce cellular membrane damage.

Clinical manifestations. The onset of autoimmune acquired hemolytic anemia is usually insidious and is characterized by anorexia, lethargy, progressive pallor, low-grade fever, and the gradual appearance of icterus. Darkening of the urine may be noted by the parents as an early finding. In severe cases the onset may be abrupt, with high fever, rapid development of pallor, marked icterus, and occasionally hemoglobinuria. Splenomegaly of moderate degree is usually detectable, and slight hepatomegaly is a frequent accompaniment. Enlargement of lymph nodes is not seen except in circumstances where an underlying or antecedent disease is responsible.

Laboratory findings. The degree of anemia is variable, but the evidences of hemolysis are usually quite apparent. The red cells reveal *anisocytosis, poikilocytosis,* and *polychromasia. Spherocytosis* is common and may equal in degree that seen in hereditary spherocytosis. Distorted and fragmented erythrocytes may also be seen. *Normoblasts* may appear in the peripheral blood in instances of severe anemia. *Reticulocytosis* is usually marked except in rare instances where, apparently, damage to the marrow erythroid elements occurs in addition to the circulating erythrocytes. In this circumstance depletion of the red cell precursors in the marrow may be found. Usually, however, marked erythroid hyperplasia in the marrow accompanies the hemolysis. The white cell count is usually elevated and platelets are normal in number. In severe cases, however, both may be reduced ("Evans' syndrome"). Thrombocytopenic purpura has been found in 13 percent of patients in one large series. Bilirubinemia is predominantly of the indirect variety. Fecal and urinary urobilinogen are elevated.

The direct *Coombs' antiglobulin test* is usually positive, and circulating free antibody may be detected by the coating of normal erythrocytes in the indirect Coombs' test. The antibody coating of the patient's cells leads to their spontaneous agglutination, thus making difficult red cell counting, blood typing, and cross matching. Not infrequently the patient's true blood type may remain in doubt and all attempts at cross matching may indicate incompatibility. In over two-thirds of the cases the antibody appears to react nonspecifically against red cells of all types. In about one-third of the cases the antibody reacts with specific red cell antigens usually in the Rh system. Patients with cold antibodies also demonstrate a positive Coombs' test.

Course and treatment. The course of autoimmune acquired hemolytic anemia is very variable. In some children the disease is extremely brief and self-limited even in the absence of any treatment. In others a single transfusion appears to terminate the process. Usually the disease is more chronic and requires therapy for at least several weeks. At present, corticosteroids represent the treatment of choice, with splenectomy reserved only for those cases failing to respond to medical management. Prednisone is administered initially at a dose of 2 mg per kilogram of body weight per day in four divided doses. Hematologic response is often dramatic, with a rapid rise in red cell count and hemoglobin concentration, disappearance of jaundice, and fall in reticulocyte count to normal levels.

The effects of steroid therapy, however, vary greatly in different patients, and several types of responses may be noted: (1) There may be a return of hematologic values to normal and a disappearance of the positive Coombs' test, in which case treatment may usually be terminated without recurrence of illness; (2) Blood values may return to normal, but the Coombs' test may remain positive. After 3 to 4 weeks of treatment, steroids may be tapered cautiously. In some children, hematologic normality may continue despite a positive Coombs' test; in others evidence of hemolysis may return; (3) Hematologic improvement may occur but with evidence of continuing hemolysis. In such instances continued steroid therapy is required; (4) Hematologic response may be inadequate despite administration of corticosteroid in doses which would ordinarily be regarded as more than adequate

(i.e., 2 mg/kg). Under such circumstances, splenectomy was usually considered indicated. During the past few years, however, cases have been reported of children who did not benefit from usual doses of prednisone but who did respond to very large doses. One patient on our own service failed to respond until a dose of 6 mg/kg/day was reached. Other observers have reported favorable responses to ACTH in some patients who failed to respond to corticosteroids.

In the absence of improvement following treatment with steroids and transfusion, splenectomy is advised. Following surgery, some of the patients recover completely with reversion of the Coombs' test to negative; others show continuing hemolysis but compensate to the degree that no additional treatment is needed; still others require continued steroid therapy to maintain an adequate hemoglobin concentration. Some children may show evidence of ongoing disease for more than a year before recovery eventually takes place. The majority of children appear to make a complete and permanent recovery, and the mortality rate is probably quite low.

Immunosuppressive agents (6-mercaptopurine, cyclophosphamide, azathiaprine) have been used in treatment of cases of chronic autoimmune acquired hemolytic anemia, with success in some instances. Because of the toxicity of these agents, added experience is required before they may be recommended for use in children. Two cases have also been reported in which thymectomy was followed by recovery in young infants who failed to respond to corticosteroids, splenectomy, and transfusion. The basis for the operation was the known relationship of the thymus to the development of immunologic competence. Here, too, the evidence relating to benefits and hazards of thymectomy in young infants is too fragmentary to permit any conclusions concerning the place of this operation in hemolytic anemia or any other disease of childhood.

The frequent uncertainty in blood typing and cross matching in autoimmune acquired hemolytic anemia makes transfusion hazardous. Transfusion should be given only when anemia is severe, and then only after careful cross matching. If no blood appears compatible and transfusion is urgently needed, group O, Rh-negative blood may be administered slowly and cautiously, with constant attention for the development of reactions. Because the response to steroids may be very rapid, it is often advisable to withhold transfusions even in the face of fairly severe anemia, providing the patient's clinical condition permits this and the blood demonstrates evidence of active regeneration.

Drug-Induced Hemolytic Anemias Associated with a Positive Coombs' Test

Administration of a variety of drugs to susceptible individuals can produce a Coombs'-positive hemolytic anemia otherwise indistinguishable from idiopathic autoimmune anemia as described in the preceding section. These drugs have included quinine, quinidine, stibophen, aminosalicylic acid, phenacetin, sulfonamides, penicillin, and cephalothin.

Several different mechanisms appear to be responsible for these reactions. With a majority of the agents the drug appears to act as a hapten, and combines with serum protein to elicit antibody production. In the presence of the drug, antigen-antibody complexes form and become attached to the red cell surface, in most cases together with complement. The latter produces damage to the cell membrane leading to premature destruction of the erythrocyte. The specific role of a suspected drug can usually be confirmed by the demonstration of a positive indirect Coombs' test using serum from the patient together with red cells from a compatible donor. The test will be positive only when the specific drug is added. In some cases Coombs' serum which is specific for the detection of complement will yield a positive reaction while anti-IgG Coombs' serum may not.

Hemolytic anemia which occurs with methyldopa is a common complication of the administration of this drug and has been reported to occur in approximately 20 percent of patients who receive it. Although the Coombs' test is positive in these patients, the presence of the drug does not appear to be necessary for the hemolytic reaction to occur once antibody formation has taken place. It has been shown that a majority of patients receiving cephalothin also develop a positive Coombs' but apparently by a nonimmunologic mechanism. It appears that the drug causes plasma proteins to adhere to the red cells to produce a positive agglutination test when Coombs' serum is added.

In most cases the anemia will subside rapidly after the offending drug is discontinued, and additional therapy is rarely necessary.

Hypersplenism

Significant and protracted enlargement of the spleen is commonly associated with anemia due to accelerated rates of destruction of the erythrocytes. The spleen may be enlarged in many situations, the most common being obstruction to the outflow of splenic venous blood (as in cirrhosis of the liver with portal hypertension, or portal vein or splenic vein obstruction), infiltration with foreign cells (Gaucher's disease, Hand-Schüller-Christian disease), proliferation of neoplastic cells (Hodgkin's disease, lymphosarcoma), accumulation of products of red cell destruction (chronic hemolytic anemias), and acute and chronic infections. Splenic enlargement produces alteration in the splenic circulation, with the result that the amount of time the red cell spends within the spleen is significantly lengthened. This, in turn, induces osmotic and metabolic changes in the red cells which lead to their premature destruction. While some of the red cells are actually "trapped" and destroyed in the spleen, the hemolytic anemia results in greater part from the metabolic damage done to the erythrocytes in the course of the prolonged abnormal circulation through the organ. Since white cells and platelets are also adversely affected by the abnormal splenic circulation, anemia due to splenic enlargement is frequently accompanied by some degree of leucopenia and thrombocytopenia. Hypersplenism will be discussed in more detail in the chapter on the spleen.

Accelerated Hemolysis Due to Intravascular Red Cell Destruction

Hemolysis Associated with Heart Valve Prostheses. Mechanical disruption of red cells has been found to occur in some patients following surgical repair of valvular defects and has been attributed to the development of abnormal intracardiac turbulence of the blood. The hemolytic process occurs intravascularly, and is associated with hemoglobinemia and excretion of large amounts of iron into the urine in the form of hemosiderin. The latter is thought to represent the metabolism of free hemoglobin by the kidneys. Because of the renal iron excretion, iron deficiency often develops in these patients. Other findings may include persistent fever, splenomegaly, and petechiae. With mild degrees of hemolysis a compensated hemolytic state can often be maintained by continuous administration of iron. When hemolysis is more severe, surgical revision of the valve prosthesis sometimes becomes necessary.

Microangiopathic Hemolytic Anemia. In a variety of pathologic states accompanied by disseminated intravascular coagulation (see p. 1242), hemolytic anemia is frequently present together with reticulocytosis and morphologic evidence of red cell fragmentation. The accelerated hemolysis appears to result from intravascular red cell damage due to the action on the cells of fibrin deposits in the microvasculature. Therapy is directed toward the abnormal coagulation changes.

Idiopathic Pulmonary Hemosiderosis. This disorder is characterized by repeated episodes of intrapulmonary blood sequestration or hemorrhage associated with respiratory distress, anemia, hemoptysis, jaundice, and iron deficiency. The etiology is not understood and the disorder is uncommon. This diagnosis should be considered, however, in a child having an acute onset of anemia with concomitant pulmonary symptoms. Radiographic abnormalities in the chest usually consist of diffuse or patchy infiltration, but the chest film in some cases may be entirely normal. The diagnosis is established by gastric washing or lung biopsy to demonstrate the presence of macrophages which contain hemosiderin granules. The course of the disease is unpredictable with frequent recurrences of the acute episodes, often with a fatal outcome. Corticosteroid therapy may be of value in some cases.

Paroxysmal Nocturnal Hemoglobinuria. This form of hemolytic anemia, which is rare in children, appears to be due to an acquired red cell defect. The affected erythrocyte exhibits increased susceptibility to hemolysis by complement or antibody, or at low pH. Hemolysis occurs intravascularly and is accompanied by hemoglobinuria and hemosiderinuria. Leucocyte alkaline phosphatase activity is typically depressed. Leucopenia and thrombocytopenia may also be present and the disorder may be associated with the syndrome of acute or acquired aplastic anemia. The diagnosis is established by demonstrating increased hemolysis of red cells incubated at 37° C in acidified normal serum (Ham test). Therapy is supportive.

Other Extracorpuscular Causes of Hemolytic Anemia

The development of isotopic techniques for measurement of red cell longevity has led to the finding that the anemia accompanying a variety of disease states is due, at least in part, to accelerated red cell destruction. This has been documented in uremia, various types of acute and chronic liver disease, rheumatoid arthritis, and burns; while the mechanism of red cell alteration has not been clarified in these instances, it is likely that membrane damage is a common denominator.

Infantile pyknocytosis, described by Tuffy et al., is the designation given to a condition occurring in the early weeks of life, characterized by the appearance in the peripheral blood of dense, irregularly contracted erythrocytes with spiny projections, and a hemolytic anemia with jaundice and splenomegaly. The cause is unknown and the condition is self-limited, although exchange transfusions have occasionally been needed to control jaundice. Pyknocytes are not limited to this order but appear as well in uremia, liver disease, hemolytic-uremic syndrome, and burns, suggesting an extrinsic cause of red cell membrane damage in all.

A moderately severe form of hemolytic anemia has been described in premature infants having vitamin E deficiency. The anemia is associated with reticulocytosis, and irregularly contracted erythrocytes may be present in peripheral blood smears. Platelet counts are frequently elevated in these infants. Severe edema unassociated with cardiovascular dysfunction or hypoproteinemia has also been observed in a group of these infants. The anemia is unresponsive to iron therapy, but administration of vitamin E as alpha-tocopherol produces a rapid reversal of all of the associated abnormal findings.

Erythroblastosis Fetalis (Hemolytic Disease of the Newborn)

Erythroblastosis fetalis is a hemolytic disorder of the fetus and newborn. It is based on an antigenic difference between the red cells of the fetus and those of the mother, on the development by the mother of antibodies which can react with and lead to destruction of the red cells of the fetus, and on the entrance of such an antibody into the fetal circulation.

The clinical manifestations of the disease vary greatly. In many cases there is no more than trifling anemia, with or without jaundice. On the other hand, there may be fetal death, generalized edema (*hydrops fetalis*), severe anemia at or shortly after birth (*anemia neonatorum*), or rapidly developing, deep jaundice (*icterus gravis*) which is sometimes fatal. These last three syndromes, differing so widely clinically, were thought to be separate diseases until 1932 when Diamond, Blackfan, and Baty after intensive study concluded that the three were closely related and were dependent on a dysfunction of erythrocyte production or "erythroblastosis fetalis." This term, first used to describe a hypothetical dysfunction, was soon taken over as the name of the clinical disease itself.

In 1940 Landsteiner and Wiener discovered the rhesus or Rh blood group factor. They found that it is present in the red cells of about 85 percent of people of the white race and that it is inherited as a Mendelian dominant. In 1941 Levine, Katzin, and Burnham suggested that erythroblastosis fetalis results from the hemolytic action of maternal isoantibodies on the red cells of the fetus, the appearance of excessive numbers of nucleated erythrocytes in the infant's peripheral blood being a compensatory response. Later in the year they, with Vogel, adduced evidence that about 93 percent of cases of gross erythroblastosis result from isoimmunization of an Rh-negative mother by the Rh factor in the red cells of her fetus. While subsequent studies have fully confirmed their basic hypothesis, new techniques have proved that an antibody or antibodies of the ABO system cause disease even more often than do Rh antibodies, but that the disease so produced is usually mild and inconsequential. At the same time the newer studies have confirmed the conclusion reached by Levine and his co-workers that the vast majority of examples of the classic disease are due to the first discovered Rh antigen, now known as D or Rh_o, and its corresponding antibody. Disease due to this antigen-antibody combination will be discussed first.

ETIOLOGY. *Distribution and Inheritance of the D Antigen.* Although, as will be seen later, the Rh gene, antigen, and antibody situation is complex and open to more than one interpretation, many of the complexities are of interest chiefly to the geneticist or serologist and are of little practical importance to the physician. A single Rh antigen and its antibody account for all but a few cases of Rh erythroblastosis. This antigen or factor is called D—or Rh_o in the alternative nomenclature—and its antibody anti-D or anti-Rh_o. The anti-D antibody serves to divide people into two classes: those whose red cells it agglutinates are termed Rh-positive, and those whose cells it does not agglutinate, Rh-negative. In nearly every instance in which erythroblastosis occurs because of antigen differences in the Rh system the mother is Rh-negative and the infant Rh-positive, the infant having inherited the Rh-positive factor from the father.

The inheritance is on a simple mendelian basis. A person receives from each parent either the Rh-positive factor D or a corresponding negative factor d. He therefore has a pair of factors, DD or Dd or dd. DD and Dd are Rh-positive, dd Rh-negative, DD being homozygous Rh-positive, and Dd heterozygous Rh-positive. It follows that there are two possible patterns of inheritance for the children of an Rh-negative woman married to an Rh-positive man, depending on whether he is homozygous or heterozygous:

	Wife				*Wife*	
	d	d			d	d
Husband	D	Dd	Dd	*Husband*	D	Dd	Dd
homozygous				heterozygous			
	D	Dd	Dd		d	dd	dd

The man in the first case produces sperm all of which carry the Rh-positive gene, so all his children will be Rh-positive (Dd). The man in the second case produces equal numbers of sperm carrying the Rh-positive gene and of sperm carrying the Rh-negative gene. No matter which type of sperm has caused fertilization in past conceptions, it will be a matter of chance which type will fertilize his wife's Rh-negative ovum in the next conception; there is always at every conception an equal chance of the embryo being Rh-positive or Rh-negative.

Since only an Rh-negative woman can bear a child suffering from an anti-D erythroblastosis, the frequency of the disease in different populations will vary with the frequency of Rh-negative persons in those populations. In a mixed Caucasoid (white) population about 17 percent are Rh-negative, but the proportion rises to about 35 in Basques and falls to about 7 in Jews in North America. In Negroids in Africa the frequency is close to 5 percent; in those of America, a little higher. In Mongoloids and their derivative peoples such as the American Indian and Eskimo the percentage falls practically to zero; they are almost 100 percent Rh-positive. Erythroblastosis is commonest in Caucasoids, quite uncommon in Negroids, practically unknown in Mongoloids.

Modes of Sensitization with the Rh Antigen; Development and Persistence of Antibodies. So far as we know, Rh sensitization occurs only through the introduction of Rh-positive red cells into an Rh-negative person. The most certain way of introduction and of sensitization is by transfusion or injection. The most common way is through the passage of red cells from a fetus to its mother; it has been shown that a small amount of their infants' Rh-positive blood is often present in the blood of Rh-negative mothers immediately after delivery. That cells of the fetus commonly enter the mother's circulation before the onset of labor is now also known.

An amount of Rh-positive blood as small as that demonstrable in the blood of a woman at delivery has been proved experimentally to be antigenic. About 50 percent of Rh-negative volunteers develop anti-D after a single injection of such quantity, about 90 percent after repeated injections, while about 10 percent are unresponsive. Women appear to respond in a comparably variable way to the antigen of their fetuses. Of all women who are found to have developed antibodies, about 40 percent will have them in their second pregnancy, 30 percent in the third, and 30 percent not until the fourth pregnancy or later. Some mothers, however, will have many Rh-positive pregnancies without producing detectable antibody; they appear to be unresponsive to the antigen.

Women vary not only in the number of stimuli required to cause the development of an antibody but also in the strength of the response. Some will, from a single stimulation, produce antibody lethal to the fetus or infant; others will produce antibody in inconsequential amount, carrying it through several Rh-positive pregnancies. In most instances two or three stimuli appear to invoke maximum response. Once a woman develops an Rh antibody she will probably carry it for life, although in a few women its titer becomes in time so low that it is almost impossible to detect. This is particularly true of a woman who, following sensitization, carries a series of Rh-negative fetuses.

Rh antibodies exist in two major forms or states: one is called the albumin, albumin-active, hyperimmune, late immune, incomplete, blocking, monovalent, or conglutinating antibody; the other, the saline, saline-active, early immune, complete, divalent, or agglutinating antibody. We prefer the terms "albumin" and "saline" as being simple, noncommittal as to the nature of the differences between the antibodies, and indicative only of the common methods used in their demonstration. The nature of the physicochemical differences between the two is not known beyond the fact that the molecular weight of the saline antibody is greater than that of the albumin. Only the latter passes the placental barrier.

Frequency of Disease; Factors Affecting Such Frequency. If one includes every degree of disease, from the clinically inapparent to intrauterine death, the frequency of Rh erythroblastosis in a mixed white population is about 1 in every 150 pregnancies, whereas in such a population 1 mating in 7 is that of an Rh-positive man with an Rh-negative woman. Some of the circumstances which account for the discrepancy between the observed frequency of disease and that which one might expect are the following:

1. Antibodies practically never develop during a first pregnancy, so that except for women who have previously received Rh-positive cells by transfusion or injection, the only Rh-negative women whose infants can develop erythroblastosis are those in a second or later Rh-positive pregnancy. Pregnancies

of this latter category make up about 1 in 15 to 20 of all pregnancies.

2. When there is ABO incompatibility between husband and wife—e.g., wife O, husband A or B— an Rh-negative woman is less likely to produce Rh antibodies than when there is no such incompatibility. Several hypotheses have been put forward to account for this fact; the most credible is that fetal cells entering such a mother's circulation are destroyed before they can stimulate Rh antibody production. Experimentally it is difficult to make group O, Rh-negative recipients produce Rh antibodies by the injection of A or B Rh-positive cells. About one-third of all matings are ABO incompatible.

These circumstances account in part for the fact that disease is less common than one might expect. There are two known factors which increase the frequency: transfusion of Rh-negative girls and women with Rh-positive blood, and difficult labor. In the latter case it is probable that more fetal red cells than usual enter the maternal circulation, the increased frequency then depending on dosage of antigen.

PATHOGENESIS. When a pregnant woman has antibodies they may enter the circulation of her fetus as early as the sixth week. How soon they begin to do harm is not known; they do not cause fetal death earlier than 16 weeks. When disease does set in, the only certainly known pathologic process that takes place is accelerated destruction of fetal red cells. The fetus responds with increased production of erythrocytes. New islands of blood formation appear—notably in the liver and spleen, although they may develop in any organ or tissue. If the rate of destruction is very rapid, more and more younger and younger cells enter the circulation.

With red cell destruction, hemoglobin is released. Most is converted to indirect-reacting bilirubin and appears as such in the plasma, but some appears as oxyhemoglobin, methemalbumin, and perhaps other heme pigments. Some portion of the pigments is cleared by the fetal kidney into the amniotic fluid, some by the liver, and possibly some by the placenta. Clearance, however, is imperfect, so that the plasma bilirubin concentration is raised, usually to between 3 and 4 mg per 100 ml at birth, but occasionally as high as 12 mg. In the latter case some of the bilirubin is likely to be direct-reacting. Less is known about the level of heme pigments, which does not parallel that of bilirubin and may be high when the bilirubin concentration is relatively low. In spite of the high level of bilirubin in the plasma, little escapes into the tissues of the fetus: the intima of the blood vessels is not commonly yellow at birth, and the skin is rarely even faintly jaundiced; the body fluids, on the other hand, and the Wharton's jelly of the cord and the loose connective tissue around the large vessels on the fetal surface of the placenta are usually yellow.

Some information on the development of the pathologic process in the fetus has been obtained by prenatal examination of amniotic fluid. If it is ana-lyzed serially commencing at about 20 weeks, bilirubin and, later, heme pigments may be found. When the latter pigments are present prior to 32 weeks, death is likely to ensue. It is evident that in these cases excessive hemolysis is going on, with the production of much pigment and the excretion of some through the kidney. We may assume that the appearance of heme pigments indicates unusually rapid hemolysis. Even if this is true, we cannot conclude that death is due to hemolysis and the resulting anemia, rather than to some other cause.

Some fetuses develop generalized edema (*hydrops fetalis*) with ascites, occasionally with hydrothorax or hydropericardium. The placenta is also edematous, and hydramnios is present. Edema in the fetus is commonly ascribed to anoxia and cardiac failure. Most, but not all, hydropic liveborn infants have a very low red cell count, a large fraction of the cells being reticulated or nucleated. How much of the apparent anemia is due to excessive hemolysis and how much to dilution of the blood is not clear. The bilirubin concentration in the infant's plasma is raised but is rarely very high.

At birth the infant with erythroblastosis has some Rh antibodies in his plasma, some attached to his red cells, and some in undefined extravascular areas. The titer in cord plasma is usually lower than in the mother's plasma, the ratio varying from 1:1 to about 1:128. There is no evidence that an increased amount of antibody is expressed from the maternal into the fetal circulation during delivery. Destruction of red cells continues after birth, while, as in the normal infant, red cell formation slows down. In most cases the result is a progressive anemia which reaches its nadir at two to six weeks, following which a reticulocytosis occurs with a slow, spontaneous rise in red cell and hemoglobin levels. In some cases blood formation apparently stops completely within a day or two after birth; the red cell count may then fall at a rate of 1,000,000 per mm^3 per day. Occasionally depression of erythropoiesis persists for three or four months.

In the liveborn erythroblastotic infant the plasma bilirubin concentration rises rapidly after birth, increasing by as much as 3 mg per 100 ml per hour in the first hours. The rate of rise is usually nearly constant for 12 to 24 hours, then tapers off, the peak being reached commonly at about 72 hours in the mature infant. In immature infants the curve may continue to rise for three or four days longer. Before bilirubin can be excreted by the liver it must be conjugated in that organ with glucuronic acid through an enzymatic process. Unconjugated bilirubin is synonymous with indirect or indirect-reacting bilirubin, conjugated with direct or direct-reacting. The mechanism of conjugation is incompletely developed at birth, requiring perhaps two or three days in the normal mature infant to become efficient, and five to seven days in an immature one. In the normal newborn with the usual rate of red cell destruction and bilirubin formation this temporary inadequacy of function is evidenced by physiologic jaundice. In the erythroblastotic infant with increased red cell destruction and bilirubin formation this same inadequacy leads rapidly to jaundice, which generally becomes more intense and persists somewhat longer than does physiologic jaundice. Some erythroblastotic patients continue to be jaundiced for several weeks or months; in such infants an obstructive factor is present in the biliary passages, as shown by the fact that a large portion of the bilirubin is direct-reacting or conjugated. Occasionally during the acute phase of the disease the plasma bilirubin concentration may reach a plateau, then rise abruptly.

Bilirubin produced by the cells of the reticuloendothelial system is at first a relatively high concentration in the circulating plasma, but tends to leave the bloodstream rapidly and to establish equilibrium with its concentration in extravascular fluid. This phenomenon is not peculiar to erythroblastotic infants but must be borne in mind in the interpretation of the clinical picture in hemolytic disease of the newborn. Within a day or two after the hemolytic process has passed its peak there is more bilirubin outside the vascular bed than in it. As the level of plasma bilirubin falls, the extravascular bilirubin, which in the acute phase of erythroblastosis fetalis is indirect-reacting or unconjugated, rapidly returns to the bloodstream. Such replenishment of the plasma bilirubin is seen particularly following exchange transfusion.

PATHOLOGY.   Most of the lesions found at autopsy appear to be evidence of: (1) accelerated blood destruction (iron in reticuloendothelial, liver, and kidney cells); (2) accelerated blood formation (expanded areas of hematopoiesis with enlargement of the organs involved, especially spleen and liver); (3) anemia (cardiac hypertrophy, vascular distention, and edema); or (4) hyperbilirubinemia (jaundice and kernicterus). However, some lesions cannot be so explained on the basis of present knowledge; they suggest an active reaction on the part of the fetus which goes far beyond the seemingly simple hematopoietic response to blood destruction. Thus, although the thymus is normal in infants who die of kernicterus, it tends to be small in those who are stillborn and in those who die of anemia or hydrops at birth. Lymphoid tissue everywhere is diminished and the follicles of the spleen are unrecognizable. The adrenals, normal in size in kernicteric infants, are markedly hypertrophied in some of those born with severe anemia. Cells of the fetal cortex are distended with fat in stillborn and hydropic infants, less so in the anemic, scarcely at all in the kernicteric. This lesion has not been described in stillborn fetuses other than those who have suffered from erythroblastosis; we have seen it in infants dying of hydrops and erythroblastemia of unknown origin. In some erythroblastotic infants the islands of Langerhans are hypertrophied. Hemorrhages may be found in the lungs or elsewhere. The bones are often dense; the long bones may have transverse zones of greater and lesser density near their ends; the skull bones may encroach on the fontanels. The bony lesion is not specific.

The Macerated Stillborn Fetus. Since prognosis for future Rh-positive pregnancies is bad once a fetus has died of the disease in utero, proof that a macerated fetus has or has not suffered from erythroblastosis is important. The diagnosis may be made from the following evidence. In gross appearance there are opaque, yellowish white radial streaks in the cortex of the adrenals; the spleen is always relatively heavy, the heart often so, and the thymus is always lighter in weight than normal. Microscopically, the streaks in the adrenals stain with scharlach R or Sudan III, indicating neutral fat; large, young erythroblasts are demonstrable in pulmonary capillaries. Serologically, red cells taken from clots in the large vessels on the fetal surface of the placenta give a positive direct Coombs' test.

Kernicterus; Nuclear Jaundice. The term "kernicterus" was originally applied to the pathologic lesion in the brain of an infant dying with severe jaundice; today it is often applied to the disease process or to the clinical manifestations of the lesion. The surface of the brain is pale yellow. Bright yellow staining may be seen in the hippocampal and adjacent olfactory areas of the cerebral cortex, the subthalamic nuclei of Luys, the globus pallidus, putamen and thalami, roof nuclei, vestibular nuclei, flocculus of the cerebellum, anterior horns of the cord. The yellow pigment is indirect-reacting bilirubin. In children dying after a few months there is no trace of yellow staining. Microscopic changes are rarely found in infants dying in the first 24 hours after birth. On the second day and after, nerve cells in the yellow areas of the brain have pyknotic or degenerated nuclei. In older patients there is marked paucity of nerve cells, loss of medullated nerve fibers, and cellular gliosis.

Pathogenesis of kernicterus. The exact pathogenesis of kernicterus has yet to be elucidated. The basic disturbance is injury of nerve cells in brain and medulla; and whether the injured cells as seen at autopsy are visibly stained or not, several facts point to unconjugated or indirect bilirubin as the material which causes the damage. The pigment in the brain tissue of infants dying of kernicterus between the second and seventh days after birth has been identified as bilirubin by spectrophotometric measurement. Day, Waters, and others have shown that the presence of measurable amounts of bilirubin in the brains of experimental animals interferes with oxygen utilization by cerebral tissue. The fact that nerve cells of the brain of erythroblastotic patients dying within the first day after birth show little or no morphologic evidence of injury may mean either that not enough bilirubin has reached them or that it requires time to show its effect. Strong support is given to the theory of brain damage by indirect bilirubin from the favorable results of timely administration of exchange transfusion. Whenever the plasma concentration of indirect bilirubin has been consistently held below 20 mg per 100 ml in mature infants, while at the same time interfering drugs have been withheld, the incidence of brain damage in erythroblastosis has been kept close to nil. Moreover, kernicterus has appeared in patients with the Crigler-Najjar syndrome who suffer a congenital lack of the enzyme system which normally conjugates bilirubin with glucuronic acid and facilitates its excretion. In these circumstances kernicterus ensues when the plasma concentration of indirect bilirubin has reached a harmful level. On the other hand, it is not possible in the light of existing knowledge to specify a threshold of plasma bilirubin concentration above which brain damage is sure to ensue. Exceptional patients have been observed who survived a plasma indirect bilirubin concentration greater than 40 mg per 100 ml without evidence of injury to the central nervous system.

In order for indirect bilirubin to injure nerve cells, it must migrate from the plasma to the brain; it must cross the blood-brain barrier. Ordinarily the barrier is high enough so that the central nervous system remains intact when the plasma bilirubin concentration stays below about 25 mg per 100 ml, and a rough correlation exists between the level to which the indirect bilirubin rises in the infant's plasma and the probability that he will develop kernicterus. Several factors, however, have the capacity to lower the threshold and to permit kernicterus to appear at lower levels of plasma bilirubin. A facilitating effect of this kind has been suspected in prematurity and clearly demonstrated in bacterial infections such as congenital pneumonia and so-called birth sepsis, and after administration of certain drugs—notably sulfisoxazole (Gantrisin) and certain synthetic forms of vitamin K (Synkavit). Sulfonamide drugs dissociate the bilirubin from the albumin to which it is attached and thus facilitate the transfer of bilirubin across membranes, as Odell has shown. The solubility of indirect bilirubin in lipid material favors its transport across membranes in a manner not well understood. Two or more of these threshold-lowering factors may operate simultaneously, possibly synergistically. Some authorities believe that anoxia or asphyxia per se will lower the blood-brain barrier for indirect bilirubin, but the supporting evidence is not convincing. The fact that heme pigments other than bilirubin are found in the plasma of some patients who later go on to show the typical picture of kernicterus may mean that these substances are capable of damaging nerve cells directly, as claimed by Abelson and Boggs, or may indicate their facilitating action on the transfer of bilirubin, or may be simple concidence.

Kernicterus is not limited to patients with erythroblastosis fetalis but has until recently been attributable more frequently to incompatibility of the D antigen than to any other single factor or group of factors. Zuelzer and Kaplan have described a number of cases which they ascribed to ABO incompatibility. With the popularization of exchange transfusion, kernicterus due to erythroblastosis of all kinds decreased,

while those cases attributable to prematurity and infection did not.

Direct or conjugated bilirubin appears to have no such harmful effect on nerve cells. In addition, it is usually excreted by the kidneys before its concentration in body fluids reaches levels as high as those attained by indirect bilirubin in the plasma of erythroblastotic patients.

SYMPTOMS. If the fetus dies in utero the mother generally experiences no symptoms save the cessation of movement. Occasionally, unusual activity shortly precedes death. If the fetus becomes hydropic, hydramnios also develops, the mother's weight increases rapidly, and she may have abdominal distress. She may herself develop edema, either limited to the legs or generalized, without hypertension and with or without mild albuminuria. The diagnosis may be confirmed by x-ray examination of the fetus in utero: the fetus cannot flex its legs and arms over its fluid-stretched abdomen and assumes the so-called Buddha position; rarely, edema of the scalp throws a halo around the fetal skull; enlargement of the placenta may be demonstrable, as may increased density of the fetal skeleton.

Most liveborn hydropic infants are born between the twenty-eighth and thirty-fourth weeks of gestation, though some are carried to term. The infant is exceedingly pale, the abdomen swollen, and there is general subcutaneous edema. Characteristically the mouth is open, the tongue protruding, but the face may be so distorted by massive edema that a diagnosis of congenital malformation is entertained. Most of these infants make no visible attempt to breathe, dying a few minutes after birth. A few live long enough to be treated.

Infants with severe anemia, with cord blood hemoglobin of 6 g or less per 100 ml, are well developed and may be above average in size, stocky, with heavy jowls, short neck, and broad chest. The abdomen protrudes. There is mild edema. The skin is pale, sometimes faintly yellow, often flecked with hemorrhage. The liver and spleen are palpably, often visibly, much enlarged. There is wide variation in the vigor of these infants immediately after birth; some cry strongly at once, but most lie limp and unmoving, whining feebly, their breathing labored, and their heartbeat rapid and forcible. Their condition may change for the worse in a few minutes. Breathing becomes irregular and gasping; frothy mucus bubbles from the lips; the infants neither move nor cry. Lacking prompt treatment they die.

Nearly all the remaining infants are surprisingly vigorous at birth, including even many with cord blood hemoglobin as low as 7 g per 100 ml. They cry as do other newborn infants. Their color varies depending in part upon the degree of anemia and in part upon the degree of peripheral vasoconstriction or relaxation; many are red or pink at birth, but pale one or two hours later. There is rarely edema, and then of the slightest degree. The spleen may or may not be palpable, in a few cases extending 1 or possibly

2 cm below the rib margin. When the cord plasma bilirubin concentration is less than 4 or 5 mg per 100 ml, jaundice of the skin is not present; above this level there may be a faint trace discernible when the blood is expressed from the skin and the infant examined in white light. The umbilical cord is always yellow if the plasma bilirubin is higher than 3 mg per 100 ml, and may be yellow at slightly lower levels.

This last group of infants lies along a scale from trifling, subclinical disease to disease which, left untreated, may maim or kill. As in the normal infant, the red cell count and the hemoglobin level rise above those of the cord blood a few hours after birth. There may be no appreciable fall for 48 to 96 hours. Thereafter in the milder cases the hemoglobin may diminish by about 50 percent in four to six weeks, to be succeeded by a slow but steady rise. At the other extreme, after the first rise and brief steady state there is a precipitous fall in hemoglobin concentration; fatal anemia may develop in a week. Between these extremes lies a large group whose rate of fall is intermediate and whose developing anemia is masked by jaundice. These are the infants in danger of kernicterus.

If at the height of the jaundice kernicterus develops, symptoms referable to the central nervous system may be seen. These may be no more than somnolence, refusal to suck, a cretinoid, expressionless appearance of the face, or fixed, downward rotation of the eyeball—the "setting sun" sign—or there may be a hardening and rigidity of the muscles, opisthotonus, or rarely convulsions, with or without fever. The Moro reflex is almost always abnormal and often absent. The signs may be fleeting and are easily missed; none of them is specific. Many of the full-term infants with kernicterus die on the third to the fifth day, the prematures on the fifth to the seventh. They are prone to bleed into their lungs in the hours before death, bloody froth oozing from the nose and mouth, while at the same time the plasma bilirubin level falls, sometimes precipitously.

Those infants who survive kernicterus will in time practically all show evidence of brain damage. For a few weeks or even months many of them appear normal. Then they are noticed to be a little slow; they do not hold their heads up as early as they should, do not respond to advances in the normal way. Muscular incoordination and hypertonicity may appear. Finally, in the majority there is fully developed athetoid cerebral palsy. In the most severely damaged, the infant is essentially decerebrate and usually dies before his second birthday; in the months before death he is prone to recurrent bouts of unexplained fever, often with clinical signs simulating meningitis.

The extent of damage and the course that will be followed in the years to come cannot be foretold from the severity of the signs in the first week; some infants with evanescent signs later develop severe palsy, others with major early signs have minor residua. Broadly, the earlier the onset of signs of

kernicterus the worse the prognosis. High-tone deafness is common; in a few survivors of erythroblastosis fetalis, it is the only persisting symptom.

Following intense jaundice, with or without kernicterus, the deciduous teeth may be greenish and their enamel defective.

In a few cases jaundice persists for several weeks or months and then spontaneously disappears. Usually it is a light, muddy yellow, but it may be quite intense. The plasma bilirubin is largely direct-reacting; bilirubin is present in the urine, while the stools are pale. Cirrhosis of the liver has been observed in these children as a late manifestation. Pigment stone in the bile ducts is a rare complication.

DIAGNOSIS. *Foreknowledge.* Erythroblastosis can occur only if an antibody capable of reacting with the cells of the fetus is present in the mother's blood. The presence of such an antibody can and should be known before the birth of the baby; the watchful physician will see to it that the blood of every Rh-negative woman married to an Rh-positive man is adequately examined for antibodies in every pregnancy. The physician will also have the blood of any pregnant woman who has ever had a transfusion examined for antibodies (other than anti-A and anti-B) that react with the red cells of her husband and might therefore react with those of her fetus; and he should do this whether she be Rh-negative or Rh-positive. One who is forewarned of the possibility of disease will be alert to detect it and to treat it if necessary.

Amniocentesis. In the past, serial measurements of the maternal titer of anti-Rh antibody have served as guides to the presence of an affected baby in utero and to the degree of severity. Excessively high titers and sudden increase in the titer have been interpreted as indicating severe disease and imminent intrauterine death and have, together with past history of stillbirths, hydrops, or severe disease, been accepted as indications for early interruption of pregnancy. It has been evident, however, that the correlation between maternal titer and status of the infant is inexact. In some cases high titers have been found in situations where the infant proves to be Rh negative; in reverse, low titers have been found with very severely affected infants. Examination of the amniotic fluid, with quantitative measurement of bilirubin pigments, has proved to be a valuable guide to management during pregnancy. Amniotic fluid is obtained by transabdominal puncture and the fluid examined spectrophotometrically. The optical density is plotted against wavelength throughout the range of 300 to 800 mμ. When the optical density of normal amniotic fluid is so plotted on a logarithmic scale, a straight line is formed. In the presence of bilirubin pigments, however, a bulge in the optical density is found at 450 mμ. The rise in optical density from the straight-line portions of the curve has been found to correlate with the severity of disease in the infants. Detailed studies by Liley, carried out at serial intervals after 28 weeks of gestation, have produced data on the results of amniotic fluid examinations which provide a very valuable guide to the presence of erythroblastosis in the fetus, its severity, and the need for interruption of pregnancy. Bowman and Pollock recently reported a 96.8 percent accuracy in predicting the severity of disease in utero with amniotic fluid examination. These authors recommend that initial amniocentesis be performed at 30 to 32 weeks of gestation. However, if the past history indicates that early intrauterine death may occur, amniocentesis is performed as early as 22 weeks. Indications for amniocentesis include past history of stillbirth or severe disease, a first immunized pregnancy in which the maternal antibody titer exceeds 1:8 in albumin by 32 weeks' gestation, and all second and subsequent pregnancies where the previous Rh-positive infant did not need treatment and in which the titer rises above 1:8 in albumin. Amniocentesis is repeated at 2- to 3-week intervals in order to follow the progress of disease. When the optical density at 450 mμ reaches the serious zone for the gestational age, induction of labor is undertaken, at or after 32 weeks of gestation. Hazards of amniocentesis include fetal hemorrhage, hemoperitoneum, infection, and premature induction of labor.

Clinical Diagnosis. In erythroblastosis diagnosis must go hand in hand with assessment of the degree of disease present and with decision as to the need for treatment. In the delivery room the diagnosis of hydrops is self-evident from the appearance of the infant and the placenta. The latter weighs 2 pounds or more, is pale, exceedingly soft and friable, and exudes much pale, pinkish yellow fluid. The diagnosis of severe anemia too is usually self-evident if one bears in mind what has been said of the clinical picture; the placenta is large, up to 1½ pounds, just a little pale, of normal consistency, and has thick, protruding marginal cotyledons. In the presence of either hydrops or severe anemia the need for treatment is urgent. For the remaining infants the slightly jaundiced cord, the rare faint jaundice of the skin, and the sometimes palpable enlargement of the spleen are the best clinical telltales; the placenta is normal in size and appearance. The combination of a trace of jaundice in the skin at birth or a readily palpable spleen with a positive direct Coombs' test * on the infant's blood provides adequate indication for treatment.

* *The Coombs' Test.* This test, so far as it applies to erythroblastosis, detects the presence of antibody globulin attached to red cells. There are two forms of the test, the direct and the indirect.

The direct test is made on the red cells of the infant. A positive test indicates that maternal antibody globulin is attached to the cells; it does not indicate the specificity of the antibody. Among newborn infants it is strongly positive in those suffering from Rh erythroblastosis of any degree. In Rh-positive infants the test may remain positive up to approximately three months if there are Rh-positive red cells in circulation.

The indirect test is used to demonstrate the presence of antibody in plasma or serum. Appropriate normal cells are exposed to the plasma or serum and the cells then tested for the presence of globulin attached to them. It is a standard method for demonstration and titration of antibodies in pregnant women.

The direct Coombs' test is the most important laboratory test in the diagnosis of erythroblastosis caused by incompatibility with the D antigen; if it is positive the disease is present; if it is negative the disease is absent. It says nothing about the degree of disease or, in itself, about the need for treatment. In the absence of determining clinical signs as given above, the need for treatment will depend on history, on additional laboratory investigation, or on the clinical progress of the infant.

If the mother has had an infant sick with the disease, it is wiser to treat her next Coombs'-positive infant rather than carry the assessment farther or await developments. When there is no such history, one turns, if possible, to the laboratory for guidance. Many centers have made it a rule to treat all Coombs'-positive mature infants whose cord blood hemoglobin concentration is 13.0 g or less per 100 ml and whose cord plasma bilirubin concentration is 3.5 mg or more per 100 ml, and likewise all Coombs'-positive premature infants unless the cord plasma bilirubin level is 1.5 mg or less per 100 ml. The measurement of bilirubin, however, is notoriously unreliable, and in many hospitals it cannot be made.† Under these circumstances one may have to arrive at a decision on the basis of the Coombs' test and the cord blood hemoglobin alone, treating all mature infants who are Coombs'-positive and have a hemoglobin of 13 g or less per 100 ml, and treating all prematures who are Coombs'-positive. If one decides against treatment immediately after birth, a careful watch must be kept on the onset and progress of jaundice and, if possible, on the plasma bilirubin level. Either readily visible jaundice within 12 hours or a plasma bilirubin concentration of 15 mg per 100 ml within 24 hours constitutes indication for immediate treatment. It is not helpful to follow hemoglobin levels during this time; it always rises after birth and usually does not begin to fall appreciably for two or three days.

DIFFERENTIAL DIAGNOSIS. Differential diagnosis includes consideration of the various causes of fetal death, hydrops, anemia, jaundice, and diseases of the central nervous system.

Diagnosis in the stillborn fetus rests with the pathologist and serologist. Hydrops occurs occasionally in the absence of demonstrable blood group incompatibility; in such cases the spleen is small, and the prognosis for future pregnancies is unimpaired. Hydrops also occurs in association with some congenital anomalies.

In the delivery room the newborn infant with severe anemia due to erythroblastosis must be promptly differentiated from one in shock and from one suffering from anemia of hemorrhage, usually concealed. The quickest method of differentiation is palpation of the abdomen; the baby with erythro-

† The distinction between direct and indirect bilirubin is even more unreliable than measurement of the total bilirubin. The physician is advised to consider all bilirubin as indirect in any infant during its first week when he is using the plasma bilirubin level as an indication for or against replacement transfusion.

blastosis has a huge liver and spleen, the others do not. A positive direct Coombs' reaction or the presence of many erythroblasts as well as normoblasts and reticulocytes in the infant's blood will confirm the diagnosis of erythroblastosis, but rarely does the clinical emergency allow sufficient time to wait for a laboratory report. The infant suffering from anemia due to hemorrhage may have many normoblasts and reticulocytes in the blood, but rarely erythroblasts.

Anemia developing soon after birth must be differentiated from congenital hypoplastic anemia (erythrogenesis imperfecta), the anemia of sepsis, and that of hemorrhage. If the anemia is due to erythroblastosis there will be a history of greater than average jaundice in the first week, while a positive direct Coombs' test on the infant's blood will make the diagnosis certain. Red cell morphology may be helpful to some degree in differentiation. The presence of nucleated red cells and reticulocytes rules out hypoplastic anemia and that due to sepsis. On the other hand, such cells are not infrequently absent in the anemia that develops after birth in erythroblastosis, while they are usually present when the anemia is due to hemorrhage; neither their presence nor their absence helps to differentiate between these two conditions.

In the differential diagnosis of jaundice the time of onset is important. The jaundice of erythroblastosis practically always develops in the first 24 hours in full-term infants; in prematures it may not be perceptible until the second day. Physiologic jaundice is rare before the second day. The jaundice of hepatitis, cytomegalic inclusion disease, toxoplasmosis, and nonhereditary hemolytic anemia may be present on the day of birth, whereas that of sepsis, syphilis, familial spherocytosis, and nonhemolytic familial jaundice rarely appears before the latter half of the first week and usually develops later. In congenital absence of the bile ducts and in galactosemia, jaundice is often not noticed until the second week. Differentiation must be by careful history, examination of the patient and his excreta, and appropriate laboratory tests. The Coombs' test is of great importance, being positive in the newborn period only in erythroblastosis.

Beyond the first week or two, erythroblastosis must always be considered in the differential diagnosis of a persisting jaundice. If the onset of the jaundice and the blood group and serologic findings are typical, the jaundice should be considered as due to erythroblastosis until proved otherwise.

Differentiation between kernicterus and other diseases of the central nervous system may be called for in the neonatal period or in later infancy or childhood. Kernicterus is the presumptive diagnosis in an intensely jaundiced newborn exhibiting the above-described clinical signs, or in an older patient with cerebral palsy or high-tone deafness who has a history of severe neonatal jaundice. If a patient has both athetoid cerebral palsy and high-tone deafness it is practically certain that these are the sequelae of neonatal kernicterus. In any suspected case confirmatory evidence may be sought in the presence of an antibody in the blood of the patient's mother which agglutinates the patient's red cells.

PROGNOSIS. Prognosis must be considered from three points of view: for a present fetus, for a future fetus, and for an infant already born.

As concerns the fetus, in the first Rh-positive pregnancy in which maternal antibodies are shown to be present one may expect about 70 percent of the infants to have mild disease requiring no treatment, 25 percent to require treatment, and 5 percent to be stillborn or have hydrops. The expectation for subsequent Rh-positive fetuses is in part related to the degree of disease in those already affected. If the maximum degree of disease in any previous infant has been mild, that in future infants is likely to be mild; if it has been moderately severe, that in future infants may be the same or may be more severe; severe disease—i.e., extreme anemia at birth, hydrops, or stillbirth—is almost always followed by hydrops or stillbirth if the pregnancy is allowed to go to term. Exceptionally an infant with mild erythroblastosis will be born to a woman who has had a stillborn or hydropic erythroblastotic fetus.

Antibody titer, if measured at regular intervals during pregnancy, may be of prognostic value. The earlier the antibody is present in a first sensitized pregnancy, the less good the prognosis; in subsequent pregnancies it is always present from the very beginning of pregnancy. In the course of pregnancy the titer may rise, fall, or remain constant. If it is constant at a low level a liveborn infant at term may be expected. If constant at a high level, fetal death or marked disease at term may be expected if the fetus is Rh-positive. A rising titer nearly always indicates that the fetus is Rh-positive, an abrupt rise that it is dangerously ill. A steadily falling titer usually indicates that the fetus is Rh-negative, certainly that it will not be seriously ill. It is not possible to give figures for high, low, or intermediate titers since the measurement of titer varies from one laboratory to another.

The prognosis for an infant already born depends on the degree of disease and on the treatment given. Nearly all those with hydrops die within a few minutes after birth. If they live longer they may be treated successfully. Infants with severe anemia at birth are also likely to die if treatment is not instituted at once. Apart from those with hydrops, the overall death rate should not be more than 2 percent for term infants; for prematures, particularly those delivered early because a previous infant had been stillborn or had hydrops, the mortality will be higher. Treatment has almost eliminated kernicterus, although it still occurs occasionally under even the most careful observation and with the most painstaking treatment: If under careful observation no neurologic signs appear in the first week, the prognosis for normal development is excellent.

TREATMENT. If possible, a woman expected to give birth to an infant suffering from erythroblastosis should be delivered in a hospital with a staff experienced in the disease. Only in this way are infants suffering from hydrops or from severe anemia at birth likely to be saved, while disease in the remainder can be assessed and dealt with with greater certainty. The general care of the infant does not differ materially from that of others of the same weight. Breast feeding, far from being contraindicated, should be recommended as for any infant. No drug is required as a rule.

The general indications for treatment have been given under diagnosis and assessment. The aim of specific treatment is to prevent death from heart failure on the first day of life in the severely anemic, death or brain damage from hyperbilirubinemia on the second to the seventh day, and death from acute anemia in the second or third week.

In the past it was assumed that elevated venous pressure in infants with severe anemia at birth was indicative of an expanded blood volume associated with actual or impending cardiac failure. Several authors have recommended immediate withdrawal of 30 to 70 ml of blood in order to lower the venous pressure to 8 to 10 cm of water. However, studies by Phibbs, Johnson, and Tooley have shown that the elevated venous pressure observed in some severely anemic infants is not associated with an expanded blood volume and that lowering of the venous pressure may follow correction of acidosis alone. These findings indicate that severely anemic infants require careful evaluation and that caution must be exercised before deciding to withdraw substantial amounts of blood. In the presence of severe respiratory distress and elevated venous pressure, it is recommended that 10 to 20 ml of blood be withdrawn and then a partial exchange transfusion be performed using packed red cells, in an attempt to correct the anemia. Attempts to correct acidosis are also made at this time. Complete exchange transfusion is delayed until the infant's general condition improves. Digitalization has been recommended by some authors, but its value in the circumstances described is doubtful.

Replacement, exchange, or substitution transfusion—the terms are synonymous—for the prevention of kernicterus was largely developed and popularized by Diamond and his associates. By 1950 their results suggested that if exchange transfusion were properly used kernicterus could be prevented in almost all cases. Mollison and Walker in controlled trials carried out in several centers in Great Britain fully confirmed the value of exchange transfusion.

Details of this method of treatment will be found in articles and in monographs on erythroblastosis. Rh-negative blood is generally used, although a few advocate Rh-positive blood. With Rh-negative blood the intent is to replace a large proportion of the patient's sensitized Rh-positive red cells with Rh-negative cells which the anti-Rh antibody cannot attack, thus minimizing red cell destruction and consequent bilirubin formation. At the same time some of the bilirubin already formed and some of the circulating antibody are removed. To be effective, treat-

ment must be given before the brain has been damaged.

Even though it is still not certain that unconjugated bilirubin is the sole noxious agent that damages the brain, the level of this pigment in the plasma is, at present, the best guide to treatment. Except in the presence of other heme pigments, damage is very unlikely to occur if the level is kept below 20 mg per 100 ml. It is easier to keep it below this concentration if the transfusion is given while the bilirubin is still low. Transfusion is less effective when the plasma bilirubin level is high because, as shown by Brown and her associates, most of the bilirubin is outside the vascular system, and the little removed by transfusion is quickly replaced from extravascular areas.

It is common practice to perform a "two-volume" exchange (170 ml/kg), that is to say, to use two times as much donor blood as the estimated blood volume (85 ml/kg) of the infant. For infants with severe anemia at birth, particularly if they are premature, two and sometimes three replacements of one to one and a half volumes each in the first 24 hours may be required. A two-volume exchange is calculated to remove 85 percent of the blood which was in circulation at the beginning of the transfusion, and will lower the level of circulating bilirubin and anti-Rh antibody by about 60 percent.

Following exchange transfusion the level of plasma bilirubin almost always rises again. This is due to a combination of inflow of extravascular bilirubin, of continued release and destruction of the infant's own red cells, of death of the effete cells in the donor blood, and probably other undetermined factors. In most cases this rise tapers off rapidly and the subsequent level does not reach 20 mg per 100 ml. In those cases in which it does reach this level, or in which the projection of the rising curve indicates that it will go well above 20, exchange transfusion is usually repeated. It is sometimes difficult to know when to stop, the rebound of bilirubin occurring again and again. Projection of the bilirubin curve based on measurements made at short intervals is the best indicator; if from these repeated determinations it appears that the peak will be little more than 20, replacement may be withheld.

Exchange transfusion involves certain risks and is not to be undertaken lightly. Even in the hands of experienced operators deaths due to the procedure itself occur occasionally, while in the hands of the beginner it carries a very appreciable risk. As with any prolonged procedure involving intravenous injection, the chance of introducing infection cannot be completely eliminated. Unless care is taken during passage and manipulation of the plastic catheter in the umbilical vein, its tip may readily be introduced into the heart and cause disturbance of the heartbeat; as a rule, such mechanical irritation evokes nothing more than a few inconsequential extrasystoles, but in rare instances ventricular fibrillation has been produced. The risk of overloading the infant's circulation can be kept to a minimum by measuring periodically the venous pressure in the ductus venosus or the inferior vena cava and removing blood as indicated; by keeping an accurate record of the amount of blood exchanged, making certain that the total volume removed always exceeds the total volume injected; or by carrying out the transfusion with the infant on a sensitive balance so that one can guard against excessive injection of blood. When bank blood is used, as is usually the case, it must be not older than one week and free from hemolysis, to insure that the material injected will not have a dangerously high concentration of potassium. In order to protect the infant's plasma from depletion of its ionized calcium by combination with excess of citrate in the donor blood, it is customary to inject intravenously and very slowly 1 ml of 10 percent calcium gluconate solution for each 100 ml of blood exchanged. If heparinized donor blood is used, this last precaution may be omitted.

A single, simple transfusion of packed, group-compatible, Rh-negative red cells is occasionally called for in the second or third week because of the development of anemia. It should be given only if the blood hemoglobin level falls below 7 g per 100 ml or if the infant is not thriving. There is no point in trying to keep the infant's hemoglobin level within the normal range by repeated transfusions.

Intrauterine Transfusion. In an attempt to salvage severely erythroblastotic infants who would die in utero before 32 to 34 weeks of gestation, Liley developed the technique of intrauterine transfusion. In this procedure Rh-negative red cells are introduced into the peritoneal cavity of the fetus in utero. Based upon history and findings on amniocentesis which indicate that intrauterine death will occur before 34 weeks, intrauterine transfusion is performed at 28 to 31 weeks of gestation, or even earlier, and is repeated at intervals of 1½ to 3 weeks until the infant is delivered at 34 to 35 weeks of gestation. Exchange transfusion is usually required after delivery. Intrauterine transfusion is a difficult and potentially hazardous procedure which should be undertaken only by those experienced in its use. There seems little doubt that in experienced hands some infants who would otherwise have died in utero have been saved. Further experience with the technique and its results should provide valuable knowledge.

Other Forms of Treatment. ACTH and adrenal corticosteroids have been used with and without exchange transfusion. They have not been proved to be beneficial. Cremer and others have shown that white light decreases cutaneous jaundice and may lower the plasma bilirubin level, but the effect is insignificant in severe erythroblastosis. Odell and coworkers have supplemented exchange transfusion by a priming injection of plasma albumin given intravenously an hour or two before the exchange. Their results indicated a substantial increase in the amount of bilirubin removed.

PREVENTION. Recent research and well-controlled clinical studies appear to justify the hope that erythroblastosis may be prevented and almost totally eliminated. The studies followed evidence which demonstrated that passage of fetal cells into the maternal circulation occurred to the greatest extent at the time of delivery, and that sensitization of Rh-negative women occurred most commonly after the delivery of the first Rh-positive infant. Furthermore, it was known that group A, Rh-positive infants produced less sensitization of group O, Rh-negative mothers than of group A, Rh-negative mothers. The explanation was that the group A infant cells were rapidly destroyed in the group O mothers' circulation and, therefore, did not stimulate antibody formation. Attempts to mimic the latter situation by the injection of potent anti-Rh antibody to Rh-negative mothers within 36 hours after delivery provided the rationale for the studies on the prevention of maternal immunization. While it now seems likely that the injected antibody works by directly inihibiting antibody production rather than by destroying the antigen-containing cells, there is little doubt that the technique has had striking success in reducing the frequency of Rh sensitization of Rh-negative women and, consequently, in their Rh-positive offspring. At present the recommended procedure is to inject one vial of anti-Rh antibody (RhoGam, Ortho) intramuscularly within 72 hours after each delivery in all Rh-negative women who have not previously been immunized.

ERYTHROBLASTOSIS DUE TO BLOOD FACTORS OTHER THAN D (RH$_o$). Shortly after the Rh blood group system was discovered, several additional systems involved in hemolytic disease were brought to light. More than 20 antigen-antibody combinations in these systems have been proved to cause erythroblastosis, but most of them are exceedingly rare. Apart from D in the Rh system and A and B in the ABO system (which will be described separately later), the commonest antigens associated with the disease are c, E, and C of the Rh system, in that order, and K of the Kell system. When disease follows sensitization by the K antigen, it is likely to be severe; fetal death and hydrops are common.

The Rh System. Two systems of nomenclature are in use, reflecting two immunologic and genetic hypotheses. In one (Fisher-Race, or CDE) there are thought to be sets of three main, and some subsidiary, genes at closely linked loci, each gene controlling development of an antigen; in the other (Wiener, or Rh-Hr) there are thought to be multiple allelic genes at a single locus, each such gene controlling the inheritance of what is termed an agglutinogen, which in turn carries qualities termed factors. The distinctions are not for the uninitiated. Some of the correpondences between the two systems are set out in Table 4.

In the CDE section of Table 4 each gene combination above the horizontal line differs from its place-mate below the line in possessing D, the Rh-positive factor; all four of the combinations above the dividing line are Rh-positive. The common gene complexes in a mixed white population are CDe

TABLE 4. *Units of Inheritance, Antigens, Agglutinogens, Factors, and Reacting Antibodies in the Rh System**

	According to CDE Hypothesis			According to Rh-Hr Hypothesis		
Abbreviation	Genes and Antigens or Agglutinogens	Reacting Antibodies	Genes	Corresponding Agglutinogens	Characterizing Factors	Reacting Antibodies
R_1	CDe	anti-C, D, and e	R_1	Rh_1	Rh_0 rh' hr"	Correspond with the Factors
R_2	cDE	anti-c, D, and E	R_2	Rh_2	Rh_0 rh" hr'	
R_0	cDe	anti-c, D, and e	R_0	Rh_0	Rh_0 rh' hr"	
R_z	CDE	anti-C, D, and E	R_z	Rh_z	Rh_0 rh' rh"	
R'	Cde	anti-C anti-e	r'	rh'	rh' hr"	
R"	cdE	anti-c anti-E	r"	rh"	rh" hr'	
r	cde	anti-c anti-e	r	rh	hr' hr"	
R_y	CdE	anti-C anti-E	r_y	rh_y	rh' rh"	

*Since 1958 genes in the CDE nomenclature have been distinguished from antigens and agglutinogens by italic type.

(41 percent), cDE (14 percent), and cde (39 percent); all others, 6 percent. Every person carries a pair of gene complexes; the frequencies of the pairs are set out in Table 5.

Just as an Rh-negative woman lacking the antigen D may be sensitized by this antigen and produce anti-D antibody, so a woman lacking the antigen c or E—for example, one who is of genotype CDe.CDe or CDe.Cde—may be sensitized by either or both of these antigens and produce anti-c or anti-E or both; equally, a woman of genotype cDE.cDE or cDE.cdE may produce anti-C or, rarely, anti-e or both. Disease resulting from these antibodies usually is not severe.

If an *Rh-positive* woman gives birth to an infant with erythroblastosis, treatment by exchange transfusion usually cannot be safely postponed until the causative antibody is identified. In these circumstances group O, Rh-positive blood is nearly always safe to use. If time permits, an attempt may be made to select a donor whose cells do not react with the mother's serum by the indirect Coombs' technique.

ABO Erythroblastosis. For some years after it became known that an anti-Rh antibody could cause erythroblastosis there was doubt that antibodies of the ABO system could do so. It is now clear that antibodies of many group O women and of some A_2 women, though not of A_1 or B women, do commonly pass the placental barrier and become attached to the cells of the fetus if it is group A_1 or B, but that disease of clinical importance is infrequent.

This form of hemolytic disease of the newborn then occurs in group A_1 or B infants of group O mothers, very rarely in B or A_1 infants of group A_2 mothers. The patient, often a first baby, is usually seen because of early and progressive jaundice. Anemia is rarely more than minimal; the percentage of nucleated red cells and of reticulocytes in the infant's peripheral blood is generally little if any beyond the normal range. The spleen and liver are almost never palpably enlarged. Upon occasion the infant may be faintly jaundiced at birth, but the plasma bilirubin concentration does not then necessarily tend to rise above physiologic levels. An assured diagnosis is often difficult to reach. The following laboratory findings together confirm the diagnosis: first, free antibody in the infant's serum that reacts strongly by the

TABLE 5. *Genotype Frequencies in an Average Mixed White Population (Adapted from Race and Sanger.)*

Antigenic Structure	Abbreviation	Percent	Zygosity
cde.cde	rr	15	Homozygous Rh-negative (dd)
CDe.CDe	R_1R_1	16 ⎫	
CDe.cDE	R_1R_2	11 ⎬ 29	Homozygous Rh-positive (DD)
cDE.cDE	R_2R_2	2 ⎭	
CDe.cde	R_1r	32 ⎫ 43	Heterozygous Rh-positive (Dd)
cDE.cde	R_2r	11 ⎭	
	R'r, R"r, R'R"	2	Homozygous Rh-negative (dd)
All other	R_1R_0, R_2R_0, R_1R_z etc.	5	Homozygous Rh-positive (DD)
	$R_0r, R_0R', R_0R"$ etc.	6	Heterozygous Rh-positive (Dd)

Total Rh-negative 17%; total positive 83%. Homozygous positive 34%; heterozygous positive 49%. Of all Rh-positive 40% are monozygous, 60% heterozygous.

indirect Coombs' technique with adult cells of the same group—i.e., an A_1 infant with the disease will have anti-A in his serum which reacts with adult A_1 cells, and a B infant will have anti-B which reacts with adult B cells; second, many more microspherocytes than normal in the blood; third, an increased osmotic fragility; fourth, the direct Coombs' test applied to the infant's cells gives a negative result by standard methods, a weakly positive result by specially sensitive methods. Estimation of the anti-A or anti-B titer in the mother's serum is not helpful; disease may occur with almost any concentration of antibody and no disease in the presence of exceedingly high concentrations. On the other hand, failure of the mother's serum to hemolyze adult red cells of the same group as the infant's argues strongly against the diagnosis. The serologic reactions of the infant's cells and serum are rarely demonstrable after the fourth day.

Differential diagnosis is the same as for jaundice due to Rh incompatibility. The greatest difficulty is likely to arise in distinguishing disease due to ABO incompatibility from hereditary spherocytosis or disease due to some of the rare antigen-antibody combinations.

Rapidly developing anemia is rare in ABO erythroblastosis and the need for exchange transfusion is usually determined by the rate of rise of serum bilirubin. As with the erythroblastosis, exchange transfusion should be performed to prevent the serum bilirubin from reaching 20 mg/100 ml. Since the rate of rise in bilirubin concentration is usually fairly slow, serial measurements of serum bilirubin will most often identify the infant who will need exchange transfusion, and it is only the rare baby who will require treatment immediately after birth. Most authors recommend exchange transfusion if the bilirubin reaches 12 mg/100 ml in the first 24 hours of life. Recently phototherapy has been employed to control the hyperbilirubinemia in those infants whose bilirubin concentration is rising more slowly. In such circumstances phototherapy is generally begun when the bilirubin reaches 10 mg/100 ml. Careful monitoring of bilirubin concentration must be done in order to prevent potentially dangerous levels from developing. If, despite phototherapy, a rise of bilirubin concentration to 20 mg/100 ml seems probable, exchange transfusion should be carried out.

The blood used in exchange transfusion for ABO erythroblastosis should be group O, Rh-type specific, or group O-Rh negative. The same principles as described for exchange transfusion in Rh erythroblastosis should be followed.

Succeeding infants in a family in which one baby has had ABO erythroblastosis will not be more seriously affected than was the first one and may be less so.

REFERENCES

HEREDITARY SPHEROCYTOSIS

Erlandson, M. E., Schulman, I., and Smith, C. H. Studies on congenital hemolytic syndromes; rates of destruction and production of erythrocytes in hereditary spherocytosis. Pediatrics, 23:462, 1959.

Gasser, C. Aplasia of erythrohopoiesis; acute and chronic erythroblastopenias or pure (red cell) aplastic anaemias in childhood. Pediat. Clin. N. Amer., p. 445, May, 1957.

Jacob, H. S. Hereditary spherocytosis: a disease of the red cell membrane. Seminars Hemat., 2:139, 1965.

—— and Jandl, J. H. Increased cell membrane permeability in the pathogenesis of hereditary spherocytosis. J. Clin. Invest., 43:1704, 1964.

Shapiro, C. M., Josephson, A. M., Rozengvaig, S., and Kauffman, A. Hereditary spherocytosis in the neonatal period. J. Pediat., 50:308, 1957.

Stamey, C. C., and Diamond, L. K. Congenital hemolytic anemia in the newborn; relationship to kernicterus. Amer. J. Dis. Child., 94:616, 1957.

Young, L. E. Hereditary spherocytosis. Amer. J. Med., 18:486, 1955.

—— Izzo, M. J., and Platzer, R. F. Hereditary spherocytosis; clinical, hematologic and genetic features in 28 cases, with particular reference to the osmostic and mechanical fragility of incubated erythrocytes. Blood, 6:1073, 1951.

—— Platzer, R. F., Evin, D. M., and Izzo, M. J. Hereditary spherocytosis: observations on the role of the spleen. Blood, 6:1099, 1951.

HEREDITARY ELLIPTOCYTOSIS

Cutting, H. O., McHugh, W. J., Conrad, F. G., and Marlow, A. A. Autosomal dominant hemolytic anemia characterized by ovalocytosis; a family study of seven involved members. Amer. J. Med., 39:21, 1965.

De Grunchy, G. C., Loder, P. B., and Hennessy, I. V. Haemolysis and glycolytic metabolism in hereditary elliptocytosis. Brit. J. Haematol., 8:168, 1962.

Ozer, L., and Mills, G. C. Elliptocytosis with haemolytic anaemia. Brit. J. Haemat., 10:468, 1964.

Weiss, I. H. Hereditary elliptocytosis with hemolytic anemia; report of six cases. Amer. J. Med., 35:455, 1963.

CONGENITAL STOMATOCYTOSIS

Lock, S. P., Smith, R. S., and Hardisty, R. M. Stomatocytosis: a hereditary red cell anomaly associated with haemolytic anaemia. Brit. J. Haematol., 7:303, 1961.

Miller, G., Townes, P. L., and MacWhinney, J. B. A new congenital hemolytic anemia with deformed erythrocytes (? "stomatocytes") and remarkable susceptibility of erythrocytes to hemolysis in vitro. Pediatrics, 35:906, 1965.

Zarkowsky, H. S., Oski, F. A., Sha 'afi, R., Shohet, S. B., and Nathan, D. G. Congenital hemolytic anemia with high sodium, low potassium red cells. New Eng. J. Med., 278:593, 1968.

ERYTHROCYTE ENZYME ABNORMALITIES

Baughan, M. A., Valentine, W. N., Paglia, D. E., Ways, P. O., Simons, E. R., and DeMarsh, Q. B. Hereditary hemolytic anemia associated with glucosephosphate isomerase (GPI) deficiency—a new enzyme defect of human erythrocytes. Blood, 32:236, 1968.

Beutler, E. Drug-induced blood dyscrasias. III. Hemolytic anemia. J.A.M.A., 189:143, 1964.

——— Glucose-6-phosphate dehydrogenase and nonspherocytic congenital hemolytic anemia. Seminars Hemat., 2:91, 1965.

Bowdler, A. J., and Prankerd, T. A. J. Studies in congenital nonspherocytic haemolytic anaemias with specific enzyme defects. Acta Haemat., 31:65, 1964.

De Leeuw, N. K. M., Shapiro, L., and Lowenstein, L. Drug-induced hemolytic anemia. Ann. Int. Med., 58:592, 1963.

Jandl, J. H. Symposium on disorders of the red cell. Amer. J. Med., 41:657, 1966.

Kirkman, H. N., and Riley, H. D., Jr. Congenital nonspherocytic hemolytic anemia. Amer. J. Dis. Child., 102:313, 1961.

Necheles, T. F., Boles, T. A., and Allen, D. M. Erythrocyte glutathione-peroxidase deficiency and hemolytic disease of the newborn infant. J. Pediat., 72:319, 1968.

——— Finkel, H. E., Sheehan, R. G., and Allen, D. M. Red cell pyruvate kinase deficiency. The effect of splenectomy. Arch. Int. Med., 118:75, 1966.

——— Maldonado, N., Barquet-Chediak, A., and Allen, D. M. Homozygous erythrocyte glutathione-peroxidase deficiency: Clinical and biochemical studies. Blood, 33:164, 1969.

Newton, W. A., Jr., and Bass, J. C. Glutathione sensitive chronic non-spherocytic hemolytic anemia. Amer. J. Dis. Child., 96:501, 1958.

Oort, M., Loos, J. A., and Prins, H. K. Hereditary absence of reduced glutathione in the erythrocytes—a new clinical and biochemical entity? Vox Sang., 6:370, 1961.

Oski, F. A., and Diamond, L. K. Erythrocyte pyruvate kinase deficiency resulting in congenital non-spherocytic hemolytic anemia. New Eng. J. Med., 269:763, 1963.

Paglia, D. E., Valentine, W. N., Baughan, M. A., Miller, D. R., Reed, C. F., and McIntyre, O. R. An inherited molecular lesion of erythrocyte pyruvate kinase. Identification of a kinetically aberrant isozyme associated with premature hemolysis. J. Clin. Invest., 47:1929, 1968.

Prins, H. K., Oort, M., Loos, J. A., Zürcher, C., and Beckers, T. Congenital nonspherocytic hemolytic anemia, associated with glutathione deficiency of the erythrocytes. Hematologic, biochemical, and genetic studies. Blood, 27:145, 1966.

Schneider, A. S., Valentine, W. N., Hattori, M., and Heins, H. L., Jr. Hereditary hemolytic anemia with triosephosphate isomerase deficiency. New Eng. J. Med., 272:229, 1965.

Tanaka, K. R., and Valentine, W. N. Pyruvate kinase deficiency. *In* Beutler, E., ed., Hereditary Disorders of Erythrocyte Metabolism. New York, Grune and Stratton, Inc., 1968, p. 229.

Tarui, S., Kono, N., Nasu, T., and Nishikawa, M. Enzymatic basis for the coexistence of myopathy and hemolytic disease in inherited muscle phosphofructokinase deficiency. Biochem. Biophys. Res. Commun., 34:77, 1969.

Valentine, W. N., Hsieh, H. S., Paglia, D. E., Anderson, H. M., Baughan, M. A., Jaffé, E. R., and Garson, O. M. Hereditary hemolytic anemia associated with phosphoglycerate kinase deficiency in erythrocytes and leukocytes. A probable X-chromosome-linked syndrome. New Eng. J. Med., 280:528, 1969.

——— Oski, F. A., Paglia, D. E., Baughan, M. A., Schneider, A. S., and Naiman, J. L. Hereditary hemolytic anemia with hexokinase deficiency. Role of hexokinase in erythrocyte aging. New Eng. J. Med., 276:1, 1967.

SICKLE-CELL ANEMIA

Diggs, L. W. The crisis in sickle cell anemia; hematologic studies. Amer. J. Clin. Path., 26:1109, 1956.

Erlandson, M. E., Schulman, I., and Smith, C. H. Studies on congenital hemolytic syndromes; rates of destruction and production of erythrocytes in sickle cell anemia. Pediatrics, 25:629, 1960.

Hughes, J. G., and Carroll, D. S. Salmonella osteomyelitis complicating sickle cell disease. Pediatrics, 19:184, 1957.

Ingram, V. M. Gene mutations in human haemoglobin: the chemical differences between normal and sickle cell haemoglobin. Nature, 180:326, 1957.

Jenkins, M. E., Scott, R. B., and Baird, R. L. Studies in sickle cell anemia. XVI. Sudden death during sickle cell anemia crises in young children. J. Pediat., 56:30, 1960.

Keitel, H. G., Thompson, D., and Itano, H. A. Hyposthenuria in sickle cell anemia; a reversible renal defect. J. Clin. Invest., 35:998, 1956.

Kunz, H. W., Pratt, E. I., Mellin, G. W., and Cheung, M. W. Impairment of urinary concentration in sickle cell anemia. Pediatrics, 13:352, 1954.

Pauling, L., Itano, H. A., Singer, S. J., and Wells, J. C. Sickle cell anemia, a molecular disease. Science, 110:543, 1949.

Scott, R. B. Sickle cell anemia; pathogenesis and treatment. Pediat. Clin. N. Amer., 9:649, 1962.

——— Banks, L. O., Jenkins, M. E., and Crawford, R. P. Studies in sickle cell anemia; clinical manifestations of sickle cell anemia in children. J. Pediat., 39:460, 1951.

Watson, R. J., Burko, H., Megas, H., and Robinson, M. The hand-foot syndrome in sickle cell disease in young children. Pediatrics, 31:975, 1963.

HEMOGLOBIN C DISEASE

Charache, S., Conley, C. L., Waugh, D. F., Ugoretz, R. J., and Spurrell, J. R. Pathogenesis of hemolytic anemia in homozygous hemoglobin C disease. J. Clin. Invest., 46:1795, 1967.

Kaplan, E., Zuelzer, W. W., and Neel, J. V. Further studies on hemoglobin C; the hematologic effects of hemoglobin C alone and in combination with sickle cell hemoglobin. Blood, 8:735, 1953.

Ranney, H. M. Observations on the inheritance of sickle

cell hemoglobin and hemoglobin C. J. Clin. Invest., 33:1634, 1954.

River, G. L., Robbins, A. B., and Schwartz, S. O. S-C hemoglobin; a clinical study. Blood, 18:385, 1961.

Thomas, E. D., Motulsky, A. G., and Walters, D. H. Homozygous hemoglobin C disease; report of a case with studies on the pathophysiology and neonatal formation of hemoglobin C. Amer. J. Med., 18:832, 1955.

OTHER ABNORMAL HEMOGLOBINS

Conley, C. L., and Charache, S. Mechanisms by which some abnormal hemoglobins produce clinical manifestations. Seminars Hematol., 4:53, 1967.

Fairbanks, V. F., Opfell, R. W., and Burgret, E. O., Jr. Three families with unstable hemoglobinopathies (Köln, Olmsted and Santa Ana) causing hemolytic anemia with inclusion bodies and pigmenturia. Amer. J. Med., 46:344, 1969.

Lehmann, H., and Huntsman, R. G. Man's Haemoglobins. Philadelphia, J. B. Lippincott Co., 1968.

Ranney, H. M. Clinically important variants of human hemoglobin. New Eng. J. Med., 282:144, 1970.

THE THALASSEMIA SYNDROMES

Caffey, J. Cooley's anemia; a review of the roentgenographic findings in the skeleton. Amer. J. Roentgen., 78:381, 1957.

Conley, C. L., Weatherall, D. J., Richardson, S. N., Shepard, M. K., and Charache, S. Hereditary persistence of fetal hemoglobin; a study of 79 affected persons in 15 Negro families in Baltimore. Blood, 21:261, 1963.

Pearson, H. A., Shanklin, D. R., and Brodine, C. R. Alpha-thalassemia as cause of nonimmunological hydrops. Amer. J. Dis. Child., 109:168, 1965.

Second Conference on the Problems of Cooley's Anemia. Ann. N.Y. Acad. Sci., Vol. 165, 1969.

Shields, G. A., Wethers, D., Gavis, G., and Watson, R. J. Hemoglobin-S-thalassemia disease. Amer. J. Dis. Child., 91:485, 1956.

Singer, K., Josephson, A. M., Singer, L., Heller, P., and Zimmerman, H. S. Studies of abnormal hemoglobins; hemoglobin S-thalassemia disease and hemoglobin C-thalassemia disease in siblings. Blood, 12:593, 1957.

Smith, C. H., Erlandson, M. E., Schulman, I., and Stern, G. Hazard of severe infections in splenectomized infants and children. Amer. J. Med., 22:390, 1957.

――― Erlandson, M. E., Stern, G., and Schulman, I. The role of splenectomy in the management of thalassemia. Blood, 15:197, 1960.

――― Erlandson, M. E., Stern, G., and Hilgartner, M. W. Postsplenectomy infection in Cooley's anemia; an appraisal of the problem in this and other blood disorders with consideration of prophylaxis. New Eng. J. Med., 266:737, 1962.

Weatherall, D. J. The Thalassemia Syndromes. Oxford, Blackwell Scientific Publications, 1965.

AUTOIMMUNE ACQUIRED HEMOLYTIC ANEMIA

Crosby, W. H., and Rappaport, H. Autoimmune hemolytic anemia; analysis of hematologic observations with particular reference to their prognostic value; a survey of 57 cases. Blood, 12:42, 1957.

Dacie, J. V. The autoimmune haemolytic anaemias. Amer. J. Med., 18:810, 1955.

Dameshek, W., Schwartz, R., and Oliner, H. Current concepts in autoimmunizations: an interpretive review. Blood, 17:775, 1961.

Githens, J. H., and Hathaway, W. E. Autoimmune hemolytic anemia and the syndrome of hemolytic anemia, thrombocytopenia and nephropathy. Pediat. Clin. N. Amer., 9:619, 1962.

Karaklis, A., Valaes, T., Pantelakis, S. N., and Doxiadis, S. A. Thymectomy in an infant with autoimmune haemolytic anaemia. Lancet, 2:778, 1964.

Laski, B., Wake, E. J., Bain, H. W., and Gunson, H. H. Autohemolytic anemia in young infants. J. Pediat., 59:42, 1961.

Miller, G., Shumway, C. N., Jr., and Young, L. E. Autoimmune hemolytic anemia. Pediat. Clin. N. Amer., p. 429, May, 1957.

Oski, F. A., and Abelson, N. M. Autoimmune hemolytic anemia in an infant. J. Pediat., 67:752, 1965.

Ritz, M. D., and Haber, A. Auto-immune hemolytic anemia in a 6-week old child. J. Pediat., 61:904, 1962.

Schwartz, R., and Dameshek, W. The treatment of autoimmune hemolytic anemia with 6-mercaptopurine and thioguanine. Blood, 19:483, 1962.

Shulman, N. R. Mechanism of blood destruction in individuals sensitized to foreign antigens. Trans. Ass. Amer. Physicians, 76:72, 1963.

DRUG-INDUCED HEMOLYTIC ANEMIAS WITH POSITIVE COOMBS' TEST

Dacie, J. V. The Haemolytic Anaemias. New York, Grune and Stratton, Inc., 1967, Part IV, p. 1078.

Huguley, C. M., Jr., Lea, J. W., Jr., and Butts, J. A. Adverse hematologic reactions to drugs. Progr. Hemat., 5:105, 1966.

Lo Buglio, A. F., and Jandl, J. H. Nature of the alphamethyldopa red-cell antibody. New Eng. J. Med., 276:658, 1967.

Molthan, L., Reidenberg, M. M., and Eichman, M. F. Positive direct Coombs' test due to cephalothin. New Eng. J. Med., 277:123, 1967.

Petz, L. D., and Fudenberg, H. H. Coombs-positive hemolytic anemia caused by penicillin administration. New Eng. J. Med., 274:171, 1966.

Robinson, M. G., and Foadi, M. Hemolytic anemia with positive Coombs' test association with isoniazid therapy. J.A.M.A., 208:656, 1969.

MISCELLEANOUS EXTRACORPUSCULAR CAUSES OF HEMOLYTIC ANEMIA

Bull, B. S., Rubenberg, M. L., Dacie, J. V., and Brain, M. C. Microangiopathic haemolytic anaemia; Mechanisms of red-cell fragmentation; in vitro studies. Brit. J. Haemat., 14:643, 1968.

Crosby, W. H. Hypersplenism. Ann. Rev. Med., 13:127, 1962.

Gilman, P. A., and Zinkham, W. H. Severe idiopathic pulmonary hemosiderosis in the absence of clinical or radiologic evidence of pulmonary disease. J. Pediat., 75:118, 1969.

Ham, T. H., Shen, S. C., Fleming, E. M., and Castle, W. B. Studies on the destruction of red blood cells—

thermal injury: action of heat in causing increased spheroidicity, osmotic and mechanical fragilities and hemolysis of erythrocytes; observations on the mechanisms of destruction of such erythrocytes in dogs and in a patient with a fatal thermal burn. Blood, 3:373, 1948.

Hsia, D. Y-Y., and Gellis, S. C. Portal hypertension in infants and children. Amer. J. Dis. Child., 90:290, 1955.

Jandl, H. J., Jacobs, H. S., and Daland, G. E. Hypersplenism due to infection; a study of 5 cases manifesting hemolytic anemia. New Eng. J. Med., 264:1063, 1961.

Miller, D. R., Baehner, R. L., and Diamond, L. K. Paroxysmal nocturnal hemoglobinuria in childhood and adolescence. Pediatrics, 39:675, 1967.

Oski, F. A., and Barness, L. Vitamin E deficiency: A previously unrecognized cause of hemolytic anemia in the premature infant. J. Pediat., 70:211, 1967.

Repetto, G., Lisboa, C., Emparaza, E., Ferretti, R., Neira, M., Etchart, M., and Meneghello, J. Idiopathic pulmonary hemosiderosis. Pediatrics, 40:24, 1967.

Ritchie, J. H., Fish, M. B., McMasters, V., and Grossman, M. Edema and hemolytic anemia in premature infants. A vitamin E deficiency syndrome. New Eng. J. Med., 279:1185, 1969.

Sigler, A. T., Forman, E. N., Zinkham, W. H., and Neill, C. A. Severe intravascular hemolysis following surgical repair of endocardial cushion defects. Amer. J. Med., 35:467, 1963.

Tuffy, P., Brown, A. K., and Zuelzer, W. W. Infantile pyknocytosis, a common erythrocyte abnormality of the first trimester. Amer. J. Dis. Child., 98:227, 1959.

Wallerstein, R. O., and Aggeler, P. M. Acute hemolytic anemia. Amer. J. Med., 37:92, 1964.

ERYTHROBLASTOSIS FETALIS

Abelson, N. M., and Boggs, T. R., Jr. Plasma pigments in erythroblastosis fetalis. I. Spectrophotometric absorption patterns. Pediatrics, 17:452, 1956.

Allen, F. H., Jr., and Diamond, L. K. Erythroblastosis Fetalis—Including Exchange Transfusion Technique. Boston, Little, Brown & Co., 1957.

Boggs, T. R., Jr., and Abelson, N. M. Plasma pigments in erythroblastosis fetalis. II. The level of heme pigment; an early guide to management of erythroblastosis fetalis. Pediatrics, 17:461, 1956.

Bowman, J. M., and Friesen, R. F. Multiple intraperitoneal transfusions of the fetus for erythroblastosis fetalis. New Eng. J. Med., 271:703, 1964.

—— and Pollock, J. M. Amniotic fluid spectrophotometry and early delivery in the management of erythroblastosis fetalis. Pediatrics, 35:815, 1965.

Brown, A. K., Zuelzer, W. W., and Robinson, A. R. Studies in hyperbilirubinemia. II. Clearance of bilirubin from plasma and extravascular space in newborn infants during exchange transfusion. Amer. J. Dis. Child., 93:274, 1957.

Clarke, C. A., and Sheppard, P. M. Prevention of Rhesus haemolytic disease. Lancet, 2:343, 1965.

Cremer, R. J., Perryman, P. W., and Richards, D. H. Influence of light on the hyperbilirubinaemia of infants. Lancet, 1:1094, 1958.

Day, R. L. Inhibition of brain respiration in vitro by bilirubin: reversal of inhibition by various means. Proc. Soc. Exp. Biol. Med., 85:261, 1954.

Finn, R., Clarke, C. A., Donohoe, W. T. A., McConnell, R. B., Heppard, P. M., Lehane, D., and Kulke, W. Experimental studies on the prevention of Rh hemolytic disease. Brit. Med. J., 1:1486, 1961.

Freda, V. J., Gorman, G. J., and Pollack, W. Successful prevention of experimental Rh sensitization in man with an anti-Rh gamma-globulin antibody preparation; a preliminary report. Transfusion, 4:26, 1964.

—— Gorman, J. G., and Pollack, W. Rh factor: prevention of isoimmunization and clinical trials on mothers. Science, 151:828, 1966.

Gorman, J. G., and Freda, V. J. Prevention of Rh hemolytic disease. Progr. Hemat., 6:121, 1969.

Hsia, D. Y-Y., Allen, F. H., Jr., Gellis, S. S., and Diamond, L. K. Erythroblastosis fetalis; studies of serum bilirubin in relation to kernicterus. New Eng. J. Med., 247:668, 1952.

Liley, A. W. Intrauterine transfusion of foetus in haemolytic disease. Brit. Med. J., 2:1107, 1963.

—— The use of amniocentesis and fetal transfusion in erythroblastosis fetalis. Pediatrics, 35:836, 1965.

Mollison, P. L., and Cutbush, M. Haemolytic disease of the newborn; criteria of severity. Brit. Med. J., 1:123, 1949.

Odell, G. B. Studies in kernicterus. I. The protein binding of bilirubin. J. Clin. Invest., 38:823, 1959.

—— Cohen, S. N., and Gordes, E. H. Administration of albumin in the management of hyperbilirubinemia by exchange transfusions. Pediatrics, 30:613, 1962.

Phibbs, R. H., Johnson, P., and Tooley, W. H. Circulatory changes in newborns with erythroblastosis fetalis with and without hydrops. Atlantic City, N.J., Proc. Soc. Ped. Res., April 1967, p. 10 (abstract).

Waters, W. J. The prevention of bilirubin encephalopathy. J. Pediat., 52:559, 1958.

—— and Porter, E. Indications for exchange transfusion based upon the role of albumin in the treatment of hemolytic disease of the newborn. Pediatrics, 33:749, 1964.

Zipursky, A., Pollock, J., Yeow, R., Israels, L. G., and Chown, B. Studies on the pathogenesis and prevention of Rh-isoimmunization in pregnant women. J. Pediat., 69:902, 1966 (abstract).

Zuelzer, W. W., and Kaplan, E. ABO heterospecific pregnancy and hemolytic disease; study of normal and pathologic variants. IV. Pathologic variants. Amer. J. Dis. Child., 88:319, 1954.

17.4
ANEMIAS DUE TO BLOOD LOSS

GEORGE R. HONIG and
IRVING SCHULMAN

The symptoms and laboratory findings in the various anemias secondary to loss of blood are influenced by both the rapidity and the duration of hemorrhage.

In infancy and childhood, acute hemorrhage may result from trauma, from primary bleeding disorders such as idiopathic thrombocytopenic purpura or hemophilia, from rupture of esophageal varices in association with portal hypertension, or from complications of such diseases as leukemia or malignant tumors in which bone marrow metastases have taken place. The first symptoms of acute blood loss of severe degree are those of shock; until adjustment of circulatory dynamics takes place, which may require a number of hours, the red blood cell count and hemoglobin may remain at normal levels. In time, as extravascular fluid enters the circulation, the manifestations of anemia—pallor, fatigue, weakness, dyspnea, tachycardia, and, in some instances, congestive heart failure—appear. When loss of blood is less sudden, there is no shock phase, and symptoms of anemia are the first to appear. The anemia is normocytic and normochromic in type. A rising reticulocyte count within a relatively short period after the onset of hemorrhage gives evidence of increased red blood cell regeneration. Within the first few days the reticulocyte count may reach a peak of 20 percent or more. If severe loss of blood has occurred, the infant or child will require immediate attention. Whole blood transfusions should be given without delay. As much as 20 ml per kilogram can be safely administered. If red cell transfusions are used, 15 ml per kilogram is generally recommended.

Chronic loss of blood may be the cause of severe anemia in both infants and children. It is commonly associated with lesions of the gastrointestinal tract, particularly polyps of the large bowel and esophageal varices. It may be also caused by intestinal parasitism. Examination of the stools for occult blood should be considered part of the routine work-up for any anemia of the iron-deficiency type, whether or not a history of poor dietary iron intake can be obtained. The onset of symptoms is insidious, and anemia may progress to a severe degree before the patient comes to the attention of the physician. Even then pallor may be the only presenting symptom. It is remarkable how great is the degree of compensation even when the hemoglobin falls to levels as low as 3 g percent. In infants the spleen may be slightly enlarged, but in older children it is usually of normal size. The anemia is typical of that due to deficiency of iron. The red blood cells are microcytic and hypochromic, and anisocytosis and poikilocytosis are marked. The reticulocyte count is low unless iron or large amounts of iron-containing foods have been given recently. The bone marrow shows normoblastic hyperplasia. Correction of the anemia is obviously dependent upon elimination of the underlying cause of blood loss. Immediate return of the red blood cell and hemoglobin levels to near normal figures by means of blood transfusions is not essential and should await completion of the diagnostic investigation. Provided the cause of blood loss has been eliminated, an adequate response of the anemia to the oral administration of iron is to be expected; only if the anemia is particularly severe or if special circumstances, such as the need for immediate surgery, exist is it necessary to use blood transfusions.

Other Red Cell Disorders

17.5
POLYCYTHEMIA AND ERYTHROCYTOSIS

GEORGE R. HONIG and
IRVING SCHULMAN

An increased total circulating red cell mass may occur during childhood as a primary disorder or may be secondary to a number of unrelated conditions.

Polycythemia vera (primary polycythemia, Vaquez-Osler disease), as described in adults, is extremely rare in children. It is thought to be a panmyeloproliferative disorder, but the cause is unknown. The condition results in marked plethora, splenomegaly, thrombosis, and hemorrhage and is characterized by elevated values for all of the formed elements of the blood and a hyperplastic bone marrow. The course of polycythemia vera is chronic and progressive. The usual treatment is phlebotomy or administration of radioactive phosphorus.

Primary erythrocytosis is a more common childhood disorder and differs from polycythemia vera in several respects. It is benign, frequently familial, and although characterized by an increased total red cell mass, it is not accompanied by elevation of white blood cells or platelets. Affected children are usually asymptomatic except for their ruddy appearance but may have minor manifestations, such as headache, dizziness, lethargy, or easy fatigability. Slight splenomegaly may be present. The disorder may be discovered by the finding of an elevated hemoglobin, hematocrit, or red cell count on a routine examination. Measurement of total circulating red cell mass is recommended, since some instances of elevated hemoglobin or hematocrit values may not be associated with true erythrocytosis. The bone marrow is normal. Although the absence of leucocytosis and thrombocytosis excludes the possibility of polycythemia vera, confirmation of the diagnosis requires investigation of possible causes of secondary erythrocytosis.

Since most children with primary erythrocytosis are asymptomatic, treatment usually is unnecessary, but phlebotomy may be useful in relieving minor manifestations. Few long-term observations are available, but the benign nature of the disorder in affected adults suggests that the prognosis is good.

Secondary erythrocytosis may result from a variety of disorders including cardiac or pulmonary abnormalities leading to oxygen desaturation; methemoglobinemia; uterine, renal, hepatic, or brain tumors; Cushing's disease; and in association with an abnormal hemoglobin (Chesapeake). Such disorders should be ruled out by appropriate studies before making the diagnosis of primary erythrocytosis.

REFERENCES

Abildgaard, C. F., Cornet, J. A., and Schulman, I. Primary erythrocytosis. J. Pediat., 63:1072, 1963.

Auerback, M. L., Wolff, J. A., and Mettier, S. R. Benign familial polycythemia of childhood. Report of two cases. J. Pediat., 21:54, 1958.

Knock, H. L., and Githens, J. H. Primary erythrocytosis of childhood. Amer. J. Dis. Child., 100:189, 1960.

Diseases of the White Blood Cells

IRVING SCHULMAN

The total number of white cells in the circulating blood and the relative proportions of the individual cell types in the differential count are valuable aids in the diagnosis of many childhood illnesses and important guides in treatment and prognosis. Both the total and differential cell counts vary with age, and therefore interpretation of results must be made against the background of the normal values for the age of the patient. During the first three days of life the total white count is high, averaging 20,000/mm³. During this period granulocytes comprise 55 to 70 percent of the cells, and immature forms, including metamyelocytes and myelocytes, are readily found. By two weeks of age, however, the total cell count normally falls to about 12,000/mm³, immature granulocytes disappear, and a reversal between the proportions of granulocytes and lymphocytes takes place. The normal total white cell count falls slowly during early childhood, reaching an average of about 8,000/mm³ by the fourth year of life. The relative proportion of granulocytes rises gradually, and it is not until two years of life that the percentage of granulocytes and lymphocytes equalizes. Not until after the fourth year does a clear-cut predominance of granulocytes become evident.

Granulocytes, which include the neutrophilic, eosinophilic, and basophilic leucocytes, are produced in the bone marrow through orderly maturation from undifferentiated precursors, a process believed to require from 6 to 10 days. A large pool of mature neutrophils exists in the marrow and constitutes a reserve equaling 20 to 25 times the number of blood neutrophils which can be released if needed. In the circulation neutrophils are found in the blood itself, but an equal number, in equilibrium with the circulating cells, are located along the inner surfaces of capillaries and venules (marginal pool). This pool may be mobilized, in situations of stress, without requiring additional release of cells from the marrow. The granulocytes, which are motile and phagocytic, and whose granules contain a variety of proteolytic enzymes, play a major role in response to infection and tissue injury. They accumulate at the site of infection or tissue injury where they phagocytize bacteria and other foreign particles which are then digested by enzymes released by rupture of the granules, now known to be pockets of enzymes (lysosomes). While the granulocytes themselves die in the process, they release enzymes and bactericidal materials into the tissues which are required for control of infection and ultimate healing. Neutrophilic leucocytosis may occur in response to a variety of stresses but most commonly as a result of bacterial infections with cocci. Together with an increase in total white cell count there is an increase in percentage of neutrophils, appearance of immature granulocytes, and a reduction in eosinophils and lymphocytes. During recovery the immature cells decrease, the total white count falls, and the percentage of neutrophils returns to normal levels. Early in the recovery phase from acute infections a moderate monocytosis appears and later eosinophilia and lymphocytosis. In addition to its occurrence in pyogenic infections, neutrophilic leucocytosis is seen in burns, acidosis, hemolysis, hemorrhage, poisoning, anoxia, infarction, and the recovery phase after leucopenia. Severe infection causes changes not only in the number of neutrophils but in their appearance. "Toxic granulation" refers to the larger, more basophilic granules which appear in neutrophils in severe infection. In very severe infection, particularly with septicemia, vacuolization of neutrophils may be seen as well. Overwhelming infections, particularly in small infants, may paradoxically induce neutropenia.

Infants and children tend to release immature granulocytes into the circulation in response to infection and other stimuli, listed above, more readily than adults. Occasionally the total white count may reach such high levels (over 50,000/mm³) and the shift to the left may be so marked that leukemia may be suggested. These leukemoid reactions may usually be distinguished from leukemia by the absence of anemia, thrombocytopenia, hepatosplenomegaly, and lymphadenopathy. Furthermore, the leucocyte alkaline phosphatase is high in leukemoid reactions while virtually absent in granulocytic leukemia.

Lymphocytes are produced in the lymph nodes, spleen, thymus, tonsils, Peyer's patches of intestine, bone marrow, and lymphocytic foci widely scattered throughout the body. It is now generally accepted that the lymphatic structures of the body are formed from lymphocytes which take origin in the thymus and seed to the other areas early in embryonic life. The small, mature lymphocytes found in the peripheral blood are of two types, though morphologically indistinguishable. A small population has a life-span of 3 to 4 days, while the larger proportion has a very long life-span of 100 to 200 days. The lymphocytes are intimately involved with immunologic competence and with the development of delayed hypersensitivity. These cells are involved with immunity at the tissue level, while the plasma cells are responsible for synthesis of circulating gamma globulin and, therefore, humoral immunity. Sex-linked agammaglobulinemia is associated with a moderate lymphopenia and hypoplasia of lymphoid tissue. The so-called Swiss type of agammaglobulinemia which stems from thymic agenesis is associated with alymphocytosis and virtual absence of lymphatic tissue throughout the body. Increases in lymphocytes in the peripheral blood are usually relative and occur in situations where there is a decrease in granulocytes. This is most common in a wide variety of viral infections, particularly rubella, measles, chickenpox, roseola infantum, influenza, but also in enteric bacterial infections such as typhoid and paratyphoid fevers. Absolute increases in lymphocytes are found in infectious lymphocytosis, infectious mononucleosis, tuberculosis, and pertussis. In the course of viral infections large, young lymphocytes appear in the circulation in small numbers and may suggest infectious mononucleosis. The fact that the total white count is not elevated and that the large lymphocytes are few in number helps to distinguish the two conditions.

Eosinophils represent normally 1 to 4 percent of the total white cells. Increases occur in allergic disorders, parasitic infestation, particularly with dog and catariaris (*Toxocara canis* or *cati*), during the recovery phase of infections, following radiation, and as a genetically determined familial trait. Increases in eosinophils may also be found in granulocytic leukemia and Hodgkin's disease.

Basophils number normally less than 0.5 percent of the total white count. They contain histamine and heparin and apparently play some role in allergic reactions. They are increased in granulocytic leukemia, in recovery from some infections, and after radiation and splenectomy.

Monocytes derive from cells of the reticuloendothelial system and normally number 5 to 10 percent of the total leucocyte count. They are phagocytic cells which can ingest and digest a variety of bacteria and chemical substances, particularly lipids. Monocytes increase during the recovery phase of acute infections, in active tuberculosis, subacute bacterial endocarditis, Hodgkin's disease, and various lipoidoses such as Niemann-Pick disease. In the latter disorder lipid-containing monocytes may be seen in the peripheral blood. Striking increases in monocytes may occur during dissemination of tuberculosis.

17.6
LEUCOPENIAS

IRVING SCHULMAN

Leucopenia is said to exist when the total white count is below the lower limit of normal for the age of the patient, usually below 4,000/mm^3. With very few exceptions, leucopenias result from decrease in the number of neutrophils and, therefore, are more properly termed *neutropenias*. These may be based upon failure of production due to impaired maturation, to marrow damage or to replacement, or to increased destruction of the neutrophils after delivery to the circulation. The latter may have an immunologic basis or result from increased sequestration of the leucocytes, as in splenic neutropenia.

As indicated in earlier discussion, transient leucopenia may occur in the course of a variety of infections, particularly of viral origin. In these situations the decrease in circulating neutrophils is rarely severe enough to lead to symptoms. Leucopenia also occurs as one facet of overall marrow failure, as in aplastic or hypoplastic anemia, leukemia, or metastatic disease of the marrow. A variety of disease states have been recognized in which there is isolated decrease in neutrophils and in which the levels reached are low enough to cause impairment of resistance to bacterial infections and of appropriate inflammatory responses. These have included acute, chronic, and recurrent varieties, some of which are obviously genetically determined, while others are acquired. With most, the exact mechanisms leading to the neutropenia are still unclear.

Drug-Related Neutropenias

As the number of drugs available for clinical use has increased, the list of agents capable of inducing granulocytopenia in recipients has been extended steadily. Some drugs will produce neutropenia in all recipients provided the dose and duration of administration are sufficient. Included in this group are the cytotoxic agents employed in treatment of leukemia and lymphomas (6-mercaptopurine, amethopterin, nitrogen mustards, azathioprine, vinca alkaloids). With a variety of other drugs now in general use, only a small percentage of recipients will develop neutropenia irrespective of the dose and duration of treatment. It is likely that more than one mechanism is involved in the pathogenesis of the various drug-related neutropenias.

With agranulocytosis due to aminopyrine and its derivatives there is no longer any doubt that the basic mechanism is immunologic. There is good evidence that the drugs combine with a serum protein to form a complex which is antigenic to some individuals. The antibody formed becomes attached to the leucocytes which then become agglutinated and destroyed when antigen is introduced. Thus in aminopyrine granulocytosis minute amounts of the drug will induce fulminating destruction of circulating white cells, within hours, in patients who have become sensitized.

With other drugs, primarily the phenothiazines and thiouracil derivatives, neutropenia occurs more gradually and there is no evidence of immunization. The individuals who develop neutropenia from such agents are believed to handle the drugs metabolically in a different manner from those who can take the drugs with impunity. While the aminopyrine drugs produce rapid destruction of circulating white cells, agents such as the phenothiazines and antithyroid drugs are believed to cause neutropenia by gradual destruction of white cell precursors in the marrow.

Some drugs now known to cause neutropenia may induce their effect through different mechanisms in different individuals. Drugs which have been identified as being associated with leucopenia are as follows: *tranquilizers* (chlorpromazine and other phenothiazines); *antipyretics and analgesics* (aminopyrine, dipyrone, and other amidopyrine derivatives); *sulfonamides; antithyroid drugs* (thiouracil and derivatives, carbimazole, methimazole), *anticonvulsants* (trimethadione [Tridione], diphenylhydantoin sodium [Dilantin]; *chloramphenicol; others* (phenylbutazone, gold, dinitrophenol, tolbutamide).

The distinction between those drugs which cause neutropenia by an immunologic mechanism and those which do not is of more than academic interest. In the former group (e.g., aminopyrine and dipyrone) agranulocytosis occurs as a sudden rapidly progressive event, is not dose or time related, and therefore even frequent blood counts during treatment will not serve to identify the patient in danger. With the more slowly acting agents progressive neutropenia may be detected in time to stop the offending agents before symptoms appear.

While all forms of severe neutropenia may be regarded as agranulocytosis, the term historically has usually been applied to the syndrome characterized by the acute onset of chills, fever, prostration, necrotizing ulceration of the mucous membranes of the mouth, throat, and elsewhere, in association with marked granulocytopenia and a very high mortality. This syndrome was recognized in 1922, and by 1934 it was clearly evident that it resulted from the use of aminopyrine. With appreciation of this relationship the use of aminopyrine decreased throughout the world, as did the incidence of agranulocytosis. During the past 10 years, however, agranulocytosis has reappeared in the United States, and deaths among children have been reported with increasing frequency. This reappearance has resulted from the use of dipyrone (Pyralgan), an antipyretic which is the sodium-sulfonate derivative of aminopyrine. This

agent has apparently achieved widespread popularity because it is an effective antipyretic which may be given parenterally. However, the danger of agranulocytosis is so great that use of such agents in children must be condemned. The treatment of agranulocytosis involves prompt cessation of the offending drug and the use of antibiotics to control infection until the granulocytes return.

Periodic (Cyclic) Neutropenia

This rare disorder is characterized by the regular development of marked neutropenia, usually at 21-day intervals but occasionally with shorter or longer cycles. The cyclic episodes of neutropenia are believed to result from disappearance of myeloid elements from the marrow which return when recovery from a cycle ensues, usually in about 10 days. Coincident with the neutropenia, patients demonstrate fever, oral mucous membrane ulcerations, frequently furunculosis, and other types of infection. The syndrome may begin in infancy or childhood and persists throughout life. The cause is unknown.

Chronic Neutropenias

A variety of chronic neutropenias have been described in childhood. Some appear to be genetically determined, and instances of both recessive and dominant modes of inheritance have been described. In other cases no hereditary pattern has been discernible. Most of the affected patients demonstrate increased susceptibility to infection, particularly in the hereditary forms which tend to appear in early infancy (infantile genetic agranulocytosis). In more benign varieties the patients appear able to increase their blood granulocyte count in response to infection and have a relatively mild course. In some of the cases with chronic benign granulocytopenia, spontaneous remissions have occurred. The entire group is rather ill-defined, and the underlying mechanisms leading to the granulocytopenia (failure of production, increased destruction) are still unclear in most instances.

Neonatal Agranulocytosis

Granulocytopenia occurring in the neonatal period in successive siblings has been described. The evidence suggested isoimmunization of the mother to the infant's leucocytes. Recovery occurred in 3 to 4 weeks.

Splenic Neutropenia

Enlargement of the spleen due to various causes may lead to neutropenia due, apparently, to increased sequestration of leucocytes in the enlarged organ.

Anemia and thrombocytopenia frequently accompany the leucopenia. In such cases the terms secondary splenic neutropenia or secondary hypersplenism are commonly applied. Cases have been reported with splenomegaly and neutropenia of unknown cause (primary splenic neutropenia), in which the hematologic abnormality has been cured by splenectomy. This diagnosis should be made with great care and with considerable reluctance, particularly since splenectomy in childhood may be followed by increased susceptibility to infection.

Neutropenia in Pancreatic Insufficiency

Shwachman and co-workers have described neutropenia, anemia, and thrombocytopenia in infants with pancreatic insufficiency, diarrhea, and failure to thrive but with normal sweat electrolytes. Marrow hypoplasia appeared to be the underlying cause of the pancytopenia.

Chediak-Higashi Syndrome

This disorder, which is transmitted as an autosomal recessive trait, is characterized by the presence of large blue to green granules in the cytoplasm of granulocytes and lymphocytes. Affected patients demonstrate depigmentation of skin, photophobia, excessive sweating, decreased production of tears, hepatosplenomegaly, and lymphadenopathy. There are progressive granulocytopenia and increased susceptibility to infection. Pathologically, histiocytic infiltration of lymph nodes, spleen, and brain, suggesting malignant lymphoma, has been found.

Disorders of Leucocyte Function

Specific disorders of leucocyte function which lead to recurrent infections have been identified. The first of these to be described was *chronic granulomatous disease,* a syndrome characterized by recurrent suppurative infections with bacteria of low virulence and ubiquitous distribution in man, such as *Staphylococcus aureus, Staphylococcus epidermidis, Serratia marcescens,* and *Aerobacter.* Associated with the suppurative infection is chronic granuloma formation. The most common clinical manifestations are lymphadenopathy, hepatosplenomegaly, recurrent pneumonitis, osteomyelitis, pleural effusion, and visceral abscess formation. Affected patients have been found to have normal humoral immunity and normal delayed hypersensitivity. The total leucocyte count responds appropriately to infection, and phagocytosis by the leucocytes is normal. The basic defect appears to lie in the impaired ability of the polymorphonuclear leucocytes (PMN's) to kill and digest bacteria after phagocytosis. Associated with the defect in bacterio-

cidal capacity of the PMN's are impaired respiration, NADH oxidase activity, and diminished hydrogen peroxide formation in response to phagocytosis. These metabolic abnormalities provide the basis for a sensitive test to identify the disorder, since the leucocytes of affected patients fail to reduce the dye nitro-blue tetrazolium to blue formazan during phagocytosis.

Most of the reported cases have been in boys, and family studies as well as results of a quantitative nitro-blue tetrazolium test have indicated that the disorder is usually transmitted as an X-linked recessive trait. However, studies of several cases reported in girls suggest that the condition may also be transmitted as an autosomal recessive trait.

A second type of leucocyte dysfunction leading to recurrent infection has been termed the *"lazy-leucocyte syndrome."* Affected patients exhibit recurrent stomatitis, otitis, gingivitis, and low grade fever. Severe peripheral neutropenia exists in the face of normal numbers of mature PMN's in the marrow. As in chronic granulomatous disease, humoral and cellular immunity and phagocytosis are all normal. In addition, in this disorder, bacteriocidal activity of the leucocytes is also normal. The only functional abnormality demonstrated thus far is an impaired random mobility of the PMN's and decreased response to chemotaxis. The basic defect appears to be an inability to release and mobilize neutrophils in response to bacterial stimuli. The disorder has been reported in both boys and girls.

17.7
ACUTE INFECTIOUS LYMPHOCYTOSIS

IRVING SCHULMAN

This disease was first described as a clinical entity by Smith in 1941. It is characterized by a mild clinical course with accompanying lymphocytosis of the peripheral blood.

ETIOLOGY. The disease appears to be contagious as well as infectious. Institutional outbreaks have been reported. Marked lymphocytosis may be found in asymptomatic patients on hospital wards, where known cases have occurred, or in asymptomatic members of families of children with the disease. To date no viral or bacterial agent has been isolated as the cause of the condition. The majority of cases have been reported in children.

SYMPTOMS. Many patients are entirely asymptomatic. In others, varied complaints have been reported. Gastrointestinal symptoms such as vomiting, diarrhea, or abdominal pain may occur. Fever is usually slight or absent. Symptoms of upper respiratory infection have been observed in some patients at the onset of the disease. A morbilliform eruption has been reported in one case, and in several others signs simulating central nervous system disease were noted. Even when symptoms are present, manifestations are generally of short duration, subsiding in a few days. Enlargement of liver, spleen, or lymph nodes is rare.

The characteristic finding is an absolute increase in the number of lymphocytes in the peripheral blood. The total white blood cell count is generally greater than 40,000. White blood cell counts over 100,000 have been reported. As the increase in white blood cells is the result of an absolute increase in lymphocytes, the lymphocyte percentage is high, in most cases being greater than 70 percent. The lymphocytes are small in size and normal in appearance. Anemia and thrombocytopenia do not occur. The heterophil agglutinin titer is normal. Apart from an increase in the percentage of lymphocytes, bone marrow is normal.

DIAGNOSIS. From the hematologic point of view the disease must be differentiated from acute leukemia, infectious mononucleosis, and lymphocytosis accompanying certain infections, particularly pertussis. Acute leukemia may be suspected initially, but the mildness of the clinical course, lack of splenic or lymph node enlargement, and absence of anemia or thrombocytopenia serve to distinguish the two conditions. Moreover, bone marrow examination fails to reveal the characteristics of acute leukemia. The normal appearance of the lymphocytes in the blood smear, as well as the normal sheep cell agglutination titer, differentiates this condition from infectious mononucleosis. Absence of the characteristic clinical symptoms of pertussis helps to distinguish acute infectious lymphocytosis from this disease.

In cases with abdominal manifestations, marked lymphocytosis should warn against erroneous diagnosis of an acute surgical condition.

PROGNOSIS. Clinical manifestations are of short duration, and the prognosis excellent. The lymphocytosis may persist for many weeks and in a few reported cases has lasted several months.

TREATMENT. Symptomatic therapy is the only treatment indicated.

Infectious Mononucleosis

This disease is discussed in the chapter on infectious diseases (Sec. 14.30).

REFERENCES

LEUCOPENIAS AND LYMPHOCYTOSIS

Cartwright, G. E., Athens, J. W., and Wintrobe, M. M. The kinetics of granulopoiesis in normal man. Blood, 24:780, 1964.

Cronkite, E. P., and Fliedner, T. M. Granulocytopoiesis. New Eng. J. Med., 270:1347, 1403, 1964.

deVaal, O. M., and Seynhaeve, V. Reticular dysgenesia. Lancet, 2:1123, 1959.

Donohue, W. L. Alymphocytosis. Pediatrics, 11:129, 1953.

Gitlin, D., Vawter, G., and Craig, J. M. Thymic alymphoplasia and congenital aleukocytosis. Pediatrics, 33:184, 1964.

Huguley, C. M. Drug induced blood dyscrasias. In Disease-a-Month. Chicago, Year Book Publishers, October, 1963.

Huguley, C. M., Jr. Agranulocytosis induced by dipyrone; a hazardous antipyretic and analgesic. J.A.M.A., 189:938, 1964.

Kauder, E., and Mauer, A. M. Neutropenias of childhood. J. Pediat., 69:147, 1966.

Kostmann, R. Infantile genetic agranulocytosis. Acta Paediat., 45(Suppl. 105):1, 1956.

Krill, C. E., Jr., and Mauer, A. M. Congenital agranulocytosis. J. Pediat., 68:361, 1966.

—— Smith, H. D., and Mauer, A. M. Chronic idiopathic granulocytopenia. New Eng. J. Med., 270:973, 1964.

Lang, J. E., and Cutting, H. O. Infantile genetic agranulocytosis. Pediatrics, 35:596, 1965.

Page, A. R., Berendes, H., Warner, J., and Good, R. A. The Chediak-Higashi syndrome. Blood, 20:330, 1962.

—— and Good, R. A. Studies on cyclic neutropenia; a clinical and experimental investigation. Amer. J. Dis. Child., 94:623, 1957.

Payne, R. Neonatal neutropenia and leukoagglutinins. Pediatrics, 33:194, 1964.

Shwachman, H., Diamond, L. K., Oski, F. A., and Khaw, K-T. The syndrome of pancreatic insufficiency and bone marrow dysfunction. J. Pediat., 65:645, 1964.

Smith, C. H. Infectious lymphocytosis. Amer. J. Dis. Child., 62:231, 1941.

—— Acute infectious lymphocytosis; specific infection; report of four cases showing its communicability. J.A.M.A., 125:342, 1944.

Zuelzer, W. W. "Myelokathexis"—a new form of chronic granulocytopenia. New Eng. J. Med., 270:699, 1964.

—— and Bajoghli, M. Chronic granulocytopenia in childhood. Blood, 23:359, 1964.

DISORDERS OF LEUCOCYTE FUNCTION

Baehner, R. L., and Nathan, D. G. Quantitative nitroblue tetrazolium test in chronic granulomatous disease. New Eng. J. Med., 278:971, 1968.

Bridges, R. A., Berendes, H., and Good, R. A. A fatal granulomatous disease of childhood. The clinical, pathological and laboratory features of a new syndrome. Amer. J. Dis. Child., 97:387, 1959.

Holmes, B., Quie, P. G., Windhorst, D. B., and Good, R. A. Fatal granulomatous disease of childhood. An inborn abnormality of phagocytic function. Lancet, 2:1225, 1966.

Miller, M. E., Oski, F., and Harris, M. B. Lazy-leukocyte syndrome. A new disorder of neutrophil function. Lancet, 1:665, 1971.

Quie, P. G. Chronic granulomatous disease of childhood. Advances Pediat., 16:287, 1969.

17.8
ACUTE LEUKEMIA

JOANN M. CORNET

Acute leukemia is characterized by a rapid, uncontrolled and abnormal proliferation of leucocytes which, untreated, leads invariably to a fatal outcome.

ETIOLOGY. At the present time the cause of human leukemia is unknown. Although viral etiology has been unequivocally established in avian and murine leukemias, and numerous reports of viruslike particles seen by electron microscopy in human leukemic tissues have appeared, etiologic proof of human leukemogenic viruses is lacking. Despite evidence suggested by the reported occasions of increased incidence within certain families, and the description of geographic leukemic "clusters," the fact remains that neither vertical nor horizontal transmission of human leukemia has been demonstrated.

The influence of such factors as ionizing radiation, chemical agents, and genetic influences must also be considered. Studies of atomic bomb survivors and patients heavily radiated for ankylosing spondylitis indicate that radiation, in sufficient dosage, is leukemogenic for man. The leukemogenic potential of intrauterine radiation and repeated or prolonged diagnostic procedures is uncertain and precise threshold dosages remain to be defined. No chemical carcinogens have been identified for childhood leukemia as with chronic benzol exposure in adults or phenylbutazone administration to elderly patients with arthritis. Retrospective studies on drugs administered during pregnancy to women whose children later developed leukemia have been negative; prospective studies, however, might be enlightening. Interest in the possible role of genetic background in leukemogenesis has stemmed from the following observations: (1) occasional reports of leukemia occurring in sibships; (2) the increased likelihood (1:5) of leukemia developing in the monozygous twin within weeks or months after the co-twin develops the disease; (3) the recognition of a significant increase in frequency of leukemia developing in children with Down's syndrome (trisomy 21 or G trisomy); (4) the increased incidence of leukemia and lymphoma in children with known genetically determined diseases such as congenital agammaglobulinemia either alone or in association with ataxia-telangiectasia, Fanconi's anemia, and Bloom's syndrome; (5) reports of cytogenetic abnormalities in leukemic children without congenital abnormalities; (6) demonstration of an abnormal chromosomal (Ph^1 or Philadelphia chromosome) configuration in 85 percent of patients with the adult form of chronic myelogenous leukemia (this deletion of the long arm of the chromo-

some occurs on the G or 21 group, the same site of abnormality as in Down's syndrome). Whether the genetic abnormalities are acquired as a result of leukemogenic influences or are inherited and thus make the host more susceptible to these influences is not clear on the basis of present information. However, it would appear that genetic aberrations may have important etiologic implications.

INCIDENCE. Acute leukemia may occur at any time throughout the pediatric age group, the peak incidence being between the ages of 2 and 5 years. With approximately 4,000 new cases occurring each year, the overall incidence in childhood is about 4 cases per 100,000 population. The risk of acute leukemia in white children during the first 10 years of life is 1 in 2,880. There is a definitely higher incidence of leukemia in white children as compared with black children in the United States, and there is a slight predilection for males.

TYPES OF ACUTE LEUKEMIA. In approximately 90 percent of children with acute leukemia, the predominating abnormal cell in the bone marrow and peripheral blood is the primitive lymphoblast. The term lymphoblastic leukemia is often used synonymously with stem-cell leukemia, because of the morphologic similarity between the stem cell and early lymphoblast, the frequent lymphoid hyperplasia, relative lymphocytosis in the peripheral blood, and the sensitivity to lympholytic agents. The majority of the remaining 10 percent of acute childhood leukemias consist of acute granulocytic leukemia and acute monocytic leukemia. Eosinophilic, basophilic, megakaryocytic, and erythroleukemias are extremely rare. Although chronic lymphocytic leukemia does not occur in children, the chronic granulocytic variety accounts for approximately 2 percent of childhood leukemias.

PATHOLOGY. The basic pathologic changes consist of the proliferation of leukemic cells within the bone marrow with replacement of the normal myeloid elements. Lymph nodes, liver, and spleen are consistently infiltrated. Other organs, especially the kidneys, central nervous system, gastrointestinal tract, and gonads may be involved, depending on the duration of the disease. Distortion of architecture of these organs is commonly seen. Secondary changes resulting from disturbance in function may include areas of hemorrhage and foci of infection.

CLINICAL MANIFESTATIONS. The symptoms of acute leukemia are attributable to the rapid proliferation of leukemic tissue, disturbance in production of normal bone marrow elements, and organ enlargement. The onset may be insidious and a frequent history is that of fever, loss of vigor, and moderate pallor in a previously healthy child. Rarely is the antecedent history that of a child regarded as chronically ill or with an unusual number of major or minor illnesses. Symptoms and signs may be more severe and specific depending on the degree of bone marrow involvement, and initial manifestations may include headache, marked pallor, extreme fatigability, tachycardia, and dyspnea from profound anemia; fever, extensive upper respiratory infection, and ulcerations of the buccal mucosa coincident with diminished granulopoiesis; petechiae, easy bruising, and mucous membrane bleeding secondary to thrombocytopenia. Anorexia, vomiting, and abdominal pain may ensue from hepatic and splenic enlargement. Bone pain and arthralgia may be striking due to extensive osseous involvement and may suggest the diagnosis of rheumatic fever or rheumatoid arthritis. Although marked lymph node enlargement is an infrequent initial symptom, moderate painless adenopathy can often be detected on physical examination. Symmetric enlargement of the salivary and lacrimal glands (Mikulicz syndrome) is a rare occurrence. While hepatosplenomegaly is a common finding, massive enlargement is rare. Leukemic infiltration of the skin (leukemia cutis) appearing as small discrete yellow nodules is an uncommon finding.

LABORATORY DATA. The peripheral blood count may be extremely variable. Normal or low white blood counts are present in about 70 percent of cases. Differential counts, especially in leucopenic individuals, may be misleading in that blast cells may be scant or absent. In such instances a relative lymphocytosis of small mature lymphocytes is usually encountered. When total white blood counts are greater than 10,000 per mm³, blasts are usually abundant. Platelets are diminished or absent on smear with actual platelet counts depressed below 50,000 per mm³ in most cases. Hemoglobin levels may be moderately to markedly low and reflect a normocytic normochromic anemia. Although the diagnosis of leukemia often appears obvious after examination of the peripheral blood smear, bone marrow aspiration from the iliac crest or vertebral spinal process should be performed in every instance, since absolute identification of cell type is mandatory for proper selection of subsequent chemotherapy. Acute promyelocytic and monocytic leukemias may become apparent only after examination of the marrow. Sternal aspiration is usually unwarranted in children since this approach is frightening, potentially dangerous, and offers no diagnostic advantage over other sites.

Examination of the bone marrow in acute lymphoblastic leukemia reveals an increase in blast forms which usually accounts for 80 to 90 percent of the total nucleated cells. There is a concomitant reduction of normal erythroid and granulocytic precursors; megakaryocytes are usually sparse or absent. Occasionally hypocellularity of the marrow may be encountered which suggests the diagnosis of aplastic anemia. However, careful search of an adequate specimen will reveal an increased number of blast cells. Other abnormal laboratory determinations may be an elevation in BUN and serum uric acid.

A variety of radiographic abnormalities may be present. Enlargement of liver, spleen, kidneys, and mediastinal nodes may be seen. Skeletal lesions are present in the majority of children and consist of

four types: (1) generalized rarefaction; (2) radiolucent bands occurring in the metaphysis adjacent and parallel to the epiphyseal lines in long bones and beneath the cortex in flat bones such as the ilium and ischium, or transverse lines of increased density ("growth arrest lines") in the metaphyses of long bones; (3) osteolytic lesions; and (4) cortical and periosteal lesions.

DIFFERENTIAL DIAGNOSIS. Many of the clinical manifestations and laboratory findings of acute leukemia are common to a variety of disorders which should be considered in differential diagnosis. These include: leukemoid reactions, idiopathic thrombocytopenia purpura (ITP), aplastic anemia, infectious lymphocytosis, infectious mononucleosis, rheumatic fever, rheumatoid arthritis, reticuloendotheliosis, Hodgkin's disease, and other malignancies, such as metastatic neuroblastoma. Leukemoid reactions accompanying infection may be associated with a marked shift to the left of the granulocytes, but blast cells are not seen and anemia and thrombocytopenia are usually absent. The hemorrhagic manifestations of ITP may suggest leukemia, but bone marrow examination is normal. Although leukemia is sometimes mistaken for aplastic anemia because of failure to identify correctly the increased blasts in the marrow, the diagnosis of aplastic anemia is usually established without difficulty since there is lack of hepatosplenomegaly and absence of leukemic cells in the peripheral blood and marrow. Infectious lymphocytosis lacks significant clinical manifestations and the increased lymphocytes are normal mature cells. Infectious mononucleosis may have several features in common with leukemia (lymphadenopathy, hepatosplenomegaly, abnormal-appearing cells), but the atypical lymphocytes can be distinguished from blasts and the bone marrow is normal.

Skeletal involvement from leukemic proliferation may mimic inflammatory and traumatic arthropathies and may lead to confusion with rheumatic fever and rheumatoid arthritis. The localization of pain and exquisite tenderness to bones should suggest the osseous manifestations of leukemia. Hodgkin's disease, other lymphomas, and the reticuloendotheliosis may all have varying degrees of adenopathy, hepatosplenomegaly, anemia, and leucopenia. However, these diseases are not associated with lymphoblastic proliferation in the bone marrow.

THERAPY OF ACUTE LYMPHOBLASTIC LEUKEMIA. Treatment should be initiated as soon as the diagnosis has been established. Transfusion of packed cells to restore normal hemoglobin levels is desirable if values are below 10.0 g percent since effective erythropoiesis cannot be anticipated until remission is induced. At the present time there are six chemotherapeutic agents of proven effectiveness available for general use: prednisone, 6-mercaptopurine, amethopterin, cyclophosphamide, vincristine, and cytosine arabinoside. (Table 6) Each agent is capable of inducing clinical and hematologic remission when used alone. However, accumulated experience has

TABLE 6.   *Chemotherapeutic Agents Effective in Acute Lymphoblastic Leukemia*

Compound	Dose	Toxicity
Prednisone	2 mg/kg/day orally for 4-6 weeks	Cushingoid manifestations Osteoporosis
Amethopterin (Methotrexate)	20-30 mg/m^2 twice a week orally, intramuscularly, or intravenously	Oral ulcerations GI ulcerations Myelosuppression
6-Mercaptopurine (Purinethol)	2.5 mg/kg/day orally	Myelosuppression
Cyclophosphamide (Cytoxan)	2.5 mg/kg/day orally	Alopecia Leucopenia Hemorrhagic cystitis
Vincristine (Oncovin)	0.05-0.075 mg/kg intravenously weekly for 4-6 doses	Neurotoxicity (jaw pain, paraesthesia, loss of DTR's) Constipation Alopecia Injection site irritation
Cytosine arabinoside (Cytosar)	Intravenously or intramuscularly. Optimal dosage route and schedule undetermined	Myelosuppression

indicated that the additive effect of the combined use of certain of these drugs results in higher remission rates without concomitant increase in toxicity. At present a regimen utilizing prednisone and vincristine for induction is employed in most centers. Prednisone, 2 mg/kg/day orally in four divided doses, and vincristine, 0.05 to 0.075 mg/kg intravenously once weekly, are given and can be expected to produce remissions in approximately 90 percent of children in 4 to 6 weeks. Since vincristine is extremely toxic locally, producing tissue necrosis, extreme caution must be exercised in preventing extravasation during administration. If remission does not occur within this time, continuation beyond 6 weeks rarely produces remission and may result in serious neurotoxicity. Once remission is documented by the presence of normal bone marrow constituents, prednisone is gradually discontinued over a 7-day period, vincristine is withheld, and Methotrexate, 20 to 30 mg/m^2 orally twice a week, is given for the maintenance phase. That maintenance therapy is indicated is based on the findings that relapse usually occurs within several weeks if chemotherapy is interrupted, and that increase in survival time is directly related to time spent in remission. As long as remission persists, Methotrexate is continued. The median duration of remission is approximately 10 to 12 months. When relapse occurs on Methotrexate, the drug should be discontinued and an attempt to reinduce remission should ensue promptly. Reinduction of remission can be again achieved in about 75 percent of patients with combined prednisone and vincristine. With remission, 6-mercaptopurine (2.5 mg/kg) as a single oral daily dose is given for maintenance. With subsequent relapse, reinduction with prednisone and vincristine can be attempted, and cyclophosphamide (2.5 mg/kg) as a single daily oral dose given for maintenance. The most recently developed chemotherapeutic agent, cytosine arabinoside (Cytosar), has been shown to produce remissions in approximately 35 percent of patients refractory to other agents. Because of its potent myelosuppressive effect and the variability in time to produce remission, close supervision of the peripheral blood count is critical when this drug is employed. The optimal dosage, sequence, route, and frequency of administration are being determined at this time. With each successive relapse, remission induction becomes more difficult to achieve, although as many as six remissions have been reported in a few cases. It should be emphasized that although prednisone and vincristine are excellent remission inducers, they should not be used for maintenance chemotherapy because rapid development of resistance occurs usually with severe associated toxicity.

Although the previously described approach for induction and maintenance of remission has been effective in lengthening survival, constant effort is being directed toward achieving still further increases in survival. Numerous regimens in which the dose, schedule, and route of administration are varied are currently undergoing evaluation in many clinics. Numerous regimens utilizing the combination of four or more agents administered at regular intervals in an attempt to eradicate totally the leukemic cell population have been employed. The results of these efforts indicate that median survival has been prolonged significantly, and in about 15 percent of children complete remissions of 4 to 5 years have occurred. These schemes using massive combined chemotherapy are confined presently to investigative centers where complex supportive care is readily available, and the patient's environment can be controlled during periods of risk from infections.

New agents for clinical trial are slowly but consistently emerging from animal screening. Two compounds which have shown definite antileukemic effect in humans are daunomycin and L-asparaginase. These compounds, not presently available for general use, are currently undergoing clinical investigation in several centers as well as in cooperative study groups. Their principal effectiveness, however, appears to be limited to induction of remission rather than to maintenance. When dosage, route, schedule, sequence, and toxicity of these agents have been thoroughly evaluated and production of these compounds increased, their release for general use can be anticipated.

In the past decade there has been an increasing interest in immunotherapy as an adjunct to chemotherapy. Preliminary clinical trials with the administration of either pooled radiated allogenic leukemic cells or repeated immunization with BCG vaccine as a nonspecific stimulus to host immunity have indicated that further reduction of leukemic cells can be accomplished subsequent to intensive chemotherapy. Attempts to cure leukemia through total body radiation followed by allogenic marrow grafting have been fraught with difficulties. However, as knowledge concerning basic immune mechanisms and histocompatibility increases and supportive care becomes more effective, advances in this technique may be anticipated.

PROGNOSIS. At present remission can be induced in approximately 90 percent of children with acute lymphoblastic leukemia; 50 percent of these patients can be expected to survive 20 to 22 months and 10 percent about 45 months. The best response to therapy and longest survival occurs in children between ages 3 and 6 years, with minimal adenopathy and organ enlargement, and low initial white blood cell counts. Although the exact number of children considered cured from leukemia is unknown, they constitute less than 1 percent of the total cases. Recent attention has been focused on the implication derived from long-term survivors as studied by Burchenal for the Acute Leukemia Task Force Registry. Of 127 children in the registry surviving over 5 years, 87 were reported alive and well without evidence of disease; most of the recurrences occurred in the fifth to ninth year after diagnosis. It appears reasonable to assume from this data that children who survive 7 years after diagnosis and who have had no evidence of disease for 4 years have been cured. Whether the factors contributing to the few apparent cures reside in the leukemic cell or in the hosts' response is not known, nor is it known whether relapse occurring after extremely long remissions is related to delayed emergence of drug resistance or reinduction of the original leukemic process.

COMPLICATIONS. Several complications may arise during the course of the disease which require particular attention both diagnostically and therapeutically.

Extramedullary Leukemic Involvement. With prolongation of survival as a result of advances in both chemotherapy and supportive therapy, extramedullary sites of leukemic involvement have become increasingly apparent. The organs most frequently involved are the central nervous system and the testes. Kidneys, ovaries, bowel, liver, and lung are involved with less frequency. Development of progressive leukemic foci in these areas is thought to result from insufficient concentration of chemotherapeutic agents at these sites. Meningeal leukemia can be explained on this basis for it is well recognized that the blood-brain barrier prevents all of the routinely employed antileukemic drugs from reaching the CNS in sufficient concentrations to be effective, with the exception of the adrenocortical steroids.

Central nervous system leukemia. This occurs in approximately 40 to 50 percent of children with acute lymphoblastic leukemia. Half of the cases develop in the presence of complete hematologic remission. Although CNS involvement may occur as early as the third month, it is unusual until the disease has been present for more than 6 months, the median time being about 10 to 12 months. The areas most frequently involved are the meninges, occasionally the sixth and seventh cranial nerves; less frequently, the second and third cranial nerves, and lumbar spinal nerves. The pathology of CNS leukemia consists of diffuse infiltrations of the leptomeninges, dura, and perivascular spaces, as well as deeper structures, e.g., the choroid plexus, hypothalamus, and tuber cinereum. Grossly the meninges appear opaque and thickened and evidence of an obstructive hydrocephalus may be seen in long-standing disease. Headache, irritability, or vomiting may be present singly or in combination and physical examination may reveal nuchal rigidity, increased head size, papilledema, and specific cranial nerve palsies.

The diagnosis is confirmed by radiographic evidence of widening of the sutures and by examination of the cerebrospinal fluid which shows increased pressure, pleocytosis of mononuclear cells (blasts), elevation of protein, and often reduction of glucose. Although the lumbar puncture itself may be of benefit in producing symptomatic relief, recurrence of symptoms is prompt in the absence of treatment. Fortunately, this particular complication of acute leukemia is quite responsive either to intrathecal chemotherapy or radiation. Methotrexate, 0.5 mg/kg intrathecally every other day for two to five doses, can be expected to alleviate symptoms rapidly and effect the return of normal spinal fluid findings in 90 percent of patients, even if marrow relapse has occurred previously on this agent. Since intrathecal Methotrexate can be absorbed systemically it is advisable to discontinue oral administration during the period of treatment. Radiation to the skull and spine in doses ranging from 1,000 to 1,200 r over a 2-week interval can also be expected to eradicate signs and symptoms of meningeal leukemia in the majority of patients treated. However, because of the attendant temporary alopecia as well as the necessity for repeated hospital visits, intrathecal therapy is preferable, unless there is evidence of deep cerebral or spinal nerve root involvement or if Methotrexate toxicity develops.

In the occasional patient in whom symptoms are severe, e.g., the sudden onset of blindness, additional benefit may be obtained from the oral administration of dexamethasone, 0.30 mg/kg/day in divided doses. Recurrence of central nervous system leukemia within 2 to 4 months is common, and a single patient may have several episodes, each responding to the therapy previously described. Recently it has been shown that utilization of higher dose radiation (2,500 r) during hematologic remission appears to be effective in preventing or delaying the development of CNS leukemia in children who are long-term survivors following combined intensive chemotherapy.

Testicular involvement. Testicular involvement is less common than CNS leukemia and is manifest by painless, progressive enlargement of the testis. This complication may also occur during a period of hematologic remission. Simultaneous enlargement of both testes is rare. Response to oral prednisone, 2 mg/kg/day in divided doses, usually occurs; however, recurrence is common and localized radiation (1,200 r) to the affected gonad may be necessary. Ovarian enlargement is seldom clinically appreciated.

Renal involvement. Bilateral renal infiltration by leukemic cells is frequent and may result in palpable enlargement of the kidneys. While infiltration of the kidneys occurs usually late in the course of leukemia, marked renal enlargement has also been noted at the time of diagnosis. Although abnormalities may be seen by pyelography, renal dysfunction can rarely be demonstrated even in the presence of palpable renal masses. Azotemia is unusual, but when present, inhibition of renal excretion of certain chemotherapeutic agents may lead to drug toxicity. Both local radiation and systemic chemotherapy can result in diminution of renal enlargement.

Uric acid nephropathy is another renal complication which may occur. Although far less frequent than the complications already described, prompt recognition of this disturbance can result in lifesaving therapy. Since uric acid is an end-product of purine metabolism, breakdown of leukemic cells can result in hyperuricemia (serum uric acid greater than 10 mg percent) and place the patient at risk from renal tubular obstruction which may progress to internal hydronephrosis and ultimately renal failure. This is most likely to occur in the patient with a high white count (greater than 20,000/mm^3) with marked adenopathy (especially mediastinal) and massive hepatosplenomegaly. Prevention of this complication, especially during the

period of induction of remission, can best be achieved by insuring good hydration and thus a high urinary output. In the presence of rising uric acid levels, alkalination of the urine by administration of sodium bicarbonate is advisable. In addition, the xanthine oxidase inhibitor, allopurinol (Zyloprim), effectively blocks the conversion of the more soluble hypoxanthine-xanthine to uric acid producing relief of hyperuricemia within 2 to 48 hours. Since potentiation of the effects of 6-MP occurs, the dosage of this drug should be reduced to 25 percent during administration of allopurinol. In the presence of oliguria, fluid administration should be restricted. Mannitol infusions may be effective in promoting diuresis. Rarely, peritoneal or hemodialysis may be necessary if renal failure is impending despite the institution of the other measures described.

Infection. During leukemic relapse increased susceptibility to infection results from diminished humoral and cellular defense mechanisms secondary to neutropenia and the administration of immunosuppressive drugs. Severe infection accounts for approximately 70 percent of deaths in leukemic children. Most of these deaths are due to septicemia, with pneumonitis, meningitis, and peritonitis less common. With the development of effective antibiotics against the penicillinase-producing *Micrococcus,* gram-negative organisms, usually enteric saprophytes, and fungi have assumed clinical significance. The most prevalent organism, accounting for approximately 50 percent of fatal bacterial infections, is *Pseudomonas;* various coliforms as well as opportunist bacteria such as *Mima* and *Herellea,* have also emerged as pathogens in leukemic children. As in other conditions where host defenses are impaired, severe clinical infection can result from ubiquitous organisms, such as *Pneumocystis carinii* and cytomegalic virus. Although the diagnosis of diseases from these organisms is difficult, they should be suspected in severe or refractory pneumonitis. Lung aspirates prepared with a silver stain will usually be diagnostic if *Pneumocystis carinii* is the causative organism. Effective treatment of this infection has resulted from the administration of pentamadine isethionate. Similarly, the identification of intranuclear inclusions in the characteristic giant cells in the sputum obtained by tracheal aspiration may lead to the diagnosis of cytomegalovirus infection for which the antiviral compound floxuridine has been efficacious.

The significance of fever in the leukemic child depends to a large extent upon the stage of the disease at which it appears. In early disease temperature elevation is common and appears to result from the hypermetabolism of leukemic proliferation rather than from infection. However, late in the disease and especially during relapse, fever is usually due to underlying infection. Thus the index of suspicion must be high since the classic signs of localizing infection may not be present. Nuchal rigidity, rales, muscle spasm, and abscess formation may all be diminished in the absence of a normal polymorphonuclear inflammatory response. Cultures should be obtained without delay and antibiotic therapy begun promptly. Nafcillin or oxacillin and kanamycin in maximum therapeutic doses administered intravenously appear to be the drugs of choice prior to bacteriologic identification. A cephalosporin may be an effective alternative. The use of pooled human gamma globulin is not effective either prophylactically or therapeutically against bacterial infections. A more rational approach for providing effective antibodies would appear to be the use of specific convalescent plasma as a therapeutic adjunct in severe gram-negative infections. In the granulocytopenic individual, *Pseudomonas septicemia* has been almost universally fatal despite the use of polymyxin, colistin, and gentamycin. A new semisynthetic penicillin, carbenicillin, has been shown to be effective even in the absence of normal circulating granulocytes. Although the collection of effective numbers of leucocytes for replacement therapy has not been feasible by the usual plasmaphoresis techniques, a recently developed blood cell separator enables rapid collection and harvesting of the leucocytes contained in 15 units of blood processed from a single donor.

Exposure of the leukemic child to chicken pox should be avoided, even during periods of remission, since fatal varicella infections can occur. The course of the disease which is frequently although unpredictably severe, and protracted in the leukemic child may be modified occasionally by the administration of gamma globulin within three days of exposure. The recommended dosage schedule is 0.6 ml/lb in three divided doses over a 24-hour period. When the newly developed zoster-immune-globulin (ZIG) becomes commercially available, complete prevention of varicella in the exposed susceptible patient may be accomplished.

Hemorrhage. Hemorrhage ranks second to infection as a cause of death and accounts for considerable morbidity. As a result of thrombocytopenia either due to lack of platelet production in the presence of leukemic relapse or to drug suppression, severe and often life-threatening hemorrhage may occur. Although epistaxis is the most frequent source of profuse hemorrhage, significant bleeding may occur throughout the gastrointestinal tract as well as the kidneys and CNS. The site and extent of bleeding determines treatment. For epistaxis, local measures consisting of digital pressure or anterior packing with Gelfoam soaked in topical thrombin may be effective, but posterior nasal packing is often necessary. In the child with massive bleeding, restoration of blood volume as well as platelets is critical. The most available type of replacement therapy is freshly drawn whole blood which may, however, produce circulatory overload without actually raising the platelets to levels where hemostasis is effective. Platelet-rich plasma (PRP) or platelet concentrates (PC) are quite useful in avoiding this problem. PRP has the advantage of being quickly prepared from freshly drawn blood by centrifuging at low speed for 3 minutes. The remaining packed cells can then be stored for future use. PC is prepared from PRP by high speed centrifugation. With plasmaphoresis techniques the use of PC is practical and valuable. Since the platelets from one donor are contained in a 15 to 25 ml volume, effective hemostasis can be achieved in most situations without risk of overloading the circulation. Although the administration of 1 unit of PC per 10 pounds of body weight every 48 hours usually prevents or corrects thrombocytopenic bleeding, higher daily doses may be necessary in the child with fever, infection, and/or splenomegaly since platelet survival is shortened in these individuals. Both PRP and PC should be obtained from ABO and Rh compatible donors. If HL-A typing is available, proper matching can preclude the development of the immune response to donor platelet transfusions.

GENERAL SUPPORTIVE THERAPY. During remission, the leukemic child does not appear to be in excessive risk to either infection or hemorrhage and normal childhood activity may be maintained. Unnecessary exposure to the common diseases of childhood should be avoided, but not at the expense of placing the child in a strict overprotective environment. Regular attendance at school and participation in the normal peer associated activities lessen anxiety both for parents and children. Parents should be encouraged to treat their child as they had prior to his developing leukemia. Overpermissiveness and overindulgence are considered by many parents as their only means of lessening the burden for a child with a fatal disease. However, consistency in parental attitudes promotes a happier more secure environment for the child.

The use of prophylactic antibiotics serves no purpose and is dangerous in that it suppresses normal bacterial flora. Hospitalization should be as brief as possible and procedures kept to the necessary minimum. Good general pediatric and preventive dental care is important. There are no dietary restrictions or additions to be advocated. The use of vitamin supplements containing folic acid is not recommended because of their possibile interference with the effect of some of the antimetabolites. Live vaccines are definitely contraindicated. There is evidence that the altered immune mechanism existing in the leukemic child may impair his ability to handle such antigenic stimuli and, therefore, inactivated vaccines should be employed. Despite demonstrated inadequacies in elevating antibody titers in children receiving immunosuppressive agents, some degree of protection is afforded with killed vaccines, especially if booster doses are given.

Other Types of Acute Leukemia

Neonatal Leukemia

Congenital leukemia may be apparent at delivery or develop during the first few weeks of life. The clinical manifestations of purpura and hepatosplenomegaly are usually present. However, anemia may not be a striking feature in the newborn. Examination of the peripheral blood reveals increased numbers of early granulocytic forms (blast cells, promyelocytes, and early myelocytes) and platelets are markedly reduced. Sepsis, congenital syphilis, erythroblastosis, congenital thrombocytopenia, toxoplasmosis, congenital rubella, and cytomegalic inclusion disease must be differentiated. Negative cultures, normal serology and the absence of blood incompatibilities in the presence of bone marrow findings of decreased or absent megakaryocytes, absolute increase of immature granulocytes, and diminished leucocyte alkaline phosphatase content confirm the diagnosis. Except for the absence of the Philadelphia (Ph[1]) chromosome this form of leukemia morphologically resembles chronic myelogenous leukemia in the adult. In addition to the increased incidence of acute lymphoblastic leukemia in Mongolism, acute and chronic granulocytic leukemia have been reported with increased frequency in newborn infants with Down's syndrome. However, recent reports have appeared describing spontaneous remission of the hematologic abnormalities in some of these infants thought to have congenital leukemia. Although the pathogenesis of this leukemoid proliferation has not been established, it is suggested that the abnormal hematopoiesis may be related to trisomy of chromosome number 21. The course of leukemia in the non-Mongol neonate is generally much more fulminant, with survivals beyond 6 months of age unusual. Response to chemotherapy is almost universally poor; remissions with 6-mercaptopurine or cytosine arabinoside can occasionally be effected.

Acute Granulocytic Leukemia

This type of acute leukemia which usually occurs in the older child (over 8 years), may be manifest in two forms; the more frequent type being promyelocytic, the other a more mature myelocytic variety. In many instances the latter may evolve into the former during the course of the disease. Diagnosis is based on bone marrow examination which reveals a predominance of promyelocytes, which may contain Auer rods, and early myelocytes in the absence of a normal complement of mature granulocytes, lymphocytes, erythroid precursors, and megakaryocytes. Resistance to therapy and attendant hemorrhagic complications pose difficult problems in management. In addition to profound thrombocytopenia, fibrinogen, and Factors V, VIII, and X deficiencies have been reported and may indicate the presence of disseminated intravascular coagulation contributing to the bleeding diathesis. Remission induction may be achieved in approximately 25 percent of patients with cytosine arabinoside. Combination of this agent with vincristine and cyclophosphamide has resulted in a 50 percent remission rate. Maintenance of remission is generally brief with relapse occurring within several months. Adrenocortical steroids probably exert little specific benefit, but may be of some value in the critically bleeding patient. Recent trials using massive combined chemotherapy indicate that a higher remisson rate can be achieved if adequate supportive therapy is concomitantly available. Daunomycin, which is currently limited to investigational use, has produced some remissions in children unresponsive to other agents.

A variant of acute granulocytic leukemia which may be seen is myelomonocytic leukemia. In this condition the peripheral blood may reveal a well-defined monocytosis while the marrow exhibits predominant myeloblastic proliferation with variable degrees of reticuloendothelial proliferation. Treatment, which is as described for acute granulocytic leukemia, is usually ineffective.

Chronic Granulocytic Leukemia

Chronic granulocytic leukemia is infrequently seen in childhood. However, when it occurs in the older child, differentiation from the hyperleucocytosis of leukemoid reactions may be difficult, since thrombocytopenia and anemia may be minimal or absent and immature granulocytes infrequent. The presence of splenomegaly, decreased levels of leucocyte alkaline phosphatase, and demonstration of the Philadelphia chromosome serve to confirm the diagnosis. Although prolonged remissions with busulfan (Myleran) can be achieved, reversion to acute leukemia manifested by a blastic crisis, anemia, and thrombocytopenia is a common outcome. In the younger child chronic granulocytic leukemia is characterized by a greater lymphadenopathy, less splenomegaly, a lower total leucocyte count, thrombocytopenia, and absence of the Philadelphia chromosome. The response to therapy in these children tends to be poor.

Acute Monocytic Leukemia

This form of acute leukemia is similar to the other types of childhood leukemias in its clinical features except for a tendency to manifest gum infiltrations. The cells of the peripheral blood and marrow type resemble monocytes, reticuloendothelial cells, or histiocytes, suggesting relationships to reticulum cell sarcoma. The clinical course is usually rapidly progressive and poorly responsive to chemotherapy. Remission rates are low, but partial and even complete remissions may occasionally be achieved with 6-mercaptopurine, vincristine, or cytosine arabinoside. The combined use of these agents with adrenocortical steroids may be advantageous. Isolated case reports suggest Methotrexate or cyclophosphamide may also be of benefit.

Informing Parents of the Diagnosis of Leukemia

As soon as the diagnosis has been confirmed, it is essential that the parents be informed and the proposed therapy and prognosis frankly discussed. There are few pediatric diseases which carry such a grave prognosis or represent a more tragic situation for parents and family to face. While a small number of long-term survivors or possible cures have been adequately documented, it would seem both unreasonable and unfair to give parents the impression that curability is likely in the light of present knowledge. It is reasonable, however, to cite the investigative efforts currently under way directed toward more effective treatment and to permit optimism engendered by the hope that prolongation of life can perhaps enable an individual to take advantage of some future advance in therapy.

There is great variability among parents in their understanding of the disease and their ability to accept the diagnosis. In general, parents of leukemic children are relatively young and often have had no personal experience from which either to consider the concept or to cope with the reality of death. The initial reaction by parents can be misleading, and may mask basic underlying feelings. Awareness of this on the part of the physician should prompt him to allow sufficient opportunity for parents to discuss their questions and express their anxieties. The physician must be prepared to reassure parents that there is nothing that they could have done to prevent the disease, that it is definitely not contagious, and that the likelihood of other children in the family developing leukemia is extremely remote. It is not unusual for parents to question information released by mass media regarding new or unusual forms of therapy. When this arises the physician should recognize the feelings of despair that can prompt parents to search for anything hopeful. The physician should firmly and decisively negate unfounded therapeutic approaches and should cooperate in investigating the possibilities of application of bona fide information. When parents are confident that their child is receiving optimal care, many of their fears, suspicions, and guilt feelings abate and they are better able to accept the events of a terminal illness.

REFERENCES

Brunell, P. A., Ross, A., Miller, L. H., and Kuo, B. Prevention of varicella by zoster immune globulin. New Eng. J. Med., 280:1191, 1969.
Burchenal, J. H. Long-term survivors in acute leukemia and Burkitt's tumor. Cancer, 21:595, 1968.
Evans, A. E. If a child must die . . . . New Eng. J. Med., 278:183, 1968.
George, P., Hernandez, K., Hustu, O., Borella, L., Holton, C., and Pinkel, D. A study of "total therapy" of acute lymphocytic leukemia in children. J. Pediat., 72:399, 1968.
Haghbin, M., and Zuelzer, W. A long-term study of cerebrospinal leukemia. J. Pediat., 67:23, 1965.
Hardisty, R. M. The treatment of acute leukaemia. Practitioner, 204:127, 1970.
——— Granulocytic leukaemia in childhood. Brit. J. Haemat., 10:551, 1964.
Henderson, E. S. Treatment of acute leukemia. Seminars Hemat., 6:271, 1969.
Hersh, E. M., Bodey, G. P., Nies, B. A., and Freireich, E. J. Causes of death in acute leukemia. J.A.M.A., 193:105, 1965.
Mauer, A. M. Pediatric Hematology. New York, McGraw-Hill Book Co., 1969.
McAllister, R. M. On the role of viruses in human cancer. J. Pediat., 69:175, 1966.
Pierce, M. I., Borges, W. H., Heyn, R., Wolff, J. A., and Gilbert, E. S. Epidemiological factors and survival experience in 1770 children with acute leukemia. Cancer, 23:1296, 1969.
Report of cooperative study of acute leukemia group B. Acute lymphocytic leukemia in children. J.A.M.A., 207:923, 1969.
Ross, J. D., Moloney, W. C., and Desforges, J. F. Ineffective regulation of granulopoiesis masquerading as congenital leukemia in a mongoloid child. J. Pediat., 63:1, 1963.
Smith, C. H. Blood Diseases of Infancy and Childhood. St. Louis, C. V. Mosby Co., 1966.
Thomas, L. B., Forkner, C. E., Frei, E., III, Besse, B. E., and Stubenau, J. R. The skeletal lesions of acute leukemia. Cancer, 14:608, 1961.
Viola, M. V. Acute leukemia and infection. J.A.M.A., 201:923, 1967.

Disorders of the Blood-Forming Organs

17.9
THE SPLEEN

IRVING SCHULMAN

POSITIONS AND METHODS OF EXAMINATION. The thin abdominal wall of young children renders palpation of the spleen easier than in adults. Palpation is a much more satisfactory method of examination than is percussion. Under ordinary conditions the spleen can easily be felt when it is sufficiently enlarged to be of diagnostic importance. Occasionally it is readily palpable when of normal size.

When moderately enlarged, the lower border of the spleen is an inch or so below the free border of the ribs; when greatly enlarged, it forms a tumor which may nearly fill the left half of the abdomen. A tumor in the left hypochondriac region is recognized to be the spleen by the sharpness of its mesial border, at about the middle of which a notch may be felt, and by the fact that it rides along the anterior abdominal wall, superficial to the descending colon, and can be readily displaced mesially, laterally, or upward. Only when greatly enlarged does it extend sufficiently far posteriorly to be felt in the left costovertebral angle.

A renal or adrenal tumor is occasionally mistaken for an enlarged spleen. In such instances the relation of the mass to the colon is helpful in diagnosis, the colon being anterior to masses of retroperitoneal origin. An enlarged and distorted left lobe of the liver may be mistaken for an enlarged spleen.

CIRCULATION IN THE SPLEEN. Blood enters the spleen through the splenic artery, which branches promptly into a trabecular artery. This enters the white pulp, which is made up of masses of lymphocytes. Some of the arterioles end here, but others continue and branch into the red pulp. The red pulp is made up of open vascular spaces (splenic sinuses) separated by cellular cords (splenic cords or cords of Billroth). In the past there was much discussion over whether the splenic circulation was "open" or "closed." Those favoring the open theory believed that blood entered the cords and then moved into the sinuses for final return to the veins. The closed theory stated that the blood never left a vessel and went directly from arteriole to sinus to vein. Current evidence indicates that both mechanisms operate, some of the blood passing directly through the organ while some goes through the cords first and thence to the sinuses. Electron microscopy has demonstrated free connections between cords and sinuses. Whether the open or closed form or splenic circulation is predominant depends upon whether the spleen is functioning normally or abnormally. Under normal circumstances blood passes rapidly through the spleen, and the cord compartment is comparatively small because of the relatively small number of abnormal cells removed for destruction. When the spleen is enlarged and functioning abnormally, the amount of blood in the cords increases, and the amount of time a blood cell remains within the spleen is lengthened significantly. This alters cell metabolism and may lead to premature cell destruction as discussed in earlier sections. The splenic vein enters the portal vein, and it is important to stress that neither vein contains valves. Therefore the pressure in the red pulp is the same as that in the portal system.

FUNCTIONS OF THE SPLEEN. In fetal life the spleen is a principal site of blood formation until about the sixth month, and the Malpighian corpuscles constitute an important source of lymphocyte formation. The organ preserves these potentialities and, when need arises, can resume hematopoiesis at any age throughout the period of growth, though more readily

in infancy than in childhood. Severe anemia or anoxemia may constitute stimuli which lead to persistence or reappearance of foci of extramedullary blood formation in the spleen.

The spleen has important effects on circulating red cells. In passage through the spleen immature red cells absorb water, become more spherical, and decrease their surface area. When the spleen is removed, red cells become thinner and tend to become target-shaped. Reticulocytes which reach the circulation are temporarily held up in the spleen until they mature; thus, after splenectomy, an increase in reticulocytes in the blood is common, not because of greater production but because of failure of removal. The spleen also selectively retains red cells containing nuclear fragments, denatured protein, and iron granules and can remove these particles without injuring the red cell. After splenectomy erythrocytes containing granules and particles are found in the blood. Finally the spleen removes aged and damaged red cells. When the spleen is removed, other reticuloendothelial organs promptly take over the latter function, and thus the life-span of normal erythrocytes is not prolonged after splenectomy. On the other hand, no organ but the spleen appears capable of developing an abnormality leading to the capacity to destroy normal cells.

The spleen is an important source of lymphocytes, plasma cells, and monocytes and also selectively eliminates damaged white cells and platelets. There is no evidence that the spleen exerts any controlling function over formation of red cells and white cells in the marrow. Whether it has some regulatory function over platelet formation is still uncertain.

Both the reticuloendothelial cells of the spleen and its tissue macrophages are stimulated to active phagocytosis when particulate matter, such as carbon or bacteria, is injected intravenously. Phagocytic activity is probably more concentrated in the spleen than in any other organ, even the liver or lungs. The readiness with which cells of the spleen take up malarial parasites, tubercle bacilli, histoplasma, and *Treponema pallidum* is familiar to pathologists. When exposed to suitable antigens, the spleen is capable of responding by formation of specific antibodies, as shown both in tissue culture and in spleen slices in vitro; consequently it has been inferred that, through the sequence of phagocytosis and antibody production, the organ plays a significant role in humoral defense against infectious agents which have in some manner gained access to the bloodstream. That this is an important function of the spleen is now universally conceded. At the same time, the exact value of the spleen's role in the defense mechanisms of the body as a whole is difficult to weigh and is probably dependent to some extent on an age factor. Results of splenectomy indicate that the importance of the spleen in protection against infection is relatively great in early infancy, becoming much less in childhood, and possibly tapering off into insignificance in the mature subject.

The question of increased tendency to infection after splenectomy has been controversial but has been clarified by recent studies. Several points should be emphasized: (1) The increased susceptibility is not represented by an increase in all types of infections but varies with specific types of infection, namely overwhelming and frequently fatal sepsis and meningitis, predominantly due to pneumococcus. (2) There is no apparent decrease in general immunity and no evidence of decrease in gamma globulin or of impaired antibody formation. The hazard of overwhelming bacterial infection appears to be due to removal of the filtering function of the spleen. (3) The degree of susceptibility is related to the underlying problem which led to splenectomy. This relationship was made clear in studies by Robinson and Sturgeon. These investigators divided splenectomized patients into two groups. One group was designated as "nonpredisposed" and consisted of normal individuals whose spleens were removed for traumatic rupture or patients whose basic disease was not accompanied by lowered resistance and was usually cured by the operation, e.g., hereditary spherocytosis and idiopathic thrombocytopenic purpura. In this group the incidence of sepsis and meningitis was 3.2 percent. The second group, the "predisposed" group, consisted of patients whose underlying diseases were severe and chronic, were accompanied by a general decrease in resistance, and were palliated but not cured by operation, e.g., thalassemia, sickle-cell anemia, cirrhosis, lipoidoses, and lymphomas. In this group the incidence of sepsis and/or meningitis rose to 20.8 percent.

It is important to point out that even in the "nonpredisposed" group the incidence of sepsis and meningitis rose to almost 15 percent where splenectomy was performed in infants under 1 year of age.

The majority of cases of sepsis or meningitis following splenectomy are caused by pneumococci, but instances due to meningococcus, *Salmonella,* and other gram-negative rods have also been reported. Over 70 percent of cases occur within two years after splenectomy, but cases occurring many years later have been observed. Penicillin prophylaxis for two years after splenectomy has been advised by Smith.

MALFORMATIONS OF THE SPLEEN. Accessory spleens are found so frequently in the region of the splenic hilus as to justify their being regarded as a normal variant rather than a true malformation. Following surgical removal of the spleen, any remaining splenic tissue is prone to undergo compensatory hypertrophy and to take over the spleen's functions. When splenectomy is undertaken as a therapeutic measure, as in some of the blood dyscrasias, removal of accessory spleens is essential for lasting success.

Because the anlage of the embryonic spleen, situated in the dorsal mesogastrium, lies close to the cephalic portion of the developing mesonephric system, it is not uncommon to find splenic tissue fused with ovary or testis.

Congenital absence of the spleen has been recorded a number of times. It may occur alone or, more commonly, in association with partial situs inversus or anomalies of the heart and great vessels or with both of these together. Boys are more often involved than girls, especially in the triple malformation. The particular lesions of the heart most frequently associated with this condition are ostium atrioventriculare commune (cor biloculare), atresia or stenosis of the pulmonary artery, and atrial septal defects. Congenital absence of the spleen produces changes in the peripheral blood which have in several instances permitted the anomaly to be identified during early life. The most characteristic change is the occurrence of Heinz bodies in from 5 to 20 percent of the erythrocytes. In addition, an erythroblastosis of from 2,000 to 40,000 per mm^3 may be present, together with an unusual frequency of Howell-Jolly bodies and target cells; decreased osmotic fragility of the red cells may be demonstrable.

INJURY OF THE SPLEEN. Falls, sledding injuries, and automobile accidents are the principal causes of rupture of the spleen. Several case reports have appeared of splenic injury following relatively minor trauma in instances where the spleen was enlarged in the course of some illness such as infectious mononucleosis. Immediately after injury the patient may faint, but he usually revives within a short time and often appears to suffer from nothing more than superficial contusions. Within the next few hours there is persistent or increasing abdominal pain, thirst, and sometimes fever and vomiting. The seriousness of the situation may not be appreciated, and some of these patients have been brought to the hospital walking.

Although the physical findings vary greatly according to the nature and severity of the injury, abdominal tenderness is a constant feature. In most instances this is especially marked in the left upper quadrant, but it usually extends in some degree to the entire abdominal area and at times is not appreciably localized. There are often rebound tenderness and muscle spasm. Pain in the left shoulder may be constant or may be elicited only on abdominal palpation. Few of these patients show shifting dullness or other signs of free fluid, even when the amount of blood recoverable at operation is as great as 500 ml. A leucocytosis of about 20,000 is commonly found.

If the patient is seen soon after the accident, when both shock and internal hemorrhage are present, accurate diagnosis of rupture of the spleen is exceedingly difficult; at this stage, however, it is of secondary importance, since treatment of shock is the immediate consideration. At a later stage, the differential diagnosis between contusion of the abdominal parietes and splenic laceration depends chiefly on the demonstration of internal hemorrhage. The patient shows increasing thirst and tachycardia, and the local abdominal signs remain unchanged or even increase. For 24 hours or more there may be no significant fall in the hemoglobin or hematocrit level, after which it drops rapidly. The blood pressure, after recovery from the initial shock syndrome, is usually well sustained. In most cases the diagnosis can be made before the development of significant anemia, air hunger, and hypotension.

In some instances, an initial trauma lacerates the spleen without complete rupture. The patient may complain of symptoms of moderate severity at the time of injury. A few days to a few months later a subsequent trauma, sometimes very mild, produces delayed rupture with all the symptoms of the acute abdominal catastrophe.

Rupture of the spleen is occasionally observed in the newborn from trauma suffered during either delivery or resuscitation. The objective symptoms are similar to those described. Abdominal hemorrhage may be suspected when there are evidences of collapse, progressive anemia, and abdominal distension with rigidity.

Splenectomy is the only treatment for rupture of the spleen, since without it death from shock and hemorrhage will almost certainly ensue. Following splenectomy the platelet count in the peripheral blood rises sharply for a few days to a week, remains high for an indefinite interval, and then gradually returns to normal level. The appearance of showers of normoblasts in the peripheral blood for some time following splenectomy is a familiar phenomenon of no clinical importance. The behavior of the leucocyte count is unpredictable.

Either at the time of the original injury or in the course of operation, splenic tissue may be seeded more or less widely throughout the peritoneal cavity, forming implants which thrive under the stimulus of splenectomy. The condition, commonly called splenosis, is of no clinical significance but may produce a bizarre picture at subsequent laparotomy.

ENLARGEMENT OF THE SPLEEN. In a study of 1,060 normal newborn infants, Akerren observed that the spleen was palpable in approximately one-third, with a peak incidence of 45 percent on the third day of life. In 113 older infants less than 3 months old, 17 percent had palpable spleens; 15 percent of 67 infants 3 to 6 months old had such a condition. From then on there is a gradually diminishing incidence of palpable spleens in normal subjects up to 3 or 4 years of age.

Moderate splenomegaly is seen in many infections and sometimes in allergic states. A palpable spleen is of diagnostic importance in syphilis, typhoid fever, malaria, infectious mononucleosis, subacute bacterial endocarditis, miliary tuberculosis, histoplasmosis, and a number of other infections. Great enlargement is to be expected in chronic malaria, schistosomiasis, and kala-azar (leishmaniasis). Splenomegaly is found in amyloidosis and in many cases of rheumatoid arthritis. Enlargement from venous

congestion is found in cardiac insufficiency and polycythemia; a more marked degree of splenomegaly occurs as a result of portal hypertension due to a localized obstruction of the splenic vein or other parts of the portal system, a condition which is discussed below.

Splenomegaly occurs in various blood diseases—in hemolytic anemias in general, in myelophthisic forms accompanied by extramedullary hematopoiesis as in osteopetrosis, in leukemia, and in some instances of purpura. In Gaucher's disease, Niemann-Pick disease, and in acute reticuloendotheliosis (Letterer-Siwe disease), splenomegaly is often the presenting symptom. The spleen is enlarged in many cases of Hodgkin's disease and other lymphomas.

It is often stated that rickets causes enlargement of the spleen. In our experience this has not been the case unless marked anemia has been present as well. The spleen is, however, more readily palpable in rickets, owing to the weak abdominal musculature and the flaring of the costal margins. Most of the conditions associated with enlargement of the spleen are discussed elsewhere.

CONGESTIVE SPLENOMEGALY (PORTAL HYPERTENSION). Obstruction of the venous return from the spleen leads to enlargement, which may reach an enormous degree. The mechanisms underlying congestive splenomegaly are conventionally divided into intrahepatic and extrahepatic causes, which are of approximately equal frequency. Cirrhosis of the liver, which may have a variety of etiologic derivations, is the principal intrahepatic cause. Among extrahepatic causes may be mentioned congenital stenosis of the venous channels, adhesions or fibrous bands constricting the vessels from without, and thrombosis of the splenic or the portal vein. A rare cause is so-called cavernous transformation of the portal vein, the pathogenesis of which is still obscure; it may represent a congenital malformation or the end result of thrombosis incurred in early life, perhaps in the course of neonatal infection.

In response to venous obstruction, anastomotic venous channels form as a means of evading it. A network of vessels extends along the gastric and esophageal walls, attaining great prominence and complexity in cases of long standing and leading to the formation of varices. When large, these dilated vessels may project into the lumen of the esophagus or, more rarely, the fundus of the stomach. In young subjects, the collateral venous anastomosis which develops in the effort to bypass the splenic or portal vein block is seldom conspicuous in the round ligament and periumbilical vessels. Consequently, formation of a caput medusae is rare and clinically detectable dilatation of hemorrhoidal veins is virtually unknown. Venous pressure in the splenic-portal system is usually greater than 200 mm of water and may even exceed 450 mm. The spleen in the early stages is soft and spongy and drips dark blood abundantly when cut. Later, as fibrosis and proliferation of reticular tissue advance in response to persistent back pressure and stasis, it becomes firmer, paler, and more dry. Hemosiderin deposits may be present but are not prominent.

In the first months or even years following the establishment of splenomegaly from venous obstruction, decompression from the escape of blood into the esophageal or gastric lumen through rupture of a varix may cause a striking reduction of the spleen's size within a few hours, so that overnight the organ, formerly conspicuous, becomes no longer palpable. With transfusions the portal system's pressure and the size of the spleen may be quickly brought back to the levels existing before hemorrhage took place. If the lost blood is not replaced by transfusion, the spleen gradually enlarges again over the course of weeks after bleeding has stopped. The cycle of blood loss, spleen shrinkage, and restoration may be repeated a number of times before the spleen, now involved in a progressive fibrotic process, fails to undergo significant shrinkage following hemorrhage. With long-standing congestion, the characteristic features of hypersplenism may be found in the peripheral blood. Reduction of the platelet count is in these cases the most troublesome component of hypersplenism, since it aggravates the risk of massive blood loss from a bleeding varix, and since it also lends itself poorly to correction by transfusion or, indeed, by any therapeutic device short of splenectomy. With repeated bouts of bleeding, many of these patients suffer from chronic iron-deficiency anemia and bone marrow exhaustion. Patients with intrahepatic portal obstruction may display some of the disturbances which at times accompany hepatic cirrhosis: ascites, reduction of serum albumin concentration, elevation of serum bilirubin, and other measurable expressions of depressed liver function.

The condition may be found as early as the second year but is more frequent at school age. It develops insidiously and may be well advanced by the time help is sought. Hemorrhage is the commonest symptom which brings the patient to a physician; it usually involves the sudden vomiting of a cupful or more of blood, or perhaps the passage of tarry or even bloody-looking stools. In some instances the enlarged spleen is the first feature noticed. There may be attacks of pain due to perisplenitis. Other patients are brought because of pallor, weakness, and fatigability.

As a rule the diagnosis is strongly suggested by the finding of a greatly enlarged spleen in a patient who gives a history of bloody vomitus or blood loss in the stools. In those patients seen early, whose spleen has shrunk from decompression following hemorrhage, correct diagnosis may not be possible until the spleen has had time to enlarge again. Identification of the cases associated with intrahepatic venous obstruction is often possible on the basis of physical findings alone, when the liver is hard and perhaps enlarged as well; or a battery of liver function tests may be required before the liver can be incriminated. The peripheral blood and bone marrow should be carefully studied in order to assess the results of blood loss and the severity of secondary hypersplenism. Barium swallow may reveal filling defects caused by esophageal varices (Fig. 12), although roentgenographic changes are not always present. Recent hemorrhage not infrequently deflates esophageal varices in the same way as it may allow the spleen to shrink. Direct search for esophageal or gastric varices by endoscopy requires superior technical skill and gentleness in order to avoid provocation of additional serious hemorrhage. In a few patients who fail to give a clear history of blood loss in vomitus or stools, repeated testing of feces for occult blood may supply this important evidence of alimentary tract bleeding. Other causes of splenomegaly with bleeding, such as leukemia or Gaucher's disease, can usualy be identified directly.

The splenic and portal venous circulations can be effectively mapped out roentgenographically after intrasplenic injection of radiopaque material suitable for intravenous administration. Since the procedure is not devoid of risk, it is best reserved for patients about to undergo operation for the establishment of a shunt between the portal and caval systems.

The duration of congestive splenomegaly is variable but is usually measured in years. In those cases secondary to hepatic disease, the prognosis is determined largely by the functional integrity of the liver. In those with extrahepatic venous obstruction, blood loss constitutes an increasingly grave threat, but hardly ever are the first few hemorrhages fatal; with proper management there should be plenty of time to establish the diagnosis and to plan corrective treatment. Progress in blood vessel surgery has greatly improved the outlook.

Treatment may be divided into supportive and operative measures. Acute blood loss may call for transfusion, and chronic blood loss usually requires supplementation of a generous diet by addition of medicinal iron. Dangerous bleeding from esophageal varices may be checked by passage of a Sengstaken balloon, a device which permits controlled intraluminal pressure to be applied at the desired level within the esophagus. In some instances esophageal bleeding has been stopped by cauterization through an esophagoscope or by injection of a sclerosing agent directly into the bleeding varix. Since definitive vascular surgery depends in part for its success on the size of the vessels involved, it is at times necessary to withhold operation for a long period, sometimes for several years. In these circumstances the full battery of palliative measures may have to be called on.

Various operations have been devised for bypassing the venous obstruction. In a splenorenal shunt the spleen is resected and the splenic vein joined to the left renal vein in an end-to-side anastomosis, leaving the kidney itself intact. Occasionally a large left adrenal vein permits an end-to-end anastomosis that is satisfactory. The splenorenal operation is but one form of portocaval anastomosis, others joining some portion of the portal vein itself directly to the

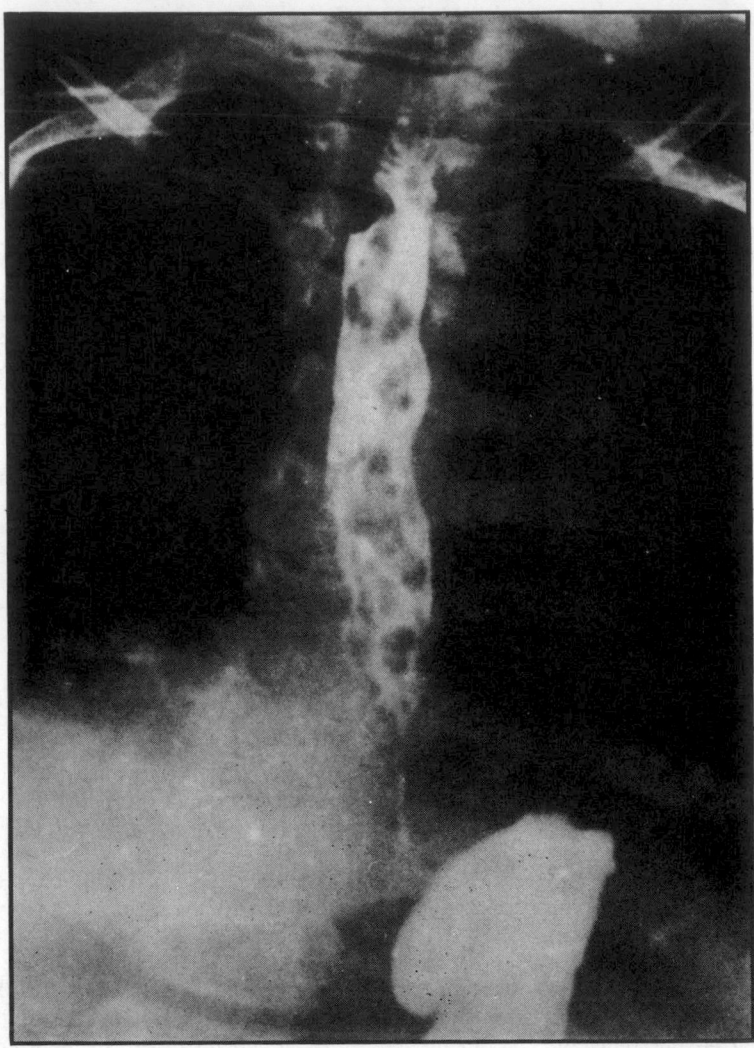

Fig. 12. Esophageal varices in cirrhosis of liver. Esophagram with barium meal.

inferior vena cava; the choice depends on the size, accessibility, and mobility of the structures at hand in the individual case. In patients with extrahepatic obstruction, a bypassing maneuver may well bring about a lasting cure with complete cessation of bleeding from esophageal or gastric varices. Even in those with intrahepatic obstruction, considerable temporary improvement may be realized, although the liver lesion may be expected to determine the outcome.

Simple splenectomy usually cures the untoward manifestations of hypersplenism in the bone marrow and peripheral blood but, except in the very rare instances of localized thrombosis of the splenic vein, does nothing to relieve the venous obstruction. It should therefore be condemned, save as an initial step in one of the venous shunt operations. The results of ligation of the hepatic and splenic arteries, as a means of controlling blood loss from venous anastomotic channels, have on the whole been disappointing.

HYPERSPLENISM.   For years it has been recognized that many hemolytic anemias, thrombocytopenic states, and neutropenias, occurring separately or in combination, respond favorably to removal of an enlarged spleen. The hypothesis by which such a sequence of events may be explained assumes that the alteration found in the peripheral blood represents an exaggeration of the normal functions of the spleen in controlling the concentration of the cellular components in circulation. The term "hypersplenism" epitomizes this hypothesis by focusing responsibility squarely on the spleen. Virtually any condition which leads to chronic splenic enlargement may be incidentally associated with such manifestations of presumably excessive splenic activity. Any of three cellular components—erythrocytes, neutrophils, or platelets—may be affected singly or in various combinations; when all three are involved, pancytopenia ensues. The bone marrow usually shows hypercellularity, with increased numbers and younger forms of the progenitors of the cells which are decreased in the peripheral blood. While some observers claim that instances of primary or so-called idiopathic hypersplenism occur, progressive improvement in diagnostic methods supports more and more the view that it is a secondary phenomenon. No constant or characteristic anatomic change is found in the spleen or elsewhere. The condition obviously constitutes a syndrome, not a disease entity.

Hypersplenism may be documented by demonstrating the rapid destruction of normal transfused erythrocytes as well as the patient's own red cells tagged with isotopes such as chromium[51] and the accumulation of excess radioactivity in the spleen. In conditions where the cells causing splenic enlargement also accumulate in the marrow (e.g., Gaucher's disease) such studies are necessary to determine the relative contribution to the hematologic picture of marrow invasion versus splenic destruction of circulating red cells, white cells, and platelets.

In circumstances where the hematologic abnormalities are due solely to the splenic enlargement (e.g., portal or splenic vein thrombosis), splenectomy will relieve them completely. In the more common conditions associated with splenomegaly, removal of the organ will eliminate only that portion of the hematologic abnormality resulting from the secondary splenic enlargement but will not affect the underlying disease (e.g., sickle-cell anemia, thalassemia, lymphomas). As indicated earlier, the hazard of postsplenectomy infection in just such patients demands that splenectomy be undertaken only when indications are definite and when the benefits anticipated outweigh the dangers imposed.

REFERENCES

Akerren, Y. On the occurrence of palpable spleens in healthy newborn babies and healthy infants. Acta Paediat., 34:184, 1947.
Blaustein, A. (ed.). The Spleen. New York, McGraw-Hill Book Co., 1963.
Bush, J. A., and Ainger, L. E. Congenital absence of spleen with congenital heart disease. Pediatrics, 15:93, 1955.
Crosby, W. H. Normal functions of the spleen relative to red blood cells; a review. Blood, 14:399, 1959.
——— Hypersplenism. Ann. Rev. Med., 13:127, 1962.
Hsia, D. Y-Y., and Gellis, S. C. Portal hypertension in infants and children. Amer. J. Dis. Child., 90:290, 1955.
Ivemark, B. I. Implications of agenesis of the spleen on the pathogenesis of conotruncus anomalies in childhood. Acta. Paediat., 44(Suppl. 104):1, 1955.
Mazel, M. S. Traumatic rupture of the spleen with especial reference to its characteristics in young children. J. Pediat., 26:82, 1945.
Motulsky, A. G., Brown, G. O., Jr., and Finch, C. A. Anemia and the spleen. New Eng. J. Med., 259:1164, 1958.
Murphy, J. W., and Mitchell, W. A. Congenital absence of the spleen. Pediatrics, 20:253, 1957.
Robinson, T. W., and Sturgeon, P. Post-splenectomy infection in infants and children. Pediatrics, 25:941, 1960.
Smith, C. H., Erlandson, M. E., Schulman, I., and Stern, G. Hazard of severe infections in splenectomized infants and children. Amer. J. Med., 22:390, 1957.
——— Erlandson, M. E., Stern, G., and Hilgartner, M. W. Postsplenectomy infection in Cooley's anemia; an appraisal of the problems in this and other blood disorders, with a consideration of prophylaxis. New Eng. J. Med., 266:737, 1962.

17.10
THE LYMPH NODES

IRVING SCHULMAN

It is characteristic of infancy and childhood that the lymphoid tissues respond to infection with a marked degree of swelling and hyperplasia. Moreover, the enlargement may persist for a long time after the primary exciting cause has subsided. This tendency is met with in all parts of the body. In the upper respiratory tract it manifests itself by the familiar hypertrophy of the tonsils and adenoids, but any of the external or internal lymph nodes exhibit this same tendency.

As age advances, retrogressive changes take place in the various lymphoid structures, and the response of regional nodes to acute infections tends to diminish. Those connected with the digestive tract begin to subside after the second year, and by the fifth or sixth year the enlargement has almost disappeared. The tonsils, adenoids, and cervical nodes tend to diminish in size around the seventh or eighth year and may undergo marked atrophy at the time of puberty.

The prominent lymphoid response in early life has been attributed to the fact that the child lacks acquired resistance toward many infectious agents. It is characteristic not only of tuberculosis but of many pyogenic infections that a first infection meets with little resistance at the portal of entry; it travels rapidly to the regional lymph nodes, where it may cause considerable reaction. A subsequent infection with the same organism finds the body with a certain degree of acquired resistance; the infectious agent encounters difficulty in getting beyond the portal of entry and may never reach the regional lymph nodes.

Heredity seems to play an important part in resistance to infections in general; this is borne out by the behavior of the lymphoid tissues. Enlarged tonsils and adenoids and marked cervical adenitis are often found in every member of a large family; frequently the parents, during childhood, had been similarly affected.

Inflammatory Adenitis

Acute Adenitis

A certain amount of secondary involvement of the lymph nodes accompanies practically all inflammatory processes. In young patients it not infrequently outlasts the original infection or greatly overshadows it in clinical importance, and in infants acute adenitis often comes close to being a disease in itself. This is particularly true during the first two years of life.

The condition most commonly follows infections of the upper respiratory tract, with involvement of the cervical nodes; it may also be seen in the occipital nodes in scalp infections, in the preauricular and postauricular nodes, in the nodes of the submental region, the axilla, and the groin, or even in internal nodes like the mesenteric and retroperitoneal groups. Suppuration of internal nodes is fortunately exceedingly rare. With acute cervical adenitis the responsible organism may or may not be recovered from pharyngeal cultures. Unless an abscess forms, one does not learn with certainty what organism is responsible or whether viable organisms are present at all. In the majority of cases of acute suppurative adenitis, beta hemolytic streptococci are found, but pneumococci, staphylococci, and other organisms occur, depending on the location and specific nature of the primary process. Some of the respiratory viruses cause enlargement and tenderness of regional lymph nodes; in these infections suppuration occurs, as a rule, only with secondary bacterial contamination.

Some swelling accompanies the primary infection, but it may increase even after this has completely healed, sometimes reaching, after two or three weeks, the size of a walnut or a hen's egg. Size alone does not indicate whether the node will eventually break down. There is great variation in individual cases in the time occupied by the increase and subsequent diminution in size, but the total duration of the process is hardly ever less than a week; in many cases the gland does not return to normal for weeks or even months. In primary infections of the throat the ensuing adenitis is often bilateral, particularly in young patients, and more than one gland may be involved on each side. Cervical adenitis often causes stiffness of the neck as a protective reaction that may be as definite as in meningitis. With great swelling the soft tissues of the lateral pharyngeal wall may be displaced medially, simulating peritonsillar or retropharyngeal abscess, and the voice may be affected. In the most acute examples of adenitis there is marked inflammation of the periglandular tissues, with pain, tenderness, and local heat. In many the node remains firm throughout; in others it becomes so soft at the height of the swelling as to suggest fluctuation; in still others it actually breaks down. If suppuration occurs it is generally evident in the latter part of the second week, but sometimes it may be as late as the third or even the fourth week. In general the cases with the most rapid enlargement are accompanied by the most severe general reaction, though there are exceptions.

Untreated cases run their course with slight fever and few general symptoms; but in young infants the constitutional reaction is often severe, particularly in the first week, and the physician may be in doubt whether the local process is sufficient to explain it. A sustained high temperature is not uncommon at the onset of severe cases. Later it becomes remitting in type, with wide fluctuations during the course of 24 hours. Daily swings from $98°$ F in the morning to $103°$ or $104°$ F by late afternoon may be repeated for as long as four weeks, even in cases in which the infection does not go on to frank abscess formation. Many of these patients show relatively little concomitant anorexia and malaise. Suppuration, when it occurs, develops earlier in infants than in older children. In a number of instances acute hemorrhagic nephritis is seen as a complication.

The course of acute adenitis has been greatly altered by chemotherapy. Prompt systemic treatment of adenitis will usually prevent suppuration and as a rule will control constitutional symptoms within 48 hours. Penicillin will cope successfully with most infections caused by hemolytic streptococci or pneumococci. For staphylococcal infections other agents are often required. Local application of cold may give some relief from pain until defervescence commences. Surgical intervention is not indicated unless suppuration has occurred. Spreading of the infection to adjacent nodes or the development of diffuse cellulitis is often the result of premature surgical intervention.

Chronic Adenitis

The commonest cause of chronic lymphadenitis is persistent pyogenic infection within the area drained: familiar examples are cervical adenopathy secondary to repeated upper respiratory infections; enlargement of the preauricular, occipital, and cervical nodes in eczema of the face and scalp; and palpability of the epitrochlear nodes in many nail-biters who develop digital infections. Unexplained generalized enlargement of the lymph nodes should suggest syphilis. It may be due to infectious mononucleosis, leukemia, lymphosarcoma, or acute reticuloendotheliosis. Tuberculous adenitis of superficial nodes is usually confined to the neck. The possibility of Hodgkin's disease, lymphogranuloma venereum, tularemia, or cat scratch disease should not be overlooked. In some instances all of the causes mentioned can be excluded, and the diagnosis remains obscure even after biopsy.

The Malignant Lymphomas

JOANN M. CORNET

The malignant lymphomas of clinical significance in the pediatric age group are Hodgkin's disease and the lymphosarcomas. In contrast to adults, these malignant lymphoproliferative disorders are relatively rare in children and constitute about 8 to 10 percent of all childhood neoplasms.

Hodgkin's Disease

Hodgkin's disease is characterized by a progressive, painless enlargement of regional lymph nodes. It is considered to be unicentric in origin, arising in a single node or anatomic group of nodes, with predictable extensions to contiguous nodes being the usual mode of progression. Subsequent involvement of other tissues including spleen, liver, bone marrow, lung, and CNS occurs in the natural history of the disease and accounts for many of the protean manifestations.

ETIOLOGY AND DISTRIBUTION. Although an infectious agent has been suggested because of the granulomatous appearance of the involved lymphoid structures, the etiology is unknown. Despite certain clinical manifestations and laboratory abnormalities which suggest an inflammatory process, the majority of opinion is that Hodgkin's disease is a neoplastic process.

The occurrence of Hodgkin's disease in patients with immunologic disorders such as SLE and rheumatoid arthritis and the frequent demonstration of impairment of lymphocyte-mediated immune response have led to an intense search for common or related predisposing factors. Additionally, the infrequent but apparently causal relationship between administration of hydantoin derivatives and the development of pseudolymphoma has long been noted. Although this type of lymphoid hyperplasia has certain histologic features common to Hodgkin's disease and lymphosarcoma, the absolute criteria for malignancy have been lacking, and regression of the lymphadenopathy has occurred following withdrawal of the offending agent. More recently, however, a group of patients receiving anticonvulsant therapy has been described in whom definite criteria of malignant lymphoma were established and who had persistence and progression of lymphoid pathology following cessation of antiscizure therapy. Whether the atypical hyperplasia observed during anticonvulsant therapy is precancerous or whether the agents are truly carcinogenic in certain sensitive individuals requires further clarification.

There is a male predominance of cases at all ages, and in childhood 60 percent of cases occur in males. The onset of the disease is rarely seen before the age of 5, after which there is a gradual rise in incidence through age 11, followed by a striking increase through adolescence and persisting through age 30.

PATHOLOGY. The cervical nodes are involved in over 50 percent of cases; axillary, inguinal, mediastinal, and retroperitoneal nodes are also frequently involved. Enlargement is usually discreet and the capsule intact. However, lymph nodes from mediastinal involvement, in widespread disease, or following extensive radio- and chemotherapy are usually adherent. Diagnosis is based upon the distinctive histopathology of the involved area. There may be varying degrees of proliferation of lymphocytes, eosinophils, histiocytes or reticulum cells, collagen and fibrous tissue, but the essential feature is the presence of *Reed-Sternberg* cells. These are large, often pleomorphic, multinucleated cells with a well-defined nuclear membrane and prominent nucleoli. Classification into three types has been made: (1) In paragranuloma, seen in 9 percent of cases, normal architecture is well preserved, normal-appearing lymphocytes are abundant, and Reed-Sternberg cells are scant. (2) Granuloma, the classic pathologic lesion accounting for 90 percent of cases, consists of loss of normal architecture from replacement by pleomorphic cellular elements including abundant Reed-Sternberg cells. (3) Sarcoma represents the most destructive form of the disease in which necrosis is present and cellular elements have been totally replaced by fibrosis and extremely pleomorphic Reed-Sternberg cells. Although this nomenclature of Hodgkin's disease originally described by Jackson and Parker has been of long-standing use, a revised classification has been recently advocated by Lukes and Butler based upon a more precise histologic description: (1) lymphocyte predominance; (2) nodular sclerosis; (3) mixed cellularity; and (4) lymphocyte depletion. These four histologic types have been considered to reflect the immunologic state of the host and to be an expression of the host's dynamic response, and may, therefore, impart a more reliable general basis for prognosis. According to this concept, the importance of the lymphocyte is recognized in relation to the immunologic defect described in Hodgkin's disease, manifested by an inability to develop delayed hypersensitivity and a delay in homograft rejection.

CLINICAL MANIFESTATIONS. The signs and symptoms depend upon the site and extent of involvement. Most commonly the initial manifestation is a painless, progressive enlargement of a superficial lymph node, or group of nodes, especially in the neck, where 60 percent of cases occur primarily. Axillary and inguinal adenopathy occur less frequently. Mediastinal adenopathy may be suggested by persistent nonproductive cough, although this site of involvement may be initially asymptomatic. Unexplained abdominal pain may be attributed to enlargement of retroperitoneal nodes. Systemic symptoms of intermittent fever (Pel-Ebstein), anorexia, nausea, and weight loss are usually absent when the disease is localized; pruritus is infrequently a complaint in children even with extensive involvement. The presence of hepatosplenomegaly signifies that the disease has extended beyond the regional lymph nodes.

Differential diagnosis of the adenopathy includes chronic pyogenic and tuberculous adenitis, cat scratch disease, infectious mononucleosis, hydantoin hypersensitivity, as well as other malignant lymphomas, reticuloendothelioses, or metastatic tumors, especially arising in the head and neck (e.g., nasopharynx or thyroid). With elimination of specific causes, diagnosis depends upon histologic examination. Although nodal aspiration may reveal typical Reed-Sternberg cells, definite diagnosis should be made on excisionally biopsied material. Proper selection of the node for biopsy is critical, and the node showing the greatest involvement may not necessarily be the most accessible one. Nodes in the inguinal region should be avoided whenever possible since lymphadenopathy is common in this area as a result of minor infections and trauma. If the disease is confined to intrathoracic nodes, a scalene biopsy or thoracotomy may be necessary. Once the diagnosis has been established, definition of anatomic extent or clinical staging should be done.

CLINICAL STAGING. As will be discussed subsequently, the staging of Hodgkin's disease offers a reasonable basis for determining therapy and defining prognosis. The following staging definitions are based on the original classification by Peters which have been recently modified by Kaplan and others.

Stage I. Disease limited to one anatomic region or to two contiguous anatomic regions on the same side of the diaphragm.

Stage II. Disease in more than two anatomic regions or in two noncontiguous regions on the same side of the diaphragm.

Stage III. Disease on both sides of the diaphragm, but not extending beyond the involvement of lymph nodes, spleen and/or Waldeyer's ring.

Stage IV. Involvement of the bone marrow, lung parenchyma, pleura, liver, bone, skin, kidneys, gastrointestinal tract, or any tissue or organ in addition to lymph nodes, spleen, or Waldeyer's ring.

All of the above stages are further subclassified into "A" or "B" to indicate absence or presence of documented, unexplained systemic symptoms of fever, night sweats, and/or pruritus.

Careful clinical, laboratory, and radiographic evaluation is mandatory for accurate staging. In addition to a detailed history and thorough physical examination, a complete blood count, urinalysis, postero-anterior and lateral chest film, skeletal survey, excretory urogram via an inferior venacavogram, bipedal lymphangiogram, liver function tests including BSP, and bone marrow aspiration should be obtained. In the presence of hilar adenopathy, whole lung tomograms should be performed. During the past few years utilization of these diagnostic procedures has permitted a more accurate definition of localized disease. Lymphangiography has been of exceptional value in that 10 percent of patients with cervical adenopathy thought to be clinically Stage I were found to have retroperitoneal node involvement and, therefore, were actually Stage III; the presence of occult disease is even greater in clinical Stage II-B disease.

It should be emphasized that in children lymph-

angiography may be exceedingly difficult to perform, and under age 6 a lymphangiogram may be impossible to obtain. Recently there has been considerable interest in further refining staging techniques by performing an abdominal laparotomy on patients with Stage I and II disease. Using this approach, biopsy of superior and inferior periaortic and mesenteric nodes can be done, in addition to liver biopsy and splenectomy. In adults this additional histologic sampling has resulted in reclassification from Stages I or II to Stages III or IV in approximately 40 percent of patients; in children, where lymphangiograms are unsuccessful, identification of disease below the diaphragm has occurred in about 50 percent of patients explored. Although this extensive approach may be regarded as being extremely aggressive for the child who seems well except for a single pathologic node in the neck, the positive correlation between accurate staging, proper selection of subsequent therapy, and ultimate prognosis appears to justify the procedure.

HEMATOLOGIC FINDINGS. There is no characteristic hematologic abnormality. In localized disease, the complete blood count is usually normal. With more extensive disease, however, anemia is common, and a high percentage of patients will have polymorphonuclear leucocytosis; leucopenia and lymphopenia often occur in advanced disease in which a few Reed-Sternberg cells may occasionally be seen in the peripheral blood. Because these cells are infrequently found in bone marrow aspirates, bone biopsy is usually necessary to document the presence or absence of bone involvement, and is recommended for children with Stage III disease.

TREATMENT AND PROGNOSIS. In the past decade it has been recognized that Hodgkin's disease is not invariably fatal as has been the previous concept. The 30 to 40 percent overall curability has been largely the result of aggressive radiotherapy to localized Stage I and II disease. Both radiotherapy and chemotherapy have produced significant palliation and have increased length of survival in Stage III and IV disease.

At the present time in many centers the recommended treatment of Stage I and II disease above the diaphragm is intensive wide field megavoltage radiotherapy. Using this technique 3,500 to 4,000 r are delivered over a 3- to 4-week period to all contiguous node-bearing areas of the neck, axillae, and mediastinum. This form of therapy is well tolerated and is designed to prevent recurrence of disease at the original site as well as to eradicate existing microscopic foci in contiguous groups of nodes. Results of this extended field therapy indicate that Stage I and II disease, which accounts for approximately 30 percent of cases, is about 70 to 80 percent curable.

There is insufficient evidence on which to recommend chemotherapy in addition to radiotherapy in localized disease. Additionally, the implications of the effect of immunosuppression on a host with presumed existing immunologic incompetence have resulted in the withholding of chemotherapy to Stage

I and Stage II disease patients by the majority of persons involved with their management.

Although sufficient long-term analysis is lacking, it now appears that patients with Stage III-A disease have a significant chance of curability when radiotherapy is extended to the node-bearing areas of the groin and retroperitoneum. In this situation, prior removal of the spleen coincident to staging at laparotomy affords the advantage of a narrower port thus sparing the left lower lung and left upper kidney from the adverse effects of radiation.

While inclusion of Stage III-B patients into programs of widespread radiotherapy has been attempted, it remains to be seen if this approach offers curability in addition to the significant palliation reported from some centers.

At the present time the mainstay of therapy for Stage III-B and IV patients is chemotherapy, where often complete or partial but temporary remissions can be effected in a high percentage of patients. As in acute leukemia, survival appears to be related to length of time spent in complete remission; consequently vigorous therapeutic management is indicated.

For initial therapy the drug of choice is vinblastine (Velban) which is an alkaloid of the periwinkle plant. Dosages of 0.075 to 0.20 mg/kg intravenously once weekly are given. Since this agent produces bone marrow depression, a complete blood count should be performed prior to each administration of the drug. When remission occurs, maintenance of the drug should be continued since relapse develops considerably sooner if therapy is discontinued. Vincristine (Oncovin), another periwinkle alkaloid, is as effective in Hodgkin's disease but its usefulness may be restricted by development of serious neurotoxicity with prolonged administration. However, since vincristine produces minimal bone marrow depression it may be substituted for vinblastine for short periods when leucopenia results from the latter. The weekly intravenous dosage of vincristine is 0.05 to 0.075 mg/kg. Another chemotherapeutic agent which has produced remissions and which is not cross-resistant in patients refractory to the periwinkle derivatives is the alkylating agent cyclophosphamide (Cytoxan). This drug can be given as an intravenous course, 7.5 mg/kg/day, daily, for 5 to 7 days. When remission is obtained, oral daily maintenance, 2.5 mg/kg is advisable. Other agents which have been effective in some cases are nitrogen mustard (Mustargen), chlorambucil (Leukeran), and procarbazine (Matulane). This latter compound, developed most recently, is a potent myelosuppressive but appears to have no cross-resistance with the other alkylating agents.

Local radiotherapy for palliation of symptoms can be beneficial, especially for extensive mediastinal involvement. General supportive therapy for infectious and hemorrhagic complications is identical to measures discussed in the previous section on acute leukemia. The value of corticosteroids appears to be nonspecific and probably contributes little to suppression of the basic disease process.

The prognosis for Stage III and IV disease has been extremely poor, with only 10 to 15 percent 5-year survival and less than 5 percent 5-year survival respectively. Recent efforts directed toward improving remission rate and survival consist of intensive courses of chemotherapy utilizing four agents (prednisone, vincristine, procarbazine, and cyclophosphamide or nitrogen mustard), in combination or in sequence. At the present time utilization of these approaches is limited to investigational centers where complex equipment and supportive care are readily available.

When prognosis is evaluated in terms of the histopathology of the Hodgkin's lesion, it is evident that lymphocyte depletion with diffuse fibrosis, or extreme abundance and pleomorphism of Reed-Sternberg cells is associated with a poor prognosis, and is most frequently present in Stage III and IV disease.

There are few diseases in children where the cooperation between medical specialists is more necessary, complex, and demanding, The desired precision in staging requires the coordinated expertise of the pediatrician, radiologist, pathologist, and surgeon; subsequent radiotherapy employing wide fields and high dosages makes special demands on the radiotherapist and his equipment to minimize radiation injury to growth centers. The use of chemotherapeutic agents requires considerable judgment in the selection and balance of therapeutic effectiveness and toxicity. Although the child and adolescent appear to have an advantage in their tolerance to all treatment modalities, meticulous attention must be focused on their overall physical and emotional development and nutritional requirements.

COMPLICATIONS AND IMMUNOLOGIC STATUS. The increased susceptibility of patients with Hodgkin's disease to a variety of infections has been frequently observed. The most common infectious complications are the usual bacterial infections. However, there is also a high incidence of tuberculosis and unusual fungal diseases such as histoplasmosis, cryptococcosis, aspergilliosis, and nocardiosis; herpes zoster, varicella, cytomegalic infections, as well as toxoplasmosis and pneumocystis disease are also more frequent. In an effort to explain this increased susceptibility, considerable information has been gathered regarding the immunologic status of the patient with Hodgkin's disease. It appears that early in the disease there is a depression of cell-mediated or delayed hypersensitivity, manifest by loss of preexisting hypersensitivity (cutaneous anergy) to PPD and *Candida* antigen, in addition to inability to develop sensitivity to dinitrochlorobenzene. Since lymphopenia is rarely present in the early stage of disease it is proposed that functional or qualitative deficiencies of the lymphocyte are responsible for the impairment of delayed immunologic capacity. Serum immunoglobins are usually normal in localized disease.

In disseminated Hodgkin's disease the immunologic defect is progressive, less specific, and more complex. The relative contributions of the marked lymphocyte and leucocyte depletion and hypogammaglobulinemia are difficult to define. Both the extent of the disease and the consequences of immunosuppressive therapy also contribute to the profound depression of host defense mechanisms.

Lymphosarcoma

Lymphosarcoma is a primary malignant tumor of lymphoid structures. It may arise within regional lymph nodes as well as in extranodal sites. The gastrointestinal tract is a frequent area of initial involvement. In contrast to Hodgkin's disease, localization of lymphosarcoma is unusual and a multicentric origin is presumed.

Cases may occur at any time in the pediatric age group, with no striking age peak as is seen in the acute leukemias. A 2.5:1 male predominance of cases is well recognized.

ETIOLOGY. Although as in acute leukemia a viral etiology has been postulated, the true stimulus to the development of the neoplastic process remains undetermined. The increased incidence of lymphosarcoma seen in children with primary immunologic deficiency states (agammaglobulinemia, ataxiatelangiectasia, Bloom's, Wiskcott-Aldrich, Chediak-Higashi syndromes) has prompted investigation of possible common pathogenetic mechanisms in the development of lymphoma and immunologic impairment. As discussed in the section on Hodgkin's disease, the relationship between certain drugs, notably hydantoins, and benign and malignant lymph node hyperplasia remains to be elucidated.

PATHOLOGY. Lymphosarcomatous tumors can originate within and outside the lymph nodes in any region where lymphoid tissue is present. Two distinct types are recognized histologically. The most frequent form of lymphosarcoma, accounting for approximately 70 percent of cases, is comprised of small lymphocytes of varying degrees of maturity. The second type, in which the predominant cell is a large immature reticulum cell, is referred to as reticulum cell sarcoma. It is not unusual, however, for absolute morphologic distinction to be difficult especially in highly undifferentiated tumors. In addition, lymphoblastic and mixed lymphocyte and reticulum cell types have been described.

CLINICAL MANIFESTATIONS. The presenting symptoms depend upon the site of involvement. Peripheral lymph nodes are most commonly involved, particularly in the cervical area. Enlargement is often rapid, usually painless, and unaccompanied by systemic manifestations of fever or weight loss. Abdominal lymphosarcoma is the second most frequent site of initial involvement and accounts for approximately one-third of the cases. These tumors may occur retroperitoneally or anywhere along the gastrointestinal tract, especially the ileum, and may cause obstructive symptoms including intussusception in addition to abdominal pain, nausea, and vomiting. Rarely, persistent unexplained fever may be the only symptom of intra-abdominal lymphosarcoma. The mediastinum is a relatively common site of lymphosarcoma, and the initial manifestation may be persistent cough. Progression of mediastinal involvement is often rapid and dyspnea accompanied by clinical signs of superior vena cava obstruction may progress to an immediately life-threatening situation within a short period of time. Another less common area of involvement is the oronasopharynx where the primary tumor may be small and relatively asymptomatic, with the cervical adenopathy being metastatic. For this reason adequate visualization of the oronasopharynx should occur prior to biopsy of any neck mass.

LABORATORY DATA. In the majority of cases the initial peripheral blood count is normal. Absolute diagnosis is based upon histologic description of excisionally biopsied accessible lymph nodes. Lymphangiography may be expected to demonstrate retroperitoneal involvement in a high percentage of cases. Although staging of disease appears to be of less prognostic value than in Hodgkin's, it is a useful method for defining extent of disease and in planning of subsequent radiotherapy and chemotherapy.

LEUKEMIC TRANSFORMATION. Leukemic transformation occurs in approximately 40 percent of children with lymphosarcoma. This is seen in both the peripheral blood and bone marrow where complete or partial replacement of normal elements by blast or immature cells occurs. The median time for developing this complication is about 6 months. Although the morphology of the abnormal cells is most frequently indistinguishable from acute lymphoblastic leukemia, the leukemic transformation of reticulum cell sarcoma may occasionally resemble acute monoblastic or monomyelocytic leukemia. There is no apparent relationship to original site of involvement or extent of disease.

TREATMENT AND PROGNOSIS. Initial therapy of lymphosarcoma depends upon the site and extent of disease. Since this disease is often widespread at the time of diagnosis, surgical excision and/or local or extended field radiotherapy cannot be anticipated to be curative as in Hodgkin's disease. Exceptions to this poor prognosis may occasionally be seen in the following situations: reticulum cell sarcoma presenting as a solitary bone lesion; lymphosarcoma or reticulum cell sarcoma arising in a solitary nodal focus high in the neck or extranodally in the skin of the cheek, the nasopharynx, or within the gastrointestinal tract. In such instances in the presence of normal hematologic findings, a negative chest x-ray and a negative lymphangiogram, a potentially curable situation may be defined. Obliterative local radiotherapy, 3,000 to 4,000 r given over a 3- to 4-week period, is the treatment of choice unless surgical extirpation is feasible.

In the majority of instances radiotherapy is only palliative. However, it may produce prompt and effective relief of symptoms in superior mediastinal involvement. At the present time for generalized nodal diseases prednisone, vincristine, and cyclophosphamide (Cytoxan) appear to be the most effective chemotherapeutic agents. Although oral administration of cyclophosphamide is efficacious, the intravenous route is preferable initially in order to achieve a more rapid response. The usual dosage is 7.5 mg/kg/day intravenously for five consecutive days, followed by an oral daily maintenance dose of 2.5 mg/kg. During the initial course of therapy, adequate hydration is essential since hyperuricemia may occasionally occur. For the acutely ill patient additional benefit may be obtained from simultaneous administration of prednisone 2 mg/kg/day in four divided oral doses.

When leukemic transformation occurs, chemotherapy is given as previously described for acute lymphoblastic leukemia. Prednisone and vincristine are the agents of choice for induction of remission. Although it has been indicated recently that by using these two drugs complete remission can be achieved in 85 percent of children, the majority of experience has shown a remission rate of only 25 to 50 percent. Similarly, the duration of remission is shorter in these children as compared with children with primary acute leukemia. Although conventional chemotherapy has not been effective in preventing leukemic transformation, recent evidence suggests that combined induction chemotherapy and radiotherapy to detectable tumor sites followed by continued concurrent courses of prednisone, vincristine, 6-mercaptopurine, Methotrexate, and cyclophosphamide may result in long remission and prevent or delay the development of leukemia.

From the foregoing it is obvious that the prognosis for both lymphosarcoma and reticulum cell sarcoma is grave. Survival figures for children are much less favorable when compared with adults with these diseases. Excluding the rare patient with localized disease and utilizing conventional therapy, the median survival is approximately 10 months.

As in the treatment of acute leukemia it appears that vigorous intensive administration of radiotherapy and/or chemotherapy has unquestionably resulted in prolongation of remission time and median survival time, and in effecting, in some instances, cure of malignant lymphoma. Since these therapies usually require readily available supportive care during induction of remission or as a consequence of the myelosuppression which often accompanies or follows intensive therapy, there is a growing opinion that treatment be initiated in institutions staffed and equipped for handling these complex problems. Once remission is achieved, however, return of the child to his local environment is both necessary and desirable. Ongoing care and follow-up can be mutually achieved through the cooperation of the referring physician and the medical center based specialists.

Burkitt's Tumor

Although the Burkitt lymphoma was originally thought to be confined to regions of tropical central Africa and New Guinea where it is endemic, it is now known to occur sporadically throughout the world including the United States. This lymphoreticular neoplasm is best classified as malignant lymphoma, undifferentiated, Burkitt type.

The presenting clinical manifestations are that of a rapidly growing multicentric extranodal tumor involving one or more sites and most commonly the pelvic or abdominal viscera, retroperitoneal soft tissues, facial or long bones. Although abnormal cells are rarely seen in the peripheral blood, significant numbers of undifferentiated lymphoreticular cells may be seen in both the bone marrow and CSF. In contrast to African children, the sporadic cases are usually older (median age 10 years) and have a lower frequency of jaw tumors and a higher incidence of peripheral lymphadenopathy and pleural effusions.

Untreated, the disease is rapidly progressive and fatal. However, a prompt and dramatic response has been seen in approximately 75 percent of non-African children given repeated courses of cyclophosphamide (Cytoxan) in high doses. Similar treatment of a group of African patients resulted in unmaintained remissions in about 20 percent.

The demonstration of high levels of herpeslike virus (HLV) antibodies in sera of affected patients and the indirect evidence of malignant transformation in tissue culture by HLV strongly suggest an oncogenic potential for an infectious agent. In endemic areas, arthropod-borne transmission of the virus may occur. Previous challenge to the reticuloendothelial system by malaria parasites appears to be related to the high incidence of Burkitt's tumor in tropical countries. The relationship of these findings to the HLV or Epstein-Barr virus associated with infectious mononucleosis remains to be elucidated. Although depressed IGG levels and impaired antibody response have been demonstrated in some patients, the determinants of host susceptibility and response to therapy have not been clarified.

REFERENCES

HODGKIN'S DISEASE

Aisenberg, A. C. Primary management of Hodgkin's disease. New Eng. J. Med., 278:93, 1968.

Billmeier, G. J., and Holton, C. P. Procarbazine hydrochloride in childhood cancer. J. Pediat., 75:892, 1969.

Frei, E., III, DeVita, V. T., Moxley, J. H., and Carbone, P. D. Approaches to improving the chemotherapy of Hodgkin's disease. Cancer Res., 26:1284, 1966.

Glatstein, E., Guernsey, J. M., Rosenberg, S. A., and Kaplan, H. S. The value of laparotomy and splenectomy in the staging of Hodgkin's disease. Cancer, 24:709, 1969.

Hyman, G. A., and Sommers, S. C. The development of Hodgkin's disease and lymphoma during anticonvulsant therapy. Blood, 28:416, 1966.

Jenkin, R. D. T., Peters, M. V., and Darte, J. M. M. Hodgkin's disease in children. Amer. J. Roentgen., 100:222, 1967.

Kaplan, H. S. Long-term results of palliative and radical radio-therapy of Hodgkin's disease. Cancer Res., 26:1250, 1966.

Lukes, R. J., and Butler, J. The pathology and nomenclature of Hodgkin's disease. Cancer Res., 26:1063, 1966.

Ultmann, J. E. The clinical picture of Hodgkin's disease. Cancer Res., 26:1047, 1966.

LYMPHOSARCOMA AND RETICULUM CELL SARCOMA

Borella, L. Reticulum cell sarcoma in children. Cancer, 17:26, 1964.

Carbone, P. P., Berard, C. W., Bennett, J. M., Ziegler, J. L., Cohen, M. H., and Gerber, P. Burkitt's tumor. Ann. Intern. Med., 70:817, 1969.

Hoogstraten, B., Owens, A. H., Lenhard, R. E., Glidewell, O. J., Leone, L. A., Olson, K. B., Harley, J. B., Townsend, S. R., Miller, S. P., and Spurr, C. L. Combination chemotherapy in lymphosarcoma and reticulum cell sarcoma. Blood, 33:370, 1969.

Hyman, G. A., and Cassileth, P. A. Efficacy of cyclophosphamide in the management of reticulum cell sarcoma. Cancer, 19:1386, 1966.

Jones, B., and Klingberg, W. G. Lymphosarcoma in children. J. Pediat., 63:11, 1963.

Sullivan, M. P. Leukemic transformation in lymphosarcoma of childhood. Pediatrics, 29:589, 1962.

Disorders of Hemostasis

17.11 MECHANISMS OF HEMOSTASIS

CHARLES F. ABILDGAARD
and IRVING SCHULMAN

The arrest of bleeding is achieved by the complex interaction of blood vessels, platelets, and the coagulation system. The functional interrelationships of these components are difficult to separate and in many instances not fully understood. A diagrammatic scheme of a current concept of hemostasis is shown in Figure 13.

Normally the structural integrity of the vascular wall is able to prevent spontaneous extravasation of blood, and bleeding does not occur from the minor traumas of ordinary activity. Interference with normal vascular integrity resulting in bleeding may be due to congenital abnormalities of structure or function of the vessels, nutritional deficiencies (scurvy), anoxia, inflammatory disease, allergic disorders, thrombocytopenia, or degenerative vascular conditions (aging). In addition to the passive role of containment, the vasculature responds to injury by reflex vasoconstriction of precapillary arterioles, leading to slowing of blood flow. This is accomplished in smaller capillaries by actual endothelial collapse. Reinforcement of local vasoconstriction follows release of serotonin from platelets. Significant slowing of flow in larger blood vessels may occur only after the systemic blood pressure has decreased. Restriction of blood vessels by the pressure of extravasated blood within the limits of surrounding tissues also may contribute to hemostasis, varying greatly with the anatomic location of bleeding.

In addition to the vascular responses to trauma and bleeding, the initial phase of hemostasis requires adequate numbers of normally functioning platelets. Following vascular injury, platelets immediately adhere to the site of endothelial damage and to one another, with prompt aggregation into a platelet plug which serves as the initial hemostatic seal (prior to fibrin formation). The stimulus for initial platelet adhesiveness is probably related to connective tissue or collagen in the injured endothelium. Formation

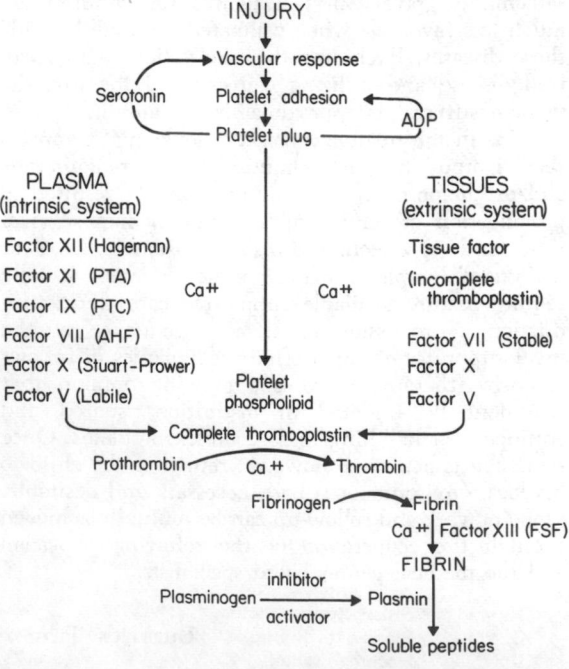

Fig. 13. Current concept of the hemostatic process.

of the tightly packed platelet plug is accelerated by thrombin, by adenosine diphosphate from red blood cells, and by a self-perpetuating cycle secondary to release of ADP from the aggregating platelets. An as yet unidentified plasma protein, which appears to be deficient in Von Willebrand's disease, is also essential for normal platelet adhesiveness. In addition, platelets may be intrinsically defective, lacking one or more of their normal properties necessary for hemostasis (the thrombasthenias). Concurrent with platelet plug formation, serotonin is released which stimulates local vasoconstriction; platelet phospholipid (platelet Factor III) is made available for participation in the coagulation process; and a factor promoting clot retraction is released from the platelets.

The final phase of hemostasis is achieved by the formation of a mesh of fibrin strands incorporating red blood cells, white blood cells, and platelets to form a more permanent seal than that provided by the initial platelet plug. Conversion of plasma fibrinogen to insoluble fibrin is the end result of a series of interactions involving several plasma proteins, calcium, platelet phospholipid, and a tissue factor. The international nomenclature for coagulation factors (Table 7) will be used hereafter except for Factors I, II, and IV, for which the more common terms fibrinogen, prothrombin, and calcium will be retained. As indicated in Figure 13, blood clotting may proceed from within the plasma (intrinsic system) or at the tissue level (extrinsic system). Within the vascular system interaction of Factors V, VIII, IX, X, XI, and XII plus platelet phospholipid and calcium leads to the formation of complete thromboplastin. In the extrinsic system, tissue factor (an incomplete thromboplastin) in combination with Factors V, VII, and X also may result in formation of complete thromboplastin. Thus, clotting may proceed at the tissue level in the absence of Factors VIII, IX, XI, and XII. Complete thromboplastin from either source acts to convert prothrombin to thrombin in the pres-

ence of calcium. In the final step, thrombin converts fibrinogen to fibrin which is rendered insoluble by the action of Factor XIII (fibrin-stabilizing factor). The fibrin clot ultimately retracts under the influence of thrombosthenin, a factor released from platelets. Thrombin has been shown to have additional important accelerating actions on both platelet aggregation and the activation of earlier coagulation factors. Thus the formation of a small amount of thrombin greatly increases the velocity of the coagulation process.

Several factors are important in maintaining fluidity of blood and include an intact vascular endothelium, natural inhibitors of coagulation factors such as antithrombin and heparin, and the neutralization of thrombin by adsorption on fibrin. An additional control or protective mechanism is the fibrinolytic system, which is capable of dissolving fibrin clots. Circulating plasminogen may be converted to plasmin, an active fibrinolysin, by a variety of tissue activators. This reaction ordinarily occurs locally, within the fibrin clot, since potent inhibitors of plasmin and plasminogen activator are present in the circulation. Because plasmin is an enzyme capable of destroying a wide range of substrates, including several coagulation factors (Factor V, Factor VIII, fibrinogen), imbalance of the fibrinolytic system may lead to serious hemorrhagic problems.

17.12
DIAGNOSIS OF HEMORRHAGIC DISORDERS

CHARLES F. ABILDGAARD
and IRVING SCHULMAN

A functional classification of hemorrhagic disorders is presented in Table 8. A careful history is probably the most important single diagnostic aid available to the physician evaluating a patient with abnormal bleeding. The type of bleeding manifestation may actually indicate the nature of the underlying disorder. For example, bleeding in the skin and from mucous membranes (petechiae, epistaxis) is commonly observed in disorders of the platelet hemostatic mechanism due to faulty platelet plug formation. Such bleeding frequently occurs in thrombocytopenia from any cause and in von Willebrand's disease. Since the platelet mechanism is usually normal in disorders due to congenital lack of specific clotting factors, such superficial bleeding manifestations are rarely seen in the hemophilias. In contrast, the latter are more commonly associated with episodes of deeper bleeding such as hemarthrosis and large hematoma formation. Detailed family history is essential, since many coagulation factor deficiencies are hereditary disorders. Specific symptoms that may be of importance include bleeding after circumcision, spontaneous bruising or petechiae, hematoma forma-

TABLE 7. *International Nomenclature for Coagulation Factors*

Factor	Common Terms
I	Fibrinogen
II	Prothrombin
III	Tissue factor, tissue thromboplastin (incomplete)
IV	Calcium
V	Labile factor, proaccelerin, accelerator globulin
VI	Accelerin (no longer in use)
VII	Stable factor, proconvertin
VIII	Antihemophilic factor (AHF), antihemophilic globulin (AHG)
IX	Plasma thromboplastin component (PTC), Christmas factor
X	Stuart-Prower factor
XI	Plasma thromboplastin antecedent (PTA)
XII	Hageman factor
XIII	Fibrin-stabilizing factor (FSF)

TABLE 8. *Classification of Hemorrhagic Disorders*

Disorders Due to Abnormal Structure or Function of the Blood Vessels

Congenital
    Hereditary hemorrhagic telangiectasia
    Cutis hyperelastica (Ehlers-Danlos syndrome)
    Idiopathic pulmonary hemosiderosis

Acquired
    Scurvy
    Septic or toxic angiitis
    Anaphylactoid purpura (Henoch-Schönlein syndrome)

Disorders of the Platelet Hemostatic Mechanism

The thrombocytopenias
    With normal or increased megakaryocytes
        Idiopathic thrombocytopenic purpura
        Neonatal thrombocytopenic purpura
        Familial thrombocytopenic purpura
        Immunologic drug purpura
    With splenomegaly
    With giant hemangioma
    With cyanotic congenital heart disease
        Secondary to syndromes associated with intravascular clotting (purpura fulminans, thrombotic-thrombocytopenic purpura, hemolytic-thrombocytopenic-uremic syndrome)
        Aldrich's syndrome
        Deficiency of thrombopoietic factor

    With decreased or absent megakaryocytes
        Secondary to marrow replacement (leukemia, tumors)
        Secondary to marrow damage by drugs, chemicals, or radiation
        Aplastic, hypoplastic anemias

Abnormal platelet hemostatis with normal platelet count
    Functional platelet disorders (thrombasthenias)
    Von Willebrand's disease (pseudohemophilia)

Disorders of the Coagulation Process

Congenital coagulation factor deficiencies
    The hemophilias
        Factor VIII deficiency (classical hemophilia)
        Factor IX deficiency (Christmas disease)
        Factor XI deficiency

    Other congenital disorders
        Afibrinogenemia, hypofibrinogenemia
        Hypoprothrombinemia
        Factor V deficiency (parahemophilia)
        Factor VII deficiency
        Factor X deficiency
        Factor XIII deficiency
        Associated with congenital hypothyroidism (deficiency of Factors VII and IX)
        Combined coagulation factor deficiencies

Transient neonatal coagulation factor deficiency
    Hemorrhagic disease of the newborn (combined deficiency of prothrombin and Factors VII, IX, and X)

Acquired coagulation factor deficiencies
    Liver disease (prothrombin and Factors V, VII, IX, and X)
    Coumarin-induced (prothrombin and Factors VII, IX, and X)
    Vitamin K deficiency (prothrombin and Factors VII, IX, and X)
    Factor V deficiency occurring postoperatively or due to malignancy
    Associated with hypothyroidism (deficiency of Factors VII and IX)
    Anticoagulants
        In lupus erythematosus (antithromboplastin, antithrombin)
        Anticoagulants against specific factors
        Heparin (extrinsic or intrinsic)

    Fibrinolysis
        Primary (malignancy)
        Secondary (intravascular clotting, shock)

Intravascular coagulation with consumption of clotting factors
Open-heart surgery

tion after injections such as routine immunizations, hemarthroses, large soft tissue hemorrhages, epistaxis, gastrointestinal bleeding, hematuria, and excessive bleeding following spontaneous loss of deciduous teeth, dental extractions, trauma, or operative procedures, particularly tonsillectomy. History of abnormal bleeding after tonsillectomy and/or adenoidectomy should always suggest the presence of an underlying hemorrhagic disorder and indicates the need for thorough investigation. Such bleeding is often the first manifestation of mild hemophilia. Although the absence of bleeding following tonsillectomy suggests a normal hemostatic mechanism, it does not rule out the presence of a bleeding problem, just as failure to bleed after circumcision does not rule out the possibility of hemophilia.

The common occurrence of epistaxis during childhood leads to the need for frequent evaluation of this complaint. A detailed history is of particular value. If epistaxis is the only bleeding manifestation it is rarely, if ever, due to an underlying hemorrhagic disorder. On the other hand, if epistaxis is accompanied by other bleeding manifestations in the patient or other family members, complete evaluation is indicated, and frequently leads to the diagnosis of a bleeding disorder such as von Willebrand's disease.

To establish a specific diagnosis in a patient with bleeding manifestations or a suspicious history, a variety of laboratory tests are useful. It is now well recognized that reliance on certain limited combinations of "routine coagulation tests" such as the bleeding time and clotting time alone may lead to gross errors in screening for hemorrhagic disorders. Initial laboratory evaluation of such a patient requires the use of a combination of screening tests sensitive enough to detect defects in all phases of hemostasis.

TABLE 9. *Results of Screening Tests for Detection of Hemorrhagic Disorders*

(N = normal, A = abnormal)

	Platelet	Bleeding Time	Prothrombin Time	Partial Thromboplastin Time
Vascular disorders	N	N/A	N	N
Platelet hemostatic disorders				
Thrombocytopenias	A	A	N	N
Thrombasthenias	N	A	N	N
Von Willebrand's disease	N	N/A	N	N/A
Coagulation factor deficiencies				
Fibrinogen	N	N/A	N/A	N/A
Prothrombin	N	N/A	A	A
Factor V	N	N/A	A	A
Factor VII	N	N/A	A	N
Factor X	N	N	A	A
Factor VIII	N	N	N	A
Factor IX	N	N	N	A
Factor XI	N	N	N	A
Factor XII	N	N	N	A
Factor XIII	N	N	N	N

A minimal effective combination of tests should include (1) platelet count and/or visualization of platelets on a stained blood smear, (2) bleeding time, (3) prothrombin time, and (4) activated partial thromboplastin time. As indicated in Table 9, use of this combination will detect an abnormality in one or more tests in all disorders of hemostasis except those on a purely vascular basis and deficiency of Factor XIII. Methods are available to perform all of these tests using capillary blood. However, most laboratories prefer the use of carefully obtained venous blood to avoid contamination of plasma with tissue factor. Several other tests (tourniquet test, prothrombin consumption test, thromboplastin generation test, recalcification time, clotting time, etc.) may reveal abnormalities in certain hemorrhagic states; however, they are not useful screening tests because they lack specificity or sensitivity, or are too time-consuming.

Detection of an abnormality in one or more of the recommended screening tests rarely provides a specific diagnosis. Depending on the results observed, further tests are usually necessary to identify a specific defect. For example, the finding of a decreased platelet count nearly always requires a bone marrow examination to aid in identifying the cause. A prolonged bleeding time usually indicates defective platelet hemostasis, but may accompany some coagulation factor defects (congenital deficiency of prothrombin, Factor V, or Factor VII). As an isolated abnormality, a prolonged bleeding time is often an indication of von Willebrand's disease or, rarely, thrombasthenia. An abnormal prothrombin time most often indicates a decreased level of one or more of the factors that make up the extrinsic system of thromboplastin formation or the so-called prothrom-

bin complex. These are prothrombin, Factor V, Factor VII, and Factor X. Specific assays or correction studies using artificial reagents are required to identify a specific defect. A circulating fibrinogen level of less than 100 mg per 100 ml also may be a cause of a prolonged prothrombin time; conversely, a normal prothrombin time indicates the absence of severe fibrinogen depletion. An abnormal partial thromboplastin time may result from a deficiency of one or more or all of the clotting factors except Factor VII. The combination of an abnormal partial thromboplastin time and a normal prothrombin time narrows the possibilities to the early coagulation factor reactants (Factors VIII, IX, XI, and XII) and is typical of hemophilia. Again, further tests are required for identification of the specific defect.

Additional studies such as clot retraction, measurement of platelet phospholipid activity, tests for platelet adhesiveness, fibrinogen determination, and tests for fibrinolytic activity may be of value in the identification of some bleeding disorders. The use of these and other more specific tests will be discussed in relation to the various clinical disorders.

17.13
CLINICAL ASPECTS OF HEMORRHAGIC DISORDERS

CHARLES F. ABILDGAARD
and IRVING SCHULMAN

Disorders Due to Abnormal Structure or Function of the Blood Vessels

A variety of disorders occur in which a hemorrhagic tendency seems to be related to increased fragility and permeability of the small arterioles, venules, and capillaries in the absence of any underlying defect in coagulation or the platelets. In some of these conditions congenital morphologic abnormalities of the vessels may be demonstrated. In many, however, the impaired vascular integrity is secondary to a variety of acquired diseases.

HEREDITARY HEMORRHAGIC TELANGIECTASIA. Also called Rendu-Osler-Weber disease, this disorder is characterized by multiple small angiomas involving the skin and mucous membranes with a tendency to bleed either spontaneously or as a result of trauma. It is transmitted as a simple dominant affecting the sexes equally. The individual lesions consist of multiple dilations of capillaries and venules from 1 to 4 mm in size, which are slightly raised, bright red, and fade partially on firm pressure. The telangiectases are present in childhood and tend to increase in number and distribution with age. Bleeding may occur from any involved site and is frequently manifested as recurrent epistaxis in childhood. Gastrointestinal, pulmonary, and urinary bleeding also occur. Tests of hemostatic function are usually normal; however, decreased platelet adhesiveness has been described. Treatment of bleeding is by topical hemostatic agents when accessible. Blood loss may require treatment of anemia with transfusions or iron.

CUTIS HYPERELASTICA. Also known as Ehlers-Danlos syndrome, this is a congenital abnormality of connective tissue formation with excessive proliferation of elastic tissue and abnormal collagen. There is marked hyperelasticity of the skin and hyperextensibility of the joints. The skin is fragile and splits on slight trauma. Prolonged bleeding may occur as a result of gaping wounds and inadequate tissue support for small blood vessels. Wound healing is slow, and the scars are thin and weak. There is no generalized bleeding tendency, and tests of hemostatic function are normal. No effective therapy is known, but an attempt should be made to increase subcutaneous fat to provide greater protection from trauma.

IDIOPATHIC PULMONARY HEMOSIDEROSIS. This is a disorder characterized by repeated intraalveolar hemorrhages often leading to chronic iron-deficiency anemia. It occurs most often in children and young adults. There is no generalized bleeding tendency, and tests of hemostatic function are normal. Hypotheses regarding the pathogenesis include (1) an isolated defect of alveolar epithelial cells resulting in localized hemorrhage and (2) an immunologic reaction caused by an unknown sensitizing agent which induces formation of autoantibodies that react with lung tissue. Some investigators have suggested that milk proteins may lead to such sensitization and recommend a trial of a milk-free diet in all patients with the diagnosis of idiopathic pulmonary hemosiderosis.

SECONDARY VASCULAR PURPURAS. Increased vascular permeability unassociated with platelet or coagulation abnormalities may lead to hemorrhagic manifestations in diabetes and hypertension. Increased vascular permeability also occurs in uremia and may be associated with abnormal platelet adhesiveness. In scurvy, bleeding occurs in the skin, mucous membranes, soft tissues, and as painful subperiosteal hemorrhages. The increased vascular permeability of scurvy is a direct result of ascorbic acid deficiency which is essential for the formation of the "intercellular cement" of the vascular endothelium.

SEVERE INFECTIONS. Severe infections may produce pupura as a result of platelet depression or toxic injury to capillaries. Meningococcemia is often associated with widespread purpura in the absence of thrombocytopenia and should always be considered when cutaneous hemorrhages coexist with fever and severe toxicity. When these findings include a decreased platelet count, the presence of intravascular clotting should be investigated; the implications of the latter will be considered in a later section. Subacute bacterial endocarditis due to *Streptococcus viridans* is also frequently associated wtih petechiae or purpuric eruptions apparently resulting from bacterial embolization. (See Section 20.14.)

ANAPHYLACTOID PURPURA (HENOCH-SCHÖNLEIN SYNDROME, ALLERGIC PURPURA). Anaphylactoid purpura usually occurs as a hemorrhagic rash in association with gastrointestinal symptoms (Henoch's purpura), joint manifestations (Schönlein's purpura), and renal involvement. It is a generalized vascular disorder resulting from acute aseptic vasculitis involving arterioles and capillaries. The inflammatory lesions in and around the vessel walls are similar to those found in periarteritis nodosa and other conditions seemingly related to hypersensitivity. The disorder is most common in children from 4 to 15 years and affects both sexes.

Etiology and Pathogenesis. Although anaphylactoid purpura is generally considered to be related to hypersensitivity, a definite allergen is rarely identified. A few patients have a history of antecedent infection with a beta hemolytic streptococcus, and in several cases recurrences of this syndrome have been associated with streptococcal infection. In rare instances specific foods, such as milk, eggs, pork, wheat, and tomatoes, have been implicated. Drug idiosyncrasy is occasionally responsible. A definite allergic history, however, is relatively uncommon.

Clinical Manifestations. These depend upon the sites involved by the widespread vasculitis. The most frequent areas of involvement are skin, joints, gastrointestinal tract, and kidneys, with rash, abdominal pain, and joint pain the most common presenting manifestations. The rash is variable, but usually progresses from recurrent crops of urticarial lesions to pink or red maculopapules which become hemorrhagic, then fade, leaving a brownish discoloration of the skin which may persist for several weeks. The distribution of the rash is quite characteristic, usually involving the buttocks, posterior thighs, and extensor surfaces of the arms and legs, while sparing the face, trunk, palms, and soles. The tips of the ears are frequently involved. Marked, painful edema of the scalp may occur, especially in younger patients. The joints, single or multiple, are puffy, warm, painful, and tender. The swelling is due to periarticular involvement rather than intraarticular bleeding. Recurrent colicky abdominal pain, vomiting, and melena are common and result from edema and hemorrhage of intestinal walls. Perforation may occur, and there is a predilection to intussusception. Occasionally the abdominal symptoms may precede the development of the typical rash. Renal involvement occurs frequently and may be manifested as gross or microscopic hematuria.

Laboratory Findings. Anemia and leucocytosis may occur as a result of blood loss. Eosinophilia is rare. Tests of hemostatic function are normal. Urinary abnormalities are most important and include hematuria, proteinuria, and increased casts. Since the renal involvement may not be manifested until late in the disease, urinalysis should be repeated at intervals for several months.

Diagnosis. The normal platelet count differentiates the Henoch-Schönlein syndrome from the thrombocytopenic purpuras. Likewise, the entirely normal coagulation studies distinguish this disorder from the primary hemorrhagic disorders. When the characteristic rash is present, the diagnosis may frequently be made on inspection. In some instances, however, the rash may be atypical or the visceral and joint manifestations may precede the appearance of the rash. In such situations an acute surgical abdomen may be suggested by patients with abdominal pain or acute rheumatic fever by patients with articular manifestations. In patients with high fever and a more petechial type of eruption, meningococcemia may be suspected. The subsequent appearance of a multiform skin eruption usually indicates the correct diagnosis.

Course and Prognosis. In most instances the disease is limited to a single episode which subsides in 4 to 6 weeks. The course is variable, however, and some children have repeated episodes with remissions and exacerbations recurring for months to years. Renal involvement appears to be the most serious aspect of the disorder. While the majority of children make a complete recovery, some develop chronic nephritis and eventual renal failure (see Sec. 22.8).

Treatment. At the time of the acute episode, nasopharyngeal cultures should be obtained and appropriate antibacterial therapy initiated to eliminate any pathogens recovered. Treatment is primarily symptomatic and supportive. Short-term steroid therapy (prednisone 1 to 2 mg/kg) may be useful in the presence of marked scalp edema, persistent joint pain, or severe abdominal colic. Some investigators feel that in the latter instance steroids may help prevent the development of intussusception by decreasing edema and hemorrhage in the bowel. Steroid therapy does not influence the course of the skin rash nor does it alter the incidence of renal involvement. Skin testing and elimination diets, while often employed to detect specific allergens, are rarely rewarding.

Disorders of the Platelet Hemostatic Mechanism

IDIOPATHIC THROMBOCYTOPENIC PURPURA. Etiology and Pathogenesis. Idiopathic thrombocytopenic purpura (ITP), characterized by a generalized hemorrhagic tendency due to a marked decrease in the number of circulating blood platelets, probably includes several disorders of differing causation and possibly different pathogenetic mechanisms. Although there is general agreement that the thrombocytopenia is primarily the result of increased platelet destruction, there is also evidence that the basic pathogenetic mechanism frequently involves the megakaryocytes, leading to some decrease in normal platelet production. The relative importance of these two mechanisms remains uncertain for many of the clinically observed forms of ITP. Although it has been clearly demonstrated that an antiplatelet factor with characteristics of an antibody is present in the plasma of many patients with ITP (primarily adults), attempts to identify such a factor regularly by in vitro tests have led to variable and often negative results (especially in children). Despite the failure of present methods to demonstrate antiplatelet antibody consistently in ITP, most investigators believe that the basic mechanism is an immunologic response. This mechanism probably varies depending upon the triggering agent (virus, drug, unknown factors) but results in sensitization or alteration of the platelets in such a manner that they are prematurely destroyed or removed from the circulation.

The spleen appears implicated in ITP in two ways: (1) as a site for removal of "sensitized" platelets from the circulation and (2) as a source of antibody production. In the presence of severe platelet sensitization, the liver also functions as a major organ of platelet sequestration.

While ITP occurs in both children and adults there are significant differences in the disease in the two age groups. The incidence is much greater in children, and there is no sex difference, compared to a 3:1 predominance of females in adults. ITP in children follows antecedent viral infections (rubella, rubeola, varicella, miscellaneous respiratory infections) in up to 80 percent of the cases. Prompt spontaneous remission occurs in 80 to 90 percent of children in contrast to a high incidence of chronic ITP in adults.

Clinical Manifestations. Bleeding into the skin, either spontaneous or following minor trauma, is the most common feature of ITP. The onset is often abrupt. The lesions may be widespread and range from pinpoint petechiae to large ecchymoses. Nosebleeds and bleeding from other mucous membranes frequently accompany the purpura and may lead to significant blood loss. Central nervous system bleeding, the most serious complication, may occur early in the course of the disease but is quite uncommon. Joint hemorrhage is rare.

Physical examination, apart from evidences of hemorrhage, is generally unrevealing. Enlargement of the spleen and lymph nodes is very uncommon; its presence requires a careful search for causes of secondary thrombocytopenia such as leukemia, Gaucher's disease, or lupus erythematosus.

Laboratory Findings. Thrombocytopenia, with platelet counts usually below 60,000 per mm³, is the most significant finding. The reduction in platelet number may be confirmed by the sparsity of platelets on the stained blood smear, where the few platelets seen are often single, large, and abnormal in shape. Although the bleeding time and tourniquet test are characteristically abnormal, these determinations are unnecessary for the diagnosis. Clot retraction is poor to absent. The whole blood clotting time, prothrombin time, and partial thromboplastin time are normal. Evidence of a disturbance in the coagulation mechanism in ITP is demonstrated by an abnormal prothrombin consumption test, which is indicative of impaired thromboplastin formation (a result of a decrease in available platelet phospholipid). Bone marrow examination is essential for accurate diagnosis and usually reveals an increased number of megakaryocytes, which are often immature in structure and do not appear to be forming platelets. Increased marrow eosinophils are sometimes seen, but the remainder of the marrow cells are normal. Erythroid hyperplasia may be noted in response to significant blood loss.

Course and Prognosis. ITP is a self-limited disease in the majority of children. Approximately 80 percent (up to 90 percent in one recent series) make a spontaneous recovery, usually within three months from the onset of illness. Relapses are relatively uncommon but may occur as long as several years following the initial episode. In 10 to 15 percent of the cases the disease becomes chronic and hemorrhagic symptoms persist. In the chronic state the severity of bleeding manifestations is quite variable and often is not correlated directly with the platelet count.

Treatment. Significant blood loss should be replaced with packed red cells or fresh whole blood. Active bleeding may respond to platelet transfusions, but this provides only temporary benefit and is rarely necessary. Restriction of activity during the acute phase is advisable.

Because of the high incidence of spontaneous recovery from ITP in children, conservative management is frequently recommended. Treatment with prednisone, cortisone, or ACTH has been widely used, but there is no evidence that the incidence of overall recovery is influenced by such therapy. It has been recognized that even low doses of prednisone may result in a decrease in the bleeding tendency before the platelet count has returned to normal. This effect is thought to result from alteration of vascular permeability. Because of these observed responses to steroid treatment, many have recommended routine use of prednisone during the initial phase of ITP in children with the aim of preventing serious bleeding manifestations. Although the most active bleeding tends to occur early in the course of the illness, the incidence of central nervous system bleeding is very low and may, in some reported cases, have actually been related to other thrombocytopenic states (such as thrombotic-thrombocytopenic purpura). Finally, the prolonged use of prednisone has been documented as capable of suppressing platelet response and actually prolonging the duration of thrombocytopenia. At the present time the definitive role of steroid therapy in ITP remains unsettled, and its routine use is open to question. A reasonable approach to the problem would appear to be individualization of each case, limiting the use of prednisone to those children presenting with extensive active bleeding manifestations, particularly mucous membrane, subconjunctival, or retinal hemorrhages, patients with only easy bruising and scattered petechiae or minimal epistaxis being followed conservatively. When prednisone is used it should be given in doses of 1 to 2 mg/kg for three weeks, then tapered and stopped during the fourth week regardless of the platelet-count response, thus avoiding the possibility of suppression. Failure to achieve spontaneous recovery within three or four months (whether prednisone was used initially or not) may warrant a similar or repeat course of treatment, since some patients appear to become more responsive after the disease has been present for a few months.

Persistence of thrombocytopenia beyond 6 months indicates a chronic state, and 6 to 12 months of disease has been used commonly as an indication for splenectomy. Splenectomy results in recovery in approximately two-thirds of the children who develop chronic ITP. In recent years it has been observed that spontaneous remission may occur as late as two years or longer from the onset of the illness. Because of this possibility it may be justified to delay splenectomy at least two years in any child who is tolerating the thrombocytopenic state without serious clinical bleeding problems.

The ultimate percentage of remissions that will be achieved by delaying splenectomy is unknown but appears to be significant. Recurrence of life-threatening bleeding or other complications may, on the other hand, justify the operation at a much earlier stage of the disease. In essence, the patient should be treated, not the platelet count.

Transfusion of fresh normal human plasma in a dose of 30 ml/kg (given in divided doses) has been observed to result in permanent return of platelets to normal levels within five days in a number of children with acute ITP and in a few with chronic ITP. This has been a purely experimental approach and the mechanism of action is unknown. The response may result from the effect of an excess of thrombopoietic factor from the transfused plasma; however, ITP does not result from lack of thrombopoietin. Further investigation of this phenomenon may lead to additional possibilities of treatment of ITP in children.

FAMILIAL THROMBOCYTOPENIC PURPURA. Chronic thrombocytopenia occurs rarely as an inherited disorder. Sex-linked recessive and autosomal dominant transmission has been described. Bleeding manifestations usually begin in infancy or childhood. Prednisone or transfusion with fresh plasma has not been of value, and the response to splenectomy has varied in reported cases.

NEONATAL THROMBOCYTOPENIC PURPURA. Thrombocytopenic purpura occurs in about half of the newborn infants of women who have or have had ITP, including mothers who have been cured by splenectomy. The disease in the infant apparently results from transplacental transmission of antiplatelet factors from mother to infant. Congenital thrombocytopenic purpura also occurs in infants born to mothers who have never had ITP. In these instances there is evidence that the mother is sensitized to the infant's platelets, which are presumably of a different immunologic type. Maternal antibodies, directed against the infant's platelets, are produced during pregnancy and cross the placenta causing thrombocytopenia in the newborn infant (a mechanism analogous to isoimmunization of red blood cells in erythroblastosis fetalis). In both types of neonatal thrombocytopenia the firstborn infant may be affected and the disease tends to occur in subsequent infants. Hemorrhagic manifestations appear within minutes to hours after birth and include skin, mucous membrane, vaginal, and central nervous system bleeding. Bleeding is most severe during the first few days and may result in death. Examination of the bone marrow in neonatal purpura may reveal decreased megakaryocytes. However, in the absence of associated disease, this finding does not alter the favorable prognosis, and megakaryocytes subsequently appear.

Recommendations for treatment have varied and include simple observation, transfusion with fresh blood or platelets to manage bleeding, routine administration of steroids, and exchange transfusion to remove circulating antibody. Although the routine use of steroids remains a debated issue, as in ITP, the apparent greater risk of serious bleeding in neonatal thrombocytopenia probably warrants this approach. Steroids are instituted as soon as the diagnosis is established and are continued for three weeks unless a platelet response occurs earlier. Intramuscular hydrocortisone, 10 mg every 12 hours, is used for the first few days, followed by oral prednisone, 1 to 2 mg/kg/day, thereafter. The disease is self-limited and in the absence of complications the prognosis is excellent. The majority of infants achieve a normal platelet count within 6 to 8 weeks.

Thrombocytopenia in the neonatal period may be secondary to a variety of systemic diseases including severe erythroblastosis fetalis, sepsis, cytomegalic inclusion disease, toxoplasmosis, congenital leukemia, and congenital aplastic or hypoplastic anemia.

Infants born to women who have rubella during the first trimester of pregnancy have a high incidence of moderate to severe thrombocytopenia. The majority of these infants also have a variety of associated defects (the congenital rubella syndrome). The thrombocytopenia may last for many weeks but usually improves spontaneously. Affected infants may carry the virus for several months and should be considered sources of infection.

A rare type of congenital thrombocytopenia is associated with bilateral absence of the radius. Megakaryocytes are decreased in the marrow, and a transient leukemoid blood picture may suggest congenital leukemia. Despite persistence of thrombocytopenia these infants tend to do well if they escape fatal bleeding during the neonatal period.

SECONDARY THROMBOCYTOPENIC PURPURA. Thrombocytopenia may occur at any age as a manifestation of a primary disease or secondary to known causative agents. In this group it is useful to distinguish those disorders associated with normal or increased megakaryocytes from those with decreased or absent megakaryocytes.

Immunologic Drug Purpura. A variety of drugs are capable of sensitizing certain individuals so that subsequent exposure to the drug leads to acute thrombocytopenia. It has been suggested that the antibody formed reacts with the specific drug and that subsequent absorption of this antigen (drug)–antibody complex onto the platelet surface leads to destruction of the latter. Lysis of platelets may be demonstrated in vitro and requires (1) the specific drug, (2) serum from the drug-sensitive patient, (3) platelets from any donor, and (4) complement. Several tests are available to detect drug sensitization. Drugs that may induce such a response in susceptible individuals include Sedormid, quinidine, quinine, digitoxin, chlorothiazide derivatives, chlorpropamide, meprobamate, phenylbutazone, sulfonamides, and antihistaminics. Thrombocytopenia resulting from this process usually resolves spontaneously on elimination of the offending drug.

Splenomegaly. A variety of conditions resulting in splenomegaly are associated with thrombocytopenia, presumably due to sequestration or destruction of platelets by the enlarged spleen. Megakaryocytes are plentiful in the marrow in most of these disorders, which include congestive splenomegaly with portal hypertension (Banti's syndrome), sickle-cell anemia, thalassemia, Gaucher's disease, reticuloendotheliosis, Hodgkin's disease, and others. Splenectomy may attenuate the thrombocytopenia in many instances even though the underlying disease is not affected.

Giant Hemangioma. Sequestration of platelets leading to severe thrombocytopenia and bleeding may occur secondary to giant hemangioma in infants. Recovery follows surgical removal, radiation, or spontaneous regression of the hemangioma.

Cyanotic Congenital Heart Disease. Thrombocytopenia frequently occurs in children over one year of age with severe cyanotic congenital heart disease whose hematocrits are over 65 percent and whose arterial oxygen saturation is below 65 percent. These children usually have little bleeding during corrective surgery which, if successful, is followed by improvement of the platelet count.

Intravascular Clotting. Thrombocytopenia is seen in several syndromes associated with intravascular clotting (thrombotic-thrombocytopenic purpura, hemolytic-thrombocytopenic-uremic syndrome, purpura fulminans, overwhelming sepsis, and others), which will be discussed in more detail in the section on acquired coagulation defects.

Aldrich's Syndrome. Thrombocytopenia, severe eczema, and increased susceptibility to infections due to an immunologic deficit comprise a rare syndrome that occurs in male infants and is transmitted as a sex-linked recessive. Normal megakaryocytes are present in the marrow. Splenectomy does not improve the thrombocytopenia and may increase susceptibility to overwhelming infection. No effective therapy is known, and these infants usually die from infection or hemorrhage in the first few years of life.

Thrombopoietin Deficiency. Chronic congenital thrombocytopenic purpura refractory to corticosteroids and splenectomy, but regularly responding to infusions of fresh or fresh-frozen plasma, has been reported in a child and is thought to be due to a congenital deficiency of a platelet-stimulating factor (thrombopoietin).

Disorders Involving the Bone Marrow. Replacement of the marrow by leukemia, metastatic neuroblastoma, lymphosarcoma, or other malignancies may result in severe thrombocytopenia due to decreased megakaryocytes. Aplastic or hypoplastic anemias, whether congenital, idiopathic, or secondary to drugs, chemical toxins, or irradiation, are also commonly associated with amegakaryocytic thrombocytopenia. Agents known to cause thrombocytopenia by damaging the bone marrow include benzol, chloramphenicol, DDT, gold salts, neomycin, nitrogen mustards, organic arsenicals, organic hair dyes, phenobarbital, streptomycin, tridione, and many others. Treatment of these bone marrow disorders is discussed in other sections.

Acute Infections and Other Disorders. Thrombocytopenia has been found in association with sepsis, tuberculosis, typhoid, measles, rubella, varicella, scarlet fever, endocarditis, infectious mononucleosis, and other infectious diseases. The mechanism of the thrombocytopenia in these acute conditions may differ from that in the usual ITP following infection. Thrombocytopenia is a common manifestation of lupus erythematosus and may accompany acquired autoimmune hemolytic anemia (Evan's syndrome).

FUNCTIONAL PLATELET DISORDERS. A group of hemorrhagic states exists in which the platelets are numerically normal but functionally abnormal. All are characterized by a prolonged bleeding time and a bleeding tendency based upon faulty platelet plug formation.

Thrombasthenia is a rare, hereditary disorder, transmitted as an autosomal recessive, in which platelets fail to aggregate in response to ADP. The bleeding time, platelet adhesiveness, and platelet phospholipid availability are all abnormal. Transfusion of normal platelet concentrates is effective in controlling bleeding.

Thrombopathias are functional platelet disorders in which platelets fail to release ADP in response to contact with collagen. This disorder may be congenital, secondary to acquired disease (e.g., uremia), or the result of exposure to a variety of antiaggregation agents among which are aspirin and other nonsteroidal anti-inflammatory agents, phenothiazines, and glycerol guaiacolate.

The functional platelet disorders described above may now be diagnosed with a high degree of accuracy as a result of new techniques for studying platelet aggregation in vitro.

VON WILLEBRAND'S DISEASE (PSEUDOHEMOPHILIA). Von Willebrand's disease is a hereditary bleeding disorder occurring in both sexes and inherited as an autosomal dominant trait. It is characterized by a prolonged bleeding time and a variable deficiency of Factor VIII (antihemophilic factor). Although less common than hemophilia, this disorder is being recognized with increasing frequency. The clinical manifestations of von Willebrand's disease are, unlike hemophilia, characterized by skin and mucous membrane bleeding. Nosebleeds and easy bruising are the most common manifestations, while hemarthrosis is rare. Menorrhagia may be a serious problem. Bleeding following dental extraction and operative procedures is extremely variable but may be serious. The severity of the disorder in terms of laboratory findings and clinical manifestations varies considerably among families, among different affected members of the same family, and, at times, in the same individual on different occasions.

The hemostatic defect in von Willebrand's disease is thought to result primarily from the deficiency of a plasma factor necessary for normal *platelet adhesiveness*. The resulting impairment of platelet plug formation is responsible for the bleeding tendency and the long bleeding time. The relationship of the observed variable deficiency of Factor VIII to the primary hemostatic defect is not well defined.

The diagnosis of von Willebrand's disease may be suspected on the basis of a history of typical bleeding manifestations involving several members of a family. Symptoms usually begin at 3 or 4 years of age and may decrease significantly during adult life, so that the childhood histories of parents and grandparents should be reviewed in detail. The most useful diagnostic test is the bleeding time. In the more severely affected patients, the Duke bleeding time (performed on the ear lobe) may be consistently prolonged. In the mildly affected patients, this test is more variable and the Ivy bleeding time or a modification thereof (performed on the forearm with a blood pressure cuff at 40 mm) is more likely to reveal the abnormality. Tests for platelet adhesiveness (both in vivo and in vitro) may reveal an abnormality in these patients but probably are no more useful clinically than the bleeding time. Screening tests for coagulation defects (prothrombin consumption test, partial thromboplastin time) may be abnormal depending upon the degree of Factor VIII deficiency. Assay of Factor VIII is necessary for specificity and may be the only means of revealing mild defects. Both the bleeding time and the Factor VIII level may vary in the individual patient and may, in fact, be within normal limits on some occasions in mildly affected patients. It may be necessary to repeat such studies several times in patients with a suggestive history whose initial studies are normal.

Local hemostatic measures are usually effective in stopping nosebleeds. However, nasal packing and replacement of blood loss may be necessary occasionally. Serious bleeding is best treated by transfusion of fresh whole blood or fresh plasma collected in plastic bags. Although this treatment may result in only transient correction of the bleeding time, it is usually effective in controlling hemorrhage. Preparation for dental extraction or elective surgery in the severely affected patient may be accomplished by transfusion of fresh plasma in a dose of 10 ml/kg immediately prior to the procedure. Commercially available Factor VIII concentrates do not correct the bleeding tendency in von Willebrand's disease. However, recent studies suggest that cryoprecipitate prepared from fresh plasmas may be effective. Since the cryoprecipitate avoids the hazard of overexpansion of the plasma volume, if available it should be used in preference to whole plasma. The finding of a normal Duke bleeding time (ear), either following plasma therapy or in a mildly affected patient (whose modified Ivy bleeding time may still be abnormal), has been used as an indication of adequate hemostatic capability of the patient to tolerate elective procedures such as dental extraction. The use of epsilon

amino caproic acid (an inhibitor of fibrinolysis) has shown promise in the treatment of bleeding in von Willebrand's disease but is still under investigation.

Familial disorders similar to von Willebrand's disease have been described in which the laboratory abnormalities consist of a prolonged bleeding time associated with mild to moderate deficiency of Factor IX (PTC) or of Factor XI (PTA). The relationship of these cases to classical von Willebrand's disease is not known.

Disorders of the Coagulation Process

The Hemophilias

Prior to 1952 the term hemophilia was reserved for a well-defined, severe hemorrhagic disorder of males due to congenital deficiency of Factor VIII (antihemophilic factor). Since that time it has been recognized that specific hereditary deficiencies of two additional coagulation proteins, Factor IX (PTC) and Factor XI (PTA), are associated with similar hemorrhagic manifestations, and the term hemophilia is now used to describe all three disorders.

FACTOR VIII DEFICIENCY (CLASSICAL HEMOPHILIA, AHF DEFICIENCY). Classical hemophilia is the most common hereditary coagulation factor deficiency. It has been estimated to have an incidence of 1 in 10,000 white male births in the United States and occurs probably with similar frequency in most races. It is transmitted by the female as a sex-linked recessive trait. The female carrier is usually asymptomatic, but in most instances can be shown to have a subnormal level of Factor VIII (30 to 50 percent). A small percentage of known carrier females have normal levels of Factor VIII (50 to 200 percent), in accordance with the Lyon hypothesis. In the affected male, deficiency of Factor VIII may be severe (less than 1 percent) to mild (5 to 25 percent). The severity of clinical manifestations is directly related to the circulating Factor VIII level, which remains fairly constant in the individual patient and among affected males in the same family.

Clinical Manifestations. Severe Factor VIII deficiency is demonstrable at birth and may lead to serious hemorrhage following circumcision. Failure to bleed excessively after circumcision does not rule out the diagnosis, since the procedure is tolerated without bleeding in a significant number of hemophilic infants, probably due to the activation of the extrinsic system of thromboplastin formation by tissue factor. In the absence of trauma, significant hemorrhagic symptoms may not occur until the infant begins to walk, when excessive bruising is usually noted. Thereafter recurrent bleeding, both spontaneous and following minor trauma, is a lifelong problem. Hemorrhage may occur in any area but most often leads to soft tissue bleeding and painful hemarthroses, particularly involving the knees, ankles, and elbows. Acute bleeding into a joint space produces severe pain, swelling, heat, tenderness, and limitation of motion. Repeated joint hemorrhages may result in extensive damage to synovial membranes, articular surfaces, epiphyseal plates, and metaphyses with ultimate contracture, ankylosis, and severe crippling if proper therapy is neglected. Bleeding may also occur into the skin, muscles, solid viscera, gastrointestinal tract, peritoneal cavity, retroperitoneal area, central nervous system, and from mucous membranes. Hematuria is a frequent manifestation. Nosebleeds occur but are rarely troublesome (in contrast to disorders involving platelets). Severe trauma or surgical procedures may lead to extensive bleeding. It is not uncommon for phases or cycles of increased incidence of apparent spontaneous bleeding episodes to occur in individual patients. Although recognized, this phenomenon is not explained. Physical examination is unrevealing in the absence of hemorrhagic manifestations, unless chronic deformities have resulted from previous bleeding episodes.

Diagnosis. Laboratory tests are essential for the detection and proper identification of hemophilia. Tests measuring platelet number and function are all normal (platelet count, bleeding time, platelet adhesiveness, clot retraction), as are the prothrombin time and fibrinogen concentration. The whole blood clotting time is markedly prolonged in severe hemophilia of all three types. However, in milder deficiencies the clotting time is entirely normal. For example, only 1 to 2 percent of normal Factor VIII level will produce a normal clotting time. Detection of milder deficiencies requires more sensitive tests, the simplest and most sensitive being the *partial thromboplastin time (PTT)*, which will usually detect levels of Factor VIII below 30 percent of normal. The thromboplastin generation test, although fairly sensitive, is difficult and time-consuming. The prothrombin consumption test is less sensitive than the PTT and may be normal in the presence of 5 to 10 percent Factor VIII.

Identification of a deficiency detected by an abnormality of the clotting time or PTT may be achieved by specific assay for coagulation factors or by correction studies using the PTT. The defect in Factor VIII deficiency is corrected by normal adsorbed plasma or plasma from a Factor IX deficient patient, whereas Factor IX deficient plasma is corrected by normal serum or plasma from a known classical hemophiliac. The prolonged PTT of Factor XI deficient plasma may be corrected with either normal absorbed plasma or serum.

Treatment. Acute bleeding episodes in the hemophilic patient vary greatly, depending upon the severity and location of the hemorrhage. Therefore, individualization of therapy is required to meet the needs of each bleeding episode. Local measures may be beneficial but most often constitute an addition to, rather than a substitute for, specific transfusion therapy. Local pressure and topical application of hemostatic agents (thrombin, Oxycel, Surgicel) may be useful in treating superficial abrasions or very minor lacerations. Suturing should be avoided where possible. Cauterization is always contraindicated. Immobilization of an affected limb and application of cold will often add to the comfort of the patient.

Specific treatment of acute bleeding depends on providing the patient with an amount of Factor VIII that will achieve and maintain hemostasis until the particular hemorrhagic manifestation has subsided. Replacement of Factor VIII is achieved by transfusion of fresh, fresh-frozen, or lyophilized plasma, fresh whole blood, or a concentrate of Factor VIII. Regardless of the source of Factor VIII, the in vivo longevity in the hemophilic patient is similar and is illustrated for nonbleeding patients in Figure 14. Within 8 hours following transfusion of Factor VIII, approximately half of the peak activity disappears, probably by equilibration in the extravascular space. Following this initial equilibration, Factor VIII has a biologic half-life of about 15 hours. The presence of active bleeding, fever, infection, or a circulating inhibitor of Factor VIII may increase rates of disappearance. The Factor VIII level needed to stop hemorrhage regularly is not known for many types of bleeding, but serious bleeding, as from open wounds or due to severe trauma, requires maintenance of a level of 20 to 30 percent of normal. Lesser episodes (soft tissue hemorrhages) may subside after a single dose of 10 ml/kg of plasma which rarely achieves a peak level of greater than 20 percent. Still lower levels of Factor VIII (5 to 10 percent) are probably effective in avoiding spontaneous bleeding during general activity.

Because newer forms of Factor VIII are available in which activity can be quantitated, it may be helpful to consider the dose in terms of units of Factor VIII (one unit being defined as the Factor VIII activity in one milliliter of average fresh normal plasma; in other words, a plasma assayed to contain 100 percent Factor VIII activity would contain 1 unit per milliliter). In these terms the average fresh plasma should contain 1 unit per milliliter (ranging from 0.5 to 2.0, since normal Factor VIII levels may vary from 50 to 200 percent). Fresh-frozen plasma or lyophilized antihemophilic plasma may contain less than 1 unit per milliliter, since there is some loss in preparation.

One of the most useful Factor VIII concentrates is the cold-precipitable fraction of plasma described by Pool which can be prepared in any blood bank. It is obtained by quick-freezing fresh plasma, thawing it in the cold, then separating the cold precipitate which can be stored frozen and later be redissolved in about 15 ml of the original plasma or saline at room temperature. This process yields 50 to 70 percent of the Factor VIII present in the original volume of plasma (125 to 175 units from 250 ml of plasma), resulting in a concentration of 8 to 11 units per milliliter. A commercially available preparation (AHF Concentrate—Human, Hyland Laboratories) has a comparable concentration of Factor VIII and is stored in the lyophilized state. Although a pure Factor VIII preparation is not available, the above concentrates have many advantages over plasma. Because of the small volumes required, high levels of Factor VIII may be achieved in the patient without fear of overexpansion of the plasma volume. By use of plasmapheresis programs it is possible to stockpile large amounts of cold-precipitated Factor VIII for an individual patient from a single donor, thereby reducing the risk of hepatitis. The commercial concentrate also provides a convenient, potent source of Factor VIII, but is more expensive and is associated with greater risk of hepatitis. An additional source of Factor VIII is Cohn's fraction I, prepared from fresh plasma (AHF-rich fibrinogen, Fibro-AHF, Merck Sharp & Dohme) which, although not truly a concentrate, does avoid overexpansion of the plasma volume when high levels of Factor VIII are required.

As a general rule, transfusion of 1 unit of Factor VIII per kilogram body weight should result in a 2 percent rise of Factor VIII in the recipient. This is a useful guide regardless of the source of Factor VIII. To treat an acute bleeding episode with plasma (whether fresh, fresh-frozen, or lyophilized) a dose of 10 units (10 ml) per kilogram is transfused within a 30-minute period (Factor VIII in plasma deteriorates rapidly at room temperature, so that plasma should not be transfused slowly over long periods of time). Such a dose should achieve an immediate peak level of approximately 20 percent Factor VIII and should be adequate to stop most simple cases of soft tissue bleeding.

Acute joint bleeding should be treated without delay. Plasma (10 ml/kg) given initially and repeated in smaller doses (5 ml/kg) on the second and third days usually provides adequate hemostasis. Using concentrated Factor VIII (AHF Concentrate—Human, Hyland Laboratories) to achieve an initial level of 40 to 50 percent in patients with acute hemarthrosis, preliminary studies have indicated that most patients respond well without the need for additional replacement therapy. Traction or splinting to prevent contractures, cold compresses, and analgesics may be indicated. Quick has presented data which suggest that aspirin may aggravate the bleeding tendency in hemophilia. Aspiration of the acute hemarthrosis is recommended by some but is probably an unnecessary risk if prompt and adequate replacement therapy is given. Rapid relief of joint pain usually follows adequate plasma therapy long before objective improvement in the joint is detectable. Rehabilitative measures should be planned to prevent muscular atrophy during periods of bed rest and to maintain functional position of the affected extremity. Gradual return to normal activities is usually possible as pain and swelling subside. The orthopedist and physical therapist may provide valuable guidance in rehabilitation.

In treating more severe bleeding manifestations —such as hemorrhage into the pharynx or neck leading to dyspnea or dysphagia, central nervous system bleeding, suspected retroperitoneal bleeding, or bleeding from deep lacerations—or in preparing a patient for necessary surgical procedures, it is necessary to achieve an initial level of Factor VIII adequate for hemostasis and to maintain hemostatic levels for longer periods of time (up to two weeks after major surgery). Although this may be attempted using plasma in a dose of 10 ml/kg initially and 5 ml/kg every 4 to 6 hours thereafter, such a regimen, at best, will maintain the patient's Factor VIII level between 10 and 20 percent of normal. Since initial levels of 50 to 100 percent may be required to achieve hemostasis and levels of 20 to 30 percent may be needed to maintain hemostasis, particularly after surgery, it is apparent that plasma therapy is inadequate and could rapidly lead to overexpansion of the plasma volume. Intensive replacement therapy of the desired degree can be achieved only with use of cryoprecipitate or one of the commercially available Factor VIII concentrates. A tentative dosage schedule can be estimated considering the half disappearance time and biologic half-life of Factor VIII as shown in Figure 14. It is useful to monitor levels of Factor VIII in the patient by assay or by following correction of the patient's PTT as a guide.

Hematuria may be successfully treated without plasma. Spontaneous hematuria, unassociated with known severe trauma, will usually subside on treatment with prednisone, 2 mg/kg for five days. Gross hematuria often disappears within 48 hours of steroid therapy. Prednisone has also been recommended for the rehabilitation period following acute hemarthrosis or for chronic "effusions" in joints, but its effect in these situations has not been objectively evaluated.

Patients requiring dental extractions (especially of permanent teeth) have usually been pretransfused with plasma and given maintenance plasma for several days. Despite this precaution, bleeding is not uncommon. There is now evidence that careful local packing of the socket with thrombin-soaked Oxycel or Surgicel and protection of the area for two weeks

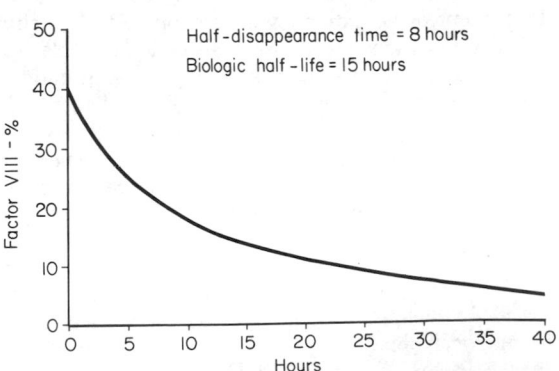

Fig. 14. In vivo longevity of Factor VIII in a hemophilic patient.

with a carefully made acrylic splint may provide hemostasis without the use of plasma in many patients. This approach is still under investigation.

Epsilon amino caproic acid (EACA) is being investigated for treatment of various types of bleeding in hemophilia. Although effective in stopping hematuria, EACA, is contraindicated for this purpose, since its use has been associated with intrarenal obstruction and decreased renal function. Continuous administration of EACA to patients with hemophilia has not decreased the incidence of bleeding manifestations.

Continuous prophylactic replacement of Factor VIII in severe hemophiliacs has not been successful using plasma. As new concentrates are developed this goal may be realized, since short-term maintenance of normal Factor VIII levels is already possible with presently available concentrates.

A rare complication of hemophilia is the development of a specific circulating inhibitor of Factor VIII, thought to be an antibody. There is no evidence that the development of such an inhibitor is related to the number of transfusions a patient receives. Therefore, transfusion therapy of acute bleeding episodes should never be withheld for fear of inducing an inhibitor. In the presence of an inhibitor, transfused Factor VIII is rapidly destroyed and transfusions should be avoided if possible. The inhibitor usually subsides with time. Prednisone has been used in treatment but does not appear to have been effective. The use of immunosuppressive drugs, such as Imuran, is now being evaluated in several centers. In dire circumstances exchange transfusion followed by large doses of concentrated Factor VIII may be lifesaving.

In addition to specific treatment for bleeding episodes, complete care of the hemophilic child should include prophylactic dental measures and routine immunizations (oral when possible). Careful counseling of parents and child regarding the limitations and requirements of hemophilia is most important in attempting to prevent the emotional invalidism and disturbed parent-child relationships that may arise.

FACTOR IX DEFICIENCY (PTC DEFICIENCY, CHRISTMAS DISEASE). Factor IX deficiency is transmitted as a sex-linked recessive trait and accounts for about 15 percent of all patients with hemophilia. The clinical manifestations are indistinguishable from classical hemophilia, and the disorder also occurs in mild to severe forms. Female carriers may be detected by Factor IX assay, but some have normal levels. Details of laboratory diagnosis have been discussed.

The principles of therapy are essentially the same as for Factor VIII deficiency except for the sources of Factor IX. Since the latter is stable in refrigerated plasma or blood, it is not necessary to use freshly drawn blood for transfusions. Plasma up to 21 days of age will provide Factor IX. Fresh-frozen or lyophilized plasma may also be used, but there is some loss of Factor IX in their preparation. The dosage of plasma is the same as in classical hemophilia. Despite the fact that Factor IX has a

biologic half-life of 30 hours (twice that of Factor VIII), the initial disappearance rate is similar and the need for repeated doses of plasma to treat severe bleeding episodes is the same as described for Factor VIII deficiency.

Concentrates containing Factor IX are being investigated but are not available for general use. A specific inhibitor of Factor IX is a rare complication of this form of hemophilia.

FACTOR XI DEFICIENCY (PTA DEFICIENCY). This least common form of hemophilia differs from the other two in several respects. Deficiency of Factor XI is transmitted as an autosomal recessive trait and occurs in both sexes. The carrier has only a mild deficiency and rarely develops clinical bleeding. The homozygote manifests severe Factor XI deficiency which is associated with hemorrhagic problems similar to those present in severe Factor VIII or IX deficiencies, but the symptoms are usually considerably milder. Diagnostic studies have been described. Treatment of bleeding episodes is by plasma transfusion as in Factor VIII deficiency. The use of fresh blood or plasma is recommended.

Other Congenital Coagulation Factor Deficiencies

AFIBRINOGENEMIA. Congenital afibrinogenemia is a rare disorder in which the blood is virtually incoagulable due to absence of fibrinogen. It occurs in both sexes and is transmitted as an autosomal recessive trait. Clinical manifestations include bruising, epistaxis, and bleeding following trauma, but may be quite mild. Congenital hypofibrinogenemias also occur in which clotting is delayed and the clot eventually formed is very small.

Treatment of acute hemorrhagic episodes or preparation for surgery is best accomplished by transfusion of concentrated human fibrinogen (Cohn's fraction I). Since bleeding usually occurs only with fibrinogen levels below 60 to 80 mg per 100 ml (normal 150 to 400 mg per 100 ml) transfusion is aimed at achieving a level of greater than 80 mg per 100 ml. A dose of 100 mg of fibrinogen per kilogram body weight may be expected to elevate the plasma level by approximately 200 mg per 100 ml in afibrinogenemia. Fifty percent of the administered fibrinogen disappears within 48 hours; thereafter the biologic half-life is approximately four or five days. Whole blood or plasma may also be used for therapy.

CONGENITAL DEFICIENCIES OF PROTHROMBIN, FACTOR V, FACTOR VII, AND FACTOR X. Isolated hereditary deficiencies of prothrombin (hypoprothrombinemia), Factor V (parahemophilia), Factor VII or Factor X (Stuart-Prower factor deficiency) are rare hemorrhagic disorders. Combined congenital deficiencies of some of these factors have also been reported. An abnormal prothrombin time is found in each disorder, but specific assays are required to establish the diagnosis. Treatment of bleeding episodes is by use of fresh whole blood or plasma. Vitamin K is of no value in treatment of the congenital deficiencies of K-dependent factors.

FACTOR XIII DEFICIENCY (FIBRIN-STABILIZING FACTOR DEFICIENCY). Congenital deficiency of Factor XIII is a rare familial hemorrhagic disorder and is probably transmitted as an autosomal recessive trait. Prolonged umbilical bleeding (after the cord has fallen), bruising, hematoma formation, and central nervous system hemorrhage are the most frequent manifestations. All of the usual tests of hemostatic function are normal. The defect is detected by testing for solubility of the patient's fibrin clot in 5 M urea, normal clots being insoluble while Factor XIII deficient clots are readily dissolved. Hemorrhagic symptoms respond readily to transfusion with whole blood or plasma.

FACTOR XII DEFICIENCY (HAGEMAN TRAIT). Deficiency of Factor XII is not a hemorrhagic disorder but is mentioned here to note the severe laboratory abnormalities associated with this hereditary trait. The homozygous state is associated with severe lack of Factor XII, which results in marked abnormalities of several coagulation tests (clotting time, prothrombin consumption test, PTT, and others). Since these patients are not subject to abnormal bleeding, specific identification of their deficiency (which is usually found as a result of an abnormal screening test) is important. This may be accomplished by assay or various correction studies. Factor XII is required for contact activation of the coagulation process in vitro; however, the in vivo significance of Factor XII is not known.

FACTORS VIII AND IX DEFICIENCIES ASSOCIATED WITH CONGENITAL HYPOTHYROIDISM. Moderate deficiencies of Factors VIII and IX have been observed in congenital hypothyroid patients and have been associated with bleeding following operative procedures or dental extractions. Treatment of the hypothyroid state has corrected the coagulation factor deficits.

COMBINED COAGULATION FACTOR DEFICIENCIES. Rare cases of a variety of combined coagulation factor deficiencies have been reported. These include Factors V and VIII, Factors VIII and IX, and several other combinations.

TRANSIENT COAGULATION FACTOR DEFICIENCIES IN NEWBORN INFANTS. Moderate deficiency of the vitamin K-dependent factors (prothrombin, Factor VII, Factor IX, and Factor X) develops in all newborn infants. During the first 48 to 72 hours of life the levels of these factors fall significantly. This decrease is followed by a gradual rise to birth levels by 7 to 10 days of age. A similar but more severe and prolonged deficiency occurs in premature infants. This transient phenomenon is thought to result from several factors: lack of vitamin K in the mother, immaturity of the liver, and absence of normal bacterial flora of the intestine responsible for synthesis of vitamin K. However, the deficiency of vitamin K-dependent clotting factors is rarely severe enough to result in spontaneous bleeding manifestations or "hemorrhagic disease of the newborn."

Administration of vitamin K in a single small dose (1 mg) either intramuscularly or orally at the time of birth will prevent the fall of prothrombin and Factors VII, IX, and X in full-term infants. This measure is recommended as prophylaxis for hemorrhagic disease of the newborn in full-term infants but is not uniformly effective in preventing a similar fall in premature infants. The natural oil-soluble preparations of vitamin K are preferred for this purpose, since large doses of the synthetic water-soluble preparations have been associated with hyperbilirubinemia and kernicterus. Hemorrhagic disease of the newborn may be effectively treated with 5 mg of vitamin K_1 intravenously. Serious bleeding may require transfusion of fresh whole blood, since several hours may be required for the effects of vitamin K.

FACTOR XI DEFICIENCY. A transient relative deficiency of Factor XI unresponsive to vitamin K has been described in normal newborn infants. In rare cases this deficit may be associated with hemorrhagic symptoms requiring transfusion with fresh whole blood or fresh-frozen plasma.

Acquired Disorders of Coagulation

VITAMIN K-DEPENDENT COAGULATION FACTORS. Combined deficiencies of the vitamin K-dependent factors (prothrombin and Factors VII, IX, and X) frequently result from interference with vitamin K intake, absorption, or utilization, as in liver disease, malabsorption syndromes, altered bowel flora, or coumarin treatment. Such deficiencies are readily detected by a prolonged prothrombin time; the degree of individual factor depression may be measured by specific assays. Treatment with vitamin K may reverse such deficiencies unless parenchymal liver disease is severe. Blood or plasma may be required to manage hemorrhagic symptoms.

FACTOR V DEFICIENCY. In severe liver disease significant Factor V deficiency may accompany that of the vitamin K-dependent factors; however, Factor V does not require vitamin K for synthesis and does not respond to similar therapy. Isolated severe deficiency of Factor V occurs rarely as a post-operative complication and may lead to serious bleeding. Treatment of bleeding due to Factor V deficiency requires transfusion of fresh blood or plasma, since this factor is quite labile on storage.

SECONDARY TO HYPOTHYROIDISM. As in congenital hypothyroidism, moderate deficiencies of Factors VIII and IX may be seen in acquired hypothyroid states and are reversible following thyroid replacement therapy.

ANTICOAGULANTS. Circulating anticoagulants are normally present in plasma and play a role in maintaining equilibrium of the overall hemostatic mechanism. Imbalance of hemostatic homeostasis leading to hemorrhagic manifestations may result from pathologic anticoagulants arising spontaneously or associated with a variety of disease states. Anticoagulants against specific clotting factors (Factors VIII, IX, and XI) occur in the hemophilias (as mentioned earlier), and an anticoagulant against Factor VIII may develop in otherwise normal individuals (particularly postpartum women and older adults). The latter circumstance results in an acquired hemophilialike state with marked decrease in Factor VIII secondary to the specific anticoagulant.

Circulating anticoagulants occur in a small percentage of patients with lupus erythematosus. These anticoagulants tend to act as antithromboplastins and antithrombins, and may be detected by noting prolongation of the clotting time, prothrombin time, and PTT of mixtures of the patient's plasma with normal blood or plasma. Significant hemorrhage is uncommon despite these activities, and the anticoagulants frequently subside following steroid treatment of the lupus.

Heparinlike anticoagulants have been reported with urticaria pigmentosa and mast-cell leukemia.

FIBRINOLYSIS. Pathologic activity of the fibrinolytic system may result in severe hemorrhagic manifestations (*fibrinolytic purpura*) by several mechanisms. These include primary breakdown of fibrin clots, enzymatic destruction of coagulation factors (fibrinogen, Factor V, and Factor VIII), and inhibition of coagulation by breakdown products of fibrinogen and fibrin. Abnormal fibrinolysis may accompany shock, major surgical procedures, liver disease, and a number of malignancies including leukemia. Increased fibrinolysis may also be secondary to disseminated intravascular clotting in a variety of diseases. Accurate differentiation of the two processes may be difficult but is important in planning effective therapy.

Screening tests for the presence of increased fibrinolysis include the whole blood or plasma clot lysis time, the euglobin clot lysis time, and fibrinogen measurement. More specific tests are available to detect fibrin and fibrinogen breakdown products and to measure plasminogen, plasminogen activator, and inhibitors of plasmin and antiplasmin.

Clinical bleeding documented as resulting from a primary increase in fibrinolysis may be effectively treated with epsilon amino caproic acid, an inhibitor of plasminogen activator. Transfusion of fibrinogen may be required to provide adequate levels for hemostasis. However, in the presence of fibrinolysis secondary to intravascular clotting, both of the above therapeutic measures may be detrimental to the patient. Inhibition of fibrinolysis eliminates a protective mechanism for removal of intravascular fibrin, and fibrinogen administration provides additional substrate for further intravascular coagulation. In such situations it is of primary importance to halt the process of intravascular clotting (usually with heparin) before initiating treatment aimed at blocking the fibrinolytic

process. This problem will be discussed further in the next section.

INTRAVASCULAR CLOTTING WITH CONSUMPTION OF COAGULATION FACTORS. The phenomenon of disseminated intravascular clotting leading to widespread fibrin deposition in small blood vessels and ultimately to diffuse hemorrhagic symptoms secondary to marked depletion of coagulation factors is thought to be a basic pathogenetic mechanism in a wide variety of disorders. These include purpura fulminans, thrombotic-thrombocytopenic purpura, the hemolytic-thrombocytopenic-uremic syndrome, complications of sepsis (particularly meningococcemia), complications of pregnancy such as amniotic fluid infusion and retained fetus, severe shock, and a number of other diverse conditions. Many of these disorders have findings similar to the generalized Shwartzman reaction, which occurs in rabbits following two intravenous doses of bacterial endotoxin. This reaction has been shown to result from intravascular clotting leading to widespread fibrin deposition, which results in cortical necrosis of the kidneys. Marked utilization of clotting factors, particularly Factors V and VIII, prothrombin, and fibrinogen, has been documented in those animals developing the Shwartzman reaction.

In many clinical conditions associated with intravascular clotting, increased fibrinolysis may occur as a secondary phenomenon. As indicated earlier, the accurate identification of these two processes has important therapeutic implications. Further complicating the problem is the frequent explosive course of some of the conditions associated with intravascular clotting and fibrinolysis. Rapid decisions may be necessary if effective therapy is to be given before irreversible complications occur. Unfortunately, there is no reliable single test known to make the differentiation and careful interpretation of a variety of studies is required. The initial approach to this problem should include a screening test for fibrinogen, a thrombin time, a prothrombin time and/or PTT, a platelet count, and a test for fibrinolysis. The presence of thrombocytopenia, decreased fibrinogen, prolonged prothrombin time, and PTT in the absence of marked fibrinolysis indicates intravascular clotting as the primary disturbance. However, there is considerable overlap of results, and more comprehensive references should be consulted for a fuller understanding of the problems of laboratory diagnosis.

Clinical experience with anticoagulant therapy in this group of disorders is limited and, in some, remains investigational. However, detection of significant intravascular clotting should lead to serious consideration of the use of heparin, particularly before treatment with fresh blood, fibrinogen, or fibrinolytic blocking agents is instituted. If used for this indication heparin should be given intravenously in a dose of 1 mg (100 units) per kilogram every 4 hours. Treatment is best monitored by obtaining the whole blood clotting time prior to each intravenous dose. Adequate heparin should result in a clotting time of 30 minutes or greater 3 to 4 hours after the previous dose. In the presence of severe renal disease, excess heparin may accumulate. Other laboratory tests should be followed to determine the effectiveness of heparin in halting the process of intravascular clotting. However, this may require neutralization of heparin in the patient's plasma before accurate clotting studies (prothrombin time, PTT, specific factor assays) can be performed. This can be accomplished using an appropriate concentration of protamine. Cessation of intravascular clotting should be followed by return to normal of depressed coagulation factors (over a period of hours), with thrombocytopenia responding more slowly. Duration of heparinization must be judged in terms of the individual syndrome and its cause.

Purpura Fulminans. Purpura fulminans is an acute, frequently fatal, disorder characterized by sudden appearance of large ecchymotic areas which are commonly located on the lower extremities and are often symmetric. The syndrome is usually preceded (several days to a month) by an infectious disease, scarlet fever or varicella being the most frequent. The lesions rapidly enlarge and may become gangrenous. The edges of the lesions are usually sharply demarcated, and central bullae may develop. Progression may lead to gangrene of an entire extremity. Fever, vomiting, and oliguria are usually present, and the patient may develop shock. Laboratory evidence of intravascular clotting may be detected. Widespread microthrombi involving many organs including the kidney have been demonstrated. The mortality rate is high, and amputation and plastic repair often have been required in survivors. Therapeutic recommendations have included steroids and heparinization. Although not extensively evaluated, heparin should be seriously considered if evidence of intravascular clotting is detected.

Thrombotic-Thrombocytopenic Purpura. Thrombotic-thrombocytopenic purpura is characterized by fever, thrombocytopenic purpura, hemolytic anemia, and variable symptoms of neurologic involvement. The red blood cells often show irregular fragmentation, distorted shapes, and burr cells (pyknocytosis) with occasional spherocytosis. The Coombs' test is negative. Hematuria, proteinuria, and azotemia are common. Transient neurologic manifestations (such as paresthesias and personality disorders), convulsions, and coma may occur. Pathologic findings include widespread occlusive fibrin deposition in small arteries, arterioles, and capillaries. Destructive lesions of the vessel walls and endothelial proliferation have been described. The disorder is nearly always fatal but corticosteroids have been recommended. To date, no case has been reported in which the coagulation changes typical of intravascular clotting have been found. Should such changes be identified, heparin therapy may be indicated.

Hemolytic-Thrombocytopenic-Uremic Syndrome. The hemolytic-thrombocytopenic-uremic syndrome has many similarities to thrombotic-thrombocytopenic purpura. Hemolytic anemia associated with pyknocytosis, significant thrombocytopenia, and severe renal impairment leading to uremia make up the clinical syndrome. It has occurred frequently in young infants following a diarrheal illness. Pathologic renal findings may be striking and have ranged from proliferative and exudative changes of the glomeruli to bilateral cortical necrosis. A fatal outcome is not uncommon and may occur during the acute phase or as a result of irreversible renal damage. The initial therapy requires careful fluid and electrolyte management (Sec. 22.4). Evidence of intravascular clotting may indicate the use of heparin (see Sec. 22.9).

Sepsis. Sepsis, due to a variety of microorganisms, has been recognized as a cause of intravascular clotting. Infections due to staphylococci, streptococci, and several gram-negative organisms, including meningococci, have been associated with the occurrence of Shwartzmanlike reactions in the human. As in the previous syndromes, suspicion of such a reaction in a patient with sepsis should lead to search for evidence of intravascular clotting and, if detected, may indicate the use of heparin as an adjunct therapeutic measure.

OPEN-HEART SURGERY. Variable deficiencies of coagulation factors and platelets have been observed following extracorporeal perfusion during open-heart surgery. However, there has been poor correlation between degree of the postoperative bleeding and the abnormality of coagulation studies. Significant blood loss is most often a result of faulty technical hemostasis and is usually an indication for reexploration of the operative site. Some investigators have identified a significant increase in fibrinolytic activity and have recommended the use of epsilon amino caproic acid for control of excess fibrinolysis.

REFERENCES

Abildgaard, C. F., Cornet, J. A., Johnson, H., and Schulman, I. Screening tests for disorders of thromboplastin formation. Pediat. Clin. N. Amer., 9:819, 1962.

——— Simone, J. V., Corrigan, J. J., Seeler, R. A., Edelstein, G., Vanderheiden, J., and Schulman, I. Treatment of hemophilia with glycine-precipitated factor VIII. New Eng. J. Med., 275:471, 1966.

——— Corrigan, J. J., Seeler, R. A., Simone, J. V., and Schulman, I. Meningococcemia associated with intravascular coagulation. Pediatrics, 40:78, 1967.

Allen, D. M., Diamond, L. K., and Howell, D. A. Anaphylactoid purpura in children (Schönlein-Henoch syndrome); review with a follow-up of the renal complications. Amer. J. Dis. Child., 99:833, 1960.

Baldini, M. Idiopathic thrombocytopenic purpura. New Eng. J. Med., 274:1245, 1301, 1360, 1960.

Barrow, E., and Graham, J. B. Von Willebrand's disease. Progr. Hemat., 4:203, 1964.

Biggs, R., and Macfarlane, R. G. Human Blood Coagulation and Its Disorders, 3rd ed. Philadelphia, F. A. Davis Co., 1962.

Blomback, M. Jorpes, J. E., and Nilsson, I. M. Von Willebrand's disease. Amer. J. Med., 34:236, 1963.

Brinkhous, K. M., ed. The Hemophilias. International Symposium, Washington. Chapel Hill, Univ. North Carolina Press, 1964.

Gaston, L. W. The blood-clotting factors. New Eng. J. Med., 270:236, 290, 1964.

Gilchrist, G. S., Ekert, H., Shankbrom, E., and Hammond, D. Evolution of a new concentrate for the treatment of Factor IX deficiency. New Eng. J. Med., 280:291, 1969.

Hardisty, R. M., and Ingram, G. I. C. Bleeding Disorders, Investigation and Management. Philadelphia, F. A. Davis Co., 1965.

Hoag, M. S., Johnson, F. F., Robinson, J. A., and Aggeler, P. M. Treatment of Hemophilia B with a new clotting factor concentrate. New Eng. J. Med., 280:581, 1969.

Hjort, P. F., and Rapaport, S. I. The Shwartzman reaction: pathogenic mechanisms and clinical manifestations. Ann. Rev. Med., 16:135, 1965.

——— Rapaport, S. I., and Jorgensen, L. Purpura fulminans. Report of a case successfully treated with heparin and hydrocortisone. A review of 50 cases from the literature. Scand. J. Haemat., 1:169, 1964.

Horowitz, H., and O'Leary, D. Von Willebrand's disease. A critical evaluation of diagnostic criteria. New York J. Med., 65:2236, 1965.

Ingram, G. I. C. Blood-coagulation factor VIII: genetics, physiological control and bioassay. Advances Clin. Chem., 8:189, 1965.

Johnson, S. A., ed. Blood Platelets. Boston, Little, Brown & Co., 1961.

Lusher, J. M., and Zuelzer, W. W. Idiopathic thrombocytopenic purpura in childhood. J. Pediat., 68:971, 1966.

Marcus, A. J., and Zucker, M. B. The Physiology of Blood Platelets, Recent Biochemical, Morphological and Clinical Research. New York, Grune & Stratton, Inc., 1965.

Merskey, C., Johnson, A. J., Pert, J. H., and Wohl, H.

Pathogenesis of fibrinolysis in defibrination syndrome: Effect of heparin administration. Blood, 24:701, 1964.

Pool, J. G., and Shannon, B. S. Production of high-potency concentrates of anti-hemophilic globulin in a closed-bag system. New Eng. J. Med., 273:1443, 1965.

Quick, A. J. Salicylates and bleeding: the aspirin tolerance test. Amer. J. Med. Sci., 252:265, 1966.

Reiguam, C. W., and Prosper, J. C. Fresh plasma transfusion in the treatment of idiopathic thrombocytopenic purpura. J. Pediat., 68:880, 1966.

Rodriquez-Erdman, F. Bleeding due to increased intravascular coagulation. Hemorrhagic syndromes caused by consumption of blood-clotting factors (consumption coagulopathies). New Eng. J. Med., 273:1370, 1965.

Salzman, E. W., and Britten, A. Hemorrhage and Thrombosis. Boston, Little, Brown & Co., 1965.

Schulman, I. Pediatric aspects of the mild hemophilias. Med. Clin. N. Amer., 46:93, 1962.

——— and Smith, C. H. Coagulation disorders in infancy and childhood. In Levine, S. Z., ed., Advances in Pediatrics. Chicago, Year Book Publishers, 1957, Vol. 9.

——— Pierce, M., Lukens, A., and Currimbhoy, Z. Studies on thrombopoiesis. I. A factor in normal human plasma required for platelet production; chronic thrombocytopenia due to its deficiency. Blood, 16:943, 1960.

——— Abildgaard, C. F., Cornet, J., Simone, J. V., and Currimbhoy, A. Studies on thrombopoiesis. II. Assay of human plasma thrombopoietic activity. J. Pediat., 66:804, 1965.

Sharp, A. A. Present status of platelet aggregation. New Eng. J. Med., 272:89, 1965.

Simone, J. V., Abildgaard, C. F., and Schulman, I. Blood coagulation in thyroid dysfunction. New Eng. J. Med., 273:1057, 1965.

Verstraete, M., Vermylen, C., Vermeylen, J., and Vandenbroucke, J. Excessive consumption of blood coagulation components as a cause of hemorrhagic diathesis. Amer. J. Med., 38:899, 1965.

chapter 18

THE RETICULOENDOTHELIOSES AND SARCOIDOSIS

ARNOLD H. EINHORN

18.1

THE NONLIPID RETICULOENDOTHELIOSES

Cells of the reticuloendothelial system are derived from the mesenchymal tissue. Their distribution is widespread; their functions and morphology are varied. This ubiquitous system encompasses the histiocytes of the loose connective tissue; the reticulum cells and the cells lining the sinuses of the lymph nodes and the sinusoids of the liver, the spleen, and bone marrow; the adventitial and endothelial cells of the blood vessels; the mesothelial cells of the serous cavities; the "dust" cells of the lungs; the myocytes of the heart; the oligodendroglia of the brain; and the supporting structures of the adrenal gland. Reticuloendothelial cells possess marked phagocytic properties and are able to ingest inert particulate matter, chemical substances, erythrocytes, and pathogenic organisms. They play an important role in hematopoiesis, antibody formation, and local as well as systemic reaction to infection.

DEFINITION. The term reticuloendotheliosis has been applied to two groups of relatively rare disease complexes: the *lipidoreticuloses* (see Sec. 8.10) and the *nonlipid reticuloendothelioses*, which have in common a systemic proliferation of the cellular elements of the reticuloendothelial system. The group of lipidoreticuloses or sphingolipidoses described in another section consists of hereditary storage diseases, autosomally transmitted, in which an inborn error of metabolism constitutes the primary defect.

The nonlipid reticuloendothelioses are characterized by an inflammatory histiocytic proliferation, sometimes with formation of granulomatous lesions. Three syndromes, thought originally to represent separate disease entities, are recognized in this group: *acute reticuloendotheliosis* (Letterer-Siwe disease), *Hand-Schüller-Christian syndrome*, and *eosinophilic granuloma*. Because of a similarity in the underlying basic pathology, they are now commonly regarded as stages of a single disease process in which the clinical manifestations are diversified, ranging from an isolated benign osteolytic lesion to a fulminating systemic disease.

PATHOLOGY. The histiocytic hyperplasia is the unifying feature of the three conditions, which are often grouped together under the name of *histiocyto-*

sis X. While the etiology and the nature of the process remain obscure, the evolution of the pathologic lesions has been well established. In the earliest stage, the lesions consist of a proliferation in sheetlike masses of nonvacuolated mononuclear histiocytes, without eosinophilic infiltration. At a later stage, eosinophils, lymphocytes, plasma cells, and multinucleated giant cells accumulate in the lesions. Concurrently clear vacuoles, shown to represent cholesterol, appear within the histiocytes. In instances where the process is fulminating, there is widespread visceral infiltration of histiocytes, and death may supervene before vacuolization has occurred. Vacuolated histiocytes ("foam cells") intermingled with eosinophils are found only in cases lasting several months or more. In the chronic stage the eosinophils disappear and fibroblasts invade the lesion, which at this stage is a typical xanthoma; it may continue for years or eventually heal with scarring.

The histology of the individual lesions does not determine the clinical grouping, the extent of the disease, or the patient's chances of survival. Differences in clinical expression and ultimate prognosis depend upon the location of the lesions, the degree of dissemination, and, in part, the age of the patient at the onset of the disease. Extensive visceral involvement and localization of lesions to organs whose functions are vital augur a somber prognosis. It has been noted that the lower the age of the child at the onset, the wider in general is the dissemination of the processes, hence the poorer the outlook. Data derived from carefully conducted correlative clinicopathologic studies suggest that involvement of the skin portends an unfavorable outcome. Localization of the lesions to the skeleton may be regarded as denoting a more favorable outcome, especially if the processes remain entirely confined to the bones.

CLASSIFICATION. The original subdivision of the disease complex into three distinct groups, while somewhat artificial, is nevertheless acceptable if used broadly to indicate the extent of initial involvement and the pattern of clinical progression of the disease. Eosinophilic granuloma designates a localized stage and benign disease with one or several lytic lesions confined to the skeleton, leaving all other systems and organs apparently intact. The term Hand-Schüller-Christian disease is linked with multiple skeletal, cutaneous, and visceral lesions and implies dissemination, chronicity, and uncertain prognosis; the name

Letterer-Siwe disease refers to the entity in which there is diffuse involvement of skin and organ systems without bone lesions initially. The latter term connotes an acute course, rapid dissemination, and unfavorable outcome. It must be recognized, however, that considerable clinical and histologic overlapping makes a distinction among the three disease variants often difficult to establish. Clinical pictures occupying intermediate or transitional positions are observed with increasing frequency, and sequences of the three morbid pictures in one patient on consecutive biopsies have been reported.

ETIOLOGY. A considerable amount of speculation has arisen relative to the etiology of these complex disorders. There are no clinical, pathologic, or epidemiologic data to support any one particular hypothesis. The incidence is about equally divided between both sexes. The theory once prevalent that attributed the pathogenesis of reticuloendotheliosis to a basic disturbance of intracellular lipid metabolism involving cholesterol is no longer accepted. Because of the malignant nature of the acute cases, a neoplastic process has been conjectured. A report of a patient with Letterer-Siwe disease whose illness terminated in a monocytic leukemia suggests a possible relationship with monocytic leukemia or lymphoreticulosarcoma. There is no conclusive evidence to substantiate this hypothesis. Efforts to demonstrate an infectious agent have been unsuccessful, although features shared with the infectious reticuloses have been described, especially those of histoplasmosis.

Heredity and genetic factors in these diseases have not been satisfactorily elucidated. In his original definition, Siwe specified that the acute disseminated reticuloendotheliosis is neither hereditary nor familial, yet there are documented reports of more than 10 families in which more than one child was affected with this disease. It is also conceivable that *Farquhar's familial hemophagocytic reticulosis* and *Nelson's familial lymphohistiocytosis* actually represent familial occurrences of histiocytosis X. These two rare, fatal, nonlipid reticuloendothelioses were described as entities distinct and separable from Letterer-Siwe's disease.

Acute Disseminated Histioreticuloendotheliosis
(Letterer-Siwe Disease)

Letterer-Siwe disease, the least common and usually the most malignant variant of the disease complex, affects mostly infants and younger children. Instances in newborn have been reported in literature. Among our own patients we have seen the disease present at birth in one newborn infant, and the development of lesions has occurred within the first days of life in two other infants. Clinical manifestations, however, are very rarely seen in the neonatal period.

A study of the mortality from Letterer-Siwe's disease in the United States in a five-year period from 1960 through 1964 revealed a striking concentration of deaths in the first two years of life, with a peak of mortality under 1 year of age. The aggregation of deaths in siblings other than twins appeared far greater for this disease than any childhood neoplasm. The risk of Letterer-Siwe in the sibling of a child with that ailment was estimated to be about 1,400 times normal. These findings are regarded as an indication of neonatal origin of Letterer-Siwe's disease.

CLINICAL MANIFESTATIONS. Characteristically, widespread involvement of viscera and skin is present at the onset without demonstrable skeletal lesions initially. In general, though not always, progression and dissemination of the morbid process is rapid, even fulminating. Early fatal termination is the rule rather than the exception.

Typical cases feature a characteristic cutaneous eruption; enlargement of spleen, liver, and lymph nodes; a febrile systemic illness; and hypoplastic anemia, leucopenia, thrombocytopenia, and a hemorrhagic tendency. Skeletal changes may occur if the course of the disease is less acute. Widespread visceral histiocytic infiltration not suspected during the child's life may be found at autopsy.

The *skin eruption* is often the first manifestation to attract attention. Cutaneous involvement is rarely the only manifestation. The rash (Fig. 1) commonly starts at the hairline, and then tends to become generalized, remaining usually most marked over the trunk, on the scalp, and in the skin folds. The individual lesions are greasy, scaly, crusted maculopapules, sometimes considerably elevated. Although they blanch under pressure, their color appears often dark red or purplish, simulating hemorrhagic vesicles. Later in the disease, with the development of thrombocytopenia, localized or generalized *petechiae* may be observed. The infiltrative exanthema may also become the site of hemorrhages and even ulcerate. A nonhemorrhagic rash does not, however, preclude the existence of diminished platelets. The skin eruption may be very pruriginous in character, and its appearance may suggest eczema or seborrheic dermatitis. However, the presence of petechiae, the distribution of the lesions, and a tenacious eruption persisting despite adequate therapy for seborrheic dermatitis or eczema, distinguishes clinically the infiltrative histiocytosis from atopic dermatitis.

As a rule, generalzed *lymphadenopathy*, moderate to marked *splenomegaly*, and *hepatomegaly* are present. Obstructive jaundice produced by a portal lesion may be the reason for seeking medical advice.

Clinical, radiologic, and pathologic evidence of *pulmonary involvement* is frequently demonstrable. Respiratory difficulties may actually herald the onset of the disease. Small infiltrative nodules, interstitial pneumonitis, and lung cysts are not uncommonly observed. Radiographic studies of the chest may reveal bilateral diffuse reticulonodular densities. When cysts are present the typical roentgenologic appearance of

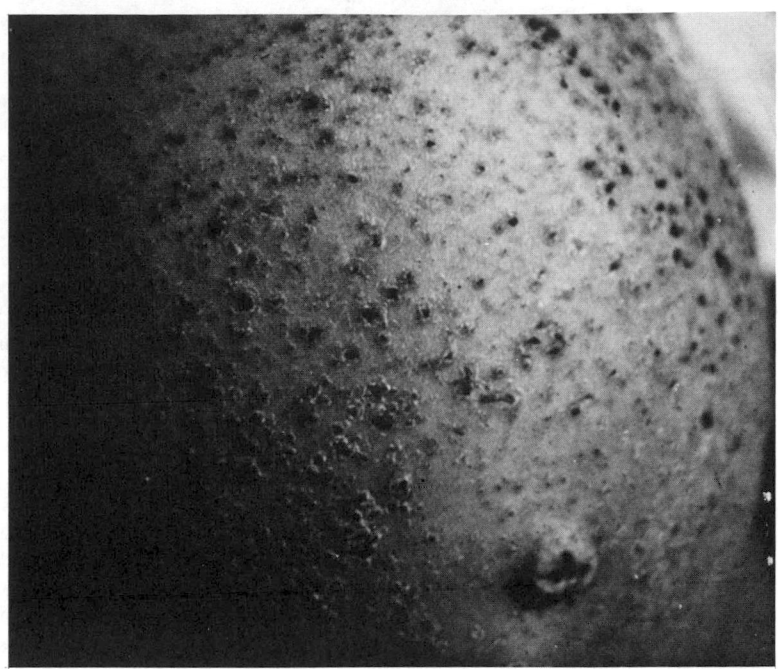

Fig. 1. Scaly and crusted cutaneous lesions on abdomen of 8-month-old infant with Letterer-Siwe disease.

"honeycomb lungs" is produced. The occurrence of pneumothorax following the rupture of subpleural lung cysts represents a typical complication in the course of Letterer-Siwe disease. In two of our patients, death was directly attributable to this complication. The combination of honeycomb lung and recurrent episodes of pneumothorax should suggest the possibility of reticuloendotheliosis.

In patients whose disease runs a subacute course, localized *osseous defects* may be found in the skull and other bones. Roentgenograms may reveal characteristic areas of rarefaction comparable to those seen in Hand-Schüller-Christian disease.

Anorexia and failure to thrive are common and at times the presenting complaints; in other cases daily temperature elevations, anemia, or hemorrhagic manifestations may be prominent features. In most instances, regardless of the mode of onset, the disease tends to run a downhill course. The child's nutritional state deteriorates, the lesions progress, and hemorrhagic manifestations, respiratory difficulties, or intercurrent infections are likely to terminate the picture. The entire duration of the disease is usually measured in months. Some cases run a more protracted and milder course. Exceptionally, arrest and complete recovery have been observed even in infants.

HISTOLOGIC DIAGNOSIS. When the disease is suspected on the basis of a typical skin rash or other findings, the diagnosis is most readily confirmed by biopsy of skin lesions or lymph nodes. Early in the disease there is a proliferation of mononuclear histiocytes without vacuolization and with minimal surrounding reaction. When survival has lasted several months the lesions tend to become granulomatous,

with "foam cells," eosinophils, and multinucleated giant cells. A *touch preparation*, made of the serous material exuding from a skin lesion after scraping the overlying epidermis with a scalpel, a simple and rapid procedure described by Moore, may facilitate the diagnosis when skin lesions are present.

TREATMENT. Efforts to arrest the disease are rarely successful. A wide variety of therapeutic agents have been used. Some measure of success has been reported from the effects of antimetabolites, corticosteroids, radiation, antibiotics, alkylating agents, or vinca alkaloids given singly or in combination. Results are, however, not striking and too often only transient. Vinblastine sulfate administered intravenously in doses of 0.15 to 0.20 mg per kilogram daily, in combination with steroid therapy in the range of 20 mg per kilogram per day of hydrocortisone, has produced apparently good remissions in some children with acute disseminated histiocytosis. Effectiveness of therapy is, however, difficult to evaluate, and the question usually remains open as to whether these patients are saved by treatment or whether their illness abated spontaneously.

The Hand-Schüller-Christian Syndrome

Originally this syndrome described a classic triad: *exophthalmos, membranous bone defects,* and *diabetes insipidus;* it was seen in older children or young adults and often followed a comparatively benign course. It is now appreciated that in this particular entity, typical lesions may be found in virtually every organ of the body. The concept of this syndrome has been broadened to include all instances of the disease complex in which skeleton, viscera, and soft tissues are affected at the onset, regardless of the patient's age.

PATHOLOGY.   While skin, middle ear, and bones are most conspicuously affected, most other soft tissues and organ systems are also commonly involved. Granulomatous lesions originating in the base of the skull, exerting pressure on the pituitary and the tuber cinereum, are responsible for the diabetes insipidus. Lesions in the orbit produce the exophthalmos. Involvement of the mastoid or petrous portion of the temporal bone cause the chronic otitis media, while displacement or extrusion of teeth results from granulomata of the mandible or maxilla.

Histologically, the lesions when fully developed are xanthomas. In their early stage the infiltrating histiocytes contain no visible lipids, and some eosinophils can be observed. The typical xanthomatous granuloma is yellowish, of miliary size, contains lipid-filled "foam cells," and is surrounded by a zone of fibrosis of variable width. With the aging of the lesion, some lipid-containing cells disintegrate, and free cholesterol crystals and giant cells may be seen in the center. Eventually, only a fibrous scar remains if healing takes place.

CLINICAL MANIFESTATIONS.   The clinical manifestations of the Hand-Schüller-Christian syndrome are most varied. The disease begins most commonly during early or late childhood; the time of onset is rarely in infancy. Any or all of the three original manifestations of the classic triad may be absent; in fact, the combination of all three is exceedingly rare. A cutaneous eruption sometimes in crops, a chronic ear dis-

charge, and diabetes insipidus are the commonest reasons for seeking medical advice. Dental loosening, loss of teeth, or ulcerative lesions of the gum may be the first symptom to attract attention. Fever may be present but is inconstant. Stunting of growth, a prominent feature in one of our patients, may be considerable in this disease.

Exophthalmos is the feature of the triad most rarely encountered. Single or multiple granulomatous lesions may be present in the orbit without producing proptosis.

Skin lesions in their early stage are often similar to seborrheic dermatitis or may present the greasy, scaly, crusted, and reddish maculopapular appearance identical with the picture described in acute reticuloendotheliosis. In the course of months, however, the reddish-brown lesions turn yellow and, microscopically, cholesterol droplets appear in the cells.

Visceral manifestations are likely to become more striking in the very young children. Enlargement of the spleen, liver, and lymph nodes may be considerable; jaundice may occur. In some instances lymph nodes are sufficiently prominent to suggest lymphoma. At times splenomegaly, hepatomegaly, or adenopathy is moderate or may not be observed at all. There may be a miliary, mottled, or patchy infiltration of the lung fields, often relatively asymptomatic. Thyroid lesions have been found at autopsy or in biopsy material even without clinical evidence of enlargement of the gland. In fatal cases miliary xanthomatous lesions are found in nearly every organ of the body, including the brain.

Skeletal lesions are most striking. Flat bones as well as long bones are affected. The calvarium of the skull is the most common site of involvement. De-

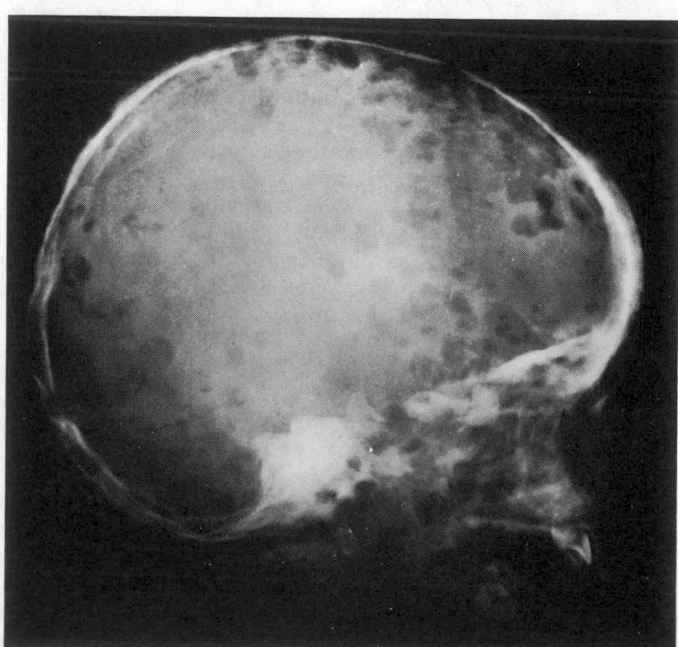

Fig. 2.   Roentgenogram of skull in reticuloendotheliosis, showing multiple defects. Patient 3½ years of age.

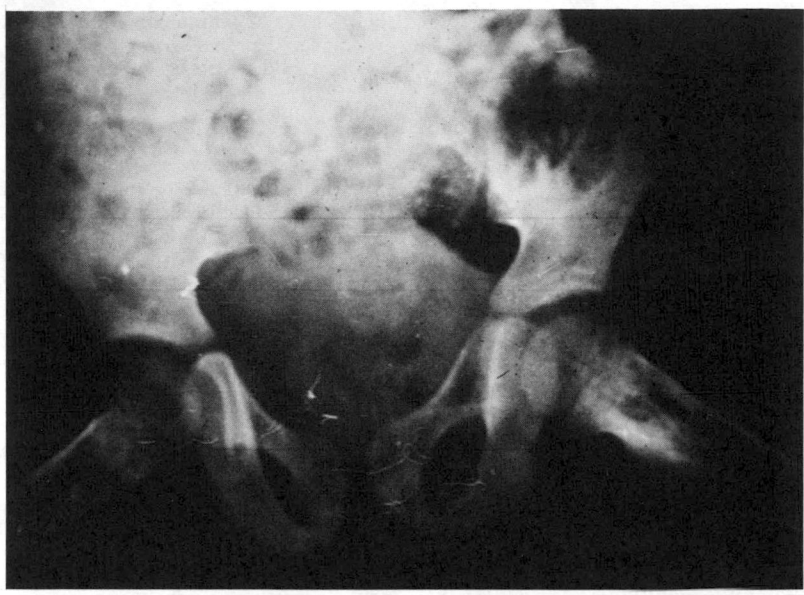

Fig. 3.   Radiographic study of 7½-year-old boy with Hand-Schüller-Christian syndrome. Destructive lesions are discernible in upper end of both femurs; note healed fractures on the right.

fects of the skull can be discovered clinically or can be palpated as soft tissue nodules overlying lytic lesions demonstrable radiographically (Fig. 2). In long bones, pathologic fractures may lead to the discovery of destructive foci (Fig. 3). The bone lesions are responsible for the exophthalmos, the *diabetes insipidus,* the chronic otitis media, and dental problems. They may produce neurologic manifestations. In flat bones, the osseous lesions present a typical radiologic appearance featuring sharply defined punched-out areas, round or ovoid, with no reaction in the surrounding bone. In long bones, however, involvement of the cortex results in a destructive lesion with periosteal new bone formation, which may suggest a neoplasm, tuberculosis, or late syphilis. The bone defects may heal spontaneously or persist for many years.

LABORATORY FINDINGS. Radiologic studies and histologic examinations of biopsy specimens of skin lesions, bone lesions, or lymph nodes constitute the only laboratory diagnostic aids. Blood lipids are characteristically not elevated. Eosinophilia has been reported but is inconstant. Anemia, leucopenia, and thrombocytopenia may be present but are observed less commonly than in acute reticuloendotheliosis.

COURSE AND THERAPY. The course is extremely variable. Some children recover completely from the disease even after lesions have continued to occur in new sites for several years. In others, diabetes insipidus may persist after the disappearance of cranial bone lesions. The polydipsia and polyuria usually respond to variable doses of vasopressin. Those in whom the disease is fatal may survive several months to several years. The course is often shorter and more progressive in younger children. In patients older than 10 years of age the prognosis for arrest of bone lesions

is excellent. Treatment is of limited value. Radiotherapy, adrenal cortical steroids, and antifolic compounds, singly or in combination, may cause retrogression of the lesions, but the response is inconsistent and often only temporary.

Eosinophilic Granuloma

This condition, as originally described, was a circumscribed bone lesion, usually solitary, seen in older children and running a benign course. Microscopically it was characterized by infiltration of round cells with no vacuoles and no fibrosis. In some instances eosinophilia was present.

The relation of this clinical variant to the other forms of reticuloendotheliosis has been known since Lichtenstein. Green and Farber described the evolution of these lesions, which is characterized by vacuolization of the histiocytes, disappearance of eosinophils, and appearance of fibrosis. Eosinophilic granuloma is now generally regarded as one mode of onset of granulomatous reticuloendotheliosis rather than as a separate disease.

Fortunately the clinical expression of this condition does not progress beyond the stage of solitary, circumscribed bone lesion in most instances. Clinically, the bone lesion may be tender; in some instances local pain or swelling may attract attention. A fracture may be the presenting complaint. The x-ray findings are identical with the description of the lesions in Schüller-Christian disease.

Treatment. Curettage is the recommended treatment because it constitutes definitive therapy, provides a specimen for pathologic examination, and avoids the hazards of irradiation. Complete healing occurs often after local curettage; and relapses after surgery are exceedingly rare. Only if the size, the location, or the number of lesions make surgery impractical, or if the operative procedure entails a risk of considerable disability, is radiotherapy indicated. The lesion is relatively radiosensitive.

Other Forms of Reticuloendotheliosis

Several varieties of reticuloendotheliosis have been reported which actually constitute atypical variants of, or diseases related to, histiocytosis. In spite of some differences in clinical expression and histologic findings there appears to be no valid reason to separate these entities from the nonlipid acute reticuloendothelioses.

Nelson and his group reported a disease fatal in three siblings, termed *generalized lymphohistiocytosis* and characterized by fever, anemia, leukopenia, thrombocytopenia, lymphadenopathy, hepatosplenomegaly, pneumonia, and meningitis. Histologically, there was extensive visceral infiltration of many organs and tissues by large lymphocytes and histiocytes. The leptomeninges, the central nervous system, and neurohypophysis were involved. The bones and skin were not affected. Involvement of the central nervous system was given as one of the grounds for separating this condition from Letterer-Siwe disease.

Almost identical clinical features were reported by Farquhar in *familial erythrophagocytic lymphohistiocytosis (familial hemophagocytic reticulocytosis)*, also a multisystem and familial disease. Clinical and pathologic findings included splenomegaly and hepatomegaly; pancytopenia and atypical lymphocytes in the peripheral blood; and associated infiltration of the bone marrow, spleen, liver, and lymph nodes by histiocytes showing active phagocytosis of erythrocytes and leukocytes.

Subsequently cases were reported of Farquhar's disease with central nervous system involvement; on the other hand, lesions of the central nervous system have also been found in Letterer-Siwe disease. Consequently, the diffuse infiltrative characteristics of both Nelson's and Farquhar's reticulosis remain the only features which still distinguish them from the granulomatous lesions of Letterer-Siwe disease.

REFERENCES

Ahnquist, G., and Holyoke, J. B. Congenital Letterer-Siwe disease (reticuloendotheliosis) in a term stillborn infant. J. Pediat., 57:905, 1960.

Avery, M. E., McAfee, J. G., and Holyoke, J. B. Course and treatment of reticuloendotheliosis (eosinophilic granuloma, Schüller-Christian disease and Letterer-Siwe disease). Amer. J. Med., 22:636, 1957.

Batson, R., Shapiro, M., and Christie, A. Acute nonlipid disseminated reticuloendotheliosis. Amer. J. Dis. Child., 90:323, 1955.

Beier, F. R., Thatcher, L. G., and Lahey, M. E. Treatment of reticuloendotheliosis with vinblastine sulfate. J. Pediat., 63:1087, 1963.

Bell, R. J. M., Brafield, A. J. E., Baines, N. D., and France. Familial haemophagocytic reticulosis. Arch. Dis. Child., 43:601, 1968.

Esterly, N. B., and Swick, H. M. Cutaneous Letterer-Siwe disease. Amer. J. Dis. Child., 117:236, 1969.

Farquhar, J. W., and Claireaux, A. E. Familial haemophagocytic reticulosis. Arch. Dis. Child., 27:519, 1952.

Freud, P. Treatment of reticuloendotheliosis—use of corticoids and antifolic compounds. J.A.M.A., 175:82, 1961.

Glass, A. G., and Miller, R. W. U.S. mortality from Letterer-Siwe disease, 1960-1964. Pediatrics, 42:364, 1968.

Green, W. T., and Farber, S. "Eosinophilic or solitary granuloma" of bone. J. Bone Joint Surg., 24:499, 1942.

Hertz, C. G., and Hambrick, G. W. Congenital Letterer-Siwe disease. Amer. J. Dis. Child., 116:553, 1968.

Lahey, M. E. Prognosis in reticuloendotheliosis in children. J. Pediat., 60:664, 1962.

Lichtenstein, L. Histiocytosis X: Integration of eosinophilic granuloma of bone, "Letterer-Siwe disease," and "Schüller-Christian disease" as related manifestations of a single nosologic entity. Arch. Path., 56:84, 1953.

Merman, A. C., and Dargeon, H. W. The management of certain nonlipid reticuloendothelioses. Cancer, 8:113, 1955.

Miller, D. R. Familial reticuloendotheliosis: concurrence of disease in five siblings. Pediatrics, 38:986, 1966.

Moore, T. D. A single technique for the diagnosis of nonlipid histiocytosis. Pediatrics, 19:438, 1957.

Nelson, P., Santamaria, A., Olson, R. L., and Nayak, N. C. Generalized lymphohistiocytic infiltration. Pediatrics, 27:931, 1961.

Oberman, H. A. Idiopathic histiocytosis. A clinical study of 40 cases and review of the literature on eosinophilic granuloma of the bone, Hand-Schüller-Christian disease and Letterer-Siwe disease. Pediatrics, 28:307, 1961.

Omenn, G. S. Familial reticuloendotheliosis with eosinophilia. New Eng. J. Med., 273:427, 1965.

Roland, A. S., et al. Recurrent spontaneous pneumothorax: A clue to the diagnosis of histiocytosis. New Eng. J. Med., 270:73, 1964.

Rogers, D. L., and Benson, T. E. Familial Letterer-Siwe disease. J. Pediat., 60:550, 1962.

Schoeck, V. W., Peterson, R. D. A., and Good, R. A. Familial Letterer-Siwe disease. Pediatrics, 32:1033, 1963.

Siegel, J. S., and Coltman, C. A. Histiocytosis X: Response to vinblastine sulfate. J.A.M.A., 197:403, 1966.

18.2
SARCOIDOSIS

Sarcoidosis, often referred to as Boeck's sarcoid, is a chronic granulomatous process of unknown cause which may affect any one or any number of organs and systems. It produces in general only mild symptoms despite extensive tissue involvement. Characteristically, the disease tends to progress slowly with relapses and remissions, ultimately burning itself out in the course of years. The clinical manifestations are due mainly to pressure phenomena exerted by enlarged structures.

EPIDEMIOLOGY, INCIDENCE, AND ETIOLOGY. The disease is rarely observed in children. In 1956, in McGovern and Merritt's first comprehensive review of childhood sarcoidosis compiled from the world literature through 1953, only 113 cases were reported in children less than 15 years of age; 135 additional cases have been subsequently documented in children. However, there is growing evidence that clinically silent forms of this disease occur more frequently in children than is generally suspected. In these asymptomatic forms bilateral hilar adenopathy, often combined with pulmonary parenchymal lesions, can be demonstrated radiographically. An increasing number of such cases have been detected primarily in countries where mass radiographic surveys have been performed on children.

Epidemiologic studies have provided no clues concerning etiology or pathogenesis of this disorder. There appears to be no clear-cut difference in sex distribution. Cases affecting siblings have been reported but have occurred so rarely that, although not excluded, a genetic factor is unlikely. The distribution of the disease is universal; the highest known prevalence rate is in Sweden. In the United States it is more common among Negroes. There are areas with high attack rates of sarcoidosis in the South Atlantic and the Gulf States, and endemic areas in New England and the Midwest. The unusually high incidence of the disease in one rural county in Virginia among workers handling peanuts and peanut products is striking but unexplained.

The possibility of an infectious causative agent has been raised because of the occasionally febrile course, because of the resemblance of the histologic lesions to tubercles, and because, in some families, more than one member has been affected, sometimes simultaneously. However, there is usually no evidence of contact, and efforts to recover an infectious agent have been unsuccessful. The belief, once prevalent, that the disease is a form of tuberculosis in an anergic subject now has few adherents. A distinct feature of the disease is the patient's inability to react to tuberculin and to other delayed hypersensitivity skin tests in the presence of normal circulating antigen-antibody production. Observations that patients who were positive reactors to tuberculin before the onset of sarcoidosis but did not react during the course of the illness and regained tuberculin sensitivity on recovery, led to the suggestion that the depressed skin reactivity possibly results from impaired immunologic mechanisms caused by the disease. Persistence of insensitivity to tuberculin after recovery has also been reported. The latter observation may lend support to an alternative hypothesis that the inability to develop and maintain delayed hypersensitivity is a constitutional immunologic defect which precedes the disease and may be a prerequisite to its development.

PATHOLOGY. The fundamental pathologic lesion, which may be found in virtually any organ or tissue, consists of granulomata of tuberclelike structure composed principally of epithelioid cells, together with varying number of Langhans'-type giant cells, and surrounded by lymphocytes. Central necrosis is inconspicuous or absent. Giant cells often contain refractile, stellate, basophilic inclusions. Tubercle bacilli cannot be found, either by acid-fast staining of tissue sections or by culture. In the course of time, the lesion may be replaced by fibrosis or hyalinization or both. The tissues most frequently involved are lymph nodes, lungs, skin, eye, and bones, especially of the hands and feet.

CLINICAL MANIFESTATIONS. The clinical picture is extremely variable. The most striking feature of sarcoidosis is the *multisystem involvement*. Signs and symptoms depend on the organs and tissues affected, hence the great diversity of clinical manifestations. As a rule the onset of symptomatic sarcoidosis is insidious. In the child as well as in the adult, cough, chest pain, and weight loss are symptoms that occur most frequently. Constitutional symptoms such as fever, anorexia, fatigability, and malaise are usually absent, although they may have been observed. The enlargement of one or more peripheral lymph nodes, the presence of skin lesions, parotid swelling, pain in the extremities, or a disturbance of vision, may be the presenting complaint, but may also indicate that the disease process is well advanced.

The *lymphadenopathy* may be generalized, the involved nodes discrete and not tender, the spleen and liver may be enlarged. Specific *skin lesions* are found in more than a third of patients with systemic sarcoidosis. They represent dermal sarcoid granulomata and are capable of wide variations in clinical appearance. They occur most often on the face, as yellowish waxy miliary papules or larger somewhat lichenoid conglomerates, or as flat, smooth, purplish, or deep pigmented papules 1 cm or more in diameter. Typical erythema nodosa lesions are not uncommon.

Ocular manifestations may result in severe impairment of vision. The eye involvement may take the form of keratitis, iritis, iridocyclitis, uveitis, glaucoma, or rarely retinitis. Flame-shaped hemorrhages in the retina have also been observed. Excessive lacrimation with involvement of the eyelids and lacrimal glands may be present. The formation of synechiae sometimes interferes with normal contraction of the pupils. When the lesions affect the eye, fibrotic uveitis may produce partial or total blindness, which makes the involvement of this organ one of the most dreaded complications of this disease. A characteristic syndrome of sarcoidosis is the so-called *uveoparotid fever*, in which tender swelling of the parotid or other salivary glands is associated with uveitis and sometimes with fever or peripheral facial paralysis.

Pulmonary and osseous lesions most frequently cause no symptoms and are discovered only through careful radiologic studies. In the bones the classical lesions are sharply defined punched-out areas of rarefaction in the phalanges or other small bones. The radiographic findings observed in the lung vary considerably. Bilateral hilar adenopathy may exist alone or in combination with parenchymal mottling. The pulmonary densities, if present, may consist of flocculent infiltrations, miliary nodules, focal streaking, or pulmonary reticulations. The most common manifestations of sarcoidosis in the lungs closely simulate the radiographic picture of miliary tuberculosis. With massive enlargement of hilar nodes, the patient may have shortness of breath on exertion. Extensive pulmonary disease can be associated with pneumothorax. Respiratory function studies in sarcoidosis have shown little correlation between functional abnormalities and radiologic changes. Impaired diffusion and reduced lung compliance were the most common findings and correlated closely with both decreased vital capacity and duration of illness. The dyspnea, if present, appeared to be secondary to diminished vital capacity.

Joint involvement clinically resembling rheumatoid arthritis has been described. Joint manifestations quite distinct from those of rheumatoid arthritis have also been reported. In such instances, the distinguishing features of the sarcoid arthritis consist of the large "boggy" effusion, with thickening of joint membranes, involvement of tendon sheaths, minimal pain and limitation of motion, and the absence of osteoporosis which is unusual in rheumatoid arthritis. Rheumatoid factor has been found in the sera of a number of patients with sarcoidosis. The presence of this factor appears unrelated to the presence or absence of joint symptoms and to be of little prognostic significance.

Other systems. Sarcoid granulomas can involve the myocardium and exceptionally the pericardium. The most frequent manifestations of sarcoid heart disease, excluding cor pulmonale, are conduction defects ranging from complete heart block to supraventricular and ventricular arrhythmias.

Symptoms of diabetes insipidus and amenorrhea due to pituitary lesions have been reported, but are exceedingly rare. The central nervous system is rarely affected, but in a small number of children paralysis of the facial nerve has been associated with uveoparotid fever. Striated muscle sarcoidosis can produce muscle weakness or pseudohypertrophy. Deafness can be the presenting symptom; in one child hoarseness was associated with the presence of a sarcoid nodule on the vocal cords.

The kidneys are among the less frequently affected organs in childhood sarcoidosis. However, several instances of kidney involvement with various degrees of renal failure have been recorded, some in association with polyarthritis. The most common findings are proteinuria, pyuria, hematuria, intermittent glycosuria, and granular casts. Clinical symptoms are usually mild and do not correlate with the severity of histologic lesions observed on biopsy or autopsy. Persistent hypertension is exceptional. Since parenchymal renal granulomas are often microscopic, they are not thought to be the cause of the impairment of renal function. The hypercalcemia of sarcoidosis with or without nephrocalcinosis or nephro-

lithiasis is believed to be primarily responsible for the renal complication of this disease. A fairly good correlation appears to exist between the severity of renal symptoms and the duration and degree of hypercalcemia. Renal insufficiency is usually associated with hypercalcemia.

Course and complications. Sarcoidosis runs a chronic course characterized by remissions and exacerbations with a tendency to ultimate healing in the child. Fatalities are infrequent. Childhood sarcoidosis could be considered essentially a benign disease but for three troublesome complications: pulmonary fibrosis, fibrotic uveitis, and nephrocalcinosis. Unsuspected tuberculosis has complicated the course of some patients and has caused their death. *Cryptococcus neoformans meningitis* has been responsible for the fatal outcome in one child with diffuse systemic Boeck's sarcoid.

LABORATORY FINDINGS AND DIAGNOSIS. The diagnosis can be established by an assessment of the clinical manifestations, the radiographic findings in lungs and bones, in combination with certain laboratory abnormalities, and the histologic features of a biopsy specimen. Most patients have an elevated serum protein due to an absolute increase of serum globulins, with elevation of α_2 and γ globulins and reversal of the albumin/globulin ratio. Serum complement activity may be increased. Hypercalcemia occurs quite commonly and is an important complicating factor in sarcoidosis. The course of hypercalcemia is believed to be due to a hypersensitivity to vitamin D. Eosinophilia is found more frequently in children than in adults. There are no other characteristic changes in blood count, blood chemistries, or sedimentation rate.

The tuberculin test is negative except in some, but not all, patients who have both sarcoidosis and tuberculosis. Depression of delayed type hypersensitivity is also demonstrable with other antigens including pertussis and mumps. Dissociation between defective cellular antibodies and the normal circulating antibody response may be used as a diagnostic aid in sarcoidosis. A negative mumps skin test with a positive mumps complement-fixation test, although not specific for sarcoidosis, can nonetheless be considered significant in support of this diagnosis.

The diagnosis is most readily confirmed by biopsy and histologic examination of a lesion. An enlarged peripheral lymph node, the scalene fat pad, a skin lesion, or muscle are tissues most suitable and most accessible for biopsy.

The *Nickerson-Kveim skin test* is helpful in differentiating sarcoidosis from other granulomatous diseases, provided the test is carried out under rigid control, with confirmation by biopsy. The test is based on the reaction that follows the intracutaneous injection of 0.2 ml of antigen prepared from sarcoid tissue. Material used for the test must be adequately tested on known cases of sarcoid before it can be used for diagnosis. The test is positive when a sarcoid lesion forms at the injection site in the course of a few weeks. It must be interpreted by histologic examination of the papule, removed by punch biopsy six or eight weeks after the injection. Although a positive Kveim test offers strong confirmation of the diagnosis, a negative result does not exclude sarcoidosis. Irregularities in response to the test depend in large part on differences in the properties of the antigenic material used.

TREATMENT. There is no specific therapy for sarcoidosis. The indications for treatment with steroids and the magnitude of the benefits derived from such therapy are still the subject of controversy. The true value of any treatment in a disease with such a high spontaneous remission rate is difficult to assess. However, there is general agreement that the adrenal corticosteroids alleviate symptoms and decrease the extent of organ involvement, at least temporarily. Therapy with adrenal corticosteroids is recommended for patients with active ocular disease, persistent hypercalcemia, central nervous system or myocardial involvement, disfiguring skin lesions, and progressive pulmonary disease. Both symptoms and lesions may improve or disappear completely under the influence of steroid therapy, but often recur when such treatment is terminated. However, relapses after withdrawal of therapy are often only temporary and may be followed by lasting improvement without reinstitution of the corticosteroids. A low-calcium diet may lower the hypercalcemia, but in the majority of cases, diet alone, or in combination with sodium sulfate, is not effective. Corticosteroids have been successful in resolving the hypercalcemia, followed by a striking and permanent return to normal renal function.

REFERENCES

Bautista, A. Childhood sarcoidosis involving joints and kidneys. Amer. J. Dis. Child., 119:259, 1970.

Beier, F. R., and Lahey, M. E. Sarcoidosis among children in Utah and Idaho. J. Pediat., 65:350, 1964.

Israel, H. L., and Jones, M. Immunologic defect in patients recovered from sarcoidosis. New Eng. J. Med., 273:1003, 1965.

James, D. G. Immunology of sarcoidosis. Lancet, 7515:526, 1967.

——— Treatment of sarcoidosis. Lancet, 7464:633, 1966.

Jasper, P. L., and Denny, F. W. Sarcoidosis in children. J. Pediat., 73:499, 1968.

Kendig, E. L. Sarcoidosis among children, a review. J. Pediat., 61:269, 1962.

Kogut, M. D., and Newman, L. L. Renal involvement in Boeck's sarcoidosis. Pediatrics, 28:40, 1961.

Lepow, H., Rubinstein, L., Chu, F., and Chandra, J. *Cryptococcus neoformans* meningoencephalitis complicating Boeck's sarcoid. Pediatrics, 19:377, 1957.

Lofgren, S. Concepts of sarcoidosis. *In* 3rd International Conference on sarcoidosis. Acta Med. Scand., 425:1, 1964.

McGovern, J. P., and Merritt, D. H. Sarcoidosis in childhood. Advances Pediat., 8:97, 1956.

Oreskes, I., and Siltzbach, L. E. Changes in rheumatoid factor activity during the course of sarcoidosis. Amer. J. Med., 44:60, 1968.

Scholz, D. A. Effect of steroid therapy on hypercalcemic and renal insufficiency in sarcoidosis. J.A.M.A., 169:682, 1959.

Shiff, A. D., Blatt, C. J., and Colp, C. C. Recurrent pericardial effusion secondary to sarcoidosis of the pericardium. New Eng. J. Med., 281:141, 1969.

Siltzbach, L. E., and Greenberg, G. M. Childhood sarcoidosis—a study of 18 patients. New Eng. J. Med., 279:1239, 1968.

Ting, E. Y., and Williams, M. H. Mechanics of breathing in sarcoidosis of lung. J.A.M.A., 192:123, 1965.

chapter 19

THE PULMONARY SYSTEM

WILLIAM H. TOOLEY, Associate Editor

Respiratory Function and Pulmonary Diseases of the Newborn

19.1
RESPIRATORY FUNCTION
IN THE NEWBORN

MARSHALL H. KLAUS

The Lung of the Fetus

The developing lung originates as an outgrowth of cells from the gut endoderm at 24 days of gestation. This collection of cells develops into the epithelial portion of the lung, while the rest of the lung is probably of mesodermal origin. During the next months, there are growth and branching of the solid endodermal bud. At the twentieth week, the solid core of cells becomes canalized and the lung is traversed by thick connective tissue septa but is not well vascularized. By the twenty-eighth week, the internal surface area and vascularization of the lung have developed sufficiently for the lung to exchange oxygen and carbon dioxide in amounts adequate to sustain life. At the time of birth, the lung of the full-term infant has grown to contain an internal surface area of about 2.8 square meters and 24 million alveolar units. In utero the lung is not completely collapsed but is partially filled with fluid. Though the volume of fluid produced in the lung and its ultimate fate are not known, its presence increases alveolar and bronchiolar radii. This has the useful effect of lowering the opening pressure required for the first inflation. There is continuity between the amniotic cavity and the lung, as demonstrated by the appearance of radiopaque material in the lung several hours after its injection into the amniotic sac. This does not necessarily imply intrauterine respiration or a large flow from the amniotic sac into the lung. In fact, lung fluid from the fetal lamb differs chemically from both umbilical vein blood and amniotic fluid. The total CO_2 content and pH of the lung fluid are lower, while its chloride and sodium concentration are higher, than those of amniotic fluid. Intermittent rhythmic respiratory movements of the fetus have been observed by many investigators. Their significance is not understood but the movements vary in intensity throughout pregnancy.

Before delivery the ribs are horizontal and the diaphragm rests very high in the chest cage. Pulmonary artery blood flow is only 10 to 15 percent of the combined output of the right and left ventricles. Flow through the bronchial arteries has not been determined.

As the infant passes through the birth canal, the chest cage is compressed. When the face is delivered and the mouth is at atmospheric pressure, the increased intrathoracic pressure produced by the chest compression (the big squeeze) forces fluid out of the lung. With delivery and recoil of the chest cage, a small amount of air replaces the lost fluid (Fig. 1).

The First Breath
(See also Sec. 2.9)

Many factors may stimulate the newborn to take his first breath. Among these are (1) low arterial Po_2 tension, (2) high arterial Pco_2 tension, (3) low arterial pH, (4) cutaneous stimulation that occurs with evaporative cooling, (5) increased airway pres-

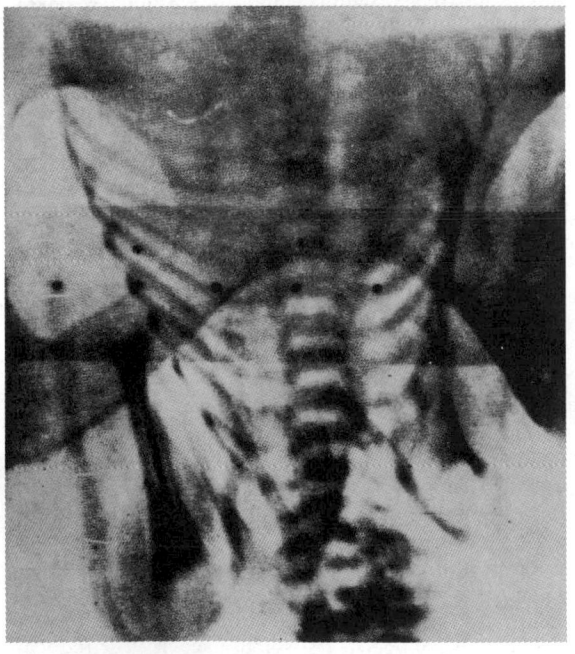

Fig. 1. Radiogram of a fetus passing through the birth canal. Note how the chest cage is compressed. (From Borell and Fernstrom. *Acta Obstet. Gynec. Scand.*, 41:213, 1962.)

sure produced by frog breathing which would stimulate a gasp reflex, and (6) a change from the weightless intrauterine state stimulating proprioceptive receptors. Though none of these alone always produces the first breath, they may in some fashion operate together. Very high pressures are required to fill the lung with air for the first time. Intrathoracic pressures as great as 40 to 70 cm of H_2O below atmospheric pressure have been recorded with the first breath. These high pressures overcome the high viscous resistance produced in moving the fluid column in the airways and the forces of surface tension as a large air-water interphase is formed for the first time. The lung tissue itself offers only minimum resistance to deformation. The first several breaths require a large change in intrathoracic pressure. The infant creates a negative pressure of some 60 cm H_2O with the first breath. Succeeding breaths are accomplished with smaller negative pressures until by 5 minutes of age the pressure change during quiet breathing is 6 to 8 cm H_2O.

Other remarkable changes occur in the lung in the first minutes of life. During the first few respirations probably more than half of the fluid contained in the lung is absorbed. The remaining fluid is absorbed during the first day. In the lamb, pulmonary blood flow increases eight- to tenfold following delivery. This increase is secondary to a decrease in pulmonary vascular resistance and other physiologic changes converting the circulation from a parallel arrangement to a series circuit. The high vascular resistance in the fetal lung is due to vasoconstriction rather than to kinking and twisting of small blood vessels, as previously believed, since very small injections of either acetylcholine or histamine into the pulmonary artery of the fluid-filled fetal lung produce a five-fold increase in pulmonary blood flow. Inflating the lung with oxygen also causes dilation of the pulmonary arterioles. With delivery and inflation of the lung with air, pulmonary vascular resistance decreases markedly.

The elastic recoil of the infant lung can be divided into two components: the first is due to the connective and elastic tissue elements; the second is the result of surface tension forces at the air-water interphase. Surface tension forces are significant because of the small alveolar radii. The pressure produced by surface forces tending to collapse the alveolar unit can be calculated from the Laplace relationship:

$$\text{Pressure} = \frac{2 \times \text{surface tension}}{\text{radius}}$$

If we substitute in this formula an alveolar radius of 50 μ and the surface tension of plasma (50 dynes/cm), the pressure tending to collapse the unit due only to the forces of surface tension of the lining of the lung would be 20 cm H_2O. The intrathoracic pressure at end-expiration would have to be more negative than -20 cm H_2O or the alveolar unit would collapse. However, the internal surface of the

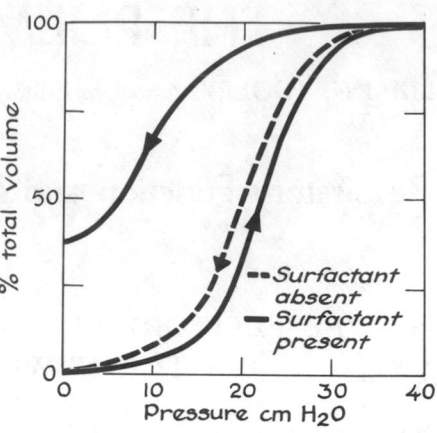

Fig. 2. An air pressure volume curve of a lung with and without pulmonary surfactant. When the surfactant is present, the lung contains more air during deflation. (Adapted from Radford, Ferris, and Kriete. New Eng. J. Med., 251:877, 1954.)

lung is lined by a highly surface-active material (lung surfactant) that markedly reduces the forces of surface tension at the air-water interphase and thereby lowers the pressure, tending to collapse the alveolus. The lung surfactant, a lipoprotein, also acts as an antiatelectasis factor by equalizing the forces of surface tension in units of varying sizes. The effects of the surfactant are illustrated in Figure 2, where air inflation and deflation pressure-volume curves are plotted with surfactant, and a deflation curve without surfactant. When the surfactant is present, during deflation the lung contains a larger volume of air at any given pressure than on inflation. Inspection of the pleural surface with a microscope reveals that large and small alveolar units remain open and empty together. However, when the lung surfactant is altered or deficient, the deflation pressure-volume curve follows the inflation curve. Inspection of the pleural surface in these conditions reveals that the small air-containing units empty first as the pressure is lowered, and only large units remain aerated at the end of deflation. When the surfactant is present, there are a large number of small units open on deflation. If the surface tension in large and small units were the same, the small alveoli would collapse into the large when the pressure is reduced as illustrated in Figure 3. However, this effect is prevented by the surfactant, which decreases the forces of surface tension as the surface concentration is increased. If large and small units can be simplified as shown in Figure 3, and each unit has three molecules of surfactant/cm², then as the small unit empties into the large, the surface concentration of the surfactant is markedly increased in the small unit with corresponding lowering of surface tension. The greater relative area change in the small alveolar unit reduces the surface tension more in the small unit and prevents collapse. In this way, the surfactant stabilizes the lung volume.

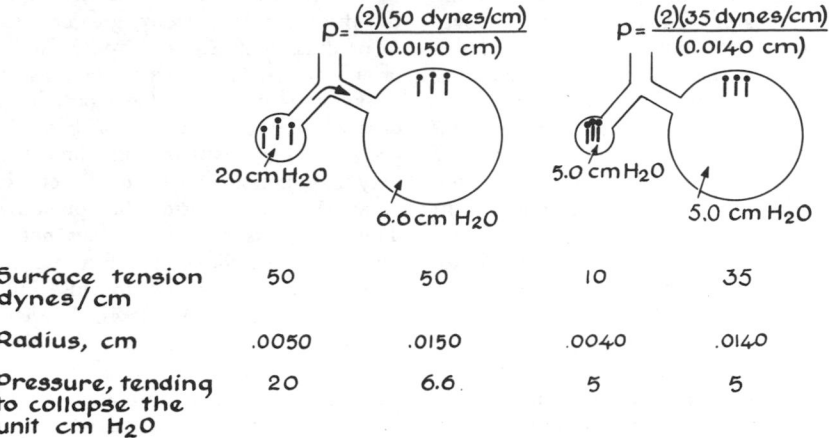

Surface tension dynes/cm	50	50	10	35
Radius, cm	.0050	.0150	.0040	.0140
Pressure, tending to collapse the unit cm H_2O	20	6.6	5	5

Fig. 3. An explanation for the manner in which pulmonary surfactant stabilizes alveolar units of varying size. As the lung deflates, the small alveolar unit has a greater decrease in area than the large unit. The surface concentration becomes greater in the small unit resulting in a lower surface tension. The pressures are thus equalized in both units. Calculations are shown for the large alveolar unit.

The surfactant, a solid, first appears in the lungs of infants weighing about 200 g and is probably necessary for survival. In the range of normal breathing lung volumes, the elastic recoil produced by the tissue and surface forces is nearly equal.

Pulmonary Function in the First Days of Life

Studies of pulmonary physiology in the newborn period have outlined the changes that occur after delivery. Table 1 is a comparison of physiologic measurements in the adult and full-term newborn infant. The mean alveolar diameter of the infant lung is half that of the adult lung, but the infant has only one-thirteenth the number of alveoli. It is apparent from the table that the infant lung is not a miniature of the adult lung.

a. Lung Volumes and Pulmonary Ventilation. In the first minutes of life an adequate functional residual capacity FRC (volume of air in the lungs at end-expiration) is attained. There is only a small increase in the FRC from 30 minutes to 5 days of age. Vital capacity increases until 24 hours of age and then remains stable.

In both the infant and the adult, the distribution of alveolar ventilation throughout the lung is uniform. Although some portions of the lung receive a much larger percentage of each tidal volume than other areas, at 1 hour of age the distribution of each breath in the newborn is already very similar to that observed in the young adult.

TABLE 1.   *A Comparison of Normal Values for Pulmonary Function in the Infant and Adult*

	Infant	Adult	Adult/Infant
Body surface area, m^2	0.21	1.70	8.1
Body weight, kg	3	70	23
O_2 consumption, ml/min	18.0	250	13.8
Lung surface area, m^2	4	80	20
Number of alveoli, $\times 10^6$	24	300	12.5
Mean alveolar diameter, cm	0.0150	0.0280	1.88
Alveolar ventilation, ml	360	4,200	12
Functional residual capacity, ml/kg	100	3,000	30
Vital capacity, ml/kg	125	4,800	25
Anatomic dead space, ml/kg	8.0	150	21
Tidal volume, ml/kg	20	500	25
Lung compliance, ml/cm H_2O	6.0	180	40
Specific lung compliance, ml/cm H_2O/ml	0.06	0.06	1.0
Airway resistance, cm H_2O/L/sec	18.0	1.9	0.105

b. Mechanics of Respiration. Lung compliance is a measure of lung distensibility, and its units are in milliliters of air per centimeter of H_2O pressure change. Within the first hours of life, there is a brisk increase in lung distensibility. The mean lung compliance is 4.5 ml/cm H_2O at 2 hours but 5 to 6 ml/cm at 24 hours. These changes are not completely understood but may be related to alterations in the elastic elements following repeated stretching, the removal of fluid from the lung, or changes in the lung surfactant.

c. Respiratory Reflexes. The chemical control of respiration in the newborn infant and adult is different. The infant responds to hypoxia by a decrease in ventilation in a cool environment, and by only a brief period of hyperventilation followed by a decrease in ventilation in a neutral thermal environment. Only after the first two weeks of life does he behave as an adult with sustained hyperventilation on exposure to an hypoxic environment. In an environment of 100 percent oxygen the newborn infant hypoventilates as early as 1 hour of age. Thus, the newborn infant has active peripheral chemoreceptor reflexes at birth but his responses are modified, possibly by central depression, during the first two weeks of life. The central chemoreceptor reflex activity, as judged by response to CO_2, of the newborn infant is the same as in the adult and is unaffected by environmental temperature or postnatal age.

The response of the infant to inflation of the lung is different from that of the adult. In the first day or two of life, the typical response to an inflation of the lung with a pressure of 10 to 15 cm of water is a gasp and a very prolonged apnea (Hering and Breuer inflation reflex), as shown in Figure 4. By the third and fourth day, greater pressure is required to produce the gasp and apnea, and a large number of infants no longer gasp. The significance of these responses is not understood, but the parodoxical gasp observed in the first day of life with low inflation pressures may explain the clinical observation that very low pressures (10 to 15 cm H_2O) are often effective in resuscitating the apneic newborn at birth. The low pressure applied does not inflate the lung but stimulates the gasp reflex, which reduces intrathoracic pressure enough to cause inflation.

d. Arterial Blood Gases. Arterial blood gases are a reflection of the pulmonary, cardiac, and metabolic status of the newborn. They may also indicate whether the infant suffered any asphyxial episode before delivery. The partial pressure of carbon dioxide in arterial blood ($Paco_2$) measures the ability of the lung to remove carbon dioxide. The HCO_3- concentration is controlled by the kidney. When the pH and HCO_3- are determined, the arterial Pco_2 can be calculated using the Henderson-Hasselbalch equation:

$$pH = 6.8 + \log \frac{HCO_3-}{Paco_2 \times sol.}$$

If only the pH is measured, the cause of the acidosis or alkalosis cannot be determined. With metabolic acidosis HCO_3- is decreased and in compensation for this, the infant hyperventilates, lowering arterial Pco_2. With pulmonary disease, apnea, or hypoventilation, the arterial Pco_2 increases. In the adult, the kidney attempts compensation by retaining HCO_3-

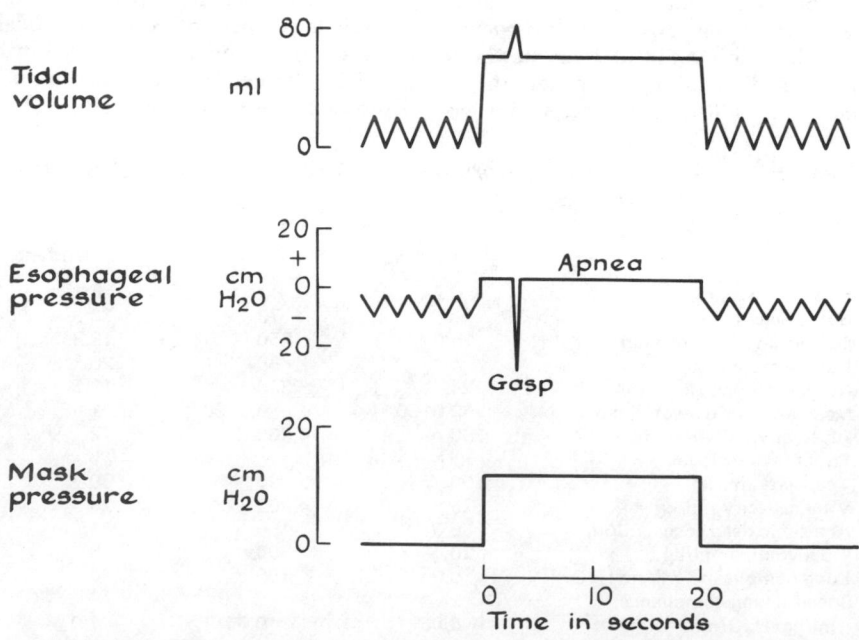

Fig. 4. The reflex response to a positive pressure inflation in the first days of life. Note the long apnea.

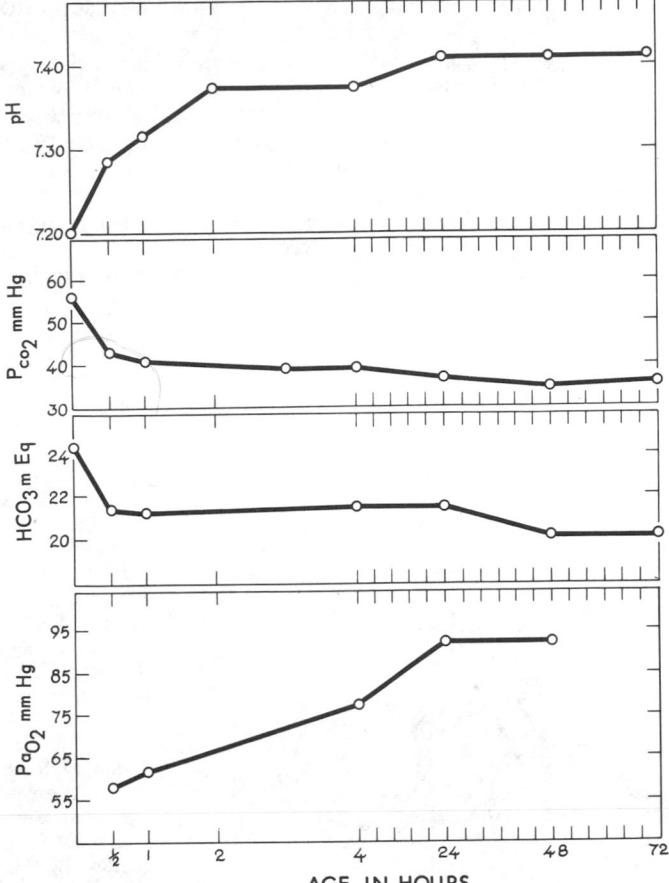

Fig. 5. The arterial Pco$_2$, HCO$_3$—, pH, and Po$_2$ during the first hours and days of life. (Adapted from Oliver et al. *Acta Pediat. Scand.*, 50:346, 1961; Prod'hom et al. *Pediatrics*, 33:682, 1964; and Weisbrot et al. *J. Pediat.*, 52:395, 1958.)

and excreting hydrogen ions. This mechanism is not well developed in the newborn infant. Only by measuring the Paco$_2$ and HCO$_3$— as well as the pH can the cause of an abnormality in acid-base balance be determined, although if two of the three are measured the third can be calculated (Sec. 3.7). Figure 5 illustrates the arterial pH, Pao$_2$ and Paco$_2$, and bicarbonate in the early hours and days of life. The normal newborn quickly regulates his pH to near adult values. The low arterial Pco$_2$ of the newborn infant during the first week of life is similar to the maternal values in the last months of pregnancy and may be the result of hyperventilation caused by the increased blood levels of progesterone. The arterial Pco$_2$ tension measured in conjunction with the mixed alveolar Pco$_2$ is also useful in determining whether all areas of the lung that are ventilated with air are also perfused with blood (Fig. 6). If, as shown in Figure 6B, one area of the lung is ventilated but not perfused, the alveolar Pco$_2$ will be less than the arterial Pco$_2$. In the normal newborn all areas of the lung that are ventilated are also perfused with blood.

The partial pressure of oxygen (Pao$_2$) in the arterial blood is dependent not only on the ability of the lung to transfer oxygen but is modified by

shunting of venous blood into the systemic circulation through the heart or lungs. Breathing 100 percent oxygen for 15 to 30 minutes will correct desaturation secondary both to diffusion abnormalities and to inadequate ventilation. Measurements of arterial Po$_2$ with 100 percent oxygen breathing are therefore useful diagnostically in determining whether arterial O$_2$ desaturation is caused by a right-to-left shunt, diffusion abnormalities, or inadequate ventilation. If no right-to-left shunt is present the arterial Po$_2$ after breathing 100 percent oxygen is equal to the atmospheric pressure minus the partial pressures of alveolar carbon dioxide and water vapor. The right-to-left shunt of venous blood when breathing 100 percent oxygen can then be calculated using the equation:

$$\frac{Q_s}{Q} = \frac{Cao_2 - Cco_2}{Cvo_2 - Cco_2}$$

Where Q_s = amount of cardiac output shunted from right to left, Q = cardiac output, Cao_2 = arterial oxygen content, Cvo_2 = mixed venous oxygen content, Cco_2 = end capillary oxygen content. When these measurements are made in the newborn infant during the first days of life, they reveal that 20 percent of the cardiac output is shunted from right

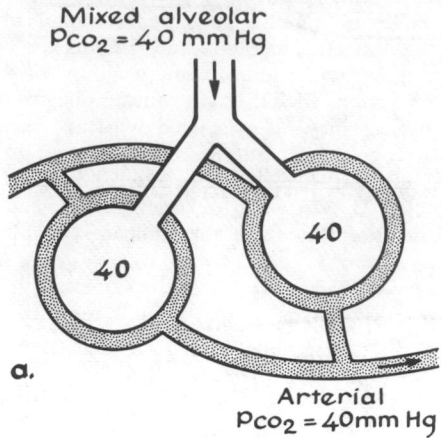

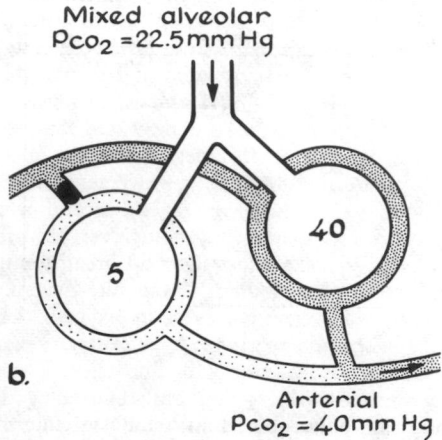

Fig. 6. Mixed alveolar and arterial P_{CO_2}, with normal and altered blood flow through the lung. A. When pulmonary blood flow matches ventilation mixed alveolar and arterial P_{CO_2} are nearly equal. B. If one area of the lung is not perfused, the mixed alveolar P_{CO_2} is reduced below the arterial P_{CO_2}. (Adapted from Comroe et al. 1962. *The Lung.* Courtesy of Year Book Publishers.)

to left. It is not known whether the shunt is in the heart or lungs but it is most likely that it occurs through the foramen ovale or ductus arteriosus. In the normal adult the shunt from right to left is about 5 percent of the total cardiac output.

In summary, before birth the lung is a fluid-filled organ receiving 10 to 15 percent of the total cardiac output. Within the first minutes of life, a large proportion of the fluid is absorbed, the lung fills with air, and the blood flow through the lung increases eight- to tenfold. By the end of the first hour of life, perfusion of the lung is distributed in proportion to the distribution of ventilation. The speed with which pulmonary ventilation and perfusion are uniformly distributed is an indication of the remarkable adaptive capabilities of the newborn infant for the maintenance of homeostasis.

RESUSCITATION. Though the newborn infant has a greater tolerance than the adult for withstanding an asphyxial episode, any delay or difficulty in the initiation of respiration should be managed promptly. The method of evaluating the status of the infant at birth and the necessity for resuscitation are discussed in Section 2.9.

REFERENCES

THE LUNG OF THE FETUS

Adams, F. H., Fujiwara, T., and Rowshan, G. The nature and origin of the fluid in the fetal lamb lung. J. Pediat., 63:881, 1963.

Dunnill, M. S. Postnatal growth of the lung. Thorax, 17:329, 1962.

Setnikar, I., Agostoni, E., and Taglietti, A. The fetal lung, a source of amniotic fluid. Proc. Soc. Exp. Biol. Med., 101:842, 1959.

Sorokin, S., Padykula, H. A., and Herman, E. Comparative histochemical patterns in developing mammalian lungs. Develop. Biol., 1:125, 1959.

THE FIRST BREATH

Agostoni, E., Taglietti, A., Agostoni, F., and Setnikar, I. Mechanical aspects of the first breath. J. Appl. Physiol., 13:344, 1958.

Avery, M. E., Frank, N. R., and Gribetz, I. The inflationary force produced by pulmonary vascular distention in excised lungs. The possible relation of this force to that needed to inflate the lungs at birth. J. Clin. Invest., 38:456, 1959.

Boston, R. W., Humphreys, P. W., Reynolds, E. O. R., and Strang, L. G. Lymph-flow and clearance of liquid from the lungs of the foetal lamb. Lancet, II:473, 1965.

Clements, J. A. Surface phenomena in relation to pulmonary function (Sixth Bowditch Lecture). Physiologist, 5:11, 1962.

Cook, C. D., Drinker, P. A., Jacobson, H. N., Levison, H., and Strang, L. B. Control of pulmonary blood flow in the foetal and newly born lamb. J. Physiol., 169:10, 1963.

Dawes, G. S., and Mott, J. C. The vascular tone of the foetal lung. J. Physiol., 164:465, 1962.

James, L. S. Onset of breathing and resuscitation. Pediat. Clin. N. Amer., 13:621, 1966.

Pattle, R. E. Properties, function, and origin of the alveolar lining layer. Proc. Roy. Soc., 148:217, 1958.

Strang, L. G. Uptake of liquid from the lungs at the start of breathing. Ciba Foundation Symposium, Development of the Lung. J. A. Churchill Ltd., London, 1966, p. 348.

LUNG FUNCTION IN NORMAL NEWBORN INFANT

Avery, M. E. The Lung and Its Disorders in the Newborn Infant, 2nd ed. Philadelphia, W. B. Saunders Co., 1968.

Comroe, J. H., Forster, R. E., DuBois, A. B., Briscoe, W. A., and Carlsen, E. The Lung. Chicago, Year Book Publishers, 1962.

Cook, C. D., Sutherland, J. M., Segal, S., Cherry, R. B., Mead, J., McIlroy, M. B., and Smith, C. A. Studies of respiratory physiology in the newborn infant. J. Clin. Invest., 36:440, 1957.

Cross, K. W., Klaus, M., Tooley, W. H., and Weisser, K. The response of the newborn baby to inflation of the lungs. J. Physiol., 151:551, 1960.

Klaus, M., Tooley, W. H., Weaver, K. H., and Clements, J. A. Lung volume in the newborn infant. Pediatrics, 30:111, 1962.

Koch, G., and Weldel, H. Adjustment of arterial blood gases and acid base balance in the normal newborn infant during the first week of life. Biol. Neonat., 12: 136, 1968.

Ledbetter, M. K., Homma, R., and Farhi, L. E. Readjustment in distribution of alveolar ventilation and lung perfusion in the newborn. Pediatrics, 40:940, 1967.

Nelson, N. M. Neonatal pulmonary function. Pediat. Clin. N. Amer., 13:769, 1966.

—— Prod'hom, L. S., Cherry, R. B., Lipsitz, P. J., and Smith, C. A. Pulmonary function in the newborn infant. II. Perfusion-estimation by analysis of the arterial-alveolar carbon dioxide differences. Pediatrics, 30:975, 1962.

—— Prod'hom, L. S., Cherry, R. B., Lipsitz, P. J., and Smith, C. A. Pulmonary function in the newborn infant: The alveolar-arterial oxygen gradient. J. Appl. Physiol., 18:534, 1963.

Oliver, T. K., Demis, J. A., and Bates, G. D. Serial blood-gas tensions and acid-base balance during the first hour of life in human infants. Acta Paediat. Scand., 50:346, 1961.

Prod'hom, L. S., Levison, H., Cherry, R. B., Drorbaugh, J. E., Hubbell, J. P., and Smith, C. A. Adjustment of ventilation, intrapulmonary gas exchange and acid-base balance during the first day of life. Pediatrics, 33:682, 1964.

Rudolph, A. M., and Yuan, S. Response of the pulmonary vasculature to hypoxia and H ion concentration changes. J. Clin. Invest., 45:399, 1966.

19.2
PULMONARY DISEASES
OF THE NEWBORN

Marshall H. Klaus

A number of signs and symptoms associated with diseases of the respiratory system (cyanosis, tachypnea, tachycardia, grunting, intercostal retractions, nasal flaring) may also be observed in diseases of other organ systems, such as metabolic acidosis and hypovolemia following neonatal asphyxia; cardiac failure; diseases of the nervous system (e.g., intraventricular hemorrhage). It is necessary to identify which organ system is mainly involved; in many "high-risk" infants several problems may coexist.

Idiopathic Respiratory Distress Syndrome
(Hyaline Membrane Disease)

Hyaline membrane disease is the major cause of mortality during the newborn period and occurs in 0.5 to 1.0 percent of all deliveries. In the United States it probably accounts for 25,000 to 40,000 deaths each year. About 10 percent of all premature infants have the disease and it is common in the infants of diabetic mothers and infants delivered from mothers with antepartum vaginal bleeding. Cesarean section in otherwise uncomplicated full-term deliveries may be associated with an increased incidence. The largest number of cases occur in prematures with birth weights between 1,000 and 1,500 g. Reducing the number of premature births will reduce the mortality from the idiopathic respiratory distress syndrome.

CLINICAL COURSE. Most of the affected infants have difficulty in instituting normal respiration. It was previously believed that after birth a free interval existed before the onset of symptoms. However, if infants are observed closely and examined carefully, symptoms are usually noted immediately after birth. Expiratory grunting or whining (observed when the infant is not crying), sternal and subcostal retractions, nasal flaring, rapid respirations (greater than 70/minute), and low body temperatures are the most striking clinical features. Grunting appears to be the most important and useful clinical sign and may be the only indication early in the disease in large infants; a decrease in grunting is often the first sign of improvement. The prolonged expiration of the grunt takes a second or more, so that when an infant grunts with every breath his respiratory frequency is less than 60 breaths/minute. Most infants are cyanotic in room air. Severely affected infants are cyanotic even in oxygen. Auscultation of the chest reveals poor air entry, decreased breath sounds, and occasionally fine rales. The arterial blood pressure is sometimes reduced and the extremities are slightly edematous. Bowel sounds are often absent in the early hours of the illness. Urine output is low during the first two or three days of life. As the disease progresses chest retractions become more marked, see-saw respirations ensue (on inspiration the anterior chest wall retracts and the abdomen protrudes; on expiration, the sternum rises), peripheral edema increases, and muscle tone decreases. As cyanosis increases, body temperature tends to drop and short periods of apnea are noted. Except for episodes of bradycardia with periods of severe cyanosis and grunting, the heart rate is often fixed. Many symptoms are related to asphyxia which, when severe, depresses the respiratory center, produces apneic episodes, changes the distribution of blood throughout the body (resulting in a pale gray skin color), and decreases the rate of heat production. About 50 to 70 percent of all infants survive after treatment.

LABORATORY DATA. A chest x-ray must be taken immediately to rule out other conditions that produce symptoms similar to the idiopathic respiratory distress syndrome, such as a diaphragmatic hernia, pneumothorax, or heart failure. The typical chest x-ray shows a diffuse reticulogranular pattern of radiodensities and an air bronchogram as shown in Figure

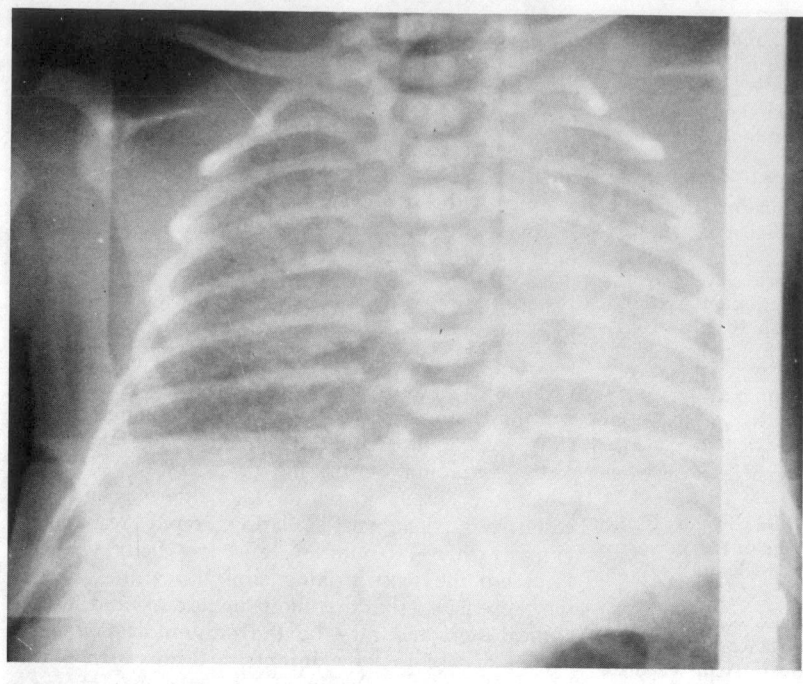

Fig. 7. Radiogram of an infant with respiratory distress syndrome, showing the characteristic findings of a diffuse haziness and the air bronchogram. (Courtesy of Dr. Harold Goldman.)

7. The reticular pattern may not be equal bilaterally. In the first hour of life the x-ray may be normal, but as the disease progresses the lung appears smaller and generalized haziness increases. Arterial or venous hematocrit as well as intraarterial blood pressure should be obtained to rule out hypovolemia, a situation which can mimic or lead to the idiopathic respiratory distress syndrome. Blood pressures are determined from an indwelling umbilical artery catheter. The technique, precautions, and complications of this procedure have been described by Kitterman et al. (1970). The pulmonary and systemic arterial pressures are slightly reduced. The exchange of oxygen and carbon dioxide and measurement of blood gases usually reveal hypoxemia and a moderately severe respiratory acidosis, with carbon dioxide tensions ranging from 50 to 90 mm Hg. Some infants also have evidence of a metabolic acidosis, secondary to hypoxia (pH 7.1 to 7.3). Severely affected infants have a large right-to-left shunt. Effective pulmonary blood flow is reduced and as much as 40 percent of the lung may be ventilated but not perfused with blood, resulting in large differences between alveolar and arterial carbon dioxide tensions (Fig. 6B). Lung compliance is reduced to one-fifth of normal, while functional residual capacity is slightly decreased. The abnormal lung elasticity and grunting greatly increase the work of breathing.

PATHOLOGY. At autopsy the lungs are liverlike and heavy. On microscopic examination the most striking finding is the absence of air in all parts of the lung except for the large dilated alveolar ducts and terminal bronchi. Pink-staining, homogenous, hyaline-like membranes line the terminal bronchioles, alveoli, and alveolar ducts. The pulmonary capillaries are engorged, the lymphatics increase in size, and pulmonary hemorrhage is common. If the infant dies in the first hours of life the membranes are not seen. Leucocytic infiltration is usually observed in infants dying after 48 hours. Histochemical and electron microscopic studies reveal the membrane to be composed of products from the infant's blood. The alveolar epithelial cells are damaged and the basement membrane is discontinuous.

Pressure volume curves of the lung differ distinctly from those in the lungs of infants dying from nonpulmonary causes. Even at the highest inflation pressure, the hyaline lung contains less air and, significantly, as the pressure is reduced the deflation curve follows the inflation curve closely (Fig. 8). The abnormal pressure-volume curves are associated with alterations in the highly surface-active alveolar lining. Lung extracts prepared from infants dying with the respiratory distress syndrome fail to reduce surface tension below 20 dynes/cm, while extracts prepared from the lungs of infants dying from other pulmonary causes reduce surface tension to 1 to 2 dynes/cm. Biochemical studies of the lung show a quantitative decrease in the highly surface-active phopholipid fraction. The alveolar surfactant is necessary for alveolar stability and its deficiency in this disease probably explains in part the decreased lung compliance and atelectasis noted during life, as well as the abnormal air pressure volume curves found at autopsy.

Study of the vasculature of the lung reveals the pulmonary vascular resistance to be markedly increased. The muscular layer of the walls of the

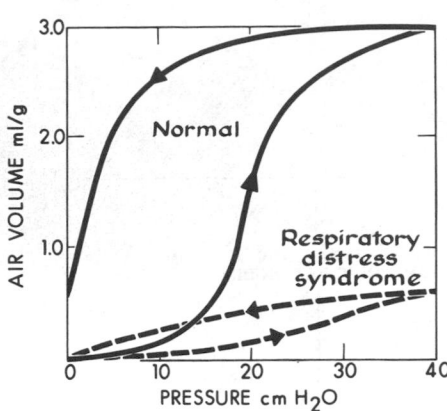

Fig. 8. Air pressure volume curves of a normal and ab-normal lung. Volume is expressed as milliliters of air per gram of lung. The lung from an infant with the respiratory distress syndrome accepts a smaller volume of air at all pressures. Note also the deflation pressure volume curve fol-lows closely the inflation curve. (Adapted from Gribetz et al. *J. Clin. Invest.*, 38:2168, 1959.)

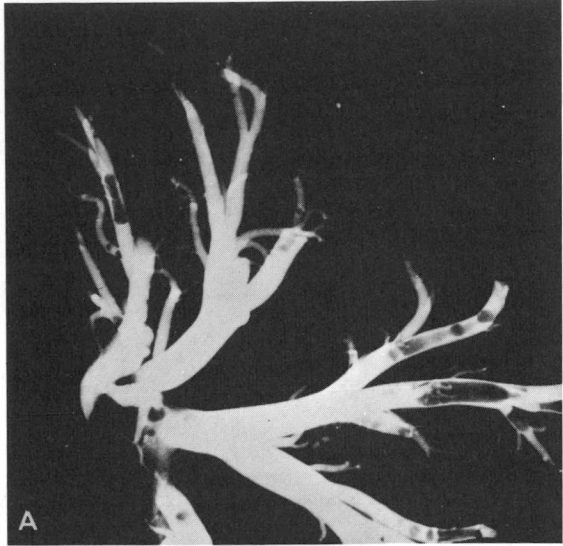

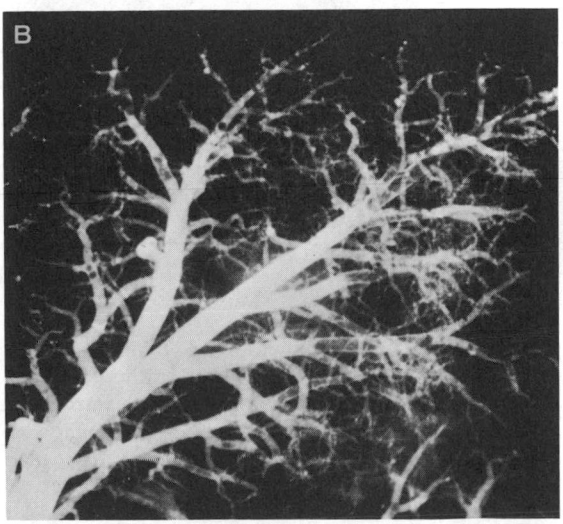

Fig. 9. Microradiographs following an injection at autopsy of a suspension of barium sulfate into the pulmonary artery at a pressure of 80 mm Hg. A. Lung from an infant with hyaline membrane disease. (From Lauweryns. *Arch. Dis. Child.*, 40:618, 1965.) B. A normal neonatal lamb lung. Note that in Fig. 9A only the main pulmonary arteries and some small muscular arteries are filled. No arteriolar or capillary filling is observed. In Fig. 9B there is complete filling of the pul-monary arterial bed.

pulmonary arterioles appears like those of unex-panded fetal lungs, even in an infant who lives for many hours. Perfusion of the vascular network of the lung, using barium sulfate as a contrast medium, shows markedly narrowed pulmonary arterioles with blockage (Fig. 9A and B). Thus, both the alveolar surface and the vasculature of the lung are affected. Subependymal and intraventricular hemorrhages are also sometimes observed at autopsy.

ETIOLOGY. Numerous theories have been proposed and rejected to explain the respiratory distress syn-drome. At present, the following theories are under active exploration, examination, and debate:

1. Alteration in the fibrinolytic enzyme system in the lung or blood was first suggested when hyaline membranes were noted to contain fibrin. This idea is supported by studies showing an inhibitor to plasminogen activator in diseased lungs. However, some investigators find no qualitative abnormality in the fibrinolytic system. Clinical trials with fibrino-lysins have been conducted but the results are in-conclusive.

2. Absence or alteration of the pulmonary sur-factant was proposed when extracts from the lungs of infants dying with hyaline membrane disease were shown to have a high surface tension. The in-creased surface tension correlated with the reduced lung compliance measured during life and the abnor-mal air-pressure volume curves found at autopsy. Fa-voring this theory is the high incidence of the disease in prematures weighing 1,000 to 1,500 g, a stage when the development of surfactant may not be com-plete. A high surface tension at the alveolar surface would lead to the sequence of events shown in Figure 10, starting with position "S", and explain most of the observed physiologic abnormalities. A high sur-face tension would cause a decreased lung compli-

ance, atelectasis, and an increase in the work of breathing. Ventilation would decrease as the infant tired. Asphyxia would develop, which would cause pulmonary vasoconstriction. Blood would bypass the lung through the foramen ovale and ductus arteriosus, lower pulmonary blood flow, and lead to more intense pulmonary vasoconstriction and further reduction in pulmonary blood flow. The resulting ischemia would interfere with lung metabolism and limit the produc-tion of surfactant.

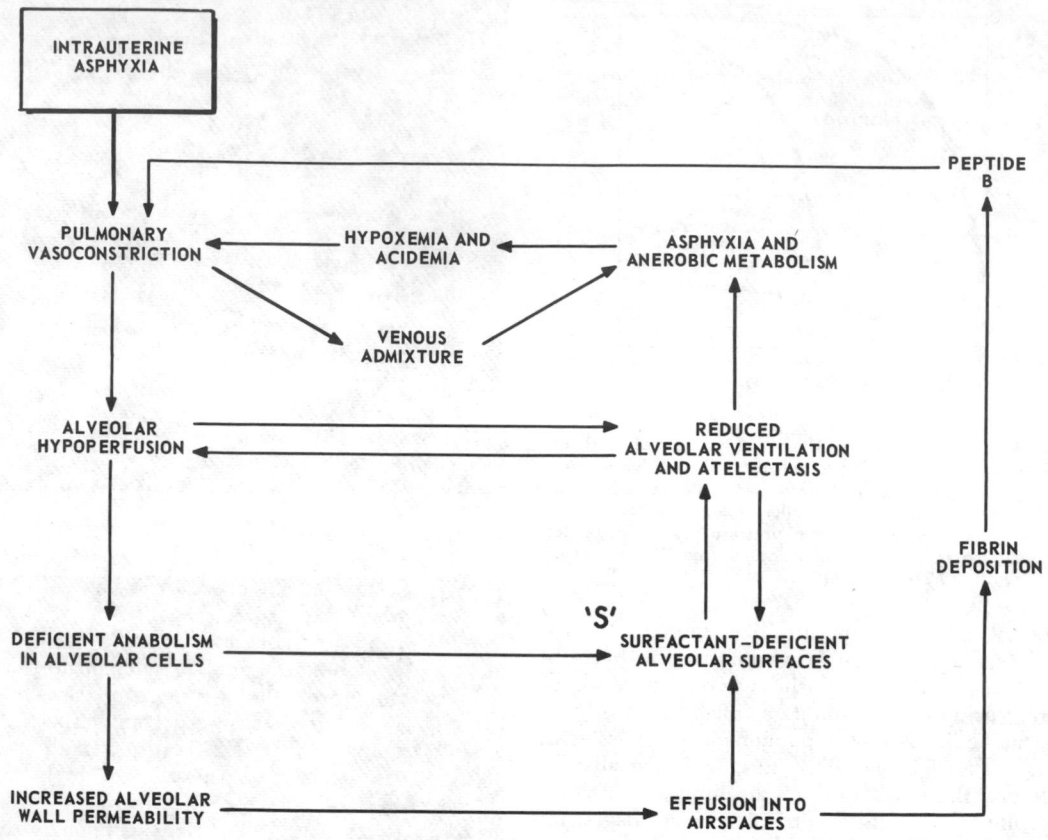

Fig. 10. Alveolar function in the respiratory distress syndrome.

3. An alternate hypothesis is that the primary lesion is pulmonary hypoperfusion rather than surfactant deficiency. This cycle begins with intrauterine asphyxia (Fig. 10), which increases pulmonary vascular resistance and promotes shunting of blood returning to the heart through the ductus arteriosus and foramen ovale and away from the lung. The kidney and gastrointestinal tract may also become ischemic. Pulmonary ischemia would damage the alveolar lining cells that produce surfactant, and explain (1) the loss of surfactant, and (2) the effusion of plasma and red cells into airspaces. When the fibrinogen is transformed to fibrin, peptides are formed. Peptide B is a potent pulmonary vasoconstrictor and its presence could potentiate and continue the pulmonary vasoconstriction. Findings which lend support to the notion that pulmonary hypoperfusion is central to this disease are: (1) the marked increase in pulmonary vascular resistance observed in the fetal lung when animal fetuses are asphyxiated; (2) large areas of the diseased lung that are ventilated with air but not perfused with blood; (3) the intense pulmonary arteriolar vasoconstriction observed when perfusion studies are performed at autopsy in lungs with hyaline membranes; (4) the increase in effective pulmonary flow, gas exchange, and clinical improvement following therapeutic measures that dilate the pulmonary arterioles; and (5) the abnormally large mass of pulmonary arteriolar muscle found in infants delivered from diabetic or latent diabetic mothers.

TREATMENT.   Although much of the pathophysiology has been described and a multitude of treatments suggested, and in some cases partially studied, no single therapeutic regimen has been demonstrated to be superior. During this period of doubt and continued study, the following approach appears most reasonable: for infants not moribund with the disease, the treatment should call for minimal risk to the infant and be based on known physiologic principles. Therapeutic regimens with increased risk, e.g., respiratory therapy, should be used only in those infants who might not otherwise survive.

Table 2 is an outline of suggested minimal risk treatments and their physiologic basis.

The care of the infant with more severe respiratory distress is most easily accomplished in those hospitals which have developed special units for the care of the high-risk infant. In such units, the patient/nurse ratio is small, with one nurse caring for from one to three infants. A physician is on duty 24 hours a day. Arterial blood gas measurements which

TABLE 2. *Minimal Risk Therapy and its Physiologic Basis*

Treatment	Physiologic Basis
Avoid maternal hypoxia, acidemia, and systemic hypotension. Prompt ventilatory resuscitation with high oxygen	Prevent fetal and neonatal asphyxia
Avoid cooling in the delivery room	Prevent metabolic acidosis and pulmonary vasoconstriction
Metabolic correction for severe neonatal asphyxia (NaHCO₃ or THAM)	Increase myocardial contractility, induce pulmonary arteriolar vasodilation, and possibly reduce brain damage
Maintain infant in a neutral thermal environment.	Reduce oxygen requirements to a minimum
Intravenous fluid and glucose	Meet metabolic requirements and reduce hyperbilirubinemia
If not well in 1 hour: 1. Increase environmental concentrations of oxygen by hood and umbilical catheterization to monitor arterial Po_2 and pH	Increase myocardial contractility, induce pulmonary arteriolar vasodilation and possibly reduce brain damage
2. NaHCO₃ to correct acidosis	

determine the amounts of both alkali and oxygen administered can be made every two to four hours as indicated. Here there are facilities for respiratory and cardiac monitoring, as well as close temperature regulation. Assisted ventilation for the respiratory distress syndrome has been developed in such units. There is general agreement that this therapy should be used only when supportive measures, as outlined above, have been unsuccessful.

Table 3 outlines a scoring procedure for determining if assisted ventilation should be used. The most valuable prognostic laboratory measurement appears to be the arterial oxygen tension. An arterial oxygen tension below 50 mm Hg with the infant breathing 100 percent oxygen is a strong indication for ventilatory therapy; at this oxygen tension, the chance of survival without ventilatory assistance is probably less than 10 percent. Four forms of assisted ventilation have been utilized: (1) positive pressure with or without an endotracheal tube; (2) tank-type respirator with intermittent negative pressure; (3) intermittent mask and bag therapy; and (4) continuous positive airway pressure delivered through an endotracheal tube. The prerequisites before embarking on any type of assisted ventilation are: a trained staff, including nurses, inhalation therapists and physicians, and the availability of arterial blood gas determinations on a 24-hour basis. In several centers

using these indications for ventilatory therapy, survival of the severely ill patient was between 30 and 80 percent.

COMPLICATIONS. The most common complications following respirator therapy are inflammatory or mechanical, e.g., pneumothorax, pneumonia, and tracheal stenosis. A recently recognized complication of respirator therapy which has occurred with positive pressure ventilators and the use of high oxygen (greater than 80 percent) for periods of greater than five to six days is a chronic pulmonary disease designated as bronchopulmonary dysplasia. Figure 11 shows the x-ray changes in this disease. Table 4 compares this disease with pulmonary dysmaturity.

Respirator therapy should be used only when the measures in Table 2 are unsuccessful. If the arterial oxygen tension drops, respirator therapy should be used, but only when arterial blood gas measurements, intensive care nursing, and trained physician support are available on a 24-hour basis.

Transient Tachypnea of the Newborn

This syndrome usually follows an uneventful term pregnancy and is first detected in the nursery when the infant is noted to have persistently high respiratory rate. Cyanosis is not prominent, although a few

TABLE 3. *Scoring Procedure for Determining if Artificial Ventilation* Should Be Used*

		0	1	2	3
Pao₂ (100% O₂)	(mm Hg)	>70	50-70	*	*<50
pH		>7.30	7.20-7.29	7.0-7.19	<7.0
Paco₂	(mm Hg)	<60	60-70	71-80	>80

*Indications for artificial ventilation are: (1) total score of 3 or greater; (2) an arterial oxygen tension lower than 50 mm Hg; or (3) two apneic episodes longer than 45 seconds.

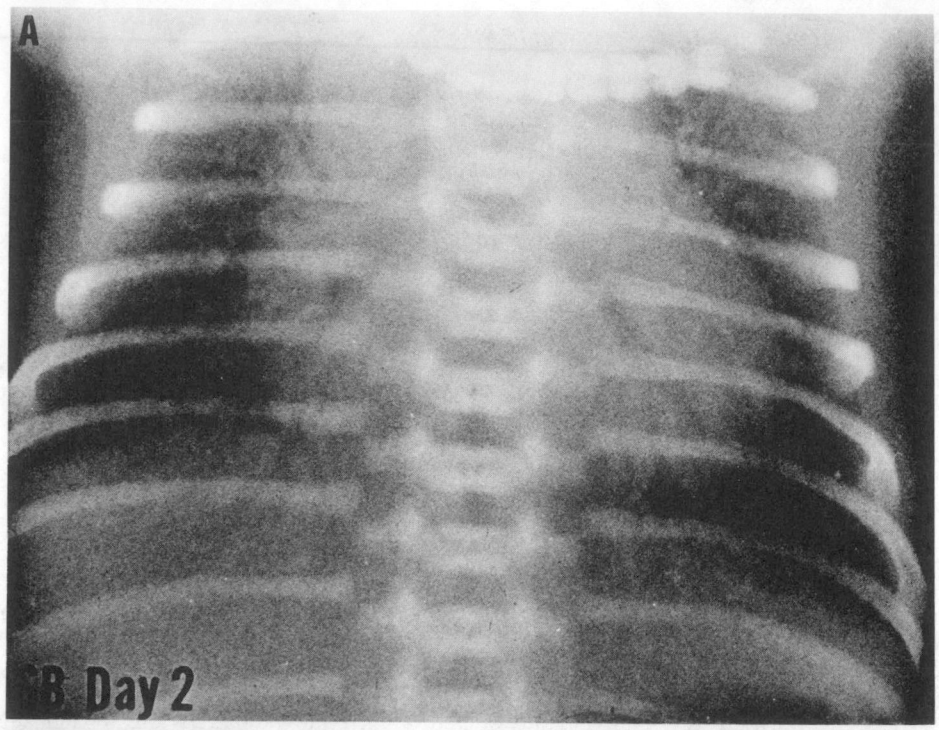

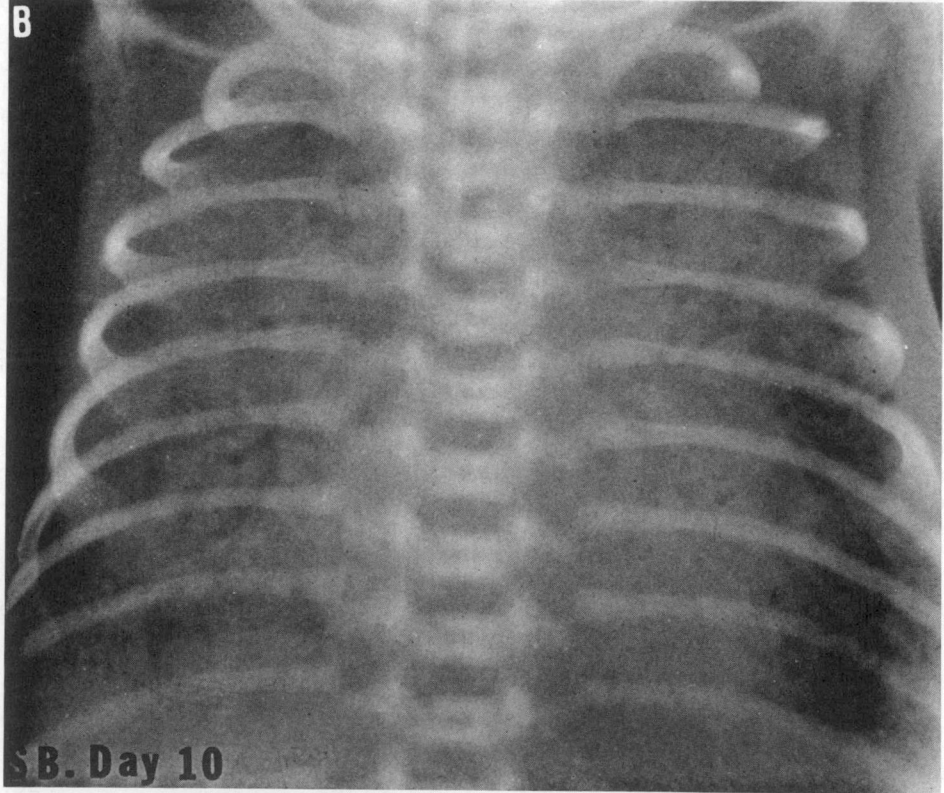

Fig. 11. Radiographic stages of bronchopulmonary dysplasia. *A.* Typical respiratory distress syndrome. *B.* Lung fields are nearly opaque as infant is weaned from the respirator. *C.* Cystlike areas of lucency in both lung fields (26 days of age). *D.* Remarkable clearing of the lung fields at 2 years of age. (From Northway and Rosan. *Radiology,* 91:49, 1968.)

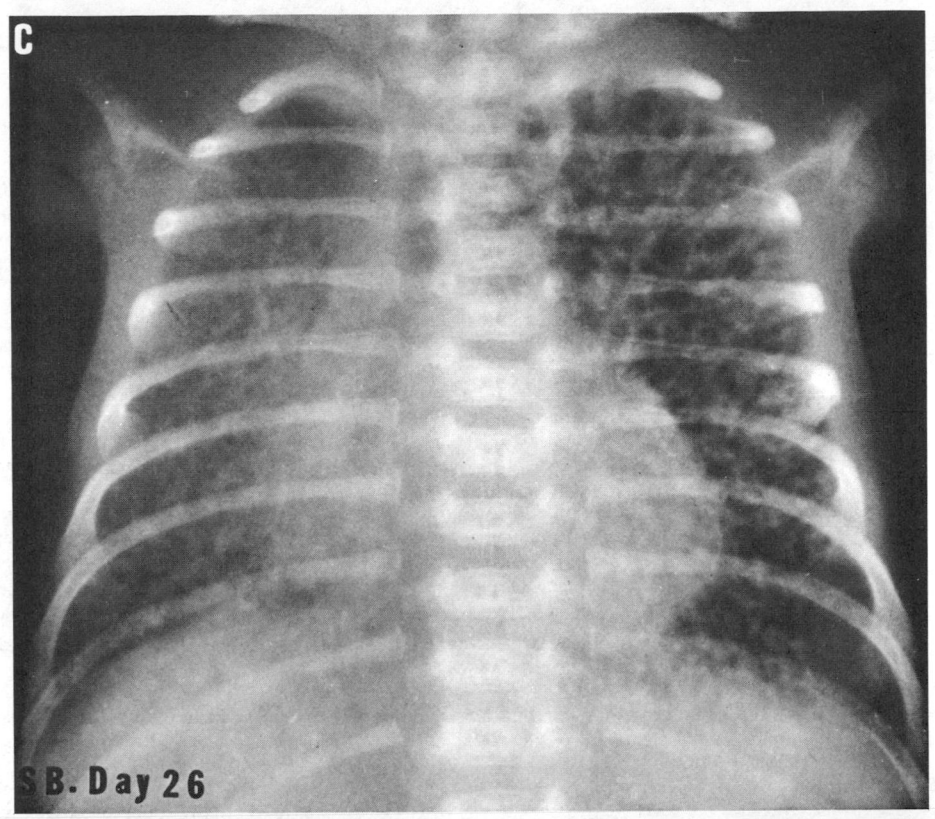

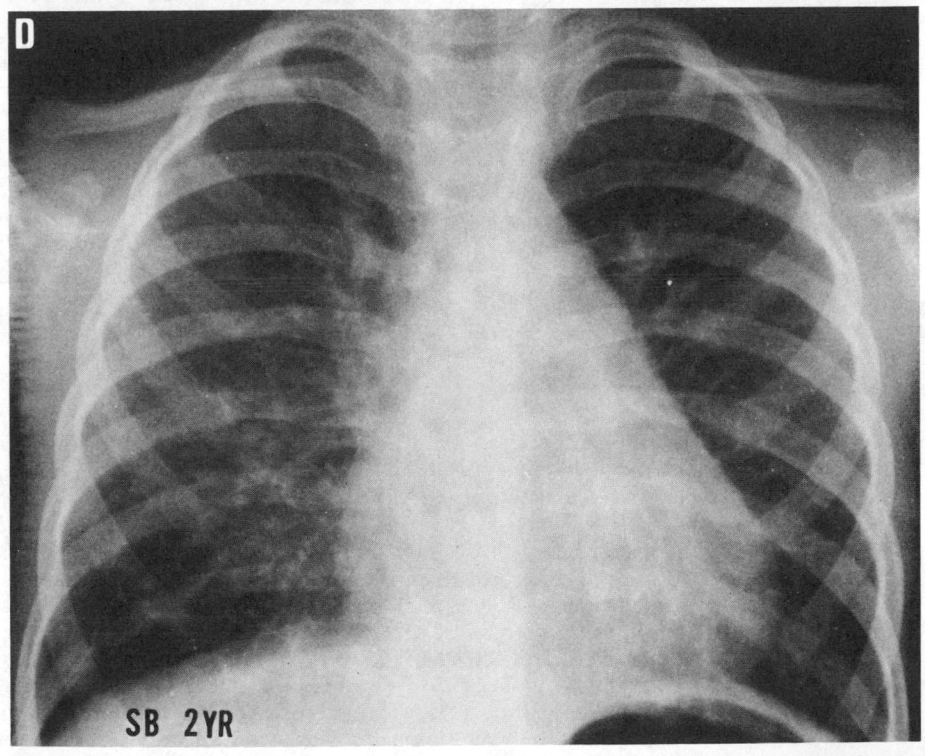

Fig. 11 (Cont.) See legend on facing page.

TABLE 4.   *A Comparison of Pulmonary Dysmaturity and Bronchopulmonary Dysplasia*

	Pulmonary Dysmaturity (Mikity-Wilson)	Bronchopulmonary Dysplasia (Oxygen Toxicity)
1. Birth weight	Usually under 1,500 g	Not specific
2. Etiology	Unknown (occurs in very immature infants, some of whom have received no additional O_2)	Probably oxygen toxicity. Preceded by severe respiratory distress syndrome, usually treated for a minimum of 5-6 days in an environment containing greater than 70% O_2
3. Chest radiograph	1. Often normal in the first few days of life 2. Small cystlike foci with diffuse coarse and lacelike pattern of infiltrates noted throughout the lung usually at 1 to 3 weeks of life (similar to those seen in cystic stage of bronchopulmonary dysplasia). Fig. 12 3. Usually complete clearing in 2-12 months; base of the lung clearing before apex	Following 4 stages are observed: 1. Typical ground glass appearance of the respiratory distress syndrome. Fig. 11A 2. Marked opacity of the lungs. Fig. 11B 3. Small rounded areas of radiolucency distributed throughout the lung (similar to the cystic stage of pulmonary dysmaturity). Fig. 11C 4. Strands of increased pulmonary parenchymal density which often clear completely. Fig. 11D
4. Pulmonary pathology a. Gross	Hyperaerated foci, separated by depressed gray-blue areas of atelectasis, often has a cobblestone appearance	
b. Light microscopy 1. Bronchiolar mucosa	Sometimes contains a few mononuclear cells	Necrosis and metaplasia with patchy loss of ciliated cells. Later irregular peribronchiolar muscular thickening
2. Bronchiolar lumen	Normal	Partially blocked with eosinophilic exudate and patchy squamous metaplasia
3. Alveolar region	Normal, or on occasion mild to moderate fibrosis	Early there is necrosis and repair of alveolar epithelium, later an increase in alveolar macrophages with alveolar coalescence. Focal thickening of the basement membrane and remnants of hyaline membranes, with sheetlike masses of histiocytes and macrophages filling some alveoli

infants require 35 to 40 percent oxygen to achieve pink color. Air exchange is good, with no rales or rhonchi: an expiratory grunt is not heard, intercostal retractions are minimal, and arterial pH and $Paco_2$ measurements are within normal limits. The chest x-ray reveals central perihilar streaking fluid in the interlobar fissures and the cardiac silhouette is often slightly enlarged. This x-ray picture can be distinguished easily from meconium aspiration or the respiratory distress syndrome. Only symptomatic treatment is necessary, but it is important not to attempt any nipple-feeding while the infant is breathing rapidly. If fluids are required they can be given by the intravenous route or gavage into the stomach. In most cases, respirations slow gradually during the first 24 hours of life, and the infants are usually able to go home when their mothers are discharged from the hospital. The pathogenesis has not been clarified; however, it has been suggested that this syndrome may be secondary to slow absorption of lung fluid. The syndrome appears to be self-limited and there have been no reported complications.

Pulmonary Dysmaturity (Wilson-Mikity Syndrome) (See also p. 1316)

This is a pulmonary disease of premature infants, first described by Wilson and Mikity in 1960. Most of the affected infants have a birth weight below 1,500 g. The usual clinical course is marked by an insidious onset of mild respiratory symptoms after the first week of life, most commonly noted around 3 weeks of age. The first signs are usually tachypnea, periods of apnea, and slight cyanosis. X-ray films at this time usually appear far more abnormal than might be apparent from the clinical findings. Chest radiographs show a diffuse, bilateral, coarse, and lacelike pattern of infiltrates with alternating cystlike foci of hyperaeration, as seen in Figure 12. There is usually no fever and the blood count is within normal limits. Moderate osteoporosis, with rib fractures, is sometimes found. In infants with severe

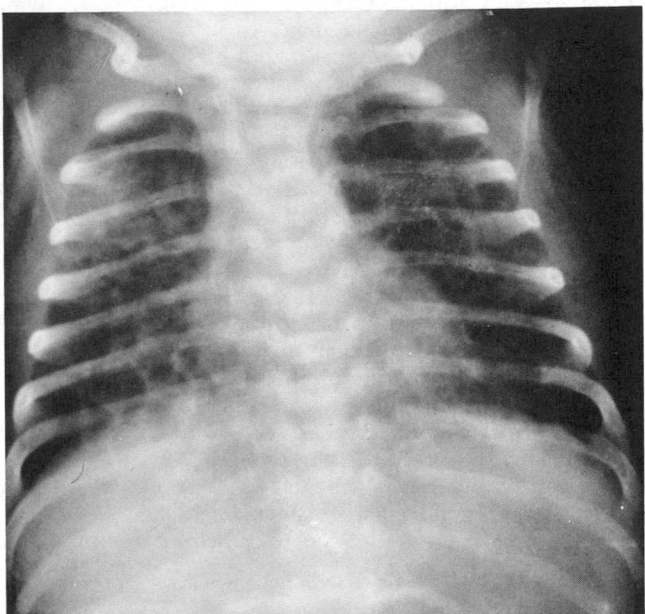

Fig. 12. Radiogram of an infant with pulmonary dysmaturity (Wilson-Mikity syndrome) showing typical cystic appearance. (Courtesy of Dr. Harold Goldman.)

disease, arterial blood gas determinations show elevated $Paco_2$ (60 to 80 mm Hg) with cyanosis in 20 to 40 percent oxygen. Pulmonary function studies show a reduced functional residual capacity and vital capacity, an increased resistance to air flow especially during expiration, and an increased work with breathing. Symptoms become increasingly severe and reach a maximum intensity usually four to eight weeks after onset. In the reported series, the fatality rate varies between 25 to 50 percent. In surviving infants the symptoms gradually disappear over weeks and months. During the recovery phases hyperaeration is first observed by x-ray at the lung bases. In six months to two years the chest x-ray becomes normal.

The cystic stage of this disease is sometimes confused with bronchopulmonary dysplasia (a chronic pulmonary disease that develops following respirator therapy with high oxygen). Table 4 compares the x-ray findings, pathology, and etiology in both diseases.

PATHOLOGY. Surprisingly, light and electron microscopic studies from lung biopsies and autopsy specimens have not shown any characteristic cellular changes. Mild pulmonary fibrosis has been noted on occasion. Sections of inflated and fixed lung specimens show an uneven pattern of aeration with overexpansion in some areas (Fig. 13).

ETIOLOGY. The studies of Burnard have suggested a working hypothesis. He demonstrated an increased distensibility of the bronchial tree with decreasing gestational age. Partial airway obstruction might easily occur following the aspiration of a small quantity of milk as a result of an undeveloped gag reflex. In the small premature infant, during any respiratory effort, transpulmonary pressures could easily collapse the

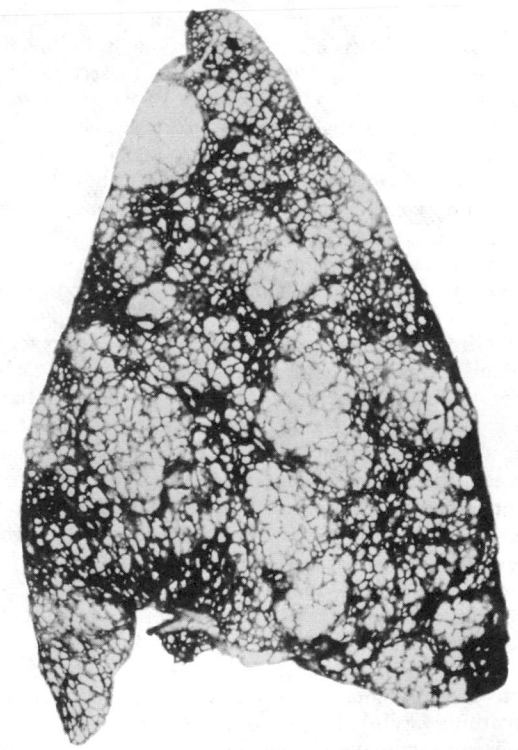

Fig. 13. A section of lung from an infant dying with pulmonary dysmaturity. The lung was inflated at 15 cm of water and fixed in formalin for 48 hours. Note the uneven aeration. (From Hodgman et al. *Pediatrics*, 44:179, 1969.)

airways. With partial obstruction following aspiration, these pressures would increase, increasing the tendency to collapse. The small radius of the bronchi of the premature infant in conjunction with the increased collapsibility would make these infants prone to unequal distribution of inspired gas.

TREATMENT. Therapy at present is symptomatic and not specific. In view of the possible association of aspiration, oral feedings should be closely monitored and gavage feedings continued until the gag reflex is complete (32 to 34 weeks). The volume of each feeding should be such that spitting does not occur after feedings. An increase in concentration of oxygen and a neutral thermal environment are useful. Digitalis may be helpful if right heart failure develops. It is important not to become discouraged if no radiologic improvement is seen over a period of several weeks of life. Even though the arterial CO_2 remains high, most infants will recover with diligent medical and nursing care. At present there is no evidence that the use of steroids helps; the rare occurrence of pulmonary fibrosis does not support their general use.

Pneumonia

Pneumonia is the largest pulmonary cause of death in infants dying after 48 hours; it is noted in as many as 22 percent of all newborn autopsies. Two peaks in incidence are observed. One is in the first 12 hours of life and is most probably secondary to maternal infection. The second peak occurs after 48 hours of life, probably from infections acquired in the nursery. The most common route of infection is aspiration of infected amniotic fluid, though some infections come from hematogenous spread through the placenta. The organisms usually found are *E. coli*, staphylococci, or streptococci.

CLINICAL COURSE. Symptoms are often not easily localized to the lung. The presenting signs may be delay in the onset of respiration, lethargy, hypotonia, hypothermia, and pallor. Cyanosis, tachycardia, tachypnea, flaring of alae nasae, and irregular respirations, with periods of apnea are often observed. Fine rales are usually heard, though a deep breath is sometimes necessary to bring them out. When the infant is kept at neutral environmental temperature, there may be some increase in body temperature. Just as often there is a drop in body temperature; the more premature the infant, the more often a drop in temperature is observed. Chest roentgenograms usually reveal irregularly shaped densities bilaterally. For early diagnosis, inspection of frozen sections of the cord and placenta has been recommended. This is sometimes useful, but pneumonia can be present in an infant without any evidence of infection of the cord and placenta. Aspiration and staining of gastric contents for polymorphonuclear leucocytes is helpful in alerting the physician to the possibility of infec-

tion. For accurate bacteriologic diagnosis nose, throat, and blood cultures should be taken.

PATHOLOGY. A diagnosis of pneumonia from gross examination of the lung can rarely be made. Microscopic examination reveals debris from the amniotic fluid and a diffuse infiltration with polymorphonuclear leucocytes. Pleural reactions are rarely seen.

TREATMENT. Successful therapy depends on early recognition and treatment. Because the disease is often rapidly overwhelming, it is recommended by some (including the author) that prophylactic antibiotic treatment be given to infants who appear normal but are delivered from mothers with infected amniotic fluid. Others advise against routine treatment under these circumstances, although they insist on watching such infants closely and treating at the earliest sign of possible illness. There is also not complete agreement on the choice of antibiotics. Combinations of penicillin and colistin, or penicillin and gentamicin have been suggested. Aqueous crystalline penicillin 20,000 to 40,000 units/kg/day in divided doses and streptomycin 10 mg/kg/12 hours is a reasonable combination, but does not cover adequately infection with gram-negative organisms. Kanamycin, colistin, or gentamicin should be used in treating a gram-negative infection. Oxygen and a neutral environmental temperature are valuable supportive measures.

Meconium Aspiration

Meconium is present in the amniotic fluid in 10 percent of all infants at birth and suggests that the infants had an asphyxial episode prior to birth. Since squamous cells are found in the lungs of most infants who die during the first week of life, it is difficult to determine whether the aspiration of large amounts of amniotic fluid is also associated with the disease. It is doubtful that amniotic fluid alone can produce any obstruction, although pulmonary disease is definitely observed in infants who have obtained meconium. While meconium can be aspirated from the trachea, in 60 percent of all infants who are born covered with meconium, only 20 to 25 percent of them will develop symptoms of respiratory distress or pulmonary radiographic changes.

CLINICAL FINDINGS. Because asphyxia is often the basis for the presence of meconium in the amniotic fluid, the infant who aspirates meconium at birth is often depressed and requires some resuscitation. Positive pressure resuscitation should be avoided until adequate laryngotracheal cleansing has been performed to prevent pushing meconium further into the small airways. Gasping respirations are sometimes observed, the chest is enlarged—especially in the anterior-posterior diameter, respirations are rapid, and rales may or may not be heard. A chest x-ray is helpful diagnostically and will show areas of increased density and overexpansion irregularly distributed throughout the lung. One complication of the partially blocked overexpanded areas of lung is rupture with pneumothorax. This should be suspected if the clinical status of the infant deteriorates rapidly. Pneumothorax has been observed as a complication in approximately 10 percent of all infants who are covered with meconium at delivery.

TREATMENT. If upper airway obstruction is observed, immediate suctioning of the trachea sometimes removes a large meconium plug. The stomach should also be suctioned to remove any swallowed meconium. Increased oxygen is indicated to prevent cyanosis. As in other pulmonary diseases in which gas exchange is limited, the thermal environment should be neutral to reduce oxygen consumption and carbon dioxide production to a minimum. Any metabolic acidosis should be treated with sodium bicarbonate. Marked recovery is usually noted after 48 hours of life but a small number of infants with meconium aspiration recover only after a prolonged period. It is of interest that the lung can absorb meconium rapidly.

Pneumothorax

An asymptomatic pneumothorax is found in about 1 percent of all routine examinations of newborn chest radiography. Considering the very high intrathoracic pressures recorded during the first minutes of life, it is surprising that pneumothorax is not a more frequent occurrence. Macklin described the path of the air after rupture. Air from the ruptured alveolus dissects up the vascular sheath into the pleural cavity. In some series, half of the symptomatic patients aspirated meconium or blood. This suggests that obstruction with a ball-valve action may be the basis for the rupture. Pneumothorax should be suspected in any newborn with respiratory distress, and a chest radiograph should be taken quickly, since adequate therapy is available.

CLINICAL FINDINGS. Cyanosis, tachypnea, grunting, and flaring of the alae nasae are often observed. Percussion is sometimes helpful, but shift of the apical impulse is usually more easily noted. A typical chest film is shown in Figure 14.

TREATMENT. If the pneumothorax is asymptomatic no specific therapy is necessary, but the infant's color, heart rate, and respiratory rate should be closely observed. If severe respiratory distress is noted, a catheter should be placed in the pneumothorax and a continuous suction of 10 to 20 cm H_2O placed on the catheter. Usually only 24 hours of suction are necessary. Because the air in the pneumothorax is absorbed by the pleural capillaries, breathing 100 percent oxygen will markedly hasten the absorption of the pneumothorax and can be lifesaving. Table 5 shows the total pressure of gases in the pneumothorax and capillary blood when breathing air or 100 percent oxygen. Since the pressure in the pneumothorax is always close to 760 mm Hg, the very

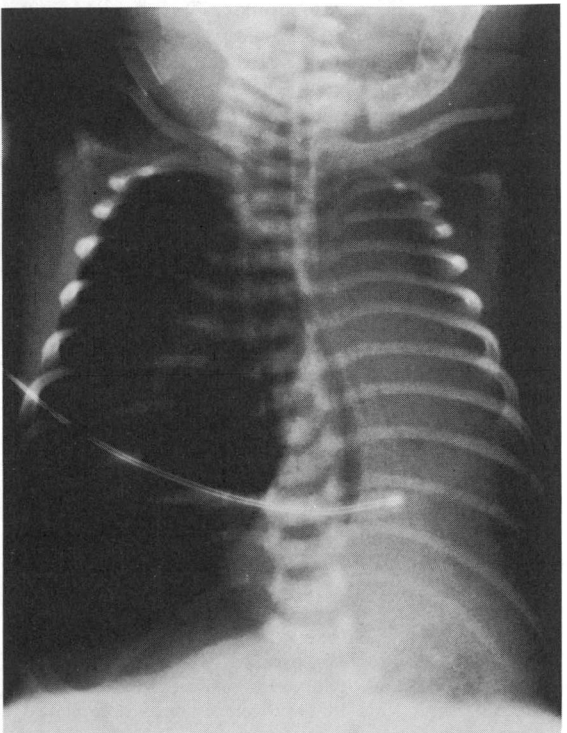

Fig. 14. Radiogram of an infant with a pneumothorax.

low capillary pressure produced with oxygen breathing hastens the absorption considerably, because gas flows from a high to low pressure. A sixfold increase in the rate of absorption of a pneumothorax has been observed with 100 percent oxygen breathing. However, because of the toxic effects of oxygen on the retina and lung, the complete effects of this mechanism cannot be utilized.

Pulmonary Hemorrhage

Pulmonary hemorrhage is commonly seen in autopsies performed in infants dying in the first week of life. Its incidence varies from 1 to 4 in 1,000 live births and is most often observed in infants who are

TABLE 5. *Total Pressure of Gases (mmHg) in the Pneumothorax and Capillary Blood*

		In Room Air	In 100% O_2
Total pressure exerted by gases	Pleural capillary blood bathing the tissue	710	155
	Pneumothorax	760	760

small for gestational age. It is found in association with pneumonia, severe anoxia, and hyaline membrane disease. When only intraalveolar hemorrhage is observed, the possibility of aspiration as the source of blood should be considered. Pulmonary hemorrhage is also noted with hemorrhagic disease of the newborn, kernicterus, and cold injury. Why pulmonary hemorrhage is seen with cold injury is not understood, but in one series, five out of eight infants dying from cold injury were found to have large pulmonary hemorrhages. X-rays are not diagnostic and vary from coarse nodular densities to reticulogranular appearance of large confluent densities.

TREATMENT. Treatment is symptomatic. Small transfusions of fresh whole blood are helpful and should be given promptly if any clotting abnormalities are found.

REFERENCES

IDIOPATHIC RESPIRATORY
DISTRESS SYNDROME

Ambrus, C. M., Weintraub, D. H., Dunphy, D., Dowd, J. E., Pickren, J. W., Niswander, K. R., and Ambrus, J. L. Studies on hyaline membrane disease. I. The fibrinolysin system in pathogenesis and therapy. Pediatrics, 32:10, 1963.

Avery, M. E., and Mead, J. Surface properties in relation to atelectasis and hyaline membrane disease. Amer. J. Dis. Child., 97:517, 1959.

—— and Oppenheimer, E. H. Recent increase in mortality from hyaline membrane disease. J. Pediat., 57:553, 1960.

Behrman, R. E. Commentary: The use of assisted ventilation in the therapy of hyaline membrane disease. J. Pediat., 76:169, 1970.

Boston, R. W., Geller, F., and Smith, C. A. Arterial blood gas tensions and acid-base balance in the management of the respiratory distress syndrome. J. Pediat., 68:74, 1966.

Bruck, K., Parmalee, A. H., and Bruck, M. Neutral temperature range and range of "thermal comfort" in premature infants. Biol. Neonat., 4:32, 1962.

Brumley, G. W., Hodson, W. A., and Avery, M. E. Lung phospholipids and surface tension correlations in infants with and without hyaline membrane disease and in adults. Pediatrics, 40:13, 1967.

Burnard, E. D., and James, L. S. Failure of the heart after undue asphyxia at birth. Pediatrics, 28:545, 1961.

Campiche, M., Jaccottet, M., and Juillard, E. La pneumonose à membranes hyalines. Observations au microscope électronique. Ann. Pediat., 199:74, 1962.

Chu, J., Clements, J. A., Cotton, E. K., Klaus, M. H., Sweet, A. Y., and Tooley, W. H. Neonatal pulmonary ischemia. Pediatrics (Suppl.), 40:709, 1967.

—— Clements, J. A., Cotton, E. K., Klaus, M. H., Sweet, A. Y., Thomas, M. A., and Tooley, W. H. The pulmonary hypoperfusion syndrome. Pediatrics, 35:733, 1965.

Cort, R. L. Renal function in the respiratory distress syndrome. Acta Paediat. Scand., 51:313, 1962.

Gitlin, D., and Craig, J. M. Nature of the hyaline membrane in asphyxia of the newborn. Pediatrics, 17:64, 1956.

Gribetz, I., Frank, N. R., and Avery, M. E. Static volume-pressure relations of excised lungs of infants with hyaline membrane disease, newborn and stillborn infants. J. Clin. Invest., 38:2168, 1959.

Gruber, H. S., and Klaus, M. H. Intermittent mask and bag therapy: An alternative approach to respirator therapy for infants with severe respiratory distress. J. Pediat., 76:194, 1970.

Heese, H. de V., Harrison, V. C., Klein, M., and Malan, A. F. Intermittent positive pressure ventilation in hyaline membrane disease. J. Pediat., 76:183, 1970.

Karlberg, P., Cook, C. D., O'Brien, D., Cherry, R. B., and Smith, C. A. Studies of respiratory physiology in the newborn infant. II. Observations during and after respiratory distress. Acta Paediat. Scand. (Suppl. 100), 43:397, 1954.

Kitterman, J. A., Phibbs, R. H., and Tooley, W. H. Aortic blood pressure in normal newborn infants during the first 12 hours of life. Pediatrics, 44:959, 1969.

—— Phibbs, R. H., and Tooley, W. H. Catheterization of umbilical vessels in newborn infants. Pediat. Clin. N. Amer., 17(4):895, 1970.

Lauweryns, J. M. Hyaline membrane disease. Arch. Dis. Child., 40:618, 1965

—— Pulmonary arterial vasculature in neonatal hyaline membrane disease. Science, 153:1275, 1966.

—— Claessens, St., and Boussauw, L. The pulmonary lymphatics in neonatal hyaline membrane disease. Pediatrics, 41:917, 1968.

Naeye, R. L. Pulmonary arterial abnormalities associated with hyaline membrane disease. Amer. J. Path., 48:869, 1966.

Nelson, N. M., Prod'hom, L. S., Cherry, R. B., Lipsitz, P. J., and Smith, C. A. Pulmonary function in the newborn infant. II. Perfusion-estimation by analysis of the arterial-alveolar carbon dioxide differences. Pediatrics, 30:975, 1962.

Normand, I. C. S., Reynolds, E. O. R., Strang, L. G., and Wigglesworth, J. S. Flow and protein concentration of lymph from lungs of lambs developing hyaline membrane disease. Arch. Dis. Child., 43:334, 1968.

Northway, W. H., Rosan, R. C., and Porter, D. Y. Pulmonary disease following respirator therapy. New Eng. J. Med., 276:357, 1967.

Prod'hom, L. S., Levison, H., Cherry, R. B., and Smith, C. A. Adjustment of ventilation, intrapulmonary gas exchange, and acid base balance during the first day of life: infants with early respiratory distress. Pediatrics, 35:662, 1965.

Rudolph, J., Desmond, M. M., and Pineda, R. G. Clinical diagnosis of respiratory difficulty in the newborn. Pediat. Clin. N. Amer., 13:669, 1966.

Shepard, F. M., Johnston, R. B., Jr., Klatte, E. C., Burko, H., and Stahlman, M. Residual pulmonary findings in clinical hyaline membrane disease. New Eng. J. Med., 279:1063, 1968.

Silverman, W. A., and Sinclair, J. C. Temperature regulation in the newborn infant. New Eng. J. Med., 274:146, 1966.

—— Sinclair, J. C., Gaudy, G. M., Finster, M., Bauman, W. A., and Agate, F. J. A controlled trial of management of respiratory distress syndrome in a body-enclosing respirator. I. Evaluation of safety. Pediatrics, 39:740, 1967.

Sinclair, J. C. Prevention and treatment of the respiratory distress syndrome. Pediat. Clin. N. Amer., 13: 711, 1966.

Stahlman, M. T., Battersby, E. J., Shepard, F. M., and Blankenship, W. J. Prognosis in hyaline membrane disease. New Eng. J. Med., 276:303, 1967.

——— Malan, A. F., Shepard, F. M., Blankenship, W. J., Young, W. C., and Gray, J. Negative pressure assisted ventilation in infants with hyaline membrane disease. J. Pediat., 76:174, 1970.

Strang, L. B., and MacLeish, M. H. Ventilatory failure and right-to-left shunt in newborn infants with respiratory distress. Pediatrics, 28:17, 1961.

Thomas, D. V., Fletcher, G., Sunshine, P., Schafer, I. A., and Klaus, M. H. Prolonged respirator use in pulmonary insufficiency of the newborn. J.A.M.A., 193:183, 1965.

Usher, R. The respiratory distress syndrome of prematurity. Pediat. Clin. N. Amer., 8:525, 1961.

PNEUMONIA

Bernstein, J., and Wang, J. The pathology of neonatal pneumonia. Amer. J. Dis. Child., 101:350, 1961.

Blanc, W. A. Pathways of fetal and early neonatal infection. J. Pediat., 59:473, 1961.

Briggs, J. N., and Hogg, G. Perinatal pulmonary pathology. Pediatrics, 22:41, 1958.

PNEUMOTHORAX

Charnick, V., and Avery, M. E. Spontaneous alveolar rupture in newborn infants. Pediatrics, 32:816, 1963.

Lubchenco, L. O. Recognition of spontaneous pneumothorax in premature infants. Pediatrics, 24:996, 1959.

Macklin, C. C. Transport of air along sheaths of pulmonic blood vessels from alveoli to mediastinum. Arch. Intern. Med., 64:913, 1939.

PULMONARY HEMORRHAGE

Ahvenainen, E. K., and Call, J. D. Pulmonary hemorrhage in infants. A descriptive study. Amer. J. Path., 28:1, 1952.

Esterly, R., and Oppenheimer, E. H. Massive pulmonary hemorrhage in the newborn. I. Pathologic considerations. J. Pediat., 69:3, 1966.

Mann, T. P., and Elliott, R. I. K. Neonatal cold injury due to accidental exposure to cold. Lancet, 1:229, 1957.

McAdams, A. J. Pulmonary hemorrhage in the newborn. Amer. J. Dis. Child., 113:255, 1967.

Rowe, S., and Avery, M. E. Massive pulmonary hemorrhage in the newborn. II. Clinical considerations. J. Pediat., 69:12, 1966.

PULMONARY DYSMATURITY

Aherne, W. A., Cross, K. W., Hey, A. M., and Lewis, S. R. Lung function and pathology in a premature infant with chronic pulmonary insufficiency (Wilson-Mikity syndrome). Pediatrics, 40:962, 1967.

Baghdassarian, O. M., Avery, M. E., and Neuhauser, E. B. D. A form of pulmonary insufficiency in premature infants. Amer. J. Roentgen., 89:1020, 1963.

Burnard, E. D. The pulmonary syndrome of Wilson and Mikity, and respiratory function in very small premature infants. Pediat. Clin. N. Amer., 13:999, 1966.

——— Grattan-Smith, P., Picton-Warlow, C. G., and Gravaug, A. Pulmonary insufficiency in prematurity. Aust. Paediat. J., 1:12, 1965.

Hodgman, J. E., Mikity, V. G., Tatter, D., and Cleland, R. S. Chronic respiratory distress in the premature infant: Wilson-Mikity syndrome. Pediatrics, 44:179, 1969.

Swyer, P. R., Delivoria-Papadopoulos, M., Levison, H., Reilly, B. J., and Balis, J. U. The pulmonary syndrome of Wilson and Mikity. Pediatrics, 36:374, 1965.

Wilson, M. G., and Mikity, V. G. A new form of respiratory disease in premature infants. Amer. J. Dis. Child., 99:489, 1960.

TRANSIENT TACHYPNEA

Avery, M. E., Gatewood, O. G., and Brumley, G. Transient tachypnea of newborn. Amer. J. Dis. Child., 111:380, 1966.

Respiratory Function and Pulmonary Disease in Older Infants and Children

WILLIAM H. TOOLEY

Respiration is the sequence of physical and chemical steps needed to supply oxygen for oxidative metabolism and to remove carbon dioxide formed in energy-producing reactions. The lungs and circulation subserve this process. The lungs consist of a distribution system (the airways) and millions of small sacs (alveoli) with a large surface area where the exchange of oxygen and carbon dioxide between air and blood is accomplished by diffusion across a thin barrier composed of the alveolar and capillary walls (the parenchyma). The movement of gas in and out of the lungs is effected by the contraction and relaxation of the diaphragm and the intercostal and abdominal muscles which increase and decrease the volume of the thorax.

19.3
THE AIRWAYS

Defective structure, foreign bodies, tumors, and inflammation can decrease the internal diameter of the airway and obstruct the flow of gas. Since the signs, symptoms, physiologic consequences, and principles of treatment for all airway obstructions are similar, regardless of the proximate cause, the general problem of airway blockage will be considered before detailing particular diseases.

Anatomy

The nose, pharynx, larynx, and the upper part of the trachea, which is outside of the thorax, will be considered as the upper airway; the lower airway includes the lower part of the trachea and the bronchi and their subdivisions to the level of the respiratory bronchioles.

The airways receive their blood supply from vessels derived from the third and fourth embryonic aortic arches: the larynx from the external carotid (third arch); the extrathoracic trachea from the subclavian (fourth arch); and the lower airway from the aorta (fourth arch) via the bronchial arteries. The motor nerves of the larynx come from the recurrent branches of the vagus and the sensory nerves from the superior laryngeal branch of the vagus. Sympathetic and parasympathetic fibers from the vagus supply the entire lower airway.

Squamous cells line the larynx; equal numbers of ciliated columnar and goblet cells line the trachea, bronchi, and larger bronchioles; and ciliated cuboidal cells and occasional goblet cells line the smaller bronchioles. There are numerous mucous glands in the submucosal and muscular layers of the trachea and bronchi, but these are not present in the smaller bronchi. The bases of the cilia are covered with a serous fluid, and their free ends extend into a mucous sheet which coats the entire tracheobronchial tree.

Three single and three paired articulated cartilages, which are connected by elastic tissue and muscles, make up the framework of the larynx. The muscles operate upon the paired cartilages, widening and narrowing the opening of the larynx into the lower pharynx. The dorsal ends of the cartilaginous crescents which support the trachea and bronchi are connected by muscle and connective tissue. These rings of muscle and cartilage are irregular and may split or fuse, particularly at the carina, whose framework may be membranous or cartilaginous. In the medium- and small-sized bronchi only fragments of cartilage remain, and the muscle forms a loose sheath which operates independently of the cartilage. In the bronchioles, muscle bundles spiral in helical turns and are proportionately thicker than in the larger airways.

The cartilage, other supporting structures, and glandular tissue are present at all ages, but the amount, strength, and distribution vary with growth. The ciliated cells are well developed at birth, but there are few goblet cells and mucous glands in the bronchi. After the first few months, goblet cells increase rapidly in number; the mucous glands increase in number and size and are abundant by 1 year of age. The growth in the cross-sectional area and tissue mass for the subdivisions of the airway is not uniform. The rate of increase in diameter of the trachea and bronchi is accelerated in the early years and during puberty, whereas after an initial growth spurt, the bronchiolar diameter increases slowly (Fig. 15). From birth to the completion of growth, the weight of the lungs and the total lung capacity increase twentyfold, while the airway diameters increase only two- to threefold. In the newborn, the trachea and bronchi have relatively little cartilage, elastic tissue, connective tissue, or muscle and the ratio of the diameter of the lumen to the wall thickness is large. The muscle is thin in the smaller airways in the neonatal period and enlarges only slightly in the first year of life, but after the fourth year, it increases in thickness in proportion to the growth of the lungs. From birth to 15 years, the diameter of large bronchioles doubles, the thickness of their walls triples, and the amount of supporting tissue increases four- or fivefold (Fig. 16).

Function

The airway warms or cools, moistens, and purifies incoming air and protects the lung against foreign

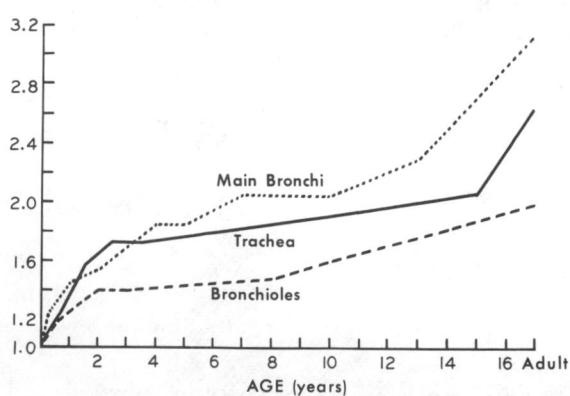

Fig. 15. The relative change in diameter of the principal components of the airway plotted against age. The diameter of the trachea doubles at about 15 years, that of the bronchi at 6 years. After an increase in diameter of 40 percent by 2 years, the bronchioles grow slowly and in adult life are twice the diameter at birth. (From Engel, 1962. *Lung Structure*. Courtesy of Charles C Thomas, Publ.)

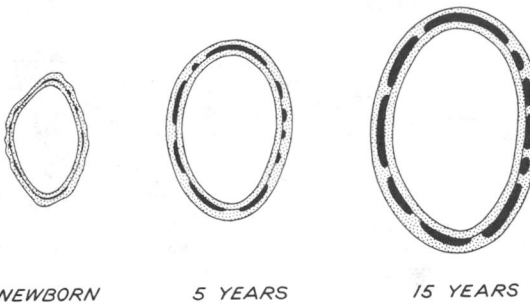

NEWBORN   5 YEARS   15 YEARS

Fig. 16. Diagrammatic representation of a large bronchiole at three ages. With growth, muscle, as depicted by thick black lines within the wall, increases in amount and thickness. The diameter of the lumen and the ratio of wall thickness to luminal diameter also increase.

bodies. It regulates the resistance to gas flow and its own volume by altering the width of its lumen. By regional changes in resistance, the amount of gas going to different regions of the lungs can be varied. This provides more ventilation to those regions with a small blood flow, thus matching ventilation to perfusion.

The large and vascular surface of the nose and pharynx adds water and changes the temperature of inspired air to body temperature. During quiet breathing, even at extremes of environmental temperature and humidity, air is at body temperature and saturated with water when it reaches the larynx. When airflow is increased and cold, hot or dry air is breathed, or when breathing through an endotracheal or tracheotomy tube, temperature and humidity control is shared by the trachea and bronchi. Most large particles are blocked by nasal hairs, caught on the tortuous nasal passages, or carried by mucus into the pharynx and swallowed. Aspiration of food, foreign bodies, and mucus is prevented by closure of the larynx. Smaller particles settle on the airway's mucous blanket, which is constantly moved upward toward the pharynx by the cilia and keeps the alveoli free of almost all foreign matter. The propulsion of mucus is so rapid that it moves the length of the airway in a few hours. The airway in newly born

and young infants is well adapted for air conditioning. However, the scarcity of mucus-producing elements may interfere with production of the mucous blanket, make the surface of the airway more susceptible to infection, and deprive the alveoli of some of their protection from bacteria and other foreign material. On the other hand, the hazard of clogging or blocking small passages because of excess production of mucus is reduced. Mucus does, however, block the small airways of some infants, as in cystic fibrosis, for example.

Since there is little exchange of gas between the lumina of the airways and blood, their volume is respiratory dead space. For efficiency, dead space must be substantially smaller than the volume of each respiration (the tidal volume). In older children and adults, the ratio of dead space to tidal volume is about 0.3; i.e., two-thirds of the volume of each breath reaches the alveolar ducts and alveoli, and one-third is left behind to fill the dead space. In the premature baby this ratio is about 0.5; in the full-term baby and young infant, about 0.4 (Table 6). The relatively large volume of the airway is a disadvantage to the infant and requires movement of proportionally more gas in and out of his lungs each minute (minute volume). However, since the lumina are comparatively wide, the work of breathing is not excessive.

The pressure of a gas is determined by the number of molecules present in a given volume. When the diaphragm contracts and the thorax enlarges, the volume of the lungs increases, the intrapulmonary gas expands, and its concentration decreases. The pressure within the lungs is then less than at the mouth, and since gas moves from regions of relatively high to relatively low pressure, inspiration occurs. The amount of air which moves along the airway in a given period of time (flow) is approximately proportional to this pressure difference and to the radius of the airway raised to the fourth power, and inversely proportional to the length of the airway and the viscosity of the gas. Of these factors, the pressure change and width of the airway can vary the most. For example, doubling the pressure will double the flow, while if the pressure is constant and the radius doubled, this will increase flow 16 times. If the airway is small, the pressure difference must be large

TABLE 6.   *Respiratory Function*

	Newly Born	5 Years	10 Years	15 Years	Adult
Frequency (breaths/min)	30	24	20	16	12
Tidal volume (ml)	20	100	225	375	450
Dead space (ml)	8	35	75	125	150
Minute volume (ml/min)	600	2,400	4,500	6,000	6,000
Dead space/tidal volume	0.4	0.35	0.33	0.33	0.33
Alveolar ventilation (ml/min)	360	1,560	3,000	4,200	4,200
Maximal inspiratory pressure (cm H_2O)	100		100		125
Maximal expiratory pressure (cm H_2O)	150		200		250
Maximal inspiratory flow (L/min)	8	75	160	325	400
Maximal expiratory flow (L/min)	10	110	210	400	500

to sustain a given flow, and the work of breathing will be great. The strength of the muscles of inspiration and the capacity of the thorax to enlarge will limit the extent to which the intrapulmonary pressure will fall below atmospheric pressure. The maximal pressure difference that the newborn can achieve is about 100 cm H_2O during inspiration and about 150 cm H_2O during expiration (maximal inspiratory and expiratory pressures). These transient pressure gradients are almost as large as in the adult (Table 6).

Respiratory maneuvers alter the airway diameter. During inspiration the pressure in the intrapleural space is less than atmospheric, and in each segment of the airway from the mouth to alveoli the pressure is less than in that portion immediately proximal to it. With inspiration, the larynx and extrathoracic trachea tend to collapse, since their intraluminal pressures are less than that in the surrounding tissues; the intrathoracic trachea, bronchi, and bronchioles dilate, since their intraluminal pressures are higher than the pressure in the surrounding lung. The collapse of the trachea and dilation of the bronchi with inspiration are greater when structural support is weak, as in the first years of life (Fig. 17). The dilation of most of the airway with inspiration increases the dead space and accounts, in part, for the infant's large dead space to tidal volume ratio. In order to maintain a given minute volume when the larynx is partially obstructed, the flow of air across the obstruction is rapid, the pressure in the trachea distal to the obstruction is significantly less than atmospheric, and the tendency of the extrathoracic trachea to collapse is exaggerated (Fig. 18).

Conversely, during expiration, the intraluminal pressures in each portion of the intrathoracic airways are less than those of the surrounding tissue, while

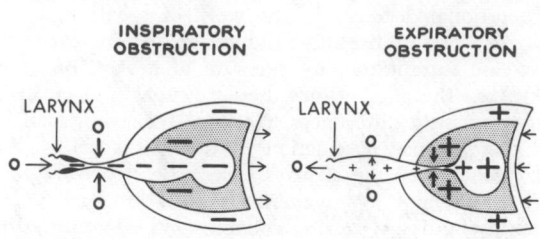

Fig. 18. When the upper airway is obstructed by a foreign body, mucus, or inflammation, the transtracheal pressure gradient is large during inspiration and the tendency of the trachea to collapse is exaggerated. With obstruction of the smaller airways, the transbronchial pressure gradient is large and the forces which tend to collapse the larger bronchi increase. When, as in the infant and small child, the cartilaginous, muscular, and elastic support is weak, the collapse of the trachea and large bronchi may significantly add to the obstruction.

the pressures within the extrathoracic trachea and larynx are greater. These transmural pressure gradients cause compression of the lower airway (Fig. 17) and dilation of the upper airway. Accelerated airflow past a bronchial obstruction may result in almost complete occlusion of the infant's weak-walled bronchi (Fig. 18). These passive mechanical consequences of respiration affect the trachea and bronchi more than the bronchioles, since the latter are supported in part by the pulmonary parenchyma.

The trachea and bronchi are also actively narrowed by contraction of their muscles, which pull together the dorsal ends of the cartilaginous crescents. These muscles are small and weak in the infant and young child; however, at this age the cartilages are also weak, so that, as in the adult, muscular contraction narrows the larger airways. Contraction of the spirally oriented muscle fibers reduces the diameter of the bronchioles without decreasing their length. Since the bronchioles are relatively large (Fig. 15) and have few muscle bundles (Fig. 16) in the first years of life, their potential for constriction during this period is proportionally less than in the adult.

In summary:

1. The chance of obstruction of the infant's airway by mucus may be reduced because the small amount of glandular tissue in the infant's airway may produce little mucus, but as a result, his lungs may be more susceptible to infection. However, the absolute cross section of the airway in infants and children is smaller than that in adults and hence more easily occluded by small amounts of foreign bodies, mucus, and debris. The small diameter of the young child's bronchi may dispose him to diseases which cause obstruction, such as asthma. By one year, the lining of the airway resembles that of the adult.

2. The airway is proportionally larger in the infant and young child than in the older child and adult. This causes a proportional increase in the

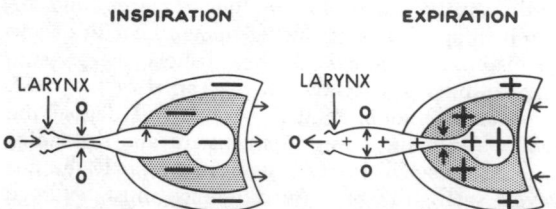

Fig. 17. The pressures along the airway and in the lung and intrapleural space during inspiration and expiration are represented by the size of the minus and plus signs. Atmospheric pressure is indicated by 0. The size of the arrows point out the magnitude of forces. The thin outline of the infant's airway indicates weak support. With inspiration there is a gradual change from atmospheric pressure at the mouth to subatmospheric pressure in the alveoli. The extrathoracic trachea tends to collapse, since the pressure is less in the lumen than in the surrounding tissue, while the intrathoracic airway dilates. With expiration pressure gradually changes from above atmospheric in the alveoli to atmospheric at the mouth. The intrathoracic airway tends to collapse and the extrathoracic trachea to dilate. In the infant, whose airways are weak and poorly supported, these phenomena may be marked.

respiratory dead space and minute volume, but a proportional decrease in the work of breathing.

3. The infant and child are able to increase and decrease intrapulmonary pressure to nearly the same extent as the adult. Since they are capable of creating large pressure differences, maximal breathing maneuvers may cause obstruction in the first years of life at a time when the airways have little structural support. This may aggravate the obstruction in diseases like laryngitis by causing collapse of the extrathoracic trachea.

4. Bronchiolar muscle is sparse at birth and increases in bulk throughout the first five years of life. Since the infant's small airways have little muscle, and since the ratio of wall thickness to diameter is relatively less than in adults, obstruction due to active reduction in diameter is limited. However, a little reduction in size by contraction of these muscles may go a long way toward obstructing the young child's bronchi, as in asthma. This inability to constrict may impair regional regulation of ventilation and result in some areas of the lung with reduced pulmonary blood flow getting a disproportionately large amount of ventilation.

Obstruction

SIGNS AND SYMPTOMS. *Anxiety and Restlessness.* The inability to breathe with ease creates anxiety. A decrease in the oxygen (hypoxemia) and an accumulation of carbon dioxide (hypercarbia) in the arterial blood accentuate this feeling. Restlessness, agitation, and vigorous respiratory efforts may accompany this sensation of strangulation and be the first signs of hypoxemia. The fatigued infant with obstruction and labored breathing who suddenly becomes more active may not be improving; he may be much worse and his increased activity may be a sign of respiratory failure.

Cyanosis. When obstruction is marked, even maximal respiratory efforts cannot deliver sufficient oxygen to the alveoli to saturate the arterial blood. As the young child increases his respiratory efforts, his airway collapses and increases the obstruction, which further reduces ventilation and augments the hypoxemia. When the child is anemic significant hypoxemia may be present without cyanosis. Also, the degree of cyanosis is difficult to estimate when there is peripheral vasoconstriction as in shock and acidosis; hence, cyanosis may not be a good index of hypoxemia under these circumstances.

Respiratory Sounds. The various abnormal breath sounds which occur with obstruction are influenced by the depth of breathing, the velocity of airflow, the position of the patient, and the size and location of the airway which is obstructed. They are a composite of the vibrations produced by the movement of air. The pitch of the breath sounds depends upon the size of the orifices or the diameter of the tube; the smaller the orifice or tube, the higher the pitch. The intensity of the breath sounds varies with the velocity of airflow, an increase in the tidal volume or rate of flow accentuating them.

Masses at the base of the tongue and in the posterior pharynx cause a gargling or snoring sound. Breathing through an obstruction of the larynx produces a relatively high-pitched, harsh noise called *stridor.* Since laryngeal obstruction is augmented during inspiration and reduced during expiration, laryngeal stridor is predominantly inspiratory. Masses at the base of the tongue and in the anterior pharynx are more likely to obstruct the larynx and cause stridor when the patient is on his back. An obstruction of the extrathoracic trachea creates noises of somewhat higher pitch during inspiration. The sounds of obstruction of the intrathoracic trachea and bronchi are predominantly expiratory.

Partial blockage of the smaller airways hinders the inflow and outflow of gas. Wheezes are heard during inspiration but are more prominent during expiration.

Cough. A cough is an explosive expiration. After a deep inspiration the glottis is closed and the muscles of expiration contract, compressing the lung and raising the intrapulmonary pressure above atmospheric pressure. The glottis then opens and gas is expelled at a rapid rate. A cough may be voluntary or reflex. The cough reflex is initiated by the irritation of nerve endings in the mucosa by dusts, chemicals, inflammation, or mucus. Rapid changes in airway volume with deep breaths stimulate other nerves in the wall of the airway and start another cough reflex. A cough, started by local irritation, will rapidly change the caliber of the airway and produce additional coughs. The infant and child have well-developed cough reflexes. A series of coughs following one inspiration is called a paroxysm and is common in pertussis and cystic fibrosis. When foreign bodies and excess mucus are present, coughing is useful. However, the rapid expiratory flow collapses and may obstruct the flabby airway of the young child. When there is no mucus or debris to be expelled, coughing may be harmful and suppression of the cough reflex helpful.

Hyperinflation. Since disease of the lower airway obstructs expiration more than inspiration, more gas enters than leaves the lung, and the volume of the lung at the end of expiration (functional residual capacity) enlarges. When overinflated, the chest is tympanitic on percussion, the anterior-posterior diameter of the chest is large, and the lungs appear radiolucent by x-ray. The term "emphysema" is frequently used to describe this type of overdistension. However, emphysema implies an irreversible process, and its use should be limited to degenerative disease characterized by irreversible breakdown of alveolar septa, decrease in pulmonary elastic tissue, and atrophy of bronchial walls. The enlargement of the lungs in asthma and bronchiolitis is *reversible* and should be called hyperinflation.

Hemoptysis. In most instances, blood in the upper airway comes from the oropharynx and esophagus. However, erosion of the airway by injury or inflammation, as occurs with foreign bodies, or inflammation as in cystic fibrosis, may cause bleeding.

Pain. Tissue damage from trauma, inflammation, or bacterial and viral invasion stimulates nerve endings by increasing tissue tension or releasing chemical agents. Irritation of the trachea and bronchi causes pain which can be abolished by vagotomy. Only the larynx, trachea, and major bronchi have sensory innervation; these nerves are probably present and functioning from birth.

Foreign bodies in the larynx and extrathoracic trachea cause continuous sharp pain in the anterior neck. Inflammation or foreign bodies in the intrathoracic trachea and large bronchi cause substernal sharp or aching pain, which is increased with coughing. The pain is usually referred to the ipsilateral side of the anterior chest wall and helps to localize the process.

Retractions. The nonrigid parts of the chest wall tend to balloon out when intrathoracic pressure is high and tend to retract when intrathoracic pressure is subatmospheric. Retraction of the sternum and suprasternal and intercostal spaces occurs during normal respiration in the small infant whose sternum and intercostal tissues are weak. In the older infant and child with a stronger chest wall, retractions reflect the large negative intrapleural pressures created during inspiration through an obstructed airway, or which are necessary to inflate a stiff or airless lung.

Secretions. Inflammation and the inhalation of particulate foreign matter, such as smoke, dusts, milk, or blood, increase the secretory activity of the mucous glands and goblet cells. The secretions are swept toward the mouth either by the action of the cilia or by coughing. Secretions clean the airway, but if abundant, they may block it. The infant's airways are small, and although the production of mucus may not be large, the likelihood of obstruction by mucus is great.

Circulatory Changes. The circulatory changes with obstruction vary with the magnitude of the respiratory effort and the degree of asphyxia. An increase in the depth and rate of breathing and anxiety causes tachycardia. Asphyxia may cause peripheral vasoconstriction, hypertension, and bradycardia or tachycardia depending upon the duration. Cyanosis and acidosis impair myocardial function and increase pulmonary vascular resistance, which increases right ventricle pressure and work. With chronic upper airway obstruction, as with greatly enlarged tonsils, pulmonary hypertension and cor pulmonale may occur. An increased work load for a damaged myocardium may lead to cardiac failure. Coughing raises the mean intrathoracic pressure, decreases venous return to the heart, lowers cardiac output, and may cause syncope. Prolonged coughing, as in pertussis, may raise the pressure in the superior vena cava and cause bleeding into the central nervous septum.

Acidosis and Dehydration. Severe airway obstruction impairs the elimination of the carbon dioxide formed by tissue metabolism. The $Paco_2$ (partial pressure of carbon dioxide in arterial blood) and the carbonic acid and hydrogen ion (H^+) concentrations rise and the pH falls. H^+ enters cells, potassium ions (K^+) leave, and the plasma K^+ and urinary excretion of K^+ increase, thus causing depletion of total body potassium. The kidneys respond to respiratory acidosis by increasing the tubular reabsorption of bicarbonate (HCO_3^-). The resulting increase in plasma HCO_3^- is "compensating" in the sense that the degree of acidosis is lessened. When the child's airway obstruction is removed or his ventilation assisted, the $Paco_2$ falls, pH rises, K^+ reenters cells and its concentration in plasma falls. However, a rapid decrease in $Paco_2$ when the plasma HCO_3^- concentration is high may cause a state of alkalosis. This may be striking if large amounts of additional HCO_3^- have been given. The low total and circulating K^+ impairs the renal excretion of HCO_3^- and delays the correction of the alkalosis. An abnormally high plasma HCO_3^- and pH may complicate the child's recovery in three ways: (1) respiration is inhibited and the time necessary to lower $Paco_2$ to normal is prolonged; (2) disconnecting the ventilator after controlled respiration may cause apnea; and (3) alkalosis may produce, as part of tetany, laryngeal spasm and bronchial constriction.

Many children with obstructive airway disease have an inadequate fluid intake and may lose weight because of a reduction in total body water, causing the circulating blood volume to decrease. Hypovolemia, acidemia, and hypoxemia constrict the vessels supplying muscle, skin, and kidney, decreasing the blood flow to these tissues. Hypoxemia and a regional reduction in perfusion decrease oxidative metabolism and increase lactic acid production. As a consequence, some degree of metabolic acidosis is present in most of these patients.

DIAGNOSTIC PROCEDURES. *Laryngoscopy and Bronchoscopy.* Visualization of the airway by laryngoscopy is useful in diagnosis of airway obstruction and is an essential procedure for the removal of foreign bodies. Laryngoscopy is not difficult. Bronchoscopy in infants and children requires great skill and must be done under general anesthesia, which suppresses coughing. The procedure irritates the upper airway, increases mucus production, and adds upper airway obstruction to lower airway disease. Premedication and atropine decrease bronchial secretion, relax bronchial smooth muscle, and may prevent postinstrumentation laryngospasm. A topical decongestant like Neo-Synephrine, systemic cortisone, and the breathing of warm moist air may limit the reaction. Careful suctioning and postural drainage following bronchoscopy are essential.

Radiography, Bronchography, Fluoroscopy. In children, anteroposterior and lateral films of the neck, while the arms are down and the back of the head is up and the neck extended, and posteroanterior films of the chest will show the shape of the air-filled larynx, trachea, or major bronchi and may reveal the sites of obstruction or distortion. Compression or exaggerated dilation of these structures with respiratory maneuvers can be determined with fluoroscopy; cinefluoroscopy is particularly useful, since the film can be viewed in slow motion.

If films and cinefluorography do not indicate the type and location of the obstruction, contrast material may be placed in the airway for visualization. An aqueous solution of propyliodone (Dionosil) is thick enough to cling to the walls of the airway, is rapidly removed by ciliary action, and is not very irritating. However, only small amounts should be injected, since an excess of Dionosil will occlude rather than outline the airway. Sufficient iodine may be absorbed to cause malaise, fever, and salivary gland swelling.

Most of the methods for the introduction of contrast material require general anesthesia. This has the disadvantages of suppressing the cough reflex and prohibiting spontaneous respiratory maneuvers. Local laryngeal anesthesia, used before supraglottic instillation of contrast material, may permit aspiration.

The conscious child can inhale nebulized Dionosil, although visualization of the smaller airways is difficult with this technique. However, with the development of ultrasonic nebulizers, particles of contrast material of appropriate size for reaching and settling on the small airways can now be made.

We have outlined the airways by injecting Dionisil through a polyethylene tube of small lumen which, after anesthetizing the larynx, was passed into the bronchi. More recently, we have used powdered tantalum. Nadel and his associates have described its use. It is nonirritating, does not obstruct, is rapidly cleared, and outlines the small airways with great clarity (see Fig 27).

Blood Gases, pH, Electrolytes. The pH, P_{CO_2}, HCO_3^-, and other electrolytes in blood drawn from a vein which drains a poorly perfused area of the body may reflect only severe regional hypoxemia and acidemia. Measurements of P_{aCO_2} and pH in venous blood do not indicate the efficiency of ventilation. An accurate assessment of ventilation, acid-base regulation, and the electrolyte changes which accompany acidosis and hypoxemia requires the analysis of arterial blood. Depending upon the age of the child, one of four sampling sites is usually available. In the young infant with a small amount of scalp tissue, the temporal artery is easily palpated and entered with a 23- or 24-gauge needle as described by Thomsen. In older infants and children, after local infiltration with 1 percent xylocaine, the femoral, brachial, or radial artery can be punctured with a 20-gauge Cournand needle or smaller regular needles. When a sample directly from an artery is unobtainable, arterialized capillary blood can be used. Warming a heel or finger in a water bath at 45° C for 20 minutes accelerates local blood flow so that the pH and blood gases of capillary and arterial samples are almost the same.

Microbiologic Samples. The identification of specific infectious agents includes appropriate sampling, isolation in culture, and presence of antibodies in the blood.

Organisms cultured from nasopharyngeal material may be responsible for upper but not for lower airway disease. There are numerous procedures for obtaining samples from the lower airway: collection of sputum; irritation of the larynx with a swab to provoke a cough; aspiration through a tracheal catheter, with or without tracheal lavage using normal saline; and direct puncture of the lung through the chest wall. This last procedure has been recommended by Klein in three groups of children: (1) the critically ill child in whom a specific etiologic diagnosis is of major importance to guide antimicrobial therapy; (2) the child who has deteriorated while on therapy and in whom an etiologic agent is not available from the usual upper respiratory tract culture; and (3) the child with pneumonia complicated by underlying disease or by drugs which limit normal host-defense mechanisms. In these circumstances the advantages of having a specific diagnosis are greater than the small risk from pneumothorax.

The isolation of a potentially pathogenic organism does not always mean that it is the cause of the disease, since many agents may be harmless inhabitants of the respiratory tract. An increase in antibodies to a specific bacterium or virus, as well as the isolation of an organism in culture, is desirable for diagnosis.

Pulmonary Function Tests. There are numerous tests of function available for assessing the amount of airway obstruction and the extent of the physiologic abnormality which the obstruction causes. The partial pressures of carbon dioxide and oxygen in arterial blood indicate whether ventilation is adequate and are essential measurements for the evaluation of the severity of the illness and the effectiveness of treatment. The measurement of dead space, functional residual capacity, the maximal volume of gas that can be expelled from the lungs by forceful effort after a maximal inspiration (the vital capacity), the resistance to gas flow through the airway (airway resistance), the maximal flow rates, and the maximal inspiratory and expiratory pressures all aid in establishment of the diagnosis and the objective evaluation of therapy.

The vital capacity and an analysis of the forced inspiratory and expiratory flow patterns require only a spirometer and a rapidly moving kymograph. These tests are simple, repeatable, and can easily be done in the office and at the bedside. With expiratory obstruction, the amount of gas in the lungs after a maximal expiration (residual volume) increases. As the residual volume enlarges, the vital capacity becomes smaller. The flow rates separate inspiratory and expiratory difficulties. Figure 19 illustrates the shape of the forced expiratory vital capacity and various types of analyses. The timed vital capacity and the maximal and midexpiratory flow rates measure the speed of pulmonary emptying and are delayed by obstruction on expiration. All of them, but particu-

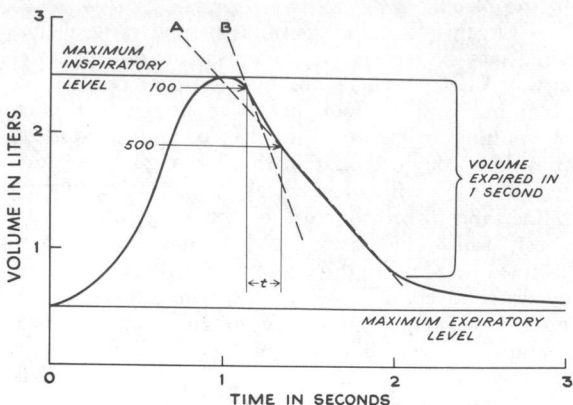

Fig. 19. This is the pattern of a forced expiration with four methods of analysis. (1) The 1-second timed vital capacity. The volume expired in 1 second divided by the vital capacity (in this example: 1.7 L/2.0 L = 85 percent). (2) The peak expiratory flow rate. Slope B parallels the rapid initial part of the expiration (Example: Volume expired in 0.05 second is 200 ml; flow rate is 240 L/minute). (3) The midexpiratory flow rate. Slope A parallels the slower mid portion of the expiration (Example: Volume expired in 0.1 second is 200 ml; flow rate is 120 L/minute). (4) The maximal expiratory flow rate. After the first 100 ml is expired, this is calculated from the time in seconds (t) needed to expire 0.5 L of gas (Example: t = 0.2 second; flow rate is 0.5 L × 60/0.2 = 150 L/minute).

larly the peak flow rate, are affected by the cooperation of the subject and the strength of the muscles of respiration and reflect the maximal expiratory force. Comroe et al. give a lucid and detailed description of these and other pulmonary function tests. Engström et al., Helliesen et al., DeMuth et al., and Weng and Levison provide normal values for most of these tests in children.

TREATMENT. The removal of obstruction and the maintenance of adequate ventilation are the primary goals of treatment. When a foreign body causes the obstruction, it is removed by aspiration; tumors, cysts, and other masses which occlude or compress the airway are excised. With other types of obstruction one or more of the following may be required.

Tracheal Intubation and Tracheotomy. Marked narrowing of the larynx by structural anomalies, spasm, or inflammation must be bypassed by introducing an endotracheal tube or by performing a tracheotomy; occasionally these procedures are also necessary for the adequate performance of positive pressure breathing devices. When the vital capacity and tidal volumes are very small, as in progressive severe bronchiectasis and chronic obliterative bronchitis, a tracheotomy may increase the efficiency of respiration by reducing the respiratory dead space. However, this drastic procedure should never be used to reduce dead space in acute diseases of the airways.

Tracheotomy has many complications: dislodgment of the tube during spasms of coughing; emphysema of the neck and mediastinum; pneumothorax; and the difficulty of decannulation. For laryngeal bypass during acute obstruction, the use of a nasotracheal tube as described by Allen and Steven appears preferable. This technique involves direct laryngoscopy and the passage of a tube made of some nonirritating material and of suitable size through one nostril into the pharynx, from which it is guided through the larynx. The child is lightly anesthetized. This is easily done even in the newborn.

Tracheotomies and endotracheal tubes impair the cleansing action of the mucous lining of the airway, make coughing difficult, and eliminate the filtering and air conditioning provided by the nose and the pharynx. Management must include the warming and moistening of inspired air and frequent suctioning of the trachea and bronchi. The method described by Segal for suctioning through an endotracheal tube is useful. During the procedure airway pressure is kept positive, which distends the airway and permits deeper suctioning without collapse of the bronchi. It also allows ventilation to continue during suctioning.

Tracheotomy or nasotracheal intubation may be lifesaving and should not be delayed when upper airway obstruction is severe and progressive.

Management of Secretions. When irritated, the epithelium of the airway releases large quantities of mucus which entraps foreign bodies and debris. If the amount of mucus does not exceed the capacity of the cilia to clear the airway, this reaction helps to maintain the patency of the bronchial tree. When production is too great, mucus adds to the obstruction; when too little is made, foreign bodies and inflammatory exudate block the airway; if the mucus is too thick, the cilia have difficulty moving it and the mucous stream is slowed. The slower the movement of mucus, the longer it is exposed to the gas which moves in and out of the airway. The mucus dehydrates, becomes more viscid, and slows further. If gas flow is rapid, dehydration is accelerated. Dehydrated and moving slowly, the mucus forms crusts, and the underlying cilia are destroyed. The aim of expectorant therapy is to balance the quality and quantity of mucus against the capacity of coughing and ciliary action to remove it.

Coughing. Coughing accelerates the movement of accumulated mucus, and cough reflexes should not be depressed except when there is little mucus to be evacuated. Coughing also aggravates the obstruction. Codeine (0.5 mg/kg of body weight repeated three to four times a day) suppresses the cough reflexes but also depresses respiration. Drugs like dextromethorphan (0.5 mg/kg of body weight repeated three to four times a day) are just as effective antitussive agents, do not depress respiration, and are not addictive. Mild exercise, change in position, and deep breaths may initiate coughing. They also make coughing more effective by freeing aggregations of mucus from the bronchial walls.

Postural drainage. Gravity speeds the flow of mucus from the upper lobe bronchi when the patient is sitting or standing. By varying the position of the chest in relation to the mouth, drainage of the other major bronchi can also be facilitated by gravity. The use of postural drainage is of particular usefulness in removing localized intrabronchial obstructions. When mucous obstruction is generalized, the child should be placed for 5 to 10 minutes in each of the various positions necessary for optimal drainage of the major bronchi.

Alteration of the viscosity of mucus. Belladonna and its derivatives decrease secretory activity and ciliary motion and increase the viscosity of the mucous blanket. Antihistaminics are weakly parasympatholytic and have the same action. These drugs may be useful in upper airway disease, but their use in lower airway disease should be restricted to the control of the irritation which accompanies bronchoscopy.

To prevent drying of mucus, the larynx and trachea should be kept warm and moist when airflow is rapid, as it is in all obstructive diseases. Numerous vaporizers and croup tents are available for this purpose. When mucus production is low and mucus is thick, tenacious, or crusted, it is more easily expelled by coughing and moved by cilia if it is diluted. Secretions in the lower airway may be moistened by inhaling an aerosol with droplets of a suitable size for deposition in smaller airways (about 5 μ). The use of an aerosol of one-half normal sodium chloride is reported to be particularly helpful and is widely used to liquefy the sticky secretions which accumulate in cystic fibrosis of the lungs. It is said to be most effective in children with this disease when delivered by an ultrasonic nebulizer all night, every night. Not everyone agrees that nebulized or aerosilized saline solutions are beneficial in the treatment of obstructive airway disease and there is some evidence that they may be harmful.

Potassium iodide given orally (5 mg/kg body weight in milk every 3 to 4 hours) produces bronchorrhea and may thereby decrease the viscosity of mucus.

Among other agents whose action is said to decrease the viscosity of mucous secretions are crystalline trypsin, desoxyribonuclease, streptokinase, hyaluronidase, lysozyme, acetylcysteine, and pimetine hydrochloride. Some of these drugs are effective in fibrin lysis, others split disulfide bonds, but only lysozyme clearly dissolves normal mucus. There is no convincing evidence that any of them affect the thick secretions of chronic airway diseases such as bronchiectasis. Some, if not all, of them irritate the mucosa, cause smooth muscle constriction, and increase obstruction.

Bronchodilators. Since the smooth muscle of the airways has tone, the inhalation of bronchodilator aerosols decreases airway resistance by about 25 percent, even in individuals with normal lungs. Bronchodilation is useful in all lower airway diseases where the normal tone is augmented by irritation with foreign bodies, dusts, chemicals, cold air, and inflammation. Drugs which relax bronchial smooth muscle can be given orally, intracutaneously, subcutaneously, intramuscularly, intravenously, or introduced locally into the respiratory tract as an aerosol.

Epinephrine (0.01 ml/kg intradermally or 0.02 ml/kg subcutaneously of a 1:1,000 solution every 2 to 3 hours) is a potent bronchodilator, but it also has a slight constrictor effect on the pulmonary arterioles, increase systolic blood pressure, widens the pulse pressure, increases cardiac work, and may decrease ciliary activity and the production of mucus. It should be used with caution in the asphyxiated child, whose circulating endogenous catecholamines are increased and whose circulation is already stressed.

Ephedrine (0.5 mg/kg orally every 4 to 6 hours) is the best bronchodilator for oral administration. It relaxes bronchial smooth muscle slightly less than epinephrine, but its action is more sustained. It is not as vigorous a constrictor of the pulmonary arterioles, it does not depress ciliary motion, and its effect on secretory mechanisms is not prominent. Because of its central nervous excitatory effect, it is often combined with phenobarbital.

Aminophylline (10 mg/kg orally every 4 to 6 hours or 3 to 5 mg/kg every 8 hours intravenously) is less effective than ephedrine and epinephrine as a bronchodilator, but it has a less striking effect on the circulation and probably decreases pulmonary arteriolar resistance. It may be effective when epinephrine is not. It is frequently combined with ephedrine and phenobarbital in the treatment of asthma. However, it causes gastrointestinal irritation which prevents its use over long periods of time. Intravenous aminophylline may decrease airway resistance dramatically. However, it is necessary to continue treatment in order to prevent recurrence. Aminophylline should *not* be given as a suppository since its absorption is erratic and deaths associated with gastrointestinal bleeding, extreme hyperpyrexia, and shock have been reported from its administration in this manner.

Isoproterenol (5 drops of a 1:200 solution in 1 ml of saline as an aerosol three to four times a day) is the most effective bronchodilator for local administration. It is a congener of epinephrine with an increase in inhibitory and a decrease in excitatory sympathetic activity. It causes marked dilation of bronchial smooth muscle, decreases pulmonary vascular resistance, stimulates the myocardium, and increases cardiac output. But, since it dilates the renal, mesenteric, femoral, and pulmonary vascular beds, it does not increase blood pressure. An isoproterenol aerosol should contain particles small enough to reach the small bronchioles (less than 5 μ) but large enough to coalesce into drops (greater than 2 μ) which can fall onto the wall of the airway. While holding his nose and breathing through his mouth, the patient empties his lungs. He then slowly breathes in the aerosol mixture, from a nebulizer held in his mouth, to his maximum inspiratory capacity and holds his breath for five seconds. He repeats the maneuver four to six times or until there is a paroxysm of coughing or evidence of systemic drug effect

1282 CH. 19: THE PULMONARY SYSTEM

such as tachycardia. The slow, maximal inspiration is important to assure delivery of the drug to poorly ventilated airways; breath-holding allows time for droplets to form and settle onto the bronchial walls. This is a difficult maneuver for children under five years. When obstruction is severe and ventilation rapid, aerosols may not be effective, but intravenous isoproterenol is usually very effective. It is administered by continuous intravenous infusion in a starting dose of 0.1 μg/kg/minute. Heart rate and blood pressure should be closely monitored. If the heart rate exceeds 200 per minute, or if the blood pressure decreases significantly, the rate of administration should be decreased.

Decongestants. *Phenylephrine* (Neo-Synephrine—1 drop of a 1 percent solution per kilogram every 3 to 4 hours) increases systolic and diastolic blood pressure, decreases heart rate, constricts the pulmonary arteries, does not change cardiac output, but increases cardiac work. It has only weak bronchodilator activity; however, delivered locally it is a good decongestant. As an aerosol it relieves lower airway obstruction by decreasing mucosal edema. It is often included in the mixtures which are vaporized and blown over young children in croup tents.

Anti-Inflammatory Agents. Hydrocortisone (2 mg/kg orally in divided doses), or equivalent doses of other corticosteroids, suppresses the reactivity of connective tissue to injury, inhibits fibroblast formation, probably blocks the constriction of bronchial smooth muscle by histamine, and reduces edema. Its anti-inflammatory action could benefit most forms of obstruction associated with inflammation. Four to six hours elapse between administration of hydrocortisone and its maximum action. Antibiotics should also be given when it is used in conditions in which bacterial infection may be present. Inflammation is a more important cause of obstruction in the young infant than bronchoconstriction. The anti-inflammatory action of cortisone is particularly useful in increasing the size of the airway lumen in this age group.

Oxygen. When hypoxemia and cyanosis are present, increasing the oxygen concentration in inspired gas will reduce anxiety and the forceful inspiratory or expiratory efforts which augment obstruction, decrease the work of breathing, decrease pulmonary vascular resistance, and improve cardiovascular function. An inspired oxygen concentration of 30 to 100 percent may be necessary to bring oxygen partial pressure in arterial blood to normal levels and remove the symptoms of oxygen lack.

There are several methods for delivering oxygen to children, the choice depending upon the amount needed. A tent has a large volume and many leaks, and even at high flow rates, an oxygen concentration of 40 percent is rarely achieved; oxygen flowing at 4 to 5 L/minute through a 4- to 5-L plastic hood placed over an infant's head will produce a concentration of close to 100 percent; oxygen flowing

through a nasal catheter into the nasopharynx at 4 L/minute will provide a concentration of about 50 percent; the inspired gas may be 100 percent if a tight-fitting oxygen mask is used. Since cold, dry oxygen is irritating, it should be warmed and moistened, regardless of the mode of delivery.

Oxygen breathing may depress respiration and aggravate respiratory acidosis. On the other hand, a decrease in pulmonary arteriolar constriction may permit greater pulmonary blood flow to some units which had been ventilated but not perfused. This increases elimination of carbon dioxide even though total ventilation may be decreased. Oxygen therapy in infants with acute airway obstruction usually causes a fall in arterial carbon dioxide by reducing anxiety, decreasing forceful respiration, and improving the circulation. In any event, since the prompt use of mechanical respirators can correct hypoventilation, oxygen should not be withheld from any child with hypoxemia.

Normal adults breathing 100 percent oxygen for prolonged periods of time may develop tracheobronchitis, fatigue, and vomiting. Although inhaling 50 percent oxygen for long periods of time eliminates these symptoms of oxygen toxicity, the possibility that they may occur with 100 percent oxygen should not preclude its use when necessary. Atelectasis is more apt to occur if the gas trapped behind an obstruction of the lower airway is 100 percent oxygen rather than 80 percent nitrogen. However, as the child recovers, spontaneous deep breaths and sighs are usually sufficient to correct this.

Fluids and Electrolytes. Small amounts of water should be offered frequently during acute obstruction, and generous quantities of warm broth and fruit juices at room temperature should be provided after removal of the obstruction; 100 ml/kg of fluid per day usually prevents dehydration. Children in whom acute laryngotracheitis, bronchitis, asthma, and bronchiolitis cause severe respiratory distress should be given 5 percent glucose in 0.5 normal saline by vein (100 ml/kg/day). Sodium bicarbonate should be added to intravenous solutions in an amount sufficient to correct acidosis. A pH of 7.25 or less should always be raised by infusing bicarbonate. As ventilation improves, calcium gluconate (250 mg/kg/day) and potassium chloride (1 mEq/kg/day) should be added to the oral or intravenous fluids.

Sedation. The use of sedatives in the treatment of obstructive airway disease in children has usually been condemned, since they depress the respiratory center and tend to decrease respiration. However, one of the objects of therapy is to reduce the force and speed of inspiration and expiration and limit the airway collapse, which in children may be a more significant cause of obstruction than the primary blockage. Sedatives, by relieving anxiety and slightly depressing respiration, will diminish the rate of airflow but will often increase minute volume.

Phenobarbital (1 mg/kg every 4 to 6 hours) depresses respiratory drive and relieves anxiety. *Meprobamate* (10 mg/kg every 6 hours), *ethanol* (1 ml of a 40 to 50 percent solution/kg), and *chloral hydrate* (50 mg/kg every 8 hours) are excellent drugs for controlling anxiety and have only a minor effect on ventilation. *Aspirin* (10 mg/kg every 4 hours) depresses the cortex and may allay anxiety, but it stimulates the medullary center and stimulates respiration.

Direct Instillations into the Trachea. Although tracheal lavage and suction through an endotracheal tube may mobilize tenacious mucus and help clear the airway, the procedure usually requires a general anesthetic and is not easily repeated. However, if a tracheotomy or endotracheal tube is in place for long periods of time, periodic lavage with normal saline can be carried out. The specific treatment of *Pseudomonas* and fungal infections is often done best by delivering appropriate antibiotics directly onto the walls of the airways through an endobronchial tube.

When an endotracheal tube is unnecessary for ventilation, local bronchial medication and normal saline can be introduced through an indwelling tracheobronchial catheter placed as described under methods for bronchography. These small polyethylene catheters are immobilized with adhesive tape and left plugged except when antimicrobial drugs or saline are introduced. They have been left in place for months without difficulty.

Assisted Ventilation. If the child tires and arterial CO_2 tension rises, positive pressure can be used to assist ventilation by an apparatus which is attached to a tightly fitting mask over the child's face or to a cuffed endotracheal tube. Children usually tolerate a mask if they are properly sedated; if an endotracheal tube is used, they must usually be heavily sedated or anesthetized. The amount of dead space between the airway and the source of fresh air must be small, bearing in mind that the child's dead space is about 1 ml per pound of body weight. If the dead space of the mask and attachments approaches the volume of the child's dead space, the effectiveness of ventilation for CO_2 removal will be impaired, and arterial CO_2 tension will rise even though oxygenation is adequate. If the arterial P_{CO_2} rises to 60 mm Hg, ventilation should be assisted.

Radford, Ferris, and Kreite's nomogram gives the frequency and tidal volume necessary to provide a basal minute volume for children of various sizes. However, most positive pressure ventilators are designed to deliver a given pressure and not a fixed volume, and there is no guarantee that high pressure will affect an adequate minute volume. Pressure, rate, and flow should be set to provide sufficient alveolar gas exchange to keep the arterial CO_2 at normal levels. Frequent measurement of arterial P_{CO_2} is necessary to assure adequate performance.

REFERENCES

AIRWAY ANATOMY AND FUNCTION

American Physiological Society. Washington, D.C. Handbook of Physiology, Sec. 3: Fenn, W. O., and Rahn, H., eds. Respiration. Baltimore, Williams & Wilkins Co., 1964, Vol. I, II.

Avery, M. E. Mechanics of respiration. *In* Fomon, S., ed. Normal and Abnormal Respiration in Children, Report 37th Ross Conf. on Pediatric Research. Columbus, Ohio, Ross Laboratories, 1961, pp. 15-46.

Bucher, U., and Reid, L. Development of the mucus-secreting elements in human lung. Thorax, 16:219, 1961.

Butler, J., Caro, C. G., Alcala, R., and DuBois, A. B. Physiological factors affecting airway resistance in normal subjects and in patients with obstructive respiratory disease. J. Clin. Invest., 39:584, 1960.

Comroe, J. H., Jr. Physiology of Respiration. Chicago, Year Book Publishers, 1965.

Cudmore, R. E., Emery, J. L., and Mithal, A. Postnatal growth of the bronchi and bronchioles. Arch. Dis. Child., 37:481, 1962.

Engel, S. Lung Structure. Springfield, Ill., Charles C Thomas Co., 1962.

Loosli, C. G., and Potter, E. L. Pre- and postnatal development of the respiratory portion of the human lung. Amer. Rev. Resp. Dis., 80:5(Suppl.), 1959.

Miller, W. S. The Lung, 2nd ed. Springfield, Ill., Charles C Thomas Co., 1947.

Scammon, R. E. The respiratory system. *In* Abt, I. A., ed. Pediatrics, 1st ed. Philadelphia, W. B. Saunders Co., 1923, Vol. 1, pp. 335-352.

von Hayek, H. The Human Lung. New York, Hafner Publishing Co., 1960.

Walker, J. E. C., and Wells, R. E., Jr. Heat and water exchange in the respiratory tract. Amer. J. Med., 30:259, 1961.

DIAGNOSIS AND TREATMENT FOR OBSTRUCTION

Allen, T. H., and Steven, I. M. Prolonged endotracheal intubation in infants and children. Brit. J. Anaesth., 37:566, 1965.

Avery, M. E., Galina, M., and Nachman, R. Mist therapy, Pediatrics, 39:160, 1967.

Briscoe, W. A., and DuBois, A. B. The relationship between airway resistance, airway conductance and lung volume in subjects of different age and body size. J. Clin. Invest., 37:1279, 1958.

Comroe, J. H., Jr., Forster, R. E., II, DuBois, A. B., Briscoe, W. A., and Carlsen, E. The Lung, 2nd ed. Chicago, Year Book Publishers, 1962.

Dautrebande, L. Physiological and pharmacological characteristics of liquid aerosols. Physiol. Rev., 32:214, 1952.

DeMuth, G. R., Howatt, W. F., and Hill, B. The growth of lung function. Part V. Forced flow rates. Pediatrics, 35:200 (Suppl.), 1965.

Engström, I., Karlberg, P., and Kraepelien, S. Respiratory studies in children. I. Lung volumes in healthy children 6-14 years of age. Acta Paediat. Scand., 45:277, 1956.

Farinas, P. L. Bronchography by atomization. Radiology, 51:491, 1948.

Harter, J. G., Reddy, W. J., and Thorn, G. W. Studies on an intermittent corticosteroid dosage regimen. New Eng. J. Med., 269:591, 1963.

Helliesen, P. J., Cook, C. D., Friedlander, L., and Agathon, S. Studies of respiratory physiology in children. I. Mechanics of respiration and lung volumes in 85 normal children 5 to 17 years of age. Pediatrics, 22: 80, 1958.

Klein, J. O. Diagnostic lung puncture in the pneumonias of infants and children. Pediatrics, 44:486, 1969.

Marshall, R. The physical properties of the lungs in relation to the subdivisions of lung volume. Clin. Sci., 16:507, 1957.

Modell, J. H., Smith, B. E., Williams, D., Weibley, T. C., and Jalowayski, A. Tolerance of mice to ultrasonic aerosol exposure. Amer. J. Dis. Child., 115:322, 1967.

Moffet, H. L. Bacteria recovered from distilled water and inhalation therapy equipment. Amer. J. Dis. Child., 114:7, 1967.

Myers, R. N., Shearburn, E. W., and Haupt, G. J. Prevention and management of pulmonary complications by percutaneous polyethylene tube tracheostomy. Amer. J. Surg., 109:590, 1965.

Nadel, J. A., Wolfe, W. G., Graf, P. D., Youker, J. E., Zamel, N., Austin, J. H. M., Hinchcliffe, W. A., Greenspan, R. H., and Wright, R. R. Powdered tantalum: a new contrast medium for roentgenographic examination of human airways. New Eng. J. Med., 283:281, 1970.

Nolke, A. C. Severe toxic effects from aminophylline and theophylline suppositories in children. J.A.M.A., 161:693, 1956.

Radford, E. P., Jr., Ferris, B. G., Jr., and Kriete, B. C. Clinical use of a nomogram to estimate proper ventilation during artificial respiration. New Eng. J. Med., 251:877, 1954.

Segal, S. Endobronchial pressure as an aid to tracheobronchial aspiration. Pediatrics, 35:305, 1965.

Thomsen, A. Arterial blood sampling in small infants. Acta Paediat. Scand., 53:237, 1964.

Waring, W. W., and Killelea, D. E. Bronchography in infants and children. I. A non-fluoroscopic technique. Pediatrics, 30:378, 1962.

Weng, T-R., and Levison, H. Standards of pulmonary function in children. Amer. Rev. Resp. Dis., 99:879, 1969.

Whittenberger, J. L., ed. Artificial Respiration: Theory and Applications. New York, Hoeber Med. Div., Harper & Row, 1962.

19.4
SPECIFIC DISEASES CAUSING OBSTRUCTION

Inspiratory Obstruction

Inspiratory stridor, hoarseness, and suprasternal and intracostal retractions are the signs of partial obstruction of the larynx and extrathoracic trachea. If the obstruction is severe, agitation, cyanosis, acidosis, and circulatory collapse also occur. The principal goals of therapy are removal of the obstruction, alleviation of cyanosis, correction of acidosis, and support of the circulation.

Structural Defects

LARYNGEAL APLASIA. There were only 16 cases of this anomaly reported to 1965. If the infant is born alive, there are vigorous inspiratory efforts and marked cyanosis. The only treatment is immediate tracheotomy.

TRACHEAL APLASIA. This is an even rarer anomaly, with nine cases reported to 1963. It is a hopeless condition, unless the aplasia is limited to the upper trachea or is associated with a tracheoesophageal fistula, when tracheotomy may be lifesaving.

LARYNGEAL STENOSIS. Congenital stenosis, due to thickening of the subglottal structures 2 to 3 mm below the true cord, is usually due to anomalies of the cricoid cartilage. It causes severe inspiratory and expiratory stridor and the usual signs of obstruction, from birth. A tracheotomy is usually necessary, and since the stenotic cartilage may not grow, a permanent tracheostomy may be required.

TRACHEAL STENOSIS. There were 23 cases of this anomaly reported by 1957: 12 were caused by regional absence of the membranous part of the trachea, with the tracheal cartilages forming a complete small ring; the other cases were associated with absent or incomplete cartilaginous rings. Inspiratory stridor occurs with extrathoracic stenosis; inspiratory and expiratory stridor accompany intrathoracic stenosis. The symptoms are present from birth. If there is a cartilaginous ring present and the stenotic segment is short, it should be excised. Regional areas of weakness due to cartilaginous insufficiency become strengthened by stiffening as the infant grows and obstruction disappears.

LARYNGEAL WEB. Persistent fusion of the developing glottis produces this more common problem. The web, which may be very thin or moderately thick, usually extends between the vocal cords across the anterior quarter to two-thirds of the glottis. When it covers the entire larynx, it represents an emergency. The newborn makes vigorous inspiratory efforts but rapidly becomes cyanotic; and if he is to survive, the web must be perforated immediately. If the obstruction is moderate, repeated dilatation of the larynx is sufficient for correction. While inspiratory stridor is present from birth, it may vary in severity, since the web may intermittently swell and the obstruction wax and wane.

LARYNGOMALACIA (CONGENITAL LARYNGEAL STRIDOR). This is a relatively common condition in which the weak laryngeal structure of the newborn is exaggerated and causes more than the usual amount of collapse with inspiration. Stridor is present from birth and may be consistent or intermittent, depending upon the vigor of inspiration and the position of the child. There is often a pectus excavatum, which is usually transient and may be due to the newborn's relatively compliant sternum, which is pulled dorsally during a vigorous inspiration. The epiglottis appears curled and is drawn down into the larynx with inspiration. Specific therapy is usually not necessary, since the larynx strengthens with age and symptoms disappear by the first or second year of life. Upper respiratory infections or other conditions which may cause only a minor degree of obstruction, but which will cause an acceleration of inspiratory airflow and promote laryngeal collapse, aggravate the obstruction and should be treated with sedation, decongestants, and, if appropriate, antibiotics.

TRACHEOMALACIA.   This condition may be regional or generalized. When there is local delay in development of tracheal cartilages or other structural support, there will be a functional stenosis which obstructs inspiration if it is in the upper part of the trachea, or obstructs expiration if it occurs in the lower half of the trachea. The involved tracheal rings may harden with age, but resection may be required. Generalized tracheomalacia produces severe obstruction when there are other causes of partial proximal airways obstruction such as upper respiratory infection; these should be treated vigorously. There is no specific treatment for generalized tracheomalacia, which is usually self-limited.

TRAUMA.   Vocal cord paralysis following birth injury, local surgery, or other injury and dislocation of the cricothyroid or the cricoarytenoid articulations at birth or later may lead to marked inspiratory obstruction.

Tumors

Laryngeal papillomas and fibroleiomyomas, and tracheal leiomyomas and adenocarcinomas occur in childhood. The signs and symptoms of obstruction depend on the size of the tumor and the size and strength of the larynx related to the age of the child. These tumors require surgical excision.

There are 20 cases of subglottic hemagiomas reported. These are frequently associated with angiomas elsewhere. Signs and symptoms are intermittent, depending upon the degree of vascular engorgement. Hydrocortisone may cause a striking improvement. They also respond to irradiation, but this may cause laryngeal damage. Tracheotomy is often necessary.

Compression by External Masses

Cystic masses, such as cystic hygroma and lingual cysts; tumors, such as teratoma of the tonsil and nasopharyngeal angiofibroma; and oropharyngeal abscesses may obstruct the glottis. These must be removed surgically. Micrognathia, macroglossia, and glossoptosis may also obstruct the airway above the glottis (see Sec. 28.3). These may be so severe that the tongue

must be sutured forward or a tracheostomy performed. Large tonsils and adenoids occasionally cause inspiratory obstruction and may cause severe hypoventilation and cor pulmonale.

Thyroglossal duct cysts and thyroid adenomas and teratomas may obstruct the trachea.

Metabolic Disorders

Rickets with tetany or other metabolic problems associated with hypocalcemia or alkalosis promote laryngeal constriction and obstruction of the upper airway, which responds to calcium treatment.

Laryngeal Abscess

This is a rare complication of infections of the larynx and of the neck, usually streptococcal in origin. The abscess forms in the areolar tissue anterior to the epiglottis between it and the hyothyroid membrane. There is progressive dyspnea and aphonia, retraction of the neck, and a palpable mass in the midline above the thyroid cartilage which moves with the larynx. Aspiration and drainage are indicated.

Inflammation

CROUP.   Croup is usually a benign condition which occurs in infants and young children between 6 months and 3 years of age. In some children, who seem particularly susceptible, it is recurrent. Croup is usually preceded by an upper respiratory infection. The first symptoms—a barking cough associated with inspiratory stridor and marked retractions—usually occur at night. The patient awakes with extreme anxiety and attempts violent inspiratory efforts. The symptoms continue for three or four days, being most prominent at night. The amount of laryngeal obstruction, as judged from the symptoms, may be marked, although the degree of inflammation and edema of the larynx is not striking. The inflammation is probably infectious; hemadsorption virus I and II of the myxovirus group have been isolated in some cases (Sec. 14.31).

Treatment in most cases includes only inhalation of warm moist air, sedation, and decongestants. Differentiation from potentially serious bacterial infections is not always made readily, and in some circumstances antibiotics are indicated. Cold air, moist or dry, aggravates the obstruction.

Case I: *M. C., a 6-year-old male, had a two-day history of clear nasal discharge and mild coughing. On the second night of the illness he awoke with a barking cough. Within three hours he was restless, and inspiratory stridor was prominent. By morning his symptoms were less troublesome, and pulmonary function studies were performed. His vital capacity was small, his inspiratory flow rate was low during*

TABLE 7.   *Croup (M.C.)*

		During Disease	One Week After Recovery
Vital capacity (% normal)		55	110
Functional residual capacity (% normal)		110	100
Arterial blood gas tensions (mm Hg)	Po$_2$ (rest)	70	100
	Po$_2$ (coughing)	50	
	Pco$_2$ (rest)	50	36
	Pco$_2$ (coughing)	58	
Expiratory flow rates (% normal)	Maximal effort	80	90
	Moderate effort	100	100
Inspiratory flow rates (% normal)	Maximal effort	25	80
	Moderate effort	50	100

a normal inspiration and strikingly reduced with a forced inspiration, and his expiratory flow rate was normal (Table 7). The partial pressure of oxygen (Pao$_2$) was low, and the partial pressure of carbon dioxide in arterial blood (Paco$_2$) was high during quiet breathing—hypercarbia and hypoxemia were accentuated by coughing. He was given sedation and a cough suppressant containing codeine and placed in a croup tent with moist, warm air. His symptoms, which were most marked at night, persisted for three days. One week following recovery his vital capacity and his blood gases and flow rates during quiet and forced breathing were normal. The low inspiratory and normal expiratory flow rates indicated that the obstruction was inspiratory and located in the extrathoracic airway. Codeine and sedation helped to limit the additional obstruction caused by coughing and maximal inspiratory efforts.

CHRONIC LARYNGITIS.   A catarrhal inflammation of the larynx may persist for many months in the presence of chronic infection in the nose or paranasal sinuses. Enlargement of the adenoids is usually associated. Removal of the focus of infection is often followed by prompt disappearance of the laryngeal symptoms. Other causes of chronic laryngitis are tuberculosis, syphilis, neoplasm, and foreign body.

Tuberculous laryngitis is rare in young children; it is usually associated with advanced pulmonary disease and often with tracheitis. The symptoms are in no way characteristic, but ragged ulcerations can be seen with the laryngoscope; the ulcerations are superficial as contrasted with those found in adults. Tubercle bacilli are found in the gastric washings.

Syphilitic laryngitis is common in early congenital syphilis. There is nothing characteristic about the laryngitis clinically except its protracted course. The inflammation is a catarrhal one.

EPIGLOTTITIS.   This life-threatening disease occurs in children of all ages but is most severe in the young infant. After a one- or two-day history of upper respiratory infection, the child may develop progressively severe inspiratory stridor and hoarseness associated with a moderate fever. The symptoms become more severe over two to three days and are not usually more marked at night. When the inflammation is caused by bacteria, the course is fulminating; and the progress from stridor to life-threatening obstruction is rapid. The temperature rises to 102° to 104° F, and dyspnea becomes striking. There is usually a leucocytosis, predominantly polymorphonuclear in type. There are reddening and swelling of the mucous membranes of the epiglottis and glottis, with thick superficial secretions. The appearance of the larynx is similar to that seen after exposure to flame and smoke. *H. influenzae* type B is the most common cause, but pneumococci, streptococci, and staphylococci may be responsible.

When the disease is caused by a virus the signs and symptoms are less fulminating but are similar to those caused by bacterial inflammation. There is usually less fever and leucocytosis. Viral inflammation is primarily subglottal and produces an obstructing fibrinous exudate on the tracheal wall. Influenza, parainfluenza, ECHO, adeno, and respiratory syncytial viruses have been isolated from patients with laryngotracheitis.

An environment which is warm and moistened is necessary in all cases; oxygen is required when symptoms are severe and cyanosis present. Fluid and electrolytes must be provided intravenously when obstruction is marked. Digitalis is useful when cardiac function is inadequate. Since bacterial and viral infections are difficult to distinguish clinically, all treatment programs should include an antibiotic. Ampicillin, effective against *H. influenzae*, is probably the best agent.

Since the accompanying anxiety and vigorous inspiratory efforts augment the obstruction, mild sedation may be given. However, great care must be taken not to depress the patient excessively. There is considerable controversy on the use of corticosteroids. However, the weight of evidence indicates they are not efficacious. Nasotracheal intubation or tracheotomy is mandatory in any case of rapidly increasing obstruction which is not relieved by more conservative therapy.

Lower Airway Obstruction

Figure 20 shows some of the mechanisms which cause obstruction. Foreign bodies, inflammation, or edema may occlude the airway. In addition, the child's poorly supported large airways collapse normally during a forced expiration (Fig. 17), as with crying and when expired gas flow is accelerated in order to pass a partially occluded segment of the large bronchi. If the lumina of the smaller airways narrow, gas flow accelerates through the small bronchi, the pressure difference across the walls of the larger bronchi increases, and the force tending to buckle the walls is greater (see Fig. 18).

After complete obstruction of an airway, there is absorption of gas distal to the blockage. Depending upon the location of the block, atelectasis may include a respiratory bronchiole and its alveolar ducts and alveoli or a mainstem bronchus and the whole lung. Usually pulmonary blood flow to the occluded unit decreases or stops within 24 hours. Initially, the involved segment of the lung is small and, in some instances, such as asthma, may remain so. In patients with blockage due to a foreign body, after a few days the atelectatic area may enlarge as it fills with mucus. Deprived of blood flow and the cleansing action of the cilia and mucous lining, infection flourishes in the mass of accumulating mucus. Abscesses may form or chronic inflammation may slowly erode and destroy the wall of the airway, causing bronchiectasis. Weeks after occlusion, blood flow increases through the atelectatic segment and the mucus becomes absorbed.

Partial obstruction causes air trapping. If the obstruction is generalized as in asthma, bronchitis, or bronchiolitis, there will be uniform hyperinflation.

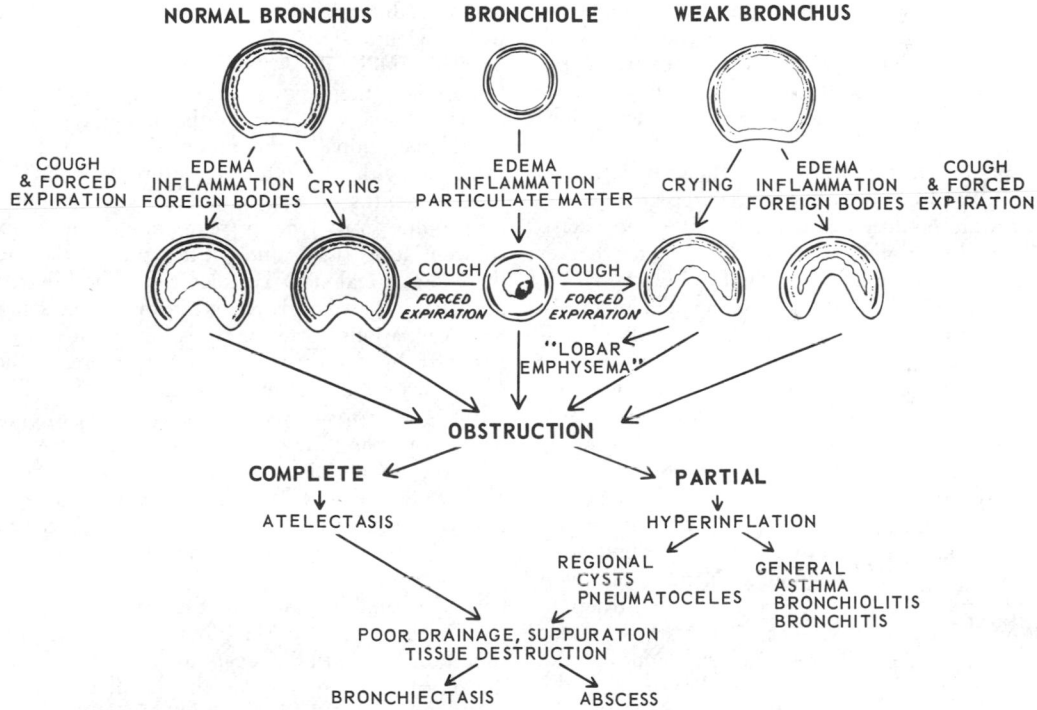

Fig. 20. A scheme showing some of the factors which cause obstruction and the consequences of the obstruction. The child's bronchus has proportionately little intrinsic support (normal bronchus). Segments or all of the bronchi in some children may be particularly weak (weak bronchus). Partial occlusion of the bronchioles increases the velocity of gas flow and provokes coughing; the pressure difference across the wall of the bronchi becomes greater and the bronchial walls buckle. The weak bronchus buckles more than the normal one. Crying and primary bronchial occlusion also invaginate the walls of the bronchi. Obstruction is either complete or partial—if complete the lung becomes atelectatic; if partial the lung becomes hyperinflated. A small, weak segment of bronchus may collapse with forced or even normal expiration and overdistend a lobe or smaller subdivision of the lung causing idiopathic lobar emphysema. Asthma, bronchiolitis, and bronchitis partially occlude most of the airway structures and cause generalized hyperinflation. If a bronchiole is partially blocked, cystic dilation of the structures distal to the block may occur producing cysts or pneumatoceles. If these become infected, abscesses may be formed. Areas of the lung with partially or completely obstructed airways drain poorly and become infected. If the process is long standing, suppuration and bronchiectasis may develop.

If the obstruction is localized, the lung distal to the obstruction will expand, and occasionally cystic lesions may develop which may become infected.

In all of these conditions, if the bronchus is less sturdy than normal because of regional anomalies, delayed maturation, or destructive processes, expiratory obstruction is accentuated.

Aspiration

In a review of over 1,000 cases of endobronchial foreign bodies, Hollinger lists the following objects as most commonly found: bones (20 percent), hardware (15 percent), nuts (14 percent), coins (14 percent), and safety pins (11 percent).

When the trachea, major bronchi, and their subdivisions divide, one of the two divisions is larger. The angle of take-off of the smaller branch is more acute than that of the larger. Large inspired particles tend to follow the path of the larger subdivisions and lodge in the lower lobe of the right lung. In the infant with diaphragmatic breathing, the lumina of the ventral and lateral bronchi are narrow, while the basilar bronchi are wide. As a consequence, foreign bodies most frequently occlude the superior, lateral, and basilar segments of the right lobe; they occlude the basilar and lateral segments of the left lower lobe less often.

Inspiration distributes small particles in a random manner. Large foreign bodies block large airways and cause acute respiratory distress, with either atelectasis or localized hyperinflation, depending upon whether the occlusion is complete or partial. There is an explosive onset of coughing and dyspnea. Hemoptysis, purulent sputum, fever, and leucocytosis develop if the foreign body lacerates the airway or if there is infection. If there is partial obstruction and overdistension, the unit may rupture, causing mediastinal emphysema or pneumothorax. Foreign bodies rarely erode into the interstitial space and produce mediastinal emphysema. If the foreign bodies are radiopaque, they are easily diagnosed by x-ray and can be removed by bronchoscopy. Nuts and other nonopaque material are less easily diagnosed. Peanuts, pumpkin seeds, and popcorn often cause partial obstruction. Infants who have inhaled these items often present with acute respiratory distress, hyperinflation of the ipsilateral lung with shift of the mediastinum to the contralateral side. *Small children should not be given peanuts, pumpkin seeds, or popcorn.*

Smaller foreign bodies block small bronchi, and a mild cough may be the only symptom. However, if not treated, fever, cough with the production of purulent sputum, and the other symptoms of pulmonary suppuration occur. Indeed, these are often the first indication of a previous aspiration. Inhaled vegetable matter is particularly likely to produce a local inflammatory reaction and distal infection with abscess formation. Even after foreign bodies are removed, patients may have cough, excessive bronchial secretions, residual bronchial inflammation, and endobronchial granulation with more or less permanent obstruction.

Barbed grass heads are an especially troublesome problem. They anchor themselves to the wall of the airway, causing a marked local inflammatory reaction. They are not easily coughed up or moved by ciliary action and remain in the bronchi until removed by bronchoscopy. Some have such acute barbs that respiratory movements may carry them through the bronchus into the parenchyma, toward the pleura, and create bronchopleural fistulas.

Structural Defects

Rarely, the entire tracheobronchial tree is deficient in cartilage and elastic tissue. When such a defect occurs, the airway is markedly dilated and all segments collapse easily during expiration. Symptoms are wheezing, hyperinflation of the lungs, and intermittent pulmonary infection. There is no cure; however, avoiding forceful expiration, as occurs with crying, is desirable. Intercurrent respiratory infection should be treated vigorously.

"LOBAR EMPHYSEMA." This condition is an acute respiratory emergency. Tachypnea, retractions, and cyanosis usually appear in the first days of life although occasionally the onset of symptoms is more insidious with the clinical picture most marked at 2 or 3 months of age. There is hyperinflation localized to one lung, lobe, or segment, which compresses adjacent lung tissue and pushes the mediastinum to the contralateral side. Histologically, the lung consists of distended alveoli, ruptured intraalveolar septa, and large cavitations. Often there is fibrosis of the remaining intraalveolar tissue, which may represent healing of concurrent or intercurrent inflammation. External pressure by *anomalous* vessels, cysts, or tumors may be responsible. Stanger, Lucas, and Edwards have reviewed the association between acyanotic congenital cardiac disease and lobar emphysema and point out that compression of a bronchus by a distended pulmonary artery or the left atrium may cause this syndrome. Most cases are probably due to intrinsic weakness of a small segment of the airway.

In cases where symptoms are severe and the condition appears life-threatening, surgical removal of the obstructed segment and hyperinflated pulmonary tissue is mandatory. Some authors recommend transthoracic needling for intermittent decompression of the overdistended lung. The high incidence of pneumothorax makes this procedure of doubtful value. When the symptoms are less marked, a trial of bronchodilation, moderate sedation, and prevention of upper respiratory tract infections would seem indicated.

Case II. *D.M. was normal until two weeks of age, when intermittent wheezing, intercostal retractions, and cyanosis occurred with a minor upper re-*

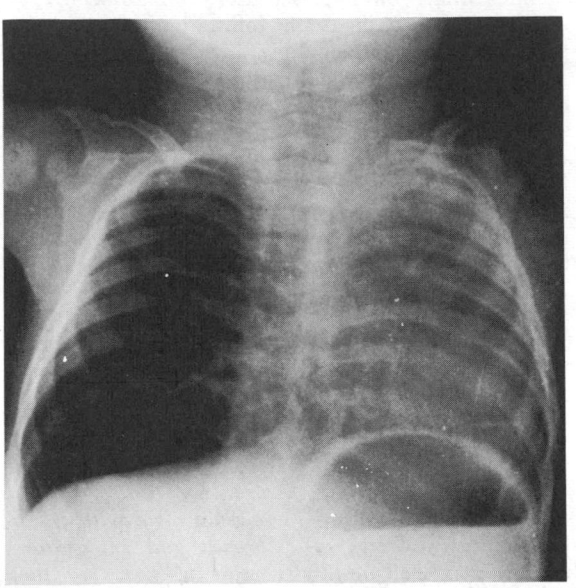

Fig. 21. Chest radiogram of patient D. M. The right lung is hyperinflated and the mediastinum is shifted to the left.

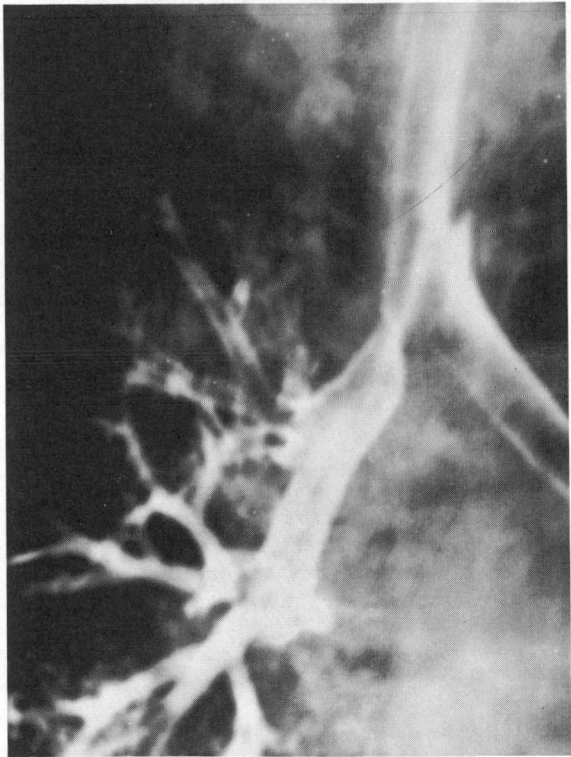

Fig. 22. Patient D. M. A small segment of the right mainstem bronchus just below the carina is narrow on forced expiration. (From a cinebronchogram.)

spiratory infection. These symptoms progressed, and he was admitted to the hospital at the age of 10 months with a diagnosis of "collapsed left lung." Figure 21 shows the airless left lung and a hyperinflated right lung. After instillation of radiopaque material through a transtracheal catheter, cinebronchograms were done. During a normal expiration, a 1 cm area of the proximal right mainstem bronchus collapsed partially (Fig. 22); crying completely occluded the segment. During inspiration, the bronchus was well filled without evidence of obstruction. The patient was given an oral bronchodilator, sedation, and tetracycline for 10-day periods with each upper respiratory tract infection. He had little respiratory distress for four years. Cinebronchography repeated at one-year intervals showed that the "weak" segment collapsed less as the child grew, and at five years no collapse with forced expiration occurred. This course would suggest that some cases of "lobar emphysema" can be conservatively treated and that the structural defect is corrected with time.

Tumors and External Compression

Sixteen cases of partial obstruction of the bronchus due to bronchial adenoma were reported to 1961. Cysts arising in bronchial walls or lymphatic tissue may occlude the airway. These may occur in any part of the lung but are most commonly found in the posterior mediastinum. Adenomas and cysts usually cause wheezing, repeated episodes of infection, and hemoptysis. If they obstruct a large airway, they cause dyspnea, retractions, and cyanosis. Adenomas usually obstruct bronchi but may occlude the trachea. In bronchial adenoma, respiratory symptoms are typically relieved by flexing the neck and are aggravated by hyperextension. Cysts, because of their posterior placement, ordinarily cause anterior displacement and compression of the major bronchi or trachea. The differential diagnosis of localized airway obstruction includes bronchial adenoma and cysts. The only appropriate treatment is surgical removal.

Stridor, wheezing, and intermittent pulmonary infections may also be caused by extrinsic compression of the trachea or bronchi by vascular anomalies. A double aortic arch is the most common, but respiratory symptoms may occur with right aortic arch and anomalous innominate and pulmonary arteries. Occasionally, a patent ductus arteriosus displaces the left pulmonary artery posteriorly and compresses the left upper lobe bronchus. Wheezing, cough, and intermittent complete obstruction with infection are usually present from birth. Occasionally, without surgical correction, the symptoms disappear as the child grows. However, prolonged compression of the trachea or bronchus by vascular or other extrinsic masses may produce a permanent softening of the airway segment, which may continue to collapse during expiration after surgery. Therefore, surgical correction of these anomalies is best done early in life.

Acute Bronchitis (Asthmatic Bronchitis)

Acute bronchitis usually begins after one to two days of upper respiratory tract infection with the gradual onset of cough. In the young infant there are wheezing, hyperinflation of the lungs, and acute respiratory distress. The cough is usually moderately productive, and often there are mild fever, leucocytosis, and a rapid sedimentation rate. Early there are rhonchi and, later, coarse rales throughout the lungs. The signs and symptoms persist for a week or 10 days. Occasionally, if there is complete obstruction, there is atelectasis. Pneumonitis is not unusual after several days of bronchitis. Radiologic examination of the chest shows diffuse hyperinflation with some increased peribronchial markings radiating from the hilum.

When bacteria cause acute bronchitis, beta hemolytic streptococcus, *Hemophilus influenzae*, and *Staphylococcus aureus* are commonly cultured from sputum. Many cases are probably caused by viral infection (Sec. 14.31). Bed rest, fluids, mild sedation, warm, moist air, and bronchodilators are adequate for most cases. Expectorants may be used. Drugs which depress ciliary activity or dry and decrease bronchial secretions must be avoided. If the infecting agent is bacterial, an appropriate antibiotic should be given.

Chronic Bronchitis

A persistent cough, wheezing, and coarse rales which last for two weeks or longer characterize chronic bronchitis. There are frequent exacerbations. Children with chronic bronchitis have a very sensitive bronchial tree which responds with vigorous constriction to small amounts of acetylcholine and histamine. This response is blocked by bronchodilator drugs such as isoproterenol. In this respect these children are similar to those with asthma. Chronic bronchitis may persist for years and cause destruction of lung tissue and pulmonary insufficiency. In chronic irritation of the airway and chronic bronchitis, goblet cells in the bronchial mucosa proliferate and crowd out ciliary cells. This effect makes bronchial drainage difficult. Prolonged inflammation thickens and distorts the bronchial wall. This state is often called "pseudobronchiectasis" or "tubular bronchiectasis." The process is usually reversible.

Bacteria rarely cause chronic bronchitis. Viral infection may or may not be responsible for the chronic disease, but certainly acute exacerbations are regularly associated with recovery of virus. Prominent agents in recurrent attacks of bronchitis are the respiratory syncytial, influenza, parainfluenza, Q fever, and adenoviruses.

Many cases of chronic bronchitis seem to be manifestations of hypersensitivity. Chronic hypersensitivity bronchitis with infiltration of the peribronchial space, eosinophils, and small round cells appears to be a distinct entity. Treatment consists of postural drainage, moist, warm air at night, and suppression of intercurrent bacterial infections. The use of steroids has been recommended in chronic bronchitis. Young infants and children may respond rapidly to prednisone therapy, even after several months or years of repeated episodes of wheezing, coughing, and progressive respiratory insufficiency.

Chronic Obliterative Bronchiolitis

A chronic inflammation of the peribronchiolar tissue may cause disease characterized by progressive dyspnea and respiratory failure.

Case III. *K.M., an 11-year-old male with insidious onset of shortness of breath and intermittent cough, was well until 10 years of age. He then developed in succession giant urticaria, glomerular nephritis, and Henoch-Schönlein's purpura. Four months after the symptoms appeared, he had a markedly distended chest, pronounced inspiratory effort, poor breath sounds, and striking subcutaneous and mediastinal emphysema, as shown in Figure 23A. Figure 23B, a chest film taken 10 days later, shows hyperinflated lungs, marked peribronchial thickening radiating from the hilum, and an enlarged right heart. His vital capacity and expiratory flow rates were reduced, his inspiratory flow rates were normal, and his functional residual capacity greatly increased. He had arterial desaturation and respiratory acidosis at rest (Table 8). There was no difference in expiratory flow rates when maximal or moderate effort was made, suggesting that the airways did not collapse with expiration. After six months of treatment with steroids, there was an increase in his vital capacity, reduction in his functional residual capacity, and improvement in his blood gases, but very little increase in the expiratory flow rates. Despite continuous steroid therapy his vital capacity remained low, and hypercarbia and hypoxemia increased. Two years after his symptoms began, he had a tracheotomy and required assisted ventilation for the six months prior to his death. At postmortem, his lungs were markedly inflated and did not collapse when the chest was opened. The parenchyma was normal. Only the medium- and small-sized bronchi and the bronchioles were abnormal. Figure 24 shows the marked enlargement of the peribronchiolar structures and the partial occlusion of the bronchial lumen.*

This type of chronic obliterative bronchiolitis may respond to steroid therapy, but occasionally, as with K.M., it progresses despite the use of antiinflammatory agents.

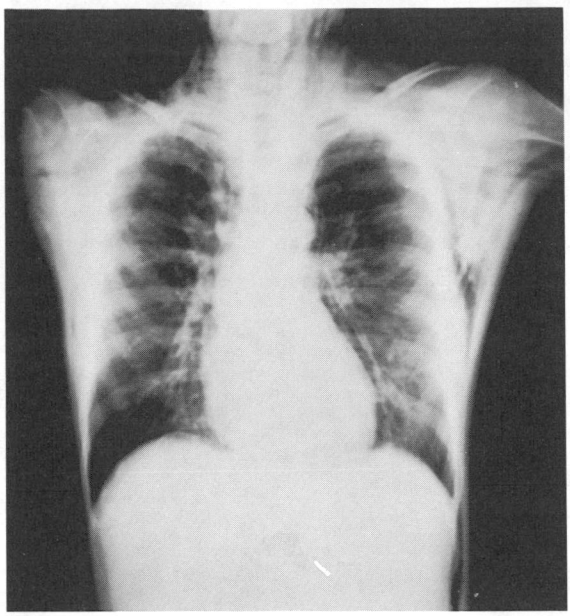
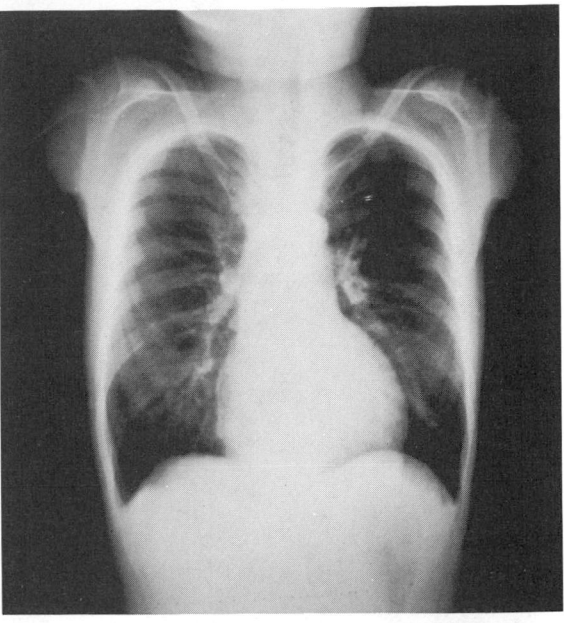

A   B

Fig. 23. Patient K. M. Posteroanterior chest radiogram of patient with chronic obliterative bronchiolitis. A. There is generalized peribronchial opacity and hyperinflation of the lungs. B. PA chest film 10 days after A. There is free gas in the pleural space, mediastinum, and soft tissues of the neck.

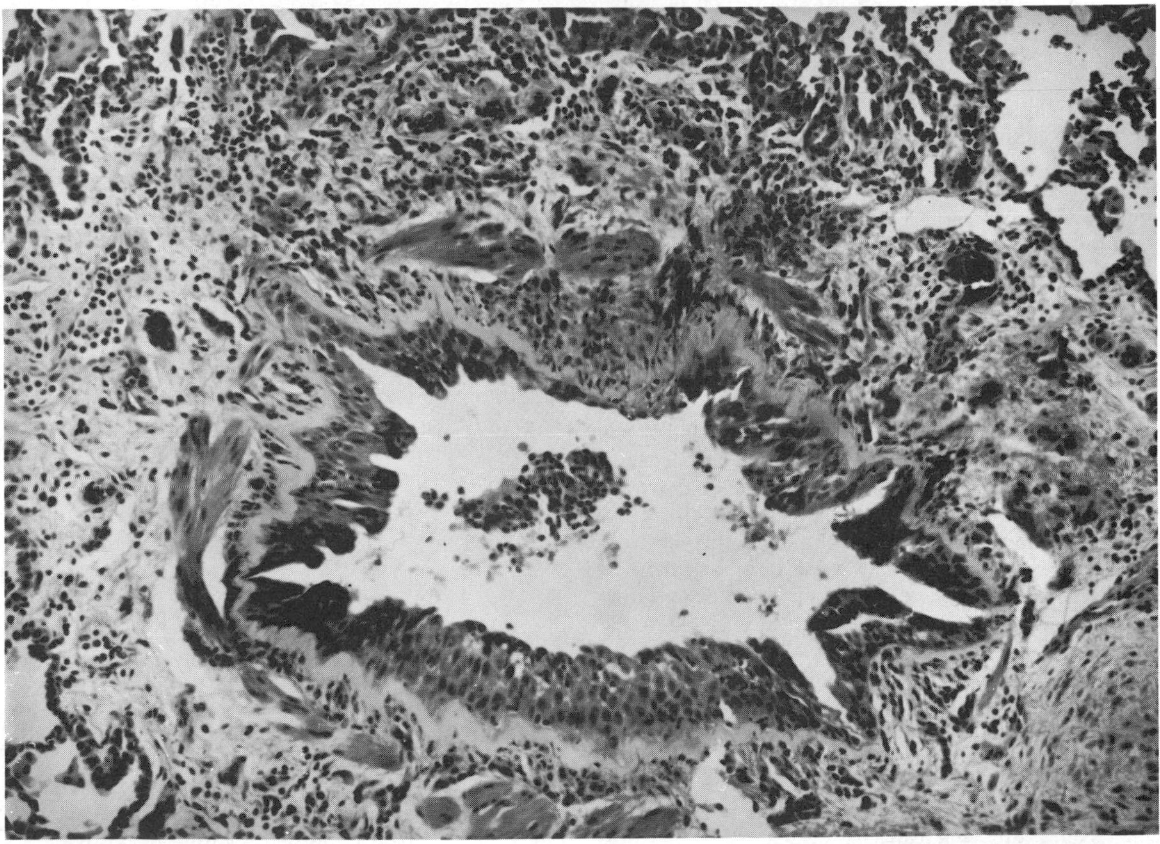

Fig. 24. Patient K. M. The wall of this small bronchus is thick and edematous and contains fibrous tissue and chronic inflammatory cells; the basement membrane is thick; and there is marked peribronchial inflammation. Plasma cells, lymphocytes, and a few eosinophils fill the lumen. H & E ×72

TABLE 8.   *Chronic Obliterative Bronchiolitis (K.M.)*

		Age		
		12 Years	12 Years (Prednisone)	14 Years (Prednisone and Tracheotomy)
Vital capacity (% normal)		29	50	30
Functional residual capacity (% normal)		231	150	240
Arterial blood gas tensions (mm Hg)	P_{O_2} (rest)	64	75	34
	P_{O_2} (very moderate exercise)	52	63	
	P_{CO_2} (rest)	51	43	78
	P_{CO_2} (very moderate exercise)	60	51	
Expiratory flow rates (% normal)	Maximal effort	15	25	12
	Moderate effort	15	25	12
Inspiratory flow rates (% normal)	Maximal effort	70	100	60
	Moderate effort	80	110	70

Bronchiolitis

Bronchiolitis is a disease of infants and young children most commonly seen in winter and spring and often occurring in epidemics. After a period of upper respiratory tract infection, lasting one to several days, there is an abrupt onset of accelerated respiratory rate and intercostal and subcostal retractions, associated with the rapid development of hyperinflation of the lungs. In addition to the respiratory symptoms, infants with bronchiolitis have tachycardia, cyanosis with an increase in pulmonary vascular resistance, and occasionally right heart failure. In a review of 1,230 cases, Heycock reports a 5.5 percent overall mortality and a 6.5 percent mortality in infants under 6 months of age. Most large series of cases report a mortality of under 1 percent. Leer et al. report no deaths in 297 patients treated in five hospitals during a control study on the use of steroids.

The walls of the small bronchi and bronchioles are thick and infiltrated with inflammatory cells. The lumina are often completely occluded with leucocytes and debris. There are also inflammation and partial occlusion of the medium-sized bronchi, and this probably is responsible for most of the expiratory obstruction. Bacteria or viruses may cause bronchiolitis. Sell states that most cases are due to *H. influenzae*. However, the majority of reports indicate that viruses, principally the respiratory syncytial, influenza B, and parainfluenza viruses, are responsible (Sec. 14.31). Elderkin and co-workers isolated viruses or demonstrated a rise in virus anitbody in two-thirds of infants with bronchiolitis.

There is marked obstruction to expiration with gas trapping. The functional residual capacity increases and the vital capacity decreases. Lung compliance also decreases as the lung is overdistended. Late in the disease, the patient may hypoventilate and develop respiratory acidosis and hypoxemia.

The patient should be sedated, usually with chloral hydrate, and should not be disturbed. The majority of patients have desaturation of the arterial blood and require warm, moist oxygen. Since the young infant has little bronchiolar muscle, bronchodilators are not very effective; intravenous bronchiodilators may even be dangerous. Hydration and electrolyte replacement are important. If there is reason to suspect that bronchiolitis is due to bacterial infection, ampicillin and/or kanamycin should be given.

Since most of the bronchiolar obstruction is inflammatory, many authors advocate the use of an anti-inflammatory agent. McGeorge suggests the use of 100 mg hydrocortisone every 4 hours. However, several recent controlled studies show no benefit from cortisone (see Connolly et al., 1969; Leer et al., 1969). In extremely ill infants, tracheostomy has been advocated. However, the complication rate from tracheostomy, in a disease with less than 1 percent mortality, argues against the procedure. If respirations must be assisted, and if tracheal intubation is necessary for efficiency in operating a ventilator and to reduce dead space, nasotracheal intubation is probably preferable.

Asthma
(See also Sec. 11.5)

Asthma is characterized by paroxysmal attacks of wheezing, dyspnea, and cough, with or without the production of sputum. These episodes are frequently preceded by symptoms of mild upper respiratory tract infections. Occasionally, respiratory distress is severe, the retractions and tachypnea become more marked, and there may be a rapid deterioration in the patient's condition with a precipitous fall in arterial oxygen tension and a dramatic rise in arterial carbon dioxide tension.

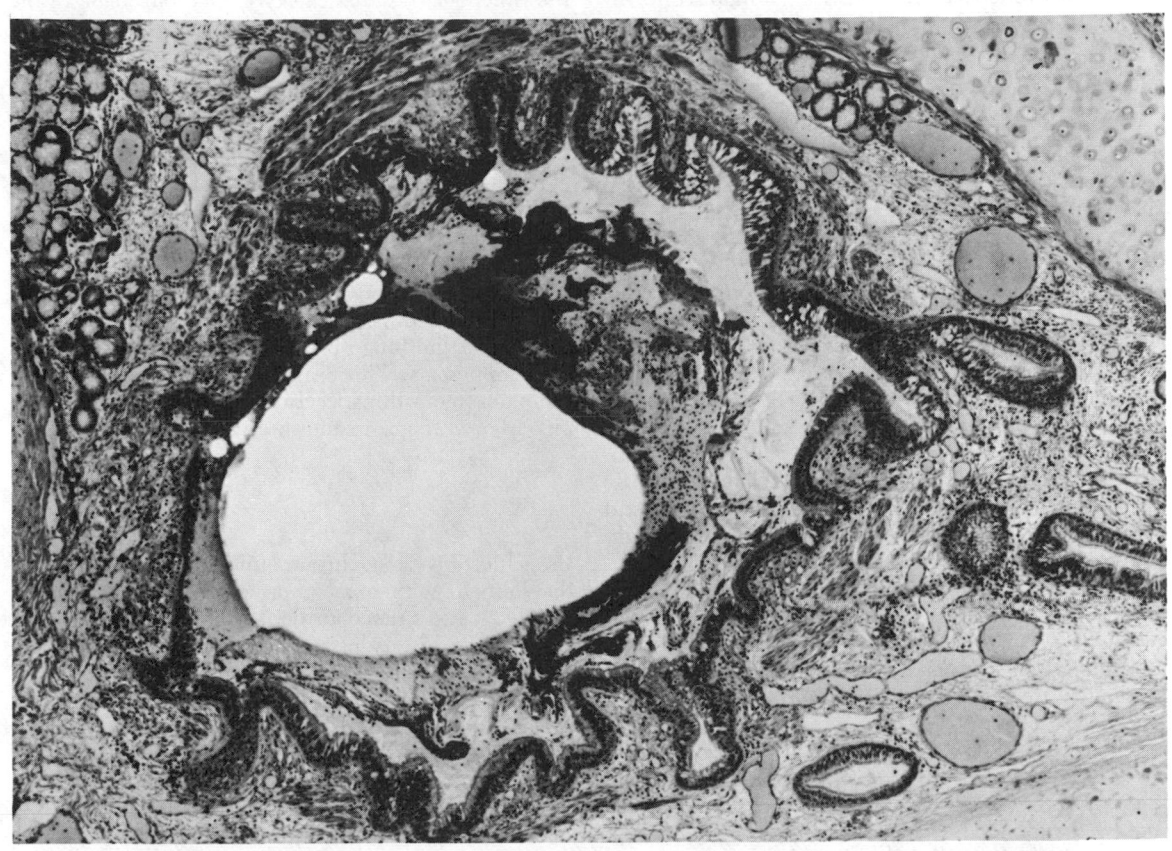

Fig. 25. Asthma. A small bronchus partly filled with mucus and epithelial and inflammatory cells. The bronchial wall is hyperemic, edematous, and filled with eosinophils. The mucous glands and goblet cells are distended with mucus. The smooth muscle is prominent. H & E ×40

The airways in individuals with asthma are extremely sensitive to airborne or blood-borne excitants, both physical and chemical. Whatever the proximate cause of the irritation, there is local release of histamine and slow-reacting substances which cause edema of the bronchial walls, excess secretion of mucus by the bronchial glands, and constriction of the bronchi. Leucocytes, predominantly eosinophils, surround the bronchi, invade their walls, and appear in the lumen of the bronchi (Fig. 25).

The edema, mucopurulent material, and the muscular constriction reduce the size of the bronchial lumen and increase the resistance to airflow. The larger airways tend to collapse during forced expiration, and the combination of large and small airway obstruction leads to air trapping and hyperinflation of the lungs. As the lungs become larger, the vital capacity decreases and the work of breathing increases. There is a decrease in alveolar ventilation, a decrease in arterial oxygen tension, and an increase in arterial carbon dioxide tension.

The air trapping, hyperinflation of the lungs, and uneven distribution of inspired gas in asthma are usually reversible. Rackemann, in a review of 449 adults who developed asthma before the age of 13 years, reported that 30 percent were cured, 20 percent had no asthma but had other allergic symptoms, 20 percent had occasional episodes of wheezing, 28 percent still had severe recurrent episodes of wheezing, and 2 percent died. Asymptomatic children with asthma can have significant airway obstruction between acute attacks and it is possible that prolonged airway obstruction may lead to irreversible pulmonary damage.

Early treatment is essential. When wheezing begins, prompt administration of bronchodilators, by inhalation of aerosols or by oral, subcutaneous, or intramuscular routes, and rest and quiet will abort many attacks. *If the symptoms become worse and there is acute respiratory failure with cyanosis and acidosis, management must be vigorous.* Aerosol bronchodilators, such as isoproterenol, and oxygen should be given with positive pressure through a tight-fitting mask with a small dead space. Aminophylline and/or isoproterenol intravenously are often necessary but, when used, continuous monitoring of the patient's cardiovascular status is essential. Aminophylline should be continued until airway obstruction has been completely relieved, since bronchoconstriction often rapidly recurs if therapy stops too soon.

When intravenous therapy ceases, aminophylline by mouth and aerosol bronchodilators should be continued for at least one week. Ample fluid and appropriate electrolytes must be provided, as previously discussed.

If, despite these measures, respiratory failure persists and arterial oxygen is below 50 mm Hg while breathing room air, or arterial CO_2 tension is above 60 mm Hg, orotracheal intubation with controlled ventilation is necessary. Since acidosis decreases myocardial efficiency, increases pulmonary vascular resistance, alters the distribution of K+ between intracellular and extracellular spaces, and may affect smooth muscle tone, correction of the pH is desirable when the pH is below 7.25. Sodium bicarbonate and tromethamine (THAM) often provide dramatic improvement when given intravenously. With a severe episode of asthma requiring hospitalization, the patient's status must be frequently assessed by measuring the tensions of oxygen and carbon dioxide in arterial blood. *There is no substitute for the frequent analysis of arterial blood.*

It has been suggested that in asthmatic children bronchodilator therapy be used continuously between attacks in order to minimize the danger of permanent lung damage. Isoproterenol aerosol is the usual bronchodilator used for such therapy.

Case IV: J.M., a 14-year-old boy, had a history of asthma since the age of 2½ years. He received intermittently steroids, aminophylline, and ephedrine by mouth for his recurrent episodes of wheezing. He required hospitalization on 10 occasions and lived in a convalescent home for one period of 18 months. Between acute episodes he had no disabling symptoms, but he became short of breath while swimming and playing tennis. His chest was large and hyperresonant, and a short expiratory wheeze was audible during a series of forced expirations. His chest film showed his lungs to be hyperinflated (Fig. 26). His pulmonary function (Table 9) was measured when he was symptom-free. These studies showed a decrease in vital capacity, an increase in the functional residual capacity, and a decrease in the expiratory and inspiratory flow rates. His arterial blood gas tensions were normal at rest; and with moderately severe exercise, oxygen tension fell and CO_2 tension rose. These functional abnormalities were completely reversed after one week of vigorous bronchodilator therapy with isoproterenol by aerosol and aminophylline and ephedrine orally.

This case illustrates that airway obstruction due to asthma can be completely removed by vigorous therapy. This response suggests that prolonged obstruction in asthmatic children with persistent overinflation of the lung need not cause tissue destruction and emphysema. This example also illustrates that the symptom-free asthmatic child may have considerable airway obstruction in the interval between attacks.

Bronchiectasis

Bronchiectasis is a chronic inflammatory disease of the bronchi with a more or less continuous cough, which produces mucopurulent sputum. There is often a preceding history of pneumonia, aspiration of foreign bodies, measles, or pertussis. Bronchiectasis is frequently associated with sinusitis and asthma. Most cases of bronchiectasis in childhood are associated with cystic fibrosis. Chronic irritation of the airways by infection probably makes them more sensitive to other stimuli.

Cough productive of mucopurulent sputum is the principal symptom; but, particularly in young infants, there are also stridor and wheezing. Gas exchange is often impaired, causing cyanosis and respiratory acidosis. Intermittent fever, hemoptysis, and signs of pneumonia are common. The chest is large, and rales of various types are heard diffusely through the lungs. Clubbing of the fingers is frequently seen. Children with bronchiectasis fatigue easily, have reduced exercise capacity, and have delayed physical growth. Bronchograms (with airways outlined by tantalum) show widely dilated bronchi (Fig. 27).

TABLE 9.   *Chronic Asthma (J.M.)*

		Symptom-free	After One Week Vigorous Bronchodilator Therapy
Vital capacity (% normal)		75	100
Functional residual capacity (% normal)		180	110
Arterial blood gas tensions (mm Hg)	Po_2 (rest)	90	98
	Po_2 (exercise)	75	97
	Pco_2 (rest)	42	38
	Pco_2 (exercise)	46	34
Expiratory flow rates (% normal)	Maximal effort	40	120
	Moderate effort	50	120
Inspiratory flow rates (% normal)	Maximal effort	45	110
	Moderate effort	55	110

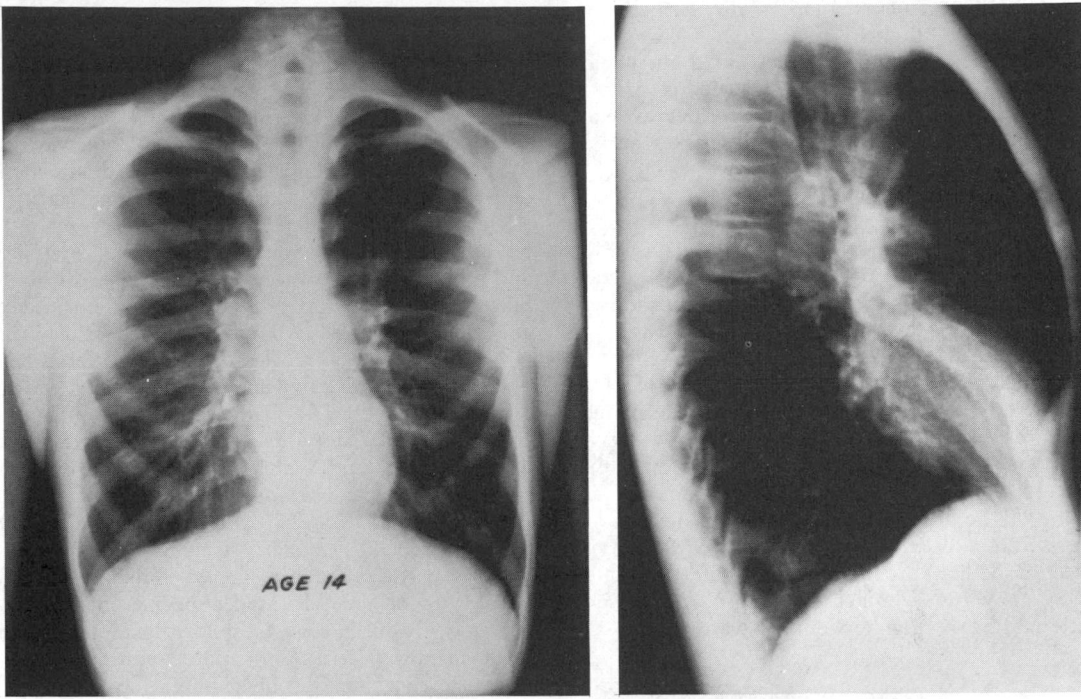

Fig. 26. Asthma. Chest radiogram of patient J. M. The lung is hyperinflated and the anteroposterior diameter of the chest is greater than normal. There are few lung markings and the enlargement of the lung makes the heart appear small.

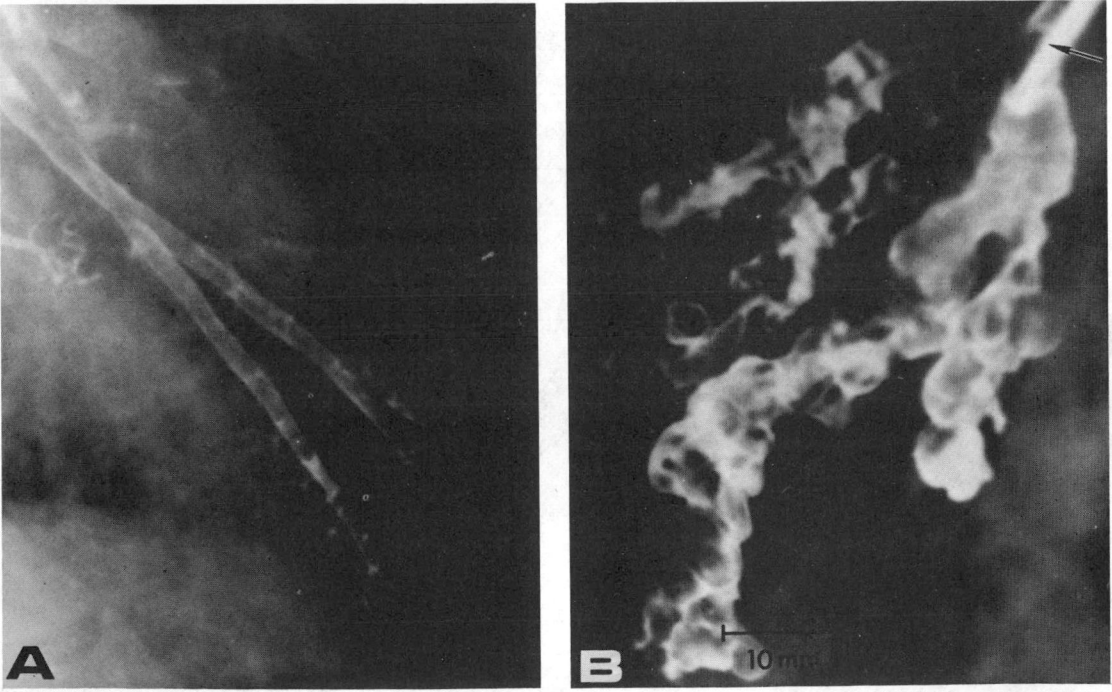

Fig. 27. A. Normal right lower lobe bronchi outlined with tantalum. B. The same patient's left lower lobe bronchi outlined with tantalum showing the dilation of the bronchi characteristic of bronchiectasis. (Courtesy of Dr. J. A. Nadel.)

Bronchiectasis is characterized by dilation, chronic purulent inflammation, and destruction of the walls of the bronchi (Fig. 28). Complete or partial obstruction decreases bronchial drainage and increases the infection. When obstruction is complete, there is atelectasis and abscess formation; when obstruction is partial there is overdistension and regional hyperinflation.

Twenty percent of the reported cases in children begin under one year of age, and 75 percent begin prior to 5 years of age. This early onset suggests that some infants may be predisposed to ectasia and hints at a relationship to the narrow lumina and weak structure of the infant's bronchi.

Some authors have implied that bronchiectasis is congenital and due to general weakness of all of the airways. However, congenital bronchiectasis need not be diffuse, since some airways may be weaker than others, and some may mature more slowly than others. In these, minor persistent inflammation and irritation of the bronchioles, such as with measles and pertussis infection and after inhalation of some types of foreign bodies, producing cough and forced expiration, may cause bronchial collapse and promote infection. The normal tendency toward airway collapse in the young infant makes regional obstruction with foreign bodies or infection more hazardous and leads to suppuration. The left lung is more often involved than the right. This one sided predominance may reflect the more favorable drainage from the right lung (see previous discusson of aspiration).

Children with bronchiectasis usually have a large total lung capacity, large functional residual capacity, and a small vital capacity. There is an increase in airway resistance and a decrease in flow rates, particularly the forced expiratory flow rate. Ventilation and pulmonary perfusion are unevenly distributed. Some areas of the lung may have little ventilation and a large blood flow. This has the effect of a right-to-left shunt and causes desaturation of arterial blood. Other areas of the lung may receive little blood flow but be relatively well ventilated. This tends to increase the respiratory dead space, decrease ventilatory efficiency, and increase the work of breathing.

Treatment consists of increasing the drainage from the dilated and partially or completely obstructed bronchi. Aerosol or systemic bronchodilators, vigorous postural drainage, and nebulization, particularly at night, are essential. Specific infections are treated with antibiotics. Occasionally prolonged antibiotic therapy is useful to suppress chronic infection, as with cystic fibrosis. The regimen recommended by Matthews et al. for cystic fibrosis is applicable to all cases of bronchiectasis.

If bronchiectasis is localized and does not heal with conservative treatment, surgical excision of the involved area is recommended. The mortality from segmental or lobar resections is less than 1 percent. Unfortunately, many children have more generalized disease than is suspected, and recurrences following resection are not unusual.

Case V. R.O., a 12-year-old boy, had an onset of intermittent fever and a cough which produced mucopurulent sputum at the age of 15 months. In the first 11 years of his life he had 13 hospitalizations for pneumonia of the right lower lobe and the lingular segment of the left upper lobe. A bronchogram showed that there was widespread saccular dilation of all the bronchi in the right lower lobe and lingula. He had a marked decrease in vital capacity, an increase in functional residual capacity, and reduction in the expiratory flow rate during a maximal expiratory effort. He also had arterial oxygen desaturation and carbon dioxide retention at rest; these were more marked during exercise (Table 10). There was no difference in inspiratory flow when maximal or moderate efforts were used. The increased flow rate on expiration with moderate effort suggests that with rapid airflow there was collapse of the airways.

After one month of chloramphenicol treatment for H. influenzae grown in culture from his sputum, postural drainage, nebulization at night, and vigorous bronchodilation therapy with isoproterenol aerosol every two hours, his vital capacity increased, his functional residual capacity decreased, and his blood

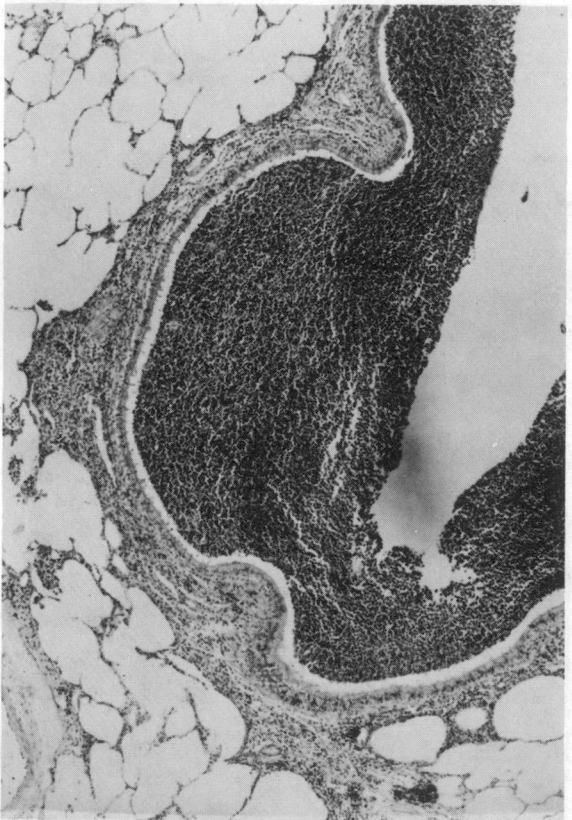

Fig. 28. R. O. Bronchiectasis. The bronchus is dilated and filled with exudate. Fibrosis and chronic inflammatory cells replace most of the normal structure of the bronchial wall. H & E ×40

TABLE 10.   *Bronchiectasis (R.O.)*

		Before Therapy	After Vigorous Bronchodilation and Antibiotic Therapy	After Surgery
Vital capacity (% normal)		40	70	65
Functional residual capacity (% normal)		250	150	75
Arterial blood gas tensions (mm Hg)	Po_2 (rest)	85	90	90
	Po_2 (exercise)	60	80	86
	Pco_2 (rest)	50	40	40
	Pco_2 (exercise)	60	45	35
Expiratory flow rates (% normal)	Maximal effort	30	50	60
	Moderate effort	60	90	90
Inspiratory flow rates (% normal)	Maximal effort	60	75	85
	Moderate effort	60	75	85

gases approached normal. However, he still had a marked decrease in expiratory flow rate.

He had a right thoracotomy with removal of the right lower lobe, and six weeks later a left thoracotomy with removal of the lingula. One year following surgery, the patient's vital capacity and functional residual capacity were normal, when allowance was made for removal of lung tissue, and blood gases at rest and exercise were normal. However, expiratory flow rates were still slightly reduced.

Medical management improved but did not cure this patient. Surgical removal of the right lower lobe and lingula caused a marked improvement in pulmonary function, although the persistent decrease in flow rates suggests either residual bronchiectasis or other intercurrent airway disease.

REFERENCES

INSPIRATORY OBSTRUCTION

Blattner, R. J. Acute laryngotracheobronchitis, comments on current literature. J. Pediat., 62:288, 1963.

Campbell, J. S., Wiglesworth, F. W., Latarroca, R., and Wilde, H. Congenital subglottic hemangiomas of the larynx and trachea in infants. Pediatrics, 22:727, 1958.

Cox, M. A., Schiebler, G. L., Taylor, W. J., Wheat, M. W., and Krovetz, L. J. Reversible pulmonary hypertension in a child with respiratory obstruction and cor pulmonale. J. Pediat., 67:192, 1965.

Fox, H., and Cocker, J. Laryngeal atresia. Arch. Dis. Child., 39:641, 1964.

Holinger, P. H., Johnston, K. C., and Schild, J. A. Congenital anomalies of the tracheobronchial tree and of the esophagus; diagnosis and treatment. Pediat. Clin. N. Amer., 9:1113, 1962.

Houston, I. B., and Mackie, D. G. Congenital tracheal stenosis. Thorax, 16:94, 1961.

Leer, J. A., Green, J. L., Heimlich, E. M., Hyde, J. S., Moffet, H. L., Young, G. A., and Barron, B. A. Corticosteroid treatment in bronchiolitis, a controlled collaborative study in 297 infants and children. Amer. J. Dis. Child., 117:495, 1969.

McIntosh, R., and Nichol, K. D. Abscess of the larynx in infants: Report of 5 cases. J.A.M.A., 90:2095, 1928.

McLean, D. M., Edwards, H. E., McQueen, E. J., and Petite, H. E. Myxovirus infections in acute laryngotracheobronchitis (Toronto, 1961-1962). Canad. Med. Ass. J., 87:998, 1962.

Pimpinella, R. J. The nasopharyngeal angiofibroma in the adolescent male. J. Pediat., 64:260, 1964.

Wilson, T. G. Discussion on stridor in infants. Proc. Roy. Soc. Med., 45:355, 1952.

Witzleben, C. L. Aplasia of the trachea. Pediatrics, 32:31, 1963.

LOWER AIRWAY OBSTRUCTION

Aspiration

Clery, A. P., Ellis, F. H., Jr., and Schmidt, H. W. Problems associated with aspiration of grass heads (inflorescences). J.A.M.A., 171:1478, 1959.

Bloomer, W. E. Trauma to the chest. In Lindskog, G. E., Liebow, A. A., and Glenn, W. W. L., eds. Thoracic and Cardiovascular Surgery with Related Pathology. New York, Appleton-Century-Crofts, 1962, pp. 26-29.

Holinger, P. H., Andrews, A. H., Jr., and Anison, G. C. Pulmonary complications due to endobronchial foreign bodies. Illinois Med. J., 93:19, 1948.

Inhaled foreign bodies. Brit. Med. J., 5440:943, 1965 (leading article).

Jewett, T. C., and Butsch, W. L. Infection from timothy grass. J. Thorac. Cardiov. Surg., 50:124, 1965.

Structural Defects, Tumors, and External Compression

Brünner, S., Poulsen, P. T., and Vesterdal, J. Cysts of the lung in infants and children. Acta Paediat. Scand., 49:39, 1960.

Campbell, J. S., Wiglesworth, F. W., Latarroca, R., and Wilde, H. Congenital subglottic hemangiomas of the larynx and trachea in infants. Pediatrics, 22:727, 1958.

Derrick, J. R., and Stoeckle, H. Bronchial obstruction secondary to an aberrant pulmonary artery. Amer. J. Dis Child., 99:830, 1960.

Levin, S. J., Adler, P., and Scherer, R. A. Collapsible trachea (tracheomalacia): a non-allergic cause of wheezing in infancy. Ann. Allergy, 22:20, 1964.

Litt, R. E., Mencia, L. F., and Altman, D. H. Congenital stenosis of the right mainstem bronchus. Amer. J. Roentgen., 89:1017, 1963.

Mustard, W. T., Trimble, A. W., and Trusler, G. A. Mediastinal vascular anomalies causing tracheal and esophageal compression and obstruction in childhood. Canad. Med. Ass. J., 87:1301, 1962.

Opsahl, T., and Berman, E. J. Bronchiogenic mediastinal cysts in infants: case report and review of the literature. Pediatrics, 30:372, 1962.

Pontius, R. G. Bronchial obstruction of congenital origin. Amer. J. Surg., 106:8, 1963.

Sloan, H. Lobar obstructive emphysema in infancy treated by lobectomy. J. Thorac. Surg., 26:1, 1953.

Soderlund, S., Robertson, B., and Borlenghi, R. Infantile lobar emphysema. Acta Paediat. Scand. (Suppl.), 159:89, 1965.

Stanger, P., Lucas, R. V., Jr., and Edwards, J. E. Anatomic factors causing respiratory distress in acyanotic congenital cardiac disease: special reference to bronchial obstruction. Pediatrics, 43:760, 1969.

Van Epps, E. F., and Davies, D. H. Lobar emphysema. Amer. J. Roentgen., 73:375, 1955.

Weisel, W., and Lepley, D. Tracheal and bronchial adenomas in childhood. Pediatrics, 28:394, 1961.

Bronchitis

Carilli, A. D., Gohd, R. S., and Gordon, W. A virologic study of chronic bronchitis. New Eng. J. Med., 270:123, 1964.

de Vries, K., Witkop, J., Hensen, J. F., and Sluiter, H. J. Hormonal treatment of chronic bronchitis. In Orie, N. G. M., and Sluiter, H. J., eds. Bronchitis (International Bronchitis Symposium, Groningen, Netherlands, 1960). Springfield, Ill., Charles C Thomas Co., 1961, pp. 323-335.

Fletcher, C. M. Chronic bronchitis: factors in pathogenesis and their clinical application. Lancet, 1:271, 1954.

Bronchiolitis

Canby, J. P., and Redd, H. J. Tracheotomy in the management of severe bronchiolitis. Pediatrics, 36:406, 1965.

Connolly, C., Field, C. M. B., Glasgow, J. F. T., Slattery, C. M., and MacLynn, D. M. A double blind trial of prednisolone in epidemic bronchiolitis due to respiratory syncytial virus. Acta Paediat. Scand., 58:116, 1969.

Elderkin, F. M., Gardner, P. S., Turk, D. C., and White, A. C. Aetiology and management of bronchiolitis and pneumonia in childhood. Brit. Med. J., 2:722, 1965.

Heycock, J. B., and Noble, G. C. 1230 cases of acute bronchiolitis in infancy. Brit. Med. J., 2:879, 1962.

James, J. A. Dexamethasone in croup, a controlled study. Amer. J. Dis. Child., 117:511, 1969.

Leer, J. A., Green, J. L., Heimlich, E. M., Hyde J. S., Moffet, H. L., Young, G. A., and Barron, B. A. Corticosteroid treatment in bronchiolitis, a controlled collaborative study in 297 infants and children. Amer. J. Dis. Child., 117:495, 1969.

McGeorge, M. Severe obstructive bronchiolitis in infancy: treatment with hydrocortisone. Clin. Pediat., 3:11, 1964.

Phelan, P. D., and Williams, H. E. Sympathomimetic drugs in acute viral bronchiolitis. Their effect on pulmonary resistance. Pediatrics, 43:493, 1969.

Reynolds, E. O. R., and Cook, C. D. The treatment of bronchiolitis. J. Pediat., 63:1205, 1963.

Sell, S. H. W. Some observations on acute bronchiolitis in infants. Amer. J. Dis. Child., 100:7, 1960.

Wright, F. H., and Beem, M. O. Diagnosis and treatment: management of acute viral bronchiolitis in infancy. Pediatrics, 35:334, 1965.

Asthma

Addis, G. J. Bicarbonate buffering in acute exacerbation of chronic respiratory failure. Thorax, 20:337, 1965.

Bocles, J. S. Status asthmaticus. Med. Clin. N. Amer., 54:493, 1970.

Engström, I. Respiratory studies in children. XI. Mechanics of breathing, lung volumes and ventilatory capacity in asthmatic children from attack to symptom-free status. Acta Paediat. Scand., 53(Suppl.):155, 1964.

Kraepelien, S. Respiratory studies in children. IV. The effect of bronchodilator drugs on the lung volumes in symptom-free asthmatic children. Acta Paediat. Scand., 47:547, 1958.

Levin, S. J., and Scherer, R. A. Allergic tracheitis: a problem in pediatric allergy. Ann. Allergy, 22:26, 1964.

McFadden, E. R., and Lyons, H. A. Serial studies of factors influencing airway dynamics during recovery from acute asthma attacks. J. Appl. Physiol., 27:452, 1969.

Middleton, E., Jr. The anatomical and biochemical basis of bronchial obstruction in asthma. Ann. Int. Med., 63:695, 1965.

Mithoefer, J. C., Runser, R. H., and Karetzky, M. S. The use of sodium bicarbonate in the treatment of acute bronchial asthma. New Eng. J. Med., 272:1200, 1965.

Rackemann, F. M., and Edwards, M. C. Asthma in children. New Eng. J. Med., 246:815, 1952.

Richards, W., and Patrick, J. R. Death from asthma in children. Amer. J. Dis. Child., 110:4, 1965.

———— and Siegel, S. C. Status asthmaticus. Pediat. Clin. N. Amer., 16:9, 1969.

Tooley, W. H., DeMuth, G., and Nadel, J. A. The reversibility of obstructive changes in severe childhood asthma. J. Pediat., 66:517, 1965.

Bronchiectasis

Avery, M. E., Riley, M. C., and Weiss, A. The course of bronchiectasis in childhood. Bull. Hopkins Hosp., 109:20, 1961.

Field, C. E. Bronchiectasis: a long-term follow-up of medical and surgical cases from childhood. Arch. Dis. Child., 36:587, 1961.

Iacocca, V. F., Sibinga, M. S., and Barbero, G. J. Respiratory tract bacteriology in cystic fibrosis. Amer. J. Dis. Child., 106:315, 1963.

Matthews, L. W., and Doershuk, C. F. Mist therapy in the obstructive lesions of cystic fibrosis. Pediatrics, 39:176, 1967.

———— Doershuk, C. F., Wise, M., Eddy, G., Nudelman, H., and Spector, S. A therapeutic regimen for patients with cystic fibrosis. J. Pediat., 65:558, 1964.

Ramirez, R. J. Pulmonary aspergilloma: endobronchial treatment. New Eng. J. Med., 271:1281, 1964.

Williams, H., and Campbell, P. Generalized bronchiectasis associated with deficiency of cartilage in the bronchial tree. Arch. Dis. Child., 35:182, 1960.

19.5
THE PARENCHYMA

Anatomy

The parenchyma includes the respiratory bronchioles, alveolar ducts, alveoli, pulmonary capillaries, lymphatics, and their interstitial supporting tissue. The respiratory bronchioles, which have a somewhat greater diameter than the terminal bronchioles, divide into alveolar ducts from which numerous alveoli protrude. These structures are nourished by the pulmonary arterial circulation. They probably have no nerve supply, but the smooth muscle in the walls of the respiratory bronchioles and surrounding the openings of the alveoli reacts to locally applied stimuli.

Ciliated and nonciliated cuboidal cells line the respiratory bronchioles. This epithelium is continuous with the flat, nonciliated cells lining the alveolar ducts and alveoli. The nuclei of the alveolar lining cells lie in depressions in the capillary walls and are widely spaced, occupying only about one-tenth of the surface of the alveoli. Their cytoplasmic attenuations cover the remainder of the surface. There are no mucous cells in the respiratory bronchioles. However, a deposit resembling mucus, which is continuous with an acellular layer covering the alveolar cell cytoplasm, covers the respiratory bronchiolar epithelium.

Just as the lumen of the bronchioles is continuous with the alveoli, the supporting elements of the bronchiolar tree are continuous with the framework of the alveoli. Helical turns of smooth muscle proceed from the terminal bronchioles to surround the respiratory bronchioles. The muscle mass gradually decreases as the blind ends of the alveolar ducts are approached, and the residual strands of smooth muscle terminate by forming rings around the mouths of the alveoli. The loose interstitial tissue between the respiratory bronchioles contains many small lymph vessels and small divisions of the pulmonary arteries and veins. Elastic, collagen, and reticular tissue also course through the interstitial space between the parenchymal structures and tend to localize at the mouths of the alveoli. The collagen fibers form wavy bundles when the lung is at a small volume, but are pulled straight when the lung is expanded and limit the volume to which the lung can be inflated. Expansion of the lung stretches the elastic and reticular fibers. At the end of inspiration these fibers return to their original length, facilitating expiration.

There is a large amount of interstitial tissue in the lung of the newly born. It is composed principally of vascular tissue, elastic and collagen tissue being present in proportionately smaller amounts than in the adult lung. Elastic fibers increase in number and size until about four years of age when their distribution and concentration are similar to those in the adult lung. The elastic tissue in the lung of the newly born has different staining qualities from mature elastic tissue, so that there may be a qualitative as well as quantitative distinction. The staining characteristics of elastic tissue change little in the first months, but by one year of age they are similar to the adult.

The lung is divided into four primary volumes and four capacities, each of which includes two or more primary volumes (Fig. 29):

Volumes

1. Tidal volume (TV) is the volume of gas inspired or expired during each respiratory cycle.
2. Inspiratory reserve volume (IRV) is the maximal amount of gas that can be inspired after a normal inspiration.
3. Expiratory reserve volume (ERV) is the maximal amount of gas that can be expired after a normal expiration.
4. Residual volume (RV) is the volume of gas remaining in the lungs at the end of a maximal expiration.

Capacities

1. Total lung capacity (TLC) is the amount of gas in the lung at the end of a maximal inspiration.
2. Vital capacity (VC) is the maximal volume of gas that can be expelled from the lungs by forceful effort following a maximal inspiration.
3. Inspiratory capacity (IC) is the maximal volume of gas that can be inspired after a normal expiration (resting expiratory level).
4. Functional residual capacity (FRC) is the volume of gas that can be inspired after a normal expiratory level.

The lung grows by increasing the size and number of alveoli. Dunhill calculated that there are 24 million alveoli at birth, 250 million at four years of age, and 296 million in the adult. These figures suggest that lung growth may be due principally to generation of new units in infancy; but in childhood, growth is probably the result of an increase in size of units, since their diameters continue to increase until adulthood. Lung growth is alinear in respect to age, but from infancy to adulthood the size of the lung is proportional to body height, and the relative sizes of the primary lung volumes and capacities are the same at all ages: the residual volume is approximately 25 percent, the functional residual capacity approximately 40 percent, and the tidal volume during normal respiration about 8 percent of the total lung capacity.

Function

The parenchyma permits exchange of carbon dioxide and oxygen between air and blood and maintains a

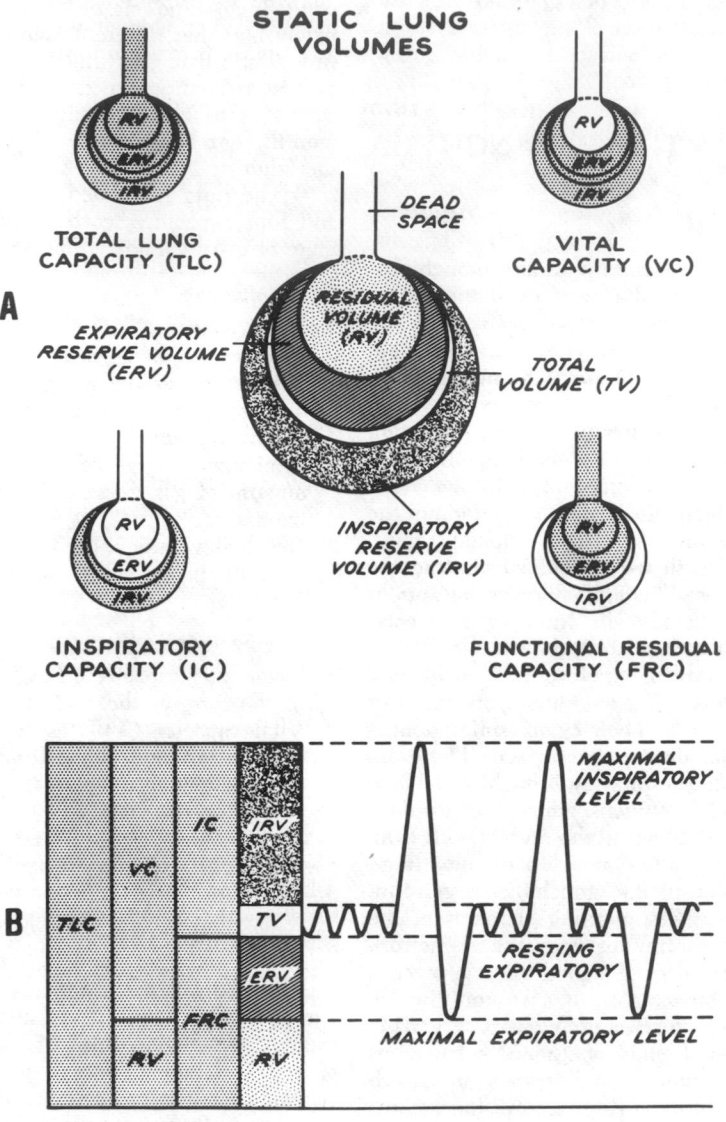

Fig. 29. A. The large central diagram illustrates the four primary lung volumes and their approximate magnitude. The outermost line indicates the greatest size to which the lung can expand; the innermost circle (residual volume) indicates the volume that remains after a maximal expiration. The shaded areas in the smaller diagrams represent the four lung capacities. B. Lung volumes as they appear on a spirogram tracing; shading in the vertical bar next to the spirogram tracing corresponds to that in the central diagram. The relation of the lung capacities to the spirogram are also indicated. (From Comroe et al. *The Lung*, 2d ed. Courtesy of Year Book Publishers.)

barrier between gas and liquid which prevents undissolved gas from entering the interstitial space and fluid from entering the alveolar lumina. Phagocytosis and the mouthward movement of the acellular alveolar lining prevent the accumulation of foreign material.

The amount of oxygen and carbon dioxide exchanged depends upon the volume of fresh air reaching the alveoli each minute (ventilation), the difference between their partial pressures in alveolar gas and capillary blood, the alveolar surface area, the amount and distribution of pulmonary blood flow,

and the depth of the tissue separating blood and gas. **VENTILATION.** The amount of air reaching the alveoli is determined by *the dead space, the resistance to gas flow, the resistance of the lung to deformation, the size of the lung, the work capacity of the respiratory system,* and *reflexes* which increase or decrease the respiratory drive. Dead space and resistance to gas flow were considered in the section on airways. When the tissue is rigid and resists deformation, it has a high elasticity or a low compliance; compliance is the change in volume effected by a given change in intrapleural pressure and is expressed as liters/cm H_2O. The amount of force needed to increase the lung volume depends upon the resistance of the tissue and the tension of the internal surface of the lung. The alveolar surface has a low surface tension when its area is small as when the lung is at its functional residual capacity, but surface tension rises rapidly when, during inspiration, the area of surface is expanded. The low surface tension at FRC tends to keep the alveoli from collapsing when the distending pressure is low and prevents atelectasis; the relatively high tension which develops during inspiration is the major part of the tissue resistance which must be overcome during respiration. At the end of inspiration, about two-thirds of the lung's elastic recoil is provided by surface forces and one-third by tissue forces. Since the young infant and child exert maximal inspiratory forces equivalent to the adult (Table 6), change in volume is governed by lung size, tissue composition, and surface tension. When the lung is small, the change in volume for a given pressure change will be small. The lung of the newly born infant has a compliance of 0.006 L/cm H_2O and a vital capacity of 200 ml (Table 11). The compliance is small when compared with the child or adult, but when it is divided by the FRC, it is 0.06 L/cm H_2O/L at all ages. The vital capacity is about twice the FRC in infancy and adulthood. Although the amount and composition of tissue elements alter with growth, the elasticity of the lungs does not seem to be affected. It is probable that in normal lungs the alveolar lining, which is apparently the same at all ages, is the predominant determinant of tissue elasticity. When airway resistance, functional residual capacity, the chest wall, and inspiratory force are normal, the vital capacity is a good index of lung compliance.

ALVEOLAR-PULMONARY CAPILLARY OXYGEN AND CARBON DIOXIDE PRESSURE DIFFERENCE. The larger the differences in partial pressures between the air and blood phase, the more gas is exchanged; thus the maximum flux occurs when the partial pressure of oxygen is high in the alveolus and low in precapillary blood, and the opposite is true of the partial pressure of carbon dioxide. When ventilation is greater than normal, partial pressure of oxygen in the alveoli is high and that of carbon dioxide is low, whereas when

ventilation is too low, the reverse is true. When respiratory dead space is large, alveolar oxygen pressure may be normal but carbon dioxide partial pressure is high. When cardiac output is diminished, or when the uptake of oxygen and production of carbon dioxide by the body's tissues are increased, the partial pressure of oxygen is low and the partial pressure of carbon dioxide is high in blood entering the pulmonary capillaries. Conversely, when cardiac output is excessive or tissue oxygen uptake and carbon dioxide production are small, partial pressure of oxygen in precapillary blood is high and that of carbon dioxide is low. At high altitude the partial pressure of oxygen in the alveoli is low.

ALVEOLAR SURFACE AREA. The normal adult lung has a surface area of about 80 square meters or approximately 1 square meter per kilogram. The surface area of the lung in the newly born is 4 square meters, also about 1 square meter per kilogram. Surface area appears to remain proportional to body size throughout childhood. It is not, however, proportional to metabolic requirements. The relatively large oxygen uptake of the infant requires an increase in total ventilation.

PULMONARY BLOOD FLOW. Venous return to the heart and the magnitude of right-to-left shunt determine total pulmonary blood flow. Cardiac output and pulmonary blood flow increase when either oxygen utilization, ventilation, or both increase, and when arterial oxygen tension is low. Ventilation and pulmonary blood flow are controlled by reflexes which can increase or decrease ventilation and cardiac output depending upon the amount of gas exchange needed. Changes in airway and vascular resistance are caused by alterations in pH and oxygen tension; when the pH or oxygen tension is low, the small airways dilate and the pulmonary arterioles constrict; when the pH or oxygen is high, the airways constrict and the pulmonary arterioles dilate. These reactions, which are dependent on the environment of the tissue, tend to match regional ventilation and blood flow and lead to an increase or decrease in ventilation to areas where blood flow is high or low, and an increase or decrease in perfusion to areas where ventilation is large or small. Thus when regional blood flow is reduced suddenly, carbon dioxide tension in the alveoli and surrounding tissue falls, the pH of

TABLE 11. *Ventilation*

	Newly Born	5 Years	10 Years	15 Years	Adult
Compliance (L/cm H_2O)	0.006	0.045	0.075	0.15	0.18
Compliance/FRC (L/cm H_2O/L)	0.06	0.06	0.06	0.06	0.06
Vital capacity (ml)	200	1,300	2,300	4,000	5,000
Functional residual capacity (FRC) (ml)	100	750	1,250	2,500	3,000
Diffusion capacity for carbon monoxide (ml/min/mm Hg pressure of CO_2)	1.5	7.5	15	25	30

the tissue rises, the bronchioles constrict, and ventilation to this region decreases. These mechanisms maintain partial pressures of 100 and 40 mm Hg, respectively, for oxygen and carbon dioxide in arterial blood during periods of widely varying metabolic demands and activity and in some instances in the presence of cardiopulmonary disease.

DIFFERENCE BETWEEN ALVEOLAR GAS AND CAPILLARY BLOOD. Carbon dioxide diffuses readily; in normal infants, children, and adults its partial pressure is only 1 to 2 mm Hg higher in arterial blood than in the alveoli. Oxygen diffuses less easily; when the partial pressure of alveolar oxygen is 100 mm Hg, pulmonary venous oxygen partial pressure depends upon the length of time blood is in the pulmonary capillaries and exposed to alveolar gas and upon the depth of tissue between gas and blood. In normal adults, the difference in partial pressure of oxygen between alveolar gas and arterial blood is less than 10 mm Hg; in infants it is greater. This difference may be due to several factors: rapid blood flow through short capillaries, proportionally large amount of interstitial tissue in the infant, uneven distribution of ventilation and perfusion, or intrapulmonary right-to-left shunts. The large amount of loose interstitial tissue in the infant may be increased further with pulmonary edema and inflammation which markedly widen the diffusion distance. In infants, children, and adults the uptake of carbon monoxide from the alveoli has been used to measure diffusion capacity. In the newborn it appears low; in older children as in adults, it is closely related to total lung capacity (surface area).

THE BARRIER FUNCTION OF THE PARENCHYMA. Alveolar cells and their protoplasmic processes delimit the interstitial space and, by regulating their permeability, keep tissue fluid from entering the alveoli. With maximal breaths and hypoxia, the cells are attenuated and diffusion distance is decreased; also the alveolar walls are more permeable to fluids and red blood cells. In the young infant, when undissolved gas enters the interstitial space, it can easily dissect between the loosely supported vessels and airways toward the hilum and the periphery. This process probably explains why pneumomediastinum, interstitial emphysema, and pneumothorax are common in infancy and childhood.

PHAGOCYTIC FUNCTION OF THE PARENCHYMA. When foreign particles are present in the alveoli, alveolar cells divide, free themselves from the wall, and act as phagocytes. The acellular layer lining the alveoli is continuous with the mucous lining of the airways, and particles caught on its surface are swept up the airway.

Diagnostic Procedures

BIOPSY. Biopsies of the lung or of regional lymph nodes are often necessary to diagnose localized or diffuse parenchymal disease. Biopsies are particularly useful in sarcoidosis and other granulomatous conditions, in proliferative interstitial reactions to beryllium and other irritative agents, and in unusual chronic diseases due to hypersensitivity or infection. When there is suppurative lung disease, biopsies should be avoided, since there is considerable danger of producing empyema or pneumothorax. There are several procedures: percutaneous needle biopsy, transbronchoscopic biopsy, open-lung biopsy, and lymph node biopsy.

Percutaneous needle biopsy with the Vim-Silverman or Franklin-Silverman needle is a relatively benign procedure. Krumholz and Weg reported no major complications in 60 consecutive percutaneous biopsies. However, 20 percent of their cases developed pneumothorax, and half of these required decompression by thoracostomy.

Anderson and Harrison did transbronchoscopic lung biopsies on 32 patients and were usually able to obtain satisfactory specimens from more than one area of the lung. There were no serious complications reported, although 6 of the 32 patients developed minor pneumothoraces. Multiple biopsies are desirable, since in most diffuse diseases of the lung, there are areas of normal lung tissue.

Open-lung biopsy is a commonly used procedure. We inflate the lung with an intrapulmonary pressure of 10 cm H_2O, place two clamps across the segment to be biopsied, cut between the clamps, and immediately place the clamped specimen in a rapidly penetrating fixative. This procedure usually preserves the architecture of the lung as it is during life. In 105 open-lung biopsies reviewed by Gaensler et al., there was one operative death and two major complications.

The fatty tissue overlying the scalenus anticus muscle in the neck usually contains a number of small lymph nodes into which lymph drains from the lungs. In 1949 Daniels suggested the removal and examination of these nodes for the diagnosis of malignant and nonmalignant pulmonary lesions such as sarcoidosis, tuberculosis, silicosis, and histoplasmosis. Complications are rare, but pneumothorax due to puncture of the apical pleura, hemidiaphragmatic paralysis following accidental section of the phrenic nerve, air embolism, hemorrhage, and infection occur occasionally.

PULMONARY FUNCTION TESTS. Diseases of the lung parenchyma may decrease lung volume, increase the amount of tissue between alveoli, partially or completely occlude bronchioles, and interrupt the pulmonary circulation. Depending on the type and distribution of the process, there will be decreases in the vital capacity, lung compliance, pulmonary diffusion capacity, and the partial pressure of oxygen in arterial blood; and increases in dead space ventilation and the partial pressure of carbon dioxide in arterial blood. Comroe and his associates have described in detail the various types of pulmonary function tests which may be useful in parenchymal diseases.

Since the maximal inspiratory force is constant in childhood (Table 6), an increase in tissue elasticity or a decrease in lung volume will also decrease the vital capacity, so that in those cases where compliance is low, vital capacity will also be reduced. Vital capacity maneuvers are easily performed with a spirometer and kymograph, which can also be used for measuring timed vital capacity and maximal expiratory flow rates (Figs. 29 and 19). It is the most useful single test for evaluating the stiffness of the lung. In most children the efficiency of gas exchange and the quality of lung tissue can be determined by measuring the vital capacity and the partial pressure of oxygen and carbon dioxide in arterial blood at rest and during exercise.

REFERENCES

Cook, C. D., and Hamann, J. F. Relation of lung volumes to height in healthy persons between the ages of 5 and 38 years. J. Pediat., 59:710, 1961.

DeMuth, G. R., and Howatt, W. F. The growth of lung function. Part III. Pulmonary diffusion. Pediatrics, 35:185, 1965.

Dunhill, M. S. Postnatal growth of the lung. Thorax, 17:329, 1962.

Engström, I., Karlberg, P., and Kraepelien, S. Respiratory studies in children. I. Lung volumes in healthy children 6 to 14 years of age. Acta Paediat. Scand., 46:277, 1956.

Stahlman, M. T. Pulmonary ventilation and diffusion in the human newborn infant. J. Clin. Invest., 36:1081, 1957.

Strang, L. B. Measurements of pulmonary diffusion capacity in children. Arch. Dis. Child., 35:232, 1960.

DIAGNOSIS

Anderson, H. A., and Harrison, E. G., Jr. Transbronchoscopic lung biopsy in diffuse pulmonary disease. Ann. Otol., 74:1113, 1965.

Comroe, J. H., Jr., Forster, R. E., DuBois, A. B., Briscoe, W. A., and Carlsen, E. The Lung, 2nd ed. Chicago, Year Book Publishers, 1955.

Daniels, A. C. A method of biopsy useful in diagnosing certain intrathoracic diseases. Dis. Chest, 16:360, 1949.

Gaensler, E. A., Moister, M. V. B., and Hamm, J. Open-lung biopsy in diffuse pulmonary disease. New Eng. J. Med., 270:1319, 1964.

Krumholz, R. A., and Weg, J. G. Percutaneous needle biopsy of the lung. J.A.M.A., 195:38, 1966.

19.6
DISEASES CAUSING REDUCTION OF THE PARENCHYMA

Reduction in Parenchyma Because of Absence of Tissue

AGENESIS OF THE LUNG. In the embryo the respiratory system begins as a median ventral diverticulum of the foregut, from which the epithelium and glands of the trachea, bronchi, and alveoli originate. This diverticulum grows into the mesoderm on the ventral surface of the foregut, which provides mesenchymal support, and divides into two lung buds. Each bud contains one tube, or bronchus, which divides dichotomously, until there are usually 18 generations at birth. Inhibition or aberrations in the sprouting of the bronchial tree may produce complete absence of bronchi and parenchyma (agenesis or aplasia) or underdeveloped lung, varying in degree from conditions in which the bronchus is present as a small outpocketing of the trachea to small lungs with normal architecture, hypoplasia. Absence of both lungs or of one lobe is very rare. Agenesis of one lung is more common.

In 1955 Valle reviewed 120 cases of unilateral pulmonary aplasia. Symptoms are usually present from birth, but occasionally the condition is asymptomatic. There are labored breathing, cyanosis, and cough. The thorax is usually symmetric, but there may be some scoliosis. Breath sounds from the aplastic lung are absent or bronchial in quality. The mediastinum shifts toward the affected side, and there is overinflation of the contralateral lung. X-ray of the chest shows a dense, homogeneous shadow with narrowing of the intercostal spaces. The appearance resembles massive atelectasis, and this is usually the initial diagnosis. In about one third of the 73 cases described by Oyamada et al. there were other congenital anomalies. This condition is compatible with life and may not produce symptoms—an unsuspected aplastic lung was found at autopsy in a 72-year-old woman.

Some authors believe that an agenesis of the pulmonary artery is primary, followed by failure of the development of the main bronchus and its subdivisions. However, since the vascularization of the lung follows the initial branching of the mainstem bronchus, it seems likely that there is primary failure of the lung bud.

HYPOPLASIA OF THE LUNG. Hypoplasia of the lung may be primary or secondary to a reduction in intrathoracic volume, as occurs with congenital diaphragmatic herniation. In the 24 cases of congenital diaphragmatic hernia described by Roe and Stephens, there were 10 hypoplastic lungs. In the primary cases not associated with thoracic space-occupying masses, the pulmonary artery is small and the hypoplasia may be due to failure of bronchial branching or secondary to hypoplasia of the pulmonary artery.

The signs, symptoms, and radiologic appearance of the chest in hypoplasia of the lung are similar to those in agenesis. The diagnosis is made by bronchography and pulmonary angiography.

LOBECTOMY AND PNEUMONECTOMY.   Segmental resections and the removal of lobes or whole lungs are done for a variety of reasons in childhood. When the excision is done for localized diseases such as cysts and aspiration of foreign bodies with atelectasis, there is usually no residual disease in the remaining parts of the lung. In these patients there is no apparent tendency for compensatory increase in volume or number of remaining lung units or pulmonary capillary bed. When a localized area of a generalized disease such as tuberculosis or bronchiectasis is removed, the remaining lung may still be diseased. In these patients there is usually a slight decrease in lung volume, an increase in resistance to airflow, and overdistension of the remaining units.

Reduction in Parenchyma Because of Space-Occupying Lesions

CYSTS OF THE LUNG.   There are a number of conditions in which sharply defined fluid or air-filled cysts with definite walls are found within the lung. About one third of all cases reported have been in children.

Pulmonary cysts in children often produce no symptoms. However, if they are large and compress adjacent airways, they may cause coughing, wheezing, and other signs and symptoms of obstructive airway disease. If they reduce markedly the amount of pulmonary tissue available for gas exchange, there will be cyanosis. When symptoms are present, there is usually a decrease in the vital capacity, a decrease in the maximal expiratory flow rates, and some arterial desaturation.

Some cysts are secondary to obstruction of an airway, as previously noted. These may become very large and require surgical excision. Other cysts result from purulent pneumonias, particularly staphylococcal pneumonias. These lesions are rarely large, are almost always asymptomatic, and do not require surgical excision. They usually regress spontaneously. However, cysts are occasionally found when there is no evidence of preceding obstruction or infection. These are probably congenital, since they commonly appear in children under 1 year of age, and when removed there is no pathologic evidence of inflammation of the bronchi, vessels, or alveoli. The high incidence in some ethnic groups, as reported by Baum et al., suggests that some may be inherited. If congenital cysts are large, infected, and cause symptoms, they should be removed. If they are small, not infected and do not produce symptoms, they should be observed.

CONGENITAL CYSTIC ADENOMATOID MALFORMATION OF THE LUNG.   These are hamartomas or nonneoplastic, tumorlike malformations with abnormal mixtures of pulmonary tissues. Kwittken and Reiner reviewed 32 cases. In the involved lung there are large numbers of cystic terminal respiratory structures which communicate with each other and are lined with pseudostratified ciliated columnar epithelium or respiratory cuboidal epithelium. There is an increase in elastic tissue, polypoid configuration of the mucosa, and commonly mucogenic cells lining the alveoli. There is usually no cartilage present and no evidence of inflammation.

These structures usually cause severe respiratory distress and cyanosis beginning at a few days or weeks of age. X-ray of the chest shows an increase in the size of the affected lobe with some areas of radiolucency. About one half of the affected newborn infants are hydropic, and there is a history of polyhydramnios in 20 percent of cases. Since these lesions are large, prompt diagnosis and surgical excision are required.

ACCESSORY LOBES AND SEQUESTERED LUNG.   Accessory lobes are small, usually located in the inferior portion of the left thorax, and are often associated with diaphragmatic defects. They may or may not have a communication with the bronchial tree, but they receive blood only from the bronchial arteries. They are usually asymptomatic, but if there is a bronchial connection, they may become infected and bronchiectasis may develop.

Sequestered lung segments are cystic, intrapulmonary lesions which have no direct communication with the bronchial tree and receive their blood supply from the systemic circulation. They are usually asymptomatic and are diagnosed incidentally druing routine chest films.

PULMONARY TUMORS.   The majority of the intrathoracic tumors in childhood are in the mediastinum. There are only a few cases of benign intrapulmonary tumors such as fibromas, lipomas, and hemangiomas reported. They are usually small and asymptomatic. Intrapulmonary malignant tumors such as neuroblastomas, sarcomas, lymphoblastomas, ganglioneuromas, and endotheliomas are somewhat more common.

Primary bronchogenic carcinoma of the lung is rare. McAldowie reported the first case in 1876. In 1954 Anderson reviewed 16 cases of carcinoma of the lung in children of 10 months to 14 years of age. They were all adenocarcinomas or undifferentiated carcinomas and occurred with equal frequency in both sexes. As with other malignancies of childhood, carcinomas of the lung grow rapidly and metastasize early. All of the patients reported by Anderson died. The mean survival time after diagnosis was six months, which is less than half the period of survival reported in adults.

PULMONARY ARTERIOVENOUS FISTULAS.   Large channels connecting a branch of the pulmonary artery to a pulmonary vein may be congenital or due to trauma. In 1957 Purriel and Muras reviewed 170 cases. Of these, 37 percent were in children. In 75 percent of those diagnosed in adults symptoms were present prior to the age of 15 years; 14 percent of the cases had had symptoms from infancy.

In some cases arteriovenous fistulas are asymptomatic and are discovered accidentally. In about 85 percent there is clubbing of the fingers and toes, cyanosis, and polycythemia; many patients have hemoptysis. A bruit is often present. A radiograph of the chest shows one or several large, irregular, lobulated densities in the mid or lower portion of the lung.

About 70 percent of patients with arteriovenous fistulas have cutaneous telangiectases. Telangiectases are small localized arteriovenous capillary connections that are actually tiny AV fistulas. They form groups of ruby-red lesions in the skin of the face and body and on the lips and may occur in all organs of the body. When they bleed they cause hemoptysis, hematuria, and gastrointestinal hemorrhage. Telangiectases are inherited. Hodgson and his colleagues found 129 cases of hereditary hemorrhagic telangiectasia (often called Rendu-Osler-Weber syndrome) in one family with 330 members; 15 percent of these 129 cases had AV fistulas. Since most pulmonary AV fistulas are one manifestation of hereditary telangiectasia, they should always be looked for when cutaneous telangiectases are present. When pulmonary AV fistulas cause symptoms, they should be removed.

CONGENITAL PULMONARY LYMPHANGIECTASIS (CONGENITAL DILATION OF THE PULMONARY LYMPHATICS). Laurence first described this rare condition which he considered a primary developmental abnormality of the pulmonary lymphatics. It is a generalized disease of the lung, causing cysts in the subpleural and interlobular connective tissue which are rarely more than 10 μ in diameter. There is abundant connective tissue in the septa which appears to be embryonic.

There were 22 cases reported until 1963, all of whom died under 2 weeks of age. In 1963 Javett and his co-workers reported an infant alive at 9 months of age. This infant had severe respiratory distress with retractions, prolonged expiration, and progressive cyanosis. X-ray of the chest showed voluminous lungs which did not alter in size with respiratory maneuvers. There is no known treatment.

Reduction in Parenchyma Because of Inflammation

Inflammation may involve the intraalveolar and interalveolar spaces, as in the bacterial and mycotic pneumonias, or be confined principally to the interalveolar tissue, as in viral pneumonias and pulmonary hypersensitivity diseases.

THE BACTERIAL PNEUMONIAS. Hospitalization for bacterial pneumonias has declined during the past three decades. In 1934, 4.8 percent of all the outpatients seen at the Harriet Lane Home had pneumonia, and 49 percent of them were hospitalized. In 1958, 3.3 percent of the outpatients had pneumonia, but only 18 percent of them were hospitalized (Ravitch and Fein, 1961). Early treatment of respiratory infections with antibiotics is probably the principal cause of this reduction in incidence. However, particularly in the winter months, bacterial pneumonias continue to be an important cause of severe illness.

Thirty years ago more than half of the pneumonias in childhood were caused by the *Diplococcus pneumoniae*. Today, with the widespread use of antibiotics, the frequency with which various organisms produce pneumonia is constantly changing. Pneumococcal pneumonias are still seen, but pneumonias due to *Staphylococcus aureus* have become much more common, and there has been an apparent increase in fungal and viral pneumonias.

The acute primary bacterial pneumonias have many common features. Their distribution is typical of pulmonary infections due to inhalation, and they usually locate in one or more of the following lobes or segments: the middle lobe, the lingula, the posterior and anterior segments of the upper lobes, or the superior segments of the lower lobes. As lobes or segments become consolidated and airless, the vital capacity decreases and the work of breathing increases—reflected in young infants and children by intercostal *retractions* and *flaring* of the alae nasae. The vital capacity and lung compliance are usually lower than would be predicted from the extent of consolidation. These changes are probably the result of congestion and an increase in parenchymal rigidity in the apparently normal areas of the lung. When the lung is extremely stiff, or if inspiration is inhibited by pleurisy and pain, the patient is unable to maintain an adequate ventilation, and oxygen tension falls and carbon dioxide tension rises in arterial blood. Blood which continues to flow through the consolidated areas of the lung cannot be oxygenated, which adds to the arterial desaturation.

Patients with bacterial pneumonias should be placed in bed and given adequate fluids (at least 100-120 ml/kg/day). When cyanosis is present, oxygen should be provided by tent or nasal catheter. Oxygen, so often used unnecessarily in other diseases, is a very important therapy in pneumonia. Aspirin will usually reduce the agitation and apprehension associated with fever and the discomfort caused by pleurisy. If pleuritic pain is severe, codeine (0.5 mg/kg body weight) should be given. Codeine will slightly depress the respiratory center, but by reducing splinting of the chest wall allows deeper breaths and often permits an increase in ventilation.

Pneumococcal Pneumonia. The pneumococcus rarely causes a primary infection, but usually invades the lung after the respiratory tract has been damaged by an unrelated viral or chemical agent. Initially, pneumococcal pneumonia is characterized by a rapidly mounting inflammatory edema and exudation of serum and red blood cells into the alveoli. Quickly, within 24 to 48 hours, the alveoli are filled with fibrin, leucocytes, red cells, and large numbers of pneumococci (red hepatization).

The onset of pneumococcal pneumonia is abrupt with fever, chills, chest pain, and dyspnea. These symptoms are usually preceded by an upper respiratory tract infection. Cough, which produces blood-tinged sputum, is present early but may disappear with lobar consolidation. The child appears acutely ill, and physical examination reveals tachypnea, tachycardia, and limited depth of inspiration. There is dullness to percussion over the affected segment of the lung, breath sounds are diminished, and bronchial breathing and pleural friction rubs may be heard. There are usually no rales until later in the course of the disease. Small, sterile, pleural effusions found by x-ray are common, and empyema may be a late complication. Thoracentesis may be necessary to distinguish between these two complications.

Penicillin is the specific treatment for pneumococcal pneumonia. Although there are reports of the successful use of oral preparations, we prefer procaine penicillin G administered intramuscularly (10,000 units/kg every 8 hours). Treatment should continue for at least two days after the patient's temperature becomes normal. Erythromycin (5 to 10 mg/kg every 6 hours) may be given to those children who are sensitive to penicillin. Although they may persist for several weeks, sterile effusions usually resolve without treatment. Complicating empyemas require closed-suction drainage.

The pneumococcus does not produce a true exotoxin, and the antigen of the polysaccharide capsule does not cause tissue necrosis. Consequently there is usually no residual lung damage following pneumococcal pneumonia.

Streptococcal Pneumonia. Pneumonia caused by Group A hemolytic streptococci usually follows one of the childhood exanthemas, particularly rubeola, varicella, and scarlet fever. Pneumonias due to the streptococcus are uncommon, but they accounted for 13 percent of 93 children hospitalized with pneumonia in the Boston Children's Hospital in 1959. All of these children developed empyema; all but three had received antibiotics before the diagnosis was made. The streptococcus first invades the upper respiratory tract. Local inflammatory reaction may block lymphatic vessels, after which there is retrograde extension of the infection through the lymphatics to the bronchi, lung parenchyma, and pleural surface. In the early stage most of the inflammatory reaction is often interstitial and resembles that of interstitial pneumonias caused by viruses or pleuropneumonialike organisms. The small bronchi may become partially obstructed if there is peribronchiolar inflammation. Distal to the obstruction, poorly ventilated, hyperinflated regions of the parenchyma may become the site of abscess or pneumotocele formation. In other cases there is a rapid accumulation of edema

fluid in the interstitial spaces, which enters the alveoli. The interstitial spaces and the bronchial walls are infiltrated with leucocytes, and there is shedding of the alveolar epithelium. During the healing phase of streptococcal pneumonias, the intraalveolar edema fluid, red blood cells, fibrin, and other debris may coalesce and produce hyaline membranes.

Streptococcal pneumonia characteristically follows the sudden onset of sore throat with hoarseness, fever, chest pain, cough, and marked respiratory distress. The child appears acutely ill. Leucocytosis is usually present. There is dullness to percussion over the affected lung. If an effusion is present and if the pneumonia is localized to a segment or lobe, crepitant rales and pleural friction rubs are usually heard. A radiograph of the chest may show segmental involvement, diffuse peribronchiolar densities, or effusion. The x-ray findings may resemble those in interstitial pneumonia caused by viruses or the purulent pneumonias with abscess formation and pneumatoceles seen with staphylococcal lung infections. In addition to abscess formation, the most common complication is empyema. Less commonly, pericarditis, peritonitis, systemic streptococcal disease, and purpura fulminans occur.

Large doses of intravenous or intramuscular penicillin G (100,000 units/kg/day or more) are necessary to treat streptococcal pneumonia effectively. The clinical response, the decrease in the white cell count, and the disappearance of the streptococcus may proceed slowly after initiating penicillin therapy; three to four weeks of treatment may be required. Empyema requires closed-suction drainage.

Staphylococcal Pneumonia. During the past decade the staphylococcus, particularly phage type 80-81, has become a common cause of suppurative pneumonia, especially in infants. The organisms first produce a diffuse inflammation in one or more segments of the lung, which may early—and deceptively—resemble pneumonitis of viral etiology. The right lung is more often affected than the left. Inflamed bronchi become partially occluded and pneumatoceles are formed beyond the obstruction. The bacteria grow rapidly and produce a necrotizing toxin, which causes tissue destruction. Microabscesses form around small bronchi and in pneumatoceles. Pneumatoceles and abscesses extend toward the pleural space and frequently rupture into it, causing empyema and pneumothorax.

Staphylococcal pneumonias are usually characterized by the rapid development of fever, tachypnea, dyspnea, tachycardia, and cyanosis. The onset is often preceded by an upper respiratory infection for which antibiotics have been given. The child with staphylococcal pneumonia may be lethargic or irritable and usually appears acutely ill. Ileus and abdominal distension are common. The physical signs reflect the progress of the disease. There may be evidence of inflammation and consolidation, hyperinflation if pneumatoceles are large, pneumothorax, or pleural effusions. The chest x-ray may show a lobar distribution of radiodensities, effusion, or pneumo-thorax; most characteristic are discrete areas of over-inflation and distinct pneumatoceles.

Staphylococcal pneumonia must be treated with maximal doses of a penicillin or other antibiotic for no less than four weeks. If the staphylococcus is sensitive to penicillin, the drug of choice is penicillin G (150,000 units/kg/12 hours). If the staphylococcus is resistant to penicillin, the drug of choice is sodium dimethoxyphenyl penicillin (50 mg/kg/6 hours). Pneumothorax, which occurs in the first or second day of the disease, must be decompressed, but large pneumatoceles may resemble a pneumothorax so that caution must be exercised not to enter inadvertently a pneumatocele, causing a pneumothorax and inducing an empyema. However, pneumatoceles are part of the healing process and are seen three to four days after treatment has begun. If empyema is present, it must be promptly treated by closed-suction drainage. Surgical decompression is most urgent in infancy.

Huxtable, Tucker, and Wedgwood followed, for an average of 43 months, 22 children who had recovered from staphylococcal pneumonia. There was complete radiologic resolution in 19 and only minimal residua in 3. All had normal exercise tolerance and growth following recovery.

THE MYCOTIC INFECTIONS. Pulmonary infections with fungi appear to be increasing in frequency. The mycoses tend to infect debilitated patients, especially those with leukemia or chronic pulmonary disease. Patients receiving prolonged steroid therapy or long-term antibiotic therapy are particularly susceptible to fungal infections. Some pulmonary mycotic infections, such as histoplasmosis and coccidioidomycosis, are extremely common in certain circumscribed geographic areas. (See also Sec. 14.43.)

Histoplasmosis. Primary infection of the lung with *Histoplasma capsulatum* is very common in endemic areas and usually produces no symptoms. Occasionally, histoplasmosis is a disseminated systemic infection; 10 cases under 10 years of age are included in the Communicable Disease Center's Co-operative Mycosis Study (1963). Rarely, an acute rapidly progressing pulmonary inflammation occurs and is associated with fever, anorexia, malaise, tachypnea, tachycardia, and rales. X-rays of the chest show enlargement of the hilar nodes with perihilar parenchymal opacities. In children the chronic progressive form of pulmonary histoplasmosis is very uncommon. The only effective treatment for disseminated or progressive pulmonary histoplasmosis is intravenous amphotericin B (0.5 to 1.0 mg/kg/day until a total dose of at least 25 mg/kg has been reached).

Coccidioidomycosis. Primary infection of the lungs with *Coccidioides immitis* is also very common in endemic areas, especially in arid regions of the southwest United States, Mexico, and other parts of Central America. In 1963, 35,000 new cases were reported, most of them asymptomatic. Many of these had a low-grade fever, minimal lung involvement,

and erythema nodosum typical of "valley fever." Occasionally there is progressive primary lung inflammation, which must be treated vigorously. The only effective treatment is intravenous administration of 1 mg/kg/day of amphotericin B for a total dose of 50 mg/kg. Occasionally much larger doses are required. Ziering and Rockas in 1964 reported starting an apparently successful course of treatment in a 3-month-old infant with disseminated pulmonary coccidiodomycosis. A total dose of 2 g of amphotericin B was given over an 18-month period.

Aspergillosis. Aspergilli, particularly *A. fumigatus,* are commonly found in the sputum of patients with chronic pulmonary disease. They may be harmless saprophytic commensals but may be responsible for a primary disease process. The most common manifestations of pulmonary aspergillosis are mycetomas or fungus balls. These usually form in previously existing bronchiectatic cavities such as occur in cavitary histoplasmosis.

Rarely, in previously normal children, aspergilli cause an acute pneumonia which is usually fatal. Strelling and his co-workers described two cases and reviewed four others. These children had an acute onset of dyspnea, fever, cough, diminished breath sounds, and rales. Chest x-ray showed widely distributed, fluffy opacities.

Pulmonary aspergillosis occasionally produces migratory pulmonary lesions, eosinophilia, and other evidences of acute pulmonary or systemic hypersensitivity. One case of secondary Henoch-Schönlein purpura from this cause was reported by Mann and Pasha in 1959. The allergic aspect of aspergillosis must be emphasized. Some physicians feel that aspergillosis pneumonia occurs only in patients with asthma.

Aspergillosis pneumonia should be treated with intravenous amphotericin B (1 mg/kg/day to a total dose of 25 mg/kg). Localized mycetomas should be excised if the remainder of the lung is normal, or treated with the local instillation of amphotericin B as described by Ramirez. The allergic manifestations of aspergillosis may be dramatically relieved by prednisone.

Case VI. *R.B. is a 16-year-old boy who had moderately severe asthma for which he received intermittent corticosteroid therapy from the age of 4 years. At 11 years of age a right upper lobe lobectomy was performed for bronchiectasis. At 15 years of age he was admitted to the hospital with cough, dyspnea, weight loss, and a chest x-ray showing typical aspergilli mycetomas (Fig. 30).*

Pulmonary function studies revealed a reduction in vital capacity, decreased inspiratory and expiratory flow rates, an increase in functional residual capacity, and normal arterial oxygen and carbon dioxide tensions at rest. Arterial oxygen tension fell, and carbon dioxide tension rose, with moderate exercise (Table 12). Since he had bronchiectasis of the right middle and both lower lobes, excision of the mycetomas in the left upper lobe was not undertaken. He received a total dose of 3 g of amphotericin B intravenously

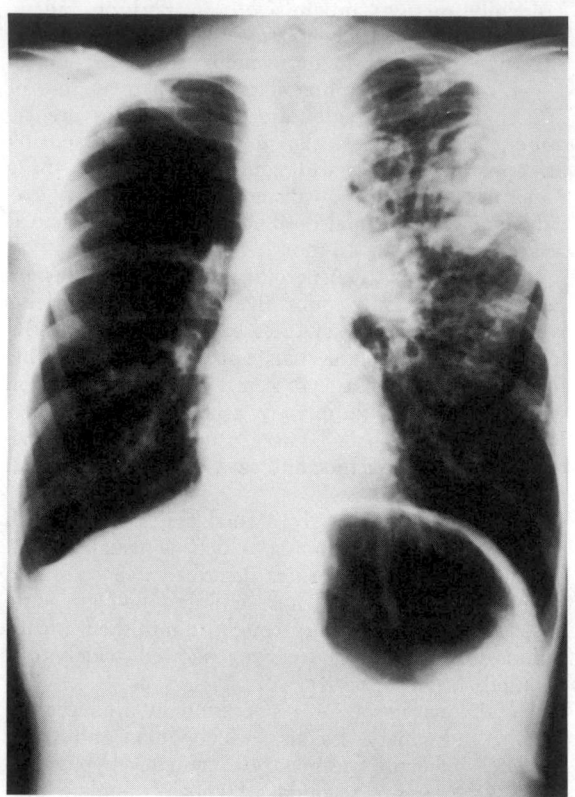

Fig. 30. Chest radiogram showing typical aspergilli mycetomas.

Actinomycosis. Actinomycosis is a chronic mycotic infection which tends to be suppurative and forms abscesses and sinus tracts in the cervicofacial area. Pulmonary infections are not uncommon in adults. In children, actinomycosis is apparently rare. Paul, however, reported two children from one hospital with widespread pneumonia caused by actinomycosis. She successfully treated these children with one million units of intramuscular penicillin G per day for two months. Penicillin in generous dosage appears to be the therapy of choice.

Nocardiosis. This chronic and suppurative disease resembles actinomycosis. Abscesses and sinuses are less common, however, and in children the lung is more often involved. It may occur as a complication of immune-deficient disease, such as fatal granulomatous disease. Seventeen cases of pulmonary nocardiosis have been reported in children. There is persistent cough, intermittent septic fever, hepatosplenomegaly, and progressive pulmonary insufficiency. Treatment with a combination of sulfadiazine and tetracycline has been effective. Localized abscesses, when they occur, should be excised.

Blastomycosis, Cryptococcosis, Candidiasis, Sporotrichosis. Blastomyces, cryptococci, and candidae have all caused pulmonary inflammation in children, and for these amphotericin B, although quite toxic, appears to be the only effective agent. Sporotrichum has been occasionally identified as the organism responsible for chronic pulmonary inflammation. This infection responds to some extent to therapy with potassium iodide, but again amphotericin B is probably the drug of choice.

REFERENCES

DISEASES CAUSING REDUCTION IN PARENCHYMA BECAUSE OF ABSENCE OF TISSUE

Booth, J. B., and Berry, C. L. Unilateral pulmonary agenesis. Arch. Dis. Child., 42:361, 1967.
Cook, C. D., and Bucci, G. Studies of respiratory physiology in children. IV. The late effects of lobectomy on pulmonary function. Pediatrics, 28:234, 1961.
Ferencz, C. Congenital abnormalities of pulmonary vessels and their relation to malformations of the lung. Pediatrics, 28:993, 1961.
Filler, J. Effects upon pulmonary function of lobectomy

over a three-month period without improvement in his clinical condition, pulmonary function, or his x-ray. A small polyethylene catheter was then passed into the trachea through the cricothyroid membrane and placed into the left upper bronchus. Amphotericin B (0.5 mg in 2 ml 0.9 percent sodium chloride) was instilled through this catheter into the area of the mycetomas daily for 12 months. After three months of this treatment, the mycetomas disappeared and his pulmonary function improved (Table 12). However, widespread bronchiectasis remains and is probably responsible for the low vital capacity, hyperinflation, and reduced expiratory flow rate.

TABLE 12.   *Aspergillosis (R. B.)*

		Before Therapy	18 Months After Therapy
Vital capacity (% normal)		70	80
Functional residual capacity (% normal)		174	133
Arterial blood gas tension (mm Hg)	Po_2 (rest)	85	88
	Po_2 (exercise)	72 (200 kg-m/6 min)	85 (300 kg-m/6 min)
	Pco_2 (rest)	39	40
	Pco_2 (exercise)	46 (200 kg-m/6 min)	41 (300 kg-m/6 min)
Expiratory flow rates (% normal)		25	50
Inspiratory flow rates (% normal)		50	90

performed during childhood. Amer. Rev. Resp. Dis., 89:801, 1964.

Giammona, S. T., Mandelbaum, I., Battersby, J. S., and Daly, W. J. The late cardiopulmonary effects of childhood pneumonectomy. Pediatrics, 37:79, 1966.

Landing, B. H. Anomalies of the respiratory tract. *In* Symposium on Respiratory Disorders. Pediat. Clin. N. Amer., Feb., 1957, p. 73.

Oyamada, A., Gasul, B. M., and Holinger, P. H. Agenesis of the lung. Report of a case, with a review of all previously reported cases. Amer. J. Dis. Child., 85:182, 1953.

Roe, B. B., and Stephens, H. B. Congenital diaphragmatic hernia and hypoplastic lung. J. Thorac. Surg., 32:279, 1956.

Valle, A. R. Agenesis of the lung. Amer. J. Surg., 89:90, 1955.

DISEASES CAUSING REDUCTION IN PARENCHYMA BECAUSE OF SPACE-OCCUPYING LESIONS

Anderson, A. E. Bronchogenic carcinoma in young men. Amer. J. Med., 16:404, 1954.

Baum, G. L., Racz, I., Bubis, J. J., and Molho, M. Cystic disease of the lung. Report of 88 cases, with an ethnologic relationship. Amer. J. Med., 40:578, 1966.

Caffey, J. On the natural regression of pulmonary cysts during early infancy. Pediatrics, 11:48, 1953.

Hodgson, C. H., Burchell, H. B., Good, C. A., and Clagett, O. T. Hereditary hemorrhagic telangiectasia and pulmonary arteriovenous fistula. New Eng. J. Med., 261:625, 1959.

Javett, S. N., Webster, I., and Braudo, J. L. Congenital dilatation of the pulmonary lymphatics. Pediatrics, 31:416, 1963.

Kwittken, J., and Reiner, L. Congenital cystic adenomatoid malformation of the lung. Pediatrics, 30:759, 1962.

Laurence, K. M. Congenital pulmonary lymphangiectasis. J. Clin. Path., 12:62, 1959.

McAldowie, A. M. Primary cancer of the lungs in a child five and a half months old. Lancet, 2:570, 1876.

Osler, W. On a family form of recurring epistaxis, associated with multiple telangiectases of the skin and mucous membranes. Bull. Hopkins Hosp., 12:333, 1901.

Pinney, C. T., and Salyer, J. M. Bronchopulmonary sequestration. J. Thorac. Surg., 33:791, 1957.

Purriel, P., and Muras, O. Aneurismas arteriovenosos depulmon. Torax, 6:101, June, 1957.

Rendu, M. Epistaxis répétées chez un sujet porteur de petits angiomes cutanés et muqueux. Soc. Med. Hôp. Paris, Bull. Mem., 13:731, 1896.

Weber, F. P. Multiple hereditary developmental angiomata (telangiectases) of the skin and mucous membranes associated with recurring haemorrhages. Lancet, 2:160, 1907.

THE BACTERIAL PNEUMONIAS

Gourlay, R. H. Staphylococcal pneumonia and empyema in infants and children. Canad. Med. Ass. J., 87:1101, 1962.

Huxtable, K. A., Tucker, A. S., and Wedgwood, R. J. Staphylococcal pneumonia in childhood. Long-term follow-up. Amer. J. Dis. Child., 108:262, 1964.

Johnson, J. R., and Bauer, L. E. Segmental consolidation of the lung. Amer. J. Med., 30:147, 1961.

Kevy, S. V., and Lowe, B. A. Streptococcal pneumonia and empyema in childhood. New Eng. J. Med., 264:738, 1961.

Marshall, R., and Christie, R. V. The visco-elastic properties of lungs in acute pneumonia. Clin. Sci., 13:403, 1954.

Middelkamp, J. N., Purkerson, M. L., and Burford, T. H. The changing pattern of empyema thoracis in pediatrics. J. Thorac. Cardiov. Surg., 47:165, 1964.

Ravitch, M. M., and Fein, R. The changing picture of pneumonia and empyema in infants and children. J.A.M.A., 175:1039, 1961.

Witt, R. L., and Hamburger, M. The nature and treatment of pneumococcal pneumonia. Med. Clin. N. Amer., 47:1257, 1963.

MYCOTIC INFECTIONS

Blattner, R. Pulmonary aspergillosis in children. J. Pediat., 70:139, 1967.

Carlile, W. K., Holley, K. E., and Logan, G. B. Fetal acute disseminated nocardiosis in a child. J.A.M.A., 184:477, 1963.

Furculow, M. L. Communicable disease cooperative study: Comparison of treated and untreated severe histoplasmosis. J.A.M.A., 183:823, 1963.

———— The use of amphotericin B in blastomycosis, cryptococcosis, and histoplasmosis. Med. Clin. N. Amer., 47:1119, 1963.

Mann, B., and Pasha, M. A. Allergic primary pulmonary aspergillosis and Schönlein-Henoch purpura. Brit. Med. J., 1:282, 1959.

Paul, F. M. Two cases of thoracic actinomycosis in children. Arch Dis. Child., 38:276, 1963.

Peabody, J. W., and Seabury, J. H. Actinomycosis and nocardiosis. A review of basic differences in therapy. Amer. J. Med., 28:99, 1960.

Ramirez, R. J. Pulmonary aspergilloma—endobronchial treatment. New Eng. J. Med., 271:1281, 1964.

Ridgeway, N. A., Whitcomb, F. C., Erickson, E. E., and Law, S. W. Primary pulmonary sporotrichosis. Amer. J. Med., 32:153, 1962.

Strelling, M. K., Rhaney, K., Simmons, D. A. R., and Thomson, J. Fatal acute pulmonary aspergillosis in two children of one family. Arch. Dis. Child., 41:34, 1966.

Tesh, R. B., Shacklette, M. H., Diercks, F. H., and Hirschl, D. Histoplasmosis in children. Pediatrics, 33:894, 1964.

Utz, J. P. Chemotherapeutic agents for the systemic mycoses. New Eng. J. Med., 268:938, 1963.

Winn, W. A. Coccidioidomycosis and amphotericin B. Med. Clin. N. Amer., 47:1131, 1963.

Ziering, W. H., and Rockas, H. R. Coccidioidomycosis. Long term treatment with amphotericin B of disseminated disease in a three month old baby. Amer. J. Dis. Child., 108:454, 1964.

pulmonary infections. A history of severe, recurrent infections of the lung should alert the physician to the possibility of the presence of these diseases.

19.7
PNEUMONITIS

Immunologic Defects Predisposing to Recurrent Pulmonary Infections

Recurrent sinopulmonary infections are characteristic of several immunologic deficiency diseases. These include agammaglobulinemia, "acquired" hypogammaglobulinemia, ataxia-telangiectasia, and Wiskott-Aldrich syndrome. Methotrexate and treatment with other immunosuppressive drugs also predispose to

Diseases Causing Interalveolar Inflammation

Viral and certain parasitic infections, chemical irritants, allergic reactions, and some diseases of unknown origin cause an interstitial inflammation. The reaction may be acute, with histamine release, which causes bronchospasm and pulmonary edema; or it may be subacute, with the accumulation of round cells and the formation of granulomas in the interalveolar spaces. After injury of this type there is a proliferation of fibroblasts, and healing is often accompanied by fibrosis.

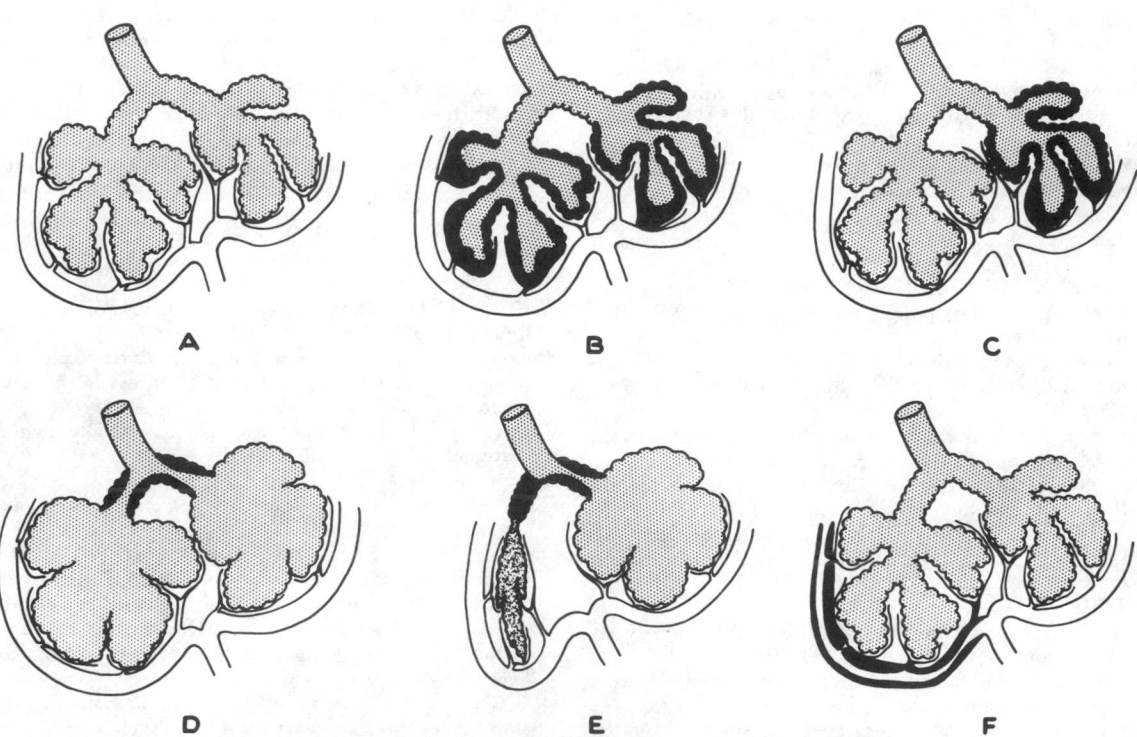

Fig. 31. A schematic representation of the possible sites of interalveolar inflammation. A. Normal portion of lung with a narrow space between the alveolar and capillary walls and uniform distribution of both ventilation and blood flow. B. An inflammatory process spread out evenly between the alveoli and pulmonary capillaries—lung volume, vital capacity, lung compliance, and diffusion capacity are low; there is arterial desaturation with exercise; the distribution of ventilation and perfusion is uniform. C. Part of the lung is normal and part is affected—again, lung volume, vital capacity, lung compliance and diffusion capacity are low; there is arterial desaturation but in this instance the distribution of ventilation and perfusion is not uniform. D. An inflammatory reaction surrounding all the small bronchi—lung volume is large, vital capacity low, and diffusion capacity normal; there may be arterial desaturation with exercise; the distribution of ventilation and perfusion is uniform. E. Peribronchial inflammation partially occluding some small airways causing hyperinflation and completely occluding other small airways producing atelectasis—lung volume may be normal or low; vital capacity and lung compliance are low; diffusion capacity is normal when related to the volume of lung ventilated, but is low in absolute terms. There is arterial desaturation at rest and with exercise; the distribution of ventilation and perfusion is not uniform. F. Only the perivascular area of the parenchyma is involved—lung volume, vital capacity and lung compliance are normal; diffusion capacity is low, the apparent physiologic dead space is large; there is arterial desaturation with exercise and there may be some at rest; the distribution of ventilation is uniform but the distribution of perfusion is not uniform.

The signs, symptoms, and pathophysiology of these diseases vary, depending upon the localization of the inflammation. Figure 31 displays some of the possible sites of interstitial infiltration. If the process is confined to the boundary between alveoli and capillaries, the lung will be stiff, the vital capacity reduced, the pulmonary diffusion capacity low, and there will be desaturation of the arterial blood with exercise or, in severe cases, at rest. Such localization and pure "alveolar-capillary block" probably does not occur. Infiltration about small airways produces the signs and symptoms of airway obstruction with a decrease in vital capacity, a decrease in expiratory flow rates, and an increase in the work of breathing. When inflammation surrounds the pulmonary vessels, vital capacity may be normal but diffusion capacity will be low, and the apparent physiologic dead space large. Most interstitial diseases of the lung affect the alveolar-capillary boundary and the peribronchial and perivascular spaces and cause signs, symptoms, and physiologic changes which are a combination of those seen in "alveolar-capillary block" and obstruction of the airways and pulmonary vessels.

Interstitial Pneumonitis Caused by Infectious Agents

THE VIRAL PNEUMONIAS. The viruses of the childhood exanthemas, such as varicella, rubeola, and most of the respiratory viruses, may cause interstitial pneumonitis. With the use of tissue culture and the determination of antibody titers, specific agents have been identified in up to 50 percent of cases. The respiratory syncytial viruses, the myxoviruses, and adenoviruses are the most common organisms, but the frequency with which they affect the lung varies from year to year.

Viral pneumonitis is characterized by the sudden onset of tachypnea, nonproductive cough, substernal discomfort, low-grade fever, and malaise after several days of an upper respiratory tract or exanthematous infection. The pharynx is reddened, and there is a slight nasopharyngeal mucous discharge. There may be dullness over the lung, diminished breath sounds, and fine, crepitant rales. Often, however, there are no physical signs of lung disease, even though there are diffuse perihilar and parenchymal infiltrations seen on the chest x-ray.

No specific therapy is available. Treatment includes rest, adequate fluid intake, and aspirin. If airway obstruction is present, bronchodilators and the other measures outlined previously for diseases of the airway should be used. If there is cyanosis, oxygen should be given.

The mortality rate is low, but convalescence is often prolonged. Neurasthenia lasting for several weeks is common.

Psittacosis Pneumonitis. The signs and symptoms of infection with Bedsoniae organisms, particularly the psittacosis virus, are indistinguishable from those associated with other viral infections of the lung. A history of contact with birds (especially psittacine birds) should suggest this agent. Psittacosis virus is best treated with one of the tetracyclines. We have recently seen a case in a 2-week-old infant following a visit to his grandmother who had infected parakeets.

Q-Fever. *Rickettsia burneti* causes an acute pneumonitis characterized by an infiltration of the peribronchiolar and perivascular spaces with plasma cells and lymphocytes. The disease usually begins with severe headache which is followed by the gradual onset of chills, fever, malaise, nonproductive cough, and substernal chest pain. The clinical and x-ray picture is similar to other viral infections of the lung. The diagnosis must be made by recovery of the virus from the blood or by specific serologic tests. *Rickettsia burneti* is sensitive to the tetracyclines and chloramphenicol, and infections respond to therapy with either.

MYCOPLASMA PNEUMONIAE (EATON AGENT) PNEUMONIA. The pleuropneumonialike organisms (PPLO) cause an acute, self-limited interstitial pneumonitis and necrotizing bronchiolitis. After about a two-week incubation period the onset of symptoms is abrupt, with malaise, generalized aches, and a paroxysmal, nonproductive cough. There are few physical findings, but rales are usually heard at the bases of the lung late in the disease. As in the viral pneumonias, the absence of physical signs is in contrast to the x-ray appearance of marked perihilar densities and diffuse, mottled, parenchymal infiltrations. A specific diagnosis can be established by culturing *Mycoplasma pneumoniae* from sputum or blood, although this is technically difficult. In addition, serum from these patients contains a macroglobulin which in an environment of $0°$ to $10°$ C agglutinates human, type O red cells (cold agglutination). Infections with this organism are best treated with tetracyclines, especially dimethylchlortetracycline.

THE PARASITIC PNEUMONIAS. *Pneumocystis carinii Pneumonitis.* In 1938, Ammich described a peculiar interstitial pneumonitis of premature infants. This disease is characterized by a diffuse, interalveolar infiltration of histiocytes which greatly widens the alveolar septa. There is sloughing of the alveolar lining and the accumulations of a granular, foamy eosinophilic material within the alveoli. In 1951 Vanek described *Pneumocystis carinii* within the intraalveolar macrophages. These organisms are best visualized by Giemsa stain. In the past three decades many cases of *Pneumocystis carinii* pneumonitis in infants have been reported from Europe and a very few in the past decade from the United States.

In premature infants, the onset of *Pneumocystis carinii* pneumonitis is insidious and usually starts at 4 to 6 months of age. The infant looks ill, becomes restless or languid, and his respiratory rate increases. After two or three weeks, marked respiratory distress develops with sternal and intercostal retraction and severe cyanosis. Physical examination may reveal areas of fine, crepitant rales, particularly after coughing. If the infiltrative process is peribronchial, the small bronchi may become partially occluded and cause overinflation of lung tissue distal to the obstruction. These areas of hyperinflation may rupture into the pleural space, causing pneumothorax, or rupture within the lung allowing air to dissect through the interstitial tissue to the mediastinum causing mediastinal emphysema. Chest x-ray shows areas of hyperinflation alternating with areas of opacification.

In older children *Pneumocystis carinii* causes a diffuse pulmonary inflammation, with marked cyanosis and minimal constitutional symptoms. The disease usually occurs in patients with low or absent immunoglobulins or following prolonged administration of corticosteroids or other suppressants of immunity. It may be seen in association with salivary gland virus infections.

Spontaneous cures in infants and children have been reported, although the mortality is about 50 percent. Recently hydroxystilbamide (4 mg/kg/day for 2 weeks) or pentamidine isethionate (4 mg/kg im per day for 2 to 3 weeks) has been used successfully in treatment of this disease.

Toxocara canis Pneumonitis (Visceral Larva Migrans). Infestation with *T. canis* usually occurs in children under 4 years of age with a history of pica. The parasite is swallowed, invades the intestine, and is carried by the portal circulation to the liver. In 7 of 17 cases reported by Snyder (1961), there was pulmonary involvement. The disease is characterized by recurrent fever, cough, lassitude, anorexia, and weight loss. There is usually hepatomegaly. Eosinophilia of greater than 30 percent is a constant feature of the disease. The chest film shows a diffuse, parenchymal infiltration and occasionally miliary nodules similar to those seen in miliary tuberculosis. The organism can be directly identified only by liver or lung biopsy. Treatment with diethylcarbamazine (20 mg/kg/day for a month) and corticosteroids may be effective.

Filaria Pneumonitis (Tropical Eosinophilia). Tropical eosinophilia is a common cause of pneumonitis in India and some areas of Central America and southeast Asia. Most of the cases are in children under 10 years of age. The disease is characterized by diffuse interstitial edema and interalveolar infiltration of eosinophils. The onset is insidious with a low-grade fever, hacking dry cough, wheezing, and nocturnal respiratory distress. Rales may be heard at the bases of the lungs. Chest x-ray shows diminished translucency with an increase in hilar markings. The eosinophil count is always elevated to at least 2,500 cells per mm^3. Treatment with diethylcarbamazine (6 mg/kg three times per day for five days) is usually successful.

Interstitial Pneumonitis Caused by Chemical Agents

Silo-Fillers' Disease. In 1956 Lowry and Schuman described an acute pneumonitis in adults following exposure to freshly filled silos. The disease is caused by inhalation of nitrogen dioxide. The interalveolar septa become edematous, widened, and filled with an accumulation of mononuclear cells and fibroblasts; the alveolar epithelium becomes hyperplastic. In 1964, Olson reported a typical case in a 6-year-old boy.

At the time of exposure to nitrogen dioxide there are cough and dyspnea followed by a period of several days in which there are no symptoms. After the symptom-free interval, there is an abrupt onset of chills, fever, dyspnea, cyanosis, and cough. There are rales throughout the lungs, and chest x-ray shows diffuse pulmonary infiltration. Corticosteroids have been used in treatment. However, the course is usually fulminating and the mortality is high.

Kerosene Pneumonia. (See also Sec. 13.6) Kerosene can be aspirated during the vomiting and gagging which follows its accidental ingestion, or it can be absorbed from the intestine and excreted through the lungs. It produces acute interalveolar edema and mononuclear cell infiltration with exudation into the alveoli. This condition is characterized by the sudden onset of dyspnea, cyanosis, and high fever. The clinical course is often alarming, but most patients recover. Chest x-ray shows diffuse pulmonary infiltrations. Treatment is symptomatic. Antibiotics may be useful to prevent secondary bacterial infection.

Pneumonitis Caused by Ingestion of Long-Chain Hydrocarbons. Old English and Red Cedar furniture polishes may cause very severe pneumonitis. Ingestion of these and similar compounds are now a more common cause of pneumonitis than inhalation or ingestion of kerosene. Patients ingesting furniture polish are hospitalized more frequently, for longer periods of time, and have a higher death rate than those ingesting kerosene. These patients present with high fever, lethargy, cyanosis, tachypnea, and cough. Their lungs are filled with rales and x-rays of the chest show diffuse mottled radiodensities. Treatment includes antibiotics, oxygen, and steroids. *Old English, Red Cedar, and other furniture polishes are so toxic to children that unless they can be locked in cupboards out of reach, they should not be kept in the home.*

Pneumonitis from Other Chemicals. Many chemicals, if inhaled in high concentrations, may cause acute interalveolar edema and mononuclear infiltration and intraalveolar exudation with a sudden onset of cough, substernal pain, and cyanosis. Prolonged exposure to lower concentrations of the same agents may cause a chronic interstitial pneumonitis, characterized by interalveolar granuloma formation similar to that seen in sarcoidosis. Organic compounds such as shellac, gum arabic, and polyvinylpyrrolidone (a macromolecular substance found in hair spray), and inorganic substances such as beryllium, mercury vapors, and chlorine may cause this reaction. Corticosteroids reduce the inflammatory process and may prevent fibrosis.

Interstitial Pneumonitis Due to Hypersensitivity

Sarcoidosis
(See also Sec. 18.2)

Sarcoidosis is a generalized disease of unknown cause which may affect the lungs, eyes, skin, lymph nodes, liver, and other tissues. In the lung there are interalveolar, peribronchiolar, and periarteriolar granulomas characterized by nests of epithelioid cells and Langhans' giant cells surrounded by a thin wall of lymphocytes. The granulomas are rarely necrotic and never show central caseation. Diffuse infiltration of the interalveolar space with mononuclear cells precedes the formation of granulomas. The periarteriolar granulomas are relatively vascular and are often surrounded with hyalinelike material. This stage of the disease resembles polyarteritis nodosa. Late in the disease the granulomas may be replaced by fibroblasts and fibrous tissue.

The onset of sarcoidosis is insidious, with anorexia, fatigue, lethargy, and weight loss. There may be a dry, hacking cough with mild dyspnea. Physical findings related to the lung are usually minimal. The presence of the disease in other organs is responsible for most of the symptoms—particularly the eyes, with iritis, uveitis, and keratitis; the parotid gland, with uveoparotid fever; and the kidneys, with acute glomerulonephritis. The serum globulins, particularly the α_2 globulins, are elevated, serum albumin is low, and occasionally there is hypercalcemia. Initially, the chest film shows enlargement of hilar nodes, followed by a diffuse pulmonary infiltration after weeks or months. Diagnosis is best made by scalene node or lung biopsy.

Sarcoidosis is probably a delayed hypersensitivity reaction, and the worldwide distribution suggests that many agents may be responsible. In the southern United States the disease is attributed to exposure to the loblolly pine (Cummings, 1956) or peanuts.

Long-term therapy of the kind used in diseases known to be due to hypersensitivity is usually followed by a dramatic remission of symptoms. Both corticosteroids (2 mg/kg every other day) and chloroquine (5 to 10 mg/kg twice a day) have been used successfully.

Hypersensitivity to Inhaled Organic Material
(Farmers' Lung, Pigeon Breeders' Lung, Maple-Bark Strippers' Disease, Bagassosis)

In 1932 Campbell reported an acute pneumonitis in farm workers following exposure to moldy hay (farmers' lung). The inflammation is subacute with accumulations of lymphocytes, plasma cells, epithelioid cells, and Langhans' giant cells which widen the interstitial space. An identical reaction occurs in some individuals following exposure to pigeons (pigeon breeders' lung, Fig. 32), maple-bark (maple-bark strippers' disease), redwood tree bark and moldy sugar cane bark (bagassosis). In farmers' lung, the specific antigen is hay mold; in pigeon breeders' lung, pigeon feathers and droppings; in maple-bark strippers' disease, the fungus *Cryptostioma corticale;* in redwood tree exposure, the redwood fungus of the genus *Graphium;* and in bagassosis, sugar cane mold. New cases of farmers' lung in children have been reported but there are no reported cases of maple-bark strippers' disease or bagassosis in children as yet. However, Stiehm and his colleagues (1966) have collected five cases of pigeon breeders' lung in a short period, and it is likely that these and similar parenchymal diseases of hypersensitivity are common causes of pneumonitis in childhood.

Acute, subacute, and chronic stages have been distinguished in these diseases, but usually one stage merges imperceptibly into the next. Acute episodes begin several hours after exposure and are characterized by dyspnea, fever, and chest pain. Physical findings are minimal and consist only of a few moist rales and occasional wheezes. X-ray of the chest is normal. If exposure to the antigen continues, there is severe dyspnea, nonproductive cough, cyanosis, and the chest x-ray shows a diffuse, fine, mottled infiltration, usually most marked in the lower part of the lung. There is a marked reduction in vital capacity and diffusion capacity, and there is arterial desaturation with rest and with exercise. Hypergammaglobulinemia with elevation of the γG, γM, and γA fractions is common, but serum complement is normal.

The subacute course, the granulomatous reaction, hypergammaglobulinemia, and the normal serum complement suggest that these diseases are due to delayed hypersensitivity. A specific diagnosis can be made by the demonstration of specific precipitins or by the appearance of induration and hemorrhage 24 hours or more after the intradermal injection of the responsible antigen.

Since pulmonary fibrosis may develop, vigorous treatment is desirable. Immediate removal of the specific antigen from the patient's environment and treatment with corticosteroids (2 mg/kg hydrocortisone daily for one to six months, or equivalent doses of other corticosteroids) usually produces a rapid disappearance of the signs and symptoms and radiologic abnormalities.

The Collagen Diseases
(See also Chap. 12)

The collagen diseases involve many organ systems and include polyarteritis nodosa, rheumatoid arthritis, lupus erythematosus, scleroderma, and rheumatic fe-

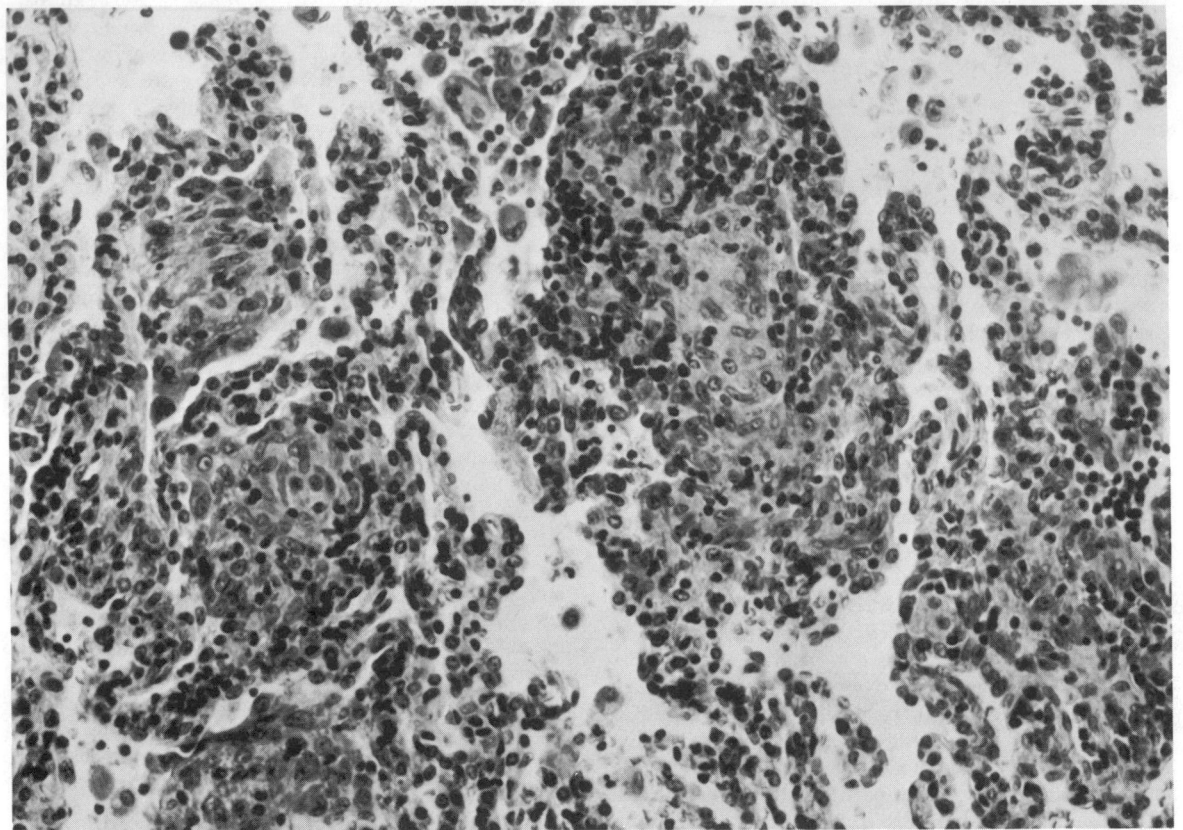

Fig. 32.   Pigeon breeders' lung—granulomatous interstitial pneumonitis. There is diffuse leucocytic infiltration of the alveolar septa. Interspersed with the lymphocytes are focal accumulations of histiocytes forming noncaseating granulomas. There is no fibrosis.

ver. The cellular pattern of the pulmonary lesions in these conditions is similar and resembles the changes in interstitial tissue of other organs. In the initial stages there is an accumulation of mucopolysaccharides, water, and granular eosinophilic material in the interstitial spaces, which widens the interalveolar septa. Lymphocytes, monocytes, and plasma cells invade the interstitial space, particularly the peribronchiolar and periarteriolar regions. Later, there is a poliferation of fibroblasts and the formation of fibrous tissue.

When the collagen diseases involve the lung, the principal signs and symptoms are dyspnea, cyanosis, nonproductive cough, clubbing of the fingers, and occasional basilar rales. Chest x-rays show a nonspecific, diffuse parenchymal infiltration. The vital capacity, lung compliance, and arterial oxygen saturation are usually reduced. The use of corticosteroids (1 to 2 mg/kg/day) may be successful in the treatment of the pulmonary manifestations of collagen disease when the interstitial inflammation is acute. However, corticosteroids are of little value in the later stages when there is widespread fibrosis.

Polyarteritis nodosa produces leucocytic infiltration and a fibrinoid reaction within the media of muscular arteries. When the lungs are involved, there

are usually associated accumulations of round cells and epithelioid cells which form giant cells in the interalveolar spaces.

Brinkman and Chaikof (1959) reported pulmonary involvement in one 13-year-old child with *rheumatoid arthritis*. The lungs at autopsy were honeycombed in appearance and filled with small cysts lined with cuboidal epithelium. There was interalveolar fibrosis and some infiltration of round cells but no giant cell formation. The disease in this case was in a late stage and did not respond to corticosteroid therapy.

In *systemic lupus erythematosus* lung lesions are not as marked as renal, cardiac, skin, and joint lesions. However, in more than half of the cases studied at autopsy there is interstitial pneumonitis, pulmonary hemorrhage or edema, or pleuritis. Since the lesions are more often proliferative than fibrotic, lupus erythematosus is particularly responsive to corticosteroid therapy. Ziff and co-workers (1958) report that the addition of chloroquine appeared to increase the effectiveness of corticosteroid therapy.

Scleroderma usually affects the lung. Progressive sclerotic involvement of the muscles of the chest wall may limit respiration and cause hypoventilation but this is not the main source of the respiratory insufficiency. When the lungs are involved, there is a diffuse, interstitial fibrosis which may thicken the alveolar walls and obliterate the alveoli or partially obstruct small airways, overdistend alveoli, and cause cysts. The pulmonary blood vessels may be encased in collagenous sheaths which obliterate their lumina.

Desquamative Interstitial Pneumonitis

This disease was described by Liebow in 1965 and one of the original 18 cases was a 16-year-old boy. Since that time, a few additional cases have been reported in children and it may be a relatively common cause of chronic lung disease in childhood. The disease begins with shortness of breath, which is progressive. Nonproductive cough and weight loss are common. Clubbing is severe. Rales are rarely heard. There is no fever. The chest x-ray shows a "ground-glass" appearance at the bases of the lung, with large ill-defined densities at the hilar and the posterior portions of the lung. The microscopic lesions are characterized by massive proliferation and desquamation of large alveolar cells and thickening of the walls of the distal air spaces.

Most cases respond to steroid therapy, usually with stabilization and sometimes by remission of clinical symptoms and roentgenographic changes. We have followed for 13 years a remarkable case which has responded to chloroquine therapy (Case VII).

Case VII. *A 13-year-old white female was well until 3 years of age, after which she gradually developed shortness of breath, cyanosis, nonproductive cough, and clubbing of the fingers and toes. At 4 years of age she was deeply cyanotic in room air at rest and was unable to walk more than 50 feet. She had tachycardia, tachypnea, and intercostal retractions. There were no abnormalities noted on examination of her chest, but chest x-ray showed diffuse infiltration, particularly in the perihilar region (Fig. 33A). Her vital capacity was 50 percent of normal (Table 13). A lung biopsy showed marked interstitial pneumonitis with interalveolar accumulations of lymphocytes and multinucleated giant cells. Many of the small pulmonary arterioles were surrounded by dense collections of lymphocytes, and some of them showed fibrinoid degeneration. These morphologic findings were considered to be consistent with pulmonary collagen disease of an undifferentiated type. She was placed on hydrocortisone (2 mg/kg/day), and her clinical condition improved gradually. However, at 6 years of age her vital capacity was still below normal; her diffusion capacity was low; there was arterial desaturation at rest; maximal flow rates and functional residual capacity were normal. At 6 years of age, cortisone was stopped and chloroquine (60 mg twice a day) was started. At 8 years of age her vital capacity, pulmonary diffusion capacity, and arterial saturation at rest were normal, although moderate exercise (200 kg-m for six minutes on a bicycle ergometer) resulted in arterial desaturation. (See Fig. 33B for chest x-ray.) We stopped chloroquine at age 10 years, and at age 11 years both vital capacity and pulmonary diffusion were low and the arterial desaturation present at rest was more marked with exercise. After breathing 100 percent oxygen for 20 minutes, the arterial oxygen tension was lower than normal (normal over 600), indicating a small (about 10 percent) right-to-left shunt, probably intrapulmonary. We resumed chloroquine therapy at age 11, and at age 13 vital capacity, functional residual ca-*

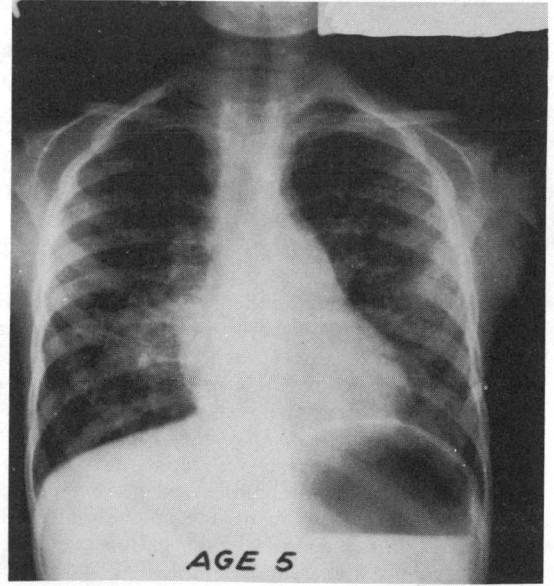

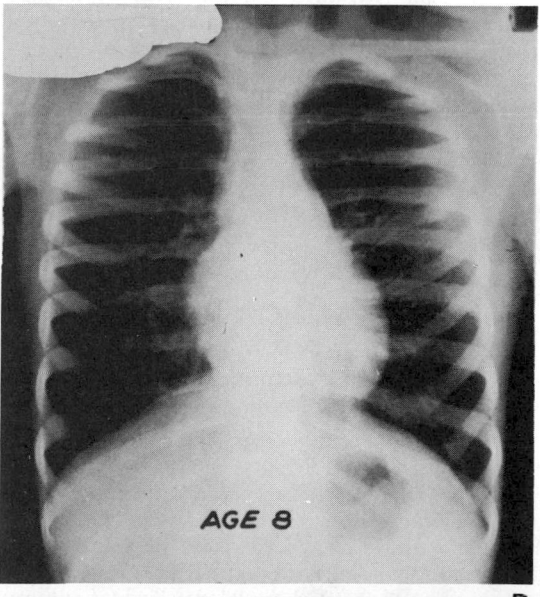

A **B**

Fig. 33. Desquamative interstitial pneumonitis. Chest radiograms of Case VII. A. Before treatment (age 5 years). B. After treatment (age 8 years).

TABLE 13. *Desquamative Interstitial Pneumonitis*

	4 Years	6 Years (On Cortisone)	8 Years (On Chloroquine)	11 Years (Off Chloroquine)	13 Years (On Chloroquine)
Vital capacity (% normal)	50	75	100	81	95
Functional residual capacity (% normal)		95	110	105	120
Diffusion capacity (% normal)		46	100	38	57
Arterial blood gas tensions (mm Hg) — P_{O_2} (rest-air)		65	85	66	87
P_{O_2} (rest-100% O)				532	595
P_{O_2} (200 kg-m/6 min—air)			75	51	73
P_{O_2} (200 kg-m/6 min—100% O)					615
P_{CO_2} (rest-air)		38	30	39	37
Expiratory flow rate (% normal)		80	85	75	100
Inspiratory flow rate (% normal)		80	85	80	100

pacity, and maximal flow rates were normal; there was no evidence of right-to-left shunt. However, diffusion capacity remained low, and there was arterial desaturation with exercise. Her chest x-ray showed diffuse, interstitial opacification consistent with chronic fibrosis. At 18 years of age she still takes chloroquine, her x-ray is normal and, except for a low diffusion capacity, her pulmonary function is normal.

The preceding case illustrates that with time or specific therapy, some of the evidences of pulmonary insufficiency caused by desquamative interstitial pneumonitis disappear. However, the persistent reduction in diffusion capacity and the finding of arterial desaturation with exercise suggest that the disease may have permanently reduced the size of the pulmonary vascular bed, even though the alveolar volume and surface area were capable of normal growth (normal vital capacity).

Chronic Interstitial Pneumonitis of Unknown Etiology

Idiopathic Interstitial Pneumonitis of Premature Infants
(Wilson-Mikity Syndrome, Cystic Emphysema, Pulmonary Dysmaturity)

In 1960 Wilson and Mikity described five premature infants who slowly developed tachypnea, retractions, and cyanosis one to five weeks following birth. Their chest x-rays showed a coarse pulmonary infiltration and small areas of hyperinflation which appeared cystic. Three of these infants died; at autopsy, their lungs showed accumulations of mononuclear cells, fibroblasts, and fibrosis in the interalveolar

space. In 1963 Butterfield and his associates described eight premature infants who had onset of respiratory distress at 13 to 82 days of age and whose chest x-rays showed bilateral areas of "consolidation and pneumatocele formation." ECHO type 19 virus was isolated in one of the infants who died. They proposed the name "cystic emphysema" for this condition. In 1963 Baghdassarian and her associates reported six premature infants who had respiratory distress and chest films showing a diffuse, bilateral, coarse, lacelike pattern of infiltrates with alternating cystlike foci. The onset of symptoms in five of their cases was at birth. They proposed the term "pulmonary dysmaturity." In all these infants the clinical course was similar and the x-ray and morphologic descriptions identical.

The disease is characterized by a sudden onset at birth or an insidious onset in the first month of life. The infants become progressively cyanotic even in 100 percent oxygen. Intercostal retractions are marked; the chest is usually hyperresonant to percussion; rales are uncommon. Chest x-rays show a diffuse reticular distribution of radiodensities interspersed with areas of radiolucency. Pulmonary function studies reveal arterial oxygen desaturation and a reduction in vital capacity and lung compliance. The microscopic appearance of the lung is consistent with chronic interstitial inflammation of nonspecific type (Fig. 34). Somewhat similar chest x-ray and morphologic changes have been observed in newborn infants with severe idiopathic respiratory distress who have required prolonged positive-pressure ventilation. This suggests that the reaction may represent healing following severe damage to pulmonary tissues caused by pulmonary ischemia or prolonged positive-pressure ventilation with 100 percent oxygen. Chronic infection, aspiration of maternal blood, gastric contents or milk, a congenital anatomic abnormality, and delayed pulmonary development have been proposed as causing this disease. Since injury to the lung parenchyma by almost all the toxins, infections, and hypersensi-

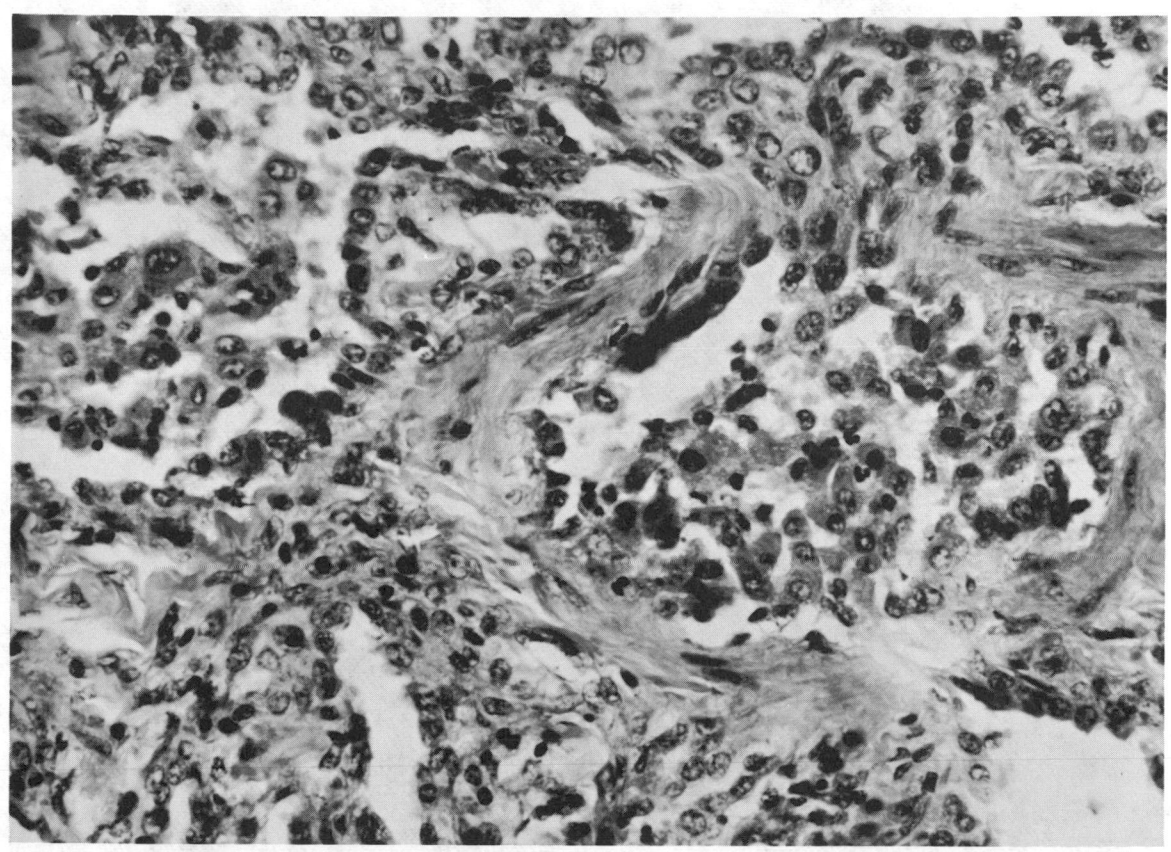

Fig. 34. Interstitial pneumonitis of the newborn. Lung tissue obtained by biopsy demonstrates a subacute process with thickened alveolar septa caused by edema, lymphocytes, histiocytes, and fibroblasts. There is some interalveolar fibrosis. There is hypertrophy of the alveolar lining cells; macrophages fill the alveolar lumina.

tivity reactions (described in the earlier part of this section) cause this type of interalveolar inflammation with fibroblastic proliferation and fibrosis, it is likely that the syndrome has no one specific cause. Rather, it is probably the nonspecific healing process following pulmonary damage.

Treatment must include oxygen in a concentration sufficient to maintain adequate arterial saturation. For the first two to three weeks, 100 percent oxygen is usually required. Digitalis may improve cardiac function if there is pulmonary hypertension, right ventricular hypertrophy, and cardiac failure. Corticosteroids have been used (Swyer et al., 1965, and Bucci et al., 1966) with apparent success. As there is always interstitial proliferation early in the disease and since the prevention of fibrosis should be the goal of therapy, corticosteroids (1 mg/kg prednisone every other day for 1 to 12 months) are recommended.

The mortality in this syndrome is not very high. Whether permanent pulmonary damage results is not known, although at 3 years of age, two of the cases reported by Swyer and his colleagues had residual radiologic abnormalities.

Case VIII. *A 4-year-old white male weighed 1,500 g at birth and developed tachycardia, tachypnea, intercostal retractions, and cyanosis at the age of 2 weeks. At 8 weeks of age his respiratory rate was 80; intercostal retractions were marked; vital capacity and lung compliance were low; arterial Po_2 was low when breathing room air and less than normal breathing 100 percent oxygen (indicating a right-to-left shunt of about 35 percent); he had a moderately severe respiratory acidosis (Pco_2 58); maximal flow rates were normal (Table 14). An x-ray of his chest revealed diffuse reticular densities throughout both lung fields (Fig. 35A). He required an environmental oxygen concentration of 80 to 100 percent for three months in order to prevent cyanosis. At 5 months of age he began to improve, and the environmental oxygen was slowly lowered until at 7 months of age there was no cyanosis when breathing room air. At 2½ years of age he was of normal height, had apparently normal exercise tolerance, and his lung compliance and arterial blood gas tensions were normal. However, the radiologic appearance of his lungs remained abnormal, with hyperinflation and some persistent linear radiodensities (Fig. 35B).*

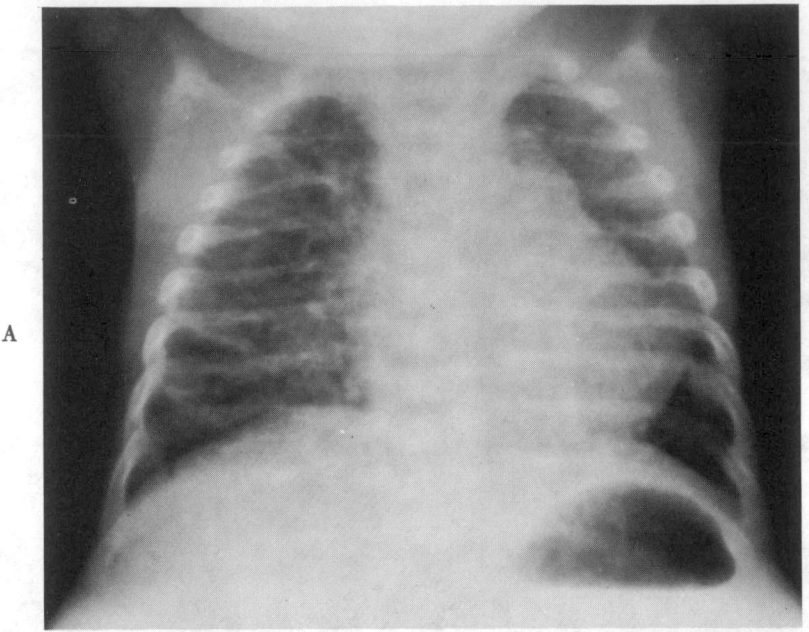

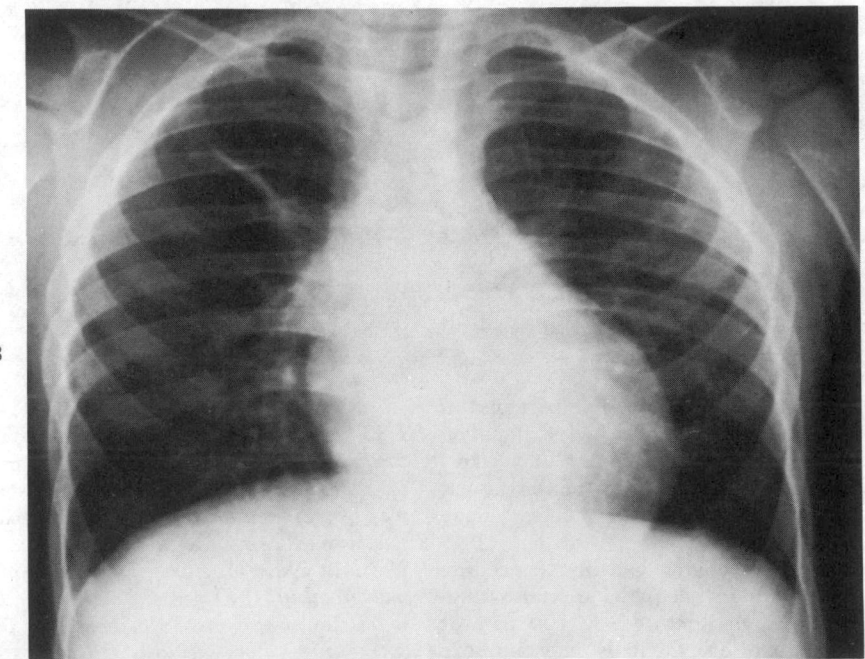

Fig. 35. Interstitial pneumonitis of the newborn. *Top.* At 7 weeks. There are diffuse radiodensities which form a recticular pattern. The airless portions of the lung alternate with overinflated areas. The heart is enlarged. *Bottom.* At 2½ years. There is uniform hyperinflation of the lung and a linear opacification in the right upper lobe; the heart is slightly enlarged.

Chronic Fibrosis of the Lung
(Hamman-Rich Syndrome)

Klopstock (1908) appears to have reported the first case of interstitial pulmonary fibrosis. His patient was a 10-year-old girl whose lungs at autopsy showed masses of fibrous tissue in the interalveolar septa which compressed the surrounding alveoli; there was hypertrophy of the alveolar epithelium and normal bronchi and bronchioles. Since the report of Hamman and Rich (1944) of several cases of diffuse interstitial fibrosis of the lung, the clinical syndrome and characteristic pathology have been well defined. It is undoubtedly not a specific disease, but probably repre-

TABLE 14.   *Idiopathic Interstitial Pneumonitis of the Premature Newborn Infant*

		8 Weeks	6 Months	2½ Years
Vital capacity (%)		46	—	—
Lung compliance (%)		20	60	90
Arterial blood gas tensions (mm Hg)	Po_2 (room air)	40	65	82
	Po_2 (100% O_2)	120	240	490
	Po_2 (5 min running-room air)	—	—	80
	Pco_2 (air)	58	38	39
Expiratory flow rate (% normal)		100	—	—
Inspiratory flow rate (% normal)		160	—	—

sents the end stage of chronic interstitial pneumonitis.

The clinical manifestations vary. Dyspnea, cyanosis, and clubbing of the fingers and toes are the most common features. Increasing cyanosis, respiratory distress, and cardiac failure are seen in the terminal stages of the disease. The vital capacity and lung compliance are usually very low; there is arterial desaturation at rest and with exercise; but there is usually no increase in airway resistance. The chest x-ray shows extensive, bilateral radiodensities that may appear miliary, linear, nodular, or confluent.

At autopsy the lungs are firm and rubbery and sink in water. Most of the interalveolar space is occupied by dense fibrous tissue, but there are usually scattered areas of chronic inflammation (Fig. 36). Inspection of Figures 32, 34, and 36 illustrates the progression of acute to chronic interstitial inflammation.

Treatment of this disease with corticosteroids is usually unsuccessful, since only those parts of the lung which show chronic pneumonitis might be expected to resume normal function. Oxygen and other

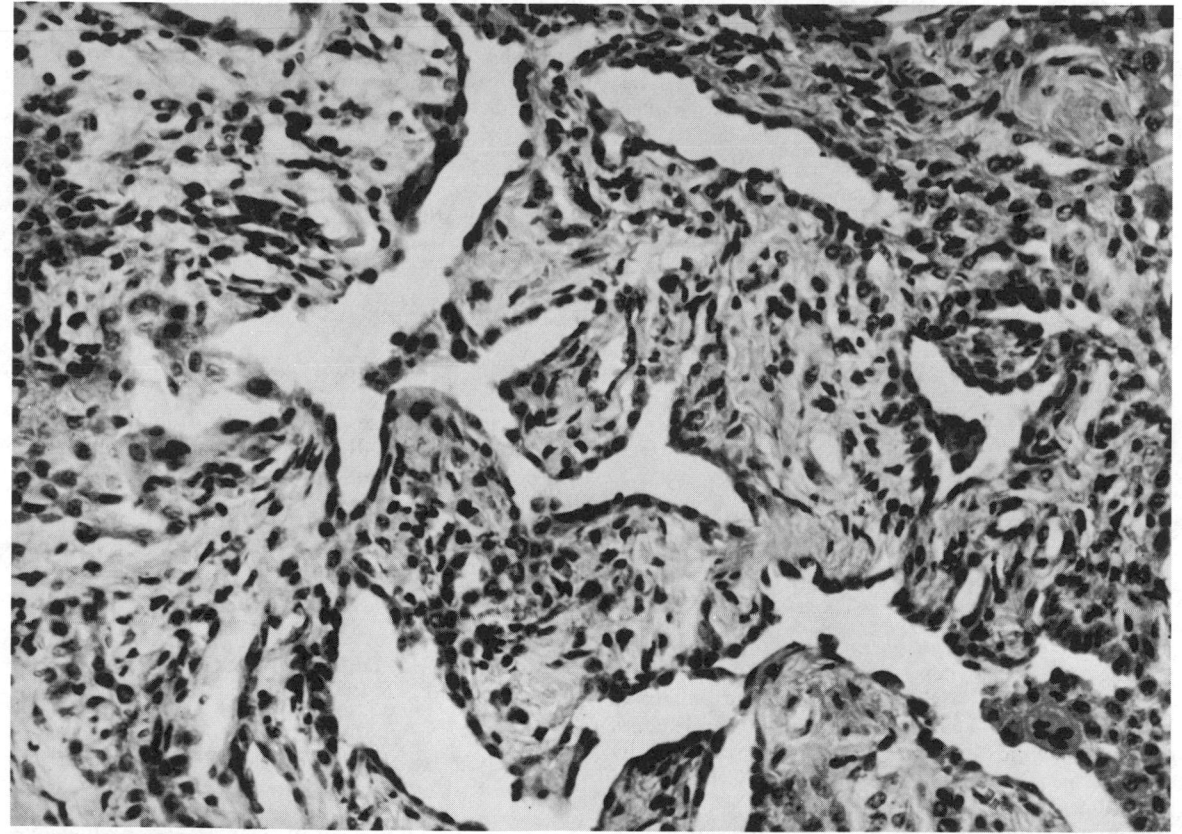

Fig. 36.   Lung tissue obtained at autopsy from a 2-year-old child with chronic interstitial pneumonitis and fibrosis. There is marked thickening of the alveolar septa with fibrous tissue and lymphocytes. There is little active inflammation.

supportive measures may provide temporary improvement. The poor prognosis in pulmonary fibrosis emphasizes the importance of utilizing corticosteroids in the earlier stages of proliferative interstitial pulmonary disease in order to prevent permanent damage.

Idiopathic Pulmonary Hemosiderosis

This is a relatively rare disease, although Soergel and Sommers (1962) reviewed 112 patients, 80 percent of whom were under 16 years of age, the youngest being 4 months of age. It is characterized by continuous, mild intrapulmonary bleeding. Early, the principal symptoms may be malaise and anemia, and the chest film may show blotchy pulmonary infiltrations. After several weeks or several years a brisk hemoptysis may occur followed by marked anemia, tachycardia, and tachypnea. Physical examination at this time may reveal fine rales and dullness over the lower lobes. Chest x-ray will show cardiac enlargement and multiple poorly defined confluent pulmonary infiltrations throughout the lung. Episodes of bleeding may recur many times and eventually lead to pulmonary hemosiderosis and fibrosis. Most of the patients who survive for several years suffer from symptoms of chronic respiratory distress indistinguishable from chronic pulmonary fibrosis. In some cases, pulmonary hemorrhages cease for many years; these may represent permanent remissions. There are no distinctive laboratory features, although there may be an elevation in the a_2 globulin. The prognosis is poor, but about 20 percent of the cases reported have had an apparently spontaneous remission.

The causation of the disease is unknown. Autosensitization of lung tissue has been suggested repeatedly, but no autoantibodies to lung have been demonstrated. Soergel and Sommers suggest that the pathogenic mechanism is primarily an abnormality of alveolar epithelial growth and function which affects the mechanical stability of the alveolar capillaries.

Treatment is symptomatic. Corticosteroids have been reported to be useful (Cooper, 1960; Irvin and Snowden, 1957).

Miscellaneous Parenchymal Diseases

Pulmonary Alveolar Proteinosis

This is a chronic disease of the lung in which there is an intraalveolar deposition of PAS-positive proteinaceous material rich in lipids. Twenty-six cases were described in 1958 by Rosen and his colleagues; one was a child. The condition is characterized by dyspnea associated with a cough which is productive of yellow sputum, fatigue, and weight loss. Physical examination may reveal a few scattered rales and, rarely, clubbing of the fingers and toes. Chest x-rays show a fine, diffuse perihilar, radiating, feathery, or vaguely nodular density similar to that seen in pulmonary edema. The outlook is unfavorable: 30 percent of the cases originally reported died within five years of diagnosis. There is no specific therapy.

Lipid Pneumonia

This is a chronic pulmonary disease which follows the aspiration of fats or oils. Laughlen directed attention to it in 1925, and a number of cases were reported over the next decade. The use of oily nose drops was responsible for most of the cases. Lately, this condition has become increasingly rare, since the risk of using oily nose drops has become generally appreciated.

The pathologic changes depend to some extent on the type of oil aspirated. Fats which have a high content of free fatty acids cause an intense, acute inflammatory reaction in the lung which may result in localized abscesses or areas of gangrene. More characteristic is the picture produced by bland oils, such as mineral oil. These cause an outpouring of mononuclear phagocytes, which absorb the oil until they are filled with fine droplets, giving them a foamlike appearance. These cells then enter the interalveolar septa and are carried up the lymphatics to the hilar lymph nodes. There is a proliferation of the alveolar epithelium, and occasional interalveolar giant cells are formed.

The onset of the condition is insidious. Often there are no symptoms, the condition being discovered accidentally by x-ray. There may be a dry, unproductive cough, tachypnea, and weight loss. Physical examination may show nothing abnormal, or there may be signs typical of bronchitis or pneumonitis. Chest x-ray shows radiodensities of a nonspecific nature.

The prognosis of uncomplicated lipid pneumonia is good. There is no specific therapy.

Pulmonary Alveolar Microlithiasis

This is a rare disease (66 cases were described up to 1963) in which small deposits of calcium are present uniformly throughout the lung. The disease has a slow progressive course, with increasing cyanosis and respiratory distress. It is always fatal and there is no known therapy.

References

IMMUNOLOGIC DEFECTS PREDISPOSING TO RECURRENT PULMONARY INFECTION

Ammann, A. J., Cain, W. A., Ishizaka, K., Hong, R., and Good, R. A. Immunoglobulin E deficiency in ataxia-telangiectasia. New Eng. J. Med., 281:469, 1969.

Barandun, S., Riva, G., and Spengler, G. A. Immunologic deficiency diagnosis, forms and current treatment. Birth Defects, Original Article Ser., 4:40, 1968.

Cain, W. A., Ammann, A. J., Hong, R., Ishizaka, K., and Good, R. A. IgE deficiency associated with chronic sinopulmonary infection. J. Clin. Invest., 48:12A, 1969.

Cooper, M. D., Chae, H. P., Lowman, J. T., Krivit, W., and Good, R. A. Wiskott-Aldrich syndrome: immunologic deficiency disease involving afferent limb of immunity. Amer. J. Med., 44:499, 1968.

Robbins, J. B., Eitzman, D. V., and Ellis, E. F. Immunochemical evidence for development of "acquired" hypogammaglobulinemic state. New Eng. J. Med., 274:607, 1966.

South, M. A., Cooper, M. D., Wollheim, F. A., and Good, R. A. IgA system. II. Clinical significance of IgA deficiency: studies in patients with agammaglobulinemia and ataxia-telangiectasia. Amer. J. Med., 44:168, 1968.

INTERSTITIAL PNEUMONITIS CAUSED BY INFECTIOUS AGENTS

Ammish, O. Uber die nichtsyphilitische interstitielle pneumonie des ersten kindesalters. Virchow's Arch., 302:539, 1938.

Clyde, W. A., and Denny, F. W., Jr., The etiology and therapy of atypical pneumonia. Med. Clin. N. Amer., 47:1201, 1963.

——— and Denny, F. W., Jr. Mycoplasma infections in childhood. Pediatrics, 40:669, 1967.

Deamer, W. C., and Zollinger, H. U. Interstitial "plasma cell" pneumonia of premature and young infants. Pediatrics, 12:11, 1953.

Herlinger, H. Pulmonary changes in tropical eosinophilia. Brit. J. Radiol., 36:889, 1963.

Hilleman, M. R., Hamparian, V. V., Ketler, A., Reilly, C. M., McClelland, L., Cornfeld, D., and Stokes, J., Jr. Acute respiratory illnesses among children and adults. Field study of contemporary importance of several viruses and appraisal of the literature. J.A.M.A., 180:445, 1962.

Kingston, J. R., Chanock, R. M., Mufson, M. A., Hellman, L. P., James, W. D., Fox, H. H., Manko, M. A., and Boyers, J. Eaton agent pneumonia. J.A.M.A., 176:118, 1961.

May, J. B. Eaton agent pneumonia, current status. N. Carolina Med. J., 26:15, 1965.

Robbins, J. B., Miller, R. H., Arean, V. M., and Pearson, H. A. Successful treatment of *Pneumocystis carinii* pneumonitis in a patient with congenital hypogammaglobulinemia. New Eng. J. Med., 272:708, 1965.

Snyder, C. H. Visceral larva migrans. Pediatrics, 28:85, 1961.

Vanek, J. Atypicka ("intersticialni") pneumonie deti, vyvolana pneomocystis carinii (atypical interstitial pneumonia of infants produced by pneumocystis carinii). Cas. Lek. Cesk., 90:1121, 1951.

INTERSTITIAL PNEUMONITIS CAUSED BY CHEMICAL AGENTS

Daeschner, C. W., Jr., Blattner, R. J., and Collins, V. P. Hydrocarbon pneumonitis. Pediat. Clin. N. Amer., p. 243, Feb. 1957.

Haggerty, R. J. Toxic hazards: furniture polish. New Eng. J. Med., 260:835, 1959.

Hatthes, F. T., Kirschner, R., Yow, M. D., and Brennan, J. C. Acute poisoning associated with inhalation of mercury vapor. Report of four cases. Pediatrics, 22:675, 1958.

Huxtable, K. A., Bolande, R., and Klaus, M. Experimental furniture polish pneumonia in rats. Pediatrics, 34:228, 1964.

Jiminez, J. P., and Lester, R. G. Pulmonary complications following furniture polish ingestion, report of 21 cases. Amer. J. Roentgen., 98:323, 1966.

Lesser, L. I., Weens, H. S., and McKey, J. D. Pulmonary manifestations following ingestion of kerosene. J. Pediat., 23:352, 1943.

Lowry, T., and Schuman, L. M. Silo-fillers' disease—a syndrome caused by nitrogen dioxide. J.A.M.A., 162:153, 1956.

Lund, J. S., and Feldt-Rasmussen, M. Accidental aspiration of talcum (report of a case in a 2-year old). Acta Paediat. Scand., 58:255, 1969.

Olson, E. T. Occurrence of silo-fillers' disease in children, J. Pediat., 64:724, 1964.

INTERSTITIAL PNEUMONITIS DUE TO HYPERSENSITIVITY

Sarcoidosis

Beier, F. R., and Lahey, M. E. Sarcoidosis among children in Utah and Idaho. J. Pediat., 65:350, 1964.

Cummings, M. M., Dunner, E., Schmidt, R. H., Jr., and Barnwell, J. B. Concepts of epidemiology of sarcoidosis: preliminary report of 1,194 cases reviewed with special reference to geographic ecology. Postgrad. Med., 19:437, 1956.

Kendig, E. L. Sarcoidosis among children, a review. J. Pediat., 61:269, 1962.

Löfgren, S. Concepts of sarcoidosis, in 3rd International Conference on Sarcoidosis. Acta Med. Scand., 425 (Suppl.):1, 1964.

McGovern, J. P., and Merritt, D. H. Sarcoidosis in childhood. Advances Pediat., 8:97, 1956.

Morse, S. I., Cohn, Z. A., Hirsch, J. G., and Schaedler, R. W. The treatment of sarcoidosis with chloroquine. Amer. J. Med., 30:779, 1961.

Siltzbach, L. E., and Greenberg, G. M. Childhood sarcoidosis—a study of 18 patients. New Eng. J. Med., 279:1239, 1968.

Winnacker, J. L., Becker, K. L., and Katz, S. Endocrine aspects of sarcoidosis. New Eng. J. Med., 278:427, 483, 1968.

PNEUMONITIS DUE TO HYPERSENSITIVITY

Banaszak, E. F., Thiede, W. H., and Fink, J. N. Hypersensitivity pneumonitis due to contamination of an air conditioner. New Eng. J. Med., 283:271, 1970.

Campbell, J. M. Acute symptoms following work with hay. Brit. Med. J., 2:1143, 1932.

Emanuel, D. A., Wenzel, F. J., Bowerman, C. I., and Lawton, B. R. Farmer's lung: clinical, pathologic and immunologic study of twenty-four patients. Amer. J. Med., 37:392, 1964.

——— Wenzel, F. J., and Lawton, B. R. Pneumonitis due to *Cryptostroma corticale* (maple-bark disease). New Eng. J. Med., 274:1413, 1966.

Hughes, W. F., Mattimore, J. M., and Arbesman, C. E. Farmer's lung in an adolescent boy. Amer. J. Dis. Child., 118:777, 1969.

Lunn, J. A., and Hughes, D. T. D. Pulmonary hypersensitivity to the grain weevil. Brit. J. Industr. Med., 24:158, 1967.

Rankin, J., Jaeschke, W. H., Callies, Q. C., and Dickie, H. A. Farmer's lung: physiopathologic features of the acute interstitial granulomatous pneumonitis of agricultural workers. Ann. Intern. Med., 57:606, 1962.

Reed, C. E., Sosman, A., and Barbee, R. A. Pigeon-breeders' lung: a newly observed interstitial pulmonary disease. J.A.M.A., 193:261, 1965.

Stiehm, E. R., Reed, C. E., and Tooley, W. H. Pigeon breeders' lung in children. Pediatrics, 39:904, 1967.

COLLAGEN DISEASE

Baker, L. A., and David, D. Pulmonary manifestations of collagen diseases. Med. Clin. N. Amer., 43:145, 1959.

Brinkman, G. L., and Chaikof, L. Rheumatoid lung disease: report of a case which developed in childhood. Amer. Rev. Resp. Dis., 80:732, 1959.

Goldring, D., Behrer, M. R., Brown, G., and Elliott, G. Rheumatic pneumonitis. Part II. Report on the clinical and laboratory findings in twenty-three patients. J. Pediat., 53:547, 1958.

Ziff, M., Esserman, P., and McEwen, C. Observations on the course and treatment of systemic lupus erythematosus. Arthritis Rheum., 1:332, 1958.

DESQUAMATIVE INTERSTITIAL PNEUMONITIS

Gaensler, E. A., Godd, A. M., and Prowse, C. M. Desquamative interstitial pneumonia. New Eng. J. Med., 274:113, 1966.

Liebow, A. A., Steer, A., and Billingsley, J. G. Desquamative interstitial pneumonia. Amer. J. Med., 39:369, 1965.

CHRONIC IDIOPATHIC PNEUMONITIS OF PREMATURE INFANTS

Baghdassarian, O. M., Avery, M. E., and Neuhauser, E. B. D. A form of pulmonary insufficiency in premature infants; pulmonary dysmaturity? Amer. J. Roentgen., 89:1020, 1963.

Bucci, G., Iannaccone, G., Scalamandre, A., Savignoni, P. G., and Mendicini, M. Observations on the Wilson-Mikity syndrome; diffuse cyst-like emphysema of premature infants. Ann. Paediat., 206:135, 1966.

Butterfield, J., Moscovici, C., Berry, C., and Kempe, C. H. Cystic emphysema in premature infants, a report of an outbreak with the isolation of Type 19 ECHO virus in one case. New Eng. J. Med., 268:18, 1963.

Swyer, P. R. Deliveria-Papadopoulos, M., Levison, H., Reilly, B. J., and Balis, J. U. The pulmonary syndrome of Wilson and Mikity. Pediatrics, 36:374, 1965.

von Hottinger, A., Kaufman, H. J., Weisser, K., and Werthemann, A. Uber eine seltene Lungenerkrankung Frühgeborener. Ann. Pediat., 201:13, 1963.

Wilson, M. G., and Mikity, V. G. A new form of respiratory disease in premature infants. Amer. J. Dis. Child., 99:489, 1960.

CHRONIC FIBROSIS OF THE LUNG

Bradley, C. A., III. Diffuse interstitial fibrosis of the lungs in children. J. Pediat., 48:442, 1956.

Hamman, L., and Rich, A. R. Acute diffuse interstitial fibrosis of lungs. Bull. Hopkins Hosp., 74:177, 1944.

Klopstock, F. Uber eine eigentümliche Form totaler produktiver interstitieller Pneumonie neben subakuter Leberatrophie im Kindesalter. Virchow Arch. Path. Anat., 192:254, 1908.

Talner, N. S., Howatt, W. F., DeMuth, G. R., Dickinson, D. G., and Stern, A. M. The syndrome of alveolar-capillary block. Pediatrics, 27:227, 1961.

IDIOPATHIC PULMONARY HEMOSIDEROSIS

Cooper, A. S. Idiopathic pulmonary hemosiderosis. New Eng. J. Med., 263:1100, 1960.

Danigelis, J. A., and Markarian, B. Pulmonary proteinosis, including pulmonary electron microscopy. Amer. J. Dis. Child., 118:871, 1969.

Irvin, J. M., and Snowden, P. W. Idiopathic pulmonary hemosiderosis. Amer. J. Dis. Child., 93:182, 1957.

Soergel, K. H., and Sommers, S. C. Idiopathic pulmonary hemosiderosis and related syndromes. Amer. J. Med., 32:499, 1962.

PULMONARY ALVEOLAR PROTEINOSIS

Rosen, S. H., Castleman, D., and Liebow, A. A. Pulmonary alveolar proteinosis. New Eng. J. Med., 258:1123, 1958.

LIPID PNEUMONIA

Bromer, R. S., and Wolman, I. J. Lipoid pneumonia in infants and children. Radiology, 32:1, 1939.

Goodwin, T. C. Lipoid cell pneumonia. Amer. J. Dis. Child, 48:309, 1934.

Laughlen, G. F. Studies on pneumonia following nasopharyngeal injections of oil. Amer. J. Path., 1:407, 1925.

PULMONARY ALVEOLAR MICROLITHIASIS

Clark, R. B., and Johnson, F. C. Idiopathic pulmonary alveolar microlithiasis. Pediatrics, 28:650, 1961.

Rotem, Y., Solomon, M., and Hertz-Frankenhuis, M. Pulmonary alveolar microlithiasis. Ann. Pediat., 201:4, 1963.

19.8
THE CHEST WALL

ROBERT H. GREGG

Function of the Chest Wall

Ventilation of the lungs follows changes in the intrathoracic pressure, which in turn follows changes in intrathoracic volume. Initiation of these volume changes is the principal function of the chest wall.

The Rib Cage

The motion of the rib cage has been carefully studied in adults but not in children. In the adult the principal, and probably only, motion of a rib is rotation of its head at the point of articulation with the spine. This rotary motion of the head occurs around the axis of the neck of the rib. Because the ribs slope downward and forward, this motion raises the sternum and increases the anteroposterior diameter of the rib cage (Fig. 37). This effect is most prominent in the upper six ribs. Rotation of the heads of the seventh through the tenth ribs results in a slight depression of the lower sternum, but these ribs effectively increase the intrathoracic volume by increasing the lateral diameter of the chest.* These motions can be verified by feeling one's own chest during breathing, noting the greater lateral motion in the lower chest and the greater anterior expansion in the upper chest.

The Respiratory Musculature

DIAPHRAGM. The diaphragm is the most important of the respiratory muscles and its action accounts for approximately two-thirds of the tidal exchange during quiet breathing. As the diaphragm contracts the central portion moves downward like a piston. The pistonlike descent is limited by the increasing intra-abdominal pressure. At this point the diaphragm retains its domed shape while much of the muscle runs in a nearly vertical direction along the chest wall. As contraction continues, upward traction is exerted on the costal margin, enlarging the rib cage as described previously. Whether the chest expands more than the abdomen, or the abdomen more than the chest, depends on the relative compliance of these structures, not on which muscles are active. Therefore, the terms "diaphragmatic breathing" and "abdominal breathing" usually applied to newborn infants have little meaning.

INTERCOSTAL MUSCLES. The external intercostals which contract during quiet inspiration, slant downward and forward between the ribs. When they contract they raise the ribs (Fig. 37). The internal intercostals, which are active only during forced expiration, run in the opposite direction; when they

---

* The angle of the rib neck and the course and curvature of the ribs which account for this effect are not easy to visualize without a three-dimensional model. Such a model can be improvised by making a semicircle with the thumb and forefinger. Let the thumb tip represent the head of the rib at the articulation with the spine. Let the tip of the forefinger represent the sternal end of the rib. The ribs slope downward and forward, so the head of the rib at the spine (the thumb) is higher than the sternal end (the finger). Now rotate the semicircle on the thumb tip around the long axis of the distal phalanx of the thumb and note that the motion raises and lowers the "sternal" end of the model and represents the motion of the upper ribs. The action of the lower ribs is illustrated when the interphalangeal joint of the thumb is flexed. Note that the direction of the axis of the distal phalanx of the thumb has changed and now rotate the model on the thumb *tip* around this new axis. The "rib" motion now approximates a "bucket-handle" effect responsible for the increase in the lateral diameter of the chest.

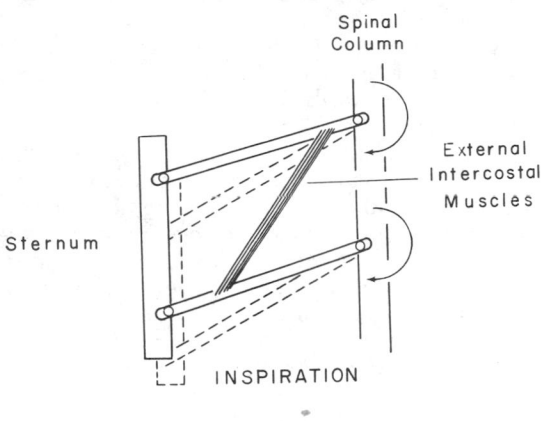

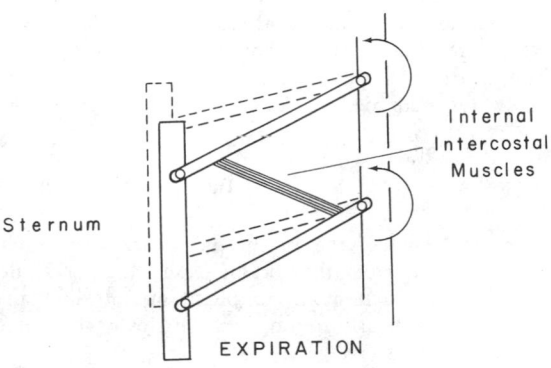

Fig. 37. Action of the upper ribs and the intercostal muscles. Inspiration: Contraction of the external intercostal muscles elevates the ribs and sternum and increases the anteriorposterior diameter of the chest. Expiration: With expiration the sternum descends and with forced expiration the internal intercostal muscles contract. (Modified from Fenn. *Sci. Amer.*, 202:142, 1960.)

contract, the ribs are forced downward and the thoracic volume is decreased.

Mechanics of Thoracic Motion

Inspiration is always an active process; during quiet breathing only small pressure changes are required and the energy consumed is only a small fraction of the basal metabolic needs. The motive force for quiet inspiration is supplied by the diaphragm and the external intercostals. When forceful inspiration is required, there is augmented contraction of the diaphragm and the external intercostals, and the accessory muscles of inspiration are utilized. The most important of these are the sternocleidomastoid and strap muscles of the neck. Additional chest expansion can be achieved by extension of the trunk. This mechanism is used when the ventilatory needs are great. In patients with extreme respiratory distress, the platysma becomes active, but its contraction is ineffectual in increasing ventilation. It does, however, distort the mouth with each breath, causing the sign called "fishmouthing."

Quiet expiration is passive, powered only by the elastic recoil of the lung. During forceful expiration the internal intercostals contract (Fig. 37). In cases of severe expiratory obstruction or increased ventilatory needs the musculature of the abdominal wall is also used. These muscles increase the intraabdominal pressure and push the diaphragm up. In addition, they decrease intrathoracic volume by flexing the trunk and by pulling the lower costal margins toward the midline. These are strong muscles capable of sustaining an intraabdominal, and hence, intrathoracic, pressure of 100 mm Hg. A transient rise to 200 or 300 mm Hg occurs with vigorous coughing and is a necessary part of this protective reflex. In children with acute illnesses causing cough or expiratory obstruction, pain and tenderness of the abdominal wall are common due to muscular cramps. In children with chronic respiratory obstruction or cough, the musculature of the abdominal wall is often visibly and palpably hypertrophied.

Changes with Growth

The chest wall of the infant differs in several anatomic respects from that of an older child or adult. The wall is much more compliant and flexible, the shape is more nearly round, and the ribs have a more horizontal course.

These anatomic differences impose no apparent functional handicap. Although the mechanics of chest wall motion have not been well studied in the infant, the ability of a newborn baby, even one with diaphragmatic paralysis or hernia, to survive the difficult respiratory adjustments of birth, attests to the reserve of the system.

The rounded shape of the chest present at birth changes rapidly to the flattened ellipse found in older children and adults. The lateral diameter of the chest increases more rapidly than does the anterior-posterior dimension. The ratio of the anterior-posterior diameter and the lateral diameter is 0.93 at birth, 0.78 at one year of age, and by the age of two years it approaches the value of 0.69 found in older children.

REFERENCES

Agostini, E. Volume-pressure relationships of the thorax and lung in the newborn. J. Appl. Physiol., 14:909, 1959.

———— Action of respiratory muscles. In Fenn, W. O., and Rahn, H. eds. Handbook of Physiology, Sec. 2, Respiration. Washington, D.C., Amer. Physiol. Soc., 1964, Vol. 1.

———— and Magnoni, P. Deformation of the chest wall during breathing efforts. J. Appl. Physiol., 21:1827, 1966.

Campbell, E. J. M. The Respiratory Muscles and the Mechanics of Breathing. London, Lloyd-Luke, Ltd., 1958.

Howatt, W., and DeMuth, G. Configuration of the chest. Pediatrics (Suppl.), 35:177, 1965.

Jordanglou, J. Rib movements in health, kyphoscoliosis and ankylosing spondylitis. Thorax, 24:407, 1969.

Richards, C. C., and Bachman, L. Lung and chest wall compliance of apneic paralyzed infants. J. Clin. Invest., 40:273, 1961.

19.9
DISEASES OF THE CHEST WALL AND PLEURAL DISEASES

Neuromotor Diseases Which Impair Ventilation (See also Sec. 15.13)

Some decrease in ventilatory capacity occurs when the nerve supply of any of the respiratory muscles is lost, or when these muscles are unable to respond to neural stimulation. Neuromotor weakness limits the ability of the respiratory musculature to expand the thorax, and will decrease the vital capacity. Since a large reserve of ventilatory capacity is present normally, small losses of effective muscle strength are not clinically evident but they will reduce the maximum voluntary ventilation. An impairment of neuromotor function reduces the ability to cough effectively. The weakened muscles cannot generate the large increase in intrathoracic pressure necessary for forceful coughing and secretions may accumulate in the airway and cause atelectasis.

If the disability becomes more severe, an increased effort is required to maintain the tidal volume at the normal level and the patient finds it easier to breathe rapidly and shallowly. Rapid, shallow breathing, without occasional deep breaths or sighs, leads to the development of focal areas of atelectasis, and the compliance of the lungs decreases. As the lungs become more "stiff," expansion is even more difficult, the tidal volume decreases further, alveolar hypoventilation occurs, and the carbon dioxide tension of the blood increases. Hypoventilation and a shuntlike effect originating in the atelectatic areas decrease the oxygen tension in arterial blood. Physical examination shows an anxious, frightened child with an increased blood pressure and pulse rate. Cyanosis and mental confusion are late signs. These signs are easily recognized and the diagnosis can be confirmed by arterial blood gas analysis.

Slowly progressive ventilatory failure can be difficult to diagnose. Initially, attention may be drawn away from the respiratory tract since chronic hypoxemia may cause pulmonary hypertension and right-sided heart failure, polycythemia, or even symptoms suggestive of neurasthenia. However, a careful history, physical examination, and arterial blood gas analysis should identify the organ system primarily involved.

Poliomyelitis

Respiratory paralysis caused by poliomyelitis is now, happily, uncommon, particularly when contrasted with the frightening epidemics of the preimmunization years. The respiratory paralysis occurs during the acute phase of the infection, either while the patient is febrile or shortly after the fever subsides. The extent of the paralysis varies greatly from patient to patient, ranging from slight involvement to almost complete loss of function of the respiratory muscles. Characteristically, the paralysis is spotty and asymmetric and thus no single pattern of breathing can be expected. The diaphragm is often involved, either partially or completely. Intercostal muscle paralysis is apt to be incomplete since the innervation of these muscles originates from 12 spinal cord segments. Paralysis of the accessory muscles is randomly distributed. The physiologic changes common to other forms of respiratory paralysis are also seen.

Management is described in Section 14.35.

Guillain-Barré Syndrome

Respiratory paralysis occurs occasionally in this syndrome and is the usual cause of death in the fatal cases. This condition is now probably a more common cause of respiratory paralysis than is poliomyelitis. The onset of respiratory paralysis is gradual, often insidious, and difficult to detect in the early stages. The paralysis usually follows an ascending path and involves the intercostals before it involves the diaphragm. Symmetric involvement is the rule in this illness, in contrast to the spotty paralysis of poliomyelitis. Complete recovery is expected in the Guillain-Barré syndrome.

The management is the same as that suggested for poliomyelitis.

Progressive Infantile Spinal Atrophy
(Werdnig-Hoffman Syndrome)

Progressive loss of anterior horn cells leading to paralysis of respiratory and other musculature is the hallmark of this lethal disease of infancy and early childhood. Death usually occurs before 5 years of age from ventilatory failure. The intercostal muscles are severely involved while diaphragmatic function is comparatively well preserved giving the affected child a characteristic appearance. During inspiration the chest wall collapses, and the upper abdomen protrudes markedly, producing a "see-saw" or paradoxical pattern of breathing (Fig. 38). The child's cry is weak, and his cough is feeble and ineffective. As the disease progresses, the chest gradually becomes

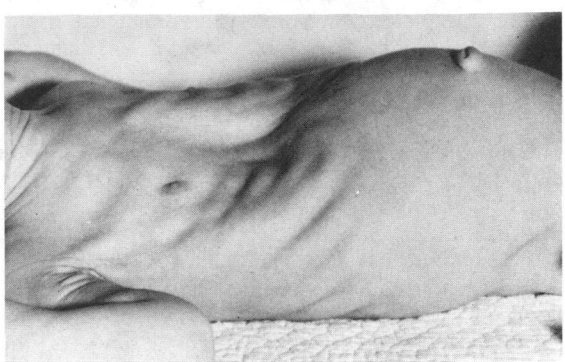

Fig. 38. A child with advanced infantile spinal atrophy during an inspiratory effort. Note that the diaphragm has descended and is distending the abdomen but the absence of effective intercostal muscle contraction has allowed the chest to collapse partially. The anterior-posterior diameter is decreased. From Dekabon. 1959. *Neurology of Infancy.* Courtesy of The Williams & Wilkins Co.)

flattened in the anteroposterior diameter. This flattening, usually symmetric, is a particularly striking finding since normal children of this age have a rounded chest.

Long-term mechanical support of respiration is not recommended since recovery cannot occur. However, short-term respiratory support during an acute infection might be used even though the course of the disease cannot be changed.

Spinal Cord Injury

Cord transections are an infrequent cause of childhood respiratory paralysis. A high cervical transection causes paralysis of both diaphragm and the intercostals and is incompatible with prolonged survival. Transection between C5 and D1 will permit continued diaphragmatic function but will result in intercostal paralysis. With the diaphragm active and the intercostals paralyzed, the chest collapses and the abdomen protrudes on inspiration, as seen in children with spinal muscular atrophy.

Diaphragmatic Paralysis

Paralysis of one leaf of the diaphragm is noted occasionally in the newborn infant, particularly after difficult breech deliveries. If the phrenic nerve has been subjected to a stretch injury, the paralysis may be temporary; if actual avulsion of the roots of nerves from C3, C4, and C5 has occurred, the paralysis is permanent. Injuries of the brachial plexus are commonly associated with phrenic nerve injuries and are caused by the same type of birth traumas. Diaphragmatic paralysis may also occur as a rare complication of pneumonia.

When one leaf of the diaphragm is paralyzed,

it moves higher in passive response to the subatmospheric intrapleural pressure. After prolonged denervation the muscle fibers atrophy and the diaphragmatic leaf moves still higher. After atrophy, when the diaphragm is inert and flaccid, paradoxical motion occurs quite regularly; on fluoroscopic examination the diaphragm is seen to move up with inspiration and down with expiration. This abnormal motion may be absent if some muscle tone remains or if the paralysis is incomplete.

On physical examination there is an increased flaring motion of the lower costal margin on the involved side. This increase in motion on the paralyzed side is caused either by the absence of the diaphragmatic contraction which normally opposes this flaring motion, or by a compensating increase in intercostal activity. Paralysis of the diaphragm also eliminates the normal protrusion of the epigastrium which occurs when the diaphragm contracts and descends. The combination of abnormal and asymmetric movements of the epigastrium and the rib margins should suggest the diagnosis to the careful observer.

The loss of function resulting from diaphragmatic paralysis is variable. Healthy adults and older children tolerate complete paralysis of one leaf of the diaphragm without distress and some newborn infants with diaphragmatic paralysis are also asymptomatic; such cases may be discovered by study of infants with brachial palsy. However, several authors have reported major respiratory symptoms in the first few months of life in infants with paralysis of one diaphragmatic leaf, and several deaths have been attributed to isolated, unilateral diaphragmatic paralysis. If respiratory distress does occur and the diaphragm is high and moving paradoxically, surgical imbrication of the paralyzed leaf is reported to be of great benefit.

Eventration of the Diaphragm

A defect in the diaphragmatic muscle allowing a limited herniation of abdominal contents is called an eventration. Small eventrations are minor anomalies, but when all of the muscle of one leaf of the diaphragm is missing the remaining membrane is elevated and moves paradoxically. In this severe form of eventration the functional handicap is the same as that seen in diaphragmatic paralysis of long duration, and it is often impossible to differentiate the two conditions. Surgical repair of these defects is rarely required.

Occasionally in the newborn infant, an extremely large eventration may closely resemble a congenital diaphragmatic hernia, may cause severe respiratory symptoms, and does require surgical intervention.

Muscular Dystrophy

Respiratory failure caused by muscular dystrophy occurs late in the course of the disease, most often involving adolescent or young adult patients. Patients with the myotonic form of muscular dystrophy may have a nearly normal vital capacity, even when alveolar hypoventilation and hypercapnea are present. This unusual combination of findings might be expected in this disease since loss of the muscle's ability to relax precedes muscular atrophy. In the nonmyotonic forms of muscular dystrophy, seen more often in childhood, the vital capacity and maximum voluntary ventilation are markedly reduced. Arterial oxygenation is maintained only by increased effort and by decreasing metabolic needs through inactivity.

Myasthenia Gravis

Myasthenia gravis can cause ventilatory failure at any age. In the usual form of this disease, ventilatory failure occurs only after ptosis and generalized weakness have been present for a prolonged period.

A transient form of myasthenia gravis sometimes occurs in newborn infants whose mothers have the disease. Respiratory failure may result in the infant's death a few hours after birth; but if the infant can be kept alive with proper drug therapy, respiratory support recovery can be expected in a few weeks (15.13).

Structural Abnormalities of the Thorax (See also Sec. 25.3)

Structural abnormalities of the thorax may limit thoracic motion. If the limitation is severe, alveolar hypoventilation can occur, just as it does when neuromuscular failure results in inadequate thoracic motion. All the structural abnormalities discussed here restrict ventilation to some degree.

Pectus Excavatum (Funnel Chest)

Pectus excavatum is a funnel-shaped depression of the anterior thorax caused by posterior displacement of the lower sternum. This common, often familial, deformity is usually inconspicuous or absent at birth, but develops over a period of months or years because of mechanical stresses caused by abnormal diaphragmatic attachments.

The clinical importance of pectus excavatum has been the subject of much debate, but the objective data now available suggest that it is rarely, if ever, a cause of major cardiopulmonary disability. Small decreases of 10 percent or less in total lung capacity, vital capacity, and maximum voluntary ventilation are found in children with this defect. These changes are not severe enough to cause symptoms. Similar minor decreases have been observed in adults with pectus excavatum so it is unlikely that the pulmonary disability increases with age. Surgical repair of the deformity did not result in improvement of pulmonary function in the reported cases in which pulmonary function tests were done both before and after the operation.

Several findings in pectus excavatum are superficially suggestive of cardiac disease. The heart is displaced to the left by the sternum and may appear to be enlarged on an anterior-posterior roentgenogram. The change in cardiac position is also responsible for electrocardiographic abnormalities. A parasternal systolic murmur is heard in most children with pectus excavatum. Despite these findings the patients show little if any evidence of cardiac disease. Cardiac catheterizations are not recommended since studies on a number of children with this deformity have shown no hemodynamic malfunction. Most patients are asymptomatic.

Since there is no evident physiologic handicap, the only reason for surgery is the correction of the cosmetic defect. However, the risks and discomfort of the operation should be carefully considered before surgical correction is done for cosmetic reasons alone.

A funnel chest is not always the result of a congenital malformation; sometimes it is an acquired abnormality. Persistent sternal depression develops in children who have respiratory tract obstruction or parenchymal disease of the lung requiring forceful inspiratory efforts and retractions of the sternum for a prolonged period. This secondary deformity is most apt to occur in young infants with a soft, compliant thoracic wall. If the obstruction is relieved, or the lung disease clears, the sternal depression will disappear—rapidly in the infant and more slowly in an older child.

Pectus Carinatum

The "pigeon breast" deformity is less common than pectus excavatum and has not been as well studied. There is no evidence that this deformity causes cardiopulmonary disabilities, and treatment, if any, should be based on the need for cosmetic repair.

Thoracic Deformity Due to Bone Dysplasia

In several forms of generalized bone dysplasia the thorax is small and causes neonatal asphyxia when the abnormality is severe. The interrelationships of this group of diseases are not clear. Achondroplasia is not included. This condition causes nasal obstruction and hence some respiratory distress, particularly in the newborn infant, but the chest is probably not abnormally small.

The *Asphyxiating Thoracic Dystrophy of Juene*, described in 1956, is now being quite frequently recognized. Children with this genetically determined condition have a small, bell-shaped thorax, and at postmortem examination, somewhat small lungs as well. Respiratory insufficiency may occur in the new-

born period or in association with intercurrent infections in older infants. The affected children seem to improve with age and growth; if they survive the hazards of infancy their respiratory limitations may decrease. The other features of this illness are polydactyly, dysplasia of the pelvis, short stature, and sometimes an unusual and severe form of renal disease (Fig. 39).

Similar thoracic deformities are seen in *chondroectodermal dysplasia*, or the Ellis-van Creveld syndrome, which is another form of generalized bone dysplasia and dwarfism. The distal portions of the extremities are foreshortened more than the proximal segments. The nails are dystrophic, and the teeth and hair are hypoplastic. The thorax is small and bell-shaped, much like that described in patients with the thoracic dystrophy of Juene. Since these children seem to improve with age some authorities have tentatively suggested sternal splitting procedures to increase the intrathoracic volume. However, as yet there has been little experience with this procedure.

Thanatophoric dwarfism causes neonatal death (thanatophoric = death-bringing) from asphyxia. The chest is tiny, rigid, and bell-shaped, a combination that produces inadequate aeration of the lung. Although the general body configuration suggests an

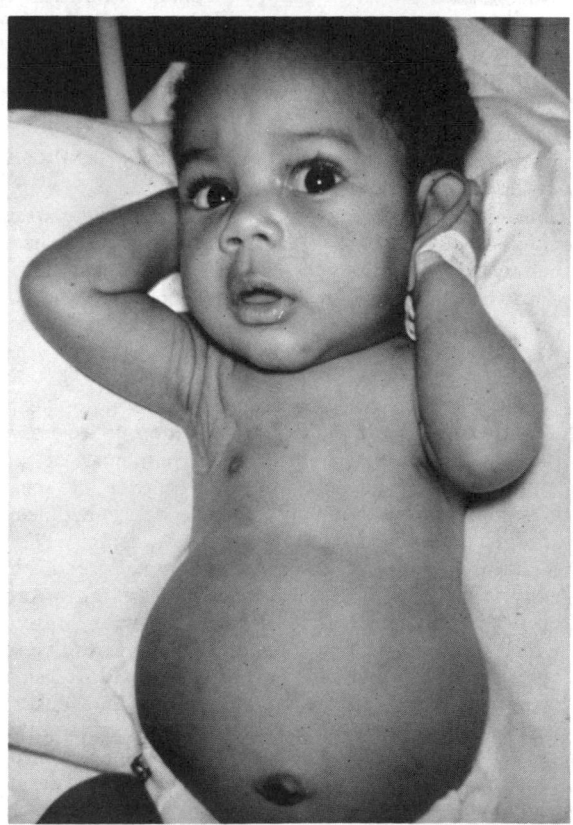

Fig. 39. Infant, age 4 months, with thoracic dystrophy. He has a very small chest, 33 cm in circumference. He had severe respiratory distress at the time of a respiratory infection but was asymptomatic before and after. (From Hanissian et al. *J. Pediat.*, 71:855, 1967.)

extreme form of achondroplasia, thanatophoric dwarf-ism seems to be a different disease. Some of the neo-natal deaths attributed to achondroplasia may, in fact, be caused by this disease.

Other Congenital Anomalies of the Thorax

The sternum is formed by midline fusion of paired sternal bands. A failure of fusion of the upper por-tion of the sternum leaves the mediastinum covered only by skin and subcutaneous tissue which moves paradoxically with respiration. The absence of sup-porting bone allows this area to be forced inward with inspiration and to protrude with expiration. Surgical repair is advised to protect the upper me-diastinum and to improve the child's appearance. Repair is most easily done in young infants.

Severe defects of sternal fusion exposing the heart, ectopia cordis, are often associated with other major cardiovascular malformations and are usually fatal.

Occasionally, congenital absence of portions of ribs leaves an area of the chest wall unsupported by bone; such areas move paradoxically with respiration much like the sternal cleft defects. Children who have large defects that cause functional disability are candidates for surgical repair. However, in most in-stances the bony defects are small, the children are asymptomatic, and surgical correction is unnecessary.

Kyphoscoliosis

The chest may be deformed by forward angulation (kyphosis) or curves (scoliosis) of the spine. These are relatively common in childhood and result from neuromuscular disease, vertebral anomalies, neuro-fibromatosis, or from unknown causes. These de-formities become progressively more severe as the child grows, and tend to stabilize only after growth ceases. Patients with kyphoscoliosis have several car-diopulmonary handicaps. The total lung volume and the vital capacity are reduced. The compliance of the lungs is also reduced, probably because of focal atelectasis and the inability to take occasional deep breaths. The chest wall remains surprisingly com-pliant in children but becomes abnormally rigid in early adult life. These changes increase the work of respiration and lead to rapid, shallow breathing, which minimizes energy expenditure but results in alveolar hypoventilation. The carbon dioxide tension of arterial blood increases and arterial oxygen tension decreases. Oxygen tension is further decreased by shunts through atelectatic areas. Hypoxemia causes constriction of the pulmonary arterioles, increase in pulmonary arterial pressure, and right ventricular hypertrophy. Cardiopulmonary failure and death may occur in the late stages of this condition. If cardio-pulmonary failure is to be prevented, treatment must be started in childhood when the severity of this deformity is increasing most rapidly.

In patients with severe deformity the vital ca-pacity is progressively decreased. Cardiopulmonary failure may occur when the vital capacity is less than 60 percent of normal. Serial measurements of vital capacity are important in assessing the severity of the disease and should be performed on all children with kyphoscoliosis at regular intervals.

Although use of braces and cases may slow or halt the progression of idiopathic scoliosis, a decreas-ing vital capacity is an indication for surgical cor-rection of the deformity. This will not restore the vital capacity to normal but will often interrupt the progress of the illness and prevent cardiopulmo-nary failure.

In the postoperative period, respiratory function may be impeded by immobilization or by application of body casts. Therefore, the patient's respiratory re-serve will limit the surgeon's choice of corrective pro-cedures.

Cardiopulmonary Failure and Obesity
(Pickwickian Syndrome)

This bizarre syndrome consists of cyanosis, poly-cythemia, and somnolence; it is a complication of extreme obesity and is rarely seen in children. The events leading to this condition begin with massive deposition of fat on the chest and in the abdomen. The fat deposits make these structures less compliant than normal and increase the work of breathing. Al-though this problem is common to all obese subjects, for unknown reasons some develop alveolar hypo-ventilation. The carbon dioxide retention causes som-nolence; the hypoxemia causes polycythemia, pulmo-nary hypertension and, occasionally, heart failure may ensue. Eventually, deep cyanosis and coma may occur. Restoration of adequate ventilation may require the use of mechanical ventilators. Oxygen should not be withheld, even though it may decrease the ventila-tory drive.

Reduction in weight is the only satisfactory ther-apy and after sufficient weight loss these patients have normal cardiopulmonary function.

Connective Tissue Diseases that Affect the Chest Wall

Rheumatoid spondylitis, infrequently seen in children, may, in its severe form, cause complete immobility of the spine and the rib cage. The chest becomes fixed in a position of partial inspiration, so that the functional residual volume is increased and the vital capacity is decreased. When the thorax is rigid the diaphragm becomes solely responsible for ventilation. No specific therapy is necessary since diaphragmatic contraction is ordinarily capable of maintaining ade-quate ventilation.

Scleroderma, or progressive systemic sclerosis, may be associated with a rapid respiratory rate, breathlessness, and a decrease in compliance of the lungs. Since there is an increase in elasticity of the soft tissues it has been suggested that the respiratory symptoms are caused by a "hidebound" chest. This suspicion is not substantiated by careful studies which indicate that parenchymal involvement is the principal abnormality responsible for the loss of compliance.

Trauma

Multiple fractures of the ribs or costal cartilages from crushing chest trauma may cause a "flail" chest. The rib cage loses its rigidity and its ability to function as the framework of the respiratory bellows; chest wall motion is paradoxical; the crushed section collapses on inspiration and bulges on expiration. Although the chest wall of a child is resilient and resistant to trauma, crush injuries do occur when the injuring force is large.

Adequate ventilation may require the use of an intermittent, positive pressure respirator. The positive pressure inflates the lungs and the inflated lung serves as an internal splint for the crushed chest wall. Contusion of the lung, causing a fluffy shadow on the radiograph, may occur in the absence of rib fractures.

Pleural Diseases

Pleural disease may restrict ventilation in two ways. Collections of fluid or air in the pleural space may compress one or both lungs, or scarring of the pleura, following hemothorax or empyema, may envelop the lung in a rigid fibrous coating which severely limits expansion. The ventilatory restriction in pleural disease is often marked even when the radiographic abnormality is not striking.

Empyema

Empyema was once frequent and usually followed pneumococcal pneumonia. It is now infrequent and when it does occur it is apt to be a complication of pneumonia due to staphylococcus, streptococcus, or *H. influenzae* infections. Staphylococcal empyema, the most severe type, and *H. influenzae* empyema occur most often in infants under one year of age; streptococcal empyema is most often seen in older children. More boys are affected than girls. The onset of the major symptoms is abrupt. The babies are usually seriously ill at the time they are first seen and appear grey, lethargic, tachypneic, and anxious. The nostrils flare with inspiration and an expiratory grunt is almost always present. The physical signs of empyema are easily recognized. The chest is dull to percussion throughout the involved side and the breath sounds are diminished on that side.

Pneumothorax occurs frequently in staphylococcal pneumonia and empyema, usually in the first day or two of hospitalization. A sudden increase in respiratory distress or rapid deterioration of the child's condition should suggest this possibility. If it does occur, prompt removal of the trapped air by needle aspiration may be momentarily helpful but in all such cases a catheter should then be inserted through the anterior chest wall into the pleural space and connected to a closed drainage system.

Whenever purulent fluid accumulates in the pleural space it should be removed promptly. Early in the course of an infection, if the pleural fluid is watery, it may be evacuated by thoracentesis, but thick, purulent material cannot be adequately drained through a needle; catheter drainage of the intrapleural space is needed. The catheter should be placed in a dependent position and connected to a water-sealed drainage system. The mechanics of the drainage system require careful and continuing attention, since the catheters often become obstructed by thick pus or may drain only a small and loculated portion of the pleural cavity. Inadequate or delayed drainage may leave purulent material in the pleural space which organizes into a thick fibrous coating, obliterates the pleural space, and restricts motion of the lung and thorax. The fibrous scar can be successfully removed surgically by a decortication procedure; however, if the diagnosis can be made early in the course of the illness, and antibiotics and pleural drainage properly used, decortication procedures should rarely be needed.

Hemothorax

Collections of blood in the pleural space are almost always caused by trauma. Blood is mildly irritating to the pleural surfaces and is not completely absorbed. If the blood is not removed, pleural scarring and fibrothorax follow.

Pneumothorax

Pneumothorax occurs most often in newborn infants and in children with asthma, cystic fibrosis, and staphylococcal pneumonia. It also occurs in apparently healthy children. Four out of five of these spontaneous cases are in older boys. The cause of these air leaks is not always known, but minor congenital anomalies of the lung are sometimes seen and must always be suspected. Cough or vigorous exercise may be the immediate cause but even these "explanations" are not always available, since some episodes begin during sleep or quiet breathing.

Spontaneous pneumothorax does not always cause a very serious illness. Sudden chest pain or discomfort occurs at the onset, and is the usual reason for seeking medical care. Dyspnea, if present, is not severe. No active treatment is required, early recovery can be expected, and recurrence is unlikely.

Unfortunately, spontaneous pneumothorax is not always so benign. Collapse of the lung on the involved side may be complete, air in the pleural space may be trapped under pressure, the contralateral lung compressed, and nevous return to the heart impeded. Death may occur if the trapped pleural air is not removed promptly. Aspiration of air from the pleural cavity by thoracentesis will provide effective relief if no further air leak occurs; however, in cases of tension pneumothorax, a continuing leak is to be expected and the pleural air should be removed through a catheter inserted into the pleural cavity and connected to water-sealed drainage.

If a patient has recurrent episodes of pneumothorax, a thoracotomy should be performed in order to resect the source of air leak if it can be identified, and to obliterate the pleural space. Either procedure should be effective in preventing further recurrences.

Chylothorax

A leak in the thoracic duct or in the major lymph channels of the mediastinum which transport fat absorbed from the gut allows chyle to accumulate in the intrapleural space. Lymph which leaks from the lungs or pleura is clear, and does not contain the fat characteristic of chyle. Chylothorax is unusual in childhood but is least rare in the neonatal period. The clinical manifestations are those of any hydrothorax. As the pleural fluid gradually increases in volume, respiratory distress becomes more severe.

Chylothorax may be caused by surgical or other trauma to the mediastinal structures and has also been reported as a complication of mediastinal tumors. However, since this condition is most common in the newborn infant, birth trauma is probably an important factor in these cases. Trauma alone is apparently not the sole cause since, in some cases, the chylothorax is already present at the time of birth and in others is associated with lymphatic abnormalities elsewhere, such as lymphedema and chylous ascites. Congenital anomalies of the lymph vessels probably make them unusually susceptible to the trauma of birth.

Chylothorax may not appear for several days or weeks after birth or other trauma. In these instances the initial chyle leak may be into the mediastinal tissues with delayed rupture into the pleural space.

The chyle leak usually stops spontaneously and abruptly after an unpredictable interval of several days, weeks, or months. Repeated thoracentesis or closed chest drainage is the suggested interim treatment. A diet based on casein and medium-chain triglycerides may be tried since the latter are transported through the portal circulation and not through the thoracic duct. In one reported case prompt clearing followed use of such a diet in a child who had required repeated thoracenteses over a period of four months.

When other methods fail the thoracic duct should be ligated and the pleural space obliterated. Such procedures are usually successful.

REFERENCES

POLIOMYELITIS

Affeldt, J. E. Neuromotor paralysis. *In* Fenn, W. O., and Rahn, H., eds. Handbook of Physiology, Sec. 3, Respiration. Washington, D.C., Amer. Physiol. Soc., 1965, Vol. II, p. 1509.

Ferris, B. G., Mead, J., Whittenberger, J. L., and Saxton, G. A. Pulmonary function in convalescent poliomyelitis patients. III. Compliance of lungs and thorax. New Eng. J. Med., 247:390, 1952.

Spencer, W. A. Treatment of Acute Poliomyelitis. Springfield, Ill., Charles C Thomas, Publ., 1954.

SPINAL CORD LESIONS

Sandor, F. Diaphragmatic respiration: A sign of cervical cord lesion in the unconscious patient ("horizontal paradox"). Brit. Med. J., 1:465, 1966.

MUSCULAR DYSTROPHY

Kilburn, K. H., Eagan, J. T., Sieker, H. O., and Heyman, A. Cardiopulmonary insufficiency in myotonic and progressive muscular dystrophy. New Eng. J. Med., 261:1089, 1959.

DIAPHRAGMATIC PARALYSIS

Bishop, H. C., and Koop, C. E. Acquired eventration of the diaphragm in infancy. Pediatrics, 22:1088, 1958.

McCredie, M., Lovejoy, F. W., and Kaltreider, N. L. Pulmonary function in diaphragmatic paralysis. Thorax, 17:213, 1962.

Richard, J., Chevalier, V., Capelle, R., Cavrot, E., Content, J., and Delforge, J. La paralysie diaphragmatique obstetricale, A propos de dix cas. Arch. Franc. Pediat., 14:563, 1957.

Riley, E. A. Idiopathic diaphragmatic paralysis, a report of 8 cases. Amer. J. Med., 32:404, 1962.

Shifrin, N. Unilateral paralysis of the diaphragm in the newborn infant due to phrenic nerve injury, with and without associated brachial palsy. Pediatrics, 9:69, 1952.

MYASTHENIA GRAVIS

Namba, T., Brown, S. B., and Grob, D. Neonatal myasthenia gravis. Report of 2 cases and review of literature. Pediatrics, 45:488, 1970.

PECTUS EXCAVATUM

Fink, A., Rivin, A., and Murray, J. F. Pectus excavatum. An analysis of twenty-seven cases. Arch. Intern. Med., 108:427, 1961.

Orzalesi, M. M., and Cook, C. D. Pulmonary function in children with pectus excavatum. J. Pediat., 66:898, 1965.

Reusch, C. S. Hemodynamic studies in pectus excavatum. Circulation, 24:1143, 1961.

Weg, J. G., Krumholz, R. A., and Harkleroad, L. E.

Pulmonary dysfunction in pectus excavatum. Amer. Rev. Resp. Dis., 96:936, 1967.

THORACIC DYSTROPHY

Ellis, R. W. B., and Van Creveld, S. A syndrome characterized by ectodermal dysplasia, polydactyly, chondrodysplasia and congenital morbus cordis. Arch. Dis. Child., 15:65, 1940.

Hanissian, A. S., Riggs, W. W., Jr., and Thomas, D. A. Infantile thoracic dystrophy—a variant of Ellis-van Creveld syndrome. J. Pediat., 71:855, 1967.

Jeune, M., Beraud, C., and Carron, R. Dystrophie thoracique asphyxiante de caractère familial. Arch. Franc. Pediat., 12:886, 1955.

Maroteaux, P., Lamy, M., and Robert, J. M. Le nanisme thanatophore. Presse Med., 75:2519, 1967.

Pirnar, T., and Neuhauser, E. B. D. Asphyxiating thoracic dystrophy of the newborn. Amer. J. Roentgen., 98:359, 1966.

THORACIC ANOMALIES

Bernhardt, L. C. Bifid sternum. J. Thorac. Cardiovasc. Surg., 55:758, 1968.

Ravitch, M. M. Atypical deformities of the chest wall—absence and deformities of the ribs and costal cartilages. Surgery, 59:438, 1966.

KYPHOSCOLIOSIS

Bergofsky, E. H. Quantitation of the function of respiratory muscles in normal individuals and quadriplegic patients. Arch. Phys. Med., 45:575, 1964.

—— Turino, G. M., and Fishman, A. P. Cardiorespiratory failure in kyphoscoliosis. Medicine, 38:263, 1959.

Caro, C. G., and DuBois, A. B. Pulmonary function in kyphoscoliosis. Thorax, 16:282, 1961.

Cook, C. D., Barrie, H., DeForest, B. A., and Helliesen, P. J. Pulmonary physiology in children. III. Lung volumes, mechanics of respiration and respiratory muscle strength in scoliosis. Pediatrics, 25:766, 1960.

Makley, J. T., Herndon, C. H., Inkley, S., Doershuk, C., Matthews, L. W., Post, R. H., and Littell, A. S. Pulmonary function in paralytic and non-paralytic scoliosis before and after treatment. J. Bone Joint Surg. (Brit.), 50A:1379, 1968.

Westgate, H. D., and Moe, J. H. Pulmonary function in kyphoscoliosis before and after correction by the Harrington instrumentation method. J. Bone Joint Surg. (Brit.), 51:935, 1969.

PICKWICKIAN SYNDROME

Barrera, F., Reidenberg, M. M., and Winters, W. L. Pulmonary function in the obese patient. Amer. J. Med. Sci., 254:785, 1967.

Cayler, G. G. Cardiorespiratory syndrome of obesity (Pickwickian syndrome) in children. Pediatrics, 27:237, 1961.

Cherniak, R. M. Management of cardiopulmonary disorders in the obese patient. Mod. Treatm., 4:1162, 1967.

Finkelstein, J. W., and Avery, M. E. The Pickwickian syndrome, studies on ventilation and carbohydrate metabolism. Case report of a child who recovered. Amer. J. Dis. Child., 106:251, 1963.

CONNECTIVE TISSUE DISEASE

Travis, D. M., Cook, C. D., Julian, D. G., Crump, C. H., Helliesen, P., Robin, E. D., Bayles, T. B., and Burwell, C. S. The lungs in rheumatoid spondylitis, gas exchange and lung mechanics in a form of restrictive pulmonary disease. Amer. J. Med., 29:623, 1960.

SCLERODERMA

Adhikari, P. K., Bianchi, F. A., Boushy, S. F., Sakamoto, A., and Lewis, B. M. Pulmonary function in scleroderma. Its relation to changes in chest roentgenogram and in the skin of the thorax. Amer. Rev. Resp. Dis., 86:823, 1962.

TRAUMA

Brewer, L. A. The management of crushing injuries of the chest. Surg. Clin. N. Amer., 48:1279, 1968.

EMPYEMA

Hendren, W. H., and Haggarty, R. J. Staphylococcal pneumonia in infancy and childhood. J.A.M.A., 168:1, 1958.

Hertzler, J. H., Miller, A. E., and Tuttle, W. M. Present concepts in the treatment of empyema in children. A.M.A. Arch. Surg., 68:838, 1954.

Smith, P. L., and Gerald, B. Empyema in childhood followed roentgenographically: Decortication seldom needed. Amer. J. Roentgen., 106:114, 1969.

Wise, M. B., Beaudry, P. H., and Bates, D. V. Long-term follow-up of staphylococcal pneumonia. Pediatrics, 38:398, 1966.

PNEUMOTHORAX

Cran, I. R., and Rumball, C. A. Survey of spontaneous pneumothoraces in the Royal Air Force. Thorax, 22:462, 1967.

Stradling, P., and Poole, G. Conservative management of spontaneous pneumothorax. Thorax, 21:145, 1966.

CHYLOTHORAX

Lichter, I., Hill, G. L., and Nye, E. R. The use of medium-chain triglycerides in the treatment of chylothorax in a child. Ann. Thorac. Surg., 5:352, 1968.

Maloney, J. V., Jr., and Spencer, F. C. The nonoperative treatment of traumatic chylothorax. Surgery, 40:121, 1956.

McKendry, J. B. J., Lindsay, W. K., and Gerstein, M. C. Congenital defects of the lymphatics in infancy. Pediatrics, 19:21, 1957.

Randolph, J. G., and Gross, R. E. Congenital chylothorax. A.M.A. Arch. Surg., 74:405, 1957.

chapter 20

THE CIRCULATORY SYSTEM

ABRAHAM M. RUDOLPH, Associate Editor

The mammalian circulation undergoes continuing change from the time of embryonic differentiation to the death of the organism. The main process affecting the circulation in adult life is that of aging, during which fibrous replacement of elastic and smooth muscle components of the vascular system produces primarily structural changes. The most dramatic changes in the circulation occur at the time of birth, however, when the functions of gas exchange, which were carried out by the placenta in utero, are taken over by the lungs, requiring a complete reorientation of the circulation. Some of these adjustments occur rapidly, but others are prolonged over several weeks or months.

In order to appreciate the effects of circulatory disorders, it is important to consider the age of an infant or child and to understand normal physiologic adjustments after birth. Furthermore, it should be realized that the same anatomic or pathologic lesions may produce entirely different physiologic disturbances, depending on the degree of maturation of the circulation.

ventricle. This arrangement provides blood of relatively high oxygen saturation to the heart, head and neck, and upper trunk. The remaining portion of inferior vena caval blood is distributed in the same way as superior vena caval return.

Almost all superior vena caval blood passes through the tricuspid valve and is ejected by the right ventricle into the pulmonary artery. Most of this blood, 80 to 90 percent, passes through the ductus arteriosus to the descending aorta, the remainder entering the lungs.

DISTRIBUTION OF BLOOD FLOW IN THE FETUS. The ductus arteriosus provides a communication between the pulmonary artery and aorta almost large enough to equilibrate pressures in the pulmonary and systemic circulations. In such a hydrodynamic system, distribution of flow is regulated by the local resistance to blood flow in each organ.

Placental vascular resistance is very low, thus permitting a large proportion, 40 to 50 percent, of total cardiac output, to enter this organ. Pulmonary vascular resistance, however, is very high, and blood

20.1

THE FETAL CIRCULATION AND CIRCULATORY ADJUSTMENTS AFTER BIRTH

ABRAHAM M. RUDOLPH

To understand the circulatory adjustments after birth, it is necessary to review briefly the fetal circulation, which is discussed in greater detail elsewhere (Sec. 2.11). The arrangement of the fetal circulation is shown diagrammatically in Figure 1.

VENOUS RETURN TO THE FETAL HEART. Placental blood returns to the fetus through the umbilical vein, which, just distal to the liver, is joined by the portal vein. A variable portion, 20 to 80 percent, of umbilical venous blood, which has a relatively high oxygen saturation, passes through the liver; the remainder bypasses the liver through the ductus venosus and enters the inferior vena cava directly.

Inferior vena caval blood, comprising blood returning from the lower body as well as the total umbilical venous return, is in part deflected directly through the foramen ovale to the left atrium and

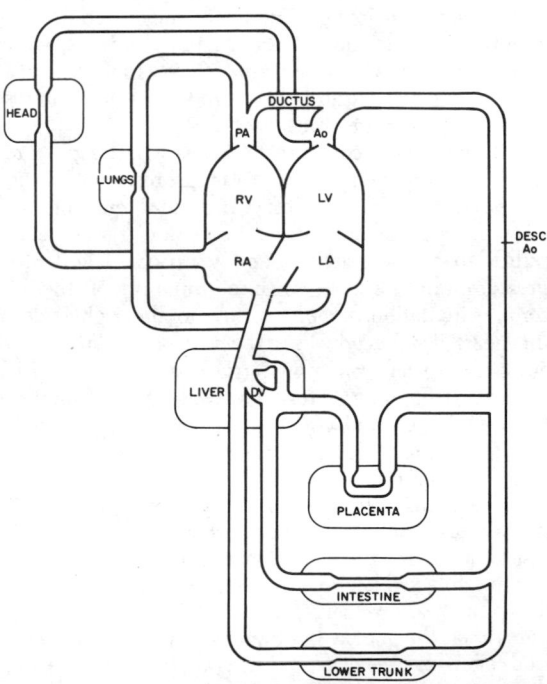

Fig. 1. Fetal circulation.

flow through the lungs is thus very small. The small blood vessels in the fetal lung have a thick muscular medial layer, in marked contrast to the arterioles of the adult lung, which have thin walls with negligible amounts of muscle. In addition, the fetal pulmonary vessels are very reactive, showing marked vasoconstrictor responses both to decreased arterial oxygen tension and to reduced pH of the perfusing blood.

The two major transformations occurring after birth are expansion of the lungs with air and elimination of the placental circulation. Expansion of the lungs produces a marked decrease of pulmonary vascular resistance, with an increase in pulmonary blood flow. Although this increase may be related partly to a simple physical process associated with expansion of the lungs, it has been shown that the major change is due to the effects of oxygen on the pulmonary arterioles. The inhalation of gas containing relatively high concentrations of oxygen results in a relaxation of the hypoxemia-induced pulmonary vasoconstriction of the fetal lung. The resulting vasodilation of the precapillary vessels is almost certainly related to a direct effect of oxygen diffusion from surrounding alveoli and not, as formerly held, to a reflex phenomenon arising beyond the capillaries.

Eliminating the placental circulation removes a low-resistance circuit, causing a marked rise in systemic vascular resistance. There is thus a reorientation of resistances, and should the ductus arteriosus remain patent, blood would flow in a left-to-right direction from aorta to pulmonary artery. The ductus arteriosus usually does remain patent for several hours after birth, and a small to moderate left-to-right shunt occurs, resulting in a high pulmonary blood flow. Increased oxygenation of the arterial blood stimulates constriction of the ductus arteriosus, which is functionally closed within 10 to 15 hours after birth. Organic closure by thrombosis and fibrosis takes place within three weeks.

Two factors combine to increase left atrial pressure: (1) higher systemic vascular resistance causes increased resistance to left ventricular ejection, and (2) increase in pulmonary blood flow raises venous return to the left atrium and ventricle. Right atrial pressure falls because, with elimination of the placental circulation, venous return to the right side of the heart is reduced. This reversal of pressure gradient between left and right atria causes an apposition of the left flap of the foramen ovale, with functional closure of the atrial communication.

The initial decrease in pulmonary vascular resistance after birth is related to the relief of pulmonary vasoconstriction induced by hypoxemia. When the ductus arteriosus closes and pulmonary vascular resistance falls, the circulatory pattern characteristic of the adult has begun to appear. A further change in the pulmonary vessels occurs as the muscular component of the media gradually disappears over a period of 7 to 14 days; within about 3 to 4 weeks the histologic appearance of the vessels is similar to that in the adult. Associated with these maturational changes is a decrease in pulmonary arterial and right ventricular pressure. Also, the prenatal dominance of the right ventricle is reversed, and left ventricular weight increases rapidly, whereas right ventricular weight is first stationary and then slowly increases.

The maturational changes of the pulmonary vessels have a profound influence in determining the clinical course and hemodynamic manifestations of many congenital heart lesions; and in turn, the presence of congenital heart disease may affect the normal postnatal changes in the pulmonary vessels. The reactivity of the pulmonary circulation in the neonatal period is extremely important in any condition which may induce hypoxia and acidosis, since marked pulmonary vasoconstriction with interference in pulmonary blood flow may occur.

20.2
THE SIGNS AND SYMPTOMS OF CARDIOVASCULAR DISEASES IN INFANTS AND CHILDREN

ROBERT F. CASTLE

It cannot be overemphasized that a correct interpretation of a careful history and physical examination is the most important means of evaluating patients with cardiovascular diseases. There has been an increasing tendency to stress the importance of detailed cardiac catheterization studies, which include such methods as cineangiocardiography, dye dilution methods, and radioisotope techniques. To be sure, these tools have furnished a great deal of information concerning the pathophysiology of congenital and acquired heart disease, and they are especially important in the diagnosis of complicated and unusual anomalies. Fortunately, we have been able to apply much of the knowledge gained from catheterization techniques to the clinical evaluation of the patient, so that an accurate diagnosis based on history, physical examination, EKG, and plain x-rays is now possible in a great majority of patients. Phonocardiography and vectorcardiography, which represent extensions of auscultation and electrocardiography, respectively, are also valuable techniques capable of furnishing important diagnostic data at no additional risk to the patient. Therefore, it is possible not only to reach a correct diagnosis in most patients but also to estimate the severity of many lesions readily through clinical evaluation alone. Through understanding the pathophysiology of congenital and acquired heart disease and correlating this knowledge with the clinical picture presented by the patient, one can avoid overreliance on cardiac catheterization. However, since clinical diagnosis in the infant with congenital heart disease is at present not as accurate as in the older child, cardiac catheterization is frequently required.

The spectrum of signs and symptoms of cardiac disease in infants and children differs considerably from that in adults. Not only does the pediatrician often deal with different diseases than does the internist, but in infants and children congenital and acquired diseases are superimposed on the changing cardiovascular system of the immature and growing organism.

As a general rule, the existence of genuine symptoms referable to the cardiovascular system implies the presence of a hemodynamically significant lesion that may ultimately require detailed evaluation and, quite likely, surgical repair if feasible from an anatomic and physiologic standpoint. However, a lack of symptoms does not necessarily imply a negligible lesion, especially in the case of obstructive lesions such as isolated pulmonic and aortic stenosis and coarctation of the aorta.

The Manifestations of Congenital Heart Disease in Infants and Children

Cardiac Failure

In the early neonatal period serious cardiovascular malformations may present in a form indistinguishable clinically from so-called idiopathic respiratory distress syndrome. One should be especially alert to the possibility of an underlying cardiac defect in the full-term infant who appears normal at birth but develops tachypnea, cyanosis, grunting respirations, marked tachycardia, and hepatomegaly in the early hours or days of life. A variety of congenital cardiac defects, all of serious proportion and many interfering with the establishment of an effective systemic circulation, may cause such difficulties in the neonatal period. In the first week of life the underlying lesion is most likely to be aortic atresia or some other form of the hypoplastic left heart syndrome. However, anomalies such as transposition of the great vessels, coarctation of the aorta, patent ductus arteriosus, isolated severe pulmonary stenosis, and other lesions may also be responsible.

In infants 1 week to 1 month of age the frequency with which various cardiac malformations cause respiratory distress and congestive failure differs somewhat. Although the majority of infants with coarctation of the aorta are not symptomatic, this lesion is the most common cause of failure at this age. The next most frequent lesions causing failure are transposition of the great vessels and endocardial fibroelastosis. Various forms of left-to-right shunts may also cause difficulty at this age.

In infants beyond the immediate neonatal period, signs of respiratory distress also point to cardiac decompensation. Tachypnea, dyspnea, tiring, and fretfulness during feeding often antedate other manifestations of congestive failure. However, these signs are frequently missed or misinterpreted because the physician is unaware that they may represent early signs of failure. Often the diagnosis of congestive failure is not made until, in addition to the respiratory symptoms of left heart decompensation, the infant exhibits many of the florid signs of right heart failure. However, even in the presence of hepatomegaly, peripheral edema is usually mild and may involve only the eyelids. It should be emphasized that the infant in failure frequently appears dusky or frankly cyanotic because of poor cardiac output and peripheral stasis. This may occur in the presence of a large left-to-right shunt and does not necessarily indicate a central right-to-left shunt. Infants in borderline or frank congestive failure often perspire excessively; the mechanism of this is not understood. Sweating is an especially prominent sign in infants with left-to-right shunts. In infants with large left-to-right shunts, precordial fullness and hyperactivity are also frequently called to the physician's attention by the parents.

The vast majority, perhaps 95 percent, of patients with congenital heart disease who will exhibit congestive failure during childhood do so by the time they are a year of age. In only a few situations is congestive failure apt to appear for the first time in later childhood. Occasional patients with endocardial cushion defects may develop failure in later childhood. Decompensation may also occur in patients with previously well-compensated lesions who develop superimposed bacterial endocarditis, pneumonia, severe anemia, or a serious arrhythmia.

In general, there is a tendency for the manifestations of congestive failure to lessen or even to disappear if the infant can be successfully managed beyond the critical first 6 to 12 months of life. This generalization applies to infants with large left-to-right shunts (with the exception of occasional patients with endocardial cushion defect) and also to many infants who develop failure secondary to an obstructive lesion, particularly coarctation of the aorta. Most children with large left-to-right shunts are remarkably symptom-free beyond the second year. True, many continue to exhibit retardation in growth, but exercise tolerance usually improves and the only symptom may be mildly increased fatigability.

Pulmonary Infections

Lower respiratory tract infections frequently complicate the clinical course of infants and children with congenital heart disease. Often it is very difficult to separate the manifestations of a pulmonary infection from those related to the underlying cardiac condition. Such infections are common in patients with large left-to-right shunts and in those cyanotic conditions associated with excessive pulmonary blood flow. They afford a considerable hazard to these patients, particularly in the first 6 to 12 months of life.

Many infants with heart disease develop lower

respiratory tract infections in the presence of existing congestive failure. At times, a pulmonary infection may precipitate overt manifestation of cardiac failure in a previously compensated infant. However, another group exists in which frequent bouts of lower respiratory tract infections occur but cardiac decompensation is not a problem.

One should be alert to the possibility of undiagnosed heart disease in infants with frequent pulmonary infections. This problem does not usually present itself in infants with large left-to-right shunts, since these patients very commonly have prominent murmurs and cardiomegaly, which point to an underlying cardiac abnormality. However, murmurs may be inconspicuous at times in patients in severe congestive failure. A basic cardiac disorder is more apt to be overlooked in a few conditions not always associated with murmurs, including patients with coarctation of the aorta, anomalous origin of the left coronary artery from the pulmonary artery, endocardial fibroelastosis, glycogen storage disease, and severe pulmonary hypertension, either isolated or associated with congenital heart disease. In such conditions cardiomegaly on x-ray examination and EKG abnormalities may provide the clue to an underlying cardiac disorder.

Expiratory wheezing is frequently a prominent feature in respiratory infections occurring in infants with heart disease. Syndromes representing or resembling bronchiolitis are common. Such illnesses, particularly if recurrent or persistent, should alert the physician to the possibility of a basic cardiac condition.

Growth Disturbances

Not infrequently, congenital heart disease is associated with growth retardation. In general, infants with large left-to-right shunts at the ventricular or pulmonary artery levels are most likely to show growth retardation. Most infants who have severe obstructive lesions, such as pulmonary or aortic stenosis, exhibit normal growth and development. In fact, patients with severe pulmonary stenosis are often robust or even obese during infancy.

Most children with cyanotic conditions do not thrive. This includes patients with transposition of the great vessels, tricuspid and pulmonary atresia, more severe forms of endocardial cushion defects, persistent truncus arteriosus, and Ebstein's malformation; many patients with tetralogy of Fallot grow normally. Infants with these conditions, in whom some sort of surgical procedure is hemodynamically helpful, may show improvement in growth following surgery. However, such improvement rarely occurs spontaneously. In contrast, some children with large left-to-right shunts show growth retardation during the first 6 to 12 months, and then show slow improvement in rate of weight gain during the second and subsequent years, even in the absence of surgical alleviation of their abnormality.

In most, but not all, abnormally small children with congenital heart disease the cardiac lesion is the dominant factor underlying the growth disturbance. General syndromes—such as Down's syndrome, Turner's syndrome, and the various trisomy states—are frequently associated with congenital cardiac lesions, but these syndromes are also characterized by growth retardation in their own right. Moreover, isolated noncardiac anomalies may also adversely affect growth. Furthermore, some patients with congenital heart disease appear to be constitutionally small, some being truly dwarfed. In the latter groups, surgery even if totally corrective does not result in any significant improvement in growth.

Special Manifestations in Cyanotic Conditions

Occasionally an infant is brought to the physician with a presenting complaint of cyanosis, but the clinical presence or absence of a cardiac disorder may be very difficult to determine with certainty. Depending on the severity of the lesion, clinically evident cyanosis may not be apparent until 6 months of age or even later. Moreover, moderate degrees of arterial desaturation are associated with a ruddy or plethoric appearance rather than outright cyanosis. Many normal young infants have peripheral acrocyanosis due presumably to peripheral stasis associated with immature vasomotor control mechanisms regulating peripheral blood flow. Also, normal infants and some older children exhibit peripheral cyanosis along with transient blueness of the mucous membranes and perioral regions following exposure to cold, during fright, and during prolonged crying, especially when there is associated breath holding. The physician should be able to recognize these patients easily. They do not have other signs or symptoms pointing toward cardiovascular disease. They have normal exercise tolerance, and they do not become cyanotic with usual vigorous physical activity and exercise in the absence of cold exposure.

Most infants with cyanotic congenital heart disease have a delayed and diminished fall in hemoglobin levels from the high values normal in the immediate neonatal period. Thus, persisting polycythemia may be a more sensitive index of arterial oxygen desaturation than any objective physical sign. In older infants with cyanotic congenital heart disease, therapy of iron deficiency may ameliorate anoxic symptoms, although cyanosis may become much more striking.

Most patients with cyanotic congenital heart disease have symptoms of anoxia and/or congestive failure, as manifested by clubbing of the fingers and toes, growth and motor retardation, restlessness, heat intolerance, irritability, a preference for the knee-chest position in infants, squatting in older children, and hyperventilation with minimal exertion (e.g., during feeding). Hemiparesis secondary to cerebral thrombosis may occur in cyanotic infants during the first two years, whereas brain abscess is the most common central nervous system complication in these children beyond the second year. Overt hypercyanotic spells may appear and occur with no apparent inciting cause, although a frightening experience, anger, feeding, or attempt to perform some physical activity often seem to initiate these episodes. Such spells may be relatively mild when they first occur, but they tend to become progressively more severe with the passage of time. As a spell begins, the patient becomes more dyspneic and tachypnea increases. Cyanosis deepens and prolonged crying may occur. The patient often becomes quite hypotonic, may lose consciousness, and in severe cases may convulse. Such episodes demand early treatment, since a severe spell may terminate fatally. Such attacks are characteristic of, but not entirely specific for, the tetralogy of Fallot and are a strong indication for surgical intervention whenever possible.

Congestive heart failure is extremely uncommon in the tetralogy of Fallot, unless a complicating factor, such as severe anemia or bacterial endocarditis, supervenes. However, in many other cyanotic conditions, manifestations of heart failure as well as those of anoxia contribute to the patient's disability. Cyanotic conditions associated with congestive failure include transposition of the great vessels, tricuspid atresia, persistent truncus arteriosus, total anomalous pulmonary venous return, severe forms of endocardial cushion defect, and some cases of Ebstein's malformation.

Special Manifestations in Obstructive Conditions

Some infants with obstructive lesions such as aortic and pulmonic stenosis and coarctation of the aorta exhibit congestive failure, frequent lower respiratory tract infections, and growth retardation. However, these manifestations are not seen in most patients, and the lesion is discovered as an incidental finding in an apparently healthy infant or child. Older children and adolescents with moderate to severe isolated pulmonary stenosis may experience increased fatigability and may rarely complain of exertional angina, but they are generally able to lead active lives. However, such symptoms demand further investigation and consideration of surgery. Children with severe aortic stenosis may also complain of angina and dyspnea on exertion. They may also experience syncopal attacks. It must be emphasized that symptomatology of this type in aortic stenosis indicates the presence of severe obstruction and is a prompt and clear indication to further evaluation and probably corrective surgery. Congenital aortic stenosis is the congenital lesion most frequently associated with sudden death, and careful questioning of the patient and his parents is imperative in the evaluation of this lesion. Unfortunately, sudden death may occasionally occur in this disease in the absence of any previous symptoms.

In older children with coarctation of the aorta,

headaches may be a complaint. These are presumably a reflection of the high arterial pressure proximal to the aortic obstruction. Another rather infrequent complaint in coarctation is intermittent exertional claudication involving the legs.

The Asymptomatic Group

A great many congenital cardiac defects are initially detected as incidental findings in completely asymptomatic children. In most of these patients a careful physical examination plus simple ancillary studies such as routine x-rays and the electrocardiogram give considerable assistance to the physician as he attempts to identify the lesion and estimate its severity. However, many children have no abnormalities other than the presence of a cardiac murmur. In this group, the physician is forced to decide on the presence or absence of a lesion by the characteristics of the murmur itself. Here, the physician must be well aware of the characteristics of the common innocent murmurs as well as the abnormal murmurs associated with congenital defects.

The Manifestations of Acquired Heart Disease in Infants and Children

Acquired heart disease in early infancy is relatively uncommon. However, acute myocarditis does occur. In most patients it is thought to be of viral origin, particularly from viruses of Coxsackie Group B. This infection may be acquired from the mother, who may give a history of a mild grippelike illness in the immediate prepartum or postpartum state. Affected infants may develop severe congestive heart failure in a very short period of time. These babies are usually critically ill, and many succumb very quickly to the disease, despite intensive therapy. Older, previously normal infants and children may also develop primary myocarditis, with signs of left and right heart failure dominating the clinical picture.

Secondary myocarditis may occasionally occur as a complication of practically any infection—bacterial, viral, rickettsial, protozoan, fungal, or helminthic in origin. Although such involvement is usually mild and may be detected only through transient changes in the EKG, notable exceptions do occur. Diphtheria deserves special emphasis. Moreover, in other infections myocarditis may be severe and life-threatening.

Endocardial fibroelastosis, a disease of uncertain causation, may cause sudden or gradual appearance of cardiac decompensation in apparently normal infants. These infants may present with respiratory distress, particularly syndromes resembling bronchiolitis, with mild to moderate expiratory wheezing. However, cardiomegaly is often noted radiographically. Signs of congestive failure are present initially or develop over the ensuing days or weeks.

In children beyond age 5 or 6 years, rheumatic fever and rheumatic heart disease make up the overwhelming majorty of patients with acquired cardiac conditions. The manifestations of this disease are considered elsewhere (Sec. 12.1). It should be emphasized that in patients with acute rheumatic fever, myocarditis is of greatest importance in contributing to disability and evidence of cardiac failure. Valvar lesions are of relatively minor hemodynamic importance in the acute phase. However, with the passage of time and the development of the chronic phase, the functional impairment resulting from the valvar lesion assumes greater importance. In children with chronic rheumatic heart disease, mitral and aortic insufficiency are the dominant valvar lesions. However, when failure develops in these children, reactivation of acute rheumatic fever must be searched for. In the absence of congestive failure, these lesions may be associated with relatively few symptoms except for some dyspnea on exertion and easy fatigability.

Severe valvar mitral stenosis may occur in the pediatric age group, although it is rare. In this situation dyspnea on exertion, paroxysmal nocturnal dyspnea, hemoptysis, and frank bouts of pulmonary edema are frequent. Acquired aortic stenosis is extremely rare in children.

A variety of arrhythmias may appear in infants and children. These range from simple atrial and ventricular premature beats to much more serious arrhythmias such as ventricular tachycardia. In simple premature beats, symptoms are usually minimal, although the patient may occasionally complain of a peculiar sensation in the chest, usually associated with the vigorous postextrasystolic contraction. In the more sustained arrhythmias a sensation of rapid heart action, nausea, vomiting, respiratory distress, cyanosis, shock, and evidence of congestive failure may appear.

Paroxysmal supraventricular tachycardia of infancy deserves special mention. This entity is characteristically superimposed upon a normal heart, although occasionally these patients have an underlying Wolf-Parkinson-White pattern in the EKG. These infants, usually previously healthy males, rapidly develop signs of congestive failure with hepatomegaly, marked dyspnea, and peripheral and central cyanosis. Examination usually shows a heart rate of 280 to 330 per minute. These infants respond well to therapy with digitalis, but prompt recognition of this entity is mandatory.

Cardiac involvement may occur in a variety of diseases, those of particular importance being severe anemias, acute nephritis, the collagen diseases, neuromuscular dystrophies, and hyperthyroidism and hypothyroidism.

REFERENCES

Gasul, B. M., Arcilla, R. A., and Agustsson, M. H. Bedside diagnosis of congenital malformations of the heart. Med. Clin. N. Amer., 46:717, 1962.

Keith, J. D. Congestive heart failure. Pediatrics, 18:491, 1956.
—— Rowe, R. D., and Vlad, P. Heart Disease in Infancy and Childhood. New York, The Macmillan Co., 1958.
Nadas, A. S. Pediatric Cardiology. Philadelphia, W. B. Saunders Co., 1963.
Wood, P., McDonald, L., and Emanuel, R. The clinical picture correlated with physiological observations in the diagnosis of congenital heart disease. Pediat. Clin. N. Amer., 5:981, 1958.

20.3
CARDIOVASCULAR SOUNDS

ROBERT F. CASTLE

In recent years, there has been renewed interest in cardiac auscultation and phonocardiography. The latter technique affords a method for recording in a permanent, visual form the heart sounds and murmurs. Phonocardiography is also a very valuable teaching tool since it enables the physician to correlate findings on auscultation with documentary evidence presented by the phonocardiogram. However, phonocardiography is no substitute for thorough auscultation, and the physician who practices auscultation in a carefully disciplined manner should be able to predict in a great majority of cases what will be recorded on the phonocardiogram. Beyond its usefulness as a teaching device and its function as an objective and permanent record, the phonocardiogram is valuable as a diagnostic tool in its own right. In certain situations it can be helpful in assisting the physician to quantitate, at least in a rough fashion, the severity of certain lesions.

The human ear can normally perceive sounds ranging from 20 to 16,000 cycles per second. However, sensitivity is greatest in the range of 1,000 to 2,000 cycles per second. Heart sounds occupy a much lower range and consist of vibrations below the lower limit of audibility, as well as audible components from 20 to 200 cycles per second. Cardiac murmurs are of somewhat higher frequency, but rarely exceed 1,000 cycles per second. Unlike the human ear, most phonocardiographic systems are quite sensitive to lower frequencies. In fact, filtering circuits, high-frequency response microphones, and other methods of decreasing the sensitivity of the system to low-frequency vibrations must be incorporated into the phonocardiographic apparatus lest high frequencies be masked. This is accomplished with varying degrees of success in different systems. Nevertheless, consistent recording of high-pitched murmurs is often difficult.

Many different phonocardiographic systems are available. These vary considerably in their sensitivity, complexity, and expense. Regardless of the type of system employed, a variety of simultaneous reference tracings should be recorded so that one may correlate the phonocardiographic findings with the electrical and mechanical events of the cardiac cycle. Commonly used reference tracings include the electrocardiogram, respiration, carotid and jugular pulses, and the apex cardiogram. Phonocardiograms may also be recorded at the time of cardiac catheterization along with simultaneous intravascular and intracardiac pressure tracings.

Generally, phonocardiographic tracings are recorded over the following precordial areas: (1) cardiac apex (mitral area); (2) lower left sternal border (tricuspid area); (3) middle left sternal border (secondary aortic area); (4) upper left sternal border (pulmonic area); and (5) upper right sternal border (primary aortic area). The sensitivity of the apparatus is kept constant so that the intensity and configuration of the heart sounds and murmurs may be compared in the various areas. The phonocardiographic characteristics of the heart sounds and murmurs are discussed and illustrated in the subsequent sections.

Heart Sounds

Phonocardiographic studies aid in the analysis of individual heart sounds. These techniques are of particular value in timing sounds in relation to the electrical and mechanical events of the cardiac cycle. Furthermore, they also assist in documenting the intensity of the heart sounds and their components in the various recording areas.

FIRST HEART SOUND. The first heart sound is related to mechanical events surrounding the onset of ventricular contraction, closure of the atrioventricular valves, and opening of the semilunar valves with ejection of blood into the great arteries. The relative importance of left- versus right-sided phenomena has been an area of controversy, but most investigators now believe that in normal individuals right-sided events do not contribute significantly to the first heart sound. Opening of the pulmonic and aortic valves and the onset of flow into the great vessels occur shortly after mitral and tricuspid closure. In the normal heart, opening of the semilunar valves represents a minor contribution to the formation of the first sound complex.

Phonocardiography is of great value in timing the components of the first sound complex and aiding in their identification. For example, in mitral stenosis the apical first sound is delayed in relation to the QRS complex of the electrocardiogram (Fig. 2). The interval between the onset of the Q wave of the EKG and the onset of the first sound is termed the Q-1 time. In mitral stenosis this interval is prolonged and the degree of prolongation correlates roughly with the severity of the stenotic process.

Another situation in which the phonocardiogram is helpful is in the identification of early systolic ejection clicks. These sounds represent pathologic accentuation of the ejection components of the

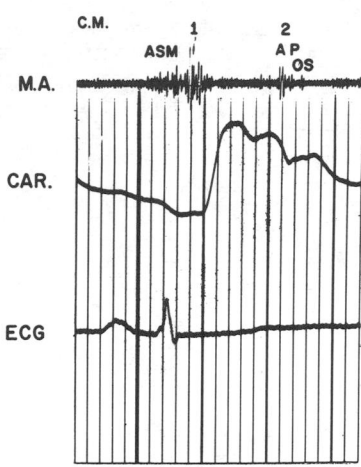

Fig. 2. Severe mitral stenosis. A presystolic or atrial systolic murmur (ASM) precedes a delayed and rather intense first heart sound at the apex or mitral area (MA). A mitral opening snap (OS) occurs in early diastole.

first sound. They occur in situations associated with fibrosis and/or stenosis of the aortic or pulmonic valve or with dilation of a great vessel distal to either a stenotic or normal valve. Ejection sounds are illustrated in Figures 3 and 4.

SECOND HEART SOUND. The second heart sound arises from the separate and successive closure of the aortic and pulmonary valves, resulting in splitting of the second sound. In normal individuals, pulmonic valve closure is a relatively low-energy sound which is heard and recorded best over the pulmonic area and radiates only moderately well down the left sternal border, but not to the cardiac apex except in very small children or those with an unusually thin chest wall. Consequently, splitting of the second sound is normally best evaluated over the upper left sternal border. Ordinarily, splitting varies from 0.02 to 0.04

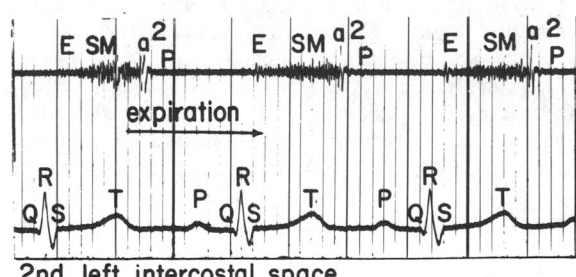

2nd left intercostal space

Fig. 3. Severe pulmonic stenosis. Note the brief ejection sound (E) which becomes more prominent on expiration. A kite-shaped systolic murmur (SM) reaches peak intensity in late systole and continues to the first (aortic) component of the second sound (a). The pulmonic component (p) is markedly delayed and of very low amplitude. The last peaking of the systolic murmur and the very wide splitting suggest severe obstruction to right ventricular outflow.

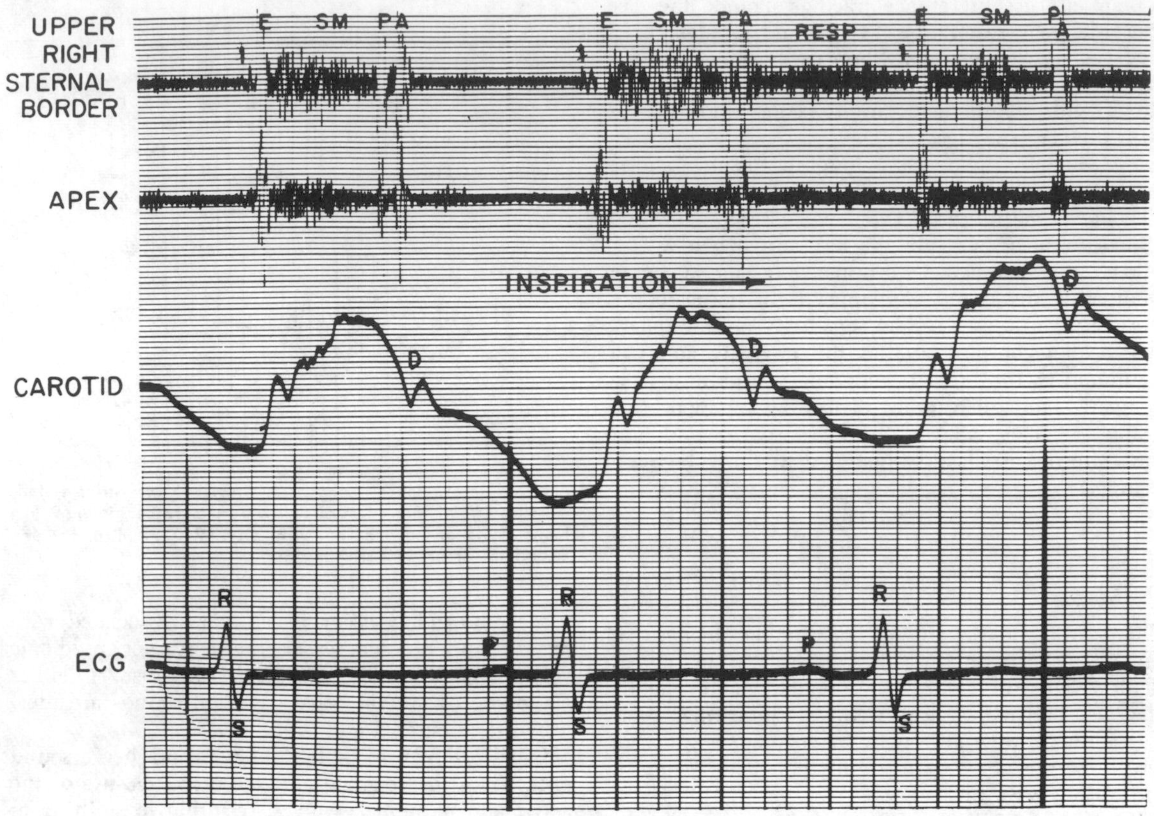

Fig. 4. Severe aortic stenosis. A prominent ejection sound or click (E) is noted. These are common in valvar aortic stenosis and they are often maximal at the apex in this condition. An intense crescendo-decrescendo systolic murmur (SM) is maximal over the upper right sternal border. This patient has paradoxical splitting of the second heart sound. The carotid dicrotic notch (D) uniformly follows aortic valve closure by 0.01 to 0.02 seconds and a simultaneous carotid pulse tracing is very useful in defining the aortic component of the second sound. Note that second sound splitting decreases during inspiration.

seconds, depending on phases of respiration. During inspiration, intrathoracic negative pressure increases and blood is aspirated into the great veins and right heart. This increased systemic venous return augments right heart stroke volume during inspiration, thus prolonging right ventricular systole and increasing the splitting of the second sound. At normal respiratory rates, the augmented volume of blood in the pulmonary circuit reaches the left ventricle during the succeeding expiration. Thus, during expiration left ventricular systole is slightly prolonged, right ventricular systole is shortened, and splitting decreases. In most normal subjects, the respiratory variation in splitting is more marked in standing and sitting positions. This may reflect greater respiratory variation in venous return to the heart in the upright position.

The phonocardiogram may be helpful in documenting departures from the normal pattern of second sound splitting. The sequence of ventricular contraction may be altered in complete right and left bundle branch block. In right bundle branch block,

right-sided events are delayed and splitting of the second sound increases, although the normal sequence of valve closure is retained. In left bundle branch block, left-sided events are delayed so that the aortic component of the second sound may follow the pulmonic. In this situation, inspiration results in a decrease in second sound splitting or so-called paradoxical splitting.

The pattern of second sound splitting is altered in a variety of congenital and acquired lesions. In atrial septal defects, right ventricular stroke volume is large and remains relatively constant at all phases of respiration. This typically results in wide and fixed splitting of the second sound (Fig. 5). However, this appears to be an acquired age-dependent phenomenon and many children do not exhibit wide, fixed splitting of the second sound until after they are 5 to 6 years of age. Nevertheless, when present, this finding may be very helpful in pointing to the existence of an atrial defect. In isolated pulmonary stenosis, the obstruction to ventricular outflow results in prolongation of right ventricular systole and

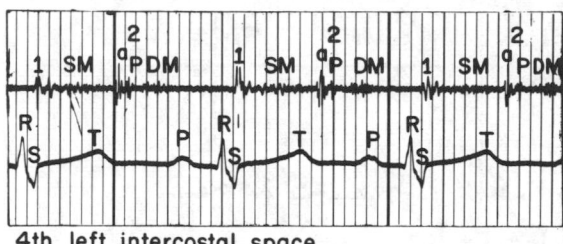

4th left intercostal space

Fig. 5. Atrial septal defect. A low frequency, low amplitude, systolic ejection murmur (SM) is recorded. The second sound is split constantly at 0.05 second. A low frequency protodiastolic murmur (DM) is present. This is a flow murmur and reflects the high volume of blood traversing the tricuspid valve in early diastole.

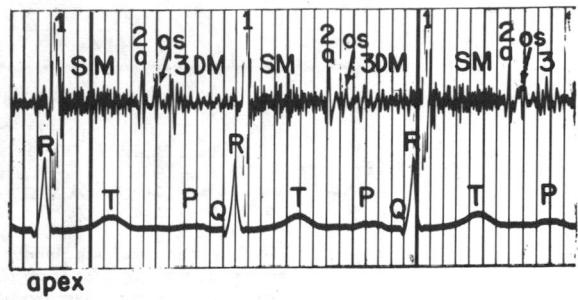

apex

Fig. 7. Mitral regurgitation (with mild mitral stenosis). An intense first sound is recorded which introduces a holosystolic murmur (SM) of slightly variable configuration. An opening snap (OS) is recorded. A third sound (3) is present, as is a low frequency diastolic rumble (DM). The third sound results from rapid ventricular filling in early diastole and is not recorded in dominant mitral stenosis. The diastolic murmur in this case results from a large flow across a slightly stenotic mitral valve.

wide splitting (Fig. 3). Here the extent of prolongation of the interval between aortic and pulmonic valve closure correlates with the degree of valvar narrowing, and the phonocardiogram can be valuable in the assessment of the severity of the stenotic process. In the presence of a ventricular septal defect or mitral regurgitation, splitting is often accentuated, probably due to earlier closure of the aortic valve (Fig. 6). Conversely, in aortic stenosis, left ventricular systole may be prolonged. Occasionally in this condition the order of valve closure may be reversed (paradoxical splitting). This is rare in children but when present indicates very severe obstruction (Fig. 4).

In patients with pulmonary hypertension, the pulmonic component of the second heart sound increases in intensity. The splitting intervals tend to narrow in patients with interventricular septal defects or patent ductus arteriosus who develop pulmonary hypertension. Wide splitting tends to persist in patients with atrial septal defects and pulmonary hypertension.

THIRD AND FOURTH HEART SOUNDS. A brief low-pitched third heart sound is heard and recorded in many normal children. It is associated with rapid inflow of blood into the left and possibly right ventricles in early diastole and occurs 0.12 to 0.18 seconds after the second sound. The third sound may be accentuated in situations associated with increased velocity and volume of blood flow into the left ventricle (Fig. 7). This occurs in ventricular septal defects and patent ductus arteriosus. It also occurs in rheumatic heart disease, particularly with mitral and aortic insufficiency. High output states such as anemias and thyrotoxicosis may also be associated with prominent third sounds.

Fourth sounds are related to atrial contraction and they may be noted in normal children although they are less frequent than third sounds. They tend to appear or become accentuated in the presence of systolic hypertension within the respective ventricle. Therefore, fourth sounds may be noted in patients with severe pulmonary and aortic stenosis, coarctation of the aorta, and pulmonary and systemic hypertension. Documented existence of a fourth sound in a patient with aortic stenosis should alert the physician to the presence of a severe obstruction.

Heart Murmurs

The phonocardiogram assists in the analysis of murmurs in respect to their intensity, frequency, duration, and timing. Moreover, diagnostically significant data may be contained in the configuration of murmurs and the interrelationships of murmurs with the heart sounds and simultaneous reference tracings.

SYSTOLIC (VENTRICULAR) EJECTION MURMURS. Systolic (ventricular) ejection murmurs arise from the normal, antegrade ejection of blood into a great vessel. Such murmurs may be recorded regularly within the main pulmonary artery in normal individuals by means of intracardiac phonocardiography. The same normal murmurs are often audible externally over the upper left sternal border; this is especially common during adolescence. Innocent pulmonic ejection murmurs make up one of the larger groups of so-called functional murmurs. They are early to mid-

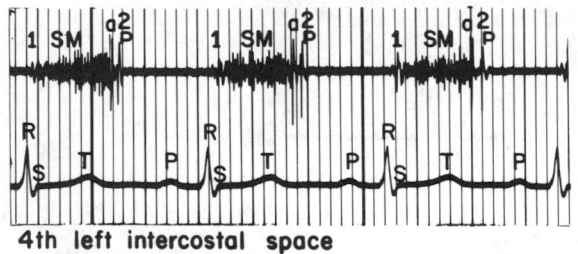

4th left intercostal space

Fig. 6. Ventricular septal defect. An intense holosystolic murmur is recorded. The murmur continues to the first or aortic component of the second sound (a²). Both components of the second sound are well shown.

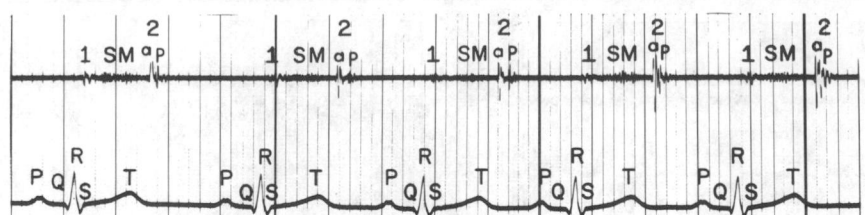

Fig. 8. Innocent pulmonic ejection murmur. Innocent pulmonic ejection murmur recorded over the upper left sternal border. This systolic murmur (SM) is of low amplitude and is crescendo-decrescendo in configuration. It arises in association with the rapid ejection of blood into the pulmonary artery (see text). Note also the normal respiratory variation in splitting of the second heart sound.

systolic in timing, blowing in quality, and of relatively low frequency. Typically, they have a low amplitude, crescendo-decrescendo configuration on the phonocardiogram (Fig. 8). Pulmonary ejection murmurs become more prominent in situations where there is an increase in volume or velocity of blood flow into the pulmonary artery and/or where there is decreased blood viscosity. Thus, they may be accentuated by exercise or other high-output states (e.g., thyrotoxicosis) and also by anemia.

In the presence of a left-to-right shunt at the atrial level (e.g., atrial septal defects and anomalies of pulmonary venous return), there is increased flow through the right ventricular outflow tract and pulmonary valve and accentuation of the physiologic ejection murmur (Fig. 5). Differentiating such patients from individuals with normal pulmonic ejection murmurs is not always easy. Careful anlaysis of the second heart sound is very helpful in this situation, since wide, constant splitting of the second sound favors the presence of an atrial defect in older children and adults, whereas normal variable splitting in this age group accompanies the innocent ejection murmur. Immediate disappearance of a pulmonary ejection murmur with the Valsalva maneuver strongly favors the presence of an innocent murmur. Here, however, a lack of cooperation may limit the usefulness of this test in smaller patients.

The left-sided counterpart of the pulmonary ejection murmur is another important innocent murmur of childhood. This murmur is frequently termed the vibratory murmur (also known as the "twanging string" murmur or Still's murmur). This murmur is also early to midsystolic in timing, and it has a characteristic low-pitched, musical, groaning quality. It produces on the phonocardiogram a series of evenly spaced, "picket fence" deflections which reflect its musical nature (Fig. 9). This murmur is typically maximal along the lower left sternal border, although it is often most intense in a somewhat more lateral location. Intracardiac phonocardiographic studies have established the origin of this murmur in the outflow region of the left ventricle. It is common in young children and is often first heard at the time of a preschool examination.

Systolic ejection murmurs may be pathologically accentuated in the presence of organic obstruction of either ventricle (see Figs. 3 and 4). Organic ejection murmurs, particularly when resulting from valvar stenosis, are frequently introduced by an ejection click (see above). These murmurs are noisy, usually intense, and of diamond-shaped configuration on the phonocardiogram. However, the latter description is often only an approximation. For example, in severe pulmonic stenosis, the crescendo portion of the murmur may be much longer than the decrescendo portion, tending to produce a kite-shaped murmur. In general, the murmur of pulmonary stenosis tends to be higher-pitched, longer, and reaches peak intensity later in systole in the more severe degrees of obstruction. Such a predictable pattern is not seen in aortic stenosis. Here, the length and peaking time of the murmur do not bear a well-defined relationship to the severity of obstruction.

DIASTOLIC (ATRIAL) EJECTION MURMURS. Diastolic ejection murmurs may also occur. An example is the

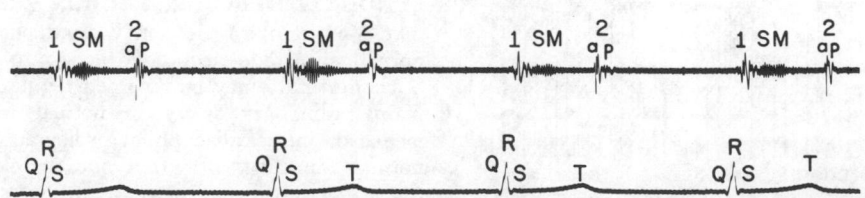

Fig. 9. Vibratory murmur. Vibratory or Still's murmur recorded over the lower left sternal border. The evenly spaced "picket fence" deflections comprising the early to midsystolic murmur (SM) are characteristic and reflect the low frequency, musical quality of this murmur.

presystolic murmur of mitral stenosis, which arises during the antegrade ejection of blood from the left atrium through the stenotic mitral valve into the left ventricle. In the presence of first-degree heart block, when there is a delay between atrial and ventricular contraction, this murmur can clearly be shown to possess a crescendo-decrescendo configuration on the phonocardiogram similar to that seen in systolic (ventricular) ejection murmurs. However, this observation is not usually made in mitral stenosis, since with normal P-R intervals the first sound cuts off the presystolic murmur near its midpoint, tending to give one the impression of only a crescendo, presystolic murmur (Fig. 2).

SYSTOLIC REGURGITANT MURMURS. Systolic regurgitant murmurs arise from the retrograde passage of blood. The murmur of mitral regurgitation is a classic example (see Fig. 7). Likewise, the murmur of interventricular septal defect represents a special case in which a similar murmur arises from the passage of blood from the high pressure left ventricle to the relatively lower pressure right ventricle (see Fig. 6). Regurgitant murmurs are classically holosystolic (i.e., beginning with the first heart sound and ending with the second sound), but they may be plateau-shaped, decrescendo, crescendo-decrescendo, or crescendo.

Although regurgitant murmurs are typically holosystolic, this is not always the case. Certain patients with mitral regurgitation appear to have only mid- or late-systolic murmurs, sometimes introduced by single or multiple high-pitched systolic clicks. This type of mitral regurgitation is nonrheumatic, but may develop secondary to congenital or acquired abnormalities of the papillary muscles and/or the chordae tendineae.

There is a group of patients with small ventricular septal defects in whom the murmur is high-pitched and present only in early to midsystole. Here, late-systolic disappearance of the murmur may be related to functional closure of the defect during the latter portion of systole. In occasional patients, a series of phonocardiograms during infancy and early childhood may give documentary evidence for functional closure of an interventricular septal defect. In this situation a holosystolic murmur may be noted in infancy. Later, late-systolic attenuation of the murmur may appear. Finally, if functional closure of the defect becomes complete, no murmur will be recordable. Similar late-systolic attenuation or even total disappearance of the systolic murmur may occur in the patient with a large interventricular septal defect who develops progressive pulmonary vascular obstruction. However, a consideration of the total clinical picture should allow easy differentiation of these two groups of patients.

DIASTOLIC REGURGITANT MURMURS. Diastolic regurgitant murmurs originate at either the aortic or pulmonic valves. Aortic insufficiency most commonly is a manifestation of rheumatic heart disease, but it may have a variety of other causes, both congenital

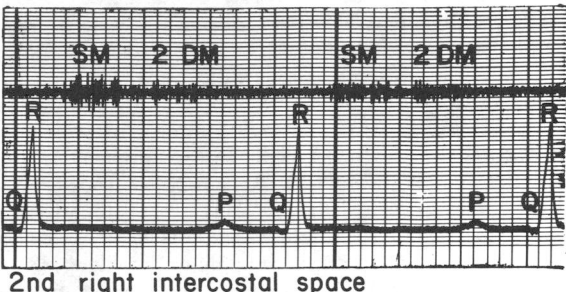

2nd right intercostal space

Fig. 10. Aortic regurgitation (with mild aortic stenosis). A crescendo-decrescendo systolic murmur (SM) is noted. The murmur reaches maximal intensity in midsystole and ends before the second sound (2). A decrescendo diastolic murmur (DM) begins with the second heart sound and continues through diastole. The systolic murmur is an aortic ejection murmur, reflecting increased left ventricular stroke volume. Such murmurs are commonly seen in dominant aortic regurgitation and do not necessarily reflect the presence of organic narrowing at the aortic valve.

and acquired. Characteristically, the murmur of aortic regurgitation is of high frequency and decrescendo in configuration (Fig. 10). It is often holodiastolic, recorded maximally over the third left intercostal space, and well transmitted down the left sternal border. It is less intense in the primary aortic area. Nonrheumatic types of aortic regurgitation may have an atypical pattern of transmission, often along the right sternal border. The high-frequency diastolic murmur of mild to moderate degrees of aortic insufficiency is difficult to record with many of the commonly employed phonocardiographic machines. Careful auscultation may establish the presence of this murmur when it cannot be documented phonocardiographically.

The murmur of pulmonary regurgitation is not uncommon in children. Causes for this murmur include complete congenital absence of the pulmonary valve or lesser degrees of congenital valvar insufficiency. This may occur as an isolated condition, but it is usually associated with other defects. Acquired pulmonary regurgitation may result from dilation of the pulmonary valve ring in patients with pulmonary hypertension, or it may follow pulmonary valve surgery. In contrast to aortic regurgitation, the murmur of pulmonary insufficiency has less tendency to be decrescendo in configuration, and it tends to be lower-pitched and shorter in duration except when associated with severe pulmonary hypertension. Murmurs of pulmonary regurgitation are characteristically maximal over the upper and middle left sternal border.

FLOW MURMURS. This term has become popular recently and generally refers to diastolic murmurs arising at the mitral or tricuspid valve from increased volumes of blood flowing across a normal or, at most, only mildly stenotic valve. The resultant murmurs are of low frequency and in most circumstances are confined to the early or rapid filling phase of diastole.

Mitral flow murmurs may be observed in patients with congenital heart disease associated with large left-to-right shunts at the ventricular (or great vessel) level. Serial phonocardiograms in patients with ventricular septal defects may show disappearance of the apical diastolic murmur. This indicates a decrease in the left-to-right shunt and may result from several causes: (1) It can occur because of partial or complete functional closure of the defect. (2) Infundibular pulmonic stenosis may progress with a resultant decrease in pulmonary blood flow. (3) Rarely, and most ominously, pulmonary hypertension may progress, and blood flow through the lung decreases owing to elevation of the pulmonary vascular resistance.

Short apical diastolic rumbles may also be noted in patients with rheumatic heart disease who have dominant mitral regurgitation with or without minimal mitral valve narrowing (Fig. 7). A similar murmur, the so-called Carey-Coombs murmur, occurs in acute rheumatic carditis. Here, dilation of the left ventricle probably adds to the relative mitral stenosis. During convalescence this murmur tends to shorten and often disappears.

Tricuspid flow murmurs also occur (Fig. 5). These may often be recorded in patients with large atrial septal defects or partial or total anomalous pulmonary venous drainage. Rarely, such murmurs may occur on the basis of intrinsic tricuspid valve involvement in rheumatic heart disease.

CONTINUOUS MURMURS. A continuous murmur classically arises at the site of a communication between a high- and a low-pressure vessel or chamber. In this situation, a pressure gradient is present throughout the cardiac cycle and there is a resultant continuous, crescendo-systolic, decrescendo-diastolic murmur. Patent ductus arteriosus is the best known example, and it is typically associated with a so-called machinery or Gibson murmur (Fig. 11). Many other types of arteriovenous fistulas can result in murmurs of similar configuration. In some patients, the diastolic components of these murmurs may be of high frequency and difficult to record.

In patients with a large patent ductus, the murmur may be purely systolic in timing due to the presence of pulmonary arterial hypertension. In some patients, the typical continuous murmur may not develop until the child is several years of age. In others, a previously continuous murmur may shorten or even disappear as pulmonary hypertension progresses.

Continuous murmurs should be distinguished from to-and-fro murmurs. In the latter group, the systolic and diastolic components have a separate origin. An example is an interventricular septal defect associated with aortic insufficiency. Here, the hemodynamic lesions responsible for the systolic and diastolic components of the murmur are different, and both murmurs have their own separate characteristics.

REFERENCES

Castle, R. F. Variables affecting the splitting of the second heart sound in atrial septal defect. Amer. Heart J., 73:468, 1967.
———— . and Craige, E. Auscultation of the heart in infants and children. Pediatrics, 26:511, 1960.
Gamboa, R., Hugenholtz, P. G., and Nadas, A. S. Accuracy of the phonocardiogram in assessing severity of aortic and pulmonic stenosis. Circulation, 30:35, 1964.
Luisada, A. A., and Shah, P. M. Controversial and changing aspects of auscultation. I. Areas of auscultation. II. Normal and abnormal first and second sounds. Amer. J. Cardiol., 11:774, 1963.
———— and Shah, P. M. Controversial and changing aspects of auscultation. III. Diastolic sounds. IV. Intervals. V. Systolic sounds. Amer. J. Cardiol., 13:243, 1964.
McKusick, V. A. Cardiovascular Sound in Health and Disease. Baltimore, The Williams and Wilkins Co., 1958.
Nadas, A. S., and Ellison, R. C. Phonocardiographic analysis of diastolic flow murmurs in secundum atrial septal defect and ventricular septal defect. Brit. Heart J., 29:684, 1967.
Sutton, G., Harris, A., and Leatham, A. Second heart sound in pulmonary hypertension. Brit. Heart J., 30:743, 1968.
Tavel, M. Clinical Phonocardiography and External Pulse Recording. Chicago, Year Book Medical Publishers, Inc., 1967.
Wennevold, A. The origin of the innocent "vibratory" murmur studied with intracardiac phonocardiography. Acta Med. Scand., 181:1, 1967.

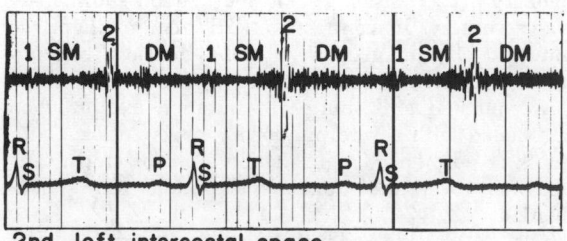

2nd left intercostal space

Fig. 11. Patent ductus arteriosus. A continuous murmur is recorded which is of maximal intensity at the time of the second sound. This represents a machinery or Gibson murmur. It is typically found in patent ductus arteriosus, but may arise at any arteriovenous fistula.

20.4

RADIOGRAPHY AND FLUOROSCOPY

ROBERT F. CASTLE

The teleroentgenogram gives accurate information about the size and contour of the heart and the vascularity of the lung fields. Being a permanent record, it is valuable for comparison with previous and subsequent films of the patient. Fluoroscopy is of added value in allowing additional observation of the dynamics of the various chambers of the heart, the aorta, and the pulmonary vessels. The cardiac silhouette should be studied not only in the frontal view but also in both oblique views. Barium swallow is used for delineation of heart or vascular structures impinging on the esophagus, the position of the aortic arch, anomalous position of other vessels as in a "vascular ring," and the size of the left atrium.

Accurate measurement of heart size can be made from a teleroentgenogram, a film taken with the x-ray tube 6 feet from the patient in the erect position. At this distance error in width of the heart shadow due to divergence of the rays is negligible. Distortion in roentgenograms taken at shorter distance may erroneously suggest enlargement. The most valuable cardiac measurement is the total transverse diameter of the heart as compared with the maximal transverse diameter of the chest. The ratio of heart width to that of the internal diameter of the chest, measured at the upper level of the right diaphragm—the cardiothoracic index—is 0.40 to 0.50 except in newborn infants, in whom it can normally be as high as 0.55. In a child whose diaphragm is elevated for any reason, the heart can be so horizontally placed that the index may be higher than normal without signifying true cardiac enlargement. The estimation of heart size is subject to certain limitations. The outline of the heart varies in different phases of the cardiac cycle; even more striking is the change in the breadth and contour of the heart with different phases of respiration, the transverse diameter of the heart shadow being decreased during inspiration. For purposes of comparison the films must be accurately centered and the exposure made in moderate inspiration. Satisfactory films may be difficult to obtain in young infants, and fluoroscopy may be more helpful. However, because of the increased risk of excessive irradiation inherent in fluoroscopy, this procedure is limited to those situations where satisfactory information cannot be obtained in conventional roentgenograms.

The contour of the cardiovascular shadows gives valuable information. Certain differences between the adult contour and that of infants and children should be noted. In evaluating the structures at the base of the heart, it must be remembered that normally in early infancy a broad thymic shadow in this area is frequently present. Also the relatively high diaphragm in infants causes transverse position of the heart with widening of the shadow of the great vessels. Relative prominence of the pulmonary artery in the cardiac silhouette of the children is frequently present; it does not necessarily imply the presence of heart disease, since it may result from clockwise rotation of the heart.

The three standard positions for cardiac roentgenography are (1) posteroanterior; the patient stands facing the cassette or fluoroscopic screen with his chest pressed firmly against it; (2) left anterior-

oblique, attained by rotating the patient approximately 45 degrees so that his left shoulder is toward the cassette or screen; (3) right anterior-oblique, obtained by rotating the patient 45 degrees so that his right shoulder is pressed against the cassette or screen.

In the posteroanterior view *the right heart border is formed by the right atrium. The superior vena cava is seen extending upwards as a longitudinal band. Dilatation of the ascending portion of the aorta may cause a convexity to the right of the upper sternum. When the left atrium is enlarged its shadow may extend beyond the right heart border above that of the right atrium.*

The aortic knob is the upper shadow of the left border. This is relatively small in children. The aortic shadow may be prominent and hyperdynamic when viewed by fluoroscopy in the presence of a patent ductus arteriosus or of aortic insufficiency. Normally the second convexity on the left is that of the main stem of the pulmonary artery. This area is enlarged with advanced mitral disease and also with certain congenital anomalies. There may be a poststenotic dilation with little pulsation in the presence of pulmonic valvar stenosis. Enlargement with increased pulsations is associated with those conditions which cause shunting of blood into the right heart or pulmonary artery. Concavity at the level of the pulmonary segment is seen in pulmonary stenosis of the infundibular type. The lower two-thirds of the left border is caused by the ventricular shadow. Enlargement of either ventricle may be the cause for increasing prominence of this area. In pronounced right ventricular hypertrophy the apex is raised above the diaphragm, whereas it is displaced outward and downward by left ventricular dilatation.

In the left anterior-oblique view (Fig. 12A) *the region of the right ventricle lies anteriorly and that of the left ventricle posteriorly, making this radiographic position of particular value in analyzing specific ventricular enlargement. When the right atrium is enlarged the shadow of its appendage is seen as a shelflike prominence in the upper third of the anterior contour. The ascending portion of the aortic arch is the uppermost anterior shadow. The lowest posterior shadow is that of the inflow tract of the left ventricle. Normally with inspiration the ventricle should clear the vertebral bodies by 55 degrees of rotation from the frontal plane. Enlargement of this area is seen with mitral insufficiency or with increased volume of pulmonary blood flow returning to the left ventricle in certain congenital anomalies. The left atrium constitutes the upper portion of the posterior shadow. Notable enlargement of this chamber causes elevation and compression of the left main bronchus. In congenital anomalies with pulmonary artery hypoplasia or markedly diminished blood flow through this vessel there is an abnormal translucency in the region of the "pulmonary window," which lies just below the arch of the aorta at the level of the bifurcation of the trachea.*

In the right anterior-oblique view (Fig. 12B) *the*

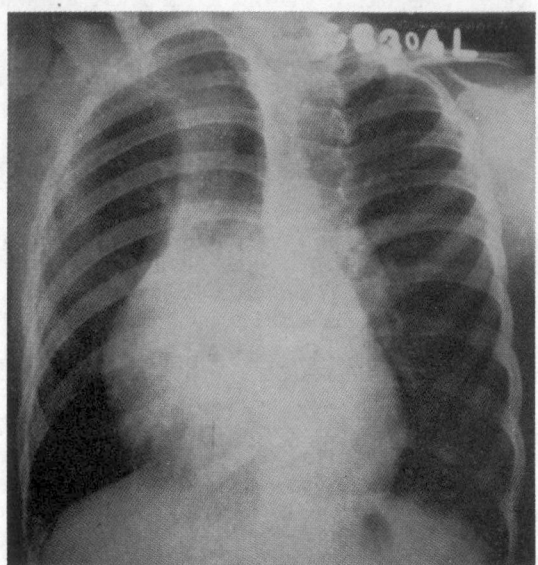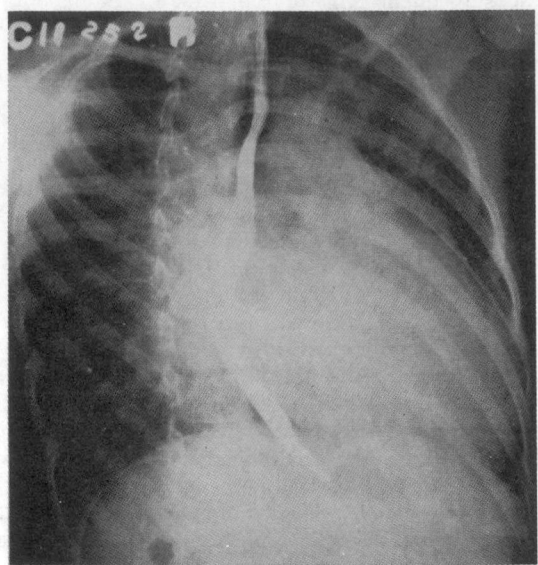

Fig. 12. A. (Left) Posterior enlargement of the left ventricle. Left anterior oblique view shows the lower dorsal cardiac shadow overlapping the vertebral column in a case of mitral insufficiency. B. (Right) Roentgenogram taken in right anterior oblique position showing posterior displacement and compression of esophagus due to enlargement of the left auricle caused by severe rheumatic heart disease.

upper anterior shadow is that of the main stem of the pulmonary artery and the conus of the right ventricle. In some cases this may be the optimal position for evaluation of these areas. The ventricular chambers form the lower portion of the anterior curve. The right atrium when enlarged protrudes posteriorly above the diaphragm but does not impinge on the esophagus. Evaluation of the size of the left atrium is dependent on study with barium swallow. Enlargement of this chamber causes posterior compression with or without displacement of the middle third of the thoracic esophagus, which can be observed in this oblique or in the left lateral view.

Evaluation of the vascularity of the lung fields is an important part of every roentgenographic study. In those congenital abnormalities in which pulmonary flow is decreased the lung fields appear abnormally clear, especially in the peripheral areas. Increased pulmonary flow due to an arteriovenous shunt causes enlargement of the pulmonary artery and its branches, giving a congested appearance to the lung fields. Increased amplitude of pulsations in the hilar vessels ("hilar dance") seen in fluoroscopy is usually most prominent in cases of atrial septal defect. When pulmonary hypertensive changes occur, as for example in some cases of ventricular septal defect, the vascular markings in the periphery of the lung fields may become less prominent although hilar vessels remain large.

REFERENCES

Caffey, J. Pediatric X-Ray Diagnosis, 4th ed. Chicago, Year Book Publishers, 1961.

McIntosh, C. B., and Jackson, R. L. Angles of clearance. Amer. J. Dis. Child., 71:357, 1946.
Roesler, H. Clinical Roentgenology of the Cardiovascular System, 2nd ed. Springfield, Ill., Charles C Thomas, 1947.
Schwedel, J. B. Clinical Roentgenology of the Heart. New York, Harper & Row, 1946.

20.5
THE ELECTROCARDIOGRAM AND VECTORCARDIOGRAM

MADISON S. SPACH

Pediatric electrocardiography has assumed increasing importance during the past decade. Its use, initially limited to the cardiologist, is now widespread among all physicians caring for children. The main requirement for becoming proficient in the interpretation of electrophysiologic tracings is repeated exposure to and use of electrocardiography. Burch and Winsor have presented an excellent primer of electrocardiography, and Grant admirably discusses the vector approach to the scalar electrocardiogram.

Since the conventional electrocardiogram (EKG) and vectorcardiogram (VKG) both record events of electrical activation of cardiac muscle, the term *electrocardiography* is used to include both techniques, which use different formats for data presentation. To interpret such tracings properly, it is helpful to re-

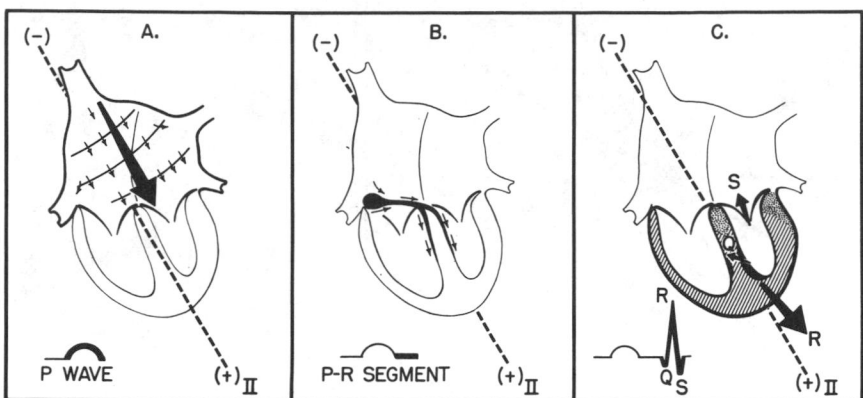

Fig. 13. Relationship of normal pattern of electrical activation of heart to lead II electrocardiogram. A. Atrial depolarization is initiated in the SA node. The electrical wave front spreads over the atria downward and to the left. The resultant vector of this electrical activity inscribes an upright P wave in lead II. B. There is very slow transmission of the electrical impulse through the AV node with subsequent rapid transmission through the bundle of His and bundle branches to the ventricles. The electrical forces generated in the conduction system are too small to be recorded in the peripheral electrocardiogram (P-R segment). C. Ventricular activation begins with depolarization of both septal surfaces, starting slightly earlier on the left side and involving a larger septal surface than on the right, thus generating an electrical force oriented to the right and superiorly (Q wave in lead II). The ventricular free walls then are depolarized in an endocardial-to-epicardial direction, with a resultant vector oriented slightly to the left and downward (R wave). Finally, the last areas of ventricular activation are located in the upper ventricular septum and basal left ventricular free wall with a resultant electrical vector oriented superiorly (S wave).

view the normal pattern of electrical activation of the heart (Fig. 13) (Scher and Young, Spach et al). Depolarization is initiated in the SA node, and the wave front spreads down and leftward over the auricles. This generates a small potential on the body surface (P wave), which can be represented by a vector (i.e., an electrical force with direction) pointing inferiorly and to the left (Fig. 13A).

The biochemical and electrical characteristics of the AV node, easily influenced by metabolic abnormalities, impart a very slow speed to the transmission of the electrical impulse (P-R interval, Fig. 13B); thereafter, the impulse is transmitted rapidly to the ventricles via the bundle of His and bundle branches. The activation of ventricular muscle (QRS) begins with depolarization of both sides of the ventricular septum; however, a wide area on the left begins slightly earlier than a small area on the right side (Q wave). The wave fronts then invade both ventricular free walls in an endocardial-to-epicardial direction (R wave). Finally, the last areas to be depolarized are the high ventricular septum and basal left ventricular free wall (S wave). The anatomic position of the ventricles and the sequence of activation greatly influence the orientation of the electrical tracing recorded on the body surface. Figure 13C shows the early (Q), middle (R), and late (S) vector positions for these three periods of normal ventricular activation. After the rapid process of ventricular depolarization, there follows the slower process of repolarization (T wave), which requires metabolic work to restore the cellular resting potential (Page).

Abnormal metabolic states most readily influ-

ence the sensitive AV node and the process of repolarization (T wave). Ventricular hypertrophy primarily affects the pattern of ventricular depolarization (QRS). Also, if a ventricle is severely "overloaded," there may be an abnormal pattern of repolarization (T wave changes).

Electrocardiographic Methods

ELECTROCARDIOGRAM. The conventional scalar lead tracing presents a graph of voltage (1 millivolt = 10 mm deflection) against time. A paper speed of 25 mm per second usually is employed; however, recording of 50 mm per second permits more detailed analysis. For each lead, an upright deflection indicates that electrical activity is approaching the positive terminal, and a negative deflection indicates receding activity. One needs to memorize the position of the axis of each lead and its positive terminal (Fig. 14). For all V leads, the positive terminal is the exploring electrode at its designated position, and the negative terminal may be considered to be the theoretical electrical center of the heart.

VECTORCARDIOGRAM. The newer vectorcardiogram probably will never replace the scalar electrocardiogram. Since it is a plot of voltage against voltage, it does not permit estimation of time unless the oscilloscopic beam is moving. Additionally, since the P and T loops are quite small on the vectorcardiogram, they must be amplified for detailed analysis and easier interpretation in the scalar tracing. For rate and interval determination, the scalar tracing is essential

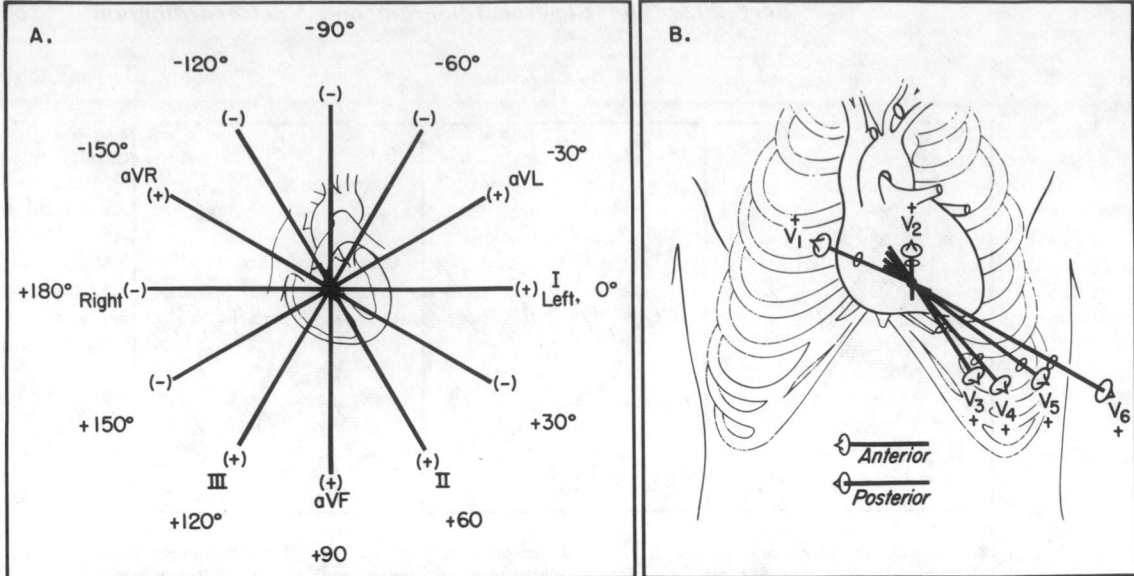

Fig. 14. Orientation of lead axes used for recording the scalar electrocardiogram. *A.* Limb leads. The six limb leads view the electrical activity of the heart in the frontal plane (see Fig. 15). Note that the positive terminal of AVR, AVL, and AVF is located at the right arm, left arm, and foot respectively. *B.* Commonly used precordial leads. The positive terminal is located at the designated position (designated by circle) of each of the V leads. Note that the axis of lead V₂ is positioned in an almost direct anterior-posterior orientation.

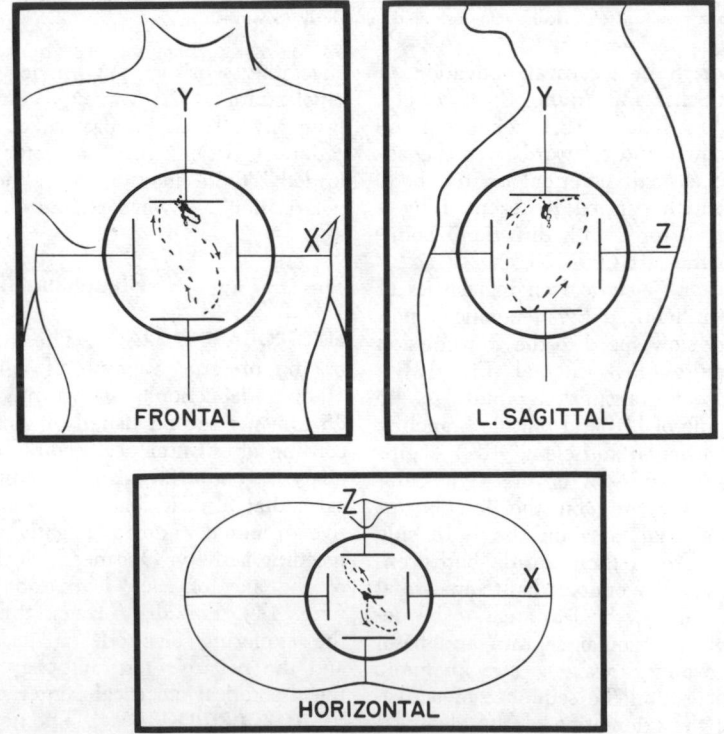

Fig. 15. Three planes used in vectorcardiographic presentation of QRS loop with connections to oscilloscopic plates from representative body areas. Many lead systems are available for applying electrode connections to the patient. All of these systems utilize preamplifiers to enlarge the electrical signal and apply the resultant voltage to the horizontal and vertical plates of an oscilloscope. Thus, the electrical activity can be recorded in three mutually perpendicular axes. The frontal plane utilizes the X (right-left) and Y (inferior-superior) axes. The sagittal plane utilizes the Y and Z (anterior-posterior) axes. The horizontal plane uses the X and Z axes. By recording the electrical activity in the three planes shown, the QRS "loop" can be viewed three dimensionally. The QRS loop shown is that of a normal 12-year-old boy (tetrahedron reference lead system).

in the diagnosis of arrhythmias and ventricular conduction disturbances (e.g., bundle branch block). However, the vectorcardiogram allows a more precise analysis of the details of the QRS complex (loop). Thus, the two techniques are complementary, each having advantages and disadvantages.

There are approximately 32 different lead systems available for recording the vectorcardiogram. Presently, it appears that the Frank lead system may evolve as the standard one for children. The leads are connected to the patient so that cardiac electrical activity can be recorded in three mutually perpendicular axes (X, right-left; Y, inferior-superior; and Z, anterior-posterior). Figure 15 illustrates a normal QRS loop of a 12-year-old child as viewed in three planes with the connections to the oscilloscopic plates from representative body areas. By connecting two mutually perpendicular leads to the vertical and horizontal oscilloscopic plates, a QRS "loop" is inscribed, which can be visualized three-dimensionally.

DIGITAL COMPUTER ELECTROCARDIOGRAPHY. At present, reports of the use of tape recording of the electrocardiogram with analysis by computers has been limited to adults (Pipberger et al., Caceres et al.); however, studies are under way in in children. This method probably will be refined for practical use and offers advantages over present techniques for screening purposes and quantitative analysis.

Electrocardiographic Approach

Electrocardiography plays an essential role in the diagnosis of (1) cardiac arrhythmias, (2) ventricular conduction disturbances, (3) ventricular and atrial hypertrophy, (4) myocardial changes associated with myocarditis and electrolyte disturbances, (5) myocardial infarction, and (6) specific cardiac abnormalities (e.g., atrioventricular canal defects). The maximum amount of clinical information should be available for optimal interpretation of the electrocardiogram. Knowledge of the patient's age, clinical history, drug administration, physical findings, and radiologic features is especially valuable. The diagnosis of an electrocardiographic abnormality (e.g., premature ventricular beats) may occur in a normal child. Also, a normal electrocardiogram may be obtained in the presence of marked cardiac abnormality (e.g., acute rheumatic myocarditis).

The routine measurements include auricular and ventricular rate and rhythm, P-R interval, and QRS interval. The tracing then is inspected sequentially for abnormalities of P, QRS, and T waves. In general, ventricular hypertrophy is visualized best in the precordial leads and in the vectorcardiogram.

Normal Electrocardiogram and Vectorcardiogram

It is most difficult to memorize the normal values for all the scalar leads; therefore, it is helpful to have references such as Ziegler's available for review. The normal P wave has a maximum height of 2.5 mm in any limb lead. The average P-R interval of 0.10 second during the first month gradually increases to 0.16 second at 12 years of age. Ziegler has published

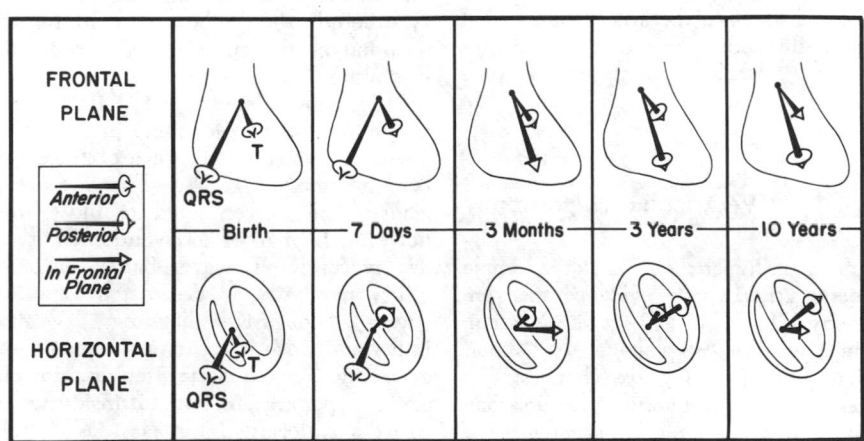

Fig. 16. Average axis of QRS and T wave in normal children from birth through childhood. The QRS axis at birth usually is oriented to the right and anteriorly. Within three months, this axis shifts leftward and is oriented at approximately 60 degrees in the frontal plane (see Fig. 10). Usually it remains in this position in the frontal plane throughout childhood as there is a gradual further shift posteriorly. The schematic representation of the QRS vector emphasizes the average position for normal children; some normal children may retain slight right axis deviation or develop left axis deviation after 10 years of age. At birth, the T wave is oriented anteriorly and quickly shifts posteriorly within 24 hours. Thereafter, there is a gradual shift of the T wave vector in a posterior-anterior direction so that usually at the age of 10 years, the T wave is oriented in the frontal plane. The shift of the T wave throughout childhood progresses at different rates in normal children. Some children retain posterior orientation of the T wave vector throughout childhood. In the frontal plane, the T wave is oriented at approximately 60 degrees throughout childhood.

tables showing variations in the P-R interval with heart rate. A few normal children have permanently prolonged P-R intervals. The average QRS duration of 0.06 (maximum 0.08) second in the infant gradually increases to 0.08 (maximum 0.10) second in the normal adolescent.

Changes with age of the QRS complex for the limb and precordial leads can be visualized best from a vector approach (Fig. 16). At birth, right axis deviation and anterior orientation of the QRS are associated with the prominent right ventricle. The average QRS shifts leftward and is oriented in a position of 60 degrees in the frontal plane from approximately three months of age throughout childhood. The anterior orientation of QRS gradually shifts posteriorly through childhood, with the greatest change occurring during the first three years. Voltage criteria for normality in the precordial leads are quite variable. Ziegler found that the average R wave deflection of 15 mm (maximum 30 mm) in lead V_1 in the newborn gradually diminishes to 5 mm (maximum 15 mm) in the teen-ager; also, the average 6 mm (maximum 21 mm) R wave in lead V_6 in the newborn increases to an average of 15 mm in older children. Rarely, normal adolescents may have an R wave deflection of up to 30 mm in lead V_6.

The T wave vector is positioned slightly to the left at approximately 60 degrees in the frontal plane (Fig. 16). It is oriented anteriorly at birth, giving rise to an upright T wave in lead V_1. Within 24 hours, the T wave usually shifts posteriorly and is associated with a negative T wave deflection in lead V_1. Thereafter, the T vector gradually shifts in an anterior direction throughout childhood. There is much variation in the anterior movement of the T vector, so that some children retain posterior orientation with negative T waves in the anterior precordial leads throughout childhood; a few may develop an anterior position by 9 years with an upright T wave in lead V_1.

Ventricular Hypertrophy

The EKG diagnosis of hypertrophy is not a simple matter. Six general criteria give evidence for ventricular hypertrophy (Table 1): (1) axis deviation; (2) abnormal increase in QRS voltage; (3) abnormal QRS configuration; (4) T wave changes; (5) P wave changes; and (6) abnormal vectorcardiographic QRS loop. It is rare for all criteria to be positive in the diagnosis of hypertrophy, and the relative importance of positive criteria must be weighed at various ages. Abnormal right or left axis deviation is generally the weakest criterion. Nadas has emphasized caution in the diagnosis of hypertrophy based solely on abnormal QRS voltage.

RIGHT VENTRICULAR HYPERTROPHY (RVH). Because of the anatomic relationship of the ventricles, electrical predominance of the right ventricle tends to orient the QRS to the right and anteriorly (Fig. 17). This results in right axis deviation, prominent R waves in the anterior precordial leads, and increased S waves in lead V_6. Mild RVH, with or without chamber dilatation, is evidenced by a rsR' pattern in lead V_1 (terminal R is more prominent than initial r). This is the so-called incomplete right bundle branch block pattern; although this term is a misnomer, as pointed out by Boineau and co-workers, it is used clinically to indicate mild hypertrophy and/or dilation of the right ventricle. There is a reciprocal relationship of the T wave to the height of the R wave in lead V_1. Infants often demonstrate an upright T wave in lead V_1 (anterior T wave vector) as the major evidence of moderate RVH as, for example, in tetralogy of Fallot (Ziegler). Severe right ventricular hypertrophy presents a tall (> 30 mm), upright QRS complex with a deeply negative T wave in V_1. Digitalis may produce similar T waves in the presence of moderate RVH, since digitalis T wave changes result in the T vector being directed away from the hypertrophied ventricle.

In the absence of tricuspid stenosis or atresia, right atrial hypertrophy occurs only in the presence of right ventricular hypertrophy or dilation. Thus, right atrial enlargement, which generates tall (> 2.5 mm), peaked P waves in leads II and V_1, presents indirect evidence of RVH.

LEFT VENTRICULAR HYPERTROPHY (LVH). Since the left ventricle becomes the dominant chamber after a few months of life, and since LVH is a further accentuation of this dominance, the configuration of the QRS loop in the presence of LVH may appear normal. This diagnosis primarily rests upon voltage measurements of QRS components. The text by Guntheroth should be consulted for a detailed description of the criteria used for diagnosis of LVH in children.

In mild to moderate LVH there is accentuation of the Q wave (> 4.5 mm) in leads V_5 and V_6, and a summation of the R wave of these two should exceed 55 mm. (Fig. 18.) The T wave in these two leads becomes accentuated in mild to moderate LVH; however, in marked left ventricular hypertrophy, the left precordial T waves flatten or become inverted (this frequently is designated as "left ventricular strain"). The EKG diagnosis "LV strain" is quite important, since it occurs in so few conditions in children—e.g., severe aortc stenosis, coarctation of the aorta, hypertension, and intrinsic myocardial disease such as endocardial fibroelastosis. Rarely, it is seen with patent ductus and aortic insufficiency with marked left ventricular dilation. Since digitalis may cause similar T wave changes, it is important to obtain an electrocardiogram prior to digitalis administration. An increase in the depth of the S wave in lead V_2 is quite helpful also in detecting left ventricular hypertrophy; S waves greater than 30 mm are occasionally seen as the main evidence of LVH

TABLE 1. *Criteria for Right, Left, and Combined Ventricular Hypertrophy*

Right Ventricular Hypertrophy	**Left Ventricular Hypertrophy**	**Combined Ventricular Hypertrophy**
Axis deviation *1. RAD > 120° (R/S ratio in lead a VR > 1). Most valuable over age 2 years.	Axis deviation *1. LAD > −30° (R/S ratio lead II < 1). Most valuable under age 10 years.	***1. Positive criteria for RVH and LVH. **2. Positive criteria for RVH with normal R voltage V_6. **3. Positive criteria for LVH with R/S ratio > 1 in lead V_1. *4. Very large R and S waves in V_3 (Katz-Watchel phenomenon).
Abnormal QRS voltage *1. R wave in V_1 > 15 mm (over age 12 months). **2. S wave in V_6 > 9 mm (over age 1 month).	Abnormal QRS voltage **1. R wave V_6 > 35 mm. **2. S wave V_1 > 20 mm. **3. Sum of R wave V_6 and S wave V_1 > 45 mm.	
Abnormal QRS configuration ***1. qR pattern in V_1. **2. rsR' pattern V_1 with R' taller than initial r (dilation with or without mild hypertrophy). ***3. Onset of intrinsicoid deflection V_1 > 0.03 sec (onset of downward deflection from peak of R wave). **4. Totally upright deflection (R) V_1 (after 1 year). *5. R/S ratio V_1 > 1 after 10 years. **6. R/S ratio V_6 < 1 after 6 months.	Abnormal QRS configuration ***1. QS configuration V_1. **2. Deep Q wave (>4.5 mm) V_6.	
T wave changes ***1. Upright T wave V_1 after 4 days until 9 years. **2. Deeply coved negative T waves associated with tall R wave V_1.	T wave changes **1. Tall thin peaked T wave V_6 (volume overload of left ventricle). ***2. Inverted T wave V_6.	
P wave changes (right atrial enlargement) ***1. P wave > 2.5 mm lead II. ***2. Upright P wave > 3.0 mm lead V_1.	P wave changes (left atrial enlargement) ***1. P wave with 2 peaks 0.04 sec apart in lead I, II, or V_6. ***2. Biphasic P wave V_1 with large terminal negative deflection.	
Abnormal QRS loop ***1. Initial forces oriented to left and posteriorly. ***2. QRS loop oriented to right and anteriorly (over age 6 months).	Abnormal QRS loop **1. Counterclockwise frontal plane QRS loop under age 6 months. **2. QRS loop oriented markedly posterior.	

The relative importance of each finding is indicated by asterisks (the greater the number of asterisks, the more reliable the criterion). Voltage and R/S ratio criteria assume relatively greater importance the more they exceed normal values. Many of the criteria listed are those of Nadas and Keith, et al. RAD = Right axis deviation. LAD = Left axis deviation. The intrinsicoid deflection is the rapid downward deflection after peak of the R wave.

in the absence of positive voltage criteria in the left precordial leads. Left atrial enlargement is indicative of LVH (in the absence of mitral stenosis) and is evidenced by widely notched P waves ("P mitrale") in leads I, II, and/or V_6; also, lead V_1 shows a diphasic P wave with a large terminal negative deflection.

Qualitative interpretation of vectorcardiographic QRS loops particularly is helpful in detecting left ventricular hypertrophy in the infant. A counterclockwise loop in the frontal plane in a child under six months of age is quite suggestive of left ventricular hypertrophy with dilatation of this chamber (Fig. 18A). LVH with "systolic overload" (e.g., aortic stenosis, endocardial fibroelastosis) usually produces a normally oriented frontal plane QRS loop. In the future, digital computer measurements of selected spatial vectorcardiographic parameters may offer improved diagnostic criteria for detection of LVH; however, at present, changes in the precordial leads provide the most helpful data for the evaluation of LVH. **T WAVE ABNORMALITIES AND ELECTROLYTE EFFECTS.** ST segment and T wave changes are due to abnormal ventricular repolarization which occur secondary to: (1) abnormal sequence of ventricular depolarization; (2) myocardial ischemia; and (3) abnormal metabolic states, which include electrolyte disturbances and changes secondary to drugs.

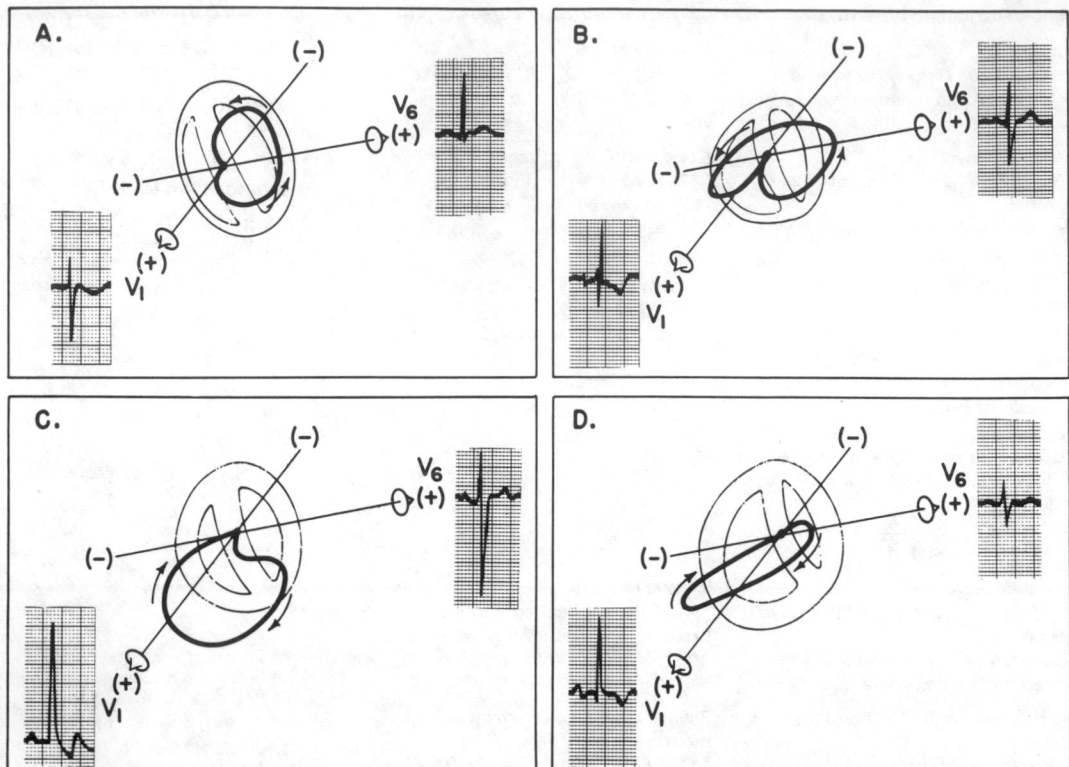

Fig. 17.   Electrocardiographic and vectorcardiographic changes with right ventricular hypertrophy. The horizontal plane vectorcardiographic QRS loop is shown as the darkened line with arrows indicating the direction of rotation. For orientation purposes, this is superimposed over a background picture of the heart as it anatomically relates to the horizontal plane of the vectorcardiogram. The scalar tracing in leads V_1 and V_6 are shown with the orientation of the lead axes as related to the QRS loop and ventricles. The tracings shown were obtained in the following conditions: A. Normal 6-year-old child; B. Atrial septal defect in a 7-year-old child; C. Tetralogy of Fallot in a 4-year-old child; and D. Total anomalous pulmonary venous drainage in a 3-year-old child. A. Normal horizontal plane QRS loop and scalar leads for a 6-year-old child. The QRS loop initially is directed slightly to the right and anteriorly and rotates leftward and posteriorly. Scalar lead V_1 shows an initial upright deflection associated with the anterior orientation of the QRS loop. Thereafter, the negative deflection in lead V_1 (S wave) is associated with the leftward and posterior position of the QRS loop as electrical activity is directed away from the anterior chest. B. Mild right ventricular hypertrophy and/or dilation. The initial portion of the QRS loop is inscribed normally; however, the terminal part of the loop is directed to the right and anteriorly. The terminal anterior and rightward vector is associated with a large R' deflection in lead V_1 and a prominent negative deflection in lead V_6. The rsR' pattern shown in lead V_1 is the "incomplete right bundle branch block pattern." C. Moderately severe right ventricular hypertrophy. The QRS loop is oriented far anteriorly and to the right due to the right ventricular predominance. This is associated with the prominent R wave deflection in lead V_1 and marked S deflection in lead V_6. D. Marked predominance of right ventricle. The initial forces of the QRS loop are oriented posteriorly and to the left. The loop then rotates far to the right and anteriorly. This type of QRS loop is associated with a qR deflection in lead V_1 and an RS deflection in lead V_6.

In the presence of abnormal ventricular depolarization, repolarization is altered and the T vector is abnormally oriented and directed away from the ventricle, which is delayed in depolarization; e.g., in left bundle branch block, the T wave is negative in lead V_6 and positive in lead V_1. In the presence of mild right ventricular hypertrophy with dilation, as occurs in atrial septal defect, frequently there are prominent negative T waves over the entire anterior precordium. In the severe hypertrophy of either ventricle, secondary T wave changes occur with the T wave pointing away from the severely overworked chamber; e.g., in severe pulmonary stenosis with marked right ventricular hypertrophy, the T wave in leads V_1 and V_2 becomes markedly inverted.

Inflammatory conditions of the heart produce T

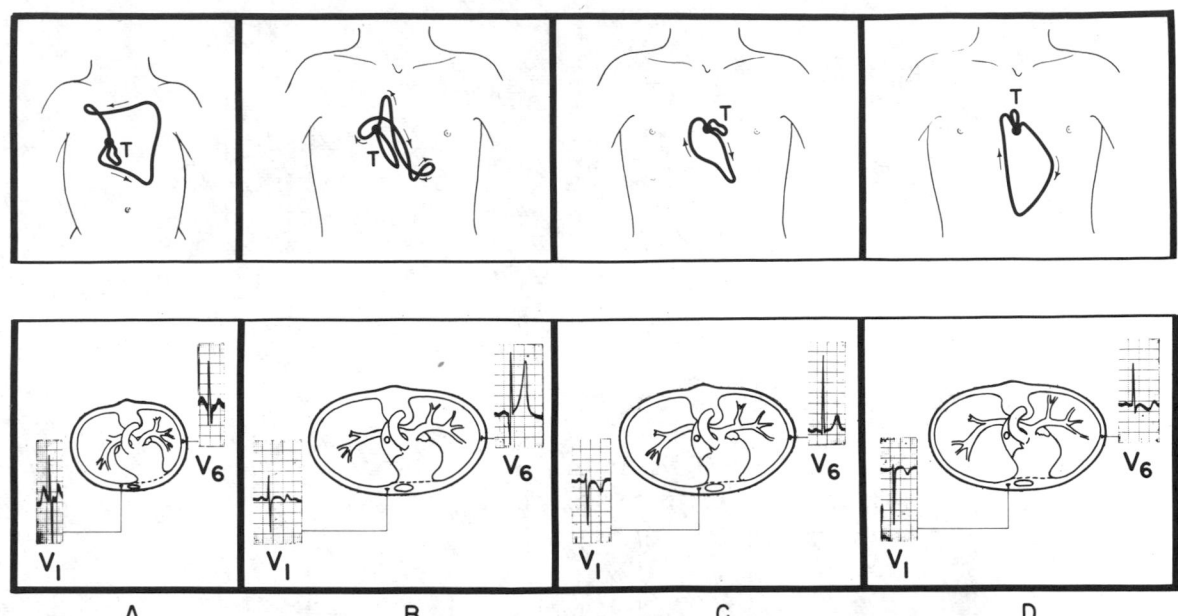

Fig. 18. Frontal plane vectorcardiographic (*top*) and precordial EKG manifestations (*bottom*) of left ventricular hypertrophy. A. Infant with LVH secondary to large left-to-right shunt due to ventricular septal defect. The frontal plane QRS loop is oriented to the left and superior with counterclockwise rotation. Right ventricular hypertrophy is manifested by the upright T wave in lead V$_1$. LVH is manifested in V$_6$ by the prominent Q wave and the R wave of normal amplitude. B. Ten-year-old child with LVH due to large volume of left ventricle (VSD). The QRS loop in the frontal plane is nonspecific but the T loop is quite prominent. LVH is manifested in lead V$_6$ by the deep Q wave, tall QRS, and tall, thin, peaked T wave. C. Nine-year-old with LVH secondary to moderately severe aortic stenosis. LVH is manifested in lead V$_6$ by the tall QRS complex (3.6 mv). Note that the frontal plane QRS loop appears normal. D. Ten-year-old with severe aortic stenosis. The frontal plane vectorcardiogram shows a normal QRS loop with the T wave abnormally oriented in a superior direction. In the precordial leads, LVH is manifested by the deep S wave in lead V$_1$ and the depressed ST-T wave in lead V$_6$.

wave abnormalities, as seen in acute pericarditis, with depressed ST-T waves over the left precordium. Myocarditis also produces T wave changes.

Pure hyponatremic or hypernatremic states have little effect upon the electrocardiogram, but such disturbances usually are associated with other electrolyte disturbances. Low serum calcium is evidenced by prolongation of the period of repolarization with prolonged S-T segment and increase in the Q-T interval. Hypercalcemia results in shortening of the S-T segment and Q-T interval.

In the detection of electrolyte disturbances, the electrocardiogram classically has been most helpful in the presence of potassium abnormalities. With *hypokalemia*, there is depression of the S-T segment with resultant diphasic T waves; frequently a U wave develops giving the appearance of a prolonged Q-T interval. When the potassium level falls below 3 mEq/L, the QRS S-T junction frequently appears as a "checkmark" due to marked depression of the S-T segment. *Hyperkalemia* of mild degree is evidenced by increased prominence of the T wave, espe-

cially in the midprecordial leads. Since "prominent" T waves over the midprecordium are common in children, the evaluation of hyperkalemic EKG changes is often difficult without a base line tracing. With increasingly severe hyperkalemia, varying degrees of atrioventricular block occur with prolongation of the P-R interval and ultimate disappearance of P waves; this is often associated with broadening of the QRS complex. The presence of prolongation of the QRS is evidence of severe hyperkalemia.

Characteristic Electrocardiograms

Although the EKG must be interpreted in relation to the clinical findings, certain tracings correlate extremely well with specific cardiac diagnoses. In endocardial cushion defects (atrioventricular canal abnormalities), the QRS is oriented in a superior direction with a counterclockwise frontal plane QRS loop (Fig. 19). Characteristic Q wave (lead I, aVL,

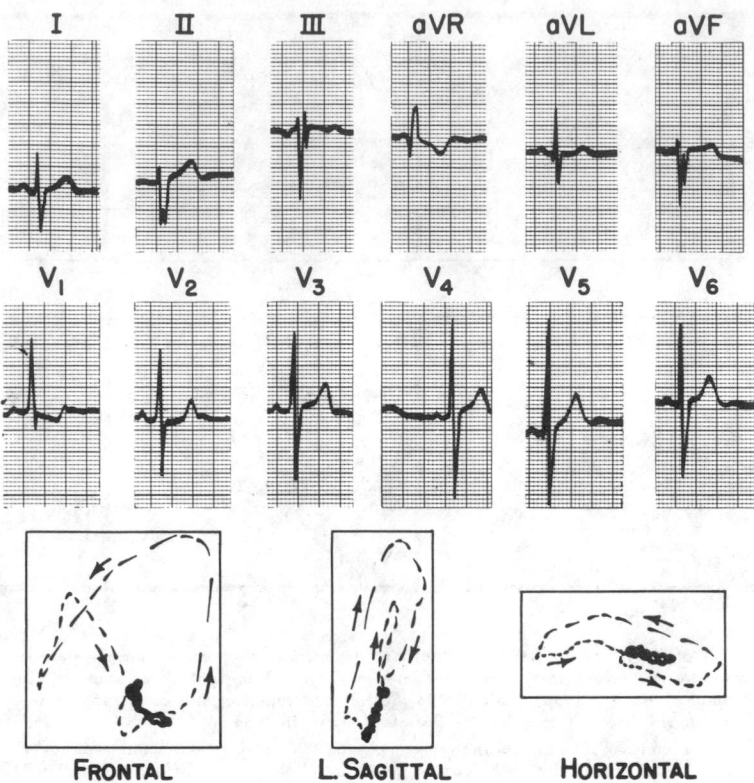

Fig. 19. Characteristic electrocardiogram and vectorcardiogram (tetrahedron system) in endocardial cushion defect. The above tracings were obtained in a 6-year-old child with an ostrium primum atrial septal defect, with mild mitral regurgitation. The frontal plane QRS loop is oriented mostly superiorly with counterclockwise inscription of the loop. This is correlated with the predominantly negative QRS deflection in scalar lead aVF. The terminal activity of the QRS loop is oriented to the right and is associated with a predominantly upright deflection in lead V_1 (moderate RVH). This type of vectorcardiogram and electrocardiogram is most unusual in children, except in the presence of various types of atrioventricular canal abnormalities.

and V_6) and ST-T changes occur in infants with myocardial infarction secondary to anomalous origin of the left coronary artery from the pulmonary artery. The combination of right axis deviation, "P pulmonale," and an R wave greater than 30 mm with deeply coved negative T waves in lead V_1 is most rare except with pure pulmonary stenosis and a systolic pressure higher in the right ventricle than in the left ventricle.

Arrhythmias

When the rate and rhythm are not completely controlled by the sinoatrial node, an abnormal arrhythmia is present. Final diagnosis rests with the electrocardiogram, and the vectorcardiogram provides no assistance. There are two general types of arrhythmias: (1) cardiac irritability with extra beats and tachycardia, and (2) varying degrees of depression of atrioventricular conduction with resultant dropped beats or ventricular bradycardia when there is no transmission of the impulse from the atria to the ventricles. The arrhythmias are discussed in detail elsewhere (p. 1368).

REFERENCES

Boineau, J. P., Spach, M. S., and Ayers, C. R. Genesis of the electrocardiogram in atrial septal defect. Amer. Heart J., 68:637, 1964.

Burch, G. E., and Winsor, T. A Primer of Electrocardiography. Philadelphia, Lea & Febiger, 1955.

Caceres, C. A., Steinberg, C. A., Abraham, S., Carbery, W. J., McBryde, J. M., Tolles, W. E., and Rikli, A. E. Computer extraction of electrocardiographic parameters. Circulation, 25:356, 1962.

Frank, E. An accurate, clinically practical system for spatial vectorcardiography. Circulation, 13:737, 1956.

Grant, R. P. Clinical Electrocardiography; The Spatial Vector Approach. New York, McGraw-Hill Book Co., Blakiston Division, 1957.

Guntheroth, W. A. Pediatric Electrocardiography. Philadelphia, W. B. Saunders Co., 1965.

Keith, J. D., Rowe, R. D., and Vlad, P. Heart Disease in Infancy and Childhood. New York, The Macmillan Co., 1958.

Nadas, A. S. Pediatric Cardiology. Philadelphia, W. B. Saunders Co., 1957.

Page, E. The electrical potential difference across the cell membrane of heart muscle. Circulation, 26:582, 1962.

Pipberger, H. V., Stallman, F. W., Yano, K., and Draper, H. W. Digital computer analysis of the normal and abnormal electrocardiogram. Progr. Cardiovasc. Dis., 5:378, 1963.

Scher, A. M., and Young, A. C. The pathway of ventricular depolarization in the dog. Circ. Res., 4:461, 1956.

Spach, M. S., Huang, S., and Ayers, C. R. Electrical and anatomic study of the Purkinje system of the canine heart. Amer. Heart J., 65:664, 1963.

Ziegler, R. F. Electrocardiographic Studies in Normal Infants and Children. Springfield, Ill., Charles C Thomas, 1951.

—— The importance of positive T waves in the right precordial electrocardiogram during the first year of life. Amer. Heart J., 52:533, 1956.

20.6
CARDIAC CATHETERIZATION

MADISON S. SPACH

Clinical Role of Cardiac Catheterization

Cardiac catheterization has played an essential role in the diagnostic and surgical therapeutic advances in heart disease in children over the past decade. The correlation of the clinical manifestations of many cardiac defects with physiologic and anatomic (angiocardiographic) data obtained in the catheterization laboratory has placed clinical cardiology on a very firm basis. Indeed, most defects now can be diagnosed accurately by review of the patient's history, physical examination, x-rays, and electrocardiogram. The increasing ability of the surgeon to successfully correct or palliate many complicated cardiac lesions has placed greater demands upon the clinician for a *complete* cardiac diagnosis, which often is achieved only by laboratory methods. Thus, laboratory methods for diagnosis have become an integral part of clinical pediatric cardiology, and the clinician must become familiar with catheterization techniques, types of data obtained, and their value and limitations. Although cardiac catheterization provides vital information, laboratory findings must be evaluated in conjunction with all the clinical data in arriving at a final diagnosis and decision as to the advisability of surgical intervention.

Most children undergo cardiac catheterization to obtain otherwise unavailable information which pertains to cardiac surgery. The indications for surgery vary from one center to another; and likewise, there are no set criteria as to the indications for cardiac catheterization. Rapid improvements in catheterization techniques and their increased safety, on the one hand, and improved clinical diagnostic accuracy, on the other, make it clear that the indications will be changing constantly in the future. However, catheterization is indicated especially in symptomatic infants with large left-to-right shunts and in those children with cyanotic heart disease. Most patients have catheterization prior to cardiac surgery, but there is a trend to forego studies in patients with the typical clinical findings in secundum and primum type atrial defects, valvar pulmonary stenosis, and ventricular septal defects without pulmonary hypertension. Uncomplicated patent ductus arteriosus and coarctation of the aorta rarely require catheterization.

Clinical Approach to Cardiac Catheterization

The purpose of catheterization is to provide information related to the unknown or unproven. The recent advent of the creation of an interatrial septal defect by balloon septostomy, introduced by Rashkind, has added a therapeutic role to the procedure in selected patients.

The procedure must be planned carefully in light of the clinical findings, diagnostic possibilities, and the patient's status. In the laboratory, the procedure should be approached as a precise physiologic and anatomic study to prove or disprove the clinical assumptions and to rule out associated lesions. There are four general types of abnormalities, singly or in combination, that require clarification at catheterization:

1. Intracardiac and extracardiac shunts: Such shunts should be detected, localized, and quantitated. The pulmonary vascular resistance should be estimated in the presence of pulmonary hypertension, and the anatomic nature of the underlying defect may require clarification.

2. Obstructive lesions: The site of obstruction must be determined, the anatomic nature of the narrowing clarified, and its hemodynamic severity evaluated.

3. Valvar insufficiency: Regurgitation should be localized and its severity estimated.

4. Abnormal position or structure of vessels, cardiac chambers, and valves: A record of accurate anatomic data requires the use of angiocardiographic techniques.

Equipment Used to Obtain Data

The value of the procedure is related directly to the ability of the laboratory to provide accurate and complete physiologic and anatomic data. Several excel-

Fig. 20. Equipment used in a cardiac catheterization laboratory. A. The equipment is arranged in the laboratory so that the catheter position may be visualized on the television screen (5) while monitoring intracardiac pressures and the electrocardiogram on the oscilloscope (4). The x-ray image of the image intensifier (6) is detected by a closed-circuit television network and viewed on the television screen. The x-ray unit shown employs two image amplifiers (6) positioned at right angles for simultaneous recording of movies (biplane cineangiocardiography). The recording ensemble (2) consists of a group of preamplifiers and a photographic recorder for obtaining a permanent record of electrocardiographic, indicator-dilution, and pressure data. A multichannel tape recorder (1) is connected to the recording ensemble so that data may be recorded in "live" form when desired. Equipment used for recording radioisotope dilution curves for external monitoring of the heart, lungs, and head is performed with the use of two scintillation detectors (7) which are connected to count rate meters (3) and these, in turn, are connected to the recorder (2). Intracardiac pressures are determined by connecting the catheter to pressure sensing devices (transducers —8) which generate electrical voltage depending upon the pressure to which they are exposed. Not shown is a Lown Cardioverter which is used for emergency treatment of severe arrhythmias (e.g., ventricular tachycardia and fibrillation) by delivering a high voltage DC shock to the chest wall for cardioversion. B. Equipment used for measurement of blood gases and for recording dye dilution curves is shown. The hemoglobin oxygen saturation can be determined by passing blood through a cuvette (2) which employs photocells operating at different wavelengths of light. The electrical output of the photocell-sensing device will depend upon the relative amounts of reduced and oxyhemoglobin. These electrical signals are relayed to the control panel (1) and the ratio of reduced-to-oxyhemoglobin is read from a galvanometer scale located by the cuvette (2). The blood gas and pH analyzing system (4) utilizes special electrodes for determining the partial pressure (mm Hg) of oxygen and carbon dioxide and blood pH.

lent reviews are available which present a detailed analysis of catheterization methodology. Since right and left heart catheterization can be performed at any age, the limitations in data acquisition involve (1) the ability of the cardiologist to manipulate the catheter to a desired position and (2) the availability of adequate techniques to obtain and record the desired information. Angiocardiographic apparatus is essential for complete diagnoses in many patients, especially in infants with complex lesions.

All pediatric cardiac laboratories should use an image intensifier for x-ray visualization, since radiation exposure is significantly reduced as compared to that received from conventional fluoroscopes (Spach

and Capp). Additionally, cineradiography requires the use of an image intensifier. Visualization studies following selective injection of contrast media (e.g., Hypaque) utilize either biplane angiocardiography (serial x-ray films) or cineangiocardiography (movie film). The x-ray film method has the advantage of depicting more excellent detail than is available in motion pictures, whereas the cine method offers the advantages of the demonstrating motion and of producing less radiation exposure.

Equipment should be available to (1) record the electrocardiogram, (2) record intracardiac and vascular pressures, (3) perform oxygen analysis of blood samples, and (4) perform indicator dilution studies. Intracardiac phonocardiography is also quite useful for the detection of multiple defects. One must be prepared to utilize all of the facilities available to achieve a complete evaluation in complicated cardiac lesions, whereas one or two methods may afford a complete diagnosis in simple lesions. Figure 20 demonstrates the types of equipment used in a cardiac catheterization laboratory. It is apparent that the cardiologist in the laboratory must, of necessity, become familiar with the use of electronic and x-ray apparatus.

A special notation is in order concerning the performance of balloon septostomy in infants. This is indicated in selected patients, especially small critically ill newborns with transposition of the great vessels. The prime requisite is a probe-patent foramen ovale which allows passage of the balloon-tipped catheter into the left atrium. The catheter passage must be from below; therefore, it is of prime importance in patients who are potential candidates for this procedure that the femoral vessels not be used for venipunctures so that these vessels are maintained for catheter passage.

Technique of Obtaining Information

APPROACH TO THE HEART. The catheter is passed to the heart via vessels in the arms, axilla, or groin region. The groin approach is especially useful in cyanotic patients, in whom the foramen ovale usually remains probe-patent, making possible the performance of both right and left heart catheterization via a single vein. If left heart catheterization cannot be achieved by this method, one may use (1) the transseptal atrial needle (usually restricted to older children), (2) retrograde aortic approach to the left ventricle, and (3) percutaneous direct anterior chest or subxiphoid left ventricular approach with a needle.

DETECTION OF SHUNTS. There are five currently available methods which can be used for the detection and localization of shunts: (1) blood oxygen analysis; (2) dye dilution curves; (3) ascorbic acid or hydrogen dilution curves; (4) radioisotope dilution curves; and (5) selective angiocardiography. In most laboratories, only oxygen data and dye dilution curves allow quantification of the magnitude of the shunt.

The most commonly used and traditional method for arteriovenous shunt detection is blood oxygen analysis. In the absence of a left-to-right shunt, the blood oxygen tension, saturation, and content remain rather constant throughout the right side of the heart. In progressing from a proximal to a more distal chamber or vessel, a sudden large increase in blood oxygen strongly suggests the presence of a left-to-right shunt. Table 2 summarizes the use of oxygen data for the detection, localization, and quantification of cardiac shunts. Initially, blood oxygen was analyzed by the gasometric method of Van Slyke and Neill. Although this is an excellent method, it has been replaced in many laboratories by the use of spectrophotometric methods, oximetry, or direct measurement of oxygen tension (polarographic and potentiometric methods). These latter methods have the inherent advantages of requiring smaller aliquots of blood and of allowing rapid analysis with quickly available results. The future development of fiber optic catheters may make possible direct intracardiac oximetry.

The greatest disadvantage of blood oxygen data is the relative insensitivity of the method; small shunts may be missed. One of the indicator dilution methods should be available when oxygen data present equivocal results. Arterial dye dilution curves are recorded by withdrawing blood through a densitometer (light sensing device) during the intracardiac injection of indocyanine dye. Normally a curve is inscribed as shown in Figure 21A. In the presence of a left-to-right shunt (Fig. 21B), there is pulmonary recirculation during the initial passage of dye from the heart, and this produces distortion of the disappearance phase of the arterial dye curve because of runoff of the shunted blood from the lungs.

Dye dilution curves may be used to localize the site of the left-to-right shunt by variation of the injection site, as shown in Figure 22. Small left-to-right shunts may be missed by oxygen saturation data and by peripheral arterial dye curves following right-sided injections. Another sensitive method utilizes the injection of ascorbic acid as the indicator and a platinum electrode potentiometric or polargraphic device for the detection system (Bargeron et al.). Following injection into the pulmonary artery, a left-to-right shunt is indicated by early recirculation of the indicator into the pulmonary artery.

The diagnosis of a right-to-left shunt most commonly is suggested when the systemic arterial oxygen saturation is less than 95 percent. Pneumonia and hypoventilation, which may produce reduced pulmonary venous saturation, must be excluded as complicating features. Indicator dilution studies are used to confirm and locate the site of the shunt (Fig. 23). Following injection of an indicator into the right ventricle, a right-to-left shunt is indicated by an early appearance time at a peripheral body site of the indicator involved in the venoarterial shunt.

PRESSURE DATA. Recording of intracardiac pressures is an integral part of the catheterization procedure. Pulmonary and systemic resistance calculations depend upon determination of mean aortic and pulmonary artery pressures. Average normal values for pressures are given in Table 3. The type of pressure change obtained as the catheter is withdrawn from the pulmonary artery is helpful in the diagnosis of several types of pulmonary stenosis (Fig. 24). With retrograde left ventricular catheterization, the presence and site of obstructive lesions are clarified by the type of pressure change noted while withdrawing the catheter into the aorta. (Fig. 25).

SELECTIVE ANGIOCARDIOGRAPHY. One of the major advances in cardiac catheterization has been

TABLE 2.   *Summary of the Use of Blood Oxygen Data*

Minimal hemoglobin oxygen saturation step-up suggestive of left-to-right shunt (single blood sample).

	Step-up
Superior vena cava to right atrium	10%
Right atrium to right ventricle	7%
Right ventricle to pulmonary artery	5%

The minimal values are shown which suggest a left-to-right shunt. Increased mixing of blood at more distal sites accounts for the diminution in magnitude of the step-up required to suggest a left-to-right shunt.

Estimation of magnitude of shunts (using hemoglobin saturation or oxygen content).

(1) Left-to-right shunt:

$$\frac{PA - MVB}{Art. (PV) - MVB} = \% \; Qp \text{ comprised by L-R shunt.}$$

(2) Right-to-left shunt:

$$\frac{PV - Art.}{PV - MVB} = \% \; Qs \text{ comprised by R-L shunt.}$$

In estimating the magnitude of left-to-right shunts, the equation indicates that the size of the calculated shunt depends upon the saturation of shunted blood (pulmonary venous) as well as that of the mixed venous blood. A right-to-left shunt is suggested if the systemic arterial oxygen saturation is less than 95%; however, pulmonary venous saturation should be measured to rule out pulmonary causes of decreased arterial saturation.

Calculation of blood flow.

(1) Qs (L/min) $= \dfrac{O_2 \text{ consumption (ml/min)}}{Art. \; O_2 \text{ content (ml/L)} - MVB \; O_2 \text{ content (ml/L)}}$

(2) Qp (L/min) $= \dfrac{O_2 \text{ consumption (ml/min)}}{PV \; O_2 \text{ content (ml/L)} - PA \; O_2 \text{ content (ml/L)}}$

(3) Left-to-right shunt = $Qp - Qs$

(4) Right-to-left shunt = $Qs - Qp$

(5) Calculation of flow in the presence of bidirectional shunting:

Qep (L/min) $= \dfrac{O_2 \text{ consumption (ml/min)}}{PV \; O_2 \text{ content (ml/L)} - MVB \; O_2 \text{ content (ml/L)}}$

Left-to-right shunt = $Qp - Qep$
Right-to-left shunt = $Qs - Qep$

Oxygen consumption must be measured and blood oxygen content determined to calculate quantitative flow (liters/minute). Because of the difficulties in determining oxygen consumption in infants and small children, "assumed" values often are used for this calculation. The "assumed" calculations have obvious quantitative deficiencies, but the data can be used accurately to estimate the pulmonary-to-systemic resistance ratio (vide infra).

Calculation of resistance.

(1) $Rs = \dfrac{Art. \text{ mean pressure (mm Hg)} \times 960 \times 1.36 \times 60}{Qs \text{ (ml/sec)}}$

(dyne-seconds per cm^5)

$Rs = \dfrac{Art. \text{ mean pressure} - RA \text{ mean pressure}}{Qs \text{ (L/min)}}$

(mm Hg/L/min)

(2) $Rp = \dfrac{PA \text{ mean pressure (mm Hg)} - PV \text{ mean pressure (mm Hg)} \times 960 \times 1.36 \times 60}{Qp \text{ (ml/sec)}}$

(dyne-seconds per cm^5)

$Rp = \dfrac{PA \text{ mean pressure} - PV \text{ mean pressure}}{QP \text{ (L/min)}}$

(mm Hg/L/min)

TABLE 2.   (continued)

Calculation of resistance (continued)

Calculation of pulmonary and systemic resistance is useful in evaluation of patients with pulmonary hypertension. Either of the two equations shown may be used for estimation of vascular resistance. Pulmonary resistance normally is 1 to 3 mm Hg/L/min (100 to 250 dyneseconds per cm^5). Resistance ratios (Rp/Rs) greater than 0.3 are abnormal, and values greater than 0.7 indicate marked pulmonary vascular obstruction.

Art. = systemic artery; MVB = mixed venous blood; PA = pulmonary artery; PV = pulmonary vein; Qep = effective pulmonary blood flow; Qp = pulmonary blood flow; Qs = systemic blood flow; RA = right atrium; Rp = pulmonary vascular resistance; and Rs = systemic vascular resistance. Many of the values and calculations listed are summarized from Rudolph and Cayler. *Pediat. Clin. N. Amer.*, 5:907, 1958.

the incorporation of selective angiocardiography as an integral part of the procedure. Pressure, oxygen, and indicator dilution data are invaluable for the detection, localization, and quantification of shunts and for detecting various types of diagnostic abnormal circulatory patterns (e.g., transposition of the great vessels and total anomalous pulmonary venous drainage); however, selective angiocardiography is required for complete cardiac diagnosis in complicated cardiac lesions (e.g., single ventricle). Also, it is most helpful in the clarification of the nature of many

cardiac defects, such as the various types of endocardial cushion defects, anomalous pulmonary venous drainage, truncus arteriosus, and transposition of the great vessels. Figure 26 demonstrates a biplane cineangiocardiogram which was helpful in clarifying the diagnosis in a 3-month-old infant with Type I truncus arteriosus.

Biplane angiocardiography currently is used in several catheterization laboratories to estimate left ventricular and atrial volumes, left ventricular mass, and ejection fractions. This method, which requires

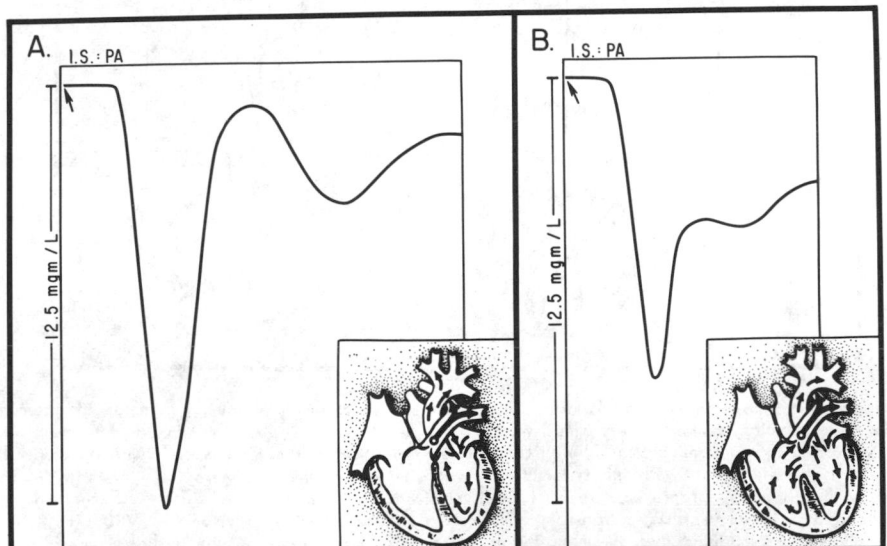

Fig. 21.   Arterial dye curves: Normal curve and curve indicating left-to-right shunt. The curves were recorded by injecting indocyanine dye into the pulmonary artery (I.S.: PA) while withdrawing femoral artery blood through a densitometer. A. Normal curve. This was recorded in a 4-year-old child with aortic stenosis. This indicates that following the initial passage of dye through the systemic circulation, the concentration falls almost to base line levels and is followed by a prominent recirculation curve. B. Arterial dye curve in the presence of a left-to-right shunt. These curves were recorded in a 3-year-old child with a moderately large left-to-right shunt due to a VSD. This shows distortion of the disappearance phase due to run-off of the blood shunted through the lungs. The arrow below the base line of the dye curve indicates the time of injection of dye through the catheter. Within the cardiac inserts, the solid lines indicate the course of flow immediately following injection and the interrupted arrows indicate the course of flow following pulmonary venous return to the heart.

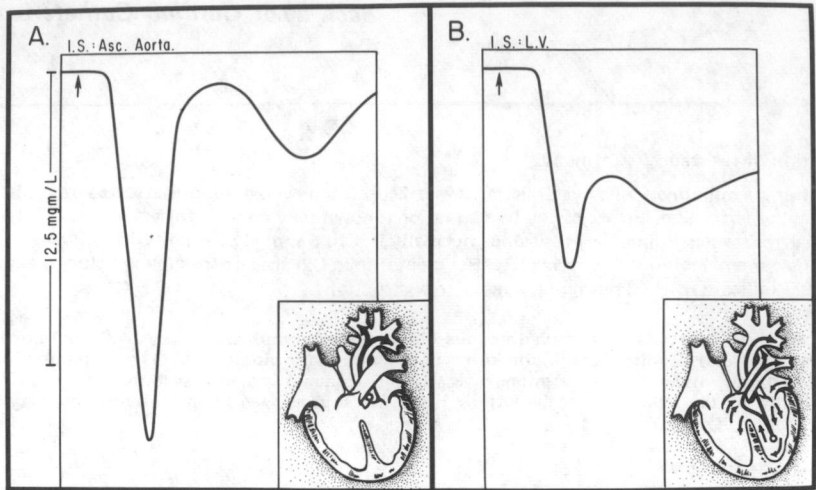

Fig. 22. Localization of the site of the left-to-right shunt with arterial dye curves. These curves were recorded by injecting indocyanine dye in (A) the ascending aorta and (B) the left ventricle while withdrawing femoral arterial blood through a densitometer. Following injection of dye in the ascending aorta (A) there is a rapid and large deflection since all of the dye was transmitted to the systemic circuit. The curve recorded after injection into the left ventricle (B) shows distortion of the disappearance phase, which indicates run-off of blood shunted to the lungs. The pattern of left-to-right shunting following injection into the left ventricle and the absence of left-to-right shunt following aortic root injection localizes the shunt of the ventricular level (VSD).

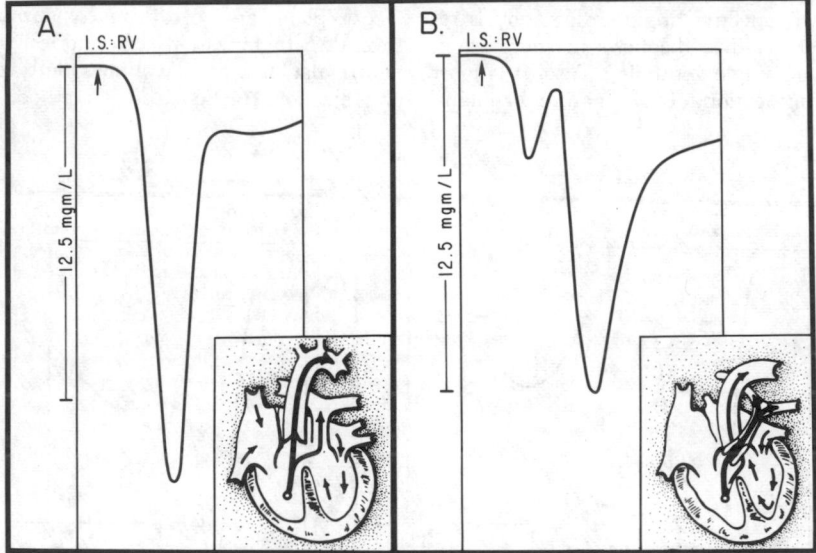

Fig. 23. Arterial dye curves in cyanotic heart disease. These curves were recorded following injection of indocyanine dye into the right ventricle while sampling femoral artery blood through the densitometer. The arrow indicates the time of injection of dye. A. This curve was recorded in a 3-month-old infant with complete transposition of the great vessels with an associated VSD. It indicates a very large right-to-left shunt with the systemic circulation being supplied mostly by the right ventricle. The venoarterial shunt is indicated by the early appearance time of dye following injection into the right ventricle. The schematic insert illustrates the pattern of flow from the right ventricle in transposition of the great vessels with an associated VSD. The solid line indicates that immediately following injection of dye, the majority of flow occurs into the aorta, with a slight amount of blood shunting across the ventricular septal defect into the left ventricle and pulmonary artery. The interrupted arrows indicate return from the lungs and early recirculation from the body. B. This arterial dye curve indicates a small right-to-left shunt (mild tetralogy of Fallot). The right-to-left shunt in the dye curve is indicated by the early appearance time of the initial small deflection caused by that dye which has traversed the VSD to the aorta, without initial passage through the lungs. The "double bump" curve with early appearance time is characteristic of a right-to-left shunt of small to moderate magnitude. The small early initial deflection represents that portion of the indicator involved in the right-to-left shunt, and the second large deflection represents the remainder of the bolus of indicator which traversed the lungs before flow to the peripheral circulation occurred. The schematic insert shows the pattern of flow from the right ventricle in the presence of a VSD and infundibular pulmonary stenosis with a small right-to-left shunt. The solid lines indicate that the major portion of flow occurs into the pulmonary artery from the right ventricle and a small amount of blood is shunted through the ventricular septal defect into the aorta. The interrupted arrows indicate the pattern of flow following pulmonary venous return to the left heart.

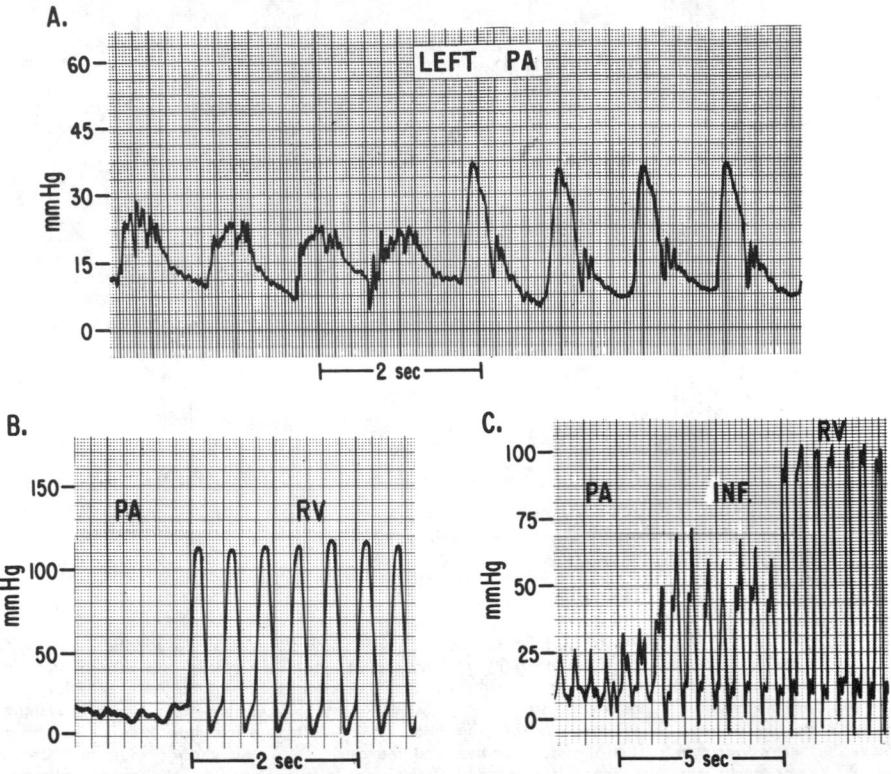

Fig. 24. Use of pressure data in the diagnosis of various types of pulmonary stenosis. A. Pressure tracing characteristic of peripheral stenosis of the pulmonary artery: As the catheter was withdrawn from the left pulmonary artery, the sudden increase in systolic pressure and mild fall in diastolic pressure indicated a constriction of this vessel. Subsequent cineangiocardiographic studies delineated the site of narrowing near the junction of the main pulmonary artery and the left pulmonary artery. B. Typical pressure change in valvar pulmonary stenosis. As the catheter was withdrawn from the pulmonary artery, there was a sudden increase in systolic pressure as the catheter traversed the pulmonary valve, thus localizing the site of the obstruction to the valve. C. Pressure changes associated with valvar and infundibular pulmonary stenosis. This type of pressure tracing is frequently obtained in patients with tetralogy of Fallot. Note the rise in systolic pressure as the catheter traversed the valve with a second rise between the infundibulum and the body of the right ventricle.

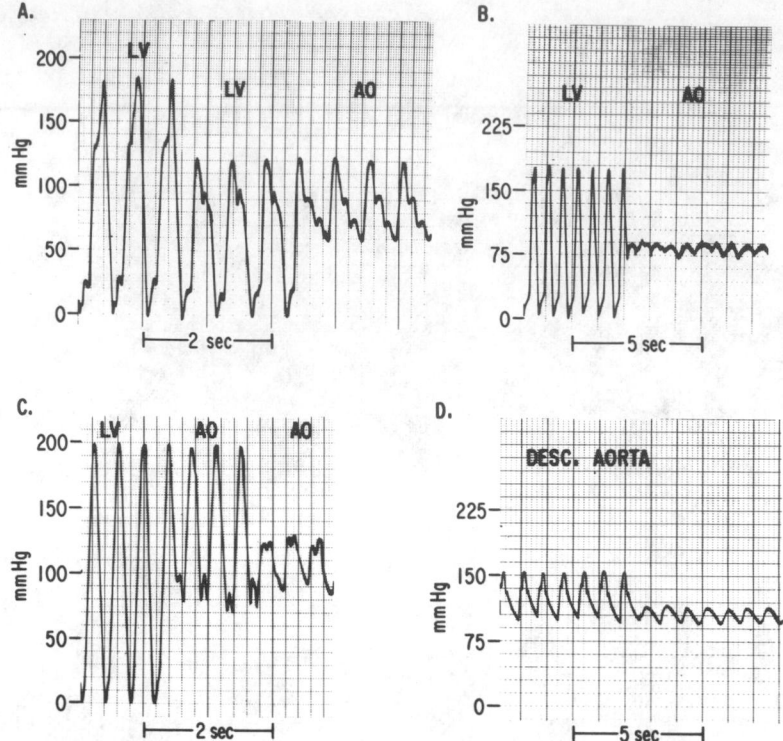

Fig. 25. Localization of the site of obstruction in the left ventricle and aorta. The localization of the site of obstructive lesions on the left side can be determined by passing the catheter in a retrograde fashion into the left ventricle. The type of pressure change found upon withdrawal of the catheter from the left ventricle into the aorta is characteristic for the various types of obstruction. A. Subaortic stenosis: There is a drop in systolic left ventricular pressure as the catheter is withdrawn from the body of the left ventricle into the outflow portion of the left ventricle. Further withdrawal across the aortic valve into the aorta shows no change in systolic pressure at the valve level. B. Valvar aortic stenosis: There is a sudden drop in systolic pressure as the aortic valve is traversed. Note that the simultaneous fall in systolic pressure and rise in diastolic pressure indicates that the site of obstruction is located at the valve. C. Supravalvar aortic stenosis: The withdrawal of the catheter from the left ventricle across the aortic valve into the proximal aorta is indicated by the sudden rise in diastolic pressure. The systolic pressure in this area indicates no valvar stenosis. Further withdrawal into the aorta shows a drop in systolic pressure (without change in diastolic pressure) indicating a narrowing immediately above the aortic valve. D. Coarctation of the aorta: Withdrawal of the catheter from the descending aortic arch into the thoracic aorta shows an abrupt drop in systolic pressure indicating the site of the obstruction of the coarctation.

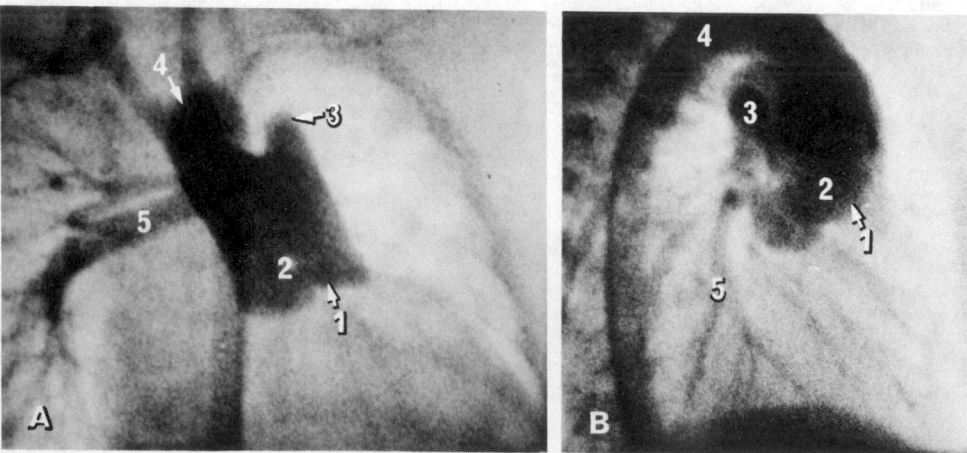

Fig. 26. Biplane cineangiocardiogram in Type I truncus arteriosus. A. Anterior-posterior view. B. Right-lateral view. Contrast media was injected with the catheter positioned in the ascending aortic arch area. These pictures demonstrate the origin of the aorta (4) and pulmonary artery (3) from a common trunk (2). Also demonstrated is the single semilunar valve (1) of the truncus which appears to be tricuspid in the lateral view. The right pulmonary artery (5) can be seen to arise from the main pulmonary artery in the lateral view. This study shows that the pulmonary artery arises from the truncus and this connection is situated in the position found in a Type I truncus arteriosus.

TABLE 3. *Average Normal Range of Cardiovascular Pressure (in mm Hg)*

	Infants and Children	Newborn Period
Right atrium	a* = 3-7 v* = 2-5 m* = 1-5	m = 0-3
Right ventricle	$\frac{15\text{-}30}{2\text{-}5}$	$\frac{35\text{-}65}{1\text{-}5}$
Pulmonary artery	$\frac{15\text{-}30}{5\text{-}10}$	$\frac{35\text{-}65}{20\text{-}40}$
	m = 10-20	m = 25-40
Pulmonary capillary wedge	a = 3-7 v = 5-15 m = 5-12	
Left atrium	a = 3-7 v = 5-15 m = 5-10	m = 1-4
Left ventricle	$\frac{80\text{-}130}{5\text{-}10}$	
Systemic artery	$\frac{90\text{-}130}{60\text{-}90}$	
	m = 70-95	

*a and v refer to pulse waves; m to mean pressure. Zero reference point at midthoracic level. Modified from Rudolph and Cayler. *Pediat. Clin. N. Amer.*, 5:907, 1958.

numerous measurements of the chamber silhouette, may receive more widespread use as its clinical role continues to be evaluated in the future.

RISKS OF CARDIAC CATHETERIZATION. There is risk associated with any catheterization procedure, and the danger generally increases with the severity of the underlying cardiac lesion. The main danger of catastrophic events (e.g., penetration of the heart with the catheter and air embolism) usually can be avoided by constant vigilance in the handling of the catheter. Arrhythmias are common, and the sudden onset of ventricular fibrillation, although rare, almost always can be successfully corrected by immediate electric countershock measures with instruments such as the Lown Cardioverter. The development of systemic hypotension may require treatment with vasopressor agents, particularly in the presence of pulmonary hypertension or severe pulmonary stenosis. The added risk of selective angiocardiography remains to be clarified; however, blood hyperosmolarity and increased plasma volume occur transiently following injection of hypertonic contrast media.

REFERENCES

Bargeron, L. M., Jr., Clark, L. C., Jr., and Lyons, C. Modern methods in the diagnosis of congenital heart disease. Med. Clin. N. Amer., 46:1555, 1962.

Nadas, A. S. Pediatric Cardiology. Philadelphia, W. B. Saunders Co., 1963.

Rashkind, W. J., and Miller, W. W. Creation of an atrial septal defect without thoracotomy: A palliative approach to complete transposition of the great vessels. J.A.M.A., 196:991, 1966.

Rudolph, A. M., and Cayler, G. G. Cardiac catheterization in infants and children. Pediat. Clin. N. Amer., 5:907, 1958.

Spach, M. S., and Capp, M. P. Radiation exposure in children: Diagnostic studies for congenital heart disease. Amer. J. Dis. Child., 103:750, 1962.

Wood, E. H., ed. Symposium on use of indicator-dilution technics in the study of the circulation. Circ. Res., 10:377, 1962.

Zimmerman, H. A., ed. Intra Vascular Catheterization. Springfield, Ill., Charles C Thomas Co., 1959.

20.7
DISORDERS OF THE HEARTBEAT

WARREN G. GUNTHEROTH

Abnormalities of rate, rhythm, and mechanism * are relatively common in the pediatric age group, and for the most part are relatively benign. They deserve attention, however, because they may indicate more serious cardiac disorders. Abnormalities of mechanism which do not alter the rate or rhythm cannot be diagnosed from the pulse, although careful auscultation of the first heart sounds may suggest the presence of the abnormality. Although prowess with the stethoscope is laudable, it is foolhardy to make a firm diagnosis of disturbances of rate, rhythm, or mechanism without an electrocardiogram. Interpretation of the electrocardiogram, however, may require considerable experience, in addition to a pair of calipers, a long continuous strip, and a flair for mathematical puzzles. Although the history and physical examination alone are rarely sufficient for diagnosis, they sometimes give very substantial grounds for a diagnosis in the face of an equivocal electrocardiogram. For example, if massage of the carotid sinus slows the heart rate, the arrhythmia is probably not of ventricular origin, since the vagus has little effect on ventricular pacemakers.

A general observation is in order here, relative to therapy. The great majority of disorders of the heartbeat in children are benign. Abolition of an arrhythmia with some drugs or techniques may be attended by a greater mortality and morbidity than are inherent in the disorder. The decision is then what *should* be done, not what *can* be done. The classification presented here considers first those disorders of rate or rhythm which can be observed clinically.

* Mechanism is generally used to designate the anatomic origin of an electrocardiographic complex. Normally, the mechanism is "sinus," indicating origin of the beat in the sinus node.

Rapid Rates, Regular Rhythm

Sinus tachycardia cannot be considered an abnormality without consideration of age and the state of a patient. The physician dealing with children is immediately confronted with the arbitrary definition of tachycardia as a rate over 100 per minute, whereas a rate under 100 in an infant is slower than "normal." Normal rates for age similarly are of little value unless wakefulness, fever, crying, and activity are defined. Nadas considers the average sleeping pulse rate in infants to be 120 per minute, decreasing gradually with age to less than 100 at 6 years, and less than 80 by puberty. Sinus tachycardia generally is not a primary disorder and does not require treatment except for the underlying process. In rare instances of chronic sinus tachycardia, a small dose of reserpine (0.1 mg twice a day) may be effective.

Paroxysmal atrial tachycardia (PAT) is probably the single most important disturbance of rate in pediatrics. It frequently occurs in otherwise normal infants and children, and can lead to serious difficulties if not diagnosed and treated properly. It may escape attention in the infant because of the nonspecific symptoms and findings: poor feeding, irritability, tachypnea, and pallor. In young infants, the rates may be over 300 per minute under which circumstances, according to Langendorf and Pick, there is no significant difference between PAT and *atrial flutter.* The rate is characteristically unvarying, and does not slow gradually, but will abruptly change to either a normal rate, or occasionally to one-half of its previous rate, if atrioventricular (AV) block occurs. Signs of congestive failure are usually present if the PAT has been present for over 48 hours.

The EKG is helpful, but sometimes less diagnostic than the knowledge of abrupt onset or termination of the tachycardia (Fig. 27). Distinguishing an atrial from a nodal pacemaker in some instances is practically impossible, and in such cases they may be labeled "supraventricular tachycardia." Similarly, when supraventricular tachycardia is accompanied by ventricular conduction disturbances, the arrhythmia may be difficult to distinguish from *ventricular tachycardia.* The disturbance may be of the ventricular preexcitation type (Wolff-Parkinson-White syndrome) or may involve right or left bundle branch block or "arborization" block (Fig. 28). The recognition of preexcitation syndrome has prognostic significance, since these patients are prone to repeated attacks of PAT, whereas PAT uncommonly recurs after the first year in infants without preexcitation.

Treatment of PAT is usually rewarded with fairly prompt reversion to sinus rhythm. Although treatment should be prompt and vigorous, the situation usually is not desperate and there is time for deliberate action. A brief trial of vagal stimulation may be in order, particularly if the child is not in vascular collapse. Unilateral carotid body massage, eyeball pressure, deep breathing or Valsalva maneuver, and gagging induced physically or vomiting with syrup of ipecac have all been successful at times in reverting PAT to sinus rhythm. However, most pediatric experience with the first three has been disappointing, and eyeball pressure has been reported to cause permanent, serious damage and is inadvisable. Pharmacologic equivalents of these maneuvers are more effective, but also more dangerous, particularly the longer-acting parasympathomimetics such as mecholyl. Prostigmin, 0.05 to 1 mg (0.5 mg/m²), subcutaneously, has been advocated by Nadas. Acetylcholine has a considerable advantage over mecholyl in that it is much safer. It produces a brief, vigorous effect, allowing repetition and increase of subsequent dosage. Langendorf and Pick suggest starting with 1 mg intravenously and increasing subsequent dosage by 1 mg. Atropine should be ready in a syringe in the event of cardiac arrest. We prefer intravenous phenylephrine (Neo-Synephrine) 0.10 mg initially, increasing if necessary up to the adult dose of 1 mg. Phenylephrine, a relatively pure alpha adrenergic agent, increases the systemic blood pressure, which is thought to produce a reflex vagal effect

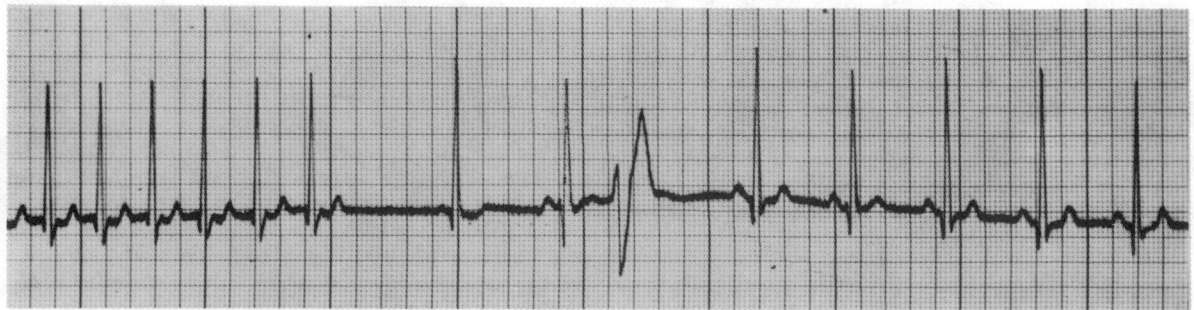

Fig. 27. A continuous recording of lead II during reversion of paroxysmal atrial tachycardia to sinus arrhythmia. At the point of interruption of the PAT, there is a long pause, followed by a beat which is probably nodal, judging from the short P-R interval. The beat following this is of sinoatrial origin, and the next beat is a ventricular premature contraction, with an associated compensatory pause. (From Guntheroth. *Pediatric Electrocardiography.* Courtesy of W. B. Saunders Co., 1965.)

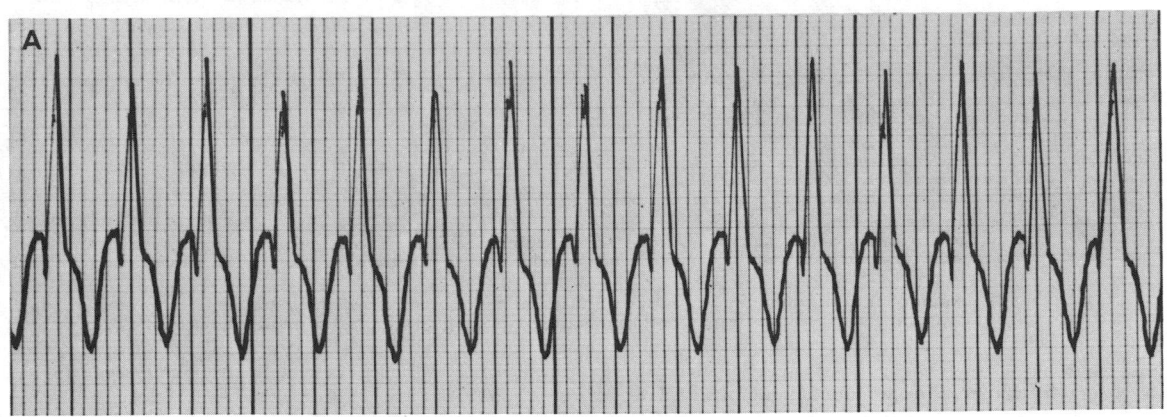

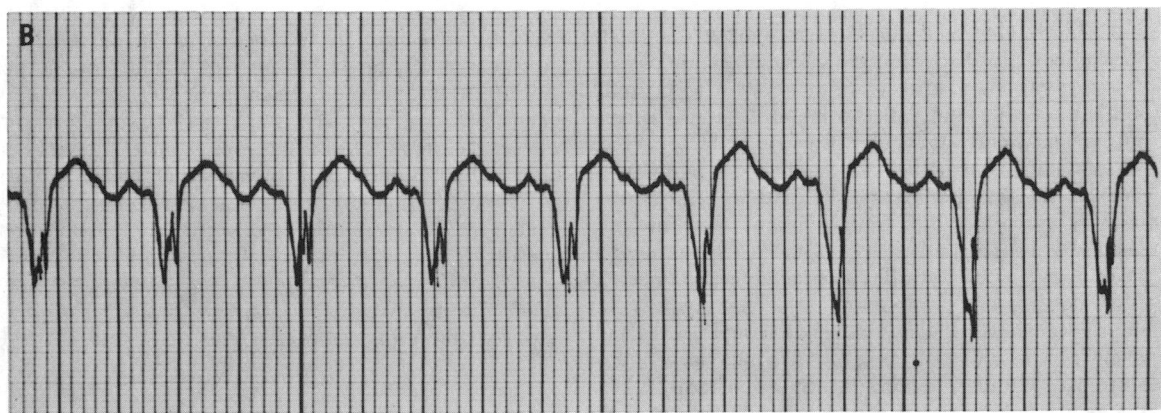

Fig. 28. **A.** Paroxysmal atrial tachycardia with aberrant ventricular conduction. The P waves are superimposed on the T waves, and the record is similar to ventricular tachycardia. **B.** The same patient after conversion to sinus rhythm, with preexcitation syndrome (Wolff-Parkinson-White). Both records are from the same EKG lead. Note the difference in ventricular conduction during the tachycardia.

through the baroreceptors (Youmans et al). Since coronary perfusion pressure is obviously maintained or increased, giving phenylephrine has an advantage over the use of parasympathomimetics, which lower the systemic pressure.

The mainstay of therapy for PAT is digitalis. For the severely affected child, intravenous digoxin may be indicated. The total digitalizing dose, intravenously, for children under 2 years is 40 μg/kg; over 2 years, 30 μg/kg; average adult dose 1.35 mg; 0.8 mg/m². In each case, one-half the total digitalizing dose may be given at once, and one-fourth is given at 6-hour intervals, twice. If the doses are given orally, the dose must be increased by multiplying by 1.7. Maintenance digoxin should be one-eighth of the digitalizing dose twice a day. Even if reversion does not occur immediately, the patient's general status almost invariably benefits because of improvement in cardiac function. Also, digitalis appears to sensitize the heart of vagal action, and repeating the maneuvers listed above under vagal stimulation will often be successful after digitalization. After success-

ful reversion of a patient, there is the problem of how long to continue digitalis. For the first attack, one month of digitalis therapy seems reasonable, but for recurrences it should be given for 6 months or more.

Frequent recurrences of PAT may be a challenging therapeutic problem. If the patient is digitalized, most of the attacks will spontaneously revert after a few hours, and rarely continue to the point of decompensation. Additional drugs may be successful in reducing the frequency of attacks. Reserpine, 0.1 mg two to three times a day, will help in some patients. Propranolol has been advocated, but its value is uncertain (Hurst and Myerburg). Quinidine has been useful and safe in moderate dosage: 6 mg/kg every 6 hours, according to Gold.

Quinidine also may be useful in the acutely ill patient that has not responded to digitalis or phenylephrine. However, pushing quinidine to toxicity is more hazardous than the use of cardioversion. If the patient appears to be deteriorating, cardioversion with DC countershock is indicated, starting with 25 watt-

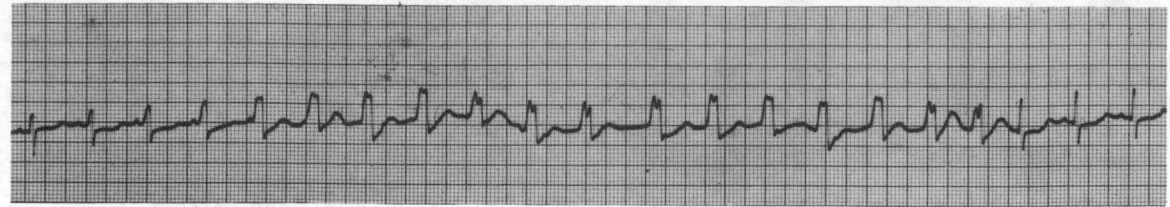

Fig. 29. Ventricular tachycardia in a 13-year-old boy. At the end and beginning of the record, sinus rhythm is present. The ventricular pacemaker captures, and there is dissociation between the P and QRS.

seconds in smaller children, measuring up to 100 for older patients. Intravenous diazepam (Valium) just prior to cardioversion is relatively safe and effective for narcosis.

Ventricular tachycardia is recognized by wide, bizarre-looking QRS complexes (Fig. 29) and, when P waves can be identified, they are seen to be independent of the ventricular complexes. The dissociation of atrial and ventricular beats is the factor which distinguishes ventricular tachycardia from PAT with preexcitation syndrome, or PAT with aberrant intraventricular conduction. Since digitalis is contraindicated in ventricular arrhythmias, establishing the mechanism of tachycardia associated with widened QRS complexes is important, and may require an esophageal lead. Records from an esophageal lead, taken at the right atrial level, produce large atrial complexes which help to determine whether there is a regular relationship between atrial and ventricular excitation. If the P waves regularly follow the QRS complexes, or are completely independent, PAT is ruled out. Ventricular tachycardia in the acute form requires prompt attention since it may be followed by ventricular fibrillation and death. Lidocaine (Xylocaine) is usually given rapidly intravenously, 1 to 2 mg/kg, or in a slow drip over a period of hours. Although side effects are fewer than with procaine amide (Pronestyl), respiratory depression or seizures can be produced. Cardioversion is not usually indicated, although DC defibrillation should be on standby in the event of fibrillation.

We have treated three patients with chronic ventricular tachycardia over a period of several years with quinidine, 6 mg/kg four times a day. They remain asymptomatic as long as the rate is kept below 150, and attempts to convert them with a variety of drugs, including propranolol, have been unsuccessful.

Nodal tachycardia may behave like either ventricular tachycardia or PAT in different patients. Digitalis frequently causes worsening, and in one of our patients, was almost catastrophic. In these patients, the P waves usually follow the QRS complexes at short intervals. If the QRS complexes are broad and slurred, there is no practical way to differentiate, with certainty, nodal tachycardia with aberrant ventricular conduction from ventricular tachycardia. However, the treatment is the same.

Slow Rates, Regular Rhythm

Sinus bradycardia in the pediatric age is relatively uncommon if the definition of a rate of 60 per minute or less is used. Such rates suggest markedly increased vagal tone, if a sinus mechanism is present. A regular bradycardia, however, may represent a *nodal rhythm* secondary to sinoatrial block (failure of impulse formation or transmission from the sinus node), or *complete AV block* (Fig. 30). The latter usually is a congenital condition, and rarely occurs as a manifestation of digitalis intoxication or rheumatic carditis, which led Grant to consider it a qualitatively different disorder from first- and second-

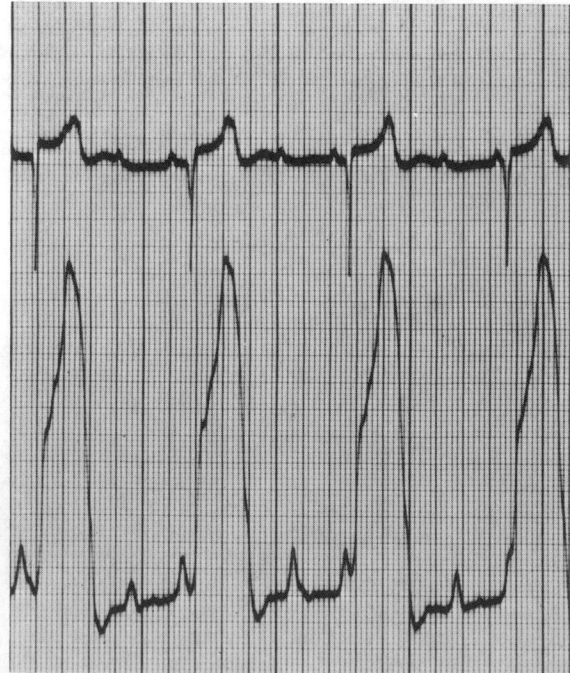

Fig. 30. Complete atrioventricular block. The pressure tracing is from the left ventricle, and demonstrates the effect of atrial contraction.

degree AV block. However, it is not unusual to see third-degree (complete) AV block occur transiently during cardiac catheterization, in the operating room under halothane anesthesia, under hypothermia, and in hypoxic states. Permanent block may occur as a serious complication of surgical correction of endocardial cushion defects and ventricular septal defects. Whereas congenital AV block rarely causes symptoms during childhood, the acquired form is attended by a significant mortality in the first few months.

There is no really satisfactory treatment for complete heart block. Isoproterenol is helpful in increasing the nodal rate, but a sustained action is difficult to obtain. Implantable pacemakers are certainly not indicated in the congenital form unless there are serious symptoms such as syncope or congestive failure. Difficulties due to unexpected battery failure, broken wires, and other failures are still all too common. The newer type of pacemaker which responds to atrial excitation is more physiologic but necessarily has more components with attendant failure risks. In our opinion, implanted, transvenous pacing is preferable to epicardial electrodes which require thoracotomy.

Stokes-Adams attacks are remarkably rare in childhood, and the great majority of syncopal or convulsive disorders are not related to arrhythmias.

Normal Rate, Regular Rhythm, Abnormal Mechanism

These are relatively subtle disorders, usually diagnosed with the electrocardiogram. *Wandering pacemaker* is generally regarded as a benign variant of normal, with a gradual shift of the P vector due to shift of the pacemaker between an upper and lower focus in the right atrium, usually accompanied by slight shortening of the P-R interval.

First-degree AV block is defined as prolonged atrioventricular conduction, with no dropped beats. Although a soft first heart sound may suggest this diagnosis, it is essentially an EKG diagnosis, based upon a prolonged P-R interval, relative to statistically defined limits for age and rate established by Ashman and Hull. The great majority of children with this condition are perfectly normal, and the significance

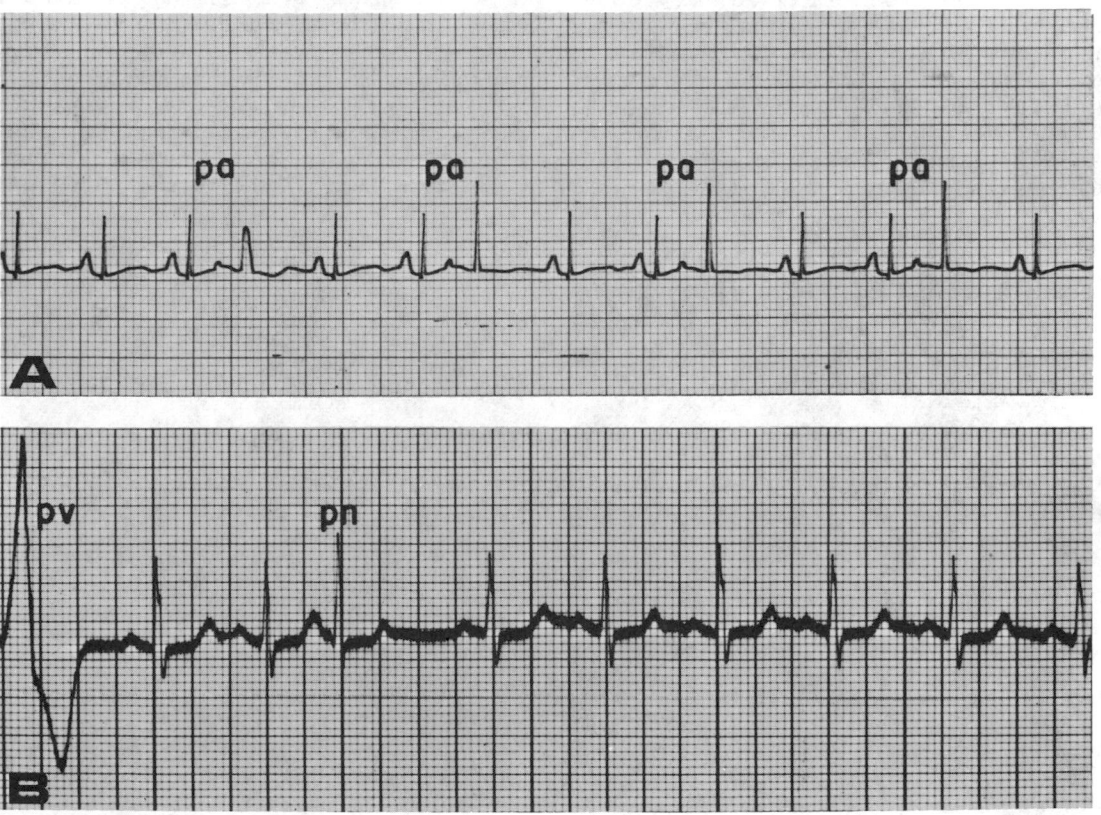

Fig. 31. A. Atrial premature contractions occurring in a patient whose dominant rhythm is sinus tachycardia. Ventricular conduction is somewhat abnormal in all four beats following the atrial premature contraction, but the abnormality is most marked in the first premature contraction. Note the lack of a compensatory pause following the premature contraction. B. The two premature contractions in this strip are ventricular (PV) and nodal (PN). Both are followed by a compensatory pause, which indicates that the nodal contraction did not conduct in a retrograde fashion to excite the atria, and therefore the following atrial contraction occurred on time, and was not conducted to the ventricle, which is the basis for the compensatory pause.

of a prolonged P-R interval depends upon its acquisition in association with a specific illness or drug. There is nothing specific about P-R prolongation in relation to rheumatic fever; similar findings occur with a variety of childhood viral disorders. On the other hand, P-R prolongation is the earliest reliable sign of digitalis effect in infants and children; this situation clearly requires a "control" EKG before digitalization.

Arrhythmias: Relatively Infrequent, Single Beats

Extrasystoles are a frequent source of complaint in adults, but children rarely seem aware of them unless physicians or parents are concerned about them. They may arise in the atrium (Fig. 31A), in the atrioventricular node, or in the ventricle (Fig. 31B). Ventricular premature beats are relatively common; probably everyone has them at one time or another during a lifetime. They may be diagnosed by the subsequent "compensatory pause," which is longer than the normal interval between beats (Fig. 31B). This pause indicates that the atria are not excited as a consequence of the ventricular extrasystole, and they respond to the next sinus beat on time. However, the ventricles are refractory to this first sinoatrial beat after the extrasystole, so that the next ventricular beat does not occur until after the second sinoatrial beat. The EKG is necessary to be certain about the origin of the extrasystole since occasionally there is retrograde conduction into the atria, which resets the rhythm and eliminates the long pause. Conversely, the ventricular extrasystole may fall exactly between two normal beats during a relatively slow sinus rhythm, and the ventricle may be responsive to the next sinus beat without pause. *Nodal extrasystoles* may or may not be associated with a compensatory pause, depending upon retrograde activation of the atria. *Atrial extrasystoles* (Fig. 31A) logically should never produce a compensatory pause unless the premature atrial contraction is not conducted by the AV node.

Although most children with extrasystoles do not have heart disease, it is wise to perform a careful history and physical exam and obtain chest radiograms and an electrocardiogram. In addition, vigorous exercise should be monitored by apical pulse or EKG; an increased frequency of extrasystoles suggests heart disease, whereas in the benign cases the extrasystoles will either disappear or remain the same in frequency. Treatment is rarely necessary. If necessary, quinidine is the favored drug in modest doses.

Interference dissociation may resemble nodal or atrial extrasystoles on auscultation. If the sinus pacemaker is unusually slow, the node may take over as pacemaker. The AV node may "escape" for one or two beats if there is an unusually long interval between sinoatrial beats (Fig. 32A). Nodal escape is a relatively benign disorder. However, if there is nodal tachycardia, the AV node may become the dominant pacemaker. In that case, a transient increase in sinoatrial rate may permit the sinoatrial pacemaker to interfere by capturing the ventricles for one or two beats and the resulting arrhythmia is

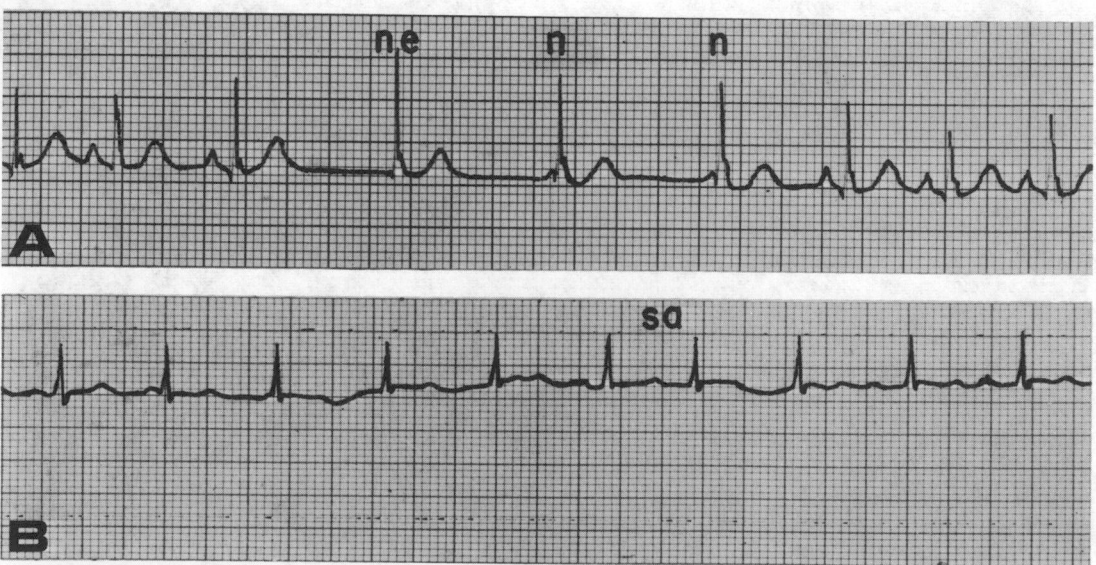

Fig. 32. A. Sinus arrhythmia with nodal escape (ne) which is maintained as nodal rhythm for three beats, and followed by a return to a sinus pacemaker. An example of atrioventricular dissociation, without block. B. A basically nodal rhythm with atrial interference occurring at the seventh beat, with return to a nodal rhythm immediately after the one conducted sinoatrial contraction (sa). An example of interference dissociation.

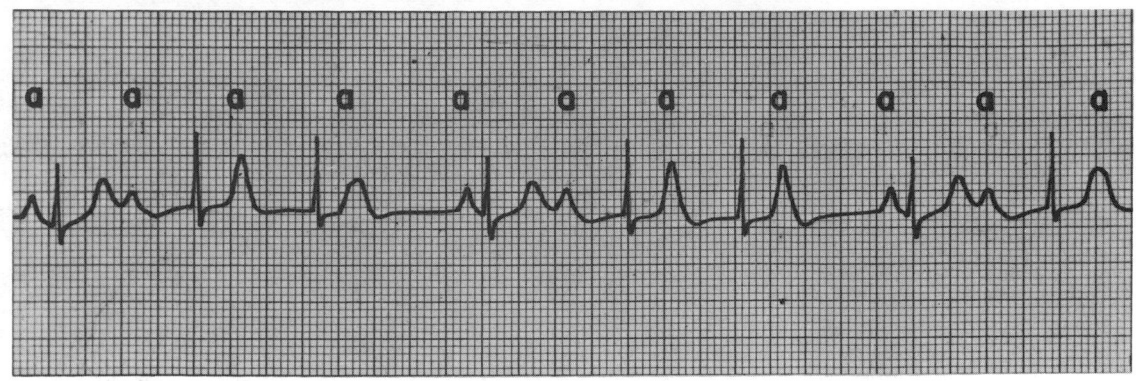

Fig. 33. Second–degree AV block, with progressive prolongation of AV conduction (Wenckebach phenomena). The fourth and eighth atrial contractions are "dropped," with no ventricular response.

interference dissociation (Fig. 32B). This arrhythmia is not threatening per se, but it frequently indicates a significant cardiac disorder such as acute rheumatic carditis. It is also seen in digitalis intoxication, although in association with prolonged AV conduction. Treatment is directed at the underlying disorder.

Occasional dropped beats are due either to sinoatrial block or pause, or more commonly, partial AV block, in particular, Wenckebach's phenomenon (Fig. 33). The former is benign, but the latter is almost invariably a sign of cardiac disease. Wenckebach's phenomenon represents cycles of increasingly delayed AV conduction finally resulting in failure to conduct one sinoatrial beat; the resulting pause apparently allows recovery of the AV node, and the succeeding beat demonstrates a relatively normal P-R interval, and the cycle begins again. An additional characteristic is the successive shortening of the P-R interval starting after the dropped atrial beat. This arrhythmia may be suspected by auscultation, since the varying interval between atrial and ventricular contractions causes variations in the first heart sound, the shorter the P-R the louder the sound. Treatment of the arrhythmia is unnecessary, but the underlying disorder usually deserves careful attention.

REGULAR ARRHYTHMIAS. *Sinus arrhythmia* is the rule, rather than the exception, in infants and children at rest. With longer periods of observation, particularly during sleep, Morgan and co-workers found sinus arrhythmia in almost every infant. The degree of arrhythmia present in normal children may be quite marked.

Bigeminy is an unusual arrhythmia in childhood. The common occurrence of bigeminy in adults as a sign of digitalis intoxication probably is related to the empirical association of bigeminy with atrial fibrillation. Atrial fibrillation is a rare condition in the pediatric age group and bigeminy is only rarely a useful sign of digitalis intoxication in children. (Guntheroth, 1964). Bigeminy usually consists of coupled ventricular extrasystoles although nodal and atrial forms occur. Symptoms are rarely a problem in children, but the association of this disorder with serious disorders which may lead to ventricular tachycardia may warrant treatment with quinidine.

IRREGULAR ARRHYTHMIA. The only two causes of totally irregular pulse are *atrial flutter* with varying

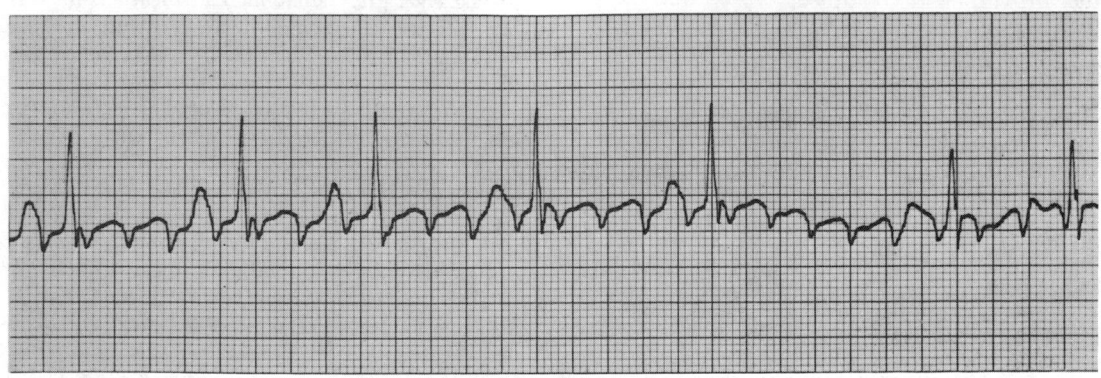

Fig. 34. Atrial flutter, with varying AV block.

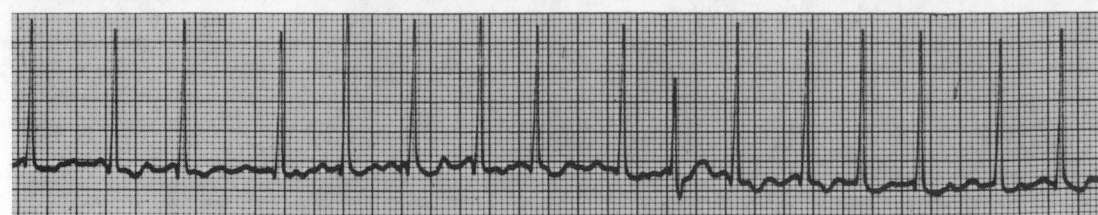

Fig. 35. Atrial fibrillation with rapid ventricular response. Note the marked irregularity of ventricular response.

AV block (Fig. 34) and *atrial fibrillation* (Fig. 35). As noted above, both are remarkably rare in children. Atrial fibrillation is generally associated with marked enlargement of the atria, as found in severe rheumatic heart disease, or Ebstein's anomaly. The exact mechanism of this arrhythmia is still being debated, although Scherf has presented very convincing evidence that "circus movement" is unlikely as an explanation for either atrial fibrillation or flutter, and argues for a single focus of rapid depolarization. In some instances, however, circus movement seems well documented. Digitalis is universally accepted as the drug of choice. The drug is pushed to the point of what would otherwise be a sign of toxicity, partial AV block, in order to slow the ventricular response. It seems prudent to use a short-acting digitalis preparation such as digoxin. Reversion to sinus rhythm by means of quinidine or external countershock is usually temporary unless the arrhythmia is recently acquired or unless surgical relief of the underlying lesion has been accomplished. Relative small shocks are necessary, 25 watt-seconds or even less, preferably delivered immediately after the QRS, from a synchronized DC discharge (Lown). Quinidine, at least for a day prior to conversion, is recommended. **NO PULSE.** The ultimate in serious arrhythmias, no apical pulse, may represent either *cardiac arrest* or *ventricular fibrillation*. The latter requires defibrillation with external countershock, usually 50 watt-seconds or more. Both conditions require support by closed chest massage and ventilation until the nature of the arrhythmia is confirmed.

REFERENCES

Ashman, R., and Hull, E. Essentials of Electrocardiography. New York, The Macmillan Co., 1941.

Gold, H. Quinidine in Disorders of the Heart. New York, Paul B. Hoeber, Inc., 1950.

Grant, R. P. Clinical Electrocardiography. New York, McGraw-Hill Book Co., 1957.

Guntheroth, W. G. Digitalis in pediatrics. Pediat. Dig., 6:41, 1964.

——— Pediatric Electrocardiography. Philadelphia, W. B. Saunders Co., 1965.

Hurst, J. W., and Myerburg, R. J. Cardiac arrhythmias: evolving concepts. Mod. Conc. Cardiovasc. Dis., 37:79, 1968.

Langendorf, R., and Pick, A. Cardiac arrhythmias in infants and children. Pediat. Clin. N. Amer., Feb., 1954, p. 215.

Lown, B. Cardioversion of arrhythmias. Mod. Conc. Cardiovasc. Dis., 33:863, 1964.

——— Ehrlich, L., Lipschultz, B., and Blake, J. Effect of digitalis in patients receiving reserpine. Circulation, 24:1185, 1961.

Morgan, B. C., Bloom, R. S., and Guntheroth, W. G. Cardiac arrhythmias in premature infants. Pediatrics, 35:658, 1965.

Nadas, A. S. Pediatric Cardiology, 2nd ed. Philadelphia, W. B. Saunders Co., 1963.

Scherf, D., and Schott, A. Extrasystoles and Allied Arrhythmias. New York, Grune and Stratton, Inc., 1953.

Weinstein, L. Cardiovascular manifestations in some of the common infectious diseases. Mod. Conc. Cardiovasc. Dis., 23:229, 1954.

Youmans, W. B., Goodman, M. J., and Gould, J. Neosynephrine in treatment of paroxysmal supraventricular tachycardia. Amer. Heart J., 37:359, 1949.

20.8
PATHOPHYSIOLOGY OF CONGENITAL HEART DISEASE

JULIEN I. E. HOFFMAN

Congenital anomalies of the heart and great vessels may be classified in many ways, depending upon which aspects of anatomy and physiology are emphasized. Purely anatomic classifications have some merit because the anatomic abnormalities may give rise to some of the clinical features and indicate what needs to be done during surgical correction of the lesion. However, other aspects of diagnosis and treatment are not well served by this type of classification because, despite the large number of anatomic abnormalities which can occur, there are only a limited number of pathophysiologic responses. It is therefore possible for lesions with quite different anatomic features to resemble each other clinically and physiologically; for this reason a classification based on both anatomic and physiologic features will be used here. There may, of course, be overlapping in any classification because a single lesion may be classified in more than one group or because a patient may have several lesions which are in different groups.

Obstructive Lesions

A congenital obstruction to the flow of blood may occur in any part of the cardiovascular system, certain sites being affected more often than others. If the obstruction is complete because a portion of the heart has not developed, it is termed an "atresia": for example, in mitral atresia there is no passage from left atrium to left ventricle; in pulmonary atresia, none from right ventricle to pulmonary artery. Because of these major abnormalities, blood has to flow through abnormal pathways; these complex lesions will be discussed later (p. 1379). If the obstruction is incomplete, blood can flow along normal pathways; the basic anatomy of the cardiovascular system is normal, but an unusually high pressure proximal to the obstruction is needed to force blood through the narrowed region. There is thus an increased pressure load on the involved portions of the heart.

In general the sites of partial obstruction are similar on the right and left sides of the heart and can be listed in orderly fashion by following the flow of blood into and through the heart.

1. There may be partial obstruction near or at the entry of the great veins into their respective atria. A diaphragm with a small hole in it has been found high in the inferior cava. On the left side similar diaphragms or narrowed (stenotic) segments have been found in one or more pulmonary veins near their entry into the left atrium. These are all rare obstructions.

2. There could be some obstruction to flow of blood through the atria, although this is almost unheard of in the right atrium. Congenital tumors are a possible cause. Similar tumors might occur in the left atrium, although a diaphragm which divides the left atrium into upper and lower chambers connected by a small orifice is commoner. This lesion is rare and is called *cor triatriatum.*

3. Flow of blood from atrium to ventricle through an atrioventricular valve may be impeded by partial fusion of the valve cusps (*tricuspid* or *mitral stenosis*). Both of these are rare as congenital lesions but occur as consequences of rheumatic fever.

4. Obstruction to flow of blood in the body of the ventricles is uncommon, although abnormal muscle bundles in the right ventricular body dividing it into inflow and outflow portions have been reported.

5. All the lesions referred to so far have been rare. By contrast, partial obstruction to flow of blood out of the ventricles is very common, due to narrowing in the outflow tract or semilunar valves. Thus in the right ventricle, outflow tract obstruction may be due to hypertrophy of the infundibular muscle, to a fibrous or fibromuscular ring below the pulmonary valve; rarely it may be due to a valvelike structure which during systole is pushed into the outflow tract or to an aneurysm or muscle mass projecting from the ventricular septum into the right ventricular outflow tract. None of these is common as an isolated lesion, but they are frequently associated with ventricular septal defects. On the other hand, partial fusion of the pulmonary valve cusps (valvar pulmonic stenosis) is one of the common congenital heart lesions.

The outflow tract of the left ventricle may be obstructed by an abnormal mitral valve leaflet which balloons into the outflow in systole, by muscular hypertrophy of the ventricular septum, or by subvalvar fibrous or fibromuscular rings or fibrous diaphragms. Subvalvar stenosis is more common as an isolated lesion in the left ventricle than in the right. Partial fusion of the aortic valve cusps (valvar aortic stenosis) is also common.

6. The arteries leaving each ventricle may be narrowed beyond the semilunar valves. There may be one or several stenotic areas in the pulmonary arteries; mild stenoses are common, severe ones unusual. On the left side the aorta may be constricted just above the aortic valves (supravalvar aortic stenosis), narrowed for a fairly long segment of its ascending and arch portion (hypoplastic aortic arch), or constricted somewhere in the arch or descending aorta (coarctation of the aorta).

7. Should the pulmonary or systemic vascular beds have an abnormally high resistance to flow, there would be a pressure load on the right and left ventricles respectively. This rarely happens as an isolated congenital lesion but may occur in the pulmonary vascular bed in association with other congenital heart lesions—e.g., large communications between the systemic and pulmonary circulations.

Physiologic Effects of a Pressure Overload

LEFT VENTRICLE. The effects of acute pressure load on the left ventricle can be studied experimentally by partially occluding the ascending aorta. As soon as the aorta has been narrowed, the systolic pressure rises in the left ventricle and its stroke volume falls, probably because at that instant the left ventricle cannot produce enough energy to raise pressure high enough to overcome the obstruction. Therefore the amount of blood left in the ventricle at the end of systole (residual or end-systolic volume) is increased. In the next ventricular diastole the left ventricle fills normally from the left atrium, so that at the end of diastole the left ventricular volume is greater than it was in the preceding beat. Its muscle fibers are therefore slightly stretched and, as shown first by Frank and by Starling, the ventricle can produce more contractile energy and do more work. Diastolic inflow into the left ventricle will exceed its outflow for several beats, thereby causing more ventricular dilation. As a result, more and more contractile energy can be made available; ultimately an equilibrium is reached with the normal stroke volume being ejected at a higher systolic pressure by a ventricle with increased end-diastolic and end-systolic volumes.

One of the immediate results of ventricular dilation is a rise in tension in its wall, much as tension rises in an elastic band which is stretched. In an intact heart this increased tension is reflected by a raised pressure at the end of diastole. Because the relationship of fiber length to end-diastolic pressure is not linear there is at first a small rise in end-diastolic pressure for marked increases in fiber length (or ventricular volume); subsequently, with further increase in fiber length, there is a disproportionately great rise ·in end-diastolic pressure. This may be stated differently by saying that as the ventricle dilates it becomes less distensible.

In addition to this primary method of increasing contractile force there are at least three other mechanisms which may come into action. There is an intrinsic mechanism whereby cardiac muscle fibers, after initial distension, can somehow produce more contractile energy from shorter fiber lengths and with lower end-diastolic pressures; the importance of this mechanism in the intact animal is not known. Secondly, increased sympathetic nervous stimulation of the heart produces greater contractile force and rate of ejection, shortens systole, and lowers end-diastolic pressure. Finally, after an obstruction has been present for some time there is hypertrophy of the myocardium; the increased muscle mass allows more cardiac work to be done without marked ventricular dilation and high end-diastolic pressures. Should the obstruction be too severe or the compensating mechanisms fail, then the left ventricle will dilate and its end-diastolic pressure will rise excessively.

LEFT ATRIUM. Once the left ventricle has become less distensible and has a high end-diastolic pressure, it obstructs the outflow of blood from the left atrium just as if there were mitral stenosis or a left atrial tumor. The left atrial response is similar to that described for the left ventricle—i.e., it dilates, hypertrophies, and probably has increased sympathetic nervous stimulation. Also, like the left ventricle, its systolic pressure rises to help overcome the obstruction, and later its diastolic and mean pressures also rise.

PULMONARY VEINS. When either the left atrial pressure is raised or there is an anatomic obstruction to pulmonary venous drainage, the pulmonary venous pressure rises, the increased tension in the vein walls being due to stretching of muscle and elastic fibers. With this rise in pressure there is increased transudation of fluid through the capillary walls into the interstitial spaces of the lung, from where it passes into the alveoli or the lymphatics. Should the lymphatic drainage be inadequate, fluid will accumulate in the alveoli.

An increased pulmonary vascular resistance is commonly associated with a high pulmonary venous pressure. The mechanisms producing this effect are not clear, although reflexes from the distended left atrium or pulmonary veins, changes due to pulmonary

venous hypoxia, or mechanical compression of small vessels by edema fluid are the most likely factors. With the high pulmonary vascular resistance, pulmonary arterial pressure will rise and there will be a pressure overload on the right ventricle.

RIGHT VENTRICLE. Whether the pressure load is due to a high pulmonary vascular resistance or to obstruction of the right ventricular outflow tract, the response of the right ventricle is similar to that described for the left ventricle. Right ventricular systolic pressure will rise, some dilation will be followed by hypertrophy, sympathetic nervous stimulation of the myocardium will increase and, if the load is too great, the end-diastolic pressure will rise.

RIGHT ATRIUM. Decreased distensibility of the right ventricle with a raised end-diastolic pressure or obstruction at the tricuspid valve places a pressure load on the right atrium which responds as did the left atrium. When right atrial pressure rises, blood is dammed back in the systemic veins until they are sufficiently stretched for their pressure to rise; peripheral organs, particularly the liver and spleen, will become congested and perhaps enlarged, and increased transudation of fluid into interstitial tissues may cause edema.

CLINICAL FEATURES. The clinical features of pressure overloading of each part of the cardiovascular system can be understood from what has been described. The left ventricular response is manifested by left ventricular hypertrophy, which can be inferred from a slow, forceful heave of the left ventricular apex. Hypertrophy by itself does not significantly enlarge the heart, for the increased wall thickness may only be a few millimeters, but if there is associated dilation then the left ventricular apex will be displaced to the left and downward. The heart may or may not be enlarged on x-ray, although even if not enlarged there may be a slightly more rounded left ventricular contour than is normally seen. There is no specific change in the first or second heart sounds due to left ventricular hypertrophy, but a third heart sound may appear; if there is systemic hypertension, aortic closure will be loud. Electrocardiographic manifestations will be increased left, inferior, and posterior forces on the vector or scalar electrocardiograms. The mean frontal QRS axis, it should be noted, remains normal with pure left ventricular hypertrophy, since an inferiorly placed ventricle with a normal sequence of depolarization cannot produce the left superior axis which is commonly spoken of as left axis deviation.

Left atrial pressure loading may be inferred clinically by hearing a well-marked fourth heart sound, which suggests more forceful contraction by a hypertrophied atrium. Electrocardiographically there may be a widely notched P wave in lead II and in leads V_5 and V_6, and the P wave in V_1 may be enlarged and biphasic or negative. On x-ray the typical signs of left atrial dilatation may be seen if the atrium is sufficiently enlarged.

An increased pulmonary venous pressure may be

manifested in many ways. With congestion of the pulmonary veins and an increased amount of interstitial fluid the lungs become stiffer (less compliant). Resting ventilation is then achieved by faster rate and shallower depth, thus producing the tachypnea so common in left ventricular failure. Should exertion require more ventilation, the rate of breathing will increase but a greater tidal volume may also be needed; to achieve a greater tidal volume with stiffer lungs requires greater contraction of the diaphragm and intercostal muscles so that there will be subjective symptoms (dyspnea) and, particularly in infants, retraction of the supra-, inter-, and subcostal regions. In some people this chain of events is also associated with diffuse bronchospasm, so that expiration becomes prolonged and wheezing; if, in addition, there are also increased bronchial secretions, there will be rhonchi, and the clinical picture will resemble closely that due to bronchiolitis or bronchial asthma with parenchymal infection.

Right ventricular hypertrophy manifests itself by a forceful, slow lift felt along the left sternal border and behind the xiphisternum, and perhaps an associated tapping left ventricular apex beat if the left ventricle is normal. If there is associated pulmonary hypertension, the pulmonary artery may be felt to pulsate in the third interspace at the left sternal border, the pulmonic component of the second heart sound will be accentuated, and there may be a systolic click at the base. The right ventricle will appear enlarged on x-ray only if dilated; even if the heart is not enlarged the apex may be tipped up. If there is pulmonary hypertension the main pulmonary artery may be enlarged. Electrocardiographically there may be right axis deviation of the mean frontal QRS axis, the right precordial leads will show tall R waves or perhaps a qR complex, and sometimes there may be T wave changes consisting of upright T waves at an age when they should be inverted, or deep asymmetric inversions of the right-sided T waves, which have been described as a strain pattern.

Right atrial pressure loading reflects itself in perhaps a right atrial fourth heart sound, some dilation of the right atrium on x-ray, and tall peaked P waves in leads II and V_1 of the electrocardiogram. Should the systemic venous pressure be elevated, then the characteristic enlargement of liver and spleen and edema of the soft tissues may be found. At times the mean venous pressure is not raised but a large "a" wave may be seen.

It should be noted that a raised pulmonary venous pressure is more commonly the result of the left ventricular failure than of primary obstruction of the left atrium or the pulmonary veins. Similarly pressure loading of the right atrium is usually the result of right ventricular failure. Furthermore, right ventricular pressure loading is frequently the result of pulmonary hypertension due to a raised pulmonary vascular resistance which, in turn, follows left ventricular failure; the dictum that left ventricular failure is the most common cause of right ventricular failure

is as true in children as in adults. However, it is not unusual to get left ventricular failure without right ventricular failure, and the two must be diagnosed independently. Finally, since a left ventricular pressure overload, as in coarctation of the aorta, can cause a right ventricular pressure overload via a raised pulmonary vascular resistance, it is possible for the clinical picture to be dominated by the right ventricular signs; electrocardiographic signs of "pure" right ventricular hypertrophy may be seen when the only lesion is on the left side, especially in young infants.

Left-to-Right Shunts and Regurgitant Lesions

A left-to-right shunt is said to occur when oxygenated blood recirculates through the lungs (i.e., bypasses the peripheral tissues) because of an abnormal communication between the greater and lesser circulations. Sometimes left-to-right shunts are found in complex malformations, such as transposition of the great arteries, which also have right-to-left shunts, but these will not be considered further in this section.

Left-to-right shunts may be classified anatomically by noting where each portion of the greater circulation may join the lesser circulation:

A. Connection between the aorta and the lesser circulation
  1. To pulmonary artery:
     Patent ductus arteriosus
     Aortopulmonary window
     Anomalous origin of the left coronary artery
  2. To right ventricle or
  3. To right atrium:
     Fistula from sinus of Valsalva
     Coronary arteriovenous fistula
  4. To systemic veins:
     Arteriovenous fistula
B. Connection between left ventricle and the lesser circulation
  1. To right ventricle:
     Ventricular septal defect
  2. To right atrium:
     Left ventricular-right atrial communication
C. Connection between left atrium and lesser circulation
  1. Incompetent foramen ovale
  2. Atrial septal defect—ostium secudum type, with or without partial anomalous pulmonary venous connection
  3. Atrial septal defect—ostium primum type
D. Connection between pulmonary veins and lesser circulation
  1. Partial anomalous pulmonary venous connection without an atrial septal defect

There may be combinations of any of these lesions.

The physiologic effects and clinical features of many of the lesions with left-to-right shunts are similar to those noted in regurgitant lesions. A *regurgitant lesion* may be defined as one in which blood ejected from an atrium or ventricle returns to that chamber through incompetent semilunar or atrioventricular valves. Thus it is possible to have aortic, mitral, pulmonic, and tricuspid regurgitation as congenital lesions, although they are all much commoner as acquired lesions. In addition, blood may return from the aorta or its branches to left atrium or ventricle through fistulas, and these lesions will also be considered here.

GENERAL PHYSIOLOGY AND CLINICAL FEATURES. While the exact site of the defect determines some of its clinical features, specific diagnoses often have to be made or confirmed by cardiac catheterization and angiocardiography. Many of these lesions resemble each other closely, and their effects depend more on the size of the left-to-right shunt and on which ventricle bears the load than on the specific lesion present. Shunts from the aorta to the pulmonary artery cause the left ventricle to put out greater stroke and minute volumes; there is never a volume overload of the right ventricle, but should the pulmonary arterial pressure rise there will be a pressure load on the right ventricle. Similar effects may follow aortic or mitral regurgitation or left-sided arterioventricular or arterioatrial fistulas. Shunts from the aorta or left ventricle to the right ventricle or atrium produce the same effects as those just mentioned but, in addition, cause an increase in right ventricular volume work. By contrast, shunts between the atria or from pulmonary veins to right atrium cause an increased volume load of the right but not the left ventricle; less commonly they may also increase right ventricular pressure work. Right ventricular volume overload may also result from pulmonic or tricuspid regurgitation.

The effects of an acute or chronic volume load on the left ventricle are similar to those noted with a pressure load, but with certain important exceptions. The primary stimulus to dilation of the ventricle is the increased amount of blood which has to be ejected, and the stretching of the muscle fibers allows the ventricle to eject a larger than normal stroke volume at normal pressure. There is more dilation with volume loads as compared with pressure overload. Clinically the left ventricle will be dilated and thus enlarged to the left. Its apex beat will be forceful, but unlike the precordial activity with a pressure load, the left ventricle will feel very hyperactive (if the left-to-right shunt is large). If there is much pulmonary hypertension there will also be the signs of a right ventricular pressure load. Third and fourth heart sounds due to rapid left ventricular inflow in early diastole and to left atrial hypertrophy respectively may be heard. The types of murmurs present will depend on the exact lesion, but when there are large left-to-right shunts, marked mitral regurgitation, or aortoatrial shunting, there is usually a low-frequency rumbling middiastolic murmur at or near the apex. This murmur is due to increased blood flow through the mitral valve in diastole. A similar diastolic murmur may be heard in marked aortic regurgitation and is then called an Austin Flint murmur. It is thought to be due to either increased turbulence of blood flow through a normal mitral valve into a dilated left ventricle or to vibration of the aortic cusp of the mitral valve as it is moved between diastolic streams of blood entering the left ventricle from the left atrium and from the aorta as a regurgitant jet.

Dilation and hyperactivity of the left ventricle and atrium will be noted on fluoroscopy, and additionally there may be right ventricular dilation. An increased pulmonary blood flow appears on fluoroscopy as pulsation of the pulmonary arteries extending out into the lung fields, and on both fluoroscopy and x-ray the pulmonary vessels will be wider than normal and will be prominent all the way out to the periphery of the lung fields. This sign, it should be realized, is indirect. It implies that when there is an increased pulmonary arterial blood flow the pulmonary arteries will be dilated. This is often true, but should the pulmonary arterial pressures be low and the arteries relatively undistensible, a large blood flow could take place without any vascular dilation. This can be understood if one considers that increased flow through a rigid pipe could occur without any widening of the pipe. Occasionally these conditions are met, so that a large pulmonary blood flow occurs without there being any significant vascular dilation.

Should there be marked pulmonary venous congestion the pulmonary veins may also be seen to be distended, and pulmonary edema will show up as hazy opacification, often most marked in the perihilar regions; at times there will be an air bronchogram. These findings are typical of pulmonary edema whether there is a large left-to-right shunt or not.

Electrocardiographic signs of left ventricular dilation without hypertrophy are scarce. Alterations in the T waves in the left precordial leads have been described but are not specific.

A right ventricular volume overload occurs when there is a left-to-right shunt between the atria, between the pulmonary veins and the right atrium, and also with pulmonic or tricuspid regurgitation. It also occurs in combination with left ventricular volume overload when a shunt from the aorta or left ventricle passes into the right ventricle or atrium. The physiologic responses and adaptations to acute and chronic volume overloads are identical with those in the left ventricle and atrium, but in general there can be a large right-sided volume load with little or no rise in right ventricular end-diastolic pressure. This may be due to the right ventricular wall being thinner and more distensible than that of the left ventricle so that more distension is needed to achieve any given end-diastolic pressure. It could also be due to the fact that the right ventricle normally ejects into a low-pressure system; this would be expected to allow the ventricle to empty more completely by the end of systole so that when there is a massive inflow in diastole the end-diastolic volume is not as great as it would have been had the end-diastolic volume been large. If the ventricle does become overstretched or if its distensibility falls, then right-sided end-diastolic and atrial pressures rise and systemic venous pressure rises; this increased pressure may be detected by careful examination of the neck veins, by hepatomegaly, and by peripheral edema.

The clinical signs of a right-sided volume load are a hyperactive right ventricular impulse behind the left sternal border and xiphoid process and (in pretricuspid shunts or tricuspid regurgitation) a rumbling middiastolic murmur best heard at the right or left lower sternal border due to increased flow through the tricuspid valve in diastole. On radiologic examination the right ventricle is dilated and hyperactive, and the signs of increased pulmonary blood flow will be present if there is a large left-to-right shunt. On the electrocardiogram there will often be right axis deviation and clockwise rotation, and the right-sided chest leads often show an rSr' or rSR' pattern.

The size of the left-to-right shunt depends upon the resistance to flow from the greater to the lesser circulation, and this resistance may occur at the communication between the two circulations, in the small pulmonary vessels or, for shunts into the right atrium and systemic veins, in the right ventricle. At birth the small pulmonary arteries of the full-term infant have thick walls and narrow lumina, thereby offering high resistance to flow through them. Pulmonary arterial pressure is therefore high, almost as high as in the aorta, so that no matter how large the communication between the two circulations, the left-to-right shunt will be small. At this stage there will be little or no evidence of extra volume work done by either ventricle or of excess blood flow through the lungs, and there may or may not be a significant murmur. After birth the muscle in the media of the small pulmonary arteries begins to involute so that these vessels come to have a thin wall and a wide lumen. The rate of involution varies widely and may be slower when there is pulmonary hypertension due to a large communication between greater and lesser circulations or to hypoxia; without these, the resistance falls to near normal within two or four weeks after birth. At this time the amount of left-to-right shunting will depend on the size of the defect and, for atrial and systemic venous shunts, on the right ventricular distensibility. If the defect is small, thus offering high resistance to flow through it, the left-to-right shunt will always be small, and though there may be characteristic murmurs, there will be little or no evidence of a volume load on either ventricle or of an increased pulmonary blood flow.

If the defect is large, however, the falling pulmonary vascular resistance permits an increasing left-to-right shunt. As mentioned before, the right ventricle is seldom affected by a large left-to-right shunt. The left ventricle can sustain a moderate volume load without an excessive rise in end-diastolic pressure. The patient will then have evidence of a hyperkinetic left ventricle with an increased pulmonary blood flow, but at rest there will be only minor symptoms, or none at all. Exertion, however, calling for a greater blood flow and thus causing a rise in left ventricular end-diastolic pressure may produce the characteristic tachycardia, tachypnea, and dyspnea. If the defect is very large the left-to-right shunt will be great, and overt left ventricular failure may occur.

The time course of these changes varies from patient to patient, but since the lowering of pulmonary vascular resistance takes some weeks it is rare to find frank heart failure from uncomplicated left-to-right shunts in the first month of life. From then until six months is a period of high risk of heart failure, precipitated not only by the fall in pulmonary vascular resistance but also by the postnatal drop in hemoglobin, by infections, and by the increased demands for blood flow as the child becomes more active. In premature infants the time course may be modified because at birth the pulmonary arterioles have not yet developed their characteristic thick muscular walls. Therefore the pulmonary vascular resistance is not very high at birth and soon falls to very low levels after involution has begun. If there is a large defect a big left-to-right shunt can occur early, and overt heart failure may occur within the first two months after birth; the anemia of prematurity and the increased susceptibility to infection are probably additional factors in the early onset of heart failure.

When the communication is between the atria or between the pulmonary veins and the right atrium the amount of left-to-right shunt depends not only on the size of the defect and the pulmonary vascular resistance but also on the distensibility of the right ventricle. Since there is no high pressure forcing blood into the right atrium, the amount of blood shunted into the right ventricle depends on the ease with which the ventricle can be distended in diastole. At birth the two ventricles have equally thick walls and are probably equally distensible; the right ventricle cannot accept large amounts of blood. As time goes by, the left ventricular wall becomes much thicker than that of the right ventricle, so that more blood can be accepted by the more distensible right ventricle. An analogy would be blowing air into a Y tube connected to two balloons, one thin-walled and the other inelastic; more air would go into the thinner and more distensible balloon. For a large left-to-right shunt to occur with these lesions, there must be a large communication, low resistance to filling of the right ventricle, and a low pulmonary vascular resistance. The need for this combination probably explains in part why large left-to-right shunts and heart failure rarely occur in young children with these lesions.

PULMONARY VASCULAR DISEASE. Sometimes a sequence of histologic changes narrows or occludes the small pulmonary arteries and causes a rise in pulmonary vascular resistance. The earliest alteration (stage I) is thickening of the medial muscle and slight narrowing of the lumen; it occurs after 2 months of age whenever there is pulmonary hypertension from any cause. Then, in stage II, the intima becomes thickened and cellular, and more vascular narrowing occurs; this change is seldom seen in the first year of life but is common after the second year. In stage III the intima becomes acellular and hyaline, the lumen becomes narrower and may be partly or completely occluded by thrombosis. Stages IV and V are denoted by the addition of plexiform and angiomatoid lesions and stage VI (rarely seen) is defined by the onset of acute arteritis.

These changes are common with pulmonary hypertension and a big pulmonary blood flow, for example, with a large ventricular septal defect or patent ductus arteriosus, truncus arteriosus, transposition of the great arteries with a large ventricular defect or tricuspid atresia, or atrioventricularis communis. They may also occur without an excessive pulmonary blood flow, as in mitral stenosis, or in transposition of the great arteries without a ventricular septal defect and without severe pulmonary hypertension. Finally, similar changes without the medial hypertrophy of stage I occur with large atrial septal defects, though seldom under 20 years of age.

There appear to be at least two mechanisms involved in these changes. The medial hypertrophy is a response to maintained pulmonary hypertension and is similar to the work hypertrophy seen in response to an increased load by cardiac and skeletal muscle or the smooth muscle of the bowel or ureter. The intimal changes are probably due to damage from excessive shearing forces created by rapid flow of blood past the stationary arterial wall. Therefore the earliest and most severe vascular damage occurs in lesions like big ventricular defects where the medial hypertrophy narows the small arteries so that the large pulmonary blood flow creates high flow velocities and great shearing forces. Similar flows through wide arteries, as in atrial septal defects, have lower velocities, lesser shearing forces, and so produce damage more slowly.

Right-to-Left Shunts

These are said to occur when blood bypasses the lungs so that unoxygenated blood enters the systemic arterial circulation. By convention, impaired ventilation-perfusion relationships in the lungs are not included under this heading, although they certainly cause arterial desaturation and have to be considered in the differential diagnosis. The lesions found in this group can be the most complex in all congenital heart disease, and often multiple anomalies occur in the same heart. Nevertheless the main groups of anomalies which may be seen can be classified as follows:

A. Communication between the greater and lesser circulations; high resistance to flow at some site in the lesser circulation; normal connections of great vessels to the heart.

In this group the communication between the two circulations is a patent ductus arteriosus or aortopulmonary window, a ventricular septal defect or an atrial septal defect of the secundum or primum type, or even a patent foramen ovale. A left-to-right shunt does not occur, because high resistance to flow through the right side raises right-sided resistances and pressures so much that some blood passes through the defect into the left side. Thus a greatly raised pulmonary vascular resistance will cause a right-to-left shunt through any of the defects, and so will marked peripheral pulmonary arterial stenosis. Severe valvar, subvalvar, or infundibular stenosis, on the other hand, will not cause a right-to-left shunt through a patent ductus arteriosus which is distal to the obstruction but will cause right-to-left shunts through ventricular or atrial defects which are proximal. The shunt at ventricular level is easily understood because the high outflow resistance causes the right ventricular systolic pressure to rise to systemic levels, and it is easier for some blood to go through the defect into the left side than to go through the obstructed region. The reason for the right-to-left shunt when an atrial opening is present is that when there has been a sufficient pressure load on the right ventricle to make it less distensible and raise its end-diastolic pressure, the right atrial pressure will rise and force blood into the left atrium. Finally, any impairment of atrial emptying like tricuspid stenosis or Ebstein's disease, or any cause of a raised atrial pressure such as gross tricuspid regurgitation, will permit a right-to-left shunt through an atrial opening but not through more distal defects.

Two anatomic subgroups require further description; in one, the communication between the two circulations is unusually large, while in the other there is an atresia, or complete obstruction to blood flow.

In some patients the atrial or ventricular septum is almost completely missing, so that there is, in effect, a single atrium or single ventricle. Physiologically these behave like large atrial or ventricular septal defects; however, since blood can mix more easily in the common chamber there may be right-to-left shunts without marked obstruction to blood flow out of the right heart chambers. Comparable mixing after blood leaves the ventricles occurs in truncus arteriosus, an anomaly in which both ventricles empty through a single valve ring into a single great artery which supplies both the systemic tissues and the lungs. Here systemic arterial blood is always desaturated, the degree varying with the pulmonary vascular resistance.

In other patients, obstruction at the pulmonary or tricuspid valves is complete—pulmonary or tricuspid atresia. With tricuspid atresia all systemic venous return passes across an atrial septal defect into the left atrium, where it mixes with the pulmonary venous return. This combined venous return passes through the mitral valve into the left ventricle. From there it is distributed to the body via the aorta and to the lungs via a ventricular septal defect, the right ventricle, and the pulmonary artery. The right ventricle is almost always very small, and blood flow into the lungs may be markedly restricted by a very small pulmonary valve or by a ventricular septal defect that is too small.

Pulmonic atresia prevents blood from passing directly from the right ventricle into the pulmonary artery. If there is no ventricular septal defect, then systemic venous blood passes from right atrium to left atrium, thence to left ventricle and aorta, and reaches the lungs through a patent ductus arteriosus or bronchial arteries. If there is a ventricular septal defect, then right ventricular blood passes into left ventricle and aorta, from where it reaches the lungs through one of the two routes just mentioned.

B. A large group of cyanotic congenital heart diseases have abnormal connections between the great vessels and the cardiac chambers.

1. Complete transposition of the great arteries, with the aorta arising from the right ventricle and the pulmonary artery from the left ventricle. In this condition, systemic venous blood enters the right atrium and ventricle and then passes into the aorta, while pulmonary venous blood enters the left atrium and ventricle and then passes back into the lungs through the pulmonary artery. For the patient to survive there must be a patent ductus arteriosus or ventricular or atrial openings for the exchange of blood between the two circuits.

2. Partial transposition of the great arteries: (a) aorta from right ventricle, pulmonary artery overriding a ventricular septal defect, and so coming from both ventricles (Taussig-Bing syndrome); (b) pulmonary artery and aorta from right ventricle, with aorta close to a ventricular septal defect (double outlet right ventricle). Usually, because the aorta lies over the ventricular septal defect, aortic saturation is normal unless there is also pulmonic stenosis.

3. Total anomalous pulmonary venous drainage into the right atrium. Here all systemic and pulmonary venous blood returns to the right atrium, from where some goes normally through the tricuspid valve into right ventricle while the rest passes through an atrial septal defect into the left atrium.

4. Partial or complete transposition of the systemic veins so that one or more of them enters the left atrium.

C. Miscellaneous.

1. Aortic atresia, in which blood from the left ventricle passes across a ventricular septal defect into the right ventricle, pulmonary artery, and through a patent ductus arteriosus into the aorta.

2. Mitral atresia, in which blood passes from the left to the right atrium and right ventricle, from where it reaches the aorta via a ventricular septal defect or a patent ductus arteriosus.

3. Pulmonary arteriovenous fistula, in which systemic venous blood bypasses the alveoli in one or more channels, which thus carry desaturated blood into the pulmonary veins.

BASIC PHYSIOLOGY OF RIGHT-TO-LEFT SHUNTS. Some desaturated venous blood bypasses the lungs and is not oxygenated, so that there is arterial desaturation Whether this is detectable clinically as cyanosis depends on the arterial saturation and the hemoglobin concentration. It is said that cyanosis appears when there is about 5 g of reduced hemoglobin per 100 ml of blood in the skin vessels, so that with marked anemia, cyanosis is unlikely to be seen unless arterial desaturation is extreme; conversely, polycythemic babies can look cyanotic even though their arterial oxygen saturations are normal. Knowledge of the hemoglobin concentration is therefore essential when interpreting presence or absence of arterial desaturation from changes in skin color. The color changes are usually well shown in the nailbeds but should be confirmed in the lips, tongue, and conjunctivae; if cyanosis is peripheral, due to cold or a slow peripheral circulation, then the nailbeds will be blue but the warm central areas will be pink. It is also necessary to remember that occasionally cyanosis is due to methemoglobinemia.

When there are right-to-left shunts the arterial oxygen saturation depends chiefly upon the pulmonary blood flow and not, as is generally thought, on the size of the right-to-left shunt. With the same magnitude of right-to-left shunt a big pulmonary blood flow will produce a relatively high arterial oxygen saturation while a small pulmonary blood flow will give a low arterial oxygen saturation. In other words, the arterial saturation is determined by how much the almost fully saturated pulmonary venous blood is diluted by unsaturated systemic venous blood; since the pulmonary blood flow in these anomalies varies much more than does the amount of right-to-left shunting, the pulmonary flow becomes the chief determinant of arterial saturation. For this reason, too, most palliative operations for these lesions are concerned with increasing a diminished pulmonary blood flow rather than reducing any right-to-left shunting.

In general, no matter what the precise anatomic lesions may be, there are four physiologic syndromes which patients with this group of lesions may show.

1. There may be a massive pulmonary blood flow, as in transposition of the great arteries with a ventricular septal defect, tricuspid atresia with a transposition, tricuspid atresia and a very large ventricular septal defect, or truncus arteriosus. These patients are not very desaturated and may not even appear cyanotic. Their difficulties are due, not to hypoxemia, but to the huge volume load on the left ventricle with resultant left ventricular failure. In this sense they resemble patients with a large patent ductus arteriosus or ventricular septal defect; they require vigorous medical treatment for their heart failure and, if this fails, the volume overload of the left ventricle will have to be reduced by banding the pulmonary artery.

2. There is a group with moderate pulmonary blood flow. They are more desaturated than the previous group and are usually mildly or moderately cyanotic; however, the desaturation is not severe enough to produce hypoxemia symptoms, nor is the pulmonary blood flow high enough to cause left ventricular failure. These patients do reasonably well for many years, although they usually have some limitations on exertion. Sooner or later they will need corrective surgery, if possible, or else palliative surgery to permit them to do more than their current pulmonary blood flow allows; indications for surgery will be considered in the discussion of each separate lesion.

3. There is a third group in which pulmonary blood flow is very low and there is obstruction to the pulmonary venous return which is usually the cause of the low pulmonary blood flow. Here there is some obstruction between the pulmonary veins and the left atrium, as when the pulmonary veins form a common trunk which drains by various routes into the right atrium and is either long and narrow or else has a stenotic orifice. Note that pulmonary venous obstruction not associated with anomalous pulmonary venous drainage and communications between the two sides of the heart would have all the features of pulmonary venous obstruction, but would not have right-to-left intracardiac shunts. Obstruction to pulmonary venous drainage and right-to-left shunting also occur when there is obstruction to left atrial outflow with intracardiac communications; thus they are seen in mitral atresia with too small an interatrial opening. The right-to-left shunt would not be seen in mitral stenosis or cor triatriatum unless there were also a patent ductus arteriosus or a ventricular septal defect and severe pulmonary hypertension.

These patients are deeply cyanotic because of the low pulmonary blood flow and the right-to-left shunt; the consequences of this will be discussed in the next section. In addition, they also have the effects of a raised pulmonary venous pressure, particularly pulmonary edema. As a result they are very ill, and treatment must be directed to relieving the pulmonary venous obstruction. Almost always, successful relief of the obstruction will increase pulmonary blood flow.

4. In the final group the pulmonary blood flow is severely reduced because venous blood is diverted from the lungs, as in tetralogy of Fallot, transposition of the great arteries without an adequate intracardiac communication, tricuspid atresia without a large ventricular septal defect, and severe pulmonic stenosis or atresia with an intact ventricular septum. These patients are markedly desaturated and cyanotic, and their symptoms are related to severe hypoxemia. Since the supply of oxygen to the tissues is inadequate, the patients, usually infants, are tachypneic at rest and have a very low exercise tolerance; feeding may cause fatigue and caloric intake may be disturbed. Any exertion increases the cyanosis. If hypoxemia is severe, the child usually seems feeble. Because oxygen supply to metabolizing tissues is inadequate, profound metabolic acidosis develops owing to anaerobic metabolism. In most patients with metabolic acidosis, hyperventilation lowers arterial carbon dioxide tension and so brings arterial pH to or near normal. Patients with cyanotic heart disease and metabolic acidosis, however, are denied this compensation; while they do hyperventilate, so little blood passes through the lungs that arterial carbon dioxide tension remains normal and pH falls markedly.

Most of these infants have markedly diminished pulmonary vascular markings on x-ray; however, in transposition of the great arteries and sometimes in other lesions where there has been an adequate flow through the ductus arteriosus the lung fields may show normal sized vessels. Usually the heart is small, and enlargement occurs only as a terminal event. The combination of severe cyanosis with the other symptoms, and the x-ray findings described, indicate that severe disease is present and that further studies should be done immediately. There should never be any delay in making these studies, for two main reasons. If there is a metabolic acidosis it needs to be corrected before more harm is done, and at this stage even a few hours delay may be fatal. Even more important is the fact that in the very young infants the major portion of the already very low pulmonary blood flow may be coming from the aorta through the patent ductus arteriosus. If this begins to close, as it usually does at some time, hypoxemia will rapidly become worse. It is possible that some of the deterioration which occurs so often in the first few days or weeks is due to this closing down of a vital source of pulmonary blood flow.

GENERAL PRINCIPLES OF TREATMENT.   Any patient in this fourth group has very severe heart disease and, particularly in infancy, the results of either medical or surgical treatment are poor. As soon as the patient is seen he should be put into an atmosphere of high oxygen, though the limitations of this must be stressed. It is difficult to attain 100 percent oxygen unless a tight-fitting face mask is used; the common practice of allowing oxygen to flow into an Isolette seldom raises the oxygen concentration within the Isolette above 50 to 60 percent even at flow rates of 10 to 20 L/minute. Better results can be expected of hyperbaric oxygen chambers, but these are not likely to be in general use, are associated with complications, and cannot be used for more than a few hours at a time. The main problem with supplying oxygen to these patients is that, because of the small pulmonary blood flow, the amount of extra oxygen introduced into the body will be very small at best. In most of these patients the hemoglobin that does get into the lungs is normally and fully oxygenated; therefore all that can be done by increasing alveolar oxygen tension in a hyperbaric oxygen chamber is to increase the amount of oxygen which is dissolved in the plasma. This is small, and in general the amount of extra oxygen introduced into the body by hyperbaric oxygenation is only about 20 percent more than is taken up while breathing room air.

In addition to oxygen, the metabolic acidosis

must be treated. Once the arterial pH is known, infusions of sodium bicarbonate can be given, or TRIS buffer may be used with due precautions. Undiluted molar sodium bicarbonate containing 44.5 mEq in 50 ml is given intravenously in 5 ml amounts. After each injection arterial or mixed venous pH should be checked, and the time and amount of subsequent injections should be based on the response. Very large quantities of sodium bicarbonate may have to be given rapidly to these small babies, and this entails giving large quantities of sodium and water. However, these infants are often dehydrated, so that there is little risk of causing congestive heart failure; in any event that risk must be taken to combat the acidosis. It must be emphasized that treatment of metabolic acidosis and oxygen therapy are only temporary palliations, and as a rule are used only until surgical treatment can be carried out. Once these hypoxemic symptoms and signs occur they can usually be relieved only by increasing the pulmonary blood flow. The child should also be kept at an optimal temperature (skin temperature about 36.5° C) to minimize oxygen needs. Furthermore, these infants are so ill that they often have acute dilation of the stomach; therefore not only should they not be given oral fluids but removal of the stomach contents may prevent aspiration.

Palliative medical treatment is usually done while preparing the patient for surgery, and part of this preparation may consist of cardiac catheterization. If the diagnosis is not clinically certain, then limited catheterization studies are needed to guide the surgeon, since different operations are needed for different anatomical entities. These procedures may be briefly listed:

1. Pulmonary venous obstruction with total anomalous pulmonic venous drainage can be relieved by anastomosing the common pulmonary trunk to the left atrium.

2. A larger opening in the atrial septum is made when there is mitral atresia with pulmonary venous obstruction, tricuspid atresia with too small an atrial opening, or transposition of the great arteries without a large intracardiac communication.

3. If there is obstruction to the right ventricular outflow tract, then it may be possible to widen the valve orifice or partly resect the infundibular obstruction and so increase pulmonary blood flow. Whether this can be done depends upon the exact anatomy (usually determined by angiocardiography) and the experience of the surgeon.

4. If a direct attack on the obstruction is not possible then pulmonary blood flow can be increased by anastomosing the aorta or subclavian artery to the pulmonary artery or else by anastomosing the superior vena cava to the pulmonary artery.

Impaired Myocardial Contractility

There is a miscellaneous group of diseases characterized by impaired myocardial contractility in the absence of a pressure or a volume overload. The impaired contractility may be associated with known causes, such as infections of the myocardium by Coxsackie B virus or *Trypanosoma cruzi*; enzyme defects like glycogen storage disease; chronic degenerative nervous system diseases like Friedreich's ataxia; and disorders like sickle-cell anemia or hemochromatosis. Often, however, there is extxensive myocardial damage or endocardial thickening of no known cause.

In all these diseases the load imposed by a normal cardiac output at normal pressures cannot be handled without ventricular dilation and hypertrophy. Sooner or later, therefore, ventricular enddiastolic pressures rise with the consequences already discussed.

Clinically these diseases show no pathognomonic features. The heart is enlarged and a hypertrophied left ventricle may be felt. There is often a prominent third heart sound, but no significant murmurs are present unless ventricular dilation causes mitral or tricuspid regurgitation. Electrocardiograms sometimes show ventricular hypertrophy, usually left-sided, and there are often marked T wave changes out of proportion to the degree of hypertrophy. On x-ray the heart usually shows enlargement of all chambers, though at times the left atrium and ventricle may be predominantly affected.

Since all these findings are nonspecific, antemortem diagnosis can be made only, it at all, by detecting associated lesions or enzyme defects or occasionally by demonstrating infection with a specific organism. More often than not diagnosis can only be made postmortem.

20.9
OBSTRUCTIVE LESIONS OF THE CIRCULATION

MARY ALLEN ENGLE

Malformations which obstruct blood flow through or out of the heart usually occur alone but may be found in combination with another obstructive lesion or another anomaly, such as a septal defect. Whether the involvement is on the right or the left side of the heart, certain similarities exist. The obstruction is more often valvar than sub- or supravalvar. The semilunar valves are affected more often than the atrioventricular valves, and the valves on the right side more often than those on the left. Obstruction in the two great arteries has been recognized far more frequently in the aorta (coarctation) than in the pulmonary artery, but recent advances in selective angiocardiography and cardiac catheterization are revealing increasing numbers of instances of stenosis of the peripheral pulmonary arterial tree.

Obstruction to Venous Return

Obstruction to inflow of venous blood into the heart occurs chiefly as a consequence of a more distal obstruction or of ventricular failure; however, isolated obstruction of systemic or pulmonary venous drainage may be encountered.

OBSTRUCTION TO SYSTEMIC VENOUS DRAINAGE. Restriction of superior vena caval flow is evidenced by dilation of the superficial venous channels visible in the skin and distention of veins in the neck. Edema of the head, neck, and upper extremities as well as cyanosis in these areas occur in severe obstruction. Venous angiography opacifies these dilated channels and may disclose the cause of the obstruction: extrinsic pressure; intrinsic narrowing as by a clot; obstruction at anastomosis of superior vena cava to right pulmonary artery (Glenn procedure for uncorrectable anomalies of the right heart); or obstruction to right atrial inflow or outflow (e.g., tumor, tricuspid stenosis, or right ventricular failure). Obstruction of superior vena caval flow is encountered far more often in adults than in children.

Absence of the inferior vena cava is noted chiefly in those rare syndromes with visceral heterotaxy and abnormalities of cardiac position. Venous drainage then is via an enlarged azygous system, and it may be obstructed. Thrombosis of the inferior vena cava or its tributaries may occur following trauma or manipulation with a catheter or at surgery. Engorgement of the veins caudad to the point of occlusion occurs, and edema follows. If the obstruction in the inferior vena cava is near the heart, hepatomegaly is present. Constrictive pericarditis may be responsible for signs of caval obstruction because of involvement of the caval orifices in the process and because of impairment of myocardial function.

PULMONARY VENOUS OBSTRUCTION. The most common cause of obstruction of pulmonary venous drainage is left ventricular failure. Other causes include obstruction or marked insufficiency of the mitral valve; restriction of the left ventricular cavity, as with a tumor or the hypoplastic left heart syndrome; a mass or diaphragm within the left atrium; stenoses of normally draining pulmonary veins; and obstruction in the course of anomalously draining pulmonary veins. This last situation is the chief cause of respiratory distress and early death of babies born with total anomalous pulmonary venous drainage, wherein a point of stenosis exists between the confluence of pulmonary veins and their ultimate point of entry into the right atrium. Obstructed pulmonary venous drainage is the rule with infradiaphragmatic pulmonary venous return but it also occurs in the supradiaphragmatic forms.

In addition to the symptoms and signs of respiratory distress, there are striking radiologic features of obstructed pulmonary veins; a fine, reticular, stip-

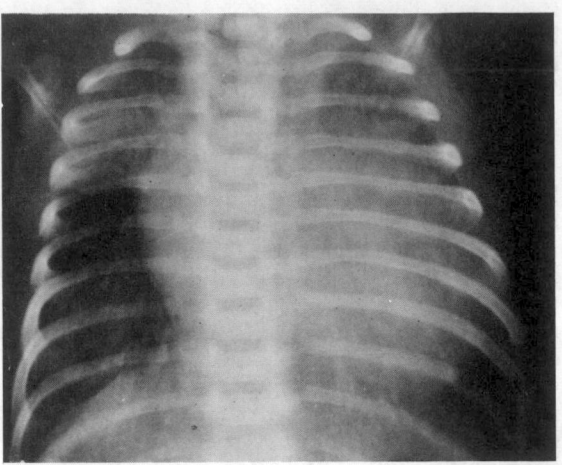

Fig. 36. Pulmonary venous obstruction secondary to severe valvar aortic stenosis in 5-week-old infant with left-sided congestive cardiac failure. Note the especially hazy density of the right upper lobe. There is less edema of the right lower lobe. The left lung field is hidden by the massively enlarged heart. This baby successfully underwent open-heart surgery with relief of the stenosis.

pling maximal in the hilar areas but radiating into the midlung fields and sometimes even into the periphery. (See Fig. 61, Sec. 20.11.) In infants with left-sided cardiac failure there are often variations in the degree of haziness in the two lungs, suggesting regional differences in adequacy of pulmonary venous drainage (Fig. 36). Pressure measurements at cardiac catheterization of the pulmonary "capillary" or wedge pressure and of pressures in the left atrium and beyond, together with contrast visualization, permit localization of the side and cause of pulmonary venous obstruction.

When pulmonary venous return is obstructed, the factors that determine the function, the symptomatology, and the surgical possibilities in that patient are (1) the severity of obstruction, (2) presence of a shunt proximal to, at the same level, or distal to the obstruction, and (3) the presence of other cardiovascular malformations. Complete cardiologic evaluation by catheterization and contrast visualization is necessary to assess each of these.

Obstruction at or near Atrioventricular Valves

Physiologic adaptation to obstructive lesions about the atrioventricular valves include elevation in mean pressure and in the a wave of the pressure pulse, increase in the size of the chamber and the thickness of the wall of the affected atrium, and elevation of pressure in the veins draining into that atrium. With a severe grade of tricuspid stenosis, pulsations at the margin of the liver may be detected at the time of

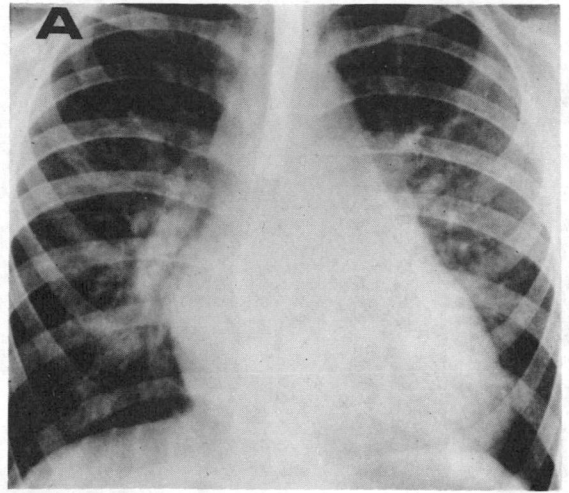
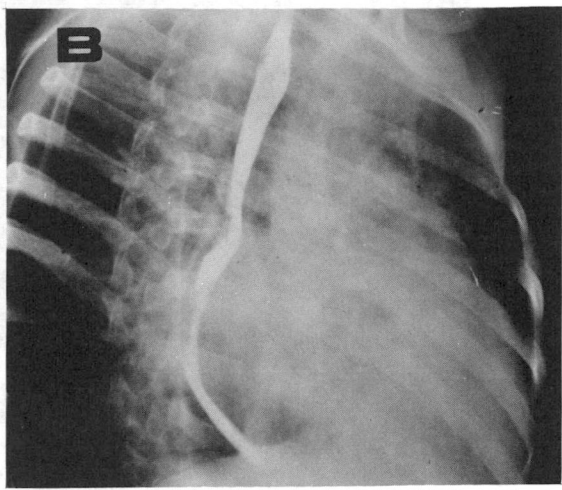
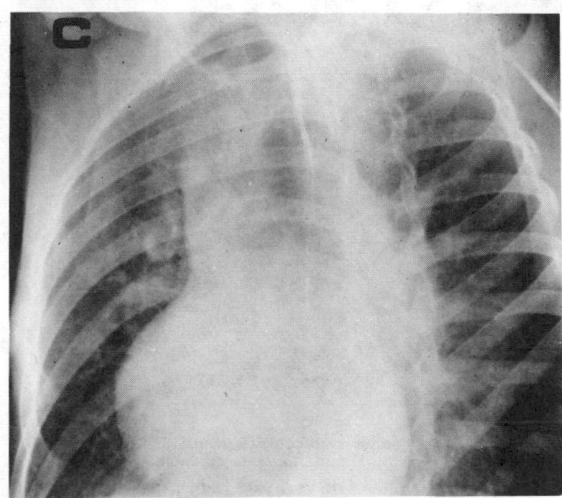

Fig. 37. Congenital mitral stenosis, coarctation of aorta, and patent ductus arteriosus. Roentgenograms in frontal (A), RAO (B), and LAO (C) views of 6-year-old girl. Note displacement of barium-filled esophagus in frontal and RAO views by markedly enlarged left atrium. (From Freundlich et al. *Pediatrics*, 27:427, 1961.)

atrial systole. The liver becomes engorged, veins of the neck distended, and peripheral edema may appear. If the obstruction involves the mitral valve, radiologic evidence of distended pulmonary veins may be noted, and the patient may experience shortness of breath on exertion or when supine, and may suffer from attacks of pulmonary edema, episodically or on effort. Long-standing or severe elevation of pulmonary venous and capillary pressures results in elevation of pressure in the main pulmonary artery and in systolic hypertension of the right ventricle.

The chief auscultatory sign of stenosis of an atrioventricular valve is a late diastolic (presystolic) rumbling murmur. This is maximal at the apex if there is mitral stenosis or at the lower left sternal border if there is tricuspid stenosis. The first heart sound, which is produced by closure of the AV valves, becomes delayed and accentuated. An opening snap may be heard shortly following the second sound.

The roentgenogram with barium swallow in frontal (Fig. 37A) and oblique views (Fig. 37B and C) gives evidence of enlargement of the atria. Right atrial enlargement is best seen in the frontal view as a fullness of the right lower cardiac shadow. Left atrial enlargement is best detected by displacement of the barium-filled esophagus in the right anterior-oblique and frontal views. Enlargement of these chambers is seen when their volume is increased. Hypertrophy of the atrial walls may occur to a marked degree without these radiologic changes. Atrial hypertrophy is reflected best in the waves in the electrocardiogram: P waves are high and peaked if the abnormality is right atrial, and low, broad, and notched if left atrial.

Anatomically the obstruction is usually at the valve, in the form of atresia or stenosis. Less often a complete or partial obstruction occurs as a supravalvar or subvalvar diaphragm.

TRICUSPID STENOSIS. As a congenital anomaly this lesion rarely occurs alone. More often it is associated with pulmonic stenosis, atrial and sometimes ventricular septal defect, and an underdeveloped right ventricle. The patient is then cyanotic, with de-

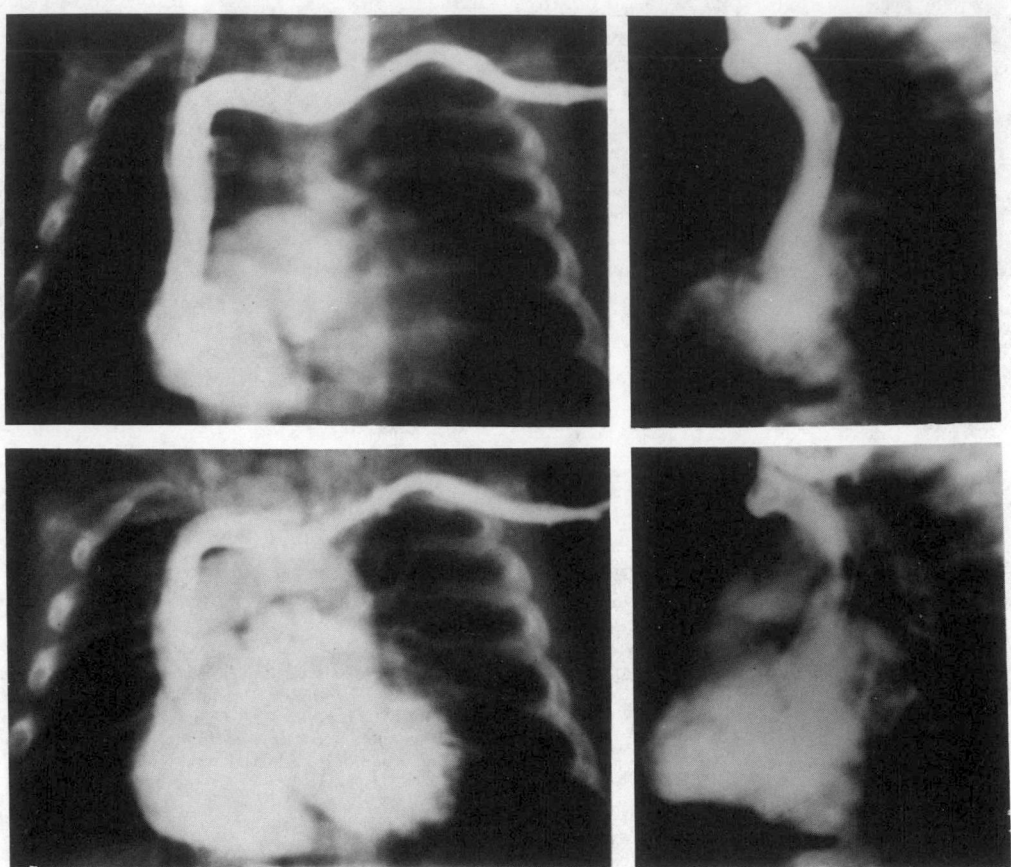

Fig. 38.   Tricuspid atresia, with course of circulation demonstrated by venous angiocardiograms in frontal (on left) and lateral views. Contrast medium from left arm opacifies superior vena cava, right atrium and the left atrium in upper films. In the lower films the contrast has entered the left ventricle and aorta, then by way of a patent ductus arteriosus (lateral view) into the pulmonary artery branch. The centrally located triangular radiolucency in both frontal projections at the level of the diaphragms is due to unopacified right ventricle. This cyanotic baby was benefited by surgical creation of a shunt between the base of the aorta and the right pulmonary artery (Waterston procedure).

creased pulmonary blood flow. Clinically it is difficult to distinguish from that of tricuspid atresia (see below), but at cardiac catheterization the distinction is made by the passage of the catheter or contrast medium through the stenosis but not the atresia. A tumor in the right atrium and chronic constrictive pericarditis may simulate tricuspid stenosis. Contrast visualization and analysis of pressure tracings help in the differential diagnosis.

TRICUSPID ATRESIA.   Agenesis of the tricuspid valve occurs in association with a patent foramen ovale or atrial septal defect. Blood that is obstructed at the normal right atrial outlet passes through an opening in the atrial septum into left atrium and ventricle. When the great arteries are in their normal relationship, this mixed venous and arterial blood enters the aorta. Blood reaches the lungs via a patent ductus arteriosus of other collateral channels to the pulmonary artery (Fig. 38), or by way of a ventricular

septal defect to a small right ventricle and thus to the pulmonary artery. The usual effect is that of diminished pulmonary blood flow, either because the ventricular septal defect is small and restrictive or the ductus and collateral pathways are inadequate. In severe forms there are three or more areas of obstruction to systemic venous return before it can reach the lungs for oxygenation: (1) the atretic tricuspid orifice; (2) a foramen ovale or atrial septal defect that is so small that it limits right atrial outlet; (3) a restrictive ventricular septal defect; and (4) a hypoplastic or atretic pulmonary valve and artery. The patient is deeply cyanotic and quite limited in exercise tolerance.

Pulmonary blood flow may be adequate or even excessive with tricuspid atresia, however, if the ventricular septal defect is large or if the great arteries are transposed. In the latter condition, mixed venoarterial blood from the left ventricle readily enters the posteriorly placed pulmonary artery. The aortic flow occurs via a ventricular septal defect into the rudimentary right ventricle and anteriorly placed aorta. Patients with tricuspid atresia and excessive pulmonary flow have minimal, if any, cyanosis, but often present in cardiac failure. (Refer to right-to-left shunts, p. 1406 for further details of diagnosis and treatment.)

MITRAL STENOSIS. This rare lesion may occur as an isolated anomaly or may be associated with endocardial fibroelastosis, ventricular septal defect, atrial septal defect (Lutembacher's syndrome), with patent ductus arteriosus and/or coarctation of the aorta (Fig. 33). The congenitally malformed mitral valve may take a variety of forms, from one resembling a normal valve with fused commissures, or a diaphragm with multiple perforations, to an elongated windsac which protrudes into the left ventricle. When the condition produces marked symptoms, the valve orifice may sometimes be increased in size at open-heart surgery by plastic repair, valvotomy, or valve replacement. The obstruction is rendered functionally more severe when it occurs together with a left-to-right shunt, as through a ventricular septal defect or patent

ductus. Then the increased pulmonary blood flow augments pulmonary venous return across the mitral valve.

Conditions mimicking mitral stenosis in their effect include *constricting ring* just proximal or distal to the valve; *left atrial tumor,* especially myxoma; and *cor triatriatum.* In the last named, failure of resorption of the common pulmonary vein results in a partitioning of the left atrium into two parts, so that there seem to be three atria. The pulmonary veins drain into the proximal chamber, which communicates through an opening, variably restricted in size, with the distal portion of the left atrium. The latter is connected to the atrial appendage and the mitral valve. A defect in the atrial septum may be present as a communication between the right atrium and the distal or proximal part of the left atrium. When proximal, the atrial septal defect relieves some of the obstruction to pulmonary venous drainage but the patient then has the effects of a left-to-right shunt at atrial level.

Diagnosis of the condition can be made by a combination of pressure measurements and selective angiocardiography. If pressures can be measured in

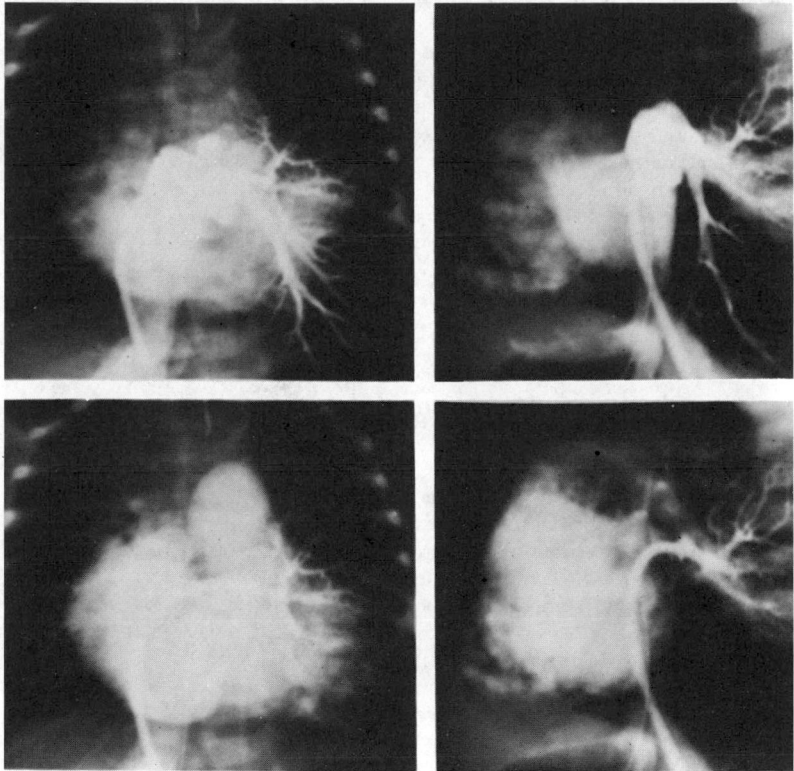

Fig. 39. Mitral atresia and aortic atresia with hypoplasia of the left ventricle in a 3-day-old baby. Angiocardiogram in simultaneous frontal view on left and lateral view on right side. Selective injection of contrast medium into the left atrium in the upper films fills the left pulmonary veins but does not pass into a left ventricle. Instead it passes through an atrial septal defect into the large right atrium and refluxes into the inferior vena cava. In the lower films the right ventricle, pulmonary artery, and patent ductus fill. Not seen because the structure was so small is a stringlike aortic arch filled retrogradely by way of the ductus.

the distal left atrium and in the pulmonary wedge position and are found to be elevated in the latter while normal in the former, then obstruction to drainage of pulmonary veins exists, either at the point of entrance to the left atrium (*congenital stenoses of pulmonary veins*) or at the diaphragm of a cor triatriatum. Injection of contrast medium into the pulmonary artery completes the differentiation by demonstrating an upper atrial chamber and a lower one with the atrial appendage attached. Surgical excision of the diaphragm at open-heart surgery can correct the anomaly.

MITRAL ATRESIA. When there is aplasia of the mitral valve or atresia of the tissue just above or below it, blood returning from the lungs leaves the left atrium via a defect in the atrial septum or, rarely, via an anomalous pulmonary venous connection, so that it mixes in the right atrium with systemic venous drainage. The left ventricle is underdeveloped and functions only if there is a ventricular septal defect to direct blood back into it from the right ventricle. Aortic valve hypoplasia or atresia commonly coexists. The presence of a patent ductus arteriosus allows blood to flow into the aorta in retrograde fashion as the right ventricle pumps blood to the lungs (Fig. 39). Life expectancy is rarely beyond the newborn period, unless there is some means for establishing adequate aortic blood flow (as with a large ventricular septal defect or when the aorta is transposed to the right venticle). If the aorta is adequate in size to permit cerebral and coronary blood flow, life expectancy in this malformation may be increased by creation of a large atrial septal defect to permit pulmonary venous blood to exit unobstructed from the left atrium whose natural outlet is blocked. At the same operation some obstruction to the excessive pulmonary blood can be created by banding the pulmonary artery.

Obstruction at or near Semilunar Valves

In contrast to the preceding obstructing conditions, which are rare, obstruction to ventricular outflow is quite common. As with other congenital anomalies, adaptations to stenosis depend on the severity of the narrowing. Mild pulmonic or aortic stenosis may be tolerated for a full life-span without evidence of cardiac disability other than a susceptibility to bacterial endocarditis. On the other hand, marked obstruction in either area may lead to death from congestive heart failure as early as the newborn period.

Proximal to the obstruction the systolic pressure becomes elevated, while distally, the systolic pressure is lower and in severe circumstances may be well below normal, with a narrow arterial pulse pressure. When obstruction is severe, right ventricular systolic pressure may rise as high as 250 mm Hg and left ventricular pressure may reach 300 mm. Hypertrophy of the wall of the ventricle accompanies the systolic

work load and with severe overload. There is elevation of end-diastolic pressure and dilation of the chamber. Withdrawal of the cardiac catheter across the narrowed region localizes the level of obstruction. For example, in supravalvar pulmonic stenosis, when the catheter is withdrawn from distal to proximal pulmonary artery across the obstruction, the systolic pressure rises while the diastolic pressure remains constant in the artery, or may drop slightly; as the catheter is further withdrawn across the valve, the diastolic pressure drops to that of a ventricular chamber. If the systolic pressure gradient occurs at the same time that the diastolic pressure changes from that of an artery to that of a ventricle, the stenosis is at the valve. If the systolic pressure drop is recorded when the diastolic pressure has already dropped to that of the ventricular level, the obstruction is subvalvar. The same principles apply to aortic stenosis except that usually the catheter is withdrawn from the ventricle across the valve and into the aorta. Illustrations of these pressure changes may be seen in Figures 24 and 25 (Sec. 20.6). Selective injection of contrast medium proximal to the obstruction gives visual proof of the type of obstruction and its hemodynamic effects.

Auscultatory evidence of pulmonic or aortic stenosis is an ejection-type murmur, with peak intensity in mid, early, or late systole (Fig. 40). A thrill usually overlies the point of maximal intensity of the murmur. An early systolic ejection sound is often heard when the stenosis is valvar and is mild or moderately severe, and the artery beyond is dilated.

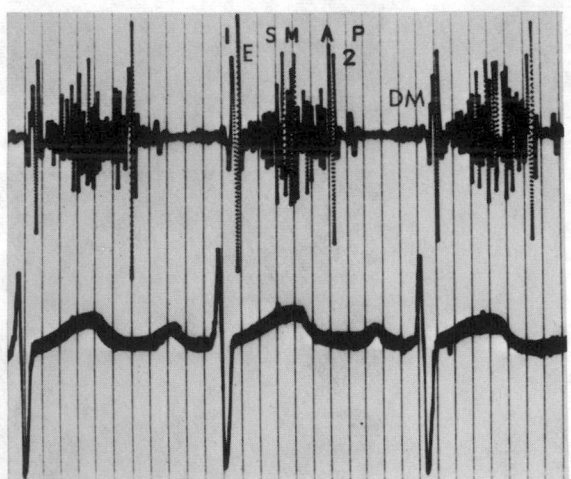

Fig. 40. Phonocardiogram recorded from second left interspace of infant with severe valvar pulmonic stenosis and congestive heart failure. A diamond-shaped ejection-type murmur with peak intensity in midsystole is followed by a widely split second sound, the pulmonic component (P) being both diminished and delayed. An early systolic ejection sound (E) follows closely after the first heart sound. The late diastolic murmur is unusual unless pulmonic stenosis is severe; it may be related to the altered atrial hemodynamics during congestive heart failure. (Time lines 0.04 second. Recording at 120/500 cycles per second.)

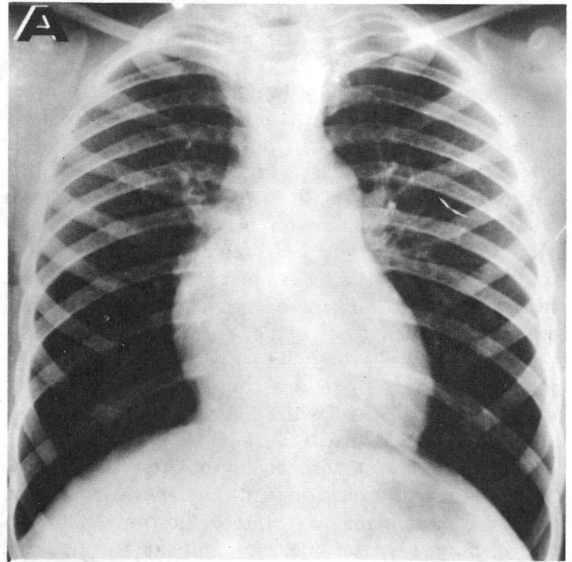
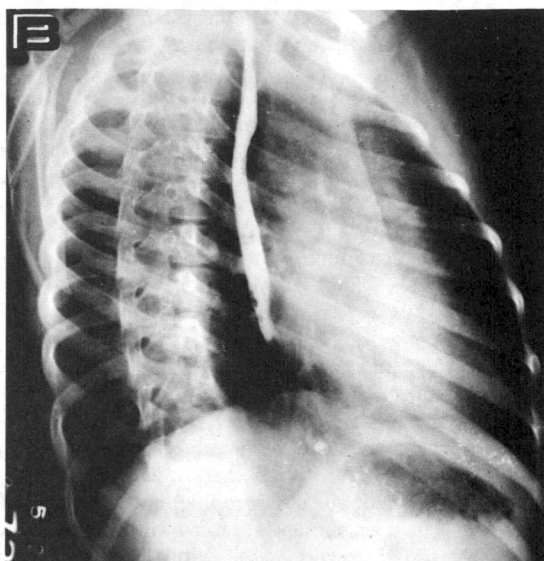
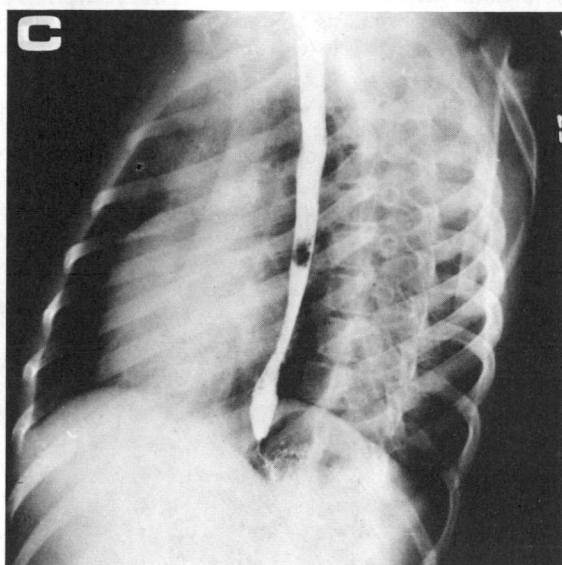

Fig. 41. Valvar pulmonic stenosis, moderately severe, in 7-year-old boy. Cardiac series of films in (A) frontal, (B) RAO, and (C) LAO views. Note prominent main pulmonary artery (poststenotic dilatation) as well as enlargement of right atrium in frontal view. Pulmonary vascularity is decreased in periphery of lungs. Enlargement of right ventricle is indicated in LAO view by the anterior bulge of the cardiac shadow. Pressures preoperatively were 96/6 in RV and 14/3 mm Hg in PA; 18 months after open pulmonary valvotomy, they were 28/4 in RV and 20/4 mm Hg in PA.

When stenosis is valvar or subvalvar, the component of the second heart sound contributed by closure of that semilunar valve is diminished and delayed. However, when the stenosis is supravalvar, that component of the second sound is often accentuated.

Supravalvar stenosis, whether aortic or pulmonic, may be part of the supravalvar syndrome in which the facial features are coarse, with large, protuberant upper lip and malformed teeth, strabismus, mental retardation, sometimes together with physical retardation, inguinal hernias, skeletal anomalies, and hypercalcemia. Supravalvar stenosis is also found in the congenital rubella syndrome. In addition, it may occur as an isolated anomaly or as a familial cardiovascular defect.

Although it is the severity of the obstruction, rather than its precise location, that determines the patient's disability, it is important to define the site of stenosis before undertaking cardiac surgery for relief of moderate or severe obstruction to ventricular outflow. The region of stenosis may be judged by clinical findings, such as point of maximal intensity of the murmur and presence or absence of an ejection click and poststenotic dilation of the main pulmonary artery (Fig. 41), an infundibular chamber or the aorta. The area of obstruction can be defined still more precisely by analysis of pressure curves and by recording a systolic pressure gradient across the obstruction. Selective injection of contrast medium further localizes the stenosis, while cineangiocardiography indicates whether the narrowing is fixed or variable during the phases of the cardiac cycle.

PULMONIC STENOSIS.   Pulmonic stenosis may occur below, at, or above the valve. In *subvalvar* stenosis the obstruction is in the body of the ventricle and is due to an anomalous muscle bundle that divides the right ventricle into two parts, or is in the outflow tract, where a fibrous concentric ring or muscular mass causes infundibular stenosis. Unless the obstruction is immediately beneath the valve or is elongated and diffuse, an infundibular chamber exists between the point of stenosis and the valve ring.

Valvar pulmonic stenosis is due to fusion of the valve cusps into a thick, dome-shaped structure. The lines of fusion of the commissures are usually visible on the pulmonary arterial side; they serve as useful guidelines for incision when the surgeon performs a valvotomy. Sometimes hypertrophic muscular infundibular stenosis accompanies severe valvar pulmonic stenosis; it usually regresses following successful open valvotomy. Poststenotic dilation of the main pulmonary artery is characteristic of valvar stenosis (Figs. 41 and 42). The degree of dilation bears no direct relationship to the severity of stenosis, but in general the artery is more dilated with mild obstruction than with marked valvar pulmonic stenosis.

Supravalvar pulmonic stenosis takes the form of a constricting ring (coarctation) in the main pulmonary artery. More distal narrowing may occur as single or multiple constrictions with poststenotic dilation in the branches of the pulmonary artery. (See peripheral pulmonary artery stenosis, p. 1389.) Since the systolic pressure is elevated up to the point of constriction, the pressure at which the pulmonary valve closes is higher than normal, and the sound of pulmonary valve closure is accentuated. If the supravalvar stenosis is severe, it is possible for the surgeon to resect such a coarctation of the main pulmonary artery or major right or left branch and reanastomose the cut ends of the arteries, just as for coarctation of the aorta, or to perform a plastic procedure to enlarge the lumen. Iatrogenic supravalvar pulmonic stenosis is created when the surgeon bands the main pulmonary artery to reduce the excessive pulmonary blood flow of babies with ventricular septal defect and intractable cardiac failure.

In pulmonic stenosis at any of these sites, symptoms are usually lacking unless stenosis is severe. Then the patient may experience shortness of breath on exertion, easy fatigue, or right-sided congestive cardiac failure.

Pulmonic stenosis is recognized when a crescendo-decrescendo systolic murmur is heard in the second left interspace, overlying the pulmonary artery. When the stenosis is mild, the pulmonic (second) component of the second heart sound (S_2) in the second left interspace is of average intensity, but with increasing severity of valvar or subvalvar obstruction, the pulmonic component is increasingly

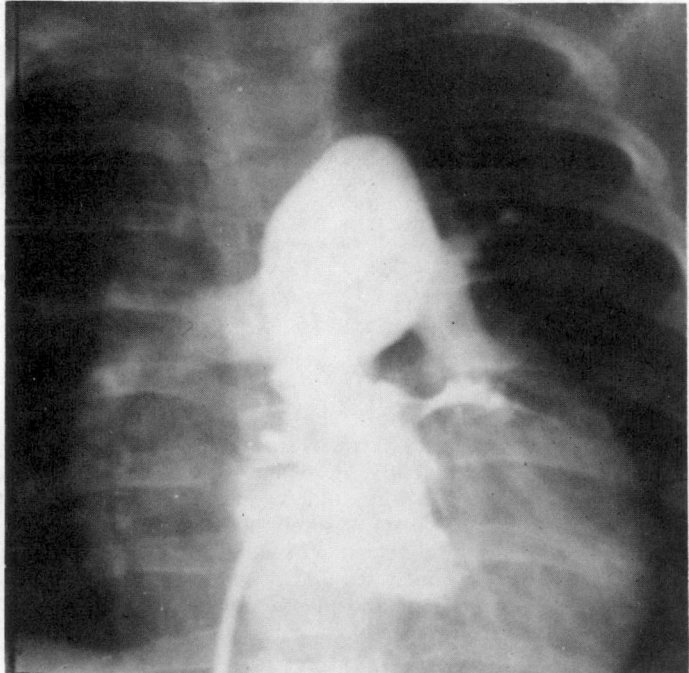
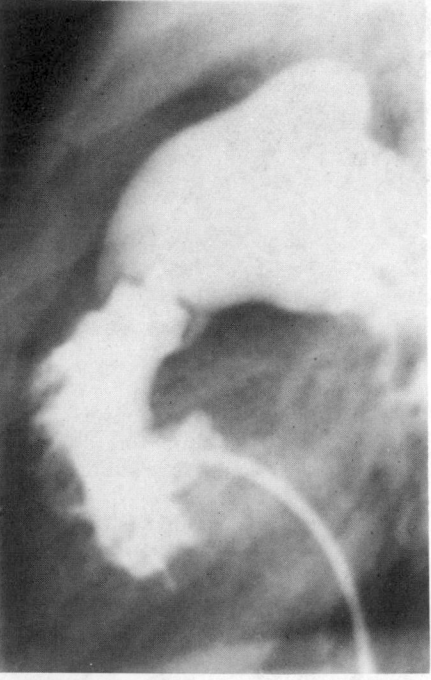

Fig. 42. Valvar pulmonic stenosis, severe, in an infant. Selective right ventricular angiocardiogram in frontal (on the left) and lateral views shows coarse trabeculations of the hypertrophied right ventricle. Better seen in the lateral view is the thick radiolucent dome of a stenosed pulmonic valve with a central jet of contrast medium passing through it into the markedly dilated main pulmonary artery.

delayed, so that S_2 is abnormally widely split and diminished, even to the point of inaudibility (refer to Fig. 40). The murmur transmits along the course of pulmonic blood flow, over the lung fields. When stenosis causes enlargement of the right ventricle, one may palpate a right ventricular tapping impulse and observe a precordial bulge along the lower left sternal border.

Electrocardiograms are useful in estimating the burden on the right ventricle. With increasing degrees of hypertrophy, the electrocardiogram shows in the right precordial leads a conduction disturbance (incomplete right bundle branch block), then increasing amplitude of the R wave (right ventricular hypertrophy), and last, deep inversion of T waves and depression of S-T segments ("strain").

The electrocardiogram is more helpful than the roentgenogram in judging severity of stenosis, for the cardiothoracic ratio may be normal even though the obstruction is marked. If the right ventricle is enlarged, however, one may be sure the stenosis is at least moderately severe. Poststenotic dilation of the pulmonary artery in valvar pulmonic stenosis is seen best in the frontal and right anterior-oblique position (Figs. 41 and 42). An infundibular chamber is seen in the same views as a bulge in the outflow tract of the ventricle below the level of the main pulmonary artery.

Cardiac catheterization and selective angiocardiography identify the area of stenosis and measure the systolic pressure gradient across the obstruction.

Open-heart surgery for relief of stenosis is indicated promptly when the obstruction is severe (right ventricular systolic pressure greater than systemic pressure) and is indicated electively for moderately severe stenosis, but for those with milder obstruction (right ventricular systolic pressure below 70 mm Hg) surgery is not indicated. Instead, that patient should be observed regularly, especially during the growth period, because the obstruction might increase.

PULMONIC ATRESIA. If there is aplasia of the pulmonary valve, usually there is a ventricular septal defect with overriding aorta and vessels of collateral circulation from the aorta to the branches of the pulmonary artery. This is a form of tetralogy of Fallot, often referred to as "pseudotruncus arteriosus." It is

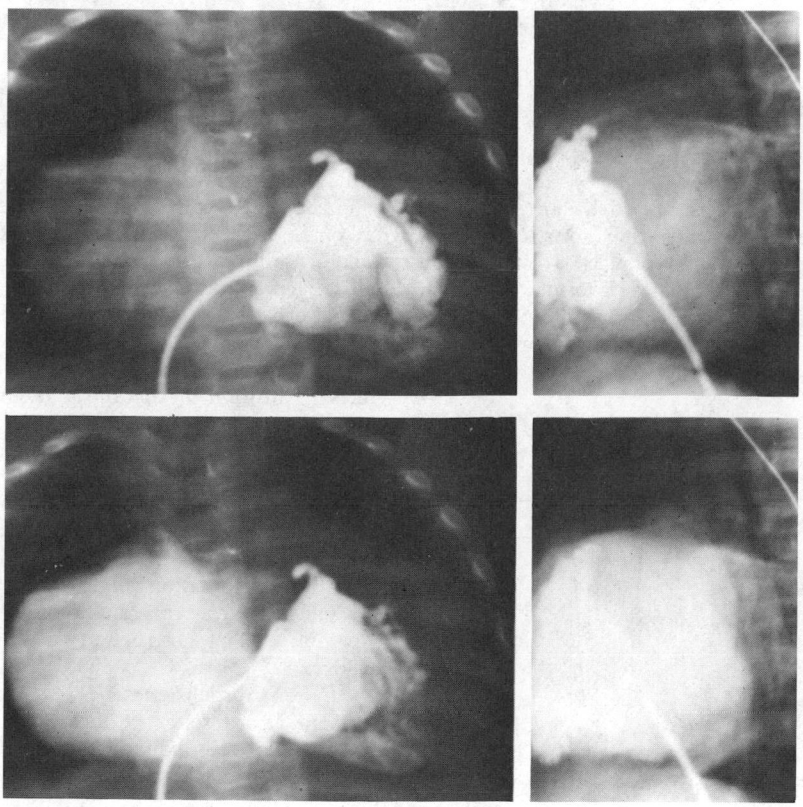

Fig. 43. Pulmonic atresia with intact ventricular septum, tricuspid regurgitation, and small defect in atrial septum. A patent ductus arteriosus (not seen here) supplied mixed venoarterial blood to the lungs. In the frontal (on the left) and simultaneous lateral views (on the right) of a selective right ventricular angiocardiogram can be seen the failure of forward flow of blood through the atretic pulmonic valve. Blood regurgitates into the tremendously dilated right atrium, which is well filled in the lower film while contrast is still dense in the right ventricle. Exit of blood from the right atrium into the left atrium was slow and is faintly evident in the lower film.

discussed in the chapter on Cyanotic Congenital Heart Disease (20.11).

Rarely, the ventricular septum is intact in the presence of pulmonic atresia and the patient survives only if there is an outlet in the atrial septum for exit of systemic venous blood. The cavity of the right ventricle may then be small, with a thick wall if most of the blood from the right atrium passes through a large atrial septal defect into the left side of the heart. At the opposite extreme, the right ventricle may be enormously dilated if blood does enter the right ventricle through the tricuspid valve and then regurgitates during ventricular systole through the same route to the right atrium (Fig. 43). The pulmonary circulation is supplied from the aorta through a patent ductus arteriosus. This inefficient arrangement usually ends in death in early infancy; neither medical nor surgical treatment is very effective. (See Sec. 20.11.)

AORTIC STENOSIS. *Subvalvar aortic stenosis* is caused by a fibrous constricting ring, by hypertrophied muscle bundles, and by obstruction of a ballooning aortic leaflet of the mitral valve. Though the last condition has been reported chiefly in young adults, it may be present even in infancy. The quick upstroke of the aortic pressure curve and the development of a systolic gradient as ventricular systole proceeds are characteristic of muscular hypertrophic subaortic stenosis (Fig. 44).

Valvar aortic stenosis is due to fusion of two or three cusps. Warty excrescences may protrude from the thick valve tissue.

Supravalvar stenosis is caused by an encircling, constricting ridge in the ascending aorta. The aorta may be dilated or may be hypoplastic distal to the obstruction. The blood pressure is often higher in the right arm than in the left. Since the obstruction is distal to the aortic valve, the aortic component of

the second heart sound is not diminished; it may be exaggerated. Selective aortography combined with pressure measurements establish the diagnosis (Fig. 45).

Certain features characterize aortic stenosis, regardless of its exact site. Although some patients who have high-grade obstruction experience syncope or congestive heart failure and even sudden death during exertion or at quiet activity, it is usually the presence of a heart murmur in a well-developed individual, rather than symptoms, that calls the physician's attention to the condition. The systolic murmur is crescendo-decrescendo in form and is maximal at the second right interspace or in the suprasternal notch with transmission into the carotid arteries. However, in some patients with muscular subaortic stenosis and in some infants, the murmur is heard best low along the left sternal border. If the stenosis is severe, the sound of aortic closure is delayed. It may coincide with the pulmonic component of the second heart sound or may even follow the pulmonic component. In the latter situation, S_2 narrows with inspiration and widens with expiration (paradoxical splitting). An early systolic ejection sound indicates that the stenosis is valvar in origin. A decrescendo diastolic murmur of aortic insufficiency may be heard in patients with valvar as well as sub- and supravalvar stenosis. When the stenosis causes left ventricular enlargement, a lift of the apex may be felt. In young subjects with severe obstruction, the left ventricular enlargement produces a precordial bulge in the anterior axillary line.

The electrocardiogram is less sensitive as an index of severity of obstruction in aortic stenosis than it is in pulmonic stenosis. When abnormalities of S-T segments and T waves ("strain") are added onto the pattern of left ventricular hypertrophy, the stenosis is usually severe. That patient merits early cardiac catheterization with contrast visualization for precise definition of the site and severity of obstruction.

If there is left ventricular enlargement on roentgenograms of the chest, the stenosis is moderate to severe. Poststenotic dilation of the aorta is best seen in left anterior-oblique and frontal views; its presence favors the diagnosis of valvar stenosis.

The combination of left heart catheterization and selective left ventricular angiocardiography defines the level of obstruction as well as measures its severity.

When aortic stenosis is severe, open-heart surgery can afford relief of most forms of obstruction, at the valve, or proximal or distal to it, but there is a risk of creating aortic insufficiency in the attempt. Aortic insufficiency occasionally occurs spontaneously or following bacterial endocarditis.

AORTIC ATRESIA. Functionally, this lesion resembles the situation in which there is mitral atresia, an underdeveloped left ventricle, atrial and ventricular septal defects, and a patent ductus arteriosus (Fig. 39). Aortic atresia is the most limiting feature and

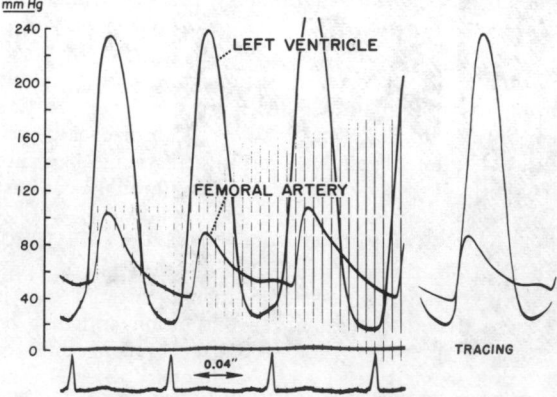

Fig. 44. Muscular subaortic stenosis due to hypertrophied musculature in infant with glycogen storage disease of myocardium. Pressure tracings from left ventricle and femoral artery show the initial synchronous rise in pressure and the development of a marked systolic gradient as ventricular systole proceeds. (From Ehlers et al. *Circulation*, 25:96, 1962.)

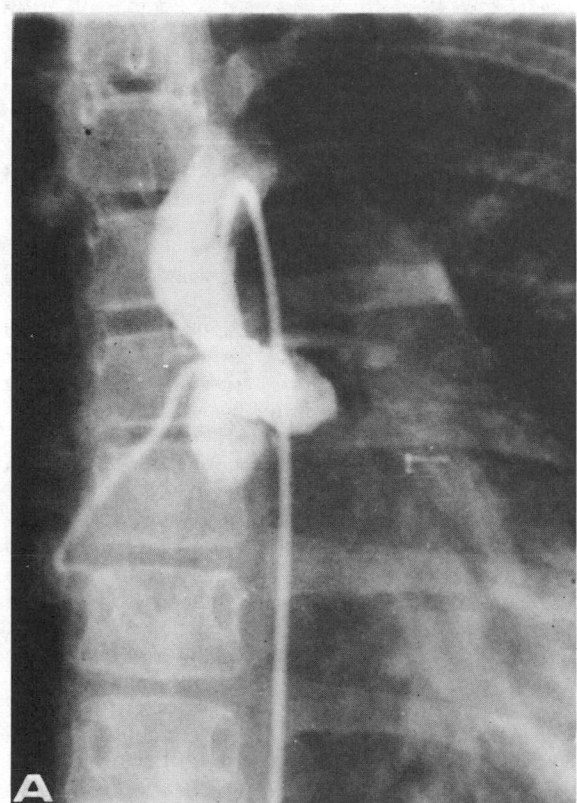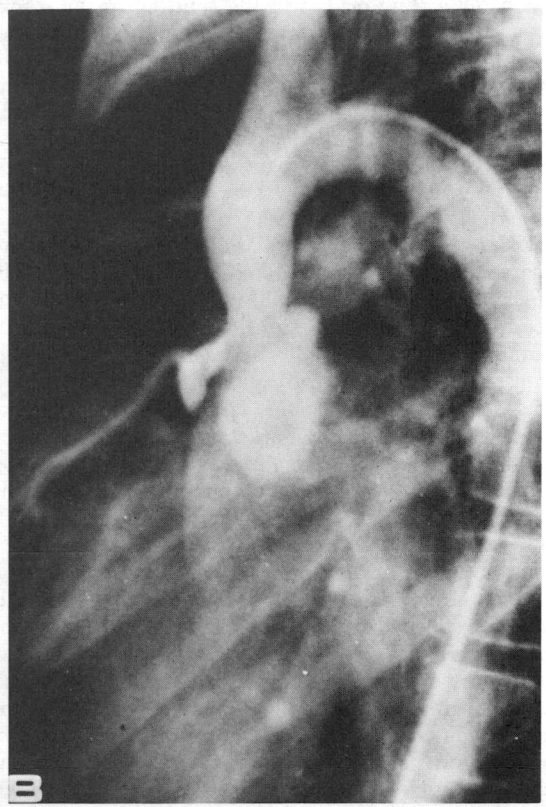

Fig. 45. Supravalvar aortic stenosis in 10-year-old girl with the supravalvar stenosis syndrome. Selective aortogram shows three aortic sinuses of unequal size and the origin of the coronary arteries proximal to the supravalvar area of narrowing with poststenotic dilation of the ascending aorta and innominate artery. A. Frontal view. B. Lateral view. (From Engle and Ehlers. *Theory and Practice of Auscultation*, 1963. Courtesy of F. A. Davis Co., pp. 238-53.)

the most uncorrectable aspect of the hypoplastic left heart syndrome. Rarely is there survival beyond the first days of life. The condition should be suspected when a newborn infant becomes dusky, exhibits respiratory distress, and has very weak pulses in arms and neck. (See Sec. 20.11.)

Obstructive Lesions of Major Arteries

In addition to supravalvar pulmonic and aortic stenosis, discussed above, single or multiple areas of narrowing and poststenotic dilation may occur in the branches of the main pulmonary artery or in the aorta and its branches. Though coarctation of the aorta has been well known for a long time, it has been only since the development of techniques of selective pulmonary arteriography and aortography that obstructive lesions of the pulmonary arterial tree and aortic branches (especially the renal artery) have been appreciated.

PULMONARY ARTERY BRANCH AND PERIPHERAL PULMONARY ARTERY STENOSIS. Branch stenosis or stenoses may be the only cardiovascular malformation

but more often, the obstruction is detected during evaluation of another cardiac anomaly, such as a septal defect. The association of branch stenosis with patent ductus arteriosus and the rubella syndrome is now well recognized.

Branch stenosis may cause an ejection-type, soft systolic murmur or a continuous murmur, audible over one or both lung fields more than over the precordium. The diagnosis is made at cardiac catheterization, either through recording a systolic pressure gradient across the obstruction or through contrast visualization of the narrowing.

PRECAPILLARY PULMONARY ARTERIAL OBSTRUCTION. Obstruction to blood flow through the precapillary branches of the pulmonary arterial tree is associated with pulmonary hypertension and may be primary (idiopathic) or secondary to congenital or acquired heart disease or to pulmonary disease. The pathologic findings range in severity from medial hypertrophy to intimal proliferation thrombosis, and recanalization with adventitial reaction and plexiform lesions.

The important finding on physical examination concerns the second sound in the second left interspace: the pulmonic component is audibly and often palpably accentuated, and the splitting of the second sound is narrow or absent. Often a high-pitched decrescendo diastolic murmur of pulmonic insufficiency can be heard along the left sternal border. There may be a short, early or midsystolic murmur in the second left interspace. A right ventricular tap is felt in the lower left parasternal area.

Electrocardiography shows right ventricular hypertrophy and sometimes "strain." Roentgenograms of the chest show enlargement of the main pulmonary artery and the right and left branches in the hilar regions with scant vascular markings in the peripheral lung fields. The right ventricle and atrium are enlarged. The diagnosis is confirmed by pressure measurements at cardiac catheterization.

Whether primary or secondary, the prognosis with severe pulmonary arterial obstruction is poor. Patients experience dyspnea on exertion, syncope, congestive cardiac failure, cyanosis if there is a right-to-left shunt route, and sudden death.

COARCTATION OF THE AORTA. Most often coarctation occurs as a localized narrowing of the aorta with a circumferential internal diaphragm just distal to the left subclavian artery at the level of the ligamentum arteriosum. Coarctation may also occur at other sites: in the transverse aortic arch or in the thoracic or abdominal aorta. The old terms, infantile and adult-type coarctation, do not include all varieties of coarctation. It is preferable, instead, to define the coarctation by its location and extent as well as by its relation to the ductus if that structure is patent. If the ductus is patent, its aortic end can be proximal to, distal to, or at the level of the coarctation.

Wherever the coarctation is situated, the pulse is stronger and the blood pressure higher in those arteries proximal to the coarctation than in the more distal vessels. The diagnosis is made on the basis of such a discrepancy between the two arms or between the upper and lower extremities. Although there is usually hypertension in the arms, the blood pressure there may be in normal limits if the coarctation is slight or collateral circulation is rich. Auscultation over the back, along the course of the aorta, usually reveals a systolic murmur over the point of narrowing. In older children or teen-agers one may see and palpate on the chest wall dilated arteries of collateral circulation.

Symptoms, if present, include headache and pains in the legs on exercise. Severe obstruction leads to congestive cardiac failure, especially in the young infant and particularly if he has an associated ventricular septal defect or patent ductus.

Radiologic signs of coarctation in the usual area depend on recognizing the poststenotic dilation of the descending aorta in the frontal view, where one sees a "3 sign," and on barium swallow in the frontal and left anterior-oblique view, where one notes an "E sign" of esophageal displacement by the dilated segment of aorta distal to the coarctation (Fig. 46). Notching of the undersurfaces of the ribs is not often found in infants or young children. Angiocardiography or aortography defines the site and extent of constriction as well as the size of the adjacent aorta and arteries (Fig. 47).

Infants with coarctation who develop congestive cardiac failure usually have one or more coexistent and sometimes even more physiologically significant defects, such that the signs of the coarctation may be masked by the other lesions. Many infants in

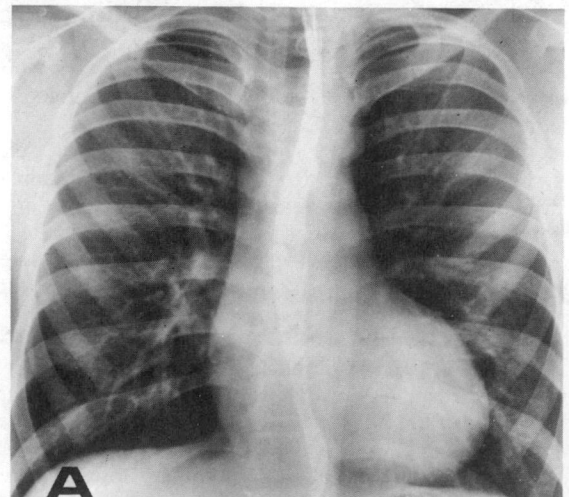
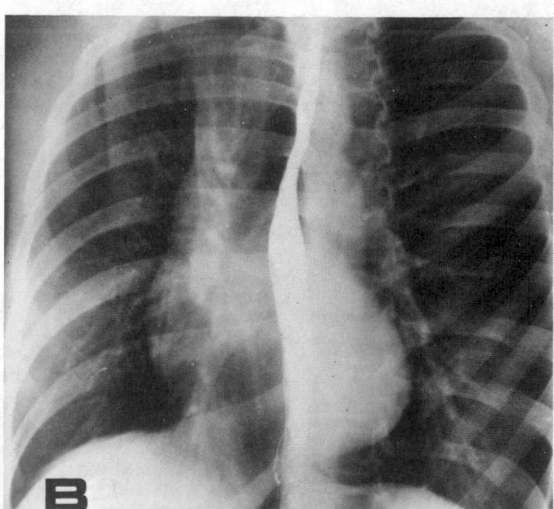

Fig. 46. Coarctation of aorta in 8-year-old boy. Frontal view (A) shows E sign of barium-filled esophagus, the upper curve being due to displacement by the left aortic arch and the lower one, displacement by the postcoarctation dilation of descending aorta. The area of dilated aorta proximal and distal to the constriction can be seen on the upper left heart border in the frontal view (3 sign) and superimposed on the vertebrae in the LAO projection (B). Anterior displacement of barium-filled esophagus by the postcoarctation segment of aorta is seen in LAO view. Left ventricle is enlarged in both views.

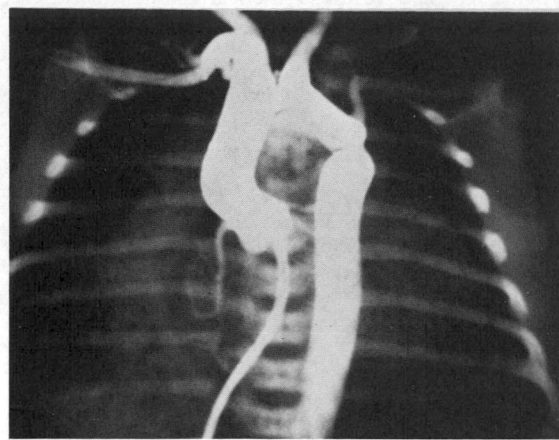

Fig. 47. Coarctation of aorta in infant with evidence of a small patent ductus. Aortic injection shows the coarctation in the descending arch of the aorta at the level of the opacified left subclavian artery. Note the narrowing of the transverse aortic arch between the innominate and the left carotid arteries as well as the greater than normal length of descending aorta between the left carotid and subclavian arteries. In this infant there is no evidence of collateral circulation.

failure respond to intensive medical management and enter the benign period of the childhood years when there is rarely disability due to the lesion. Resection of the coarctation and end-to-end anastomosis of the aorta is indicated for those babies who fail to improve on medical management and for older children

around the age of 10 years. Because of the frequent coexistence of some abnormality of the aortic valve, such as bicuspid aortic valve, aortic stenosis, or aneurysm of the sinus of Valsalva, it is well to protect the postoperative patient against bacterial endocarditis at times of predictable risk, just as one does the unoperated patient with coarctation.

INTERRUPTION OF ISTHMUS OF AORTA. There is aplasia of a portion of the descending arch of the aorta, which may be represented by a fibrous cord or actual absence of tissue. The left ventricle sends blood only to those brachiocephalic and vertebral arteries arising from the aortic arch. The descending aorta is supplied via a patent ductus arteriosus with blood from the right ventricle and pulmonary artery. Hence the patient has cyanotic toes (a sign of "reverse flow ductus") and pink fingers and face. The diagnosis is made by contrast visualization, selectively injected to opacity the ascending and the descending aorta. The condition can be surgically corrected by anastomosing the aortic arch to the descending aorta, directly or with use of a graft.

PERIPHERAL SYSTEMIC ARTERIAL STENOSIS (RENAL ARTERY STENOSIS). Now recognized as one cause of hypertension of otherwise unexplained etiology, stenosis of the renal artery is a physiologically significant form of peripheral aortic branch stenosis. The diagnosis is made by selective aortography (Fig. 48). Contrast medium is injected through a catheter placed in the descending aorta with its tip near the origin of the renal artery. Resection of the area of stenosis, or if this is not possible, removal of the affected kidney if the other is normal, may result in relief of hypertension. (See Sec. 21.6.)

REFERENCES

OBSTRUCTION TO VENOUS RETURN

Vena Caval Obstruction

Effler, D. B., and Groves, L. K. Superior vena caval obstruction. J. Thorac. Cardiovasc. Surg., 43:574, 1962.
Skinner, D. B., Salzman, E. W., and Scannell, J. G. The challenge of superior vena cava obstruction. J. Thorac. Cardiovasc. Surg., 49:824, 1965.

Pulmonary Venous Obstruction

Carter, R. E. B., Capriles, M., and Noe, Y. Total anomalous pulmonary venous drainage. Brit. Heart J., 31:45, 1969.
Mody, M. R., Gallen, W. J., and Lepley, D. Total anomalous pulmonary venous drainage below the diaphragm. Amer. J. Cardiol., 34:575, 1969.
Nakib, A., Moller, J. H., Kanjuh, V. I., and Edwards, J. E. Anomalies of the pulmonary veins. Amer. J. Cardiol., 20:77, 1967.
Robinson, A. E., Chen, J., Bradford, W., and Lester, R. Kerley B lines in total anomalous pulmonary venous connection below the diaphragm (type III). Amer. J. Cardiol., 24:436, 1969.

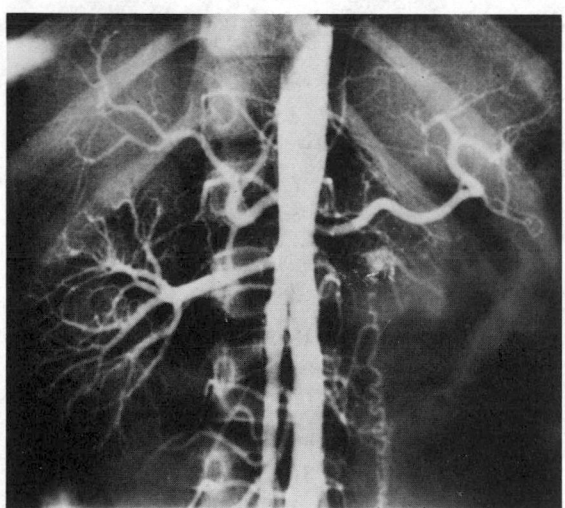

Fig. 48. Renal artery stenosis in 10-year-old girl with hypertension and congestive heart failure. Selective aortogram shows opacification of abdominal aorta, both suprarenal arteries and the right renal artery. Absence of opacification of origin of left renal artery, due to stenosis; an artery of collateral circulation in region of left ureter is seen, along with scant opacification of distal renal artery. Following left nephrectomy, she has had full relief of congestive heart failure and hypertension. (From Jabloner and Engle. *Heart Bull.,* 13:84, 1964.)

Snellen, H. A., van Ingen, H. C., and Hoefsmit, E. Ch. M. Patterns of anomalous pulmonary venous drainage. Circulation, 38:45, 1968.

Cor Triatriatum

Grondin, C., Leonard, A. S., Anderson, R. C., Amplatz, K. A., Edwards, J. E., and Varco, R. L. Cor triatriatum: a diagnostic surgical enigma. J. Thorac. Cardiovasc. Surg., 48:527, 1964. Abstr., Circulation, 32:152, 1965.

Jeiger, W., Gibbons, J. E., and Wigglesworth, F. W. Cor triatriatum: clinical, hemodynamic and pathologic studies: surgical correction in early life. Pediatrics, 31:255, 1963.

ATRIOVENTRICULAR VALVE OBSTRUCTION

Tricuspid Stenosis and Atresia

Guller, B., and Titus, J. L. Morphological studies in tricuspid atresia. Circulation, 38:977, 1968.

Marcano, B. Z., Riemenschneider, T. A., Ruttenberg, H. D., Goldberg, S. J., and Gyepes, M. Tricuspid atresia with increased pulmonary blood flow: an analysis of 13 cases. Cirrculation, 40:399, 1969.

Mitral Stenosis

Castaneda, A. R., Anderson, R. C., and Edwards, J. E. Congenital mitral stenosis resulting from anomalous arcade and obstructing papillary muscles. Report of correction by use of ball valve prosthesis. Amer. J. Cardiol., 24:237, 1969.

Daoud, G., Kaplan, S., Perrin, E. V., Dorst, J. P., and Edwards, F. K. Congenital mitral stenosis. Circulation, 27:185, 1963.

Wooley, C. F., Klassen, K. P., Leighton, R. F., Goodwin, R. S., and Ryan, J. M. Left atrial and left ventricular sound and pressure in mitral stenosis. Circulation, 38:295, 1968.

Atrial Tumor

Goldberg, H. P., Glenn, F., Dotter, C. T., and Steinberg, I. Myxoma of the left atrium. Diagnosis made during life with operative and postmortem findings. Circulation, 6:752, 1952.

SEMILUNAR VALVE OBSTRUCTION

Pulmonic Stenosis

Engle, M. A., Ito, T., and Goldberg, H. P. The fate of the patient with pulmonic stenosis. Circulation, 30:554, 1964.

―――― Ito, T., Lukas, D. S., and Goldberg, H. P. Electrocardiographic evaluation of pulmonic stenosis. J. Pediat., 57:171, 1960.

―――― Holswade, G. R., Goldberg, H. P., Lukas, D. S., and Glenn, F. Regression after open valvotomy of infundibular stenosis accompanying severe valvular pulmonic stenosis. Circulation, 17:862, 1958.

Gale, G. E., Barlow, J. B., and Heinmann, K. W. Double-chambered right ventricle. Brit. Heart J., 31:291, 1969.

Lucas, R. V., Jr., Varco, R. L., Lillehei, C. W., Adams, P., Jr., Anderson, R. C., and Edwards, J. E. Anomalous muscle bundle of the right ventricle—hemodynamic consequences and surgical considerations. Circulation, 25:443, 1962.

Vogelpoel, L., and Schrire, V. Auscultatory and phonocardiographic assessment of pulmonary stenosis with intact ventricular septum. Circulation, 22:55, 1960.

Pulmonic Atresia

Cole, R. B., Muster, A. J., Lev, M., and Paul, M. H. Pulmonary atresia with intact ventricular septum. Amer. J. Cardiol., 21:23, 1968.

Davignon, A. L., Greenwold, W. E., DuShane, J. W., and Edwards, J. E. Congenital pulmonary atresia with intact ventricular septum; clinicopathologic correlation of two anatomic types. Amer. Heart J., 62:591 and 690, 1961.

Kieffer, S. A., and Carey, L. S. Radiological aspects of pulmonary atresia with intact ventricular septum. Brit. Heart J., 25:655, 1963.

Aortic Stenosis

Beuren, A. J., Schulze, E., Eberle, P., Harmjanz, D., and Apitz, J. The syndrome of supravalvular aortic stenosis, peripheral pulmonic stenosis, mental retardation, and similar facial appearance. Amer. J. Cardiol., 13:471, 1964.

Bentall, H. H., and Morrow, A. G. The place of surgery in hypertrophic obstructive cardiomyopathy. J. Thorac. Cardiovasc. Surg., 51:49, 1966.

Braunwald, E., Goldblatt, A., Aygen, M. M., Rokoff, S. D., and Morrow, A. G. Congenital aortic stenosis. I. Clinical and hemodynamic findings in 100 patients. Circulation, 27:426, 1963.

Campbell, M. The natural history of congenital aortic stenosis. Brit. Heart J., 30:514, 1968.

Cohen, J., Effat, H., Goodwin, J. F., Oakley, C. M., and Steiner, R. E. Hypertrophic obstructive cardiomyopathy. Brit. Heart J., 26:16, 1964.

Cooley, D. A., Beall, A. C., Jr., Hallman, G. L., and Bricker, D. L. Obstructive lesions of the left ventricular outflow tract. Surgical treatment. Circulation, 31:612, 1965.

Frank, S., and Braunwald, E. Idiopathic hypertrophic subaortic stenosis. Circulation, 37:759, 1968.

McGoon, D. C., Geha, A. S., Scofield, E. L., and DuShane, J. W. Surgical treatment of congenital aortic stenosis. Dis. Chest, 55:388, 1969.

Morrow, A. G., Goldblatt, A., and Braunwald, E. Congenital aortic stenosis. II. Surgical treatment and the results of operation. Circulation, 27:450, 1963.

Schwartz, L. S., Goldfischer, J., Sprague, G. J., and Schwartz, S. P. Syncope and sudden death in aortic stenosis. Amer. J. Cardiol., 23:647, 1969.

Varghese, P. J., Izukawa, T., and Rowe, R. D. Supravalvular aortic stenosis as part of rubella syndrome, with discussion of pathogenesis. Brit. Heart J., 31:59, 1969.

OBSTRUCTION OF GREAT ARTERIES

Peripheral Pulmonary Artery Stenosis

Baum, D., Khaury, G. H., Ongley, P. A., Swan, H. J. C., and Kincaid, O. W. Congenital stenosis of the pulmonary artery branches. Circulation, 29:680, 1964.

Perloff, J. K., and Lebauer, E. J. Auscultatory and phono-cardiographic manifestations of isolated stenosis of the pulmonary artery and its branches. Brit. Heart J., 31: 314, 1969.

Rios, J. C., Walsh, B. J., Masumi, R. A., Sims, A. J., and Ewy, G. A. Congenital pulmonary artery branch stenosis. Amer. J. Cardiol., 24:318, 1969.

Rowe, R. D. Maternal rubella and pulmonary artery stenosis. Pediatrics, 32:180, 1963.

Precapillary Pulmonary Arterial Obstruction

Hood, W. B., Jr., Spencer, H., Lass, R. W., and Daley, R. Primary pulmonary hypertension: familial occurrence. Brit. Heart J., 30:336, 1968.

Luke, J. J., Mehrizi, A., Folger, G. M., Jr., and Rowe, R. D. Chronic nasopharyngeal obstruction causing cor pulmonale. Pediatrics, 37:762, 1966.

Rao, B. N. S., Moller, J. H., and Edwards, J. E. Primary pulmonary hypertension in a child: response to pharmacologic agents. Circulation, 40:583, 1969.

Thilenius, O. G., Nadas, A. S., and Jockin, H. Primary pulmonary vascular obstruction in children. Pediatrics, 36:75, 1965.

Coarctation of Aorta

Ibarra-Perez, C., Castaneda, A. R., Varco, R. L., and Lillehei, C. W. Recoarctation of the aorta. Nineteen year clinical experience. Amer. J. Cardiol., 23:778, 1969.

Schuster, S. R., and Gross, R. E. Surgery for coarctation of the aorta: review of 500 cases. J. Thorac. Cardiovasc. Surg., 43:54, 1962.

Sinha, S. N., Kardatzke, M. L., Cole, R. B., Muster, A. J., Wessel, H. U., and Paul, M. H. Coarctation of the aorta in infancy. Circulation, 40:385, 1969.

Tawes, R. L., Berry, C. L., and Aberdeen, E. Congenital bicuspid aortic valves associated with coarctation of the aorta in children. Brit. Heart J., 31:127, 1969.

Renal Artery Stenosis

Halpern, M., and Evans, J. A. Coarctation of the renal artery with "notching" of the ureter. A roentgenologic sign of unilateral renal disease as a cause of hypertension. Amer. J. Roentgen., 88:159, 1962.

20.10
LEFT-TO-RIGHT SHUNTS

JULIEN I. E. HOFFMAN

Connections between the Aorta and the Pulmonary Artery

Patent Ductus Arteriosus

THE NORMAL DUCTUS ARTERIOSUS. In fetal life the ductus arteriosus carries blood from the pulmo-

nary artery into the aorta, thus bypassing the high resistance of the pulmonary vascular bed. Immediately after birth when the lungs have expanded, the pulmonary vascular resistance drops; at the same time the systemic vascular resistance rises after the low resistance of the placental circulation has been eliminated. These changes cause the ductus arteriosus to carry blood from the aorta to the pulmonary artery —i.e., a left-to-right shunt occurs—and this has been demonstrated in normal children during the first day of life. By the end of the first day no shunts can normally be detected, but this is due to functional and not anatomic closure of the ductus arteriosus, as shown by the reopening of the ductus after certain stimuli, such as hypoxia, and by finding anatomic patency of the ductus arteriosus in autopsies of infants who died from a wide variety of causes. Anatomic obliteration of the ductus arteriosus is slower but is usually complete by three weeks.

THE ABNORMAL PATENT DUCTUS ARTERIOSUS. *Etiology.* Maternal rubella in the first trimester is often followed by persistent patency of the ductus arteriosus, but in most patients no known cause can be established. The lesion is said to be more common in children born at high altitudes, but it is not known if this is due to some influence on the formation of the ductus arteriosus prenatally or if it is due to a postnatal response to persistent hypoxemia.

Anatomy. Usually the ductus arteriosus connects the aorta just beyond the left subclavian artery to the left pulmonary artery near the bifurcation of the main pulmonary artery. The ductus may be long and thin or short and wide; at times, the two vessels appear to have a side-to-side anastomosis.

Physiology and Clinical Features. The size of the left-to-right shunt, and therefore the clinical features, depends on the resistance to flow offered by the ductus arteriosus and the pulmonary vascular bed. If the ductus is long and narrow so that resistance to flow through it is very high, then a large left-to-right shunt will never develop no matter how low the pulmonary vascular resistance falls. Because the aortic pressure soon exceeds the pulmonary arterial pressure throughout the cardiac cycle, there will be a left-to-right shunt through the ductus in systole and diastole. Therefore, there will be a murmur continuously throughout the cardiac cycle, and its maximal intensity occurs late in systole, because of the time taken for the peak of pressure to travel round the arch of the aorta to the ductus. This murmur has a typical grinding, machinery, or echoing quality and is usually heard best at the second left intercostal space under the left clavicle. Sometimes, however, the murmur has no distinguishing quality and may be better heard at the lower left sternal border.

When the shunt is small, no other murmurs are present, and the heart sounds are normal. Since there is little extra burden on the left ventricle, there may be no detectable hypertrophy or dilation, and the slightly increased pulsation of the ventricular apex may not be obvious. This combination of the typical continuous murmur without signs of significant cardiac involvement is strongly suggestive of a small patent ductus arteriosus.

When the ductus arteriosus is larger but still offers some resistance to flow through it, then a large left-to-right shunt can develop as soon as the pulmonary vascular resistance falls. In addition to the typical murmur, the signs and symptoms of a left ventricular volume overload will appear, but pulmonary arterial pressure will be normal or only slightly elevated, so that there will be no right ventricular pressure overload. Thus there will be clinical, electrocardiographic, and radiologic evidence of left ventricular dilation and hypertrophy and of pulmonary plethora; there may be a middiastolic apical rumbling murmur due to increased flow through the mitral valve; and there will be a bounding or collapsing pulse with a rapid rise to a high systolic pressure and a rapid fall to a low diastolic pressure. The rapid rise to a high systolic pressure is due to the rapid ejection of a large left ventricular stroke volume into the aorta; the rapid fall to a low diastolic pressure is due to rapid runoff of blood through the ductus into the pulmonary artery as well as a rapid peripheral runoff through a lowered systemic vascular resistance, possibly related to reflex inhibition of arterial baroreceptors.

When the ductus arteriosus offers no resistance to blood flow because it is so large and short, then the pulmonary arterial pressure remains the same as the systemic pressure. When the pulmonary vascular resistance falls a large left-to-right shunt can occur. The pulmonary vascular resistance may, however, decrease more slowly than usual in these patients. The clinical features may be the same as those described for the moderate-sized ductus, with two main exceptions. Because of the high pulmonary arterial pressure there will be evidence of right ventricular pressure overload, and this can at times dominate the clinical and electrocardiographic picture. Another consequence of the high pulmonary arterial pressure is that the diastolic murmur may disappear, leaving only a systolic murmur and making the clinical diagnosis of patent ductus arteriosus difficult.

When the left-to-right shunt puts so much load on the left ventricle that compensatory mechanisms fail, all the consequences of a high pulmonary venous pressure are found. The infant may present with tachypnea, especially on feeding; poor weight gain; tachycardia; excessive sweating, again often with feeding; and cough and wheezing. Examination of the child will usually lead to the diagnosis, providing that certain features are borne in mind. Right heart failure is not infrequently absent, and the mistake is often made of diagnosing the syndrome of tachypnea, tachycardia, wheezing, and rales as being due to bronchiolitis or bronchopneumonia and not to left ventricular failure; the latter should always be considered if there is the slightest suggestion of heart disease.

From these considerations it will be realized that the small or moderate-sized patent ductus arteriosus seldom presents any difficulties in clinical diagnosis. The large patent ductus arteriosus with pulmonary hypertension, however, may be very hard to diagnose clinically. There may be only a systolic murmur, which is usually not pathognomonic of a patent ductus arteriosus and, if it is heard lower down than usual, might easily be mistaken for the murmur of a ventricular septal defect. In some infants and young children this systolic murmur is irregular in quality, having high-pitched clicks interspersed with vibrations of lower frequency. The resulting quality is easy to detect though hard to describe but, if present, helps to distinguish the systolic murmur of a patent ductus arteriosus from that of a ventricular septal defect. Another cause of difficulty in diagnosis is the change in physical signs which sometimes occurs during severe heart failure. The cardiac output may fall markedly and lead to peripheral systemic vasoconstriction; the heart will then not be hyperactive, the murmur becomes softer, and the pulses will not be bounding. It is easy to understand how the diagnosis of a patent ductus with a large left-to-right shunt might be missed in these circumstances. After digitalization leads to clinical improvement in these cases, most or all of the classical physical signs may reappear.

A persistent patent ductus arteriosus occurs in about 14 percent of premature infants; it is commoner if there has been much respiratory distress. These ductuses can cause congestive heart failure, and a common error is to assume that the symptoms are due to the lung disease and so ignore the cardiac lesion. The physical and radiologic signs of a patent ductus arteriosus are usually present, but at times cardiac catheterization is needed to make the diagnosis. Spontaneous closure of these ductuses in premature infants is frequent and can occur even if there has been heart failure. However, if the infant does not improve with medical treatment the ductus should be closed surgically, provided the doctors and nurses are experienced in surgical and postoperative care of premature infants.

While the clinical diagnosis of this lesion is usually simple, there are times when it cannot be differentiated from truncus arteriosus, ventricular septal defect with aortic regurgitation, fistula from aortic sinus of Valsalva to right atrium or ventricle, and coronary arteriovenous fistula. Whenever there is doubt, the patient should be catheterized in a center with experience in this field. Since surgical closure of the ductus can be lifesaving, this diagnosis should be suspected in any infant who might have heart disease and should be proven if need be by cardiac catheterization. If the child is in difficulty, he should be operated on at any age. If the ductus is not big and the patient has no symptoms, then surgery is better deferred until it can be done with greater safety. This will usually be at about 2 or 3 years of age. Spontaneous closure of patent ductus arteriosus has been reported, most often in premature infants, but as the frequency of closure does not appear to be high in older children and surgical closure of the defect has negligible mortality, operation should be advised in most. Even if there is no hemodynamic load on the heart, there is always a risk of bacterial endocarditis; and since surgical closure of the ductus prevents the development of subacute bacterial endocarditis, it should be recommended in all patients beyond infancy.

In a few patients the pulmonary vascular resistance is so high that a right-to-left shunt through the ductus arteriosus occurs. This usually happens after the pulmonary vessels have been affected by long-continued high flows and pressures from large left-to-right shunts, though in rare instances it may result from primary congenital vascular changes. These patients have the signs of right ventricular pressure load, with very loud pulmonic closure, sometimes a pulmonic regurgitant murmur, and a heaving right ventricle and pulmonary artery; there may also be a systolic click at the base. The typical ductus murmur is replaced by a soft systolic murmur or no murmur at all, and the bounding pulses disappear. Because the right-to-left shunt passes into the aorta at or below the origin of the left subclavian artery, there is often differential cyanosis—i.e., the toes are cyanotic while the fingers are not. Unless the cause for the high pulmonary vascular resistance can be reversed, the ductus should not be closed surgically. The operation has a high mortality and, even if successful, leaves the patients with severe pulmonary arterial hypertension in which a safety valve has been removed. These patients may live for several years but tend to die in progressive right ventricular failure. Some may succumb suddenly, particularly with exertion, probably because of inability to maintain an adequate cardiac output. No treatment for this condition is known.

AORTOPULMONARY FENESTRATION. This rare abnormality is due to partial failure of separation of the primitive truncus arteriosus into aorta and pulmonary artery, so that the two vessels communicate just above the semilunar valve as if a side-to-side anastomosis had been done. Because the defect is usually wide, the left-to-right shunt is almost invariably large and there is marked pulmonary arterial hypertension. Physiologically it acts like a large patent ductus arteriosus. Clinically there may be a continuous murmur like that of a patent ductus arteriosus, but best heard at the third and fourth intercostal spaces along the left sternal border; at other times there may be only the systolic component of the murmur so that it resembles the murmur of a ventricular septal defect.

The diagnosis of a large left-to-right shunt with pulmonary arterial hypertension is usually made, and definitive diagnosis has to be made by cardiac catheterization and angiocardiography. The defect can be closed relatively easily with the aid of cardiopulmonary bypass.

ANOMALOUS ORIGIN OF THE LEFT CORONARY ARTERY. This term is applied when the left coronary artery is attached to the pulmonary artery, while the right coronary artery arises normally from the aorta. In fetal life, when pulmonary arterial pressure is high, blood perfuses the myocardium normally. After birth the left coronary artery still perfuses its myocardium, although with desaturated blood, and collateral vessels from the right coronary artery may help this perfusion. Then when pulmonary arterial pressure drops to its low normal level and there are big collaterals, blood can flow from the right coronary artery through collateral vessels and then through the left coronary artery into the pulmonary artery without perfusing the myocardium of the anterolateral wall of the left ventricle. The low-resistance left coronary artery steals blood from the high-resistance myocardial bed.

The clinical features reflect these physiologic changes. In early infancy there is usually no detectable disability. As the left ventricular myocardium becomes less well perfused there may be episodes of myocardial ischemia, and these infants characteristically have attacks of screaming, as if with pain, and pallor. With further left ventricular damage the pattern of anterolateral infarction appears on the electrocardiogram; the presence of large Q waves in leads I and AVL should make one suspicious of the diagnosis in any infant with a suggestive history. The left ventricle enlarges and hypertrophies, and there may be episodes of left ventricular failure or congestive heart failure. The myocardial damage may involve the papillary muscles, resulting in mitral insufficiency.

Diagnosis can be strongly suspected by history and electrocardiography and should be confirmed by cardiac catheterization and angiocardiography. Treatment in most patients consists of ligation of the anomalous left coronary artery if there is flow from the coronary artery into the pulmonary artery. This prevents the runoff and so permits perfusion of the surviving myocardium via the collaterals. In general the results of this procedure have been good, although ultimate prognosis depends on how much heart muscle has been infarcted. Recently some have suggested that it might be better to anastomose the left coronary artery to the aorta, but the results have not been evaluated. Should there be a large ventricular aneurysm and persistent heart failure, excision of the aneurysm should be considered. If pulmonary arterial pressure is high, as occurs when there is a complicating mitral stenosis, ligation of the anomalous artery is not indicated.

Connection between Aorta and Right Ventricle or Atrium

FISTULAS FROM SINUS OF VALSALVA. These fistulas may be congenital or may follow rupture of a congenital aneurysm of the sinus of Valsalva into one of the cardiac chambers; the latter may be suspected if there is a history of the sudden appearance of a murmur or of symptoms postnatally. These fistulas most commonly enter the right atrium or ventricle, but can also enter the left atrium or ventricle. If they enter the left side they display the features of aortic regurgitation, do not cause a left-to-right shunt, and are not associated with excessive pulmonary blood flow.

The fistulas which enter the right heart produce physiologic changes similar to those of patent ductus arteriosus, the size of the shunt depending on the pulmonary vascular resistance and the resistance of the fistula. The physical signs are similar to those of the patent ductus arteriosus, but in addition there is an increased volume load on the right heart which is hyperactive and dilated. The murmur is usually continuous or to and fro, and the site of maximum intensity is along the left lower sternal border. The diastolic component of the murmur may be more prominent than in a patent ductus arteriosus because of the large pressure gradient between the aorta and the right atrium or right ventricle in disastole. There is a rumbling middiastolic murmur in the mitral area and, if the shunt enters the right atrium, in the tricuspid area also.

Differentiation from other members of this group can only be made by cardiac catheterization and angiocardiography. Surgical closure of the fistula is usually simple with the aid of cardiopulmonary bypass.

Fistulas entering the left side should be considered whenever aortic regurgitation appears to be present, for they are easier to treat than are lesions of the aortic valves.

CORONARY ARTERIOVENOUS FISTULA. This is also rare. Large fistulous communications pass from one or both coronary arteries to enter the right atrium through the coronary sinus or else plunge directly through the muscle into any of the cardiac chambers. Usually the fistulas enter the right atrium or ventricle. Because the communications usually connect high- and low-pressure systems, the murmur is commonly continuous. There is left ventricular hyperactivity and increased pulse pressure; there may or may not be right-sided hyperactivity, depending on where the fistula enters the heart. Diagnosis depends on cardiac catheterization and angiocardiography, and surgical ligation of the fistula is usually possible.

ARTERIOVENOUS FISTULA. Congenital communications may occasionally form between any major systemic arteries and their related veins—e.g., femoral artery and vein, a cerebral artery and vein. Locally there may be systolic or continuous murmurs at the site of the fistula, occasionally a pulsatile mass may be felt, and sometimes there is abnormal function of the region whose blood supply is affected.

The cardiac effects of these fistulas, if they are large, depend on the low-resistance shunt which allows blood to run off from the arterial to the venous system. In general, blood flow to body tissues is normal, so the added amount of blood shunted imposes a volume load on both ventricles. As in a big patent ductus arteriosus, there is usually a high systemic systolic pressure and a low diastolic pressure, with bounding or collapsing pulses and a hyperactive heart. If the venal vessels are involved there will be diastolic hypertension.

If the volume load is excessive, these patients may exhibit pulmonary edema and congestive heart failure; and should heart failure cause the cardiac output to fall and systemic arteriolar vasoconstriction to occur, then precordial hyperactivity will diminish. The pulses will no longer be collapsing. In these circumstances the diagnosis may be missed until digitalization restores the typical physical signs.

When the arteriovenous fistula occurs in the region of the great vein of Galen there is usually a large aneurysm of this vein seen on cerebral angiography. Infants with this condition commonly develop severe heart failure within the first few weeks after birth and are often very cyanotic.

Diagnosis of these lesions is confirmed by cardiac catheterization and angiography. Surgical ligation or excision of the fistula or the involved arteries and veins is usually effective, although sometimes, especially in the brain, there may be damage to the region supplied by the ligated vessels.

Connection between Left Ventricle and Lesser Circulation

Ventricular Septal Defect

This is one of the commonest of all congenital heart lesions. It may be the only lesion, and as an isolated lesion occurs in about 2 out of every 1,000 livebirths. It may also occur combined with any other congenital heart lesion and often occurs in certain specific combinations like tetralogy of Fallot and certain cases of transposition of the great arteries.

ANATOMY. The commonest site of the defect is in the membranous septum, but it may also be anywhere in the muscular septum. Sometimes multiple defects are present. In some patients the defect lies poseteriorly and may or may not be part of an endocardial cushion defect with cleft mitral and tricuspid valves and an ostium primum defect of the atrial septum. In a few patients the defect may be in its usual position, but the aorta and the pulmonary artery both arise from the right ventricle. Sometimes there is associated infundibular or valvar stenosis of the right ventricular outflow tract, and sometimes aortic regurgitation is present. One other unusual but important association is with corrected transposition (ventricular inversion), in which a ventricular septal defect is the most frequent added lesion.

PHYSIOLOGY AND CLINICAL FEATURES. The clinical physiology has already been described and is similar to that of patent ductus arteriosus. There is evidence of a left ventricular volume overload if the lesion is big enough, and there may be some signs of a right ventricular volume overload as well, since the left-to-right shunt passes into the right ventricle before passing out into the pulmonary artery. If there is pulmonary arterial hypertension, there is in addition evidence of right ventricular pressure load. The symptoms are as expected for each of these patterns of overload and have already been described for patent ductus arteriosus.

The murmur of a ventricular septal defect is typically a harsh, holosystolic murmur maximal at the left lower sternal border but widely transmitted. There is no correlation between the intensity of the murmur and the size of the defect, and some of the loudest murmurs are found with hemodynamically insignificant defects (maladie de Roger). At times the murmur is crescendo-decrescendo (diamond-shaped), usually when the defect is small. When there is pulmonary arterial hypertension due to a greatly raised pulmonary vascular resistance, the murmur may be short and less harsh. Recently cardiologists have begun to recognize a high-pitched, whistling systolic murmur along the left sternal border as being due to a very small ventricular defect, but this may be difficult to separate from an innocent murmur. With big shunts there is a middiastolic rumbling murmur at the apex. The heart sounds are not unusual unless pulmonary hypertension causes a loud pulmonic closure or infundibular stenosis causes a widely split second heart sound.

· Those patients with small ventricular septal defects have little overload on the ventricles, and their main risk is of bacterial endocarditis. Those with moderate-sized defects can develop large shunts when the pulmonary vascular resistance falls but they do not have associated pulmonary hypertension, while those with very large defects have large shunts and marked pulmonary hypertension. When there are large left-to-right shunts, symptoms and cardiac failure may occur, most commonly under six months of age. In full-term infants cardiac failure seldom develops under two months of age unless precipitated by severe anemia or massive infection, but in premature infants severe cardiac failure can occur below two months of age. This time sequence is probably related to the time taken for pulmonary vascular resistance to fall and for anemia to become marked. Perhaps other compensatory mechanisms fail after this period of time.

When there are symptoms the child should be catheterized to prove the diagnosis and assess the size of the defect. Treatment of these patients by medical means is usually effective in all but the biggest defects, and it is worthwhile to try intensive medical treatment before advising surgery, unless the child's life is in immediate danger.

The principal complications of ventricular septal defects are cardiac failure from excess volume load, bacterial endocarditis, and pulmonary vascular disease. Bacterial endocarditis may occur with small as well as large defects and is rare in the pediatric age group; one should not rush to surgery merely to combat this risk, and it is by no means certain that it is completely abolished by closing the defect, because foreign material, such as sutures or a patch used to close the defect, in the circulation may form a nidus for subsequent infections. Pulmonary vascular disease probably results from stimuli associated with high pressures and flows in the pulmonary arteries and also from high left atrial pressures. In the majority of patients with big defects the pulmonary vascular resistance falls after birth, possibly more slowly than normal, and then may rise again if the necessary stimuli are present. The rise can occur as early as nine months after birth, and if it occurs, surgical closure of the defect or banding of the pulmonary artery should be done to prevent irreversible pulmonary vascular damage.

Set against these complications is the tendency for spontaneous closure of the defects, which may occur in 50 percent or more of all ventricular septal defects. Another 30 percent of defects become smaller but may not close completely. Most of this spontaneous improvement appears to take place within the first three years, but examples of late closure have been reported. Because of this high incidence of spontaneous improvement, and because most children with ventricular septal defects do well without surgery, there is no need to rush to early surgery in most of these patients; this is fortunate because the younger the child, the higher the operative mortality.

Based on these considerations, a rational approach to the treatment of ventricular septal defects can be suggested. When the defect is small and does not cause any symptoms, no specific medical therapy is needed. The child should be treated as a normal child with the sole exception that he should be given prophylactic penicillin at the time of dental treatment. Surgery should not be advised, with the hope that the defect will close by itself. Only when he is over 10 years old and has a defect of sufficient size, as evidenced by a pulmonary blood flow about twice systemic blood flow, should surgical closure be considered.

At the other extreme is the child with a huge defect who is in cardiac failure which does not respond well to intensive medical treatment. This child should be operated on to avoid death from cardiac failure. Between these two extremes are the children who have big defects and have been in cardiac failure but have responded to medical treatment. These should be followed carefully and should be catheterized to define the pulmonary flows, pressures, and vascular resistances. Then, some six months or so later, they should be recatheterized to determine whether the defect is getting smaller or the resistance is rising. It must be emphasized that early changes in pulmonary vascular resistance cannot be detected clinically and that by the time clinical changes are apparent the pulmonary vascular lesions may have become irreversible. If the vascular resistance has risen, they should be operated on without further delay.

The choice of operation depends upon the surgical skill available and the age of the child. Open-heart closure of the defect can be done in experienced centers with acceptably low mortality in children about 3 years and older, but in most hands there is still a high mortality in infants. It is therefore probably better in these cases to band the pulmonary artery, thus reducing pulmonary flow and pressure. This relieves cardiac failure and reduces or abolishes the risk of pulmonary vascular disease. When the child is older the defect can be closed and the band removed. However, since even banding of the pulmonary artery carries a high mortality in infants, it should not be undertaken without good reason.

COMPLICATED VARIETIES OF VENTRICULAR SEPTAL DEFECT. 1. When it is part of a total atrioventricular canal, the lesion places a load on both ventricles and has the features of a ventricular septal defect as well as an atrial septal defect; mitral and tricuspid regurgitation may also be added. This lesion is considered further on page 1400.

2. Both the aorta and the pulmonary artery may arise from the right ventricle. Clinically this resembles a ventricular septal defect with pulmonary hypertension, although some have left axis deviation in the electrocardiogram. There need not be cyanosis in the absence of pulmonary stenosis, because blood streaming through the defect from the left ventricle may pass out into the aorta with minimal mixing with right ventricular blood. The lesion can be diagnosed only by angiocardiography.

3. Aortic regurgitation may develop and is thought to be due to prolapse of a valve cusp which has no support because of the defect below it. It may progress to massive regurgitation. Surgical closure of the defect and repair of the valve can be done by open-heart procedures but may require valve prosthesis. Sometimes, however, closing of the ventricular defect alone may improve the aortic insufficiency.

4. Corrected transposition is a complex in which commonly the right atrium drains into an anatomic left ventricle which ejects into the pulmonary artery, while the left atrium drains into an anatomic right ventricle which empties into the aorta. Blood flow thus follows its normal physiologic pathways. The importance of the anomaly is that it is often associated with many other lesions, the commonest of which is a ventricular septal defect. The chief reasons for separating this from other types of ventricular septal defect are that the coronary arteries may run abnormally and may cross the right ventricle where during surgery the ventriculotomy would normally be placed to expose the defect; there may be a variety of arrhythmias, particularly various types of atrioventricular block; and there may be abnormalities of the left-sided atrioventricular valve producing functional mitral regurgitation, which may

need to be repaired or considered at the time of surgery.

Left Ventricular-to-Right Atrial Shunt

The septal leaflet of the tricuspid valve is partly attached to the middle of the membranous portion of the ventricular septum, so that the upper part of the membranous ventricular septum forms a small section of the wall of the right atrium. A defect here would therefore allow blood to pass from the left ventricle to the right atrium. These lesions are rare. Clinically and physiologically they resemble ventricular septal defects but in addition have large volume loads on the right atrium and ventricle. These chambers may therefore be larger than is usual with a ventricular septal defect, and there is often a tricuspid diastolic flow murmur heard in the region of the xiphisternum. Pulmonary arterial pressures are seldom very high, so that there is little pressure loading of the right ventricle.

These lesions are usually diagnosed only at cardiac catheterization and can be corrected by open-heart surgery.

Connection between Left Atrium and Lesser Circulation

Atrial Septal Defects

EMBRYOLOGY AND ANATOMY. At about the third or fourth week of fetal life the two atria are partly separated by the septum primum, which has in its posterior and inferior portion an opening, the ostium or foramen primum. The inferior margin of this opening is formed by the endocardial cushions from which the atrioventricular valves develop. If development is interfered with at this stage there will be an ostium primum defect which is low in the atrial septum and has no inferior rim of atrial septal tissue. This lesion is usually associated with abnormalities of the mitral and/or tricuspid valves; often there is also defective formation of the upper part of the ventricular septum.

If normal development continues beyond this stage the ostium primum closes, and another opening, the ostium or foramen secundum, forms in the upper part of the septum primum. This opening allows blood to pass from one atrium to the other, and should development stop at this stage there will be an ostium secundum defect of the atrial septum.

Finally, another septum, the septum secundum, grows down on the right atrial side of the septum primum. This septum forms a crescent which covers the foramen secundum but allows blood to pass through it by a valvelike action. The residual opening is known as the foramen ovale.

Incompetent Patent Foramen Ovale

In fetal life the foramen ovale allows blood to pass from the inferior vena cava and right atrium to the left atrium. After birth left atrial pressure rises so that the valve covering the foramen is pressed against the atrial septum and prevents a left-to-right shunt. A right-to-left shunt does not normally occur since right atrial pressure is lower than left atrial pressure; however, catheters can usually be passed from the right to the left atrium and, should right atrial pressure rise for any reason, right-to-left shunting can occur.

In some infants the valve does not completely cover the foramen ovale, either because the flap is too short or because the left atrium has become dilated and the foramen ovale has enlarged; left-to-right atrial shunting of varying magnitude may then occur. Usually these children have no symptoms, though they may have cardiac murmurs. In most cases of patent foramen ovale, spontaneous closure occurs, even when large left-to-right shunts have been present. Clinically a shunt through an incompetent foramen ovale presents no specific features, but may resemble an atrial septal defect. The only importance to be attached to it is the realization that, if found at cardiac catheterization in infancy, it may well disappear with growth.

Secundum Atrial Septal Defects

When the septum secundum does not form, the ostium secundum is left unsealed. It is an opening of variable size anywhere in the atrial septum, but always has a rim of atrial tissue separating it from the atrioventricular valves.

When this opening is present, blood passes from left to right because of the lower distensibility and therefore higher filling resistance of the left ventricle (see p. 1373 in left-to-right shunt classification). The magnitude of the shunt depends on the resistance to flow offered by the size of the atrial opening, the distensibility of the right ventricle, and pulmonary vascular resistance. Small atrial defects do not permit large shunts; large defects would allow large left-to-right shunts, provided the right ventricle is distensible and the pulmonary vascular resistance is low. As a rule, pulmonary vascular resistance in secundum atrial septal defects is very low in childhood and does not limit flow. The variations in right ventricular distensibility have not been measured, but in infancy when the right ventricular wall is relatively thick it may be relatively less distensible, and so limit the shunt.

Clinically, a large atrial septal defect places a large volume load on the right atrium and ventricle (see p. 1374). These chambers are enlarged clinically and on x-ray, and the right ventricle and pulmonary arteries are hyperactive. Characteristically, the second heart sound is widely split and there is little respiratory variation in the width of splitting. This is one of the cardinal physical signs of atrial septal defect, but it is important to realize that it may not be present. The second sound is often normally split if the defect is small or in infants and young children no matter how large the defect is. Furthermore, if there is marked pulmonary hypertension, with little or no left-to-right shunt, the second sound may be narrowly split, and pulmonic closure is very loud.

Murmurs are not diagnostic in these lesions. If the left-to-right shunt is fairly large, there is often a rumbling early or middiastolic murmur due to increased flow through the tricuspid valve. There is usually a moderately loud, blowing systolic murmur, often ejection in type, maximal at the upper left sternal border. Although this murmur is produced by turbulent blood flow in the pulmonary artery, it may be differentiated from the innocent pulmonary flow murmur by its response to a Valsalva maneuver. When this maneuver raises intrathoracic pressure, systemic venous return is immediately reduced, right ventricular stroke volume falls, and the innocent pulmonary flow murmur suddenly decreases in intensity. With a large atrial septal defect enough blood from the lungs returns continuously to the right side to maintain right ventricular stroke volume for several beats, so that little change occurs in intensity of the murmur.

Radiologically there may be an enlarged and hyperactive right ventricle with dilated, pulsatile main and branch pulmonary arteries. On electrocardiogram there is moderate right axis deviation and right ventricular hypertrophy with rSr' or rSR' patterns in the right precordial leads.

Secundum atrial septal defects are often associated with partial anomalous pulmonary venous drainage. One or more pulmonary veins, usually from the right lung, may enter the superior vena cava or right atrium. Clinically there is no way of detecting these abnormal veins, although occasionally their presence may be suggested by unusual opacities along the heart border. Diagnosis is usually made at cardiac catheterization or surgery.

One particular variety of the secundum atrial septal defect is the sinus venosus defect. This is a secundum defect occurring superiorly and posteriorly just below the entrance of the superior vena cava into the right atrium. Because of its position some of the superior vena caval return may enter the left atrium and cause mild arterial desaturation. There is also usually anomalous drainage of the upper right pulmonary vein into the right atrium.

Pulmonary vascular changes causing an early rise in pulmonary vascular resistance are seldom found with this lesion. However, after many years of high flow, intimal changes may develop in the pulmonary arteries, and these changes may then progress to thrombosis, pulmonary hypertension, and secondary medial hypertrophy. This complication occurs usually beyond the age of 20 years, and it may cause rapid and irreversible vascular changes leading to cyanosis, heart failure, and death.

Treatment of secundum atrial septal defects consists of surgical closure of the defect and diversion of any anomalous pulmonary venous flow into the left atrium. Selection of patients for operation is not easy because so few of them have any significant symptoms. Bacterial endocarditis is rarely seen with this lesion, so that closure of the defect to prevent this complication is not justifiable. In most patients, the decision to operate is based on belief that a sufficiently large left-to-right atrial shunt ultimately endangers the patient's heart and pulmonary vasculature. There is an increasing incidence of cardiac arrhythmias, especially atrial fibrillation, and of cardiac failure and pulmonary vascular obstructive disease after the second decade. Since the operative mortality and morbidity are very low in uncomplicated secundum atrial septal defects, most cardiologists recommend surgery for moderate or large left-to-right atrial shunts when patients are about 5 to 10 years old. The exact size of the left-to-right shunt for which surgery should be definitely recommended has not been determined. In general, if the shunt is large enough to cause cardiomegaly and increased pulmonary vascularity, it is probably large enough to warrant operation.

Ostium Primum Defects

The physiology of ostium primum defects of the atrial septum is similar to that described for secundum atrial defects; both these groups of patients have hyperactive right ventricles, increased pulmonary blood flow, basal systolic ejection murmurs, tricuspid middiastolic murmurs, and widely split, fixed second heart sounds. In addition, ostium primum atrial septal defects may have features due to associated mitral or tricuspid regurgitation or a ventricular septal defect and also have a characteristic electrocardiogram.

If mitral regurgitation is present, there is a blowing, apical pansystolic murmur and often an apical middiastolic rumbling murmur. Should the amount of regurgitation be large, there is left ventricular and left atrial hypertrophy, and there may even be left ventricular failure with pulmonary edema. Tricuspid regurgitation may manifest as a pansystolic murmur in the tricuspid area or as systolic pulsation of the jugular veins. It is important to realize that although cleft mitral valves are almost always found with ostium primum defects of the atrial septum, mitral regurgitation is rare. This is because the different sections of the mitral valve may all coapt during systole and not allow any significant regurgitation. As a result, only a minority of these patients have any of the signs or symptoms of mitral regurgitation.

Some patients have a more complex lesion, with an ostium primum atrial septal defect, a cleft mitral valve, and a cleft tricuspid valve. As a rule it is the septal leaflets of the mitral and tricuspid valves which are cleft, each septal leaflet being divided into anterior and posterior segments. The anterior segments of each septal leaflet are joined through the defect, and so are the posterior segments. As a result there are crossing the defect an anterior mitral-tricuspid valve leaflet and a posterior mitral-tricuspid valve leaflet, hence the name "common atrioventricular valve." Alternative names are "partial endocardial cushion defect," since the valves are formed from the primitive endocardial cushions, and "partial atrioventricular canal," since it is this canal which is now not completely separated by the endocardial cushions. There may or may not be mitral and/or tricuspid regurgitation.

In this variety of endocardial cushion defect the upper part of the ventricular septum is almost always deformed, but in some patients there is actually a large communication between the two ventricles below the valves. The combination of ostium primum atrial septal defect, common atrioventricular valve, and ventricular septal defect is called a complete atrioventricular canal and imposes the greatest loads on the heart. There may or may not be mitral or tricuspid regurgitation, but the ventricular septal defect behaves like any other ventricular septal defect in producing a volume load on the left ventricle and, if large, causing pulmonary hypertension and a pressure load on the right ventricle. The characteristic ventricular septal defect murmur is also present.

Some infants with an atrioventricular canal may have congestive heart failure in the first few weeks or months of life and may have marked pulmonary arterial hypertension despite having no or only a small shunt at the ventricular level. Both these facts contrast strongly with what occurs in secundum atrial septal defects. Sometimes these differences are due to the added loads imposed by mitral and tricuspid regurgitation. In other patients, however, the main reason for the severity of the lesion may result from there being a large shunt from the left ventricle to the right atrium with minimal mitral regurgitation. Because of the large pressure gradient between left ventricle and right atrium there can be a large shunt which is not limited by either a high pulmonary resistance or low right ventricular distensibility. Furthermore, since there can be a very large shunt immediately after birth, pulmonary hypertension can persist and in its turn cause medial hypertrophy sufficient to raise pulmonary vascular resistance and produce a pressure load on the right ventricle. It is possible that these patients are those who might respond poorly to banding of the pulmonary artery, though at this age there is very little else to offer them if medical treatment fails. This physiologic sequence may also explain why children with this lesion may develop pulmonary vascular disease very early.

An important diagnostic criterion of any of the ostium primum defect group is that the QRS axis in the frontal plane, as judged by the limb leads, almost invariably shows marked left (superior) axis deviation. In almost all these cases the mean electrical axis ranges from $-60°$ to $-120°$. It is unrelated to the amount of right or left ventricular hypertrophy and appears to be caused by an associated conduction anomaly. This electrocardiographic axis is not completely pathognomonic of endocardial cushion defects; it can occur with some ventricular septal defects, particularly with a double outlet right ventricle; it may be seen in some transpositions of the great arteries with or without single ventricles; it occurs in tricuspid atresia or pulmonary atresia with a hypoplastic right ventricle. Occasionally the axis may extend as far left as $-60°$ in a secundum atrial septal defect. Conversely, a few endocardial cushion defects have been reported with normal or right axis deviation. Nevertheless, the left axis deviation is an essential part of the diagnosis, which should seldom be made in its absence. It is of interest that children with Down's syndrome often have endocardial cushion defects, which is the commonest congenital heart lesion in these patients.

Treatment consists of surgical closure of the atrial and ventricular septal defects and repair of the valve lesions, only if these are producing regurgitation. Operative closure of the defects often has to be undertaken early because of the risks of cardiac failure and pulmonary vascular disease. The results are fairly good except in those with total atrioventricular canals. Because of the nature of the valve anomalies in the latter group, repair is difficult and operative mortality high.

Connection between Pulmonary Veins and Lesser Circulation

Partial anomalous venous connection without an atrial septal defect is a rare lesion. Clinically the lesion resembles secundum atrial septal defect except that in most the second heart sound has been reported as being normally split. Usually the veins of the right lung drain anomalously into the right atrium or superior vena cava. The diagnosis is made at cardiac catheterization, and surgical treatment is planned according to the anatomy of the anomalous pulmonary veins.

20.11
CYANOTIC CONGENITAL HEART DISEASE

MILTON H. PAUL

Cyanotic congenital heart lesions represent anatomic and physiologic abnormalities which allow for shunting of systemic venous blood directly into the systemic arterial circulation without it being oxygenated by prior passage through the lungs. The most apparent physiologic consequence of this right (venous) to left (arterial) shunting of blood is systemic arterial oxygen desaturation, and the clinical result is cyanosis. Cyanosis refers to a dusky, blue-purple color resulting from the presence of an excessive amount of reduced hemoglobin in the circulating blood, and it is most readily apparent in superficial capillary-rich sites such as the lips, mucous membranes, and nailbeds. The term "percentage arterial oxygen saturation" refers to the percentage of arterial hemoglobin that is in the form of oxyhemoglobin, the range of normal values being from 94 to 98 percent. Most physicians recognize definite cyanosis at levels of arterial oxygen saturation less than 85 percent. Cyanosis is less likely to be apparent clinically in patients with severe anemia because concentration of total circulating reduced hemoglobin in the capillary bed may be severely limited by the anemia. Conversely, apparent cyanosis may occur in association with normal arterial oxygen saturation when the peripheral circulation is so abnormally slow or the total blood volume is so increased as to result in an increased concentration of reduced hemoglobin in the distal capillary beds. This form of peripheral cyanosis is commonly noted in the normal newborn infant and characteristically is limited distally to the hands and feet, with normal color in the proximal portion of the limbs and the lips and the tongue. Rarely, transient cyanosis and plethora are present in a newborn with clinical findings of transient cardiovascular strain, and this appears related to neonatal polycythemia and hypervolemia resulting from excessive transfusion of placental blood at delivery. Spontaneous improvement generally occurs.

In the differential diagnosis of cyanosis, pulmonary causes must be considered as being very common; they include airway obstruction, atelectasis, pneumonia, respiratory distress syndrome in the newborn, congenital diaphragmatic hernia, and tracheoesophageal fistula. Other conditions which must be included are vasomotor instability in the newborn with peripheral cyanosis, septicemia and severe infections, intracerebral damage at birth resulting in alveolar hypoventilation, and methemoglobinemia of either congenital or acquired origin.

In addition to the specific clinical (cyanosis) and physiologic (systemic arterial oxygen unsaturation) manifestations of right-to-left shunting of blood, several associated abnormalities are often present in the patient with cyanotic congenital heart disease.

Clubbing or hypertrophic osteoarthropathy of the fingers ordinarily does not appear until 1 or 2 years of age in the cyanotic child, and only rarely it may be associated with a noncardiac abnormality such as lung abscess, subacute bacterial endocarditis, or a familial causation.

Polycythemia with increased hemoglobin and hematocrit values is another consequence of arterial oxygen unsaturation; this represents an adaptation of the hematopoietic system to the anoxic stimulus. The increased oxygen content achieved by this compensatory mechanism is advantageous until the polycythemia reaches hematocrit levels of about 70 to 75 percent, when the hemodynamic stresses of the associated high blood viscosity probably outweigh the advantages of the increased circulating oxyhemoglobin. It is of considerable clinical importance to recognize that relative hypochromic anemia should be diagnosed in the severely cyanotic patient in the presence of high erythrocyte counts and normal hemoglobin and hematocrit levels, and that this can be easily corrected by oral iron administration.

The increased blood viscosity in severe cyanotic polycythemia may be responsible for cerebral, mesenteric, renal, or pulmonary thromboses. Cerebral thromboses are the most common and generally occur in the infant under 2 years of age. Dehydration greatly increases the danger of thrombosis in this age group, and an adequate fluid intake is imperative, particularly in hot weather or during febrile illnesses.

Brain abscesses represent a significant complication in cyanotic patients with venous-arterial shunts, since bacteria which are normally filtered out in the pulmonary circulation may be shunted directly into the systemic circulation (see tetralogy of Fallot).

Cyanotic patients with long-standing and severe polycythemia may have changes in several factors of the blood-clotting mechanism. Thrombocytopenia is commonly present, and in the older patient with long-standing polycythemia caution is advised in regard to the occurrence of excessive postoperative bleeding.

Extreme degrees of hypoxemia in infants with severe cyanotic congenital heart disease may result in severe metabolic acidosis caused by a relatively anaerobic tissue metabolism and lactate accumulation. Therapy directed toward the correction of the uncompensated metabolic acidosis with intravenous administration of sodium bicarbonate or amine buffers is particularly important in the severely cyanotic infant with an acute prolonged hypoxemic-dyspneic spell and clinical deterioration.

The prolonged and severe hypoxemia of cyanotic congenital heart disease frequently results in retarded physical growth, about 40 percent of the children with transposition of the great arteries, tricuspid atresia, and tetralogy of Fallot being below the third percentile in body weight.

Tetralogy of Fallot

Tetralogy of Fallot is the most common cyanotic heart lesion encountered in patients with cyanotic congenital heart disease who survive beyond infancy. The four structural abnormalities that constitute tetralogy of Fallot are pulmonary stenosis, ventricular septal defect, dextroposition of the aorta, and right ventricular hypertrophy. Although these four elements are generally present, there is a wide anatomic varia-

tion with resultant physiologic and clinical variation. (See Fig. 49B and C.)

MORPHOLOGY. The primary site of obstruction to blood flow is in the outflow tract of the right ventricle (infundibular stenosis), but other elements of the pulmonary outflow tract are usually involved, the pulmonary valve being stenotic and the pulmonary arteries hypoplastic. In the most severe form, often termed pseudotruncus, the distal infundibular outflow tract and pulmonary valve are atretic and the main pulmonary arteries are severely hypoplastic. The ventricular septal defect is usually large and is located just below the crista and is in close proximity to the tricuspid and aortic valves. The aorta arises directly over the ventricular septal defect, and this overriding of both ventricular cavities (dextroposition) is a much discussed feature of the malformation. The degree of overriding varies greatly and can be best evaluated by angiography (Fig. 50). An important secondary anatomic feature is the frequent occurrence (20 to 25 percent of cases) of a right-sided aortic arch in tetralogy of Fallot.

HEMODYNAMICS. In tetralogy of Fallot, right ventricular contraction is unable to eject the entire systemic venous return into the pulmonary circulation because of the pulmonary outflow tract stenosis or atresia. Varying amounts of venous blood are shunted across the ventricular septal defect and into the aorta, resulting in cyanosis. As a result of the pulmonary outflow tract obstruction the pulmonary artery pressure and pulmonary blood flow are reduced.

Because the ventricular septal defect in tetralogy of Fallot is usually large, right ventricular peak systolic pressure equals that in the left ventricle and aorta, and the right and left ventricular pressure contours are essentially similar. Rarely, the ventricular septal defect is anatomically or functionally small due to the apposition of a tricuspid valve leaflet to the defect. Right ventricular pressures will then exceed left ventricular pressures, a finding usually associated with severe pulmonary valve stenosis with an intact ventricular septum.

The clinical status in tetralogy of Fallot depends in hemodynamic terms primarily upon the magnitude of the pulmonary blood flow which in turn depends upon: the anatomic severity of right ventricular outflow tract obstruction; the relative resistances to ventricular outflow imposed by the systemic and pulmonary circulations; and the presence of systemic to pulmonary collateral blood supply via bronchial arteries or a persistent patent ductus arteriosus.

The fall in systemic vascular resistance associated with peripheral vasodilation during exercise in tetralogy of Fallot results in a marked increase in right to left shunting and in cyanosis. The acute, severe episodes of hypoxemia, termed "blue spells," that occur in some infants with tetralogy of Fallot often upon awakening, may result from decreased systemic venous return resulting in diminished right ventricular output and pulmonary blood flow.

CLINICAL MANIFESTATIONS. The clinical findings vary with the severity of the pulmonary stenosis, but

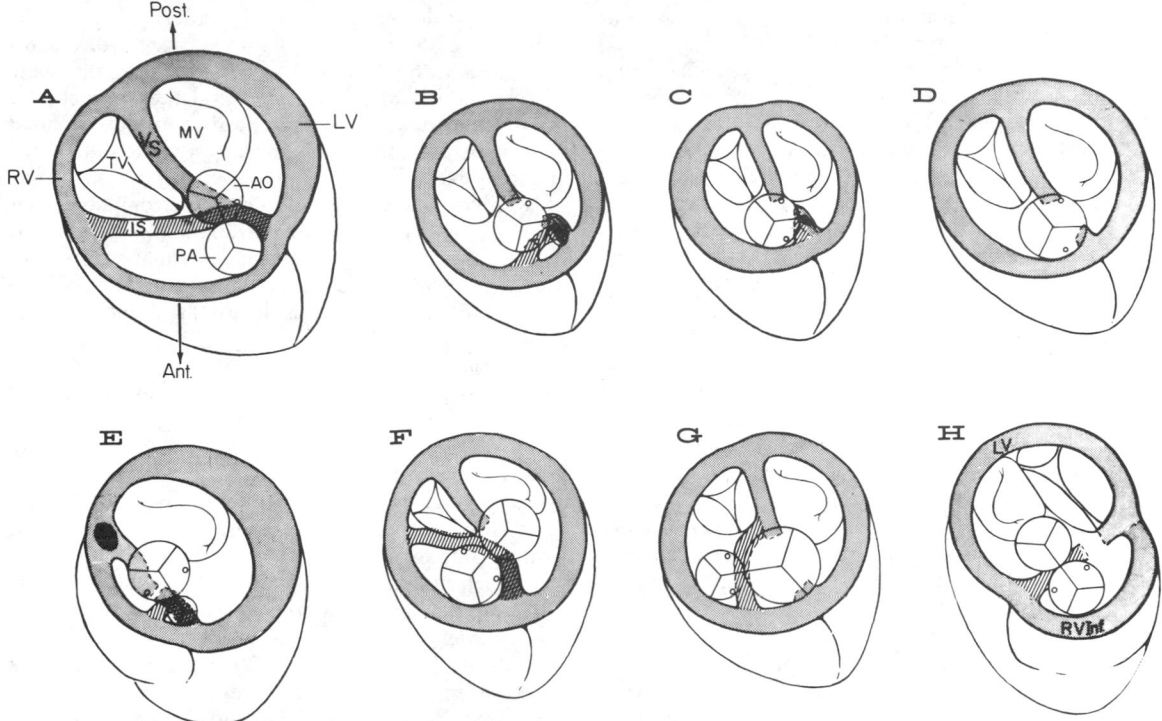

Fig. 49. Relatively frequent forms of cyanotic congenital heart disease. Hearts viewed from above, diagrams minimally schematic, atria (in normal locations) not shown. A. Normal heart. B. Tetralogy of Fallot with moderate pulmonary stenosis. C. Tetralogy of Fallot with pulmonary atresia. D. Truncus arteriosus communis. E. Tricuspid atresia with normally related great arteries. F. Complete transposition of the great arteries. G. Taussig-Bing malformation. H. Single left ventricle with an infundibular outlet chamber and "corrected" l-transposition. Ant.—anterior; Post.—posterior; RV—morphologically right ventricle; RV Inf.—right ventricular infundibulum; LV—morphologically left ventricle; PA—valve of pulmonary artery; AO—valve of aorta; TV—tricuspid valve; MV—mitral valve; VS—ventricular septum; and IS—infundibular septum (crosshatched).

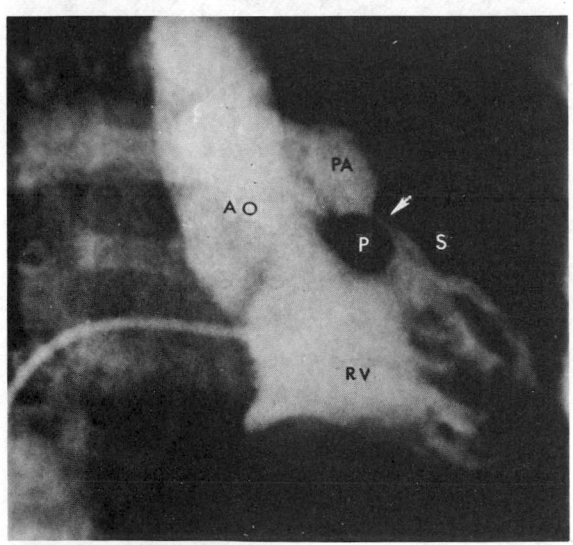

Fig. 50. Angiocardiogram, tetralogy of Fallot. Right ventricular (RV) selective injection showing severe infundibular obstruction (arrow) and early filling of aorta (AO); PA, pulmonary artery; P, parietal, and S, septal muscle bands forming crista supraventricularis.

few children with tetralogy of Fallot remain asymptomatic. Cyanosis may not be present at birth, for as long as the ductus arteriosus remains patent there may be adequate pulmonary blood flow. In the infant, attacks of paroxysmal hyperpnea and increased cyanosis may occur spontaneously or following early morning feedings or prolonged crying. The attacks may last only a few moments and have no significant sequelae; may be more prolonged and followed by limpness, deep exhaustion, or sleep; or rarely may end fatally. In the older child, exercise tolerance usually varies in proportion to the severity of the cyanosis. Many children with tetralogy of Fallot and limited exercise tolerance exhibit a characteristic squatting position after exertion, and this maneuver results in an increased arterial oxygen saturation.

Without surgical intervention, the clinical course and prognosis vary with the severity of the right ventricular outflow tract obstruction. Infants with pulmonary atresia usually require some form of palliative surgical intervention in the first few months of life. Approximately one-third of the patients with tetralogy of Fallot begin to have severe anoxic spells by 4 or 5 months of age, and many of these infants require surgical intervention quite promptly. The others remain severely cyanotic but the frequency of serious spells diminishes, presumably as a result of development of collateral circulation. About one-third of the patients show only moderate cyanosis during infancy and have infrequent and brief episodes of paroxysmal dyspnea. These children fatigue easily on moderate physical exertion, often demonstrate characteristic squatting, and usually begin to show increasing difficulties when school age is reached. The final group of patients with tetralogy of Fallot are better characterized clinically as ventricular septal defects with pulmonary stenosis in infancy and early childhood; these patients often show little or no evidence of cyanosis for several years ("acyanotic tetralogy of Fallot"). These patients do not have anoxic spells and usually do not exhibit squatting, but cyanosis on exertion becomes more manifest as they grow older, and occasionally rapid clinical change toward the classical tetralogy of Fallot occurs.

Major complications associated with tetralogy of Fallot include the occurrence of brain abscess, cerebral thrombosis with hemiplegia, and bacterial endocarditis. The diagnosis of a brain abscess should always be considered whenever signs and symptoms pointing to involvement of the central nervous system develop in a patient with congenital heart disease and a right-to-left shunt. Patients with brain abscess are usually over the age of 2 years as opposed to those with cerebral thrombosis. The onset of the illness is frequently insidious with headache, low-grade fever, and personality changes often preceding any focal neurologic lesion or convulsion. Cerebral thrombosis is more common in the presence of extreme cyanosis and polycythemia and can be precipitated by dehydration. Bacterial endocarditis is not common in tetralogy of Fallot before shunt surgery is performed, but a significant incidence of bacterial endocarditis (about 5 percent) is seen in older children with systemic-pulmonary shunts. Prophylactic antibiotic therapy should be given to all patients when surgical procedures involving the teeth, throat, and ear are undertaken.

PHYSICAL FINDINGS.   Growth and development are generally delayed in proportion to the degree of cyanosis and reflect the extent of systemic arterial oxygen unsaturation. The heart is not hyperactive, but a right ventricular systolic heave may be present along the lower left sternal border. A systolic thrill may be felt in some children along the lower left sternal border but is absent in the presence of the more severe forms of infundibular obstruction and in pulmonary atresia. At auscultation the first heart sound is normal. In some patients with severe cyanosis the first heart sound is followed by an early systolic click which is aortic in origin and maximal at the left sternal border and apex. A single loud second heart sound is generally heard, corresponding to aortic valve closure, at the lower left sternal border. When closure of the pulmonary valve is audible it is delayed and quite diminished in intensity. The systolic murmur is frequently loud and harsh, may be ste-

notic or pansystolic in quality, and is best heard at the mid or lower left sternal border. This systolic murmur in tetralogy of Fallot always stops short of the second heart sound. In general the more severe the obstruction to pulmonary blood flow, the shorter the murmur; and in extreme pulmonary outflow tract stenosis or pulmonary atresia only a short faint murmur may be heard. A faint continuous murmur may be audible over the anterior or posterior chest, particularly in patients with pulmonary atresia, and this represents enlarged bronchial collateral vessels. Rarely, a significant continuous murmur of persistent patent ductus arteriosus is heard at the upper left sternal border.

ROENTGENOGRAPHY.   In the anteroposterior chest view tetralogy of Fallot (Fig. 51) is characterized by a relatively normal-sized heart of right ventricular contour and a poorly vascularized lung field resulting from diminished pulmonary circulation. The main pulmonary artery segment is usually hypoplastic, and there is a concavity at the upper left margin of the cardiac silhouette instead of the normal convexity. A characteristic coeur-en-sabot or boot-shaped heart may be present, particularly in cases of extreme pulmonary stenosis or pulmonary atresia. The aorta is generally large and in 20 to 25 percent of the cases a right-sided aortic arch is present and can easily be recognized by observing a right-sided rather than left-sided indentation on the air tracheogram or a barium esophagram.

ELECTROCARDIOGRAM.   In the older infant and child the electrocardiogram clearly shows the anticipated right axis shift and right ventricular hyper-

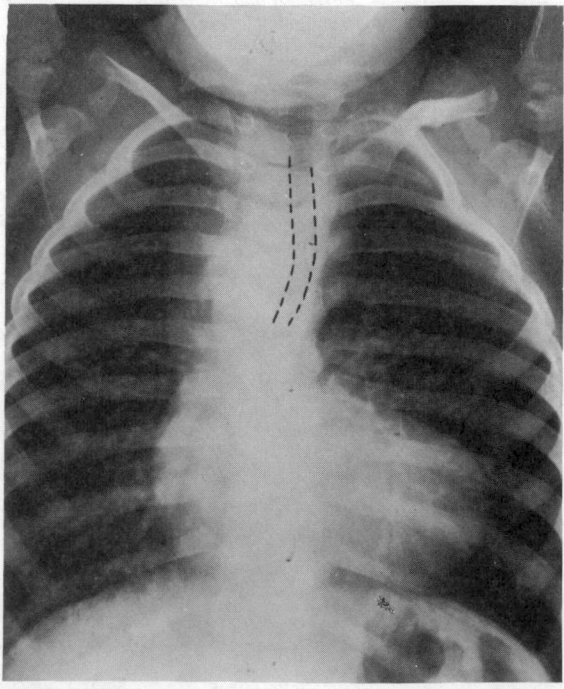

Fig. 51.   Anteroposterior chest view in tetralogy of Fallot (see text).

trophy patterns of predominant R wave over the right precordium and S wave over the left precordium. In the newborn and young infant, however, the diagnosis of pathologic right ventricular hypertrophy by electrocardiogram is somewhat more difficult because of the normal right ventricular dominance at this age. A persistent (beyond 72 hours) upright T wave in V_1 in a newborn infant may constitute the only evidence of right ventricular hypertrophy. In the acyanotic forms of tetralogy of Fallot combined ventricular hypertrophy may be noted with transition into right ventricular hypertrophy as cyanosis appears and progresses.

CATHETERIZATION AND ANGIOCARDIOGRAPHY. In the majority of patients, careful evaluation and correlation of the clinical findings, x-ray, and electrocardiogram will suffice to establish a diagnosis. A number of complex cyanotic heart lesions, however, including transposition complexes with pulmonary stenosis, single ventricle complexes with pulmonary stenosis and corrected transposition complexes with pulmonary stenosis, can be confused with tetralogy of Fallot, and careful selective angiocardiography is the diagnostic tool of most assistance. When surgery is contemplated, catheterization and particularly angiocardiography provide significant and relevant information. Catheterization substantiates overriding of the aorta with ventricular septal defect by easy passage of the catheter from the right ventricle into the aorta. Pulmonary stenosis is confirmed by systolic hypertension in the right ventricle and by a drop in the systolic pressure as the catheter enters the right ventricular infundibular chamber or pulmonary artery. The systolic pressures are usually equal in the right ventricle, the left ventricle, and the aorta. Blood samples generally reveal no significant left-to-right shunting of blood except in the acyanotic tetralogy of Fallot and provide means for quantitating the right-to-left shunt.

Selective angiocardiography with injection of contrast media into the right ventricle is of prime importance and will (1) demonstrate the anatomy of the outflow tract obstruction in detail, (2) show early filling of the aorta with passage of contrast medium across the ventricular septal defect into the left ventricle, (3) clarify the relationship of the aorta to the ventricular septal defect (overriding), and (4) evaluate the adequacy of the pulmonary artery and its branches in regard to corrective surgery (Fig. 50).

TREATMENT. Medical management is directly mainly toward the relief of paroxysmal dyspnea and cyanotic spells and the prevention of complications. An attack of paroxysmal dyspnea may be treated by placing the infant on his abdomen in a knee-chest position or by holding the child over the shoulder with the legs flexed upon the abdomen. Oxygen may be administered to lessen the dyspnea and cyanosis. The administration of morphine sulfate in the dose of 1 mg per 5 kg of body weight is especially effective for prolonged or severe attacks.

In infancy these attacks may be precipitated by a relative iron deficiency, since one of the adaptive mechanisms to cyanosis is an increase in oxygen-carrying capacity of the blood by the development of polycythemia. Patients with symptoms who have a hypochromic anemia are best treated with iron until the hematocrit reaches 65 to 70 percent. Further increase in the hematocrit will result in a considerable rise in blood viscosity with possible resultant impediment to blood flow.

SURGICAL MANAGEMENT. The indications for surgery for tetralogy of Fallot and the type of surgery, extracardiac palliative or intracardiac corrective, vary with the age of the patient and the anatomic nature and severity of the pulmonary stenosis.

In an *infant* with severe tetralogy of Fallot or a pulmonary atresia form of tetralogy of Fallot (pseudotruncus), paroxysmal dyspnea, deep cyanosis, and failure to gain weight are indications for early palliative surgery. A systemic to pulmonary anastomosis, by increasing pulmonary blood flow, will relieve the cyanosis and hypoxemic symptoms. In the younger infant, about 1 year of age and less, an aortic-pulmonary anastomosis is preferred to a subclavian-pulmonary anastomosis (Blalock-Taussig), since the former tends to function and remain patent in a larger number of infants. The ascending aorta to right pulmonary artery anastomosis (Waterston-Cooley) is more frequently used now than the descending aorta to left pulmonary artery anastomosis (Potts-Smith-Gibson). In the older infant and child, the subclavian-pulmonary anastomosis is preferred whenever technically feasible, because of the greater difficulty of obliterating an aortic-pulmonary anastomosis at the time of subsequent open-heart corrective surgery. The surgical mortality rate in infants under 2 years of age is about 10 to 15 percent. At the present time the surgical risk of open-heart repair in infants with severe tetralogy of Fallot appears to be prohibitive.

The indications for surgery in the *young child* (2 to 5 years of age) with tetralogy of Fallot depend on the persistence of paroxysmal episodes of dyspnea, frequency of squatting, presence of extreme polycythemia, and degree of limitation in physical activity. In general, a systemic-pulmonary anastomosis is the operation of choice if the clinical and angiocardiographic studies indicate the presence of pulmonary atresia, marked hypoplasia of the pulmonary annulus or pulmonary arteries, or extreme overriding of the aorta. Anastomotic surgery in this older age group carries an extremely low surgical risk of approximately 2 to 6 percent.

In *late childhood* or *early adolescence*, open-heart surgical correction of the malformation is in general the preferred surgical recommendation, unless extreme polycythemia or extreme pulmonary artery hypoplasia is present. In these instances, at the present time, it remains preferable to view complete surgical correction as a staged procedure and first perform a systemic-pulmonary shunt.

For surgical correction to be successful, the patient must have a relatively typical tetralogy of Fallot complex with a suitable outflow tract anatomy. While the patient's circulation is temporarily maintained by an artificial heart-lung machine, the pathology in the right ventricles is exposed through a right ventricular incision. The infundibular stenosis is resected, coexistent valvar pulmonary stenosis is corrected, and the ventricular septal defect closed. If indicated, the outflow tract of the right ventricle may be enlarged by placing a plastic or pericardial prosthesis in the anterior ventricular wall to enlarge the roof of the pulmonary outflow tract. The current overall mortality rate with open-heart corrective procedures for tetralogy of Fallot is approximately 10 percent in most experienced centers. The specific application of data on surgical risks is quite difficult in view of the wide spectrum of pathology ranging from the acyanotic form of tetralogy of Fallot to the extreme form with complete atresia of the right ventricular outflow tract.

Recently, intracardiac repair of tetralogy with pulmonary atresia has been accomplished by fashioning a conduit between the right ventricle and the arteries to the lungs after the ventricular septal defect is closed. The conduit materials used in this outflow tract reconstruction include pericardium, woven Dacron, or a homograft of the aorta with its aortic valve. After a successful systemic-pulmonary anastomosis procedure there is a marked decrease in symptoms, exercise tolerance is increased, squatting is discontinued, the cyanosis and clubbing diminish considerably or disappear. A machinery-type continuous murmur is detected on the side of the operation and is indicative of a functioning shunt. Long-term results after a Blalock-Taussig or Potts-Smith-Gibson anastomosis indicate that good clinical improvement can be maintained in the majority of patients for at least 10 years. In a significant number, as many as 30 percent, of patients with Blalock-Taussig anastomosis a second surgical anastomosis is necessary after some years because of reappearance of symptoms as the shunt ceases to be adequate. Complications after anastomotic procedures include subacute bacterial endocarditis, brain abscess, congestive heart failure usually associated with too large an aortopulmonary anastomosis, and an occasional instance of pulmonary hypertension and progressive pulmonary vascular disease.

In cyanotic patients undergoing successful corrective surgery there is usually an early and dramatic improvement in exercise tolerance, growth, and development; and the long-term prognosis in these cases with suitable pulmonary outflow antomy should be excellent.

Tricuspid Atresia

Tricuspid atresia is a much less frequent cause of cyanotic congenital heart disease than transposition of the great vessels or tetralogy of Fallot. In tricuspid

orifice atresia the only outlet for systemic venous blood from the right atrium to the left atrium is an interatrial communication (usually a patent foramen ovale), and there is mixing of the pulmonary venous and systemic venous return in the left atrium. (See Fig. 49E.) The left ventricular output is then distributed directly to the aorta and indirectly through a ventricular septal defect or a patent ductus arteriosus to the pulmonary artery. The pulmonary blood flow is almost always severely diminished in tricuspid atresia because of the narrow, restrictive opening of the ventricular septal defect and because of a stenotic underdeveloped right ventricular infundibular chamber and pulmonary outflow tract. Increased pulmonary blood flow is infrequently encountered in tricuspid atresia but can occur when either (1) the ventricular septal defect is large and not restrictive and the pulmonary outflow tract of the right ventricle is well developed, or (2) transposition of the great arteries is present and the pulmonary artery arises directly from the left ventricle without any associated pulmonary stenosis.

Cardiac catheterization will confirm the total right-to-left passage of blood at the atrial level, demonstrate the prominent presystolic contraction waves in the right atrium, and show a right-to-left interatrial mean pressure gradient. Angiocardiography demonstrates the sequential opacification of right atrium, left atrium, and left ventricle (Fig. 52). The intraventricular septal defect leads to subsequent opacification of the obstructive right ventricle infundibulum and the pulmonary artery trunks.

CLINICAL MANIFESTATIONS. Intense cyanosis, dyspnea, and anoxic spells are common symptoms in the

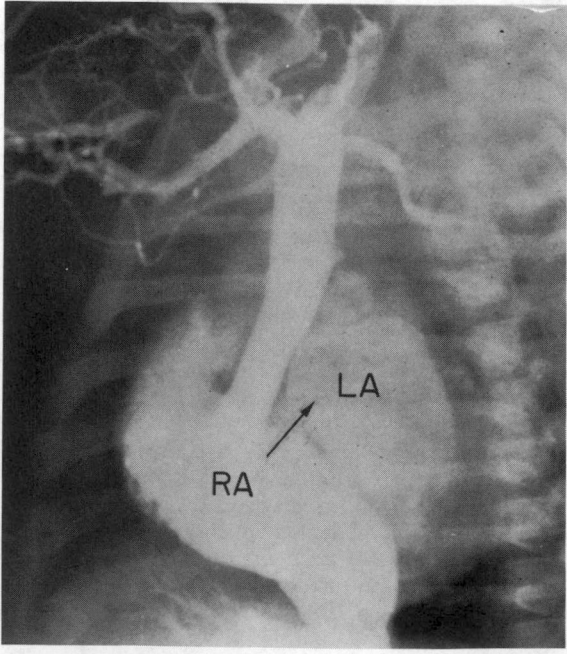

Fig. 52. Sequential opacification of right atrium, left atrium, and left ventricle in tricuspid atresia.

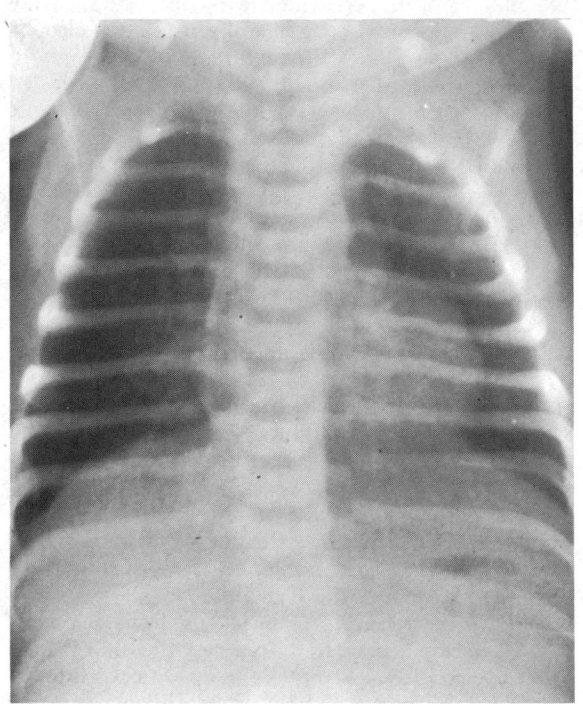

Fig. 53. Roentgenogram showing characteristic features of tricuspid atresia.

infant with tricuspid atresia. Right heart failure, manifested by hepatomegaly, occasionally with presystolic pulsations, is dependent upon the ease with which right-to-left shunting occurs at the patent foramen ovale or atrial septal defect level. Clubbing, polycythemia, and squatting, as well as poor physical development, are apparent in the older infant. However, only a few infants survive beyond 6 months of age without surgical assistance.

There is usually a harsh systolic murmur representing the ventricular septal defect and right ventricular infundibular stenosis, audible along the left sternal border but murmurs may be minimal *if* there is pulmonary atresia or no significant ventricular septal defect. The second heart sound is usually single with only aortic valve closure audible. Liver enlargement and presystolic liver pulsations are seen in about half of the cases when the interatrial communication is limiting.

The x-ray findings in the usual form of tricuspid atresia include diminished pulmonary vasculature and a heart shape that is often distinctive with a rounded or "apple" configuration, resulting from a deficiency of the right ventricular and pulmonary artery segments. (See Fig. 53.)

The electrocardiographic findings of left axis shift and left ventricular hypertrophy in tricuspid atresia are highly diagnostic of this lesion, since this is one of the few cyanotic heart lesions with diminished pulmonary vasculature which does not have evidence of right axis shift and right ventricular hypertrophy. The left ventricular myocardium is dominant in tricuspid atresia with underdeveloped right ventricle. There is often right atrial hypertrophy manifested by prominent peaked P waves in lead II.

MANAGEMENT. The treatment of infants with tricuspid atresia is surgical, and it is particularly important to note that the occurrence of severe anoxic spells in an infant about 4 or 5 weeks of age often heralds a closing patent ductus arteriosus and the elimination of the major or only source of pulmonary blood flow. A grave prognosis is generally evident at this point, and some form of systemic-pulmonary or superior vena cava-pulmonary artery shunt is urgently indicated to direct additional blood to the lungs. A right-sided or left-sided aortopulmonary shunt procedure can be performed in most of these very young infants, with about 20 percent overall surgical mortality, and a good 5- to 10-year clinical result has been noted in two-thirds of the survivors.

The venous shunt operation between the superior vena cava and right pulmonary artery (Glenn) has a higher surgical risk for infants less than 6 months of age, but has been performed in an increasing number of older infants and children with excellent palliative results.

Occasionally the interatrial communication (patent foramen ovale type of atrial septal defect) is small and obstructive to blood flow and results in a large pulsating liver, large right atrium by x-ray, and a large pressure gradient between the two atria. Enlargement of the atrial septal defect by balloon catheter septostomy at cardiac catheterization (viz., transposition of the great arteries) or by surgical septectomy may be indicated.

Pulmonary Atresia or Stenosis with Intact Ventricular Septum

A number of lesions with dominant right-to-left shunt at the atrial level must be differentiated from the usual tricuspid atresia anatomy. In pulmonary atresia with intact ventricular septum the hemodynamics resemble to some extent those in tricuspid atresia, since essentially all the right atrial blood is shunted into the left atrium, left ventricle, and aorta. The right ventricular chamber size varies considerably, but in most instances the right ventricle is diminutive as is also the tricuspid valve orifice. Occasionally extreme pulmonary valve stenosis rather than pulmonary valve atresia with intact ventricular septum will be present. In pulmonary atresia with intact ventricular septum the pulmonary circulation is supplied and life sustained primarily through a patent ductus arteriosus.

The clinical symptoms in infants with intact ventricular septum and pulmonary atresia or extreme stenosis are similar to those in tricuspid atresia. However, the clinical status of such infants often deteriorates extremely rapidly, with intense hypoxemia and dyspnea and early death within a few days after birth unless adequate pulmonary blood flow can be surgically provided.

Infants with pulmonary atresia and intact ventricular septum differ from tricuspid atresia in that often little or no cardiac murmur is heard, and the cardiac murmur that may be heard is soft and blowing and probably represents insufficiency of the hypoplastic tricuspid valve. Although patency of the ductus arteriosus is obligatory for life, a continuous murmur is rarely heard. The second sound at the pulmonary area is single, reflecting aortic valve closure.

Tricuspid atresia and pulmonary atresia with intact ventricular septum or extreme pulmonary stenosis with intact ventricular septum may show similar x-ray appearances. The most important differential finding is related to the electrocardiogram; the mean QRS axis in tricuspid atresia is shifted to the left, whereas in pulmonary atresia it is usually normal or occasionally to the right. In the early days or weeks of life left ventricular hypertrophy may be noted in some infants with pulmonary atresia or extreme pulmonary stenosis and intact ventricular septum, but right ventricular hypertrophy becomes evident in the electrocardiogram as the right ventricular muscle thickens, if the infant survives beyond the first few months of life. A closed pulmonary valvotomy, as described by Brock, can be performed if the ventricular cavity size and infundibular anatomy permit surgical puncture of the atretic pulmonary valve dome. When the ventricular cavity is diminutive or the infundibulum is completely obstructed, an aorto-pulmonary shunt can be attempted. As in tricuspid atresia, enlargement of the interatrial septal defect by balloon catheter septostomy is indicated during the initial diagnostic cardiac catheterization procedure.

Ebstein's Anomaly

In Ebstein's anomaly of the heart, the tricuspid valve attachments are abnormal and are characterized by downward displacement and anomalous attachment of the posterior and septal leaflets to the ventricular wall. The abnormally situated tricuspid valve now divides the right ventricle into a proximal "atrial" segment and a distal functional ventricle. This "atrial" segment and the right atrium are usually enormously dilated, and there is evidence of anatomic tricuspid incompetence.

The hemodynamic abnormalities in this anomaly are related primarily to the small size of the functioning right ventricle and to the usual presence of tricuspid regurgitation with varying degrees of right-to-left shunting of blood through a patent foramen ovale.

The clinical symptoms vary in severity depending upon the extent of the downward displacement of the tricuspid valve. Rarely in the most severe

cases, cardiorespiratory difficulties are prominent during the neonatal period and early infancy with advanced cyanosis and congestive heart failure. Usually the hemodynamic status improves and the cyanosis gradually diminishes as the infant grows older. In the majority of instances with less severe anatomic and physiologic abnormalities, symptoms are not commonly present in infancy. Slight cyanosis is usually manifested in later childhood. There is often little limitation of activity during childhood, but exercise tolerance becomes limited eventually. Attacks of paroxysmal supraventricular tachycardia are not uncommon.

There is a characteristic, usually pathognomonic, auscultation in Ebstein's anomaly. A triple or quadruple heart sound rhythm is associated with a soft systolic murmur of tricuspid regurgitation and a soft, scratchy middiastolic murmur at the lower left sternal border and apex. The second heart sound is widely split.

The roentgenographic findings include moderate or marked cardiomegaly with gross enlargement of the right atrium and normal or diminished pulmonary vascular markings (Fig. 54).

The electrocardiogram is also characteristic, demonstrating right atrial hypertrophy and incomplete or complete right bundle branch block patterns. The Wolff-Parkinson-White electrocardiographic pattern is also a relatively frequent finding.

Cardiac catherization may be complicated by an increased incidence of induced arrhythmias. Car-

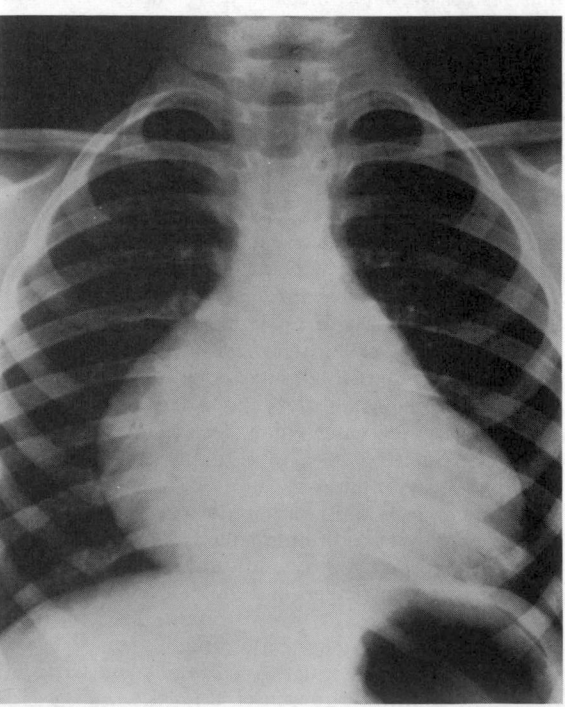

Fig. 54. Roentgenogram showing cardiomegaly, a characteristic finding in Ebstein's anomaly.

diac catheterization, to be diagnostic, must demonstrate that a portion of the right ventricle functions as right atrium because of the abnormal distal location of the tricuspid valve. This "atrialization" of a portion of the right ventricle is best confirmed by simultaneous intracardiac electrocardiogram-pressure recordings or detailed angiocardiography.

The life expectancy of the patient with Ebstein's anomaly varies considerably depending upon the severity of the malformation, the usual cause of death being congestive heart failure in the second or third decade of life. In the critically-ill cyanotic infant it is essential not to mistake Ebstein's anomaly for pulmonary atresia or severe pulmonary stenosis with intact ventricular septum and submit the Ebstein infant to surgical treatment. It is conversely equally disastrous to defer surgical intervention in pulmonary atresia. In older patients, moderate congestive heart failure can be effectively treated with digitalis and diuretics. Surgical maneuvers directed at realigning the tricuspid leaflets to their true annulus, resection of redundant atrialized tissue, or placement of a prosthetic valve have been attempted. In some instances there has been improvement, but long-term results have not yet been assessed.

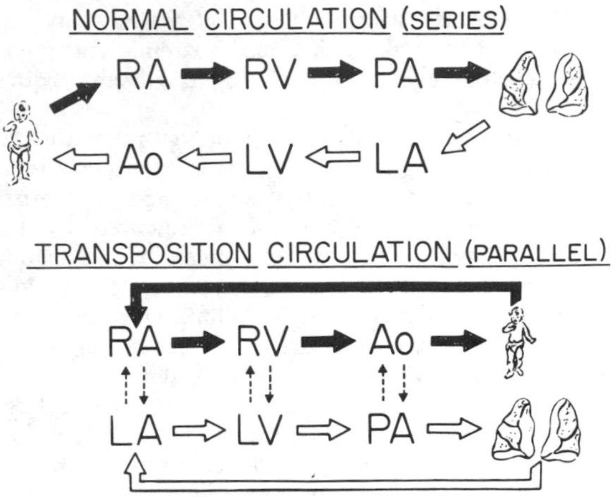

Transposition of the Great Arteries

Transposition of the great arteries (complete transposition of the great arteries with normal cardiac chamber relationships) is one of the most significant cardiac lesions encountered in the newborn period. It represents (1) the most common cardiac cause of cyanosis in the newborn period, (2) the most common cause of congestive heart failure within the first 2 months of life, and (3) the most common cause of death in infants with cyanotic congenital heart disease.

MORPHOLOGY AND PHYSIOLOGY. In transposition of the great arteries, the aorta arises from the right ventricle and the pulmonary artery from the left ventricle. In a literal sense "transposition" of the great arteries is present when the aorta and pulmonary artery are "placed across" the ventricular septum so that they arise from the inappropriate ventricles. The developmental abnormality (Fig. 49F) also results in abnormal relationships between the great arteries themselves and replacement of the normal aortic-mitral valve fibrous continuity with pulmonary-mitral valve fibrous continuity.

Anatomic communications must exist between the pulmonary and systemic circulations to permit some oxygenated pulmonary venous blood to enter the systemic arterial circuit and some systemic venous blood to enter the pulmonary arterial circuit (see Fig. 55). An incompetent dilated patent foramen ovale or secundum atrial septal defect is almost always present at the atrial level, and a patent ductus arteriosus is present in over half of the autopsied specimens. A ventricular septal defect is present in about one-half

Fig. 55. In the normal heart the systemic and pulmonary circulations function in series and the systemic tissues and organs utilize the oxygen absorbed into the pulmonary circulation. In transposition of the great arteries the two circulations function in parallel and are relatively independent of each other. Shunting of blood ⇄ (atrial septal defect, ventricular septal defect or patent ductus arteriosus) is essential for postnatal survival and provides oxygenated pulmonary venous blood to the systemic circuit and unoxygenated mixed venous blood to the pulmonary circuit. RA, right atrium; LA, left atrium; RV, right ventricle; LV, left ventricle; PA, pulmonary artery; AO, aorta.

of the infants with transposition of the great vessels. Common atrioventricular canal, atrioventricular valve atresia, severe pulmonary valve stenosis or atresia, or right aortic arch are *rarely* present in transposition of the geat arteries with normal cardiac chamber relationships, dextrotransposition, but are *commonly* associated with the much less frequent levotransposition complexes.

The primary physiologic consequences of transposition of the great arteries are (1) severe hypoxemia and (2) congestive heart failure. These physiologic consequences of complete transposition of the great vessels are extremely serious, since the resultant separation of pulmonary and systemic routes of blood flow are not compatible with prolonged life. The right ventricle now functions as the systemic ventricle and delivers primarily unoxygenated mixed venous blood to the coronary and systemic arteries. The level of arterial oxygen saturation is dependent upon the transfer of oxygenated pulmonary venous blood to the systemic circuit, and this is a function of (1) the number and size of the shunting defects (foramen ovale, ostium secundum defect, ventricular septal defect, and patent ductus arteriosus) and (2) the hemodynamic consequences of associated significant pulmonary stenosis or increased pulmonary vascular resistance which effect a greater transfer of left-sided pulmonary venous blood to the right-sided aorta.

The separation of the venous and arterial routes of blood flow also results in high cardiac output levels for both the right and left ventricles with consequent early cardiac dilatation and myocardial failure.

CLINICAL MANIFESTATIONS. Although the clinical course in transposition of the great arteries can vary as a result of the above-described anatomic and physiologic factors, the clinical picture is generally quite uniform.

Two basic clinical patterns emerge related to the primary physiologic consequences of transposition of the great arteries—i.e., hypoxemia and congestive heart failure. One extreme is represented by the severely cyanotic infant with minimal communication between the pulmonary and systemic circulations (intact ventricular septum and limiting patent foramen ovale). The other extreme is represented by the mild or moderately cyanotic infant with prominent congestive heart failure symptoms who has a large communication (usually ventricular septal defect) between the pulmonary and systemic circulations.

Most infants become critically ill in the first few weeks or months of life. Cyanosis is usually present at birth and dyspnea, congestive heart failure, and failure to thrive become apparent very early. Paroxysmal dyspneic (anoxic) spells are common, particularly in infants with an intact ventricular septum, and these signify urgent need for palliative intervention.

FINDINGS. Cyanosis is usually intense but the systemic arterial oxygen saturation can vary from as low as 10 to 20 percent to as high as 75 to 85 percent, depending upon the associated anatomic and physiologic shunting mechanisms. Growth and muscular development are seriously impaired in the older surviving infant but may appear normal in the seriously ill newborn infant. In contrast to the findings in tetralogy of Fallot, heart failure is common and manifestations of both left (pulmonary rales) and right (hepatomegaly) ventricular failure may be seen.

A loud, usually single second heart sound representing aortic valve closure is heard along the entire left sternal border. A harsh systolic murmur is often present representing either (1) the presence of a ventricular septal defect or (2) functional left ventricular outflow tract stenosis resulting from the increased pulmonary artery blood flow characteristic of transposition physiology. In the former instance the murmur is pansystolic and maximal along the mid and lower left sternal border, and in the latter instance the murmur has a stenotic quality and is often maximal at the upper right sternal border. In about one-half of the infants a rumbling, middiastolic murmur is heard at the apex (left ventricular inflow murmur of functional mitral stenosis).

When transposition of the great arteries is associated with preductal coarctation of the aorta, increased pulmonary vascular resistance, and patent ductus arteriosus, flow through the ductus occurs from the pulmonary artery to the descending aorta, resulting in differential cyanosis, with the upper body more cyanotic than the lower.

The roentgenogram is the most helpful single observation in establishing the diagnosis since a cyanotic infant with cardiac enlargement and pulmo-

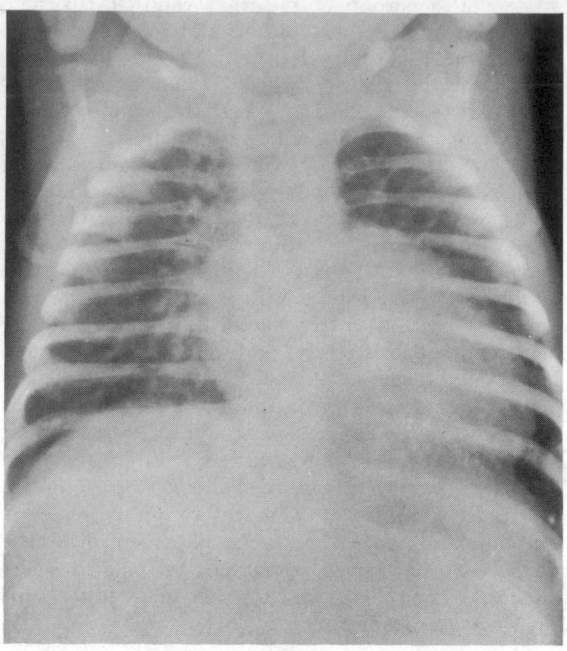

Fig. 56. Roentgenogram showing egg-shaped cardiac silhouette in a patient with transposition of the great arteries.

nary vascular enlargement is likely to have transposition of the great arteries. The classical egg-shaped or oval cardiac silhouette (Fig. 56) is highly diagnostic, but it is present in only about one-third of the infants.

The electrocardiogram usually shows right axis shift; right atrial hypertrophy is common. Right ventricular hypertrophy is more commonly present in transposition of the great arteries with intact ventricular septum or with associated significant pulmonary stenosis, whereas combined ventricular hypertrophy is usually present when a ventricular septal defect and pulmonary hypertension are present.

Cardiac catheterization and angiocardiography (Fig. 57) are valuable in confirming the diagnosis and establishing the presence of associated lesions (ventricular septal defect, pulmonary stenosis, infantile coarctation). Extensive laboratory confirmation in the extremely ill, cyanotic newborn carries a significant risk unless an optimal technique is employed to avoid cardiorespiratory depression from sedation, hypothermia, and excessive angiocardiographic media.

MANAGEMENT. The medical management in transposition of the great arteries is directed toward the control of congestive heart failure, the treatment of pulmonary infections, and the relief of paroxysmal dyspnea. Only about 10 percent of the infants with this lesion survive beyond 6 months of life without surgical therapy. However, if the clinical status is stable, these infants may be managed conservatively until an age (18 to 24 months) that is now considered satisfactory for open-heart corrective surgery. Most infants, however, become critically ill before 2

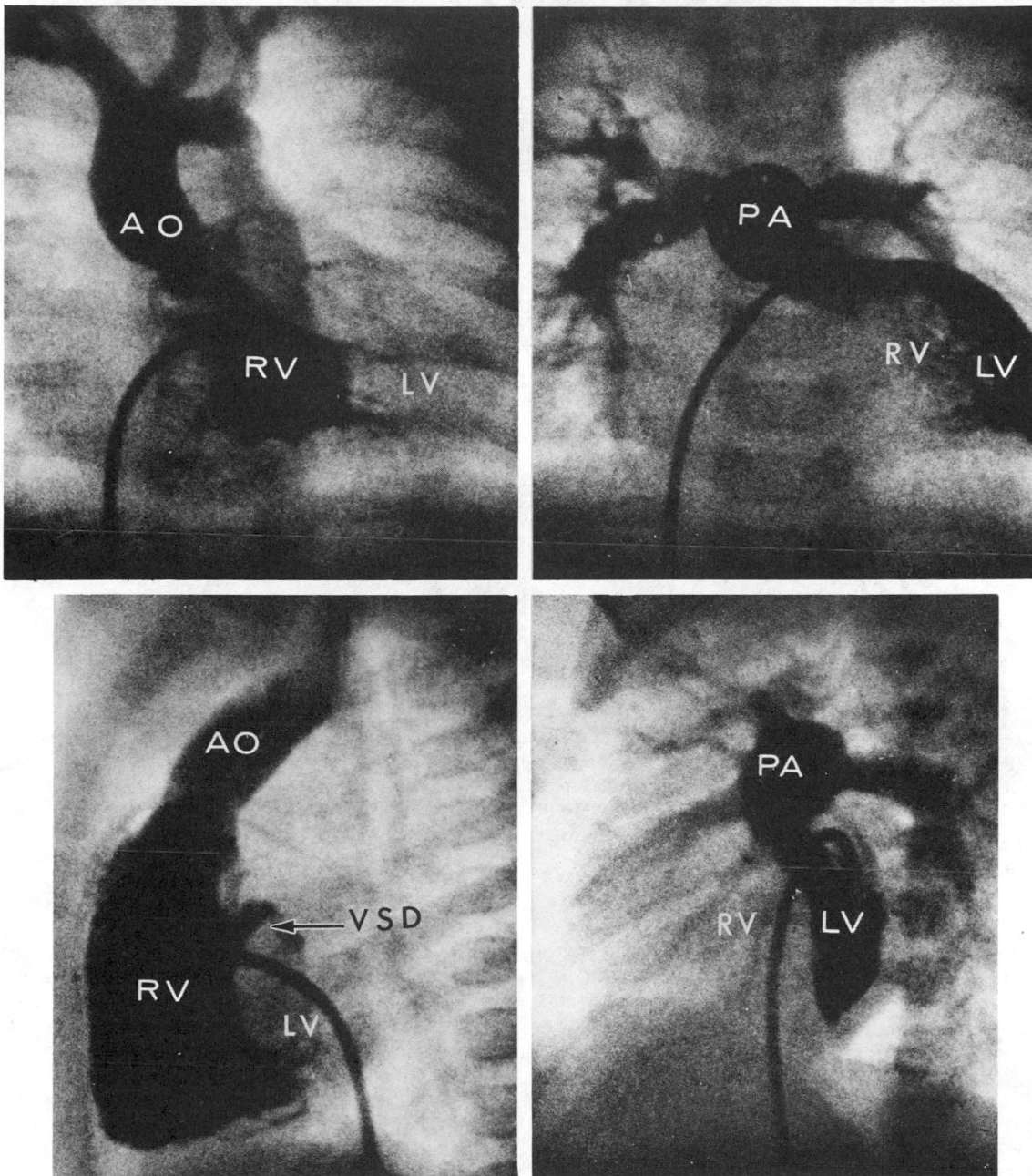

Fig. 57. Selective right and left ventricular angiocardiograms in infant with transposition of the great arteries and small ventricular septal defect. *Top.* Anteroposterior views. *Bottom.* Lateral views. RV, right ventricle; LV, left ventricle; AO, aorta; PA, pulmonary artery; VSD, ventricular septal defect.

to 3 months of age and require prompt palliative therapy if they are to survive.

The recent innovation of a nonsurgical technique to rupture the shunt-limiting valve of the foramen ovale by repeatedly withdrawing an inflated balloon-tipped catheter from the left atrium to the right atrium across the patent foramen ovale provides a means of enlarging the interatrial communication by cardiac catheterization techniques (Fig. 58). Significant increases in the systemic arterial oxygen saturation and dramatic clinical improvement have been noted, particularly in the severely hypoxemic infant with intact ventricular septum and high left atrial pressures.

The surgical creation of a large interatrial septal defect can be recommended for all severely anoxemic

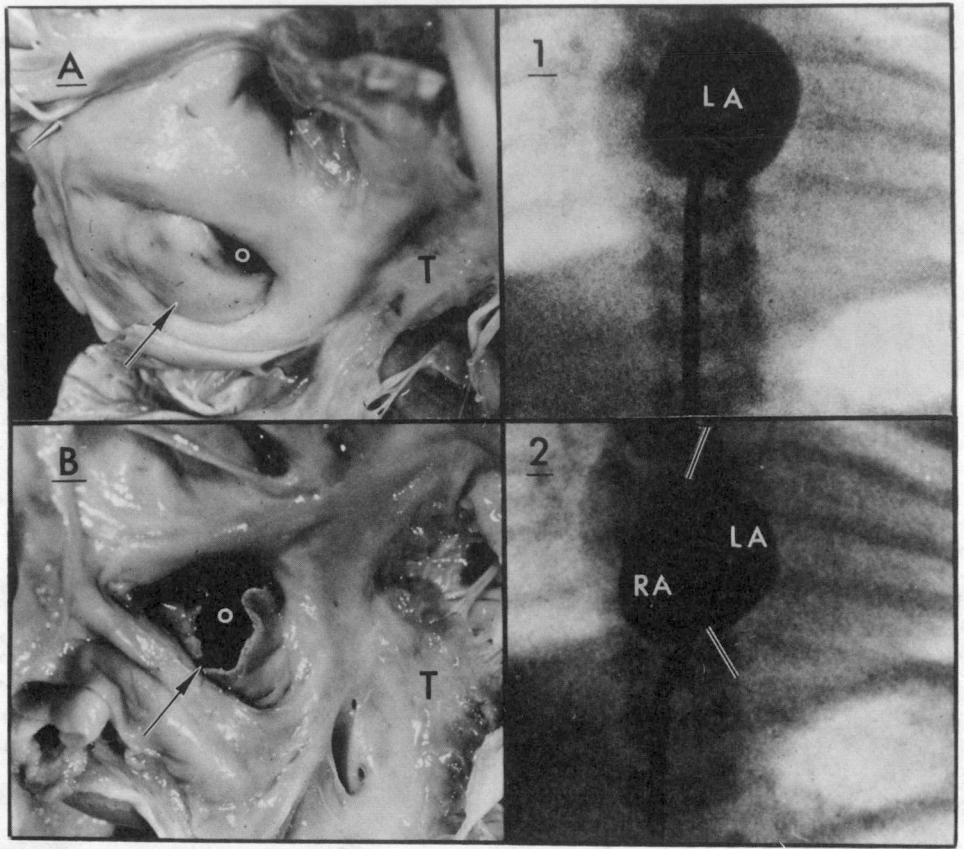

Fig. 58. Balloon-catheter atrial septostomy. A., B. Right atrial view of foramen ovale. A. Oval opening, patent foramen ovale (o). B. Long, linear tear in septum primum flap produced by balloon-catheter septostomy. 1, 2. Individual cine frames illustrating balloon-catheter septostomy. LA, left atrium; RA, right atrium.

infants with transposition of the great arteries when there is continuing evidence for inadequate intracardiac shunting. The purpose of these procedures is to provide for increased mixing of systemic venous and pulmonary venous blood to sustain life and increase the chances of survival with a view to complete operative repair at a later age. These palliative operations are applicable in the newborn period and generally carry a 20 to 30 percent operative mortality. Dramatic clinical improvement with occasional increases in systemic arterial oxygen saturation up to 85 percent have been noted in most of the survivors.

Total surgical correction of transposition of the great arteries can be effected now in the older infant and child with an acceptable surgical risk by redirection of the total systemic venous and pulmonary venous return to the appropriate ventricles with construction of an interatrial pericardial tube (Mustard operation).

Total Anomalous Pulmonary Venous Drainage

Total anomalous pulmonary venous drainage is characterized by the absence of any direct communication between the pulmonary veins and the left atrium. The pulmonary veins are connected either directly to the right atrium or to venous vessels draining toward the right atrium, such as the left superior vena cava and innominate vein, the coronary sinus, the portal vein, or the ductus venosus. The most common form involves the drainage pathway via the left superior vena cava and innominate vein, comprising 40 percent of all cases. The clinical and physiologic features of a special group of infants with total anomalous pulmonary venous drainage are dictated by the presence of anatomic pulmonary venous obstruction. This obstruction occurs most commonly in infants with infradiaphragmatic drainage of the common pulmonary vein, which enters either the portal vein or the ductus venosus. Supradiaphragmatic drainage pathways with pulmonary venous obstruction can occur because of constriction of the anomalous left superior vena cava or because of termination of the main pulmonary veins in a "blind" sac.

HEMODYNAMICS. All of the pulmonary venous and systemic venous blood returns to and eventually mixes in the right atrium. A variable proportion then passes from the right atrium (1) through an interatrial communication, usually a patent foramen ovale, to the left ventricle and aorta, and (2) through the tricuspid valve into the right ventricle and pulmonary artery.

Systemic arterial oxygen unsaturation is always present and results from the obligatory shunting of blood at the atrial level. The arterial oxygen saturation varies widely in different infants, depending upon the ratio of pulmonary to systemic blood flow.

Three hemodynamic and clinical patterns are evident and can be related to (1) the pulmonary vascular resistance and pulmonary blood flow, and (2) the adequacy of the interatrial communication.

In the majority of infants, pulmonary hypertension is associated with high pulmonary blood flow and relatively low pulmonary vascular resistance. These infants generally survive the first few months of life and succumb to severe congestive heart failure during the first year of life unless partial or complete surgical correction is successful. A second, smaller group of infants have severe pulmonary hypertension and restricted pulmonary blood flow associated with an anatomic obstruction to the pulmonary venous blood flow. In this group the pulmonary artery pressures are usually higher than systemic pressures, and death is common in the first weeks of life. A third, much smaller group of children, by contrast, have increased pulmonary blood flow and near normal pulmonary artery pressures and usually a large interatrial communication. This group does relatively well clinically throughout childhood and adolescence. Complete rerouting of the pulmonary venous drainage to the left atrium, with closure of the atrial defect and obliteration of the systemic venous drainage pathway surgically, is also well tolerated in this latter group.

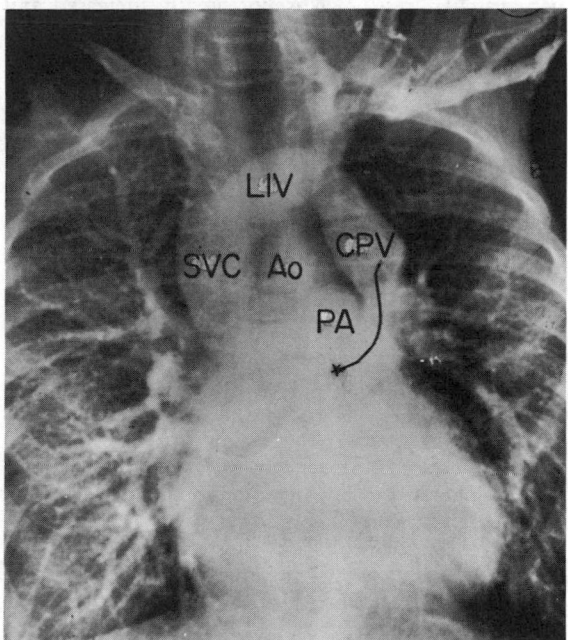

Fig. 59. Abnormal pulmonary venous pathways in total anomalous pulmonary venous drainage.

Cardiac catheterization indicates that the oxygen saturation of blood samples in the right and left atria and ventricles and in the pulmonary artery and aorta is more or less equal. This results from the common mixing of the pulmonary venous and systemic venous blood return proximal to, or in, the right atrium, and this oxygen saturation is significantly higher than that of the peripheral systemic venous return. The anomalous pulmonary venous pathway may be suspected from an unusual position of the probing catheter (in the left superior vena cava or common pulmonary vein) and the observation of an unusually highly oxygen-saturated blood sample in a normally-situated anatomic structure (in the coronary sinus, inferior vena cava, or right superior vena cava). Angiography may outline the abnormal pulmonary venous pathways (Fig. 59). The presence of severe pulmonary hypertension and markedly increased pulmonary vascular resistance usually indicates that a significant anatomic obstruction is present in the pulmonary venous drainage pathway.

CLINICAL FEATURES. About 80 percent of all patients develop symptoms early in infancy and manifest tachypnea, congestive heart failure, and failure to thrive. In the group without pulmonary venous obstruction cyanosis may be minimal, but as congestive heart failure progresses, cyanosis may become striking. The heart is hyperdynamic and large. A quadruple gallop heart rhythm is frequently heard. A soft, ejection-type systolic murmur is heard along the left sternal border, and a middiastolic inflow rumble is usually present at the lower left sternal border and apex. A continuous murmur is occasionally heard at the base and is a venous hum originating in the large venous channel.

The roentgenologic examination shows pulmonary vascular engorgement with cardiac enlargement. In the type in which the pulmonary veins enter the persistent left superior vena cava, a pathognomonic configuration termed "figure-of-eight" or "snowman" may be recognized (Fig. 60).

The electrocardiogram uniformly shows right ventricular hypertrophy, and there is often right atrial hypertrophy.

In these infants with the unobstructed form of total anomalous pulmonary venous drainage, the prognosis is poor when cogestive heart failure is advanced. Surgical correction provides a direct pulmonary venous return pathway into the left atrium. This is accomplished by anastomosis of the common pulmonary vein directly to the left atrium or by opening the roof of the coronary sinus into the left atrium. These surgical procedures can provide effective and dramatic restoration of the circulation pathways, but they carry a moderately high risk in the infant age group. When pulmonary venous obstruction is present, usually associated with infradiaphragmatic drainage, a characteristic clinical syndrome is evident. There is a very early onset of severe dyspnea, considerably more cyanosis than in the unobstructed form, a characteristic chest roentgenogram

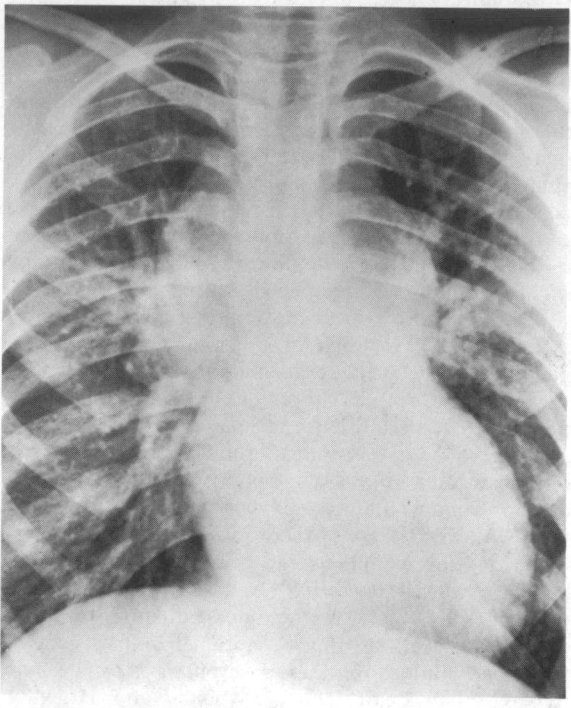

Fig. 60. Roentgenogram showing "figure-of-eight" configuration in total anomalous pulmonary venous drainage into persistent left superior vena cava.

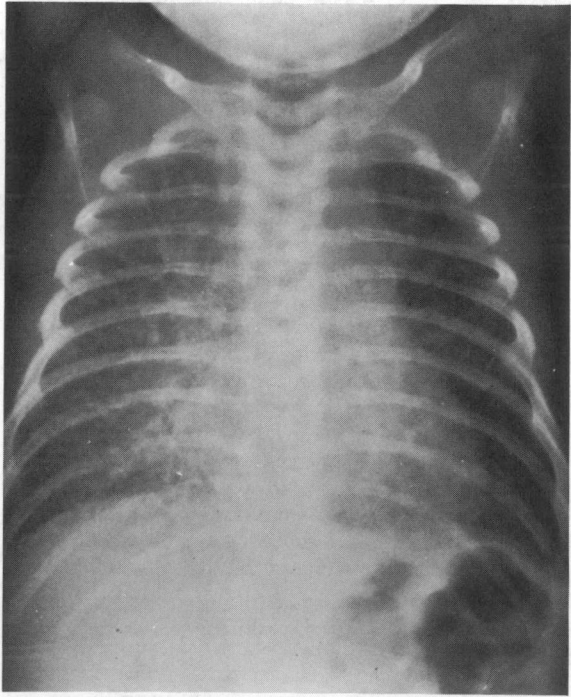

Fig. 61. Chest roentgenogram showing minimal cardiac enlargement and reticulated peripheral lung fields in total anomalous venous drainage with pulmonary venous obstruction.

with minimal cardiac enlargement, and diffusely hazy, reticulated peripheral lung fields (Fig. 61). This obstructed form is characterized by rapid clinical deterioration and early death in the first weeks of life. Surgery has dramatically, but rarely, effected a correction of this form of total anomalous pulmonary venous drainage.

Truncus Arteriosus

Truncus arteriosus is characterized by the emergence of only a single arterial trunk from the ventricular portion of the heart, and this vessel gives rise directly to the coronary, pulmonary, and systemic circulations. (See Fig. 49D.) A ventricular septal defect is present, and the pulmonary arteries arise as a single vessel or as two separate vessels from the ascending portion of the truncus. Truncus arteriosus must not be confused with the relatively common tetralogy of Fallot with pulmonary atresia (pseudotruncus), which is characterized by a single vessel, the aorta, arising from the heart but always accompanied by a remnant of an atretic pulmonary artery leaving the right ventricular outflow region. There is a high incidence (25 percent) of right aortic arch in truncus arteriosus.

HEMODYNAMICS. The systemic (left) and venous (right) ventricles discharge blood at a systemic pressure into the common arterial trunk; thus, the coronary arteries, pulmonary arteries, and aorta are delivered a mixture of venous and arterial blood at systemic pressure. The pulmonary blood flow is generally greatly increased in infancy, since the pulmonary vascular resistance is not greatly increased and there are usually adequate-sized primary pulmonary artery branches. Consequently, cyanosis is minimal and the general hemodynamics as well as the clinical picture are those of a large left-to-right shunt. The pulmonary circulation is restricted in a small number of patients by obstructive increased pulmonary vascular resistance (older child or young adult) or rarely by hypoplastic or stenotic pulmonary arteries arising from the truncus.

Symptoms usually appear in the first weeks or months of life, and the cardiac findings and symptoms are those of a large left-to-right shunt with left-sided failure, including dyspnea, wheezing, frequent respiratory infection, and poor physical development. In the infant, cyanosis is often not apparent or is minimal at rest, since the pulmonary blood flow is greatly increased. The heart is hyperdynamic, and the peripheral pulses are prominent but not collapsing. The second heart sound is loud and single due to the presence of a single set of semilunar valves. A harsh systolic murmur is heard best along the mid-left sternal border, and a continuous murmur is heard at the base or lateral chest wall. In infants only the systolic murmur may be heard, but in most older children the continuous murmur is also audible. If the pulmonary blood flow is restricted either is unusual, and only a systolic murmur of low intensity may be heard.

The roentgenographic findings also depend upon the size of the pulmonary arteries and the pulmonary blood flow pattern, but in the majority of infants there is considerable cardiac enlargement with increased pulmonary vascular markings. The electrocardiogram uniformly demonstrates right ventricular hypertrophy or combined ventricular hypertophy.

The diagnosis is best confirmed by catheterization and selective angiocardiography from the ventricular chambers or the truncus, since angiocardiography reveals the common trunk arising from the heart and the origin of the pulmonary arteries from the truncus (Figs. 62 and 63).

The prognosis is variable, depending to a considerable degree upon the pulmonary blood flow pattern, but the majority of infants die within the first 6 months of life from heart failure. Surgical pulmonary artery banding (constriction) to reduce the pulmonary blood flow to an optimal level has been helpful in selected patients. A recent surgical advance provides complete physiologic correction of the abnormal circulation in truncus arteriosus. The pulmonary arteries are excised from their common truncus origin and the ventricular septal defect is closed with a patch. A portion of the right ventricular wall is excised for attachment of an aortic homograft, which functions as a valved right ventricular outlet conduit to the pulmonary arteries.

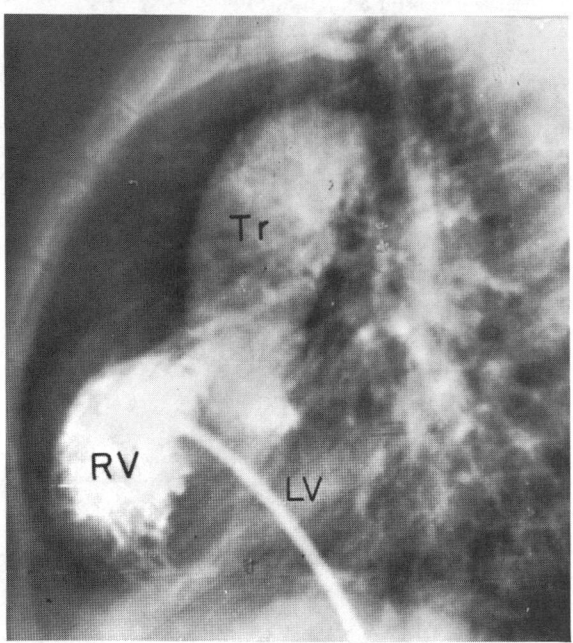

Fig. 62. Angiogram showing common trunk (see text).

by high pulmonary vascular resistance or by stenotic or hypoplastic pulmonary arteries, the clinical findings are significantly altered due to the lower pulmonary blood flow. Cyanosis is more severe, failure

Hypoplastic Left Heart Complex

Hypoplastic left heart complex is a broad term referring to a characteristic arrangement of defects consisting of marked underdevelopment of the entire left side of the heart, including the ascending aorta, aortic valve, left ventricle, mitral valve, and left atrium. In contrast, the right side of the heart is grossly dilated and hypertrophied, with a widely patent ductus arteriosus which delivers blood into the aorta. The specific anatomic abnormalities include aortic valve atresia or severe aortic stenosis with or without mitral stenosis and combined aortic and mitral atresia.

The essential hemodynamic abnormality centers about the absence or inadequacy of left ventricular function due to the above structural abnormalities. The pulmonary venous blood is shunted from the left atrium via an interatrial communication (patent foramen ovale) to the right atrium. The right ventricle functions as a systemic as well as pulmonary ventricle by delivering blood into the aorta through a widely patent ductus arteriosus. The pulmonary vascular resistance must be systemic or greater to provide for this essential systemic function of the right ventricle. The patent foramen ovale is often quite small and restrictive, resulting in severe left atrial and pulmonary venous hypertension.

Infantile coarctation of the aorta in which a tubular construction is proximal to the entrance of

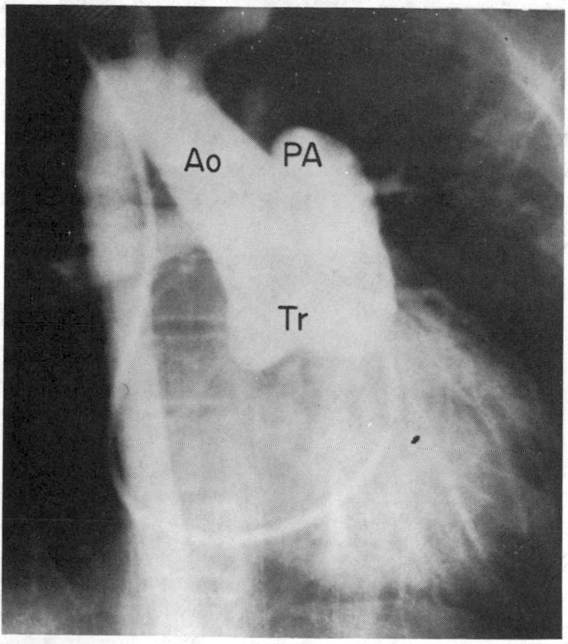

Fig. 63. Angiogram showing origin of the pulmonary arteries from the truncus.

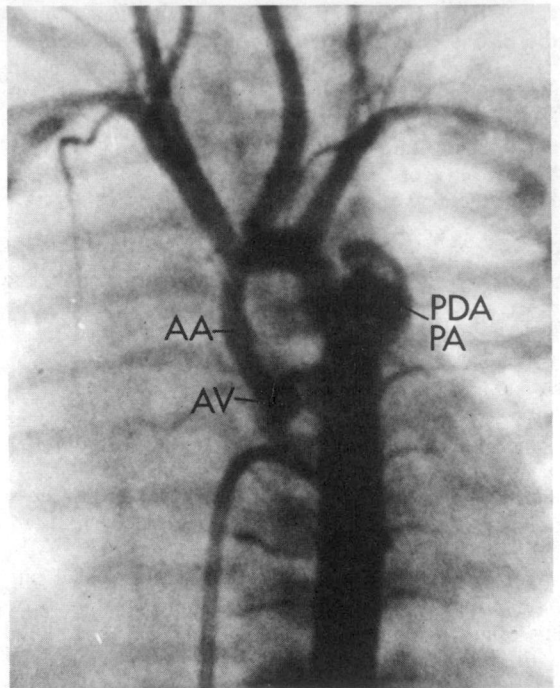

Fig. 64. Hypoplastic left heart complex; aortic and mitral valve atresia. Anteroposterior cineaortogram showing small aortic valve ring (AV), hypoplastic ascending aorta (AA) with patent ductus arteriosus (PDA), and large main pulmonary artery (PA).

the ductus arteriosus resembles this complex in many of these hemodynamic respects; however, the aortic and mitral valve and the ascending aorta are essentially normal. (See p. 1390.)

Most infants with hypoplastic left heart complex are acutely ill with signs of congestive heart failure in the first days or weeks of life, and those with aortic atresia usually succumb within the first few days of life.

On physical examination there are signs and symptoms of severe right-sided and left-sided heart failure, cyanosis of varying degree, pallor, and often poor peripheral pulses. On auscultation murmurs are not a prominent finding, but a soft systolic murmur and middiastolic rumble may be present. The second heart sound (pulmonary valve closure) is single and accentuated unless clinical deterioration is advanced.

The roentgenogram shows striking generalized cardiac enlargement even shortly after birth, with increased pulmonary vascular markings. Pulmonary venous congestion may be prominent. The electrocardiogram without exception shows right ventricular hypertrophy and usually right atrial hypertrophy. These infants are critically ill, and intracardiac diagnostic procedures are difficult. Angiocardiography offers a direct method of diagnosis revealing much of the pathology on an aortogram, which will show the hypoplastic ascending aorta filling in a retrograde

fashion (Fig. 64) as well as a large patent ductus arteriosus entering a huge pulmonary artery.

Supportive therapy with oxygen and digitalis is only of limited benefit, and survival beyond the first days or weeks of life is rare. Since functional closure of the patent ductus arteriosus and restriction to left atrial emptying are prominent physiologic obstructions to the circulatory pathways, palliation has been recently attempted by surgical creation of an atrial septal defect and an aortic-pulmonary anastomosis combined with banding of the pulmonary artery branches.

Anomalies of the Aortic Arch

Abnormal development of the large arterial trunks from the primitive aortic arch system results in anomalies in the position or course of the aortic arch or of the vessels arising from the arch. A right arch with descent of the aorta on the right side causes no symptoms but casts a prominent roentgenographic shadow on the right side of the mediastinum that may be mistaken for enlarged nodes or a tumor mass. There is a right aortic arch in about 20 percent of cases of the tetralogy of Fallot. Correct diagnosis of the position of the arch in this condition is important in relation to surgical shunt procedure. Right aortic arch is also frequent in cases of truncus arteriosus.

A right aortic arch with a taut left ligamentum arteriosum, a double aortic arch, or an anomalous origin of one of the main vessels from the arch may

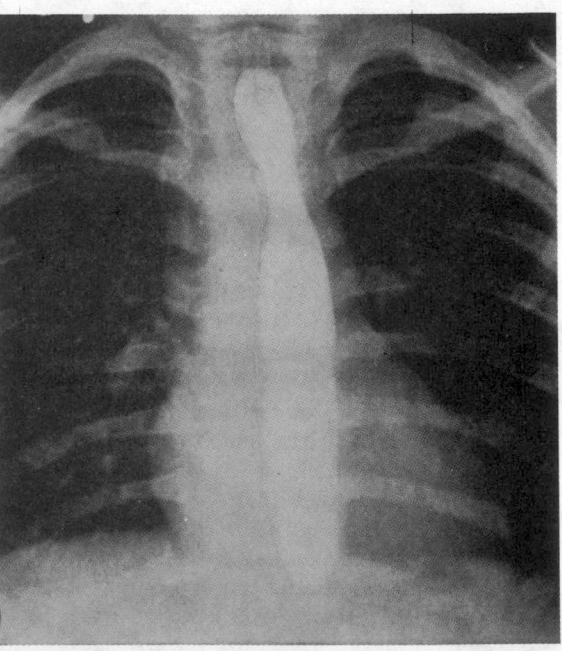

Fig. 65. Right aortic arch. Note impingement of aorta on right side of the barium-filled esophagus.

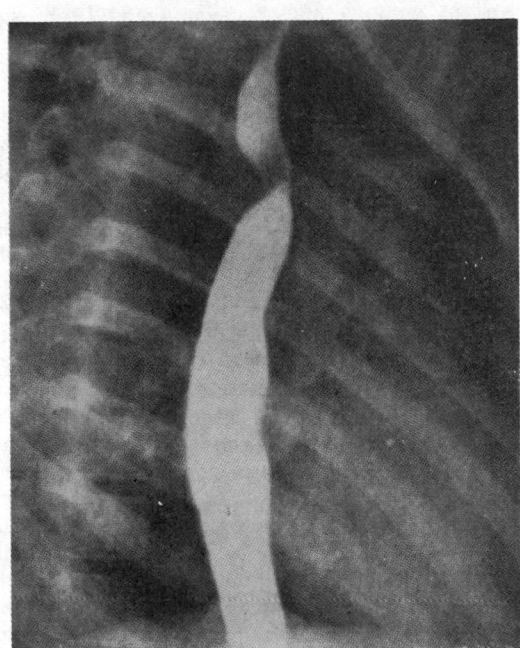

Fig. 66. Right aortic arch with left descending aorta. Right anterior oblique view showing anterior displacement of barium-filled esophagus.

impinge in varying degree on either the esophagus or trachea or both. The degree of pressure may be so slight as to produce no symptoms, the presence of the anomaly being a chance finding on x-ray or even at autopsy. In a certain number of these cases, especially those in which there is encirclement ("vascular ring"), sufficient compression is present to be of serious import, especially in infants. Symptoms are difficulty in swallowing, dyspnea or stridor, cyanosis and choking while feeding, and a tendency to extend the neck.

Clinical diagnosis of these anomalies is made by study of the outline of the trachea and of the barium-filled esophagus as seen under the fluoroscope or in roentgenograms taken in frontal and oblique or lateral views. The ascending portion of a right aortic arch indents the right side of the esophagus as seen in the anterior view (Fig. 65). The normal left aortic arch indents the left side of the esophagus. Where a right aortic arch crosses behind the esophagus to descend on the left, in the oblique views the signs are anterior displacement and transverse posterior compression of the barium-filled esophagus at the level of the third or fourth thoracic vertebra (Fig. 66). The course of a right subclavian artery with anomalous origin from the left side of the aortic arch is seen as a diagonal filling defect running obliquely behind the upper part of the esophagus. When these anomalies cause serious symptoms, which is most likely to occur in infants, early surgical intervention is indicated. Release of the "ring" with relief of pressure is accomplished by division of the

ligamentum arteriosum or patent ductus on the left or of the smaller of the two segments of a double aortic arch. An anomalous constricting subclavian artery can be divided.

REFERENCES

Cole, R. B., Muster, A. J., Lev, M., and Paul, M. Pulmonary atresia with intact ventricular septum. Amer. J. Cardiol., 21:23, 1968.

Cooley, D. A., Hallman, G. L., and Leachman, R. D. Total anomalous pulmonary venous drainage. Correction with the use of cardiopulmonary bypass in 62 cases. J. Thorac. Cardiovasc. Surg., 51:88, 1966.

Ebstein, W. Uber einen sehr seltenen Fall von Insufficienz der Valvula tricuspidalis, bedingt durch eine angeborene hochgradige Missbildung derselben. Arch. Anat. Physiol., 33:238, 1866.

Fallot, A. Contributions a l'anatomie pathologique de la maladie bleu (cyanose cardiaque). Marseille Med., 25:77, 138, 207, 270, 341, 403, 1888.

Genton, E., and Blount, S. G., Jr. The spectrum of Ebstein's anomaly. Amer. Heart J., 73:395, 1967.

Guntheroth, W. G., Morgan, B. C., and Mullins, G. L. Physiological studies of paroxysmal hyperpnea in cyanotic congenital heart disease. Circulation, 31:70, 1965.

Lev, M., and Eckner, F. A. O. The pathologic anatomy of tetralogy of Fallot and its variations. Dis. Chest, 45:251, 1964.

Liebman, J., Callum, L., and Belloc, N. Natural history of transposition of the great arteries—Anatomy and birth and death characteristics. Circulation, 40:237, 1969.

Noonan, J. A., Nadas, A. S., Rudolph, A. M., and Harris, G. B. C. Transposition of the great arteries. A correlation of clinical, physiologic and autopsy data. New Eng. J. Med., 263:592, 1960.

Paul, M. H., Miller, R. A., and Potts, W. J. Long-term results of aortic pulmonary anastomosis for tetralogy of Fallot: an analysis of the first 100 cases of 11 to 13 years after operation. Circulation, 23:525, 1961.

Plauth, W. H., Jr., Nadas, A. S., Bernhard, W. F., and Gross, R. E. Transposition of the great arteries: clinical and pathological observations on 74 patients treated by palliative surgery. Circulation, 37:316, 1968.

Rashkind, W. J., and Miller, W. W. Transposition of the great arteries: Results of palliation by balloon atrioseptostomy in thirty-one infants. Circulation, 38:453, 1968.

Riker, W. L., Potts, W. J., Grana, L., Miller, R. A., and Lev, M. Tricuspid stenosis or atresia complexes. J. Thorac. Cardiovasc. Surg., 45:423, 1963.

Sinha, S. N., Rusnak, S. L., Sommers, H. M., Cole, R. B., Muster, A. J., and Paul, M. H. Hypoplastic left ventricle syndrome. Analysis of thirty autopsy cases in infants with surgical considerations. Amer. J. Cardiol., 21:166, 1968.

Snellen, H. A., Van Ingen, H. C., and Hoefsmit, E. Ch. M. Patterns of anomalous pulmonary venous drainage. Circulation, 38:45, 1968.

Stewart, J. R., Kincaid, O. W., and Edwards, J. E. An atlas of vascular rings and related malformation of the aortic arch system. Springfield, Ill., Charles C Thomas, Publ.. 1964.

Subramanian, S., Carr, I., Waterson, D. J., and Bonham-carter, R. E. Palliative surgery in tricuspid atresia: forty-two cases. Circulation, 32:977, 1965.

Tandon, R., Hauck, A. J., and Nadas, A. S. Persistent truncus arteriosus. A clinical, hemodynamic and autopsy study of nineteen cases. Circulation, 28:1050, 1963.

Van Praagh, R., and Van Praagh, S. The anatomy of common aorticopulmonary trunk (truncus arteriosus communis) and its embryologic implication. A study of 57 necropsied cases. Amer. J. Cardiol., 16:406, 1965.

20.12
ABNORMALITIES OF CHAMBER AND GREAT VESSEL LOCALIZATION

MILTON H. PAUL

The apex of the heart is normally directed to the left side of the chest, and the left ventricle is to the left of and posterior to the right ventricle. Abnormalities of the position of the ventricles and of the origin of the aorta and pulmonary artery from the ventricles are occasionally encountered. Terms such as dextrocardia, dextroversion, isolated levocardia, and corrected transposition have been applied to some of these disturbances of position. These terms are often ill-defined and confusing. Recently, Van Praagh has presented a classification based on embryologic development of the primitive cardiac tube, which helps in the understanding of these anomalies. (Fig. 67).

ATRIAL POSITION. The heart and great arteries and veins embryologically develop from a straight tube. The ultimate positions of the left and right atria are closely related to the position of the abdominal viscera. The abdominal systemic veins eventually become confluent to form the sinus venosus and right atrium. They are related to the position of the liver and stomach. If the major liver development is on the right, the inferior vena cava and right atrium will be on the right; this is the normal pattern and is termed situs solitus. If the liver is mainly on the left, the "right" or systemic venous atrium will be on the left; this is called situs inversus. Occasionally, the position of the liver is central and the atria are indeterminate, and the term situs symmetricus has been used. In this condition the spleen is usually absent, and it has often been called the "asplenia" syndrome.

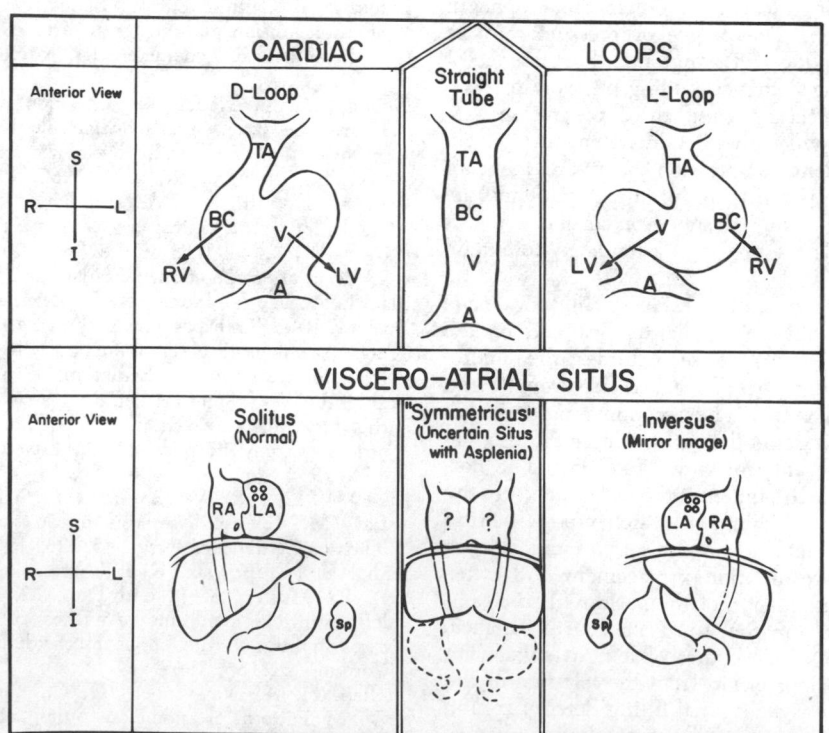

Fig. 67. Abnormalities of chamber and great vessel localization. S, superior; I, inferior; R, right; L, left; TA, truncus arteriosus; BC, bulbus cordis; V, primitive ventricle; A, atrium; RV, right ventricle; LV, left ventricle; RA, right atrium; LA, left atrium; SP, spleen.

VENTRICULAR POSITION. As rapid differential growth of the primitive cardiac tube occurs, it loops forward and the loop protrudes to one side. Normally, the bulbus cordis region of the tube is directed to the right, and this area eventually forms the outflow tract or infundibulum of the right ventricle. This has been termed a *d* (dextro)-loop. If the cardiac tube swings to the left, however, an *l* (levo)-loop is formed. The bulbus cordis region would be carried to the left and developed into a left-sided but morphologic right ventricle.

In situs solitus, a *d*-loop is the normal developmental pattern, whereas in situs inversus normal cardiac development is associated with an *l*-loop. In both these circumstances, the loop is termed concordant. If, however, an *l*-loop occurs in situs solitus or a *d*-loop occurs in situs inversus, it is discordant.

GREAT ARTERY POSITION. After cardiac development is completed, in *d*-loop hearts the aortic valve normally lies to the right of the pulmonary valve, and this relationship is reversed in the *l*-loop heart. Normally the aorta originates from the morphologic left ventricle and the pulmonary artery from the morphologic right ventricle. When the origin of the great arteries is disturbed so that the aorta arises from the morphologic right venticle, the condition of transposition exists. This may occur in either *d*-loop or *l*-loop hearts.

In the common type of complete transposition of the great arteries, there is a *d*-loop, and the ventricles have their usual anatomic relations, but the aorta arises from the right or venous ventricle.

In the condition known as "corrected transposition" there is an *l*-loop and the aorta arises from the morphologic right ventricle, which in this situation is, however, a functional left ventricle.

Using this classification, it is then possible to define the vast majority of abnormalities of chamber or great artery positions in terms of three parameters, namely: (1) *Concordant or discordant;* (2) d-*loop or l-loop;* and (3) *Normal or transposed great arteries.*

REFERENCES

Van Praagh, R., Ongley, P. A., and Swan, H. J. L. Anatomic types of single or common ventricle in man. Morphologic and geometric aspects of 60 necropsied cases. Amer. J. Cardiol., 13:867, 1964.

———— and Van Praagh, S. Anatomically corrected transposition of the great arteries. Brit. Heart J., 29:112, 1967.

———— Van Praagh, S., Vlad, P., and Keith, J. D. Anatomic types of congenital dextrocardia. Diagnostic and embryologic implications. Amer. J. Cardiol., 13:510, 1964.

20.13
CONGESTIVE HEART FAILURE IN INFANCY AND CHILDHOOD

EUGENIE F. DOYLE

Congestive heart failure exists when the heart is unable to supply a cardiac output adequate for tissue needs or to expel an excessive venous return. The clinical syndrome of congestive heart failure in the pediatric age group is caused by a wide variety of congenital cardiac malformations, primary myocardial diseases, and disturbed myocardial states secondary to anemia or to renal or pulmonary disease. Most instances of heart failure in infancy (Table 4) are due to severe forms of congenital heart disease; of these

TABLE 4. *Leading Causes of Heart Failure in Infancy*

Congenital Malformations
    Large left-to-right shunts
        Ventricular septal defect
        Patent ductus arteriosus
        Endocardial cushion defects
        Total anomalous pulmonary venous drainage
        Truncus arteriosus with increased pulmonary vascular flow
        AV fistula (especially cerebral)
        Common atrium
        Aortic pulmonary fenestration

    Large right-to-left shunts
        Complete transposition of great vessels
        Hypoplastic left heart syndrome with patent ductus arteriosus
        Tricuspid atresia

    Obstructive lesions
        Coarctation of aorta (usually associated with patent ductus arteriosus)
        Aortic stenosis or atresia
        Pulmonic stenosis
        Mitral stenosis
        Cor triatriatum
        Pulmonary venous obstruction

Endomyocardial Diseases
    Endocardial fibroelastosis
    Myocarditis (especially Coxsackie B)
    Ectopic origin of left coronary artery from pulmonary artery
    Medial necrosis of coronary arteries
    Cardiac form of glycogen storage disease

Arrhythmias
    Paroxysmal atrial or ventricular tachycardia
    Paroxysmal atrial flutter

Circulatory Congestion
    Overtransfusion or overhydration
    Diminished renal function

TABLE 5.   *Leading Causes of Heart Failure in Childhood*

Myocarditis
    Rheumatic fever
    Viral infections (especially Coxsackie B)

Rheumatic Valve Disease
    Mitral insufficiency
    Mitral stenosis
    Aortic insufficiency

Bacterial Endocarditis
    Primary (rare)
    Secondary to congenital or rheumatic heart disease

Congenital Cardiac Defects
    Complicated by
        Surgical ventriculotomy
        Pulmonary vascular obstruction
        Infection
        Arrhythmias
    Incompletely relieved by surgery
        Transposition of great vessels
        Atrioventricular canal

Arrhythmias
    Atrial fibrillation
    Complete heart block
        Postoperative
        Congenital (rare)

Anemia
    Chronic, severe, especially Cooley's

Systemic Hypertension Secondary to
    Acute or chronic renal disease
    Pheochromocytoma

Hyperthyroidism

Cor Pulmonale Secondary to
    Extensive pulmonary disease
    Severe chest deformity

Endomyocardiopathy
    Chronic myocarditis
    Tuberous sclerosis
    Tumor
    Hurler's disease

transposition of the great arteries, ventricular septal defect, patent ductus arteriosus, coarctation of the aorta, and hypoplastic left heart syndrome are the most frequent. Another important cause of failure at this age is endocardial fibroelastosis. If failure due to congenital cardiac defects does not occur during early infancy, it is unlikely to become evident until the child is considerably older, when complications such as infection, progressive pulmonary hypertension, or arrhythmias may increase the myocardial burden or when, during the postoperative period following ventriculotomy, myocardial efficiency may be temporarily impaired.

In childhood, rheumatic fever, rheumatic heart disease, renal disease, and complicated forms of severe congenital malformations are the most frequent causes of failure (Table 5).

MECHANISM AND SYMPTOMS.   The different physiologic mechanisms causing myocardial failure in various congenital cardiac defects are discussed in Section 20.8. Impaired myocardial performance from any cause results in a reduction in cardiac output. The heart soon attempts to compensate by increasing its stroke volume; a rise in *end-diastolic pressure* in the ventricles is achieved by increases in atrial and venous pressures. *Cardiac enlargement* almost invariably results, the exceptions being some small infants with decreased ventricular compliance. When cardiomegaly is marked, the myocardium is stretched, so that it is functioning on the descending limb of the stroking curve and stroke volume begins to fall. *Tachycardia*, due probably to sympathetic nervous system stimulation, also occurs so that even with a diminishing stroke volume the cardiac output may be adequate for some time. Eventually the compensatory tachycardia becomes inadequate as the stroke volume decreases further or as the tachycardia itself causes further myocardial burden by impairing coronary filling or by increasing myocardial oxygen consumption. The release of catecholamines by the sympathetic nervous system also attempts to compensate by its ionotropic effect on myocardial contractility, by increasing systemic vascular resistance and venous tone, and by decreasing cutaneous, splanchnic, and renal blood flow. *Reduced urinary output* and enhanced *sweating* occur. As compensatory mechanisms fail, the cardiac output decreases further. The patient senses increasing *fatigue*, and *pallor* appears. The infant may evidence *difficulty in feeding*: though hungry, the effort of sucking produces ready fatigue; he will doze from exhaustion; however, the small food intake per feeding will make him awaken soon, hungry, anxious to suck vigorously, but promptly tiring again. This type of feeding history is very characteristic of the infant with poor cardiac output. *Failure to thrive* is a consequence.

Further rises in left and right atrial pressures are reflected in the pulmonary venous and systemic venous beds, respectively, causing the symptomatology of left and right heart failure.

Left Heart Failure.   *Dyspnea*, first on exertion and later at rest, is due partly to decreased compliance of the lung secondary to pulmonary venous congestion and edema; stimulation of stretch receptors in the left atrium and pulmonary veins may also play a role. The stimulation of chemoreceptors by hypoxia and hypercapnia secondary to the presence of transudate between alveoli and capillaries is not usually an important mechanism but may play a role in severe or advanced cases.

Tachypnea is frequently the earliest sign of cardiac failure in infants with obstructive left heart lesions as well as in those with large left ventricular volume overloading. It is frequently stressed that hepatomegaly is one of the first signs of failure in infancy; however, this may occur only late, or not at all when the left ventricle fails first. Since left heart failure is common in infants, the importance of respiratory distress as the first evidence of failure must be stressed.

Orthopnea, relief of dyspnea in the sitting position, is related to the fact that, in this position, venous return to the heart is reduced, thereby decreasing the pulmonary blood volume. Pulmonary edema is caused by marked pulmonary venous congestion causing excessive filtration of fluid through the pulmonary capillaries; alveolar fluid accumulates with resulting impairment in alveolar gas exchange. Increasing *rales, bloody frothy sputum, wheezing,* and *progressive cyanosis* may occur. *Chronic hacking cough* may result from congestion of the bronchial mucosa secondary to increased pulmonary venous pressure. *Hoarseness* may be caused by pressure on the left recurrent laryngeal nerve by the enlarged left pulmonary artery or left atrium.

Pulmonary function studies in patients with left heart failure have shown reduced lung compliance, which increases the work of breathing, especially in infants. Though tachypnea increases energy demands, it appears the rapid shallow respirations are the most economic breathing pattern for infants in failure. Vital capacity and total lung capacity are usually diminished.

Right Heart Failure. Signs of right heart failure result from systemic venous hypertension. The most common manifestation is *hepatomegaly,* which is the most reliable manifestation of right heart failure in infancy and childhood. With sudden right-sided failure, the liver is usually quite tender from capsular distension, and the liver edge is rounded. *Anorexia* and *abdominal pain* may be present. When congestive failure is chronic, the liver may be quite firm with a sharp edge and without associated tenderness. *Splenomegaly* usually indicates severe elevation of venous pressure and generally occurs only after failure has been present for a period of several weeks. *Distension of neck veins* may be evident in children but is rarely discernible in infants, whose necks are short. *Venous pressure elevation* may be measured in older cooperative children; in the agitated child it is valueless. Frank *edema* is a relatively uncommon manifestation in infants and children, occurring only with severe right heart failure. The edema in cardiac failure probably results partly from the increased venous pressure exceeding the oncotic pressure of the plasma proteins. Since the lymph flow is impaired by the increased systemic venous pressure, there is an increased production and a slower removal of interstitial fluid. Also increased renal reabsorption of sodium and water plays an important role in the fluid retention associated with congestive heart failure. Both hemodynamic and neurohumoral mechanisms are considered responsible for enhanced sodium retention which follows the drop in renal blood flow. Hypersecretion of aldosterone results when the re-

duced renal blood flow stimulates the secretion of renin from the juxtoglomerular apparatus. Following conversion of renin to angiotension II, the adrenals are stimulated to release aldosterone, which promotes sodium reabsorption by its effect on the distal renal tubules. Renal mechanisms involved in edema formation are discussed in detail in Section 22.10.

Ascites is seen only in children with chronic right heart failure in which hepatic parenchymal necrosis caused by congestion and hypoxia leads to fibrotic displacement. *Sweating* is a very common and important sign of cardiac failure at all ages; it is especially common in infants. The sweat contains relatively low amounts of sodium. The increased perspiration is probably due to increased sympathetic activity. The mother will frequently complain that the infant's head is always sweaty, that the pillow is damp after naps, and that the patient has chronic heat rash. *Pallor* is another common finding, particularly when failure is severe; it is probably due to vasoconstriction of skin vessels as a sympathetic response to the decreased cardiac output and lowered blood pressure.

It is not uncommon to find right- or left-sided failure in pure form in children with congenital heart disease. For instance, in cases of coarctation of the aorta and aortic stenosis, left-sided failure alone may be seen early in the course of decompensation. Also right-sided failure alone may be encountered with tricuspid valve disease, pulmonic stenosis, or large atrial septal defects. More commonly, however, signs of left and right heart failure occur concomitantly.

TREATMENT. The patient in acute congestive heart failure presents a medical emergency. Vigorous measures should be used for the immediate problem while diagnostic measures to detect the patient's underlying disease are undertaken. The aims of therapy are: (1) improvement in myocardial efficiency; (2) removal of accumulated fluid and sodium; (3) decrease in energy requirements; and (4) improved tissue oxygenation. Measures used include digitalis preparations, diuretics and low-sodium diet, enforced bed rest, and oxygen.

Digitalis. The principal effect of digitalis on the heart is an improvement in the force of systolic contraction. It also increases vagal tone at the SA node and the AV node, causing a slowing of sinus rhythm when therapeutic doses are employed and degrees of conduction delay when near-toxic and toxic dosage is used.

In general, infants and children require larger amounts of digitalis per unit weight than do adults for full digitalization and maintenance. The explanation for this relatively higher dosage requirement in infants cannot be explained by differences in absorption, tissue fixation, or excretion. Available studies show that the absorption, tissue concentrations, and urinary and fecal excretion of digoxin in the infant are in the same range as in the adult. Digitalis is beneficial for most cases of heart failure seen in infants and children. The exceptions are newborns with the severest forms of cardiac defects, such as

TABLE 6.   *Digitalis Preparations: Initial Digitalization and Maintenance*

Drug	Route of Administration	Initial Digitalization Dose mg/kg			Dose Division	Maintenance
		Under 1 yr*	1-2 yr	Over 2 yr		
Digoxin	Oral	0.07	0.06	0.04-0.05	50-70% stat; remainder in 2 doses at 6-8 hour intervals	30% digitalizing dose
	Parental	75% of above	75% of above	75% of above	as above	30% dose
Digitoxin	Oral and parenteral	0.035	0.03	0.02-0.025	as above	10-20% initial dose
Lanatoside C	iv	0.035	0.03	0.025		

*The response of newborn infants is variable, and only 75% of the above dosages is recommended.

Note: Digoxin and digitoxin are both available in pediatric liquid solution, tablet form, and pediatric parenteral form, so that precise dosage can be readily employed even for premature infants.

hypoplastic left heart syndrome, where the anatomy is incompatible with postnatal existence, and children with severe anemia or thyrotoxicosis, where the myocardium is already expelling a higher than normal cardiac output.

A wide variety of digitalis preparations is available. The fast-acting glycosides used most frequently in pediatric practice are listed in Table 6. Digoxin is the most widely used in pediatrics. It is a highly satisfactory agent because it is rapidly absorbed, well tolerated, and rapidly excreted. The latter feature is a great advantage if toxicity occurs. The advantage of digitoxin is that the dosage by oral or parenteral route is the same. However, both the onset of effect and its elimination are slow. These features are helpful in maintaining stable control of heart failure when the patient has chronic heart disease, but disadvantageous if rapid digitalis effect is required or if toxicity occurs. In emergency situations either intravenous digoxin or lanatoside C is preferred because of the rapid onset of their action, which is evident within 5 to 10 minutes of administration.

There is a great need for caution in prescribing digitalis preparations. The glycosides are very potent drugs, and fatalities have resulted from careless prescriptions. Mistakes in dosage are less likely to occur if pediatricians become thoroughly familiar with one or two forms of digitalis preparations. The dosage schedule listed in Table 6 is recommended for the average case. Note that smaller starting doses are recommended for newborn infants of all birth weights.

It should be appreciated that the "correct" dose of digitalis is that which is adequate to relieve the evidences of failure without producing toxicity. Although Table 6 provides guidelines for therapy, occasionally patients require considerably larger doses. Also some patients may develop signs of toxicity with doses as small as 50 percent or less of that recommended. The latter is especially apt to be noted when acute myocarditis is present, when the patient already has prolonged AV conduction, or when hypokalemia exists.

Every patient being digitalized should be closely observed for his clinical response to the drug. As soon as failure subsides, a maintenance dosage can be started. If there is no response after the full digitalizing dose has been administered, additional doses of one-quarter the calculated digitalizing dose can be given every 8 hours for several doses until a clinical response or early toxicity is obtained. Before increasing the dose to the point of full toxicity, however, ancillary measures to control the failure should be used.

Clinical response to digitalis is shown by subsidence of dyspnea, reduction of pulse and respiratory rate toward normal, weight loss, reduction in cardiomegaly and hepatomegaly, and whatever other signs of failure the patient may have presented initially. Manifestations of clinical toxicity to digitalis are nausea, vomiting, bradycardia, and arrhythmias.

Electrocardiographic responses to digitalis are listed in Table 7. A base line EKG should be obtained before digitalization is started and should be repeated when the calculated dose is completed, or sooner if clinical signs of toxicity occur. It must be stressed that there is no strict correlation between the presence or absence or the degree of abnormality of the EKG findings and the therapeutic effect of digitalis on heart muscle. Therapeutic effects of digitalis are gauged by evaluation of the patient, not the EKG, which is only an aid in detecting toxicity.

Digitalis toxicity demands cessation of the drug. The management of digitalis toxicity (see Table 8) varies with the manner in which overdosage occurred. Accidental excessive oral intake requires rapid gastric lavage. Intramuscular overdosage may be treated by measures aimed at slowing absorption from the injec-

TABLE 7. *Electrocardiographic Responses to Digitalis*

Digitalis effect:	Shortening of the Q-T interval, slowing of the sinus rate, S-T segment depression, flattening or inversion of the T wave, slight prolongation of P-R interval.
Excessive digitalis effect (early toxicity):	Marked depression of the S-T segment, moderate prolongation of the P-R interval, occasional premature ventricular contractions. (Digitalis may be continued cautiously at a lower dose.)
Digitalis toxicity:	Markedly prolonged P-R interval, second- and third-degree block, frequent premature ventricular contraction, digeminy, trigeminy, paroxysmal tachycardia, flutter, fibrillation.

tion site. If patients receiving digitalis are kept under careful medical supervision, toxicity is usually detectable early and severe toxicity can be prevented. If arrhythmias are present, administration of potassium chloride is indicated. Potassium is most effective when there is some degree of hypokalemia, which may occur after prolonged diuretic therapy. Intravenous Dilantin, lidocaine (Xylocaine), and propranolol have been used effectively in some cases. In instances where toxicity is manifested by marked sinus bradycardia or AV block, atropine rather than potassium is indicated. If atrial fibrillation or severe ventricular arrhythmias occur, external electric countershock may be helpful.

Epinephrine or Isoproterenol. Epinephrine infusion is another method of improving myocardial efficiency which has proved useful in some infants with large left-to-right shunts who failed to respond satisfactorily to other measures. An accurately controlled infusion of 0.5 to 0.9 μg per kg per minute of epinephrine hydrochloride may effect improvement, due apparently to the direct effect of epinephrine on the myocardium and possibly to enhanced systemic vasoconstriction and coronary artery dilatation. This measure, though helpful in some cases, is not without risk and should be used selectively and with great care. It may be helpful in an acute situation preliminary to emergency surgery. Similar results have been obtained with intravenous infusion of isoproterenol in doses of 0.1 μg/kg/minute.

Diuretics. Diuretics are important adjuncts to digitalis therapy, especially when there is considerable pulmonary or peripheral edema. These agents aid in restoring extracellular fluid volume to normal by interfering with tubular reabsorption of electrolytes, notably sodium and potassium, and of water. Since all diuretic agents can cause considerable electrolyte imbalance, concentrations of serum electrolytes should be checked periodically when the drugs are used over an extended period. The *mercurial diuretics* have been highly efficacious, with low toxicity, for infants and children. They are particularly helpful in acute failure; their disadvantage is that they must be given parenterally. Patients receiving mercurials may develop hypochloremic alkalosis and become refractory to further therapy. The administration of ammonium chloride or lysine hydrochloride to these patients raises low serum chloride levels and restores responsiveness to further mercurial diuretics. The *chlorothiazide derivatives* are also extremely effective. Since they are given orally they are particularly helpful in patients in chronic failure. Potassium chloride supplements are usually necessary when chlorothiazides are prescribed. *Spironolactone,* an aldosterone inhibitor, has proved a useful diuretic; because of its potassium sparing effect, it is especially effective when combined with mercurials or chlorothiazides. It is

TABLE 8. *Management of Digitalis Toxicity*

A. Stop further digitalis!

B. If excessive oral Intake: gastric lavage
   If excessive intramuscular dosage: cold compress locally; tourniquet on extremity

C. Medications:
   Anti-arrhythmic agents (continuous monitoring essential):

KCL: iv (severe cases):	0.3-0.5 mEq/kg/hour (40 mEq in 500 ml 5% glucose solution)
oral (mild cases):	1-1.5 mEq/kg/day (3 divided doses)
Dilantin:	2 mg/kg iv repeat PRN
Lidocaine (Xylocaine)	1 mg/kg iv repeat PRN
Propranolol:	0.025-1 mg/kg iv slowly
Procaine amide:	3-5 mg/kg slowly iv

   Chelating agent (to mobilize calcium):
   EDTA: 15 mg/kg/hour in 5% glucose solution. Total dose should not exceed 60 mg/kg/day

D. Electric countershock (for ventricular fibrillation only):
   Direct current countershock is currently the method of choice. Initial discharge set at 15 joules in infants and 50-100 joules in children. In case of failure to revert, stronger shocks increased in stepwise fashion are used.

TABLE 9.   *Diuretics Available for Pediatric Use*

Agent	Route	Dosage
Mercurials:		
Meralluride	im	0.1-0.25 ml infants
Mercaptomerin	im	0.3-1 ml children
Chlorothiazide	oral	25 mg/kg (not over 500 mg/day)
Hydrochlorothiazide	oral	2.5 mg/kg
Spironolactone	oral	1.5-3 mg/kg/day
Aminophylline	oral	10 mg/kg/dose
	rectal	5 mg/kg/dose
	iv or im	3 mg/kg every 6 hours
Ethacrynic acid	iv or oral	0.5-1 mg/kg

particularly helpful when ascites is present. *Aminophylline* may also be used jointly with mercurials for an enhanced diuresis. It is a very useful agent in the presence of pulmonary edema.

Recent experience with *ethacrynic acid,* a derivative of phenoxyacetic acid, has demonstrated it to be a potent, rapid-acting, fairly safe diuretic that can be administered orally or intravenously. It appears to block sodium reabsorption at all sites where the sodium ion is transported. Ethacrynic acid has an advantage over the mercurials in acutely ill patients because of its fast action and its independence of serum chloride concentration for efficacy. Dosage schedules for these agents are listed in Table 9.

Salt Restriction.   During acute heart failure salt restriction is indicated. Low-sodium milk is available for infant feeding, and salt restriction to less than 1 g daily is advised for children. Because a low-salt diet is unpalatable and usually low in protein, prolonged salt restriction is not advisable; a moderate salt intake and an oral diuretic are usually preferable in cases of chronic failure.

Rest.   The work load required of the failing heart is considerably eased if the patient is kept as basal as possible. Bed rest in a comfortable propped position is preferred. Sedation should be given if the infant is fretful or the child apprehensive. The amount of handling and examination should be the minimum consistent with good medical care. Small frequent feedings may be advisable.

Antibiotics.   Antibiotics also have a role in the treatment of congestive heart failure when the added burden of infection, usually respiratory, pushes the patient in borderline compensation into frank failure. In small infants, especially those with large left-to-right shunts, it is often difficult to distinguish left heart failure from bronchopneumonia. Whenever infection is a possibility antibiotics should be used.

Oxygen.   Oxygen is clearly indicated if the patient is visibly desaturated. Even in the absence of cyanosis, however, labored respirations are frequently eased when the patient is put in a cool humidified tent with a concentration of 50 percent oxygen.

TREATMENT OF THE UNDERLYING DISEASE.   As mentioned earlier the presence of congestive heart failure requires therapy irrespective of the underlying disease. Although alleviation of failure can usually be achieved through a combination of the measures listed above, ultimate cure will depend upon therapy of the basic illness. Diagnostic measures to differentiate congenital cardiac defects should be undertaken once failure is controlled. Fortunately most of the congenital cardiac defects causing failure are amenable to surgery. Specific forms of treatment for other causes of heart failure, such as rheumatic fever, hypertension, arrhythmias, thyrotoxicosis, and myocarditis, are discussed elsewhere.

REFERENCES

MECHANISMS

Aviado, D. M., Jr., and Schmidt, C. F. Reflexes from stretch receptors in blood vessels, heart and lungs. Physiol. Rev., 35:247, 1955.

Aygen, M. M., and Braunwald, E. Studies on Starling's law of the heart. VIII. Mechanical properties of human myocardium studied in vivo. Circulation, 26:516, 1962.

Gaffney, T. E., and Braunwald, E. Importance of the adrenergic nervous system in the support of circulatory function in patients with congestive heart failure. Amer. J. Med., 34:320, 1963.

Laragh, J. H. Hormones and the pathogenesis of congestive heart failure: vasopressin, aldosterone, and angiotenson II. Circulation, 25:1015, 1962.

Pittman, J. G., and Cohen, P. The pathogenesis of cardiac cachexia. New Eng. J. Med., 271:403, 453, 1964.

Rushmer, R. F. Cardiovascular Dynamics. Philadelphia, W. B. Saunders Co., 1961.

Talnor, N. S. Congestive heart failure. *In* Moss, A. J., and Adams, F. H., eds., Heart Disease in Infants, Children and Adolescents. Baltimore, The Williams and Wilkins Co., 1968, pp. 1004-1027.

Turino, G. M., and Fishman, A. P. The congested lung. J. Chron. Dis., 9:510, 1959.

THERAPY

Engle, M. A. Treatment of the failing heart. Pediat. Clin. N. Amer., 2:247, 1964.

Keith, J. D., Rowe, R. D., and Vlad, P. Heart Disease in Infancy and Childhood, 2nd ed. New York, The Macmillan Co., 1967, pp. 1020-1048.

Rudolph, A. M., Mesel, E., and Levy, J. M. Epinephrine in the treatment of cardiac failure due to shunts. Circulation, 28:3, 1963.

Serratto, M., and Miller, R. A. Congestive Heart Failure. *In* Watson, H., ed., Paediatric Cardiology. St. Louis, C. V. Mosby, 1968, pp. 909-931.

Sparrow, A. W., Friedberg, D. Z., and Nadas, A. S. The use of ethacrynic acid in infants and children with congestive heart failure. Pediatrics, 42:291, 1968.

DIGITALIS: PHARMACOLOGY AND TOXICITY

Eliot, R. S., and Blount, S. G., Jr. Calcium Chelates and digitalis: a clinical study. Amer. Heart J., 62:7, 1961.

Fowler, R. S., Rathi, L., and Keith, J. D. Accidental

digitalis intoxication in children. J. Pediat., 64:188, 1964.

Hernandez, A., Burton, R. M., Pagtakhan, R. D., and Goldring, D. Pharmacodynamics of ³H-Digoxin in infants. Pediatrics, 44:418, 1969.

Levine, O. R., and Blumenthal, S. Digoxin dosage in premature infants. Pediatrics, 29:18, 1962.

Lown, B., Kleiger, R., and Williams, J. Cardioversion and digitalis drugs: Changed threshold to electric shock in digitalized animals. Circ. Res., 17:519, 1965.

20.14
INFECTIONS OF THE HEART

SIDNEY BLUMENTHAL

Pericarditis

Pericarditis is usually a manifestation of a systemic disease. It may occur as the principal manifestation of such disease, be subordinate to other manifestations, or be clinically unsuspected. Its features depend upon the etiology and pathologic characteristics of the pericardial involvement.

ETIOLOGY. Rheumatic fever is the most common cause of pericarditis in childhood. Less common causes include rheumatoid arthritis and other collagen diseases, viral agents, pyogenic organisms, tuberculosis, uremia, trauma, and certain severe hereditary anemias. Rarely myxedema, neoplastic invasion, mycotic or protozoan agents, Friedreich's ataxia, or ulcerative colitis result in pericarditis. Not infrequently, the cause remains obscure.

PATHOLOGY. Acute pericarditis may be of the dry, fibrinous variety or result in effusion which is serous, exudative, hemorrhagic, or purulent. The myocardium is usually involved in the disease process. Chronic pericarditis causes a fibroplastic proliferation which may result in adhesions between parietal and visceral surfaces of the pericardium and in calcium deposition.

Acute pericarditis occurring as a complication of meningococcemia frequently progresses rapidly from a purulent effusion to a thick fibrinous exudate to constricting pericarditis. In inadequately treated patients or in those receiving suppressive agents for other disease processes, this transition to constrictive pericarditis can occur in one to two weeks.

PERICARDITIS WITHOUT EFFUSION. *Clinical Manifestations.* The cardinal signs of dry pericarditis are pain, pericardial friction rub, and alterations in the electrocardiographic pattern. The diaphragmatic pericardium and lower portion of the parietal pericardium are supplied with nerve fibers, while none are found in the visceral pericardium or upper portion of the parietal pericardium. Lack of pain is not unusual. When present, the pain is commonly precordial, constant, sharp, and not infrequently relieved by leaning forward or turning to the side. It may be referred to the neck, tip of the shoulder, or left arm. Some-

times the pain is pleural, varying in intensity with respiration. Pain on swallowing may be noted because of the proximity of the esophagus to the pericardium.

A friction rub is best heard when the diaphragm of the stethoscope is held firmly against the chest wall. It may vary with change in position of the patient or with changes in respiration. Rubs are most commonly heard in the fourth interspace at the left sternal margin, but can be heard at any point over the precordium. They sound superficial, often resembling the creaking of leather. They vary in intensity and in timing, may or may not be to-and-fro in nature, but are consistently in phase with the heart sounds.

Electrocardiographic Findings. The characteristic electrocardiographic changes result from the pericarditis, without regard to cause. The changes, being progressive in nature, are best evaluated from serial tracings. Within a week of onset of the pericarditis, there occurs concordant upward displacement of the S-T segment without T wave inversion. Within a few days, the S-T segments return to normal or become depressed, while the T waves become flattened and then inverted. The T wave changes may persist for months. QRS voltages may be low. The S-T segment and T wave changes are not localized to any particular leads, and there is no reciprocal relationship between leads I and II. If serial tracings are not available, differentiation from digitalis effect or myocardial disease may be difficult.

PERICARDIAL EFFUSION. *Clinical Findings.* Pericardial effusion may cause sufficient stretching of the pericardium to cause precordial discomfort, cough, or dyspnea. Rapid enlargement of the cardiac silhouette results in an increase in cardiac dullness while the precordium remains quiet. A friction rub is often present despite large effusions, while the heart sounds commonly become muffled. The peripheral pulses and venous pressure remain normal unless tamponade occurs. The electrocardiographic changes are similar to those already described, although low voltage of the QRS complexes is more frequent with large effusions. Radiographs confirm the presence of a large cardiac silhouette, which may be "water bottle" or "pear" shaped. Distinction from enlargement of the cardiac shadow due to dilation associated with heart failure is often difficult. Congested lung fields are usually not present in patients with large pericardial effusions, while severe pulmonary congestion is common when cardiac failure is marked. Cardiac fluoroscopy is also not helpful, as the large cardiac silhouette is quiet in both effusion and dilation.

Cardiac tamponade results from increased intrapericardial pressure due to a rapid accumulation of pericardial fluid and/or inadequate stretching of the pericardium. As intrapericardial pressure increases, cardiac filling is impaired and circulatory embarrassment ensues. An elevated venous pressure is required to maintain cardiac filling. Tachycardia and reflex vasoconstriction compensate for the diminished stroke volume and lowered blood pressure. If the compensatory adjustments are inadequate, circulatory impairment with shock results.

On examination, the patient appears extremely ill and anxious with cold, clammy extremities. Peripheral edema, distended neck veins, and hepatomegaly are noted. The pulse is rapid and difficult to palpate. Arterial pressures are low with a decreased pulse pressure. Pulsus paradoxus (a drop of more than 10 mm Hg pressure on deep inspiration) is a valuable diagnostic sign.

Confirmatory Diagnosis. In order to arrive at a correct diagnosis, it may be necessary to utilize other procedures. Some of the techniques which have been used are intravenous injection of carbon dioxide, echocardiography, radioactive scanning, cardiac catheterization, and angiocardiography.

Injection of carbon dioxide is a simple, safe method of visualizing the thickness of the pericardium. With the patient lying on his left side, 100 percent carbon dioxide is given rapidly by intravenous injection while rapid serial radiographs are obtained. The gaseous bubble clearly outlines the right atrial border, enabling one to measure accurately the thickness of the pericardium. The right atrial wall can also be demonstrated by an intracardiac catheter or by angiocardiography.

Echocardiography is a simple, safe procedure for outlining the anterior and posterior walls of the pericardium utilizing ultrasound recording. Sufficient experience with this method has demonstrated its clinical usefulness where the technique is available.

Radioactive scanning avoids the risk of intracardiac manipulations or of angiography. Radioactive iodinated serum albumin is injected intravenously, and after it has equilibrated throughout the blood, a scan of radioactivity over the chest is made. The heart cavity is outlined and compared with the cardiac density observed radiographically.

Pericardial paracentesis should be performed if there is any possibility that the fluid contains bacteria or if tamponade is suspected. The xiphoid approach should be used with electrocardiographic monitoring. The needle serves as the exploring unipolar electrode; when it touches the myocardium, abnormal complexes will be seen. Equipment for resuscitation, including a defibrillator, should be available.

Treatment. Treatment of acute pericarditis is aimed at its cause. Pericardial effusion does not usually require any specific treatment other than therapy of the cause of the effusion. However, if signs of cardiac tamponade are present, treatment is urgent and lifesaving. It consists of removal of pericardial fluid by paracentesis. The patient should be carefully monitored and if tamponade recurs, an open pericardiotomy is indicated. This is most apt to occur in patients with meningococcemia. It should be recognized that an elevated central venous pressure is an important compensatory mechanism to insure adequate venous filling; phlebotomy is strongly contraindicated. Vasoconstricting agents and intravenous fluids may be useful adjutants.

Chronic Constrictive Pericarditis

Chronic constrictive pericarditis is an uncommon complication of acute pericarditis in which fibrous proliferation has been extensive. The fibrous tissue contracts and thickens markedly, often with calcium deposition, resulting in the development of an adherent, unyielding pericardium.

ETIOLOGY. Tuberculosis is considered to be the most frequent cause of chronic constrictive pericarditis. However, in many of the reported instances of this complication, the tuberculin test was negative, and there was no other evidence of tuberculosis. Constrictive pericarditis may result from hemorrhagic or pyogenic infusions, and also from myxedema, rheumatoid arthritis, and viral pericarditis. Acute rheumatic fever rarely causes chronic constrictive pericarditis.

PATHOLOGIC PHYSIOLOGY. The constricting pericardium interferes with diastolic filling as well as emptying of the ventricles. As the tricuspid valve opens, a sudden rush of blood into the right ventricle occurs. This is reflected in a sudden drop in venous and right atrial pressure with an abrupt rise in right ventricular pressure. The rigid pericardium limits right ventricular capacity so that a prompt rise in right atrial and right ventricular diastolic pressure follows. The venous and atrial pressure tracings show a dominant Y descent and trough, while the ventricular tracing shows a conspicuous dip in early diastole. Associated myocardial insufficiency is present in most patients with constrictive pericarditis.

CLINICAL MANIFESTATIONS. The onset is insidious. Ascites becomes severe, accompanied by marked hepatic enlargement often simulating nephrosis or cirrhosis of the liver. Peripheral edema, if present, is minimal compared to the ascites and hepatomegaly. Precordial pain and friction rub are not usual. The heart is often described as normal in size or slightly enlarged, but in some cases marked cardiomegaly occurs. The pulse is rapid, the precordium quiet, and there is neck vein distension and elevated venous pressure. The distended jugular veins reveal the Y trough or X depression, and pulsus paradoxus is present. The electrocardiogram reveals a low-voltage QRS pattern with T wave flattening or inversion. Prominent bifid P waves are common.

It may not be possible to differentiate chronic constrictive pericarditis from diffuse myocardial disease, including obscure myocardiopathies and myocarditis, despite the characteristic features of peripheral and intracardiac pressure traces. Furthermore, in those patients with proved mechanical restriction due to an unyielding pericardium, myocardial insufficiency plays an important role in the altered hemodynamics.

Specific Etiologic Types of Pericarditis

RHEUMATIC PERICARDITIS. The incidence of rheumatic fever and the severity of rheumatic heart disease are declining in the United States. Rheumatic pericarditis is seen less frequently than a decade ago; however, it remains the most common cause of pericarditis in childhood.

Pericarditis occurs during the acute exudative phase of the rheumatic infection and is part of a pancarditis. Auscultatory evidence of endocardial involvement is always present. If the effusion is massive or the friction rub loud, masking apical sounds, a murmur may be difficult to hear. If murmurs are not present, other causes of pericarditis should be considered.

The incidence and severity of chronic rheumatic heart disease are related directly to the severity of carditis during the acute infection, regardless of treatment. Pericarditis is a manifestation of severe acute carditis with a serious prognosis.

ACUTE NONSPECIFIC PERICARDITIS (ACUTE BENIGN). This infection usually affects previously healthy individuals, children and adults. The onset is acute, often following a respiratory infection. Pain, fever, and malaise are noted, and a friction rub, not accompanied by murmurs, is heard. Leucocytosis and an elevated sedimentation rate are present. The electrocardiogram is typical of pericarditis. The clinical course, measured in weeks, is self-limited. Although relapses are common, ultimate recovery is complete without residua.

The amount of effusion varies, rarely being extensive. Although viruses (Coxsackie B, influenza) have been implicated as the etiologic agent in some cases, usually no cause is identified. Treatment is symptomatic. Adrenocortical steroids have been advocated by some in severe cases.

PURULENT PERICARDITIS. This is a rare, serious complication of a systemic disease in which the pericardium is "seeded" as a result of bacteremia. Occasionally, the pericarditis results from direct extension from the pleural space. *Staphylococcus aureus, Hemophilus influenzae,* and meningococci are the most common causal organisms.

Patients usually have a severe systemic reaction to the infectious process with prominent signs of pericarditis. The entire clinical picture may be masked in patients receiving steroids for other systemic diseases. Tamponade and constrictive pericarditis may occur as complications in an unusually rapid sequence.

Treatment, which includes antibiotics and adequate drainage, depends upon the clinical recognition of this complication, laboratory identification of the offending organism, and awareness of the likelihood of the development of tamponade and constrictive pericarditis.

PERICARDITIS IN RHEUMATOID ARTHRITIS. Pericarditis is the most common cardiac complication of juvenile rheumatoid arthritis. It is clinically recognized in 7 percent of patients with this disease; however, a higher incidence is reported from data derived from postmortem examinations. Patients with this complication may be asymptomatic, a friction rub being an incidental finding. More often patients complain of pain, and clinical findings identical with other forms of pericarditis are noted.

Pericarditis may occur at any age, unrelated to the age of onset or the severity of the arthritis. It usually occurs after the onset of arthritis, but may be concomitant with or, rarely, precede it. The clinical course of the pericarditis is usually short and benign. Tamponade is rare. Constrictive pericarditis may be a late complication.

There is no clear evidence that adrenocortical steroids alter the course of pericarditis. Treatment should be directed toward control of the systemic disease.

TUBERCULOUS PERICARDITIS. Tuberculous pericarditis has been reported in children and is believed to be due to direct infection of the pericardium from the lungs, mediastinal lymph nodes, or pleura. The onset is insidious and the course chronic, with vague symptomatology. Tuberculous pericarditis is considered to be the most frequent cause of chronic constrictive pericarditis. Antituberculous chemotherapy has markedly improved the prognosis.

UREMIC PERICARDITIS. Uremic pericarditis is usually asymptomatic with minimal signs and is seen in the end stages of renal insufficiency. The mechanisms responsible for its production are unknown.

TRAUMATIC PERICARDITIS. Hemorrhage into the pericardium may result from penetrating or nonpenetrating wounds. The clinical features depend upon the amount of bleeding. Tamponade can occur.

PERICARDITIS WITH CHRONIC ANEMIA. Pericarditis occurs as a complication of thalassemia and congenital hypoplastic anemia. Its pathogenesis has not been clearly delineated, nor is the significance of hemosiderin deposition well understood. This complication usually occurs late in the course of the disease and is of serious prognostic importance.

POSTPERICARDIOTOMY SYNDROME. Postpericardiotomy syndrome may occur as a complication of any operation in which the pericardium is opened. Its cause is unknown; hypersensitivity, sterile inflammatory response to blood in the pericardium, and viral infection have been suggested. The syndrome is characterized by fever, chest pain, pleural and/or pericardial friction rub, roentgen evidence of pleural or pericardial reaction, and less often electrocardiographic evidence of pericarditis.

The onset usually occurs in the third or fourth postoperative week, but may begin from 3 days to 3 months (rarely 6 months) following surgery. The syndrome is self-limited, usually subsiding in 10 to 20 days; marked variations in severity of symptoms have been noted. Recurrences are common often at 2- to 3-week intervals.

Treatment is symptomatic, including bed rest, aspirin, and sedation when indicated. Adrenocortical steroids may be of value if symptomatic treatment is ineffective. It has been suggested that the incidence and severity of the syndrome can be reduced by strict limitation of physical activity when signs of inflammatory reaction of the pleura or pericardium are present in the early postoperative period.

Myocarditis

The most common forms of myocardial disease are inflammatory in nature, resulting from disorders of connective tissue or systemic infection. Myocardial dysfunction may be secondary to anemia or endocrine or metabolic disturbances, or result from an infiltrative process. At times the myocardium is affected without evidence of associated disease.

Acute or chronic myocarditis may occur as the only feature or the principal feature of a systemic disease, while in other situations the manifestations of the myocarditis are entirely masked by the nature of the systemic disease. In some instances, the inflammatory process in the heart is confined to the myocardium (isolated myocarditis), while in others, myocarditis is part of a pancarditis, as in acute rheumatic carditis.

The most common cause of myocarditis in children is acute rheumatic fever. Other causes include diseases due to bacteria, viral agents, and rickettsia, and collagen diseases. Not infrequently the etiologic agent remans unidentified.

CLINICAL MANIFESTATIONS. The onset is often sudden with temperature elevation, dyspnea, and a rapid pulse rate out of proportion to the temperature elevation. The heart sounds are indistinct, dull, or muffled. There may be equalization of the duration of systole and diastole with a tic-tac rhythm. Cardiac dilation occurs, often causing masked enlargement of the cardiac shadow on x-ray. Congestive heart failure may result. The electrocardiogram reveals nonspecific changes, including atrioventricular conduction defects and S-T segment and T wave changes. Not uncommonly, the first clinical manifestation is cardiomegaly or congestive heart failure.

TREATMENT. Treatment should be directed toward control of the underlying disease causing the myocarditis. Agents capable of eliminating the cause of the myocardial process may result in dramatic improvement. In other circumstances where the disease process runs a self-limiting course, agents that suppress the inflammatory process are of value. Adrenocortical steroids are beneficial in connective tissue disorders, not by their curative effect, but by their action in suppressing the disease process. In view of deleterious side effects which have been encountered, they should be used only in situations which are considered life-threatening.

If heart failure complicates myocarditis, a cardiotonic regimen is indicated. This includes the use of oxygen, sedation, diuretics, and digitalis. These are supportive measures and should not be expected to result in the dramatic changes which can be achieved if the cause of the myocarditis is corrected or the inflammatory process suppressed.

PROGNOSIS. Prognosis following recovery from acute myocarditis is generally considered to be good; however, this depends upon the severity of the inflammatory process. In some patients extensive residual myocardial fibrosis may be the explanation for subsequent myocardial insufficiency or cardiac enlargement of "unknown cause."

Specific Diseases Causing Myocarditis

RHEUMATIC CARDITIS. Acute rheumatic carditis is discussed in Section 12.1. The reported incidence of carditis in rheumatic fever varies considerably, from 10 to 50 percent. It is difficult to obtain a reliable figure, in view of the difficulty in diagnosing rheumatic fever without cardiac involvement. Carditis is an early complication, apparent during the first week of the disease in 75 percent and in the first 4 weeks in over 90 percent of cases in which it occurs. In this disease, myocarditis is part of a pancarditis; it does not occur as an isolated event. Heart failure resulting from rheumatic carditis is always associated with clear clinical evidence of endocardial as well as myocardial involvement. Significant cardiac enlargement, pericarditis, and heart failure are manifestations reflecting severe carditis. Prognosis regarding ultimate chronic rheumatic heart disease is closely related to the existence of carditis and its severity during the acute attack.

DIPHTHERIA. Diphtheria is a relatively uncommon disease in the United States. Myocarditis is one of its most serious complications and occurs in severe forms of the disease, being found at autopsy in 50 percent of the patients dying from diphtheria. Toxins affect the myocardium, causing degenerative changes with frequent involvement of the conduction system. Evidence of cardiovascular disturbance may be seen in the first week or as late as the sixth week of the disease. The first evidence of cardiac dysfunction is usually a change in the quality of the first heart sound, often accompanied or followed by disturbances of rhythm, ectopic beats, or conduction defects of varying severity including complete heart block. The electrocardiogram reveals nonspecific S-T segment depression and T wave flattening or inversion, as well as the abnormalities in rhythm and conduction. Ventricular tachycardia and fibrillation may occur. Heart failure may result from the myocardial involvement. At times, the initial manifestation of carditis is sudden death resulting from ventricular tachycardia, fibrillation, or complete heart block.

The prognosis is grave, the mortality rate approximating 30 to 50 percent. In those who survive, recovery is usually complete, although permanent conduction defects have been reported.

Therapy is directed toward specific treatment of diphtheria and support of the myocardium. The latter includes strict bed rest and, if evidence of heart failure is detected, digitalis.

Sudden onset of circulatory collapse, seen in some patients, has a very grave prognosis. It has been reported as being a result of severe changes in the adrenal cortex. Treatment of the shock includes the use of intravenous plasma, norepinephrine or phenylephrine infusion, and adrenocortical steroids.

MEASLES. Measles myocarditis is rare. It results in gallop rhythm, indistinct heart sounds, cardiac dilation, and heart failure. Electrocardiographic changes include first-degree heart block. T wave changes are present in almost 20 percent of patients with measles. These are generally considered to be nonspecific and are not manifestations of myocarditis.

MUMPS. Mumps is rarely complicated by myocarditis. When present, severe conduction defects are common. It is usually a mild, self-limited disease, and complete recovery is the rule.

ACUTE POLIOMYELITIS. Focal myocarditis has been observed at autopsy in patients dying of this disease. Evidence of myocarditis is uncommonly recognized clinically because of the more dramatic neurologic manifestations. Minor electrocardiographic alterations have been reported. Systemic hypertension results from central nervous system involvement and is not a reflection of myocardial involvement. Bulbar lesions affecting the vasomotor center cause tachycardia, arrhythmias, low pulse pressure, and marked fluctuations in blood pressure, followed by circulatory collapse.

COXSACKIE GROUP B VIRUS. Coxsackie Group B virus has been isolated from the myocardium and proved to be a causative agent of myocarditis alone or associated with encephalitis in newborn infants. This agent should be suspected as a possible cause whenever myocarditis occurs in infants, particularly when illness due to this agent amongst adults is prevalent. The severity of the myocarditis varies markedly, complete recovery occurring in some, whereas others have a rapidly fatal course. This virus has also been reported as a cause of myocarditis and/or pericarditis in older children. Treatment is supportive in nature. Some have advocated the use of adrenocortical steroids, while others have suggested that these agents may be harmful.

Endocarditis

Acute and subacute bacterial endocarditis are terms which have been in common use for almost a century. With the advent of the antibiotic era and subsequent alteration of the clinical course of bacterial endocarditis, these terms have outlived their usefulness. It is preferable to make the diagnosis of bacterial endocarditis and designate the specific etiologic organism. Rarely, bacterial endocarditis may develop in the heart with no preexisting disease, but most frequently it is superimposed on an already diseased endocardium.

Bacterial Endocarditis in Children with Heart Disease

Bacterial endocarditis occurs in patients with heart disease as a consequence of implantation of bacteria upon damaged endocardial surfaces. The clinical course is dependent upon the characteristics of the invading organism and the nature and severity of the preexisting heart disease.

INCIDENCE. Bacterial endocarditis is not a rare complication of heart disease in childhood, accounting for approximately 0.25 patients per 1,000 admissions to active pediatric centers. The hospital admission rate has been sustained, possibly reflecting the greater interest in heart disease in children and the increase in admissions of patients for diagnosis and treatment of congenital malformations of the heart. Bacterial endocarditis in patients with heart disease is primarily a disease of young adults, but all ages, including infants, may be affected. In children it is a complication of congenital heart disease in about two-thirds of the cases and rheumatic heart disease in the remaining one-third. The most common anomalies predisposing to bacterial endocarditis are those which result in the development of a significant pressure gradient across the defect, or where the deformed valve produces jet lesions upon the endocardium. These include ventricular septal defect, patent ductus arteriosus, coarctation of the aorta, bicuspid aortic valve, pulmonic or aortic stenosis, and tetralogy of Fallot.

PATHOGENESIS. Transient, innocuous bacterial invasion of the bloodstream occurs in normal persons. Bacterial endocarditis is a complication of this bacteremia in a patient with heart disease. Portals of entry include teeth and gums, tonsils and adenoids, bronchi, gastrointestinal and genitourinary tracts, and the skin. Organisms present in the bloodstream are implanted upon a damaged endocardial surface. It has been suggested that hemodynamic trauma to the endocardium or the existence of abnormally thickened valves predisposes to collagenous tissue degeneration, or that the impact of the jet-streaming effect on the endocardial or endothelial surfaces results in fibrous tissue overgrowth with deposition of blood elements at that site. An attractive nidus for the establishment of circulating organisms is present. Vegetations develop in which viable bacteria may be present for long periods. Fragments of the vegetations have a tendency to break off and to embolize. If the fragment contains viable bacteria, an abscess or mycotic aneurysm may develop. Inflammatory myocardial changes are often present in addition to endocardial changes.

BACTERIOLOGY. The most common causative organism is the alpha streptococci (viridans), accounting for about 80 percent of cases, while *Staphylococcus aureus* is next in frequency among children. The enterococcus group of streptococci, which are common invaders in adults, are relatively rarely encountered in children. Other organisms which are infrequently implicated include *Escherichia coli*, *Pseudomonas*, and *Aspergillus*. *Staphylococcus albus* has been reported as the usual causative agent following open-heart surgery.

CLINICAL FEATURES. The clinical picture is varied, resulting from infection, embolization, and intrinsic cardiac damage. The onset is usually insidious, with signs of general infection, such as fever and malaise, predominating in the early phase of the disease. Symptoms due to embolization may occur at any time, but, like heart failure, are usually found late in the course of the disease.

Common symptoms are fever, malaise, and fatigue. Anorexia, headache, myalgia or arthralgia, and weight loss are often noted, while chills, chest pain, and night sweats are rather uncommon. The most frequent findings, fever and a murmur, are present in almost all patients. Splenomegaly and petechiae are commonly noted but not invariably present. Abnormal laboratory findings include an elevated sedimentation rate and microscopic hematuria, while anemia and significant leucocytosis are less common findings.

Not infrequently, the only history is that of unexplained fever and fatigue in a child known to have heart disease. Additional symptoms often reflect the nature of the underlying heart disease. In a child with cyanotic congenital heart disease, increasing cyanosis, progressive exercise intolerance, paroxysmal dyspnea, and syncope occur.

PROGNOSIS. The most important factors affecting prognosis are the nature of the infecting organism and age of the patient. The recovery rate approximates 100 percent when infection is due to sensitive viridans streptococci, while the mortality rate remains relatively high in infections due to *Staphylococcus aureus*. Delay in treatment due to failure to consider and investigate the possibility of bacterial endocarditis, particularly in infancy and early childhood, accounts for a conspicuous mortality rate. The duration of symptoms prior to onset of treatment is of less significance than accurate identification of the offending organism. The severity of the underlying heart disease, development of congestive heart failure, and a poor nutritional state, considered important prognostic factors in adults, are of less significance in the pediatric age group.

MANAGEMENT. A high index of suspicion of bacterial endocarditis is necessary in the evaluation of patients with heart disease who develop unexplained fever and malaise. Blood cultures should be obtained before treatment is started in order to identify the infecting organism and to determine its sensitivity to antibiotics. Six samples of at least 10 ml for each culture are recommended, preferably drawn during a 48-hour period. If the patient has recently received antibiotics, it is suggested that these drugs be discontinued and blood cultures be obtained over a 3- to 4-day period. Blood should be cultured in anaerobic as well as aerobic media and the cultures observed for 3 weeks before being considered negative.

The choice of antibiotics to be used in treatment depends upon identification of the causative agent and the results of in vitro sensitivity tests. Antibiotics may be used singly in the treatment of drug-sensitive organisms, and in combination for drug-resistant organisms. In choosing a drug, consideration should be given to its bactericidal or bacteriostatic activity and its ability to penetrate the depths of the fibrin matrix of the vegetation. Penicillin meets these criteria and has been proved to be a very effective drug alone or in combination for the management of serious infections. New drugs should be carefully evaluated before they replace penicillin. Bacteriostatic agents should not be given without bactericidal agents despite the results of sensitivity testing.

Cases will be encountered at times where treatment must be instituted without knowledge of the causative organism or confirmation of the diagnosis, because of the critical condition of the patient. Under these circumstances, the safest course is to treat the patient as if he had an infection due to a resistant organism resulting, unavoidably, in treatment for a prolonged period of some patients who do not have bacterial endocarditis.

In the treatment of endocarditis due to viridans streptococci, penicillin is the drug of choice; it is given in a dose of 10 million units intravenously per day for 5 days followed by one million units twice a day intramuscularly for a total period of 4 weeks. Although penicillin-resistant strains are rarely encountered in childhood, when they occur, penicillin should be continued and streptomycin added in doses of 50 mg/kg/day intramuscularly for 1 week and then 25 mg/kg/day for an additional 3 weeks.

Endocarditis may be due to coagulase-positive or coagulase-negative drug-sensitive or drug-resistant staphylococci. Penicillin is bactericidal through its action on the cell wall of the staphylococcus. Resistance to penicillin is most often due to the production of penicillinase by the microorganism. Less often, resistance is due to some other inherent characteristic which results in the production of "persisters." These are important considerations in planning a treatment regimen. Penicillinase-resistant penicillins are of value in destroying those microorgansms which produce penicillinase. Treatment should be started with a penicillinase-resistant penicillin such as nafcillin or methicillin, given intravenously in doses of 100 mg/kg/day for 7 to 10 days, after which time 50 mg/kg/day is given intramuscularly for a total treatment period of 6 weeks and for at least 2 weeks after all evidence of infection has subsided. Cephalothin is an effective substitute in patients who are allergic to penicillin. In patients in whom the infection is not controlled by these agents, consideration should be given to the addition of a drug, such as chloramphenicol, erythromycin, or lincomycin, whose primary actions are at the cellular level. The dose for chloramphenicol is 100 mg/kg/day to a maximum of 2 g/day, erythromycin 50 mg/kg/day to a maximum dose of 1 g/day, and lincomycin 40 mg/kg/day (every 8 or 12 hours) to a maximum of 500 mg/day.

Endocarditis due to coagulase-negative staphylococci are usually encountered in patients with an intracardiac foreign body such as suture material, valve prosthesis, or a ventriculoatrial shunt catheter. Treatment consists of the use of drugs for resistant organisms. Almost invariably, successful therapy will not be achieved until the foreign body has been removed.

In the treatment of endocarditis due to other organisms, the choice of drugs, which should be used in combination, depends upon the demonstrated degree of sensitivity of the organisms by in vitro sensitivity tests.

Where large doses of penicillin are being used, the inadvertent administration of excessive amounts of potassium should be avoided. Potassium penicillin G contains about 1.7 mEq of potassium per million units. One is apt to produce dangerous elevations of serum potassium after rapid injections of large doses and in patients with impaired renal function.

The efficacy of intermittent peak concentrations of antibiotics is still a debatable issue. The use of the continuous intravenous method supplemented by additional rapid injections to produce peak concentrations should be considered in the management of the difficult case. Probenecid is effective in increasing blood levels of penicillin, with any given dose of the antibiotic. Probenecid, 250 to 500 mg every 6 hours, results in a twofold increase in penicillin blood levels.

In addition to optimal antibiotic therapy, supportive measures are utilized as necessary. These include maintenance of good nutrition, adequate vitamin intake, and correction of secondary anemia. A cardiotonic regimen is utilized if evidence of congestive heart failure occurs. Anticoagulants and adrenal corticosteroids have no place in the management of these patients.

PROPHYLAXIS. The concept of drug prevention of bacterial endocarditis in children with organic heart disease is accepted medical practice. Prophylaxis is advised for any manipulative procedure in an infected area. The aim of prophylaxis is the elimination of bacteremia before microorganisms can be implanted upon an abnormal endocardium. A high blood level of antibiotic is necessary to achieve these results. Sterilization of the operative site is not attempted. The choice of antibiotic depends upon the nature of the operative intervention and the anticipated invading organism. Operative intervention in the oropharynx results in bacteremia due to viridans streptococci, while genitourinary or gastrointestinal manipulation is followed by invasion by enteric organisms. Prophylaxis aimed at controlling viridans streptococci requires the use of large doses of penicillin; sulfonamides are ineffective for this purpose. One suggested regimen is intramuscular penicillin 1 million units (250,000 units crystalline potassium penicillin G, plus 750,000 units aqueous procaine penicillin G) given 2 to 3 hours before surgery, followed by daily intramuscular injection of 600,000 units of aqueous procaine penicillin G for 2 to 3 days. For prevention of anticipated invasion with enteric organisms, 1 million units of penicillin G (combined crystalline potassium penicillin G and

procaine penicillin G) with streptomycin (10 to 15 mg/kg/day) may be given 2 to 3 hours before surgery, followed by daily procaine penicillin (600,000 units/day) and streptomycin (10 to 15 mg/kg/day) for 2 to 3 days.

Bacterial Endocarditis in Children without Preexisting Heart Disease

This is a rare complication of septicemia which may be due to any pathogenic microorganism. *Staphylococcus aureus*, beta hemolytic streptococci, pneumococci, *Escherichia coli*, and meningococci have been described as causative agents in children. Large vegetations invade the endocardium, resulting often in severe destruction, ulceration, and perforation.

The clinical picture is predominantly that of an overwhelming sepsis, usually overshadowing evidence of endocarditis. The appearance of a loud murmur may be the first and only sign of cardiac involvement. Organisms can usually be recovered from the bloodstream. Treatment is that of the septicemia with supportive measures as indicated for cardiac complications.

REFERENCES

PERICARDITIS

Benzing, G., III, and Kaplan, S. Purulent pericarditis. Amer. J. Dis. Child., 106:289, 1963.

Bishop, L. H., Jr., Estes, E. H., Jr., and McIntosh, H. D. The electrocardiogram as a safeguard in pericardiocentesis. J.A.M.A., 162:264, 1956.

Deterling, R. A., and Humphreys, G. H., II. Factors in the etiology of constrictive pericarditis. Circulation, 12:30, 1955.

Feigenbaum, H., Waldhausen, J. A., and Hyde, L. P. Ultrasound diagnosis of pericardial effusion. J.A.M.A., 191:711, 1965.

Ito, T., Engle, M. A., and Goldberg, H. P. Post-pericardiotomy syndrome following surgery for non-rheumatic heart disease. Circulation, 17:549, 1958.

Lietman, P. S., and Bywaters, E. G. L. Pericarditis in juvenile rheumatoid arthritis. Pediatrics, 32:855, 1963.

Lukash, W. M. Massive pericardial effusion due to meningococcic pericarditis. J.A.M.A., 185:598, 1963.

McGuiness, J. B., and Taussig, H. B. The post-pericardiotomy syndrome: Its relation to ambulation in the presence of "benign" pericardial and pleural reaction. Circulation, 26:500, 1962.

Moschocowitz, E. Pathogenesis of constrictive pericardium. J.A.M.A., 153:194, 1953.

Moss, A. J., and Bruhn, F. The echocardiogram. An ultrasound technic for the detection of pericardial effusion. New Eng. J. Med., 274:380, 1966.

Nadas, A. S., and Levy, J. M. Pericarditis in children. Amer. J. Cardiol., 7:109, 1961.

Rosenthal, L. Detection of pericardial effusion by radioisotope heart scanning. Canad. Med. Ass. J., 90:447, 1964.

Shea, D. W., Kirklin, J. W., and DuShane, J. W. Chronic constrictive pericarditis in children. Amer. J. Dis. Child., 93:430, 1957.

MYOCARDITIS

Benirschke, K., and Pendleton, M. E. Coxsackie virus infection; an important complication of pregnancy. Obstet. Gynec., 12:305, 1958.

Boyer, N. H., and Weinstein, L. Diphtheritic myocarditis. New Eng. J. Med., 239:913, 1948.

De La Chapelle, C. E., and Kossman, C. E. Myocarditis. Circulation, 10:747, 1954.

Javett, S. N., et al. Myocarditis in the newborn infant. A study of an outbreak associated with Coxsackie group B virus infection in a maternity home in Johannesburg. J. Pediat., 48:1, 1956.

Kibrick, S., and Benirschke, K. Severe generalized disease (encephalohepatomyocarditis) occurring in the newborn period and due to infection with Coxsackie virus, group B; evidence of intrauterine infection with this agent. Pediatrics, 22:857, 1958.

Morgan, B. C. Cardiac complications of diphtheria. Pediatrics, 32:549, 1963.

Rosenbaum, H. D., Nadas, A. S., and Neuhauser, E. B. D. Primary myocardial disease in infancy and childhood. Amer. J. Dis. Child., 86:28, 1953.

Rosenberg, H. S., and McNamara, D. G. Acute myocarditis in infancy and childhood. Progr. Cardiovasc. Dis., 7:179, 1964.

Spain, D. M., Bradess, V. A., and Parsonnet, V. Myocarditis in poliomyelitis. Amer. Heart J., 40:336, 1950.

BACTERIAL ENDOCARDITIS

Bennett, I. L., Jr., and Belson, P. B. Bacteremia: A consideration of some experimental and chemical aspects. Yale J. Biol. Med., 26:241, 1954.

Blumenthal, S. Bacterial endocarditis. In Gellis, S. S., and Kagan, B. M., eds., Current Pediatric Therapy. Philadelphia, W. B. Saunders Co., 1966-67, pp. 189-192.

——— Griffiths, S. P., and Morgan, B. C. Bacterial endocarditis in children with heart disease. A review based on the literature and experience with 58 cases. Pediatrics, 26:993, 1960.

Committee report on prevention of rheumatic fever and bacterial endocarditis through control of streptococcal infections. Circulation, 21:151, 1960.

20.15
MYOCARDIAL DISORDERS

SYDNEY BLUMENTHAL

Endocrine Disturbances

Hypothyroidism is associated with myxedematous changes which affect the myocardium. This results in diminished cardiac output, bradycardia, and narrow pulse pressure. Radiologic signs of cardiomegaly and low voltage in the electrocardiogram are usual findings. *Hyperthyroidism* causes tachycardia, an increased cardiac output, and wide pulse pressure. On occasion, the cardiac changes are the initial manifestation of hyperthyroidism in the adolescent.

Pheochromocytoma results in paroxysmal or, more frequently in children, sustained systemic hypertension. Severe, long-standing hypertension results in left ventricular hypertrophy and left heart failure. Sudden death has been reported. Marked fluctuations in blood pressure occur following surgical removal of such tumors, necessitating careful blood pressure monitoring in the operative and immediate postoperative period.

Congenital adrenal hyperplasia of the salt-losing variety may, in early infancy, cause severe hyperkalemia, which in male infants may be the only manifestation of this syndrome. Elevated serum potassium seriously affects myocardial function. Hyperkalemia causes conduction defects affecting atrial, atrioventricular, and intraventricular conduction, which may result in cardiac standstill. The first electrocardiographic manifestation consists of tall peaked T waves. As serum potassium increases the P waves become broadened, P-R interval prolonged, and QRS and T waves widen. Further increase results in a sinusoidal QRS pattern which precedes cardiac arrest.

Infiltrative Cardiomyopathies

Glycogen storage disease of the heart (type 2 glycogen storage) is a rare familial disease resulting in marked cardiomegaly in early infancy (Sec. 8.8). The structure of the glycogen is apparently normal. Alpha-1-glycosidase (acid maltase) is deficient in these tissues. Tremendous stores of glycogen infiltrate the myocardium as well as other striated muscle. Patients present with large, quiet hearts without significant murmurs. Skeletal muscle involvement causes generalized hypotonia and enlargement of the tongue. Death from intercurrent infection or heart failure usually occurs before 1 year of age.

Cardiac hemochromatosis is seen in older children with signs of diffuse extracardiac hemochromatosis. The myocardial changes result in myocardial insufficiency. Arrhythmias are late manifestations. Pericarditis may be associated with myocardial infiltration.

Tumors of the heart, primary or metastatic, are rare in childhood. *Myxomas* are benign endocardial tumors which arise from the atrial septum. They are often pedunculated with attachment to the septum in the region of the foramen ovale. They are found in either atrium, much more commonly in the left than the right; intermittent obstruction to either the mitral or tricuspid valve may occur. Embolization of myxomatous tissue has been observed. Systemic embolization from a left atrial tumor may result in a clinical picture resembling bacterial endocarditis or acute rheumatic fever including fever, elevated erythrocyte sedimentation rate, and local pain at the site of embolization. Right atrial tumors may cause pulmonary embolization in addition to varying degrees of tricuspid obstruction. *Rhabdomyoma* is seen most often in infants, associated with tuberous sclerosis. Arrhythmias are often present. *Sarcoma* of the heart, usually infiltrative in nature, has been described. Such tumors result in cardiomegaly, vena caval obstruction, and congestive failure.

Miscellaneous Cardiomyopathies

Friedreich's ataxia is complicated by cardiac involvement in about one-third of afflicted patients. Myocardial fibrosis and coronary artery changes have been reported resulting in cardiomegaly, arrhythmias, and myocardial and coronary insufficiency. The electrocardiogram demonstrates arrhythmias and nonspecific T wave changes.

Muscular dystrophy, as a complication of any primary muscle disease, may affect myocardial as well as skeletal muscles, resulting arrhythmias, myocardial insufficiency, and heart failure.

Homeostatic mechanisms secondary to *severe anemia* consist of tachycardia and elevated central venous pressure resulting in an increased cardiac output. In acute anemia, cardiac dilation and circulatory collapse represent failure of these homeostatic mechanisms. In chronic anemia, cardiac hypertrophy is still another homeostatic mechanism which is effective in maintaining an increased cardiac output. It is often difficult or impossible to differentiate between the tachycardia, the elevated venous pressure, cardiomegaly, and edema due to chronic anemia and that resulting from heart failure. Treatment of the anemia with repeated slow transfusions of packed red cells results in prompt improvement in cardiac function.

Systemic lupus erythematosus results in some form of cardiac involvement in 50 percent of the cases. However, systemic symptoms and those due to involvement of other organ systems, especially the kidneys, are the outstanding clinical features of this disease, overshadowing evidence of myocarditis, endocarditis, or pericarditis.

Rheumatoid arthritis rarely affects the myocardium. Pericarditis is the usual form of cardiac involvement in the juvenile form of this disease.

Myocardial Disease Due to Acute Nephritis

Cardiac involvement which may complicate acute nephritis is usually manifested by the sudden appearance of congestive heart failure early in the course of the renal disease. It is more frequently seen in patients with systemic hypertension, but it also occurs without accompanying hypertension.

Heart failure is probably due to multiple factors, though its exact cause remains obscure. Hypervolemia secondary to sodium and water retention appears to be the major mechanism. Left ventricular strain resulting from systemic hypertension may also play a role. Although systemic hypertension alone is not the cause of left heart failure in this syndrome, an increased blood volume may account for both hypertension and failure. Whether or not myocardial insufficiency due to pathologic changes in the myocardium contributes to the heart failure in acute nephritis is uncertain.

Recognition and treatment of heart failure as a medical emergency may be lifesaving. Treatment consists in the use of a cardiotonic regimen and control of systemic hypertension. Digitalization should be achieved with a relatively rapidly excreted glycoside such as digoxin. Because of impaired renal function, the possibility of digitalis intoxication should be considered and the digitalizing dose should be somewhat less than in other patients of similar age and weight. The sudden onset of pulmonary edema necessitates venesection or application of tourniquets. Systemic hypertension should be treated as described in Section 21.12.

Cardiomyopathy of Obscure Cause

Primary endocardial fibroelastosis is a disease of unknown cause resulting in symptoms which usually appear before the age of 1 year. It has been suggested that this is a congenital, metabolic defect, often familial in nature. Endocardial and subendocardial fibroelastic proliferation accompanied by marked hypertrophy of myocardial fibers results in a large, thick-walled heart. The endocardium has a milky appearance and is thickened. The pathologic process involves primarily the left atrium and left ventricle, though right-sided involvement has been described. The fibroelastosis may extend to involved mitral and aortic valves. Associated extracardiac anomalies are rare.

Symptoms first become apparent when congestive heart failure develops. These are initially due to myocardial failure of the left ventricle, followed by failure of both ventricles. Murmurs are absent or insignificant.

Radiographic examination reveals marked cardiomegaly, and the electrocardiogram confirms the presence of left ventricular hypertrophy. T wave changes may be noted. Treatment consists in the use of a cardiotonic regimen for control of heart failure. If the response is satisfactory, digitalis should be continued for a long period.

The clinical picture of primary endocardial fibroelastosis, with a markedly enlarged, quiet heart without murmurs, is often impossible to differentiate from other forms of primary myocardial disease, particularly acute myocarditis. Fundamentally, primary endocardial fibroelastosis is a pathologic diagnosis which can only be suspected on clinical grounds.

Secondary endocardial fibroelastosis may be seen in cardiac anomalies which result in hypoxia, marked stretching of the endocardium, or localized injury to the endocardium secondary to jet effect. The location of the endocardial lesions is specific for each anomaly. The clinical picture is that of the underlying anomaly. In this syndrome the endocardial changes are secondary to an intracardiac anomaly.

Idiopathic cardiac hypertrophy has, in the past, been used to described a syndrome in which there is marked cardiac enlargement without significant murmurs. It is now appreciated that these cases often are due to acute myocarditis, primary endocardial fibroelastosis, aberrant origin of the left coronary artery, glycogen storage disease of the heart, or medial necrosis of the coronary arteries. In some instances, the cause of the myocardial hypertrophy remains obscure, so that a diagnosis of idiopathic cardiac hypertrophy continues to seem desirable. The number of cases fitting this diagnostic category should continue to decrease until ultimately the term will be discarded.

Aberrant Origin of the Coronary Arteries

Origin of the right coronary artery from the pulmonary artery usually does not result in any significant disturbance of cardiac function and is compatible with survival to adulthood. A continuous murmur may be produced by flow of blood from the left coronary artery through dilated collaterals into the right coronary artery and then into the pulmonary artery.

Origin of the left coronary artery from the pulmonary artery is usually associated with early onset of symptoms and early death (under 6 months of age). Episodes of pallor, crying, and perspiration, often associated with feeding, reflect coronary insufficiency. The electrocardiogram characteristically shows deep Q waves in leads I and AVF.

Recognition is important, as many good results have been reported following ligation of the anomalous left coronary artery to improve perfusion from the right coronary artery through collateral channels.

REFERENCES

CARDIOPATHY DUE TO ENDOCRINE DISTURBANCES

Baratz, J. J., and Bronstein, I. P. The heart in children with thyroid deficiency. Amer. J. Dis. Child., 64:471, 1942.

Iversen, T. Congenital adrenocortical hyperplasia with disturbed electrolyte regulation, "Dysadrenocorticism." Pediatrics, 16:875, 1955.

INFILTRATIVE CARDIOMYOPATHIES

di Sant' Agnese, P. A., Andersen, D. H., Mason, H. H., and Baumann, W. A. Glycogen storage disease of the heart. I. Report of two cases in siblings with chemical and pathologic studies. Pediatrics, 6:402, 1950.

———— Andersen, D. H., and Mason, H. H. II. Critical review of the literature. Pediatrics, 6:607, 1950.

Wilson, R. A., and Clark, N. Endocardial fibroelastosis associated with generalized glycogenosis. Pediatrics, 26:86, 1960.

TUMORS OF THE HEART

Engle, M. A., and Glenn, F. Primary malignant tumor of the heart in infancy; case report and review of the subject. Pediatrics, 15:562, 1955.

Goldberg, H. P., and Steinberg, I. Primary tumors of the heart. Circulation, 11:963, 1955.

Pratt-Thomas, H. R. Tuberous sclerosis with congenital tumors of heart and kidney. Amer. J. Path., 23:189, 1947.

THE HEART IN MUSCULAR DYSTROPHY

Kilburn, K. H., Eagan, J. T., Sieker, H. O., and Heyman, A. Cardiopulmonary insufficiency in myotonic and progressive muscular dystrophy. New Eng. J. Med., 261:1089, 1959.

Manning, G. W., and Cropp, G. J. The electrocardiogram in progressive muscular dystrophy. Brit. Heart J., 20:416, 1958.

Rubin, I. L., and Buchberg, A. S. Heart in progressive muscular dystrophy. Amer. Heart J., 43:161, 1952.

MISCELLANEOUS CARDIOMYOPATHIES

The Heart in Friedreich's Ataxia

Nadas, S. A., Alimrung, M. M., and Sieracki, L. A. Cardiac manifestations of Friedreich's ataxia. New Eng. J. Med., 244:239, 1951.

The Heart in Anemia

Porter, W. B., and James, G. W., III. The heart in anemia. Circulation, 8:111, 1953.

Shubin, H., Levinson, D. C., and Griffith, G. C. Endocarditis due to coagulase-positive Staphylococcus pyogenes var. aureus. J.A.M.A., 167:1218, 1958.

Systemic Lupus Erythematosus and the Heart

Cook, C. D., Wedgewood, R. J. P., Craig, J. M., Hartmann, J. R., and Janeway, C. A. Systemic lupus erythematosus. Description of 37 cases in children. Pediatrics, 26:570, 1960.

Harvey, A. M., Shulman, L. E., Tumulty, P. A., Conley, C. L., and Schoenrich, E. H. Systemic lupus erythematosus; review of the literature and clinical analysis of 138 cases. Medicine, 33:291, 1954.

Gribetz, D., and Henley, W. Systemic Lupus Erythematosus. New York, Grune and Stratton, Inc., 1959, p. 65.

THE HEART IN ACUTE NEPHRITIS

Derow, H. A. The heart in renal disease. Circulation, 10:114, 1954.

Etteldorf, J. N., Smith, J. D., and Johnson, C. The effect of reserpine and its combination with hydralazine on blood pressure and renal hemodynamics during the hypertensive phase of acute nephritis in children. J. Pediat., 48:129, 1956.

CARDIOMYOPATHIES OF OBSCURE CAUSE

Andersen, D. H., and Kelly, J. Endocardial fibroelastosis. I. Endocardial fibroelastosis associated with congenital malformations of the heart. II. A clinical and pathological investigation of those cases without associated cardiac malformations, including report of two familial instances. Pediatrics, 18:513, 539, 1956.

Dennis, J. L., Hansen, A. E., and Corpening, T. M. Endocardial fibroelastosis. Pediatrics, 12:130, 1953.

chapter 21

SYSTEMIC ARTERIAL HYPERTENSION

M. DONALD BLAUFOX, Associate Editor

21.1
REGULATION OF BLOOD PRESSURE

The maintenance of systemic arterial pressure within normal limits is essential for adequate perfusion of the vital organs of the body. Physiologic alterations in blood pressure occur with exercise, time of day, postural changes, and advancing age. Under basal conditions, however, the systolic and diastolic blood pressures of a given individual fluctuate between relatively narrow limits. The range of normal pressure is maintained by the interplay of a number of physiologic factors, the most important of which are cardiac output, total peripheral resistance, and blood volume.

Cardiac output and peripheral vascular resistance both are subject to neural and hormonal influences. Augmented sympathetic nervous activity, originating mainly from the medulla oblongata, increases sympathetic tone with resultant increases in heart rate, cardiac output, and peripheral vascular resistance, all of which act in the direction of elevating the blood pressure. Norepinephrine plays a dual role in the sympathetic system as a circulating hormone and as the major neural transmitter. The addition of norepinephrine to the circulation causes a rise in both systolic and diastolic blood pressure as a result of peripheral vasoconstriction. These peripheral effects are accompanied by a bradycardia of vagal origin which tends to reduce cardiac output and thus to restore normal blood pressure. Increased circulating epinephrine results in tachycardia and increased cardiac output. The net effects of neural and humoral factors on blood pressure are detected by the carotid sinus, resulting in a final neural regulation. Although circulating angiotensin may play a role in the hormonal regulation of normal blood pressure, its relative importance is not clear.

Regulation of plasma volume is complex and becomes significant in blood pressure control in pathologic states of abnormal renal and pituitary function. Under normal circumstances, however, the circulating plasma volume is maintained relatively constant and contributes little to day to day variations in arterial pressure.

Alterations in any of these mechanisms of control may cause hypertension. Their relative importance in specific disease entities is discussed below.

The consistent finding in hypertension, however, is an increase in the total peripheral vascular resistance.

21.2
MEASUREMENT OF THE BLOOD PRESSURE

An adequate definition of hypertension constitutes a major problem in diagnosis, due in part to difficulties in measuring the actual arterial pressure. In adults, most physicians accept consistent blood pressure recordings of greater than 140 millimeters of mercury systolic and 90 millimeters of mercury diastolic in a patient at rest with a normal pulse rate to be diagnostic of systemic arterial hypertension. Hypertension in children unquestionably occurs at levels below these, since the normal range of mean arterial pressure in childhood is significantly lower than that of adults. Several extensive surveys have been conducted to define the limits of normal blood pressure in children of different ages, and numerous tables may be found in the monograph of Moss and Adams. These data were recorded in large outpatient populations using arm pressures in children and the flush method in infants. Recently Kass has studied the blood pressure in a group of children in the home using an automated monitoring system that permits more objective criteria. His data, given in Table 1, show a continuing rise in pressure throughout life. Although an automatic monitoring system such as the one used by Kass may provide the most objective and reproducible means of measurement of the blood pressure, this type of apparatus is not practical for routine office use at present. Clinical evaluation of blood pressure, therefore, usually must be based on either the auscultatory or flush method.

The child should be examined in a quiet room and be as relaxed as possible. The reading usually is taken, therefore, toward the end of the physical examination. The pulse rate should also be determined, since tachycardia increases the blood pressure. An appropriate-sized cuff and its proper application are essential. The blood pressure cuff should cover approximately two-thirds of either the upper arm or thigh. The cuff should be applied tightly and inflated and deflated several times before a reading is

TABLE 1.   *Blood Pressure in Children**

Age Group	N	Male Systolic		Diastolic		N	Female Systolic		Diastolic	
		$\bar{x}$	s	$\bar{x}$	s		$\bar{x}$	s	$\bar{x}$	s
2-4	34	95.23	10.46	63.14	7.56	22	95.36	7.91	65.27	7.84
5-6	24	97.17	9.38	66.75	9.12	25	96.76	13.83	67.04	10.33
7-8	35	103.20	10.25	69.37	9.38	42	102.57	11.57	71.07	9.75
9-10	25	106.24	10.88	72.28	8.87	39	104.67	9.76	72.72	10.95
11-12	24	107.96	13.79	72.67	11.42	17	111.41	11.78	72.11	12.16
13-14	18	107.22	11.28	70.94	8.73	21	105.71	10.64	69.43	12.38
	160					166				

$\bar{x}$ = mean

s = standard deviation

*Data obtained in the home using an automated monitoring system. (Kass, E.H., and Zinner, S.H. How early can the tendency toward hypertension be detected? *In* The Milbank Memorial Fund Quarterly, Preventive Approaches to Chronic Diseases 47: 143-152, 1969, part 2.)

taken. The pressure is then increased to a level of 20 to 30 mm Hg above the systolic pressure and the air is released very slowly. The appearance of the first sound is easily detected and occurs when the pressure in the cuff approximates the systolic blood pressure. The diastolic level is correlated best with the disappearance of vascular sounds. If the vascular sounds persist to zero, the point of muffling of sound is also recorded as a rough estimate of the true diastolic pressure. In some individuals hemodynamic changes may alter the sounds so that the diastolic pressure cannot be determined by auscultation. Measurements with a mercury manometer are preferable to those obtained with an aneroid, which frequently requires adjustment and may give misleading values.

In infants the vascular sounds may be extremely difficult or impossible to hear in the antecubital fossa, and an attempt should be made to determine the pressure in the legs instead of the arms. If the sounds cannot be heard in the popliteal fossa, the flush method provides a useful alternative to the auscultatory method. The infant is placed supine and a proper-sized arm cuff is applied above the wrist or the ankle. The extremity is compressed distal to the cuff with an elastic material such as an Ace bandage and the cuff is rapidly inflated to about 200 mm Hg. Compression is then removed and the air is gradually released until the blanched portion of the extremity distal to the cuff flushes. The values obtained by this method correlate roughly with the mean arterial pressure. The flush method should be used only if all attempts at auscultation fail. In cases involving serious therapeutic decisions it may be necessary to determine the blood pressure by direct arterial puncture.

21.3
PREVALENCE OF CHILDHOOD HYPERTENSION

Although the prevalence of hypertensive arterial disease in adults approaches 15 to 20 percent, it is so uncommon in children that reliable data concerning its frequency are not available. In two surveys, elevations of the blood pressure were noted in 1.4 percent of 1,795 ambulatory subjects between 12 and 21 years of age, and in 2.3 percent of 1,473 children. Interpretation of such figures is complicated especially by the difficulties in measurement and in defining normal ranges for blood pressure in children of different ages.

There is a striking difference between children and adults in the distribution of the causes of hypertension. In adults only 5 to 10 percent of hypertensive individuals can be shown to have remediable lesions, the remainder being classified as idiopathic or essential. In contrast, essential hypertension is the final diagnosis probably in less than 20 percent of hypertensive children. Diseases associated with systemic arterial hypertension in children are listed in Table 2.

TABLE 2.   *Most Common Diseases Associated with Systemic Arterial Hypertension in Children*

1. Renal parenchymal disease
2. Renal arterial disease
3. Coarctation of the aorta
4. Pheochromocytoma
5. Adrenogenital syndrome
6. Primary hyperaldosteronism
7. Renal tumor
8. Cushing's syndrome
9. Brain tumor

The high incidence of secondary hypertension in children is emphasized by the study of Still and Colton who reported an incidence of underlying pyelonephritis in 59 percent of children with severe hypertension. The wide diversity of causes of hypertension in childhood, listed in Table 2, and the fact that many of these causes are remediable constitute an adequate and demanding indication for extensive investigation of any child in whom the blood pressure has been found to be consistently above the normal for his age.

21.4
EVALUATION OF THE HYPERTENSIVE CHILD

A blood pressure recording more than two standard deviations above the reported mean for a given age group is reason to suspect hypertension, and readings above these values on two or three successive examinations at rest are adequate justification for further studies. Elevated pressure in the arms is a mandatory indication to include in the physical examination a blood pressure recording from the legs. A corresponding elevation of the blood pressure in the legs makes a diagnosis of coarctation of the aorta unlikely. Other simple procedures to seek a rapid diagnosis may be performed immediately. These include examination of the ocular fundi, auscultation of the abdomen for a vascular bruit, and examination of the urinary sediment.

The funduscopic examination in the hypertensive child usually is normal. The presence of arteriolar spasm, exudates, and/or hemorrhages, however, confirms the suspicion of persistent significant hypertension. Papilledema indicates a hypertensive emergency with an urgent need for institution of therapy.

The grading of hypertensive retinal changes in childhood has not been studied as thoroughly as in adults, but the criteria of Keith and Wagener still may be applied (Table 3). The level of the arterial pressure has some prognostic significance for a population, but is of limited value for evaluation of a given individual.

The presence of an abdominal bruit in a hypertensive subject makes the likelihood of renovascular disease high. The bruit is usually continuous, high pitched, and best heard in the periumbilical area or flank. Aortic bruits may be misleading.

Examination of the urinary sediment should be performed to evaluate the possibility of underlying acute or chronic renal disease, both of which are associated frequently with hypertension. A very careful search should be made for red blood cells and red cell casts to rule out the possibility of glomerulonephritis. White cells and white cell casts or granular casts in the urine are suggestive of pyelonephritis. The presence of proteinuria may indicate underlying primary renal disease; however, proteinuria also occurs in nephrosclerosis and thus may be secondary to the hypertension.

The simple procedures discussed above define the limits of what may be accomplished during a routine office examination. Following this the concentrations in serum of urea nitrogen, creatinine, Na, K, and CO_2 should be determined. A twenty-four hour urine specimen should be collected for quantitative determination of vanillin mandelic acid (VMA) and catecholamines, to rule out the possibility of pheochromocytoma. Urinary excretion of adrenal cortical steroids may also be evaluated on this urine specimen.

If the urinalysis is suggestive of renal disease and a review of the history suggests that the patient has acute glomerulonephritis, it can be anticipated that with or without treatment the blood pressure will return to normal within a short time (see Sec. 22.8). If the clinical diagnosis is chronic renal dis-

TABLE 3.   *Grading of Hypertensive Retinal Changes*

| Group | Sclerosis | Arteriolar Narrowing | | Hemorrhage | Exudate | Papilledema |
		General	Focal			
1	−	+	−	−	−	−
2	±	±	+	±	−	−
3	±	±	±	±	+	−
4	±	±	±	±	±	+

− = not present
+ = must be present
± = may be present or absent

This chart is a modified classification used by the author. A higher group is associated with a worse prognosis. Group 4 requires emergency therapy and Group 3 requires urgent therapy. The presence of hemorrhages in Group 2 probably indicates a greater severity of disease than Group 2 changes without hemorrhage.

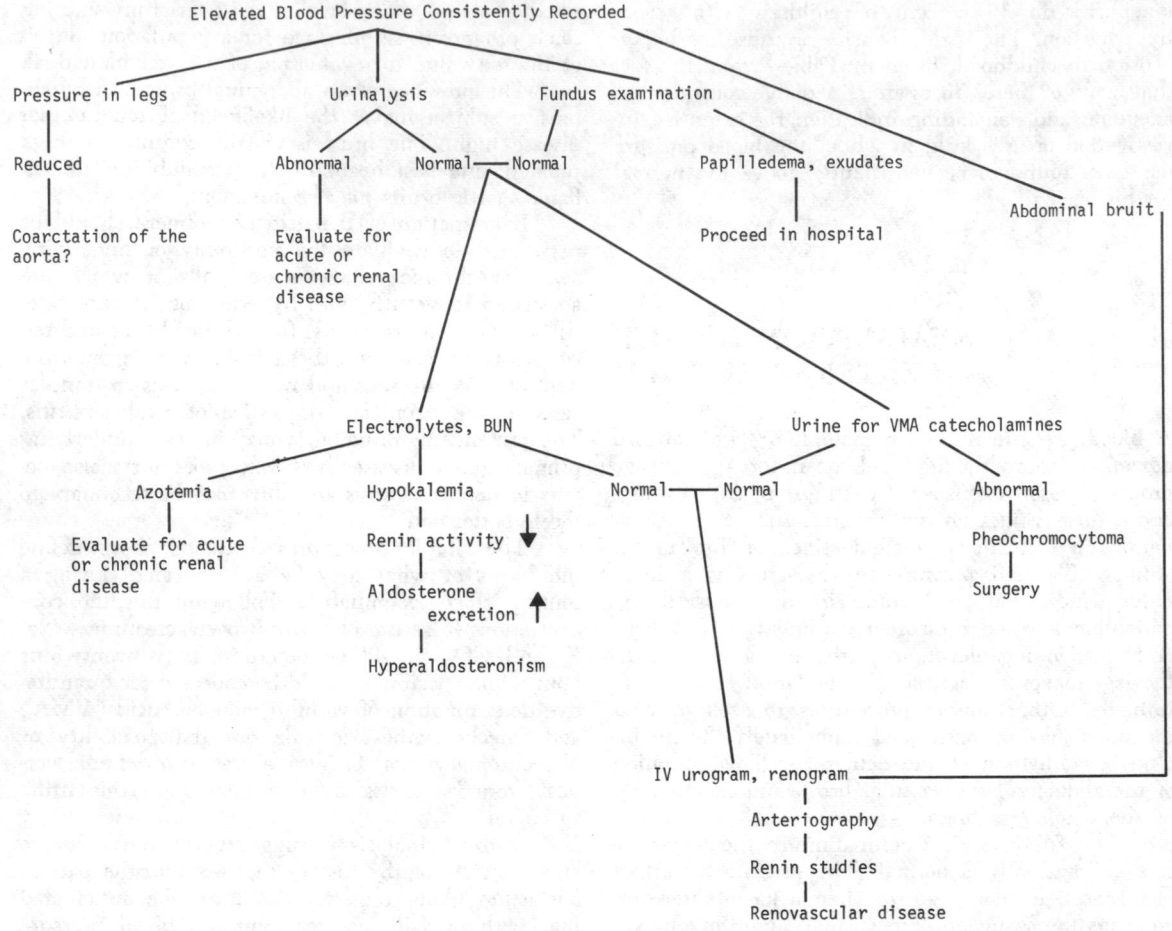

Fig. 1. The flow scheme illustrated above is intended to serve as a guide in the evaluation of the hypertensive child and is discussed in detail in the text. The work up for hypertension should be complete, proceeding from simple office tests to more complicated examinations. Although a thorough systematic approach should be developed, it should also be flexible and modified according to the history and physical findings of the individual patient.

ease the next step should be intravenous urography to rule out a possible anatomic lesion.

A normal intravenous urogram with accumulating evidence of chronic renal disease should lead the physician to consider renal biopsy for definitive diagnosis. The biopsy carries some risk and the benefits to the patient must be considered carefully in terms of evaluation of prognosis and therapy. The blood pressure must be controlled well with antihypertensive therapy before a renal biopsy can be done safely.

In a child with well-documented, persistent hypertension and no evidence of medical renal disease, the possibility of a renal vascular lesion must be investigated by arteriography and renin studies.

Persistent hypertension and a negative work-up suggest a diagnosis of essential hypertension, but plasma renin activity and aldosterone excretion should be assayed to rule out the possibility of primary hyperaldosteronism, which may occur with normokalemia.

This general outline describes briefly a method of approach to the hypertensive patient in the pediatric age group. At any point a positive finding either may cause the physician to change direction or to proceed more vigorously with the next step. Figure 1 presents a flow scheme summarizing the steps which may be followed in evaluating the hypertensive patient. Each of the more common causes of hypertension which may be encountered is discussed separately in more detail in the following sections.

References

Guyton, A. C., Coleman, T. G., Fourcade, J. C., and Navar, L. G. Physiologic control of arterial pressure. Bull. N.Y. Acad. Med., 45:811, 1969.

Kass, E. H., and Zinner, S. H. How early can the tendency toward hypertension be detected? Milbank Mem. Fund Quart., Preventive Approaches to Chronic Diseases. Vol. 47, Part 2, pp. 143-152, July 1969.

Loggie, J. M. H. Hypertension in children and adolescents. I. Causes & diagnostic studies. J. Pediat., 74:331, 1969.

Londe, S. Blood pressure in children as determined under office conditions. Clin. Pediat., 5:71, 1966.

Masland, R. P., Jr., Heald, F. P., Goodale, W. T., and Gallagher, J. R. Hypertensive vascular disease in adolescence. New Eng. J. Med., 255:894, 1956.

Moss, J. A., and Adams, J. H. Problems of Blood Pressure in Childhood. Charles C Thomas, 1962.

Rubin, M. I. Systemic hypertension. Pediat. Clin. N. Amer., 11:431, 1964.

Still, J. L., and Cottom, D. Severe hypertension in childhood. Arch. Dis. Child., 43:34, 1967.

21.5
ESSENTIAL HYPERTENSION

The diagnosis of essential hypertension can be made with confidence only after exclusion of all of the causes listed in Table 2 and discussed in detail below. It is not a very satisfactory diagnosis, and it is likely that within the large group of adults and the smaller number of children classified as having essential hypertension there are multiple causes.

A variety of etiologic factors has been implicated in essential hypertension. There is a well-established familial occurrence which is statistically greater than the incidence expected for the general population. Previously unsuspected elevations in blood pressure have been reported by Kass to occur as early as the second and third years of life in children of high risk families. An individual with one hypertensive parent has an increased chance of becoming hypertensive, and one with two hypertensive parents is at very high risk. Although genetic predisposition alone might explain the familial occurrence of hypertension, among populations of similar genetic background a greater prevalence has been found in groups with a high salt intake. A genetic predisposition for hypertension combined with salt sensitivity has been documented in strains of rats that are sensitive to salt and become hypertensive when exposed to relatively low dietary sodium intake. Other strains have been reported that are resistant to hypertension regardless of the salt intake. These data suggest that a combination of genetic and environmental factors may play a significant role in some forms of hypertension.

The relationship between stress and elevation in the blood pressure has been recognized for many years. There is clearly a neurogenic role in the regulation of blood pressure, and many investigators have suggested the possibility that essential hypertension is the result of a neurologic abnormality. Although the characteristic hypertensive individual is reported to be nervous, tense, and driving, there is certainly a very significant number of patients with essential hypertension who appear to be placid and calm and yet equally hypertensive.

Another factor in hypertension appears to be obesity and poor physical conditioning. Hypertension is more common among obese people and a greater than expected proportion of hypertensives are obese. Weight reduction may lower the blood pressure and improve their prognosis.

The hemodynamics of juvenile essential hypertension (age 14 to 35 years) have been studied by several groups who report normal cardiac index with increased peripheral vascular resistance in mild fixed hypertension and increased cardiac output with normal peripheral resistance in labile hypertension. Some of these hemodynamic changes may be reversed with good physical conditioning and regular exercise programs, but hypertension may also occur in athletes.

The complexities of studies that have attempted to elucidate the true etiology of essential hypertension are such that Page has suggested a mosaic theory which takes into account all of the multiple factors known to play a role in the normal physiologic regulation of blood pressure. He has suggested that it is an abnormal interaction of these factors that may produce the patient with essential hypertension.

Elevation of the mean arterial pressure of even a relatively small degree is associated with clear-cut decreases in life expectancy of adults. Although few studies are available of mild hypertension in the pediatric age group, there appears to be a definite and highly significant reduction of life expectancy in children also. Hypertension should be regarded as a serious disease, and its cause should be pursued vigorously before accepting the diagnosis of essential hypertension.

REFERENCES

Chiang, B. N., Perlman, L. V., and Epstein, F. H. Overweight and hypertension. Circulation, 39:403, 1969.

Dahl, L., Heine, M., and Tassinari, L. Role of genetic factors in susceptibility to experimental hypertension due to chronic excess salt ingestion. Nature, 194:480, 1962.

Eilertsen, E., and Humerfelt, S. The observer variation in the measurement of arterial blood pressure. Acta Med. Scand., 184:145, 1968.

Frohlich, E. D., Tarazi, R. C., and Dustan, H. P. Reexamination of the hemodynamics of hypertension. Am. J. Med. Sci., 257:9, 1969.

Kannel, W. B., Brand, N., Skinner, J. J., Jr., Dawber, T. R., and McNamara, P. M. The relation of adiposity to blood pressure and development of hypertension. Ann. Intern. Med., 67:48, 1967.

Keith, N. M., Wagener, H. P., and Barker, N. W. Some different types of essential hypertension: their course and prognosis. Am. J. Med. Sci., 197:332, 1939.

Kuramoto, K., Murata, K., Yazaki, Y., Ikeda, M., and Nakao, K. Hemodynamics in the juvenile hypertension with special reference to the response to propranolol. Jap. Circ. J., 32:981, 1968.

Miall, W. E., and Lovell, H. G. Relation between change of blood pressure and age. Brit. Med. J., 2:660, 1967.

Oberman, A., Lane, N. E., Harlan, W. R., Graybiel, A., and Mitchell, R. E. Trends in systolic blood pressure in the thousand aviator cohort over a twenty-four period. Circulation, 36:812, 1967.

Page, I. The mosaic theory of arterial hypertension—its interpretation. Perspect. Biol. Med., 10:326, 1967.

Perera, G. The course of primary hypertension in the young. Ann. Intern. Med., 49:1348, 1958.

Prior, I. A. M., Evans, J. G., Harvey, H. P. B., Davidson, F., and Lindsey, M. Sodium intake and blood pressure in two Polynesian populations. New Eng. J. Med., 279:515, 1968.

Roland, A. S., Hildreth, E. A., and Sellers, A. M. Occult primary renal disease in the hypertensive patient. Arch. Intern. Med., 113:101, 1964.

Sasaki, N. High blood pressure and the salt intake of the Japanese. Jap. Heart J., 3:313, 1962.

Sokolow, M., Werdegar, D., Kain, H. K., and Hinman, A. T. Relationship between level of blood pressure measured casually and by portable recorders and severity of complications in essential hypertension. Circulation, 34:279, 1966.

Tseng, W. P. Blood pressure and hypertension in an agricultural and a fishing population in Taiwan. Amer. J. Epidem., 86:513, 1967.

21.6
RENOVASCULAR HYPERTENSION

The proportion of hypertensive children with renovascular disease varies in reported series from 5 to 20 percent. Among 35 patients with definite or probable renovascular hypertension whom we have studied with Dr. Arthur Goldman, two (ages 7 and 12) were less than 26 years of age. The disease also has been reported to occur in infancy.

Renovascular hypertension may be caused by many different abnormalities of the renal vasculature (Table 4). The site of the abnormality may be extrarenal, involving the main renal artery, or intrarenal, involving branches of the renal artery. Major disease entities included within this broad classification are fibromuscular dysplasia of the renal artery, which is an abnormality of the blood vessel wall, stenosis of the renal artery caused by an arteriosclerotic plaque or other malformation, impingement on the renal artery by cyst or tumor, and occlusion of the renal artery by embolism.

TABLE 4.   *Causes of Renovascular Hypertension*

Fibromuscular dysplasia
Arteriosclerosis
Congenital stricture
Renal artery aneurysm
Renal artery thrombus
Arteriovenous fistula
Compression of the renal artery

An experimental model for renovascular hypertension was first described by Goldblatt in 1934 who reported that constriction of the renal artery in dogs after contralateral nephrectomy resulted in sustained systemic arterial hypertension. Subsequently Goormaghtigh reported that hyperplasia of the juxtaglomerular apparatus occurs in the kidney ipsilateral to an arterial constriction. The granules contained in the juxtaglomerular apparatus are increased in renovascular hypertension and are rich in renin activity.

Renin has been characterized as an enzyme of molecular weight somewhere between 40,000 and 50,000 which acts upon an α_2 globulin in the blood stream to form angiotensin I, a decapeptide with a terminal histidine-leucine group. In the presence of chloride ion and a converting enzyme found in plasma and in lung tissue, angiotensin I is rapidly converted to angiotensin II, an octapeptide formed by splitting off the terminal histidine-leucine from angiotensin I. Angiotensin II is a potent vasopressor substance with an extremely short biologic half-life, due to the widespread occurrence both in plasma and tissue of angiotensinases which destroy its biologic activity. Angiotensin II provides a major hormonal stimulus to the adrenal gland for the release of aldosterone. Rapid and prompt rises in renin occur with sodium deprivation and changes in posture, associated with slower increases in aldosterone secretion and conservation of "effective" plasma volume.

An increase in renin secretion has been noted in animals and in patients with renovascular hypertension, and it is postulated that renal artery stenosis produces a stimulus to the kidney resulting in increased release of renin. The nature of the stimulus may be a pressure change, or a change in the glomerular filtration rate and the delivery of sodium to the macula densa. After an increased rate of renin release is achieved, angiotensin II may act as a pressor agent in mediating the subsequent hypertension. Most experiments have failed to confirm the occurrence of prolonged increased renin activity in experimental hypertension. A more consistent role of renin has been described in the regulation of plasma volume in relation to sodium intake.

The diagnosis of renovascular hypertension requires evaluation of many functional variables. These specific investigations should be undertaken only after ruling out other conditions which are more easily diagnosed or if an abdominal bruit is present. The most innocuous screening test for this disease is the ^{131}I-orthoiodohippurate renogram which characteristically reveals a reduced uptake and a delayed excretion of radioactivity by the involved kidney. This test detects unilateral renal disease and is not specific for renovascular disease. Approximately 80 percent of patients with renovascular hypertension may have an abnormal renogram; however, approximately 15 to 20 percent of all hypertensive patients also have an abnormal renogram associated with unilateral renal disease which is not the cause of the hypertension.

Intravenous urography has been performed extensively as a screening test and many technical variations have been suggested. The rapid-sequence intravenous urogram with 30-second, 1-, 2-, 3-, and 5-minute films is probably the most useful modification proposed. The use of urea and mannitol infusions also has been suggested to exaggerate the differences between the involved and normal kidney. The characteristic findings of renovascular disease on intravenous urography are a delayed appearance of opaque contrast agent and a prolonged nephrogram effect on the involved side. A significant difference in renal size also suggests unilateral disease, since normally differences in kidney length rarely exceed 10 percent. This test, like the radiorenogram, has a diagnostic accuracy of about 80 percent; when the two procedures are combined, nearly 90 percent of all patients with renovascular hypertension may be detected.

The diagnosis of renovascular hypertension is especially difficult in patients with either segmental or bilateral lesions. In all patients the presence of an abnormal intravenous urogram or renogram greatly strengthens the justification for aortography. Since the prevalence of renovascular disease is relatively so high in children, aortography should be considered even in the presence of normal urography and renograms after other forms of secondary hypertension have been ruled out. The aortogram is definitive in demonstrating the presence or absence of a renal vascular abnormality; however, the presence of a renal artery abnormality is not by itself adequate justification for surgery. Measurement of bilateral renal vein renin activity at the time of aortography is useful. The ratio of the higher to lower value of renin activity in the renal veins in the normal population as well as in patients with essential hypertension in our experience is 1.35 ± 0.21 SD. Patients with renovascular hypertension have a renal vein renin activity on the involved side that is usually at least twice and often more than three times that of the uninvolved side. Elevated peripheral renin activity is also suggestive of renovascular disease. It should be appreciated that renal vein renin activity on the involved side may be within the normal range in patients with renovascular hypertension. In addition, multiple problems arise in renal vein sampling, including the possibility of dilution of the specimen from vena caval or gonadal vein blood. Nevertheless, the diagnostic and prognostic accuracy of bilateral renal vein sampling for renin activity appears to be greater than 90 percent.

Renal funcion studies of each kidney have also been used extensively to diagnose unilateral disease; however, the accuracy is probably the same as that of renin measurements, and morbidity from the procedure is much greater. Proper performance of a "split-function study" is extremely difficult and this test should not be undertaken casually. Optimally, the patient should be salt-loaded prior to the test; however, this should not be done in patients with accelerated or malignant hypertension or in those who have been on a severely restricted sodium diet. Under these circumstances salt-loading is dangerous and may exacerbate the hypertension. Catheters are placed in each ureter, and following a suitable equilibration period of not less than 45 to 60 minutes, at least three urine collections are obtained over a period of 20 to 30 minutes each. It is not necessary to obstruct both ureters since bladder leakage can be corrected using criteria suggested by Rapaport. Several modifications of the test permit catheterization of only one ureter. Measurements are made of para-aminohippurate (PAH), inulin, and creatinine clearances, urinary sodium concentration, and urinary osmolality at the time of the split-function study. The character istic finding in renovascular hypertension is a reduction in the rate of urine flow of greater than 50 percent and a decrease in urinary sodium concentration of greater than 20 percent on the involved compared with the opposite side. Urine osmolality and PAH, creatinine, and inulin concentrations are increased on the involved side.

Even after renovascular hypertension has been clearly diagnosed, there still remains the problem that present surgical methods result in cure rates of only 50 to 75 percent. An additional problem in children is that patients who are operated on at a very young age may require reoperation because of recurrent stenosis at the graft site. Finally, in a significant number of patients subjected to renal vascular surgery nephrectomy may result. Results in children, however, seem reasonably good and the gains of curing the hypertension merit serious consideration of remedial surgery.

REFERENCES

Amsterdam, E. A., Couch, N. P., Christlieb, A. R., Harrison, J. H., Crane, C., Dobrzinsky, S. J., and Hickler, R. B. Renal vein renin activity in the prognosis of surgery for renovascular hypertension. Amer. J. Med., 47:860, 1969.

Blaufox, M., Birbari, A., Hickler, R., and Merrill, J. Peripheral plasma renin activity in renal homotransplant recipients. New Eng. J. Med., 275:1165, 1966.

Combined Staff Clinics of the College of Physicians and Surgeons, Columbia University, and the Presbyterian Hospital, N.Y. Recent advances in hypertension. Amer. J. Med., 39:616, 1965.

Coran, A. G., and Schuster, S. R. Renovascular hypertension in childhood. Surgery, 64:672, 1968.

Foster, J. H., Pettinger, W. A., Oates, J. A., Rhamy, R. K., Klatte, E. C., Burko, H. C., Bolasny, B. L., Gordon, R., Puyau, F. A., and Younger, R. K. Malignant hypertension secondary to renal artery stenosis in children. Ann. Surg., 164:700, 1966.

Goldblatt, H., Lynch, J., Hanzal, R. F., and Summerville, W. W. Studies on experimental hypertension: I. The production of persistent evaluation of systolic blood pressure by means of renal ischemia. J. Exp. Med., 59:347, 1934.

Goormaghtigh, N. Histological changes in the ischemic kidney with special reference to the juxtaglomerular apparatus. Amer. J. Path., 16:409, 1940.

Kirkendall, W. M., Fitz, A. E., and Lawrence, M. S. Renal hypertension. New Eng. J. Med., 276:479, 1967.

Ljungqvist, A., and Wallgren, G. Unilateral renal artery stenosis and fatal arterial hypertension in a newborn infant. Acta Paediat. Scand., 51:575, 1962.

Maxwell, M. H., Gonick, H. C., Wiita, R., and Kaufman, J. J. Use of rapid-sequence intravenous pyelogram in diagnosis of renovascular hypertension. New Eng. J. Med., 270:213, 1964.

—— Lupu, A. N., and Franklin, S. S. Clinical and physiological factors determining diagnosis and choice of treatment of renovascular hypertension. Suppl. II to Circulation, Res. 20 and 21:201, 1967.

Mickelakis, A. M., Foster, J. H., Liddle, G. W., Rhamy, R. K., Kuchel, O., and Gordon, R. D. Measurement of renin in both renal veins. Arch. Intern. Med., 120:444, 1967.

Page, I., and McCubbin, J., eds. Renal Hypertension, 1st Edition. Chicago, Yearbook Medical Publishers, 1968.

Rapoport, A. Modification of "Howard Test" for detection of renal artery obstruction. New Eng. J. Med., 263:1159, 1960.

Shapiro, A. P., Perez-Stable, E., Scheib, E. T., Bron, K., Moutsos, S. E., Berg, G., and Misage, J. R. Renal artery stenosis and hypertension. Amer. J. Med., 47:175, 1969.

Stamey, T. A., Nudelman, I. J., Good, P. H., Schwentker, F. N., and Hendricks, F. Functional characteristics of renovascular hypertension. Medicine, 49:347, 1961.

21.7
RENAL HYPERTENSION

In addition to renovascular hypertension, renal hypertension includes a wide variety of other conditions; it implies the occurrence of systemic hypertension associated with parenchymal renal disease, which may be acute or chronic. A few patients with chronic parenchymal renal disease have associated elevations of peripheral plasma renin activity; however, the majority do not. Patients undergoing chronic hemodialysis with refractory hypertension and elevated renin activity are relieved of their hypertension after bilateral nephrectomy, suggesting an etiologic role of renin in these few cases. The majority of patients with renal hypertension, however, have either normal or low peripheral renin activity and the renin-angiotensin system cannot be implicated. Furthermore, there is a marked increase in peripheral renin activity and an almost complete absence of hypertension in patients with acute renal failure, raising further doubt concerning the etiologic role of increased renin-angiotensin activity in hypertension of renal parenchymal origin.

The prostaglandins may play a role in the maintenance of normal blood pressure. Prostaglandin E_2 is probably secreted by the kidney, which contains high concentrations of this material in the medulla. A lack of this vasodepressor lipid has been suggested as a causative factor in the hypertension of chronic renal disease. Multiple other factors are important; an abnormality of sodium regulation and expansion of plasma volume may be of considerable importance in patients with hypertension and renal disease. In patients with acute glomerulonephritis with edema and hypertension, urinary sodium usually falls to extremely low levels. Plasma expansion plays a significant role in the hypertension of acute glomerulonephritis; however, the blood pressure may be extremely labile and the disease can present acutely as hypertensive encephalopathy prior to the development of manifest edema. This sudden and accelerated change in blood pressure cannot be explained on the basis of volume expansion alone and as yet no satisfactory explanation exists. Patients with the nephrotic syndrome are rarely hypertensive unless there is underlying progressive glomerulonephritis. The plasma volume in these individuals with hypoproteinemia is variable.

Acute pyelonephritis is not associated with significant changes in blood pressure. In contrast, chronic pyelonephritis is often associated with hypertension of severe degree. Unilateral atrophic pyelonephritis or hypoplastic kidney may occasionally represent curable forms of hypertension; however, hypertensive patients with unilateral pyelonephritic changes without associated parenchymal atrophy usually will not respond to nephrectomy. In our experience, renal vein renin is of little value in the evaluation of unilateral atrophic kidney. These patients probably should be treated medically, reserving nephrectomy only for those patients who do not respond or in whom the involved kidney does not contribute significantly to overall renal function.

The diagnosis and treatment of acute glomerulonephritis and other acute and chronic renal diseases is discussed in Section 22.8. Reliance on intravenous urography, blood chemical values, and careful examination of the urinary sediment is invaluable. Any patients in the pediatric age group with hypertension and no apparent etiology must be suspected as having possible chronic parenchymal renal disease. Treatment of the hypertension of chronic renal disease differs little from that of essential hypertension, and is discussed below.

21.8
PHEOCHROMOCYTOMA

Pheochromocytoma is an adrenal medullary tumor which causes hypertension through secretion of variable amounts of norepinephrine and epinephrine. The action of these agents on blood pressure is discussed in the section on blood pressure regulation (p. 1437). The tumor commonly occurs within the adrenal gland or in the sympathetic chain along the aorta. Approximately 10 percent are bilateral, approximately 10 percent are ectopic, and approximately 10 percent are malignant. They have been reported to occur in children of all ages and both sexes and have been implicated in malignant hypertension.

The clinical picture may include a history of tachycardia, blanching of the fingertips, pounding headache, and sweating. These symptoms may be associated with either paroxysmal or sustained hypertension, although the occurrence of intermittent periods of increased secretion of catecholamines by these tumors is relatively rare. Hypersecretion is usually continuously present, although acute attacks may be superimposed. This continuous secretion of catecholamines makes reliable diagnosis possible by determination of urinary catecholamines and their metabolites, metanephrine and vanillin mandelic acid. Normal values for the rate of urinary excretion of the end products of norepinephrine and epinephrine metabolism vary with the age of the child. The excretion is expressed best in relation to creatinine excretion, and decreases from 6.9 micrograms of VMA per milligram of creatinine during the first year of life to 1.34 at age 15 to 18. Other diagnostic tests are less reliable; they include the intravenous administration of histamine, tryamine, or glucagon to provoke a blood pressure response. These are particularly useful in the rare patient with intermittent secretion. They must be compared with a base-line cold pressor test for adequate interpretation. The hazards of such tests should be appreciated. An ampul of phentolamine (Regitine) should always be available to block the blood pressure response. An occasional patient has been reported in whom palpation over the site of the tumor or a change in posture provoked a hypertensive episode. Regitine may be used as a diagnostic test in the patient with sustained hypertension.

Localization of the tumor may be accomplished by arteriography or retroperitoneal air inflation, both of which may carry significant hazard. Treatment is surgical and requires delicate handling of rapid fluctuations of blood pressure during the operation.

REFERENCES

Gitlon, S. E., Mendlowitz, M., Wilk, E. K., Wilk, S., Wolf, R. L., and Bertani, L. M. Excretion of catecholamine catabolites by normal children. J. Lab. Clin. Med., 72:612, 1968.

Insley, J., and Smallwood, W. C. Pheochromocytoma in children. Arch. Dis. Child., 37:606, 1962.

Rossi, P., Young, I. S., and Panke, W. F. Techniques, usefulness, and hazards of arteriography of pheochromocytoma. J.A.M.A., 205:547, 1968.

Sheps, S. G., and Maher, F. T. Histamine and glucagon tests in diagnosis of pheochromocytoma. J.A.M.A., 205:895, 1968.

Primary hyperaldosteronism was first described in 1954 by Conn in a 34-year-old female patient with recurrent episodes of weakness and paralysis, hypernatremia, hypokalemia, alkalosis, and decreased urinary concentrating ability. Primary hyperaldosteronism may present as benign essential hypertension, or in rare instances, as malignant hypertension. It occurs in children as well as in adults. The actual prevalence of the disease is currently a subject of intense controversy. Approximately 20 percent of hypertensive patients have small adrenal cortical adenomas at post-mortem examination. Based on this finding and the low renin activity noted frequently in patients with essential hypertension, it has been suggested that as many as 10 to 20 percent in the adult age group have primary aldosteronism. However, this possibility remains unproved and the total number of patients with documented primary hyperaldosteronism is relatively small.

Primary hyperaldosteronism is usually caused by a unilateral tumor of the adrenal cortex, although adrenal hyperplasia and carcinoma have been associated with the syndrome. There is increased secretion of aldosterone, which acts upon the renal tubule, producing retention of sodium and excessive wastage of potassium. There is usually only a small weight gain, with a trace of edema, as a result of so-called DOCA escape.

Associated with the hypersecretion of aldosterone are hypernatremia, hypokalemia, alkalosis, expanded plasma volume, suppressed plasma renin activity, and hypertension. The hypertensive syndrome cannot be reproduced easily in experimental animals by the administration of either aldosterone or mineral corticoids alone, so that other factors may also play a role. The biochemical abnormalities associated with primary aldosteronism extend to organs besides the kidney and the blood vessels. Increased secretion of potassium in the saliva and reduction of sweat sodium have been reported. The presenting symptom may be hypokalemic paralysis, but the majority of patients are discovered because of hypertension and asymptomatic hypokalemia. The normokalemic patient may develop hypokalemia after administration of sodium or diuretics. However, hypokalemia in essential hypertension is not uncommon, and most patients who exhibit hypokalemia during diuretic therapy do not have primary hyperaldosteronism.

As a screening test, peripheral plasma samples are obtained for measurement of renin activity after the patient has been standing two or three hours. Under these circumstances in normal subjects the plasma renin activity is usually elevated; however, in patients with primary hyperaldosteronism, because of the increased aldosterone secretory rate and maximum sodium retention, plasma renin activity is suppressed and even maximum stimuli such as upright posture and diuretics cause no increase in renin activity. Recent reports suggest that as many as 20 percent of patients with essential hypertension may have fixed low levels of plasma renin activity. In our experience, however, all patients with essential hypertension studied on a metabolic balance ward reveal a renin response to stimuli such as upright posture and diuretics. Thus fixed low levels of renin activity are very suggestive of the diagnosis of primary aldosteronism. However, since low renin activity alone cannot be considered diagnostic of primary hyperaldosteronism, this finding should lead to measurement of aldosterone excretory or secretory rates. Conversely, renin activity as well as aldosterone should be measured in patients with essential hypertension who may have secondary hyperaldosteronism. Elevation of plasma renin activity in these patients easily differentiates them from those with primary hyperaldosteronism. Secondary aldosteronism occurs either as a response to sustained elevated renin secretion by the kidney or as a result of decreased metabolism of aldosterone, as occurs in patients with cirrhosis. The serum sodium concentration in these patients usually is reduced.

After the diagnosis of primary hyperaldosteronism is established, an attempt should be made to localize the tumor, for which retroperitoneal pneumography and aortography have been used. Bilateral adrenal vein catheterization may reveal an elevation in aldosterone on one side. Aldosteronomas have also been localized successfully by adrenal phlebography.

The treatment of choice is surgery; if the lesion cannot be localized, bilateral exploration of the adrenal glands may be necessary. Spironolactone, an aldosterone antagonist, may be used both as a therapeutic test and for treatment of primary aldosteronism; in high dosages (up to 600 mg/day in adults) it may successfully control the hypertension and the hypokalemia. Medical therapy has been used for a relatively short time and little is known concerning the long-term effects of spironolactone in the continued presence of an aldosterone-secreting tumor. Patients in whom the evidence of primary hyperaldosteronism is equivocal and in whom the tumor cannot be localized may be treated with spironolactone therapy until the lesion is delineated. However, if an aldosteronoma is clearly demonstrated by biochemical findings, surgery is the treatment of choice, especially in the pediatric age-group.

REFERENCES

Conn, J. W. Presidential address, Part I. Painting background, Part II. Primary aldosteronism, A new clinical syndrome. J. Lab. Clin. Med., 45:3, 1955.

——— Rovner, D. R., Cohen, E. L., Bookstein, J. J., Cerny, J. C., and Lucas, C. P. Preoperative diagonsis of primary aldosteronism. Arch. Intern. Med., 123:113, 1969.

Ehrlich, E. N. Aldosterone, the adrenal cortex, and hypertension. Ann. Rev. Med., 19:373, 1968.

Kaplan, N. M. Hypokalemia in the hypertensive patient. Ann. Intern. Med., 66:1079, 1967.

Melby, J. C., Spark, R. F., Dale, S. L., Egdahl, R. H., and Kahn, P. C. Diagnosis and localization of aldosterone-producing adenomas by adrenal-vein catheterization. New Eng. J. Med., 277:1050, 1967.

Spark, R. F., and Melby, J. C. Aldosteronism in hypertension. Ann. Intern. Med., 69:685, 1968.

21.10

COARCTATION OF THE AORTA

Coarctation of the aorta is reported to occur in about 10 percent of children with hypertension. The role of the kidney in hypertension has been controversial; however, in a recent investigation renin activity was normal in 9 of 10 patients.

The diagnosis may be suspected if a discrepancy of blood pressure readings is discovered between the arms and legs, with diminution in the intensity of the arterial pulses of the lower extremities. Rib notching may be seen on radiographs of the chest. Definitive diagnosis is made by aortography. The treatment is surgical.

REFERENCES

Kirkendall, W. M., Culbertson, J. W., and Eckstein, J. W. Renal hemodynamics in patients with coarctation of the aorta. J. Lab. Clin. Med., 53:6, 1959.

Timmis, G. C., and Gordon, S. A renal factor in hypertension due to coarctation of the aorta. Preliminary observations. New Eng. J. Med., 270:814, 1964.

Wernig, C., Schonbeck, M., Weidmann, P., Baumann, K., Gysling, E., Wirz, P., and Siegethaler, W. Plasma renin activity in patients with coarctation of the aorta. Circulation, 40:731, 1969.

21.11

MISCELLANEOUS CAUSES OF HYPERTENSION

Hypertension in *Cushing's syndrome* is associated with primary disease of the adrenal or the therapeutic administration of corticosteroids. Hypertension in this condition is associated with vasculitis and may be severe and difficult to treat. Hypertension as the sole presenting symptom is extremely rare but does occur. In children with the adrenogenital syndrome and a C_{11}-hydroxylase deficiency there is impaired conversion of 11-deoxycorticosterone to corticosterone. This results in the accumulation of 11-deoxycorticosterone, which is a mineral corticoid and the cause of the associated hypertension.

Wilms' tumor or other vascular tumors of the kidney may present with hypertension. These neoplasms behave like arteriovenous fistulae and the elevation of blood pressure characteristically is systolic with a wide pulse pressure. In our experience measurements of renin activity in these patients have not confirmed a renovascular component. *Neuroblastoma* may be associated under rare circumstances with secretion of catecholamines, or may be located in such a position as to partially obstruct the renal artery.

Finally, mercury poisoning; radiation of the kidney; genitourinary surgery; burns; brain tumors, especially tumors of the third ventricle and other conditions associated with increased intracranial pressure; Stevens-Johnson syndrome; Guillain-Barré syndrome; poliomyelitis; acute bacterial endocarditis; and arteritis all have been associated either transiently or during their entire course with elevations of systemic arterial pressure.

Because of the wide variety of conditions that may be associated with hypertension, any patient in whom an abnormality of blood pressure is found should be evaluated thoroughly. Only after one is reasonably certain that none of the rarer diseases associated with hypertension nor any of the more common underlying causes is present can a diagnosis of essential hypertension in childhood be made. Even then it is worthwhile to consider reevaluation at some later date. Diseases such as fibromuscular dysplasia of the renal artery may be extremely difficult to detect. We have seen recently one individual who had apparently normal aortography despite consistently abnormal renograms five years prior to admission to our hospital. Aortography was repeated using a magnification technique with selective arterial catheterization on the suspected side, and fibromuscular dysplasia was demonstrated.

21.12 THERAPY

Therapy of hypertension may be divided into hypertensive emergencies, which require immediate parenteral administration of antihypertensive medication, and nonemergency treatment of hypertension, in which the blood pressure may be reduced safely over a period of days or weeks. It is inadvisable to permit any individual to be subjected to prolonged periods of elevated systemic arterial pressure. Papilledema with the presence or high risk of convulsions and encephalopathy is the most urgent indication for antihypertensive therapy.

The many effective antihypertensive medications which are available today make the selection of therapy partially objective and partially a matter of personal preference and experience. Patients will often exhibit differing responses to antihypertensive drugs, both in therapeutic effectiveness and side effects, and it is important that any physicians responsible for the care of patients with hypertension be familiar with several antihypertensive drugs. The dosages used in pediatrics are highly empirical since so little experience has been accumulated. The major drugs used, with recommended starting dosages and mode of action, are listed in Table 5. All of the drugs may be used in virtually any form of hypertension, whether it be essential or secondary; however, special caution should be exercised in the drug therapy of pheochromocytoma.

Wide divergence of opinion exists concerning the benefits of antihypertensive therapy; however, the majority of reports in the literature suggest that therapy is of value even when hypertension is mild

TABLE 5. *Antihypertensive Therapy in Outpatients*

Drug	Site of Action	Onset of Action	Dose	Side Effects
Chlorothiazide	Arteriolar smooth muscle, sodium depletion	One week	10-20mg/kg daily	Hyperglycemia, potassium depletion, hyperuricemia, dehydration
Hydralazine	Arteriolar smooth muscle	2-4 hours	0.2-0.6mg/kg every 4-6 hours	Lupus, headache, palpitation, anorexia, rheumatoid state
Reserpine	Peripheral catecholamine depletion, central nervous system	Three days to one week	0.005-0.015mg/kg daily	Nasal congestion, sedation, bradycardia, depression
Methyldopa	Unknown	4-6 hours	10-60mg/kg daily	Hemolytic anemia, fever, leukopenia, abnormal liver function
Guanethidine	Postganglionic sympathetic blockade	36 to 48 hours	0.2-2.5mg/kg daily	Potentiates norepinephrine, postural hypotension, bradycardia
Spironolactone	Aldosterone antagonist	One week	1.0-10mg/kg daily	Hyperkalemia

or moderate. In malignant or accelerated hypertension, antihypertensive therapy definitely results in a significant prolongation of life. Although firm data are not available, it seems reasonable to recommend that any child with a consistent elevation of diastolic pressure to 100 mm Hg or greater and a systolic pressure of greater than 140 mm Hg should receive antihypertensive therapy. Undoubtedly, levels below this should be treated in some individuals.

Treatment of Hypertensive Emergencies

A hypertensive emergency may be defined as any situation in which sudden and alarming elevation of the blood pressure constitutes a threat to life. In a patient with papilledema and encephalopathy and elevation of the blood pressure, the dangers of the situation and the urgency of treatment are obvious. Hemorrhages and exudates in the eye grounds indicate that the hypertension is of severe degree but may not require as urgent therapy. The level of the blood pressure itself is not a completely reliable guide to the urgency of therapy, although severe elevations of blood pressure carry with them the dangers of congestive heart failure, cerebral vascular accident, and renal damage. The sudden onset of proteinuria and renal insufficiency may also indicate acceleration of hypertension and increasing urgency for therapy. Several modalities of therapy are available. The drugs should be administered parenterally in an attempt to return the arterial pressure to normal or near normal levels within a matter of hours.

Intravenous administration of diazoxide is the simplest and probably the safest mode of therapy in a hypertensive emergency. This drug presumably acts upon the arterial vasculature directly and results in a lowering of the mean arterial pressure by 25 percent within a few seconds. It is not associated with significant side effects when used in acute therapy and will not reduce the pressure below normal. For this reason, we consider it the treatment of choice in hypertensive emergencies, although approval by the Federal Drug Administration for general use is still pending. Diazoxide, in a dose of 5 mg per kg body weight, is given rapidly intravenously, in order to avoid the effects of protein binding.

Reserpine when given parenterally may have an effect within a few hours but usually reaches a maximum in four to six hours. A dose as high as 0.2 mg per kg has been recommended as an initial emergency dose in pediatrics; however, this is significantly higher than the amount usually given as a test dose in adults. The need for a test dose is supported by the observation that parenteral administration may be associated with the sudden release of catecholamines into the circulation and production of a hypertensive emergency, or the patient may suffer severe hypotension requiring norepinephrine for support. A total test dose for children probably should not exceed 0.2 mg. This may be followed after approximately four hours by .02 mg per kg, with an absolute limit of 0.5 mg. If no significant hypotensive effect has been achieved four hours later, the dose may be doubled and then doubled again every six hours until the desired level of blood pressure is reached.

Hydralazine may be administered intramuscularly, with an expected onset of action within about 15 to 20 minutes. The maximum effect is seen in about two hours and the dose can be adjusted at intervals of four to six hours depending upon the response. The undesirable side effect of producing a tachycardia with reduced coronary blood flow usually is not a serious consideration in children.

Intravenous methyldopa has been used in the treatment of hypertensive emergencies; however, its action is relatively mild and it depends largely upon postural changes to produce its hypotensive effect. Therefore, we limit the use of methyldopa to ambulatory patients receiving medication by the oral route.

Patients with severe hypertension resistant to all other modalities may require ganglionic blocking drugs such as trimethaphan and pentolinium for blood pressure control. These drugs require special nursing care. Sodium nitroprusside is probably the most potent antihypertensive drug that has been described; however, like the ganglionic blocking agents it requires moment to moment monitoring of blood pressure in order to provide adequate control with a carefully regulated intravenous drip.

Chronic Hypertension

The therapy of chronic hypertension depends completely upon the individual patient. The two drugs that seem most desirable for initiation of antihypertensive therapy in children are thiazides and hydralazine, both of which are relatively well tolerated by most individuals and have a significant hypotensive effect in mild hypertension. Reserpine, although it has several undesirable side effects, may be of value, especially in combination with hydralazine, where the bradycardia produced by reserpine tends to ameliorate the tachycardia which results from the other drug. Methyldopa also is a convenient drug to administer and is well tolerated by most patients.

The initial therapy of choice in the pediatric age-group, therefore, is diuretic therapy followed by the addition of first hydralazine, and then methyldopa if necessary. In the absence of adequate effects the logical choice is the addition of reserpine. Guanethidine, which has the greatest number of side effects, is probably the most potent drug available for antihypertensive therapy of the ambulatory patient, excluding the ganglionic blocking agents which have very severe side effects and are highly impractical. The use of monamide oxidase inhibitors is associated with an alarming number of serious side effects and should be avoided in pediatric practice.

REFERENCES

Colwill, J. M., Dutton, A. M., Morrissey, J., and Yu, P. N. Alphamethyldopa and hydrochlorothiazide. New Eng. J. Med., 271:696, 1964.

Etteldorf, J. N., Smith, J. D., Tharp, C. P., and Tuttle, A. H. Hydralazine in nephritic and normal children with renal hemodynamic studies. Amer. J. Dis. Child., 89:451, 1955.

Finnerty, F. A., Jr., Davidow, M., and Kakaviatos, N. Hypertensive vascular disease. Amer. J. Cardiol., 19:377, 1967.

Freis, E. The value of antihypertensive therapy. Bull. N.Y. Acad. Med., 45:951, 1969.

Goldberg, L. I. Monoamine oxidase inhibitors. J.A.M.A., 190:132, 1964.

Hansen, J. Hydrochlorothiazide in the treatment of hypertension. Acta Med. Scand., 183:317, 1968.

Horwitz, D., Pettinger, W. A., Orvis, H., Thomas, R. E., and Sjoerdsma, A. Effects of methyldopa in fifty hypertensive patients. Clin. Pharmacol. Thera., 8:224, 1967.

Loggie, J. M. H. Hypertension in children and adolescents. II. Drug therapy. J. Pediat., 74:640, 1969.

Smith, W. M., Damato, A. N., Galluzzi, N. J., Garfield, C. F., Hanowell, E. G., Stimson, W. H., Thurm, R. H., Walsh, J. J., and Bromer, L. The evaluation of antihypertensive therapy cooperative clinical trial method. Ann. Intern. Med., 61:829, 1964.

Veterans Administration cooperative study group on antihypertensive agents: Effects of treatment on morbidity in hypertension. J.A.M.A., 202:1028, 1967.

Wolf, R. L., Mendlowitz, M., Roboz, J., Styan, G. P. H., Kornfeld, P., and Weigl, A. Treatment of hypertension with spironolactone. J.A.M.A., 198:1143, 1966.

chapter 22

THE KIDNEYS AND URINARY TRACT

CHESTER M. EDELMANN, JR., Associate Editor

22.1
MORPHOLOGIC DEVELOPMENT

JAY BERNSTEIN *

The development of the metanephros or definitive kidney begins in the fifth week of embryonic life, when a diverticulum of the Wolffian or mesonephric duct establishes contact with the caudal mesenchyme of the nephrogenic cord. This diverticulum, the ureteric bud, develops into the renal collecting system, including the ureter, pelvis, calyces, and collecting ducts. The mesenchyme or metanephric blastema forms the renal secretory system, including glomeruli, convoluted tubules, and loops of Henle.

The ureteric bud divides into the first generation of branches, the primary cranial and caudal pole tubules, which eventually give rise to the major calyces. Subsequent branching gives rise to the minor calyces and collecting ducts of the renal pyramids. Secretory activity of the first nephrons causes dilatation and consequent remodeling of the metanephric duct and its branches to form the pelvis and calyces, the outflow of urine possibly being temporarily impeded by epithelial septa at the caudal end of the ureter. The relationship of continuing formation and accumulation of urine to subsequent organogenesis is not clear; that the former may have a profound effect on development is suggested by the frequent association of congenital urinary tract obstruction with parenchymal maldevelopment of the kidney.

Proliferation of and differentiation within the metanephrogenic mesenchyme lead to the development of glomeruli and tubules in juxtaposition to the growing collecting ducts. A condensation of mesenchyme appears near the growing end, at the ampulla of the collecting tubule, and this cellular mass is transformed into a nephric vesicle by the development of a lumen. As it grows, the vesicle becomes kinked into an S-shaped structure, in which a glomerulus is formed at the blind, free end and continuity with the collecting system is established

at the other. Capillaries grow into the cleft at the free end of the kinked vesicle to form the glomerular vessels, establishing circulation through blood vessels in the adjacent mesenchyme. Basement membrane material appears between juxtaposed endothelial and epithelial cells, to become a progressively thicker, better-defined structure with advancing age. In its definitive form, the glomerulus is composed of a rete or network of freely anastomosing capillaries. These assume with age a lobulated appearance, although numerous intercapillary connections persist. The solid central portion of the glomerulus is referred to as the stalk. It contains cells morphologically different from capillary endothelium; they are believed to function in phagocytosis and secretion, and they respond to mineralocorticoid deficiency by developing granules similar to those in cells of the juxtaglomerular apparatus.

Continued growth of the vesicle leads to further elongation and coiling, with development of the proximal and distal convoluted tubules and the intervening loop of Henle. The first portion of the distal convolution remains in close proximity to the hilar arterioles of the glomerulus, and the two undergo specialization to form the complex known as the juxtaglomerular apparatus. The epithelial cells in that part of the distal convolution differentiate into the macula densa, and specialized cells develop between and in the walls of the afferent and efferent arterioles. Secretion of renin has been attributed to granular epithelioid cells in the walls of the hilar arterioles. Agranular "lacis" cells form the juxtaglomerular cell mass and are continuous with and morphologically similar to the mesangial cells of the glomerular stalk. In early infancy this complex is poorly developed; it does not appear as a well-defined structure before the age of 2 years.

Nephrogenesis proceeds at the periphery, and the growth of the kidney is thus centrifugal. The central portion of the cortex near the corticomedullary junction contains the developmentally older glomeruli, whose loops of Henle dip into the medulla and whose efferent arterioles form the arteriolae rectae of the medulla. The peripheral cortex contains the more recently formed glomeruli and tubules. These are the cortical nephrons, whose loops of Henle do not reach into the medulla. The deeper glomeruli are also larger than those developing more peripherally, and a number, particularly around the arcuate vessels, normally undergo sclerosis, involu-

---

* In addition to the sections appearing under his name, all the discussions of renal pathology were written by Dr. Bernstein.

tion, and resorption in the early neonatal period. The difference in size between central and peripheral glomeruli is most marked in early infancy. Continued development of the outer glomeruli leads toward greater homogeneity, but differences may persist or reappear in certain diseases, such as sickle-cell anemia.

As nephrogenesis in the inner cortex proceeds, new nephrons are formed at the growing ampullary end of the collecting duct in more or less successive fashion. By differential growth, distal convoluted tubules of earlier nephrons maintain their points of attachment on the terminal segments of the succeeding nephrons. The nephrons thus form arcades, draining peripherally, generally in groups of four to seven, the last segment of the "collecting tubule" finally entering the collecting duct. Beyond the arcades, subsequent nephrons are attached individually and directly to the ends of the branching collecting ducts in the peripheral cortex.

Knowledge of the postnatal growth and maturation of the kidney is fragmentary. Physical growth during organogenesis depends upon the formation of new units and enlargement of existing units. Formation of new nephrons ordinarily ceases before full fetal maturity, but it continues for a variable period of time postnatally in premature infants. Cessation of nephrogenesis postnatally in prematurely born infants may, however, come earlier than it would have, had the fetus remained in utero. Nephrogenesis may also occasionally cease prematurely in normally developing fetuses, and babies of low birth weight probably present a degree of nephrogenesis commensurate with their gestational age rather than their size. It is not known whether or not these factors affect subsequent renal development. Renal growth during infancy and childhood ordinarily follows a predictable allometric curve, and the size of the kidneys correlates to a strikingly high degree with both age and the usual parameters of somatic growth. However, in patients with intrinsic renal disease, cerebral abnormalities, and some forms of congenital heart disease, renal size may be considerably less than expected.

Maturation of the kidney has been assessed both by the histologic appearance of glomeruli and by the size and disposition of the tubules. The rate of glomerular maturation is variable, and immature forms are present normally for months after birth. Superimposed diseases, such as inflammation and urinary tract obstruction, may lead to a persistence of abnormally primitive forms and even to regressive changes in normally formed glomeruli. Glomerular size, which also follows a regular growth curve in childhood, may be either retarded or accelerated by certain diseases. Cyanotic congenital heart disease, for example, is often associated with striking glomerular enlargement. Glomerular function increases during early infancy, but it is quite clear that even immature glomeruli can function once capillary circulation has been established. Increasing glomerular filtration rate in childhood seems to be related to increasing

glomerular size and surface area of the capillary bed, but the mechanics of filtration, as judged by the distributions of electron-dense tracers, undergo changes during glomerular maturation.

Tubular maturation has been assessed in morphometric studies of microdissected specimens. The number of nephrons that reside entirely in the cortex is greatest in newborns and declines with continued growth as Henle's loops extend to the medulla. As tubules increase in length and volume, the convolutions become more coiled and the tubular length becomes more uniform. Glomerular size, which at birth had been more uniform than tubular size, also tends with age toward even more uniformity. The composite glomerular-tubular ratio decreases, approaching the greater homogeneity of the adult kidney. The functional counterpart of this relative diversity of "glomerulotubular balance" in immature kidneys might be tubular "insufficiency" relative to the adult, and the presence of numerous cortical nephrons almost certainly would result in poorer concentrating ability than in the adult.

Histochemical studies of developing and immature kidneys have in general shown enzymatic activity increasing with maturation, and some shifts in distribution also occur. Activity in the nephrogenic zone of the cortex is weak or absent, and greater activity can be demonstrated in the more mature tubules of the inner cortex. Enzymic induction postnatally appears, however, to be more dependent upon increased metabolic work load than on structural maturation. The distribution of certain isozymes in the formed nephrons of immature kidneys follows approximately the same pattern as in adult kidneys. Ultrastructural studies have shown that subcellular structures are present in fetal cells and that they become more complex during subsequent development. Observations on passage of large molecules through the glomerulus indicate that differences in the filtration barrier between mature and immature glomeruli may reside in the degree of endothelial fenestration. These observations suggest that renal maturation may be related in part to continual differentiation of individual cells, but that a major contribution comes from physical growth of the organ with changing anatomic relationships of nephrons and ducts and with more efficient functional integrity.

REFERENCES

Bernstein, J., and Meyer, R. Some speculations on the nature and significance of developmentally small kidneys (renal hypoplasia). Nephron, 1:137, 1964.

DuBois, A. M. The embryonic kidney. In Rouiller, C., and Muller, A. F., eds., The Kidney. New York, Academic Press, Inc., 1969, Vol. 1, Ch. 1, p. 1.

Fetterman, G. H. Microdissection in the study of normal and abnormal renal structure and function. In Sommers, S. C., ed., Pathology Annual. New York, Appleton-Century-Crofts, 1970.

—— Shuplock, N. A., Philipp, F. J., and Gregg, H. S. The growth and maturation of human glomeruli and proximal convolutions from term to adulthood; studies of microdissection. Pediatrics, 35:601, 1965.

Oliver, J. Nephrons and Kidneys. A Quantitative Study of Developmental and Evolutionary Mammalian Architectonics. New York, Hoeber Medical Division, Harper & Row, 1968.

Osathanondh, V., and Potter, E. L. Development of human kidney as shown by microdissection. I-III. Arch. Path., 76:271, 277, 290, 1963.

Zamboni, L., and De Martino, C. Embryogenesis of the human renal glomerulus. I. A histologic study. Arch. Path., 86:279, 1968.

22.2
PHYSIOLOGY AND FUNCTIONAL DEVELOPMENT OF THE KIDNEY

ADRIAN SPITZER

The limited variability of the internal environment required for the development and subsequent maintenance of the organism is in large part the result of the activity of the kidneys. As stated by Homer Smith, father of modern renal physiology, "In the last analysis, composition of the plasma is determined not by what the body ingests but by what the kidneys retain and what they excrete." Hence, it is probably correct to say that the excretory function of the kidney is only incidental to its regulatory function. Conceptually, however, the regulatory and excretory functions of the kidney should not be considered identical. The kidney of the newborn, for instance, has an excretory capacity which is entirely adequate under usual circumstances, but its ability to respond to changes is slow and quantitatively limited. At any age excretory rates of the diseased kidney may be normal at a time when regulatory function is significantly deficient, as evidenced by distortions in the composition of the body fluids.

A thorough understanding of the mechanisms underlying the excretory and regulatory functions of the kidney, and knowledge concerning the capacity of the organ to fulfill its role at different ages and in various states of disease, are of paramount importance in providing optimal medical care of the child.

Fetal Kidney

Morphologic Characteristics

From the end of the second month until the end of the eighth month of embryonic life, nephrogenesis proceeds in a centrifugal pattern, accounting for the relative maturity of the medullary and juxtamedul-lary nephrons as well as for the high degree of structural and functional heterogeneity which characterizes the developing kidney.

About 20 percent of the nephrons are formed by 3 months of gestation and about 30 percent by 5 months. Formation of new nephrons ceases when the fetus reaches a length of 46 to 49 cm and a weight of 2,100 to 2,500 g. In the prematurely born infant with a weight well below 2,500 g, nephrogenesis continues after birth, but probably for a shorter period of time than if the fetus had remained in the uterus.

At the end of a full-term gestation, each kidney contains 850,000 to 1,000,000 nephrons. As a result of the centrifugal pattern of development, the ratio of the height of the cortex to that of the medulla is about 1:5 in the newborn, compared to about 1:2.4 in the adult. The glomeruli are small, their average diameter being 100 μ or about half the adult size. The total area for filtration, relative to body weight, is, however, higher than that at any other age. The thickness of the glomerular basement membrane is only half that of an adult, but its capacity to ultrafilter does not seem to be affected since the urine is "free" of protein even in prematurely born babies. The tubules, especially the proximal convolutions, are short and their differentiation is incomplete. Electron micrographs of the proximal tubule reveal a less complex brush border and smaller mitrochondria as compared to the adult structure. About 20 percent of the loops of Henle are still within the cortex.

Postnatal growth depends almost exclusively on enlargement of existing units and follows a predictable allometric curve which correlates linearly with age and body surface area. Within the kidney, however, the various structural components grow at different rates, with the proximal tubules accounting by far for most of the kidney enlargement with age.

A variety of factors can interfere with the normal development of the kidney, both during intra- and extrauterine life. Adrenocorticosteroids, for instance, have been shown to induce cystic transformation in the subcortical area. Inflammatory disease processes and obstruction of the urinary tract may lead to persistence of abnormally primitive nephrons or even to regressive changes of normally formed ones. Cyanotic heart disease is often associated with striking glomerular enlargement.

Despite this susceptibility to noxious stimuli, the capacity of the kidney to compensate for injury is greater in childhood than later in life. A number of observations suggest that this is due to the activity of normal growth mechanisms in addition to the processes accounting for compensatory growth.

Functional Development

During intrauterine life the kidney is able to perform most of the functions which characterize the adult organ. The development of the mammalian fetus, however, does not seem to depend on the capacity of the kidneys to retain or excrete substances, these regulatory and excretory functions being assumed by the placenta. This conclusion is supported by the fact that children with bilateral renal agenesis may be born without other abnormalities.

Renal plasma flow, as determined in experimental animals, is low during intrauterine life, and renal vascular resistance is high. This might contribute to the low tubular secretory rates observed during this period, although immaturity of the secretory mechanisms per se is of major importance.

Formation of urine by the human fetal kidney begins toward the end of the first trimester. This coincides with the differentiation of the brush border in the proximal tubules and the onset of transport by the renal tubular epithelium, as evidenced, for instance, by accumulation of dyes in tubular segments isolated from human fetuses. No information is available regarding rates of glomerular filtration (GFR) or urine flow in the human fetus. In the sheep, however, in which formation of urine starts around 2 months of gestation, there is a progressive increase in the rate of both glomerular filtration and urine flow up to about 4 months of intrauterine life. During the remaining month of gestation, despite a continuing increase in GFR, a decrease in urine flow occurs. This is likely to be the result of the onset of function of the newly formed loops of Henle, which have a high capacity to reabsorb salt and water.

Fetal urine is hypotonic to plasma, as a result of low concentrations of electrolytes and urea. The fetus is able to excrete an acid urine, with a pH of about 6, but the capacity of the kidney to increase the excretion of H^+ following administration of an acid load has been found to be limited.

The Neonatal Kidney

Following placental separation, there is a prompt increase in renal blood flow. The mechanism which underlies this adaptation is still controversial, although it is probably the consequence of a sudden decrease in renal arteriolar resistance. Morphologic evidence for such a mechanism is offered by the presence in the precapillary branches of the so-called "dormant organs" (lung, gut, kidney) of turgid epithelioidal cells which shrink immediately after birth. The stimulus for this change is entirely unknown. Accompanying the increase in renal blood flow, there is a marked increase in functional capacity. However, definite limitations in many renal functions persist during the newborn period and, to a lesser degree, during most of the remainder of infancy.

Glomerular Function

The first step in the formation of urine is ultrafiltration of plasma across the semipermeable membranes of the glomerular capillaries. Micropuncture studies in single nephrons of experimental animals have shown that at arterial pressures comparable to those found in adult man, glomerular capillary pressure is around 60 mm Hg. Opposing filtration is the pressure in the proximal tubule, about 14 mm Hg, and the colloid osmotic pressure of the plasma proteins, approximately 25 mm Hg. Thus the effective hydrostatic pressure for filtration is 20 to 25 mm Hg. These forces, together with the size of the glomerular capillary area and the permeability characteristics of the capillary membrane, determine the rate of glomerular filtration.

In young infants glomerular filtration rates have been found to be low compared to the adult, even when corrected for kidney weight or body surface area. Moreover, it has been suggested that in the immature kidney not all the glomeruli participate equally in the process of filtration. The more recently formed glomeruli, located in the superficial cortex, probably have a lower filtration rate than the deeper and more mature ones. During the first week of life the mean value for total kidney GFR is 35 ml/minute/1.73 m^2. A steady progression occurs, so that at the end of the first year the corrected values for GFR are close to those found in adults. Because of the wide range of normal variation, however, individual measurements of GFR during infancy may be difficult to interpret. The search for an explanation for the low rates of glomerular filtration during infancy points toward a multicausal phenomenon.

One of the factors found to play a role in experimental animals is a relatively high resistance in the afferent arterioles. For example, an 88 percent decrease in intrinsic renal vascular resistance was found to occur in the piglet during the first 6 weeks of extrauterine life.

Low capillary permeability is another contributing factor. The clearance of dextran with a molecular weight of 15,000 is close to zero in the newborn infant whereas the adult is able to filter dextran molecules up to a weight of about 50,000. The calculated effective pore radius is 20 Å in the newborn compared to 40 Å in the adult. The net result is a low hydrostatic pressure available to move fluid through the glomerular capillary membrane (effective filtration pressure). An increase in filtration pressure together with an increase in the surface area of the filtering membrane have been shown recently to account quantitatively for the changes in GFR observed during development.

Not yet defined is the role that the tubule may play in controlling glomerular filtration. Experimental evidence points toward the existence of a regulatory mechanism whereby a low tubular reabsorptive capacity results in a low rate of filtration. Since, during most of infancy, striking limitations exist in the reabsorptive capacity of the tubules, such a mechanism might have a significant influence on the rate of glomerular filtration.

Tubular Function

REABSORPTIVE MECHANISMS. The daily rate of urinary output represents only a small fraction of the glomerular ultrafiltrate. In adult man, about 175 liters of filtrate, which contain some 25,000 mEq of sodium chloride, are reabsorbed daily, compared with about 9 liters of fluid and 1,300 mEq of sodium chloride reabsorbed by the kidney of the newborn. Expressed relative to body weight or the size of the extracellular compartment the rates in the newborn and the adult are similar, representing a turnover of about four times the total body content of sodium and water.

In the mammalian nephron about 70 to 75 percent of the filtered sodium chloride and fluid is reabsorbed in the proximal convolution. Simultaneous measurements of electrochemical potential gradients and the direction and magnitude of net ion movement permit characterization of the nature of these reabsorptive mechanisms (Fig. 1). When net transport takes place against an electrochemical gradient, and requires energy, it is called active. Active transport excludes, therefore, passive diffusion or bulk movement of fluid. It includes, on the other hand, carrier-mediated transport along an electrochemical gradient, provided the process is energy consuming and the rate of transport exceeds that expected to occur as a result of the electrochemical forces operating at the level of the respective membrane. Substances actively reabsorbed by the proximal tubule include sodium, amino acids, calcium, phosphorus, potassium, organic anions, and vitamin D.

Sodium diffuses from the proximal tubule into the cell along an electrochemical gradient, but its extrusion from the cell takes place against such a gradient. Potassium is transported actively across the luminal cell boundary against an electrochemical potential, while net movement across the peritubular cell border occurs by passive diffusion. Chloride ions

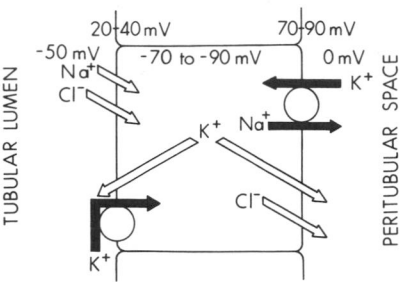

Fig. 2. Ion transport by a distal tubular cell. See legend, Figure 1.

are reabsorbed passively in proximal tubules but the exact nature of the process at the luminal membrane is not known, and may be ionic diffusion or carrier mediated transport. Transport of chloride out of the cells occurs along an electrochemical gradient.

In the loop of Henle about 15 percent of the filtered sodium is reabsorbed, mainly in relationship to the concentrating and diluting mechanism (see below). The remaining 10 to 15 percent is reabsorbed in the distal tubule. Virtually all filtered potassium is reabsorbed in the proximal tubule, the excreted moiety being added to the distal tubular fluid by active secretion. The nature of chloride transport in the distal nephron is still controversial, some evidence suggesting an active mechanism.

Whereas the proximal tubule reabsorbs most of the substances present in the glomerular filtrate, either in an indiscriminate fashion or with only gross regulation, the distal nephron (distal convoluted tubule and collecting duct) performs the "fine tuning" which allows the kidney to fulfill its regulatory function (Fig. 2).

SECRETORY MECHANISMS. Two mechanisms for active tubular secretion of organic substances, both in the proximal tubule, have been characterized. One serves as a transport pathway for a variety of organic acids, including creatinine, para-aminohippurate (PAH), and penicillin. The other one transports organic bases such as guanidine, choline, and histamine.

Knowledge concerning the capacity for transport of the tubule in the developing kidney is limited. One micropuncture study in young rats showed a low capacity for sodium reabsorption by the proximal tubule when compared to the adult animal. The Tm^* for glucose has been found to be 59 ± 11 mg/minute/1.73 m^2 in the newborn, 175 ± 19 at 3 months of age, and 364 ± 35 and 303 ± 29 in adult

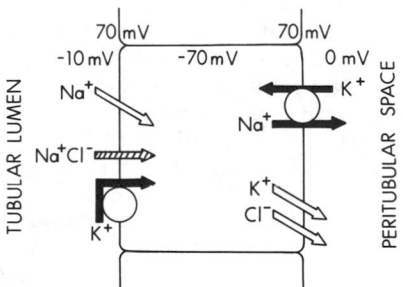

Fig. 1. Ion transport by a cell of the proximal tubule. Open arrows represent passive diffusion, hatched arrows carrier-mediated passive transfer, and solid arrows active transport. The figures represent electrical potential differences.

---

* An extensively used method to evaluate renal functional capacity is to determine the highest rate at which a given substance can be reabsorbed or secreted by the tubule. This is called the "tubular transport maximum" or the Tm of that substance.

men and women respectively. The maximum secretory capacity for para-aminohippurate has been found to be 20 ± 6 mg/minute/1.73 m^2 in full-term infants. The mean increases to 40 at 3 months of age, and to 50 at 6 months. In the adult it is 80 ± 16 mg/minute/1.73 m^2.

Glomerulotubular Interrelations

It is well established that under varying experimental conditions a proportionality is maintained between the amount filtered and the amount reabsorbed at the level of the whole kidney as well as at the level of individual nephrons. As an example of this, the fraction of sodium which is reabsorbed in the proximal tubule is constant over a wide range of filtration rates. This phenomenon has been named glomerulotubular balance.

During infancy the kidney undergoes both morphologic and functional changes which affect to varying degrees different parts of the nephron and of the kidney, altering the relationship between the glomerulus and the tubule, i.e., between the capacity to filter and the capacity to handle the filtered load. The consequence is a continually changing state of glomerulotubular balance.

Studies performed almost half a century ago have shown a strong predominance of glomerular tissue over tubular tissue in the newborn animal. More recently, this finding has been confirmed in the human. In one study in a full-term infant the diameter of the glomeruli averaged 116 μ and the length of the proximal tubule 1.79 mm. This compares to a glomerular diameter of about 200 μ and a proximal tubular length of about 20 mm in the adult. Thus, whereas the increase in glomerular size is less than twofold, the increase in proximal tubular length exceeds tenfold. The mean ratio of glomerular surface to proximal tubular volume has been found to be 27.8 in a full-term infant, 13.4 in a 3-month-old infant, and 3.1 in an adult. This indicates that in the infant the glomeruli are disproportionately large relative to the proximal tubules. Nephron heterogeneity also characterizes the developing kidney, with tubules varying in length over a tenfold range, but with a rather small variation in glomerular size. The fact that these morphologic features are more prominent in the renal cortex, which is onto- and phylogenetically newer than the medullary area, and that they disappear with age, proves their developmental origin.

Both glomerular preponderance and nephronic heterogeneity are expressed at the functional level. Tm_{PAH} in the infant is about 0.10 mg per gram of kidney weight compared to about 0.30 mg per gram in the adult. Therefore, from a functional point of view, there is only one-third as much proximal tissue per unit weight in the kidney of the newborn as there is later in life. This relatively low level of maturation of the tubular capacity for transport, together with a relatively higher capacity for glomerular filtration, i.e., glomerular preponderance, accounts for certain characteristics of kidney function in infancy.

Serum concentrations at which glucose and bicarbonate appear in the urine are lower in infancy than later in life. The net percent tubular reabsorption of amino acids and phosphate is low. The average penicillin to inulin ratio in the urine has been found to be 2.2 in premature infants and 4.2 in older children. Since penicillin is actively secreted by the tubule and inulin concentration is a measure of glomerular filtration rate, this finding supports the hypothesis of greater immaturity of tubular than glomerular function in early life.

Simultaneous measurements of glomerular filtration rate and effective renal plasma flow in early infancy have revealed values of filtration fraction (GFR/ERPF) ranging from 0.32 to 0.34 compared to a range of values of 0.19 to 0.20 in adult man. These data initially were interpreted as providing additional evidence for glomerular preponderance. Subsequently the extraction ratio of PAH was found to range between 0.50 and 0.80 during the first three months of life, which represents on the average 30 percent less than the adult value of 0.95. Correction for this extraction ratio yields a mean filtration fraction of 0.23, a value which is only slightly higher than that observed in the adult.

More recent studies on the intrarenal distribution of blood flow suggest that a significant part of the blood going to the cortex at this age may represent nutrient flow which is not filtered. In addition a higher proportion of the total renal blood flow is distributed to the juxtamedullary nephrons. The fraction of postglomerular flow that passes through the vasa recta thus bypasses the secretory sites of the proximal tubules. Under these circumstances the ratio of GFR to ERPF does not represent an index of the balance between glomerular and tubular function and the filtration fraction does not have the generally accepted physiologic meaning.

Although morphologic characteristics play an important role in the overall picture of glomerulotubular imbalance in early life, this is by no means the only contributing factor. Progress in histochemistry has made possible the mapping of enzymatic activity in the developing kidney of experimental animals. In agreement with the finding of structural immaturity of the outer cortex, little enzymatic activity has been found in this area. Even in tubules which have reached morphologic maturity, the activity of mitochondrial ATPase and of succinic dehydrogenase is less than in the adult. In contrast, there is greater activity in the medulla of enzymes of mitochondrial origin, the activity being even greater than in the adult kidney.

The mechanism(s) responsible for enzymatic maturation are yet to be determined. One possible contributing factor is substrate-induced stimulation. Several studies have shown that the capacity to secrete PAH increases significantly following ingestion of a high-protein diet. The capacity of the tubules to transport organic acids can be enhanced by administration of penicillin, which, as already mentioned, is excreted by active secretion.

In summary, during intrauterine life glomerular development prevails over tubular development and medullary development precedes and exceeds cortical development. In early postnatal life, glomerular filtration rates are low, as a result of relatively impermeable basement membranes, high intrarenal vascular resistance, and low net driving force for filtration. However, since tubular transport capacity proportionally is even lower, a state of glomerulotubular imbalance, characterized by glomerular preponderance, exists during infancy. This is expressed in a limited capacity of the nephrons to handle the filtered load, which results in urinary losses of substances such as glucose, amino acids, phosphate, and calcium. Furthermore, working under conditions close to maximum transport capacity, the kidney is limited in its ability to adapt under conditions of stress.

Renal Control Mechanisms

The complex systems that control homeostasis are of two principal types: steady state and negative feedback. In a steady-state system a change in one variable is minimized by a change in one or more covariables. Only the variable and the effector organ are involved in such a mechanism, and the degree of control achieved is not very tight. The concentrations in plasma of urea and creatinine seem to be under the control of a simple steady-state mechanism in which the glomeruli represent the end organs.

The negative feedback systems are much more complex and are able to provide a much finer degree of control. They can be located within the effector organ itself or be remote from it. In a negative feedback system the change in the controlled variable determines a change in a servo-elementlike mechanism which causes a change in the opposite direction in the effector organ. The metabolism of salt and water and, probably in part, acid excretion are controlled by such systems.

In general, the steady-state systems are better developed in infancy than the more complex feedback systems. In the following sections the mechanisms controlling three essential body constituents will be considered: those for water, sodium, and hydrogen ion.

CONTROL OF WATER EXCRETION. Under usual circumstances about 99 percent of the water filtered by the glomeruli is reabsorbed passively by the tubules, as a result of the active transport of sodium. In order to maintain the osmolality of the body fluids, in face of wide variations in intake and extrarenal loss, the amount of water excreted per unit of urinary solute can be varied over a tremendous range. The mature kidney is able to produce a urine as dilute as 50

mOsm/L under conditions of water diuresis and as concentrated as 1,300 mOsm/L during antidiuresis.

There are three distinct areas for water movement along the nephron: the proximal tubule, where the amount of water reabsorbed is totally dependent on the reabsorption of sodium, and both the reabsorbate and the fluid delivered into more distal parts of the nephron are always isosmotic; the distal tubule, including the loops of Henle, where the amount of water that is reabsorbed varies, but is always somewhat less than the rate of reabsorption of sodium, the tubular fluid ultimately becoming hypotonic; and the collecting duct, where the amount of water reabsorbed is determined not only by the rate of sodium reabsorption and the permeability characteristics of the membrane, but also by the capacity of the medulla to concentrate solute. The two latter segments, namely the distal nephron (including the loops of Henle) and the collecting duct, are involved in the process of urinary concentration and dilution, and need to be considered in more detail.

In order to understand this process some knowledge about countercurrent multipliers is necessary (Fig. 3). The descending and ascending limbs of the loops of Henle are arranged as two parallel tubes connected in a hairpin manner, in which flow takes place in opposite directions. This structure, which is able to transport sodium actively, has therefore the characteristics of a countercurrent multiplier. In such a system small differences in gradients can be multiplied as a function of length. In the particular instance of the kidney, the active transport of sodium out of the ascending limb of the loops of Henle coupled with the relative impermeability to water of this site produces hypertonicity of the interstitium, causing passive movement of water out of and net movement of sodium into the descending limb. A steady state is reached in which the interstitium and the fluid in the descending limb become more and

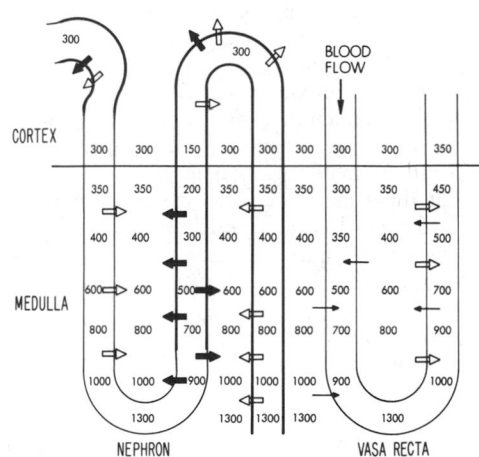

Fig. 3. Countercurrent multiplication and countercurrent exchange in the formation of hypertonic urine. Solid arrows indicate active transport of sodium, open arrows passive movement of water, and thin arrows passive diffusion of sodium.

more concentrated from the cortex to the medullary tip, and fluid in the ascending limb becomes more and more dilute on its way up toward the cortex.

This system allows for both urinary dilution as well as concentration. In the absence of ADH, the distal and collecting ducts are impermeable to water, and the dilute fluid that leaves the ascending limb of the loops of Henle becomes progressively more dilute as additional solute is removed in these structures. Maximal water diuresis, therefore, represents maximal trapping of water within the nephron, coupled with maximal pumping of sodium out.

Increase in the tonicity of blood is a stimulus for secretion of ADH, which acts to render the collecting duct permeable to water. Hypotonic fluid leaving the loops of Henle and the distal convolution becomes isotonic as it equilibrates with the interstitium of the cortex. Concentration of the urine occurs during its passage through the collecting duct as it traverses the medulla, passive outward movement of water being induced by the progressively increased hypertonicity of the interstitium.

Urinary concentration and dilution obviously are not all or none phenomena, the rate of urine flow, i.e., the rate of excretion of water, varying inversely with the amount of ADH present as a continuous function.

During the first few days of life the newborn does not respond to a water load. By the end of the first week the response to a decrease in plasma osmolality is prompt and the degree of urinary dilution achieved is comparable to that observed in the adult. However, the rate of urinary flow is lower, and the infant stops excreting water at an accelerated rate before the entire load has been eliminated. This suggests an immaturity of the underlying control mechanism and renders the infant more vulnerable to excess administration of water.

The capacity to concentrate the urine in response to water deprivation matures more slowly than the diluting capacity. Following maximal stimulation, young infants usually are unable to concentrate their urine to more than 700 mOsm/L, compared to 1,300 mOsm/L in the older child or adult. One of the contributing factors in this limitation is the shortness of the loops of Henle and, probably, a low capacity of the tubules to reabsorb sodium. Of even greater importance, however, may be the infant's low rate of excretion of urea, resulting from the strongly anabolic state which characterizes this period of life. When infants are fed urea or high-protein diets, their ability to concentrate the urine approaches adult values.

Information concerning the rate of release of antidiuretic hormone and the sensitivity of the end organ to it is controversial. During osmotic diuresis, urines hypotonic to plasma have been observed in infants, possibly indicating incomplete equilibration between tubular and interstitial fluid. This could be due to relative impermeability of the tubules, unavailability or impaired responsiveness to ADH, or a combination of both.

It should be emphasized that the limitation in concentrating capacity observed during the first few weeks of life does not significantly jeopardize the well-being of the infant. Due to his relatively large surface area, the infant loses large amounts of water via nonrenal routes (skin and lungs). In view of this, an increase in concentrating capacity to mature levels would save only trivial amounts of water.

CONTROL OF SODIUM EXCRETION. Sodium is the major cation of the extracellular fluid and, therefore, is directly linked to variation in extracellular volume. Its reabsorption and excretion are tightly controlled by a complex mechanism which is only partially defined. No secretory mechanism for sodium exists; sodium is excreted to the degree that the amount reabsorbed is smaller than the amount filtered. The latter is directly proportional to the rate of glomerular filtration, which is controlled through the sympathetic nervous system and unidentified intrarenal and extrarenal mechanisms. Tubular reabsorption is controlled by the adrenal cortex, peritubular physical factors, and other mechanisms related to variations in intravascular volume or filling.

The lack of a secretory mechanism for sodium has been explained on the basis of the phylogenetic need of terrestrial vertebrates to conserve, rather than to excrete, sodium. Since ontogenesis repeats phylogenesis, one would expect to find the newborn better equipped to withstand the stress of sodium deficiency than that of sodium excess. The response of infants to sodium restriction has not been tested adequately. Considerable data are available, however, suggesting significant limitations in response to sodium loading.

When a sodium solution is administered intravenously to an adult there is an almost immediate increase in urine volume, the excess fluid being excreted within 2 or 3 hours. A proportionately similar volume of saline infused into an infant elicits after a much longer delay only a small increase in the rate of urine flow; the excretion of the excess load takes three to four times longer.

Infants fed diets with high sodium content develop a measurable expansion of their extracellular compartment and, switched abruptly to such a regimen, they may become edematous. No careful study has been done in order to test the capacity of the infant to adjust to relatively small changes in sodium intake. The tolerance to variation in intake arising from the differences in sodium content of proprietary formulas suggests that the newborn is able to handle an intake of sodium varying between 5 and 20 mEq per day. For an older infant, receiving a diversified diet, the amount can increase to 50 mEq per day. Recent evidence indicates, however, that when an infant between 5 and 7 months of age is given a diet with a sodium content in excess of 50 mEq per day he starts retaining sodium. It is not known to what degree sodium is retained before a new steady state is reached. It is likely that a relatively high degree of expansion is needed in order to elicit a response of the control mechanism.

ACID-BASE REGULATION. The important role played by the bicarbonate-carbonic acid buffer system in acid-base homeostasis derives not from its high buffering capacity, since this is restricted by its pK which is remote from the normal pH of the blood, but rather from the fact that its two components are regulated by very effective physiologic systems: the concentration of carbonic acid is controlled by the respiratory system and the concentration of bicarbonate is controlled by the kidney.

The net effect of intermediary metabolism is the production of a hydrogen ion load which must be neutralized by an equivalent amount of buffer, approximately 50 to 100 mEq/1.73 m²/24 hours. This is accomplished by the active secretion of hydrogen ion by the renal tubular cells (Fig. 4), which results in reabsorption of filtered bicarbonate, and thus its conservation, and formation of new bicarbonate by net excretion of hydrogen into the urine in combination with a number of buffers. Hydrogen ion that is excreted following titration within the tubule of filtered substances such as phosphate and creatinine is referred to as titratable acid. Additional hydrogen ion is excreted as ammonium (NH_4^+), following titration of ammonia (NH_3), which is synthesized by the tubule from glutamine and other amino acids and secreted into the distal nephron.

Although immediately following birth the newborn seems to be in a state of relative acidemia when compared to his mother, blood samples collected at 1 day of age from the left atrium of full-term infants have been found to have a mean pH of 7.40. This does not hold true for premature infants, whose blood pH can remain acid for several weeks. The main feature of this "acidotic" state is a relatively low concentration of bicarbonate in plasma, secondary to the inability of the immature kidney to con-serve this ion. In the adult the threshold for bicarbonate, i.e., the plasma concentration below which urine is bicarbonate free, ranges between 25 and 27 mmoles per liter; during the first year of life, in contrast, it is in the range of 21.5 to 22.5. Furthermore, depending on their dietary intake, young infants may excrete little phosphate in their urine and, as a consequence, be limited in their capacity to excrete titratable acid. Production of ammonia by the kidney in response to administration of acidifying salts also is low by adult standards. After 1 month of age, however, infants fed cow's milk formulas excrete hydrogen ion at rates comparable to those observed in older children. They are unable, however, to increase these rates substantially in response to acid loading, which suggests again that the kidney is working close to its maximum capacity. This fact, added to the low threshold for bicarbonate, explains why the ability of the infant to maintain the pH of the body fluids within the normal range is so often overtaxed during states of disease.

REFERENCES

Barnett, H. L. Kidney function in young infants. Pediatrics, 5:171, 1950.
Edelmann, C. M., Jr., and Spitzer, A. The maturing kidney. J. Pediat., 75:509, 1969.
——— and Spitzer, A. The kidney. In Smith, C. A., and Nelson, N. M., eds., The Physiology of the Newborn Infant, 4th ed. Springfield, Ill., Charles C Thomas, Publisher, 1972.
McCance, R. A. Age and renal function. In Black, D. A. K., ed., Renal Disease. Philadelphia, F. A. Davis Co., 1962, p. 157.
Pitts, R. F. Physiology of the Kidney and Body Fluids, 2nd ed. Chicago, Year Book Medical Publishers, Inc., 1968.
Smith, H. W. Renal function in infancy and childhood. In The Kidney. New York, Oxford University Press, 1951, p. 492.
Vernier, R. L., and Smith, F. G., Jr. Fetal and neonatal kidney. In Assali, N. S., ed., Biology of Gestation. New York, Academic Press, Inc., 1968, Vol. II, p. 225.
Vogh, B., and Cassin, S. Correlations of renal function and morphogenesis in the embryo and neonate. In Sunderman, F. W., and Sunderman, F. W., Jr., eds., Laboratory Diagnosis of Kidney Diseases. St. Louis, Warren H. Green, Inc., 1970, p. 21.

22.3

CLINICAL EVALUATION OF RENAL FUNCTION

ADRIAN SPITZER

No single test is able to provide comprehensive information about the status of the kidney. The tests available measure specific aspects of regulation· and

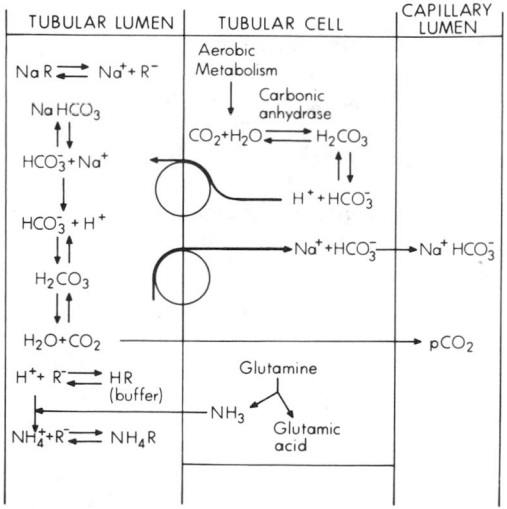

Fig. 4. Mechanisms involved in reabsorption of filtered bicarbonate and in excretion of hydrogen ion in urine.

of urine production; several may be necessary in order to define adequately the clinical condition of the patient.

Urine Analysis

Prompt examination of a freshly voided *random urine specimen* is of great value in the examination for renal disease. If urine is not examined soon after voiding, formed elements may have disappeared. Thus, although the first urine specimen in the morning has the advantage of being concentrated, it may not be possible in the nonhospitalized patient to perform the appropriate examinations without undue delay.

Urine should be free of protein when tested with 10 percent sulfosalicylic acid or with paper strips impregnated with bromphenol blue (Albustix). Both these methods detect as little as 5 to 10 mg of protein per 100 ml of urine. It should be recognized that if the urine is very dilute significant degrees of proteinuria can escape detection. Not infrequently proteinuria is found on a single examination in an apparently healthy child. Repeat examination usually is negative. Persistently positive results, even if proteinuria is minimal, necessitate further investigation.

Examination of the urinary sediment following centrifugation of 10 ml of urine for 5 minutes should reveal no more than 2 to 4 white blood cells per high-power field, usually no red cells, and rarely any casts. Casts are cylindrical masses of agglutinated material formed in the distal parts of the nephron, from protein or from protein and cells. The presence of more than a few cellular casts in the sediment is indicative of renal disease. Red cell casts are pathognomonic of glomerulonephritis, but not specific for any type.

Bacteriuria is evaluated by direct examination of the urinary sediment for the presence of organisms, as well as by cultural methods. These are discussed on page 1541.

The *Addis count* was devised in order to examine urine quantitatively, making it possible to express results as *rates* of excretion of cells and casts rather than *concentrations*. In addition, the Addis count specimen may be used conveniently to determine rates of excretion of protein and as a test of concentrating performance.

The child is instructed to have a normal noon meal and then, except for a dry supper, to thirst and fast totally until the following morning. Starting in the evening, just prior to going to bed, the bladder is emptied and the time of this "discard" specimen is noted. A timed collection of urine is then begun, which includes all urine passed during the night (if any) as well as the first urine voided the next morning. Under these conditions urinary osmolarity in healthy children aged 2 to 16 averages 1,090 mOsm/L with a range of 870 to 1,310 (mean ±2

SD). Data in children below 2 years of age are limited, but a concentration of at least 800 mOsm/L should be achieved by subjects between 3 months and 2 years of age. During the period 1 week to 3 months, an osmolarity of 700 or more is expected.

Good correlation is found under most circumstances between concentrating performance and GFR. Significant impairment in concentrating ability in association with normal GFR may be indicative of an acquired disorder, such as pyelonephritis (p. 1540), potassium deficiency (p. 1508), or hypercalciuria (p. 1508). It may be found also in specific diseases, such as sickle-cell anemia (p. 1510), diabetes insipidus (Sec. 16.12), or nephronophthisis (p. 1515).

The great majority of Addis count specimens reveal no protein when tested by conventional chemical methods. Up to 50 mg of protein per 12 hours is usually considered normal in the adult, although data from our laboratory suggest that 10 to 20 mg may be the upper limit of normal in children.

The numbers of cells and casts in a measured aliquot of urine are estimated quantitatively in a counting chamber. An amount of urine equivalent to that passed in a period of 20 minutes is centrifuged for 5 minutes at 3,500 rpm and the sediment is resuspended in a volume of 1 ml. All nine large squares on one side of a standard counting chamber (0.9 mm^3) are examined. The sum of each element times 40,000 represents the rate of excretion of that element per 12 hours.* Up to 1 million white blood cells and 0.25 million red blood cells are considered normal in children, with perhaps up to 0.5 to 0.75 million red blood cells in adults. Since no more than 5,000 casts per 12 hours are excreted by normal subjects, under the conditions outlined for the Addis count, casts usually are not found in the absence of disease.

Tests of Renal Function

PLASMA UREA AND CREATININE. The elimination of most waste products from the bloodstream depends on the adequacy of the filtering process. In dehydration, circulatory failure, and intrinsic renal disease, the rate of glomerular filtration drops, and the concentrations of the excretory products in the blood rise. The concentrations of urea and creatinine in plasma or serum, therefore, commonly are used to

---

* The volume of the aliquot is calculated as follows:

$$\text{aliquot volume} = \frac{20 \times \text{total volume}}{\text{length of collection (minutes)}}$$

This fraction represents one thirty-sixth of a 12-hour period. The volume in which the cells are counted is 0.9 mm^3. The number of cells per 1.0 ml is calculated by multiplying the actual count by $\frac{1,000}{0.9}$. Therefore, actual cell count $\times 36 \times \frac{1,000}{0.9} =$ cell count per 12 hours.

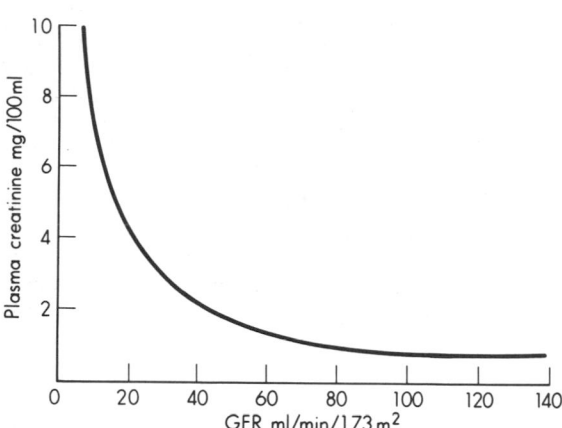

Fig. 5. Relationship between concentration of creatinine in the serum and rate of glomerular filtration. A similar correlation applies to urea.

assess renal function. When the production rate is constant the relationship between plasma levels and GFR is hyperbolic, as seen in Figure 5. It should be appreciated that filtration rate can be less than 50 percent of normal with the urea or creatinine level still within what is considered "normal limits." This is explained by the relatively wide range of values in the normal population as well as by the inherent variability of the methods of chemical analysis. The issue is further complicated by changes in plasma concentrations which occur with age. It is frequently overlooked that the urea nitrogen and creatinine concentrations of a 1-year-old child are usually not more than 10 and 0.5 mg per 100 ml, respectively. Levels of urea and creatinine well within the accepted normal range for older children and adults might, therefore, signify in infants a substantial impairment in glomerular filtration.

CLEARANCE METHODS. The rate of excretion of a substance by the kidney is not a measure of intrinsic excretory capacity since the rate of excretion depends also on the intake or rate of production. A better estimate of renal capacity is gained from the amount of blood (or plasma) that would have had to have been cleared completely of the substance per unit time to provide for the rate of excretion observed in the urine. This value, referred to as the renal clearance, is given by the formula:

$$\frac{U \times V}{P} = C$$

in which U and P are, respectively, concentrations in urine and plasma (or serum) of the substance under consideration, V is the rate of urine flow, and C is the renal clearance of that substance. Conventionally, clearances are expressed in milliliters per minute related to some unit of body size, usually 1 or 1.73 m² of body surface area.

GLOMERULAR FILTRATION RATE (GFR). Estimates of GFR probably provide a better assessment of the progression of renal disease than any other test of renal function. A substance used to measure the rate of glomerular filtration should not be bound by plasma proteins, should be freely filtered at the glomerular level, must be neither secreted nor reabsorbed by the tubule, and must be physiologically inert. *Inulin*, a polymer of fructose, has been found to fulfill all these requirements and consequently its clearance is used as the reference for measurement of glomerular filtration rate. The drawbacks in its use are the necessity for continuous intravenous infusion and the rather elaborate chemical analysis required. Clearance of inulin in the adult male and female are, respectively, 127 (21.5)* and 117 (16.4) ml/minute/1.73 m². In the first few days of life, GFR in full-term infants may be as low as 25 to 30 ml/minute/1.73 m². It reaches 50 to 60 by several weeks, from which point it gradually increases, reaching adult levels by 12 to 18 months of age.

Although each has its limitations, both *urea* and *creatinine clearances* provide reasonable estimates of GFR. At rates of urine flow above 2 ml/minute/ 1.73 m², approximately 60 percent of filtered urea is excreted. Since the portion excreted falls unpredictably when the rate of urine flow is below 2 ml/ minute, it is essential to maintain rates above this level throughout the collection periods. To this end the subject is given water to drink at a rate of 20 ml per kg over a period of 60 to 90 minutes. The bladder is emptied and three 20-minute collection periods are carried out. Following voiding of the third specimen, a single blood sample is obtained. Since serum urea changes very little in the postabsorptive state and GFR in man is not influenced by diet, breakfast need not be withheld. It is important, however, that the child remain supine at quiet bed rest throughout the test.

Assuming that under these conditions 60 percent of filtered urea is excreted, the normal rate of urea clearance is 0.6 times 127 ml/minute/1.73 m², or 75 ml/minute/1.73 m². The lower limit of normal is 60 ml/minute/1.73 m².

Creatinine clearance has the advantage of being much less dependent on rate of urine flow. The clearance can be performed as described above for urea, or it can be performed on 12- or 24-hour urine specimens, minimizing collection and timing errors. Since creatinine is filtered as well as secreted into the urine its clearance is greater than the true GFR. However, because of the presence of interfering chromogens in the plasma, the plasma level of creatinine usually is overestimated and hence the clearance comes close to the true GFR.

In chronic renal disease, when GFR has fallen to 25 ml per minute or below, urea and creatinine

---

* Here and in the following text, values are given as the mean followed in parenthesis by the value of one standard deviation.

clearances provide a very accurate estimate of GFR. At this stage of disease, as discussed in the next chapter, there is marked hyperperfusion of the residual nephrons, resulting in excretion of close to 100 percent of filtered urea. At the same time, filtered creatinine provides most of the creatinine excreted, with relatively little coming from tubular secretion. Thus, urea clearance is just below the true GFR, creatinine clearance is just above it, and the mean is equal to GFR.

Recent progress has made possible the use of *isotope methodology* and mathematical analysis of *plasma disappearance curves* for measurements of GFR. This method obviates the need for urine collections and substitutes isotope counting for tedious and often inaccurate chemical determinations. Because of their short half-lives and the fact that they are excreted solely by glomerular filtration, ^{125}I-iothalamate and ^{51}Cr-EDTA are suitable isotopes. The amount of radiation from one procedure is about 40 μr which is, e.g., only one-fifth the amount of daily background radiation in New York City.

RENAL BLOOD FLOW. Since almost all the postglomerular blood perfuses the renal tubules before entering the venous drainage, certain substances that are actively secreted by the tubules, such as *p*-aminohippurate (PAH), are removed almost completely from the blood on one passage through the kidney. At plasma levels of PAH below 4 to 5 mg per 100 ml, an average of only 10 percent of the renal arterial concentration is found in renal venous blood. Arterial minus venous concentration, divided by arterial concentration, termed the extraction ratio, ranges from 0.85 to 1.0. Measurement of the clearance of PAH provides therefore a close estimate of renal plasma flow (RPF). Renal blood flow (RBF) can be calculated with knowledge of the hematocrit:

$$RBF = \frac{RPF}{1 - hct}$$

Values of PAH clearance in adult males and females are, respectively, 643 (140) and 585 (128) ml/minute/1.73 m². The average value for children aged 2 to 12 has been found to be 654 (120). In patients with renal disease PAH extraction varies widely and unpredictably and thus its clearance is an unreliable measure of renal plasma flow. Therefore, although PAH clearance has been of great value in physiologic investigation, it has limited use in clinical assessment.

A single injection method based on the analysis of the plasma disappearance curve of ^{131}I-orthoiodohippurate can be used for measurement of RPF. It has the advantages previously mentioned with regard to isotope techniques. The procedure results in about 14 μr of total body radiation.

The fraction of renal plasma flow filtered is referred to as the filtration fraction, FF; it is calculated from the ratio of C_{In} to C_{PAH}. Values of 0.20 (0.03), 0.21 (0.04), and 0.20 (0.04) have been found in adult males, adult females, and children aged 2 and over, respectively. Since values for PAH clearance in young infants range from 20 to 50 percent of adult values, FF at this age has been calculated to be as high as 0.5. However, even at low concentrations of PAH in plasma, the extraction ratio in young infants may be considerably below 0.9, resulting in falsely low values of RPF and proportionately high values of FF.

EXCRETION OF HYDROGEN ION. Tests of renal acidifying mechanisms are useful in evaluating patients either with specific tubular abnormalities or with generalized disturbances in tubular functions.

Total CO_2 and pH are measured in blood and in one or two 1-hour collections of urine. A dose of ammonium chloride calculated to reduce blood total CO_2 by 4 to 6 mmoles/L is administered orally over the next hour. This dose is calculated on the assumption that total body water is 60 to 70 percent of body weight. For example, a patient weighing 10 kg is to be tested. His blood CO_2 is 23 mmoles/L and it is planned to lower this to 18. The dosage of ammonium chloride required is $0.7 \times 10 \times (23 - 18)$ = 35 mEq or 1.8 g of ammonium chloride (1.0 mEq of ammonium chloride = 53 mg).

Urine is collected at hourly intervals for the following 4 to 5 hours. Maximal values in normal infants and children are shown in Table 1.

TABLE 1.   *Excretion of Hydrogen Ion*

	Infants During First Year of Life	Children 3 to 15 Years
Urine pH	$\leqq 5.0$	$\leqq 5.5$
Titratable acid $\mu Eq/min/1.73$ m²	62 (43-111)	52 (33-71)
Ammonium $\mu Eq/min/1.73$ m²	57 (42-79)	73 (46-100)

Total acid excretion is impaired in chronic renal failure, hypercalcemia, potassium deficiency, and tubular disorders (notably distal tubular acidosis), although ammonium excretion is normal in potassium deficiency and most tubular disorders. In early chronic renal failure, on the other hand, ammonium excretion may be impaired at a time when total acid excretion is normal.

Radiography of the Kidney

A film of the abdomen is a simple and valuable procedure in the investigation for disease of the kidney. The normal organ has a smooth outline. An irregular edge may be indicative of scarring following infection or of vascular obstruction. It should be differentiated from lobulation which is characteristic of the fetal kidney but can persist into ex-

TABLE 2. *Kidney Size**

Surface Area	Right Kidney	Left Kidney
m²	cm	cm
0.2	6.2	6.0
0.3	6.6	6.6
0.5	7.6	7.6
0.7	8.5	8.6
1.0	9.9	10.2
1.2	10.8	11.3
1.5	12.2	12.8

*The length of the kidneys as a function of body surface area. The range around each mean is approximately ±1 cm. (From Olbing. *Harnwegsentzündungen bei Kindern und Jugendlichen*, 1971. Courtesy of Thieme, Stuttgart.)

trauterine life. The size of the kidney varies with age (Table 2). A large kidney may be the result of hypertrophy or hydronephrosis. A small kidney, in the pediatric age group, is in most instances a congenitally dysplastic or hypoplastic organ. Since 90 percent of renal calculi are radiopaque, radiographic examination should be done in all patients with renal colic. Occasionally nephrocalcinosis will be seen, the most common cause in children being distal renal tubular acidosis.

Intravenous and retrograde pyelography, cystography, renal angiography, and renography are discussed in the sections on urogenital disorders (p. 1549) and hypertension (Sec. 21.4).

Percutaneous Renal Biopsy

Percutaneous needle biopsy has been applied extensively in the past decade to the diagnosis and study of renal disease. Its value for both clinical and research purposes is now firmly established.

When renal biopsy was first introduced as a diagnostic tool very careful selection of patients for the procedure was made. Currently, however, as both its safety as well as its importance have become recognized, it is included more and more as part of the routine diagnostic work-up of patients with parenchymal renal disease.

Examination of renal tissue is of value to the clinician in the resolution of diagnostic problems, as in children discovered fortuitously to have proteinuria and microscopic hematuria; as a guide to therapy, as in patients with the nephrotic syndrome unresponsive to adrenocortical steroid therapy; as a means of determining progression of disease; and in determining prognosis.

To insure minimal risk to the patient and maximal likelihood of obtaining tissue adequate for study, percutaneous renal biopsy should be done only by those thoroughly trained in the procedure. Contraindications for biopsy include the presence of only one functioning kidney, pyelonephritis, dysplastic-

hypoplastic and cystic disorders, and obstructive urologic conditions. Hypertension must be controlled with appropriate therapy before a renal biopsy is attempted. Adequate studies must be done to ensure absence of any type of bleeding disorder. Following the procedure, the patient should be kept in bed under close observation for 24 hours or as long as significant hematuria persists. Transient microscopic hematuria occurs in most patients; gross hematuria is observed rarely.

REFERENCES

Barnett, H. L., and Sereny, F. Kidney function tests in infants and children. Pediat. Clin. N. Amer., 2:191, 1955.

Lippman, R. W. Urine and Urinary Sediment, 2nd ed. Springfield, Ill., Charles C Thomas, Publ., 1957.

Reubi, F. C. Clearance Tests in Clinical Medicine. Springfield, Ill., Charles C Thomas, Publ., 1963.

Sunderman, F. W., and Sunderman, F. W., Jr., Laboratory Diagnosis of Kidney Diseases. St. Louis, Warren H. Green, Inc., 1970.

22.4
UREMIA: PATHOPHYSIOLOGY AND TREATMENT

CHESTER M. EDELMANN, JR.

Uremia is conveniently discussed under the headings *acute renal failure* and *chronic renal failure*. This section will deal with the pathophysiology and treatment of each, without regard to specific diagnostic entities.

Acute Renal Failure

The term acute renal failure is applied to the clinical syndrome of oliguria and sudden loss of renal homeostasis. Oliver's pathologic studies following traumatic and toxic injury revealed the presence of cellular necrosis in the proximal tubules when the syndrome followed exposure to certain toxins (mercuric ion, arsenic, carbon tetrachloride, diethylene glycol, and sulfonamides), in addition to the more characteristic widespread but patchy disruption of the basement membrane throughout the nephron. The latter lesion may be the only change observed when this syndrome follows a number of heterogeneous incidents, such as thermal burns, crush injury, incompatible blood transfusion, prolonged anesthesia, surgical shock, utilization of the pump oxygenator, and possibly severe diarrheal dehydration. No correlation can be shown between the clinical features and the histologic abnormalities. Moreover, in children with acute renal failure, postmortem examination of the kidneys frequently reveals no significant morphologic abnormality. The common denominator in all of these conditions may be prolonged ischemia.

In the absence of significant morphologic changes in the glomeruli, the reduced inulin clearance and the oliguria of acute renal failure have been attributed to fairly complete reabsorption of glomerular filtrate, but may alternatively be due to glomeruli which are perfused with blood but do not filter.

Acute renal failure may be caused also by extensive glomerular damage, as in acute glomerulonephritis, rapidly progressive glomerulonephritis, Goodpasture's syndrome, and the hemolytic-uremic syndrome, and is seen in association with bilateral occlusion of the renal arteries, sickle-cell crisis, myoglobinuria, and a number of other diseases.

Acute cortical and tubular necrosis is not observed commonly in the pediatric age group. Most cases have been reported in the newborn, and are attributed to obstetric complications, asphyxia, erythroblastosis, sepsis, dehydration, and hemorrhage. Recently, acute papillary necrosis following administration of radiographic material has been reported. Scattered reports of renal cortical and medullary necrosis in older infants and children have been attributed to the usual factors, including circulatory collapse, infection, nephrotoxins, vascular disease, burns, and transfusion reactions.

DIAGNOSIS. The diagnosis of acute renal failure may at times be extremely difficult. It is important early to rule out two conditions which may mimic true renal failure and which frequently are amenable to specific therapy. The first of these, termed prerenal failure, refers to decreased renal blood flow and glomerular filtration rate, and oliguria secondary to cardiovascular insufficiency. Initially, the process is rapidly reversible and there may be no renal parenchymal lesions, although if renal ischema persists, renal damage may be severe. Prerenal failure is seen in association with vascular collapse, blood loss, hypotension, and severe dehydration.

Postrenal failure refers to absence of urine secondary to urinary tract obstruction. Radiographic studies and ureteral catheterization may be necessary to make the diagnosis.

True renal failure is seen infrequently in childhood. It is observed most commonly during the course of various types of acute glomerulonephritis. The most difficult aspect of diagnosis is ruling out prerenal and postrenal causes.

The alert physician, aware of situations in which renal failure may develop, should watch the urinary output in order to detect significant oliguria which is not a response to dehydration. In general, a urine output of less than 400 ml/m²/day (approximately 15 ml/kg) in a well-hydrated individual indicates some degree of renal failure.

The excretion of small quantities of isotonic or hypotonic urine is highly suggestive of acute renal failure. Unfortunately, a moderately concentrated urine may be elaborated during the early stages.

When this is the case, fluids should be administered cautiously until better hydration is established. Urine should be collected hourly, through an indwelling catheter if necessary. If urine flow and clinical status are evaluated at hourly intervals, the situation is usually more clearly defined within 2 to 3 hours, provided arterial hypotension does not exist. Potassium salts should not be administered in rehydration therapy until the possibility of acute renal failure has been excluded.

TREATMENT. No effective measure for reversing the acute pathologic process is available. Not infrequently, congestive heart failure and death are consequent to attempts at "flushing out" the kidney. The physician's therapeutic role is to maintain normal body composition while awaiting spontaneous recovery.

Efforts should be directed toward restoration of blood and extracellular volume, if deficient. Administration of fluids to differentiate between oliguria due to dehydration and true renal failure has been discussed above. Infusion of intravenous fluid, 10 to 15 ml per kg body weight, usually will suffice.

The use of intravenous mannitol in the prevention of acute renal failure has been proposed. Current evidence indicates that when given early in the course of prerenal failure it may prevent development of renal lesions and progression to true renal failure.

Water Balance. During renal failure, water requirement is limited to that needed to replace urinary output plus insensible loss. From this must be subtracted metabolic water available from the high rate of tissue catabolism that is usually present. Water intake thus should be limited to 200 to 300 ml/m²/day, plus urinary output. The most accurate gauge of adequacy of water balance is careful daily measurement of body weight. A weight loss of about 0.5 percent per day indicates an appropriate water intake.

Electrolyte Balance. Urine output and sodium concentration should be measured daily. Provided that overhydration has not occurred, sodium losses should be replaced, preferably with sodium lactate or bicarbonate, to combat or prevent acidosis. Replacement of other electrolyte losses need not occasion concern; the problem is to prevent their accumulation in excess. Hyponatremia is unlikely to be a sign of sodium deficiency but rather an indication of water excess.

Serious acute hyperkalemia usually can be avoided by adherence to the principles of management of acute renal failure. Serum potassium levels should be followed closely in conjunction with frequent use of the electrocardiogram. If serum potassium rises above 6 mEq/L or if the sequential changes of potassium intoxication are seen in the electrocardiogram, therapy with a cation exchange resin should be instituted (see below). The emergency treatment of advanced potassium intoxication consists of administration of intravenous sodium bicarbonate or hypertonic glucose and insulin. These measures are only temporary and should be followed promptly by dialytic management.

Caloric Requirements. Tissue catabolism, with release of intracellular potassium and of phosphate and other acid products, may be prevented in large part by maintaining good nutrition. This is done with the use of nonprotein, electrolyte-free foods, although attainment of full caloric intake is almost an impossible task in the face of severe renal failure. At least one-fourth and preferably one-half of the calories should be provided as carbohydrate. Fat may be given in moderate amounts to the oliguric patient, but protein is best avoided. Ethyl alcohol, given orally or intravenously, can be used to supplement caloric intake. There is recent evidence to suggest that the use of anabolic agents such as norethandrolone may aid in minimizing protein catabolism.

Infection. The most common cause of death in patients with acute renal failure is infection, particularly of the respiratory or urinary tract. So-called prophylactic antibiotics should not be used, but rather patients should be observed closely for development of infection and treated vigorously if it occurs.

Dialysis. Dialytic therapy can be done, when indicated, even in the smallest infant. Further details concerning performance of peritoneal and extracorporeal dialysis are given below. Indications for this procedure include renal failure extending beyond 7 to 10 days, or severe volume overload, acidosis, or hyperkalemia. Blood urea nitrogen in excess of 100 to 150 mg percent usually indicates a degree of uremia that warrants dialysis.

Recovery Phase. Recovery from acute renal failure is frequently accompanied by a period of obligatory diuresis during which modification of the glomerular filtrate appears to be impaired. Adequate and appropriate fluids must be provided to prevent sodium depletion, hypovolemia, and acidosis. Following cessation of the diuretic phase, evidence of renal tubular defects (e.g., isosthenuria, renal tubular acidosis) may persist for many months.

Chronic Renal Failure

PATHOPHYSIOLOGY. The functional disturbances of chronic renal insufficiency appear to be explainable on the basis of total renal function being assumed by a small number of residual nephrons. A growing body of evidence suggests that the residual nephrons function in a qualitatively normal fashion and that their inadequate number accounts for the quantitative disturbances in overall function of the kidney, particularly the reduced capacity to excrete ammonium, total hydrogen ion, sodium, phosphate, and other anions.

In the diseased kidney, the residual nephrons are hyperperfused, i.e., there is a marked increase in rate of glomerular filtration per nephron. Although this functional adaptation may enhance the excretory capacity of the kidney, it appears to contribute to the concentrating defect and to the inability to conserve sodium.

The functional characteristics of the diseased kidney are incompletely understood. Of great importance in therapy, however, is appreciation of the reduced capacity both to excrete and to conserve, although within these narrowed limits, the kidney qualitatively may be able to function normally.

TREATMENT. Treatment of patients with chronic renal insufficiency is nonspecific unless there is a recognizable and treatable underlying condition. It is extremely important, therefore, whenever possible, to make a precise diagnosis of the cause of chronic renal insufficiency. Successful treatment of infants and children with impairment of renal function due to pyelonephritis, particularly when associated with correctable forms of obstructive uropathy, provides a striking example of the importance of this principle.

Diet. Regulation of the diet is a primary means of treating disturbances, such as chronic uremia, in which there is a decreased ability to handle some of the end products of the metabolism of foods. Unfortunately such regulation usually involves reduction of the intake or intestinal absorption of certain foods which, in the infant or child, are important for growth. Therefore, arbitrary, unnecessary restrictions should be avoided. Although these patients frequently grow very slowly, a palatable, well-balanced diet, adequate to meet caloric and other nutritional needs, should be provided.

In the asymptomatic infant or child with chronic renal insufficiency, no change should be made in the usual well-balanced diet. Patients with more severe degrees of renal insufficiency do require dietary regulation involving particularly intake of protein, osmotically active solutes, and certain electrolytes and minerals such as sodium, calcium, and phosphate.

Each 100 g of dietary protein, essential in the maintenance of a positive nitrogen balance, requires renal excretion of approximately 70 mEq of acid. In order to provide essential protein and yet not induce metabolic acidosis in patients with severe renal insufficiency, dietary protein should be limited initially to 0.3 to 0.5 g per kg of body weight per day. This amount can be increased empirically as tolerated. Protein-containing foods should be limited to those of high biologic value, i.e., providing a rich mixture of essential amino acids. These include meat, fish, eggs, cheese, and milk. The intake of high-protein vegetables, particularly those of the bean family, should be markedly curtailed. Cow's milk is an excellent source of high-biologic-value protein, but owing to its high sodium, potassium, and phosphate content it is best restricted or completely removed from the diet.

Remarkable clinical improvement has been reported in patients with advanced chronic uremia given a diet constructed to provide a minimal intake of protein in the form of essential amino acids. Although further clinical trials with this type of low-protein diet are needed, the experience reported has been successful enough to warrant clinical application. It should be noted that several authors have emphasized the failure of adults to adhere to strict, unpalatable dietary regimens. We have applied the principles underlying this type of therapy with success to infants and small children, using naturally available foods and less vigorous attempts at dietary control. Low-protein, low-electrolyte products such as Controlyte * and Resource Baking Mix * are of considerable value in providing caloric intake in the form of bread, cookies, milk shakes, etc. Infants with severe renal insufficiency often do very well on formulas with low concentrations of both electrolytes and protein.†

Arbitrary restriction of dietary sodium is one of the commonest errors in treatment of patients with renal disease. The child with hypertension, edema, or obvious salt intolerance needs restriction of dietary sodium to as little as 0.2 mEq per kg per day, whereas certain patients with chronic renal disease tend to be salt-losers and require sodium supplementation. In the absence of these complications, a normal sodium intake should be allowed. Certain milks with low sodium content (for example Lonolac, Mead Johnson Laboratories), excellent for infants and children with cardiac impairment, may be dangerous in children with renal disease owing to their high potassium content.

Most patients with renal insufficiency can be allowed to ingest water ad libitum, their water intake being regulated by their own thirst mechanisms. There may be a decrease, however, in the renal ability to conserve water requiring the provision of adequate water to prevent dehydration and hemoconcentration, particularly in hot weather and during febrile illnesses. Children allowed free access to water usually present no problem, but disturbances in water balance may occur in the infant or the sick child whose water intake is regulated by the parent or the physician.

Anorexia, nausea, and vomiting are frequent disturbances in chronic uremia. Early in the course of renal insufficiency, gastrointestinal symptoms usually respond well to simple restriction of dietary protein; in the more advanced stages, they may be exceedingly resistant to treatment. Phenothiazines, such as prochlorperazine (0.4 mg/kg/24 hours) or chlorpromazine (2 mg/kg/24 hours) given in three or four oral doses, may be very effective.

Acidosis. Patients with mild degrees of acidosis are usually asymptomatic and require no therapy other than modification of diet. The child who remains acidotic despite restriction in dietary protein may require more specific therapy.

Correction of acidosis requires administration of alkali, given usually in a dosage of 1 to 3 mEq/kg/day. After prolonged ingestion of diets low in protein and high in carbohydrate, patients with chronic acidosis may develop potassium depletion and therefore may require a mixture of sodium and potassium salts, as in the following formula, which provides 25 mEq of each cation per 15 ml:

Sodium citrate ($Na_3C_6H_5O_7 \cdot 5H_2O$), 97 g
Potassium citrate ($K_3C_6H_5O_7 \cdot H_2O$), 90 g
Water, quantum sufficit 500 ml

If there is severe reduction in glomerular filtration rate, potassium depletion is less likely and the potassium load of this solution may be excessive. In these instances, a solution of sodium citrate alone can be given.* Aluminum hydroxide, used primarily to correct hyperphosphatemia, may also serve to correct acidosis. A dosage of 50 to 150 mg/kg/day may be given.

Respiratory compensation of metabolic acidosis, resulting in low Pco_2 in blood, may be of extreme importance in preventing severe acidosis in the patient with impaired renal mechanisms for hydrogen ion excretion. Interference with alveolar ventilation secondary to pneumonia, sedatives, or thoracic surgery may result in profound acidosis and sudden death.

Disturbances in Handling of Water and Solutes. The rare patient requiring sodium supplementation to combat excessive salt losses has been mentioned. Much more common, however, is the child whose ability to excrete sodium is reduced to the level where ingestion of normal amounts of dietary sodium is excessive and results in edema. Frequently, correction is achieved by restriction of sodium intake to 0.2 to 1 mEq/kg/day. When this measure is not successful, diuretic therapy may be given. Hydrochlorothiazide appears to be the drug of choice and is given in a dosage of 2 to 4 mg/kg/day. Recent experience with furosemide in children suggests that it is a most useful diuretic. We have used it in a dose of 1 to 2 mg/kg given orally once or twice a day.

Hyperkalemia and Hypokalemia. Significant elevation of extracellular potassium concentration is not a common finding in patients with chronic renal insufficiency unless there is a marked reduction in glomerular filtration rate, oliguria, or acidosis. In these instances, exogenous sources of potassium such as drugs and antibiotics, candy, and fruits, must be carefully controlled. Diuretics may be useful in promoting urinary losses of potassium. Kayexalate (so-

---

* D. M. Doyle Pharmaceutical Co., Minneapolis, Minn.
† Two such preparations, PM 60-40 (Ross Laboratories) and SMA New Formula S-26 (Wyeth Laboratories) are commercially available.

* Although not tolerated by all patients, some find sodium bicarbonate (baking soda) to be a convenient form of therapy. One gram contains 11.9 mEq of sodium. One measuring teaspoon is approximately 3.7 g, and thus provides about 44 mEq.

dium polystyrene sulfonate, Winthrop Laboratories), a sodium-potassium exchange resin, is especially effective. It can be given orally or rectally in a starting dosage of 0.5 to 1.5 g/kg/day, with subsequent adjustment of the dosage according to need. One gram will exchange approximately 1 mEq of potassium.

Hypokalemia, due to anorexia, diarrhea, vomiting, or the injudicious use of diuretic drugs, also occurs in patients with chronic uremia. Increase in potassium intake is a simple corrective measure and may be given in a dosage calculated to provide a daily supplement of 3 to 5 mEq per kg.*

Hypocalcemia and Bone Disease. Hypocalcemia is commonly seen in patents with chronic renal disease. Although it usually causes no symptoms, muscle cramps, weakness, tetany, and convulsions may be seen occasionally. Therapy is aimed at symptomatic control and consists of a diet low in phosphate and oral administration of aluminum hydroxide and calcium. The calcium is usually given in the form of calcium lactate,† calculated to provide 10 to 20 mg of calcium per kg per day. Without supplemental vitamin D, patients with chronic renal insufficiency usually remain in negative calcium balance despite oral calcium supplementation, although recent evidence suggests that the use of calcium carbonate may obviate the need for pharmacologic doses of the vitamin.

The hypocalcemia of chronic renal disease has been attributed at least in part to relative vitamin D resistance, and therefore the use of vitamin D to promote calcium absorption from the gut has been advocated. Vitamin D may induce hypercalcemia and metastatic calcification, however, and therefore should be used with caution. Widespread arterial calcification in the absence of hypercalcemia has been reported. We recommend its use in patients in whom other measures have not been successful and then only with careful monitoring of concentrations of calcium and phosphate in serum. The serum calcium times phosphorus product should not be allowed to exceed 70. A dosage of 25,000 to 50,000 units of vitamin D daily may be given initially, but dosage levels as high as 400,000 units per day may be necessary.

Recent studies suggest that in uremic patients there may be either a deficit in the conversion of vitamin D to its active metabolite, 25-hydroxycholecalciferol (25-HCC), or an increased rate of destruction of 25-HCC. Treatment with 25-HCC rather than vitamin D, although still experimental, may prove to be effective and nontoxic.

The quantitative importance of acidosis in the pathogenesis of uremic osteodystrophy is unclear, but it seems to play some role. Correction of acidosis, therefore, is an integral part of therapy.

The bone disease of chronic renal insufficiency generally falls into one of two categories: rickets (or osteomalacia) or osteitis fibrosa. Vitamin D is the treatment of choice for the former. In osteitis fibrosa, serum calcium levels may be normal or slightly reduced, suggesting that an unusually severe degree of secondary hyperparathyroidism may play a major role. Doses of vitamin D adequate to cause healing may result in dangerous degrees of hypercalcemia. Partial parathyroidectomy has been carried out in a number of adult patients and a few children with apparently beneficial results.

Hypertension. Control of hypertension can be a large factor in prolonging survival in patients with chronic renal disease. Therapy is empirical, the particular drug and effective dose being determined by trial in each patient.

Hydrochlorothiazide, discussed previously, may be successful in controlling mild elevations of blood pressure, especially in patients with a tendency toward sodium retention.

Reserpine is perhaps the safest and simplest antihypertensive agent available. A dosage of 0.01 to 0.02 mg/kg/day in one or two divided doses is often effective and usually completely without side effects, although somnolence, headaches, nasal stuffiness, and diarrhea may be seen at higher levels. When reserpine alone does not yield normotension, hydralazine is given in addition. The effective dosage of this drug varies enormously. Therapy should be initiated at low dosage levels and adjusted over a period of days to weeks until the desired response or side effects are noted. An initial dosage of 1 or 2 mg/kg/day in four divided doses can be tried with careful monitoring of the blood pressure. Doses as high as 20 mg per kg may be required. Side effects include nausea, hypotension, headaches, and tachycardia. If blood pressure has not returned to normal levels with those agents, guanethidine or alpha-methyldopa can be given, in starting dosages of 0.2 to 0.3 mg per kg per day and 10 mg per kg per day, respectively. Guanethidine is given as a single daily dose; alpha-methyldopa is divided into two or three doses daily.

Anemia. The anemia of chronic renal disease is rarely symptomatic, although it may be persistent and severe. There is no specific therapy, assuming that iron deficiency and other nutritional lacks, such as vitamin D, folic acid, and vitamin B_{12}, have been ruled out. Blood transfusions are only of temporary value, depress the bone marrow, and are not without hazards. Sudden, unexpected, and unexplained deaths have followed transfusions of whole blood in patients with chronic renal insufficiency. Sensitization of patients from administration of blood may be of importance when subsequently considering renal transplantation. If anemia is severe and symptomatic, we recommend the infusion of washed red blood cells, which appear to cause fewer reactions than whole blood and are relatively free of leucocytes.

---

* One gram of potassium chloride contains 13.4 mEq of potassium. Potassium Triplex (Lilly) is a palatable liquid preparation which contains 15 mEq per 5 ml.

† One gram of calcium lactate, Ca $(C_3H_5O_3)_2 \cdot 5H_2O$, contains 130 mg of calcium. A variety of proprietary preparations is available.

The transfusion must be given slowly and with extreme caution, since patients with renal insufficiency may be very sensitive to small changes in vascular volume; severe hypertension may be noted after administration of blood. Concomitant administration of a potent diuretic, such as furosemide, has been advocated.

Growth Failure. The cause of growth failure in chronic renal disease is uncertain, although poor nutrition, chronic acidosis, negative calcium balance, and chronic infection may play important roles. Therapy is directed toward each separate problem or complication in an attempt to provide as healthy a milieu as possible for growth. The possible beneficial effect of growth hormone or of anabolic steroids has not been established.

Neuromuscular and Psychologic Disturbances. It is important to realize that the irritative neuromuscular phenomena commonly seen in patients with chronic uremia, including muscle twitching and convulsions, are rarely due to hypocalcemia and thus respond poorly to calcium therapy. This is probably due to the protective effect of the associated acidosis and elevated level of serum magnesium. Other than the rare instance in which hypocalcemia can be implicated, therapy is nonspecific and unsatisfactory, consisting merely of sedation.

Other types of neuromuscular disturbances include a variety of mental symptoms, ranging from depression to psychosis, and peripheral neuropathy. Treatment other than dialysis is not available.

Management of a child with chronic renal insufficiency must include psychologic support not only of the child but also of his family. Considerable understanding of child development and of the defenses used by children of different ages is required for this aspect of treatment. As in other serious diseases in which the cause is not known, the parents and older patients need to be reassured repeatedly that they are not responsible for the disease. In an illness such as chronic uremia in which medical treatment is usually so inadequate, it is important also for the physician to examine repeatedly how his own feelings may be affecting his relationship with the patient and his family.

The Effect of Chronic Uremia on Unrelated Intercurrent Disturbances. The presence of chronic renal insufficiency in an infant or child must be taken into account in the treatment of unrelated intercurrent disturbances. For example, toxic amounts of potassium may inadvertently be given in the form of potassium penicillin, and the concentration of other drugs excreted by the kidneys may reach abnormally high levels if they are given in the usual dosage. Kunin has provided excellent data concerning appropriate dosages of antibiotics in patients with renal failure. Finally, there is the recurrent and difficult problem of trying to assess how much chronic renal insufficiency may be contributing to such common events as recurrent respiratory infections and particularly psychologic disturbances.

Immunosuppressant Drugs. At present there are only limited data concerning the value of these drugs in the treatment of patients with chronic renal insufficiency. Earlier experience indicated that adrenocortical steroids were of little, if any, value and there was even some suspicion that in addition to their known undesirable side effects they accelerate loss of kidney function in some patients. Other reports have indicated that unexpected improvement has occurred in some patients given adrenocortical steroids. There is suggestive evidence that treatment with other immunosuppressant drugs, such as 6-thioguanine, azathioprine, and cyclophosphamide, may arrest or retard progression of chronic renal impairment in certain patients with various types of chronic glomerulonephritis. The data are preliminary and general recommendations regarding use of these drugs cannot be given. Children considered candidates for such therapy should be evaluated by investigators actively engaged in studying the effects of these drugs in patients with chronic renal disease.

Dialysis. Peritoneal dialysis has been used frequently in the treatment of infants and children with acute renal failure and to a much lesser degree in patients with chronic renal failure. The procedure, which is technically simpler than hemodialysis, is tolerated even by small infants. The 2-liter exchanges commonly employed in adults are too large for children. In older children a 1-liter exchange is used. In younger children and infants 50 to 100 ml per kg per exchange has been recommended. Commercially available catheters are suitable for use in children and are inserted after distending the abdomen by installation through a No. 18 needle of a volume of fluid equal to one exchange. This permits positioning the catheter within the peritoneal cavity so that free return of fluid is obtained. Commercial dialysis fluid with or without added potassium is used, with 5 mg of heparin per liter.

Usually 1.5 percent glucose dialysis fluid is employed. If it is desired to remove additional fluid from the patient, a mixture of equal parts of 1.5 percent and 7 percent glucose may be employed. We have avoided the use of 7 percent glucose dialysis fluid alone, to avoid excessively rapid transfer of fluid.

Peritoneal urea clearances relatively greater than those obtained in adults have been reported in children. It has been suggested that this is due to greater permeability of the peritoneal membrane or to the fact that the peritoneal surface area is greater relative to body size than in adults.

Dialysis can be maintained continuously for periods of 48, 72, or more hours, as needed clinically, with the risk of peritonitis increasing as the duration of dialysis is prolonged. In one child, whom we maintained with a single catheter for a period of more than 3 months, peritonitis did occur but was controlled with antibiotic therapy.

A major disadvantage of peritoneal dialysis is the large loss of protein and amino acids in the peritoneal fluid. This may be particularly troublesome in patients being maintained chronically.

Adults with terminal renal failure have been maintained with chronic hemodialysis for periods of several years. Attempts at such therapy in children although initially discouraging, more recently have met with considerable success. The technical problems are greater than in adults, particularly with regard to maintenance of cannulas. Recent experience with surgically created internal arteriovenous fistulas, which obviate the need for cannulization, is encouraging. In children, special attention must be paid to nutritional requirements, and in many instances nutritional supplements may be necessary. Despite the improved success with chronic hemodialysis in children, its major role, apart from the treatment of acute renal failure, remains the maintenance and preparation of children for renal allotransplantation.

The techniques of hemodialysis in children are essentially the same as in adults. Descriptions of techniques applicable to the pediatric age group have been presented by Lee and Sharpstone, Chamberlain et al., Kallen et al., and Fine et al.

Transplantation. As survival figures following renal homotransplantation steadily improve, this procedure becomes more and more the one of choice in the management of terminal renal failure. This is particularly true for children, in whom chronic dialysis as definitive therapy generally has not been successful. The seventh report of the kidney transplant registry showed that kidneys donated by living close relatives have a 1-year survival of 87 percent and a 2-year survival of 77 percent, whereas kidneys from cadaver sources have a 1-year survival of 42 percent and 2-year survival of 40 percent. Recent experience indicates that even better results can be anticipated when the donor is a living relative who is matched for histocompatibility antigens. Since children are likely to have healthy, young parents to serve as donors, transplantation may turn out to have its greatest success in the pediatric age group. In addition, children may experience less toxicity during immunosuppressive therapy and they are likely to be free from diseases of other body systems.

The decision regarding renal transplantation cannot be undertaken lightly; not all children with chronic uremia can be considered suitable candidates. Nevertheless, after careful evaluation of all the medical, social, and psychologic aspects, with regard both to the patient and to his family, the procedure should be considered in certain children, in whom it can be a most profitable undertaking.

REFERENCES

Anderson, J., Lee, H. A., and Stroud, C. E. Haemodialysis in infants and small children. Brit. Med. J., 1:1405, 1965.

Berlyne, G. M., Shaw, A. B., and Nilwarangkur, S. Dietary treatment of chronic renal failure. Experiences with a modified Giovanetti diet. Nephron, 2:129, 1965.

Bernstein, J., and Ruben, M. Congenital abnormalities of urinary system: II. Renal cortical and medullary necrosis. J. Pediat., 59:657, 1961.

Brescia, M. J., Cimino, J. E., Appel, K., and Hurwich, B. J. Chronic hemodialysis using venipuncture and a surgically created arterio-venous fistula. New Eng. J. Med., 275:1089, 1966.

Brèt, A. J., Dubois, J. P., and Demay, C. Cortical necrosis and renal thrombosis in the newborn. Arch. Franc. Pediat., 21:101, 1964.

Bricker, N. S., Klahr, S., Lubowitz, H., and Rieselbach, R. E. Renal function in chronic renal disease. Medicine, 44:263, 1965.

——— Wessler, S., and Avioli, L. V. Renal osteodystrophy. Therapy based on mechanism. J.A.M.A., 211:97, 1970.

Cameron, J. S., and Miller-Jones, C. M. H. Renal function and renal failure in badly burned children. Brit. J. Surg., 54:132, 1967.

Chamberlain, M. J., Shackman, R., Smith, E. K. M., and Wrong, O. M. Haemodialysis in young children. Brit. Med. J., 1:1610, 1965.

Clapp, W. M., Holmes, J., and O'Brien, D. Extracorporeal hemodialysis in children. Amer. J. Dis. Child., 104:45, 1962.

Clarkson, E. M., McDonald, S. J., and DeWardener, H. E. The effect of a high intake of calcium carbonate in normal subjects and patients with chronic renal failure. Clin. Sci., 30:425, 1966.

Collins, D. L., and Esperanca, M. G. A miniature disposable artificial kidney. J. Pediat., 66:103, 1965.

de St. Jeor, S. T., Carlston, B. J., and Tyler, F. H. Planning low-protein diets for use in chronic renal failure. J. Amer. Diet. Ass., 54:34, 1969.

Doxiadis, S. A. Azotaemia in infancy. Arch. Dis. Child., 23:50, 1948.

Editorial. Mannitol and renal function. Lancet, 1:1183, 1968.

Feldman, W., Baliah, T., and Drummond, K. N. Intermittent peritoneal dialysis in the management of chronic renal failure in children. Amer. J. Dis. Child., 116:30, 1968.

Fine, R. N., DePalma, J. R., Lieberman, E., Donnell, G. N., Gordon, A., Maxwell, M. H. Extended hemodialysis in children with chronic renal failure. J. Pediat., 73:706, 1968.

——— Korsch, B. M., Grushkin, C. M., and Lieberman, E. Hemodialysis in children. Amer. J. Dis. Child., 119:498, 1970.

——— Rosoff, L., Grushkin, C. M., Donnell, G. N., and Lieberman, E. Total parathyroidectomy in the treatment of renal osteodystrophy. J. Pediat., 76:32, 1970.

——— et al. Renal homotransplantation in children. J. Pediat., 76:347, 1970.

Fleisher, D. Cation exchange resin therapy for hyperkalemia in infants and children. J. Pediat., 58:486, 1961.

Franklin, S. S., and Merrill, J. P. Acute renal failure. New Eng. J. Med., 262:711, 1960.

Gianantonio, C. A., Vitacco, M., Mendilaharzu, J., Mendilaharzu, F., and Rutty, A. Acute renal failure in infancy and childhood. Clinical course and treatment of 41 patients. J. Pediat., 61:660, 1962.

Giovanetti, S., and Maggiore, Q. A low nitrogen diet

with proteins of high biological value for severe chronic uremia. Lancet, 1:1000, 1964.

Glassock, R. J., Feldman, D., Reynold, E. S., Dammin, G. J., and Merrill, J. P. Human renal isografts: a clinical and pathologic analysis. Medicine, 47:411, 1968.

Hill, R. B., Jr., Dahrling, B. E., II, Starzl, T. E., and Rifkind, D. Death after transplantation. Amer. J. Med., 42:327, 1967.

Holliday, M. A. Diagnosis and treament: Acute renal failure. Pediatrics, 35:478, 1965.

Hutchings, R. H., Hickman, R., and Scribner, B. H. Chronic hemodialysis in a preadolescent. Pediatrics, 37:68, 1966.

Jones-Boulton, J. M., et al. Treatment of terminal renal failure in children by home dialysis and transplantation. Arch. Dis. Child., 46:457, 1971.

Kallen, R. J. A method for approximating the efficacy of peritoneal dialysis for uremia. Amer. J. Dis. Child., 111:156, 1966.

——— Zaltzman, S., Coe, F. L., and Metcoff, J. Hemodialysis in children: Technique, kinetic aspects related to varying body size, and application to salicylate intoxication, acute renal failure and some other disorders. Medicine, 45:1, 1966.

Katz, A. I., Hampers, C. L., and Merrill, J. P. Secondary hyperparathyroidism and renal osteodystrophy in chronic renal failure. Medicine, 48:333, 1969.

Kessel, M., and Pann, W. Alwall's artificial kidney modified for the treatment of infants. Pediatrics, 35:123, 1965.

Kunin, C. M. A guide to use of antibiotics in patients with renal disease. A table of recommended doses and factors governing serum levels. Ann. Intern. Med., 67:151, 1967.

——— More on antimicrobials in renal failure. Ann. Intern. Med., 69:397, 1968.

Kwittken, J. Acute tubular nephrosis in the newborn infant, a manifestation of anoxia. Pediatrics, 33:380, 1964.

LaPlante, M. P., et al. Kidney transplantation in children. Pediatrics, 46:665, 1970.

Lauler, D. P., Schreiner, G. E., and David A. Renal medullary necrosis. Amer. J. Med., 29:132, 1960.

Lee, H. A., and Sharpstone, P. Haemodialysis in pediatrics. Acta Paediat. Scand., 55:529, 1966.

Lilly, J. R., et al. Renal homotransplantation in pediatric patients. Pediatrics, 47:548, 1971.

Lloyd-Still, J. D., and Atwell, J. D. Renal failure in infancy with special reference to the use of peritoneal dialysis. J. Pediat. Surg., 1:466, 1966.

Makoff, D. L., Gordon, A., Franklin, S. S., Gerstein, A. R., and Maxwell, M. H. Chronic calcium carbonate therapy in uremia. Arch. Intern. Med., 123:15, 1969.

Mallick, N. P., and Berlyne, G. M. Arterial calcification after vitamin-D therapy in hyperphosphataemic renal failure. Lancet, 2:1316, 1968.

Manley, G. L., and Gollipp, P. J. Renal failure in the newborn. Treatment with peritoneal dialysis. Amer. J. Dis. Child., 115:107, 1968.

Mauer, S. M., and Nogrady, M. B. Renal papillary and cortical necrosis in a newborn infant: Report of a survivor with roentgenologic documentation. J. Pediat., 74:750, 1969.

Merrill, J. P. The Treatment of Renal Failure: Therapeutic Principles in the Management of Acute and Chronic Uremia. New York, Grune and Stratton, Inc., 1955.

——— Uremia. New Eng. J. Med., 282:953, 1014, 1970.

Oliver, J., MacDowell, M., and Tracey, A. The pathogenesis of acute renal failure associated with traumatic and toxic injury; renal ischemia, nephrotoxic damage and the ischemuric episode. J. Clin. Invest., 30:1307, 1951.

Potter, D., Belzer, F. O., Rames, L., Holliday, M. A., Kountz, S. L., and Najarian, J. S. The treatment of chronic uremia in childhood. I. Transplantation. Pediatrics, 45:432, 1970.

——— et al. Treatment of chronic uremia in childhood. II. Hemodialysis. Pediatrics, 46:678, 1970.

Pratt, E. L. Treatment of anuria. Amer. J. Dis. Child., 76:14, 1948.

Proceedings of the Conference of the Nutritional Aspects of Uremia. Amer. J. Clin. Nutr., 21:349, 1968.

Reisman, L. E., and Pathak, A. Bilateral renal cortical necrosis in the newborn associated with fetomaternal transfusion and hypermagnesemia. Amer. J. Dis. Child., 111:541, 1966.

Rennie, I. D. B., and Cameron, J. S. Peritoneal dialysis for traumatic renal failure in a three-week old infant. Guy's Hosp. Rep., 115:449, 1966.

Riley, C. M. Thoughts about kidney homotransplantation in children. J. Pediat., 65:797, 1964.

Robinson, G. C., and Wong, L. C. Acute tubular necrosis in infancy and childhood. Amer. J. Dis. Child., 95:417, 1958.

Segar, W. E., Gibson, R. K., and Rhamy, R. Peritoneal dialysis in infants and small children. Pediatrics, 27:603, 1961.

Schreiner, G. E., and Maher, J. F. Uremia: Biochemistry, Pathogenesis, and Treatment. Springfield, Ill., Charles C Thomas, Publ., 1961.

Scribner, B. H. Dialysis. In Black, D. A. K., ed., Renal Disease, 2nd ed. Philadelphia, F. A. Davis Co., 1967, p. 446.

Stewart, B. H., and Straffon, R. A. Human kidney transplantation: present status and projected future. Maryland Med. J., 18:61, 1969.

Stohlman, F., Jr. The kidney and erythropoiesis. New Eng. J. Med., 279:1437, 1968.

Thomas, M. A. Perinatal hemorrhagic necrosis of renal pyramids. Amer. J. Dis. Child., 108:13, 1964.

Tiddens, H. A. W. M. Growth-limiting factors in renal disease. Boerhaave Course for Post-Graduate Medical Teaching. In Van Der Werff Ten Bosch, J. J., ed., Somatic Growth of the Child. Springfield, Ill., Charles C Thomas Co., Publ., 1966, p. 215.

Williams, A. V., Hargest, T. S., and Wohltmann, H. J. Chronic hemodialysis of a 2-year-old child. Pediatrics, 43:116, 1969.

22.5
RENAL ABNORMALITIES IN THE NEWBORN

JAY BERNSTEIN

Renal disease in the newborn may present as an obvious congenital malformation, an abdominal mass with hematuria or evidence of infection, or nonspecifically as failure to thrive. The majority of infants with renal disease have a congenital malformation or some form of gross obstructive uropathy. Acquired disorders such as pyelonephritis, circulatory disturbances, or vascular occlusions also are observed. Neoplasms are rare, although Wilms' tumor may manifest itself in the neonate.

A characteristic mode of presentation of renal disease in the newborn is the *large kidney-hematuria syndrome.* It should be apparent from the following discussion that this is a totally nonspecific clinical syndrome that may reflect any one of a variety of underlying disorders, either acquired or congenital. Certain diseases of the kidney assume particular importance in the newborn period because of unique clinical or pathologic manifestations, and certain congenital abnormalities are lethal shortly after birth.

Congenital Abnormalities

The most readily recognized renal malformation clinically is *bilateral agenesis,* i.e., complete absence of the kidneys. This anomaly is associated with oligo-hydramnios and amnion nodosum, a peculiar facies, and misshapen and low-set ears, a collection of malformations that has come to be known as Potter's syndrome. Oligohydramnios and abnormal ears are seen, however, with other forms of renal maldevelopment. The former results from decreased urination during intrauterine life, and the latter have been recognized in individuals of all ages with relatively minor renal anomalies.

Infantile polycystic disease is often evident in the newborn period. This condition, a form of parenchymal maldevelopment, customarily is accompanied by polycystic changes of the liver and pancreas and sometimes by cystic malformation of the lungs. In some of these infants the abdomen may be greatly distended by relatively huge kidneys, which characteristically are uniformly enlarged. Grossly they have a diffusely spongy appearance, and histologic examination shows generalized, more or less uniform dilatation of collecting tubules. Glomeruli and convoluted tubules are less regularly involved. This disease is familial, apparently a genetically recessive disorder. Its relationship to other forms of polycystic disease in childhood is at the moment not settled, and it does appear to be distinct from classic, autosomal dominant, adult polycystic disease (p. 1478).

Another type of parenchymal maldevelopment is *renal dysplasia,* which results from altered development and differentiation of both the collecting system and nephrons. Among the important types or patterns of dysplasia in the newborn period is the condition of severe dysplastic hypoplasia, often referred to as "aplasia," in which only a small nubbin of renal tissue is grossly identifiable. Multicystic dysplasia (Fig. 6) is closely related, being distinguished grossly by numerous, often large renal cysts, and is almost always associated with ureteropelvic occlusion. This is, incidentally, the most common

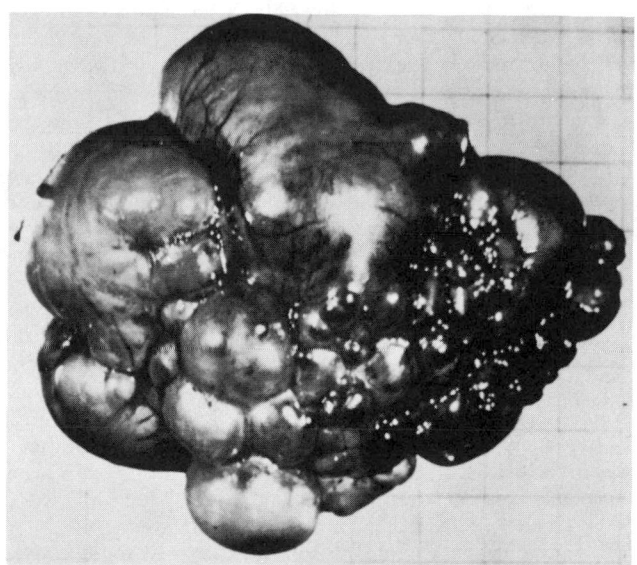

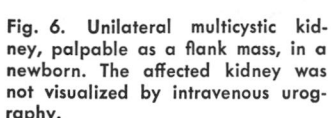
Fig. 6. Unilateral multicystic kidney, palpable as a flank mass, in a newborn. The affected kidney was not visualized by intravenous urography.

form of cystic disorder in newborns. Bilateral involvement in either condition may be accompanied by stigmata of Potter's syndrome and is lethal within the first few days of life. The enlarged multicystic kidneys usually are palpable on abdominal examination. The bladder is hypoplastic, and the infant does not pass urine. Unilateral multicystic kidney, either in newborns or older children, is discovered most often as an abdominal or flank mass, and excretory urography fails to demonstrate renal function on the affected side. Such kidneys are usually subjected to surgical extirpation.

Posterior urethral valves in newborns often are accompanied by renal dysplasia, the severity of which appears to be related to the degree of urinary obstruction. Severe valvar obstruction can be the cause of bladder dilatation and hydroureter very early in life and may be a cause of anuria in the newborn (Fig. 7). In this regard, the presence of bilateral renal masses and a midline suprapubic mass in a newborn male should be taken as prima facie evidence of urethral or bladder neck obstruction until appropriate diagnostic measures can be undertaken.

Acquired Abnormalities

Several types of *nephritis,* including chronic glomerulonephritis and the nephrotic syndrome (p. 1506), have been described in newborns. Although they are listed here with the acquired disorders, they may in fact be congenital diseases.

Acute pyelonephritis in the newborn is a severe infection. It occurs most often in males and results from coliform septicemia. Clinical or anatomic evidence of an underlying anomaly of the urinary tract only occasionally is present. The initial sign often is jaundice due to conjugated hyperbilirubinemia, presumably resulting from toxic injury to the liver. Irritability and anorexia are common, and the recognition of renal involvement may be delayed because of anuria. The infection responds to prompt and vigorous antibiotic therapy, but in severe cases the course is rapid and the child may be moribund before the gravity of his illness is appreciated. The effect of infection on subsequent renal development and function is not known. Acute infections can and do occur in infants who have anatomic urologic abnormalities. In such cases the outcome may hinge on the prevention of recurrent or chronic pyelonephritis; surgical relief of the underlying lesion is mandatory.

The most common forms of acquired renal disease in the newborn fall into the general category of *circulatory disturbances.* Some are clearly the result of ischemia and anoxia, such as infarction of the kidney following vascular occlusion. Others, such as cortical necrosis, presumably result from transient or functional alterations in renal blood flow. This group of renal abnormalities presents an ill-defined clinical problem, in which recognition of the anatomic lesion

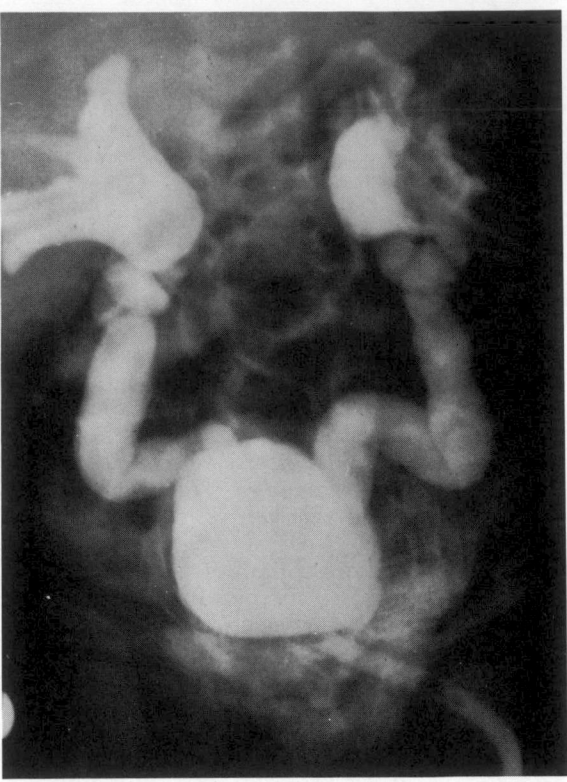

Fig. 7. Bilateral hydroureter and hydronephrosis secondary to a posterior urethral valve in a newborn. The greatly enlarged kidneys and bladder were easily palpable on physical examination.

is not often possible. Any of these lesions may be present in an infant with enlarged kidneys, azotemia, and hematuria, although these findings are equally compatible with the diagnosis of a congenital malformation of the urinary tract.

Vascular occlusion may result from either *arterial* or *venous thrombosis.* The former (p. 1533) usually is embolic from a primary thrombus lying within the ductus arteriosus. Renal infarction may be unilateral, but aortic occlusion or multiple emboli can cause bilateral necrosis. Flank masses and hematuria are the clinical evidences of renal involvement. Embolic lesions also appear in the extremities, gastrointestinal tract, and head, and portions of the thrombus that extend into the pulmonary artery can embolize to the lungs.

Renal vein thrombosis (p. 1534) occurs more commonly, involving the major vessels, their tributaries, or both. Renal infarction often ensues, particularly when the intrarenal vessels are occluded, thereby providing another variant of the "large kidney-hematuria syndrome." Prompt surgical extirpation has been advocated in the treatment of unilateral infarction, but in recent years several observers have favored more conservative therapy. There are several reports of recovery after caval embolectomy, and some after nonsurgical management of bilateral infarction. In many newborns, as in older children, venous thrombosis has been a complication of diarrhea and dehydration. In recent years, however, the incidence of idiopathic or "primary" thrombosis has increased, often occurring in babies born to diabetic mothers. Some evidence has been presented that despite their appearance these babies are hypovolemic and are in a sense, therefore, dehydrated. The intrauterine origin of the lesion has been amply demonstrated. It also occurs in newborns who have polyuria and dehydration from other causes, such as anencephaly. Therapeutic measures include rehydration and anticoagulation, although the latter is not without hazard and its therapeutic efficacy is unknown.

Anoxic lesions of the kidney in which vascular occlusion cannot be demonstrated include *cortical* (Fig. 8), *medullary* (Fig. 9), and *tubular necrosis*. These conditions in the past have been reported infrequently, but the descriptions of "hemorrhagic nephritis" and "hemorrhagic infarction" of the kidneys in newborns probably include many examples of cortical and medullary necrosis. Cortical necrosis has been confounded also with infarction due to renal vein thrombosis on the grounds that they are different stages of the same process, but there is no evidence that the two are related. Both cortical and medullary necrosis in newborns are associated with anemic or asphyxial shock. Blood loss may have resulted from uteroplacental hemorrhage or hemolytic disease. Ma-

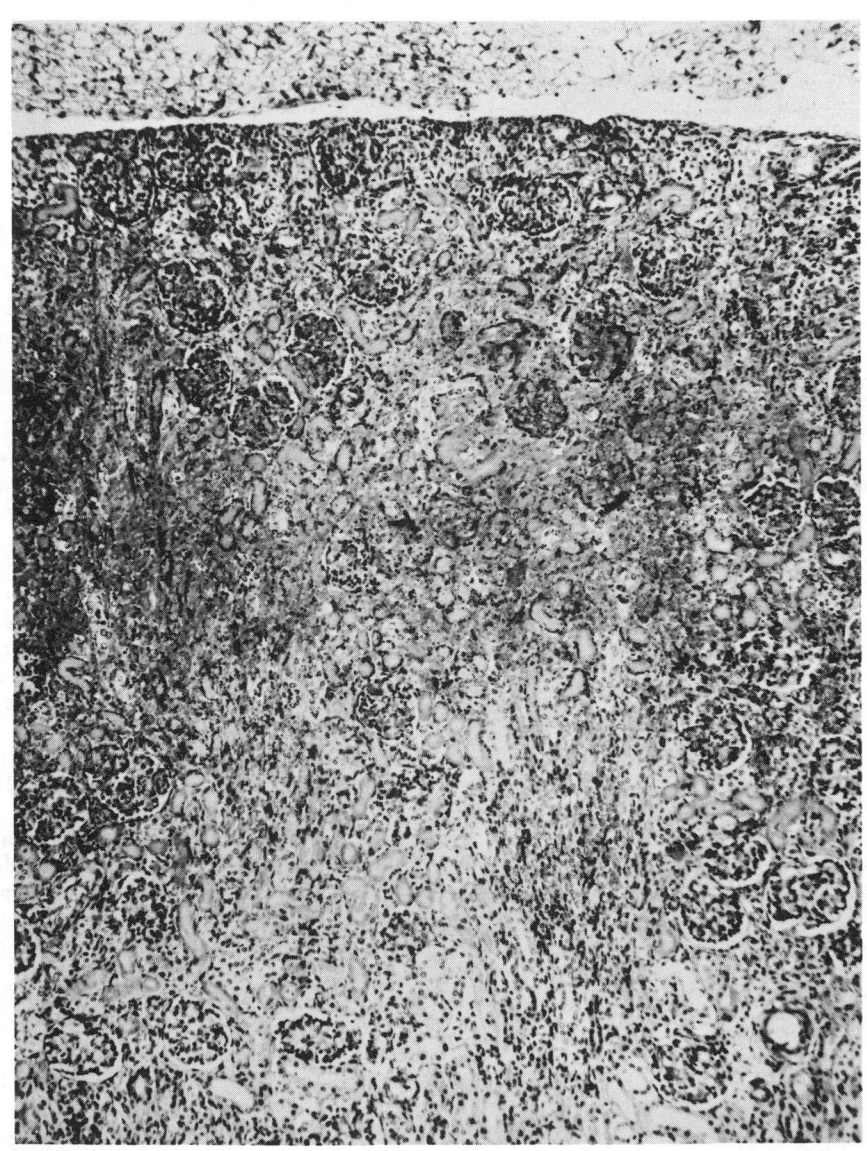

Fig. 8. Renal cortical necrosis in a newborn. All elements in the central portion of the cortex have undergone ischemic necrosis and a zone of subcapsular sparing is present. H&E ×120.

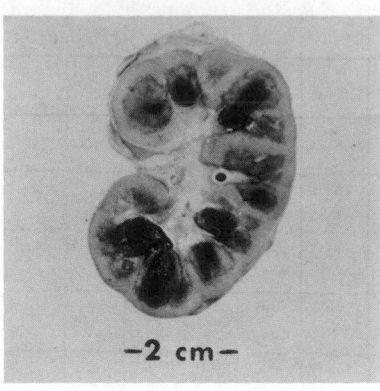

Fig. 9. Renal medullary necrosis in a newborn. The medullary pyramids are partially hemorrhagic; the cortex is not involved.

ternal toxemia has been relatively frequent among the babies suffering fom fetal asphyxia. Cortical necrosis has been observed in stillborn infants, and a variable degree of cortical involvement accompanies medullary necrosis. Both conditions usually are bilateral, and both can be responsible for renal enlargement and hematuria. Cortical necrosis is sometimes accompanied by an unexplained thrombocytopenia, and clinical or histopathologic evidence of intravascular coagulation has been found on occasion, although relatively few cases of documented disseminated intravascular coagulation have had renal cortical necrosis.

Tubular lesions consisting of fatty infiltration, cellular degeneration, and necrosis also have been described in asphyxiated infants. These morphologic changes would appear to form a spectrum that reflects the degree of cellular injury, but an interrelationship of this sort has not in fact been demonstrated. Some newborns with presumed tubular injury have had azotemia, cylindruria, and oliguria or anuria, but precise clinicopathologic correlations are lacking. Increased urinary excretion of casts and cells has been demonstrated in surviving asphyxiated infants. Studies of renal function in infants with the respiratory distress syndrome have shown depressed glomerular filtration rates, diminished urea clearances, and low urine volumes; these findings suggest a decreased renal blood flow, an interpretation supported by postmortem vascular studies. These functional abnormalities possibly are due to hypovolemia, which in distressed infants seems to result from a shift of fluid into the extravascular space. More detailed studies of renal morphology and function in the newborn clearly are in order, but there does seem to be some justification for linking clinical and pathologic renal abnormalities with perinatal asphyxia.

References

Bernstein, J., and Meyer, R. Congenital abnormalities of the urinary system. II. Renal cortical and medullary necrosis. J. Pediat., 59:657, 1961.

Brough, A. J., and Zuelzer, W. W. Renal vascular disease. Pediat. Clin. N. Amer., 11:533, 1964.

Cort, R. L. Renal function in the respiratory distress syndrome. Acta Paediat., 51:313, 1962.

Halvorsen, S., and Aas, K. Observations on the urine of asphyxiated and dysmature infants. Acta Paediat., 51: 417, 1962.

Royer, P., Habib, R., and Mathieu, H. Le syndrome "gros rein-hématurie" transitoire du nouveau-né. In Problèmes Actuels de Néphrologie Infantile. Paris, Éditions Médicales Flammarion, 1963, pp. 336-339.

Rubenstein, M., Meyer, R., and Bernstein, J. Congenital abnormalities of the urinary system. I. A postmortem survey of developmental anomalies and acquired congenital lesions in a children's hospital. J. Pediat., 58: 356, 1961.

Takeuchi, A., and Benirschke, K. Renal venous thrombosis of the newborn and its relation to maternal diabetes. Biol. Neonat., 3:237, 1961.

22.6

ABNORMALITIES OF RENAL DEVELOPMENT: HYPOPLASIA AND DYSPLASIA; CYSTIC DISORDERS AND POLYCYSTIC DISEASE

JAY BERNSTEIN

Developmental disturbances of the kidneys include various forms of hypoplasia (reduction of mass), dysplasia (abnormal differentiation), and polycystic disease. The genetic basis of some conditions, such as bilateral polycystic disease, is widely accepted, but heritable conditions account for only a fraction of these structural abnormalities (Table 3). Most human malformations occur without overt evidence of either abnormal inheritance or exogenous injury to the fetus. Renal dysplasia may, however, be related to developmental abnormalities of the urinary tract, and in this sense the maldevelopment is conditioned by environmental factors. Also, maturation continues during the postnatal development of the kidney, and the reactions of immature structures to injury can mimic antenatal developmental abnormalities.

The practice of regarding all kidneys that contain cysts as "polycystic" does not appear to be justified. Cysts of the renal parenchyma are encountered in both dysplastic and polycystic kidneys. Cysts also may be encountered in conditions that clearly are acquired rather than developmental, e.g., cystic arteriolar nephrosclerosis in the adult, and in conditions in which they seem to be secondary to another renal abnormality, e.g., tubular cysts in the congenital nephrotic syndrome. Cysts do not appear to be of specific pathogenetic significance, and they may develop in normally formed, dysplastic, atrophic, or scarred nephrons (Table 4).

TABLE 3. *Classification of Inherited Renal Structural Abnormalities*

I. Polycystic disease
  A. Infantile polycystic disease
    1. Polycystic disease of early infancy
      a. Neonatal polycystic disease ("Potter type 1," rein d'éponge)
      b. Meckel's syndrome
    2. Polycystic disease of childhood
      a. Medullary tubular ectasia
      b. Congenital hepatic fibrosis
  B. Adult polycystic disease

II. Cortical cysts
  A. Tuberous sclerosis complex
  B. Lindau's disease
  C. Micromulticystic disease and cystic infantile nephrosclerosis
    1. Cerebrohepatorenal syndrome (Zellweger)
    2. Autosomal trisomy syndromes, D and E
    3. Multiple malformation syndromes

III. Medullary sponge kidney

IV. Hereditary and familial dysplasia
  A. Cystic and medullary dysplasia with cerebral and ocular maldevelopment
  B. Beckwith's syndrome
  C. Lenz's microphthalmia syndrome

V. Hereditary hydronephrosis and agenesis

TABLE 4. *Classification of Renal Cysts* Based on Clinical, Radiologic, and Pathologic Correlation*

I. Renal Dysplasia
  A. Multicystic kidney
  B. Focal and segmental cystic dysplasia
  C. Multiple cysts associated with lower urinary tract obstruction

II. Polycystic Disease
  A. Infantile polycystic disease
    1. Polycystic disease of the newborn
    2. Polycystic disease of childhood
      a. Congenital hepatic fibrosis
      b. Medullary tubular ectasia
  B. Adult polycystic disease

III. Cortical Cysts
  A. Trisomy syndromes
  B. Tuberous sclerosis complex
  C. Simple cysts
    1. Solitary
    2. Multiple
  D. Multilocular cysts

IV. Medullary Cysts
  A. Medullary sponge kidney
  B. Medullary cystic disease
  C. Medullary necrosis
  D. Pyelogenic cyst

V. Miscellaneous Intrarenal Cysts
  A. Inflammatory
    1. Tuberculosis
    2. Calculous disease
    3. Echinococcus disease
  B. Neoplastic—cystic degeneration of carcinoma
  C. Traumatic—intrarenal hematoma

VI. Extraparenchymal Renal Cysts
  A. Parapelvic cyst
  B. Perinephric cyst

*From Elkin and Bernstein. *Clin. Radiol.*, 20:65, 1969.

Renal Hypoplasia

Renal hypoplasia, in which there is a diminution of otherwise normally developed parenchyma, may take several forms. Unilateral hypoplasia, the "dwarf" kidney, is in early infancy an incidental finding, although it has been regarded as a predisposing factor in the development of hypertension and chronic pyelonephritis. Consequently, the presence of inflammation and scarring in small kidneys makes it very difficult to differentiate hypoplasia from secondary atrophy, the shrunken kidney. A localized or segmental form of hypoplasia associated with hypertension in children and young adults has come to be known as the *Ask-Upmark kidney.* This abnormality is distinguished by transverse grooves on the capsular surface, marking the sites of hypoplastic lobes that overlie elongated, calyxlike recesses of the renal pelvis. The hypoplastic lobes are aglomerular and contain atrophic, thyroidlike tubules and sclerotic vessels. However, the lesion may very well be an acquired, localized atrophy, rather than a developmental abnormality. The degree of associated arterial hypertension is often very severe, many patients passing into a malignant or accelerated phase. Nephrectomy is curative in a minority of cases, possibly because of bilateral involvement or possibly because of secondary vascular alterations in the opposite kidney that sustain the hypertension.

Bilateral hypoplasia has been observed in a few infants who apparently had had difficulty in concentrating urine despite severe dehydration of extrarenal origin. The functional significance of bilateral hypoplasia is far from established; chronic renal failure and growth retardation, tubular insufficiency with acidosis and cation-wasting, and inability to respond to water deprivation are possible complications. A distinctive form of bilateral hypoplasia, known as *oligoméganéphronie,* is associated with a reduction of nephrons and marked hypertrophy of those that are present. The kidneys are extremely small and contain a reduced number of pyramids. These children suffer from impaired concentrating ability, polyuria and polydypsia, and dehydration, beginning in the first weeks or months of life. Growth retardation and anemia are followed by the characteristic findings of uremia. Other, associated malformations are rare. The condition is undoubtedly congenital, but a familial incidence has not been observed.

Renal Dysplasia

Renal dysplasia is defined as abnormal development of nephronic and ductal structures, resulting in total or partial renal malformation. The abnormalities under consideration must be differentiated from cystic disease on the one hand and hypoplasia with structurally normal parenchyma on the other. Dysplastic kidneys contain abnormally differentiated structures that have a fetal or primitive appearance (Fig. 10). Histologic examination of a typical dysplastic kidney discloses conglomerates of seemingly disorganized epithelial structures, surrounded by abundant fibrous tissue and often containing islands of cartilage. Structures that can be regarded as resulting from embryonic maldevelopment are (1) primitive ducts, which are lined by relatively tall columnar epithelium, often ciliated, and surrounded by fibromuscular collars, and (2) nests of metaplastic cartilage. The former, located frequently in the medulla, appear to be altered derivatives of the metanephric duct; the latter, principally cortical, derive from metanephric blastema. Primitive nephronic elements (glomeruli and tubules) are generally present, and cysts, which may or may not be present, are regarded as coincidental findings.

The association of renal dysplasia with other anomalies of the urinary tract is on the order of 90 percent. It is believed that the significance of this association lies in the obstructive nature of most ureteral and lower urinary tract anomalies. Patterns of malformations correlate to a degree with the nature and severity of the obstructive lesion. Unilateral ureteral anomalies are associated with ipsilateral and lower urinary tract anomalies with bilateral dysplasia. Severe degrees of urinary tract obstruction, as in posterior urethral valves, are associated with renal dysplasia, but less severe obstruction rarely is. Cortical dysplasia is generally most marked and sometimes present only in the outer portion, that is in the part of the cortex formed late in development after urinary excretion in the inner portion has already commenced. The association of dysplasia and urinary tract obstruction may be coincidental, but the patterns that have been observed do support the hypothesis that a causal relationship exists.

CLINICAL FORMS OF DYSPLASIA. The majority of dysplastic kidneys are sporadic malformations, without evidence of heritable causation; a very small minority are familial; and trisomy syndromes may

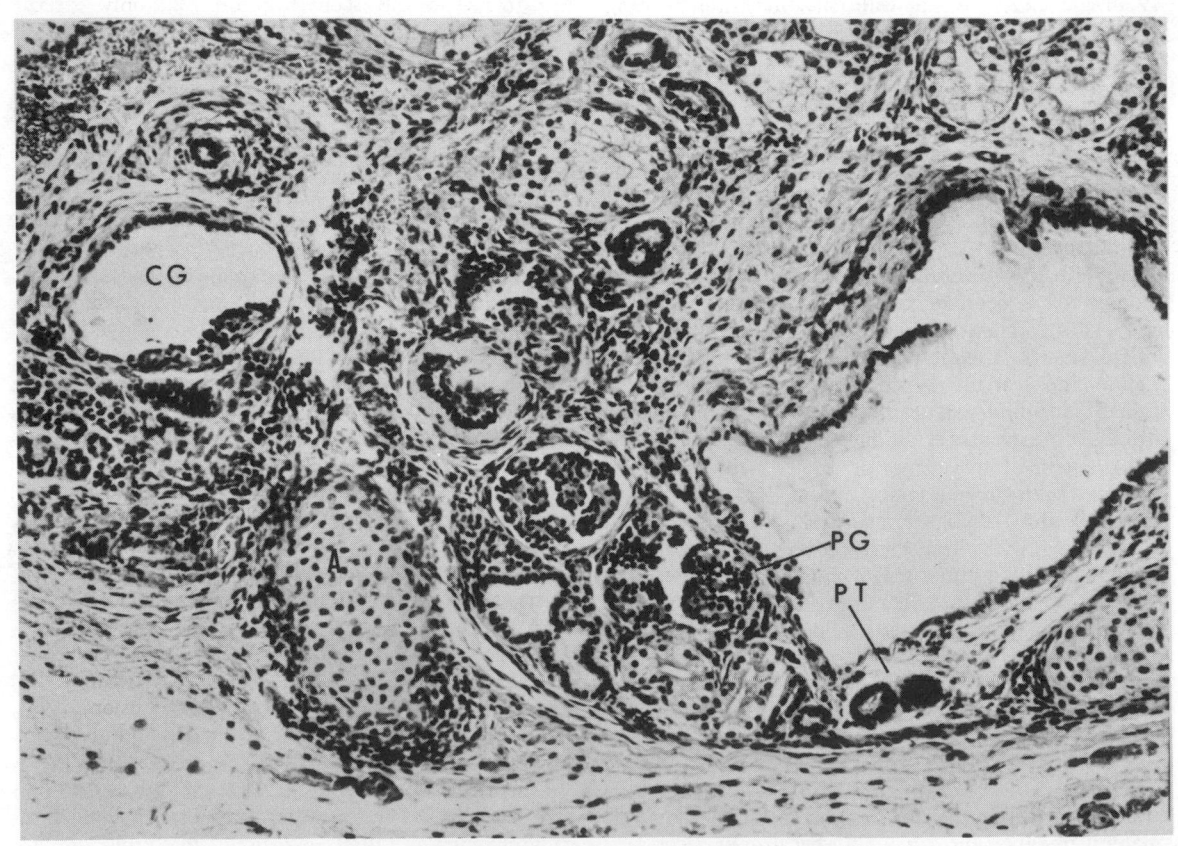

Fig. 10. Cortical dysplasia, showing the presence of heterotopic cartlage (A), primitive tubules (PT), primitive glomeruli (PG), and cystic glomeruli (CG). H&E ×190.

include a relatively minor degree of renal maldevelopment. Several types of dysplasia can be recognized as clinicopathologic entities, although a sizable
group remains unclassified.

Multicystic kidneys and *aplastic kidneys* differ
only by the occurrence in the former of gross cysts.
They are similar malformations, both commonly unilateral and encountered at all ages, and both occurring bilaterally in newborns as lethal malformations.
Bilateral multicystic dysplasia is the single most common cystic disorder of the newborn. Unilateral aplasia
may be associated with a variety of vague signs and
symptoms, some of which probably are related to
recurrent infection. Hypertension is an important
complication. Of particular interest in children is
the unilateral multicystic kidney, which presents as
an abdominal mass and may be associated with nonspecific complaints. Abnormalities of the other kidney
are relatively common and do impair the prognosis,
but multicystic dysplasia is not a progressive disease
that will eventually involve the opposite side. It is
rarely associated with hypertension, at least in pediatric practice. Males predominate, and the lesion is
somewhat more common on the left. The kidney
does not function, and invariably there is ureteropelvic occlusion. The lesion seems to be innocuous,
but surgical extirpation is the preferred treatment,
possibly because of the difficulty in differentiating
it from Wilms' tumor.

General dysplasia is the term used to describe
small malformed kidneys that retain a semblance of
normal architecture and a limited ability to function.
Most clinical studies of "renal hypoplasia" have dealt
with this type of malformation. There are fewer lobes
than normal, a feature apparent grossly and radiographically, and radiographic studies often delineate
pyelocalyceal deformities. Symptoms, in addition to
those deriving from renal insufficiency, are related
to infection, occurring in two-thirds, and lithiasis,
in one-third of cases. Hypertension develops in 20
to 25 percent, though not always as the result of
pyelonephritis. Multiple congenital malformations are
often observed in infants with bilateral dysplasia.

Cortical dysplasia is seen in association with
lower urinary tract obstruction, its incidence being
in general related to the severity of obstruction. Extensive cortical dysplasia may nullify surgical relief
of posterior urethral valves. Medullary dysplasia, another associated abnormality, may be partly responsible for a diminished ability to concentrate urine
after surgical reconstruction.

Instances of *familial dysplasia* are quite uncommon, a few having been described in association
with cerebral and ocular maldevelopment. These patients suffered from chronic renal insufficiency, often
in early infancy. A form of medullary dysplasia,
characterized by widely separated, immature ducts
and an increase in stroma, is a usual concomitant of
Beckwith's syndrome of macroglossia, omphalocele,
and visceromegaly. The kidneys are considerably enlarged, but the functional significance of the ab-

normality has not as yet been studied. Renal parenchymal abnormalities encountered in the autosomal
trisomy and multiple malformations syndromes are
generally cystic and have usually been classified with
forms of polycystic disease.

Cystic Disorders of the Kidney

Cystic conditions of the kidney comprise a heterogeneous group of heritable and acquired conditions
that defy classification on purely morphologic or
purely clinical grounds (Table 4). Among the cystic
disorders important in the pediatric age group are
polycystic disease and certain lesions encountered in
association with several constellations of congenital
malformations. These two groups of cystic disease
encompass, incidentally, the great majority of inherited renal structural abnormalities.

POLYCYSTIC DISEASE. Most studies have supported
the division of polycystic disease into infantile and
adult forms. Certain morphologic features overlap
and are held in common, and the interrelationships
of the different subtypes have remained in question
despite more than a half-century of speculation. Morphologic studies have been dominated by concern for
the cysts, often to the exclusion of clinical and genetic
features. It would seem a priori that only careful
differentiation by all available criteria could lead to
meaningful correlations and generalizations.

Microdissection of cystic kidneys has provided
a means of localizing the cysts, of determining their
relationships to each other and to other parts of the
nephron, and of measuring them and other parts of
the nephron. The results of such studies in polycystic disease have, however, been subjected to over-
interpretation. It is debatable whether these observations, without clinical, genetic, and other morphologic
data, will provide an adequate basis for classification
or even whether the generalizations derived from
them can be transposed to histologic studies of cystic
kidneys. It is also quite uncertain that the pathogenesis of the diseases or even of the cysts can be derived
from such observations.

Infantile polycystic disease encompasses at least
two major subgroups and appears to be a heterogeneous collection. Most workers have tended to
differentiate, despite morphologic and clinical overlapping, (1) the large, spongy kidneys usually encountered in newborns and accompanied by involvement of the liver and other viscera, and (2) the
predominantly medullary disease in older children,
commonly asymptomatic and usually accompanied by
hepatic involvement and portal hypertension. This
separation may, however, be artificial, and the subdivision into fewer or more categories will depend
ultimately upon extended clinical and genetic studies.

The first group includes those designated elsewhere as "hamartomas," "rein d'éponge," and "Potter
type i." The kidneys are greatly enlarged and diffusely spongy, and the usual gross landmarks are

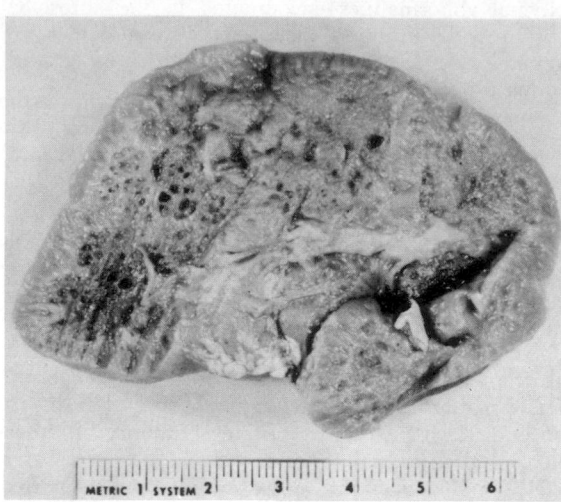

Fig. 11. Polycystic disease in a newborn infant, showing preservation of cortex and medullary pyramids; note gross medullary ectasia.

preserved apart from minor obliteration of the corticomedullary junctions. Slightly increased connective tissue may be present among the tubular elements, but significant fibrosis ordinarily is not present. Microdissection studies have indicated that the most consistent and prominent site of dilation is in the collecting tubules, and histologic examination may also show dilation of glomerular spaces and convoluted tubules. The medullary ducts characteristically are dilated, and ectasia of the collecting ducts may be seen at the papillae. The condition is usually associated with cystic changes in the liver and sometimes with changes in the pancreas and other organs. Massive enlargement of the kidneys can produce sufficient abdominal distention in the fetus to result in dystocia. The majority of liveborn infants die within the first few days of life, although survival into infancy has been described. The condition appears either sporadically or in more than one sibling of a single generation. It has not been reported in the offspring of unaffected sibs, nor has consanguinity been noted in the parents. The sibling involvement and horizontal familial transmission are consistent with an autosomal recessive abnormality.

The second type may very well lack clinical or pathologic homogeneity. Renal cortical involvement is irregular, and medullary tubular ectasia predominates (Fig. 11), often to the point of being detectable by excretory urography. Involvement of the liver is associated with considerably more fibrosis than in the early infantile type, and these cases have been designated as "congenital hepatic fibrosis." Portal hypertension is often the principal clinical problem, renal involvement being an incidental radiographic finding. Whether the early infantile and later types of polycystic disease are distinct entities or stages in the evolution of one entity is still a matter of debate.

The *adult type of polycystic disease* does on occasion occur in childhood. These patients may have large flank masses, proteinuria, and various formed elements in the urine. Hypertension and the classical evidence of progressive renal failure do occur. Adult polycystic disease can be differentiated pathologically from the infantile type. The familial character of the disorder is quite typical, with repetition in several generations, demonstrating an autosomal dominant mode of inheritance.

RENAL CORTICAL CYSTS. Multiple cortical cysts are encountered in several malformation syndromes. They cannot be regarded as either polycystic disease or renal dysplasia. Microcysts, principally in the peripheral cortex, involve both collecting tubules and portions of the nephron. Similar lesions have been seen in the cerebrohepatorenal syndrome, autosomal trisomy syndromes D and E, the lissencephaly syndrome, the oral-facial-digital syndrome, the Schwartz-Jampel syndrome, Ivemark's syndrome, and Jeune's syndrome, among others. They have rarely been of clinical significance. It is not clear whether they are inherent features of the genetically determined syndromes. The practice of applying the term "polycystic" indiscriminately to this miscellany has little more than descriptive value. *Tuberous sclerosis* may be singled out as distinctive. Renal cysts are variably present. They are generally of tubular origin, lined by hyperplastic cells, and are often of sufficient size to produce radiographic distortion and to be associated with renal functional impairment.

REFERENCES

Bernstein, J. Developmental abnormalities of the renal parenchyma—Renal hypoplasia and dysplasia. *In* Sommers, S. C., ed., Pathology Annual. New York, Appleton-Century-Crofts, 1968, Ch. 3.

———— and Meyer, R. Some speculations on the nature and significance of developmentally small kidneys (renal hypoplasia). Nephron, 1:137, 1964.

Elkin, M., and Bernstein, J. Cystic diseases of the kidney—Radiological and pathological considerations. Clin. Radiol., 20:65, 1969.

Lundin, P. M., and Olow, I. Polycystic kidneys in newborns, infants, and children. Acta Paediat., 50:185, 1961.

Osathanondh, V., and Potter, E. L. Pathogenesis of polycystic kidneys. Arch. Path., 77:459, 1964.

Royer, P., Habib, R., Mathieu, H., and Courtecuisse, V. L'hypoplasie rénale bilatérale congénitale avec réduction du nombre et hypertrophie des néphrons chez l'enfant. Ann. Pédiat., 9:133, 1962.

22.7

POSTURAL PROTEINURIA

CHESTER M. EDELMANN, JR.

Postural, or orthostatic, proteinuria, is a condition in which significant protein excretion occurs in the upright position, particularly in hyperlordosis, but disappears or is reduced to normal levels (less than 25 mg per 24 hours) during recumbency.

The incidence of orthostatic proteinuria is not known, but the condition is said to be common, occurring in as many as 2 to 5 percent of adolescents. In the survey of Randolph and Greenfield of almost 4,000 children ranging in age from 3 weeks to 16 years, who were screened for urinary tract disease, proteinuria was observed on at least one occasion in more than one-third. However, reexamination of the children with one positive test revealed no persistent, intermittent, or postural proteinuria in the entire group. Wagner et al. detected proteinuria on initial testing in 5.4 percent of 4,807 children aged 5 to 18 years. Only 1.1 percent had a positive second test. A number of these were thought to have orthostatic proteinuria.

The pathophysiology is not fully understood. Increased glomerular filtration of protein has been suggested, although diminished tubular reabsorption cannot be excluded. Elevated inferior vena caval pressure has been observed concomitant with orthostatic protein excretion, but artificial elevation of the pressure in recumbency fails to reproduce this effect. Proteinuria has been induced in susceptible individuals by the application of tourniquets to the legs and by norepinephrine administration. Alternatively, it has been suggested that the protein may be derived from renal papillary lymph, although other studies strongly suggest a vascular derivation.

Orthostatic proteinuria has been shown to be nonselective, similar to the slight proteinuria present in normal subjects, suggesting that orthostatic proteinuria may simply reflect an exaggeration of the normal state. However, the technical difficulties in determining selectivity in normal subjects in the presence of very minimal proteinuria, and the possibility of nonrenal sources of protein make this interpretation uncertain.

The erect posture and ambulation usually increase the rate of protein excretion in patients with renal disease. If renal abnormalities are mild, proteinuria may be demonstrable only in the erect or lordotic position. Therefore, proteinuria cannot be classified as "benign" simply because it can be made to disappear during recumbency. King reported that one-third of 191 apparently healthy young males with postural proteinuria had developed constant proteinuria when examined 5 to 8 years later. Robinson and co-workers, in a study of army recruits with what they termed fixed and reproducible orthostatic proteinuria, demonstrated significant abnormalities on renal biopsy in one-half.

Light microscopy generally has revealed either no abnormalities or minimal alterations in glomerular structure; focal abnormalities in the glomeruli have been seen with electron microscopy. Lange et al. have reported the finding of gamma globulin and complement, suggesting the presence of immune complexes. Thus, considerably more attention must be directed toward this condition than has been recommended in recent years, and all such patients should be investigated thoroughly. Long-term follow-ups of many patients are needed before the true significance of postural proteinuria can be determined.

Herdman et al. reported cessation or diminution of proteinuria in four of five patients with orthostatic proteinuria and suggested that a diagnostic trial of steroid therapy in this condition might separate out patients with benign disease from those with a poorer prognosis.

The diagnosis of postural proteinuria is easily established by comparison between rates of excretion of protein in a timed overnight specimen (e.g., an Addis count) and in a specimen obtained in the erect and, preferably, lordotic position. If postural proteinuria is found, patients should have appropriate investigation to discover specific etiology and pathology. In the absence of demonstrable abnormality, patients should be followed for possible subsequent development of overt renal disease.

REFERENCES

Herdman, R. C., Michael, A. F., and Good, R. A. Postural proteinuria. Response to corticosteroid therapy. Ann. Intern. Med., 65:286, 1966.

King, S. E. Albuminuria (proteinuria) in renal diseases. II. Preliminary observations on the clinical course of patients with orthostatic albuminuria. New York J. Med., 59:825, 1959.

———— Postural adjustments and protein excretion by the kidney in renal disease. Ann. Intern. Med., 46:360, 1957.

———— and Baldwin, D. S. Renal hemodynamics during erect lordosis in normal man and subjects with orthostatic proteinuria. Proc. Soc. Exp. Biol. Med., 86:634, 1954.

———— and Baldwin, D. S. Production of renal ischemia and proteinuria in man by the adrenal medullary hormones. Amer. J. Med., 20:217, 1956.

Lange, K., Treser, G., Sagel, I., Ty, A., and Wasserman, E. Routine immunohistology in renal diseases. Ann. Intern. Med., 64:25, 1966.

Lathem, W. Renal circulatory dynamics and urinary protein excretion during infusions of l-norepinephrine and l-epinephrine in patients with renal disease. J. Clin. Invest., 35:1277, 1956.

———— Roof, B. S., Nickel, S. F., and Bradley, S. E. Urinary protein excretion and renal hemodynamic adjustments during orthostasis in patients with acute and chronic renal disease. J. Clin. Invest., 33:1457, 1954.

Lecocq, F. R., McPhaul, J. J., and Robinson, R. R. Fixed and reproducible orthostatic proteinuria. V. Results of a 5 year follow-up evaluation. Ann. Intern. Med., 64:557, 1966.

Lowgreen, E. Studies on benign proteinuria with special reference to the renal lymphatic system. Acta Med. Scand. (Suppl.), 300, 1966.

MacLean, P. R., and Robson, J. S. Unselective proteinuria in acute ischemic renal failure. Clin. Sci., 30:91, 1966.

Randolph, M. F., and Greenfield, M. Proteinuria. A six-year study of normal infants, preschool and school-age populations previously screened for urinary tract disease. Amer. J. Dis. Child., 114:631, 1967.

Robinson, R. R., and Glenn, W. G. Fixed and reproducible orthostatic proteinuria. IV. Urinary albumin excretion by healthy human subjects in the recumbent and upright postures. J. Lab. Clin. Med., 64:717, 1964.

——— Glover, S. N., Phillippi, P. J., Lecocq, F. R., and Longelier, P. R. Fixed and reproducible orthostatic proteinuria. I. Light microscopic studies of the kidney. Amer. J. Path., 39:291, 1961.

Rowe, D. S., and Soothill, J. F. The proteins of postural and exercise proteinuria. Clin. Sci., 21:87, 1961.

Ruckley, V. A., MacDonald, M. K., Maclean, P. R., and Robson, J. S. Glomerular ultrastructure and function in postural proteinuria. Nephron, 3:153, 1966.

Slater, R. J., O'Doherty, N. J., and DeWolfe, M. S. Studies on human proteinuria. I. The mechanism of postural proteinuria. Pediatrics, 26:190, 1960.

Wagner, M. G., Smith, F. G., Jr., Tinglof, B. O., and Cornberg, E. Epidemiology of proteinuria. A study of 4,807 school children. J. Pediat., 73:825, 1968.

22.8
GLOMERULONEPHRITIS

CHESTER M. EDELMANN, JR.

Glomerulonephritis is a term used to include a number of diseases of the kidney which affect primarily the glomeruli. These diseases are distinguished from primary vascular disorders, nephropathies associated with systemic diseases, toxic and infectious disorders of the kidneys, congenital parenchymal malformations, and so forth. Although they are considered collectively, since they exhibit many similarities in their clinical courses and histologic abnormalities, it should be emphasized that these diseases undoubtedly represent diverse etiologies, and their nosologic relationships are unclear.

Addis considered that all forms of glomerulonephritis began with an acute stage, even though the disease at that stage might not have been clinically apparent. Longcope and Ellis subsequently divided glomerulonephritis into two groups, depending on whether the onset was acute or insidious. They recognized that recovery was the common course following acute glomerulonephritis, whereas failure to recover was most common when the onset was insidious.

In addition to these clinical classifications, attempts have been made to classify glomerulonephritis on the basis of the histologic changes within the kidney. Most recently, classifications based on underlying immunologic mechanisms have been proposed. It is apparent, however, that no classification, clinical, pathologic, or immunologic, is completely satisfactory. The same disease may present clinically with an abrupt explosive onset and be labeled "acute glomerulonephritis" or may be detected fortuitously and ultimately be labeled "chronic progressive glomerulonephritis." Conversely, patients presenting with any given clinical picture may have a wide variety of underlying histologic lesions.

Unfortunately, too little is known of the cause of most forms of glomerulonephritis to make possible a classification based on etiology. The classification used here, therefore, is based mainly on the various clinical syndromes which have been identified. This of necessity must result in some degree of confusion and redundancy. For example, lupus erythematosus, hereditary nephritis, and membranoproliferative glomerulonephritis all may present with a clinical picture indistinguishable at onset from acute postinfectious glomerulonephritis. As described here, however, acute glomerulonephritis refers to the latter condition. The various diseases which may present clinically with the nephrotic syndrome are mentioned in the discussion under that heading. Nevertheless the bulk of the section on the nephrotic syndrome deals with the idiopathic form commonly observed in children. Without this somewhat arbitrary restriction, many forms of progressive glomerulonephritis would need to be discussed under each of the headings acute glomerulonephritis, the nephrotic syndrome, and chronic progressive glomerulonephritis.

Attempts have been made to point out the interrelationships between the various clinical and pathologic syndromes, but the reader should be aware that distinctions often are arbitrary and a certain degree of compromise cannot be avoided.

REFERENCES

Heptinstall, R. H. Glomerulonephritis: Historical outline and classification. In Pathology of the Kidney. Boston, Little, Brown, and Co., 1966, p. 235.

White, R. H. R. Glomerulonephritis in children. Brit. J. Hosp. Med., p. 746, May 1970.

Etiology and Pathogenesis

CLARK D. WEST

Currently, many forms of glomerulonephritis are considered to have their origin in an immune reaction. In brief, the sequence of the reaction is thought to be formation or lodgement of an antigen-antibody complex in the glomerulus, activation of the complement system by the immune complex, with the complement reaction in turn producing the inflammation which generates the glomerular lesion. Because of the diverse morphologic characteristics of the glomerular lesions in the various nephritides, it is felt that the nature and site of the immune reaction, and perhaps the nature of the antibody itself, vary significantly from one type of nephritis to the other.

For a better understanding of the origin of the differences in the various types of glomerular immune reaction, its constituent parts can be considered separately. The *antigen*, which reacts with antibody to make up the immune complex, has differing origins in the various types of nephritis. In acute poststreptococcal nephritis, for example, there is evidence that the antigen is a constituent of the plasma membrane of the streptococcus, although this has not been definitely established. In lupus nephritis and in the nephritis accompanying chronic septicemia, the antigen is present in the circulation. In lupus, it consists of nuclear material, and in chronic septicemia of antigens found in the invading organism. Antigen fixed in the glomerulus also can be the target of antibody. Thus, in Goodpasture's syndrome and in certain types of rapidly progressive nephritis the antigen is the protein of the glomerular basement membrane. In the remainder of the nephritides listed below the nature and origin of the antigen is not known.

A second requirement in the pathogenesis of immunologically determined glomerulonephritis is the presence of *antibody*, which, in all types of human nephritis, is made by the host. In types in which the antigen is present in the circulation, antibody formation apparently is stimulated in the same manner as by any soluble antigen in the circulation. If conditions are right, including a state of slight antigen excess, *soluble immune complexes* are formed and remain for a period in the circulation. Subsequently these complexes become attached to the glomerular capillary walls. Why the attachment occurs in this capillary bed as opposed to other sites in the body is not completely understood. Attachment may be at this site because of an inherent stickiness of the endothelium or because of the large volume of fluid being filtered from plasma in this bed.

In Goodpasture's syndrome, in which the target of antibody is part of the structure of the glomerular capillary wall, it seems likely that the antigen which stimulates antibody production is part of the basement membrane of the lungs and that the antibody produced cross-reacts with an antigen in the glomerular basement membrane. Thus, renal involvement usually follows the pulmonary manifestations.

More and more, the characteristics of the antibody are being recognized as important determinants in the development and the severity of the nephritis. For instance, recent studies have indicated that the complement-fixing activity of the antibody correlates closely with the presence of nephritis; in disseminated lupus erythematosus, signs of nephritis were present only in those patients who had antinuclear antibody with high complement-fixing activity.

The next step in the pathogenesis of nephritis is the reaction of the immune complex with *complement*. In recent years great advances have been made in our knowledge of the complement system, but to make it pertinent to nephritis, much more information is needed. The complement system, which contains nine components, reacts like a row of dominoes, in that activation of one component causes activation of the next ad seriatum until all nine components have reacted.

In most types of nephritis, the initiating event is thought to be activation of C1 by reaction with the immune complex. C1 in turn activates C2 and C4. These components then combine to form the complex C42, which is usually attached to a structure and in turn reacts with C3. The events to this point constitute the *activation mechanism* of the complement system. The reaction of subsequent components is known as the *attack mechanism*. This nomenclature has evolved from the observation that many of the components which react subsequently, namely C3 through C9, have the ability to initiate events which lead not only to lysis of red blood cells but also to production of an inflammatory reaction. Thus, when activated, C3 liberates a low-molecular-weight anaphylatoxin, which also has chemotactic properties. In addition, on its attachment to a structure, C3 confers on that structure the property of immune adherence, so called because other small particles, even if devoid of complement, will stick to the C3-coated structure. C5, the component reacting after C3, when activated also forms a low-molecular-weight fragment which has the properties of anaphylatoxin; the complex of C5, C6, and C7, formed in the course of the complement reaction, has chemotactic properties. Finally, C8 and C9 have the ability to produce an ultrastructural lesion in the wall of erythrocytes and other cells.

The extent of the contribution of the above factors to *glomerular inflammation* in nephritis is currently not established. Low-molecular-weight fragments with chemotactic or anaphylatoxic properties may be swept away from their site of formation in the glomerulus and be ineffective, as compared to their effectiveness at sites of inflammation in soft tissue, where there is less fluid movement. Immune adherence of polymorphonuclear leucocytes to glomerular capillary walls through the presence of C3 is thought by some investigators to be the sole contribution of the complement system to the inflammatory reaction. Further work is needed to assess specifically the role of complement in nephritis and to identify the components or fragments involved.

There is evidence that there are mechanisms for activation of complement other than by the immune complex. Thus, it has been found that in cobra venom there is a factor which will activate C3, and that the activated C3 will in turn cause activation of subsequent components. Thus, the attack mechanism is activated and the need for the immune complex and for C1, C4, and C2 is bypassed. There is evidence that a similar factor may be present in the plasma of hypocomplementemic patients with membranoproliferative nephritis, but its role in producing the glomerular inflammation has not been established.

A brief discussion of the evidence that immune complex and complement participate in producing the glomerular inflammation of nephritis is in order. One of the main items of evidence is the frequent detection in patients with nephritis of IgG and components of complement, particularly the third component, in the glomerular capillary wall. Using immunopathologic methods, with fluorescein-labeled antibody, both IgG and complement, or complement alone, have been observed in nearly all types of nephritis. These proteins cannot be detected in normal kidneys or in the kidneys of patients with so-called nil disease or lipoid nephrosis. The pattern of fluorescence correlates to some extent with the site of the antigen-antibody reaction. For instance, in acute poststreptococcal nephritis, and usually in lupus nephritis, the IgG and complement components are in granular deposits in the capillary walls, representing aggregates of these proteins which are immunologically nonspecific with regard to specific sites within the kidney, whereas in Goodpasture's disease and certain types of rapidly progressive nephritis there is a thin delicate line of fluorescence which represents the cut surface of the glomerular basement membrane, the specific site of the antigen-antibody reaction.

Identification of glomerular immune complexes is also possible by electron microscopy. They are recognized as electron-dense masses, located close to the basement membrane either on the endothelial or epithelial side. Their position and distribution usually correlate with the pattern of fluorescence.

A second point favoring participation of immune complex and complement in the pathogenesis of nephritis is the fact that serum complement levels often are low in certain types of nephritis and that breakdown products of complement may be found in the circulation in these cases. Whereas this suggests an ongoing complement reaction, certain reservations as to the meaning of the hypocomplementemia should be kept in mind. Thus, in many types of nephritis, abundant IgG and complement may be detectable in the glomeruli, yet serum complement has never been found to be reduced. Secondly, recent studies have shown that in membranoproliferative nephritis, the hypocomplementemia is not dependent on the kidneys; in patients maintained in the anephric state after bilateral nephrectomy, the hypocomplementemia continues unabated. Ancillary studies give evidence that complement breakdown in these patients is occurring in the circulation. Thus, the significance of hypocomplementemia as indicating an intrarenal complement reaction needs further evaluation.

The final point of evidence for the immune-complex origin of nephritis is the fact that antibody specific for basement membrane can be eluted from the kidneys of patients with Goodpasture's syndrome and certain other types of rapidly progressive nephritis. The eluted antibody can be shown to react in vitro with the glomerular basement membrane of normal kidney and, on injection into monkeys, produces a fulminating nephritis. Antinuclear-reacting gamma globulin also has been eluted from the glomeruli in lupus nephritis.

In summary, an immune origin of many, if not most, types of glomerulonephritis has been suggested by the presence in the glomerular lesions of components of complement and often also of IgG, supposedly as the antibody portion of an immune complex. The glomerular inflammation is thought to be the result of the activation of the complement system by reaction with the immune complex.

In only a few types of nephritis, namely that associated with Goodpasture's syndrome, lupus erythematosus, chronic septicemia, and possibly acute poststreptococcal nephritis, has the antigen with which the antibody reacts been identified. In membranoproliferative nephritis, the requirement for antigen may be bypassed altogether, and the hypocomplementemia may not even be indicative of a glomerular immune reaction. In all other types of nephritis, the origin and nature of the immune reactions are not known, and the presence of IgG and complement in the lesions is the only evidence that an immune reaction is responsible for the inflammation.

REFERENCES

Coahrane, C. C. Mediation of immunologic glomerular injury. Transplant. Proc., 1:949, 1969.

Dixon, F. J. Tissue injury produced by antigen-antibody complexes. In Grabar, P., and Meischer, P., eds., Mechanisms of Cell and Tissue Damage Produced by Immune Reactions. II. International Symposium on Immunopathology. New York, Grune and Stratton, Inc., 1961.

Koffler, D., Schur, P. H., Kunkel, H. G., and Grat, M. Evidence for the renal deposition of antigen-antibody complexes in patients with systemic lupus erythematosus. In Grabar, P., and Meischer, P., eds., Immunopathology: Mechanisms of Inflammation Produced by Immune Reactions. 5th International Symposium. New York, Grune and Stratton, Inc., 1967.

Müller-Eberhard, H. J. Complement. Ann. Rev. Biochem., 38:389, 1969.

Tojo, T., and Friou, G. J. Lupus nephritis: varying complement-fixing properties of immunoglobulin G antibodies to antigens of cell nuclei. Science, 161:904, 1968.

Acute Glomerulonephritis

CHESTER M. EDELMANN, JR.

Acute glomerulonephritis is characterized by the sudden onset of proteinuria and hematuria one or two weeks following a respiratory infection, in association with a variable degree of edema, hypertension, and oliguria. Performance of percutaneous renal biopsies soon after the onset of what appears clinically to be acute glomerulonephritis has led to the recognition that many of the chronic progressive glomerulopathies may be initiated or exacerbated by a syndrome that is indistinguishable clinically from acute postinfectious glomerulonephritis. It is the latter disease that will be discussed in this section.

ETIOLOGY. Experimental work and clinical observations both suggest that acute nephritis most commonly represents an altered tissue reaction following infection with Group A beta hemolytic streptococci. Other infectious agents, including other bacteria and viruses, have been implicated, and it is likely that there are diverse etiologies. Differences in clinical course and renal histology dependent upon etiology have not been established and only acute poststreptococcal nephritis will be described here in detail.

Although infection with Group A streptococci precedes the acute episode in most instances, the rate of attack varies widely. It has been possible to demonstrate a rise of antistreptolysin O titer in 70 to 90 percent of afflicted children. It has been shown that most of the infections which precede acute nephritis are caused by type 12 or 4 hemolytic streptococci; less frequently other types (types 1, Red Lake, and 25) are implicated. The infection is usually followed by a latent period before the nephritis becomes evident.

It is now generally accepted that acute glomerulonephritis is a form of "immune-complex disease," the antigenic component of the immune complex being related somehow to the streptococcus. Most attempts at demonstrating streptococcal components or products in the deposits in the kidney, however, have been unsuccessful. Recently, Lange and associates demonstrated in the serum of patients with acute glomerulonephritis antibody that reacted with the glomerular capillary wall of patients with early acute glomerulonephritis. The antibody appeared to be specific for streptococcal plasma membrane, and presumably was reacting in the glomerulus with streptococcal material.

INCIDENCE.   The incidence of acute nephritis in children is difficult to assess. Systematic examination of the urine in children recovering from streptococcal infections has provided clinical evidence that many patients with acute glomerulonephritis are not diagnosed because they are either asymptomatic or have such mild symptoms that the disease is not suspected and the urine is not examined. The performance by Dodge and co-workers of percutaneous renal biopsies in family contacts of patients with acute glomerulonephritis has now confirmed the diagnosis in such children not suspected of having the disease. Although the proportion of patients who may be undiagnosed cannot be estimated with any assurance, the figure is probably high enough that any epidemiologic studies must be interpreted with the knowledge that the population being described is the empirical one composed of recognized or manifest cases. Reports of patients with poststreptococcal glomerulonephritis with minimal or no urinary findings, which may be more frequent in children than adults, complicate epidemiologic analyses even further.

An analysis of the age of onset of clinically recognizable acute glomerulonephritis in 214 children during their first 12 years of life showed a peak incidence between 6 and 7 years with about 60 percent of cases occurring between 5 and 10 and 90 percent between 2 and 12 years of age (Fig. 12). Although it does occur, the disease is rare under 1 year of age, probably because of the low prevalence of streptococcal infections during that period. The high incidence during early school years may be related to the correspondingly high prevalence of streptococcal infections during that time.

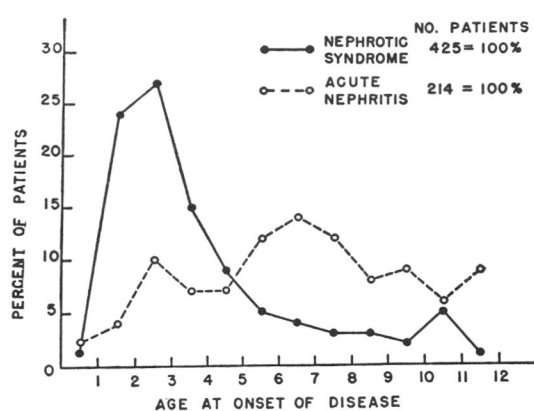

Fig. 12.   Age of onset of acute nephritis in 214 patients and of the nephrotic syndrome in 425 patients. (From Barnett, Forman, and Lauson. *Advances Pediat.*, 5:53, 1952.)

There is a distinct predominance of males over females, in some series as high as two to one. Familial incidence is not conspicuous. In this country climate seems to have a negligible influence on the incidence. Seasonal incidence is directly related to that of respiratory infections.

CLINICAL FEATURES.   Clinical manifestations of acute glomerulonephritis usually occur after an asymptomatic period following infection, rarely while the acute infection is still present. The latent period ranges from 1 to 2 weeks, the mean interval being 10 days. The preceding infection is usually one involving the upper respiratory tract, such as tonsillitis, otitis media, or cervical adenitis. Not infrequently, particularly in warm climates, infections of the skin, notably impetigo, precede glomerulonephritis. In some instances there is no knowledge of a preceding infection. Coexistence of active rheumatic fever and acute glomerulonephritis is rare, although it does occur; it was observed twice in one series of 140 patients.

There is marked variation in the intensity and distribution of symptoms and signs at the onset and during the early stage of acute nephritis. In many instances the symptoms and the urinary findings are so mild that, unless specially looked for, the disease is unrecognized. It is probable that the number of such unrecognized cases greatly exceeds those recognized.

The usual clinical manifestations of acute nephritis are a mild degree of edema, urinary abnormalities (hematuria, proteinuria, and cylindruria) and varying degrees of hypertension. The possibility of a child presenting with minimal or even no urinary abnormalities must not be overlooked. In one group of 144 hospitalized patients, 77 percent had urinary abnormalities, edema, and hypertension; 9 percent had urinary abnormalities and edema; 6 percent had urinary abnormalities and hypertension; and only 8 percent had urinary abnormalities alone.

Abdominal pain is present in more than one-half of patients. Other less frequent symptoms are low-grade fever, anorexia, vomiting, and headache. Evidences of the preceding infection may persist in the respiratory tract or skin.

The early phase of acute nephritis in children is made perilous by three possible complications: hypertensive encephalopathy, cardiac failure, and acute renal failure. Early recognition and prompt treatment of these complications are of greatest importance. Although usually present soon after the onset of disease, they may develop several days later, a fact which necessitates close observation.

Edema is present in most patients, although fluid retention may not be apparent until the patient has lost several pounds of weight in association with a diuresis. Edema is almost certainly due to primary renal retention of salt and water; the theory attributing it to generalized increased vascular permeability has been discarded.

Symptoms and signs referable to the heart occur in many patients with acute nephritis, and heart failure dominates the clinical picture in some. Paroxysmal or persistent dyspnea, orthopnea, apical gallop rhythm, cardiac enlargement, venous engorgement, enlarged liver, and pulmonary edema may appear suddenly during the course or may be the first manifestation of the disease. Radiographic evidence of pulmonary edema is seen in as many as 60 percent of cases. The cause of heart failure in acute nephritis is not certain but it is probably attributable to an increase in blood volume secondary to retention of sodium and water. Although cardiac work may be aggravated by accompanying hypertension, it seems clear that failure is not due to hypertension per se. Evidence for myocarditis is lacking.

Hypertensive encephalopathy is characterized by headache, vomiting, irritability or apathy, convulsions, transitory paralyses, and coma. Temporary, complete blindness occurs occasionally. Cause of the elevated blood pressure is unknown. The hypertension of acute nephritis is attributed to expanded vascular volume or to vasospasm, the cerebral symptoms being caused by cerebral ischemia and anoxia. Papilledema may or may not be present. Blood pressure may be as high as 160 to 200 systolic and 100 to 140 diastolic.

Severe renal failure (p. 1463) is a less common complication of acute nephritis in children. It is characterized by marked oliguria or anuria.

LABORATORY FINDINGS. Although urinary abnormalities may be minimal, proteinuria is almost always present, ranging from 1+ to 4+. Quantitatively, there is usually not more than 1 g of protein in a 12-hour overnight collection and there may be as little as 25 or 50 mg.

Gross or microscopic hematuria is almost always present, the urine usually being reddish-brown or smoky in appearance. The supernatant usually is brownish, indicating hemolysis and release of hemoglobin which has been converted to acid-hematin.

The urinary sediment also contains many white blood cells and epithelial cells, and hyaline, granular, and red blood cell casts. Early in the disease, white blood cells in the urine may predominate and suggest a urinary tract infection. These urinary abnormalities may vary independently in severity and duration.

The antistreptolysin O titer is usually elevated, the degree and duration of the elevation being related to hemolytic streptococcal infection rather than to the severity or duration of glomerulonephritis..

Hypocomplementemia is almost always demonstrable and is very useful in the differential diagnosis. With the exception of lupus erythematosus, the finding of a transiently low complement level in a patient presenting clinically with acute nephritis almost assures the diagnosis of postinfectious glomerulonephritis.

Mild hypoalbuminemia is commonly found, which is usually dilutional in origin. Occasionally it is caused, at least in part, by severe proteinuria. Almost one-half of children have moderate degrees of hypercholesterolemia, as part of a generalized hyperlipidemia. The cause of these elevations is unknown. Hypoalbuminemia and hyperlipidemia, in association with proteinuria and edema, may lead initially to the diagnosis of the idiopathic nephrotic syndrome.

Moderate elevation of the body temperature and leucocytosis may be present during the first few days. Mild anemia is usually present, being attributable to expansion of the vascular volume. Hemolysis and bone marrow depression are absent or play only minor roles. Unexplained thrombocytopenia has been reported, and may be related to the preceding infection, although this finding should alert the physician to the possibility of a hemolytic-uremic syndrome. Elevation of the erythrocyte sedimentation rate develops during the course of acute glomerulonephritis.

Transient electrocardiographic changes consisting of premature beats, T wave inversion, and prolongation of the P-R interval may occur.

Renal functional impairment is usually present from the onset. The most characteristic alteration is reduction in glomerular filtration rate. Urea clearance is usually depressed, with the blood urea and nonprotein nitrogen correspondingly increased. Renal plasma flow is usually normal or slightly increased, rarely decreased. The filtration fraction characteristically is low. This low filtration fraction indicates that the functional alteration, like the morphologic one, is predominantly glomerular. Ability to excrete water may be maintained but frequently is impaired. Maximal concentrating capacity is retained throughout in about 40 percent of patients with acute glomerulonephritis; in the remainder it may be impaired either early or late. The few observations on other tubular functions, such as extraction ratio of paraaminohippurate and maximal rates of tubular transport of PAH and glucose, indicate that these functions frequently are impaired to some degree. Return of the various renal functions to normal generally lags behind clinical improvement; decreased glomerular filtration and impaired concentrating capacity may persist after blood pressure has returned to normal and edema has disappeared.

RENAL PATHOLOGY. Acute glomerulonephritis is a nonsuppurative inflammatory disease of the kidney, in which the primary lesion resides in the glomeruli. Poststreptococcal glomerulenophritis is characteristically diffuse, involving virtually all glomeruli. The most striking abnormality of the glomeruli is hypercellularity, compounded of swelling and proliferation of the capillary endothelial cells, proliferation of the mesangial or intercapillary cells, and variable leucocytic infiltration. The glomeruli are usually enlarged, sometimes considerably, and they are ischemic despite the presence of leucocytes within the capillary lumens. Electron microscopic studies have in addition shown swelling of the basement membrane and subepithelial deposits of electron-dense material, forming localized bumps or "humps" that contain immunoglobulin and complement. Deposits of basement membranelike material are also found among the mesangial cells in the glomerular stalks. Changes in epithelial cells, consisting of variable swelling, increased vacuolization, and occasional fusion of the foot processes, are believed to be secondary to alterations in endothelial cells and basement membrane that affect the permeability of the glomerular capillaries. More severe degrees of glomerular inflammation include crescent formation and focal thrombosis. Tubular necrosis and disruption are occasionally seen in association with severe glomerular inflammation.

Despite the occasional predominance of either exudative or proliferative changes, subclassifying the disease into these two traditional histologic types contributes little to the clinical evaluation of the patient. The severity of the histologic lesion seems to be correlated in a general way with the severity of the clinical course, and permanent renal impairment is found among those children who had initially severe disease.

Resolution of the inflammatory process in acute diffuse glomerulonephritis appears to be a protracted process. Most cases go on to complete recovery, with perhaps only focal glomerular scarring. The mesangial cells, which had been diffusely increased, aggregate in clusters in the stalks, where they are associated with the deposits of fibrillary, periodic acid-Schiff-positive, basement membranelike material and with focal deposits of immunoglobulin. These abnormalities may persist long after the patient's clinical status has reverted to normal. Endothelial and mesangial cells eventually return to normal, and the deposits are resorbed. Some adhesions also may persist, but even severe exudative lesions, such as crescents, are capable of resolution. Severely damaged glomeruli may, on the other hand, undergo obsolescence, with fibrosis and hyalinization, and the loss of a sufficient number of glomeruli can lead to a functional deficit

or to permanent glomerular insufficiency. It is not known whether the latter is static, once the initial inflammatory process has subsided, or if glomerular damage is progressive, leading to diffuse glomerular depletion and the findings of chronic glomerulonephritis.

DIFFERENTIAL DIAGNOSIS. The onset of the classical manifestations of acute glomerulonephritis, urinary abnormalities, edema, and hypertension, following infection in a child usually establishes the diagnosis without difficulty. When there are only urinary abnormalities, the diagnosis is more difficult. Transient urinary abnormalities may occur in the course of dehydration, heart failure, infections, and drug intoxications. Their persistence for a week without other explanation suggests the diagnosis of nephritis, which may be supported by the demonstration of renal functional impairment. Differentiation from postural proteinuria may require careful observation.

Urinary tract infection should be considered in the differential diagnosis even in the absence of specific symptoms. Urine cultures, with quantitation of bacteriuria, serve to establish the diagnosis. Benign recurrent hematuria may mimic acute nephritis in every respect, and is differentiated on the basis of the clinical course (p. 1507).

Not infrequently the onset of some type of progressive glomerulonephritis, particularly membranoproliferative disease, mimics acute glomerulonephritis. Exacerbation of preexisting chronic nephritis also may easily be mistaken for acute disease. The history and prior urinalyses, in addition to renal biopsy close to the onset of recognized disease, are of value in the differential diagnosis. Additional conditions which have to be considered are renal disease associated with Henoch-Schönlein syndrome, systemic lupus erythematosus, and periarteritis nodosa.

It should be emphasized that despite typical clinical and laboratory findings, the diagnosis of acute poststreptococcal glomerulonephritis cannot be established with certainty without histologic examination of the kidney. A renal biopsy should be performed, therefore, in all atypical cases, all cases that are unusually severe, and in patients in whom recovery is not following the expected course.

TREATMENT. The preventive treatment of acute nephritis consists in the prevention of streptococcal infections. An epidemic of acute nephritis at Red Lake, Minnesota, was promptly terminated by mass prophylaxis with benzathine penicillin. However, once the infection is clinically evident, the incidence of nephritis can be decreased only slightly, if at all, despite early and adequate treatment with antibiotics. After the nephritis itself has developed, antibiotics fail to affect its course. They are indicated only when there is evidence of persistent streptococcal infection.

No therapeutic measure has been demonstrated to influence favorably the course of acute glomerulonephritis. Prompt recognition and treatment of the early complications, based on sound understanding of the disturbed physiology, constitute the most urgent aspects of treatment.

Edema and Congestive Failure.   Salt restriction is the most important and frequently the only measure required in the therapy of edema. Patients demonstrating severe degrees of edema and oliguria may require management including dialysis, as described under *acute renal failure* (see p. 1463). Diuretics are usually totally ineffective, although a trial of furosemide or ethacrynic acid may be warranted. Patients with evidence of circulatory congestion and pulmonary edema may respond well to elevation of the head of the bed, phlebotomy, rotating tourniquets, positive pressure oxygen, and morphine. The value of digitalis is debated, but it probably should be given in the desperately ill patient.

Hypertension.   When there is evidence of rising blood pressure, or when the diastolic value exceeds 90 mm Hg, antihypertensive therapy should be given. Magnesium sulfate has been used widely for the treatment of hypertension, but with development of more effective and less toxic agents, it no longer is indicated. In our opinion a combination of reserpine (80 to 150 μg per kg) and hydralazine (250 to 500 μg per kg) given intramuscularly constitutes the treatment of choice. Often only a single dose is necessary, but the drugs should be given repeatedly as needed, with appropriate modification of dosage (see Sec. 21.12).

In situations with marked rises in blood pressure, requiring more urgent control, ganglionic blocking agents, such as pentolinium tartrate, or the veratrum alkaloids may be of value. Given parenterally, these agents may produce a drop in blood pressure within a few minutes.

Bed Rest.   Although traditional therapy of acute glomerulonephritis has included prolonged bed rest, a much less restrictive policy is now generally recommended. Bed rest is indicated as long as there are clinical manifestations of active disease, such as edema, hypertension, or gross hematuria. These usually subside within 2 or 3 weeks, after which the patient feels quite well. At this stage it is our policy to allow the patient up, activity gradually being resumed. Within a few weeks most children are back in school, but exhausting and competitive activities are prohibited until the Addis count returns to normal. This policy of early ambulation is well supported by many observations, especially the controlled studies of Akerrén and Lindgren in Sweden.

Diet.   Although protein restriction has been advocated in the past, present evidence indicates that it is without value. Illingworth et al. treated 42 cases by allocating them randomly to two dietary regimens, severe protein restriction and ordinary ward diet. Each patient was observed for a minimum period of one year and strict criteria of cure were applied. Their investigation failed to reveal any advantage in restricting protein. Similarly, Mortensen placed 44 patients alternately on low- and high-protein diets. Evaluation of these patients two years after discharge revealed that those on the high-protein diet recovered more rapidly than those on the restricted diet. It appears, then, that the only time that protein need be restricted is if acute renal failure occurs during the initial stage of acute nephritis. The same principle applies to the salt content of the diet, which should be that of a normal diet except during the period of hypertension, edema, and oliguria.

Antibiotics.   Recommendations vary concerning the prevention and treatment of infections in children recovering from acute nephritis. Although continuous prophylactic administration of antibiotics has been recommended, we do not believe this is justified. As has been pointed out, second attacks are rare. The situation differs from rheumatic fever in that the number of nephritogenic types of streptococci is limited; the great majority of attacks are caused by type 12, and a permanent immunity to this type results from an attack.

Other Therapy.   There is no convincing evidence that tonsillectomy, renal decapsulation, adrenocortical steroids, or immunosuppressive agents have any favorable influence on the course of acute glomerulonephritis.

COURSE AND PROGNOSIS.   In the great majority of instances the course of acute glomerulonephritis in children is benign. In the past the majority of deaths were due to extension of the preceding streptococcal infection, congestive heart failure, or hypertension with central nervous system complications. Deaths from these causes are now rare. In a prospective study of 362 children with acute glomerulonephritis, there were no deaths attributable to them. Early deaths are due now almost exclusively to acute renal failure, which appears to be more frequent and more severe in adults than in children.

In the course of 1 to 3 weeks, edema, gross hematuria, and hypertension, if they have been present, ordinarily have disappeared and the patient usually feels quite well. Abnormal laboratory findings usually last somewhat longer. Functional impairment, as shown by azotemia or impaired clearances of urea, creatinine, or inulin, may persist for 1 or 2 months, occasionally as long as 6 months. Addis counts remain abnormal somewhat longer, usually not more than 6 months but sometimes for more than a year. If renal function has returned to normal, one can confidently predict that the urinary abnormalities will do so, though somewhat later, and permanent recovery is practically assured (Fig. 13). The probability of a second attack is less than the probability of a first attack in the population at large, for permanent immunity develops against the particular nephritogenic strain of streptococcus that has caused the attack.

The proportion of patients who fail to heal following what appears clinically to be acute glomerulonephritis is generally estimated to range from 30 to 50 percent in adults and from 0 to 10 percent in children. These estimates, based previously on clinical

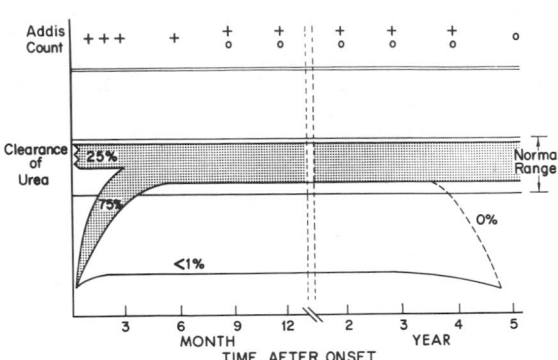

Fig. 13. Schematic representation of the course of acute glomerulonephritis in children.

data alone, must be reexamined to include the relationship between the clinical and pathologic features of the disease. Understanding the nature and course of the disease(s) in these patients requires additional information on several important questions. The one which has been argued most extensively is whether acute glomerulonephritis in children is an antecedent of chronic nephritis in adults. Prospective studies have revealed complete healing in such a high proportion of children that a relationship with chronic nephritis in adults seems very unlikely. However, at least two possible situations could negate this suggestion. Acute glomerulonephritis in children whose clinical features are so mild that the disease is not recognized could, unlike the recognized form, lead to latent disease first manifested as chronic nephritis of unknown cause in adults. However, our experience and that of most though not all other pediatric nephrologists suggests that the severity of the clinical manifestations correlates with the severity of the pathologic change in the glomerulus and with the patient's prognosis. It seems unlikely, therefore, that complete healing would occur less frequently in children with the mildest clinical disease.

The preceding discussion does not exclude completely the second possibility, that what appears clinically to be complete healing may be associated histologically with pathologic processes which might lead to future disease after a long latent period. Persistent histologic alterations observed in renal biopsy of children who clinically have recovered completely provide tentative support for this concept. However, until much more evidence is at hand it does not seem reasonable to assume that there is a relationship between acute glomerulonephritis in children and chronic nephritis of unknown cause in adults.

Another important unanswered question concerns the nature of the disease(s) in children with apparent acute glomerulonephritis which *does* fail to heal. Percutaneous renal biopsy has shown that some patients in these groups had preexisting glomerular disease, the proportion being lower in children than in adults. Such exacerbations of preexisting renal disease may follow streptococcal as well as other infections, which in itself does not establish the diagnosis of acute poststreptococcal glomerulonephritis. In other patients what appears to be acute glomerulonephritis is, in fact, the onset of one of the many types of progressive glomerulonephritis.

Excluding these patients, there remains a very small number of patients with typical acute poststreptococcal glomerulonephritis who do develop chronic renal disease. In our experience these children have had severe symptoms initially with depressed renal function which, though it may improve, does not return to normal. They "progress," therefore, from what appears to be acute glomerulonephritis directly to chronic renal insufficiency over a period of months or years. Renal biopsies suggest that in these children so many glomeruli were destroyed in the initial episode that chronic renal insufficiency developed even though there was no continuing activity of the initial disease process.

We have not seen children develop chronic nephritis after a latent stage of several years during which renal function was normal and Addis counts abnormal. If children go through such a course it must be extremely rare, and no justification exists for trying to explain on such a sequence the large number of cases of chronic nephritis seen in adults.

REFERENCES

Addis, T. Glomerular Nephritis; Diagnosis and Treatment. New York, The Macmillan Co., 1948.

Akerrén, Y., and Lindgren, M. Investigation concerning early rising in acute haemorrhagic nephritis. Acta Med. Scand., 151:419, 1955.

Albert, M. S., Leeming, J. M., and Scaglione, P. R. Acute glomerulonephritis without abnormality of the urine. J. Pediat., 68:525, 1966.

Bates, R. C., Jennings, R. B., and Earle, D. P. Acute nephritis unrelated to group A hemolytic streptococcus infection. Amer. J. Med., 23:510, 1957.

Blumberg, R. W., and Feldman, D. B. Observations on acute glomerulonephritis associated with impetigo. J. Pediat., 60:677, 1962.

Burke, E. C., and Titus, J. L. Poststreptococcal acute glomerulonephritis in children. Med. Clin. N. Amer., 50:1141, 1966.

Callis, L., Castelló, F., and Garcia, L. Histopathological aspects of acute diffuse glomerulonephritis in children. Helv. Paediat. Acta, 22:(Suppl.)16, 1967.

Cohen, J. A., and Levitt, M. F. Acute glomerulonephritis with few urinary abnormalities. Report of two cases proved by renal biopsy. New Eng. J. Med., 268:749, 1963.

Daeschner, C. W., Moyer, J. H., Bell, W. R., and Clark, J. L. Parenteral administration of reserpine in the treatment of hypertension due to acute and chronic nephritis; clinical and renal hemodynamic studies. Pediatrics, 19:566, 1957.

Derrick, C. W., Reeves, M. S., and Dillon, H. C., Jr. Complement in overt and asymptomatic nephritis after skin infection. J. Clin. Invest., 49:1178, 1970.

Dodge, W. F., Daeschner, C. W., Jr., Brenman, J. C., Rosenberg, H. S., Travis, L. B., and Hopps, H. C. Percutaneous renal biopsy in children. II. Acute glomerulonephritis, chronic glomerulonephritis, and nephritis of anaphylactoid purpura. Pediatrics, 30:297, 1962.

——— Spargo, B. H., Bass, J. A., and Travis, L. B. The relationship between the clinical and pathologic features of poststreptococcal glomerulonephritis. A study of the early natural history. Medicine, 47:227, 1968.

Edelmann, C. M., Jr., Greifer, I., Barnett, H. L. The nature of kidney disease in children who fail to recover from acute glomerulonephritis. J. Pediat., 64:879, 1964.

Etteldorf, J. N., Smith, J. D., and Johnson, C. The effect of reserpine and its combination with hydralazine on blood pressure and renal hemodynamics during the hypertensive phase of acute nephritis in children. J. Pediat., 48:129, 1956.

Feldman, J. D., Mardiney, M. R., and Shuler, S. E. Immunology and morphology of acute post-streptococcal glomerulonephritis. Lab. Invest., 15:283, 1966.

Fish, A. J., Herdman, R. C., Michael, A. F., Pickering, R. J., and Good, R. A. Epidemic acute glomerulonephritis associated with type 49 streptococcal pyoderma. II. Correlative study of light, immunofluorescent and electron microscopic findings. Amer. J. Med., 48:28, 1970.

Fleisher, D. S., Voci, G., Garfunkel, J., Purugganan, H., Kirkpatrick, J., Jr., Wells, C. R., and McElfresh, A. E. Hemodynamic findings in acute glomerulonephritis. J. Pediat., 69:1054, 1966.

Greifer, I. Clinicopathology and natural history of acute glomerulonephritis. In Metcoff, J., ed., Acute Glomerulonephritis, 17th Annual Conference on the Kidney. Boston, Little, Brown, and Co., 1967, p. 165.

Grupe, W. E. IgG-β1c cryoglobulins in acute glomerulonephritis. Pediatrics, 42:474, 1968.

Harrington, J. T., and Senior, G. Recovery following 36 days of oliguria in a child with acute glomerulonephritis. Amer. J. Dis. Child., 115:611, 1968.

Herbert, H. J. Acute glomerulonephritis in childhood, a study of the late prognosis of twenty-seven cases. J. Pediat., 40:549, 1952.

Herdson, P. B., Jennings, R. B., and Earle, D. P. Glomerular fine structure in poststreptococcal glomerulonephritis. Lab. Invest., 15:283, 1966.

Heymann, W., and Wilson, S. G. F. Hyperlipemia in early stages of acute glomerular nephritis. J. Clin. Invest., 38:186, 1959.

Hoyer, J. R., Michael, A. F., Fish, A. J., and Good, R. A. Acute poststreptococcal glomerulonephritis presenting as hypertensive encephalopathy with minimal urinary abnormalities. Pediatrics, 39:412, 1967.

Hutt, M. S. R., Pinniger, J. L., and DeWardener, H. E. The relationship between the clinical and the histological features of acute glomerular nephritis. Based on a study of renal biopsy material. Quart. J. Med., 27:265, 1958.

Illingworth, R. S., Philpott, M. G., and Rendle-Short, J. A controlled investigation of the effect of diet on acute nephritis. Arch. Dis. Child., 29:551, 1954.

Jennings, R. B., and Earle, D. P. Poststreptococcal glomerulonephritis: histopathologic and clinical studies of the acute, subsiding acute, and early chronic latent phases. J. Clin. Invest., 40:1525, 1961.

Joseph, M. C., and Polani, P. E. The effect of bed rest on acute hemorrhagic nephritis in children. Guy Hosp. Rep., 107:500, 1958.

Kandall, S., Edelmann, C. M., Jr., and Bernstein, J. Acute poststreptococcal glomerulonephritis. A case with minimal urinary abnormalities. Amer. J. Dis. Child., 118:426, 1969.

Lewy, J. E., Salinas-Madrigal, L., Pirani, C., and Metcoff, J. Clinical and morphological correlates in acute glomerulonephritis. Pediat. Res., 2:318, 1968.

Lieberman, E., Donnell, G. N. Recovery of children with acute glomerulonephritis. Amer. J. Dis. Child., 109:398, 1965.

McCluskey, R. T., Vassalli, P., Gallo, G., and Baldwin, D. S. An immunofluorescent study of pathogenetic mechanisms in glomerular diseases. New Eng. J. Med., 274:695, 1966.

McCrory, W. W., Fleisher, D. S., and Sohn, W. B. Effects of early ambulation on the course of nephritis in children. Pediatrics, 24:395, 1959.

Metcoff, J., ed. Acute Glomerulonephritis. 17th Annual Conference on the Kidney. Boston, Little, Brown and Co., 1967.

Michael, A. F., Jr., Drummond, K. N., Good, R. A., and Vernier, R. L. Acute poststreptococcal glomerulonephritis: Immune deposit disease. J. Clin. Invest., 45:237, 1966.

Minkowitz, S., Wenk, R., Friedman, E., Yuceoglu, A., and Berkovich, S. Acute glomerulonephritis associated with varicella infection. Amer. J. Med., 44:489, 1968.

Neustein, H. B., and Davis, W. Acute glomerulonephritis. A light and electron microscopy study of eight serial biopsies. Amer. J. Clin. Path., 44:613, 1965.

Perlman, L. V., Herdman, R. C., Kleinman, H., and Vernier, R. L. Poststreptococcal glomerulonephritis: a ten-year follow-up of an epidemic. J.A.M.A., 194:175, 1965.

Potter, E. V., Siegel, A. C., Simon, N. M., McAninch, J., Earle, D. P., Poon-King, T., Mohammed, I., and Abidh, S. Streptococcal infections and epidemic acute glomerulonephritis in South Trinidad. J. Pediat., 72:871, 1968.

Risdon, R. A., Sloper, J. C., and DeWardener, H. E. Relationship between renal function and histological changes found in renal-biopsy specimens from patients with persistent glomerular nephritis. Lancet, 2:363, 1968.

Roy, S., III, Wall, H. P., and Etteldorf, J. N. Second attacks of acute glomerulonephritis. J. Pediat., 75:758, 1969.

Rubin, M. I., Rapoport, M., and Bruck, E. Renal function studies in acute glomerulonephritis in children. J. Pediat., 41:823, 1952.

Tina, L. U., D'Albora, J. B., Antonovych, T. T., Bellanti, J. A., and Calcagno, P. L. Acute glomerulonephritis associated with normal serum β1C-globulin. Amer. J. Dis. Child., 115:29, 1968.

Treser, G., Ehrenreich, T., Ores, R., Sagel, I., Wasserman, E., and Lange, K. Natural history of "apparently healed" acute poststreptococcal glomerulonephritis in children. Pediatrics, 43:1005, 1969.

——— Semar, M., McVicar, M., Franklin, M., Ty, A., Sagel, I., and Lange, K. Antigenic streptococcal components in acute glomerulonephritis. Science, 163:676, 1969.

Vernier, R. L., Worthen, H. G., Wannamaker, L. W.,

and Good, R. A. Renal biopsy studies of the acute exacerbation in glomerulonephritis. Amer. J. Dis. Child., 98:653, 1959.

Wilson, S. G. F., and Heymann, W. Acute glomerulonephritis with the nephrotic syndrome. Pediatrics, 23: 874, 1959.

Yuceoglu, A. M., Berkovich, S., and Minkowitz, S. Acute glomerulonephritis associated with ECHO virus type 9 infection. J. Pediat., 69:603, 1966.

Rapidly Progressive Glomerulonephritis

CHESTER M. EDELMANN, JR.

Rapidly progressive glomerulonephritis refers to a severe form of glomerulonephritis that follows a very rapid course, varying from a few weeks to a few months, and ending commonly in death from uremia. The etiology is unknown but it appears to be an entity that is different from acute poststreptococcal glomerulonephritis. The condition is considered by some investigators to be a form of antiglomerular basement membrane disease.

Most reports have been in young adults, but a number of children have been described as well. The clinical onset may be acute or insidious. Proteinuria and hematuria are present, and azotemia progresses rapidly. Histologic examination of the kidneys reveals severe hypercellularity and hyperlobulation of the glomeruli. Crescents are a very prominent feature, and glomerular scarring is progressive.

Differential diagnosis includes acute poststreptococcal glomerulonephritis, hypersensitivity angiitis, lupus erythematosus, hemolytic-uremic syndrome, and Henoch-Schönlein nephritis.

No treatment has been demonstrated to be effective, although claims have been made for the beneficial effects of both heparin and immunosuppressive agents.

Chronic Progressive Glomerulonephritis of Nonspecific Etiology

CHESTER M. EDELMANN, JR.

Chronic nephritis represents a group of many diseases, rather than a single entity. It is characterized by bilateral, nonsuppurative disease of the kidneys, with continued loss of nephrons, progressive reduction in renal function, and ultimate renal insufficiency. Considered here are those conditions without known etiology. Progressive glomerular diseases with known etiologies or associated with systemic diseases, such as anaphylactoid purpura; metabolic diseases, such as diabetes mellitus; and collagen diseases, such as lupus erythematosus, are discussed elsewhere. It is difficult to estimate the frequency with which chronic nephritis in children is associated with these various conditions. It would appear, however, that in most instances it arises de novo. The end stage comprises the pathologic features of glomerular obsolescence, tubular atrophy, and cortical fibrosis. Secondary vascular changes and chronic inflammation complicate the histologic picture. Occasionally remnants of the active process provide a clue to the initial lesion. Much more information can be obtained by studying renal biopsies during the course of disease.

ETIOLOGY AND MORPHOLOGIC CLASSIFICATION. In children, as in adults, chronic nephritis may develop insidiously in the absence of any evidence of previous kidney disease, it may manifest with a nephrotic syndrome, or it may begin with what appears to be acute nephritis.

It has been suggested that a common cause of chronic nephritis in adolescents and adults is acute poststreptococcal glomerulonephritis in childhood, usually unrecognized. However, there is no convincing evidence for the progression, following a prolonged latent phase, of acute to chronic glomerulonephritis in either children or adults (see p. 1486).

The etiology of most forms of chronic glomerulonephritis is unknown, although recent evidence suggests that immune mechanisms may play a major role (see p. 1480). Renal biopsy has served to group the various nephritides into a number of histologic patterns, even though it is most likely that each morphologic type has a number of etiologies. There is a tendency for some of the histologic types to have a somewhat characteristic clinical course, and therefore it is useful to consider these individually.

A common histologic pattern found in children is *diffuse proliferative glomerulonephritis*, with crescent formation and hyalinization and sclerosis of glomeruli. The clinical features in such patients are extremely variable. They usually progress insidiously and may be detected fortuitously; they may present with what appears to be acute glomerulonephritis; uncommonly in children the first manifestation is the nephrotic syndrome; other children present for the first time in terminal renal failure. The pathogenesis of disease is entirely unknown, and there is no specific laboratory test. The course of these patients may be slow or rapid. They do not appear to be affected by any form of therapy.

Focal glomerulonephritis refers to a histologic pattern in which only some of the glomeruli reveal abnormalities, in contrast to the diffuse involvement seen in most types of nephritis. This form of glomerular disease has been found in association with collagen disease, may occur as a complication of bacteremia, and apparently may occur without known cause. Focal glomerulonephritis also occurs during the course of certain infections, particularly in patients with bloodstream invasion by pathogenic organisms such as the staphylococcus, gonococcus, and pneumococcus. These focal lesions result in urinary abnormalities but do not produce renal insufficiency. They are considered to be a manifestation of bacteremia and not a specific renal disease entity. Renal involvement occurs concomitant with infection, and not after a latent phase, as in acute poststreptococcal glomerulonephritis.

The lesions of periarteritis, systemic lupus erythematosus, and the Henoch-Schönlein syndrome may be focally distributed. In addition, focal glomerulonephritis may be found on renal biopsy in patients with asymptomatic proteinuria, asymptomatic hematuria, clinical acute glomerulonephritis, recurrent hematuria, or the nephrotic syndrome, suggesting not a single, but a group of diseases, with similar histologic abnormalities.

There are no distinctive clinical or laboratory features. Urinary findings vary from minimal abnormalities to massive proteinuria and gross hematuria. Reduction in renal function is usually only moderate, and may be entirely absent. Evidence of preceding streptococcal or other infection is lacking.

Differential diagnosis consists simply of ruling out known specific renal disease. In the absence of identifiable etiology, and with the histologic demonstration of focal renal involvement, the diagnosis of focal glomerulonephritis is made.

Some cases appear to be self-limiting, although since focal glomerulonephritis is a pathologic diagnosis associated with a variety of diseases, its course is extremely variable. Renal failure is reported, although the disease may continue for many years. Treatment is entirely symptomatic unless a specific etiology is determined.

Membranoproliferative glomerulonephritis is a specific type of disease in children that often is associated with persistent hypocomplementemia, although not all patients with hypocomplementemia have this histologic lesion. It appears to be the same disease as described under the term lobular glomerulonephritis. It commonly presents with the nephrotic syndrome, but may develop insidiously or have an abrupt onset similar to and causing it to be confused with acute poststreptococcal glomerulonephritis. This lesion is characterized by large, hyperlobulated glomeruli. The capillary walls are thickened, containing deposits that disrupt the basement membrane, which appears to be fragmented and split around them. The glomeruli contain beta-1C globulin, but immunofluorescence has shown relatively little IgG. The pattern of deposition is suggestive of immune-complex disease, but the antigenic stimulus is unknown. The course may be rapidly progressive, but it usually extends over a period of many years, with ultimate loss of renal function, progressive uremia, and death. It has been pointed out that patients may have normal function and be totally asymptomatic over a period of years, a circumstance not to be misinterpreted as indicating a good prognosis. At times the serum complement level may return to normal, despite clinical and histologic evidence of continued, active disease.

Pure membranous nephropathy is only rarely encountered in childhood. It usually is detected during the investigation of a child with the nephrotic syndrome, but may be found in patients with minimal, asymptomatic proteinuria. The course of this disease usually is quite protracted and patients characteristically are well for many years prior to their ultimate downhill course.

In patients with the nephrotic syndrome, complete clinical and biochemical remission may occur; patients with proteinuria as the only manifestation may have a return to an entirely normal urine; nevertheless, renal biopsy demonstrates steady progression of disease and recovery is not to be anticipated. Recent evidence suggests that this may be another example of immune-complex disease, although the nature of the antigen is not known (see p. 1480).

CLINICAL FEATURES.   As noted above, patients with chronic nephritis may have few if any symptoms for long periods of time. Indeed, the condition may be detected by the chance finding of asymptomatic proteinuria or hematuria. If it has been preceded by the nephrotic syndrome, there is often a period of months or even years during which the tendency toward edema subsides and the proteinuria decreases.

Hypertension, with significant elevation of diastolic pressure, often is present, although apparently less frequently than in adults with chronic nephritis. Ophthalmoscopic examination in patients with hypertension shows constricted retinal vessels, edema, exudates, or hemmorhages. Even with persistent reduction of kidney function, children may continue to grow through midchildhood and begin to have symptoms only during adolescence. When symptoms do develop, lassitude and fatigability are common and anemia is almost invariably present. There may be headache, restlessness, and insomnia. Muscular pains and twitchings are frequent, and there may be convulsions associated with hypertension. Rickets may become clinically manifest, and tetany may be present. Pericarditis is unusual in children.

As the condition advances the patient tends to become drowsy, he may develop Cheyne-Stokes respiration, and death follows, usually preceded by coma. The nature of the factors responsible for these manifestations remains obscure. Acidosis and dehydration play a limited part in the symptomatology. Nitrogen retention may be marked, but the symptoms cannot be attributed to or correlated with the level of any known nitrogenous constituent of the blood. Despite this uncertainty, it seems likely that retention of some end product of metabolism is responsible.

LABORATORY FEATURES.   As stated by Relman, "The cardinal laboratory finding in chronic glomerulonephritis and the sine qua non for the diagnosis is proteinuria." The degree of proteinuria is extremely variable and, particularly in the late stages of the disease, it may be minimal. The urinary sediment contains abnormal numbers of red blood cells and leucocytes, and as the disease progresses, large, broad renal failure casts appear.

Renal functional impairment may be minimal

early, but it becomes marked as the disease progresses. Gradually all the clinical and laboratory features of uremia develop (p. 1465).

PATHOPHYSIOLOGY. The disturbed physiology of chronic glomerulonephritis can be related directly to the process of progressive nephron destruction and production of renal insufficiency. The consequences of the resulting uremia have been discussed in an earlier section (p. 1465).

DIFFERENTIAL DIAGNOSIS. The findings of persistent proteinuria and hematuria in association with reduced renal function are suggestive of chronic glomerulonephritis, but are not sufficient to rule out other conditions. A search must be made for specific diseases, such as hereditary nephritis, lupus erythematosus, and renovascular hypertension. Urine cultures are essential in excluding pyelonephritis, radiographic examination of the urinary tract may be necessary to rule out obstructive uropathy and congenital malformations, and renal biopsy may be extremely helpful in diagnosing other conditions.

COURSE AND PROGNOSIS. Recovery does not occur once a child has passed into the hypertensive, uremic phase of the disease. Occasional patients who have had proteinuria for years, however, have apparently healed completely. Without histopathologic examination, the nature of the disease in such patients remains uncertain.

Chronic glomerulonephritis has an extremely variable course, making estimates of its duration very uncertain. The onset of azotemia usually indicates death from renal insufficiency within 5 to 10 years, but survivals well beyond this period have been reported. Hypertension is a serious prognostic sign, particularly when diastolic levels exceed 100 to 110 mm Hg. The association of hypertension and uremia indicates usually that death will occur within 3 to 5 years.

Some estimate of the course of the disease may be obtained from serial determinations of serum levels of urea or creatinine, or from estimates of glomerular filtration rate. When function falls below 10 to 15 percent of normal, patients are usually near the terminal phase of their disease.

TREATMENT. There is still no form of therapy which appears to reverse the course of chronic nephritis. However, during much of the course, and often over a period of many months or years, symptomatic treatment can be of great importance to the patient. Details of treatment are given in the discussion of uremia (p. 1465).

Prolonged restriction of activity is not recommended unless demanded by the symptomatic state of the patient. The child should be encouraged to attend school and to participate in other activities within his limitations. No special changes in diet are needed early in the course of chronic nephritis and needless restrictions should be avoided.

The evidence to date of favorable effects from treatment with adrenocortical steroids or other immunosuppressant therapy is not conclusive. Individual case reports suggest that in some patients the process of progressive nephron destruction may be slowed or even halted by such therapy.

REFERENCES

RAPIDLY PROGRESSIVE
GLOMERULONEPHRITIS

Bacani, R. A., Velasquez, F., Kanter, A., Pirani, C. L., and Pollak, V. E. Rapidly progressive (non-streptococcal glomerulonephritis). Ann. Intern. Med., 69:463, 1968.

Heptinstall, R. H. Rapidly progressive glomerulonephritis. *In* Pathology of the Kidney. Boston, Little, Brown and Co., 1966, p. 275.

Urizar, R. E., Tinglof, B., McIntosh, R., Litman, N., Barnett, E., Wilkerson, J., Smith, F., Jr., and Vernier, R. L. Immunosuppressive therapy of proliferative glomerulonephritis in children. Amer. J. Dis. Child., 118:411, 1969.

Kincaid-Smith, P., Saker, B. M., and Fairley, K. F. Anticoagulants in "irreversible" acute renal failure. Lancet, 2:1360, 1968.

CHRONIC PROGRESSIVE
GLOMERULONEPHRITIS

Adams, D. A., Gordon, A., and Maxwell, M. H. Azathioprine treatment of immunological renal disease. J.A.M.A., 199:459, 1967.

Bacani, R. A., Velasquez, F., Kanter, A., Pirani, C. L., and Pollak, V. E. Rapidly progressive (nonstreptococcal) glomerulonephritis. Ann. Intern. Med., 69:463, 1968.

Burke, E. C. Chronic nephritis in children: A diagnostic enigma. Proc. Mayo Clinic, 34:591, 1959.

Clark, N. S. Nephritis in childhood. A clinical assessment of the Ellis classification. Arch. Dis. Child., 31:12, 1956.

Corley, C. C., Jr., Lessner, H. E., and Larsen, W. E. Azathioprine therapy of "autoimmune" diseases. Amer. J. Med., 41:404, 1966.

Drummond, K. N., Hillman, D. A., Marchessault, V. J. H., and Feldman, W. Cyclophosphamide in the nephrotic syndrome of childhood. Canad. Med. Ass. J., 98:524, 1968.

Edelmann, C. M., Jr., Greifer, I., and Barnett, H. L. The nature of kidney disease in children who fail to recover from apparent acute glomerulonephritis. J. Pediat., 64:879, 1964.

Editorial. Treatment of steroid-resistant nephrotic syndrome. Lancet, 1:644, 1966.

——— Immunosuppressive or anti-inflammatory. Brit. Med. J., 1:650, 1967.

——— Immunosuppressive drugs and chronic renal disease. Lancet, 1:1093, 1967.

——— Recurrent haematuria and focal nephritis. Lancet, 1:413, 1966.

Grupe, W. E., and Heymann, W. Cytotoxic drugs in steroid-resistant renal disease. Amer. J. Dis. Child., 112:448, 1966.

Halikowski, B., Kucharska, K., Garwicz, S., Wyszkowski, J., and Sancewicz-Pach, K. The results of immunosuppressive therapy in chronic renal diseases in children and the assessment of erythroblasts behaviour. Acta Pediat. Scand., 59:44, 1970.

Heptinstall, R. H., and Joekes, A. M. Focal glomerulonephritis. A study based on renal biopsies. Quart. J. Med., 28:329, 1959.

Herdman, R. C., Edson, J. R., Pickering, R. J., Fish, A. J., Marker, S., and Good, R. A. Anticoagulants in renal disease in children. Amer. J. Dis. Child., 119: 27, 1970.

—— Pickering, R. J., Michael, A. F., Vernier, R. L., Fish, A. J., Gewurz, H., and Good, R. A. Chronic glomerulonephritis associated with low serum complement activity (chronic hypocomplementemic glomerulonephritis). Medicine, 49:207, 1970.

McCrory, W. W. A new cause for an old disease—chronic nephritis. J. Pediat., 72:912, 1968.

Michael, A. F., Vernier, R. L., Drummond, K. N., Levitt, J. I., Herdman, R. C., Fish, A. J., and Good, R. A. Immunosuppressive therapy of chronic renal disease. New Eng. J. Med., 276:817, 1967.

Northway, J. D., McAdams, A. J., Forristal, J., and West, C. D. A "silent" phase of hypocomplementemic persistent nephritis detectable by reduced serum β_{1c} globulin levels. J. Pediat., 74:28, 1969.

Okuda, R., Watanabe, Y., Yamamoto, Y., and West, C. D. The origin of membranoproliferative nephritis. Evidence against an origin from acute poststreptococcal nephritis. Amer. J. Dis. Child., 119:291, 1970.

Risdon, R. A., Sloper, J. C., and DeWardener, H. E. Relationship between renal function and histological changes found in renal biopsy specimens from patients with persistent glomerular nephritis. Lancet, 2:363, 1968.

Ross, J. H. Recurrent focal nephritis. Quart. J. Med., 29:391, 1960.

Swanson, M. A., and Schwartz, R. S. Immunosuppressive therapy. New Eng. J. Med., 277:163, 1967.

Urizar, R. E., Tinglof, B., McIntosh, R., Litman, N., Barnett, E., Wilkerson, J., Smith, F., Jr., and Vernier, R. L. Immunosuppressive therapy of proliferative glomerulonephritis in children. Amer. J. Dis. Child., 118:411, 1969.

Vernier, R. L., Farquhar, M. G., Brunson, J. G., and Good, R. A. Chronic renal disease in children. Correlation of clinical findings with morphologic characteristics seen by light and electron microscopy. Amer. J. Dis. Child., 96:306, 1958.

West, C. D., Holland, N. H., McConville, J. M., and McAdams, A. J. Immunosuppressive therapy in persistent hypocomplementemic glomerulonephritis and lupus nephritis. J. Pediat., 67:1113, 1965.

—— and McAdams, A. J., Serum β_{1c} globulin levels in persistent glomerulonephritis with low serum complement: variability unrelated to clinical course. Nephron, 7:193, 1970.

—— McAdams, A. J., McConville, J. M., Davis, N. C., and Holland, N. H. Hypocomplementemic and normocomplementemic persistent (chronic) glomerulonephritis; clinical and pathological characteristics. J. Pediat., 67:1089, 1965.

—— McAdams, A. J., and Northway, J. D. Focal glomerulonephritis in children. J. Pediat., 73:184, 1968.

White, R. H. R. "Silent" nephritis. Guy Hosp. Rep., 113:190, 1964.

—— Cytotoxic drug therapy in steroid resistant glomerulonephritis. Proc. Roy. Soc. Med., 60:1164, 1967.

—— Cameron, J. S., and Trounce, J. R. Immunosuppressive therapy in steroid-resistant proliferative glomerulonephritis accompanied by the nephrotic syndrome. Brit. Med. J., 2:853, 1966.

22.9
GLOMERULONEPHRITIS IN SYSTEMIC DISEASE

CHESTER M. EDELMANN, JR.

Henoch-Schönlein Syndrome

The Henoch-Schönlein syndrome is discussed in detail elsewhere (Sec. 17.13). This section will treat only the renal manifestations.

Anaphylactoid purpura appears to be more common in children than adults, with a peak incidence in childhood around 3 to 5 years. Cases in infants as young as 6 months have been reported. Most series report more males than females, but a higher incidence in females also has been reported. Most cases occur during the winter and spring months. A history of preceding respiratory infection is common, but there is no convincing evidence that the condition is related to antecedent streptococcal infection.

Reports in the literature vary considerably with regard to the frequency of renal involvement in this disease, but probably one-fourth to one-half of children have obvious renal disease. In our recent experience with 24 children with Henoch-Schönlein syndrome, only 6 had abnormal urines, as judged by repeated Addis counts, whereas 21 demonstrated histologic abnormalities on biopsy.

The pathogenesis of the syndrome is unknown. The multiorgan involvement and diffuse vasculitis suggest the possibility of a hypersensitivity reaction to drugs, foods, or infectious agents.

Renal involvement usually becomes apparent within a few days to a few weeks after the onset of the skin, joint, and gastrointestinal manifestations. The clinical features vary from minimal urinary abnormalities to severe, rapidly progressive nephritis and often are indistinguishable from acute glomerulonephritis, the diagnosis of Henoch-Schönlein nephritis being suggested by the accompanying joint, skin, or gastrointestinal involvement.

Serum concentration of beta-1C globulin is consistently normal. Infrequently a nephrotic syndrome is seen.

Renal biopsy early in the course of the disease reveals most commonly a focal proliferative glomerulonephritis. In those children with progressive disease, subsequent biopsies may be indistinguishable from nonspecific, progressive glomerulonephritis.

Immunofluorescent studies have shown prominent deposits of fibrin, in addition to IgG and beta-1C globulin, in the glomeruli.

Most series suggest that more than 90 or 95 percent of children with Henoch-Schönlein nephritis recover completely. Reports indicating a poorer prognosis are probably due to selection of patients with the most severe degree of renal involvement. Even in severe cases the course is usually a self-limiting one, with return of urine to normal over a period of a few weeks to a few months. Some children are seen, however, with a chronic course, with repeated remissions and exacerbations. Renal damage may be extensive enough to cause permanent reduction in renal function and renal insufficiency.

Although adrenocortical steroids cause prompt remission of most manifestations of the disease, they have not been shown to have a beneficial effect on the renal disease in the child with severe nephritis or the nephrotic syndrome. A few patients appear to have benefited from azathioprine or cyclophosphamide but an adequate evaluation has not been done.

Systemic Lupus Erythematosus (SLE)

Infection and renal failure continue to constitute the major causes of death in children with SLE. General aspects of the disease are discussed in detail elsewhere (Sec. 12.3). The discussion here will focus on the renal involvement.

ETIOLOGY AND PATHOGENESIS. Twenty years after the discovery of the LE cell by Hargraves it was shown that the LE cell phenomenon was the result of alteration of cellular nuclei by a humoral factor, shown to be antinuclear antibody, and of the subsequent phagocytosis of the altered nuclear material.

Lupus erythematosus glomerulonephritis is now recognized as an example of immune-complex disease (p. 1480); a variety of nucleoproteins serve as the antigens and can be found in the circulation associated with antinuclear antibody in the form of soluble immune complexes. These complexes, together with complement, have been demonstrated in the kidneys of patients with glomerulonephritis, and presumably are causative of the disease in that organ.

It would appear that lupus arises from a combination of genetic and environmental factors. A major environmental factor is sunlight. A number of drugs, including hydralazine, isoniazid, several anticonvulsants, and several antibiotics, also may be included as environmental factors, although there is some question whether "spontaneous" and drug-induced lupus are identical. The origin of the nucleoprotein and the relationship to environmental factors is not known. The sera of patients with SLE contain a variety of antibodies, implicating a number of different antigens.

INCIDENCE. SLE occurs in all races and in children of all ages, with a peak in adolescence. The ratio of girls to boys is about 4 to 1. Only 42 patients with SLE age 15 or under were encountered at the hospitals of New York University over an 18-year period. Hagge and associates reported on 41 children seen at the Mayo Clinic from 1945 to 1967. Although no precise data are available concerning the incidence of SLE in the pediatric age group, these experiences provide some idea of the uncommonness of the disease, which, nevertheless, maintains an important place among the various nephritides which may progress to renal failure.

CLINICAL FEATURES. Meislin and Rothfield reported a mean time between onset of disease and diagnosis of 3.3 years, evidencing the insidious manner in which SLE may present. Often an erroneous initial diagnosis, such as rheumatic fever or rheumatoid arthritis, is made.

Half of children present with joint involvement and many with either skin manifestations or neurologic symptoms. At times asymptomatic proteinuria and/or hematuria may be the presenting complaint, but usually by the time renal involvement is apparent, the diagnosis of SLE is readily established.

Renal disease occurs in two-thirds or more of children with lupus. A clinical picture of acute or progressive glomerulonephritis may be present, and rapidly progressing uremia is encountered occasionally. Most patients with renal involvement have the nephrotic syndrome at some point in the course of their disease.

In the absence of therapy, lupus nephritis is an ultimately fatal process, terminal uremia occurring after a period of months to many years. Meislin and Rothfield reported 70 percent survival 5 years after diagnosis in children without renal disease at onset, 45 percent in children with renal disease. At 10 years these figures fell to 55 and 20 percent, respectively, and by 20 years to 30 and 5 percent.

PATHOLOGY. Histologic examination in cases with renal involvement shows generalized or focal glomerulonephritis. Severe glomerular lesions may be associated with fibrinoid degeneration and focal necrosis. Crescents are common. Subendothelial deposits in the capillary wall lead to focal segments of marked thickening known as "wire loops." Immune complexes are readily identified within the glomeruli by specific immunofluorescence. A granular deposition on the capillary wall has been correlated with symptomatic renal injury, whereas linear and mesangial deposits have not been associated with clinical evidence of renal disease. The presence of renal involvement correlates in general with other clinical evidence of activity. Renal lesions may be progressive, although minimal lesions respond to therapy and often show little progression over periods of several years.

THERAPY. There is accumulating evidence that patients with lupus nephritis benefit from administration of adrenocortical steroids or other cytotoxic, immunosuppressant drugs. Treatment may not only suppress clinical and laboratory manifestations of disease, but in addition produce both functional and histologic improvement. Currently we recommend that patients be treated initially with steroids alone. If nontoxic doses are not successful in producing complete control of disease, as judged by examination of the urine and of serum factors, other drugs, such as azathioprine or cyclophosphamide, are added to the regimen.

Shur and Sandson have reported on the usefulness of immunologic factors in judging activity of disease in patients with SLE. They found that very low complement levels and high titers of complement-fixing antibodies to DNA were always associated with active disease, whereas the absence of these abnormalities usually indicated inactive renal disease. A 50-percent fall in serum complement level usually accompanied or preceded the onset of active nephritis. Thus serial immunochemical observations may be of value as guides to therapy.

Polyarteritis Nodosa

This disease is rare in children, although it occurs at all ages, including infancy. The male to female ratio is approximately 2 to 1. The kidneys are involved in 75 to 85 percent of cases.

Lesions within the kidney include the typical vasculitis found also in other organs, as well as a type of glomerulitis with capillary microthrombi, focal fibrinoid necrosis, and crescent formation.

Etiology and pathogenesis are not known, but the disease is thought to be one of hypersensitivity. In the so-called chronic (or macroscopic) form, medium-sized vessels are involved, and often several organ systems are affected. Renal involvement may manifest as flank pain and gross hematuria, or as subacute glomerulonephritis. Hypertension is frequent. The course varies from months to years.

At times polyarteritis follows an acute fulminating course, beginning with a clinical syndrome resembling severe acute glomerulonephritis. Progression to terminal uremia may occur within a few weeks. Involvement of small-caliber arteries has led to its designation as the *microscopic form* of polyarteritis.

In infants, polyarteritis presents with fever, rash, conjunctivitis, and rhinitis. Although the kidneys are involved in most cases, death usually occurs from lesions of the coronary arteries.

There is evidence that corticosteroid therapy is of benefit in adult subjects, but the experience in children has been too limited to evaluate its usefulness.

Goodpasture's Syndrome

A form of glomerulonephritis associated with diffuse pulmonary hemorrhage was reported by Goodpasture in 1919. Patients are usually young adults, with only rare reports in children; males predominate 5 or 6 to 1. The reported cases have provided no evidence for streptococcal etiology. Patients present with cough, dyspnea, and hemoptysis, followed in days, weeks, or months by the clinical and laboratory features of severe acute glomerulonephritis.

Blood pressure initially is usually normal and edema is uncommon. Rales, rhonchi, and wheezes usually are present and anemia is evidenced by pallor.

Pulmonary infiltrates are seen radiographically, and at autopsy the alveoli are distended with red blood cells and hemosiderin-laden macrophages. Histologic examination of the kidneys reveals severe, proliferative glomerulonephritis. The lesion initially may be focal and associated with capillary thrombosis and deposition of fibrin in the glomerular tuft. Progression of the lesion leads to more diffuse involvement and marked crescent formation, as in rapidly progressive glomerulonephritis. Glomerular fibrosis and sclerosis ensue.

Immunofluorescent examination has shown linear deposits of IgG and beta-1C globulin on the basement membranes of the alveoli, alveolar capillaries, and glomerular capillaries. Lerner et al. have eluted the immune globulins from the kidneys of patients, and, by injection into monkeys, have induced nephritis with a similar pattern of linear deposition, thus confirming the hypothesis that this syndrome is caused by autoantibodies to glomerular and alveolar basement membranes. Although antiglomerular basement membrane antibodies are present in all cases, the mechanism of immunization and the source of the immunizing antigen is unknown.

Differential diagnosis includes acute glomerulonephritis with pulmonary congestion, uremic pneumonitis, pneumonia complicated with nephritis, polyarteritis nodosa, and idiopathic pulmonary hemosiderosis. There is a difference of opinion, however, as to whether the last entity is, in fact, different from Goodpasture's syndrome.

In the review by Benoit, the mean duration of survival in those who died was 15 weeks. In the series reported by Proskey et al. it was 41 weeks, and only 13 of 56 patients survived.

Treatment with adrenocortical steroids and various immunosuppressant agents has been tried, but most cases progress to death in uremia, unless the course is interrupted with dialysis and transplantation.

Hemolytic-Uremic Syndrome

This condition has been described for several decades under a variety of names, but the term hemolytic-uremic syndrome was first used by Gasser and associates, who reported five children with the sudden onset of intravascular hemolysis and acute renal failure. It is of note that four of the five were infants, since it has been recognized subsequently that the disease is seen predominantly in young infants and only rarely after the age of 2 years. There is no sex predilection.

The hemolytic-uremic syndrome is an uncommon condition, but occasional outbreaks and a number of instances of close association with various infectious agents have suggested that infectious disease may be a common precedent. The wide geographical variation in incidence is unexplained.

Many features of the disease have suggested an immune process, but the Coombs' tests usually is negative, serum complement levels are not depressed, and immunoglobulins have not been demonstrated in the kidney.

Many aspects of the hemolytic-uremic syndrome are similar to those of the Shwartzman reaction: the occurrence in young subjects, the onset following infection, the finding of fibrin in glomerular capillaries and arterioles, and the selective involvement of the kidneys. These observations have led to the hypothesis that intravascular coagulation is the initial event in the disease, although primary damage to blood cells or blood vessels cannot be ruled out. The following sequence of events has been proposed. Following the onset of diffuse intravascular clotting, fibrin is deposited in the glomerular capillaries and arterioles, resulting in patchy fibrinoid necrosis. Red blood cells and platelets passing through these damaged vessels are injured, resulting in hemolytic anemia, platelet destruction, and thrombocytopenia. If the process is not too severe, gradual recovery may take place, otherwise death in renal failure will ensue.

The course of the disease is quite characteristic. Following several days of acute gastroenteritis, an infant or young child, previously well, develops the clinical features of acute glomerulonephritis. In addition, a severe hemolytic anemia is present from the onset or develops within a few days. Thrombocytopenia and its complications also are usually present. The course is one of prolonged renal failure with repeated hemolytic episodes.

Mild to severe neurologic signs, including irritability, ataxia, convulsions, and coma, commonly are seen. The disease may either progress to death (in 10 to 50 percent) or gradually abate over a period of several weeks. Both neurologic and renal sequelae are seen, the incidence relating apparently to the severity of the initial process.

In the reports of Gianantonio and associates, complete recovery was observed in 60 percent of those considered initially to be mild, in contrast to fewer than 15 percent of those considered severe. Of 76 patients followed for 1 to 8 years, healing was observed in only 33. Another 20 appeared to be in the process of stabilization or recovery; seven had died or were uremic; and there were signs of progressive renal disease in the remainder.

Renal lesions in this syndrome fall into two overlapping general categories. The patients described originally by Gasser et al. had cortical necrosis; those reported by Royer et al. had a form of severe glomerulitis, termed thrombotic microangiopathy. Fibrinoid necrosis and thrombosis of arterioles and glomeruli are seen in both. Electron microscopy discloses subendothelial deposits of fibrillary and granular material, believed to be at least in part fibrin.

The glomeruli in thrombotic microangiopathy are the site of striking endothelial and mesangial swelling. Focal or partial glomerular necrosis is often observed, suggesting a transition stage to cortical necrosis. Renal biopsies in survivors may show patchy glomerular scarring and residual vascular lesions, and the possibility of subsequent chronic progressive glomerulonephritis cannot be excluded.

Therapy remains unsatisfactory. The management of acute renal failure, which may require dialysis, is discussed on p. 1463. Severe hemolysis may necessitate blood transfusions. Corticosteroids, although not adequately evaluated, do not appear to be of value. On the basis of the similarity to the Shwartzman reaction, therapy with heparin has been proposed, and a number of authors have suggested that this form of therapy may reduce the acute mortality. Others have had less success, and until controlled clinical trials are conducted, the utility of heparin in this condition will remain unknown.

Thrombotic Thrombocytopenic Purpura (TTP)

TTP is a generalized vascular or hematologic disease characterized by fever, purpura, and neurologic manifestations. It is described fully in the section on hemorrhagic disorders (Sec. 17.13) and therefore only those aspects relating to the kidney will be discussed here. The kidneys are often involved in TTP, examination of the urine revealing proteinuria, gross or microscopic hematuria, white blood cells, and casts. Renal function varies from normal to severely depressed, but some degree of azotemia is usually present. Pathologic examination reveals large, bland, thrombotic masses in intralobular arterioles and glomeruli. A focal proliferative glomerulitis is occasionally present in addition to the vascular leison, but we have not seen the striking endothelial alterations of the hemolytic-uremic syndrome.

Differential diagnosis includes the hemolytic-uremic syndrome and systemic lupus erythematosus. The cause of TTP is unknown. It runs a chronic or fulminating course; therapy is not available; and the outcome is invariably fatal.

Septicemia

Since the advent of the antibiotic era, pyelonephritis and renal abscess formation, which may occur as suppurative complications in patients with sepsis, have become uncommon. This type of disease will not be considered further in this section, which focuses on the nonsuppurative involvement of the kidney during bloodstream infection.

Chronic bacteremia has been implicated as the precursor of severe renal disease in a variety of clinical situations, including bacterial endocarditis, infected prosthetic devices placed in the circulation such as ventriculoatrial shunts, malaria, and syphilis. In addition, transient urinary abnormalities and acute glomerulonephritis have been reported in association with a large number of viral diseases, although a clear-cut causal relationship has not been established for most. It is of interest, nevertheless, that severe progressive renal disease in many species is a common consequence of viral infection.

There is considerable evidence that the renal disease that may occur during the course of chronic bacteremia (which may present as acute glomerulonephritis, progressive nephritis, or the nephrotic syndrome) is immunologically determined and not the consequence of septic emboli. The mechanism appears to be the formation in the circulation of soluble antigen-antibody complexes which deposit in the glomerular capillary walls, so-called immune-complex renal disease (see p. 1480). In patients with the nephrotic syndrome secondary to *Plasmodium malariae* infection, specific antigen and IgG, IgM, and beta-1C globulins have been demonstrated in the glomeruli. In a patient with an infected ventriculoatrial shunt, *Micrococcus* antigen was present, along with immune globulin and complement. In many of these patients, serum complement is reduced.

Treatment consists of eradication of the infection, which does not, however, preclude the possibility of progressive renal disease. Immunosuppressive therapy has been without effect.

REFERENCES

HENOCH-SCHÖNLEIN

Allen, D. M., Diamond, L. K., and Howell, D. A. Anaphylactoid purpura in children (Schoenlein-Henoch Syndrome). Amer. J. Dis. Child., 99:833, 1960.

Ayoub, E. M., and Hoyer, J. Anaphylactoid purpura: Streptococcal antibody titers and β_1c-globulin levels. J. Pediat., 75:193, 1969.

Bergstrand, A., Bergstrand, G., and Bucht, H. Kidney lesions associated with anaphylactoid purpura in children. Acta Paediat., 49:57, 1960.

Bouissou, H., Dupont, H. G., and Régnier, Cl. L'atteinte rénale au cours du syndrome de Schönlein-Henoch. Arch. Franc. Pédiat., 16:7, 1959.

Dodge, W. F., Travis, L. B., and Daeschner, C. W. Anaphylactoid purpura, polyarteritis nodosa and purpura fulminans. Pediat. Clin. N. Amer., 10:879, 1963.

Gairdner, D. Schönlein-Henoch syndrome (anaphylactoid purpura). Quart. J. Med., 17:95, 1948.

Grupe, W. E., and Heymann, W. Cytotoxic drugs in steroid-resistant renal disease. Amer. J. Dis. Child., 112:448, 1966.

Kobayashi, O., Wada, H., Kanasawa, M., and Kamiyama, T. The anaphylactoid purpura-nephritis in childhood. Acta Med. Biol., 13:181, 1965.

Lewis, I. A. The Schönlein-Henoch Syndrome (anaphylactoid purpura) compared with certain features of nephritis and rheumatism. Arch. Dis. Child., 30:212, 1955.

Michael, A. F., Vernier, R. L., Drummond, K. N., Levitt, J. I., Herdmann, R. C., Fish, A. J., and Good,

R. A. Immunosuppressive therapy of chronic renal disease. New Eng. J. Med., 276:817, 1967.

Oliver, T. K., Jr., and Barnett, H. L. Incidence and prognosis of nephritis associated with anaphylactoid (Schoenlein-Henoch) purpura in children. Amer. J. Dis. Child., 90:544, 1955.

Philpott, M. D., and Briggs, J. N. Treatment of the Schönlein-Henoch syndrome with adrenocorticotrophic hormone (ACTH) and cortisone. Arch. Dis. Child., 28:57, 1953.

Roberts, F. B., Slater, R. J., and Laski, B. Prognosis of Henoch-Schönlein nephritis. Canad. Med. Ass. J., 87:49, 1962.

Royer, P., Habib, R., and Mathieu, H. Les néphropathies du purpura rheumatoide. In Problèmes Actuels de Néphrologie Infantile. Paris, Editions Médicales Flammarion, 1963, Vol. I, p. 72.

Sterky, G., and Thilén, A. A study on the onset and prognosis of acute vascular purpura (the Schönlein-Henoch syndrome) in children. Acta Paediat., 49:217, 1960.

Urizar, R. E., Michael, A., Sisson, S., and Vernier, R. L. Anaphylactoid purpura. II. Immunofluorescent and electron microscopic studies of the glomerular lesions. Lab. Invest., 19:437, 1968.

Vernier, R. L., Worthen, H. G., Peterson, R. D., Colle, E., and Good., R. A. Anaphylactoid purpura. I. Pathology of the skin and kidney and frequency of streptococcal infection. Pediatrics, 27:181, 1961.

Wedgwood, R. J. P., and Klaus, M. H. Anaphylactoid purpura (Schoenlein-Henoch Syndrome); a long-term follow-up study with special reference to renal involvement. Pediatrics, 16:196, 1955.

White, R. H. R., Cameron, J. S., and Tounce, J. R. Immunosuppressive therapy in steroid-resistant proliferative glomerulonephritis accompanied by the nephrotic syndrome. Brit. Med. J., 2:853, 1966.

SYSTEMIC LUPUS ERYTHEMATOSUS

Ackerman, G. L. Alternate-day steroid therapy in lupus nephritis. Ann. Intern. Med., 72:511, 1970.

Adams, D. A., Gordon, A., and Maxwell, M. H. Azathioprine treatment of immunological renal disease. J.A.M.A., 199:459, 1967.

Comerford, F. R., and Cohen, A. S. The nephropathy of systemic lupus erythematosus. An assessment of clinical, light, and electron microscopic criteria. Medicine, 46:425, 1967.

Cook, C. D., Wedgwood, R. J. P., Craig, J. M., Hartmann, J. R., and Janeway, C. A. Systemic lupus erythematosus. Description of 37 cases in children and a discussion of endocrine therapy in 32 of the cases. Pediatrics, 26:570, 1960.

Corley, C. C., Jr., Lessner, H. E., and Larsene, W. E. Azathioprine therapy of "autoimmune diseases." Amer. J. Med., 41:404, 1966.

Gary, N. E., Maher, J. F., and Schreiner, G. E. Lupus nephritis. Renal function after prolonged survival. New Eng. J. Med., 276:73, 1967.

Grupe, W. E., and Heymann, W. Cototoxic drugs in steroid-resistant renal disease. Amer. J. Dis. Child., 112:448, 1966.

Hagge, W. W., Burke, E. C., and Stickler, G. B. Treatment of systemic lupus erythematosus complicated by nephritis in children. Pediatrics, 40:822, 1967.

Hanson, V., and Kornreich, H. Systemic rheumatic disorders in childhood. Bull. Rheum. Dis., 17:435, 1967.

Holman, H. Systemic lupus erythematosus. A review of certain recent developments in the study of this disease. J. Pediat., 56:109, 1960.

Jacobs, J. C. Systemic lupus erythematosus in childhood: Report of 35 cases. Pediatrics, 32:257, 1963.

Kellum, R. E., and Haserick, J. R. Systemic lupus erythematosus: Statistical evaluation of mortality based on consecutive series of 299 patients. Arch. Intern. Med., 113:200, 1964.

Koffler, D., and Kunkel, H. G. Mechanisms of renal injury in systemic lupus erythematosus. Amer. J. Med., 45:165, 1968.

———— et al. Variable patterns of immunoglobulin and complement deposition in the kidneys of patients with systemic lupus erythematosus. Amer. J. Path., 52:305, 1969.

Kornreich, H. K., Drexler, E., and Hanson, V. Antinuclear factors in childhood rheumatic disease. J. Pediat., 69:1039, 1966.

Maher, J. F., and Schreiner, G. E. Treatment of lupus nephritis with azathioprine. Arch. Intern. Med., 125:293, 1970.

Meislin, A. G., and Rothfield, N. Systemic lupus erythematosus in childhood. Analysis of 42 cases, with comparative data on 200 adult cases followed concurrently. Pediatrics, 42:37, 1968.

Michael, A. F., Vernier, R. L., Drummond, K. N., Levitt, J. I., Herdman, R. C., Fish, A. J., and Good, R. A. Immunosuppressive therapy of chronic renal disease. New Eng. J. Med., 276:817, 1967.

Peterson, R. D. A., Vernier, R. L., and Good, R. A. Lupus erythematosus. Pediat. Clin. N. Amer., 10:941, 1963.

Pollak, V. E., and Pirani, C. L. Renal histologic findings in systemic lupus erythematosus. Mayo Clin. Proc., 44:630, 1969.

———— Pirani, C. L., and Kark, R. M. Effect of large doses of prednisone on the renal lesions and life span of patients with lupus glomerulonephritis. J. Lab. Clin. Med., 57:495, 1961.

———— Pirani, C. L., and Schwartz, F. D. Natural history of renal manifestations of systemic lupus erythematosus. J. Lab. Clin. Med., 63:537, 1964.

Ritchie, R. F. Antinuclear antibodies: Their frequency and diagnostic association. New Eng. J. Med., 282:1174, 1970.

Schur, P. H. ANA. (Editorial). New Eng. J. Med., 282:1205, 1970.

———— and Sandson, J. Immunologic factors and clinical activity in systemic lupus erythematosus. New Eng. J. Med., 278:533, 1968.

Smith, F. G., Jr., Litman, N., and Latta, H. Lupus glomerulonephritis. The effect of large doses of corticosteroids on renal function and renal lesions in two children. Amer. J. Dis. Child., 110:302, 1965.

Soffer, L. J., Souther, A. L., Weiner, H. E., and Wolf, R. L. Renal manifestations of systemic lupus erythematosus: A clinical and pathological study of 90 cases. Ann. Intern. Med., 54:215, 1961.

Symposium on Systemic Lupus Erythematosus. Mayo Clin. Proc., 44:579-696, 1969.

West, C. D., Holland, N. H., McConville, J. M., and McAdams, A. J. Immunosuppressive therapy in persistent hypocomplementemic glomerulonephritis and in lupus nephritis. J. Pediat., 67:1113, 1965.

Zweiman, B. et al. The prognosis of lupus nephritis. Ann. Intern. Med., 69:441, 1968.

POLYARTERITIS NODOSA

Arroyave, H. C., Quiroga, Z. G., Gordillo, P. G., and Bessodo, M. Y. L. Polyarteritis nodosa. Bol. Med. Hosp. Infantil Mexico, 24:549, 1967.

Fager, D. B., Bigler, J. A., and Simonds, J. P. Polyarteritis nodosa in infancy and childhood. J. Pediat., 39:65, 1951.

Frohnert, P. P., and Sheps, S. G. Long-term follow-up study of periarteritis nodosa. Amer. J. Med., 43:8, 1967.

Harrison, C. V., Loughridge, L. W., and Milne, M. D. Acute oliguric renal failure in acute glomerulonephritis and polyarteritis nodosa. Quart. J. Med., 33:39, 1964.

Roberts, F. B., and Fetterman, G. H. Polyarteritis nodosa in infancy. J. Pediat., 63:519, 1963.

GOODPASTURE'S SYNDROME

Beirne, G. J., Octaviano, G. N., Kopp, W. L., and Burns, R. O. Immunohistology of the lung in Goodpasture's Syndrome. Ann. Intern. Med., 69:1207, 1968.

Benoit, F. L., Rulon, D. B., Theil, G. B., Doolan, P. D., and Watten, R. H. Goodpasture's syndrome. A clinicopathologic entity. Amer. J. Med., 37:424, 1964.

Dixon, F. J. The pathogenesis of glomerulonephritis. Editorial. Amer. J. Med., 44:493, 1968.

Duncan, D. A., Drummond, K. N., Michael, A. F., and Vernier, R. L. Pulmonary hemorrhage and glomerulonephritis. Report of six cases and study of the renal lesion by the fluorescent antibody technique and electron microscopy. Ann. Intern. Med., 62:920, 1965.

Goodpasture, E. W. The significance of certain pulmonary lesions in relation to the etiology of influenza. Amer. J. Med. Sci., 158:863, 1919.

Lerner, F. A., Glassock, R. J., and Dixon, F. J. The role of antiglomerular basement membrane antibody in the pathogenesis of human glomerulonephritis. J. Exp. Med., 126:989, 1967.

O'Connell, E. J., Dower, J. C., Burke, E. C., Brown, A. L., Jr., and McCoughey, W. T. E. Pulmonary hemorrhage-glomerulonephritis syndrome. Relationship to Goodpasture's syndrome with report of case in 9-year-old girl. Amer. J. Dis. Child., 108:302, 1964.

Powell, A. H., and Bettez, P. H. Goodpasture's syndrome. Pulmonary hemosiderosis with glomerulonephritis. Canad. Med. Ass. J., 90:5, 1964.

Proskey, A. J., Weatherbee, L., Easterling, R. E., Greene, J. A., Jr., and Weller, J. M. Goodpasture's syndrome. A report of five cases and review of the literature. Amer. J. Med., 48:162, 1970.

Scheer, R. L., Grossman, M. A. Immune aspects of the glomerulonephritis associated with pulmonary hemorrhage. Ann. Intern. Med., 60:1009, 1964.

Sturgill, B. C., and Westervelt, F. B. Immunofluorescence studies in a case of Goodpasture's syndrome. J.A.M.A., 194:914, 1965.

HEMOLYTIC-UREMIC SYNDROME

Abildgaard, C. F. Recognition and treatment of intravascular coagulation. J. Pediat., 74:163, 1969.

Barnard, P. J., and Kibel, M. Hemolytic-uremic syndrome of infancy and childhood. Report of 11 cases. Cent. Afr. J. Med., 11:4, 1965.

Chan, J. C. M., Eleff, M. G., and Campbell, R. A. The hemolytic-uremic syndrome in nonrelated adopted siblings. J. Pediat., 75:1050, 1969.

Edelmann, C. M., Jr. The hemolytic-uremic syndrome. New Eng. J. Med., 281:1072, 1969.

Editorial. Haemolytic-uraemic syndrome. Lancet, 2:271, 1968.

Gasser, C., Gautier, E., Steck, A., Siebenmann, R. E., and Oechslin, R. Hämolytisch-urämische Syndrome. Schweiz. Med. Wschr., 85:905, 1955.

Gianantonio, C. A., Vitacco, M., Mendilaharzu, F., and Gallo, G. The hemolytic-uremic syndrome. Renal status of 76 patients at long-term follow-up. J. Pediat., 72:757, 1968.

——— Vitacco, M., Mendilaharzu, F., Rutty, A., and Mendilaharzu, J. The hemolytic-uremic syndrome. J. Pediat., 64:478, 1964.

Gilchrist, G. S., Ekert, H., Lieberman, E., Fine, R. N., and Grushkin, C. Heparin therapy in the haemolytic-uraemic syndrome. Lancet, 1:1123, 1969.

Habib, R., Mathieu, H., and Royer, P. Le syndrome hémolytique et urémique de l'enfant. Nephron, 4:139, 1967.

Hammond, D., Lieberman, E., Wright, H. T., Jr., Heuser, E. T., and Rapaport, S. I. Hemolytic-uremic syndrome. Amer. J. Dis. Child., 114:440, 1967.

Javett, S. N., and Senior, B. Syndrome of hemolysis, thrombopenia, and nephropathy in infancy. Pediatrics, 29:209, 1962.

Katz, J., Lurie, A., and Kaplan, B. Haemolytic-uraemic syndrome and heparin therapy. Lancet, 2:700, 1969.

Lanzkowsky, P., and McCrory, W. W. Disseminated intravascular coagulation as a possible factor in the pathogenesis of thrombotic microangiopathy (hemolytic-uremic syndrome). J. Pediat., 70:460, 1967.

Lieberman, E., Heuser, E., Donnell, G. N., Landing, B. H., and Hammond, G. D. Hemolytic-uremic syndrome. Clinical and pathological considerations. New Eng. J. Med., 275:227, 1966.

McLean, M. M., Jones, C. H., and Sutherland, D. A. Hemolytic-uremic syndrome. A report of an outbreak. Arch. Dis. Child., 41:76, 1966.

McQuiggan, M. C., Oliver, W. J., Littler, E. R., and Cerny, J. C. Hemolytic-uremic syndrome. J.A.M.A., 191:787, 1965.

Mettler, N. E. Isolation of a microtatobiote from patients with hemolytic-uremic syndrome and thrombotic thrombocytopenic purpura and from mites in the United States. New Eng. J. Med., 281:1023, 1969.

Piel, C. F., and Phibbs, R. H. The hemolytic-uremic syndrome. Pediat. Clin. N. Amer., 13:295, 1966.

Royer, P., Habib, R., and Mathieu, H. La micro-angiopathie thrombotique du rein et syndromes apparentés. In Problèmes Actuels de Néphrologies Infantile. Paris, Editions Médicales Flammarion, 1963, p. 103.

Schumway, C. N., and Terplan, K. L. Hemolytic anemia, thrombocytopenia and renal disease in childhood. The hemolytic-uremic syndrome. Pediat. Clin. N. Amer., 11:577, 1964.

Shinton, N. K., Galpine, J. F., Kendall, A. C., and Williams, H. P. Haemolytic anaemia with acute renal disease. Arch. Dis. Child., 39:455, 1964.

Vasalli, P., and McCluskey, R. The coagulation process and glomerular disease. Amer. J. Med., 39:179, 1965.

Vitsky, B. H., Suzulei, Y., Strauss, L., and Churg, J. The hemolytic-uremic syndrome. Amer. J. Path., 57:627, 1969.

THROMBOTIC THROMBOCYTOPENIC PURPURA

Amorosi, E. L., and Ultmann, J. E. Thrombotic thrombocytopenic purpura. Report of 16 cases and review of the literature. Medicine, 45:139, 1966.

McCutcheon, S. W., Rupe, C. E., Barnhart, M. I., and Fine, G. A case of renal thrombotic thrombocytopenic purpura. With comments on coagulation and immunofluorescent studies. Henry Ford Hosp. Med. Bull., 16:239, 1968.

MacWhinney, J. B., Packer, J. T., Miller, G., and Greendyke, R. M. Thrombotic thrombocytopenic purpura in childhood. Blood, 19:181, 1962.

Wile, S. A., and Sturgeon, P. Thrombotic thrombocytopenic purpura. Pediatrics, 17:882, 1956.

SEPTICEMIA

Adeniyi, A., Hendrickse, R. G., and Houbou, V. Selectivity of proteinuria and response to prednisolone or immunosuppressive drugs in children with malarial nephrosis. Lancet, 1:644, 1970.

Allison, A. A. C., Houba, V., Hendrickse, R. G., de Petris, S., Edington, G. M., and Adeniyi, A. Immune complexes in the nephrotic syndrome of African children. Lancet, 1:1232, 1969.

Braunstein, G. D., Lewis, E. J., Galvanek, E. G., Hamilton, A., and Bell, W. R. The nephrotic syndrome associated with secondary syphilis. Amer. J. Med., 48:643, 1970.

Burch, G. E., Chu, K. C., Colcolough, H. L., and Sohal, R. S. Immunofluorescent localization of Coxsackievirus B antigen in the kidney observed at routine autopsy. Amer. J. Med., 47:36, 1969.

Editorial. Viruses and renal disease. J.A.M.A., 204:219, 1968.

Falls, W. F., Jr., Ford, K. L., Ashworth, C. T., and Carter, N. W. The nephrotic syndrome in secondary syphilis. Report of a case with renal biopsy findings. Ann. Intern. Med., 63:1047, 1965.

Kaufman, D. B., Logan, L., and McIntosh, R. M. The nature of the antibody in a patient with immune complex renal disease. Pediat. Res., 3:363, 1969.

Kibukamusoke, J. W. Malaria prophylaxis and immunosuppressant therapy in management of nephrotic syndrome associated with Quartan malaria. Arch. Dis. Child., 43:598. 1968.

Michael, A. F., Herdman, R. C., Fish, A. J., Pickering, R. J., and Vernier, R. L. Chronic membranoproliferative glomerulonephritis with hypocomplementemia. Transplant. Proc., 1:925, 1969.

Papaioannou, A. C., Asrow, G. G., and Schuckmell, N. H. Nephrotic syndrome in early infancy as a manifestation of congenital syphilis. Pediatrics, 27:636, 1961.

Rames, L., Wise, B., Goodman, J. R., and Piel, C. F. Renal disease with staphylococcus albus bacteremia. A complication in ventriculoatrial shunt. J.A.M.A., 212:1671, 1970.

Stickler, G. B., Shin, M. H., Burke, E. C., Holley, K. E., Miller, R. H., and Segar, W. E. Diffuse glomerulonephritis associated with infected ventriculoatrial shunt. New Eng. J. Med., 279:1077, 1968.

Taitz, L. S., Isaacson, C., and Stein, H. Acute nephritis

associated with congenital syphilis. Brit. Med. J., 2: 152, 1961.

Ward, P. A., and Kibukamusoke, J. W. Evidence of soluble immune complexes in the pathogenesis of the glomerulonephritis of quartan malaria. Lancet, 1:283, 1969.

22.10
THE IDIOPATHIC NEPHROTIC SYNDROME OF CHILDHOOD
(Lipoid Nephrosis)

CHESTER M. EDELMANN, JR.

The nephrotic syndrome is characterized by proteinuria, hypoproteinemia, lipidemia, and edema. In contrast with the experience in adults, the nephrotic syndrome in children usually occurs in the absence of recognizable systemic or preexisting renal disease, and as such is referred to as *pure lipoid nephrosis* or the *idiopathic nephrotic syndrome of childhood*. These terms will be used here interchangeably.

Rarely in children, although commonly in adults, the nephrotic syndrome may occur in the course of various systemic disorders (Henoch-Schönlein syndrome, lupus erythematosus, sickle-cell anemia, cyanotic congenital heart disease, malaria, syphilis, tuberculosis, diabetes mellitus, amyloidosis, multiple myeloma), following renal vein thrombosis, or as a result of drug toxicity (Tridione, mercurials, penicillamine, tolbutamide, bismuth, gold salts). Whether the nephrotic syndrome which follows a bee sting or exposure to poison oak or poison ivy is different from the idiopathic disease is unknown. Of considerable importance, however, is that a nephrotic syndrome may occur in children during the course of various types of progressive glomerulonephritis, due, at least to a major extent, to nonspecific basement membrane damage and development of heavy proteinuria.

Almost 80 percent of children who develop the nephrotic syndrome have neither recognizable associated disease (as judged by all laboratory examinations, including renal biopsy) nor evidence of exposure to known toxic agents. A significant number of such children have, in addition to the characteristics of the nephrotic syndrome, one or more nephritic manifestations, such as hematuria, reduced kidney function, or hypertension, a fact which has led some observers to consider that *all* instances of the nephrotic syndrome not associated with recognizable systemic disease represent a stage of glomerulonephritis. However, the demonstration in these children of "minimal change" pathology on percutaneous renal biopsy has substantiated the view of most pediatricians that the idiopathic nephrotic syndrome as seen in children is unrelated to acute and chronic forms of glomerulonephritis. Furthermore, it has not been useful prognostically to subdivide these children into two groups on the basis of whether or not nephritic manifestations are present, the outcome almost uniformly being good.

With the onset of the nephrotic syndrome in childhood, 20 percent of patients demonstrate focal, proliferative, or membranous changes on renal biopsy, representing, therefore, a nephrotic stage of the various forms of progressive glomerulonephritis. In contrast to patients with idiopathic or minimal change disease, these patients usually fail to respond to therapy and have a grave prognosis.

This section will deal primarily with the idiopathic nephrotic syndrome of childhood, with only passing reference to the syndrome as encountered as a feature of a systemic disease or during the course of some form of glomerulonephritis.

INCIDENCE. The incidence of the nephrotic syndrome in children in the United States has been estimated variously to be 1.9, 2.3, and 2.8 cases per 100,000 white children below 10 years of age. Schlesinger et al. reported an incidence of 1.9 cases per 100,000 white children and 2.8 cases per 100,000 nonwhite children under 16 years of age. These authors found the number of active cases to be 15.7 per 100,000 children below the age of 16.

The age of onset peaks at 2 to 3 years of age, with more than half the cases between 1 and 4 and three-quarters less than 7 years of age. Our recent experience with more than 200 patients agrees precisely with that of Barnett, Forman, and Lauson that 60 percent of the patients are males.

ETIOLOGY. The cause of the nephrotic syndrome is unknown. Even when it occurs in association with some systemic disorder or following toxic exposure, the pathogenic relationship is not clear and the association is not a consistent one. Many nephrologists consider the idiopathic nephrotic syndrome a disease of hypersensitivity, related to a poorly understood antigen-antibody reaction involving the kidneys. Evidence in favor of this formulation includes the apparently increased incidence of allergic disease in patients and their families, production of a similar disease in experimental animals using a variety of immunologic techniques, and the favorable effects of adrenocortical steroids and other immunosuppressant drugs. It must be recognized that none of these constitutes a firm basis for including lipoid nephrosis among the diseases of immune origin. Furthermore, serum complement activity in these patients is normal and neither gamma globulin nor components of the complement system are found deposited in renal tissue. Finally, the mechanism of action of none of the drugs found useful in these patients is understood.

FAMILIAL FORMS OF THE NEPHROTIC SYNDROME. The occurrence of the nephrotic syndrome in siblings or in consecutive generations of the same family is infrequent. Two forms of heritable nephrosis can be identified. One form, congenital or infantile nephrosis (p. 1506), differs from idiopathic childhood nephrosis by its appearance before 3 months of age and often at or shortly after birth, and by its lack of responsiveness to steroid therapy, poor prognosis, and distinctive morphologic appearance. The other form, familial childhood nephrosis, simulates sporadic childhood nephrosis in clinical picture and pathologic findings. The possibility that it is a heritable disorder arises only when the syndrome occurs in more than one member of the same family and follows a similar clinical course.

CLINICAL FEATURES. The most important clinical feature is proteinuria, although edema is the symptom commonly calling attention to the disease. The onset of edema usually is insidious, but it may be abrupt. It is usually noted first about the eyes and often is more apparent to the parents than to the physician. The edema may progress slowly or rapidly; not uncommonly, however, it tends to subside and reappear over a period of weeks. The first evidence of periorbital edema is often attributed to a cold, although frank respiratory symptoms are usually wanting. If may be misinterpreted as allergic in origin. Sooner or later the edema becomes generalized, with ascites and occasionally pleural effusion, and the true nature of the disease becomes apparent.

The presence of clinical edema is not necessary for the diagnosis of the nephrotic syndrome, and it should be considered as a secondary manifestation of the disease. The degree and duration of edema are very variable. Untreated, some children remain edematous, whereas others have repeated remissions and exacerbations.

Significant findings on physical examination generally are limited to those associated with edema. Marked skin pallor may be present. The large abdomen produced by ascites is common, and labial or scrotal swelling is often seen. More severe degrees of edema may be associated with dilated veins of the anterior abdominal wall, umbilical hernia, and rectal prolapse. The liver is enlarged in many children during the active stage; it decreases in size with recovery. Treatment with adrenocortical steroids has dramatically altered the clinical course of nephrosis. If initiated early, it may prevent the appearance of massive edema and in many cases will prevent its recurrence after a remission.

Susceptibility to infection is increased during periods of edema. Peritonitis, which may be accompanied by bacteremia and cellulitis, is the commonest of these. In the past, pneumococcal infection was common, but infections with other organisms are now more frequent. The presence of ascites may mask the classical signs of peritonitis, which must be suspected, therefore, whenever an edematous child develops fever and looks sick.

Minor skin irritations and infections are commonly seen during periods of massive edema. These occur around the genitalia, the eyes, and other areas where swelling causes pressure on opposing skin surfaces. A curious erysipeloid infection of the skin is occasionally encountered. It differs from erysipelas in having less induration and no very sharp edge; the infectious agent in such cases is not known.

Malnutrition is common in children in whom the active stage of the disease is prolonged. Poor appetite and loss of protein in the urine are responsible. Malnutrition and consequent reduction in muscle mass tend to be obscured by the edema, although changes in the quality of the hair may reveal it. Striking changes also may be observed in the cartilage of the ear. Despite the poor nutrition, which now only in rare instances may persist for many months, there is apparently no residual growth impairment if recovery from the disease occurs and prolonged high dosage steroid therapy has not been required.

Gastrointestinal disturbances not associated with infections are frequently observed. Diarrhea is especially common during periods of massive edema and has been attributed to edema of the intestinal mucosa.

Respiratory difficulty resulting from abdominal distention, with or without pleural effusion, may be disturbing and occasionally alarming.

The fact that children in the active stage of the nephrotic syndrome are sometimes irritable and depressed is less surprising than that they are ever otherwise. Even in the presence of massive edema, which appears so uncomfortable to others, many children remain in remarkably good spirits.

LABORATORY FEATURES. With the exception of edema, the nephrotic syndrome is characterized by altered laboratory examinations, and these play a major role in establishing the diagnosis and evaluating prognosis, and as guides to treatment.

Proteinuria is consistently present during the active stage, the daily output varying from as little as 50 mg to 15 g or more per day. This protein is predominantly albumin, reflecting its small molecular size. Nevertheless, tests of urinary protein selectivity, which reflect clearance ratios of various molecular weight proteins, have yielded variable results. Most children with lipoid nephrosis have highly selective proteinuria, i.e., almost exclusively albuminuria, in contrast to those with glomerulonephritis who more often have nonselective proteinuria, i.e., excretion of low- and high-molecular-weight proteins. Thus there is a rough correlation between the selectivity index on the one hand and either the likelihood of steroid response or the histologic classification on the other. However, exceptions to the rule that highly selective proteinuria indicates a steroid-responsive, minimal-change patient and poorly selective proteinuria a steroid-unresponsive patient with glomerulonephritis are too numerous to make this test very helpful clinically.

Fifty percent of children have hematuria at the onset. In most this is minimal, ranging from one-half to several million red blood cells per 12-hour overnight specimen. Exceptionally, however, gross hematuria is encountered.

Hypoproteinemia, hypoalbuminemia, and hyperlipemia are characteristic, cholesterol being the only lipid which is commonly measured. Total serum protein averages 4.0 g per 100 ml with most values falling between 3 and 5; albumin averages 1.5 g per 100 ml, with a range of 0.5 to 2.5. Characteristically, alpha-2 and beta globulins are markedly elevated and gamma globulin is depressed. Cholesterol, which in one series averaged 730±81 mg per 100 ml, may vary from normal to as high as 1,500.

Serum calcium concentration is uniformly reduced, often to as low as 6 mg per 100 ml, but the deficit is largely in the protein-bound fraction, so that tetany almost never occurs. The sedimentation rate is usually markedly elevated. The beta-1C component of complement is normal in children with lipoid nephrosis, although it is low in about 5 to 7 percent of all children presenting with the nephrotic syndrome. When found to be depressed it reflects underlying glomerulonephritis and almost always augurs a poor prognosis.

Tests of renal function yield variable results. Maximum concentrating ability and acidification of the urine usually are retained, and as a rule frank azotemia is absent. The urea clearance, glomerular filtration rate, and renal plasma flow are generally within the normal range, although they may be depressed, particularly during severe exacerbations. The occasional observation of urea and inulin clearances significantly above normal remains unexplained.

RENAL PATHOLOGY. Studies of renal biopsies have led to the separation of patients who develop the nephrotic syndrome in the absence of systemic diseases into three pathologic subgroups: "minimal change" or "nil disease" in about 80 percent, glomerulonephritis in 15 to 20 percent, and membranous nephropathy in only a few childhood cases. All categories will be considered here.

Despite the finding in children with the idiopathic nephrotic syndrome of minimal changes or normal histology, the condition is nonetheless believed to result from glomerular abnormality. The minimal changes that can be seen comprise slight stalk hypercellularity, slight leucocytosis, slight increase of mesangial matrix, and an occasional sclerotic glomerulus. Biopsies showing focal or segmental glomerular sclerosis, commonly accompanied by tubular atrophy, have in recent studies been grouped separately and have been associated with significantly poorer responsiveness to steriod therapy and with a poorer ultimate prognosis. Electron microscopic study of biopsies with minimal change has consistently shown, as in all other types of the nephrotic syndrome, fusion of foot processes of the glomerular epithelial cells (podocytes). Evidence has been presented to show that fusion is secondary to excessive glomerular filtration of protein, but it has also been suggested that fusion is a reflection of a primary abnormality in the epithelial cells that alters their ability to maintain the basement membrane. Immunofluorescent studies for glomerular deposits of immunoglobulin and complement generally have been negative. "Minimal change" disease has usually, though not invariably, been associated with a good initial response to therapy and a good prognosis. Focal glomerular sclerosis and involution developing in cases of initially normal histology may, however, progress to chronic nephritis and renal failure.

Membranous nephropathy is distinctly less common in children than in adults. The lesion is characterized by marked thickening of capillary walls (Fig. 14). Staining of the basement membrane by the periodic acid-silver methenamine technique shows that the outer surface of the basement membrane has a striated or "picket-fence" appearance. Electron microscopy reveals subepithelial deposits, which are initially separated by spikelike projections of basement membrane and are later incorporated into the greatly thickened membrane. Immunofluorescence discloses a uniform, finely granular deposition of IgG and the beta-1C component of complement. There is no evidence that the membranous lesion is a stage in the progression of "minimal change" disease. Rather, membranous thickening seems to be present at the onset, increasing with duration of disease and progressing to capillary collapse and glomerular involution. This lesion is commonly associated with hematuria at the onset of disease, with poor responsiveness to steroid therapy, and with progressive renal insufficiency. Although clinical improvement has been

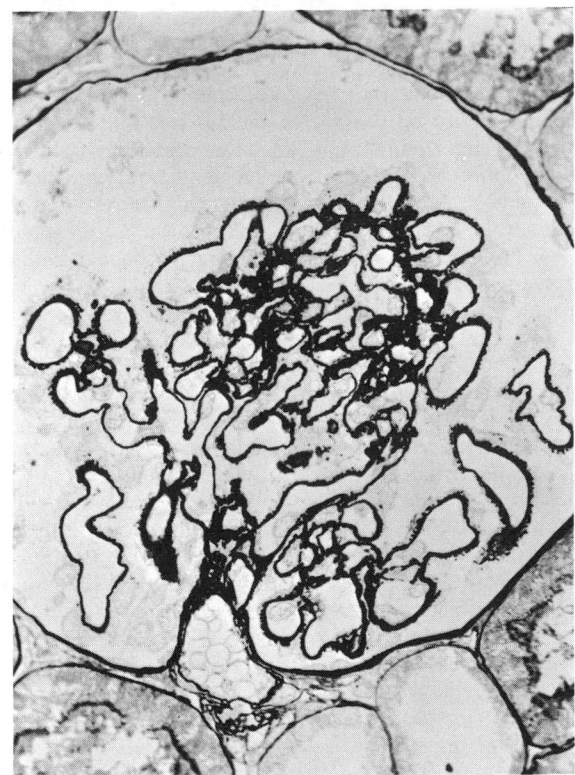

Fig. 14. Membranous nephropathy in idiopathic nephrotic syndrome: note thickening of basement membrane, with subepithelial "spikes." Jones' periodic acid-silver methenamine stain. ×350.

observed in as many as one-fourth of cases, it has been doubted that histologic resolution takes place.

Some patients have glomerulonephritis. Among the several patterns observed have been exudative, proliferative, chronic sclerosing, and membranoproliferative (mesangiocapillary) glomerulonephritis. The first, which may indeed be poststreptococcal, has a tendency to undergo rapid, often spontaneous cure. The others are noted for steroid-unresponsiveness, although the proliferative lesion may in time resolve and allow for lengthy, possibly permanent remission. Membranoproliferative glomerulonephritis has been associated with persistent hypocomplementemia and chronic disease. Patients commonly develop the nephrotic syndrome, either at the beginning of clinical illness or during its course. If the nephrotic syndrome can develop as an intercurrent "phase" in any form of chronic nephritis, the presence of a chronic sclerosing lesion in a previously asymptomatic patient could be evidence of prior subclinical disease.

PATHOPHYSIOLOGY.   There are striking changes in nephrosis in the metabolism of protein, lipids, electrolytes, and water. However, a great deal of evidence points to increased glomerular membrane permeability to protein as the basic disturbance in this condition.

Membrane Permeability.   It is generally accepted that abnormal permeability of the glomerular basement membrane to normal plasma protein accounts for the proteinuria of the nephrotic syndrome. Decreased tubular reabsorption of filtered protein may play a secondary role but cannot adequately explain the amounts of protein encountered clinically. Although increased passage of protein through a defective basement membrane is associated morphologically with obliteration of the foot processes and formation of vacuoles and hyaline droplets, the nature of the glomerular lesion is entirely unknown.

Protein Metabolism.   Although it is generally agreed that proteinuria is the major cause of hypoproteinemia, increased rates of catabolism of protein also occur and apparently explain some of the discrepancies between intensity of proteinuria and degree of hypoalbuminemia. Protein loss through the gastrointestinal tract, as in protein-losing enteropathy, has been reported in a few patients.

The usual pattern of hypoproteinemia is low albumin, normal or low alpha-1 globulin, elevated alpha-2 and beta globulins, and low gamma globulin. Occasional patients show increase in the gamma globulin fraction, particularly those with systemic lupus erythematosus.

Lipid Metabolism.   Patients with the nephrotic syndrome exhibit marked hyperlipemia. In addition to the elevation in serum cholesterol, there are proportional increases in the concentration of phospholipids and even more marked increases in the concentration of triglycerides, which is the primary cause of the lactescent appearance of serum. All of the serum lipids exist in association with proteins as lipoproteins.

The cause of hyperlipidemia remains obscure. Markedly elevated cholesterol is rarely seen in the presence of normal serum albumin. However, normal or only moderately elevated levels of cholesterol are commonly observed in association with hypoalbuminemia.

Electrolyte and Water Balance.   The mechanism of edema formation in patients with the nephrotic syndrome is complex. Hypoproteinemia, specifically hypoalbuminemia, causes a reduction in the colloid osmotic pressure of the plasma, thus permitting a shift of water from the intravascular to the interstitial space with a resultant decrease in the vascular volume and the formation of edema. The continued accumulation of edema fluid is due to a relative increase in tubular reabsorption of sodium chloride and water. Although increased excretion of aldosterone has been observed during periods of edema, recent data suggest that the decreased circulating volume stimulates an increase in tubular reabsorption of sodium through nonadrenal mechanisms also. Vascular contraction stimulates release of antidiuretic hormone as well, leading to retention of water. A reduction in renal plasma flow and GFR, which occurs in some patients, may also contribute to sodium and water retention.

Renal Tubular Function.   Defects in tubular function, including amino-aciduria, phosphaturia, glycosuria, polyuria, renal tubular acidosis, and concentrating defects, have been described. Since these are absent in the majority of patients with the nephrotic syndrome, it is uncertain whether they represent abnormalities that develop during the course of prolonged proteinuria, or whether they represent instances of primary damage to both glomeruli and tubules.

DIFFERENTIAL DIAGNOSIS.   The combination of edema, proteinuria, hypoproteinemia, and hyperlipemia defines the nephrotic syndrome; differential diagnosis concerns the underlying diseases with which it may be associated. All the conditions mentioned above, including the various types of glomerulonephritis, must be considered. In the clinically typical patient with normocomplementemia and no evidence of either systemic disease or glomerulonephritis, the diagnosis of "minimal change" disease can be established with reasonable certainty by demonstrating a complete clinical and laboratory response to adrenocortical steroid therapy. When there is evidence of systemic disease or glomerulonephritis, and in all steroid nonresponsive patients, diagnostic investigation should include histologic examination of tissue obtained by percutaneous renal biopsy, to permit morphologic as well as clinical classification.

TREATMENT.   Nephrosis is a trying disease for the physician, the family, and the patient himself. Treatment must include measures directed toward control of the outstanding clinical feature, edema, and, more importantly, toward attempts to modify favorably the course of the disease and its ultimate prognosis. In addition, because of the chronicity of the disease and the uncertainty of the outcome, the child with nephrosis, and his parents, need more than the usual amount of psychologic support from the physician.

In recent years there have been several major advances in the treatment of children with the nephrotic syndrome. First was the development of antibacterial agents, which have almost eliminated the severe infections which were the principal cause of death in these children. Another advance was the development of the therapeutic use of adrenocortical steroids, which in most instances permits complete control of the edema and does appear to modify favorably the underlying disease and the ultimate outcome. The availability of potent diuretic agents constitutes another advance, permitting the control of severe edema in patients prior to their response to adrenocortical steroid therapy and in those who are refractory to such therapy. Finally, it now appears that other immunosuppressant or cytotoxic drugs may be effective in the management of steroid-responsive, but steroid-toxic, children.

General Measures. The *diet* of the nephrotic child is that suitable for the normal child. Salt needs to be restricted only during periods of edema, at which time foods are not salted during cooking, a shaker is not provided, and excessively salty foods are avoided. The protein content of the diet is not altered. No restrictions are placed on the *activity* of the child beyond those which he himself may impose during periods of edema. It is important to maintain associations with other children, but because exacerbations of proteinuria and edema may follow common *upper respiratory tract infections,* some limitations are advisable. For example, when contacts with other children during visits or playtimes are planned, more than the usual amount of attention is paid to the possibility of infection in the other children. Although exposure to large groups is best avoided, patients are encouraged to attend kindergarten and regular school classes.

Serious intercurrent infections are a real hazard for the nephrotic child. Although continuous prophylaxis with antibiotics is not recommended, it is advisable to administer antibiotics after definite exposure to bacterial infection and to use these agents promptly and more liberally for therapy of possible bacterial infection, particularly during periods of edema. In the past, most serious infections were due to pneumococcus, but at present they are caused more frequently by other organisms, particularly gram-negative bacilli and staphylococci. Until the infecting organisms can be identified, a broad-spectrum antibiotic is indicated.

Adrenocortical Steroids. Although recommendations for specific adrenocortical steroids and dosage schedules vary considerably, the basic aim of all regimens is to maintain the patient free from proteinuria* with the minimal dosage of adrenocortical

---

* Daily determination of urinary protein concentration is performed at home by the parents on the first urine specimen in the morning using 10 percent sulfosalicylic acid or Albustix. This test constitutes the simplest assessment and yet the most important manifestation of disease activity. It has been extremely valuable in judging adequacy of treatment.

steroids. We are not convinced that any one of the suggested therapeutic regimens for adrenocortical steroids has any clear advantage over the others, including the following plan which we currently use. This plan is relatively easy to follow, it utilizes one of the less expensive drugs, and it involves oral medication exclusively.

Initial Treatment. Adrenocortical steroid therapy is started as soon as the diagnosis is established, prednisone being given orally for 28 days in a dosage of approximately 60 mg per m² per day. For older children, a daily dosage of 80 mg usually is not exceeded. With this regimen, diuresis will occur in the majority of patients within 7 to 21 days and the urine will become free from protein (less than 5 to 10 mg per 12-hour night specimen). Following completion of this 28-day course of therapy, daily dosage is reduced to 40 mg per m² and is given 3 consecutive days out of each week for an additional 4 weeks. Patients receive no additional prednisone unless there is a return of proteinuria.

Treatment of refractory patients. Our experience has been that, with rare exception, patients who do not respond to an initial treatment of four weeks of daily therapy and four weeks of intermittent therapy do not respond to continuing steroid therapy alone, even when given in higher dosage. Our recommendation, therefore, is that treatment of such patients with an immunosuppressant drug be considered at this time.

Treatment of recurrences. Patients showing recurrences of proteinuria lasting more than two or three days are begun again on their initial dosage of prednisone, which is continued until the urine is free from protein for three days. Therapy is then changed to the lower dosage, given on an intermittent basis for an additional four weeks, as during the initial course of therapy. If this fails to prevent frequent recurrences, patients are considered for combined therapy with an immunosuppressant agent.

Alternate-day steroid therapy, in which a single dose, equivalent to twice the usual daily dose, is given once every 48 hours, has not been successful in our experience, although good results have been claimed by others. Properly designed, controlled clinical trials have not been done. Until the therapeutic efficacy and the supposed freedom from steroid toxicity of this dosage schedule has been tested against other dosage schedules, we do not recommend that it be used.

In addition to hypothalamic-pituitary-adrenocortical suppression, other side effects of steroid therapy are frequently seen in children with the nephrotic syndrome who are treated with relatively high dosages over prolonged periods of time. Extensive experience indicates, however, that with proper precautions, serious side effects, such as vertebral compression fractures, arrested growth, and severe Cushing's syndrome, are not seen more frequently in children with the nephrotic syndrome than in children receiving steroids for other reasons.

An occasional child is encountered in whom

tapering of steroids after many months of therapy at high dosage is associated with symptoms of headache, lethargy, weakness, anorexia, and vomiting. Treatment is accomplished by providing the minimal dosage of steroid which is adequate to alleviate the symptoms. After a period of two to three months, therapy is stopped. If symptoms reappear, treatment is given for another period of two to three months. In rare instances, supportive therapy may be required for as long as one year before treatment can be discontinued completely.

The nephrotic syndrome related etiologically to certain drugs, such as Tridione, usually resolves after discontinuation of the offending agent. If not, it is questionable whether or not adrenocortical steroids should be used. At present, we would tend not to give them until several weeks or even months after the drug has been stopped. Drugs implicated in producing the nephrotic syndrome should be withheld permanently since their repeated administration may subsequently result in irreversible disease.

Diuretics. Sodium restriction, though capable of slowing accumulation of edema during an exacerbation of the nephrotic syndrome, is usually not successful in eliminating edema. In recent years numerous diuretic agents have become available which, combined with moderate sodium restriction, contribute significantly to control of edema.

Since the majority of patients diurese quite satisfactorily within two to three weeks after beginning adrenocortical steroid therapy, diuretic agents are not given initially. But in refractory patients, or before diuresis has occurred in very edematous patients who become more edematous during treatment, diuretics may provide important symptomatic relief.

Hydrochlorothiazide in a dosage of 2 to 4 mg per kg per day is the agent used initially in patients whose edema is not severe. The thiazide drugs are relatively nontoxic. Hypokalemia is usually not seen if a child is eating a normal diet, but may be avoided by giving potassium supplements. Elevated concentration in serum of uric acid is frequently found. The other side effects, including thrombocytopenia, skin rashes, jaundice, pancreatitis, and hyperglycemia, are either extremely rare or have not been reported in children.

In patients with severe degrees of edema, we have developed the following schedule of diuretic therapy, which has proved extremely successful. In hypoalbuminemic patients, salt-poor human albumin is given first, in a dosage of 0.5 g per kg for patients whose serum albumin is between 1.5 and 2.0 g per 100 ml, and 1 g per kg if the serum albumin is lower. The albumin is infused slowly over the course of 1 hour. Furosemide is given by intravenous injection after an additional 30 to 60 minutes of equilibration, in a dose of 1 mg per kg. This entire course may be repeated every 4 to 6 hours as needed.

Immunosuppressant-Cytotoxic Drugs. The use of drugs such as nitrogen mustard, cyclophosphamide, chlorambucil, methotrexate, 6-thioguanine, and aza-thioprine has been advocated in the treatment of patients refractory to other forms of therapy. The value of these agents in such patients has not been established, they do not appear to be very promising, and recommendations regarding their use are under constant revision.

There has been considerable recent experience with steroid-responsive, frequently relapsing children in whom prednisone therapy has resulted in serious complications, including vertebral compression fractures, arrested growth, and severe Cushing's syndrome. Treatment with the drugs mentioned above, and particularly with cyclophosphamide, either alone or in combination with low-dosage prednisone, has been successful in inducing and maintaining remissions, permitting gradual resolution of steroidal side effects. The use of these drugs in appropriately selected patients may prove to be a major advance in the management of these steroid-dependent children.

Since the use of the newer immunosuppressant and cytotoxic drugs must still be considered experimental, patients considered candidates for such treatment should be managed by or in consultation with investigators actively engaged in studying the effect of these drugs in patients with the nephrotic syndrome.

COURSE AND PROGNOSIS. There are indications that steroid therapy has modified the outcome of the nephrotic syndrome quite apart from its diuretic effect. In the antibiotic era before the introduction of steroids, a group of 60 children showed the following figures: 33 (55 percent) were recovered or recovering, 18 (30 percent) had died during the active stage, and 9 (15 percent) had developed renal insufficiency, of whom 3 had died. Riley and coworkers have since collected data on 779 nephrotic children from 18 clinics. They were followed for a 5-year period in an effort to evaluate the effect of prolonged and intensive steroid therapy. The survival rate in the control group was 60 percent as compared with 75 percent in the intensive steroid therapy group. A longer period of observation is needed before a final evaluation of the outlook can be made, since patients who appear to be doing well at the end of 5 years of steroid therapy may subsequently do less well and ultimately develop renal insufficiency. The situation is further obscured by the fact that in neither of these series is it possible to separate patients with lipoid nephrosis from those with glomerulonephritis.

Ninety-five percent of children with the idiopathic nephrotic syndrome have a total response to initial adrenocortical steroid therapy, with loss of all clinical and laboratory evidences of disease. The subsequent course in these children tends to follow one of three general paterns: (1) Twenty-five percent do not again develop evidence of disease and appear, therefore, to have recovered; (2) Forty-five percent do relapse from time to time, but infrequently; (3) The remainder have frequent relapses, and are referred to by some authors as being steroid dependent. Relapses in the latter two categories may occur over a period of many years, patients continuing to respond, however, to repeated courses of treatment, and presumably going on to ultimate recovery. Patients who relapse infrequently require relatively little steroid therapy and generally do not get into difficulty with steroid toxicity. In contrast, patients who relapse often may require such frequent treatment that severe steroid toxicity becomes their major problem.

Fortunately only 5 percent of children with lipoid nephrosis fail to attain a complete remission in response to initial steroid therapy. The prognosis in these patients is grave, renal insufficiency usually ensuing over a period of months or years. Much less often a patient previously steroid responsive becomes nonresponsive after one or more successfully treated relapses. Recent evidence suggests that at least some of these patients may respond to cyclophosphamide and subsequently be amenable once more to steroid treatment.

It is not possible early in the course of disease to predict which course a given child will follow. It is now recognized that the various laboratory tests which are abnormal more often in patients who are steroid-resistant and who do poorly serve to identify patients with glomerulonephritis, rather than to determine prognosis in patients with minimal-change disease. In the latter group, we have found no correlation between the subsequent course and age, sex, or the presence or absence of hematuria or poorly selective proteinuria.

Perhaps the best prognostic feature at the onset of disease other than the findings on renal biopsy is initial response to adrenocortical steroid therapy. Complete cessation of proteinuria following treatment with steroids indicates a favorable prognosis; incomplete or absent response is usually associated with a grave outcome.

Finally, *criteria of recovery* must be considered in formulating therapy and must be included as an important aspect of discussions with the family. Recovery from the nephrotic syndrome must be defined as permanent subsidence of all the manifestations of the disease. Although one can never be absolutely certain that proteinuria may not recur at some future date, if two or three years have elapsed on a steroid-free regimen without recurrence of proteinuria, permanent recovery is almost virtually assured.

REFERENCES

Abramowicz, M., Arneil, G. C., Barnett, H. L., et al. Controlled clinical trial of azathioprine in children with nephrotic syndrome. Lancet, 1:959, 1970.

Ackerman, G. L., and Nolan, C. M. Adrenocortical responsiveness after alternate-day corticosteroid therapy. New Eng. J. Med., 278:405, 1968.

Arneil, G. C. Management of the nephrotic syndrome. Arch. Dis. Child., 43:257, 1968.

——— and Lam, N. C. Long-term assessment of steroid therapy in childhood nephrosis. Lancet, 2:819, 1966.

Barnett, H. L., Forman, C. W., and Lauson, H. D. The nephrotic syndrome in children. Advances Pediat., 5:53, 1953.

Browth, R. B., Burke, E. C., and Stickler, G. B. Studies in nephrotic syndrome. 1. Survival of 135 children with nephrotic syndrome treated with adrenal steroids. Mayo Clin. Proc., 40:384, 1965.

Calcagno, P. L., and Rubin, M. I. Physiologic considerations concerning corticosteroid therapy and complications in the nephrotic syndrome. J. Pediat., 58:585, 1961.

Cameron, J. S., and Blandford, G. The simple assessment of selectivity in heavy proteinuria. Lancet, 2:242, 1966.

——— and White, R. H. R. Selectivity of proteinuria in children with the nephrotic syndrome. Lancet, 1:463, 1965.

Churg, J., Habib, R., and White, R. H. R. Pathology of the nephrotic syndrome in children. Lancet, 1:1299, 1970.

Cornfield, D., and Schwartz, M. W. Nephrosis: A long-term study of children treated with corticosteroids. J. Pediat., 68:507, 1966.

Cornwell, D. G., Nakasato, D., Oncley, J. L., Hughes, W. L., Jr., and Janeway, C. A. Studies on the metabolism of plasma proteins in the nephrotic syndrome. II. The lipoproteins. J. Clin. Invest., 37:172, 1958.

Davis, R. A., Fertig, J. W., and Berger, A. P. Nephrosis of childhood: statistical evaluation of the effect of adrenocortical-active therapy. J. Chronic Dis., 3:640, 1956.

Drummond, K. N., Hillman, D. A., Marchessault, V. J. H., and Feldman, W. Cyclosphosphamide in the nephrotic syndrome of childhood. Canad. Med. Ass. J., 98:524, 1968.

——— Michael, A. F., Good, R. A., and Vernier, R. L. Nephrotic syndrome of childhood. Immunologic, clinical and pathologic correlations. J. Clin. Invest., 45:620, 1966.

Duffy, J. L., Cinque, T., Grishman, E., and Churg, J. Intraglomerular fibrin, platelet aggregation, and subendothelial deposits in lipoid nephrosis. J. Clin. Invest., 49:251, 1970.

Editorial. Treatment of steroid-resistant nephrotic syndrome. Lancet, 1:644, 1966.

Etteldorf, J. N., Shane, R., III, Summitt, R. L., Sweeney, M. J., Wall, H. P., and Burton, W. M. Cyclophosphamide in the treatment of idiopathic lipoid nephrosis. J. Pediat., 70:758, 1967.

Gitlin, D., Cornwall, D. G., Nakasato, D., Oncley, J. L., Hughes, W. L., Jr., and Janeway, C. A. Studies on the metabolism of plasma proteins in the nephrotic syndrome. II. The lipoproteins. J. Clin. Invest., 37:172, 1958.

——— Janeway, C. A., and Farr, L. E. Studies on the metabolism of plasma proteins in the nephrotic syndrome. I. Albumin, gamma-globulin and iron-binding globulin. J. Clin. Invest., 35:44, 1956.

Goldbloom, R. B., Hillman, D. A., and Santulli, T. V. Arterial thrombosis following femoral venipuncture in edematous nephrotic children. Pediatrics, 40:450, 1967.

Gootman, N., Gross, J., and Mensch, A. Pulmonary artery thrombosis. Pediatrics, 34:861, 1964.

Gotoff, S. P., Fellers, F. X., Vawter, G. F., Janeway, C. A., and Rosen, F. S. The beta-1-C globulin in childhood nephrotic syndrome. New Eng. J. Med., 273:524, 1965.

Grupe, W. E., and Heymann, W. Cytotoxic drugs in steroid-resistant renal disease. Amer. J. Dis. Child., 112:448, 1966.

Harter, J. G., Reddy, W. J., and Thorn, G. W. Studies on an intermittent corticosteroid dosage regimen. New Eng. J. Med., 269:591, 1963.

Hayslett, J. P., Krassner, L. S., Bensch, K. G., Kashgarian, M., and Epstein, F. H. Progression of "lipoid nephrosis" to renal insufficiency. New Eng. J. Med., 281:181, 1969.

Heymann, W., Nash, G., Gilkey, C., and Lewis, M. Studies on the causal role of hypoalbuminemia in experimental nephrotic hyperlipemia. J. Clin. Invest., 37:808, 1958.

Hooft, C., and van Acker, K. J. The natural history of the idiopathic nephrotic syndrome in childhood. Ann. Paediat. (Basel), 207:1, 1966.

Janeway, C. A. Studies on the pathogenesis of nephrotic edema. J. Pediat., 58:640, 1961.

Korsch, B., and Barnett, H. L. The physician, the family, and the child with nephrosis. J. Pediat., 58:707, 1961.

Lagru, G., Bariéty, J., Canlorbe, P., Vassal, J., and Milliez, P. La chimiothérapie dite immunodépressive dans les syndromes néphrotiques primitifs de l'enfant. Presse Med., 75:1773, 1967.

Lawson, D., Moncrief, A., and Payne, W. W. Forty years of nephrosis in childhood. Arch. Dis. Child., 35:115, 1960.

Lieberman, E., Heuser, E., Gilchrist, G. S., Donnell, G. N., and Landing, B. H. Thrombosis, nephrosis, and corticosteroid therapy. J. Pediat., 73:320, 1968.

Livanou, T., Ferriman, D., and James, V. H. T. Recovery of hypothalamo-pituitary-adrenal function after corticosteroid therapy. Lancet, 2:856, 1967.

MacLean, P. R., and Robson, J. S. A simple method for determining selectivity of proteinuria. Lancet, 1:539, 1967.

McCrory, W. W., and Fleisher, D. S. The nephrotic syndrome. In Gairdner, D. M. T., ed., Recent Advances in Pediatrics, 2nd ed. Boston, Little, Brown and Co., 1958, p. 227.

Metcoff, J., and Janeway, C. A. Studies on the pathogenesis of nephrotic edema. J. Pediat., 58:640, 1961.

Michael, A. F., Vernier, R. L., Drummond, K. N., Levitt, J. I., Herdman, R. C., Fish, A. J., and Good, R. A. Immunosuppressive therapy of chronic renal disease. New Eng. J. Med., 276:817, 1967.

Morris, H. G., Jorgensen, J. R., Elrick, H., and Goldsmith, R. E. Metabolic effects of human growth hormone in corticosteroid-treated children. J. Clin. Invest., 47:436, 1968.

Northway, J. D., and West, C. D. Successful therapy of trimethadione nephrosis with prednisone and cyclophosphamide. J. Pediat., 71:259, 1967.

Oliver, W. J., and Collins, W. R. Combined familial proteinuria and hyper-cholesteremia. Amer. J. Dis. Child., 99:261, 1960.

Poth, J. L., Sharp, G. S., and Schrier, S. L. Cold agglutinin disease and the nephrotic syndrome. J.A.M.A., 211:1989, 1970.

Riley, C. M., Davis, R. A., Fertig, J. W., and Barger, A. P. Nephrosis of childhood: Statistical evaluation of the effect of adrenocortical-active therapy. J. Chronic Dis., 3:640, 1956.

Rothenberg, M. B., and Heymann, W. The incidence of the nephrotic syndrome in children. Pediatrics, 19: 446, 1957.

Saxena, K. M., and Crawford, J. D. The treatment of nephrosis. New Eng. J. Med., 272:522, 1965.

Schlesinger, E. R., Sultz, H. A., Mosher, W. E., and Feldman, J. G. The nephrotic syndrome. Its incidence and implications for the community. Amer. J. Dis. Child., 116:623, 1968.

Sonnenschein, H., Minsky, A. A., and Kramer, B. The nephrotic syndrome in children. Differentiation into two clinically recognizable groups. Clin. Pediat., 5: 527, 1966.

Soyka, L. F. The nephrotic syndrome. Current concepts in diagnosis and therapy; advantages of alternate day steroid regimen. Clin. Pediat., 6:77, 1967.

———— and Saxena, K. M. Alternate-day steroid therapy for nephrotic children. J.A.M.A., 192:225, 1965.

Symchych, P. S., and Perrin, E. V. Thrombosis of the main pulmonary artery in nephrosis. Thromboembolism as a complication of nephrosis. Amer. J. Dis. Child., 110:636, 1965.

Thorn, G. W. Clinical considerations in the use of corticosteroids. New Eng. J. Med., 274:775, 1966.

Todd, R. McL., and Bouton, M. J. Nephrosis: A clinical and histological study of 38 children. Arch. Dis. Child., 40:659, 1965.

Trygstad, C. W., McCabe, E., Francyk, W. P., and Crummy, A. B. Renal vein thrombosis and the nephrotic syndrome: A case report with protein selectivity studies. J. Pediat., 76:861, 1970.

Volhard, F., and Fahr, T. Die Brightsche Nierenkrankheit. Berlin, Springer, 1914.

West, C. D., Hong, R., and Holland, N. H. Effect of cyclophosphamide on lipoid nephrosis in the human and on aminonucleoside nephrosis in the rat. J. Pediat., 68:516, 1966.

———— McAdams, A. J., McConville, J. M., Davis, N. C., and Holland, N. H. Hypocomplementemic and normocomplementemic persistent (chronic) glomerulonephritis; clinical and pathoolgical characteristics. J. Pediat., 67:1089, 1965.

White, R. H. R. Cytotoxic drug therapy in steroid-resistant glomerulonephritis. Proc. Roy. Soc. Med., 60:1164, 1967.

———— Cameron, J. S., and Trounce, J. R. Immunosuppressive therapy in steroid-resistant proliferative glomerulonephritis accompanied by the nephrotic syndrome. Brit. Med. J., 2:853, 1966.

———— Glasgow, E. F., and Mills, R. J. Clinico-pathologic study of nephrotic syndrome in childhood. Lancet, 1:1353, 1970.

Wittig, H. J., and Goldman, A. S. Nephrotic syndrome associated with inhaled allergens. Lancet, 1:542, 1970.

22.11
MISCELLANEOUS NEPHROPATHIES

CHESTER M. EDELMANN, JR.

Infantile Nephrosis
(Congenital Nephrosis)

The nephrotic syndrome occurs infrequently during the first year and particularly during the first three months of life; when it does it presents certain characteristic features: a high familial incidence, almost complete resistance to therapy, and a fatal outcome. Many of these cases have occurred in newborn and premature infants.

At least 112 families with congenital nephrosis have been described, with the great majority coming from Finland or occurring in families of Finnish origin. From a genetic study of 57 Finnish families, Norio concluded that the disease is transmitted as an autosomal recessive.

Hallman, Norio, and Kouvalainen pointed out features of the disease which indicate an onset during intrauterine life: almost without exception the placenta is very large; the birth weight is low, at least partly because of prematurity; proteinuria and characteristic changes in serum proteins are seen immediately after birth in a great majority of cases; wide cranial sutures at birth indicate that the ossification process already is delayed in utero; polycythemia and especially the advanced erythroblastosis occasionally seen in newborns with congenital nephrosis probably derive from impaired function of the large edematous placenta.

The pathologic findings have been variable, and some contradictory observations have been reported. The glomeruli often have been said to be normal, but hypercellularity and basement membrane thickening, progressing to glomerular sclerosis and hyalinization, also have been described, particularly in older infants. Most electron microscopic studies have shown fusion of foot processes and slight thickening of the basement membranes by electron-dense accumulations. As in older children with the nephrotic syndrome, the evidence seems to favor a primary glomerular lesion, which may, however, be histologically inconspicuous in its early stages. A very striking feature in many of these children, approximately 50 percent, is the presence of marked dilatation of the cortical tubules, most severe near the corticomedullary junction. In some cases, this cystic degeneration has been striking enough to prompt the suggestion that these children have a form of congenital renal tubular dysplasia, a "microcystic disease," that results in local tubular atrophy, occlusion, hyperplasia, and cyst formation. The finding of glomerular lesions in most studies suggests, however, that the tubular abnormalities are secondary reactions in immature kidneys to the primary glomerular disease. The localization by fluorescent-antibody techniques of gamma globulin and complement fractions in the glomeruli has suggested that the disease is an immune process. Kouvalainen and co-workers transplanted skin from infants born with congenital nephrosis to the mother and obtained an accelerated rejection, suggesting previous sensitization of the mother to the fetus.

The clinical picture and laboratory findings in congenital nephrosis do not differ from the nephrotic syndrome in older children, except for the age of the patients. Most of them have developed edema during the first month of life; exceptionally it has been present at birth. Although the serum cholesterol is usually elevated in these infants as in children and adults with the nephrotic syndrome, the distribution of values is shifted to the left due to the developmentally lower values in young infants.

Susceptibility to infection and to water and electrolyte imbalance is exaggerated by the young age of these patients. Steroid therapy fails to induce a remission and may complicate the management of the disease. Most patients survive but a few months, succumbing as a rule to renal failure. Exceptionally an infant who develops the disease toward the latter part of the first year will show the favorable response seen in the older child. Successful therapy with a combination of immunosuppressive drugs has not been reported, but additional experience with this form of treatment is needed. If the disease is in fact primarily renal, these infants should be considered as candidates for renal allotransplantation.

Benign Recurrent Hematuria

This is an entity characterized by multiple episodes of gross hematuria which occur over a period of months or years. By definition the prognosis for recovery is good, since evidence of progressive renal disease automatically excludes the designation "benign."

The onset commonly mimics acute poststreptococcal glomerulonephritis, although hypertension, reduced renal function, and edema usually are absent. However, instead of following the expected course for acute nephritis, recurrent bouts of gross hematuria ensue, often with considerable proteinuria. The acute episodes usually are preceded by a viral respiratory infection, and abdominal symptoms may be striking. In between episodes the patient is asymptomatic, the only abnormality being residual microscopic hematuria, with or without minimal or moderate proteinuria. In some patients, urinalysis is reported to have returned to normal during asymptomatic periods.

Histologic changes in the kidney are limited to minimal to moderate proliferative glomerulonephritis, which may be focal in distribution. Some biopsies have revealed normal histology.

Benign hematuria has been reported as a familial disease, although in such instances great caution must be exercised in making this diagnosis, since familial nephritis of the form that progresses to uremia may be present for many years without evidence of renal damage. Since even minimal urinary abnormalities may be evidence of severe, progressive renal disease, the diagnosis of benign hematuria should not be made in familial or nonfamilial cases without thorough examination, including renal biopsy.

The clinical course may be as long as 10 years. During this time no loss of renal function is noted and scarring and glomerular obsolescence are not seen on renal biopsy. Apparently, complete recovery ultimately ensues, although longer follow-up of many patients is needed to determine this with certainty.

Balkan Nephropathy

A peculiar form of renal disease has been reported in recent years in certain rural areas of Bulgaria, Rumania, and Yugoslavia. Several members of one family may be affected, but the disease is seen rarely in children. Urinary findings are minimal, hypertension is unusual, and there is a striking loss of concentrating capacity. Patients progress slowly but relentlessly to chronic uremia, without passing through a nephrotic stage. Pathologically, the tubules seem to be primarily involved, exhibiting degenerative changes with severe interstitial fibrosis. Ultimately, the kidneys are extremely contracted with extensive fibrosis and almost total absence of recognizable nephric elements in the outer part of the cortex. There is no clue to etiology. Although therapy is not available, those moving out of an endemic area appear to escape the disease.

Hyperuricemia and Gout

It is estimated that as many as two-thirds of patients with gout have renal involvement. This disease, however, has been reported only rarely in childhood and few of these patients have had overt renal manifestations. Rosenthal and associates described an infant from a gouty family with elevated levels of uric acid in the blood and symptoms of uremia at age 2 months. Several adolescents are included in the report by Duncan and Dixon of familial gout and renal disease with hypertension. Hyperuricemia and uric acid nephropathy is also observed following prolonged diuretic therapy and in patients having acute cytolytic therapy for malignant disease, such as leukemia.

Renal damage occurs primarily from parenchymal deposition of urates, particularly in the renal pyramids, and precipitation within the tubules, with subsequent nephron loss. In addition, stones are present in approximately one-fifth of patients. Finally, patients with gout seem to be unusually prone to development of pyelonephritis.

Hypercalcemia and Hypercalciuria

Hypercalcemia and/or hypercalciuria are seen in a variety of clinical situations, including immobilization, vitamin D intoxication, idiopathic hypercalcemia of infancy, hyperparathyroidism, hyperthyroidism, sarcoidosis, multiple myeloma, and malignancy. Nephrocalcinosis with severe, generalized renal damage and ultimate renal insufficiency may result.

In the absence of demonstrable nephrocalcinosis and prior to depression of glomerular filtration rate, characteristic changes in renal function may be noted. The most prominent of these is a rapidly developing and equally rapidly reversible concentrating defect, produced apparently by impairment of production of the usual medullary gradient of hyperosmolality. Another finding in patients with hypercalcemia, with the notable exception of hyperparathyroidism, is metabolic alkalosis. Parathormone release appears to lower the renal threshold for bicarbonate. Parathormone inhibition due to hypercalcemia, therefore, might be the cause of the alkalosis. Other patients with calcium nephropathy, particularly those with idiopathic hypercalcemia and vitamin D intoxication, develop the features of renal tubular acidosis.

Treatment consists of determining and correcting the underlying causes of hypercalcemia or hypercalciuria. Early changes of calcium nephropathy, including degenerative and necrotic changes in the tubular epithelium of Henle's loop, distal convoluted tubule, and collecting duct, are reversible. As the process advances, calcium is deposited interstitially and changes of chronic inflammation may be noted. Ultimately glomeruli may be sclerosed, apparently because of tubular obstruction and nephrocalcinosis.

Potassium Depletion

Potassium depletion severe enough to cause renal impairment is not often encountered in infants and children, but it does occur, particularly under two circumstances: in chronic gastrointestinal loss and secondary to hyperadrenalism.

It appears that potassium depletion must be of fairly long duration and of considerable magnitude before the kidney is affected, although there are instances in which abnormalities have occurred apparently after only a few days of potassium loss. Potassium depletion in man is associated with characteristic histologic changes in the kidney, namely swelling and degeneration of tubular epithelial cells, particularly in the proximal convolution. This contrasts with the rat, in which the predominant lesion is in the collecting ducts. Although the renal lesions appear to be reversible, there are reports of anatomic changes of pyelonephritis and interstitial nephritis in a few instances of chronic potassium loss.

The physiologic consequences of potassium nephropathy include (1) a concentrating defect, (2) limitation in production of a hydrogen ion gradient, and (3) increase in the renal bicarbonate threshold. It has been suggested recently, however, that the elevation in renal bicarbonate threshold and resulting metabolic alkalosis seen in patients with potassium depletion is due in most instances to an accompanying deficiency of sodium chloride.

An additional consequence of potassium depletion, demonstrated primarily in rats, is a marked increase in susceptibility to pyelonephritis. The role of potassium depletion as a predisposing factor for pyelonephritis in man requires further study.

Treatment generally consists of administration of potassium, which must be given cautiously, particularly in patients with impaired renal function. Conditions such as primary hyperaldosteronism must receive specific therapy before potassium repletion can be accomplished.

Drugs, Metals, and Other Nephrotoxins

Renal damage may occur from a variety of pharmacologic and toxic agents. Damage may be either mild and reversible or so severe that acute or chronic renal failure occurs.

A number of agents have been shown to have their effect on the proximal tubule and to produce features of the Fanconi syndrome. These include tetracycline, oxalic acid, and lead and other heavy metals (including mercury, cadmium, uranium, copper, and bismuth). In addition, heavy metals may cause either acute tubular necrosis or chronic nephropathy.

A variety of organic solvents are capable of producing severe renal damage by a number of different mechanisms. The most common of these is carbon tetrachloride, which causes acute proximal tubular necrosis and oliguric renal failure. Recovery in children usually is complete. Ethylene glycol is metabolized partially to oxalate; deposition of calcium oxalate crystals causes proximal tubular obstruction and dilatation. Propylene glycol causes acute intravascular hemolysis and consequent renal damage. Diethylene glycol causes severe renal cortical necrosis.

Certain antimicrobials are nephrotoxic. Sulfonamides cause obstructive uropathy by crystallization within the tubules or ureters. Streptomycin, vancomycin, kanamycin, neomycin, polymyxin, colistin, bacitracin, amphotericin B, and dimethoxyphenyl penicillin are all toxic to the renal tubular epithelium. Hematuria, proteinuria, or both give the first indication of renal toxicity, generally preceding development of azotemia. Discontinuation of treatment usually leads to a fairly prompt return of urine to normal, but the nephrotoxicity of neomycin, amphotericin B, and bacitracin may be permanent.

The nephrotic syndrome has been attributed to ingestion of a variety of drugs and metals, including trimethadione, tolbutamide, penicillamine, gold, bismuth, mercury, and thallium.

A great deal of attention has been directed in recent years to analgesic nephropathy. Severe interstitial nephritis with extensive renal damage apparently does occur, although the dosage must be tremendous and given over very long periods. Earlier reports focused on phenacetin as the major toxic agent, but it is likely that a number of other analgesics can be implicated as well.

Finally, there have been a number of reports of acute oliguric renal failure secondary to the intravascular administration of various media in the course of radiographic studies. Infants appear to be particularly susceptible.

Diabetes Mellitus

Prior to the discovery of insulin, renal deaths in patients with diabetes mellitus were not reported. Renal failure now accounts for more than half the deaths in such patients. However, in the pediatric age group significant clinical signs of renal involvement in patients with diabetes mellitus are extremely rare, so-called diabetic nephropathy taking usually 10 years or so to develop, despite notable exceptions. Nevertheless, even young patients with diabetes mellitus may be found to have minimal proteinuria if carefully tested, and renal abnormalities have been demonstrated histologically early in the course of the disease, as well as in patients with so-called prediabetes. The nephrotic syndrome has developed occasionally in diabetic children, possibly a chance occurrence. In a study of 123 children with diabetes mellitus, Moss reported a tendency for blood pressure to increase significantly at about 13 years of age, as compared to normal controls, and postulated that this reflected a prehypertensive state due to subclinical renal vascular disease.

There is still controversy as to the possible correlation between the degree of clinical and biochemical control of diabetes and the likelihood of emergence of renal and other complications. There is no question, however, that diabetic nephropathy may develop even in the patient with the best control of disease.

The renal lesions of diabetes mellitus are numerous, comprising a severe nephropathy that affects glomeruli, tubules, vessels, and interstitium. Renal lesions in childhood diabetes are, however, relatively mild. Biopsy studies disclose focal thickening of the glomerular basement membranes and stalks, and hyaline deposits appear at the vascular poles. Electron microscopy in the earliest stages shows thickening of basement membranes and the accumulation of hyaline or basement membranelike material beneath endothelium and among mesangial cells—changes that appear to be progressive. Similar abnormalities have been detected in renal biopsies of diabetic children with the nephrotic syndrome.

The high prevalence of pyelonephritis in patients with diabetes mellitus was originally interpreted as reflecting an unusual susceptibility of these patients to bacterial infection of the urinary tract. It is now recognized that the frequency of infection is due probably to the frequency of urethral catheterization rather than the diabetic process per se. However, an unusually severe complication of pyelonephritis, necrotizing renal papillitis, is much more common in the diabetic than in the nondiabetic population. This condition, which represents ischemic necrosis of the papilla, develops during an episode of acute infection. Papillary tissue that is sloughed may be recovered in the urine. Characteristic filling defects can be observed radiographically.

The only treatment of diabetic nephropathy, apart from optimal clinical management of the diabetes per se, is treatment of urinary tract infection. Established diabetic nephropathy is treated as is any type of chronic renal insufficiency (p. 1465).

Sickle-Cell Disease

Patients with sickle-cell disease have functional and morphologic abnormalities involving many organ systems. Renal manifestations include a concentrating defect, hematuria, the nephrotic syndrome, and a peculiar type of progressive nephropathy which may lead to renal insufficiency. Priapism, a common urologic complication in adults, is rare in children.

The incidence of sickle hemoglobin in American Negroes has been estimated to be 8 percent, and 2 to 3 percent of these have sickle-cell disease. The proportion demonstrating renal involvement is unknown, but the concentrating defect and hematuria are seen in patients with SA and SC hemoglobin as well as patients with sickle disease. Progressive nephropathy apparently is limited to the latter group.

CLINICAL AND LABORATORY FEATURES. During the first few years of life, GFR and RBF in patients with sickle-cell disease tend to be normal or elevated for age, similar to the findings in patients with other types of chronic anemia. These functions subsequently decrease, however, so that characteristically they are reduced to below normal by early adult life.

Studies in adults have suggested that as many as one-third of affected patients may have hematuria; although this abnormality is not uncommon in children, precise figures are not available. Hematuria may be unilateral or bilateral in origin. The left kidney is involved four times as often as the right and a similar male to female ratio of 4:1 has been described. Passage of clots may lead to renal colic.

The concentrating defect is not present early in life but is almost constant after 2 or 3 years of age. Initially, this abnormality may be reversible but by adolescence it appears to be a permanent defect.

Reports of the nephrotic syndrome associated with sickle-cell disease are rare, but it is probably not an uncommon disorder since we have seen several instances in the past few years. This form of the nephrotic syndrome is totally resistant to steroid therapy and we have had one patient in whom severe sickle crisis was produced by administration of prednisone.

Chronic renal insufficiency and uremia secondary to sickle-cell disease, with all clinical and laboratory manifestations of chronic glomerulonephritis, also have been reported, although rarely. We have treated four children with this condition and have found evidence of early renal insufficiency in a number of other children. This suggests that generalized renal damage secondary to sickle-cell disease may be more common than realized.

PATHOLOGY. Pathologic studies of young patients show certain abnormalities that can be correlated with the known alterations of renal function. Scarring and tubular obliteration in the inner medulla, presumably the result of anoxic injury, may be responsible for the irreversible concentrating defect that appears in late childhood. A more severe, acute lesion is papillary necrosis, which occurs in both the homozygous and heterozygous forms of the disease. Pelvic and medullary hemorrhages are particularly common and often are the only pathologic findings in kidneys removed for gross unilateral hematuria. These lesions presumably result from vascular stasis, a state that would be enhanced by the tendency of erythrocytes to undergo sickling in the hypoxic and hypertonic environment of the medulla.

Changes are also present in the cortex, where the glomeruli are markedly congested. During childhood the glomeruli, particularly in the inner cortex, appear to undergo striking, progressive enlargement, considerably in excess of normal growth. This finding is undoubtedly related to the increased glomerular filtration rate seen in the same age group. However, increased vascularity gives way to progressive ischemia and sclerosis, apparently leading in some individuals to glomerular obliteration and chronic renal insufficiency. Less severe changes probably underlie the decline of glomerular filtration in older patients. Other abnormalities include focal tubular necrosis and scarring, tubular hemosiderosis, and cortical infarcts. The nephrotic syndrome, which seems to occur with increased frequency in hemoglobin S disease, is associated with nonspecific ultrastructural changes in glomerular capillary wall and mesangium; electron-dense deposits of iron-protein complex are found in the mesangium.

PATHOPHYSIOLOGY. The etiology of hematuria in the patient without generalized renal damage or chronic renal insufficiency is probably related to papillary congestion and necrosis secondary to red cell sickling, stasis, and hypoxia. Similarly, the concentrating defect appears best explained by sickling of erythrocytes in the vasa recta during descent into the hypertonic, relatively hypoxic, renal medulla. Vascular stasis may exaggerate the normal degree of hypoxia and thus interfere with medullary sodium transport in the loop of Henle or impair countercurrent exchange mechanisms of the vasa recta. Osmotic diuresis with its associated increase in medullary blood flow might be expected to reverse intravascular sickling in the kidney, by lessening medullary hypoxia and decreasing medullary hypertonicity. Thus it is of interest that the maximal rate of reabsorption of free water during osmotic diuresis in patients with sickle-cell anemia is normal or close to normal, supporting the hypothesis that the concentrating defect is caused by intravascular sickling. Further evidence relating disturbed function specifically to the sickling phenomenon is correction of the concentrating defect in young subjects by administration of multiple blood transfusions.

The pathogenesis of the nephrotic syndrome and renal insufficiency in patients with sickle-cell disease is unknown, but the latter may result from the occurrence of multiple small infarctions over the course of many years. The tendency for renal insufficiency to occur with advancing age lends support to this suggestion.

Radiation Nephritis

Radiation nephritis results usually from inclusion of the kidneys in the field of x-ray therapy. The most frequent circumstance in children is following abdominal irradiation for Wilms' tumor. Luxton has established the following classification of the various patterns of disease: acute radiation nephritis; chronic radiation nephritis; benign hypertension; late malignant hypertension. Although other authors have not found it possible to fit all patients into this scheme, and there does appear to be a considerable degree of overlap, the classification has clinical usefulness.

Acute radiation nephritis occurs within a few months to a year following x-ray exposure; it may be manifested by abnormal urine, symptoms of uremia, or hypertension. Death may occur from malignant hypertension or uremia. If recovery is to take place, improvement is usually noted within several months of onset. Even with recovery there is usually residual renal damage. *Chronic radiation nephritis* may occur as a sequel to acute radiation nephritis or evolve asymptomatically following irradiation of both kidneys. *Benign essential hypertension* with minimal renal abnormalities may occur within a year following x-ray therapy. *Late malignant hypertension* has been seen up to several years following irradiation, in patients with chronic radiation nephritis, and in patients with exposure of just one kidney. The prognosis is ominous.

In a long-term follow-up of children who had undergone nephrectomy and radiation for malignant disease, Mitus and associates concluded that normal renal function can be preserved if x-ray exposure is kept below 1,200 r. This figure agrees well with the finding of Luxton that adults are able to tolerate 1,700 r to both kidneys. Avioli and associates found that renal plasma flow and glomerular filtration rate decreased progressively as radiation dosage exceeded 400 r. At dosages of 2,000 to 2,400 r a progressive decrease in glomerular filtration rate was observed which persisted up to 12 months after radiation.

The renal lesion progresses from the acute stage of cortical edema and glomerular ischemia to the chronic lesion of glomerular sclerosis, tubular atrophy, and cortical fibrosis. The kidney becomes small and atrophic. Vascular changes are usually prominent. The small vessels undergo fibrinoid necrosis, medial fibrosis, and hyalinization. However, hypertension is common, and secondary vascular changes

may be superimposed on the primary lesions. Tubular atrophy generally parallels the degree of glomerular sclerosis, though on occasion the former is present to an excessive degree.

Hepatorenal Syndrome

Renal failure is encountered frequently in patients with terminal liver disease. Morphologic lesions in the kidneys have been variable and involve both glomeruli and tubules. However, the low glomerular filtration rate and renal blood flow appear to be due to altered hemodynamics rather than a specific anatomic or biochemical defect. This view is supported by the prompt functioning of kidneys from patients with the hepatorenal syndrome when transplanted into recipients without hepatic disease.

The functional pattern of oliguria, azotemia, low concentration of sodium in serum and urine, and high urinary specific gravity is similar to that observed experimentally during decreased renal perfusion. In most patients with cirrhosis, cardiac output is adequate and plasma volume is normal or increased. Despite this there appears to be a general hypoperfusion of all vital organs, including the kidneys, as is seen in congestive heart failure or hypovolemia. The cause of renal hypoperfusion is unknown, and Papper has suggested that other mechanisms, such as abnormalities in the intrarenal circulation, should be considered in the pathogenesis of renal failure.

No specific treatment is available. Transient improvement has been noted in response to volume expansion, and reversal of renal failure has been reported following portacaval shunting.

REFERENCES

INFANTILE NEPHROSIS

Fetterman, G. H., and Feldman, J. D. Congenital anomalies of renal tubules in a case of "Infantile Nephrosis." Amer. J. Dis. Child., 100:319, 1960.

Grupe, W. E., Cuppage, F. E., and Heymann, W. Congenital nephrotic syndrome with interstitial nephritis. Amer. J. Dis. Child., 111:482, 1966.

Hallman, N., Norio, R., and Kouvalainen, K. Main features of the congenital nephrotic syndrome. Acta Paediat. Scand. (Suppl.), 172:75, 1967.

Hansen, M. F., and Coye, R. D. Congenital nephrosis with renal arteriolar hypertrophy. Amer. J. Dis. Child., 102:28, 1961.

Kouvalainen, K. Immunological features in the congenital nephrotic syndrome. A clinical and experimental study. Ann. Paediat., 9:(Suppl.)22, 1963.

———— Vaino, T., Hjelt, L., and Hallman, N. Behavior of skin grafted from infants to mother in congenital nephrosis families. Ann. Paediat., 8:173, 1962.

Lange, K., Wachstein, M., Wasserman, E., Alptekin, F., and Slobody, L. B. The congenital nephrotic syndrome. An immune reaction? Amer. J. Dis. Child., 105:338, 1963.

Laron, Z., Yonis, Z., Tissibov, R., and Boss, J. Infantile nephrosis in two siblings. Case report. Ann. Paediat., 195:337, 1960.

Norio, R. Heredity in the congenital nephrotic syndrome. A genetic study of 57 Finnish families with a review of reported cases. Ann. Paediat., 12:(Suppl.) 27, 1966.

Oliver, J. Microcystic renal disease and its relation to "Infantile Nephrosis." Amer. J. Dis. Child., 100:312, 1960.

Parker, R. A., and Piel, C. F. The nephrotic syndrome in the first year of life. Pediatrics, 25:967, 1960.

Vernier, R. L., Brunson, J., and Good, R. A. Studies in familial nephrosis. I. Amer. J. Dis. Child., 93:469, 1957.

Worthen, H. G., Vernier, R. L., and Good, R. A. Infantile nephrosis. Amer. J. Dis. Child., 98:731, 1959.

BENIGN RECURRENT HEMATURIA

Ayoub, E. M., and Vernier, R. L. Benign recurrent hematuria. Amer. J. Dis. Child., 109:217, 1965.

Bodian, M., Black, J. A., Kobayashi, N., Lake, B. D., and Shuler, S. E. Recurrent hematuria in childhood. Quart. J. Med., 34:359, 1965.

Editorial. Recurrent haematuria and focal nephritis. Lancet, 1:413, 1966.

Ferris, T. F., Gorden, P., Kashgarian, M., and Epstein, F. H. Recurrent hematuria and focal nephritis. New Eng. J. Med., 276:770, 1967.

Johnston, C., and Shuler, S. Recurrent haematuria in childhood. A five-year follow-up. Arch. Dis. Child., 44:483, 1969.

Lannigan, R., and Insley, J. Light and electron microscope appearances in renal biopsy material from cases of recurrent haematuria in children. J. Clin. Path., 18:178, 1965.

Livaditis, A., and Ericsson, N. O. Essential hematuria in children—prognostic aspects. Acta Paediat., 51:630, 1962.

Marks, M. I., and Drummond, K. N. Benign familial hematuria. Pediatrics, 44:590, 1969.

McConville, J. M., West, C. D., and McAdams, A. J. Familial and nonfamilial benign hematuria. J. Pediat., 69:207, 1966.

Singer, D. B., Hill, L. L., Rosenberg, H. S., Marshall, J., and Swenson, R. Recurrent hematuria in childhood. New Eng. J. Med., 279:7, 1968.

Travis, L. B., Daeschner, C. W., Dodge, W. F., Hopps, H. C., and Rosenberg, H. S. "Idiopathic" hematuria. J. Pediat., 60:24, 1962.

BALKAN NEPHROPATHY

Editorial. The Balkan Nephropathy. Lancet, 1:304, 1966.

Hall, P. W., III, Dammin, G. J., Griggs, R. C., Fajgolj, A., Zimonjic, B., and Gaon, J. Investigation of chronic endemic nephropathy in Yugoslavia. II. Renal pathology. Amer. J. Med., 39:210, 1965.

Wolstenholme, G. E. W., and Knight, J. The Balkan Nephropathy. Boston, Little, Brown and Co., 1967.

HYPERURICEMIA AND GOUT

Decker, J. L., and Vandeman, P. R. Renal calculi preceding gouty arthritis in a child. Amer. J. Med., 32:805, 1962.

Duncan, H., and Dixon, A. St. J. Gout, familial hyperuricaemia, and renal disease. Quart. J. Med., 29:127, 1960.

Editorial. Gout and the kidney. Lancet, 1:961, 1968.

Gutman, A. B., and Yü, T. F. Uric acid nephrolithiasis. Amer. J. Med., 45:756, 1968.

Rosenthal, I. M., Gaballah, S., and Rafelson, M. E., Jr. Metabolic studies in a young child with elevated serum uric acid levels. Amer. J. Dis. Child., 102:631, 1961.

——— Gaballah, S., and Rafelson, M. E., Jr. Gout in infancy manifested by renal failure. Pediatrics, 33:251, 1964.

Smythe, C. M., and Cutchin, J. H. Primary juvenile gout. Amer. J. Med., 32:799, 1962.

HYPERCALCEMIA AND HYPERCALCIURIA

Edwards, N. A., and Hodgkinson, A. Studies of renal function in patients with idiopathic hypercalciuria. Clin. Sci., 29:327, 1965.

Ferris, T. F., Kashgarian, M., Levitin, H., Brandt, I., and Epstein, F. H. Renal tubular acidosis and renal potassium-wasting acquired as a result of hypercalcemic nephropathy. New Eng. J. Med., 265:924, 1961.

Gill, J. R., and Bartter, F. C. On the impairment of renal concentrating ability in prolonged hypercalcemia and hypercalciuria in man. J. Clin. Invest., 40:716, 1961.

Heinemann, H. O. Metabolic alkalosis in patients with hypercalcemia. Metabolism, 14:1137, 1965.

Manitius, A., Levitin, H., Beck, D., and Epstein, F. H. The mechanism of impairment of renal concentrating ability in hypercalcemia. J. Clin. Invest., 39:693, 1960.

Richet, G., Ardaillou, R., and Amiel, C. Alcalose métabolique rénale de l'hypercalcémie. In Hamburger, J., ed., Actualités Néphrologiques de l'hôpital Necker, 1963. Paris, Editions Médicales Flammarion, 1963, p. 145.

Schlesinger, B. E., Butler, N. R., and Black, J. A. Severe type of infantile hypercalcemia. Brit. Med. J., 1:127, 1956.

Stark, H., Barnett, H. L., and Edelmann, C. M., Jr. Renal effects of hypercalciuria in immobilized children. Proc. Soc. Exp. Biol. Med., 118:870, 1965.

POTASSIUM DEPLETION

Holliday, M. A., Segar, W. C., Bright, N. H., and Egan, T. The effect of potassium deficiency on the kidney. Pediatrics, 26:950, 1960.

Kassirer, J. P., and Schwartz, W. B. Correction of metabolic alkalosis in man without repair of potassium deficiency. Amer. J. Med., 40:19, 1966.

Leaf, A., and Santos, R. F. Physiologic mechanisms in potassium deficiency. New Eng. J. Med., 264:335, 1961.

Manitius, A., Levitin, H., Beck, D., and Epstein, F. H. On the mechanism of impairment of renal concentrating ability in potassium deficiency. J. Clin. Invest., 39:684, 1960.

Relman, A. S., and Schwartz, W. B. The kidney in potassium depletion. Amer. J. Med., 24:764, 1958.

Welt, L. G., Hollander, W., Jr., and Blythe, W. B. The consequences of potassium depletion. J. Chronic Dis., 11:213, 1960.

DRUGS, METALS, AND OTHER NEPHROTOXINS

Abramowicz, M., and Edelmann, C. M., Jr. Nephrotoxicity of anti-infective drugs. Clin. Pediat., 7:389, 1968.

Balslov, J. T., and Jorgensen, H. E. A survey of 499 patients with acute anuric renal insufficiency. Amer. J. Med., 34:753, 1963.

Editorial. Phenacetin. Lancet, 2:717, 1968.

Emmerson, B. T. Metals and the kidney. *In* Black, D. A. K., ed., Renal Disease. Philadelphia, F. A. Davis Co., 1967, p. 561.

Gilberg, E. F., Khoury, G. H., Hogan, G. R., and Jones, B. Hemorrhagic renal necrosis in infancy: Relationship to radiopaque compounds. J. Pediat., 76: 49, 1970.

Gilman, A. Analgesic nephrotoxicity. A pharmacologic analysis. Amer. J. Med., 36:167, 1964.

Gruskin, A. B., Oetliker, O. H., Wolfish, N. M., Gootman, N. L., Bernstein, J., and Edelmann, C. M., Jr. Effects of angiography on renal function and histology in infants and piglets. J. Pediat., 76:41, 1970.

Hollenberg, N. K., Adams, D. F., Oken, D. E., Abrams, H. L., and Merrill, J. P. Acute renal failure due to nephrotoxins. Renal hemodynamic and angiographic studies in man. New Eng. J. Med., 282:1329, 1970.

Kunin, C. M. Nephrotoxicity of antibiotics. J.A.M.A., 202:204, 1967.

Mavromatis, F. Tetracycline nephropathy. J.A.M.A., 193:191, 1965.

Robinson, G. C., and Wong, L. C. Acute tubular necrosis in infancy and childhood. Amer. J. Dis. Child., 95:417, 1958.

Schreiner, G. E., and Maher, J. F. Toxic nephropathy. Amer. J. Med., 38:409, 1965.

DIABETES MELLITUS

Daysog, A., Jr., Dobson, H. L., and Brennan, J. C. Renal glomerular and vascular lesions in prediabetes and in diabetes mellitus: A study based on renal biopsies. Ann. Intern. Med., 54:672, 1961.

Klein, R., and Laron, Z. Current problems in diabetes. Pediatrics, 18:983, 1956.

Marble, A. The future of the child with diabetes. J. Amer. Diet. Ass., 33:569, 1957.

Moss, A. J. Blood pressure in children with diabetes mellitus. Pediatrics, 30:932, 1962.

Rosenbaum, P., Kattine, A. A., and Gottsegen, W. L. Diabetic and prediabetic nephropathy in childhood. Amer. J. Dis. Child., 106:83, 1963.

Urizar, R. E., Schwartz, A., Top, F., Jr., and Vernier, R. L. The nephrotic syndrome in children with diabetes mellitus of recent onset. Report of five cases. New Eng. J. Med., 281:173, 1969.

SICKLE-CELL DISEASE

Barnett, H. L., and Bernstein, J. Clinical pathological conference. J. Pediat., 73:936, 1968.

Berman, L. B., and Schreiner, G. E. Clinical and histologic spectrum of the nephrotic syndrome. Amer. J. Med., 24:249, 1958.

———— and Tublin, I. The nephropathies of sickle-cell disease. Arch. Intern. Med., 103:602, 1959.

Bernstein, J., and Whitten, C. F. A histologic appraisal of the kidney in sickle-cell anemia. Arch. Path., 70:407, 1960.

Calcagno, P. L., McLavy, J., and Kelley, T. Glomerular filtration rate in children with sickle-cell disease. J. Pediat., 5:127, 1950.

Etteldorf, J. N., Smith, J. D., Tuttle, A. H., and Diggs, L. W. Renal hemodynamic studies in adults with sickle-cell anemia. Amer. J. Med., 18:243, 1955.

Harrow, B. R., Sloane, J. A., and Liebman, N. C. Roentgenologic demonstration of renal papillary necrosis in sickle-cell trait. New Eng. J. Med., 268:969, 1963.

Heinemann, H. O., and Cheung, M. W. Renal concentrating mechanism in sickle-cell anemia. J. Lab. Clin. Med., 49:923, 1957.

Keitel, H. G., Thompson, D., and Itano, H. A. Hyposthenuria in sickle-cell anemia: a reversible renal defect. J. Clin. Invest., 35:998, 1956.

Knochel, J. P. Hematuria in sickle-cell trait. Arch. Intern. Med., 123:160, 1969.

Kunz, H. W., Mellin, G. W., Cheung, M. W., and Pratt, E. L. Impairment of urinary concentration in sickle-cell anemia. Amer. J. Dis. Child., 86:512, 1953.

Levitt, M. F., Hauser, A. D., Levy, M. S., and Polimeros, D. The renal concentrating defect in sickle-cell disease. Amer. J. Med., 29:611, 1960.

McCoy, R. C. Ultrastructural alterations in the kidney of patients with sickle-cell disease and the nephrotic syndrome. Lab. Invest., 21:85, 1969.

Mostofi, F. K., Vorder Bruegge, C. F., and Diggs, L. W. Lesions in kidneys removed for unilateral hematuria in sickle-cell disease. Arch. Path., 63:336, 1957.

Perillie, P. E., and Epstein, F. H. Sickling phenomenon produced by hypertonic solutions: a possible explanation for the hyposthenuria of sicklemia. J. Clin. Invest., 42:570, 1963.

Plunket, D. C., Leiken, S. L., and LoPresti, J. M. Renal radiologic changes in sickle-cell anemia. Pediatrics, 35:955, 1965.

Redman, J. F., and Mobley, J. E. Sickle-cell disease: Renal colic and microscopic hematuria. J. Urol., 100:594, 1968.

Schlitt, L. E., and Keitel, H. G. Renal manifestations of sickle-cell disease: a review. Amer. J. Med. Sci., 239:773, 1960.

———— and Keitel, H. G. Pathogenesis of hyposthenuria in persons with sickle-cell anemia or the sickle-cell trait. Pediatrics, 26:249, 1960.

Sharpe, A. R., Jr., Fox, P. G., Jr., and Dodson, A. I., Sr. Unilateral renal hematuria associated with sickle-cell disease and sickle-cell trait: study of five patients and review of literature. J. Urol., 81:780, 1959.

Suster, G., and Oski, F. A. Enuresis in sickle-cell anemia. Amer. J. Dis. Child., 113:311, 1967.

Sweeney, M. J., Dobbins, W. T., and Etteldorf, J. N. Renal disease with elements of the nephrotic syndrome associated with sickle-cell anemia. J. Pediat., 60:42, 1962.

Van Eps, L. W. S., Pinedo-Vells, C., de Vries, G. H., and de Koning, J. Nature of concentrating defect in sickle-cell nephropathy. Microangiographic studies. Lancet, 1:450, 1970.

Vernier, R. L. Hematuria as a manifestation of sickle-cell anemia in children. Amer. J. Dis. Child., 89:221, 1955.

Whitten, C. F., and Younes, A. A. A comparative study
of renal concentrating ability in children with sickle-
cell anemia and in normal children. J. Lab. Clin. Med.,
55:400, 1960.

Zarafonetis, C. J. D., Steiger, W. A., Molthan, L.,
McMaster, J., and Colville, V. F. Renal defect asso-
ciated with sickle-cell trait and sickle-cell disease. J.
Lab. Clin. Med., 44:959, 1954.

RADIATION NEPHRITIS

Avioli, L. V., Lazor, M. Z., Cotlove, E., Brace, K. C.,
and Andrews, J. R. Early effects of radiation on renal
function in man. Amer. J. Med., 34:329, 1963.

Luxton, R. W. Radiation nephritis. A long-term study of
54 patients. Lancet, 2:1221, 1961.

———— and Kunkler, P. B. Radiation nephritis. Acta
Radiol., 2:169, 1964.

MacKay, E. V., and Biggs, J. S. G. Late sequelae of
radiotherapy for Wilms' tumour in infancy. Aust.
Radiol., 10:356, 1966.

Mitus, A., Tefft, M., and Fellers, F. X. Long-term follow-
up of renal functions of 108 children who underwent
nephrectomy for malignant disease. Pediatrics, 44:912,
1969.

O'Malley, B., D'Angio, G. J., and Vawter, G. F. Late
effects of roentgen therapy given in infancy. Amer. J.
Roentgen., 89:1067, 1963.

Zuelzer, W. W., Palmer, H. D., and Newton, W. A., Jr.
Unusual glomerulonephritis in young children; prob-
ably radiation nephritis; report of three cases. Amer. J.
Path., 26:1019, 1950.

HEPATORENAL SYNDROME

Editorial. Renal resurrection. New Eng. J. Med., 280:
1414, 1969.

Koppel, M. H., Coburn, J. W., Mims, M. M., Goldstein,
H., Boyle, M. D., and Rubini, M. E. Transplantation
of cadaveric kidneys from patients with hepatorenal
syndrome. Evidence for the functional nature of renal
failure in advanced liver disease. New Eng. J. Med.,
280:1367, 1969.

Papper, S., and Vaamonde, C. A. Renal failure in cirrhosis—role of plasma volume. Ann. Intern. Med., 68:
958, 1968.

Reynolds, T. B., Lieberman, F. L., and Redeker, A. G.
Functional renal failure with cirrhosis. The effect of
plasma volume expansion. Medicine, 46:191, 1967.

Schroeder, E. T., Numann, P. J., and Chamberlain, B. E.
Functional renal failure in cirrhosis. Recovery after
portacaval shunt. Ann. Intern. Med., 72:923, 1960.

Shear, L., Kleinerman, J., and Gabuzda, G. J. Renal
failure in patients with cirrhosis of the liver. I. Clinical
and pathologic characteristics. Amer. J. Med., 39:184,
1965.

22.12
HEREDITARY NEPHROPATHIES

JAY BERNSTEIN

Diffuse nephritis occurs in several familial and
inherited diseases, and in some it is the primary ab-

normality. Our awareness and knowledge of hereditary nephritis have increased greatly in the last decade, and the list of variants and subgroups has grown
accordingly. The recognition of hereditary hematuria
does, however, date back to Guthrie's studies at the
turn of the century; the relation between hereditary
nephritis and deafness was recognized by Alport in
1927. Other nephropathies have been identified and
studied, among them Fanconi's nephronophthisis,
which has in recent years been identified tentatively
with medullary cystic disease. At least part of the
recent, rapid upturn has been due to greater accuracy
in differentiating hereditary nephritis from acquired
disease, which in the individual case may be difficult
both clinically and pathologically.

Hereditary Nephritis

Hereditary nephritis occurs both with and without
nerve deafness; the former might properly be termed
Alport's syndrome. A number of large families have
been studied through several generations, demonstrating the frequent concurrence of renal disease and
deafness, although some individuals may have had
only one or the other. A high incidence of ocular
abnormalities, among them lens deformities and cataracts, also has been seen. Whether hereditary nephritis in families without nerve deafness is a subgroup
of the more complete syndrome or a separate disease
is not clear; another subgroup is hereditary nephritis
with polyneuropathy. An apparently distinct condition is the uncommon familial association of nephropathy with hyperprolinemia and mental retardation,
perhaps representing the coexistence of two separable abnormalities. A diffuse nephropathy has been
encountered also in hereditary lipodystrophy, in hereditary osteolysis, and in the nail-patella syndrome
(osteo-onychodysplasia). The last has been described
as a relatively benign, rarely fatal condition, transmitted as an autosomal dominant. The hereditary
transmission of hereditary nephritis with nerve deafness is, on the other hand, far from clear.

Hereditary nephritis with nerve deafness and
ocular abnormalities characteristically begins in childhood with episodic hematuria. Attacks often are precipitated by streptococcal and other infections, and, as
with typical acute glomerulonephritis, clinical manifestations include edema, mild oliguria, and azotemia.
Hypertension is said to be relatively uncommon. Attacks are not associated with reduction of the serum
concentration of complement. Other laboratory findings are not different from other types of nephritis.
Proteinuria, pyuria, cylindruria, and hematuria variably persist after the initial attack, and the course
may be complicated by infection, with dysuria and
bacteriuria.

Males are affected earlier and more severely
than females, although a clinical study of a kindred
will often uncover a greater number of females,
many with mild or subclinical disease. Males die
from renal failure by the third or fourth decade,

whereas many females often remain asymptomatic, their disease being discovered only on screening urinalysis or audiometric testing. These and other observations on the sex ratios of affected sibships have led to the suggestion that the condition is transmitted as a partially X-linked dominant, a proposal not universally accepted. An autosomal dominant inheritance, perhaps male-limited with nonrandom segregation and preferential association with the X-chromosome, also has been proposed, but the matter remains unresolved.

Both the renal disease and deafness are progressive, the two being more commonly associated in older patients. Renal failure in males commonly develops in the second or third decade of life, but a rapid course and fatal outcome are seen also in childhood, the pattern among members of a single kindred usually being strikingly similar. Deafness, beginning in childhood, occurs mostly, though not exclusively, in patients with renal disease, affecting an estimated half of patients with renal failure. The deafness results from abnormality in the eighth nerve or possibly in the organ of Corti, and it is not, therefore, helped very much by prosthetic devices. The disease in females, as noted, is typically milder, although there clearly are exceptions to this rule. Exacerbations, with proteinuria, edema, and even hypertension, occur during pregnancy.

The pathogenesis of the renal lesion is not known. Histopathologic studies have demonstrated progression from a minimal early lesion to severe renal atrophy. Biopsies early in the course of disease may disclose focal glomerular lesions, consisting of stalk sclerosis, epithelial immaturity, and thickening of the capsular basement membrane. Apparent progression leads to capsular proliferation with crescents, and, typically, periglomerular fibrosis. Focal cortical fibrosis and tubular atrophy become more severe and are associated with infiltrates of chronic inflammatory cells. A characteristic, but by no means specific, finding is numerous interstitial, lipid-containing foam cells, particularly in the inner cortex. Their presence, even in the absence of other findings, is suggestive of hereditary nephritis. The end stage is diffuse chronic nephritis, combining elements of glomerular and interstitial nephritis.

Therapy is limited to supportive measures, except that intercurrent infections are treated specifically. Steroids and immunosuppressive agents have not been helpful.

Nephronophthisis and Medullary Cystic Disease

The diseases described as *medullary cystic disease* and as *familial juvenile nephronophthisis* hold many features, both anatomic and clinical, in common, and they cannot be readily differentiated in the evaluation of any given case. It has been proposed, therefore, that they constitute a single clinical entity, a familial nephropathy in which cysts of the renal medulla are at times prominent though inconstantly present. Other studies have indicated, however, that familial medullary cystic disease with an adult onset is transmitted as a dominant trait, whereas juvenile nephronophthisis beginning in childhood is transmitted as a recessive. The clinical condition does indeed appear to be composed of several genetically heterogeneous abnormalities, some associated with retinal abnormalities. There is little reason to regard the renal lesion as an embryologic, developmental abnormality, and the cysts appear to be unnecessary to either the clinical state or pathologic progression of the disease.

Clinical studies in both conditions are characterized by the early findings of polyuria, growth retardation, and normochromic anemia. Proteinuria and formed elements in the urine are uncommon, and other clinical signs and symptoms are often minor prior to the stage of renal failure. Anemia, however, is often severe, out of proportion to the degree of renal failure. Functional studies show impaired concentrating ability, and renal failure develops insidiously and inexorably. An inability to conserve sodium ion may lead to hyponatremia. The history of familial involvement and of polyuria are strong clues to the diagnosis.

Pathologic studies have shown extensive interstitial and tubular changes. Tubular atrophy is marked, and there is cystic dilatation of Henle's loops and of collecting ducts. Microdissection reveals numerous diverticula of the distal convoluted tubule, descending limbs, and collecting ducts. Localized ductal dilatation, particularly in the medullary portions of collecting ducts, reach gross proportions. Glomeruli are at first normal, but periglomerular fibrosis progresses to glomerular sclerosis. Interstitial fibrosis and inflammatory cell infiltrates are prominent, causing confusion with chronic interstitial nephritis.

Treatment is supportive, including provision of adequate amounts of fluid and electrolyte.

REFERENCES

Alexander, F., and Campbell, S. Familial uremic medullary cystic disease. Pediatrics, 45:1024, 1970.

Alport, A. C. Hereditary familial congenital hemorrhagic nephritis. Brit. Med. J., 1:504, 1927.

Antonovych, T. T., Deasy, P. F., Tina, L. U., D'Albora, J. B., Hollerman, C. E., and Calcagno, P. L. Hereditary nephritis: Early clinical, functional, and morphological studies. Pediat. Res., 3:545, 1969.

Broberger, O., Winberg, J., and Zetterström, R. Juvenile nephronophthisis. I. A genetically determined nephropathy with hypotonic polyuria and azotaemia. Acta Paediat., 49:470, 1960.

Cassady, G., Brown, K., Cohen, M., and DeMaria, W. Hereditary renal dysfunction and deafness. Pediatrics, 35:967, 1965.

Chappell, J. A., and Kelsey, W. M. Hereditary nephritis. Amer. J. Dis. Child., 99:401, 1960.

Fanconi, V. G., Hanhart, E., Albertini, A., Von Uhlinger, E., Dolivo, G., and Prader, A. Die familiäre juvenile Nephronophthise (Die idiopathische parenchymatöse Schrumpfniere). Helv. Paediat. Acta, 6:1, 1951.

Gardner, K. D. Evolution of clinical signs in adult-onset cystic disease of the renal medulla. Ann. Int. Med., 74:47, 1971.

Giselson, N., Heinegard, D., Holmberg, C-G., Lindberg, L-G., Lindstedt, E., Lindstedt, G., and Schersten, B. Renal medullary cystic disease or familial juvenile nephronophthisis: a renal tubular disease. Amer. J. Med., 48:174, 1970.

Goldbloom, R. B., Fraser, F. C., Waugh, D., Aronovitch, M., and Wiglesworth, F. W. Hereditary renal disease associated with nerve deafness and ocular lesions. Pediatrics, 20:241, 1957.

Goldman, R., and Haberfelde, G. C. Hereditary nephritis: report of a kindred. New Eng. J. Med., 261:734, 1959.

Herdman, R. C., Good, R. A., and Vernier, R. L. Medullary cystic disease in two siblings. Amer. J. Med., 43:335, 1967.

Hobolth, N. Hereditary nephropathy with haematuria. Acta Paediat., 52:581, 1963.

Ivemark, B. I., Ljungqvist, A., and Barry, A. Juvenile nephronophthisis. Part II. A histologic and microangiographic study. Acta Paediat., 49:480, 1960.

Kaufman, D. B., McIntosh, R. M., Smith, F. G., Jr., and Vernier, R. L. Diffuse familial nephropathy: A clinicopathological study. J. Pediat., 77:37, 1970.

Knepshield, J. H., Roberts, P. L., Davis, C. J., and Moser, R. H. Hereditary chronic nephritis complicated by nephrotic syndrome. Arch. Intern. Med., 122:156, 1968.

Kopelman, H., Asatoor, A. M., and Milne, M. D. Hyperprolinemia and hereditary nephritis. Lancet, 2:1075, 1964.

Ljungqvist, A., Victorin, L., and Winberg, J. Atypical nephronophthisis. A clinico-pathologic study of juvenile patients without hypotonic polyuria. Acta Paediat., 56:164, 1967.

Mangos, J. A., Opitz, J. M., Lobeck, C. C., and Cookson, D. U. Familial juvenile nephronophthisis: an unrecognized renal disease in the United States. Pediatrics, 34:337, 1964.

McCrory, W. W., Shibuya, M., and Worthen, H. G. Hereditary renal glomerular disease in infancy and childhood. Advances Pediat., 14:253, 1966.

Mongeau, J. G., and Worthen, H. G. Nephronophthisis and medullary cystic disease. Amer. J. Med., 43:345, 1967.

Pedreira, F. A., Marmer, E. L., and Bergstrom, W. H. Familial juvenile nephronophthisis and medullary cystic disease. J. Pediat., 73:77, 1968.

Perkoff, G. T. The hereditary renal diseases. New Eng. J. Med., 277:79, 1967.

Reyersbach, G. C., and Butler, A. M. Congenital hereditary hematuria. New Eng. J. Med., 251:377, 1954.

Rome, L., Cuppage, F. E., and Vertes, V. Familial hematuric nephritis. Pediatrics, 38:808, 1966.

Schafer, I. A., Scriver, C. R., and Efron, M. L. Familial hyperprolinemia, cerebral dysfunction and renal anomalies occurring in a family with hereditary nephropathy and deafness. New Eng. J. Med., 267:51, 1962.

Strauss, M. B., and Sommers, S. C. Medullary cystic disease and familial juvenile nephronophthisis. Clinical and pathological identity. New Eng. J. Med., 277:863, 1967.

Wallace, I. R., and Jones, J. H. Familial glomerulonephritis and aminoaciduria. Lancet, 1:941, 1960.

Whalen, R. E., and McIntosh, H. D. The spectrum of hereditary renal diseases. Amer. J. Med., 33:282, 1962.

22.13

DISORDERS OF RENAL TUBULAR FUNCTION

JUAN RODRIGUEZ SORIANO

Renal tubular disorders may be defined as conditions in which specific tubular dysfunctions exist in association with little or no impairment of glomerular function. This definition applies only to the early stages of disease, since secondary glomerular damage may appear later, as in the Fanconi syndrome with cystinosis, or in renal tubular acidosis with nephrocalcinosis and secondary pyelonephritis. In addition, decreased glomerular function and elevation of blood urea may be seen as prerenal phenomena early in the disease if a tubular defect in the conservation of water or solute is present (p. 1464).

Defects of tubular function may be single or multiple. Analysis of the disorder may be complicated by the fact that a defect may not represent a primary, specific abnormality, but rather a secondary, functional one. For example, a concentrating defect may be due to potassium deficiency; hyperkaliuria may be caused by secondary hyperaldosteronism; hypercalciuria may result from acidosis; an increased phosphate clearance may be due to acidosis itself or result from secondary hyperparathyroidism. The reversibility of the abnormality when the primary cause is corrected establishes the defect as functional, but such a clear distinction between functional and specific defects is not always possible.

The cause of many renal tubular disorders is unknown, but in most a hereditary or acquired etiology may be traced. Genetic disorders may modify renal function in two ways: through a primary abnormality in a specific tubular function (e.g., primary renal glycosuria), or secondarily by the toxic effect on the renal tubule of accumulated metabolites consequent to an extrarenal metabolic block (e.g., galactosemia). Both primary and secondary causes may present with identical symptomatology and be indistinguishable on the basis of functional and urinary findings. For this reason a descriptive rather than an etiologic classification is followed in this section.

Renal Glycosuria

Primary renal glycosuria results from a defect in proximal tubular reabsorption of glucose. Glomerular filtration rate and other tubular functions are normal. Most cases are believed to be inherited as an autosomal dominant characteristic, but in one family both parents were normal, suggesting an autosomal recessive trait.

This condition undoubtedly is present at birth but its discovery may be delayed until adult life. It is a benign condition and patients generally are asymptomatic, except for the rare occurrence of hypoglycemia. The presence of glucose in the urine concurrent with normal blood levels establishes the diagnosis. In the obvious case, glycosuria is constant, even during fasting, but in some cases it can be detected only postprandially.

Two types of renal glycosuria have been recognized. In so-called type A or "renal diabetes," both the renal plasma threshold and the maximal rate of glucose reabsorption (glucose Tm) are low (see p. 1455). This is believed to represent a true tubular defect, although the abnormality in the transport mechanism is completely unknown. This type of renal glycosuria may occur as an isolated defect but more often is associated with other tubular abnormalities as part of the Fanconi syndrome.

In type B or "pseudorenal diabetes," the Tm of reabsorption is normal, but there is a low renal plasma threshold, with a resultant marked splay of the titration curve of glucose reabsorption. This type may represent an exaggerated heterogeneity of the nephron population, either functional or anatomic or both. The overall rate of glucose reabsorption is normal at high plasma levels, but at lower levels a disparity exists in the saturation of glucose transport in individual nephrons.

Type B glycosuria is said to be present only as an isolated abnormality without other tubular defects. However, in glucoglycinuria (Sec. 8.2) this type of glycosuria is seen, and we have studied one child with this defect who had a similar abnormality in bicarbonate reabsorption.

The separation of types A and B as two different entities is still a matter of speculation. It is now known that, at least in the rat, the splay of the titration curve of glucose reabsorption increases when the extracellular volume is expanded, a factor not controlled in most studies. Moreover, in one pedigree studied by Elsas and Rosenberg, both types A and B coexisted in the same family, suggesting the possibility of different degrees of the same inherited defect rather than two distinct types of disease.

It is known that some amino acids share the same transport processes in the renal tubule and the intestinal mucosa. In renal glycosuria the glucose tolerance test is frequently flattened, suggesting a defect in the transport of glucose through the intestine. However, studies in one family, utilizing the in vitro incubation of jejunal mucosa with radioactive glucose, failed to show an abnormality in cellular uptake. In contrast, in glucose-galactose malabsorption, a familial disease with defective intestinal absorption of both of these sugars (Sec. 23.5), an abnormality in the renal tubular transport of glucose has been demonstrated. These studies suggest that at least two mechanisms are responsible for glucose transport, and that only one is shared by both the gut and the kidney.

In the few cases of renal glycosuria studied, the kidney was histologically normal. However, Monasterio et al. have reported alterations in the structure of proximal tubular cells when observed by the electron microscope.

The differentiation of renal glycosuria from diabetes mellitus is essential in order to avoid dangerous therapeutic errors. The glucose oxidase test will differentiate other types of mellituria.

Therapy is not indicated. The amount of glucose in the urine is independent of the carbohydrate intake and no dietary restrictions are needed.

Amino-Acidurias

The amino acids present in the glomerular filtrate normally are reabsorbed almost completely in the proximal tubule. Urine of the normal adult contains less than 1 percent of the filtered amino nitrogen, mainly in the form of glycine, taurine, histidine, and glutamine, which are the only amino acids detected when urine is analyzed by paper chromatography. However, it can be demonstrated by ion exchange chromatography that most of the plasma amino acids are present in urine, although in very small amounts. The rate of excretion of amino acids in infants and children is comparatively greater than in adults. Healthy children excrete alpha-amino nitrogen at a rate of about 2.5 mg per kg body weight per day, infants as much as 8.5 mg per kg. The pattern of urinary excretion of amino acids in children is similar to that in adults, but may differ markedly in small infants, especially prematures, who excrete predominantly threonine, serine, proline, glycine, and alanine. The percentage tubular reabsorption of all amino acids is lower in infancy, reflecting their state of glomerulotubular imbalance (see p. 1456).

Tubular reabsorption of amino acids is accomplished by a number of specific, energy-dependent, active transport processes. The efficiency of tubular reabsorption of individual amino acids is related to their chemical structure, steric configuration, and concentration in plasma. Although the knowledge of these transport mechanisms is still limited, it appears that there are several distinct transport sites for individual or groups of amino acids and that competitive and noncompetitive mechanisms of inhibition of uptake occur at the various sites.

Transport sites common to more than one amino acid have been identified on the basis of physiologic studies or characteristic findings in patients with specific diseases. The first site involves the dibasic amino acids (lysine, arginine, and ornithine). This transport system is defective in cystinuria, an inherited disorder leading to impaired intestinal absorption and marked urinary hyperexcretion of cystine as well as the dibasic amino acids (Sec. 8.2). In a recently described condition called hyperdibasic amino-aciduria, the defect is limited to the dibasic amino acids, without involvement of cystine (Sec. 8.2). This suggests that there are two renal mechanisms for dibasic amino acid transport, only one of which includes cystine.

A second transport mechanism involves the acidic amino acids (glutamic and aspartic acids). This transport site has been identified only in the dog.

Imino acids (proline and hydroxyproline) and glycine are involved in a transport system which is defective in familial imino-glycinuria. Affected individuals excrete excessive amounts of all three compounds (Sec. 8.2).

Neutral amino acids, other than glycine and the imino acids, share a common transport mechanism since they are all characteristically increased in Hartnup disease (Sec. 8.2).

The beta-amino compounds (beta-alanine, beta-amino isobutyric acid, and taurine) share a transport system distinct from that transporting alpha-amino acids, as has been shown in patients with beta-alaninemia.

In many instances the absorption of amino acids at the level of the jejunal mucosa appears to involve mechanisms similar to those in the renal tubule, since identical defects in transport have been identified. For example, in cystinuria and in Hartnup disease, intestinal and tubular absorption of the same group of amino acids is defective. However, in familial imino-glycinuria, in vitro studies using intestinal biopsy specimens revealed no defect in mucosal uptake. It is possible, as in cystinuria, that further study of this disorder will reveal the presence of more than one genetic type.

Increased urinary excretion of amino acids is due to one of the following mechanisms:

1. *Saturation* of tubular transport due to an increased filtered load, the plasma level of the amino acid or acids involved being elevated (overflow amino-aciduria).
2. *Competition* between the reabsorption of amino acids sharing a common transport site, when the concentration in plasma of one of them is increased (combined amino-aciduria).
3. *Selective abnormaltiy* leading to a specific defect in the reabsorption of an individual or a group of amino acids (specific renal amino-aciduria).
4. *Generalized abnormality* involving a large and heterogeneous group of amino acids due to nonspecific dysfunction of the proximal tubule (nonspecific renal amino-aciduria).

In the renal amino-acidurias, specific or nonspecific, the plasma levels characteristically are normal. Only these types will be considered in this section.

CYSTINURIA. The importance of this defect is that patients are prone to urolithiasis. Tubular reabsorption of cystine, lysine, arginine, and ornithine is ab-

normal. (See also Section 22.15.) This disorder is discussed in detail in Section 8.2.

HARTNUP DISEASE. This is a disorder in which there is abnormal tubular transport of the neutral amino acids, with the exception of the imino acids and glycine. A peculiar rash is present and there are central nervous system manifestations. The disease is described in detail in Section 8.2.

DIBASIC AMINO-ACIDURIA. This condition was described by Whelan and Scriver in 13 of 33 members of a French Canadian family. The proband was an 18-month-old girl studied because of small stature and a mild malabsorption syndrome. Neither defect could be linked confidently to the amino-aciduria, which appeared to be a dominantly inherited trait. Affected individuals, mostly asymptomatic, excrete excessive amounts of lysine, ornithine, and arginine; cystine, which is excreted in abnormal amounts along with the dibasic amino acids in classical cystinuria, is excreted normally. Plasma values are normal after oral administration of cystine but are lower than in control subjects after administration of lysine, indicating a concomitant defect in the intestinal absorption of the dibasic amino acids.

FAMILIAL IMINO-GLYCINURIA. This entity results from the defective tubular reabsorption of proline, hydroxyproline, and glycine. Only a few families, mostly of Jewish origin, have been described. The disease is inherited as an autosomal recessive. Patients are generally asymptomatic but a few subjects have been mentally retarded. The original case presented with convulsions and high spinal fluid protein.

In the homozygotes the urinary excretion of proline, hydroxyproline, and glycine is increased. Heterozygotes for the defect have hyperglycinuria only, without concomitant hyperimino-aciduria. This suggests that there is more than one renal transport system for glycine and the amino acids: one common for all three compounds, and two (or more) responsible for a selective absorption of glycine or the imino acids. In the homozygotes the common system is severely affected, the selective system permitting partial reabsorption of glycine and the imino acids; in the heterozygotes the activity of the common system appears to be less affected, permitting reabsorption of virtually all the filtered proline and hydroxyproline but only part of the glycine.

The intestinal transport of glycine and imino acids in this condition has been found to be normal by most authors, but it was impaired in two patients, most likely indicating the presence of more than one genetic type.

HEREDITARY GLYCINURIA. This condition has been described by DeVries and co-workers in a single family, transmitted as an autosomal dominant, and present in three consecutive generations. The only clinical manifestations were associated with recurrent nephrolithiasis. Urinary excretion of glycine was markedly elevated; plasma level was normal. Chemical analysis of one calculus revealed primarily calcium oxalate, but 0.5 percent of free glycine also was found. Jejunal transport of glycine was not investigated.

GLUCOGLYCINURIA. This condition was described by Käser et al. in 14 members of a single family. Type B renal glycosuria was present in association with a marked excretion of glycine. The patients were asymptomatic except for the propositus who had cystic fibrosis.

LATE VITAMIN D-RESISTANT RICKETS WITH HYPER-GLYCINURIA. This entity is similar to the more common *familial hypophosphatemia* (Sec. 3.5) except for the presence of excessive urinary excretion of glycine and its late onset in adolescence and early adulthood. In a case of Scriver and associates, glycinuria and hyperphosphaturia were associated with renal glycosuria and abnormal excretion of glycylproline.

The relationship, if any, between the various entities of abnormal excretion of glycine is unknown. Differentiation from *idiopathic hyperglycinemia* (Sec. 8.2), in which the hyperglycinuria depends on an overflow mechanism, is important.

BETA-AMINO-ISOBUTYRIC ACIDURIA. This finding has no clinical significance. The urinary excretion of the metabolite is of interest as a genetic marker.

NONSPECIFIC RENAL AMINO-ACIDURIAS. The presence of a generalized amino-aciduria is indicative of nonspecific tubular damage and generally is associated with other tubular abnormalities. This type of amino-aciduria usually is not characteristic, most of the plasma amino-acids being present in the urine in excessive amounts. However, some differences in the pattern of amino-aciduria may be found depending on the etiology of the tubular dysfunction. Thus cystine is characteristically increased in Wilson's disease, proline in cystinosis, and lysine and tyrosine in Lowe's syndrome.

Generalized amino-aciduria is characteristically present in vitamin D-deficiency rickets and may be found as an isolated tubular abnormality in cases of congenital lactose intolerance, hereditary intolerance to fructose, galactosemia, Wilson's disease, heavy metal poisoning, and malnutrition.

Disorders of Phosphate Transport

Between 85 and 95 percent of filtered phosphate normally is reabsorbed in the proximal tubule. Rate of reabsorption is controlled by parathyroid hormone, which acts to inhibit reabsorption and thus to enhance urinary excretion. Calcitonin, a recently discovered hormone which has an effect on serum calcium opposite to that of parathyroid hormone, also increases the urinary excretion of phosphate.

Variation in phosphate reabsorption is poorly reflected by urinary excretion of phosphate, which is dependent mainly on oral intake and plasma concentration. Determination of phosphate clearance, or better, the coefficient of tubular reabsorption of phosphate (TRP), is necessary.* Since TRP varies with the concentration of phosphate in plasma, the latter value must be taken into consideration when the TRP is interpreted. This is the basis of the *phosphate excretion index* (PEI) which is calculated from the regression between the percent of filtered phosphate that is excreted and the concentration of phosphate in serum. Children 2 to 15 years of age have lower values of PEI than adults, reflecting a higher reabsorption of phosphate at the same plasma concentration (see Nordin and Fraser).

Although these calculations are useful in clinical medicine, the range of values obtained in normal subjects is very large, overlapping with that of patients with proved hypo- and hyperparathyroidism. The maximum rate of tubular reabsorption of phosphate ($Tm_{phosphate}$) would seem to be a more precise means of assessment, but its calculation requires a phosphate infusion and determination of glomerular filtration rate. The same disadvantage applies to determination of the "theoretical renal phosphate threshold." In this test a progressive increase in serum

---

* The formula for calculation of TRP is derived as follows:

$$(1) \qquad TRP = \frac{\text{Reabsorbed Phosphate}}{\text{Filtered Phosphate}} \times 100$$

$$(2) \qquad TRP = \frac{\text{Filtered Phosphate} - \text{Excreted Phosphate}}{\text{Filtered Phosphate}} \times 100$$

$$(3) \qquad TRP = [\,1 - \frac{\text{Excreted Phosphate}}{\text{Filtered Phosphate}}\,] \times 100$$

Filtered phosphate is calculated as the product of glomerular filtration rate (GFR) and plasma concentration of phosphate, and GFR usually is estimated from creatinine clearance. Therefore, substituting in (3):

$$(4) \qquad TRP = [\,1 - (U_p V \div \frac{U_{cr} V}{P_{cr}}\, P_p)\,] \times 100$$

$$(5) \qquad TRP = [\,1 - \frac{U_p P_{cr}}{U_{cr} P_p}\,] \times 100$$

where U_p, P_p, U_{cr}, and P_{cr} are, respectively, urine and plasma concentrations of phosphate and creatinine, and V is rate of urine flow. It can be seen that the value for V cancels out in the final equation, signifying that TRP can be calculated without knowing rate of urine flow, and therefore an untimed urine specimen can be used.

phosphate is produced by infusing buffered sodium phosphate in increasing amounts over a period of 3 hours. The regression of urinary phosphate on serum phosphate is calculated, and the point at which the regression line cuts the abscissa is defined as the "theoretical" renal phosphate threshold. This technique seems especially useful in patients with osteomalacia, to test the sensitivity of the renal tubule to a physiologic dose of vitamin D.

Decreased tubular reabsorption of phosphate is found in both hyperparathyroidism and specific tubular dysfunctions involving phosphate transport. The distinction between these two conditions may be difficult, since secondary hyperparathyroidism often accompanies renal tubular abnormalities. An increase in phosphate reabsorption during induced hypercalcemia or during low phosphate intake favors the primacy of the hormonal mechanism.

An isolated defect in renal tubular transport of phosphate was believed to constitute the primary abnormality in *hereditary hypophosphatemia* (familial vitamin D-resistant rickets). However, this view is not accepted by many authors who believe the primary abnormality to be intestinal malabsorption of calcium and phosphorus, with secondary hyperparathyroidism. Recent studies have suggested, however, that the disease arises from a metabolic defect causing a reduction in 25-hydroxycholecalciferol, a metabolite of vitamin D.

Decreased phosphate clearance or increased TRP is present in primary hypoparathyroidism and in *pseudohypoparathyroidism,* a disorder characterized by congenital unresponsiveness of the proximal tubule to parathyroid hormone (Sec. 3.5).

Multiple Dysfunction of the Proximal Renal Tubule
(Fanconi Syndrome)

The name Fanconi syndrome or DeToni-Debré-Fanconi syndrome is given to a group of disorders involving multiple functional disturbances of the proximal tubule, including defects in the reabsorption of glucose, amino acids, and phosphate. Tubular proteinuria, acidosis, inadequate renal conservation of sodium and potassium, and a defect in maximum renal concentrating ability may all be present. The term Fanconi syndrome was originally given to the idiopathic form of the disorder. However, cystinosis was soon found to be the most common etiology of the "primary" form in children, and many other causes or entities with an associated Fanconi syndrome have been disclosed. In current terminology, the designation Fanconi syndrome is given to any nonspecific, complex, proximal tubular dysfunction, complete or partial, regardless of etiology (Table 5).

PATHOPHYSIOLOGY; CLINICAL AND LABORATORY FEATURES. The Fanconi syndrome probably is caused by nonspecific enzymatic damage to the proximal tubule. The multiple toxins, endogenous and exogenous, producing this syndrome, and the experimental production by administration of an enzyme inhibitor, maleic acid, sustain this hypothesis. Details concerning specific etiologies are discussed below.

The histology of the kidney is normal or shows nonspecific lesions of tubular damage. In cases of

TABLE 5. *Fanconi Syndromes*

Primary	Glyco-suria	Amino-Aciduria	Hyper-phos-phaturia	Rickets, Osteo-porosis	Tubular Acidosis	Hypo-kalemia	Hypo-calcemia	Concen-tration Defect
Primary								
Cystinosis	++	++	++	++	+	+	−	+
Idiopathic	++	++	++	++	+	+	−	+
Luder-Sheldon syndrome	++	++	+	+	+	−	−	−
Lowe's syndrome	±	++	++	++	+	−	−	±
Secondary								
Tyrosinemia	++	++	++	++	+	+	−	+
Galactosemia	±	++	−	−	±	−	−	−
Glycogen storage disease	±	±	±	±	−	−	−	−
Wilson's disease	±	++	±	±	±	−	−	−
Fructose intolerance	−	+	−	−	+	−	−	−
Nephrotic syndrome with tubular dysfunction	++	++	+	+	++	++	++	+
Heavy metals	++	++	±	±	−	−	−	−

++ almost always present
 + often present
 ± rarely present
 − absent

cystinosis all gradations from normal structure to chronic renal disease can be found. Clay and associates found by microdissection a straight, short proximal tubule ("swan neck") in both childhood cases of cystinosis and adult cases of the idiopathic type. They believed it represented a congenital malformation directly responsible for the tubular dysfunction. This interpretation is questionable, recent evidence indicating that the anomaly represents an atrophic, secondary change. Vacuolization of distal tubular cells can be found in cases with potassium deficiency.

The clinical picture varies depending on both the degree of tubular dysfunction and the etiology. However, characteristic symptomatology is common to all forms with complete dysfunction of long-standing duration. Failure to thrive and growth retardation are constant. Bone lesions of rickets, osteoporosis, or both, are frequent, despite adequate intake of vitamin D, and may dominate the clinical picture. Polyuria is found occasionally and in the early months of life may cause unexplained fever, dehydration, and constipation. Muscular weakness and paralysis caused by potassium deficiency may also be present.

Serum analysis reveals hypophosphatemia and normal levels of calcium. Alkaline phosphatase is increased if there are active osteomalacic lesions. Hyperchloremic acidosis and hypokalemia are frequently present. Rarely, a patient may present with metabolic alkalosis due to chronic renal loss of sodium and potassium. Serum levels of amino acids are normal.

The urine contains glucose, and there is a generalized amino-aciduria of "nonspecific renal type." Rate of execretion of phosphate in urine may be normal, but an increased phosphate clearance or decreased coefficient of phosphate reabsorption (TRP) is found. Tubular proteinuria frequently is present.

The urine pH is 6.0 or higher and rates of excretion of titratable acid and ammonium are low. However, most patients are able to elaborate an acid urine and to excrete adequate hydrogen ion when appropriately stimulated, indicating that the acidosis is of the proximal type, i.e., caused by a defect in bicarbonate reabsorption (p. 1459). Both the plasma threshold and maximal rate of reabsorption of bicarbonate have been found low in cases of Fanconi syndrome of varied etiologies.

Hypercalciuria is not constant, and when present it depends probably more on the rate of sodium excretion than on the existence of a metabolic acidosis. Even when hypercalciuria is present, nephrocalcinosis and lithiasis are exceptional, in contrast with distal renal tubular acidosis. A defect in maximum concentrating ability may be present; it probably results from the potassium deficiency and hypercalciuria rather than from a specific tubular defect.

Treatment. The course, prognosis, and specific treatment of the Fanconi syndrome depend on etiology. Secondary dysfunctions will, in general, disappear after withdrawal of the offending cause or treatment of the primary disease. Some general thera-peutic measures, applicable to all types of the disease, will be considered here.

The bone lesions of rickets and osteomalacia are resistant to vitamin D and require doses in excess of 25,000 IU per day. Some children require as much as 400,000 IU per day and often remineralization cannot be achieved even with these large doses. Careful monitoring of concentration of calcium in blood and rate of excretion in urine is necessary to avoid vitamin D toxicity. Correction of the acidosis is an important measure, but, in contrast with distal renal tubular acidosis, rachitic lesions will not heal until vitamin D is given. The amount of sodium and potassium citrate or bicarbonate necessary to control the acidosis is generally much larger than required in distal renal tubular acidosis. It should be given every 2 to 4 hours, day and night, in a dose sufficient to keep the blood pH and total CO_2 within the normal range. As much as 10 mEq per kg per day of citrate or bicarbonate may be required. Rampini and associates have shown recently that the correction of the acidosis is greatly facilitated by the administration of hydrochlorothiazide, which probably acts by causing sodium loss with a consequent decrease in extracellular volume, resulting in increased proximal tubular reabsorption of sodium, and concurrently, bicarbonate. Unpublished observations have demonstrated the same effect with other potent diuretics. Surprisingly the bone lesions also may heal rapidly during diuretic therapy, even in the absence of vitamin D administration, perhaps reflecting increased reabsorption of both phosphate and calcium. The administration of potassium is mandatory if hypokalemia is present. In these cases, the administration of diuretics may be dangerous. When polyuria is present, water requirements should be evaluated carefully, especially during infancy. Finally, it must be realized that in spite of all these measures, growth and development often remain poor.

PRIMARY FANCONI SYNDROMES. *Idiopathic Fanconi syndrome* is most often seen in adults but it occurs occasionally in children. About 50 cases have been reported. In a few cases there is a suggestion of an autosomal recessive inheritance, but in one family the complete syndrome was observed in two generations, indicating transmission as an autosomal dominant. The onset is often between the first and second years of life and the clinical picture is that of the complete Fanconi syndrome. In contrast with cystinosis, glomerular function may not be affected during its evolution and patients may attain adult life, although severely retarded in growth. In many cases clinical onset is delayed until adulthood. Exclusion of cystinosis is obligatory in any isolated Fanconi syndrome appearing in childhood, since the diagnosis of cystinosis implies a fatal prognosis. Only after a repeatedly negative search for cystine, including examination of leucocytes, can a Fanconi syndrome be labeled idiopathic.

Luder-Sheldon syndrome was described in a family with glucoamino-aciduria in three generations of the same family. Over the course of many years the three affected members of the last generation developed vitamin D resistant rickets and tubular acidosis.

Cerebro-oculo-renal dystrophy (Lowe's syndrome) was described in 1952 by Lowe, Terrey, and MacLachlan. It associates the Fanconi syndrome with mental retardation and severe congenital ocular abnormalities.

It is a hereditary condition, transmitted by a sex-linked recessive gene, all the affected members being males. A few cases of Lowe's syndrome in females have been reported; they probably represent a metabolically similar but genetically different entity. The initial demonstration of development of cataracts in female carriers has not been confirmed. Chromosomal analyses have been normal, and no specific metabolic block has been detected. Abnormalities of amino acid excretion during ornithine administration have been reported, but the significance is unknown.

The age of onset is variable, ranging from early months of life to late childhood. The presence of cataracts is almost constant and they frequently coexist with congenital glaucoma (hydrophthalmos). Nystagmus is common and is probably secondary to blindness. The involvement of the nervous system is very characteristic and combines severe mental retardation with marked muscular hypotonia and tendinous arreflexia. Paralyses are never found. Patients may emit a continuous, distressing cry. Cryptorchidism is reported in one-fourth of the cases.

A peculiar type of Fanconi syndrome is seen: tubular proteinuria is always present, glycosuria is rare, amino-aciduria is only moderate, a concentrating defect is exceptional, and hypokalemia has never been found. Lowe and co-workers reported a characteristic organic aciduria; however, this finding has not been confirmed. Osteoporosis is the most frequent bone lesion, but rickets also may be present. Retardation in growth and development becomes evident during the evolution of the disease. Development of glomerular insufficiency does not occur, but the prognosis nevertheless remains poor due to severe mental retardation and poor vision.

The differential diagnosis includes other conditions in which there is an association of cerebral, ocular, and renal abnormalities. A frequent error is the indiscriminate diagnosis of Lowe's syndrome in a severely retarded child with rickets, amino-aciduria, and ocular anomalies. In many such cases, rickets is due to deficiency of vitamin D from inadequate nutrition and lack of sunlight.

There is no specific therapy, but adequate measures to control bone lesions and acidosis should be undertaken.

SECONDARY FANCONI SYNDROMES. *Cystinosis.*

This disease is an inborn error of metabolism first recognized at autopsy by Abdehalden in 1903, and established as a clinical entity by Lignac in 1924. It is also known under the names of Lignac-Fanconi syndrome or cystine storage disease. The disorder is characterized by the existence of the Fanconi syndrome in association with deposits of cystine crystals in many tissues of the body. Tubular dysfunction represents a secondary abnormality, but often appears to be a "primary" condition, the cystine storage being undetected.

The incidence is estimated to be between 1 in 20,000 and 1 in 40,000 of the general population. In one-third of reported cases there is a familial distribution, the disorder being inherited as an autosomal recessive.

Recent studies have shown that the defect in cystinosis is the excessive storage and subcellular compartmentalization of cystine in the lysosomes, and not a defect in the normal degradation of cystine, as formerly believed. Plasma cystine levels are normal, but the cellular content of cystine is markedly elevated, as much as 100 times normal in peripheral leucocytes or fibroblasts cultured from cystinotic patients. Leucocytes and fibroblasts obtained from parents of these children average five or six times the normal content of free cystine, permitting the first biochemical identification of the heterozygote. The tubular dysfunction is believed to represent a toxic effect of the stored cystine on sulfhydryl-containing enzymes, since the clinical prognosis seems to be related to the degree of cystine storage.

The clinical symptomatology arises from involvement of kidney, intestine, eyes, liver, spleen, and lymph nodes. Three phenotypes are recognized: a fatal "infantile" form, described here, a benign "adult" form, and an "adolescent" form of intermediate clinical severity. Children with the "infantile" form present a clinical picture dominated by the tubular symptomatology, with progressive glomerular insufficiency and death in uremia. The clinical onset occurs in the first months of life, but in rare cases may be delayed until late childhood ("adolescent" form). The earliest abnormality, detected in the apparently normal siblings of affected children, is the appearance of amino-aciduria. Soon thirst, vomiting, constipation, chronic dehydration, unexplained fever, and failure to thrive become evident. Growth retardation becomes more and more severe, and signs of rickets may become predominant. When renal function is studied during the early stage, glomerular filtration rate is normal, but multiple tubular dysfunctions usually are found. Sometimes only isolated abnormalities are present: glycosuria, amino-aciduria, or hyperchloremic acidosis. Death may occur during this stage from acute hypokalemia, acidosis, or overwhelming infection. Hepatomegaly, lymphadenopathy, and, rarely, splenomegaly may appear. Photophobia, if noted, should suggest strongly the diagnosis of cystinosis. This has been attributed to the presence of refractile bodies in the cornea and conjunctiva, but probably is due to a peripheral pigmentary retinopathy which is almost always present in the severe form. In the benign "adult" form, corneal deposits are present but photophobia is rare.

After a variable period, glomerular insufficiency becomes evident and tubular symptomatology improves or disappears. This amelioration is only apparent and is due to the progressive destruction of nephrons. After a number of years the glomerular insufficiency becomes so severe that the symptomatology is dominated by the uremic syndrome. Death occurs usually before puberty.

Cystine crystals are rectangular or hexagonal and they are easily seen under polarized light in peripheral leucocytes, bone marrow aspirates, rectal mucosa, liver, spleen, or lymph nodes. In about 80 percent of cases they can be seen by slit-lamp examination of the cornea and conjunctiva. Cystine is soluble in aqueous solution and in formalin, and, therefore, an alcoholic fixative should be chosen for pathologic studies. The absence of cystine crystals in a single bone marrow aspiration does not exclude the condition, and repeated trials may be necessary. The best way to diagnose this entity is by a determination of the cystine content of peripheral leucocytes; an increase is pathognomonic for cystinosis.

Treatment is symptomatic. The use of diuretics facilitates markedly the correction of the acidosis and the healing of bone lesions, but careful attention must be paid to the development of severe hypokalemia. The initial impression of the usefulness of penicillamine has not been confirmed, and the possible beneficial effect of a diet poor in cystine and methionine also remains controversial. The recent demonstration that dithiothreitol removes cystine from cultured cystinotic fibroblasts opens a new approach to treatment, if similar results are obtained in patients. A few patients with cystinosis at the stage of severe uremia have received an allotransplant, but the follow-up is still too short to know if the disease will occur in the grafted kidney.

Congenital Cirrhosis with Fanconi Syndrome and Tyrosinuria ("Tyrosinemia"). This entity, first reported by Baber in 1956, consists of congenital cirrhosis of the liver and multiple tubular dysfunctions. Tyrosine is present in abnormal amounts in blood and urine and the term "tyrosinemia" has been suggested. A high degree of consanguinity has been reported. The disease appears to be inherited as an autosomal recessive. Gentz and associates suggest that the condition is an inborn error of tyrosine metabolism associated with lack of p-hydroxyphenylpyruvic acid oxidase. p-hydroxyphenylpyruvic acid is increased in the urine, suggesting an identity with the condition "tyrosinosis" described by Medes (Sec. 8.2). However, on both clinical and biochemical grounds the conditions appear to be different.

In cases with very early onset the clinical picture is dominated by liver involvement and is similar to that of galactosemia and hereditary fructose intolerance. It can be especially confused with the latter disease, in which blood tyrosine levels frequently are elevated. In less severe cases, the Fanconi syndrome is the predominant feature. Hepatomegaly is constant. Death may occur during the early months

of life from hepatic insufficiency or be delayed several years, in which case the development of a malignant hepatoma has been reported. Differential diagnosis also must include Wilson's disease, in addition to other tubular disorders. The finding of tyrosinemia and tyrosinuria is not adequate to establish the diagnosis, which should be made, if possible, by demonstration of the enzymatic deficiency.

The outcome of the disease invariably is fatal. The effects of a diet low in phenylalanine and tyrosine are very promising, with excellent results reported on tubular dysfunction and rate of growth. The effect on hepatic function, however, is very poor and the early forms continue to have a very severe prognosis.

Galactosemia. (Sec. 8.6) This is an inborn error of galactose metabolism caused by an absence of galactose-1-phosphate uridyl transferase. The accumulation of galactose-1-phosphate has toxic effects in many body tissues, especially liver, brain, lens, and kidney. The renal toxic effect is primarily an isolated amino-aciduria, but tubular proteinuria, true glycosuria, and tubular acidosis also may present. The tubular abnormalities disappear quickly when a diet without lactose and galactose is instituted.

Glycogen Storage Disease. (Sec. 8.8) Occasionally a patient with the hepatorenal form of glycogen storage disease may demonstrate tubular dysfunction, as in the original case of Fanconi and Bickel, who presented with gluco-amino-phosphaturia. Tubular dysfunction is probably dependent on accumulation of glycogen in the renal proximal tubular cells.

Wilson's Disease. (Sec. 8.11) The most frequent renal abnormality is amino-aciduria. Glycosuria, increased phosphate and urate clearances, and hyperchloremic acidosis may also be found. Hypercalciuria is very frequent and urinary lithiasis has been reported in adult cases. The tubular abnormalities probably depend on toxic accumulation of copper. Treatment of the disease by D-penicillamine improves the hepatic and neurologic symptoms but the effect on tubular dysfunction is less evident.

Hereditary Intolerance to Fructose. (Sec. 8.6) Amino-aciduria and hyperchloremic acidosis may be present in this disease. A defect in bicarbonate reabsorption has been documented by Morris. The toxic substance is probably fructose-1-phosphate.

Nephrotic Syndrome. The presence of tubular abnormalities during the evolution of the idiopathic nephrotic syndrome is exceptional. Only 13 cases of a complete Fanconi syndrome have been described in children. It is not known if these patients represent a specific entity or a particular evolution of a noncharacteristic idiopathic nephrotic syndrome.

The clinical picture is rather uniform. During the initial period the nephrotic syndrome is uncomplicated and normal renal histology and function are present. Later, tubular function becomes progressively affected with marked hypokalemia and tetany. In a later stage, glomerular insufficiency is severe and all reported cases have died in uremia. The administration of steroids has been ineffective.

Exogenous Toxins. Proximal tubular damage may follow the exposure to many toxic substances. Heavy metals, including lead, cadmium, uranium, and mercury, are especially notorious. Chisolm and Leahy found that amino-aciduria and glycosuria were almost constant in lead poisoning in children and reported a case with associated increased phosphate clearance and rickets. Other potentially toxic substances include lysol, methyl-3-chromone, and some antibiotics, including outdated tetracycline and amphotericin B. The tubular abnormality disappears after removal of the toxic substance.

Renal Tubular Acidosis

Although renal acidosis is always tubular in origin, it can be classified conveniently into glomerular or tubular on the basis of the underlying pathophysiology. Glomerular acidosis is present in patients with chronic renal insufficiency and is part of the uremic syndrome. Tubular acidosis is a condition in which glomerular function either is normal or is relatively less impaired than tubular function. Used in this general sense, renal tubular acidosis (RTA) represents a syndrome and includes varied etiologies.

Two mechanisms are involved in renal excretion of acid (p. 1459): (1) reabsorption of filtered bicarbonate, which is primarily a proximal function, and (2) excretion of hydrogen ion in the form of titratable acid and ammonium, which is primarily a distal function. Abnormalities of these mechanisms will be associated, therefore, with (1) loss of bicarbonate into urine due to a defect in bicarbonate reabsorption, termed proximal renal tubular acidosis, (2) impaired excretion of hydrogen ion as titratable acid or ammonium, or both, termed distal renal

tubular acidosis, or (3) a combination of (1) and (2) (Table 6).

PROXIMAL RENAL TUBULAR ACIDOSIS. In this condition hyperchloremic acidosis results from a depression in the renal threshold of excretion of bicarbonate, caused by a defect in reabsorption of bicarbonate in the proximal tubule. Under ordinary circumstances, virtually all filtered bicarbonate is reabsorbed. If the concentration of bicarbonate in plasma exceeds the level of the renal threshold, bicarbonate reabsorption is incomplete and urinary excretion gradually lowers the concentration to a level below the threshold. At this point the excretion of bicarbonate ceases and a new steady state is reached. The level of the bicarbonate threshold changes with age: in adults bicarbonate begins to be excreted in urine when the concentration in plasma exceeds 25 to 26 mmoles per liter, whereas in infants bicarbonate is present in urine when the plasma level exceeds 22 mmoles per liter. Patients with proximal RTA have bicarbonate thresholds below normal for age. Therefore bicarbonate is present in the urine when the concentration in plasma is below that found in normal individuals; a steady state is maintained with the plasma bicarbonate in the acidemic range. This can be increased into the normal range only by giving large amounts of bicarbonate orally or intravenously, although this is associated with large losses of bicarbonate in the urine. When therapy is stopped the acidemia quickly reappears, due not only to continued loss of bicarbonate into the urine, but also to inhibition of the distal mechanisms of hydrogen ion secretion, as the distal tubule is flooded with bicarbonate-rich fluid. Only by giving large amounts of bicarbonate on a continuous basis can levels of bicarbonate in plasma be elevated to and maintained within the normal range.

TABLE 6.   *Renal Tubular Acidosis*

	Proximal	Distal
Primary	Idiopathic	Idiopathic

Secondary	Fanconi syndrome
	Cystinosis
	Lowe's syndrome
	Hereditary intolerance
	   to fructose
	Various states of renal
	   insufficiency
	Lightwood's syndrome (?)
	Others
		Primary hyperpara-
		   thyroidism
		Vitamin D intoxication
		Amphotericin B nephropathy
		Hyperglobulinemias
		Medullary sponge kidney
		Renal tubular necrosis and
		   renal transplantation
		Lightwood's syndrome (?)
		Others

Urine pH	4.5 to 7.8 depending on
	   level of plasma bicarbonate
		Always above 6.0 regardless of
		   level of plasma bicarbonate

Bicarbonate threshold	Decreased	Normal

Hydrogen
   excretion
	Normal, below bicarbonate
	   threshold
		Impaired, below bicarbonate
		   threshold

Therapy	Resistant to alkali therapy Effect of diuretics	Sensitive to alkali therapy No effect of diuretics

An important feature of these patients is their unimpaired ability to lower urinary pH and to excrete adequate amounts of titratable acid and ammonium when their bicarbonate concentration in plasma is below their threshold. As a consequence they may easily be overlooked by the usual methods of detecting RTA.

The exact nature of the defect is unknown. A deficiency of carbonic anhydrase appears to be excluded, as judged by a normal response to the administration of the enzyme inhibitor acetazolamide. The condition may be due to a primary defect in bicarbonate reabsorption or may be due to an abnormality in sodium reabsorption in the proximal tubule, leading secondarily to impaired bicarbonate reabsorption.

Primary proximal renal tubule acidosis refers to the occurrence of hyperchloremic acidosis due to an isolated defect in bicarbonate reabsorption, in the absence of any other abnormality in glomerular or tubular function. The only clinical manifestation is retarded growth; the complications observed in patients with distal RTA, such as interstitial nephritis, bone lesions, nephrocalcinosis, nephrolithiasis, polyuria, and hypokalemia are absent. Most patients with this condition have been males.

Functional evaluation of these patients reveals the presence of a low bicarbonate threshold. When distal acidifying capacity is examined at levels of serum bicarbonate below the renal threshold, all subjects excrete a urine of strongly acid pH, with rates of excretion of titratable acid and ammonium in the normal range.

Treatment consists of administration of sodium bicarbonate or citrate in amounts adequate to maintain the plasma concentration within the normal range. The starting dosage is 5 to 10 mEq per kg per 24 hours, given in fractional doses spread over as much of the 24-hour period as is practical.

The prognosis of these patients seems to be good; all the patients we have studied have been taken off therapy after several years of treatment without reappareance of the acidosis. During administration of adequate alkali therapy, there is usually slow but progressive catch-up growth.

Secondary proximal renal tubular acidosis has been demonstrated in association with other tubular dysfunctions, in patients with idiopathic or secondary Fanconi syndrome (cystinosis, Lowe's syndrome, tyrosinemia, glycogen storage disease, Wilson's disease, hereditary fructose intolerance, nephrotic syndrome, multiple myeloma, renal amyloidosis, and toxicity to outdated tetracycline, methyl chromone, and heavy metals), in patients with vitamin D-deficient rickets, medullary cystic disease, or following renal transplantation.

In 1953 Lightwood et al. described a transient form of renal tubular acidosis in infants with anorexia, vomiting, constipation, and failure to thrive. Rickets and nephrocalcinosis usually were absent radiologically. Most of the infants were male. The response to alkali therapy was dramatic and the patients were said to recover by 2 years of age.

The pathophysiology of the acidosis in these infants was unclear since few precise studies of hydrogen ion excretion were performed. Latner and Burnard presented considerable evidence for a defect in bicarbonate reabsorption in six patients, but on the basis of other evidence the defect was generally accepted as an inability to acidify the urine. Lightwood's syndrome thus became recognized as a transient, self-limited form of distal RTA in infants.

It is of interest that these patients were mainly males, nephrocalcinosis and rickets were strikingly absent, and very high dosage therapy was required to maintain their blood bicarbonate within the normal range. These features can now be recognized as characteristic of proximal and not distal RTA. In addition, although a large number of these infants were diagnosed in various parts of Great Britain in the late forties and early fifties, the disease subsequently all but disappeared, suggesting that its frequency at that time was the result of some unrecognized environmental factor. There is evidence that this may have been vitamin D intoxication, or toxicity to sulfonamides or mercury.

It seems reasonable to conclude, therefore, that in most instances Lightwood's syndrome represented a *secondary* form of *proximal* RTA. This is of considerable importance since it implies that the diagnosis of *primary distal* RTA in an infant most likely establishes the existence of a permanent defect.

DISTAL RENAL TUBULAR ACIDOSIS. In this type of RTA the primary defect is an inability to establish adequate gradients of hydrogen ion between blood and tubular fluid, despite low levels of serum bicarbonate. The inability to lower urinary pH to less than 7.0 or 6.5 is the most distinctive feature.

Primary distal renal tubular acidosis (Butler-Albright Syndrome) is a disorder that occurs predominately in females (about 70 percent) and usually is not diagnosed until after 2 years of age, frequently not until adult life. However, several cases unquestionably have begun in infancy, presenting with vomiting, constipation, anorexia, polyuria, dehydration, and failure to thrive. The majority of cases are sporadic, but at least 18 families with RTA have been reported. Inheritance appears to be of the dominant type, with a variable degree of expression.

Growth retardation is most evident beyond early infancy and may represent the only clinical abnormality. Bone lesions are frequent although they usually are absent early in life. Rickets and osteomalacia often are present during childhood and adolescence, accompanied by generalized bone demineralization. Nephrocalcinosis is an almost constant finding and may be demonstrated radiographically. Calcium deposits preferentially in the renal medulla, which can become completely petrified. Urolithiasis also is common, but occurs less frequently in children than in adults. The intravenous pyelogram otherwise is normal if obstructive uropathy caused by the lithiasis is not present.

Analysis of blood reveals a low pH and low concentration of bicarbonate, with elevation of the chlo-

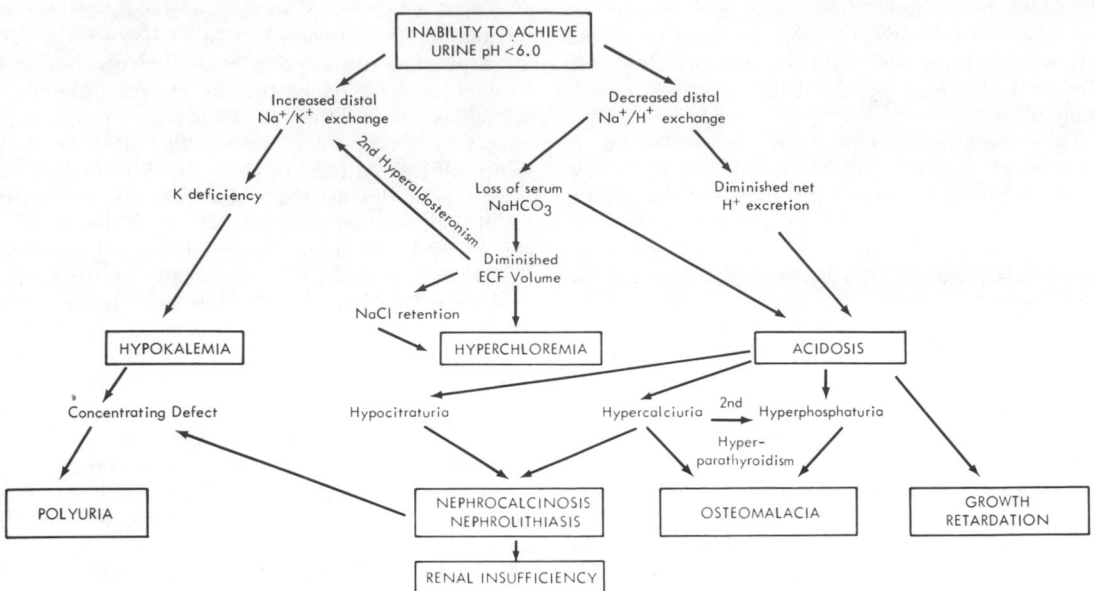

Fig. 15. Interrelationship of the metabolic complications of distal RTA. (From Rodriguez-Soriano and Edelmann. *Ann. Rev. Med.,* 20:363, 1969.)

ride. Moderate hyponatremia and hypokalemia may be present, although the serum potassium is not a good index of the degree of potassium deficiency, due to the associated acidemia. Periodic paralysis caused by severe potassium deficiency is not exceptional. The concentration of phosphate in blood is low, with normal or even high levels of calcium. The alkaline phosphatase level may be elevated if active osteomalacic lesions are present. Glomerular filtration rate is normal in the young child but a progressive decrease may occur over the years as a consequence of progressive parenchymal damage. It should be noted that evaluation of glomerular function is best performed after prolonged administration of alkali therapy, and correction of the contracted extracellular space.

Urinary pH is usually above 6.0 or 6.5, with low rates of excretion of titratable acid and ammonium. A small degree of proteinuria may be found. Leucocyturia is frequent and may accompany sterile urines or be secondary to urinary tract infection. Polyuria due to a concentrating defect is marked. In the early stages, the hyposthenuria may be corrected by adequate control of the acidosis and potassium deficiency, but subsequent to nephrocalcinosis and tubular damage, it becomes fixed.

The phosphate clearance is increased either as a direct consequence of the acidemia or as a manifestation of secondary hyperparathyroidism. Hypercalciuria is a constant feature when acidosis is present and reverts completely to normal after adequate alkali therapy. Hyperkaliuria results mainly from secondary hyperaldosteronism triggered by sodium depletion. A

low excretion of citrate is characteristic and is probably secondary to intratubular acidosis and potassium deficiency. Normal urinary levels of citrate can be obtained only after persistent administration of alkali and potassium. Hypercalciuria, hypocitraturia, and alkaline urine are important factors in the development of nephrocalcinosis. The pathophysiologic interrelations in this disease are schematized in Figure 15.

Other tubular functions usually are normal. Amino-aciduria is usually not found although there are two reports noting its presence, with disappearance following correction of the acidosis and hypokalemia.

The histology of the kidney is normal in the early stages, but later variable degrees of calcium deposition and interstitial nephritis are observed.

The prognosis of primary distal RTA is good if the diagnosis is established early enough to prevent the development of nephrocalcinosis, secondary pyelonephritis, and tubular damage.

Treatment consists of correction of the acidemia, following which the bone lesions heal, without need for large doses of vitamin D, and growth rate accelerates, patients often regaining their earlier normal growth pattern or even evidencing catch-up growth. Calcium excretion reverts to normal and further calcium deposits may be prevented. Potassium needs to be given regardless of the level of serum potassium; in instances of severe hypokalemia, potassium should be given prior to the correction of acidemia. A useful mixture is a solution of sodium and potassium citrate: 100 g of each salt diluted in 1 liter of water provides approximately 2 mEq per ml. A dose of 2 to

5 mEq per kg is adequate, but it must be adjusted in each case according to changes in blood pH and bicarbonate and rate of excretion of calcium in urine. In some cases correction of the acidemia may permit continued excessive excretion of calcium, resulting in further calcium deposition. Calcium excretion falls to normal with increased intake of citrate.

Secondary distal renal tubular acidosis may be associated with a number of systemic or renal conditions including starvation, malnutrition, hyperparathyroidism, hyperthyroidism, vitamin D intoxication, amphotericin B nephropathy, hypergammaglobulinemic states (idiopathic hypergammaglobulinemia, hyperglobulinemic purpura, Sjögren syndrome, cryoglobulinemia, active chronic hepatitis, sarcoidosis), hepatic cirrhosis, medullary sponge kidney, and a variety of genetically transmitted disorders (hereditary fructose intolerance with nephrocalcinosis, Ehlers-Danlos syndrome, Fabry's disease, hereditary elliptocytosis), and probably also after renal tubular necrosis and renal homotransplantation.

Idiopathic Hypercalciuria

Idiopathic hypercalciuria is a frequent cause of recurrent lithiasis in adults. It occurs less frequently in children, however, and few cases have been described. The most frequent presenting symptom is growth retardation in association with renal abnormalities such as proteinuria and decreased concentrating capacity. Clinical manifestations also include urolithiasis, nephrocalcinosis, and vitamin D-resistant rickets.

Calcium excretion exceeds 5 mg per kg per day. Acidemia is not present and hypercalciuria does not decrease after administration of sodium bicarbonate. Serum calcium is normal and serum phosphorus may be normal or low. Renal histology is normal or shows variable degrees of interstitial nephritis. In the cases studied, intestinal absorption of calcium was normal, pointing to a renal tubular abnormality as the cause of the hypercalciuria.

There is no specific therapy. Thiazide diuretics, which are known to decrease calcium excretion, remain under evaluation. Decrease in calcium excretion has been noted following restriction of dietary sodium, constituting, at present, the most effective method of treatment.

Sodium-Losing Disorders

PSEUDOHYPOALDOSTERONISM. This entity, first described by Cheek and Perry in 1958, is believed to represent a failure of the renal tubule to respond to aldosterone, with secondary excessive loss of sodium in the urine, hyponatremia, and hyperkalemia. The five cases reported were all males, suggesting a sex-linked genetic transmission.

Affected infants are normal at birth, but after one or two weeks exhibit vomiting, anorexia, failure to thrive, and, if treatment is delayed, severe marasmus, with delayed skeletal and psychomotor development. During episodes of dehydration, often triggered by intercurrent infection, patients may have marked collapse or even coma.

The concentration of sodium in plasma is low, and moderate hyperkalemia is present. Despite dehydration and hyponatremia, a high rate of excretion of urinary sodium continues. The excretion of 17-ketosteroids and 17-hydroxysteroids is normal but the excretion of aldosterone is abnormally high, up to 900 μg per 24 hours. The administration of DOCA or aldosterone fails to modify the urinary excretion of sodium.

Differentiation from the salt-losing forms of congenital adrenal hyperplasia and adrenal insufficiency is clinically difficult and depends upon appropriate investigation of steroid metabolism. Hypertrophic pyloric stenosis, cystic fibrosis, inappropriate ADH secretion, and other salt-losing nephropathies (see below) also should be considered.

The administration of supplementary sodium chloride is the treatment of choice. A dose of about 5 g per day is required, following which there is usually a dramatic decrease in vomiting, weight gain, and enhanced skeletal and psychomotor development. There is some evidence that after some months or years, the need for supplementary sodium chloride decreases, but sufficient data from long-term follow-ups are not yet available.

SALT-LOSING NEPHROPATHIES. Excessive urinary loss of sodium occurs together with other tubular abnormalities in the Fanconi syndrome, in distal renal tubular acidosis, and in other tubulopathies; it is also found in association with generalized renal disease. Limitation of renal capacity to conserve sodium is common in most cases of uremia, but usually a balance between input and output is maintained, urinary wastage becoming evident only under conditions of salt deprivation. However, in exceptional cases, termed "salt-losing nephritis," the urinary loss of sodium is so marked during periods of normal intake that patients may appear to have Addison's disease. This syndrome has usually been associated with chronic pyelonephritis, medullary cystic disease, and hereditary polycystic disease.

The condition apparently is rare in children, the youngest patient reported being an adolescent. Urinary sodium loss of lesser degree is seen, however, in children with bilateral renal hypoplasia or dysplasia, obstructive uropathy, juvenile nephronophthisis, and interstitial nephritis.

It is important to realize that the salt-losing defect associated with tubular or generalized renal disease is often unrecognized. Dehydration may be minimal and the serum sodium may be normal due to compensatory contraction of the extracellular space. However, even in such patients, administration of extra sodium is followed by improved well-being, weight gain, and increases in rates of glomerular filtration and renal plasma flow.

Potassium-Losing Disorders

PSEUDOHYPERALDOSTERONISM (LIDDLE'S SYNDROME). This hereditary condition, probably transmitted as an autosomal dominant, was described in 1964 by Liddle, Bledsoe, and Coppage in six siblings with hypertension, hypokalemic alkalosis, and negligible aldosterone secretion. The disorder seems to be caused by an unusual tendency of the kidney to reabsorb sodium and excrete potassium even in virtual absence of mineralocorticoids. These patients differ from normal subjects and from patients with primary aldosteronism in that their electrolyte excretion is unaffected by giving either an inhibitor of aldosterone synthesis or an aldosterone antagonist. Giving both an inhibitor of tubular sodium transport (Triamterene) and supplementary potassium chloride serves to normalize the blood pressure and correct the hypokalemia.

HYPERPLASIA OF THE JUXTAGLOMERULAR APPARATUS WITH HYPERALDOSTERONISM AND HYPOKALEMIC ALKALOSIS (BARTTER'S SYNDROME). Bartter and associates, in 1962, reported a new syndrome characterized by hypokalemic alkalosis, hyperaldosteronism with normal blood pressure, and hyperplasia of the juxtaglomerular apparatus. About 25 cases have been reported in the literature under such varied names as renal tubular alkalosis, congenital hyperaldosteronism, chronic idiopathic hypokalemia, and congenital hypokalemia. Several familial cases have been described; it is probably inherited as an autosomal recessive.

Symptoms first occur during infancy but the diagnosis may be delayed for many years. The earliest symptoms are polyuria, polydipsia, tendency toward dehydration, constipation, vomiting, and anorexia. Growth retardation is constant, becoming more marked as the child gets older. Muscular weakness is frequent and very often recurrent tetany is present. A dilated viscus (megacolon, dilated ureter) is often found. The blood pressure characteristically is normal. The outstanding biochemical feature is the marked hypokalemia, often accompanied by hyponatremia, hypochloremia, and metabolic alkalosis. Hypomagnesemia, hypercalcemia, and hyperlipemia may also be found. Aldosterone secretion and excretion rates are markedly elevated if potassium deficiency has been corrected previously. Cortisol and corticosterone production are normal. Plasma renin activity and angiotensin level are characteristically elevated. The response to expansion of intravascular volume by means of albumin infusion or high sodium load, which inhibits the angiotensin-aldosterone system, is paradoxical in some cases: neither secretion of aldosterone nor plasma renin activity is changed by these measures. However, in other cases, a normal, although somewhat blunted response has

been reported. Angiotensinase levels are significantly reduced.

Renal pathology is characteristic. The glomeruli reveal marked hypertrophy of the juxtaglomerular apparatus, and a variable degree of hyalinization. The tubular lesions of potassium deficiency may be present. The zona glomerulosa of the adrenal gland is hypertrophic, with marked lipid infiltration.

The pathogenesis of this syndrome remains obscure. Bartter and associates believed that the primary defect was an inability of the vascular wall to respond to angiotensin, the subsequent increase in angiotensin leading to increased aldosterone secretion and potassium loss. A central point in this hypothesis was the normotension and the decreased response to administration of angiotensin. However, this resistance to the pressor effect of angiotensin may be secondary to the hyperreninemia (tachyphylaxis), since it has been found in many other patients with conditions producing chronically elevated renin levels (malignant or renovascular hypertension, liver cirrhosis with ascites, and sodium depletion).

An alternative explanation more recently proposed suggests that the primary cause is a renal tubular defect in proximal reabsorption of sodium with increased delivery of sodium into the distal nephron and enhanced exchange with potassium, even after correction of secondary hyperaldosteronism. The capacity of these patients to conserve sodium normally is explained by a compensatory increase in distal sodium reabsorption. This theory explains the absence of hypertension on the basis of chronically decreased intravascular volume despite increased aldosterone secretion rate and plasma renin activity, and the persistence of hypokalemia despite correction of the hyperaldosteronism.

Differential diagnosis includes primary aldosteronism; the very high levels of renin and angiotensin in Bartter's syndrome differentiate the two conditions. The more rare tumor in the juxtaglomerular apparatus causes autonomous oversecretion of renin, but hypertension is constantly observed. Patients with secondary hyperaldosteronism due to renovascular or malignant hypertension or associated with edematous states should be differentiated easily. Other potassium-losing disorders such as the Fanconi syndrome, distal renal tubular acidosis, Liddle's syndrome, and some types of pyelonephritis must also be considered.

The prognosis is poor and death may occur suddenly due to acute electrolyte imbalance or intercurrent infection. There is some evidence that progressive glomerular insufficiency may appear over the course of years.

Therapeutic administration of potassium is mandatory, but if given alone it is quickly lost in the urine without correction of the hypokalemia. The best results are obtained by the simultaneous administration of spironolactone (Aldactone) with sodium and potassium supplements. Dosage must be adjusted to obtain an equilibrium between intake and excretion. Partial adrenalectomy is without effect and should not be done.

Nephrogenic Diabetes Insipidus
(See also Sec. 16.12)

Nephrogenic diabetes insipidus (NDI) is a hereditary disorder characterized by insensitivity of the renal tubule to antidiuretic hormone (ADH). Most of the affected patients are male, suggesting a sex-linked transmission. Heterozygous females may exhibit some degree of polyuria with limitation of concentrating ability. This type of inheritance contrasts with ADH-deficient diabetes insipidus which, when genetically determined, is transmitted as an autosomal dominant.

NDI appears shortly after birth. Polyuria and polydipsia generally are not appreciated, and the infant presents with a nonspecific picture of vomiting, anorexia, constipation, unexplained fever, recurrent dehydration, and failure to thrive. In some of these infants thirst is virtually absent (occult diabetes insipidus). A marked retardation in psychomotor development is often present; it has been attributed both to the chronic hyperelectrolytemia and to the lack of environmental stimulation, most of the infant's time being spent in drinking and sleeping.

In older children, beyond 3 or 4 years of age, polyuria, polydipsia, and retarded growth persist, but a more normal balance between intake and output is possible and secondary complications generally are absent.

Examination of the serum, especially in infants, reveals increased concentrations of sodium, chloride, and urea, secondary to the negative water balance. Despite dehydration and hemoconcentration, urine is dilute, with a specific gravity between 1.001 and 1.005 (40 to 200 mOsm/kg). During severe dehydration, with very decreased glomerular filtration rate, urinary osmolality may increase, but rarely to even slightly hypertonic levels. Administration of vasopressin changes neither the volume nor concentration of the urine. A water deprivation test to assess maximum urinary concentrating ability is not necessary for the diagnosis; it is hazardous and should be avoided.

Insensitivity to ADH is the only primary tubular abnormality in NDI, but during dehydration proteinuria and amino-aciduria may be present. Glomerular filtration rate is normal if hydration is adequate.

In most cases the intravenous pyelogram is normal. Although marked bladder distension and hydronephrosis have been attributed to the high rate of urine flow, such findings should suggest the diagnosis of obstructive uropathy with secondary diabetes insipidus and adequate urologic studies should be done.

Histologically the kidney is normal, although a shortened proximal segment has been demonstrated by microdissection by Darmady and co-workers; this finding needs confirmation. In one case studied by electron microscopy, glomerular immaturity and mitochondrial changes in the tubules were noted, suggesting an abnormality in mitochondrial membrane lipids.

The exact pathogenesis of NDI is unknown. Antidiuretic hormone is present in blood and urine and neurohypophyseal lesions are not found. It is believed at present that the intracellular intermediate in the action of vasopressin is cyclic 3′,5′-AMP, the formation of which is stimulated by the action of vasopressin on the adenyl cyclase system. An abnormality in the cellular production of cyclic AMP could account for the tubular insensitivity to the hormone, similar to the mechanism that has been described in patients with tubular insensitivity to parathyroid hormone.

Differential diagnosis includes the hereditary form of ADH-lack diabetes insipidus, which also may start very early in life. The response to vasopressin serves to separate these conditions. Several renal disorders may present with a syndrome of vasopressin-resistant diabetes insipidus: obstructive uropathies, hypercalcemia, hypercalciuria with or without renal tubular acidosis, potassium-losing disorders, and a special group of chronic renal diseases which includes bilateral renal hypoplasia, medullary cystic disease, and familial nephronophthisis. It also may be present in renal periarteritis nodosa, renal amyloidosis, and Sjögren syndrome. Some adults with malignant hypertension present with nocturnal diabetes insipidus only; during the day the urine is hypertonic to plasma and the patient is oliguric.

The prognosis is favorable if the diagnosis is made early in life and adequate therapy is instituted. However, between 5 and 10 percent of patients die in infancy and in some cases both mental and physical growth is irreversibly retarded.

Therapy consists in giving water in amount and frequency necessary to compensate for the obligatory urinary loss. In older children this aim is easily attained, but great difficulties may be encountered in infancy, especially when thirst is absent. Administration of solute-poor milk reduces urinary water requirements and helps to maintain an adequate water balance.

The discovery that thiazide diuretics decrease urinary output has facilitated enormously the management of these patients, especially during infancy. The decrease of urinary volume observed following administration of the diuretic is accompanied by an increased concentration of urinary solute and decreased clearance of free water. It has been shown that the effect is mediated through sodium depletion, with increased proximal reabsorption of sodium and water and decreased delivery of fluid to the distal tubule. Giving sodium chloride interferes with the antidiuretic effect, which is maximal on a low-sodium intake. Furthermore, the effect can be produced by other diuretics and is not an exclusive property of the thiazides. An antidiabetic agent, chlorpropamide, has an antidiuretic effect in ADH-lack diabetes insipidus, but is without effect in the nephrogenic form.

REFERENCES

RENAL GLYCOSURIA

Elsas, L. J., and Rosenberg, L. E. Familial renal glycosuria: a genetic reappraisal of hexose transport by kidney and intestine. J. Clin. Invest., 48:1845, 1969.
——— Hillman, R. E., Patterson, J. H., and Rosenberg,
L. E. Renal and intestinal hexose transport in familial
glucose-galactose malabsorption. J. Clin. Invest., 49:
576, 1970.
Krane, S. M. Renal glycosuria. In Stanbury, J. B., Wyn-
gaarden, J. B., and Fredrickson, D. S., eds., The Meta-
bolic Basis of Inherited Disease. New York, McGraw-
Hill Book Co., 1966, p. 1221.
Marble, A. Renal glycosuria. Amer. J. Med. Sci., 183:
811, 1932.
Monasterio, G., Oliver, J., Muiesan, G., Pardelli, G.,
Marinozzi, V., and MacDowell, M. Renal diabetes as
a congenital tubular dysplasia. Amer. J. Med., 37:44,
1964.
Reubi, F. C. Glucose titration in renal glycosuria. In
Lewis, A. A. G., and Wolstenholme, G. E. W., eds.,
Ciba Foundation Symposium on the Kidney. London,
J. and A. Churchill, Ltd., 1954, p. 96.

AMINO-ACIDURIAS

Brodehl, J., and Gellissen, K. Endogenous renal transport of free amino acids in infancy and childhood.
Pediatrics, 42:395, 1968.
Boström, H., and Hambraeus, L. Cystinuria in Sweden.
VII. Clinical, histo-pathological, and medico-social aspects of the disease. Acta Med. Scand. (Suppl.), 411,
p. 7, Vol. 175, Stockholm, 1964.
Chisolm, J. J., Jr., and Harrison, H. E. Amino-aciduria.
Pediat. Clin. N. Amer., 7:333, 1960.
——— and Harrison, H. E. Aminoaciduria in vitamin D
deficiency states, in premature infants and older infants with rickets. J. Pediat., 60:206, 1962.
DeVries, A., Kochwa, S., Lazebnik, J., Frank, M., and
Djaldetti, M. Glycinuria. A hereditary disorder associated with nephrolithiasis. Amer. J. Med., 23:408,
1957.
Ghadimi, H., and Schwachman, H. Evaluation of amino-
aciduria in infancy and childhood. Amer. J. Dis.
Child., 99:457, 1960.
Henneman, P. H., Dempsey, E. F., Carroll, E. L., and
Henneman, D. H. Acquired vitamin D resistant osteomalacia: a new variety characterized by hypercalcemia,
low serum bicarbonate and hyperglycinuria. Metabolism, 11:103, 1962.
Käser, H., Cottier, P., and Antener, I. Glucoglycinuria,
a new familial syndrome. J. Pediat., 61:386, 1962.
Milne, M. D., Crawford, M. C., Girao, C. B., and
Loughridge, L. The metabolic abnormality of Hartnup
disease. Biochem. J., 72:308, 1959.
Pruzanski, W. Cystinuria and cystine urolithiasis in
childhood. Acta Paediat. Scand., 55:97, 1966.
Rosenberg, L. E., Durant, J. L., and Elsas, L. J. Familial
iminoglycinuria. An inborn error of renal tubular transport. New Eng. J. Med., 278:1407, 1968.
Scriver, C. R. Hartnup disease. A genetic modification
of intestinal and renal transport of certain neutral
alpha-amino acids. New Eng. J. Med., 273:530, 1965.
——— Use of human genetic variation to study membrane transport of amino acids in kidney. Amer. J.
Dis. Child., 117:4, 1969.
——— Efron, M. L., and Schafer, I. A. Renal tubular
transport of proline, hydroxyproline, and glycine in
health and in familial hyperprolinemia. J. Clin. Invest.,
43:374, 1964.
——— Goldbloom, R. B., and Roy, C. C. Hypophosphatemic rickets with renal hyperglycinuria, renal glucosuria, and glycyl-prolinuria. Pediatrics, 34:357, 1964.
Tancredi, F., Guazzi, G., and Auricchio, S. Renal imino-
glycinuria without intestinal malabsorption of glycine
and imino acids. J. Pediat., 76:386, 1970.
Whelan, D. T., and Scriver, C. R. Hyperdibasicamino-
aciduria: an inherited disorder of amino acid transport.
Pediat. Res., 2:525, 1968.

DISORDERS OF PHOSPHATE TRANSPORT

Albright, F., Burnett, C. H., Parson, W., Reifenstein,
E. C., Jr., and Roos, A. Osteomalacia and late rickets:
the various etiologies met in the United States with
emphasis on that resulting from a special form of renal
acidosis; the therapeutic indications for each etiological
sub-group and the relationship between osteomalacia
and Milkman's syndrome. Medicine, 25:399, 1946.
De Deuxchaisnes, C. N. M. D., and Krane, S. M. The
treatment of adult phosphate diabetes and Fanconi syndrome with neutral-sodium phosphate. Amer. J. Med.,
43:508, 1967.
Dent, C. E., and Harris, H. Hereditary forms of rickets
and osteomalacia. J. Bone Joint Surg., 38B:204, 1956.
——— and Stamp, T. C. B. Theoretical renal phosphorus threshold in investigation and treatment of
osteomalacia. Lancet, 1:857, 1970.
Editorial. Plasma phosphate and tubular reabsorption of
phosphate. Lancet, 1:820, 1970.
Harrison, H. E., and Harrison, H. C. Hereditary metabolic bone diseases. Clin. Orthop., 33:147, 1964.
Nordin, B. E. C., and Fraser, R. Assessment of urinary
phosphate excretion. Lancet, 1:947, 1960.
Royer, P. Étude sur les rachitismes vitamino-résistants
hypophosphatémiques idiopathiques. Acta Clin. Belg.,
15:499, 1960.
Tapia, J., Stearns, G., and Ponseti, I. V. Vitamin D resistant rickets—A long-term clinical study of eleven
patients. J. Bone Joint Surg., 46A:935, 1964.
Thalassinos, N. C., Leese, B., Latham, S. C., and Joplin,
G. F. Urinary excretion of phosphate in normal children. Arch. Dis. Child., 45:269, 1970.
Vaandrager, G. J., and Weyers, H. A. Primary vitamin
D refractory rickets. II. The calcium infusion test as
a means of determining the calcium avidity of the
skeleton (Calcium retention test). Ann. Paediat., 201:
185, 1963.
Winters, R. W., Graham, J. B., William, T. F., McFalls,
V. W., and Burnett, C. H. A genetic study of familial
hypophosphatemia and vitamin D resistant rickets with
a review of the literature. Medicine, 37:97, 1958.

FANCONI SYNDROME

Abbassi, V., Lowe, C. U., and Calcagno, P. L. Oculo-
cerebro-renal syndrome. A review. Amer. J. Dis. Child.,
115:145, 1968.
Baber, M. D. A case of congenital cirrhosis of the liver
with renal tubular defects akin to those of the Fanconi
syndrome. Arch. Dis. Child., 31:335, 1956.

Bickel, H., et al. Cystine storage disease with aminoaciduria and dwarfism (Lignac-Fanconi syndrome). Acta Paediat. Scand., 42(Suppl. 90), 1952.

Chisolm, J. J., Jr., and Leahy, N. B. Aminoaciduria as a manifestation of renal tubular injury in lead intoxication and a comparison with patterns of aminoaciduria seen in other diseases. J. Pediat., 60:1, 1962.

Clay, R. D., Darmady, E. M., and Hawkins, M. The nature of the renal lesion in the Fanconi syndrome. J. Path. Bact., 65:551, 1953.

Crawhall, J. C., Lietman, P. S., Schneider, J. A., and Seegmiller, J. E. Cystinosis. Plasma cystine and cysteine concentrations and the effect of D-penicillamine and dietary treatment. Amer. J. Med., 44:330, 1968.

Darling, S., and Mortensen, O. Aminoaciduria in galactosemia. Acta Paediat., 43:337, 1954.

Dent, C. E., and Harris, H. Hereditary forms of rickets and osteomalacia. J. Bone Joint Surg., 38B:204, 1956.

Fanconi, G. Der Frühinfantile nephrotisch-glykosurische Zwergwuchs mit hypophosphatamischer Rachitis. Zeit. Kinderheilk., 147:299, 1936.

———— and Bickel, H. Die chronische Aminoacidurie (aminosaure Diabetes oder nephrotisch-glykosurischer Zwergwuchs) bei Glykogenose und der Cystin Krankheit. Helv. Paediat. Acta, 4:359, 1949.

Gentz, J., Jagenburg, R., and Zetterström, R. Tyrosinemia. J. Pediat., 66:670, 1965.

Goldman, H., Scriver, C. R., Aaron, K., and Pinsky, L. Use of dithiothreitol to correct cystine storage in cultured cystinotic fibroblasts. Lancet, 1:811, 1970.

Holmes, L. B., McGowan, B. L., and Efron, M. L. Lowe's syndrome: a search for the carrier state. Pediatrics, 44:358, 1969.

Houston, I. B., Boichis, H., and Edelmann, C. M., Jr. Fanconi syndrome with renal sodium wasting and metabolic alkalosis. Amer. J. Med., 44:638, 1968.

Hunt, D. D., Stearns, G., McKinley, J. B., Froning, E., Hicks, P., and Bonfiglio, M. Long-term study of family with Fanconi syndrome without cystinosis (DeToni-Debré-Fanconi syndrome). Amer. J. Med., 40:492, 1966.

Leaf, A. The syndrome of osteomalacia, renal glycosuria, aminoaciduria and hyperphosphaturia (The Fanconi Syndrome). In Stanbury, J. B., Wyngaarden, J. B., and Fredrickson, D. S., eds., The Metabolic Basis of Inherited Disease. New York, McGraw-Hill Book Co., 1966, p. 1205.

Lowe, C. U., Terrey, M., and MacLachlan, E. A. Organic-aciduria, decreased renal ammonia production, hydrophthalmos, and mental retardation. Amer. J. Dis. Child., 83:164, 1952.

Luder, J., and Sheldon, W. A familial tubular absorption defect of glucose and amino acids. Arch. Dis. Child., 30:160, 1955.

Morris, R. C., Jr. An experimental renal acidification defect in patients with hereditary fructose intolerance. I. Its resemblance to renal tubular acidosis. J. Clin. Invest., 47:1389, 1968.

———— An experimental renal acidification defect in patients with hereditary fructose intolerance. II. Its distinction from classic renal tubular acidosis; its resemblance to the renal acidification defect associated with the Fanconi syndrome of children with cystinosis. J. Clin. Invest., 47:1648, 1968.

Oetliker, O., and Rossi, E. The influence of extracellular fluid volume on the renal bicarbonate threshold. A study of two children with Lowe's syndrome. Pediat. Res., 3:140, 1969.

Rampini, S., Fanconi, A., Illig, R., and Prader, A. Effect of hydrochlorothiazide on proximal renal tubular acidosis in a patient with idiopathic "DeToni-Debré-Fanconi syndrome." Helv. Paediat. Acta, 23:13, 1968.

Rodriguez Soriano, J., Houston, I. B., Boichis, H., and Edelmann, C. M., Jr. Calcium and phosphorus metabolism in the Fanconi syndrome. J. Clin. Endoc., 28:1555, 1968.

Richards, W., Donnell, G. N., Wilson, W. A., Stowens, D., and Perry, T. The oculo-cerebro-renal syndrome of Lowe. Amer. J. Dis. Child., 109:185, 1965.

Royer, P., Habib, R., and Mathieu, H. Le syndrome oculo-cérébro-rénal de Lowe et les maladies apparentées. In Problèmes Actuels de Néphrologie Infantile. Paris, Editions Médicales Flammarion, 1963, p. 205.

———— Mathieu, H., and Habib, R. Les syndromes néphrotiques avec insuffisance tubulaire grave. In Problèmes Actuels de Néphrologie Infantile. Paris, Editions Médicales Flammarion, 1963, p. 216.

Schneider, J. A., Wong, V., Bradley, K., and Seegmiller, J. E. Biochemical comparisons of the adult and childhood forms of cystinosis. New Eng. J. Med., 279:1253, 1968.

Seegmiller, J. E., Friedmann, T., Harrison, H. E., Wong, V., and Schneider, J. A. Cystinosis. Ann. Intern. Med., 68:883, 1968.

Seip, M., Steen-Johnsen, J., Vellan, J. E., and Gjessing, L. R. Dietary treatment of cystinosis. Acta Paediat. Scand., 57:409, 1968.

Sheldon, W., Luder, J., and Webb, B. A familial tubular absorption defect of glucose and amino acids. Arch. Dis. Child., 36:90, 1961.

Stickler, G. B., Hayles, A. B., Power, M. H., and Ulrich, J. A. Renal tubular dysfunction complicating the nephrotic syndrome. Pediatrics, 26:75, 1960.

Uzman, L. L., and Denny-Brown, D. Amino-aciduria in hepatolenticular degeneration (Wilson's disease). Amer. J. Med. Sci., 215:599, 1948.

RENAL TUBULAR ACIDOSIS

Albright, F., Burnett, C. H., Parsons, W., Reifenstein, E. C., Jr., and Roos, A. Osteomalacia and rickets: The various etiologies met in United States with emphasis on that resulting from a special form of renal acidosis; the therapeutic implications for each etiological subgroup and the relationship between osteomalacia and Milkman's syndrome. Medicine, 25:399, 1946.

Elkinton, J. R., McCurdy, D. K., and Buckalew, V. M., Jr. Hydrogen ion and the kidney. In Black, D. A. K., ed., Renal Disease. Oxford, England, Blackwell Scientific Publications, 1967, p. 110.

Györy, A. Z., and Edwards, K. D. G. Renal tubular acidosis. A family with an autosomal dominant genetic defect in renal hydrogen ion transport, with proximal tubular and collecting duct dysfunction and increased metabolism of citrate and ammonia. Amer. J. Med., 45:43, 1968.

Huth, E. J., Webster, C. D., and Elkinton, J. R. The renal excretion of hydrogen ion in renal tubular acidosis. III. An attempt to detect latent cases in a family; comments on nosology, genetics, and etiology of the primary disease. Amer. J. Med., 29:586, 1960.

Latner, A. L., and Burnard, E. D. Idiopathic hyperchloremic renal acidosis of infants: Observations on the site and nature of the lesion. Quart. J. Med., 19:285, 1950.

Lightwood, R., and Butler, N. Decline in primary infantile renal acidosis: Aetiological implications. Brit. Med. J., 1:855, 1963.

—— Payne, W. W., and Black, J. A. Infantile renal acidosis. Pediatrics, 12:628, 1953.

McCrory, W. W. Growth disorders associated with renal acidosis. J. Pediat., 57:5, 1960.

Morris, R. C., Jr. Renal tubular acidosis. Mechanisms, classification and implications. New Eng. J. Med., 281:1405, 1969.

—— and Fudenberg, H. H. Impaired renal acidification in patients with hypergammaglobulinemia. Medicine, 46:57, 1967.

Randall, R. E., Jr. Familial renal tubular acidosis revisited. Ann. Intern. Med., 66:1024, 1967.

—— and Taggart, W. H. Familial renal tubular acidosis. Ann. Intern. Med., 54:1108, 1961.

Relman, A. S. Renal acidosis and renal excretion of acid in health and disease. Advances Intern. Med., 12:295, 1964.

Reynolds, T. B. Observations on the pathogenesis of renal tubular acidosis. Amer. J. Med., 25:503, 1958.

Rodriguez Soriano, J., Boichis, H., and Edelmann, C. M., Jr. Bicarbonate reabsorption and hydrogen ion excretion in children with renal tubular acidosis. J. Pediat., 71:802, 1967.

—— Boichis, H., Stark, H., and Edelmann, C. M., Jr. Proximal renal tubular acidosis: a defect in bicarbonate reabsorption with normal urinary acidification. Pediat. Res., 1:81, 1967.

—— and Edelmann, C. M., Jr. Renal tubular acidosis. Ann. Rev. Med., 20:363, 1969.

Royer, P., and Broyer, M. L'acidose rénale au cours des tubulopathies congénitales. In Actualités Néphrologiques de l'Hôpital Necker. Paris, Editions Médicales Flammarion, 1967, p. 73.

—— Lestradet, H., Nordmann, R., Mathieu, H., and Rodriguez Soriano, J. Étude sur quatre cas d'acidose tubulaire chronique idiopathique avec hypocitraturie. Sem. Hôp. Paris (Ann. Pediat.), 38:808, 1962.

Seldin, D. W., and Wilson, J. D. Renal tubular acidosis. In Stanbury, J. B., Wyngaarden, J. B., and Fredrickson, D. S., eds., The Metabolic Basis of Inherited Disease. New York, McGraw-Hill Book Co., 1966, p. 1230.

Wrong, O., and Davies, H. E. The excretion of acid in renal disease. Quart. J. Med., 28:259, 1959.

IDIOPATHIC HYPERCALCIURIA

Beilin, L. J., and Clayton, B. E. Idiopathic hypercalciuria in a child. Arch. Dis. Child., 39:409, 1964.

Fanconi, A. Idiopatische Hypercalciurie im Kindersalter. Helv. Paediat. Acta, 18:306, 1963.

Jeune, M., Gilly, R., Hermier, M., Frédérich, A., Collombel, C., and Raveau, J. L'hypercalciurie idiopathique de l'enfant. Pédiatrie, 1:22, 1967.

Royer, P., and Balsan, S. Effet d'un regime pauvre en chlorure de sodium dans le "syndrome d'hypercalciurie idiopathique avec nanisme et troubles rénaux" de l'enfant. Schweiz. Med. Wschr., 96:412, 1966.

—— Balsan, S., and Mathieu, H. Hypercalciurie idiopathique avec nanisme et atteinte rénale chez l'enfant. In Actualités Néphrologiques de l'Hôpital Necker. Editions Médicales Flammarion, Paris, 1966, p. 245.

—— Mathieu, H., Gerbeaux, S., Frédérich, A., Rodriguez Soriano, J., Dartois, A. M., and Cuisinier, P. L'hypercalciurie idiopathique avec nanisme et atteinte rénale chez l'enfant. Sem. Hôp. Paris (Ann. Pédiat.), 38:767, 1962.

SODIUM-LOSING DISORDERS

Cheek, D. B., and Perry, J. W. A salt wasting syndrome in infancy. Arch. Dis. Child., 33:252, 1958.

Donnell, G. N., Litman, N., and Roldan, M. Pseudo-hypoadrenalcorticism. Renal sodium loss, hyponatremia, and hyperkaliemia due to a renal tubular insensitivity to mineralocorticoid. Amer. J. Dis. Child., 97:813, 1959.

Royer, P., Habib, R., and Mathieu, H. Le pseudohypo-minéralocorticism. In Problèmes Actuels de Néphrologie Infantile. Editions Médicales Flammarion, Paris, 1963, p. 147.

Thorn, G. W., Koepf, G. F., and Clinton, M., Jr. Renal failure simulating adrenocortical insufficiency. New Eng. J. Med., 231:76, 1944.

POTASSIUM-LOSING DISORDERS

Bartter, F. C., Pronove, P., Gill, J. R., Jr., and MacCardle, R. C. Hyperplasia of the juxtaglomerular complex, with hyperaldosteronism and hypokalemic alkalosis. Amer. J. Med., 33:811, 1962.

Beilin, L. J., Schiffman, N., Crane, M., and Nelson, D. H. Hypokalaemic alkalosis and hyperplasia of the juxtaglomerular apparatus without hypertension or edema. Brit. Med. J., 4:327, 1967.

Brackett, N. C., Jr., Koppel, M., Randall, R. E., Jr., and Nixon, W. P. Hyperplasia of the juxtaglomerular complex with secondary aldosteronism without hypertension (Bartter's syndrome). Amer. J. Med., 44:803, 1968.

Bryan, G. T., MacCardle, R. C., and Bartter, F. C. Hyperaldosteronism, hyperplasia of the juxtaglomerular complex, normal blood pressure and dwarfism: report of a case. Pediatrics, 37:43, 1966.

Camacho, A. M., and Blizzard, R. M. Congenital hypokaliemia of probable renal origin. Amer. J. Dis. Child., 103:535, 1962.

Cannon, P. J., Leeming, J. M., Sommers, S. C., Winters, R. W., and Laragh, J. H. Juxtaglomerular cell hyperplasia and secondary hyperaldosteronism (Bartter's syndrome): A re-evaluation of the pathophysiology. Medicine, 47:107, 1968.

Cheek, D. B., Robinson, M. J., and Collins, F. D. The investigation of a patient with hyperlipemia, hypokalemia and tetany. J. Pediat., 59:200, 1961.

Goodman, A. D., Vagnucci, A. H., and Hartroft, P. M. Pathogenesis of Bartter's syndrome. New Eng. J. Med., 281:1435, 1969.

Greenberg, A. J., Arboit, J. M., New, M. I., and Worthen, H. G. Normotensive secondary hyperaldosteronism. J. Pediat., 69:720, 1966.

Imai, M., Yabuta, K., Murata, H., Takita, S., Ohbe, Y., and Sokabe, H. A case of Bartter's syndrome with abnormal renin response to salt load. J. Pediat., 74:738, 1969.

Liddle, G. W., Bledsoe, T., and Coppage, W. S., Jr. A familial renal disorder simulating primary aldosterone secretion. In Baulieu, E. E., and Robel, P., eds., Aldosterone. Oxford, Blackwell Scientific Publications, 1963, p. 353.

Royer, P., Habib, H., and Mathieu, H. L'hypokaliémie chronique idiopathique avec hyperkaliurie. In Problèmes Actuels de Néphrologie Infantile. Editions Médicales Flammarion, Paris, 1963, p. 159.

Visser, H. K. A., Degenhart, H. J., Desmit, E., and

Cost, W. S. Mineralocorticoid excess in two brothers with dwarfism, hypokalemic alkalosis, and normal blood pressure. Acta Endoc., 55:661, 1967.

NEPHROGENIC DIABETES INSIPIDUS

Abelson, H. Nephrogenic diabetes insipidus. A study of the fine structure of the kidney in a seven-month-old male. Pediat. Res., 2:271, 1968.

Berlyne, G. M., Nilwarangkur, S., Janabi, K., and Cooper, M. Nocturnal nephrogenic diabetes insipidus. Quart. J. Med., 34:463, 1965.

Crawford, J. D., and Kennedy, G. C. Chlorothiazide in diabetes insipidus. Nature, 183:891, 1959.

Darmady, E. M., Offer, J., Prince, J., and Stranack, F. The proximal convoluted tubule in the renal handling of water. Lancet, 2:1254, 1964.

Earley, L. E., and Orloff, J. The mechanism of antidiuresis with the administration of hydrochlorothiazide to patients with vasopressin-resistant diabetes insipidus. J. Clin. Invest., 41:1988, 1962.

Forssman, H. On hereditary diabetes insipidus with special regard to a sex-linked form. Acta Med. Scand. (Suppl.), 159:1, 1945.

Friis-Hansen, B., Skadhauge, E., and Zetterström, R. Fluid and electrolyte metabolism in nephrogenic diabetes insipidus. Acta Paediat. (Suppl.), 146:57, 1963.

Gautier, P. E., and Prader, A. Un cas de diabète insipide néphrogène chez un nourrisson avec absence initiale de soif (diabète insipide occulte). Helv. Paediat. Acta, 11:45, 1956.

——— and Simpkiss, M. The management of nephrogenic diabetes insipidus in early life. Acta Paediat., 46:354, 1957.

Holliday, M. A., Burstin, C., and Hurrah, J. Evidence that the antidiuretic substance in the plasma of children with nephrogenic diabetes insipidus is antidiuretic hormone. Pediatrics, 32:384, 1963.

——— Egan, T. J., Morris, R. C., Jarrah, A. S., and Harrah, J. L. Pitressin-resistant hyposthenuria in chronic renal disease. Amer. J. Med., 42:378, 1967.

Lestradet. H. Diabète insipide nephrogenique idiopathique héréditaire. In Modern Problems in Pediatrics. Basel, Karger, 1960, Vol. VI, p. 376.

Lobeck, C. C., Barta, R. A., and Mangos, J. A. Study of sweat in pitressin-resistant diabetes insipidus. J. Pediat., 62:868, 1963.

Orloff, J., and Burg, M. B. Vasopressin-resistant diabetes insipidus. In Stanbury, J. B., Wyngaarden, J. B., and Fredrickson, D. S., eds., The Metabolic Basis of Inherited Disease. New York, McGraw-Hill Book Co., 1966, p. 1247.

Robinson, M. G., and Kaplan, S. A. Inheritance of vasopressin-resistant ("nephrogenic") diabetes insipidus. Amer. J. Dis. Child., 99:164, 1960.

Ruess, A. L., and Rosenthal, I. M. Intelligence in nephrogenic diabetes insipidus. Amer. J. Dis. Child., 105:358, 1963.

Schoen, E. J. Renal diabetes insipidus. Pediatrics, 26:808, 1960.

Schotland, M. G., Grumbach, M. M., and Strauss, J. The effect of chlorothiazides in nephrogenic diabetes insipidus. Pediatrics, 31:741, 1963.

22.14
CIRCULATORY DISTURBANCES

CHESTER M. EDELMANN, JR.

Renal Cortical Necrosis

In childhood this disorder is seen most frequently in association with dehydration, infection, and shock. The clinical picture is that of acute renal failure. Patients early are usually described as feeling well with no physical findings. Blood pressure usually remains normal. Total anuria is not uncommon, as distinguished from acute tubular necrosis. The urine is grossly abnormal, with protein, red blood cells, white blood cells, and less commonly casts. The course and treatment is of the uremic syndrome. Most reported cases have ended fatally, although it is very likely that there is an appreciable survival among less severely affected patients.

Pathologic examination shows patchy or diffuse ischemic necrosis of the cortex, occasionally accompanied by medullary necrosis. The necrosis is often hemorrhagic and is usually bland. Vascular occlusion of arterioles and glomeruli by fibrinous masses is sometimes seen, but thrombi cannot be demonstrated in all cases.

The pathogenesis of renal cortical necrosis, with its severe cortical destruction and almost total sparing of the medulla, is unknown. The initiating factor, toxic or other, may cause vasospasm of the small renal vessels, but there is considerable evidence that intravascular coagulation, as part of a spontaneous Shwartzman reaction, is responsible.

Renal Artery Occlusion

Renal artery occlusion has been reported rarely in infants and children. The usual etiology is either infection or trauma, and one or both renal arteries may be involved. Other etiologies include neurofibromatosis, compression by neoplasm, the vasculitis of lupus erythematosus and polyarteritis nodosa, aneurysm, and embolic occlusions.

Clinical manifestations vary with the etiology and specific circumstances. Pain, fever, nausea, and vomiting are frequently seen. The kidney is often palpably enlarged. Hypertension may or may not be present. Woodard et al. have called attention to the occurrence in infants of hypertension and congestive heart failure, in the absence of renal enlargement.

The urine usually contains red blood cells and protein, but may be normal. Gross hematuria is rare. Function of the involved kidney usually is severely impaired. London et al. have reported elevation in serum and urinary lactic dehydrogenase in adults with renal artery occlusion, and this may be a worthwhile examination in infants and children. Definitive diagnosis, of course, is established by renal arteriography.

In the absence of early diagnosis, cortical necrosis or renal infarction with irreversible damage may ensue. Treatment is surgical: thrombectomy, arterial reconstruction, or nephrectomy.

Renal Vein Thrombosis

Renal vein thrombosis with hemorrhagic infarction of the kidney, first described by Rayer in 1837, is not a rare occurrence in children. In most instances the diagnosis has been made postmortem, but increasing awareness of the condition has permitted clinical diagnosis in many instances.

Thrombosis of the renal vein leading to hemorrhagic infarction is seen most frequently in newborn infants, in association with diarrhea, vomiting, and dehydration. Suggested explanations for the higher prevalence in infants have included a greater tendency toward dehydration, the low blood pressure characteristic of the newborn infant, a low rate of renal blood flow, the frequency of septicemia, birth trauma, and anomalous venous circulation. However, the condition may occur under a variety of situations in every age group; when there is no apparent predisposing cause it has been referred to as primary renal vein thrombosis. A number of reports suggest an increased incidence in infants of toxemic and diabetic or prediabetic mothers. In adult subjects, renal vein thrombosis occurs as a complication of renal amyloidosis and diabetes mellitus. This association is not seen in children.

In somewhat less than one-half of the cases in infants and young children the thrombosis is bilateral. In unilateral cases in girls, though apparently not in boys, it occurs more frequently on the left than on the right side. Combined thrombosis of renal veins and inferior vena cava has been reported, but is far less frequent than renal vein thrombosis alone.

In cases in which renal vein thrombosis has been recognized clinically, the diagnosis has depended on the sudden appearance of a mass in the flank, accompanied by gross hematuria. However, hematuria and albuminuria are not essential to the diagnosis, since the urinary findings may be quite trivial and even absent. Fever, leucocytosis, vomiting, diarrhea, and dehydration may precede or follow the appearance of the mass, but again, may be absent. Anemia is common; thrombocytopenia has been observed in some cases. Hypertension commonly is recorded in older subjects. In the cases reported in infants, blood pressure usually has not been recorded although there are instances of hypertension. Isolated proteinuria, or massive edema and the nephrotic syndrome, common forms of presentation in adults, appear to be the result of gradual thrombosis of the renal veins. These forms of presentation are extremely rare in the pediatric age-group.

The major laboratory aids to diagnosis are an excretory urogram or radioisotopic scan, which reveal nonfunctioning of the kidney, and an inferior vena cavagram. Renal arteriography, with particular attention to the venous phase, has been advocated.

Differential diagnosis includes Wilms' tumor, hydronephrosis, multicystic kidney, and retroperitoneal hemorrhage.

Renal thrombosis is a serious condition; more than 95 percent of infants may be expected to die unless promptly treated. Nephrectomy is considered by most to be the best form of treatment in unilateral cases, although it has been suggested recently that recovery may take place, even with full return of renal function, with intensive medical therapy alone. Extension of the thrombus to involve the contralateral kidney is often given as a reason for nephrectomy, but this sequence is not well documented in the literature. Medical therapy is the only course in instances of bilateral involvement, and a number of cases of this type have recovered.

If renal vein thrombosis is diagnosed early in its development, thrombectomy may be of value, although the thrombus frequently extends far intrarenally. Indeed, many authors feel that the thrombus may begin in the arcuate and interlobular vessels and then extend to involve both smaller and larger veins.

Anticoagulant therapy to prevent dissemination of the clot and fibrinolytic therapy to promote dissolution have not been evaluated adequately, but may be of value.

Renal Arteriovenous Fistula

This rare abnormality occurs as a congenital defect and may also arise secondary to trauma. In a review in 1967, Malloy et al. found 24 cases of congenital fistula in the literature and added three more. There have now been several instances of fistula secondary to the trauma of needle biopsy.

The clinical picture includes hypertension, congestive heart failure, local thrill and bruit, and hematuria. The diagnosis is established by angiography and the treatment is surgical, in most instances nephrectomy.

REFERENCES

CORTICAL NECROSIS

Bernstein, J., and Meyer, R. Congenital abnormalities of the urinary system. II. Renal cortical and medullary necrosis. J. Pediat., 59:657, 1961.

Eskeland, G., and Skogrand, A. Bilateral cortical necrosis of the kidneys in infancy. Acta Pediat. Scand., 48:278, 1959.

Lindqvist, B., Erlanson, P., and Brun, A. A case of renal cortical necrosis probably caused by a human equivalent of the Shwartzman reaction. Acta Med. Scand., 173:561, 1963.

Mauer, S. M., and Nogrady, M. B. Renal papillary and cortical necrosis in a newborn infant: Report of a survivor with roentgenologic documentation. J. Pediat., 74:750, 1969.

Reisman, L. E., and Pathak, A. Bilateral renal cortical necrosis in the newborn. Associated with fetomaternal transfusion and hypermagnesemia. Amer. J. Dis. Child., 111:541, 1966.

Rieselbach, R. E., Klahr, S., and Bricker, N. S. Diffuse bilateral cortical necrosis. A longitudinal study of the functional residual nephrons. Amer. J. Med., 42:457, 1967.

Wells, J. D., Margolin, E. G., and Gall, E. A. Renal cortical necrosis. Clinical and pathologic features in twenty-one cases. Amer. J. Med., 29:257, 1960.

RENAL ARTERY OCCLUSION, RENAL VEIN THROMBOSIS, AND ARTERIO-VENOUS OCCLUSION

Avery, M. E., Oppenheimer, E. H., and Gordon, H. H. Renal vein thrombosis in newborn infants of diabetic mothers. New Eng. J. Med., 256:1134, 1957.

Beck, A. D., and Marshall, V. F. Renal venous thrombosis in children. Aust. New Zeal. J. Surg., 38:35, 1968.

Belman, A. B., Susmano, D. F., Burden, J. J., and Kaplan, G. W. Nonoperative treatment of unilateral renal vein thrombosis in the newborn. J.A.M.A., 211:1165, 1970.

Brough, A. J., and Zuelzer, W. W. Renal vascular disease. Pediat. Clin. N. Amer., 11:533, 1964.

Bruns, W. T. Ascending thrombosis involving inferior vena cava and renal veins. Amer. J. Dis. Child., 99:276, 1960.

Debré, R., Royer, P., Fauré, C., Pellerin, D., Habib, E., and Habib, R. L'aneurysme congénital de l'artere rénale avec hypertension artérielle grave chez l'enfant. Arch. Franç. Pédiat., 14:1, 1957.

Eliahou, H. E., Boichis, H., and Eden, E. Traumatic renal infarction in a solitary kidney. J. Urol., 90:16, 1963.

Fein, R. L., Chait, A., and Leviton, A. Renal vein thrombectomy for the treatment of renal vein thrombosis associated with the nephrotic syndrome. J. Urol., 99:1, 1968.

Gold, D., Latts, E. M., and Wexler, H. M. Congenital arteriovenous fistulae of kidney. A case report and review of the literature. Arch. Intern. Med., 115:208, 1965.

Habib, R., and Habib, E. C. Les lésions vasculaires de la neurofibromatose de Von Recklinghausen. Arch. Anat. Path., 10:47, 1962.

Jorgensen, L., Neset, G., Kjoerheim, A., and Mageroy, K. Renal vein thrombosis in the newborn. Acta Path. Microbiol. Scand. (Suppl.), 148:19, 1961.

Karafin, L., and Stearns, T. M. Renal vein thrombosis in children. J. Urol., 92:91, 1964.

Lackner, H., Walker, W. C., and Tillack, T. W. Calcified intrarenal arteriovenous fistula with spontaneous rupture: A case report. J. Urol., 97:997, 1967.

London, I. L., Hoffsten, P., Perkoff, G. T., and Pennington, T. G. Renal infarction. Elevation of serum and urinary lactic dehydrogenase. Arch. Intern. Med., 121:87, 1968.

Maldonado, J. E., Sheps, S. G., Bernatz, P. E., DeWeerd, J. H., and Harrison, E. G., Jr. Renal arteriovenous fistula. A reversible cause of hypertension and heart failure. Amer. J. Med., 37:499, 1964.

Malloy, T. R., Leberman, P. R., and Murphy, J. J. Renal arteriovenous fistula. J. Urol., 98:40, 1967.

McFarland, J. B. Renal venous thrombosis in children. Quart. J. Med., 34:269, 1965.

Miller, H. C., and Benjamin, J. A. Acute idiopathic renal vein thrombosis in infants. Pediatrics, 30:247, 1962.

Morris, G. C., Jr., DeBakey, M. E., Cooley, D. A., and Crawford, E. S. Experience with 200 renal artery reconstructive procedures for hypertension or renal failure. Circulation, 27:346, 1963.

Nilsson, C. G., and Ross, R. J. Bilateral renal arteriovenous fistulas and decreased blood pressure following renal biopsies. J. Urol., 97:176, 1967.

Oppenheimer, E. H., and Esterly, J. R. Thrombosis in the newborn: Comparison between infants of diabetic and nondiabetic mothers. J. Pediat., 67:549, 1965.

Rayer, P. F. O. Traite des Maladies des Reins. Paris, J. B. Bailliere, 1837.

Seeler, R. A., Kapadia, P., and Moncado, R. Nonsurgical management of bilateral renal vein and inferior vena cava thrombosis in a neonate. Clin. Pediat., in press.

Smith, G. H., Remmers, A. R., Dickey, B. M., Sarles, H. E. Intrarenal arteriovenous fistula and systemic hypertension following percutaneous renal biopsy. Report of a case. Nephron, 5:24, 1968.

Stark, H. Renal vein thrombosis in infancy. Recovery without nephrectomy. Amer. J. Dis. Child., 108:430, 1964.

Takeuchi, A., and Benirschke, K. Renal venous thrombosis of the newborn and its relation to maternal diabetes. Report of 16 cases. Biol. Neonat., 3:237, 1961.

Tveteraas, E., and Rudström, P. Renal thrombosis in the newborn: Report of "primary" case successfully treated by surgery. Acta Paediat. Scand., 45:545, 1956.

Verhagen, A. D., Hamilton, J. P., and Genel, M. Renal vein thrombosis in infants. Arch. Dis. Child., 40:214, 1965.

Wegner, G. P., Crummy, A. B., Flaherty, T. T., and Hipona, F. A. Renal vein thrombosis. A roentgenographic diagnosis. J.A.M.A., 209:1661, 1969.

Wilkey, J. L., Rowe, F. H., Brown, J., and Gersack, J. Intrarenal arteriovenous fistula. J. Urol., 93:663, 1965.

Woodard, J. R., Patterson, J. H., and Brinsfield, D. Renal artery thrombosis in newborn infants. Amer. J. Dis. Child., 114:191, 1967.

22.15
UROLITHIASIS

MARTIN A. NASH

The precipitation and growth of crystalline material in the genitourinary tract has fascinated and puzzled medical scientists since antiquity. A fairly common occurrence in adults, urinary stones in the pediatric population are relatively rare, at least in the United States. In some areas of the world urinary lithiasis in children is endemic and presents a major health problem. For example, a recent survey from two hospitals in New Delhi disclosed stones in 600 children occurring over a 2-year period. Sixty percent were bladder calculi. The etiology of these is elusive, but their occurrence appears to be more frequent in the lower socioeconomic classes, suggesting an environmental or dietary factor related to poverty. In the United States bladder stones are exceedingly rare in the absence of a neurogenic bladder or foreign body.

Urinary stone disease occurs more frequently in males, although this sex preponderance is not borne out in all surveys. Williams' large experience suggests that the majority in children occur under 4 years of age with a peak in the second and third years.

Calculi are composed of a crystalline fraction imbedded in an organic matrix, which comprises 2.5 to 10 percent of the stone by weight and consists of various proteins. The crystalline fraction is composed of one or more of the following: calcium phosphate, calcium oxalate, or magnesium ammonium phosphate; less commonly uric acid and cystine; and rarely xanthine. The analysis of calculi traditionally has been performed by chemical means, which serve to identify chemical radicles but not crystalline structure. The recent application to stone analysis of the tools of mineralogy and crystallography has demonstrated the large number and great complexity of crystals which precipitate as calcium salts in human stone disease.

PATHOGENESIS AND PROPHYLAXIS. Theories of the pathogenesis of stone formation have revolved around the two components of calculi, matrix and crystal. At the present time it appears that although the protein matrix, acting as an adhesive, is important in the growth of stones, disturbances in these urinary proteins are not inciting events in their formation.

Consideration of the explanation for precipitation of crystals in urine can be approached usefully through an examination of the behavior of urine as an aqueous solvent. It is clear that far greater amounts of calcium, phosphate, oxalate, uric acid, and cystine can be held in solution in urine than in distilled water. This superiority of urine to water as a solvent can be explained to a great extent by an examination of the factors which determine the capacity of an aqueous solvent. The application of these factors to the pathogenesis and treatment of urinary stones is discussed in the following paragraphs.

Quantity of Solvent. Obviously the greater the quantity of solvent for a fixed amount of solute, the more dilute the solution and the lesser the probability of precipitation. The quantity of solvent, i.e., the rate of urine flow, has been implicated in some cases of endemic stone formation in dry climates where water drinking is minimal, and in areas where chronic gastroenteritis with subsequent dehydration and oliguria is prevalent. The virtues of increasing fluid intake in stone formers is apparent.

Concentration of Ions. For a fixed quantity of solvent the greater the amount of a specific solute, the greater the likelihood that the solubility constant will be exceeded and precipitation will occur. However, it is not the molecular *concentration* per se that is important but the molecular *activity,* and the chance of two molecules interacting is decreased by the presence of other particles. Many substances in urine (Na^+, Cl^-, $SO_4^=$, Mg^{++}, urea) contribute to the total molecular strength, and thus enhance solubility. An increased quantity of solute in the urine is of prime importance in many diseases. For example, in hyperparathyroidism, vitamin D intoxication, distal renal tubular acidosis, immobilization, thyrotoxicosis, and sarcoidosis the rate of calcium excretion may be increased over normal. The quantity of uric acid for excretion is augmented in gout, the Lesch-Nyhan syndrome, and the leukemias, especially while under treatment with cytotoxic drugs. Oxalate excretion is increased in hyperoxaluria of both types and in hyperglycinuria. There is a marked elevation of cystine excretion in cystinuria. There are a few reports of xanthine stones associated with the metabolic disorder xanthinuria. Theoretically there may be an increase in the occurrence of xanthine stones with the wide use of the xanthine oxidase inhibitor, allopurinol, although this has not been seen thus far as a complication of therapy. Although 50 percent of children and adults with urinary stones do not have an associated identifiable disease, approximately one-half of these patients are hypercalciuric, either constantly or intermittently.

Treatment directed toward decreasing the amount of solute excreted includes limiting the intake of foods containing high amounts of calcium, purine (uric acid), or sulfoproteins (cystine). However, since 60 percent or more of oxalic acid is produced endogenously, decreasing oxalate intake is of little benefit. Other approaches include decreasing the formation of uric acid by inhibiting the enzyme xanthine oxidase with the drug allopurinol, and converting cystine into a more soluble disulfide by the administration of penicillamine. Recent evidence suggests that some patients with a familial occurrence of calcium stones demonstrate an augmented excretion of calcium after a glucose load. This work must be confirmed, however, before carbohydrate limitation can be recommended as therapy.

pH. Solubility varies markedly with changes in pH. Calcium phosphate and magnesium ammonium phosphate are more soluble at a pH less than 6 and uric acid at a pH greater than 6. Cystine demonstrates little increase in solubility up to pH 7, but further increases in pH greatly augment its solubility.

The importance of pH as a pathogenetic factor is suggested in several clinical situations. The majority of uric acid stone-formers show neither hyperuricemia nor increased uric acid excretion, but as a group these patients have a lower mean urine pH than controls, producing a favorable environment for uric acid precipitation. Therapy is directed at alkalinization of the urine by administration of sodium bicarbonate or citrate. The vast majority of patients with magnesium ammonium phosphate stones have urinary tract infection with a urea-splitting organism (such as *Proteus*), releasing ammonia which renders the urine alkaline and favors magnesium ammonium phosphate precipitation. Treatment is directed toward eradication of infection and acidification of the urine by administration of ammonium chloride, ascorbic acid, or methionine. The frequent occurrence of urolithiasis in distal renal tubular acidosis may be related partially to persistent urine alkalinity. Although there is no way to acidify the urine, due to the nature of the intrinsic defect, treatment of systemic acidosis decreases the rate of excretion of calcium. In urine, as opposed to water, the solubility of oxalate is increased with alkalinization, related most likely to a consequent absolute decrease in calcium excretion, and an increase in both the rate of excretion and the degree of ionization of citrate. Urinary alkalinization in this instance has not been evaluated as a therapeutic measure.

Presence of Substances Having a Particular Solubilizing Action. Magnesium ions have been shown to exert a greater influence on solubility than can be explained by their contribution to the total ionic strength. This action is presumably due to the formation of complex ions which further reduce the activities of precipitable ions. Citrate has been found to have a similar virtue to an even greater degree, probably due to the same mechanism. Pyrophosphate can be shown to increase the solubility of calcium oxalate and calcium phosphate; two small peptides have been identified recently which increase calcium phosphate solubility, presumably by inhibiting the aggregation of tiny clusters of ions.

Some patients with idiopathic calcium phosphate stones have been shown to have a decreased ratio of urinary Mg^{++} to Ca^{++}. Rats on Mg^{++}-deficient diets show an increased incidence of calcium deposition in the proximal tubules. There are several reports of patients with recurrent calcium lithiasis who have remained stone-free on oral magnesium therapy. This treatment may be useful for those patients with a decreased urinary Mg^{++} to Ca^{++} ratio, but controlled studies are needed before a recommendation can be made. The concentration of citrate in urine is decreased in patients with distal renal tubular acidosis, but there is no practical way to increase it since oral citrate is quickly metabolized to bicarbonate. Oral phosphate will increase urinary pyrophosphate, but favorable results from this therapy are not universal, and recent evidence suggests that in some patients it may be deleterious.

Time. Time has an adverse effect on solubility. Precipitates often are seen, e.g., in urine specimens which have been allowed to stagnate in their collection bottles. The factor of time is important in situations where urinary stasis may occur, such as ureteropelvic obstruction, megaureter, and neurogenic bladder. Treatment consists of relief of obstruction and establishment of adequate drainage.

Presence of a Nidus. A precipitate may be induced in a saturated solution by addition of a crystal of the solute or, under some circumstances, by addition of a nonspecific particle. An important factor in stone formation is the presence of a nidus on which crystallization may take place, such as an indwelling catheter, a postoperative or self-introduced foreign body, or debris from infection. Two-thirds of patients with stones are infected either primarily or secondarily, *Proteus* and *E. coli* being the predominant organisms. Treatment of a nidus obviously involves removal with either surgery or antibiotics.

The relative frequency with which the factors discussed above are important etiologically in children with stones is uncertain. Approximately 30 percent of stones are associated with significant anomalies of the genitourinary tract, and 10 percent are related to metabolic disorders, leaving 50 to 60 percent idiopathic. This percentage will decrease as more knowledge is gained concerning the factors affecting urine as a solvent.

CLINICAL PICTURE. Two-thirds of children with stones are discovered incidentally or during a work-up for urinary tract infection. Presenting symptoms in the remainder are hematuria, fever, flank pain, recurrent urinary tract infection, or persistent pyuria. It should be noted that the symptoms attributed to trigonitis (frequency, dysuria, terminal hematuria) are the same symptoms presented by patients with bladder calculi, in both cases symptoms being produced by irritation of the trigonal area.

DIAGNOSIS. The diagnosis of urinary tract stone should be entertained in any child with the above symptomatology or urinary findings. The approach to etiology in a child with a stone will be based more profitably on a consideration of abnormalities in the nature of urine as a solvent, rather than on the perfunctory elimination of named diseases. These factors, as discussed above, are summarized in Table 7, along with some of the underlying diseases. The evaluation should include a search for a family history of stones or metabolic diseases, urine culture, radiographic examination of the urinary tract (uric acid and xanthine stones are the only radiolucent ones), determination of the capacity for urinary acidification (administering ammonium chloride if necessary), multiple analyses of 24-hour rates of excretion of calcium (normal $\leq$ 2 to 4 mg/kg on a usual diet, $\leq$200 mg in adults), oxalate (normal = 10 to 25 mg/24 hours in adults and proportionately less in children as corrected for surface area), and cystine * (normal < 70 mg/g creatinine). Analysis of urine for citrate and magnesium is interesting but not essential for treatment. The serum should be analyzed for urea nitrogen and creatinine, as indices of renal function, as well as for calcium, phosphorus, alkaline phosphatase, uric acid, and electrolytes (with special attention to bicarbonate as an indication of acidosis). A urea or creatinine clearance is helpful

---

* The nitroprusside test on a random urine specimen will give an adequate indication of markedly increased cystine concentration. To 5 ml of urine are added a few drops of ammonium hydroxide and 2 ml of fresh 5 percent NaCN. After 10 minutes for equilibration a few drops of 5 percent sodium nitroprusside are added. A deep purple color indicates a positive reaction. False-positives occur from ketonuria.

TABLE 7. *Factors Contributing to Stone Formation*

Composition of Stone	Contributory Factors
Calcium phosphate	Hypercalciuria
	Hyperparathyroidism
	Vitamin D intoxication
	Distal renal tubular acidosis
	Immobilization
	Thyrotoxicosis
	Sarcoidosis
	Idiopathic
	High calcium diet (in susceptible individuals) (?)
	Alkaline urinary pH
	Decreased urinary citrate
	Decreased urinary pyrophosphate (?)
	Decreased urinary Mg^{++}/Ca^{++} ratio (?)
	Foreign body
	Urinary stasis
Calcium oxalate	All of above except pH
	Hyperoxaluria
	Types I and II hyperoxaluria
	Hyperglycinuria
	Ethylene glycol poisoning
	Pyridoxin deficiency (?)
Magnesium ammonium phosphate	Infection with urea-splitting organism
	Alkaline urine
	Foreign body
	Urinary stasis
Uric acid	Hyperuricosuria
	Gout
	Lesch-Nyhan syndrome
	Hematologic malignancies
	High-purine diet
	Acid urine
Xanthine	Xanthinuria
	Acid urine
	Allopurinol therapy (?)
Cystine	Cystinuria
	Acid urine

as an estimate of renal damage and as a basis for later evaluation of renal function. Of primary importance is a chemical analysis of stone composition. It should be noted that a small uric acid stone may lead to obstruction, infection, and subsequent stone growth by deposition of magnesium ammonium phosphate. Failure to recognize the composition of the nucleus would lead to misdirected and deleterious pH therapy.

TREATMENT. Treatment of urinary stones too large to pass spontaneously is surgical removal. Prophylaxis to prevent recurrence involves appropriate alteration of urine composition by the methods discussed above. Stones secondary to a metabolic disorder can be expected to recur unless the underlying abnormality is treated. In contrast to adults, recurrence of stones of the idiopathic variety in children appears to

be infrequent. Severe and irreversible renal damage unfortunately is the occasional result of silent urinary stone disease but should be preventable by early detection and treatment.

REFERENCES

Aberle, B. Die Nierensteinkronkheit beim Kind. Urologe, 7:279, 1968.

Aurora, A. L., Ramalingaswami, V., and Gaitonde, P. D. Bladder stone disease in children in Delhi area. J. Urol., 91:347, 1964.

———— Taneja, O. P., and Gupta, D. N. Bladder stone disease of childhood. Acta Paediat. Scand., 59:177, 1970.

Bass, H. N., and Emanuel, B. Nephrolithiasis in childhood. Clinical and etiologic considerations. Clin. Pediat., 5:79, 1966.

Borden, T. A., and Lyon, E. S. Effects of magnesium and pH on experimental calcium oxalate stone disease. Invest. Urol., 6:412, 1969.

Daeschner, C. W., Singleton, E. B., and Curtus, J. C. Urinary tract calculi and nephrocalcinosis in infants and children. J. Pediat., 57:721, 1960.

Davis, H. Metabolic causes of renal stones in children. J.A.M.A., 171:2199, 1959.

DeVries, A., Frank, M., and Atsmon, A. Inherited uric acid lithiasis. Amer. J. Med., 33:880, 1962.

———— Kochwa, S., Lazebnik, J., Frank, M., and Djaldetti, M. Glycinuria, a hereditary disorder associated with nephrolithiasis. Amer. J. Med., 23:408, 1957.

Eckstein, H. B. Endemic urinarylithiasis in Turkish children. A clinical study of 119 cases. Arch. Dis. Child., 36:137, 1961.

Eckstein, V. H. B. Harnsteine in Kindesalter. Z. Kinderheilk., 2:451, 1965.

Elliot, J. S., Ribeira, M. E., and Euscbia, E. Effect of oral phosphate upon urinary excretion of oxalic acid. Invest. Urol., 7:528, 1970.

Fleisch, H. F., and Bisaz, S. Isolation from urine of pyrophosphate, a calcification inhibitor. Amer. J. Physiol., 203:671, 1962.

Gershoff, S. N. The formation of urinary stones. Metabolism, 13:875, 1964.

Knox, W. E. Cystinuria. In Stanbury, J. B., Wyngaarden, J. B., and Fredrickson, D. J., eds., The Metabolic Basis of Hereditary Disease, 2nd ed. New York, McGraw-Hill Book Co., 1966, p. 1262.

Lattimer, G. K., and Hubbard, M. Pediatric urologic admissions. J. Urol., 66:289, 1951.

Lemann, J., Jr., Piering, W. F., and Lennan, E. J. Possible role of carbohydrate-induced calciuria in calcium oxalate kidney-stone formation. New Eng. J. Med., 280:232, 1969.

Lyon, E. S., Borden, T. A., Ellis, J. E., and Vermuelen, C. W. Calcium oxalate lithiasis produced by pyridoxine deficiency and inhibition with high magnesium diets. Invest. Urol., 4:133, 1966.

Melick, R. A., and Henneman, P. H. Clinical and laboratory studies of 207 consecutive patients in a kidney stone clinic. New Eng. J. Med., 259:307, 1958.

Miller, G. H., Vermuelen, C. W., and Moore, J. D. Calcium oxalate solubility in urine. Experimental urolithiasis XIV. J. Urol., 79:607, 1968.

Moore, C. A., and Bunce, G. E. Reduction in frequency

of renal calculus formation by oral magnesium administration. Invest. Urol., 2:7, 1964.

Myers, N. A. A. Urolithiasis in childhood. Arch. Dis. Child., 32:48, 1957.

Oxeopoulos, D. G., Soyannwa, M. A. O., and McGeown, M. G. Magnesium/calcium ratio in urine of patients with renal stone. Lancet, 2:420, 1968.

Pak, C. Y. C. Physicochemical basis for formation of renal stones of calcium phosphate origin: calculation of the degree of saturation of urine with respect to brushite. J. Clin. Invest., 48:1914, 1969.

Powell, T. O., and Mickelson, J. C. Urinary calculi in children. Surg. Gynec. Obstet., 66:300, 1958.

Prien, E. L. Studies in urolithiasis. II. Relationship between pathogenesis, structure, and composition of calculi. J. Urol., 61:821, 1949.

—— and Frondel, C. Studies in urolithiasis. I. The composition of urinary calculi. J. Urol., 57:949, 1947.

—— and Prien, E. L., Jr. Composition and structure of urinary stone. Amer. J. Med., 45:654, 1968.

Pruzanski, W. Cystinuria and cystine urolithiasis in childhood. Acta Paediat. Scand., 55:97, 1966.

Vermeulen, C. W., Lyon, E. S., and Fried, F. A. On the nature of the stone-forming process. J. Urol., 94:176, 1965.

—— Lyon, E. S., and Miller, G. H. Calcium phosphate solubility in urine as measured by a precipitation test: Experimental urolithiasis XIII. J. Urol., 79:596, 1958.

Wenzl, J. E., Burke, E. C., Stickler, G. B., and Utz, D. C. Nephrolithiasis and nephrocalcinosis in children. Pediatrics, 41:57, 1968.

Williams, D. I., and Eckstein, H. B. Urinary lithiasis. *In* Williams, D. I., ed., Pediatric Urology. London, Butterworths, 1968, p. 323.

Williams, H. E., and Smith, L. H. L-Glyceric aciduria. New Eng. J. Med., 278:233, 1968.

Zinsser, H. H. Urinary calculi. J.A.M.A., 174:2062, 1960.

22.16
INFECTIONS OF THE URINARY AND GENITAL TRACTS

MARK ABRAMOWICZ

Cystitis and Pyelonephritis

The urinary tract is one of the most common sites of infection. Although there is considerable variability in clinical presentation, site of infection, and extent of involvement, the feature common to all urinary tract infections is the presence in the urine of significant numbers of bacteria. Bacteriuria per se may not always indicate active infection of the urinary tract, but it defines the population at risk and therefore, for practical purposes, should be considered synonymous with urinary tract infection.

Clinically, it is usually not possible to localize infection specifically to the bladder or to the kidney.

Therefore, in this section, the term urinary tract infection (UTI) will be used to refer to either or both conditions.

INCIDENCE AND PREVALENCE.   Less than 1 percent of apparently healthy newborns have UTI. Underlying congenital malformations are rare in these infants. Although sex distribution varies, there appears to be a slight preponderance of males. As many as 1 or 2 percent of females and 0.5 percent of males beyond the neonatal period, but below 2 years of age, have UTI. In contrast to newborns, as many as 80 percent of these patients have associated congenital malformations or malfunctions of the urinary tract.

In the survey of school-age children by Kunin and co-workers, bacteriuria was found in 1.2 percent of girls and 0.03 percent of boys. Most of these children were asymptomatic, but 40 percent had positive radiographic findings, most commonly caliectasis. This abnormality in 13 percent of those with asymptomatic bacteriuria suggests that this condition sometimes is associated with pyelonephritis. In girls the cumulative rate of bacteriuria over the first 7 years of school was 2.9 percent, with an annual mean conversion rate of 0.3 percent. If further study finds no change in the conversion rate in adolescence, it can be projected that 5 percent of girls will have bacteriuria by the time of graduation from high school.

ETIOLOGY.   The bacteria responsible for most urinary tract infections are enteric organisms, including *E. coli, A. aerogenes, B. proteus, Pseudomonas aeroginosa,* and enterococci; less than 10 percent of infections are caused by gram-positive cocci.

E. coli accounts for approximately one-half to three-fourths of initial infection and a lower proportion of recurrent infections. Certain *E. coli* serotypes, namely, 04, 06, 02, 01, and 75, commonly cause UTI; however, this relationship reflects their ubiquity rather than a particular pyelopathogenicity. Enteropathogenic *E. coli* serotypes are rare in urinary tract infection.

Pure cultures are the rule; it is even uncommon to find more than one serotype of *E. coli* infecting urine at one time, although several strains are usually present in feces. A mixed flora in urine is most often the result of contamination, but truly mixed infections may be seen in patients with chronic or complicated infections, especially after instrumentation. In the majority of patients the organism cultured from the urine can also be isolated from the stool.

Most recurrences of UTI are associated with a new serologic type of *E. coli* or another species altogether. This makes it unlikely that protoplasts of *E. coli* play an important role in recurrent infection, despite the fact that these L-forms have been cultured from infected renal tissue.

Circulating antibodies often can be demonstrated in patients who have evidence of pyelonephritis. Usually, no antibody response is seen when infection is limited to the lower urinary tract. However, lack of understanding of the complex relationship between antibody formation, recovery, resistance, and protection from reinfection precludes valid conclusions with clinical implications. Assessment of antibody response, therefore, is of value mainly in implicating a specific organism and in helping to localize the site of infection within the urinary tract.

The role of viruses in the pathogenesis of urinary tract infection is still not convincingly demonstrated. Type II adenovirus has been implicated as an etiologic agent in acute hemorrhagic cystitis in children.

PATHOGENESIS. Bacteria usually invade the urinary tract by an ascending route. Hematogenous spread is probably a rare event, since most urinary tract infections are with gram-negative organisms, all of which are potent pyrogens, and since most cases of bacteriuria, symptomatic or not, do not follow an obvious bacteremia. Gram-positive infections with staphylococci and enterococci are more likely to be blood-borne. Lymphatic spread from the gastrointestinal tract or from the bladder upward has never been proved.

The normal bladder in some way rids itself of invading bacteria. Voiding and dilution probably play important roles in this, although there is always a small amount of urine left in the bladder, and bacteria multiply there very easily. In patients with obstruction or bladder dysfunction, this bladder clearance mechanism fails. Vesicoureteral reflux may occur, and ureteral peristalsis may be disturbed.

Other factors besides obstruction that are associated with frequent and persistent urinary tract infections include stasis, abnormal renal vasculature, calculi, or the presence of islets of dysplastic tissue. All of these possess a potential for causing obstruction of some degree, but a purely mechanistic view of the pathogenesis of urinary tract infection is not adequate to explain all the observations. In experimental animals partial obstruction of a ureter does not necessarily produce infection localized to the obstructed side; complete obstruction does tend to localize infection, but bacteria injected into a completely obstructed kidney usually disappear.

The reported incidence of underlying uropathy in patients with bacteriuria varies widely, depending on the criteria for selection of patients, the choice of diagnostic tests, and their interpretation. However, some of the more reassuring reports with regard to absence of uropathy come from studies in which true bacteriuria was not convincingly documented.

Certain systemic disorders, as well as pregnancy, are associated with an increased incidence of UTI, although in most the cause is not apparent; these include cirrhosis of the liver, hypertension, hypokalemia, and perhaps diabetes mellitus.

Chronic pyelonephritis may follow either single or multiple acute infections. In the absence of urologic abnormality, it is not known why the infection resolves rapidly in some patients, whereas in others it persists. The possible roles of immune mechanisms in the host and transformation of L-forms of bacteria both have aroused speculation from observations in experimental pyelonephritis, but there are few data

relevant to human disease. The role of bacterial infection in the pathogenesis of chronic pyelonephritis has been questioned because of the frequent failure to elicit a history of infection or to demonstrate bacteriuria in such patients. Using immunofluorescent techniques, Aoki and associates have been able to identify bacterial antigen in the kidneys of patients with so-called abacterial pyelonephritis, suggesting that renal infection in fact did play a role in the pathogenesis of their disease.

CLINICAL AND LABORATORY FEATURES. Infants with *acute pyelonephritis* usually present with nonspecific symptoms, including fever, anorexia, vomiting, diarrhea or constipation, jaundice, and anemia. Examination of the urine leads to the correct diagnosis. The classic description of acute pyelonephritis in older children includes rigors, chills, and high fever; suprapubic, abdominal, and flank pain; vomiting and malaise; and occasionally central nervous system signs such as meningismus, stupor, delirium, or convulsions. However, this clinical picture is rare, and in most instances the symptoms of pyelonephritis are less severe. Urinalysis usually reveals proteinuria, leucocyturia, microscopic hematuria, and almost invariably bacteriuria.

Chronic pyelonephritis combines the features of chronic infection with those of progressive renal insufficiency; in addition, symptoms of acute pyelonephritis may occur during exacerbations. In many instances, chronic pyelonephritis is limited to one kidney or to one renal pole, and the symptomatology is that of acute and chronic infection without evidence of renal insufficiency.

Leucocyturia may be continuous, intermittent, or absent. Significant bacteriuria is not always present. In cases with reduced renal function it can be inferred that the disease process is bilateral and diffuse, and renal biopsy may contribute to the diagnosis. Intravenous urogram (IVU) may reveal impaired function and general or local contraction and narrowing, the kidney appearing compressed medially against the vertebral column, with calyces, pelvis, and ureter lying in one straight vertical line. The calyces may appear either blunted and clubbed or narrowed and elongated. There is an irregular diminution of parenchyma. When the disease process is unilateral there usually is hypertrophy of the contralateral kidney.

Infections of the lower urinary tract cause few systemic signs other than fever; local symptoms include painful urination, burning, frequency, urgency, low abdominal or suprapubic pain, and retention which may be secondary to pain. Enuresis, hematuria, and foul-smelling urines are also frequently present.

Many cases of urinary tract infection evolve insidiously with almost total absence of symptoms. In retrospect one may uncover suggestive signs, such as unexplained bouts of fever, malaise, or abdominal pain of low-grade intensity.

PATHOPHYSIOLOGY. In acute pyelonephritis, glomerular filtration rate usually remains normal. A decreased capacity to concentrate urine has been described, persisting for 4 to 6 weeks after subsidence of clinical symptoms. Extremely severe metabolic acidosis has been observed in infants with acute pyelonephritis, suggesting the possibility of a defect in urinary acidification. A systematic study of the effect of pyelonephritis on urinary acidification is needed.

In chronic pyelonephritis, as the disease progresses, diminution in total renal function ensues, until the complete picture of chronic renal insufficiency has evolved. At any given level of glomerular filtration rate, however, concentrating capacity and ability to excrete hydrogen ion in pyelonephritis usually are lower than in other forms of chronic renal disease.

PATHOLOGY. Except in young infants, the kidney in acute infections is usually enlarged with a smooth capsular surface, which only rarely is marred by superficial abscesses. The pelvic mucosa may be involved and wide yellow streaks may radiate from pelvis to capsule. Microscopically there is edema, congestion, polymorphonuclear infiltration of the interstititum, abscess formation, and distended tubules, filled with exudate consisting of leucocytes, bacteria, and debris. Excessive tubular dilatation may result in necrosis. The brunt of the inflammation is borne by the medulla. However, glomeruli may be involved either in the exudative process or by periglomerular fibrosis.

At a later phase, plasma cells and lymphocytes replace the polymorphonuclear leucocytes, and, when healing occurs, an interstitial scar is formed. In fatal cases the inflammation extends producing a swollen kidney studded in its entirety with abscesses and disrupted tubules.

In chronic pyelonephritis the kidney is usually contracted and has an irregularly scarred surface and an adherent thickened capsule. The calyces and pelvis are fibrosed and distorted by wedge-shaped parenchymal scars. The thickness of the parenchyma is diminished, often unevenly. Glomeruli show proliferation, crescents, and hyalinization, and are surrounded by intense pericapsular fibrosis. They are clustered together in wedges by the interstitial scarring. Bands of fibrosis and nests of lymphocytes, eosinophils, and plasma cells disrupt the renal architecture. Tubules are atrophied and dilated and may contain "colloid" casts. Productive endarteritis, hyperplastic arteriosclerosis, or fibrinoid arteriolar necrosis may be present, as well as foci of calcification.

DIAGNOSIS. Regardless of which collection technique is employed, a negative culture usually can be considered a valid result, since under ordinary conditions, in a patient who is not under treatment, a false-negative urine culture is rare. When the culture reveals bacteria, the number of organisms in the urine specimen must be quantitated in order to distinguish contaminated from truly infected urine. In toilet-trained children infected urines contain more than 10^5 organisms per ml, in contrast to contaminated urines, which contain fewer than 10^3 organisms per ml. Counts between 10^3 and 10^5 are of equivocal

significance. In younger children and infants, the possibility that urine does not remain in the bladder long enough to allow bacteria to enter a logarithmic growth phase cannot be excluded, so that lower counts of plausible organisms may represent true infection and should be repeated. However, in younger children and infants who have convincing nonbacteriologic evidence of infection, bacterial counts are seldom less than 10^5.

Urine obtained by suprapubic puncture or from the upper urinary tract by retrograde catheterization should not contain any bacteria if sterile technique is employed. Therefore, any growth from these sources may be important, but it should be noted that low counts in bladder aspirates are rare in patients with other evidence of true infection.

Low bacterial counts or sterile urine in the presence of true infection may be seen with rapid urine flow, urine pH of less than 5.0 or more than 8.5, the presence of an antibiotic or chemotherapeutic agent in the urine, or complete ureteral obstruction.

Of the many ways proposed for circumventing the tedious performance of quantitative bacterial cultures, examination of the gram-stained urinary sediment has proved of value; it also provides immediately available information. Bacteria seen in the smear of an uncentrifuged urine specimen indicate more than 10^5 organisms per ml; few or no organisms, less than 10^5. Following centrifugation, many bacteria on smear reflect counts over 10^5; few or no organisms represent less than 10^3. A simple and inexpensive culture technique which uses agar-coated microscope slides for quantitative culture was recently described and has been found to be highly reliable. A number of other tests have been proposed, based on color alteration of an indicator in the presence of products derived from bacterial metabolism. Correlation between the results of these tests and bacterial counts, however, has shown them to be inadequate, even for screening, since they yield an unacceptable number of false-negative results. Measurement of urinary glucose concentration, using a newly devised paper strip, appears to be of value in screening, a concentration of glucose less than 2 mg percent reflecting bacterial metabolism and indicating significant bacteriuria.

Since an increased rate of excretion of white blood cells is present in many cases of UTI, leucocyturia should suggest this diagnosis. However, "pus cells" may be absent in as many as 20 percent of cases of true infection, and their presence may be related to other causes, such as vaginal contamination, glomerulonephritis, nephrocalcinosis, or urolithiasis, or may result from a functional renal disturbance secondary to dehydration or hypotension. White blood cell casts suggest renal involvement, and when these are accompanied by significant bacteriuria, the combination favors a diagnosis of pyelonephritis.

Red blood cells may appear in urine in infection of either the lower or upper tract. Microscopic hematuria is found in urethritis and hemorrhagic cystitis, or may be due to an underlying urologic abnormality such as hydronephrosis, duplication, ureterocele, or lithiasis.

Proteinuria in urinary tract infection is usually of small magnitude, ranging from trace to 2+. Interestingly, regardless of its magnitude, the electrophoretic pattern is typical: globulins predominate and are equally distributed among alpha, beta, and gamma.

TREATMENT. Oral sulfonamides are most often used for initial treatment of acute infection with sensitive organisms or before sensitivities are known. Ampicillin and tetracyclines are alternative choices for oral treatment of acute infections, but there is no evidence that these agents are more effective than sulfonamides in patients with fever or other toxic signs. Tetracyclines should not be given to children less than 3 years old when an alternative is available, since mottling of permanent teeth has been reported after the use of tetracyclines in this age group.

Subsequent treatment is guided by response to therapy and the results of the culture and antibiotic sensitivity test (Sec. 14.1). If the patient responds to initial therapy, a sensitivity report of resistance to the drug can be ignored, since disks that evaluate sensitivity simulate antibiotic concentrations in blood, and urine concentrations are much higher when the antibiotic is excreted by the kidney. Infections can be cured by sterilizing the urine alone, so that agents with little or no tissue activity, such as acidifying drugs or nitrofurantoin, can eradicate bacteriuria, even when there is evidence of renal involvement. Although some laboratories report sensitivities for neomycin, this drug should never be given parenterally because of its severe ototoxicity.

In chronic or complicated infections sensitivity tests should be used to guide therapy. The usual organisms in such difficult cases are *Klebsiella-Aerobacter, Proteus, Pseudomonas,* and resistant strains of *E. coli.* When infecting organisms are resistant to kanamycin, colistin, ampicillin, and other well-established antimicrobials, two newer drugs may be useful. Carbenicillin is effective in urinary tract infections caused by *Pseudomonas* or by strains of *Proteus* that are resistant to ampicillin. Gentamicin has a broad gram-negative spectrum that includes *Pseudomonas.* Since wide use of these newer agents will undoubtedly result in an increase in the number of resistant strains, they should be reserved for infections that are resistant to other drugs.

In patients with diminished renal function, dosage schedules must be altered if the drug to be used is excreted by the kidneys. Specific recommendations for these alterations have been published by Kunin and others.

In acute, uncomplicated infections controlled studies have demonstrated that 10 days of treatment are as effective as 2 months of treatment in eradicating bacteriuria and preventing recurrences. Most initial infections will show clinical improvement within 24 hours and sterile urine within a few days.

A "cure" is determined by several negative cultures following discontinuation of therapy.

The patient should be followed with repeated urinalysis and cultures for at least 2 years, since symptomatic or asymptomatic recurrences of bacteriuria are common. The optimal duration of therapy for recurrent or chronic infections has not been established, but many authorities recommend a period of 1 to 6 months. If long-term prophylaxis is to be used, acidifying agents have the advantage of not promoting superinfection.

Recognition and treatment of an associated urologic abnormality are mandatory; complete radiologic and urologic evaluation should be undertaken in every patient shown to have significant bacteriuria. IVU may be performed within a week of diagnosis. Voiding cystourethrogram should not be done until the urine is sterile, to avoid obtaining positive results which may be due to the infection rather than to an intrinsic abnormality. In patients with obstructive or other urologic anomalies, there may be no response to therapy until the underlying lesion has been corrected. It should be emphasized that restricting the radiographic investigation to patients who have had pyuria or symptoms or a past history of infection will result in overlooking children with important and correctable urologic abnormalities.

There is no unanimity of opinion on what should be done when certain urologic or radiographic abnormalities are found. Perhaps the most controversial of these is the presence of ureteral reflux, which can be transient or medically reversible and which is not invariably corrected by surgical intervention. The best indications for surgery in a patient with reflux would seem to be loss of renal parenchyma, progressive ureteral dilatation, or infection that does not respond to adequate medical therapy. Certainly it has become clear that the surgical correction of apparent bladder neck obstruction often is of no benefit to the patient, and major surgery of uncertain value should be reserved for the most difficult cases or those in whom anatomic obstruction is unquestionable. In the case of distal urethral obstruction, a controlled trial of meatotomy in girls with meatal stenosis demonstrated no effect of the procedure in lowering the recurrence rate of UTI.

COURSE AND PROGNOSIS. A UTI may represent (1) an isolated single episode of infection of the upper or lower urinary tract, (2) one of many recurrent acute infections, or (3) an acute episode in the course of chronic infection.

The symptomatic, uncomplicated UTI responds quickly to therapy or may improve spontaneously. Nevertheless, one-third or more may relapse within 1 year. Although UTI associated with uropathy may not be curable until there is correction of the underlying abnormality, subjective symptoms and urinary findings may disappear with treatment, only to return when therapy is discontinued.

Although some studies have indicated that the severity rather than the rate of recurrence is related to the presence or absence of underlying uropathy, a much higher rate of recurrence has been observed in most studies of patients with urologic abnormality. In the great majority of recurrences the infective organism differs from the initial one. Thus recurrence usually represents new infection rather than relapse of latent infection. Several retrospective studies suggest that the prognosis of even single urinary tract infections is guarded in that an appreciable proportion of patients will have asymptomatic, continued bacterial infection, leading eventually to chronic pyelonephritis.

Although the urine will be rendered sterile by treatment in 75 to 80 percent of patients with chronic pyelonephritis, the infection almost always recurs, and patients with bilateral disease may progress ultimately to renal failure. In cases of unilateral chronic pyelonephritis, with either hypertension or severe recurrent disease, nephrectomy may be curative.

Xanthogranulomatous Pyelonephritis

In this disease the renal parenchyma is wholly or regionally replaced by inflammatory tissue, consisting of masses of lipid-laden histiocytes, surrounded by mononuclear infiltrates and fibrosis. Several cases have been reported in childhood. Etiology is unknown. The disease usually is preceded by long-term, low-grade urinary infection, often with *B. proteus,* with local suppuration, microobstruction, and lithiasis. The clinical signs are those of UTI and of an increasing renal mass. On x-ray an enlarged nonfunctioning kidney is found, usually with calyceal deformity. Treatment consists of nephrectomy.

Renal Tuberculosis

Tuberculosis is now a rare form of pyelonephritis in childhood. It occurs by hematogenous spread from primary lesions in the lungs or infected cervical nodes; however, the primary lesion may heal before renal involvement is evident.

Initially tubercles form in the glomeruli of both kidneys. Most of these heal spontaneously. Only 4 to 5 percent of lesions progress to the point of slough, with shedding of organisms and white blood cells in the urine. With progression, the medulla is colonized; this secondary lesion is usually unilateral. Tubercles coalesce and caseate and, as their contents slough, a paracalyceal cavity becomes evident on IVU and there is marked increase in the excretion of white cells, red cells, and organisms in the urine. The time lag from initial seeding to demonstrable calyceal deformity may range from months to years. Gradually an entire pyramid may become caseated; if the caseum is retained it creates a roundish, solidified, sometimes calcified bulge; if the caseum is evacuated, a jagged cavity appears. With time, the cavity may contract and a capsular indentation will mark its emplacement.

The infection may spread across the pelvic cavity to other calyces or down to the ureter and bladder. Involvement of the ureter may cause stricture, rigidity, and proximal dilatation. Tuberculous cystitis occurs in most patients with moderately advanced renal tuberculosis, producing typical trigonitis and disseminated ulceration. If the inflammation penetrates through the mucosa into the muscle, fibrosis will result in a rigid, contracted malfunctioning bladder.

In male children with advanced renal tuberculosis the prostate, vas, and epididymis may be infected. Presenting symptoms are dysuria, loin pain, or painless hematuria.

Tuberculosis of the urinary tract often evolves insidiously; over a quarter of pediatric cases are asymptomatic and are discovered by the incidental finding of leucocyturia; in others it is discovered by doing routine urine cultures following pulmonary or miliary tuberculosis.

Treatment is usually medical. Even nonfunctioning kidneys are now left in situ and observed, provided the urine can be sterilized. Hypertension, secondary infection of advanced tubercular lesions, or intractable pain are indications for surgery.

During therapy, urinalysis, ESR, cultures, and IVU should be repeated every 4 to 6 months; similar tests are done at yearly intervals following cessation of therapy. Improved general state, return of urine to normal, and repeated negative cultures indicate success of treatment. Following a 2-year course of therapy over 85 percent of cases remain negative for 5 to 10 years.

Perinephritis and Perinephric Abscess

Perinephritis is an infection of the tissue surrounding the kidney; it is usually unilateral, and may occur at any age. There is a slight preponderance of females.

ETIOLOGY.   Perinephritis probably represents the result of hematogenous spread. However, it may occur after blunt local trauma, or by extension from a renal abscess, pyelonephritis, or an adjacent osteomyelitic focus.

CLINICAL MANIFESTATIONS.   Onset may be abrupt, with chills, high fever, and prostration, or insidious, with a variable period of flank tenderness, pain, low-grade fever, and the gradual development of psoas spasm. At the height of disease there is marked lumbar pain, spasm, lameness, persistent flexion of the thigh, indefinite local swelling, and a fluctuating temperature. If untreated the symptoms may persist for many weeks, followed by spontaneous resolution. In two-thirds of cases suppuration occurs with formation of an abscess, which may rupture into the peritoneal cavity, viscera, thorax, urinary tract, iliocostal space, or groin.

DIAGNOSIS.   Urinary abnormalities are present mainly in cases which occur as a complication of pyelonephritis. Radiography may show edema around the kidney, an obliterated psoas shadow, scoliosis with concavity facing the affected side, and sometimes atelectasis and pleural fluid in the corresponding hemithorax. The kidney usually is displaced anteriorly, caudally, and laterally. On fluoroscopy there may be a decreased diaphragmatic excursion on the affected side, and IVU reveals markedly decreased renal excursion and sometimes pelvic deformation. Diagnosis may be confirmed by needle aspiration.

TREATMENT. Treatment consists of analgesics and appropriate chemotherapy. If the responsible organism has not been identified by culture of blood or urine, antibiotics covering a broad range of organisms including staphylococci should be administered. Surgical drainage may be required. Prognosis usually is excellent.

Balanoposthitis

Balanoposthitis is an inflammation of the glans and of the prepuce which may occur at any age. It originates from poor local hygiene, infected regional dermatitis, or urethritis; it may also follow a combination of mechanical and infectious factors, such as phimosis, forceful manipulation of the foreskin, and masturbation.

The inflamed glans and prepuce are red, painful, edematous, and purulent. The meatus may be narrowed or encrusted, with resultant dysuria. The infection usually does not extend into the urinary tract.

Treatment consists of sitz-baths, irrigations, and local applications of antibiotics in solution or ointment. Systemic therapy rarely is necessary. A dorsal slit of the foreskin may be required when the edema is such that the preputial cavity cannot be exposed. Circumcision may be advisable but only after recovery from the acute episode.

Urethritis

Urethritis usually presents as an inflammation of the distal two-thirds of the urethra, with dysuria, frequency, leucocyturia, and urethral discharge. Urine voided initially is positive, while midstream specimens may be negative. Similarly, a comparison of spontaneously voided urine with that obtained by catheterization may confirm the diagnosis.

Most instances of urethritis are nonspecific or nonbacterial, but gonococcal urethritis is not uncommon. It may be seen in infants although most cases occur in patients over 7 years of age. Infection in older patients in nearly all cases is the result of direct sexual encounter or handling of the genitalia by an infected person. The symptoms of gonococcal urethritis are more severe than those of nonbacterial urethritis. Extension up the urethra may produce cystitis, prostatitis, or epididymitis. Reiter's triad

(conjunctivitis, arthritis, and urethritis) is very rare in children. Gonococcal vaginitis is also seen.

Diagnosis is made by stained smear and culture of urethral discharge, and occasionally urine culture and stain may also be positive. Treatment consists of appropriate antibiotic therapy.

Prostatitis and Prostatic Abscess

Prostatitis is a rare entity in childhood. It may occur as an extension of tuberculosis or gonococcal urethritis, or be of nonspecific bacterial origin. Presenting symptoms are frequency, dysuria, leucocyturia, terminal hematuria, perineal pain, and fever. Diffuse edema and tenderness are evident on rectal examination. Cultures of the uretheral discharge should be obtained, preferably following prostatic massage.

Prostatic abscess occurs mainly in infancy and is believed to originate by hematogenous spread. The causative organisms are usually staphylococci or coliforms. Treatment consists of incision and drainage combined with chemotheraphy.

Nonspecific Vulvo Vaginitis

This term is applied to a group of infections affecting the vulva, vagina, and often the urethra. Nonspecific vaginitis may be seen at any age, even in infancy, but is most frequent after the second year of life. A local cause is usually responsible, such as pinworms, scabies, a local lesion of varicella, or, most commonly, poor hygiene. It may follow local trauma, especially from the introduction of foreign bodies. Masturbation may be a contributing cause. Unexplained self-limited attacks frequently occur in otherwise healthy girls.

Urinary frequency or enuresis is sometimes seen and may be the presenting symptom. The disease generally begins as a subacute catarrhal inflammation, the discharge being the first and often the only symptom. It is white or yellowish and rarely profuse; in some cases a foul odor is present. Blood-stained discharge often results from a foreign body. When the discharge is abundant, there may be excoriations of the labia and the skin of the thighs. The mucous membranes are swollen and red. Microscopic examination of the discharge usually shows fewer pus cells and more epithelial cells than in gonorrhea. Organisms may be numerous or comparatively infrequent, and it is common to observe several types in a single preparation, i.e., both cocci and bacilli, gram-positive as well as gram-negative. Diphtheroids and *E. coli* are found in the great majority of cases, with a doubtful pathogenic role. Among the organisms of etiologic significance occasionally encountered are beta hemolytic and other forms of streptococci, *Staphylococcus aureus,* and trichomonas. With hemolytic streptococcal infections the same strain is at times recovered from the nose and throat in association with a respiratory infection.

Simple cleansing measures consisting of sitz-baths and local irrigations with warm saline solution should be prescribed. In some cases these alone will cause the condition to disappear within a few days. Antibacterial agents given by mouth may be dramatically effective in cases which accompany a respiratory infection; they should be used also in cases with associated lymph node enlargement and those resistant to local therapy. Specific local therapy includes instillation of acidifying solutions, such as dilute acetic acid (vinegar) and introduction into the vagina of urethral suppositories of 0.2 percent nitrofurazone or aminoacridine. The latter treatment is especially effective against trichomonas. Mycotic infections may be treated with topical administration of 0.5 percent gentian violet or nystatin. In refractory or recurrent cases the possibility of a foreign body must be investigated thoroughly.

REFERENCES

Allen, T. D. Pathogenesis of urinary tract infections in children. New Eng. J. Med., 273:1421, 1472, 1965.

Andersen, H. J., Hanson, L. A., Lincoln, K., Orskov, I., Orskov, F., and Winberg, J. Studies of urinary tract infections in infancy and childhood. IV. Relation of the coli antibody titre to clinical picture and to serological type of infecting *Escherichia coli* in acute, uncomplicated urinary tract infections. Acta Paediat. Scand., 54:247, 1965.

Andriole, V. T., and Epstein, F. H. Prevention of pyelonephritis by water diuresis: evidence for the role of medullary hypertonicity in promoting renal infection. J. Clin. Invest., 44:73, 1965.

Aoki, S., Imamura, S., Aoki, M., and McCabe, W. R. "Abacterial" and bacterial pyelonephritis. Immunofluorescent localization of bacterial antigen. New Eng. J. Med., 281:1375, 1969.

Bank, N., and Bailine, S. H. Urinary beta-glucuronidase activity in patients with urinary tract infection. New Eng. J. Med., 272:70, 1965.

Beeson, P. B., and Rowley, D. Role of natural inhibitors in mechanisms of localization of bacteria in kidney. *In* Quinn, E. L., and Kass, E. H., eds., Henry Ford Hospital International Symposium on the Biology of Pyelonephritis. Boston, Little, Brown and Co., 1960, p. 433.

Bulger, R. J., and Kirby, W. M. M. Simple tests for significant bacteriuria. Arch. Intern. Med., 112:742, 1963.

Cohen, S. N., and Kass, E. H. A simple method for quantitative urine culture. New Eng. J. Med., 277:176, 1967.

Cox, C. E., and Hinman, F., Jr. Experiments with induced bacteriuria, vesical emptying and bacterial growth on mechanism of bladder defense to infection. J. Urol., 86:739, 1961.

DeLuca, F. G., Fisher, J. H., and Swenson, O. Review of recurrent urinary tract infections in infancy and early childhood. New Eng. J. Med., 268:75, 1963.

Etzwiler, D. D. Incidence of urinary-tract infections among juvenile diabetics. J.A.M.A., 191:81-83, 1965.

Grossi, M. T., and Buchman, M. I. Vaginitis in children. Amer. J. Dis. Child., 97:613, 1959.

Hatch, C. S., and Cockett, A. T. K. Xanthogranulomatous pyelonephritis. J. Urol., 92:585, 1964.

Hauschka, M. S., Netter, E., and Rubin, M. I. Urinary tract infection in children. II. Identification of Escherichia Coli O antibodies in serum of patients. Amer. J. Dis. Child., 109:238, 1965.

Hodges, C. V. Chronic urethritis in girls. J.A.M.A., 149:753, 1952.

Hodgman, J. E., Schwartz, A., and Thrupp, L. D. Bacteriuria in the premature infant. Pediat. Res., 1:303, 1967.

Hodson, C. J. Coarse pyelonephritic scarring or "atrophic pyelonephritis." Proc. Roy. Soc. Med., 58:785, 1965.

——— Radiologic diagnosis of renal involvement. *In* O'Grady, F., and Brumfill, W., eds., Urinary Tract Infection. London, Oxford Univ. Press, 1968, Chap. 13.

Holland, N. H., and West, C. D. Prevention of recurrent urinary tract infections in girls. Amer. J. Dis. Child., 105:560, 1963.

Houston, I. B. Pus cell and bacterial counts in diagnosis of urinary tract infection in childhood. Arch. Dis. Child., 38:600, 1963.

——— Urinary white cell excretion in childhood. Arch. Dis. Child., 40:313, 1965.

Kalmanson, G. M., and Guze, L. B. Role of protoplasts in pathogenesis of pyelonephritis. J.A.M.A., 190:1107, 1964.

Kunin, C. M. Emergence of bacteriuria, proteinuria, and asymptomatic urinary tract infections among a population of school girls followed for 7 years. Pediatrics, 41:968-976, 1968.

——— The natural history of recurrent bacteriuria in school girls. New Eng. J. Med., 282:26, 1970.

——— Deutscher, R., and Paquin, A., Jr. Urinary tract infection in school children: an epidemiologic, clinical and laboratory study. Medicine, 43:91, 1964.

——— and McCormack, R. C. An epidemiologic study of bacteriuria and blood pressure among nuns and working women. New Eng. J. Med., 278:635-642, 1968.

——— Southall, I., Paquin, A. J. Epidemiology of urinary tract infections. New Eng. J. Med., 263:817-823, 1960.

——— Zacha, E., Paquin, A. J. Urinary tract infections in school children. I. Prevalence of bacteriuria and associated urologic findings. New Eng. J. Med., 266:1287-1296, 1962.

Lattimer, J. K. Current concepts—renal tuberculosis. New Eng. J. Med., 273:208, 1965.

Lincoln, K., and Winberg, J. Studies of urinary tract infection in infancy and childhood. II. Quantitative estimation of bacteriuria in unselected neonates with special reference to the occurrence of asymptomatic infections. Acta Paediat., 53:307, 1964.

——— and Winberg, J. Studies of urinary tract infection in infancy and childhood. III. Quantitative estimation of cellular excretion in unselected neonates. Acta Paediat., 53:447, 1964.

Lystad, A., and Gardborg, O. Quantitative bacteriological examination of urine in children with urinary tract infection. Acta Paediat., 52:277, 1963.

Macauley, D., and Sutton, R. N. P. The prognosis of urinary infections in childhood. Lancet, 2:1318, 1957.

MacDonald, R. A., Levitin, H., Mallory, G. K., and

Kass, E. H. Relation between pyelonephritis and bacterial counts in the urine. New Eng. J. Med., 256: 915, 1957.

Matsaniotis, N., Danelatou-Athanassiadou, C., Katerelos, C., Hartokalis, P., and Apostolopoulou, E. Low urinary glucose concentration: A reliable index of urinary tract infection. J. Pediat., 78:851, 1971.

McCabe, W. R., and Jackson, G. G. Treatment of pyelonephritis—bacterial, drug and host factors in success or failure among 252 patients. New Eng. J. Med., 272:1037, 1965.

McCarthy, J. M., and Pryles, C. V. Clean voided and catheter neonatal urine specimens. Bacteriology in the male and female neonate. Amer. J. Dis. Child., 106: 473, 1963.

Moore, T., and Hira, N. R. The role of the female urethra in infections of the urinary tract. Brit. J. Urol., 37:25, 1965.

Nelson, J. D., and Peters, P. C. Suprapubic aspiration of urine in premature and term infants. Pediatrics, 36:132, 1965.

Netter, E. Bacteriology and immune response in urinary tract infections. Pediat. Clin. N. Amer., 2:517, 1964.

Neumann, C. G., and Pryles, C. V. Pyelonephritis in infants and children: autopsy experience at the Boston City Hospital 1933-1960. Amer. J. Dis. Child., 104: 215, 1962.

Norden, C. W., and Kass, E. H. Bacteriuria of Pregnancy—A critical appraisal. Ann. Rev. Med., 19:431-470, 1968.

North, A. F. Bacteriuria in children with acute febrile illness. J. Pediat., 63:408-411, 1963.

O'Brien, N. G., Carroll, R., Donovan, D. E., and Dundon, S. P. Bacteriuria and leucocyte excretion in the newborn. J. Irish Med. Ass., 61:267, 1968.

O'Grady, F., and Brumfill, W., eds. Urinary Tract Infection. London, Oxford Univ. Press, 1968.

Pawlowski, J. M., Bloydorf, J. W., and Kimmelstiel, P. Chronic pyelonephritis—a morphologic and bacteriologic study. New Eng. J. Med., 268:965, 1963.

Pometta, D., Rees, S. B., Younger, D., and Kass, E. H. Asymptomatic bacteriuria in diabetes mellitus. New Eng. J. Med., 276:1118-1121, 1967.

Pryles, C. V. The diagnosis of urinary tract infection. Pediatrics, 26:441, 1960.

——— Atkin, M. D., Morse, T. S., and Welch, K. J. Comparative bacteriologic study of urine obtained from children by percutaneous suprapubic aspiration of the bladder and by catheter. Pediatrics, 24:983, 1959.

——— and Luden, D. The bacteriology of the urine in infants and children with gastroenteritis. Pediatrics, 28:877, 1961.

——— and Steg, N. Specimens of urine obtained from young girls by catheter versus voiding. A comparative study of bacterial cultures, gram stains, and bacterial counts in paired specimens. Pediatrics, 23:441, 1959.

——— Wherrett, B. A., and McCarthy, J. M. Urinary tract infections in infants and children. Long term prospective study: interim report on result of six weeks chemotherapy. Amer. J. Dis. Child., 108:1, 1964.

Randolph M. F., and Greenfield, M. The incidence of asymptomatic bacteriuria and pyuria in infancy. J. Pediat., 65:57, 1964.

——— and Greenfield, M. Lower urinary tract obstruction in normal male children. Amer. J. Dis. Child., 110:523, 1965.

Rollestan, G. L., Shannon, F. T., and Utley, W. L. F. Relationship of infantile vesico-ureteric reflux to renal damage. Brit. Med. J., 1:460-463, 1970.

Saeed, S. M., and Fine, G. Xanthogranulomatous pyelonephritis. Amer. J. Clin. Path., 39:616, 1963.

Sanford, J. P., and Barnett, J. A. Immunologic responses in urinary tract infection. Prognostic and diagnostic evaluation. J.A.M.A., 192:587, 1965.

Shannon, F. T. Vesico-ureteric reflux and renal papillary necroses. Presented at Symposium on Pyelonephritis, Melbourne, Australia, March, 1970.

Smellie, J. M., Hodson, C. J., Edwards, D., Normand, I. C. S. Clinical and radiological features of urinary infection in childhood. Brit. Med. J., 2:1222-1226, 1964.

Spark, H., Travis, L. B., Dodge, W. F., Daeschner, C. W., Jr., and Hopps, H. C. The prevalence of pyelonephritis in children at autopsy. Pediatrics, 30:737, 1962.

Steele, R. E. Jr., Leadbetter, G. W., Jr., and Crawford, J. D. Prognosis of childhood urinary tract infection. The current status of patients hospitalized between 1940 and 1950. New Eng. J. Med., 269:883, 1963.

Tallgren, L. G., and von Bonsdorff, C. H. The effect of varying the pH level upon sensitivity of urinary bacteria to antibiotics. Acta Med. Scand., 178:543, 1965.

Tidstrom, B. Urinary protein in glomerulonephritis and pyelonephritis. Acta Med. Scand., 174:385, 1963.

Wechsler, H. Renal tuberculosis. In Strauss, M. B., and Welt, L. G., eds., Diseases of the Kidney. Boston, Little, Brown and Co., 1963, p. 980.

Winberg, J. Renal function studies in infants and children with acute non-obstructive urinary tract infections. Acta Paediat. Scand., 48:577, 1959.

22.17

UROLOGY

SELWYN B. LEVITT

Congenital Urogenital Pathology

General Considerations

CLINICAL PRESENTATION. The nature of the anomaly and the age of the child are the most important factors determining the mode of presentation of congenital urogenital disorders. Anomalies of the external genitalia, such as hypospadias (Fig. 16), epispadias (Fig. 17), extrophy (Figs. 18 and 19), and ambiguous genitalia (Figs. 20 and 21), are strikingly obvious at birth. Internal anomalies, however, are much less simple to diagnose and the physician must be aware of the associated conditions that should arouse suspicion of their possibile presence.

The genitourinary tract is involved in as many as 30 to 40 percent of children with congenital anomalies of other systems. Oligohydramnios should suggest the possibility of renal agenesis, severe hypoplasia, or complete bladder outflow obstruction,

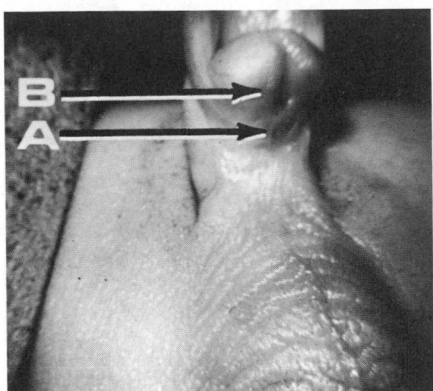

Fig. 16. Hypospadias. Distal penile meatus (A) with blind glandular sinus (B), chordee, and dorsal preputial hood (classical cobra-head appearance).

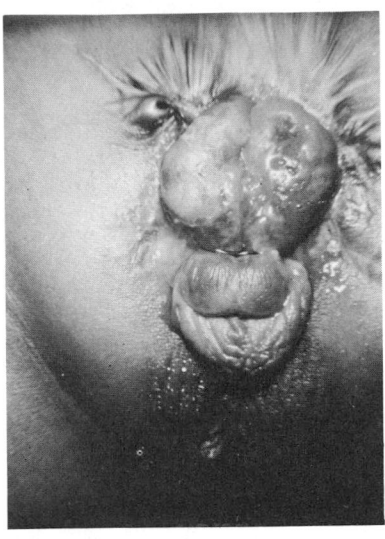

Fig. 18. Exstrophy. Epispadias in a male.

since fetal urine contributes significantly to the formation of amniotic fluid. The classic Potter facies (Fig. 22), characterized by low-set ears, hypertelorism, pronounced epicanthal folds, flattened nose, and micrognathos, may also be present in these patients.

Small deformed ears are a common concomitant of renal anomalies, often on the ipsilateral side if the renal lesion is unilateral. A single umbilical artery, estimated to occur in 0.52 percent of infants, was shown by Feingold and associates to be associated with urinary tract anomalies in 33 percent of the cases they studied with intravenous urography.

Absent abdominal musculature together with undescended testes are associated consistently with marked dilation of the urinary tract; these constitute the triad of the "prune belly syndrome" (Fig. 23). An infant with a major anomaly, such as an anorectal malformation, abnormality of the cloaca, or tracheoesophageal fistula, should be investigated for associated urologic anomalies. Myelomeningoceles and sacral deformities are often accompanied by neurogenic vesical dysfunction; if three or more segments of the sacrum are absent, the association is invariable. A lax anus with absent anocutaneous reflex confirms this suspicion.

Kidneys in the normal neonate are palpable, owing to their low lumbar position and to the minimal resistance of the abdominal wall. Large kidneys suggest either cystic disease of the kidneys or, less frequently, hydronephrosis; neoplasms occur but are much less common.

The most common presentation of an obstructive anomaly in the neonate or older infant is unexplained fever, often associated with vomiting and

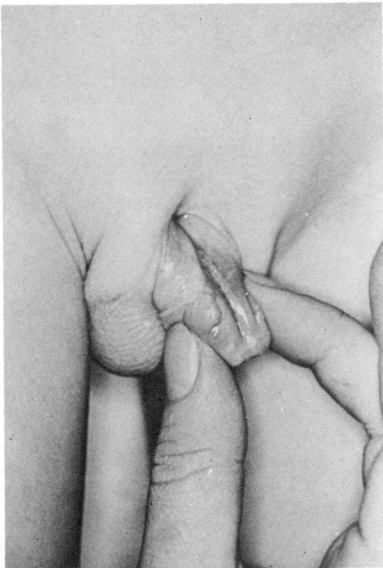

Fig. 17. Penopubic variety of epispadias in a patient with urinary incontinence.

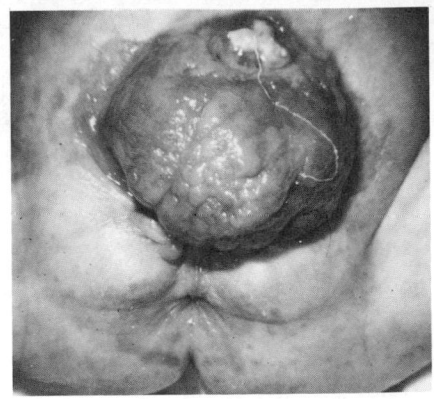

Fig. 19. Exstrophy. Epispadias in a female.

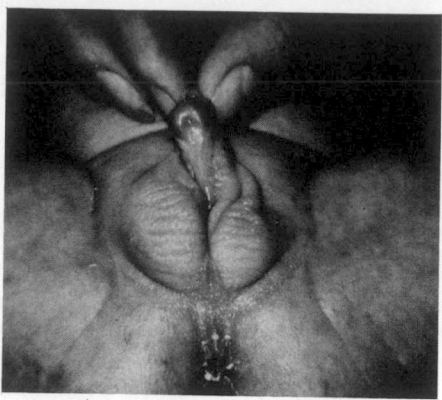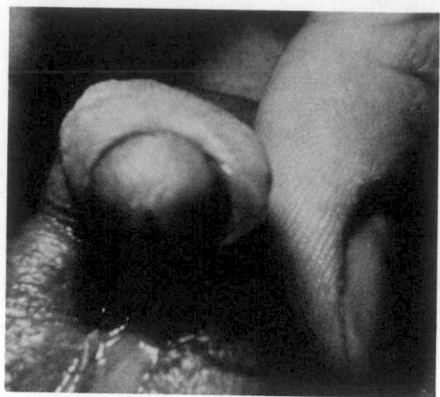

Fig. 20 (*Left*) and 21 (*Right*). Ambiguous genitalia, showing bifid scrotum or rugated labia majora, penis with chordee, and scrotal hypospadias or hypertrophied clitoris with urogenital sinus.

diarrhea. Symptoms and signs of obstruction per se are rare modes of presentation before toilet training has been achieved. The child's stream is rarely observed by the parent and diapers conceal the normal intermittent pattern of micturition because they are usually wet. Thus the opportunity to observe a poor urinary stream or dribbling may be missed. Even in the older child or teen-ager, congenital obstructions frequently are not recognized since the individual has *never* micturated with a normal, uninterrupted stream and thus may not recognize his abnormal pattern of voiding.

Obstructive anomalies not detected at birth often present later with signs and symptoms of urinary tract infection. Initial treatment of these infections may produce a good symptomatic response, satisfying both patient and physician. Unsuspected underlying pathology may then continue to take its toll and to progress silently until either frequent reinfection or evidence of renal failure leads to further investigation. If the lesion had been detected at the time of

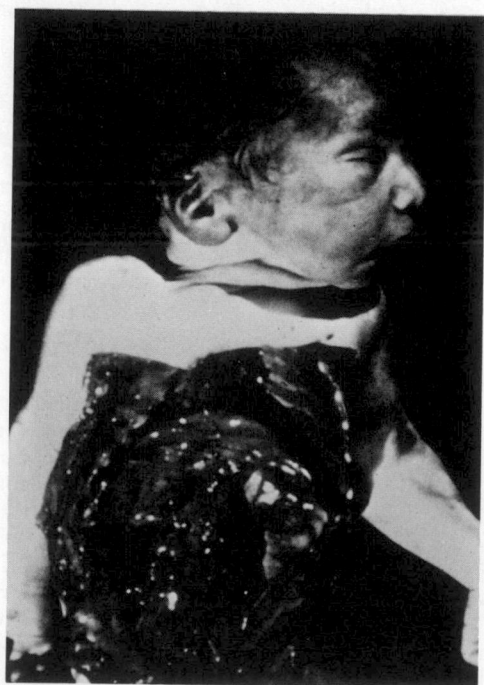

Fig. 22. Potter facies in a patient with renal agenesis, showing low-set ears, pronounced epicanthal folds, flattened nose, and micrognathos.

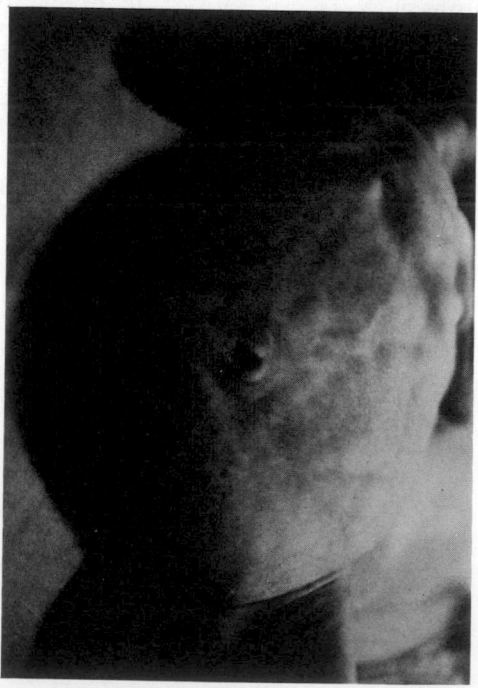

Fig. 23. Prune belly syndrome, showing distended abdomen with wrinkling of the skin.

the original infection it might have yielded admirably to corrective surgery, with a good anatomic and functional result. Thus, despite opinions to the contrary, it is our strong belief that intravenous urography and voiding cystourethrography are mandatory studies in any child, male or female, who has had a documented urinary tract infection.

DIAGNOSTIC PROCEDURES. Intravenous urography is used routinely for evaluation of the urinary tract and is a safe procedure at all ages. Mortality is extremely rare; for example, only one death has occurred in the vast experience at the Hospital for Sick Children, London, in the past 30 years.

In performing urography, the intravenous route of injection is preferable; subcutaneous injection, such as in the subscapular region, occasionally may be necessary but it should be appreciated that the quality of visualization may be lost with this technique. Positioning is important in order to move gas-filled bowel away from the renal areas. Prone films and filling of the stomach with a feed or carbonated drink often are helpful. When there is poor visualization with a standard dose, urography should be repeated with a larger dose. Films taken immediately after injection, during the vascular phase of the study, show a total bodygram effect from opacification of vascular tissue. Masses which are highly vascular opacify whereas cystic lesions are outlined by a negative shadow. This technique is useful also in demonstrating parenchymal thickness in hydronephrosis.

Formerly, the finding on conventional urography of one "nonfunctioning" and one normal kidney led to ablative surgery rather than plastic reconstruction. Better visualization with demonstration of adequate parenchymal thickness has led to more conservative reconstructive procedures with very encouraging results. When using a high dose, it must be recognized that the rapid injection of a large amount of contrast material, with its large osmolar load, may be hazardous to the patient with cardiac impairment, due to volume overload, and to the dehydrated infant, in whom vascular collapse may occur during the diuretic phase of the study.

Voiding cystourethrography should be regarded as an obligatory part of the radiologic work-up of any child with a documented urinary tract infection or with suspected obstructive uropathy. It is preferable, although not always possible, to do the study in the unanesthetized child. Some physicians feel that in the acutely ill or uremic child with suspected obstructive uropathy, antibiotics should be administered 24 to 48 hours before the cystourethrogram, in an attempt to prevent acute exacerbations of pyelonephritis and gram-negative septicemia. A number 5 or 8 pediatric feeding tube makes an ideal catheter for infants or toddlers of either sex; it is simple to pass and is atraumatic. In older children a Foley catheter may be more appropriate. Lubasporin is a satisfactory antibiotic-impregnated lubricant. A 12 to 15 percent solution of a water-miscible contrast medium such as diatrizoate is used. Fluoroscopy provides maximum information regarding vesicoureteral reflux, bladder configuration and function, as well as urethral anatomy; properly done it also involves the least amount of radiation. The initial specimen of urine obtained by catheterization during this procedure should be cultured.

Voiding cystourethrography has emerged as the best and most accurate indicator of urethral pathology in the male. In the female, however, the urethral configuration as seen on a single voiding film may be overinterpreted as indicative of obstructive disease. Urethral patterns in the female previously regarded as obstructive have been found to correlate poorly with other indications of obstruction, such as residual urine, bladder trabeculation, bougie á boule urethral calibration, and pressure-flow studies. Sequential voiding with spot films, which show dynamic changes in the urethra, has provided an explanation for many of the urethrographic variations described as pathologic when recorded on a single film.

Ascendant lipiodol, a low-density contrast material in oily solution, can be injected together with the water-miscible contrast material when performing the cystogram. Since it floats on top of the urine rather than mixing with it, any residual noted on a film taken the following day suggests incomplete bladder emptying.

Aortography and selective renal angiography may be helpful in the differential diagnosis of abdominal masses. Inferior vena cavography has little value in pediatric urology; it may be useful in the diagnosis of renal vein thrombosis or to help to determine the extent of an abdominal mass.

Cystoscopy and retrograde urography in children must always be done under general anesthesia. It should be noted that high-dose urography may obviate the need for retrograde studies. The smallest possible instruments should be used in the male to prevent postendoscopy edema and difficulty with micturition. With the miniature instruments now available, no child should be denied a full urologic evaluation when it is indicated.

The Bladder and Urachus

EMBRYOLOGY. The urorectal septum divides the cloaca into a ventral vesicourethral segment and a dorsal rectal moiety. The upper half of the vesicourethral canal, which is continuous with the allantois, forms the definitive bladder. Normally the allantois undergoes retrogressive changes with complete obliteration of its lumen, the residual fibrous cord or *urachus* passing from the apex of the bladder to the umbilicus. Anomalous closure of the allantois most often results in a *patent urachus*, which appears clinically as a urinary fistula opening at the umbilicus. A small uncomplicated patent urachus may close spontaneously, but should it persist extraperitoneal excision and bladder closure is required. Other abnormalities include a urachal cyst, if the lumen is obliterated at both ends, a blind-ending urachal sinus, or a urachal diverticulum.

ANATOMY AND PHYSIOLOGY. The bladder detrusor is composed of interlacing bundles of smooth muscle fibers and elastic tissue which extend down into the posterior urethra. The muscular arrangement at the vesicourethral junction constitutes the bladder neck, which is no longer considered to be a true sphincter but rather an integral portion of the detrusor mechanism, the only true sphincter being the skeletal muscle of the urogenital diaphragm or external urinary sphincter.

Both the autonomic pelvic nerves and the somatic internal pudendal nerves emanate from the conus medullaris, which lies at the level of the first lumbar vertebra in the adult and slightly lower in the child. The conus contains the sacral segments of the spinal cord and is the integrating center for the spinal reflex for micturition (Fig. 24). This simple segmental reflex is modified by voluntary and involuntary impulses descending from the suprasegmental level; these may be facilitatory or inhibitory.

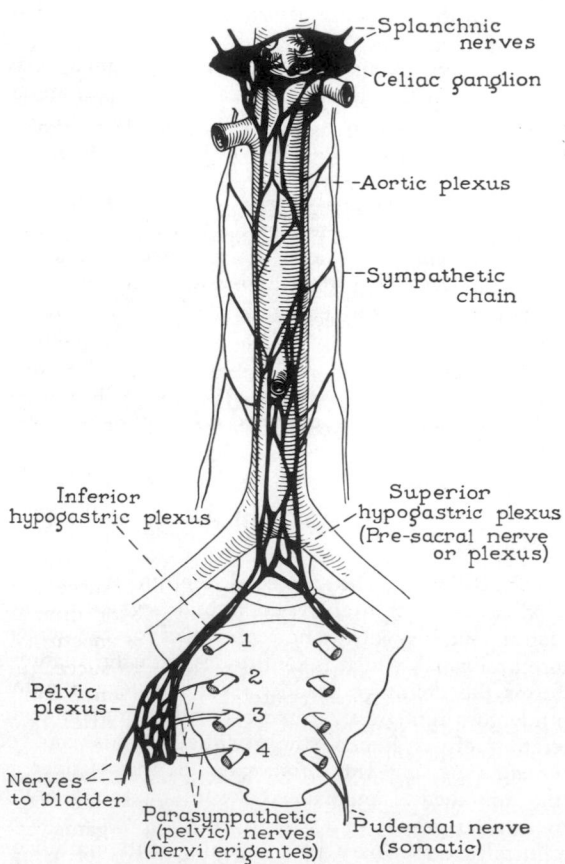

Fig. 24. Nerve supply of the bladder. (From Campbell and Harrison. *Urology*, 3rd ed., Vol. 1, p. 112. Courtesy of W. B. Saunders Company.)

Motor innervation to the detrusor is autonomic, predominantly parasympathetic, and is derived from sacral spinal segments 2, 3, and 4, which reach the bladder as the pelvic nerve or nervi erigentes. The sympathetic system from the lower thoracic and upper lumbar cord plays only a minor role. Proprioceptive (appreciation of bladder fullness) and exteroceptive (hot and cold sensation) impulses are carried by afferent fibers which return to the cord in the pelvic nerve. The somatic internal pudendal nerve (S 3 and 4) contains the afferent and efferent supply to the striated external sphincter and posterior urethra.

Normal bladder function, in which the bladder is emptied completely and voluntarily at intervals, depends upon an intact nerve supply as well as the inherent properties of the bladder muscle and elastic tissue. Reflex activity and sensation are under nervous control, whereas tone and rhythmic contractility do not require participation of the central nervous system.

During the first years of life the child's bladder empties reflexly at intervals varying from 30 minutes to 3 hours. Bowel actions and penile erections occur similarly. The infant who is always wet, whose diapers are damp within a few minutes of changing, and who is never seen to project his urine with force may have an abnormality in bladder function. Micturition following instillation of cold water into the bladder, the "ice water" test of Bors, indicates an intact autonomic reflex arc. An intact somatic arc is confirmed by a normal anocutaneous and bulbocavernosus reflex. Cystometry provides information concerning residual urine, bladder capacity, accommodation, and the threshold and force of the detrusor contraction.

URINARY RETENTION. In the newborn, urinary retention must be differentiated from true anuria. The neonate may not pass urine for 24 to 48 hours. The exact cause of this is undetermined but it may be related to deposition of urates or Tamm-Horsfall proteins in the renal tubules. The bladder does not become distended and no treatment is required. True retention in the male infant is most often due to temporary obliteration of the urethral meatus with epithelial debris, particularly when there is a coronal hypospadias associated with meatal stenosis. Probing of the meatus on the glans dorsal to the hypospadiac opening may reveal a blind sinus, which extends for a variable distance. Membranous or posterior urethral atresia as a cause of urinary retention is suspected by the inability to pass a catheter. Posterior urethral valves, though only an occasional cause of acute retention in the newborn, often will allow easy retrograde passage of a catheter. Voiding cystourethrography is the most accurate means of demonstrating the nature and site of these obstructions. In the female, hydrocolpos secondary to obstructing vaginal septae or an imperforate hymen occasionally may produce acute urinary retention.

In the older infant or toddler, acute retention is due to a variety of causes, including painful meatal ulcers in boys, fecal impaction with rectal distension, urethral strictures, vesical or urethral diverticuli, impacted urethral calculi, or urethral prolapse of lobules of a bladder tumor. Acute inflammatory lesions of the prostate or a prostatic abscess occasionally may be responsible.

Chronic retention of urine usually presents as overflow incontinence with a painless, overdistended, easily palpable suprapubic mass. Often renal failure or complicating infection is the factor that draws attention to the condition.

ENURESIS. All children lack voluntary bladder control during the first year or two of life. Daytime control is gained before nighttime continence, and by age 4 years most children have attained full control.

Enuresis is the repeated involuntary passage of urine beyond the age at which voluntary control is expected. It may be nocturnal or diurnal or both. It is termed primary when the child has never been dry for a sustained period of time, or termed acquired when control has been gained and then lost. Organic enuresis implies a recognizable underlying abnormality; functional or psychogenic enuresis implies its absence.

Functional nocturnal enuresis is an extremely common disorder, with an estimated prevalence in the United States of five million children. Blaufield and Douglas followed 5,380 children from birth and found that at age 6, 1.3 percent of boys and 4.1 percent of girls were still wet by day; 11.9 percent of boys and 8.4 percent of girls were bedwetters. Two years later nocturnal enuresis persisted in 8 percent of boys and 6.4 percent of girls. It is of interest that Levine reported that 1.2 percent of navy recruits were enuretic.

At all age levels, nocturnal enuresis is more common in boys. A familial factor is common. Gregor found one parent to have been enuretic in 47 percent of his cases; in 35 percent a sibling had enuresis. Socioeconomic factors also may play a role.

Children still enuretic at age 5 or 6 require careful evaluation to exclude organic causes. A detailed history will determine whether the child's only symptom is bedwetting. These cases fall almost exclusively into the functional group. Many enuretics, although wet only at night, have daytime urgency and frequency. Infection and bladder calculi must be considered, the latter being suggested by painful micturition. Other causes of frequency include chronic renal failure and diabetes mellitus and insipidus. Dribbling incontinence due to retention with overflow is excluded by abdominal palpation. Neurogenic bladders which never fill because of poor resistance at the bladder outlet are almost always associated with other somatic neurologic signs, such as perineal anesthesia and absent or poor rectal tone; bowel control also may be impaired, and footdrop and disturbances in gait are often evident. An absent sacrum is readily apparent, and other forms of spinal dysraphism such as diastometamyelia may be revealed by a pit or hairy mole on the back. An ectopic ureter

produces dribbling incontinence despite normal micturition at regular intervals. Incontinence associated with coughing or straining (stress variety) is uncommon in children but may occur with some forms of neurogenic bladder, epispadias, or following operations to relieve bladder neck or urethral obstruction.

A great number of theories have been advanced to explain the etiology of functional enuresis. These range along a spectrum beginning with subtle organic GU pathology as the causal agent in virtually every case, through theories that consider enuresis to be a neurologic or endocrine diathesis, to hypotheses that maintain that the symptom is related exclusively to psychiatric or sociologic factors (see Chap. 6).

Minor degrees of urethral and bladder neck obstruction have been described by some urologists. However, improper development of bladder capacity and uninhibited detrusor contractions as determined by cystometry are the urologic lesions most frequently cited. Abnormal detrusor function has been ascribed to delayed development of inhibitory control of the bladder reflex arc consequent to delayed myelinization of the central or peripheral nerves. Arnold believes that certain children have an "inborn familial diathesis toward uninhibited bladder contractions which expresses itself in the absence of tranquility of cerebral process."

Immature electroencephalographic patterns have been found in enuretic children. Some with electroencephalographic evidence of seizure activity were reported to have the most severe degrees of enuresis, and thus it has been suggested that enuresis in some cases may be an epileptic equivalent.

Inadequate nocturnal increase in ADH also has been postulated as a cause of enuresis. Breneman is of the conviction that food allergy is an important factor.

The behaviorists state that enuresis is a symptom of deficit and is due to a failure of conditioning. On the other hand, many psychiatrists consider enuresis a manifestation of antisocial aggressive behavior.

The numerous theories concerning the etiology of functional enuresis are matched by the diversity of treatments that have been proposed. These include bladder training with fluid restriction at night, drug therapy (including dilantin, dextroamphetamine, propantheline, and imipramine), psychotherapy, and urologic manipulation. The most uniformly successful treatments appear to be timed training for diurnal enuresis and alarm-bell conditioning for nocturnal wetting. Tofranil (imipramine) is the most successful drug for the functional enuretic. It is given 1 hour before bedtime in a dose of 25 to 50 mg. After 1 to 2 months, the dosage is gradually reduced.

In cases thought to be functional, intravenous urogram and voiding cystourethrogram are performed initially to exclude underlying organic pathology. Endoscopic and surgical methods of treatment are reserved for cases in which unquestionable pathology has been demonstrated. Such treatment thus is directed specifically at elimination of obstruction and only incidentally at the eradication of enuresis. Psychiatric treatment should be reserved for those children exhibiting other manifestations of behavior disorders and evident emotional disturbance.

It is wise to maintain a certain scepticism with regard to all methods of treatment. Barbour and colleagues found that 75 percent of children were cured over a period of 5 years but that the cure was not related to any particular type of treatment.

NEUROGENIC BLADDER. The most common cause of neurogenic bladder dysfunction in children is myelomeningocele. The incidence of spina bifida cystica in the United States has been reported to vary from 1.1 to 2.5 per 1,000 births; approximately 25 percent of these are stillborn. If immediate closure of the myelomeningocele is accomplished, more than 70 percent will survive one year and most will live into the second decade.

Although myelodysplasia is the commonest type of neurogenic bladder dysfunction occurring in children, other causes must not be overlooked. Agenesis of three or more sacral segments is associated invariably with severe loss of pelvic nerve supply. Operative trauma from excision of a sacrococcygeal tumor or from an abdominal-perineal pull-through procedure for Hirschsprung's disease or anorectal anomaly is not an uncommon cause of neurogenic bladder. Spinal dysraphism, traumatic paraplegia, extradural spinal cord metastases, and abscesses are rare causes. Neurogenic bladders occasionally develop after measles or other forms of viral encephalitis as well as following tuberculous meningitis.

More than 90 percent of myelomeningoceles involve the lumbosacral spine. Extensive myelodysplasia affects the whole sacral outflow, thus destroying the bladder reflex arc and rendering it an autonomous or lower motor type neurogenic bladder. In the complete form of this lesion there is no vesical sensation, no voluntary micturition, and no reflex bladder emptying. Detrusor contractions are initiated by bladder distension, are myogenic in nature, poorly coordinated, and result in inadequate bladder emptying. However, the extent of neural involvement in myelomeningocele is variable, seldom resulting in as complete a lesion as in traumatic paraplegia, so that some afferents and efferents usually are intact. When the sensory elements are more severely affected than the motor, there may be features of the atonic bladder. If the long tracts of the spinal cord are dysplastic above the level of the overt lesion, features of the uninhibited or upper motor neuron bladder may be present in addition.

Various classifications of the neurogenic bladder resulting from myelodysplasia have been offered. Two main types are recognized. In the first the bladder is flaccid, thin-walled, and free of trabeculations. Urethral resistance is low and does not allow the bladder to distend. Manual expression permits easy bladder expressibility. The upper tract usually is not dilated and infection is easily controlled. In the second type the bladder is grossly hypertrophied and

trabeculated and urethral resistance is high, so that manual expression is difficult and incomplete. The upper tract commonly is dilated and reflux frequently is present. Infection may be difficult to control. Many cases fall between these extremes, and the features of a given patient may change with time, in some instances as a result of secondary infection.

Examination should attempt to elicit a sensory level but in the newborn this is often difficult. Absence of perineal sensation and the anocutaneous reflex, with poor rectal tone, indicates efferent or motor denervation. However, preservation of perineal sensation does not necessarily mean that the efferents are intact.

Since renal failure is an important cause of death in these patients, treatment is directed toward preventing obstruction and infection. An intravenous urogram is done as soon as the back wound is healed. This examination identifies associated upper tract anomalies, which have been reported to be present in 20 percent of cases; in addition it establishes a base line for subsequent studies, which are done yearly until the child is stabilized and then biennially. A voiding cystourethrogram is done prior to the IVU to exclude reflux. Urine cultures are performed every 3 months. Suprapubic aspiration is the most reliable method of obtaining the urine. This procedure is particularly applicable in these children, since most have anesthesia of the suprapubic area.

Infections are treated with appropriate short courses of antibiotics. Long-term therapy is reserved for infections which recur frequently. The usual cause in such cases is inadequate bladder emptying due to high outlet resistance. This can be managed in a variety of ways; endoscopic resection of the bladder neck or YV plasty, external sphincterotomy, and overdilation of the urethra in the female are all accepted modes of therapy. The site of obstruction is usually at the external sphincter rather than the bladder neck and thus sphincterotomies in the male and overdilation in the female seem to be the most appropriate procedures. Urinary diversion is indicated in the patients with progressive upper tract dilation or in those with repeated severe infection with vesicoureteral reflux who have failed to respond to more conservative treatment.

Treatment is aimed not only at prolonging life, but also at improving the quality of life. This involves producing a bladder which will provide adequate dry periods between voidings. Constant wetting with its attendant malodour, excoriation, and bedsores will reduce patients to miserable social outcasts. If adequate dry periods cannot be attained with bladder training, including voiding on schedule, crede, and the surgical procedures mentioned, males are fitted with a penile collecting device. There is, of course, no adequate collecting device for females and thus in these patients, as well as in males who cannot tolerate an external device, a procedure to divert the urine must be performed. The optimum time for this is just before school age. The site of the stoma must be carefully chosen so as not to interefere with orthopedic appliances. The isolated ileal or sigmoid conduit is the best form of diversion but cutaneous ureterostomies may be preferable when the ureters are grossly dilated. Hip surgery, if indicated, should precede diversion since management of the stoma in a child with a double hip spica can present a formidable problem.

The Penis

PREPUCE. The preputial skin normally is redundant. In newborns the visceral surface frequently is adherent to the glans penis; these adhesions usually resolve spontaneously during infancy. Accumulation of smegma from the preputial glands admixed with retained urine may produce chemical irritation or become infected secondarily, resulting in balanitis or balanoposthitis. In such cases the adhesions are lysed, allowing retraction of the prepuce; release of the retained infected smegma and resolution of the inflammation with local treatment is then readily accomplished. Recurrent episodes of balanoposthitis or balanitis associated with inability to retract the prepuce because of a narrow preputial opening (phimosis) is best treated by elective circumcision after the acute inflammation has subsided.

Paraphimosis results in a patient with mild phimosis when the prepuce is retracted behind the glans, becomes edematous, and then cannot be reduced. If left untreated vascular obstruction results and gangrene of the glans can occur. Older children must be sedated in order to reduce the paraphimosis. Occasionally a dorsal slit through the constricted preputial ring is necessary. Circumcision should be delayed until the edema has resolved.

Circumcision is the commonest urologic operation performed in infancy and childhood. Extreme phimosis with ballooning of the prepuce on micturition, phimosis with complicating balanoposthitis, and an episode of paraphimosis are indications for circumcision. Campbell reported five fatalities in children with severe phimosis and secondary obstructive uremia.

Ritualistic circumcision of the neonate is practiced by Jews, among whom, it is interesting to note, carcinoma of the penis is virtually nonexistent. The prevalence of carcinoma of the cervix in the female partners of circumcised men also seems to be lower but this claim has not been confirmed.

Circumcision is not altogether a benign procedure. Complications include postoperative hemorrhage, which is not uncommon and may be alarming. Medical and religious authorities consider a recognized familial bleeding tendency as a definite contraindication. Partial or even complete amputation of the glans is not unknown, and extensive burning and subsequent sloughing of part of the penis may follow the use of diathermy. Excessive removal of penile skin can lead to scarring and contractures. Insuffi-

cient removal of mucosa can result in recurrent phimosis. Deeply placed sutures have produced urethral fistulae. Meatal ulcers due to ammoniac dermatitis and diaper rash are much more common in circumcised boys and may lead to meatal stenosis. Circumcision is contraindicated in boys with hypospadias or genital anomalies which might require preputial skin for later surgical reconstructions. The anesthetic risk for the older infant is low but cannot be disregarded. In a series of 90,000 circumcisions Gardner found a mortality rate of 0.018 percent.

HYPOSPADIAS. Hypospadias is a common urogenital anomaly in which the external urethral meatus lies on the ventral aspect of the penis proximal to the normal site (Fig. 16); it occurs in approximately 1 in 160 male children. The urethral groove normally closes ventrally by progressive fusion of the urogenital folds from behind forward. In patients with hypospadias it fails to complete its development. Because the posterior urethra develops from a separate embryologic anlage (the urogenital sinus), continence is never deficient. More than 50 percent of cases are of the minor glandular and subcoronal type. Penile, penoscrotal, and scrotal hypospadias account for 30 to 40 percent, and the remaining small number are of the perineal type. The minor forms frequently are associated with meatal stenosis. Other features include lack of normal ventral preputial skin, and chordee or the presence of fibrous bands which produce ventral curvature of the glans and penile shaft (Fig. 25). Together these features give the penis a hooded or cobra-head appearance. When the urethral meatus opens proximal to the penoscrotal junction, the scrotum remains incompletely fused; in the perineal type it is completely bifid.

There is a tendency for hypospadias to be familial. Other congenital anomalies of the urinary

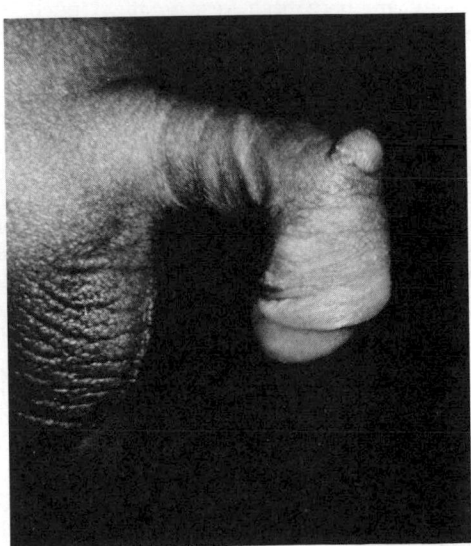

Fig. 25. Hypospadias. Erect penis showing marked chordee.

tract frequently are present and should be investigated by intravenous urography. Cryptorchidism occurs in about 15 percent of cases and often is bilateral. The severe forms of hypospadias, especially with incomplete scrotal fusion and undescended testes, should be evaluated carefully to exclude problems of intersex (see Sec. 16.11).

Treatment of glandular hypospadias initially is aimed at alleviating meatal stenosis if present. A dorsal meatotomy should be done as soon as the condition is diagnosed. In the neonate no anesthesia is required and the procedure can be done in the nursery simply by dividing the septum between the dorsal blind pit and the urethra itself. If there is no chordee nothing further need be done. However, excision of the redundant dorsal hood (a modified circumcision) will improve the cosmetic appearance of the penis considerably.

Patients with chordee require subsequent straightening of the penis, which is performed usually between 12 and 18 months of age. Urethroplasty to advance the urethral meatus is deferred until 3½ to 4½ years. This usually permits complete reconstruction before the child attends school. However, the parents must be cautioned that often more than two stages are required since fistulae and strictures are not uncommon.

The ultimate goal is a straight penis with a urethral meatus placed sufficiently distal to allow the child to stand when urinating and to direct his stream without difficulty. Such a result will permit normal coitus and the cosmetic appearance of the penis should be satisfactory.

EPISPADIAS-EXSTROPHY COMPLEX. Classical exstrophy of the bladder with epispadias is the commonest manifestation of a series of anomalies ranging from simple mild epispadias to complete cloacal exstrophy (Figs. 17, 18, 19). It occurs once in every 30 to 50,000 births and thus about 100 children with exstrophy are born each year in the United States. The ratio of males to females is 2 to 1. There is no prominent familial predisposition, although isolated cases of exstrophies occurring in the same family, in siblings, and in twins have been reported.

The anomaly results from a failure of midline fusion of the mesodermal structures in the infraumbilical abdominal wall. Muecke has reproduced the anomaly in chicks by placing a minute plastic disc over the cloacal membrane, obstructing mesodermal migration. Multiple organ systems in the lower abdomen are involved, including the genitourinary, musculoskeletal, and in the severest forms, the intestinal tract. In all there is shortening in the sagittal plane as well as midline failure, so that the umbilicus is displaced downwards, the anus forwards, and the scrotum is somewhat anteriorly situated and typically flat. The bladder is completely everted and the ureteral orifices can be seen to efflux urine, constantly bathing the abdominal wall and perineum. The penis is short and flat and the urethra appears as a short mucosal strip on the dorsum of the penis. The symphysis pubis and the recti muscles are widely diastased. There is almost always an umbilical hernia, and inguinal hernias are common. The weak pelvic floor commonly allows rectal prolapse, which may be severe. Upper urinary tract anomalies are unusual.

Treatment is aimed at preserving renal function, preventing the complications of continued incontinence which no appliance can control, construction of a penis in the male, and improving the appearance of the child. The continual incontinence and ulcerated inflamed exposed bladder renders most children with untreated exstrophy very irritable and bad tempered, which serves to accentuate their hernias and aggravate their rectal prolapse.

Pyelonephritis usually does not occur in early infancy, but with time infection and obstruction take their toll in untreated patients, about two-thirds dying before their twenty-first year. Those who survive have an increased liability to neoplastic change in the exposed bladder epithelium.

Early treatment consists of measures to protect the skin of the perineum and abdominal wall from excoriation. Vaseline gauze and various barrier creams in addition to frequent diaper changes are important. Definitive treatment involves primary closure of the bladder (with or without osteotomies) or urinary diversion. Bladder reconstruction results in good urinary control in only about 5 to 15 percent, and most of these subsequently require diversion for deterioration of the upper tracts secondary to obstruction, persistent infection, and bladder calculi. However, since in boys incontinence occasionally can be controlled with an external collecting device, closure may represent a reasonable compromise for those whose upper tracts remain stable and free of major infection. For boys who cannot be fitted with an incontinence device and for the incontinent girls, urinary diversion into an isolated ileal or sigmoid loop is the treatment of choice.

Children with uncomplicated epispadias usually are incontinent. Reconstructive bladder neck surgery together with closure of the urethra should be attempted. Williams reported on 27 such children in 1965; he achieved successful control in 70 percent of the girls and 47 percent of the boys. For those few children with epispadias but no incontinence, simple closure of the urethra suffices and a good cosmetic and functional result can be obtained.

The Testis

CRYPTORCHIDISM. The testes develop from the medial aspects of the urogenital ridges which extend from the thorax to the sacrum. By differential growth, with cranial degeneration and caudal differentiation, the testes come to lie opposite the internal inguinal rings by the sixth month of gestation. In the last trimester they traverse the inguinal canals and reach the scrotum. Scorer, on the basis of 1,700 examinations, defined a descended testis in the full-term neonate as one that with gentle traction can be coaxed 4 cm below the pubic arch, with 2½ cm as the minimum distance in prematures. Most testes descend fully within 6 weeks after birth in full-term infants and within 3 months in prematures. With this definition, he found the prevalence of cryptorchidism to be 30 percent in prematures, 4 percent in term infants, and 0.66 percent at 1 year of age. Since the prevalence of cryptorchidism in adults is between 0.28 and 0.8 percent, the formerly widely held concept that undescended testes frequently descend spontaneously and completely at puberty is untenable. Spontaneous complete descent after infancy is uncommon and even if it does occur the testis will have suffered degenerative changes proportionate in severity to its delay in reaching the scrotum. Late spontaneous descent, therefore, is neither to be expected nor desired.

Cryptorchidism is more common on the right side and is bilateral in approximately 20 percent of cases. There are two main types. In the incompletely descended variety the testis stops somewhere along its normal path of descent and may be found anywhere between the abdomen and upper part of the scrotum. Most of these are located at the superficial inguinal ring or within the inguinal canal. The second variety is the ectopic testis which is located most commonly in the superficial inguinal pouch between scarpas fascia and the external oblique aponeurosis. However, it may also be found in pubic, femoral, or perineal locations.

It is important to differentiate undescended testes from retractile testes since no treatment is required for the latter condition. In childhood an active cremasteric reflex elevates the testis in response to cold, stress, or merely palpation; however, careful examination reveals that it can be manipulated into the bottom of the scrotum. Failure to differentiate retractile from undescended testes has invalidated many statistical analyses of the prevalence of testicular undescent, its spontaneous resolution, and the response to gonadotropins.

Embryologic studies suggest that descent is controlled by production of testosterone by the testis under the influence of gonadotropic hormone of chorionic and possibly of fetal pituitary origin. The pathogenesis of nondescent is obscure. The occurrence of undescended testes in siblings as well as in fathers and sons suggests a genetic etiology. Hormonal deficiencies have been postulated, but seem unlikely in view of the absence of other endocrinopathy, and the poor response of the unilateral undescended testis to exogenous gonadotropin. In the majority of instances hormonal stimulation appears adequate, and the testis either fails to respond because of an intrinsic deficiency, or is prevented from descending by an anatomic hindrance. Fibrous bands, a narrow inguinal canal, and inadequate length of the spermatic vessels frequently are noted at surgery, but are just as likely to be the result as the cause of the condition.

Histologic examination of the undescended testis after age 5 reveals a lag in development as compared with the normally descended contralateral organ. At and after puberty the undescended testis degenerates rapidly. Fertility is unusual in untreated bilateral cryptorchid men, and indeed many reports show a fertility rate of less than 30 percent in patients with the untreated unilateral variety. In contrast, Gross reported a rate of fertility exceeding 80 percent in his treated bilateral cryptorchids and the figures for fertility in patients treated for unilateral undescent are even more encouraging.

Torsion, trauma, and malignancy are more common in undescended than in normal testes. The increased risk for malignancy overall is about 20-fold, and abdominal varieties are probably even more prone to develop neoplastic change. However, perspective must be maintained despite these alarming statistics since testicular tumors are rare. Although the cryptorchid has about a 1.5 percent chance of developing a tumor, the majority of these are seminomas, with an excellent prognosis. Orchidopexy, although it does not change the malignant potential, does allow easy examination and prompt recognition should a tumor develop. Where malignancy has developed, the average delay before presentation has been 15 years. The bilateral cryptorchid is particularly at risk, a tumor in one testis indicating a chance of malignancy in the other of 1 in 4.

The incidence of urinary tract anomalies has been reported to be 13 percent in cryptorchid individuals screened with intravenous urography. Approximately half of these anomalies were considered significant. Infants with bilateral undescended testes should have buccal smears to exclude cases of congenital adrenal hyperplasia with complete fusion of the urogenital folds and a normally appearing penile urethra.

Treatment of the true undescended and ectopic unilateral testis is surgical; the optimum age is 5 years. The writer does not recommend a trial of hormonal treatment in boys with a unilateral undescended testis, as advocated by some. However, patients with bilateral undescended testes may benefit from a course of gonadotropin. Dougherty reported success in bringing about descent in one-third of such patients using Follutein (chorionic gonadotropin, Squibb) in three doses of 3,300 units each over a 10-day period. Patients who do not respond should have surgical exploration. Failure to locate a testis in the groin should direct the surgeon to a thorough exploration of the pelvis and abdomen on that side, since agenesis accounts for only 2 percent of impalpable undescended testes. An abdominal testis may require a two-stage orchiopexy to bring it into good position within the scrotum.

TORSION. In the absence of trauma, the sudden or gradual onset of groin pain associated with testicular swelling and scrotal edema must be considered to be testicular torsion until proved otherwise. Mumps orchitis and epididymo-orchitis must be differentiated but they are rare conditions in the prepubertal child. Torsion of Müllerian and Wolffian duct vestiges may mimic testicular torsion. However, excision of these gangrenous twisted appendages results in less morbidity than if they are treated conservatively. Idiopathic testicular infarction is a rare condition that may simulate torsion. Its etiology is obscure and it may involve only a portion of the testis.

Torsion of the spermatic cord may be supravaginal where the tunica vaginalis has only a loose attachment to the scrotal wall; this variety predominates in infancy. The intravaginal type occurs where the tunica covers the whole epididymis and extends unusually far up the spermatic cord. The testis and epididymis are suspended from the tunica by a narrow vascular pedicle which can readily twist. This is the more common variety in older children. Torsion of a redundant mesoorchium where wide separation of the testis and epididymis occurs is a rarer abnormality which results in testicular strangulation without epididymal involvement.

Treatment consists of prompt exploration, detorsion, and fixation of the testis to the scrotum. Since the predisposing anomaly is bilateral in at least 50 percent of cases, fixation of the opposite side should be accomplished during the same operation.

HYDROCELE. Primary vaginal hydrocele in children is the result of incomplete obliteration of the processus vaginalis. It is always communicating even though the very small connection with the peritoneal cavity may be difficult to demonstrate. Spontaneous cure is likely and usually occurs within the first few months of life. However, some may take as long as a year to close, and unless the hydrocele is very large when first seen or continues to enlarge, or is associated clinically with a hernia, no treatment is required in the first year.

Encysted hydroceles of the cord have the same pathogenesis. They can be differentiated from vaginal hydroceles by the fact that the testis is palpable distally. They are distinguished from tumors of the cord by transillumination and by their fluctuant cystic feel. Treatment is the same as for vaginal hydroceles.

Female Genitalia

Examination of the female genitalia may reveal significant abnormalities. *Vaginal aplasia* may be recognized by an absent vaginal opening or a shallow depression. Associated serious upper urinary tract anomalies have been reported in 30 to 50 percent of cases.

Epispadias, although extremely rare without associated exstrophy, can occur as an isolated anomaly.

Vaginal cysts, which derive from the epoöphoron or Gartner's duct, may present at the level of the hymen. Differential diagnosis includes a paraurethral cyst, a urethral diverticulum, an ectopic ureterocele, or hydrocolpos associated with a bulging obstructing

hymen. Suprapubic and rectal examinations are done to exclude the pelvic mass of hydrocolpos and probing of the vagina assures its patency. Ureteroceles are usually associated with duplications of the upper tract, and thus intravenous urography and voiding cystourethrography are helpful.

Hydrocolpos most often results from vaginal obstruction above the hymen, and no bulging or cystic mass is visible. Septa most commonly occur at the junction of the upper and middle thirds of the vagina and result from failure of fusion between the sinovaginal bulbs of the urogenital sinus and the fused Müllerian ducts.

Adherent labia minora is not a congenital condition but results from mild trauma in the presence of the hypoestrogenic state of childhood. Vulvovaginitis may be the precipitating factor. The adhesions are readily lysed and recurrence is prevented by the application of dienestrol cream.

Urethral prolapse is occasionally seen in children following a period of coughing or straining. Resection or ligation of the prolapsed mucosa may be required. There is little or no tendency for stenosis to occur.

Hymeneal polyps occur not infrequently. Very rarely mesonephric carcinoma or sarcoma botryoides will be detected by the discovery of a similar-appearing vaginal mass.

Girls with anorectal anomalies may have rectovaginal or rectovesical *fistulas.* Low anorectal anomalies in the female are associated only occasionally with urinary tract abnormalities, whereas these are present in two-thirds of patients with high anomalies.

Obstructive Uropathy and Anomalies of the Kidneys and Ureters

Obstructive uropathy refers to an impedance to normal urinary flow, which may be located anywhere along the course of the urinary drainage system. It may be organic or functional, and in neonates, infants, and children is usually congenital.

Ureteropelvic Obstruction

Hydronephrosis due to obstruction at the ureteropelvic junction is the commonest upper tract obstruction encountered in children. It is slightly more common in boys than girls. When unilateral the left side is more commonly involved than the right. Bilateral involvement has been reported in 11 to 25 percent, and in infants is more common than unilateral involvement. In some patients the pathology in the opposite kidney becomes overt only some time after surgery on the first side.

Hydronephrosis is encountered at all ages but most often during the first 6 months of life, when it is discovered most frequently as an abdominal mass. In later childhood, abdominal or flank pain or hematuria following minor trauma is the more common mode of presentation. In infants transillumination in a darkened room using a fiberoptic light source may reveal the cystic nature of the mass. The diagnosis may be made with high dose intravenous urography, with early films to outline the parenchymal thickness and later films to delineate the site of obstruction and extent of pyelocaliectasis. Occasionally differentiation from multicystic kidney and tumor is difficult.

The basic cause of the obstruction is still in dispute. Compression of the ureter by aberrant vessels has been implicated frequently. Fibrous bands, a high insertion of the ureter into the pelvis, and organic stenoses account for some cases. The most widely held explanation, however, suggests a functional obstruction, peristaltic waves from the renal pelvis failing to be transmitted to the ureter across the ureteropelvic junction. Murnaghan explains this dysfunction on the basis of an interruption of the circular element of the musculature. Vesicoureteral reflux must be excluded as a cause of ureteropelvic obstruction, particularly in patients with infection, since secondary acquired obstructions may result.

The treatment is surgical and involves plastic repair of the ureteropelvic junction. Nephrectomy may be required but conservative procedures generally should be tried first, since most kidneys are salvageable and contralateral kidney disease is not uncommon. Often the radiographic appearance of the grossly dilated pelvis and calyces changes little postoperatively, but progression of disease is prevented. Excellent clinical response including absence of pain, infection, and complicating calculi can be expected.

Horseshoe Kidney

Horseshoe kidney occurs in about 1 in every 600 individuals. It results from incomplete ascent, failure of rotation, and fusion of the two metanephric blastemal masses. The isthmus is at the lower pole in more than 90 percent of cases and ureteral duplication as well as obstruction, particularly at the ureteropelvic junction, is fairly common. Many children experience vague abdominal pain which is difficult to explain in the absence of complicating infection, hydronephrosis, or calculi. Surgical division of the isthmus for relief of pain has been advocated but its efficacy is dubious. Many horseshoe kidneys function normally and require no treatment at all. Those with obstruction should have appropriate corrective surgery. Horseshoe kidneys have been reported with increased frequency in Turner's syndrome.

Ectopic Kidney

An ectopic kidney is usually associated with a normally placed contralateral kidney. It derives its importance from the frequent association with ureteropelvic or ureteral obstruction. The usual site is pelvic or sacroiliac but rare cases of a thoracic kidney have been reported. The lower abdominal location renders the organ easily palpable on abdominal or bimanual examination. It can be differentiated from a ptotic kidney, which is rare in children, by its anomalous short vessels and short ureter. Should the ectopic organ cross the midline during embryologic development, fusion usually results, and is termed crossed fused ectopia. The crossed organ in such situations lies below and medial to the normally placed one.

Pelvic ectopia is not uncommonly associated with anorectal abnormalities and may be found incidentally at the time of an abdominal-perineal pull-through procedure for anorectal agenesis.

Obstruction of the Ureter and the Ureterovesical Junction

Megaureter or megaloureter is literally a large, dilated ureter. However, the term in urologic parlance generally implies chronic ureteral dilatation without overt organic obstruction. *Hydroureter,* in contrast, is a dilated ureter consequent to organic obstruction, either of the ureter itself or of the bladder or urethra.

Megaureters may be divided into those with free vesicoureteral reflux, and those without reflux in which there is an impediment to emptying of the lower ureter of a functional nature. In the latter, referred to as *primary obstructive megaureter,* the basic pathology is unexplained, and the ureter is dilated in all but its terminal segment. Cases with other congenital anomalies, such as ureteral duplication, ectopia, and ureterocele, are not included in this definition, although the obstructive element may be very similar.

Primary obstructive megaureter is primarily a disease of early life; males predominate, the left side is much more frequently involved than the right, and bilateral disease is common, particularly during infancy. Infection is the most common complication. However, pain, hematuria, or uremia may be the presenting features.

Management is conservative in those with mild disease. Failure to clear infection or progression of the dilatation radiographically necessitates excision of the obstructing segment and ureteral reimplantation. If the disease is unilateral and the kidney has been destroyed by hydronephrotic atrophy, nephroureterectomy is the preferred treatment. Severe bilateral disease may require urinary diversion.

Vesicoureteral reflux on occasion is associated with massive ureteral dilatation, referred to as the *refluxing megaureter.* The distinction between simple and massive dilatation is somewhat arbitrary but suggests certain characteristics. These ureters show marked permanent dilatation on intravenous urography, as well as on retrograde cystography, distinct from the distensibility of ureters that is often seen during reflux in which the dilatation is transitory and disappears rapidly with ureteral emptying. Cinegraphic studies reveal ineffective peristalsis and the ureter is slow to empty. Severe hydronephrosis and marked parenchymal atrophy are the rule. Refluxing megaureters are usually encountered in early infancy, and the kidneys, in addition to hydronephrotic atrophy, may show dysplastic areas containing primitive tubules and glomeruli.

The bladder, particularly when both ureters are involved, may be of large capacity, leading to the designation *megaureter-megacystis* syndrome. The walls of the bladder are smooth and there are no trabeculations. The trigone may be large and the ureteral orifices widely spread apart. Despite the large capacity of the bladder it is able to empty completely, although it may refill rapidly by return of refluxed urine from the megaureters. The large bladder capacity in megacystis syndrome is thought to develop as a result of the usually large volumes of urine which the viscus is required to accommodate. Swenson and Brenner suggested that megacystis syndrome was analagous to Hirschsprung's disease, but exhaustive histologic studies by Liebowitz and Bodian showed that the ganglion cells in the bladder wall are normal in number and distribution.

Treatment is dependent upon the amount of remaining renal function and the capacity of the ureters to regain their tone. Preliminary temporary diversions may be required to assess these factors before embarking on reconstructive surgery or deciding upon permanent urinary diversion.

Ureteral Anomalies: Duplication, Ectopia, Ureterocele

The ureter develops embryologically as an outgrowth or bud from the Wolffian duct. It then grows toward the caudal end of the nephrogenic cord, divides successively to form the pelvocalyceal system and collecting tubules, and in the process induces differentiation of the metanephric blastema to form the definitive kidney.

Early division of the ureteric bud results in incomplete *ureteral duplication,* whereas an accessory bud arising directly from the Wolffian duct produces complete duplication, with each ureter opening separately into the bladder or onto an ectopic site. Both buds grow into the undivided metanephrogenic mass, so that the resulting duplicated kidney is one continuous parenchymal structure with two collecting systems.

The incidence of duplication is one per 150 births. The process frequently is bilateral. The sex incidence is equal but females are recognized more frequently owing to complicating urinary tract infections. Ureteral duplication must be distinguished from a bifid renal pelvis, which is a normal variant occurring in 10 percent of the population.

Many duplicated ureters function normally. However, complications are not uncommon. The bifid ure-

ters in the incomplete variety may show dilatation above their points of juncture as a result of abnormal peristalsis. In complete duplications where both ureters open into the trigone, the ureter opening cephalad and lateral, which serves the lower moiety of the duplicated kidney, has a shorter submucosal tunnel than its fellow and is thus more prone to reflux. Chronic pyelonephritis in the lower element thus is not uncommon. In such cases ureteral reimplantation or heminephroureterectomy may be necessary.

The complications and mode of presentation of *ectopic ureters* vary with the sex of the child and the position of the ectopic opening. In females, where the orifice usually is at the bladder neck, infection is often the first evidence of abnormality. When the orifice opens into the distal urethra, vagina, or vestibule, persistent wetting associated with normal micturition is the rule. In the male the ectopic ureter enters the posterior urethra, ejaculatory duct, or vas. Epididymitis or urinary tract infection is the first evidence of abnormality. Intravenous urography, voiding cystourethrography, and endoscopy confirm the diagnosis. The ectopic ureter and renal segment which it subserves is usually markedly dilated and dysplastic; treatment is excision.

The ectopic ureter may be complicated by a ureterocele, which refers to ballooning of the submucous portion of the ureter within the bladder. Females are affected seven times more commonly than males. Both sides are equally affected and bilateral disease occurs in about 10 percent. The renal element involved characteristically is small and dysplastic while the ureter is grossly dilated. The ureterocele may be so large as to obstruct both ureters as well as the bladder neck. Prolapse may occur in girls and appear as a pink swelling at the urethral meatus. Complicating infection is generally the mode of presentation. Standard treatment includes uncapping of the ureterocele and heminephroureterectomy.

The *simple ureterocele,* involving the termination of a single, normally situated ureter, results from stenosis of the ureteric orifice. It produces flank pain and may become infected. Diagnosis is established by intravenous urography, which demonstrates a typical cobra-head appearance at the ureteral termination. Cystoscopy confirms the diagnosis. Treatment requires ureteral reimplantation by an antireflux technique.

Obstruction of the Bladder Neck and Urethra

Minor degrees of *obstruction to bladder outflow in the female* are difficult to diagnose. Indeed many question whether obstruction is even a factor in children who present to the pediatrician or urologist with recurrent urinary tract infection, enuresis, or difficulty with urination. Voiding cystourethrograms in girls are difficult to interpret even when multiple films are taken during the act of micturition. Bougie á boule calibration of the urethra is often not diagnostic since the range of normal is large. Furthermore, correlation with the findings on voiding cystourethrography is inconstant. Urethral calibration as a method of diagnosing obstruction has been criticized by those who regard the obstructive element as functional rather than organic. Endoscopic methods are notoriously inaccurate in demonstrating minor degrees of obstruction. Physiologic methods of testing, including measurement of detrusor pressures, flow rates, and calculations of urethral outflow resistances, have such wide variations, even in normal subjects, that they are of limited value. Obstructions due to meatal stenosis, distal urethral stenosis, and bladder neck contraction do exist, but their prevalence rate remains in great dispute.

Urethral meatal stenosis is probably the most common *outlet obstruction in the male child*, particularly in circumcised infants. Most are acquired, secondary to meatitis and meatal ulcers. Diagnosis is made by observation of the voided stream, which is narrowed and forceful. Calibration confirms the stenosis. Ventral meatotomy may be required. The congenital variety is usually associated with glandular and subcoronal hypospadias. Dorsal meatomy will relieve the obstruction in these cases.

Meatal stenosis results rarely in serious outlet obstruction, the most severe examples of which in early infancy are caused by *posterior urethral valves*, saillike mucosal folds which arise from the lower aspect of the verumontanum. Their cusps extend laterally and downwards to become attached to the walls of the urethra (Fig. 26). The resulting obstruction is severe, with elongation and dilatation of the posterior urethra and gross trabeculation of the bladder with cellules and saccules. Marked ureteral dilation, elongation, and tortuosity are the rule. Hydronephrotic renal atrophy is often severe and various degrees of cystic dysgenesis complete the picture. The majority of cases present within the first year of life and more than half of these in the first 3 months. Infants presenting in the neonatal period usually represent the most severe cases and have a high mortality.

Presentation within the first week is usually due to signs of renal failure or secondary infection. Anuria sometimes occurs. The bladder is distended and typically is very firm owing to gross hypertrophy of the detrusor muscle. Hydronephrotic kidneys may be palpable.

The status of the upper tracts is demonstrated with high-dose intravenous urography and with tomography if necessary. A voiding cystourethrogram will demonstrate the classic picture of valves. Other less common causes of obstruction to be ruled out include urethral diverticulae, anterior urethral valves, posterior urethral polyps, trigonal cysts, Marion's disease (bladder neck obstruction), and urethral fibroelastosis.

Perineal urethrostomy and transurethral fulguration of the valves are done after preparation for surgery, which involves rehydration and correction of

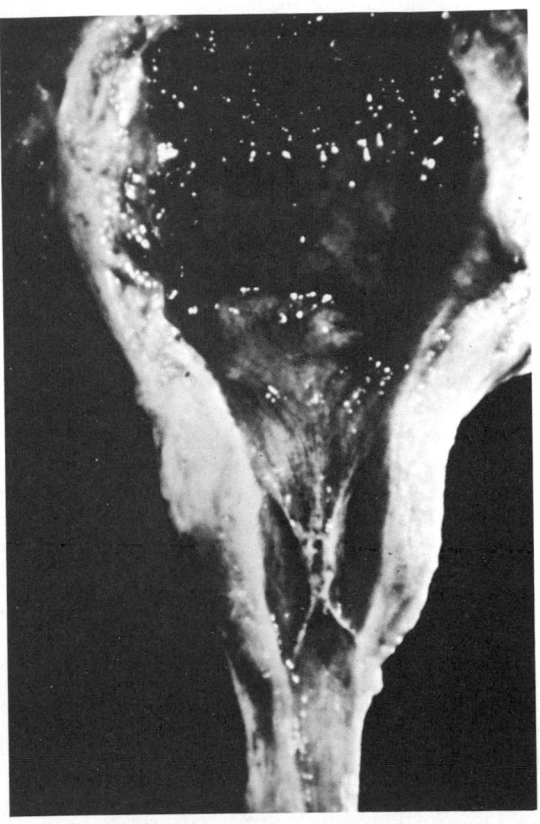

Fig. 26. Posterior urethral valves. Coronal section through the hypertrophied bladder and dilated posterior urethra.

electrolyte imbalance and may require 24 hours or more; a period of peritoneal dialysis may be needed. When infection is present, or in those with serious renal functional impairment or massive hydronephrosis, it is safer simply to divert the urine by nephrostomy or high-loop ureterostomy, definitive surgery being performed at a later date.

Prune Belly Syndrome
(*Triad Syndrome*)

This syndrome is characterized by absence of the anterior abdominal musculature, dilatation of the urinary tract, and cryptorchidism. The wrinkled skin over the abdomen gives the appearance of a wizened prune. Later, as the subcutaneous tissue increases, the abdomen is more appropriately described as "pot belly." The associated uropathy is so severe that 20 percent of reported infants are stillborn or die within the first month, and 50 percent are dead within 2 years.

Other features include flared lower ribs, flattened diaphragm, and talipes equinovaris. Anomalies of the GI tract are common, particularly malrotation.

The urinary tract abnormalities include a very large-capacity bladder, with its apex attached to the umbilicus. A urachal diverticulum may be present. The bladder neck and posterior urethra are widely dilated and taper down to a membranous urethra of normal caliber. In most cases no organic obstruction can be demonstrated. A few have urethral atresia; reflux is almost always present, the ureters showing massive irregular dilatation; renal dysplasia often is found. Treatment is difficult, reconstructive surgery usually being unsuccessful. Urinary diversion, usually by cutaneous ureterostomy, may be necessary for those with uncontrolled infection, progressive dilatation, or decreasing renal function.

Vesicoureteral Reflux

Reflux of urine from the bladder into the ureter is abnormal at any age. The anatomic and functional features that characterize the normal flap-valve mechanism include an oblique entry of the intramural ureter into the bladder, adequate length of the intramural ureter and especially the submucosal segment (the ratio of submucosal length to the diameter should be approximately 5 to 1), good support from the bladder musculature, adequate distal fixation to a normal trigone by the ureterotrigonal ligaments, and normal ureteral flexibility and peristalsis.

Reflux may be suspected on intravenous urography but is best demonstrated during voiding cystourethrography. Minor reflux occurs only on voiding (i.e., high-pressure reflux) and may be present at one examination and absent on the next. More severe reflux occurs during filling of the bladder as well as during voiding (low-pressure type) and is less likely to disappear spontaneously, especially if associated with ureteral dilatation.

Primary reflux is the most common variety in children and is due to a congenitally anomalous ureterovesical junction. With time a number of these junctions mature and reflux ceases spontaneously.

Secondary reflux follows severe obstruction of the bladder outlet, neurogenic bladder, and inflammation secondary to infection, with edema and rigidity of the submucosal ureter and interference with the contractility and tone of the ureterotrigonal muscle. Frequently infection is superimposed upon a primarily defective valve. Reflux may also result from iatrogenic causes, such as following decompression of a ureterocele or reimplantation of a ureter into the bladder by a faulty technique.

The clinical significance of reflux lies in the fact that it provides a ready avenue to convert a lower urinary tract infection into pyelonephritis. Reflux over long periods of time may damage the ureteral and pelvic musculature, causing dilatation, loss of elasticity, and impaired peristalsis. It is thought by some that reflux per se, without associated infection, does not cause renal functional deterioration; however, this point remains debatable.

Focal chronic pyelonephritis is a serious and frequent complication that occurs in as many as 30 percent of children with reflux. Reflux itself may predispose the child to recurrent infection by virtue of the refluxed urine returning to the bladder and acting as a residual after voiding. Younger children tend to have a relatively low incidence of pyelonephritis as detected radiographically. However, with time an increasing number develop scarring, reflecting continued exposure to infection, which may occur with mild as well as severe degrees of reflux.

Treatment is directed toward keeping the urine sterile and eliminating reflux. Antibacterial agents, adequate fluid intake, and regular double voiding will accomplish this goal in about 50 percent of patients with mild reflux. Smellie has presented strong arguments for long-term chemotherapy for as long as reflux is observed. She has been able to maintain 76 percent of 84 children with reflux completely free from infection. Even more important, follow-up examinations in 24 of 26 refluxing children who initially had normal urograms showed normal renal growth, and no fresh scars.

Continued reflux after an adequate trial of conservative therapy, inability to render the urine sterile with antibacterials, fresh scarring, and follow-up urograms showing marked ballooning of the ureter and pelvis indicate the need for antireflux surgery.

More severe degrees of reflux with abnormally located or patulous ureteral orifices seldom achieve a spontaneous cure with conservative measures and, in these, early surgery may be indicated.

The rate of success of antireflux surgery in experienced hands for relatively normal or moderately dilated ureters varies from 70 to 95 percent. In advanced, severely dilated ureters the success rate drops precipitously. Success implies absence of reflux with no further dilatation of the collecting system. Sterile urine is achieved without antibiotics in more than two-thirds of these children within a year of surgery. In children who continue to have recurrent bacteriuria infection seems to be localized to the lower tract, since follow-up urography usually shows no evidence of progressive pyelonephritic scarring.

Neoplasms of the Genitourinary Tract

The genitourinary tract is the primary site in 6 to 10 percent of all malignant tumors in children. The prognosis for tumors treated before they have spread beyond the confines of the involved organ is encouraging. Malignant tumors of the genitourinary tract in infants and children can be classified into three groups. The renal tumor encountered most frequently is the nephroblastoma or Wilms' tumor. Sarcoma botryoides or rhabdomyosarcoma arising from the urogenital sinus is less common and more lethal. The third group comprises the gonadal tumors, which are usually benign teratomas but can behave malignantly.

therapy are generally not helpful in tumors untreatable by radical surgery.

Nephroblastoma

Wilms' tumor is the most common malignant tumor of the genitourinary tract. The majority present between 6 months and 3 years of age. Sex incidence is equal. The tumor is bilateral in 5 to 10 percent of cases. Associated anomalies include aniridea, congenital hemihypertrophy, and genitourinary malformations.

A firm abdominal mass is the presenting sign in most children. Pain related to rapid growth and hemorrhage into the tumor are not infrequent. Hematuria occurs in about 30 percent. Fever is often seen and hypertension has been reported in up to 60 percent. Spontaneous rupture with presenting signs of an acute abdomen may occur. Some evidence of spread is present in 30 to 40 percent of cases when first seen.

The intravenous urogram demonstrates a renal mass lesion, usually with calyceal distortion. Nonfunction is unusual and calcification is present in about 10 percent. Differential diagnosis includes hydronephrosis, cystic kidney disease, other renal tumors, and neuroblastoma. Transabdominal exploration should be performed as soon as the work-up is completed. Nephrectomy, paraaortic lymph node dissection, and thorough inspection of the contralateral kidney should be performed. Actinomycin D, in a daily dosage of 15 μg per kg for 5 days, is given once the diagnosis is confirmed on frozen section. Radiotherapy to the tumor bed also is recommended, usually within 3 to 10 days after surgery. It has been suggested to give repeated courses of actinomycin D 6 weeks after surgery and then every three months for 15 months. Children under 1 year of age are usually not given actinomycin or radiotherapy. Radiotherapy to the lung is given for metastases, and if disappearance of an isolated lesion is not complete, surgical excision should be performed.

The overall rate of recovery is about 60 percent. Most can be regarded as cured if there has been no recurrence within 2 years. Neonatal tumors are rarely true Wilms' tumors but rather fibromatous variants, with an excellent prognosis following nephrectomy alone.

Tumors of the Urogenital Sinus

Rhabdomyosarcoma arises in the base of the bladder, posterior urethra, or vagina. Presenting symptoms and signs include stranguria, urinary retention, and the passage of grapelike masses. Hematuria is uncommon but vaginal bleeding sometimes occurs. Radical surgical extirpation has resulted in an overall cure rate of 53 percent for tumors in the vagina and base of the bladder, although those in the prostate carry a very poor prognosis. Radiotherapy and chemo-

Testicular Tumors

These tumors constitute about 3 percent of urologic neoplasms in children. They present as scrotal swellings which must be differentiated from hydroceles, hernias, torsion, and hemorrhagic infarctions. Teratomata are the commonest variety. They are slow-growing and benign but can become malignant in later life. Sertoli cell tumors and interstitial cell tumors usually are benign. Orchidoblastoma, however, is a tumor peculiar to children and may metastasize rapidly. Paratesticular tumors are embryonic sarcomas. They grow rapidly and have a high mortality.

Ovarian Tumors

These tumors are often difficult to diagnose. Vague abdominal pains are usual but on occasion torsion is encountered. Teratomas are the most common types and most are benign. Granulosa cell tumors may present with isosexual precocity. Dysgerminomas occur in later childhood. Treatment of these tumors is salpingo-oophorectomy. Invasive lesions require wider excision, including the uterus and both appendages, followed by radiation.

Trauma

Renal trauma in childhood is generally due to direct blunt trauma from blows or automobile accidents. The kidney is prone to trauma in the young because of the small perinephric fat pad. In addition its lower situation allows it less protection from the rib cage than in the adult. Other viscera are often injured in conjunction with the renal injury.

Preexisting renal disease is found in 15 to 25 percent of children. Hydronephrosis is the most commonly discovered incidental lesion but Wilms' tumor and cystic kidney also are encountered.

The kidney may be contused or lacerated. Lacerations may be incomplete, involving the parenchyma and capsule only, or complete, with involvement of the pelvocalyceal system. The most serious injury is the shattered fragmented kidney. Deceleration injuries, such as those which occur with falls from a height, can result in avulsion of the vascular pedicle; these children often present in shock.

Diagnosis is based on history, hematuria, loin pain, bruising, and tenderness. Significant bleeding and urinary extravasation result in a flank mass. Intravenous urography shows decreased concentration in contused kidneys or frank extravasation from lacerations. Vascular injuries produce spasm and thrombosis resulting in nonvisualization on the intravenous urogram. In such cases angiography and selective renal arteriography are of great value, and help to differentiate vascular spasm from thrombosis. Demonstration of a thrombotic renal artery occlusion should be followed by prompt transabdominal exploration, thrombectomy, and repair of the vessel.

Most renal injuries respond to conservative therapy, including strict bed rest and careful monitoring of vital signs. An expanding flank mass, severe continuous or persistent hematuria, ureteral avulsion, and shattered kidneys are indications for prompt surgical intervention. Angiography, if available, is very helpful in these cases and increases the chances of partial or total salvage of the kidney, since excellent delineation of the extent of the lesion, including its remaining intact vascularity, is obtained.

Following conservative treatment or reparative surgery of a renal injury, careful clinical and radiologic follow-up is mandatory. Scarring may produce obstructive uropathy or a parapelvic pseudocyst. Ischemia may result later in hypertension. These complications almost invariably become apparent within the first year following the trauma.

Penetrating injuries are unusual in children but occasionally occur. The ureter is more likely to be involved in this type of injury. Exploration is usually required to control hemorrhage.

Bladder injuries may result in intraperitoneal or extraperitoneal rupture. The former usually occurs as a result of blunt trauma applied to a full bladder, rupture occurring at the bladder dome. Extraperitoneal extravasation is usually associated with a pelvic fracture. Children with hematuria resulting from indirect trauma, especially when the trauma is poorly localized, as in automobile accidents, must have a retrograde cystogram in addition to intravenous urography. Ruptures of the bladder are easily overlooked on the latter examination.

Treatment consists of prompt cystostomy, local drainage, and suture of the laceration.

Urethral injuries usually result from instrumentation and pelvic fractures. Most cases involve males. Rupture of the urethra above the urogenital diaphragm results from serious crush injuries with pelvic fracture dislocations. The puboprostatic ligaments are ruptured and the posterior urethra becomes avulsed at the prostatic apex. Complete separation of bladder and urethra can occur. These children are usually severely shocked and have marked bruising, swelling, and lower abdominal tenderness. Large pelvic hematomas and urinary extravasation is the rule. There is inability to void, and catheterization of the bladder is not possible. Cystostomy, drainage, and reapproximation of the severed, avulsed urethral segments must be undertaken promptly. Posterior urethral strictures are a common and serious complication.

Anterior urethral lacerations result from instrumentation or occasionally from straddle injuries. Treatment involves catheter drainage for partial lacerations. Complete lacerations require diversion by cystostomy and urethral repair.

Penile injuries with pants zippers are fairly common. Local anesthesia generally is sufficient to allow removal of the clothing but on occasion surgical removal under general anesthesia is required. Iatrogenic injuries from circumcision are discussed on page 1553.

Contused testes may occur from direct blows. Minor blows are often held responsible for testicular symptoms caused by torsion. Trauma is treated with elevation, immobilization, and application of ice packs. Exploration is required in cases of rupture.

REFERENCES

Arnold, J. H. Cystometry and enuresis. J. Urol., 96:38, 1966.

Backhouse, K. M. The Gubernaculum testis hunteri: testicular descent and maldescent. Ann. Roy. Coll. Surg., 35:15, 1964.

Barbour, R. F., Borland, E. M., Boyd, M. M., Miller, A., and Oppe, T. E. Enuresis as a disorder of development. Brit. Med. J., 2:787, 1963.

Berdon, W. E., Levitt, S. B., Baker, D. H., Becker, J. A., and Uson, A. C. Hydronephrosis in infants and children—value of high dosage excretory urography in predicting renal salvageability. Amer. J. Roentgen., 109:2, 1970.

Blomfield, J. M., and Douglas, J. B. Bedwetting prevalence among children 4-7. Lancet, 1:850, 1956.

Boyarsky, S. The Neurogenic Bladder. Baltimore, The Williams and Wilkins Co., 1967.

Breneman, J. C. Nocturnal enuresis. A treatment regimen for general use. Ann. Allerg., 23:185, 1965.

Browne, D. Diagnosis of undescended testicle. Brit. Med. J., 2:168, 1938.

Campbell, E. B., and Young, J. D., Jr. Enuresis and its relationship to electroencephalographic disturbances. J. Urol., 96:947, 1966.

Campbell, M. F. Urology, 2nd ed. Philadelphia, W. B. Saunders Co., 1963.

Caucci, M. Clinical and statistical appraisal of seven hundred orchidopexies, operative technique and follow-up. Int. Surg. (Chicago), 45:218, 1966.

Chrispin, A. R. The pyelogram following angiocardiography in children with congenital heart disease. Proc. Roy. Soc. Med., 58:419, 1965.

DeLeon, G., and Mandell, W. A comparison of conditioning and psychotherapy in the treatment of functional enuresis. J. Clin. Psychol., 22:326, 1966.

Ditman, K. S., and Blinn, K. A. Sleep levels in enuresis. Amer. J. Psychiat., 111:913, 1955.

Dougherty, L. J., and Lattimer, J. K. Unpublished data presented before the committee on pediatric urology of the American Academy of Pediatrics. October, 1964.

Ehrlich, R. M., Dougherty, L. J., Tomashefsky, P., and Lattimer, J. K. Effect of gonadotropin in cryptorchidism. J. Urol., 102:793, 1969.

Feingold, M., Fine, R. N., and Ingall, D. Intravenous pyelography in infants with single umbilical artery. New Eng. J. Med., 270:1178, 1964.

Felton, L. M. Should intravenous pyelography be a routine procedure for children with cryptochism or hypospadias? J. Urol., 81:335, 1959.

Gairdner, D. Fate of foreskin. Brit. Med. J., 2:1433, 1949.

Gilbert, J. B., and Hamilton, J. B. Studies in malignant

testis tumors. III. Incidence and nature of tumors in ectopic testes. Surg. Gynec. Obstet., 71:731, 1940.

Gleason, D. M., Bottaccini, M. R., and Lattimer, J. K. What does the bougie á boule calibrate? J. Urol., 101:41, 1969.

Gravier, L. Hydrocolpos. J. Pediat. Surg., 4:5, 1969.

Griscomb, N. T. The roentgenology of neonatal abdominal masses. Amer. J. Roentgen., 93:447, 1965.

Gross, R. E. The Surgery of Infancy and Childhood. (Asian ed.) Philadelphia, W. B. Saunders Company, 1967, p. 480.

Hallgren, B. Enuresis, a clinical and genetic study. Acta Psychiat. Scand. (Suppl.), 114:32:1, 1957.

Hallman, D. S., and Blackman, N. Enuresis, firesetting and cruelty to animals; a triad predictive of crime. Amer. J. Psychol., 122:1431, 1966.

Hamilton, W. J., Boyd, J. D., and Mossman, H. W. Human Embryology, 3rd ed. Cambridge, England, W. Heffer and Sons, 1962.

Hicks, W. R., and Banes, E. H. A double blind study of imipramine on enuresis in 100 naval recruits. Amer. J. Psychiat., 120:812, 1964.

Hilson, D. Malformation of ears as sign of malformation of genitourinary tract. Brit. Med. J., 2:785, 1957.

Johnson, N. Torsion of the testis—a plea for bilateral exploration. Med. J. Aust., 1:653, 1960.

Johnston, J. H. Reconstructive surgery of megaureter in childhood. Brit. J. Urol., 39:17, 1967.

Kunin, C. M. The natural history of recurrent bacteriuria in schoolgirls. New Eng. J. Med., 282:26, 1970.

Lattimer, J. K. Congenital deficiency of the abdominal musculature and associated genitourinary anomalies: a report of 22 cases. J. Urol., 79:343, 1958.

——— and Vernon Smith, M. J. Exstrophy closure. A follow-up on 70 cases. Trans. Amer. Ass. Genitourin. Surg., 57:1965.

Levine, A. Enuresis in the Navy. Amer. J. Psychiat., 100:320, 1943.

Liebowitz, S., and Bodian, M. A study of vesical ganglia in children. J. Clin. Path., 16:342, 1963.

Linderholm, B. E. The cystometric findings in enuresis. J. Urol., 96:718, 1966.

MacCollum, D. W. Clinical study of the spermatogenesis of undescended testicles. Arch. Surg. (Chicago), 31:290, 1935.

MacGregor, M. Pyelonephritis Lenta. Arch. Dis. Child., 45:240, 1970.

McDonald, P., and Hiller, H. G. Angiography in abdominal tumors of childhood. Clin. Radiol., 19:1, 1968.

McGovern, J. H., and Marshall, V. F. Congenital deficiency of the abdominal musculature and obstructive uropathy. Surg. Gynec. Obstet., 108:289, 1959.

Marshall, V. F., and Muecke, E. C. Variations in exstrophy of the bladder. J. Urol., 88:6, 1962.

Martin, C. R. A. A New Approach to Nocturnal Enuresis. London, A. K. Lewis and Co., Ltd., 1966.

Martin, L. W., and Pedro, M. R. An evaluation of 10 years' experience with retroperitoneal node dissection for Wilms tumor. J. Pediat. Surg., 4:6, 1969.

Muecke, E. C. The role of the cloacal membrane in exstrophy: the first successful experimental study. J. Urol., 92:659, 1964.

Muellner, S. R. Primary enuresis in children. A new concept of its causes and treatment. J. Kentucky Med. Ass., 63:253, 1965.

Murnaghan, G. F. Experimental aspects of hydronephrosis. Brit. J. Urol., 31:370, 1959.

Murphy, S., Jackson, N., and Hammar, S. Neurological evaluation of adolescent enuretics. J. Pediat., 45:2, 1970.

Nash, D. F. E. Urinary problems of spina bifida. Develop. Med. Child Neurol., 11:106, 1969.

Nation, E. F. Duplication of the kidney and ureter—a statistical study of 230 new cases. J. Urol., 51:456, 1944.

O'Connor, J. F., and Neuhauser, E. B. D. Total body opacification in conventional and high dose intravenous urography in children. Amer. J. Roentgen, 90:63, 1963.

Oppe, T. E. Enuresis. Clin. Proc., Nov. 1966.

Potter, E. L. Bilateral renal agenesis. J. Pediat., 29:68, 1946.

——— Pathology of the Fetus and the Newborn. Chicago, Year Book Publ., 1952.

Rickham, P. P., and Johnston, J. H. Neonatal Surgery. London, Butterworths, 1969.

Ruch, T. C., and Patton, H. D. Urinary bladder. In Physiology and Biophysics. Philadelphia, W. B. Saunders Co., 1965, p. 1010.

Scorer, C. G. A treatment of undescended testicle in infancy. Arch. Dis. Child., 32:520, 1957.

Scott, J. The volume and circulation of the liquor amnii: Clinical observations. Proc. R. Soc. Med., 59:1128, 1966.

Shopfner, C. E. Modern concepts of lower urinary tract obstruction in pediatric patients. Pediatrics, 45:194, 1970.

Smallpeice, V. Urinary Tract Infection in Childhood and its Relevance to Disease in Adult Life. St. Louis, The C. V. Mosby Co., 1969.

Smellie, J. M. Medical aspects of urinary infections in children. J. Roy. Coll. Physicians (London), 1:2, 1967.

——— and Normand, I. C. S. Urinary Tract Infection. Symposium. London, Oxford Univ. Press, 1968.

Smith, D. Spina Bifida and the Total Care of Spinal Myelomeningocoele. Springfield, Ill., Charles C Thomas, 1965.

Smith, D. R. Repair of hypospadias in the preschool child: a report of 150 cases. J. Urol., 97:97, 1967.

Smyth, B. T., and Forsythe, I. W. Hypospadias and associated anomalies of the genitourinary tract. J. Urol., 82:109, 1959.

Sohval, A. R. Testicular dysgenesis as an etiologic factor in cryptorchidism. J. Urol., 72:693, 1954.

——— Testicular dysgenesis in relation to neoplasm of the testicle. J. Urol., 75:285, 1956.

Starfield, B. Functional bladder capacity in enuretic and non-enuretic children. J. Pediat., 70:5, 1967.

Stein, Z. A., and Susser, M. W. Socio-medical study of enuresis among delinquent boys. Brit. J. Prev. Soc. Med., 19:174, 1965.

——— Susser, M. W., and Wilson, A. E. Families of enuretic children. Develop. Med. Child. Neurol., 7:658, 1965.

Stephens, F. G. Congenital Malformations of the Rectum, Anus and Genito-urinary Tracts. Edinburgh, E. & S. Livingstone, 1963.

Swenson, O., and Brenner, R. Aggressive approach to the treatment of Wilms' tumor. Ann. Surg., 166:4, 1967.

Treffert, D. A. An evaluation on imipramine in enuresis. Amer. J. Psychiat., 121:178, 1964.

Uson, A. C., Cox, L. A., and Lattimer, J. K. Hydronephrosis in infants and children. J.A.M.A., 205:6, 1968.

——— Levitt, S. B., and Lattimer, J. K. Giant hydronephrosis in children. Pediatrics, 44:2, 1969.

Wiles, P. Family tree showing hereditary undescended right testicle and associated deformities. Proc. Roy. Soc. Med., 28:157, 1934.

Williams, D. I. The chronically dilated ureter. Ann. Roy. Coll. Surg., 14:107, 1954.

——— Pediatric Urology. London, Butterworths, 1968.

——— and Burkholder, G. V. The prune belly syndrome. J. Urol., 98:244, 1967.

——— and Hulme-Moir, I. Primary obstructive megaureter. Brit. J. Urol., 42:140, 1970.

——— and Karlaftis, C. M. Hydronephrosis due to pelviureteral obstruction in the newborn. Brit. J. Urol., 38:138, 1966.

——— and Woodard, J. R. Problems in the management of ectopic ureteroceles. J. Urol., 92:635, 1964.

——— and Young, D. G. Malignant tumors of the genitourinary tract in childhood. Practitioner, 200: 678, 1968.

Woodburne, R. T. Structure and function of the urinary bladder. J. Urol., 84:79, 1960.

Young, C. Conditioning treatment of enuresis. Develop. Med. Child Neurol., 7:557, 1965.

chapter 23

THE GASTROINTESTINAL TRACT

MURRAY DAVIDSON, Associate Editor

23.1
ANATOMY, PHYSIOLOGY, AND BIOCHEMISTRY OF THE NORMAL GASTROINTESTINAL TRACT

MURRAY DAVIDSON

Digestion and Assimilation

Digestion, absorption, and assimilation of foodstuffs in infants is similar to that in adults. However, in certain respects the infant's gastrointestinal capacity and digestive ability are limited and his gastrointestinal tract is more easily upset. During periods of stress, particularly those imposed by infection, the infant's intestinal tolerance may be impaired to such an extent that nutrition cannot be maintained through the usual pathways for digestion and assimilation. By 2 years of age, most of these limitations are no longer operative.

Gastrointestinal Motility

Sucking and Swallowing

Opening and closing movements of the mouth have been demonstrated prenatally in human fetuses as young as 8½ weeks. Newborn infants weighing more than 1,500 g usually have little difficulty coordinating sucking and swallowing. Consecutive sucks occur in small bursts of 3 to 4 in the neonate and in more efficient groupings of 10 to 30 after several days of life. The mechanism has been studied by recording pressures in the oral cavity and by cineroentgenographic techniques with both artificial and natural nipples coated with radiopaque materials. The infant grasps the nipple between tongue and hard palate and alternate suction and compression help pass the milk to the pharynx. Suction is created by withdrawing the tongue from the hard palate and compression by its reapposition to that surface. The infant can breathe during this process since continuity of the respiratory tract is not interrupted. With onset of swallowing there is sudden elevation of the posterior part of the tongue, which forces the contents of the posterior pharynx into the esophagus while the epiglottis simultaneously closes the entry to the larynx

and the muscles of the soft palate the entry to the nose. When the act of swallowing is initiated, a variable amount of air is present in the posterior pharynx. A portion of this air is swallowed and propelled by the bolus of food acting as a piston. By the age of 6 months the average child is no longer able to coordinate sucking and swallowing with breathing. The pattern at this age becomes more like that of the adult, in whom breathing and swallowing occur at different times. Attempts to do both simultaneously may result in aspiration.

Attempts of the young infant to move semisolid food to the back of his mouth with his tongue are clumsy during the early weeks of life; by the age of 3 months he is usually able to do this easily. For this reason efforts to administer such foods prior to this age sometimes meet with failure. Newborn infants generally exhibit no difficulty in passing swallowed material to the stomach, despite the fact that records made in the first days of life demonstrate incoordinate esophageal peristaltic activity. In most infants the pattern rapidly becomes normal, although in mental retardates uncoordinated and delayed swallowing patterns may persist for several weeks.

Gastric Motility

Interpretation of data on emptying of the infant's stomach is difficult, because of variations in techniques of study by different authors. Influences such as the state of health of the infant, his degree of hunger at the time of study, the type of meal fed, the times and volume of feeding, possible psychic stresses induced during roentgenographic studies, and positions in which studies are performed are variables which have been largely uncontrolled. Air has been demonstrated to traverse the pylorus within minutes after birth. The pylorus will open almost immediately as feedings reach it; in one study the average time for opening of the pylorus after a barium meal reached the cardia was 90 seconds. Infants fed in the upright position or on their right sides displayed the shortest interval between the time the barium meal entered and left the stomach. However, in other positions emptying was only slightly longer. Air was also less likely to pass to the duodenum when the infants were fed upright than in other positions.

The motility of the stomach is markedly affected by the addition of fat to a meal. When fat first enters the duodenum and absorption begins, it evokes the elaboration of enterogastrone, a hormone which inhibits gastric motility and secretion. As a result, a fatty meal stays in the stomach much longer than a fat-free meal.

Saturated fatty acids are particularly effective in delaying stomach emptying. Among other ingested materials, large milk curds or chunks of solid food also delay opening of the pylorus. Emptying is retarded if the stomach contains increased amounts of mucus or when the muscular tone of the organ is lax, conditions normally present in low-birth-weight infants and induced in larger infants and children by fever, infection, and states of malnutrition.

Factors contributing to earlier emptying are feedings of larger volume and of increased carbohydrate content, greater degree of denaturation or fragmentation of protein particles, and low temperature of foods. Osmolality of ingested food also plays an important role. Relatively isosmotic material passes through the pylorus more readily than extremely hypotonic or hypertonic foods. Studies of emptying time of the stomach in low-birth-weight infants by use of aqueous or milk mixtures with barium have demonstrated significant emptying in 3 to 4 hours on all feedings; complete emptying occurs by 5 hours with aqueous mixtures and by 7 to 8 hours with milk. Variations ranging from 1½ to 25 hours have been reported for complete emptying in full-term infants.

Intestinal Motility

Transit time through the intestines has been measured in only a limited number of children using relatively crude techniques such as feeding of colored markers, manometry, and radiography. Wide variations are reported in all age ranges. Lönnerblad found that the small intestinal transport time of a barium meal varied from ½ to 6 hours in patients less than 1 year old. Radiographs of the small intestine in infants differ from those seen in older children and adults in that the contrast medium progresses more slowly, appears in clumps, and usually does not produce the feathery appearance caused by the intestinal mucosa. Explanation of this difference is a matter of dispute, attributed by some to an increased secretion of mucus in early life, by others to difficulty in fat assimilation. Development of the normal adult pattern commonly takes place by the end of the first year, but is delayed in the presence of the "malabsorption syndrome" (Fig. 1).

Two types of motility occur in the large intes-

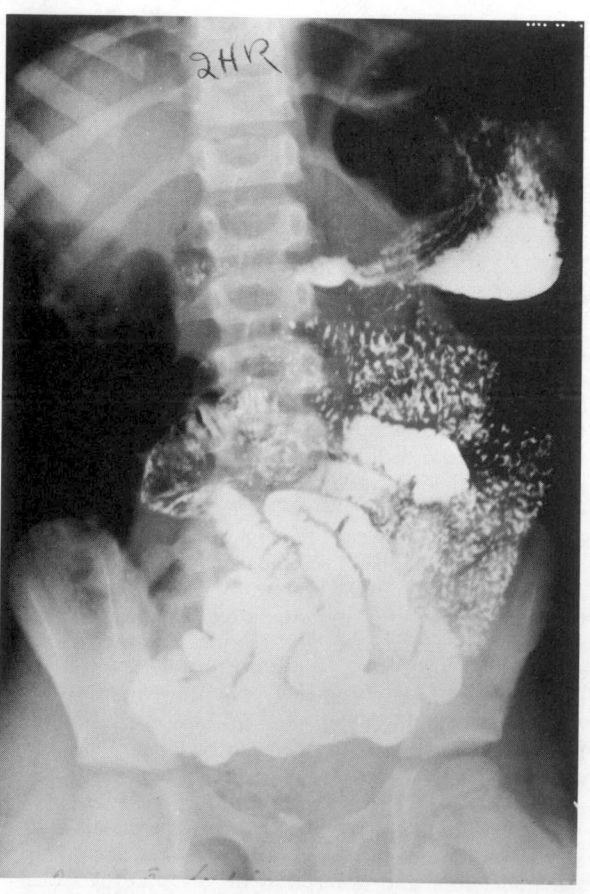

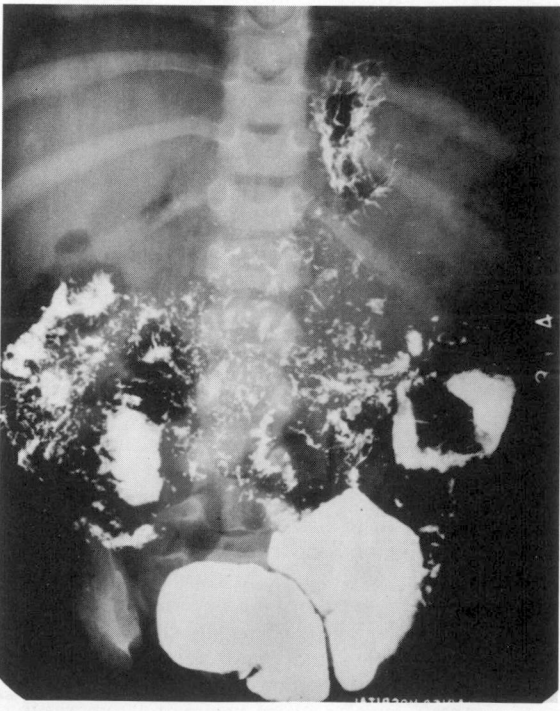

Fig. 1.   *Left.* Intestinal pattern of a normal child 2 years of age two hours after ingesting a barium meal. *Above.* Intestinal pattern in a 19-month-old patient with the celiac syndrome two hours after ingesting a barium meal.

tine. Closely approximated segments may simultaneously be engaged in different types of "resting" activity, involving mixing of contents or exchanges of fluid, electrolytes, and nutriments. In other periods these local patterns are diminished and coordinated propulsive motility supervenes to push the colonic contents analward. Such coordinated mass movements occurring during feeding produce the gastrocolic reflex. Fluid introduced into the sigmoid or descending colon induces a propulsive state toward the terminal rectum, while fluid introduced into the rectum produces immediate relaxation and accommodation by this intestinal segment slowly followed by patterns associated with fluid absorption.

Defecation

Although passage of material through the gastrointestinal tract from the upper esophagus to lower colon is under autonomic control, defecation is entirely a voluntary act. Though not sufficiently well studied, it may be possible that peristalsis in the colon induced by feedings results in bowel movements in infants. However, normal individuals do not usually defecate involuntarily beyond the initial months of life irrespective of the vigor of colonic peristalsis. Instead, material projected into the rectum distends that organ. If the volume is appreciable or if the process occurs when there is a particularly resistant state of rectal muscular tone, receptors in the lower rectal mucosa are activated to set up the reflex urge to defecate. Voluntary expulsion occurs following increase in intraabdominal pressure by the Valsalva maneuver, during which there is descent of the diaphragm and contraction of the rectus muscles. It is necessary that direction of this increased force against the pelvic contents be coordinated with simultaneous squatting and application of leverage to the feet in order to pinch off the upper rectum from the rest of the colon by action of the pelvic sling muscles. If such leverage is not applied, squeezing of the rectal contents may aid in retention with gradual subsidence of the urge to defecate and additional drying of the mass.

Digestive Secretions and Absorption

Mouth and Pharynx

The normal adult secretes from 1 to 2 liters of saliva daily; accurate measurements of daily volume of saliva are not available in infants and children. The parotid component is relatively watery, whereas the submaxillary gland produces both aqueous and mucinous fractions. Electrolyte levels are always hypotonic to serum but have been shown to rise with increased secretory rates and to be somewhat higher in the neo-

natal period. The protein content is mainly from amylase and mucopolysaccharides, including the blood group fractions. The quantities of saliva and of salivary amylase are reported to be small for several weeks after birth, but apparently adequate for the needs of the infant's digestion. Beyond 3 months of age amylase is found in increasing amounts, particularly if starch is fed.

Stomach

Coagulation of casein is an important gastric function usually attributed to rennin. However, this enzyme, present in newborn calf gastric juice, has not been demonstrated in the human infant. Gastric acidity aids in milk curdling, the solubility of casein being minimal at the isoelectric point (pH 4.7). Gastric pepsin also has milk-clotting properties. The curd of breast milk, which is low in casein, is soft and friable, in contrast to that of raw cow's milk, which is tough and less easily broken up and digested. Measures to influence the character of the curd have played a large part in the history of artificial feeding.

The volume of gastric secretion and its acidity have been measured early in life and are at adult levels in a considerable proportion of both low-birth-weight and full-term newborn infants. However, beyond the first days of life the ability to secrete acid is impaired for a number of weeks, especially among infants of low birth weight or in malnourished children of higher weights. The increase in volume and acidity of gastric secretion in response to histamine stimulation in older children has been found similar to that of adults, using weight or surface area as a standard of reference.

Proteolytic digestion is thought not to occur appreciably in the infant's stomach since pH levels beyond the immediate newborn period are commonly above 4.0 in the breast-fed infant and over 5.0 among those who are bottle-fed. At these levels of acidity conversion of pepsinogen to pepsin is impeded, since peptic digestion is effective only at a pH below 3.0. Nevertheless, some gastric proteolysis does occur at the higher pH that prevails in early life. This activity may be attributed either to the higher plasma pepsinogen levels of the first weeks of life resulting apparently from supplemental maternal corticosteroids, or to the presence of the enzyme cathepsin, which is effective over a wider range of pH extending from 2.0 to 5.0. Pure cathepsin has not been isolated but its activity has been demonstrated to be distinct by heating and inactivating pepsin at 70° C.

Small Intestine

Most protein hydrolysis is accomplished by the peptidases of pancreatic juice, which are secreted in inactive "zymogen" forms and are activated by a variety of agents, including enterokinase from the duodenal mucosa. The active peptidases of the pancreas include trypsin, chymotrypsin, and the carboxypeptidases. At least four other enzymes with effects on digestion of protein or nucleic acids have been isolated from pancreatic secretions: pancreatic elastase, pankrin, ribonuclease, and deoxyribonuclease. Although the precise kinetics of the individual enzymes has not been studied in infants, proteolytic activity has been demonstrated even in young low-birth-weight infants. Failure of protein hydrolysis is virtually confined to situations in which insufficient pancreatic secretions enter the intestine. The most frequent cause in children is cystic fibrosis of the pancreas (see Chap. 9). It may also occur in rare cases of congenital atresia of the common bile duct in which the pancreatic duct empties into the atretic bile duct. Failure to activate the precursor forms of the peptidases because of a congenital enterokinase deficiency may infrequently simulate conditions in which pancreatic secretions are excluded. Unsplit protein may also appear in the stools as a result of tough curd formation in the stomach, from inadequate mastication of solid foods, or in states of hyperperistalsis.

Controversy has prevailed as to whether proteins are completely broken down to amino acids before absorption or whether in the course of digestion certain polypeptide complexes are absorbed intact. Although it has been shown that biologic traces of unsplit protein are absorbed and it may be presumed that the same is true of peptides, their importance as nutrients has not been demonstrated. Peptide levels in portal blood are negligible. However, high titres of enzymes capable of protein hydrolysis are found in mucosal cells, and polypeptides can be shown to disappear from the intestinal lumen before digestion. Thus, although the hydrolysis of proteins to amino acids in the digestive tract is believed to be virtually complete under normal conditions, there is limited evidence suggesting auxiliary avenues of digestion. Absorption of amino acids occurs in the upper small intestine. The L-forms in low concentration may be absorbed against a concentration gradient, suggesting an active transport mechanism. In high concentration, absorption may occur principally by simple diffusion.

Salivary and pancreatic amylase digestion of starch and glycogen results in splitting of more than 90 percent of these substrates into maltose (1-4 alpha-linked diglucose) and the remainder, which comes from the branching points of chains in the polysaccharide structures, into isomaltose (1-6 alpha-linked diglucose). Pancreatic amylase is delayed in development; it reaches full activity at 4 to 6 months of age. Maltose, isomaltose, and two disaccharides which occur naturally, sucrose (cane sugar, 1-2 alpha-linked glucose-fructose) and lactose (milk sugar, 1-4 beta-linked galactose-glucose), together with other rare disaccharides, are hydrolyzed by specific disaccharidases into their component monosaccharides. The disaccharidases are located in the outer cell layer of

epithelium of the intestinal villi, mainly, though not entirely, concentrated in the brush border. Complete hydrolysis probably takes place at this membrane, although some may occur within the mucosal cell after absorption of the disaccharide.

At least four (and perhaps five) individual disaccharidases are present which are capable of digesting maltose. Two of these are also able to split sucrose and one can hydrolyze isomaltose. Two beta glycosidases capable of hydrolyzing lactose are described, one concentrated in the brush border and the other in the cytoplasm of the mucosal cells. Significant sucrase and isomaltase activities are demonstrable in the 12-week fetus. Maltase activity develops more slowly, but all of the alpha glycosidase activities are comparable to those of adults by 6 to 7 months of fetal life. The beta glycosidases develop more slowly, and reach normal levels of activity only at the end of gestation. Babies born prematurely usually display decreased lactase activity during the first 3 days of life. On a comparative basis maltase activity is about three times as great as that for sucrase-isomaltase and six to eight times greater than that for lactase in the normal child. Lactase activity usually decreases gradually after the first year of life, and only rarely is the level of activity of this early period maintained into adult life. The enzymes are distributed relatively evenly over the entire small intestine, but activities are somewhat lower in the duodenum and terminal ileum.

Glucose and galactose are absorbed against a concentration gradient by an active transport mechanism which is energy and sodium dependent. It is generally believed that fructose is absorbed by passive diffusion; however some authors believe that it, too, is absorbed by an active process of a very low order of magnitude. The absorption of monosaccharides facilitates absorption of water and sodium (solvent drag).

Although faulty splitting of disaccharides with their appearance as such in stools is rare and confined to disaccharidase deficiency states (see below), starch may escape digestion to a variable extent under normal circumstances. "Intracellular starch," present in vegetable cells unruptured by processing, is often demonstrable in normal stools. Starch which is extracellular, i.e., from ruptured vegetable cells, often appears in stools of young infants. Unfortunately such starch is often regarded as indicative of incomplete digestion due to inadequate amylase activity; however, it has been shown that it results from release of starch is often regarded as indicative of incomplete ings in which it was encased when it passed to the lower colon.

Balance studies of carbohydrate digestion and absorption do not provide valid information since the unabsorbed carbohydrate is fermented in the intestine. Holt and Somersalo overcame this difficulty by feeding ^{14}C-tagged carbohydrate; they found more than 98 percent absorption of ingested starch, even by low-birth-weight infants.

A negligible amount of fat splitting occurs in the stomach although some emulsification results from mechanical activity there. Lipase from the pancreatic juice is activated by the bile acids and hydrolyzes triglycerides, ultimately to monoglycerides, long-chain fatty acids, and glycerol; this occurs by a stepwise process with the intermediate formation of diglycerides. The end products form micelles with bile salts. These are polar complexes which are more lipid soluble at one end and more water soluble at the other; they are thus more readily absorbable by the mucosa of the upper small intestine. The products of triglyceride digestion are also absorbed here whereas the bile salts are passed back into the lumen and then to the ileum, where they are reabsorbed to enter the bloodstream and be reexcreted in the bile. This recirculation of conjugated bile salts is referred to as the enterohepatic circulation.

Absorbed fatty acids and monoglycerides are reesterified in the upper intestinal mucosa to triglycerides; they become encased by lipoproteins, cholesterol, and phospholipids to form chylomicrons, and pass through the mucosal cells to the lacteals and the lymphatic system in this form. It is believed that triglycerides of fatty acids below 10 carbons (short- and medium-chain) are able to be absorbed intact and to pass directly into the portal circulation.

Overall fat digestion and absorption is readily measured by means of fat balance. After the neonatal period, 95 percent of the intake of most fats is absorbed. Slightly lower figures are often obtained during the early weeks of life, and markedly reduced figures are encountered in premature infants. The chemical constitution of the fat affects the ease of absorption, short-chain fats and those containing unsaturated linkages being more readily assimilated. The premature commonly absorbs from 40 to 85 percent of the intake of butter fat. In the belief that the difficulty of fat absorption in premature infants might be limited to absorption through the lacteals, Snyderman and her associates fed fats with extremely short chains—tributyrin and triaxetin—and found that these materials were absorbed almost completely.

The assimilation of fat in conditions of malabsorption is favored by finer mechanical subdivision or by surface-active agents such as bile salts; however, the effect is very small. Treatment with surface agents seems indicated only in patients in whom bile salts are deficient, such as those with biliary atresia or with surgical removal of the ileum, which is the site of bile salt reabsorption. In patients with other forms of malabsorption, the use of fats with higher proportions of short-chain fatty acids or of unsaturated fatty acids may improve absorption. According to Holt, an even more effective method of increasing fat absorption is simply to give more fat, since the percentage of ingested fat which is absorbed is appreciably influenced by the intake. Hence, even though the stool loss is increased by increasing the intake, the absolute quantity of fat absorbed is also increased correspondingly.

Fluid Exchange and Colonic Function

There is no portion of the gastrointestinal tract of man in which the mucosa may be regarded as impermeable to movement of water in either direction. Net changes in amounts of water at any point are dependent on a multiplicity of factors which include (1) the state of hydration of the individual, (2) the quantities of water available in the intestinal tract, (3) the effects of feeding, (4) the osmolality of gastrointestinal contents, (5) the nature of the lumenal solutes and their normal mechanisms of digestion and absorption, (6) the site within the intestinal tract, and (7) the tonus of the intestinal musculature.

Techniques devised to assess these multiple factors have suffered from lack of specificity and precision. Balance studies are relatively crude and have been done often under unphysiologic conditions. Investigations using "isolation" of segments between balloons are subject to undetected errors such as leaks. Many calculations are based on assumptions of unidirectional flux in a system which almost constantly undergoes multidirectional flux, i.e., into and out of the mucosal cells. Finally, it is not possible to assess the constant influences on lumenal contents of additions from and losses to the adjacent segments of the intestinal tract.

The handling of water appears to be passively linked to that of solutes in terms of both quantity and rate of movement. Expressed in terms of unit serosal surface area, the rates of influx of water from isotonic solutions are approximately equal in the jejunum and ileum; both appear to be more rapid than in the colon. However, limited measurements have indicated that the mucosal surface area, per unit length or per unit serosal surface, is greater in the jejunum than in the ileum. This ratio is also considerably higher in all areas of the small intestine than in the colon. This implies that the unidirectional flow rates per unit mucosal surface are faster in the colon than in the small bowel and faster in the ileum than in the upper small intestine. However, the osmotic permeability of all areas of the small and large intestine is sufficiently high that solute transport from isotonic solutions is quickly followed by flow of enough water to maintain isotonic conditions in the gut lumen.

Although the underlying mechanism for absorption of isotonic solutions is not entirely defined, most workers infer from available data that it is based on active sodium transport. Various studies indicate that sodium and water absorption are facilitated by the solvent drag effect of active glucose absorption in the upper small intestine. These effects seem less influential in the lower ileum or colon. Differences in patterns of sodium and water movements are also apparent from studies with adrenal hormones. Levitan and co-workers were unable to show any effect of aldosterone on ileal water and electrolyte composition, but found significant increases in colonic sodium absorption. In our own studies of colonic absorption of sodium we have observed that the absence of intralumenal potassium produces a movement of potassium out of the mucosa while sodium from isotonic fluids moves in the opposite direction, though the exchange is not stoichiometric. The mechanism is probably responsible for the fact that the ratio of sodium to potassium in ileal water is reported at 12 to 20 to 1, whereas in the stool the ratio is less than 1 to 3. Chloride absorption and bicarbonate secretion in the small and large intestine have a similar relationship, but are influenced considerably by intralumenal pH and by serum potassium levels. With hypokalemia and tissue potassium depletion the permeability of gut mucosa to chloride is adversely affected.

The colon of the normal adult normally absorbs about 400 ml of water per day; the figure for infants is probably proportionately higher. Various calculations have shown that this colonic activity represents less than 20 percent of the total fluid and electrolyte absorbing capacity, and suggest why resection of extensive portions of the colon is usually followed rapidly by readjustment and fairly normal stool formation.

Material arriving in the rectum is usually semiliquid. This portion is the final area for water absorption and the consistency of the stool passed is determined largely by the activity of the segment. The young infant has a smaller capacity for retention of material in the rectum than the older child and adult; this results in stools which have a smaller volume, an increased water content, and which are passed more frequently.

Intestinal Bacteria and Stool

Bacteria are usually absent from the gastrointestinal tract at birth, but invade it quickly via both mouth and anus within the first hours of life. By the end of 24 hours an intestinal flora is firmly established. The duodenum, particularly the first portion, is usually sterile, a phenomenon attributed to the discharge of acid chyme from the stomach. Farther down the intestinal tract, organisms are found in increasing numbers, being most abundant in the colon. Aerobic cultures reveal the ever-present coliform organisms and many varieties of lactobacilli, streptococci, and staphylococci. Yeasts are often found when special efforts are made to cultivate them. By far the most frequent organisms, in infants as well as adults, are various members of the Bacteroides group; these are pleomorphic, gram-negative, nonspore-bearing organisms which, being anaerobic, are not usually reported in stool cultures. The bacterial flora is influenced to a considerable extent by the diet. In the breast-fed infant, lactobacilli are always conspicuous, and a gram-positive flora predominates; in artificially fed infants the proportions of protein and sugar in the formula affect the bacterial flora, a relatively high-protein intake favoring the growth of the coliform organisms. Fatty acids tend to check the growth of a number of organisms, notably staphylococci. When fat is completely removed from the infant's diet the stools tend to become loose and mushy for a variable length of time. What part the bacterial flora plays in this change is not clear.

The role of the intestinal bacteria in the maintenance of health would seem to be an important one, as has been demonstrated by studies of germ-free animals. Bacteria appear to be important for the synthesis of essential nutrients and also as natural sources of antibiotics which protect against pathogenic microorganisms. The known B vitamins are all synthesized by the intestinal bacteria, particularly by coliform organisms. It is not clear whether these are essential for human nutrition. However, useful synthesis occurs for folic acid and biotin and there is evidence that synthesis in the intestine may be an important source of vitamin K in the early days of life.

In ruminant animals and in certain other herbivora the bacteria of the gut perform functions which they do not perform in man; enzymes which they produce are capable of hydrolyzing cellulose and of synthesizing ascorbic acid as well as certain essential amino acids.

Many intestinal microorganisms elaborate substances which inhibit the growth of other organisms. The colon bacilli are particularly noteworthy in this respect and elaborate a variety of so-called colicins, the most powerful of which is colicin K. The fact that L. bifidus is conspicuous in the flora of the breast-fed infant and that in circumstances of poor hygiene the breast-fed infant tends to suffer less from infection has led to the view that this organism possesses specific virtue in combating infections. A number of attempts have been made to encourage an abundant L. bifidus flora in infants. However, evidence is still awaited that a predominant growth of these organisms has virtue.

The intestinal bacteria may under certain circumstances exert untoward effects. They may compete with the body for available nutrients and some of them, particularly certain types of E. coli, are potential pathogens to debilitated and small infants. Several strains with specific antigenic structure have been incriminated as etiologic agents in epidemics of infantile diarrhea. The presence of such strains in the stools of infants is not necessarily associated with disease, for they are at times found in healthy carriers. Whether such strains arise from mutations of nonpathogenic colon bacilli or whether they are invariably acquired by contact is not clear.

The increasing use of antibiotics and the popularity of high-protein diets have tended to destroy the balance of the intestinal flora, suppressing some organisms and permitting others which are potential pathogens to flourish. The emergence of resistant staphylococci and of the pathogenic strains of coliform organisms may well be related to these practices.

Although the importance of the stools as a guide to the feeding of infants was overemphasized in the past, there is no doubt that valuable information concerning the infant's digestion can be obtained from this source.

The first rectal discharges after birth consist of meconium. It is composed of bile and intestinal secretions high in nitrogenous and mucopolysaccharide content, with squamous epithelial cells and hair that have been swallowed in utero. The absence of epithelial cells in meconium may be of diagnostic aid in intestinal obstruction in the newborn. Normal meconium contains representative amounts of the amylolytic, tryptic, and lipolytic activities secreted by the pancreas. Bacteria are absent from meconium in the first hours of life. A dark brownish-green semisolid, it is usually passed four to six times a day for the first two or three days. When the milk supply becomes well established, the appearance changes to that of normal milk feces.

The stools of a healthy breast-fed infant may have the color of egg yolk but are usually paler and often green. The quantity passed in one day usually ranges from 30 to 45 g (1 to 1½ ounces). They are seldom entirely smooth and homogeneous but contain, in general, a large number of small, light yellow particles. Their consistency is sometimes pasty, often rather loose although never watery under normal conditions. They have a slightly sour but not unpleasant odor. The reaction is acid, usually between pH 4.5 and 5.1. This acidity is due largely to the presence of organic acids but partly also to carbon dioxide, the loss of which accounts for the reaction becoming less acid on standing. The number of stools passed by most breast-fed infants in the early weeks of life is from two to four daily. After the first month the usual number is two or three per day, although many infants have only one and others have four or more. The average child passes approximately 100 to 150 g of stool per day during the first 5 years of life. Stool water content may be up to 80 percent of a formed stool and is rarely less than 70 percent. Total osmolality of a normal stool ranges from 200 to 250 mOsm/L, the values increasing as stool becomes softer. Values for sodium and chloride are variable, but always, except in severe and prolonged diarrhea, they are considerably lower than simultaneous concentrations of these electrolytes in serum.

The stools of an infant fed on cow's milk are usually firmer, more homogeneous, and less frequent than in the breast-fed infant. However, the stools of infants on low-protein formulas may more closely resemble the stools of breast-fed babies. The color of the stools of cow's milk-fed infants is likely to be paler, and the odor more unpleasant. The reaction is less constant and tends to be more alkaline, the pH ranging between 4.6 and 8.3. The undigested masses appearing in the stools of infants taking milk are usu-

ally spoken of as "curds." In infants given raw cow's milk these may take the form of bean-sized lumps composed of coagulated casein with an envelope of soap; they are of no pathologic importance. A different type of curd, which is small, white or yellowish-white, and consists almost entirely of fat, is seen in conditions where fat is not being digested completely.

In the past, alterations in the gross characteristics of the stool were interpreted as indications of impairments in the digestion of protein, fat, or carbohydrate—a foul odor pointing to indigestion of protein with overgrowth of putrefactive bacteria, the presence of gross fat indicating fat indigestion, and presence of vegetable material or of a frothy stool suggesting carbohydrate indigestion. Although these changes in the gross appearance of the stool do suggest incomplete digestion of specific foodstuffs, they give only qualitative information and none concerning the quantity that is being digested. They should not be used as indications for withdrawing specific foods from the diet as was done formerly.

The *pigment* of infants' stools shows variations which are not seen in later childhood. Partly because of air swallowing and partly because of the peculiarities of the intestinal flora on a milk diet, the reducing power of the infant's intestinal contents is distinctly less than in later life and is subject to greater variations. As a consequence, the bilirubin of the bile is incompletely reduced to stercobilin; a variable amount of bilirubin is excreted as such, and bilirubin crystals can sometimes be identified in the stools microscopically. Bilirubin is readily oxidized by the oxygen of the air to the green biliverdin. Frequently one sees a yellow stool become green on standing, due to such oxidation.

Absence or diminution of biliary secretion results in pale stools. However, a pale stool in an infant does not necessarily mean that bile pigment is absent; it may be due to the fact that nearly all of the pigment exists as the colorless stercobilin. Such stools will darken on standing and are thus easily distinguished from acholic stools. The normal fecal color in older children is due mainly to dipyrrole pigments and to pigments formed in the intestine by bacterial action.

Abnormal pigments may be found in the stool after ingestion of various vegetables. Black stools may result from bleeding in the upper intestine; they may occur with the administration of any heavy metal which forms a black sulfide, iron being the commonest of these. Bacteria may contribute to stool color, e.g., red staining of stools and diapers in the presence of *B. serratio.* Streaks of blood due to small anal fissures may be associated with constipated stools. In dysentery, flecks of blood and mucus are found. Larger hemorrhages may occur with any type of ulcerative lesion of the intestine. In intussusception the stools contain blood and mucus without appreciable quantities of fecal matter.

Microscopic examination of the stools gives little information that cannot be obtained on inspection,

Chemical examination, however, has yielded information of fundamental importance in regard to the absorption of both organic and inorganic foodstuffs. The chief clinical value of stool analyses is in the disorders of fat assimilation. An excess of fat in the stools may be evident as gross steatorrhea, but the appearance is often deceptive since chemical studies may reveal a marked loss of fat which has not been suspected. Impairment of fat assimilation cannot be accurately assessed by measuring the percentage of fat in individual stools since this is subject to considerable variation. It may be recognized by balance studies or by measuring the total fat excreted over a minimum period of 3 or 4 days. Normally from 2 to 3 g of lipids are excreted per day by infants and young children; a daily excretion in excess of 4 g is evidence of poor absorption. When there is marked interference with absorption the feces may contain more than 10 g per day. Defective fat absorption is seen in diarrheal states, in many acute and chronic infections, in prematurity, in celiac disease, in disorders of pancreatic secretion, and in bile salt deficiency syndromes.

Absence of significant quantities of proteolytic enzymes in the stool occurs in cystic fibrosis of the pancreas and at times in other pancreatic disorders (Chap. 9).

REFERENCES

Ames, M. D. Gastric acidity in the first ten days of life of the prematurely born baby. Amer. J. Dis. Child., 100:252, 1960.

Ardran, G. M. A cineradiographic study of breast feeding. Brit. J. Radiol., 31:156, 1958.

—— and Kemp, F. H. A correlation between sucking pressures and movements of the tongue. Acta Paediat. Scand., 48:261, 1959.

—— and Lind, J. A cineradiographic study of bottle feeding. Brit. J. Radiol., 31:11, 1958.

Borgstrom, B., Lindquist, B., and Lundh, G. Digestive studies in children. Amer. J. Dis. Child., 101:454, 1961.

Caffey, J. Pediatric X-Ray Diagnosis, 4th ed. Chicago, Year Book Publishers, 1961.

Ebers, D. W., Smith, D. I., and Gibbs, G. E. Gastric acidity on the first day of life. Pediatrics, 18:800, 1956.

Fordtran, J. S., Levitan, R., Bikerman, V., Burrows, B., and Ingelfinger, F. J. The kinetics of water absorption in the human intestine. Trans. Ass. Amer. Physicians, 74:195, 1961.

Frazer, A. C., French, J. M., and Thompson, M. Radiographic studies showing induction of segmentation pattern in small intestine in normal human subjects. Brit. J. Radiol., 22:123, 1949.

Goebel, W. F., and Barry, G. T. Colicine K. II. The preparation and properties of a substance having colicine K activity. J. Exp. Med., 107:185, 1958.

Grayzel, H. G., Elkan, B., Moghazeh, M., Schneck, L., and Garza, S. Plasma pepsinogen levels in the newborn. Amer. J. Dis. Child., 103:759, 1962.

Gryboski, J. D. The swallowing mechanism of the neonate. I. Esophageal and gastric motility. Pediatrics, 35:445, 1965.

—— Thayer, W. R., and Spiro, H. M. Esophageal motility in infants and children. Pediatrics, 31:382, 1963.

Hirsch, J., Ahrens, E. H., and Blankenhorn, D. H. Measurements of the human intestinal length in vivo and some causes of variation. Gastroenterology, 31:274, 1956.

Holt, L. E., Jr. Role of Carbohydrates in Infant Feeding. Advances in Chemistry, Series XII. New York, Interscience Publishers, 1955, p. 104.

—— The adolescence of nutrition. Arch. Dis. Child., 31:427, 1956.

Hood, J. H. Effect of position on amount and distribution of gas in the intestinal tract of infants and young children. Lancet, 2:107, 1964.

Hunt, J. N. The osmotic control of gastric emptying. Gastroenterology, 41:59, 1961.

Jones, D. V., and Work, C. E. Volume of a swallow. Amer. J. Dis. Child., 102:527, 1961.

Kron, R. E. J., Ipsen, J., and Goddard, K. E. Consistent individual differences in the nutritive sucking behavior of the human newborn. Psychosom. Med., 30:151, 1968.

Lönnerblad, L. Transit time through the small intestine; a roentgenologic study of normal variability. Acta Radiol. (Suppl.), 88, 1951.

Northrop, J. H. Isolation and properties of pepsin and trypsin. In Harvey Lectures, 1934-35. Baltimore, Williams and Wilkins Co., 1936, Vol. 30, p. 229.

Olsen, E. Studies on Intestinal Flora of Infants. Copenhagen, Munksgaard, 1949.

Silverio, J. Gastric emptying time in the newborn and the nursling. Amer. J. Med. Sci., 247:732, 1964.

Snyderman, S. E., Morales, S., and Holt, L. E., Jr. The absorption of short chain fats by premature infants. Arch. Dis. Child., 30:83, 1955.

Strawczynski, H., Beck, I. T., McKenna, R. D., and Nickerson, G. H. The behavior of the lower esophageal sphincter in infants and its relationship to gastroesophageal regurgitation. J. Pediat., 64:17, 1964.

Symposium on physiology and pathology of digestion in infancy. Bibliotheca Paediatrica, Ann. Paediat., Suppl. 64. Basel, S. Karger, 1957.

Törnwall, L., Lind, J., Peltonen, T., and Wegelius, C. The gastrointestinal tract of the newborn. I. Cineradiographic findings. Ann. Paediat. Fenn., 4:209, 1958.

Symptomatic Conditions of the Gastrointestinal Tract:
Diagnosis and Treatment

23.2
VOMITING

MURRAY DAVIDSON

In infants and young children, vomiting may occur from a great variety of causes; although some of these are trivial, vomiting may also indicate serious disease. A distinction is sometimes made between regurgitation, in which a mouthful or two of food is brought up at one time with little effort or distress, and true vomiting, in which the stomach virtually empties itself. As a rule regurgitation results from minor feeding disorders. Vomiting of larger volumes need not necessarily indicate serious disease, but if persistent and recurrent, the symptom requires investigation.

The pathophysiologic mechanism of vomiting is often misunderstood and therefore symptomatically mistreated. In virtually all instances the stomach is atonic and distended and the force for vomiting is supplied by strong contractions of the abdominal musculature. The column of food is usually not held up at the pylorus, but in the duodenum, which is in spastic contraction during nausea and vomiting; the afferent stimuli to the vomiting center in the central nervous system arise from the duodenum.

Only in those rare instances in which there is obstruction at the pylorus does vomiting occur from a stomach in which vigorous contractions are taking place. Thus, hypertrophic pyloric stenosis is one of the few conditions in infants in which the stomach empties by reverse peristalsis, a condition which usually induces projectile vomiting.

VOMITING IN THE NEONATAL PERIOD. In the newborn, vomiting may be benign and self-limited, probably caused by irritating material swallowed during the birth process. The presence of blood requires determination of the type of hemoglobin by alkaline denaturation (Apt test) to indicate its probable origin, i.e., maternal or infant. Intracranial pathology, septicemia, and certain metabolic abnormalities, particularly those associated with chronic acidosis, may result in persistent and projectile vomiting by a newborn. With congenital anomalies of the gastrointestinal tract vomiting is common. Specific obstructive lesions are discussed later in this chapter. A history of polyhydramnios in the mother or finding of a single umbilical artery at delivery should alert the physician to an increased likelihood of one of the congenital gastrointestinal anomalies. Bile-stained or fecal vomiting virtually always indicates gastrointestinal obstruction. Generally speaking, the higher the level of obstruction the earlier symptoms appear. In malformations of the ileum, colon, or rectum, vomiting is less constant and appears later.

OVERDISTENTION OF THE STOMACH. Gastric overdistension is especially common in infants, resulting from the swallowing of air and/or from the ingestion of too large a volume of food. The vomiting is not accompanied by other evidence of disease. It occurs effortlessly within a few minutes after nursing; it may be produced by moving the infant or by undue pressure upon the stomach. Air swallowing, as previously explained, is normal. Excessive amounts of gastric air is one of the most common causes of overdistention and of vomiting in the first 6 months of life. Breast-fed infants may swallow excessive air when the supply of milk is small or when the nipples are retracted. In bottle-fed infants it may result from feeding with a nipple with inadequate aperture. With both breast- and bottle-fed infants prolonged feeding time causes excessive air ingestion. Some infants swallow air between feedings; this habit may be encouraged by the use of pacifiers or by sucking the thumb or fingers. Hunger may at times lead to vomiting because the infant is apt to suck other objects within reach and thereby swallow considerable air between feedings. However, in general, the mother is more likely to believe that the infant's cry of discomfort is due to hunger and not to distention with air; this may lead to too frequent feedings of excessive quantities of milk. Infants may not always indicate that they are satiated and will often respond to stimulation by the breast or bottle by sucking, even if this ultimately aggravates their discomfort. In artificially fed infants, the bottle should be held in a position which will keep the neck of the bottle always filled with liquid. Regurgitation due to air swallowing can be prevented by feeding the infant in the semierect position to maintain the air bubble at the cardiac end of the stomach, by limiting sucking periods to approximately 20 minutes, by encouraging intervals of about 4 hours between feedings, and by patiently holding the infant upright over the shoulder for a few minutes after feeding and patting him gently on the back until belching occurs. In general, it is wise to interrupt a feeding at least once for this purpose. Persistent cases of such functional vomiting may require thickening of liquid feedings by adding two tablespoonsful of infant cereal to an eight-ounce bottle of milk, and in some instances it may be necessary to switch to formulas containing a vegetable oil. The addition of the latter offers two advantages. Vegetable oil may pass from stomach to small intestine more easily and may result in less malodorous vomitus, in the event that the child continues to regurgitate despite all efforts. Sedation and antispasmodics are unphysiologic because of the atonic stomach, and are usually ineffective.

Gastric vomiting, when due to mechanical factors only, is usually not associated with nausea; the infant's appetite remains good.

INFECTION. Vomiting is seen in association with many infections, both enteric and parenteral; it may occur at the onset of any acute febrile disease. The vomiting may or may not persist; it may also outlast the underlying disease. Infants and young children may develop vomiting even with a common cold or an attack of otitis media. Severe vomiting with such vigorous (anterograde) gastric peristalsis as to suggest pyloric stenosis may be observed in neonates with infection of the urinary tract. Vomiting due to infection often bears no definite relation to the intake of food; it may be delayed for some hours after a meal. In general, when vomiting results from parenteral infection or other systemic disease, desire for food may be impaired. The ingestion of toxic substances or of food which is contaminated by bacterial toxins may also lead to vomiting. Treatment in instances associated with infections is usually not specific, and is directed to parenteral rehydration, whenever the patient's condition requires it.

As children grow older, vomiting due to improper feeding technique or parenteral infections becomes less frequent. Dietary indiscretions and acute febrile illness may lead to short-term bouts of emesis which are usually self-limited.

Epidemics of nausea and vomiting, thought to be due to a viral infection, affect adults as well as children. The specific diagnosis and its infectious etiology are usually not established; the latter is merely postulated from the presence of many cases of vomiting in the community at the same time. Many affected individuals suffer the complete picture of nausea, vomiting, diarrhea, abdominal pain, slight elevation of temperature, and often moderate pharyngeal hyperemia. The condition is more severe in children, who may have an explosive onset and more persistent periods of vomiting. Frequently they suffer intense thirst but vomit as soon as they drink any amount of liquid. In this condition, the stomach is atonic and gastric secretions are diminished. The latter slows the rate at which the water achieves isotonicity, which is required for its passage to the duodenum. Proper management is based on severe restriction of intake, which should be limited to very small amounts (one ounce per hour) of carbonated sodas, fruit punch, or sweetened weak tea until at least 8 to 10 hours have passed without nausea and vomiting. The symptoms usually subside completely after 24 to 72 hours.

CENTRAL NERVOUS SYSTEM DISEASES. Vomiting is a feature of organic nervous system disease with increased intracranial pressure or hemorrhage. Cerebral vomiting is usually forcible or projectile and may bear no relationship to meals. In meningitis, the effects of parenteral infection and disease of the central nervous system are combined, and vomiting is rarely absent. Vomiting among children may also be reflex from irritation of the pharynx. It may be excited by paroxysms of coughing, particularly in pertussis.

Acute attacks of *abdominal epilepsy* (Sec. 15.10) as a cause of vomiting are probably diagnosed more frequently than warranted. The diagnosis should require that the child have an abnormal electroencephalographic tracing and other features of epilepsy, and that the attacks may be aborted by administration of parenteral barbiturates. Dilantin is very effective prophylactically as long-term therapy. *Abdominal migraine* is equally difficult to diagnose with accuracy. In such patients, progression of a beginning attack may be interrupted in older children by oral administration of 1 to 2 mg of ergotamine tartrate combined with 50 mg of caffeine. These medications are usually ineffective once the attack is established, but their efficiency in preventing progression of early symptoms is a valuable diagnostic test.

METABOLIC CAUSES. Vomiting is common in advanced renal insufficiency, adrenocortical insufficiency associated with congenital adrenal hyperplasia, diabetic acidosis, renal tubular acidosis, lactic acidosis, isovaleric acidosis, and congenital galactosemia.

DRUGS. Vomiting may be caused by many drugs, including digitalis, sulfonamides, broad-spectrum antibiotics, acetylsalicylic acid, various anesthetic agents, and a variety of poisons.

HABIT VOMITING AND CYCLIC VOMITING. Habit is a potent factor in causing vomiting to continue when for any reason it has occurred frequently. There is no question that some infants and children vomit far more readily than do others. Habitual vomiting may be encouraged by injudicious attitudes on the part of the parents in regard to the child's meals, especially when food is forced because of the mistaken notion that a child must be fed a stated quantity of food at a stated time, disregarding his own inclinations. This form of habitual vomiting commonly makes its appearance early in the second year of life. Prompt diagnosis of the causes with adequate explanation and orientation to proper parental attitudes are necessary (Chap. 6).

If habitual vomiting goes untreated and symptoms become pernicious, it may be difficult to distinguish the condition from cyclic vomiting. The latter syndrome, also known as recurrent, periodic, or acetonemic vomiting, is characterized by attacks of vomiting which recur at irregular intervals without apparent cause. The attacks usually begin between the ages of 2 to 4 years, but they may date from infancy. Almost invariably the condition subsides before puberty. The attacks are of variable length, some lasting only a few days and others more than a week. They usually occur several times a year and are separated by intervals during which the child is entirely normal. Children with the fixed-habit type of vomiting are less likely to have such long symptom-free periods. Children with either habit or cyclic vomiting do not have any demonstrable underlying pathology.

Severe bouts of cyclic vomiting are often associated with ketosis, dehydration, and fever. In some instances headache, general malaise, and anorexia may occur as prodromal symptoms. The vomiting may be so persistent and severe that it leads rapidly to prostration. Parenteral treatment with appropriate electrolyte solutions is sometimes necessary. The cycle may be broken with one of the phenothiazine derivatives, given rectally or by injections. These agents are especially useful in this type of vomiting but must be prescribed with caution because of their serious side effects. Unfortunately, they are also too frequently prescribed in less severe vomiting of infants and children, in which case their potential toxicity outweighs any possible benefits. Perphenazine (Trilafon), chlorpromazine (Thorazine), or prochlorperazine (Compazine) may be given as rectal suppositories in doses of 0.2 mg per kg body weight. Medication is repeated at 8-hour intervals in lower dosages with a maximum daily dose of 0.4 mg per kg for children up to 40 kg and 16 mg per day for those over that weight. These agents tend to induce drowsiness which may be initially useful in overcoming the vomiting. They may also cause undesirable extrapyramidal manifestations. However, these side effects occur rarely with the dosages recommended; they include generalized muscular rigidity, facial grimacing, torticollis, inability to control the tongue, difficulty with swallowing, and drooling. Withdrawal of the drugs will usually result in disappearance of these untoward symptoms within 24 hours with no additional therapy. The slow intravenous administration of 10 to 75 mg of diphenhydramine hydrochloride (Benadryl) over a period of 5 to 10 minutes often dramatically reverses the extrapyramidal signs. The injection is terminated as the patient begins to respond. Although chlorpromazine is less likely to induce extrapyramidal symptoms than are the other phenothiazine derivatives, administration of this agent is more frequently associated with obstructive jaundice.

Cyclic vomiting should probably not be regarded as a disease entity. In some instances it appears to be precipitated by nonspecific stimuli, such as infection, emotional upset, or fasting, in susceptible individuals who also may possess an unusual tendency to develop ketosis and hypoglycemia. For many of these children small frequent feedings and a late evening snack are suggested to forestall early morning exacerbations. In other instances the mechanism appears to be quite different; such diverse causes as food allergy and partial intestinal obstruction have been implicated. Millichap and his associates have described a group of patients in whom they attributed cyclic vomiting to an episodic disorder arising in the brain and believe that it should be classified as an autonomic epilepsy. Vomiting in patients with familial dysautonomia may be of this type.

CHALASIA OF THE ESOPHAGUS. Vomiting and regurgitation may arise from disturbances in the esophagus. Congenital surgical problems leading to ob-structive vomiting are described elsewhere in this section (pp. 1604–1607). A rare congenital problem is chalasia, or an abnormally relaxed cardiac orifice. In this condition ingested material is refluxed effortlessly into the esophagus after its passage to the stomach. The functional abnormality is readily demonstrated by fluoroscopic examination with barium. Unless there is marked pyloric obstruction, hiatal hernia, or severe peptic esophagitis from acid reflux, the condition is self-limited and disappears after the first few months of life. The only treatment usually required is to maintain the infant almost constantly in a vertical position. If hiatus hernia or severe pyloric obstruction accompany chalasia, surgical repair may be necessary before the symptoms subside.

ACHALASIA (CARDIOSPASM). Although slightly more frequent than chalasia, this lesion is still extremely rare in children; it is more common in adults. In children, symptoms usually first appear some time after 5 years of age. In this condition there is gradual distintegration of the myenteric ganglia of the lower end of the esophagus. The nervous elements that remain provide disorganized peristalsis and, with parasympathomimetic stimulation, respond maximally as per Cannon's law; spasm of the entire esophagus results. This pathophysiologic mechanism explains the symptomatology. Swallowing difficulties and vomiting occur intermittently and during the early period of slow insidious onset there may be no difficulties for days at a time. Occasionally the primary difficulty is caused mainly by the spasm and functional narrowing at the lower end of the esophagus, where a chunk of swallowed food, usually meat, may lodge and produce substernal fullness. Such obstructions are usually relieved by washing down the impacted

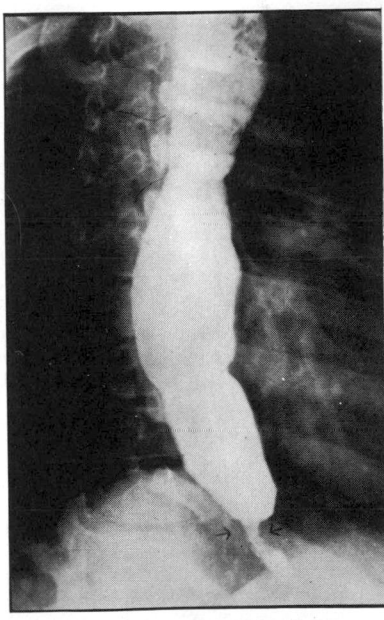

Fig. 2. Achalasia of the esophagus. Right anterior view after barium swallow.

food with fluids. In other patients, disordered motility and spasm produce the sensation of substernal pain and difficulty even when they swallow water or their own saliva. Vomiting is never forceful but consists of drooling and regurgitation after a variable length of time. With passage of time, a megaesophagus develops, with a typical funnel-shaped narrowing at the cardiac end of the esophagus (Fig. 2). In advanced cases esophagitis with pressure necrosis and ulceration of the esophageal mucosa are seen. Some patients suffer repeated bouts of pneumonia from aspiration and may develop bronchiectasis or lung abscesses.

Anticholinergic and antispasmodic drug therapy are usually ineffective. Medical management includes maintaining nutrition with high-calorie liquid diets when necessary. Most patients ultimately require dilation with bougies. Pneumatically controlled application of pressure from a rubber balloon to "fracture" the stenosing lower esophageal fibers, or a pyloromyotomy of the lower esophagus (Heller procedure) is sometimes necessary. In all patients who have had surgical splitting of muscle fibers at the cardioesophageal junction or pyloromyotomy, interruption of vagal fibers and postprandial vertical positioning of the patient are advised to minimize the undesirable effects of the incompetent lower esophagus with its tendency to reflux.

SURGICAL CONDITIONS INVOLVING ABDOMINAL ORGANS.   Vomiting is a prominent symptom in surgical conditions such as appendicitis, peritonitis, intussusception, volvulus, abdominal trauma, internal herniations, incarcerated hernias, and twisted ovarian cysts. These conditions are discussed under their appropriate headings elsewhere in this chapter.

REFERENCES

Adams, H. D. Esophageal amyenteric achalasia. Surg. Gynec. Obst., 119:251, 1964.

Benedict, E. B. Bougienage, forceful dilatation, and surgery in treatment of achalasia; a comparison of results. J.A.M.A., 188:355, 1964.

Berenberg, W., and Neuhauser, E. B. D. Cardio-esophageal relaxation (chalasia) as a cause of vomiting in infants. Pediatrics, 5:414, 1950.

Cassella, R. B., Brown, A. L., Sayre, G. P., and Ellis, F. H., Jr. Achalasia of the esophagus: pathologic and etiologic considerations. Ann. Surg., 160:474, 1964.

Craig, W. S. 1961. Vomiting in the early days of life. Arch. Dis. Child., 36:451, 1961.

Forshall, I. The cardio-oesophageal syndrome in childhood. Arch. Dis. Child., 30:46, 1955.

Gamble, J. L. Chemical anatomy, physiology and pathology of extracellular fluid. A Lecture Syllabus, 6th ed. Cambridge, Mass., Harvard University Press, 1958.

Hoyt, C. C., and Stickler, G. B. A study of 44 children with the syndrome of recurrent (cyclic) vomiting. Pediatrics, 25:775, 1960.

Hughes, J. G. The etiology of vomiting in infancy and childhood. Pediat. Clin. N. Amer., 2:483, 1955.

Kanner, L. Child Psychiatry, 3rd ed. Springfield, Ill., Charles C Thomas, Publ., 1957.

Millichap, J. G., Lombroso, C. T., and Lennox, W. G. Cyclic vomiting as a form of epilepsy in children. Pediatrics, 15:705, 1955.

Redo, S. F., and Bauer, C. H. Management of achalasia in infancy and childhood. Surgery, 53:263, 1963.

Riley, C. M., Day, R. L., Greeley, D. McL., and Langford, W. S. Central autonomic dysfunction with defective lacrimation. Pediatrics, 3:468, 1949.

Shaw, E. B., Dermott, R. V., Lee, R., and Burnbridge, T. N. Phenothiazine tranquilizers as a cause of severe seizures. Pediatrics, 23:485, 1959.

Sorsdahl, O. A., and Gay, B. B., Jr. Esophageal achalasia in childhood. Amer. J. Dis. Child., 109:141, 1965.

Soveri, V. Der Verlauf der luft durch den verdauungskanal des Säuglings. Acta Paediat. Scand., 23:(Suppl. 3) 1969.

Swenson, O. S., and Oeconomopoulos, C. T. Achalasia of the esophagus in children. J. Thorac. Cardiovasc. Surg., 41:49, 1961.

Thomson, J. Neuro-muscular incoordination of the cardia in the newborn. Arch. Dis. Child., 25:52, 1950.

23.3

RUMINATION SYNDROME
(MERYCISM OR MERYCASM)

ARNOLD H. EINHORN

Some young infants acquire the aptitude of inducing at will the regurgitation of previously ingested food, much in the manner of ruminant animals. In Latin the term *ruminare* means chewing the cud. This singular habit is seen primarily in infants from extremely underprivileged homes. When it develops into a regular pattern it leads to weight loss, growth failure, severe malnutrition, dehydration, and electrolyte imbalance. If the process is not recognized and arrested, it may even progress to death from starvation.

The habit of rumination commences usually between the ages of 3 and 6 months, and may persist for many months. The onset has been reported to occur exceptionally as early as the fifth week, and as late as the twelfth month of life. Among 43 of our own patients with infantile rumination, this syndrome started before 3 months of age in two infants only. Both infants had undergone surgery at birth for upper airway obstruction, were breathing via tracheostomy tubes, and were being fed exclusively through gastrostomy. At the ages of 8 and 11 weeks respectively, these two infants began bringing up voluntarily part of their stomach contents, mouthing the material vigorously before reswallowing it, seemingly seeking to recapture the oral gratification of feeding, of which they were being deprived.

In the early decades of the twentieth century this syndrome was quite common, reports on the subject in the literature were numerous, and mortality rates were estimated to be in the vicinity of

20 percent. Although in present times its incidence has considerably declined, it still occurs probably more frequently than the scarcity of reports in the current literature would indicate. The prevalance of this syndrome in the past was apparently related to the general social and economic deprivation of the time. Richmond suggests that overall improvement of infant care may account for its decreased incidence.

Numerous speculations have been made concerning the nature and etiology of this entity. The illness is generally regarded as psychosomatic in nature and constitutes an emotional derangement secondary to a distressful environment. It does not appear to be the result of any organic abnormality, anatomic or physiologic. Lack of stimulation, and disruption or deprivation of a close mother-infant relationship are the major etiologic factors of the rumination syndrome. Such conditions are fostered especially by adverse environmental circumstances which are found primarily in homes with precarious social and economic conditions. Surroundings equally unsuitable for appropriate parent-infant interaction may prevail in instances of profound and chronic familial disharmony, maternal psychopathology, and prolonged institutionalization.

The following observations were made by us on 43 infant ruminators hospitalized in our service and followed until well after recovery from their aberrant behavior. The ratio of males to females was approximately 2:1. All were offspring of parents living in ghetto slums. However, nine infants, including the two patients previously mentioned who had neonatal surgery, had never left the hospital before the onset of their rumination. Seven of these infants, abandoned by their parents, remained in the hospital after birth pending foster home placement. Custodial care of these "social boarders" was good, but was given in a depersonalized hospital setting by varied staff members without any attempt to create surrogate-mother figures. In this group of patients, total lack of parent-infant interaction was coupled with incomplete deprivation. The remaining 35 infants were all hospitalized after failing to thrive in a home environment of extreme poverty. All but one of the 43 infants were born out of wedlock. Even where both parents were living together, this arrangement was at best temporary and the emotional climate pervading each home was extremely insecure. Drug addiction, admitted to by seven mothers, existed probably in several others, and also in some of the fathers. The only married parents were both narcotic users. Some of the mothers of our ruminators appeared either very dull, apathetic, or immature; in some, frank psychopathology was documented. Evidence of child battering in other siblings, alcoholism, and prostitution were apparent or admitted to by several mothers.

The episodes of rumination in the afflicted infant take place at any time between feedings, provided the infant is alone and not in the proximity of objects likely to attract or occupy his attention. Since the infants do not usually ruminate when distracted, it is often difficult to observe them performing their deliberate regurgitation. Even the parents of these infants seldom witness it. Typically, the following sequence of events occur in rapid succession during the act. Motionless at first, as if plunged in deep meditation, the infant frowns and grimaces, curls his lower lip, protrudes his tongue and projects his mandible forward. His head slightly extended, he arches his back and stiffens his abdominal muscles, making at the same time rhythmical chewing movements until food is brought up with evident ease, a mouthful at a time. A portion of the regurgitated stomach contents is rechewed and partially reswallowed. Variable quantities of this material ejected to the outside without force run along the corner of the mouth onto the infant's shirt, which remains constantly wet and sour smelling, usually around one side of the neck. The losses of fluids, electrolytes, and nutrients may be considerable. Some infants introduce one or several fingers or objects into their mouths to help them accomplish the rumination. The infants often show obvious signs of satisfaction as if the rumination procedure produced a sense of accomplishment. We have observed occasionally, fleeting, but frank, smiles on the faces of these habitually unsmiling youngsters upon the successful completion of their regurgitation.

The disorder may go unrecognized for long periods of time if the diagnosis is not systematically considered in evaluating infants with failure to thrive. Physicians who are unfamiliar with the relatively rare rumination syndrome tend to mistake it for habitual vomiting. Rumination should be strongly suspected in any emaciated young infant from an economically disadvantaged home who has "vomitus" constantly plastered over his chin, neck, and upper shirt, yet is actually never seen vomiting. Once the suspicion is aroused the diagnosis can be readily confirmed by furtive observation. In rumination the regurgitation is self-induced and is followed by rechewing and reswallowing the expelled material. Vomiting is distressing and involuntary; rumination is effortless and accomplished with evident control. Furthermore, the infantile ruminator, far from suffering the discomforts related to the act of vomiting, evidently derives sensory pleasure from sucking and mouthing the regurgitated matter. In addition to the state of malnutrition of variable severity, the outward appearance of infantile ruminators is striking. These infants are quiet, sad, and singularly wide-eyed. When alone and not engaged in their odd practice they seem lost in inner contemplation. They may continue to produce sucking movements even though their mouths are empty. While they may lie immobile for hours with a vacant gaze and seem detached from their surroundings, any external stimulation evokes a rapid change in comportment and draws their immediate and clinging attention. Intensely, searchingly, untiringly, and often without turning their heads, they follow every gesture or movement of any bystander or any unaccustomed moving object. The melancholy of their facial expression and the alertness, inquisitiveness, and intensity of their foraging gazes, paired with the gauntness and ascetic quality of their features, produce in these infants the appearance of "wise old men." Associated neurotic traits such as autistic posturing, excessive genital and fecal play, body rocking, and head rolling and banging have been reported by Richmond to be more frequent in ruminating infants.

The rumination syndrome may be exceedingly difficult to control. Mechanical devices such as chin straps, and a variety of physical treatments including aversive conditioning by electric shock, have been recommended as means of preventing or inhibiting rumination. Such methods have proved worthless; those of a punitive nature are at best undesirable. The use of thickened feedings or solid food is sometimes effective in milder cases. In instances where infants are able to ruminate only when they use a finger, toy, or some other object, elbow restraints can be of value. The most successful results are obtained by distracting the patient after feedings, holding him, and providing him with attention during and after nursing. When the continued presence, comfort, and physical contact of the mother or any other adult cannot be constantly assured, distraction with multicolored or moving objects and the company of other children can greatly contribute toward the infant's improvement. Permanent control of the habit may be anticipated only by furthering or reestablishing a close, warm, and comfortable maternal-child relationship or its closest equivalent. Major emphasis must be placed upon the correction of the social, emotional, or educational deficiencies in the human environment of the infant which carry the responsibility for the deprivation and the disruption in mother-infant relationship.

REFERENCES

Cameron, H. C. Forms of vomiting in infancy. Brit. Med. J., 1:872, 1925.

Fullerton, D. T. Infantile rumination. Arch. of Gen. Psychiat., 9:593-600, 1963.

Hollowell, J. G., and Gardner, L. I. Rumination and growth failure in male fraternal twins, associated with disturbed family environment. Pediatrics, 36:565-571, 1965.

Gaddini, R. D. B., and Gaddini, E. Rumination in infancy. In Jessner, L., and Pavenstedt, E., eds., Dynamic Psychopathology in Childhood. New York, Grune and Stratton, Inc., 1959, pp. 166-185.

Luckey, R. E., Watson, C. M., and Musick, J. K. Aversive conditioning as a means of inhibiting vomiting and rumination. Amer. J. Ment. Defic., 73:139, 1968.

Menking, M., Wagnitz, J. G., Burton, J. J., Coddington, R. D., and Sotos, J. F. Rumination—A near fatal psychiatric disease of infancy. New Eng. J. Med., 280:802-804, 1969.

Patton, R. J., and Gardner, L. I. Influence of family and environment: "The syndrome of maternal deprivation." Pediatrics, 30:957, 1967.

Richmond, J. B., Eddy, E., and Green, M. Rumination:

A psychosomatic syndrome of infancy. Pediatrics, 22:49, 1958.

Rothney, W. B. Rumination and spasmus nutans. Hosp. Practice, 4:102-106, Sept. 1969.

Stein, M. L., Rausen, A. R., and Blau, A. Psychotherapy of an infant with rumination. J.A.M.A., 171:2309, 1959.

23.4
GASTROINTESTINAL BLEEDING

MURRAY DAVIDSON

HEMATEMESIS. Vomited blood is not uncommon in the newborn period. True gastric hemorrhage may occur from ulcers in states of anoxemia, in septicemia, in hemorrhagic disease of the newborn, and in hiatus hernia of the stomach from erosion of the esophageal mucosa by regurgitated gastric juice.

Vomited blood in newborns is not necessarily from the infant's stomach. Vomiting of blood swallowed during the birth process may be delayed up to two or three days. The most reliable means for distinguishing maternal from infant's blood is the semiquantitative test for fetal hemoglobin by alkali denaturation. Trauma to the nasopharynx caused by a suction tube is another source of vomited blood in newborn infants. Infants at the breast may draw blood from a fissure or ulcer in the mother's nipple. Alarmingly large amounts of blood may be vomited in these circumstances, yet the child's condition remains good. Examination of the mother will generally reveal the source of the trouble. It may sometimes be noted that vomiting of blood follows nursing from one breast and not from the other.

In older infants and children, too, vomited blood may come from a source other than the gastrointestinal tract. The nose and pharynx are the most common sources, especially with nosebleeds and after tonsillectomy. Although peptic ulceration is the most common cause of true upper gastrointestinal bleeding in all age groups, a very important cause of hematemesis in children is rupture of *esophageal varices.* These varices develop as a collateral venous network in portal hypertension due to cirrhosis of the liver or obstruction of the extrahepatic portal vein system. These lesions may be congenital or acquired. The acquired form may be due rarely to cavernomatous transformation of the portal vein or frequently to pyelothrombophlebitis. The latter may be secondary to infection of the umbilical cord or may follow catheterization of the vessel. Hematemesis is usually the first sign of the condition; the varices may rupture without warning, and bleeding may be massive. Episodes of hemorrhage recur unless the portal hypertension is corrected surgically by some type of portacaval shunt. Other less common causes of bleeding from the esophagus in children are erosions of the mucosa associated with hiatus hernia, regurgitation of gastric juice as in chalasia (p. 1575), and thoracic gastrointestinal duplications which open into the esophagus and are lined by secreting gastric mucosa.

As in adults, children who bleed from peptic ulcers may have displayed no previous signs of ulcer, and bleeding may continue to the point of exsanguination. Abscesses and neoplasms of the stomach may cause hemorrhages. Hemorrhage is seen with various systemic conditions such as thrombocytopenia, leukemia, scurvy, hemophilia, purpura, and rarely in infections such as malaria and hemorrhagic measles. Liver poisons, such as phosphorous, may lead to hypoprothrombinemia and bleeding. Fatal hemorrhage has been reported to occur some time after the swallowing of a foreign body.

If the hemorrhage is rapid and vomiting prompt, the blood may be bright red; if blood has been in the stomach for a period of time it is dark brown and black, resembling coffee grounds. The stools, which invariably contain blood if there is bleeding from the stomach, are black and tarry in appearance if considerable blood is present; otherwise the presence of blood is detected only by chemical tests. Whether or not symptoms of shock are present will depend upon the amount and rapidity of blood loss.

A vital part of management of gastrointestinal hemorrhage is to keep the patient quiet and immobilized; sedation with morphine may be necessary. If a good deal of blood has been lost, supportive transfusions with whole blood to replace cells and blood volume are required. Hematocrits must be followed frequently and regularly to evaluate continuing losses of blood. The pulse should be carefully watched; if there are signs of vascular collapse, transfusion is urgently indicated. Whether food or water should be given by mouth during the period of hemorrhage and observation depends on the diagnosis; if in doubt, no feedings should be given. With known peptic ulcerations, frequent small amounts of antacids or milk are useful. If bleeding is due to esophageal varices, food should be withheld for at least 24 hours after the hemorrhage has been controlled. Fluids should be given parenterally as indicated. Gastric cooling has been employed for control of upper gastrointestinal hemorrhage in adults with some success; there has been little experience with this procedure in children.

Specific treatment should be directed toward the primary condition causing the hematemesis.
HEMATOCHEZIA AND MELENA. Hematochezia, appearance of gross blood in the stool, is usually associated with bleeding from the lower intestines. Melena, or tarry stool, indicates presence of blood from the upper gastrointestinal tract which has been altered by secretions as it passed to the rectum. However, massive gastric bleeding may be followed by recognizable unaltered blood in the stool, whereas slow oozing of blood from the lower ileum may occasionally result only in tarry stools. Blood losses up to about 15 ml per day may occur from any point in the intestinal tract without a gross change in appearance of the stool of children, although tests for occult blood would be strongly positive.

Conditions associated with hematemesis usually lead to melena or occult blood in the stool. Intussusception is associated with bloody stools, the blood being characteristically mixed with mucus, without stool, to give the classic currant jelly stool. In acute dysentery, diarrhea and gross bleeding are common.

The presence of blood in the stools in children is a prime example of the principle that the diagnostic implications of symptoms and findings in children may be quite different than in adults. The possibility that such bleeding in an adult is from a malignancy dictates an attitude of immediacy in approach. The probability of a malignancy in a child with this finding is so remote that the same attitude should not prevail. A number of reported series of children admitted to hospitals for investigation of rectal bleeding indicate that in a considerable percentage no etiologic diagnosis is established despite repeated sigmoidoscopic, radiographic, and other examinations. Since fissure in ano often accounts for more than 50 percent of children with rectal bleeding in whom a diagnosis is established, one may safely postpone more extensive investigations while a course of mineral oil therapy is prescribed. This therapeutic approach to rectal bleeding is probably more important for evaluation than are repeated instrumentations and barium enemas. If bleeding persists after a few weeks of treatment with oral doses of liquid petrolatum, investigation is warranted.

The data in Table 1 are compiled from a number of sources. The 13 causes of rectal bleeding in children are listed in order of the ages at which they initially are encountered. The frequency of occurrence is indicated semiquantitatively by the number of (+) signs, or by a (−) if of negligible incidence. Thus, although swallowed blood may be a source of rectal bleeding at other ages than in the newborn period, its occurrence is so rare at these times as to

TABLE 1.   *Rectal Bleeding in Children*

Causes	Newborn	1 wk-2 yr	2-13 yr
1. Swallowed blood	+++*	−	−
2. Trauma to rectum	+*	±	−
3. Milk allergy	+	+*	−
4. Bleeding diathesis	++*	+*	+*
5. Peptic ulceration	++*	++*	+*
6. Developmental anomalies	±	++*	+*
7. Meckel's diverticulum	−	++*	+*
8. Intussusception	−	++*	+*
9. Fissure in ano	−	++++ ++++	++++
10. Polyps	−	++*	+++*
11. Portal hypertension	−	+*	++*
12. Ulcerative colitis	−	±*	+++*
13. Cancer	−	−	−

*Bleeding may be massive.

deserve a (−) sign. On the other hand fissure in ano is so much more common a cause of rectal bleeding than all others, that it is graded eight (+) in the 1-week to 2-year age group. The chart makes clear that cancer is not a serious problem and repeated definitive studies are therefore not indicated for this possibility. Most of the conditions in this table are discussed individually elsewhere in this chapter.

REFERENCES

Abrams, B., and Lynn, H. B. Rectal bleeding in children. Amer. J. Surg., 104:831, 1962.

Brayton, D. Gastrointestinal bleeding of "unknown origin"; a study of cases in infancy and childhood. Amer. J. Dis. Child., 107:288, 1964

Gross, R. E. Rectal bleeding in infants and children. In Surgery of Infancy and Childhood. Philadelphia, W. B. Saunders Co., 1953, pp. 369-376.

Spencer, R. Gastrointestinal hemorrhage in infancy and childhood: 476 cases. Surgery, 55:718, 1964.

23.5

DIARRHEA

MURRAY DAVIDSON

PHILIP SUNSHINE and
NORMAN KRETCHMER
(Disaccharide and Oligosaccharide Malabsorption)

Acute Diarrhea

The subject of acute diarrhea and its causes and management are discussed elsewhere in detail (Sec. 3.8). Certain supplemental general features of the subject, especially those related to gastrointestinal function, are discussed in this section. They are also related to the problem of chronic diarrhea, which is discussed principally in this chapter.

PATHOLOGIC CHEMISTRY AND PHYSIOLOGY. The mechanism responsible for the hyperperistalsis of acute diarrhea is not known accurately. Apart from the pathogenic organisms there is no convincing evidence that the intestinal contents contain a direct irritant. The initial treatment of purging, formerly suggested, to remove such irritants is no longer recommended. The loss of nutrients in diarrhea is due only in part to hyperperistalsis which prevents adequate time for absorption; there may be disturbances in enzyme functions, impairment of the inherent assimilatory mechanisms, and also disturbances in fluid and electrolyte movements. These factors do not necessarily operate simultaneously. In some severe cases fluid absorption may be impaired to such an extent that symptoms of shock appear some hours before diarrhea is evident. Likewise, with recovery, balance studies have shown that it is not uncommon for poor assimilation of fat to persist for days or even weeks after hyperperistalsis has subsided. The extent to which assimilation of individual nutrients is impaired varies widely in individual cases. Of the calorigenic foodstuffs, protein assimilation is relatively little affected; even moribund infants with severe diarrhea may continue to absorb and retain nitrogen. Assimilation of fat is usually affected and may be markedly impaired in severe cases. It is readily measured by balance studies; in cases of moderate severity only 50 to 70 percent of the intake may be absorbed, whereas in the most severe cases absorption may fall to 20 percent of the intake or even less. A flat postabsorptive blood sugar curve and the passage of considerable flatus are commonly regarded as evidence of impaired carbohydrate absorption. These findings, however, do not necessarily indicate a serious defect of absorption; the postabsorptive sugar curve is related to rate rather than to completeness of absorption. The only accurate method of measuring carbohydrate absorption involves balance studies with labeled carbohydrate in which the intake and stool output of tagged carbon are measured. This method has not been applied to infants with diarrhea. In exceptional infants failure of carbohydrate assimilation may be based on temporary deficiencies of the appropriate digestive secretions, especially lactase (p. 1592).

Most serious for the welfare of the infant are the disturbances in water and electrolyte balance in diarrhea. The loss of water and electrolyte in the stools is promptly reflected by a reduction of blood volume and of interstitial fluid volume. The loss of extracellular fluids is responsible for a series of pathologic processes, discussed elsewhere (Sec. 3.7). Stool losses of water in severe cases of diarrhea may range from 250 to 500 ml or more per day, amounting to 10 to 15 times the normal, and electrolyte losses may also approach a tenfold increase over normal. In some instances, a relative deficit of water predominates and *hyperelectrolytemia* develops. This condition and the opposite disturbance, *hypoelectrolytemia*, are discussed in detail elsewhere (Sec. 3.7).

PATHOLOGY. Except in shigella infections, in which ileocolitis is often found, and in patients with staphylococcal enterocolitis, in which ulcerations may occur (Sec. 14.6), nothing striking is usually seen grossly in the gastrointestinal tract of children with acute diarrhea. The intestines are likely to be distended but otherwise normal. Parenteral infection may be present but frequently is absent. Although melena or hematemesis may have occurred, the site of bleeding is seldom demonstrated. Anatomic changes from dehydration, loss of fluid from the subcutaneous tissues, and reduction of muscle volume are less conspicuous at autopsy than during life. In long-standing cases evidences of malnutrition are prominent. Fatty liver is a fairly frequent finding. Thrombosis of the cerebral venous sinuses is found in some fatal cases, and subdural effusions and hemorrhages have been described. A rare lesion is calcification of the renal epithelium.

"NUTRITIONAL" TREATMENT. Parenteral fluid and electrolyte therapy of hospitalized patients with diarrhea is discussed in Section 3.8. The home treatment of infants with mild diarrhea should be expectant; patients should be observed especially closely for the development of constitutional symptoms. Special attention should be paid to the intake of fluids, which in young infants should not be allowed to fall below 150 ml per kg per day. However, feeding should be infrequent and of relatively large amounts each time, rather than the small frequent feedings which are often ordered; the latter tend to induce frequent bowel movements. Lowering the fat content of the milk presumably serves to shorten the course of mild diarrhea and to lessen the chance of a mild attack increasing in severity. This concept has not been studied adequately and has been challenged by some who recommend that an infant with mild diarrhea be offered usual amounts of its normal diet. If diarrhea remains mild or if moderate diarrhea subsides rapidly, parenteral therapy may not be required. Charcoal, kaolin, pectin, apple pulp, carrot soup, carob flour, and synthetic resins have been suggested in an effort to diminish the number of stools. In our experience these remedies are of limited value. In the hope of arresting the diarrhea, oral solutions of glucose and of electrolytes are often substituted for the milk feeding. There is no objection to this procedure if properly used and isotonic solutions of glucose should be encouraged, but excessive or improper use of electrolyte mixtures has been held responsible for the apparent increase in the incidence of hypernatremia (hyperelectrolytemia) in dehydrated infants. This applies especially if the use of such a solution is in addition to milk.

Controversy prevails as to the desirability of restricting oral food in infants with acute diarrhea who require hospitalization for parenteral fluid and electrolyte management. In cases with vomiting it must obviously be withheld. The debatable question arises when vomiting is not a problem. There is no question that the administration of feedings to a patient with an intolerant intestine increases the volume of diarrheal stools and that the reduction of oral intake decreases them. This finding has been generally interpreted as indicating that the administration of oral food decreases the tolerance of the intestine, and that resting the intestine promotes recovery. The procedure followed by those who interpret the evidence in this way is to omit all oral food for a period of 24 hours or perhaps longer, postponing its resumption until dehydration has been brought under control and the stools have become less voluminous and watery. It is then cautiously introduced in a stepwise manner. Should the stools again become increasingly loose and frequent, the conclusion is drawn that the introduction of oral food was premature and a second period of oral starvation is instituted. Various modifications of this general plan are used. In the belief that only caloric food is harmful some physicians give water and electrolytes by mouth from the start; others give glucose, water, and electrolytes, withholding only protein and fat. The belief prevails that the attack of diarrhea is shortened by such dietary management.

A different point of view was expressed by Park in 1924, who advocated disregarding the stools and thinking rather of the assimilation of the food by the child. His view, however, did not gain wide acceptance in the absence of physiologic data on different regimens. Chung undertook such studies in 1948, obtaining results which supported Park's views. He and his co-workers were able to show that although administration of oral food increased stool losses in patients with infantile diarrhea as well as in those with other forms of intestinal intolerance, it also increased the quantities absorbed of nitrogen, fat, and electrolytes. They further made a comparison of the duration of diarrhea in a group of infants with summer diarrhea in which half the cases were subjected to early fasting while the other half were allowed an adequate oral intake from the start. Their findings are shown in Table 2, in which the duration was measured by the time required before the infant could take a full diet without evidence of diarrhea. The interpretation drawn from these results was that oral feedings merely demonstrated intolerance rather than adding to it and did not delay recovery. These investigators inclined to view instances in which patients had deteriorated under oral feeding as compared with parenteral fluid therapy as due not to any noxious effect of the oral food, but rather to the fact

TABLE 2. *Duration of Infantile Diarrhea**

Regimen	Duration (Days)								Total Cases
	1-2	3-4	5-6	7-8	9-10	11-12	13-14	Over 14	
Early oral starvation	0	14	10	10	3	3	7	3	50
Early oral feeding	4	19	12	9	2	4	1	2	53

*From Chung. *J. Pediat.*, 33:14, 1948.

that oral food was substituted for parenteral therapy rather than used as a supplement to needed parenteral fluid.

Oral feedings are less controversial if they are relied on simply as a source of calories and nutriment, but are *expected to induce additional losses of fluid and electrolyte,* in the recovery phases of acute diarrhea. Adoption of such an attitude permits earlier institution of oral feedings, with simultaneous prolonged administration of intravenous fluids, properly designed for daily maintenance needs, as well as for replacement of losses induced by the feedings. Use of combined oral feeding and parenteral fluid and electrolyte regimens has been successfully employed by us in a number of instances of protracted diarrhea with resistant infections. Parenteral therapy can only be relaxed in the combined oral-intravenous treatment when it is clear that sufficient fluids are being *absorbed* from the oral intake.

Parenteral Nutrition. The majority of fatalities in diarrhea occur in long-standing cases in which profound inanition develops. Combined oral nutrition with prolonged parenteral fluid therapy is usually successful in forestalling this dire result. Some investigators have tried to sustain both nutrition and fluid-electrolyte metabolism by the parenteral route alone. Emulsified fat suitable for intravenous use has been made available from time to time. Although it is the most potent source of calories and it has been shown that it is rapidly burned, the difficulty has been the occurrence of reactions in a considerable percentage of cases, usually attributable to the emulsifying agent. Fat emulsions in small quantities can be given subcutaneously and do not seem to have any harmful effects, but are not useful for long-term management. Commercial protein hydrolysates and amino acid mixtures are nonantigenic and can be given safely intravenously. Although these preparations are effective sources of nitrogen, positive nitrogen balance cannot be achieved unless sufficient calories are simultaneously supplied from other sources to prevent their conversion by gluconeogenesis to sources of energy. Amino acid mixtures are excellent culture media and care must be used to avoid contamination. Cloudy solutions should never be used and it is a good precaution to add penicillin to the solution to prevent bacterial growth in the infusion bottle.

Currently, there is increasing interest in and success with parenteral "hyperalimentation." This form of therapy is not new in principle, but the practice is novel. Deep veins are cannulated so that hypertonic glucose solutions may be successfully administered without fear of venous thrombosis. This calorie source together with amino acid mixtures and adequate fluid and electrolyte offers both parenteral "feeding" and fluid-electrolyte replacement. It is indicated much more frequently following surgery for congenital lesions of the gastrointestinal tract than in persistent diarrhea, since in our experience the latter group does just as well with combined nutritional feedings orally and fluid-electrolyte administration parenterally. Morbidity is lower with this combined treatment than with the deep venous alimentation.

Neonatal Necrotizing Enterocolitis

Necrotizing enterocolitis is a virulent form of diarrhea among neonates; it is particularly prevalent among low-birth-weight infants. The etiology is unknown, but mesenteric vascular ischemia with resultant hypoxia of the intestinal mucosa has been suggested as the probable pathogenetic mechanism. Initially the condition is not remarkably different from other types of diarrhea in the neonate. The lethargy, irritability, distension, anorexia, vomiting, and poor body temperature regulation are not unusual among low-birth-weight infants with diarrhea from any cause. However, the history of difficulty with aeration at birth, increased apneic episodes, and blood in the stools should alert the physician to the possibility of this serious condition. Pneumatosis intestinalis, the presence of air in the submucosa and/or subserosal surfaces of the colon, is virtually always present and is pathognomonic. Increased air in the bowel lumen or in the peritoneum (indicating perforation of gangrenous bowel) may be seen but are not specific signs of necrotizing enterocolitis. Barium examination is not necessary for demonstration of any of the radiographic findings associated with the condition; it is actually contraindicated since it may lead to perforation.

Once suspected, oral feedings are discontinued, and a regimen of parenteral fluid therapy is instituted, with intermittent or continuous gastric suction. Antibiotic therapy is given, using combinations of penicillin and kanamycin. Plain and upright radiograms of the abdomen should be obtained every 6 to 12 hours to follow the progress of the infant. In some, the symptoms will regress after 48 to 72 hours. However, the mortality is above 50 percent in most series, and there is an increasing tendency to approach the situation aggressively. If deterioration occurs with medical management, surgery may be indicated even in the absence of signs of perforation. Resection and primary anastomosis are carried out for localized lesions; in more extensive cases resection and exteriorization with ileostomy or colostomy are recommended. The extensive nature of the surgical procedure in many instances dictates a prolonged period of parenteral alimentation, this being one type of infantile diarrhea in which this method of treatment may be lifesaving.

Chronic Diarrhea

Persistence of acute diarrhea may presage a chronic problem in any individual case. More frequently chronic diarrhea tends to develop insidiously. Rational therapy of chronic diarrhea depends to a large extent on precise knowledge of its etiology and pathophysiology. The underlying process in a patient with acute diarrhea is much more likely to be self-limited than in one with chronic symptoms.

Although, as in acute diarrhea, loose or watery stools may result from a disorder of the normal fluid and electrolyte balance in the distal colon, involvement of this area by the disease occurs in only a limited number of types of chronic diarrhea. In many instances, the disturbance of colonic function is secondary to small bowel malfunction; for example, inflammatory exudates may be passed from the small intestine into the colon and have a deleterious effect on colonic salt and water absorption; or in patients with disaccharidase deficiencies excess disscharides may exert an osmotic effect and withdraw colonic fluid. In each of these instances there may be little or no objective evidence to suggest disease of the colon, yet the small intestinal disease may produce chronic watery diarrhea of the type usually associated with large bowel diseases. In other forms of chronic diarrhea the stools, instead of being watery or loose, are more likely to be large, bulky, and somewhat softer than normal stools. In these patients the only defect in intestinal function might be a profound disturbance in fat digestion or absorption, with little or no alteration in the handling of other nutriments or of water and electrolytes.

The inflammatory diseases which are associated with chronic diarrhea may involve either small or large intestine, or both; they include regional enteritis, ulcerative colitis, and pseudomembranous enterocolitis of congenital megacolon. Other forms of chronic diarrhea include the various malabsorption syndromes and functional chronic diarrhea.

Malabsorption Syndrome
(Celiac Syndrome)

In 1888 Gee described a chronic nutritional disorder of children characterized by abdominal distention and persistent diarrhea with large, greasy, foul-smelling stools, which he referred to as "the celiac affection" and which subsequently was called "celiac disease." Unfortunately, a wide variety of entities, differing from each other in causation and in course, but presenting in common the symptom of persistent or recurrent diarrhea, were ultimately ascribed to this term and gathered under the title of "the celiac syndrome," synonymous with "malabsorption syndrome."

Since "celiac *disease*" is a single clearly identifiable clinical and pathologic entity, the time has arrived to discard the term "celiac *syndrome*." It has been demoted to the position of a secondary title in this edition of the textbook, and hopefully will be dropped entirely from popular usage in the future. Clinical entities which have been distinguished in the malabsorption syndrome are usually classified into

groups based either on the mechanism of the defect, such as digestive, absorptive, or exudative, or on the specific types of foodstuffs (fat, protein, carbohydrate) which are primarily involved in the absorption defect. In the following presentation the division is by foodstuffs.

Lipid Malabsorption

Historically, the major defect in the patients described by Gee in 1888 was probably in absorption of lipids. The disease entities which involve the defect of fat absorption make up a group in which many of the fundamental defects in absorption tend to remain constant throughout the life-span, and mechanisms of studying the disorders are equally applicable to children and adults. Digestive ability for fat is evaluated by both direct and indirect means. Measured meals have been fed, digestive and assimilative activities permitted to occur, and the residue measured in material aspirated from tubes terminating at specific locations in the gastrointestinal tract, or from stools which are collected for varying periods. The usual balance study technique involves collection of stools for 72 to 96 hours from a subject on a measured fat intake. Some authors utilize 5-day collections and discard those of alternate days, pooling the samples of days 1, 3, and 5 for the determination of average fat losses in the stool. Fat absorption is also assessed after feeding measured amounts of radioiodine which has been incorporated into either specific saturated and unsaturated, long- and short-chain fatty acids, into triglycerides of known fatty acid composition, or into fatty mixtures (Lipiodol). Although a disadvantage of such procedures results from the need to employ isotopes in young children, differential studies with a group of such agents make it possible in some instances of doubt to pinpoint whether a defect exists primarily in digestive or absorptive activity. The measurement of split and unsplit fat in the stool and the ratio of saturated to unsaturated fatty acid patterns have been utilized as indications of fat digestion and of the amount of exogenous versus endogenous fat in the specimen. These techniques are useful in a semiquantitative sense, but cannot be interpreted with certainty when the results are not clear-cut. Perhaps amplification with more precise methods such as gas-liquid chromatography will make this type of study even more valuable in the future.

A variety of "tolerance" curves is employed in study of fat digestion and absorption. A chylomicron count is a crude measurement using the number of fat particles in the bloodstream visible under the microscope, after ingestion of a fatty meal. It was formerly popular to test for the differential effects of both water-miscible and fat-soluble preparations of vitamin A. Vitamin A levels in blood are measured at 1 and 5 hours after feeding of either water-miscible or oily preparations of the vitamin. In the normal individual, a significant rise over the base line is expected from both. In those individuals in whom there is a defect in the digestion of vitamin A but not in absorption, as with pancreatic insufficiency, the fat-soluble preparation is not absorbed, but the tolerance curve for the water-soluble form is normal. In individuals with absorptive defects, feeding either form of vitamin A yields a low tolerance curve. Some authors do not carry out a tolerance test but simply interpret a low fasting carotene level as indicating malabsorption. However, this interpretation is less reliable in children than in adults since supplementation of the diet with water-miscible preparations may maintain a normal fasting carotene level even in patients with malabsorption.

Disorders of lipid "absorption" may be due to abnormalities of lipolysis, of mucosal cell transport, or of lymphatic transport of fat. However, it is difficult to pinpoint the precise mechanism causing steatorrhea in premature infants or in patients with conditions such as neurogenic tumors with increased catecholamine secretion, or dysgammaglobulinemia.

ABNORMALITIES OF LIPOLYSIS AND SOLUBILIZATION OF LIPIDS. Abnormalities of lipolysis are due principally to pancreatic insufficiency, which in children is virtually restricted to *cystic fibrosis of the pancreas* (Chap. 9). However, isolated deficiencies of specific pancreatic enzymes, including lipase, have been described in rare patients. Also pancreatic lipase may be destroyed by the acid pH of the upper small intestine in patients with hypersecretion of gastric acid.

In those conditions in which normal hepatic function is impaired, or in which there is obstruction to flow of bile into the duodenum, the critical levels of conjugated bile salts essential to the formation of micelles may not be reached and solubilization will be impaired. In addition to liver diseases, this problem may occur in those instances in which chronic stasis of the small bowel results in bacterial overgrowth of this region with resultant deconjugation of the bile salts by the organisms. Such bacterial overgrowth is encountered in a variety of conditions including decreased acidity, as with achlorhydria following resections of the stomach, malrotations, multiple small intestinal strictures, and jejunal diverticula and duplications. Another factor which interferes with the effectiveness of conjugated bile salts in micellar formation is disturbance in the enterohepatic circulation resulting from extensive disease of the distal small bowel, or absence of this segment after surgery for a congenital obstruction or an acquired inflammatory disease.

ABNORMALITIES OF MUCOSAL-CELL TRANSPORT. *Idiopathic Celiac Disease (Gluten-Induced Enteropathy).* Idiopathic celiac disease is a relatively rare condition characterized by malabsorption of fat. In this disease, in contrast to cystic fibrosis of the pancreas, there does not appear to be any deficiency in lipolysis. The major clinical manifestations, as well as the physiologic and biochemical abnormalities observed in patients with idiopathic celiac disease, can be attributed to the malabsorption of fat and the

resulting malnutrition. In virtually all respects idiopathic celiac disease in children is identical with nontropical sprue as seen in adults, and the latter term has now generally been abandoned in favor of celiac disease in all age groups.

Etiology. At the present time the exact cause and pathogenesis of celiac disease must be considered to be unknown. There is some evidence that a genetic constitutional factor may play a role; in some families it has occurred in more than one child. Symptoms suggesting celiac disease during early childhood have been reported in the medical history of a number of adults.

In addition to the possible genetic factor, there is evidence that intolerance to certain proteins plays a part in most instances of the disease. A close correlation is observed between the ingestion of wheat flour and exacerbations of the disease. The disturbing factor in wheat lies in a protein moiety, gluten, particularly its gliadin component. Oral administration of glutamine, the amino acid which comprises 43 percent of the nitrogen of gliadin, has no demonstrable effect on a patient with celiac disease, but the feeding of various peptide fractions of gliadin is deleterious to the patients. Patients with celiac disease have been described who showed no sensitivity to gluten but who demonstrated steatorrhea following the ingestion of small amounts of cow's milk beta-lactoglobulin. These observations suggest the possibility that a variety of proteins may play specific roles in individual patients.

A variety of nonspecific stresses may initiate or aggravate symptoms in a child with celiac disease. Chief among these are parenteral infections, the effect of which on intestinal assimilation of fat appears to be no different from that seen in many normal infants; what differentiates the patient with celiac disease are the prolonged duration of his response, the often minor nature of the infections, and the persistence of the pattern beyond infancy. In this sense, the difference between the normal and the celiac subject is one of degree. One child passes through acute infections, even in infancy, without any disturbance of digestion; another develops diarrhea which may outlast evidence of infection for a week or two; in a third, whom we label a "celiac," the disturbance of assimilation persists for months and the tendency to it extends beyond the age of infancy.

Among pediatricians with wide experience in celiac disease there are conflicting opinions concerning other precipitating factors. Most agree that emotional stress may initiate or aggravate the symptoms in the absence of infections. As discussed below, opinions are more disparate concerning the effect of the fat content of the diet.

Pathology. A major advance in the diagnosis of celiac disease has been the introduction of the peroral biopsy technique. A variety of tubes and capsules is employed. Each operates differently in practice, but the principle common to all involves the sucking in of a small knuckle of upper intestinal

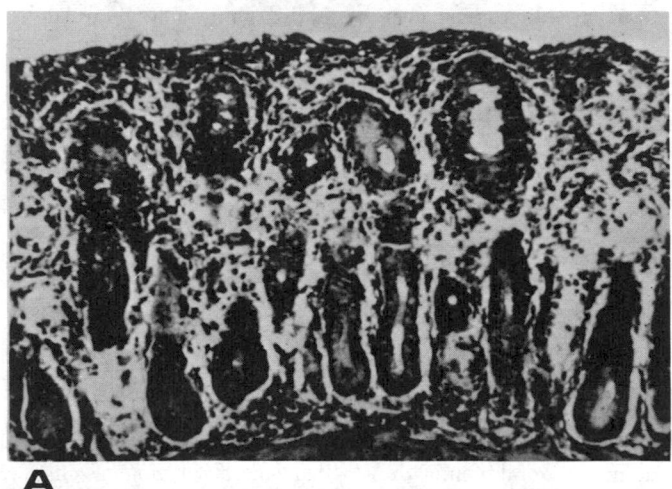

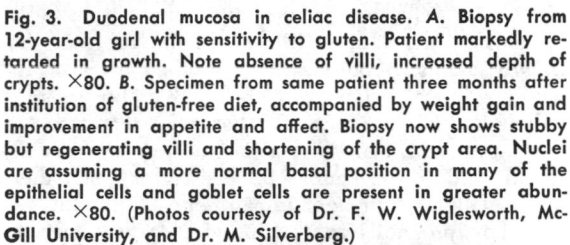

Fig. 3. Duodenal mucosa in celiac disease. A. Biopsy from 12-year-old girl with sensitivity to gluten. Patient markedly retarded in growth. Note absence of villi, increased depth of crypts. ×80. B. Specimen from same patient three months after institution of gluten-free diet, accompanied by weight gain and improvement in appetite and affect. Biopsy now shows stubby but regenerating villi and shortening of the crypt area. Nuclei are assuming a more normal basal position in many of the epithelial cells and goblet cells are present in greater abundance. ×80. (Photos courtesy of Dr. F. W. Wiglesworth, McGill University, and Dr. M. Silverberg.)

mucosa, amputation of it relatively atraumatically, and the ability to withdraw it for examination. Although rare instances of protracted bleeding or perforation are encountered, thousands of biopsies have been performed without incident, and the procedure is now relatively routine. The tissue recovered may be examined by light and electron microscopy, studied chemically for enzymes and other constituents, or assayed for immune substances. Microscopic examination is of particular value for the diagnosis and follow-up of patients with celiac disease (Fig. 3).

Children with celiac disease suffer mucosal lesions of the small intestine which are apparent on gross and microscopic examination. Loss of villi with obliteration of intervillous spaces can be demonstrated by light microscopy. The mucosal cells tend to become more cuboidal than columnar and there is disturbance in the normal basal position of their nuclei. The crypts are deeper and increased mitoses can be observed in the cells which line them. The monocellular population of the lamina propria is also increased. Electron micrographs reveal loss of brush borders in the epithelial cells. The changes can be shown to be reversible in patients treated by exclusion of gluten from the diet. The specificity of the lesion for celiac disease is sometimes questioned, since similar changes in villi may occur in some inflammatory conditions and in other instances of malnutrition. However, among such patients the findings are usually not as generalized, and are less intense than those observed so uniformly in all patients with untreated celiac disease.

Other anatomic changes observed in a limited number of autopsies are those of inanition. There is conspicuous atrophy of fat, lymphoid tissue, and muscle; a small heart is not an uncommon finding. Evidence of infection or of specific deficiencies may be encountered. There may be a fatty liver.

Pathologic physiology. The view that starch ingestion has an adverse effect on celiac disease is no longer widely held. It is the specific protein of flour rather than the starch which is responsible. Starch itself is reasonably well absorbed, and the presence of extracellular starch granules in the stools carries no sinister significance. A flat or nearly flat blood sugar curve following oral ingestion of glucose, or of the pentose sugar xylose, is commonly found in idiopathic celiac disease. It is by no means specific for this condition, since it is also encountered in severe malnutrition of any cause and in some chronic disorders affecting hepatic function. Using isotopically labeled glucose in tolerance tests on patients with celiac disease, Somersalo was able to demonstrate that the absorption of glucose was minimally affected; the flat tolerance curve was attributed to delay in the rate of absorption.

The assimilation of protein is affected relatively little in the celiac patient. Except during episodes of diarrhea, from 80 to 90 percent of the nitrogen intake is absorbed, and blood amino acid curves after a test dose of casein or gelatin follow a normal pattern. However, hypoproteinemia and nutritional edema are sometimes encountered. In some of these cases it has been possible to demonstrate that the hypoproteinemia results from excessive losses of serum proteins into the gastrointestinal lumen. In others, the hypoproteinemia may reflect overall malnutrition. It has been our impression that the hydrolability which is often seen in these patients is related to hypoproteinemia. Such patients when affected by an intercurrent acute digestive upset may lose weight so precipitously and develop alarming symptoms of dehydration so rapidly as to justify the term "celiac crises."

The fundamental defect in celiac disease is malabsorption of fat, the unabsorbed fat of the feces being virtually completely split. As in the normal subject, the unsaturated and short-chain fats are more readily absorbed; the unabsorbed fecal fats are therefore the longer chain saturated fatty acids. To what extent or how the atrophic changes described in the intestinal villi are responsible for the deficit in absorption is not known. The earlier view that the fat intolerance was induced by fat and could be ameliorated by limiting the fat intake has little support.

Symptoms. In most patients with celiac disease the symptoms begin during infancy, although rarely before 6 months of age. Only exceptionally does the process begin later than the third year. Though breast feeding will not prevent the development of celiac disease, it has a tendency to postpone the time of appearance of symptoms, probably because many breast-fed infants are introduced to solid foods, including wheat cereal, at a later time. The development of the frank clinical picture is inevitably insidious but often follows one or more acute episodes. A common story is that the infant suffered from one or more attacks of acute diarrhea, perhaps associated with respiratory infections and accompanied by vomiting. Recovery from these symptoms seems to be incomplete. The appetite is not restored and normal weight gain is not resumed. The stools, though numbering only one to three a day, tend to be mushy and unusually bulky; they are foul and often frothy.

If the condition persists, the picture of chronic malnutrition becomes established. There is loss of subcutaneous fat, particularly conspicuous in the buttocks (Fig. 4). Muscular activity is diminished, and the muscles lose their tone; the abdomen becomes distended, and there is a change in disposition, the child becoming fretful. Sleep is often disturbed.

Exacerbations of the acute digestive disturbances occur at irregular intervals. Often they are precipitated by obvious infections; at other times these may not be as apparent and other causes may be implicated. In those patients in whom sensitivity to protein has been demonstrated, relatively minor dietary indiscretions may produce exacerbations of the disease. During these episodes acute diarrhea may develop, sometimes of alarming severity; vomiting may

also occur, and loss of weight may be precipitous, obliterating several months' gain. The hydrolability and marked anorexia of these patients is often very striking.

With persistence of the celiac state evidence of malnutrition becomes more conspicuous and specific deficiencies may make their appearance. Anemia is one of the commonest; usually it is microcytic, but occasionally the macrocytic type more characteristic of adults is encountered. There may be hypoproteinemia and nutritional edema. Symptoms due to deficiency of fat-soluble vitamins may develop in severe and long-standing cases. Tetany and rickets as complications of celiac disease, apparently more common in Europe, are seen rarely in this country. Osteoporosis may be the only expression of vitamin D deficiency. The osteoporotic bones are fragile, and fractures of the long bones may occur. Hypoprothrombinemia due to deficient absorption of vitamin K is occasionally seen, but hemorrhage is rare. Frank vitamin A deficiency is virtually unknown in celiac patients in the United States, despite the fact that it is a common complication in other parts of the world. Clinical deficiencies of the B group are rare, although thiamine deficiency has been reported. Delay in growth and in skeletal maturation is commonly found, and if the condition persists for years there may be some permanent impairment of growth.

The prognosis in the individual case must be based largely on prolonged observation of the patient. There is generally a period of quiescence in late childhood and adolescence even without treatment, which is referred to as the latent period. However, evidence is accumulating that mucosal lesions, mild degrees of steatorrhea, and less than optimal growth may be the result of failure to adhere to a strict diet during this age period. Intellectual development is not permanently impaired by the nutritional disturbance. Although celiac patients frequently appear dull, they progress normally with convalescence.

Diagnosis. In the presence of chronic malnutrition and typical stools, steatorrhea must be established before the diagnosis of celiac disease can be made. Steatorrhea is most accurately measured by a complete fecal collection for a period of several days. Children with celiac disease absorb less than 90 percent of the ingested fat, and show fecal loss of fat greater than 3 to 5 g per day. There has been an unfortunate tendency to make the diagnosis in many children who suffer one or more acute digestive upsets from which they may recover entirely, or for the diagnosis to be made in many children with the irritable colon syndrome (see below). To label such children as celiac often results in their being placed on sharply restricted diets and becoming the objects of undue concern. Once steatorrhea has been demonstrated in the individual patient, other causes of this condition must be ruled out before the diagnosis of idiopathic celiac disease is tenable.

Of special importance to the differential diag-

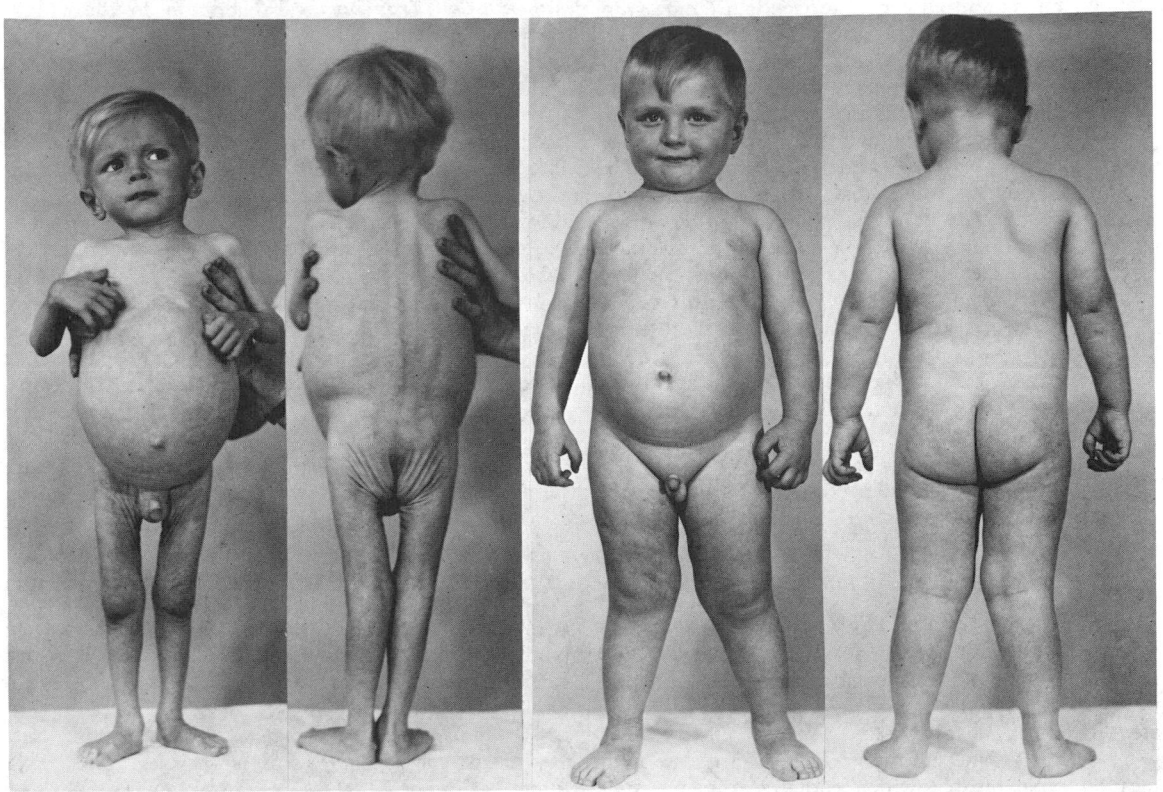

Fig. 4. Celiac disease. *Left.* Age 2 years, 10 months. *Right.* Age 4 years, 1 month. William K. weighed 6½ pounds at birth and, though never breast-fed, thrived normally until the age of 11½ months when, following a cold, he began to experience anorexia, abdominal distention, flatulence, occasional vomiting, and the passage of five or six frothy, light-colored, foul-smelling stools each day. He lost weight and his extremities became spindly. The diagnosis of celiac disease was made when he was 13 months old, but his parents for a time refused hospital care. At 15 months he had an attack of bronchopneumonia, following which his digestive symptoms increased. Despite restriction of his diet with sharp limitation of his intake of fat and starch, his abdominal distention persisted or even increased, he gained little weight, and his disposition became progressively more irritable. At 2 years, 10 months, he weighed 7,500 g (16½ pounds), was markedly wasted with feeble musculature and tympanitic distention of the belly and had slight periorbital edema. Treatment was begun with a protein milk formula, banana, vitamin concentrates, and for a time daily infusions of plasma, followed by a transfusion of 200 ml of whole blood. Within a week his appetite had improved, and beef, gelatin, and cottage cheese were added to his diet. The first photographs (*left*) were taken after 12 days in the hospital. As his appetite increased and his disposition became less fretful he began to gain weight and strength, and his stools became fewer in number and less foul. At the age of 3 years he weighed 11 kg (24 pounds, 3 ounces) and was sent home to continue on a high-protein, low-fat, low-starch diet, on which he continued to thrive. At 4 years, 1 month, he was chubby, active and cheerful, weighing 18.5 kg (40 pounds, 11 ounces); all findings were normal (*right*).

nosis is the demonstration that apathy, negativism, anorexia, and evidences of abnormal absorption may be reversed after a short period of intake of a gluten-free diet. The abnormalities observed on peroral biopsy specimens of the upper intestinal mucosa are also reversible, but only after a number of months on a gluten-fee diet.

Roentgen studies of the small intestine in celiac disease usually reveal a clumping segmentation pattern, similar to that seen in the normal young infant. Such a pattern is abnormal, however, when seen after the first year; its presence is not confined to celiac disease, but its absence would make one question that diagnosis. Roentgen studies are employed,

in addition, to rule out the possibility of a short-circuiting congenital anomaly which might result in steatorrhea.

Treatment. Successful therapy in celiac disease depends on maintaining the patient's nutrition from the point of view of calories and specific nutrients and of treating intercurrent complications, especially infections. Attempts should be made to avoid excessive psychologic stress.

In those patients sensitive to wheat gluten the complete elimination of this protein from the diet and the substitution of corn, rice, soybean, or buckwheat flour for wheat and rye flour often have a striking effect. It has been our experience that in such children strict adherence to such an elimination regimen has permitted complete freedom from symptoms. The efficacy of an elimination diet has been well demonstrated also in instances of sensitivity to the beta-lactoglobulin of cow's milk. Patients should otherwise receive a nutritious diet, rich in proteins.

The view that carbohydrates are not well tolerated by patients with celiac disease can probably be attributed to the occasional instance in which extreme mucosal changes result in temporary acquired disaccharidase deficiency or glucose-galactose intolerance. In these instances, until successful regeneration of villi has occurred in response to a gluten-free diet, it may be necessary to avoid lactose or sucrose for a time.

Restriction of fat has been widely advocated with a view to decreasing fecal losses and with the hope that partial rest of the disordered function of fat assimilation will promote recovery. On the other hand, those who have employed generous fat intakes, even prior to the introduction of the gluten-free diet, have not been impressed with unfavorable effects on tolerance. Balance studies carried out by Macrae, by Morris, and by Chung et al., have shown that even high levels of fat do not affect the percentage absorbed; they increase the fecal loss of fat but also increase the absolute amount absorbed by the patient, and they produce no consistent effect upon the assimilation of other foodstuffs. When fats are to be given there is some advantage in replacing butter in part by vegetable oil, which contains a higher proportion of the more readily assimilable unsaturated fatty acids. Feeding of medium-chain triglycerides, which contain fatty acids ranging from 8 to 12 carbons, yields virtually quantitative absorption, presumably directly into the portal circulation.

Fat-soluble vitamins should be provided in increased quantities to compensate for impaired absorption. Anemia should be watched for and treated appropriately with iron if it is of the usual microcytic variety, or with folic acid when it is macrocytic. Other drugs play little part in therapy.

Some patients, especially those with hypoproteinemia, seem to be unusually hydrolabile and may develop alarming symptoms of fluid loss and shock with great rapidity. The management of these acute episodes differs in no way from that of hypovolemic shock in general (Sec. 3.7).

The psychologic disturbances of the celiac patient should not be overlooked. Patients who are markedly undernourished are often petulant and difficult to manage, requiring a combination of sympathy and firmness that is not always available. Emotional tensions in the family may compromise the environment needed for convalescence and recovery and exercise an unfavorable influence on the child's digestion. Mothers of these patients are often tense, apprehensive, and overprotective. The attitude of mystery conveyed to the lay mind by the term "celiac" and the rigid systems of control often employed may perpetuate an attitude of invalidism, which must be guarded against.

Other Nonspecific (Generalized) Disorders of Mucosal-Cell Transport. In addition to the villous atrophy and mucosal cell disorganization associated with ingestion of specific proteins, such as gluten in celiac disease, a wide variety of additional noxious agents is associated with a similar effect on the small intestinal mucosa. In most instances the clinical manifestations and the laboratory tests for steatorrhea are similar to those in celiac disease. The condition is, however, not improved by feeding of a gluten-free diet, although in some instances authors report some crossover between onset from another cause and worsening of the disease with gluten ingestion.

Tropical sprue is a condition similar to celiac disease described among patients from warm countries. In tropical sprue there is a greater monocellular and eosinophilic infiltration of the lamina propria of the blunted villi. Reported improvement with long-term antimicrobial therapy has suggested an infectious etiology. Additional beneficial effects of withdrawal of gluten from the diet are also observed in certain instances. In addition, megaloblastosis is the rule in tropical sprue and folic acid therapy is beneficial. This is in contrast to children with celiac disease, in whom there is depression of serum folate levels but rarely a macrocytic anemia.

Malabsorption of lipids occurs in certain skin diseases, particularly *dermatitis herpetiformis* (Sec. 26.4) and *acrodermatitis enteropathica,* and in a limited number of these instances abnormal upper intestinal mucosal biopsies are reported. These diseases are not related to gluten ingestion. Acrodermatitis enteropathica is probably associated with immunoglobulin insufficiency, and is improved by feeding of unpasteurized human milk, a source of secretory IgA; adrenocorticosteroids may also be beneficial. Additional causes of upper intestinal mucosal abnormalities are infiltration with parasites, particularly *Giardia lamblia,* prolonged or intensive irradiation or treatment with drugs of the antifole group, and infiltration of the bowel wall by tumors or by inflammatory diseases. Circulatory disturbances, chiefly vascular occlusions or chronic heart failure, have also been observed to lead to villous atrophy and impaired lipid absorption.

Specific Mucosal-Cell Transport Defects: A-Beta-Lipoproteinemia (Acanthocytosis). In this rare hereditary condition there is a congenital deficiency in the ability to synthesize beta lipoprotein. These patients demonstrate abnormalities of the central nervous system, ocular defects, and red blood cell membrane deficiencies (Sec. 8.9). It is from the latter abnormality that the secondary name of acanthocytosis is derived.

The gastrointestinal manifestations in this disease are associated with the inability to transport absorbed fat from the intestinal mucosa. Since the intestinal mucosal cells cannot synthesize beta lipoprotein they are unable to invest the triglycerides reconstituted after fatty acid absorption with a protein envelope containing this substance. This limits

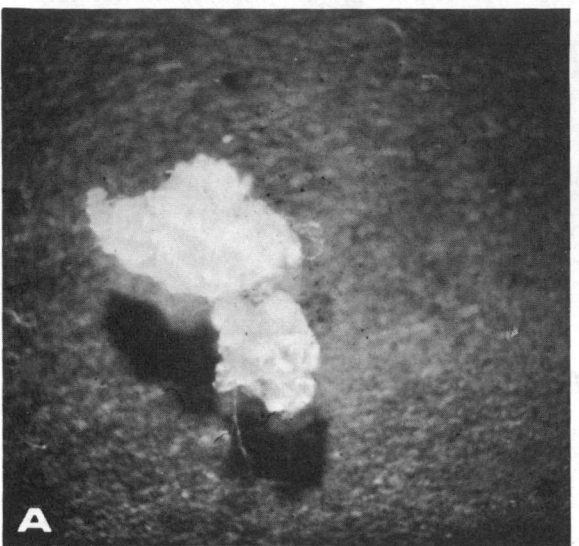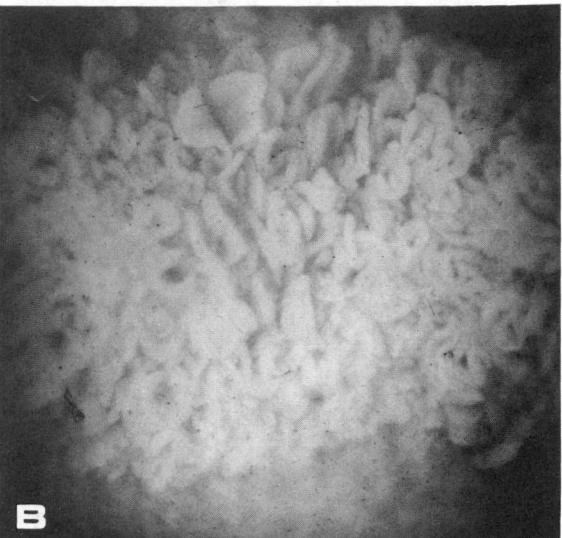

Fig. 5. A-beta-lipoproteinemia. *A.* Gross appearance of biopsy specimen illustrates the "frosted cake" opaque appearance from lipid-laden epithelial cells. *B.* Dissecting microscopic appearance (×28) showing details of this change of villi. (Photo courtesy of Dr. F. W. Wiglesworth, McGill University, and Dr. M. Silverberg.)

chylomicron formation and lipid cannot be transported into the lymphatic system or bloodstream. However, carbohydrate tolerance tests are normal, differing from most of the other diseases with fat malabsorption. Peroral intestinal biopsy specimens have a characteristic frosted appearance imparted by heavy fat stores (Fig. 5). The site of pile-up in the mucosal cell is easily demonstrated on light microscopic examination of specimens stained for fat (Fig. 6).

Treatment consists of a low-fat diet. Feeding of medium-chain triglycerides results in decrease in steatorrhea, and improved general nutrition. However, this treatment does not improve the basic defect and has no influence on the ocular, red blood cell, or central nervous system lesions.

ABNORMALITIES OF INTESTINAL LYMPHATIC TRANSPORT. Mechanical blockage of the lymphatics is encountered in a number of conditions and is associated with steatorrhea. Increased pressure on the intestinal lymphatics results in dilation of the lacteals in the villi. In many of these diseases fat losses are of less importance than the exudation of protein (see below).

Among the many acquired diseases in which this abnormality may occur are lymphomas, leukemia, infectious lymphadenopathy (as in tuberculosis or parasitic infestations), and scarring of the submucosa after irradiation. Widespread congenital obstructive abnormalities of the lymphatic system (*Milroy's disease*) may be associated with dilation of intestinal lacteals; the disease may also be confined to lym-

Fig. 6. Sudan black stain of jejunal biopsy showing that location of lipid in patient with hypobeta-lipoproteinemia is restricted to mucosal layer. (×80). (Photo courtesy of Dr. F. W. Wiglesworth, McGill University, and Dr. Mervin Silverberg.)

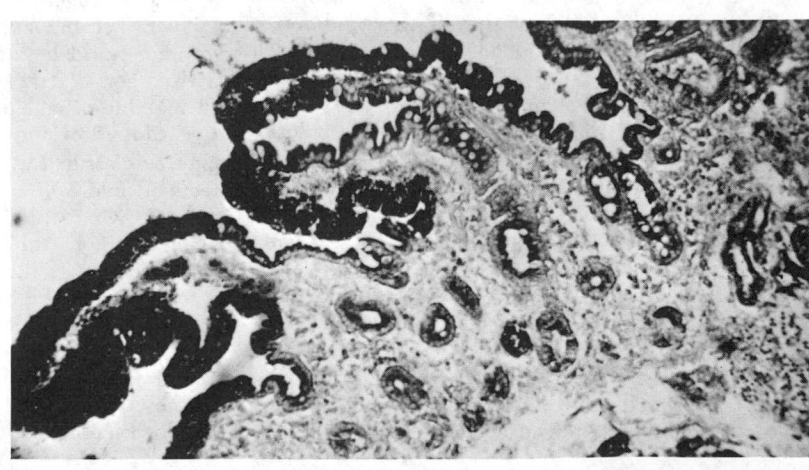

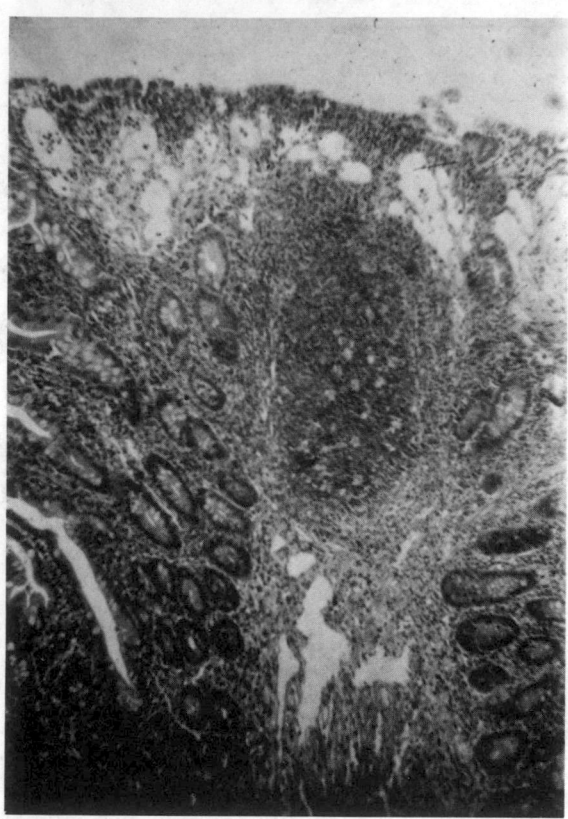

Fig. 7. Ileum in congenital intestinal lymphangiectasia. Surgical specimen from 10-year-old girl with history of diarrhea, steatorrhea, protein depletion, and tetany from early in life. Microscopic H & E section (×80) shows dilated lacteals of lamina propria of mucosa. (Photo courtesy of Dr. F. W. Wiglesworth, McGill University, and Dr. Mervin Silverberg.)

phatics of the mucosa. The latter condition is known as congenital lymphangiectasia and may be widespread over the intestine or confined to a localized segment of small bowel. The peroral biopsy is characteristic (Fig. 7).

Administration of a low-fat diet or of medium-chain triglycerides in the diet reduces protein loss and steatorrhea in these patients. If the condition is secondary to a primary disease which can be ameliorated with reduction of the pressure in the intestinal lymphatics, the symptoms improve or subside. Occasionally it can be demonstrated radiographically that the lymphangiectasia is confined to a limited area of the intestine in which the mucosal patterns are strikingly disordered; in such instances surgical excision of the affected region affords complete cure.

Carbohydrate Malabsorption

POLYSACCHARIDES—STARCH INTOLERANCE? The concept of starch intolerance is not a useful one. In his initial report of celiac disease in the United States in 1908, Herter reported that the children were made worse by ingestion of certain starchy foods. However, he clearly did not believe that this was intolerance to starch, since, on the basis of his empiric observations, he did not advise withholding starch but rather recommended substitution of certain starchy foods for others. With the demonstration of the pathogenetic role of the protein complex gluten from wheat and rye, the lack of any effect of starch in this disease is established. Nevertheless, in the 40 years between Herter's report and the elucidation of the role of gluten, pediatricians focused their attentions on starch and have made the diagnosis of "starch intolerance" in many children who were treated with rigid starch-poor diets. The routine microscopic examination of stools for starch has become the standard "test" to establish the diagnosis. It has been established that this test is not reliable, and that many normal children pass undigested starch in their stools. The diagnosis of starch intolerance is not tenable by the criteria currently in use and should not be made. Virtually all children diagnosed as having starch intolerance have the condition termed irritable colon of childhood (see below). Occasionally children with sucrase-isomaltase deficiency might be expected to be intolerant to starches. However, isomaltose only makes up a small fraction of most starches and the rare clinical problems are relatively minor when they do occur, and are limited only to the early months of life.

DISACCHARIDE AND OLIGOSACCHARIDE MALABSORPTION. Abnormalities of sugar digestion and absorption have been recognized for many years, but it was not until 1958 that Durand described an infant who suffered from vomiting, diarrhea, and failure to thrive, and who had both lactosuria and amino-aciduria. The following year Holzel and co-workers described siblings who were unable to hydrolyze lactose and who had fermentative diarrhea. These observations led to the recognition first of lactose and subsequently to sucrose-isomaltose malabsorption as distinct entities in infants and children which could cause failure of growth and development. Initially all of these defects were thought to be related to a congenital deficiency of the disaccharidases. It soon became apparent that carbohydrate malabsorption could be an acquired abnormality associated with other defects that could damage or alter the normal intestinal epithelia.

Classification. Sugar malabsorption syndromes may be classified as either congenital or acquired defects (Table 3).

Congenital abnormalities. Glucose-galactose malabsorption. Although these patients may have normal activities of intestinal disaccharidases, they have a congenital inability to absorb actively either glucose or galactose. The defect is inherited as an autosomal recessive disease and affects both the intestine and the kidney. Ingestion of either glucose or galactose by these patients will produce severe watery diarrhea, but intravenous infusions of either glucose or galac-

TABLE 3. *Classification of Sugar Malabsorbtion*

I. Congenital Abnormalities
   A. Glucose-galactose malabsorption
   B. Sucrose-isomaltose malabsorption
   C. Lactose malabsorption

II. Acquired or Secondary Disaccharide Malabsorption Associated With:
   A. Infectious diarrhea in infancy and childhood
   B. Kwashiorkor or severe malnutrition
   C. Gluten-induced enteropathy
   D. Cystic fibrosis
   E. Ulcerative colitis or granulomatous enterocolitis
   F. Blind-loop syndrome
   G. Severe Giardia infestation
   H. Beta lipoprotein deficiency
   I. Extensive resection of the small intestine
   J. Drug ingestion
      1. Colchicine
      2. Neomycin
      3. Birth control medication

tose are metabolized normally. The patients also have a decreased urinary clearance of these monosaccharides, and glucosuria is a common finding. The mucosal morphology is normal, but the accumulation of either glucose or galactose by the intestinal cells is defective. Sodium absorption, sodium activation of invertase, Na^+-K^+-dependent ATPase activity, and the absorption of l-amino acids are all normal. The basic defect appears to be the inability of the microvilli to bind either of the monosaccharides. Fructose is absorbed normally, and may be used as the source of carbohydrate in the diet of these infants.

Transient malabsorption of monosaccharides has been found in patients who have had resection of portions of their small intestine, and in certain infants who have had acute episodes of gastroenteritis. Often the infants will not tolerate any feeding which contains more than 1 to 2 percent carbohydrate. If the basic pathophysiology can be corrected, these patients will begin to tolerate normal carbohydrate intake after several weeks or months.

Sucrose-isomaltose malabsorption. This defect of carbohydrate malabsorption is due to congenital deficiencies of both intestinal sucrase and isomaltase. It is inherited as an autosomal recessive disorder. The defect is much more common than congenital lactose malabsorption. In many patients the clinical manifestations of the disorder are not severe. Most infants ingest either breast milk or formulas which contain lactose and will not have any clinical manifestations until sucrose or starch-containing foods are added to their diets. If the infant is fed a proprietary formula containing sucrose, the clinical signs may be manifested in the early neonatal period. Cereals, especially those with added sucrose, are poorly tolerated. Although isomaltose constitutes only 4 or 5 percent of dietary starch, the presence of this sugar in starch-containing foods was thought to be responsible for producing diarrhea in these patients. These patients do not hydrolyze oligosaccharides such as maltotriose or even maltotetrose readily, and the presence of these sugars in the intestinal lumen will accentuate the diarrhea.

As the children mature, they are able to tolerate increasing amounts of sucrose and starch despite the fact that the specific activities of both sucrase and isomaltase remain decreased. The morphology of the small intestine is normal by light microscopy and the activities of trehelase, beta-galactosidases, and various other digestive enzymes are within normal ranges.

Sucrose-isomaltose malabsorption is one of the rare genetic disorders in which two enzymatic activities are affected. There are many investigators who believe that only one enzyme is involved, and that the enzyme has two active sites for hydrolysis of both disaccharides.

Attempts to identify two separate enzymes by ion-exchange, gel-filtration, or trypsin-inhibition techniques have not been successful, and heat inactivation offers the only tenuous data indicating that there are two separate enzymes.

Congenital lactose malabsorption. This defect is rare, and few cases have been documented in the neonatal period wherein the defect persists into late infancy and childhood. Many patients appear to have either a delay in development or maturation of intestinal lactase, or an acquired defect secondary to mucosal damage. Because of the difficulty in diagnosing the entity precisely, the exact incidence of the defect or the mode of inheritance have not been elucidated. Although the incidence of congenital lactose malabsorption is low, the prevalence of lactose malabsorption in adults is quite high. Approximately 10 percent of Caucasians, 60 to 70 percent of American Negroes, and a larger percentage of Orientals will manifest lactose malabsorption as adults, even though these patients had been able to tolerate milk as infants. Although not definitely proved, there are circumstantial data to suggest that many tribes of American Indians are likewise affected.

The mechanism by which the persons of the various ethnic groups lose their capability of hydrolyzing lactose has not been elucidated. In 1967, Cook investigated 72 children from Baganda and found that newborns were able to hydrolyze lactose normally. By the age of 3 or 4 years, there was a significant decrease in the ability of these children to hydrolyze lactose. In another study it was demonstrated that the Baganda and other Bantu tribes of Uganda had a very high incidence of lactose malabsorption, while the Hamitic group, which include the Hima of Uganda and the Tussi of Rwanda, have a low incidence of lactose malabsorption despite the fact that they consume little milk in the postinfancy period.

The capability of these various groups to hydrolyze lactose may be dependent upon one or a multitude of factors. These could include: (1) Some ethnic groups have an increased incidence of infections or parasitic infestations which damage the intestinal mucosa and inhibit the activity of lactase; (2) Various factors in the diet may inhibit or destroy the disacchariddase; (3) The amount of milk in the diet may alter the activity of lactase; (4) There is a genetic characteristic that is associated with the decrease in the activity of lactase. Each of these factors may have an effect upon the activity of intestinal lactase, but the importance of each factor has not been evaluated carefully.

Secondary or acquired carbohydrate malabsorption. The acquired defects of carbohydrate absorption constitute the problems observed in the greatest number of patients. It appears that any disorder which can damage the intestinal cell can produce disaccharide malabsorption. This is especially true in patients with gluten-induced enteropathy or infections which damage the small intestine. Lactase appears to be the digestive enzyme most readily affected and is usually the last to reappear after the small intestine has returned to normal function. The enzyme is usually low in activity as compared to sucrase and maltase, and any disorder which affects the small intestine usually will affect lactase primarily. In adults, the intestine has a rapid turnover rate, which in normal patients may be between 48 and 72 hours. If the intestine is damaged, the turnover rate may be prolonged. Although conclusive data in humans are lacking, there are indications in laboratory animals that the turnover rate in suckling animals is markedly prolonged over that of adult animals, and may approach six to seven days. Thus any damage to the mucosa in suckling animals would require almost twice as long to repair as would the adult mucosa, and the activities of intestinal disaccharidases, especially lactase, might be depressed for a greater period of time.

Cystic fibrosis. Approximately 15 percent of patients with cystic fibrosis have lactose malabsorption. The mechanism by which this interesting occurrence takes place has not been evaluated. This disacchariddase deficiency occurs even when the intestinal morphology appears to be grossly normal.

Drugs. Certain drugs such as colchicine and neomycin have a unique capability of depressing the activity of various disaccharidases, especially lactase, even though the gross morphology of the intestine may not be affected. In laboratory animals, small amounts of colchicine appear to exert their effect directly upon the differentiated cell of the villus without affecting cellular renewal or proliferation.

Pathophysiology. When patients with carbohydrate malabsorption ingest the sugar to which they are intolerant, a watery fermentative diarrhea ensues. The sugar which is not hydrolyzed remains in the lumen of the intestine; and although small amounts may passively diffuse across the cell membrane, most of the unhydrolyzed sugar will pass through the small intestine unchanged. The sugar will act as an osmotic hydrogogue and cause an increased amount of fluid to accumulate in the intestinal lumen. In the distal ileum and colon, bacteria ferment the sugar to lactic and acetic acids, and these molecules can act so as to increase the water content within the lumen of the bowel. Lactic and acetic acid may be irritating to the colon as well, and perpetuate the water loss. The stool is watery, of low pH (4.0 to 5.0), and irritating to the rectoanal area.

The unhydrolyzed sugar which passively diffuses into the intestinal cell is usually excreted unchanged in the urine. Although not proved, it appears that the disaccharide or oligosaccharide is toxic both to the intestinal cell and to the renal tubular cells. Other sugars as well as various amino acids are, in turn, poorly reabsorbed from the renal tubule, and significant melituria and amino-aciduria may result.

Clinical Manifestations. The clinical manifestations of carbohydrate malabsorption are fairly characteristic and do not depend upon the specific disaccharide or oligosaccharide involved. However, the earlier in infancy the disorder becomes manifest, the more serious are the complications. Infants with lactose malabsorption are the most severely affected because of marked fluid and electrolyte imbalance, and also it takes longer for the intestine to recover normal function. Severe fermentative diarrhea associated with abdominal cramping, dehydration, and acidosis are common findings in these patients. Although not mentioned widely in the literature, another common finding in infancy is vomiting, which occasionally may be present in the absence of diarrhea. Initially the infants may demonstrate a voracious appetite in order to compensate for intestinal losses, but after a period of time, the infants become lethargic, irritable, and anorexic. Steatorrhea is encountered in some patients with carbohydrate intolerance and is usually a sign that the small intestine has suffered significant damage. It is usually not encountered in patients with congenital defects early in the course of their disease.

If the disorder is unrecognized in infancy, dehydration, acidosis, and mucosal damage will result, and irreversible damage to the small intestine will ensue. The infant can develop protein-losing enteropathy and intractable and unrelenting diarrhea, and may succumb in a severely malnourished state.

Older infants and children do not seem to have a protracted course, and many patients with sucrose-isomaltose malabsorption appear to tolerate these sugars more readily as they mature.

The patients who have acquired carbohydrate malabsorption usually regain their ability to hydrolyze the carbohydrate to which they are intolerant when the basic pathophysiology has returned to normal.

Adults usually have minimal signs and symptoms of carbohydrate malabsorption, which include bloating, abdominal cramps, and loose stools. In fact some adults who recognize their intolerance will use milk or lactose as a cathartic.

Diagnosis. If a patient is suspected of having carbohydrate malabsorption, diagnostic procedures should be performed without delay. Screening pro-

TABLE 4. *The Composition of Carbohydrates in Various Milks*

Milk	Carbohydrate				
	Lactose	Sucrose	Glucose	Maltose	Dextrin or Starch
Human milk	x				
Cow's milk	x				
Goat's milk	x				
Evaporated milk	x				
Alacta	x				
Olac	x			x	x
Similac	x				
Enfamil	x				
Nutramigen		x			x
Probana	x		x		x
Soyolac		x	x	x	x
Prosobee		x	x	x	x
Mullsoy		x			x
Baker's	x		x	x	x
Isomil		x	x	x	x
Meat-base		x			x
Portagen	x	x			x
CHO-Free (Either dextrose, sucrose, or lactose may be added)					

cedures such as examining fresh stools or rectal swabs for acidity and reducing substances have been advocated, but are not helpful and are often misleading in very young patients. If the patient has not ingested the carbohydrate to which he is intolerant, the changes in the stool may not be detected.

Disaccharide and monosaccharide tolerance tests are useful as screening procedures, although there is a great deal of debate as to their validity. If the emptying time of the stomach is delayed, a very slow rise in blood glucose may be noted. Also, measurements of glucose concentration in capillary blood tend to be greater than those of venous blood and may, therefore, alter interpretation of results.

In most instances, an increase in the concentration of glucose in blood greater than 25 mg per 100 ml within one hour after ingestion of 2.0 to 2.5 g disaccharide per kg body weight, indicates that significant hydrolysis of sugar has occurred. The patient should be carefully observed for the development of abdominal cramps or watery diarrhea within 2 to 6 hours following ingestion of the test substance. If a patient has a normal elevation in the concentration of glucose in blood and no symptoms following the ingestion of the sugar, the diagnosis of carbohydrate malabsorption cannot be made. However, if the rise in the concentration of glucose in blood is less than 25 mg per 100 ml, a diagnosis may be suspected.

Radiographic techniques utilizing lactose in a barium mixture have been utilized to demonstrate marked outpouring of fluid into the lumen of the colon in patients with lactose malabsorption. This increased fluid loss occurs in the area of the splenic flexure.

Several authors have attempted to identify patients with congenital lactose malabsorption and separate them from those patients with acquired lactose malabsorption by searching for the presence of lactosuria. If lactosuria were present, the patient was diagnosed as having the acquired form of the disease. Data from laboratory animals as well as affected adults would tend to mitigate the diagnostic significance of this finding. The presence of lactosuria depends not only upon the mucosal structure and function, and the activity of the disaccharidase, but also on the amount of substrate presented to the mucosa.

Biopsies of the mucosa of the small bowel and direct assay of the disaccharidases are the best methods of correctly diagnosing the disorder. Initially research tools, the biopsies and assays have now been adapted for clinical diagnosis. If biopsies are taken from the duodenum, or jejunum which has been damaged, the activities of the enzymes are decreased. If ratios of activities such as sucrase:lactase or isomaltase:lactase are used, the interpretations may be made with greater validity. Although the techniques for biopsy and assay are the most reliable diagnostic tools available, there are rare occasions when the results may be misleading. Therefore, one must use the clinical features, laboratory diagnosis, and mucosal assays to arrive at a correct diagnosis.

Treatment. Treatment is almost always dietary in nature, and consists of removing the offending sugar or sugars from the diet. Patients who have glucose-galactose malabsorption are the most difficult patients to treat, and fructose must be the only sugar in their diet. Patients with lactose malabsorption will thrive on a diet in which milk intake is reduced. They usually do not have to be placed on a milk-

and milk-product–free diet, but will thrive if they do not drink milk with meals. Newborns and small infants must be fed formulas which do not contain lactose, and will grow and develop if they are fed soybean, meat-base, or other formulas in which sucrose, glucose, or maltose has been substituted for lactose (Table 4). On occasion the infants will tolerate little or no carbohydrate, and a carbohydrate-free formula will have to be given to them. Infrequently, a patient will have such extensive mucosal damage that an intractable diarrhea will result. These patients have to be maintained on hypercaloric intravenous feedings which contain 15 to 25 percent glucose, 3 to 5 percent hydrolyzed protein or amino acids, vitamins, and electrolytes. They can then be fed very small amounts of oral nutriments until they regain their ability to digest and absorb food normally. Sometimes this treatment may require several months before any oral feedings are tolerated.

Patients with sucrose-isomaltose malabsorption can be managed quite well by just omitting sucrose-containing foods from their diets. A starch-free diet is usually not necessary, as the infants and children may tolerate a small to moderate amount of this substance without difficulty. The parents can usually titrate the amount of starch their child can tolerate by observing the effect of diet on the frequency and amount of stool excreted by the patient. As these children mature, the amount of starch they can tolerate increases so that they can usually ingest a fairly normal diet.

Protein Malabsorption

Gastric achylia is uncommon in children, but in rare instances in which partial or total gastrectomy is performed for tumors or congenital defects, achlorhydria may result. Although gastric achlorhydria primarily induces disordered protein digestion, secondary problems of malabsorption often complicate the deficiency. The lack of hydrochloric acid may lead to decreased pancreatic secretion or to excessive multiplication of upper small intestinal flora. These effects result in further decrease of proteolysis and disturbed lipid digestion and absorption.

Deficiency of exocrine secretion of the pancreas results in an assimilatory defect caused by incomplete splitting of protein. In the United States pancreatic insufficiency of this type in children occurs almost exclusively in *cystic fibrosis of the pancreas*, a congenital condition in which deficiency of the exocrine secretion of the pancreas represents only one part of a more generalized disorder (Chap. 9). The pancreatic insufficiency of this disease represents by far the most common cause of malabsorption among children. Patients have been described with isolated pancreatic deficiencies associated with bone marrow insufficiencies which result in neutropenia, anemia, and thrombocytopenia. Some of these patients display

marked growth retardation and radiologic evidence of metaphyseal dysostosis. Among children with this syndrome who have died, postmortems showed extensive replacement of pancreatic tissue with fat, hence the alternative name of *congenital lipomatosis* of the pancreas.

Isolated *deficiencies of trypsinogen* have also been reported in rare instances. The latter deficiency may be identical to a lesion first described by Hadorn, *enterokinase deficiency*. These patients exhibit a defect, apparently congenital, in the secretion of the intestinal enzyme enterokinase. Although activation of trypsin from trypsinogen is autocatalytic, some active trypsin is initially necessary, and this usually results from the action on trypsinogen of enterokinase. Although patients with this deficiency behave from birth as if their pancreatic secretory function were impaired and respond favorably to feedings of pancreatic extracts, it can be shown that the salutary effects of such extracts is in the activation of the patient's own trypsinogen. This can be demonstrated in vitro by addition of either trypsin or enterokinase to the duodenal fluid from an affected child. Duodenal secretions of such patients are otherwise normal in volume, electrolyte and bicarbonate content, and in lypolytic and amylolytic activities. They can be stimulated with secretin and pancreozymin. Intestinal morphology on examination of peroral biopsy is normal. Symptoms which are most frequent are those of hypoproteinemia, anemia, and failure to thrive because of decreased protein digestion. Patients respond to feedings of hydrolyzed proteins or to small supplements of pancreatic extracts with meals.

EXUDATIVE ENTEROPATHY: PROTEIN-LOSING GASTROENTEROPATHY. Excessive leakage of plasma proteins into the gastrointestinal tract has been demonstrated as a cause of hypercatabolic hypoproteinemia. The condition has been described in association with a variety of anatomic abnormalities: giant hypertrophy of the gastric mucosa, obstruction and dilatation of the lymphatic drainage of the intestinal mucosa (lymphangiectasia), granulomatous diseases of the intestine, and ulcerative colitis. Exudative enteropathy has been attributed to cow's milk protein ingestion, has been demonstrated in gluten-induced enteropathy, and has been observed by us in a patient with a secreting neuroblastoma.

Children with this condition suffer from edema. Often where generalized lymphatic abnormalities play a role, edema may be unequally distributed. Disturbances of growth are frequent and gastrointestinal complaints inconstant. The disease is usually suspected when hypoproteinemia is found without proteinuria. Definitive diagnosis rests on demonstration that the protein losses are into the intestine. Intravenous injection of ^{131}I-labeled albumin has limitations, since intestinal enzymatic activity splits the exuded albumin with variable reabsorption of the resultant amino acids and radioactive iodine. In one technique which overcomes this difficulty, resins

—Amberlite IRA-400 or Deacidite FF (Permutit)—are fed orally to bind the exuded radioiodine. Another technique substitutes a synthetic, ^{131}I-labeled polyvinyl pyrrolidone, but variations in molecular size and properties not entirely similar to those of serum albumin limit the effectiveness of the test. We prefer injection of 20 to 30 μc of ^{51}Cr-labeled albumin. The radioactive chromium is poorly absorbed after digestion and is readily assayed in four-day stool collections. Patients with the disease demonstrate excretion well in excess of the normal daily rate of 0.01 to 0.1 percent of the injected dose. However, because of greater stability of the iodinated albumin, chromated albumin should only be used for quantitating albumin leaks; ^{131}I albumin is a better measure of total albumin turnover.

The picture varies with the specific cause, but patients generally display greater depression of serum albumin than of the globulins, except for gamma globulin, which may be specifically depressed. Diarrhea and steatorrhea are inconstant findings. Where the primary condition may be alleviated, as in *localized* intestinal mucosal abnormalities, in gluten-induced enteropathy, or in inflammatory diseases such as regional enteritis and ulcerative colitis, the hypoproteinemia improves. For the majority of patients therapeutic efforts are generally not rewarding. Diuretics, salt restriction, and periodic injections of albumin are employed for symptomatic relief. In patients with lymphangiectasia and steatorrhea, the use of low-fat diets or diets in which medium-chain triglycerides have been substituted for long-chain saturated fatty acid fats are of considerable value, not only in improving steatorrhea, but also in reducing protein losses.

Milk-associated Gastroenteropathy. Wilson and his co-workers have reported children with increased protein loss associated with red cell transudation and iron-deficiency anemia which responded to withdrawal of cow's milk protein from the diet. As these children matured, they regained their tolerance for whole milk. Waldmann et al. have added additional findings in children who probably suffer from the identical problem and have labeled the condition *allergic gastroenteropathy.* Their patients suffered diarrhea, steatorrhea, growth retardation, anemia, hypoproteinemia and edema, respiratory and/or skin allergies, and peripheral eosinophilia. Studies of the gastrointestinal tract revealed it to be the site of red cell and protein losses. Microscopic examination of peroral biopsies reveals normal villous architecture with increased amounts of eosinophils and plasma cells in the lamina propria. We have confirmed their finding that not all children improve simply with withdrawal of milk and milk products from their diets. In certain instances beef must also scrupulously be avoided in all forms. Corticosteroids are helpful, but unnecessary if proper dietary eliminations have been carried out.

Cow's milk may also be involved in other gastrointestinal disorders. Occasional infants display a marked intolerance during the first weeks of life which expresses itself in vomiting, or in rectal bleeding which may be profound and associated with severe diarrhea, simulating ulcerative colitis. Tolerance for cow's milk is usually normal by the end of the first year of life in these patients. In a patient in whom we observed steatorrhea related to the ingestion of cow's milk beta lactoglobulin, there was ultimate spontaneous improvement. On the other hand Kuitenan and co-workers observed patients who had malabsorption induced by ingestion of cow's milk and whose intestinal mucosa had blunted villi. Others have suggested that gluten intolerance, presumably a permanent defect, may develop secondarily in similar children.

Amino Acid Malabsorption

The various hereditary amino-acidopathies are presented in detail elsewhere (Sec. 8.2). A number of these involve disturbances of specific digestive and absorptive functions in the small intestine. If patients with *phenylketonuria* and *maple syrup urine disease* are fed a diet rich in tryptophan, they do not achieve anticipated serum levels, and they pass excessive amounts in the stool and excrete elevated amounts of indoles in the urine. The latter quite certainly arise from intestinal bacterial breakdown of the unabsorbed tryptophan by intestinal bacteria, since their appearance in urine can be suppressed with oral feeding of neomycin. In *cystinuria* the renal tubular defect in transportation of cystine, cysteine, hemocysteine, ornithine, lysine, and arginine is also shared by the intestinal villi, and has been confirmed in in-vitro studies. The defect in absorption is especially important for lysine. It has been reported that the combination of excessive urinary losses and the poor absorption of this essential amino acid may be an important factor in the below-normal growth exhibited by patients with cystinuria.

Hartnup disease is a recessive condition in which the transport mechanism for the mono amino-mono carboxylic amino acids is deficient. These include alanine, serine, threonine, phenylalanine, lysine, tryptophan, histidine, and citrulline. Findings with tryptophan are the same as in phenylketonuria, i.e., poor absorption, excessive indole formation, and so forth. In addition it is postulated that the neurologic signs which these patients demonstrate may be due to absorption from the colon of decarboxylated products of some of these amino acids: histamine, phenylalanine, tryptamine, and tyramine. In *Oasthouse syndrome* malabsorption for amino acids may be less important than excessive losses of methionine and branched-chain amino acids into the stool. Diarrhea results from irritation by products of bacterial degradation of the excessive intraluminal methionine, and the symptoms improve with antibiotics or with a low-methionine diet.

Irritable Colon Syndrome
of Childhood
(Chronic Nonspecific Diarrhea)

This syndrome, by no means uncommon in pediatric practice, is characterized by recurrent episodes of loose stools, occurring for the most part in children from 6 months to 3 years of age. Steatorrhea and malabsorption of protein do not occur, and although accurate studies of carbohydrate absorption are wanting, the normal growth of these children belies any significant loss of this foodstuff either. The fundamental difficulty appears to be irritability of the colon.

The cause of the condition is unknown. There is a strong familial tendency, often with a similar history in siblings, and not infrequently adults in the family suffer from an irritable colon. Various stresses may initiate diarrheal episodes; mild infections, usually of the respiratory tract, allergic reactions, and emotional stresses can often be identified as precipitating factors. In other instances such factors are not apparent. The possibility that unrecognized viral infections are involved remains to be investigated. Pathogenic bacteria have not been identified in the stools.

The episodes of diarrhea are commonly observed toward the end of the first year, before which there may have been a history of constipation. The onset is often insidious but may be dramatic. A diarrheal attack may last a few days or may continue for weeks, the intervals between attacks showing great variability. Constitutional symptoms, such as fever and leucocytosis, are absent and the appetite remains unaffected. In fact, except for the looseness of the bowels the child seems altogether well, and unless his diet is restricted he continues to gain weight normally. The number of stools varies from 3 to 10 a day. Frequently all, or a majority of them, will be passed within the space of a few hours in the early part of the day, and during the remainder of the day the child is free of symptoms. Apart from the fact that they tend to be loose, the stools are not abnormal. Mucus is often present, and in the more severe cases there may be excoriation of the buttocks. In a few instances in which balance studies have been carried out the only defect of absorption was found to be that of water. The presence of extracellular starch granules in the stools carries no untoward significance, nor does stainable fat in the feces imply that fat absorption is defective.

Diarrheal episodes usually cease between 3 and 4 years of age; only in rare instances do they occur after the age of 5 years. During interludes between diarrheal exacerbations, and especially following their complete cessation, the child frequently has chronic constipation.

The chief importance of this condition lies in its differentiation from the various causes of the malabsorption syndrome. Unless the diet has been unduly restricted, evidence of malnutrition is not present, nor can steatorrhea be demonstrated by chemical means. Pathogenic bacteria are not recovered from the stools, which contain neither pus nor blood. The characteristic features of cystic fibrosis of the pancreas are wanting. In our experience gastrointestinal allergy has played little part; we have not encountered instances in which the stools contained abundant eosinophils. The diagnosis is rarely difficult. We have, however, encountered occasional instances of low-grade salmonella infection which have simulated it closely.

The treatment is largely expectant. Reassurance that the condition does not involve loss of nutrients, is not caused by the food, and requires no special diet will do much to allay needless parental concern and to avoid invalidism on the part of the child. It can be confidently predicted that the condition will improve with time although it may not disappear altogether, even in adult life. The avoidance of stress situations, if this can be accomplished, may be expected to lessen the activity of the colon. Little can be accomplished by diet. We have observed during motility studies that the ingestion of ice water, which normally does not induce propulsive activity in the colon, does so in individuals suffering from diarrheal diseases, and specifically in children with this syndrome who have been so studied. We therefore advocate avoidance of iced foods in these children. Cohlan and his co-workers showed that diiodohydroxyquinoline (diodoquin) decreased the number of stools in a considerable number of patients, as contrasted with a placebo. The mechanism of action of this agent in amelioration of the condition is unknown.

References

MALABSORPTION SYNDROME

Andersen, D. H. Celiac syndrome. VI. The relationship of celiac disease, starch intolerance, and steatorrhea. J. Pediat., 30:564, 1947.

Anderson, C. M. Histologic changes in duodenal mucosa in coeliac disease: reversibility during treatment with wheat gluten-free diet. Arch. Dis. Child., 35:419, 1960.

——— Intestinal malabsorption in childhood. Arch. Dis. Child., 41:571, 1966.

——— Townley, R. R., Freeman, M., and Johansen, P. Unusual causes of steatorrhea in infancy and childhood. Med. J. Aust., 2:617, 1961.

Boyer, P. H., and Andersen, D. H. A genetic study of celiac disease. Amer. J. Dis. Child., 91:131, 1956.

Chung, A. W., Morales, S., Snyderman, S. E., Lewis, J. M., and Holt, L. E., Jr. Studies in steatorrhea: Effect of the level of dietary fat upon the absorption of fat and other foodstuffs in idiopathic celiac disease and cystic fibrosis of the pancreas. Pediatrics, 7:491, 1951.

Clark, P. A. The use of d-xylose excretion test in children. Gut, 3:333, 1962.

Collins, J. R. Small intestinal mucosal damage with villous atrophy—a review of the literature. Amer. J. Clin. Path., 44:36, 1965.

Cortner, J. A. Giardiasis, cause of celiac syndrome. Amer. J. Dis. Child., 98:311, 1959.

Davidson, M. Clinical conference: The celiac syndrome. Pediatrics, 21:508, 1958.

———— and Bauer, C. H. The value of microscopic examination of the stool for extracellular starch in the diagnosis of starch intolerance. Pediatrics, 21:565, 1958.

———— Burnstine, R. C., Kugler, M. M., and Bauer, C. H. Malabsorption defect induced by ingestion of beta lactoglobulin. J. Pediat., 66:545, 1965.

Donaldson, R. M., Jr. Studies on the pathogenesis of steatorrhea in the blind loop syndrome. J. Clin. Invest., 44:1815, 1965.

Fernandes, J., van de Kamer, J. H., and Weijers, H. A. Differences in absorption of the various fatty acids studied in children with steatorrhea. J. Clin. Invest., 41:488, 1961.

Frazer, A. C. Fat metabolism and the sprue syndrome. Brit. Med. J., 2:769, 1949.

Gee, S. On the coeliac affection. St. Bartholomew's Hosp. Rep., 24:17, 1888.

Green, M., Cooke, R. E., and Lattanzi, W. Occurrence of chronic diarrhea in three patients with ganglioneuromas. Pediatrics, 23:951, 1959.

Herbst, J. J., Sunshine, P., and Kretchmer, N. Intestinal malabsorption in infancy and childhood. Advances Pediat., 16:11, 1969.

Herskovic, T., Sinawer, S. J., Goldsmith, R., Klein, R., and Zamcheck, N. Intestinal lymphangiectasia. Pediatrics, 40:345, 1967.

Herter, C. A. On Infantilism from Chronic Intestinal Infection. New York, The Macmillan Co., 1908.

Holt, L. E., Jr. Celiac disease, What is it? J. Pediat., 46:369, 1955.

Hooft, C., Kriekemans, J., VanAcker, K., Devos, E., Traen, S., and Verdonk, G. Sjögren-Larsson syndrome with exudative enteropathy. Helv. Paediat. Acta, 22:447, 1967.

Isselbacher, K. J., Scheig, R., Plotkin, G. R., and Caulfield, J. B. Congenital betalipoprotein deficiency: an hereditary disorder involving a defect in the absorption and transport of lipids. Medicine, 43:347, 1964.

Kuitunen, P., Visakorpi, J. K., and Hallman, N. Histopathology of duodenal mucosa in malabsorption syndrome induced by cow's milk. Ann. Paediat. Fenn., 205:54, 1965.

Lamy, M., Frezal, J., ·Polonovski, J., Druez, G., and Rey, J. Congenital absence of beta-lipoproteins. Pediatrics, 31:277, 1963.

MacDonald, W. C., Dobbins, W. O., III, and Rubin, C. E. Studies of the familial nature of celiac sprue using biopsy of the small intestine. New Eng. J. Med., 272:448, 1965.

Macrae, D., and Morris, N. Metabolism studies in coeliac disease. Arch. Dis. Child., 6:75, 1931.

Margileth, A. M. Acrodermatitis enteropathica. Amer. J. Dis. Child., 105:285, 1963.

MacMahon, R. A. Massive resection of intestine in infancy. Aust. N. Zeal. J. Surg., 35:202, 1966.

Mistilis, S. P., and Skyring, A. P. Intestinal lymphangiectasia. Amer. J. Med., 40:634, 1966.

Möllerberg, H., and Soderhjelm, L. The D-xylose test in healthy infants and children. Acta Soc. Med. Upsal., No. 1 and 2, 70:41, 1965.

Robertson, A. F., and Putz, J. Serum and erythrocyte fatty acids in case of acrodermatitis enteropathica. J. Pediat., 70:279, 1967.

Rubin, C. E., and Dobbins, W. O., III. Peroral biopsy of the small intestine. A review of its diagnostic usefulness. Gastroenterology, 49:676, 1965.

Salt, H. B., Wolf, O. H., Lloyd, J. K., Fosbrooke, A. S., Cameron, A. H., and Hubble, D. V. On having no beta-lipoprotein. A syndrome comprising a-beta-lipoproteinemia, acanthocytosis, and steatorrhoea. Lancet, 2:325, 1960.

Samloff, M., Davis, J. S., and Schenk, E. A. A clinical and histochemical study of celiac disease before and during a gluten-free diet. Gastroenterology, 48:155, 1965.

Schick, B., and Wagner, R. Über eine Verdauungsstörungen jenseits des Kindersalter. II. Z. Kinderheilk., 35:263, 1923.

Sheehy, T. W., Artenstein, M. S., and Green, R. W. Small intestinal mucosa in certain viral diseases. J.A.M.A., 190:1023, 1964.

Sheldon, W., and Tempany, E. Small intestine peroral biopsy in coeliac children. Gut, 7:481, 1966.

Somersalo, D. Quoted by Holt, L. E., Jr. Nuevas puntas de vista en la alimentacion del niño. Rev. Espan. Pediat., 60:741, 1954.

Stickler, G. B., Hallenbeck, G. A., Flock, E. V., and Rosevear, J. W. Catecholamines and diarrhea in ganglioneuroblastoma. Amer. J. Dis. Child., 104:598, 1962.

Véghelyi, P. V. Giardiasis. Amer. J. Dis. Child., 59:793, 1940.

Visakorpi, J. K., Immonen, P., and Kuitunen, P. Malabsorption syndrome in childhood. The occurrence of absorption defects and their clinical significance. Acta Paediat. Scand., 56:1, 1967.

Wells, G. C. Skin disorders in relation to malabsorption. Brit. Med. J., 2:937, 1962.

Weijers, H. A., and van de Kamer, J. H. Coeliac disease. I. Criticism of the various methods of investigation. Acta Paediat. Scand., 42:24, 1953.

———— and van de Kamer, J. H. Celiac disease and wheat sensitivity. Pediatrics, 25:127, 1960.

———— van de Kamer, J. H., and Dicke, W. K. Celiac disease. In Advances in Pediatrics. Chicago, Year Book Publishers, 1957, Vol. 9, p. 277.

Winawer, S. J., Broitman, S. A., Wolochow, D. A., Osborne, M. P., and Zamcheck, N. Successful management of massive small bowel resection based on assessment of absorption defects and nutritional needs. New Eng. J. Med., 274:72, 1966.

CARBOHYDRATE MALABSORPTION

Auricchio, S., Rubino, A., and Mürset, G. Intestinal glycosidase activities in the human embryo, fetus and newborn. Pediatrics, 35:944, 1965.

Bayless, T. M., and Rosensweig, N. S. A racial difference in incidence of lactase deficiency. J.A.M.A., 197:968, 1966.

Cook, G. C. Lactase activity in newborn and infant Baganda. Brit. Med. J., 1:527, 1967.

Crane, R. K. A perspective of digestive-absorptive function. Amer. J. Clin. Nutr., 22:242, 1969.

Dahlqvist, A. Specificity of the human intestinal disaccharidases and implications for hereditary disaccharide intolerance. J. Clin. Invest., 41:463, 1962.

———— and Lindberg, T. Development of the intestinal disaccharidase and alkaline phosphatase activities in the human foetus. Clin. Sci., 30:517, 1966.

Davidson, M. Disaccharide intolerance. Pediat. Clin. N. Amer., 14:93, 1967.

Deren, J. J., Broitman, S. A., and Zamcheck, N. Effect of diet upon intestinal disaccharidases and disaccharide absorption. J. Clin. Invest., 46:186, 1967.

Doell, R. G., and Kretchmer, N. Studies of small intestine during development. I. Distribution and activity of β-galactosidase. Biochim. Biophys. Acta, 62:353, 1962.

Durand, P. Lattosuria idiopathica in una paziente .con diarrea cronica ed acidosi. Minerva Pediat., 10:706, 1958.

Eggermont, E., and Loeb, N. Glucose-galactose intolerance. Lancet, 11:343, 1966.

Gray, G. M. Carbohydrate digestion and absorption. Gastroenterology, 58:96, 1970.

——— Santiago, N. A., Colver, E. H., and Genel, M. Intestinal β-galactosidases. II. Biochemical alteration in human lactase deficiency. J. Clin. Invest., 48:729, 1969.

Haemmerli, U. P., et al. Acquired milk intolerance in the adult caused by lactose malabsorption due to a selective deficiency of intestinal lactase activity. Amer. J. Med., 38:7, 1965.

Hamilton, J. D., and McMichael, H. B. Role of the microvillus in the absorption of disaccharides. Lancet, 11:154, 1968.

Herbst, J. J., Hurwitz, R., Sunshine, P., and Kretchmer, N. Effect of colochicine on intestinal disaccharidases: Correlation with biochemical aspects of cellular renewal. J. Clin. Invest., 49:530, 1970.

——— Sunshine, P., and Kretchmer, N. Intestinal malabsorption in infancy and childhood. Advances Pediat., 16:11, 1969.

Holzel, A., Schwarz, V., and Sutcliffe, I. W. Defective lactose absorption causing malnutrition in infancy. Lancet, 1:1126, 1959.

Huang, S. S., and Bayless, T. M. Milk and lactose intolerance in healthy orientals. Science, 160:83, 1968.

Knudsen, K. B.. Bradley, E. M., Lecocq, F. R., Bellamy, H. M., and Welsh, J. D. Effect of fasting and refeeding on the histology and disaccharidase activity of the human intestine. Gastroenterology, 55:46, 1968.

Koldovsky, O. Development of the Functions of the Small Intestine in Mammals and Man. Basel, New York, S. Karger, 1969.

——— and Sunshine, P. Effect of cortisone on the development pattern of the neutral and acid β-galactosidase of the small intestine of the rat. Biochem. J., 117:467, 1970.

——— Sunshine, P., and Kretchmer, N. The digestion of carbohydrates during postnatal development. Gastroenterology, 50:596, 1966.

Kretchmer, N., and Sunshine, P. Intestinal disaccharidase deficiency in the sea lion. Gastroenterology, 53:123, 1967.

Meeuwisse, G. W., and Dahlquist, A. Glucose-galactose malabsorption: A study with biopsy of the small intestinal mucosa. Acta Paediat. Scand., 57:273, 1968.

Paes, I. G., Searl, P., Rubert, M. W., and Faloon, W. W. Intestinal lactase deficiency and saccharide malabsorption during oral neomycin administration. Gastroenterology, 53:49, 1967.

Plotkin, G. R., and Isselbacher, K. J. Secondary disaccharidase deficiency in adult celiac disease (nontropical sprue) and other malabsorption states. New Eng. J. Med., 271:1033, 1964.

Prader, A., and Auricchio, S. Defects of intestinal disaccharide absorption. Ann. Rev. Med., 16:345, 1965.

Simoons, F. J. Primary adult lactose intolerance and the milking habit: A problem in biological and cultural interrelations. Amer. J. Dig. Dis., 14:819, 1969.

Sunshine, P., and Kretchmer, N. Studies of small intestine during development. III. Infantile diarrhea associated with intolerance to disaccharides. Pediatrics, 34:38, 1964.

Townley, R. R. W., Khaw, K. T., and Shwachman, H. Quantitative assay of disaccharidase activities of small intestinal mucosal biopsy specimens in infancy and childhood. Pediatrics, 36:911, 1965.

PROTEIN MALABSORPTION

Bookstein, J. J., French, A. B., and Pollard, H. M. Protein-losing gastroenteropathy: concepts derived from lymphangiography. Amer. J. Dig. Dis., 10:573, 1965.

Burch, G. E., and Phillips, J. H., Jr. Protein-losing gastroenteropathy. Amer. J. Med. Sci., 245:109, 1963.

Burke, V., and Anderson, C. M. Chronic volvulus as a cause of hypoproteinemia, edema and tetany. Austr. Paediat. J., 2:114, 1966.

Burns, B., and Gay, B., Jr. Menétrier's disease of the stomach in children. Amer. J. Roentgen., 103:300, 1968.

Degnan, T. J. Idiopathic hypoproteinemia. J. Pediat., 51:448, 1957.

Holt, P. R. Dietary treatment of protein loss in intestinal lymphangiectasia: the effect of eliminating dietary long chain triglyceride on albumin metabolism in this condition. Pediatrics, 34:629, 1964.

Jeffries, G. H., Chapman, A., and Sleisenger, M. H. Low-fat diet in intestinal lymphangiectasia: its effect on albumin metabolism. New Eng. J. Med., 270:761, 1964.

Pittman, F. E., Harris, R. C., and Barker, H. G. Transient edema and hypoproteinemia. Possible Menétrier's disease. Amer. J. Dis. Child., 108:189, 1964.

Rosen, F. A., Smith, D. H., Earle, R., Janeway, C. A., and Gitlin, D. The etiology of hypoproteinemia in a patient with congenital chylous ascite. Pediatrics, 30:696, 1962.

Waldmann, T. A., Steinfeld, J. L., Dutcher, T. F., Davidson, J. D., and Gordon, R. S. The role of the gastrointestinal system in "idiopathic hypoproteinemia." Gastroenterology, 41:197, 1961.

Yssing, M., Jensen, J., and Jarnum, S. Dietary treatment of protein-losing enteropathy. Acta Paediat. Scand., 56:173, 1967.

MILK-ASSOCIATED GASTROENTEROPATHY

Davidson, M., Burnstine, R. C., Kugler, M. M., and Bauer, C. H. Malabsorption defect induced by ingestion of beta lactoglobulin. J. Pediat., 66:545, 1965.

Fallström, S. P., Winberg, J., and Andersen, H. P. Cows' milk induced malabsorption as a precursor of gluten intolerance. Acta Paediat. Scand., 54:101, 1965.

Kuitunen, P., Visakorpi, J. K., and Hallman, N. Histopathology of duodenal mucosa in malabsorption syndrome induced by cow's milk. Ann. Paediat. Fenn., 205:54, 1965.

Waldmann, T. A., Wochner, D. R., Laster, L., and Gordon, S., Jr. Allergic gastroenteropathy—a cause of excessive gastrointestinal protein loss. New Eng. J. Med., 276:761, 1967.

Wilson, J. F., Heiner, D. C., and Lahey, M. E. Milk-induced gastrointestinal bleeding in infants with hypochromic microcytic anemia. J.A.M.A., 189:568, 1964.

AMINO ACID MALABSORPTION

Hooft, C., Carton, D., Snoeck, J., Timmermans, J., Anterner, I., van den Hende, C., and Oyaert, W. Further investigations in the methionine malabsorption syndrome. Helv. Paediat. Acta, 23:334, 1968.

Rosenberg, L. E., Crawhall, J. C., and Segal, S. Absorption—Intestinal transport of cystine and cysteine in man: evidence for separate mechanisms. J. Clin. Invest., 46:30, 1967.

IRRITABLE COLON SYNDROME

Cohlan, S. Q. Chronic nonspecific diarrhea in infants and children treated with diiodohydroxyquinoline. Pediatrics, 18:424, 1956.

Davidson, M., Sleisenger, M. H., Almy, T. P., and Levine, S. Z. Studies of distal colonic motility in children. I. Non-propulsive patterns in normal children. II. Propulsive activity in diarrheal states. Pediatrics, 17:807, 1956.

—— and Bauer, C. H. The value of microscopic examination of the stool for extracellular starch in the diagnosis of starch intolerance. Pediatrics, 21:565, 1958.

—— and Wasserman, R. The irritable colon of childhood (chronic nonspecific diarrhea syndrome). J. Pediat., 69:1927, 1966.

Prugh, D. G., and Schwachman, H. Observations in "unexplained" chronic diarrhea in early childhood. Proc. combined meeting Amer. Pediat. Soc., Brit. Paediat. Ass., Soc. Pediat. Res., and Canad. Pediat. Soc. Amer. J. Dis. Child., 90:496, 1955.

23.6
ABDOMINAL PAIN

MURRAY DAVIDSON

Recurrent abdominal pain represents a common complaint in pediatric practice; it has been estimated that approximately 1 in 10 school-age children suffer with the problem. An organic cause for the condition is found in less than 10 percent of these children. Although repeated and potentially harmful investigations are to be avoided, the diagnosis of serious or treatable conditions causing recurrent abdominal pain must be made without delay. Certain guidelines are useful for suggesting how diligent the diagnostic work-up should be.

Organic causes are more likely if the pain is sharply localized and constant, especially if it occurs during the night and awakens the child from sleep. Severity of pain is not a good guide, since more emotional children and parents may subjectively exaggerate a symptom, while more phlegmatic patients may minimize a complaint. Pains which are generalized over the periumbilical area or in the middle of the lower abdomen are less likely to be organic than those which are lateralized. Presence of anemia, persistent or recurrent fevers, elevation of erythrocyte sedimentation rates, marked loss of appetite, vomiting, or weight loss may point to an organic cause of abdominal pain, and such findings should be explained adequately. It is sometimes pointed out that patients with pain in multiple parts of the body, such as limb pain or headaches in addition to abdominal pains, are less likely to have an organic disease. This is generally true, but regional enteritis (see below) and other inflammatory or immunologic disorders may present with such multiple and not easily definable symptoms. Similarly, obviously disturbed interpersonal relationships between parents and children often suggest a primary emotional cause for the complaint; however, when severe, the child's disability may be the cause of great frustration, especially where there have been recurrent ineffective reassurances by physicians that the problem is not organic.

The major organic cause for recurrent abdominal pain is usually disease of the urinary tract, and every patient with the complaint deserves urinalysis. Within the gastrointestinal tract a number of conditions, such as peptic ulcer, regional enteritis, Meckel's diverticulum, gastrointestinal tumors, and ulcerative colitis, may present with chronic abdominal pain as the major symptom. We have observed abdominal pain as a severe and unexplained prodromal complaint in at least two children who subsequently developed unequivocal diabetes mellitus.

Psychogenic causes vary and careful interview is necessary. Among the predominating ones are guilt and anxiety in the child with respect to parental discord, physical or emotional illness of a parent, or overwhelming family financial problems which have been allowed to worry the child. School or learning difficulties, inability to handle hostile feelings toward parents or siblings, age-related problems, such as sexual feelings in early adolescence, may all be transposed into abdominal pain. The major avenues for treatment lie in patient counseling by the interested pediatrician after he has become thoroughly acquainted with the basis of the symptoms. In some instances psychiatric referral is indicated.

An important type of recurrent abdominal pain, which we believe is often present and which tends to bridge the gap between the psychologic and organic, is related to the tendency to constipation. Colicky or paroxysmal abdominal pain results from distension of the intestine when exaggerated peristalsis occurs in the presence of some degree of obstruction. Among individuals genetically predisposed to constipation there is increased tone in the distal colon, which may progress in some to unremitting spasm when they are under physical or emotional stress. If such individuals simultaneously are troubled by flatulence, and trapping of gas which they are unable to pass, severe pain may result. In some instances certain foods to which patients are allergic or otherwise intolerant may increase intestinal gas production. A number of such patients who have been severely troubled over long periods with such symptoms have been relieved when managed by the type of regimen described below for patients with constipation.

Acute abdominal pain is associated with such surgical problems as appendicitis, volvulus, or intussusception. In acute mesenteric adenitis pain is usually present. However, it is doubtful that diagnoses such as chronic appendicitis and chronic mesenteric adenitis, which were formerly frequently applied, are at all tenable in modern pediatrics.

Paroxysmal Fussing
(Infantile Colic)

This is defined as a symptom complex of early infancy characterized by evidence of intermittent abdominal pain of varying degrees of severity for which no organic or obvious physiologic cause can be demonstrated. It is an ill-defined condition which seems to consist primarily of pain associated with symptoms ranging in degree from general fussiness to paroxysms of agonized crying. The symptoms usually start after feeding and become worse late in the day. Besides the typical unhappiness, as exemplified by clenching the fists and flexing the legs, the infant often makes sucking movements and appears to be searching for food. Usually these infants have a great deal of gas, manifested by excessive belching, flatus, and rumbling. The passage of gas occasionally is followed by temporary relief, supporting the theory that loops of intestine distended from collected air cause colic. It is most common in the first-born, usually starting at 2 to 4 weeks of age and lasting through the third or fourth month. It is difficult to state what percentage of infants have colic, since a certain amount of fussiness is natural, and crying that may be considered normal in one household or in one infant might be regarded as intolerable in another.

There is little agreement as to the cause of infantile colic. Physiologic immaturity of the intestinal tract, a constitutional predisposition to hypertonicity, hunger, improper feeding, allergy, or a reaction to tenseness in the home have all been described as etiologic factors. A careful history is important, not only for obvious medical reasons but also to provide an opportunity for the mother to discuss her attitudes and feelings. A thorough physical examination must exclude such conditions as disease of the central nervous system, detectable congenital defects of the gastrointestinal or genitourinary tracts, and other organic causes. This investigation should include a rectal examination, since gentle dilatation of a "tight" rectal sphincter frequently will give rather spectacular and sometimes permanent relief. The finding of such spasm on rectal examination suggests that this type of colic may be related to a predisposition to later constipation and to functional gastrointestinal problems, and that the difficulty may have a pathogenesis not unlike the colic described in the section immediately preceding. Except for a very questionable psychologic advantage to the parents, changing the formula is useless except in the rare instances of milk allergy or flatulence from lactose intolerance.

Treatment of infantile colic is often not very satisfactory. Stress should be laid on feeding in the upright (sitting) position and on careful burping to prevent as much swallowed air as possible from entering the intestines. Most physicians restrict the use of drugs to severely disturbed patients. Among the drugs that have been recommended are paregoric, phenobarbital, and various anticholinergic agents. In a number of instances we have been impressed that 10 to 15 drops of an alcoholic beverage, given in 2 ounces of warm, slightly sweetened water, has been associated with passage of flatus and temporary relief of symptoms. Applications of heat to the abdomen and stimulation of the rectum with a vaseline covered thermometer tip or glycerine suppository appear to have the same effect. Until an exact cause can be found, drug therapy should be secondary, and sympathetic support for family is of utmost importance. The pediatrician must give parents adequate time and display a patient and interested attitude. Despite the fact that treatment often does not meet with success, the doctor's interest will serve to help the parents and the infant through a trying but self-limited experience.

REFERENCES

Aldrich, C. A., Sung, C., and Knop, C. The crying of newly born babies. III. The early period at home. J. Pediat., 27:428, 1945.

Apley, J. The Child with Abdominal Pains. Blackwell Scientific Publications, Oxford, England, 1959, p. 86.

——— The child with recurrent abdominal pain. Pediat. Clin. N. Amer., 14:63, 1967.

Green, M. Diagnosis and treatment: psychogenic, recurrent, abdominal pain. Pediatrics, 40:84, 1967.

Jorup, S. Colonic hyperperistalsis in neurolabile infants; studies in so-called dyspepsia in breast-fed infants. Acta Pediat. Scand., 41:Suppl. 85, 1952.

Marshall, D. G. Diagnosis and treatment: recurrent abdominal pain in children—a surgeon's viewpoint. Pediatrics, 40:84, 1967.

Rambar, A. C. Colic in infants—general considerations. Pediatrics, 18:829, 1956.

Wessel, M. A., Cobb, J. C., Jackson, E. B., Harris, G. S., Jr., and Detwiler, A. C. Paroxysmal fussing in infancy, sometimes called colic. Pediatrics, 14:421, 1954.

——— Use of methyl scopolamine nitrate in the treatment of paroxysmal fussing (colic) in infancy. New Eng. J. Med., 257:14, 1957.

Winsey, H. S., and Jones, P. F. Acute abdominal pain in childhood: analysis of a year's admissions. Brit. Med. J., 1:653, 1967.

23.7
CONSTIPATION

MURRAY DAVIDSON

Constipation is defined as a state in which bowel movements are hard, infrequent, and difficult to pass. These attributes are commonly related, since colonic stasis causes infrequent stools and, by allowing more time for water absorption, predisposes to hard stools, which are difficult to pass. Infrequent defecation and difficult defecation may, however, occur independently. A marked reduction in food intake may result in infrequent but easy passage of feces; on the other hand, anal stenosis or fissure may cause a soft stool to be passed with difficulty. Such conditions should not be regarded as constipation.

Constipation in children may result rarely from disturbances in propulsion of material into the lower colon due to hypothyroidism, diabetes, neuromuscular disorders, prolonged bed rest, or obstruction by space-occupying lesions. However, an infrequent but important anatomic anomaly which does cause constipation by interfering with peristalsis in the colon is Hirschsprung's disease or congenital aganglionosis (see below).

In the most common form of constipation, so-called functional constipation, there is excessive drying of rectal contents associated with difficulty in evacuation. The tendency to suffer with this problem is probably constitutional and hereditary, as evidenced by frequent strong family histories, by greater concordance among monzygous than dizygous twins, and by the fact that some infants display constipation from the first days of life even though they are ingesting formulas identical with those which do not evoke this symptom in the vast majority. Motility studies of the distal colon have demonstrated that certain children with constipation have increased frequency of pressure wave patterns presumed to be associated with altered fluid absorption; they also display the ability to resist development of propulsive activity following parasympathomimetic drug stimulation. Ziskind and Gellis showed that constipated children absorb increased amounts of water from their rectums.

Infants fed on cow's milk, with its higher content of casein and calcium salts, tend to have bowel movements that are harder and less frequent than those of breast-fed infants. When higher protein feedings are used, such as unmodified cow's milk, protein milk, or formulas fortified with calcium caseinate, the constipating effect is more striking. In older children overemphasis on milk may result in diminished intake of residue foods; conversely, children who tend to be constipated may have diminished appetites and prefer milk to other foods. Two factors, therefore, tend to aggravate the symptoms of constipation: first, smaller boli reach the rectum as a result of low intake of roughage; second, individuals who are disposed to constipation reduce the quantity of rectal contents by excessive water resorption. Both mechanisms result in a lessened urge and further drying of the mass into small, pelletlike formations.

SYMPTOMS. Passage of constipated stools may be accompanied by rectal pain, and if anal fissures result, the surface may be streaked with blood. Infrequently, excessive straining with constipated stools may be associated with rectal prolapse; in adults it is believed to lead more commonly to hemorrhoids.

With developing awareness that evacuation is under voluntary control, children may begin deliberately to withhold the stool in the latter part of the first year of life. Such children, by grunting, turning red, and "squeezing," appear to make attempts to defecate but are actually able to accomplish withholding by diminishing the effectiveness of the feet as a fulcrum; they develop a personal pattern whereby they avoid squatting and/or they do not rest both feet squarely on the ground when the intraabdominal pressure is raised. Both of these activities are necessary for normal defecation (Sec. 23.1). Gradual distension of the rectum by the retained stool results in increased ability to withhold larger quantities before urgency is experienced. This leads to abdominal distension, decreased frequency of stool passage, increased pain, and difficulty in passing the larger and firmer stool masses. The decreased appetite frequently observed in constipated individuals is exaggerated at this stage. Parents complain that the stool is often large and firm enough to interfere with the toilet plumbing. Frequent involuntary passage of the relatively liquid material which slithers around the large bolus of hard material may result in paradoxical diarrhea, or encopresis, after a number of days without bowel movement. Children rarely exhibit symptoms such as headache and general malaise often reported by adults with fecal impactions.

DIFFERENTIAL DIAGNOSIS. Infants who strain and pass small stools must have digital examinations of their rectums. Rarely, a firm constriction will be encountered at the anus, dilation of which by the examining finger may be followed by copious passage of stool. If the rectal examination has permitted ready entry of the finger, it usually implies that the tightness was due to muscle spasm rather than to the extremely rare instance of a sphincteric anomaly. In addition, if the examining finger palpates stool in the rectum, organic and neurogenic obstructions above this level are virtually ruled out.

In the older child in whom chronic constipation has led to the development of large, infrequent stools, the question of Hirschsprung's disease may be raised. The mistaken impression has been created that either early onset of symptoms or marked infrequency of bowel movements favors the diagnosis of Hirschsprung's disease and does not occur in chronic constipation. We believe that the presence or absence of the urge to defecate is a more reliable differential diagnostic criterion. Since the proprioceptors which initiate this reflex "call" are located just proximal to the internal sphincter, failure of patients with congenital aganglionic megacolon to propel material to this site results in rare activation of this reflex. Also, presence or absence of stool on rectal examination will suggest the proper diagnosis. In doubtful cases a trial period of therapy with large doses of mineral oil, as outlined later, may be of diagnostic benefit, since patients with Hirschsprung's disease will not respond. The barium enema and biopsy findings diagnostic of Hirschsprung's disease are described in a separate section below.

TREATMENT. In the infant the objective should be to alter the consistency of the feces in such a way that they can be readily passed. In most instances this objective can be accomplished by increasing the concentration or changing the type of carbohydrate in the formula. Lactose appears to be slightly more laxative than cane sugar; malt-dextrin preparations per se exert no laxative effect. Substitution of certain carbohydrate preparations such as honey, molasses (dark cane syrup is preferable to light), brown sugar, and malt soup extract is effective. The addition of solid foods to the infant diet, especially prunes, apricots, and fibrous vegetables, may be of some benefit.

Although often recommended, additional water probably has the effect merely of increasing urinary rather than stool water. However, nonabsorbable hygroscopic substances, which to some extent retain water in the gut, may be given to soften the stool. One teaspoonful of agar sprinkled in the food once or twice daily or the surface-active agent dioctyl sodium sulfosuccinate (Colace), in a dosage of 5 mg per kg per 24 hours divided into 3 or 4 doses, is widely used for this purpose.

The question of the desirability of regular bowel habits is often argued. It has clearly been demonstrated that retention of fecal material for more than 24 hours, and indeed for considerably longer, produces no untoward results. For the majority of children who are not constipated, daily movements are not necessary, and parents should be reassured in this regard. However, the inherent tendency to be constipated beyond infancy is best combated by development of regular bowel habits; this is possible only in children above 3 years of age who may be motivated and trained in this direction. Attempts at toilet training at too early an age (before 2½ to 3 years) may result in voluntary withholding and should be discouraged. During training, the use of a "potty" chair which sits on the floor is preferable to the seat which is attached to the adult toilet because the former provides better leverage for evacuating hard stools. Even those attachable seats which provide a foot rest are not suitable since they do not permit the small child properly to bend the knees and "squat."

Older children who exhibit symptoms of chronic constipation, with or without significant resistance to bowel movement and development of fecal impactions, require a more thorough regimen, described in three phases:

In the first phase, hypertonic phosphate enemas (1 ounce for every 20 pounds of body weight to a maximum of 4 ounces) are given morning and evening in pairs, one hour apart. When the second enema of a pair yields clear returns, evacuation of preexistent impactions is assumed to be complete. Saline enemas may be substituted, but tap water enemas must be avoided because of the hazard of water intoxication.

Mineral oil given orally is prescribed on an individual basis. Children receiving sufficient amounts of mineral oil should pass three to five large, loose, unformed bowel movements daily but should not have leakage of oil between times. In fact, "overflow" soiling of oil due to retention of solid fecal masses is an indication of inadequate doses of oil; paradoxically such soiling subsides when the dose is increased. It is our general practice to start with approximately 1 to 2 ounces daily for every 10 pounds of body weight and to increase the dose by ½ to 1 ounce daily until the desired response is achieved. The mineral oil is preferably chilled and taken directly from a glass. Half the total dose is given in the morning and the other half at bedtime, in order to interfere as little as possible with the absorption of fat-soluble vitamins and lipids from meals taken during the day. Children are permitted to drink sweetened fluids or juice immediately after taking the medication to eliminate the oily sensation from their mouths.

Youngsters who develop three to five soft bowel movements daily during the first phase of management are continued on the same doses of oil for a second period of approximately three months duration while they develop a regular daily pattern. Following this phase, the oil is withdrawn gradually; to insure lasting success the physician must continue to offer interest, encouragement, and patient handling of overanxious parents for considerable periods. In a few instances continuance of symptoms beyond the second phase of management may indicate a deep-seated emotional problem for which psychiatric help is necessary. In the majority of cases, however, the development of regularity is the end of the problem for the remainder of childhood and adult life.

The continuing use of laxatives, suppositories, and enemas should be discouraged and children should not be made dependent on them. Little may be expected from involved and restrictive dietary management of chronic constipation. Nevertheless, in the continuing management of constipation, daily intake of prunes and bran flakes, with reduction in milk intake to 1 pint daily to reduce casein and calcium intake, and substitution of adequate fruit juices and water may be of some value.

REFERENCES

Brazelton, T. B. Child-oriented approach to toilet training. Pediatrics, 29:212, 1962.
Davidson, M., Kugler, M. M., and Bauer, C. H. Diagnosis and management in children with severe and protracted constipation and obstipation. J. Pediat., 62:261, 1963.
Mercer, R. D. Constipation. Pediat. Clin. N. Amer., 14:175, 1967.
Ziskind, A., and Gellis, S. S. Water intoxication following tap-water enemas. Amer. J. Dis. Child., 96:699, 1958.

23.8
RECTAL INCONTINENCE AND PRURITIS ANI

THOMAS V. SANTULLI and
MURRAY DAVIDSON

The most important cause of inability to control fecal evacuations by children is the "overflow soiling" which follows overdistension of the rectum from prolonged chronic constipation and fecal impactions. Not infrequently the condition appears rather suddenly among children who are over 5 years of age and in whom the underlying constipation and gradually increasing periods between bowel movements have previously gone unnoticed. If such patients are not adequately examined to establish the true nature of the condition, the focus of diagnosis and management may often be misdirected toward "improving" the children's attitudes and motivating them to exert better control and to pay more attention to local cleanliness. Unable to satisfy such wishes because of the involuntary nature of the symptom, such youngsters may take to hiding their soiled undergarments; when this act is discovered it is regarded as further proof of the psychogenic origin of the soiling and of the contrariness of the patients, with reprimands, bribery, or vain attempts at psychotherapy becoming poor and frustrating substitutes for treatment that may be curative, i.e., the type of management of extreme constipation discussed above.

Other less common causes of rectal incontinence are paraplegia due to myelitis following injury to or disease of the spinal cord, spina bifida, and comatose states. The condition may also occur from chronic stretching of the sphincter by rectal prolapse of long standing, or it may be the result of scarring at the sphincter following surgery in the area for imper-

forate anus or congenital megacolon. Treatment of this assorted group of conditions is often unsatisfactory. For incontinence of neurogenic origin the best chance for improvement lies in surgical correction of the underlying lesion, if this is possible. For local problems at the anus or sphincter it is important to determine whether incontinence is due to poor control or to too tight an outlet with resultant retention and overflow. In the latter states sphincterotomy may be helpful. Many operative procedures involving muscle and tendon transplants have been tried for loose sphincters but none has been completely satisfactory. It is seldom necessary to treat this group of conditions by the establishment of a permanent colostomy. Most of these patients for whom no definitive procedure is available can be managed best by symptomatic treatment consisting of local cleanliness, constipating foods, avoidance of fecal impactions, use of bulk type laxatives such as psyllium seed, agar, or methyl cellulose, and periodic enemas as needed to maintain an empty rectum and lower colon.

Anal itching may result from moist underclothing and overflow soiling. Pruritis ani is also associated with hemorrhoids, fissures, and oxyuriasis. It results in scratching, restlessness, and irritability. Anal pruritis of nocturnal periodicity is almost always due to pinworm infestation. Treatment consists of local cleanliness and removal of the underlying cause. The anal area should be cleansed by washing or wiped with soft cotton rather than with toilet tissue. Drying powders or hydrocortisone ointment are beneficial.

REFERENCES

Ellison, F. S. Anal fissure occurring in infants and children. Dis. Colon Rectum, 3:61, 1960.
Mentzer, C. G. Anorectal disease. Pediat. Clin. N. Amer., 3:113, 1956.
Santulli, T. V. Miscellaneous anal diseases. *In* Benson, C. D., et al., eds., Pediatric Surgery. Chicago, Year Book Publishers, 1962, p. 854.
Turell, R., Pomeranz, A. A., and Denmark, S. M. The colon and anorectum in pediatric practice. Int. Abstr. Surg., 103:209, 1956.

Malformations of the Gastrointestinal Tract

23.9
ABNORMALITIES OF DEVELOPMENT CAUSING OBSTRUCTION

MURRAY DAVIDSON

Gastrointestinal symptoms based on congenital malformations may initially appear at any age. Most lesions of major significance are associated with symp-

toms occurring early in life, often in the newborn period. Manifestations of gastrointestinal tract obstruction are the most common complaints. Atresias and severe degrees of stenosis of the lumen cause intrinsic obstructions, while the accessory lumena produce extrinsic pressure; i.e., cysts, diverticula, or duplications are obstructing when they become distended with secretions or trapped intestinal contents and impinge on the main tract. The higher the lesion and the more complete the obstruction, the earlier do obstructive symptoms appear in an infant. Interpretation of objective signs is the same as for older individuals; e.g., whether vomitus contains bile depends on whether on obstruction lies above or below the biliary tract outflow into the duodenum.

Radiographic findings of intestinal obstruction in infants are similar to those in older children, and introduction of contrast medium is sometimes helpful for delineating the level of obstruction. The newborn provides a special situation in that swallowing of air and its normal passage through his gastrointestinal tract represents introduction of a contrast medium since that tract was not aerated before birth. It is almost always unnecessary in newborns to complicate the diagnosis and management by introducing barium or a similar material. Another important difference between the neonate and older individuals is that, despite presence of a complete obstruction, at least 50 percent of newborns with atresias as low as the terminal ileum may pass meconium, and the presence or absence of stools becomes a reliable guide to diagnosis only after the initial meconium stools have been passed.

Atresia of the gastrointestinal tract was formerly presumed to occur in utero as a malfunction of a normal ontogenetic mechanism. During the early stages of fetal life the mucosa lining the developing gut cavity tends to proliferate and to occlude the lumen, with subsequent recanalization and appearance of mucosal and submucosal elements appropriate for the particular segment. It was accepted for a long time that failure to complete the recanalization process would lead to stenosis or atresia, and this mechanism probably still accounts for some of the fore- and hindgut abnormalities. However, the midgut has not been shown to develop the solid stage, and there is a strong body of evidence to indicate that most small intestinal lesions probably arise from compromise of the fetal circulation to part of the developing gut, as might result from an intrauterine volvulus. The resulting gangrenous loop of intestine is ultimately resorbed and may leave an atretic segment connecting two patent areas as the only evidence of this fetal accident. In some cases evidence of intrauterine peritonitis may be seen.

REFERENCES

Dykstra, G., Sieber, W. K., and Kiesewetter, W. B. Intestinal atresia. Arch. Surg. (Chicago), 97:175, 1968.

Louw, J. H. Jejunoileal atresia and stenosis. J. Pediat. Surg., 1:8, 1966.

23.10
ESOPHAGEAL MALFORMATIONS

JOSE M. FERRER, JR.

A great variety of congenital malformations of the esophagus are encountered, including diverticula,

TABLE 5.   *Congenital Atresia of the Esophagus and Tracheoesophageal Fistula. Types of Anomaly with Numbers and Percentages in Babies Hospital Series*

		Number of Cases	Percent
Type I.	Absence of esophagus	0	0
Type II.	Atresia without fistula	8	6
Type III.	Tracheoesophageal fistula		
	A. Fistula from upper esophageal segment with blind or absent lower segment	1	
	B. Fistula from lower esophageal segment with blind upper segment	122	
	C. Fistulas to both upper and lower esophageal segments	3	
	Total Type III	126	93
Type IV.	Fistula without atresia	1	1
	Total	135	100

fistulous communications, stenoses, atresias, duplications, and congenital shortening.

Esophageal Atresia

The most common esophageal anomaly is atresia with tracheoesophageal fistula. There are three forms of this anomaly, as shown in Table 5 and in Figure 8, but by far the most frequent is that in which the upper part of the esophagus terminates in a blind pouch and the lower part communicates with the trachea (Fig. 8) at or near the bifurcation, or with a primary bronchus.

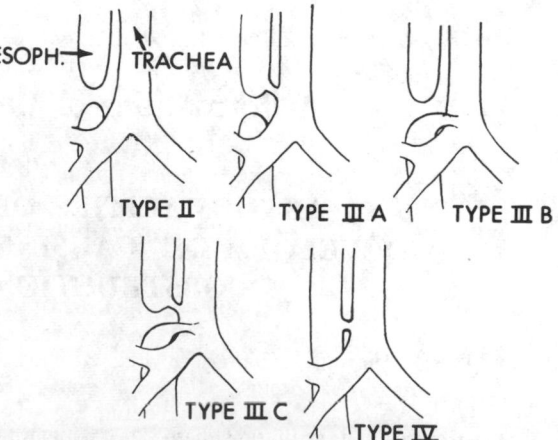

Fig. 8. Types of esophageal atresia with and without tracheoesophageal fistula.

As a result of this high obstruction, attempts at feeding the infant result in prompt regurgitation, often through the nose as well as the mouth. Indeed, there is inability to swallow even saliva, and drooling is often a conspicuous sign. Cyanotic choking and coughing attacks occur as the result of the inevitable aspiration of food and saliva, and occasionally following a feeding there may be sudden suffocation with a fatal outcome. Physical signs of atelectasis or pneumonia are usually present, particularly in the right upper lobe, as a result of repeated aspiration. In the presence of any of the above signs or symptoms in a newborn infant, the existence of this anomaly should be suspected. Prompt diagnosis can easily be made by passing a soft rubber stomach tube. If atresia is present, the tip of the tube will be checked at the bottom of the blind pouch or will double back and reappear in the pharynx. Radiographic confirmation of the diagnosis may be obtained by introducing air or 2 ml of liquid contrast material through the tube to outline the upper blind esophageal pouch. Overfilling of the pouch with contrast agent will result in aspiration and should be avoided because these agents are irritants in the lung. The presence of gastric tympany plus radiographic demonstration of air in the upper gastrointestinal tract confirm the presence of the tracheoesophageal communication.

Without surgical treatment, the outlook is hopeless, the infant seldom surviving beyond the seventh day of life. In recent years, treatment has become increasingly successful because of early diagnosis, advances in anesthesia and thoracic surgery, accumulated experience in dealing with the postoperative problems, and the control of infection with antibiotics. In the Babies Hospital of the Columbia-Presbyterian Medical Center in New York, the survival rate following operation for the years 1953 through 1962 was 61 percent (Table 6). The chances of survival are enhanced if the operation can be performed during the first 48 hours of life, before atelectasis or pneumonia has occurred. Once the diagnosis is made, nothing should be given by mouth, and the pharynx should be suctioned every 20 minutes. Hydration and electrolyte balance should be maintained or restored by parenteral fluids. Penicillin should be given to prevent pulmonary bacterial infection. The infant should be kept in an incubator supplied with humidified oxygen.

The preferred surgical approach is retropleural via a right posterior thoracotomy incision through the fourth rib bed. A transpleural intercostal incision is also satisfactory and perhaps a little faster. After division of the fistula and closure of its tracheal end, the esophageal segments are joined by end-to-end anastomosis, using two layers of fine silk. A sleeve of upper pouch muscularis is developed and used as the second layer to reinforce the primary mucosal suture line. A temporary gastrostomy is often advisable in order to start early feeding. Oral feeding may be started in small amounts on the twelfth to fourteenth day after surgery and increased gradually. In selected cases with ideal anastomoses, gastrostomy may be

TABLE 6. *Congenital Atresia of the Esophagus. Survival Rates—Babies Hospital*

Dates	No. of Patients Operated Upon	No. of Survivors	Percent of Survivors
1903-52*	101	33	33%
1953-62	102	62	61%
Total			
1903-62	203	95	47%
1961-62	23	18	78%

*N.B. 1903-52, 38 cases not operated and all died.

omitted and oral feedings started early. Subsequent dilation and calibration of the anastomotic site with bougies is always helpful and sometimes mandatory. The early postoperative care is extremely important. The infant should be promptly returned to an incubator with humidified, oxygen-enriched atmosphere. Frequent pharyngeal suctioning is continued. Fluid and electrolyte requirements must be carefully calculated and maintained by parenteral routes for the first few days until gastrostomy or oral feedings are adequate. It is essential to avoid overhydration as well as dehydration in these cases. Appropriate antibiotics and vitamins, including vitamin K, should be administered. Contrast roentgenograms should be made at the end of the second postoperative week to determine the patency of the anastomosis (Fig. 9). Other major anomalies, if present, greatly decrease the chances of survival. Low birth weight also militates against survival (Table 7).

In some cases with a long segment of atresia, there is insufficient length for direct end-to-end anastomosis. In these, the safest procedure is to exteriorize the upper blind pouch in the neck, close the tracheal fistula and the lower segment, and immediately perform a gastrostomy. Subsequently, the esophagus can be reconstructed by interposing a segment of colon or jejunum to bridge the gap between esophagus and stomach or between the upper and lower esophageal segments. These reconstructive procedures carry a very high mortality in newborn infants and should not be undertaken until the age of 2½ to 3 years.

In about 7 percent of cases of congenital esophageal atresia, no tracheal fistula exists or there is a fistula only from the upper pouch to the trachea; in these cases the stomach and intestines contain no gas and the lower esophageal segment is rudimentary or absent. Diagnosis and treatment are the same as outlined above. The rare H type of tracheoesophageal fistula without atresia is difficult to diagnose because the child swallows normally; however there are periodic attacks of coughing and choking associated with bouts of aspiration pneumonia. When the diagnosis is made, surgical closure of the fistula is indi-

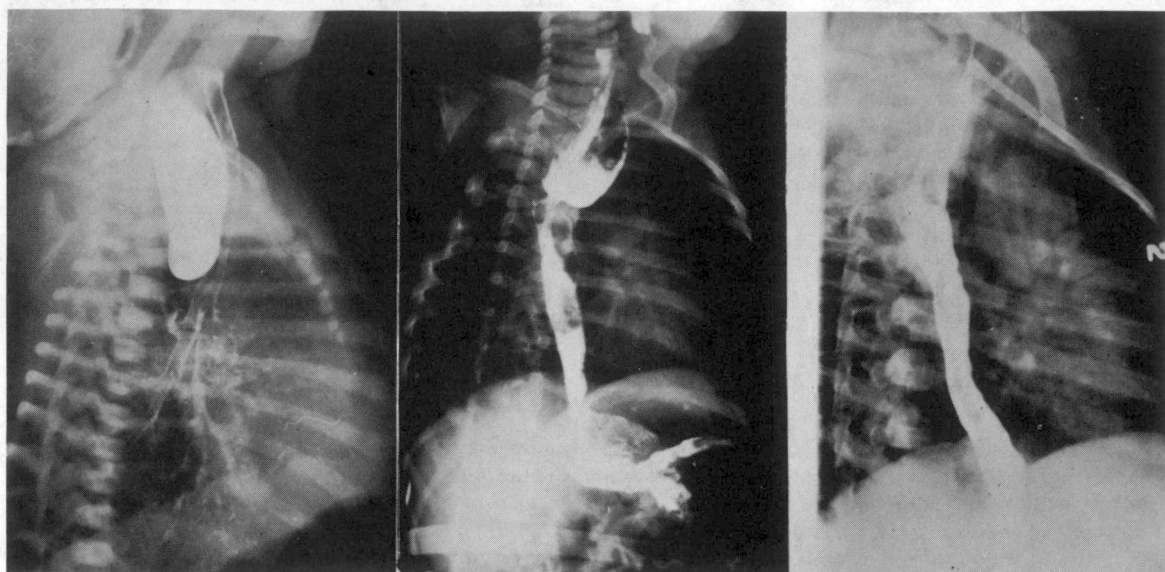

Fig. 9.   Contrast roentgenograms in esophageal atresia.

TABLE 7.   *Congenital Atresia of the Esophagus. Survival by Birth Weight—Babies Hospital*

Birth Weight (g)	No. of Cases	No. of Survivors	Percent of Survivors
<1,500	8*	0	0%
1,501-2,000	15	3	20%
2,001-2,500	27	19	70%
>2,500	55	40	73%
	105*	62	59%

*Includes 3 patients not operated upon.

cated. Cinefluorography is of particular value in diagnosing this anomaly.

The commonest postoperative complication and cause of death in infants with esophageal atresia and tracheoesophageal fistula is atelectasis with pneumonia. The second most frequent complication is a leak at the esophageal anastomosis with resulting mediastinal abscess and esophagopleural fistula with empyema, requiring secondary surgical procedures which often prove fatal. Postoperative stricture of the anastomosis can almost invariably be handled satisfactorily by dilations.

Congenital Esophageal Stenosis

Stenosis of the esophagus without fistula often responds to repeated dilations, but severe cases, particularly those with long segments of stenosis, usually require surgical correction. These strictures are often complicated by an element of spasm, which may cause marked variation in the severity of the symptoms, notably regurgitation and a feeling of substernal fullness or sticking of food. The amount of spasm, and therefore the degree of obstruction, may vary with the emotional state of the child. Parental attitude toward the child's abnormality is extremely important in evaluating the symptoms and deciding on therapy. Often, despite the complaint of severe vomiting, the child may be very well nourished and should not be subjected to extensive dilation or to surgical intervention. A reassuring relationship between physician and parents, with instructions about a soft and nutritious diet which is used temporarily during periods of difficulty, will often alleviate the anxiety of parents and patients and control the problem.

Congenital Duplication of the Esophagus

This may occur at any level, but is seen more often in the lower two-thirds. It is a rare anomaly and usually manifests itself either by compression of the esophageal lumen with dysphagia or by hemorrhage. It is treated by resection with end-to-end anastomosis of the esophagus.

Congenital Shortening of the Esophagus

This is a rare malformation. It is discussed in the section on esophageal hiatal hernia. Esophageal obstruction caused by "vascular ring" anomalies is described in Section 20.11.

Esophageal Hiatal Hernia

This condition has been recognized with increasing frequency in recent years as a cause of vomiting in the first year of life. The abnormal position above the diaphragm of the gastric cardia and proximal stomach results in incompetency of the cardiac sphincter mechanism. The symptom of neonatal vomiting in hiatal hernia is similar to that seen in chalasia, and, as in the latter, the maintenance of the infant in the vertical posture is often the only treatment needed to relieve the emesis. Indeed, the hernia itself may become smaller or even disappear with postural therapy alone.

Much more serious than vomiting, however, is the reflux into the esophagus of acid peptic gastric juice. This produces peptic esophagitis with its dangerous sequelae of ulceration, hemorrhage, and stricture formation and is a common cause of hematemesis in the young infant. There is disagreement regarding the relative frequency of congenital esophageal stenoses and stenoses secondary to peptic esophagitis.

The diagnosis of esophageal hiatal hernia may be made by esophagram, preferably with cinefluorography. Reflux from stomach to esophagus can best be demonstrated by this technique and is an essential part of the diagnosis. Since most of these hernias are of the sliding type and many are small, they may not appear on all films; multiple films or repeated examinations may be necessary.

Congenitally short esophagus has been thought to be the cause of these hernias. However, true congenital shortening of the esophagus or congenital intrathoracic stomach is a rare anomaly. Much more often, the esophageal shortening is due to spasm and is secondary to the herniation of stomach and cardia. If the hernia is repaired early, before the scarring of advanced esophagitis produces permanent shortening, the esophagus always stretches easily to permit replacement of the cardia below the diaphragm.

If postural therapy does not relieve vomiting or if hematemesis or obstruction due to spasm or early stricture occurs, transthoracic repair of the hernia should be undertaken promptly. This operation is associated with an extremely low mortality and morbidity, even in the newborn period. Esophageal dilations are usually not an effective cure and carry a real danger of perforation. They further tend to delay definitive repair until the inflammatory and cicatricial changes are no longer reversible. When this happens, simple repair of the hernia will not effect a cure.

In the presence of advanced and long-standing esophagitis with repeated hemorrhage or severe cicatricial stenosis, resection of the esophagus and cardia must be performed with the interposition of a jejunal segment to reestablish continuity. This operation carries a high mortality and morbidity and should not be performed during the first 2 years of life.

Paraesophageal hernias are infrequent as compared to the sliding type. They are usually much larger, but the cardia remains in its normal position and is competent. Therefore, reflux esophagitis does not occur. The symptoms of this hernia are obstructive and are successfully relieved by surgical repair.

REFERENCES

Astley, R., and Carre, I. J. Gastro-oesophageal incompetence in children. Radiology, 62:351, 1954.

Burke, J. B. Partial thoracic stomach in childhood. Brit. Med. J., 2:787, 1959.

Carre, I. J., and Astley, R. The fate of partial thoracic stomach in children. Arch. Dis. Child., 35:484, 1960.

Chepley, J. J., and Kurtzman, R. S. Isolated keterotaxy of the stomach. Amer. J. Roentgen., 91:770, 1964.

DeBoer, A., and Potts, W. J. Congenital atresia of the esophagus with tracheo-esophageal fistula. Surg. Gynec. Obst., 104:475, 1957.

Filler, R. M., Randolph, J. G., and Gross, R. E. Esophageal hiatus hernia in infants and children. J. Thorac. Cardiovasc. Surg., 47:551, 1964.

Forshall, I. The cardio-oesophageal syndrome in childhood. Arch. Dis. Child., 30:46, 1955.

Haight, C. Some observations on esophageal atresias and tracheooesophageal fistulas of congenital origin. J. Thoracic Surg., 34:141, 1957.

Holder, T. M., Cloud, D. T., Lewis, J. E., Jr., and Pilling, G. P., IV. Esophageal atresia and tracheoesophageal fistula. A survey of its members by the Surgical Section of the American Academy of Pediatrics. Pediatrics, 34:542, 1964.

Humphreys, G. H. The surgical treatment of congenital atresia of the esophagus. Surgery, 15:801, 1944.

——— Ferrer, J. M., and Wiedel, P. D. Esophageal hiatus hernia of the diaphragm. J. Thorac. Cardiovasc. Surg., 34:749, 1957.

——— Hogg, B. M., and Ferrer, J. M. Congenital atresia of the esophagus. J. Thorac. Cardiovasc. Surg., 32:332, 1956.

——— Wiedel, P. D., Baker, D. H., and Berdon, W. E. Esophageal hiatus hernia in infancy and childhood. Pediatrics, 36:351, 1965.

Husfeldt, E. Hiatus hernia in infants and adults. Great Ormand Street J., 6:71, 1953.

Johnston, J. H. Hiatus hernia in childhood. Arch. Dis. Child., 35:61, 1960.

Koop, C. E., and Verhagen, A. D. Early management of atresia of the esophagus. Int. Abstr. Surg., 113:103, 1961.

Ladd, W. E., and Swenson, O. Esophageal atresia and tracheoesophageal fistula. Ann. Surg., 125:23, 1947.

Longino, L. A., Woolley, M. M., and Gross, R. L. Esophageal replacement in infants and children with use of a segment of colon. J.A.M.A., 171:1187, 1959.

Martin, L. W. Management of esophageal anomalies. Pediatrics, 36:342, 1965.

Meredino, K. A., and Thomas, G. I. The jejunal interposition operation for substitution of the esophagogastric sphincter. Surgery, 44:1112, 1958.

Robb, D. Hiatus hernia in infants and children. New Zeal. Med. J., 56:238, 1957.

Swyer, P. R. Partial thoracic stomach and esophageal hiatus hernia in infancy and childhood. Amer. J. Dis. Child., 90:421, 1955.

Wayson, E. E., Garnjobst, W., Chandler, J. J., and Peterson, C. G. Esophageal atresia with tracheoesophageal fistula: lessons of a quarter century's experience. Amer. J. Surg., 110:162, 1965.

23.11
GASTRIC MALFORMATIONS

THOMAS V. SANTULLI

The stomach is sometimes in the thoracic cavity in cases of diaphragmatic hernia or eventration of the diaphragm. In such instances the cardia is usually in its normal position, while the greater curvature protrudes through the diaphragmatic defect or occupies the dome of the eventration. In other cases the upper part of the stomach protrudes into the thoracic cavity through a congenitally enlarged diaphragmatic hiatus, constituting an esophageal hiatal hernia. In these patients the esophagus itself is of normal length, but the stomach has not completed its descent in embryonic development. Varying degrees of this abnormality are seen. Examples of congenitally short esophagus, though rare, are at times encountered; in them the stomach tends to occupy a vertical position, with its upper portion fixed at a supradiaphragmatic level. In situs inversus the stomach may be situated on the right side of the abdomen.

Malformations of the stomach are much less frequent than those of other parts of the alimentary tract. Duplication of the stomach may cause hematemesis, or produce a cystic mass that is palpable in the epigastrium or is seen during fluoroscopy to impinge on the gastric lumen, causing partial obstruction. Very rarely a constriction is found near the middle of the organ, dividing it into compartments. Diverticula are sometimes seen, usually associated with a defect in the muscular coat, so that the wall locally consists only of mucosa and serosa. Rarely, there may be congenital atresia of the pylorus. This may cause persistent vomiting, and unless the condition is recognized and appropriate treatment instituted, death supervenes in a few days from starvation and dehydration. Ectopic gastric mucosa may be found in Meckel's diverticulum or elsewhere in the intestine and may cause peptic ulceration and hemorrhage.

Congenital Hypertrophic Pyloric Stenosis

This is a relatively common condition characterized by persistent vomiting, constipation, failure to gain or actual loss of weight, marked visible gastric peristalsis, and usually a palpable pyloric mass. Unless recognized early and treated properly it may result in prolonged morbidity. It is seen in early infancy, usually in the first 2 months of life but seldom in the first 2 weeks; only in exceptional instances do symptoms appear in the first few days after birth. Fully four-fifths of the cases occur in male infants, and first-born children are more commonly affected. There is some evidence for a genetic factor; when one of identical twins is affected, the other is usually affected also, while the same is not true of nonidentical twins. Reports have appeared of multiple cases in one family or in successive generations in the same family. The incidence of pyloric stenosis apparently varies in different parts of the world. According to Wallgren, the incidence in Sweden in live births is 1 in 150 boys and 1 in 775 girls. Comparatively large numbers of cases are reported in North America, England, and northern Europe, while reports are scanty from Latin America, and the condition is said to be rare among native infants in Africa. A large proportion of cases occurs in nursing infants, although it is not infrequent in artificially fed infants.

PATHOGENESIS AND PATHOLOGY. The pathogenesis of the stenosis is obscure. Markedly hypertrophied pyloric muscle has in rare instances been found in stillborn infants, indicating an inception of the process before birth. On the other hand, Wallgren, who gave barium feedings to 1,000 unselected newborn infants for fluoroscopic examination of the stomach and the duodenum, was unable to find any sign of obstruction or pyloric hypertrophy at that age. Five of these infants subsequently developed pyloric stenosis. Such evidence suggests a postnatal onset. Earlier writers usually argued that hypertrophy of the muscle appeared first and spasm later. A point in favor of this view is the marked variation in the intensity of spasm encountered from one case to another. On the other hand, the development of hypertrophy of smooth muscle secondary to spasm is a more familiar sequence, and the primary role of spasm is further supported by the favorable outcome of cases treated with antispasmodic drugs. Several investigators have found in infants with pyloric stenosis certain degenerative changes in the nerve cells of the myenteric plexus of the pylorus which have been interpreted as a response to excessive vagal stimulation. The nature of the stimulus is not known.

The appearance of the pylorus is remarkably uniform. It constitutes a hard, whitish mass about 2 cm long and about 1.5 cm in diameter. Its lumen may be so narrow as barely to admit a fine probe, while the normal pylorus will usually admit a No. 21 sound, French scale. Frequently water cannot be forced through the stenosed pylorus, owing probably to the fact that the mucous membrane is thrown into folds. The walls of the stomach are hypertrophied, especially toward the pyloric end. The stomach is dilated; its lower border may extend well below the level of the umbilicus. On section the pylorus is much thickened and considerably elongated; the lower end may project into the duodenal lumen somewhat as the uterine cervix projects into the vagina. On microscopic examination the thickening is seen to be chiefly of the muscle of the circular layer, which is increased to two or three times its normal width. The other coats are thickened but to a much lesser degree.

The hypertrophied smooth muscle cells contain a large amount of glycogen.

Although some authorities believe in the existence of cases of pure pylorospasm unaccompanied by hypertrophy, the uniformity with which the pylorus is found to be enlarged at operation argues against this view. We are inclined to think that the two conditions are in reality one and that failure to palpate the pylorus in atypical cases does not justify the conclusion that hypertrophy is absent.

CLINICAL FEATURES. In the majority of instances the clinical picture evolves in a typical sequence. Symptoms usually appear between the second and third weeks of life, rarely in the first few days, and may appear up to 12 weeks after birth. A delay in onset is seen more commonly in premature infants. The typical history is that of an infant who, having been nursing and gaining weight regularly in the first week or two, begins to vomit without evident cause.

Vomiting. Initially vomiting occurs occasionally, then repeatedy. The manner of vomiting is characteristic, as in a short time it becomes more forceful and then projectile. It is more forcible than that seen in any nonobstructive condition. An infant will often fairly shoot out the contents of the stomach, sometimes to a distance of 3 or 4 feet; food is often regurgitated through the nose. Vomiting usually occurs directly after feeding and characteristically nursing is resumed with avidity.

The vomitus usually consists only of food; it does not contain bile. The absence of bile is a critical point in establishing the level of the obstruction above the ampulla of Vater. In some, coffee-ground vomitus appears as a consequence of gastritis. In these instances the partially digested blood should not be confused with the green staining of gastric secretions which occurs with reflux of bile into the stomach. Vomiting does not usually occur at night unless the infant is nursed at that time. In general, the bulk of a feeding is expelled at one time; however, the amount vomited may be greater than the feeding just taken, indicating considerable retention. In spite of marked retention, frequent regurgitation of small amounts of feeding is unusual in contrast to vomiting from several other causes. Some of these patients vomit regularly after every feeding, while others retain two or three feedings in succession. The frequency of vomiting varies from once or twice to six or eight times a day.

Owing to loss of fluid the infant may become markedly dehydrated; the skin becomes dry and inelastic, and the urine is scanty. Excessive loss of acid in the gastric secretions may lead to alkalosis, hypokalemia, and occasionally to tetany. The usual electrolyte picture includes marked reduction of plasma chloride and elevation of bicarbonate (Sec. 3.7).

Stools. Constipation is the rule and follows a reduction in the volume of food reaching the intestine because of the excessive vomiting. Occasionally even when vomiting is severe, there may be frequent small stools consisting mostly of bile-stained mucus.

Weight. Progressive deterioration in the nutritional status is one of the most striking features, and close observation of the weight is one of the best guides to the progress of the baby. The subcutaneous fat is depleted more than is muscle, so that the patient, in spite of his small size, may present a muscular appearance. If the loss amounts to as much as one-fourth of the maximum body weight previously attained, the condition should be considered critical. In such instances, the body temperature may be subnormal.

Peristalsis. On examination of the abdomen the epigastrium is usually prominent in contrast to the lower half of the abdomen, which may be sunken. The characteristic gastric peristaltic waves are best seen immediately after taking a feeding and if the patient is observed in a strong light directed almost horizontally, to bring out changes in the contour of the anterior abdominal wall. If the waves do not appear spontaneously, they can often be excited by gentle friction or tapping of the epigastrium. The wave begins in the left upper quadrant as a ball-like prominence and slowly moves toward the right, proceeded by a depression or trough. The wave may progress past the midline and fade as it approaches the obstructed pylorus. Sometimes one wave is quickly followed by another. Typical gastric contractions are rarely mistaken for anything else and are virtually pathognomonic of pyloric or duodenal obstruction.

Pyloric Mass. Palpations of the infant's abdomen for the pyloric hypertrophy or "tumor" requires both patience and experience. The examination is facilitated if the stomach is empty and a pacifier is used to relax the abdominal muscles; also by taking care that the palpating fingers are warm. Compressing the stomach with the opposite hand may help displace the pylorus under the examining finger. The hardened pylorus can be felt in most instances about 3 to 5 cm below the right costal margin and just lateral to the right rectus muscle, sometimes quite superficially. The mass feels about as big as a medium-sized olive. It may be obscured by distention of the stomach or by enlargement of the liver. The pylorus may be displaced on its duodenal attachment by the gastric enlargement which occurs in cases of long standing. In spite of its excursion the direction and course of the peristaltic waves aid the examiner in finding it. The mass may be felt only during active gastric peristalsis, and when it contracts actively under the examining finger its identity is unmistakable. The character of the tumor is thus more important than its position. It is best felt after vomiting or after emptying the dilated stomach. If the tumor cannot be felt from the right side, the examiner should attempt palpation from the baby's left side. Palpation of the tumor has been reported in 68 to 100 percent of patients with pyloric stenosis, depending on the thoroughness, patience, and experience of the examiner.

Gastric Retention. Prolonged retention of food in the stomach is one of the characteristic features of pyloric stenosis. In healthy nursing infants the stomach is found virtually empty at the end of 3

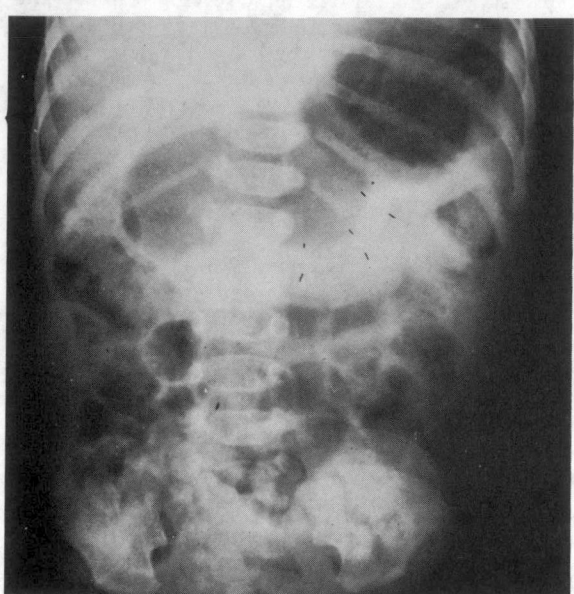

Fig. 10. Plain roentgenogram in hypertrophic pyloric stenosis illustrating the dilation of the gas-filled stomach. Note also the marked degree of thickening of the gastric wall and the peristaltic wave, best seen along the greater curvature.

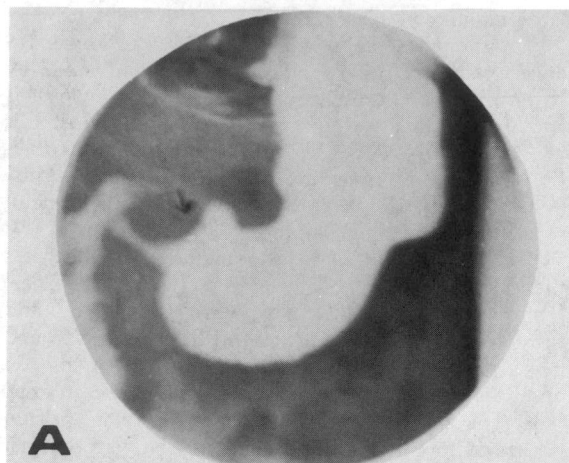

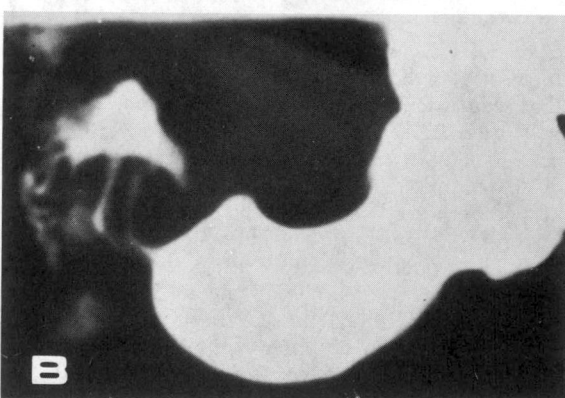

Fig. 11. Barium contrast study in hypertrophic pyloric stenosis. A. A peristaltic contraction is seen ending abruptly in the antrum near its junction with the pyloric canal. The narrowing and elongation of the pyloric channel is illustrated by the stringlike appearance of the barium. B. The double tracks of barium in the pyloric channel noted in this case are related to asymmetric narrowing of the lumen of the canal. (The single track of barium usually seen, as in A, results from more concentric narrowing of the pyloric lumen). The barium also outlines the duodenal bulb which is indented and tilted superiorly. The duodenal lumen forms a circumferential cuff or fornix around the projecting pyloric muscle tumor resulting in the umbrellalike appearance of the bulb.

hours, often at the end of 2 hours. If pyloric stenosis is present, food in considerable amount is invariably found after 3 hours and, unless vomiting has occurred, usually after 4 hours. A large gastric residue, which consists of both food and gastric secretions, may persist even after vomiting or fasting for many hours. Gastric retention may be estimated by aspiration of the stomach contents by means of a catheter and gentle suction.

DIAGNOSIS. This is usually easy after a few days of observation. The history of postnatal onset, with almost uninterrupted progression of symptoms and absence of bile in the vomitus, is characteristic. The presence of visible gastric peristaltic waves and a palpable pyloric mass establishes the diagnosis and allows the initiation of treatment early in the course of the disease.

In atypical cases and in those infants where the tumor cannot be palpated with certainty, roentgen examination may be necessary. A plain film of the abdomen often shows a large gas-filled stomach (Fig. 10). Roentgenograms using contrast material show elongation and narrowing of the pyloric channel with delayed opening. The gastric emptying time is usually, but not always, prolonged, and gastric peristaltic waves are easily visualized. The base of the duodenal bulb is frequently indented and tipped superiorly (Fig. 11). If roentgenologic examination is carried out using a cine technique, the pyloric channel appears poorly distensible and peristaltic waves cannot be identified with certainty, suggesting a reduction in the compliance of the surrounding hypertrophied muscle.

Pyloric stenosis has been mistaken for cerebral disease because of the projectile nature of the vomiting, but usually there are other signs of a central nervous system disorder in the latter. In general, the only difficulty is to distinguish it from vomiting associated with improper feeding or with parenteral infecton. In the former case, projectile expulsion of the food usually does not occur, and the other essential features of pyloric stenosis are lacking; in the latter, anorexia and other evidences of infection are often present.

Congenital obstruction of the duodenum or other part of the small intestine may lead to persistent, forcible vomiting and, if the obstruction is high up, even to visible gastric peristalsis. In these cases, whether due to stenosis or duodenal compression from congenital bands, the symptoms appear soon after birth and the vomitus contains bile, except in the very rare instance of supraampullary obstruction.

COURSE. In severe cases, peristalsis and vomiting are little influenced by changes in feeding. Unless proper treatment is instituted the loss of weight is continuous, amounting to 50 to 100 g a day, and the condition generally proves fatal in from 4 to 6 weeks.

In mild cases the symptoms, though characteristic, are much less marked. Gastric peristalsis and the palpable pyloric mass are present, but the vomiting may be only occasional, the loss of weight is not so relentless, and there may be periods of improvement in which the infant gains weight. In this group some of the patients do well with medical treatment, the symptoms gradually abate, and by the age of 6 to 8 months all evidence of obstruction has disappeared. The muscular hypertrophy recedes less rapidly. Pyloric muscle enlargement has been found at autopsy in children dying of intercurrent disease as long as 6 months after the disappearance of all symptoms. A chronic form of infantile stenosis which persists into later childhood has been reported but is extremely rare.

TREATMENT. In most American clinics, operative correction of all patients with hypertrophic pyloric stenosis is regarded as the treatment of choice. Uniform success is expected, with almost immediate relief of symptoms, gain in weight beginning within a week, and a short hospital stay. Experience in many of the larger pediatric centers now indicates a mortality of less than 1 percent. It should be emphasized, however, that successful treatment requires facilities which are specially adapted for the preoperative and postoperative care of these infants.

Medical treatment has peen reported to yield a degree of success comparable to that of early surgery. Considerable skill and effort are needed to bring this about, and the hospital stay is greatly prolonged compared to surgical treatment. The choice of procedure is therefore influenced to a considerable extent by experience with the method employed and by the medical and surgical talent available. In a controlled study, Mellin et al., of Babies Hospital, compared the results of medical and surgical therapy and concluded that operative treatment was preferable in experienced hands.

Surgical Treatment. The current low operative risk has been achieved by proper preparation of the patient, especially by the correction of dehydration and metabolic derangements.

The Fredet-Ramstedt operation is the accepted procedure. The pyloric mass is incised along its longitudinal axis, and the hypertrophied muscle layers are split along the entire length of the tumor. The divulsion is extended into the contiguous antrum for a short distance, and the muscle fibers are separated down to the submucosa without opening the lumen of the stomach. The intact mucosal and submucosal layers pout between the disrupted smooth muscle, thereby maintaining the opening in the pyloric channel.

Postoperative treatment is important. Parenteral fluids are given until oral intake is adequate. The following scheme of feedings is used at the Babies Hospital: Nothing is given orally for the first day. Thereafter, 30 ml of 5 percent glucose water are given, and repeated every 3 hours. After three or four such feedings, milk is started consisting of 30 ml of half-strength evaporated milk formula which is progressively increased. The infant is held semiupright for all feedings, following which he is placed flat in his crib, lying on one side or the other. Larger quantities of a sweetened evaporated milk formula providing two-thirds of a calorie per milliliter are given according to the following schedule:

40 ml every 3 hours for 8 feedings
50 ml every 3 hours for 8 feedings
60 ml every 3 hours for 8 feedings
75 ml every 3 hours for 8 feedings
90 ml every 4 hours for 6 feedings
105 ml every 4 hours for 6 feedings
120 ml every 4 hours for 6 feedings

Subsequent increases or other modifications are made according to individual requirements. The customary vitamin supplements are withheld during the immediate postoperative period and are resumed usually on the fifth day after operation.

Any vomiting during the first few days after operation almost always stops, and the infant does well after the stomach has been evacuated by tube. Complications are rare but include perforation of the duodenum at the time of operation, persistent obstruction due to incomplete separation of the circular muscle, intestinal obstruction due to postoperative adhesions, and dehiscence of the abdominal wound. Most patients resume daily weight gain early in the postoperative period and are ready for discharge from the hospital 3 to 7 days after surgery.

Medical Treatment. This is carried out on the theory that the pylorus will in time open up spontaneously if nutrition can be maintained and the patient kept alive until then. Several routine measures are helpful, refeeding being the most effective. When a feeding has been vomited, food will often be retained if the infant is immediately refed, which can be done a second or third time. Feedings should be made small, perhaps slightly more concentrated than breast milk and not too close together. Stomach washing has little effect.

Treatment with antispasmodics to relax the pylorospasm is the medical alternative to operation. Atropine methyl nitrate (Eumydrin) has been used and great success has been claimed for it. It is said to be much less toxic than atropine itself. Eumydrin is used in aqueous (1:10,000) or alcoholic (0.6 percent) solution. The alcoholic solution is preferable, in that it can be applied dropwise to the base of the infant's tongue, where it is absorbed locally, and the amount used can be accurately determined. The aqueous solution is given by mouth, but it deteriorates rapidly and must be freshly prepared each week. The infant should first be treated with fluids in a manner analogous to preoperative preparation. The drug is then given 15 to 20 minutes before each feeding, starting with doses of about 0.05 mg and working up quickly to amounts of about 0.3 mg. Immediate effects upon the vomiting are infrequent, but usually there is some improvement by the fourth day. Some weight gain should show itself in the first week. The dosage of Eumydrin is adjusted to the individual patient and may be increased when the response is not adequate. Parenteral fluids may be given if necessary. Expert nursing care is essential; the situation is not necessarily beyond the scope of a cooperative mother, but she should be carefully instructed and constantly supervised.

It is by no means clear that the pharmacologic effect of Eumydrin must be continuously maintained for medical treatment to be effective. Good results have been obtained in typical cases when the drug was given only once a day or when it was discontinued after only a week or two of therapy. The reason for this is not fully understood, but it is possible that a vicious circle is interrupted by Eumydrin treatment. Thus, the optimal length of time that treatment should be continued is not known.

Eumydrin produces toxic effects, which include mydriasis, flushing, dry mouth, and fever. These effects are easily handled by omitting the next dose. A more serious symptom is abdominal distention due to gastric atony or paralytic ileus, which may supervene in spite of improvement in the vomiting. Fatalities have occurred when the drug was continued in the presence of distention.

Comparable success has been reported with the use of methyl scopolamine nitrate (Skopyl, Skopolate), a pharmacologically related drug which exerts its principal effect by decreasing gastric tone. Its toxic action is somewhat less conspicuous than that of atropine derivatives.

Our experience with medical treatment, carried out as described, is that a small proportion of the cases respond rapidly and can be discharged from the hospital as quickly as operated cases. For the majority, however, the situation is only slowly brought under control, and four or five weeks of close observation in a hospital are needed to achieve success. A few respond poorly, and it is only by the most skillful efforts that they can be carried through with this regimen. The treatment adopted in the individual case will, as pointed out, depend in large part upon the experience of the medical and surgical personnel at hand. When skilled surgical talent is available it would seem preferable to give medical treatment no more than a brief trial in mild cases; certainly it should be abandoned if the weight cannot be maintained.

REFERENCES

Becker, J. M., Schneider, K. M., and Fischer, A. E. Pyloric atresia. Arch. Surg., 87:413, 1963.
Donovan, E. J., and Santulli, T. V. Duplication of the alimentary tract. Ann. Surg., 126:289, 1947.
Gross, R. E., Holcomb, G. W., Jr., and Farber, S. Duplications of the alimentary tract. Pediatrics, 9:449, 1952.
Nisson, S. Duplications of the stomach. Amer. J. Surg., 100:59, 1960.

CONGENITAL HYPERTROPHIC PYLORIC STENOSIS

Alarotu, H. The histopathologic changes in the myenteric plexus of the pylorus in hypertrophic pyloric stenosis of infants (pylorospasm). Acta Paediat., 45:579, 1956.
Benson, C. D., and Lloyd, J. R. Infantile pyloric stenosis. Amer. J. Surg., 107:429, 1964.
Clark, M. B., and Norman, J. N. Alkalosis in pyloric stenosis. Lancet, 1:1244, 1964.
Day, L. R. Medical management of pyloric stenosis. J.A.M.A., 207:948, 1969.
Donovan, E. J. Congenital hypertrophic pyloric stenosis. Ann. Surg., 124:703, 1946.
Freisen, S. R., Boley, J. O., and Miller, D. R. The myenteric plexus of the pylorus: Its early normal development and its changes in hypertrophic pyloric stenosis. Surgery, 39:21, 1956.
Lynn, H. B. The mechanism of pyloric stenosis and its relationship to preoperative preparation. Arch. Surg., 81:453, 1960.
Mellin, G. W., Santulli, T. V., and Altman, H. S. Congenital pyloric stenosis. J. Pediat., 66:649, 1965.
Nielsen, O. S. Histological changes of the pyloric myenteric plexus in infantile pyloric stenosis: Studies on surgical biopsy specimens. Acta Paediat., 45:636, 1956.
Scharli, A., Seiber, W. K., and Kiesewetter, W. B. Hypertrophic pyloric stenosis at the Children's Hospital of Pittsburgh from 1912 to 1967. J. Pediat. Surg., 4:108, 1969.
Wallgren, A. Preclinical stage of infantile hypertrophic pyloric stenosis. Amer. J. Dis. Child., 72:371, 1946.

23.12

MALFORMATIONS OF THE SMALL INTESTINE

MARK M. RAVITCH

A wide variety of congenital malformations may lead to neonatal intestinal obstruction. The presenting signs and symptoms are frequently similar. Plain films of the entire baby, contrast enema and physical examination, and observation of the vomitus will generally provide the diagnosis of intestinal obstruction and frequently of the specific kind and location. In general, it is immaterial whether the obstruction is complete or incomplete, since even incomplete obstruction will require early operative relief.

Normal newborn babies regurgitate readily, but seldom vomit, and almost never do they vomit bile. Although distention is usual in neonatal intestinal obstruction, it may not occur with high obstructions, since vomiting appears early and may evacuate the obstructed proximal bowel. In the presence of vomiting in the newborn, whether or not bile is present, and whether or not the baby is distended, roentgenograms in the supine and the upright positions should be taken at once. The roentgenogram usually establishes the diagnosis of obstruction or frequently indicates its nature. With complete obstruction, the proximal loops are usually dilated and there is absence of air in the colon. Barium swallow is rarely necessary, may be hazardous, and may actually give less information than a plain film. On the other hand, an *enema* of thin barium or of a water-miscible contrast solution will tell whether the colon is distal to the obstruction or not and will also indicate the presence of incomplete rotation of the intestine. In any instance in which there is a high probability that intestinal obstruction exists, a gastric tube is placed for constant suction, intravenous fluids are started, and operation undertaken.

Atresia and Stenosis

ETIOLOGY OF INTESTINAL ATRESIA AND STENOSIS. Intrinsic obstructions of the intestine may vary from narrowing of the lumen for shorter or longer distances, or partial occlusion by a crescentic diaphragm, to complete occlusion by a diaphragm, or actual solid replacement of a segment or several segments of the bowel, or even to a total deficiency of a segment or several interrupted segments of bowel and their mesentery. There is abundant evidence that atresia, at least beyond the ligament of Treitz, derives from an intrauterine pathologic process which results in destruction of a portion of the bowel. The causative lesions which have been demonstrated in pathologic material or in the experimental laboratory, operating upon mammalian fetuses in utero, are occlusions of mesenteric vessels, intussusceptions, volvulus, herniation, and strangulation in abdominal wall defects (gastroschisis). The clinical demonstration in children, with one or several complete interruptions of the bowel, that segments between interruptions, or distal to interruptions, contain bile or squames of the vernix caseosa, or lanugal hairs, and the same demonstration in the meconium of children with intestinal atresias, all are evidence that the bowel was patent from end to end, and functioning before the development of the atresia. In the duodenum, actual absence of a segment is much rarer than in the distal bowel and a complete membrane is the commonest form of obstruction. Here it is still conceivable that the old theory of a failure of canalization of the once completely obstructing epithelial plug is the mechanism

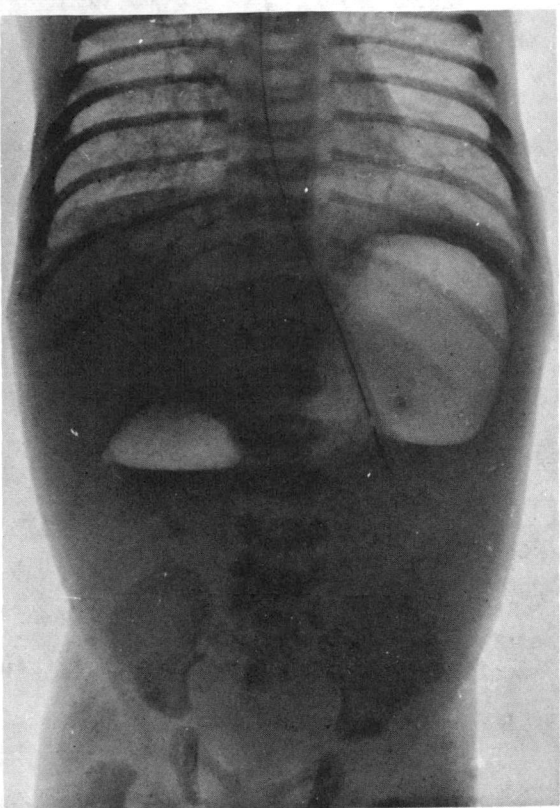

Fig. 12. Duodenal atresia. Note the "double bubble" sign, the huge dilation of the duodenum, and the absence of air in the rest of the intestinal tract. This child, like a quarter to a third in most series, demonstrated Down's syndrome or mongolism. Correction of duodenal atresia is by duodenoduodenostomy or duodenojejunostomy.

involved. Neonatal intestinal obstruction, as a result of a lesion extrinsic to the bowel, is seen in annular pancreas, in malrotation or nonrotation, and in herniation, particularly diaphragmatic hernia.

Neonatal Duodenal Obstruction

The classical sign of *duodenal atresia* (Fig. 12) is the double bubble radiologic sign showing one fluid level on the left, in the stomach, and another on the right, in the hugely dilated duodenum, with absence of air beyond. In the vast majority of cases, the obstruction is distal to the ampulla of Vater, and the vomitus contains bile. The common mechanism is a diaphragm of mucosa, which may or may not have a tiny central perforation or be incomplete and crescentic. In all series a substantial proportion of patients, in some up to 35 percent, show Down's syndrome. Vomiting begins within a few hours of birth, except in children with incomplete obstructions. *Annular pancreas* (Fig. 13) causes duodenal obstruction by encircling the duodenum with a ring-

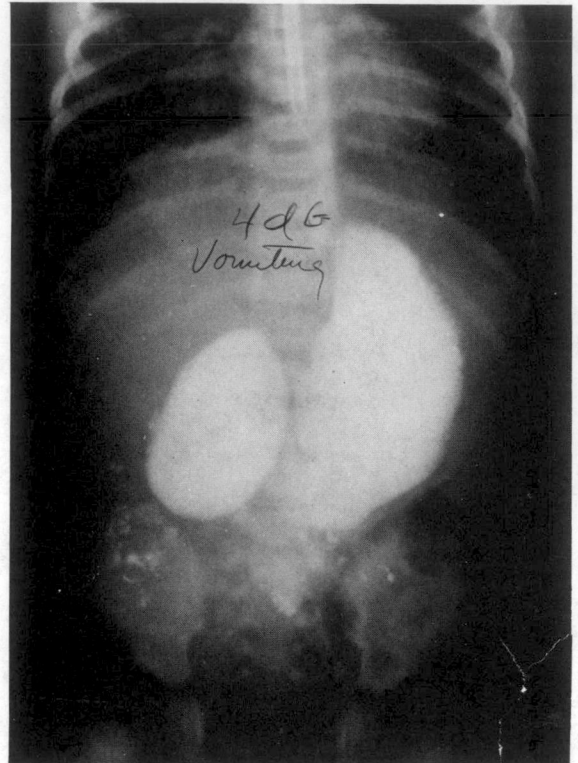

Fig. 13. Annular pancreas. Ordinarily a contrast meal is not required for diagnosis. Note the hugely dilated duodenum and the incomplete obstruction demonstrated by the passage of barium and air into the distal bowel. Treatment is duodeno-duodenostomy or duodenojejunostomy. The pancreatic ring is not to be disturbed.

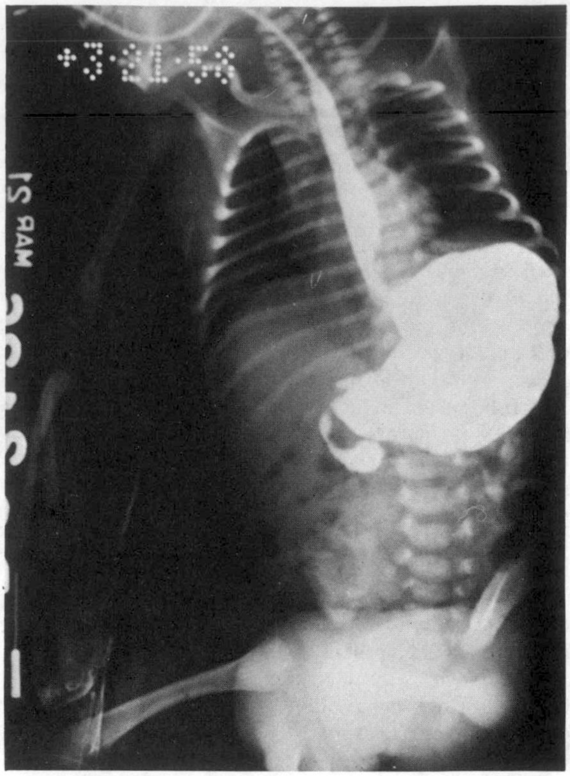

Fig. 14. Duodenal obstruction due to malrotation and Ladd's bands. The obstruction is in the duodenum which is not as dilated as in duodenal stenosis or atresia or annular pancreas, the obstruction is incomplete, there is a suggestion that the small bowel gas is all on the right side and the colonic gas all on the left side, and barium enema confirmed this. Treatment is the division of constricting peritoneal bands and derotation of the mesentery if there is a volvulus, which is not the case in this instance.

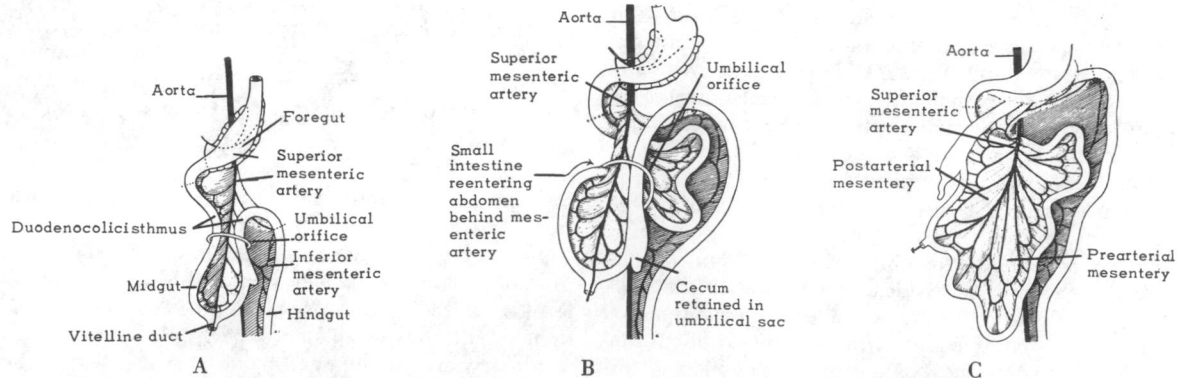

Fig. 15. Developmental rotation of the intestinal tract in embryonic life. A. At about the eighth week of intrauterine life most of the small intestine and part of the large intestine occupy the cavity of the umbilical cord, lying outside the abdominal cavity. Turning on the axis of the superior mesenteric vessels, the midgut loop has rotated about 90 degrees, so that the proximal portion lies to the right, the distal portion to the left of the midsagittal plane. (First stage of rotation.) B. At about the tenth week, as this extruded portion of the gut is returned to the abdominal cavity, the proximal coils pass from behind the superior mesenteric vessels; the distal portions of the intestine leave the umbilical cord last, coming to lie in the right half of the abdominal cavity. (Second stage of rotation.) C. At the completion of the second stage of rotation, the transverse colon lies anterior to the superior mesenteric vessels, which in turn lie anterior to the duodenum; the duodenojejunal junction is at the left of the midsagittal plane. (Modified from Dott. From Gardner and Hart, Arch. Surg., 29:942, 1934.)

like constricting mass of pancreatic tissue which results from fusion of the dorsal and ventral pancreatic anlagen. Curiously, the condition may cause no disturbance until adult life. In a substantial proportion of the cases, symptomatic in the neonatal period, an intrinsic obstruction of the duodenum is associated. The radiologic picture is similar to that of duodenal atresia, but the site of obstruction is usually in the third portion of the duodenum and the obstruction may be complete or incomplete.

Duodenal atresia is treated best either by duodenojejunostomy or duodenoduodenostomy, making sure in either instance, by passing a catheter in both directions, that one is not dealing with two mucosal diaphragms, a not uncommon situation. Gastrojejunostomy leads to anastomotic ulcers and should not be performed. Annular pancreas is treated similarly by duodenoduodenostomy or duodenojejunostomy. In the first place there is frequently an intrinsic obstruction, and in the second place, operative division of the pancreatic ring has proved to be unsatisfactory because: (1) the pancreas may be closely adherent to the duodenum or even intramural; (2) pancreatitis or pancreatic fistula may result; and (3) inflammation resulting upon the division of the pancreas may cause a secondary inflammatory obstruction.

Duodenal Obstruction by "Ladd's Bands"

Peritoneal bands from the nonrotated or incompletely rotated cecum in the left upper quadrant to the peritoneum in the right upper quadrant, traversing and obstructing the duodenum, may produce a picture which is principally that of duodenal obstruction, generally incomplete (Fig. 14). The contrast enema injection, which is a regular part of the study in almost all children with neonatal obstruction in which the etiology is not clear, will show the incomplete rotation of the colon and alert the operator to the possibility of this factor in the obstruction.

Anomalies of Rotation

ETIOLOGY. The portion of the intestine extending from the duodenum to the middle of the transverse colon is formed from the embryonic midgut loop. In early fetal life, this loop projects into the exocoelom in the umbilical cord, receding in about the ninth or tenth week into the endocoelom, the true abdominal cavity. As is shown in Figure 15, the reentering gut normally rotates in a counterclockwise direction about its nutrient vessel, the superior mesenteric artery, coming to lie with duodenum behind, and the transverse colon in front. The mesentery of the midgut subsequently fuses with the peritoneum of the posterior abdominal wall, forming a diagonal line of attachment extending from the duodenojejunal fossa in the left upper quadrant downward and to the

right. This complicated process may in a number of ways fail to be completed properly. The midgut, or a portion of it, may remain caught in the umbilical cord, producing an omphalocele with a small or large separation of the recti, the herniated viscera being covered only by translucent amniotic membrane. In such instances atresias of the intestine are common and anomalies of rotation invariable. Anomalies of rotation, which may occur independently of omphalocele, consist of incomplete rotation, nonrotation, or reverse rotation. Intestinal obstruction occurring as a result of incomplete rotation may be caused by the peritoneal bands passing from the cecum in the left upper quadrant to the posterior parietal peritoneum on the right across the duodenum, which is not rotated and which passes straight down on the right. Alternatively, and much more ominously, the obstruction may be due to a volvulus of the entire small bowel, whose mesentery has no fixation, so that the bowel hangs free on the mesenteric stalk. Since the volvulus is of the entire small bowel, the obstruction is high. In this case, distended small bowel loops do not appear, for when the baby vomits, the proximal intestine empties. Distention may thus not occur until the circulation of the twisted bowel has been compromised and a mass of engorged and necrotic bowel becomes visible and palpable as the baby goes into shock. A delay of several hours before operation in a vomiting baby who turns out to have volvulus of the midgut may be the difference between reduction of viable bowel, or the near-hopeless problem of resecting the entire small intestine, and perhaps right colon, for gangrene.

An interesting and often confusing picture is produced by children in whom duodenal bands, associated with incomplete rotation, do not obstruct the duodenum sufficiently to bring the patient to operation in infancy, or in whom the volvulus of the entire small bowel on its mesentery fails to produce complete intestinal obstruction or complete vascular occlusion. Such children may struggle through months or even years of malnourished life, being diagnosed as psychoneurotic, malabsorption syndrome, and so forth, before the diagnosis is made, and relief given by operation. This condition has often been mistaken for cyclic vomiting of metabolic origin. At other times the picture simulates celiac syndrome, with abdominal distention and malnutrition erroneously attributed to a disturbance of digestion rather than to a mechanical abnormality. The barium swallow in these chronic cases will usually show the duodenum coming straight down from the pylorus without the usual C loop and may show an oblique irregularity of the bowel which is the effect of the twist of the volvulus. Barium enema will show the abnormal position of the colon.

In the neonate, the treatment of intestinal obstruction due to an anomaly of rotation is urgent operation. Rapid evisceration permits appraisal of the situation, derotation of an existing volvulus, and division of abnormal bands constricting the duodenum.

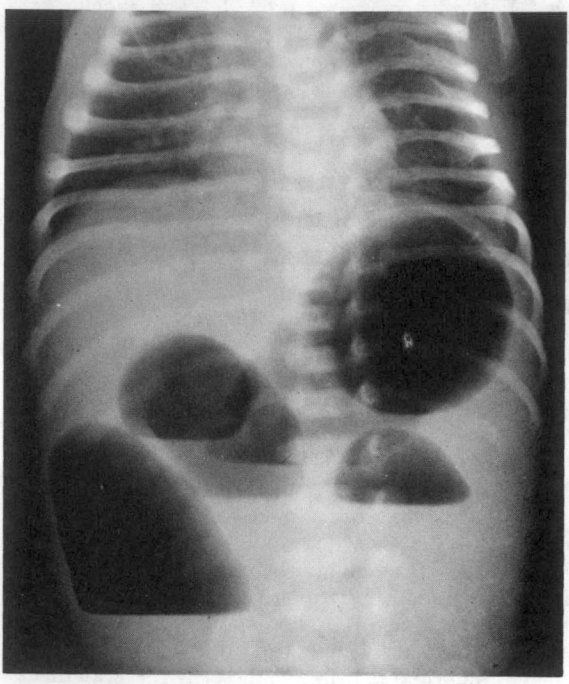

Fig. 16. Jejunal atresia is diagnosed by the dilation of a modest number of loops of small bowel. The enormous discrepancy in size between this dilated bowel and the contracted, unused neonatal distal bowel presents a technical problem in the restoration of continuity.

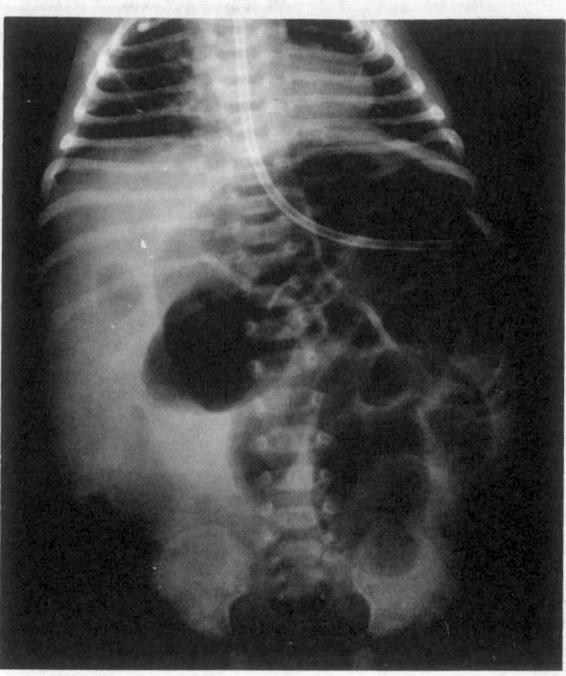

Fig. 17. Meconium ileus. The numerous dilated loops of bowel suggest that the obstruction is well down in the ileum. The speckled radiolucencies in the otherwise empty right side of the abdomen are the tell-tale bubbles of air in the viscid meconium impacted in the terminal ileum. Colonic irrigation with gastrographin may successfully dislodge the meconium and avoid the necessity for a laparotomy.

Atresia of the Jejunum and Ileum

The picture in atresia of the jejunum and ileum (Fig. 16) is the nonspecific one of neonatal intestinal obstruction, bilious vomiting, distention, and absence of stools. The higher the obstruction, the earlier the onset of vomiting; the lower the obstruction, the greater the distention and the more numerous the loops of dilated bowel. Hydramnios is common with any congenital obstruction of the alimentary tract. Occasionally the obstruction is incomplete, due to a local stenosis, while in other children the bowel may be missing or occluded in one or several segments. Immediate operation is the treatment and may be made difficult by the enormous disproportion between the dilated proximal bowel and the tiny unused distal bowel. Survival of 70 to 80 percent of patients can be expected, depending upon the size of the infant, the association of other anomalies, and delay in operation. Louw from South Africa reported 94 percent survival in 33 successive infants.

Meconium Ileus

The clinical picture in the infant with meconium ileus (Fig. 17) (see Chap. 9) is essentially that of

neonatal intestinal obstruction. Radiographically the granular appearance of the characteristically viscid meconium in the right side of the abdomen, speckled with tiny air bubbles, the "rabbit pellets" of inspissated meconium in the colon, also frequently visible on the roentgenogram, and particularly the knowledge that previous siblings have had this condition, all make the diagnosis. A variety of operative treatments—enterotomy and evacuation, enterotomy and irrigation with acetylcysteine, resection of the terminal ileum containing the obstructing mass of meconium, and either anastomosis or double-barreled enterostomy—have all yielded substantial salvage in various reported series. Most exciting is the recent observation that the irrigation of the colon in the unoperated baby with 15 or 20 ml at a time either of a dilute 4 percent acetylcysteine solution or of the radiocontrast material gastrographin, which contains a small amount of the detergent Tween-80, will liberate the adherent meconium in the terminal ileum and allow the babies to be relieved without operation. This is not to be recommended in babies who present radiologic evidence of massive distension, since it is in these babies that there probably is some additional complicating factor resulting from the intrauterine obstruction, viz., meconium peritonitis, volvulus, or atresia. The ultimate prognosis is that of any child with cystic fibrosis of the

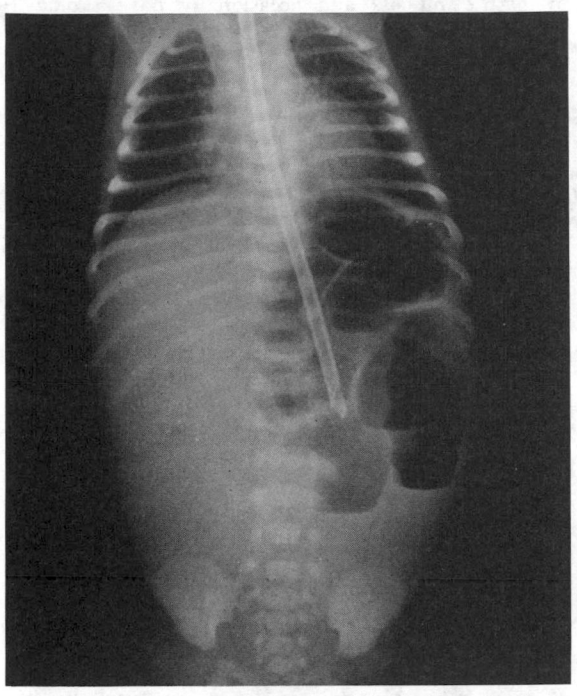

Fig. 18. Jejunal atresia with meconium peritonitis. The diffuse opacity is altered in the right lower quadrant by a minute speckled calcification indicating that the dilated bowel ruptured into the peritoneal cavity, decompressing itself, at least several days before birth so that calcification had time to occur in the fetal peritoneum. The perforation has usually sealed over by the time of birth, but the intense inflammatory reaction complicates the problem of dealing with the atresia.

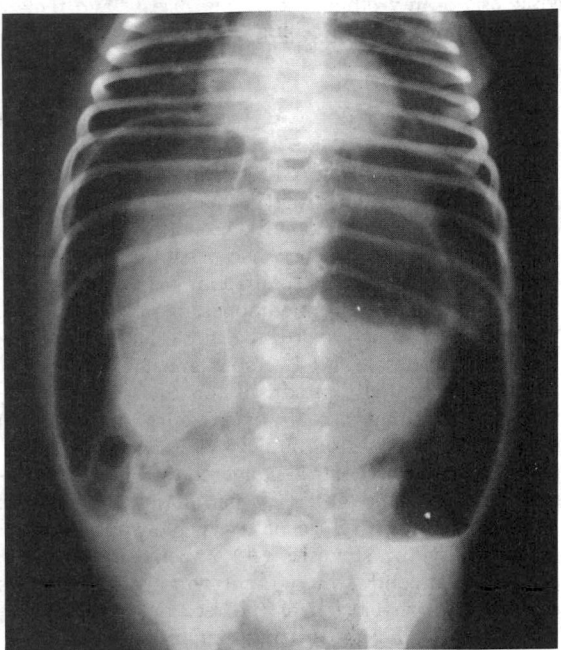

Fig. 19. Neonatal perforation in a 7-day-old infant who refused his feedings and suddenly became distended, due to a perforated gastric ulcer which was successfully closed. Perforated duodenal ulcer or neonatal gastric rupture, without ulceration, could easily have been the cause.

pancreas and apparently neither worse nor better than for children with cystic fibrosis who do not present in infancy with meconium ileus.

Meconium Peritonitis

Meconium peritonitis (Fig. 18) is the result of an intrauterine rupture of the intestine with escape of the contents into the peritoneal cavity. The initiating obstruction may have been an atresia or may have been meconium ileus in association with mucoviscidosis. Often by the time of birth the perforation has resealed and, in a rare case, no cause for the initiating obstruction is found. Attention will have been directed to the child in the first place because of intestinal obstruction, and operation undertaken to correct the cause of the intestinal obstruction. In an infant with neonatal intestinal obstruction in whom the roentgenogram shows obvious calcification, varying from speckles to sheets, in an area where there are no gas-filled loops, one may confidently make the diagnosis of meconium peritonitis. With a widespread inflammatory reaction, operation may be extremely difficult. In what has been termed the cystic form of meconium peritonitis, the extruded meconium becomes encapsulated in the neighborhood of the per-

foration and it is possible to resect, en masse, the sac of meconium and the malformed bowel which has perforated.

Hirschsprung's Disease

This condition is characterized by intestinal aganglionosis. It may manifest itself in the newborn as an incomplete or a total intestinal obstruction and occasionally with perforation of the distended proximal bowel. The films show numerous dilated loops of small bowel and in the infant it is notoriously difficult to be certain whether a distended loop is colon or small intestine. Contrary to earlier impressions, it is now demonstrated that a carefully done contrast enema may be diagnostic, showing a narrow rectum and sigmoid and dilated proximal colon. The enema in any case will likely lead to the discharge of inspissated meconium and yield temporary relief. (See Sec. 23.13.)

Meconium Plug

In some infants with neonatal intestinal obstruction a diagnostic contrast enema leads to discharge of a large, formed meconium cast of the distal bowel, following which all symptoms are relieved. Occasionally the obstructing meconium plug is in the transverse colon or the splenic flexure. If gastrographin irrigations do not succeed in dislodging it, operation is required. These children prove not to have muco-viscidosis or any other underlying disease and remain perfectly well after the plug has passed.

Neonatal Intestinal Perforation

Occasionally an infant who seems not to be doing well, who rejects feedings, or perhaps has vomited only once or twice, suddenly becomes massively distended. One should suspect the possibility of neonatal intestinal perforation. A plain film may show an extraordinary degree of pneumoperitoneum (Fig. 19). Operation obviously is to be undertaken at once. The possibilities are: (1) "spontaneous" rupture of the stomach, usually proximally on the greater curvature, which may actually represent rupture from emetic force, or perforation by a gavage tube, probably not indicative of a congenital anatomic weakness as earlier thought; (2) perforation of a gastric or duodenal ulcer; (3) a postnatal blow-out proximal to an atresia or stenosis; (4) a perforation of the cecum or appendix in a child with Hirschsprung's disease; (5) perforation of the rectum by thermometer or rectal tube; or (6) perforation of the small or large bowel on an unexplained basis.

Duplications of the Intestinal Tract (Enteric Cysts)

These lesions are spherical or tubular structures with serosal covering, mucosal lining, and usually a muscular wall in common with the segment of bowel to which they are attached. The smallest ones may be submucosal, protruding into the lumen, and may cause intussusception. Symptoms otherwise are produced by the distension, size, and displacement of a large blind cyst, by obstruction from compression of the attached bowel, or from bleeding when a cyst lined by gastric mucosa communicates with the neighboring bowel and produces a peptic ulcer. Treatment is by resection of the cyst with the attached bowel, although in certain locations, particularly if a tubular cyst is very long and would require resection of a long segment of bowel, it may be preferable to peel the mucosa from the cyst. Cysts behind the duodenum, which are not susceptible of extirpation, may be treated by anastomosing to the duodenum. The explanation frequently suggested for formation of enteric cysts is that they result from incomplete canalization of the intestine following the stage of epithelial cords, so that as vacuoles form and coalesce in the epithelial mass, one vacuole remains to form a cyst. However, the duplications are usually separated from the lumen of the bowel by a heavy muscular wall and occasionally are entirely detached. None of the embryologic explanations thus far offered appears to be valid. In the mediastinum so-called duplications of the esophagus occur, which although

closely attached to the esophagus, are, in fact, lined by gastric mucosa and occasionally have prolongations passing down through the diaphragm, communicating with the lumen of the small intestine. These cysts are almost invariably associated with thoracic vertebral malformations, and not uncommonly the same patients have duplications of the ordinary variety within the abdomen. Complete duplication of the colon is also usually associated with vertebral malformations as well as with duplications of the bladder and urethra, and with external anal orifices and/or fistulas. The multiple duplications and associated vertebral anomalies that are encountered with esophageal and colonic duplications suggest a more complicated origin for these lesions than for the more commonly encountered isolated enteric cysts. Incomplete caudal twinning has been suggested to be the genesis of such complex duplications of the colon.

Meckel's Diverticulum and Persistent Vitelline Duct

The omphalomesenteric duct, or vitelline duct, connects the midgut of the embryo to the yolk sac. From the seventh to the twelfth week of fetal life the duct gradually becomes obliterated and ordinarily no connection with the bowel persists. However, any or all portions of the omphalomesenteric duct may persist. Figure 20 shows some of the possible types of vitelline duct remnants. Symptoms are related to the nature of the persistence. No more than a fibrous cord representing the omphalomesenteric vessels may persist, connecting the small intestine to the umbilicus, and this may serve as the focal point for a volvulus or as a band under which another loop of bowel may be caught. At times a cyst of intestinal structure occurs in the umbilical cord, removed some distance from the umbilicus, and is treatable by mere ligation and division of the cord. At the other extreme the ileum may connect widely with the umbilicus by a side arm of bowel, forming a fecal fistula (Fig. 21). In some instances a portion of the mucosa may persist at the umbilicus, presenting either as a cherry-red mass, which simulates a peculiarly stubborn granuloma, or as a mucosal cyst under the umbilicus, with or without an external communication. At times the cordlike remnant of the vitelline vessels between the intestine and the umbilicus may contain, in its midportion, a cyst lined by intestinal mucosa.

Most important is the true Meckel's diverticulum, an outpouching of the ileum which occurs anywhere from the ileocecal valve to a point, in the adult, three feet or more proximal to the valve (Fig. 20). The incidence of Meckel's diverticulum is variously given as 1 to 2 percent. It may be a slender process, like a vermiform appendix, or a bell-shaped out-pouching several inches wide at the base and several inches long. Symptoms arise from two circum-

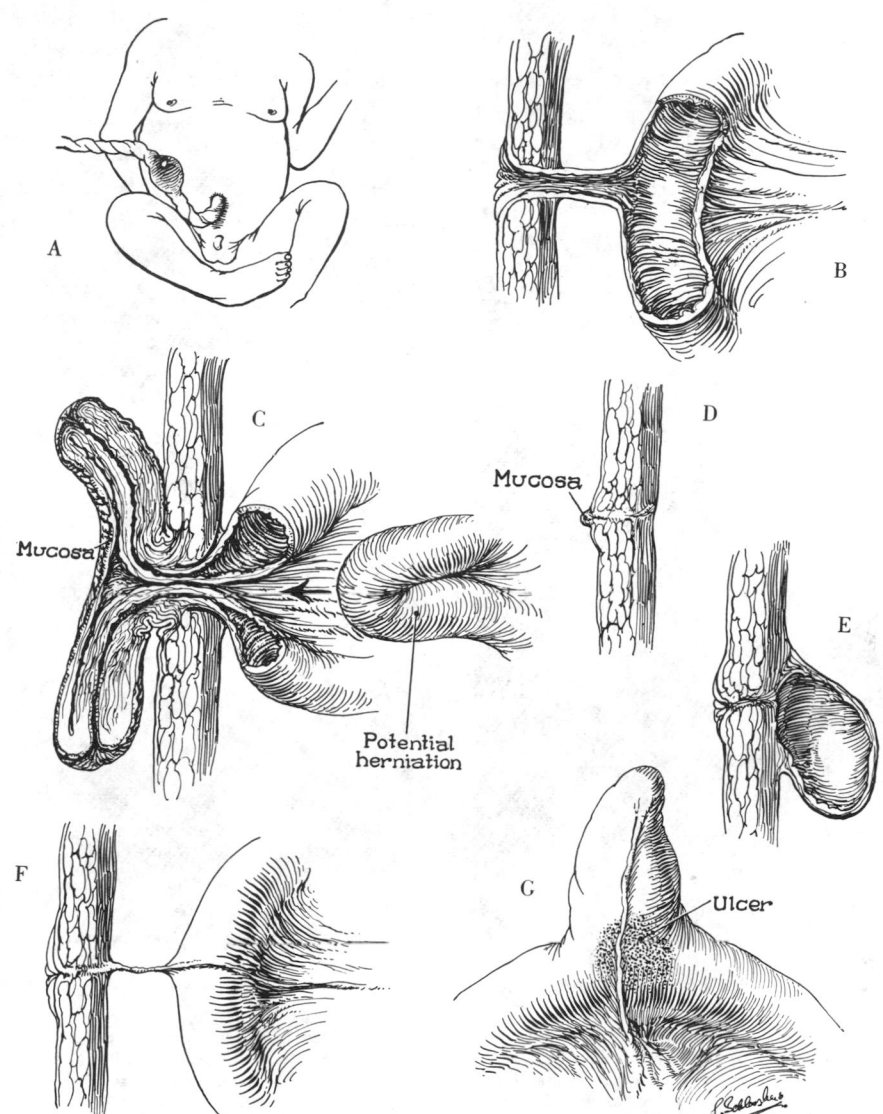

Fig. 20. Some of the possible types of vitelline duct (omphalomesenteric duct) remnants. A. Epithelial cyst in the cord—rare type. Cysts in this position may also be due to collections of Wharton's jelly. B. Patent omphalomesenteric duct connecting ileum with umbilicus and constituting a fecal fistula. C. Prolapse of proximal and distal loops of ileum through the orifice shown in B. This may be complicated by a hernia between the prolapsed loops. D. Mucosal polyp or pouch in external surface of umbilicus, often confused with an umbilical granuloma. E. Extraperitoneal mucosal cyst which may communicate with the surface, in which case there is a continuous discharge of mucus. F. Persistence of the vitelline artery which may act as a band to obstruct another loop or bowel or may serve as the focal point for a volvulus. At times an epithelium-lined cyst occurs in the middle of such a band. G. Meckel's diverticulum showing the characteristic vascular supply. A peptic ulcer is indicated.

stances: (1) Slender diverticula resemble vermiform appendices, and "diverticulitis" in them produces a disease which is indistinguishable from appendicitis and is treated in the same way. (2) Many of the diverticula contain ectopic gastric mucosa, and peptic ulcers develop in the neighboring ileal mucosa. Such ulcers occasionally perforate, but more commonly bleed.

In infants and children, painless intestinal bleeding—the passage of large quantities of fresh blood in the stool in the absence of hematemesis—is strongly suggestive of a peptic ulcer associated with a Meckel's diverticulum. The hemorrhage is rarely exsanguinating but may be extremely severe. Fresh blood may alternate with changed blood. A massive hemorrhage leads to rapid evacuation of bright red blood, to be

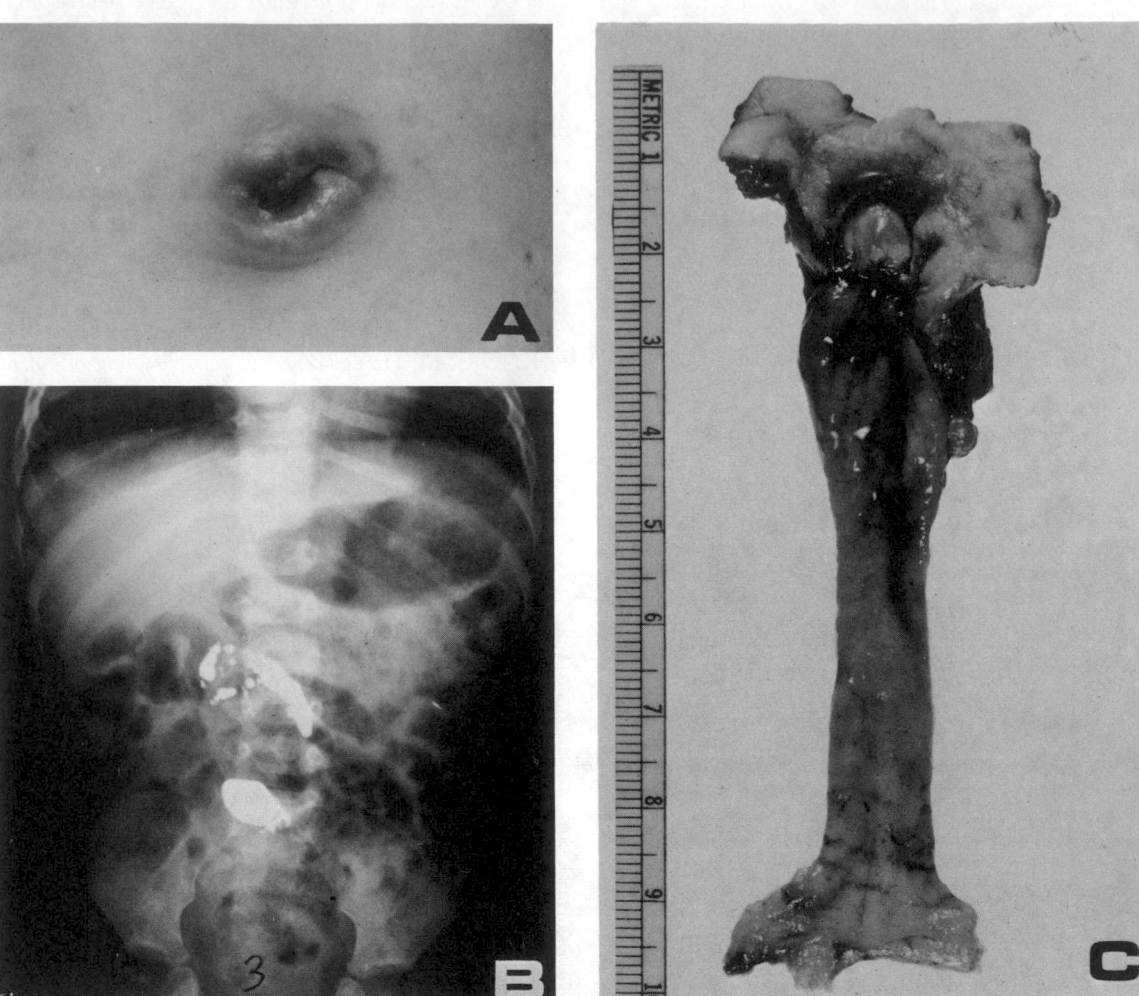

Fig. 21. Infant with persistent mucoid drainage from umbilicus since birth. No feces or air observed to have been discharged. *A*. Obvious sinus leading down from the somewhat inflamed umbilicus which was covered by a glairy fluid. *B*. Injection of the sinus tract with contrast material showed free passage into a bowel-like structure leading from the umbilical sinus to the antimesenteric border of the ileum. *C*. Note in the opened specimen the umbilical skin at left, the smooth granulating lining of the subcutaneous portion of the tract, the thick, raised, obviously gastric mucosa of the distalmost intraabdominal portion of the tract, and the smooth intestinal lining of the remainder, merging indistinguishably at the bowel end with the mucosa of the ileum.

followed, as bleeding subsides, by slow evacuation of changed blood. Repeated hemorrhage is common, and operation is performed in chronic cases on suspicion, after the stomach and colon have been studied and found normal. Meckel's diverticula are rarely found by roentgenography. In acute cases, operation for massive hemorrhage may have to be performed without these studies. Resection of the diverticulum is curative, but at times a broad attachment of the diverticulum to the intestine may require resection of a segment of bowel. Occasionally Meckel's diverticula do not bleed until later in life. Hemangiomas of the bowel, isolated or diffuse, or duplications of the gut may give rise to intestinal hemorrhage simi-

lar to that from a Meckel's diverticulum. Meckel's diverticulum is one of the more common mechanical lesions which lead to intussusception.

Ordinarily, if a Meckel's diverticulum is encountered in the course of operation for another purpose, it is resected if the basic condition is such as to make this seem reasonable.

Mesenteric Cysts

Cysts of the mesentery produce symptoms mechanically, obstructing the bowel either by direct infringement upon and compression of the lumen or by initiating volvulus. They may be chylous, filled with opaque, creamy material, or lymphatic. Lymphatic cysts are usually unilocular and thin-walled, but occasionally appear as diffuse lymphangiomas of omentum or mesentery. Diagnosis is seldom made before operation because the cysts are usually so soft and flabby as not to be palpable. Symptoms arise either from compression or twisting of the bowel, causing obstruction, or from inflammation in the cyst, clinically simulating appendicitis. The attachment to the bowel is frequently so intimate as to require resection of the bowel with mesenteric cyst.

REFERENCES

Abrami, G., and Dennison, W. M. Duplications of the stomach. Surgery, 49:794, 1961.

Amadeo, J. H., Ashmore, H. W., and Oponte, G. E. Neonatal gastric perforation caused by congenital defects of the gastric musculature. Surgery, 47:1010, 1960.

Basu, R., Forshall, I., and Rickham, P. P. Duplications of the alimentary tract. Brit. J. Surg., 47:477, 1960.

Beardmore, H. E., and Wiglesworth, F. W. Vertebral anomalies and alimentary duplications. Pediat. Clin. N. Amer., 96:457, 1958.

Benson, C. D., and Linkner, L. M. The surgical complications of Meckel's diverticulum in infants and children. Arch. Surg., 73:393, 1956.

—— and Lloyd, J. R. Atresia and stenosis of the jejunum and ileum. *In* Pediatric Surgery, 2nd ed. Chicago, Year Book Publishers, 1969.

—— Bentley, J. F. R., and Smith, J. R. Developmental posterior enteric remnants and spinal malformations. Arch. Dis. Child., 35:76, 1960.

Cullen, T. E. Embryology, Anatomy and Disease of the Umbilicus. Philadelphia, W. B. Saunders Co., 1916.

deLorimier, A. A., Fonkalsrud, E. W., and Hays, D. M. Congenital atresia and stenosis of the jejunum and ileum. Surgery, 65:819, 1969.

Donald, J. G., et al. Unusual manifestations of aganglionic disorder in the newborn. Surgery, 56:144, 1964.

Dykstra, G., Sieber, W. K., and Kiesewetter, W. B. Intestinal atresia and stenosis of the jejunum and ileum. Surgery, 64:661, 1968.

Feggetter, S. A review of the long-term results of operations for duodenal atresia. Brit. J. Surg., 56:68, 1969.

Handlesman, J. C., and Ravitch, M. M. Chylous cysts of the mesentery in children. Ann. Surg., 140:1, 1954.

Holsclaw, D. A., Eckstein, H. B., and Nixon, H. H. Meconium ileus—A 20 year review of 109 cases. Amer. J. Dis. Child., 109:101, 1965.

Jackson, J. M. Annular pancreas and duodenal obstruction in the neonate. Arch. Surg., 87:379, 1963.

Kiesewetter, W. B. Meckel's diverticulum in children. Arch. Surg., 75:914, 1957.

Kittle, C. F., Jenkins, H. P., and Dragstedt, L. R. Patent omphalo mesenteric duct and its relation to the diverticulum of Meckel. Arch. Surg., 54:10, 1947.

Louw, J. H., and Barnard, C. N. Congenital intestinal atresia, observations on its origin. Lancet, 2:1065, 1955.

Lynn, H. B. Duodenal obstruction: Atresia, stenosis and annular pancreas. *In* Pediatric Surgery, 2nd ed. Chicago, Year Book Publishers, 1969.

Martin, L. W. Meconium ileus. Amer. J. Dis. Child., 109:99, 1965.

Mellish, R. W., and Koop, C. E. Clinical manifestations of duplication of the bowel. Pediatrics, 27:397, 1961.

Moore, T. C., and Battersby, J. S. Congenital cysts of the mesentery. Ann. Surg., 145:428, 1957.

Parrish, R. A., et al. Spontaneous rupture of the gastrointestinal tract in the newborn. Ann. Surg., 159:244, 1961.

Pollock, W. F. Intestinal obstruction in the newborn. Surg. Gynec. Obst., 119:104, 1964.

Ravitch, M. M. Hindgut duplications, doubling of colon and genitourinary tracts. Ann. Surg., 137:588, 1953.

—— Pediatric Surgery, 2nd ed. Chicago, Year Book Publishers, 1969.

Rogers, C. S. R. Pneumoperitoneum in the newborn. Surgery, 56:842, 1964.

Santulli, T. V. Meconium ileus. *In* Pediatric Surgery. Chicago, Year Book Publishers, 1969.

—— and Blanc, W. A. Congenital atresia of the intestine; pathogenesis and treatment. Ann. Surg., 154:939, 1961.

Snyder, W. H., Jr., and Chaffin, L. Embryology and pathology of the intestinal front-presentation of 48 cases of malrotation. Ann. Surg., 140:368, 1954.

—— and Chaffin, L. Malrotation of the intestine. *In* Pediatric Surgery. Chicago, Year Book Publishers, 1969.

Spencer, R. The various patterns of intestinal atresia. Surgery, 64:661, 1968.

Swischuk, L. E. Meconium plug syndrome: A cause of neonatal intestinal obstruction. Amer. J. Roentgen., CIII:339, 1968.

Wang, C. A., et al. Anomalies of intestinal rotations in adolescents and adults. Surgery, 54:839, 1963.

Wilmore, D. W., Groff, D. B., Bishop, H. C., and Dudrick, S. J. Total parenteral nutrition in infants with catastrophic gastrointestinal anomalies. J. Pediat. Surg., 4:181, 1969.

Young, D. G., and Wilkinson, A. W. Abnormalities associated with neonatal duodenal obstruction. Surgery, 63:832, 1968.

23.13
CONGENITAL AGANGLIONIC MEGACOLON
(HIRSCHSPRUNG'S DISEASE)

MURRAY DAVIDSON and
MERVIN SILVERBERG

Congenital aganglionic megacolon or Hirschsprung's disease is a malformation of the parasympathetic system, characterized by absence of the intramural ganglion cells of the submucosal (Meissner's) and myenteric (Auerbach's) plexuses, and producing a disorder of stool propulsion. As a result of obstruction by the abnormally innervated distal colon, the proximal normal bowel becomes distended; i.e., megacolon develops and the distal segment is narrowed.

The pathophysiology of the narrowed bowel is not entirely clear. Some authors believe that it is not "spastic,' but simply fails to participate in normal peristalsis. Others suggest that the obstruction which this segment is associated with may be due in part to tonic contraction of its smooth muscle, since adrenergic innervations appear to be disturbed. The entire rectum is usually involved, but the proximal extent of the defect above this segment is variable. In more than half the patients aganglionosis extends to the midsigmoid colon. In others, varying lengths of the colon are abnormal. Ten to 15 percent of all cases extend beyond the left side of the colon, and in rare instances part or all of the small bowel may be aganglionic. Segmental involvement has been reported on one occasion. In other instances, very short segments of aganglionosis, not even reaching to the rectosigmoid, have been associated with the picture of megarectum, colonic dilation extending virtually to the anal canal.

The incidence in the general population is reported to be higher than 1 in 5,000. Support for the role of genetic factors in the pathogenesis of this condition is derived from evidence that there is a familial incidence of 2 to 4 percent, a preponderance of affected males, and an association with Down's syndrome. Additionally, a hereditary disease which has been related to specific gene defects and which is analogous to that of man occurs in the mouse. Hair changes result from reduced numbers of pigment cells in the mouse's coat, and the bowel changes are initially identical and are associated with absence of colonic ganglion cells.

The most common early clinical presentation is that of delay in passage of meconium, associated with abdominal distention, in the first days of life. This apparent intestinal obstruction may be complicated by perforation of the proximal colon, cecum, or appendix, if these structures are distended and have thinned-out walls. Digital examination of the small-caliber rectum often results in a copious gush of meconium or fecal material with apparent relief of the obstructive features. These cases may be confused with the so-called self-limited meconium plug syndrome. They should be followed closely for signs of continuing fecal retention as a clue to the possible presence of congenital aganglionic megacolon.

A second common presenting syndrome in the first weeks of life is severe persistent or recurrent diarrhea, due to secondary enterocolitis. The condition arises more commonly among infants with long segments of aganglionic bowel. Peritonitis, mucosal ulceration, and septicemia develop frequently in this condition, and the mortality rate is about 75 percent. In older children enterocolitis is rare, and they display the more characteristic symptoms of Hirsch-sprung's disease, i.e., persistent abdominal distention and stool retention. Malnutrition, anemia, rectal bleeding due to ulcers from colonic stasis, protein-losing enteropathy, and recurrent systemic infections have all been reported as complicating features of the disease.

Physicians frequently are assured that the symptoms of this disease may readily be distinguished from those of chronic voluntary stool withholding because the patients with congenital megacolon have a history of difficulty going back to the neonatal period. It is apparent from the foregoing that some children may present no such history, others may have had diarrhea, and only some will have been constipated. Conversely, children with voluntary withholding may have had a prior history of colic and bowel difficulty which goes back to birth. The most important distinguishing features in differential diagnosis were pointed out above in the discussion of constipation and are reiterated here. The stool, which is retained in patients with Hirschsprung's disease, generally does not reach the distal area of the rectum. This produces two major differential findings. Since the proprioceptors which initiate the "call to defecate" are located just proximal to the internal sphincter, this reflex is rarely activated in children with congenital aganglionic megacolon. Secondly, on repeated digital examinations of their rectums this segment is virtually always found to be empty despite large amounts of retained material.

The mainstays of diagnosis are the barium enema and rectal biopsy. Radiocontrast studies before the age of 6 weeks will often not show a *transition zone*. In the young child, especially if frequent enemas have been given to decompress the colon, sufficient time may not have elapsed to permit the segment proximal to the aganglionic area to become dilated. Failure to evacuate barium adequately after examination should alert the radiologist to the correct diagnosis even in the absence of the typical transition zone (Fig. 22). Excessive amounts of administered barium may obscure the typical appearance in the older infant and child. Total colonic aganglionosis is often associated with an apparently normal barium enema, i.e., no transition zones or dilated areas are visualized, although narrowing and shortening of the normal-caliber colon with rounding of the flexures should be apparent in such a colon, and these signs may be considered presumptive evidence of the disease. If there is any reasonable doubt and the infant's clinical condition permits temporizing, a rectal biopsy should be done. Wedge biopsies taken deep enough to contain elements of the intramuscular plexus are preferred, since these ganglion cells are more easily identifiable. To obviate administration of general anesthesia and any of the rarely encountered postoperative complications such as stricture, bleeding, or sepsis in very ill infants, simple rectal suction biopsy has become popular. In experienced hands, demon-

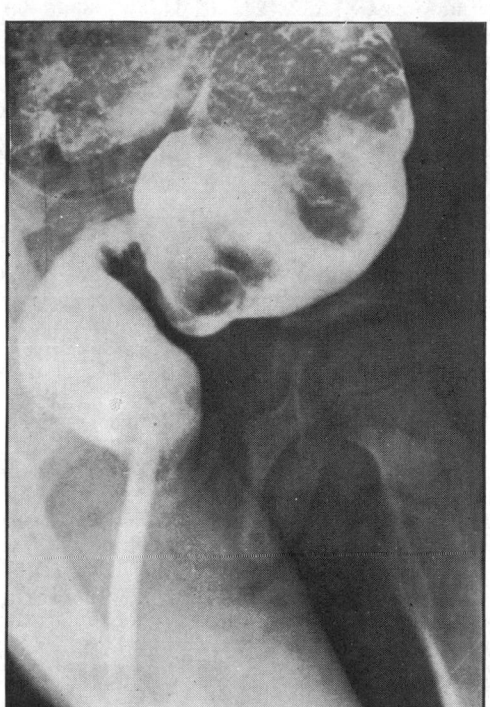

Fig. 22. Congenital megacolon in a boy of 7 years, 11 months. Transition segment at rectosigmoid junction.

stration of submucosal ganglia (Meissner's plexus) is adequate to exclude the diagnosis in many cases. However, absence of ganglia from tissue secured by this technique should not be considered diagnostic of Hirschsprung's disease, since such biopsy specimens

may be too small, too superficial, or taken from areas too close to the internal sphincter, wherein there is usually a paucity of ganglia. Manometric diagnostic studies show dissociation of stimulated motility between the normally innervated and aganglionic segments, and abnormal contractile responses of the internal sphincter to rectal distention.

Treatment of aganglionic megacolon may be either symptomatic or definitive. In the acutely ill and distended child, emergency correction of fluid and electrolyte imbalance and hypoproteinemia with appropriate treatment of sepsis are mandatory. Following restoration of reasonable homeostatic balance the patient is provided with an emergency colostomy, in a segment in which normal ganglia have been identified on pathologic review of frozen sections. In less urgent situations the obstipated patient may be helped to evacuate by mechanical means using enemas. Only small isotonic enemas should be used since serious complications have followed the use of tap-water, hypertonic phosphate solutions, or large saline enemas. With severe impaction frequent mineral oil or warm saline instillations, retrograde or through a colostomy, are useful.

Definitive surgical procedures are designed to establish regular and spontaneous defecation, maintain complete continence, and avoid problems of ultimate sexual potency. A number of different surgical techniques is employed, each intended best to serve the operative objectives and yielding optimal results in the hands of its originator (Fig. 23). All the methods now include some form of sphincterotomy or sphincter dilation to correct the sphincteric achalasia, which is demonstrable on motility study. The individual procedures contribute very little to overall mortality. A majority of deaths are due to irremediable imbalances in the nutritional or fluid-electrolyte conditions of patients preoperatively, the

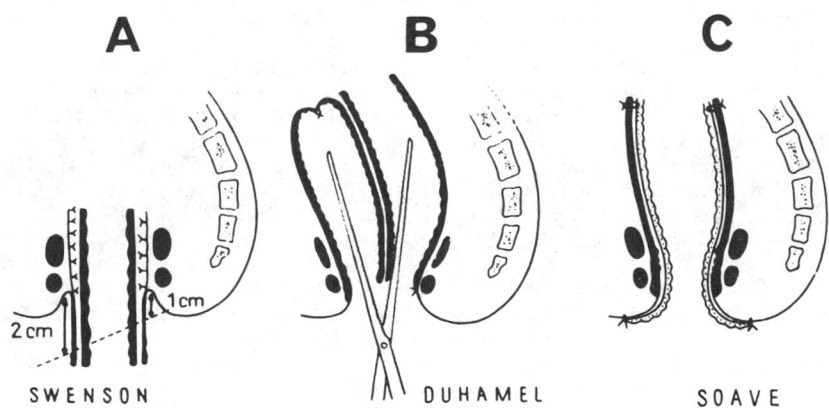

Fig. 23. Descriptions of surgical procedures for Hirschsprung's disease. A. Swenson's modified abdominoperineal pull-through procedure includes resection of most of aganglionic segment with an oblique anastomosis to preserve more of the anterior rectal wall. B. Duhamel makes a high posterior rectal incision and a side-to-side colorectal anastomosis using crush clamps. C. Soave removes the cylinder of rectal mucous membrane and pulls normal colon through the muscular sleeve. (Reproduced courtesy of Dr. George B. Jerzy Glass from *Progress in Gastroenterology*, Vol. 2. Grune & Stratton, Inc.)

most important factor in death being the development of pseudomembranous enterocolitis. The latter condition is not an infrequent complication in the postoperative period and its precise cause and treatment are unknown.

A number of disorders simulate aganglionic megacolon clinically and have often been considered collectively as pseudo-Hirschsprung's diseases. Abnormal, decreased, or absent intramural ganglion cells are noted in *Chagas' disease,* immaturity of ganglion cells, and a number of unnamed conditions. *Segmental dilation of the colon, achalasia of the distal colon* with normal ganglia, and colonic disorders associated with congenital colonic anomalies, vascular insufficiency of the colon, hypothyroidism, and central nervous system diseases, usually simulate aganglionosis but normal ganglion cells may be demonstrated. Ehrenpreis has postulated that one mechanism for postnatal degeneration of ganglion cells in the myenteric plexuses, and a possible cause of congenital aganglionosis, is a vascular accident which results in poor oxygenation of the affected segment.

REFERENCES

Aldridge, R. T., and Campbell, P. E. Ganglion cell distribution in the normal rectum and anal canal. A basis for the diagnosis of Hirschsprung's disease by anorectal biopsy. J. Pediat. Surg., 3:475, 1968.

Atias, A., Neghme, A., Mackay, L. A., and Jarpa, S. Megaesophagus, megacolon, and Chagas' disease in Chile. Gastroenterology, 44:432, 1963.

Bill, A. H., Jr., and Chapman, N. D. The enterocolitis of Hirschsprung's Disease. Its natural history and treatment. Amer. J. Surg., 103:70, 1962.

Bodian, M., and Carter, C. O. A family study of Hirschsprung's Disease. Ann. Hum. Genet., 26:261, 1963.

———— Carter, C. O., and Ward, B. C. H. Hirschsprung's Disease. Lancet, 1:302, 1951.

Bowden, D. H., Goodfellow, A. M., and Munn, N. D. Hirschsprung's Disease in the neonatal period; a report of five cases, four of which involved the small intestine. J. Pediat., 50:321, 1957.

Boley, S. J., Lafer, D. J., Klienhaus, S., Cohn, B. D., Mestel, A. L., and Kottmeirer, P. K. Endorectal pull-through procedure for Hirschsprung's disease without primary anastomosis. J. Pediat. Surg., 3:258, 1968.

Davidson, M. Congenital aganglionosis. *In* Code, C. F., ed., Handbook of Physiology—Alimentary Canal. Washington, D.C., Amer. Physiol. Soc., 1968, Chap. 134, p. 2783.

———— and Bauer, C. H. Studies of distal colonic motility in children. IV. Achalasia of the distal rectal segment despite presence of ganglia in the myenteric plexuses of this area. Pediatrics, 21:746, 1958.

———— Sleisenger, M. H., Steinberg, H., and Almy, T. P. Studies of distal colonic motility in children. III. The pathologic physiology of congenital megacolon (Hirschsprung's disease). Gastroenterology, 29:803, 1955.

Dobbins, W. O., and Bill, A. H., Jr. Diagnosis of Hirschsprung's disease excluded by rectal suction biopsy. New Eng. J. Med., 272:990, 1965.

Duhamel, B. New operation for treatment of Hirschsprung's disease. Arch. Dis. Child., 35:38, 1960.

Ehrenpreis, T. Long-term results of rectosigmoidectomy for Hirschsprung's disease, with a note on Duhamel's operation. Surgery, 49:701, 1961.

———— Pseudo-Hirschsprung's disease. Arch. Dis. Child., 40:177, 1965.

———— Acquired megacolon as a complication of rectosigmoidectomy for Hirschsprung's disease. Arch. Dis. Child., 40:180, 1965.

———— Some newer aspects on Hirschsprung's disease and allied disorders. J. Pediat. Surg., 1:329, 1966.

Emanuel, B., Padorr, M. P., and Swenson, O. Familial absence of myenteric plexus (congenital megacolon). A study of six families. J. Pediat., 67:381, 1965.

———— and Padorr, M. P. Mongolism associated with Hirschsprung's disease. J. Pediat., 66:437, 1965.

Fraser, G. C., and Berry, C. Mortality in neonatal Hirschsprung's disease: with particular reference to enterocolitis. J. Pediat. Surg., 2:205, 1967.

Graivier, L., and Sieber, W. K. Hirschsprung's disease and mongolism. Surgery, 60:458, 1966.

Hiatt, R. B. The pathologic physiology of congenital megacolon. Ann. Surg., 133:313, 1951.

———— The surgical treatment of congenital megacolon. Ann. Surg., 133:321, 1951.

———— The physiologic basis for surgery in congenital megacolon. Surg. Clin. N. Amer., 38:561, 1958.

Koop, C. E. The choice of surgical procedures in Hirschsprung's disease. J. Pediat. Surg., 1:523, 1966.

Lawson, J. O. N., and Nixon, H. H. Anal canal pressures in the diagnosis of Hirschsprung's disease. J. Pediat. Surg., 2:544, 1968.

McElhannon, F. N. Experimental production of megacolon resembling Hirschsprung's Disease. Surg. Forum, 10:218, 1960.

Moriarty, L. R., and Ramsey, B. W. Membranous colitis in two cases of Hirschsprung's disease treated with large doses of antibiotics. Pediatrics, 15:438, 1955.

Moseley, P. K., and Segar, W. E. Fluid and serum electrolyte disturbances as a complication of enemas in Hirschsprung's disease. Amer. J. Dis. Child., 115:714, 1968.

Nixon, H. H. Seminar on pseudo-Hirschsprung's disease. Proc. Brit. Ass. Paediat. Surg. Edinburgh. Arch. Dis. Child., 41:147, 1965.

Passarge, E. The genetics of Hirschsprung's disease. Evidence for heterogeneous etiology and a study of 63 families. New Eng. J. Med., 276:138, 1967.

Soave, F. Hirschsprung's disease: a new surgical technique. Arch. Dis. Child., 39:116, 1964.

Swenson, O. A new surgical treatment for Hirschsprung's disease. Surgery, 28:371, 1950.

———— Follow-up on 200 patients treated for Hirschsprung's disease during a ten year period. Ann. Surg., 146:706, 1957.

———— Neuhauser, E. B. D., and Picket, L. K. New concepts of the etiology, diagnosis and treatment of congenital megacolon (Hirschsprung's disease). Pediatrics, 4:201, 1949.

Tobin, F., Reid, N. C. R. W., Talbert, J. L., and Schuster, M. M. Non-surgical test for the diagnosis of Hirschsprung's disease. New Eng. J. Med., 278:188, 1968.

Zuelzer, W. W., and Wilson, J. L. Functional intestinal obstruction on a congenital neurogenic basis in infancy. Amer. J. Dis. Child., 75:40, 1948.

23.14
ANORECTAL MALFORMATIONS

THOMAS V. SANTULLI

Malformations of the anus and rectum, frequently referred to as "imperforate anus," are among the most common of congenital anomalies, occurring about once in every 5,000 births. They consist of a variety of lesions ranging from a mild congenital stenosis of the anus which requires simple dilation for cure to complex deformities which present some of the most vexing and discouraging problems in management.

Four main types of malformations were originally described by Ladd and Gross. Recently, it has been necessary to modify this classification in order more directly to relate clinical appearance with embryologic derivation and certain anatomic features. Chief among these features is the relationship of the termination of the bowel, even as a fistula, to the puborectalis sling of the levator ani musculature. The newer classification retains the four general types as originally described but subdivides the Type III malformations into (A) a "low anomaly" group, or anal agenesis, and (B) a "high anomaly" group, or rectal agenesis (Fig. 24). This distinction is important since, generally, the "high anomaly" carries a far greater mortality and morbidity and is accompanied by a much higher incidence of urologic and vertebral malformations than the "low anomaly." In the "low anomaly" the termination of the bowel has passed through the puborectalis sling and has been generally associated with a far better functional result than in the high group, in which the bowel has not traversed the sling. Figures 25 and 26 show the various fistulous terminations of the bowel in females and males and the relationships of these terminations to the puborectalis sling.

Types I, II, and III A represent abnormalities in the embryologic formation of the anus and/or perineum. Type III B is an embryologic malformation of the rectum and anus. Type IV is probably not an embryologic defect. It should be considered an acquired malformation since it can best be explained as a secondary atresia in the fetus resulting from a vascular accident to an already normally formed bowel.

The diagnosis can usually be made soon after birth by careful examination of the perineum. In Types I and IV the anal opening is normally located, but digital examination will disclose the diagnosis. The normal anal site may be imperforate as in the extremely rare Type II anomaly (imperforate anal membrane) and in Types III A and III B. In these, there is usually a depression (anal dimple) where one would expect to find the anus. In most cases the anal dimple is sharply defined, in others it may be

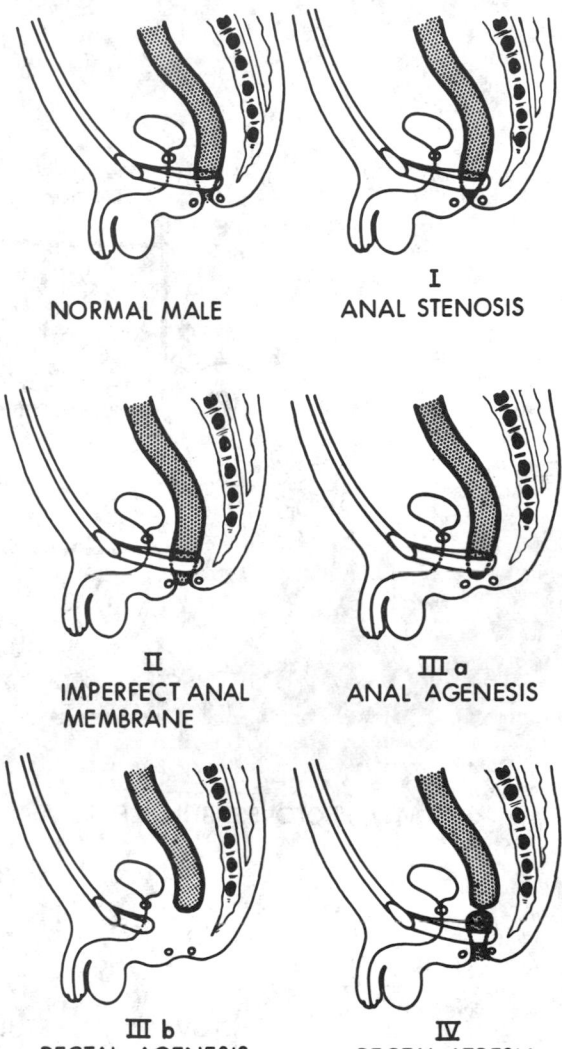

NORMAL MALE | I ANAL STENOSIS

II IMPERFECT ANAL MEMBRANE | III a ANAL AGENESIS

III b RECTAL AGENESIS | IV RECTAL ATRESIA

Fig. 24. The types of malformations of the anus and rectum schematically represented and compared with the normal male. Possible fistulous connections are omitted. Note the relationship of the termination of the bowel to the puborectalis sling of the levator ani muscle. (From Santulli et al. *Surg. Clin. N. Amer.*, 45:1253, 1965.)

less evident. The skin is more deeply pigmented than the surrounding skin and the skin lines appear to converge to a central point within the external anal sphincter muscle which surrounds the dimple. Puckering can be seen at this point when the muscle contracts. Over three-quarters of the patients have an ectopic opening of the bowel (fistula) in the perineum, vagina, urethra, or bladder (Fig. 25 and 26). Careful search should be made for a fistula in every case. In the male, passage of flatus or meconium from the urethra indicates the presence of a recto-urinary communication.

The various malformations, including their fistulous connections, are listed in Table 8. Types III A

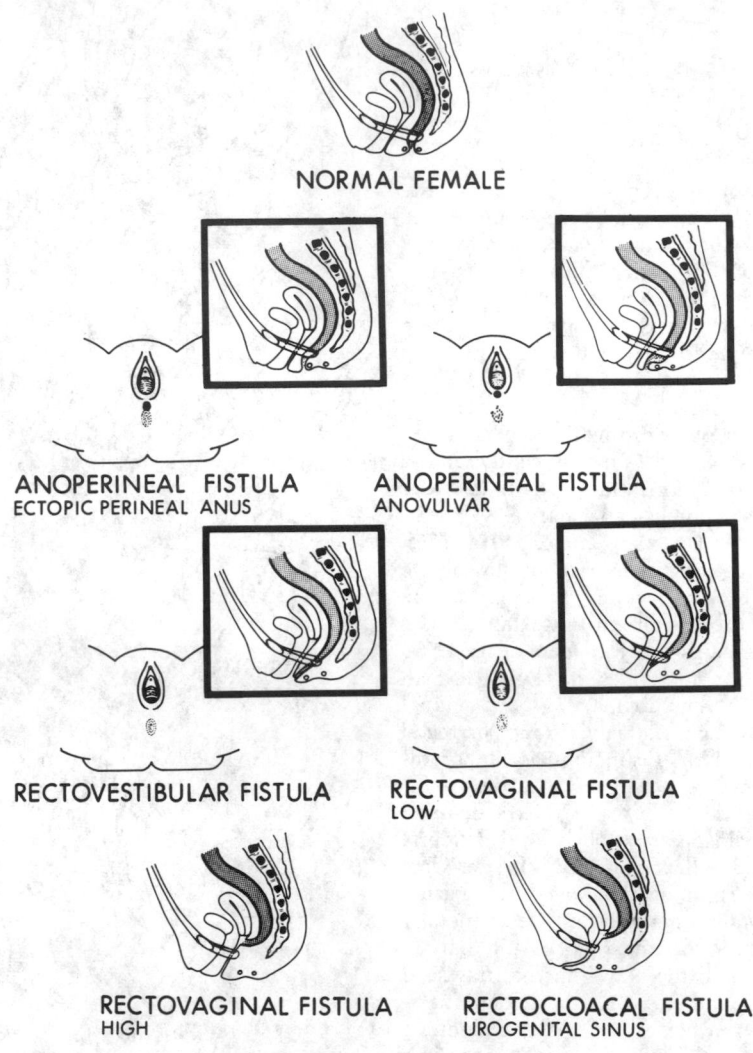

NORMAL FEMALE

ANOPERINEAL FISTULA
ECTOPIC PERINEAL ANUS

ANOPERINEAL FISTULA
ANOVULVAR

RECTOVESTIBULAR FISTULA

RECTOVAGINAL FISTULA
LOW

RECTOVAGINAL FISTULA
HIGH

RECTOCLOACAL FISTULA
UROGENITAL SINUS

Fig. 25. Drawings of fistulas in the female compared with the normal. Anoperineal fistulas present as either an *ectopic perineal anus* which is in the fourchette. The rectovestibular fistula lies within the vestibule of the vagina (fossa navicularis). Its course is directly cephalad, paralleling the posterior vaginal wall, instead of posterior as in the anovulvar fistula wherein the bowel is relatively superficial to the skin. *Rectovaginal fistulas* are usually low but may be located at any level in the posterior vaginal wall. The *rectocloacal fistula* occurs as a high communication in a urogenital sinus, which is represented by a single external orifice. (From Santulli et al. *Surg. Clin. N. Amer.*, 45:1253, 1965.)

and III B (anal and rectal agenesis) constitute about 90 percent of the lesions. Nearly all of the females have a fistula communicating with the perineum or the vagina but not with the urinary tract. A fistula to the perineum or the urinary tract (usually urethral, rarely vesical) may be found in 70 percent of the males.

Outlining the rectal pouch by roentgenograms taken with the baby held in the upside down position was once considered important in determining the level of the termination of the bowel, and therefore valuable in planning the surgical approach. However, these x-ray studies are of limited value,

particularly in view of recent experience with cinefluoroscopy, which has shown the level of termination of the bowel to vary widely in the same patient depending on the state of contraction of the perineal and pelvic musculature.

The most important contribution of radiology to the evaluation of patients with imperforate anus lies in the detection of accompanying vertebral and urologic abnormalities. Some abnormality of the lumbosacral spine may be found in over 50 percent of the "high anomaly" (Type III B) group, and the accompanying neurologic defects may significantly affect the functional end results in these patients. It

FISTULAS IN MALE

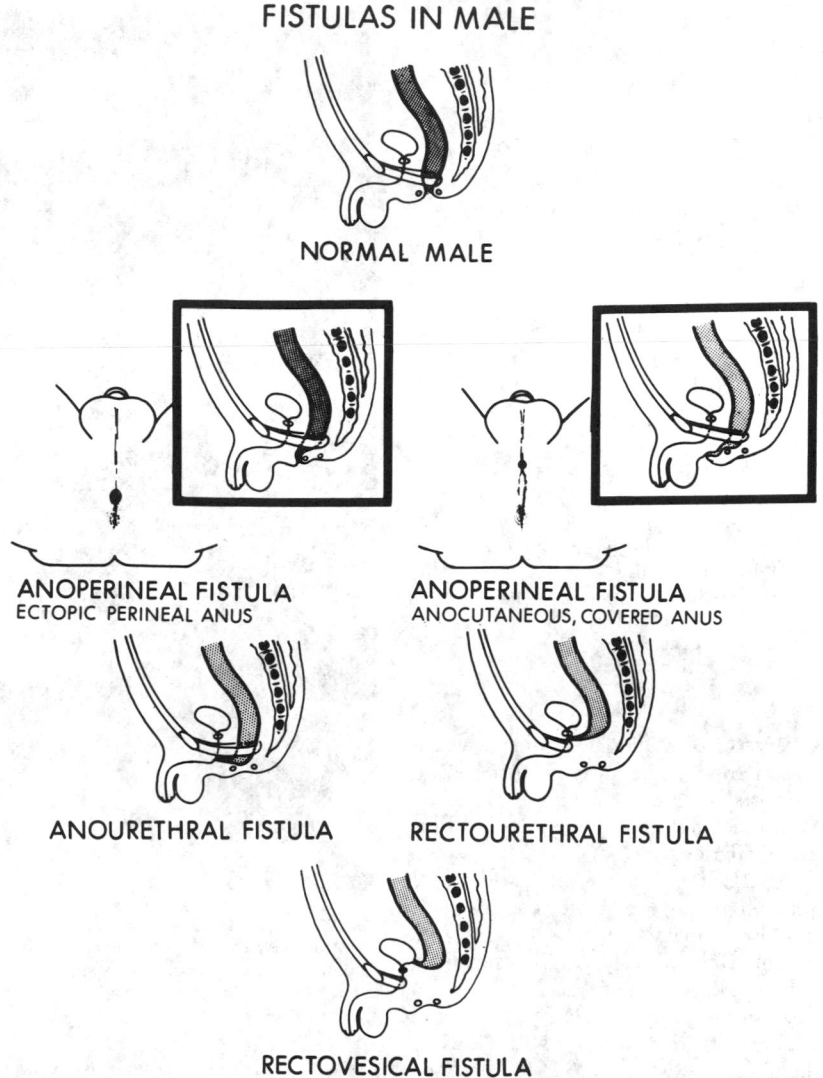

NORMAL MALE

ANOPERINEAL FISTULA
ECTOPIC PERINEAL ANUS

ANOPERINEAL FISTULA
ANOCUTANEOUS, COVERED ANUS

ANOURETHRAL FISTULA

RECTOURETHRAL FISTULA

RECTOVESICAL FISTULA

Fig. 26. Drawings of fistulas in the male compared with the normal. The anoperineal fistulas may be located anywhere between the perineosacral junction and the anal dimple. In the *ectopic perineal anus* the opening resembles a normal anus. In the *anocutaneous fistula* or *covered anus* the orifice may be small and resemble the end of a cutaneous tract of meconium in a thickened perineal skin which is sometimes represented as a median band (see Fig. 25). The anourethral fistulas are rare malformations in which the bowel has passed through the puborectalis sling as in the previous anomalies and opens as a fistula in the bulbar or in the membranous urethra.

should be emphasized that when the lower spine is abnormal, the incidence of urologic abnormalities is high and may exceed 70 percent. Hence, early intravenous pyelography should be done in all patients with imperforate anus (Fig. 27).

About 40 percent of the patients have other developmental anomalies and half of these may be serious. The most commonly associated major anomalies are congenital heart disease, atresia of the esophagus, hydronephrosis, and malformations of the spine.

The treatment is determined by the specific type of anomaly present. For the Type I anomaly (anal stenosis) it is relatively simple. Daily dilations with rubber bougies, catheters, or finger are instituted and gradually decreased in frequency as the stricture softens and the anus remains supple. The parents are instructed on the technique of dilations, which are usually continued several times a week for 3 to 6 months. Rarely, in severe strictures, an anoplasty may be necessary.

The Type II anomaly (imperforate and membrane) is extremely rare and becomes apparent soon

TABLE 8.   *Malformations of the Anus and Rectum*

I.   Anal Stenosis

II. Imperforate Anal Membrane

III. Anal and Rectal Agenesis
    A. Anal Agenesis
       Female 1. With fistula
             a. Anoperineal
                1. Ectopic perineal anus
                2. Anovulvar
             2. Without fistula
       Male   1. With fistula
             a. Anoperineal
                1. Ectopic perineal anus
                2. Anocutaneous (covered anus)
             b. Anourethral (bulbar or membranous)
             2. Without fistula
    B. Rectal Agenesis
       Female 1. With fistula
             a. Rectovestibular
             b. Rectovaginal
             c. Rectocloacal (urogenital sinus)
             2. Without fistula
       Male   1. With fistula
             a. Rectourethral
             b. Rectovesical
              2. Without fistula

IV. Rectal Atresia

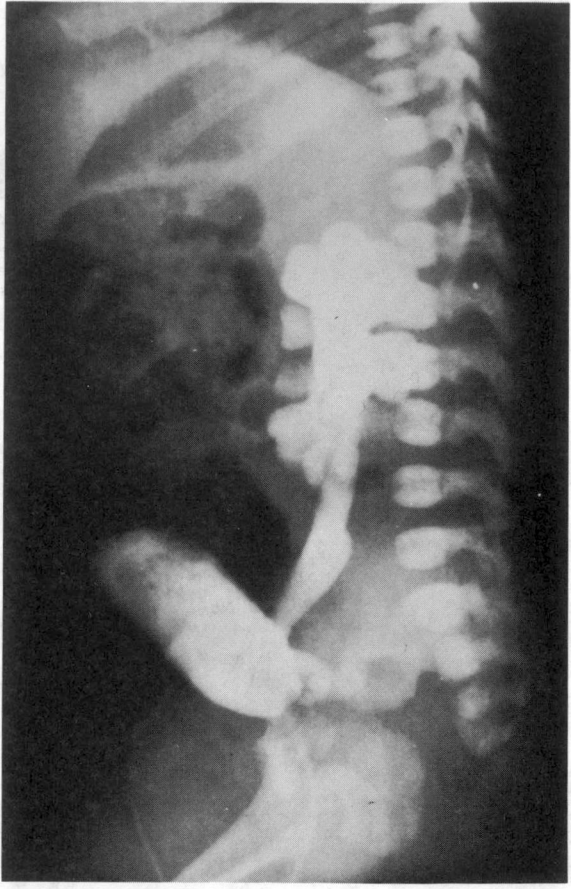

Fig. 27. Lateral roentgenogram of a female infant with Type III B malformation (high anomaly) illustrating an abnormal "stubby" sacrum. Intravenous pyelogram shows severe hydronephrosis. There was also evidence of ureteral reflux on this study.

after birth as a very thin, bulging membrane which looks dark because of the meconium lying just behind it. Treatment consists of either making a cruciate incision through the membrane or excising it. This is followed by anal dilations.

For the Type III anomalies of anal and rectal agenesis the treatment may be more complicated. The infant with a "low anomaly" can often be treated simply, and sometimes definitively, in the newborn period by what is known as a "cutback" procedure. In the female with an anovulvar fistula (Figs. 25 and 28) and in the male with the "covered anus" variety of anoperineal fistula (Figs. 26 and 29), the opening can be made larger by incising through the skin directly back to the anal dimple, beneath which lies an adequate anal canal. Continence will not be compromised, even if it is necessary to divide the anterior commissure of the external sphincter muscle, since the bowel has come through the puborectalis sling of the levator ani muscle in these low anomalies. This is followed by daily dilations. If the anomaly in either male or female is an ectopic perineal anus (Figs. 28 and 29), either no treatment or dilations only will be required.

In general, the baby with a "high anomaly" should have a preliminary divided sigmoid colostomy performed in the newborn period, followed by an abdominoperineal procedure at from 9 to 12 months of age, carefully bringing the bowel through the puborectalis sling of the levator ani muscle. This is particularly important in male infants who do not present a visible perineal opening. In almost 50 percent of these male infants there is a fistula to the urethra or bladder; exploration of the perineum in these infants is to be avoided.

For the Type IV anomaly (rectal atresia) the treatment is a preliminary colostomy in the newborn period, followed by an abdominoanal pull-through procedure at the age of 9 to 12 months.

Regardless of the form of treatment utilized it is essential that these children be followed closely for many years and great care be taken to guard against stricture, impaction, and resulting rectal inertia. Dilations, cathartics, stool softeners, and cleansing enemas are all adjuncts which may be used advisedly and under medical supervision to insure good bowel function.

The overall mortality is about 10 percent; surgical procedures to correct the malformations account for 2 percent of the deaths, prematurity and associ-

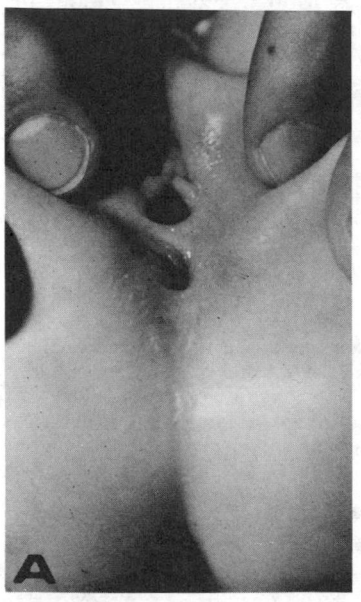

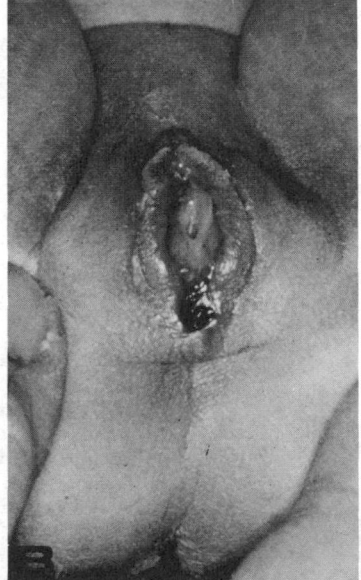

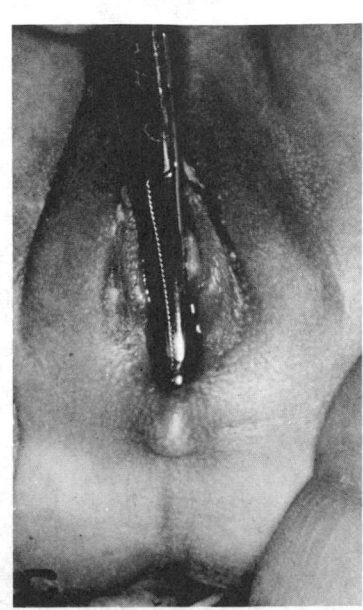

Fig. 28. Photographs of fistulas in the female. *A.* In the *ectopic perineal anus* the opening of the bowel is in the perineum between the fourchette and the anal dimple, and resembles a normal anus. *B.* Anovulvar fistula at the fourchette. Note the radial skin lines converging towards the site of the anal dimple. *C.* Clamp in anovulvar orifice illustrating posterior direction of the fistula; the bowel lies relatively close to the skin. *D.* A *rectovestibular fistula* is seen in the vestibule of the vagina. Its posterior (dorsal) circumference is not visible beneath the skin of the intack fourchette. *E.* The external appearance in the *rectocloacal* or urogenital sinus malformation. Note the single external orifice and the flattened appearance of the perineum due to the absence of a natal cleft. In these patients the urethra and vagina share a common passageway and the rectal fistula is located high in the posterior vaginal wall (Fig. 21), usually just distal to a bicornuate or double uterus. (Modified from Santulli et al. *Surg. Clin. N. Amer.,* 45:1253, 1965.)

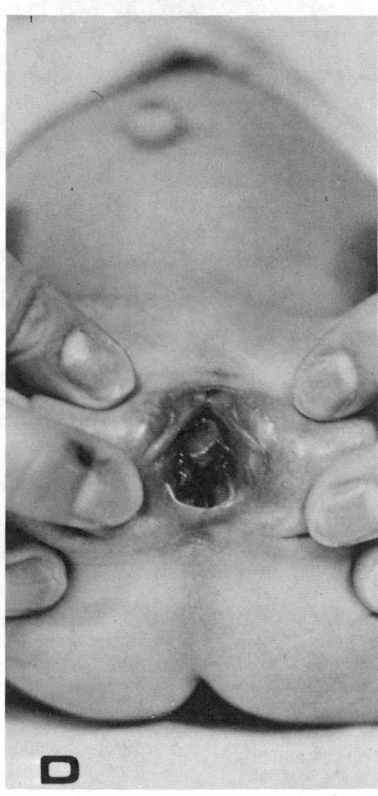

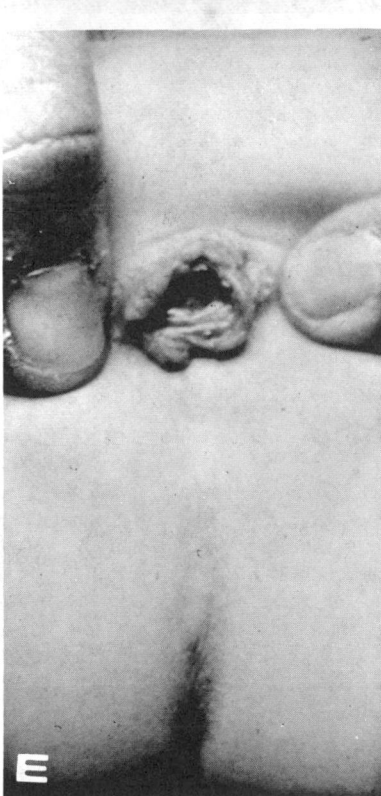

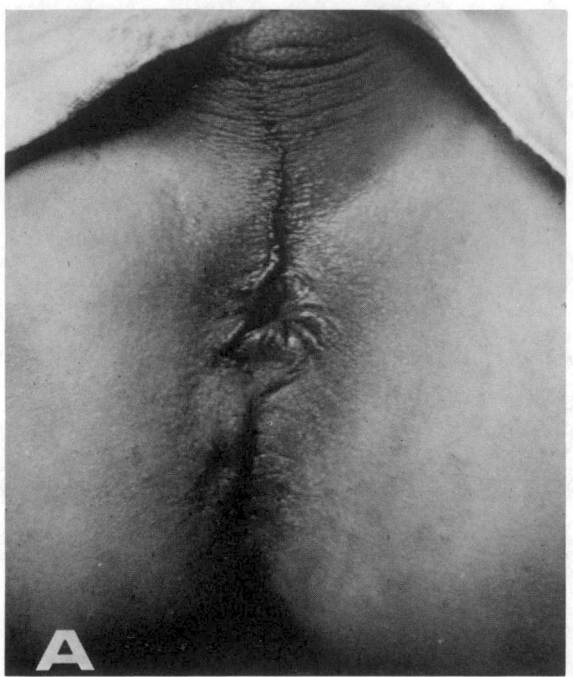

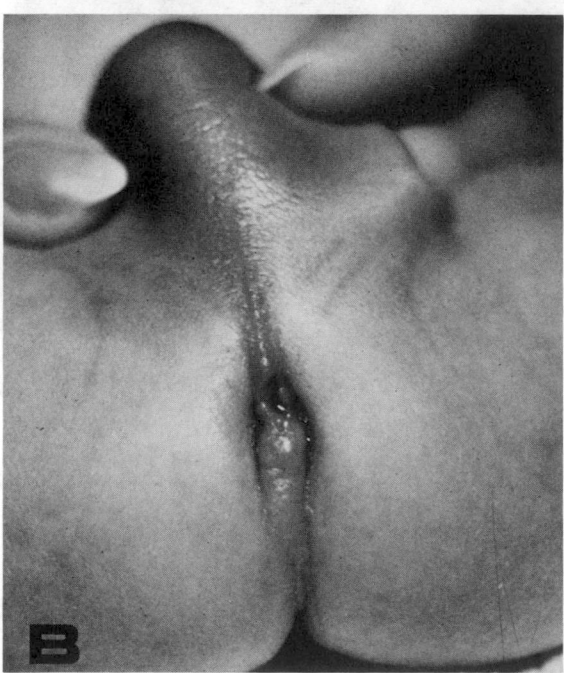

Fig. 29. Photographs of the perineum in the male with: A. Ectopic perineal anus. The orifice, which is between the anal dimple and the perineoscrotal junction, resembles a normal anus. Note the radial skin lines posterior to the fistula converging to the anal dimple. (From Santulli et al. Surg. Clin. N. Amer., 45:1253, 1965.) B. An anocutaneous fistula or covered anus may appear anywhere in the midline anterior to the anal dimple. Note the thickened perineal skin (or median band) leading back to the anal dimple.

ated anomalies for the remainder. About three-quarters of the survivors should have satisfactory anal function. The first definitive operation is the most important one; subsequent corrective procedures yield progressively poorer results. The functional results in the low anomalies are far better than in the high anomalies, as one would expect from the anatomic considerations and the associated sacral malformations with the accompanying nerve deficits in the latter group.

REFERENCES

Berdon, W. E., Baker, D. H., Santulli, T. V., and Amoury, R. The radiologic evaluation of imperforate anus. An approach correlated with current surgical concepts. Radiology, 90:466, 1968.

Bill, A. H., Jr. Common denominators in rectal anomalies on both sides of the Atlantic. Arch. Dis. Child., 39:149, 1964.

Hiatt, R. B., and Santulli, T. V. Important factors influencing the treatment of imperforate anus. Dis. Colon Rectum, 5:110, 1962.

Kiesewetter, W. B., Turner, C. R., and Sieber, W. K. Imperforate anus: Review of sixteen year experience with 146 patients. Amer. J. Surg., 107:412, 1964.

Louw, J. H. Congenital abnormalities of the rectum and anus. In Current Problems in Surgery. Chicago, Year Book Medical Publishers Inc., 1965.

Nixon, H. H. Imperforate anus. In British Surgery Practice and Surgery Progress. London, Butterworths, 1961.

Rehbein, F. Imperforate anus: Experiences with abdomino-perineal and abdomino-sacral-perineal pull-through procedures. J. Pediat. Surg., 2:99, 1967.

Santulli, T. V. "Imperforate anus." In Mustard, W. T., et al., eds., Pediatric Surgery, 2nd ed. Chicago, Year Book Publishers, 1969, p. 983.

——— Schullinger, J. N., Amoury, R. A., and Berdon, W. E. Malformations of the anus and rectum. Surg. Clin. N. Amer., 45:1253, 1965.

Smith, E. I., and Gross, R. E. The external anal sphincter in cases of imperforate anus: A pathologic study. Surgery, 49:807, 1961.

Stephens, F. D. Congenital Malformations of the Rectum, Anus and Genitourinary Tracts. Edinburgh and London, E. and S. Livingstone, 1963.

Swenson, O., and Grana, L. Long term results of surgical treatment of imperforate anus. Dis. Colon Rectum, 5:13, 1962.

23.15
MALFORMATIONS OF THE ABDOMINAL PARIETES

THOMAS V. SANTULLI

Umbilical Hernia

Unlike omphalocele this is a very common lesion in infants and children and, while a source of much

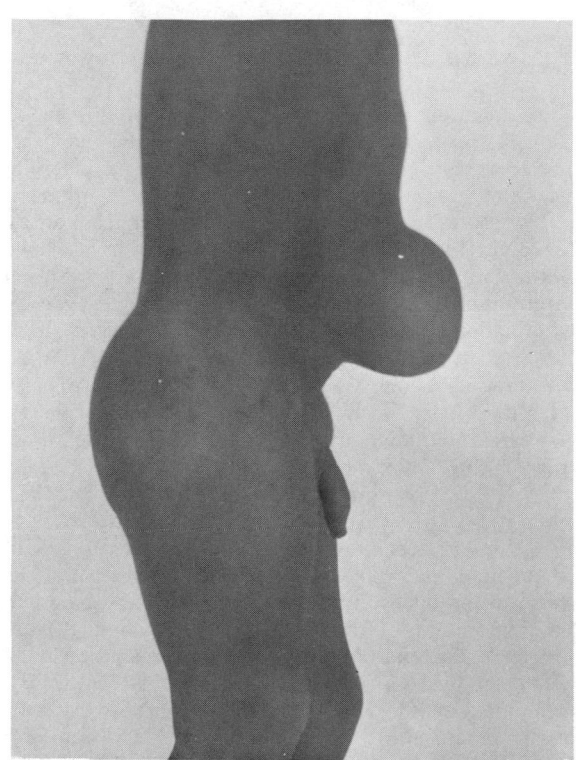

Fig. 30. Unusually large umbilical hernia in a 5-year-old boy which required surgical repair.

annoyance, is rarely serious. It results from a muscular and fascial defect of the abdominal wall where the wall was pierced by the blood vessels of the umbilical cord. The peritoneum which protrudes through this defect is completely covered by skin (Fig. 30). Although separation of the rectus muscles, if present, is usually confined to this region, the separation may extend upward and downward in the midline (diastasis recti). The hernia is seen especially in infants born prematurely, and in those who are poorly nourished or suffer from rickets or cretinism. It is more frequent among Negroes than in other races and is about twice as common in girls as in boys.

The protruding mass is usually from 1 to 2 cm in diameter. It can be easily reduced; the edge of the hernial ring and fascial defect may be felt. With larger masses and a larger ring there may be local tympany, and a gurgling sound is heard on reduction. Incarceration of the contents (omentum or intestine) is extremely rare, but it does occur.

In a great majority of patients, the fascial ring gradually becomes smaller and the hernia disappears spontaneously; even fairly large hernias will close. The value of adhesive strapping, once widely practiced, is open to question. If the hernia has not disappeared by the end of the fourth year, operation may be necessary.

Inguinal Hernia, Hydrocele

This is a common condition which is seen much more frequently in boys than in girls. The great majority are of the indirect variety; direct inguinal hernia is uncommon in infancy and childhood. About 60 percent are found on the right side, 20 percent on the left, and 20 percent are bilateral.

Embryologically, as the testis descends through the inguinal canal a projection of peritoneum (processus vaginalis) is carried downward into the scrotum. Normally, the lowermost part of this process, which lies in the scrotum alongside the testis, is pinched off to form the tunica vaginalis, while the remainder closes off up to the internal ring and atrophies. Any portion of the processus vaginalis may remain patent. If all of it stays open a complete congenital hernia results; when only the upper part is patent the hernia is said to be incomplete, as the sac is not in continuity with the tunica vaginalis. Central portions of the processus vaginalis may persist and give rise to hydrocele of the spermatic cord (or canal of Nuck in the female). Combinations of hernia and hydrocele are common.

Most hernias in the pediatric age-group contain small bowel; female infants may have an ovary or fallopian tube in the sac. A sliding type of hernia in the female infant involving ovary or fallopian tube is relatively common.

Inguinal hernias appear at any age, frequently soon after birth or during the first few months of life. There is a history of recurrent swelling in the inguinal area or scrotum which is usually easily reduced (Fig. 31). If the mass is not present during physical examination the diagnosis can be made from the characteristic history and from palpable thickening of the spermatic cord. In infants and young children the diagnosis cannot be made by palpation of an enlarged internal ring through the invaginated scrotum as in the adult, since the ring is too small to admit the tip of the finger. Gentle palpation of the lower part of the inguinal area near the pubis will frequently give the sensation of rubbing silky surfaces together if a hernial sac is present (the silk sign).

A history of incarceration can be obtained in about 20 percent of children with an inguinal hernia up to 1 year of age. It may occur anytime but is most common in the first 3 months of life. When this complication develops the inguinal mass is usually painful and the child is fretful. Vomiting occurs and there may be abdominal distention. Although uncommon, strangulation does occur and infarction of the small bowel, ovary, or testis (most common) may result.

All inguinal hernias are potentially dangerous and should be surgically corrected early in life. Operation is deferred only in the premature infant and in the infant with a serious associated illness which

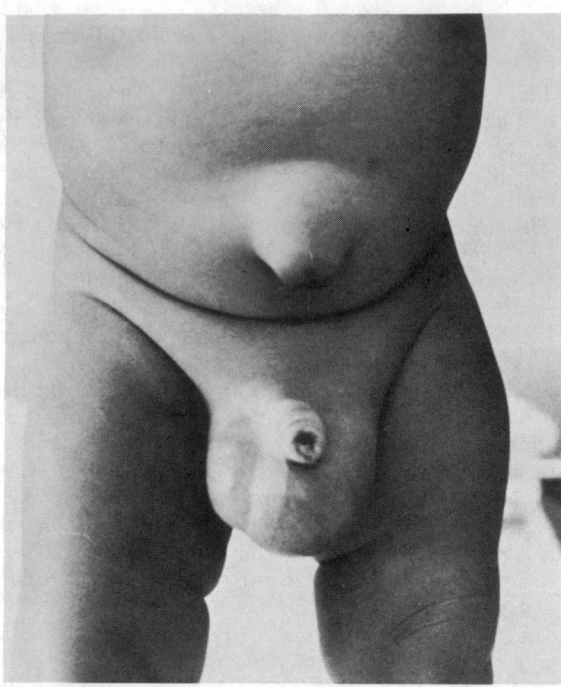

Fig. 31. A 1-year-old boy with a large left inguinal hernia which extends into the scrotum. There is also a smaller right inguinal hernia and an umbilical hernia.

would contraindicate surgery, in which case the hernia may be temporarily treated by some form of truss (yarn truss or elastic belt with a rubber pad over the inguinal region). For incarceration reasonable attempts should be made to reduce the hernia. This is best accomplished by adequate sedation, Trendelenburg position, and gentle taxis. If these measures are unsuccessful or if there are signs of strangulation, immediate operation is indicated.

The results of surgical treatment are excellent; recurrence is rare, morbidity and mortality are extremely low.

Femoral Hernia

This is very rare in the pediatric age group. The hernia protrudes through the femoral canal below the inguinal ring. Surgical repair is necessary.

Epigastric Hernia

This is an unusual hernia of the linea alba which is due to a midline fascial defect above the umbilicus. It varies from a few millimeters to several centimeters in diameter and occurs anywhere between the xiphoid and the umbilicus. The lesion may be painful; it is frequently tender. A small subcutaneous mass can be felt, which usually represents properitoneal fat

herniated through a defect in the linea alba. Surgical repair is usually indicated.

Eventration of the Diaphragm

Less common than diaphragmatic hernia, this condition is due to an abnormal thinness of the diaphragmatic muscle; in some instances there is complete absence of the muscle layer in a part of the diaphragm. This results in stretching of the diaphragm, allowing abdominal viscera to ascend into the hemithorax. Two forms are generally recognized. In true congenital eventration, the phrenic nerve is normal; Faradic stimulation, however, does not cause contraction of the muscular elements of the diaphragm. Acquired eventration is due to unilateral phrenic nerve palsy resulting from birth injury to the brachial plexus; Faradic stimulation in acquired cases causes contraction of the diaphragm.

If the diaphragm is markedly elevated and compresses the ipsilateral lung there is acute respiratory embarrassment in the newborn period, with dyspnea, cyanosis, and shift of the mediastinal structures to the opposite side; the symptoms and roentgen findings may be indistinguishable from those of true diaphragmatic hernia. In less severe cases there may be a combination of respiratory and gastrointestinal symptoms in later life. Treatment is usually not necessary in the mild case. When symptoms are present, surgical intervention is indicated. Plication operations are usually successful in repairing localized defects; in rare instances of extensive muscle deficiency the use of mersilene or other synthetic prosthesis has been successful.

Diaphragmatic Hernia

Diaphragmatic hernia is a protrusion of abdominal organs into the chest through a defect in the diaphragm. It occurs in two forms, the congenital and the posttraumatic; the latter is exceedingly uncommon in early life. In the congenital type, which occurs more frequently on the left side, the defect is caused by a failure of fusion of the various parts of the embryonic diaphragm and may appear in one of several areas of the diaphragm. Most commonly it occurs in the posterolateral portion along the pleuroperitoneal canal or the foramen of Bochdalek; less frequently at the esophageal hiatus or in the retrosternal areas (the foramen of Morgagni). In most instances of hernia through the posterolateral defect there is free communication between the thoracic and abdominal cavities; rarely there may be a thin peritoneal sac covering the abdominal viscera in the chest. The small intestine, right side of the colon, stomach, and spleen may be found in the thoracic cavity. There is usually an associated malrotation with nonfixation of the intestine. With right-sided hernias a part of the liver may be in the thorax. The homolateral lung is usually completely collapsed and may be hypoplastic, the mediastinal structures are shifted to the opposite side of the chest, and the contralateral lung is often partially compressed and may also be hypoplastic. Hernias at the esophageal hiatus usually have a peritoneal sac which greatly limits the upward progress of abdominal viscera; the sac rarely contains more than the stomach. Retrosternal hernias (through the foramen of Morgagni) have a sac in about half of the cases; only a part of the transverse colon, stomach, or liver may be herniated.

Usually symptoms are present at birth; in some instances the patient may be several weeks or months old before any significant abnormality is suspected. There may be respiratory, circulatory, or digestive disturbances. In severe cases cyanosis is evident immediately after birth; it may be constant or intermittent and usually deepens as distention of the intrathoracic intestine increases. There is rapid respiration, dyspnea, overdistention of the involved chest, and a sunken abdomen. Other symptoms may at times suggest intestinal obstruction; occasionally acute, but more often chronic or intermittent, vomiting is prominent. In milder cases the condition may not be recognized for a long time; the first sign to attract attention may be anemia. Pain is seldom complained of, but there may be unexplained episodes of anorexia and dyspnea. The physical signs are variable, and in some cases no abnormality may be detected, even when the condition is known to be present. Sometimes the findings suggest pneumothorax; at other times, there is so much dullness and suppression of breath sounds as to suggest pleural fluid. The heart may be displaced to the opposite side. In infants intestinal peristaltic sounds are not usually heard over the involved side, as they commonly are in older patients.

The diagnosis can be made by plain roentgenograms of the chest which demonstrate a shift of the heart to the opposite side, the characteristic mottled appearance of air-filled loops of intestine in the involved hemithorax, and the relative absence of intestinal shadows in the abdomen (Fig. 32A and B). Ingestion of barium or other radiopaque medium is usually not necessary to establish the diagnosis; indeed this should be avoided if possible. Rarely, when the diagnosis is not clear on plain roentgenograms, barium may be required to differentiate congenital lung cyst or postpneumonic pneumatoceles. In the less frequent esophageal hiatal hernia and retrosternal hernia, which show little if any respiratory symptoms, roentgen studies of the gastrointestinal tract with contrast media are necessary.

Respiratory acidosis may occur from the diminished ventilatory capacity of the lungs resulting from compression and incomplete development (hypoplasia);

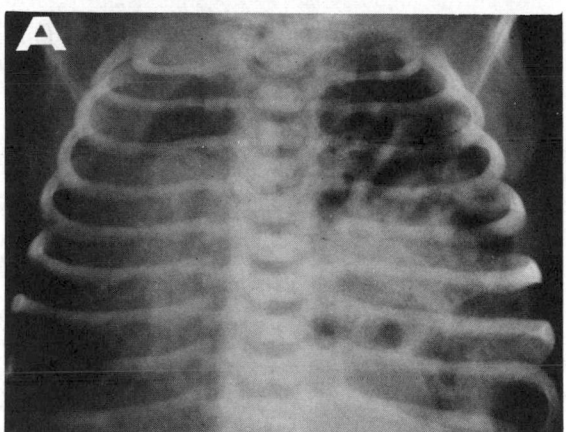

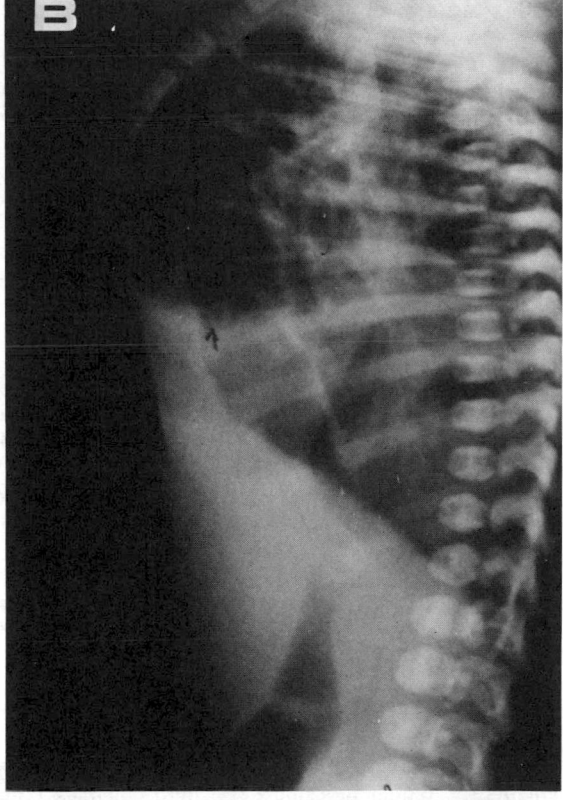

Fig. 32. Left diaphragmatic hernia in a newborn infant with marked respiratory distress and cyanosis. A. Plain roentgenogram of chest in anteroposterior projection illustrates air-filled intestinal loops in left hemithorax and shift of mediastinal structures to the right. B. Lateral projection showing intestines in the thoracic cavity. Note the scaphoid abdomen and minimal intestinal shadows in the peritoneal cavity. Emergency operation revealed a posterolateral defect of the left diaphragm (foramen of Bochdalek) which was repaired after placing the intestine in the peritoneal cavity.

there is frequently an accompanying severe metabolic acidosis which requires correction with sodium bicarbonate. These acid-base disturbances and the response to treatment are most conveniently determined by serial microstudies of arterialized capillary blood (see Sec. 3.7).

The urgent need for surgical repair must be emphasized; with conservative therapy 75 percent of patients have been reported to have died before the end of the first month, most of these deaths occurring within the first few days of life. Expectant treatment is dangerous because of the threat of sudden distention of the intrathoracic intestine which may lead to acute respiratory distress and death. Except for small esophageal hiatal defects which are asymptomatic at the time, all congenital diaphragmatic hernias should be operated upon as soon as the condition is recognized, regardless of the extent of the herniation and the condition of the child. Even in asymptomatic cases operation should be done early in order to avoid the serious complications of intestinal obstruction or incarceration.

Omphalocele and Gastroschisis

Omphalocele (hernia into the umbilical cord, exomphalos) is a rare and serious anomaly which consists of a herniation of abdominal viscera into the base of the umbilical cord. The covering of the protruding mass is thin and translucent, consisting of a fusion of the peritoneum and the amniotic membrane; it is not covered by skin as is the umbilical hernia (Fig. 33). The mass varies in size from a small protrusion to complete eventration in which nearly all the abdominal organs are outside the body. The defect in the abdominal wall may be quite small, measuring up to 2 cm in diameter, or it may be enormous, extending to the flanks. Malrotation of the portion of the alimentary tract supplied by the superior mesenteric artery is commonly associated.

The condition must be recognized at the time of delivery in order to avoid injury to the contained viscera when ligating the umbilical cord. Treatment consists of immediate coverage of the mass by sterile gauze moistened with warm saline, since the thin sac will soon dry and rupture, which may lead to infection and death. Operation is urgently required. Small omphaloceles are simple to repair; the sac is excised, its contents placed in the abdomen, and the defect in the abdominal wall closed. Large omphaloceles, especially those containing the liver, may be extremely difficult to treat. Furthermore, there is a relatively high incidence of associated anomalies, such as intestinal atresia, which may affect the prognosis. However, some of these large lesions may be successfully repaired by multiple operations. The first procedure consists of extensive mobilization of the skin of the abdominal wall in order to cover the mass and its sac which must be kept intact. Silastic, mersilene, or similar type of synthetic material is used

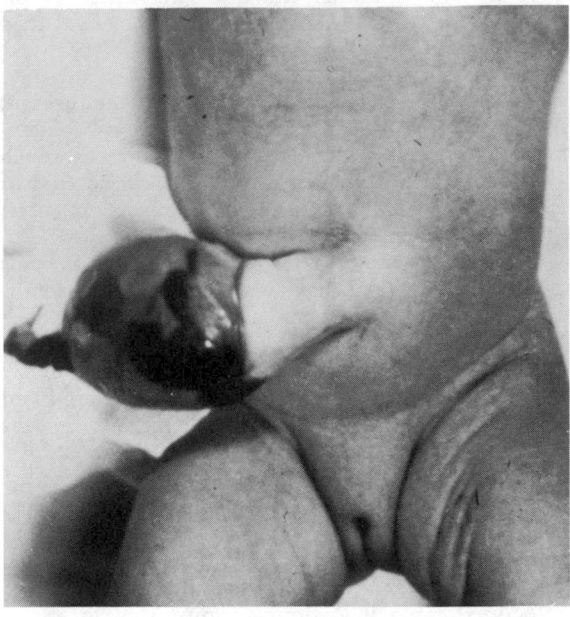

Fig. 33. Omphalocele or hernia into the base of the umbilical cord. The thin sac covering the viscera consists of a fusion of the peritoneum and amniotic membrane.

to cover the viscera if the sac has been ruptured. Later, when the peritoneal cavity has sufficiently enlarged to contain the viscera, the large defect of the abdominal wall (ventral hernia) is corrected by a second operation.

In giant omphaloceles, nonoperative treatment occasionally may be successful. Care must be taken to keep the sac intact. The application of 2 percent aqueous solution of Merthiolate to the sac several times a day may be beneficial. In time the herniated mass diminishes in size as the viscera gradually recede into the enlarging abdominal cavity, and epithelization of the sac occurs.

Gastroschisis is a defect in the abdominal wall similar to omphalocele but occurring at a point other than the umbilicus. The umbilicus is normally inserted, the viscera protruding through an extraumbilical defect. There is no membranous covering of the exteriorized intestine, which is thickened, imbedded in a mass of adhesions, and covered with a gelatinous exudate. The lesion may be successfully treated by covering the viscera with silastic or similar type of synthetic material which is sutured to the edges of the peritoneal and fascial defect in the abdominal wall. Gradual and progressive manual compression of the protruding mass of viscera is accomplished over a period of days or weeks, and final closure of the abdominal wall defect is achieved when all of the viscera has been reduced into the enlarging peritoneal cavity.

REFERENCES

UMBILICAL HERNIA

Benson, C. D. Umbilical hernia. *In* Mustard, W. T., et al., eds., Pediatric Surgery, 2nd ed. Chicago, Year Book Publishers, 1969, p. 689.

Halpern, L. J. Spontaneous healing of umbilical hernia. J.A.M.A., 182:851, 1962.

Sibley, W. L., III, Lynn, H. B., and Harris, L. E. Infantile umbilical hernia. Minn. Surg., 55:462, 1964.

INGUINAL HERNIA

Clatworthy, H. W., Jr., and Thompson, A. G. Incarcerated and strangulated inguinal hernia in infants: A preventable risk. J.A.M.A., 154:123, 1954.

De Boer, A., and Potts, W. J. Inguinal hernias in children. Arch. Surg., 86:1072, 1963.

Fonkalsrud, E. W., deLorimier, A. A., and Clatworthy, H. W., Jr. Femoral and direct inguinal hernias in infants and children. J.A.M.A., 192:597, 1965.

Fosburg, R. D. Femoral hernias in children. Amer. J. Surg., 109:470, 1965.

Kiesewetter, W. B., and Parenzan, L. When should hernia in the infant be treated bilaterally? J.A.M.A., 171:127, 1959.

Koop, C. E. Inguinal herniorrhaphy in infants and children. Surg. Clin. N. Amer., 37:1675, 1957.

Potts, W. J., Riker, W. L., and Lewis, J. E. The treatment of inguinal hernia in infants and children. Ann. Surg., 132:566, 1950.

Santulli, T. V., and Shaw, A. Inguinal hernia: Infancy and childhood. J.A.M.A., 176:110, 1961.

Snyder, W. H., Jr., and Greaney, E. M., Jr. Inguinal hernias. *In* Mustard, W. T., et al., eds., Pediatric Surgery, 2nd ed. Chicago, Year Book Publishers, 1969, p. 692.

Sparkman, R. S. Bilateral exploration in inguinal hernia in juvenile patients. Surgery, 51:393, 1962.

Swenson, O. Diagnosis and treatment of inguinal hernia. Pediatrics, 34:412, 1964.

EVENTRATION OF THE DIAPHRAGM

Bisgard, J. D. Congenital eventration of the diaphragm. J. Thorac. Surg., 16:484, 1947.

Bishop, H. C., and Koop, C. E. Acquired eventration of the diaphragm in infancy. Pediatrics, 22:1088, 1958.

Chin, E. F., and Lynn, R. B. Surgery of eventration of the diaphragm. J. Thorac. Surg., 32:6, 1956.

Sanford, M. C. Eventration of the diaphragm repaired utilizing tantalum mesh. J. Thorac. Surg., 25:422, 1953.

DIAPHRAGMATIC HERNIA

Baffes, T. F. Diaphragmatic Hernia. *In* Mustard, W. T., et al., eds., Pediatric Surgery, 2nd ed. Chicago, Year Book Publishers, 1969, p. 342.

Gross, R. E. Congenital hernia of the diaphragm. *In* The Surgery of Infancy and Childhood. Philadelphia, W. B. Saunders Co., 1958, p. 428.

Jackson, T. M. Congenital diaphragmatic hernia. Arch. Surg., 95:102, 1967.

Meeker, I. A., Jr., and Kincannon, W. N. The role of ventral hernia in the correction of diaphragmatic defects in the newborn. Arch. Dis. Child., 40:146, 1965.

Ravitch, M. M., and Handleman, J. C. Lesions of the thoracic parietes in infants and children. Surg. Clin. N. Amer., 32:1397, 1952.

Snyder, W. H., Jr., and Greaney, E. M., Jr. Congenital diaphragmatic hernia; 77 consecutive cases. Surgery, 57:576. 1965.

Thompson, S. A. Diphragmatic hernia in infancy and childhood. Surg. Clin. N. Amer., 34:997, 1954.

OMPHALOCELE AND GASTROSCHISIS

Allen, R. G., and Wrenn, E. L., Jr. Silon as a sac in the treatment of omphalocele and gastroschisis. J. Pediat. Surg., 4:3, 1969.

Gilbert, M. G., Mencia, L. F., Brown, W. T., and Linn, B. S. Staged surgical repair of large omphaloceles and gastroschisis. J. Pediat. Surg., 3:702, 1968.

Grob, M. Conservative treatment of exomphalos. Arch. Dis. Child., 38:148, 1963.

Gross, R. E. A new method for surgical treatment of large omphaloceles. Surgery, 24:277, 1948.

Moore, T. C., and Stokes, G. E. Gastroschisis. Surgery, 33:112, 1953.

Rickham, P. Rupture of exomphalos and gastroschisis. Arch. Dis. Child., 38:138, 1963.

Inflammatory Diseases

23.16

ESOPHAGUS

JOSE M. FERRER, JR.

Acute Esophagitis

It is quite remarkable, considering the frequency of infections in the pharynx, that they so rarely extend to the esophagus. Thrush, when very extensive in the pharynx, may involve the esophagus, but there it gives rise to no new symptoms. Diphtheria of the pharynx may invade the esophagus, but this is rare and produces no symptoms by which it can be diagnosed during life. In infants succumbing during the first weeks of life, from whatever cause, erosion and cellular infiltration of the lower part of the esophagus may occasionally be encountered as an unexpected postmortem finding. The origin of these lesions is obscure, but is believed to be related to chemical digestion by regurgitated gastric secretions in the last hours or days preceding death. Peptic esophagitis often complicates hiatal hernia or chalasia. Stasis and esophagitis with ulceration may complicate congenital or acquired stenosis or cardiospasm. The symptoms are quite indefinite, and this lesion is often found at autopsy when its presence was not suspected during life.

Corrosive Esophagitis

Severe burns and inflammation of the esophagus result from chemical trauma. These cases are most frequently encountered between the ages of 18 months and 5 years; nearly all of them result from the swallowing of lye, although they may be due to other chemicals, such as ammonium hydroxide, permanganate, or sodium hypochlorite (Clorox). Strong solutions of lye which are employed for cleaning drains are often within reach of young children, who readily mistake them for milk, especially if they are stored in containers previously used for beverages, such as soda bottles.

The damage will depend upon the quantity and concentration of the corrosive. Burns in the mouth and pharynx are always present and are responsible for the early symptoms. There is burning pain in the throat, thirst, and prostration; there may be great dysphagia with spasm of the pharynx on attempts to swallow. The principal danger at this stage is from supraglottic edema with respiratory obstruction, and tracheostomy is occasionally necessary. These acute inflammatory changes rarely last more than a few days, and the patient is thought to have recovered until the symptoms of esophageal stricture develop, generally from one to three months after the injury. The injury to the esophagus is usually confined to the mucosa and submucosa; only rarely is the muscular layer affected. Healing gradually occurs by granulation and cicatrization, contraction of the cicatrix leading to stricture with partial or, in a few instances, complete obliteration of the esophageal lumen (Fig. 34).

Prompt treatment, faithfully carried out, will prevent stricture in nearly every case. Where prophylaxis has been properly applied, the incidence of strictures has decreased from approximately 50 percent to less than 10 percent of the cases.

Immediately following the injury one should attempt to neutralize the caustic in order to limit corrosive action in the stomach. Stricture prophylaxis should be commenced within 24 hours. No greater mistake can be made than to wait until the acute inflammation has subsided for fear of damaging the esophagus by treatment. The extent of esophageal injury should be determined early by careful and skilled esophagoscopy. In the early days it is inadvisable to rely on the esophagram for determination of injury.

The Salzer-Bokay treatment consists of daily in-

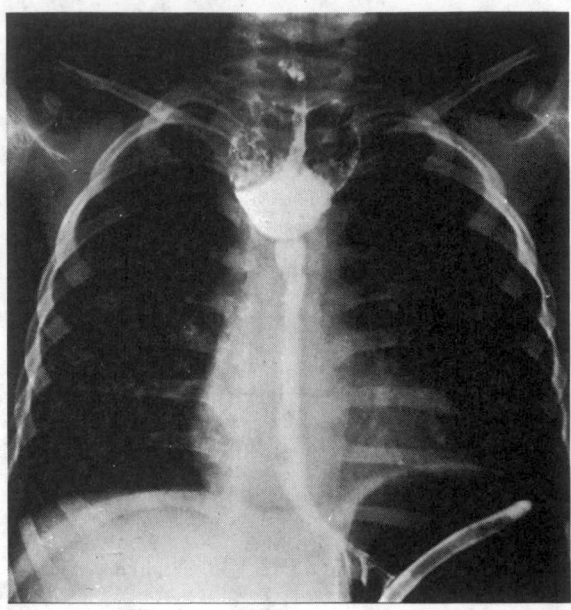

Fig. 34.   Cicatricial stenosis of esophagus following lye burn.

troduction of large catheters, sealed at both ends and filled with small shot or mercury. In all children with demonstrable esophageal lesions the catheters are passed daily through the esophagus into the stomach with the child in a vertical position. These bougies should be lubricated before passing. They should not be forced; if bleeding occurs it is best to discontinue treatment for the day. One should first attempt to pass a No. 14 or 16 French and increase the size up to a No. 28 or No. 30, depending on the age of the child. Each bougie is left in place for a minute or more. On the next day, treatment is begun with a bougie smaller than the largest one previously passed, and the size is increased progressively. The routine followed in the Babies Hospital consists in daily bouginage for the first two weeks, followed by three times a week for two weeks, then twice a week for another two weeks, and once a week for the next month. The frequency is gradually decreased, but should be at least once a month until a year has passed, and every few months for three to five years. If any evidence of stricture develops, daily dilatations should be resumed. Fluoroscopy of the esophagus is desirable at some time during the early months of the treatment. The patient must be impressed with the need for regularity in continuing the treatment despite the absence of symptoms. In severe lye strictures, dilation with a guide string may have to be combined with a gastrostomy.

The treatment of strictures that fail to respond to dilatation is surgical and may be successfully accomplished by esophagoplasty, resection with end-to-end anastomosis, or preferably by interposition of a jejunal or colonic segment graft to replace the scarred esophagus.

Some observers have reported that the use of corticosteroids in association with early bouginage has further reduced the incidence of stricture formation.

Periesophageal Mediastinal Abscess

Retroesophageal abscess is a rare occurrence in infancy, the pathologic process being similar to that in retropharyngeal abscess. In early life lymphoid tissue located between the esophagus and the vertebral column on either side of the midline may be the seat of acute inflammation with or without suppuration. An abscess may result from suppuration of such a node or from extension of a retropharyngeal abscess; it may be caused by tuberculosis of the lower cervical or upper thoracic spine.

However, most mediastinal abscesses result from esophageal perforation caused by a foreign body or by instrumentation. These perioesophageal abscesses may perforate into the pleura or pericardium.

The symptoms are largely respiratory, including an irritative cough or spasmodic inspiratory dyspnea, although dysphagia and regurgitation may be observed. These abscesses are too low to be reached by digital exploration of the pharynx, although they may be high enough to cause swelling at the side of the neck. The crepitus of subcutaneous emphysema may be felt in the neck or supraclavicular areas due to the dissection upward of air leaking into the mediastinum. Prognosis is grave. Recovery has been observed rarely after spontaneous drainage into the esophagus. If left alone, the abscess may burrow into the abdominal cavity. Some patients have succumbed to a sudden attack of asphyxia. Most commonly the abscess ruptures into the pleura, and emphysema or pyopneumothorax results, often with the formation of an esophagopleural fistula. Vigorous use of broad-spectrum antibiotics plus early surgical drainage of the mediastinum and of the pleura provide the best chance for recovery.

Mediastinal abscess should be suspected whenever the possibility of esophageal perforation exists and when there is unexplained fever with or without respiratory signs or symptoms. This condition should be considered as an unusual cause of paroxysmal dyspnea, particularly in tuberculous patients, and confirmatory evidence sought by roentgenogram. Roentgenography, often with the use of a small amount of swallowed liquid contrast material, should be used to demonstrate free air in the mediastinum or pleura or a leak from the esophagus. Tuberculous abscesses should, if possible, be handled conservatively; the pressure symptoms may subside if the spinal caries is appropriately treated. The mode of drainage of nontuberculous abscesses depends on their location. Both cervical and intrathoracic abscesses may be drained externally, and while fistulas of the esophagus may develop, they seldom persist. A temporary gastrostomy should be performed if evidence of fistula develops.

REFERENCES

Bill, A. H., Jr., Mebust, W. K., and Sauvage, L. R. Evaluation of technics of esophageal dilatation in relation to danger of perforation; study of 441 dilatations of benign strictures in children. J. Thorac. Cardiovasc. Surg., 45:510, 1963.

Cleveland, W. W., Chandler, J. R., and Lawson, R. B. Treatment of caustic burns of esophagus; early esophagoscopy and adrenocortical steroids. J.A.M.A., 186:262, 1963.

Gellis, S. S., and Holt, L. E., Jr. Treatment of lye ingestion by the Salzer method. Ann. Otol., 51:1086, 1942.

Gruenwald, P., and Marsh, M. R. Acute esophagitis in infants. Arch. Path., 49:1, 1950.

Haller, J. A., and Bachman, K. The comparative effect of current therapy on experimental caustic burns of the esophagus. Pediatrics, 34:236, 1964.

Hopkins, W. A., and Ziviren, G. T. Colon replacement of the esophagus in children. J. Thorac. Cardiovasc. Surg., 46:346, 1963.

Humphreys, G. H., Ferrer, J. M., and Wiedel, P. D. Esophageal hiatus hernia of the diaphragm. J. Thorac. Surg., 34:749, 1957.

Longino, L. A., Woolley, M. M., and Gross, R. L. Esophageal replacement in infants and children with use of a segment of colon. J.A.M.A., 171:1187, 1959.

Martin, J. M., and Arena, J. M. Lye poisoning and stricture of the esophagus; a report of 50 cases. Southern Med. J., 32:286, 1939.

Merendino, K. A., and Thomas, G. I. The jejunal interposition operation for substitution of the esophagogastric sphincter. Surgery, 44:1112, 1958.

Ray, E. S., and Morgan, D. L. Cortisone therapy of lye burns of the esophagus. J. Pediat., 49:394, 1956.

Vandever, H. W., Ellis, F. H., Jr., and Hyles, A. B. Suppurative mediastinitis secondary to traumatic perforation of the esophagus. Mayo Clin. Proc., 30:288, 1955.

Viscomi, G. J., Beekhuis, G. J., and Whitten, C. F. An evaluation of early esophagoscopy and corticosteroid therapy in the management of corrosive injury of the esophagus. J. Pediat., 59:356, 1961.

23.17
STOMACH

THOMAS V. SANTULLI

Acute Gastritis

Inflammatory lesions of the stomach are comparatively uncommon in early life. They may occur in severe gastroenteritis, in parenteral infections, or from the introduction of irritant drugs or poisons. In contrast to the situation in adults, hyperacidity is rarely the cause.

Corrosive gastritis usually results from the swallowing of caustic alkalis. Less frequently ammonia, carbolic acid, hypochlorite solutions (Clorox), and other corrosives are responsible. Some cases have been caused by a too strong solution of calcium chloride. The lesions in the stomach are much influenced by the quantity and concentrations of the irritant and by the quantity of food in the stomach. Strong caustics usually act more intensely in the pharynx and esophagus, since spasms of the muscles of these parts often prevents the agent from reaching the stomach. The gastric lesions may affect the mucous membrane diffusely or may produce irregular ulcerations, especially along the greater curvature. Perforation may occur. In severe cases death takes place within a few hours; dark, ragged ulcers are found, the surrounding mucosa being intensely congested, with extravasations in places. If death is delayed there is intense inflammation often with the production of pseudomembrane. Recovery may result in a cicatricial contraction of the stomach with partial obstruction.

The immediate symptoms are intense pain, a sense of constriction in the throat, and vomiting, sometimes of blood. The effects of the caustic may be seen in the mouth. Collapse follows rapidly. If the patient survives, acute gastritis persists for some time and often esophagitis and enteritis as well. Dehydration may be a serious problem.

Treatment consists in early gastric lavage. However, if an hour or more has elapsed, lavage is quite useless, and therapy should be confined to the treatment of pain and shock and the prevention of esophageal stricture, especially after the swallowing of lye (p. 1636).

Membranous gastritis is occasionally found in association with diphtheria, bacillary dysentery, or streptococcal infections of the phaynx. *Candida* infection of the mouth may extend down the esophagus and involve the gastric mucosa. These lesions are usually first detected at postmortem examination.

Gastric Ulcer

Acute erosions of the mucosa of the stomach are not uncommonly found at postmortem examination in marasmic infants and in those with bacteremia. Peptic ulcers in infancy and childhood occur more frequently than was formerly believed. They are located somewhat more often in the upper duodenum than in the stomach. "Stress" ulcers of the stomach may complicate various severe illnesses or trauma; Curling's ulcer, which is seen in major burns, is an example.

23.18
PEPTIC ULCER

MERVIN SILVERBERG

Peptic ulcers in infants and children are reported with remarkably variable frequencies from different parts of the United States. In most large pediatric centers the condition is viewed as relatively uncommon, the average number of new cases being about two per year per center. Pain attributed to peptic ulceration is often indistinguishable from functional abdominal pain which is so ubiquitous in children. The major diagnostic aids are radiographic signs of an ulcer crater or of deformity from scarring or other evidences of ulcer complications. Presumptive x-ray features such as spasm and thickened folds of the duodenum are of controversial value, particularly in the apprehensive child. Gastric acid studies in children, including the augmented histamine stimulation test, show an unusually broad range of normal values without consistently significant differences from ulcer patients. Four varieties of peptic ulcer disease are recognized:

1. *Acute infantile ulcers* are restricted to the infant. Hemorrhage and perforation are common presenting manifestations. Lesions occur with equal frequency in the stomach and duodenum. The newborn infant is particularly vulnerable in the first 48 hours of life. This may be the result of stress or hypoxia, and the increased gastric acidity and parietal cell mass normally observed during this period probably play a contributing role.

2. *Acute childhood ulcers* occur at any age between infancy and adolescence. The major presenting manifestations vary with the age of the child. Many younger children complain more of periumbilical than epigastric pain. The relationship of symptoms to the ingestion of food is variable. Pain is often aggravated by eating and is frequently accompanied by vomiting, instead of the characteristic relief of pain reported by adults with ulcer when they take feedings. Pyloric canal ulcers are rare, but in these instances vomiting may be particularly severe and prolonged due to pylorospasm. Adolescents more often report symptoms like those of adults, their pain being localized to the epigastrium, and they usually are relieved with food intake.

The acute ulcer in children is located in the duodenum in 90 percent of cases, the posterior wall of the bulb being a particularly predilected site. The male to female ratio for incidence is approximately 1.5:1. About 20 percent of children experience bleeding leading to anemia and this is mainly painless and occult, although melena is occasionally encountered. Significant or characteristic emotional problems are relatively common; these children are often described as anxious, intense, and introverted. A family history of ulcer diathesis is found in at least one case in four.

Most children respond well to an antiulcer regimen and are free of complaints within three months. However, when followed for periods exceeding one year, up to 50 percent are reported to develop recurrences with a typical chronic history of episodic or intractable discomfort, bleeding, or obstruction.

3. *Secondary ulcers* occur with greater frequency in children than in adults. Ulcers of the stomach or duodenum occur in association with severe infections, burns (Curling's ulcer), neurologic disorders (Rokitansky-Cushing ulcer), and ulcerogenic drugs such as corticosteroids. Other disorders associated with peptic ulcers in greater numbers than would be expected by chance are cirrhosis of the liver, chronic pulmonary disease, hypoglycemia, and congenital pyloric stenosis. These children frequently present with severe gastrointestinal bleeding or perforation, and the morbidity is compounded by the underlying illness.

4. *Zollinger-Ellison syndrome and related disorders.* Severe peptic ulcer disease is associated with non-beta cell islet adenomas secreting a gastrinlike material. These patients do not have hyperinsulinemia. Most patients demonstrate gastric hypersecretion of such magnitude that histamine augmentation does not increase the acid output. These ulcers are usually single, located in the duodenum, and are associated with intractable and persistent symptoms which are usually resistant to amelioration by medical therapy. Severe watery diarrhea and steatorrhea due to excessive gastric secretions may complicate the already difficult course of these patients.

A related syndrome with multiple endocrine adenomas involving the parathyroid, pancreatic islets, and pituitary glands is associated with multifocal peptic ulcers resistant to medical therapy. These adenomas may be hormonally active in various combinations.

Therapeutic measures vary according to the type of ulcer. Acute ulcers in older children respond best to regular frequent neutralization of gastric acidity by foods and antacids. Initially, the dietary and antacid regimen is introduced on an hourly basis, the intervals are spread as the symptoms improve, and a normal dietary regimen is introduced once the patient becomes asymptomatic. Postcibal anticholinergic agents are prescribed three times a day and at bedtime. They are continued for at least one year and antacids are prescribed whenever ulcer complaints recur. Severe bleeding is treated with blood volume replacement, cold saline gastric lavages, and nasogastric suction. Surgical procedures have been restricted to emergency complications of perforation, severe hemorrhage, and obstruction. That the child with chronic complaints would benefit from earlier surgical intervention has been suggested by some authors but remains to be proved. Vagotomy and pyloroplasty or antrectomy give best results in both

emergency and elective surgery. Patients with ulcerogenic tumor syndromes must be carefully explored and the tumor(s) removed. Even when this is practical, but especially if such a tumor is difficult to locate or has metastasized, or in cases where islet tissue is diffusely involved, total gastrectomy has been reported to be the operation of choice for direct treatment of the ulcer. Infants and children with resected stomachs have been shown to thrive under careful dietary management.

REFERENCES

Baidan, M., McIntyre, J. A., and Dietel, M. Peptic ulcer in children and adolescents. Arch. Surg. (Chicago), 99:15, 1966.

Barber, K. W., Jr., Lynn, H. B., DuShane, J. W., and Priestley, J. T. Surgical treatment of complicated duodenal ulcer in childhood. Postgrad. Med., 35:175, 1964.

Boley, J. S., Krieger, H., Schwartz, S., Harandian, D., and Pearlman, B. The effect of operations for peptic ulcer on growth and nutrition of puppies. Surgery, 57:441, 1965.

Collins, D. L., Black, J. H., and Mullinger, M. M. Gastrectomy in early childhood. Amer. J. Dis. Child., 109:149, 1965.

Donovan, E. J., and Santulli, T. V. Gastric and duodenal ulcers in infancy and in childhood. Amer. J. Dis. Child., 69:176, 1945.

Fällström, S. P., and Reinard, T. Peptic ulcer in children. Acta Paediat. Scand., 50:431, 1961.

Habbick, B. F., Melrose, A. G., and Grant, J. C. Duodenal ulcer in childhood: A study of predisposing factors. Arch. Dis. Child., 43:23, 1968.

Jackson, R. H., Blair, E. L., Dawson, P. J., Reed, J. D., and Watts, W. P. T. Gastrin activity of tumour tissue in a child with the Zollinger-Ellison syndrome. Lancet, 2:908, 1963.

Karlstrom, F. Peptic ulcer in children in Sweden during the years 1953-1962. Ann. Paediat. (Basel), 202:218, 1964.

Lucas, C., and Benson, C. D. Chronic bleeding duodenal ulcer in childhood managed by hemigastrectomy and vagotomy. Surgery, 61:478, 1967.

McAleese, J. J., and Sieber, H. K. The surgical problem presented by peptic ulcer of the stomach and duodenum in infancy and childhood. Ann. Surg., 137:334, 1953.

Michener, W. M., Kennedy, R. L. J., and DuShane, J. W. Duodenal ulcer in childhood. Amer. J. Dis. Child., 99:135, 1960.

Milliken, J. C. Duodenal ulceration in children. Gut, 6:25, 1965.

Muggia, A., and Spiro, H. M. Childhood peptic ulcer. Gastroenterology, 37:715, 1959.

Raffensperger, J. G., Condon, J. B., and Greengard, J. Complications of gastric and duodenal ulcers in infancy and childhood. Surg. Gynec. Obstet., 123:1269, 1966.

Ravitch, M. M., and Duremdes, G. D. Operative treatment of chronic duodenal ulcer in childhood. Ann. Surg., 171:641, 1970.

Romas, A. R., Kirsner, J. D., and Palmer, W. L. Peptic ulcer in children. A.M.A. J. Dis. Child., 99:135, 1960.

Rosenlund, M. L. The Zollinger-Ellison syndrome in

children. A review. Amer. J. Med. Sci., 254:884, 1967.

Schuster, S., and Gross, R. E. Peptic ulcer disease in childhood. Amer. J. Surg., 105:324, 1963.

Shaw, A., Symonds, F., Bush, J., and Wardlaw, L. Surgical management of Curling's ulcer in children. J.A.M.A., 197:922, 1966.

Singleton, E. B., and Faykus, M. H. Incidence of peptic ulcer as determined by radiological examinations in the pediatric age group. J. Pediat., 65:858, 1964.

Tudor, R. B. Peptic ulceration in childhood. Pediat. Clin. N. Amer., 14:109, 1967.

Wilson, S. D., and Ellison, E. H. Total gastric resection in children with the Zollinger-Ellison syndrome. Arch. Surg. (Chicago), 91:165, 1965.

23.19
INTESTINES

MARK M. RAVITCH

Appendicitis

Acute appendicitis is the most common lesion requiring laparotomy in children. It occurs in all age groups. It is rare in the youngest infants, although a number of cases have been reported occurring in the first few days of life. Males are more commonly affected than females in the ratio of more than 2:1.

ETIOLOGY AND PATHOLOGY. The exciting cause of acute appendicitis is usually obscure. In occasional instances acute enteritis seems to merge into appendicitis. This is a particularly dangerous sequence in mass outbreaks in schools and summer camps, where the appendix of the one unfortunate child whose enteritis does not "clear up" may go on to perforation before the superimposed appendicitis is recognized. Acute upper respiratory infections at times precede an attack of appendicitis. In a number of cases a fecalith or a worm plays an obvious role by obstructing the lumen of the appendix and setting in motion a train of consequences attributable to distension of the appendix and obstruction of its blood supply. The anatomic structure of the appendix, a long, narrow intestinal diverticulum supplied by a single artery, explains its predisposition to disease. Mucosal inflammation produces edema and resultant obstruction of the lumen. Distension follows, the intraluminal tension increases, and the blood supply is interfered with. Ulceration, infection, and gangrene result. At times the lumen may remain free of obstruction, and the frequent instances of spontaneous recovery from appendicitis are probably attributable to the absence of obstruction in those cases. In infants, necrosis and perforation are more common than in older patients. This is probably accounted for by the more delicate structure of the appendiceal wall in younger children, as well as by infants' lower resistance to infection in general. The relatively smaller omentum of the infant increases the seriousness of perforation.

SYMPTOMS. When the complete succession and array of symptoms of appendicitis are present—anorexia, cramplike abdominal pain beginning in the epigastrium and migrating to the right lower quadrant, vomiting, localized pain and tenderness, and muscular rigidity—the diagnosis is readily made. However, in a great many instances, particularly in children under 5 years of age, the symptoms are atypical or difficult to elicit because of the inability of the patient to cooperate. Abdominal pain is probably the most invariable symptom. The early generalized cramplike pain is frequently dismissed in children as mere colic. Vomiting is a common early sign. Either constipation or diarrhea may be present. If the appendix is long enough to dip down into the pelvis there may be pain on urination—usually at the end of micturition when the bladder has contracted, pulling away from the inflamed tissues.

Abdominal palpation in an infant with an acute abdominal disorder calls for the exercise of the greatest gentleness and patience. The response of a child to a single abdominal palpation is not to be trusted, and it may be necessary to draw a chair up to the bed and to sit for 10 or 15 minutes or longer, repeatedly examining the child until he is quiet. Muscle spasm is frequently absent or undetectable in infants. Rebound tenderness is an important sign, particularly useful in infants. The two evidences of rebound tenderness in an infant are the sudden cry or grimace when the hand is released, and an involuntary flexion of the right thigh. Rectal examination is of the greatest importance. After the finger has been fully introduced the child should be allowed to settle down before manipulation is begun. There may be merely tenderness localized in the right side, or a fogginess in the cul-de-sac, suggesting a diffuse peritonitis with exudation of a considerable quantity of pus, or palpation of a mass may reveal the presence of an appendiceal abscess. Abdominal distension is a late sign and indicates peritonitis rather than appendicitis. Fever is more likely to be present than in adults and likely to be higher, but its presence is important chiefly as a nonspecific indication of the presence of an acute infectious process. The leucocyte count tends to be elevated, but it is not to be relied upon. The chief advantage of the finding of leucocytosis is the attendant realization that some acute inflammatory process must be present and that the child may not be dismissed until its source has been discovered.

It is not at all rare for an infant or child with an illness allegedly of one or two days' duration to be brought in with a well walled-off appendiceal abscess obviously of greater duration. Appendicitis may be confounded with colic or indigestion, and, in infants, with intussusception. Differentiation from an acute gastrointestinal upset is always difficult and may be impossible. In gastrointestinal upsets the pain is likely to be less severe, while repeated vomiting and diarrhea are likely to be prominent. The possibility of a strangulated inguinal hernia should always be considered in infants with abdominal pain and vomiting. In older children an iliac adenitis which drains a trivial infection of the foot may very closely mimic appendicitis. In infants with abdominal pain and tenderness radiologic examination of the chest is a wise diagnostic measure. Pneumonia may be difficult to differentiate from appendicitis, and the abdominal signs may be remarkably like those of appendicitis at a time when the pulmonary physical signs are still obscure. Fever, leucocytosis, and prostration all tend to be more marked with pneumonia than with appendicitis, and accessory evidences of pulmonary disease such as dyspnea and dilation of the alae nasi are helpful signs. However, we have seen an instance in which a child in the hospital with veritable right-sided lobar pneumonia developed appendicitis which was permitted to go on to abscess formation before this diagnosis was made. The abdominal pain which accompanies acute rheumatic fever may frequently precede the appearance of joint pains and of evidences of carditis and is readily confused with appendicitis. The crises of sickle-cell anemia may simulate appendicitis. The condition called mesenteric adenitis closely resembles appendicitis clinically. The so-called Brennemann syndrome is a frequent source of diagnostic difficulty. In this condition patients with acute upper respiratory infections, particularly tonsillitis, develop abdominal pain, tenderness, muscular rigidity, and even rebound tenderness of such a degree as to overshadow the primary pharyngeal infection, which is sometimes not discovered until after a negative abdominal exploration. Primary bacterial peritonitides may be confused with appendicitis. In these conditions, high fever and prostration are likely to be present and diarrhea is common. If there is any likelihood that one of these conditions is present, as in a child with nephrosis or with vaginal discharge, an attempt should be made to establish the diagnosis by aspiration of pus from the peritoneal cavity with a short-beveled needle. If the diagnosis of a primary peritonitis can thus be established by a smear showing only pneumococci or only gonococci, operation is unnecessary and the treatment may be left to antibiotics. If mixed or gram-negative organisms are found, it is good evidence of peritonitis of perforative origin, requiring operation. A large number of other abdominal conditions, such as torsion of an ovarian or mesenteric cyst, pyelitis, and the onset of acute nephritis, may be confused with appendicitis. The acute exanthematic diseases are occasionally ushered in by abdominal pain indistinguishable from appendicitis, and at times appendicitis occurs in association with other diseases. Abdominal allergy and abdominal epilepsy are occasionally responsible for acute attacks of pain.

The fundamental point in the differential diagnosis is this: while every attempt should be made to arrive at an accurate diagnosis, the clinical picture of appendicitis is so varied and uncertain that more harm will result from too rigid adherence to fixed diagnostic criteria than from ready resort to operation. *If a child has abdominal tenderness and if his history and physical examination do not disclose features incompatible with appendicitis, operation should be performed.* The safest approach is to operate at once whenever there is a reasonable possibility that a child may have appendicitis. The mortality from appendectomy, if the appendix is normal, or inflamed but unruptured, is almost nil. Further, it must not be forgotten that appendicitis does not spare children with known rheumatic fever, sickle-cell anemia, or other acute or chronic diseases, and that in general the removal of a normal appendix will do little harm to such a patient. If two of every three unruptured appendices removed are acutely inflamed, one may probably be satisfied. Hypercritical attempts at diagnostic accuracy before resort to operation invite perforation of the appendix and grave complications or death.

So long as the patient remains a diagnostic problem, opiates are to be avoided for fear of obscuring surgical signs. Cathartics should never be given to patients with abdominal pain. An enema will frequently relieve colonic distension which may mimic appendicitis. In remote areas where operation is impossible, penicillin in large doses, as shown by the war experience, may tide the patient over. Apart from such instances one should operate whenever the diagnosis of appendicitis is made. If children are brought in late in the disease suffering from dehydration and loss of fluids, two or three hours before operation may profitably be spent in intubating the intestine, restoring fluid balance with transfusions of blood and plasma and infusions of electrolytes, and administering antibiotics.

In the postoperative treatment of patients with perforated appendices the mortality, morbidity, and length of hospitalization have been greatly lowered by the use of antibiotics, indwelling intestinal tubes, and large transfusions of blood plasma to replace the protein-rich fluids which are lost into the lumen of the intestine, the wall of the intestine, and the peritoneal cavity. These measures should be employed prophylactically in such patients without waiting for paralytic ileus, hemoconcentration, and electrolyte imbalance.

After a simple appendectomy through a McBurney incision, the patient may be allowed to be up and about as soon as he wishes after recovering from anesthesia, and may be permitted unrestricted activity at once. The child may eat a normal diet as soon as he desires it, and enemas may be given at any time. Prophylactic appendectomy is not advised as a routine measure but is justifiable for children who are about to be taken to remote areas for a protracted stay.

Although appendicitis characteristically is a recurrent disease (if not treated by appendectomy), we do not recognize a condition in which the appendix is chronically mildly inflamed and produces vague symptoms and "a rundown condition." When a child has appendicitis he either recovers spontaneously or gets worse. If he recovers spontaneously, the appendix causes no symptoms until the next acute attack.

Mesenteric Adenitis

This name is given to a condition which produces an acute illness characterized by abdominal pain, nausea, and vomiting, often in association with an upper respiratory infection. The pain may be severe, but the patient is generally not particularly ill. Pain and tenderness are usually more diffuse than in appendicitis, while rebound tenderness and muscle spasm are likely to be absent. Fever and leucocytosis are common. At operation the appendix is found to be normal; the mesenteric lymph nodes at the ileocecal junction and along the terminal ileum are enlarged and often appear succulent, with occasional edema of the mesentery and a little clear, free fluid. On section the nodes show a nonspecific hyperplasia. Cultures for viruses and pathogenic bacteria have either been reported to be negative or have yielded so wide a variety of organisms as to lose significance. Mesenteric adenitis is not a well-defined entity; no specific etiology or pathognomonic lesion has been demonstrated, and the symptoms are nonspecific. Moreover, autopsies on children dying of any cause, including violent trauma, frequently show large mesenteric lymph nodes.

REFERENCES

Aird, I. Acute non-specific mesenteric lymphadenitis. Brit. Med. J., 2:680, 1945.

Benson, C. D., Coury, J. J., Jr., and Hagge, D. R. Acute appendicitis in infants; a 15-year study. Arch. Surg., 64:561, 1952.

Brennemann, J. The abdominal pain of throat infections. Amer. J. Dis. Child., 22:493, 1921.

——— Abdominal pain in children. J.A.M.A., 127:691, 1945.

Campbell, E. H., Jr. Acute abdominal pain in sickle-cell anemia. Arch. Surg., 31:607, 1935.

Firor, H. V., et al. Perforating appendicitis in infants. Surgery, 56:581, 1964.

Hoefer, P. F. A., Cohen, S. M., and Greeley, D. M. Paroxysmal abdominal pain, an epileptic equivalent. Trans. Amer. Neurol. Ass., 75:183, 1950.

Hurwitt, E. S. Acute appendicitis occurring during the course of other diseases. New Eng. J. Med., 236:20, 1947.

Longino, L. A., Holder, T. M., and Gross, R. E. Appendicitis in childhood; a study of 1,358 cases. Pediatrics, 22:238, 1958.

Minervini, F., and Santulli, T. V. Acute appendicitis in early childhood. J. Pediat., 52:324, 1958.

Postlethwait, R. W., and Campbell, F. H. Acute mesenteric lymphadenitis. Arch. Surg., 59:92, 1949.

Potts, W. J. Acute appendicitis in children. Amer. J. Dis. Child., 55:511, 1938.

Scott, H. W., Jr., and Ware, P. F. Acute appendicitis in childhood. Arch. Surg., 50:258, 1945.

Shaw, E. B. Appendicitis in childhood. Pediatrics, 22:235, 1958.

Stanley, Brown, E. G. Acute appendicitis during the first five years of life. Amer. J. Dis. Child., 108:1348, 1964.

23.20
REGIONAL ENTERITIS

MERVIN SILVERBERG and
MURRAY DAVIDSON

This chronic nonspecific enteritis is characterized by one or more combinations of noncaseating granulomata, necrotizing or cicatrizing inflammation, and external or internal strictures and fistulas. The inflammatory process usually involves all layers of the gut wall, often including the subtending mesentery and regional lymph nodes. Although there are many earlier references in the literature, the full importance of the disease was not recognized until the publication by Crohn, Ginzburg, and Oppenheimer in 1932 which described the lesion limited to the ileum, hence their term "terminal ileitis," referring to its principal location in over 80 percent of cases. Since that time the disease process has been shown to involve all areas of the gastrointestinal tract, continuously or serially, from esophagus to anus. When confined to the colon alone the condition may be difficult to distinguish from chronic ulcerative colitis, and it is estimated that 20 percent of all patients with chronic inflammatory disease of the colon suffer from regional enteritis.

Ten to 15 percent of patients are reported to have onset of disease below the age of 15 years; although a considerable proportion of these are in the early adolescent age group, some cases may start as young as 1 year of age. A slight male preponderance has been noted and in 4 to 5 percent of the cases a familial incidence is reported. Pathogenesis of the disease is unknown.

The onset is abrupt in less than 10 percent of children, in whom the pathology is restricted to the terminal ileum, and it simulates acute appendicitis or intestinal obstruction. These patients are usually diagnosed at laparotomy, half of them undergoing an uneventful and apparently permanent recovery. The remainder develop the clinical picture of chronic regional enteritis, frequently involving other areas of the intestine, within weeks to months of the surgery. Although certain of the clinical manifestations vary with the anatomic site and extent of involvement, abdominal pain is the rule, and children most commonly present with chronic constitutional complaints, e.g., failure to thrive, persistent or recurrent fevers, weight loss, and anorexia. The type of anemias encountered with chronic inflammations, in which both serum iron concentration and total iron binding capacity are low, is found in most cases and occasionally may be the presenting problem. Diarrhea, although not infrequent, is usually intermittent, and rarely explosive, bloody, or accompanied by steatorrhea. Patients often are troubled by borborygmi, bloating, and flatulence.

Perianal or perirectal abscesses and fistulae occur somewhat less frequently than in adults, but when they do these lesions may antedate any other systemic or abdominal complaints of the disease. Digital clubbing, apthous stomatitis, erythema nodosum, arthritis, and pyoderma gangrenosum are associated abnormal findings and in some cases may present before the gastrointestinal manifestations. Growth failure and sexual infantilism are major concerns in the adolescent, and an otherwise asymptomatic patient may seek help primarily for these complaints, with gastrointestinal disease developing later. Fistulous connections often develop between adjacent involved loops of intestine and, occasionally, between a diseased area and normal colon, the bladder, or the abdominal wall. Free perforation with diffuse peritonitis, amyloidosis, and protein-losing enteropathy are less frequent complications.

Roentgenographic changes in the prestenotic phase of the disease are often subtle and difficult to recognize. Radiograms may be completely normal for one to two years. Early abnormalities affect the ileocecal valve area, resulting in thickened mucosal folds with some rigidity and separation of the bowel loops. Eventually a cobblestone pattern is noted. The progressive constriction of affected segments results in the final picture of rigid pipe-stems or "string signs," with skip areas of apparently normal intestine intervening.

Therapeutic regimens utilized over three decades suggest that medical management is the major form of treatment, with surgical intervention restricted to specific complications. This approach is mainly due to the high incidence of recurrence of disease and complications which ranges between 50 to 75 percent. Supportive measures are important to maintain nutrition, hydration, and comfort. Except during exacerbations, when it may be prudent to reduce the intake of raw fruits and vegetables or of highly seasoned foods, an ad lib diet is best ordered to avoid compounding the severe anorexia. Supplements of 5,000 IU vitamin A, 400 IU of vitamin D, and 50 to 200 mg of ascorbic acid are prescribed daily. Additional vitamin D may be indicated when there is need to improve calcium absorption. Electrolyte and mineral losses, mainly of potassium and calcium, may be excessive with severe diarrhea and/or with adrenocorticosteroid therapy, and supplementation is often necessary. Extensive ileal involvement may result in bile salt deficiencies due to interruption of the enterohepatic circulation, with resultant steatorrhea. Prescription of a diet in which half of the ingested fat has been replaced by a source of medium-chain triglycerides may not only lessen steatorrhea, but also may result in significant weight gains among such patients. Anticholinergic drugs such as methantheline bromide (Banthine), 6 to 7 mg per kilogram per day, or propantheline bromide (Probanthine), 2 to 3 mg per kilogram per day, each administered every four hours and at bedtime, are often helpful for relief of abdominal discomfort. Selected patients experience improvement of most of their complaints after administration of a nonabsorbable sulfonamide such as salicylazosulfapyridine (Azulfidine), in divided doses totalling 2 to 8 g per day. Many patients respond only transitorily to these measures and some not at all. Corticosteroids are eventually required for a majority. Initially, prednisone is administered in a dose of 2 mg per kilogram per day for 10 to 14 days and then withdrawn very slowly over a period of 6 to 8 weeks. Occasionally the child may exacerbate repeatedly during attempts to taper doses of prednisone, and 10 to 40 U daily of intramuscular ACTH may be introduced to facilitate steroid withdrawal. Short 14 to 21 day courses of prednisone may be useful for subsequent relapses; although Azulfidine may not be dramatic in its salutary effects on a severe bout of the disease, once a child has improved with steroids this sulfonamide may be helpful in maintaining a better state of health and may permit more prolonged intervals between steroid therapy. Other immunosuppressive agents such as 6-mercaptopurine and azothioprine have been reported to be beneficial in a limited number of complicated cases, but these drugs cannot as yet be recommended for general use in a vast majority of patients. Diarrhea, if prominent, usually subsides with general improvement of the patient.

As a rule, 75 percent of these patients suffer chronic indolent courses with variable degrees of debilitation and incapacitation. The requirements for and hazards of long-term steroid therapy together with the high risk of postoperative recurrences emphasize the therapeutic dilemma in treating many patients with this disease.

References

Barber, K. W., Waugh, J. M., Beahrs, O. H., and Saner, I. W. G. Indication for and the results of the surgical treatment of regional enteritis. Trans. Amer. Surg. Ass., 80:146, 1962.

Chrispin, A. R., and Tempeny, E. Crohn's disease of the jejunum in children. Arch. Dis. Child., 42:631, 1967.

Crohn, B. B., Ginsburg, L., and Oppenheimer, G. D. Regional ileitis, a pathologic and clinical entity. J.A.M.A., 99:1323, 1932.

—— and Yarnis, H. Regional Ileitis, 2nd ed. New York, Grune and Stratton, Inc., 1958.

Davidson, M. Ulcerative colitis anrd regional enteritis. *In* Green and Haggerty, eds., Ambulatory Pediatrics. Philadelphia, W. B. Saunders Co., 1968, pp. 696-707.

Silverman, F. N. Regional enteritis in children. Austr. Paediat. J., 2:207, 1966.

Sobel, E. H., Silverman, F. N., and Lee, C. M., Jr. Chronic regional enteritis and growth retardation. Amer. J. Dis. Child., 103:569, 1962.

van Heerden, J. A., Sigler, R. M., and Lynn, H. B. Regional enteritis in children: surgical aspects. Mayo Clin. Proc., 42:100, 1967.

Winkelman, E. Regional enteritis in adolescence. Pediat. Clin. N. Amer., 14:141, 1967.

23.21
ULCERATIVE COLITIS

MURRAY DAVIDSON and
MERVIN SILVERBERG

Ulcerative colitis is the most common chronic inflammatory disease of the bowel. The mucosa of the colon is friable and often frankly ulcerated and covered with exudate. The primary complaints are abdominal pain and diarrhea, frequently associated with rectal bleeding. The disease may involve either the entire large intestine or portions of it, and the clinical course is variable. *Proctitis* is a form of the disease limited to the segment distal to the rectosigmoid junction. This clinical variety is different at different ages. It is not very common in children, but when present it usually heralds spread to full-blown disease in more proximal areas of the colon. In adults this limited form of disease is a frequent finding and virtually always augurs well for the patient.

ETIOLOGY. The exact pathogenesis of the disease remains obscure. Common presence of elevated white blood count and sedimentation rate, fever, and pus cells in the stool suggests that the disease may be an infectious process. In some patients the initial presentation has been associated with a well-documented bacterial or amebic dysentery infection which then persisted beyond the period when the specific infection cleared. However, despite frequent and diligent attempts to prove a relationship with bacteria or viruses, no specific pathogenic organism has been demonstrated.

Focus on the gastrointestinal tract as a major central and peripheral lymphoid organ has been accompanied by a great deal of work attempting to relate ulcerative colitis to some immunologic or hypersensitivity disorder. The sera of patients contain circulating antibodies to many different antigens, but they do not appear to be related to the severity, duration, or extent of the disease. Furthermore, these antibodies are neither tissue- nor species-specific, are often found in normal individuals, and persist after colectomy, suggesting that their presence is a secondary event with only questionable relationship to pathogenesis. The possible cytotoxic effects of lymphocytes and bacterial antigens in patients with ulcerative colitis has been investigated with inconclusive results. Milk allergy has been suggested as an important pathogenic factor, but results of clinical studies are contradictory. Circulating immunoglobulins IgA, IgM, and IgG do not consistently differ from those of control subjects, and studies of tissue-fixed immunoglobulins have not been revealing.

Although there is general agreement that psychologic factors are important in children with ulcerative colitis, there are differences of opinion concerning their role in etiology. Many of the patients are dependent, passive, rigid, and oversensitive, with an excessive need for love, and with mothers who are domineering, punitive, and lack warmth. Failure of all patients and all mothers to show these characteristics has led to the impression that these features may not be of primary importance. It is likely that there are multideterminants, including personality patterns of both mother and child as well as environmental influences such as separation phenomena, which play an etiologic role. Whichever emotional factors are important, there is little question that once the disease is established exacerbations and remissions are often associated with changes in emotional state.

SYMPTOMS. *Diarrhea and abdominal pain* are the most common presenting features, often with rectal bleeding and occasionally with tenesmus. In rare cases the rectal bleeding precedes any changes in fecal consistency. Characteristically, the stools are loose to watery and contain small amounts of feces mixed with variable quantities of pus and mucus. The bowel movements occur mainly during the night and early morning hours, but in severe attacks they are continuous throughout the day.

Clinically apparent dehydration and depletion of electrolytes occurs only in severe attacks. However, patients with milder but persistent diarrhea may display marginal insufficiences which are easily thrown into severe depletion states during brief exacerbations.

Anemia is common in ulcerative colitis, although there is disagreement as to its etiology and relationship to rectal bleeding. Many patients suffer from iron-deficiency anemia, while others with persistent bleeding have little or no red cell deficit. In some children, particularly in those with a chronic continuous course of illness, anemia is related to defects in hematopoiesis and iron transport capabilities, often in the face of minimal blood loss per rectum. This type of anemia may be further compromised by excessive protein exudation into the gastrointestinal tract and as a rule responds poorly to oral or parenteral iron administration. In a small number of cases excessive hemolysis has been demonstrated, presumably due to absorbed bacterial toxins, medication such as sulfonamides, or autoimmune processes such as microangiopathic hemolytic anemia.

Significant *liver disease* is an uncommon complication in children, although mild abnormalities of liver function tests are frequently reported. Fatty metamorphosis is the most common histologic finding and has been attributed to nutritional deficiencies or absorption of toxic materials. Hepatitis acquired by parenteral therapeutic measures, or due to an immunologic disturbance, is the second most common lesion. Pericholangitis and biliary or postnecrotic cirrhosis have been noted in long-standing cases, but are unusual in children.

Erythema nodosum occurs in about 1 to 2 percent of cases, and although it usually is noted during an attack, the lesions occasionally precede all gastrointestinal manifestations. *Pyoderma gangrenosum, erythema multiforme, papulonecrotic lesions,* and *erythematous plaques* are encountered in an appreciable number of children. *Uveitis* and *arthritis,* which often coexist with *apthous ulcerations* and skin lesions during exacerbations of the disease, may be more troublesome to the patient than the colonic symptoms.

DIAGNOSIS. Before making the diagnosis of idiopathic nonspecific ulcerative colitis, it is important to rule out other identifiable causes of colonic inflammation and diarrhea. Repeated stool examinations for amebic and bacterial infections must be performed. On the other hand, the diagnosis of ulcerative colitis should be considered in patients with early onset of painless rectal bleeding without diarrhea.

The two most important tools for diagnosis of ulcerative colitis are sigmoidoscopy and barium enema. With sigmoidoscopy a friable, easily bruised mucosa is seen more commonly than are frank ulcers or exudates. In many instances no abnormalities are observed until the epithelial surface is gently swabbed with a cotton pledget, following which a shower of petechiae and small bleeding points develops. This finding is associated with microscopic evidence of mucosal inflammation and cellular infiltration of the small vessels of the bowel wall. Among patients with long-standing disease, muscular spasm, as well as shortening and narrowing of the colonic lumen, may make sigmoidoscopy difficult. A rectal biopsy adds little to the diagnosis, although in rare cases histologic study of grossly normal-appearing mucosa may demonstrate pathology, e.g., increased cellularity of the lamina propria, microscopic abscesses, or granulomas.

Barium enema may appear entirely normal for periods as long as two to three years after the onset of the disease. Conversely, the first examination, within days or weeks of onset, may show evidence of advanced disease. Minimal lesions are represented simply by loss of mucosal integrity, progressing to the pseudopolypoid appearance. Decrease of colonic haustrations with marked shortening and narrowing to a "pipestem" lumen are later findings. It has been demonstrated that in some patients the colon has a remarkable potential for returning toward a normal appearance when the clinical picture improves.

Patients with this illness generally should have sigmoidoscopy performed annually and barium enema every one to two years before adolescence, with semiannual examinations after this age because of the dangers of complications. The clinical picture in individual patients may require deviation from this schedule, making it desirable to examine some children more frequently or to postpone studies in others because of illness.

Two pathogenic entities are described, one granulomatous and the other nonspecific. Almost every aspect of the disease has been examined for possible clues to help distinguish these types and a great deal of emphasis is placed on radiologic differences. In nonspecific ulcerative colitis the disease is essentially mucosal with almost invariable involvement of the rectum, as compared to granulomatous disease which is usually transmural, discontinuous, and often spares the rectum. Roentgenologic differences are useful in selected cases although interpretation is often based on a great deal of personal bias. A normal rectum, cecal deformity, strictures, fistulae, cobblestone appearance of the mucosa, and longitudinal ulcerations which are presumably submucosal in location are all suggestive of granulomatous disease. The differential diagnosis is greatly facilitated in that 10 percent of patients with granulomatous disease in whom small bowel disease is simultaneously demonstrable.

CLINICAL COURSE. Two clinical patterns are observed in children. Remitting colitis is the more common type and is associated with recurrent relapses which are often stormy and are interspersed between periods free of symptoms. Patients with this pattern of disease usually present with bloody diarrhea and may experience considerable rectal bleeding even during diarrhea-free periods. In the second pattern, referred to as chronic continuous colitis, there are no complete remissions at any time. The diarrhea is usually deceptively mild and more tolerable than the complications which develop in patients with this type of disease. Despite frequent absence of rectal bleeding, intractable anemia and other signs of poor nutrition such as hypoproteinemia and failure to gain weight are problems. These patients are more prone to bouts of fever and development of arthritis, fistulas, and abscesses than are those with the remitting pattern. Children with the remitting pattern of the disease usually either appear to be entirely well after two or three years or they develop the chronic continuous type. Although many of the clinical features of the chronic continuous pattern of disease are common to those attributed to granulomatous colitis, histopathologic examinations of surgical specimens often does not reveal granulomas. Conversely, some patients whose biopsies or surgical specimens do not support the diagnosis of granulomatous disease subsequently develop clear-cut ileocolitis. Both granulomatous and nonspecific ulcerative colitis have been reported to occur in the same family and they have similar epidemiologic and genetic characteristics. Colitis is a familial disease and together with regional enteritis most large series report that approximately 10 percent of patients have affected relatives. The disease occurs in Jews about 10 times as often as in all other groups combined, and is encountered with lowest frequency among nonwhites.

Some patients, though not all by far, suffer one or the other of the various *colonic complications.*

Enterocolic fistulas or abnormal communications between bowel and skin, usually anorectal fistulas, occur. Some patients develop the ominous complication referred to as *toxic megacolon,* with acute dilation and stasis. The exact cause of this complication is unknown, but it is likely that electrolyte imbalance is an important contributing factor.

There is no increased tendency to develop adenomatous polyps in these patients. Heaped up remnants of colonic mucosa which remain between the ulcers of this disease lead to a *"pseudopolypoid"* appearance on roentgenographic examination. These lesions are inflammatory and are not premalignant. *Cancer* of the colon occurs in an appreciable percentage of children with ulcerative colitis. Although the factors which predispose to development of carcinoma are unknown, its occurrence appears to be particularly related to duration of disease for more than 5 to 10 years and to onset in early childhood.

THERAPY. *Dietary restrictions* are often imposed, but their value is questionable. Patients are frequently treated with diets free of highly seasoned foods and roughage. There are few clinical or experimental data to indicate that these foods make the disease worse. Studies of concurrent lactase deficiency in the small intestine have been conflicting. Tolerance tests can be used to determine the presence of specific sugar intolerance in individual patients. More frequently, an initial short-term trial of milk and milk product withdrawal is arbitrarily attempted during the acute phase of illness to observe for possible relationship between either lactose intolerance or "allergy" to cow proteins and the pathogenesis of symptoms. Such a relationship has not been observed by us very often, and milk is reintroduced after one to two months. Children are otherwise permitted a free intake, keeping in mind that unnecessary dietary manipulations compromise the already capricious intake of these ill children. The ideal self-chosen diet is rich in calories, high in protein, and supplemented with 5,000 IU vitamin A, 400 IU vitamin D, and 50 to 200 mg vitamin C each day, particularly during anorectic periods.

As in many other chronic diseases in children, excessive *restriction of physical activity* is both unnecessary and frustrating to both physician and patient. While hospitalization is useful for the initial evaluation, and a brief period of increased rest may be helpful in aborting attacks in patients who have been in remission, children generally do better if allowed free choice of activity.

Psychotherapy is an important consideration in ulcerative colitis, but there is need for individualization. A majority of patients can be managed by their personal physician alone if he is sensitive to the damaging effects of diagnostic procedures, the fears of the chronically ill child, and the anxieties and helpless feelings of parents. He must be a good listener and spend time in gaining the confidence of the child and family. As a rule, the constant availability of one sympathetic physician who explains, is honestly optimistic, is reassuringly frank, and is attuned to problems of individual families, will maintain an ideal doctor-patient relationship and is sufficient for chronic care of the child. For the very immature, labile child whose parents may be unable to cope with his needs, a team approach with psychiatric help is sometimes desirable.

Antispasmodic agents are used to control abdominal pain. Methantheline bromide (Banthine), 6 to 7 mg per day, or the more easily tolerated propantheline bromide (Probanthine), 2 to 3 mg per kg per day, are prescribed before meals and at bedtime, with optimal results obtained when atropine side effects are noted. *Antidiarrheal drugs* are frequently prescribed but do not produce much effect as long as the inflammatory process remains active. Diphenoxylate hydrochloride (Lomotil, 2.5 to 5.0 mg, 3 or 4 times daily) or preparations containing opiates (Donnagel-PG, Tincture of Paregoric, and so forth) are the preparations most often utilized. One must be aware of the danger of possible intestinal atony from overdosage with these agents.

The anemic child requires *iron supplements* or *blood replacement,* as indicated. Oral ferrous sulfate is used in appropriate doses except when gastrointestinal intolerance necessitates the intramuscular or intravenous administration of the iron-dextran complex, Imferon. Patients with the granulomatous and chronic continuous forms of colitis are often unable to utilize exogenous iron. They are best treated with small transfusions of packed red blood cells if anemia becomes severe.

Nonabsorbable sulfonamide preparations, particularly salicylazosulfapyridine (Azulfidine) or sulfasuccidine, 2 to 8 g per day, are useful and constitute the initial therapy in most patients. Their mode of action is not clear but these drugs have been shown to suppress symptoms for prolonged periods in individual patients. Although not dramatic in aborting severe attacks, these agents may be used for "maintenance" therapy to reduce the frequency of relapses. Soluble, absorbable sulfonamides, penicillin and streptomycin, or chloramphenicol may be prescribed in usual therapeutic doses for periods of one to two weeks during acute febrile periods, especially if steroids are being given.

Anti-inflammatory and *immunosuppressive drugs* provide the most certain control of acute and deteriorating symptomatology. Prednisone administered over a period of 6 to 8 weeks is used most frequently by us. Dosage is 2.0 mg per kg per day in divided doses for 10 to 14 days, followed by a slow withdrawal for the duration of treatment. In up to 30 percent of patients other authors report more prolonged periods of therapy. Complications of steroid administration such as osteoporosis, hypertension, excessive weight gain, and hypokalemia must be anticipated in such patients, and they are treated prophylactically, or at the time they arise. Attempts to avoid steroid side effects by alternate-day administration have not been universally successful in this disease. Rectal instillations of corticosteroids at bedtime are advocated by some workers and may be an adjunct in patients with severe urgency and frequency of defecation. It is preferable that enemas not be prescribed for chronic home use since this may develop into an important point of contention between mother and child.

Corticotropin (ACTH, 20 to 80 U) is usually restricted to specific hospitalized cases or to patients in whom steroid withdrawal repeatedly results in exacerbation of the disease. Unfortunately, children often find frequent regular injections of the aqueous or gel preparations objectionable, and prolonged use is therefore undesirable.

Conclusions vary from unbridled enthusiasm to pessimistic caution with regard to the use of 6-mercaptopurine or azathioprine. Adequately controlled studies are not available and the hazards of bone marrow depression, malignancy, and a high rate of relapse are very real.

In both acute and chronic disease there is wide divergence of opinion as to the indications for surgical intervention and the nature of the operation to be employed. Fulminant ulcerative colitis requiring early surgical management is fortunately rare in childhood. Perforation, impending perforation, and the presence of cancer are undisputed indications. Severe hemorrhage is uncommon and surgery is rarely, if ever, indicated. Criteria for elective surgery are usually based on degree of clinical disability, failure of growth and development, and, in those patients with disease exceeding 10 years' duration, the fear of cancer. The criterion of surgery for a prolonged duration of clinical symptomatology varies with different authors from 1 to 9 years. Although still unproved, we believe that patients with chronic continuous disease in whom there is no concomitant small intestinal involvement may benefit from early surgery.

When considering surgery in long-standing cases, it is necessary to take into account the high risk of carcinoma, which outweighs the small mortality from elective colectomy.

Total colectomy and permanent ileostomy is the operation most likely to produce a cure. Most appliances that can be utilized with an abdominal ileostomy now make it possible for such a patient to lead a normal life. With proper preparation, patients with the disease make an excellent emotional adjustment to surgery. There is usually marked physical improvement, disappearance of complications, and a complete change for the better in the emotional status of all the members of the family.

REFERENCES

Bargen, J. A., and Kennedy, R. L. J. Chronic ulcerative colitis in childhood. Postgrad. Med., 17:127, 1955.

Barr, M., Devava, S., and Zetterstrom, R. Studies of the anemia in metabolism. Acta Paediat., 44:62, 1965.

Broberger, O., and Lagercrantz, R. Ulcerative colitis in childhood and adolescence. Advanced Pediat., 14:9, 1966.

Davidson, M. Management of ulcerative colitis in children. Amer. J. Surg., 107:3, 1964.

———— Current concepts: juvenile ulcerative colitis. New Eng. J. Med., 277:1408, 1967.

———— Ulcerative colitis and regional enteritis. *In* Green and Haggerty, eds., Ambulatory Pediatrics. Philadelphia, W. B. Saunders Co., 1968, pp. 696-707.

———— Bloom, A., and Kugler, M. Chronic ulcerative colitis of childhood: An evaluative review. J. Pediat., 67:3, 471, 1965.

Ehrenpreis, T. Surgical treatment of ulcerative colitis in childhood. Arch. Dis. Child., 41:137, 1966.

———— Ericson, N. O., Billing, L., Lagercrantz, R., and Rudhe, W. Surgical treatment of ulcerative colitis in children. Acta Paediat. Scand., 49:810, 1960.

Engel, G. L. Studies of ulcerative colitis. II. The nature of the somatic processes and the adequacy of psychosomatic hypothesis. Amer. J. Med., 16:416, 1954.

———— Studies of ulcerative colitis. III. The nature of the psychologic process. Amer. J. Med., 19:231, 1955.

Flood, C. A., Lepore, M. J., Hiatt, R. B., and Karush, A. Prognosis in chronic ulcerative colitis. J. Chron. Dis., 4:267, 1956.

Goldberg, H. I., Carbone, J. V., and Margulis, A. R. Roentgenographic reversibility of ulcerative colitis in children treated with steroid enemas. Amer. J. Roentgen., 103:365, 1968.

Jackson, D. D., and Yalom, I. Family research on the problem of ulcerative colitis. Arch. Gen. Psychiat. (Chicago), 15:410, 1966.

Kirsner, J. B., Rasking, H. F., and Palmer, W. L. Ulcerative colitis in children. Amer. J. Dis. Child., 90:141, 1955.

Korelitz, B. I., Gribetz, D., and Danziger, I. The prognosis of ulcerative colitis with onset in childhood. I. The presteroid era. Ann. Int. Med., 57:582, 1962.

———— Gribetz, D., and Danziger, I. The prognosis of ulcerative colitis with onset in childhood. II. The steroid era. Ann. Int. Med., 57:592, 1962.

———— Gribetz, D., and Kopel, F. B. Granulomatous colitis in children: a study of 25 cases and comparison with ulcerative colitis. Pediatrics, 42:446, 1968.

Lagercrantz, R., Hammerstrom, S., and Perlmann, P. Autoimmunity in ulcerative colitis. Acta Paediat. Scand. (Suppl.), 177, 111, 1967.

McDermott, J. F., Jr. Children with ulcerative colitis. Their own perception of the disease. Psychosomatics, 7:163, 1966.

Michener, W. M. Ulcerative colitis in children. Problems in management. Pediat. Clin. N. Amer., 14:159, 1967.

———— Gage, R. P., Sauer, W. G., and Stickler, G. B. The prognosis of chronic ulcerative colitis in children. N. Eng. J. Med., 265:1075, 1961.

Prugh, D. G. Childhood experience and colonic disorder. Ann. N.Y. Acad. Sci., 58:355, 1954.

Schneider, K. M., Becker, J. M., Korelitz, B. I., Krasna, I. H., and Kark, A. E. The surgical treatment of ulcerative colitis in childhood—a study of 38 cases. J. Pediat. Surg., 3:12, 1968.

Tumen, H. J., Valdes-Dapena, A., and Haddad, H. Indications for surgical intervention in ulcerative colitis in children. Amer. J. Dis. Child., 116:641, 1968.

23.22
ANORECTAL CONDITIONS

THOMAS V. SANTULLI

Anorectal Abscesses

Perianal abscesses are relatively common in infancy. Deeper ischiorectal abscesses may also occur. They usually occur from infection of an anal crypt. Anal inflammation and infection may also originate in the preformed anal ducts and glands. Primary infection of these glands, which usually empty into the crypts of Morgagni, may cause perianal suppuration with subsequent formation of anal fistulas.

There is a painful swelling overlying the perianal area or ischiorectal fossa with redness, heat, and induration. Fluctuation occurs late. Treatment consists of early incision and drainage followed by warm baths and local cleanliness. In about one-half of the cases of surgical or spontaneous drainage of these abscesses, a fistula in ano will result.

Fistula in Ano

Fistula in ano is the end result of progression of an abscess which originates in an anal crypt of Morgagni. The diagnosis is based on the presence of an opening in the perianal area which usually can be probed upward into the involved anal crypt within the anus. A history of one or more episodes of perianal drainage, spontaneous or surgical, with intermittent purulent discharge is common. In some cases recurrent fistulas may communicate with an abscess in the lower pelvic or perirectal area. Such abscesses originally arise from internal fistulous tracts from the appendix, small intestine, cecum, or sigmoid and may indicate a chronic inflammatory disease, e.g., regional enteritis. Treatment consists of incision with wide exposure of the entire tract, including the internal opening.

23.23
PERITONITIS

THOMAS V. SANTULLI

Inflammation of the peritoneum may be classified as acute or chronic, primary or secondary, localized or diffuse, bacterial or nonbacterial.

Acute peritonitis may occur at any time in infancy and childhood. In the newborn period it is usually but one manifestation of generalized sepsis (Sec. 14.2). It may also occur from perforation of the intestine with spilling of meconium into the peritoneal cavity.

Acute Primary Peritonitis

Acute primary or idiopathic peritonitis has almost disappeared since effective antibacterial agents have been available. The organisms responsible for most of these infections—some type of pneumococcus or hemolytic streptococcus—are effectively controlled by early antibacterial treatment. Both sexes are about equally affected with acute primary peritonitis; most of the cases occur in children from 1 to 6 years of age. The peritonitis is diffuse, involving the general peritoneal cavity; localized abscesses are not as common as in secondary peritonitis. The fluid is generally thin and contains large amounts of fibrin which eventually causes many adhesions between loops of intestine.

The onset is usually sudden, the child becoming acutely ill with fever as high as 105° F and prostration. Sometimes there has been a preceding upper respiratory infection. An older child experiences diffuse abdominal pain and tenderness with boardlike rigidity; in younger patients the abdomen may be soft and doughy. Anorexia and vomiting are rarely absent. Leucocytosis is marked (sometimes as high as 50,000), with 80 to 90 percent polymorphonuclear leucocytes.

When there are no localizing signs to indicate a secondary type of peritonitis, some have advocated needle aspiration of the peritoneal fluid to establish the diagnosis. If streptococci or pneumococci are seen on microscope smear, in the absence of *E. coli*, the diagnosis of primary idiopathic peritonitis is made and appropriate chemotherapy is instituted. Blind needle aspiration always carries the risk of perforating a loop of intestine which may be adherent to the abdominal wall. It may be safer to take the child to the operating room, where a very small incision is made in the right lower quadrant of the abdomen, preferably under local anesthesia, in order to obtain some fluid for smear which can be immediately examined. If the character of the fluid and morphology of the organisms establish the presence of primary peritonitis, the procedure is terminated. If secondary peritonitis is found, as indicated by the character of the fluid and the presence of *E. coli* in the smear, the incision is enlarged and appropriate surgical treatment is carried out as described below.

The mortality from primary peritonitis should be very low if antibiotic treatment is instituted early in the disease.

Acute Secondary Peritonitis

This is much more common than primary peritonitis. The most frequent cause is appendicitis with perforation, which should always be suspected when peritonitis appears without obvious explanation. Other important causes are primary inflammations of other abdominal viscera from which extension to the peritoneum may occur, as in volvulus, intussusception, Meckel's diverticulum, perforating ulcers, and rupture of a viscus. The infection is caused by a variety of organisms; the commonest, in order of frequency, are some type of *E. coli*, nonhemolytic streptococci, staphylococci, and *Cl. perfringens* (welchii).

The fluid is usually purulent, and in rapidly progressing cases there is an extensive exudation of fibrin with formation of pockets containing pus among the coils of intestine. The process may become localized and result in a peritoneal abscess which may be found in the pelvis, the subhepatic area, subphrenic space, or among loops of small intestine. In children, pelvic abscesses frequently rupture spontaneously into the rectum.

As in adults, the symptoms in older children are usually well marked and sufficiently characteristic to enable one to recognize the disease easily, but this is not so in infants, in whom the symptoms are often obscure. In some cases the acute toxemia and hypovolemia resulting from peritoneal exudation cause rapid prostration and death, and the disease may be found at autopsy when not suspected during life.

As a rule, the signs of the preceding abdominal illness, usually appendicitis, increase in severity, the temperature rises, usually between 101° and 106° F, and ileus and dehydration are invariably present; vomiting and constipation ensue. Older children complain of pain which may be localized or general; in younger ones pain is indicated by crying and fretfulness. The abdomen becomes distended and tympanitic. There is marked tenderness on pressure and rebound tenderness as well as rigidity of the abdominal wall which may be both localized and diffuse.

The general symptoms are those of a serious disease; the pulse is weak, rapid, and compressible. In severe cases there may be hiccough, cold extremities, and collapse. In infants convulsions may occur. A polymorphonuclear leucocytosis of 10,000 to 25,000 is almost invariably present but may be absent in some cases of the gravest type.

In the most severe forms of diffuse peritonitis the course is short; without treatment these patients may succumb within a few days. In other cases the course is slower and the process more apt to be localized. Development of a peritoneal abscess is indicated by continued fever, often spiking in nature, with chills and sweating. The inflammatory mass may be palpable externally or by rectum.

Residual adhesions, persisting after the infection has been overcome, sometimes give rise to obstructive symptoms later, and operation may be necessary to relieve intestinal obstruction.

Treatment consists of correction of hypovolemia and electrolyte imbalance with blood, fluids, and electrolytes, early operation, and antibiotics; aspiration of intestinal contents through a Miller-Abbott intestinal tube is indicated for paralytic ileus. A period of preoperative preparation is important, but this should not be prolonged.

Localized Peritonitis

Local collections of exudate or *abscesses* may form in the pelvis, subhepatic area, subphrenic space, or among loops of intestine which delay recovery; some eventually absorb or rupture into the bowel, usually the rectum; others need to be drained. *Subphrenic abscess,* usually on the right side, is an uncommon condition in children. Although the most common cause is a focus of suppuration in the abdomen, such as perforated appendicitis with peritonitis, it may represent metastasis from a more remote infection by way of the bloodstream, or in rare instances, direct extension of pneumonia or empyema downward through the diaphragm. The symptoms and physical signs may resemble those of empyema, but more often the symptoms appear as a gradual exacerbation of the primary intraperitoneal disease. There may be higher elevation of the temperature, increasing malaise, anorexia, and upper abdominal pain. Hiccough may occur. Tenderness and spasm are found over the upper abdomen or costal margin on the right or left side, and a mass or local bulging with edema may be present. Roentgenograms in the upright position may show haziness in the lower lung field, with an indistinct diaphragmatic shadow and a collection of pleural exudate or, less frequently, a fluid level with gas just beneath the diaphragm. Diagnostic aspiration of the abscess is often unreliable and may be dangerous; contamination of the pleura is to be avoided. Incision and drainage, usually employing the posterior or extraperitoneal approach, as well as appropriate antibiotic treatment are necessary.

Chronic Peritonitis

The most common form of chronic peritonitis is tuberculous (Sec. 14.20).

Other less common types include: the widespread adhesive peritonitis that sometimes follows acute diffuse peritonitis, calcified meconium peritonitis with extensive adhesions resulting from perforation of the intestine in the prenatal period, and nonspecific inflammatory peritonitis accompanying chylous ascites or ascites due to portal hypertension.

REFERENCES

Gross, R. E. Primary peritonitis. *In* The Surgery of Infancy and Childhood. Philadelphia, W. B. Saunders Co., 1953, p. 384.

Harvey, H. D., and Meleney, F. L. Peritonitis: Collective review of significant literature for 6½ years. Surg. Gynec. Obstet., 67:339, 1938.

Ladd, W. E., and Swan, H. Subdiaphragmatic abscess in children. New Eng. J. Med., 229:1, 1943.

Miscellaneous Surgical Topics

23.24
FOREIGN BODIES OF THE GASTROINTESTINAL TRACT

THOMAS V. SANTULLI and
RAYMOND A. AMOURY

Between the ages of 1 and 4 years particularly, the habit of swallowing foreign substances is a very common one. The variety of objects swallowed includes all those articles which the young child can reach and put into his mouth. The most common are detached parts of toys, marbles, pebbles, buttons, and coins. Not only are such smooth articles swallowed but also, with equal readiness, sharp ones such as pins of every variety, bits of glass, fragments of bone, nails, and small toy knives and forks; extraordinary objects are sometimes swallowed. At the time of swallowing, choking or coughing attacks, severe pharyngeal pain, and sometimes slight hemorrhage may occur.

Foreign bodies in the *esophagus* are, in general, the most difficult to manage. Only large objects and those with sharp edges and angles are apt to become impacted; others pass into the stomach and rarely give trouble. A foreign body may become impacted at any point in the esophagus, most commonly in its upper portion, about the level of the fourth cervical vertebra. If allowed to remain it may lead to ulceration or perforation. The ulceration may occur into the trachea or into the posterior mediastinum, producing retroesophageal or mediastinal abscess. A tracheoesophageal communication leads to aspiration pneumonia and sometimes to lung abscess.

If the foreign body lodges in the throat it may give rise to gagging. In the esophagus itself it may cause dysphagia, vague sensations of discomfort, or no symptoms at all. In many cases respiratory symptoms predominate, such as dry cough and tracheal gurgling, and little or no obstruction to swallowing is observed. Some patients will tolerate liquid foods perfectly well, while attempts to take solid or semi-solid foods precipitate attacks of choking or vomiting. When there is laceration of the esophagus, ulceration and inflammation are likely to follow. In such instances there is pain and soreness on swallowing. It is well to remember that foreign bodies or, indeed, a food bolus is much more likely to become impacted in the esophagus if a preexisting stricture is present.

Opaque foreign bodies can be localized accurately by radiography (Fig. 35). A flat object, like a coin, will usually lie in the frontal plane if it is in the esophagus and in the sagittal plane if in the larynx. All foreign bodies that lodge in the esophagus should be removed. Sounding is valueless and may cause further impaction of the object; the removal should be left to the specialist in esophagoscopy. Clumsy attempts to remove an object impacted in the entrance of the esophagus not infrequently result in its aspiration into the larynx, with resulting asphyxiation. Most foreign bodies can be withdrawn with the esophagoscope, although sometimes it is more convenient to push them down into the stomach.

Once foreign bodies have entered the *stomach,* 90 to 95 percent of them will pass uneventfully through the gastrointestinal tract. During passage of the object through the intestine there may be complaints of pain, but in the great majority of instances

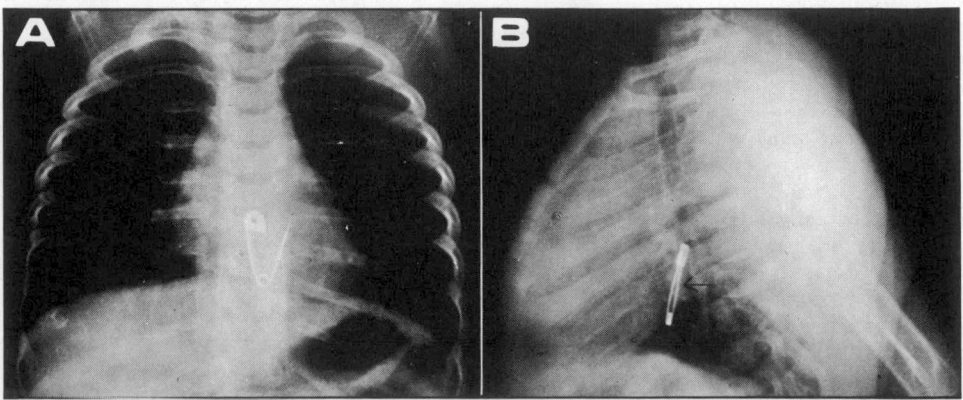

Fig. 35.   Safety pin in esophagus. A. Anteroposterior view. B. Left lateral view.

there are no symptoms whatever, even with sharp or angular bodies. Impaction and perforation, while possible, are rare. Progress may be impeded at the pylorus, the horizontal part of the duodenum, the duodenojejunal junction, and the ileocecal area. The usual time required for a foreign body to traverse the intestinal tract is from 2 to 12 days, but it may be considerably longer. We have known a safety pin to be retained in the intestinal tract for 8 months without producing any symptoms and then to be passed spontaneously; its presence in the stomach was demonstrated by x-ray two hours after it was swallowed. If the body swallowed is a smooth one, it passes through the anus without difficulty; sharp bodies may produce severe anal pain and sometimes rectal bleeding.

Diagnosis is often a matter of much difficulty, and without roentgen examination positive verification is impossible. Often when the physician is called because this condition is suspected by parents the alarm turns out to be a false one; the object thought to have been swallowed is discovered in the child's crib.

Although most foreign bodies, including open safety pins, pass through the *intestinal tract* without causing any symptoms whatever, certain objects are potentially dangerous enough to justify interference. The relation between the size of the foreign body and the size of the child is important. Objects over 5 or 6 cm in length may be expected to cause trouble in the younger child, and their progress should be observed carefully; these may include some bobby pins, hairpins, and long needles. If such a foreign body has already passed the pylorus, roentgen observations of its progress should be made periodically; if it remains stationary for a week or 10 days, there is cause for some concern. Operation is indicated at the first sign of perforation—tenderness, rigidity, fever, nausea, and vomiting. With the more innocuous foreign bodies, especially those that are disc-shaped, expectant treatment is almost always successful. The diet need not be changed. No emetics or cathartics should be administered.

Bezoars. Quite distinct from such accidental swallowing of foreign bodies as has just been described is the practice of pulling off and swallowing hair, fur from rugs, wool from toys or blankets, shreds from clothing, and a great variety of other substances. In infants the quantity of the substance is generally small, and usually it provokes vomiting or the material is speedily passed by rectum. It occasionally happens that the substance does not pass in the stools and accumulates to form an intestinal mass which may be associated with obscure and sometimes severe symptoms of long duration. More often the mass forms in the stomach. These gastric tumors, or *bezoars,* are usually composed of hair from the patient's own head, although hair from toys, brushes, and other sources is occasionally found in them. They are more frequently seen in older children than in infants, and usually in girls on account of their long

hair. The habit of trichophagia may continue for years, until a mass of considerable size has formed, sometimes attaining 2 or 3 pounds in weight.

The symptoms of such a hair ball in the stomach (*trichobezoar*) are usually indefinite. Epigastric pain or vague gastric distress is common, but vomiting is not especially marked. The general health may suffer but little for a long time. Foul breath is not infrequent. On palpation the abdominal mass is readily felt. The tumor may be mistaken for malignancy, a displaced spleen or kidney, fecal impaction, or a mesenteric cyst. Roentgen examination may show an extensive filling defect. A correct diagnosis may not be made until operation is performed. In a few instances the tumor has disappeared after catharsis, but the risk involved is obvious. With surgical removal the outcome is almost always favorable.

In sharp contrast to the hair balls are the food balls (*phytobezoars*) sometimes found in the stomach. These form quite suddenly as a result of the ingestion of some mucilaginous material which adheres to whatever food happens to be present in the stomach, producing a heterogeneous solid mass. Such tumors have followed the ingestion of varnish, shellac, tar, or powdered agar. A more frequent cause in this country is the persimmon; this fruit, particularly if not quite ripe, forms a mucilaginous product on reaching the stomach. Instances are recorded in which a persimmon debauch has been followed within a few hours by symptoms of gastric distress as the result of a large persimmon bezoar occupying the entire stomach. The drug salol, once popular as an intestinal antiseptic, also has a tendency to produce these bezoars.

Mineral concretions (*gastroliths*) occasionally occupy the stomach in young subjects. They have been observed after the administration of magnesium, bismuth, or iron salts. We have recently seen one which consisted largely of barium sulfate employed for a contrast meal some weeks before. The conditions responsible for their formation are obscure.

REFERENCES

Benson, C. D., and Lloyd, J. R. Foreign bodies in the gastrointestinal tract. *In* Mustard, W. T., et al., eds., Pediatric Surgery, 2nd ed. Chicago, Year Book Publishers, 1969, p. 825.

Biehusen, F. C., and Pulaski, E. J. Lead poisoning after ingestion of a foreign body contained in the stomach. New Eng. J. Med., 254:1179, 1956.

Friedlander, F. C., and Kushlick, P. Trichobezoar. Arch. Dis. Child., 29:556, 1954.

Grekin, T. C., and Musselman, M. M. The management of foreign bodies in the alimentary tract. Ann. Surg., 135:528, 1952.

Holinger, P. H., and Johnston, K. C. Foreign bodies in the air and food passages. Pediat. Clin. N. Amer., 1:827, 1954.

Laff, H. S., and Allen, R. P. Management of foreign bodies in the alimentary tract. J. Pediat., 48:563, 1956.

23.25
ESOPHAGEAL VARICES

JOSE M. FERRER, JR.

These varicose veins occur in the lower esophagus and cardia and are caused by portal hypertension (Sec. 24.10). They can be the source of severe exsanguinating hemorrhage. These varices should be suspected as the cause of upper gastrointestinal bleeding whenever there is evidence of intrahepatic or extrahepatic portal vein obstruction. The diagnosis of esophageal varices is made by esophagoscopy ad esophagram. The hemorrhage is best controlled by the Blakemore-Sengstaken balloon and tube or by the use of esophageal and gastric hypothermia. Recurrent hemorrhage can be prevented by performing some form of portacaval venous shunt to relieve the portal hypertension.

23.26
DILATION OF THE STOMACH; GASTRIC PERFORATIONS

THOMAS V. SANTULLI

Acute Dilation
(Gastric Paralysis)

This is a rare condition in childhood; though it may occur in infancy, most of the cases we have seen have been in older children. It is encountered in association with dilation of the intestine in severe infections, such as pneumonia or typhoid fever, in states of extreme inanition, in hypokalemia, and also postoperatively. The disturbance is probably neurogenic in origin, normal peristalsis being inhibited; secretion, however, continues actively. The condition is characterized by progressive prostration and collapse, by upper abdominal distention, and by the vomiting of large amounts of fluid, which is usually colorless although sometimes bile-stained or darkened by the presence of changed blood. Acute dilation of the stomach is a serious, often fatal complication. Treatment consists in keeping the stomach empty by continuous gastric suction and in maintaining fluid balance. Transfusion may be required to combat shock. We have seen the condition subside and recur again within a few days. Great caution must be used in resuming oral feeding after such an episode.

Chronic Dilation

This may be obstructive or atonic in origin, or it may result from overfeeding. Pyloric stenosis and congenital malformations of the duodenum are the most common causes of obstruction. Atonic dilation may be encountered in severe rickets as a manifestation of general muscular atony; it is also seen in older subjects with visceroptosis. Some degree of dilation is not uncommon in the digestive disorders of infancy.

Symptoms will depend upon the cause of the dilation. When the stomach does not empty in the normal time and when the amount vomited exceeds the quantity of food taken at the last meal, one may assume that dilation is present. The stomach can usually be outlined by percussion; if its lower border is below the umbilicus, dilation may be assumed. Occasionally a dilated colon is mistaken for it. More accurate information is obtained by roentgenographic study.

The ultimate prognosis in chronic dilation is good, provided the underlying factors can be dealt with, although the dilation may persist for months.

Gastric Perforations

Spontaneous perforation or rupture of the stomach in newborn infants has been reported in the literature since 1825. Although not a common lesion, its occurrence must be considered seriously in any infant, premature or full-term, who in the first few days of life exhibits respiratory distress and rapidly increasing abdominal distention. An *upright* roentgenogram of the abdomen will usually show considerable quantities of free air in the peritoneal cavity and will establish the diagnosis of perforated viscus (Fig. 36). If the pneumoperitoneum is massive, the stomach is the most likely source.

Abdominal exploration with closure of the perforation and performance of a gastrostomy should be carried out as soon as possible after the diagnosis is made. Nasogastric suction, vitamin K by intravenous administration, oxygen, and systemic antibiotics should be promptly administered. If respiratory embarrassment secondary to sudden abdominal distention is severe, a 19 or 20 gauge needle inserted through the upper abdominal wall will allow for escape of air from the peritoneal cavity and may dramatically improve the infant's condition while preparations are being made for emergency operation. It should be emphasized that multiple perforations may occur, and that several deaths have been caused by failure to recognize all sites at the time of exploration.

In extremely rare instances, perforation of the stomach may be associated with total distal obstruction, such as in pyloric or upper duodenal atresia. However, the exact cause of so-called spontaneous perforation or rupture is unknown. It is probably related in some way to sudden increases in intragastric pressure. The amount of pressure required to rupture the stomach is variable and dependent upon the degree of prematurity of the infant and factors which

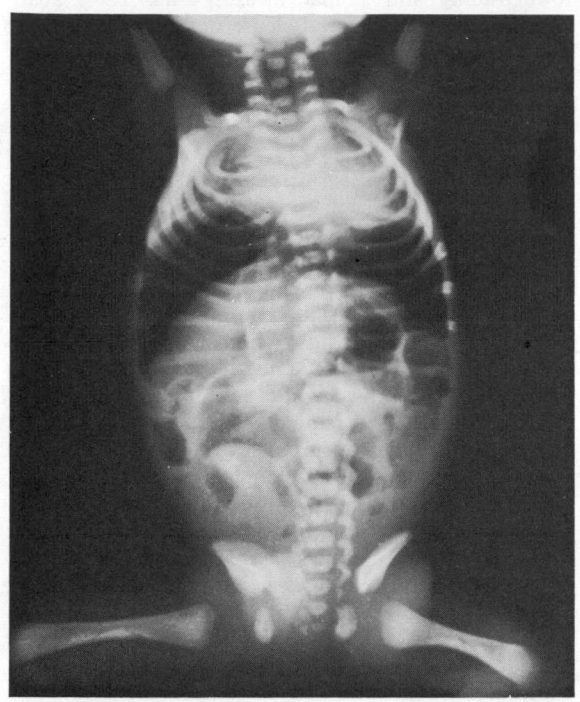

Fig. 36. Plain roentgenogram of a premature infant taken in the *upright* projection illustrating massive pneumoperitoneum due to gastric perforation.

23.27
INTESTINAL OBSTRUCTION
AFTER THE
NEONATAL PERIOD

MARK M. RAVITCH

The term ileus denotes intestinal obstruction of all kinds. *Mechanical ileus* may be due to a variety of causes: compression by a neoplastic or inflammatory mass; constriction in a herniation through a natural orifice or beneath adhesive bands; twists or angulations due to adhesions; volvulus due to abnormal fixation of the bowel at one point or to complete lack of fixation; intussusception; tumors involving the bowel; ingested foreign bodies; fecal concretions; masses of ascarids; congenital atresias and stenoses; meconium ileus; or aganglionosis. The order of probability in the differential diagnosis of intestinal obstruction varies with the age of the patient. In the newborn, atresia, malrotation, aganglionosis, meconium ileus, and meconium plug are chief possibilities. In the first two years after the neonatal period, incarcerated hernia and intussusception are the most common causes of mechanical ileus; thereafter the field broadens.

The onset of mechanical ileus is characterized by intestinal pain which is severe, griping, and periodic. Borborygmi offer corollary evidence of increased peristalsis. In an uncommunicative child, periodic restlessness associated with simultaneous increase in intestinal noises is diagnostic. In general, in low obstruction, distension appears early and the onset of vomiting may be delayed; in high obstruction, vomiting is an early symptom and death may occur without distension. The rapid loss of great quantities of fluid and electrolytes in high obstruction is one of its principal dangers. However, the fluid which backs up in the bowel in low obstruction is just as effectively lost to the body as if it had been vomited. Mechanical intestinal obstruction is an acute surgical emergency. The diagnosis should be made and treatment instituted on the basis of cramps and vomiting in a child in whom another cause is not established for these symptoms. Distension, obstipation, persistent failure to pass either feces or flatus, absence of peristaltic sounds, the presence of intestinal patterns, dehydration, electrolyte disequilibrium and tachycardia, and radiographic evidence of dilated loops and fluid levels are late results of obstruction, seen only in neglected patients. A mass is felt only when ileus is caused by a palpable tumor or when strangulated bowel, as in volvulus, becomes sufficiently engorged and distended to be palpable. Tenderness appears when the bowel is becoming gangrenous or is perforating. Plain x-ray films of the abdomen with the patient erect and recumbent are of great value

may weaken the gastric wall, such as intubation, sepsis, and peptic ulceration. Recent evidence casts some doubt on the widely accepted theory that a congenital deficiency of muscle fibers in the stomach wall is the underlying cause of "spontaneous" gastric rupture.

REFERENCES

Castleton, K. B., and Hatch, F. F. Idiopathic perforation of the stomach in the newborn. Arch. Surg., 78:874, 1958.

Inouye, W. Y., and Evans, G. Neonatal gastric perforation: A report of six cases and a review of 143 cases. Arch. Surg., 88:471, 1964.

Linkner, L. M., and Benson, C. D. Spontaneous perforation of the stomach in the newborn: Analysis of thirteen cases. Amer. J. Surg., 149:525, 1959.

MacGillivray, P. C., Stewart, A. M., and MacFarlane, A. Rupture of the stomach in newborn infants due to congenital defects in gastric musculature. Arch. Dis. Child., 31:56, 1956.

Rees, J. R., and Redo, F. S. Neonatal gastric necrosis and perforation treated by gastrectomy and esophagogastric anastomosis. Surgery, 64:472, 1968.

Shaw, A., Blanc, W. A., Santulli, T. C., and Kaiser, G. Spontaneous rupture of the stomach in the newborn: A clinical and experimental study. Surgery, 58:561, 1965.

Vargas, L. L., Levin, S. M., and Santulli, T. V. Rupture of the stomach in the newborn infant. Surg. Gynec. Obstet., 101:417, 1955.

in revealing distended loops long before they are discovered by physical examination. The presence of fluid levels and distended loops is corroborative evidence of intestinal obstruction, but not required. The barium swallow has no place in the study of this condition.

Treatment is operative and immediate. It is impossible to determine clinically whether one is dealing with a mechanical obstruction which will produce gangrene (volvulus, adhesive bands), or one which may not (intrinsic tumors, kinks due to adhesions), and the surgeon is rarely justified in temporizing. If obstruction is incomplete, there may be some justification for delay and study in spite of the ever-present risk that the obstruction will become complete. The stomach must be emptied before induction of anesthesia, and a Cantor or Miller-Abbott indwelling intestinal tube is best inserted at once. Before operation, rehydration should be started with electrolyte solution; blood and plasma may be needed. Large doses of penicillin and streptomycin have been found to ameliorate the effects of experimental strangulating obstruction. Administration of antibiotics is therefore begun as soon as the diagnosis has been made, and while preparations for operation are under way. Dependence on indwelling tubes for relief of mechanical intestinal obstruction is dangerous and rarely defensible.

After operation, no food or water is given by mouth until passage of feces and flatus demonstrates the patency and muscular sufficiency of the alimentary canal. The period of intravenous alimentation may last a week or more. Particularly in infants, this period will tax the ingenuity of the physician in supplying water, electrolytes, nitrogen, and calories (in that order) without producing anasara or cardiac failure. Fluid removed by intestinal intubation must be replaced parenterally in addition to the calculated daily requirements, and allowance must be made for the loss of protein-containing fluid into edematous bowel wall and into the peritoneal cavity. In infants, early resort is made to parenteral nutrition through centrally placed silastic catheter.

Paralytic ileus may occur in massive peritonitis, after extensive operative procedures, following release of a low mechanical obstruction late in the disease, or in severe bodily injuries or overwhelming infections. The abdomen is greatly distended. There is absence of peristaltic waves, cramps, and borborygmi, and the pain is only a constant dull ache from distension. Intestinal tonus has been destroyed and the alimentary stream is stagnant. Treatment is directed at relief of the primary condition, at decompression of the intestine with indwelling tubes and enemas, and at maintenance of fluid balance. If the bowel is not completely paralyzed, pharmacologic stimulation may be attempted with Pitressin, Prostigmin, or Mecholyl. Pharmacotherapy is most likely to be effective early, before extreme distension has destroyed the tonus of the bowel. These drugs all have potent side effects and must be administered with caution.

Operative intervention is not employed, and resort to ileostomy and similar measures has been abandoned. As in mechanical ileus, nothing is given by mouth until intestinal function has been restored.

Intussusception

Intussusception consists in the invagination of one portion of the intestine into another. Characteristically it affects infants in the first two years of life, although in some parts of the world, as in Nigeria, a later onset is common. In 152 cases seen at the Johns Hopkins Hospital from 1893 to 1948, 61 percent occurred in children from the fourth through the tenth month of life, and the peak of incidence was in the seventh, eighth, and ninth months. It affects males more frequently than females in the ratio of 3:2, and white children more often than Negro children. Most of the victims are well nourished and in good health up to the time of onset. A large number of the patients seem to occupy late positions in their mothers' obstetric careers.

The cause is rarely clear. An area of thickening in the intestinal wall, or a mass incorporated in it, could conceivably act like a foreign body and be propelled by the normal peristaltic activity of the gut. However, in less than 10 percent of the cases, and in only 2.5 percent of those under the age of 2 years, does a polyp, Meckel's diverticulum, nodule of ectopic pancreatic tissue, or other local lesion serve as the exciting cause. The marked development of the lymphoid nodules of the intestine, coinciding as it does with the age incidence of intussusception, has been thought by some to be a contributing factor. Peyer's patches enlarged to tumorlike proportions have been found in some instances. It has been pointed out that in infancy the disproportion between the calibers of cecum and ileum is greater than in later life, facilitating the occurrence of intussusception. Attempts have been made to correlate the incidence of adenovirus in the stools and the occurrence of intussusception, with results which are equivocal.

Of 123 cases in which data were available, in 103 the intussusception began at or near the ileocecal valve, in 14 well up in the small bowel, and in 6 in the colon. Attempts at greater precision in localization are apt to be inaccurate, and the use of compound anatomic designations tends to obfuscation.

PATHOLOGY. Once an intussusception forms, it is clear that the leading point or intussusceptum is constant (Fig. 37), any increase in length occurring at the expense of the sheathing or receiving loop, the intussuscipiens. Compression of the mesenteric vessels between the two inner layers, and the U-shaped angulation of the mesenteric vessels at either end of the intussusceptum (Fig. 38), leads to venous stasis, engorgement, edema, exudation, further vascular compression, and ultimately gangrene. Discharge of blood is one of the first results, and the early evacuation

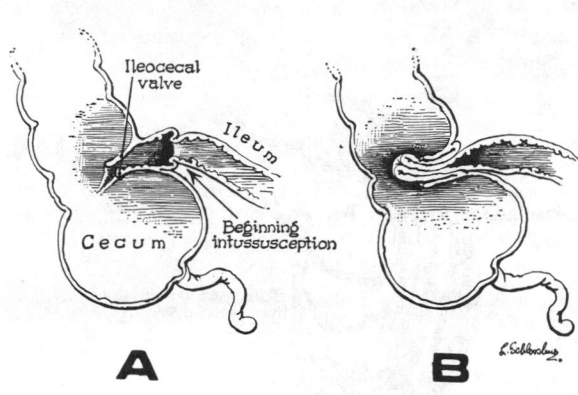

Fig. 37. Onset of intussusception. Diagram of intussusception beginning just proximal to the ileocecal valve, probably the most common site. At A the process is just commencing; at B it has advanced into the ascending colon. The leading point of the intussusception does not change, no matter how far the intussusception progresses.

of quantities of mucus is correlated with the appearance of great numbers of goblet cells in the mucosa of the intussusceptum. The tension of the mesentery on the intussusceptum tends to arch the bowel in a curve with its center at the mesenteric root. Edema and compression produce intestinal obstruction, although most patients should be relieved of their intussusception before they have come to suffer from ileus. The rapidity of appearance of gangrene is highly variable. At times the bowel is viable and reducible after a week, whereas at other times an intussusception may become irreducible within 24 hours. Spontaneous sphacelation of the intussusception and passage of the slough through the rectum is a rarity of chiefly historic interest.

SYMPTOMS.   The clinical picture of acute intussusception is so striking and so characteristic that once seen it should be easily recognized thereafter. A well-nourished infant between 4 and 11 months of age suddenly cries out with obvious abdominal colic and vomits. The attacks of colic recur regularly, in the intervals leaving a flaccid or prostrated infant, but rarely one who appears normal. There is usually one normal stool, evacuating the colonic contents. Thereafter, only blood or blood and mucus are passed. Lassitude or collapse increases. The abdomen is relaxed, soft, and nontender except, at times, directly over the palpable intussusception. Signs of ileus—distension, vomiting, and tachycardia—gradually supervene.

The initial symptom in almost half of the cases is *abdominal pain* and in the other half *vomiting*. In a few cases bloody rectal discharge is the first recognized symptom, but this occurs chiefly in infants in the first year of life who have failed to attract attention with their less dramatic earlier symptoms. The pain is characteristically episodic and cramplike, and at first very severe. Pain may appear to decrease in intensity late in the course of intus-

susception, when intestinal dilation produces atony.

Vomiting appears initially as a reflex symptom but, if the patient has been neglected, takes on the character of the vomiting in intestinal obstruction. In one study, 141 of 152 patients, or 93 percent, vomited before treatment was begun, and 75 percent of infants under 1 year of age who vomited began to vomit in the first three hours of disease. It is of interest that in 8 percent of the cases studied, the patients took and retained food after the onset of symptoms, and in 42 percent they accepted food but were unable to retain it.

Bloody stools are the telltale sign of intussusception. In all, blood was seen in 138 out of 152 cases, or 91 percent. In 95 percent of patients under 2 years of age blood was observed in the stool or in the rectum, but only in 65 percent of those older than 2 years. Frequently one normal stool is passed, after which obstruction becomes complete and no feces or flatus appears. Characteristically, blood is passed admixed with mucus in the classical currant jelly stool, but at times only a thin bloody fluid (prune juice stool) appears. Feces continue to be mixed with the blood in enough instances to warrant caution in making the diagnosis of dysentery solely on the basis of bloody diarrhea, particularly since, in a small number of cases of intussusception, the obstruction is incomplete and there is continuing diarrhea. In many cases blood is first observed on the examining finger, emphasizing the importance of rectal examination.

PHYSICAL EXAMINATION.   The child is characteristically listless and apathetic or even prostrate. The abdomen is flaccid and flat until signs of obstruction supervene and distension appears. More than a third of the patients present with a temperature of 101° F or higher. Fever is more common and higher in the younger infants. Pulse and respiratory rates tend to be elevated. In three-fifths of the cases there is a leucocyte count of over 12,000.

Prostration is present in over half the cases. Great torpor and severe depression are indicative of grave progression of the disease. *Dehydration* is dependent on the extent of the vomiting and of the intestinal obstruction. Surprisingly early in the disease the infant may be severely dehydrated with lax skin and deeply sunken eyes.

Examination of the Abdomen.   The abdomen is at first flat or scaphoid, and in this condition the mass formed by the intussusception may be visible. The abdomen is soft and nontender, although palpation of the mass itself may elicit a little tenderness and muscular resistance. Early in the progress of intussusception the mass passes into the hepatic flexure, behind the liver and right costal margin, and may be difficult or impossible to feel for a time. The mass is most readily felt when thrown into prominence by vigorous peristalsis during a cramp, and is usually described as tubular or sausage-shaped. In almost 90 percent of the cases the mass is felt abdominally or rectally. In six of a group of 152 pa-

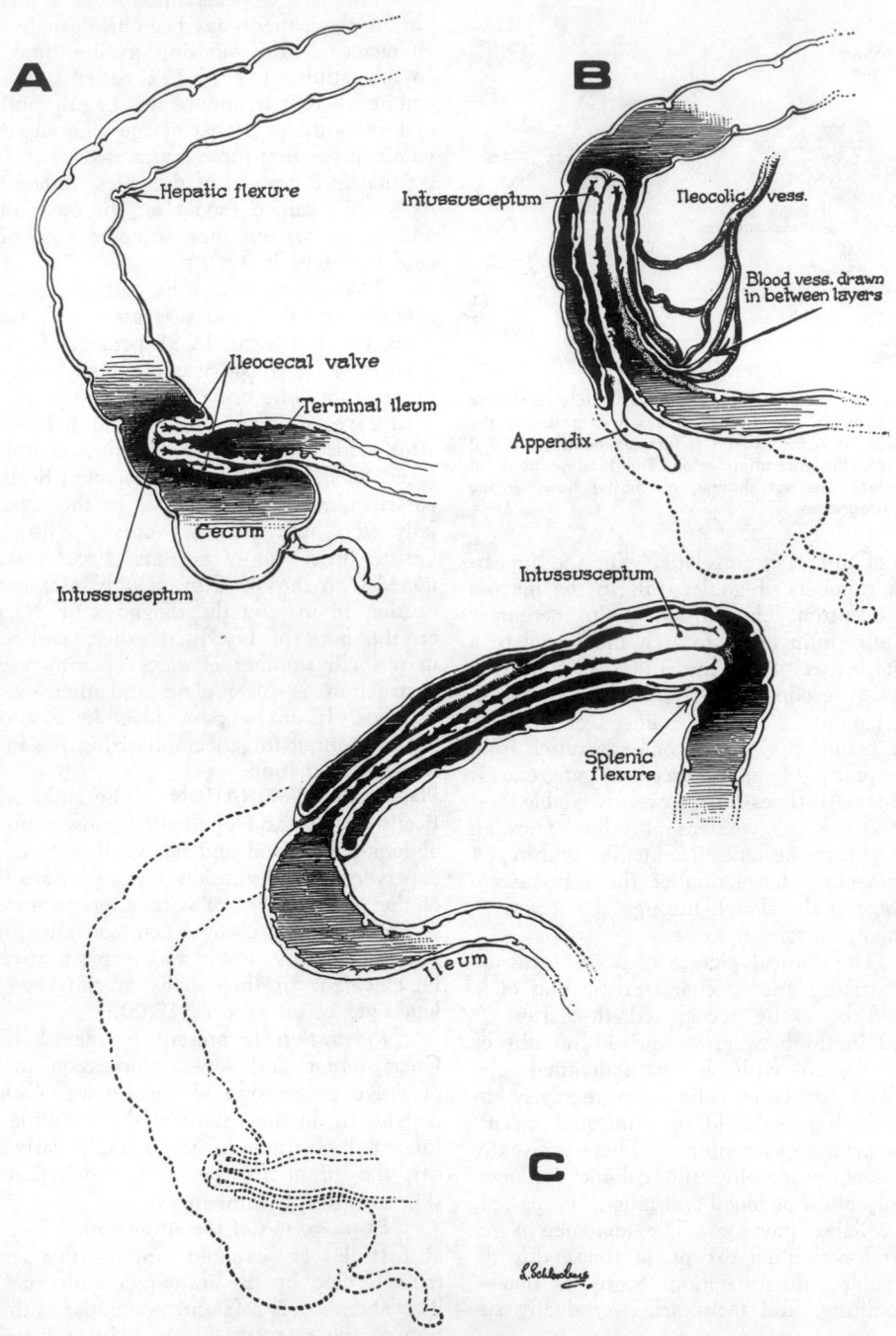

Fig. 38. Progress of intussusception. As the intussusception is passed along by peristaltic action, the appendix is drawn in between its layers (B) and the telescoping of the bowel pulls it away from its normal position (C).

tients, a mass was felt rectally when none was palpable on abdominal examination. In 11 patients, or 7.2 percent, the intussusception presented through the anus.

PROGNOSIS. The duration of the pathologic process is an obvious determining factor in the production of necrosis of the bowel; death is rare in cases recognized and treated in the first 24 hours. Today, death

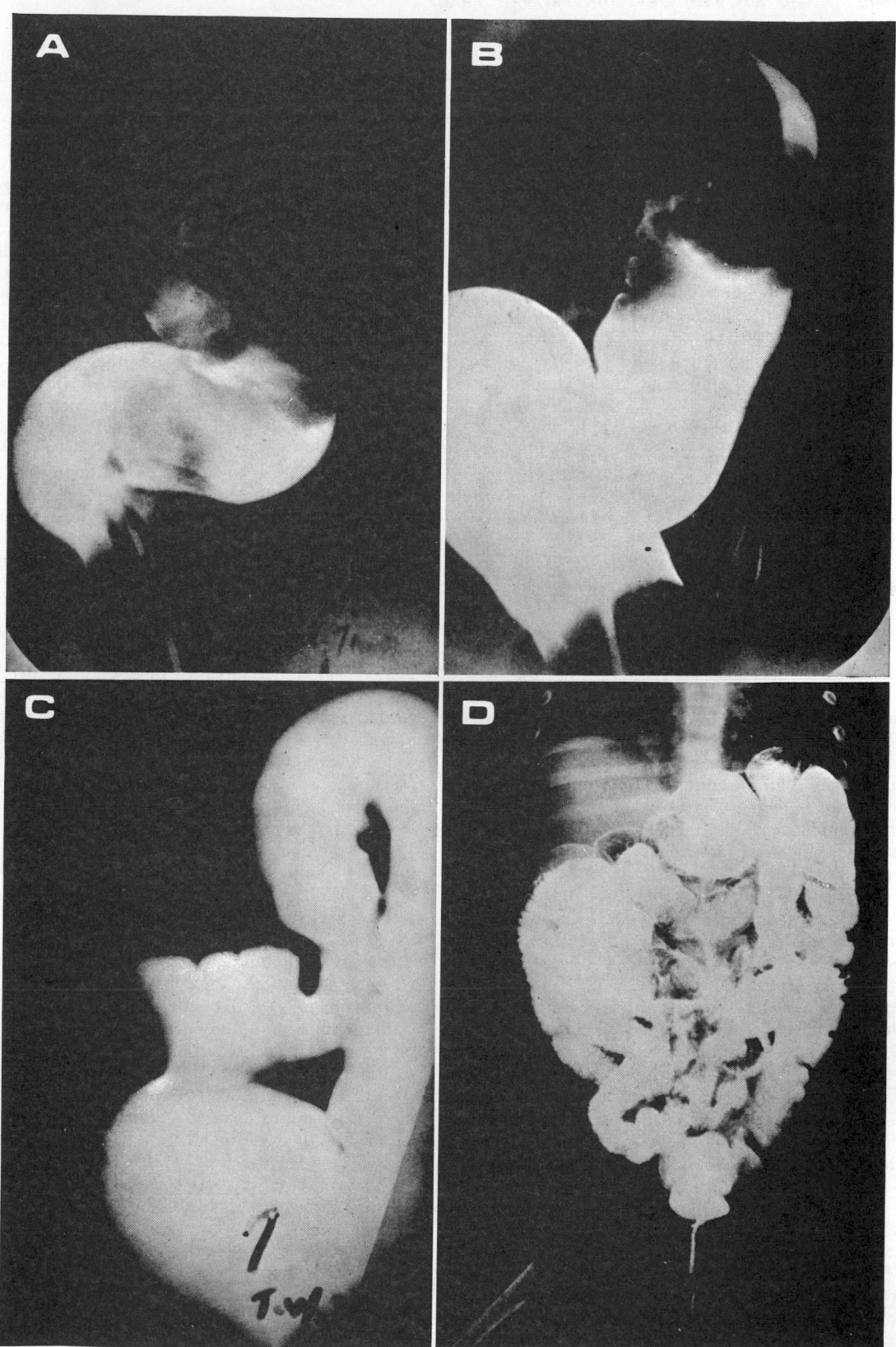

Fig. 39. Hydrostatic pressure reduction in treatment of intussusception. (For details see text.)

from intussusception is altogether a rarity. The mortality rises with the duration of symptoms until one passes 96 hours, at which point there emerge a number of cases of nonstrangulating chronic intussusception which lower the mortality figures. Intussusception may reduce itself spontaneously; we have several records of children with clear histories of repeated episodes precisely like those in which an intussusception was found and treated. High fever is of grave prognostic significance, although in a third of our fatal cases the temperature was below 101° F on admission. Dehydration likewise indicates dangerous progression of the disease. Until fairly recently mortality reports of 20 to 30 percent were common. In most large clinics there has been a steady downward progression in mortality rates from intussusception, and one should now expect no deaths except in patients moribund when first seen.

TREATMENT. Definitive treatment should be instituted at once, subject only to the necessity for administration of fluid or blood to combat dehydration or shock. If the patient is to be operated upon initially, the administration of blood, fluids, and antibiotics is more important than rushing him to the operating room. If he is to be treated by hydrostatic pressure reduction, fluids or blood may be administered at once and reduction begun as the fluids drip into the vein.

The pioneer work of Hirschsprung, the massive statistics of the Scandinavian and Australian groups, our own experience, and the increasing experience of others, indicate hydrostatic pressure reduction to be the method of choice in the treatment of intussusception. The discomfort of hydrostatic pressure reduction is much less than that of operative reduction; the complications, in the absence of anesthesia or incision, are fewer, and the period of hospitalization much shorter.

The operating room should be advised to prepare for operation as soon as the diagnosis of intussusception is made or suspected. As in any intestinal obstruction a tube is passed into the stomach for constant suction. Blood or electrolytes are administered as indicated. The infant is taken at once to the fluoroscopic room and a Foley bag catheter with a 45 ml balloon is inserted into the rectum just beyond the sphincters, and the balloon is distended. The catheter is left ungreased so that it can be expelled only with difficulty, and the buttocks are tightly strapped with adhesive. A barium suspension, from a height of 3 feet above the table, is permitted to run into the bowel under fluoroscopic observation. The barium will usually be seen to run rapidly into the rectum and colon until the head of the barium column meets the point of the intussusceptum (Fig. 39). At this point, the rounded head of the advancing barium column suddenly becomes concave, forming a meniscus around the point of the intussusceptum much as a column of barium in the vagina would outline the cervix. As pressure increases, the meniscus lengthens, the horns extending until suddenly the intussusceptum is pushed back and the meniscus flattens out again. This process is continued until the entire colon fills readily and until barium can be seen to flow freely into the ileum. So long as reduction continues, however slowly, the flow of barium should be uninterrupted and the reduction continued. Successful reduction is denoted by the following criteria: (1) the free flow of barium well into the small bowel; (2) disappearance of the mass; (3) passage of feces or flatus; (4) clinical relief of the patient; and (5) recovery in the stool of charcoal given by mouth. The intussusception can almost invariably be reduced at least to the cecum; and, if there is doubt about complete reduction, it is necessary only to make a small McBurney incision either to confirm the reduction or to complete it by pushing the last small tip of ileum through the ileocecal valve. In a series of 101 patients treated since 1939 by barium enema reduction, there have been two deaths. In the first instance barium enema reduction failed to move the intussusception and operation was immediately undertaken. From the operative note it is apparent that nonviable bowel was reduced and not recognized, and death ultimately resulted. In the other, the barium enema was successful but the child had cystic fibrosis and pneumonia and died from pulmonary causes. In 68, barium enema alone reduced the intussusception while in 33 operative completion was undertaken. In most of these the intussusception was found to have been reduced to the cecum, and in 8 the intussusception was found to have been reduced by the enema.

Reduction of an intussusception by hydrostatic pressure is a surgical procedure to be instituted under the direction of the surgeon while the operating room is held in readiness.

At the completion of successful reduction of the intussusception the child is sent to the ward. Charcoal is instilled in the stomach through a tube and recovered by enema in six hours, further to confirm reduction. As a prophylactic against enteric infection neomycin is administered for several days. Recurrence (2 to 6 percent) is apparently no more likely after hydrostatic pressure reduction than after manual operative reduction; although the adhesions after operation might make recurrence less likely, they are responsible for a significant number of cases of subsequent intestinal obstruction. Resection is more common in patients treated primarily by operation. Clinical and experimental evidence indicates that with 3 feet of pressure, rupture of the bowel does not occur and gangrenous bowel will not be reduced. The incidence of specific pathologic lesions causing intussusception is so low, and the lesions in themselves usually so innocent, that no concern need be felt over the possibility that such a lesion might be missed unless a second intussusception occurs.

REFERENCES

Benson, C. D., Lloyd, J. R., and Fischer, H. Intussusception in infants and children. Arch. Surg., 86:745, 1963.

Gross, R. E., and Ware, P. E. Intussusception in childhood: experiences from 61 cases. New Eng. J. Med., 239:645, 1948.

Hirschsprung, H. Hundertundsieben Fälle von Darminvagination bei kinder, behandelt im könighin louisen-kinderhospital in Köpenhagen wahrend der jahre, 1871-1904; kurze tabellarische darstellung. Mitt. Grenzgeb. Med. u. Chir. (Gena), 14:555, 1905.

Ravitch, M. M. Intussusception in Infants and Children. Springfield, Ill., Charles C Thomas, Publ., 1959.

Wangensteen, O. H. Intestinal Obstruction, 3rd ed. Springfield, Ill., Charles C Thomas, Publ.

23.28
RECTUM AND ANUS

THOMAS V. SANTULLI

Prolapse of the Rectum

Prolapse is the abnormal descent or protrusion through the anus of one or more coats of the rectum. When mucous membrane alone descends, the prolapse is said to be partial or incomplete; if all coats of the bowel are involved, it is complete (procidentia). In the latter, the mucosal folds of the protruding mass are concentric; in partial prolapse they are arranged radially. In infancy, the rectal mucosa, which is loosely attached to the underlying muscularis, may be normally redundant. Mucosal prolapse is frequently seen under the age of 3 years, most of the cases occurring in the first year. Certain anatomic features in the young age group predispose to prolapse: the nearly vertical course of the rectum, which has little of the lateral and anteroposterior curves of the adult organ, the flat surfaces of the infantile sacrum and coccyx, the relatively low position of the rectum in relation to other pelvic organs, and the lack of support furnished by the levator ani muscles. Spontaneous cure usually results with increasing age and normal growth, as the pelvis loses its vertical plane, the sacrum becomes hollowed out, the muscular layers of the rectum and its supports are better developed, and the mucosal redundancy disappears.

Any condition which increases the intraabdominal pressure may precipitate prolapse—the straining effort at stool as in constipation, diarrhea, polyps, worms, phimosis, whooping-cough, and excessive vomiting. Malnutrition with consequent absorption of the ischiorectal fat is a contributing factor. Repeated episodes of prolapse of the rectum occur frequently in infants and young children with fibrocystic disease of the pancreas, probably related to the frequent stools and malnutrition. Prolapse usually disappears with improved dietary control. It has been stated that cystic fibrosis of the pancreas is the most common cause of prolapse of the rectum in the pediatric age group, and its repeated occurrence in a patient known to have a ravenous appetite is suggestive of the disease. Complete prolapse sometimes occurs in debilitated or malnourished patients. It may also be seen in children with meningomyeloceles as a result of partial or complete sphincter paralysis and in patients with exstrophy of the urinary bladder.

The protrusion usually comes on gradually at stool and recedes spontaneously. When recurrent, it often remains permanently extruded and, rarely, may become strangulated or gangrenous. Blood and mucus may be passed by rectum due to the engorgement. Secondary inflammatory changes occur in the mucosa, resulting in ulceration.

Although most prolapses reduce spontaneously, some may require manual replacement. The lesions usually regress with growth of the child. They can frequently be managed by simple measures or by correcting the cause. Constipation should be controlled by stool softeners; paregoric may be helpful in checking tenesmus in diarrhea; polyps should be removed. In severe and chronic cases operative intervention may be necessary, consisting of excision of the prolapsed mucosa, or temporary packing of the presacral space with gauze through a posterior approach in order to produce adherence of the rectum to the sacrum. Rarely are more radical procedures necessary in children.

Fissure in Ano

Anal fissure or anal ulcer is a superficial tear in the anal canal at the mucocutaneous junction. It occurs commonly in infancy as the result of trauma from the passage of a hard, bulky stool or explosive diarrhea. In infancy, the lesions are usually multiple and occur in any part of the anus; in older children and adults, they are usually located posteriorly, sometimes anteriorly, but rarely in the lateral quadrants. In the acute fissure, the base is shallow and the edges are clean, soft, and usually sharply defined. In the more chronic form, as the edges become thickened and undermined, there will frequently be found a tag of edematous skin at the peripheral or distal end of the fissure, the "sentinel pile." Severe pain on defecation and bleeding are the cardinal symptoms. The blood is characteristically bright red, streaking the surface of the stool. Constipation may be the cause or the result of a fissure in ano.

Almost all of the fissures in this age group will heal with conservative measures consisting of warm baths, drying and anesthetic ointments, and treatment of constipation with stool-softeners. The instillation of warm olive or mineral oil before defecation, and gentle dilation of the external and sphincter are helpful. Treatment should be continued for several weeks after the apparent healing and disappearance of symptoms. If these simple measures fail and the fissure assumes a chronic appearance with fibrosis and undermined skin edges, surgical excision is necessary.

Hemorrhoids

Hemorrhoids are not often seen in children but may be found in patients with chronic constipation. True internal hemorrhoids are rare; external hemorrhoids and tags are more common. Pain, protrusion, and bleeding are the usual symptoms. Conservatism with treatment of the underlying constipation will usually correct the condition. Operation is rarely necessary but may be needed for acute external thrombosed hemorrhoids.

REFERENCES

di Sant'Agnese, P. A., and Vidaurreta, A. M. Cystic fibrosis of the pancreas. J.A.M.A., 172:2065, 1960.
Fowler, R. Anatomy and treatment of rectal prolapse in childhood. Austr. Paediat. J., 3:90, 1967.
Kulczycki, L. L., and Schwachman, H. Studies in cystic fibrosis of the pancreas: Occurrence of rectal prolapse. New Eng. J. Med., 259:409, 1958.
Santulli, T. V. Prolapse of the rectum. In Mustard, W. T., et al., eds., Pediatric Surgery, 2nd ed. Chicago, Year Book Publishers, 1969, p. 1007.

23.29
ASCITES

THOMAS V. SANTULLI

Ascites denotes an excessive collection of fluid in the general peritoneal cavity. The term is usually confined to noninflammatory extravasations with a low specific gravity containing few cellular elements. The fluid is amber and usually clear. It is seen in nephrosis, heart failure, constrictive pericarditis, portal hypertension due to cirrhosis of the liver or thrombosis of the portal or hepatic veins, and nutritional edema. It may accompany any condition causing pressure on the inferior vena cava above the entrance of the hepatic veins. Fluid accumulation within the peritoneal cavity is also encountered in some cases of tuberculous peritonitis and advanced abdominal malignancy.

The symptoms consist of abdominal distention, fullness, and discomfort due to the fluid accumulation. Small amounts of fluid in the peritoneal cavity are difficult to detect. Large amounts are, as a rule, easy to identify. The abdomen is moderately or greatly distended, the skin of the abdominal wall is tense or shiny, and the umbilicus is often pouting. There is dilation of the superficial veins, especially about the umbilicus. With significant accumulations a fluid wave can be elicited. In infants and children shifting

dullness alone is not pathognomonic of ascites, since it may be caused by a change in position of the intestinal contents.

Cysts of the omentum or mesentery, celiac syndrome with conspicuous abdominal distention, and, occasionally, severe megacolon are to be differentiated from ascites. Rarely, hydronephrosis may be difficult to distinguish.

The prognosis and treatment depend on the cause.

Chylous Ascites

This is a rare form of ascites in which the abdominal fluid contains fat. The color may be bluish-white, milky, or creamy, and the fluid after standing will have at its surface a lipid layer, the thickness of which serves as a rough measure of total fat content; after a diet rich in fat, the content has been as high as 5 percent in some cases.

Cases which appear in the first year of life are usually due to congenital malformation of the central or peripheral lymph channels. Acquired cases are due to obstruction of the thoracic duct, which may result from neoplasm, inflammation, or obstruction to the intestine, as in malrotation or incarcerated inguinal hernia. Other causes are filariasis with obstruction of the thoracic duct by the parent worm, trauma to the thorax or abdomen, or surgical injury of the duct.

The diagnosis of chylous ascites, or chyloperitoneum, is made by aspiration and inspection of the fluid. The fat content of the fluid varies directly with the quantity of fat in the diet; its protein content usually remains more or less constant at 2 or 3 gm per 100 ml.

The treatment is directed at the cause of the condition if this is known. In the absence of obvious cause, conservative management consisting of a low-fat, high-protein, high-vitamin diet and aspiration of the fluid is indicated. In most cases the fluid reaccumulates rapidly and repeated paracenteses may be necessary. In some instances the patient may recover after several aspirations without the cause ever being known. When many aspirations are necessary, the loss of fat may be minimized by a low-fat diet or medium-chain triglycerides; but loss of protein, which is considerable, is less easily controlled, and hypoproteinemia may result. In most cases, surgical exploration is indicated to search for the cause.

REFERENCES

Gribetz, D., and Kanof, A. Chylous ascites in infancy. Pediatrics, 7:632, 1951.
Nix, J. T., Albert, M., Dugas, J. E., and Wendt, D. L. Chylothorax and chylous ascites; a study of 302 selected cases. Amer. J. Gastroent., 28:40, 1957.
Vasko, J. S., and Tapper, R. I. The surgical significance of chylous ascites. Arch. Surg., 95:355, 1967.
Warwick, W. J., Holman, R. T., Quie, P. G., and Good,

R. A. Chylous ascites and lymphedema. Amer. J. Dis. Child., 98:317, 1959.

Wegner, E. S. Congenital chylous ascites, apparently cured by Routte's operation (venous peritoneal anastomosis). Amer. J. Dis. Child., 47:586, 1934.

Whittlesey, R. H., Ingram, R. P., and Riker, W. L. Chylous ascites in childhood, report of five cases. Ann. Surg., 142:1013, 1955.

23.30
NEOPLASMS OF THE ALIMENTARY TRACT

MARK M. RAVITCH and
THOMAS V. SANTULLI

Benign polyps are the most common intestinal tumors. They usually are confined to the colon, and the most frequent symptom is bleeding. The blood is generally bright red and may be present either on the surface of the stool, mixed with the stool, or occasionally passed free into the toilet bowl; the character of bleeding is determined to some degree by the distance of the lesion from the anus. Rarely is the bleeding in large amounts. Diagnosis is made by digital examination of the rectum or by proctosigmoidoscopy; occasionally the lesion may protrude at the anus.

Peculiar to children are juvenile polyps; they are usually single, occasionally multiple, but only under exceptional circumstances are they numerous. They may be sessile or pedunculated, and may reach a size of 2 or 3 cm. They are most commonly found in the rectum. Grossly they are smooth and spherical, and histologically the surface is covered by only a single layer of flattened cells which have frequently been entirely abraded. The stroma of the polyp is composed of a loose myxomatous tissue in which there are numerous large mucus lakes, lined by tall columnar cells. Serial section of such a polyp shows that these mucus lakes communicate with the surface, and the histologic appearance is entirely different from the arborization, with numerous irregular clefts, of a true adenomatous polyp. Juvenile polyps are self-limited and possibly inflammatory in origin. They do not lead to the development of malignancy, and they frequently become infarcted and are expelled. The differential diagnosis between a juvenile and an adenomatous polyp cannot be made radiologically. If one is within reach of the sigmoidoscope and removed in this manner and found to be a juvenile polyp, there is no need for operation to identify the nature of other more proximal polyps in the same child.

Adenomatous polyps in the rectum are of chief interest because of bleeding and occasional prolapse. In the small bowel they are of interest chiefly because of their propensity for causing intussusception, the usual cause of their discovery. They may cause painless bleeding and diarrhea. Polyps are occasionally multiple, and repeated operations for intussusception have been recorded in some patients with numbers of polyps. There are a number of syndromes of familial involvement with intestinal polyps. One of the best known is the Peutz-Jeghers syndrome, in which scattered polyps of colon, small intestine, and stomach occur in association with the characteristic melanin pigmentation of the lips, buccal mucosa, tongue, palms, and soles. The Peutz-Jeghers polyps are hamartomatous and have almost never been known to lead to malignant degeneration.

On the other hand, *polypoid adenomatosis of the colon,* one of several familial syndromes associated with colonic polyps, invariably leads to the development of cancer if the colon or entire colonic mucosa is not removed by one or another operation. Bloody diarrhea is the usual presentation. Symptoms of familial polyposis rarely become apparent until after the first decade. Carcinomatous degeneration in childhood has been reported.

Lipomas, myomas, angiomas, and other tumors of the small bowel occur infrequently. The first two manifest themselves chiefly by obstructive symptoms, and the angiomas by bleeding. Occasionally the angiomatous process may be so diffuse as to involve the entire small intestine and make resection impossible. At operation the angiomas may be remarkably innocent, showing only unimpressive telangiectatic vessels on the serosal surface and a questionable thickening and darkening of the mucosa here and there.

Any resectable tumor of the bowel should be removed, since even benign tumors may have serious consequences by serving as the focal point of intussusception. Carcinoids, or tumors of the argentaffin cells of Kultchitsky in the mucosa of the small intestine, are of low-grade malignancy, late to metastasize, and often cured by simple resection. In children they are most likely to be discovered accidentally in a resected appendix, the most common sites for such tumors being the appendix and the terminal ileum. In the usual situation the carcinoid is not recognized at the time of the appendectomy and is discovered by the pathologist. Under these circumstances no further operation need be undertaken, for carcinoids of the appendix are rarely malignant.

Lymphosarcoma is the most common malignant tumor of the bowel in childhood. It is an insidious tumor, usually extending to the point of total infiltration of the intestine and becoming incurable before causing any symptoms, which are chiefly those of intestinal obstruction. Bleeding is a rare symptom. In the terminal ileum, the site of predilection for this lesion, lymphosarcoma tends to produce chronic intussusception into the cecum, the occurrence of which, after infancy, should lead to suspicion of the correct diagnosis. Resection of the primary mass, subsequent roentgen therapy, and the addition of the currently available chemotherapeutic agents are followed by only occasional cures.

Ectopic pancreatic tissue occurs in the stomach, duodenum, or ileum. In many of the cases reported, the ectopic pancreatic tissue was found in a Meckel's diverticulum. Submucosal nodules of ectopic pancreatic tissue are an occasional cause of the intussusception, but rarely cause trouble otherwise.

REFERENCES

Knox, W. G., Miller, R. E., Begg, C. F., and Zintel, H. A. Juvenile polyps of the colon, a clinico-pathologic analysis of 75 polyps in 43 patients. Surgery, 48:201, 1960.

Mestel, A. L. Lymphosarcoma of the small intestine in infancy and childhood. Ann. Surg., 149:87, 1959.

Middelkamp, J. N., and Haffner, H. Carcinoma of the colon in children. Pediatrics, 32:558, 1963.

Ravitch, M. M. Polypoid adenomatosis of the entire gastrointestinal tract. Ann. Surg., 128:283, 1948.

Riner, L., Silverstein, J., and Tope, J. W. Benign neoplasms of small intestine—collective review. Int. Abstr. Surg., 102:1, 1956.

Santulli, T. V. Intestinal polyposis associated with mucocutaneous pigmentation (Peutz-Jeghers Syndrome). In Mustard, W. T., et al., eds., Pediatric Surgery, 2nd ed. Chicago, Year Book Publishers, 1969, p. 891.

Troll, M. M. Aberrant pancreatic and gastric tissue in the intestinal tract. Arch. Path., 38:375, 1944.

Wenzl, J. E., Bartholomew, L. G., Hollenback, G. A., and Stickler, G. B. Gastrointestinal polyposis with mucocutaneous pigmentation in children (Peutz-Jeghers Syndrome). Pediatrics, 28:655, 1961.

chapter 24

THE LIVER

LAWRENCE M. GARTNER and IRWIN M. ARIAS, Associate Editors

In recent years advances in biochemical and morphologic techniques and concepts have contributed greatly to the understanding of the pathogenesis, diagnosis, and treatment of liver disease in infants and children. This chapter will review these liver diseases, emphasizing their pathophysiology.

24.1

SUBCELLULAR ANATOMY OF THE LIVER PARENCHYMAL CELL

SIDNEY GOLDFISCHER and MARCUS H. MA

The introduction of electron microscopy to the study of the liver has resulted in identification of subcellular anatomic structures (organelles) which were unknown a few years ago. This section will summarize current knowledge of the ultrastructure of the hepatic parenchymal cell. Much of this knowledge has been derived from studies combining the use of electron microscopic, histochemical, biochemical, and cell fractionation techniques. For example, lysosomes, the most recently discovered class of organelles, were described by biochemists on the basis of their high levels of acid phosphatase and other acid hydrolase activities and their sedimentation characteristics in the ultracentrifuge. Their morphologic equivalent was not suspected until lysosome-rich fractions of liver were examined in the electron microscope. These fractions contained large numbers of particles previously described as pericanalicular "dense bodies." Application of a relatively simple staining procedure, which permitted visualization of the reaction product of acid phosphatase activity as a lead-phosphate precipitate, confirmed the identification of "dense bodies" as lysosomes.

There have been numerous electron microscopic studies of pathologic liver but surprisingly few studies of normal liver. Although the detail seen in electron micrographs is impressive, caution must be used in interpretation because of artifacts and inadequate sampling. Interpretation of static images must also be tempered by the consideration that the liver cell is synthesizing, conjugating, hydrolyzing, storing, excreting, secreting, and absorbing a variety of materials including proteins, lipids, carbohydrates, and heavy metals, and probably doing all of these at the same time.

The major morphologically recognized components of the parenchymal liver cell will be discussed in the following sections and are schematically represented in Figure 1 and illustrated in Figures 2 and 3.

The Plasma Membrane

The plasma membrane is not simply a container delimiting the cytoplasm of the hepatocyte, but is an active participant in the functioning of the cell. The sinusoidal, lateral, and bile canalicular portions of the plasma membrane differ in appearance and enzymatic activity. The surface area of the membranes

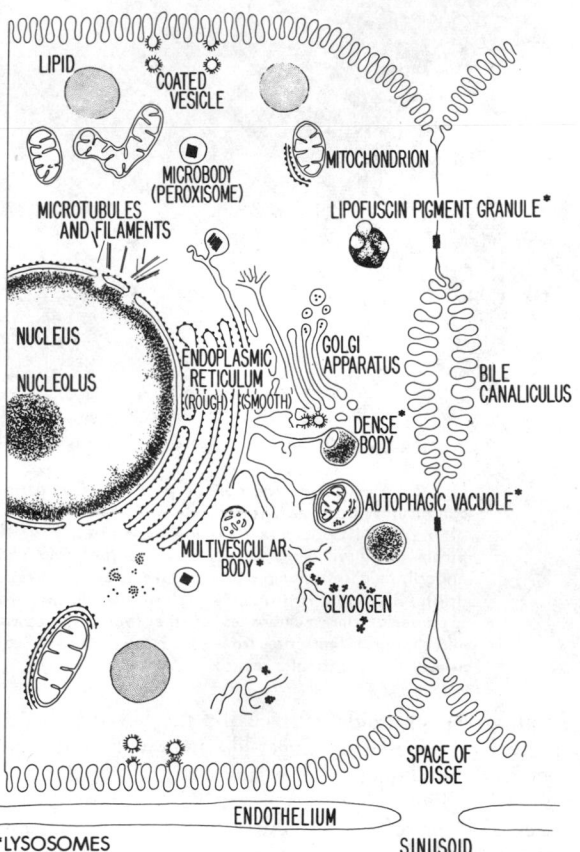

Fig. 1. Rat liver cell. The fine structure of this cell, which has been studied most extensively by electron microscopists, is similar to that of human hepatocytes. In man, the smooth endoplasmic reticulum often appears as irregularly shaped vesicles and the peroxisomes only rarely have cores.

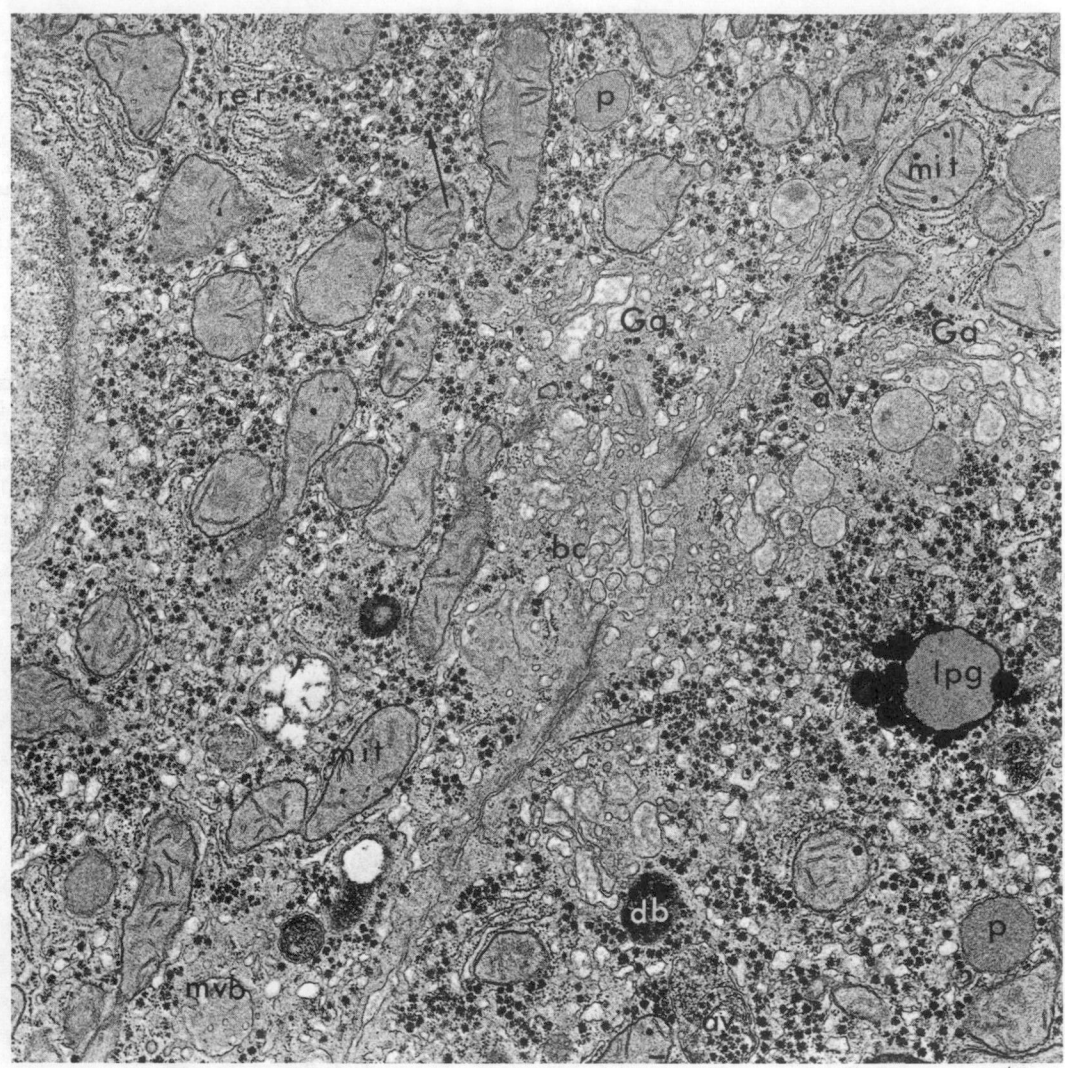

Fig. 2. Electron micrograph of portions of two normal human liver cells. Microvilli project into the bile canaliculus (bc) which is formed by invagination of adjacent plasma membranes. The saccules and vesicles of the Golgi apparatus (Ga) are most often near the bile canaliculus. Also seen in this area of the cytoplasm are four types of lysosomes: autophagic vacuoles (av) containing glycogen and fragments of the endoplasmic reticulum, dense bodies (db), multivesicular bodies (mvb), and a lipofuscin pigment granule (lpg). Glycogen is present in close association with smooth endoplasmic reticulum (arrows pointing to glycogen). The membranes of the rough endoplasmic reticulum (rer) are studded with ribosomes. The mitochondria (mit) are traversed by cristae and contain dense granules. Peroxisomes have a moderately dense, finely granular matrix.

forming the sinusoidal surface and the bile canaliculi is greatly increased by finger-like microvilli that project into the lumen of the sinusoid and canaliculus (Fig. 2). Tight junctions, formed by fusion of the external layers of the opposing plasma membranes on each side of the bile canaliculus, probably serve to limit direct exchange of material between blood and bile. The canalicular membrane has high levels of hydrolase activity toward all nucleoside phosphates, including adenosine triphosphate (ATP). Such "ATPase" activity suggests that active transport may occur in canalicular membranes. In bile secretory

failure of intrahepatic or extrahepatic origin in rats, canalicular microvilli are distorted and lose their nucleoside phosphatase activity. The lateral and sinusoidal surfaces show greatly increased "ATPase" activity, which may represent a change in polarity of hepatocellular excretory processes during bile secretory failure.

There is no acceptable morphologic evidence for the pathways by which bile constituents move out of the liver cell into the canaliculus. This suggests that the structures involved in bile secretion are beyond the resolution of current electron microscopic

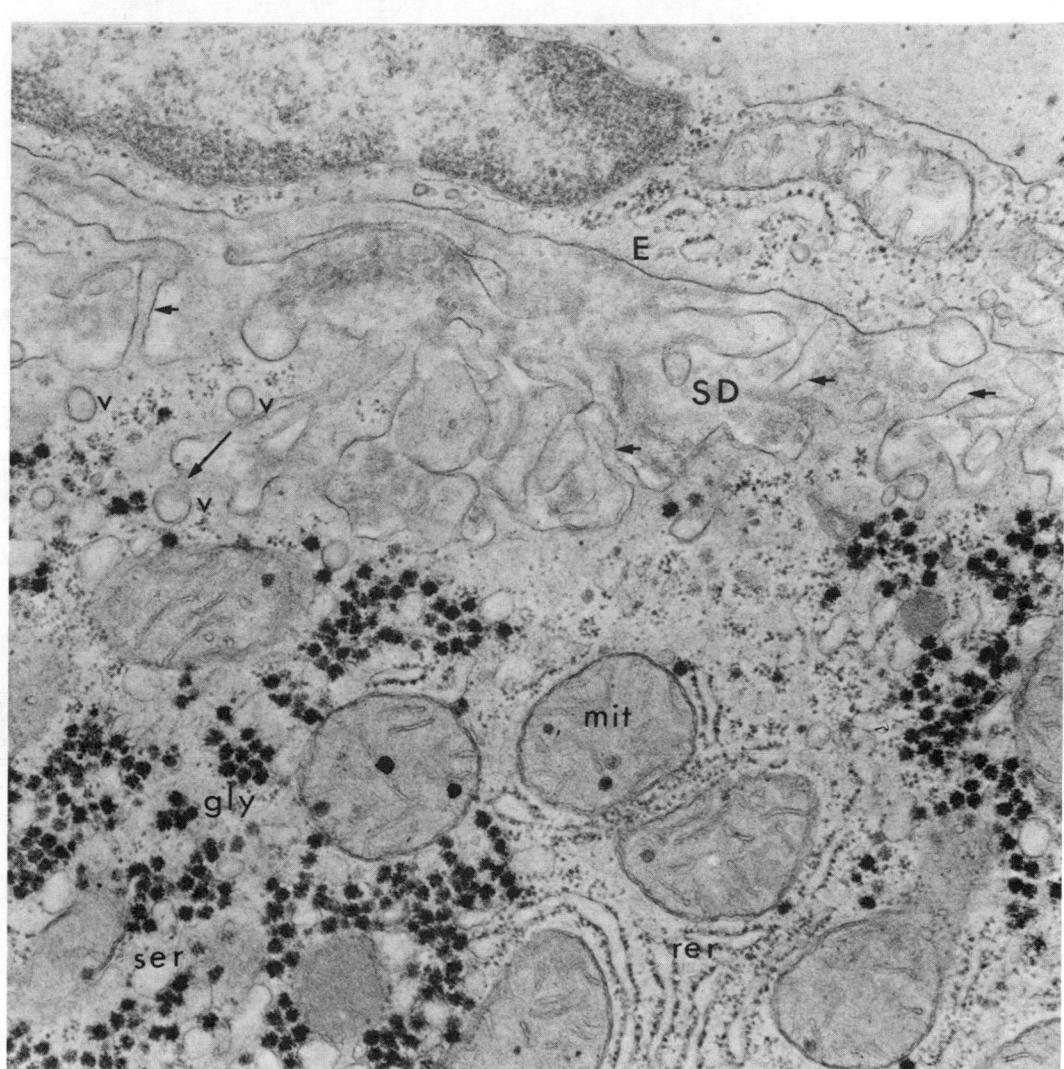

Fig. 3. Sinusoidal aspect of a normal human liver cell. Between the endothelial cell (E) and the liver cell is the space of Disse (SD). Microvilli (short arrows) project into the space of Disse. Immediately beneath the sinusoidal surface are several coated vesicles (v) one of which appears as if forming from the plasma membrane (long arrows). Mitochondria (mit), rough endoplasmic reticulum (rer), smooth endoplasmic reticulum (ser), and glycogen (gly) are also seen.

techniques. The sinusoidal surface appears to be a two-way passage. Lipids, glucose, amino acids, and other materials enter the liver across this membrane; cholesterol, albumin, and fibrinogen and the other proteins involved in coagulation are secreted into the circulation across this membrane. Small, "coated vesicles" formed from the plasma membrane probably function in transporting proteins and lipids across the sinusoidal membrane into the cytoplasm (Fig. 3).

The Nucleus

The nucleus functions as the principal site for the regulation of hereditary characteristics. The deoxyri-

bonucleic acid (DNA) of the nucleus is localized in the chromatin, which represents the chromosomes of interphase nuclei. Heterochromatin is that portion of the chromosomes that has remained condensed during interphase and is considered relatively inactive. It appears as densely stained clumps of fine fibrous material largely around the nuclear periphery and adjacent to the nucleolus. The metabolically active euchromatin, however, is poorly stained and difficult to identify in routine ultrathin sections.

Ribonucleic acid (RNA) is present in the nucleolus. The nucleolus consists of a granular and a fibrous component. Available evidence indicates that the fibrous component contains protein and DNA and the granular component contains RNA molecules

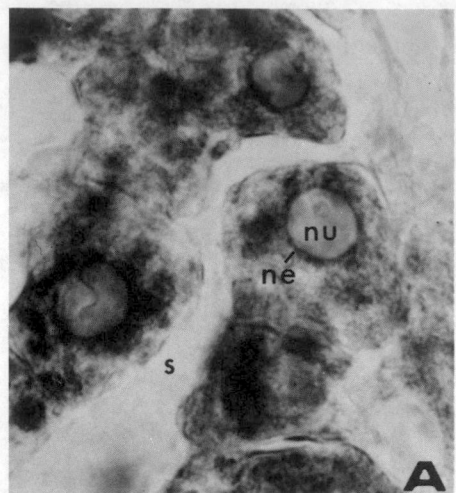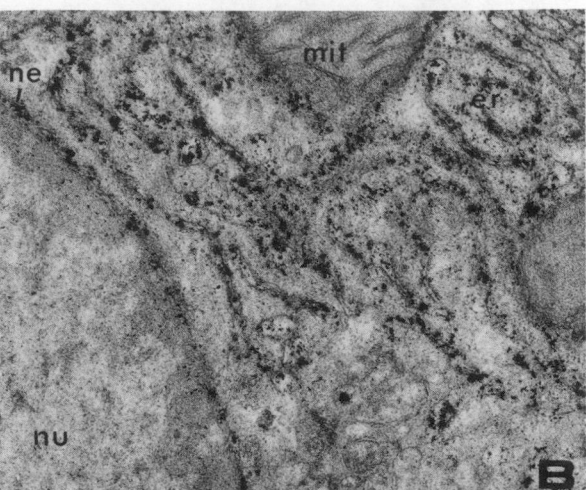

Fig. 4. Rat liver sections incubated to visualize a microsomal enzyme, glucose-6-phosphatase. Enzyme reaction product "stains" the nuclear envelope (ne), and the endoplasmic reticulum (er), indicating that glucose-6-phosphatase is present at both sites. This is seen in light (A) and electron micrographs (B). The nucleus (nu) and mitochondria (mit) are unstained. (Electron micrograph by Dr. Edward Essner.)

that are precursors to the RNA of the large ribosomal subunit.

The nucleus is surrounded by a pair of membranes which enclose a space called the perinuclear cisterna. The outer membrane is studded with ribosomes, and the nuclear cisterna is continuous with and enzymatically similar to endoplasmic reticulum (Fig. 4). The paired nuclear membranes often fuse and show discontinuities called nuclear pores. It is not known whether the "pore" represents a true hole or whether it is sealed by a "diaphragm" derived from the fused membranes.

The Endoplasmic Reticulum

The endoplasmic reticulum is a continuous system of rough (granular) and smooth surfaced (agranular) cisternae and tubules. Continuities are often found between the nuclear envelope and the rough surfaced endoplasmic reticulum, and available evidence strongly suggests that the smooth endoplasmic reticulum is formed from the rough endoplasmic reticulum (Figs. 1 and 2). The membranes of the rough endoplasmic reticulum are studded with ribosomes, which consist of ribonucleic acid and protein and are the sites at which amino acids are incorporated into protein. Free ribosomes are also seen in the cytoplasm as single granules and in ordered arrays. Studies of fetal liver suggest that the rough endoplasmic reticulum evolves from an early stage in which ribosomes are scattered freely in the cytoplasm and subsequently form "polysomes," from which membranes of the rough endoplasmic reticulum are derived.

Protein, after synthesis by ribosomes on the rough endoplasmic reticulum, is believed to be transported in the cisternae of the endoplasmic reticulum. This has been demonstrated in guinea pig pancreas by Palade et al. Triglycerides are apparently synthesized in the endoplasmic reticulum of liver from fatty acids absorbed at the cell surface. In rats fed orotic acid, β-lipoprotein synthesis is deficient. Consequently, lipid accumulates within the cisternae of the endoplasmic reticulum. This is similar to what occurs in the intestinal epithelium of children with absence of β-lipoproteins (acanthocytosis), where massive amounts of triglycerides accumulate and conversion to chylomicra does not take place. It is believed that protein and lipids move from the endoplasmic reticulum to the Golgi apparatus. The smooth endoplasmic reticulum is the main site of drug-metabolizing enzymes. In rats, many compounds such as phenobarbital appear to induce proliferation of the smooth endoplasmic reticulum. Glucuronyl transferase, which catalyzes the formation of glucuronides of bilirubin, various drugs, and endogenous steroids, is found in the smooth endoplasmic reticulum. Newborn infants metabolize various drugs poorly and have reduced enzyme activity associated with the smooth endoplasmic reticulum. Morphologic studies in newborn and fetal rats reveal comparatively little smooth endoplasmic reticulum until approximately the end of the first day of life. The smooth endoplasmic reticulum also appears to be the site at which peroxisomes (microbodies), some dense bodies, and autophagic vacuoles are formed.

The microsomal fraction of liver, obtained by ultracentrifugation, is composed mainly of endoplasmic reticulum. In addition to various drug-metabolizing enzymes and glucuronyl transferase, the microsomal fraction also contains many other enzymes including those concerned with the intermediary metabolism of proteins, lipids, and carbohydrates, and enzymes of heme biosynthesis and of an electron transport chain. It is possible to separate the microsomes into smooth and rough endoplasmic reticulum subfractions. Thus, most drug-metabolizing enzymes are localized in the smooth endoplasmic reticulum but the precise localizations of the other enzymes mentioned have not been fully elucidated. Several microsomal enzymes, including glucose-6-phosphatase, which is absent in type 1 (von Gierke's) glycogen storage disease, can be demonstrated in the endoplasmic reticulum of normal liver by cytochemical staining methods (Fig. 4).

The Golgi Apparatus

First described in 1898 by Camillio Golgi, the "internal reticular apparatus" was the subject of bitter controversy for fifty years. At a time when most cytologists concluded that the Golgi apparatus was an artifact, electron microscopy revealed the characteristic arrays of parallel saccules (Figs. 1 and 2). Although unimpressive in size, the fine structure of the hepatocyte Golgi apparatus is typical and consists of three or four parallel saccules that are dilated at the edges and associated with vacuoles and small vesicles that are probably derived from the saccules (Fig. 2).

Much remains to be learned concerning the role of the Golgi apparatus, particularly in the liver cell. In glandular epithelium, the great size and apical localization of the Golgi apparatus, and its fluctuation with the functional state of the gland, have pointed to an important role in secretion. In many types of cells secretory material is first seen in the saccules of the Golgi apparatus and becomes "packaged" as a granule within a membrane-bound vacuole, which then buds off from the terminal dilatations of the saccule. In the liver, similar packaging of lipoproteins previously formed in the endoplasmic reticulum has been demonstrated. The lipoprotein-laden vacuoles, having separated from the Golgi saccule, then move to the sinusoidal surface to discharge their contents into the space of Disse.

The predominantly pericanalicular location of the Golgi apparatus suggests that it plays a role in the elaboration and transport of bile. In bile secretory failure in the rat, the Golgi apparatus is greatly enlarged (Fig. 5). The Golgi apparatus appears to be the site in which sugars are incorporated into glycoproteins. Reasonably pure Golgi apparatus fractions have recently been isolated from rat and bovine liver and other tissues. UDP galactose, N-acetylglucosamine galactosyl transferase, and other sugar transferases are concentrated in these fractions.

Peroxisomes (Microbodies)

Highly purified preparations of intact rat liver microbodies are greatly enriched in four oxidases; three of these, uricase (urate oxidase), L-d-hydroxy acid oxidase, and D-amino acid oxidase, form hydrogen peroxide which is in turn destroyed by the fourth oxidase, catalase. This link to hydrogen peroxide metabolism has led to the suggestion that these granules be called peroxisomes.

Peroxisomes are round organelles that are slightly smaller than mitochondria and are delimited by a single membrane. They appear to be formed by the smooth endoplasmic reticulum and are distributed throughout the cytoplasm. The peroxisome of many species contains a core or nucleoid which may be crystal like. In general, a correlation exists between the presence or absence of microbody cores and the presence or absence of uricase activity, but there are exceptions. In human livers, cores are only rarely found.

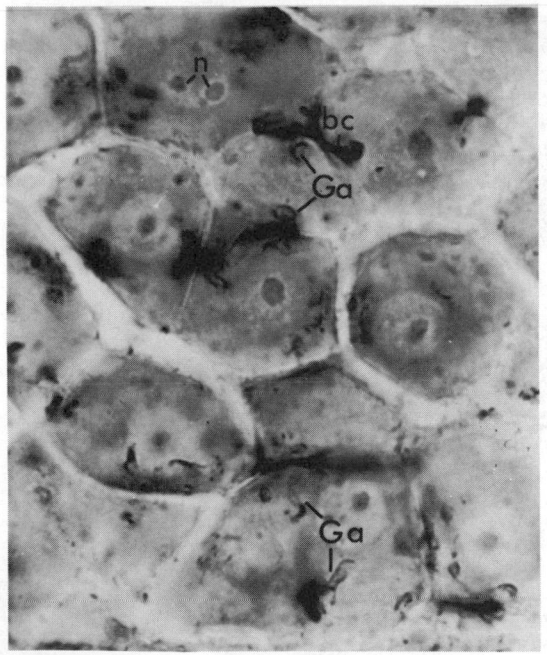

Fig. 5. Liver obtained from a rat treated with icterogenin, an alkaloid that inhibits the capacity of the liver to transport conjugated bilirubin into bile. Incubated for thiamine pyrophosphatase (TPPase) activity. The membranes of the Golgi apparatus (Ga) have high levels of TPPase activity and are visualized in this preparation. Segments of bile canaliculi (bc) also hydrolyze TPP and are seen to be wider than Golgi saccules. The Golgi apparatus appears larger than in normal animals. Nucleoli (n) are lightly stained in TPPase preparations.

Microtubules and Filaments

Thin filaments which are 40 to 50 angstroms wide and microtubules which are 250 to 300 angstroms wide are concentrated around the nucleus and bile canaliculi of the human hepatocyte. Although nothing is known of the functions of these intracellular elements, it has been suggested that they either may be contractile and responsible for intracellular movements or may represent channels for the transport of fluids.

Lysosomes

Lysosomes contain more than a dozen acid hydrolases that are capable of degrading virtually all components of the cell and are, therefore, well equipped to serve as an intracellular digestion system. Material that is taken into the cell by pinocytosis and phagocytosis (endocytosis) and cytoplasmic constituents, such as mitochondria, glycogen, and fragments of endoplasmic reticulum, may be incorporated into lysosomes. The latter phenomenon, known as autophagia, is prominent in stress situations, such as starvation and after partial hepatectomy, but also occurs in normal cells (Figs. 1 and 2). It is believed that autophagia provides the cell with a means of metabolizing its own structures under stress as well as removing organelles following damage by toxins or disease.

Lysosomes are not usually seen in light microscopic study of hematoxylin-eosin preparations. Because of their digestive function, their appearance on electron micrographs varies according to the material they contain and to the extent to which it has been degraded. Fortunately there are excellent cytochemical staining techniques for visualizing several lysosomal enzymes. Following staining for acid phosphatase, lysosomes can be identified by electron as well as light microscopy (Fig. 6A). In the liver, lysosomes are localized along bile canaliculi.

Electron dense granular and membranous materials, called dense bodies or residual bodies (Figs. 1 and 2), are found within lysosomes. They are believed to be the undigested residue of hydrolysis. Electron micrographs demonstrate that human liver lysosomes often contain an insoluble lipid and dense melaninlike pigment. Such lysosomes, called lipofuscin pigment granules, are considered to be residual bodies and appear to increase in number with aging. Lipofuscin pigment granules are yellow-brown and may be seen in routine histologic preparations. In hemosiderosis and hemochromatosis iron is deposited in lysosomes. In Wilson's disease lysosomes contain high concentrations of copper (Fig. 6B). In bile secretory failure of intrahepatic or extrahepatic causes

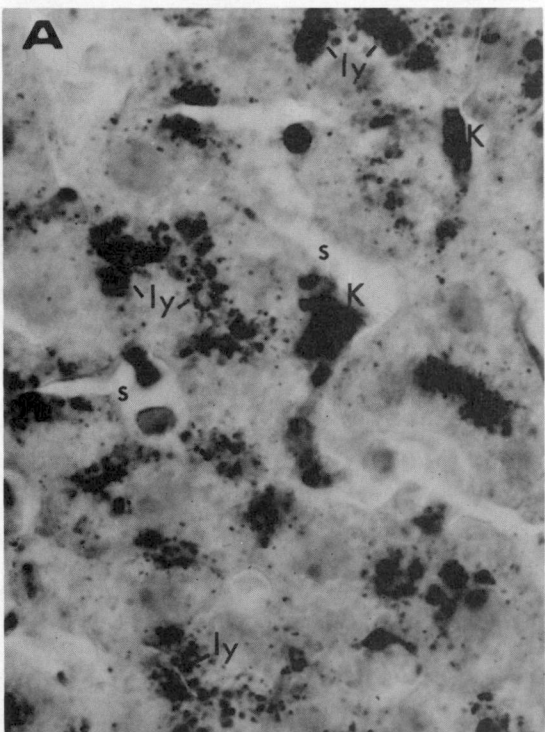
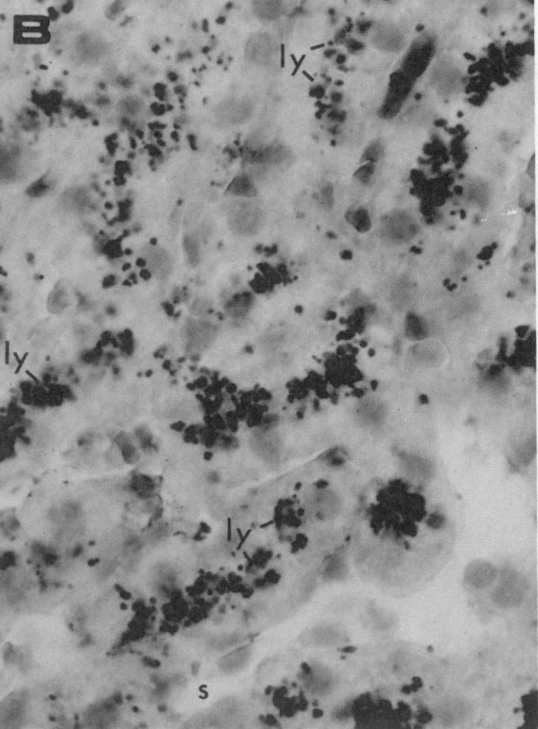

Fig. 6.   Frozen sections of a liver biopsy specimen from a 15-year-old boy with Wilson's disease. A. Incubated to visualize the activity of a lysosomal enzyme, acid phosphatase. The lysosomes of parenchymal cells (ly) have a pericanalicular localization. Kupffer cells (K) lining the sinusoids (s) show high levels of acid phosphatase activity. B. Stained to visualize copper. Stainable copper is also localized to the pericanalicular granules (ly). Red blood cells are seen within the sinusoids (s).

lysosomes contain dense material thought to be bile.

Another type of lysosome whose precise function is not known is the multivesicular body. Multivesicular bodies are membrane delimited structures containing varying numbers of small smooth vesicles that may originate from endoplasmic reticulum or the Golgi apparatus.

A number of hereditary storage diseases, including type II glycogenosis (Pompe's disease), Gaucher's disease, and metachromatic leucodystrophy, which had previously been believed to be unrelated, now appear to be "lysosomal diseases." Patients suffering from these disorders are deficient in various lysosomal hydrolases, leading to an unceasing accumulation of the appropriate substrate within lysosomes. Eventually the affected cells, filled with huge lysosomes that are distended by accumulated substrate (e.g., glycogen in Pompe's disease, kerasin in Gaucher's disease), can no longer function. Prolonged intravenous administration of the deficient hydrolase to a 3-month-old child with Type II glycogenosis has resulted in marked histologic improvement of the child's liver, with disappearance of the enormous glycogen-packed lysosomes. This type of therapy may eventually prove to be of great value.

Glycogen

Glycogen occurs in two forms within liver cells. The less common type is composed of single, roughly spherical, "beta" particles. These particles are often found within liver cell nuclei in adult patients undergoing metabolic stress; in children, "glycogen nuclei" are often found in normal specimens of liver. Cytoplasmic glycogen appears as tightly packed accumulations of particles that resemble the "beta" particles and are referred to as glycogen rosettes or "alpha" particles (Figs. 2 and 3). "Alpha" particles are present in almost all liver cells in close association with the smooth endoplasmic reticulum. There is disagreement as to whether this association reflects a role of the endoplasmic reticulum in the synthesis or phosphorolytic breakdown of glycogen.

Small amounts of glycogen are found in autophagic vacuoles (Fig. 2), a type of lysosome. This glycogen is normally degraded by a lysosomal enzyme, acid maltase, that hydrolyzes linear oligosaccharides and the outer chains of glycogen to glucose. In children suffering from one of the rarer hereditary glycogen storage diseases, type II glycogenosis (Pompe's disease), the phosphorylase enzymes are normal; however, acid maltase is absent. Consequently, in the liver glycogen accumulates within lysosomes, which become greatly distended.

Mitochondria

The mitochondrial fine structure is characteristic. They are delimited by an outer smooth membrane which is separated by a short distance from an inner membrane, folded into numerous "cristae" which project like baffles into the inner compartment (matrix) (Figs. 1–3). A few smaller dense granules that appear to be sites at which cations like calcium accumulate are scattered within the mitochondrial matrix. DNA fibrils and granules resembling ribosomes have been found in mitochondria.

It has been estimated that there are more than a thousand mitochondria in a single parenchymal liver cell. In mitochondria oxidation of a variety of substrates is coupled with esterification of inorganic phosphate to produce adenosine triphosphate (ATP). Energy is stored in the high-energy phosphate bonds of ATP and is available for essential cell functions.

The mitochondria also have several important secondary functions. For example, they are vital in gluconeogenesis from pyruvate, they are able to oxidize fatty acids, and they contain the enzyme δ-amino levulinic synthetase which catalyses the rate-controlling step in porphyrin synthesis.

Mitochondria are sensitive indicators of cell damage. Mitochondrial swelling, gigantic and bizarre-shaped mitochondria, and the formation within mitochondria of unknown crystal-like materials composed of filaments and rods have been described in various hepatic disorders. These changes are not specific and may, in fact, be seen in normal liver. The metabolic defects associated with these altered forms are not known.

References

de Duve, C. Tissue fractionation: past and present. J. Cell Biol., 50:20D, 1971.

—— and Baudhuin, P. Peroxisomes (microbodies) and related particles. Physiol. Rev., 46:323, 1966.

—— and Wattiaux, R. Functions of lysosomes. Ann. Rev. Physiol., 28:435, 1966.

Dingle, I. T., and Fell, H. B., eds. Lysosomes in Biology and Pathology. New York, John Wiley & Sons, Inc., 1969.

Essner, E., and Novikoff, A. B. Human hepatocellular pigments and lysosomes. J. Ultrastruct. Res., 3:374, 1960.

Hug, G., and Schubert, W. K. Lysosomes in type II glycogenosis. J. Cell Biol., 35:CI, 1967.

Jones, A. L., and Fawcett, D. W. Hypertrophy of the agranular endoplasmic reticulum in hamster liver induced by phenobarbital (with review of the function of this organelle in liver). J. Histochem. Cytochem., 14:215, 1966.

Loewy, A. G., and Siekevitz, P. Cell Structure and Function. New York, Holt, Rinehart & Winston, Inc., 1969.

Ma, M. H., and Biempica, L. The normal liver cell. Cytochemical and ultrastructural studies. Amer. J. Path., 62:353, 1971.

Mahley, R. W., Hamilton, R. L., and Lequire, V. S. Characterization of lipoprotein particles isolated from the Golgi apparatus of rat liver. J. Lipid Res., 10:433, 1969.

Novikoff, A. B. Mitochondria (Chondriosomes). *In*

Brachet, J., and Mirsky, A. E., eds., The Cell. New York, Academic Press, 1961, Vol. 2, p. 299.

——— and Essner, E. The liver cell. Some new approaches to its study. Amer. J. Med., 29:102, 1960.

——— Roheim, P. S., and Quintana, N. Changes in rat liver cells induced by orotic acid feeding. Lab. Invest., 15:27, 1966.

Palade, G. E. Structure and function at the cellular level. J.A.M.A., 198:143, 1966.

——— Siekevitz, P., and Caro, L. G. Structure, chemistry and function of the pancreatic exocrine cell. In deReuck, A. V. S., and Cameron, M. P., eds., Ciba Foundation Symposium, The Exocrine Pancreas. Boston, Little, Brown and Co., 1962.

Rouiller, C., and Jezequel, A. M. Electron Microscopy of the Liver. In The Liver. New York, Academic Press, 1963, Vol. I, p. 195.

Steiner, J. W., Phillips, M. J., and Miyai, K. Ultrastructural and subcellular pathology of the liver. Int. Rev. Exp. Path., 3:65, 1964.

24.2
CLINICAL-LABORATORY EVALUATION OF HEPATIC FUNCTION

KEITH S. HENLEY

Ideally, laboratory tests should help discriminate between a limited number of diagnostic possibilities which have been arrived at on the basis of history and physical examination. Clinical reality falls short of this ideal for two reasons:

1. The increasing use of automated screening procedures, already applicable to adults and older children, and likely to be available soon to children of all ages, will provide information, whether it is requested or not. It is, therefore, increasingly important for the clinician to be aware of the uses and limitations of laboratory tests, and to know how abnormalities can be confirmed. Any unexpected abnormality demands that the test be repeated.

2. Interpretations of the current armamentarium of tests of hepatic biochemistry are based on information derived from a patient population in which the diagnosis was rarely, if ever, in doubt. Although there are few studies based on patients whose diagnoses were uncertain, such studies have tended to modify widely held beliefs.

Within these limitations, laboratory tests help to determine whether the hepatic abnormality is acute, chronic, or both; they also help in monitoring the course of the disease. Functions that are most readily disturbed are those which are either relatively specific to the organ, such as the metabolism and excretion of pigments, release of enzymes which are present predominately in the liver, or manifestations of disturbed synthesis of proteins, including plasma proteins and specific factors involved in co-

agulation. Functions of the liver that are shared with other organs, such as glycolysis, respiration, and oxidative phosphorylation, do not lend themselves to organ-specific evaluation for clinical purposes.

The Metabolism of Pigments and Dyes

Measurements in Blood

The serum bilirubin becomes elevated if the pigment load presented to the liver is in excess of the capacity of the liver to remove, metabolize, or excrete the material. The metabolism of bilirubin is considered in a separate section. In anicteric patients it might seem logical to measure the ability of the liver to metabolize bilirubin by means of a bilirubin tolerance test. This is not recommended because bilirubin is almost insoluble in water and often pyrogenic and may produce venous sclerosis.

SULFOBROMOPHTHALEIN (BSP).   This dye is metabolized and excreted predominantly by the liver. It is soluble in water, heat resistant and therefore capable of being sterilized for intravenous injection, and easily measured spectrophotometrically.

Following intravenous administration of BSP the dye is partially bound to serum proteins and transferred primarily into the liver, where its tissue concentration (storage) is proportional to the concentration in the plasma. The subsequent excretory mechanism whereby BSP is transferred into bile is rate-limiting and depends, in part, on prior intrahepatic conjugation of BSP with glutathione.

Procedure.   Five mg of BSP per kg of body weight is injected intravenously as an aqueous solution. After 45 minutes a second venipuncture is performed at a different site. The intensity of the purple color obtained upon the addition of alkali to serum is compared with that of a standard solution containing 10 mg/100 ml of BSP and expressed as a percentage. It is important to be certain that the needle is securely in the vein, for a serious chemical cellulitis may result when the dye is injected extravascularly. The retained percentage of BSP at 45 minutes is less than 5 percent in normal adults and in infants and children beyond the first month of life.

In the presence of moderate to severe conjugated hyperbilirubinemia there is *usually* no purpose in performing a BSP examination, since retention of large amounts of conjugated bilirubin is associated with defective excretion of BSP.

Interpretation.   The dye may be retained for one or more of the following reasons:

1. The dose administered on a weight basis may not be appropriate. The standard of 10 mg/100 ml is based on an estimated plasma volume of

5 percent of body weight. Any discrepancy between body weight and plasma volume, such as may occur with obesity, dehydration, pathologic fluid accumulation, etc., will result in falsely high calculated BSP retention.

2. Shock, heart failure, or presinusoidal anastomoses between radicles of the hepatic artery and portal vein, as in cirrhosis, may reduce perfusion of the liver and increase plasma BSP retention.

3. Impaired uptake of BSP may be seen in febrile conditions such as pneumonia.

4. Reduced storage capacity of the liver for the dye may occur with acute or chronic hepatocellular damage and/or biliary obstruction. Impairment of conjugation of BSP with glutathione may further lower the amount of the dye taken up by the liver in the presence of inflammatory and/or obstructive disease of the liver.

5. The transport of the free and conjugated dye into the bile canaliculi is defective in parenchymal disease, in cholestatic conditions, and in extrahepatic ductal obstruction.

It follows that, with the reservations mentioned, measurement of BSP retention is a useful test for the presence or absence of liver disease but is of no value in differentiating the various inflammatory and obstructive liver diseases.

Measurements of Bile Pigments in Stool and Urine

Bilirubin in the intestine is converted by bacterial action to urobilinogen and urobilin. Some of the urobilinogen is reabsorbed and excreted in the urine, subsequently oxidizing to urobilin on standing. In clinical practice, inspection of the stool for the presence of bile pigment may be satisfactory to determine whether biliary secretion into the intestine has occurred. The rate of excretion of urinary urobilinogen is a function of urinary pH. Maximum excretion usually occurs between noon and 4 P.M., when urinary pH is generally highest.

Procedure. The urine is collected under a layer of toluene in a brown bottle and kept in the cold.

To 10 ml of urine, 1 ml of Ehrlich's reagent is added, and the solution mixed thoroughly. The presence of a detectable red color in urine diluted up to 1 in 20 is normal.

Biochemical Indicators of Acute Hepatocellular Injury

One of the fundamental functions of living matter is to establish and maintain concentration gradients between cellular compartments and between cellular and extracellular fluid. These concentration gradients may be modified as a response to injury or to physiologic changes such as muscular exercise. Enzyme activity in tissue is usually many hundreds if not thousands of times greater in cell fluids than in serum. Tissue injury is reflected, therefore, by a prompt increase in enzyme activity. Since the liver is an organ particularly rich in enzymes, both on a unit weight basis and because of its size, hepatocellular injury is easily demonstrable by increased enzyme activity in serum. Although the mechanism for removal of enzymes from serum is not well understood, the half-life is measured in hours as demonstrated by the disappearance curves of injected enzymes.

For most clinical purposes, estimations of glutamic pyruvic transaminase (GPT) and of glutamic oxalacetic transaminase (GOT) in serum suffice. Creatine phosphokinase (CPK), an enzyme present principally in muscle and also in the brain, is not helpful in the diagnosis of liver disease.

The upper limit of normal values for GOT and GPT in serum in older children and adults is 40 Karmen units. During the first two months of life, however, the upper limit is 120 Karmen units. Although unusual in childhood, serum GOT values may rise due to nonhepatic causes, such as muscle necrosis. Serum GPT elevations result only from hepatic disorders. Comparison of the relative activities of GOT and GPT is often helpful in elucidating the nature of the disease process and the magnitude of involvement of subcellular organelles. The ratio of the activities of GOT and GPT in human liver is about 1.2:1. If the enzyme pattern of the tissue is accurately reflected in serum in acute liver injury, one would expect the ratio of the two enzymes in serum to be the same. However, in acute viral hepatitis, the ratio is usually less than one. An explanation can be found in the distribution of these enzymes between cellular compartments. About 60 percent of the GOT in liver is in the cytoplasm of the cell, the remainder being in the mitochondria. On the other hand virtually all the GPT in liver is in the cytoplasm. Hence, in acute hepatocellular injury in which cellular organelles are spared, GOT increases relatively less than GPT and the ratio of GOT to GPT in serum is less than one. In protracted liver disease, such as chronic hepatitis and cirrhosis, the ratio tends to increase due to release of mitochondrial GOT. The validity of this concept is confirmed by the concomitant increase in serum glutamic dehydrogenase activity. This enzyme is exclusively localized to mitochondria.

Although the striking elevations of enzyme activities in serum so often seen in acute viral hepatitis generally indicate the magnitude of the injury, they have no bearing on prognosis. On the contrary, if, in the face of a rising serum bilirubin, a worsening clinical picture, and diminution of liver size, transaminase activity in serum declines, the prognosis is usually ominous. The mechanism for this important phenomenon is not understood. The simple explanation that there has been complete loss of enzyme from the liver has been repeatedly disproved by analysis of liver tissue at autopsy.

With the exception stated above, the acuteness and severity of liver injury is reflected in the magnitude of the increase in serum enzyme activity. Detectable increases occur during the incubation period of acute viral hepatitis and in asymptomatic hepatitis proved by biopsy. Cholestatic forms of liver disease are often associated with progressive rises of transminases in serum. These may reach a peak after hyperbilirubinemia has begun to subside. In tumors of the liver, serum transaminase activity may be elevated, but increased serum LDH is seen more frequently. These abnormalities are often associated with retention of BSP and elevation of serum alkaline phosphatase.

Increases in enzyme activities in serum are not specific; minor elevations may be seen in febrile disorders and in granulomatous processes involving the liver, such as brucellosis and miliary tuberculosis. Serum enzyme levels may be elevated in hepatocellular injury which is so slight that it is inapparent by light microscopic histology.

Serum alkaline phosphatase activity may be as high as 25 King-Armstrong units in normal growing infants and children. Elevations may be found in association with all hepatocellular diseases, including acute hepatitis and mechanical obstruction to bile flow. Variations in level of alkaline phosphatase activity will not usually discriminate among the various types of liver diseases.

Biochemical Indicators of Chronic Hepatocellular Injury

NONSPECIFIC SERUM PROTEINS. Whereas the half-life of enzymes in serum is measured in hours, the half-life of the serum proteins is measured in days or weeks. Alteration in rates of synthesis or degradation are therefore usually not reflected by changes in concentrations in serum for many days. Changes typical of chronic liver disease are reduced concentrations of serum albumin and increased concentrations of total globulins, especially of the gamma globulin fraction.

Methods. Total protein concentration is measured by the biuret reaction. The different protein moieties are then identified by their varying mobilities in an electrophoretic field. Albumin migrates most rapidly to the anode, followed in order by alpha-1, alpha-2, beta, and gamma globulin fractions, which are then quantitated and reported, usually as a percentage of the total.

The "salting out" method formerly used does not differentiate among various globulin fractions, and gives falsely high values for the total albumin concentration. The ratio of albumin to globulin based on this method is therefore not a reliable measurement. Measurement of albumin by dye binding

techniques, as used in automated methods, may give falsely low values for serum albumin when significant hyperbilirubinemia is present. Recently developed immunologic techniques offer greater accuracy and specificity and are now being used more frequently in the diagnostic laboratory.

ALBUMIN. Albumin synthesis occurs almost exclusively in the liver, and is impaired in liver disease regardless of etiology. The serum albumin concentration is determined by its rate of entry into and removal from the circulation. It is also modified by alterations of plasma volume, and a low concentration of albumin in plasma may be a dilutional phenomenon. There are, of course, many other causes of low concentration of albumin in the serum, including malnutrition and malabsorption, kwashiorkor, protein-losing enteropathies, and chronic renal disorders with albuminuria.

GLOBULINS. The increased concentration of gamma globulins is not a pathognomonic laboratory finding of chronic liver disease. Collagen diseases and chronic infections may produce similar changes. Hypergammaglobulinemia is presumed to be due to inflammatory cells, mainly plasma cells, which synthesize gamma globulins. There is, therefore, a fairly good correlation between the magnitude of the mesenchymal cell infiltrate in a liver biopsy specimen and the level of circulating gamma globulin. In chronic active hepatitis the serum gamma globulin concentration may be increased as much as five-fold.

Prolonged cholestasis, due either to an extrahepatic cause or to disorders primarily affecting the bile canaliculi, may be associated with increased concentrations in the serum of cholesterol and its transport protein, which migrates with β-globulins on electrophoresis.

Flocculation tests, such as the thymol turbidity test, were used widely in the past as indicators of hepatic parenchymal disease. They are crude methods for detection of elevated globulins and have been, or should be, replaced by the more specific techniques noted above.

FACTORS OF COAGULATION. As usually performed, the prothrombin time measures thrombin and factors V, VII, and X. Prolongation of prothrombin time is commonly seen in chronic liver disease associated with progressive hepatocellular changes, with or without jaundice. The prothrombin time is also prolonged when bile fails to reach the intestine, resulting in impairment of the absorption of fat-soluble natural vitamin K. In this condition hypoprothrombinemia is promptly corrected by parenteral administration of vitamin K or oral administration of water-soluble synthetic vitamin K, which obviates the need for emulsification by bile acids in the intestine; with severe hepatocellular injury vitamin K has no effect.

The time taken for a fibrin clot to form under standard conditions is measured and compared with a normal control. The difference is often reported as a percentage. This can be misleading unless the logarithmic nature of the calibration curve is recalled.

Prolongation of the prothrombin time by more than three seconds compared with the control is almost invariably clinically significant.

Miscellaneous Procedures

HEPATIC SCINTISCANNING. Radioiodinated rose bengal (capable of being absorbed and retained by the parenchymal cells) or radioactive gold (phago-cytosed by the cells of the reticuloendothelial system) is given intravenously and radioactivity over the liver is measured by a suitable scanner. The child has to remain immobile during the scanning procedure. Newer scanning cameras have made this procedure far less of an ordeal for the child. Larger areas, such as abscesses, hematomata, and cysts will be identified as blank areas on the scan. Only the surface of the liver is scanned effectively and only areas greater than 2 cm in diameter will be defined.

LIVER BIOPSY. Percutaneous liver biopsy in infants and children has been rendered safer and more efficient by the introduction of the suction technique utilizing the Menghini needle. With this technique and a transcostal approach, small movements of the liver during respiration may be tolerated. Sedation is helpful but must be administered with caution in the face of hepatic dysfunction. The chest should be immobilized by an assistant and the skin and chest wall anesthetized. Serious coagulation defects are an absolute contraindication; a prothrombin time in excess of three seconds' prolongation over control and/or platelet count of less than 75,000/mm³ should suggest caution and hematologic consultation before proceeding. Liver biopsy should not be performed when infection of the liver or cystic disorders of the liver are known or suspected: supradiaphragmatic biopsy in the face of ascites may result in hydrothorax. Biopsy of the liver is most helpful in diagnosis of infiltrative diseases, including neoplasms; differentiation of chronic hepatitis from cirrhosis; preoperative evaluation of portal hypertension; and differentiation of neonatal hepatitis from biliary atresia.

REFERENCES

Bourke, E., Milne, M. D., and Stokes, G. S. Mechanism of renal excretion of urobilinogen. Brit. Med. J., 2: 1510, 1965.

Henley, K. S., Schmidt, E., and Schmidt, F. W. Enzymes in Serum: Their Use in Diagnosis. Springfield, Ill., Charles C Thomas, Publ., 1966.

Mendeloff, A. I., Kramer, P., Ingelfinger, F. J., and Bradley, S. E. Studies with bromsulfalein. II. Factors altering its disappearance from the blood after a single intravenous injection. Gastroenterology, 13:222, 1949.

Menghini, G. One-second needle biopsy of the liver. Gastroenterology, 35:190, 1958.

Obrinsky, W., Denley, M. L., and Brauer, R. W. Sulfobromophthalein sodium excretion test as a measure of liver function in premature infants. Pediatrics, 9:421, 1952.

Osserman, E. F., and Takatsuki, K. The plasma proteins in liver disease. Med. Clin. N. Amer., 47:679, 1963.

Porter, M., Riley, H. D., Jr., and Graham, H. Needle biopsy of the liver in infants and children. J. Pediat., 65:176, 1964.

Watson, C. J., and Hawkinson, V. Studies on urobilinogen. VI: Further experiences with the simple quantitative Ehrlich reaction. Am. J. Clin. Path., 17:108, 1947.

Wroblewski, F. Serum enzyme alterations in diseases of the liver and biliary tract. Med. Clin. N. Amer., 44: 699, 1960.

Yudkin, S., Gellis, S., and Lappen, F. Liver function in newborn infants, with special reference to excretion of bromsulphalein. Arch. Dis. Child., 24:12, 1949.

24.3
BILIRUBIN METABOLISM

LAWRENCE M. GARTNER

Jaundice, a yellow discoloration of skin, sclerae, and other body tissues due to accumulation of bilirubin, is a sign of major importance in many pathologic and functional disorders involving the hepatic, biliary, and hematologic systems. Yellow skin may also occur in individuals ingesting excessive amounts of β-carotene-containing foods such as carrots or sweet potato; but the sclerae do not become pigmented and the serum van den Bergh reaction remains normal. In neonates, icterus of sclerae or skin is not apparent until the serum bilirubin exceeds approximately 5.0 mg/100 ml, whereas in older children and adults icterus will be clinically apparent at serum bilirubin concentrations above 2.0 mg/100 ml. Clinical evaluation of the intensity of icterus is inaccurate, and serum bilirubin concentration should be measured, particularly in the neonate. The normal total bilirubin concentration in serum after the neonatal period is less than 1.0 mg/100 ml. The normal direct-reacting bilirubin concentration in serum is less than 0.5 mg/100 ml.

BILIRUBIN PRODUCTION. Bilirubin is derived from multiple sources. Approximately 85 percent of the bilirubin excreted results from the breakdown of hemoglobin of mature, circulating erythrocytes. The circulating red blood cell has an average life span of 120 days, at which time mechanical fragility increases and the cell is lysed in the reticuloendothelial system, the spleen primarily. Hemoglobin consists of heme, an iron-porphyrin complex, combined with globin (Fig. 7). The pathway by which hemoglobin is converted to bilirubin is not known with certainty. Recent studies, however, have demonstrated that spleen and liver Kupffer's cells contain a microsomal heme oxygenase capable of oxidizing the porphyrin ring of heme at the alpha-methene bridge to form the linear tetrapyrrole biliverdin. The carbon atom

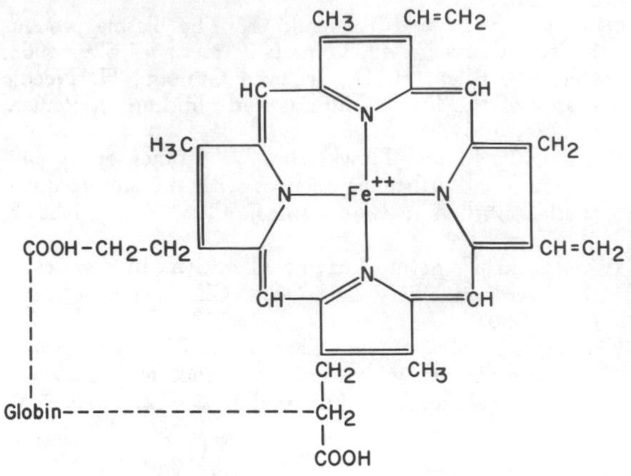

Fig. 7. The structure of hemoglobin.

of the alpha-methene bridge is oxidized quantitatively to carbon monoxide, measurement of which affords an estimation of the rate of erythrocyte hemolysis. The iron released during hemoglobin catabolism is stored as ferritin. The globin is degraded to its component amino acids for reutilization in the synthesis of proteins. Biliverdin is reduced to bilirubin in the reticuloendothelial system by the enzyme bilirubin reductase and, perhaps, nonenzymatically by various reducing substances. One gram of hemoglobin will theoretically produce 34 mg of bilirubin.

Approximately 15 percent of the bile pigment excreted into the intestine is normally derived from sources other than the destruction of mature, circulating erythrocytes. This has been termed "shunt bilirubin production" and has been further subdivided into bilirubin production resulting from pathways related to erythrocyte formation and pathways independent of erythrocyte formation. In the former pathway, heme not entering the circulation as erythrocytes can contribute to bilirubin synthesis. In the latter pathway bilirubin may be derived from nonerythrocyte heme proteins such as myoglobin, catalase, peroxidase, or cytochromes. Of the total shunt bilirubin production in man, approximately 25 percent is derived from the nonerythropoietic component.

SERUM TRANSPORT OF BILIRUBIN. Unconjugated bilirubin is nearly insoluble in serum water at physiologic pH and is transported in plasma primarily bound to albumin, with small amounts associated with other plasma proteins only at high serum bilirubin concentrations. One mole of albumin has been shown to be capable of binding at least two moles of bilirubin in vivo and three or more moles in vitro.

Thus, at a molar ratio of two, one gram of albumin will bind 16 mg of bilirubin, permitting a serum unconjugated bilirubin concentration of between 50 and 75 mg/100 ml. The first binding site is believed to afford a tighter bond than any of the subsequent binding sites. In clinical experience high concentrations of unconjugated bilirubin are rarely attained. Although bilirubin is tightly bound to albumin, organic anions such as salicylates and sulfonamides may displace bilirubin from albumin into the tissues, particularly if bilirubin is bound to sites beyond the first. As will be discussed subsequently, the albumin-bilirubin bond in neonates is a critical factor in the production of kernicterus.

UPTAKE OF BILIRUBIN BY THE LIVER CELL. The mechanism and regulation of hepatic uptake of bilirubin are not well understood, but animal studies suggest that the process may be one of facilitated diffusion of pigment from plasma across the hepatic cell plasma membrane into the cytoplasm. Bilirubin in the liver cell is not albumin-bound. Two hepatic cytoplasmic proteins, Y and Z, that function as intracellular acceptors of bilirubin, sulfobromophthalein (BSP), and other anions have been described. Reduction of these proteins may result in diminished entry of bilirubin.

BILIRUBIN CONJUGATION. Bilirubin must be made water soluble in order to be excreted into bile. This is accomplished by conjugation of bilirubin with glucuronic acid. One mole of bilirubin acquires two moles of glucuronic acid on the carboxyl groups of the propionic side chains (Fig. 8), forming an ester-linked bilirubin diglucuronide (pigment II of Cole and Lathe). Glucuronic acid used in this process is derived from uridine diphosphoglucuronic acid (UDPGA), and the transfer is catalyzed by glucuronyl transferase, an enzyme associated with the endoplasmic reticulum of the hepatocyte. Glucuronic acid is derived from glucose by the following enzymatic steps in the liver cell:

$$\text{glucose-1-PO}_4 + \text{uridine-5-(PO}_4)_3 \xrightarrow{\text{uridyl transferase}} \text{uridine diphosphoglucose (UDPG)} + \text{pyrophosphate}$$

$$\text{uridine diphosphoglucose} + \text{DPN} \xrightarrow{\text{UDPG dehydrogenase}} \text{uridine diphosphoglucuronic acid (UDPGA)} + \text{DPNH}$$

Free glucuronic acid is not a significant precursor of uridine diphosphoglucuronic acid (UDPGA).

Chromatographic examination of icteric serum and bile reveals a component identified as pigment I, which contains equimolar amounts of bilirubin and glucuronic acid, suggesting that it may be bilirubin monoglucuronide. Pigment II contains two moles of glucuronic acid per mole of bilirubin and is, therefore, bilirubin diglucuronide. The biologic existence of pigment I is uncertain. It may represent a complex of free bilirubin and bilirubin diglucuronide. The clinical importance of pigment I in icteric serum is uncertain; and for the present, its measurement should not influence treatment. Conjugated bilirubin

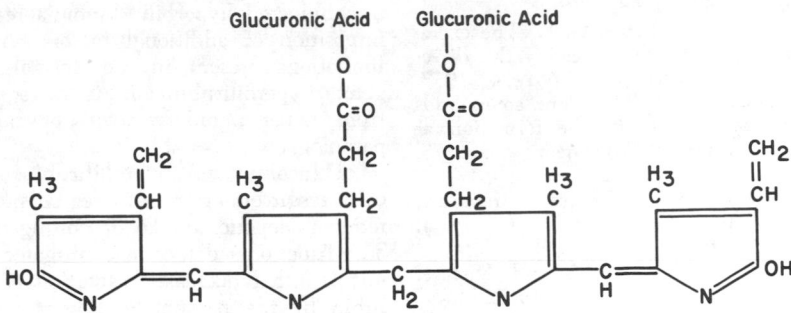

Fig. 8. The structure of bilirubin diglucuronide.

in serum is also bound to albumin. Other conjugates of bilirubin, such as sulfate and taurine, have been prepared synthetically; however, their biologic importance is uncertain.

Naturally occurring metabolites, such as thyroxine, and drugs, such as morphine, may also be conjugated with glucuronic acid, resulting in biologic inactivation and enhanced solubility in water. The latter facilitates their excretion by the liver or kidney. Whereas bilirubin is conjugated with glucuronic acid by an ester linkage, most drugs and other naturally occurring substances form an ethereal glucuronide conjugate. The question of the existence of multiple glucuronyl transferase enzymes is still not resolved.

HEPATIC CELL BILIRUBIN EXCRETION. The excretion of conjugated bilirubin from the liver cell into bile is probably energy-dependent and normally limits the overall transfer of bilirubin from plasma to bile. Other organic anions, such as BSP and cholecystographic dyes, which are rapidly transferred from the liver cell into bile, may share this excretory pathway with conjugated bilirubin. Severe reduction of hepatic excretory function or marked increase in bilirubin entering the hepatocyte will result in accumulation of conjugated bilirubin in the liver cell and plasma.

TRANSPORT OF BILIRUBIN IN THE BILE DUCTS AND INTESTINES. Conjugated bilirubin in bile is conducted via the intrahepatic and extrahepatic bile ducts into the gallbladder and ultimately into the duodenum. In the gallbladder and intestinal tract, conjugated bilirubin may be partially hydrolyzed to unconjugated bilirubin by beta glucuronidase or the alkaline intestinal pH. Unconjugated bilirubin, but not conjugated bilirubin, may be partially reabsorbed by gallbladder, bile duct, and intestinal tract epithelial cells. The quantitative importance of the enterohepatic circulation of bilirubin in the normal individual and in patients with hyperbilirubinemia is unknown. The bacteria of the small and large intestine reduce conjugated and unconjugated bilirubin to a group of colorless compounds which react with Ehrlich's aldehyde reagent and are generally grouped together as urobilinogens. These compounds are subsequently oxidized to urobilins (stercobilins), which may give the brown color to normal feces. Following administration of broad-spectrum antibiotics and sulfonamides, which substantially decrease intestinal bacterial counts, urobilinogens are not formed and bilirubin may be excreted in the feces. Normally about 75 percent of the urobilinogen formed per day is reabsorbed in the ileum and ultimately excreted by the kidney and liver. Fecal and urinary excretion of urobilinogen is usually increased in hemolytic disease. Urinary urobilinogen excretion is also increased in parenchymal liver disease but may be absent with complete biliary obstruction.

The van den Bergh Reaction

The functional classification of jaundice depends upon the biochemical nature of the serum bilirubin (i.e., whether the serum bilirubin is unconjugated or conjugated). The unconjugated and conjugated bilirubin concentrations are reasonably approximated by estimation of indirect- and direct-reacting bilirubin using the van den Bergh reaction. The reaction of bilirubin as direct or indirect is independent of protein binding. In the reaction, which was first described by Ehrlich in 1883 and applied by van den Bergh in 1913, bilirubin is coupled with diazotized sulfanilic acid to produce a red dipyrrolazo derivative which can be estimated colorimetrically. Methodologically the "direct" reaction is performed first and the intensity of the color measured one minute after addition of the reagents. An accelerator (methanol or caffeine) is then added and the color measured 10 to 30 minutes later. The difference between the "total" and "direct" is the "indirect" reacting portion. Falsely high concentrations of direct-reacting pigment may be obtained in the van den Bergh reaction if the serum contains excessive bile acids or urea.

REFERENCES

Arias, I. M. Formation of bile pigment. Handbook of Physiology. Alimentary Canal V, Chapter 110. 2347-2374, 1967.
———— Gartner, L. M., Cohen, M., Ben Ezzer, J., and Levi, A. J. Chronic nonhemolytic unconjugated hyper-

bilirubinemia with glucuronyl transferase deficiency. Amer. J. Med., 47:395-409, 1969.

Billing, B. H., Cole, P. G., and Lathe, G. H. The excretion of bilirubin as a diglucuronide giving the direct van den Bergh reaction. Biochem. J., 65:774, 1957.

Dutton, G. J., and Storey, I. D. E. Uridine compounds in glucuronic acid metabolism. I. The formation of glucuronides in liver suspensions. Biochem. J., 57:275, 1954.

Gartner, L. M., and Arias, I. M. Formation, transport, metabolism and excretion of bilirubin. New Eng. J. Med., 280:1339-1345, 1969.

Gray, C. H. Bile Pigments in Health and Disease. Springfield, Ill., Charles C Thomas Co., 1961.

Gunn, C. H. Hereditary acholuric jaundice in a new mutant strain of rats. J. Hered., 29:137, 1938.

Hymans van den Bergh, A. A., and Muller, P. Uber eine direkte und eine indirekte Diazoreaktion auf bilirubin. Biochem. Z., 77:90, 1916.

Israels, L. G. The bilirubin shunt and shunt hyperbilirubinemia. In Popper, H., and Schaffner, F., eds., Progress in Liver Diseases, Vol. III. New York, Grune and Stratton, Chap. 1, 1970.

Lemberg, R. The chemical mechanism of bile pigment formation. Rev. Pure Appl. Chem., 6:1, 1956.

Lester, R., and Schmid, R. Intestinal absorption of bile pigments. II. Bilirubin absorption in man. New Eng. J. Med., 269:178, 1963.

Levi, A. J., Gatmaitan, Z., and Arias, I. M. Two hepatic cytoplasmic protein fractions, Y and Z, and their possible role in the hepatic uptake of bilirubin, sulfobromophthalein, and other anions. J. Clin. Invest., 48:2156-2167, 1969.

London, I. M., West, R., Shemin, D., and Rittenberg, D. On the origin of bile pigment in normal man. J. Biol. Chem., 184:351, 1950.

Malloy, H. T., and Evelyn, K. A. The determination of bilirubin with the photoelectric colorimeter. J. Biol. Chem., 119:481, 1937.

Odell, G. B. The dissociation of bilirubin from albumin and its clinical implications. J. Pediat., 55:268, 1959.

Ostrow, J. D., and Schmid, R. The protein-binding of C^{14} bilirubin in human and murine serum. J. Clin. Invest., 42:1286, 1963.

Schmid, R. Hyperbilirubinemia. In Stanbury, J. B., Wyngaarden, J. B., and Fredrickson, D. S., eds., The Metabolic Basis of Inherited Disease. New York, McGraw-Hill Book Co., 1966, Chap. 37.

Tenhunen, R., Marver, H. S., and Schmid, R. Microsomal heme oxygenase. Characterization of the enzyme. J. Biol. Chem., 244:6388-6394, 1969.

With, T. K. Biologie der Gallenfarbstoffe. Stuttgart, Thieme, 1966.

24.4
JAUNDICE IN THE NEWBORN

LAWRENCE M. GARTNER

Icterus neonatorum or jaundice of the newborn is a descriptive term encompassing a large variety of diseases and physiologic variations. Moderately elevated serum unconjugated bilirubin concentrations in normal newborn infants are so common that the term "physiologic jaundice" is often used. Severe unconjugated hyperbilirubinemia results from superimposition of additional factors on the physiologic limitations present in the normal neonate. Conjugated hyperbilirubinemia is infrequent and results from hepatic, biliary tract, or rarely hematologic pathology.

Unconjugated hyperbilirubinemia can theoretically result either from increased production or from reduced hepatic uptake or conjugation of bilirubin. The functional defect in conjugated hyperbilirubinemia is either decreased excretion of conjugated bilirubin by the parenchymal liver cell or damage to the intrahepatic or extrahepatic biliary system. Whenever conjugated bilirubin is increased in serum, the concentration of unconjugated bilirubin is also increased.

Unconjugated Neonatal Hyperbilirubinemia

Physiologic Jaundice of the Newborn

Serum unconjugated bilirubin concentrations transiently exceed 2.0 mg/100 ml during the first week of life in approximately 90 percent of all newborn infants. Clinical icterus is not usually detectable during the first 24 hours of life unless there is hemolytic disease or some other superimposed disorder. The average maximum serum bilirubin concentration in normal full-term infants is approximately 6 mg/100 ml and will occur during the second to fourth days of life. In premature infants the rate of increase in serum bilirubin concentration is similar to that in full-term infants, but the higher maximal levels of 10 to 12 mg/100 ml are not reached until the fifth to seventh days of life. Serum unconjugated bilirubin concentrations attained in physiologic jaundice are not associated with kernicterus in full-term infants but may be in premature infants under certain circumstances (see below and also Sec. 15.3). Concentrations of serum bilirubin exceeding 10 mg/100 ml in full-term infants and 14 mg/100 ml in premature infants suggest that additional factors are superimposed on the normally occurring physiologic jaundice. The diagnosis of physiologic jaundice may be considered in any newborn with mild unconjugated hyperbilirubinemia, but is only established by excluding known causes of jaundice in this age group. For this reason all jaundiced newborn infants should have the following laboratory tests performed: (1) maternal blood group and Rh type; (2) infant blood group, Rh type, and Coombs test; (3) total and direct-reacting serum bilirubin concentrations; (4) hemoglobin or hematocrit determination; (5) examination of erythrocyte morphology; and, in some cases, (6) white blood cell count and urinalysis. In infants with severe hyperbilirubinemia more extensive studies are indicated.

The etiology of physiologic jaundice is not understood, although mechanisms to explain its development have been suggested. Since the bilirubin in these infants is unconjugated, four possible mechanisms can be considered: (1) increased production of bilirubin either from destruction of mature, circulating erythrocytes or from other sources; (2) impairment of uptake of bilirubin from serum by the liver cell; (3) defective hepatic conjugation of bilirubin with glucuronic acid; and (4) increased enterohepatic circulation of bilirubin.

1. Survival of circulating erythrocytes in full-term and prematurely born infants may be slightly to moderately reduced, resulting in increased bilirubin production. The degree of this increased production, however, would not alone account for the concentrations of bilirubin observed in newborns. Excessive synthesis of bilirubin from sources other than circulating erythrocytes has been postulated but not demonstrated.

2. Transport of bilirubin from serum into the liver cell has not been investigated in newborn human infants owing to inadequacy of techniques. It has been demonstrated, however, that newborn guinea pigs have markedly defective hepatic uptake of bilirubin. It has also been demonstrated that one of the hepatic cytoplasmic organic anion binding proteins, 'Y', is relatively deficient in the newborn guinea pig and monkey, suggesting that this deficiency may limit hepatic uptake of bilirubin. Reduced hepatic blood flow in neonates could also theoretically delay the transport of unconjugated bilirubin from plasma into the liver.

3. Deficiencies in the hepatic glucuronide conjugating pathways have been demonstrated in newborn infants and animals in vivo and in vitro. In newborn guinea pigs, uridine diphosphoglucose dehydrogenase activity is reduced, limiting the production of uridine diphosphoglucuronic acid (UDPGA). It is not known, however, whether the availability of UDPGA is a limiting factor in bilirubin glucuronide formation during the newborn period. Deficiency of glucuronyl transferase activity is generally considered to be the more significant factor responsible for physiologic jaundice, but definitive studies to establish the rate-limiting step in overall transfer of bilirubin from plasma to bile in newborns with physiologic jaundice have not been reported thus far. Glucuronyl transferase activity probably reaches normal adult levels during the first week of life, as judged from studies performed in both newborn guinea pigs and monkeys. The relative inability of the liver of the newborn infant to form glucuronides also accounts for impaired drug metabolism and for toxicity, such as the peripheral vascular collapse (the "gray syndrome") observed following administration of chloramphenicol to full-term neonates (Sec. 14.1). Although factors regulating maturation of glucuronyl transferase activity are unknown, inhibition of the enzyme may be biologically important. Urine and serum obtained from normal women during the second and third trimesters of pregnancy inhibit hepatic glucuronyl transferase activity in vitro. Several progestational steroids isolated from pregnancy sera competitively inhibit glucuronyl transferase activity in vitro. Attempts to correlate inhibition of glucuronyl transferase activity by normal maternal sera with the occurrence and severity of physiologic jaundice have been unsuccessful. Markedly increased serum levels of inhibition are observed, however, in the syndrome of transient familial neonatal hyperbilirubinemia. Pregnane-3(a), 20(β)-diol, an inhibitory steroid, has been isolated from the milk of certain mothers and is associated with prolonged unconjugated hyperbilirubinemia in their breast-fed infants.

4. In newborn infants, unlike the older children, bilirubin is probably not chemically reduced to urobilinogens in the intestine because of the limited number of enteric bacteria. Therefore, excess unconjugated bilirubin in the intestinal tract could theoretically result in increased absorption by the intestinal mucosa, presenting an exaggerated load of bilirubin to the liver. Oral administration of a substance such as agar, that will bind bilirubin and prevent its intestinal reabsorption, has been shown to reduce the severity of physiologic jaundice.

Kernicterus

Kernicterus, a neurologic syndrome occurring in severely jaundiced newborn infants, is characterized pathologically by bilirubin staining and necrosis of neurons in the basal ganglia, hippocampal cortex, and subthalamic nuclei of the brain. Other areas of the central nervous system are less commonly affected. The clinical syndrome and pathologic lesions result from entry of unconjugated bilirubin into the central nervous system, causing a toxic encephalopathy. Conjugated hyperbilirubinemia does not cause kernicterus.

Kernicterus may present clinically as lethargy, rigidity, opisthotonus, high-pitched cry, and convulsions; it may result in death. Survivors may show evidence of cerebral palsy, frequently of the choreoathetoid type, deafness, mental retardation, and other neurologic defects in infancy or early childhood. These late manifestations of kernicterus may occur in some infants without clinical evidence of kernicterus having been present during the newborn period. Subtle forms of brain damage, such as loss of cognitive function, may be late sequelae of bilirubin encephalopathy in the absence of any other neurologic impairments. Premature infants are particularly susceptible to this type of insult.

The acute damage due to bilirubin encephalopathy is most likely to occur during the third to seventh days of life, but it may develop at older ages including adolescence in those children with persisting severe unconjugated hyperbilirubinemia.

Statistical evidence supporting the concept of a critical serum concentration of unconjugated bilirubin above which a significant number of infants will develop kernicterus has been accumulated only for full-term infants with erythroblastosis. An unconjugated serum bilirubin concentration of 20 mg/100 ml or greater occurring during the first week of life is accepted as an indication for exchange transfusion in such infants. Critical serum bilirubin concentrations have not been established for full-term infants without hemolytic disease or for premature infants with or without hemolytic disease. In premature infants, kernicterus can occur at serum bilirubin concentrations as low as 9.0 mg/100 ml, especially when associated with asphyxia, respiratory distress syndrome, hypoglycemia, acidosis, sepsis, meningitis, and possibly hypothermia. In low-birth-weight infants with these complications, lower serum bilirubin concentrations should be taken as an indication for exchange transfusions.

Of importance in the development of kernicterus is the capacity of serum albumin to bind unconjugated bilirubin, enabling bilirubin to remain in solution in plasma. Several commonly used drugs such as sulfonamides and salicylates compete with bilirubin for albumin binding and, thus, should not be administered to mothers in late pregnancy or labor or to newborn infants. Displacement of bilirubin from albumin by these drugs results in deposition of unconjugated bilirubin in many tissues, including the brain, and in *reduction* of serum bilirubin concentrations. Physiologic derangements such as acidosis or marked increase in unesterified fatty acids due to either starvation or hypothermia may also diminish the albumin binding capacity for bilirubin. Hypoalbuminia will also result in reduced plasma binding capacity for bilirubin. Recent studies using newer techniques for estimation of plasma protein binding capacity suggest that minimal brain damage in some older children correlates with poor albumin binding reserve and moderate concentrations of unconjugated bilirubin during the newborn period.

In severe erythroblastosis the aim of therapy is to alleviate the anemia, prevent further hemolysis, restore the blood volume to normal, and prevent kernicterus by removal of unconjugated bilirubin. In the forms of hyperbilirubinemia *not* associated with hemolysis, the major object of therapy should be to prevent brain damage. Exchange transfusion has been the standard mode of therapy in both hemolytic and nonhemolytic hyperbilirubinemia for many years. The risk of the procedure and the length of time required for its performance have led to development of other means for removal of bilirubin. The administration of phenobarbital to patients with Type II glucuronyl transferase deficiency results in a marked decrease in serum bilirubin concentrations, presumably due to stimulation of the deficient conjugating enzyme. Similar treatment of pregnant women during the last trimester of pregnancy and of the infants immediately following delivery has been shown to reduce the peak concentration of bilirubin in those infants with physiologic jaundice. A dose of approximately 5 milligrams/kilogram/day has been used for the newborns and approximately 90 milligrams/day for the mothers. Treatment of the newborn infant alone, without prior treatment of the mother during pregnancy, is also effective but to a lesser degree. At least two or three days of treatment of the infant are required before any effect is observed. Thus, this is not suitable therapy for an infant who develops hyperbilirubinemia during the second or third day of life. It has been assumed that phenobarbital increases hepatic bilirubin excretion by stimulation of glucuronyl transferase activity; in fact, however, the drug has been shown to stimulate synthesis of the hepatic cytoplasmic bilirubin binding protein 'Y' in rats. Thus, phenobarbital may ameliorate jaundice of the newborn by enhancing the hepatic uptake of bilirubin from the circulation. Since phenobarbital has respiratory depressant effects, its use requires careful observation of the infants and is not without potential dangers.

The exposure of infants to increased intensities of light in the visible range, particularly blue light, results in increased oxidation of bilirubin to other products, as yet not definitively identified. Studies in animals and more limited studies in infants have demonstrated that the photo-oxidation products of bilirubin are excreted in urine and bile as water soluble materials. Increased total excretion of bilirubin metabolites has been demonstrated in congenitally jaundiced rats following light exposure. Normal full-term and premature infants exposed to fluorescent light for periods of one to three days demonstrate peak serum bilirubin concentrations approximately one-half those of infants not exposed to increased light intensities. The effectiveness of phototherapy in infants with hemolytic diseases remains to be evaluated. Although the use of phototherapy has become widespread throughout the United States, there are still many unanswered questions regarding its safety and effectiveness. The major unanswered question is whether phototherapy is effective in preventing the development of either frank kernicterus during the newborn period, or the milder forms of brain damage thought to be associated with bilirubin toxicity. Phototherapy may or may not have effects on the plasma protein binding of bilirubin, or circadian rhythms, on physical growth, and on neurologic development. Whether the light exposure should be continuous or intermittent and which intensities and wavelengths should be used also requires further evaluation. It has been generally agreed, however, that the infants' eyes must be covered during the period of light exposure to prevent possible retinal damage.

Severe or Prolonged Unconjugated Hyperbilirubinemia of the Newborn

Many factors or diseases may be superimposed on the normally occurring physiologic jaundice of the newborn, resulting in severe or prolonged unconjugated hyperbilirubinemia, sometimes with increased risk of kernicterus; among these are

1. Exaggerated erythrocyte destruction
2. Transient familial neonatal hyperbilirubinemia
3. Hepatic Glucuronyl Transferase Deficiency
   a. Type I
   b. Type II
4. Breast-feeding jaundice
5. Drug-induced jaundice
6. Maternal diabetes and jaundice
7. Pyloric stenosis and jaundice
8. Miscellaneous (hypothyroidism, anoxia, mongolism, starvation)

EXAGGERATED ERYTHROCYTE DESTRUCTION. The classic situation in which severe hyperbilirubinemia of the newborn is related to exaggerated erythrocyte destruction is erythroblastosis fetalis secondary to Rh or major blood group incompatibility between infant and mother. The pathogenesis of this syndrome is discussed elsewhere (Sec. 17.3). Although the excessive destruction of erythrocytes and production of bilirubin in this disease usually begin in utero, the serum bilirubin concentration in cord blood is either normal or slightly increased. The placenta is capable of transporting unconjugated bilirubin from fetal to maternal plasma for excretion by maternal liver. In cases of severe erythroblastosis, particularly following successful intrauterine transfusion, cord blood direct-reacting bilirubin concentrations of up to 40 mg/100 ml have been observed. Markedly elevated direct-reacting bilirubin concentrations may persist for one to two weeks in these cases. These observations suggest that the human placenta cannot efficiently transfer conjugated bilirubin, and that severe hemolytic disease with marked increase in bilirubin production either stimulates hepatic uptake and/or conjugation of bilirubin, or reduces the already limited hepatic excretory capacity for bilirubin in utero.

Infants with severe hemolytic disease become clinically icteric as early as 30 minutes after delivery. With less severe hemolysis, icterus may not be observed until after the second day of life. In some infants with significant hemolysis, jaundice does not become severe, suggesting that in these infants hepatic uptake, conjugation, and excretion are adequate.

During the newborn period hemolysis may also occur as a result of congenital spherocytosis, pyknocytosis, minor blood group incompatibilities, sepsis, and resorption of blood from hematomas. Deficiency of erythrocyte glucose-6-phosphate dehydrogenase (G6PD) activity (see Sec. 8.12) may result in episodic hemolysis during the neonatal period, particularly after exposure to certain drugs such as phenacetin or chemicals such as naphthalene, or with infection. Hemolysis may follow administration of large doses of vitamin K_3 to either mother or newborn, ingestion of mothballs containing naph-

thalene prior to parturition, or inhalation of naphthalene vapors by neonates. Hemolysis in G6PD deficient individuals may occur at any time in life, but in older individuals hemolysis may result in anemia without icterus, whereas during the neonatal period, when hepatic mechanisms are relatively deficient, icterus commonly occurs. In general, hemolysis occurring during the first week of life produces predominantly unconjugated hyperbilirubinemia. After the second week of life, hemolysis may be associated with significantly increased serum concentrations of both conjugated and unconjugated bilirubin, particularly if there is coexistent hepatic damage. The use of vitamin K_3 has been discontinued and replaced by vitamin K_1. Administration of 1.0 mg of vitamin K_1 oxide to newborns with or without G6PD deficiency does not produce hemolytic disease and yet is more than adequate to prevent hemorrhagic disease of the newborn.

Large numbers of infants with G6PD deficiency and severe neonatal hyperbilirubinemia have been described in many areas of the world. In Israel, however, where there is a high incidence of G6PD deficiency, the incidence of associated neonatal jaundice is low. This difference suggests that an additional factor may be operative in those infants who develop marked hyperbilirubinemia. In the United States there have been occasional cases of neonatal hyperbilirubinemia associated with G6PD deficiency, but not in the high frequency seen in some parts of the world. Infants with severe hyperbilirubinemia and G6PD deficiency require exchange transfusion if kernicterus is to be prevented. The diagnosis of G6PD deficiency requires demonstration of increased hemolysis and reduced erythrocyte glucose-6-phosphate dehydrogenase activity.

TRANSIENT FAMILIAL NEONATAL HYPERBILIRUBINEMIA. This is a syndrome in which all infants of a mother develop severe unconjugated hyperbilirubinemia within the first four days of life. Jaundice spontaneously subsides during the second to third week of life. These infants may develop kernicterus unless an exchange transfusion is performed.

Known causes of severe hyperbilirubinemia have been excluded in these infants. Both maternal and infant sera inhibit glucuronyl transferase activity in vitro. Sera obtained from normal women during the second and third trimesters of pregnancy and immediately following delivery also inhibit glucuronyl transferase activity in vitro. However, sera from mothers of infants with transient familial neonatal hyperbilirubinemia are four to ten times more inhibitory. During the postpartum period the inhibitory effect of sera gradually decreases, becoming normal by about the fourteenth postpartum day. Inhibition by infant sera is slightly less than that observed with maternal sera but follows a similar course. The inhibitor has not been identified; however, the association with pregnancy suggests that it is a progestational steroid. Although the syndrome is familial, inheritance of the disorder has not been demonstrated. Diagnosis requires demonstration of increased inhibition of glucuronyl transferase activity by sera from mother and infant in vitro.

BREAST MILK JAUNDICE. Occasional breast-fed infants develop severe and prolonged unconjugated hyperbilirubinemia which cannot be explained by any known cause. Unlike infants with erythroblastosis fetalis, transient familial neonatal hyperbilirubinemia, or inherited glucuronyl transferase deficiency, severe jaundice is not present in these breast-fed infants during the early days of life. Significant elevations occur on the fourth to seventh days of life. Maximum concentrations of serum unconjugated bilirubin between 15 and 25 mg/100 ml occur during the second and third weeks. Following this period, hyperbilirubinemia gradually decreases and may either disappear by the end of the third week or persist for as long as 10 weeks. Interruption of nursing for three or four days results in rapid decline in hyperbilirubinemia, while interruption of nursing for six to nine days usually returns the serum bilirubin concentration to normal. Except for jaundice, these infants appear entirely well. Approximately 75 percent of the infants nursed by these mothers will develop the syndrome. Kernicterus has not been observed in this syndrome, presumably because the peak concentrations of unconjugated bilirubin occur after the end of the first week of life. Kernicterus can occur during this time of life in full-term otherwise healthy infants but only with serum bilirubin concentrations higher than occur in this syndrome. Breast milk obtained from the mothers of infants with this syndrome contains pregnane-3(a),20(β)-diol, which competitively inhibits glucuronyl transferase in vitro. The isomer found normally in urine and serum of both pregnant and nonpregnant women but not in milk is pregnane-3(a),20(a)-diol, an equally inhibitory steroid. During lactation and only during lactation, these women excrete increased amounts of the abnormal isomer, suggesting that the actively secreting mammary tissue is the source of the abnormal steroid.

In contrast to the syndrome of transient familial neonatal hyperbilirubinemia, sera from these nursing mothers does not significantly inhibit glucuronyl transferase activity.

Despite continuation of breast feeding, hyperbilirubinemia gradually disappears in all of these infants, accompanied in some cases by a spontaneous and concurrent disappearance of inhibitor from the milk. In other cases the inhibitor remains in the milk over a prolonged period, and the disappearance of jaundice must be attributed to maturation of the infant's hepatic glucuronyl transferase activity.

Although this syndrome may be suspected on the basis of the family history and the temporal relationship of jaundice to breast feeding, a definite diagnosis requires demonstration of inhibition of glucuronyl transferase by milk in vitro. The occurrence of this syndrome in breast-fed infants should not lead to the interdiction of breast feeding either of infants

with this syndrome or of infants in general. Despite jaundice, infants with the breast-feeding jaundice syndrome are vigorous and do not suffer any sequelae from it. In those rare occasions when hyperbilirubinemia exceeds 20 mg/100 ml during the first two weeks of life, interruption of nursing for three or four days will usually result in significant reduction of hyperbilirubinemia.

INHERITED DEFICIENCY OF GLUCURONYL TRANSFERASE ACTIVITY. Two forms of glucuronyl transferase deficiency may be clearly distinguished on the basis of clinical, chemical, and genetic findings. The Type I abnormality has previously been called the Crigler-Najjar syndrome. Type II syndrome was described more recently and is often not recognized until adolescence or even later, although it may present as exaggerated neonatal jaundice. Type I glucuronyl transferase deficiency is a rare syndrome inherited as an autosomal recessive and characterized by the onset of jaundice shortly after birth. Unconjugated hyperbilirubinemia persists throughout life at serum concentrations ranging from 20 to 40 mg/100 ml as a result of an almost total inability to conjugate bilirubin with glucuronic acid in the liver. In the absence of repeated exchange transfusions most infants develop kernicterus resulting in death during the first week of life. Patients with the Type I syndrome who survive the first weeks of life usually have severe neurologic impairment. Occasional individuals reach childhood without neurologic signs, even without exchange transfusions. These rare survivors have occasionally developed signs of kernicterus later in life. Hepatic glucuronyl transferase activity measured in vitro is virtually absent in these individuals when bilirubin is used as the glucuronide receptor. With other substrates used either in vitro or in vivo, glucuronyl transferase activity is extremely low. Gallbladder bile is very light in color, containing little bilirubin and no glucuronide. Both parents have a partial deficiency in the ability to form glucuronides of bilirubin and other substrates both in vivo and in vitro, although they do not have hyperbilirubinemia. The pattern of inheritance of the syndrome indicates an autosomal recessive mode of transmission. A similar enzymatic defect has been found in a mutant strain of Wistar rats (Gunn) which also have lifelong unconjugated hyperbilirubinemia and develop kernicterus during the neonatal period. The Gunn rat has a normal capacity for the excretion of administered *conjugated* bilirubin.

The second type of glucuronyl transferase deficiency (Type II) is similar to the first but is characterized by greater variation in the serum bilirubin concentrations from one affected individual to another. The range of unconjugated serum bilirubin concentrations observed is from normal to 22 mg/100 ml. The mode of inheritance is probably that of an autosomal dominant with marked variability in penetrance, accounting for those individuals with detectable defects in glucuronyl transferase activity but normal or only mild elevations of serum bilirubin concentrations. Abnormalities of conjugation and a history of chronic jaundice are found only in members of one parental lineage. Gallbladder bile is pigmented and contains bilirubin glucuronide. In this syndrome, as in the Type I, glucuronyl transferase activity is markedly deficient. Although some of these patients do not present with icterus until adolescence, chronic hyperbilirubinemia may begin during the first days of life and kernicterus, although very rare in the Type II syndrome, has been reported in two cases. Type I and Type II syndromes are not known to have occurred in the same families.

Administration of phenobarbital in doses of 5 mg/kilogram body weight/day to children and in doses of 30 to 90 mg/day to adults with the Type II disorder of glucuronyl transferase results in dramatic decreases of the serum bilirubin concentration within one to two weeks. Similar administration to patients with the Type I disorder results in no change in the serum bilirubin concentration. The mechanism of the response to phenobarbital is uncertain although the evidence presented supports the view that enzyme induction may be occurring. The observed differences between Types I and II probably reflect differences in the structure of a single glucuronyl transferase or in the control of protein synthesis.

The administration of phenobarbital offers a relatively simple means for differentiation of the two syndromes and for reduction of hyperbilirubinemia in patients with Type II glucuronyl transferase deficiency.

DRUG-RELATED JAUNDICE. The administration of several drugs to neonates is associated with exaggerated unconjugated hyperbilirubinemia, either as a result of hemolysis or interference with hepatic conjugation of bilirubin. Vitamin K_3 given in large doses to newborns or to pregnant women at term may cause hemolysis in the newborn, especially in the presence of glucose-6-phosphate dehydrogenase deficiency. The administration of novobiocin to newborn infants increases the incidence of severe unconjugated hyperbilirubinemia approximately threefold. Novobiocin is a noncompetitive inhibitor of glucuronyl transferase in vitro. The increased frequency with which inhibitors of glucuronyl transferase produce unconjugated hyperbilirubinemia in neonates may result from the relatively low endogenous activity of the enzyme in neonatal liver. Although streptomycin and chloramphenicol also inhibit glucuronyl transferase activity in vitro, neither of these antibiotics increases the severity or frequency of jaundice in neonates.

MATERNAL DIABETES AND JAUNDICE. Compared with normal infants of the same gestational age, infants of women with either frank or gestational diabetes have an increased incidence and prolongation of neonatal unconjugated hyperbilirubinemia. These infants also have higher hemoglobin concentrations than normal, which could result in increased bilirubin formation. It is not known whether this factor or possible derangements in endocrine metabolism cause the exaggerated hyperbilirubinemia. Early feeding (prior to 12 hours of age) reduces the intensity of hyperbilirubinemia in these infants.

PYLORIC STENOSIS AND JAUNDICE. Infants with pyloric stenosis (Sec. 23.11) occasionally develop unconjugated hyperbilirubinemia coincident with the onset of vomiting, or more rarely they have persistent jaundice from birth. The serum bilirubin concentrations are usually 5 to 20 mg/100 ml. Although two infants with this syndrome have been reported to have direct-reacting hyperbilirubinemia and mechanical obstruction of the common bile duct, this has not been found in any other case. With careful search for elevated serum bilirubin concentrations in infants with pyloric stenosis, it may be found that hyperbilirubinemia is more common than was realized merely from the appearance of clinical jaundice in infants with pyloric stenosis. Chemical studies of hepatic function, radiographic studies of the bile ducts, and histologic examination of liver biopsy specimens are normal. Neither the severity of pyloric obstruction nor the degree of dehydration and electrolyte imbalance correlates with the occurrence of jaundice. Pyloromyotomy is usually followed by rapid disappearance of hyperbilirubinemia. Congenital obstruction of the duodenum and jejunum is also associated with an increased incidence of severe unconjugated hyperbilirubinemia. The mechanism by which intestinal obstruction causes jaundice is unknown.

MISCELLANEOUS CONDITIONS ASSOCIATED WITH NEONATAL UNCONJUGATED HYPERBILIRUBINEMIA. Neonatal anoxia and respiratory distress during the first few days of life may increase the incidence and severity of unconjugated hyperbilirubinemia, particularly in prematurely delivered infants. Experimental birth asphyxia in monkeys increases the severity of the normally occurring neonatal unconjugated hyperbilirubinemia.

The interval between birth and the onset of feeding may be related to the severity of unconjugated hyperbilirubinemia in premature infants. Studies on this question in premature infants are not in agreement, however, although early feeding of infants of diabetic mothers does reduce the severity of the unconjugated hyperbilirubinemia.

Prolonged and sometimes severe unconjugated hyperbilirubinemia may also be seen in infants with either congenital hypothyroidism or mongolism.

REFERENCES

Arias, I. M., Gartner, L. M., Seifter, S., and Furman, M. Prolonged neonatal unconjugated hyperbilirubinemia associated with breast feeding and a steroid, pregnane-3-(α), 20(β)-diol, in maternal milk that inhibits glucuronide formation in vitro. J. Clin. Invest., 43: 2037, 1964.

Behrman, R. E., and Hsia, D. Y. Y. Summary of a symposium on phototherapy for hyperbilirubinemia. J. Pediat., 75, 1969.

Blanc, W. A., and Johnson, L. Studies on kernicterus. J. Neuropath. Exp. Neurol., 18:165, 1959.

Boggs, T. R., Jr., and Bishop, H. Neonatal hyperbilirubinemia associated with high obstruction of the small bowel. J. Pediat., 66:349, 1965.

——— Hardy, J. B., and Frazier, T. M. Correlation of neonatal serum total bilirubin concentrations and developmental status at age eight months. J. Pediat., 71: 533, 1967.

Brown, A. K., and Zuelzer, W. W. Studies on the neonatal development of the glucuronide conjugating system. J. Clin. Invest., 37:332, 1958.

Crigler, J. F., and Najjar, V. A. Congenital familial nonhemolytic jaundice with kernicterus. Pediatrics, 10:169, 1952.

Doxiadis, S. A., and Valaes, T. The clinical picture of glucose-6-phosphate dehydrogenase deficiency in early infancy. Arch. Dis. Child., 39:545, 1964.

Gartner, L. M., and Arias, I. M. Studies of prolonged neonatal jaundice in the breast-fed infant. J. Pediat., 68:54, 1966.

——— The transfer of bilirubin from blood to bile in the neonatal guinea pig. Pediat. Res., 3:171-180, 1969.

——— and J. Bernstein. Kernicterus and prematurity: The development of nuclear jaundice at relatively low serum concentrations of bilirubin. Jewish Memorial Hosp. Bull., 10:125, 1965.

——— Snyder, R., Chabon, R. S., and Bernstein, J. Kernicterus: High incidence in premature infants with low serum bilirubin concentrations. Pediatrics, 45:906, June 1970.

Hsia, D. Y. Y., Allen, F. H., Jr., Gellis, S. S., and Diamond, L. K. Erythroblastosis fetalis. VIII. Studies of serum bilirubin in relation to kernicterus. New Eng. J. Med., 247:668, 1952.

——— Dowben, R. M., Shaw, R., and Grossman, A. Inhibition of glucuronyl transferase by progestational agents from serum of pregnant women. Nature, 187: 693, 1960.

Kernicterus. Report based on a symposium held at the IX International Congress of Pediatrics, Montreal, July, 1959. Sass-Kortsak, A., ed. Toronto, University of Toronto Press, 1961.

Lathe, G. H., and Walker, M. Inhibition of bilirubin conjugation in rat liver slices by human pregnancy and neonatal serum and steroids. Quart. J. Exp. Physiol., 43:257, 1958.

——— and Walker, M. The synthesis of bilirubin glucuronide in animal and human liver. Biochem. J., 70: 705, 1958.

Lischner, H. W. Genesis of neonatal jaundice. Biochem. Clin., 3:57, 1964.

McKay, R. J., Jr. Current status of use of exchange transfusion in newborn infants. Pediatrics, 33:763, 1964.

——— and Lucey, J. F. Bilirubin metabolism and "physiologic" jaundice. New Eng. J. Med., 270:1292, 1964.

Sutherland, J. M., and Keller, W. H. Novobiocin and neonatal hyperbilirubinemia. Amer. J. Dis. Child., 101: 447, 1961.

Taylor, P. M., Wolfson, J. H., Bright, N. H., Birchard, E. L., Derinoz, M. N., and Watson, D. W. Hyperbilirubinemia in infants of diabetic mothers. Biol. Neonat., 5:289, 1963.

Wolfson, S., Arias, I. M., Lucey, J. F., and McKay, R. J., Jr. Transient familial neonatal hyperbilirubinemia. J. Clin. Invest., 44:1442, 1965.

24.5
CONJUGATED NEONATAL HYPERBILIRUBINEMIA

JAY BERNSTEIN

Neonatal jaundice occurring after the first week of life is often characterized by an elevation of the conjugated fraction of serum bilirubin. This pattern of hyperbilirubinemia is seen in extrahepatic biliary atresia, neonatal giant-cell hepatitis, hepatitis due to known infectious agents, erythroblastosis fetalis, and certain metabolic disorders. Despite the presumption of hepatocellular damage, histologic evidence of cellular injury varies considerably, and neither inflammatory cell infiltration nor cholestasis is a constant finding.

Biliary atresia and neonatal hepatitis account for most cases of prolonged obstructive jaundice in early infancy, other conditions being relatively uncommon. Some causes of conjugated hyperbilirubinemia are amenable to specific therapy, either antibiotic or surgical, but most are not. Recognizing the former and not aggravating the latter are the principal considerations in clinical management. For the majority of infants with primary hepatic disease, the differentiation between biliary atresia and neonatal hepatitis can be made by clinical observation and a few well-chosen laboratory tests. The difficulty lies most often in those cases that combine the clinical features of both conditions. Acholic stools and the clinical picture of complete biliary obstruction in severe neonatal hepatitis, on one hand, and evidence of hepatocellular damage in biliary atresia, on the other, are the major causes of confusion. Histopathologic examination of the liver offers the most reliable means of distinguishing between the two.

Biliary Obstruction and Extrahepatic Biliary Atresia

The most common cause of conjugated hyperbilirubinemia during the early months of life is extrahepatic biliary obstruction, of which 90 percent can be attributed to ductal atresia. Atresia may be diffuse or segmental, involving all or several of the extrahepatic ducts, and may be accompanied by occlusion of intrahepatic ducts. Secondary changes in the liver are severe, progressing from portal fibrosis and bile duct proliferation to biliary cirrhosis. Progressive obliteration of intrahepatic bile ducts occurs in the later stages. Giant-cell transformation of liver cells is seen in about one-third of the cases.

Jaundice sometimes appears in the first days of life, or it may begin later in the first month. Approximately one-half of these infants are anicteric until the second week of life. Serum bilirubin concentrations in the early months of life are frequently less than 12.0 mg/100 ml, despite complete biliary obstruction. Later in life the concentration inexplicably rises. As in all cases of conjugated hyperbilirubinemia, the urine contains bilirubin. The stools are usually, but not invariably, gray or white. Urobilinogen is generally absent from stool and urine, but trace amounts are occasionally found. Both the conjugated and unconjugated fractions of serum bilirubin are increased, and the serum alkaline phosphatase, glutamic-oxaloacetic transaminase, and glutamic-pyruvic transaminase are moderately elevated. In biliary atresia there is a distinct predominance among whites, and females outnumber males; the reverse is true in neonatal hepatitis, in which there is no racial predilection and a higher prevalence in males.

The diagnosis has at times been obscured by markedly elevated serum glutamic-oxaloacetic and glutamic-pyruvic transaminase levels and mild reticulocytosis, findings more characteristic of neonatal hepatitis. These babies, in whom clinical differentiation of the two conditions is difficult, have, in addition to biliary atresia, the histologic changes of hepatitis, especially hepatocellular giant-cell transformation. Thus far, tests of liver function have not provided a satisfactory means of differentiating these cases from those of severe neonatal hepatitis.

The diagnosis of biliary obstruction, usually atresia, is suspected in a neonate with persistent conjugated hyperbilirubinemia, mild to moderately abnormal liver function studies, and acholic stools. A liver biopsy is indicated to confirm the diagnosis, in part at least to protect cases of hepatitis from unnecessary surgery. Percutaneous needle biopsy will often suffice, but a larger, open biopsy may be necessary for adequate histologic evaluation. The most characteristic histologic abnormality is proliferation of intrahepatic bile ducts, a lesion common to all forms of extrahepatic obstruction (Fig. 9). Absence of the intrahepatic ducts, a rare finding, may occur together with extrahepatic atresia or by itself as a diffuse lesion. Intrahepatic atresia, associated with a clinical syndrome of fluctuating jaundice, extreme hyperlipemia, xanthomatosis, and sometimes marked lymphedema, seems to be compatible with a relatively long life span, unlike extrahepatic atresia.

Neither clinical evaluation nor liver biopsy enables one to differentiate the several causes of extrahepatic obstruction, and surgical exploration is, therefore, clearly indicated. Other causes of extrahepatic obstruction in the newborn include choledochal cyst and obstructive plugs of inspissated bile and mucus. Both lesions are completely correctable. In about 5 percent of infants with atresia, surgery is successful in establishing biliary drainage into the intestinal tract. The disease is, however, most often fatal, with biliary cirrhosis, portal hypertension, rickets, frequent infection, and hepatic failure as the late manifestations. Although the majority of infants with this

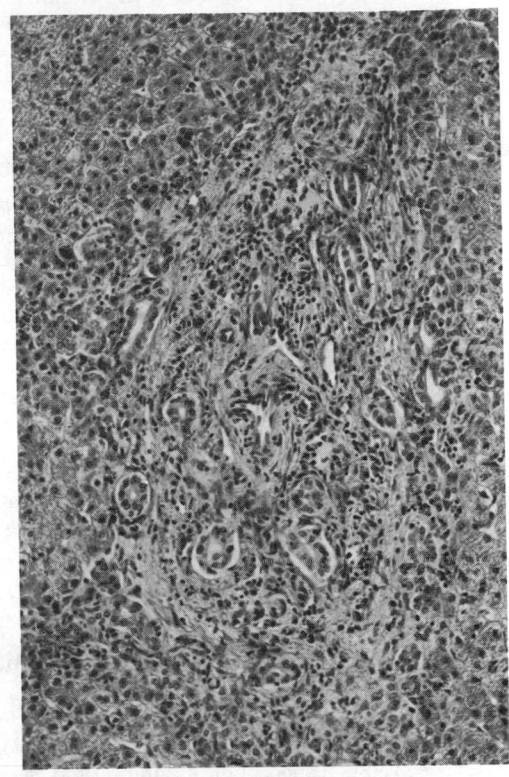

Fig. 9.   Typical changes in the portal area of a young infant with extrahepatic biliary atresia: bile duct proliferation, fibrosis, medial hypertrophy of hepatic artery. H&E ×75.

disease die during the early years of life, survivors into late adolescence have been reported.

The optimal time for surgery is uncertain, but most authorities believe that an exploratory laparotomy, operative cholangiogram, and liver biopsy should be performed during the first two months of life to repair correctable obstructions before the development of severe cirrhosis. It must be noted, however, that later reexplorations and postmortem dissections have occasionally disclosed patent ducts that had escaped earlier surgical detection. Also, spontaneous recovery in infants diagnosed at surgery and by biopsy as having atresia may mean that partial and transient obstruction does occur and that potentially patent ducts may persist. Meticulous dissection is, however, probably contraindicated, because (1) the ducts are delicate and easily injured, (2) isolating the ducts by dissection may lead to avascular necrosis and secondary stricture, and (3) prolonged anesthesia and surgery in patients with severe hepatocellular alterations or hepatitis probably increase the mortality and morbidity.

Inoperable biliary atresia admits of no specific therapy, but attention must be directed toward prevention and treatment of intercurrent infections, maintenance of good nutrition, prevention of hemorrhage by administration of vitamin K, and prevention of rickets. The last can be treated with intramuscular vitamin D in a dose of 25,000 to 40,000 units every three months. Cirrhosis and portal hypertension will develop and should be managed accordingly.

Extrahepatic biliary atresia has been considered a developmental abnormality, but more recently it has been regarded as a consequence of cholangitis and ductal injury. The morphologic evidence of obstructive cholangiolitic changes in congenital rubella suggests, for example, that atresia can follow intrauterine or perinatal viral infections that localize in and destroy the biliary epithelium. Of interest also is the observation that instances of familial disease have been described in which intrahepatic atresia, extrahepatic atresia, and hepatitis were all present in the same family. Both biliary atresia and giant-cell hepatitis have been observed with increased frequency in trisomy E. The relationship between the chromosomal abnormality and possible viral infection remains entirely conjectural. It is conceivable that atresia shares with hepatitis common etiologies, and that its distinctive histologic features represent merely the secondary effects of biliary tract obstruction.

Neonatal Hepatitis

Neonatal hepatitis simulates biliary atresia by producing an obstructive type of jaundice. Its etiology has not been established, but a viral origin seems likely. The occasional familial occurrence of neonatal hepatitis suggests that genetic factors may also play a role, and there is an unaccountably high incidence of giant-cell hepatitis in E-trisomy syndrome.

Histologically, hepatitis is accompanied by variable giant-cell transformation, in which the liver cell cords are changed into and disrupted by large, multinucleate, syncytial giant cells. Giant-cell transformation is not a specific lesion; rather it is a response to hepatocellular damage that is seen also in biliary atresia, toxic injury, and sepsis. Degenerative or toxic hepatocellular changes in hepatitis also include cytoplasmic swelling, bile stasis, pigment retention, and glycogen accumulation. Alterations in liver cells may, however, be fairly inconspicuous, and the histopathologic diagnosis depends on demonstrating an inflammatory reaction. Inflammatory cells infiltrate the lobules and portal areas, where they are usually accompanied by and may be difficult to differentiate from hematopoietic cells.

Jaundice in neonatal hepatitis may be present at birth or may not develop until several days or weeks later. Both the conjugated and unconjugated fractions of the serum bilirubin are elevated; the ratio of the two is variable and is significant only when the unconjugated fraction is high enough to cause kernicterus. The stool is frequently gray, and the urine contains bilirubin. A mild hemolytic anemia is present in most cases. The serum glutamic-oxaloacetic and glutamic-pyruvic transaminases are often markedly elevated. The level of serum enzyme activity is usu-

ally greater than in biliary atresia, but the use of these tests to differentiate the two conditions is not reliable. Radioactive rose bengal excretion studies may demonstrate passage of radioisotopes into the intestines, presumptive evidence of biliary patency. Hepatitis, unlike biliary atresia, is twice as common in males as in females.

Known infectious agents that can cause hepatitis in early infancy include toxoplasmosis, bacterial infections with syphilis and listeria, and viral infections with cytomegalovirus, rubella, herpesvirus, varicella, and Coxsackie virus. Direct liver involvement occurs in all of these diseases, varying from mild giant-cell transformation and cholangiolitis in rubella to severe zonal necrosis in herpes simplex. A specific diagnosis may require elaborate procedures, such as viral isolation or the Sabin-Feldman dye test for toxoplasmosis, but elevated serum immunoglobulin (IgM) is good presumptive evidence of antenatal infection. Testing for syphilis is mandatory, as the disease is once again increasing.

Most cases of hepatitis, however, are not caused by an identifiable agent, and a viral etiology is only presumed. Clinical studies may fail to distinguish neonatal hepatitis from biliary atresia, and great emphasis has been placed, therefore, on liver biopsy. Percutaneous needle biopsy is preferable to an open procedure, because anesthesia and surgical exploration may significantly increase mortality and morbidity. When needle biopsy fails to give sufficient information and an open biopsy is necessary, the surgical procedure should be as brief as possible, perhaps limited to the biopsy and an operative cholangiogram.

Most infants with neonatal hepatitis will recover with only supportive therapy. There is no specific treatment. A small number of infants do not recover from their hepatitis; a few develop cirrhosis and portal hypertension.

Sepsis and Jaundice

Sepsis has often been implicated as a cause of neonatal jaundice, but it is probably less commonly so than generally supposed. Conjugated hyperbilirubinemia develops de novo after the period of physiologic jaundice as a complication of enterobacterial sepsis, particularly *E. coli* pyelonephritis. Infants present with poor feeding, lethargy, and irritability. Laboratory studies show moderate azotemia, acidosis, hyperbilirubinemia, normal or only mildly elevated serum transaminase concentrations, and slight hemolysis. Adequate antibiotic therapy of the underlying infection results in abatement of jaundice. Other infections due to different organisms are less often associated with jaundice. Histopathologic studies reveal bile stasis and, sometimes, evidence of hepatocellular damage, the pathogenesis of which is unknown. The bile stasis and jaundice seen occasionally in patients with diarrhea seem more likely to be remote effects of intestinal disease than the result of ascending bacterial cholangitis.

Erythroblastosis and Conjugated Hyperbilirubinemia

Conjugated hyperbilirubinemia has long been recognized as a complication of erythroblastosis fetalis. It persists for weeks after severe erythroblastosis and initially severe unconjugated hyperbilirubinemia, but the use of exchange transfusion in treating erythroblastosis has reduced the frequency of this complication. It may be present at birth in severely anemic and hydropic babies, and it is commonly present in newborns previously treated with intrauterine transfusions. Histologic studies have shown hepatocellular necrosis and giant-cell transformation. The serum glutamic-oxaloacetic and glutamic-pyruvic transaminases are often elevated. The cause of cellular injury is not known. Anemia and hypoxemia have been implicated, but overproduction of bilirubin in utero has been postulated to induce glucuronyl transferase activity in the face of hepatocellular excretory immaturity. Finally, a mild transient conjugated hyperbilirubinemia has been seen during the recovery stage, possibly when the amount of bilirubin being conjugated exceeds the cell's excretory capacity. A similar phenomenon may also be operative in other hemolytic anemias, such as glucose-6-phosphate dehydrogenase deficiency.

REFERENCES

Alagille, D., Borde, J., Habib, E., Joannides, Z., Thomassin, N., and Kremp, L. Icteres cholestatiques familiaux de l'enfant. Rev. Int. Hepat., 18:701, 1968.

Alpert, L. I., Strauss, L., and Hirschhorn, K. Neonatal hepatitis and biliary atresia associated with trisomy 17-18 syndrome. New Eng. J. Med., 280:16, 1969.

Bennet, D. E. Problems in neonatal obstructive jaundice. Pediatrics, 33:735, 1964.

Bernstein, J., and Brown, A. K. Sepsis and jaundice in early infancy. Pediatrics, 29:873, 1962.

Brent, R. L., et al. Persistent jaundice in infancy. J. Pediat., 61:111, 1962.

Brough, A. J., and Bernstein, J. Liver biopsy in the diagnosis of infantile obstructive jaundice. Pediatrics, 43:519, 1969.

Craig, J. M., and Landing, B. H. Form of hepatitis in neonatal period simulating biliary atresia. Arch. Path., 54:321, 1952.

Dunn, P. M. Obstructive jaundice, liver damage and Rh hemolytic disease of the newborn. Jewish Memorial Hosp. Bull., 10:94, 1965.

Sass-Kortsak, A., Bowden, D. H., and Brown, R. J. K. Congenital intrahepatic biliary atresia. Pediatrics, 17:383, 1956.

Strauss, L., and Bernstein, J. Neonatal hepatitis in congenital rubella. Arch. Path., 86:317, 1968.

Thaler, M. M., and Gellis, S. S. Studies in neonatal hepatitis and biliary atresia. I-IV. Amer. J. Dis. Child., 116:257, 262, 271, 280, 1968.

24.6
JAUNDICE IN OLDER CHILDREN

IRWIN M. ARIAS

Whereas developmental aspects of bilirubin metabolism influence the pathogenesis of congenital as well as acquired jaundice in neonates, jaundice in older children results from diseases and mechanisms similar to those found in adults. Some of the syndromes seen in adults may have their onset in childhood or during adolescence. In older children and adults, the first clinical manifestation of hyperbilirubinemia is jaundice of the sclerae, which is observed when the serum bilirubin concentration exceeds approximately 2 mg/100 ml. Most acquired forms of liver disease in these age groups are manifested by an increase in the plasma concentration of unconjugated as well as conjugated bilirubin, and analysis of plasma bile pigments alone fails to differentiate various types of hepatocellular and obstructive liver disease. However, it is useful to classify some forms of clinical jaundice depending upon whether the predominance of serum bilirubin is unconjugated or conjugated.

Unconjugated Hyperbilirubinemia with Overt Hemolysis

Hemolytic disease or ineffective erythropoiesis occurring in older children with a normal liver is rarely associated with unconjugated hyperbilirubinemia in excess of 3 to 4 mg/100 ml. Hemolysis in association with liver disease, such as cirrhosis or hepatitis, results in predominantly conjugated hyperbilirubinemia with bilirubinuria.

Unconjugated Hyperbilirubinemia without Overt Hemolysis

The term "Gilbert's syndrome" has been used to describe any older child or adult with chronic unconjugated hyperbilirubinemia not attributed to overt hemolysis. All signs and laboratory tests of hepatic function are normal. The serum bilirubin fluctuates from normal to 5 or 6 mg/100 ml and is entirely unconjugated. There is no bilirubinuria. This syndrome is associated with a variety of acquired diseases and may follow viral hepatitis. The disorder is benign and liver biopsy and repeated liver function tests are not indicated. The mechanism of this syndrome and its pathogenesis continue to attract interest and remain increasingly controversial. Impaired transfer of bilirubin from plasma into the liver as well as reduced hepatic glucuronyl transferase activity have been claimed. Gilbert's syndrome results from many etiologic factors and may be classified as follows: (1) In compensated hemolytic disease, the hemoglobin concentration and reticulocyte count may be normal, but ^{51}Cr erythrocyte life span is shortened, resulting in increased bilirubin formation. (2) Rarely, patients have Gilbert's syndrome in association with increased production of bile pigment from sources other than mature circulating erythrocytes. ^{51}Cr erythrocyte life span is normal; however, there is a substantial increase in fecal urobilinogen excretion. (3) Drugs, such as novobiocin and flavaspidic acid, occasionally produce unconjugated hyperbilirubinemia in older children and adults as well as in neonates. The mechanism is uncertain; however, inhibition of glucuronyl transferase activity in vitro and competition for binding with bilirubin to Z protein have been observed. (4) Mild unconjugated hyperbilirubinemia occurs in patients with thyrotoxicosis. Jaundice disappears following successful treatment of hyperthyroidism. The mechanism is unknown. (5) Following portacaval shunt surgery in patients with cirrhosis, chronic unconjugated hyperbilirubinemia occasionally develops and disappears following splenectomy. (6) Gilbert's syndrome may occur as an inheritable disorder which appears to be transmitted as an autosomal dominant characteristic. (7) In other patients, the disorder is associated with a variety of acquired diseases, and in many patients no associated disease or inheritance can be detected.

Etiologic diagnosis of chronic unconjugated hyperbilirubinemia in older children and adults requires extensive and frequently highly specialized techniques. On the other hand, with the exception of compensated hemolytic disease, Gilbert's syndrome is a cosmetic disorder probably resulting from different genetically determined factors in the formation, transport, and disposition of bilirubin. It is the responsibility of physicians to recognize this commonly occurring benign disorder and to avoid overdiagnosis and over-energetic treatment. This syndrome is not a manifestation of chronic active liver disease or cirrhosis and rarely, if ever, requires treatment other than reassurance. Unconjugated hyperbilirubinemia regardless of etiology is accentuated by fasting, exercise, sepsis, alcohol, pregnancy, and, rarely, menstruation.

Conjugated Hyperbilirubinemia

In all cases of conjugated hyperbilirubinemia, the concentration of unconjugated bilirubin in serum also increases. The reason for this is uncertain; however, deconjugation of bilirubin glucuronide by liver β-glucuronidase has been proposed. Conjugated bilirubin in serum is bound to albumin and an alpha-1 globulin. Conjugated bilirubin is filtered into the urine bound to a low-molecular-weight, dialyzable carrier which has not been identified.

Conjugated bilirubin, as well as other organic anions such as porphyrins, various drugs, sulfobromophthalein, indocyanine green, steroids, and other metabolites, are excreted into the bile presumably by an active transport system. With the exception of bile acids, these substances are excreted by a common mechanism. Impaired biliary excretion of bile acids occurs in obstructive jaundice and bile secretory failure (cholestasis). The result is conjugated hyperbilirubinemia, bilirubinuria, increased concentrations of cholesterol and bile salts in serum, and enhanced serum alkaline phosphatase activity. Morphologically, the liver shows signs of cholestasis.

Acute viral hepatitis accounts for most cases of conjugated hyperbilirubinemia in children. This is discussed in detail in another section (Sec. 14.28). Mechanical obstruction due to calculi, abdominal tumors, enlarged lymph nodes, or primary carcinoma results in either acute or chronic conjugated hyperbilirubinemia and, if not relieved, the development of biliary cirrhosis. These entities are rare in childhood. Calculi in the bile ducts or gallbladder may occur in association with chronic hemolytic disease.

A large number of chemical substances and drugs are associated with the development of hepatic necrosis, bile stasis, and fatty degeneration. Jaundice may or may not occur, depending upon the severity of the hepatic damage. The substances most commonly associated with direct type of hepatic injury are chloroform, carbon tetrachloride, phosphorus, and arsenic. Jaundice due to bile secretory failure (cholestasis), rather than to parenchymal liver cell damage, may occur following administration of other drugs. Approximately 2 percent of individuals receiving chlorpromazine, independent of the dose administered, develop conjugated hyperbilirubinemia and elevation of serum alkaline phosphatase activity. Many of these patients also show eosinophilia. Abnormal retention of sulfobromophthalein (BSP) is regularly found. Within two weeks after withdrawal of the drug, jaundice and hepatic function usually return to normal. Hypersensitivity may be the mechanism by which chlorpromazine and several other drugs produce jaundice with cholestasis. Several synthetic steroids, including C-17 alkylated anabolic steroid and naturally occurring and synthetic estrogens, may produce conjugated hyperbilirubinemia when administered in large enough dose. Although jaundice occurs only rarely with these drugs, BSP excretion by the liver is frequently abnormal. Histologic changes demonstrating bile stasis and canalicular dilation are variable. Complete recovery occurs following withdrawal of the drug.

Recurrent familial cholestasis is a rare disorder of unknown etiology characterized by multiple episodes of conjugated hyperbilirubinemia. Pruritis also occurs and is probably secondary to retention of bile acids. Pathologically there is intense cholestasis. Remissions and exacerbations are spontaneous, and there is complete functional and morphologic return to normal during remission. A congenital origin has been postulated, based on the early age of onset and familial occurrence.

Bile secretory failure (cholestasis) may also be associated with Hodgkin's disease, cirrhosis due to any cause, and sickle-cell disease.

Two inherited disorders with mild conjugated hyperbilirubinemia are the Rotor syndrome and the Dubin-Johnson syndrome. In both, the transfer of various organic anions including bilirubin from liver to bile is defective. Bile acid excretion is normal and plasma bile acid concentrations are also normal. Chronic conjugated hyperbilirubinemia resulting from these disorders is usually detected during adolescence or early adulthood, but may be noted as early as the second year of life. Sulfobromophthalein (BSP) retention is abnormal in both syndromes, particularly if an intravenous infusion of the dye is given. Radiologic visualization of the gallbladder with iodopanoic acid is usually abnormal in the Dubin-Johnson syndrome and normal in the Rotor syndrome. Other tests of hepatic function are normal in both. The Rotor syndrome is transmitted with the characteristics of an autosomal dominant gene. The Dubin-Johnson syndrome occurs as a familial disorder with characteristics suggesting a recessive mode of inheritance. In Israel, it is seen almost entirely in Persian Jews, in whom it occurs with a gene frequency of approximately 1 per 1,400. Pathologically, cholestasis is absent in both syndromes; however, in the Dubin-Johnson syndrome, the liver cells contain a black pigment which has physical and chemical properties of melanin. The pigment probably results from accumulation, oxidation, and polymerization of metabolites which are normally excreted in bile. The life expectancy of patients with both the Dubin-Johnson syndrome and the Rotor syndrome is normal. In each of these disorders hyperbilirubinemia is usually quite mild and may be converted into overt jaundice by infection, pregnancy, oral contraceptives, alcohol, and surgery. These factors are responsible for the high frequency with which these patients are incorrectly diagnosed and subjected to inappropriate treatment.

REFERENCES

Arias, I. M. Chronic unconjugated hyperbilirubinemia without overt signs of hemolysis in adolescents and adults. J. Clin. Invest., 41:2233, 1962.
———— Effects of a plant acid (icterogenin) and certain anabolic steroids on the hepatic metabolism of bilirubin and sulfobromophthalein (BSP). Ann. N.Y. Acad. Sci., 104:1014, 1963.
Dubin, I. N. Chronic idiopathic jaundice: a review of 50 cases. Amer. J. Med., 24:268, 1958.
———— and Johnson, F. B. Chronic idiopathic jaundice with unidentified pigment in liver cells (a new clinicopathologic entity with a report of 12 cases). Medicine, 33:155, 1954.
Foulk, W. T., Butt, H. R., Owen, C. A., Whitcomb, F. F., and Mason, H. L. Constitutional hepatic dysfunction (Gilbert's disease): its natural history and related syndromes. Medicine, 38:25, 1959.
Rotor, A. B., Manahan, L., and Florentin, A. Familial non-hemolytic jaundice with direct van den Bergh reaction. Acta Med. Philipp., 5:37, 1948.
Schiff, L., ed. Diseases of the Liver. Philadelphia, J. B. Lippincott Co., 1963.
———— and Billing, B. H. Congenital defects in bilirubin metabolism as seen in the adult. Gastroenterology, 37:595, 1959.
Smetana, H. F., Hadley, G. G., and Sirsat, S. M. Infantile cirrhosis. An analytic review of the literature and a report of 50 cases. Pediatrics, 28:107, 1961.
Williams, R., Cartter, M. A., Sherlock, S., Scheuer, P. J., and Hill, K. R. Idiopathic recurrent cholestasis: a study of the functional and pathological lesions in 4 cases. Quart. J. Med., 33:387, 1964.

24.7
METABOLIC DISORDERS
OF THE LIVER

MERVIN SILVERBERG

The liver is affected by numerous metabolic disorders, but in only a few do we find significant clinical and pathologic alterations of this complex organ. These may be grouped into four general areas of metabolic disturbances: carbohydrate, protein, lipid, and a category of miscellaneous diseases in which the exact etiology has not been determined.

Disorders of Carbohydrate Metabolism

Galactosemia and hereditary fructose intolerance or fructosemia (see Sec. 8.6) show many remarkable similarities. In both, ingestion of the offending agent results in vomiting, hypoglycemia, and failure to thrive. Hepatocellular disease, as well as renal dysfunction, develops as a result of accumulation of toxic substrates, i.e., galactose-1-phosphate and fructose-1-phosphate, respectively. In galactosemia, deficiency of the enzyme uridyl transferase is responsible for the failure to metabolize galactose-1-PO_4, which may cause severe and often irreversible damage to the cornea and the central nervous system. In each case hepatomegaly and conjugated hyperbilirubinemia are noted early in infancy. In the untreated child, ascites, cirrhosis, portal hypertension, and occasionally hepatic failure will be evident before the first year of life. Hepatic manifestations are usually reversible when specific dietary restrictions are introduced before the age of 3 months. These two disorders emphasize the need for testing urine for non–glucose-reducing substances in infants and children with liver disease, failure to thrive, and other more obscure disorders.

Nine enzymatically defined glycogenoses have been described (see Sec. 8.8). They are associated with various degrees of qualitative and quantitative abnormalities of glycogen deposition in tissues, and excessive fat accumulation in the liver. Elevated serum transaminases are noted in some and, with the exception of those types involving primary skeletal muscle, hepatomegaly is common to all. Two types, III and IV, are associated with hepatocellular dysfunction and fibrosis. In the branching enzyme defect (Type IV), deficiency of amylo-1,4 → 1,6-transglucosidase results in hepatic cirrhosis and portal hypertension during early infancy. None of the three reported cases has survived beyond the fourth year of life; one milder case is known to one of the authors, (LMG), however. This 8-year-old with massive hepatomegaly has mild to moderate transaminase elevations and mild hepatic fibrosis, but normal growth and development. The hepatotoxic effect is attributed to amylopectin, the relatively insoluble plant-like glycogen with long outer chains. Patients with deficiencies of debrancher enzymes (Type III), amylo-1,6-glucosidase or oligo-1,4 → 1,4-glucotransferase, occasionally develop extensive hepatic fibrosis, but cirrhosis has never been recorded.

Disorders of Protein Metabolism

A number of phenotypes of hereditary tyrosinemia have been described varying with the age of the patient. The earliest manifestations occur in the first two months of life with signs and symptoms attributed to acute hepatic necrosis. Hypoglycemia, hypoproteinemia, and a hemorrhagic diathesis are common presenting features. A more slowly progressive phenotype may present with nodular cirrhosis, portal hypertension, and renal tubular insufficiency. Survivors of infantile hepatic necrosis may have a similar clinical picture. In the older child, complete renal tubular failure may predominate in the clinical picture. Many patients succumb to a virulent multifocal primary hepatic malignancy. The basic defect is still uncertain; deficiency of parahydroxyphenylpyruvic acid oxidase may be etiologic. Elevated serum levels of tyrosine and its keto acid derivatives are observed; hypermethioninemia also occurs and is believed to be secondary to liver damage. Careful dietary restriction of phenylalanine and tyrosine will reverse many of the hepatic and renal tubular abnormalities; it has been valuable in managing asymptomatic siblings who are homozygous for the disease.

Disorders of Lipid Metabolism

The liver has a very rapid turnover of lipids and is therefore one of the major sites of storage of excess or abnormal lipid material. Hepatosplenomegaly is found in most varieties of lipid storage diseases. Niemann-Pick disease may be associated with early cholestasis which is indistinguishable from idiopathic neonatal hepatitis. Occasional cases of Gaucher's disease develop portal hypertension, cholestasis, cirrhosis, cholelithiasis, and cholangitis, in decreasing order of frequency. Excessive storage of cholesterol esters

in liver, adrenal, and intestinal mucosa has been noted in Wolman's disease (familial visceral xanthomatosis). All patients reported have died in early infancy. Familial hepatic cholesterol ester storage disease in older children has a more benign course, but septate cirrhosis of the liver develops.

A damaged liver from any cause is prone to accumulate all lipid fractions, resulting in a nonspecific fatty liver. Cirrhosis rarely results from a fatty liver in children, but hepatomegaly and abnormal liver function tests are commonly encountered. Various disorders involving excessive mobilization of lipids may also lead to accumulations of fat in the liver (e.g., diabetes, hyperphagia, corticosteroids, and protein-calorie deficiencies). Drugs such as tetracyclines, hydrocarbons, and heavy metals interfere with lipid exit from the liver.

Reye's syndrome is a disorder characterized by fatty infiltration of the liver, brain, pancreas, and kidney, and is usually accompanied by deep coma, fever, seizures, and hematemesis. Markedly elevated serum transaminases are regularly found. Hypoglycemia is a frequent although inconstant finding. The moderately to markedly enlarged liver uniformly demonstrates fatty swelling of hepatocytes with some peripheral lobular necrosis. The brain shows fatty swelling, edema, and necrosis which results in marked elevation of serum creatine phosphokinase (CPK). The course of the disorder is brief; in two-thirds of the cases death occurs within several days. Improvement is rapid in the survivors, some of whom have neurologic residua. Within three weeks liver function is entirely restored to normal. No late hepatic sequelae have been noted.

The etiology of the disorder is unknown but epidemiologic data have suggested that it may be a sequela of viral infection. A high frequency of both chicken pox and of influenza infections have been observed in the communities in which epidemics of Reye's syndrome have occurred, and approximately 15 percent of patients with Reye's syndrome have had associated chicken pox. Also, the great majority of the patients have an antecedent upper respiratory infection. However, direct evidence for a viral infectious etiology of the syndrome is lacking.

Disorders of Undefined Etiology

Hepatic manifestations of Wilson's disease (Sec. 8.11) predominate in 80 percent of patients presenting under the age of 15; they include atypical hepatitis, portal hypertension, and cirrhosis. In rare cases, a fulminant course is observed with rapid onset of hepatic failure. Histologically, the disease progresses from fibrosis with excessive copper deposition in asymptomatic preschool patients, through subacute necrosis, to nodular cirrhosis. Liver function may improve with treatment consisting of a low copper diet and a copper chelating agent.

Asymptomatic focal hepatic fibrosis may be

found in most patients with cystic fibrosis (Chap. 9) regardless of the therapeutic status of the child. In poorly controlled cases, hepatomegaly and steatosis often occur. Rarely, the young infant may present with prolonged cholestasis attributed to inspissated bile secretions. Biliary cirrhosis resulting in portal hypertension is found in older children and adolescent patients, and occasionally may be the initial manifestations of cystic fibrosis.

Cirrhosis in infants and young children associated with *alpha-1-antitrypsin* deficiency has been reported although the causal relationship is unclear. Coexisting chronic obstructive pulmonary disease has been noted in one sibship. The enzyme deficiency may be detected in some cases by serum protein electrophoresis, since the trypsin inhibitor makes up 90 percent of the α-1 globulin. Clinical manifestations of cirrhosis develop early in life, with death occurring before 1 year of age in many cases. Hepatic coma may develop just prior to death; marked hypoprothrombinemia has been noted very early in the course and is unresponsive to vitamin K. Cirrhosis presenting later in childhood and even in young adults may also result from alpha-1-antitrypsin deficiency.

Varieties of familial intrahepatic cholestasis appear to be related to defects in bile excretion. Cholestasis, pruritis, and failure to thrive are frequently encountered. A benign recurrent form may follow neonatal hepatitis, but usually has an onset after the first year of life. A large number of these cases has been found in a geographic isolate in southern Norway. More virulent varieties have been described with death occurring in early infancy. Some of these latter patients are mentally and physically retarded; others have lymphedema and hemangiomata. Byler's disease, a disorder in the Amish, is characterized by recurrent episodes of severe cholestasis with progressively worsening liver function, leading to death before the age of 10 years.

Excessive visceral deposition of ceroid is reported to produce hepatomegaly, and occasionally cholestasis and cirrhosis. The basic defect in these patients in unknown.

The cerebro-hepato-renal syndrome of Zellweger is often associated with infantile cirrhosis. Other features are profound hypotonia, glaucoma, hypoprothrombinemia, brain anomalies, peculiar facial appearance, congenital stippled epiphyses, minor orthopedic anomalies, and cysts of the renal cortex and other tissues. The basic defect and the nature of the genetic transmission are undetermined, but may relate to a basic defect in mitochondrial metabolism.

REFERENCES

Aagenaes, O., Vander Hagen, C. B., and Refsun, S. Hereditary recurrent intrahepatic cholestasis from birth. Arch. Dis. Child., 43:646, 1968.

Bradford, W. D., and Latham, W. C. Acute encephalopathy and fatty hepatomegaly. Am. J. Dis. Child., 114:152, 1967.

Brady, R. O. The sphingolipidoses. New Eng. J. Med., 275:312, 1966.

Clayton, R. J., Iber, F. L., Ruebner, B. H., and McKusick, V. A. Byler disease. Fatal familial intrahepatic cholestasis in an Amish kindred. Am. J. Dis. Child., 117:112, 1969.

Donnell, G. N., Bergren, W. R., and Ng, W. G. Galactosemia. Biochem. Med., 1:29, 1967.

Glick, T. H., Likosky, W. H., Levitt, L. P., Mellin, H., and Reynolds, D. W. Reye's Syndrome: An epidemiologic approach. Pediatrics, 46:371, 1970.

Gray, O. P., and Saunders, R. A. Familial intrahepatic cholestasis in infancy. Arch. Dis. Child., 41:320, 1966.

Kahane, D., Berant, M., and Wolman, M. Primary familial xanthomatosis with adrenal involvement (Wolman's disease). Pediatrics, 42:70, 1968.

Levin, B., Oberholzer, V. G., Snodgrass, G. J. A. I., Stimmler, L., and Wilmers, M. J. Fructosemia. An inborn error of fructose metabolism. Arch. Dis. Child., 38:220, 1963.

Oppenheimer, E. H., and Andrews, E. C., Jr. Ceroid storage disease in childhood. Pediatrics, 23:1091, 1959.

Partington, M., Scriver, C. R., and Sass-Kortsak, A. Conference on hereditary tyrosinemia. Can. Med. Ass. J., 97:1045, 1967.

Reye, R. D. K., Morgan, G., and Baral, J. Encephalopathy and fatty degeneration of the viscera. A disease entity in childhood. Lancet, 2:749, 1963.

Scriver, C. R., Larochelle, J., and Silverberg, M. Hereditary tyrosinemia and tyrosyluria in a French Canadian geographic isolate. Am. J. Dis. Child., 113:41, 1967.

Sharp, H. L., Bridges, R. A., Krivit, W., and Freier, E. F. Cirrhosis associated with alpha-1-antitrypsin deficiency: A previously unrecognized inherited disorder. J. Lab. Clin. Med., 73:934, 1969.

Sidbury, J. B., Jr. The Glycogenoses. In Gardner, Lytt I., ed., Endocrine and Genetic Diseases of Childhood. Philadelphia, W. B. Saunders Co., 1969.

Smetana, H. F., Hadley, G. G., and Sirsat, S. M. Infantile cirrhosis. An analytic review of the literature and a report of 50 cases. Pediatrics, 28:107, 1961.

Stanbury, J. B., Wyngaarden, J. B., and Fredrickson, D. S., eds., The Metabolic Basis of Inherited Diseases, 2nd ed. New York, McGraw-Hill Book Co., 1966.

Talamo, R. C., and Hendren, W. H. Prolonged obstructive jaundice. Amer. J. Dis. Child., 115:71, 1968.

Tyson, K. R. T., Schuster, S. R., and Swachman, H. Portal hypertension in cystic fibrosis. J. Pediat. Surg., 3:271, 1968.

Wilroy, R. S. S., Crawford, E., and Johnson, W. W. Cystic fibrosis with extensive fat replacement of the liver. J. Pediat., 68:67, 1966.

24.8
HEPATITIS

IRWIN M. ARIAS

Acute infectious hepatitis and serum hepatitis are the most common forms of acute inflammatory disease of the liver causing necrosis of parenchymal liver cells. Known infectious agents such as syphilis, cytomegalovirus, and infectious mononucleosis may cause similar hepatic damage. These diseases are discussed in detail in other sections (Chap. 14). A large variety of poisons and drugs may also cause acute hepatitis. Subclinical anicteric hepatitis is extremely common; symptoms may be mild and transient; the only sign may be moderate hepatomegaly with right upper quadrant tenderness. Acute hepatitis is usually benign in children, and jaundice, if present, rarely persists for more than one to two weeks. Rarely, acute fulminating hepatitis occurs leading to the rapid onset of hepatic failure, coma, and death. The mortality in children from acute fulminating hepatitis with coma is approximately 70 percent.

Laboratory studies in acute hepatitis reveal markedly elevated serum GOT and GPT activities, direct- and indirect-reacting serum bilirubin concentrations, and serum alkaline phosphatase activity. In the initial stages, plasma proteins and prothrombin time are normal; however, later in the course of the disease, prothrombin time is elevated and unresponsive to vitamin K. In addition, serum albumin concentration decreases. In acute hepatitis, leucopenia with relative lymphocytosis occurs, the erythrocyte sedimentation rate is elevated, and moderate degrees of hemolysis accompany the disease.

There is no specific therapy for acute viral hepatitis. In the acute phase of the disease, bed rest is advised. Generally a high-protein, high-carbohydrate, and vitamin-rich diet is recommended. Since many drugs are potentially toxic to the liver, medication should be restricted as much as possible. Relapse of acute hepatitis and fulminant hepatitis have been treated with adrenocortical steroids; however, there are no control studies to evaluate their effectiveness which, in general, is in doubt. Other aspects of treatment of acute fulminant hepatitis are included in the section on treatment of liver failure (see p. 1692).

Cirrhosis or chronic active hepatitis following acute hepatitis is rare in children. Both forms of liver injury as well as recurrent attacks of acute hepatitis have been described in adolescent drug addicts.

Chronic active hepatitis is occasionally seen in children either following an episode of acute hepatitis or with an insidious onset. Children who have chronic active hepatitis may develop cirrhosis, die from rapidly developing hepatic failure, or eventually recover. The factors responsible for determining the clinical course are unknown. Mainly in adolescent girls, chronic active hepatitis is associated with various nonhepatic manifestations. These include arthritis, skin rashes, uveitis, and markedly elevated serum gamma globulin concentrations, positive tests for lupus erythematosus, and nuclear antimitochondrial or antismooth muscle antibodies. The extrahepatic manifestations of the disease usually respond dramatically to corticosteroid therapy; however, it is doubtful if the life history of the disorder is changed.

Some clarification of the relationship between infectious hepatitis, serum hepatitis, and the development of chronic liver disease has come from studies of the "Australia" or "hepatitis-associated antigen" and antibody, which are reviewed in Section 14.28.

References

Bodansky, O., Krugman, S., Ward, R., Schwartz, M. K., Giles, J. P., and Jacobs, A. M. Infectious hepatitis. Amer. J. Dis. Child., 98:166, 1959.

Gellis, S. S., and Hsia, D. Y. Y. Viral hepatitis. New Eng. J. Med., 249:400, 1953.

Havens, W. P., Jr. Viral hepatitis. Postgrad. Med. J., 39:212, 1963.

Klatskin, G. Toxic and drug-induced hepatitis. *In* Schiff, L., ed., Diseases of the Liver. Philadelphia, J. B. Lippincott Co., 1963, p. 453.

Mistilis, S. P., and Blackburn, C. R. B. Active chronic hepatitis. Amer. J. Med., 48:484, 1970.

24.9
CIRRHOSIS

IRWIN M. ARIAS

Cirrhosis of the liver occurs in stillborns and children of all ages. It is extremely common in India, the Far East, and parts of South America, where nutritional, viral, and genetic factors may be of etiologic importance. In the United States, cirrhosis is less common and usually is of the biliary type, resulting from either extrahepatic or intrahepatic biliary atresia. Various types of hepatitis are usually responsible for the majority of remaining cases. Cirrhosis may also result from syphilis, hemosiderosis, Wilson's disease, α-1-antitrypsin deficiency, cerebrohepato-renal syndrome, or galactosemia. In infants with biliary atresia, cirrhosis may occur as early as the first month of life but is usually delayed for many months. Children with fibrocystic disease develop a delayed type of cirrhosis late in their course with bile stasis and marked portal fibrosis. Cirrhosis following hepatitis may occur within several months after the onset of the acute illness; however, more commonly it is detected within one to two years.

Frequently cirrhosis is unrecognized until portal hypertension occurs although mild hepatomegaly may have been present. The first signs may be ascites or hemorrhage from esophageal varices. If the underlying disease is progressive, death from hemorrhage, infection, or coma develops. Occasionally other signs of liver failure such as spider angiomata, palmar erythema, marked muscle wasting, and loss of body hair may be seen.

The diagnosis of cirrhosis may be suspected clinically and by the results of liver function tests. The diagnosis is usually made by histologic examination of liver obtained either by percutaneous needle biopsy or by surgical biopsy. Scanning of the liver following administration of colloidal gold or technetium may reveal a characteristic "mottled appearance" associated with splenic uptake. The serum bilirubin concentration may be elevated and is predominantly of the conjugated type. Plasma albumin concentration is reduced, the gamma globulin concentration elevated, the prothrombin time prolonged, and the transaminase levels mildly elevated. BSP retention usually is abnormal.

Portal hypertension is usually manifested by splenomegaly, dilated abdominal veins, and esophageal varices which can be demonstrated radiographically or endoscopically.

Therapy is specific only in cases where bacterial or parasitic infection is the cause, as in syphilis, or where biliary obstruction can be relieved surgically. In adults a high-protein, high-caloric diet is essential for hepatic regeneration; it should be supplemented with water-soluble vitamins. The major therapeutic considerations are directed toward relief of portal hypertension, salt and water retention, and the bleeding tendency, and toward prevention of hepatic coma.

REFERENCES

Achar, S. T., Raju, V. E., and Srirmachari, S. Indian childhood cirrhosis. J. Pediat., 57:744, 1960.

Craig, J. M., Gellis, S. S., and Hsia, D. Y. Y. Cirrhosis of the liver in infants and children. Amer. J. Dis. Child., 90:299, 1955.

di Sant'Agnese, P. A., and Blanc, W. A. A distinctive type of biliary cirrhosis of the liver associated with cystic fibrosis of the pancreas; recognition through signs of portal hypertension. Pediatrics, 18:387, 1956.

Klatskin, G. Newer concepts of cirrhosis. Arch. Int. Med., 104:899, 1959.

Smetana, H. F., et al. Infantile cirrhosis; analytical review of literature and report of 50 cases. Pediatrics, 28:107, 1961.

24.10
PORTAL HYPERTENSION

LAWRENCE M. GARTNER and
IRWIN M. ARIAS

Portal venous hypertension is produced when the flow of portal blood to the liver is obstructed either within the liver or along the extrahepatic portal vein. A major cause of portal hypertension in children is thrombosis ("cavernous transformation") of the portal vein, the etiology of which is usually unknown. Omphalitis, umbilical vein catheterization, and intra abdominal infection in infancy may produce portal vein thrombosis. Hepatic function and histology are completely normal. Although thrombosis of the portal vein probably occurs in the newborn period, the onset of bleeding from esophageal varices, almost always the presenting symptom in this disorder, does not occur until 6 months to 15 years later. Variceal hemorrhage is manifested by hematemesis, melena, sudden onset of anemia, and in some cases shock. Hemorrhage is usually not fatal when hepatic function and morphology are normal. The other signs of extrahepatic portal obstruction are splenomegaly, distended abdominal veins, thrombocytopenia, leucopenia, and anemia. Following the sudden loss of a large volume of blood, the spleen may not be palpable. However, after blood transfusion or spontaneous restoration of blood volume, splenomegaly may reappear.

The second major cause of portal hypertension in children is cirrhosis, which may be postnecrotic or biliary. In biliary cirrhosis, portal hypertension follows months or years of jaundice, pruritis, and progressive deterioration of hepatic function. In postnecrotic cirrhosis of any cause, the progressive deterioration of hepatic function may be very insidious, but clinical and laboratory signs of hepatic damage are usually evident prior to clinical recognition of portal hypertension.

In schistosomiasis of the liver, hepatic function remains normal until very late in the disease, and portal hypertension and massive splenomegaly occur as initial manifestations. This sequence results from intrahepatic portal venous obstruction by schistosome eggs and the associated inflammation. Markedly elevated serum alkaline phosphatase activity is usually observed in schistosomiasis of the liver, but its cause is obscure. In endemic areas, such as northeastern Brazil, China, and Africa, schistosomiasis is the predominant cause of portal hypertension in children; it may be associated with infantilism.

A relatively rare cause of portal hypertension is the syndrome of congenital hepatic fibrosis with polycystic disease of the liver, kidneys, and/or spleen. Hepatic fibrosis may exist without hepatic cysts, however; there may also be hepatic cysts without fibrosis. Approximately one-half of the children with polycystic disease of the liver have renal polycystic disease as well. The hepatic cysts are variable in size, occasionally being large enough to be identified by hepatic scanning or angiography. The initial symptom is usually hematemesis secondary to esophageal varices, the existence of hepatic disease having been unnoticed since jaundice and laboratory evidence of liver disease are absent. Portal hypertension is thought to result from a paucity of hepatic portal venules rather than fibrosis or the cysts. Massive hepatomegaly is common, and in some young infants an enlarged abdomen may be the first indication of hepatic disease.

Although extremely rare in infants and children, obstruction of hepatic vein blood flow due to thrombosis or tumor (Budd-Chiari syndrome) may result in catastrophic illness with sudden hepatic enlargement and vascular collapse. Portal hypertension and secondary splenic enlargement result as well.

Ascites is generally absent in those causes of portal hypertension which spare hepatocellular function, such as congenital hepatic fibrosis and extrahepatic portal vein thrombosis, whereas it is common in those disorders with reduced hepatic cell function such as cirrhosis.

The diagnosis of portal hypertension requires

the demonstration of esophageal and/or gastic varices by barium swallow or endoscopy or demonstration of elevated portal venous pressure by splenic pulp manometry or umbilical venous catheterization. Percutaneous splenic venography usually demonstrates the site and extent of obstruction to the portal venous system and frequently reveals the size and location of anastomoses between the portal and systemic venous systems. The latter information is of critical importance in determining the type of surgery to be performed. When portal hypertension is secondary to cirrhosis or congenital hepatic fibrosis, percutaneous splenic venography or umbilical venography reveals dilated collateral venous channels, normal portal vein, and intrahepatic circulatory changes. Meghini needle biopsy is of considerable assistance in differentiating intrahepatic from extrahepatic causes of portal hypertension.

Surgical relief of portal hypertension offers the only means by which subsequent hemorrhagic episodes may be prevented. The decision to perform surgery and the choice of technique depend on the location of the obstruction, the frequency and severity of previous bleeding, the degree of hypersplenism, and the availability of vessels of sufficient size to permit successful anastomosis. In certain patients with severe cirrhosis the operative risks may be so great that surgery should not be undertaken. Portal venous surgery in patients with normal hepatic histology and function should result in a permanent cure of the disease without risk of hepatic damage from diversion of portal blood. However, in patients with cirrhosis, although successful surgical correction of portal hypertension may prevent subsequent bleeding from esophageal varices, hepatic function sometimes deteriorates further, resulting in death from hepatic insufficiency.

REFERENCES

Hsia, D. Y. Y., and Gellis, S. S. Portal hypertension in infants and children. Amer. J. Dis. Child., 90:290, 1955.

Oski, F. A., Allen, D. H., and Diamond, L. K. Portal hypertension—a complication of umbilical vein catheterization. Pediatrics, 31:297, 1963.

Sherlock, S. Diseases of the Liver and Biliary System, 3rd ed. Philadelphia, F. A. Davis Co., 1963.

Vorhees, A. B., Jr., Harris, R. C., Britton, R. C., Price, J. B., and Santulli, T. V. Portal hypertension in children: 98 cases. Surgery, 58:540, 1965.

24.11
HEPATIC FAILURE

LAWRENCE M. GARTNER

Hepatic failure occurs when liver cell function is no longer able to sustain the minimal needs of the patient for synthesis and detoxification of a large number of chemical substances. The syndrome is characterized initially by mild confusion, slowness of thought, slurred speech, and poor handwriting (Stage I). This stage may be followed by more severe drowsiness and bizarre behavior, as well as tremors and flapping of the hands when elevated (Stage II). Stage III is characterized by marked sleepiness, incoherent speech, mental confusion, and severe hand flap; stage IV, by complete coma and absence of hand flap. The EEG is abnormal during stages II, III, and IV. Other evidence of hepatic cellular insufficiency usually develops concomitantly with the onset of coma or pre-coma. Marked prolongation of prothrombin time occurs, as well as hypoglycemia and severe hyperbilirubinemia. Hypoalbuminemia occurs after several days. Previously elevated SGOT and SGPT values may decline abruptly with the onset of hepatic failure. The liver often decreases in size, heralding the loss of hepatic tissue and glycogen. Hepatic failure may occur with either acute hepatic damage such as viral hepatitis or toxic ingestions, or in chronic and progressive disorders of the liver, such as chronic active hepatitis. Ammonia levels in the circulating blood are usually elevated, assisting in diagnosis of hepatic failure. It is not certain whether ammonia accumulation alone or other toxic accumulations are responsible for the neurologic disturbance. The overall mortality in all patients with hepatic failure regardless of age and diagnosis is 90 percent.

Treatment of hepatic failure consists of removal of protein from the diet, prevention of absorption of protein products from the intestine by enemas, and oral administration of nonabsorbable antibiotics such as neomycin to prevent bacterial enzymatic production of ammonia. Intestinal bleeding must be prevented as well. The development of esophageal hemorrhage will often precipitate the onset of hepatic coma. Diuretics should be discontinued since these may also precipitate coma. Corticosteroids are usually used, but there is no evidence that they are effective in the treatment of hepatic failure. Hemodialysis and peritoneal dialysis have not been helpful although the blood ammonia level is reduced by these procedures. Cross circulation with animals and human volunteers has met with some success. The method currently held most effective is exchange transfusion using fresh blood equivalent to twice the patient's blood volume. Repeated transfusions may be necessary and plasmapheresis may be used to reduce the volume of fresh red cells needed. Many patients show marked improvement of neurologic status immediately following the procedure, only to deteriorate again. Experience thus far indicates a slight improvement in overall survival with the use of exchange transfusion.

REFERENCES

Chalmers, T. C. Pathogenesis and treatment of hepatic failure. New Eng. J. Med., 263:23-30, 77-82, 1960.

Cohen, M. I., Schonberg, S. K., and Witover, S. The use of plasmapheresis during exchange transfusion for hepatic encephalopathy. J. Pediat., 75:431-435, 1969.

Trey, C., and Davidson, C. S. The management of fulminant hepatic failure. *In* Popper, H., and Schaffner, F., eds., Progress in Liver Disease, Vol. III. New York, Grune and Stratton, 1970, p. 282-298, Chap. 18.

24.12
TUMORS OF THE LIVER

JAY BERNSTEIN, A. JOSEPH BROUGH, and SEYMOUR ALPERT

Primary tumors of the liver are relatively uncommon in children, accounting for 1.5 percent of all tumors. They comprise perhaps 10 percent of abdominal neoplasms. Approximately two-thirds of such tumors are discovered in the first three years of life; the peak incidence is at 1 year of age. Some hepatic tumors are present at birth.

The most common clinical abnormality is painless abdominal enlargement. Jaundice rarely occurs, and abnormalities of liver function tests are uncommon. Excretory urography is often helpful in establishing that the abdominal tumor is hepatic, rather than an extrahepatic neuroblastoma or a Wilms' tumor. Hepatic calcification, sometimes due to bone formation, can be seen radiographically, simulating metastatic neuroblastoma. Scintillation scanning, celiac axis angiography, splenoportography, cholecystography, and cholangiography are valuable in localizing areas of involvement and demonstrating important anatomic relationships that must be known if surgical therapy is considered. The specific diagnosis of a hepatic tumor can only be determined by pathologic examination of tissue obtained by needle or open biopsy. Although radiologic studies may suggest operability or inoperability, a laparotomy is necessary for determining the extent and resectability of a tumor.

Hepatocellular neoplasms constitute approximately one-half of primary hepatic tumors in childhood. Carcinomas are usually primary in the sense that they are not associated with preexisting cirrhosis. Hepatocellular tumors include both hepatoblastoma and hepatocellular carcinoma, the former a less differentiated tumor that often contains mesenchymal elements. The mesenchymal components include variable amounts of hematopoietic tissue, osteoid, bone, cartilage, and muscle. Both types of tumors are often associated with a specific serum α_2-globulin fetoprotein which has diagnostic and prognostic importance. Epithelial differentiation in hepatoblastoma can occasionally lead to squamous metaplasia, melanin production, and gonadotropin production with precocious puberty. The incidence of congenital malformations in patients with hepatoblastoma is unexpectedly high.

Both types of hepatocellular tumors are associated relatively frequently with osteoporosis and with the combination of hyperlipemia, hypercholesterolemia, and lipid histiocytosis. The prognosis in hepatoblastoma may be relatively good in comparison with the outcome in hepatic carcinoma. In at least one series, one-half of children with successfully resected tumors were long-term survivors, and our own experience has been similar. (See Table 1.) Hepatocellular carcinomas, on the other hand, generally have a poor prognosis, despite a frequently benign histologic appearance. The well-differentiated hepatocellular carcinoma cannot always be distinguished from the rare hepatic adenoma, and the usual criteria of malignancy, such as cellular atypism and vascular invasion, are often lacking. Malignant hepatomas invade local vessels and metastasize to other portions of the liver, to the lungs, to the peritoneum, and to lymph nodes. Direct extension through the vena cava also occurs.

Malignant mesenchymal tumors are rare. One in particular, an embryonal sarcoma or rhabdomyosarcoma, has been discussed extensively in the literature. It may arise in the liver or more commonly in the extrahepatic biliary tree. Growth into and along the common duct causes intermittent, mild jaundice. The tumors are similar histologically to embryonal rhabdomyosarcomas seen elsewhere. The prognosis is exceedingly poor. Chemotherapy and irradiation are only palliative.

Benign tumors of the liver include hepatocellular adenomas, hemangiomas, lymphangiomas, and so-called hamartomas. One group of adenomas is distinguished by a central fibrous core and centrally placed bile ducts within tumor nodules. Hemangiomas may grow to considerable size and produce symptoms by pressure. They may be solitary or part of a generalized visceral hemangiomatosis. They have been observed to opacify during excretory urography. Both cavernous and endotheliomatous tumors occur. Such tumors occasionally behave as arteriovenous fistulas, with an audible bruit and cardiomegaly. Thrombosis of the vascular channels can lead to consumption of clotting factors and secondary thrombocytopenia. Traumatic rupture of a vascular tumor can lead to exsanguinating hemorrhage. Lymphangiomas can become enormous, and the loculi contain

TABLE 1. *Hepatic Tumors, Children's Hospital of Michigan, 1950-1970*

	Total	Alive
Hepatoblastoma	11*	4
Hepatic carcinoma	4	0
Hepatic sarcoma	2	0
Lymphangioma	3	3
Hemangioma	6	6
"Hepatic neuroblastoma"	6†	4

*3 operative deaths, 2 tumor deaths, 2 lost-to-follow-up
†2 deaths not related to tumor

fluid indistinguishable from hepatic lymph. They may be superficial or pedunculated, and they are rarely associated with visceral lymphangiomatosis. Hamartomas contain epithelial and mesenchymal elements arranged in disorderly fashion, and they are sometimes regarded as tumorous malformations.

Hepatic cysts of biliary origin can arise as part of polycystic disease or as isolated lesions. The latter are usually unilocular and lined by biliary epithelium. They may develop as the result of localized ductal obstruction and distention. They contain mucus and bile in varying amounts and at times are surrounded by dense fibrous capsules.

Metastatic tumors of the liver are far more common than primary tumors. Of particular interest is so-called hepatic neuroblastoma, i.e., marked hepatomegaly due to extensive infiltration by neuroblastoma in very young infants. The tumor is presumed to arise in the adrenal, although demonstration of an adrenal mass is frequently lacking. The babies present with abdominal distention and mild anemia, and the diagnosis is usually established by liver biopsy and histopathologic examination. The prognosis in our experience has been extremely good. Most cases have been treated with irradiation, resulting in complete resolution of the tumor and long-term survival. Spontaneous resolution has also been known to occur without specific therapy.

Surgical extirpation of primary tumors is the accepted form of therapy at present. Resection of very large tumors involving the right or left hepatic lobes is practicable by modern surgical techniques. Benign tumors should be excised preferably in toto; partial resection may be necessary if symptoms due to enlargement or rupture occur. Hamartomas that are pedunculated can easily be excised; however, those deep within the parenchyma, producing no symptoms, may be left in situ after a definitive diagnosis has been made.

REFERENCES

Clatworthy, W. H., Boles, E. T., Jr., and Kottmeier, P. K. Liver tumors in infancy and childhood. Ann. Surg., 154:476, 1961.

Edmondson, H. S. Differential diagnosis of tumors and tumor-like lesions of liver in infancy and childhood. Amer. J. Dis. Child., 91:168, 1956.

chapter 25

THE BONES AND JOINTS

FREDERIC SILVERMAN, Associate Editor

The skeletal system is more than a structural framework designed to support and protect soft tissues and to implement their activities, as in locomotion. It is an active reservoir of elements important in homeostasis, and often accurately reflects responses to conditions that threaten functional integrity of the body as a whole. In addition, it is subject to disorders restricted to, or chiefly manifested in, bone. Certain systemic conditions with skeletal manifestations, such as scurvy, rickets, renal and metabolic disorders, infections of bone and joints, including tuberculosis and syphilis, and skeletal aspects of growth and development are described in their respective chapters and the reader is referred to them and to the index for conditions not found below. This section deals largely with primary disorders of the skeletal system and is organized on a regional basis.

25.1

THE SKULL

Congenital and Developmental Anomalies

Congenital and developmental defects of the skull may occur as isolated abnormalities or as part of a more or less clearly defined syndrome. When an unusual lesion presents in the skull, it is wise to search elsewhere for other defects.

VARIATIONS IN SIZE. An abnormally large head is properly designated *macrocranium* or *macrocephaly*. Hydrocephalus is one of the major causes of macrocranium but not an exclusive one; in the infant, an enlarging head is a common clinical sign of subdural hematoma. Primary enlargement of the brain, in which an absolute increase in weight of brain occurs, is called *megalencephaly* and is associated with enlargement of the cranial cavity. In the brain, the amount of tissue and function are poorly correlated, and, as in hydrocephalus, children with megalencephalic macrocranium frequently are mentally retarded. *Brain tumors* cause cranial enlargement by obstructing cerebrospinal fluid pathways, producing hydrocephalus. *Pseudohydrocephalus* is the disproportionate enlargement of the cranium with respect to the facial structures; it is seen most commonly in lateral projections of the skull in premature infants. A similar disproportion is observed in hypopituitary and Russell-Silver dwarfs, and in some instances of

the diencephalic syndromes. Also, in the recovery phase of privational dwarfism, when cranial growth is rapid, widened sutures may simulate those of actively increased intracranial pressure. Macrocranium is a component of some generalized hyperostotic skeletal disorders; in achondroplasia it usually indicates hydrocephalus. The head reaches adult size in early life in cerebral gigantism.

Microcrania or *microcephaly* is an abnormally small head, frequently associated with, or resulting from, a primary developmental defect of the brain, *microencephaly*. Microcrania may be due to many causes, including *premature synostosis* of all the cranial sutures, prenatal infection (toxoplasmosis, cytomegalic inclusion disease, rubella), high-dosage levels of intrauterine radiation, and other causes of brain injury during fetal life or infancy. It is a common manifestation of syndromes associated with mental retardation; almost all children with a head circumference more than two standard deviations below the mean are mentally subnormal.

VARIATIONS IN SHAPE. Macrocranium and microcranium are evaluated more adequately with the tape measure than by simple inspection or roentgen examination; however, abnormalities of shape may alter a measurable circumference while a normal cranial volume is retained as a result of compensatory changes in dimensions not usually measured. Thus, *postural flattening* due to prolonged recumbency in infancy may increase the vertical height of the skull at the expense of dimensions in the horizontal plane (Fig. 1). Mentally retarded children and those with neuromuscular defects are frequently unable or slow to sit without support and often manifest marked postural flattening. Infants with normal mentality, maintained in dorsal recumbency by virtue of any debilitating or prolonged illness, including affective deprivation, or by orthopedic appliances, may also develop postural flattening. Once the child can sit and maintain the erect position, the deformity usually disappears spontaneously. Craniosynostoses are responsible for most clinically obvious variations in cranial shape which are persistent.

Cranial bossing of *rickets (caput quadratum)* and *syphilitic hyperostoses* are now rarely seen. *Cephalhematoma* (Sec. 2.10) is the most common cause of circumscribed cranial swelling in the newborn period. Defects associated with *meningocele* or *encephalocele* are easily recognized (Sec. 15.2). Asymmetry of the skull is associated with *congenital torticollis;* in this condition, asymmetry is characterized by occipital flattening on the side opposite

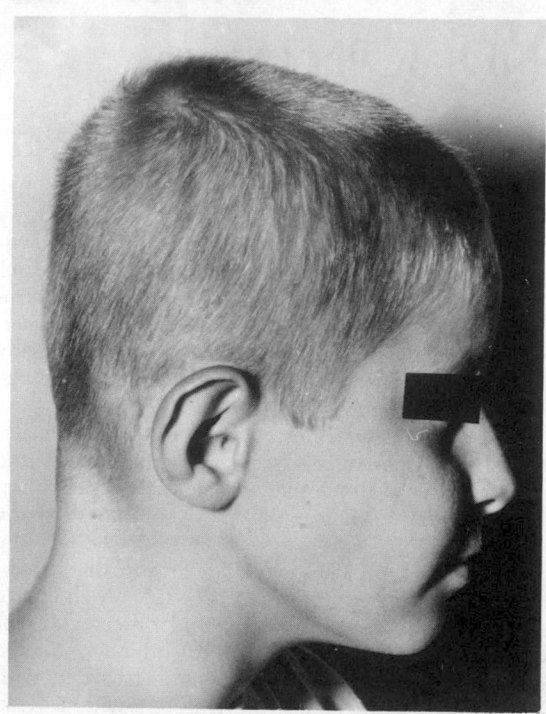

Fig. 1. Postural flattening of skull in a child with prolonged recumbency resulting from congenital cardiac disease.

the affected sternocleidomastoid muscle and downward displacement of the eye, ear, and corner of the mouth on the same side. *Polyostotic fibrous dysplasia* may also produce asymmetry of the skull. A wide cranial vault is commonly seen in *osteogenesis imperfecta* and in cleidocranial dysostosis. *Facial asymmetry* occurs in the *cri du chat* syndrome, and is progressive in *Romberg's facial hemiatrophy* (Fig. 2A and B).

Neurofibromatosis may be associated with cranial and facial asymmetry. *Hemifacial microsomia* is another cause of facial asymmetry and is considered by some to be a variant of Goldenhar's syndrome (oculo-auriculo-vertebral dysplasia).

A special form of fibrous dysplasia affecting the jaws almost exclusively is a cause of facial swelling in childhood. Known as "cherubism" or *familial fibrous dysplasia of the jaws,* it appears to result from action of a dominant gene, with 100 per cent penetrance in males and 50 to 70 percent penetrance in females. There is painless, usually symmetrical swelling of the jaws beginning at about 2 to 5 years of age and persisting until puberty, after which slow resolution takes place. Despite severe cystic changes in the jaws with marked crowding of the teeth and gross oral and facial deformity, symptoms are few and treatment is unnecessary.

Jaw cysts occur in the *basal cell nevus syndrome* where they are associated with multiple cutaneous basal cell carcinomas, small pits in the palms, rib

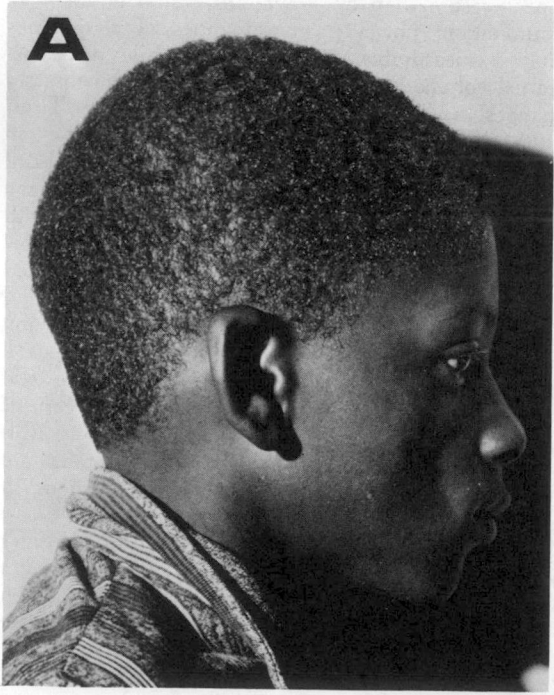

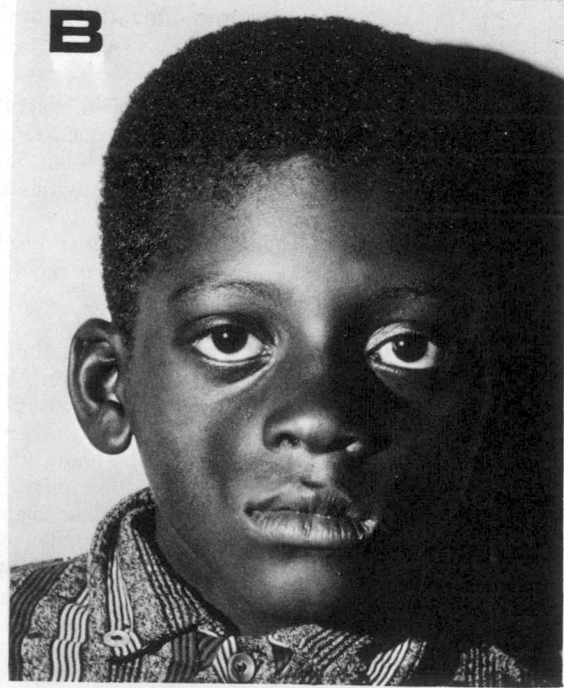

Fig. 2. (A and B) Romberg's facial hemiatrophy. The right-sided deformity was progressive during the period of growth.

and vertebral deformities, and calcification in the falx cerebri. Siblings of patients with the syndrome have presented with brain tumors which, curiously, were all medulloblastomas.

CRANIOSYNOSTOSIS. Premature union of the cranial bones may take place before birth, which is considered to be the case if manifestations are observed prior to the second decade. When intrauterine synostosis of the coronal and lambdoidal sutures is associated with congenital hydrocephalus, the newborn infant has a grotesque trilobed cranium which has been given the name of "cloverleaf skull" (Kleeblattschädel). The range of normal variation in the time of postnatal closure of sutures has not been established, but there has been an increasing tendency to consider that beginning closure may take place normally in the second decade. Findings on direct inspection of the vault are not infrequently at variance with radiographic interpretations. Nevertheless, when premature union of cranial bones takes place during an age when growth of the brain is active, distortion occurs in patterns that frequently permit analysis of the sutures affected. If growth of the bony cranium is arrested at any one site, and the cranial contents continue to enlarge, compensatory growth must occur at other sites.

Three basic assumptions, for which there is ample support, are helpful to understand the cranial distortions produced by craniosynostosis: (1) growth of the cranial vault is dependent upon growth of the brain; (2) growth occurs at the sutures in a direction perpendicular to the longitudinal axis of the suture; and (3) premature closure of one small segment of a suture is as effective in restricting growth as is involvement of the entire suture. The implication is that bony continuity across a suture may not be demonstrated radiographically even though premature union has taken place.

Craniosynostosis of the sagittal suture is the most common form, occurring in about 50 percent of recorded cases. Lateral growth of the cranium is restricted, compensatory growth takes place in length, and the skull becomes long and narrow (*scaphocephaly*) and may increase in height as well (Fig. 3). Craniosynostosis of the coronal suture is second in frequency and gives rise to a skull that is short in its anteroposterior diameter, but wide and high (*acrocephaly* or *oxycephaly*) (Fig. 4). Associated malformations are more common whenever the coronal suture is involved; segmentation errors of the hands and feet (Fig. 5) and functional or anatomic defects of the brain, facial deformity, and ocular hypertelorism are frequently present. The shallow orbits lead to proptosis, and pressure on the optic nerves

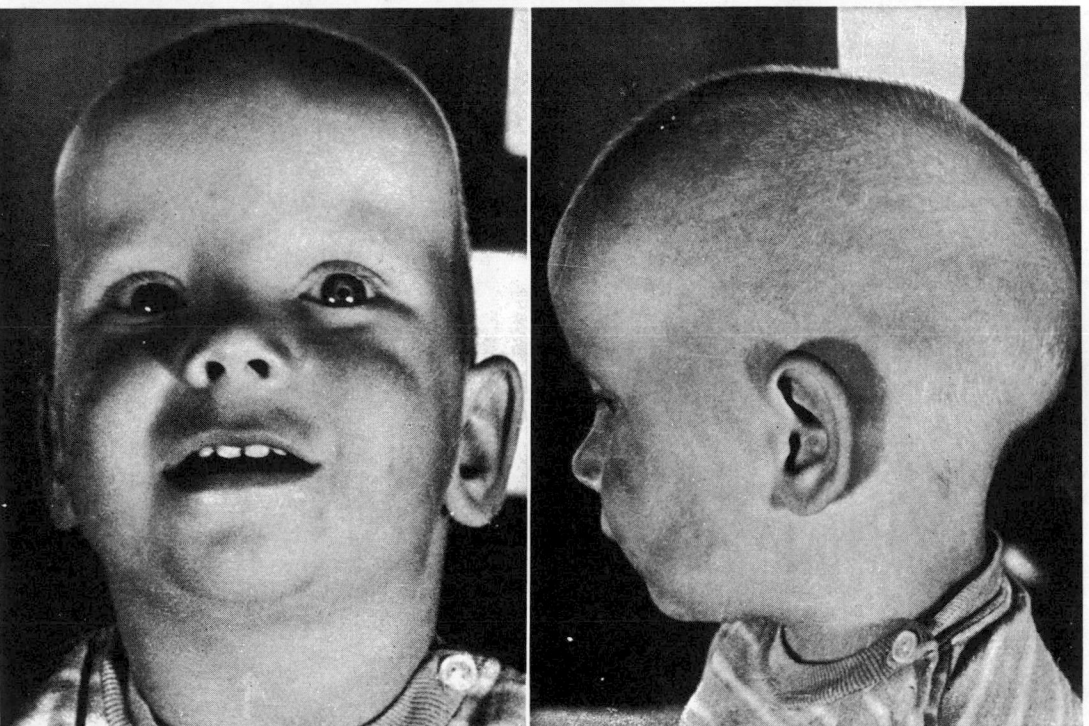

Fig. 3. Premature synostosis of sagittal suture. The cranium is narrow but high and elongated ventrodorsally. (From Silverman. *Ohio Med. J.,* 50:131, 1954.)

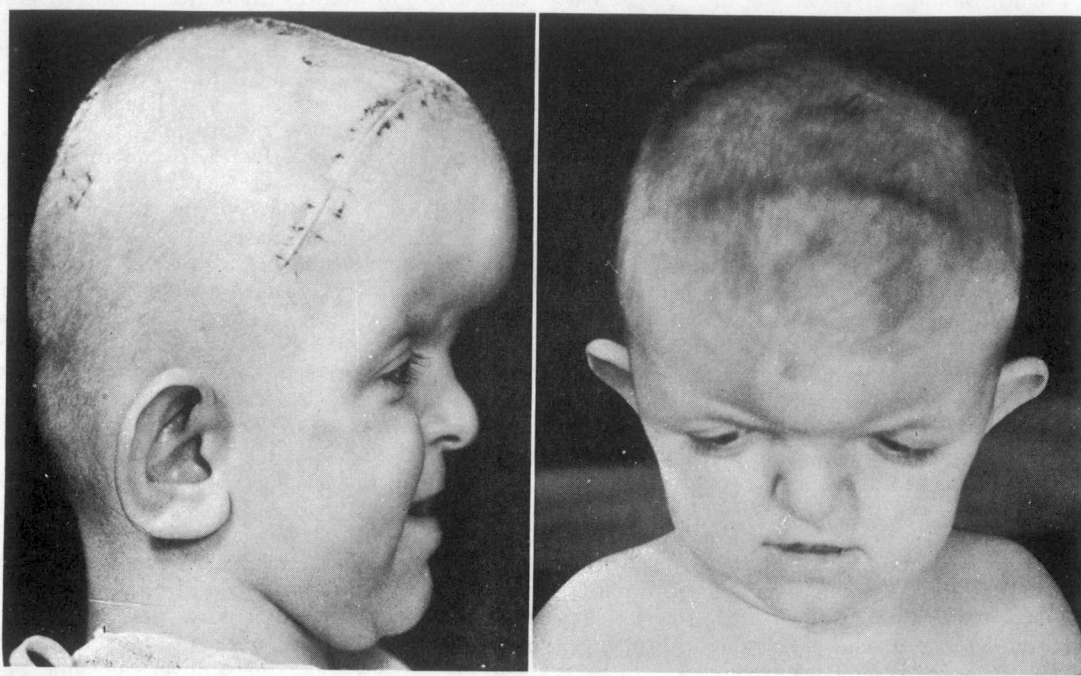

Fig. 4.   Premature synostosis of coronal suture. (Courtesy of Dr. Frank Mayfield.)

by the distorted bony structures may result in progressive blindness. Unilateral premature synostosis of the coronal suture (*plagiocephaly*) results in flattening of the forehead on the affected side with elevation of the ipsilateral orbit (Fig. 6). Pedal and manual deformities, especially syndactyly, are common when coronal suture and sagittal suture closure are combined; the combinations give rise to various forms of acrocephalosyndactylies, of which *Apert's syndrome* is perhaps the best known. They also occur with acrocephalopolysyndactylies, of which *Carpenter's syndrome* is the best example. These conditions have been confused with the *Laurence-Moon-Biedl syndrome* but can be differentiated by radial rather than ulnar polysyndactyly and by the absence of retinitis pigmentosa in the former conditions. Sagittal

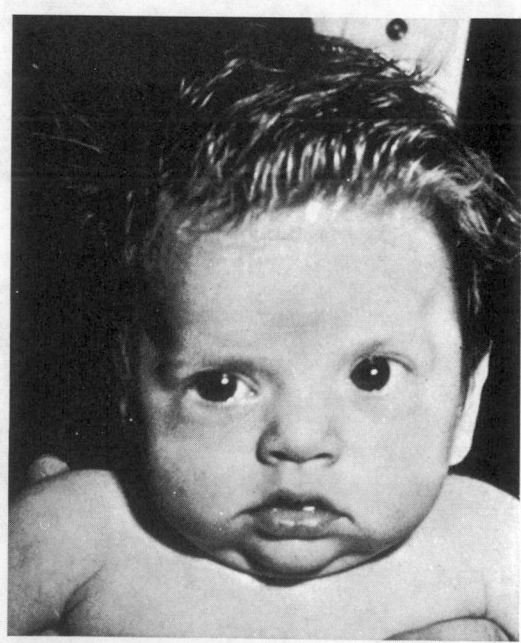

Fig. 5.   Pedal syndactyly. Foot of patient shown in Figure 3. (Courtesy of Dr. Frank Mayfield.)

Fig. 6.   Plagiocephaly. The forehead is flattened on the left side, and the left orbit is elevated, as a result of premature synostosis of the left limb of the coronal suture.

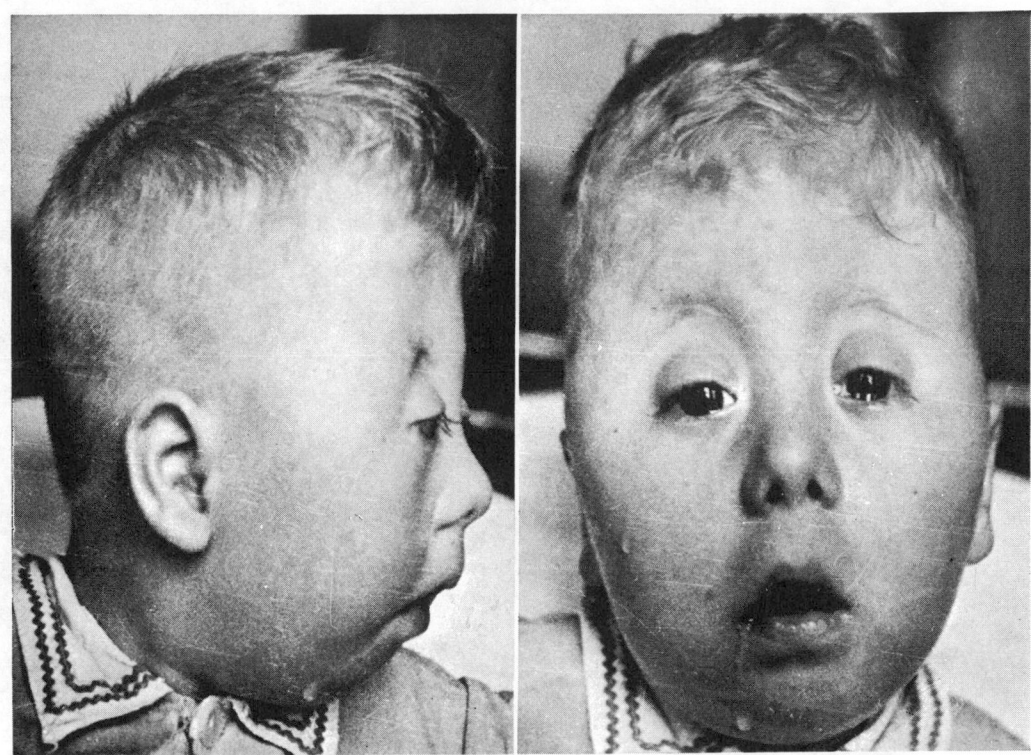

Fig. 7. Premature synostosis of coronal and sagittal sutures. (From Silverman. *Ohio Med. J.,* 50:131, 1954.)

and coronal suture involvement permits cranial growth almost exclusively in the vertical axis of the skull. The cranium is high, narrow, and almost comes to a point (Fig. 7).

Trigonocephaly, a triangular-shaped head with a keel-like protrusion of the forehead, is associated with premature obliteration of the metopic suture and with hypoplasia of the ethmoid bone which results in an abnormally narrowed distance between the medial walls of the orbits (orbital hypotelorism). A mongoloid slope to the palpebral fissures is commonly present, but only rarely is the condition associated with Down's syndrome.

In *Crouzon's disease,* the cranial deformity is associated with hypoplasia of the facial bones, producing a characteristic facies (Fig. 8) with a high, wide skull flattened anteroposteriorly, exophthalmos and external strabismus, a beaked nose, a short upper lip due to hypoplasia of the maxilla, and a protruding lower lip due to relative mandibular prognathism. When all the cranial sutures are obliterated prematurely, growth of the skull is prevented in all directions and microcrania and microcephaly result.

Premature synostosis of the cranial sutures has been observed in hypophosphatasia, idiopathic hypercalcemia, vitamin D-resistant rickets, and even in simple privational rickets. It may occur as a complication following relief of increased intracranial pressure in hydrocephalus by a ventriculojugular shunt mechanism.

In the majority of cases, the diagnosis may be made or at least suspected at birth because of obvious skull deformity or common associated deformities. Palpation of the fontanels and sutures may reveal obliteration of normally soft areas or actual heaping up of bone to form a ridge along the path of a suture. X-ray examination of the skull provides conclusive diagnosis only when bony continuity across a suture is demonstrated; otherwise, it provides only supportive evidence by the demonstration of deformities secondary to the invisible suture abnormality. In instances in which all the sutures are obliterated so that compensatory deformity cannot occur, a "hammered silver" appearance is usually present. This appearance is generally considered indicative of increased intracranial pressure, but measurements of cerebrospinal fluid pressure are infrequent in reports on craniosynostosis, and results are not always in agreement. Evidence provided by flattened gyri, diminished amounts of cerebrospinal fluid, and forceful abrupt separation of bones when the last connecting fragment of bone is removed during creation of an artificial suture, indicates that increased intracranial pressure does exist in some instances.

Postural flattening of the skull, and microcrania due to primary developmental or acquired defect of the brain, must be differentiated from craniosynostosis. In the former, there is often marked flattening in the occipital region but little or no deformity in the region of the orbits, and the coronal sutures are

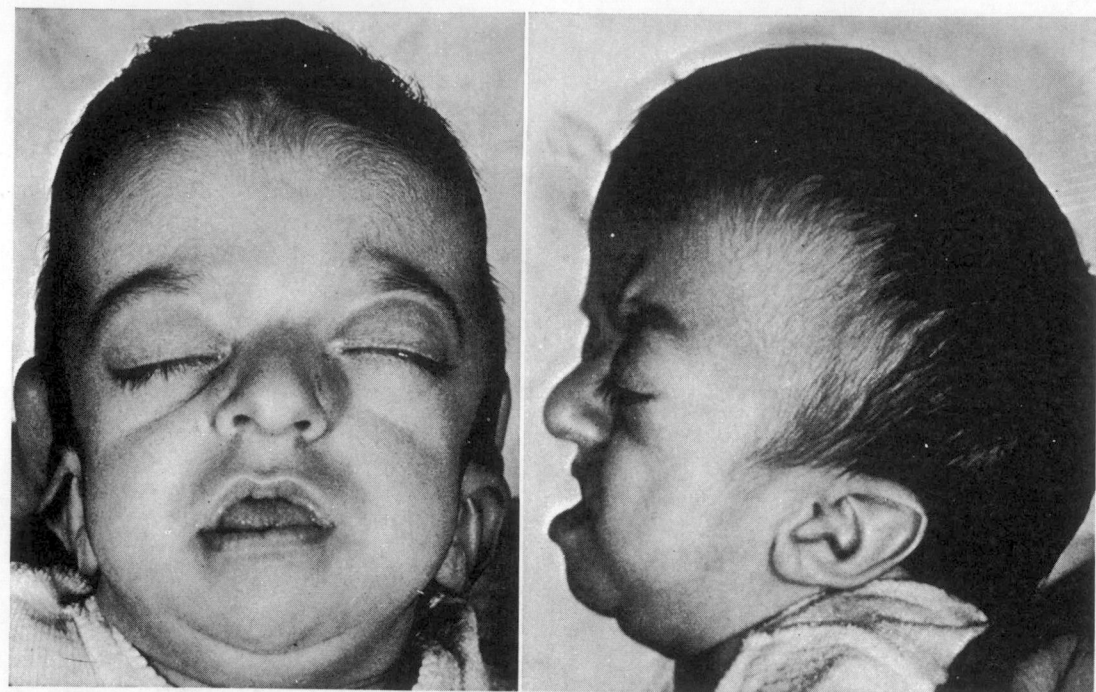

Fig. 8. Crouzon's disease. Craniosynostosis in association with hypoplasia of the maxilla and other deformities. Note the exophthalmos even with the lids closed, the prognathism and the beaked nose.

clearly open on roentgenographic examination. In microcrania, the skull is small because the stimulus of a growing brain is lacking. The sutures may close prematurely but there is little or no cranial deformity, and signs of increased intracranial pressure are absent. In addition, the cranial bones may be unusually thick, and pneumatization of the paranasal sinuses and of the temporal bone is often exaggerated.

The clinical importance of craniosynostosis is related to (1) distortion, compression, and subsequent dysfunction of the brain and its nerves; (2) associated malformations of the brain; and (3) psychologic effects of cranial and facial deformities.

The logical treatment for craniosynostosis is the surgical production of artificial sutures to permit normal, symmetric growth of the brain which may thereby attain optimal development. Surgical treatment was recommended and attempted in the late nineteenth century, fell into disfavor, but was revived in the 1930's and 1940's when radiographic identification had become established and surgical techniques had improved. At present, surgical treatment is recommended in instances of severe deformity or papilledema and in Crouzon's disease. Since the rate of growth of the brain is very rapid during the first year of life, lesser indications may be more important when the condition is recognized early. Considerable disagreement exists concerning the indications for treatment of isolated sagittal suture synostosis; some even suggest that the mental development and cosmetic results are not significantly

affected by treatment in this form of synostosis. For other forms, the division of opinion on management is not so great. Neurosurgeons reporting the largest series of cases tend to be the most enthusiastic in relation to surgical management and its results. In general, the pediatrician must be guided by the experiences of his neurosurgical colleagues, but it is well to recognize that the procedure is technically easier during the first year, and particularly during the first six months, than it is at later ages.

CRANIAL DEFECTS.   At birth, as many as six fontanels may be palpated or demonstrated radiographically in the normal infant skull (Fig. 9). Additional fontanels occur as normal variants in the metopic suture and in the sagittal suture midway between the anterior and posterior fontanels. Occasionally, continuity of unossified membrane is noted between midline fontanels in otherwise normal children; in such instances, closure of the fontanels may be somewhat retarded without any adverse clinical findings. The speed and sequence of fontanel closure are variable. The anterior fontanel usually closes clinically during the first half of the second year of life but may close earlier. The posterior fontanel is generally closed by the end of the second month and may be closed at birth. The anterolateral fontanels disappear during the first three months, and the posterolateral fontanels during the second year. In as many as 35 percent of newborn infants, local areas of softening can be palpated, particularly in the parietal bone along the lambdoidal suture. These areas, when

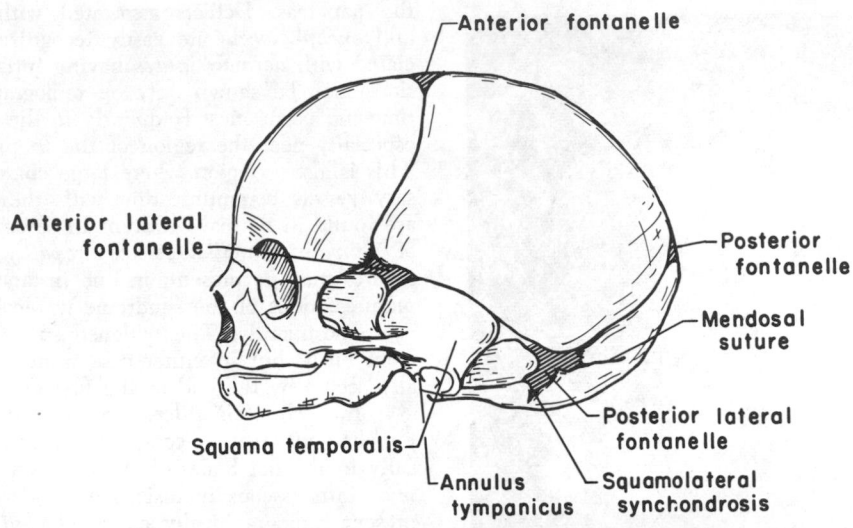

Fig. 9. Normal fontanels in newborn infant, which may be palpated or visualized roentgenographically.

pressed with the finger, give the impression of being indented in the same fashion as a table tennis ball might be indented, and the condition is known as *craniotabes*. Craniotabes occurs pathologically in rickets, hydrocephalus, and certain skeletal dystrophies, but is rare in any event after the first year.

A defect is occasionally palpated extending across the midline just anterior to the region of the posterior fontanel. With the passage of time, bone appears centrally and divides it into symmetrical, bilateral parietal defects known as *enlarged parietal foramina* (Fig. 10A and B). The defects usually occur as solitary lesions without clinical significance. They must be differentiated from defects due to meningocele, histiocytosis X, epidermoidoma, infection, primary or metastatic neoplasm, and from surgical defects. Enlarged parietal foramina often persist throughout life but require no treatment. Their oc-

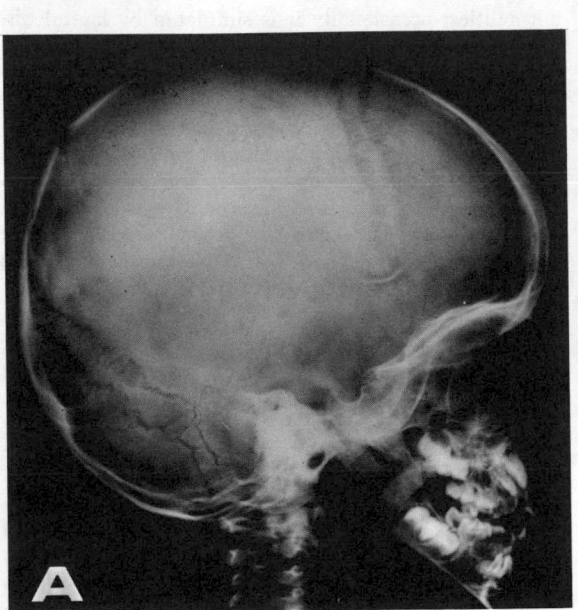

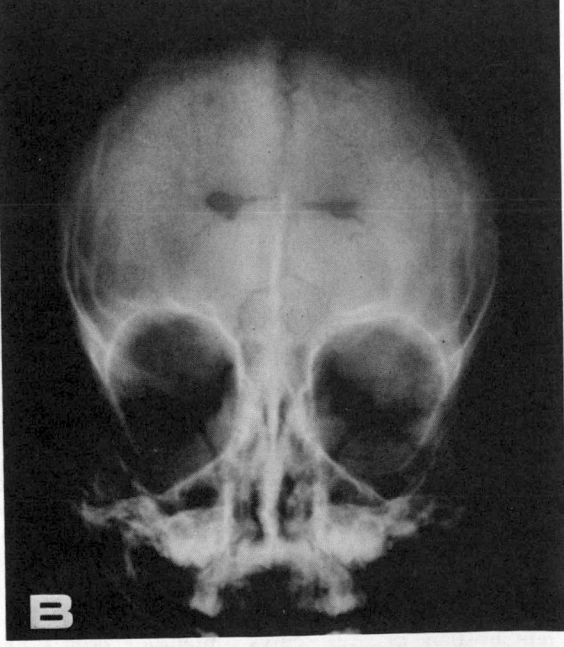

Fig. 10. (A and B) Persistent parietal foramina. Incidental finding in child examined for head injury.

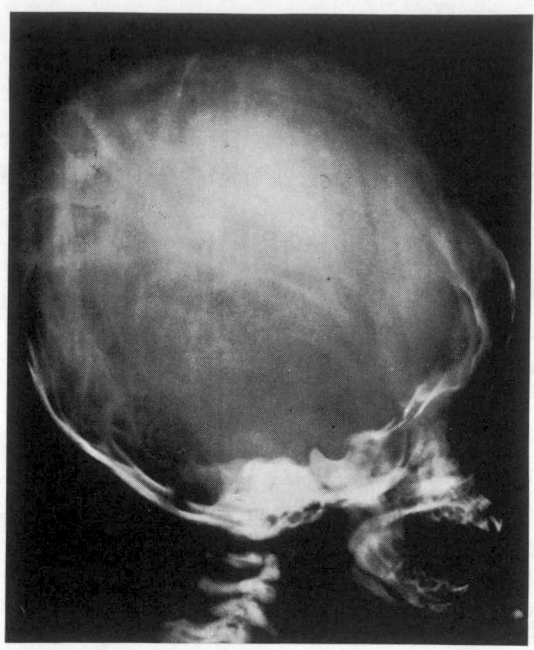

Fig. 11.   Craniolacuna (Lückenschädel).

currence is strongly familial and suggests a dominant genetic trait.

Lacunar skull (Lückenschädel) is the term used to describe the radiographic appearance of multiple large and small radiolucent areas in the infant skull (Fig. 11). It is commonly associated with spina bifida, meningocele, or meningomyelocele. The Arnold-Chiari malformation is a common associated anomaly. Although long survival is not the rule when multiple malformations are present, when lacunar skull occurs as an isolated phenomenon, the prognosis for life and for early disappearance of the irregular mineralization of the skull is good. In fact, even in association with spinal dysraphic syndromes, the soap bubble appearance usually disappears by the second half of the first year.

In osteogenesis imperfecta (p. 1729) and in cleidocranial dysostosis (p. 1731) large cranial defects are present, and at times the cranial vault may feel as if there is no bone present at all. Persistence of a large anterior fontanel with extensions into adjacent sutures may be noted in cleidocranial dysostosis even in adults. Mineralization of the cranium is also lacking in the severe, usually fatal infantile form of hypophosphatasia.

Congenital defects in the roofs and walls of the orbits may lead to cerebral herniation into the orbit (orbital encephalocele) and produce pulsating exophthalmos. In the majority of cases, neurofibromatosis is also present. Unilateral proptosis may also occur in association with retrobulbar glioma, Hand-Schüller-Christian disease, scurvy, infantile cortical hyperostosis, and, rarely, mucocele of a paranasal sinus.

The last may be a manifestation of cystic fibrosis of the pancreas. Defects associated with meningocele and encephalocele are easily recognized; those associated with dermal sinuses having intracranial extensions may be shown only on radiographic examination and occur most frequently in the occipital area, especially near the region of the torcular Herophili. This is also a region where large channels for emissary vessels communicating with the dural sinuses are found in normal children. In occasional instances of idiopathic familial osteoarthropathy, wide cranial sutures may be present; in one instance, the cranial manifestations of the syndrome were observed to develop postnatally. The widened sutures may persist from birth, but in either case mineralization generally occurs by the end of the first decade.

In Hand-Schüller-Christian · disease, focal, punched-out areas are commonly observed radiographically in the flat bones of the cranium. Epidermoidomas, intra-osseous inclusions of epidermal elements, present radiographically as radiolucent defects with sharply demarcated sclerotic borders. Vascular malformations of the epicranium are occasionally associated with clinical and radiologic defects in the calvarium underneath the soft tissue vascular swellings.

MISCELLANEOUS ABNORMALITIES. Ocular hypertelorism is a rare, occasionally inherited deformity of the anterior basilar portion of the cranium and the adjacent facial bones, characterized by a conspicuous increase in the distance between the eyes (Fig. 12). The facial deformity is said to result from overgrowth of the lesser wings of the sphenoid bone and underdevelopment of the greater wings so that there is a simulation of the fetal cranial proportions. It occurs frequently in a mild degree unassociated with functional disturbances or other anatomic abnormalities; occasionally it is simulated by lateral displacement of the inner canthus (dystropia canthorum) without underlying bony abnormality as in Waardenburg's syndrome. In the severe forms, there may be cleft lip, cleft palate, and even cleft nose; occasionally frontal lipomas or teratomas are present. The "median cleft face syndrome," as this group of malformations is known, is less frequently associated with intellectual deficit than is the group of median cleft lip deformities associated with hypotelorism. Orbital hypotelorism is a radiographic diagnosis characterized by an abnormal approximation of the medial walls of the two orbits. Clinically, a relative excess of soft tissue between the palpebral fissures may give the impression of widely spaced eyes. Epicanthal folds are frequently associated with this excessive soft tissue, and it is not surprising that a relative hypotelorism is observed in practically all patients with Down's syndrome, regardless of the chromosomal abnormality. Orbital hypotelorism is also associated with trigonocephaly and the cyclopia-arhinencephaly group of cerebral malformations which occurs frequently in the trisomy 13–15 syndrome. DeMyer and his associates have recommended the term holoprosencephaly for the group of cerebral malformations because the prosencephalon is affected, and because absence of olfactory bulbs and nerves (arhinencephaly) is not a constant manifestation. The cerebral malformations are associated with profound amentia and most affected infants die in infancy.

In the *Treacher-Collins* or *Franceschetti syndrome* (*mandibulofacial dysostosis*) (Fig. 13), the lateral portions of the facial structure, particularly the zygomatic arches, are hypoplastic or absent and the palpebral fissures have an antimongoloid slant. A coloboma is commonly present along the lower lid and the ears are deformed. The mandible is hypoplastic. It has been suggested that unilateral manifestations constitute a different entity, the first and second branchial arch syndrome. Isolated *hypoplasia of the mandible*, also known as *Pierre Robin syndrome*, may produce serious respiratory distress and even retarded physical development when the associated glossoptosis is severe. Because of the small mandible, the tongue tends to fall backward and occlude the pharyngeal airway. The respiratory and feeding difficulties associated with the small lower jaw usually respond to procedures designed to maintain the infant in the prone position. Mechanical and surgical procedures are described for those infants who do not respond to simple positional treatment. With the passage of time, enlargement of the mandible usually takes place spontaneously.

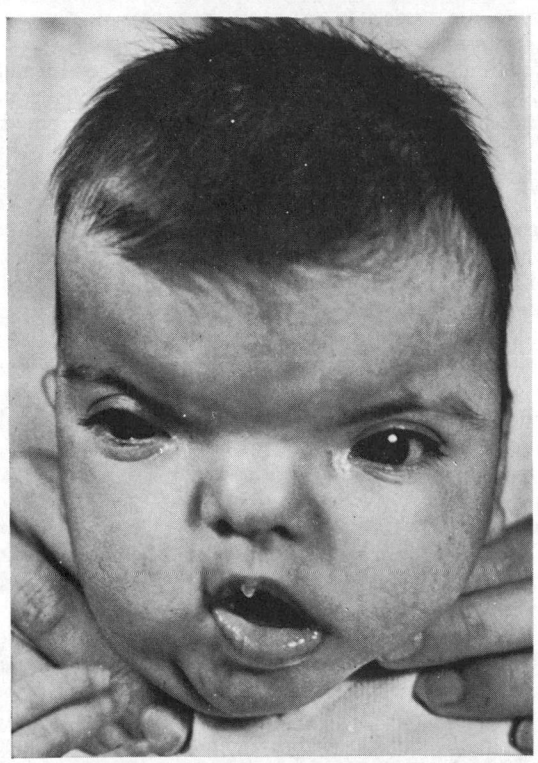

Fig. 12. Ocular hypertelorism. Child also has sagittal craniosynostosis. (Courtesy of Dr. Frank Mayfield.)

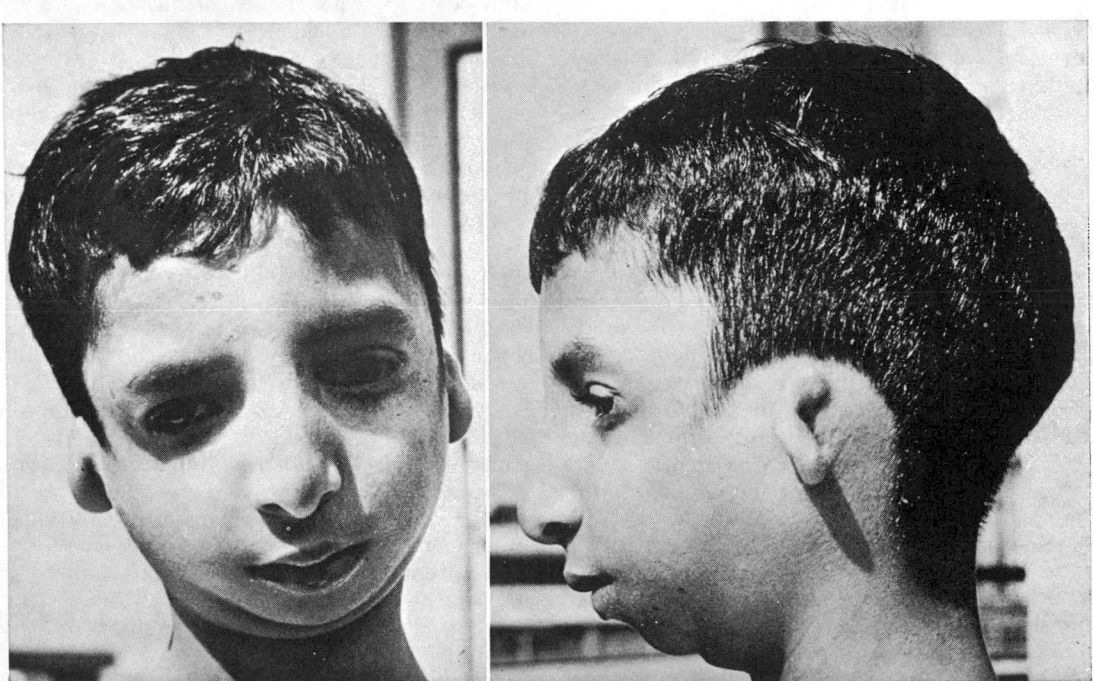

Fig. 13. *Treacher-Collins syndrome* (Franceschetti syndrome, mandibulofacial dysostosis). The deformities of the external ears and the hypoplastic mandible are clearly shown. The antimongoloid slant of the eyes can be recognized, but the defect (coloboma) of the lower lids is obscured by the heavy shadows.

Acquired Cranial Abnormalities

In its passage through the birth canal, the fetal head undergoes characteristic distortion or molding from which recovery occurs within the first few days. The distortion, which increases the vertical dimensions of the head at the expense of the horizontal, results from the following bony alterations: the occipital bone bends as on a hinge at the cartilaginous junction immediately behind the foramen magnum so that the parietal bones are squeezed superiorly, override the occipital posteriorly and the frontal anteriorly, and are widely separated from the squamosa of the temporal bones. In infants delivered by cesarean section, molding may be present only if the procedure was undertaken after the onset of labor. Prominent molding is frequently associated with *neonatal cephalhematoma*. Calcification beneath the overlying periosteum of neonatal cephalhematomas may appear radiographically as either irregular mottled densities or, when the direction of the x-ray beam is tangential to the swelling, as prominent external thickenings. Well-calcified cephalhematomas may be present at birth and probably represent sequels to intrauterine mechanical pressure of the type the promontory of the sacrum may exert against the calvarium. External thickenings of the calvarium may persist into the second decade; occasionally radiolucent areas indicate the site of fibrous rather than bony resolution of a neonatal cephalhematoma.

FRACTURES. Fractures of the skull are common in infancy and childhood, often bearing little relationship to the apparent initiating trauma. The difficulties of obtaining an adequate history of injury must always be kept in mind. Radiographic examination is of great value in the identification of skull fractures, but failure to demonstrate a fracture does not exclude its presence. Gurdjian and his associates have provided charts for the prediction of fracture sites which permit selective positioning during radiologic examination when the site of impact is known. However, the curved surface of the calvarium and the superimposition of the bones of the base, limit the usefulness of these techniques. Except in those cases where there is a depressed fracture, the significance of radiologic documentation of fracture is related to (1) the ability to indicate degrees of injury to soft parts, particularly the brain; (2) the location of the fracture with respect to vascular structures such as the dural sinuses and the middle meningeal vessels which may produce subdural or epidural intracranial hemorrhage; (3) location of the fracture with respect to the air cavities of the skull (nasopharynx, paranasal sinuses, pneumatized portions of the temporal bones, etc.) which provide direct communication with the outside and which may permit introduction of infection into the cranial cavity through the defect; and (4) linear or diastatic (gaping) characteristics of the fracture. Diastatic fractures can occur only if there are associated tears of the dura; under these circumstances, cerebrospinal fluid can escape into the subdural space or into the subgaleal space. In addition, with loss of integrity of the dura, the endocranial surface of the bone is unprotected from the pulsating activity of the underlying brain and cerebrospinal fluid, and erosions may develop in association with subdural fluid collections which act as tumor masses. Rarely, a fracture of this type enlarges progressively to form a permanent cranial defect, usually with underlying cerebral changes such as focal atrophy and with clinical sequelae such as paralyses, convulsions, and mental retardation.

Severe shock, manifested by cold clammy skin, weak and rapid pulse, subnormal temperature, and unconsciousness, is a bad prognostic sign and should be treated immediately, even before diagnostic radiographic procedures are undertaken. The duration of unconsciousness is a rough index of the severity of intracranial damage. The classical signs of epidural hemorrhage—unconsciousness, clear period, recurrence of unconsciousness—call for immediate neurosurgical intervention.

The custom of routine skull examinations for all children who have had known or suspected cranial injury may be questioned. The actual presence of a radiographically demonstrable fracture plays little role in the clinical management of a patient unless there is depression, injury to important vascular channels, or communication with the outside. In general, the clinical information is adequate to indicate those individuals in whom these complications are to be expected. Clinical evidence of depression, definite information of contact with a sharp or pointed object, bleeding from the ear or ecchymoses in the mastoid regions of orbits, and otorrhea or rhinorrhea, all constitute reasonable indications for radiologic examination of the cranium. Unconsciousness, which may be an indication of the severity of the injury, also can be considered an indication, but little is gained and much may be lost by subjecting an unconscious, hypotensive child to multiple manipulations for radiologic examinations when he is first brought to the hospital. In the absence of localizing signs, examination is best deferred until the clinical condition has stabilized. For those children who have had skull injury without unconsciousness or any of the other localizing signs, and for whom adequate clinical examination and observation is available, radiologic examinations probably are not required. In particular, the inconclusiveness of the radiologic examination of the cranium should not substitute for a careful clinical examination of any child who has been subjected to head trauma.

Sequelae of skull fracture may include headache, dizziness, disturbances of hearing, and neurologic defects inclualding epilepsy and mental retardation. Most of these are the consequences of complications of the fractures and not the fractures themselves, and the management is that of the complications.

A special form of fracture of the walls of the orbit, particularly the floor (roof of the maxillary sinus) should be noted. This is termed a *blow-out fracture* and results from the sudden increase of intraorbital pressure following a blow of a relatively blunt object such as a fist to the globe. In the most common form, a fracture of the roof of the maxillary sinus takes place with a herniation of some of the orbital contents into the sinus. If the condition is not recognized and treated promptly, enophthalmos and persistent diplopia may occur when the initial edema and hemorrhage have resolved. Clinically, the condition must be suspected when there is a history of a direct blow to the eye, and when there is diplopia, downward displacement of the eyeball, and disturbance of extraocular movements. Sensory disturbance of the skin supplied by the infraorbital nerve may be present. Radiographically, the sinus on the affected side may be clouded, but a distinct depression of bone in the roof, and particularly the associated soft tissue shadow bulging into the cavity of the sinus from the roof, are diagnostic. In many instances, laminograms are necessary to demonstrate the fracture and protrusion of orbital contents. Prompt reduction of the soft tissue herniation and elevation of the depressed bone is necessary to avoid the sequelae noted above.

CRANIAL MANIFESTATIONS OF SYSTEMIC DISORDERS.
Postural flattening and cranial bossing of rickets and syphilis have been described elsewhere. Cranial aberrations as a result of chronic hemolytic anemias are largely limited to radiologic observations. Similar changes have been observed in chronic iron-deficiency anemia. The characteristic facies of patients with Mediterranean anemia (thalassemia major) is produced by swelling of the facial bones, particularly the maxilla and the zygoma, resulting in high cheek bones and a mongoloid appearance. Infections of the cranium are discussed in relation to the specific diseases in which they occur, such as syphilis, tuberculosis, and osteomyelitis. Primary neoplasms of the cranium include rare Ewing's tumors in the vault and cartilaginous tumors in the base. More commonly, the cranium demonstrates responses to tumors of nervous tissue and its coverings, to tumors of adjacent soft tissue such as orbital or pharyngeal rhabdomyosarcomas and hemangiomas, and to metastatic lesions, particularly those of neuroblastoma. These manifestations are associated with rapid and marked widening of the sutures which may be related to increased intracranial pressure, but is definitely associated with focal proliferation of metastatic tumor in bone adjacent to the sutures.

In recent years, many reports of new "syndromes" involving cranial features have made their appearance. The reader interested in this area is referred to the monograph by Gorlin and Pindborg. For cranial features of skeletal dysplasias and other generalized disorders, the accompanying references should be consulted.

REFERENCES

GENERAL

Brailsford, J. F. The Radiology of Bones and Joints, 5th ed. Baltimore, The Williams & Wilkins Co., 1953.

Caffey, J. Pediatric X-ray Diagnosis, 5th ed. Chicago, Year Book Medical Publishers, 1967.

Fairbank, H. A. T. An Atlas of General Affections of the Skeleton. Baltimore, The Williams & Wilkins Co., 1951.

Köhler, A., by Zimmer, E. A. Borderlands of the Normal and Early Pathologic in Skeletal Roentgenology. English translation by Case, J. T., 10th ed. New York, Grune & Stratton, Inc., 1956.

McKusick, V. A. Mendelian Inheritance in Man, 2nd ed. Baltimore, The Johns Hopkins Press, 1968.

Murray, R. O., and Jacobson, H. G. The Radiology of Skeletal Disorders. Baltimore, The Williams & Wilkins Co., 1971.

Rubin, P. Dynamic Classification of Bone Dysplasias. Chicago, Year Book Medical Publishers, 1964.

CONGENITAL AND DEVELOPMENTAL ANOMALIES

Anderson, D. E., and McClendon, J. L. Cherubism—hereditary fibrous dysplasia of the jaws. I. Genetic considerations. Oral Surg., 15(Suppl. 2):5, 1962.

Burland, J. G. Cherubism: Familial bilateral osseous dysplasia of the jaws. Oral Surg., 15(Suppl. 2):43, 1962.

Capitanio, M., and Kirkpatrick, J. A. Widening of the cranial sutures. A roentgen observation during periods of accelerated growth in patients treated for deprivation dwarfism. Radiology, 92:53, 1969.

Dorst, J. P. Functional craniology: An aid in interpreting roentgenograms of the skull. Radiol. Clin. N. Amer., 2:347, 1964.

Holden, J. D. Russell-Silver dwarf. Develop. Med. Child. Neurol., 9:457, 1967.

McClendon, J. L., Anderson, D. E., and Cornelius, E. A. Cherubism—hereditary fibrous dysplasia of the jaws. II. Pathologic considerations. Oral Surg., 15(Suppl. 2): 17, 1962.

McKusick, V. A. Heritable Disorders of Connective Tissue, 2nd ed. St. Louis, The C. V. Mosby Company, 1960.

O'Connell, E. J., Feldt, R. H., and Stickler, G. B. Head circumference, mental retardation and growth failure. Pediatrics, 36:62, 1965.

Strauss, R. G., West, P. J., and Silverman, F. N. Unilateral proptosis in cystic fibrosis. Pediatrics, 43:297, 1969.

CRANIOSYNOSTOSIS

Currarino, G., and Silverman, F. N. Orbital hypotelorism, arhinencephaly, and trigonocephaly. Radiology, 74:206, 1960.

Reilly, P. J., Leeming, Joan M., and Fraser, P. Craniosynostosis in the rachitic spectrum. J. Pediat., 64:396, 1964.

Shillito, J., Jr., and Matson, D. Craniosynostosis. A review of 519 surgical patients. Pediatrics, 41:829, 1968.

CRANIAL DEFECTS

Chamberlain, D. S., Whitaker, J., and Silverman, F. N. Idiopathic osteoarthropathy and cranial defects in children (Familial idiopathic osteoarthropathy). Amer. J. Roentgen., 93:408, 1965.

Currarino, G., Tierney, R. C., Giesel, R. G., and Weihl, C. Familial idiopathic osteoarthropathy. Amer. J. Roentgen., 85:633, 1961.

Matson, D. D., and Ingraham, F. D. Intracranial complications of congenital dermal sinuses. Pediatrics, 8: 483, 1951.

O'Rahilly, R., and Twohig, M. J. Foramina parietalia permagna. Amer. J. Roentgen., 67:551, 1952.

Taybi, H., and Silverman, F. N. Congenital defect of the bony orbit and pulsating exophthalmos. Amer. J. Dis. Child., 92:138, 1956.

MISCELLANEOUS ABNORMALITIES

Gerald, B. E., and Silverman, F. N. Normal and abnormal interorbital distances, with special reference to mongolism. Amer. J. Roentgen., 95:154, 1965.

Gorlin, R. J., and Pindborg, J. J. Syndromes of the Head and Neck. New York, McGraw-Hill Book Co., 1964.

Graff, W. C. The first and second brachial arch syndrome. Plast. Reconstr. Surg., 36:485, 1965.

Kurlander, G. J., DeMyer, W., and Campbell, J. A. Roentgenology of the median cleft face syndrome. Radiology, 88:473, 1967.

Pollard, J. J., and New, P. F. J. Hereditary cutaneomandibular polyoncosis. A syndrome of myriad basal-cell nevi of the skin, mandibular cysts, and inconstant skeletal anomalies. Radiology, 82:840, 1964.

Shopfner, C. E., Jabbour, J. T., and Vallion, R. M. Craniolacunia. Amer. J. Roentgen., 93:343, 1965.

ACQUIRED CRANIAL ABNORMALITIES

Gurdjian, E. S., Webster, J. E., and Lissner, H. R. Observations on prediction of fracture site in head injury. Radiology, 60:226, 1953.

Moloy, H. C. Studies on head moulding during labor. Amer. J. Obstet. Gynec., 44:762, 1942.

Zizmor, J., Smith, B., Fasano, C., and Converse, J. M. Roentgen diagnosis of blow-out fractures of the orbit. Amer. J. Roentgen., 87:1009, 1962.

25.2
THE EXTREMITIES

Developmental Anomalies

A difference in size of the two sides of the body may result from *hemihypertrophy* or *hemiatrophy*. In some instances, it is difficult or impossible to decide whether the large or the small side is the normal one. When generalized, the asymmetry may appear as an isolated malformation, although other developmental anomalies may be present on the affected side.

Vascular or neurologic anomalies are not uncommon; although clinically silent, lymphangiectasia may be identified in the lungs by radiographic examination, and similarly in the bowel by barium studies and mucosal biopsy when the hemihypertrophy is a consequence of unilateral lymphangiectasia. Abnormalities of the lymphatic channels on the affected side may be shown by lymphangiography. Hemihypertrophy associated with diminished stature and increased excretion of urinary gonadotropins has been described as a separate syndrome by Silver. The overlap of clinical manifestations with the syndrome described by Russell has suggested "lumping" rather than "dividing" the syndromes, and the combination of dwarfism, asymmetry, craniofacial disproportion (pseudohydrocephalus), and occasional anomalies of sexual development and/or abnormal urinary excretion of gonadotropins is best categorized as *Russell-Silver dwarfism* (Fig. 14). Aniridia occurs with exceptional frequency in association with hemihypertrophy; an increased frequency of Wilms' tumors of the kidney has been noted with both hemihypertrophy and aniridia. Adrenal neoplasm and hepatoblastoma have also been reported in association with hemihypertrophy.

Localized overgrowth has been observed in association with hemangiomas, neurofibromas, and lipomatosis. Localized developmental defects of the extremities, most commonly in the form of hypoplasia or malsegmentation, are usually readily recognized although they may constitute problems in management. Care must always be taken not to overlook associated disease or malformations. Hypoplasia of the femur has been noted in newborns of diabetic

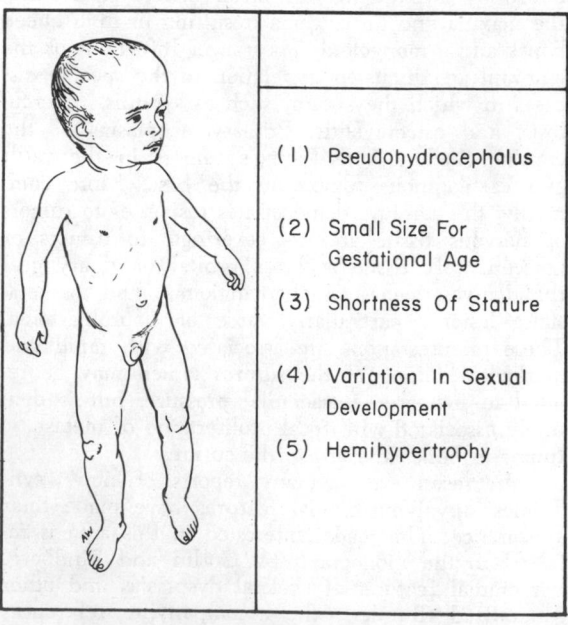

(1) Pseudohydrocephalus

(2) Small Size For Gestational Age

(3) Shortness Of Stature

(4) Variation In Sexual Development

(5) Hemihypertrophy

Fig. 14. Major criteria of Russell-Silver dwarfism. Modified from Holden.

or prediabetic mothers. Extension of this association to include instances of sacral absence or hypoplasia has given rise to the term *caudal regression syndrome.* The observation of skeletal defects (phocomelia) following exposure of the pregnant mother to thalidomide has emphasized the unknown role of chemical as well as infectious agents in the production of defects.

Complete absence of all extremities is called *amelia;* the absence of only one is called *ectromelia.* In *hemimelia,* the distal portions of the extremity are defective and a tapering stump is present. *Phocomelia* denotes absence of proximal portions of the affected member, the hand or foot seeming to arise directly from the trunk. Intrauterine amputations occur rarely; incomplete forms, in which circular grooves almost separate a digit or limb, are known as *Streeter's bands.* The causes are unknown. Hereditary factors have been implicated in some instances.

Individual bones are occasionally absent; more frequently, the defective bone is identified radiographically as a small oval or round osseous mass without functional structure. The radius, fibula, and femur are the bones most frequently affected. When the radius is absent or hypoplastic, radial deviation of the hand is present; the thumb is frequently absent or hypoplastic. Varying degrees of deformity have been observed by Fanconi and others in association with an aplastic anemia, skin pigmentation, and other anomalies. Deformities of the thumb in association with congenital heart disease, especially atrial septal defect, is known as the *Holt-Oram syndrome;* it is transmitted as an autosomal dominant trait. When the fibula is absent, the tibia is usually bowed laterally; vestiges of the fibula contribute to this bowing, and division of the dense band which represents the undeveloped fibula is important in the management of the deformity. Absence, hypoplasia, or habitual displacement of the patella is associated with the *iliac horn syndrome,* which, in its fully developed form, also includes arthrodysplasia of the elbows, ectodermal dysplasia of the nails, especially of the thumb and index finger, hornlike posterior growths on the ilium (Fig. 15), and occasionally a familial form of nephritis.

Segmentation abnormalities of the fingers and toes are not uncommon and are usually components of recognizable syndromes. *Polydactyly,* the presence of more than the usual number of digits, occurs as a hereditary trait. The most common form is that of

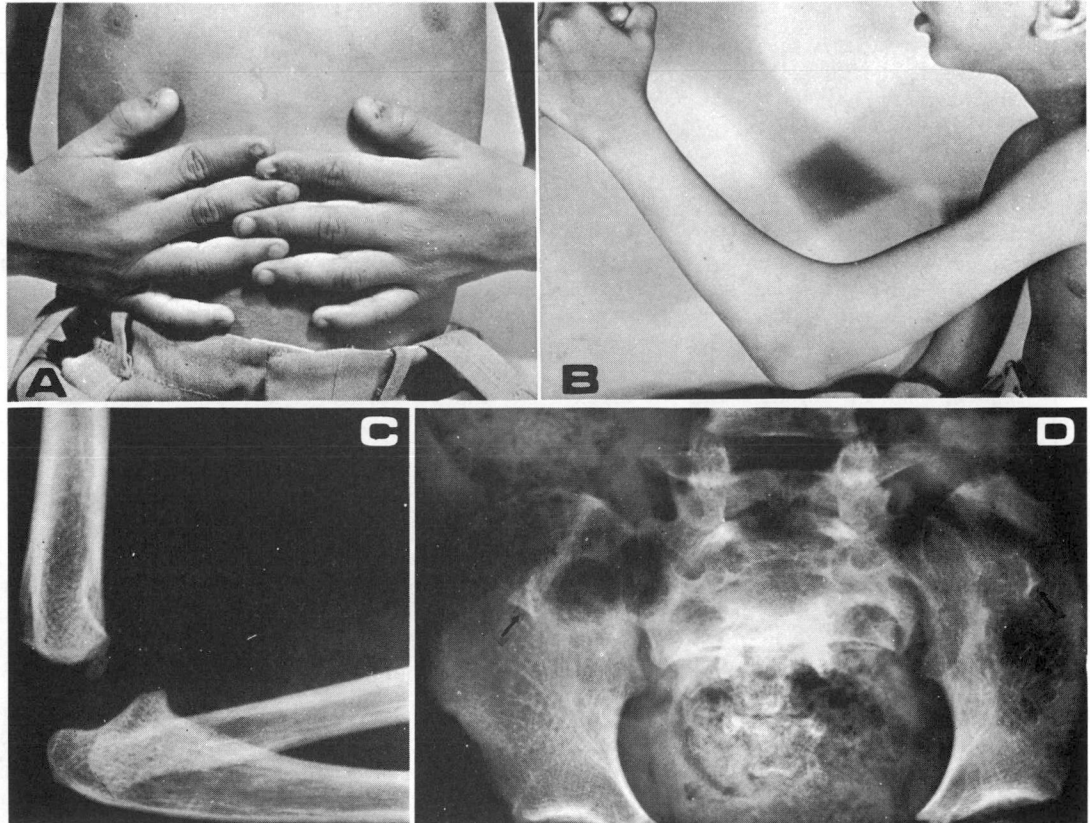

Fig. 15. Iliac horn syndrome (arthro-onychodysplasia). *A.* Defective nails on thumbs and index fingers. *B.* Maximal extension at elbow. *C.* Lateral radiograph of elbow showing dysplasia and dislocation of radial head. *D.* Arrows indicate iliac horns in film of pelvis.

a single accessory digit, often hypoplastic, attached to the ulnar side of the little finger; occasionally the thumb is duplicated. In other forms, an entire extra digit may be present; variable involvement of the several phalanges and of the associated metacarpal or metatarsal bones is observed. The dichotomy is usually more prominent distally. The location of extra digits in relation to the radial or ulnar sides of the hand is of significance in identification or exclusion of various syndromes associated with polydactyly. Polydactyly is a characteristic manifestation of the *Laurence-Moon-Biedl syndrome* in association with obesity, hypogenitalism, retinitis pigmentosa, and mental retardation. It also occurs in the *Ellis-van Creveld syndrome* (see p. 1724) in association with chondrodystrophic changes, ectodermal dysplasia, and congenital heart disease.

Syndactyly is the partial or complete fusion of digits involving the soft tissues or bony structures or both. In its mildest form, it appears as a prominent web between adjacent digits. The observation of syndactyly in a newborn infant should warrant investigation for the clinically more important craniosynostoses which are frequently associated.

In *Apert's syndrome*, the syndactyly usually involves the index, ring, and middle fingers; it is complete so that bony fusion as well as soft tissue fusion is present, and there is usually a single nail for the conjoined mass of digits. In *Carpenter's syndrome*, syndactyly is combined with polydactyly and craniosynostosis; the extra digit is on the radial side of the hand and the syndactyly is less severe than in Apert's syndrome. Individual nails are usually present for the almost completely fused digital mass. When syndactyly is also present in the Laurence-Moon-Biedl syndrome, the feature that differentiates it from Carpenter's syndrome is the location of the polydactylous digit on the ulnar or fibular side of the hand or foot respectively.

When syndactyly is associated with hypoplasia of the affected hand, the sternal head of pectoralis major is frequently missing together with the nipple on the same side. This combination of malformations is known as *Poland's syndactyly*. *Arachnodactyly* is characterized by abnormally elongated fingers and toes which are reminiscent of the legs of a spider and responsible for the descriptive name. It is commonly seen in *Marfan's syndrome* (see below) as well as in *homocystinuria*.

Abnormally short digits are found in *brachydactyly* and may result from shortness or absence of phalanges or metacarpal and metatarsal bones. Several hereditary forms have been described. Shortening of the third and fourth metacarpal bones is prominent in pseudohypoparathyroidism and is also observed in gonadal dysgenesis; it is probably much more common as an anatomic variant or as a manifestation of primary skeletal dysplasias. Brachydactyly and brachymetacarpia, occurring as isolated abnormalities, are frequently classified among the peripheral dysostoses. Hypoplasia of the proximal phalanges of the great toes occurs in *myositis ossificans progressiva* and can be observed before the soft tissue changes of the disease have made their appearance. Comparable deformities occur in the hands.

Camptodactyly is a fixed flexion contracture of one or more fingers; it may be congenital or acquired, sporadic or familial. The proximal interphalangeal joint, most frequently that of the fifth digit, is most commonly affected. In 60 to 70 percent of the individuals, the deformity is bilateral.

Clinodactyly refers to incurving of a digit, usually associated with hypoplasia of a middle phalanx (*brachymesophalangia*). Curving of the terminal phalanx of the fifth digit is a manifestation of *Kirner's anomaly,* which appears to result from abnormal growth of the epiphyseal cartilage of the distal phalanx. In diastrophic dwarfism, hypoplasia of the first metacarpal bone causes the thumb to arise at a more acute angle from the hand than usual. In somatic trisomy syndromes, various flexion contractures of fingers, with overlapping, have been described. Radial-ulnar fusions are seen in some instances of Klinefelter's syndrome.

Kaufmann first demonstrated that in children with the Duchenne type of progressive muscular dystrophy the ratio of the maximal sagittal diameter of the fibula to the minimal sagittal diameter of the tibia is greater than in normal children or in children with other neuromuscular disturbances. The disparity apparently occurs as part of the disease and is not acquired as a consequence of abnormal neuromuscular stresses. This "fibular sign" has proved to be a helpful diagnostic and differential point and its value has been supported by other workers.

McKusick's catalog of "Mendelian Inheritance in Man" is a useful, rapid reference for sources of information on these and other types of malformations.

PRENATAL BOWING OF TUBULAR BONES. Prenatal bowing of tubular bones in the extremities may be a consequence of faulty position of the fetus in utero, but the occurrence of the condition in successive pregnancies suggests that other than mechanical factors may at times be at fault. Further support for this interpretation is the observation of bowing of the long bones in association with hypophosphatasia. In most instances, an otherwise healthy infant is born with simple and multiple bowing deformities of the extremities; at the summit of the bowing, the skin may be pitted or dimpled. In some of the children with hypophosphatasia, in whom the bowing deformities and dimples were present at birth, the clinical signs of hypophosphatasia were not present at birth but developed some months later. Radiographic examination discloses bowing of the long bones with cortical thickening on the inside of the curves (Fig. 16). The milder lesions gradually disappear after birth and the affected bones are restored to normal. Moderately severe prenatal bowing of the femurs and tibias may persist as late as the seventh year. In severe cases, plastic surgery may be required.

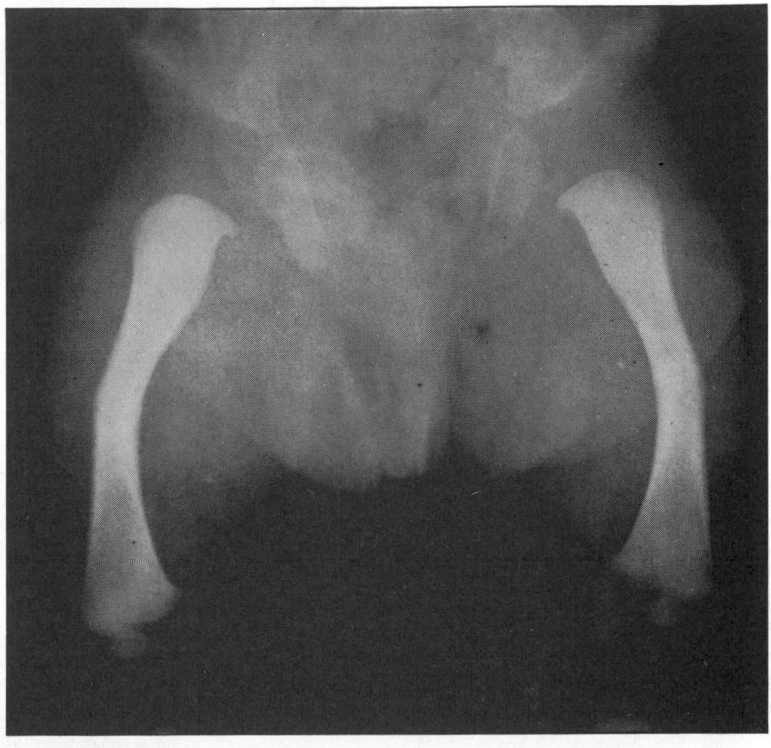

Fig. 16. Congenital bowing of tubular bones. A dimple is present over the apex of the curve on the left thigh.

Bowing is a not uncommon manifestation of congenital hypoplasia of the femur in infants born of diabetic mothers.

NONRACHITIC BOW LEGS. This is a cause of considerable parental concern if the usual history of retrogression in similarly affected siblings or antecedents is not appreciated. When the ankles are held together, there is significant separation of the medial surfaces of the knees. Often the calves are even more widely separated and exaggerate the deformity. The condition usually corrects itself spontaneously (Fig. 17); the course can be followed radiographically. Rarely, and in cases developing after the age of 6 years, the condition tends to progress to a true tibia vara which may require osteotomy for correction.

KNOCK KNEE. This deformity is the opposite of bow leg and is seldom congenital. It usually makes its appearance after the child begins to walk and may be progressive. Those cases not due to rickets or other metabolic disorders are often associated with generalized relaxation of ligamentous structures, including flatfoot deformity. During the period of growth, muscle training and minor orthopedic devices are preferable to surgical procedures in all but extreme cases. Deformities due to dystrophies and dysplasias are extremely difficult to correct. Shopfner has described the transformation of bow legs to knock knees to normal as a feature of normal growth and development.

CONGENITAL CLUBFOOT DEFORMITY. The components of congenital clubfoot deformity include adduction of the forefoot, inversion of the calcaneus under the astragalus, and plantar flexion with equinus position at the ankle joint, all associated with relative rigidity in these abnormal positions. Fixed clubfoot deformity requires orthopedic treatment. As a result of various intrauterine positions, many infants are born with one or both feet held in the "clubbed" position, or in the reverse position of abduction, eversion, and dorsiflexion. In these infants, in contrast with those with true congenital clubfoot whose deformity is relatively fixed, passive motion of the foot through the normal full range is possible although in the relaxed state the foot returns to the disturbing clubbed position. Manipulation through the full range of motion several times a day has been recommended as treatment. Clubfoot deformity developing after birth results from trauma, local disease, or neuromuscular disease such as poliomyelitis, myelodysplasia, or peroneal muscular atrophy.

FLATFOOT (PES VALGUS, FALLEN ARCH). When a child first begins to walk, the thickness of the plantar fat pads is usually such that the entire sole touches the ground when weight is put upon it. In many instances, the muscles supporting the inner side of the foot are actually weaker than their opponents, and some valgus deformity is produced by weight-bearing. This condition is so common that the term "physiologic flatfoot" has been applied to it. It requires no treatment, for it soon corrects itself as the muscles increase in strength. After the age of 3, the contour of the child's foot in weight-bearing should resemble that of an adult.

True flatfoot deformity does not develop until

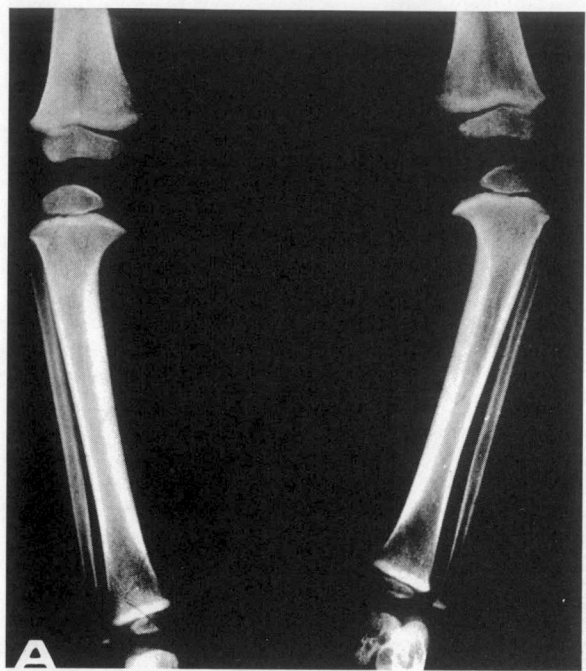

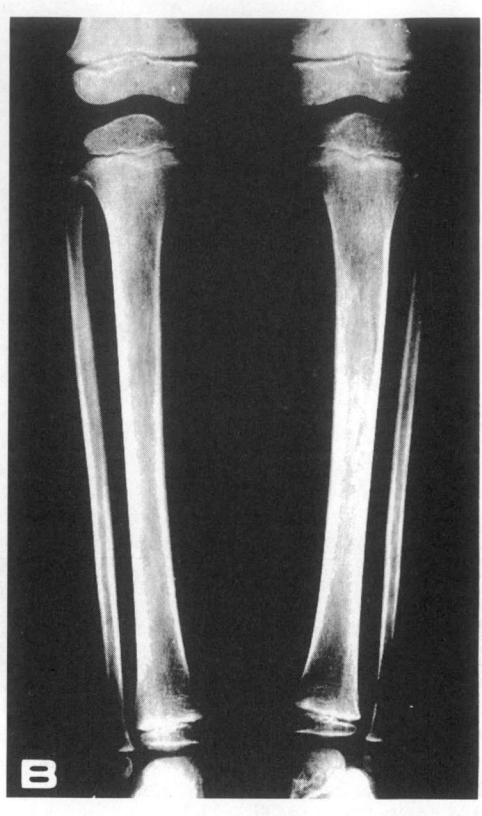

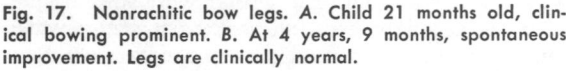

Fig. 17. Nonrachitic bow legs. A. Child 21 months old, clinical bowing prominent. B. At 4 years, 9 months, spontaneous improvement. Legs are clinically normal.

some time after weight-bearing begins, except in instances of pathologic ligamentous relaxation. The patient often complains of fatigue or pain in the feet. In addition to the conspicuous valgus position, and the fact that the heel and sole of the shoe are unduly worn on the medial side, one finds on examination a "double" internal malleolus; below the internal malleolus, there appears a second prominent bony mass, the talus. In most instances the causes of flatfoot are probably congenital peculiarities of structure. Diseases that lead to muscular weakness and relaxation of ligaments in general are doubtless responsible for some instances. The treatment is seldom difficult. An inner support on the sole or in the shoe is all that is required.

TORSION OF THE LOWER EXTREMITIES. Twisting of the lower extremities on their longitudinal axes may be partial or total, lateral or medial, and congenital or acquired. The majority of cases appear to be acquired and are quite responsive to management. All varieties of the acquired forms are believed to result from *persistent* positional stresses, such as sleeping prone in the "frog leg" position (lateral torsion of femurs) or in the "fetal position" (medial torsion of the tibias) and sitting on the floor with knees flexed and feet turned out (sitting between the feet, lateral torsion of tibias and femurs) or with the feet turned in (sitting on the feet, medial torsion of tibias). The

latter two positions are recognized as common attitudes during television viewing.

The usual clinical complaint of parents is that the children are either bowlegged or pigeon-toed in the medial torsions, or have everted and even flat feet in the lateral variety. The diagnosis is made by determining the extent of passive internal and external rotation. Normally, the entire lower extremity can be rotated equally in both directions as the child lies in the supine position; restriction of rotation is in the direction opposite to that of the torsion and is recognized by a dissociation between the position of the anterior aspect of the knees and the axis of the foot. Tibial torsion is further recognized by allowing the child to sit with the feet dangling and noting whether the feet turn in or out. Children who habitually sit on their feet may develop bony prominences over the head of the talus and the anterior external corner of the calcaneus; they may even develop callosities in these areas.

Radiologic examination usually is not helpful, as the changes are greatest in the soft tissues. In severe medial tibial torsion, a discrepancy between the positions of the upper and lower ends of the tibia and fibula may be noted; in a single frontal projection of the leg, the bones at the knee may be externally rotated while at the ankle they are internally rotated.

In very mild cases, elimination of the posture habit may be all that is necessary for treatment. In more severe cases, corrective manipulations under orthopedic guidance are recommended, and minor appliances such as bars on shoes for sleeping or even special shoes may be required. Braces are used rarely and surgical procedures are not indicated.

As a general rule, conservative management provides the greatest chance for spontaneous regression in all of the common mild developmental deformities of the extremities of infancy and childhood. However, the parents cannot be assured that the child will "outgrow" the condition, and careful serial observations are indicated in all cases.

Acquired Conditions

FRACTURES. Trauma is probably the most common single cause of skeletal disease in childhood, and fractures the most obvious manifestation. Frequently, fractures are recognized clinically by the time-honored triad of pain, swelling, and deformity; at other times, even careful radiographic examination immediately after injury may fail to disclose the skeletal abnormality. It is, nevertheless, wise to obtain competent radiographic examination in any instance when fracture is suspected clinically by virtue of symptoms or known severity of trauma. The examination should include radiographs of both the affected and the corresponding uninjured part of the skeleton, taken with the parts in identical position and in two planes at right angles to each other. The proximal and distal joints of a fractured bone should be included on the film. Current standards of management, which may carry medicolegal implications, usually require a second examination immediately after reduction of a fracture, and it is advisable to obtain a final film when healing is complete.

Fortunately, the healing of fractures in children is prompt, and reconstitution of bone takes place to a degree that can correct even major angulation deformities. The longer the period between the time the bone was fractured and the time when it ceases its growth, i.e., union of its epiphysis with the shaft, the greater is the chance of reconstitution. Rotational deformities and marked overriding or distortion require more careful correction than does angulation. Injury to an epiphysis and its radiologically invisible cartilage is more likely to produce a local disturbance of growth than is injury to the shaft.

UNRECOGNIZED TRAUMA. In certain instances, trauma to the skeleton adequate to produce fracture and reparative change may occur unknown to those responsible for the child. Examples may include the usual trauma of birth in which no inordinate problem of delivery was appreciated, or the trauma of play in which some wrenching of extremities occurs but passes unnoted. Because of lack of recognition of the initial injury, the involved part is not immobilized for protection, and repetitive injury may occur from forces not considered traumatic under usual circumstances. Repetition of injury is promoted also when the infant is merely unable to communicate the fact of the initial injury.

As a result of the repetitive injury, bizarre radiographic changes are observed, usually beginning 12 to 14 days after the initial injury (Fig. 18). Metaphyseal irregularities are found when any of a series of injuries has occurred within two to three weeks prior to radiologic examination. There are frequently massive calcifying parosteal hematomas along the shafts, almost invariably extending to the epiphyseal end of the shaft. These are similar to the calcifying hematomas of healing scurvy and are often confused with it, or even with neoplasm. The histologic picture of the new bone mass may simulate neoplasia, and serious diagnostic error may result if adequate consideration is not given to the anatomic differences between tissues of infants and those of adults. That the lesions are not due to scurvy or other nutritional or metabolic disease is indicated by the fact that an extensive lesion may be present at one end of a bone while the other, more rapidly growing end is normal. This contradiction may be true even though multiple bone involvement is the rule and though there is a tendency toward symmetry of lesions. In infants less than 6 months of age, scurvy is distinctly unusual. Moreover, when the vitamin C content of the blood has been measured, no deficiency adequate to explain the lesions has been found. Hematologic disorders have not been identified in the few cases in which they were sought.

THE BATTERED CHILD. (See also Sec. 13.12.) An important form of unrecognized trauma results when children are roughly handled by adults in play or anger. In such circumstances, the history of the initial trauma is difficult or impossible to obtain because of unawareness, reluctance to incriminate oneself, or deliberate lying. Woolley and Evans found the environmental factors surrounding infants with such lesions to vary from "unavoidable" episodes in stable households, through an unprotected environment, to one characterized by the presence of aggressive, immature, or emotionally ill adults. When removed from the traumatic environment, the children developed no new lesions and the old lesions healed. Only in cases with gross epiphyseal displacement have skeletal sequelae been observed; otherwise complete healing can be expected.

The importance of recognition of the lesions is threefold: (1) Serious disease—such as primary or metastatic bone neoplasm, polyostotic osteomyelitis, congenital syphilis—can be excluded from consideration, and dangerous, expensive, and time-consuming procedures to effect a diagnosis can be discarded. (2) The children may be removed from a potentially harmful environment. One child in Woolley and Evans' series, one in our series, and several in unreported instances which have come to our attention have returned home with lesions healed and have subsequently died under circumstances which are, to

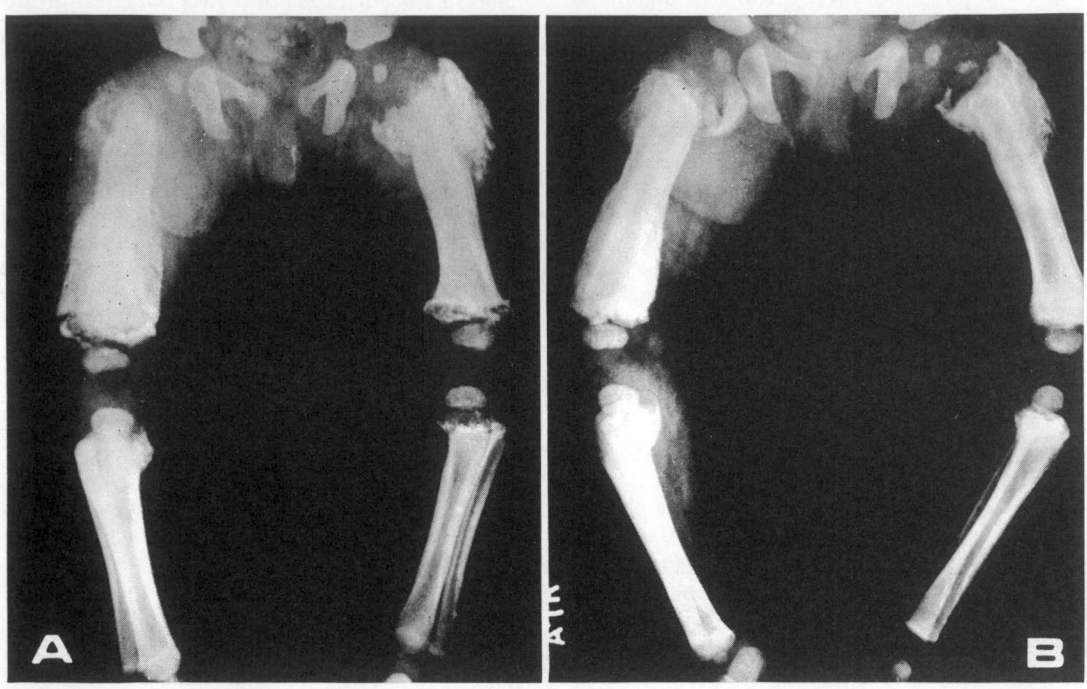

Fig. 18.   Reparative changes in unrecognized trauma in 7-month-old infant. A. May 16, 1950. B. June 17, 1950.

say the least, suspicious of recurrent injury. (3) Because of the association of similar lesions with subdural hematomas, first pointed out by Caffey, such bone lesions should call attention to the possibility of subdural hematoma, a condition with far more important sequelae than the bone lesions themselves.

The recognition of identical lesions in children with *generalized insensitivity (indifference?) to pain* supports the concept of a repetitive traumatic basis for the lesions, but also suggests a contributory mechanism in the syndrome in some instances.

SPIRAL FRACTURE OF THE TIBIA. This injury occurs with considerable frequency in childhood. Often the initiating injury is unknown, and the child merely refuses to bear weight on one extremity. At other times, there is a history of a fall while walking or running. Optimal projection of the spiral fracture line is of paramount importance, and oblique as well as anteroposterior and lateral films may have to be obtained. The fracture is generally incomplete, lacking the sign of point tenderness; and deformity or displacement seldom occurs because of the splinting action of the fibula. In cases with displacement, fracture of the opposite end of the fibula should be sought.

Stress fractures are occasionally seen in the upper third of the tibia; they also occur in the fibula, and have been described as "fatigue fractures." Both may be a cause of limping or disinclination to bear weight on an extremity.

DISLOCATIONS. Dislocations may occur with or without fractures. As a general rule, one form of injury usually seems to protect from the other. Dislocation of the radial head is more frequently a subluxation and occurs commonly when young children are dragged or lifted by the hand. The head of the radius partly escapes from the annular ligament. The child usually holds the arm in a moderately flexed position at the elbow with the forearm midway between pronation and supination. Distinct tenderness is noted over the region of the radial head. Reduction is accomplished by gentle pressure with the thumb over the radial head while gently flexing and extending the elbow and supinating the forearm. Generally, the reduction is spontaneous or occurs while the radiologic technician is attempting to obtain a film. Relief of symptoms is almost immediate, and radiographic examination is rarely useful.

EPIPHYSEAL SEPARATIONS. These are common injuries in children. A fall on an outstretched arm which would produce a Colles' fracture in the adult usually results in a posterior displacement of the distal epiphysis of the radius together with a small fragment of the adjacent metaphysis. Mechanical reduction and cast immobilization are necessary. Although the possibility of epiphyseal injury and growth disturbance is greater than in a fracture of a shaft, adverse sequelae are infrequent. In obese, preadolescent or adolescent children, epiphyseal separation of the femoral head is not uncommon; the condition may develop spontaneously and be manifested by pain or may occur with some pain following unusual activity or injury. Hip pain at the time warrants careful examination of both hips to detect demineralization of the femoral neck adjacent to the conjugating cartilage prior to any slipping deformity. Repositioning of the femoral head is often difficult, and the position is generally maintained by surgical introduction of a metallic nail along the course of the femoral neck into the femoral head. This is one of the few exceptions to the usual disinclination to utilize intramedullary pins and nails for the treatment of fractures in children. We have the distinct impression that epiphyseal separations occur with greater frequency in adolescent and preadolescent children in shoulders, wrists, and other areas as well as the hips. There is some experimental evidence which suggests that this vulnerability of the union between epiphysis and shaft is related to endocrine activity around the time of puberty. We have observed spontaneous displacement of the upper epiphysis of the humerus in a 14-year-old boy as a consequence of throwing a football. An evaluation of the metabolism of estrogens and androgens in children with slipped femoral epiphyses would be of interest.

The adolescent child who participates in athletics has an increased risk of injury to the growing epiphyses. This appears to be particularly true of obese children and tall, uncoordinated, lanky children. Sprains around weight-bearing joints in children must be carefully checked for possible epiphyseal injury. Reasonable supervision of children's athletic endeavors is important to help prevent injury.

BONE CONTUSIONS. Contusions occur as a consequence of direct injury to bony structures. Usually there are no radiographic features initially, but the subperiosteal hemorrhage which commonly accompanies the injury results in later formation of new bone under the elevated periosteum. This becomes visible radiographically about two to three weeks after the injury, often when the initial contusion has been forgotten.

BONE ATROPHY. Acquired bone atrophy results from neuromuscular disease, immobilization, or metabolic disorder. From the standpoint of pediatric importance, immobilization carries the greatest threat. When a previously active individual is totally immobilized, as by the application of a body cast, certain changes take place in the body. Among them is prompt mobilization of calcium from the now inactive bones. The resulting hypercalcemia can produce renal damage, hypertension, and convulsions. Physiotherapy to minimize inactivity is important in the prevention as well as the treatment of the "immobilization syndrome." Children with vitamin D-resistant hypophosphatemic rickets, who are receiving large doses of vitamin D, are especially susceptible to this condition when immobilized for osteotomies. Garn and his associates have demonstrated that cortical bone increases in thickness through childhood and that "atrophy" is related largely to inhibition or even reversal of this process. Cortical thickness may be a more accurate indicator of nutritional status than the size and number of the secondary ossification centers. The nutritional status of children with phenylketonuria managed by dietary restriction may be assessed by measurements of cortical thickness as adequately as by other methods of evaluation.

REFERENCES

DEVELOPMENTAL ANOMALIES

Archibald, R. M., Finby, N., and DeVito, F. Endocrine significance of short metacarpals. J. Clin. Endocr., 19: 1312, 1959.

Blank, E., and Girdany, B. R. Symmetric bowing of the terminal phalanges of the fifth fingers in a family (Kirner's deformity). Amer. J. Roentgen., 93:367, 1965.

Chang, C. H. Holt-Oram syndrome. Radiology, 88:479, 1967.

Currarino, G., and Waldman, I. Camptodactyly. Amer. J. Roentgen., 92:1312, 1964.

Dawson, J. P. Congenital pancytopenia associated with multiple congenital anomalies (Fanconi type); review of the literature and report of a 20-year-old female with a 10-year followup and apparently good response to splenectomy. Pediatrics, 14:325, 1955.

Doege, T. C., Thuline, H. C., Priest, J. H., Norhy, D. E., and Bryant, J. S. Studies of a family with the oral-facial-digital syndrome. New Eng. J. Med., 271: 1073, 1964.

Kohler, H. G. Congenital transverse defects of limbs and digits (intrauterine amputation). Arch. Dis. Child., 37:263, 1962.

Larson, R. L., and Mahon, R. O. The epiphyses and the childhood athlete. J.A.M.A., 196:607, 1968.

Miller, R. W., Fraumani, J. F., Jr., and Manning, M. D. Association of Wilms' tumor with aniridia, hemihypertrophy and other congenital malformations. New Eng. J. Med., 270:922, 1964.

Silver, H. K., Kiyasu, W., George, J., and Deamer, W. Syndrome of congenital hemihypertrophy, shortness of stature, and elevated urinary gonadotropins. Pediatrics, 30:654, 1962.

Taybi, H. Diastrophic dwarfism. Radiology, 80:1, 1963.
——— and Rubinstein, J. H. Broad thumbs and toes, and unusual facial features. Amer. J. Roentgen., 93: 362, 1965.

PRENATAL BOWING OF TUBULAR BONES

Caffey, J. Prenatal bowing and thickening of the tubular bones, with multiple cutaneous dimples in the arms and legs; a congenital syndrome of mechanical origin. Amer. J. Dis. Child., 74:43, 1947.

Conway, T. J. Prenatal bowing and angulation of long bones. Amer. J. Dis. Child., 95:305, 1958.

Kellsey, D. C. Hypophosphatasia and congenital bowing of the long bones. J.A.M.A., 179:187, 1962.

Kite, J. H. Torsion of the legs in young children. Clin. Orthop., 16:152, 1960.

ACQUIRED CONDITIONS

Caffey, J. Multiple fractures of the long bones in infants suffering from chronic subdural hematoma. Amer. J. Roentgen., 56:163, 1946.

Dodd, K., Braubarth, H., and Rapoport, S. Hypercalcemia nephropathy and encephalopathy following immobilization; case report. Pediatrics, 6:124, 1950.

Garn, S. M., Rohmann, C. G., and Nolan, P., Jr. Relations of development and aging. *In* Firren, J. E., ed., The Developmental Nature of Bone Changes During Aging. Springfield, Ill., Charles C Thomas, Publ., 1964, Chap. 4.

Griffiths, A. L. Fatgiue fracture of the fibula in childhood. Arch. Dis. Child., 27:552, 1952.

Helfer, R. E., and Kempe, C. H. The Battered Child. Chicago, University of Chicago Press, 1968.

Stark, H., Barnett, H. L., and Edelmann, C. M., Jr. Renal effects of hypercalciuria in immobilized children. Proc. Soc. Exper. Biol. Med., 118:870, 1965.

Wooley, P. V., and Evans, W. A., Jr. Significance of skeletal lesions in infants resembling those of traumatic origin. J.A.M.A., 158:539, 1955.

25.3
THE AXIAL SKELETON

Thoracic Cage

FUNNEL CHEST (PECTUS EXCAVATUM). This term is applied to a congenital depression of the lower portion of the sternum which results in a hollow of variable depth between the two sides of the lower rib cage (Fig. 19). It is thought to result from a congenitally short central tendon of the diaphragm as well as a primary growth abnormality of the costal cartilages. The depressed sternum may compress the heart; frequently the mediastinal structures are displaced posteriorly and to the left. The functional results of this deformity and its treatment are discussed in Section 19.19.

Cardiac murmurs commonly occur in association with congenital funnel chest and are generally functional in nature. Similar murmurs are noted when the thoracic spatial relationships are disturbed by an absence of the usual smooth posterior curvature of the dorsal spine. The "straight back syndrome" is characterized by an unusual straight alignment of the thoracic vertebral structures which limits the anteroposterior thoracic diameter from behind as a depressed sternum does from in front. Radiographic recognition of the straightness of the spine in lateral projection may provide an adequate explanation for cardiac murmurs that otherwise might suggest more vigorous diagnostic procedures to eliminate organic cardiac disease.

PIGEON BREAST. This condition is, in effect, the reverse of funnel chest; the anteroposterior diameter of the thorax is increased by a ventral position of the sternum and the attached cartilages, in the form of a sharp, often keel-like projection, which cosmetically may be more disturbing than funnel chest. Pigeon chest deformity occasionally occurs in association with other abnormalities, particularly of the vertebrae and ribs. It is much more common as a localized, lower sternal protrusion in association with cardiac enlargement, particularly when there is disproportionate enlargement of the right ventricle. A special form of pigeon breast deformity is associated with *premature union of the sternal segments.* Cardiac malformations and pulmonary hypertension are seen with considerable frequency in association with this anomaly.

Flaring of the lower rib cage was a common deformity when rickets was a common disease; the horizontal grooves where the flare begins are known as Harrison's grooves. In present-day practice, this flaring is seen more frequently as a result of long-standing abdominal distension, as for example in chronic megacolon or in the celiac syndrome.

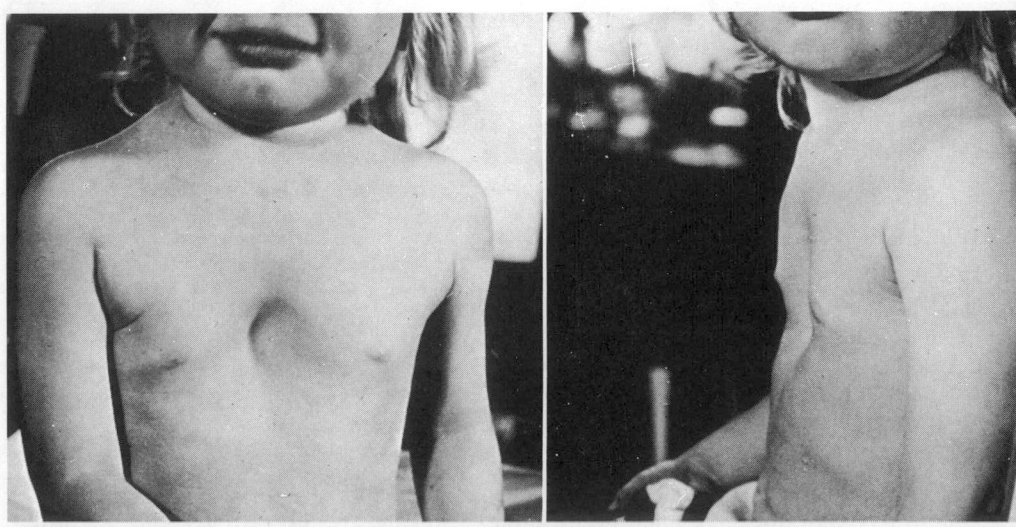

Fig. 19. Funnel chest deformity. (Courtesy of Dr. J. Helmsworth.)

SPRENGEL'S DEFORMITY. This condition is a congenital failure of descent of the scapula, usually unilateral, which produces asymmetry of structure and function at the shoulder. The involved scapula is not only higher but also more medially placed than the normal scapula. The vertebral border of the scapula, which normally parallels the spine, inclines sharply caudally toward the spine. In some cases there is an anomalous bone connecting the medial border of the scapula to the spinous process of one or more cervical vertebrae; in others, fibrous connections limit the lateral excursion of the scapula. Cervicodorsal scoliosis is almost always present, and anomalies of vertebrae (hemivertebra, vertical fusions, and spina bifida) are frequently associated. Clinically, apart from the obvious malposition of the scapula and difference of height of the shoulders, there is inability to abduct the arm and raise it above the head. Surgical removal of restricting osseous or fibrous structures may lead to both cosmetic and functional improvement.

DEFECTS AND PROTRUSIONS. Congenital defects, clinically visible and palpable as depressions in the thoracic wall, occur as a result of maldevelopment of ribs; vertebral anomalies are usually present as well. Deformity of the thoracic wall occasionally occurs in association with hypoplasia of the pectoralis major, mammary hypoplasia, and a costal cartilage defect. Rarely, failure of fusion of the lateral portions of the early fetal sternum leads to a midline defect, with retraction on inspiration. Congenital malformation of the heart may be present. A syndrome has been described, characterized by a high omphalocele (between the umbilicus and the sternum), defect of the anterior portion of the diaphragm, and defect of the pericardium. A ventricular diverticulum may extend through the defect toward or to the umbilicus and present as a pulsating mass. Other protrusions commonly result from dyschondroplasias involving the costochondral junctions. They are invisible radiographically, although obvious clinically when composed of cartilage; evidence of dyschondroplasia elsewhere should suggest the diagnosis. Extremely narrow thoraces, not infrequently associated with respiratory difficulties, are seen in *Jeune's disease* (asphyxiating thoracic dystrophy) and the *Ellis-van Creveld syndrome*.

Vertebral Column

The vertebral column forms a smooth curve in infancy when observed from the side. The several normal curves appear later as development proceeds from holding the head erect, through sitting, to ambulation. When viewed from behind, the spine is normally straight at all ages. Variations from the normal are recognized by decrease or increase of normal curves, and by the appearance of pathologic curves and protrusions.

SCOLIOSIS. An abnormal curvature, usually lateral and most obvious when viewed from behind, is a common orthopedic problem in childhood. It may result from congenital malformation of the vertebral column itself or from associated malformations, e.g., Sprengel's deformity or hypoplasia of the femur. It was formerly acquired as a result of poliomyelitis affecting spinal or extremity muscles, and it may be a complication of other neuromuscular disease such as spastic paralysis. A large number of cases occur without obvious cause and are designated as idiopathic; some of these are probably the result of clinically inapparent nervous system infections. Arteriovenous malformations have been demonstrated in some instances by aortographic techniques. Scoliosis is one of the most common skeletal abnormalities in neurofibromatosis, and it may be a manifestation of osteoid osteoma of the spine. Scoliosis is a component of several skeletal dysplasias, particularly diastrophic dwarfism, spondyloepiphyseal dysplasia, dysplasia epiphysealis punctata, and others. Kyphos occurs occasionally in achondroplasia and is an important component of metatropic dwarfism. An effective test of organic scoliosis consists in observing the effect on the spine of suspending the patient by the arms and again by the legs. When the curvature persists during these maneuvers it is not likely to improve spontaneously and is almost certain to grow worse in time.

The management of all such cases requires competent orthopedic participation. Surgical procedures such as excision of hemivertebra or spine fusion have fairly clear indications and contraindications. Radiographic control of the progress of scoliosis is indispensable for management.

Intraspinal extension of neuroblastomas must always be sought when the diagnosis of tumor is made. Films to demonstrate the intervertebral foramina should be routine even when central nervous system manifestations are lacking. Acute retention in infants may be the first manifestation of this complication of a paraspinal neuroblastoma, and the neurologic manifestations may require surgical management prior to the attack on the primary tumor.

SCHEUERMANN'S DISEASE (JUVENILE KYPHOSIS, JUVENILE ROUNDBACK DEFORMITY). This is a progressive kyphosis usually of the dorsal spine, developing during adolescence. Originally considered an epiphysitis, it is now believed by most observers to be the consequence of rupture of thinned cartilaginous plates with prolapse of intervertebral disk tissue into the cancellous bone of the vertebral bodies. A primary cause has not been established, but there does appear to be some relationship to stress. The condition is usually recognized radiographically by the fact that several adjacent vertebrae are involved, in contradistinction to the usual localization to one or two vertebrae in infectious processes. Early treatment by bracing and recumbency to minimize deformity is recommended.

CONGENITAL MALFORMATIONS. Important malformations in number and form result from vertical and horizontal errors in segmentation. Vertical fusion of cervical vertebrae is known as the *Klippel-Feil malformation*. It is associated with a short neck, the head resting on the shoulders, limitation of head motion, a low posterior hairline, and occasionally with neurologic abnormalities, particularly a tendency to mirror movements of the upper extremities. Spina bifida is commonly present at the affected level. Clinical confusion with Sprengel's deformity (discussed above) is not uncommon.

Spina bifida refers to a failure of fusion of the two lateral halves of the arch of the vertebra. In its mildest form, spina bifida occulta, the diagnosis is exclusively radiologic, and clinical signs and symptoms are lacking. The prevalence of radiographic defects in the sacral area diminishes with increasing age. For example, defects were found in 22 percent of boys and 9 percent of girls between 7 and 8 years contrasted with 4 percent in adult men and 1 percent in women. Undue importance has been attributed to the presence of lumbar spina bifida in relation to disease of the urinary tract; the condition is found as frequently as an incidental observation in asymptomatic children as it is in children with urinary disease. In more severe forms, meningeal and neural elements may protrude posteriorly; neurologic deficit is usually present when neural elements occupy the protrusion (meningomyelocele) but not in simple meningocele. In radiographs, the incomplete neural arch may be recognized; an increase in the distance between the pedicles is usually obvious. The *Arnold-Chiari malformation* and its intracranial complications should be suspected when meningomyelocele is present. Defects of union between the vertebral body and lateral masses are less readily demonstrated but may lead to anterolateral herniation of meninges at any level above the filum terminale, as a so-called anterior meningocele. Neuroenteric communications associated with duplication of the intestine have probably been mistaken for anterior meningoceles.

In some cases of spina bifida, there is a bony, cartilaginous, or fibrous protrusion into the spinal canal from a vertebral body. The protrusion may transfix the spinal cord and aggravate neurologic deficit, as longitudinal growth of the body tends to alter relationship of the transfixing object to the spinal cord. Improvement in neurologic symptoms may follow surgical removal of the offending protrusion, whose cord-splitting action is indicated by the term *diastematomyelia*.

Hemivertebra deformities result from failure of development of one of the paired chondrification centers for vertebral bodies. They usually occur in the cervical and thoracic regions and often produce scoliosis. At successive levels, one sees partially mature development occurring now on one side, now on the other, so that the final result is a jumble of malformed vertebrae, often out of line, with the vertebral bodies traversed here and there by vertical or diagonal fissures. The ribs share in the defect of segmentation; there may be 10 or 11, 13 or 14 ribs on one side, and fusion of some of the ribs is almost always found. Although there may be serious postural deformity, neurologic complications are rare. The condition is sometimes familial. A high incidence of hemivertebra is found in individuals with congenital malformations of the lungs, although in such cases the vertebral anomaly is not always at the thoracic level. Hemivertebra deformities of the lumbar spine are often associated with anomalies of the urinary tract.

Vertebral anomalies such as segmentation errors and hemivertebras occur in association with several fairly well-defined syndromes. In *Larsen's syndrome*, vertebral malformations are associated with multiple congenital dislocations and a distinctive facies characterized by widely spaced eyes and frontal bossing. In *Wildervanck's syndrome*, a cervical Klippel-Feil anomaly is associated with congenital perceptive deafness and paralysis of the sixth nerve. The condition is limited to females almost completely. Spina bifida may be a component of *cleidocranial dysostosis*. Anomalies of the spine and of the ribs are seen in *Waardenburg's syndrome* and in the *basal cell nevus syndrome*. *Goldenhar's syndrome* (oculo-auriculovertebral dysplasia) is characterized by epibulbar dermoids, auricular appendages, and vertebral anomalies including occipito-atlanto fusion, wedge and block vertebra, hemivertebra, spina bifida, and/or scoliosis. A form of dwarfism characterized by almost universal hemivertebra formation has been described under the term of *polydysspondyly*. Spinal deformities in the sacral area are common in cases of rectal atresia.

Spondylolisthesis is a horizontal slipping of one vertebra or another. It is thought to result from a congenital weakness aggravated by stress of the isthmus of the neural arch, commonly in the fifth lumbar vertebra, so that the vertebral body and pedicles bearing the weight of the trunk are forced forward while the neural arch is anchored posteriorly. Back pain is the most common symptom, and deep lumbar lordosis the most obvious physical sign. Definite diagnosis is made by radiologic examination. The presence of the defect without slipping is often an incidental finding and is called prespondylolisthesis.

FRACTURES AND DISLOCATIONS. Fracture of the cervical spine during parturition may give rise to a clinical picture similar to amyotonia congenita. The preservation of sensation and sphincter tone in the latter condition is a valuable differential sign. Compression fractures of vertebral bodies occasionally occur in tetanus or following convulsive seizures of other cause. In cervical injuries associated with marked forward flexion, the odontoid process may slowly "disappear" with an ultimate radiographic appearance simulating that of congenital absence. Local disease such as osteomyelitis, leukemic infiltration, and histiocytosis may lead to compression fractures. It is now generally agreed that Calvé's *verte-*

bra plana represents compression fracture of a vertebral body affected with eosinophilic granuloma. Fractures of the vertebral plates producing a sharply demarcated depression in their midportion occur in sickle-cell anemia and in thalassemia major. They are seldom of clinical significance. Vertical fracture of cervical vertebral bodies may occur as a result of compression injuries, as in diving, and may carry a bad prognosis because of associated cord damage; paraplegia is a common complication.

Gross dislocations are recognized radiographically with ease; subluxations are much more difficult, if not impossible to recognize. A common problem following head and neck injury is so-called *subluxation of the cervical spine* associated with acute torticollis. Townsend and Rowe showed that the radiographic appearance of subluxation may be induced at will by voluntary neck flexion mimicking torticollis. Since acute torticollis may result from various causes, including cervical adenitis, the diagnosis of subluxation is seldom if ever justified, and vigorous treatment (i.e., casts, prolonged traction, and immobilization) is wisely withheld until conservative measures have been tried. *Acute torticollis* may also be associated with *calcification of the intervertebral disks,* but a cause-and-effect relationship has not been proved in children; the latter condition is best considered an incidental observation without significance with respect to local or systemic disease.

Congenital torticollis is associated with fibrosis of a portion of a sternomastoid muscle present at birth or developing shortly thereafter; it is frequently associated with a tumor within the fibrotic muscle. The head is generally inclined to the side of the affected muscle and rotated to the opposite side. Cranial and facial asymmetry commonly accompanies the condition and both improve following relief of the torticollis. In the great majority of cases improvement in the deformities takes place with conservative management, which may include gentle manipulation to stretch the affected muscle. In children in whom recovery does not take place by 6 months of age, surgical intervention should be considered, especially if facial deformity develops.

INFECTIONS. *Tuberculosis of the spine* (Sec. 14.20) has become uncommon in recent years. Tuberculin testing is of paramount importance in diagnosis, since the clinical and radiologic features of tuberculous osteitis are practically indistinguishable from those due to *nontuberculous osteitis.* Several published reports of benign osteitis in children indicate that reliance on radiographic evidence alone for etiologic diagnosis in spinal lesions may be misleading (Fig. 20). In two of several cases observed personally, aspiration from the area of the lesion revealed hemolytic staphylococci, sensitive to available antibiotics. Recognition of a freely communicating venous plexus between the pelvic organs and the spine explains the relationship between pelvic infection or surgery and subsequent osteitis. Although these nontuberculous lesions heal spontaneously, they are favorably influenced by antibiotics and restriction of

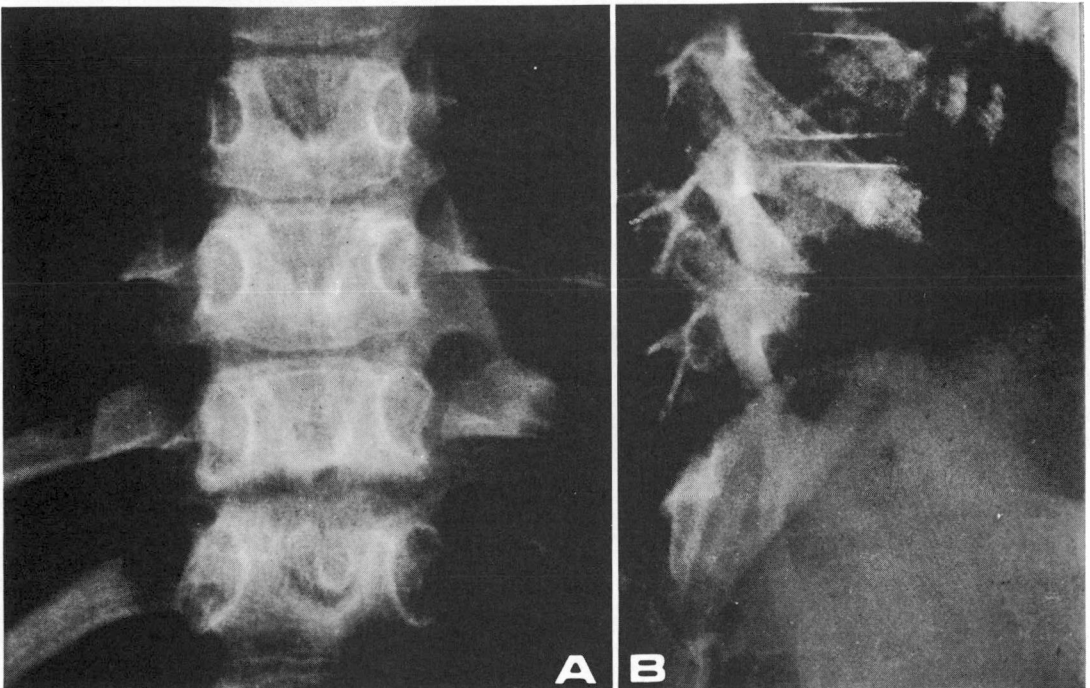

Fig. 20. Nontuberculous osteitis of the spine. *A.* Anteroposterior view. *B.* Right lateral view. Hemolytic *Staphylococcus aureus* was cultivated from material aspirated from paraspinal abscess. Note paraspinal soft tissue swelling and "tuberculous" destruction of vertebral bodies. Tuberculin test negative.

activity. Occasionally, they present with acute abdominal pain simulating intussusception or other intra-abdominal disease. Stiffness of the spine is an
important clinical clue to the diagnosis.

Pelvis

Secondary ossification centers occur in considerable
profusion in the pelvis and should not be confused
with the results of disease or injury (see below). In
girls, crestal centers at the ilia usually appear within
six months of the menarche. A corresponding developmental status may be inferred for males when
this center is first noted. Radiographically, ridging
of opposing pubic bones and "swelling" of the ischiopubic synchondroses are observed as part of normal
growth and development. Radiolucent defects separating the superior pubic ramus into medial and
lateral portions are occasionally seen in newborn infants; they have no known clinical significance.
Aseptic necroses of epiphyses in the hip are discussed under *juvenile osteochondroses* (p. 1738).
    Congenital malformations of consequence usu-
ally occur in association with systemic dysplasias or
other malformations, and are frequently of importance in definitive diagnosis. Kaufmann's monograph
is an extremely useful reference in this regard. Nonmineralization of the pubis is a manifestation of cleidocranial dysostosis in childhood; with increasing
age, progressive mineralization takes place. Nonmineralization of the pubis should not be confused with
actual pubic separation, found characteristically with
exstrophy of the bladder, but also without bladder
abnormality in some instances of diastasis recti with
ventral hernia. *Congenital absence or hypoplasia of
the sacrum* is a not uncommon severe spinal malformation. It is almost invariably associated with musculoskeletal abnormalities of the lower extremities,
and bladder or bowel dysfunction is frequent. A
relationship with diabetes in the mother has been
suggested. *Sacrococcygeal teratomas* are attached to
the tip of the coccyx and present as mass lesions of
the buttocks and presacral area. Frequently, the
greater portion of the mass is internal and the tumor
presents as a relatively small lesion externally.
    Acetabular angles and their relationship to con-
genital dislocation of the hip are discussed on page
1746. The presence of flat acetabular roofs and wide
ilia in the first six months of life is a useful diagnostic sign in Down's syndrome; steep acetabular
roofs and narrow iliums occur in the newborn with
trisomy 17–18.
    Coxa vara, once a manifestation of rickets, is
recognized more frequently as a manifestation of
metaphyseal dysostosis (p. 1725). Slipping of the
femoral epiphysis occurs about the time of adolescence, particularly in overweight males, and causes
considerable disability unless treated immediately.
The frequency of bilateral involvement warrants

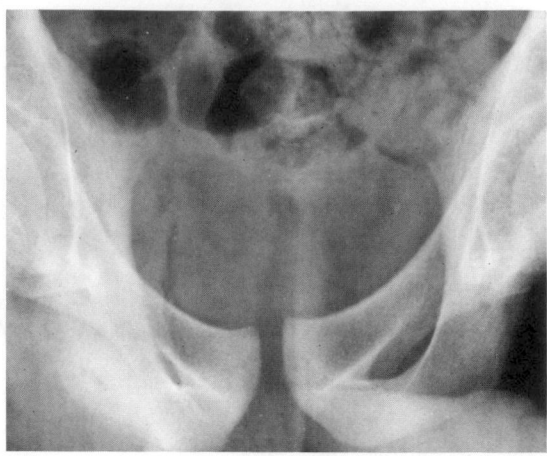

Fig. 21. Irregular bone production at site of avulsed right
ischial apophysis. This 17-year-old boy was active in track and
football; he developed pain in adductor region of thigh after a
scrimmage. Examination performed after six to seven months of
intermittent discomfort. Biopsy showed endochondral bone
repair.

careful attention to the unaffected side when an
acute slipping has been noted on one side.
    Injuries to the pelvic bones usually result from
trauma of considerable force. Apart from those involving the hip joints, in which sequelae affecting
locomotion may occur, injuries to the bony pelvis
are important by virtue of damage to adjacent soft
parts, particularly the urethra and rectum. Such
damage is suggested by the presence of blood in
urine or feces. Epiphyseal separations may occur as
a consequence of self-inflicted trauma; one of the
most common is avulsion of the un-united ossification center of the ischial tuberosity following violent
contraction of the hamstring muscles during strenuous activity in athletic teenagers. Initial local signs of
pain are quickly forgotten but recurrent pain and
tenderness may lead to radiographic examination.
The presence of irregular, and at times excessive,
new bone formation may lead to erroneous diagnosis
of neoplasm. The condition responds to conservative
management; surgical intervention is unnecessary
(Fig. 21).

REFERENCES

THORACIC CAGE

Cantrell, J. R., Haller, J. A., and Ravitch, M. M. A syn-
    drome of congenital defects involving the abdominal
    wall, sternum, diaphragm, pericardium and heart.
    Surg. Gynec. Obstet., 107:602, 1958.
Currarino, G., and Silverman, F. N. Premature oblitera-
    tion of the sternal sutures and pigeon breast deformity.
    Radiology, 70:532, 1958.
——— and Swanson, G. E. Developmental variant of
    ossification of manubrium sterni in mongolism. Radi-
    ology, 82:916, 1964.

Polgar, G., and Koop, C. E. Pulmonary function in pectus excavatum. Pediatrics, 32:209, 1963.

Ravitch, M. M. Operative treatment of congenital deformities of the chest. Amer. J. Surg., 101:588, 1961.

VERTEBRAL COLUMN

Bailey, D. K. Normal cervical spine in infants and children. Radiology, 59:712, 1952.

Begg, A. C. Nuclear herniations of the intervertebral disk: Their radiological manifestations and significance. J. Bone Joint Surg., 36B:180, 1954.

Cozen, L. The developmental origin of spondylolisthesis. Two case reports. J. Bone Joint Surg., 43-A:180, 1960.

Freiberger, R. H. Osteoid osteoma of the spine. A cause of backache and scoliosis in children and young adults. Radiology, 75:232, 1960.

Jamison, R. C., Heimlich, E. M., Miethke, J. C., and O'Loughlin, B. J. Nonspecific spondylitis of infants and children. Radiology, 77:355, 1961.

Jones, Peter G. Torticollis in Infancy and Childhood. Springfield, Ill., Charles C Thomas, Publ., 1968.

Melnick, J. C., and Silverman, F. N. Intervertebral disk calcification in childhood. Radiology, 80:399, 1963.

Moes, C. A. F., and Hendrick, E. B. Diastematomyelia. J. Pediat., 63:238, 1963.

Passarge, E., and Lenz, W. Syndrome of caudal regression in infants of diabetic mothers: Observations of further cases. Pediatrics, 37:672, 1966.

Townsend, E. H., Jr., and Rowe, M. L. Mobility of the upper cervical spine in health and disease. Pediatrics, 10:567, 1952.

Williams, H. J., and Pugh, D. G. Vertebral epiphysitis: a comparison of the clinical and roentgenologic findings. Amer. J. Roentgen., 90:1236, 1963.

Wiltse, L. I. The etiology of spondylolisthesis. J. Bone Joint Surg., 44-A:539, 1962.

PELVIS

Blumel, J., Evans, E. B., and Eggers, G. W. N. Partial and complete agenesis or malformation of the sacrum with associated anomalies. J. Bone Joint Surg., 41A:497, 1959.

Caffey, J. Achondroplasia of pelvis and lumbosacral spine. Amer. J. Roentgen., 80:449, 1958.

——— and Ross, S. E. The ischiopubic synchondrosis in healthy children. Amer. J. Roentgen., 76:488, 1956.

Kaufmann, H. J. Röntgenbefunde am kindlichen Becken bei angeborenen Skelettaffektionen und chromosomalen Aberrationen. Stuttgart, Georg Thieme Verlag, 1964.

25.4
SYSTEMIC AFFECTIONS OF THE SKELETON

Hereditary and Developmental Conditions

Skeletal Dysplasias

Although certain systemic dysplasias of the skeleton are clearly defined and obvious, others are encountered that are difficult to classify. Many of the conditions can be identified and separated from others that resemble them by virtue of (1) a constellation of findings constantly present in one and not in the others; (2) a consistent lack, in the one, of findings invariably present in the others; and (3) the character of the findings in antecedents or collaterals when familial disease is present. Morphologic similarities do not necessarily reflect relationships in etiology or pathogenesis; however, until fundamental biochemical differentiation can be accomplished, morphologic criteria coupled with inheritance patterns appear to offer the best basis for the identification of individual syndromes.

Various classifications of skeletal dysplasias have been offered and they are constantly being revised. Rubin, whose monograph should be consulted by all interested in bone dysplasias, postulates that a defect in the factors that cause bone to achieve its ultimate size, shape, and structure, results in a specific alteration. By analysis of the alterations, the defective factors can be identified, and relationships among various dysplasias can become the basis for a "dynamic classification." Rubin's classification is shown in Table 1. The inability to pigeon-hole certain conditions which have been separated from the large groups of previously unclassifiable dysplasias supports the criticism that this classification implies information on pathogenesis which we do not have. Nevertheless, it is a useful starting point for identification.

Rubin defines *dysplasia* as "a disturbance in bone form or modeling which assumes a disturbance in growth, intrinsic to bone." Depending upon the degree of growth disturbance, the dysplasia may be an aplasia, a hypoplasia, or a hyperplasia. *Dystrophy* is defined as "a disturbance in bone form or modeling which assumes a disturbance in nutrition or metabolism, extrinsic to bone." *Dysostosis* is defined as "a disturbance in bone form or modeling which assumes a disturbance or a defect in developmental ectodermal or mesenchymal tissues." These definitions are retained in the following discussion.

ACHONDROPLASIA. Achondroplasia is the most common and consequently the best known of the gen-

TABLE 1.   *Broad Classification and Terminology**

	Dysplasia		Dysostosis	Dystrophy
	Hypoplasia, Variety Congenita and Tarda	Hyperplasia		
Epiphysis	Spondyloepiphyseal dysplasia Multiple epiphyseal dysplasia	Dysplasia epiphysalis hemimelica	Diastrophic dwarfism	Hypothyroidism
Physis	Achondroplasia Metaphyseal dysostosis	Hyperchondroplasia Enchondromatosis	Chondroectodermal dysplasia Dyschondrosteose	Hypopituitarism and hyperpituitarism Hurler's syndrome
Metaphysis	Hypophosphatasia Osteopetrosis Craniometaphyseal dysplasia	Multiple exostoses		Rachitiform disease Gaucher's disease Heavy metal intoxication Hyperparathyroidism
Diaphysis	Osteogenesis imperfecta Idiopathic osteoporosis	Progressive diaphyseal dysplasia Hyperphosphatasemia	Cleidocranial dysostosis	Hormonal osteoporosis Vitamin A and D intoxication

*From Rubin. *Dynamic Classification of Bone Dysplasias*, Year Book Publishers, 1964.

eralized skeletal dysplasias. Typical examples are illustrated in ancient Egyptian, Greek, and Roman art as well as in the works of sixteenth- and seventeenth-century painters. The cause is unknown but an autosomal dominant heredity is accepted by most investigators. Poor reproductive powers as well as diminished longevity may lead to difficulties in tracing the genetic features. In addition, the fairly high spontaneous mutation rate for the condition, which compensates in part for the genetic losses, may further confuse the issue. As in many other clearly defined syndromes, affected individuals from different families resemble each other much more than they resemble their unaffected siblings. The basic morbid mechanism is a failure of normal growth of the cells in the proliferative cartilage in the zones of growth, with defective endochondral bone formation everywhere in the skeleton. As a result, the long bones are shortened, and the round and flat bones are reduced in size. Subperiosteal bone formation, in contrast, proceeds relatively normally so that cortical bone in all parts of the skeleton appears unaffected. This selective disturbance in growth of the skeleton produces an individual in whom the extremities are disproportionately short in relation to the head and trunk. In the extremities, the proximal bones, the humeri and the femora, which normally grow the most, are disproportionately shortened in relation to the distal bones, giving rise to shortening of the roots of the extremities, and hence the characterization *rhizomelic dwarfism.*

Microscopically, the most striking changes are in the cartilage (Fig. 22). The zone of proliferative cartilage is very narrow and may be absent in places; orderly cartilage columns parallel to the shaft are not formed, but instead one finds irregular nests of pro-

liferating cells with occasional columns lying diagonally or transversely. The matrix has a coarse, fibrillar appearance; calcification, however, is not interfered

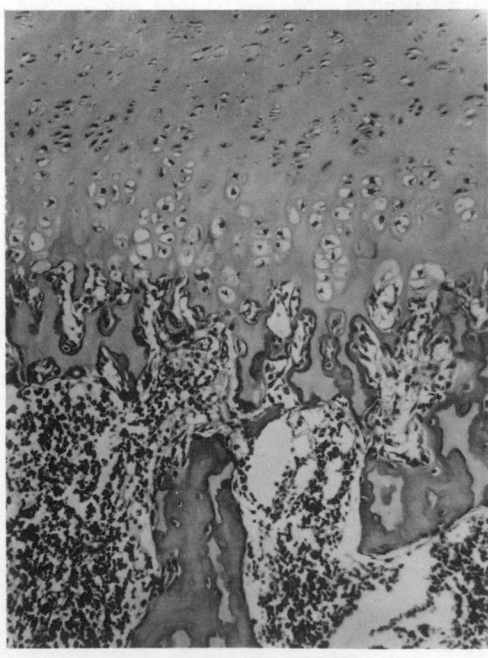

Fig. 22. Costochondral junction in achondroplasia. Note retarded cartilage growth, and irregular maturation of cartilage cells. Conversion of calcified cartilage to bone is unaffected, but the spicules of primary spongiosa are very short. H&E ×150. (Courtesy of Dr. A. J. McAdams.)

with and may occur between cartilage cells which seem to have undergone no proliferation, forming a dense and often irregular epiphyseal line. On the diaphyseal side of the epiphyseal line, one finds coarse irregular trabeculae in which remnants of cartilage are found here and there. The marked flaring of the metaphyses and the knobbed appearance of joints in some cases is considered by Rubin to be the consequence of disparity between appositional cartilage growth (width) and interstitial growth (length) of the epiphysis. The separation of cases into hypotrophic and hypertrophic forms histologically and radiographically has been challenged by the identification of *metatropic dwarfism* (see below) as a separate condition which could include all instances of "hypertrophic chondrodystrophy." Review of the drawings of the gross specimens of the bones which Kaufmann characterized as "hypertrophic chondrodystrophy" indicates that he was, in fact, dealing with metatropic dwarfism.

Cranial deformities are a constant feature of classical achondroplasia. Individuals with normal skull included in well-known monographs on "chondrodystrophy" almost certainly represent examples of

other conditions, including various forms of spondyloepiphyseal dysplasia (p. 1727), metaphyseal dysostosis (p. 1725), and even vitamin D-resistant rickets. The base of the cranium, preformed in cartilage, suffers from the same defect of endochondral bone formation as do the long bones in achondroplasia. The foramen magnum is small, a feature which may contribute to hydrocephalus and exaggerate the overgrowth of the calvarium which is necessary to accommodate the expanding brain. The forehead bulges over the base, and the nasal bone is anchored deep under the overlying forehead.

The growth of the vertebrae is affected so as to reduce the dimensions of the vertebral canal. Caffey has pointed out that, in the frontal plane, the interpediculate distance reflects this reduction, particularly in the areas (lower lumbar spine) where normally increased width is noted. The vertical height of vertebral bodies is less affected than are the sagittal and coronal diameters in the newborn period and throughout life. The restriction of space for the spinal cord makes this structure exceedingly vulnerable to trauma and to minor displacements which would have little significance in an individual of normal proportions.

Diagnostic features have been described in the pelvis by Caffey and consist primarily of diminution in vertical height of the ilia due to diminished growth of the body of the ilium. The greater sciatic notch is consequently reduced from a long smooth curve to a minute indentation in the medial border of the ilium (Fig. 23).

The most striking clinical feature in children with achondroplasia is the extreme shortness of the extremities as compared with the length of the body (Fig. 24). The short upper extremities may scarcely extend below the iliac crests instead of reaching half-

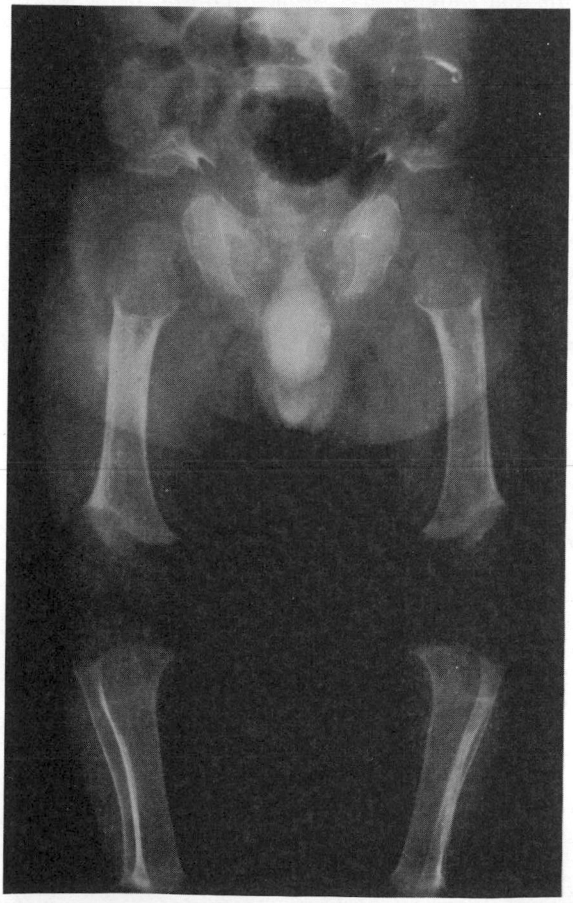

Fig. 23. Pelvis and lower extremities in achondroplasia. Note the small sacroiliac notch.

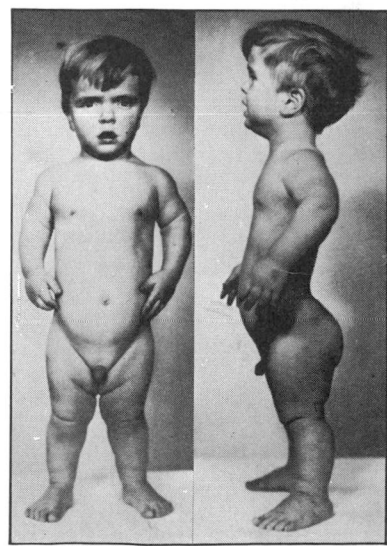

Fig. 24. Classical achondroplasia in a boy of 3 years, 11 months.

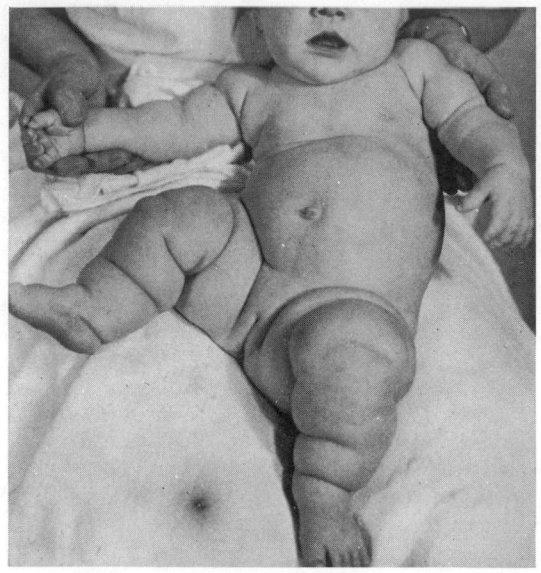

Fig. 25. Achondroplasia in an infant of 6 months, producing the riding breeches deformity. (Courtesy of Dr. Frank C. Neff.)

way to the knees. In early infancy, there appears to be too much soft tissue for the amount of bone, and the skin of the extremities is frequently thrown up into prominent folds (Fig. 25). The fingers are short, stubby, and of almost equal length; when placed on a flat surface, they tend to diverge at the proximal interphalangeal joints (Fig. 26). The cranial involvement regularly results in prominence of the forehead and a depression of the base of the nose. The lower jaw is often unusually prominent, especially with increasing age. A marked lumbar lordosis is present. The maximum height obtained by achondroplastic dwarfs is often less than three and a half feet. Some instances of hypochondroplasia, which simulates a very mild form of achondroplasia but which probably constitutes a separate disease, probably account for the great variation in the severity of the disease reported in the literature. In

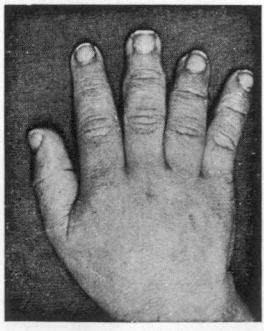

Fig. 26. Characteristic hand in achondroplasia.

achondroplasia, puberty develops normally and there is no impairment of reproductive function. In pregnant females, cesarean section is required because of the deformity of the pelvis.

The mentality of the achondroplastic dwarf is more apt to be normal than not. Most affected individuals find a normal life hampered only by the restrictions of stature and their distinctive appearance. Other forms of micromelic dwarfism may simulate achondroplasia in the newborn, including *osteogenesis imperfecta* as a result of multiple fractures, *thanatophoric dwarfism, metatropic dwarfism, dysplasia epiphysealis punctata,* and others. The differential diagnosis is usually simple when appropriate radiographs are available. Consistent involvement of the cranium and characteristic involvement of the pelvis and vertebral column serve to differentiate achondroplasia from other forms of micromelic dwarfism. Treatment of achondroplastic dwarfs with human growth hormone has not produced significant results.

THANATOPHORIC DWARFISM. The separation of this condition from classical achondroplasia is still resisted by some authorities. Nevertheless, the obligatory early demise (*thanatophoros*–affinity for death) and the extreme micromelic dwarfism are regularly associated with characteristic flat vertebral bodies (Fig. 27A and B) while apparently similar dwarfed infants who survive have distinctly taller vertebral bodies. The severity of the clinical features may separate thanatophoric dwarfism from achondroplasia, just as the mildness of the clinical features separates hypochondroplasia from it. The genetic characteristics of thanatophoric dwarfism are not known, but thus far, all parents have been apparently normal and consequently a recessive mode of inheritance is possible. Achondroplasia and hypochondroplasia appear to be transmitted as dominant traits.

METATROPIC DWARFISM. This form of dwarfism, identified by Maroteaux and his associates, probably represents the hyperplastic chondrodystrophy described by Kaufmann. Affected infants resemble children with achondroplasia at birth because of short extremities and prominent joints, but cranial involvement is questionable or lacking entirely. A small tail-like appendage at the base of the spine is usually present. Radiographs show short tubular bones with markedly expanded metaphyses. The pelvis, though abnormal, differs from the achondroplastic pelvis in the size and shape of the body of the ilium (Fig. 28A and B). The strongest argument for separation of metatropic dwarfism from achondroplasia is the evolution: achondroplastic infants become achondroplastic children and adults; children with the achondroplasia-like proportions of metatropic dwarfism at birth become kyphotic, scoliotic, misshapen individuals with a relatively short trunk and relatively long extremities (Fig. 29). The change from the long trunk-short extremity appearance in infancy justifies the name applied by Maroteaux and his associates (*metatropos*–affected by change).

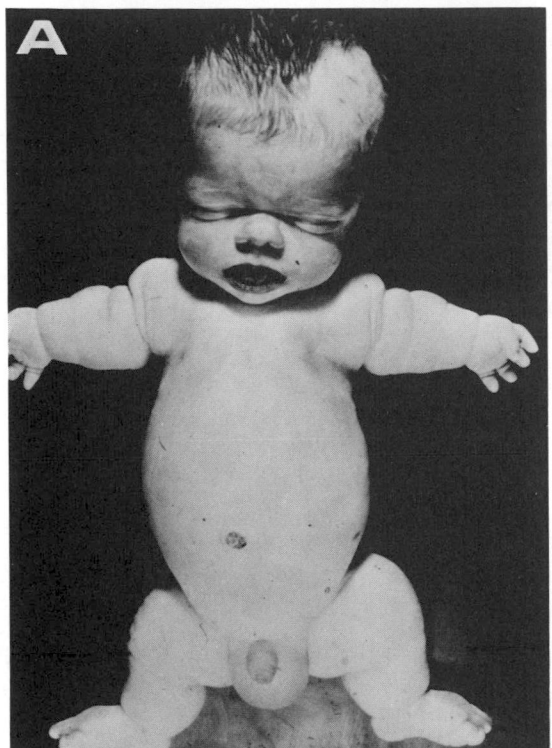
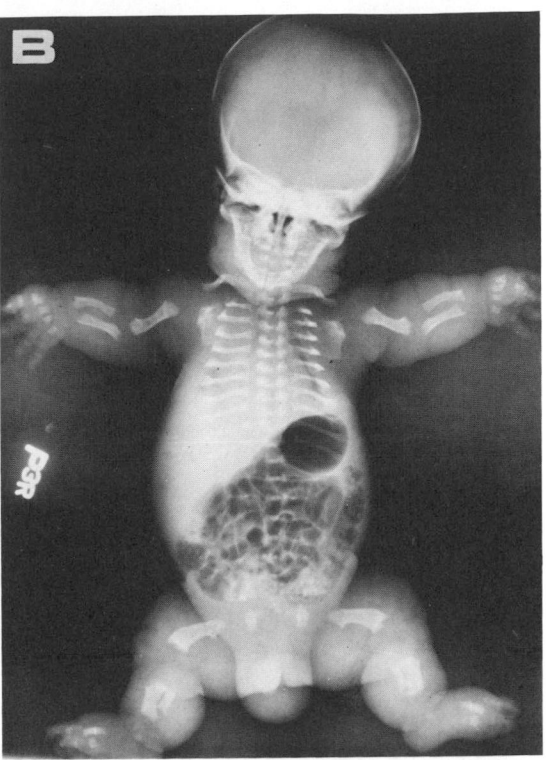

Fig. 27. (A and B) Thanatophoric dwarfism. Exaggerated "achondroplastic" features. Note flat ossification centers for vertebral bodies and bowing of the markedly shortened tubular bones.

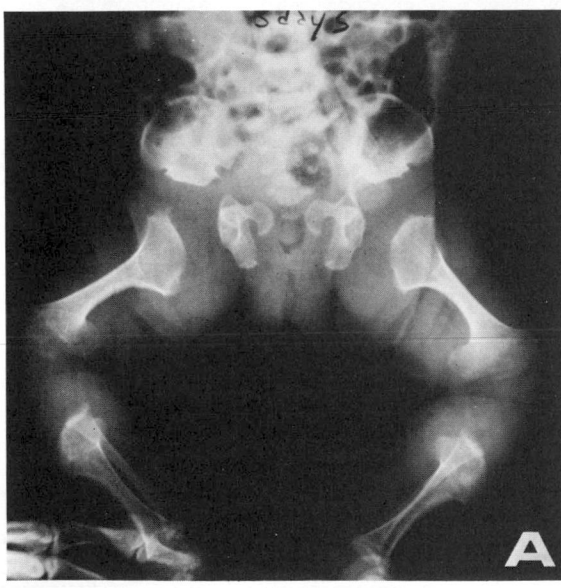

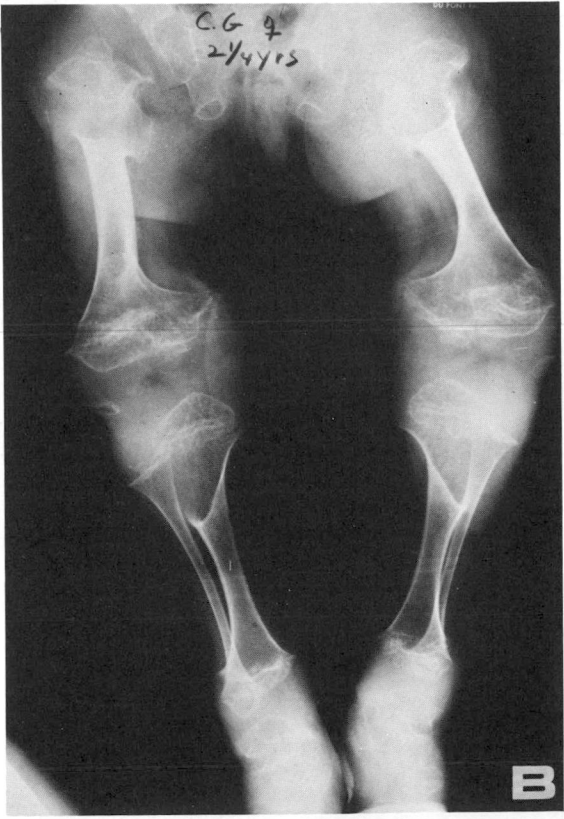

Fig. 28. A. Three-day-old infant with classical features of metatropic dwarfism. At this time, child had relatively long trunk and relatively short extremities and was thought to have achondroplasia in spite of a normal cranium. Radiographs demonstrate typical pelvic features and expanded ends of long bones characteristic of metatropic dwarfism. B. Same patient at 2¼ years. The clinical deformities in spine were becoming apparent and were reflected in the changes in thhe radiographic features of the lower extremities. (Courtesy of Dr. Chestley Yelton, Birmingham, Alabama.)

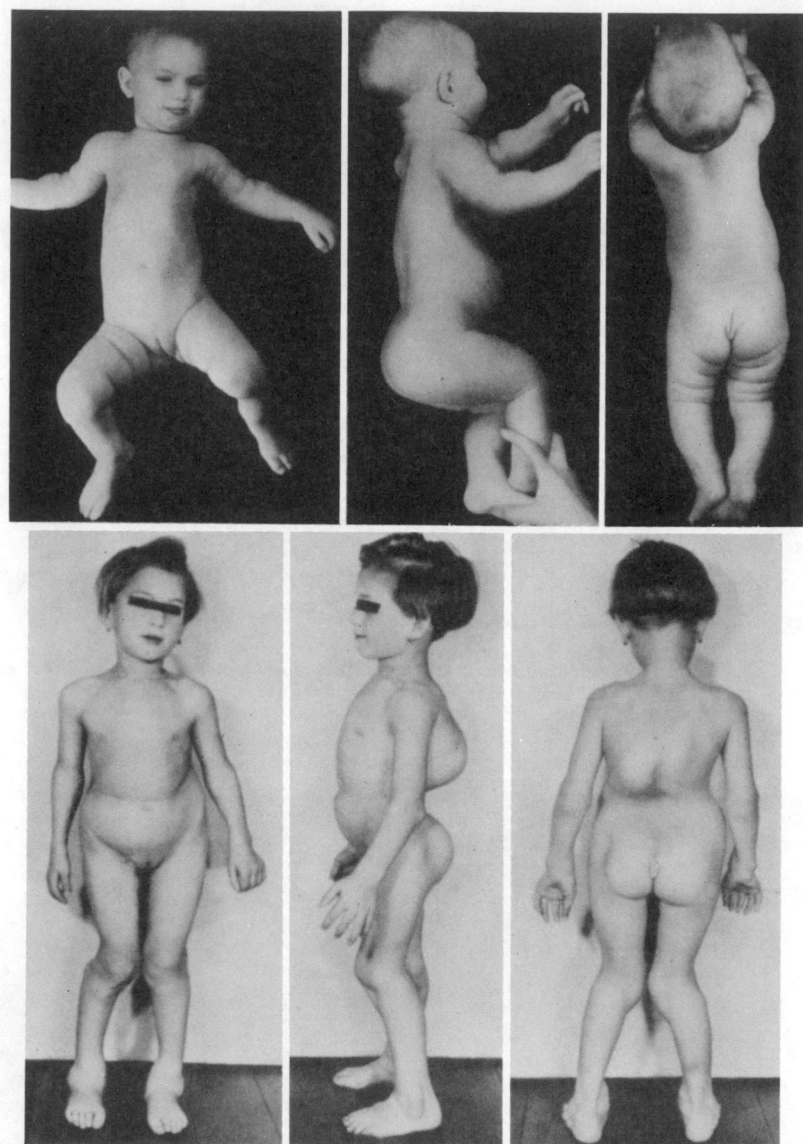

Fig. 29.   Metatropic dwarfism. Clinical features at 10 months and at 7 years of age. Initially with long trunk and relatively short extremities with normal cranium. At 7 years, progressive kyphosis caused a reversal of proportions with features resembling Morquio's disease. (Courtesy of Dr. Pierre Maroteaux and Ferdinand Enke Verlag.)

DIASTROPHIC DWARFISM. This dysplasia is distinguished from achondroplasia in the newborn by the presence of congenital clubfoot deformity, deformities of the external ears, and proximal insertion of the thumbs (due to short first metacarpal bone). There is also an absence of the characteristic cranial, vertebral, and pelvic changes of achondroplasia. With increasing age, the spine tends to become progressively scoliotic, a feature which, together with the clubfoot deformity, gave rise to the appellation diastrophic (*diastrophos*–twisted, contorted). Surgical procedures designed to prevent scoliosis or correct the foot deformity are rarely if ever successful. The condition is thought to be transmitted as an autosomal recessive trait.

CHONDROECTODERMAL DYSPLASIA. This condition is also known as the Ellis-van Creveld syndrome, and is characterized by shortening of the long bones of the extremities due to failure of cartilaginous growth simulating achondroplasia, polydactylism, and hypoplasia of the nails, teeth, and hair. In about a third of the cases, congenital heart disease is present. The diagnosis is easily made on inspection when the polydactyly and ectodermal dysplasia are noted in a child who appears to be achondroplastic. Distinct radiographic features are found in the pelvis, which resembles that of achondroplasia in the newborn period but becomes more normal with increasing age. Premature appearance of ossification centers for the femoral heads is common. In contradistinction to achondroplasia, the shortening is most prominent in the distal portions of the extremities (*acromelic* rather than *rhizomelic*). In the carpus, "fusion" of the capitate and hamate is common, and in the knee, the proximal tibial epiphysis has an eccentric ossification center. Ultimately, a normal tibial plateau is formed. The skull and vertebral column show none of the growth disturbances of achondroplasia. The heredity follows an autosomal recessive pattern.

JEUNE'S DISEASE (ASPHYXIATING THORACIC DYSTROPHY).

This disorder has many radiographic features in common with chondroectodermal dysplasia. The pelvic and rib changes are practically identical; the extremities, when involved, have varying patterns of deformity but none which resemble those characteristic of chondroectodermal dysplasia. Clinical manifestations are respiratory difficulties which can be improved by placing the child in the prone position. In severe cases, the thoracic cage is too small to permit heart and lungs to sustain life.

METAPHYSEAL DYSOSTOSIS.

Once considered a rare dysplasia, metaphyseal dysostosis is now being recognized with increased frequency. Confusion with achondroplasia has been common clinically and radiographically, and has been responsible for reports on the familial incidence of achondroplasia which were in fact describing cases of metaphyseal dysostosis. The condition is characterized radiographically by irregular and inadequate mineralization of the primary zones of calcification and of the metaphyses. Radiographically, the changes resemble rickets, and confusion with vitamin D-resistant rickets has been reported. The normal mineralization of the ossification centers and the shafts of the bones serves to identify the condition, and the normal calcium, phosphorus, and alkaline phosphatase levels of the blood exclude rickets. Metaphyseal dysostosis occurs in two major forms; a severe form with gross deformity (Jansen) and a mild form of dwarfism, coxa vara, and minor metaphyseal irregularities (Schmid). In the severest form, the marked failure of mineralization of metaphyses is reminiscent of that seen in hypophosphatasia. In several reported instances, the alkaline phosphatase level, however, has been found elevated; in others, the calcium content of the serum was elevated, but in general, diagnostic changes in chemical constituents of the blood have been lacking. It is wise to consider this systemic disorder when a child presents with bilateral coxa vara and irregular mineralization of the femoral necks.

McKusick has described a condition which he calls "cartilage-hair dysplasia" among the Amish of Pennsylvania and Ohio. The radiographic and clinical features are those of metaphyseal dysostosis, but McKusick takes issue with this term on the basis of biopsy studies of a costochondral junction in which a failure of orderly cartilage growth was found, rather than disturbed transformation of cartilage to bone (dysostosis). The hair of affected individuals is more thin than that of normal persons and lacks a central core of pigment. Metaphyseal dysostosis has also been found to occur in association with congenital pancreatic insufficiency and with cyclic neutropenia. Some of the patients with exocrine pancreatic insufficiency had siblings with diabetes mellitus.

EPIPHYSEAL DYSPLASIAS.

In this group of dysplasias are included several conditions which are related largely through disproportionate involvement of epiphyseal ossification centers in the course of their development. Variable involvement of the vertebral column is prominent in the group classified as *spondyloepiphyseal dysplasias*. Almost all conditions in both groups have associated abnormalities and are generally, but not always, associated with disturbances of longitudinal growth of bone. *Dysplasia epiphysealis punctata* (stippled epiphyses) is observed in the newborn infant. The original description by Conradi unfortunately introduced the term "chondrodystrophia calcificans congenita" in the mistaken belief that the condition was a form of achondroplasia, and that the calcifications in the sites of epiphyseal ossification centers represented premature appearance of these centers. Although some of the long bones are definitely shortened, others show no shortening (Fig. 30). Avascular tissues, including not only cartilage of epiphyses and periarticular tissues, but also cartilages of the respiratory tree, are calcified in an irregular stippled fashion. Contractures of one or more joints may be present, and cataract is common. Dyskeratotic skin lesions are fre-

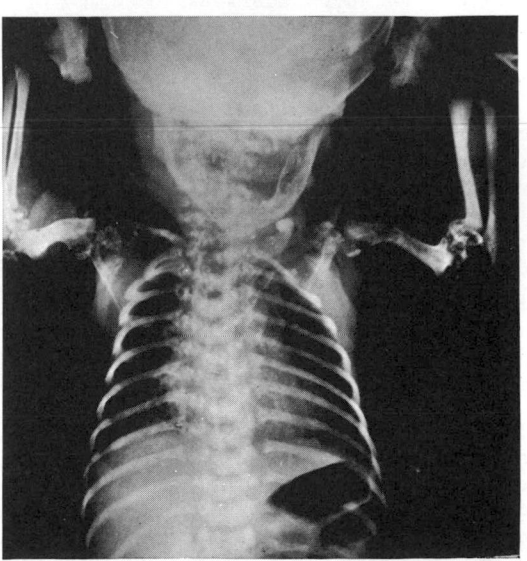

Fig. 30. Dysplasia epiphysealis punctata.

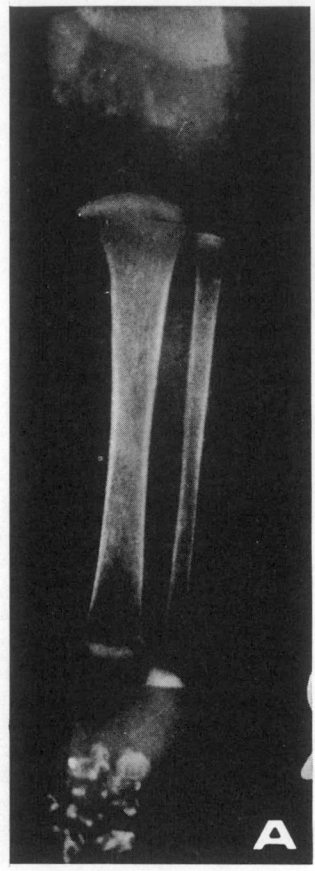
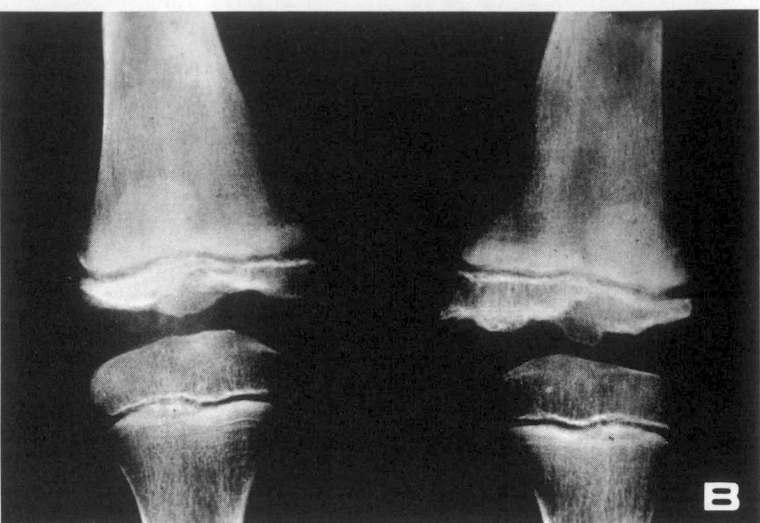

Fig. 31. *A.* Dysplasia epiphysealis punctata at 2 months of age. *B.* Same patient at 6 years. The flattened epiphyses appear like those in dysplasia epiphysealis multiplex. Comparable "transformations" were present in other areas, especially in the wrists.

quently present. Approximately 50 percent of affected children survive the first year. In those who do survive the calcification disappears and subsequent ossification is irregular, so that the ultimate form of epiphyses and round bones may be distorted (Fig. 31). Respiratory difficulties from failure of growth of the affected respiratory cartilages may contribute to the morbidity and mortality.

Dysplasia epiphysealis multiplex is generally considered a disease of older children in whom irregularities of epiphyseal ossification centers and round bones produce diagnostic changes (Fig. 32). Long-term observation of children with "stippled epiphyses" (dysplasia epiphysealis punctata) has shown them to develop features indistinguishable from dysplasia epiphysealis multiplex (see Figure 32). It has been postulated therefore that the two conditions represent extremes of a syndrome in which the manifestations are related to the severity of prenatal cartilaginous injury. It is quite probable that the two forms of epiphyseal dysplasia are separate entities, but because of the obvious inclusion of some instances of each in reports of the other condition, the criteria for separation of the two conditions are uncertain. Calcific collections in and about joints have been observed in certain unusual infections in animals and, rarely, in children. An infectious basis for

some sporadic instances of either dysplasia epiphysealis punctata or dysplasia epiphysealis multiplex has been postulated by Caffey.

Morquio's syndrome has been included as a form of epiphyseal dysplasia, and because of the spinal involvement has been classified as a *spondyloepiphyseal dysplasia*. From a morphologic standpoint, this is an acceptable point of view, although from biochemical studies, it is equally proper to classify Morquio's syndrome among the mucopolysaccharidoses. Although these conditions frequently have severe and diagnostic skeletal abnormalities recognizable by radiologic examination, Hurler's disease and related mucopolysaccharidoses are discussed in Section 8.13. Morquio's syndrome, like most of the other spondyloepiphyseal dysplasias, is not recognized at birth but only after the child first begins to walk, near the end of the first year. There is progressive deformity of the extremities with a pronounced knock-knee deformity. The severe dwarfism that develops is due in part to the involvement of the extremities and in part to the shortness or deformity of the trunk. The vertebral bodies are markedly flattened, and as a consequence of this, plus the stooped posture, the hands often reach to the level of the knees. With the shortening of the trunk, there is marked forward projection of the sternum, on which

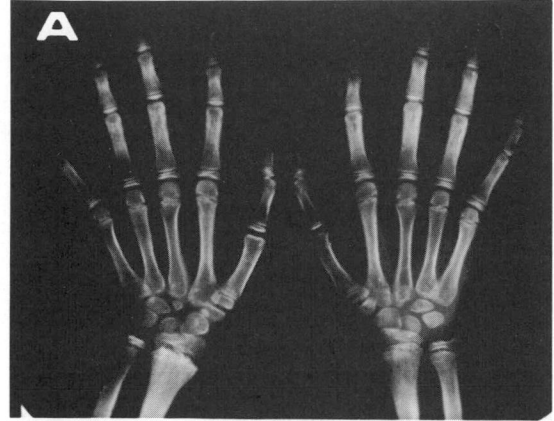

Fig. 32. A. Maldevelopment of carpal bones in dysplasia epiphysealis multiplex at 11 years. B and C. Same patient at 1 year, 5 months. Note that the "stippled" calcification predominates in distal row of carpal bones which show evidence of more severe involvement in A, than does the proximal row.

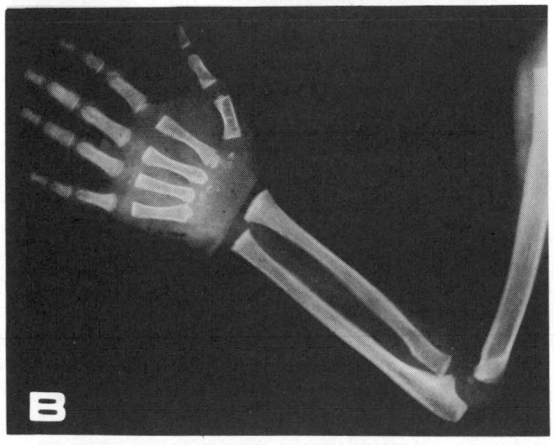

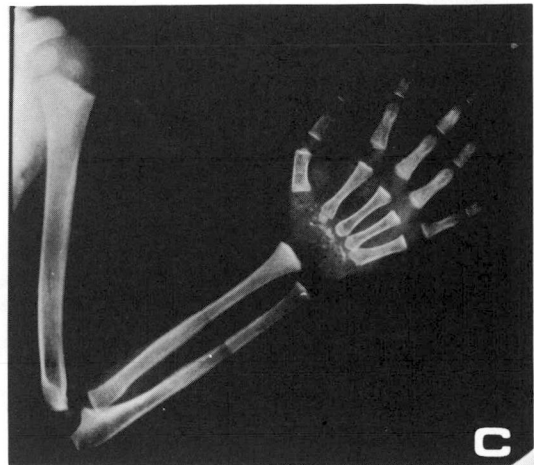

the chin frequently rests because of a short neck. The cranium is not affected. The epiphyses have multiple ossification centers and are irregular and ultimately develop bizarre articular configurations. Some of the irregularities may be adaptive reactions which may predispose to arthritic changes in adult life. The condition is generally considered to be transmitted by an autosomal recessive mechanism.

Morquio-Ullrich disease was considered a separate entity until the associated corneal opacities were shown to be present in typical Morquio's disease. Today, there is no justification for a separate classification.

A *pseudoachondroplastic form of spondyloepiphyseal dysplasia* has been described in individuals who demonstrate a marked longitudinal growth disturbance in addition to the irregularities of the epiphyses and prominent spinal dysplasia. These individuals are characterized by a normal cranium and a relatively normal pelvis (the sacroiliac notch is not shortened), by a scoliosis which may be prominent, and by pseudoachondroplastic body proportions. The onset of this condition is also not recognized clinically until after the end of the first year, in contradistinction to most instances of achondroplasia.

A *tarda form of spondyloepiphyseal dysplasia* has been described by Lamy and Maroteaux. The clinical and radiographic features are not unlike those of Morquio's disease, but the onset of the condition is not noted until the second decade of life. Furthermore, the dwarfism is less severe, although the relatively short trunk is quite characteristic. Vertebral involvement is marked, and in adults, narrowing of the interspaces and increased density of adjacent vertebral bodies simulate the appearance of calcified intervertebral disks. Approximately half of these individuals develop arthralgias in the fourth and fifth decades. Pains in the joints of the lower extremities may be the first clinical manifestation of the disease. A morphologic classification of the spondyloepiphyseal dysplasias has been proposed by Maroteaux and his associates and should be consulted in the classification of skeletal dysplasias associated with vertebral anomalies.

MULTIPLE HEREDITARY EXOSTOSES (DIAPHYSEAL ACLASIS). This condition may be considered as a disorder of cartilaginous bone formation with epiosteal manifestations. It has a strong familial tendency. The growing ends of bone are characteristically affected; fragments of the cartilaginous epiphyseal line become separated from the main body of cartilage and incorporated in the bone of the shaft. The ectopic cartilage continues to proliferate and to change to bone, forming a bony excrescence capped with

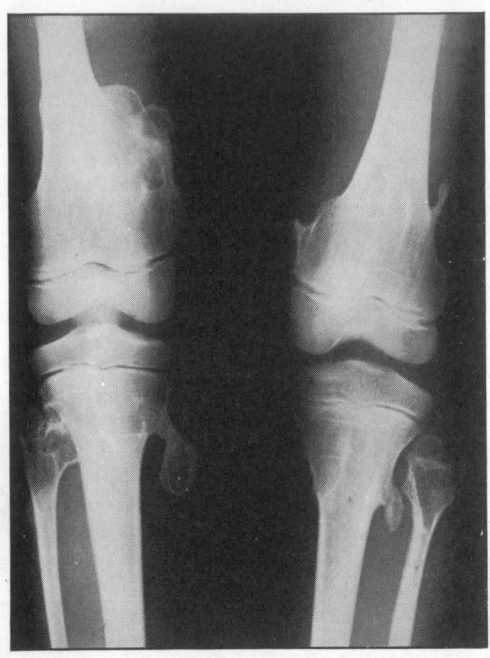

Fig. 33. Multiple cartilaginous exostoses in the femors, tibias, and fibulas of a boy 5 years of age.

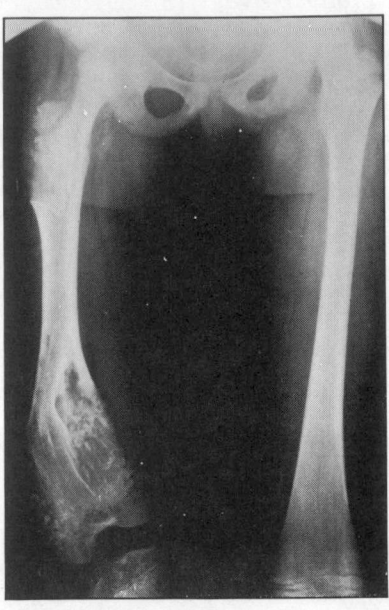

Fig. 34. Ollier's enchondromatosis in a girl 5 years of age.

cartilage, which continues to grow, invariably away from the adjacent joint (Fig. 33), until cartilaginous growth ceases throughout the body. Knees and shoulders are areas most severely involved, but any bone may be involved, including vertebrae. Signs and symptoms arise from pressure of the bony masses on adjacent structures or by interference with joint action by sheer size or position. Treatment by excision is dictated by the severity of signs and symptoms. Sarcomatous degeneration of the exostoses has been estimated to occur in 5 to 11 percent of cases. A sudden increase in growth of a tumor in the adult warrants careful evaluation for the possibility of this type of transformation. The tumors are usually not present at birth, but make their appearance by 2 or 3 years of age and progress subsequently until cartilage growth ceases. Prior to the appearance of the tumors, radiographic examination of the skeleton may demonstrate no abnormalities whatsoever.

OLLIER'S SYNDROME (ENCHONDROMATOSIS). The effects of abnormal cartilage-bone growth are more clearly understood if this condition is considered as analogous to multiple hereditary exostoses except that the masses of cartilage are proliferating within the bone rather than upon it (enostosis rather than exostosis). The enosteal masses of cartilage are predominantly unilateral in Ollier's disease, but some involvement is often present on both sides of the skeleton. The affected bones are usually short and bowed (Fig. 34). Disturbances of constriction occur and result from internal expansion of bone rather than from external excrescense (Fig. 35). Bowing deformities, at times, require surgical correction.

Maffucci's syndrome is the combination of multiple enchondromas with cavernous hemangiomas in which calcified phleboliths are commonly found on roentgen examination. The condition manifests itself at or about the time of puberty by the appearance of painless bluish nodules, commonly on the hands and feet. Progressive enlargement takes place to form monstrous deformed limbs which are scarcely recognized except for the presence of nails. The vascular and bony abnormalities are associated but separate malformations. Deformities sometimes become so marked that amputation is necessary.

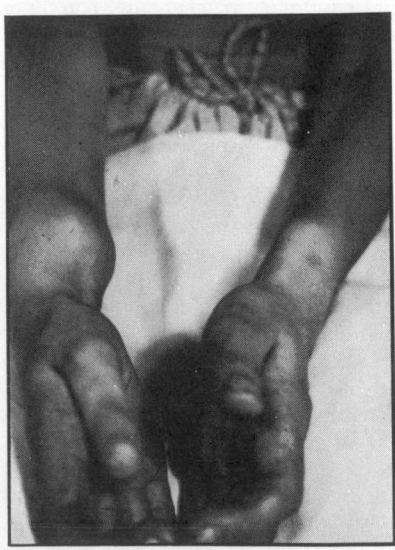

Fig. 35. Ollier's disease in a boy 11 years of age.

DYSCHONDROSTEOSIS. This hereditary bone dysplasia has an autosomal dominant mode of transmission and is characterized by mesomelic dwarfism and deformity of the distal radius and ulna resulting in wrist deformity which has been termed Madelung's deformity. It has been suggested that all instances of nontraumatic. Madelung's deformity, without other obvious skeletal dysplasia, such as hereditary exostoses and enchondromatosis, are a result of this generalized dysplasia in which the mild features elsewhere have been overlooked. Madelung's deformity is characterized by bowing and disproportionate shortening of the radius with dislocation or subluxation of the distal radio-ulnar articulation, and dorsal prominence at the distal end of the ulna.

OSTEOGENESIS IMPERFECTA (FRAGILITAS OSSIUM, LOBSTEIN'S DISEASE). This occurs in two recognizable forms: a congenital form present at birth, characterized by ribbonlike bone shadows with almost countless fractures (Vrolik's disease), and a later appearing form, osteogenesis imperfecta tarda or osteopsathyrosis (Lobstein's disease), in which bone atrophy predominates with solitary fractures of individual bones. The congenital form is more severe, almost always occurs sporadically, and is considered to be recessive in inheritance (Fig. 36). The tarda form is usually an expression of a dominant trait. Possibly because the congenital type is rarely compatible with longevity, associated abnormalities are more commonly found in the tarda form; these include ostosclerosis with deafness, dental deficiencies of enamel and dentine, and a characteristic blue color of the sclerae. The last is due to thinness or unusual translucency of the sclerae, said to be an expression of defective connective tissue, and may occur in individuals unaffected with skeletal abnormalities.

The clinical manifestations are related almost exclusively to the ease with which the bones fracture. Not only minor trauma, but the ordinary stresses of ambulation or even position change, can be associated with fracture. Fortunately, these fractures appear to cause less pain than do comparable fractures in the normal individual. As a general rule, the fractures tend to become less common after puberty. Attempts have been made, with questionable therapeutic success, to induce premature puberty by the administration of endocrine preparations. As a result of the recurrent deforming fractures, dwarfism is common and activity is often restricted. Compres-

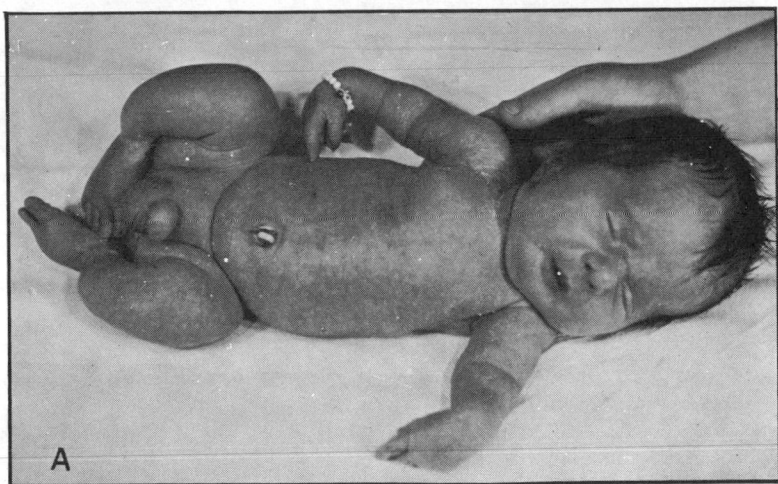

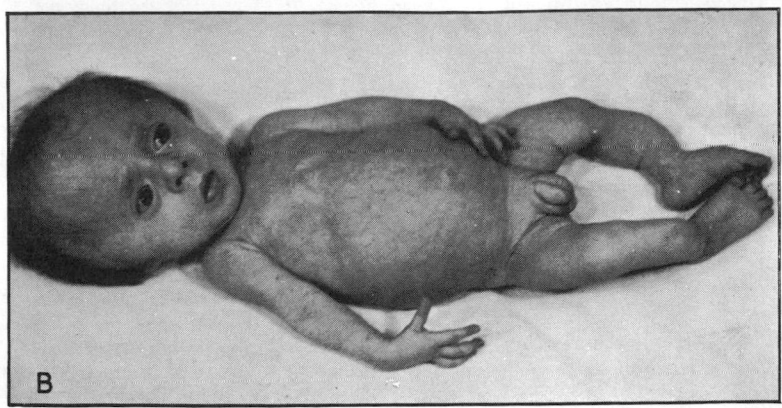

Fig. 36. Osteogenesis imperfecta, with deformities. A. Age 5 days. B. Same patient, age 9 months.

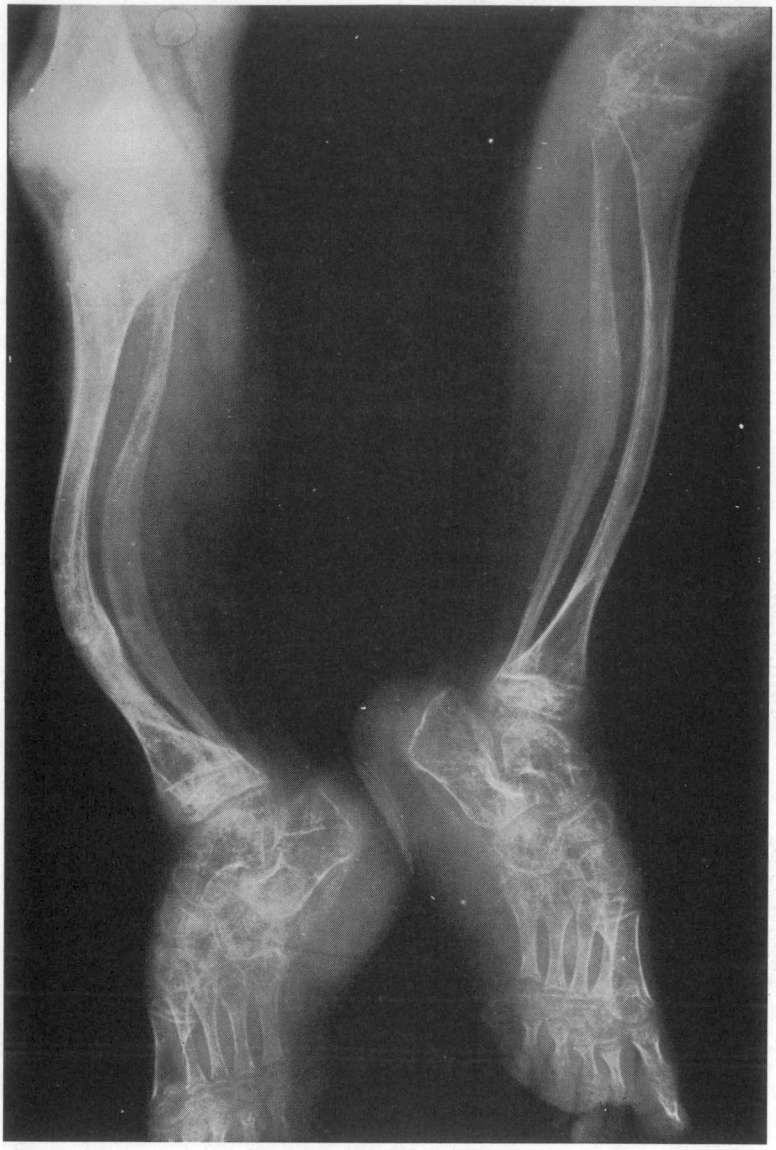

Fig. 37. Osteogenesis imperfecta in a boy 8 years of age. The bowing of the tibias and fibulas is secondary to fractures and callus formation. These changes are superimposed on a background of thin, brittle cortical walls, the primary change in osteogenesis imperfecta.

sion fractures of the vertebral bodies are common, the resulting vertebra plana contributing to the diminished stature. Involvement of the skull is manifested by lateral bulging of the calvarium. Histologic examination of the bones reveals imperfectly formed and imperfectly calcified bone trabeculae. The cortex is notably deficient, and discontinuity of cortex is observed. There is no specific change in bone cell population; fractures heal promptly, but the bone replacing the callus is deficient and bends easily or refractures. No diagnostic changes have been found in the chemical composition of the blood.

The radiologic diagnosis is usually simple. The ribbonlike bones of the congenital type can scarcely be confused with any other condition. In the tarda type, the combination of bone atrophy, bony deformity, and multiple fractures in varying stages of repair is diagnostic. However, when only one fracture is present, even in association with bone atrophy, the diagnosis may be difficult (Fig. 37). Comparable radiologic pictures may be seen with bone atrophy following paralytic diseases or in severe malnutrition. In such cases, roentgen examination of the skull has been valuable. In infancy, the skull in osteogene-

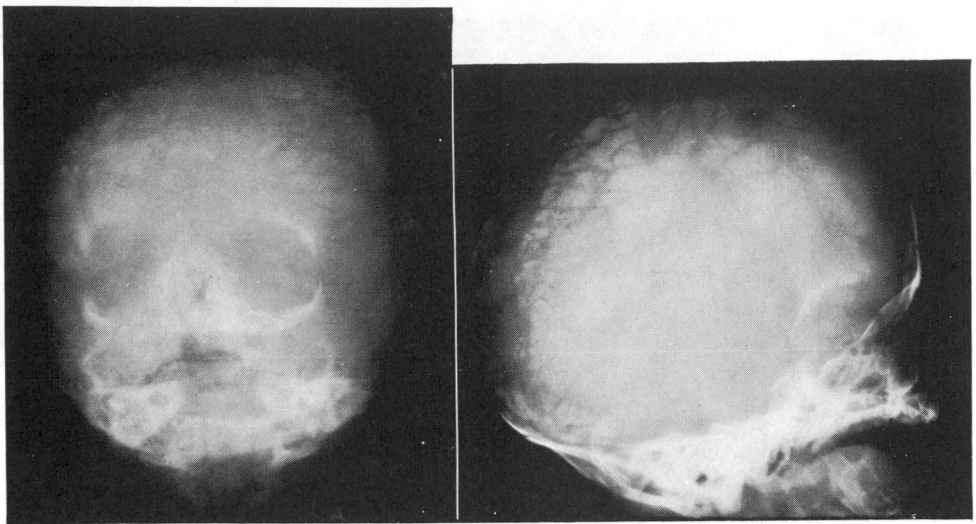

Fig. 38. Roentgenogram of skull in osteogenesis imperfecta, showing the mosaic pattern of rarefaction. Patient 1 week old.

sis imperfecta is similar to that in cleidocranial dysostasis; the soft membrane of the calvarium contains a few islands of bone formation but is otherwise unmineralized. With the passage of time, more islands appear and grow toward each other, leaving dark lines of unmineralized membrane between them, much like sutures (Fig. 38). These dark streaks may persist into adult life, providing the mosaic pattern that constitutes a radiographic hallmark of the disease. In other instances, the islands fuse and this diagnostic feature is obliterated.

Orthopedic management is generally more helpful than medical (endocrine) therapy. Sofield has devised a technique of multiple osteotomies in deformed bones which are then permitted to heal in better alignment by being transfixed on intramedullary pins.

CLEIDOCRANIAL DYSOSTOSIS. This is an unfortunate term, since involvement of structures other than clavicles and skull is thereby disregarded. In the classical case, the teeth are defective, being small and poorly formed, and deciduous teeth are retained into late adulthood. Nonmineralization of the pubis is a frequently associated observation; in adult life, mineralization takes place. Clinical signs and symptoms do not occur as a result of the nonmineralization of the pubis.

The skull may be so soft as to feel as if no bone were present in it at all. In other cases, a large fontanel is felt and tends to persist into late adolescence or early adult life. The eyes are generally widely spaced, and the cranial vault seems to bulge forward and to each side of the facial area. Radiographically, the skull shows the inadequacy of mineralization. Frequently, multiple small islands of bone density are seen within the general membrane of the skull, the margins of which simulate multiple fractures.

With the passage of time, the islands enlarge and coalesce until mineralization of the skull is complete. In some individuals, a large anterior fontanel may persist after the separate islands are fused. The relative softness of the calvarium causes it to sag around the base, producing what has been appropriately described as a "tam-o'-shanter skull."

Ossification of the clavicles may be completely absent, or diminutive ossification centers may be found. Failure of development of the clavicles accounts for the characteristic ability of affected individuals to bring the shoulders together in front of them (Fig. 39).

Ligament relaxation in other areas is not unusual, and both knock-knee deformity and genu recurvatum may occur. Spina bifida has been found frequently, and in many instances there are irregularities in the growing ends of the tubular bones, not unlike those seen in metaphyseal dysostosis. A significant diminution in stature is almost always present.

The condition may be present in individuals who demonstrate only some of the components; in fact, normal clavicles may be present. In questionable cases examination of other members of the family may assist the diagnosis since the hereditary pattern is that of an autosomal dominant trait; however, sporadic cases comprise about 25 percent of reported instances.

Miscellaneous Dysplasias

ENGELMANN'S DISEASE (PROGRESSIVE DIAPHYSEAL DYSPLASIA). This is a hyperostotic disease primarily of tubular bones, but also involving the cranium and the vertebral column in well-developed cases. Its onset usually occurs between 2 and 6 years with gait disturbance, fatigability, and failure to gain

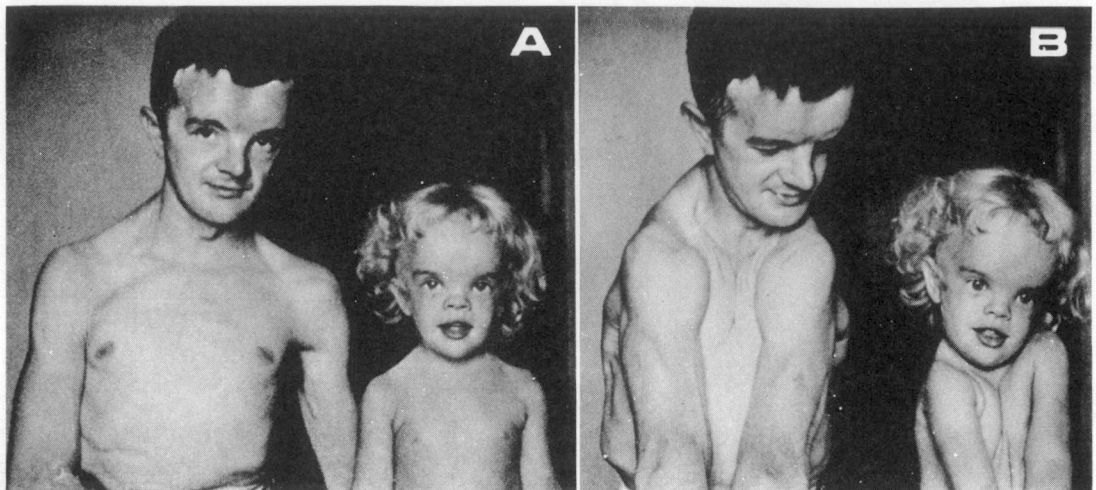

Fig. 39. A. Cleidocranial dysostosis. Father and child with condition. Note ocular hypertelorism, depression in center of father's forehead, and sloping shoulders. B. Approximation of shoulders made possible by defective formation of rudimentary clavicles.

weight. The symmetrically involved long bones are expanded as well as thickened. Caffey has pointed out the enlargement of channels for nutrient vessels in the femur and tibia in illustrations of published cases. Girdany has described a family with typical and severe cases as well as cases with only minimal external cortical thickening. He observed clinical improvement with increasing age in this family, and has suggested that primary muscular involvement may be a part of the clinical picture. The external cortical thickening involves only the shafts; metaphyses and epiphyses are generally normal. Extensive involvement of the cranium and facial bones may produce a form of leontiasis ossea.

METAPHYSEAL DYSPLASIA (PYLE'S DISEASE). The condition described by Pyle is characterized by failure of bone absorption in the metaphyses so that the ends of the long bones are splayed (Fig. 40); the tibial curving commonly presents clinically as knock knees. The affected tubular bones are longer than normal so that affected individuals are usually tall but have a normal sitting height. Fractures have occurred in some individuals. Cranial involvement was limited to slight thickening of the base of the skull in the early cases described, and involvement of the facial bones was totally lacking. Bakwin and Krida consequently termed the condition familial metaphyseal dysplasia. Subsequently, patients were reported with cranial features of leontiasis ossea with massive swelling of cranial and facial bones in addition to the typical splayed and elongated tubular bones. These patients have been classified as cranial metaphyseal dysplasia. The identity of these two conditions has not yet been proved notwithstanding the marked similarity in the manifestations in the extremities. In Pyle's patient, and in his sister, who also had the disease, cranial manifestations were still absent in follow-up examinations almost 40 years after the initial report. A daughter born to the sister of Pyle's patient is not affected.

MARFAN'S SYNDROME. Although this condition has been known in the past as arachnodactyly due to the spiderlike elongated digits, the eponymic term is preferred, as McKusick has demonstrated that the typical gracile digits may be clinically inapparent. Furthermore, elongated digits may occur without the connective tissue disorder which constitutes Marfan's syndrome. Marfan's syndrome is a generalized disorder of connective tissue with involvement of the eyes (ectopia lentis), the cardiovascular system (aortic aneurysm), and the osseous system (excessive length of tubular bones). The chief clinical features are the general elongation of the extremities. Even in individuals of stocky body build, the condition may be present and is characterized by an increase in the span (the distance between the tips of the middle fingers when the arms are fully extended at shoulder height) over that of the vertical height. The ligaments are relaxed so that joints are loose, and flat feet and scoliosis are common. Thoracic deformities (pectus excavatum and pectus carinatum) have been observed. The ectopia lentis is bilateral and associated with tremor of the iris. Aortic aneurysm, which may lead to death in early adult life, results from degeneration of the media of the great vessels. Radiographically, the narrow elongated tubular bones are suggestive, and the diagnostic features include not only an absolute increase in length but a disproportionate increase of the more distal bones; elongation of the forearms, for example, is disproportionately greater than that of the upper arms. Camptodactyly of the fifth finger occurs with some frequency. The condition is apparently transmitted as an autosomal dominant trait.

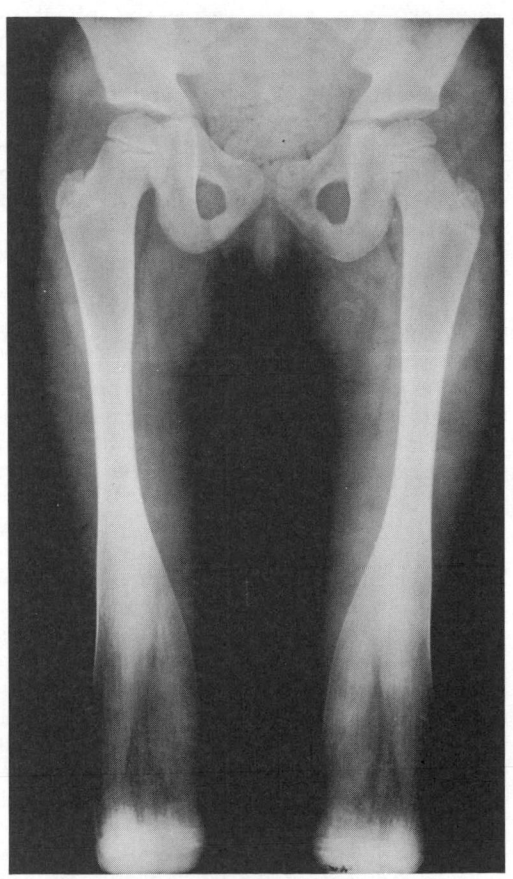

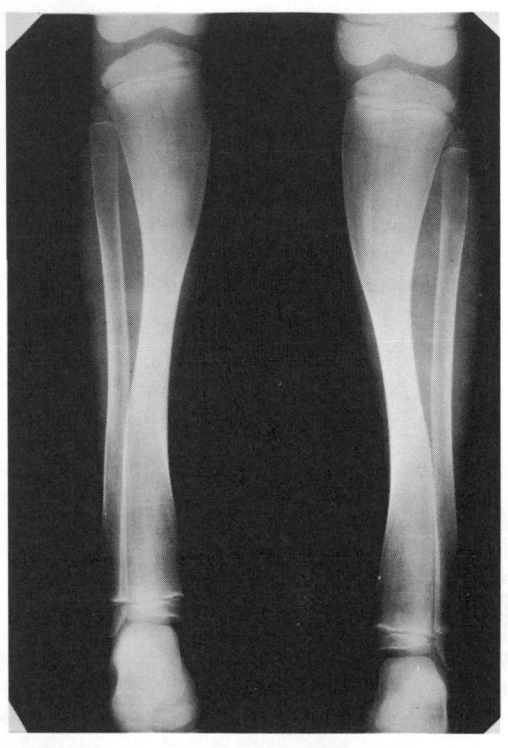

Fig. 40. Pyle's disease. Photographs from original films of cases reported by Bakwin and Krida. (Courtesy of Dr. Harry Bakwin.)

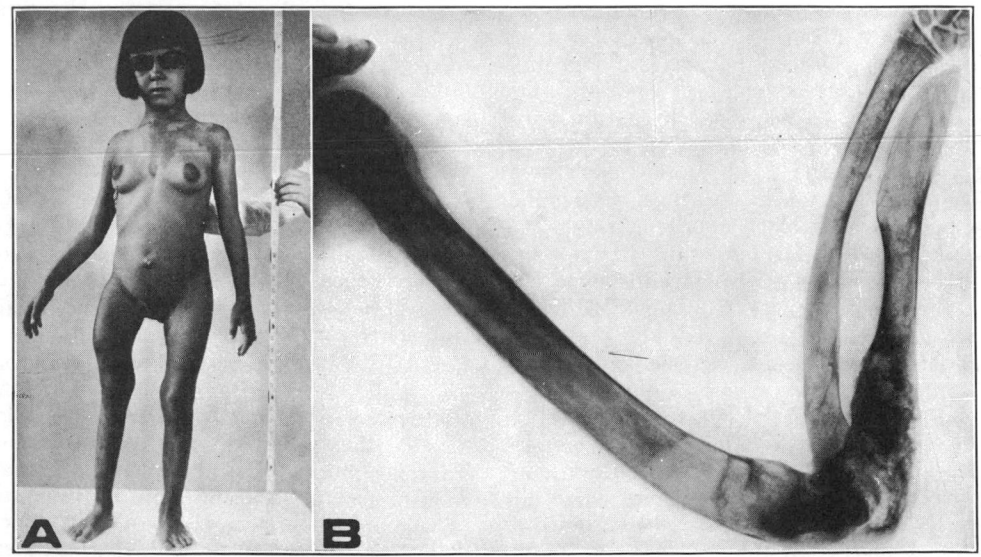

Fig. 41. Polyostotic fibrous dysplasia. A. A 5-year-old patient with precocious puberty. B. Roentgenogram of bones of arm in osteodystrophia fibrosa. (From McCune and Bruch. *Amer. J. Dis. Child.*, 54:806, 1937.)

Almost identical changes are seen in *homocystinuria;* the chief differential points are the almost universal mental retardation and the urinary excretion of homocystine in patients with homocystinuria. Homocystinuria is transmitted as an autosomal recessive trait.

POLYOSTOTIC FIBROUS DYSPLASIA (McCUNE-ALBRIGHT DISEASE). This condition may not belong properly among the skeletal dysplasias, but is included because of the interesting skeletal features which are present. Localized areas of fibrous dysplasia occur in bones, producing a washed-out uniform appearance with loss of trabecular architecture. These features are observed in several bones and are predominantly unilateral. Polyostotic fibrous dysplasia is generally associated with irregular pigmentation of the skin which is also predominantly unilateral, commonly on the side involved with the bone lesions. In the cranium, the bone tends to become thickened and increased in density; cranial asymmetry may result. Precocious puberty has been described in females affected with the disease (Fig. 41), and in some males. Pathologic fractures through the areas of fibrous dysplasia may first call attention to the disease.

NAIL-PATELLA SYNDROME (ARTHRO-ONYCHO-DYSPLASIA, ILIAC HORN SYNDROME, FONG'S SYNDROME). The condition is recognized clinically by an inability to extend the elbows in an individual who has an ectodermal dysplasia involving the nails of at least the thumb and index finger. Other nails may be involved, but become less severely affected going from the radial to the ulnar side of the hand. Inspection of the knee then demonstrates the broad flat appearance resulting from congenital absence or hypoplasia of the patellas. Radiographically, the radial heads are hypoplastic and dislocated, ossification centers for the patellas are extremely small or absent, and bony excrescences, for which there does not appear to be any mammalian homologue, extend backward from the alae of the ilia (see Fig. 15). Occasionally they can be palpated clinically. The condition appears to be transmitted by an autosomal dominant gene which is closely linked to the locus deciding the ABO blood group. Individuals with incomplete forms have been described in families demonstrating an atypical form of nephritis.

HYPOPHOSPHATASIA. It is not clear whether this is a true skeletal dysplasia or whether the hypophosphatasia which characterizes the condition results from other more basic defects. In either event, in this condition, there are characteristic low alkaline phosphatase levels in blood and tissues, defective transformation of cartilage to bone, premature shedding of the deciduous teeth (often the feature which brings the child to the physician), and an associated abnormal metabolite (ethanolamine phosphate) in the urine. The condition is most severe in the newborn infant who obviously has suffered in utero. These children are usually nonviable and have practically no mineralized bone throughout the body. In these infants, there is a failure to form primary spongiosa of an extremely severe degree. In infants over 6 months of age, the mineralization of the skeleton is appreciably better, but the children fail to thrive. Cranial sutures are separated and fontanels bulge. Bowing of the long bones is a common manifestation. If the infant survives, the clinical picture changes and the forms seen in children are recognized. These are similar to, and have been confused with, rickets because of defective gait, short stature, bow legs, enlargement of the joints, and even a "rachitic" rosary. Radiographs demonstrate irregularities of mineralization in all areas where cartilage is transforming to bone and, as in rickets, accentuation in areas of most rapid growth. Characteristically, however, irregular islands of radiolucency extend into the shaft of the bone from the irregular epiphyseal line. The disease in adults is usually found incidental to a chemical analysis of the blood when a low alkaline phosphatase level is noted. Ethanolamine phosphate is also present in the urine. There may be a history of fractures and of "rickets" during childhood. Premature closure of cranial sutures occurs in a large percentage of children with the condition. Teeth show an aplasia, hypoplasia, or dysplasia of the cementum. Premature exfoliation is believed to be related to aplasia of cementum, and may affect permanent as well as deciduous teeth.

HYPERPHOSPHATASIA. This condition is frequently referred to as juvenile Paget's disease with clinical features in the child quite comparable to those of the adult. Bowing deformity of the legs develops in childhood, and muscle weakness is prominent. Although thickening of the bones of the skull and of the face may take place, the cranial features are not as prominent clinically as in adults. Characteristically, the long bones demonstrate, in addition to the bowing, extensive cortical hyperostoses, often with the appearance of active intraosseous reorganization. The alkaline phosphatase level of the serum is markedly and consistently elevated, and serves to differentiate the condition from other hyperostotic conditions affecting the appendicular skeleton and the skull.

OSTEOPETROSIS (ALBERS-SCHÖNBERG'S DISEASE, MARBLE BONES). This is an osteosclerotic disorder commonly associated with anemia and deafness, and usually identified radiographically by marked increase in radiodensity of almost all the bones of the body, with disproportionate involvement of the long tubular bones and the base of the skull (Fig. 42). In spite of their radiodensity, the bones are relatively brittle, and fractures are common particularly in the hip. Dental sepsis has been frequent, and osteomyelitis of the mandible was a common complication before potent anti-infectious agents were available. The tubular bones are not only increased in density, but also demonstrate a disturbance in their constriction, so that flaring of the distal ends of the growing shafts is a prominent feature in childhood (Fig. 43). Variations in density of bone extending in bands

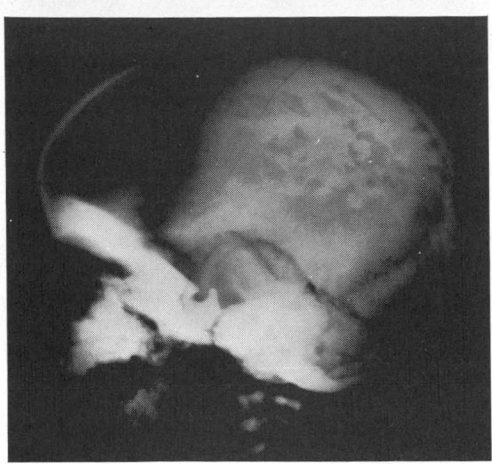

Fig. 42. Roentgenogram of skull in a boy (age 3 years, 9 months) with osteopetrosis.

across the poorly constricted metaphysis suggest that there are periods of exacerbation and remission of the disease. Individuals who have been followed into adult life, though dwarfed, frequently recover from the myelosclerotic anemia which characterizes their course in infancy and childhood. Even hepatosplenomegaly, present in childhood, tends to recede. The skeletal changes result from a persistence of primary spongiosa which is not properly eroded and remodeled. It would appear that some of the cases found in infancy represented instances of idiopathic hypercalcemia (see Sec. 3.5) rather than osteopetrosis.

The osseous lesions of pseudohypoparathyroidism (Chap. 16) and of the storage diseases (Hurler's syndrome, Gaucher's disease, Niemann-Pick's disease) are described elsewhere (Sec. 8.10).

PYCNODYSOSTOSIS. Maroteaux and Lamy have described a form of osteosclerotic dwarfism associated with fractures which has been confused with osteogenesis imperfecta as well as osteopetrosis. Because of the dense bone, the term pycnodysostosis (*pyknos*—thick) was coined to describe it. Differential features include the absence of severe anemia, loss of the angle of the mandible so that radiographs demonstrate the ascending ramus as a direct continuation of the body of the mandible, and hypoplasia of the terminal phalanges. The authors have postulated that Henri de Toulouse-Lautrec owed his short stature to this entity, and that the several fractures he was known to have had reflected this condition rather than osteogenesis imperfecta.

MEDULLARY STENOSIS. Congenital medullary stenosis is a form of proportional dwarfism characterized by self-limited bouts of clinical tetany with hypocalcemia and hyperphosphatemia. Radiographs of the skeleton demonstrate absolute decrease in size of tubular bones with disproportionately decreased shaft width. The latter is due to extreme narrowness of the medullary cavities. In the skull, calvarial bones are thin and the anterior fontanel closes late. There are no signs of disease of associated organs. Medullary stenosis in metacarpal bones occurs to some degree in the normal population; it is more common in some Central American populations than in a carefully studied North American group. The relationship of this developmental variation to the generalized disorder with systemic manifestations is not clear.

REFERENCES

HEREDITARY AND DEVELOPMENTAL CONDITIONS

Lamy, M., and Maroteaux, P. Les chondrodystrophies génotypiques. Paris, L'Expansion Scientifique Française, 1960.

McKusick, V. A. Mendelian Inheritance in Man, 2nd ed. Baltimore, The Johns Hopkins Press, 1968.

Achondroplasia

Caffey, J. Achondroplasia of the pelvis and lumbosacral spine. Amer. J. Roentgen., 80:449, 1958.

Cohen, M. E., Rosenthal, A. G., and Matson, D. D. Neurological abnormalities in achondroplastic children. J. Pediat., 71:367, 1967.

Kaufmann, E. Untersuchungen über die sogenannte foetale Rachitis (Chondrodystrophia foetalis). Berlin, Georg Reiner, 1892.

Kozlowski, K., and Zychowicz, C. Hypochondroplasie. Fschr. a. d. Geb. d. Roentgenstr., 101:531, 1954.

Maroteaux, P., Spranger, J., and Wiedemann, H.-R. Der metatropische Zwergwuchs. Arch. Kinderheilk., 173:211, 1966.

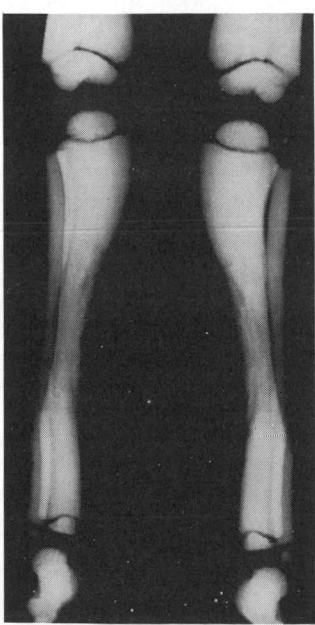

Fig. 43. Roentgenogram of lower extremities of a boy (age 3 years, 9 months) with osteopetrosis.

Silverman, F. N. A differential diagnosis of achondroplasia. Radiol. Clin. N. Amer., No. 6, 2:223, 1968.

Chondroectodermal Dysplasia

Caffey, J. Chondroectodermal dysplasia (Ellis-van Creveld disease); report of 3 cases. Amer. J. Roentgen., 68: 875, 1952.
Ellis, R. W. B., and Andrew, J. D. Chondroectodermal dysplasia. J. Bone Joint Surg., 44B:626, 1962.
———— and van Creveld, S. A syndrome characterized by ectodermal dysplasia, polydactyly, chondrodysplasia and congenital morbus cordis. Arch. Dis. Child., 15: 65, 1940.
McKusick, V. A., Egeland, J. A., Eldridge, D., and Krusen, D. E. Dwarfism in the Amish. I. The Ellis-van Creveld syndrome. Bull. Hopkins Hosp., 115:306, 1964.

Metaphyseal Dysostosis

Burke, Valerie, Colebatch, J. H., Anderson, Charlotte M., and Simons, M. J. Association of pancreatic insufficiency and chronic neutropenia in childhood. Arch. Dis. Child., 42:147, 1967.
Evans, R., and Caffey, J. Metaphyseal dysostosis resembling vitamin D refractory rickets. Amer. J. Dis. Child., 95:640, 1958.
Jansen, M. Uber atypische Chondrodystrophie (Achondroplasie) und über eine noch nicht beschriebene angeborene Wachstrumsstörung des Knochensystems: Metaphysäre Dysostosis. Z. Orthop. Chir., 61:255, 1934.
Kozlowski, K. Metaphyseal dysotosis. Amer. J. Roentgen., 91:602, 1964.
McKusick, V. A., Eldridge, R., Hostetler, J. A., Egeland, J. A., and Ruangwit, U. Dwarfism in the Amish. II. Cartilage-hair dysplasia. Bull. Hopkins Hosp., 116: 285, 1965.
Schmid, F. Beitrag zur Dysostosis Enchondralis Metaphysaria. Mschr. Kinderheilk., 97:393, 1949.
Stephens, F. E. An achondroplastic mutation and the nature of its inheritance. J. Hered., 34:229, 1943.

Epiphyseal Dysplasias

Dyggve, T. V., Melchior, J. C., and Clausen, J. Morquio-Ullrich's disease. An inborn error of metabolism? Arch. Dis. Child., 37:525, 1962.
Ford, N., Silverman, F. N., and Kozlowski, K. Spondyloepiphyseal dysplasia (pseudo-achondroplastic type). Amer. J. Roentgen., 86:462, 1961.
Lamy, M., and Maroteaux, P. Les chondrodystrophies génotypiques. Paris, L'Expansion Scientifique Française, 1961.
Maroteaux, P., and Lamy, M. La maladie de Morquio. La Presse Med., 71:2091, 1963.
———— Wiedemann, R., Spranger, J., Kozlowski, K., and Lenzi, L. Essai de Classification des Dysplasies Spondylo-épiphysaires. Lyon, France, SIMEP Editions, 1968.
Schenk, E. A., and Haggerty, J. Morquio's disease. A radiologic and morphologic study. Pediatrics, 34:839, 1964.
Silverman, F. N. Dysplasies épiphysaires: Entité protéiforme. Ann. Radiol., 4:833, 1961.

Multiple Hereditary Exostoses

Jaffe, Ч. L. Hereditary multiple exostosis. Arch. Path., 36:335, 1943.

Ollier's Syndrome and Maffucci's Syndrome

Carleton, A., Elkington, J. St. C., Greenfield, J. G., and Robb-Smith, A. H. T. Maffucci's syndrome (dyschondroplasia with haemangeiomata). Quart. J. Med., 11: 203, 1942.
Herdman, R. C., Langer, L. O., and Good, R. A. Dyschondrosteosis. J. Pediat., 68:432, 1966.
Margolis, J. Ollier's disease. Arch. Int. Med., 103:297, 1959.

Osteogenesis Imperfecta

Follis, R. J., Jr. Osteogenesis imperfecta congenita: A connective tissue diathesis. J. Pediat., 41:713, 1952.
———— Maldevelopment of corium in osteogenesis imperfecta syndrome. Bull. Hopkins Hosp., 93:225, 1953.
Sofield, H. A., and Millar, E. A. Intramedullary fixation of deformities of the long bones. J. Bone Joint Surg., 41A:1372, 1959.
Wright, P. B., Gernstetter, S. L., and Greenblatt, R. B. Therapeutic acceleration of bone age in osteogenesis imperfecta; case report. J. Bone Joint Surg., 33A:939, 1951.

Cleidocranial Dysostosis

Anspach, W. E., and Huepel, R. C. Familial cleidocranial dysostosis (cleidal dysostosis): A preosseous and dentinal dystrophy. Amer. J. Dis. Child., 58:786, 1939.
Bach, Ch., Fauré, C., Schaeffer, P., and Jolly, J. La dysostosis cléidocranienne. Etude de six observations. Association à des manifestations neurologiques. Ann. Pediat., 13:67, 1966.
Forland, M. Cleidocranial dysostosis: a review of the syndrome and report of a sporadic case with hereditary transmission. Amer. J. Med., 33:792, 1962.

MISCELLANEOUS DYSPLASIAS

Engelmann's Disease

Girdany, B. R. Engelmann's disease (progressive diaphyseal dysplasia). A nonprogressive familial form of muscular dystrophy with characteristic bone changes. Clin. Orthop., 14:102, 1959.
Joseph, J., LeFebvre, J., Guy, E., and Job, J. C. Dysplasie cranio-diaphysaire progressive. Ann. Radiol., 1:477, 1958.
Neuhauser, E. B. D., Schwachman, H., Wittenberg, M. H., and Cohen, J. Progressive diaphyseal dysplasia. Radiology, 51:11, 1948.
Singleton, E. B., Thomas, J. R., Worthington, W. W., and Hild, J. R. Progressive diaphyseal dysplasia (Engelmann's disease). Radiology, 67:233, 1956.

Metaphyseal Dysplasia

Bakwin, H., and Krida, A. Familial metaphyseal dysplasia. Amer. J. Dis. Child., 53:1521, 1937.

———— Personal communication.

Mori, P. A., and Holt, J. F. Cranial manifestations of familial metaphyseal dysplasia. Radiology, 66:335, 1956.

Pyle, E. A case of unusual bone development. J. Bone Joint Surg., 13:874, 1931.

Marfan's Syndrome

McKusick, V. A. Heritable Disorders of Connective Tissue, 2nd ed. St. Louis, C. V. Mosby Co., 1960.

Schimke, R. N., McKusick, V. A., Huang, T., Pollack, A. D. Homocystinuria: Studies of 20 families with 38 affected members. J.A.M.A., 193:711, 1965.

Polyostotic Fibrous Dysplasia

Albright, F., Butler, A. M., Hampton, A. O., and Smith, P. Syndrome characterized by osteitis fibrosa disseminata, areas of pigmentation and endocrine dysfunction, with precocious puberty in females; report of five cases. New Eng. J. Med., 216:727, 1937.

McCune, D. J., and Bruch, H. Osteodystrophia fibrosa; report of a case in which the condition was combined with precocious puberty, pathologic pigmentation of the skin and hyperthyroidism, with a review of the literature. Amer. J. Dis. Child., 54:806, 1937.

Nail-Patella Syndrome

Carbonara, P., and Alpert, M. Hereditary osteo-onychodysplasia (HOOD). Amer. J. Med. Sci., 248:139, 1964.

Doub, H. Editorial. Clinical observations and research (iliac horn syndrome). Radiology, 59:578, 1952.

Lawler, S. D., Renwick, J. H., Mosbech, J. Wildervank, L. S., and Hauge, M. Linkage tests involving the P blood group locus and further data on the ABO: nail-patella linkage. Ann. Hum. Genet., 22:342, 1958.

Hypophosphatasia

Currarino, G., Neuhauser, E. B. D., Reyersbach, G. C., and Sobel, E. Hypophosphatasia. Amer. J. Roentgen., 78:392, 1957.

McCance, R. A., Fairweather, D. V. I., Barrett, A. M., and Morrison, A. B. Genetic, clinical, biochemical and pathological features of hypophosphatasia. Quart. J. Med., 25:523, 1956.

Naki, Hisayo, Landing, B. H., and Pettit, Mary D. Distinguishing hypophosphatasia from cretinism by means of alkaline phosphatase stains of skin biopsy. Amer. J. Clin. Path., 33:115, 1960.

Ritchie, G. MacL. Hypophosphatasia: Metabolic disease with important dental manifestations. Arch. Dis. Child., 39:384, 1964.

Hyperphosphatasia

Fanconi, G., Moreira, G., Uehlinger, E., and Giedion, A.

Osteochalasia desmalis familiaris: Hyperostosis corticalis deformans juvenilis: Chronic idiopathic hyperphosphatasia: Osteo-ectasia and macrocranium. Helv. Paediat. Acta, 19:279, 1964.

Osteopetrosis

Piatt, A. D., Erhardt, G. A., and Araj, J. S. Benign osteopetrosis. Amer. J. Roentgen., 76:1119, 1956.

Pycnodysostosis

Maroteaux, P., and Lamy, M. The malady of Toulouse-Lautrec. J.A.M.A., 191:715, 1965.

Medullary Stenosis

Caffey, J. Congenital stenosis of medullary spaces in tubular bones and calvaria in two proportionate dwarfs, mother and son; coupled with transitory hypocalcemic tetany. Amer. J. Roentgen., 100:1, 1967.

25.5
JUVENILE OSTEOCHONDROSES

Irregularity of mineralization in an adult bone usually represents replacement of normally mineralized structures by pathologic material. In the child, however, irregularity of mineralization is usually a stage in the transformation of cartilage to bone. At several sites in the growing skeleton, delay in the appearance of ossification centers, or damage to centers already present, may result in structural alteration of the cartilage. Reossification then takes place over a period of many months with variable residual deformities, depending largely on local factors. These deforming lesions are called the juvenile osteochondroses. Causes and pathogenesis are both unknown, but a traumatic basis for some, at least, appears very likely. The subject has been confused by the inclusion in some series of children whose irregular mineralization, radiographically indistinguishable from that of an osteochondrosis, actually represents a stage of normal development. The absence of deformity in the final mineralized stage in such individuals has at times been attributed to various forms of treatment. It is obvious that critical reevaluation of both diagnosis and management of patients with this group of conditions is necessary.

The usual clinical signs of osteochondroses are mild local tenderness, pain, swelling, and motor disability; constitutional signs are mild or absent. The frequency of these complaints in active growing children warrants circumspection in making the diagnosis even when they are present in association with irregular mineralization. Examination of the opposite side is mandatory as the frequent bilateral symmetry of irregularities of mineralization may be helpful in the recognition of an anatomic variant masquerading

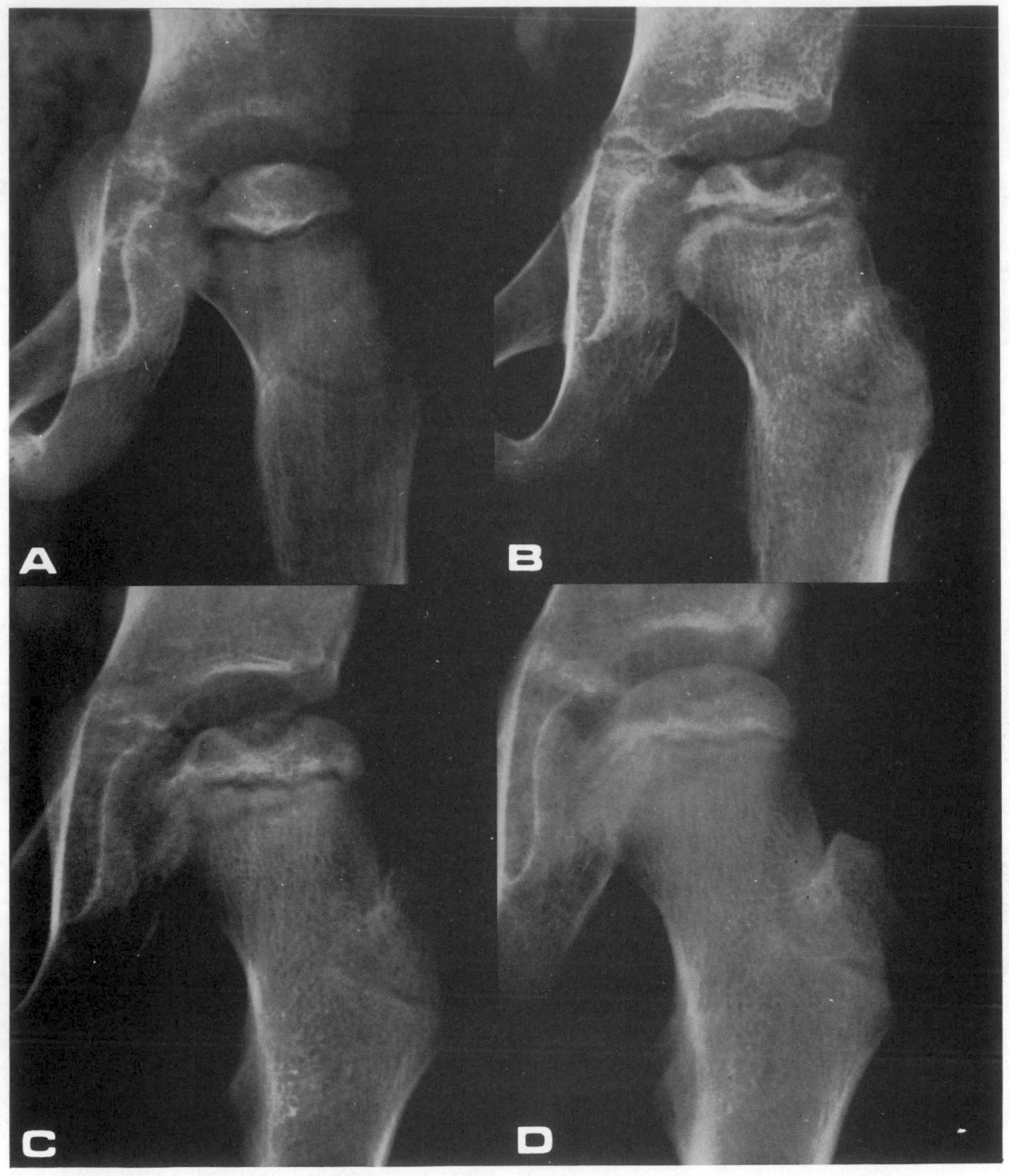

Fig. 44. Serial films at roughly yearly intervals in 7-year-old boy with coxa plana (Legg-Calvé-Perthes' disease) who had a limp for four and one half months prior to first film. Treated with bed rest for seven months followed by cast and crutches for about one year. Unrestricted activities two years, nine months after initial film.

as disease. Most of the osteochondroses have been cataloged according to the names of the individuals first to describe them. Only major and clearly defined entities will be discussed here; the bibliography should be consulted for more extensive coverage.

COXA PLANA (LEGG-CALVÉ-PERTHES' DISEASE). This is by far the most important and the most serious of the juvenile osteochondroses. Limp, usually intermittent, and mild local pain, often referred to the medial side of the ipsilateral knee, are the principal and sometimes the only clinical manifestations. Limitation of abduction and of internal rotation of the hip can often be demonstrated early during the active phase of the disease; these are usually lacking later. Constitutional signs are slight or absent. A significant percentage of cases is found incidental to radiologic examination, such as intravenous pyelograms or bowel studies which include the area of the hip. In some, the clinical signs are present for months prior to radiographic signs; in others, the radiographic features are so well advanced that the clinical history of pain of a few days' or even several weeks' duration indicates a relatively long asymptomatic period.

Coxa plana rarely develops in children younger than 3 years; it is more frequent in boys than in girls in the ratio of about 6 to 1. The condition appears to be unaffected in the speed of its development and regression by any form of treatment (Fig. 44). An active phase of approximately 18 months' duration is characterized by initial faint sclerosis of the affected femoral head with some relative or even absolute radiolucency of the subjacent neck. Not uncommonly, a curvilinear radiolucent shadow appears approximately one millimeter inside the convex projection of the subchondral aspect of the ossification center. This radiolucent shadow is often seen only in a film taken with the femur in abduction and external rotation and appears to be related to the anterior portion of the ossification center. Caffey believes that this line is the consequence of direct traumatic compression of the femoral head by its acetabular roof, and that ischemic necrosis is not the primary basis for Legg-Calvé-Perthes' disease. He has also pointed out that generalized retardation of skeletal maturation is usually present and predisposes to the initial injury.

Following the subchondral epiphyseal fracture and the associated slight but regular lateral displacement of the femoral head in the acetabulum, the ossification center gradually flattens, develops irregular sclerosis and rarefaction, and increases in width. The subjacent neck often increases in width as well, and adaptive changes in the acetabular fossa follow. Occasionally a destructive area in the femoral neck appears prior to diagnostic changes in the head. A relatively quiescent period radiographically lasting about 12 months follows the initial period of destruction, and then remineralization begins and progresses for approximately another 18 months. The ultimate shape of the femoral head is subject to wide variation, and no convincing proof is available that prolonged periods of immobilization and non-weight-bearing significantly affect the end result. Nevertheless, avoidance of weight-bearing would seem reasonable, at least during periods of clinical symptoms, and vigorous contact sports are probably best avoided. After a latent period of 10 to 20 years, osteoarthritic changes may develop in the hips if there is any degree of coxa plana or coxa magna deformity.

OSTEOCHONDROSIS OF THE TARSAL NAVICULAR (KÖHLER'S DISEASE). This disease causes pain, tenderness, and swelling on the dorsum of the foot, usually in children between the ages of 3 and 8 years. Constitutional signs or symptoms are infrequent. The characteristic radiologic findings include irregular rarefaction and sclerosis with flattening and marginal expansion. Unfortunately, the ossification center for the tarsal navicular makes its appearance during these same years and may from the very beginning have irregular sclerosis and apparent "fragmentation." Measurement of the cartilage

space between the anterior aspect of the astragalus and the cuneiform should indicate a diminution on the affected side if a pathologic process is present. Radiographic signs identical with those on an affected side are not uncommonly observed if the healthy foot is examined at the same time. It is very likely that the incidence of this disease is appreciably less than its frequent descriptions would suggest and that normal variations in development are confused with it. Progressive demineralization of a tarsal navicular bone which has been normally mineralized is perhaps the only unequivocal radiographic feature (Fig. 45).

OSTEOCHONDROSIS OF THE TUBEROSITY OF THE TIBIA (OSGOOD-SCHLATTER'S DISEASE). This condition is generally believed to be a consequence of partial avulsion of the infrapatellar tendon from its insertion in the cartilaginous tuberosity. It develops most frequently between the tenth and fifteenth years and is characterized by local swelling and tenderness, with pain on movement of the shank. In the lateral radiograph, there should be soft tissue swelling over the region of the anterior tibial tubercle, thickening of the affected infrapatellar tendon in comparison with that on the opposite side, and subsequently irregular deposition of calcium in the tendon and the adjacent tibial tubercle. Irregularity of mineralization without soft tissue swelling or thickening of the infrapatellar tendon is insufficient for a diagnosis.

OSTEOCHONDROSIS OF THE PATELLA (SINDIG-LARSON'S DISEASE. This disease should be diagnosed only if, in addition to the presence of distinct clinical signs, there are *progressive* destructive radiographic changes in the patella. Irregular mineralization of the normal patella is a rule during the first 12 to 18 months of its ossification, and ossification from two or more centers is common even in older children. Pain and tenderness at the patella are the usual clinical signs.

PSEUDO-OSTEOCHONDROSES. Important entities include *Blount's disease* (medial tibial condyle), *Calvé's disease* (single vertebral body), and *Scheuermann's disease* (several vertebrae and adjoining intervertebral disks). In Blount's disease, a failure of transformation of cartilage to bone at the medial aspect of the epiphyseal line produces a tilting of the medial half of the tibial plateau. The demineralized metaphysis beneath the epiphyseal ossification center develops a beak facing medially when viewed in the frontal plane. A marked bow-leg deformity results. In early childhood, nonrachitic deformities may develop with even a mild beak of the metaphysis; nevertheless, considerable and even complete spontaneous recovery can take place in children under 6 years of age, and osteotomy is recommended only in older children with prominent beaks and widely mineralized tibial epiphyses at the knee, for whom spontaneous correction appears to be unlikely. The radiographic appearance of destruction in the medial spur of the tibia actually represents persistence of poorly developing epiphyseal cartilage.

Calvé described collapse of a single vertebral

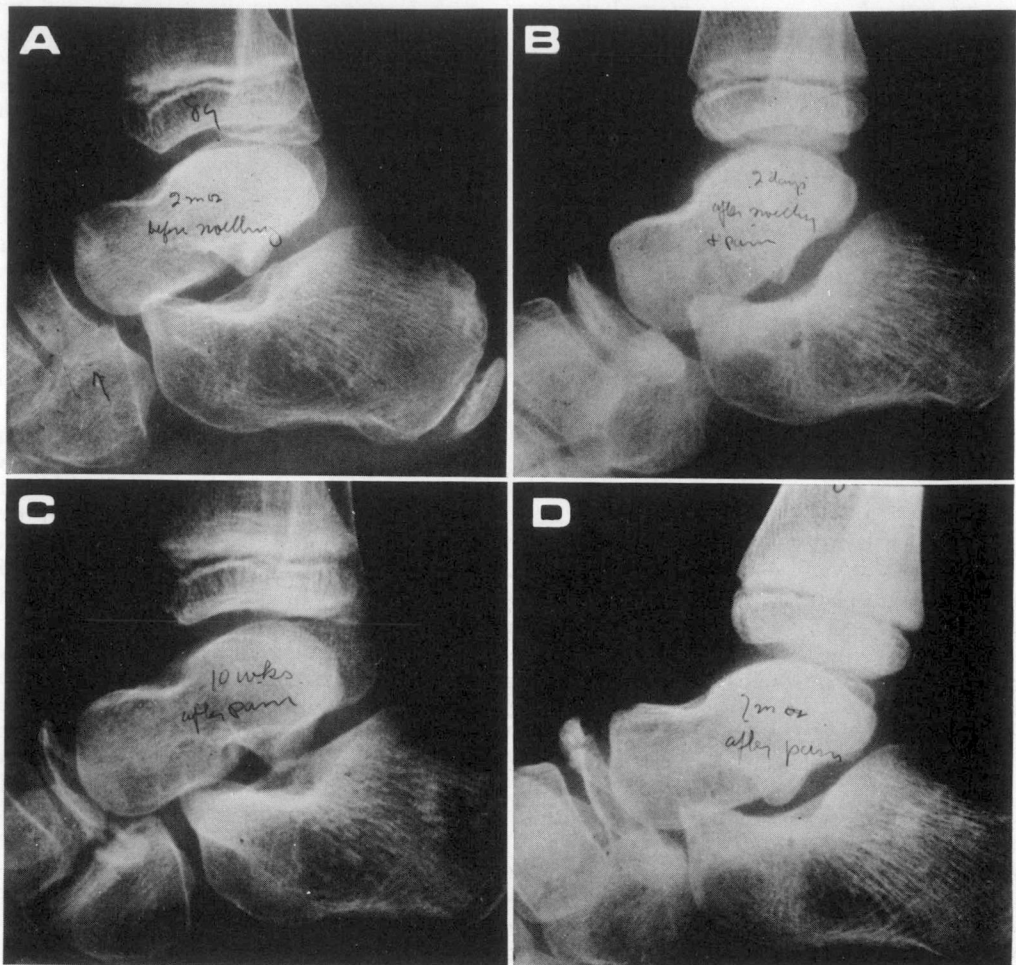

Fig. 45. Osteochondrosis of tarsal navicular. Progressive changes in the tarsal navicular in Kohler's disease; girl 8 years of age who complained of pain, tenderness, and swelling of dorsum of foot. A. Two months before onset. B. Two days after onset. C. Ten weeks after onset. D. Seven months after onset. The tarsal navicular, normal before onset, becomes progressively more flattened ventrodorsally and larger peripherally, while the cartilage spaces in front and in back of it increase in depth.

body in children between 2 and 11 years of age who had regional rigidity, tenderness, and kyphosis or scoliosis, usually in the lower dorsal or lumbar segments. The flattened vertebral body is visualized best in lateral projection and is unassociated with destructive changes in the intervertebral disks. In fact, adjacent to the anterior portion of the affected vertebra, which is compressed more than the posterior portion, the cartilage space of the intervertebral disk actually appears increased. Compere has clearly demonstrated by biopsy of collapsed vertebrae that, in young adults, this lesion has been associated exclusively with eosinophilic granuloma. When the identical lesion has been observed in children, there are frequently other granulomatous lesions in the skeleton which, if biopsied, will demonstrate the histologic features of Hand-Schüller-Christian disease or eosinophilic granuloma. Prognosis is uniformly good; com-

plete clinical recovery is the rule, although anatomic recovery of the height of the vertebral body may not be achieved.

Scheuermann's adolescent kyphosis was considered to result from ischemic necrosis of the epiphyseal ring ossification centers of the vertebral bodies, whereas Calvé's disease was originally considered an osteochondrosis of the primary center for the body. Schmorl, however, was able to demonstrate that the primary lesion in Scheuermann's disease was fracture of the cartilaginous plates of the body, followed by protrusion of nucleus pulposus into the marrow cavity of the contiguous body and associated narrowing of the affected intervertebral disk. Because the posterior vertebral joints are secure, the disk herniation causes the anterior portions of the affected bodies to approximate each other more than the posterior. This produces the characteristic round-back deformity, which can be exaggerated, as persistent unequal pressures on the vertebral bodies produce anterior wedging. The lesions of Scheuermann's disease usually develop between the tenth and twentieth years, more commonly in boys than in girls. Usually there is no pain or tenderness and the condition is first noted when parents or friends comment on "poor posture." In contradistinction to tuberculosis and Calvé's disease, several adjacent vertebrae are usually affected. Laminograms may be necessary to demonstrate the Schmorl's nodes (intravertebral herniations of the nucleus pulposus). Prognosis is unpredictable. In some, the round back progresses to severe crippling deformity; in others, the deformity stabilizes and mild deformities may actually disappear. Treatment is directed at the prevention of further deformity, sometimes with the use of braces and generally avoiding unusual physical stresses on the spine.

Postnatal and Acquired Conditions

INFANTILE CORTICAL HYPEROSTOSIS. This is a disease of the fetus and younger infant characterized by external cortical thickenings of both the long and flat bones. Its cause and pathogenesis are unknown. The presence of fever and a high erythrocyte sedimentation rate suggest that it is an infection; however, bacterial, viral, and serologic studies have failed to identify a causal agent. Hypersensitivity to milk has been suggested as a cause but this also lacks scientific support. Increased platelet counts in several instances have suggested venous thrombotic phenomena as a causal mechanism. The presence of the disease in utero and its familial occurrence have been reported. It is generally accepted that the disease is limited in onset to the fetus and infants younger than 6 months, but a chronic form of the condition may persist for years.

The disease begins in a previously healthy infant with sudden swelling of the lower part of the face, or in the thorax or extremities, with fever and hyperirritability. Salivation, refusal of food, and pallor are common. The soft tissue swellings are deep and firm, and fixed to the underlying bones, with no discoloration of the easily movable skin and no increased local heat. We have not found enlargement of regional lymph nodes in any of our patients in any phase of the disease. Positive laboratory findings in the acute phase of the disease include acceleration of the erythrocyte sedimentation rate and increased alkaline phosphatase activity in serum. The course, both of the disease in different patients and of individual lesions in a single patient, is highly variable. Unilateral proptosis simulating that due to malignant neoplasm has been reported in several instances. The disease may be limited to the lower jaw, with mild local and constitutional signs, and with complete clinical recovery after a few weeks; in other patients, most of the long bones of the body and

their contiguous soft tissues are affected, with high continuous fever and extreme hyperirritability. Each individual lesion may have its own course; one may be involuting while another is evolving. A lesion may partially subside and then suddenly enlarge with a severe local exacerbation. Complete clinical recovery is the rule after several weeks or months. However, the disease has lasted two or three years in several patients, and as long as seven years in one. Crippling residuals developed in the arms of one patient. Several patients have died of causes that are not clear.

The basic radiographic finding is an external thickening of the bony cortex (Fig. 46). In some cases, the mandible alone has been affected; in others, the mandible and practically all of the tubular bones have been involved. In severe cases one or both scapulas have been thickened and sclerotic, and in one patient, one ilium was similarly affected. Instances are recorded where misdiagnoses of malignancy have led to mutilating surgery; these have occurred when lesions have been limited to the scapula, and biopsy material has been misinterpreted. In long-standing cases, the bones may become dilated and have large medullary cavities with thin cortical walls. The disease is generally self-limited, but severely ill patients may benefit from the administration of cortisone or hydrocortisone, to which a prompt response usually can be anticipated. Recurrence of clinical signs and symptoms may be noted when steroid therapy is discontinued. Aspirin has been useful for symptomatic treatment. Caffey has recommended that steroid treatment be continued until three days after fever has subsided. Since response usually takes place within 72 hours, a period of seven days is usually adequate for the initial treatment.

Identical clinical and radiologic sequences have been reported in an infant following smallpox vaccination; material reacting like vaccinia virus was obtained from a scapular biopsy. The inability of careful workers to obtain virus from prior cases of infantile cortical hyperostosis would suggest that this infant had both infantile cortical hyperostosis and generalized vaccinia, and that a cause and effect relationship did not exist.

Subperiosteal new bone formation has been reported in normal newborn infants as a developmental feature; the frequency of unrecognized traumatic periostitis must also be considered when cortical new bone formation is observed in young infants.

HYPERVITAMINOSIS A. In chronic poisoning by vitamin A, the onset of clinical signs is gradual and is characterized by such common complaints as pruritus, anorexia, and irritability. During the early phase, the concentration of vitamin A in the blood is elevated, but there are as yet no bone lesions. The clinical picture first becomes suggestive when deep, tender, hard lumps appear in the extremities and in the occipital region of the head; at this stage, which usually occurs six months or more after the beginning

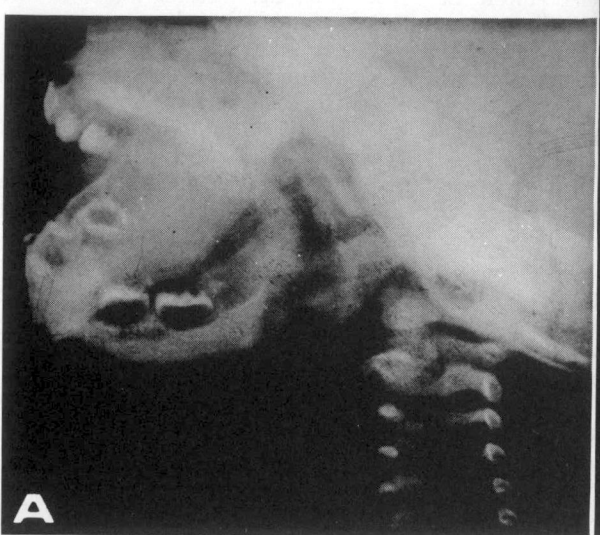
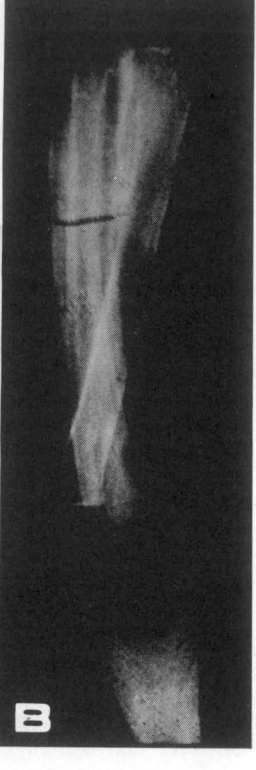

Fig. 46. Infantile cortical hyperostosis. A. Thickening of mandible in patient 3 months of age. B. New bone formation in ulna and radius in patient 4 months old.

of ingestion of excessive amounts of vitamin A, hyperostoses can be demonstrated radiographically in the underlying bones. Additional findings in some patients include fissures in the lips, loss of hair, jaundice, and enlargement of the liver. The diagnosis should be confirmed by measurement of the concentration of vitamin A in the blood, which is always increased although in variable degrees in different patients. Careful questioning usually elicits the fact that the infant or child had been receiving vitamin A in excess of 50,000 units daily. Not infrequently, the preparation has been administered for the treatment of skin disorders. Recovery from the hypervitaminosis is rapid, and the patient's subjective symptoms usually disappear within four to six days after stopping the administration of vitamin A. Preventive measures include instruction of mothers and physicians that vitamin A concentrates are potentially toxic preparations which can really do harm. Except in rare circumstances, the diet of the normally fed child contains adequate vitamin A and requires no supplementation in this respect.

Acute poisoning by vitamin A in infants is characterized by transitory bulging of the anterior fontanel. This follows a massive single dose of vitamin A, usually of several hundred thousand units. Bulging of the fontanel becomes evident after 12 hours and usually disappears after 36 hours. Vomiting is common. Although it has been said that there are no residuals, instances of premature closure of cranial sutures have been observed subsequent to

episodes of acute hypervitaminosis A. The ocular fundi and electroencephalograms are normal.

PULMONARY OSTEOARTHROPATHY. As in adults, pulmonary osteoarthropathy may occur in association with diseases associated with hypoxia, with chronic pulmonary, liver, and enteric diseases, and occasionally without any associated or predisposing condition. Clubbing of the fingers and toes is most common in cyanotic heart disease; following a predisposing lesion, such as subacute pneumonia with empyema, clubbing may develop as early as three weeks after the onset of the primary disease; it usually subsides when the causative factor is removed. Familial instances have been reported in a form associated with either delayed closure of sutures or widening and subsequent slow remineralization of normal sutures, cutaneous eczematoid lesions, and vague arthralgias. It has been suggested that the hereditary factors responsible for osteoarthropathy are activated by various conditions and by differing severities of the same condition in different individuals and, in some, are sufficiently sensitive to require no activation.

PERIOSTEAL HYPEROSTOSIS WITH DYSPROTEINEMIA. This has been reported as a clinical entity. It is manifested by febrile illness asociated with severe pain in the extremities, bone tenderness, and radiographic evidence of widespread subperiosteal new bone formation in the long bones. The plasma proteins are elevated; the alkaline phosphatase levels, however, are not. The illness may be of months' to years' duration and generally recovery is complete. Inability to walk is the common clinical manifestation.

DISEASES OF THE BLOOD. The skeletal system frequently reflects pathologic changes in the marrow. Symptoms of skeletal involvement may distract attention from the less obvious primary disease in such conditions as leukemia and sickle-cell anemia, where a rheumaticlike picture may occur. Frequently, the skeletal lesions are incidental observations, helpful in diagnosis, but occasionally they are the first indication of systemic hematologic disorder. The disorders most commonly associated with such changes are leukemia, chronic hemolytic anemias, and hemophilia. The frequency with which painful symmetrical swellings of the hands and feet occur in sickle-cell disease in infants has given rise to the term "hand-foot syndrome." Swelling appears rapidly, persists for days to weeks, is unassociated with hemolytic crises or obvious infection, and in about 75 percent of the cases, reversible destructive and productive changes occur in the underlying bones. Similar radiographic changes have been observed in salmonella infections associated with sickle-cell disease. In severe instances of iron-deficiency anemias, changes comparable to those of the hemolytic anemias may be observed in the skull.

Angular depressions of the vertebral plates into the bodies, which were thought to be specific for sickle-cell disease, have now been identified in other hemotologic disorders and probably represent fractures of the plate into vertebral bodies weakened by trabecular erosion subsequent to abnormal marrow activity.

NEOPLASMS. Neoplasms affecting the skeletal system may occur as a primary disease of skeletal structures, as neoplasia of nonosseous tissue in bone, or as a metastatic lesion from a primary neoplastic focus elsewhere in the body. The incidence of primary tumors increases with age. Certain tumors occur with greatest frequency at different ages; thus, although any tumor may occur over a fairly wide age range, the patient's age may be a helpful differential point. For example, a bone tumor in a 9-year-old boy is more likely to be a sarcoma of the Ewing type, whereas in a 16-year-old boy, an osteogenic sarcoma would be expected. In all instances, the definitive diagnosis rests on histologic examination in conjunction with the radiographic features and the biologic behavior of the tumor.

Bone cyst is a benign expanding lesion, occurring most frequently in children between 6 and 12 years of age. It is most frequently recognized as a result of pathologic fracture, or as an unsuspected finding during radiologic examination for unrelated symptoms. It is usually intimately related to a cartilaginous epiphyseal line, from which it appears to originate, but the epiphysis is not affected. Growth of the cyst continues as long as this attachment is maintained and skeletal growth continues, so that recurrence may take place after surgical treatment if this is undertaken too early. Occasionally a pathologic fracture is curative.

Giant-cell tumor occurs in a later age group than bone cyst, usually developing in the late teens. It also differs from bone cyst in that the epiphysis is involved. Because giant cells are commonly found in areas of bone destruction from whatever cause, the diagnosis of giant-cell tumor must be made with circumspection. It produces destruction of bone with little or no productive reaction. Aneurysmal bone cyst, which also produces destruction with little or no productive reaction, has been confused with giant-cell tumor when the epiphyseal involvement and the age of the patient are not considered.

Other benign destructive lesions include *nonosteogenic fibroma* and *chondromyxoid fibroma*. These occur with greater frequency in the lower extremities than in the upper; radiologic characteristics are similar and diagnosis is made by biopsy, which at times can consist of the totally excised lesion. *Fibrous cortical defects* occur with great frequency in growing bone, particularly about the knee. The genesis and course are described in detail by Caffey. As a rule, they are asymptomatic incidental lesions found on routine examination of the affected area. They are, of course, not neoplastic, but they frequently precipitate an unnecessary diagnostic fright. Multiple fibromas have been observed in the bones of infants who had cutaneous fibromatosis as well, and were thought to have neurofibromatosis with bone lesions. Several such cases have had spontaneous recovery with disappearance of the cutaneous as well as of the osseous lesions.

Osteoid osteoma is regarded by many as a tumor although others consider it infectious, notwithstanding the failure to identify any infectious agent. It is a small dense nidus of bone and osteoid tissue surrounded by vascular osteogenic tissue and capable of producing an intense productive bone reaction. Clinically, severe boring local pain, worse at night, is present; the pain is said to respond to aspirin, the administration of which is reputed to be a diagnostic test. Symptoms are commonly relieved by excision of the nidus. Many cases described in the past as Garré's sclerosing osteomyelitis are now thought to have represented examples of osteoid osteoma.

Among *malignant tumors of bone*, osteogenic sarcoma and Ewing's tumor are encountered most frequently. *Ewing's tumor* may be productive or destructive of bone. The lamellated periosteal reaction, once considered pathognomonic, has no specific diagnostic value. The tumor usually occurs in children between 5 and 10 years of age; it is associated with pain and generally with regional soft tissue swelling. Any bone may be involved. The lesion metastasizes to lungs and to other bones. Microscopically, Ewing's sarcoma has been confused with neuroblastoma, and pathologists disagree about its exact nature. Clinically and radiologically, it is most frequently confused with osteomyelitis.

Osteogenic sarcoma is more common in the 10 to 15 year age-group. It too may arise in any bone, but the ends of the shafts of the major long bones are sites of predilection. As the name indicates, it is

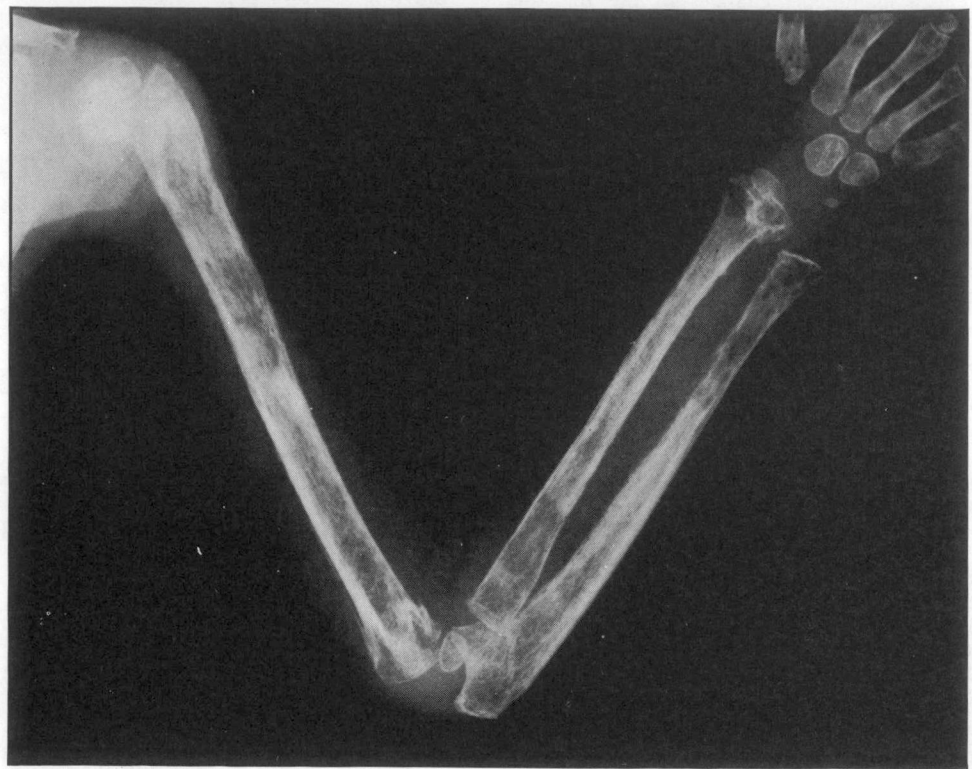

Fig. 47. Roentgenogram showing leukemic infiltration of the bones of a girl 3½ years of age.

generally a bone-producing tumor. New bone formation extends out from the affected bone into the soft tissues surrounding it. Some islands of bone are commonly found in the soft tissue but have no functional structure. In addition, destruction of preexisting bone occurs in practically every case, and in some instances may predominate in the radiographic picture. Extension of tumor in the bone and its medullary cavity is invariably greater than can be demonstrated radiographically. Radical surgery and radiation are occasionally followed by "cure," but the rates of local recurrence or metastatic lesions (chiefly pulmonary) are disappointingly high, and the tumor is almost invariably associated with a fatal outcome.

Clinical manifestations of "bone pain" and rheumaticlike symptoms occur in 50 percent of children with *leukemia*, and may precede the development of diagnostic features in the blood. Local accumulations of leukemic cells are responsible for the destructive and productive bone lesions (Fig. 47) and probably for the pain.

Leukemic lesions have been divided arbitrarily into four types: (1) transverse bands of diminished density at the growing ends of long bones and (2) focal areas of destruction, ranging from moth-eaten rarefaction to gross destruction with collapse of structure; (3) osteosclerosis; and (4) subperiosteal new bone formation. Generally, there is polyostotic involvement, and any bone may be affected; vertebral

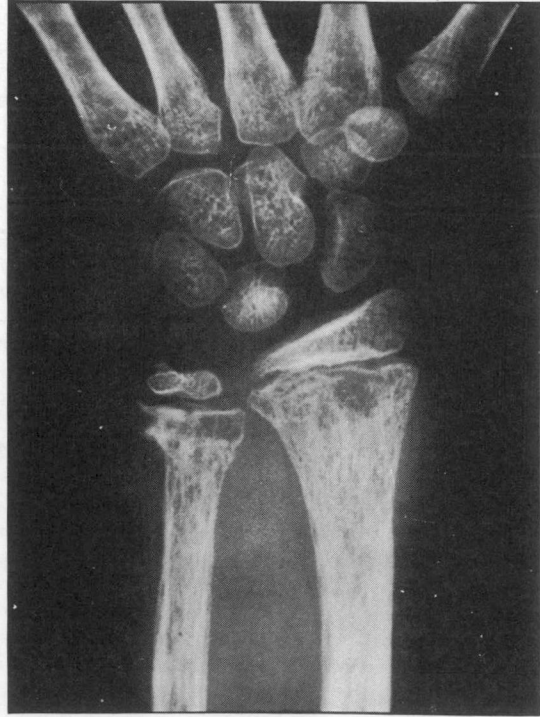

Fig. 48. Metastatic neuroblastoma in the ulna and radius of a boy 9 years of age.

body collapse has been observed as an initial manifestation of skeletal involvement. Pleural reactions may accompany rib lesions.

Neuroblastoma frequently metastasizes to bone and produces destructive and reactive lesions in the appendicular skeleton (Fig. 48) indistinguishable from those of leukemia. In the skull, signs of actively increased pressure are often seen as the bony vault is thickened inward by the metastases. *Wilms' embryoma* of the kidney may also produce irregular destructive lesions when metastases to bone occur. *Neurofibromas* and *ganglioneuromas* cause bone changes by pressure erosion. Pseudarthrosis in association with neurofibromatosis, however, generally occurs without local tumor tissue. Scoliosis is common in association with neurofibromatosis, even in the absence of obvious bone lesions. "Dumbell tumors," in which relatively large intraspinal and extraspinal masses of tumor communicate by a narrow isthmus through an intervertebral foramen, produce diagnostic enlargement of the foramen.

Metastatic embryonal rhabdomyosarcoma may produce defective mineralization in the ends of the shafts of the major long bones which can resemble the lesions of resistant rickets, metaphyseal dysostosis, or leukemia.

Tumorlike irregularities are commonly seen in the growing bones of children in the course of normal development. These are common on the posterior aspect of the distal metaphysis of the femur, where they have been mistaken for periosteal sarcoma. Tumorlike bone production in the scapula in infantile cortical hyperostosis has been noted on page 1741. Organic material such as thorns or other organic foreign bodies may produce reactions disturbingly like those of bone tumor.

REFERENCES

GENERAL

Bick, E. M., and Copel, J. W. Longitudinal growth of the human vertebra; a contribution to human osteogeny. J. Bone Joint Surg., 32A:803, 1950.

Caffey, J. The early roentgenographic changes in essential coxa plana; their significance in pathogenesis. Amer. J. Roentgen., 103:620, 1968.

Compere, E. L., Johnson, W. E., and Coventry, M. B. Vertebra plana (Calvé's disease) due to eosinophilic granuloma. J. Bone Joint Surg., 36A:969, 1954.

Eyring, E. J., Bjornson, D. R., and Peterson, C. A. Early diagnostic and prognostic signs in Legg-Calvé-Perthes disease. Amer. J. Roentgen., 93:382, 1965.

Goff, C. W. Legg-Calvé-Perthes Syndrome and Related Osteochondroses of Youth. Springfield, Ill., Charles C Thomas Co., 1954.

Harris, V. J., and Harris, W. S. Increased thickness of the fibula in Duchenne muscular dystrophy. Amer. J. Roentgen., 98:744, 1966.

Kaufmann, H. J. New roentgen finding in pseudohypertrophic muscular dystrophy. Amer. J. Roentgen., 89:970, 1963.

Langenskiöld, A. Tibia vara. (Osteochondrosis deformans tibiae); survey of 23 cases. Acta Chir. Scand., 103:1, 1952.

Schmorl, G., and Junghanns, H. The Human Spine in Health and Disease. New York, Grune & Stratton, Inc., 1959.

Shopfner, C. E., and Coin, C. G. Genu varus and valgus in children. Radiology, 92:723, 1969.

POSTNATAL AND ACQUIRED CONDITIONS

Infantile Cortical Hyperostosis

Caffey, J. On some late skeletal changes in chronic infantile cortical hyperostosis. Radiology, 59:651, 1952.

——— Infantile cortical hyperostosis: a review of the clinical and radiographic features. Proc. Roy. Soc. Med., 50:347, 1957.

Cochran, W., Connolly, J. H., and Thompson, I. D. Bone involvement after vaccination against smallpox. Brit. Med. J., 2:285, 1963.

Goldbloom, R. B., et al. Idiopathic periosteal hyperostosis with dysproteinemia. A new clinical entity. New Eng. J. Med., 274:873, 1966.

Iliff, C. E., and Ossofsky, H. J. Infantile cortical hyperostosis. An unusual cause of proptosis. Amer. J. Ophthal., 53:976, 1962.

Pickering, D., and Cuddigan, B. Infantile cortical hyperostosis associated with thrombocythemia. Lancet, 2:464, 1969.

Shopfner, C. E. Periosteal bone growth in normal infants. A preliminary report. Amer. J. Roentgen., 97:154, 1966.

Sidbury, J. B., Jr., and Sidbury, J. B. Infantile cortical hyperostosis; an inquiry into the etiology and pathogenesis. New Eng. J. Med., 250:309, 1954.

VanBuskirk, F. W., Tampas, J. P., and Peterson, O. S., Jr. Infantile cortical hyperostosis: An inquiry into its familial aspects. Amer. J. Roentgen., 85:613, 1961.

Hypervitaminosis A

Caffey, J. Chronic poisoning due to excess of vitamin A, description of the clinical and roentgen manifestations in seven infants and young children. Pediatrics, 5:672, 1950.

——— Editorial: Vitamin A poisoning. Amer. J. Roentgen., 67:818, 1952.

Knudson, A. G., Jr., and Rothman, P. E. Hypervitaminosis A; a review with a discussion of vitamin A. Amer. J. Dis. Child., 85:316, 1959.

Marie, J., and See, G. Acute hypervitaminosis A of the infant, its clinical manifestations with benign acute hydrocephalus and pronounced bulge of fontanel; clinical and biologic study. Amer. J. Dis. Child., 87:731, 1954.

Pulmonary Osteoarthropathy

Chamberlain, D. S., Whitaker, J., and Silverman, F. N. Idiopathic osteoarthropathy and cranial defects in children (familial idiopathic osteoarthropathy). Amer. J. Roentgen., 93:408, 1965.

Currarino, G., Tierney, R. C., Giesel, R. G., and Weihl, C. Familial idiopathic osteoarthropathy. Amer. J. Roentgen., 85:633, 1961.

Witherspoon, J. T. Congenital and familial clubbing of the fingers and toes, with a possibly inherited tendency. Arch. Int. Med., 57:18, 1936.

Diseases of the Blood

Caffey, J. Cooley's erythroblastic anemia: Some skeletal findings in adolescents and young adults. Amer. J. Roentgen., 65:547, 1951.

Cassady, J. P., Berdon, W. E., and Baker, D. H. The "typical" spine changes of sickle-cell anemia in a patient with thalassemia major (Cooley's anemia). Radiology, 89:1065, 1967.

Moseley, J. E. Bone Changes in Hematologic Disorders. New York, Grune & Stratton, Inc., 1963.

Shahidi, N. T., and Diamond, L. K. Skull changes in infants with chronic iron deficiency anemia. New Eng. J. Med., 202:137, 1960.

Watson, R. J., Burko, H., Megas, H., and Robinson, M. The hand-foot syndrome in sickle-cell disease in young children. Pediatrics, 31:975, 1963.

Neoplasms

Caffey, J. Fibrous defects in cortical walls of growing tubular bones; their radiologic appearance, structure, prevalence, natural course and diagnostic significance. Advances Pediat., 7:13, 1955.

——— and Anderson, D. Metastatic embryonal rhabdomyosarcoma in the growing skeleton. Amer. J. Dis. Child., 95:581, 1958.

Jaffey, H. L. Osteoid osteoma of bone. Radiology, 45:319, 1945.

Silverman, F. N. The skeletal lesions in leukemia. Amer. J. Roentgen., 59:819, 1948.

Silverstein, M. N., and Kelly, P. J. Leukemia with osteoarticular symptoms and signs. Ann. Int. Med., 59:637, 1963.

Weston, W. J. Thorn and twig-induced pseudotumors of bone and soft tissues. Brit. J. Radiol., 36:323, 1963.

25.6
THE JOINTS

Primary noninflammatory disorders of the joints are discussed in this section. Discussed elsewhere are infections of joints (Chap. 14), and involvement of the joints in the connective tissue diseases (Chap. 12) and in gout (Chap. 8).

IDIOPATHIC COXALGIA. It is not uncommon to encounter children with *acute hip pain* and limitation of motion, particularly abduction and external rotation, who are thought to have coxa plana if afebrile, or infectious arthritis if febrile. Neither leucocytosis nor radiographic change is found. The condition has been called "toxic arthritis" but, in the absence of known toxins and proved joint inflammation, the term "idiopathic coxalgia" is preferred. As a rule the symptoms abate spontaneously within 48 hours.

HEMARTHROSIS. Hemarthrosis is uncommon in childhood except in association with blood dyscrasias, particularly hemophilia (Chapter 17). Pain, swelling, limitation of motion, and even fever may simulate

infectious arthritis. Repeated episodes result in thickening of soft tissues, organization of unabsorbed blood, and deforming ankylosis. Subchondral hemorrhages directly into the bones may produce rounded defects of variable size. The chronic inflammation produces an acceleration of maturation and increase in size of the epiphyses of the affected joints.

DISLOCATION. Dislocations occur as a result of congenital malformations, anomalies of fetal position, diseases of muscles and nerves, trauma, and infection. Among those caused by trauma, the most common is subluxation of the radial head ("pulled elbow"). This is seen in children between 1 and 3 years of age following a sudden pull on the arm such as occurs in lifting. Pain is immediate and the child usually refuses to move the arm, giving the erroneous impression of a neurologic injury. The forearm is held midway between pronation and supination. There is no swelling or discoloration, and surprisingly little tenderness about the elbow. Radiographic examination is not particularly helpful, as gross dislocation is rarely present. Treatment consists in gentle flexion of the elbow to 90 degrees, application of mild pressure with the thumb over the radial head, and gentle rotation of the forearm. As the forearm is supinated, a click is often felt beneath the thumb, and prompt and complete relief of symptoms is obtained. No anesthesia is necessary and immobilization after reduction is seldom required. Spontaneous reduction may also take place, and it is not unusual for it to occur during positioning for radiographic examination.

CONGENITAL DISLOCATION OF THE HIP. Teratologic dislocation, in which there is gross congenital malformation involving the structures of the hip joint, is discussed in Section 2.10. What is generally called "congenital dislocation of the hip" is a dislocation occurring usually after the fourth month when the hips are subjected to the stresses of weight-bearing and locomotion. Prior to this time, particularly in the newborn period, the condition is more accurately described as "dislocatability of the hip."

During the past 20 years, the most popular hypothesis relating to cause and pathogenesis has been that of a congenital dysplasia of the acetabulum which predisposed to subsequent dislocation. Congenital laxity of ligamentous structures, often on a familial basis, has also been postulated as a basis for some cases. More recently, particularly in Sweden, a delay in development of enzyme systems necessary for the degradation of maternal hormones causing ligamentous relaxation, and transmitted via the placenta, has been postulated; and the results of assay of urine from newborn infants with and without the condition have been offered as support of the hypothesis. According to this theory, infants with congenital dislocatability of the hip are unable to properly degrade maternal hormones until near the end of the first week of life. As a consequence, the femoral heads can be dislocated from the acetabular cavities when the femurs are extended and adducted (swaddling

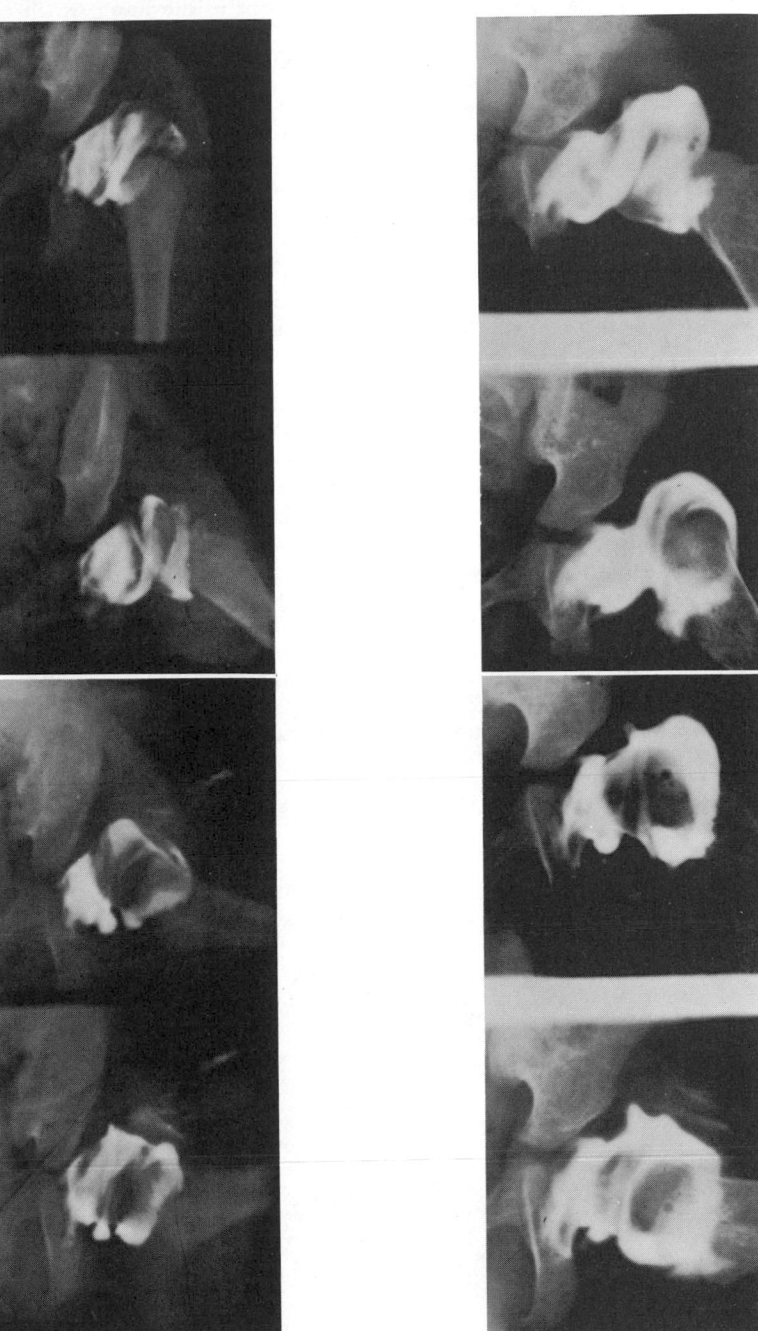

Fig. 49. Arthrograms in congenital dislocation of the hip. *Left.* Female, age 7½ weeks. Spot films taken during manipulation. From top: 1. neutral position; 2. abduction; 3. abduction and internal rotation; and 4. marked abduction and external rotation. Only in 4 is cartilaginous head seated in acetabulum. *Right.* Male, age 2 years. Hourglass contracture of capsule prevents entrance of head into acetabular cavity.

position). On flexion and abduction of the hips, the femoral heads can be induced to reenter the acetabular cavities. The entrance and exit of the femoral heads is responsible for the clicks noted in performing the Ortolani maneuver or the subluxation provocation maneuver (Palmén, Coleman). If position of the lower extremities favors dislocation of the femoral head from its acetabular cavity, and normal ligamentous resistance is regained when the delayed enzyme system begins to function in the second week, the dislocation becomes relatively fixed. Secondary atrophy of the acetabular fossa develops and the classic appearance of "acetabular dysplasia" with congenital dislocation of the femur can be observed. The variability in development of an enzyme system necessary for degradation of the maternal enzymes has a counterpart in the variability in the development of other enzyme systems (Section 2.5). Confirmation of this theory has not been forthcoming, but management based partly on the concept has been extremely successful in practically eliminating the disease as a cause of morbidity in childhood in Sweden.

Unless there is gross dislocation, radiographic examination has little to offer in the newborn period. Acetabular angles, which were once considered of great diagnostic significance, have been shown by Caffey to be so variable that little reliance can be placed upon them until at least the second half of the first year.

In cases first diagnosed after the end of the first year, and in whom simple manipulative procedures do not appear to give a firm replacement of the head in the acetabular fossa, arthrograms (Fig. 49) may demonstrate the anatomic abnormalities of the capsule and labrum which preclude a satisfactory closed reduction. In cases diagnosed even later, the acetabular cavity is shallow, the ossification center for the femoral head on the affected side is small and lies at a higher level than the normal head on the opposite side. The femoral neck is usually anteverted; the proximal end of the femur is displaced laterally with respect to the acetabulum in comparison with the opposite side. A false acetabulum may be present in the ilium which is usually hyperplastic (Fig. 50).

Clinically, the older child walks with a marked limp or even a waddling gait if both hips are involved. The lesion is six to seven times more frequent in girls than in boys, and the left hip is affected more frequently than the right. Negroes are rarely affected by the condition; the incidence in most studies of other large populations is 1.5 in 1,000 live births. Local variations have been reported, and in some geographic areas there is a high familial incidence. Local areas of high incidence of congenital dislocation of the hip may be accounted for in part by local practices such as binding or swaddling as well as by genetic factors in relation to maternal relaxing hormone production and timing of enzymatic degradation activity on the part of the newborn infant. Other cases may represent genetic factors related to congenital relaxation of ligaments as described by Carter and Wilkinson.

Shortening of the affected thigh and limitation of abduction and external rotation are important clinical findings. A positive Trendelenburg sign (lowering of the opposite gluteal fold when the patient bears his full weight on the affected limb) is easily demonstrated in older children. Asymmetry of skin folds in the thigh is so common in normal infants that this sign alone has little diagnostic value, although it does warrant further examination for dislocation or dislocatability of the hips.

From the standpoint of prevention of disability,

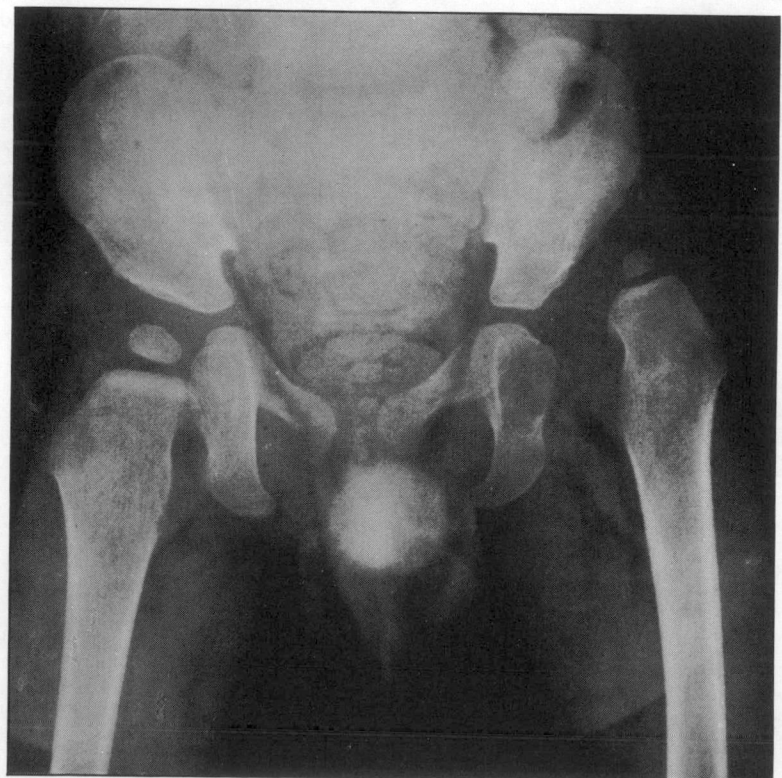

Fig. 50. Full dislocation of the left hip in a girl 17 months of age. All the components of Putti's triad are present. The acetabular roof is short and tilted upward with enlargement of the acetabular angle of 46 degrees. The femoral epiphyseal ossification center is small. The femur is displaced cephalad and laterad onto the ilial wing, where a shallow false acetabular cavity is already evident.

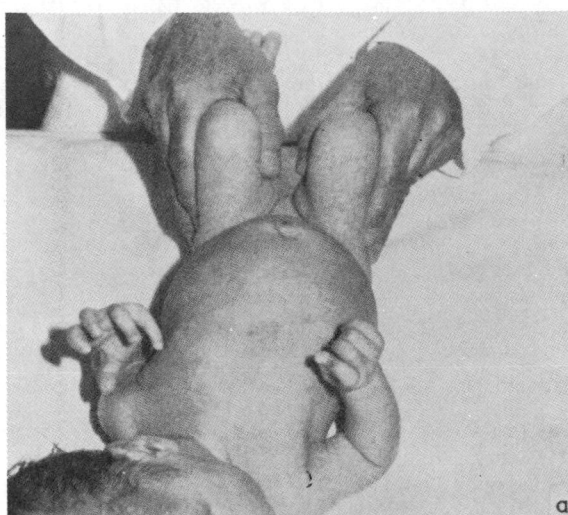

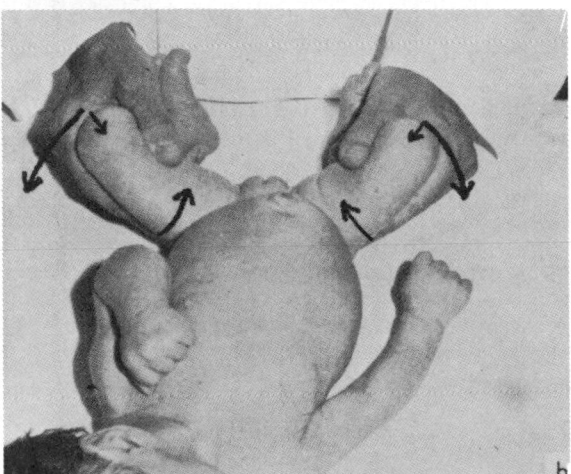

the earlier the diagnosis is made and the treatment begun, the greater is the likelihood of cure. In the newborn period, the Ortolani maneuver can identify the condition as the dislocated femoral head slips back into the acetabular fossa. In this procedure (Fig. 51), the examiner places the infant on his back on a firm surface. The legs are adducted with the hips and knees extended. The femurs are held between the thumb medially, and the index and middle fingers laterally; the tips of the latter two should press against the greater trochanter. The knee joint usually then fits in the thenar portion of the examiner's palm. The legs are then flexed to 90 degrees at the hips and the knees. With one hand holding one lower extremity in this position, the other then abducts the other lower extremity into a "frog leg" position, meanwhile pressing upward and forward with the tips of the fingers over the greater trochanter. With a normal infant, suitably relaxed, the abduction can be continued to 90 degrees without incident. In the child with a dislocated hip, a resistance may be encountered at about 60 degrees of flexion to stabilize the pelvis. Palmén and Coleman independently described a reverse procedure which would produce a dislocation not identified by the Ortolani maneuver. The initial stages of what Palmén calls the "subluxation provocation maneuver" are comparable to those of the Ortolani maneuver up to the point where abduction of the femurs is initiated. The femurs are abducted and flexed to only about 45 degrees and rotated slightly internally; the palms of the examiner are then pushed against the knees while the thumb presses outward on the internal aspect of the thighs (Fig. 52). A positive reaction is noted when the sensation of a jerk indicates that the femoral head has been displaced outward, upward, and backward from the acetabular fossa. The Ortolani maneuver then suffices for reduction.

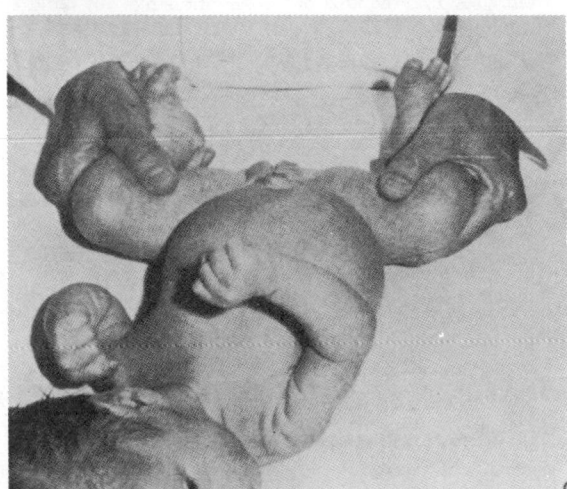

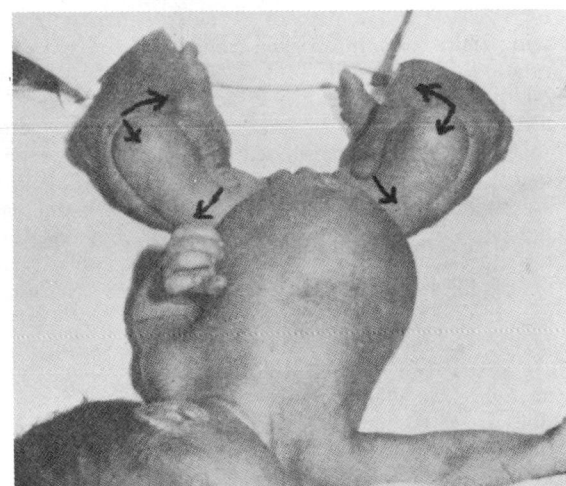

Fig. 51. Sequence of flexion and abduction of hips in the Ortolani maneuver. (With permission from Palmén. *Acta Paediat. Scand.*, 50(Suppl. 129):1, 1961.)

Fig. 52. The direction of forces exerted in the subluxation provocation maneuver. Compare with 51B. (With permission from Palmén. *Acta Paediat. Scand.*, 50(Suppl. 129):1, 1961.)

If the jerk of exit or entrance or both can be elicited in a newborn infant, the position of reduction is maintained by placing the child in a simple padded splint which holds the femurs in abduction and external rotation 24 hours a day for periods of two weeks to three months. Various splints, including the Frejka pillow splint, have been devised and are quite satisfactory. A large padded diaper may be utilized but is somewhat less secure in its effect. The splints or pads may be removed for bathing the baby but should be reapplied immediately. Usually, within two to three weeks, the entrance and exit clicks can no longer be elicited. After a period of six weeks on the average, the splints are no longer needed and the joint is stable. Only if clinical signs persist at this time is radiographic examination necessary. In premature infants, the clinical signs are extremely difficult to elicit, and it is probably wise to assess the range of motion of the hips at the time the infant is being discharged. Any limitation of abduction and external rotation, or any abnormal clicks, warrant radiographic examination.

In the treatment of older children with congenital dislocation of the hip, the soft tissues may be stretched by traction; and by subsequent manipulation under anesthesia, the femoral head can be replaced in the acetabular fossa. Plaster casts are usually required to maintain this position because by this time the acetabulum has become quite shallow. In children who do not respond to relatively gentle manipulative procedures, or whose arthrograms demonstrate complications to closed reduction, such as an hour-glass capsule, interposition of the labrum, or accumulation of fat in the acetabulum, an open reduction is usually necessary.

With extensive abduction and external rotation, the capsule of the hip is pulled tight and the vascular supply to the head may be compromised; aseptic necrosis of the femoral head has been reported in as high as 20 to 30 percent of older patients treated with rigid casts in marked abduction and external rotation. The ultimate fate of children with congenital dislocation of the hip is not known. Many who were treated by manipulative methods relatively late in childhood have developed coxa plana-coxa magna deformities and arthritic changes in middle adult life. Initial short-term follow-up of individuals treated in the newborn period by the more simple methods thus far suggests almost complete absence of complications or sequelae. The experience in Malmö, Sweden, where the Ortolani maneuver and the subluxation provocation maneuver have been utilized for over 10 years, and where children with positive signs have been treated immediately in the newborn period, suggests that nonteratogenic congenital dislocation of the hip can be recognized and treated in the newborn period and that morbidity from this condition in later childhood can practically be eliminated completely. Examination of the hips of the newborn infant for dislocatability by the maneuvers described should be as much a part of every newborn examination as counting the fingers and toes.

SLIPPED FEMORAL EPIPHYSES. This lesion is rarely encountered in children younger than 10 years or older than 17 years. Boys are more frequently affected than girls, but only slightly so. Clinical manifestations are limited to pain in the affected hip and limb. Usually, there is no conspicuous injury prior to the onset; in many cases, symptoms occur during ordinary activities such as walking and running, and sometimes the pain has appeared in the morning after several hours of sleep. Diagnosis is made on radiographic examination when the femoral head is demonstrated to be shifted medially and dorsally in relation to the end of the shaft. Often the radiolucent strip between the epiphyseal ossification center and the shaft is deepened. Some studies indicate that the primary change is fibrous degeneration of the cartilaginous plate which weakens the bone at this site and permits slipping of the epiphysis.

Treatment of slipped femoral epiphysis is surgical and is considered urgent in most clinics. Bed rest must be instituted immediately to prevent the stresses of further weight-bearing; most orthopedists insert metallic nails through the center of the femoral neck into the femoral head if it has been maintained in good position. If the femoral head has slipped appreciably, normalization of its position with respect to the femoral neck is attempted by manipulation prior to nailing. In every case, careful attention must be paid to the apparently healthy hip because bilateral disease occurs in as many as 20 percent of patients.

REFERENCES

IDIOPATHIC COXALGIA

Monty, C. P. Prognosis of "observation hip" in children. Arch. Dis. Child., 37:539, 1962.
Spock, A. Transient synovitis of the hip joint in children. Pediatrics, 24:1042, 1959.

CONGENITAL DISLOCATION OF THE HIP

Andrén, L. Instability of the pubic symphysis and congenital dislocation of the hip in newborns. Acta Radiol., 54:123, 1960.
Caffey, J., Ames, R., Silverman, W. A., Ryder, C. T., and Hough, G. Contradiction of the congenital dysplasia—predislocation hypothesis of congenital dislocation of the hip through a study of the normal variation in acetabular angles at successive periods in infancy. Pediatrics, 17:632, 1956.
Carter, C. O., and Wilkinson, J. Persistent joint laxity and congenital dislocation of the hip. J. Bone Joint Surg., 46B:40, 1964.
Coleman, S. Diagnosis of congenital dysplasia of the hip in the newborn infant. J.A.M.A., 162:548, 1956.
Palmén, K. Preluxation of the hip joint. Diagnosis and treatment in the newborn and the diagnosis of congenital dislocation of the hip joint in Sweden during

the years 1948-1960. Acta Paediat. Scand. 50 (Suppl. 129), 1961.

Silverman, F. N. Current concepts in diagnosis and management of congenital dislocation of the hip. Pediatrics, 34:554, 1964.

SLIPPED FEMORAL EPIPHYSES

Johnston, J. A., Manson, C., and Mitchell, C. L. Epiphysiolysis. Amer. J. Dis. Child., 92:337, 1956.

Klein, A., Joplin, R. J., Reidy, J. A., and Hanelin, J. Roentgenographic features of slipped capital femoral epiphysis. Amer. J. Roentgen., 66:361, 1951.

Lacroix, P., and Verbrugge, J. Slipping of the upper femoral epiphysis; a pathological study. J. Bone Joint Surg., 33-A:371, 1951.

chapter 26

THE SKIN

JOSEPH McGUIRE, Associate Editor

26.1
INTRODUCTION

Because of its unique location as a limiting membrane positioned between the individual and his milieu, the skin is one of the best-described organs of the body. Man, with relatively sparse hair, exhibits a considerable expanse of skin. The relative ease of observation has permitted the growth of a tremendous descriptive literature which, although useful to the specialist, impedes and often discourages others.

Whereas abnormalities of other organ systems are often described in terms that imply pathogenesis (e.g., pulmonary infarct, pulmonary alveolar proteinosis), dermatologic terms (acne, psoriasis, vitiligo) usually contain no such implication.

An attractive aspect of dermatology is that most diagnoses can be made from the morphology, configuration, and distribution of the lesions. Morphology refers to the description of an individual lesion and is expressed by the following words: elevated, flat, pigmented, atrophic, etc. Configuration refers to the patterning of the lesions; for example, annular, confluent, arcuate, linear. Distribution refers, of course, to the area of the body involved by the eruption.

These three types of descriptive analysis permit accurate pattern recognition of many skin diseases strictly from the clinical examination. In addition to careful inspection, histologic examination is often useful. A convenient aid to dermatologic diagnosis is the punch biopsy which, when performed with local anesthesia, is no more effort for the physician or uncomfortable for the patient than a venipuncture. The biopsy tool, which resembles a cork borer, is the only special instrument required. The site can be closed with an adhesive dressing without suturing. A core of skin 5 mm in diameter is sufficient for adequate study of tissue by a pathologist.

The skin is a bilaminar organ (Figs. 1 and 2). The outer layer, the epidermis, is a relatively impermeable membrane, the chief function of which is to retard exchange of liquids from either side. The effectiveness of this membrane is vividly demonstrated by the profuse fluid loss which follows damage to the epidermis by superficial thermal injury, pemphigus, or poison ivy dermatitis. Supporting the epidermis is the dermis, which accounts for the main bulk of the skin. It is a relatively acellular fibrous tissue containing collagen and elastin fibers. In this

chapter, diseases will be classified into those affecting primarily the epidermis (keratinization), those affecting the dermis (blistering diseases, infections, disorders of pigmentation), and a miscellaneous group. These same descriptive terms will reappear in each section:

Macules—flat lesions
Papules—raised lesions
Vesicles—blisters less than 5 mm in diameter
Bullae—blisters greater than 5 mm in diameter

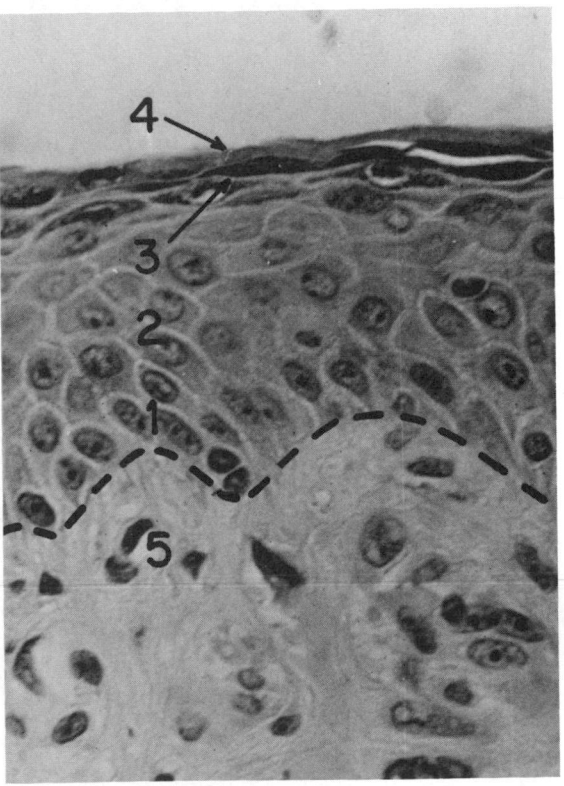

Fig. 1. Section of child's skin. ×600.
1. Basal layer—location of cycling cells, the "stem cell" population of the epidermis.
2. Malpighian layer—differentiating epidermal cells.
3. Granular layer—transitional zone between differentiating cells and stratum corneum.
4. Stratum corneum—compact layer composed of tightly adherent, dead, fully differentiated cells consisting predominantly of keratin and smaller amounts of cholesterol and phospholipid.
5. Dermis. The dermis is more cellular than normal because of the presence of a juvenile melanoma (benign).

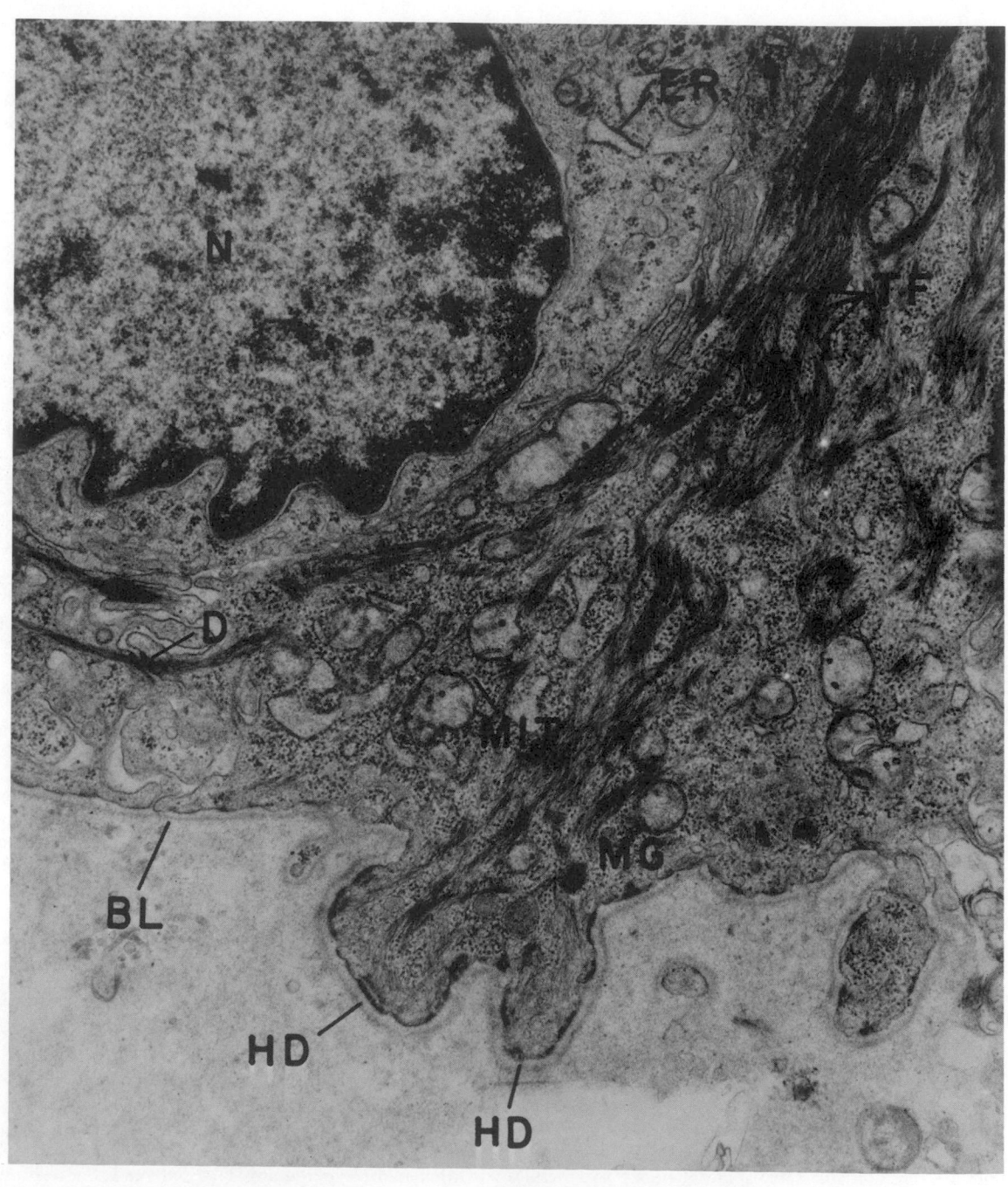

Fig. 2. Electromicrograph of basal cell from normal epidermis. BL—Basal lamina; HD—Hemi-desmosome; D—Desmosome; MIT—Mitochondria; MG—Melanin granule; TF—Tonofilaments; ER—Endoplasmic reticulum; N—Nucleus of basal cell.

No attempt has been made to provide a complete catalog of skin diseases, and the reader is encouraged to consult references for more detailed and complete information.

26.2
DISEASES OF KERATINIZATION

ROBERT G. CROUNSE

Keratinization is the term applied to the differentiation of the ectodermal tissues (hair, epidermis, and nails) into a final hardened end product. In each case, this product is eventually shed to the environment either gradually, as is the case with human epidermis, or abruptly, as is the case with snake skin. Though use of the term keratinization implies understanding of the composition and structure of the protein(s) called keratin, lack of precise biochemical information precludes the exact definition of molecular diseases of "keratin" in the same sense as is now evident, for example, for hemoglobin. It is more comfortable, therefore, to speak of disorders of the process of keratinization, the results of which will be, respectively, fragile (or absent) hair, scaling epidermis, and deformed nails. In these disorders, other ectodermal systems may be affected, including teeth and sweat glands. The observation of ectodermal disease in early life should prompt also a search for other systemic disorders, including aminoaciduria, deafness, immunologic defects, malnutrition, toxins, or other systemic disease.

The chief function of the epidermis, the paper-thin cellular outermost tissue of the skin, is to interpose a highly efficient barrier between man and his environment. Loss of sufficient amounts of this barrier, as in extensive burns, pemphigus, or toxic epidermal necrolysis, can be fatal. This barrier function is provided by a membrane composed of the fibrous protein(s) "keratin" plus lipids in the horny layer of the epidermis, the so-called stratum corneum. This layer is subject to continuous loss to the environment, and continuous regeneration from below. Imbalance in the rate of renewal, especially overproduction, results in a group of scaling or exfoliative disorders. The congenital forms are often termed ichthyosis; the acquired forms include exfoliative dermatitis, psoriasis, and seborrheic dermatitis.

Although the precise role of lipids in orderly epidermal keratinization is not understood, their importance is emphasized by the examples of disordered keratinization associated with lipid imbalance, demonstrated by essential fatty acid deficiency in animals, in children, in Refsum's disease, and in Triparanol-induced "ichthyosis" and hair loss.

Keratinization in the hair follicle is somewhat better defined biochemically. The fibrous low-sulfur protein "keratin" is responsible for the highly ordered alphahelical x-ray diffraction pattern of the hair shaft, and is, in turn, embedded in and stabilized by a group of amorphous "cementing" proteins extensively cross-linked by disulfide bonds. It is the purposeful rupture and reformation of these disulfide bonds that result in the process known as permanent waving. Alterations in the synthesis of this group of high-sulfur proteins is apparently defective in certain cases of "kwashiorkor," the widely publicized protein deficiency syndrome, and in trichoschisis, a newly discovered congenital abnormality of hair (p. 1760).

Interpretation of hair follicle disorders requires an appreciation of two extraordinary features of the hair follicle. These are (1) high rates of mitosis, metabolic activity, and protein synthesis, rendering the hair root extremely sensitive to mitotic or metabolic inhibitors such as thallium or agents used in cancer chemotherapy; (2) the phenomenon of an inevitable and occasionally dramatic hair cycle, or alternation of actively growing and totally resting phases of hair growth. Approximately 90 percent of scalp hairs in the normal scalp are growing. Major changes in the normal growing/resting ratio, such as occur after birth, after pregnancy, and sometimes after high fever, result in unusual shedding of large numbers of resting hairs, so-called telogen alopecia.

Keratinization of the nail is poorly understood biochemically; kinetic events are similar to those of ectodermal tissues, and subject to interruption by systemic events. Serious illness results in transverse lines, and local trauma to the proliferative matrix of the nail base causes nail dystrophy. The slow rate of growth of nails as compared to hair makes them less useful as a temporal guide to systemic events.

Epidermal Scaling Disorders

THE ICHTHYOSES. The precise classification of these congenital disorders of epidermal differentiation continues to be a vexing problem. Attempts to distinguish between forms by differences in epidermal cellular kinetics or inheritance patterns have been very helpful, and well summarized recently in the pediatric literature by Esterly. For the moment, most cases of ichthyosiform dermatitis appearing during the first year of life can be classified as one of the following four types.

Ichthyosis Vulgaris. Dryness and scaling on extensor surfaces characterize this well-known genetically dominant form of ichthyosis (Fig. 3). Flexural sparing, onset after 3 months of age, and an atopic diathesis are supporting features. Histologically, the granular layer is reduced or absent. The horny layer is thickened (hyperkeratosis). Epidermal renewal rate is not accelerated, in contrast to the other ichthyosiform dermatoses. Treatment is topical and symptomatic. The principle of restoration of relative flexibility to the thickened, dry stratum corneum is based

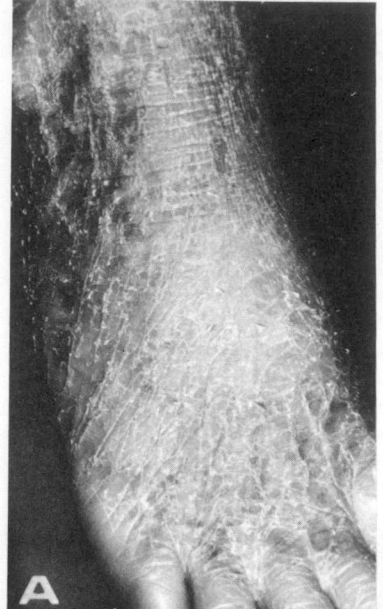

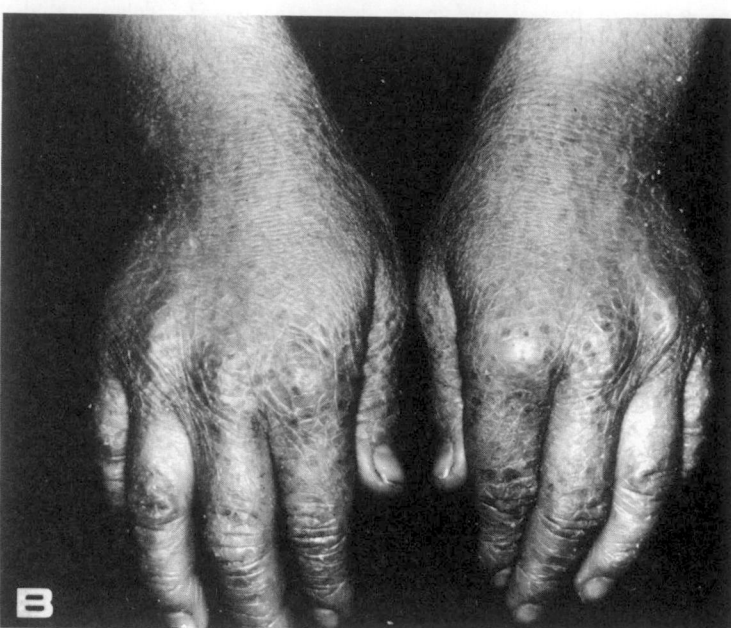

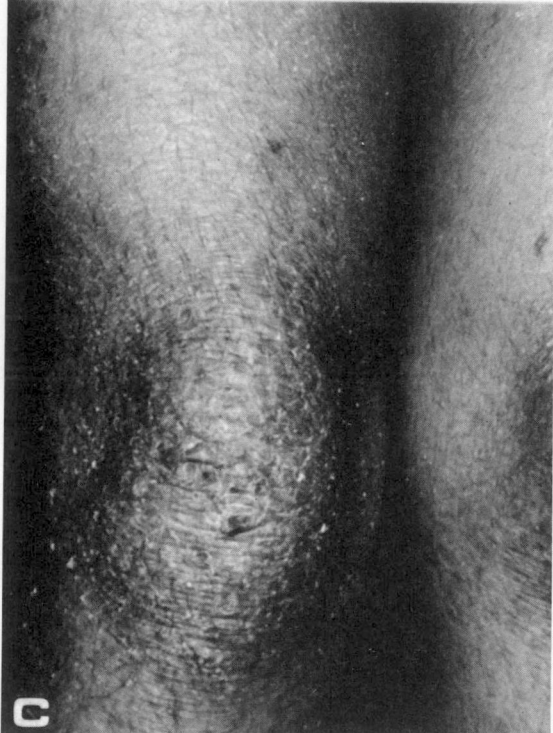

Fig. 3. Ichthyosis vulgaris in an 8-year-old girl. Ichthyosis vulgaris is a dominantly inherited disease characterized by retention of scale especially in extensor areas. This disorder is often associated with atopy and is more troublesome when the humidity is low.

upon the concept of hydration followed by the application of oil or grease to maintain hydration. The addition of an ounce or two of bath oil to the tub in theory leaves a protective coat on the hydrated skin during emergence. In practice, a comparative trial of several ointments often provides the best individual compromise between cosmetic acceptability and therapeutic effect. The simple concept of hydration often results in dramatic improvement of a previously uninformed patient. In milder cases, spontaneous reduction in severity occasionally occurs near puberty.

Bullous Congenital Ichthyosiform Erythroderma (Bullous CIE). This severe dominant disorder, also termed "epidermolytic hyperkeratosis" by Frost and

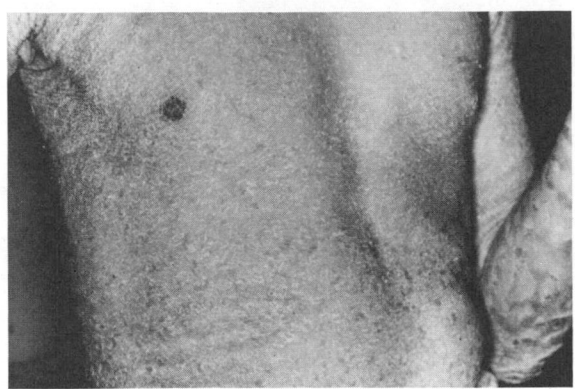

Fig. 4. Epidermolytic hyperkeratosis. The mother of this 6-year-old boy also has epidermolytic hyperkeratosis, a dominantly inherited disease.

Van Scott, is characterized by blisters, background erythema, and flexural involvement (Fig. 4). Rapid epidermal turnover renders the disease somewhat susceptible to systemic antimitotic drugs and may be disabling enough to warrant such therapy. Secondary bacterial infection of bullae requires systemic antibiotics. Lesions are frequently present at birth, but may abate spontaneously after puberty. Interestingly, some cases of severely localized forms of hyperkeratotic disorders previously termed ichthyosis hystrix (Fig. 5), linear nevus, or palmar and plantar hyperkeratosis have been shown to exhibit histologic and cellular kinetic features of bullous CIE. Electron mi-

croscopic studies are consistent with faulty or incomplete keratinization, but have not yielded any etiologic clues.

Nonbullous Congenital Ichthyosiform Erythroderma (Nonbullous CIE). This disorder, also called lamellar ichthyosis (Fig. 6), is characterized by generalized scaling and redness; when it occurs with mental retardation and spastic paralysis it is termed Sjögren-Larsson syndrome. Nonbullous CIE is a recessive disease ordinarily present at birth. In its most grave form it is apparently represented by the bizarre "harlequin fetus." Most infants with lamellar ichthyosis begin life as collodion babies with a cellophane-like covering present at birth (Fig. 7). Heavy scaling of scalp, palms, and soles is common in nonbullous CIE, as is ectropion; the latter may occur also secondary to other chronic scaling or bullous diseases. The histology is not specific; there is increased thickness of the stratum corneum, granular layer, and overall epidermis, and some retention of nuclear remnants.

Sex-Linked Ichthyosis. Careful clinical observation has separated this form of ichthyosis from those previously reported. Distinctive features include involvement of flexural areas and sides of the neck; occasionally delayed appearance (up to 1 year of age); and a classic sex-linked pattern of inheritance with exclusive male involvement. Histologic sections may be helpful in confirming the diagnosis. Therapy is symptomatic and supportive; the prognosis is benign but the course is prolonged.

HYPERKERATOSIS OF THE PALMS AND SOLES (KERATODERMA PALMARIS ET PLANTARIS). Unusual thickening of the stratum corneum of the palms and

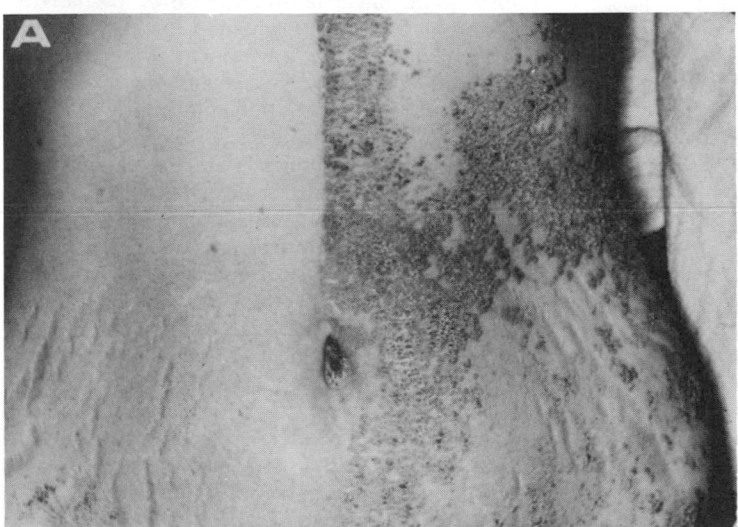
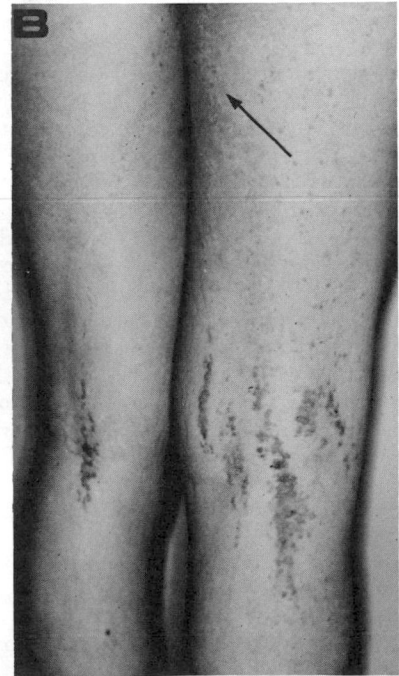

Fig. 5. Ichthyosis hystrix. A. Nevoid form of epidermolytic hyperkeratosis. Uncommon lesion in a young adult. Epidermal nevi may be linear or segmental and, although they are usually present in early childhood, they may appear or become more extensive later in life. B. Bilateral distribution of epidermal nevus.

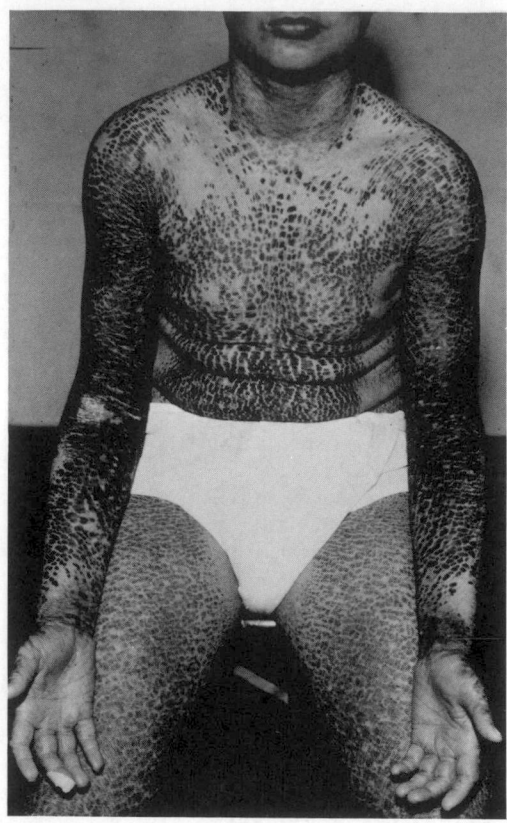

Fig. 6. Lamellar ichthyosis. Angular, brownish scales involving most of body including flexural areas. The face is scaly with ectropion formation. The clear areas on the flanks have been treated with retinoic acid.

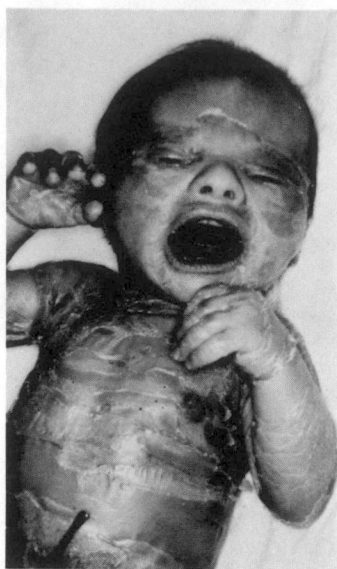

Fig. 7. Collodion baby. This newborn Puerto Rican boy, age 4 days, has only slight flexural scaling of the neck. The typical "baked apple" appearance is apparent in the photograph. The skin is taut and split. There is ectropion and contracting bands around the fingers and toes. Most of these infants later have the clinical picture of lamellar ichthyosis.

soles without other skin abnormality can occur as diffuse scaling and fissuring or as discrete punctate lesions. Both forms may occur as an autosomal dominant trait with expression during the first few years of life. Reports of successful treatment with topical vitamin A acid are encouraging. Systemic steroids may be effective but require prolonged administration with the attending hazards. Keratolytic ointments containing salicylic acid are still widely used.

The much quoted mal de Meleda refers to a recessive form of palmar and plantar hyperkeratosis traced to an inbred population on the Mediterranean island of Meleda. Lesions on extensor surfaces and nail changes differentiate this syndrome clinically. Several other syndromes of combined defects including palmar and plantar hyperkeratosis occur and have been well described by Butterworth and Strean. Pathogenesis of these peculiar localized disorders is not clear. The occurrence of keratoderma following systemic administration of a hypocholesterolemic agent reemphasizes the need to consider lipid involvement in the differentiation of tissues ordinarily associated primarily with protein synthesis.

PSORIASIS. Psoriasis is a relatively common disease; its prevalence in the United States is probably about 2 percent. Onset is common before age 10, and rare before age 3, although it has been reported just after birth. The mode of inheritance of psoriasis is not clear; proposals range from simple dominant with incomplete penetrance to a system of three interdependent genetic loci, two recessive and one sex-linked. The possibility of genetic subpopulations within the diagnosis of psoriasis is quite real.

Typical lesions of psoriasis are red plaques surmounted by a silvery-white scale, especially common about the elbows, knees, scalp, and penis (Fig. 8). In children, an acute eruptive form, often post-streptococcal, has been reported frequently. Generalized disease can occur and is severe. Major protein loss and negative nitrogen balance can result from the generalized exfoliation; enhanced transepidermal water loss and inadequate heat regulation can be significant.

The etiology of psoriasis is unknown; scaling is the result of markedly accelerated epidermal turnover. Histologic and electron microscopic changes reflect the apparently incomplete keratinization process.

Treatment is dependent upon the extent of involvement. Localized plaques are best treated with tar and ultraviolet light, topical steroids under occlusive wrap (Saran or the equivalent), or even with just bland ointments. Generalized disease may require careful attention to water and electrolyte losses with measurements of intake and output and replacement

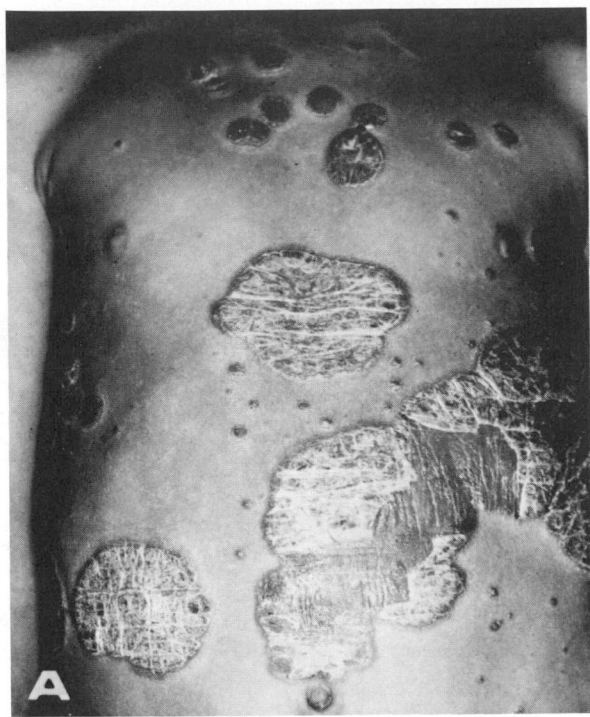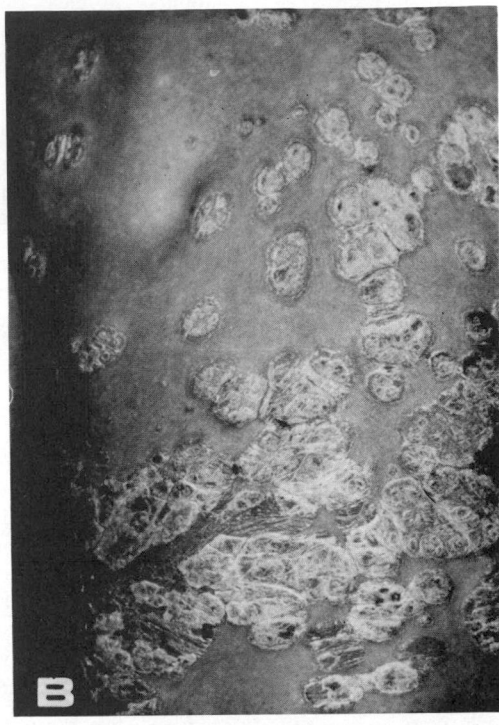

Fig. 8. Psoriasis. A. Extensive involvement in 7-year-old boy with clinical evidence of disease since birth. B. View of back of same patient.

if necessary. Systemic corticosteroids or methotrexate are occasionally required.

GENERALIZED EXFOLIATIVE DERMATITIS. Causes of generalized exfoliative dermatitis include besides psoriasis such diseases as seborrheic dermatitis, which, when generalized in infancy, is termed Leiner's disease, atopic dermatitis, and pityriasis rubra pilaris. Lymphoma or leukemia, as well as severe drug reaction, should be considered as possible causes. Pathophysiologic and therapeutic considerations described for generalized psoriasis apply to these as well. The generalized erythema and subsequent shedding of the horny layer following scarlet fever or severe measles is a benign self-limited process.

SEBORRHEIC DERMATITIS. Erythema with yellowish greasy-appearing scales characteristically localized to the scalp, eyebrows, nasolabial folds, and presternal skin is typical of seborrheic dermatitis. Extensive scalp involvement with thick crusting is often called "cradle cap." Facial involvement may suggest lupus erythematosus or photosensitivity. Heavy scaling with crusting and/or purpura should suggest Letterer-Siwe's disease. Major presternal involvement might indicate Darier's disease. However, seborrheic dermatitis is far more common than any of these. Treatment of seborrheic dermatitis is with topical medications, including corticosteroids and sulfur- or tar-containing preparations. The disorder recurs and requires continued therapy.

Hair Defects

Careful examination of hairs, collectively or individually, has become important in a variety of situations of particular interest to the pediatrician. Increasing reports of the use of scanning electronmicroscopy, physical strength measurements, and biochemical evaluation of abnormal hair shafts or plucked roots emphasize awareness of the potential value of hair examination in the detection of inherited or acquired metabolic derangement.

ABNORMALITIES OF HAIR SHAFTS. Microscopic examination of scalp hairs from individuals who complain of unusual fragility of hair or inability to perform satisfactorily ordinary cosmetic manipulations is especially important in uncovering occasional inherited metabolic defects. The abnormality called *trichorrhexis nodosa*, in which partial fracture sites of the hair shaft appear microscopically as interlocking paint brushes, has been noted in about one-half of the cases of argininosuccinicaciduria, an aminoaciduria with proved defect in the enzyme argininosuccinase. Trichorrhexis nodosa is most commonly produced by the trauma of grooming, especially in adults, but when present in a child should trigger a search for argininosuccinicaciduria or other congenital syndromes with which it has been occasionally associated. *Tri-*

choschisis, a term recently applied to clean-faced fractures of the hair shaft, was observed in a child without other abnormality other than aminoaciduria; examination of the hairs under polarized light revealed regular and alternating disappearance of the usual uniform birefringence. Amino acid analysis of this hair was compatible with a deficiency in a relatively specific group of high-sulfur amorphous hair proteins; similar proteins are known to be decreased in some cases of kwashiorkor. *Monilethrix,* alternate fusiform constriction of the hair shaft, may be associated with other minor ectodermal abnormalities; association with argininosuccinicaciduria has not been confirmed. The period of alternation has not consistently varied with any known biologic period; however, lack of accurate measurements of growth rate in individual cases often has hampered clarification of such a relationship. *Trichorrhexis invaginata* refers to an uncommon ball-and-socket "bamboo joint" defect of hair shafts, occurring often in conjunction with ichthyosis linearis circumflexa; it is occasionally associated with nonspecific aminoaciduria and an autosomal recessive inheritance has been noted. *Pili annulati* ("ringed hair") is not associated with systemic disease. The defect is characterized quite literally by "holes" in the mass of the hair shaft, apparently representing absence of cortical cells rather than medullary abnormalities as previously suggested. *Pili torti* refers to frequent and severe twisting of the hair shaft. It has been associated with a variety of ectodermal and neuroectodermal defects, the most recent of which is sensory neural hearing loss, or Bjornstad's syndrome. *"Kinky hair disease"* apparently represents pili torti and monilethrix in association with severe neurologic disease with abnormal neuronal accumulation of oxidized lipids. Diffuse thinning of hair shafts may also be a sign of "cartilage-hair hypoplasia"; focal thinning may be a sign of reversible toxicity from drugs or malnutrition.

LOSS OF SCALP HAIR. Diffuse thinning of scalp hair in children, especially if it occurs suddenly, should arouse suspicion of systemic toxicity, either iatrogenic or secondary to accidental ingestion of a poison such as thallium. Both of these circumstances result in damage to the growing, or "anagen," hair roots. Since about 90 percent of hair in the scalp normally is growing at any given time, and since they are distributed randomly, damage to all growing hairs will result in diffuse damage or loss. The injury may be quickly reversible, resulting in rapid recovery of the root and distal propagation of a constriction of the hair shaft often severe enough to cause easy breakage; if more severe there may be atrophy and rapid loss of all anagen hairs. New hairs will replace them in a period of weeks, assuming the individual survives the systemic toxic insult. Some circumstances result in a rapid conversion of a large percentage of hairs from a normal growing to a normal resting (telogen) stage; the microscopic appearance of these normal resting roots is readily differentiated from toxic atrophic roots

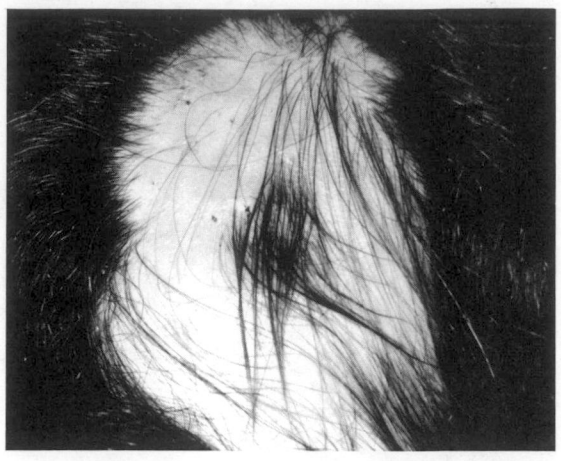

Fig. 9. Alopecia areata. Patterned nonscarring hair loss usually occurring in well-demarcated areas on scalp and in older males in beard area. Alopecia areata sometimes involves eyelashes and eyebrows.

described above. This "telogen effluvium" is most commonly secondary to high fever ("postfebrile alopecia"); it also occurs postpartum, postbirth, or following heparin therapy. *Anagen* and *telogen alopecia* can be readily distinguished by microscopic examination of the roots of hair being lost.

Focal or patterned hair loss in a child can usually be divided into scarring disorders, such as localized morphea and discoid lupus erythematosus, or sharply limited areas of hair loss without apparent scalp disease. In the latter instance, two diagnostic possibilities predominate. *Trichotillomania* refers to self-induced breaking or pulling of the hairs from the scalp. Usually a stubble of shortened hairs remains, indicative of the difficulty of breaking hairs cleanly at the scalp surface by manual manipulation. Examination with ultraviolet lamp, a microscopic potassium hydroxide preparation, and culture will rule out infection with fungus. Trichotillomania may reflect severe psychopathology; fortunately, it is more regularly associated with less serious behavior disturbances. In teenagers, a traction alopecia may result from cosmetic procedures such as tight rollers and hot combs. Irregular spreading patches of balding leaving absolutely bare and apparently normal scalp are most likely lesions of *alopecia areata* (Fig. 9). This peculiar idiopathic disorder is characterized histologically by incomplete formation of hair shaft by reasonably normal hair roots; hence it represents a true "disorder of keratinization." This disease may occur at any age. It may progress to complete loss of scalp and body hair (Fig. 10). At least in the early stages, the process is reversible, either spontaneously or secondary to locally injected or systemically administered corticosteroids. Reports of increased coincidence of vitiligo and of "organ-specific autoimmune disease," especially hyperthyroidism, have not as yet

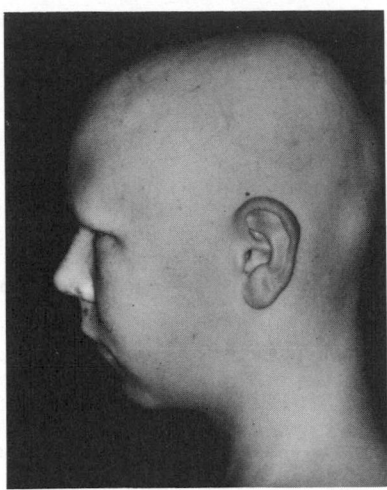

Fig. 10. Alopecia universalis. Loss of scalp hair, eyebrows, and eyelashes in a 13-year-old boy. This occurs in a small number of patients with alopecia areata.

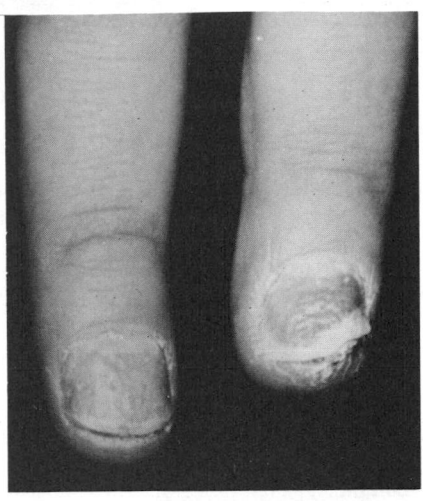

Fig. 11. Psoriasis involving nails in 6-year-old girl. This difficult therapeutic problem is characterized by pitting and lifting of the nails.

yielded specific causative factors. Peculiar patterned alopecia is seen also with several of the syndromes of trisomy; its nature has not been clarified.

HIRSUTISM. Increased hairiness, or hirsutism, is clearly a diagnosis based in part upon semantics, in that it will be dependent upon culturally determined norms. In medical usage, it commonly refers to male-pattern hairiness in a female, or adult-type hairiness in a young child. Some instances dictate a search for endocrine disturbances due to tumors, glandular hyperplasia, or iatrogenic causes, which should not be overlooked. Hirsutism has been noted frequently in the several types of mucopolysaccharidoses, in congenital erythropoietic porphyria, and in several other congenital syndromes. Focal thickening of the skin with sharply localized superimposed hirsutism, seen commonly on a wrist or forearm, is striking testimony to chronic trauma, often in a mentally defective child with a persistent habit of chewing or biting the involved area. In virtually all instances, the excess hair is simply a coarse terminal type of hair arising from the same follicle that previously produced the unnoticed or unobjectionable "vellus" or fine downy hair.

Removal of unwanted hair can be accomplished temporarily by a variety of commercially available depilatories, or permanently by electrolytic destruction of each individual hair root.

Abnormalities of the Nail

Nail deformations are common; however, both diagnosis and treatment are generally unsatisfactory. Thickened hypertrophic nails (*onychogryphosis*) may be regularly pared if desired. Spoon-shaped nails (*koilonychia*) are often congenital and idiopathic;

occasionally they, together with distal loosening of the nail plate (*onycholysis*), draw attention to hypochromic anemia, polycythemia vera, or hyperthyroidism. Although *clubbing* (hippocratic nails) is most often congenital, it prompts consideration of systemic vascular or pulmonary disorder. Discolored or crumbly nails suggest bacterial or mycotic origin; ice-pick pits suggest psoriasis (Fig. 11). Distortion of the nail with firm chronic inflammation surrounding the nail base is suggestive of Candida albicans infection. Any severe dermatitis involving the skin near the nail base and its underlying proliferative nail matrix can result in distortion of the nail. Brief systemic illnesses are frequently heralded as the cause of transverse lines or depressions propagated distally as the nail continues to grow.

References

DISEASES OF KERATINIZATION

Brown, A. C., Belser, R. B., Crounse, R. G., and Wehr, R. F. A congenital hair defect: Trichoschisis with alternating birefringence and low sulfur content. J. Invest. Derm., 54:496, 1970.

Brown, A. C., Crounse, R. G., and Winkelmann, R. K. Generalized hair follicle hamartoma. Arch. Derm., 99:478, 1969.

Crounse, R. G., and Van Scott, E. J. Changes in scalp hair roots as a measure of toxicity from cancer chemotherapeutic drugs. J. Invest. Derm., 35:83, 1960.

Gillespie, J. M. The Dietary Regulation of the Synthesis of Hair Keratin, in Symposium on Fibrous Proteins. Plenum Press, 1967.

Kligman, A. M. Pathologic dynamics of human hair loss; I. Telogen effluvium. Arch. Derm., 83:175, 1961.

McCance, R. A., and Widdowson, E. W. Calorie Deficiencies and Protein Deficiencies. Boston, Little, Brown and Co., 1968.

Menkes, J. H., Alter, M., Steigleder, G. K., Weakley, D. R., and Sung, J. H. A sex-linked recessive disorder with retardation of growth, peculiar hair, and focal cerebral and cerebellar degeneration. Pediatrics, 29: 764, 1962.

Menton, D. N. The effects of essential fatty acid deficiency on the skin of the mouse. Amer. J. Anat., 122: 337, 1968.

Mize, C. E., Herndon, J. H., Jr., Blass, J. P., Milne, G. W. A., Follansbee, C., Laudat, P., and Steinberg, D. Localization of the oxidative defect in phytanic acid degradation in patients with Refsum's disease. J. Clin. Invest., 48:1033, 1969.

Winkelmann, R. K., Perry, H. O., Achor, R. W. P., and Kirby, T. J. Cutaneous syndromes produced as side effects of triparanol therapy. Arch. Derm., 87:372, 1963.

Zaias, N. The embryology of the human nail. Arch. Derm., 87:37, 1963.

THE ICHTHYOSES

Esterly, N. The ichthyosiform dermatoses. Pediatrics, 42: 990, 1968.

Esterly, N. B., and Maxwell, E. Nonbullous congenital ichthyosiform erythroderma. A case treated with methotrexate. Pediatrics, 41:120, 1968.

Feinstein, A., Ackerman, A. B., and Ziprkowski, L. Histology of autosomal dominant ichthyosis vulgaris and X-linked ichthyosis. Arch. Derm., 101:524, 1970.

Frost, P., and Van Scott, E. J. Ichthyosiform dermatoses: Classification based on anatomic and biometric observation. Arch. Derm., 94:113, 1966.

—— and Weinstein, G. D. Vitamin A acid for ichthyosiform dermatoses and psoriasis. J.A.M.A., 207:1863, 1968.

Hirone, T. Electron microscopic studies of ichthyosis and congenital ichthyosiform erythroderma. J. Electron Micr., 18:63, 1969.

Wells, R. S., and Kerr, C. B. Genetic classification of ichthyosis. Arch. Derm., 92:1, 1965.

Wilgram, G. F., and Caulfield, J. B. An electron microscopic study of epidermolytic hyperkeratosis. Arch. Derm., 94:127, 1966.

HYPERKERATOSIS OF THE PALMS AND SOLES

Anderson, P. C., and Martt, J. M. Myotonia and keratoderma induced by 20,25 diazocholestenol. Arch. Derm., 92:181, 1965.

Butterworth, T., and Strean, L. P. Clinical Genodermatology. Baltimore, The Williams & Wilkins Co., 1962.

Heiss, H. B., and Gross, P. R. Keratosis palmaris et plantaris treatment with topically applied vitamin A acid. Arch. Derm., 101:100, 1970.

PSORIASIS

Brody, I. The ultrastructure of the epidermis in psoriasis vulgaris as revealed by electron microscopy. J. Ultrastruct. Res., 8:595, 1963.

Freedberg, I. M., and Baden, H. P. The metabolic response to exfoliation. J. Invest. Derm., 38:277, 1962.

Rothberg, S., Crounse, R. G., and Lee, J. G. Glycine-C[14] incorporation into the proteins of normal stratum corneum and the abnormal stratum corneum of psoriasis. J. Invest. Derm., 37:497, 1961.

Weinstein, G. D., and Van Scott, E. J. Autoradiographic analysis of turnover times of normal and psoriatic epidermis. J. Invest. Derm., 45:257, 1965.

HAIR DEFECTS

Altman, J., and Stroud, J. Netherton's syndrome and psoriasiform ichthyosis. Arch. Derm., 100:550, 1969.

Bradfield, R. B. Morphologic changes in human scalp hair roots during deprivation of protein. Science, 157: 438, 1967.

Brown, A. C., Belser, R. B., Crounse, R. G., and Wehr, R. F. A congenital hair defect: Trichoschisis with alternating birefringence and low sulfur content. J. Invest. Derm., 54:496, 1970.

Caputo, R., and Ceccarelli, B. Study of normal hair and of some malformations with a scanning electron microscope. Arch. Klin. Exp. Derm., 234:242, 1969.

Chernowsky, M. E., and Owens, D. W. Trichorrhexis nodosa; clinical and investigative studies. Arch. Derm., 94:576, 1966.

Comaish, S. Autoradiographic studies of hair growth and rhythm in monilethrix. Brit. J. Derm., 81:443, 1969.

Crounse, R. G., Bollet, A. J., and Owens, S. Tissue assay of human protein malnutrition using scalp hair roots. Trans. Ass. Amer. Physicians, 83:185, 1970.

Cunliffe, W. J., Hall, R., Stevenson, C. J., and Weightman, D. Alopecia areata, thyroid disease and autoimmunity. Brit. J. Derm., 81:877, 1969.

Dawber, R., and Comaish, S. Scanning electron microscopy of normal and abnormal hair shafts. Arch. Derm., 101:316, 1970.

Efron, M. L. Diseases of the urea cycle. In Stanbury, Wyngaarden, and Fredrickson, eds., The Metabolic Basis of Inherited Disease. New York, McGraw-Hill Book Co., 1966.

Gillespie, J. M. The Dietary Regulation of the Synthesis of Hair Keratin in Symposium of Fibrous Proteins. Plenum Press, 1967.

Menkes, J. H., Alter, M., Steigleder, G. K., Weakley, D. R., and Sung, J. H. A sex-linked recessive disorder with retardation of growth, peculiar hair, and focal cerebral and cerebellar degeneration. Pediatrics, 29:764, 1962.

O'Brien, J. S., and Sampson, E. L. Kinky hair disease: II. Biochemical studies. J. Neuropath. Exp. Neurol., 25:523, 1968.

Pollitt, R. J., Jenner, F. A., and Davies, M. Sibs with mental and physical retardation and trichorrhexis nodosa with abnormal amino acid composition of the hair. Arch. Dis. Child., 43:211, 1968.

Price, V. H., Thomas, R. S., and Jones, F. T. Pili annulati, optical and electron microscopic studies. Arch. Derm., 98:640, 1968.

Shih, V. E., Littlefield, J. W., and Moser, H. W. Argininosuccinase deficiency in fibroblasts cultured from patients with argininosuccinic aciduria. Biochem. Genet., 3:81, 1969.

Sims, R. T. "Beau's lines" in hair; reduction of hair shaft diameter associated with illness. Brit. J. Derm., 79:43, 1967.

Slepyan, A. H. Traction alopecia. Arch. Derm., 78:395, 1958.

Swanbeck, G., Nyren, J., and Juhlin, L. Mechanical properties of hairs from patients with different types of hair diseases. J. Invest. Derm., 54:248, 1970.

Van Scott, E. J. Morphologic changes in pilosebaceous units and anagen hairs in alopecia areata. J. Invest. Derm., 37:35, 1958.

ABNORMALITIES OF THE NAIL

Zaias, N. Psoriasis of the nail. Arch. Derm., 99:567, 1969.

26.3
DISEASES OF THE DERMIS

J. GRAHAM SMITH, JR., and
GERALD CHOTINER

The dermis consists of the fibrous proteins, collagen and elastin, embedded in an aqueous matrix known as the ground substance. Of the various dermal elements, collagen has been the most extensively studied. It is synthesized by fibroblasts and accounts for approximately 75 percent of the dry weight of the dermis. Chemically, collagen is characterized by the presence of the amino acids hydroxyproline and hydroxylysine. These two amino acids are first incorporated into the collagen peptide chains as proline and lysine respectively and are then hydroxylated. The undenatured collagen molecule is resistant to digestion by all proteolytic enzymes except amphibian, bacterial, and mammalian collagenase. Under the light microscope, the collagen fibers are coarse and wavy. The fibers are white, birefringent, and have a characteristic 700 Å periodicity. They have a high tensile strength and a high modulus of elasticity.

With increasing age the rate of collagen synthesis decreases. With certain diseases such as acromegaly and hyperthyroidism there is an increase in collagen synthesis, which is reflected in an increase in urinary excretion of hydroxyproline. In growth hormone deficient dwarfs and cretins, in whom collagen synthesis is decreased, urinary hydroxyproline excretion is also decreased.

Elastic tissue, although invariably associated with collagen, differs morphologically, physically, and chemically from collagen and is neither a member of the collagen class of proteins nor a derivative of collagen. It is assumed that elastin is synthesized by the fibroblast, but this has not yet been proved. Under the light microscope elastic fibers are delicate, straight, and branch freely. They form a latticelike pattern and generally lie parallel to the collagen fibers. The fibers are yellow, do not polarize light unless stretched, have a low tensile strength, and a low modulus of elasticity. They demonstrate fluorescence, which increases with aging. Under the electron microscope the mature elastic fiber has two morphologically different constituents, a central amorphous and a peripheral microfibrillar component. The central amorphous material has a predominance of nonpolar amino acids and has selective susceptibility to elastase digestion. The microfibrillar component has a predominance of polar amino acids, and is susceptible to the action of a number of proteolytic enzymes. During embryologic development the microfibrillar component forms an aggregate structure before any amorphous material is present. It has been suggested, therefore, that the microfibrils play an important role in the morphogenesis of the elastic fiber.

The ground substance is a complex hydrophilic mixture of various carbohydrate, lipid, and protein materials that form an amorphous, semi-fluid matrix between fibers and cells. The most extensively studied components of ground substance have been the acid glycosaminoglycans (mucopolysaccharides). The major acid glycosaminoglycans found in skin are hyaluronic acid and dermatan sulfate (chondroitin sulfate B). There is a marked decrease in acid glycosaminoglycans of the skin after the first year of life and a more gradual decrease from childhood to old age. The decrease in hyaluronic acid is greater than that of chondroitin sulfate. Diseases such as myxedema and Hurler's disease, which are associated with alterations in the ground substance, are discussed elsewhere (Sec. 8.13).

NECROBIOSIS LIPOIDICA. Necrobiosis lipoidica is a relatively uncommon disorder characterized clinically by the development of yellowish atrophic plaque-like lesions usually on the anterior lower extremities (Fig. 12). Children with necrobiosis lipoidica often have diabetes mellitus, which may, however, have its onset several years after the appearance of the typical skin lesions. Of 19 initially nondiabetic patients with necrobiosis lipoidica followed over a 10-year period, 42 percent eventually developed abnormal glucose tolerance tests and/or cortisone provocative tests. The disorder is uncommon in children, although when present the lesions are typical. The average age of onset of necrobiosis lipoidica is approximately 30 years in diabetic patients and 41 years in others. Females are affected more often than males.

Histologically, the lesions of this disorder are characterized by a peculiar alteration of the collagen called necrobiosis. The collagen fibers are swollen and homogenized, and have an affinity for hematoxylin stain. The clinical course of necrobiosis lipoidica is one of chronicity and slow progression, but in approximately 20 percent of the cases spontaneous remission occurs. Intralesional corticosteroids and excision followed by grafting are of some benefit, the latter especially when ulceration has supervened. Ulceration is rare in childhood.

GRANULOMA ANNULARE. Granuloma annulare is a fairly common disorder characterized by flesh-colored papules or nodules which by central clearing and peripheral extension form an annular lesion. These annular lesions characteristically involve the back of the hands and fingers and the extensor aspects of the arms and legs but can involve other sites. The lesions may occur at any age, but children are

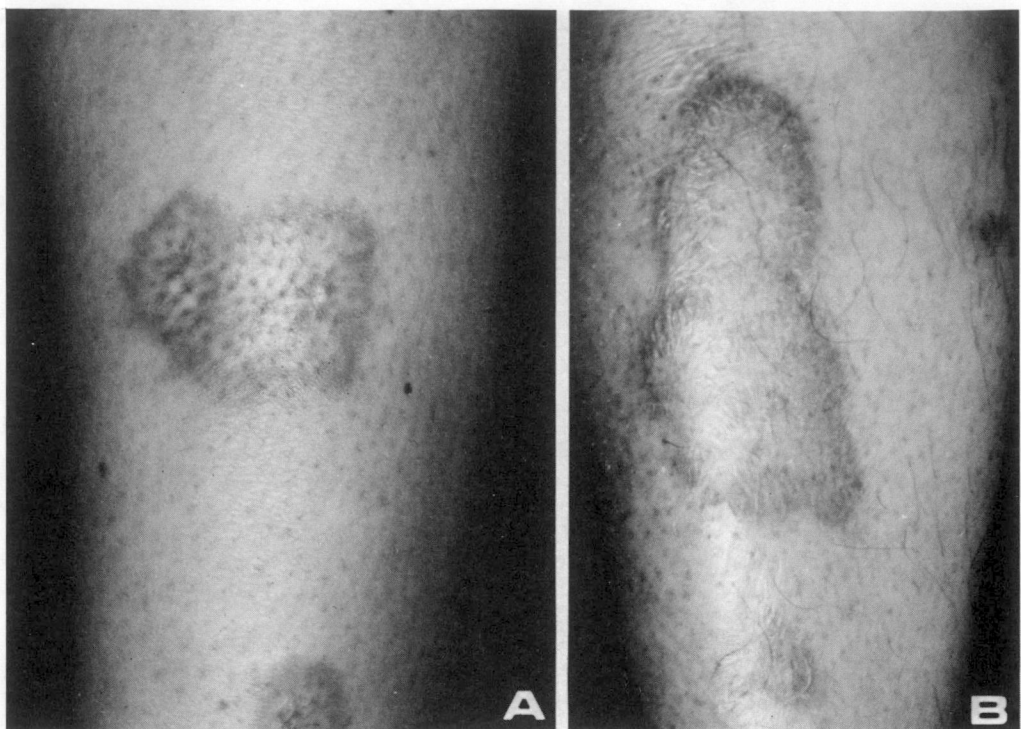

Fig. 12.   Necrobiosis lipoidica diabeticorum. A. Early lesion, not yet atrophic, in a 13-year-old girl. B. Yellowish elevated lesion on shin (a typical location). The lesion often is marked by telangiectasia and atrophy.

most frequently affected (Fig. 13). A disease that may mimic granuloma annulare is alopecia mucinosa (Fig. 14). This disease has a good prognosis in children. While the etiology is unknown, recently an association with latent diabetes mellitus has been suggested.

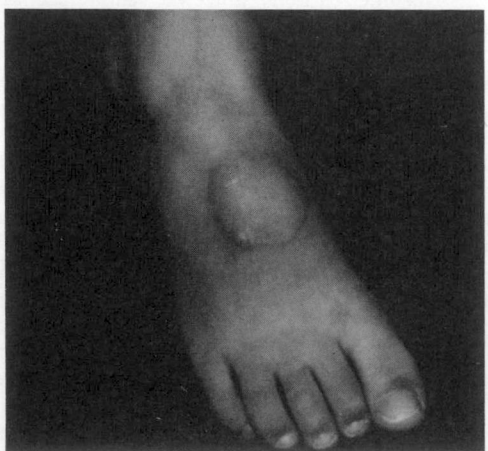

Fig. 13.   Granuloma annulare. Large annular lesion over the instep. Microscopically, there is necrobiosis and granuloma formation. The lesions heal without scarring.

Histologically, the lesions show necrobiosis of the collagen surrounded by a palisading of histiocytes. Multinucleated giant cells are uncommon and vascular changes are minimal except for perivascular lymphocyte cuffing. The lesions are asymptomatic and involute spontaneously after months or years. Treatment is difficult to evaluate because of this spontaneous involution, but intralesional corticosteroids and freezing with CO_2 or liquid nitrogen have been reported to produce regression of the lesions.

CUTIS LAXA (GENERALIZED ELASTOLYSIS).   Cutis laxa is a very rare hereditary disorder of connective tissue characterized clinically by loose pendulous skin (Fig. 15). The disease is thought to be inherited in an autosomal recessive manner, the basic defect being either the synthesis of abnormal elastic fibers, or an increased rate of degradation of the elastic tissue. The latter hypothesis is supported by the report of a deficiency of an elastase-inhibiting substance. Acquired and congenital forms of cutis laxa have been described; however, such a distinction may be artificial. In the congenital form the skin changes are present at birth or shortly afterward. In the acquired form the skin changes become manifest at or around puberty, although occasionally they do not occur until middle or old age. The loose redundant skin of cutis laxa often gives the affected child a

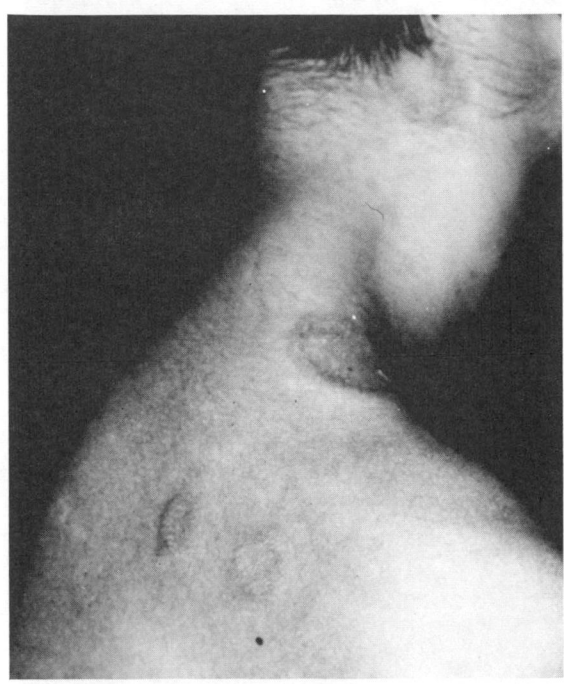

Fig. 14. Alopecia mucinosa. Annular lesions in a 6-year-old boy, which resemble granuloma annulare. There were also multiple lesions on the trunk.

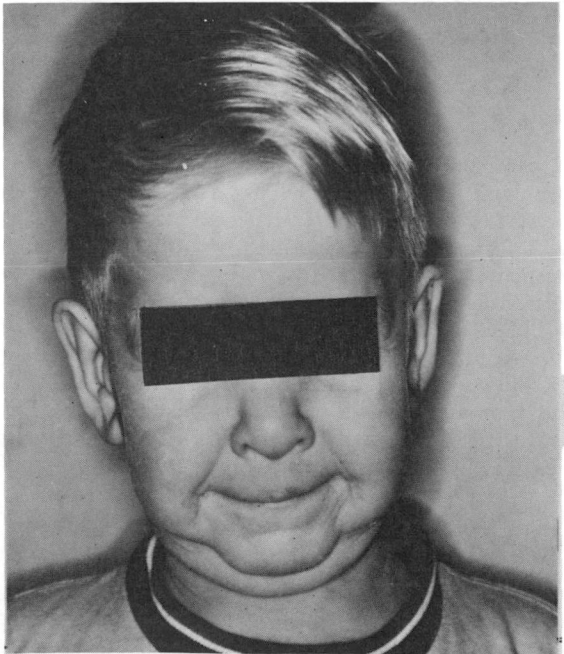

Fig. 15. Cutis laxa. Premature aged appearance of 4-year-old boy. Redundancy of skin increases with age.

progeric appearance. Pulmonary emphysema, gastrointestinal and urinary tract diverticula, and rectal and vaginal prolapse are frequently associated systemic manifestations.

Histologically, the elastic fibers are reduced in size and number and show granular changes. The collagen fibers are normal. In the absence of pulmonary emphysema the prognosis in this disorder is reasonably good. Plastic surgery is often necessary for repair of cosmetic defects, particularly ectropion of the eyelid. Frequent pulmonary function tests should be done. There is no effective medical treatment for this disorder.

EHLERS-DANLOS SYNDROME (CUTIS HYPERELASTICA). Ehlers-Danlos syndrome is another rare hereditary disorder of connective tissue. The mode of inheritance is thought to be autosomal dominant. The disorder in connective tissue is generalized and involves the skin, eye, skeleton, and vasculature. The skin is hyperextensible and extremely fragile (Fig. 16). When injured it heals poorly and forms atrophic paperlike scars. The joints are hypermobile, and subluxations occur frequently. Difficulty in walking and skeletal deformities are not uncommon. The vasculature is fragile, and hematomas and superficial soft pigmented molluscoid pseudotumors form at sites of trauma (Fig. 17). Ocular manifestations include hematomas, angioid streaks, blue sclerae, and ectopia lentis. Hernias, diverticulosis, dissecting aneurysms of large blood vessels, and pulmonary emphysema are other systemic manifestations that have sporadically been reported. Ehlers-Danlos syndrome has been associated with osteogenesis imperfecta, pseudoxanthoma elasticum, and Marfan's syndrome.

Histologically, the collagen appears to be reduced, and there is a relative increase in the elastic tissue. The pseudotumors described above are collagenous, have large numbers of blood vessels, and may contain foreign body giant cells. In later years the hyperelastic skin frequently becomes redundant and is suggestive of cutis laxa; however, unlike the skin in cutis laxa, the skin in Ehlers-Danlos syndrome remains hyperelastic. There is no treatment for this disorder, and the life-span is significantly shortened. Because of poor wound healing, surgical procedures should be avoided if at all possible.

PSEUDOXANTHOMA ELASTICUM. Pseudoxanthoma elasticum is an uncommon heritable disease of elastic tissue probably transmitted as an autosomal recessive. Although clinical manifestations become more prominent with age, many patients are aware of the changes from childhood. Flexural areas are involved, and the major sites of predilection include the neck, axilla, and crural areas. Early in the course of this disease the skin lesions consist of small white or yellowish papules which tend to increase in size up to 1 cm or more (Fig. 18). As the disease progresses, laxness of the involved skin becomes apparent. This is a systemic disease and may be associated with angioid streaks in the retina, with hemorrhages,

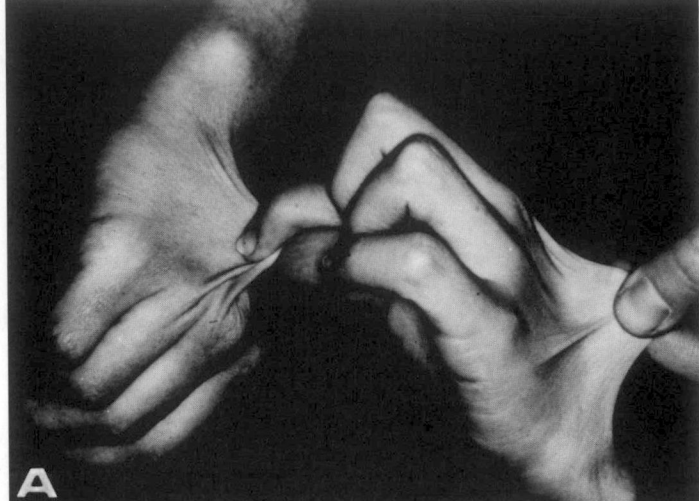

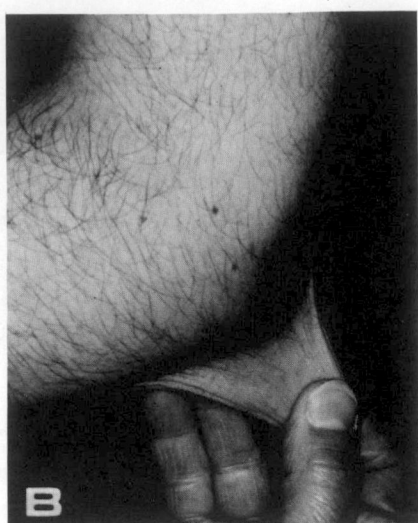

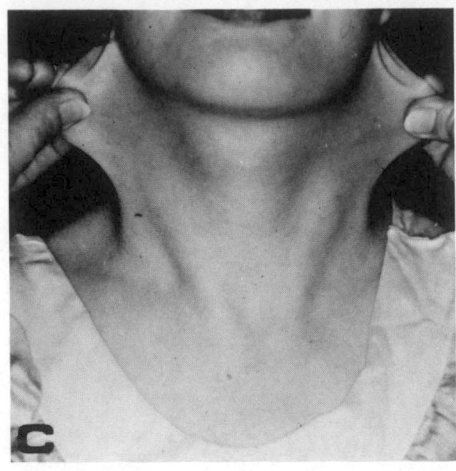

Fig. 16.   Ehlers-Danlos syndrome. Characteristic abnormal elasticity of skin.

exudation, atrophy of the choroid, and blindness. Systemic vascular disease, hypertension, and hemorrhagic phenomena, especially in the gastrointestinal tract and in the brain, occur later in life and may be fatal. It is interesting that the disease has been associated with osteitis deformans (Paget's disease), sickle-cell anemia, Marfan's syndrome, and cutis hyperelastica. In pseudoxanthoma elasticum there is an increase of dermal elastic fibers which are coated with calcium salts and acid glycosaminoglycans, particularly hyaluronic acid. The findings are most prominent in the middle third of the dermis, in contrast to actinic (senile) elastosis, where the increase in elastic fibers and acid glycosaminoglycans is in the upper third of the dermis and not associated with calcification. The changes in elastic tissue are also found in blood vessels throughout the body. The disease is slowly progressive, eventually leading to death in the latter decades. There is no treatment.

ELASTOSIS PERFORANS SERPIGINOSA.   Elastosis perforans serpiginosa is another disorder of elastic tissue

of particular interest because of its frequent association with other connective tissue disorders such as Down's syndrome, cutis hyperelastica, osteogenesis imperfecta, Marfan's syndrome, and pseudoxanthoma elasticum. The skin lesions are erythematous or skin-colored keratotic papules with a central area of scaling. The papules are frequently arranged in annular or serpiginous configuration and have a predilection for the nape of the neck, the upper extremities, and the face. The lesions are asymptomatic except for occasional pruritus. The course of this disorder is variable. Many lesions disappear spontaneously, and there seems to be no effective treatment.

Histologically, elastic tissue is seen penetrating through the epidermis. The dermis surrounding the base of the perforating elastic tissue has a granulomatous infiltrate with foreign body giant cells and histiocytes.

CHRONIC ACIDOSIS.   In either metabolic or respiratory acidosis of more than six or seven months' duration, chemical changes occurring in the connective

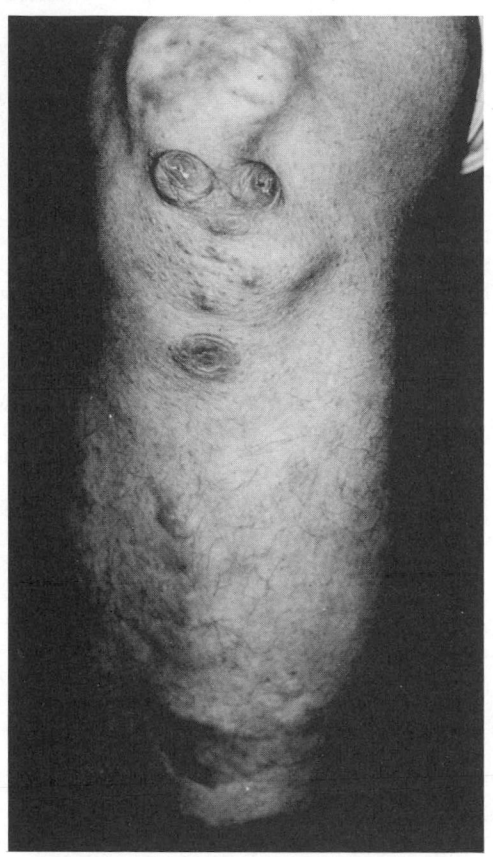

Fig. 17. Ehlers-Danlos syndrome. Knee and shin with "molluscoid pseudotumors" which are produced by trauma in the abnormal skin characteristic of this disease. Minor injuries result in broad atrophic scars present on the skin.

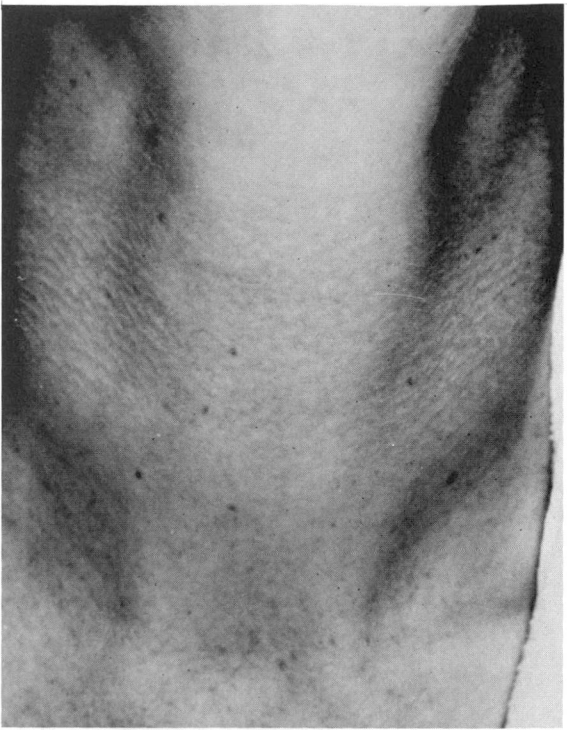

Fig. 18. Pseudoxanthoma elasticum. Characteristic yellowish reticulated papules on sides of neck also occur in the axilla.

tissue are reflected clinically. Typically, the patient shows an atrophic skin which is dry and scaly with generalized alopecia. Poor wound healing and hemorrhagic phenomena may occur, and dehiscence may follow surgical procedures in people with chronic acidosis. It has been demonstrated that the clinical findings are associated with a systemic increase of elastic tissue. There is also an apparent diminution in collagen synthesis. This decrease in production of collagen with an increase of elastic fibers may help to explain some of the clinical phenomena, since collagen provides most of the tensile strength in connective tissue. The etiology of this profound connective tissue change is not well understood.

KELOIDS. These are dense fibrous tumors, occurring with a higher frequency in Negroes than in Caucasians. The anterior surface of the chest, particularly over the sternum, is an area of predilection, but they also occur about the head, neck, and back. They are usually initiated by trauma, which may or may not be remembered by the patient. From a small papule a large, grotesque, disfiguring benign tumor may subsequently develop (Fig. 19). Children with this potential do not develop keloids following every injury. Keloidal growth follows the normal pattern of scar formation, but the various phases of healing seem to be greatly prolonged and exaggerated. An inhibitory substance which normally curtails the excessive production of collagen may be lacking. The color change is related to the vascularity of the lesion. Early lesions are heavily engorged and dark red. As fibrosis takes place, the lesions tend to become more pale or occasionally heavily pigmented. Differentiation of keloids from hypertrophic scars is usually only possible with the passage of time; the keloid grows for a longer period of time and extends beyond the area of trauma. Treatment is often unrewarding, and surgical excision may result in a larger keloid than the one excised. There are reports of varying success with prophylactic x-ray therapy given early to an area of trauma such as a surgical wound in a patient known to be a keloid former. Variable success with intralesional injection of corticosteroids has been reported.

CONNECTIVE TISSUE NEVI. Connective tissue nevi are hamartomatous lesions present at birth or appearing during the first 10 years of life which may show a predominance of collagen or elastin histologically. Their morphology varies. Flesh-colored papules, varicolored plaques, and papillomatous or verrucous lesions may occur. The plaque form, also known as

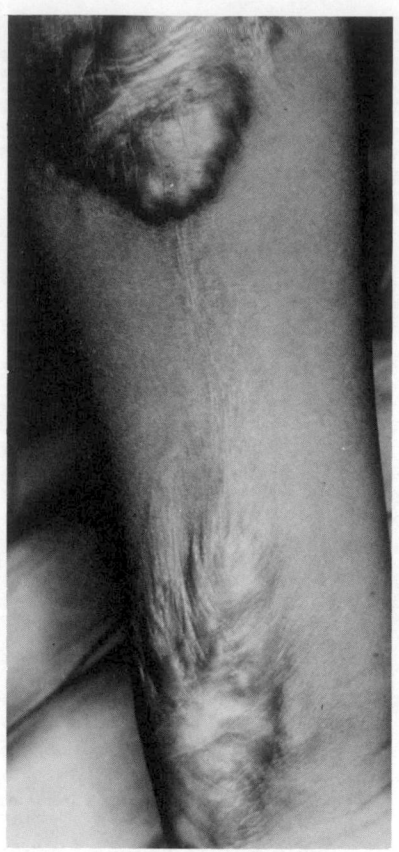

Fig. 19. Keloid on arm of a child following burn.

shagreen skin, occurs primarily in the lumbosacral area and is often associated with tuberous sclerosis.

SCLEREMA NEONATORUM. Sclerema neonatorum is a relatively uncommon disorder characterized by progressive hardening of the subcutaneous tissue. The disease usually begins in the first week of life and primarily affects either premature infants or full-term infants with major debilitating illnesses such as overwhelming pneumonitis, sepsis, or intracranial hemorrhage. Classically, the process begins over the buttocks, thighs, or hands and rapidly extends to involve the entire subcutaneous tissues, sparing only the palms, soles, and genitalia. The overlying skin is smooth, cool, tense, and mottled, and cannot be pitted, picked up, or pinched into folds. The infants are weak and may be cyanotic. A significant number have difficulty maintaining temperature control. The course generally is rapidly downhill, with the mortality rate approximating 75 percent.

The etiology is unknown, but several studies have shown an increase in the ratio of saturated to unsaturated fatty acids. Saturated fatty acids have a higher melting point than unsaturated fatty acids and could account for some of the physical changes in sclerema neonatorum. Histopathologically, sclerematous skin shows thickening of the fibrous trabeculae of the subcutaneous fat. Fat necrosis does not occur and inflammatory changes are minimal. Treatment of sclerema neonatorum is that of the underlying disease. Intensive supportive care is necessary with close monitoring of temperature and fluid and electrolyte balance. Corticosteroids have been advocated, but their effectiveness has not been substantiated.

SUBCUTANEOUS FAT NECROSIS. This disease is frequently confused with sclerema neonatorum, but its clinical separation seems to be justified. Its incidence tends to parallel the number of traumatic deliveries. Clinically, it presents in healthy-appearing term infants toward the end of the first or beginning of the second week of life; however, it may appear as early as the second day or as late as the third or fourth week. The lesions are usually located over areas prone to obstetric trauma, such as the cheeks, neck, back, shoulders, deltoid region, buttocks, and thighs. They are very firm, freely movable, occasionally slightly elevated, well demarcated, round to linear lesions which may at times have a red to blue hue. They vary in size from only a few millimeters to 10 cm. At times the lesions break down to form cysts and occasionally they ulcerate. The lesions may last from several weeks to several months; however, the patients' health remains good. The only lasting effect seems to be occasional subcutaneous calcification.

The etiology of the lesion is not well understood, except that it is often associated with obstetric trauma. Parallels have been drawn between these lesions and those of subcutaneous necrosis seen after trauma in the adult female breast. Some of the latter demonstrate calcification on healing. The lesions are also more common in infants born of primiparas older than 25 years of age, and frequently the infant weighs more than 4,000 g. Pathologically the fat lobules seem to be enlarged with a granulomatous infiltrate containing foreign body giant cells. Frequently, fat crystals can be seen within the giant cells on frozen sections. The routine process for paraffin section tends to dissolve these crystals. Although their exact chemical nature is unknown, it is thought that they may represent an alteration in fat secondary to ischemia during the trauma of delivery. This altered fat then produces a foreign body reaction in the subcutaneous tissue with subsequent development of the lesions. No definitive treatment is known for these nodules. The efficacy of corticosteroids is not well documented. Good supportive care seems adequate, since the prognosis is very good, in contrast to that of sclerema neonatorum.

WEBER-CHRISTIAN DISEASE. Weber-Christian disease, or febrile nodular nonsuppurative panniculitis, is a rare disease affecting adults primarily; cases have been reported, however, in children. The disease is characterized by the occurrence of tender subcutaneous nodules most frequently involving the extremities. These nodules, occasionally single but more commonly multiple, present initially as dull red, elevated, slightly mobile lesions 1 to 2 cm in diameter. Multiple lesions tend to coalesce, forming atrophic plaques beneath the skin. As the lesions progress, the overlying skin becomes pigmented, and the underlying subcutaneus fat becomes atrophic, resulting in a depressed hyperpigmented lesion. Occasionally, there is liquefaction of the underlying fat with the discharge of an oily yellowish-brown liquid. The lesions tend to occur in crops and each new crop is usually associated with the systemic symptoms of fever, malaise, anorexia, and pain. Not infrequently, visceral fat and bone marrow are also involved, producing unusual symptomatology.

The etiology of Weber-Christian disease remains obscure. The disease has been associated with recurrent infection, trauma, halogen ingestion, diabetes mellitus, disseminated tuberculosis, glomerulonephritis, and systemic lupus erythematosus. Histologically, the early lesions of Weber-Christian disease show fat necrosis and an inflammatory infiltrate. More mature lesions show macrophage ingestion of the fat particles (foam cells) and still older lesions show fibrosis and atrophy. Vasculitis is not uncommon. The differential diagnosis of Weber-Christian disease includes erythema nodosum, erythema induratum, subcutaneous fat necrosis, pancreatic fat necrosis, and thrombophlebitis. There is no specific treatment; corticosteroids have been tried with equivocal results. Most cases resolve within two to five years.

ROTHMANN-MAKAI OR LIPOGRANULOMATOSIS SUBCUTANEA. Rothmann-Makai or lipogranulomatosis subcutanea is another form of circumscribed panniculitis. The disease is characterized by the development of subcutaneous nodules and plaques primarily on the trunk and extremities. These nodules are firm and slightly tender on palpation and have normal or slightly hyperemic overlying skin. Occasionally these nodules liquefy and discharge an oily material, but more usually they heal without trace. In contrast to Weber-Christian disease, Rothmann-Makai affects children primarily; there are no systemic symptoms; and the lesions do not occur in crops.

Histologically the acute lesions show vasodilation, focal degeneration of fat cells, and an inflammatory infiltrate. More mature lesions show lipophagic histiocytes, and still older lesions show fibrosis. The etiology of this disorder is not known and there is no effective treatment. Fortunately the disease usually resolves spontaneously within 6 to 12 months.

REFERENCES

Finlayson, G. R., Smith, J. G., and Moor, M. J. Effects of chronic acidosis on connective tissue. J.A.M.A., 187:659, 1964.

Goltz, R. W. and Hult, A-M. Generalized elastolysis (cutis laxa) and Ehlers-Danlos syndrome (cutis hyperelastica): A comparative clinical and laboratory study. Southern Med. J., 58:848, 1965.

——— Hult, A-M., Goldfarb, M., and Gorlin, R. J. Cutis laxa—a manifestation of generalized elastolysis. Arch. Derm., 92:373, 1965.

Goodman, R. M., et al. Pseudoxanthoma elasticum: A clinical and histopathologic study. Medicine, 42:297, 1963.

Harper, F. B. The masquerade of Weber-Christian disease. Arch. Surg., 93:327, 1966.

Horsfield, G. I., and Yardley, H. J. Sclerema neonatorum. J. Invest. Derm., 44:326, 1965.

Hughes, W. E., and Hammond, M. L. Sclerema neonatorum. J. Pediat., 32:676, 1948.

Kellum, R. E., Ray, T. L., and Brown, G. R. Sclerema neonatorum—report of a case and analysis of subcutaneous and epidermal-dermal lipids by chromatographic methods. Arch. Derm., 97:372, 1968.

Laymon, C. W., and Peterson, W. C. Lipogranulomatosis subcutanea (Rothmann-Makai)—An appraisal. Arch. Derm., 90:288, 1964.

MacDonald, A., and Feirvel, M. A review of the concept of Weber-Christian panniculitis with a report of five cases. Br. J. Derm., 80:355, 1968.

Mancini, R. E., and Quaife, J. V. Histogenesis of experimentally produced keloids. J. Invest. Derm., 38:143, 1962.

Marks, M. B. Subcutaneous adipose derangements of the newborn. Amer. J. Dis. Child., 104:122, 1962.

Marshall, J., Vogelpoel, L., and Weber, H. W. Primary elastolysis. S. Afr. Med. J., 34:721, 1960.

Mehregan, A. H. Elastosis perforans serpiginosa—a review of the literature and report of 11 cases. Arch. Derm., 97:381, 1968.

Milunsky, A., and Levin, S. E. Sclerema neonatorum—clinical study of 79 cases. S. Afr. Med. J., 40:638, 1966.

Muller, S. A., and Winkelmann, R. K. Necrobiosis lipoidica diabeticorum—a clinical and pathological investigation of 171 cases. Arch. Derm., 93:272, 1966.

Rhodes, E. L., Hill, D. M., Ames, A. C., Tourle, C. A., and Taylor, C. G. Granuloma annulare—prednisone glycosuria tests in a non-diabetic group. Br. J. Derm., 78:532, 1966.

Rocha, G., and Winkelmann, R. K. Connective tissue nevus. Arch. Derm., 85:722, 1964.

Romaine, R., Rudner, E. J., and Altman, J. Papular granuloma annulare and diabetes mellitus—report of cases. Arch. Derm., 98:152, 1968.

Ross, R., and Bornstein, P. The elastic fiber—I. The separation and partial characterization of its macromolecular components. J. Cell. Biol., 40:366, 1969.

Smith, J. G., Jr. The dermal elastoses. Arch. Derm., 88:382, 1963.

Stankler, L., and Leslie, G. Generalized granuloma annulare—a report of a case and review of the literature. Arch. Derm., 95:509, 1967.

Warwick, W. J., Ruttenberg, H. D., and Quie, P. G. Sclerema neonatorum—a sign, not a disease. J.A.M.A., 184:680, 1963.

Wechsler, H. S., and Fisher, E. R. Ehlers-Danlos syndrome. Arch. Path., 77:613, 1964.

26.4

BLISTERING DISEASES

ROGER W. PEARSON

A restricted group of conditions that have blister formation as a prominent or the chief clinical feature will be discussed here. In general, the etiology of these diseases is unknown or poorly understood. Other diseases that have blistering as an occasional or regular clinical finding are discussed elsewhere. They include vesicular infectious diseases (such as certain viral infections, rickettsialpox, early congenital syphilis, bullous impetigo, and dermatophytosis), insect bite reactions, second-degree burns, incontinentia pigmenti, urticaria pigmentosa, lupus erythematosus, lichen planus, congenital ichthyosiform erythroderma, the various forms of cutaneous porphyria, drug eruptions, dyshidrotic eczema, and contact dermatitis.

The generally accepted observation that children blister more easily than adults is probably due in part to the fact that the epidermis, particularly the horny layer, is thinner in children and the connective tissue is relatively immature, containing relatively more soluble collagen and water than adult skin. There may also be special biochemical properties of young skin that leave it more susceptible to attack by certain agents. (See Toxic Epidermal Necrolysis, p. 1776.)

Epidermolysis Bullosa
(Mechanobullous Diseases)

Epidermolysis bullosa is a term applied to a group of hereditary diseases in which noninflammatory blisters develop on the skin in response to mechanical trauma. Sometimes the tendency to form blisters is so great that the trauma may be inapparent. In the past, members of this group of diseases have been considered to differ only in degree, but it is now possible to separate on the basis of clinical, histologic, and genetic findings six distinct diseases. There are some additional variant forms that defy classification because of sparsity of cases and sketchy descriptions. Since only two of the major forms of the disease show lysis of the epidermis, it seems appropriate to reintroduce the term mechanobullous diseases for the group since mechanical fragility is common to all members. The term dystrophic has resulted in frequent diagnostic errors due to the fact that dystrophic nail and teeth changes occur in JBE (see below) and in the scarring diseases. New terms have therefore been introduced for some of the diseases in the groups (Table 1).

The erythropoietic forms of porphyria, porphyria cutanea tarda, and bullous congenital ichthyosiform erythroderma are also, technically, mechanobullous diseases which may be confused with the above entities. They can usually be easily differentiated on the basis of clinical and laboratory data.

In all of the major mechanobullous diseases histologic examination of the skin gives useful information, and electron microscope examination is particularly valuable for the early establishment of the correct diagnosis. Whenever possible the lesions should be induced immediately before biopsy, by minimal mechanical trauma, since secondary alterations may destroy the diagnostic features if older lesions are taken. In instances where the skin is extremely fragile, biopsy of noninvolved skin may be adequate, the biopsy procedure itself proving sufficient trauma to produce the alterations.

EPIDERMOLYSIS BULLOSA SIMPLEX (EBS). This disease, inherited as an autosomal dominant, is characterized by the presence at birth, or development shortly thereafter, of vesicles and bullae at any site on the body following minor mechanical trauma (Fig. 20). Separation of skin layers occurs within a few minutes of injury, and frank blisters appear usually within 10 to 15 minutes. The palms and soles are usually relatively resistant to the process, especially as the child grows older. The lesions heal with remarkable rapidity and do not scar unless there has been considerable secondary infection. Heat decreases the blistering threshold, and cold raises the threshold to a near normal level. Mucous membranes are not frequently involved (when involved it is usually during infancy or early childhood), the nails not at all, and general development is normal.

Although the disease may decrease in intensity at puberty, most if not all patients can expect lifelong activity of the disease; however, if reasonable care is taken in choice of occupation and recreational activities, and the patient makes allowances for his disease, then it can be only a nuisance rather than a crippling illness.

Histologic examination of a freshly induced lesion reveals that the blisters are produced in the basal cell layer by disintegration of the cytoplasm of the cells. This process appears to be an exaggeration of the reaction pattern shown by normal basal cells in response to many types of injury. Probably the defect resides in the cytolytic enzymes or the mechanism of their activation. An alternative possibility is that the cytoplasm itself is more susceptible than normal to cytolysis (Fig. 21).

Treatment is prophylactic and consists primarily of avoidance of mechanical trauma. Most patients become expert early in life at setting their own limits of activity. Cooling of the skin immediately after injury is of great value, and air conditioning in warm climates is a wise investment. Antibiotic ointment and systemic antibiotics may be needed. Lubrication and powdering are useful in reducing friction; maceration, however, must be avoided.

TABLE 1. *Epidermolysis Bullosa*

Type	Designation	Inheritance	Location of Pathology
Epidermolysis Bullosa Simplex	EBS	Dominant	Epidermal Basal Cells
Recurrent Bullous Eruption of Hands and Feet (Weber-Cockayne)	RBEHF	Probably Dominant	Suprabasilar
Epidermolysis Bullosa Hereditaria "Letalis"	EBHL	Recessive	Dermoepidermal Junction
Dystrophic Epidermolysis Bullosa	DBD-R	Recessive	Papillary Dermis
Dystrophic Epidermolysis Bullosa	DBD-D	Dominant	Superficial Dermis
Dystrophic Epidermolysis Bullosa	DBD-A	Acquired	More Superficial than DBD-R

RECURRENT BULLOUS ERUPTION OF HANDS AND FEET (WEBER-COCKAYNE) (RBEHF). This rather uncommon condition is characterized by recurrent blisters that develop after trauma on the palms and soles; they are generally mild. They appear less commonly on the dorsum of the hands and feet and rarely elsewhere (Fig. 22). There is great variation in the intensity of trauma needed to induce the blisters. Usually the disease is first noted in early childhood, but occasionally it has a later onset. The lesions generally develop 30 minutes to 2 hours after trauma. They heal rapidly without scar formation.

The disease is usually inherited as an autosomal

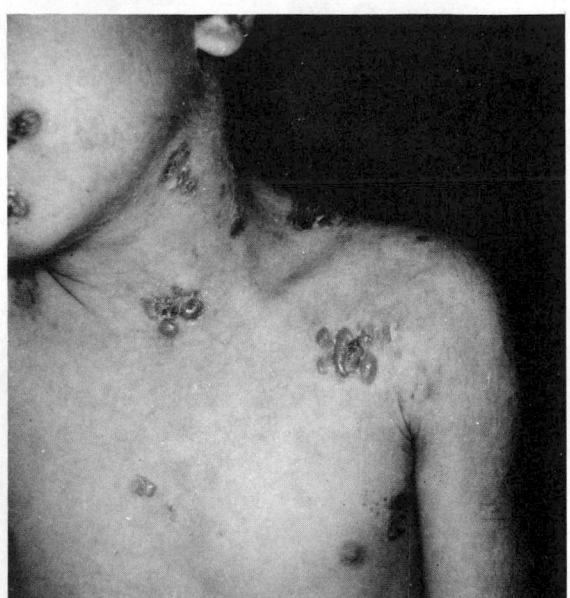

Fig. 20. Epidermolysis bullosa simplex. Typical noninflammatory blisters at various stages of development and resolution.

dominant trait, though there are some cases without an apparent hereditary basis. Relative amelioration of the process often occurs at puberty.

Although the blisters have been reported to occur at various levels within the epidermis, the histology of freshly induced lesions is characteristic. In contrast to EBS, there is lysis of cells *above* the basal layer, often extending as high as the granular layer. There is also marked dyskeratosis (Fig. 23). The pathology is identical to that found in "friction blisters" induced in normal individuals. The defect, then, would seem to be a lowered threshold for this response. Activation of cytolytic enzymes or increased substrate susceptibility, and decreased mechanical "strength" of cells are the most likely bases for the defect.

Treatment is similar to that of epidermolysis bullosa simplex (EBS). Although systemic steroid therapy has been advocated in rare severe cases, it is not advised in most instances.

JUNCTIONAL BULLOUS EPIDERMATOSIS (JBE, HERLITZ'S DISEASE, OR EPIDERMOLYSIS BULLOSA HEREDITARIA "LETALIS"). This autosomal recessive trait is apparent at birth and is characterized by vesicles, bullae, and erosions that occur following minimal trauma (Fig. 24). Blisters or erosions usually can be induced easily in clear areas. The lesions heal very slowly without scar formation, unless there has been deep infection. The mucous membranes are usually affected, and the teeth are often dystrophic. The nails are frequently dystrophic or lost. Many patients die within a few weeks, but some survive a few years, and a few survive to adulthood. It is true that some instances of alleged long survival were probably other mechanobullous diseases, but enough data is now available clearly to support the above claim. With increasing use of steroid therapy and antibiotics it is reasonable to expect more long survivals.

General development is frequently impaired, although mental function is usually normal; severe

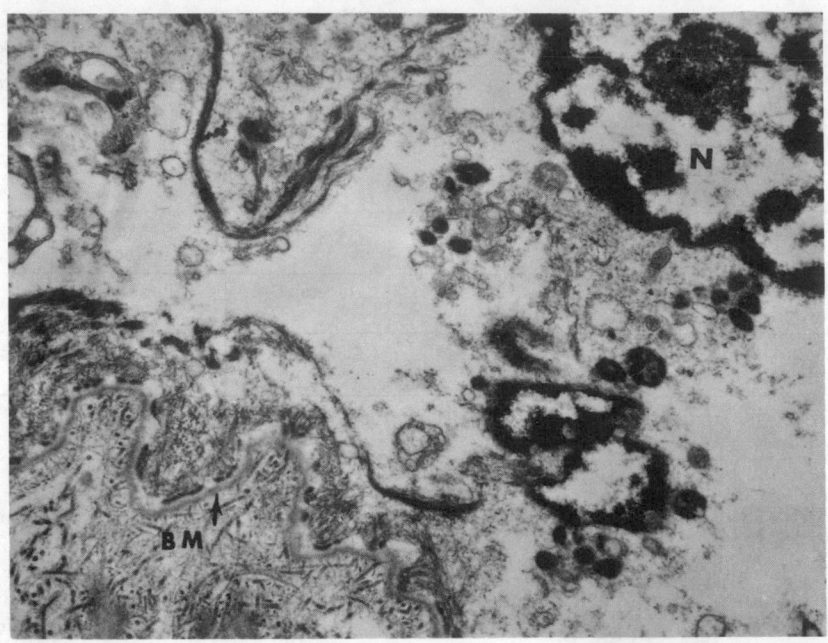

Fig. 21. Epidermolysis bullosa simplex. The dermoepidermal junction. There is marked degeneration of the cytoplasm of the basal cell resulting in early blister in the plane just beneath the intact nucleus (N). The basement membrane (BM) is intact.

anemia is often found. When death occurs the mechanism is frequently not apparent, though in some instances infection is the immediate cause.

Histologically, blisters develop at the dermoepidermal junction. There is separation between the plasma membrane of the basal cells and the basement membrane (Fig. 25).

Treatment consists of general supportive measures, air conditioning, gentleness in handling, protection from and treatment of local systemic infection, and judicious use of systemic anti-inflammatory steroids. Steroid therapy has been of value in some cases and apparently ineffective in others. Steroids are sometimes useful to help the patient through periods of increased activity of the disease. High dosage is usually required.

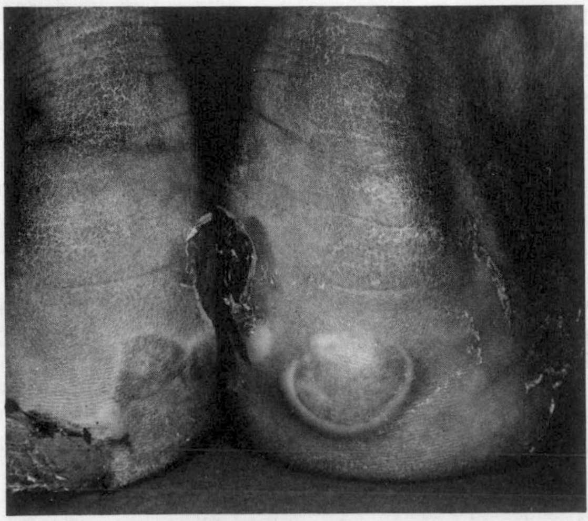

DYSTROPHIC EPIDERMOLYSIS BULLOSA (DERMOLYTIC BULLOUS DERMATOSIS). See Figures 26, 27, and 28.

Autosomal Recessive Type (DBD-R). This disease usually is present at birth and is characterized by blisters (often hemorrhagic) and erosions which tend to involve skin and mucous membranes at any location. The lesions heal slowly with scars and often with milia formation. After repeated episodes, especially on the hands and feet, there is gradual deepening of the scars. Contractures form, nails are lost, the skin of digits often fuses, and bone resorption may occur, so that marked limitation of motion results. Defects of the teeth are common. Eating may be difficult because of mucous membrane and teeth involvement. Secondary infection and anemia are common complications. General development is often slow and physical maturity may not be attained, but mental function is usually good. Some improvement often occurs at puberty and most patients reach adulthood. However, early death from infection or general debilitation or secondary amyloidosis may occur, especially in the more severely affected patients. Squamous cell carcinoma developing in scars is an occasional complication.

Fig. 22. Recurrent bullous eruption of the hands and feet (RBEHF). Blisters and thick calluses at sites of trauma.

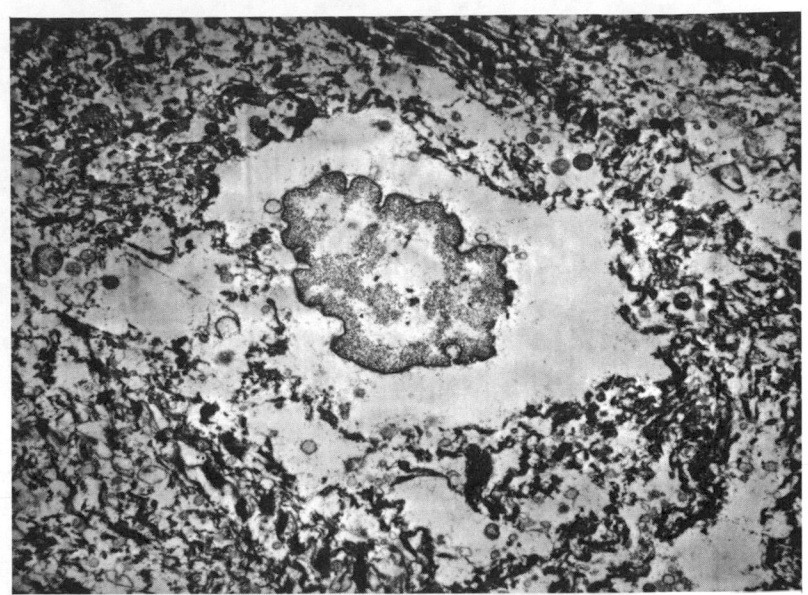

Fig. 23. RBEHF. Electron micrograph showing characteristic cytolysis and dyskeratosis of a malpighian layer cell.

In warm weather the disease is aggravated, but local cooling of the skin does not prevent experimental blister induction as can be demonstrated in epidermolysis bullosa simplex.

Histologically, the blisters are clean dermoepidermal separations. Electron microscopic examination reveals that the blisters form as a result of disintegration of the collagen of the papillary dermis. The defect in this disease is not known, but increased collagenase production in the skin of patients with DBD-R has been demonstrated. Whether the collagenase is responsible for the pathology is uncertain. An alternate possibility is that the collagen itself is defective.

Treatment consists of protection from trauma, control of infection, and general supportive measures. Surgeons generally do not attempt reconstruction of hands and feet in the presence of active disease, though recently more vigorous surgical attacks on the problem have been made. Excellent short-term improvement in mobility can be accomplished, but long-term prognosis must be guarded. Anti-inflammatory steroids have been of little or no value in small doses, but high doses are moderately effective, and useful if judiciously administered.

Autosomal Dominant Type (DBD-D). This disease presents at birth or in infancy. Vesicles and bullae occur chiefly on hands, feet, elbows, and knees. In childhood, any site on the skin may be involved. The lesions heal rather slowly with superficial scar formation and milia. Nail involvement is common, presenting typically as a clawlike dystrophy. Severe deformities of the hands and feet do not occur. Mucous membrane invovement is frequent but mild. At puberty moderate or sometimes substantial improvement occurs. General development is unaffected.

The histology in this disease is similar to that of autosomal recessive dystrophic epidermolysis bullosa but with more superficial dermal alterations.

Treatment is aimed at reducing mechanical trauma to the skin. In most instances only moderate restriction of physical activities is required.

"Acquired" Type (DBD-A). Mild dystropic epi-

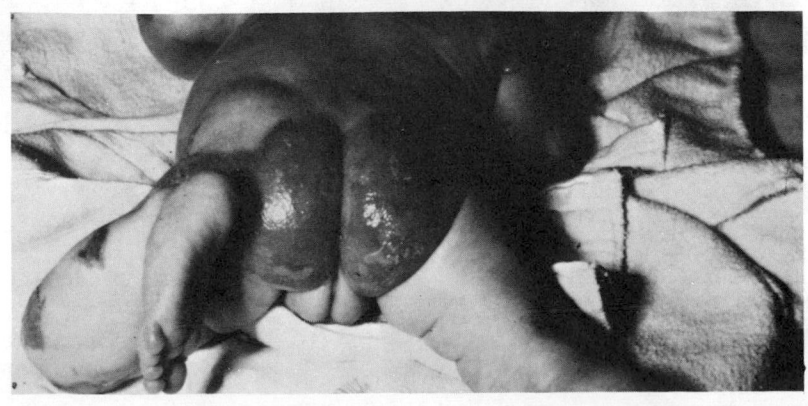

Fig. 24. Epidermolysis bullosa hereditaria "letalis" (EBHL). (Herlitz's Disease.) (Junctional bullous epidermatosis.) Infant with large erosions at sites of trauma. There is no scar formation.

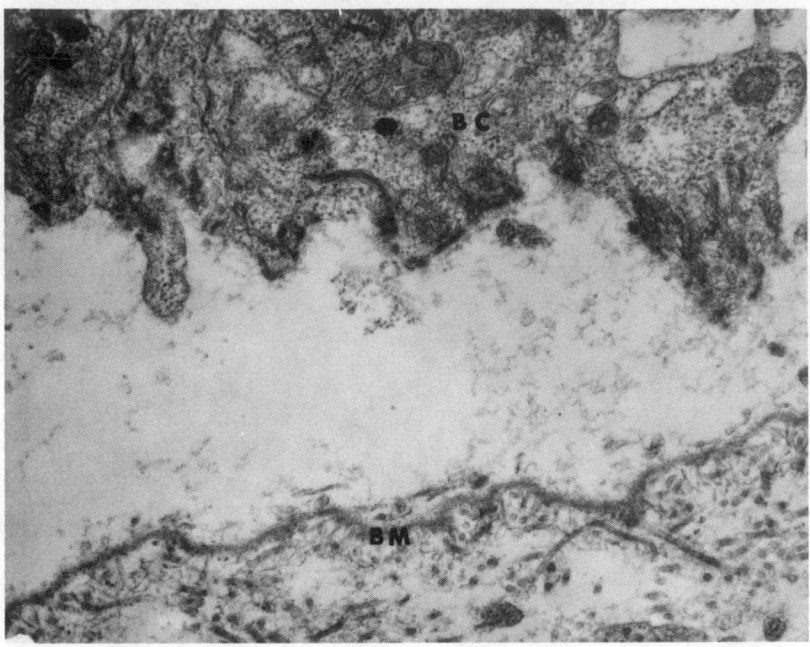

Fig. 25.   Junctional bullous epidermatosis (JBE) or epidermolysis bullosa hereditaria "letalis." Dermoepidermal junction. There is separation between the plasma membrane of the basal cell (BC) and the basement membrane (BM). The plasma membrane is apparently disrupted in some areas but some "half desmosomes" are present.

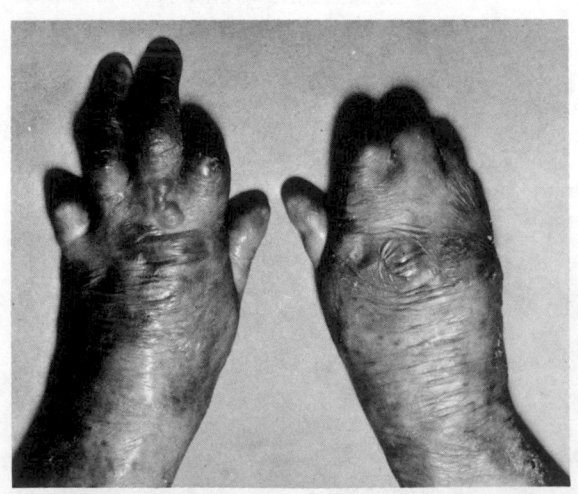

Fig. 26.   Dystrophic epidermolysis bullosa. (Dermolytic bullous dermatosis). Recessive type. Moderately severe hand lesions showing active blisters, scarring with contractures, and loss of nails.

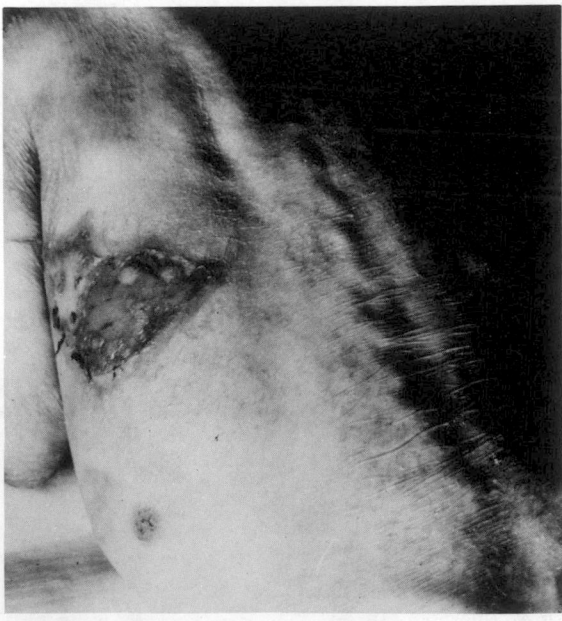

Fig. 27.   Dermolytic bullous dermatosis. Recessive type. A large erosion, massive superficial scarring, atrophy, and milia formation.

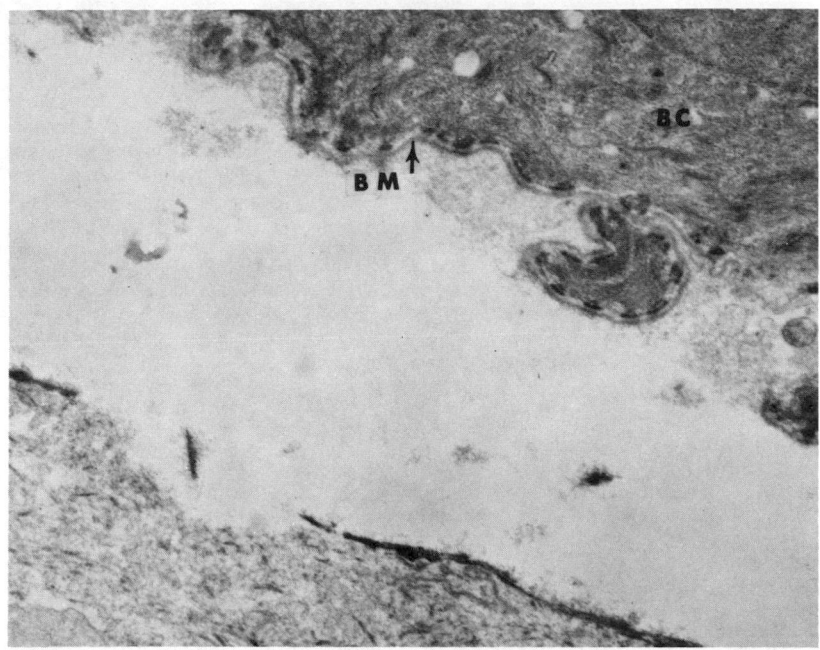

Fig. 28. Dystrophic epidermolysis bullosa. Dermoepidermal junction. The blister forms beneath the basement membrane as a result of disintegration of collagen.

dermolysis bullosa occurs occasionally without demonstrable hereditary background; it may develop during late childhood but more often in young adulthood. Some cases appear to have been induced by drugs (e.g., arsenic, sulfonamides, and most recently penicillamine). Usually the manifestations are limited to the hands, feet, elbows, and knees, but much more severe cases may occur. Blisters and erosions heal with superficial scar formation. Nail involvement is mild or absent. The pathology of the disease is similar to, but more superficial in depth than, recessive dystrophic epidermolysis bullosa. Treatment is entirely symptomatic.

Dermatitis Herpetiformis (DH)

Although this disease is most frequent in adults, it also occurs in infants or children. Its chief features are grouped, tense vesicles or bullae that usually arise on erythematous or urticarial plaques; the disease is characterized by intense, often burning pruritus and a cyclic course. The lesions are symmetrical and frequently widespread, and the elbows, knees, groin, and buttocks are sites of predilection (Fig. 29). Papular, erythematous, or urticarial lesions may predominate, especially in mild cases, causing diagnostic confusion. Spontaneous exacerbations and remissions frequently occur, although the disease tends to persist for several years. The morphology of the lesions

may change from one episode to another. Sometimes figurate patterns develop as lesions spread. Individual lesions tend to heal after a relatively short course regardless of the general activity of the disease. The patient often excoriates the lesions. Healed lesions often become hyperpigmented. There is only rarely involvement of mucous membranes. General health is usually not affected but blood eosinophilia is com-

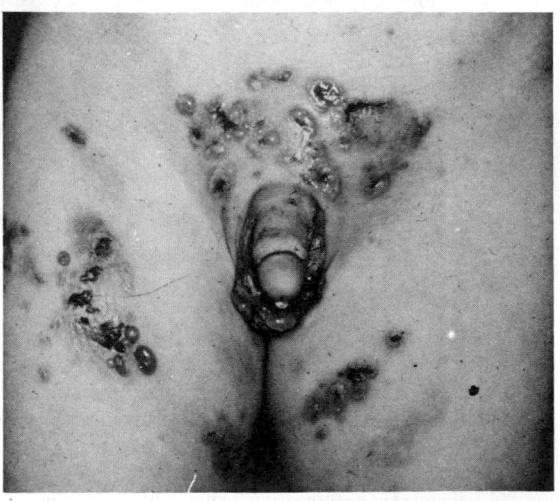

Fig. 29. Dermatitis herpetiformis. Characteristic grouped vesicles and bullae, usually on an erythematous base.

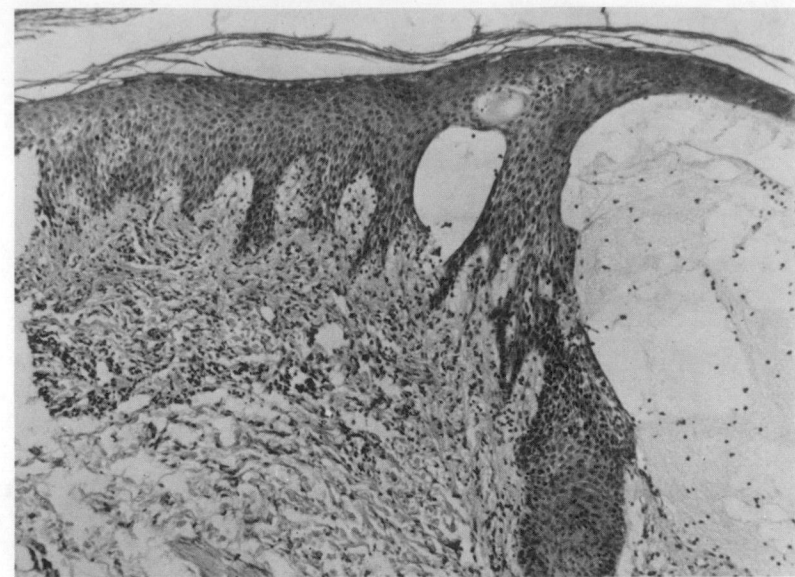

Fig. 30. Dermatitis herpetiformis. Light micrograph. Old blister at dermoepidermal junction on the right. The adjacent papillae are edematous.

mon. Small intestine abnormalities (frequently asymptomatic) are often found in patients with DH or in their relatives. The direct or indirect immunofluorescent basement membrane studies are negative.

In areas nonblistered clinically the histology of dermatitis herpetiformis is marked edema of individual dermal papillae with inflammatory cells including eosinophils. In well-developed blisters the base may be necrotic and the cavity filled with inflammatory cells, often predominantly eosinophils. The blister roof is usually not necrotic if the lesion is fresh (Fig. 30).

Treatment consists of symptomatic management of the lesions with wet compresses and antibiotic or steroid ointments, and systemic administration of sulfones or sulfapyridine. Diaminodiphenyl sulfone is probably the drug of choice. Most children respond to relatively small doses of 25 to 100 mg daily. The chief side reactions to the drug are mild hemolytic anemia and methemoglobinemia.

Toxic Epidermal Necrolysis (TEN)
(Scalded Skin Syndrome, Lyell's Disease)

This recently characterized syndrome may occur at any age but is most common in infants and young children. Formerly, examples of the syndrome were likely to be diagnosed as acute "pemphigus," erythema multiforme, or unclassified toxic bullous eruptions. It is also now apparent that Ritter's disease is TEN in the newborn.

The onset of the disease may be explosive, or a single lesion may precede by a few hours or even days generalized involvement. In children purulent nasal discharge and perinasal and perioral impetigo

are often the first lesions. In view of recent data clearly implicating a "toxin" of phage Group 2 coagulase positive staphylococci in the pathogenesis of the disease in children, cases attributed to drugs in children are perhaps coincidental. In adults, however, drugs are clearly implicated in many, if not most, cases. Erythema is followed by loosening or loss of large sheets of epidermis, but occasionally the process occurs with minimal or no erythema. Slight frictional trauma to a noneroded area will loosen or erode the epidermis at that site (Nikolsky's sign). In eroded areas flaccid blisters often develop as fluid accumulates between the loosened layers. The entire skin including palms and soles may be involved and there may be erosive mucous membrane lesions. Children often spontaneously assume the knee-chest position.

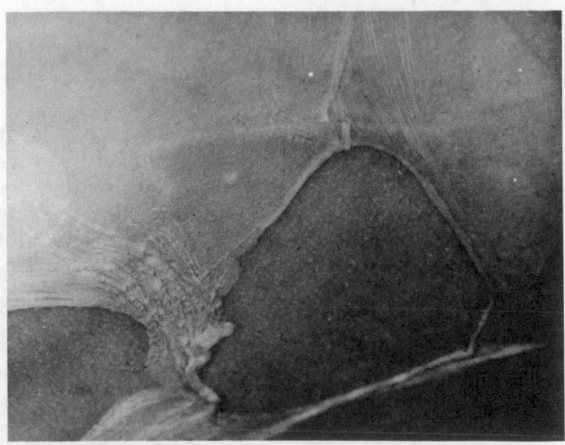

Fig. 31. Toxic epidermolysis, childhood type. Characteristic loosening of large area of epidermis.

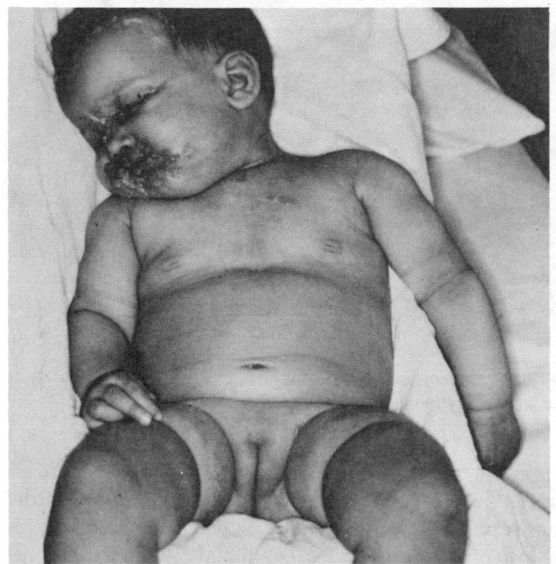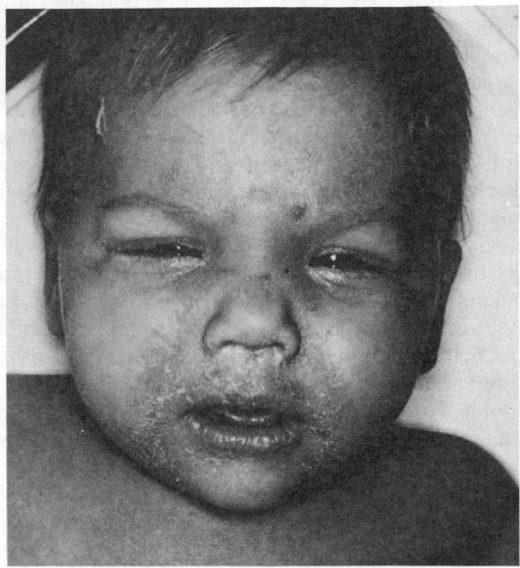

Fig. 32. Toxic epidermal necrolysis (Ritter-Lyell syndrome). *Left.* A 5½-month-old child with purulent conjunctivitis and nasal discharge for four days, impetigo about the mouth for three days and blisters for two days. Staphylococcus aureus. Phage type II was cultured for her periorbital lesions. At the time of photograph the skin was generally erythematous and tender. There were blisters on the upper chest. She responded rapidly to antibiotic therapy. *Right.* A 6½-month-old girl with three-day history of eruption nasal discharge. No bullae appeared spontaneously; however, Nikolsky's sign was positive. This child had the desquamative form of toxic epidermal necrolysis and responded rapidly to antibiotic therapy.

The skin is usually tender to light touch; fever and other signs of systemic toxicity usually are present. The active phase continues for about one week, and healing is usually complete by two weeks. Death is common in affected adults, but uncommon in children (Figs. 31 and 32).

The disease is preceded in some instances by mild upper respiratory infections or a wide variety of other infectious and noninfectious diseases or by drug intake, but in other instances such factors have been absent.

Histology reveals separation at the dermoepidermal junction as a result of necrolysis and acantholysis of basal cells, or damage higher in the epidermis at the granular layer level (Fig. 33). Most biopsy specimens from children have shown the granular layer pathology. At this higher level many cells have an acantholysislike appearance. In contrast to pemphi-

Fig. 33. Toxic epidermal necrolysis, childhood type. Blister formation at the level of the granular layer. The remainder of the epidermis is relatively intact and there is little inflammatory infiltrate.

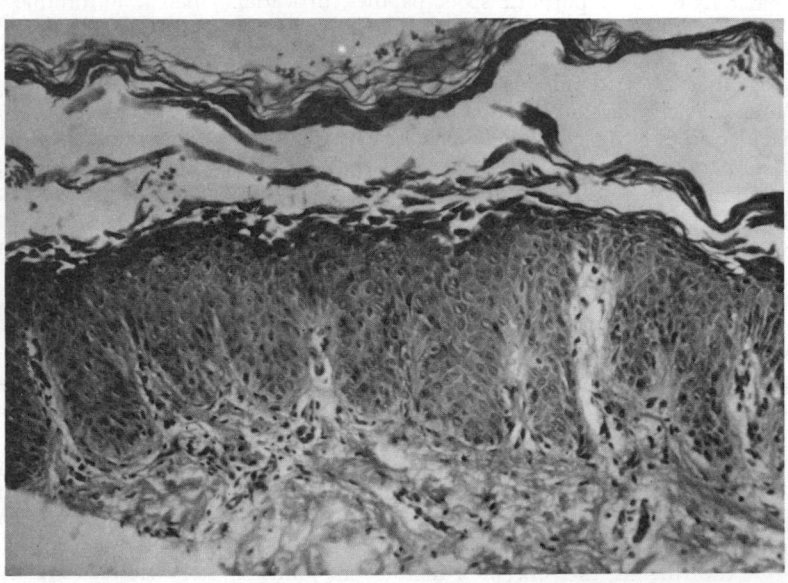

gus acantholysis, there may be actual splitting of desmosomes. When early lesions are examined, the alteration may be limited to a layer or two of cells. Later vacuolar degeneration at other levels may be seen, and in basal layer (adult) cases the entire blister roof may be necrotic. In early lesions remarkably little inflammation is seen in the dermis, suggesting that the toxic process operative in this condition is relatively specific for the epithelium. Recently it has been demonstrated that a "toxin" from coagulase positive phage Group 2 staphylococci can induce lesions in newborn mice similar clinically and histologically to childhood TEN. More mature animals are not susceptible. This finding correlates with the observation that the clinical disease occurs only in young children. It is not known whether protection from the disease in more mature individuals results from substrate resistance or "inactivation" of the "toxin."

Treatment consists of reduction of friction by removing clothes, gentle application of lubrication, treatment of any local or systemic infections, administration of prednisone in dosages as high as 4 to 6 mg/kg, and general supportive care. In children, the clinical course is characterized by spontaneous improvement. Consequently, the improvement associated with the administration of steroids is difficult to evaluate. Melish's observations on newborn mice suggest that steroids may have an adverse effect; however, steroids may be useful in selected infants and are indicated in adults whose disease is related to medications such as diphenylhydantoin.

Erythema Multiforme (EM)

This disease has an acute onset and can occur at any age. It is characterized by lesions that include erythematous macules, purpuric spots, papules, urticarial plaques, vesicles, and bullae. Individual lesions tend to develop central depressed brownish or violaceous areas that show epidermal necrosis histologically. When blisters develop, they occur on erythematous macular areas or urticarialike lesions. Concentric (iris-type) patterns of any type of lesion may develop, and spreading may result in striking polycyclic patterns (Fig. 34). Grouping may be present to some degree, causing confusion with dermatitis herpetiformis. Fortunately, the skin lesions are relatively asymptomatic. Distribution of the lesions favors the dorsum of the hands and neck, but lesions may be generalized. When mucous membrane is involved, there is usually an erosive stomatitis, often associated with fever, malaise, and other signs of systemic toxicity. When the conjunctiva and urethra are involved, the disease is sometimes called the Stevens-Johnson syndrome, especially in pediatric literature. However, it is difficult to separate this syndrome from other forms of bullous erythema multiforme.

Nevertheless, the concept of the Stevens-Johnson

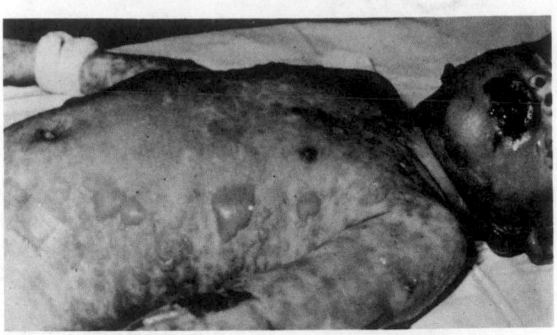

Fig. 34. Bullous erythema multiforme. Many vesicles and bullae on an erythematous base, and erosive stomatitis.

syndrome is important because of its severe clinical course, in contrast to the usual mild course of ordinary erythema multiforme. Typically, the onset is explosive, with fever, chills, malaise, and upper respiratory symptoms. Vesicles and pseudomembranous plaques that soon become hemorrhagic erosions usually develop first in the mouth, sometimes in the nasopharynx and on the lips. Most patients salivate profusely. Conjunctival involvement is generally erosive and may spread to the cornea. Severe corneal lesions may result in scar formation. When anal and urethral lesions occur they are similar to the oral lesions. Cutaneous involvement varies from none to generalized lesions of any morphologic erythema multiforme type. Maximal clinical activity occurs at 7 to 10 days; untreated, recovery occurs by 4 to 6 weeks. Milder forms of erythema multiforme usually have a somewhat shorter course. Mortality in severe erythema multiforme is usually "toxic" or due to intercurrent infection.

In some individuals regular recurrences of erythema multiforme occur, particularly in spring and fall. Occasionally recurrences may be more frequent, and chronic forms have been described; the diagnosis is especially difficult in such cases.

Erythema multiforme has been associated with a great number of systemic conditions, including infections such as mycoplasma, streptococcus, herpes simplex, deep mycoses, and tuberculosis, connective tissue diseases, and sensitization to drugs. Unfortunately, most cases are of unknown cause. The possibility that many of these may be related to mild viral or mycoplasma infections has not been studied exhaustively.

Histologically, nonblistered lesions show edema of the upper dermis, angiitis of the small vessels, and often epidermal necrosis. Blisters are subepidermal. The blister roof is often necrotic, even in early lesions. Eosinophils may be present in the blister cavity, but lymphocytes usually predominate (Fig. 35).

The treatment of erythema multiforme is dictated by the clinical state of the patient. Mild cases frequently respond to antihistamines. Anti-inflammatory steroids are indicated in cases with severe skin

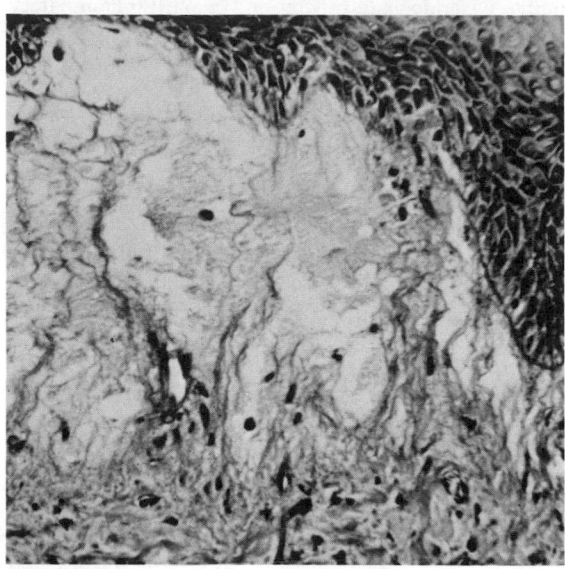

Fig. 35. Bullous erythema multiforme. Light micrograph showing early blister formation secondary to degenerative changes of the papillary dermis.

or mucous membrane involvement or when there is appreciable systemic toxicity. Prednisone, 2 to 6 mg/kg, or its equivalent may be required for control of the disease. The steroid should be reduced gradually to avoid relapse. Although response to systemic steroid administration may be dramatic, occasional patients do not respond at all. Kenalog in orabase adheres fairly well to mucosa and can be used on the oral lesions. Mouth washes with Dyclone solution reduce pain and facilitate eating.

Intravenous administration of nutrition and therapy is usually necessary in severe cases. Eye lesions are frequently responsive to local steroids, which should be used only after ophthalmologic consultation to rule out infection with herpes simplex. Skin lesions may be left alone if they are dry and asymptomatic; oozing lesions benefit from saline compresses, topical antibiotics, and/or steroids.

Bullous Pemphigoid (BP)

This disease is widely accepted as a distinct entity. It affects chiefly the elderly, but children may also be affected. The onset is often insidious. Erythematous macules and plaques may precede blister development, but blisters frequently occur in nonerythematous areas. The erythematous lesions are sometimes arranged in patterns similar to those found in erythema multiforme. The blisters characteristically are tense bullae, but vesicles also occur. There is seldom any tendency to grouping of the lesions; the distribution is usually general with some slight predilection for flexural surfaces. Rare cases of localized

disease tend to involve the legs. There is sometimes involvement of the oral mucous membranes, consisting of erosions and an occasional intact blister. Most affected patients have mild to moderate pruritus or burning, though occasionally there is severe pruritus. Notable signs of systemic toxicity attributable to the disease itself are usually absent. Individual lesions tend to heal quite rapidly, especially in children, but the natural course of the disease continues for months or years, with exacerbations and relative or complete remissions. In children the average total duration is said to be about four years. Fatal cases have occurred only in adults, and then death is usually due to complications or concurrent disease.

Histologically, blisters develop at the dermoepidermal junction and are usually accompanied by mild inflammatory changes in the dermis. Early lesions may show tiny subepidermal vacuoles or less commonly edema and inflammation of papillae, thus resembling and causing confusion with dermatitis herpetiformis. The blister roof is sometimes necrotic even in early lesions. Cells within the blister cavity may include many eosinophils, and there may be angiitis of the small vessels. The histology of bullous pemphigoid overlaps that of dermatitis herpetiformis and erythema multiforme unless very early lesions are available for study so that, in a specific case, the histology may be helpful but not absolutely diagnostic. Only bullous pemphigoid shows positive immunofluorescent staining of the basement membrane area by direct or indirect techniques. These antibodies have not yet been shown to be invoved in the pathogenic mechanism of the disease. In adults the disease is sometimes associated with malignancies or other severe systemic illness. In children it may be associated with other diseases such as ulcerative colitis.

Treatment is with corticosteroids. Moderate dosage is often sufficient, and it is frequently possible to reduce the dose to low maintenance levels or to discontinue the medication within a few weeks or months.

Bullous pemphigoid should not be confused with benign mucosal pemphigoid (ocular pemphigus, cicatricial pemphigoid), a disease that affects only adults and is characterized by erosions especially of the oral, vaginal, and conjunctival mucous membranes that frequently heal with scarring. On the skin, dermoepidermal blisters occasionally occur.

Pemphigus (P)

Pemphigus (P) has been subclassified into four types—P. vulgaris, P. vegetans, P. foliaceus, and P. erythematosus (Senear-Usher syndrome)—but the current view is that there are only two basic types: P. vulgaris and P. foliaceus. P. vulgaris is extremely rare in children, and P. foliaceus is only slightly less rare. P. vulgaris and, to a lesser extent, P. foliaceus have an apparent predilection for Jews. There is an interesting focus of the latter disease in Brazil (fogo selvagem).

P. VULGARIS. This disease usually has an insidious onset. The initial lesions may occur anywhere on the skin as flaccid blisters of any size. On the oral mucosa, they usually appear as erosions. Blisters are easily eroded, and both erosions and intact blisters often enlarge, and heal slowly. Secondary infection is common. Usually, the blisters arise from normal-appearing skin, but the base is occasionally erythematous. Mild friction applied to uninvolved areas may result in loosening of the skin (Nikolsky's sign). Symptoms are more those of general discomfort than pruritus. The natural course of the disease is slow, with almost certain death following variable exacerbations and remissions. Treatment with high doses of anti-inflammatory steroids has greatly altered the formerly dismal picture.

P. vegetans is a variant of P. vulgaris in which there is apparent increased host resistance to the disease so that progression is retarded. The prognosis is considerably more favorable than that of classical P. vulgaris. This form is characterized by verrucous vegetations with a predilection for axillae and groin. Vesicles, bullae, and pustules may also be present.

P. FOLIACEUS. As with P. vulgaris, the onset of P. foliaceus is insidious. It most often presents early as very superficial erosions and flaccid bullae arising from erythematous patches. As partial healing and new blisters or erosions occur, the sloughed layers accumulate so that the lesions are crusted and scaly. Early lesions are frequently located with a butterfly distribution on the face, the scalp, upper chest, and back (Senear-Usher syndrome). Extension of the disease occurs by spread of old lesions or the development of new ones, sometimes producing figurate patterns. Uninvolved areas may show the Nikolsky sign. Gradually the entire skin surface may become involved, and at this stage blisters are uncommon. Mucous membrane lesions are rare. Pruritis and general discomfort are usually present. The prognosis in older patients is relatively favorable when judicious treatment is given, but spontaneous remissions also occur. Young patients remain in good health and are particularly likely to have a benign course with eventual remission.

Brazilian pemphigus (fogo selvagem) is clinically similar to P. foliaceus. Children and adolescents are frequently affected. The disease is localized to a relatively small area of the country, suggesting the possibility of an infectious etiologic determinant.

Histologically the hallmark of pemphigus is acantholysis, the loss of intercellular bridges with resultant separation of cells. In P. vulgaris the process occurs chiefly at the suprabasal level, whereas in P. foliaceus the process occurs at or just beneath the granular layer. By direct or indirect immunofluorescent techniques antibodies localized between epidermal cells (or perhaps on cell membranes) may be demonstrated. The treatment of pemphigus is generally systemic administration of anti-inflammatory steroids in whatever dosage is necessary to achieve clinical control of the process. Use of an immunosuppressive is probably also effective but must be considered investigative. The long-term results in children are thought to be good.

Benign Familial Pemphigus (Hailey-Hailey Disease)

This disease is characterized by vesicles, crusts, scales, vegetations, erythematous patches, and, rarely, bullae. The eruption is generally limited to a small area of the body, usually the neck, axillae, chest, or groin. Rarely plaques or erosions are present on the oral mucous membrane. The skin lesions are commonly secondarily infected. The disease is inherited as an autosomal dominant. Of particular interest is the fact that uninvolved skin responds to a variety of experimental insults with superficial acantholysis and dyskeratosis. These are also the chief histologic features of the natural disease. It appears that the defect involves increased susceptibility of the skin to the acantholytic type of response to injury, a response that all skin is capable of showing when appropriately injured.

Onset of the disease in childhood is rare. Adolescence and young adulthood are more common times for the initial lesions to appear. Repeated exacerbations and remissions throughout life are the usual course of the disease.

Therapy is most reasonably directed against infection, which in the natural disease plays an important role. Local and systemic antibiotics, and careful hygiene are of great value. Systemic anti-inflammatory steroids are also effective in high doses, but are usually not indicated because of the relative mildness of the disease. Topical steroids are often useful.

Hailey-Hailey disease is sometimes confused with Darier's disease, which may show blisters and crusts clinically and acantholysis histologically.

References

Bean, S. F., Good, R. A., and Windhorst, D. B. Bullous pemphigoid in an 11-year-old boy. Arch. Derm., 102: 205, 1970.

Jordan, R. E., Bean, S. F., Triftshause, C. T., and Winkelmann, R. K. Childhood bullous dermatitis herpetiformis. Negative immunofluorescent tests. Arch. Derm., 101:629, 1970.

Lever, W. Pemphigus and Pemphigoid. Springfield, Ill., Charles C Thomas, Publ., 1965.

MacVicar, D. N., Graham, J. H., and Burgoon, C. F. Dermatitis herpetiformis, erythema multiforme, and bullous pemphigoid: A comparative histopathological and histochemical study. J. Invest. Derm., 41:289, 1963.

Melish, M. E., and Glasgow, L. A. The staphylococcal

scalded-skin syndrome. Development of an experimental model. New Eng. J. Med., 282:1114, 1970.

Pearson, R. W. Studies on the pathogenesis of epidermolysis bullosa. J. Invest. Derm., 39:551, 1962.

Schroeter, A., Sams, W. M., Jr., and Jordan, R. E. Immunofluorescent studies of pemphigus foliaceus in a child. Arch. Derm., 100:736, 1969.

Silver, H. F. Epidermolysis bullosa hereditaria "letalis." Report of a case surviving for two and a half years. Arch. Dis. Child., 32:216, 1957.

26.5
INFECTIONS OF THE SKIN

JOSEPH W. BURNETT

Bacterial Infections
(Pyoderma)

Streptococcal and Staphylococcal Infections

The pyodermas are a family of cutaneous infections caused primarily by *Staphylococcus aureus* and/or Group A beta hemolytic streptococci. They are classified according to their location within the skin (Fig. 36). Impetigo, the most superficial infection, involves the upper epidermis. In ecthyma, the lower epidermis and dermis are the sites of infection. Folliculitis is a superficial infection of the hair follicle, whereas furunculosis is an infection of the deeper regions of the follicle. In cellulitis the organisms invade both the dermis and subcutaneous tissues.

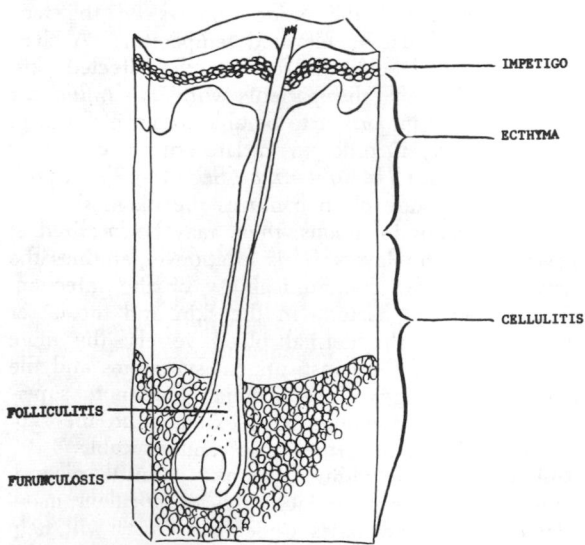

Fig. 36. The location of various pyodermas within the skin.

ETIOLOGY. Both group A beta hemolytic streptococci and staphylococci can be cultured from skin underneath most impetigo lesions. Group A beta hemolytic streptococci can be recovered from these sites in about one-half of patients, and an additional 15 percent will have serologic evidence of a recent streptococcal infection. One-third of those individuals having a streptococcus on their skin will also be nasopharyngeal carriers of the same organism. *Staphylococcus aureus* can be isolated from impetigo lesions in approximately 60 percent of the patients. These figures substantiate the futility of attempting to predict clinically whether an impetiginous lesion is caused by a streptococcus or a staphylococcus.

Pyodermas, superimposed on other dermatologic diseases, are also mixed infections caused by the Group A beta hemolytic streptococcus and *Staphylococcus aureus*. Ninety-three percent of these cases with secondarily infected eruptions have either serologic or cultural evidence of streptococcal disease, and *Staphylococcus aureus* can be recovered from the skin culture in approximately 90 percent of the same patients.

Because the lesions of folliculitis and furunculosis appear to be sharply circumscribed abscesses, they have been thought to be caused only by the staphylococcus. However, in a few instances, Group A beta hemolytic streptococci have also been recovered from purulent material in these lesions.

The deepest cutaneous infection, cellulitis, involves the dermis and subcutaneous tissues. This disease usually is caused by either the streptococcus or the staphylococcus rather than by a combination of the two. The strains of microorganisms causing pyodermas are different from those usually producing respiratory disease. In addition there may be concurrent infections due to multiple strains of the same bacterium.

INCIDENCE AND EPIDEMIOLOGY. Pyodermas are an extremely common group of diseases. Their epidemiology depends upon the nature of the bacterial pathogen, the level of the infection within the skin, and the presence or absence of bacterial infection in other regions of the body. These diseases may be spread by direct contact of susceptible individuals with either purulent material or crusts from infected lesions.

PATHOLOGY AND PATHOGENESIS. The pyodermas produce an acute inflammatory reaction in the skin. In impetigo this reaction occurs in the upper epidermis beneath the horny layer, where a vesicle containing bacteria, polymorphonuclear cells, and exudative fluid is formed. Later, the vesicle ruptures and a crust containing fibrin and leucocytes lies directly on the prickle cell layer. A similar inflammatory infiltration appears in the lower epidermis and upper dermis in ecthyma, around the hair follicle in folliculitis and furunculosis, and in the dermis and subcutaneous tissues in cellulitis.

Because streptococci and staphylococci are ubiq-

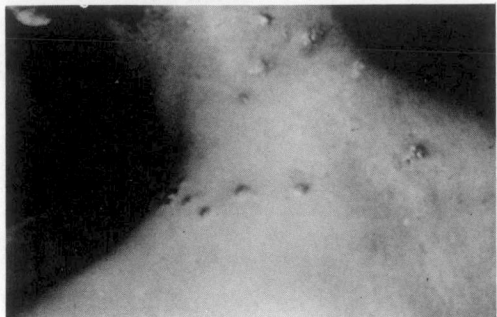

Fig. 37. Staphylococcal impetigo.

uitous, infection often occurs after trauma, which provides a foothold in the skin for the organism.

CLINICAL MANIFESTATIONS. The clinical appearance of pyodermas varies according to the location of infection in the skin. The initial lesion of *impetigo,* a vesicle, is rarely seen; however, when vesicles do appear ("bullous impetigo"), they are multiple, discrete, whitish yellow, and may or may not have a thick wall. Bullous lesions in impetigo caused by staphylococci are frequent (Fig. 37). In streptococcal impetigo or in patients whose lesions are due to a mixed streptococcal and stpahylococcal infection, the vesicles have usually ruptured, leaving a raw erythematous base covered with a yellow or honey-colored crust, the hallmark of the disease (Fig. 38). Although fever and leucocytosis are not usual, temperatures of 37.5 to 38.0° C (99.5 to 100.4° F) may be recorded. Regional lymphadenopathy can be detected in the majority of patients, especially those with streptococcal infections.

Ecthyma, an infection localized to the upper dermis and characterized by thick brown or black crusts covering raw, erythematous bases, is bacteriologically similar to impetigo and should be regarded as the same disease situated in a deeper plane of the skin.

One of the most common pyodermas occurs when preexisting dermatologic eruptions become secondarily infected (Fig. 39). In these cases the underlying eruption becomes erythematous and is covered with a purulent exudate.

Although yellow pustules surround hair follicles in both *folliculitis* and *furunculosis,* erythema, pain, and edema of the surrounding skin occur only in the lesions of furunculosis, where the focus of infection is deeper. Chronic furunculosis may be an initial symptom of underlying diabetes, lymphoma, or agammaglobulinemia; however, the vast majority of cases occur in otherwise healthy individuals. Repeated phage typing of organisms from lesions of patients with furunculosis reveals that the same type of bacterium may be recovered from different furuncles on the same individual for prolonged periods of time.

Cellulitis may appear anywhere on the body,

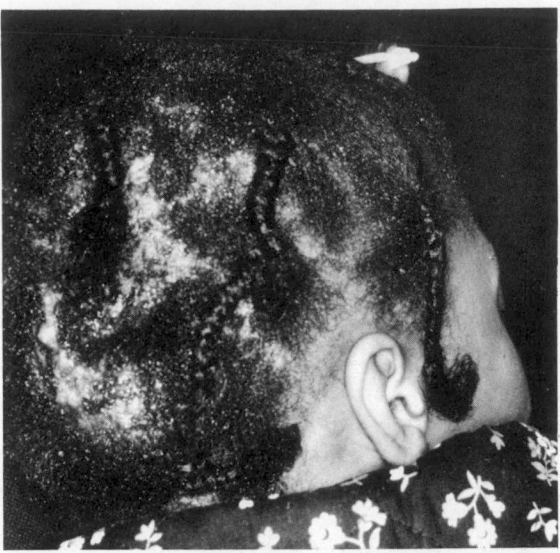

Fig. 38. Impetigo. Mixed streptococcal and staphylococcal infection of the scalp associated with temporary hair loss.

although the extremities, face, and regions around wounds are areas of predilection. Clinically, the affected skin is warm, erythematous, tender, edematous, and indurated. The patients usually have fever, malaise, and regional lymphadenopathy. The erythematous lesions of *erysipelas* are further characterized by rapidly advancing, well-demarcated borders. Occasionally vesicles or bullae may be present. Later, the lesions turn brown in color, and finally desquamate.

Cellulitis due to *Haemophilus influenzae* should be considered in children between 6 months and 2 years of age if the lesion appears on the face and the child has an elevated temperature. A characteristic purple color is seen in the affected skin in about half of the patients with *H. influenzae* cellulitis. It is important to be able to make the diagnosis promptly in order to initiate antibiotic therapy effective against *H. influenzae* (Sec. 14.18). A positive blood culture often confirms the diagnosis.

Cutaneous infections, then, may be localized at several different layers. This location determines the severity and the communicability of the infection. The deeper the bacteria in the skin and the closer they reside to the dermal blood vessels, the more marked will be the constitutional symptoms and the greater the danger of septicemia. The more superficial bacterial infections have exudates on the skin surface and are therefore more communicable.

DIAGNOSIS. In addition to the clinical picture, gram-stained smears and cultures of purulent material or of the raw bases under the crusts will help confirm the diagnosis and determine the appropriate antibiotic by in vitro sensitivity tests. Inocula for cul-

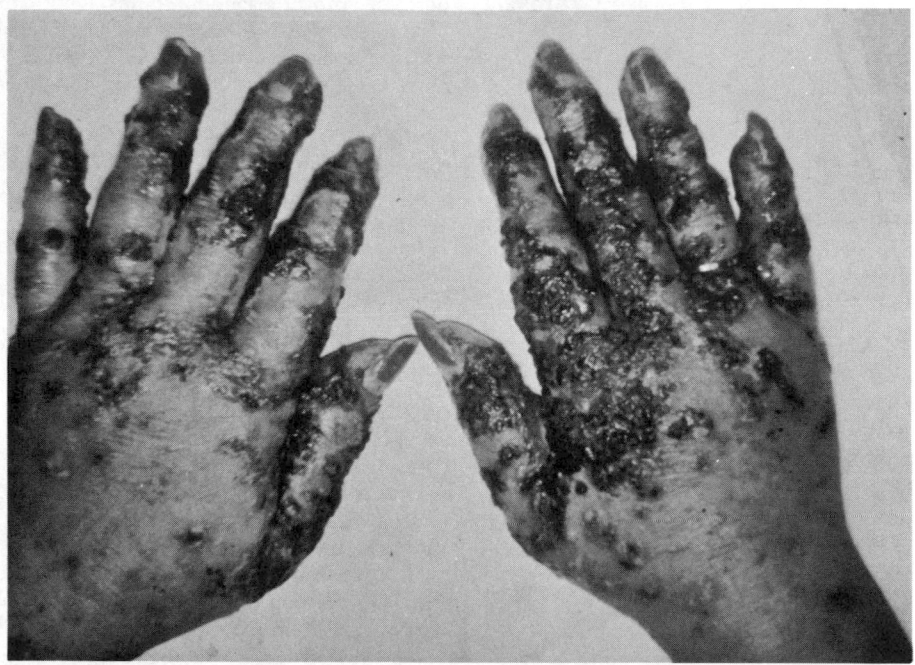

Fig. 39. Pyoderma. Superinfection of preexisting hand dermatitis.

tures in cases of cellulitis may be obtained by injecting and withdrawing sterile saline into the lesions. Serial antistreptolysin O titers are often useful in cases of suspected streptococcal infections.

DIFFERENTIAL DIAGNOSIS. Impetigo on the facial skin may be differentiated from herpes simplex by a gram smear. Cellulitis occurring on the malar region of the face may be confused with lupus erythematosus. Infected acne cysts may be misdiagnosed as simple furunculosis.

TREATMENT. In order to evaluate therapy, the natural course of these diseases must be appreciated. The bacteriologic data show that all pyodermas should be considered as mixed infections caused by both Group A beta hemolytic streptococcus and *Staphylococcus aureus.* Staphylococcal infections usually isolate themselves and may heal spontaneously. In some instances, especially in young infants, a septicemia may result, so that prompt and vigorous treatment is especially important in this age group. The course of these infections is often not so acute. Streptococcal infections tend to progress more rapidly, and early treatment is always important.

In addition to direct complications, noninfectious streptococcal sequelae must be considered. Although there is no conclusive proof that cutaneous infections cause rheumatic fever, there is evidence that streptococcal pyodermas may produce glomerulonephritis. The principles governing systemic antibiotic treatment of streptococcal and staphylococcal infections of the skin are the same as those concerning treatment of these infections elsewhere (Sec. 14.2).

Topical antibiotic preparations are not as dependable as systemic antibiotic medications in the treatment of impetigo. Because of the danger of inducing sensitivity by applying an antibiotic drug topically, the agent contained in such ointments should be one that is rarely used systemically. One popular topical antibiotic preparation contains both neomycin and bacitracin.

Scrubbing the lesions, compresses, or frequent soap baths are not sufficient therapy alone; however, simple aseptic incision and drainage may be all that is necessary for some cases of furunculosis or folliculitis. Isolation procedures, designed to prevent the spread of the infection to other individuals, should be enforced in cases where the lesions are either superficially located or draining purulent material. Family members of patients with streptococcal lesions should be examined and have throat cultures to detect carriers.

Therapy of chronic furunculosis is unsatisfactory. Staphylococcal vaccines have not been effective. An initial course of an antibiotic shown to be effective in vitro is the first step. Some experts advocate additional measures such as the institution of careful isolation practices, the application of bacitracin ointment to the nostrils, bathing with hexachlorophene soaps, and careful laundering. Techniques designed to replace virulent nasopharyngeal staphylococcal flora with relatively avirulent forms are still experimental.

Erythrasma

Erythrasma is an asymptomatic cutaneous disease appearing in the toewebs, axilla, and inguinal regions. **ETIOLOGY.** The etiologic agent of erythrasma (*Nocardia minutissima*), formerly regarded as a fungus, is now known to be a gram-positive bacillus (a Corynebacterium).

INCIDENCE AND EPIDEMIOLOGY. Erythrasma of the toewebs occurs in approximately 25 percent of the population. Axillary and pubic erythrasma is not uncommon. Generalized cutaneous erythrasma, however, is present mostly in tropical and subtropical areas. The mode of transmission is unknown.

PATHOLOGY. In erythrasma there is a mild inflammatory reaction involving only the superficial epidermis.

CLINICAL MANIFESTATIONS. The characteristic lesions of this disease include the following: scaling, fissuration, maceration of the toewebs, and dry, brown, slightly scaly, irregular, well-demarcated patches in the axillary, inguinal, submammary, and intergluteal areas. Coral red fluorescence, presumably due to porphyrins produced by these organisms, may be seen on Wood's light examination.

DIAGNOSIS. The diagnosis must be made clinically. Bacillary and coccoid forms are seen on microscopic examination of scrapings from the lesions.

Tinea pedis and various pigmentary disorders are the most common diseases confused with erythrasma.

TREATMENT. Topical salicylic acid ointment is the therapy of choice. Although the erythrasma organism is sensitive to erythromycin as well as other antibiotics, these drugs are usually not necessary to effect a cure. Some antibacterial bar soaps are effective in the prophylaxis and control of this disease.

Viral Infections

Herpes Zoster

Herpes zoster and chickenpox are infections caused by varicella-zoster (V-Z) virus, chickenpox being caused by an individual's initial exposure to this agent. The pathogenesis of herpes zoster is not known. Most experts favor the theory that zoster is caused by a reactivation of a latent varicella virus, although the possibility of reinfection cannot be excluded.

ETIOLOGY. The viruses isolated from patients with zoster and varicella are regarded as the same agent because of similarities in ultramicroscopic morphology, tissue culture propagation, and antigenic cross-reactivity. The virus of varicella-zoster is classified in the herpes virus group. It measures 200 mg in diameter, and DNA is its predominant nucleoprotein. The virus

has been isolated from both vesicular and cerebrospinal fluid. Man is the only natural or experimental host. In vitro propagation of this agent can be readily performed in tissue culture systems prepared from a number of human tissues. The highest titers to date have been obtained in primary human thyroid cell cultures.

INCIDENCE AND EPIDEMIOLOGY. Zoster occurs sporadically at any time of year. The highest age incidence of the disease is between 40 and 70 years, although cases frequently appear at an earlier age. Approximately 50 percent of the population will suffer an attack of zoster before age 75. Zoster is unusual in infants, although it has been reported in a child 3½ months of age.

Transmission of the disease is thought to occur by direct contact of susceptible individuals with infected crusts or vesicle fluids. Zoster patients are contagious for at least five to seven days after the appearance of the vesicles, since virus can be isolated from the lesions during that period. Outbreaks of varicella have been initiated by exposure of susceptible persons to zoster patients. The absence of virus from the nasopharynx and the fact that some zoster lesions are covered by clothing might explain why zoster is not so contagious as varicella.

A history of recent exposure to either zoster or varicella is usually not obtained, a finding reinforcing the concept of latent virus reactivation. Mechanical and thermal trauma have been cited as factors capable of initiating zoster attacks. The appearance of zoster in the older age groups and in patients with leukemia or lymphoma may be explained by a decrease in antiviral antibody.

PATHOLOGY AND PATHOGENESIS. The initial cytologic changes in zoster are margination of the nuclear chromatin and formation of an intranuclear inclusion body. An intraepidermal vesicle appears after the cells of the lower epidermal layers undergo balloon degeneration. A polymorphonuclear cell infiltration occurs in the corium, particularly around the blood vessels. Giant cells are seen in both the infected tissues and vesicular fluid. Similar cytologic changes may be visible in the cells of the dorsal root ganglion corresponding to the dermatome of zoster involvement. Likewise, involvement of anterior horn cells of brain tissue has been reported.

CLINICAL MANIFESTATIONS. Zoster produces a peripheral neuritis and a vesicular eruption. The latter is characterized by grouped vesicles on an erythematous base located in the distribution of the infected spinal or cranial sensory nerves (Fig. 40). Some of the vesicles may be umbilicated. Within a few days the vesicles range from a clear to a white or yellow color as cells and detritus accumulate within the vesicular fluid. Hemorrhagic vesicles appear in rare instances and are not necessarily an ominous sign. When the vesicles rupture, a yellow crust or superficial ulcer remains. Some lesions later become gangrenous and necrotic, and assume a "punched-out"

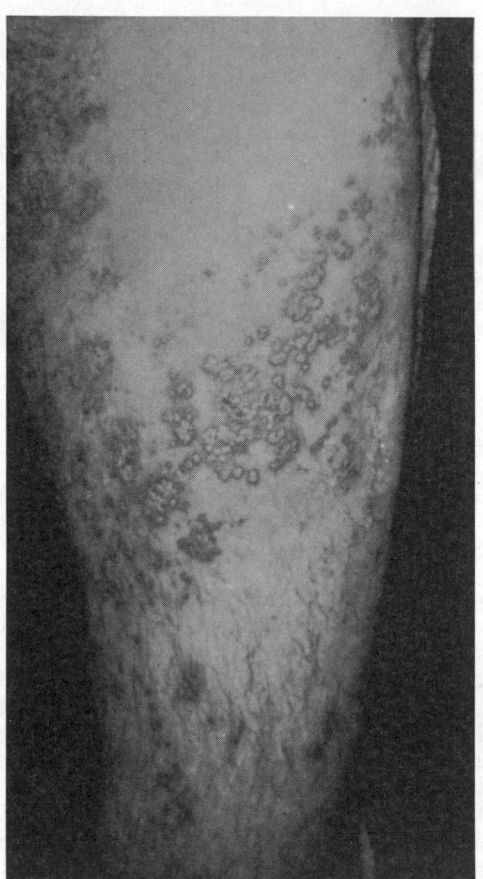

Fig. 40. Herpes zoster. Grouped vesicle restricted in location to a few contiguous dermatomes.

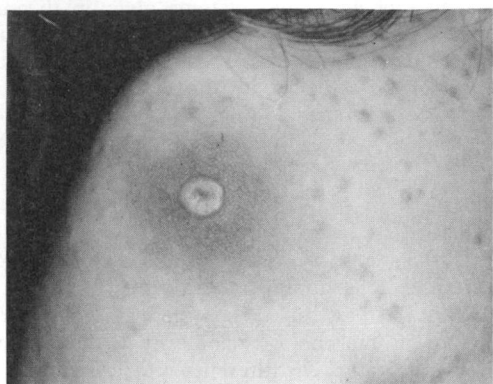

Fig. 41. Primary vaccinia. Umbilicated pustulo vesicle with surrounding erythema in a 17-month-old girl. Other papules on shoulder are probably an allergic reaction to vaccinia.

appearance. Regional lymphadenopathy, fever, and constitutional symptoms may accompany the eruption. Nerve root pain may precede, accompany, or follow the eruption; there is no correlation between the severity of the cutaneous lesion and the intensity of the pain.

Zoster may affect any area of the body. The thoracic area is involved in more than 50 percent of cases, followed by the cervical, trigeminal, and lumbar areas in that order. Vesicular lesions on the mucous membrane of the mouth and eye appear in association with cutaneous lesions in that dermatome. Vesicles located on the face between the tip of the nose and the inner canthus signify involvement of the nasociliary nerve and possibly the cornea. Trigeminal zoster is not an uncommon complication of surgery performed on the gasserian ganglion. Zoster infection of the eye is accompanied by keratoconjunctivitis, scleritis, iridocyclitis, corneal ulceration, and scarring.

The neurologic symptoms include pain, loss of sensation, and motor weakness in the involved dermatome. Approximately 25 percent of the patients have a slightly elevated protein concentration or pleocy-

tosis in their cerebrospinal fluid. Autonomic motor symptoms such as ileus or bladder paralysis have been found in cases of zoster involving the lumbosacral dermatomes. Encephalitis has been reported, usually after cases of ophthalmic zoster. Persistent or severe pain during the active disease is unusual in children. Postherpetic neuralgia is rare in childhood.

One interesting type of herpes zoster is the generalized form. In these patients the eruption is initially restricted to a few dermatomes, but within a few days scattered single vesicles appear elsewhere on the body. Pulmonary infiltrates, presumably zoster pneumonitis, are present in some cases. Although a significant number of adult patients have an underlying lymphoma or other immunologic abnormality, this relationship has not been striking in children.

DIAGNOSIS. The diagnosis of zoster may be aided by examination of a smear of vesicle fluid for giant cells and intranuclear inclusion bodies. Cultures of the vesicle fluid are the only conclusive diagnostic test. The demonstration of intranuclear inclusion bodies by biopsy is usually not necessary, but may be done to exclude smallpox infections, which are characterized by intracytoplasmic inclusions. Serologic tests for zoster are not yet generally available.

DIFFERENTIAL DIAGNOSIS. Smallpox may be differentiated from generalized zoster by physical examination, history, biopsy, and a smear of vesicular fluid. Eczema herpeticum may be confused with generalized zoster. Patients with only neuralgia before the eruption may be thought to have pleurisy or peritonitis. Rickettsialpox may be differentiated from early zoster by the appearance of an initial bite, the presence of fever before the rash, the character of the eruption, and by a complement fixation test. For discussion of vaccinia (Fig. 41) see Section 14.40.

TREATMENT. No definitive therapy is available for this disease. Symptomatic relief may be obtained with analgesics. Topical therapy is not effective. Because most zoster patients develop this disease in spite of the presence of antibodies, gamma globulin theoretically should be without benefit. Prevention of varicella after exposure of zoster patients to susceptible persons may be achieved by the prompt administration of zoster-immune globulin.

Molluscum Contagiosum

Molluscum contagiosum is a viral disease of the skin characterized by an umbilicated papule.

ETIOLOGY. Molluscum is classified as a pox virus because of its morphologic similarity with other viruses of that group. On ultramicroscopic examination molluscum particles have a dumbbell-shaped core with two surrounding envelopes. Its diameters have been estimated to be 300 by 200 mμ. Man is the only natural or experimental host. Extracts of ground molluscum lesions inoculated into cell cultures prepared from various primate tissues produce a cytotoxic reaction within 48 hours. In some cell cultures the virus is unable to replicate after successfully entering the cell. Lesions in the skin of human volunteers have been produced within two to seven weeks by subcutaneous inoculation of molluscum suspensions. Although infectious molluscum virus cannot be propagated in vitro, the production of interferon has been demonstrated in the laboratory.

INCIDENCE AND EPIDEMIOLOGY. Molluscum lesions may appear at any age, but most occur in childhood. Epidemics have been reported from institutions caring for mentally retarded children and in the populations of various Pacific islands. It is reasonable to conclude that the virus spreads by direct contact, although the exact source in most cases is unknown. Autoinoculation is common.

PATHOLOGY AND PATHOGENESIS. The well-demarcated molluscum lesion is pear-shaped and has its base in the upper dermis. As the infected cells move upward toward the center of the lesion, they become more distorted. The first changes consist of an appearance of electron dense intranuclear particles and later intracellular DNA bodies. The nucleus becomes compressed and marginated as the islands of DNA material, which contain virus, enlarge and coalesce to form inclusion bodies. The surrounding epidermis shows considerable acanthosis.

CLINICAL MANIFESTATIONS. The lesions are discrete, pearly gray, 1 to 5 mm, umbilicated papules which appear anywhere on the skin (Fig. 42) or the conjunctiva. A reactive keratitis or conjunctivitis may accompany lesions at the latter site. Usually there is no inflammation surrounding these lesions, unless they are traumatized or secondarily infected. Healing occurs without scarring in lesions free from bacterial superinfection.

DIAGNOSIS. The three best diagnostic procedures are staining smears of the expressed molluscum body, examining a biopsy specimen, or inoculating a mol-

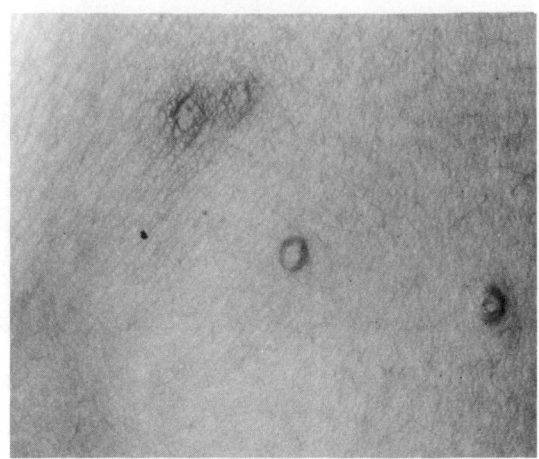

Fig. 42. Molluscum contagiosum. Typical lesions on the back of a 17-year-old boy. The umbilicated papule is produced by a virus resembling poxvirus.

luscum suspension into cell cultures in order to demonstrate the cytotoxic reaction.

The only other disease characterized by an umbilicated papule is lichen planus, which can be differentiated by its flexural distribution and purplish color. Molluscum has been confused with chickenpox, warts, papillomas, epitheliomas, furunculosis, and pyoderma.

TREATMENT. The easiest form of treatment is removal of the lesions with a sharp curette, under aseptic technique. Anesthesia is usually not necessary. Care must be taken to destroy all the lesions to prevent autoinoculation.

Limited studies suggest that isatin, a thiosemicarbazine, may be effective in decreasing spread of the virus to susceptible persons during epidemics.

Warts
(Verrucae)

Warts are a common viral disease characterized by the appearance of flesh-colored, hyperplastic papules on the skin.

ETIOLOGY. Wart virus has been classified as a papova virus with a diameter calculated to be 38 mμ. This agent is a DNA virus. Filtered wart extracts injected into the skin of volunteers have produced lesions at the inoculation site after one to six months. In vitro propagation of wart virus has not yet been satisfactorily accomplished. No serologic procedures are available.

INCIDENCE AND EPIDEMIOLOGY. Warts are one of the most common human dermatologic diseases; they are particularly prevalent in childhood but may occur at any age. The mode of transmission is unknown, but thought to be due to direct contact. Autoinoculation can occur.

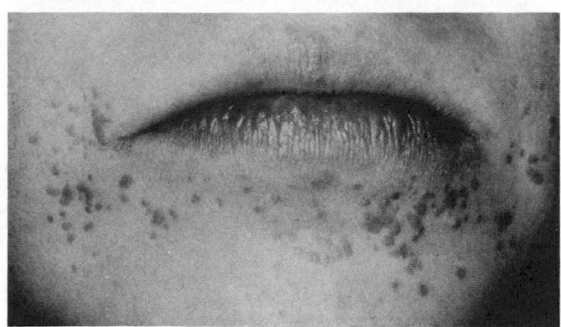

Fig. 43. Flat warts (verruca plana). These warts often occur on the face and are thought to be caused by the same virus responsible for common warts (verruca vulgaris). Flat warts are usually skin-colored or slightly hyperpigmented.

PATHOLOGY. The wart is a well-delineated hyperplastic papule extending in depth to the basal layer. There are acanthosis, parakeratosis, and hyperkeratosis within the lesion. The involved cells exhibit a progression of cellular alterations as they advance upward toward the surface. Viral packets have been discovered in both the cytoplasm and the nucleus. The "dots" grossly visible on the top of warts represent thrombosed capillaries in the long thin dermal papillae which extend high into the lesion.

CLINICAL MANIFESTATIONS. Warts are flesh-colored papules which may assume several morphologic types. Plantar and palmar warts are elevated or flat lesions which interrupt the natural skin lines and may at times be painful. Close examination may reveal punctate dots scattered over the surface. Filiform warts, commonly seen on the face and neck, are small fingerlike excrescences which protrude 1 to 10 mm above the skin surface. Flat warts are discrete, multiple, flesh-colored or slightly brown, stippled papules measuring 2 to 5 mm in diameter. These lesions appear commonly on the face or extensor arm surfaces (Fig. 43). Common warts, verrucae vulgaris, appear predominantly on the dorsal surface of the hands or periungual regions but may be seen anywhere. They measure 3 to 10 mm in diameter, are gray, brown, or flesh-colored, and are definitely elevated (Fig. 44). "Venereal" warts, verrucae accuminatae, occur on the genital regions; they are flesh-colored, wet, cauliflower papules which may be single or confluent (Fig. 45).

DIAGNOSIS. The histologic picture of warts is pathognomonic.

A plantar wart which obliterates the normal skin lines may be differentiated from a callus which does not. Periungual fibromas in tuberous sclerosis may be misdiagnosed as warts. "Venereal" warts must be differentiated from the flat, raw condyloma lata by dark field examination and by the absence of a positive serology for syphilis. Flat warts may be misdiagnosed as acne, seborrheic keratoses, epidermal nevi, or freckles.

TREATMENT. Warts are capricious in their behavior; some resolve spontaneously within a few months, but others will persist for prolonged periods of time. Cures by suggestion or hypnosis have been reported.

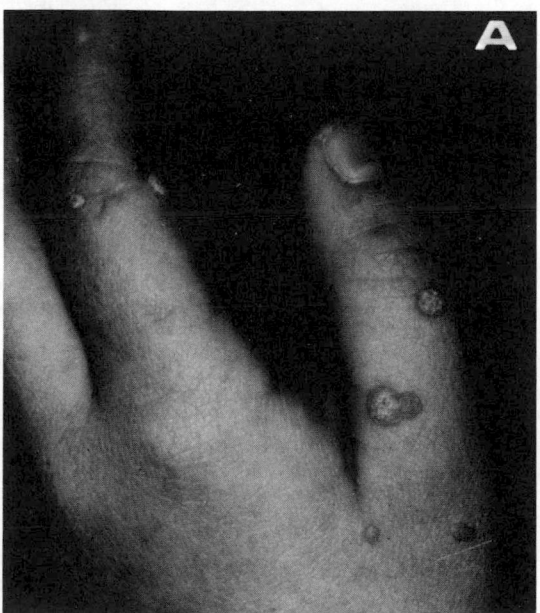
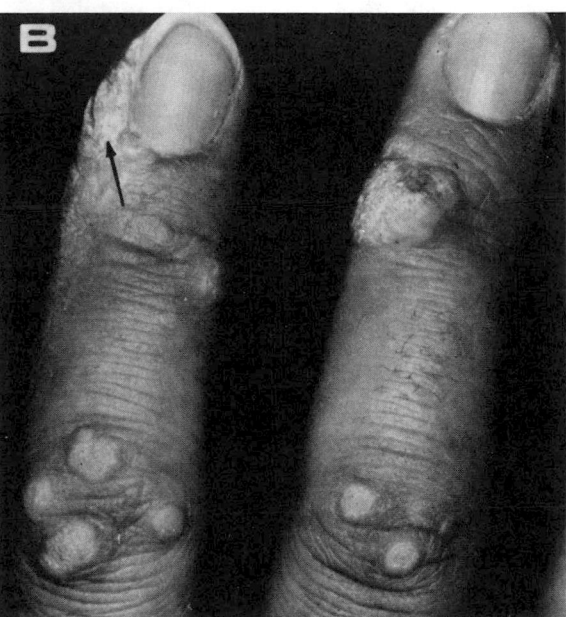

Fig. 44. Verruca vulgaris. A. Common viral warts eventually resolve spontaneously. When they occur in pressure areas, as on the sole of the foot (plantar wart), treatment is necessary. B. Warts in periungual location (arrow) sometimes produce deformity of the nail and are difficult to treat.

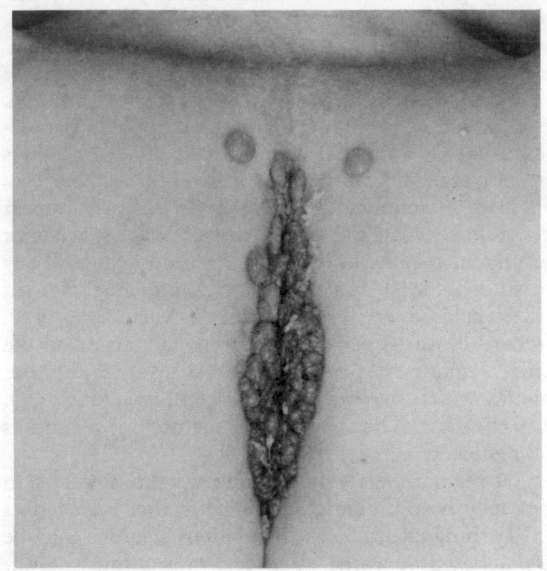

Fig. 45. Condyloma acuminatum. Perianal warts in 2-year-old boy. These genital or perianal warts are thought to be caused by the virus responsible for common warts.

In spite of this, the only satisfactory treatments for warts are destructive measures. For verruca vulgaris the topical application of strong acids such as 90 percent trichloroacetic acid is used, although application of a plaster containing 40 percent salicylic acid is preferable in children because the procedure is relatively painless. Electrodesiccation, carbon dioxide snow, and liquid nitrogen are useful but painful. The treatment of choice for plantar warts is repeated applications of the salicylic acid plaster, and for venereal warts topical podophyllin (25 percent solution in benzoin). Twelve percent salicylic acid in collodion applied twice daily may be effective against flat warts. The frequency of application for all keratolytic or acid treatments should be determined after the reaction of the patient to one application has been observed. X-ray therapy or surgical excision should not be used. Recurrences are common regardless of the therapeutic method.

Fungal Infections

Many species of fungi are pathogenic to humans. The cutaneous infections caused by these organisms are commonly classified according to the depth of the pathologic process: ultrasuperficial, cutaneous, intermediate, and subcutaneous. Those fungi which cause primary subcutaneous lesions may produce a systemic infection, and conversely, systemic fungal infections may also cause cutaneous or subcutaneous lesions. Other classification schemes are based on the species of fungus, the anatomic sites of predilection, or the morphology of the lesion. It is necessary to identify the species of invading organism as closely as possible in order to direct specific therapy and proper epidemiologic procedures.

ETIOLOGY AND CLINICAL MANIFESTATIONS. *Ultra-Superficial Fungi.* These organisms invade only the superficial skin, causing no symptoms or inflammatory reactions. *Tinea versicolor* is the cutaneous infection produced by *Malassezia furfur.* Asymptomatic, superficial, fawn or tan-colored, finely scaled lesions appear on the upper thorax, neck, axilla, and groin. In Negroes or suntanned Caucasians these lesions are hypopigmented and, except for scaling, might be misdiagnosed as vitiligo. There is no surrounding reactive erythema. The lesions are often confluent. Fungus structures consisting of round, thick-walled, refractile spherical spores and straight or curved, short or long, mycelial elements are seen microscopically.

Cutaneous Fungal Infections. Cutaneous fungal infections are caused by the "ringworm fungi" (dermatophytes). These organisms are divided into three common genera based on morphologic differences in their asexual spores (macroconidia) as seen on culture mounts. Microsporum species attack hair and skin. Epidermophyton invades nails and skin. Trichophyton may produce diseases in all three structures.

Microsporum infections. Microsporum species (*canis, audouini,* and *gypseum*) are the most common causes of tinea capitis. These fungi are characterized by single, spindle-shaped, thick-walled, rough macroconidia, and small microconidia. The latter are usually single except in the case of *M. gypseum,* where grouping may be present. The microspora are naturally found in soil and on human or animal hosts. Although *M. canis* or *gypseum* may be transmitted to man from either young animals or other humans, *M. audouini* is probably transmitted only from human to human. Hairs infected with microsporum species have mycelia within the hair shaft but spores on the hair surface (ectothrix). Microsporum infections produce well-demarcated, gray patches of partial alopecia and scaling (Fig. 46). A surrounding inflammatory reaction is more often seen in *M. gypseum* or *canis* infections than in those caused by *M. audouini.* One manifestation of the inflammatory reaction, kerion celsi, occurs after the infection has been present a few weeks. Kerions are large, localized, single or multiple, baggy, edematous lesions of the scalp containing considerable amounts of pus (Fig. 47). The hair in this region is matted to the scalp by exudate. These purulent lesions are deeper than the ordinary scaly patches and are thought to represent an immune reaction of the host to the fungi. They are regarded as a favorable sign. Slow spontaneous resolution will follow unless secondary bacterial infections intervene. Microsporum infections of

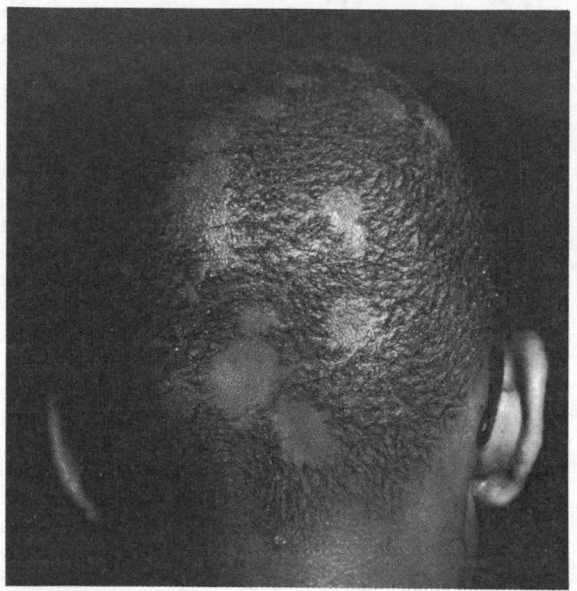

Fig. 46. Tinea capitis.

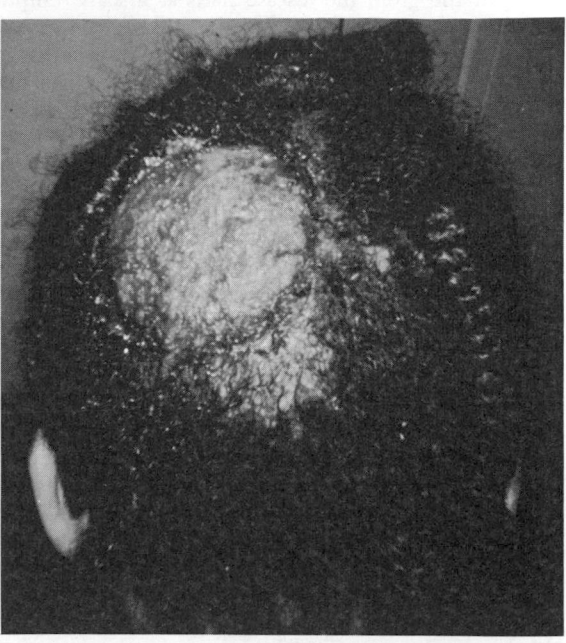

Fig. 47. Kerion celsi. A circumscribed, boggy, edematous inflammatory reaction to a fungus infection of the scalp.

the glabrous skin are characterized by oval patches with central scaling and a peripheral ring or vesicles (Fig. 48). The central scaly zone may heal as the peripheral area enlarges. These lesions are clinically indistinguishable from other causes of tinea corporis or tinea circinata. Adults are relatively resistant to these infections.

Epidermophyton infections. The genus *Epidermophyton* contains only one species, *Epider-*

mophyton floccosum. This organism, which has club-shaped, thin-walled, two- to five-celled macroconidia, is found on humans and in the soil. Epidermophyton infects nails and skin. It is one of the common causes of tinea pedis (athlete's foot) or tinea cruris. The lesions in tinea pedis commonly begin in the fourth toeweb with maceration and fissuring. Other toewebs are soon involved as the eruption spreads over the

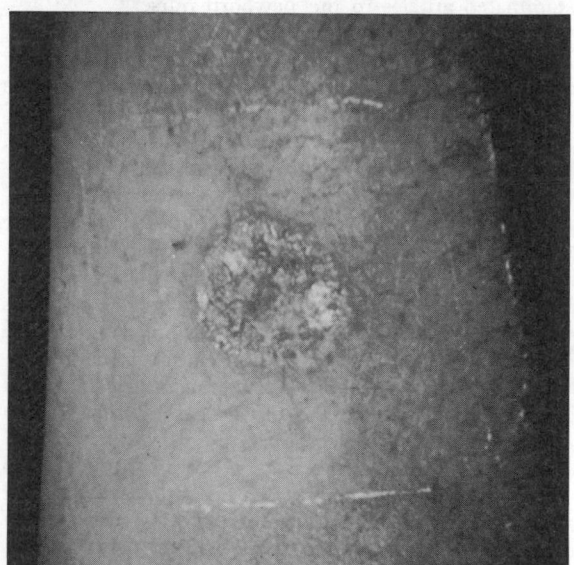

Fig. 48. Tinea circinata. A clearing central scaly area surrounded by a peripheral ring of vesicles.

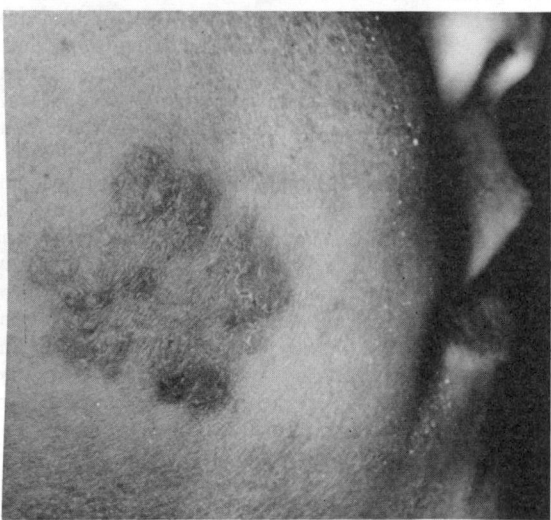

Fig. 49. Trichophyton rubrum infection on the face of a healthy 5-year-old boy.

foot. In the groin the disease starts as a scaly, elliptic patch on the inner thigh. The inguinal fold is spared initially, but within a few weeks the eruption may spread, involving both the fold and pubic area. Epidermophyton lesions may or may not exhibit clearing in the center as the patch enlarges. Later, smaller, erythematous, satellite lesions appear around the larger, primary sites. Although not common, onychomycosis and tinea pedis can be produced by this organism.

Trichophyton infections. The genus *Trichophyton* contains six important species which have smooth, thin-walled, two- to ten-celled, rounded macroconidia.

Trichophyton rubrum invades nails and epidermis, rarely hair. On the glabrous skin this organism causes dull, red, thick, scaly lesions without surrounding erythema or inflammation (Fig. 49). Complete or partial clearing of the center of the lesion is frequent except in those lesions on the palm and sole. Unilateral involvement of a palm or sole is commonly seen. Unusual skin lesions produced by this organism include unilateral papulosquamous eruptions or granulomatous lesions of the lower leg ("Majocchi-like" granulomas). *T. rubrum* may produce generalized cutaneous eruptions, some with bizarre patterns, in chronically ill patients.

Trichophyton mentagrophytes is responsible for many cases of tinea pedis and onychomycosis of the toenails. Initially the nail becomes yellow or white at the distal margin as detritus and thickened white tissue accumulate underneath. Later the process advances proximally; grooves or ridges appear on the nail plate, and finally the nail may drop off. As long as the nailbed remains free of scar, regeneration will occur. *T. mentagrophytes* may produce tinea capitis and kerion celsi. Infections due to this organism are not commonly seen in prepubertal children.

Trichophyton verrucosum, which can be acquired from cattle, horses, mice, rabbits, or man, produces an inflammatory infection. The edematous, erythematous patches with elevated borders may contain vesicles or pustules. Kerion celsi is a common complication.

T. tonsurans is a cosmopolitan fungus causing infections of the hair, skin, and nails. Because the spores of this organism are located inside the hair shaft (endothrix), the involved hairs fragment easily. These infections, known as "black dot" ringworm, appear as discrete, scattered, scaly patches containing dark stubs which remain after fragmentation of the hair. *T. tonsurans* may produce circinate, gyrate, papulosquamous eruptions, mild seborrheic-like dermatitis, perifolliculitis, folliculitis, onychomycosis, and kerion.

In this country *T. violaceum* and *schoenleini* infections have been reported from areas of Kentucky and West Virginia and in immigrants. The former organism produces primarily a "black dot" ringworm.

T. schoenleini infections ("favus") involve the scalp and are characterized by crusted, yellow lesions with upward convexity (scutula). Underneath the scutula is an erythematous base having a "mousy" odor. Because favus infections produce scarring, permanent alopecia is a common complication.

Dermatophytids are eruptions due to hypersensitivity of the host to invading fungi. These lesions appear at a site distant to the primary fungal infection. They must fulfill the following criteria: the absence of fungi in the suspected eruption, a proved fungal infection elsewhere on the skin, a positive intracutaneous tricophyton test, resolution of the suspected eruption after treatment of the distant fungal infection, and the history of appearance of the suspected "id" eruption only after irritation or inflammation of the primary fungal site. An "id" may be vesicular, lichenoid, exfoliative, erythematous, papular, or follicular. One common vesicular "id," secondary to tinea pedis, appears on the sides of the fingers.

Intermediate Fungi. *Candida albicans* causes infections of the skin and mucous membrane. It may also form granulomas and produce a disseminated disease. This organism is the most common cause of an inflammatory paronychia and a white, macerated dermatitis in the fingerwebs (Fig. 50). A generalized, erythematous, papulosquamous eruption appears in rare instances, especially in patients with hypoparathyroidism or hypoadrenalism. Candidiasis of the mucous membranes (thrush) is characterized by white patches surrounded by erythema. Thrush is a common disease in newborns. There is a direct correlation between maternal monilial vaginitis and thrush in the newborn. The disease is presumably acquired from the birth canal or by contact with children or contaminated articles in the newborn nursery.

Monilial infections occur in the mouth, rectum, vagina, and esophagus, where they may cause local pain. *Candida albicans* can cause infections of the canthi, the margins of the lips, and the skin folds of the body in the axillary, inguinal, and gluteal areas. Candida infections of the glabrous skin are characterized by sharp margins, bright erythematous color, and the appearance of satellite lesions. The satellite lesions provide an easy means to differentiate candidiasis clinically from other forms of diaper rash.

Subcutaneous Fungi. *Sporotrichum schenkii* is a pathogenic fungus found naturally on living or dead vegetation. The disease, sporotrichosis, is cosmopolitan, occurs at all ages, and is transmitted from soil or vegetation to man. No proved case of man-to-man transfer has been recorded. Cases have been commonly seen after a thorn prick or in workers who have contact with hedges, barberry bushes, or peat moss. After an incubation period of approximately 3 to 12 weeks, the initial lesion appears. It is a freely movable, pink or purple, chancriform nodule which later ulcerates. Similar satellite lesions may appear along the path of lymphatic drainage. Painless re-

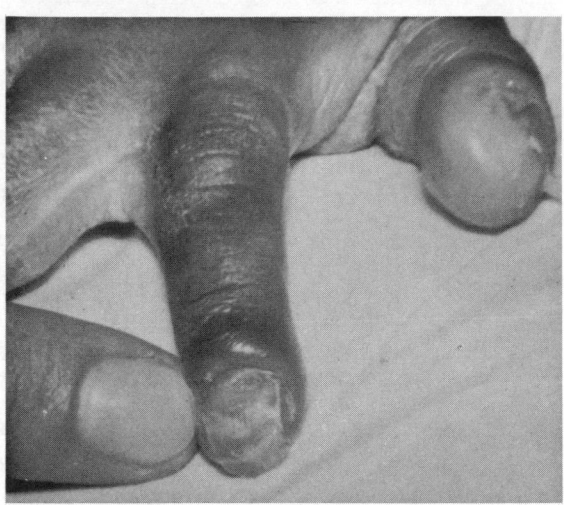

Fig. 50. Candidiasis. A macerating, fissuring dermatitis of the fingerweb and paronychia, with fungal involvement of the nail plate.

gional lymphadenopathy is present. In a few cases the lesions may become furuncular or verrucous. Similarly, a disseminated, nodular-ulcerative form of the disease has been reported.

DIAGNOSIS. All suspected fungal infections of the skin should be examined under ultraviolet light using the Wood's lamp. Blue-green fluorescence is present in eruptions due to *Microsporum audouini* and *canis* and in some lesions produced by *M. gypseum.*

Infected hairs or scrapings of the skin or nails in patients suspected of having fungal infections should be gently heated with 10 percent potassium hydroxide and examined microscopically. Specimens should be inoculated initially on Sabouraud's dextrose agar media at 25° C for four to six weeks. Once an agent has been isolated, subculturing on special media may be necessary for final identification.

In cases of suspected sporotrichosis, serologic tests and direct microscopic examination of human purulent material are not entirely dependable. The organism may be easily cultured at 25° C on blood agar or Sabouraud's dextrose agar media. Inoculation of infected material into rats or mice will produce peritonitis.

TREATMENT. The treatment of cutaneous fungal infections depends upon the species of invading organism and the depth of the pathology. All superficial and most cutaneous fungal infections can be treated primarily with keratolytic agents, 3 to 6 percent salicylic acid ointments, designed to "peel away" the infection. In special instances fungistatic preparations, such as diluted tincture of iodine, sulfur, short-chain fatty acids (undecylenic acid), tolnaftate, Castellani's paint, or Whitfield's ointment, may be used. These agents, with the exception of undecylenic acid, tolnaftate, and Whitfield's ointment, have the disadvantage of coloring the skin. For this reason salicylic acid is the main topical therapeutic preparation for these infections. Acute or exudative lesions should be initially treated with soaks or water compresses before applying keratolytic agents. Lesions superinfected with bacteria should be treated with antibiotics before antifungal therapy is initiated.

Tinea versicolor, one of the common ultrasuperficial fungal infections, responds well to tolnaftate or keratolytics such as salicylic acid ointments. Solutions of 20 percent aqueous sodium thiosulfate are also effective topically.

The cutaneous fungal infections also respond to systemically administered griseofulvin, one micronized tablet (500 mg) daily for three to five weeks. The side effects of griseofulvin include headache, gastrointestinal upsets, fatigue, insomnia, reversible proteinuria, transient and reversible leucopenia, and photosensitivity. Patients given griseofulvin for prolonged periods have been shown to have increased urinary and fecal excretion of porphyrins and porphyrin precursors. This metabolic abnormality disappears after discontinuation of the drug. Although there are no reports of patients receiving griseofulvin therapy developing photosensitivity characteristic of porphyria, it appears likely that such cases could occur. Since topical salicylic acid is inexpensive and free of side effect unless used in tremendous amounts, the use of griseofulvin should be restricted to the following clinical situations: onychomycosis, *T. rubrum* infections of the palms or soles, fungal infections involving a large proportion of the body surface, tinea capitis, or dermatophytoses unresponsive to topical therapy.

The intermediate and subcutaneous fungal infections can be treated with nystatin or amphotericin B. Oral moniliasis is best treated with nystatin, which is available in a suspension containing 100,000 units per ml. One ml is given by dropper four times a day. An ointment containing 100,000 units of nystatin per ml is effective in treating cutaneous candidiasis. When treating monilial diaper rash it is best to use the oral liquid as well as the local ointment, since oral lesions are often the initial source of infection. Generalized candidiasis is treated with systemic amphotericin B, since nystatin is not absorbed from the gastrointestinal tract and is not used in a parenteral form. Nystatin is effective only in candidiasis. Amphotericin B is used topically or parenterally for the other fungi discussed. If it is administered systemically, nephrotoxicity is a problem. Gentian violet solution is effective but discolors the skin and clothes. There is suggestive evidence that hot soaks are an effective addition to the therapeutic program in sporotrichosis; however, oral potassium iodide is the therapy of choice. Treatment should be continued for several weeks after clinical resolution of the lesion.

Parasitic Diseases

Swimmers' Itch

Swimmers' itch is a pruritic dermatitis produced by an allergic reaction to nonhuman *Schistosoma cercariae* that have penetrated the skin.

ETIOLOGY AND EPIDEMIOLOGY. The cercariae of nonhuman schistosomes are widely found in both fresh and salt water. Although the disease is probably worldwide, most reported cases are from the Great Lakes region, New England, Hawaii, and Florida.

The cercariae penetrate the skin on exposed parts of the body during or immediately after bathing. Since man is an abnormal host, the parasite remains in the skin unable to complete its life cycle.

PATHOLOGY AND PATHOGENESIS. The cutaneous eruption is thought to be due to the reaction of the human host to schistosome antigens; thus, repeated contact with the cercariae is necessary before the patient is sensitized sufficiently to become symptomatic.

Pathologic examination of biopsies from lesions of swimmers' itch reveals nonspecific chronic inflammatory changes.

CLINICAL MANIFESTATIONS. Pruritus and transient urticarial lesions appear within minutes after penetration of the cercariae. A few hours later macules may be seen which are soon replaced by papules with erythematous halos. In some instances pustular and exudative lesions may be present. The pruritus returns and becomes intensive on the second or third day. Excoriation and secondary bacterial infection are common complications. Usually spontaneous resolution is complete within two weeks.

DIAGNOSIS. The diagnosis is usually made by history and examination.

Differential Diagnosis. The other three important eruptions affecting sea bathers are cymothoidism or related conditions, seaweed dermatitis, and seabathers' eruption. The first, cymothoidism, occurs after bathing in shallow salt water and is characterized by nonpruritic hemorrhagic puncta on exposed parts of the body. Seaweed dermatitis is an eruption caused by irritation of the skin by salt-water algae; it is localized to the skin under the loose parts of the bathing suit; to date cases have been reported only from northeastern Hawaii. Seabathers' eruption is thought to be a contact dermatitis from an unknown allergen in salt water; it appears in intertriginous areas as well as on the skin under the bathing suit.

TREATMENT. Careful drying immediately after bathing is a good prophylactic measure. Antihistamines are effective in reducing pruritus, and topical emollients may provide symptomatic relief.

Creeping Eruption (*Larva Migrans*)

Creeping eruption is a disease caused by the invasion of nonhuman hookworm larvae into the human skin.

ETIOLOGY AND EPIDEMIOLOGY. The larvae of *Ancylostoma braziliense* and *A. caninum* (cat and dog hookworms) enter human skin after direct contact. These organisms are found in excreta of dogs or cats infected with the adult worms. The highest incidence of the disease is in the southeastern United States where sandy soil and warm climate provide favorable conditions for the organism. Transmission is thought to occur by direct contact of the larva and the skin.

PATHOLOGY AND PATHOGENESIS. Most of the dermal tissue reaction present in a biopsy specimen has been attributed to host hypersensitivity. However, in rare instances larvae may be found in the lower epidermis.

CLINICAL MANIFESTATIONS. The initial lesion, an erythematous papule, forms at the site of entry. Within two to three days the lesion becomes vesicular, and an erythematous, serpentine epidermal tunnel appears immediately behind the migrating larvae. As old tunnels heal, new ones are made. The eruption is present as long as the larvae remain viable, a period of days to several weeks. Approximately half of the patients have a peripheral eosinophilia. Loeffler's syndrome, presumably due to pulmonary migration of the larvae, is present in some cases.

DIAGNOSIS. The diagnosis is usually made by examination but may be proved by finding the larvae in a biopsy taken from the region of the skin immediately ahead of the advancing lesion.

The differential diagnosis includes other creeping eruptions such as myriasis or gnathostomiasis.

TREATMENT. This disease is self-limited. In cases in which only a few lesions are present, local freezing applied to the area ahead of the tunnel, where the larvae are presumed to be, may be effective. Variable results have been obtained with oral piperazine. Thiabendazole, 25 mg per kilogram twice daily for two days, is effective. In selected cases systemic corticosteroids may be required for symptomatic relief.

Infestations of the Skin

Insect Bite
(See also Secs. 11.11 and 14.53)

"Insect bite" is a term applied to a local cutaneous eruption caused by arthropods.

ETIOLOGY. A list of the habitat and characteristics of arthropods capable of inducing lesions in humans has been compiled in Table 2.

INCIDENCE AND EPIDEMIOLOGY. These eruptions are extremely common, especially in children. The epidemiology of any particular type of bite reflects the life cycle and ecology of the causative arthropod.

PATHOLOGY AND PATHOGENESIS. The pathologic features of an insect bite initially include edema and a perivascular infiltration of both mononuclear and polymorphonuclear cells. Shortly afterward, many histiocytes, eosinophils, lymphocytes, and plasma cells appear. The infiltration may be granulomatous or may become so extensive that it is difficult to distinguish from lymphoma.

Arthropods may produce human cutaneous lesions by several mechanisms. Direct tissue injury may result from biting, stinging, or burrowing. Local urticarial reactions may be produced in two ways: by venoms introduced with a bite or sting, or by contact with various arthropod secretions or integumentary structures. Vesiculation may result from contact with the integumentary fluids of certain arthropods. Necrosis has been produced by the bite of certain spiders and, in some patients, by the bite or sting of arthropods. Finally, secondary abrasions, excoriations, and bacterial infections are often superimposed upon the original lesion.

CLINICAL MANIFESTATIONS. In general, arthropod infestations localize either on exposed areas of the skin or in regions of the body where clothing fits tightly. In these areas migratory movement of the insect is impeded, and feeding or defensive biting results.

The clinical picture of an arthropod bite consists of two components: that produced by direct injury and that produced by species-specific hypersensitivity or toxicity. The latter is discussed in detail elsewhere. The mouth parts of an insect create a punctum which may be composed of single or multiple lacerations depending upon the structure of the weapon inflicting the wound. Patients who are either not sensitive or who have been "desensitized" by frequent bites will exhibit only a minimal reaction.

Papular urticaria is an eruption characterized by pruritic, papular lesions, with or without a surrounding wheal. This disease is thought to represent a papular response to an insect bite. However, in some cases the papular eruption may involve large areas of the body. Thus, it is not known whether each papule represents a bite or whether some of the lesions arise solely as a hypersensitive response.

DIAGNOSIS. The diagnosis of an eruption caused by the bite of an arthropod is made by obtaining a history of possible exposure and recognizing the presence of lesions which have central puncta, necrosis, or a series of vesicles following the line of contact with the insect.

Because many arthropods produce identical cutaneous lesions, only a careful history and a subsequent search of the patient's environment will reveal the identity of the offending arthropod. In cases with urticarial lesions this history must include the activities of the patient during the entire 48-hour span prior to the bite.

TREATMENT. Therapy of these lesions depends upon the extent of the allergic reaction, which is discussed elsewhere (Sec. 11.11).

Necrotic Arachnidism

Necrotic arachnidism is the term applied to necrotic cutaneous lesions produced by the bite of certain spiders.

ETIOLOGY. The genus *Loxosceles* includes medium-sized, yellow or brown spiders, 10 to 15 mm in length, with six eyes arranged in an arc.

INCIDENCE AND EPIDEMIOLOGY. There are two *Loxosceles* species of recognized medical importance: one indigenous to the United States, the other to South America. *Loxosceles reclusa* inhabits the south central portion of this country. It has been found in storage spaces, cellars, and closets. *Loxosceles laeta* is the South American species, which has been introduced into the United States.

PATHOLOGY. Biopsies of *Loxosceles* bites show marked inflammation and necrosis of the epidermis, dermis, and underlying tissues.

CLINICAL MANIFESTATIONS. Identical clinical pictures are caused by both *Loxosceles* species. A wheal appears at the puncture site immediately after the bite. As necrosis evolves, this area becomes violaceous. Later an eschar forms. In some patients a systemic reaction with slight fever and a generalized scarlatiniform eruption occurs. Hemolysis, shock, and renal shutdown are occasionally present. There have been two fatal cases from bites of *Loxosceles* in the United States, one in a 4-year-old boy.

DIAGNOSIS. The diagnosis can only be made by history and physical examination.

Necrotic skin lesions can also occur in any disease characterized by multiple emboli or a vasculitis.

TREATMENT. No specific treatment is currently available.

Pediculosis

Pediculosis is the disease produced from infestation of sucking lice.

ETIOLOGY. Sucking lice (Anoplura) have flattened bodies, a protrusible proboscis at the tip of the head, and legs adapted for clinging to hairs. The crab louse (*Phthirus pubis*) is light in color, measures approximately 1 mm in diameter, and has a crablike appearance. Its anterior legs are smaller than the posterior. This louse infests the pubic hairs especially, but in heavy infestations it may also be present in other hairy parts of the body, where it lays its eggs on the

TABLE 2. *Arthropods That Cause Cutaneous Lesions in Humans*

	Common Name	Size (Approx.)	Scientific Name	Habitat	Special Characteristics
	Scorpions	2-15 cm	Class—Arachnida Order— Scorpionidae	Southwestern U.S.A. Dry tropical areas Crevices	Painful
	Ticks	5 mm	Class—Arachnida Order—Acarina Family—Ixodidae Argasidae	Cosmopolitan Around grassy areas In nests or houses	Painless
	Mites Mouse mites	0.25-1.0 mm	Class—Arachnida Order—Acarina Family— Dermanyssidae	Cosmopolitan Nest parasite	Painless
	Spider mites	0.25-1.0 mm	Family— Tetranychidae	Around plants, in houses Cosmopolitan	Painless
	Chigger mites	0.25 mm	Family— Trombiculidae	Around grain, grasses, swamps, treeholes Cosmopolitan	Painless
	Follicle mites	0.25-1.0 mm	Family— Demodicidae	Cosmopolitan In man	Painless
	Grain mites	0.25-1.0 mm	Family— Pyentoidae	Cosmopolitan Around grass and straw	Painless
	Mange mites	0.25-1.0 mm	Family— Sarcoptidae	Cosmopolitan In man	Painless
	Brown spider	2.5 cm	Class—Arachnida Order—Araneidae Family— Loxoscelidae	Southern and central U.S.A. Central and So. America Crevices, storage areas	May or may not be painful; necrotic bite
	Millipedes	5.0 cm	Class—Diplopoda	Cosmopolitan Around houses, stones, crevices	Painless
	Centipedes	5.0-7.0 cm	Class—Chilopoda	Cosmopolitan Around houses, stones, crevices	Painful nocturnal feeders, produce bite with two fang marks

TABLE 2. (continued)

	Common Name	Size (Approx.)	Scientific Name	Habitat	Special Characteristics
	Buffalo gnats Blackflies	1-5 mm	Class—Insecta Order—Diptera	Widely distributed in U.S.A., especially in hilly sections with swiftly moving water streams	Painful, daytime feeders; swarm in late spring and early summer
	Biting midge Punkies "NoSeeUms" Sandfly (misnomer)	0.5-5.0 mm	Class—Insecta Order—Diptera Family— Ceratopogonidae	Salt marches of Atlantic and Gulf coasts In decayed cactus, treeholes, seepage areas, ditches	Painful, bite at dawn and dusk; weak fliers; may occur in overwhelming numbers
	Horsefly Deerfly Greenheads	7-30 mm	Class—Insecta Order—Diptera Family—Tabanidae	All over U.S.A. Breed in mud marshes	Very painful biters, daytime feeders
	Tsetse fly	6-15 mm	Class—Insecta Order—Diptera Family—Muscidae	Tropical Africa	Painful or painless; outdoor, daytime feeders
	Stable fly	6-15 mm	Class—Insecta Order—Diptera Family—Muscidae	Cosmopolitan Around large animals	Painless, daytime feeders
	Fleas	1-8 mm	Class—Insecta Order— Siphonoptera	Cosmopolitan Nest parasites	Painless, daytime or nocturnal feeders
		1 mm	Species—Tunga Penetrans	Pantropical	Female burrows in human skin to lay eggs, thereby producing blisters
	Blister beetle	1-3 cm	Class—Insecta Order—Coleoptera Family—Meloidae	Cosmopolitan	Painless; blisters form at site of bite; phototactic insects
	Caterpillar	2 cm	Class—Insecta Order— Lepidoptera	Cosmopolitan	Contact with caterpillar hairs produces urticaria
	Ants Bees Wasps Hornets	1 cm 1-3 cm 1-3 cm 1-3 cm	Class—Insecta Order— Hymenoptera	Cosmopolitan	Stinging insects
	Sandfleas	1-2 mm	Superclass— Crustacea Order—Amphipoda Isopoda	Cosmopolitan In shallow salt water	Produce hemorrhagic bites

TABLE 2. (continued)

	Common Name	Size (Approx.)	Scientific Name	Habitat	Special Characteristics
	Termites (Nasute)	3 mm	Class—Insecta Order—Isoptera	Pantropical In dead trees	Painful; ejectors of an irritant fluid
	Lice	2 mm	Class—Insecta Order—Anopleura	Cosmopolitan In man and his clothes	Painless; produces little or no reaction to biting
	Bedbugs	3-5 mm	Class—Insecta Order—Hemiptera Family—Cimicidae	Cosmopolitan Crevices, mattress seams, wallpaper	Nocturnal painless feeder
	Kissing Bug	1-3 cm	Class—Insecta Order—Hemiptera Family— Reduviidae	Widely spread south of Pennsylvania. In walls, floors, cracks, crevices, and rodent burrows	Nocturnal, may or may not be painful
	Plant bug Leafhoppers	1-3 cm	Class—Insecta Order—Hemiptera Family— Ciccadellidae Aphidae Order— Thysanoptera	Cosmopolitan Plant feeders	Painful bite
	Mosquito	2-8 mm	Class—Insecta Order—Diptera Family—Culicidae	Cosmopolitan	Painful bite
	Sandfly	1-4 mm	Class—Insecta Order—Diptera Family— Psychodidae	Present but not common in U.S.A., tropical areas, In tree-holes, rodent burrows, and crevices	Nocturnal, weak fliers; may or may not be painful

hair shaft. The head louse (*Pediculus humanus capitis*) is also light in color and 2 to 3 mm long. It infests and lays its eggs in the scalp and other hairy areas of the body. The body louse (*Pediculus humanus corporis*) spends most of its time in clothing, moving to the skin only to feed.

INCIDENCE AND EPIDEMIOLOGY. Pediculosis is not rare. Transmission of the lice occurs by direct contact of susceptible people with infected hairs or clothing containing either eggs ("nits") or adult lice.

PATHOLOGY. The major lesions in pediculosis are inflicted by the host's scratching. Only inflammatory changes are found in biopsy specimens.

CLINICAL MANIFESTATIONS. Lice produce pinpoint, flat, erythematous lesions at the feeding sites. Excori-

ations and bloody crusts are the most common lesions observed on infested patients. Secondary infections, exudation, and regional lymphadenopathy are a result of excoriation. In addition, postinflammatory hyperpigmentation may persist for several months.

Patients infested with scalp lice frequently consult physicians because of pyoderma and cervical lymphadenopathy.

DIAGNOSIS. The diagnosis of pediculosis can be made by finding the lice or eggs. In pediculosis capitis and pubis, both ova and adults can be found attached to the hairs. In cases of pediculosis corporis the adult lice are located in greater numbers in clothing seams, but a few may be found feeding on the skin.

The differential diagnosis of pediculosis corporis

includes other causes of generalized pruritus such as uremia, jaundice, malignancy, diabetes, and drug reactions. Frequently, pediculosis capitis is misdiagnosed as simple pyoderma.

TREATMENT. Benzene hexachloride (Kwell) or any of several insecticide dusts (10 percent DDT powder) may be applied to the body and clothes in the treatment of pediculosis corporis and to the infested areas of the body in cases of pediculosis capitis and pubis. Treatment of DDT-resistant lice is discussed elsewhere (Sec. 14.53).

Scabies

Scabies is a disease resulting from an infestation of the skin by the mite, *Sarcoptes scabiei*.

ETIOLOGY. The female measures 330 to 450 μ in length and 250 to 350 μ in width; the male is only about half as large.

INCIDENCE AND EPIDEMIOLOGY. Scabies is not an uncommon disease in this country. The peak seasonal incidence is during late summer and early autumn when campers and vacationers return from their trips. The mite migrates from one individual to another with facility.

PATHOLOGY AND PATHOGENESIS. Scabetic mites burrow in the skin, where the females deposit their eggs. After a few weeks the human host becomes sensitized to the antigens of the mite, and pruritus occurs. Biopsy specimens may include the mite, the ova, and the epidermal tunnel. A chronic inflammatory infiltrate is present in both the epidermis and dermis.

CLINICAL MANIFESTATIONS. Because pruritus does not occur until the patient is sensitized, the infestation is usually well advanced before symptoms appear. Nocturnal pruritus is the most common chief complaint. Small, tortuous, burrow tracts with dark plugs at the entrance are found in the afflicted sites. The genital areas and the flexural creases, particularly between the fingers, are areas of predilection, although any region of the body may be attacked. Asymptomatic or mildly pruritic hyperkeratotic lesions containing enormous numbers of acari are present in some neglected cases. In infants papulovesicular or vesiculobullous lesions are often seen, especially on the face and feet; atopic dermatitis may be mimicked. Secondary bacterial infection and excoriations are common.

DIAGNOSIS. The diagnosis of scabies may be confirmed by recovering the mite from the burrows.

Scabies must be differentiated from other causes of pruritus such as pediculosis, uremia, jaundice, diabetes, malignancy, and drug eruptions. The lesions of necrotic excoriations, although superficially resembling scabies, do not appear predominantly in flexural creases.

TREATMENT. Crotamiton cream (Eurax) or benzene hexachloride (Kwell) ointment are effective insecticide preparations which should be applied twice daily for three to four days. Fifteen percent precipitated sulfur ointments and 25 percent benzyl benzoate emulsion are also effective drugs. All members of the family should be treated and the bedclothes sprayed with insecticides.

Cutaneous Reaction to Infection

Erythema Nodosum

Erythema nodosum is a syndrome characterized by the appearance of painful, erythematous, subcutaneous nodules, usually on the extensor surfaces of the extremities.

ETIOLOGY. This syndrome is thought to be due to hypersensitivity to (1) drugs, such as iodides, bromides, penicillin, sulfonamides, and antipyrine; (2) infections, such as syphilis, lepromatous leprosy, tuberculosis, streptococcosis, meningococcic infections, lymphogranuloma venereum, cat scratch fever, coccidioidomycosis, and chancroid; and (3) miscellaneous diseases, such as sarcoidosis, ulcerative colitis, and regional enteritis. Streptococcal infections are the most common cause of this disease in American children. A great number of cases appear to occur de novo.

INCIDENCE AND EPIDEMIOLOGY. Erythema nodosum is a common syndrome in children over 6 years of age. A predominance of females has been observed in some series. Its mode of transmission is unknown.

PATHOLOGY. The pathologic alterations in this syndrome are found in the dermis, where an infiltration of mononuclear cells is present. The capillaries are dilated, and areas of thrombosis and extravasation may occur.

CLINICAL MANIFESTATIONS. Erythematous, round or elliptical, tender nodules, ranging in size from 0.5 to 3 cm, appear in crops on the extremities. Although these nodules are firm, their border is not always well delineated. After a few days the lesions become purple, then brown, in color. Constitutional symptoms may accompany the eruption. Resolution usually takes place within three weeks without ulceration and without scarring. Recurrences are not uncommon.

DIFFERENTIAL DIAGNOSIS. Periarteritis nodosa and erythema induration can be ruled out by biopsy. Erythema nodosum also may be confused with superficial, migratory thrombophlebitis and panniculitis.

TREATMENT. Treatment for this disorder depends upon the nature of the underlying disease. Analgesics are usually all that is necessary in most patients. Systemic corticosteroids and salicylates have been administered to those acutely ill patients having no conditions that would otherwise contraindicate such drugs.

Erythema multiforme is discussed elsewhere (p. 1778).

REFERENCES

BACTERIAL INFECTIONS OF THE SKIN

Burnett, J. W. Management of pyogenic cutaneous infections. New Eng. J. Med., 266:164, 1962.
———— The route of antibiotic administration in superficial impetigo. New Eng. J. Med., 268:72, 1963.
Dillon, H. C., Jr. Pyoderma and nephritis. Ann. Rev. Med., 18:207, 1967.
———— Impetigo contagiosa suppurative and non-suppurative complications. I. Clinical bacteriologic and epidemiologic characteristics of impetigo. Am. J. Dis. Child., 115:530, 1968.
Markowitz, M., Bruton, H. D., and Kultner, A. G. The bacteriologic findings, streptococcal immune responses and renal complications in children with impetigo. Pediatrics, 35:393, 1965.

ERYTHRASMA

Koostra, J. A. Prophylaxis and control of erythrasma of the toe webs. J. Invest. Derm., 45:399, 1965.
Sarkany, I., Taplin, D., and Blank, H. Erythrasma—common bacterial infection of skin. J.A.M.A., 177:130, 1961.
———— Taplin, D., and Blank, H. Incidence and bacteriology of erythrasma. Arch. Derm., 85:578, 1962.

VIRAL INFECTIONS OF THE SKIN

Herpes Zoster

Almedia, J. D., Howatson, A. F., and Williams, M. G. The morphology of varicella (chickenpox) virus. Virology, 16:353, 1962.
Brunnell, P. A., Miller, L. H., and Lovejoy, F. Zoster in children. Am. J. Dis. Child., 115:432, 1968.
———— Ross, A., Miller, L. H., and Kuo, B. Prevention of varicella by zoster immune globulin. New Eng. J. Med., 280:1191, 1969.
Gold, E., and Robbins, F. C. Isolation of cytopathogenic agents from cerebrospinal or vesicle fluid of patients with herpes zoster or varicella. Amer. J. Dis. Child., 94:545, 1957.
Mersalis, J. G., Kaye, D., and Hook, E. W. Disseminated herpes zoster. Arch. Int. Med., 113:679, 1964.
Muller, S. A. Association of zoster and malignant disorders in children. Arch. Derm., 96:657, 1967.
Weller, T. H. Varicella: Herpes zoster. In Beeson, P. B., and McDermott, W., eds., Cecil-Loeb Textbook of Medicine, 11th ed. Philadelphia, London, W. B. Saunders Co., 1963, p. 110.
———— and Witton, H. M. The etiologic agents of varicella and herpes zoster, serologic studies with the viruses propagated in vitro. J. Exp. Med., 108:869, 1958.
———— Witton, H. M., and Bell, E. J. The etiologic agents of varicella and herpes zoster, isolation, propagation and cultural characteristics in vitro. J. Exp. Med., 108:843, 1958.

Molluscum Contagiosum

Burnett, J. W., and Neva, F. N. Studies on the mechanism of molluscum contagiosum cytoxicity. J. Invest. Derm., 46:76, 1966.

Epstein, W. L., Senecal, I., Krasnobrod, H., and Massig, A. M. Viral antigens in human epidermal tumors: localization of an antigen to molluscum contagiosum. J. Invest. Derm., 40:51, 1963.
Friedman-Kien, A. E., and Vilcek, J. Induction of interference and interferon synthesis by non-replicating molluscum contagiosum virus. J. Immun., 99:1092, 1967.
Prose, P. H., Friedman-Kien, A. E., and Vilcek, J. Molluscum contagiosum virus in adult human skin cultures; an electron microscopic study. Am. J. Path., 55:349, 1969.
Sutton, J. S., and Burnett, J. W. Ultrastructural changes in dermal and epidermal cells of skin infected with molluscum contagiosum virus. J. Ultrastruct. Res., 26:177, 1969.

Warts

Almeida, J. D., Howatson, A. F., and Williams, M. G. Electron microscope study of human warts, sites of virus production and nature of the inclusion bodies. J. Invest. Derm., 38:337, 1962.
Blank, H., and Rake, G. Viral and Rickettsial Diseases of the Skin, Eyes and Mucous Membranes of Man. Boston, Toronto, Little, Brown & Co., 1955, Chap. 9, p. 156.
Chapman, G. B., Drusin, L. M., and Todd, J. E. Fine structure of the human wart. Amer. J. Path., 42:619, 1963.

FUNGAL INFECTIONS OF THE SKIN

Conant, N. F. Manual of Clinical Mycology, 2nd ed. Philadelphia, W. B. Saunders Co., 1954.
Lewis, G. M., et al. An Introduction to Medical Mycology, 4th ed. Chicago, The Year Book Publishers, 1958.
Sulton, R. L., Jr. Diseases of the Skin, 11th ed. St. Louis, C. V. Mosby Co., 1956.
Swartz, J. H. Current concepts in therapy: infections caused by dermatophytes. New Eng. J. Med., 267:1246, 1962.

PARASITIC DISEASES

Swimmers' Itch

Cort, W. W. Studies on schistosome dermatitis. XI. Status of knowledge after more than twenty years. Amer. J. Hyg., 52:251, 1950.

Creeping Eruption

Lowenthal, L. J. A. Evaluation of therapy in creeping eruption. Aust. J. Derm., 2:171, 1954.
Wright, D., and Gold, E. Löffler's syndrome associated with creeping eruption (cutaneous helminthiasis). Report of 26 cases. Arch. Int. Med., 73:303, 1946.

INFESTATIONS OF THE SKIN

Insect Bites

Benjamini, E., Feingold, B. F., and Kartman, L. Allergy to flea bites. III. The experimental induction of flea bite and by antigen prepared from whole flea extracts of Ctenocephilides felis. Exp. Parasit., 10:214, 1960.

Brook, T. Résumé of insect allergy. Ann. Allergy, 19: 288, 1961.

Gordon, R. M., and Lavopierre, M. M. J. Entomology for Students of Medicine. Oxford, Blackwell Scientific Publications, 1962.

Herms, W. B., and James, M. T. Medical Entomology, 5th ed. New York, The Macmillan Co., 1961.

Ordman, D. Desensitization to bee stings by intracutaneous injections of whole-bee extract. Brit. Med. J., 2: 352, 1958.

Necrotic Arachnidism

Atkins, J. A., Wingo, C. W., and Sodeman, W. A. Necrotic arachnidism. Amer. J. Trop. Med., 1:165, 1958.

Pitts, N. C. Necrotic arachnidism. New Eng. J. Med., 267:400, 1962.

Pediculosis

Sutton, R. L., Jr. Diseases of the Skin, 11th ed. St. Louis, C. V. Mosby Co., 1956, p. 618.

CUTANEOUS REACTION TO INFECTION

Doxiadis, S. A. Erythema nodosum in children. Medicine, 30:283, 1951.

Laurance, B., et al. Aetiology of erythema nodosum, in children. Lancet, 2:14, 1961.

26.6
DISORDERS OF PIGMENTATION

JOSEPH McGUIRE

In the basal layer of the epidermis there is a population of specialized cells, the melanocytes, which are embryonically derived from the neural crest, as are the sympathetic ganglia, Schwann cells, and adrenal medulla, inter alia. They are specialized secretory cells with complex dendritic processes through which they transfer melanin granules to keratinocytes.

Differences in skin color between the Caucasian and Negro are due to the increased amount of melanin in the epidermal keratinocytes of the latter; both races have approximately the same number of melanocytes.

The enzyme tyrosinase is present in the melanocyte and is associated with small football-shaped organelles called melanosomes. The oxidation of tyrosine to dihydroxyphenylalanine (dopa) and the oxidation of the latter to dopa quinone are catalyzed by tyrosinase. Dopa quinone is further metabolized to a polymer which is combined with a protein to form melanin. The formation of melanin in the melanosome results in a dense melanin granule which is transferred to a keratinocyte. Abnormalities in several steps of this process are reflected by clinical disease. In vitiligo and piebaldism, melanocytes are absent; however, Langerhans' cells are present not only in the normal suprabasilar position but probably also in the basilar region. In albinism, melanocytes are present; however, the melanosomes do not become pigmented because of an abnormal or missing tyrosinase.

There is a rough correlation between latitude and melanin pigmentation in the human. Tropical and subtropical populations tend to be more heavily melanized than temperate or more northerly located groups. It is, therefore, generally accepted that melanization is an important protective strategy against ultraviolet (UV) irradiation. Although the validity of this logic is unproved, melanin does protect the host from irradiation in two ways: absorption of light and absorption of radicals. The mechanism of U.V.-induced damage in biologic systems is thought to be through the generation of radicals, which produce thymine dimers in nucleic acid. These dimers are excised in a repair process.

Ultraviolet irradiation produces a greater concentration of free radicals in white skin than in nonwhite skin. Furthermore, melanin is a stable free radical and as such could function as a scavenger for the free radicals.

The destructive effects of ultraviolet light exposure are illustrated by the premature appearance of elastosis, actinic keratoses, and carcinomas in the exposed skin of albino Negroes in tropical climates. More pertinent and less generally appreciated, however, is the cumulative damage to the skin associated with chronic exposure to sunlight at temperate latitudes. Children, especially those of Celtic extraction and/or rufous complexions, can be permanently damaged by sunlight before they reach teenage. In general, the child who tans well and has brown eyes is relatively less damaged than the blue-eyed freckler. The cultural basis for sunbathing and acquisition of a suntan is obscure and is responsible not only for the actinic keratosis and many of the squamous cell carcinomas that appear later in life, but also for the prematurely aged appearance, loss of elasticity, and wrinkling in many people in the third and fourth decades of life.

Acute effects of ultraviolet irradiation are well known—erythema and blistering (Fig. 51). Chronic effects are atrophy, telangiectasia, and elastosis. In children these latter effects are definitely abnormal and are associated with xeroderma pigmentosum, the Rothmund-Thomson syndrome, and albinism. The best-known effect of ultraviolet light on skin apart from sunburn is tanning.

Although the melanocyte is the key cell in the process of pigment synthesis, the transfer of melanin granules depends on a close relationship between the melanocyte and a keratinocyte. Certain variations in skin color may represent an inability of the keratinocyte to accept granules from a normally functioning melanocyte.

Pigmentation of the skin is a multistep process with control mechanisms and abnormalities at each of the following steps: (1) melanocyte; (2) tyrosinase synthesis; (3) melanin synthesis; (4) transfer of melanin to keratinocyte.

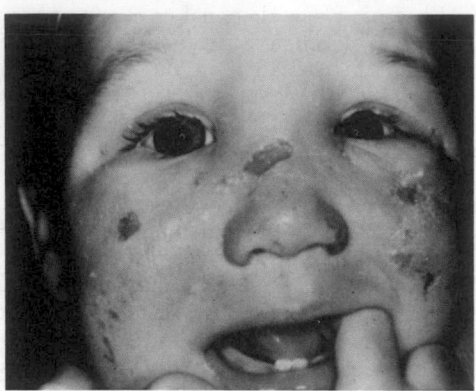

Fig. 51. Sunburn in a 1-year-old infant. There is periorbital edema, blistering, and erythema. Chronic damage from ultra-violet irradiation accounts for most of the changes associated with aging of the skin.

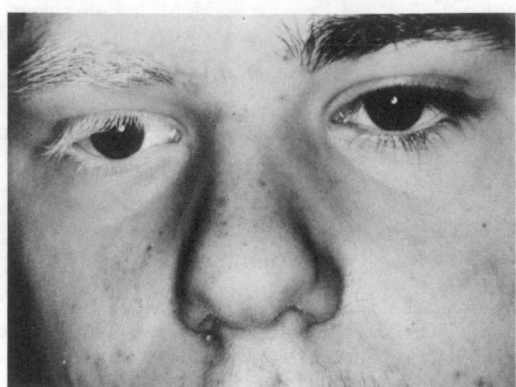

Fig. 52. Segmental vitiligo of three months' duration involving the right eyebrow and eyelash with loss of pigment of the surrounding skin—not apparent in this illustration. Note that the iris on involved side has not lost pigment.

Thus, in vitiligo and partial albinism, the melanocyte is absent or destroyed; in albinism, either no tyrosinase or an abnormal tyrosinase is synthesized; in phenylketonuria, metabolites inhibit the synthesis of melanin; and in pityriasis alba and post-inflammatory hypomelanosis, the keratinocyte is unable to accept pigment granules from the melanocyte either because the keratinocyte is abnormal or because it is dividing too rapidly.

Hormonal Control of Pigmentation

Although of considerable interest to physiologists, clinical abnormalities of pigmentation secondary to hormonal stimulation are uncommon in children. The pituitary secretes several peptides that have a direct darkening effect on the pigment cells of amphibia and, when administered systemically to man, produce darkening of the skin. Alpha and beta melanocyte-stimulating hormone (MSH) as well as ACTH in larger amounts darken human skin. In Addison's disease, loss of feedback inhibition of the pituitary gland by steroidal products of the adrenal cortex results in increased secretion of both MSH and ACTH. In Addison's disease and the ectopic ACTH syndromes, β-MSH is responsible for the generalized darkening of the skin, nevi, palmar creases, and buccal mucosa in this disease; however, ACTH may also contribute to the melanocyte stimulation. The converse of this situation is seen in panhypopituitarism, where the skin is relatively hypopigmented.

Hypopigmentation

ALBINISM.   Albinism is a classic example of an inherited defect in enzyme synthesis. It is inherited as a recessive trait and is due to absent or defective tyrosinase synthesis in the melanocyte. The melanocyte is otherwise structurally normal.

Two forms of human albinism have been described: tyrosinase negative and tyrosinase positive. Individuals with the tyrosinase negative form are more lightly pigmented, and when their hair bulbs are incubated with tyrosine, no pigment is formed. In the tyrosine positive form of albinism, cutaneous and hair pigment is diluted, the irides are not so light as in the tyrosine negative form, and when hair bulbs are incubated with tyrosine, pigment is formed. Two families have been described in which there were normally pigmented offspring from tyrosinase positive and tyrosinase negative parents. These observations indicate that the genes for the two forms of albinism are not allelic.

Affected individuals have photophobia and often nystagmus. Hair color ranges from white to blond, iris color from light blue to hazel. The protective effect of melanin is demonstrated by the accelerated aging of albino skin with the appearance of keratosis, telangiectasia, and elastosis at an early age.

There is no treatment for albinism; prophylactic measures such as protective clothing and the use of chemical sun screens (Skolex, A-fil, Uval) should be employed when sunlight cannot be avoided.

PARTIAL ALBINISM.   Partial albinism, a dominant trait, is characterized by a white forelock and circumscribed areas of depigmentation elsewhere on the body. Recently, the melanosomes contained in the melanocytes of the white forelock area have been found to resemble those found in vitiligo rather than those present in albinos. These patients do not repigment, and cosmetics may be used if the face or prominent areas are involved.

VITILIGO.   Vitiligo (Figs. 52 and 53) is a common but puzzling patchy depigmentation of the skin affecting about one percent of the people in this coun-

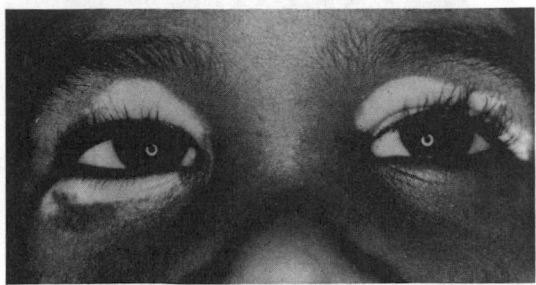

Fig. 53. Vitiligo in a Negro boy with depigmentation around eyes. Loss of pigmentation commonly occurs around body orifices, e.g., mouth, nose, nipples, eyes, navel, and on the dorsa of the hands.

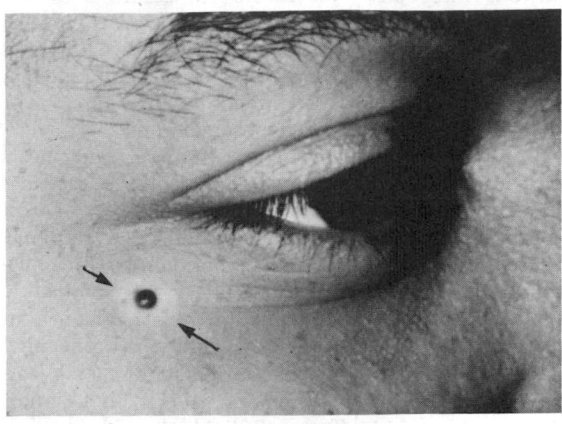

Fig. 54. Negro girl with halo nevus on right cheek. Central pigmented nevus will probably become depigmented, then area will repigment.

try. One half of these patients have relatives with vitiligo, and in half the onset is within the first two decades. Sites of trauma and pressure are often affected as well as areas around body orifices—eyes, mouth, nipples, umbilicus. The depigmented patches are usually noted during the summer, when tanning of the normal surrounding skin affords a striking contrast to the milky white area of pigment loss. Conversely, the vitiliginous patch may appear to improve in the wintertime as the surrounding suntan fades. As might be expected, the absence of melanin in vitiliginous areas results in enhanced sensitivity to sunlight. The border may be hyperpigmented. Occasionally, an intermediate degree of pigmentation may be seen between the central area of vitiligo and the normal skin. This represents partial pigment loss and heralds the progression of the depigmentation. The diagnosis can usually be made on clinical grounds; however, the use of a Wood's light facilitates identification of depigmentation in light-skinned individuals. Hair in areas of vitiligo may become depigmented or remain normal.

Basilar melanocytes are absent in well-established vitiligo; however, another type of epidermal dendritic cell, the Langerhans' cell, is present in normal or increased numbers. Ordinarily, Langerhans' cells, which can be demonstrated easily because of their ATPase activity, are present in the suprabasilar position. These dendritic cells have no desmosomes and contain racquet-shaped organelles which, unlike melanosomes, possess no tyrosinase activity. No role has yet been identified for the Langerhans' cell.

The course of vitiligo is capricious; it may progress to total depigmentation in less than a year, or it may remain relatively stable for decades. Spontaneous complete repigmentation is quite rare, although about half of the patients have some degree of repigmentation. Although vitiligo involves only the skin, it is associated with two systemic diseases—pernicious anemia and hyperthyroidism. Many patients relate their vitiligo to major trauma, either physical or emotional.

The differential diagnosis of vitiligo includes partial albinism, which, however, is present at birth; depigmentation secondary to chemical exposure (monobenzyl ether of hydroquinone); and perihalo nevus (see below). The most common condition from which vitiligo must be differentiated in childhood is pityriasis alba.

Vitiligo may be treated with the oral administration of 8-methoxypsoralen or trimethylpsoralen, which are photosensitizing agents. The medication is taken daily one to two hours before exposure to sunlight. Ordinarily, treatment is carried out through the spring, summer, and early autumn when natural sunlight is available. Because of the photosensitizing property of psoralens, exposure to sunlight must be cautious with a gradual increase in the length of exposure; otherwise a severe sunburn may result. Repigmentation occurs at the borders and within the patch of vitiligo in a perifollicular pattern. These spots coalesce to produce a fairly even pigmentation. Because of the demands made upon the patient by psoralen therapy, only highly motivated individuals should be treated. The simplest treatment is to darken the depigmented areas with dyes.

HALO NEVUS. Halo nevus is a poorly understood condition in which a halo of depigmentation appears around a pigmented nevus which itself eventually becomes depigmented and disappears (Fig. 54). The area then repigments spontaneously. Rarely, halo depigmentation may occur around a blue nevus or neurofibroma and even more rarely around a malignant melanoma.

There is a high incidence of halo nevi in vitiligo; however, they are not rare in otherwise normal children and may appear and resolve without coincident vitiligo.

CHEDIAK-HIGASHI SYNDROME. Chediak-Higashi syndrome is a rare lethal disorder associated with varying degrees of pigment dilution. In addition to apparent albinism, there are hepatosplenomegaly, recurrent infections, and severe infection or hemorrhage which usually are fatal before 10 years of age. The degree of pigment dilution in these patients as in albinos is variable, and many of the children tan, especially those of dark-skinned parents; rarely, patients may even become hyperpigmented.

Anemia and leucopenia are common, and smears of peripheral blood reveal abnormally large granules in neutrophils and eosinophils. The dilution of skin color does not represent classical albinism but may be secondary to a structural abnormality of melanosomes which are several times larger than normal.

WAARDENBURG'S SYNDROME. An uncommon form of patterned leucoderma associated with congenital deafness occurs in Waardenburg's syndrome. Waardenburg defined the syndrome in 1951 with a clinical description of 161 affected individuals with the following findings:

Lateral displacement of the medial canthi and inferior lacrimal puncta	99%
Broad nasal root	78%
Eyebrows growing together	45%
Heterochromia iridum	25%
Deafness	20%
White forelock and occasional depigmentation of eyebrows	17%

Since then, it has been estimated that 2 percent of congenitally deaf children have this syndrome. It has been suggested that a developmental abnormality in the neural crest is responsible for the pigmentary changes and the absence of the organ of Corti. Heterochromia and the white forelock may disappear in childhood.

Hyperpigmentation

PIGMENTED NEVUS. The pigmented nevus (nevus cell nevus) or mole is the most common type of hyperpigmentation seen in childhood. It is usually absent at birth and appears in the first decade, often in crops. The nevus is composed of cells closely related to melanocytes. Nevus cells may contain melanosomes and melanin, and may be dopa oxidase and tyrosinase positive, depending on their location. The presence of nonspecific cholinesterase, an enzyme not found in melanocytes, in nevus cells of intradermal nevi may indicate that nevus cells are derived from a primitive cell of neural crest origin. Nonspecific cholinesterase is present in Schwann cells, which are also derived from neural crest.

Clinically, nevi may vary considerably in morphology. They may be flat, raised, or papillomatous and tan, brown, black, or blue in color.

The earliest form of nevus may be lentigo simplex, in which there is an increased number of melanocytes and sometimes elongation or budding of

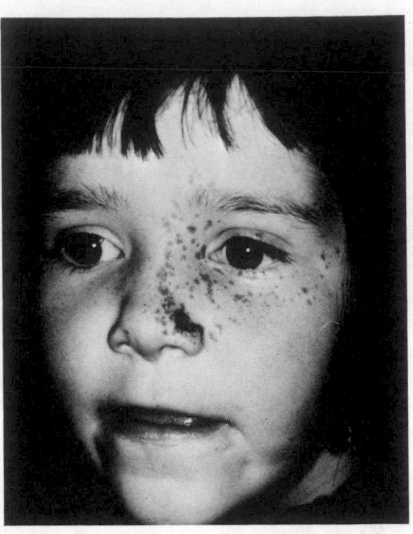

Fig. 55. Nevoid lentigo. Patterned hyperpigmentation in "nevoid" distribution.

the rete ridges. Occasionally lentiges occur in a nevoid pattern (Fig. 55).

Junctional Nevus. Most nevi seen in children are of the junctional type; they consist of an accumulation of dopa positive, melanin-containing epithelioid cells which are arranged in nests or theques in the lower epidermis and at the dermoepidermal junction. The cells are cuboidal and regular in shape. Junctional nevi are of interest because of their malignant potential, which fortunately is very small. The very large numbers of these lesions preclude their prophylactic removal. Nevi are removed for two reasons: (1) cosmetic and (2) evidence of abnormal development. They should be excised if there is bleeding or crusting, color change or speckling of pigmentation, migration of pigment outside the margins of the nevus, or rapid growth. In the natural course of junctional nevi, nevus cells migrate toward the dermis and at the same time the lesions become more dome-shaped. When nests of nevus cells occur in the epidermis as well as freely in the dermis, they are termed *compound nevi.*

Intradermal Nevus. This refers to a collection of nevus cells which are no longer associated with the dermoepidermal junction. The nevus is usually raised and may be a firm papule with varying degrees of pigmentation. The cells may contain melanin but are usually dopa negative. In the upper dermis they may be cuboidal, but in the lower dermis they are often spindle-shaped. Although the classification of nevi into junctional, compound, and intradermal types is useful clinically, a thorough search for epidermal nests of nevus cells (evidence of junctional activity) will be productive in four out of five clinically diagnosed intraepidermal nevi.

Several extensive surveys have confirmed the

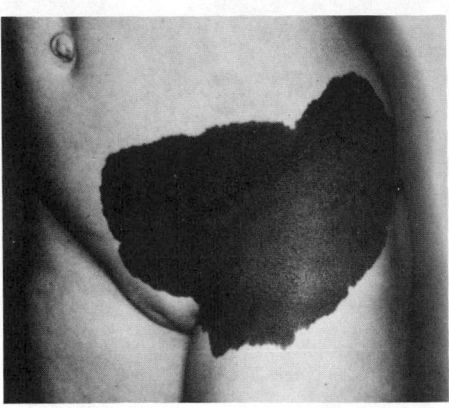

Fig. 56. Nine-year-old girl with pigmented nevus present since birth. The nevus was excised and grafted. Histologic examination revealed compound nevus and at the time of surgery a black inguinal node contained melanophages.

high incidence of junctional nevi in children, with a gradual decrease in number in older age groups. The converse relationship exists with intradermal nevi; they are rare in childhood and their incidence increases with age.

Removal of nevi for either cosmetic reasons or signs of abnormal development should be complete. Most small nevi can be removed with a punch biopsy. Larger lesions should be excised. Nevi on the palms, soles, genitalia, and sites of repeated trauma deserve special attention; however, their abundance makes wholesale removal impractical.

Extensive Pigmented Nevus. Extensive pigmented nevus (bathing trunk nevus) is a rare abnormality of pigment cell development which involves large areas of the body and is named according to its location—e.g., bathing trunk, vest, cape, stocking, sleeve (Fig. 56). It is usually present at birth, unlike most other nevus cell nevi. Most are composed histologically of dopa oxidase and tyrosinase positive cells arranged as in a compound or intradermal nevus. The skin overlying the nevus is often hairy. In addition to their disturbing appearance, they are associated with a greatly increased incidence of melanoma, and despite their size, they can and should be surgically removed.

MALIGNANT MELANOMA. Malignant melanoma (melanocarcinoma) is fortunately a rare diagnosis in children. It does, however, occur and shares the same dismal prognosis as melanoma in adults. A benign lesion, *juvenile melanoma,* which occurs in children and less commonly in adults, often causes considerable diagnostic difficulty, and must be differentiated from melanoma histologically. Clinically, juvenile melanoma may be located on any part of the body; however, there is a predilection for the face. It is smooth, elevated, usually hairless, and pink in color; however, it may be pigmented. It may resemble intradermal nevus or pyogenic granuloma. Ulceration is

rare. *Malignant melanoma* in children is clinically similar to melanoma in adults. It is usually elevated and may vary from flesh color through deep red or black. Ulceration is frequent. Treatment is unsatisfactory; however, the best approach is wide primary excision with dissection of the draining lymphatic chain. The tumor is not sensitive to x-ray or chemotherapy.

EPHILIS (FRECKLES). Freckles are absent at birth and appear in early childhood. Freckling does not occur in areas unexposed to solar irradiation. Clinically freckles are flat and vary in color from tan to black. On histologic examination they contain fewer melanocytes then the normally pigmented surrounding skin; however, the melanocytes are larger and more active.

The pigmented macules present around the mouth and across the bridge of the nose in Peutz-Jeghers syndrome are histologically identical with freckles.

MONGOLIAN SPOT. In most Mongolian and three-quarters of Negro infants, there are present one or more bluish-gray areas of discoloration over the buttocks, sacrum, or back called Mongolian spots. These are collections of dopa-positive melanocytes in the dermis which presumably have failed to migrate to the epidermis from the neural crest. They may occur on the face or trunk. Mongolian spots located on the buttocks and sacrum fade with age. They may be confused with extramedullary hematopoeisis in the newborn.

XERODERMA PIGMENTOSUM. Xeroderma pigmentosum is a rare disorder inherited as an autosomal recessive. It is characterized by a profound sensitivity of the skin to the effects of sunlight. The disease is usually apparent in the first year of life and is heralded by a sunburn out of proportion to the amount of irradiation received. The course is relentless; first there is erythema which may fade. Freckles appear, which enlarge, become more numerous, and are darkly pigmented. Telangiectasia next appears and the skin becomes dry and often atrophic. The changes resemble those of x-ray dermatitis. Tumors, benign and malignant, next appear, and the distressing appearance of these children reflects not only intrinsic changes in the skin but surgical attempts to remove ever-increasing numbers of basal cell tumors and epidermoid carcinomas. Keratoses, papillomas, and angiomas also occur. Multiple basal cell tumors and epidermal carcinomas are often present by 2 or 3 years of age.

The eyes are usually involved, with corneal ulcerations, opacities, and pterygia.

Although the skin exhibits a spectacular sensitivity to sunlight, no specific wavelength appears to be responsible for the damage. Areas that are shielded from sunlight do not deteriorate as rapidly as the skin of the face and hands.

The prognosis for patients with this disease is poor. Untreated patients usually do not survive beyond age 20, but with careful management some have lived more than 60 years. An interesting, as yet un-

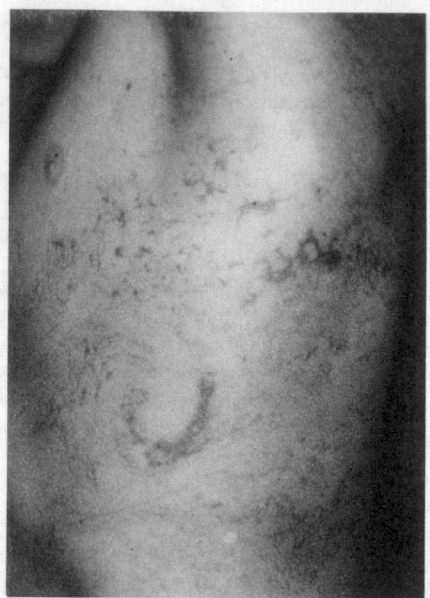

Fig. 57.   Seven-year-old girl with incontinentia pigmenti showing whorls of irregularly scattered pigmentation.

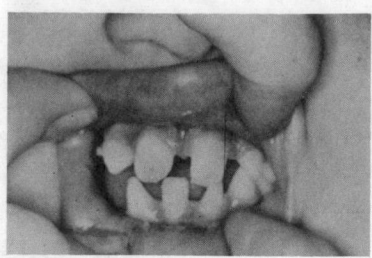

Fig. 58.   Incontinentia pigmenti showing characteristic pointed and absent teeth in 7-year-old girl.

explained abnormality in many of these patients is amino-aciduria.

A variant of xeroderma pigmentosum is the de Sanctis-Cacchione syndrome, in which there are mental deficiency, microcephaly, gonadal underdevelopment, and dwarfism.

Fibroblasts cultured from normal human skin can repair DNA (unscheduled DNA synthesis) following ultraviolet irradiation. Fibroblasts from patients with xeroderma pigmentosum are unable to participate in this repair. Similarly, exposure of normal human skin to ultraviolet irradiation stimulates unscheduled (nonmitotic) DNA synthesis in the epidermis and upper dermal fibroblasts. Patients with xeroderma pigmentosum do not show this response. It is tempting to associate the high incidence of cutaneous malignancy in patients with xeroderma pigmentosum with their inability to repair damaged DNA.

Treatment of xeroderma pigmentosum, although discouraging, is effective in prolonging comfort, acceptable appearance, and life. The chief aim is to shield the patient from all solar radiation. Sun-screen ointments are obviously not as effective as simply staying indoors during the day. Careful periodic examination and removal of tumors while they are small are extremely important measures.

INCONTINENTIA PIGMENTI.   Incontinentia pigmenti (Bloch-Sulzberger syndrome) is a rare abnormality appearing almost exclusively in infant girls. It is characterized by three separate changes in the skin: (1) inflammatory vesicles located predominantly on the extremities; (2) linear verrucous and hyperkeratotic

lesions on the extremities; and (3) irregular whorled patterns of pigmentation (Fig. 57). The pigmentation, which may have the pattern of veins in marble, often occurs in areas that are not involved by the vesicular, inflammatory, or verrucous changes.

In addition to the striking abnormalities of the skin, there are often defects of the central nervous system, teeth, or eyes. The first signs of the disease are linear or grouped vesicles usually located on the extremities. They may appear within the first two or three days after birth. New vesicles may appear and fade, to be replaced by inflammatory papules and hyperkeratotic warty lesions.

The pigmentation may be present at birth or appear within the first few years. It is brown to grayish-brown. The vesicular and verrucous lesions ordinarily resolve spontaneously within the first few years, and the pigmentation fades gradually, although usually some hyperpigmentation remains for life.

In areas of pigmentation, there are extensive dermal deposits of melanin. It is because of this apparent inability of the epidermis to retain pigment that the syndrome was named incontinentia pigmenti.

Eye changes, which occur in about one-third of the patients, include strabismus, optic atrophy, and cataract. At least a third of the children with this disorder have central nervous system involvement, which may include mental retardation, microcephaly, hydrocephalus, or seizures. Dental abnormalities are common. There may be missing teeth, delayed dentition, or conical teeth (Fig. 58). Congenital heart disease has been found in some patients. Hair loss occurs in many of these children and resembles pseudopelade (Fig. 59).

The disorder is inherited either as an autosomal dominant which is sex-linked in its expression or as a sex-linked gene on the X chromosome. In a few affected children, karotypes have been examined and found to be normal.

ACANTHOSIS NIGRICANS.   Acanthosis nigricans in children is a fairly uncommon condition in which skin markings are accentuated and the surface is velvety, rugose, and furrowed. The color may vary from tan to black. Sites of predilection are the neck,

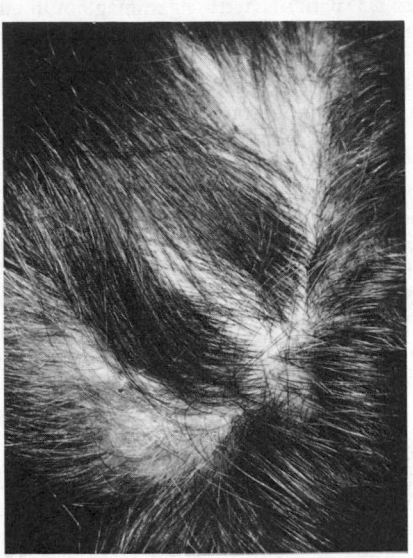

Fig. 59. Spotty alopecia occasionally present in incontinentia pigmenti. Same patient as in Fig. 57, 58.

axilla, elbows (both flexor and extensor surfaces), groin, and occasionally the buccal mucosa. Involvement is usually bilateral, and when the lesion arises unilaterally, it may be impossible to differentiate from nevus unius lateralis.

The appearance of this disease is a serious omen in adults, many of whom develop internal malignancy. In children, the association has been made only once, in a teen-age child, and no associated malignancy has been reported in younger children. Of greater significance in children is the frequent association of endocrine abnormalities of diverse types. Approximately one-third of children with acanthosis nigricans have an endocrine abnormality—diabetes, Cushing's disease, adrenocortical hyperplasia, hypothyroidism or hyperthyroidism or gigantism. Acanthosis nigricans is often present in children with lipodystrophic diabetes. Children with acanthosis nigricans in whom no endocrine abnormality can be demonstrated are regularly obese, and as techniques of endocrinologic investigation become more refined, perhaps more patients in this group will be found to have subtle endocrine abnormalities.

The sites of predilection of acanthosis nigricans are generally sites of friction and/or maceration. This suggests that a systemic predisposition can be evoked by local factors.

Familial occurrence of acanthosis associated with obesity and malignancy has been reported.

Acanthosis nigricans is chronic but often remits or improves when the obesity or underlying endocrinopathy is corrected. Local therapy has not been effective.

CAFE AU LAIT SPOT. Café au lait spots, which are a cardinal sign of neurofibromatosis (von Recklinghau-

sen's disease), may also occur in epiloia and Gaucher's disease. These macular areas of hyperpigmentation are variable in size, light tan to brown in color, and usually have a regular border. They may be present at birth and are unrelated to exposure to sun. Histologically, there is an apparent increase in the number of melanocytes demonstrated by the dopa reaction. Café au lait spots may gradually increase in size and number throughout life and often precede the appearance of neurofibromas. In addition to discrete café au lait spots, patients with von Recklinghausen's disease often have diffuse freckling and hyperpigmentation. Solitary café au lait spots have no significance; six or more café au lait spots are practically always associated with neurofibromatosis.

In Albright's disease (polyostotic fibrous displasia) there are similar patches of hyperpigmentation which, in contrast to café au lait spots in von Recklinghausen's disease, have irregular margins.

REFERENCES

Abe, K., Nicholson, W. E., Liddle, G. W., Island, D. P., and Orth, D. N. Radioimmunoassay of β-MSH in human plasma and tissues. J. Clin. Invest., 46:1609, 1967.

Cleaver, J. E. Defective repair replication of DNA in xeroderma pigmentosum. Nature, 318:652, 1968.

El-Hefnawi, H., El-Nabawi, M., and Rasheed, A. Xeroderma pigmentosum. I. A clinical study of 12 Egyptian cases. Brit. J. Derm., 74:201, 1962.

Epstein, J., Fukuyama, K., Reed, W., and Epstein, W. Defect in DNA synthesis in skin of patients with xeroderma pigmentosum demonstrated in vivo. Science, 168:1477, 1970.

Fitzpatrick, T. B., Szabo, G., Hori, Y., Sunone, A. A., Reed, W. B., and Greenberg, M. H. White leaf-shaped macules. Arch. Derm., 98:1, 1968.

Kopf, A. W., and Andrade, R. A histologic study of the dermo-epidermal junction in clinically "intradermal" nevi employing serial sections. I. Junctional theques. Ann. N.Y. Acad. Sci., 100:200, 1963.

———— Morrill, S. D., and Silberberg, I. Broad spectrum of leukoderma aquisitum centrifugum. Arch. Derm., 92:14, 1965.

Lerner, A. B. Vitiligo. J. Invest. Derm., 32:285, 1959.

———— and McGuire, J. S. Melanocyte-stimulating hormone and adrenocorticotrophic hormone, their relation to pigmentation. New Eng. J. Med., 270:539, 1964.

Reed, W. B., Dexter, R., Corley, C., and Fish, C. Congenital lipodystrophic diabetes with acanthosis nigricans. Arch. Derm., 91:326, 1965.

———— May, S. B., and Nickel, W. R. Xeroderma pigmentosum with neurological complications. Arch. Derm., 91:224, 1965.

———— Becker, S. W., Sr., Becker, S. W., Jr., and Nickel, W. R. Giant pigmented nevi, melanoma, and leptomeningeal melanocytosis. Arch. Derm., 91:100, 1965.

Windhorst, D. B., Zelickson, A. S., and Good, R. A. Chediak-Higashi syndrome: hereditary gigantism of cytoplasmic organelles. Science, 151:81, 1966.

26.7
ECZEMA
(ATOPIC DERMATITIS)
(See also Sec. 11.7)

JOSEPH McGUIRE

Eczema is a common chronic dermatitis characterized by lichenification and pruritus. It occurs in a population defined as atopic by virtue of the presence of several related conditions including asthma, seasonal rhinitis, eczema, and recurrent urticaria. The prevalence rate of atopy in the general population is unknown, but a recent survey revealed that 19 percent of a large group of dermatologic patients, who did not have eczema, had a personal history of atopy; 23 percent had a positive family history of atopy and 34 percent had either a positive personal or family history.

PHYSIOLOGY.   The skin of atopics responds abnormally to the intracutaneous injection of methacholine (mecholyl) by delayed blanching after initial erythema. In normal individuals an area of erythema appears around the site of injection and gradually fades. This paradoxical reaction was first described by Lobitz and Campbell in 1953 and is said to occur in 70 percent of patients with atopic dermatitis. Although the blanching suggests that vasoconstriction has occurred, direct examination of the capillaries does not support this assumption. Clearance measurements of ^{131}I iodoantipyrine following the injection of methacholine also reveal increased clearance of the isotope from the site of injection—an observation inconsistent with vasoconstriction. It has been suggested that a vasoconstricting substance, probably norepinephrine, is released by mecholyl; however, prior injection of the a-adrenergic blocker, pentolamine, does not block the delayed blanch. The blanch produced by the injection of epinephrine into atopic skin is associated with decreased clearance and vasoconstriction. The pharmacology of the delayed blanch, although probably an important clue to the pathogenesis of eczema, remains obscure. Atropine will block it, however, the delayed blanch will persist despite local anesthesia.

Atopic reagin appears to be identical to immunoglobulin-E, which is elevated in the sera of individuals with severe atopic dermatitis. Many individuals with moderate atopic dermatitis have normal levels of circulating IgE. It is somewhat surprising that the amount of anti-IgE necessary to produce erythema and wheal reactions when injected into the skin is no different in patients with atopic dermatitis than in control groups.

The relationship of atopic dermatitis to other mediators of the immune reaction is not so clear.

Peterson and co-workers have reported that, in a group of 23 patients with agammaglobulinemia and no detectable circulating globulin, 4 had atopic dermatitis.

PATHOLOGY.   Changes occur in both the dermis and epidermis but the alterations are so variable that the clinical features of the disease tend to be more helpful for diagnosis than the histologic features. However, microscopic examination of the skin can sometimes be of great importance in differentiating atopic dermatitis from other diseases.

Histologic changes reflect the varying clinical picture. Early changes are acanthosis and parakeratosis. The inflammatory infiltrate varies in quantity with the clinical activity of the process and consists of lymphocytes and sometimes eosinophils. Spongiosis (intercellular edema), a prominent feature of contact dermatitis, is usually not a major feature of atopic dermatitis except for the dyshidrotic form (pompholyx). Electron microscopy of exudative infantile eczema reveals lysosomes in the keratinocytes. The more chronic lichenified forms of eczema show hyperkeratosis, acanthosis, some degree of papillomatosis, and usually only scanty inflammatory infiltrate.

CLINICAL FORMS.   Long-term observations of individual patients, as well as statistical studies of large numbers of patients, both support the concept of including several clinically well-defined dermatoses within the general term atopic dermatitis. Although this "inclusive" approach to atopic dermatitis does not imply etiologic relationships, it is useful from a therapeutic standpoint and it tends to simplify an unnecessarily complicated area of dermatology. The basis for including the following clinical expressions in the category of atopic dermatitis is both the high incidence of history of atopic disease in these patients, and the changing pattern of dermatitis in a single patient (Table 3).

Infantile Eczema.   In infancy, the creases of the neck may become cracked, moist, and sometimes secondarily infected with monilia. The cheeks have a healthy, rosy appearance which, on close inspection, may be due to the presence of papules and crusting. Fissuring may occur behind the ears.

When the child becomes older, the pattern of involvement changes and becomes more scattered with extensor involvement. The lesions are usually dry and somewhat pruritic. Classic flexural involvement may occur at any age, but is most common after 4 years.

Dyshidrotic Eczema is a well established misnomer for a clinically well-defined dermatitis characterized by recurrent blistering eruptions on the palms and soles (Fig. 60). Although some of these children do have hyperhidrosis of the palms and soles, careful serial sections of the blisters establish their independence from the eccrine apparatus. This form of eczema is very pruritic and is sometimes misdiagnosed as contact dermatitis or dermatophytic infection. Opening the blisters on the hands and feet helps relieve the intense pruritus.

TABLE 3.

	Age	Site	Clinical Features
Infantile Eczema	Infancy	Cheeks, neck creases ears, scalp	Exudative, moist, cheeks are rosy: papular
Flexural Eczema	> 4 years	Antecubital popliteal areas, sides of neck, behind ears	Erythema, excoriation, skin becomes lichenified and taut
Dyshidrotic Eczema (Pompholyx)	> 2 years	Palms, soles	Intensely pruritic, blisters occur on palms, soles and sides of fingers. Blisters may be minute or large. Frequently mistaken for dermatophytic infection
Nummular Eczema	> 1 year	Extremities, trunk	Circular, papulovesicular patches, often extremely pruritic. Lesions may be sparse or numerous
Generalizes Atopic Dermatitis	> 4-5 years	Generalized	Uncommon in young children, skin is generally lichenified with slight scaling. Hands and feet are cold, the eyelids are lichenified, infraorbital pigmentation and many excoriations. Involvement is worse in flexural areas

Generalized Atopic Dermatitis. These unfortunate children itch in response to many stimuli such as heat, cold, wool, or anger. The skin becomes lichenified, taut, and scaly, and is often crossed with excoriations. Their eyelids and intraorbital folds are lichenified which gives them an apprehensive, fatigued appearance.

ANCILLARY CLINICAL FEATURES. *Ichthyosis vulgaris* (dry skin) is often associated with atopic dermatitis

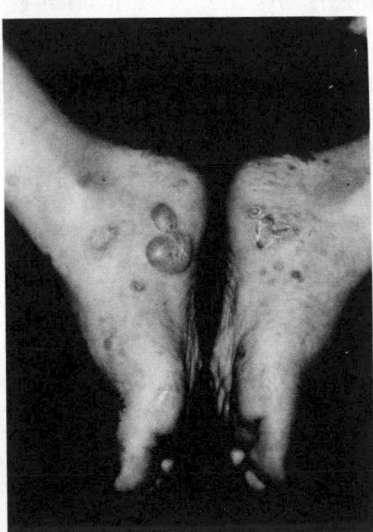

Fig. 60. Dyshidrotic eczema (pompholyx). Recurrent blistering eruption on palms and soles. These lesions are not related to sweat retention as the name suggests. Pompholyx is probably one manifestation of atopic dermatitis. This child later had characteristic atopic dermatitis.

and, even in the absence of clinically distinctive ichthyosis vulgaris, keratosis pilaris may be present. These children often have dry, chapped skin in the winter time. Prevention of scaling and chapping with local hydration and lubrication can sometimes preclude further development of eczema.

Pityriasis Alba. Pityriasis alba is a descriptive term for one or more oval or circular patches of depigmentation of varying degrees. There is often a fine scale and occasionally slight erythema. The lesions are located on the cheeks and trunk and often occur in children with evidence of atopy, especially eczema and hay fever. Pityriasis alba is thought by us to represent a form of atopic dermatitis; however, this is not a universally held concept. The lesions of pityriasis alba improve and repigment following the use of lubricants and topical steroids. In chronic eczema, there has been demonstrated a block in pigment transfer from the melanocyte to the keratinocyte. There may be a similar interference with this symbiotic relationship in pityriasis alba.

COMPLICATIONS. Atopic skin is especially susceptible to infections with microorganisms; among the more serious are herpes simplex (Fig. 61) and vaccinia. Impetigo is a common problem in these children. Because of the seriousness of Kaposi's varicelliform eruption (a vesicular eruption caused by herpes simplex or vaccinia) *these children should not be vaccinated or exposed to a freshly vaccinated individual* (see Sec. 14.40).

ASSOCIATED DISEASES. Allergic rhinitis, asthma, and vernal catarrh are frequent in children with atopic dermatitis. Cataracts occur frequently enough to be a recognized complication of the disease, although the relationship is obscure.

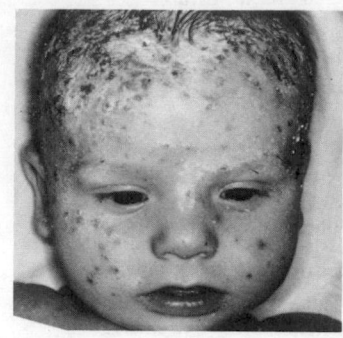

Fig. 61. Herpes simplex (eczema herpeticum). Infant with atopic dermatitis and multiple lesions of herpes simplex.

Ichthyosis vulgaris often coexists with atopic dermatitis. The Wiscott-Aldrich syndrome exhibits, in addition to atopic dermatitis, thrombocytopenia and cutaneous and pulmonary infection.

Other diseases occurring with increased frequency in children with atopic dermatitis are congenital agammaglobulinemia and phenylketonuria.

PROGNOSIS. A 20-year follow-up of 492 patients with atopic dermatitis seen at the Mayo Clinic was conducted by a questionnaire to which 45 percent responded (Table 4). The median age of onset in the mild and severe groups was 4 months; the median age of complete clearing for the two groups was 21 years. The average duration of the disease was 27 years among the mild group and 32 years in the severe group. It is apparent from this study that the prognosis for complete clearing in childhood or early adulthood is not good, especially since any patient in the "cleared" group is subject to exacerbation.

TREATMENT. The form of treatment obviously is determined by the major clinical features. Therapy for acute, weeping dermatitis differs from therapy for a chronic, lichenified dermatitis.

Pruritus is a difficult problem and must be modified in order to reduce further damage to the skin produced by scratching which, even if not aggressive enough to break the skin, will produce lichenification. Pruritus often is most severe in children around bedtime, and it is sometimes possible to administer oral antipruritic medication only before bedtime. If

TABLE 4. *Twenty-Year Follow-up of Atopic Dermatitis*

Present Condition (Percent)	Condition When First Seen	
	Mild	Severe
Completely Cleared	40	29
Better	48	55
Unchanged	1	13
Worse	11	3

necessary, the medication is given throughout the day; however, most antipruritics are somewhat sedative. Effective preparations are Hydroxyzine, Polaramine, Benadryl, and Periactin. Sometimes sedatives such as chloral hydrate or phenobarbital are required. The importance of treating pruritus is enormous in the managament of eczema; the best topical therapy without oral therapy is often ineffective.

Other aspects of treatment, including other forms of *systemic therapy, diet, desensitization,* and *hospitalization,* are discussed in Section 11.7.

REFERENCES

Lobitz, W. C., and Campbell, C. J. Physiologic studies in atopic dermatitis. Arch. Derm., 67:575-589, 1953.
Peterson, R. D., Page, A. R., and Good, R. A. Wheal and erythema allergy in patients with agammaglobulinemia. J. Allergy, 33:406, 1962.

26.8
OTHER DISEASES OF SKIN

JOSEPH McGUIRE

MILIARIA (PORAL OCCLUSION). Miliaria is a nearly universal dermatitis of infancy. The lesions result from a combination of sweating and occlusion of the intraepidermal portion of the sweat duct. If the obstruction is very superficial, then only a fraction of the epidermis is lifted away from the skin by a drop of sweat with the production of a minute transparent vesicle, miliaria crystallina, which often escapes notice. Miliaria crystallina is common in febrile illnesses and is not symptomatic. The lesions are so superficial that they may be removed by wiping the skin. This disease has no intrinsic importance and only reflects sweating and poral occlusion.

Miliaria rubra is produced by the same process occurring deeper in the sweat duct. Sweat is retained behind the deeper occlusion and causes dilation and rupture of the epidermal portion of the sweat duct with resulting swelling and inflammation. The lesions are symptomatic, often producing considerable itching and stinging—hence its familiar designation, prickly heat. The lesions appear in areas of maceration, under plastic pants, adhesive tape, and tight clothing which occlude and cause the epidermal lining of the sweat duct to swell with obstruction of the lumen. Prickly heat is especially common in hot humid weather and in febrile illnesses with associated excessive sweating.

The lesions are small (2 to 5 mm) red papules, papulovesicles, and occasionally pustules which occur most commonly on the trunk. In severe cases, the dermatitis may be generalized with a resultant decrease in sweating and evaporative heat loss. Interference with heat loss may result in temperature elevation.

Effective therapeutic measures for miliaria rubra are based on the pathogenesis of the lesion. Reduction of environmental temperature and humidity is most important. Body temperature, when this is a contributing cause, is reduced by salicylates. Lightweight absorbent clothing should be worn.

Open wet dressings with Burow's solution promote drying and heat loss. Calamine lotion is an effective drying agent. When there is secondary bacterial or monilial infection the specific antibiotic is added.

In cases of extensive involvement with anhydrosis, parenteral fluids and more active supportive measures are indicated.

PITYRIASIS RUBRA PILARIS. This rare chronic skin disease which may begin in infancy or childhood is characterized by red, horny papules which surround hair follicles. Large numbers of these papules cause the skin to appear erythematous. A characteristic clinical feature is occasional well-demarcated islands of normal skin surrounded by generalized involvement. The palms and soles are usually involved. They are red, thickened, and fissured. Papules are often present on the backs of the fingers. The scalp may be involved initially with severe seborrheic dermatitis which may also affect the face. In children, facial involvement often produces a masklike appearance.

When there is extensive involvement, the diagnosis of generalized psoriasis is often difficult to rule out. Histologic diagnosis is usually possible.

The course of the disease is persistent and fortunately asymptomatic. In a few families it appears to be inherited as a dominant trait with incomplete penetrance. Treatment consists of lubrication and the use of keratolytics such as salicylic acid. Oral vitamin A in large doses is definitely beneficial in occasional patients. Sunlight, which benefits psoriasis, has no effect on pityriasis rubra pilaris.

PITYRIASIS ROSEA. Pityriasis rosea is a papulosquamous disease occurring primarily on the trunk. It is characterized by a herald patch—an erythematous annular lesion with a scaly border which precedes the generalized eruption by about a week. Infrequently, there may be a mild prodrome of fever and sore throat. The generalized eruption occurs mainly on the trunk, and the oval lesions lie with their axes along lines of cleavage. The lesions of the generalized eruption are usually smaller than the herald patch. They enlarge and are surrounded by a collarette of fine scale. In children, the lesions may be urticarial or papulovesicular (Fig. 62).

The occasional prodrome and the usual freedom from second attacks suggest a viral causation, although this has not been proved. The disease occurs frequently in children and young adults, rarely in infants. There is no evidence that it is contagious. The disease usually lasts for six to eight weeks with or without treatment but may persist longer.

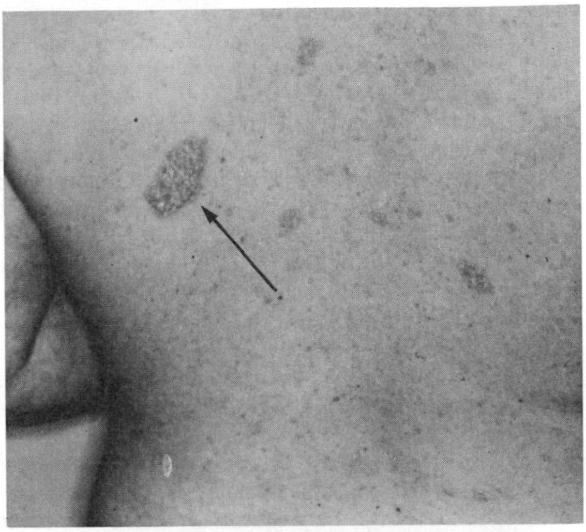

Fig. 62. Pityriasis rosea. Herald patch (arrow) precedes the generalized eruption which can be papular, urticarial, or occasionally papulovesicular.

The clincial features, the color, distribution, and morphology of the lesions are usually sufficient to establish a diagnosis. Although the disease itself is of trivial significance, it achieves distinction by being regularly misdiagnosed as tinea corporis. In older children, secondary syphilis must be ruled out.

If pruritus is troublesome, calamine lotion containing 0.5 percent phenol may be used topically. The oral administration of antihistamines is also effective for pruritus.

LICHEN PLANUS. This member of the papulosquamous group of diseases is characterized by multiple polygonal, flat-topped papules with a predilection for the flexor aspects of the wrists and forearms and the lower legs; however, any part of the body may become involved. Involvement of the buccal mucosa is frequent with a coalescence of minute white papules to form a linear or reticulated pattern. The typical lesion is usually only 1 to 2 mm in diameter; many of these may aggregate to form a plaque. Bullous forms of the disease also occur.

The disease is of unknown cause and mainly affects adults; it rarely affects children. A clinical feature shared with psoriasis is the Koebner phenomenon: new lesions appear on the skin at sites of trauma. The course of the disease is variable, often lasting a year. Lesions on the legs occasionally become hypertrophic and persist much longer.

In addition to the clinical features, which are fairly specific, there are characteristic histopathologic findings: a band of lymphocytic infiltrate immediately below the epidermis with destruction of the basement membrane of the epidermis. Differential diagnosis includes drug eruption and atopic dermatitis, in both of which there may be flat-topped papules. Oral lesions may be mistaken for thrush, and involvement of the genitalia may mimic seborrheic dermatitis or psoriasis.

Treatment is unsatisfactory and is directed toward the alleviation of pruritis, which may be severe. Topical steroids are often effective on the genitalia but usually have little effect elsewhere. The intralesional injection of triamcinolone acetonide into chronic plaques of hypertrophic lichen planus is often beneficial.

LICHEN NITIDIS. Lichen nitidis is a rare asymptomatic disease of unknown cause with no satisfactory treatment. Highly characteristic lesions permit easy diagnosis. The numerous, shiny, slightly elevated, minute, flat-topped papules may occur anywhere, but the genitalia and abdomen are most often involved. Eczema is often characterized by similar small elevated flat-topped papules, especially in the Negro. These lesions, which are associated with pruritus and friction, are easily mistaken for the relatively uncommon lichen nitidis. The course of lichen nitidis is chronic and the disease eventually resolves without residua.

MUCHA-HABERMANN DISEASE. Mucha-Habermann disease (Pityriasis lichenoides et varioliformis acuta) is an uncommon disease characterized by recurrent crops of lesions that first appear as pink papules which form a central vesicle, then crust, and sometimes undergo an area of central hemorrhagic necrosis (Fig. 63). The lesions are usually asymptomatic; however, the onset is sometimes heralded by fever and malaise. The trunk and flexor aspects of the extremities are involved, the face is usually spared. The course is unpredictable. Many patients are clear within six to eight months; however, recurrent crops of lesions may appear for years (Fig. 64).

Although the etiology is unknown, the course of the illness suggests viral etiology. The earliest histologic change is a lymphocytic infiltrate around dermal capillaries associated with epidermal edema.

There are febrile and scarring forms of the disease. Treatment is not satisfactory; systemic adenocortical steroids or tetracycline may be tried.

GIANOTTI-CROSTI SYNDROME. Gianotti-Crosti syndrome is a distinctive clinical syndrome characterized by papules one half to one centimeter in diameter located on the legs, thighs and buttocks (Fig. 65). There is usually lymphadenopathy and sometimes mild malaise. The lesions on the legs are occasionally purpuric. The disease may last up to two months. No therapy is indicated.

URTICARIA PIGMENTOSA (MASTOCYTOSIS). This disease has been classified into three groups, two of which have their onset in childhood. The lesions are characterized by collections in the dermis of tissue mast cells which stain metachromatically. Trauma or heat causes release of histamine from these cells, which leads to the formation of urticaria.

Distinguishing features of the three groups are:

I. Solitary lesion with onset in childhood
II. Multiple lesions with onset in childhood
III. Multiple lesions with onset after childhood

Group I. The lesions are often present at birth, but may appear during the first year. The lesion may be located anywhere on the trunk or extremities. Grossly, the lesions are yellow to tan in color and may range in size from a small papule to a large plaque. If a second lesion does not appear within one or two months, then the patient can be placed in group I with fair assurance. Most of these solitary

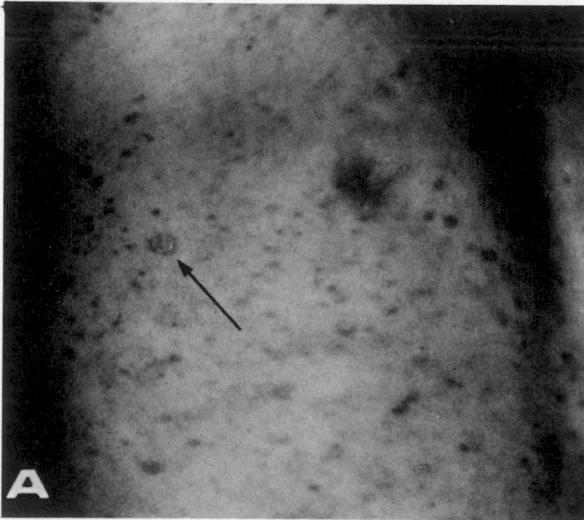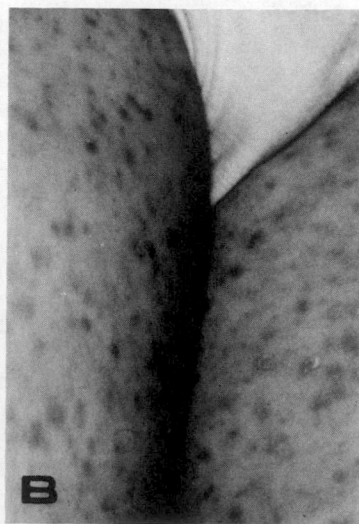

Fig. 63. Mucha-Habermann disease. A. Generalized distribution of lesions on trunk. This form of parapsoriasis is characterized by papulonecrotic lesions (arrow). B. Papular scaly lesions are distributed over extremities and trunk, usually sparing the face. The individual lesions are sometimes hemorrhagic.

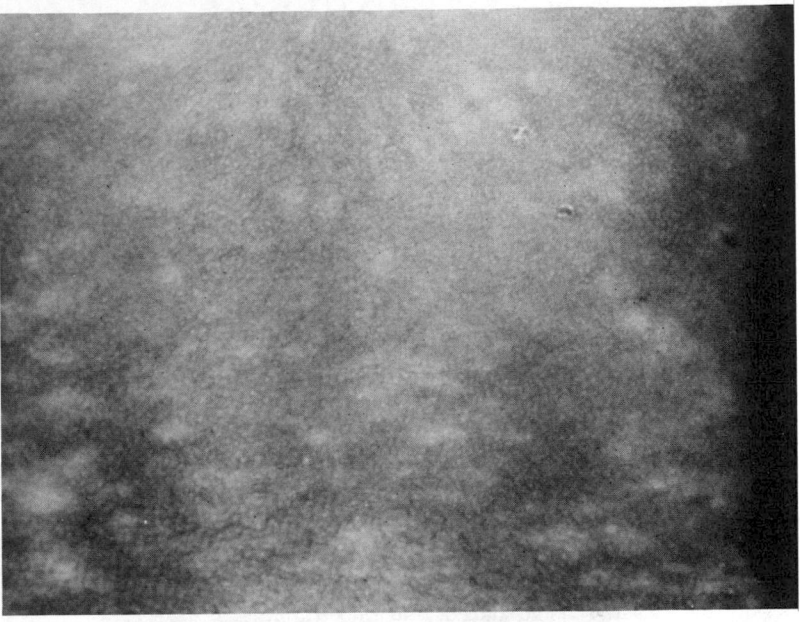

Fig. 64. Mucha-Habermann disease. The disease in this child is now quiescent and marked by postinflammatory hypopigmentation. Photograph is of back.

lesions are characterized by vesicle or bulla formation, and urticaria can be produced by rubbing (Darier's sign). These children improve spontaneously, and excision of the lesion is not indicated unless flushing or other symptoms necessitate it. Treatment is directed toward the pruritus.

Group II. The lesions are macular or maculopapular and appear from birth to age 4 years. The site of involvement is usually the trunk. They vary in size and may be pink, yellow, or brown. Vesiculation is often present, and Darier's sign is almost always positive. Pruritus is the chief symptom and may be alleviated by the use of oral antihistamines. Rarely, blistering may precede the appearance of the typical maculopapular lesions of urticaria pigmentosa. Most of these children show either marked improvement or actual disappearance of the lesions by adolescence. Rarely, the disease persists unabated into adult life.

Group III. In most of these patients, the lesions appear in adolescence or early adulthood. Located predominantly on the trunk, they are pink to brown in color and are usually macular or maculopapular.

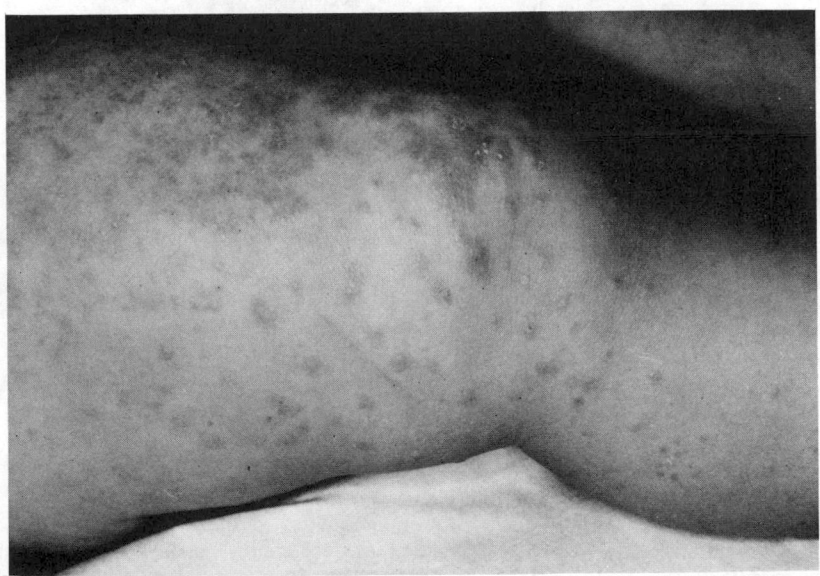

Fig. 65. Gianotti-Crosti syndrome. Red papules on legs of infant. The lesions may also occur on buttocks, extensor aspects of the arms and the face.

Darier's sign is usually positive and vesiculation is rare. These patients, in contrast to those in groups I and II, have a very chronic course.

In addition to involvement of the skin, there may be widespread and rarely fatal extracutaneous mast-cell infiltration of liver, spleen, and bone marrow. Systemic involvement is usually associated with diffuse involvement of the skin.

The cause is unknown. Thirty-one patients have been described in 14 families with pedigrees suggesting autosomal dominant form of inheritance. All three types of mastocytosis were represented in these families. Most patients, however, do not have a positive family history. Treatment is directed toward reducing pruritus with antihistamines; air conditioning is an especially effective adjunct to therapy in warm weather. The pigmentation when present is due to melanin, the formation of which is stimulated by the mast cell or its products.

NEVOXANTHOENDOTHELIOMA (JUVENILE XANTHO-GRANULOMA). This benign tumor usually appears within the first few months of life. The individual lesions are elevated, dome-shaped, and smooth. Their color is sometimes yellow-orange but can also be tan. The lesions, which are characteristically located on the scalp, may also occur elsewhere, especially in extensor areas. The lesions are usually multiple and vary in size from a few millimeters to over a centimeter in diameter.

The disease is almost always uncomplicated and resolves spontaneously. Lesions involving the iris and ciliary body may result in glaucoma. The patients are normolipemic and the disease is not related to the more sinister histiocytosis. The earliest histologic event is the accumulation of histiocytes with secondary deposition of lipids.

The lesions must be distinguished from mastocytosis which they may sometimes closely resemble.

HEMANGIOMA. Hemangiomas and pigmented-nevi are the most common developmental abnormalities of skin. They both produce considerably more apprehension than is warranted by their nature and prognosis. Hemangiomas, also termed vascular nevi, have practically no malignant potential and are of concern primarily because of their appearance, interference with function, ulceration, or hemorrhage after trauma. Most hemangiomas fall into one of the following three descriptive categories: port-wine stain (nevus flammeus), strawberry hemangioma, and cavernous hemangioma.

Port-Wine Stain. The port wine stain is pink to reddish purple and usually present at birth. The two most common sites are the nape of the neck and the center of the forehead, although the nevus may occur on any part of the body (Fig. 66). The Sturge-Weber-Dimitri syndrome includes a port-wine vascular nevus, often in the distribution of the first division of the trigeminal nerve. The lesion is composed of mature capillaries, and although those located on the face and trunk tend to regress, most

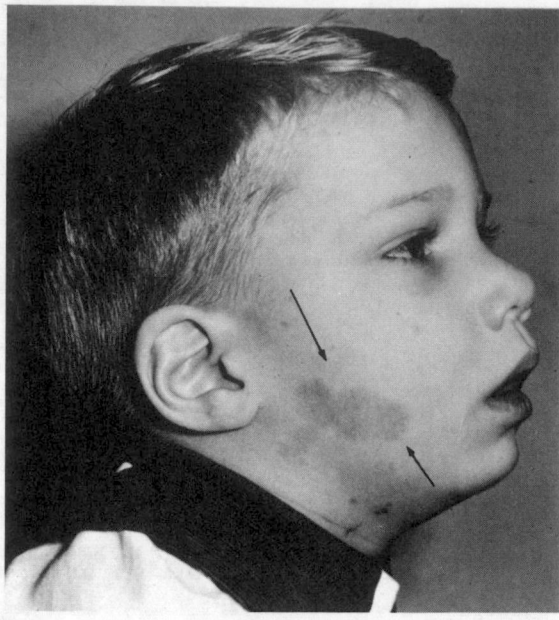

Fig. 66. Capillary hemangioma of the face. This type of hemangioma, which is more common in the midline of the forehead and the nape of the neck, consists of mature blood vessels and usually does not resolve.

grow in relation to the affected part. Occasionally, the surface of the hemangioma may become papular with age. In view of the persistent and benign course

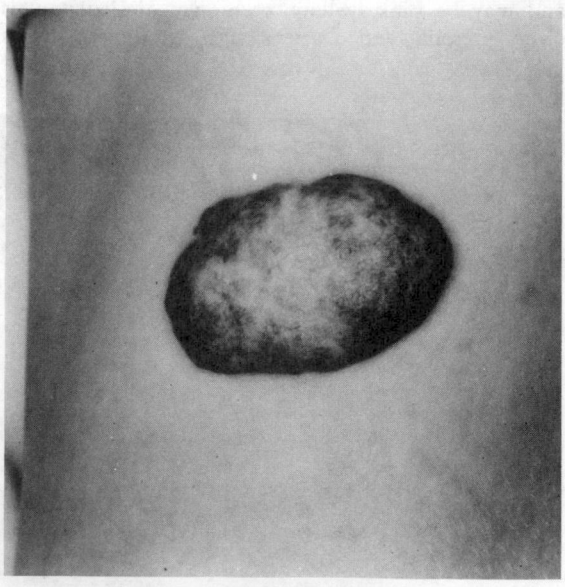

Fig. 67. Strawberry hemangioma on the thigh of an infant. These hemangiomas often undergo rapid growth in infants and, if destructive therapy is avoided, they usually resolve spontaneously with little residua. The light appearance of the center is not a highlight, but decreased vascularity that presages resolution.

of the lesion, it is best left alone unless it is disfiguring. Small lesions may be excised, but dry ice and sclerosing agents are not effective. The nevi are not radiosensitive. The most acceptable treatment is a covering cosmetic. Attempts to tattoo pigment into these nevi to lighten the color have been only partially successful.

Strawberry Hemangioma. The nevus vasculosus or strawberry mark usually appears a few days after birth as a tiny red spot. This is the only worthwhile time to interfere with its natural development; however, it is usually overlooked until after a few weeks of rapid growth. It then appears as a lobulated, elevated, bright red or red-purple, soft lesion. The lesion may persist with slow growth for several years. The color then becomes mottled and the tumor begins to involute (Fig. 67). The strawberry mark offers an almost irresistible temptation for the physician to interfere with its natural course. The ultimate cosmetic result is usually superior if impulses to treat the strawberry mark are resisted. Involution is usually nearly complete by age 6 or 7 and often occurs earlier. The dependability of this spontaneous resolution is confirmed by the absence of this lesion in adults, and there is little question that the cosmetic result is better if the lesion is not treated (Fig. 68).

In certain situations, treatment is required because the hemangioma interferes with feeding, respiration, or vision. Hemangiomas on the urethra or anus also require attention. Hemorrhage is rare and is usually the result of trauma or therapy. Ulceration is not so rare and may precede spontaneous resolution. Thrombocytopenic purpura has occurred in association with large hemangiomas, many of which are strawberry hemangiomas. The tumor apparently sequesters and destroys platelets.

The usual treatment by the application of carbon dioxide snow or dry ice is destructive and produces scarring. The strawberry hemangioma is radiosensitive, and x-ray is the preferred treatment for large lesions. Systemic steroids have been used successfully in the treatment of these nevi.

Cavernous Hemangioma. Cavernous hemangiomas are composed of mature blood vesesls and do not involute, thus differing from strawberry hemangiomas. They are almost always present at birth and do not grow except in proportion to the area of body affected. The hemangioma may be raised or flat and may be predominantly subcutaneous in location. If intervention is necessary because of the position of the hemangioma, surgery is the only effective treatment. This can sometimes be carried out in stages without the necessity of a graft. The mature blood vessels are not especially sensitive to x-ray. Several syndromes, e.g., Parkes-Weber, are associated with cavernous hemangiomas.

Other Vascular Abnormalities and Syndromes. The spider nevus or nevus araneus is a common lesion of children occurring in about one fourth of children younger than 15 years. The dorsa of the hands, forearms, and face are most commonly involved. Unlike the nevus araneus in the adult, which is a fellow traveler with Laennec's cirrhosis, the appearance of this lesion has no medical significance in the child. There is a central vessel which can often be seen to pulsate with smaller radiating vessels. Although they are of little cosmetic consequence, and often resolve spontaneously with age, electrocoagula-

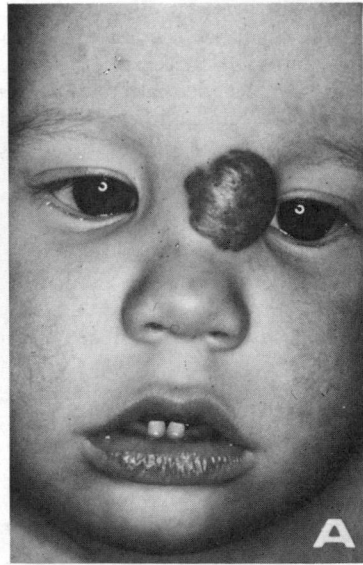 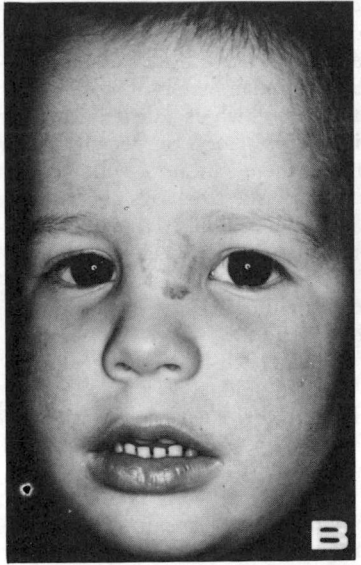

Fig. 68. Strawberry hemangioma. A. Lesion at its greatest size. B. Same lesion as in A, observed 26 months later without treatment.

tion of the central vessel will usually cause disappearance of the lesion.

There are many syndromes associated with hemangiomas.

In the Sturge-Weber-Dimitri syndrome, nevus flammeus in the trigeminal region of the face is associated with vascular abnormalities in the brain. Mental retardation, seizures, and contralateral hemiplegia are characteristic.

Parkes-Weber syndrome is a capillary or mature large vessel hemangioma on an extremity with hypertrophy of that limb.

In the von Hippel-Lindau syndrome, there are angiomas of the retina, brain, and skin. In the Maffucci syndrome, there are enchondromas of the bone associated with multiple cavernous hemangiomas. The limbs may become seriously deformed, even to the point where amputation is necessary.

A recently described syndrome is the Louis-Bar (ataxia-telangiectasia) syndrome in which there is progressive telangiectasia of the bulbar conjunctivae, ears, cheeks, and neck in association with cerebellar ataxia and retardation of growth. About half of these children have hypogammaglobulinemia; recurrent sinopulmonary infections are also characteristic of the syndrome.

The Rendu-Osler-Weber syndrome is characterized by multiple punctate small angiomas involving the tongue, nasal mucosa, lips, and fingertips. There are also telangiectases in the bowel and genitourinary tract which occasionally bleed. The syndrome is inherited as a dominant and often presents in childhood as recurrent epistaxis.

LYMPHEDEMA. Lymphedema occasionally involves the lower extremities. It is usually apparent in infancy but may not present until puberty. It involves the distal leg or the entire leg. The edema is solid and may be complicated by verrucous hypertrophy of the skin and recurrent infections. The disease may be unilateral. Lymphedema may have no apparent cause, it may be caused by postinflammatory fibrosis, or it may be a dominant trait, which is labeled Milroy's disease. Treatment is unsatisfactory. Surgery has been carried out in many of these children with considerable resultant scarring. Elastic stockings are helpful. Histologically there are greatly dilated lymph vessels in the dermis and subcutaneous tissue.

LYMPHANGIOMA. There are several benign tumors of lymphatic channels in children. The most common is lymphangioma circumscriptum, which may be present at birth or appear during childhood. The lesions may occur in any location and consist of close-set, deep vesicles which may be clear or occasionally hemorrhagic. The lesion may resolve following treatment with liquid nitrogen.

THE NEWBORN SKIN. At birth, it is vital that the skin function as a relatively impermeable membrane to protect the organism from its new, dry environment. This transition from the warm, wet intrauterine existence is usually unmarked by notable disease except for two common findings, erythema toxicum and milia. The skin of the newborn is covered by vernix caseosa. The breasts are often hypertrophic, as are the scrotum and labia majora. A few infants exhibit pigmentation of the linea alba.

Although the role of the vernix caseosa is not established, its origin appears to be fetal rather than maternal, and no demonstrably good purpose is served by its removal.

Erythema Neonatorum (Toxic Erythema of the Newborn). This eruption is ubiquitous in the newborn; its reported incidence is probably related to the frequency and care of the inspection of the infant. The early lesions are red macules that appear within the first few days of life. The macules, which may number in the hundreds, may fade or may become papules, sometimes surmounted by a small pustule which contains a large number of eosinophils. No area of the body, including the palms and soles, is spared by this peculiar common eruption.

Milia. Milia are tiny keratin inclusion cysts that occur on the nose and cheeks. Most milia disappear spontaneously; the few that persist can be easily removed by piercing the overlying skin and expressing them with a comedo extractor.

DIAPER RASH. This diagnosis includes a number of separate entities which share one feature—the site of involvement, which is the area usually covered by the diaper.

The most common clinical picture is that of scaling, erythema, and maceration. Occasionally, lesions of miliaria rubra are present in the involved area. Nodular ulcerated lesions rarely occur and may resemble lesions of secondary syphilis. Pathogenesis is probably related to maceration, moisture, and sweat retention. The appearance of this type of lesion is promoted by occlusive rubber pants and prolonged intervals between diaper changes. Diarrhea, a frequent occurrence in infants, also contributes to the maceration of the skin.

Contact dermatitis is a rare event in infants but may occur following sensitization to a detergent or disinfectant used on the diapers. More often, in children the response to these agents is a primary irritant reaction.

Seborrheic dermatitis and atopic dermatitis may also involve the diaper area and fall into the general designation of diaper dermatitis until involvement elsewhere helps establish the diagnosis.

A substantial number of eruptions in the diaper area are associated with or caused by monilia. Small red or eroded perianal satellite lesions when present strengthen the clinical impression. Positive diagnosis can be made by recovering candida from skin scrapings. Topical application of Mycostatin or Amphotericin B in combination with a topical steroid or Mycolog cream (Squibb) often dramatically improves the lesion.

Ammonia traditionally has been considered a major factor in the production of diaper rash. The evidence that ammonia generated by the bacterial decomposition of urea and other urinary substances is responsible for dermatitis is not conclusive. Other factors—maceration and irritation from feces and urine —are probably sufficient to account for most diaper rash.

The treatment of diaper rash is directed toward cleansing and drying the involved area. The diaper should be changed as soon as possible after it is soiled. The diapers furnished by commercial diaper services, in addition to their convenience, are usually cleaner and freer of residual soap and detergent than diapers washed at home. Topical steroid lotions or creams promote clearing of seborrheic and atopic dermatitis and are often helpful in diaper rash of less clearly defined causation.

ADENOMA SEBACEUM. Adenoma sebaceum is the cutaneous manifestation of a widespread abnormality involving the brain (tuberous sclerosis), retina (glioma), heart (rhabdomyoma), and kidney (angiomyolipoma). Other cutaneous signs of the disease are periungual and subungual fibromas and a characteristic slightly raised plaque, the Shagreen patch, which when present is usually located in the lumbrosacral region. Café au lait spots and a variety of pigmented and vascular nevi may also be present.

An early aid to the diagnosis of adenoma sebaceum in a patient with seizures is the presence of macular leucoderma. The pigmentation in these oval areas is usually diminished but not absent.

Epiloia refers to the triad of mental deficiency, epilepsy, and adenoma sebaceum. Most patients with adenoma sebaceum are severely retarded; rarely there is little concomitant mental retardation. Epilepsy may be of any clinical type—grand mal, petit mal, or Jacksonian.

Adenoma sebaceum is usually not present at birth but appears in the first decade as small pink or flesh-colored, dome-shaped papules in the nasolabial fold. They also commonly occur on the cheeks and chin. They may be numerous and may become pedunculated and papillomatous. The disease is inherited as an incomplete dominant. Individual lesions of adenoma sebaceum may be removed by electrodesiccation or dermabrasion.

ACNE. Acne is a common problem affecting to some degree practically every adolescent. It is characterized by comedones, papules, pustules, and cysts.

The pathogenesis of acne is closely linked to the response of the sebaceous gland to androgenic hormones, which cause hypertrophy and accompanying hypersecretion of the sebaceous glands. The permissive role of androgens in acne is further emphasized by the observation that eunuchs do not develop acne and by the rarity of acne in children up to a few years preceding pubescence. There appear to be two further requirements for the appearance of acne: (1) the formation of a comedo or blackhead (a plug of sebum and keratin in the orifice of the follicle) and (2) tissue reaction to the comedo

or to products that have accumulated behind the obstruction it creates. Large numbers of comedones may be present with very little accompanying inflammation or pustule formation. The other clinical extreme is also seen—i.e., many inflammatory papules accompanied by few comedones. Usually, however, both are present.

The role of infection in the pathogenesis of acne, though unproved, appears likely. Two organisms, *Corynebacterium acnes* and *Staphylococcus albus,* are present in practically all acne lesions whether they are open or closed comedones, papules, pustules, or cysts. Although their presence does not constitute proof of an etiologic relationship to acne, the concept is strengthened by the observation that injection of cultures of *C. acnes* into keratinous cysts causes inflammation and rupture of the cysts.

Free fatty acids are produced from sebum by the lipolytic action of *C. acnes.* Experimentally, inflammation resembling that seen in clinical acne can be produced by the intradermal injection of sebum or comedones. The free fatty acid component of sebum is especially irritating. These observations suggest that the leakage of sebum or fatty acids into the tissue is responsible in some degree for the inflammation of acne.

The significance of the lipolytic action of *C. acnes* is supported by the observation that killed *C. acnes* do not produce inflammation when injected into cysts of steatocystoma multiplex. Live cultures of *Staph. albus* are similarly without effect when injected into cysts of steatocystoma multiplex.

Clinical Investigation. The classification of clinical acne depends on the type and abundance of the several types of lesion: comedo, papule, pustule, cyst. The sites of predilection are the face, upper chest, back, and shoulders; however, the lesions may be restricted to a single area such as the forehead or upper back.

The comedo or blackhead is probably the earliest clinical expression of acne and is often unaccompanied by inflammation. Various grades of activity of acne can be defined according to the number of lesions present. Although a combination of the various types of lesion is usually present, one type, e.g., comedo, cyst, or pustule, may predominate. The comedo is easily recognized as a black dot in a patulous follicular orifice. The color is due to oxidation of lipid. A special form of excoriated acne (acne excoriée des jeunes filles) is rather common in adolescents who, acutely aware of their appearance, manipulate and excoriate otherwise imperceptible lesions, often producing a significant cosmetic problem.

Treatment. There is little evidence that therapy shortens the duration of the total course of acne. Judicious systemic and topical therapy does help control oiliness, follicular plugging, and cyst formation. The aim of therapy is to decrease in number and activity the lesions of acne and prevent scarring caused by cysts and large inflammatory pustules.

Systemic therapy. Cyclic therapy with anovulatory agents often causes clinical improvement after one or two months of treatment. This approach must be restricted to females because of the feminization produced by the estrogen.

Small maintenance doses of tetracycline, 125 to 250 mg/day, often cause dramatic improvement. Whether the effect is related to antibiosis of *Corynebacterium acnes* is not known; however, treatment with tetracycline is associated with reduction of free fatty acids in sebum.

Topical therapy. The aim of topical therapy is the reduction of oiliness and the production of mild chapping and drying. The enormous number of proprietary medications available to the physician and patient suggests that the perfect formulation has not been achieved.

One percent salicylic acid in 70 percent ethanol is an inexpensive and effective drying agent. There are many commercial variants of this type. Many commonly used preparations contain sulfur and resorcin. Pustules and cysts often respond to hot compresses with sulfur-containing solutions (Vlem-Dome). Most forms of topical therapy produce chapping, which to a small degree is desirable. During the winter when the absolute humidity is low, frequency of application must be reduced to avoid severe chapping.

Ultraviolet light. Sunlight benefits acne, although the high humidity and heat of summer may have the opposite effect. An ultraviolet lamp may be effectively used at home by the patient who, in addition to shielding his eyes, must be careful to avoid burns. The first exposure is usually limited to 15 seconds at a distance of 30 inches. The length of exposure is then increased by increments of 30 seconds until erythema is produced. Daily exposure is desirable; sporadic use of ultraviolet lamps often results in unexpected burning.

X-ray radiation is used with sharply decreasing frequency by dermatologists and has no role in pediatric practice in the treatment of acne.

Diet. The efficacy of dietary restriction in acne as in atopic dermatitis is controversial. The simplest and least punitive method of determining the effect of diet on acne is to have each patient experimentally determine to which foods, if any, he is sensitive. The foods most commonly implicated are those with high fat content: pork, french fried potatoes, potato chips, chocolate, nuts, milk. If the ingestion of these foods does not exacerbate a patient's acne, there is little reason to eliminate them from the diet. Unquestionably, there are patients in whom these foods do cause a flare-up of acne and who should avoid them; however, fatty foods should not be eliminated routinely.

Surgical. Comedones should be expressed after the face has been washed and then warmed with a hot towel. Pustules and inflamed cysts should be incised and aspirated when necessary. Cysts, especially those of a chronic nature, often resolve after the intralesional injection of triamcinolone acetonide.

Other. In some patients hygiene of the scalp and hair is related in an obscure way to the clinical activity of acne. Although it cannot be concluded that sebum from hair causes local inflammation where it touches the skin, acne of the forehead can often be improved by brushing the hair away from the forehead.

To a degree rarely seen in other diseases, encouragement, patience, and interest are effective therapeutic modalities in acne.

REFERENCES

Caplan, R. The natural course of urticaria pigmentosa. Arch. Derm., 87:146, 1963.

Kirschbaum, J. O., and Kligman, A. M. The pathogenic role of *Corynebacterium acnes* in acne vulgaris. Arch. Derm., 88:832, 1963.

Miller, R., and Shapiro, L. Bullous urticaria pigmentosa in infancy. Arch. Derm., 91:595, 1965.

Nickel, W. R. Clinical spectrum of mastocytosis (urticaria pigmentosa) in man. Arch. Derm., 96:364, 1967.

Shaw, J. Genetic aspects of urticaria pigmentosa. Arch. Derm., 97:137, 1968.

Shehadeh, N. H., and Kligman, A. M. The bacteriology of acne. Arch. Derm., 88:829, 1963.

Strauss, J. S., and Pochi, P. E. Intracutaneous injection of sebum and comedones. Arch. Derm., 92:443, 1965.

Szymanski, F. J. Pityriasis lichenoides et varioliformis acuta. Arch. Derm., 79:7, 1959.

Wenzl, J. E., and Burgert, E. O. The spider nevus in infancy and childhood. Pediatrics, 33:227, 1964.

chapter 27

THE EYES

LEONARD APT and GOODWIN M. BREININ, Associate Editors

This chapter on the eyes will consider conditions likely to be encountered by the pediatrician. He must be prepared to diagnose and treat simple inflammations of the eye and adnexae. He should also attend to superficial foreign bodies which are readily removed, but instrumentation of the eye should be avoided. In most ocular diseases other than the above, referral should be made to an ophthalmologist. For a more complete discussion of ocular disease standard texts on ophthalmology should be consulted.

27.1
EXAMINATION OF THE EYE

A systematic, detailed examination of the eyes is an indispensable part of the physical examination. An orderly sequence should be employed in which attention is directed to the ocular adnexae and to the exterior and interior of the globe. Pupillary responses should be determined and the range and character of ocular motility recorded. Proper examination of the fundus requires good pupillary dilation, which can be achieved with mydriatrics such as cyclomydril or 10 percent Neo-Synephrine. Cycloplegics such as Cyclogyl (0.5 to 2 percent), homatropine (2 to 5 percent), or atropine (0.25 to 20 percent) need not be used for mere mydriasis. In infants and some young children general anesthesia may be required to observe the fundi adequately.

The presence of vision in the infant may be inferred from pupillary reactions. Some idea of visual acuity may be gained by the ability to obtain fixation and following movements with interesting objects. Each eye should be tested separately. The presence or absence of vision and an estimate of visual acuity can be tested even in newborn infants using a rotating striped drum and observing opticokinetic nystagmus. A more precise determination of acuity is possible usually after the age of 3 years through use of such devices as E symbols of graded sizes or easily recognizable pictures subtending progressively smaller visual angles.

27.2
ANOMALIES OF THE GLOBE AND RELATED STRUCTURES

Developmental failures may involve any part of the adnexae and globe. Failure of development of the primary optic vesicles results in anophthalmos, the complete absence of an eye. Fusion of the two optic vesicles produces cyclopia, the single median eye famed in antiquity. Developmental failure at a later stage may result in microphthalmos. In *coloboma,* a frequent defect usually related to defective closure of the fetal fissure, a portion of the ocular structure is lacking. Such defects may involve the iris, lens, ciliary body, choroid, retina, or optic nerve and may produce slight or severe damage to visual function. A typical coloboma of the iris produces a keyhole defect located anteriorly. Coloboma of the choroid and retina appears as a gray area extending from the periphery to the disk, usually in the inferior quadrant. Serious eye deformities may be associated with chromosomal aberrations such as trisomy D (13-15).

Birth Injuries

Intrauterine trauma may be responsible for injury to the eyes, especially during the first trimester of pregnancy. Maternal rubella in the first trimester is a well-established cause of congenital anomalies, including cataracts. Mechanical trauma to the globe and lids may occur when there is dystocia from cephalopelvic disproportion, or even in normal deliveries when forceps are used. Usually such injuries are slight and heal rapidly, as do the more frequently observed conditions such as lid edema, ecchymoses, and conjunctival and retinal hemorrhages.

INJURIES TO THE LIDS AND ORBIT. Lagophthalmos, the inability to close an eye, occurs at times in newborn infants. It is usually unilateral and may be due to injury to the facial nerve by forceps pressure. The condition usually disappears within a week. Ointments or methylcellulose drops should be instilled to protect the exposed cornea. Traumatic ptosis occurs also in newborn infants and usually disappears in a few days.

INJURIES TO THE SYMPATHETIC NERVOUS SYSTEM. Damage to the cervical sympathetic nerve is the common cause of *Horner's syndrome,* which consists of miosis (narrowing of the pupil), ptosis, slight enophthalmos, and anhidrosis of the affected side of the face. It is often accompanied by manifestations of injury to the brachial plexus, which aids in differentiating it from intracranial hemorrhage as a cause of inequality in the size of the pupils. Depigmentation of the iris also may accompany or follow Horner's syndrome. At birth, pigmentation of the iris is incomplete, which explains the frequency of the blue-gray iris seen in newborn infants. Definitive pigmentation of the iris takes place after a few months, but in sympathetic nerve injury it may be delayed or prevented.

INJURY AFFECTING THE EXTERNAL OCULAR MUSCLES. Hemorrhage into the sheath of an extraocular muscle may lead to fibrosis with subsequent limitation of motion. If at first ocular movements are normal, later development of paralysis suggests the occurrence of hemorrhage. Differentiation from congenital strabismus is difficult at this time. Sixth nerve (abducens) palsy is the most common of the cranial nerve palsies due to its long intracranial course. Third nerve (oculomotor) palsy may occur in complete or partial form, with or without pupillary involvement. Fourth nerve (trochlear) palsy is uncommon. Paralysis of these nerves produces characteristic motor defects (Sec. 15.8), but in lesser degrees of palsy precise identification of the neurologic defects is often a matter of considerable difficulty.

INJURY TO THE OPTIC NERVE. Fracture of the orbit or hemorrhage into the optic nerve sheath may result in optic atrophy and blindness. Optic atrophy causes a blue-white appearance of the nerve head which needs to be differentiated from the grayish appearance of the optic disk seen in the normal newborn. Primary optic atrophy is manifested by a sharply defined disk margin with a blue-white appearance of the disk tissue, in which fine vessels are almost absent. In secondary atrophy the disk margin is not sharp and evidences of intraocular diseases are present.

INJURY TO THE CORNEA. Corneal haze may result from edema secondary to the birth process or from chemical injury following instillation of a solution of silver nitrate more concentrated than 1 percent. The cloudiness generally disappears within a few days or weeks. Traumatic keratitis, which is usually uniocular, must be differentiated from congenital glaucoma (p. 1825). Occasionally permanent opacities result in severe visual impairment and in such associated disturbances as amblyopia and strabismus.

INTRAOCULAR HEMORRHAGE. Retinal hemorrhages occur not uncommonly in the newborn infant; they are often bilateral. Venous congestion is the most likely cause. Capillary fragility and impaired blood coagulability may play some role, but administration of vitamin K to the mother has no significant effect. Usually the hemorrhages are of the streak or flame-shaped type, lying in the nerve fiber layer near the disk. They are absorbed within a few days, leaving no residual defect. Subhyaloid hemorrhages may occur also. Amblyopia from retinal hemorrhages in the newborn period must be extremely rare, if it occurs at all.

The ocular signs of intracranial hemorrhage in newborn infants are pupillary dilation, oculomotor palsies, and subhyaloid retinal hemorrhages, which may be present at birth or shortly thereafter. In infants, in contrast with adults, the pupillary reactions in intracranial hemorrhage are inconstant and the dilated pupil is not necessarily found on the side of the lesion.

REFERENCES

EXAMINATION OF THE EYE

Adler, F. H. Textbook of Ophthalmology, 7th ed. Philadelphia, W. B. Saunders Co., 1962.
Newell, F. W. Ophthalmology, Principles and Concepts, 2nd ed. St. Louis, C. V. Mosby Co., 1969.
Parks, M. M. Methods of Examination. In The Pediatrician's Ophthalmology. Liebman, S. D., and Gellis, S. S., eds. St. Louis, C. V. Mosby Co., 1966.

ANOMALIES OF THE GLOBE AND RELATED STRUCTURES

Cagianut, B. Ophthalmological findings in chromosomal ideases. Ophthalmologica, 155:148, 1968.
Mann, I. Developmental Abnormalities of the Eye, 2nd ed. Philadelphia, J. B. Lippincott Co., 1957.
Zellweger, H. Chromosomal aberrations and their significance for ophthalmo-otorhinolaryngology. Trans. Amer. Acad. Ophthal. Otol., 69:33, 1965.

BIRTH INJURIES

Chace, R. R., Merritt, K. K., and Bellows, M. Ocular findings in the newborn infant. Arch. Ophthal., 44:236, 1950.
Gorman, J. J., Cogan, D. G., and Gellis, S. S. An apparatus for grading the visual acuity of infants on the basis of opticokinetic nystagmus. Pediatrics, 19:1088, 1957.
Govan, C. D., Jr., and Walsh, F. B. Symptomatology of subdural hematoma in infants and in adults: Comparative study, with particular reference to the ocular signs; an observation concerning pathogenesis of subdural hematoma. Arch. Ophthal., 37:701, 1947.
McKeown, H. S. Retinal hemorrhages in the newborn. Arch. Ophthal., 26:25, 1941.
Mann, I. Developmental Abnormalities of the Eye, 2nd ed. Philadelphia, J. B. Lippincott Co., 1957.

27.3
THE LIDS

CONGENITAL ANOMALIES. The most frequent anomaly of the lids is ptosis, which may be unilateral or bilateral and when persistent is due usually to defective development or absence of the levator palpebrae superioris. It is often hereditary. Ptosis may occur alone or associated with defects of the superior rectus. Other causes include lesions of the third nerve, Horner's syndrome, and myasthenia gravis. If ptosis interferes with vision, amblyopia may develop. If bilateral, it may cause compensatory abnormal head postures. Treatment, which is surgical and usually involves shortening of the levator, should be deferred until the age of 3 or 4 years. In partial ptosis, constituting only a slight cosmetic blemish, intervention is not so urgent.

A common anomaly of the lids is *epicanthus,* a vertical semilunar skin fold extending down the side of the nose with the concavity directed toward the inner canthus. Epicanthus is a conspicuous finding in mongolism (Sec. 15.3) but is also found in normal subjects, often as a familial characteristic. It may be present in infancy and disappear when the bridge of the nose develops. Occasionally the condition persists. Its chief significance lies in its creation of an illusory appearance of convergent strabismus. In extreme cases surgical treatment may be indicated.

Anomalies of the lid margins are rare and consist chiefly of inversion (entropion) and eversion (ectropion). Should lashes rub against the cornea (trichiasis) marked damage may ensue.

Lid Infections

BLEPHAROCONJUNCTIVITIS. Two major types of this infection are encountered. The squamous form is often associated with seborrhea of the scalp. Scales and crusts line the lid margin and a low-grade staphylococcal infection may be present. The condition is often resistant to treatment, which must be prolonged and is directed at the seeding source, the scalp, and at the secondary infection. The lid margins must be cleansed of scales and crusts and antibacterial agents applied to the lids and conjunctivae. In the ulcerative form there is a purulent folliculitis with considerable discharge and loss of lashes. Ulcers may be found at the lid margin, due usually to staphylococcal infection. Expression of the meibomian glands, cleansing of the lid margins, and application of antibacterial agents constitute the most effective treatment.

HORDEOLUM (STYE). External hordeolum is the common stye, a furuncle of the lid margin arising in a ciliary follicle and its associated glands, caused by a staphylococcus. Susceptible individuals may have recurrences. The belief that refractive errors cause styes is not given much credence today. The lesion begins as a circumscribed swelling at the lid margin, although at times the onset is alarming, with marked edema of the lid, pain, and sometimes constitutional symptoms. Eventually the infection points and evacuation of the pus may occur spontaneously. This may be facilitated by epilation of involved lashes or opening with a needle. The stye should never be squeezed. Hot compresses and instillation of antibacterial agents may accelerate resolution of the infection.

CHALAZION (INTERNAL HORDEOLUM). A chalazion is a chronic granuloma caused by retention of the secretion of a tarsal gland. The lesion appears as a hard nodule under the skin. It may resorb spontaneously or progress with softening until it bursts on the conjunctival surface or occasionally on the skin surface or at the lid margin. A viscid mass extrudes for some time. Antibacterial agents are used to control secondary infection. The lesion frequently requires excision or incision and drainage with cauterization.

27.4
THE CONJUNCTIVA

CONGENITAL ANOMALIES. With the exception of pigmentation, anomalies are rare. Structural anomalies, ranging from abnormal folds and bands to complete absence of the conjunctivae, occur infrequently as do dermolipoma, angioma, and lymphangioma.

GONOCOCCAL CONJUNCTIVITIS. This was at one time common in newborn infants, from infection acquired during delivery, but due to routine prophylaxis (Sec. 2.11) it has become rare. An increase in the incidence of gonorrheal infection in the adult population in recent years has resulted in an increase in the incidence of gonorrheal ophthalmia neonatorum in many hospitals. The infection is usually bilateral and generally appears on the second or third day of life; a later onset suggests postnatal infection. Typically the inflammation is acute with marked edema of the lids, chemosis, fiery red conjunctivae, and copious discharge of pus, although occasionally a more chronic, mild catarrhal inflammation is seen. In the absence of proper treatment destructive changes are common; neglect for even a day may lead to corneal involvement which may result in opacity or perforation. The course and prognosis of the disease have been altered completely by the advent of effective antibacterial agents. With adequate treatment most cases will clear up clinically and bacteriologically in from one to four days. In addition to intramuscular penicillin given daily, a solution containing 2,500 units of penicillin per milliliter should be used locally, an instillation being given every half-hour for three hours, then every hour for 24 hours, and thereafter every two hours until the eyes are clear. Atropine drops (0.25 percent) and frequent saline irrigations are also indicated.

INCLUSION BLENNORRHEA (VIRAL CONJUNCTIVITIS). This infection is caused by a filterable virus transmitted from the genital tract of the mother during delivery. The causative organism is a large atypical virus, *Clamydia oculogenitalis,* a member of the family Chlamydiaceae, order Rickettsiales. It is now more common than gonococcal conjunctivitis. Symptoms appear between the fifth and tenth days, generally with an acute onset of swelling and redness of the lids and a profuse mucopurulent exudate in one or both eyes. Photophobia may be present, and some patients have an associated severe and persistent rhinitis. The conjunctiva of the lower tarsus and fornix is most markedly involved, and there is some congestion and thickening of the bulbar conjunctiva, although the cornea itself is not involved and the conjunctiva of the upper lid is relatively spared. The acute inflammatory stage lasts one to two weeks, gradually subsiding in the absence of treatment into a chronic papillary conjunctivitis which may last a year or more. However, vision is not disturbed and there are no sequelae. Clinically, inclusion blennorrhea differs from gonococcal conjunctivitis in the relatively milder degree of involvement of the upper tarsal conjunctiva, although clinical differentiation is difficult. The later appearance of inclusion blennorrhea is an important point, which also serves to differentiate it from silver nitrate conjunctivitis. In inclusion blennorrhea cultures show nothing characteristic. The diagnosis is made from scrapings from the conjunctiva of the lower lid, which with Giemsa stain show characteristic bluish granular cytoplasmic inclusions in the epithelial cells. Systemic and local treatment with a sulfonamide or tetracycline produces a marked abatement of the disease, although the response is not as rapid as in gonococcal conjunctivitis. Silver nitrate prophylaxis does not protect against inclusion conjunctivitis.

ACUTE CONJUNCTIVITIS DUE TO OTHER ORGANISMS. Conjunctivitis due to pneumococci, streptococci, staphylococci, or other pyogenic organisms varies greatly in its severity and duration. Acute purulent inflammations are seen, but serious complications rarely occur. Pseudomonas infections in premature infants are particularly serious. A pseudomonas infection of the conjunctiva or cornea may rapidly progress to an orbital cellulitis, panophthalmitis, and even death from septicemia. Occasionally corneal ulcers develop which are usually marginal and rarely produce permanent damage. More common complications are residual papillary hypertrophy of the conjunctiva or residual chronic conjunctivitis, particularly in staphylococcal infection.

Epidemic conjunctivitis (pink-eye) is generally due to *Haemophilus influenzae* (formerly known as the Koch-Weeks bacillus when found in the eye) or to a pneumococcus. The inflammation is usually catarrhal but associated with intense injection; petechiae may be present.

Chronic conjunctivitis may follow an acute attack or may develop insidiously; it is usually due to a staphylococcus. In some cases diphtheroids are found, and in still others cultures are sterile. The severity of the inflammation varies greatly. There may be marked hypertrophy of lymphoid follicles in the lower fornix (follicular conjunctivitis), or an associated low-grade inflammation of the lid margins (blepharoconjunctivitis). Not uncommonly recurrent styes are associated with chronic conjunctivitis. The inflammation may be limited to the angles of the eyes with an associated eczematous condition of the skin at the canthi (angular conjunctivitis caused by the diplobacillus of Morax-Axenfeld).

Treatment of both the acute and chronic forms consists of antibiotics and chemotherapy, the choice of agent depending upon the nature of the pathogenic organism. In the milder, chronic cases weak astringents, such as 0.2 percent zinc sulfate, may be tried.

ALLERGIC CONJUNCTIVITIS. The conjunctiva, like other epithelial structures, may develop a local hypersensitivity to a specific allergen. There is often no relationship between the local sensitivity of the conjunctiva and the cutaneous sensitivity to a given allergen. All the changes met with in simple allergic reactions may occur in the conjunctiva. In acute cases there is sudden vascular dilation with a boggy, exudative inflammation which disappears on removal of the irritant; in chronic cases cellular infiltration and newly formed connective tissue follow. Eosinophils are usually, but not always, present in conjunctival scrapings, and basophils are also seen.

Simple allergic conjunctivitis produces an acute, hyperemic reaction accompanied by edema of the conjunctivae and lids and profuse lacrimation with severe itching. Itching is usually far more conspicuous than in infectious conjunctivitis. The hypersensitive state of the conjunctiva can be demonstrated by instillation of the offending allergen—usually a pollen (hay fever), rarely some other vegetable or animal protein.

Local drug sensitivity may produce the same sort of reaction in the conjunctiva. Sensitivity to a drug occurs usually after repeated instillations and is most common with atropine. Once developed, this sensitivity lasts indefinitely and is often associated with cutaneous sensitivity to the drug. Treatment consists of removal of the offending agent, or if this is impossible, an attempt at desensitization to the allergen. Symptomatic relief can often be obtained with the local use of corticosteroids.

Vernal conjunctivitis (spring catarrh) is a bilateral, chronic, recurrent inflammation characterized by large, pale, flat-topped papillae in the upper palpebral conjunctivae. There is intense itching, lacrimation, and a stringy exudate containing abundant eosinophils. Although vernal conjunctivitis is generally believed to represent an allergic reaction, identification of specific allergens has been unsuccessful. It occurs during spring and summer and is primarily a disease of childhood, occurring most frequently in boys from 5 to 15 years of age. A familial history of allergy is usual. The disease is self-limited, usually lasting 8 to 10 years. Symptomatic treatment consists of frequent instillations of a drop of epinephrine, Privine, Visine, 0.06 percent Neo-Synephrine hydrochloride, or 0.25 percent acetic acid. Secondary infection is common and should be treated vigorously with antibiotics. Adrenocortical steroids have been widely used with favorable results. Corticosteroids may be applied locally in drop or ointment form and also given systemically. Antihistaminics are of little value. In severe cases radiation therapy has been employed. The occurrence of late radiation complications, however, emphatically contraindicates its use.

MEMBRANOUS CONJUNCTIVITIS. Membranes and pseudomembranes may form on the conjunctiva in the course of Stevens-Johnson disease or of any severe local infection. Diphtheritic conjunctivitis caused by *Corynebacterium diphtheriae* is now fortunately rare; it may result in significant damage to the conjunctiva and cornea.

PARINAUD'S OCULOGLANDULAR SYNDROME. Among the rarer forms of conjunctivitis seen in children is a syndrome consisting of a chronic, ulcerated, granulomatous lesion of the palpebral conjunctiva, usually unilateral, associated with marked swelling of the preauricular and cervical lumph nodes and with malaise and fever. Causative agents include various fungi, particularly leptothrix, the tubercle bacillus, *Pasteurella tularensis* (*B. tularense*), or the virus of lymphogranuloma venereum. A nonbacterial form has been described in "cat scratch disease." Recovery usually takes place within several weeks. Antibiotics and specific chemotherapy should be given; streptomycin may be effective.

TRACHOMA. The fact that trachoma exists in the United States is not generally appreciated. Imported cases occur sporadically in all parts of the country, and in certain localities it is endemic, notably in the South and Southwest and on various Indian reservations. Trachoma is caused by a virus of low infectivity, a member of the psittacosis-lymphogranuloma group of agents known as Chlamydia; it is characterized by a low-grade conjunctivitis and keratitis, which, if untreated, result in severe damage to vision.

In the early, acute stage the clinical picture is indistinguishable from catarrhal or mild purulent conjunctivitis. Cytoplasmic inclusion bodies can usually be found in epithelial scrapings, but these cannot be differentiated morphologically from the ones found in inclusion blennorrhea. The early stage is followed by a period of inflammation lasting one or two years and characterized by papillary hypertrophy and folliculosis of the conjunctiva but no scarring, with beginning vascularization of the cornea. Subsequently, evidences of scarring develop, although inflammation is still active. Opacity and superficial vascularization of the cornea gradually increase. This latter stage may persist all the patient's life, or the evidences of inflammation may subside, leaving extensive scarring of the cornea, conjunctiva, and lids.

Numerous sulfonamides and antibiotics have been found effective, systemically and locally, against the trachoma virus; sulfadiazine, streptomycin, the tetracyclines, chloramphenicol, and erythromycin have all given good results. Cortisone appears to reactivate the virus and is contraindicated.

CONJUNCTIVITIS IN ADENOVIRAL INFECTION. The adenoviruses (adenopharyngoconjunctival or APC viruses) produce two recognizable infections.

Epidemic keratoconjunctivitis is an acute, contagious disease of the conjunctiva and cornea caused most often by adenovirus type 8. Epidemics may occur by spread from contaminated eye solutions or unwashed hands. A rapid onset of acute follicular conjunctivitis with lacrimation, conjunctival chemosis, mucopurulent or purulent discharge, and preauricular adenopathy is followed in 7 to 10 days by the appearance of subepithelial infiltrates in the central corneal area. The acute inflammation subsides in several weeks, but the corneal infiltrates often persist, leaving fine scars that do not impair vision. Both eyes are usually involved. Treatment consists of local sulfonamide or broad-spectrum antibiotic drugs to prevent secondary bacterial infection, since no drug is known to inhibit the virus specifically. Isolation precautions should be taken because the disease is highly contagious.

Pharyngoconjunctival fever is encountered more often in children than in adults and is characterized by a self-limited acute follicular conjunctivitis of almost two weeks' duration, fever, malaise, sore throat, and preauricular and cervical lymphadenopathy. The disease is usually caused by adenovirus type 3. In most instances superficial punctate corneal opacities develop but disappear without sequelae as the conjunctivitis subsides. The highly contagious disease is spread by direct contact or indirectly through contaminated swimming pools, even though chlorinated. Isolation precautions and topical antibacterial eye medication to prevent secondary bacterial infection are the only treatments.

EXANTHEMATOUS CONJUNCTIVITIS. Many of the exanthems are associated with acute catarrhal conjunctivitis, and some involve the cornea. This is particularly true of measles, in which the ocular involvement precedes the skin eruption. Antibiotics are indicated only for secondary infection. Otherwise, simple ocular hygiene suffices.

Keratoconjunctivitis is a characteristic and constant finding during the acute stage of measles. Slit lamp examination for keratoconjunctivitis, however, can confirm the diagnosis of measles in the prodromal stage and establish a retrospective diagnosis as long as three months after the rash has disappeared.

Vesicles of chickenpox may occur on the conjunctiva. They rarely involve the cornea directly but may produce a late complication in the form of a shallow ulcer or bleb. These lesions usually resolve spontaneously.

In the preeruptive stage of smallpox, a catarrhal conjunctivitis often appears about the fifth day, and clears up with good hygienic treatment. Pustules are rarely found in the eye but when present may involve the deeper layers of the cornea, causing permanent scarring; if secondary infection occurs, vision may be compromised.

Vaccinial conjunctivitis is rare but does occur. It usually is due to autoinoculation. The prognosis is usually good, but in some cases serious corneal damage has occurred. The conjunctivitis should be treated with hyperimmune gamma globulin, which should either not be used or used only with caution in vaccinia keratitis.

GENERAL REMARKS. Antibiotics are routinely used in the treatment of conjunctivitis. It is, however, good practice to determine the responsible agent and its sensitivity to specific antibiotics. The tendency to administer antibiotics indiscriminately to all external inflammations may result in the development of host sensitization and resistance of the organism. A word of caution is necessary against the use of corticosteroids in conjunctivitis. Although these potent agents are highly effective in the allergic types, they are generally contraindicated in bacterial and viral inflammations. They may cause exacerbations of the disease, particularly in herpes simplex infections. Combinations of antibiotics with steroids do not altogether remove this danger.

REFERENCES

Apt, L. The eye. *In* Gellis, S. S., and Kagan, B. M., eds., Current Pediatric Therapy, 1966-1967. Philadelphia, W. B. Saunders Co., 1966.

Burns, R. P., and Rhodes, D. H., Jr. Pseudomonas eye infection as a cause of death in premature infants. Arch. Ophthal., 65:517, 1961.

Fedukowicz, H. B. External Infections of the Eye: Bacterial, Viral, and Mycotic. New York, Appleton-Century-Crofts, 1963.

Friendly, D. S. Gonococcal conjunctivitis of the newborn. Clin. Proc. Child Hosp., 25:1, 1969.

New Orleans Academy of Ophthalmology. Infectious Diseases of the Conjunctiva and Cornea; Symposium. St. Louis, C. V. Mosby Co., 1963.

Theodore, F. H., and Schlossman, A. Ocular allergy. Baltimore, The Williams & Wilkins Co., 1958.

Thygeson, P. Trachoma manual and atlas, U.S. Public Health Service Publication No. 541, Washington, D.C. 1958, U.S. Department of Health, Education, and Welfare, Division of Indian Health.

27.5
THE CORNEA

CONGENITAL ANOMALIES. The most common congenital anomalies of the cornea are those associated with defects in transparency. Corneal opacities that are poorly developed are due to contact between lens or iris and the cornea or to imperfect development of the stroma or endothelium. Pigmentary changes of the cornea occur in the endothelium or epithelium, frequently associated with melanosis of the conjunctiva. An anomaly occasionally seen is an annular peripheral opacity resembling the common arcus senilis and known as *embryotoxon*.

Variations in size may result in the cornea's being abnormally small (microcornea) or abnormally large (megalocornea). The latter may be due to an aberration of growth or may result from congenital glaucoma (buphthalmos) or congenital anterior staphyloma. The identification of congenital glaucoma is important; it is differentiated from other conditions on the basis of the elevated intraocular pressure.

Congenital dermoids of the cornea occur rarely and may involve only a small portion of, or, in severe cases, the entire cornea. These lesions are composed of fatty and fibrous tissue and are often covered with hairs.

FOREIGN BODIES. Ocular foreign bodies in children are frequently seen by the pediatrician, and those that are superficial can be safely removed by him. They usually occur beneath the upper lid on the palpebral conjunctiva which overlies the tarsus, or on the epithelium of the cornea. The symptoms of a foreign body are irritation, lacrimation, and photophobia; the complications are ulceration and infection.

For diagnosis or removal of foreign bodies, the eye is prepared with a local anesthetic such as 0.5 percent proparacaine (Ophthaine) or tetracaine (Pontocaine). Movement is prevented by placing the patient in a comfortable position or, in infants, by suitable restraint. The eye is then examined under good lighting and magnification. The lids are examined first by exploring the lower fornix and then by turning the upper lid. To facilitate eversion of the upper lid, the lash margin should be grasped between the thumb and forefinger. The tip of the other forefinger (or a toothpick applicator) is placed on the skin at the upper border of the tarsus. By pressing downward with the latter while rolling the lid out and up with the former the lid will evert readily, permitting inspection of the tarsal conjunctiva and upper fornix. The cornea should be scrutinized with care, for it is often difficult to see a small particle against a brown iris. When superficial, these foreign bodies can be simply wiped off with a moistened cotton-tipped toothpick applicator. Sharp instruments may do more harm than good and should not be used.

After removal of the foreign body, an antibiotic solution such as Neosporin should be instilled. If damage to the corneal epithelium has occurred, the eye should be patched for 24 hours to permit regeneration of the surface. It is imperative that the parents be warned to return immediately if pain persists on the following day, for this may indicate infection.

If there is any doubt about the presence of infection, perforation, or laceration, the patient should be referred immediately to the ophthalmologist.

Corneal Inflammations—Keratitis

Inflammation of the superficial layers of the cornea is a frequent accompaniment of many types of conjunctivitis. Certain organisms have a predilection for producing corneal ulcerations at the periphery or center. These may be superficial or deep. Central and deep inflammations are always serious problems.

The treatment of *marginal ulcers* is the treatment of the underlying conjunctivitis. *Central ulcers* require intensive, specific measures: antibiotics, cauterization. Pneumococcal (serpent) ulcer often produces pus in the anterior chamber (hypopyon).

Superficial punctate erosions of the cornea are not uncommon in bacterial and allergic conjunctivitis but occur particularly in certain viral infections. One of the most common viral conditions of the cornea is *dendritic keratitis,* caused by the virus of herpes simplex; it may accompany herpetic infections elsewhere on the body, or it may occur during febrile attacks of any origin or under conditions that lower the general resistance. It usually begins in the center of the cornea as a small row of vesicles which break down leaving a linear defect; the lesion then spreads in the superficial layers of the cornea until the epithelium is destroyed, forming an irregular, superficial, branching ulcer. In severe cases it may affect the deeper layers of the cornea, producing a disciform opacity. Subjectively there is pain, lacrimation, and photophobia.

Dendritic keratitis is probably the most important corneal disease leading to loss of vision in the United States. The disease should be treated by the ophthalmologist. When the infection is confined to the epithelium, treatment consists of epithelial curettage, with or without chemical cauterization, and, more commonly in recent years, with the topical use of IDU (iododesoxyuridine). This drug inhibits the viral synthesis of deoxyribonucleic acid (DNA). With stromal involvement, IDU is much less or not at all effective. *Corticosteroids are contraindicated in the epithelial form of the disease.* They have been used in conjunction with IDU in the stromal form to reduce the toxic or hypersensitive response to the virus, but there is doubt now whether corticosteroids should ever be used in the disease. Corticosteroids reduce tissue immunity and can accelerate the spread of the viral infection. Their use has led to perforation and loss of the eye. Cryotherapy has also recently been reported effective in dendritic keratitis.

INTERSTITIAL KERATITIS. The vast majority of cases of interstitial keratitis appear between the ages of 5 and 15 years, although it may occur as early as 1 year. It is most often due to congenital syphilis (tuberculosis and leprosy rarely), and serological tests are regularly positive. Other signs of late syphilis may be present. Although of frequent occurrence in former years, ocular syphilis is becoming a rarity. The condition begins as a delicate zone of opacities in the middle layers of the stroma, originating either in the center or at the periphery of the cornea. There is pericorneal injection and often edema of the epithelium, followed by vascularization of the stroma. The subjective symptoms include diminution of vision, intense photophobia, lacrimation, and pain due to involvement of the iris. After several months a stage of regression occurs lasting for many months and resulting in gradual lessening of the opacities but with resultant fine, deep scarring. Antisyphilitic medication is employed but has very little effect on the course of the disease. It may occasionally prevent the subsequent involvement of the second eye. Atropine and corticosteroids should be used to treat the accompanying iritis. Topical corticosteroids may benefit mild cases. In patients with central scarring some improvement may be brought about by grafting of corneal transplants after the inflammation has been quiescent for a period of years.

PHLYCTENULAR KERATOCONJUNCTIVITIS. The lesion (phlyctenule) consists of one or more white or grayish elevated papules, 1 to 2 mm in diameter, which may appear on the cornea or the bulbar conjunctiva but are most commonly seen at the corneoscleral junction. They are frequently bilateral. There is slight injection of the sclera in the vicinity of the excrescence. Photophobia and lacrimation are extreme. As time goes on a gray crater develops in the apex of the lesion and the nodule gradually disappears, leaving a small ulcer which then heals by epitheliazation. If the lesion is on the cornea an opacity may remain; vascularization is frequent.

Histologically the phlyctenule is a subepithelial collection of small round cells, but the pathogenesis is not altogether clear. It is usually seen in tuberculous children and has long been regarded as an allergic reaction to tuberculoprotein. However, it also occurs in sarcoid. In some cases it is thought to be an allergic reaction to various other bacteria, viruses, or fungi. The lesions usually clear up quickly in a child if he is removed from his habitual environment; but when he returns to it a new crop of phlyctenules often develops.

Antituberculous chemotherapy should be given. Topical corticosteroids are of great value along with antibiotics for secondary infection.

FUNGAL KERATITIS. The incidence of keratomycosis has risen sharply in recent years. Contributing causes are trauma and the widespread use of local corticosteroids and antibiotics. Numerous species of fungi, many saprophytic, have been isolated. The diagnosis should be considered in any persistent, slowly progressive corneal ulceration. The organism may be undetected in scrapings and cultures and be found only on histopathologic study of the enucleated eye. Treatment consists of local antifungal agents such as nystatin and amphotericin B, sulfonamides, 0.125 percent copper sulfate solution, and the oral use of sulfonamides and iodides. Many eyes respond poorly to medical treatment and require a conjunctival flap to cover the ulcer. Corneal transplantation has improved the vision of some patients after the infection has subsided.

XEROPHTHALMIA (XEROSIS). Dryness of the conjunctiva and cornea may result from local disease of the conjunctiva which destroys its mucous glands, or from systemic malnutrition with avitaminosis A. A lackluster appearance of conjunctiva and cornea, wrinkling, and Bitot spots are early signs. The latter are small, white or creamy, foamy patches lying on the conjunctiva near the limbus in the palpebral aperture. They differ from phlyctenules in that they are neither elevated nor umbilicated and are not accompanied by photophobia. Night blindness is common. In severe cases progressive corneal keratinization causes complete loss of vision, and keratomalacia with necrosis may result in loss of the eyes. Treatment consists of a nutritious diet and large doses of vitamin A.

FAMILIAL DYSAUTONOMIA (RILEY-DAY SYNDROME). Congenital absence of tearing and corneal hypesthesia or anesthesia are consistently present in familial dysautonomia (Sec. 15.13). Slight to severe corneal opacification and ulceration may occur. Mecholyl chloride, 2.5 percent eye drops, usually will cause miosis, a response consistent with parasympathetic denervation. Treatment is directed at protection of the cornea by bland drops (methylcellulose) and antibiotic ointments. Airtight goggles, occlusion with cellophane, tarsorrhaphy, and a Ridley flush-fitting scleral contact lens have also been used.

BAND KERATOPATHY. Superficial deposition of calcium in the cornea may occur primarily, or in connection with a low-grade uveitis. This is not infrequent in Still's disease and has been reported together with conjunctival crystals in hypercalcemia. Band keratopathy may be most satisfactorily treated by ionic extraction of the calcium from the cornea with a chelating agent. Preliminary curettage of the epithelium is essential, followed by application of a few milliliters of the chelating agent, such as the disodium salt of ethylene diamine tetra-acetic acid (Edathamil disodium), for a period of 15 to 20 minutes. This will usually remove most or all of the calcific opacity. Improvement in vision may be dramatic. The procedure can be reported as often as necessary.

CYSTINOSIS. In cystinosis, crystals of cystine in the cornea and conjunctiva may be revealed by the biomicroscope (slit lamp). The diagnosis can be confirmed by chemical tests on a biopsy specimen of the conjunctiva.

MUCOPOLYSACCHARIDOSIS. Corneal clouding occurs as a local manifestation of systemic mucopolysaccharidosis. Hurler's syndrome, gargoylism, is the best known of these disorders. On clinical, biochemical, and genetic grounds, McKusick grouped the mucopolysaccharide diseases into five entities. Three of the five have corneal clouding—classic Hurler's syndrome (I), Morquio's syndrome (IV), and Scheie's syndrome (V). Hunter's syndrome (II) and Sanfilippo's syndrome (III) do not have macroscopic corneal clouding. The clinical findings and the definition of the urinary mucopolysaccharide excretion pattern distinguish the foregoing corneal dystrophies from diseases such as infantile glaucoma, cystinosis, and hereditary congenital corneal dystrophy.

HEPATOLENTICULAR DEGENERATION (WILSON'S DISEASE). The Kayser-Fleischer ring is a striking diagnostic finding in Wilson's disease (Sec. 8.11). It contains copper and appears as a greenish golden annular opacity just within the limbus in the deep layers of the cornea.

27.6
THE LACRIMAL APPARATUS

OBSTRUCTION OF THE LACRIMAL DUCT (DACRYOSTENOSIS). Dacryostenosis in the newborn is manifested by tearing (epiphora) and may be observed as early as the first week of life. Contrary to prevalent opinion, most newborns do secrete tears in the first week of life. Tearing from dacryostenosis can be distinguished from that due to conjunctivitis and corneal disease by the lack of inflammatory signs, unless secondary infection of the lacrimal sac (dacryocystitis) has occurred. Infantile glaucoma must be excluded when one is confronted with the problem of tearing in young infants. Generally one side is involved. In the majority of cases the nasolacrimal duct is normally formed, and its obstruction is due to clogging with epithelial debris. Occasionally the ostium of the duct is closed by a thin membrane or by swelling of the nasal mucosa which may require probing by an ophthalmologist. However, premature probing may convert an innocent lesion into a serious one through cicatrization following the trauma of the procedure. Most cases will clear spontaneously in 6 to 12 months.

Dacryocystitis is usually associated with dacryostenosis. Some cases are localized and mild; others show marked edema of the lids and side of the nose. Pressure over the sac results in a reflux of pus through the puncta. Untreated cases may go on to abscess formation with rupture through the skin and establishment of a draining sinus. Treatment with antibiotics, locally and systemically, effectively overcomes the acute phase. A few cases persist, requiring surgical care.

27.7
THE SCLERA

By comparison with adults the normal sclera of young infants, being relatively thin, is often mistaken for "blue sclerotics," a true congenital anomaly which occurs in patients with osteogenesis imperfecta. By the end of the first year, most infants show normal opacity of the sclera.

SCLERITIS; EPISCLERITIS. Inflammation of the sclera and episclera is infrequent but has much the same etiology and therapy as uveitis. It may be a manifestation of a systemic disease, most commonly one of the so-called collagen diseases, particularly rheumatoid arthritis. Syphilis, tuberculosis, sarcoidosis, and brucellosis must be ruled out. Episcleritis is manifested as a localized, purplish, nodular area over which the conjunctiva moves easily. It is chronic, recurrent, and usually benign. Scleritis is a deeper, more diffuse, and severe inflammation which may involve the cornea. Uveitis is often associated with scleritis. Treatment consists of local vasoconstrictors, corticosteroids, cycloplegics, and treatment of the systemic disorder if known.

REFERENCES

THE CORNEA

Breinin, G. M., and DeVoe, A. G. Chelation of calcium with edathamil calcium-disodium in band keratopathy and cornea calcium affections. Arch. Ophthal., 52:846, 1954.

Cogan, D. G., and Kuwabara, T. Ocular pathology of cystinosis. Arch. Ophthal., 63:51, 1960.

Dunnington, J. H. Congenital alacrima in familial autonomic dysfunction. Arch. Ophthal., 52:925, 1954.

Garron, L. K. Cystinosis. Trans. Amer. Acad. Ophthal., 63:99, 1959.

Goar, E. L., and de la Motte, G. W. Cystine crystals in the cornea and conjunctiva. Arch. Ophthal., 51:336, 1954.

Kauffman, H. E. Chemotherapy of herpes keratitis. Invest. Ophthal., 2:504, 1963.

Klauder, J. V., and Meyer, G. P. Corticotropin, cortisone, thyroid, testosterone in syphilitic interstitial keratitis. Arch. Ophthal., 51:432, 1954.

Laibson, P. R., and Leopold, I. H. An evaluation of double-blind IDU therapy in 100 cases of herpetic keratitis. Trans. Amer. Acad. Ophthal. Otol., 68:22, 1964.

Liebman, S. D. Ocular manifestations of Riley-Day syndrome: familial autonomic dysfunction. Arch. Ophthal., 56:719, 1956.

——— Riley-Day syndrome: long term ophthalmologic observations. Trans. Amer. Ophthal. Soc., 66:95, 1968.

McLean, J. M. Oculomycosis. Amer. J. Ophthal., 56:537, 1963.

Paton, D., and McLarnen, D. S. Bitot spots. Amer. J. Ophthal., 50:568, 1960.

Thygeson, P. Herpes cornea. Amer. J. Ophthal., 36:269, 1953.

——— Observations on nontuberculous phlyctenular keratoconjunctivitis. Trans. Amer. Acad. Ophthal., 58:128, 1954.

Vaughan, D. G., Jr. Xerophthalmia. Arch. Ophthal., 51:789, 1954.

THE LACRIMAL APPARATUS

Apt, L., and Cullen, B. F. Newborns do secrete tears. J.A.M.A., 189:951, 1964.

Veirs, E. R. Lacrimal Disorders in Infants and Children. In Apt, L., ed., Diagnostic Procedures in Pediatric Ophthalmology. Boston, Little, Brown & Co., 1963.

27.8
CONGENITAL GLAUCOMA

Congenital (infantile, developmental) glaucoma is a rare disease but a serious one. The incidence has ranged from 0.008 to 0.03 percent in various reports. However, it has accounted for 5 to 13 percent of the children in the schools for the blind.

Primary developmental glaucoma is transmitted as an autosomal recessive characteristic. Although two-thirds of the patients are males, sex linkage is not common in the inheritance pattern. Three-quarters of the cases are bilateral, but the nonglaucomatous eye may show incomplete iris angle abnormalities on gonioscopic examination. In 80 to 90 percent of the cases, the disease is diagnosed by the end of the first year of life, with about 50 percent apparent at or shortly after birth.

An increase in intraocular pressure results from an interference with the drainage of aqueous humor due to a developmental anomaly in the angle of the anterior chamber. Stretching of the elastic coats of the globe is a distinctive change which can occur in the first three years of life. With a continued elevation of intraocular pressure, the globe enlarges, and thus the name buphthalmos (ox eye) is sometimes given to the disease.

Threat to vision is serious and the prognosis is poor, particularly if treatment is not promptly given. Treatment is surgical. Medical therapy with miotics or levo-epinephrine preparations is rarely if ever of value. Temporary control of ocular tension may be achieved with systemic carbonic anhydrase inhibitors such as acetozolamide (Diamox), which suppress the secretory formation of the aqueous humor. The surgical treatment of choice is goniotomy, in which an incision is made into the region of the trabecular meshwork to open a route for aqueous flow into Schlemm's canal. The operation may have to be repeated. Other surgical procedures such as goniopuncture, fistulizing operations, cyclodiathermy, and cyclocryotherapy have been less satisfactory.

The characteristic signs of infantile glaucoma are tearing, photophobia, blepharospasm, corneal haziness due to edema, and enlargement of the corneal diameter. Cupping and atrophy are late signs. Common mistaken diagnoses for congenital glaucoma are dacryostenosis and conjunctivitis.

Most infant corneas measure 10 mm or less in diameter at birth and less than 12 mm before the first year of life. A measurement of more than 11 mm in the newborn or more than 12 mm in the first year of life should arouse the suspicion of glaucoma. Megalocornea can occur as a distinct disease without an increase in intraocular pressure; it usually is a sex-linked inheritance found in males.

Other causes of corneal opacity in infants may suggest congenital glaucoma. These conditions include congenital idiopathic edema of the cornea, congenital corneal dystrophy, intrauterine or infantile inflammations of the cornea, Scheie's syndrome (mucopolysaccharidosis type V, Sec. 8.13), and the transient corneal haze seen in rubella keratitis (true congenital glaucoma may also be seen in the rubella syndrome).

Glaucoma in infants may be associated with anomalies such as aniridia, Sturge-Weber syndrome, neurofibromatosis, Lowe syndrome, Pierre Robin syndrome, microcornea, and mesodermal dysgenesis (Axenfeld's syndrome).

In the differential diagnosis of primary developmental glaucoma, one must also consider those secondary glaucomas associated with retrolental fibroplasia, intraocular tumors (e.g., retinoblastoma), uveitis, juvenile xanthogranuloma (nevoxanthoendothelioma) of the iris, and the lens complications encountered in spherophakia, Marfan's syndrome, homocystinuria, and persistent hyperplastic primary vitreous.

27.9
PHAKOMATOSES

A group of congenital syndromes affecting the eye, central nervous system, and skin have been termed phakomatoses (Sec. 15.4). They comprise the Sturge-Weber syndrome, neurofibromatosis (von Recklinghausen's disease), von Hippel-Lindau angiomatosis, and tuberous sclerosis (epiloia). Each is associated with multiple tumor formation. Vascular and neural lesions of the retina and choroid may lead to glaucoma and severe visual damage. Globes harboring such lesions have often been enucleated because of the resemblance to malignant melanoma.

27.10
THE LENS

Cataract

By definition a cataract is any opacity of the crystalline lens. However, minute opacities can be found in all lenses without impairment of vision, and sometimes marked opacities have surprisingly little effect on visual acuity.

TYPES. The term "congenital cataract" is applied to marked opacities of the crystalline lens that are present at birth, or to those that become apparent in infancy or early childhood (developmental). Congenital cataracts are usually partial and stationary. *Lamellar* or *zonular cataracts*, so called because the opacities are arranged in layers or zones around the central region of the lens, are thought to be due to nutritional deficiencies of the developing lens. They may occur in patients with rickets or hypocalcemic tetany or in other metabolic disturbances. In other cases the distribution is familial. With the ophthalmoscope one sees a circular opacity, darker at the margins than in the center, surrounded by a clear rim of cortex. Lamellar cataracts often increase in size during the first few years of life and may become mature, at which time the whole lens is opaque. *Capsular cataracts* when anterior are thought to arise

from contact between the lens and the cornea at some time during intrauterine life, or possibly as a result of birth injury. When posterior, they are usually associated with persistence of the hyaloid artery. A rarer form of capsular cataract is sometimes found in cases of mongolism, occasionally in hypothyroidism, and rarely in other pathologic conditions; these opacities are usually punctate, situated beneath the capsule, and can best be seen with the slit lamp.

Central cataracts, which are undoubtedly congenital because they are formed during intrauterine life, are frequently familial. They are small, rarely progressive, and as a rule do not interfere with vision. On ophthalmoscopic examination they are distinguished from lamellar cataracts by their central position and by their smaller size. Rubella cataract, another type of central cataract, was first described following a severe epidemic of German measles in Australia in the summer of 1940 (Sec. 14.39). In some cases the entire lens may be opaque. The anterior chamber is usually shallow in depth, and microphthalmos is common. The pupil may dilate poorly.

Nutritional cataracts can be readily produced in animals by diets containing a high proportion of lactose or galactose. Under ordinary circumstances the amount of such sugar that an infant is likely to receive need cause no concern. Only in the rare instances of *galactosemia* (Sec. 8.6) have such cataracts been observed. The earliest lens change is the appearance of a drop of oil in the center. Later a nuclear or zonular cataract develops. With no treatment the cataract becomes mature. Few if any of these cataracts regress if treatment is started after the second month of life. Cataracts have been induced in experimental animals by diets deficient in riboflavin and by deficiencies of tryptophan or other amino acids. It is uncertain what part such deficiencies play in human cataract.

Corticosteroids, given in fairly large doses (over 10 mg of prednisone) to patients with rheumatoid arthritis over a long period of time, have been reported to cause posterior subcapsular cataracts. The cataracts are bilateral and usually do not impair vision. Patients with asthma and ulcerative colitis receiving similar doses of corticosteroids have developed the cataracts much less commonly or not at all, and therefore the role of the primary disease must be taken into account.

DIAGNOSIS. Cataracts in infants and children look white to the naked eye and must be differentiated from other conditions that occur in the vitreous chamber and that give the same appearance. In rare cases retinoblastoma, or abscess in the vitreous, or a detachment of the retina caused by retrolental fibroplasia accounts for an erroneous diagnosis of cataract, but by careful examination these conditions can be seen to occur posterior to the lens. In uncontrolled congenital glaucoma lens opacities eventually result, but these are usually preceded by a general enlargement of the eye. Keratoconus (bulging forward of center of the cornea) or lenticonus (either posterior or anterior bulging of the lens) may be confused with cataract on the basis of ophthalmoscopic appearance. Retrolental fibroplasia is rarely associated with cataract formation.

TREATMENT. Although the ability to identify accurately the type of cataract may not be a necessary accomplishment of the pediatrician, the question of treatment of cataract in infancy and childhood is a problem with which he should be familiar.

In the case of total or near-total cataracts, in which the lens is entirely opaque or nearly so, operation is necessary in order that some degree of vision may be restored. It has not been proved that early operation in such cases will prevent the development of nystagmus and amblyopia. Operation has been rarely attempted before 6 months of age, and as a rule such patients are not operated upon until they are 10 or 12 months old. The prognosis is good in patients whose eyes are otherwise normal; if nystagmus, microcornea, or other abnormality is present the results are less satisfactory.

With total cataracts there is no question as to the desirability of operation, but partial and stationary cataracts present problems of judgment. The question of operation, which involves many considerations requiring consultation with an ophthalmologist, can be stated in the form of an equation: Does the visual acuity present, plus the retention of accommodation, outweigh the prospect of better visual acuity with loss of accommodative power?

Dislocation of the Lens

Dislocation of the lens into the vitreous body is usually caused by trauma. Spontaneous congenital dislocation of the lens is seen in Marfan's syndrome, spherophakia (with or without Marchesani's syndrome), and homocystinuria. Acute glaucoma may be precipitated by the dislocated lens.

27.11
THE UVEA

CONGENITAL ANOMALIES. The uveal tract, consisting of the iris, ciliary body, and choroid, is the vascular layer of the eye. The common defect, coloboma, has been described previously (p. 1817). Abnormalities occur in the number of pupils (polycoria), the shape of the pupil (dyscoria), and location of the pupil (corectopia). Persistent pupillary membranes, cysts at the pupillary border and on the iris surface, and pigment disturbances may be encountered.

Aniridia is a hereditary, dominant, bilateral disorder associated with aplasia of the macula, poor vision, nystagmus, and photophobia. Glaucoma often develops eventually. Cataracts are frequently present.

Other associated abnormalities such as oligophrenia, dyscranias, and malformations of the extremities have been described. Recent study has shown the excessive concurrence of aniridia and Wilms' tumor and, in the male, genital abnormalities.

The irides of infant, blue-eyed mongoloid imbeciles commonly exhibit a peripheral ring of small white spots called *Brushfield's spots*. These subsequently disappear in brown irides. The above changes, however, also occur in normal infants. Spotty atrophy of the iris is not uncommon in mongolism.

The *ciliary body* shows few malformations apart from coloboma. The *choroid* is a frequent site of coloboma. Rarely, the entire choroid is absent (choroideremia) except for a perimacular ring; this is associated with night blindness.

UVEITIS. Inflammation of the uveal tract is a common and important disease which has been a major cause of blindness throughout the world. In children it can often lead to severe visual impairment or blindness with few subjective complaints or obvious signs of the disease. In one pathologic study, uveitis was the third most common cause (7 percent) for enucleation in pediatric patients. Despite the advent of corticosteroid therapy, which has effected a revolutionary change in prognosis, there nevertheless continue to be seen recalcitrant forms which progress inexorably to blindness even with treatment. The fundamental problem in uveitis is the mystery of its causation. In relatively few cases can a specific organism or allergen be incriminated, such as *Toxoplasma*.

Uveitis has been subdivided into two forms, granulomatous and nongranulomatous. In the former, it is believed that the uveal tissue is actively invaded by specific organisms; the latter is considered to be an allergic response to an antigen (bacteria or their products) that may have been elaborated locally or at a remote site. These distinctions are not, however, hard and fast. Mixed involvements are often noted, the character of the reaction depending upon the degree to which hypersensitivity has been developed. Furthermore, any or all of the uveal tract may be involved, i.e., iritis, cyclitis (ciliary body inflammation), and choroiditis.

Anterior (iritis, iridocyclitis) and posterior (choroiditis) inflammations have different characteristics. In granulomatous inflammations the anterior type exhibits an insidious onset. Nodules form on the iris and keratic precipitates are abundant. Greasy exudate may cover the lens. Posterior synechiae form readily and complicated cataract ensues. Posterior uveitis is usually due to a granulomatous process and produces an exudative choroidal inflammation with formation of dense vitreous opacities.

In the nongranulomatous inflammations the anterior form is characterized by an acute onset with ciliary congestion, pericorneal flush, iris blurriness, and fine keratic precipitates. Lacrimation and photophobia may be severe. In the posterior type the choroid exhibits marked edema, but exudation into the vitreous is slight. The grayish lesion may be single or multiple. Recovery occurs with very little damage, the lesion becoming whitish with sharp, pigmented borders. In both types repeated episodes lead to posterior synechiae, iris bombé, secondary glaucoma, and complicated cataract. The anterior form, which is not common in children except when due to trauma, must be differentiated from acute conjunctivitis and acute glaucoma.

Tuberculosis, syphilis, brucellosis, toxoplasmosis, sarcoidosis, and streptococcal and viral infections may all produce granulomatous lesions. Tuberculous uveitis in children is severe and may produce a fulminating infection.

Recognition of the frequency of toxoplasmosis (Sec. 14.52) as a cause of uveitis, both congenital and adult, represents an important advance. The lesions are usually bilateral, multiple, and have a predilection for the macular areas. They tend to be large, punched out, with a dense ring of pigment when seen late. Many so-called colobomas of the macula are now considered to be due to toxoplasmic uveitis. The recent finding of toxoplasma organisms in old, adult chorioretinitic foci has increased the likelihood that this disease is a more frequent cause of uveitis than had been thought.

SYMPATHETIC OPHTHALMIA. A tragic consequence of perforating injury to one eye is the development of a bilateral, severe, granulomatous uveitis with eventual loss of both eyes. The perforation must involve uveal tissue, particularly the ciliary body. It has been suggested that sympathetic ophthalmia is due to sensitivity to uveal pigment, but this hypothesis remains unproved. All such injuries in children must be carefully observed, for the most effective prevention of sympathetic uveitis lies in prompt removal of the injured eye. As a rule such eyes are so severely damaged that retention of useful vision is unlikely, but in lesser degrees of injury the decision whether or not to remove the eye is most difficult.

The time elapsing between injury and the onset of sympathetic uveitis is quite variable, but the disease is rare before two weeks or after one year. Most cases occur in children. Once sympathetic inflammation has developed, removal of the exciting eye may prove unavailing. The onset in the sympathizing eye may be insidious with slight, irritative symptoms and mild evidences of uveitis. Eventually both eyes develop severe reactions which, in the past, led to blindness. The formerly almost hopeless prognosis, however, has been markedly improved by corticosteroid therapy. Corticosteroids suppress inflammation and thus can preserve some vision, but they do not prevent the disease. Sympathetic ophthalmia has developed in patients who were given corticosteroids promptly after injury.

All perforating injuries of the eye should be studied with great care to determine the presence of retained foreign bodies. Orbital roentgenograms must be obtained. Special procedures are available for exact localization. The removal of such foreign bodies depends on their composition, number, and location, and the prognosis is always guarded.

TREATMENT OF UVEITIS. Current treatment of uveitis consists of corticosteroids, antibiotics, and chemotherapy. Topical instillation of corticosteroids in the conjunctival sac is most effective in anterior, nongranulomatous uveitis. It is ineffective for posterior uveitis, which requires systemic steroid medication. In granulomatous uveitis corticosteroids must be used with caution for they may produce extension rather than control of the process.

Corticotropin intravenously administered is effective in sympathetic ophthalmia, but prolonged use of oral steroids is also necessary. Corticosteroids for sympathetic ophthalmia may have to be given for many months or years to suppress the uveitis.

Antimetabolite drugs have been used with some success in a small series of patients with resistant chronic uveitis including sympathetic ophthalmia. Their use has been limited by the serious drug toxicity.

In tuberculosis uveitis specific chemotherapy is indicated. Sulfonamides and pyrimethamine (Daraprim) are recommended for toxoplasmosis. Atropine is instilled locally to secure mydriasis and cycloplegia.

27.12
THE RETINA AND OPTIC NERVE

CONGENITAL ANOMALIES. Coloboma of the retina has been described elsewhere. Cysts and congenital folds are occasionally seen. The presence of medullated nerve fibers in the optic disk is quite common, giving the disk margins a feathery appearance and obscuring the vessels. An inexperienced observer is likely to mistake this picture for papilledema. Normally medullation ceases just behind the lamina cribrosa.

Displacement of the macula is a rare anomaly. In some instances it may result from retrolental fibroplasia. The optic disk also may be displaced. It sometimes appears heaped up with neuroglial proliferation (pseudoneuritis) simulating papilledema. A number of variations in shape and structure of the disk occur, such as conus and crescents.

RETINITIS PIGMENTOSA. Pigmentary degeneration of the retina is a form of abiotrophy in which the retinal neuroepithelium and pigment layer degenerate. It causes defective dark adaptation, night blindness, and visual field defects leading to severely circumscribed, tubular vision with eventual total blindness. Posterior polar cataract also occurs in time. Other genetically linked defects may be associated with it, and neurologic disturbances are not unusual, as in the Laurence-Moon-Biedl syndrome. Retinitis pigmentosa shows various patterns of inheritance and is almost always bilateral. In a well-developed case the appearance of the fundus is typical. The vessels are attenuated, the disk waxy yellow. Bone corpuscle shaped pigment is scattered around the fundus, especially in the equatorial zone. A ring scotoma of the visual field corresponds to this area. As a rule, incapacity does not develop until early adulthood, but symptoms may appear early in childhood. The prognosis is uniformly bad, and no treatment is effective.

Electroretinography is an important diagnostic aid which may reveal the existence of the disease prior to any clinical evidences. It is proving of great value in the differential diagnosis of many retinal affections with or without fundus changes.

LIPIDOSES. The general medical aspects of these diseases have been discussed elsewhere (Sec. 8.10), and therefore only the main ocular manifestations will be presented.

Xanthoma tuberosum, eyelid xanthelasmas, and arcus juvenilis appear in middle and late childhood.

The *sphingolipidoses* occur in three familial forms. (1) *Gangliosidoses.* The most common form, Tay-Sachs disease (infantile amaurotic familial idiocy) involves the nervous system only, and is characterized by decreasing vision, poor eye movements, strabismus, and characteristic ophthalmoscopic findings. These consist of a white area in the macular region approximately two disk diameters in size with a small red central area (cherry red spot); later, retinal and optic disk atrophy with blindness occurs. The white area is produced by swelling and degeneration of the ganglion cells of the ganglion layer of the retina associated with the ganglioside accumulation. By the time neurologic degeneration becomes evident, a cherry red spot is invariably present. Recently a generalized form of gangliosidosis has been recognized, and in some of these infants a cherry red spot has been observed. (2) *Sphingomyelinosis* (Niemann-Pick disease) involves the reticuloendothelial and nervous systems. Sphingomyelin accumulates in the cells of the reticuloendothelial system, producing visceromegaly, and in the ganglion cells of the retina. A cherry red spot is found in 25 to 50 percent of the cases. Decreasing vision, strabismus, and optic atrophy likewise can occur. (3) *Cerebrosidoses* are a group of rare familial disorders which involve the central nervous system and viscera or the reticuloendothelial system alone. In the pediatric form of Gaucher's disease strabismus is common. In older children and adults, large yellow-brown wedge-shaped pingueculas with their bases at the cornea may be seen. A cherry red spot in the macula area on occasion has been described in infantile Gaucher's disease.

PERSISTENT HYPERPLASTIC PRIMARY VITREOUS. This unilateral eye abnormality is caused by a failure of the tunica vasculosa lentis to regress. A white fibrous tissue mass incorporated with long ciliary processes extending to the periphery persists behind the lens. The eye usually is microphthalmic. The

abnormality is found in full-term infants. Cataract may occur; rupture of the posterior capsule will cause swelling of the lens and secondary glaucoma. The condition may suggest retinoblastoma; however, this diagnosis is usually excluded by an experienced ophthalmologist's familiarity with the appearance of the embryonic mass, the lack of calcium, its occurrence in a microphthalmic eye, and the presence of a cataract. Retrolental fibroplasia may arise in the differential diagnosis, but it is a bilateral disease and occurs in premature infants.

RETINAL DYSPLASIA. Retinal dysplasia may be an isolated uniocular abnormality, but the complete retinal dysplasia syndrome has been recently identified with the D or 13–15 trisomy chromosomal aberration. The syndrome is characterized by bilateral congenital malformations of the eyes, severe malformations of the brain, heart, and other viscera, which are usually incompatible with life, and other visible abnormalities such as harelip, cleft palate, and polydactylism. In one reported case of this trisomy, anophthalmia was present. Extensive retinal dysplasia is associated with microphthalmos, colobomas of the iris, ciliary body, and choroid, cataracts, and persistent hyperplastic primary vitreous. A pathognomonic feature of the syndrome has been found in the severely microphthalmic eyes—namely, an island of cartilage contained within a mass of fibrous connective tissue passing through the coloboma of the ciliary body of iris.

RETROLENTAL FIBROPLASIA. The meteoric rise and the equally meteoric decline of this condition are a striking example of an iatrogenic disease yielding to intensive investigation. It is discussed in detail elsewhere. Although retrolental fibroplasia can now be prevented almost completely, unfortunately there are a large number of blind and semiblind children who will require continuing medical care to retain their globes or to preserve residual vision from secondary complications such as glaucoma. No medical or surgical treatment will improve vision in the advanced case.

Although the control of oxygen therapy of prematures is clearly the major factor in the eradication of retrolental fibroplasia, other contributory elements requiring further research may be present. The disease has been encountered occasionally in premature and full-term infants who have not been exposed to oxygen. Any concentration of oxygen in excess of that in air carries the risk of producing retrolental fibroplasia.

In the past decade the more liberal use of oxygen in the treatment of respiratory distress syndrome and in the endeavor to prevent cerebral palsy has resulted in some resurgence of RLF cases. Though monitoring of arterial oxygen tension is highly advantageous when high concentrations of oxygen are given, it is not practical in most nurseries. Caution and close clinical assessment is necessary during this time. Periodic examination of the eyegrounds has been recommended as a safeguard in oxygen therapy since severe retinal vasoconstriction can be indicative of hyperoxia.

It is important to differentiate retrolental fibroplasia from other conditions giving rise to the clinical picture of a white mass in the pupil. The eyes of most infants with advanced retrolental fibroplasia exhibit bilateral structural disturbances—small eye, shallow anterior chamber, dentate (ciliary) processes in the periphery, and evidences of retinal scarring and detachment of mass formation. Mild cases may recover with no visible changes, and all degrees and grades of involvement may be found in cases of intermediate severity; myopia is frequent.

RETINOBLASTOMA. Retinoblastoma is a congenital malignant tumor arising from the nuclear layers of the retina with a marked tendency toward multiple origins in one or both eyes. The frequency of retinoblastoma seems to have increased in the past three decades and cannot be explained entirely by the increase in the number of children born from cured retinoblastoma patients. In 1931 retinoblastoma was reported to occur once in 34,000 births; in 1961 an incidence of 1:17,000 was given. Improved methods of diagnosis as demonstrated by the use of the indirect ophthalmoscope, more accurate reporting, and a true increase in the incidence of the malignancy may help to explain the change in frequency. Although the tumor is present at birth, it may not be observed until later in infancy. Occasionally the tumor is discovered in an older child and in a rare instance in an adult. Careful examination of both eyes is essential because the lesion is frequently bilateral (about 30 percent). Although the majority of cases are sporadic, a strong hereditary tendency has been noted. Evidence supports an irregular autosomal dominant mode of inheritance. When retinoblastoma has appeared in one child of healthy parents the chances for other siblings to develop the disease is small (9 percent). Recent data on the heredity of retinoblastoma suggest the following remarks. A retinoblastoma survivor with proved, hereditary retinoblastoma has a 50 percent chance that some of his children will be affected. A sporadically affected adult survivor with unilateral involvement has a 10 to 20 percent chance that some of his children will be affected; a sporadic bilateral case will pass it on to nearly 50 percent of his children.

Pathology. The most common form of tumor contains undifferentiated retinoblasts. The less frequent form is differentiated into true rosettes, although tissues intermediate between the two types are usually present. Characteristically there are areas of necrosis and degeneration with dense foci of calcium deposits. The tumor has a predilection for invasion of the optic nerve and, by extension, may reach the subarachnoid space and the brain. It is highly malignant, with a strong tendency to hematogenous dissemination. Due to local growth, secondary glaucoma and buphthalmos may occur. In a very few instances spontaneous regression has been noted.

Diagnosis. Patients are usually first observed when the tumor has grown so large that a creamy white reflex in the pupillary area is visible. At times, strabismus occurs because of impairment of vision. Therefore every young pediatric patient with strabismus should have a careful ophthalmoscopic examination. Newly formed vessels characteristically extend over the surface of the lesion. By the time the lesion is visible as a white mass in the pupil, it is far advanced. Complete retinal detachment may be present which by transillumination reveals a solid tissue. An important diagnostic point is the presence of calcium particles in the lesion. These may be grossly visible and are readily demonstrable by x-ray. Occasionally the patient may have the appearance of uveitis due to the necrosis and inflammatory response of the tumor. The globe and anterior chamber are of normal dimensions.

A number of conditions may be confused with retinoblastoma. In retrolental fibroplasia a bilateral white reflex in the pupil is usually noted within the first few months of life. A history of prematurity is present, and the globes usually show other abnormalities, such as small size and shallow anterior chamber. No calcium is present. The characteristics of persistent primary hyperplastic vitreous have been described (p. 1829). Metastatic retinitis follows lodgment of an infectious embolus in the retina and may lead to retinal detachment. Evidences of the inflammatory source of the embolus are usually present. Severe chorioretinopathies such as those caused by toxocara or toxoplasma organisms may suggest retinoblastoma. Coats' disease (massive exudative retinitis) may also require consideration. Massive retinal fibrosis may follow retinal hemorrhage.

Treatment. The only treatment of unilateral retinoblastoma is immediate enucleation. In bilateral cases treatment consists of enucleation of the more involved eye with irradiation of the other eye. Many authorities reinforce radiotherapy of the surviving involved eye by intracarotid injection of triethylenemelamine (TEM). Where the lesion is so advanced in both eyes that radiation has little to offer for conservation of vision, bilateral enucleation is necessary. Failure to treat the disease leads to inevitable fatality, with painful, grossly deformed eyes and bulky tumor masses protruding from the orbits. Photocoagulation, cyrotherapy, and ^{60}Co have been valuable adjuncts in the treatment of retinoblastoma.

Prognosis. Ellsworth reported his results of management in 192 patients. His cases were divided into five groups according to the disease stages. The cure rate ranged from 95 percent in group one to 34 percent in group five.

27.13
THE ORBIT

A number of developmental anomalies of the skull and face involve the orbit. Some have their origin in premature fusion of the cranial bones. Oxycephaly (tower skull), usually caused by fusion of both coronal and sagittal sutures, is associated with exophthalmos due to shallowness of the orbits. Divergent strabismus is common. Increased intracanial pressure leads in some cases to papilledema, followed by optic atrophy and eventually by severe visual loss. In *plagiocephaly* the ocular disturbance is usually asymmetrical. *Scaphocephaly* less frequently involves the orbits, and visual impairment is comparatively rare. *Dysostosis craniofacialis* (Crouzon's disease) is a syndrome that includes acrocephaly, marked exophthalmos, antimongoloid palpebral fissure obliquity, divergent strabismus, and in some instances optic atrophy. In *hypertelorism* there is wide separation of the eyes; strabismus and occasionally optic atrophy occur. The Treacher-Collins or *Franceschetti syndrome* (mandibulofacial dysostosis) shows a variety of defects of the lids, facial bones, and ears. The complete form includes symmetrical colobomas of the lids, antimongoloid palpebral fissures, abnormalities of lashes, parrot nose, mandibular and malar hypoplasia, malformation of the pinna and external auditory meatus, deafness, dermolipomas, and high arched palate. Many incomplete forms of this syndrome are encountered. Three other related syndromes are oculoauriculovertebral dysplasia (Goldenhar's syndrome), Pierre Robin syndrome, and Hallerman-Streiff syndrome. The four syndromes represent abnormalities of the eyes and of the structures arising from the first and second branchial arch. In general, a number of partial and atypical forms of craniostenosis and of other varieties of dysostosis occur, some of them recognized only with difficulty.

Bacterial infection of the ethmoid sinuses, originating as a complication of viral infection of the upper respiratory tract, may readily extend to the cellular tissue of the orbit, producing cellulitis and at times displacing the globe anteriorly (proptosis). Chemosis, diplopia, and fixation of the eyeball may be present. As a rule the condition responds satisfactorily to systemic antibacterial chemotherapy; actual pus formation within the orbit requiring surgical drainage is fortunately rare.

Reticuloendotheliosis of the Hand-Schüller-Christian type (Sec. 18.1) may involve the orbits, producing severe exophthalmos. In Hurler's syndrome, or gargoylism, the bones composing the orbit may be included in the disease process; corneal opacification and strabismus may occur. Unilateral exophthalmos in children has been described in fibrous dysplasia of the skull bones.

Among neoplasms which may involve the orbit, hemangioma is most common. Dermoid cysts are a common cause of proptosis in children. Neurofibroma may develop in the orbit and produce proptosis. Retinoblastoma and neuroblastoma are also rather frequent. Often the earliest clinical evidence of neuroblastoma originating in retroperitoneal tissue is unilateral or bilateral exophthalmos with ecchymoses of the lids, secondary to metastatic invasion of the orbit. Rhabdomyosarcoma is the most common malignant tumor of the orbit in children. The clinical picture is that of a rapidly growing mass in the lid or brow or progressive exophthalmos. Diagnosis is established by histologic study of a biopsy specimen. Treatment is by exenteration, irradiation, and chemotherapy. The cure rate of localized disease in recent years has increased to about 30 to 40 percent with early diagnosis and treatment.

REFERENCES

CONGENITAL GLAUCOMA

Becker, B., and Shaffer, R. N. Diagnosis and Therapy of the Glaucomas. St. Louis, C. V. Mosby Co., 1965.

Kwitko, M. L. Anterior segment anomalies. Canad. J. Ophthal., 3:116, 1968.

CATARACT

Cordes, F. C. Types of Congenital and Juvenile Cataracts. *In* Haik, G. M., ed., Symposium on Diseases and Surgery of the Lens. St. Louis, C. V. Mosby Co., 1957.

——— Retinal detachment following congenital cataract surgery. A study of 112 enucleated eyes. Amer. J. Ophthal., 50:716, 1960.

Francois, J. Congenital Cataracts. Springfield, Ill., Charles C Thomas Co., 1963.

Rubella Symposium. Arch. Ophthal., 77:427, 1967.

Scheie, H. G. Aspiration of congenital soft cataracts: a new technique. Amer. J. Ophthal., 50:1048, 1960.

Wilson, W. A., and Donnell, G. N. Cataracts in galactosemia. Arch. Ophthal., 60:215, 1958.

THE UVEA

Apt, L. Uveitis. *In* Gellis, S. S., and Kagan, B. M., eds., Current Pediatric Therapy, 1966-1967. Philadelphia, W. B. Saunders Co., 1966.

——— and Sarin, L. K. Causes for enucleation of the eye in infants and children. J.A.M.A., 181:948, 1962.

Coles, R. S. Diagnostic Procedures in Childhood Uveitis. *In* Apt, L., ed., Diagnostic Procedures in Pediatric Ophthalmology. Boston, Little, Brown & Co., 1963.

Fraumeni, J. F., Jr., and Glass, A. G. Wilms' tumor and congenital aniridia. J.A.M.A., 206:825, 1968.

Giles, C. L. Inflammatory diseases of the uveal tract. *In* Holt, L. B., ed., Pediatric Ophthalmology. Philadelphia, Lea & Febiger, 1964.

Kazdan, J. J., McCulloch, J. C., and Crawford, J. D. Uveitis in children. Canad. Med. Ass. J., 96:385, 1967.

Maumenee, A. E., ed. Toxoplasmosis, with Special Reference to Uveitis; Symposium. Baltimore, The Williams and Wilkins Co., 1962.

THE RETINA AND OPTIC NERVE

Boniuk, M., ed. Ocular and Adnexal Tumors. St. Louis, C. V. Mosby Co., 1964.

Cogan, D. G., and Kuwabara, T. Ocular pathology of the 13-15 trisomy syndrome. Arch. Ophth., 72:246, 1964.

Ellsworth, R. M. Practical Management of Retinoblastoma. Trans. Amer. Ophthal. Soc., 67:462, 1969.

Goodman, G., and Ripps, H. Electroretinography in the differential diagnosis of visual loss in children. Arch. Ophthal., 64:221, 1960.

Patz, A. Retrolental fibroplasia. Survey of Ophthal., 14:
1, 1969.
Reese, A. B. Tumors of the Eye, 2nd ed. New York,
Hoeber Medical Division, Harper & Row, 1963.
———— and Straatsma, B. R. Retinal dysplasia. Amer. J.
Ophthal., 45:199, 1959.

THE ORBIT

Blodi, F. C. Developmental anomalies of the skull affect-
ing the eye. Arch. Ophthal., 57:593, 1957.
Boniuk, M., ed. Ocular and Adnexal Tumors. St. Louis,
C. V. Mosby Co., 1964.
Cassady, J. R., Sagerman, R. H., Tretter, P., and Ells-
worth, R. M. Radiation therapy for rhabdomyosar-
coma. Radiology, 91:116, 1968.
Feingold, M., and Gellis, S. S. Ocular abnormalities
associated with first and second arch syndromes. Sur-
vey Ophthal., 14:30, 1969.
Iliff, C. E., and Ossofsky, H. J. Tumors of the Eye and
Adnexa in Infancy and Childhood. Springfield, Ill.,
Charles C Thomas, Publ., 1962.
Reese, A. B. Tumors of the Eye, 2nd ed. New York,
Hoeber Medical Division, Harper & Row, 1963.

27.14
STRABISMUS
(SQUINT)

Strabismus (crossed eyes; wall eyes) has been estimated to affect some 10 percent of the world's population. It is an important cause of visual and psychologic disability. Early recognition of strabismus is
essential for restoration of vision and the establishment of binocular visual patterns.

During the first months of life it may be difficult
to tell whether true strabismus is present. Conjugate
following movements are not firmly established until
the end of the third month. Occasionally they are
delayed some months longer, during which time
random movements of the eyes may be noted, giving
rise to transient spurious strabismus. Convergence
is not well established until 6 months of age although it may be elicited at 1 month. However,
any frequent or persistent deviation of the eyes must
be viewed with suspicion. It should be remembered
that epicanthus creates an illusion of strabismus although it may also accompany true strabismus.

ETIOLOGY. The fundamental disturbance in most
cases of strabismus is innervational, representing a
disturbance of ocular-cerebral control mechanisms
rather than of the effector organs themselves. Paretic
factors and muscular anomalies play a lesser role.
Certain types of strabismus exhibit great variability
depending upon the level of emotional reactivity of
the child. It is important, therefore, to realize that
most strabismus cannot be treated as a static anatomic entity but requires an approach that includes
insight and understanding of the organism as a
whole and, in particular, of the mental and emotional
make-up of the child.

Neither physicians nor the laity are sufficiently
aware that strabismus is one of the leading causes
of monocular blindness and that in nearly every instance this blindness is preventable. The worldwide
incidence of monocular blindness due to this cause in
men of military age during the last war was tremendous (66 percent of monocular visual loss). Loss of
vision in the deviating eye of the strabismic child is
termed amblyopia ex anopsia or, better, suppression
amblyopia. These terms indicate that the process
whereby vision is lost is an active one, engendered
in the brain, and that it serves a purpose, the eradication of troublesome double images (diplopia). The
problem is generally not one of a blind eye turning
but of a turning eye which becomes blind. The extent of visual loss in suppression amblyopia may
range from a minimal decrease in acuity to the mere
perception of light.

Suppression amblyopia treated early enough may
be reversed, thus restoring the normal level of vision
or, at least, a better level, provided the reflex patterns
of vision have not yet become completely fixed in the
developing child. In general, the age of 6 years is
critical for arresting or reversing amblyopia of this
type. Between the ages of 6 and 8 progress may
still be achieved. After the age of 8 in most instances, little if any permanent recovery of vision
will be obtained. It is commonly stated that children
will outgrow crossed eyes. While the degree of internal strabismus lessens in many cases with the
passage of time, this is usually accomplished at a
great price—the development of amblyopia.

The goal of modern ophthalmology is to obtain
a pair of eyes that not only appear cosmetically
straight but also function together in binocular single
vision. Such a functional result is not frequently obtained in a child with strabismus; but even if it is
not achieved often, the fact that it is achieved at all
is the point to be remembered. Satisfactory cosmetic
cures, however, are frequently obtained. This is generally the primary concern of the parents and, from
the psychologic viewpoint, is of great importance to
the patient. Since even an infant may develop amblyopia, the child should be examined by an ophthalmologist as soon as strabismus is suspected.

CLASSIFICATION. Strabismus embraces a number of
entities. Although paralytic factors are responsible
for a certain number of cases, most childhood strabismus is *comitant;* that is, the deviation is the same
in all fields of gaze and is not attributable to a paralytic lesion. Strabismus may be internal (convergent,
also called esotropia), external (divergent, exotropia),
vertical (hypertropia when one eye is above the visual axis, hypotropia when one eye is lower), and
occasionally torsional (cyclotropia). Frequently, horizontal strabismus is complicated by a vertical element; this reduces the likelihood of functional cure.
In most strabismus one eye is consistently deviated;
this is known as monocular strabismus. A smaller

number, termed alternators, fix equally well with either eye. In general, the monocular type is associated with amblyopia. The use of both eyes in the alternating variety permits vision development of both eyes.

Convergent Strabismus (Esotropia). Internal strabismus may be congenital or acquired. The former may be due to anatomic disturbances, neurogenic palsies, or abnormal tonic innervation. Early surgery is often required in these forms. Acquired strabismus due to abnormal tonic innervation is little influenced by any form of medical treatment and usually requires surgery. The origin of tonic deviations is poorly understood.

Approximately 50 percent of strabismus is *accommodative* in origin, indicating a disturbance in the intimate association of accommodation with convergence mediated by the cerebral cortex. In an attempt to see clearly, the child must accommodate, and in so doing exerts an abnormal degree of convergence. If the accommodative need can be satisfied in some fashion not requiring active accommodation, the associated overconvergence may be prevented. Glasses which remove the need for accommodation enable the child to see clearly and at the same time avoid the necessity for undue convergence. The fact that most children are hyperopic (farsighted), which requires greater accommodation, underlies the frequency of this form of strabismus. The onset of accommodative strabismus is from about 18 months to 4 years of age, corresponding to the maturation of the accommodative mechanism and the developing interest of the child in his environment. The child who is carried through the early formative years with suitable glasses will usually retain a normal binocular mechanism. Frequently the power of glass prescribed may be somewhat excessive as regards correction of vision but serves the purpose of preventing the crossing of the visual axes. In time such overcorrection may be cut down or glasses dispensed with altogether.

Bifocal glasses are useful in the control of accommodative squint which occurs in near vision; the prescription of an additional power of glass for near vision tends to prevent overconvergence. In time, the bifocal prescription may be decreased and eventually removed. Anticholinesterase miotics (drugs that constrict the pupil and induce ciliary spasm) reduce accommodative strabismus and may be used in conjunction with or in place of glasses. Surgery is not indicated in pure accommodative cases.

The various types of strabismus are, however, not mutually exclusive, and multiple etiologic factors —anatomic, tonic, accommodative, and fusial—may be combined in a given case. In mixed types surgery is restricted to the nonaccommodative portion of the deviation.

Divergent Strabismus. Divergent strabismus may be intermittent or constant. *Intermittent exotropia* is associated with little or no significant refractive error and has an early onset, often near birth. The deviation occurs when the child looks at distant objects or during daydreaming. Frequently he will rub his eyes when outdoors (a reaction to diplopia). Soon suppression develops and the deviation becomes more evident. Eventually it is also present at near vision, and a constant exotropia supervenes. This is the genesis of "wall-eyed" strabismus. It is usually progressive. Treatment is twofold: orthoptic, to combat suppression and build fusional amplitudes; and surgical, to correct the deviation. Early surgery is usually advisable and many functional cures result.

Constant exotropia is almost invariably a surgical problem, whether it evolves from a previously intermittent divergent strabismus or occurs as a congenital anomaly or follows the loss of vision in one eye for any reason. It is characteristic of a blind eye to become divergent in time.

Vertical Strabismus. Vertical strabismus (hypertropia or hypotropia) and torsional disturbances usually result from overaction or underaction of the vertical recti and oblique muscles. The diagnosis of vertical muscle imbalance requires a sound knowledge of the anatomy and physiology of the extraocular muscles. Treatment must be directed toward restoring physiologic function of the vertical as well as the horizontal muscles; this usually necessitates surgery.

TREATMENT OF COMITANT STRABISMUS. *Medical.* The medical treatment of strabismus consists of the prescription of glasses and miotics for the accommodative factor, the reversal of amblyopia, and the development of fusion. The latter are often referred to as orthoptic measures.

Surgical. This begins where the medical treatment ends. Only those cases which fail to respond wholly or in part to medical measures are candidates for surgery. Surgery in strabismus may be unilateral or bilateral. The decision as to monocular or binocular surgery is based on many factors. In general, where functional results are anticipated, symmetrical surgery to both eyes is employed. In predominantly cosmetic situations surgery may be restricted to one eye. As a rule, only a few days' hospitalization is necessary, and the operative risk is primarily that due to general anesthesia. Convalescence of a week to 10 days is sufficient before returning to full activity. The observation and care of the strabismic child do not end with surgery but continue through the formative years until a stable binocular relationship has been firmly established.

Paralytic Strabismus. Paralytic squint is characterized by a deviation that varies in degree according to the direction of gaze and also according to whether the patient fixates with the good eye or the affected eye. Total paralysis or partial paralysis (paresis) may affect a single muscle or group of muscles and is usually indicative of a neurogenic or myogenic lesion. Congenital anomalies and birth trauma may be causative. (See Fig. 1.)

Involvement of the lower motor neuron (nuclear and infranuclear lesions) gives rise to a deviation of the eyes accompanied by diplopia, past pointing, nausea, and vertigo. Children rapidly adapt to this

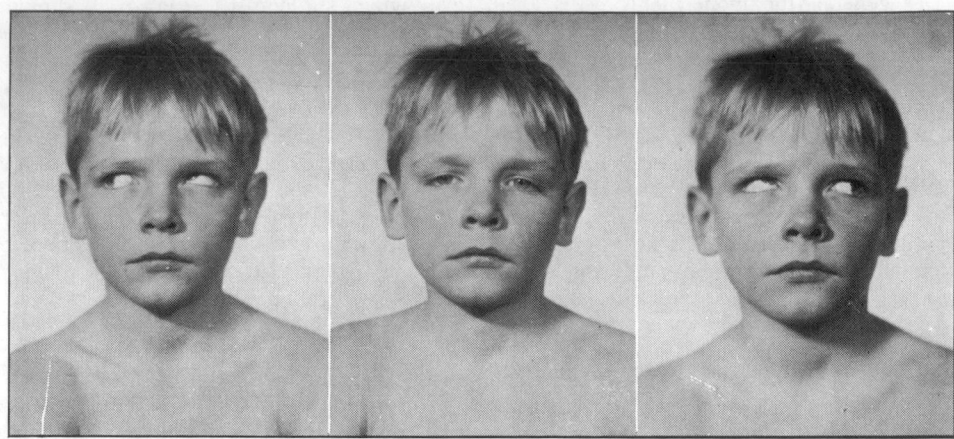

Fig. 1. Paralysis of superior rectus muscle, bilateral, with compensatory overaction of contralateral inferior oblique. On right lateral gaze the left eye rotates upward as well as medially. On left lateral gaze the right eye behaves similarly. Condition corrected by tenotomy of inferior oblique muscle on each side. Patient 8½ years old.

state with suppression of the unpleasant symptoms, an outcome rarely possible in the adult.

Supranuclear lesions, on the other hand, affect both eyes equally, with loss of associated movements or production of symmetrical, conjugate deviation of the two eyes. There is no strabismus, hence no diplopia or projectional anomalies.

Parinaud's syndrome, indicative of lesions near the corpora quadrigemina, consists of paralysis of upward and downward gaze movements with pupillary disturbances and convergence anomalies.

Internuclear lesions (medial longitudinal fasciculus syndrome) give rise to dissociated disturbances of movement wherein strabismus may be noted in one direction of gaze and not another; e.g., the medial rectus may completely fail to adduct the eye in horizontal gaze movement but can be shown to function well in convergence, providing evidence of the integrity of the lower motor neuron.

Paresis of a muscle may be evidenced by underaction as the eye rotates into its field of action (primary deviation), but more often there is noted an overaction of the yoke muscles in the good eye (secondary deviation). Surgery may be directed toward strengthening the weak muscle or weakening the overacting yoke muscle.

COMPENSATORY HEAD POSTURE (OCULAR TORTICOLLIS). In the effort to achieve binocular single vision or to assume a more favorable position of the eyes, the patient with a paretic lesion will often turn or tilt the head. (See Fig. 2.) Such head postures are often quite diagnostic. Occasionally they are due to high astigmatism or to nystagmus. In the latter case the head is usually turned to the side of the rapid component; this damps down the nystagmus and often permits better visual acuity to be obtained. Head tilts are usually due to weakness of a vertical muscle or a superior oblique, whereas head turns are

due to paresis of horizontal rotators. An important distinction should be made between ocular and congenital torticollis. Head tilts and turns based on an ocular cause may be corrected by surgery of the extraocular muscles; occasionally medical measures alone suffice (prisms, corrective lenses).

NYSTAGMUS. The origin of nystagmus may be ocular or neurogenic. Ocular nystagmus usually exhibits pendular (equal to-and-fro) movements; it is seen in albinism, spasmus nutans, congenital cataract, and other vision-impairing lesions, and congenital nystagmus. Neurogenic nystagmus is usually jerky, with a fast and a slow component; it is noted in vestibular, cerebellar, and brainstem lesions and also in congenital nystagmus.

True congenital nystagmus is observed rarely in the newborn infant, although irregular oscillating movements of the eyes are often seen. Unilateral

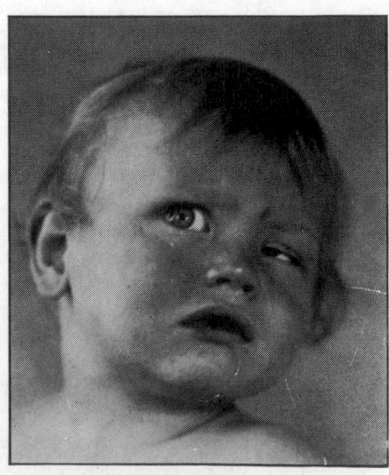

Fig. 2. Ocular torticollis in a boy of 16 months.

nystagmus usually indicates a lesion of the brainstem. The onset of nystagmus associated with ocular anomalies may be noted in the first few months after birth. Incoordinated searching movements in infants more than a month or two of age usually denote a defect of central vision.

27.15
REFRACTIVE ERRORS

Emmetropia is the term for the ideal condition in which, without accommodation, parallel rays of light (from infinity) are brought to a point focus on the retina. Very few eyes correspond to this ideal. Most infants are hyperopic; parallel rays of light would intersect behind the retina. In myopia parallel rays are brought to a focus in the vitreous in front of the retina. In astigmatism the rays are irregularly refracted in opposite meridians so that a point focus cannot be achieved. Astigmatism may be of hyperopic or myopic type.

Glasses are necessary in children to correct visually handicapped eyes (myopia, astigmatism, and the higher grades of hyperopia) or where symptoms such as headache and asthenopia are related to the refractive error. Glasses are also of great importance in reducing or correcting the deviation in accommodative strabismus.

The use of glasses does not increase a refractive error or prevent its progression. Such changes occur irrespective of the wearing of glasses. Glasses are not crutches that force the child into dependence. They serve to equalize and normalize vision and, where indicated, should be prescribed. Parental objections based on vanity or misconceptions should not be permitted to prevent the wearing of glasses by children.

REFERENCES

Bielschowsky, A. Lectures on motor anomalies of the eyes: II. Paralysis of individual eye muscles, III. Paralyses of the conjugate movements of the eyes, IV. Functional neuroses: Etiology, prognosis and treatment of ocular paralysis. Arch. Ophthal., 13:33, 569, 751, 1935.

Björk, A. Electrical activity of human extrinsic eye muscles. Experientia, 8:226, 1952.

Breinin, G. M. New aspects of ophthalmoneurologic diagnosis. Arch. Ophthal., 58:375, 1957.

────── Electrophysiologic insight in ocular motility. Amer. Orthoptic J., 7:5, 1957.

────── The nature of vergence revealed by electromyography. II. Accommodative and fusional vergence. Arch. Ophthal., 58:623, 1957.

Cogan, D. G. Neurology of the Ocular Muscles, 2nd ed. Springfield, Ill., Charles C Thomas, Publ., 1956.

Duane, A. The associated movements of the eyes: Their nerve centers, conducting paths, production, varieties and derangements. Amer. J. Ophthal., 7:16, 1924.

Holmes, G. The cerebral integration of the ocular movements. Brit. Med. J., 2:107, 1938.

Nutt, A. B., and Mein, J. Significance and management of abnormal head postures. Trans. Ophthal. Soc. Aust., 23:57, 1963.

Scobee, R. G. A Child's Eyes. St. Louis, C. V. Mosby Co., 1949.

Symposium. Accommodative esotropia. Trans. Amer. Acad. Ophthal., 61:375, 1957.

chapter 28

THE MOUTH

ARNOLD H. EINHORN

28.1
THE MOUTH OF THE NEWBORN

The oral cavity and perioral structures of the newborn infant exhibit a number of normal but distinctive and transient features which are present exclusively during the neonatal period.

Sucking pads develop soon after birth in most infants. *Sucking calluses* or corns appear frequently within days after birth on the central portion of the lips (Fig. 1). These persist only for a few weeks and consist of raised, cornified crusts or plaques protruding over the labial mucosa. Similarly, the alveolar ridges are often crowned transitorily by a thin, serrated, fringelike membrane. The frenulum of the upper lip is sometimes prominent, thick, and continued by a deep notch in the alveolar ridge of the maxilla (Fig. 2).

On or near the gum margins newborns often have small, firm, white epithelial pearls or *inclusion cysts* which are shed after a few weeks or months. Bluish, translucent *mucoceles* (see below) are also occasionally present in the mouth of the newborn. Even more commonly, white or yellow-white bodies, pinhead sized or smaller, are found on the roof of the mouth, near the junction of the hard with the soft palate, just to either side of the median raphe (Fig. 3). They are known as *Epstein's pearls* or *Bohn's pearls* and disappear quite rapidly.

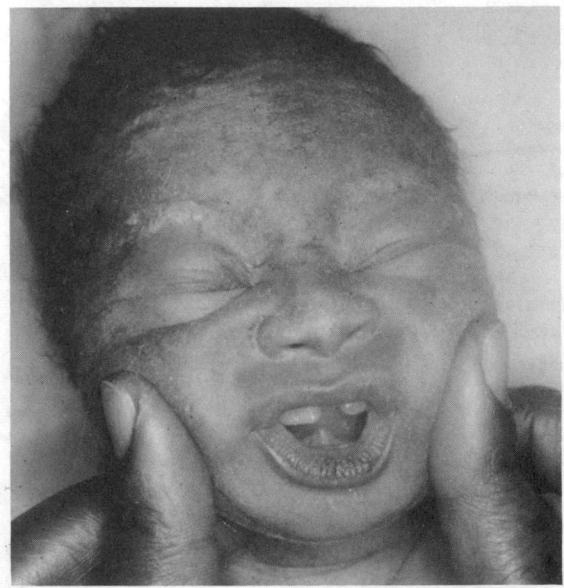

Fig. 2. Deep notched upper alveolar ridge continuing short labial frenulum.

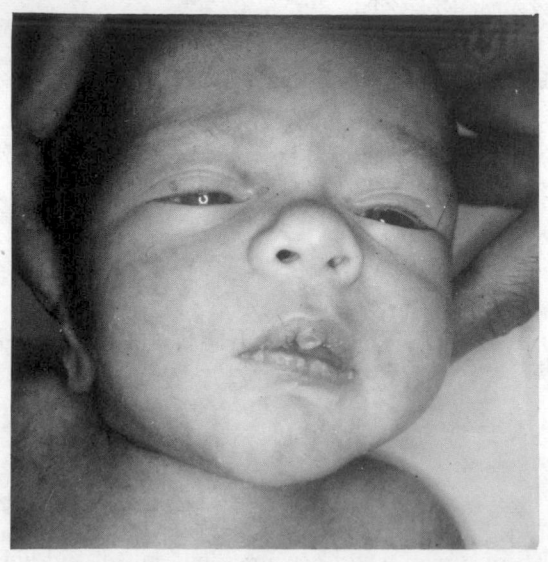

Fig. 1. Sucking calluses of the newborn.

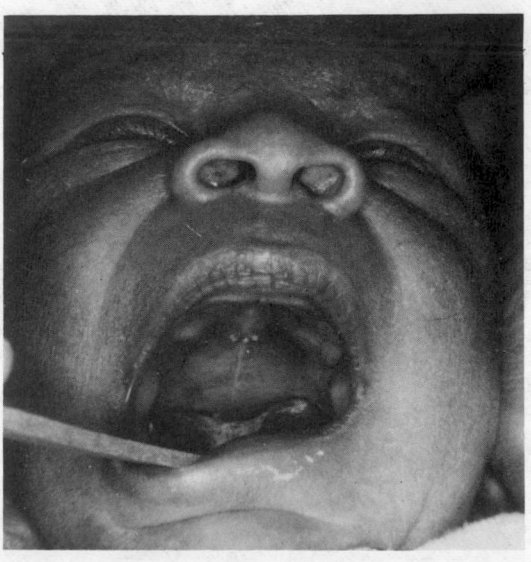

Fig. 3. Epstein's pearls.

Ulcerations of the hard palate (*Bednar's aphthae* or *pterygoid ulcers*), formerly not uncommon, are nowadays rarely observed. Although their etiology is not certain, they are generally believed to be traumatic abrasions resulting from attempts to clean the mouth at birth or from friction of the nipple. They present on the palate as superficial, elongated, oval-shaped ulcers about 1 cm or less in diameter on either side of the midline, above and somewhat medial to the tonsillar fossa. Less commonly there is a single ulcer, or a cluster of small ulcers, in the midline far back on the hard palate. As a rule these lesions are benign and disappear spontaneously within a few weeks. Petechial hemorrhages on the soft palate sometimes are also seen after birth.

Natal and Neonatal Teeth

Occasionally, one or more teeth are present at birth —*natal teeth*—or exceptionally, teeth may erupt during the neonatal period from birth through the thirtieth day—*neonatal teeth*. Usually, both natal and neonatal teeth are found in the position of the lower central incisors (Fig. 4). They are, as a rule, loosely attached to the gum margin and often shed spontaneously within a few days after birth. They may be either supernumerary or true deciduous teeth. Bodenhoff and Gorlin noted a familial incidence in approximately 15 percent of all reported instances of natal and/or neonatal teeth; in several well-documented cases there was an inheritance pattern suggesting an autosomal dominant trait.

Natal teeth have been observed in association with cleft palate, cleft lip, and other median facial defects (Sec. 15.2); chondroectodermal dysplasia

(Ellis-van Creveld syndrome) (Sec. 25.4); oculomandibulodyscephaly with hypotrichosis (Hallermann-Streiff syndrome); and pachyonychia congenita (Jadassohn-Lewandowski syndrome).

Hallermann-Streiff Syndrome (Oculomandibulodyscephaly with Hypotrichosis). In this syndrome multiple craniofacial anomalies, mental retardation, and short stature are associated with defects of hair, skin, and teeth. Dental abnormalities consist of natal teeth, subsequent dental hypoplasia, and partial anodontia. Micrognathia; microstomia; high and arched palate; hypoplasia of malar bones, mandibular rami, and nasal cartilage; microphthalmia with cataracts; and brachycephaly with cranial bossing, form a complex of oculocraniofacial malformations which produce a striking bird-headed facial appearance. The skin is atrophic; the hair is thin and rare with patchy or regional baldness and sparse body hair, eyebrows, and eyelashes. Body growth is proportionately stunted; mental and motor retardation are considerable.

Jadassohn-Lewandowski Syndrome (Pachyonychia Congenita). This disorder is a hyperhydrotic form of ectodermal dysplasia. It is transmitted as an autosomal dominant trait and affects males more commonly than females. In addition to natal teeth and intraoral leukoplakia, it features congenital thickening of the anterior portion of the nails, plantar and palmar hyperkeratosis, plantar bullae, multiple verruca, and diffusely disseminated epidermal steatocystomas.

REFERENCES

Bhaskar, S. N. Oral lesions in infants and newborn. Dent. Clin. N. Amer., 10:421, 1966.

Bodenhoff, J., and Gorlin, R. J. Natal and neonatal teeth: Folklore and fact. Pediatrics, 32:1087, 1963.

Hoefnagel, D., and Benirschke, K. Dyscephalia mandibulo-oculo-facialis (Hallermann-Streiff syndrome). Arch. Dis. Child., 40:57, 1965.

Nichamin, S. J., and Kaufman, M. Gingival microcysts in infancy. Pediatrics, 31:412, 1963.

Parmelee, A. H., Sr. The mouth of the newborn. Pediat. Clin. N. Amer., 3:847, 1956.

Soderquist, N. A., and Reed, W. B. Pachyonychia congenita with epidermal cysts and other congenital dyskeratoses. Arch. Derm., 97:31, 1968.

28.2
SOFT TISSUE LESIONS OF THE ALVEOLAR RIDGE AND FLOOR OF THE MOUTH

Eruption Cysts

These benign, bluish, compressible, raised, and fluid-filled lesions arise occasionally from the alveolar ridge

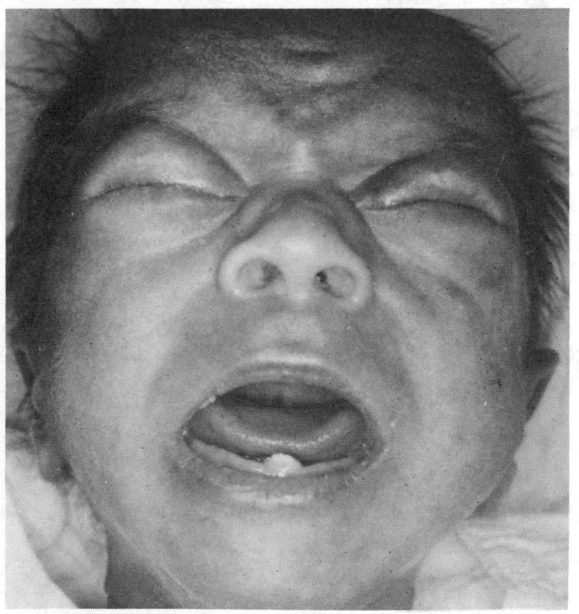

Fig. 4.   Natal tooth.

in association with erupting teeth. These cysts are believed to be, in reality, dentigerous cysts, carried to the surface by the erupting tooth. They may rupture spontaneously and heal definitively. If they persist, excision of the "roof" of the cyst may be necessary.

Mucous Cysts
(Mucoceles)

Benign, circumscribed cysts, pea-sized or smaller, are seen occasionally in any area of the oral mucous membrane containing salivary glands (Fig. 5). They are thin-walled, translucent, glistening, bluish lesions, occurring most frequently on the labial or gingival mucosa, occasionally on the buccal region or on the lower aspect of the tongue. These elevated, compressible, and fluid-filled lesions are due to the occlusion and/or traumatic rupture of minor salivary gland ducts, with secondary pooling of the saliva into the subepithelial tissue of the mucous membrane. Single or multiple, these cysts may either disappear spontaneously within a few months, or rupture, discharging a sticky mucoid material. They sometimes recur. Excision may be indicated of mucoceles which recur or of those which appear first at a later age and tend to persist.

Peripheral Giant Cell
Reparative Granuloma

Painless, hemorrhagic, soft tissue growths can arise from the interdental papilla or from areas where deciduous teeth were recently shed. These are benign lesions, probably associated with trauma and exuber-

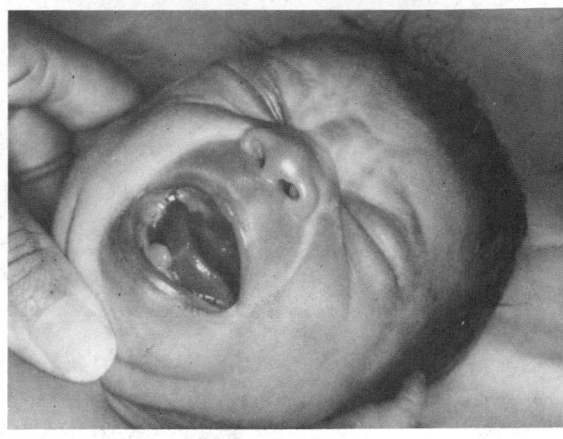

Fig. 6. Congenital epulis.

ant repair rather than with neoplasia. Since their presence may lead to displacement of adjoining teeth, they are treated by local excision.

Congenital Epulis

This lesion (Fig. 6) is a benign, slow-growing, pedunculated, and usually asymptomatic soft tissue tumor present from birth. It arises from the anterior portion of the alveolar mucosa, more commonly from the maxillary than from the mandibular ridge, and occurs far more frequently in newborn girls than in boys. Surgical excision, which is the treatment of choice, is not usually followed by recurrence.

Hemangiomas

Hemangiomas, the most common single tumor of childhood, can be seen in any of the oral soft tissue, including the tongue, the floor of the mouth, the gingiva, and the labial or buccal mucosa. These vascular anomalies may be of the cavernous or capillary type. Hemangiomas present usually as dark blue, diffuse, soft, partly raised, and compressible lesions which can be evacuated readily by stroking, remaining collapsed as long as pressure is applied, especially at the site of the feeding vessel. Their course is variable. Some may regress spontaneously. They bleed profusely when traumatized. Trauma may, however, also produce complete regression of the hemangiomas. They also vary considerably in size, ranging from small localized lesions of limited growth to extremely large tumors (Fig. 7) of rapid growth, which may interfere with function and may even be life threatening. Surgical excision is indicated for those lesions which interfere with function. Small hemangiomas may be left alone, but adrenocortical steroids may

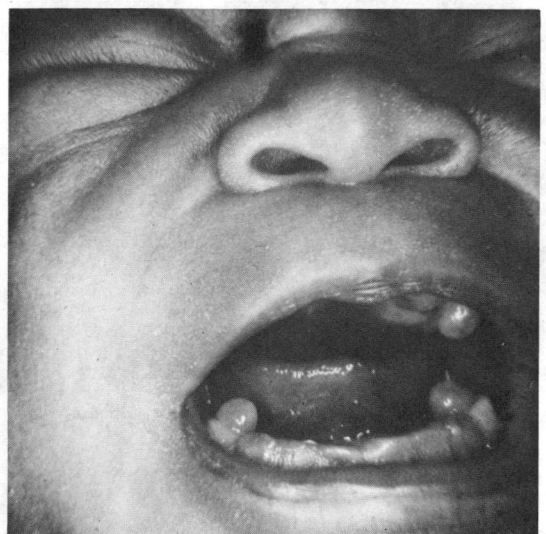

Fig. 5. Multiple oral mucoceles in a newborn infant.

be indicated if the small hemangiomas are likely to be traumatized or to cause functional impairment.

Ranula

This condition (Fig. 8) is relatively rare in children, although it can be seen even in the newborn period. It is characterized by swelling of the tissues of the floor of the mouth, which displaces the tongue forward and laterally (Fig. 8A) and may produce a visible bulge in the submandibular region. In the majority of cases, such growths represent sublingual salivary cysts; exceptionally, lymphangiomatous tissue. The treatment consists of surgical excision. However, when the size of the mass produces respiratory embarrassment, an emergency aspiration or incision and drainage may be necessary as a temporary measure, followed at a later date by the definitive excision.

REFERENCES

Bhasker, S. N. Oral tumors in infancy and childhood: A survey of 239 cases. J. Pediat., 63:195, 1963.

Firfer, H. G., and Stuteville, O. H. Congenital epulis. Oral Surg., 15:781, 1962.

Robinson, H. B. G. Oral neoplasms of children. Pediat. Clin. N. Amer., 3:854, 1958.

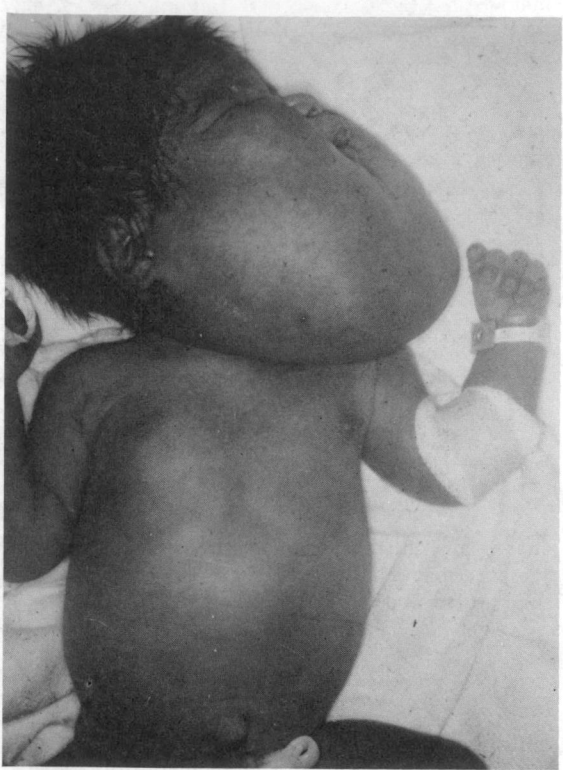

Fig. 7. Giant hemangioma of the floor of the mouth of a newborn infant.

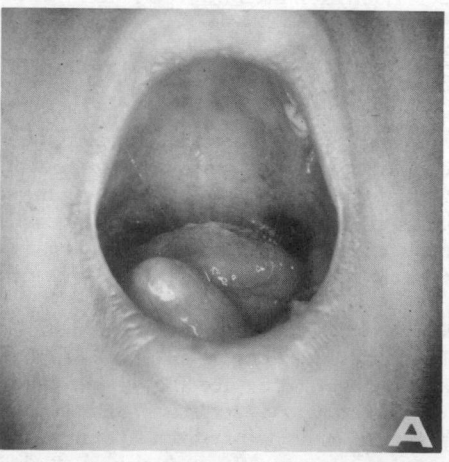
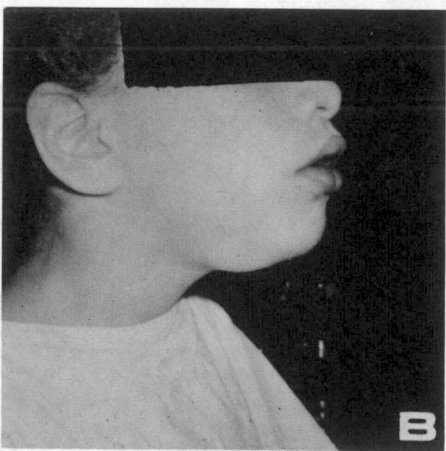

Fig. 8. Ranula. A. Protrusion of the mass with displacement of tongue. B. Visible bulge of the submandibular region due to the ranula.

28.3
MALFORMATIONS OF THE LIPS, PALATE, AND JAW

Ogival Palate

A high-arched palate without any associated defect may be seen occasionally in the normal newborn, but does not persist beyond early infancy in normal children. However, this deformity is also one of the prominent craniofacial defects commonly present in a variety of inborn skeletal abnormality syndromes. Thus, a high and narrow palate is a typical feature of those genetic affections of the skeleton which are associated with, or characterized by:

1. Hypoplasia of the lateral facial structures: mandibulofacial dysostosis of Treacher-Collins-Franceschetti (Sec. 25.1).

2. Midfacial hypoplasia without associated craniosynostosis: cleidocranial dysostosis (Sec. 25.4), arachnodactyly or Marfan's disease (Sec. 25.4), and Russel-Silver dwarfism (Sec. 25.2).

3. Midfacial hypoplasia associated with craniosynostosis: craniofacial dysostosis of Crouzon (Sec. 25.1), acrocephalopolysyndactyly or Carpenter's syndrome, and acrocephalosyndactyly or Apert's syndrome.

In *Apert's syndrome (acrocephalosyndactyly)*, a disorder of autosomal dominant inheritance, the combination of irregular craniosynostosis and considerable midfacial hypoplasia results in peculiarities of cranial shape and facial appearance. The essential craniofacial characteristics of this syndrome consist of acrocephaly, high and prominent forehead with frontal bossing, flat facies, shallow orbits, supraorbital depressions, hypertelorism, downward slanting of the palpebral fissures, short and beaked nose, and high-arched palate. The associated malformations of the extremities, which consist primarily of syndactylism of digits and toes, are described in Section 25.2. The level of intelligence is variable.

Carpenter's syndrome (acrocephalopolysyndactyly) is a clinical entity in which cranial and facial anomalies similar to those of Apert's syndrome are associated with mental retardation, obesity, and hypogenitalism. In addition to brachyturricephaly, hypertelorism, and high-arched palate there is micrognathia. Associated malformations of fingers and toes, which are discussed in detail in Section 25.2, consist of syndactyly, brachydactyly, polydactyly, and clinodactyly. The transmission of this disorder is probably autosomal recessive.

4. Midfacial hypoplasia associated with microcrania: Rubinstein-Taybi syndrome, and long-arm 18 deletion syndrome.

The *Rubinstein-Taybi syndrome* features a constellation of congenital anomalies which include short, broad, and angulated thumbs, abnormal dermatoglyphs, peculiarities of facial morphology, short stature, and mental retardation. The craniofacial defects are characterized by microcrania, midfacial hypoplasia, narrow and high-arched palate, narrow and prominent forehead, narrow and beaked nose with downward prolongation of the nasal septum, and antimongolian slanting of the palpebral fissures. There are also varied ocular defects, anomalies of the external ears, and cryptorchidism.

In *Long-arm 18 deletion syndrome,* mental deficiency, generalized hypotonia, physical growth retardation, and genital hypoplasia with cryptorchidism are associated with abnormalities of hands, feet, and dermatoglyphics; skin dimples; external ear defects and deafness; midfacial hypoplasia with high-arched palate and carp mouth; and microcephaly.

5. Diffuse hypoplasia of the face: Hallermann-Streiff syndrome (Sec. 28.1), progeria, and Seckel's bird-headed dwarfism.

Progeria is a disorder of unknown etiology and apparently sporadic occurrence. Affected individuals are short, thin, deformed, and present a striking bird-headed facial appearance with pronounced senilelike features. Body configuration and facial morphology are the result of a combination of multiple congenital defects involving skeleton, skin, subcutaneous fat, hair, teeth, nails, and blood vessels. Premature aging of the afflicted child and a short lifespan are related to the early onset in childhood of progressive arteriosclerosis leading to anginal attacks and terminally to coronary occlusion.

Skeletal anomalies in this disorder consist of generalized dysplasia and hypoplasia, and localized degenerative bone changes. Physical growth is markedly retarded. The calvarium is thin and poorly ossified; closure of the fontanel is delayed. Clavicles are characteristically short, limbs are thin, and joints are stiff and enlarged. The hips are deformed in coxa valga.

The face is hypoplastic, the chin small and receding, and the palate narrow and highly arched. The orbital cavities are relatively small and shallow, the eyes and nose are protuberant, and the scalp veins are prominent and dilated. An impression of hydrocephalus is produced by the contrast between the smallness of the face and the relative width of the forehead and cranium, further accentuated by the progressive alopecia and the absence of eyebrows and eyelashes. The skin is thin and the nails are atrophic. The teeth are delayed in eruption, irregular, crowded, and partly missing. Subcutaneous fat gradually disappears over the entire body. Intelligence is normal. There is no effective treatment for this disorder. Death usually occurs in adolescence from coronary occlusion secondary to the generalized and progressive arterial atheromatosis.

Seckel's syndome (bird-headed dwarfism) is a severely dysmorphic condition inherited as an autosomal recessive trait. Infants with this disorder are mentally retarded, have low birth weights, are small at birth, and remain short. A complex pattern of craniofacial anomalies creates a tragically grotesque bird-headed facial appearance. There is microcephaly with craniosynostosis. Facial hypoplasia involving mandible, palate, and malar bones is associated with large bulging eyes, prominent nose, receding chin, and low-set lobeless ears. The micrognathia, the beak-like protrusion of the nose, the protuberance of the eyes, the smallness of the face, and the virtual absence of forehead are all responsible for the birdlike look. There are multiple malformations of the bones and joints of the axial skeleton and of the extremities, including dislocation of the hips, hypoplasia or aplasia of one or several bones, and osseous deformities.

High-arched palate also occurs in genetic syndromes in which the skeletal component of the facial abnormalities plays a less prominent role, as in variants of the pterygium syndrome, especially Turner's OX gonadal agenesis (Sec. 16.11), leprechaunism, Cockayne syndrome, Cornelia de Lange syndrome, and Marshall's type of ectodermal dysplasia.

Leprechaunism, a rare autosomal recessive disorder is characterized by stunted physical growth, with mental and motor retardation, and extreme emaciation; small, hirsute, elfinlike, and prematurely senile facial appearance with lack of facial subcutaneous fat, beaked nose, flaring nostrils, widely spaced prominent eyes, thick lips, and narrow high-arched palate; large low-set ears; short neck; enlargement of breasts and external genitalia; and abnormalities of carbohydrate metabolism with hyperplasia of the islets of Langerhans.

Cockayne syndrome is an autosomal recessive disorder. This condition includes the following characteristic features: cachectic dwarfism with kyphosis, ankylosis, disproportionately long extremities, and large hands and feet; mental deficiency; microcranium with thick calvarium; lack of facial subcutaneous fat with prognathism, sunken eyes, and thin nose, producing a senilelike appearance; thin, pigmented, and photosensitive skin; retinal degeneration with pigmentation, optic atrophy, cataract, and pupillary sluggishness; prominent ears and partial deafness; cold, blue extremities; arteriosclerosis; ataxia and tremors; hepatosplenomegaly; and albuminuria.

Cornelia de Lange syndrome is a clinical entity which has occurred in siblings and is probably transmitted as an autosomal recessive trait. Children with this condition are short, mentally retarded, brachymicrocephalic, and hirsute. They have short extremities with tapering short fingers, oligodactyly, and proximally displaced thumbs; abnormal dermatoglyphics; defects of ribs and sternum; and hypoplastic nipples and umbilicus. Their facial appearance is striking and includes bushy eyebrows with synophris and long profuse eyelashes; flat nasal bridge with upturned tip and anteverted nostrils; increased distance from nasal base to vermilion of upper lip; midline notching of upper and lower lips; narrow high-arched palate with micrognathia; and low-set ears.

Marshall's type ectodermal dysplasia is a mildly hypohydrotic variant of ectodermal dysplasia. Additional features consist of midfacial hypoplasia with short depressed nose, low and flat nasal bridge, maxillary hypoplasia, and narrow high-arched palate; cataracts; and deafness.

Micrognathia

Isolated hypoplasia of the mandible, of various degrees of severity, may occur without associated cleft palate or any other congenital defect. The underdeveloped mandible is responsible for a characteristic "Andy Gump" or birdlike facial appearance. When the micrognathia is relatively mild, there will be no interference with breathing. In rare instances the hypoplasia is very severe and produces respiratory difficulty, requiring the same precautions as in the Pierre Robin syndrome, in which the abnormality of the jaw is associated with cleft palate and glossoptosis (see below).

Micrognathia may be one of the congenital malformations pharmacologically induced by maternal use of aminopterin during pregnancy. The anomaly is also part of several chromosomal aberration syndromes, such as 18 trisomy, long-arm 21 deletion syndrome, 13-15 trisomy, and Cri du Chat syndrome (Sec. 15.4). In a number of genetic multidefect syndromes a hypoplastic mandible also constitutes one of the typical manifestations, as in Cornelia de Lange syndrome (see above), oculo-auriculo-vertebral syndrome of Goldenhar (Sec. 25.3), progeria (see above), oculomandibulodyscephaly with hypotrichosis or Hallermann-Streiff syndrome (Sec. 28.1), Seckel's bird-headed dwarfism (see above), Russel-Silver dwarfism (Sec. 25.2), mandibulofacial dysostosis of Treacher-Collins-Franceschetti (Sec. 25.4), and Smith-Lemli-Opitz syndrome.

Smith-Lemli-Opitz syndrome is a familial disorder, probably inherited as an autosomal recessive, characterized by mental retardation, short stature, skeletal defects, and urogenital abnormalities. In addition to micrognathia the major craniofacial anomalies consist of microcephaly; low-set slanted ears; epicanthis ptosis and strabismus; broad nasal tip and anteverted nostrils: and broad maxillary ridges. Hypospadias, cryptorchidism, syndactyly of the toes, and abnormal dermatoglyphics are also part of the syndrome.

Pierre Robin Syndrome

The clinical triad of micrognathia, cleft palate, and glossoptosis is known as the Pierre Robin syndrome (Fig. 9). Because of the association of micrognathia with cleft palate, the tongue, too large for the space provided in the underdeveloped mandible, drops backward into the pharynx where it obstructs the air passage and interferes with breathing. Episodes of cyanosis, with difficulty in breathing and swallowing,

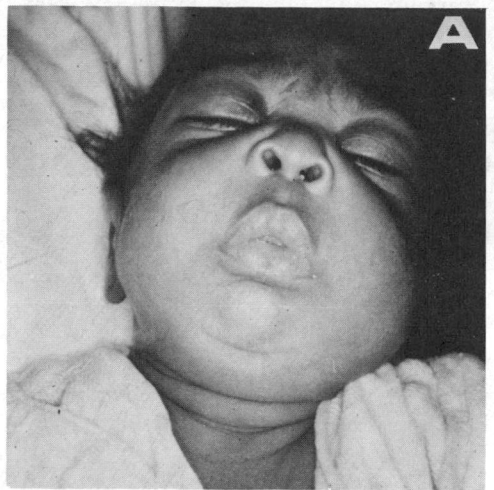

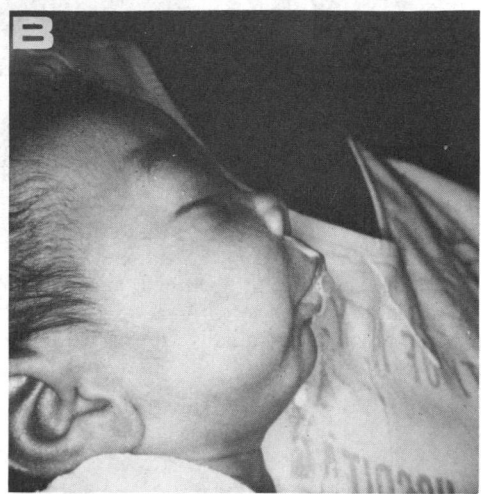

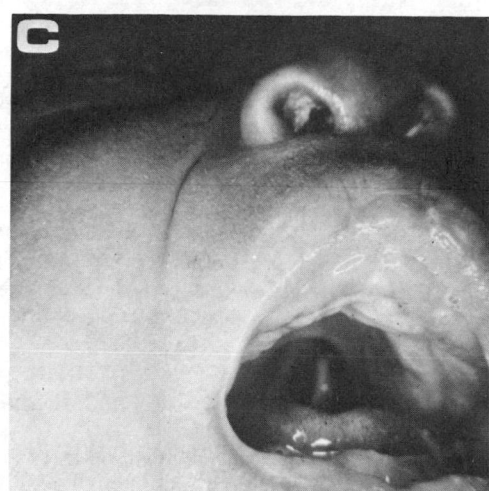

Fig. 9. Pierre Robin syndrome. A. On this anterior view, noticeable existence of respiratory distress (flaring of alae nasi, and suprasternal retractions). B. Lateral view illustrates best the micrognathia. C. Intraoral view shows wide posterior cleft palate.

often occur soon after birth especially when the infant is in the supine position. Glossoptosis may be visualized on lateral radiographs of the neck showing the encroachment of the tongue upon the pharyngeal airway. Other nasopharyngeal anomalies; ocular defects such as congenital glaucoma, congenital cataract, and retinal detachment; and a higher incidence of congenital cardiac defects have been encountered in association with the basic orofacial anomalies. The Pierre Robin anomaly may be isolated or may be part of one of the genetic dysmorphic syndromes of which cleft palate and micrognathia are characteristic features (see under Micrognathia, and Cleft Palate).

In the vast majority of cases, the respiratory distress may be alleviated by placing the infant face down. In more extreme situations, which should occur rarely if the infant is watched carefully and managed appropriately, it may be necessary to pull the tongue forward by means of a traction suture inserted temporarily through the tip of the tongue. Following such a procedure, a variety of methods have been advocated for the purpose of maintaining the forward position on the tongue during subsequent weeks or months. An artificial tongue-tie can be created either by suturing the lingual undersurface to the mucosal aspect of the lower lip, or by anchoring the tongue to the cartilaginous portion of the mandible. The desired effect can also reportedly be achieved without glossopexy, by exerting continuous traction by means of a weight upon a suture passed through the mid-body of the tongue. The use of a removable, individually constructed, acrylic palatine obturator has also been recommended as a helpful adjunct to nipple feedings. We found this device poorly tolerated. Furthermore, if the infant is carefully positioned, feeding problems are usually minor and can be handled as in any other infant with cleft palate. Most infants survive with conservative management by simple positioning, but need extremely close supervision during the first few weeks or months of life.

Cleft Lip and Cleft Palate

Cleft lip (harelip) and cleft palate are developmental anomalies of the first branchial arch of the embryo. The ensuing defects are of variable severity, some barely perceptible, others exceedingly handicapping functionally, cosmetically, and psychologically. However, even the most complex and disfiguring among these orofacial malformations is amenable to satisfactory correction, provided the numerous phases of treatment are competently planned and integrated. Successful management requires a careful and comprehensive program, optimally integrated and coordinated between the multiple disciplines involved.

Cleft Lip

Cleft lip is a frequent congenital anomaly occurring once in somewhat more than 1,000 births, either alone or in conjunction with cleft palate (see p. 1845). It is caused by incomplete fusion, during the second month of embryonic development, of the nasomedial or intermaxillary process with the more laterally placed maxillary process. Because the cleft deformity occurs during a period of intrauterine life when fetal growth is exceedingly rapid, the structures of the face and mouth develop without the normal encircling restraints of the muscles of the lips. A characteristic depression or flattening of the infant's midfacial contour may result from the disruption of normal antagonistic forces across the midline and the concomitant disturbance of growth of the facial segments involved. The facial cleft, even when not associated with cleft palate, may affect not only the lip, but also the external nose, the nasal cartilages, the nasal septum, and the alveolar process.

The cleft is usually just beneath the center of one nostril; various degrees of completeness are recognized. There may be only a slight indentation of the lip, or the fissure may extend to the nostril, causing the latter to sag and to be flattened, with the tip of the nose deviated toward the noncleft side (Fig. 10). Although cleft palate may occur without cleft lip, the failure of lip fusion by 35 days of gestational life may impair closure of the palatal shelves, which occurs later, and may be the cause for the cleft palate formation. The more complete the cleft in the lip the greater the incidence of missing, malposed, supernumerary, or malformed teeth in the line of the cleft. The defect may occur bilaterally and may be symmetrical or asymmetrical, depending on whether the lip is cleft equally on both sides. With double harelip, and particularly when cleft palate is also present, the unattached midline portion of the upper lip or *philtrum* may jut forward out of line with the rest of the lip structures. Either single or double harelip may be accompanied by cleft palate.

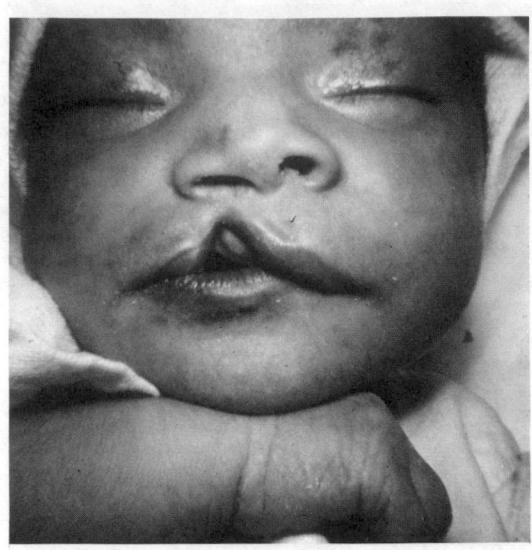

Fig. 10.   Cleft lip. Note sagging of the nostril, unilateral nasal flattening, and deviation of tip to noncleft side.

Feeding of the infant generally presents no difficulty in cases of simple cleft lip with intact palate. Nursing at breast or bottle depends mainly on the suction developed by pressing the nipple with the tongue against the hard palate, rather than on closure of the lips. It is quite unnecessary to resort to large-holed nipples, droppers, or other devices in solitary cleft lip. Feeding is also not a consideration in the timing of the primary surgical correction of the lip.

Cleft Palate

Cleft palate is often associated with harelip but may occur without it. All degrees are seen. The fissure may involve only the uvula and soft palate, or may extend forward to the nostril, involving the hard palate and the maxillary alveolar ridge. It may be unilateral or bilateral, the cleft occupying the midline posteriorly and as far forward as the alveolar process, where it deviates to the involved side, dividing the alveolar ridge usually between the tooth bud of the upper lateral incisor and that of the cuspid.

Clefts of the palate can be classified into the following four types, depending on the anatomic extent of the defect: *Type I*, cleft confined to the soft palate; *Type II*, unilateral cleft of the entire soft and hard palate; *Type III*, unilateral cleft of the entire soft and hard palate and the alveolar ridge (Fig. 11); and *Type IV*, bilateral cleft of the entire palate and alveolar ridge (Fig. 12). There may also be partial or complete lack of development of the vomer and nasal septum. In these cases the lateral palatal shelves may be quite rudimentary, leaving the nasal cavity in free communication with the oral cavity and per-

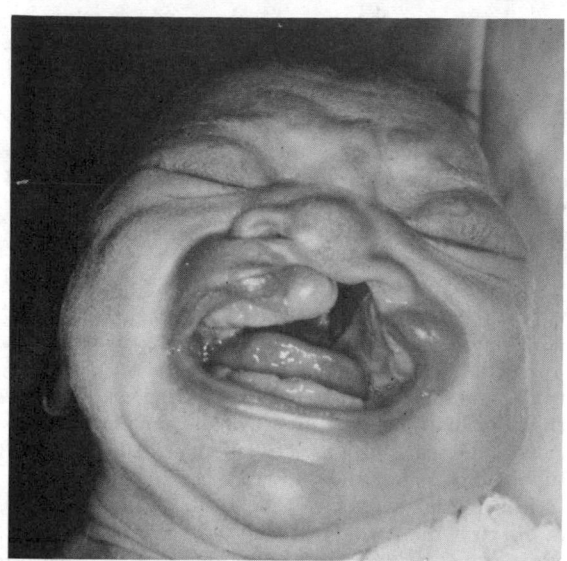

Fig. 11. Cleft palate (Type III). Complete cleft of soft and hard palates and alveolar ridge, *unilateral.*

mitting ready inspection of the turbinates, the fossa of Rosenmüller, and the adenoids. However, the philtrum, that portion of the lip just beneath the nasal septum, is almost always preserved even with extensive bilateral defects. Absence of the philtrum, when associated with hypertelorism, wide harelip, and cleft palate, should suggest the diagnosis of arhinencephaly, a "median cerebrofacial agenesis" complex in which various segmental defects occur simultane-

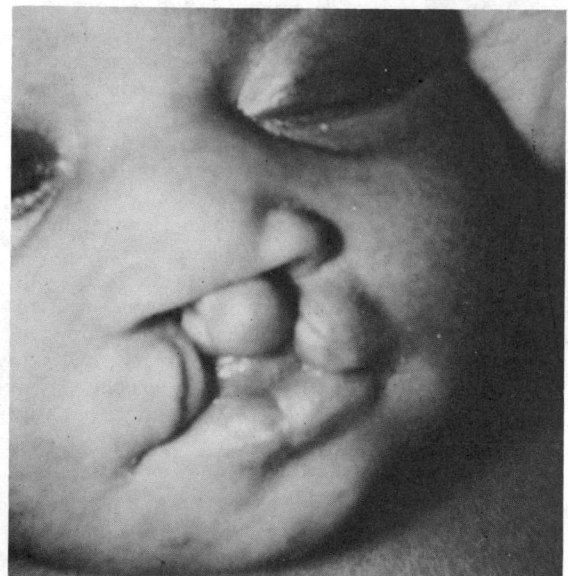

Fig. 12. Cleft palate (Type IV). Complete cleft of soft and hard palates and alveolar ridge, *bilateral.*

ously in median structures of the face and brain. (See also Sec. 15.2.)

Nutrition requires more careful consideration, and more patience is needed in feeding infants with cleft palate than with isolated cleft lip. Problems may arise from the presence of the deformity but are more often due to faulty technique or the existence of associated defects than to the cleft palate. Usually, the mechanical difficulties in sucking prevent the infant with cleft of the hard palate from establishing and maintaining an adequate supply of breast milk. However, the majority of infants readily adjust to bottle feedings in spite of their deficiencies in sucking and swallowing. In most instances, despite leakage through the nose, little difficulty is encountered if the infant is fed unhurriedly with a medicine dropper or tube-fed by gavage. Placing the infant in a sitting posture during nursing will minimize loss of fluids through the nose. We have found "cleft palate nipples" with rubber palatal flaps not only to be ineffective but also poorly tolerated, thereby enhancing the danger of aspiration of milk into the infant's lungs.

Semisolid and solid foods may be added to the nutritional regimen at the usual times; in fact, infants with cleft palate manage them somewhat more readily and efficiently than liquids.

GENETIC ASPECTS. In both cleft lip and cleft palate, a genetic pattern is suggested by the occurrence of comparable deformities among the forebears, but in some instances no such history can be obtained. Although both conditions show a familial tendency, fetal environmental factors also appear to play an important role. Breeding experiments with laboratory animals indicate that manipulations of the diet, administration of drugs, and a variety of other stresses applied to the pregnant female at the appropriate time in the gestation period will result in a relatively high incidence of analogous malformations among the young subsequently born. Comparable data regarding human experience are lacking.

Genetically, cleft lip (with or without cleft palate) and cleft palate (without cleft lip) behave as separate entities in regard to their familial distribution. Both categories appear to be etiologically heterogeneous, encompassing a variety of different types. The solitary form of cleft palate tends to be associated predominantly with other skeletal malformations, whereas harelip with or without cleft palate occurs more often in conjunction with anomalies of the central nervous system. The incidence of cleft palate is approximately two times as high in girls as in boys, whereas in most large series there is a higher incidence of harelip in males.

The incidence of cleft lip is about 1 in 1,000 births; isolated cleft palate has a frequency of approximately 1 per 2,500 births. Fraser estimates the recurrence risk of cleft lip in a sibship with one such child to be between 4 and 7 percent if neither parent is affected, and about 11 percent if one parent has the defect. With solitary cleft palate the recurrence risk for cases not associated with any other genetic malformation is probably about 3 percent if both parents are normal and one child affected, and as high as 13 percent if one parent and one child are affected.

TREATMENT.   The principle and details of surgical repair of both defects are beyond the scope of this discussion. The operative procedures employed are described in works on plastic surgery.

Many conflicting views in regard to the timing of the primary repair of the defects confront the pediatrician who assumes the responsibility of directing and coordinating the care of these children. Surgical correction of cleft lip should be done in early infancy, and here are obvious advantages to very early correction of the cleft lip, generally within the first two weeks of life. However, operation on a feeble or premature infant may well be deferred somewhat longer, at least until a steady weight gain is assured and the initial hemoglobin fall has shown an upturn. Thrush, a common complication in debilitated newborns, constitutes a threat to the success of the operation, and if it is present, surgery should be delayed. In a vigorous infant it is safe and may be advantageous to undertake the operation as early as in the first 48 hours of life. However, some surgeons prefer to wait until the infant is 1 or 2 months old.

Repair of bilateral cleft is technically more difficult, and the procedure is often performed in two steps. In experienced hands the results of surgery of cleft lip are usually quite satisfactory, although more than one operation may be required for cosmetic restitution. Great care must also be exercised to avoid excessively tight closure of the lip, which may result in a significant lingual version of the upper incisor teeth, posterior displacement of the upper lip, and exaggerated fullness of the lower lip.

Operation on cleft palate is usually done at about 18 month of age. While early intervention enhances the risk of injury or dislocation of tooth buds, deferment adds to the technical difficulty of the procedure because of the greater rigidity of the parts. The aim of the surgery is to obtain an air-tight closure of the palatal cleft and to preserve the mobility and length of the soft palate without disturbing the growing tooth buds. For cleft palate, multiple operations are required more often than in the case of simple cleft lip, and the cooperation of prosthodontist and orthodontist throughout the period of dental growth is essential for best cosmetic and functional results. Even with early closure the child may experience difficulty in sealing off the nasopharynx from the buccal cavity during deglutition and in the pronunciation of certain consonants. Speech training is almost always required.

Optimum care must also include specialized otologic and audiologic surveillance. Both before and after operation, patients with cleft palate tend to suffer from repeated and often troublesome infections of the paranasal sinuses. Hypertrophy of tonsils and adenoids is an almost invariable accompaniment, and recurrent otitis media is all too common. With chronic nasopharyngitis, the risk of tubal deafness must always be borne in mind. All efforts should be made to keep such infections down to a minimum, and when they arise they should be treated promptly with appropriate antibiotics if indicated. It must also be stressed that tonsils and adenoids may perform an essential function for intelligible speech in the child with repaired palate. An ill-considered adenoidectomy may precipitate a severe and permanent speech deterioration.

In a therapeutic situation of this nature, in which the services of several different special disciplines must be brought into effective cooperation, the pediatrician almost inevitably serves as coordinator. On his shoulders rests the responsibility for ensuring that no single aspect of the problem is overlooked. He should provide guidance, counsel, and support to both the child and parent through the various traumatic exposures. He can be of great help in allaying the parents' anxiety and the child's fears of repeated anesthetics and operations, in building up the child's confidence in himself, and in dispelling the notion that the victim of cleft palate is inferior to other children.

Familial Fibrous Dysplasia of the Jaws
(Cherubism)

This familial and hereditary variant of osseous dysplasia of childhood and adolescence affects the jaws almost exclusively and generally occurs bilaterally. Painless and firm mandibular swelling constitutes the major and usually the only symptom. The enlargement of the jaw usually begins simultaneously in both rami and extends progressively; it may start sometimes on one side, growing subsequently forward to involve the other side. The resulting osseous deformity produces characteristically a rounded "cherubic" appearance of the child's face. In typical cases the mandibular swelling becomes apparent at about 2 to 5 years of age, increases either slowly or more rapidly between the ages of 4 and 8, and remains stationary until puberty, after which slow resolution takes place. Marked dental crowding and migration of the teeth may be associated with the gross orofacial distortion, but other symptoms are unusual. Cervical and submaxillary lymphadenopathy are commonly observed. Radiography reveals multiple and frequently multioculated areas of radiolucency, which enlarge progressively with thinning and irregularity of the cortex.

The nature of this disease is still obscure. It has been suggested that cherubism represents a hereditary variant of polyostotic fibrous dysplasia. It affects boys more than girls and appears to be due to the action of a dominant gene in which the penetrance is about 10 percent in males and 50 to 70 percent in females. The course is mostly benign and the disease self-limiting; thus no treatment is necessary except if there is interference with speech and respiration. In very rare instances the growth of the bony lesion may be rapid and produce severe, even life-threatening manifestations, in which case excision is indicated.

REFERENCES

OGIVAL PALATE

Coffin, G. S. Brachydactyly, Peculiar facies and mental retardation. Amer. J. Dis. Child., 108:351, 1964.

Dekaban, A. Metabolic and chromosomal studies in leprechaunism. Arch. Dis. Child., 40:632, 1965.

Goodman, R. M., and Gorlin, R. J. The Face in Genetic Disorders. St. Louis, The C. V. Mosby Company, 1970.

Fujimoto, W. Y., Greene, M. L., and Seegmiller, J. E. Cockayne's syndrome: report of a case with hyperlipoproteinemia, hyperinsulinemia, renal disease, and normal growth hormone. J. Pediat., 75:881, 1969.

Harper, R. G., Orti, E., and Baker, R. K. Bird-headed dwarfs (Seckel's syndrome), a familial pattern of developmental, dental, skeletal, genital, and central nervous system anomalies. Pediatrics, 70:799, 1967.

Insley, J. Syndrome associated with a deficiency of part of the long arm of chromosome no. 18. Arch. Dis. Child., 42:140, 1967.

Macdonald, W. B., Fitch, K. D., and Lewis, I. C. Cockayne's syndrome, an heredo-familial disorder of growth and development. Pediatrics, 25:997, 1960.

McKusick, V. A., Mahloudji, M., Abbott, M. H., Lindenberg, R., and Kepas, D. Seckel's bird-headed dwarfism. New Eng. J. Med., 277:279, 1967.

Pashayan, H., Whelan, D., Guttman, S., and Fraser, F. C. Variability of the de Lange syndrome: report of 3 cases and genetic analysis of 54 families. J. Pediat., 75:853, 1969.

Rubinstein, J. H., and Taybi, H. Broad thumbs and toes and facial abnormalities, a possible mental retardation syndrome. Amer. J. Dis. Child., 105:588, 1963.

Salmon, M. A., and Webb, J. N. Dystrophic changes associated with leprechaunism in a male infant. Arch. Dis. Child., 38:530, 1963.

Smith, D. W. Recognizable patterns of human malformations—genetic, embryologic, and clinical aspects. In Major Problems in Clinical Pediatrics, Philadelphia, W. B. Saunders Co., 1970.

Summitt, R. L., and Favara, B. E. Leprechaunism (Donohue's syndrome): a case report. J. Pediat., 74:601, 1969.

Temtamy, S. A. Carpenter's syndrome: Acrocephalopolysyndactyly. An autosomal recessive syndrome. J. Pediat., 69:111, 1966.

Thomson, J., and Forfar, J. O. Progeria (Hutchinson-Gilford syndrome), report of a case and review of the literature. Arch. Dis. Child., 25:224, 1950.

Villee, D. B., Nichols, G., Jr., and Talbot, N. B. Metabolic studies in two boys wth classical progeria. Pediatrics, 43:207, 1969.

MICROGNATHIA AND PIERRE ROBIN SYNDROME

Berggren, R. B., and Duran, R. J. Pitfalls in the treatment of the Pierre Robin Syndrome. J. Pediat. Surg., 5:539, 1970.

Crow, M. L., Holder, T. M., McCoy, F. J., and Chandler, R. A. The use of temporary gastrostomy to prevent aspiration in Pierre Robin syndrome. Plast. Reconstr. Surg., 35:494, 1965.

Dennison, W. M. The Pierre Robin Syndrome. Pediatrics, 36:336, 1965.

Fine, R. N., Gwinn, J. L., and Young, E. F. Smith-Lemli-Opitz syndrome. Amer. J. Dis. Child., 115:483, 1968.

Goodman, R. M., and Gorlin, R. J. The Face in Genetic Disorders. St. Louis, The C. V. Mosby Company, 1970.

Goldberg, M. H., and Eckblom, R. H. The treatment of the Pierre-Robin Syndrome. Pediatrics, 30:450, 1962.

Hoffman, S., Kahn, S., and Seitchik, M. Late problems in the management of Pierre Robin syndrome. Plast. Reconstr. Surg., 35:504-511, 1965.

Oeconompoulos, C. The value of glossopexy in the Pierre-Robin syndrome. New Eng. J. Med., 262:1267, 1960.

Smith, D. W. Recognizable patterns of human malformation—genetic, embryologic, and clinical aspects. In Major Problems in Clinical Pediatrics. Philadelphia, W. B. Saunders Co., 1970.

Smith, J. L., and Stowe, F. R. The Pierre Robin syndrome. Glossoptosis, micrognathia, and cleft palate. A review of 39 cases, with emphasis on associated ocular lesions. Pediatrics, 27:128, 1961.

——— Lemli, L., and Opitz, J. M. A newly recognized syndrome of multiple congenital anomalies. J. Pediat., 64:210, 1964.

CLEFT LIP AND CLEFT PALATE

Bennett, M., Ward, R. H., and Tait, C. A. Otologic-audiologic study of cleft palate children. Laryngoscope, 78:1011, 1968.

Curtis, E. J., Fraser, F. C., and Warburton, D. Cleft lip and cleft palate. Amer. J. Dis. Child., 102:853, 1961.

Goodman, R. M., and Gorlin, R. J. The Face in Genetic Disorders. St. Louis, The C. V. Mosby Company, 1970.

Hagerty, R. F., and Hill, M. J. Midfacial contour in patient with cleft lip and cleft palate. Pediatrics, 26:387, 1960.

Landau, W., Barry, J. M., and Kock, R. Arhinencephaly. J. Pediat., 62:895, 1963.

Lis, E. T., and Pruzansky, S. Cleft lip and cleft palate: Surgical considerations. Pediat. Clin. N. Amer., 3:995, 1956.

McKenzie, J. The first arch syndrome. Arch. Dis. Child., 33:477, 1958.

McKusick, V. A. Genetics in medicine and medicine in genetics. Amer. J. Med., 34:594, 1963.

Paradise, J. L., Bluestone, C. D., and Felder, H. The universality of otitis media in 50 infants with cleft palate. Pediatrics, 44:35, 1969.

Slaughter, W. B., and Pruzansky, S. Cleft lip and cleft palate. Pediat. Clin. N. Amer., 3:1029, 1956.

Smith, D. W. Recognizable patterns of human malformation—genetic, embryologic, and clinical aspects. In Major Problems in Clinical Pediatrics. Philadelphia, W. B. Saunders Co., 1970.

Thompson, J. S., and Thompson, M. W. Genes in differentiation and development. In Genetics of Medicine. Philadelphia, W. B. Saunders Co., 1966.

CHERUBISM

Anderson, D. E., and McClendon, J. L. Cherubism: Hereditary fibrous dysplasia of the jaws, genetic considerations. Oral Surg., 15(Suppl. 2):5, 1962.

Jones, W. A. Cherubism: A thumbnail sketch of its diagnosis and a conservative method of treatment. Oral Surg., 20:648, 1965.

Thompson, N. Cherubism: Familial fibrous dysplasia of the jaws. Brit. J. Plast. Surg., 12:89, 1959.

28.4
TONGUE

Malformations of the Tongue

Macroglossia

Large, muscular tongues are occasionally familial; some orthodontists believe that these can cause malocclusion, particularly of the prognathous type. In many instances, enlargement of the tongue may be more apparent than real; a normal-sized tongue may seem larger when associated with underdevelopment of the jaws, especially in the absence of teeth.

True hypertrophy of the tongue is associated with mental retardation in cretinism, mongolism, and Cornelia de Lange syndrome; with mental deterioration, alveolar ridge hypertrophy, macrosomia, skeletal deformities, and stunted growth in generalized gangliosidosis and in Hurler's syndrome; and with macrosomia, muscular hypertrophy, omphalocele, and abnormalities of carbohydrate metabolism in Wiedemann-Beckwith syndrome.

Gross enlargement of the tongue of variable size, localized or diffuse, may be due to the presence superficially or in depth of lymphangioma or hemangioma (Fig. 13). In the latter, treatment by surgery

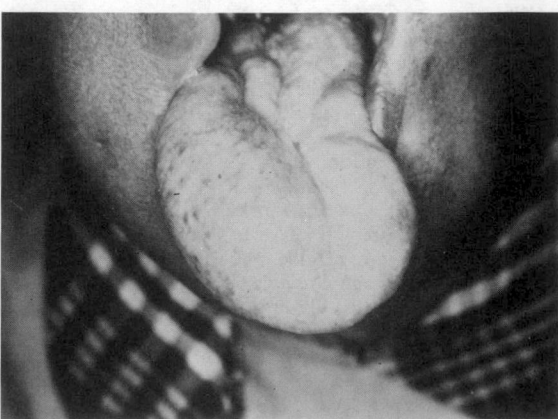

Fig. 13.   Hemangioma of the tongue.

or with adrenocortical steroids may be indicated. In rare instances neurofibromatosis has been the cause of enlargement of the tongue.

Microglossia
(Tongue Hypoplasia)

Tongue hypoplasia is a much more rare anomaly than hypertrophy. It is usually accompanied by other congenital malformations.

Aglossia Congenita
(Congenital Absence of the Tongue)

This condition is even more exceptional. It has been reported in conjunction with bony fusion of the jaws and other skeletal anomalies. In the *aglossia-adactylia syndrome,* the absence of tongue is associated with missing lower incisors, cleft or high arched palate, intra-oral bands, and abnormalities of distal portions of the limbs, especially the digits.

Tongue-tie

Congenital shortening of the frenulum interferes with protrusion of the tongue and causes a midline pucker when an effort is made to put out the tongue (Fig. 14). In all probability it should be regarded as a normal variant (Fig. 14A). The assertion is sometimes made that tongue-tie impairs an infant's ability to nurse, and it is common belief that persistent tongue-tie will eventually hamper speech, a hypothesis which, so far as we are aware, has never been properly tested. If the tongue can be protruded beyond the lips, treatment is certainly not required. When an infant's tongue is found to be more closely bound, the parents are likely to persevere and persuade someone to release it. The operation, performed by cutting the frenulum close to the undersurface of the tongue, without anesthesia, undoubtedly does no harm; whether it does any good has not been evaluated. True *ankyloglossia* (Fig. 14B), where the frenulum is replaced by a short and thickened fibrous band which restricts the range of mobility of the tongue, is rare. This condition needs appropriate surgical repair.

Geographic Tongue

This is characterized by the appearance upon the dorsum or margin of the tongue of circular, elliptical, or crescentic red patches with gray margins. These gray margins, which are slightly elevated, are apparently due to thickening of the epithelial layer and the red areas to desquamation of the epithelium. It is a common condition, probably congenital. As usually

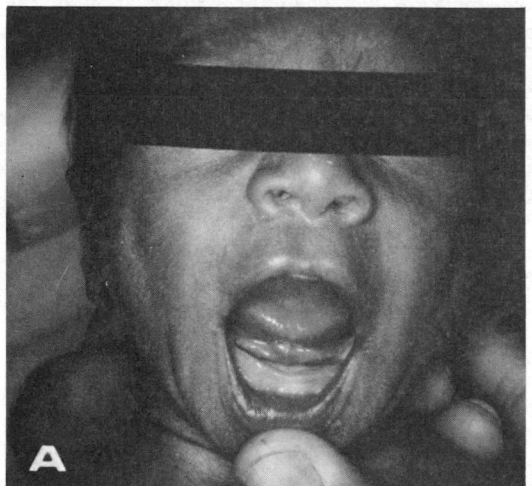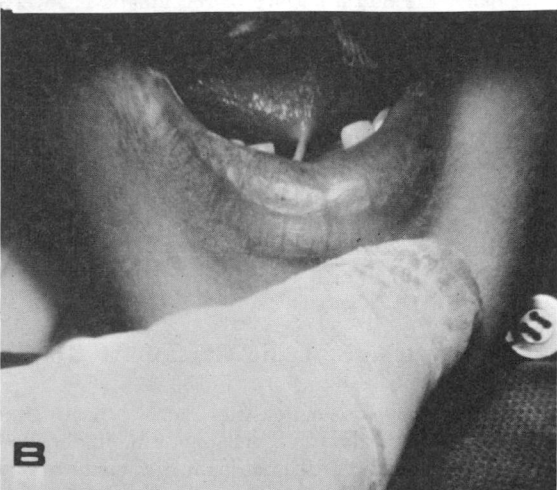

Fig. 14. Tongue-tie. A. "Normal" short frenulum of the newborn. B. True ankyloglossia.

seen, there exist upon the tongue from two to four of these red patches, surrounded by a gray border, which is 1 or 2 mm wide and slightly elevated. From day to day the configuration of the patches changes; the gray lines advance across the tongue from side to side, or from base to tip, disappearing as they reach the border or the extremity. They are followed by the red patches, and as the old ones fade away new ones form and run the same course (Fig. 15). Only the epithelium is involved, the deeper structures being unaffected. The duration of the disease is indefinite; it usually lasts for years but seems to clear up eventually. The cause is unknown. It is not accom-

panied by pain, salivation, or other symptoms of stomatitis and is of little practical importance. Treatment is unnecessary.

Fissured or Scrotal Tongue

This condition is characterized, as the name implies, by deep, irregular fissures, often several millimeters deep, upon the dorsal surface. The condition generally runs in families but is also found in mongolism. It is of no clinical significance. Evidence that it is due to vitamin deficiency is not convincing.

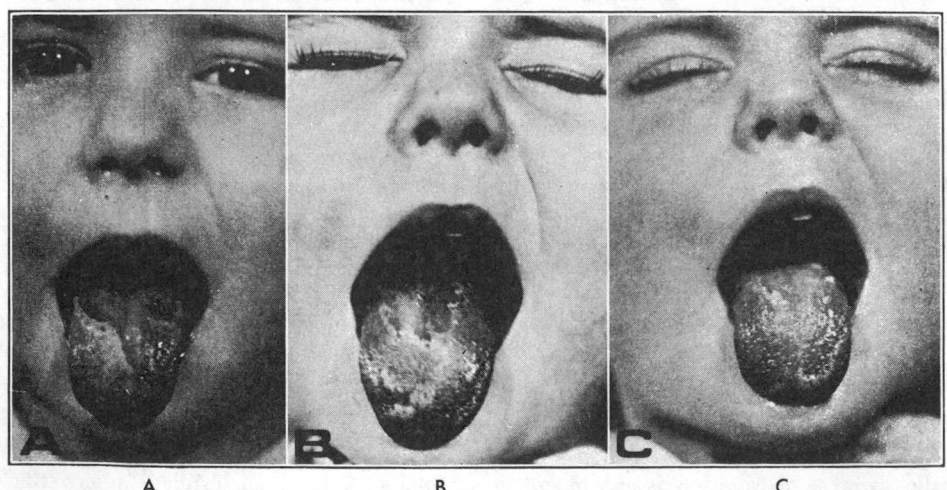

Fig. 15. Geographic tongue showing changing pattern of lesions. Patient, 2½ years of age. The interval between A and B is 14 days; between B and C, 7 days.

The Tongue in Familial Dysautonomia

Normally, the dorsal surface of the tongue is covered with conical grayish white filiform papillae. The larger and fewer red fungiform papillae are unevenly distributed near the margin and the tip. The vallate papillae are found posteriorly along the sulcus terminalis. The tongue of the patient with dysautonomia is lacking in fungiform and vallate papillae and appears uniform and smooth. The absence of these papillae, in which the taste buds are normally concentrated, explains the taste deficit found in dysautonomia patients.

Choristomatic Cyst of the Tongue

Heterotopic islands of gastric mucosa have been found within the body of the tongue or in the floor of the mouth. The area anterior to the circumvallate papillae is the usual site of involvement. The lesions present as nonulcerated, elevated, or submerged masses usually circumscribed and of slow growth. These choristomas may be asymptomatic or may interfere with feeding, deglutition, and speech. They are easily excised and usually do not recur.

Cleft Tongue

In the *orofacial digital syndrome,* an X-linked trait of dominant inheritance, limited to females and lethal to males, the tongue is characteristically cleft and lobulated. The tongue may be divided into two, three, or four lobes, and hamartomas may exist between the lobes. Other oral anomalies of this syndrome include a pseudocleft in the middle of the upper lip, a transverse cleft of the hard palate, or asymmetrical cleft of the soft palate; thick fibrous bands in the upper and lower mucobuccal folds; absence of lower, lateral incisors; malposition of teeth; and supernumerary teeth.

In *Mohr syndrome,* an autosomal recessive trait, a midline cleft of the tongue is associated with a midline cleft of the lip, conductive deafness, and facial and digital anomalies.

Thyroglossal Cyst

In the course of embryonic development, anomalies of fusion of the pharyngeal arches may cause fistulae to persist, or strands of epithelium may survive resorption and lead to the formation of cysts. The number of possible varieties of these relatively common anomalies is great. Because of its attachment to the tongue, *thyroglossal cyst,* an embryonal rest of the oral cavity, will be discussed here, although its clinical manifestations occur, in most instances, in the region of the neck, the pharynx, or the larynx.

When remnants of the thyroglossal duct persist, they may give rise to the formation of cysts, which become recognizable when the accumulation of imprisoned secretions produces a visible or palpable swelling. Such a cyst usually contains thick mucus and is lined by columnar, sometimes ciliated, epithelium; at times squamous epithelium is present, and may even predominate. The mass is generally surrounded by a thick capsule of connective tissue, and a tube or cord of epithelium with a fibrous tissue envelope often penetrates the hyoid bone and extends upward to connect with the foramen cecum at the base of the tongue.

The common site of a thyroglossal cyst is at, or near, the midpoint of the hyoid bone, usually in the midline, sometimes a little to one side. It may, however, appear at any point between the thyroid gland and the foramen cecum. As a rule, pain and dysphagia are absent, except when the contents of the cyst become infected, in which case pain, tenderness, and rapid enlargement of the overlying skin will be present. In a small infant, a thyroglossal cyst at the base of the tongue may, on rare occasions, cause breathing difficulty when the infant is in a supine position, which improves when the infant is placed on his abdomen. Not infrequently the lesion is discovered in childhood, sometimes by the parents, occasionally in the course of routine examination. It is usually quite firm, rises during swallowing, may be adherent to the overlying skin, and is almost always closely attached either to the hyoid bone or to the larynx. Transillumination often demonstrates the cystic structure but fails when the cyst contents have been rendered opaque by infection. In differential diagnosis, adenoma or abscess of the thyroid gland must be considered, although either of these is relatively rare. Since superficial cervical lymph nodes are generally situated farther toward the side of the neck, their enlargement is not apt to be mistaken for thyroglossal cyst. Lingual goiter or ectopic thyroid tissue situated high in the neck may be more readily mistaken for thyroglossal duct cysts. Such an error may lead to serious consequences if the mass is removed and proves to be the only functional thyroid tissue present. Appropriate treatment in these instances is to give adequate thyroid hormone therapy to shrink the mass sufficiently to avoid surgery.

Treatment of thyroglossal duct cyst is surgical. Care must be taken to remove not only all of the cyst but also the entire epithelial tract. This excision sacrifices usually the central portion of the hyoid bone, with amputation of the superior projection of the epithelial remnant close to the foramen cecum.

Rupture of a thyroglossal cyst following infection, or drainage by simple incision, leads to the formation of a cutaneous fistula. Cauterization is ineffectual in preventing recurrence. The entire tract must be excised.

Acquired Lesions of the Tongue

Coated Tongue

The uniform white coating seen upon the dorsal surface of the tongue in certain disease states is composed of desquamating epithelial cells, mucin, food debris, and various organisms. Under normal conditions, the saliva and the mechanical cleansing effect of mastication prevent such accumulation. In chronic mouth-breathing, and in febrile states accompanied by dehydration, especially with lack of food intake or diets limited to soft or liquid foods, such coating soon makes its appearance. No local treatment is necessary for ordinary white coating, which will disappear upon return to physiologic conditions.

In oral infections with *Candida albicans* (see Oral thrush, p. 1854), the coating appears as discrete, flaky, white patches which bleed readily on removal. In *scarlet fever* the tongue, which is heavily coated at the onset of the pharyngitis, soon clears at the tip and along its margins. The swollen, hyperemic fungiform papillae which show through the coating gave rise to the term "strawberry tongue."

The Tongue in Deficiency Diseases

In *pellagra*, the tongue and oral mucous membranes are usually inflamed and swollen; the papillae are hypertrophied; the center of the tongue may be coated although the edges are clear. Glossitis may also accompany *riboflavin deficiency* (see p. 180). The "smooth tongue" resulting from atrophy of the filiform papillae and indicative of severe nutritional deficiency is rarely seen in children.

Ulcer of the Frenulum

Friction of the tongue against the sharp edges of the lower central incisors may cause ulceration of the frenulum in infants. It occurs typically in pertussis, but also in other conditions, especially in poorly nourished and debilitated children. The ulcer may be confined to the frenum or may extend quite deeply into the tongue. It is usually about 5 to 8 mm in diameter, and of a yellowish gray color. When associated with whooping cough it persists as long as severe spasms occur. The ulcer may be touched with alum or with gentian violet. If the lesion is extensive, it may require that the child be fed by dropper or by gavage for several days. Good oral hygiene must be meticulously maintained. Treatment of any underlying chronic illness, and attempts at improving the child's nutrition are essential.

REFERENCES

GENERAL

Adran, G. M., Beckett, J. M., and Kemp, F. H. Aglossia congenita. Arch. Dis. Child., 39:389, 1964.

Bhaskar, S. N. Oral tumors of infancy and childhood: A survey of 239 cases. J. Pediat., 63:195, 1963.

Co-Te, P., Dolman, C. L., Tischler, B., and Lowry, B. Oral-facial-digital syndrome. A case with necropsy findings. Amer. J. Dis. Child., 119:280, 1970.

Goodman, R. R., and Gorlin, R. J. The Face in Genetic Disorders. St. Louis, The C. V. Mosby Company, 1970.

Gorlin, R. J., Kalmins, V., and Izant, R. J., Jr. Occurrence of heterotopic mucosa in the tongue. J. Pediat., 64:604, 1964.

——— The oral-facial-digital syndrome. Cutis, 4:1345, 1968.

Lewisohn, M. M., and Lim, D. T. Apnea in the supine position as an alerting symptom at the base of the tongue in small infants. J. Pediat., 66:1092, 1965.

Smith, A. A., Farbman, A., and Dancis, J. Tongue in familial dysautonomia: A diagnostic sign. Amer. J. Dis. Child., 110:152, 1965.

Smith, D. Recognizable patterns of human malformations—genetic, embryologic, and clinical aspects. In Major Problems in Clinical Pediatrics. Philadelphia, W. B. Saunders Co., 1970.

THYROGLOSSAL CYST

Keynes, G. Large Thyroglossal Cyst. Brit. J. Surg., 47:447, 1960.

Kottmeier, P. K., Rosenthal, S., and Minkowitz, S. Retropharyngeal abscess secondary to thyroglossal cyst. Amer. J. Dis. Child., 109:160, 1965.

Lofgren, R. H. Respiratory distress from congenital lingual cysts. Amer. J. Dis. Child., 106:610, 1963.

28.5
LESIONS OF THE GUMS AND ORAL MUCOSA

Gingival Hyperplasia

Enlargement of the gingivae is frequently observed in children and young adolescents as a consequence of unrelieved marginal gingivitis (see below). In hyperplasia of the gums seen in association with diphenylhydantoin therapy, the swollen gums are nodular, firm, and pink, presenting little or no evidence of inflammation; they almost cover the teeth. When the underlying neurologic disorder calls for continuing Dilantin therapy, the development of gingival hyperplasia is not in itself adequate justification for discontinuing the drug. In the early stages of the condition, much can be done to check its progress by close attention to oral hygiene.

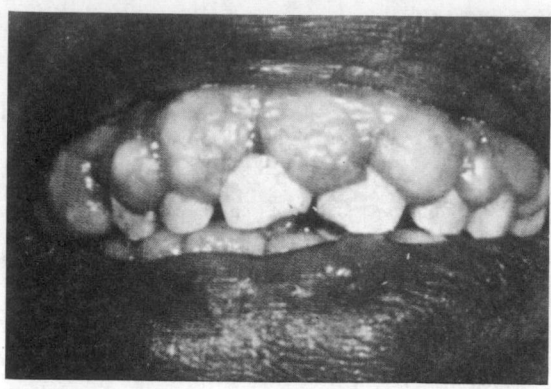

Fig. 16. Gingival fibromatosis.

In diffuse, generalized *fibromatosis of the gingivae* (Fig. 16) the teeth may be completely covered by the exuberant soft tissues, producing the appearance of anodontia. Roentgenologic studies usually show that the developing teeth have left their bony crypts, the deciduous teeth presenting evidence of resorption in normal fashion for the patient's age. The teeth seem, however, unable to pierce the gums. Surgical removal, by stages, of the overlying gum is recommended.

Inflammatory Lesions of the Oral Mucosa

Inflammation of the oral mucous membranes may occur as a primary phenomenon or as a feature of systemic disease. When localized to the gums or tongue, it is designated as gingivitis or glossitis, the term stomatitis being reserved for more generalized lesions.

In some instances the lesions are specific and their cause well identified, while in others they are less characteristic, the etiology being obscure or unknown.

The clinical manifestations may vary from a mild generalized erythema to severe inflammation accompanied by vesiculation, ulceration, or even gangrene. Some degree of secondary infection follows any break in the surface membranes. Subjective symptoms range from mild soreness with increased salivation, to pain sufficiently severe to result in dysphagia and dehydration.

Gingivitis

When inflammation involves the gums without involving the other tissues of the oral cavity, it is referred to as gingivitis. Its cause may be local or systemic. A mild gingivitis is quite common in children.

ERUPTIVE GINGIVITIS. The localized inflammatory reaction which occurs about an erupting tooth, although usually mild and transient, may assume occasionally the characteristics of a hemorrhagic cyst when the tooth has difficulty in piercing the gum.

MARGINAL GINGIVITIS. Inflammation of the gingival margin and interdental papillae, associated with a variable degree of edema, exists commonly where poor oral hygiene is maintained. The tissues bleed easily upon slight trauma, as in brushing the teeth. There are no subjective symptoms in uncomplicated cases. Removal of sources of irritation combined with daily gingival massage usually eliminates this condition readily.

Catarrhal Gingivostomatitis

Any mild, generalized, nonspecific inflammation of the oral mucous membranes is commonly referred to as catarrhal stomatitis. Local factors—chemical, traumatic, or thermal—may produce such a generalized inflammation. In sensitive individuals certain antibiotic-containing mouth-washes or lozenges may produce severe local reactions, frequently far more disturbing than the condition which they were intended to alleviate. They should not be used. Aspirin, when applied locally, may have a destructive effect upon the tissues, causing exfoliation of the mucosa and leaving a denuded surface. Habitual cheek-biting produces raw, ulcerative lesions that persist as long as the habit continues. Recovery of staphylococci, fusiform bacilli, or spirilla does not reflect the specific etiology, since these organisms frequently colonize any inflamed area of the mouth. Most cases of catarrhal stomatitis clear up spontaneously within a few days after removal of the irritant, or after recovery from the underlying infection.

Stomatitis Occurring with Infectious Diseases

In *measles,* a characteristic enanthem (*Koplik's spots*) is pathognomonic of the disease. The lesions, which may be short-lived, appear approximately one day before the rash. The surrounding buccal mucosa is inflamed, edematous, and erythematous (Sec. 14.33, pp. 730 and 732). A severe, generalized stomatitis that may become ulcerative or gangrenous has been reported as a complication of streptococcal infections. (See Sec. 14.17, p. 649.)

Diphtheria may extend onto the mucous membranes of the mouth, lips, and tongue (Sec. 14.7, p. 614). Such wide distribution of the diphtheritic pseudomembrane is seen only in the severest cases, accompanied by extensive involvement of the pharynx and tonsils. The characteristic pseudomembrane in diphtheria is whiter, more opaque, and tougher than the exudate found in other infections. The subjacent tissues show less tendency to ulcerate.

In *varicella,* vesicles may develop on the oral mucous membranes and may even appear 24 hours before the cutaneous eruption. The vesicles, which rupture readily, are surrounded by a red areola. They resemble nonspecific aphthae in appearance (See Sec. 14.25).

The term *herpangina* was coined in 1950 to describe the oral and pharyngeal manifestations of systemic infection associated with specific types of Group A Coxsackie viruses. Shortly after onset of the infection the pharynx is diffusely congested, without focal lesions. Within a day or two, small vesicles appear on the faucial pillars, the tonsils, the edge of the soft palate, or on the posterior pharyngeal wall. In contrast to herpetic stomatitis (see below and Sec. 14.29), the anterior part of the mouth is usually spared. Systemic symptoms of fever, malaise, and anorexia are more prominent than local pain. The vesicles soon rupture, leaving shallow ulcers varying from 2 to 5 mm in diameter, which persist for several days, usually outlasting the systemic symptoms. Regional adenopathy is minimal, and local complications are unknown (see Sec. 14.36, p. 751).

Herpetic Gingivostomatitis
(See also Sec. 14.29)

Primary infection with the virus of herpes simplex is by far the most common cause of severe stomatitis in children. While the incidence of the disease is greatest between the first and sixth years of life, it may occur at any age. The onset is often insidious, with general malaise sometimes accompanied by mild upper respiratory symptoms. Food and even fluids are often refused. Children old enough to communicate verbally will complain of mouth soreness, and pain on swallowing. The severity of systemic manifestations varies. Temperature elevations to between 100° and 105° F are frequently observed. Dehydration of some degree may result from the dysphagia. Regional lymphadenopathy, which is present early in the disease, persists for some time after other symptoms have subsided.

Objective findings consist characteristically of a fiery red gingiva with swollen interdental papillae. Multiple small ulcers which appear on the tongue, soft palate, and other parts of the buccal mucosa have a yellowish white center with a hyperemic border. These aphthae represent ruptured vesicles which may be noted fleetingly prior to their breakdown. Tags of gingival tissue adjacent to partially erupted teeth have a tendency to become ulcerated at their borders. The lips may develop painful fissures extending outward towards the vermilion border. Occasionally, impetiginous vesicles appear upon the cutaneous portions of the lips. Pain, malaise, and fever subside after a few days. Healing of the gingivitis and aphthae is usually complete by the tenth to fourteenth day, although lymphadenopathy may persist for two to three weeks.

Herpetic gingivostomatitis is self-limited, and its course is not greatly altered by local treatment. The use of irritating or caustic applications, such as silver nitrate, chromic acid, or sodium perborate, is contraindicated. The same is true for penicillin lozenges, which may produce glossitis. Systemic penicillin and other antibiotics have no beneficial effect and should not be given.

Herpetic gingivostomatitis should not be confused with herpangina which, despite its name, is due to Group A Coxsackie virus (see above and Sec. 14.36). The latter condition is characterized by smaller lesions confined to the faucial area, leaving the gingiva and buccal mucosa intact.

Aphthous Stomatitis

Aphthae are small, circular or oval, painful ulcers involving the oral mucosa. The lesions are usually preceded by a small transient vesicle which soon loses its friable surface, leaving a shallow ulcer, 2 to 5 mm in diameter, surrounded by a red areola. Single ulcers of this type, occurring in the buccal sulcus, are commonly referred to as "canker sores." They may appear at any age, have a sudden onset, remain painful for 5 to 10 days, and heal without scarring. There is a slight induration, but usually no adenopathy. Food intake may be somewhat troublesome, but constitutional symptoms are absent. The origin of these single lesions is still debatable; in some instances herpes virus has been recovered, but its etiologic role has not been invariably borne out by a subsequent rise in serum antibody level. Some cases have a traumatic origin. Mechanical irritation, as produced by the vigorous use of a stiff toothbrush, has often been implicated. Local applications of aqueous solution of gentian violet may prove helpful. Good oral hygiene must be maintained.

Recurrent aphthosis. Occasionally the aphthae are multiple; are distributed over the tongue, anterior pillars, buccal mucosae, and palate; and tend to recur. New lesions develop while others are regressing. Clinically, these cases closely resemble herpetic gingivostomatitis, but the temperature is seldom elevated and there is little or no regional adenopathy. Pain may be severe enough to interfere with eating and talking. Complete healing occurs within two to three weeks, only to be followed by recurrence after a variable period of remission. This type of aphthosis was also once thought to be due to herpes simplex virus, but more recent work casts doubt on this etiologic hypothesis. While a specific allergen can seldom be incriminated, some cases reportedly have improved after antihistamine therapy.

Gingivostomatitis in Metabolic Disturbances

Renal insufficiency with nitrogen retention is occasionally associated with stomatitis and gingivitis. Ulcerations may appear upon the gums, cheeks, and lips. The saliva is scant, thick, and viscid in proportion to the degree of general dehydration.

Similar lesions sometimes accompany diabetic acidosis. In poorly regulated diabetes, inflammation of the gingivae is common. The gums lose their normal texture, becoming deeply congested and edematous. Small, localized gingival abscesses are characteristic of diabetic gingivitis. The infection, in turn, makes control of the diabetes more difficult.

Gingivostomatitis in Deficiency Diseases

In *pellagra* there may be diffuse stomatitis with areas of ulceration. A characteristic form of stomatitis at the angles of the mouth (*perlèche*) is associated with *riboflavin deficiency* (Sec. 3.4, p. 180). The swollen, hemorrhagic gums of *scurvy* are described under that disease (p. 189).

Gingivostomatitis and Gingival Hemorrhage in Blood Dyscrasias

Bleeding into the gums occurs in hemorrhagic diathesis, such as thrombocytopenia, leukemia, and ascorbic acid deficiency. The gingival hemorrhagic lesions of scurvy are described in Section 3.4 (p. 189).

In the various forms of *leukemia* (Sec. 17.8) the oral lesions are quite similar. The gums become hypertrophied, ulcerated, and are pale, reflecting the progressive anemia. In the acute forms secondary infection is difficult to control and a severe gangrenous stomatitis may result. Good oral hygiene should be maintained. Parenteral injections of penicillin or other antibiotics may be required.

Agranulocytosis of any cause (Sec. 17.6) is often accompanied by ulcerations of the oral mucous membrane. The lesions, first appearing in the form of necrosis of the interdental gingival papillae, may soon involve the entire oral mucosa and pharynx, with disposition of a grayish membrane. Vincent's organisms are almost invariably present.

Dermatogingivostomatitis

Dermatogingivostomatitis is a severe, diffuse, erosive, and painful stomatitis with formation of vesicles or bullae, associated wtih typical erythematous, bullous, and virus-type lesions; involvement of conjunctival and anogenital membranes; and marked systemic symptoms. It is seen in children with *erythema multiforme exudativum* or ectodermosis erosiva pluriorificialis (Stevens-Johnson syndrome, Sec. 26.3). This syndrome may develop as a sensitivity reaction to drugs.

Oral Thrush

Thrush is a mycotic stomatitis characterized by the appearance of small white flakes or patches on the oral mucous membrane, usually on the tongue or the cheeks. It is common primarily in newborn infants, but is seen sometimes in young infants and children with malnutrition or diabetes.

ETIOLOGY. The organism which produces thrush is *Candida albicans*. The structure of the fungus is readily visualized on a slide by adding one drop of a 10 percent potassium hydroxide solution to a small quantity of buccal exudate. The presence of *C. albicans* spores is very common in dust, and in the atmosphere. Except in the newborn period, thrush is implanted with great difficulty on a healthy mucous membrane; its growth is favored by slight abrasions, lack of cleanliness, malnutrition, neoplasia, diabetes, antibiotic treatment, and hypoparathyroidism. Maternal vulvovaginal candidiasis appears to be the primary source of neonatal thrush. In utero infection of the fetus has also been reported. The infection may also be acquired from another patient, or from contaminated hands, bedding, or feeding equipment, but probably not from the air. It is relatively frequent in the first two or three months of life and also in older infants suffering from harelip, cleft palate, or any other deformity of the mouth.

PATHOLOGY. The spores lodge between the epithelial cells and gradually separate the different layers. This implantation occurs before the formation of the white pellicle. Later the disease spreads on the surface of the mucous membrane and also penetrates the deeper structures. Invasion of the blood vessels is rare, but may cause thrombosis locally or dissemination to remote parts of the body. Growth of *Candida albicans* in the buccal cavity begins usually at several discrete points on the mucous membrane, with gradual spreading until some degree of coalescence takes place; a continuous membrane may thus be formed. The acid reaction of the mouth found in thrush is presumably a result of fermentation of sugar by the organisms.

SYMPTOMS. The essential feature of thrush is the development on the oral mucosa of small white flakes which resemble deposits of coagulated milk but which differ from milk curds in that they cannot be wiped off. If forcibly removed, they usually leave bleeding points. They usually appear first on the tongue or the inner surface of the cheeks. There may be only a few scattered patches, or the mouth and pharynx may be covered. Local pain and tenderness are conspicuously absent; the mouth is sometimes dry, and occasionally there is some difficulty in swallowing.

Constitutional symptoms, if present, depend on some associated condition rather than on thrush.

DIAGNOSIS. The diagnosis is rarely difficult and in most cases is established by inspection. Manipulation with the tongue depressor readily permits differentiation between white deposits of thrush and milk curds. Coalescent thrush on the pharynx and fauces has been confused with diphtheria, although this mistake can hardly be made if all the facts are taken into consideration—the age of the patient, the involvement of the cheeks and tongue, the absence of glandular enlargement or of constitutional symptoms. In case of doubt, microscopic examination of the deposit will establish the etiology. In cultures on Loffler's medium, the large, rounded or oval spores of the fungus are easily recognized.

PROGNOSIS. The cases involving only the mouth clear up readily, leaving no scar. Thrush is rarely a dangerous disease in itself. However, in the malnourished, or in the infant with harelip or cleft palate, it may prove tenacious and troublesome—at times even serious.

TREATMENT. Oral candidiasis may be prevented to a certain degree by due attention to cleanliness of rubber nipples, bottles, and other objects which come into direct or indirect contact with the infant's mouth. Neonatal thrush is best prevented through mycologic screening and adequate therapy of all pregnant women who yield *Candida albicans* from the vagina. In infants with deformities of the mouth, and in institutional settings, the infection frequently develops despite all precautions. Local treatment is not essential, but recovery can probably be accelerated by the use of some mild antiseptic. A 1 percent aqueous solution of gentian violet on a swab may be applied several times a day. With such treatment the disease often improves; in the absence of treatment it may last several weeks. In obstinate cases, 1 or 2 ml of Nystatin U.S.P may be applied locally four times a day, in the form of a freshly prepared solution containing from 100,000 to 200,00 units per milliliter. This drug can also be administered orally at the same dosage three to four times a day with the formula.

Noma
(Gangrenous Stomatitis, Cancrum Oris)

Noma is a slow-spreading gangrene involving the mucous membranes or mucocutaneous orifices. The mouth is the site most frequently involved, but the nose, external auditory canal, vulva, prepuce, or anus may also be affected.

This disease, once invariably fatal, is now almost unknown in the United States, except in patients who live in poor conditions of hygiene and nutrition. Usually, it follows an infectious illness, most frequently measles, and often develops on the site of previous local inflammation. In the mouth it may be preceded by stomatitis, and in the auditory canal by purulent otitis media.

It is generally regarded as a malignant infection by *Borrelia* (Vincent's fusospirillar organisms) in a patient whose resistance to infection is greatly reduced by nutritional deprivation and intercurrent infection. A great variety of organisms is found in the superficial sloughs, but in areas of early necrosis fusiform bacilli and spirillar forms predominate.

The process is one of slowly spreading gangrene. Unless arrested by therapy the disease advances steadily until death occurs, often from septic complications.

The odor of the breath, or a dusky spot on the cheek or lip, may be the first symptom to attract attention. On examination of the mouth, a dark, greenish black, necrotic mass surrounded by edema is the usual finding. The cheek or lips may be two or three times their normal thickness. Externally the parts are tense and brawny from the swelling, the infiltration extending always beyond the gangrenous part. As the process extends, the teeth loosen and are extruded. Necrosis of the alveolar process of the jaw may occur, and perforation and extensive sloughing of one or both cheeks or of the lower lip may take place. The odor is very offensive; pain is rarely severe or may be absent; extensive hemorrhages are rare.

The prognosis, once extremely grave, has been markedly altered since the advent of penicillin, which usually arrests the process promptly. Without therapy the gangrenous process spreads slowly but inexorably, and the disease progresses steadily toward death.

Treatment must be prompt and vigorous. The patient should be isolated and should receive penicillin therapy in large doses, a diet rich in protein, and vitamin supplementation. Wide surgical excision, once believed to be the treatment of choice, is no longer advised. Plastic surgery may be needed after the process has been arrested.

REFERENCES

Cherry, J. D., and John, C. L. Herpangina: etiologic spectrum. Pediatrics, 36:632, 1965.
——— Hand, foot, and mouth syndrome: Report of six cases due to Coxsackie Virus, Group A, Type 16. Pediatrics, 31:637, 1966.
Dobias, B. Moniliasis in pediatrics. Amer. J. Dis. Child., 94:234, 1957.
Dodd, K., and Ruchman, I. Herpes simplex virus not the etiologic agent of recurrent stomatitis. Pediatrics, 5:883, 1950.
Hale, B. D., Rendtorff, R. C., Walker, L. C., and Roberts, A. N. Epidemic herpetic stomatitis in an orphanage nursery. J.A.M.A., 183:1068, 1963.
Kozinn, P. J., Taschadjian, C. L., and Wiener, H. Incidence and pathogenesis of neonatal candidiasis. Pediatrics, 21:42, 1958.
Lopez, E., and Aterman, K. Intrauterine infection by *Candida*. Amer. J. Dis. Child., 115:663, 1968.
Parrot, R. H., et al. Clinical and laboratory differentiation between herpangina and infectious (herpetic) gingivostomatitis. Pediatrics, 14:122, 1954.

Scott, T. F. M., Steigman, A. J., and Convey, J. H. Acute infectious gingivostomatitis: etiology, epidemiology and clinical picture of a common disorder caused by the virus of herpes simplex. J.A.M.A., 117:999, 1941.

chapter 29

TEETH

SOLOMON N. ROSENSTEIN, Associate Editor

29.1
GROWTH AND DEVELOPMENT
OF THE TEETH

Early Development

The earliest sign of tooth development, occurring during the sixth week of embryonic life, consists of unusually rapid proliferation of certain cells in the basal layer of the oral epithelium. This change takes place along the free margins of those embryonic structures that are to become the upper and lower jaw arches. The thickened line in each arch is called the dental lamina and represents the anlage of that portion of the teeth derived from the ectoderm.

As this process is taking place, additional cell proliferation produces rounded swellings at 10 different points in each arch; these are called tooth buds or germs and are the primordia of the enamel organs of the 20 primary teeth at locations that correspond to their future positions in the primary dentition. The enamel organ (Fig. 1) developing from the bud is of ectodermal origin, determines the shape of the crown of the tooth, and gives rise to its enamel. With continued growth, further structural changes take place inwardly from each arch margin. Subsequent cell proliferations occur unequally, with differentiation of outer and inner layers of cells into outer enamel epithelium and inner enamel epithelium respectively. The inner enamel cells become ameloblasts, or enamel-forming cells.

As the tooth bud undergoes cell differentiation, invagination, and further growth through the various stages of enamel organ development, the mesenchymal cells at its inner aspect become the dental papilla, the formative organ of the dentine pulp. Both the enamel organ and the dental papilla undergo further cell differentiation and proliferation with budding of capillaries; the peripheral cells of the papilla, adjacent to the inner enamel epithelium, become the odontoblasts which later form the dentine of the tooth; the structures which become the pulp arise from the inner cells.

The development of the enamel organ and the dental papilla is accompanied by that of the surrounding mesenchyme which forms the dental sac, in which cells later give rise to cementoblasts and to the fibers of the peridontal membrane (Fig. 2 and Table 1).

Later Development

PRIMARY TEETH. The inner aspect of the enamel organ becomes separated early from the adjacent dental papilla by a basement membrane, the future dentinoenamel junction. Enamel formation at any point is immediately preceded by inception of dentine formation; both develop in the enamel organ toward its periphery in a direction away from the dentinoenamel junction. Enamel formation is considered to occur in two stages: (1) formation of organic enamel matrix in which some calcium salts are present; (2) maturation, or calcification demonstrated radiographically by radiopacity. Once the inner enamel epithelial cells or ameloblasts reach the peripheral layer of outer enamel epithelial cells, the thickness of enamel is completed, constituting a united enamel epithelium, and no more enamel can be formed at that area. When this occurs over the entire contour of the enamel organ the tooth crown has reached is final stage of development, and no further enamel formation can ever be produced in that tooth.

In dentine formation odontoblasts migrate toward the middle area of the tooth; this process continues beyond the open end of the crown contributing to root formation and the lengthening of the tooth. As the odontoblasts usually remain at the inner border of the dentine, lining the pulp, dentinogenesis continues throughout the life of the tooth, with narrowing of the pulp area in the middle of the crown and root.

These structures become the 20 primary teeth, 10 in each arch, 5 in each quadrant: the central incisor next to the midline, then the lateral incisor, cuspid, first molar and second molar. This sequence represents the positions of the primary teeth in the completed dentition, but their calcification and subsequent eruption occur in different order.

PERMANENT TEETH. The dental lamina, which initiates development of the primary teeth, is similarly involved in the development of the permanent teeth. This additional function starts about the fourth to fifth month in utero and occurs in two distinct steps for two groups of permanent teeth. The permanent teeth which are the successors of the primary teeth, namely, the permanent central and lateral incisors, cuspids, and first and second bicuspids, arise from

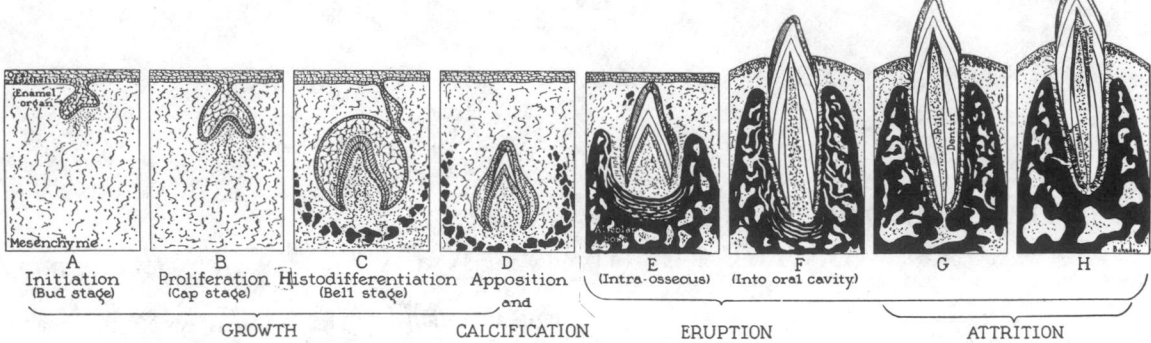

A
Initiation
(Bud stage)

B
Proliferation
(Cap stage)

C
Histodifferentiation
(Bell stage)

D
Apposition
and

GROWTH   CALCIFICATION

E
(Intra-osseous)

F
(Into oral cavity)

ERUPTION

G

H

ATTRITION

Fig. 1.   Diagrammatic representation of life cycle of the tooth. (From Schour and Massler. *J. Amer. Dent. Ass.,* 27:1785, 1940. Courtesy of the American Dental Association.)

extensions of the former laminae to the primary teeth. These extensions grow to the lingual aspect of each enamel organ of the primary teeth and become the anlage of each successor permanent tooth. This takes place at about the fifth month in utero for the permanent central incisors and continues at different times for the other permanent successor teeth until about 10 months postnatally for the second bicuspid.

The permanent molars, which later are placed distally to the primary dentition, arise from the distal extension of the posterior part of the dental lamina in each quadrant, during the development of the second primary molars. The extension that gives rise to the anlage of the first permanent molar occurs at about 4 months in utero, at about 9 to 10 months postnatally for the second, and during the fourth to fifth year for the third permanent molar.

As each permanent tooth bud is initiated, the cells of its dental lamina begin to disintegrate and disappear, each dental bud becoming thereafter an autonomously developing organ, going through the stages of development and growth described above, to its eruption and continuing growth in root length.

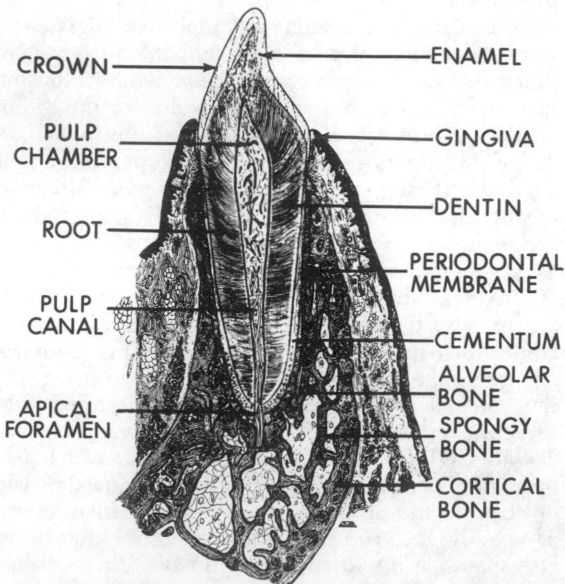

Calcification

Calcification begins in all the primary teeth before birth. It starts usually first in the central incisor crown during the fourth month, then in the other primary teeth in the following order: first molar, lateral incisor, cuspid, second molar. Calcification in the primary teeth is both prenatal and postnatal. The crowns of all the primary teeth complete their calcification after birth, during the first year of life, the central incisors within the first few months postnatally, and the second molars at about 10 to 12 months.

Calcification of the permanent teeth is a postnatal process, except for the first permanent molars where it usually begins in the tips of cusps before birth, during the eighth and ninth gestational months.

All the anterior permanent teeth except for the upper lateral incisors usually begin to calcify within the first 6 months of postnatal life; the upper central incisors, the lower central and lateral incisors, at about 3 to 4 months; the upper and lower cuspids at about 4 to 5 months. The upper lateral incisors begin to calcify later, at about the end of the first year and beginning of the second year. However, the crowns of all the incisor teeth usually complete calcification between 4 and 5 years, the cuspids at about 6 to 7 years. Disturbances in calcification in

CROWN —— ENAMEL

PULP
CHAMBER —— GINGIVA

ROOT —— DENTIN

—— PERIODONTAL
MEMBRANE

PULP
CANAL

—— CEMENTUM

APICAL
FORAMEN

ALVEOLAR
BONE

SPONGY
BONE

CORTICAL
BONE

Fig. 2.   Diagrammatic representation of the dental tissues. (From Schour. *Noyes' Oral Histology and Embryology,* 7th ed., 1953. Courtesy of Lea & Febiger.)

TABLE 1. *Classification of the Dental Tissues**

Tissue	Origin	Degree of Calcification	Function	Anatomic Classification	Regenerative Capacity	Disease	Special Fields of Dentistry
Enamel	Ectodermal	97%	Resistant to wear	Propriodontal	Nil	Enamel caries	Restorative dentistry
Dentin	Mesodermal	70%	Elastic strength	Propriodontal	Restricted	Dentin caries	Restorative dentistry
Pulp	Mesodermal	Uncalcified	Formation and vitality of dentin	Endodontal	Limited	Pulpitis	Endodontics
Cementum	Mesodermal	66%	Support	Periodontal	Good	Periodontitis Periodontosis	Periodontics
Periodontal Membrane	Mesodermal	Uncalcified	Support	Periodontal	Good	Periodontitis Periodontosis	Periodontics
Alveolar	Mesodermal	66%	Support	Periodontal	Good	Periodontitis Periodontosis	Periodontics
Gingiva	Ectodermal and mesodermal	Uncalcified	Investment and protection	Periodontal	Good	Gingivitis Gingivosis	Periodontics

*Adapted from: Schour, *Noyes' Oral Histology and Embryology*, 7th ed. Courtesy of Lea & Febiger.

these teeth cannot be attributed to pathologic disorders which occur later.

The bicuspids, or premolars, may begin to calcify between 1½ and 2½ years, although in many instances the second bicuspids may not show evidence of calcification until appreciably later. As a rule, the upper bicuspids are ahead of the lowers, and the first is ahead of the second. Their crowns are usually completed by 6 to 7 years.

The first permanent molars, which usually have begun their calcification before birth, will have crown calcification completed by about 3 years of age.

The second permanent molars usually begin calcification during the latter part of the third year and crown calcification is completed by about 7 years of age or shortly thereafter. By this time all the permanent teeth, except the third molars if present, will have completed crown calcification.

The third molars may begin calcification after the seventh year.

Eruption

The eruption of the first tooth is an important milestone for the baby and his parents; it marks the beginning of the period of the *primary dentition,* which continues until the first permanent tooth makes its appearance. The period of the *mixed dentition* follows and extends to the time of exfoliation of

the last of the primary teeth. The period of the *permanent dentition* follows.

MEAN AGES OF ERUPTION OF PRIMARY TEETH. The onset of primary dentition heralds an important change in oral and eating habits. After the earlier period of sucking and swallowing liquid and soft foods exclusively from a nipple or a spoon, the infant now learns to incise foods with the front teeth and, later, to grind them as the posterior teeth erupt. An increasing number of teeth prepares the child for eating the normal, broad variety of foods.

The successive eruption of the teeth, and the age of the child at each eruption, follows a specific pattern. The child's age at the first eruption is also an important individual developmental milestone.

A handy guide for mean ages of eruption of the primary teeth is McBride's "Rule of 4," starting with the first eruption of 6 to 7 months. Between the eruption of different types of primary teeth there is an approximate four-month interval during which the teeth of the same type erupt in the other quadrants of the mouth. The first tooth to appear is usually a lower primary central incisor, followed in short succession first by its adjacent, homologous incisor, then by an opposing upper central incisor, and finally by the homologous upper incisor. At about this time or shortly thereafter, the first of the lateral incisors will erupt and, at short intervals, will be followed by the other lateral incisors. Rather infrequently the first tooth to erupt

TABLE 2.   *Chronology of the Human Dentition**

Tooth		Calcification Begins	Crown Completed	Eruption	Root Completed	Root Resorption Begins
Primary	I	14 wk†	4 mo	6-8 mo	1½-2 yr	5-6 yr
	II	16 wk†	5 mo	8-10 mo	1½-2 yr	5-6 yr
	III	17 wk†	9 mo	16-20 mo	2½-3 yr	6-7 yr
	IV	15½ wk†	6 mo	12-16 mo	2-2½ yr	4-5 yr
	V	18-19 wk†	10-12 mo	20-30 mo	3 yr	4-5 yr
Upper Permanent	1	3-4 mo	4-5 yr	7-8 yr	10 yr	
	2	1 yr	4-5 yr	8-9 yr	11 yr	
	3	4-5 mo	6-7 yr	11-12 yr	13-15 yr	
	4	1½-1¾ yr	5-6 yr	10-11 yr	12-13 yr	
	5	2-2½ yr	6-7 yr	10-12 yr	12-14 yr	
	6	8 mo†	2½-3 yr	6-7 yr	9-10 yr	
	7	2½-3 yr	7-8 yr	12-14 yr	14-16 yr	
	8	7-9 yr	12-16 yr	17-30 yr	18-25 yr	
Lower Permanent	1	3-4 mo	4-5 yr	6-7 yr	9 yr	
	2	3-4 mo	4-5 yr	7-8 yr	10 yr	
	3	4-5 mo	6-7 yr	10-11 yr	12-14 yr	
	4	1¾-2 yr	5-6 yr	10-12 yr	12-13 yr	
	5	2¼-2½ yr	6-7 yr	11-12 yr	13-14 yr	
	6	8 mo†	2½-3 yr	6-7 yr	9-10 yr	
	7	2½-3 yr	7-8 yr	12-13 yr	14-15 yr	
	8	8-10 yr	12-16 yr	17-30 yr	18-25 yr	

*Adapted from Logan and Kronfeld; Kraus and Jordan.
†In utero (average).

may be the upper central incisor; in these children the upper lateral incisor may precede the eruption of the lowers. This slight variation occurs very seldom and does not affect the rest of the pattern of dental development.

In its normal position, the first molar, the third type of primary tooth to erupt, will appear posteriorly to a large space distal to the lateral incisor because the cuspid has not yet erupted. Parents concerned at the sight of this large tooth erupting distally to a large space should be reassured that this is normal.

The primary cuspids then erupt and are followed by the primary and second molars, often called the two-year molars.

MEAN AGES OF ERUPTION OF PERMANENT TEETH. Exfoliation of the primary teeth and eruption of permanent teeth will usually occur at average ages in children who had their primary dentitions at the usual time (Table 2). Exfoliation results from progressive resorption of the roots of the primary teeth through osteoclastic action.

Toward the end of the sixth year the lower primary central incisors begin to loosen. At 6 to 6½ years one of the permanent successor incisors erupts, followed shortly by the adjacent central incisor. At about the same time or shortly thereafter one or more permanent first molars erupt distally to the primary molars. Parents are often unaware of this posterior extension of the dentition, since the first permanent molar usually erupts uneventfully, unless

a gingival flap overlying part of the new molar becomes irritated or mildly inflamed. These first permanent molars are extremely important and must be maintained in good position and health. They provide for the future the major chewing surfaces and maintain the arch relationship when the primary molars exfoliate.

During the next half year the upper central incisor succession occurs, followed shortly by the loosening of the primary lower lateral incisors and eruption of their permanent successors at about 7 to 7½ years. Upper lateral incisor succession occurs at 8 to 8½ years.

There may appear to be a period of lessened activity at this time, during which the upper lateral incisors are continuing their eruption into normal positions in the dental arches. However, during this period intermittent resorption of the longer roots of the cuspids and the multiple roots of the primary molars is taking place. The remaining permanent successor teeth will usually erupt in order: first bicuspids erupt at about 9½ years of age, and second bicuspids at about 10½ years. In most children cuspid succession occurs after eruption of the first and second bicuspids, which erupt by 10½ years. Occasionally, cuspid succession may occur in the lower jaw prior to eruption of the second bicuspids. All these changes will happen shortly before the permanent second molars begin to erupt just distal to the permanent first molars, the lower before the upper, at about 12 years.

The third molars, if present, begin to erupt after the seventeenth year. Their emergence is usually slow, with longer intervals during which the erupting tooth is partly covered by gum tissue while bone growth occurs to provide space for it. At such times the soft tissues may become inflamed; usually gentle cleansing is sufficient to allay the troublesome condition. However, if bone growth is not sufficient to permit the tooth to reach its normal, completely erupted state, more extensive dental measures may be indicated.

NORMAL RANGE OF VARIATION IN AGES OF ERUPTION. Knowledge of the mean ages at which dentitional changes take place is useful for guidance. However, developmental phenomena such as calcification and eruption vary considerably according to individual patterns. For example, an infant who erupts his first tooth as early as 4 to 4½ months will probably erupt his first permanent molar at about 4½ years. This pattern will continue, with subsequent dental eruptions occurring at earlier ages than the average. On the other hand, the child who erupts his first tooth as late as 9 months of age will have subsequent eruptions at older ages, with the 6-year molar erupting, for example, at 7½ to 8 years. Occasionally children will not erupt the first tooth until about 1 year of age. Although such delay is observed infrequently it is still within the normal range, particularly when other pediatric developmental milestones are normal.

The multiple processes of dental development and growth are active over a long period of life, from the sixth week in utero to almost the end of childhood. In most individuals teeth grow and develop normally. Normal healthy dentition is essential for effective chewing and plays a major role in communication by speech. The social significance of attractive teeth is also a consideration of major importance.

Bone Growth

The process of tooth formation is accompanied by concomitant growth in both the maxilla and the mandible. Both jawbones develop by intramembranous ossification.

BODY OF THE MAXILLA. The maxilla is formed from three bones, the maxilla proper, the premaxilla, and the prevomer. Ossification in the maxilla is initiated early in the seventh week of embryonic development. As this bone develops it will hold all the teeth of the upper jaw except the incisors. The premaxilla forms the anterior part of the mature maxilla and holds the structures that will become the incisors. Ossification of the premaxilla begins somewhat later than in the maxilla proper and fusion of these two bones to form the primary palate occurs slightly thereafter, around the end of the eighth week. The primordia for the maxillary incisors appear in the pre-maxilla at about the middle of the eighth week. Fusion of the palatal processes of the maxillae to form the secondary palate usually starts during the ninth week.

The prevomer starts ossification at about the ninth week and is closely related to the premaxilla. It bears no teeth but participates with the premaxilla in formation of the primary palate.

BODY OF THE MANDIBLE. The mandibular arch appears during the sixth week of development as bilateral wings lateral to Meckel's cartilage. Their free ends continue to grow anteriorly toward each other and fuse by the seventh week at the future midline of the face. Fusion is usually completed during the eighth week. During the seventh week the dental lamina has formed and will give rise to the structure that will become the lower primary teeth. Ossification of the bilateral plates of the developing mandibular arch also begins in the seventh week and continues in sequence, adding to mandibular length and height, while enclosing nerves and blood vessels and the developing tooth structures.

ALVEOLAR PROCESSES. As tooth growth continues, bony septa appear between adjacent teeth. As the teeth proceed toward their eruption locations, this bone at the oral cavity portion in the maxilla and mandible extends from the body, thus enlarging the alveoli which house and support the growing roots of the teeth. This growth of alveolar processes continues with further eruption and root growth, and contributes to the increase in height, or vertical dimension, of each jawbone.

This type of bone growth must occur for development of the primary teeth, again for the successor permanent teeth, and also posteriorly to contain the roots of the permanent molars during their eruption distal to the primary dentition.

OTHER BONE CHANGES. The posterior portions of the body of the maxilla and the mandible are also the site of bone growth at ossification centers. This growth, influenced primarily by functional activity, also provides the increase in antero-posterior dimension, or length, of each arch permitting growth and eruption of the permanent molars.

As a result of these bone changes, the lower part of the face occupies a larger portion of the total head-face dimension. With further maturation facial position moves in a downward and forward direction.

Posteruptive Conditions

OCCLUSION. Upon completion of the normal eruption of both the primary and permanent dentition, normal occlusion should exist between upper and lower teeth, which consists essentially of (1) even arch form in upper and lower jaws; (2) upper anterior teeth slightly overlapping the lower anterior teeth labially; (3) the posterior upper teeth slightly overlapping the lower posterior teeth buccally; (4) cusps interdigitating with the teeth in occlusion; and

(5) the existence of a "normal" mesiodistal relation.

Marked aberrations from this pattern indicate malocclusions (see p. 1868).

MATURATIONAL CHANGES. Posteruptively, the teeth continue to undergo changes. Some of these continue events of earlier growth stages, others are manifestations of maturation and aging. Attrition, or wear of the biting surfaces secondary to function, promotes continuing dentinogenesis and other changes in the dentine and pulp. Dentinogenesis gradually narrows the coronal and root pulpal areas. Eruption does not subside even after the root of the tooth has attained its full length. To some extent this growth compensates for some of the dimensional loss in attrition, and occurs as a result of continuing deposition of cementum at the root and persisting growth of the adjacent bone.

REFERENCES

Diamond, M., and Weinmann, J. P. Enamel of Human Teeth. New York, Columbia University Press, 1940.

Kraus, B. S., and Jordan, R. E. The Human Dentition Before Birth. Philadelphia, Lea & Febiger, 1965.

Logan, W., and Kronfeld, R. Development of the human jaws and surrounding structures from birth to the age of fifteen years. J. Amer. Dent. Ass., 20:379, 1933.

McBride, W. C. Juvenile Dentistry, 5th ed. Philadelphia, Lea & Febiger, 1952.

Provenza, D. V. Oral Histology. Philadelphia, J. B. Lippincott, 1964.

Rosenstein, S. N. Dentistry for children. New York J. Dent., 22:327, 1952.

Schour, I. N. Oral Histology and Embryology, 8th ed. Philadelphia, Lea & Febiger, 1960.

Sicher, H., ed. Orban's Oral Histology and Embryology, 5th ed. St. Louis, C. V. Mosby Co., 1962.

29.2
DEVELOPMENTAL DISORDERS OF TEETH

Dental development and growth occur over a long span of years, from the sixth week of intrauterine life to the early part of the third decade of life. During this entire period, the various phenomena of tooth formation, such as cell differentiation, enamel matrix formation, calcification, eruption, and growth, are all susceptible to the influences that might affect the metabolic processes involved.

Unlike bone, which permits addition and removal of calcium salts, there is no ready metabolic inflow and outgo of calcium in any tooth structure which is already formed. During the period of tooth growth, any systemic disturbances or trauma that affects tooth germ formation, enamel matrix formation, or calcification will leave its mark on the dental structure developing at the time. Both the enamel and dentine may be affected. The extent of the en-

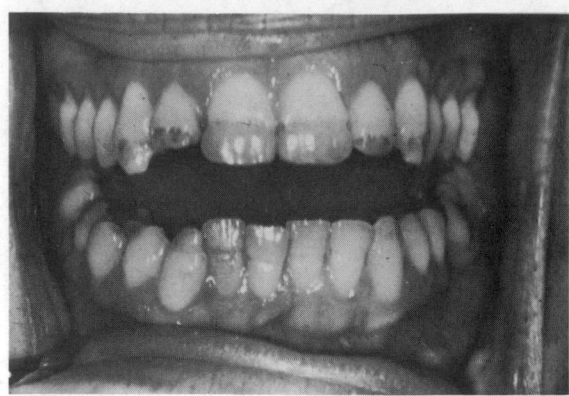

Fig. 3. Male, 31 years old. Patient had severe nephritis at 1½ years of age. Enamel hypoplasia, consisting of aplasia, pitting, and grooving present at all upper and lower incisors, cuspids, and first molars. (Courtesy of Dr. E. V. Zegarelli.)

suing anomaly will be mild, moderate, or severe, depending upon the severity and duration of the disturbance (Fig. 3). The resulting defect will usually manifest itself as some form of hypoplasia or other malstructure of the dental part that was in the formative stage at the time of the insult. When the disturbing influence is transitory the resulting mark is fixed, and normal growth resumes for the remainder of the tooth or teeth involved.

However, traumatic incidents and metabolic or other systemic disorders represent but one aspect of the total complex of developmental disorders of teeth and other oral structures. There is mounting evidence of genetic influence on tooth size and form. A number of specific abnormalities involving entire dentitions can be traced back through generations, as in odontogenesis imperfecta. Other severe developmental disorders are of such nature that a genetic influence may be suspected, but such relationship has not yet been demonstrated. Dental anomalies occur also in syndromes involving multiple developmental abnormalities; often such combinations of anomalies are associated with mental retardation and with chromosomal aberrations. (See Sec. 15.3.)

Gross disorders of development which include facial manifestation will be accompanied by dental abnormalities if such disorders occur very early and involve disturbance of ectodermal facial structures which hold developing teeth or their primordia.

The effects of systemic disturbance on formation of dental structure and the genetic influence on dental anomalies are demonstrated in the following conditions.

Prematurity; Cerebral Palsy

A high incidence of enamel hypoplasia is observed among children who were premature infants (Fig. 4). In one series this abnormality was present in 45

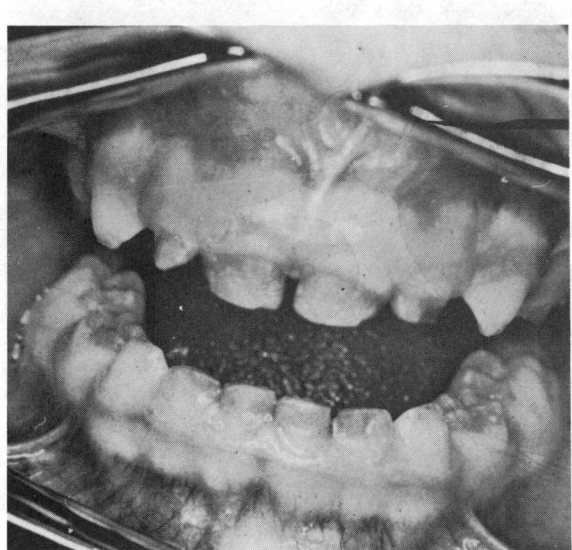

Fig. 4. Female, 3 years old, premature birth. Hypoplasia of the enamel of the primary teeth involving large areas on the incisors and first molars, tips of the cuspids, and cusps and surface enamel at the mesio-occlusal portion of the second molars.

percent of the children studied and was found to correlate significantly with neurologic, psychologic, and speech abnormalities. This finding suggests that the defects may be the result of the same insult and that the time of its occurrence could be dated from the site of the hypoplastic lesion in the prenatally formed enamel of the primary teeth, particularly the incisors.

There is a high incidence of enamel hypoplasia in patients with cerebral palsy, especially among premature infants. In one study of children with cerebral palsy 22 had been born prematurely. Of these, 41 percent had enamel dysplasia. Enamel hypoplasia was found to be more pronounced in the athetoid and severe spastic groups of children with cerebral palsy. Efforts to date the time of occurrence of enamel dysplasia in these patients indicate that the largest number of the dental abnormalities develop during the perinatal period, with a few occurrences in both the prenatal and early postnatal periods. Another significant relationship was found to exist between enamel dysplasia and blood incompatibilities.

Tooth Discoloration by Tetracycline

Administration of antibiotics of the tetracycline family during periods of tooth formation and growth may give rise to discoloration of children's teeth. The discoloration consists of darkening of the teeth. It is the result of deposition of the medication in the dentine along the incremental lines of growth (lines of Owen). Either the primary or permanent dentition or both may be affected, depending upon the

length and intensity of exposure to the drug, and the age at which the medication was given to the child. Discoloration has also been observed in primary teeth of young children who received no tetracycline therapy, but whose mothers were treated with this agent during the latter months of pregnancy.

Inherited Disorders

DENTINOGENESIS IMPERFECTA. Dentinogenesis imperfecta (odontogenesis imperfecta, hereditary opalescent dentine) is probably the most frequent of the inheritable disorders involving abnormal formations of dental structure. It is inherited as a non–sex-linked dominant characteristic. The dentine of both primary and permanent teeth is affected as a result of the failure of the odontoblasts to differentiate completely during the developmental stage of histodifferentiation. As a result dentine ground substance is formed, but the dentinal tubules may be irregularly arranged or absent. This type of dentine continues forming, with the further characteristic obliteration of pulp chambers and canals. The enamel is well formed, but root formation is usually abnormal.

Clinically, the crowns of the teeth have normal form and size. They are markedly translucent with abnormally dark color, usually grayish or bluish brown. Severe attrition occurs rapidly, with teeth frequently worn down to the gingival margins. Heroic restorative measures may be undertaken in efforts to prevent excessive attrition and early loss of teeth. In most instances full dentures are needed during the third or fourth decade.

Dentinogenesis imperfecta is found frequently as an associated condition of osteogenesis imperfecta. The dental abnormality is typical, similar to the dentinogenesis imperfecta when present alone.

AMELOGENESIS IMPERFECTA. Amelogenesis imperfecta is an inheritable anomalous condition involving the enamel. It is also a dominant characteristic, and probably non–sex-linked.

There are two types of amelogenesis imperfecta: one affects the matrix development stage and the other the maturation stage of enamel formation. Only the crowns of the teeth in both the primary and permanent dentitions are involved.

In teeth where matrix development is affected (hereditary enamel hypoplasia) the entire enamel of all the teeth is involved, probably because of the disturbance in activity of the ameloblasts. In severe cases the enamel present may be very thin, and the teeth may have a conical appearance, as if the enamel caps were missing. The exposed surfaces may be hard where some enamel is present; decay may occur.

Where the maturation stage of enamel formation is affected (hereditary enamel hypocalcification) the crowns of the teeth appear normal in size and shape, but the enamel is of poor quality, entirely opaque, and hypocalcified. The exposed structure may

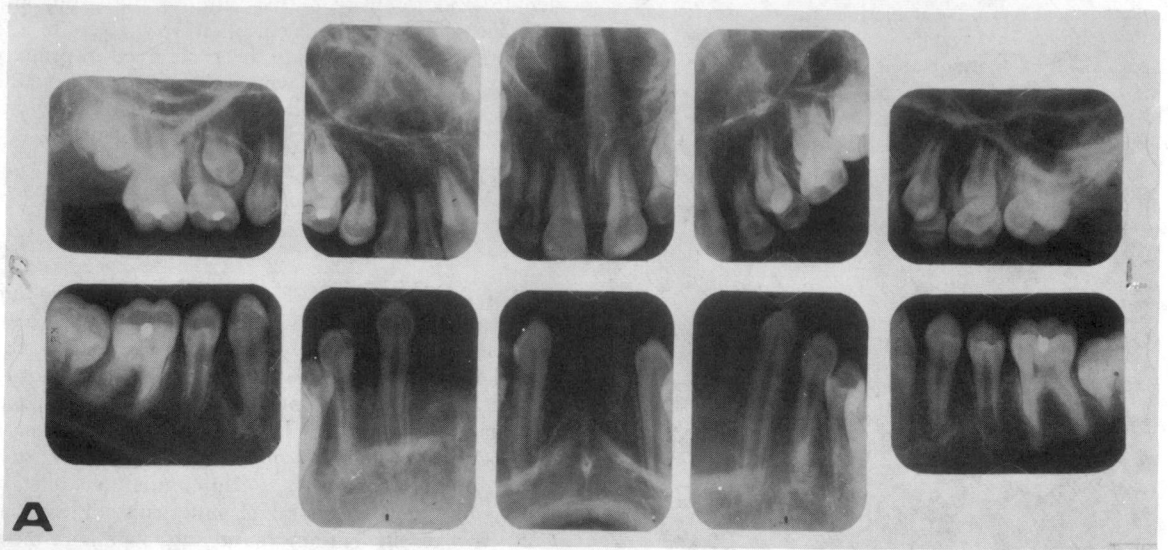

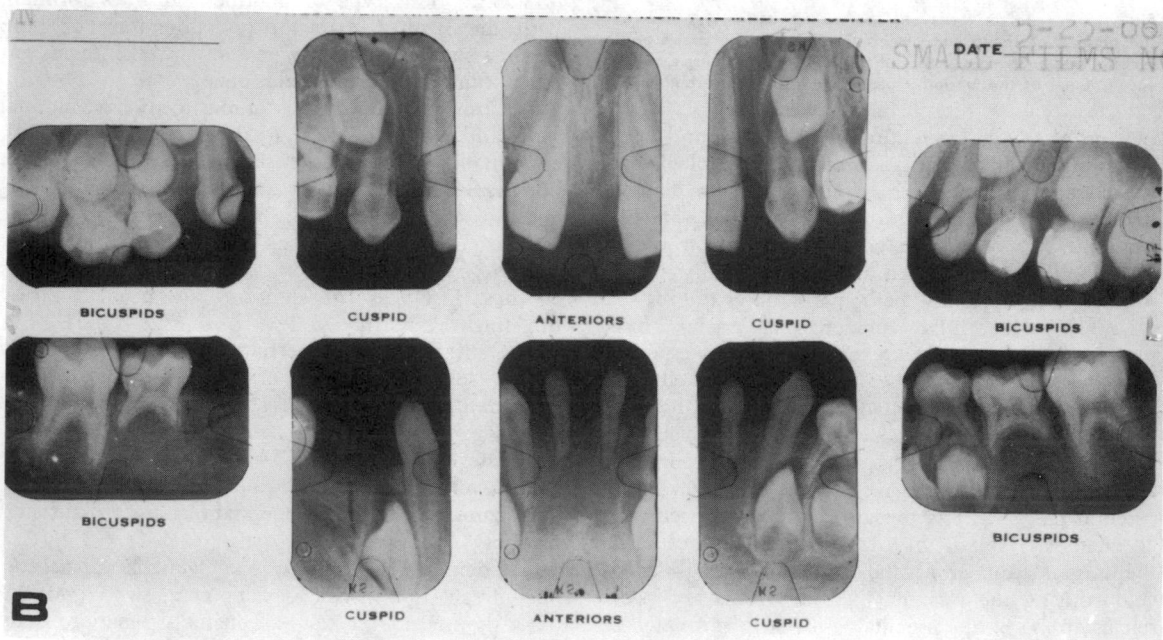

BICUSPIDS   CUSPID   ANTERIORS   CUSPID   BICUSPIDS

BICUSPIDS   BICUSPIDS

CUSPID   ANTERIORS   CUSPID

Fig. 5. Brother and sister with partial anodontia. Parents' dentitions are normal. Possible history of ano-dontia in a brother of paternal grandfather. A. Male, 11 years old. Missing lower permanent incisors and upper first bicuspids. Permanent teeth present are smaller than normal. B. Female, 7 years, 8 months. Missing upper right and left lateral incisors, left first bicuspid, right and left second and third molars, lower right and left incisors, right first bicuspid, right and left second bicuspids, second and third molars. Permanent teeth present are of normal size, but eruption is slow.

be soft, stain readily, and become rapidly abraded by mastication.

MISSING TEETH.   The term anodontia denotes the condition of congenitally missing teeth; it may be either partial or complete. A tooth or bilateral pair of teeth may be missing in the permanent dentition. The maxillary lateral incisors are involved most fre-quently, the mandibular second bicuspids slightly less frequently, and the upper bicuspids occasionally. Missing teeth may be an isolated finding or be part of a known syndrome. Where permanent lateral in-cisors or bicuspids are congenitally missing, there will often be a history of a similar occurrence in one of the parents or close relatives.

Occasionally anodontia may be more extensive; one or more primary teeth may be missing and any number of permanent teeth may be absent. Examples are shown in Figure 5.

Dental management of these situations must be based on evaluation of the distribution of teeth present. Social considerations, important especially during adolescence, often indicate the need for dental restorative procedures. Planning for these children usually requires sequential treatment at different ages because of growth changes.

HYPOPHOSPHATASIA. Hypophosphatasia, a disease of enzyme deficiency, is a recessive, genetically transmitted condition characterized by low alkaline phosphatase in the blood serum and other tissues. There is irregular and incomplete bone formation; the teeth are usually small and show abnormal root formation. (Fig. 6.) There is early root resorption in the primary and permanent teeth which, in the latter, may occur within comparatively short periods after their eruption and be followed by early loss.

DYSAUTONOMIA. This congenital syndrome is manifested by disturbances of autonomic functions (see Sec. 15.13). Several features of this condition involve the oral cavity, such as abnormal chewing and swallowing, drooling beyond the normal age, attacks of severe vomiting, insensitivity to pain, and a marked tendency to grind the teeth. Tooth grinding, noted most frequently in such patients at 2 to 3 years of age, may be so intense that primary teeth may become loosened and evulsed. Where the grinding pattern is severe, prevention of early loss of teeth may be attempted through use of a plastic "bite plate" which protects the teeth from the abnormal grinding force.

Although the severity of periodontal involvement increases frequently as these children become older, caries index is usually lower than the average for normal children. Smaller face size than in normal children has also been reported in dysautonomia. Orthodontic treatment can help to correct this aspect of growth and to improve the appearance.

The aberrant behavioral and speech patterns associated with this condition will be of concern to the dentist in his efforts to establish rapport.

OSTEOPETROSIS. Osteopetrosis, a disorder of bone formation arising during fetal life, affects the entire skeletal structure. The basilar structure of the skull and the orbits are usually affected, with involvement of the calvarium in severe cases. The facial appearance is peculiar as a result of the combination of a large skull and upper face with a very small lower face portion. The mandible is hypoplastic with irregular sclerotic areas. Some teeth may be missing; those present have areas of hypocalcification. Although the first incisors may erupt during the later part of the average first eruption period, subsequent eruptions are markedly delayed. Dental preventive measures should be instituted early to prevent caries at hypoplastic areas. Difficulty in dental management may be anticipated as a result of the impairment of vision and hearing, which are outstanding features of this condition.

CLEIDOCRANIAL DYSOSTOSIS. The congenital absence of maxillary permanent lateral incisors, sometimes accompanied by other, supernumerary teeth, may be found in cleidocranial dysostosis. This condition is inherited as a dominant factor. Other aberrant dental developmental phenomena may be unduly prolonged, with retention of primary teeth and failure or considerable delay in eruption of permanent teeth.

ECTODERMAL DYSPLASIA. Complete or almost complete anodontia is usually accompanied by other systemic signs of ectodermal dysplasia. The systemic disturbances involve all or most of the structures of ectodermal origin. Because of the absence of teeth, there is no development of alveolar processes. The body of the maxilla may be underdeveloped, but the body of the mandible is usually normal.

CHONDROECTODERMAL DYSPLASIA. In this condition the teeth that are present may be small, with many of them malformed. In the lower anterior region the teeth are frequently missing. There is also

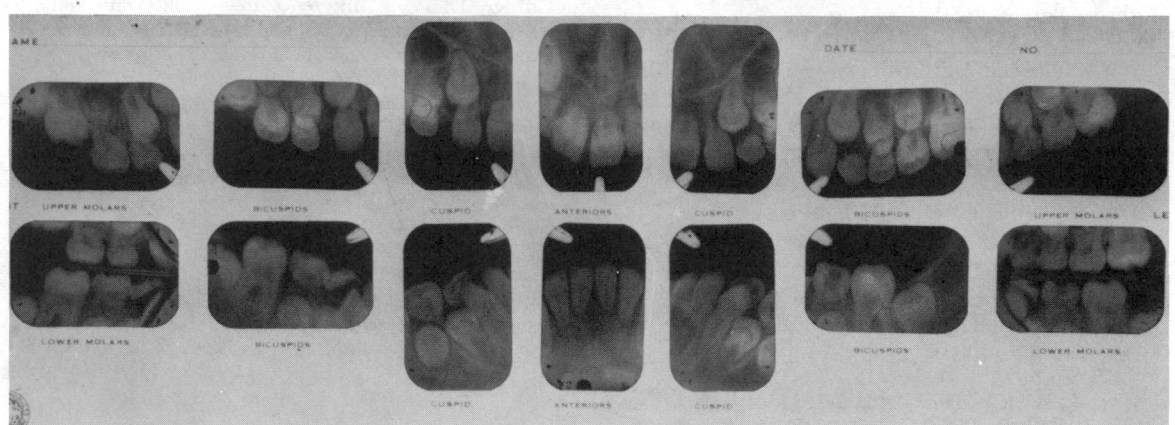

Fig. 6.   Female, 11 years old, hypophosphatasia. Oral appearance negative for age; x-rays disclose incomplete and abnormal root formation.

union of the midportion of the upper lip to the anterior maxillary gingival tissue.

ORAL CLEFTS. The genetic etiology of oral clefts is supported by a great deal of evidence. On the other hand, experimental clefts have been produced as a result of environmental influences.

The relationship between clefts and dental abnormalities varies because of differences in location and extent of the clefts. Cleft may involve the lip or the palate, or both. In cleft palate the lack of fusion may affect the soft palate only, the posterior midline section of the hard palate and the soft palate, or it may extend anteriorly to include the premaxillary bone on one or both sides, thus affecting the future anterior alveolar process.

In the latter types of cleft palate, matrix areas are affected which normally contain the primordia of future incisors. The resulting dental anomalies may involve lateral or central incisors or both, and may be manifested as malposed, malformed, missing, or supernumerary incisors. Restoration of missing teeth or removal of supernumerary teeth should be planned in accordance with stages of dentitional development. Regular dental care should be instituted early for these children to prevent premature loss of teeth and to maintain good oral health.

CHROMOSOMAL ABERRATIONS. The number of recognized syndromes involving orofacial anomalies arising from chromosomal abnormalities is increasing. It is likely that additional rare anomalous orofacial conditions which have been reported in the literature will be found to be related to chromosomal aberrations.

In *Down's syndrome* eruption of the teeth may be delayed and one or more teeth may be missing or malformed. The cuspids are most frequently malformed. Upper lateral incisors may be missing, or malformed if present, but other teeth may also be abnormal in shape and the entire dentition may be small. Periodontal disease is very common in trisomy 21, with severe bone loss occurring early in many of these patients; necrotizing gingivitis is also present in some. Malocclusion is found in a large percentage of these patients, with frequent occurrence of mandibular prognathism and posterior crossbite relationship. Cleft palate and lip have been found to occur frequently in several autosomal chromosomal syndromes, such as trisomy 6, trisomy 13–15, and trisomy 18. Other characteristic facial and cranial abnormalities also occur in these trisomies and in several sex chromosomal syndromes.

REFERENCES

Cohen, M. M. Pediatric Dentistry, 2nd ed. St. Louis, C. V. Mosby Co., 1961.

Cuttita, J. A. Kutscher, A. H., Zegarelli, E. V., and Denning, C. R. Discoloration of the teeth due to antibiotics of the tetracycline family. New York J. Dent., 35(3):89, 1965.

Finn, S. B. Clinical Pedodontics, 2nd ed. Philadelphia, Saunders, 1962.

Fraser, D. Hypophosphatasia. Amer. J. Med., 22:730, 1957.

Fraser, F. C. Experimental induction of cleft palate. In Congenital Anomalies of the Face and Associated Structures. Springfield, Ill., Charles C Thomas, Publ., 1961.

Gordon, E. J., and Rosenstein, S. N. A study of the enamel of primary teeth in cerebral palsied children. New York Dent. J., 31(6):245, 1965.

Gorlin, R. J., and Pindborg, J. J. Syndromes of the Head and Neck. New York, McGraw-Hill Book Co., 1964.

Hayward, H. L. The role of dentistry in the treatment of the cleft palate patient. New York J. Dent., 37:3, 1967.

Hirsch, K. de, and Jansky, J. J. Language investigation of children suffering from familial dysautonomia. J. Speech Hearing Dis., 25:450, 1956.

Kraus, B. S., Clark, G. R., and Oka, S. W. Mental retardation and abnormalities of the dentition. Amer. J. Ment. Defic., 72:905, 1968.

Miller, J. Dental enamel hypoplasia. Spastics' Quart. (London, Eng.), 11:26, 1962.

Public Health Service Publication No. 1487. Research Explores Cleft Palate. 1966, Government Printing Office, Washington, D.C.

Rathbun, J. C. Hypophosphatasia. Amer. J. Dis. Child., 75:822, 1948.

Reitman, A. A. An orthodontically treated case of familial dysautonomia: eight-year growth study. New York Dent. J., 35:546, 1969.

────── Blacharsh, C., and Levy, J. M. Clinical evaluation of the dental aspects of familial dysautonomia: a preliminary report. J. Amer. Dent. Ass., 71: 1436, 1965.

Riley, C. M. Familial dysautonomia. Advances Pediat., 9:157, 1957.

Rosenstein, S. N. Dental findings in 2-year-old survivors of prematurity with 2 different neo-natal antibacterial drugs. J. Dent. Child., 31:342, 1964.

Sarnat, B. G., and Schour, I. Enamel hypoplasia (chronologic enamel aplasia) in relation to systemic disease: a chronologic, morphologic and etiologic classification. J. Amer. Dent. Ass., 28:1989, 1941, and J. Amer. Dent. Ass., 29:67, 1942.

Silverman, W. A., Anderson, D. A., Blanc, W. A., and Crozier, D. N. A difference in mortality rate and incidence of kernicterus among premature infants allotted to two prophylactic antibacterial regimens. Pediatrics, 81:614, 1956.

Watson, W. O., Massler, M., and Perlstein, M. A. Tooth ring analysis in cerebral palsy. Amer. J. Dis. Child., 107:370, 1964.

Zegarelli, E. V., Kutscher, A. H., and Fahn, B. Discoloration of teeth associated with intensive tetracycline therapy in infancy. New York J. Med., 63(18): 2703, 1963.

────── Rosenstein, S. N., Kutscher, A. H., Fahn, B., Botwick, J., and Silverman, W. Discoloration of the teeth associated with oxetetracycline administration of premature birth children. J. Dent. Child., 30:69, 1963.

29.3

COMMON ACQUIRED DISORDERS OF THE TEETH

Dental Decay

Dental decay is probably the most prevalent disease of childhood. It has been reported that over 80 percent of preschool-age children and over 90 percent of school children have some decay, with an appreciable incidence of teeth lost by extraction. The dental loss gives rise in many children to severe malocclusion and such sequelae as facial disfigurement and loss of function. Most, if not all, of this disease experience can be prevented.

ETIOLOGIC CONSIDERATIONS AND PREVENTION. Susceptibility and immunity to decay involve both constitutional systemic factors and local oral environmental factors. Studies of families have demonstrated genetic and familial factors in dental decay. In one study of a large population where exposure to environmental factors was comparable for all families, mean decay experience (DMF*) of offspring was significantly correlated with the DMF of mothers.

Systemic, nutritional factors also play an important role. One of the most significant measures in this category is the fluoridation of a community water supply to the extent of 1 to 1.5 parts of fluoride to 1 million parts of water in areas where fluoride is not found naturally in water. In children born and raised in communities with fluoridation, there is over 60 percent reduction in decay associated with a marked decrease in the number of extractions required, and more children attain adolescence and adulthood with intact, complete dentitions.

A well-balanced diet is as essential for good dental and oral health as it is for optimal nutritional intake and total good health. Such a diet should include proteins, fats, carbohydrates, minerals, and vitamins. Proteins, for example, enter into formation of the protein matrix of dentine and enamel. Daily dietary minerals are required for optimal dental health. Calcium, for example, is essential in tooth and bone formation.

Vitamins also have specific roles in oral health. Vitamin A is essential for normal enamel formation, integrity of the epithelial layers of the oral soft tissues, and keratin formation. Vitamin C is necessary for normal dentine formation and for integrity of the oral soft tissues and blood vessels. Vitamin D is required for effective utilization of calcium and phosphorus in tooth formation and growth. Several vitamin B factors are involved in maintaining proper oral

---

* DMF, used as an index of total decay experience, represents the sum of decayed, missing, and filled teeth.

---

health as exemplified by the relation of riboflavin to cheilosis, of niacin to the glossitis and stomatitis of beriberi, and of pyridoxine to the oral microflora.

The beneficial effects of a well-rounded diet can be negated by neglect and unfavorable oral environmental factors, primarily poor eating habits and poor choice of foods. There is evidence that adherence to three regular meals daily and avoidance of carbohydrate snacks can result in a marked reduction in incidence of dental decay. For the growing preschool-age child and young school-age child, a snack in the middle of a long afternoon may be indicated, but should be limited to fruit, fruit juice, or a noncarbohydrate food such as cheese. Fruit is superior to other desserts at the end of a meal because it is removed more readily from tooth surfaces. Added protection is provided by toothbrushing following each meal, which eliminates food debris and microorganisms from the teeth.

Two major factors related most closely to initiation of decay in teeth are (1) microorganisms, and (2) the acidic end products of enzymatic degradation of carbohydrates. The latter products develop when carbohydrate foods are permitted to remain about the teeth following eating. Both initiating factors and their sources are removed by thorough brushing immediately after meals.

NIGHTTIME BOTTLE CARIES SYNDROME. In a large group of young children with rampant decay involving all or practically all their teeth, case histories disclosed an almost constant relationship to an earlier feeding habit. It consisted of giving to the child in the crib at naptime and nighttime, a bottle with milk, juice, or syrup and water, while falling asleep. (Fig. 7.) Often, this practice was continued until 3½ or 4 years of age, well past the age at which the child discontinued bottle use at mealtime. Infants who took the feeding completely and discarded the bottle before falling asleep did not have a high incidence of decay; those who kept the bottle in their mouth during sleep, with intermittent sucking, showed an interesting distribution of carious involvement. The lower incisors were usually unaffected, because the nipple was held in the tongue, which covered and protected the lower anterior teeth. All the upper teeth, especially the upper incisors and the lower posterior teeth, became affected by decay, the severity depending upon the length of this habit. The prolonged nighttime bottle habit had another unfavorable aspect: when these children were too old to use the feeding bottle they substituted other foods, usually carbohydrates, and became almost constant between-meal nibblers, which continued their susceptibility to widespread decay. Since the prolonged use of the bottle serves only to satisfy the need for sucking and for relaxation, rather than need for food, it should be discontinued and some other sucking aid used, such as a large nipple pacifier or a bottle with water.

PREVENTION AND TREATMENT. Regular visits to the dentist should be encouraged and should start

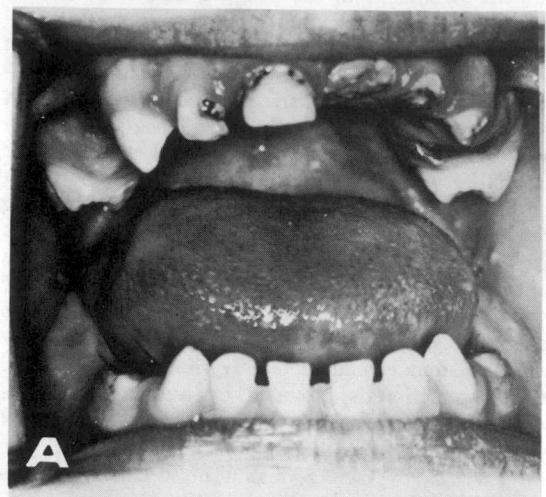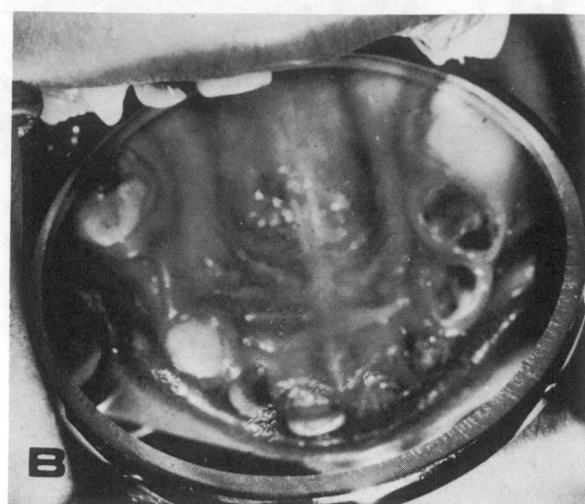

Fig. 7.   A. Labial view. B. Lingual view. Rampant decay in the primary dentition of a 4-year-old boy with history of bottle feeding during naptime and nighttime till 4 years of age. Lower anterior teeth are perfect and uninvolved because of protection from the tongue during sucking and swallowing. All upper teeth and lower posterior teeth are extensively decayed. Upper right second molar required early extraction.

shortly after the primary dentition is erupted. The dentist can detect early decay and, if present, institute corrective and preventive measures. Instructions can be given by the dentist to both the parent and the child in proper home care measures. Thus the child becomes aware early of the need for good oral health and proper home care.

Good home care measures include correct toothbrushing after meals and recommendations regarding eating habits. Through these measures the dentist can also help prevent common disorders of the oral soft tissues and to a large extent disorders of occlusion.

Common Soft Tissue Disorders

These conditions include the simple forms of gingivitis which involve usually the marginal gingivae and interdental papillae, and are the result of a lack of good oral hygiene. Proper toothbrushing and eating habits can prevent these mild conditions.

In some instances gingivitis secondary to lack of oral hygiene and other unfavorable habits may give rise to excessive hypertrophy of the gingivae at puberty. The hypertrophied tissue appears inflamed and bleeds easily. Gingival hypertrophy occurs also in children on dilantin therapy for seizures, when good oral hygiene is lacking. This type of hypertrophy is mainly fibrous and appears firm: the presence of calcified masses, apparently heteroplastic bone, in the gingival tissues has also been reported. Both types of gingival hypertrophy will improve with appropriate dental treatment followed by a regimen of good oral home care procedures. Where the dilantin hypertrophy is excessive, gingival resection

is usually indicated and should be followed by thorough instruction in suitable home care procedures. It is almost axiomatic that regular dental prophylaxis and suitable home care procedures help greatly to prevent the occurrence of these gingival changes.

Other disorders of the gingivae are discussed in the section on diseases of the mouth (Sec. 28.5).

Disorders of Occlusion

Malocclusion may become manifest in a variety of intermaxillary relationships. The child with a developing abnormality of occlusion can benefit greatly if it is detected and evaluated early by the dentist. In certain forms of developing malocclusion, early intervention can prevent the need for extensive treatment; in other forms, it may be necessary to observe the subsequent course of development and make the final decision on treatment at a later age.

A number of cases of malocclusion may be attributed to genetic factors which give rise to abnormal dimensional relationships between jawbones and the dentitions they contain. These conditions require expert observation and evaluation to determine indications for treatment. However, a large proportion of malocclusions are the result of premature loss of primary teeth and early loss of first permanent molars. Loss of these teeth and the development of this type of malocclusion can be prevented by proper care provided through early and regular visits to the dentist. Available tooth conservation procedures in children are very important preventive measures.

Other cases of malocclusion result from poor oral habits, such as thumb-sucking, lip-sucking, and tongue-thrusting. The effects of these oral habits on developing occlusions can be recognized early in the primary dentition. When they are intercepted early and proper therapy is instituted, malocclusion in the permanent dentition may be prevented or attenuated.

REFERENCES

Ast, D. B., and Fitzgerald, B. Effectiveness of water fluoridation. J. Amer. Dent. Ass., 65:581, 1962.

Brash, J. C., McKeag, H. T. A., and Scott, J. H. The Etiology of Irregularity and Malocclusion of the Teeth, 2nd ed. London, Dent. Bd. of the United Kingdom, 1965.

Gustafson, B. E., Quensel, C. E., Lande, L. S., Lundquist, C., Granen, H., Bonow, B. E., and Krasse, H. The Vipeholm dental caries study; the effect of different levels of carbohydrate intake on caries activity in 436 individuals observed for 5 years. Acta Odont. Scand., II:232, 1964.

Klein, H. The family and dental disease. IV. Dental disease (DMF) experience in parents and offspring. J. Amer. Dent. Ass., 33:735, 1946.

——— The family and dental disease. Pub. Health Rep., 62(35):1253, 1947.

Lundquist, C. Oral sugar clearance. Odont. Rev., 3: Suppl. 1, 1952.

McBeath, E. C. Vitamin D studies, 1933-1934. Amer. J. Pub. Health, 34(10):1028, 1934.

——— and Verlin, W. A. Further studies on the role of vitamin D in the nutritional control of dental caries in children. J. Amer. Dent. Ass., 29:1393, 1942.

Orland, F. J., Blayney, J. R., Harrison, R. W., Reyniers, J. A., Trexler, P. C., Ervin, R. F., Gordon, H. A., and Wagner, M. Experimental caries in germfree rats inoculated with enterococci. J. Amer. Dent. Ass., 50: 259, 1955.

Rosenstein, S. N. Systemic and environmental factors in rampant caries in young children. New York Dent. J., 32:400, 1966.

Zegarelli, E. V., and Ziskin, D. E. Bone heteroplasia in a case of dilantin hyperplastic gingivitis. Amer. J. Orthodont. Oral Surg., 29:152, 1943.

29.4

DENTISTRY FOR HANDICAPPED CHILDREN

Dentistry is an important part of the total care and rehabilitation of handicapped children. This service is necessary to prevent loss of teeth adding dental disability to their other handicaps.

The teeth of children with certain severe conditions, such as cerebral palsy, are as susceptible to decay as those of other children. Without adequate dental care, the decayed teeth soon require extraction and many teeth will be lost eventually. When they become young adults the facial disfigurement and lack of oral function resulting from extensive edentulous areas may constitute obstacles to their vocational training and habilitation and to their prospects of becoming self-supporting. Furthermore, the exten-

sive restorative procedures required at that time may be considerably more difficult and costly. These factors dictate the need for early care and preventive measures. Consequently, visits for dental care at a young age are essential for they will permit the dentist to perform dental preventive procedures, provide instruction in oral home care, and create awareness of the need for good dental care early in life.

These considerations apply equally to patients with cleft palate and lip, cardiovascular conditions, blood dyscrasias, and metabolic disorders.

Dentistry can be performed under normal conditions, using local anesthesia, on children with many types of handicapping disorders. The cooperation necessary to attain stability in the dental chair can be developed. Complete dental care can be provided for patients with neuromuscular disabilities, mental retardation, metabolic and circulatory disorders, and other conditions. These children also benefit in general ways from their visits to the dental office and from the friendly reception of the dentist and auxiliary personnel.

However, it may not be possible to develop such cooperation in the child because of his lack of ability to comprehend, excessive dyskinetic movements, or extreme emotional disturbance. In such cases preoperative administration of combinations of sedatives and muscle relaxants has been found helpful. The agents used should be safe and effective, and given in conservative dosages and proper combination. They should be eliminated rapidly, have no danger of addiction, and be discontinued after the first few visits if the patient has become oriented to the need for dental care.

Some handicapped patients may require general anesthesia for their dentistry, particularly in case of severe emotional disturbance and when there is inability to comprehend or communicate. General anesthesia may also be indicated for children with rampant decay or with deep decay in many teeth, but should be limited to the very difficult patient who cannot be managed otherwise. It provides the opportunity to complete all necessary treatment in one or two sessions, but should be performed only under optimal conditions with adequate assistance and all necessary safeguards. Subsequently, the children should visit their dentists for regular cleaning and orientation to dentistry under normal conditions.

Liaison between the dentist who treats handicapped children and their pediatrician is essential. An abstracted medical history of each child should be available to the dentist in order to assure the best general care. The dentist should be apprised of special precautions that may be required for each individual handicapped child, such as the need for protective antibiotic coverage for children with cardiovascular conditions.

The benefits of early dental care, prevention of premature tooth loss, indoctrination in home care procedures, and dental preventive measures should be made available to all handicapped children.

References

Adelson, J. J. Some selective general anesthetic techniques for the problem patient. New York J. Dent., 34(9):332, 1964.

——— The effects of dental treatment on behavior of handicapped patients. J. Amer. Dent. Ass., 71:1411, 1965.

Green, A., and Mendelsohn, M. J. Is premedication necessary for handicapped children? J. Dent. Child., 27: 40, 1960.

Rosenstein, S. N. Clinical management of the handicapped. In Institute on Mental Retardation for Physicians and Dentists. Fergus Falls, Minn., Nov. 7, 1959, p. 46, Minn. St. Health D., Minneapolis, 1959.

——— On dentistry for the handicapped. Bull. N.J. Soc. Dent. Child., 12(3):3, 1964.

——— Operative dentistry and endodontics for the physically limited patient. Cereb. Palsy J., 26:8, 1965.

chapter 30

THE NOSE, PARANASAL SINUSES, AND PHARYNX

ROBERT J. RUBEN, Associate Editor

30.1
NOSE AND PARANASAL SINUSES

Physiology

The primary function of the nose is to serve as a conduit of air to the larynx. As air travels through the nose, it is brought to body temperature, humidified, and cleared of macromolecular-sized particles by means of the anatomic properties of the nose. Three to four turbinates on each side increase the total area to which the inspired air is exposed. The nose, including the turbinates, is lined by respiratory mucosa containing *cilia* and mucus-secreting glands. The submucosal tissue covering the turbinates is a type of erectile tissue; its high vascularity is a primary factor in warming the air to body temperature.

A small carbon particle can travel 1 cm per minute by means of the cilia in the nose. The mucous glands secrete about 1 liter of mucus per day, which is usually swallowed. Many disease states of the nose and paranasal sinuses are due to malfunction of air flow, cilia activity, mucus secretion, and/or damage to the turbinates. When the nasal septum, the midline divider of the nose, is malformed, as in cleft palate and cleft lip, or distorted subsequent to a nasal injury, it can effectively distort and block the airflow. This in turn can cause changes in the mucosal flow and allow infection to develop.

Olfaction is another important function of the nose. However, the natural ability of the nose and paranasal sinuses in man for air processing, may be to the detriment of the nose as an organ of olfaction. The function of olfaction is not necessary for life in man, as demonstrated by patients who are congenitally anosmic. A separate olfactory mucosa is located in the roof of the nose under the cribiform plate. This mucosa can be destroyed either by intracranial or intranasal growths. Anosmia can be a sign of intracranial tumor.

The nose and paranasal sinuses have other important functions which are less obvious. The air space in the nose is part of the normal resonance cavity of the entire upper airway and is essential to the production of proper speech sounds.

The nose and the sinuses protect the intracranial cavity. They provide an air-filled shock absorber which can be fractured before the calvarium is fractured. The contents of the orbit can be directly affected by fractures of the sinuses. The orbit is supported superiorly by the frontal sinus, medially by the ethmoid sinus, and inferiorly by the maxillary sinus.

An understanding of the paranasal sinuses requires knowledge of the way they drain. The maxillary and frontal sinuses are large, air-filled, bony cavities lined with respiratory mucosa which drain through small ostia. The frontal sinus drains through the nasal frontal duct, which opens under the anterior portion of the middle meatus. The hiatus semilunaris is the most constant of several orifices of the maxillary sinus; it opens usually into the midportion of the nasal cavity, underneath the middle turbinate. Patency of the ostia is essential for normal functioning of the sinuses. Swelling of the mucosa due to infection causes narrowing or closure of the ostia and permits pus to accumulate in the sinus. Unless it is drained either by opening the ostia or entering the sinus, the pus will raise the pressure in the sinus. Together with the infection, this increased pressure can destroy the mucosa; it also compromises the vascular supply by cutting off the venous circulation and may cause the bone to die. The result is a chronic osteomyelitis with sequestration of bone. The pus which drains through this sequestra into the surrounding tissue may invade the epidural space, the orbit, the face, or the deep fascial planes of the neck.

Growth

At birth a rudimentary maxillary antrum air cell is present which has a volume of less than 0.5 ml. There are also rudimentary ethmoid sinus cells on each side of the nose. As the child grows, the maxillary and ethmoid sinuses grow and enlarge. The frontal and sphenoid sinuses develop as outgrowths of the superior and posterior ethmoid cells. At 3 years of age a rudimentary frontal sinus can usually be seen radiographically, and at 5 years the sphenoid sinus becomes apparent. There is significant variability from individual to individual.

The floor of the maxillary sinus in a child contains the buds of all the deciduous and permanent teeth. As the child grows, the floor of the antrum begins to occupy the space formerly utilized by the teeth. At the age of 6 or 7 years the floor of the antrum has descended to the level of the floor of the nose.

Malformations

The two most common malformations of the nose and paranasal sinuses are *cleft palate* and *choanal atresia*.

Cleft Palate

In an infant with cleft palate, the nasal cavity is exposed to food, usually causing a chronic inflammation of the mucosa of the nose and sinuses. When the palate is repaired, the nasal septum is usually found to be misplaced and grossly malformed. The ensuing anatomic and physiologic block which exists on at least one side of the nose produces a chronic rhinitis which may progress to chronic sinusitis.

The tip of the nose in many children with cleft palate is abnormally developed, with the cartilage of the tip either completely missing or grossly malformed. The consequences of this abnormality are twofold. The most obvious is the serious cosmetic defect which can contribute to the emotional problems of these children. The second effect of the malformation is on the internal configuration of the vestibule of the nose. Normal airflow through the nose depends in part on the placement of the cartilages of the vestibule. These may be congenitally absent, as in cleft palate, or may be destroyed by an abscess dissolving them. This absence of cartilage alters the airflow which serves as a functional block to one side of the nose.

Choanal Atresia

This congenital defect is described as a closure of the posterior part of the nose that is connected to the nasopharynx. Choanal atresia can be either unilateral or bilateral, bony or membranous, complete or partial. This defect is usually present in children with acrocephalosyndactylia (Apert's syndrome).

An infant with bilateral choanal atresia will present with severe difficulty in breathing and eating. Infants are preferential nose breathers and must learn to breathe through their mouth. The diagnosis is easily made by observing that the respiratory distress ceases when the mouth is held open. The infant will usually learn to breathe through its mouth. Feeding problems can be managed satisfactorily for several months by giving small feedings and allowing the child to breathe between feedings.

Children with unilateral choanal atresia are usually diagnosed after the age of 3 years when they either complain of one nostril being closed, or present with a constant drainage from one nostril.

Choanal atresia should be diagnosed radiographically using radiopaque material introduced through the nares. On a submental radiographic view the dye stops at the choana in membranous choanal atresia. In bony atresia it stops halfway, at the junction between the bony and membranous palates.

It is a common practice to test for choanal atresia by inserting a small rubber catheter into the nares. This procedure will usually perforate a membranous atresia but not rupture through a bony atresia. Rupture of the membranous atresia allows the child to breathe better temporarily but may create stenosis and make the subsequent surgical repair much more difficult. It is preferable, for this reason, to make the diagnosis by radiographic examination.

The definitive surgical repair should be planned in a meaningful way. Surgery can be done as early as several weeks of age or, when possible, deferred until 1 to 1½ years of age.

Other Malformations

Other malformations of the nose and sinuses are rarer than choanal atresia. They include clefts of the midface and nose, cysts of the sinuses, ectopic teeth, and encephaloceles. *Encephaloceles* result from herniation of the meninges through the floor of the anterior cranial fossa into the nasal sinus cavities; they may or may not contain brain tissue. An encephalocele can present as a lump in the forehead or as a mass protruding from the nose or in the nasopharynx. Although uncommon, the diagnosis should be considered whenever a mass is present in the nose, sinus, or pharynx in early infancy. The puncture or unplanned removal of such a lesion can result in an opening of the meninges with subsequent meningitis. A planned neurosurgical removal can be done successfully.

Inherited Diseases

There are several inherited diseases that affect the nose, including the dominantly transmitted "potato nose," which is a large, bulbous deformity of the tip of the nose. Of more importance is the hereditary telangiectasia of Rendu, Osler, and Weber (Sec. 17.13). This disease is inherited as an autosomal dominant abnormality. It usually appears first in older children with chronic and severe epistaxis from telangiectasia of the nasal septum. Diagnosis requires demonstration of the telangiectasia and usually a history of the inherited disease. Treatment is removal of the telangiectasia which should be considered in patients with severe and chronic epistaxis.

REFERENCES

GENERAL

Birrell, J. F. Ear, Nose and Throat Diseases of Children. Philadelphia, F. A. Davis Co., 1960.
Jackson, C., and Jackson, C. L. Diseases of the Nose, Throat and Ear, 2nd ed. Philadelphia, W. B. Saunders Co., 1969.

Choanal Atresia

Diamant, H., and Kinnman, J. Congenital choanal atresia: a report of clinical series with special references to early symptoms and therapy. Acta Paediat. (Stockholm), 52:106, 1963.
Erickson, D. L., Lodge, J. L., and Tomsovic, E. J. Medical management of bilateral choanal atresia, a report of four cases. J. Pediat., 63:561, 1963.
Flake, C. G., and Ferguson, C. F. Congenital choanal atresia in infants and children. Ann. Otol., 73:458, 1964.

Encephaloceles

Beyer, T. E., Blair, J. R., and Lipscomb, W. R. Intranasal meningocele. Laryngoscope, 61:917, 1951.
Ingraham, F. D., and Matson, D. D. Spina bifida and cranium bifidum: unusual nasopharyngeal encephalocele. New Eng. J. Med., 228:815, 1943.
Zarem, H. A., Gray, G. F., Jr., Morehead, D., and Edgerton, M. T. Heterotopic brain and nasopharynx and soft palate: report of 2 cases. Surgery, 61:438, 1967.

Tumors

Tumors of the nose usually produce one or all of four major symptoms: nasal obstruction, epistaxis, abnormal nasal discharge, and/or hyponasal speech. All these symptoms are due to occlusion of the nose and sinus airways, which may cause inability to clear bacteria, to produce voice, and to breathe through the nose.

Juvenile Angiofibroma

The most serious tumors of the nose and paranasal sinuses in children are the juvenile angiofibromas. This tumor occurs predominantly in boys from age 10 to 19, the mean age being 13 years. It can present either as a mass protruding from the nose or as chronic epistaxis. It is a benign tumor which can, however, spread locally, invade the orbit, and even produce blindness. This tumor must be removed surgically. The diagnosis can be suspected clinically from its firmness, which is greater than that of most intranasal masses, and from its occurrence

in the preadolescent male. A boy with a suspected angiofibroma should not have a biopsy until other diagnostic procedures, including arteriograms, have been done. These tumors are exceedingly vascular and a small biopsy can result in a significant hemorrhage. The biopsy should be planned as part of an operative procedure under general anesthesia with blood for transfusion readily available. The biopsy is usually done preliminary to a one-stage surgical removal of the tumor.

Polyps

The most common growths in the nose and paranasal sinuses are polyps. Polyps are soft masses made up of loose connective tissue and mucosa infiltrated with eosinophiles. They can protrude either into the choana or from either external nares. Polyps are usually associated with two general types of diseases: allergy and mucoviscidosis. Many children with marked nasal polyps have severe allergic problems. Treatment of polyps must include both surgical removal and control of the allergy by desensitization. Steroids should not be used, either topically or systemically. The polyps need to be removed to allow for normal physiology of the nose and sinuses. Severe polyposis may be associated with both chronic and acute sinusitis or with periosteal abscesses. There is also an association of polyps with asthma and chronic chest disease in adults.

The polyps seen in children with mucoviscidosis should also be removed for the maintenance of proper nasal physiology and for cosmetic reasons when they protrude from the nose. These may recur and need to be removed with each recurrence.

Mucoceles and Pyoceles

The sinuses may contain mucoceles or pyoceles. These are mucosal cysts filled with either mucus or pus, which can erode through the bony portion of the sinus and present as a soft mass on the face or periorbital region. Any mass presenting in this way demands radiologic study to determine whether or not it is of sinus origin.

Osteoma

Occasionally a slow growing bony mass is noted in one of the paranasal sinuses. These are osteomas and become apparent clinically when they occlude one of the ostia of the sinuses, causing acute or chronic sinusitis. They are occasionally noted on radiographs taken for other reasons. If they are discovered incidentally, they should be followed conservatively; they are slow growing and, usually, many years will elapse before any treatment is necessary.

Fibrous Dysplasia of Bone

Monostotic and *polyostotic* fibrous dysplasia of the nose and paranasal sinuses occur in childhood and usually lead to gross disfigurement of the child. The entire sinus may be replaced by a bony mass. Biopsy will confirm the diagnosis. Progression of the disease cannot be controlled. Patients can be treated only symptomatically for the sinus and ear conditions resulting from the occlusion of the sinus cavities and/or cavities of the middle ear. Plastic and reconstructive surgery can often reduce the cosmetic deformity later in life.

Dentigerous cysts are found in the maxilla and palate. They can grow to large size and are easily diagnosed radiographically.

Malignant Neoplasms

Cancers of the nose and paranasal sinuses are rare in children. They are usually mesodermal cancers. Metastases can also be found in the nose and paranasal sinuses, and malignancies can also invade the nose and paranasal sinuses from nearby structures, such as the tongue and nasopharynx.

REFERENCES

JUVENILE NASOPHARYNGEAL ANGIOFIBROMAS

Apostol, J. V., and Frazell, E. G. Juvenile nasopharyngeal angiofibroma: a clinical study. Cancer, 18:869, 1965.

Sternberg, S. S. Pathology of juvenile nasopharyngeal angiofibroma: a lesion of adolescent males. Cancer, 7:15, 1954.

Schwachman, H., et al. Nasal polyposis in patients with cystic fibrosis. Pediatrics, 30:389, 1962.

MALIGNANT NEOPLASMS

Berg, E. T., and Torelman, N. G. Malignant tumors of the head and neck in childhood. Acta Otolaryng. (Stockholm), 68:551, 1969.

Rush, B. F., Chambers, R. G., and Ravage, M. M. Cancer of the head and neck in children. Surgery, 53:270, 1963.

Sutow, W. W. Cancer of the head and neck in children. J.A.M.A., 190:414, 1964.

Infectious Diseases

Bacterial infection of the sinuses can occur early in infancy and throughout childhood. The infections may be symptomatically severe but are usually not dangerous unless the infectious process extends to adjacent structures.

The signs of acute maxillary sinusitis of infancy are purulent nasal discharge from one naris, associated with swelling of the cheek, the alveolar ridge, and the periorbital area. The treatment of choice is appropriate antibiotic therapy and intranasal drainage of what is, in reality, a facial abscess. Untreated acute maxillary sinusitis of infancy may result in osteomyelitis of the maxilla. The sequelae from the osteomyelitis are hypoplasia of the affected side of the face and loss of the primary and secondary dentition.

Acute maxillary, ethmoid, and/or frontal sinusitis in childhood are especially dangerous diseases. The symptoms and signs are those of fever, purulent nasal discharge, and facial and periorbital swelling. The greatest danger exists when the facial swelling is primarily periorbital, indicating that bone and periosteum are affected by the infection. The pus in the sinuses cannot escape; as a result there is necrosis of the bone, venous thrombosis, and finally, formation of bony sequestra. The first sign of this sequence is swelling of the periosteum. Extravasation of the pus from the sinus into the orbit, especially from an ethmoid cell through the lamina papyracea, can cause permanent blindness due to thrombosis of the orbital vein.

All children with periorbital edema, no matter how slight, should be investigated for sinusitis. Occasionally only one or two periorbital ethmoid cells are involved. The contents of the nose and nasopharynx must be cultured and a smear examined immediately. Appropriate antibiotic therapy must be started. Periorbital swelling will often proceed so rapidly that surgical drainage of the affected sinus cells will be necessary.

Acute frontal sinusitis may also cause orbital swelling preceded by supraorbital swelling. The infection may involve the eye and may also produce an epidural abscess secondary to erosion of the frontal sinus. Radiographs to demonstrate an acute frontal sinusitis should be taken with the child's head in upright position to demonstrate the fluid level in the sinus. If there is a fluid level and tissue swelling, the sinus should be surgically drained, since the probability that the nasal frontal duct will open spontaneously is small. At no time should the nasofrontal duct be manipulated. Drainage of the frontal sinus with irrigation of the frontal sinus cavity with antibiotics can be done through the small trephination which is put into the frontal sinus. Interference with the nasofrontal duct can cause stenosis, result in a chronic frontal sinusitis refractory to treatment, and lead to a serious cosmetic defect as well as additional medical difficulties.

Chronic sinusitis in children is very commonly overlooked. The clinical manifestations are chronic cough from the postnasal drip, constant purulent nasal discharge, cervical lymphadenopathy, and, not infrequently, chronic mild epistaxis. Chronic sinusitis may aggravate respiratory symptoms in asthmatic children. The diagnosis of chronic sinusitis is made radiographically by demonstrating mucosal thickening or complete obliteration of the sinus cavity.

Several distinct disease entities are associated with chronic sinusitis. These include cystic fibrosis, mucopolysaccharidosis, Kartagener's syndrome (sinusitis, dextrocardia, and situs inversus), allergy, intranasal masses such as polyps, immunoglobulinopathy, and, not uncommonly, self-inflicted wounds secondary to a foreign body in the nose.

The treatment of chronic sinusitis in a child is determined mainly by the cause. Simple nasal or sinus obstruction requires removal of the obstruction. However, most children with chronic sinusitis will have no readily identifiable cause. A lateral radiograph of the soft tissue of the neck should be obtained to determine the size of the adenoids, which may occlude the choana and contribute to the sinusitis and subsequent rhinitis. If nasal decongestants and systemic treatment with appropriate antibiotics fail to arrest the disease, an adenoidectomy and sinus irrigation are indicated.

External infections of the nose and face may be of great seriousness. These are usually either small staphylococcal abscesses or more widespread streptococcal infections. The venous drainage of the face is connected with the cavernous sinuses. Infections of the face and nose can cause cavernous sinus thrombosis with resulting hydrocephalus, meningoencephalitis, and neurologic sequelae. Infection of the external nose and face must be treated vigorously to prevent any of these potentially lethal sequelae.

References

SINUSITIS

Bluestone, C. D., and Steiner, R. E. Intracranial complications of acute frontal sinusitis. Southern Med. J., 58:1, 1965.

Kavanaugh, F. Osteomyelitis of superior maxilla in infants. Brit. Med. J., p. 468 (Feb. 13), 1960.

Proctor, D. F. The nose and parasanal sinuses in childhood. Springfield, Ill., Charles C Thomas, Publ., 1963.

Siedband, E. N. Roentgen-study of development of frontal sinuses: interorbital distance of half-axial view during infancy and childhood. Ann. Paediat. (Basel), 206:175, 1966.

Trauma

The nose is the part of the face that is most subject to trauma, both externally and internally. Birth injury may cause fracture of the nose with displacement and dislocation of the nasal septum. These lesions will result in both external and internal nasal deformities later in life. Trauma of the nose in childhood can cause severe fractures which are easily reduced. Untreated, these fractures may result in severe cosmetic deformities which become grossly apparent in adolescence. Almost all external fractures of the nose have an associated subluxation and/or fracture of the nasal septum. A nasal septum that occludes one side

of the nares can produce difficulty in breathing, rhinitis, and chronic sinusitis. All nasal fractures must be reduced and the septum should be repositioned.

Cosmetic correction of the external nasal and septal deformities in preadolescent children can be undertaken but should be limited to the most minimal type of correction, and then only in the most extenuating circumstances. A case in point is an 8-year-old girl, a "battered child," who had her nose so badly displaced due to multiple fractures that her cosmetic appearance was grotesque. A minimal procedure was done in order to enhance the social adjustment of this child.

A hidden, and often overlooked, injury following trauma to the nose is a nasal septal hematoma. The injury, which may or may not be associated with the fracture, has caused blood to accumulate underneath the mucosa of the nasal septum. The septum will be grossly widened and occludes one or both sides of the nares. The hematoma can either resolve or become a septal abscess. The nasal hematoma or abscess can erode the nasal septum, leaving a septal perforation. This nasal septal perforation can produce, among several other deformities, an external saddle nose deformity.

Nasal septal perforation can also cause severe epistaxis due to bleeding from the edges of the perforation which, in some instances, can be life-threatening. A nasal septal abscess can extend to form an abscess of the face. These complications can all be avoided by inspection of the nasal septum after nasal trauma. If present, a hematoma or abscess should be drained.

Fractures of the bones of the face occur in children secondary to falls, automobile accidents, or to trauma such as being hit in the eye by a baseball. The sequelae of these traumas are facial deformity; if they occur in the maxillary sinus and orbit, they produce entrapment of the extraocular muscles, which may cause diplopia. These fractures can be diagnosed radiographically and need prompt treatment. A facial fracture often overlooked is that of the orbital floor, sometimes called the blowout fracture. This usually results from blunt trauma to the eye. The orbital contents crush the floor of the orbit, which constitutes the roof of the maxillary sinus. The extraocular muscles lying on the floor of the orbit become entrapped in the fracture. If this injury is suspected, it is advisable to obtain radiographs, including tomograms, of the floor of the orbit. The extraocular muscles can be freed from such a fracture and the fracture repaired.

Manifestations of General Disease

There are a number of generalized diseases that can manifest themselves in the nose and paranasal sinuses. The mucopolysaccharidoses may present with nasal masses and/or chronic sinusitis. The child with allergy or cystic fibrosis may have nasal and/or sinus polyps with a chronic sinusitis. In cystic fibrosis the chronic sinusitis is due to the thick viscosity of the mucus and the patient's inability to process the discharge properly. Children with hypothyroidism may have nasal swelling, nasal obstruction, and secondary sinusitis. Abnormalities of the immune system, nongranulomatous uveitis, and retrobulbar neuritis may be associated with sinusitis. Children with cleft palate usually have a chronic rhinitis and sinusitis.

Special Areas

Epistaxis

Epistaxis is a relatively common occurrence in children. Most often there is a small amount of bleeding, which is easily controllable. Epistaxis usually occurs as a result of erosion of the small vessels in the anterior portion of the nasal septum, called *Kiesselbach's area*. The cause is basically rhinitis or trauma secondary to a child picking his nose. Bleeding can be controlled by placing a small cotton pledget soaked in 5 percent hydrogen peroxide, with a few drops of 1:1,000 adrenalin or 1 percent Neo-Synephrine, in the nose. Only moderate pressure is needed to control the bleeding. The use of excessive pressure or very tight nasal packing is to be avoided; it is liable to cause more erosion of the vessels or of the nasal septum, and secondary infection. Any recurrence of epistaxis should be investigated thoroughly for underlying diseases such as coagulation disorders, rheumatic fever, cystic fibrosis, and immunologic defects. Occasionally an adenoidal mass blocking the choana will cause rhinitis and chronic minimal expistaxis.

Severe epistaxis is fortunately uncommon in children and is usually the hallmark of more serious conditions in the nose or sinuses; these include juvenile angiofibromas, congenital telangiectasia, coagulation defects, leukemia, renal failure, or tumors of the nose. The management of severe epistaxis requires extensive nasal packing and possibly blood transfusion. If the nose must be packed tightly for longer than a day, the child should be hospitalized and placed on antibiotics. An intravenous solution should be maintained so that blood transfusions may be given. It is not uncommon in a severe nosebleed to lose a significant amount of the total blood volume. The back of the throat should be inspected for blood which is coming from the choana and being swallowed. In severe epistaxis more blood may be swallowed than escapes through the nose. As a result, the blood pressure may decrease suddenly, out of proportion to the amount of external bleeding from the nose. The child may also vomit blood which can be aspirated. The oropharynx should be checked periodically for continued bleeding. If the bleeding continues, a posterior pack must be placed and appropriate therapy, including blood replacement, instituted.

Foreign Bodies

Foreign bodies in the nose occur commonly in children two to five years of age. Most of these are easily removed. If an initial attempt is unsuccessful, the foreign body must be removed under general anesthesia. It is pointless to try to pull out a foreign body that has been wedged in the nose for some days, weeks, or months. If such an attempt is made, in the process of struggling with the child, several complications may occur, including destruction of one part of the internal nose, either the septum or the turbinates. The most serious complication occurs when the foreign body is pushed back into the choana and is aspirated by the struggling child. As a result, a relatively innocuous nasal foreign body is turned into a very dangerous laryngeal and/or tracheal foreign body.

Some of the more difficult intranasal foreign bodies are seeds, such as lima beans, split peas, or kidney beans. These are quite hard when inserted, but inside the nose the moisture and heat cause swelling of the beans. Whatever space remains in the nose is occupied by the mass, which must be removed piecemeal. In order to do this the child must be asleep under controlled conditions, using a spotlight for adequate visualization. Our practice with foreign bodies in the nose or ear, which are not easily removed on the first attempt, is to wait until a general anesthesia can be obtained. Removal of a foreign body is not an emergency procedure and should not be done in haste in the middle of the night. Under general anesthesia it can be easily performed with minimal physical and psychologic trauma to the child.

Headache

Children are sometimes suspected of having sinusitis or rhinitis because of headache. Although these children should be examined for sinusitis, few will be found to have it. Many of these children have the classical episodic symptoms of migraine headache associated with nausea, vomiting, general malaise, and, occasionally, photic images. A family history of migraine is significant in these children.

Nose Drops

Nose drops are commonly used for the purpose of decongesting the nose and opening the sinus ostia. They are frequently given for many days at a time. At best the effects of nose drops last for approximately an hour or two and after three or four days they are not effective. It is not infrequent for older children to acquire a nose drop "habit." The mucosa becomes so inflamed and swollen that the patient needs nose drops constantly to keep the nasal passages open. Such constant use of nose drops promotes changes in the mucosa. This condition is called rhinitis medicamentosus and is characterized by blue to reddish coloration of the nose and constant clear drainage. The normal mucosa of the nose and sinuses is changed into a polypoid type of mucosa which can no longer properly handle infections. The proper practice advised for nose drops is to use 0.25 percent Neo-Synephrine in normal saline, approximately five drops every two to three hours, for no more than two to three days. If this does not have the desired effect, one has to resort to other methods of treatment of the nasal congestion.

Systemic nasal decongestants can also be used. Their effect, like nose drops, is limited to only a few hours, and they should also be used for only a few days. After this time there is little effect on the nose and it seems pointless to continue such therapy over a prolonged period of time. Furthermore, several of these decongestants have a stimulating effect on the child and they may have other unknown effects.

REFERENCES

Connell, J. T. Effectiveness of topical nasal decongestants. Ann. Allerg., 27:541, 1969.
Kirchner, J. A. Traumatic nasal deformity in the newborn. Arch. Otolaryng., 62:139, 1955.

30.2
THE NASOPHARYNX AND OROPHARYNX

Physiology

The physiology of the naso-oral pharynx is only partially understood. Both the nasal and oral pharynx are essential in the proper production of speech sounds; these are produced by the coordinated activity of the pharyngeal, palatal, and tongue musculature closing and opening the nasopharynx. When these processes are abnormal, as in patients with cleft palate, the proper closing of the nasopharynx is prevented and air escapes through the nose, resulting in the typical nasal speech.

The nasopharynx also is the area in which the eustachian tube opens. Obstruction at the nasopharyngeal end of the eustachian tube, either mechanical or physiologic, causes otitis, which can be either inflammatory, serous, or mucoid and which can result in loss of hearing.

The musculature of the oropharynx plays a significant role in proper swallowing. Paralysis of the musculature of the oropharynx can cause abnormalities in swallowing which can result in aspiration.

The least-understood factor concerning the naso-oral pharynx is the role of the collection of lymphoid tissue which completely encircles the pharynx and is called *Waldeyer's ring*. It consists of the palatine tonsil, lymphoid deposits on the pharyngeal walls, and the lymphoid mass in the nasopharynx called the adenoids and the lingual tonsils. This tissue consists of multiple aggregations of lymphoid germinal cells which proliferate lymphocytes. The lymphoid tissue, small at birth, hypertrophies during the second to sixth year of life, and then gradually atrophies. Adults usually have very small tonsils, an almost undetectable amount of adenoid tissue, and a small amount of lymphoid tissue at the base of the tongue.

It would appear from the histology, growth pattern, and anatomic position that these lymphoid areas should play a role in the development of antibodies to ingested foods, inhalants, and organisms which might cause upper respiratory infections. These lymphoid tissues are found in other mammals but usually not as prominently as in man.

Growth

The naso-oral pharynx continues to grow until puberty. The amount of air space for speech production is variable, depending on the area occupied by the tonsils and adenoids. At puberty the adenoids and tonsils atrophy and the amount of space in the naso-oral pharynx increases. A critical aspect of this is the distance between the posterior end of the soft palate and the anterior portion of the nasopharynx in the posterior pharyngeal wall. If the soft palate cannot close this space during speech, air will escape through the nose and the resultant speech will be hypernasal. The adenoidal mass in the preadolescent fills a large part of this area allowing the soft palate to close it off. It is common to observe marked hypernasal speech or nasal escape following surgical removal of the adenoids. This will usually correct itself spontaneously, but it may require either an operative procedure or a prosthesis to correct the nasal speech.

Congenital Malformations

The most common congenital malformations of the naso-oral pharynx are those associated with *cleft palate*. These malformations occur somewhat more frequently than 1 in 1,000 births and are to some degree hereditary in nature. They can be induced in fetuses of experimental animals by a number of teratogenic agents. However, similar effects have not been documented in human beings.

The problems of cleft palate are described more thoroughly in the chapter on the mouth (see Sec. 28.3). This type of malformation consists of a spectrum of abnormalities, including cleft lip, cleft lip and palate, partial cleft of just the lip or the palate, a bifid uvula, or submucosal cleft of the palate. All of these malformations can be associated with abnormal, hypernasal speech.

Cases of *atresia* of the nasopharynx have been described. *Dermoid cysts* of the nasopharynx are seen at birth and can present as a closure or stricture of the nasopharynx. *Diverticula* of the pharynx are found. They are thought to be secondary to embryonic rests of pharyngeal tissue. If posterior, they will occur in early childhood and can simulate an esophageal atresia.

Growths

The most common growths in the naso-oral pharynx in children are the result of the natural hypertrophy of the tonsils and adenoids. The size of the lymphoid centers can at times fill the entire nasopharynx and/or occlude the upper airway. Juvenile angiofibromas, as previously described, may present as a nasopharyngeal mass. Other masses, such as polyps, can fill the nasopharynx.

Infections

The naso-oral pharynx is infected quite often by viruses and bacteria during childhood. The infant is usually relatively free from upper respiratory infections. The frequency of upper respiratory infections increases at about 2 or 3 years of age, when children start nursery school or in general come into greater contact with other children.

Acute bacterial pharyngitis associated with tonsillitis is characterized by high fever, erythema and pus on the tonsils and pharynx, cervical lymphadenopathy, and, on occasion, edema of the pharynx. The tonsils and pharyngeal walls are often speckled with white circular purulent areas, which should be cultured since an etiologic diagnosis cannot be made on clinical grounds (see Sec. 14.17). A child may have several episodes of upper respiratory infections each winter and only a few of them may be bacterial and need antibiotic therapy. There is an alarming tendency for many children to be placed on antibacterial therapy at the first sign of an upper respiratory infection, e.g., with a runny nose and mild fever. Some children are actually maintained on antibiotic therapy from October to May for various infections. Many of these are probably viral in nature and such therapy is contraindicated. Indiscriminate use of antibiotics may produce drug sensitivity and the development of resistant strains of bacteria. These consequences can become quite severe and life-threatening when a severe bacterial infection of the pharynx must be treated and the organism is insensitive to the more common antibiotics, and/or the patient is allergic to penicillin, necessitating the use of other antibiotics.

Although rare today, *diphtheria* is still seen occasionally. It is discussed in detail in Section 14.7.

Chronic infections of the pharynx are seen in children. These will usually be manifest by a chronic cervical lymphadenopathy and a granular, scarred appearance of the tonsils. The crypts of the tonsils may be filled with a caseous exudate which can be expressed by pressure on the tongue. The presence of such exudate, however, does not by itself indicate chronic tonsillitis. Most cases of so-called chronic tonsillitis are probably the late result of upper respiratory infections. Occasionally, a tonsil will be found to have an abscess within its cavity. The presence of an abscess in the body of the tonsil is compatible with the diagnosis of chronic tonsillitis.

Although most infections of the pharynx run a benign course and are easily treatable by systemic medication, there are infections whose course is quite serious. These grave infections are really complications of the superficial, mucosal, and lymphoid areas of the pharynx. When the infection escapes the confines of the tonsils or the superficial mucosa of the pharynx and infiltrates the deeper layers of the pharynx, the consequences can be grave.

The most common of these infections are those in the peritonsillar area. A *quinsy*, or *peritonsillar abscess*, presents as a mass on the superior fold of the tonsil, pushing the tonsil down toward the midline and anteriorly. The uvula is pushed away from the side of the infected tonsil. The posterior portion of the soft palate will be swollen. There is usually a collection of pus, from 1 to 5 ml, lying between the superior pillar of the tonsil and the superior portion of the palate. The pus will sometimes also be found within the body of the muscle of the soft palate. If this disease is allowed to go untreated, the abscess can perforate spontaneously. The pus can be aspirated into the lung or perforate into the deep structures of the neck and spread to the mediastinum. The treatment for peritonsillar abscess is proper antibiotic therapy and incision and drainage.

An acute pharyngitis and/or tonsillitis can also become a parapharyngeal or a posterior *pharyngeal abscess*. A collection of pus accumulates in the deep structures of the neck, either in the parapharyngeal area or the posterior pharyngeal area, and forms characteristically a mass in the neck. It also causes marked trismus due to involvement of the pterygoid muscles. The problem of rupture is very much the same as in peritonsillar abscess, except that the abscess ruptures more often into the neck with the resultant drainage into the mediastinum. A rare consequence of deep neck abscess is rupture of the carotid artery with bleeding from the ear.

Another serious complication of infection of the naso-oral pharynx is airway obstruction. An acute tonsillitis or acute pharyngitis may occlude the airway and make it quite difficult for the child to breathe. Only rarely, however, is either intubation or tracheostomy required.

Infectious mononucleosis (Sec. 14.30) is the cause of an inflammatory response in the naso-oral pharynx, especially the oropharynx. It is common to see cases of extreme tonsillar hypertrophy in patients with this disease, which is one of the few causes of spontaneous hemorrhage from the tonsils. The size of the tonsils can be so great in mononucleosis that a tracheostomy is needed in order to maintain a proper airway.

Trauma

The most common form of injury to the naso-oral pharynx is surgical trauma with bleeding, which must by controlled by suture and/or packing. The patient may be gravely ill, and much of the blood may have been swallowed. Occasionally, usually following automobile accidents, trauma to the neck will cause damage to the pharynx, especially the oropharynx. This is the type of trauma usually found in the deep neck which can result in aneurysms of the carotid artery and fractures of the mandible and maxilla protruding into the pharynx.

Manifestations of Systemic Disease

Chronic infections of the naso-oral pharynx may be the presenting complaint of patients with a variety of systemic diseases. Children with hypogammaglobulinemia are prone to infections of the naso-oral pharynx usually manifested by an increased incidence of tonsillitis or pharyngitis. The established relationship between rheumatic fever and streptococcal infections involves primarily infections of the naso-oral pharynx. Sickle-cell disease also can be manifested by repeated infections of the naso-oral pharynx.

Tonsillitis and Tonsil Surgery

Each year in the United States many hundreds of thousands of tonsillectomies are performed upon children. Many of these tonsillectomies are performed needlessly.

Tonsillectomy is an operation that has been performed ever since the beginning of recorded medical history. The indications for tonsillectomy are relatively straightforward and the dangers inherent in the operation including the psychologic trauma are also well known. The physician must weigh the risks as well as the potential benefits and decide which children should be candidates for this type of procedure.

The indications for tonsillectomy are chronic airway obstruction, pulmonary hypertension, severe and chronic tonsillitis, and/or peritonsillar abscess. Some tonsils are so enlarged that they obstruct the upper airway. Sometimes the tonsils as well as the adenoids will obstruct the upper airway enough to cause pulmonary hypertension. Once a child has had a peritonsillar abscess which has had to be incised and drained, it is likely that the tonsils are so diseased

that removal is recommended to prevent recurrence of the infection.

The problem of defining chronic tonsillitis is more difficult. At one extreme, the child who has three or four tonsillar infections each year does not have chronic tonsillitis and does not need a tonsillectomy. At the other extreme of this spectrum is the child who continually has infected tonsils from which pus can be expressed, who has severe cervical lymphadenopathy with spiking temperatures and who, even in the face of good antibiotic therapy, maintains the chronic infection. This child would benefit from a tonsillectomy. The line between chronic tonsillitis and numerous upper respiratory infections is a fine one requiring careful weighing of surgical risk as against expected benefit.

Tonsillectomy is a dangerous operation; it is essentially an operation on the vascular system within the airway with minimal control of bleeding and with a high probability of aspiration. Removal of the tonsils has been associated with a relatively high morbidity consisting of secondary infections and postoperative bleeding and an alarmingly high mortality. Various estimates are given for the number of deaths from tonsillectomy each year and a reasonable estimate may be no more than 1 in 1,000 and perhaps no less than 1 in 10,000. As noted in previous paragraphs, the palatine tonsils are just part of Waldeyer's ring, a circumferential deposit of lymphoid tissue. The function of this lymphoid tissue is not known. It is believed that it may have some connection with antibody response to foreign particles that are ingested or aspirated; however, this hypothesis is only speculative. We know from experience that it is quite easy to survive without tonsils, as many people have had their tonsils removed and have done quite well. However, numerous studies have shown that removal of tonsils in a large population of children does not significantly decrease the number of cases of infection that the children will develop. Also, most studies have shown that tonsillectomy does not affect the incidence of rheumatic fever.

It has also been well documented that the removal of tonsils during an epidemic of poliomyelitis will increase the frequency and the severity of paralysis in those children in whom the tonsils have been removed. Certainly at present a tonsillectomy should not be performed if the child has not had proper immunization against poliomyelitis.

The adverse psychologic effect of tonsillectomy has been discussed extensively and constitutes a contraindication that cannot be overemphasized.

The problem of removing the adenoids is somewhat different. The adenoids will block the eustachian tubes and will contribute to ear infection and, most importantly, to the problems of fluid in the ears which cause chronic hearing loss. The adenoids can also effectively block the choanae and cause rhinitis and sinusitis. In well-documented cases of mucoid otitis media, chronic otitis media, rhinitis, and sinusitis, adenoidectomy should be performed. The adenoidectomy, however, need not always be done in conjunction with a tonsillectomy. These are two independent procedures, for which there are very different indications.

The primary complication arising from an adenoidectomy is bleeding from the adenoid bed. This bleeding is controlled by a posterior pack which should be kept in place for 12 to 24 hours following such bleeding. The morbidity and mortality from adenoidectomy appears to be significantly less than that from tonsillectomy. However, the adverse psychologic effects may not be similarly reduced.

In summary, the indications for tonsillectomy are straightforward and few. Tonsillectomy is a dangerous procedure and should only be considered after weighing the possible benefit to the child. It is the feeling of this author that many tonsillectomies are performed for the wrong reasons. The rationale for an adenoidectomy is different from that of a tonsillectomy. The morbidity and mortality is much less than that of tonsillectomy. Consideration must be given again, however, to the operative risk versus the benefit to the patient. In addition, the speech must be checked before adenoidectomy is decided upon, for hypernasal speech may result secondary to adenoidectomy in a child with a submucosal cleft palate, bifid uvula, or a foreshortened palate. In too many instances children who have had adenoidectomies suffer postoperatively from significant speech defects which can only be corrected by secondary operations.

REFERENCES

RETROPHARYNGEAL ABSCESS

Greenwald, H. M., and Messeloff, C. R. Retropharyngeal abscess in infants and children. Amer. J. Med. Sci., 177:767, 1929.

McLean, S., and von Hofe, F. H. Retropharyngeal lymphadenitis in infancy and early childhood. Amer. J. Med. Sci., 169:543, 1925.

TONSILS AND ADENOIDS

Anderson, J. A. Poliomyelitis and recent tonsillectomy. J. Pediat., 27:68, 1945.

Anderson, G. W., and Rondeau, J. L. Absence of tonsils as a factor in the development of bulbar poliomyelitis. J.A.M.A., 155:1123, 1954.

Berner, R. E. Hazards of adenotonsillectomy in the child with cleft palate. J.A.M.A., 181:558, 1962.

Bolande, R. P. Ritualistic surgery—circumcision and tonsillectomy. New Eng. J. Med., 280, No. 11:591, 1969.

Chamovitz, R., Rammelkamp, C. H., Jr., Wannamaker, L. W., and Denny, F. W., Jr. The effect of tonsillectomy on the incidence of streptococcal respiratory disease and its complications. Pediatrics, 26:355, 1960.

Downes, J. Changes in the risk of tonsillectomy over the period 1880–1949. Milbank Mem. Fund Quart., 32:22, 1954.

Evans, H. E. Tonsillectomy and adenoidectomy. Clin. Pediat., 7:71, 1968.

Francis, T., Jr., Krill, C. F., Toomey, J. A., and Mack, W. N. Poliomyelitis following tonsillectomy in five members of a family. J.A.M.A., 119:1392, 1942.

Kaiser, A. D. Relation of tonsils and adenoids to infections in children based on a control study of 4,400 children over a ten-year period. Amer. J. Dis. Child., 41:568, 1931.

——— Significance of tonsils in the development of the child. J.A.M.A., 115:1151, 1940.

——— The tonsil and adenoid problem. In Kelly, J. C., ed. Brennemann, Practice of Pediatrics. Hagerstown, Md., W. F. Prior Co., Vol. 2, Chap. 40, 1948.

Koburg, E. Cell production and cell migration in the tonsil. In Cottier, H., ed. Germinal Centers and Immune Responses. Berlin, Springer Verlag, 1966.

Lewis, E. E. Variations of the incidence of surgery. New Eng. J. Med., 281:880, 1969.

Mertz, J. C. Tonsillectomy and respiratory illness in populations of two communities in N.Y. State. Milbank Mem. Fund Quart., 32:5, 1954.

Paton, J. H. P. The tonsil-adenoid operation in relation to the health of a group of school girls. Quart. J. Med., 12:119, 1943.

Proctor, D. F. The tonsils and adenoids in childhood. Springfield, Ill., Charles C Thomas, Publ., 1960.

Tate, N. Death from tonsillectomy. Lancet, 2:1090, 1963.

Top, F. H. Occurrence of poliomyelitis in relation to tonsillectomies at various intervals. J.A.M.A., 60:534, 1952.

VELOPHARYNGEAL INCOMPETENCE

Stool, S. E., Graham, W., and Randal, P. Velopharyngeal incompetence: pseudomental retardation and its consequence. Clin. Pediat., 8:42, 1969.

chapter 31

THE EAR

ROBERT J. RUBEN, Associate Editor

31.1
PHYSIOLOGY

The ear serves as the entry for sound to the child and it is through his ability to hear that the child learns language and is able to learn to speak. A child with impaired hearing may either suffer from only a small decrease in verbal intelligence or may appear to be mentally retarded. Many hearing problems are remediable or curable and proper treatment can have profound effects on the child's intellectual and total development.

The ear is also a frequent site of infection in infants and children and extension of infections from the ear, especially to the central nervous system, may lead to very serious, sometimes fatal, disease.

Outer Ear

The outer ear consists of the pinna and the external auditory canal; the latter serves primarily as a funnel through which airborne sound reaches the middle ear. The pinna serves in some ways as a collector for sound but it is of little physiologic significance. A normal pinna has considerable cosmetic importance. Children lacking a proper pinna will often suffer at the hands of their peers and may have severe psychologic problems as a result.

The function of the external canal is to provide and maintain an airway to the middle ear. The external canal secretes a wax called cerumen. Under normal circumstances, this cerumen is cleared by itself from the ear; when it accumulates, it can block the canal and cause a hearing loss.

Middle Ear

The middle ear is of prime importance as an acoustic transformer. It consists of the tympanic membrane; three small bones called the *malleus, incus,* and *stapes;* and two small muscles, the stapedius which is attached to the stapes and the tensor tympani which is attached to the malleus. The drum and the ossicles serve as the hydraulic transformer. The sound waves travel from the drum through the ossicles to the oval window. The latter consists of the footplate of the third little bone called the stapes. There is a surface ratio of approximately 18:1. This means that each unit of sound arriving at the small stapes has been magnified 18 times during its course through the middle ear. There is also a small lever ratio contributed by the ossicles; it amounts to approximately 1:1.2. This transformer amplification of sound is required because the inner ear is based on fluid transmission. The airborne sound must be increased in intensity to compensate for the loss due to the air fluid interface. Any interruption of the ossicular chain will result in a diminution of the amount of sound transmitted into the inner ear. An increase of mass, the breaking of an ossicle, or a change in the elasticity can produce such losses in sound transmission through the middle ear.

The middle ear cavity is lined with respiratory mucosa which comprises both mucoid secretory cells and cilia. This mucosa may become inflamed and excrete mucus and pus. Mucus and pus in the middle ear cavity cause a dampening effect upon the ossicles and a decrease in transmission of sound through the middle ear cavity. Under ordinary circumstances the cilia can remove the infected material through the eustachian tube into the nasopharynx, where it is swallowed with other secretions of the oropharynx. If the eustachian tube is blocked by large adenoids, edema, infection, or polyps, the material cannot be excreted. Blockage of the eustachian tube makes it also impossible for air to move in and out of the middle ear. Air in the middle ear will be absorbed by the tissue in the ear and result in negative pressure within the middle ear cavity. The negative pressure causes the tympanic membrane to fold in and results in the excretion of a clear, serous fluid which can turn into a very thick, mucoid type material. The negative pressure also leads to a further decrease in the amount of sound that can be conducted through the middle ear.

The eustachian tube is an essential link in the physiology of the middle ear. As long as the eustachian tube is patent, the patient can control his middle ear pressure. If the pressure becomes too high, the tube will open and equalize it. If the pressure becomes too low, the opening of the tube will, again, equalize the pressure. Opening of the tube may be difficult in infants and young children when the tube is occluded at its nasopharyngeal end by inflammation, especially adenoids when they are chronically infected. If the tube cannot be opened, pressure differentials will be allowed to go unchecked. In children, increased negative middle ear pressure results in the production of a transudate which turns into a thick, gel-like substance. This substance has been given the eponym of "glue ear."

Inner Ear

The inner ear serves as a transducer, changing acoustic energy into a useful biochemical energy which is then transmitted through the nerve of hearing into the central nervous system for comprehension. The cells that serve this function are end state cells and are grouped together under the name of organ of Corti. From animal experimentation, it appears that these cells are produced only once during life and never undergo mitosis again. It is estimated that these cells develop in the human fetus at approximately two-and-one-half months' gestation. After this time the cell differentiates and develops but never divides. If the cell dies it is not replaced.

The organ of Corti is contained in a bony structure called the cochlea and is arranged in a spatial or tonotopic organization. High-frequency tones are heard best toward the base of the cochlea and low-frequency tones are heard best toward the apex of the cochlea. Deficits in the organ of Corti at various places within the cochlea can cause partial to total hearing losses at different frequencies.

The biochemistry of the inner ear is only partly known. Most of the usual enzymes are found. The organ of Corti itself seems to have an increased amount of anaerobic enzymes and appears able to carry on its function for a short period of time in states of reduced oxygen availability.

After the inner ear has transduced the acoustic energy, it is carried along the eighth nerve into the central nervous system. The central nervous system has auditory representations bilaterally. There are numerous crossed and uncrossed auditory pathways.

The patient must have a complete and intact middle ear, inner ear, and eighth nerve and central auditory system in order to be able to respond to sound adequately. Deficiencies anywhere along this pathway will result in decrease in responsivity to sound.

31.2
GROWTH AND DEVELOPMENT

The size of the pinna and external auditory canal grow in relationship to the rest of the head during the first 10 years of life. The tympanic membrane in the young infant is located at an angle somewhat closer to horizontal than vertical; it is brought to a relatively more vertical position as the individual grows to maturity. The middle ear itself, the ossicles, and the inner ear remain the same size as at birth. The mastoid system, which is a group of air cells connected to the middle ear through a single air cell

called the aditus ad antrum, grows during childhood. At birth, the infant has only a single mastoid cell called the antrum. As the child grows, many small cells proliferate and become the mastoid cells. These mastoid cells are all connected to the middle ear. In the mature individual they extend from the mastoid tip, around the sigmoid sinus, under the middle cranial fossa into the zygomatic arch, and reach back into the medial portion of the middle cranial fossa; they also border upon the posterior cranial fossa. The proliferation of these mastoid cells opens up the possibility of infections occurring in juxtaposition to a good portion of the middle cranial and posterior cranial fossae as well as the sigmoid sinus; the anterior cells that proliferate along the zygomatic group juxtapose the carotid artery.

The eustachian tube also changes position throughout life. In the infant, the tube is almost horizontal. As the individual grows, the eustachian tube lies more vertically until it reaches its adult course at an angle approximately 15 degrees from the horizontal, starting at its highest point in the middle ear and extending to the nasopharynx.

31.3
EXAMINATION

Physical examination of the ear in infants and children is difficult. The examination should start with the pinna and posterior mastoid area. The configuration of the pinna should be noted to determine whether all of the landmarks are present including a tragus, a helix, an antihelix, and a lobule. The presence of extra tags of skin or small sinuses should also be noted. The postauricular area, the mastoid area, should be examined for fistulas, swelling, or tenderness. The ear canal itself must be seen to determine if it is patent and to note the condition of the skin. Much time should be spent in examination of the tympanic membrane, which must be viewed clearly. If the canal is filled with cerumen, it is wise to irrigate the canal out gently and then look very carefully. Irrigation should not be done if a perforated tympanic membrane is suspected. It is inadvisable to try to clean the wax out with a curette unless one can do it very skillfully. It usually causes a certain amount of pain and, in the infant or young child, will result in crying. The crying itself will distort the tympanic membrane by causing it to become hyperemic and thick. Since repeated examinations of the tympanic membrane are often necessary, it is important to avoid, if possible, conditioning the infant to the point where he starts crying immediately upon seeing the otoscope.

A normal tympanic membrane is seldom seen as so many have been the site of disease. A normal tympanic membrane is a semitranslucent to transparent, thin, delicate membrane, in the middle of which the malleus can be seen; posteriorly and superiorly the incus and incudal-stapedial joint can also be noted. There should be a triangular light reflex anteriorly, and occasionally a dark shadow can be seen anterosuperiorly and another one posteroinferiorly, representing respectively the eustachian tube and round window. The pars flaccida, which is the upper fifth of the tympanic membrane, should be noted and should be somewhat loose. Occasionally, the chorda tympani can also be seen superiorly. A view of each of these landmarks must be sought. The lack of one of them can mean an abnormal drum. Most drums in children with suspected ear disease are thick; they may either be bulging or retracted. Absence of the translucency of the tympanic membrane indicates some type of disease within either the tympanic membrane or the middle ear itself.

A useful instrument in examination of the ears is the pneumo-otoscope. This is an otoscope that has a sealed head and a small rubber bulb. Air pressure can be gently applied through the ear speculum in the closed pneumatic otoscope. If the drum moves back and forth readily, there is probably no fluid within the middle ear. If the drum does not move back and forth readily, there is a possibility that there is fluid or mucoid material behind the drum, or that the drum itself may be missing.

Examination of the hearing ability in a child depends upon the age of the child. Screening audiometry must be done on all infants and at all routine postnatal visits. This consists of determining whether the child responds to various sounds—made with some keys, a toy whistle, or a horn, on either side of the child's head and outside of the child's field of vision. The test is done with the child in the mother's lap while somebody in front of the examiner distracts the child. If the child does not react properly according to his age level, a possible hearing loss should be suspected. Failure to respond to this screening test, coupled with a history by the parents of lack of responsiveness to sound, should indicate the need for an extensive hearing evaluation of the child.

An extensive hearing evaluation is done in an audiometric setting where a trained audiologist and a technician watch the child's responses to sound under controlled conditions. This testing also has its limitations and if the tests do not show that the child has hearing within normal range, an even more extensive work-up using auditory evoked potentials should be contemplated. This test uses a potential evoked through an auditory stimulus, recorded by electroencephalography, to determine the hearing threshold of the child. Reports from some centers indicate a relatively good correlation with the child's hearing. In children with defective hearing, follow-up studies have been relatively good. However, even after extensive testing with auditory evoked potentials and other special instruments, some question may remain concerning the degree of a young infant's hearing loss. In some of these instances, a hearing loss is assumed, and the child is managed appropriately with the use of hearing aids and an infant auditory training program.

Older children may be tested by more conventional means. Toddlers from one and a half to three years of age can be tested by conditioned audiometry. The child is taught a game. Every time he hears the signal, he either puts a block in a box or takes another ring off a dowel. Using this method, an audiogram can be constructed to assess the presence and extent of hearing loss.

Audiograms are usually reported in terms of air conduction, bone conduction and, if the child has acquired language, in terms of word discrimination. If the air conduction is within normal range, the hearing is normal. If the air conduction is low but bone conduction is normal, there is some type of conductive loss, indicating some difficulty with the transformer mechanism of the middle ear. These problems are usually remediable with either medical, surgical, or prosthetic treatment. If the bone conduction and air conduction are depressed, the problem may be either within the inner ear or the central nervous system. Many of these problems are usually within the inner ear and also are remediable to a large extent by rehabilitative programs which include the use of infant auditory training and proper selection of hearing aids. As will be pointed out in the following paragraphs, hearing loss in children occurs in association with many other diseases. All children with proved hearing loss must be screened for the more common and the more serious of these diseases. If attention is focused only on the hearing, the diagnosis of other serious disorders may be overlooked.

REFERENCES

Birrell, J. F. Ear, Nose and Throat Diseases of Children. Philadelphia, F. A. Davis Co., 1960.

Eagles, E. L., et al. Hearing sensitivity and related factors in children. Monograph, University of Pittsburgh, Graduate School of Public Health. Laryngoscope, June, 1963.

Jackson, C., and Jackson, C. L. Diseases of the Nose, Throat and Ear. Philadelphia, W. B. Saunders Company, 1959.

McLellan, M. S., and Struck, A. Ear studies in the premature infant: a statistical description of otoscopic landmarks. J. Pediat., 67:122, 1965.

Ruben, R. J. Development of the inner ear of the mouse. Acta Otolaryng. (Stockholm), Supplement 220, 1967.

Shambaugh, G. E., Jr. Surgery of the Ear, 2nd ed. Philadelphia, W. B. Saunders Company, 1967.

Wever, E. G., and Lawrence, M. Physiological Acoustics. Princeton, N.J., Princeton University Press, 1954.

31.4
MALFORMATIONS

The inner ear contains not only the hearing apparatus but also the vestibular apparatus for balance. The latter includes the three *semicircular canals* and the two static organs, the *saccule* and *utricle*. The growth of the entire bony labyrinth, which includes the cochlea, the semicircular canals, and the static organs, is governed by the normal development of the brain stem. When the brain stem develops abnormally, there are usually associated bony abnormalities of the inner ear. These cover a spectrum from complete agenesis of the bony labyrinth to a lack of one semicircular canal or a decreased number of turns in the cochlea. This type of malformation can be diagnosed radiographically using a Townes and Stenver's view. The bony cochlea is easily visualized in the infant and young child, as it calcifies very early in comparison to the rest of the cranium. It is important to look for malformations of the bony labyrinth in all cases of suspected hearing loss. If such malformations exist, the clinician should consider the strong possibility that there are also malformations of the central nervous system.

These malformations are not common and probably account for only a small number of cases of congenital deafness. The commonest lesion of the inner ear resulting in deafness is the loss of the cells of the organ of Corti. The greatest number of the cells in the inner ear are end state cells. These cells are most likely laid down at two-and-one-half-month gestation time. If any disease process, either genetic, such as Waardenburg's disease, or acquired, such as rubella, interferes and destroys these cells, no new cells will develop. There will, however, be complete normal growth of the bony labyrinth. The absence of these cells cannot be detected radiographically but must be assumed once deafness is proved by clinical means using hearing tests, examination, and history.

The middle ear is subject to many types of malformations that cause a conductive hearing loss, which can be corrected either by surgical repair of the middle ear or by the use of hearing aids. Middle ear malformations run a spectrum from aplasias of the middle ear with small remnants of ossicles, as found in the Treacher-Collins syndrome, to relatively minor malformations which just cause fixation of one or two ossicles. In many cases, there is either no tympanic membrane or it has not differentiated completely and the external canal is still closed by a bony plate. Malformations of the middle ear are frequently found in conjunction with malformations of the first two branchial arches, expressed as major and minor malformations of the face and palate. The malleus and part of the incus derive from Meckel's cartilage, which is a part of the first branchial arch. The stapes comes from Reichert's cartilage, which is part of the second branchial arch. Whenever malformations such as cleft palate, bifid nose, and a small mandible are present, the possibility of a middle ear malformation with subsequent conductive hearing loss should be suspected.

Malformations in the middle ear are usually associated with malformations of the external ear. The latter include a wide variety of malformations ranging from minor deviations of the pinna to complete absence of the pinna, as well as abnormal tags of skin in and around the area of the pinna. These deformities of the external ear are frequently associated with gross kidney malformations such as horseshoe kidney or agenesis of one kidney. It is advisable to obtain an intravenous excretory urogram on all children with pinna malformations and/or middle ear malformations.

The presence of congenital middle ear malformations may make the diagnosis of ear infections difficult. Infections of the middle ear present with pain, decreased hearing loss, and discharge from the ear. Infection is very difficult to diagnose in an ear that already has a conductive hearing loss and in which there is no drum to perforate and no canal through which discharge can come. There have been reports of cases of meningitis and cholesteatoma secondary to infections in ears that have congenital middle ear malformations. Occult middle ear infections should be considered in patients with congenital middle ear malformations who have fever of unknown origin.

REFERENCES

MIDDLE EAR MALFORMATIONS

Altmann, F. Malformations of the auricle and external auditory meatus: a critical review. Arch. Otolaryng., 54:115, 1951.
——— Malformations of the eustachian tube, middle ear and its appendages: a critical review. Arch. Otolaryng., 54:241, 1951.
Ruben, R. J., Toriyama, M., Dische, M. R., Bransilver, B., and Daly, J. F. External and middle ear malformations associated with mandibulo-facial dysostosis and renal abnormalities: a case report. Ann. Otol., 78, No. 3, p. 605, 1969.

31.5
INHERITED DISEASES

It is believed that approximately 50 percent of all deafness is inherited. The number of inherited diseases of the ear, with or without other affected associated organ systems, is extremely large. Any child with a hearing loss, especially those affecting the inner ear, should be considered as a possible genetic problem if no acquired cause is found.

Inherited disorders of the outer and middle ear are usually associated with other craniofacial malformations. One of the most common of these is the Treacher-Collins syndrome which is inherited as an autosomal dominant with incomplete penetrance. This condition consists of a small mandible, small maxilla, absence of the eyelashes on the lower lids, down-slanting eyes, and rather typical abnormal facial expression. These children may also have associated gross renal anomalies such as a horseshoe kidney or agenesis of one kidney. Middle ear malformations are also commonly found in this group. Other autosomal dominant inherited diseases, such as Apert's disease and Crouzon's disease, have associated middle ear malformations.

Otosclerosis is another common disease of the middle ear. It is an autosomal dominant disease which has variable penetrance. The disease is characterized by gradual loss of hearing which can be either conductive, conductive and nonconductive, or completely nonconductive. The onset is usually not until the third or fourth decade of life. However, it is occasionally seen in young children and should be suspected in a child with middle ear hearing loss and a positive family history for the condition.

The various mucopolysaccharidoses (Sec. 8.13) may also result in middle ear hearing loss because of the excessive secretion of mucoid fluid within the middle ear.

Osteogenesis imperfecta (van der Hoeve's syndrome) is an autosomal dominant disease with a variable penetrance affecting elastic tissues; it is also associated with a high incidence of hearing loss and tinnitus. The losses may be either conductive, nonconductive, or mixed.

Hearing loss with middle ear malformations has been associated with cardiac malformation. Children with any type of inherited hearing loss, whether in the middle ear or inner ear, should have a cardiac evaluation including electrocardiogram to rule out associated cardiac anomalies.

Inherited diseases of the inner ear are also numerous. One of the most common, perhaps because of its easy identification, is the Waardenburg's syndrome. This is an autosomal dominant inherited disease with variable penetrance. The full syndrome consists of bilateral, nonconductive deafness, a white forelock of hair, heterochromia of the iris, a widened distance between the eyes, and an antimongoloid slant to the eyes. The syndrome can and does occur in all combinations and permutations. Children may be seen who are bilaterally deaf and who have only an increased distance between the eyes; others are deaf in one ear and have a white forelock. It is imperative to question and to examine all relatives in any family in which inherited hearing loss is known or suspected.

The Jervell, Lange-Nielsen syndrome is an autosomal recessive disease associated with inner ear deafness. It is characterized by severe hearing loss accompanied by a cardiac conduction defect associated with a prolonged QT interval in the electrocardiogram. These patients have been reported to have multiple episodes of syncope; unexpected death occurs in the teens. It is felt the syncopal episodes are attributed to atrial fibrillation and the sudden death to a ventricular fibrillation. This condition provides a striking example of why all children with suspected hearing loss should have electrocardiograms.

Alport's disease is an extremely important inherited disease which is most likely inherited as an autosomal dominant with variable penetrance and which occurs primarily in males. It results in a progressive inner ear hearing loss, usually beginning at the end of the first decade. However, progressive glomerulitis rather than hearing loss is the most important aspect of the disease. The first symptoms and signs are either a gradual high-frequency hearing loss in a child who is found to have microscopic hematuria, or microscopic or gross hematuria in a child who is found to have hearing loss. The renal disease progresses, especially in boys, to death from renal insufficiency (Sec. 22.12). There are other associated nephropathies with hearing loss and it is most important that all children with progressive hearing loss be rigidly screened for renal disease. Screening programs have invariably revealed a number of children with both hearing loss and the beginnings of renal involvement.

These are only a few ear diseases that are inherited. As investigations progress, it is probable that anomalies associated with deafness syndromes will be found in increasing numbers. However, there are still many patients who are either born without hearing or who have progressive disease for which no specific etiologic factor is found. It is known that each individual probably carries a number of deafness genes. The probability that both parents may have the same deafness gene is small but very real. Thus, whenever a child with sporadic deafness is seen and there is no history of either acquired or inherited disease, the deafness is thought to be genetic in origin. The family must be apprised of this possibility when planning to have other children.

31.6
GROWTHS

Tumors of the external, middle, and internal ears are not rare in children, but fortunately, they are seldom malignant. The most common growth found in the external auditory canal in children is the *aural polyp*. This mass of loose connective tissue, usually arising from the drum will often grow out from the middle ear mucosa through a perforation in the tympanic membrane and fill the canal. The polyp must be surgically removed and the middle ear and the mastoid explored, to rule out other more serious conditions. An aural polyp is usually indicative of either cholesteatoma or chronic mastoid disease.

The most dangerous among the common growths of the ear in children are those found in the middle ear and the mastoid. These growths are called *cholesteatomas* and consist of epithelial sacs which fill with debris. The sacs will grow and secrete large amounts of collagenase which causes the neighboring bone to be absorbed. Cholesteatomas are usually associated with chronic suppuration of the ear, especially with pseudomonas or other infections of the external canal and mastoid. The growth of cholesteatomas causes bony destruction of the middle ear with first a conductive hearing loss and purulent discharge, and then facial nerve paralysis; permanent inner ear loss; epidural, subdural, or brain abscess; and meningitis. There also can be thrombosis of the sigmoid sinus and drainage into the deep spaces of the neck. Cholesteatoma is the most dangerous condition seen in the middle ears of children.

Cholesteatomas are classified into three groups. The least common are the *congenital cholesteatomas*, which probably start as rests of epithelial cells. These can grow behind the drum or as part of the temporal bone. They are not necessarily associated with perforations and in many instances they present as a brain tumor, or as another primary childhood tumor of the temporal bone, the eosinophilic granuloma. However, the latter usually appears as multiple defects in the temporal bone and is not often confused with primary cholesteatoma.

There are two groups of acquired cholesteatoma, those with, and those without perforation of the tympanic membrane. Those without a perforation of the tympanic membrane, called primary acquired cholesteatomas, can present as a small outpouching of the epithelium of the pars flaccida behind the tympanic membrane. They can be quite small and cause no apparent harm in the beginning. They can be diagnosed early and should be removed before they cause wider and irreparable destruction.

The *secondary acquired cholesteatomas* associated with tympanic membrane perforations are by far the most common. The perforations of the tympanic membrane will usually be in the posterior superior surface. The perforation can be very small. Typically, one sees a small dimpling with some mucopurulent discharge and small, white, flaky material coming out from the posterior superior portion of the tympanic membrane. These patients have a hearing loss, usually conductive, but they may have a total loss of hearing secondary to labyrinthine involvement. These cholesteatomas may be confined to a sac but, in many instances, they will have left the sac and penetrated all the cells in the mastoid. These cholesteatomas must be completely removed as soon as they are diagnosed in order to prevent the more serious sequelae of brain abscess, cavernous sinus thrombosis, facial nerve paralysis, and deafness.

There are two rare growths associated with the ear. *Monostotic fibrous dysplasia* can start in any bone in the facial complex and grow into the mastoid bone. This growth usually causes a sealing off of the middle ear and tympanic membrane. The squamous cells of the tympanic membrane then form cholesteatomas and there is both a hearing loss and chronic drainage from the ear. The squamous cells must be removed so that the cholesteatomas cannot recur as the bone grows. *Acoustic neuroma,* a rare tumor of the auditory nerve as it passes from the brain stem into the internal auditory meatus, usually begins its growth in the inferior portion of the eighth nerve, which is the vestibular portion. It then progresses and will destroy the cochlear division of the eighth nerve and the facial nerve which runs in the same canal. Tumors of the eighth nerve present in a child as unsteadiness, nystagmus, and loss of hearing. In addition there is an inability to discriminate speech, which is much worse than one would expect from the loss of hearing. These tumors are seldom diagnosed as early in children as they are in adults. Any child with a history of unilateral hearing loss should be considered as possibly having an acoustic neuroma. Since these tumors are seen most commonly in association with von Recklinghausen's neurofibromatosis, a family history and examination for possible café-au-lait marking or other stigmata of this disease are indicated in any child with unilateral hearing loss.

31.7
INFECTIONS

Otitis Externa

The external ear is most commonly affected by otitis externa, which is seen most frequently in children from five years of age until young adulthood. It occurs especially in the summer months with swimming and maceration of the ear by water, with secondary infection by either staphylococcus or, in many cases, pseudomonas. The ear canal is swollen and discharges purulent material. A quasi pathognomonic sign is elicited by gently palpating the tragus; if this procedure causes pain, the diagnosis of external otitis can be made almost with certainty. Occasionally what appears to be only a chronic external otitis is in fact a manifestation of mastoiditis with infection coming from the drum and macerating the external canal.

The treatment for otitis externa is in two steps. The usual practice is first to apply Burow's solution (aluminum acetate) in a cotton wick in the external canal for 24 hours. This irrigation reduces the swelling, changes the pH which helps combat the pseudomonas infection, and also greatly relieves the pain. The external canal is then treated with local application of an antibiotic in combination with an adrenocortical steroid. This topical medication is given every three to four hours. Most cases of external otitis should resolve within two to five days. If not, another cause such as foreign body or middle ear infection should be suspected.

Viral diseases of the external auditory meatus in children are rare. The most common syndrome is the Ramsey-Hunt syndrome, due to herpes zoster virus involving vesicles on the external canal and drum and associated with facial nerve paralysis.

Otitis Media

The most common ear infection in childhood is probably simple otitis media. Many children have one or two episodes of otitis media each year. The most common organisms causing otitis media are pneumococcus and *H. influenzae*. These two organisms are treated quite well with penicillin and ampicillin. With proper treatment there will be no spontaneous drainage from the ear in most cases of otitis media. Occasionally there will be a spontaneous perforation into the canal. The majority of cases of otitis media resolve well on antibiotic therapy and need no surgical intervention or any further medication. Occasionally, the otitis media will not resolve and the child will be left with a bulging, painful drum. In rare instances where there is acute pain and high fever, a myringotomy under a general anesthetic is indicated to decompress the abscess, to relieve the pain, and also to obtain a culture.

The usual case of bacterial otitis media will resolve in approximately one week and the drum will return to normal within two to three weeks following the infection. However, in many instances a fluid is left in the ear which coalesces and becomes very thick and viscous. This condition is sometimes referred to as "glue ear"; it may result in a hearing loss which may not be suspected by the parent. This type of hearing loss, secondary to the mucoid secretion of the middle ear, can cause significant hearing impairment to the child and result in language retardation. The ears should be checked very carefully after otitis media to make sure the drum has returned to normal within two to three weeks. If there is any doubt, an audiogram should be done. Children in whom a conductive loss is persisting three to four weeks after otitis media, should be considered as possible candidates for removal of the thick mucoid material from the middle ear.

The most common complication of otitis media is that of tympanomastoiditis. More rare complications are those of labyrinthitis, facial nerve paralysis, or meningitis.

Mastoiditis

Diseases of the mastoids fall into three categories: acute, semiacute, and chronic. *Acute mastoiditis* is a rare disease. However, in a large hospital setting it is seen approximately once or twice a year. The patient, usually a young child under 3 years of age, presents with a history of drainage from the ear, pain, temperature, and retroauricular swelling which deflects the external ear downward and laterally. The swelling consists of a collection of pus which has broken through the mastoid air cells, underneath the temporalis fascia. This pus must be incised and drained, and the smaller mastoid air cells must be opened to remove the remainder of the pus. The proper therapy requires systemic antibiotics in addition to surgical incision and drainage of the abscess.

Semiacute mastoiditis. This condition usually develops in young children with a history of ear infection several weeks before the onset of signs of mastoid disease. The ear may or may not be draining and the drum may or may not show fluid behind it. What appears to happen in many of these cases is that the single air cell leading from the mastoid into the middle ear, called the aditus ad antrum, becomes distended with either swollen mucosa, pus, or dead cellular debris. The infection causes death of bone and mucosa and a breakdown of the natural barriers from the mastoid into the surrounding structures. These children will complain of tenderness behind the ear. They may have meningitis, epidural or subdural brain abscess, or they may present with meningismus. The diagnosis is sometimes difficult as the ear findings may be nonspecific. Radiographic examination of the mastoid is very important in these cases. It shows cloudiness of the entire mastoid with loss of detail of the septa of the small mastoid cells. Treatment includes exenteration of the infected cells, removal of pus and granulation from the dural spaces and adjacent areas, and systemic antibiotics in high dosages.

Chronic mastoiditis. Individuals in this group have had repeated episodes of otitis media and have developed chronic mastoiditis, which is a chronic osteomyelitis. There are many forms of this disease. One specific type is called necrotizing otitis media which is usually caused by streptococcal infection of the middle ear. Patients with chronic mastoid disease have chronically draining ears with either small or large perforations. They have conductive hearing losses and may have other signs of complications of mastoiditis. These ears not only need a mastoidectomy with removal of the infected mastoid bone, but also tympanoplasty wtih reconstruction of both the tympanic membrane and the hearing apparatus in the middle ear.

Mastoid infection is still a common disease in children. Except in rare families with genetic predisposition to mastoid disease, or in patients with cleft palate, or other underlying anomalies, mastoid disease could be prevented. Closer follow-up of children with acute otitis media, the use of myringotomy to remove thick fluid in children with chronic mucoid otitis media, and the early recognition of tympanic membrane perforation would help in decreasing the number of children with mastoid disease.

Inner Ear Infections

The inner ear is affected by both viral and bacterial disease. The most common viral disease of the inner ear is mumps. The mumps virus can cause total deafness in one or, occasionally, both ears.

Mumps is one of the most common causes of unilateral acquired deafness in children. However, any unilateral acquired deafness has to be investigated for the possibility of tumor. To assume that all cases of unilateral deafness are secondary to mumps will result in overlooking an occasional tumor or an inherited disease characterized by unilateral deafness.

Acute purulent labyrinthitis and loss of hearing due to bacterial destruction of the inner ear are uncommon. Bacteria can invade the inner ear through an otitis media extending through either the round window or the oval window. Meningitis can also cause labyrinthitis with bacteria invading through the internal auditory meatus, the endolymphatic duct and sac, or the perilymphatic aqueduct. Labyrinthitis will not only produce symptoms of hearing loss but also symptoms of gross vestibular loss, including marked dizziness and nystagmus.

Petrositis

ARNOLD H. EINHORN

The petrous pyramid, which contains the labyrinth, gradually becomes pneumatized after the first year of life; by the age of 4 this process is usually complete, the cancellous bone being replaced by air cells lined with mucous membrane which communicate with those of the mastoid process. Prior to its pneumatization, infection of the pyramid is extremely rare. After the fourth year, however, suppuration in the pyramid is encountered, nearly always as a result of extension of a mastoid infection.

The clinical picture of petrositis usually develops two to four weeks after an attack of otitis media, sometimes even in spite of mastoidectomy. The most characteristic symptom is deep orbital pain, often intermittent. The development of such pain with low-grade sepsis and a persistent mastoid or aural discharge is sufficient to make the diagnosis; involvement of the sixth nerve, causing weakness or paralysis of the external rectus, occurs in about one-third of the cases. It is an indication of involvement of the apex of the pyramid. The combination of abducens palsy, orbital pain, and aural discharge is known as the *Gradenigo syndrome*. At times other symptoms are encountered; there may be transient facial paralysis or vestibular symptoms—vertigo, nystagmus nausea, and vomiting. The location of the pain may be atypical.

In some instances the process subsides without further surgical intervention, but such a favorable outcome cannot be counted on, for there is great likelihood that the infection will extend to the superior petrosal or cavernous sinuses, causing septic thrombosis, or will perforate the dura, leading to meningitis or brain abscess. Such perforation is usually followed by relief from pain and may be mistaken for improvement. A generalized meningitis may be localized, the spinal fluid showing a moderate polymorphonuclear reaction without organisms.

If there are evidences of petrositis, surgical advice should be sought at once. Considerable help can often be obtained from roentgenograms. Drainage of the pyramid is usually indicated, a procedure which can as a rule be accomplished without destruction of the labyrinth. The incidence of petrositis has diminished greatly with the use of antibiotics.

REFERENCES

OTITIS EXTERNA

Perry, E. T. The Human Ear Canal. Springfield, Ill., Charles C Thomas, Publisher, 1957.
Senturia, B. H. Diffuse external otitis: pathogenesis and treatment. Laryngoscope, 65:313, 1955.

OTITIS MEDIA

Brennemann, J. Otitis media as a pediatrician sees it. J.A.M.A., 97:449, 1931.
Coffey, J. D., Jr., Booth, N. H., and Martin, A. D. Otitis media in the practice of pediatrics. Pediatrics, 28:25, 1966.
Friedmann, I. Pathology of otitis media. J. Clin. Path., 9:229, 1956.
——— The pathology of secretory otitis media. Proc. Roy. Soc. Med., 56, No. 8, 695, 1963.
Gronroos, J. A., Leena, V., Salmivalli, A., and Berglund, B. Coexisting viral (respiratory syncytial) and bacterial (pneumococcus) otitis media in children. Acta Otolaryng. (Stockholm), 65:505, 1968.
Harrison, K. Exudated otitis media in children (the glue ear). Practitioner, 159:744, 1967.
Holm, V. A., and Kunze, L. V. H. Effect of chronic otitis media on language and speech development. Pediatrics, 43:833, 1969.
House, H. P., Linthicum, F. H., and Johnson, E. W. Current management of hearing loss in children. Amer. J. Dis. Child., 108:677, 1964.
Howie, V. M., Ploussard, K. A., and Lefter, R. L. Otitis media: a clinical and bacterial correlation. Pediatrics, 45:29, 1970.
Olmstead, R. W. A study of the pattern of hearing in children following acute otitis media. Amer. J. Dis. Child., 100:772, 1960.
——— Alvarez, M. C., Moroney, J. D., and Eversden, M. Pattern of hearing following acute otitis media. J. Pediat., 65:252, 1964.
Paradise, J. L., Bluestone, C. D., and Felder, H. The universality of otitis media in 50 infants with cleft palate. Clin. Pediat., 44:35, 1969.
Samuels, S. S. Secretory otitis media in children. Pediatrics, 15:334, 1955.
Silverstein, H., Bernstein, J. M., and Lerner, P. I. Antibiotic concentrations in middle ear effusions. Pediatrics, 38:33, 1966.
Tilles, J. G., et al. Acute otitis media. Serologic studies and attempts to isolate viruses and mycoplasmas from aspirated middle ear fluids. New Eng. J. Med., 277:613, 1967.
Towson, E. H. Otitis media in pediatric practice. New York J. Med., 64:1591, 1964.

MASTOIDITIS

Begley, J. W., Jr. Acute and subacute mastoiditis necessitating mastoidectomy in the antibiotic era; report of 10 cases. J. Indiana Med. Ass., 48:496, 1955.

Cone, A. J. Mastoid disease: a critical review. J. Pediat., 11:706, 1937.

Fowler, E. P., Jr., and Swenson, P. C. Petrositis: roentgenologic and pathologic correlation. Amer. J. Roentgen., 41:317, 1939.

Shambaugh, G. E., Jr. Surgery of the Ear, 2nd ed. Philadelphia, W. B. Saunders Company, 1967.

PETROSITIS

Fowler, E. P., Jr., and Swenson, P. C. Petrositis: a roentgenologic and pathologic correlation. Amer. J. Roentgen., 41:317, 1939.

Symposium: Certain fundamentals in regard to suppuration of the petrosal pyramid. Ann. Otol., 44:1002, 1935.

31.8
TRAUMA

The external ear is exposed to blunt trauma. Repeated blows to the external ear may cause hematomas. These hematomas can become infected and result in a "cauliflower ear." This is occasionally seen in children with the battered child syndrome. Trauma to the external auditory canal is often self-inflicted. Either the child picks the ear or someone has attempted to remove some type of foreign body.

Trauma to the middle ear comes about from two main sources. The first is iatrogenic—induced by traumatic removal of a *foreign body* from the external ear. Foreign bodies in the external canals of young children are common; they may include wads of paper, erasers, or insects. These objects should be removed very carefully. Each year in a large medical center several children are seen in whom an attempt to remove a foreign body has caused removal not only of the foregin body but also of the tympanic membrane and most of the ossicles. The child then has a permanent hearing loss. This type of trauma must be avoided. A child with a foreign body in the ear which cannot be removed easily should be anesthetized and the foreign body removed with the use of a microscope or hand otoscope.

The other most common type of trauma to the middle ear is barotrauma. As described previously, the middle ear is very important in regulating pressure mechanisms of the ear. In airplane ascents or descents, or in springboard or scuba diving, the changes in pressure in the middle ear can become much greater than the environmental changes especially in children with large adenoids and poorly functioning eustachian tubes. The ear drum can then be perforated either by negative or positive pressure in the middle ear. These perforations usually heal quite well spontaneously although they are quite painful at the time of perforation. Water should be kept out of any ear with a perforation.

Another form of trauma that affects both the middle and inner ear are fractures of the temporal bone. There are two main types of fractures, both of which are associated with basilar skull fractures. Most fractures of the temporal bone are characterized by hearing loss and the presence of blood behind the drum. The blood can drain into the pharynx through the eustachian tube. Some patients may have marked dizziness if the fracture has gone through the vestibular portion of the inner ear; some may have paralysis of the facial nerve, if the fracture has involved the lower portion of the temporal bone. Longitudinal fractures run in the long axis of the temporal bone. These fractures usually go through the inner ear and result in permanent hearing loss. The transverse fractures go through the short axis of the temporal bone. If these are confincd to the middle ear, they will result only in a conductive hearing loss and, on many occasions, a total or partial facial nerve paralysis. This latter type of fracture should be explored early as the facial nerve will usually contain various fragments of bone and/or middle ear ossicles. The facial nerve can usually be successfully repaired.

Fractures of the temporal bone must be considered similar to skull fractures and treated accordingly. The recommended practice is to observe these patients for any neurologic sequelae. Prophylactic antibiotics are *not* indicated in these cases, unless there is an accompanying otitis media or the child develops otitis media. In this case, a culture is taken and the child is placed on appropriate antibiotic therapy. Fractures of the temporal bone do not heal as other bony fractures do. The fracture heals only by fibrous reunion whch always leaves a potential avenue for bacteria to go from the upper respiratory tract into the meninges. Thus, meningitis secondary to the fracture may develop subsequently, even many years after the fracture has occurred.

31.9
SPECIAL PROBLEMS

Deafness

The ear is one of man's most essential organs. Without hearing a person cannot easily acquire language, which is one of his most valuable attributes. An extremely important aspect of any pediatrician's practice should be a constant awareness of the possibility of hearing loss in any of his patients. Approximately

TABLE 1. *Speech, Language, and Hearing Checklist* *

This checklist outlines behavior that may be expected of a child at various age levels. If he consistently fails to respond as the checklist suggests, he may have a problem that requires further evaluation.

Average Age	Question	Average Behavior
3-6 mo	What does he do when you talk to him?	He should awaken to or quiet at the sound of his mother's voice.
	Does he react to your voice even when he cannot see you?	He should typically turn eyes and head in the direction of the source of sound.
7-10 mo	When he can't see what is happening, what does he do when he hears familiar footsteps . . . the dog barking, the telephone ringing . . . candy paper rattling . . . someone's voice . . . his own name?	He should turn his head and shoulders toward familiar sounds, even when he cannot see what is happening. Such sounds do not have to be loud to cause him to respond.
11-15 mo	Can he point to or find familiar objects or people, when he is asked to? Example: "Where is Jimmy?" "Find the ball."	He should show his understanding of some words by appropriate behavior; for example, by pointing to or looking at familiar objects or people, on request.
	Does he respond differently to different sounds?	He should jabber in response to a human voice, and is apt to cry when there is thunder, or may frown when he is scolded.
	Does he enjoy listening to some sounds and imitating them?	Imitation indicates that he can hear the sounds and match them with his own sound production.
1½ yr	Can he point to parts of his body when you ask him to? Example: "Show me your eyes." "Show me your nose."	Some children begin to identify parts of the body. He should be able to show his nose or eyes.
	How many understandable words does he use— words you are sure really mean something?	He should be using a few single words. They are not complete or pronounced perfectly but are clearly meaningful.
2 yr	Can he follow simple verbal commands when you are careful not to give him any help, such as looking at the object or pointing in the right direction? Example: "Johnny, get your hat and give it to daddy." "Debby, bring me your ball."	He should be able to follow a few simple commands without visual clues.
	Does he enjoy being read to? Does he point out pictures of familiar objects in a book when asked to? Example: "Show me the baby." "Where's the rabbit?"	Most 2-year-olds enjoy being "read to" and shown simple pictures in a book or magazine, and will point out pictures when you ask them to.
	Does he use the names of familiar people and things such as Mommy, milk, ball, and hat?	He should be using a variety of everyday words heard in his home and neighborhood.
	What does he call himself?	He refers to himself by name.
	Is he beginning to show interest in the sound of radio or TV commercials?	Many 2-year-olds do show such interest by word or action.
	Is he putting a few words together to make little sentences? Example: "Go bye-bye car." "Milk all gone."	These sentences are not usually complete or grammatically correct.
2½ yr	Does he know a few rhymes or songs? Does he enjoy hearing them?	Many children can say or sing short rhymes or songs and enjoy listening to records or to mother singing.
	What does he do when the ice cream man's bell rings, out of his sight, or when a car door or house door closes at a time when someone in the family usually comes home?	If a child has good hearing, and these are events that bring him pleasure, he usually reacts to the sound by running to look or telling someone what he hears.
3 yr	Can he show that he understands the meaning of some words besides the names of things? Example: "Make the car go." "Give me the ball."	He should be able to understand and use some simple verbs, pronouns, prepositions, and adjectives, such as "go," "me," "in," and "big."

TABLE 1. (continued)

Average Age	Question	Average Behavior
3 yr (cont'd.)	Can he find you when you call him from another room?	He should be able to locate the source of a sound.
	Does he sometimes use complete sentences?	He should be using complete sentences some of the time.
4 yr	Can he tell about events that have happened recently?	He should be able to give a connected account of some recent experiences.
	Can he carry out two directions, one after the other? Example: "Bobby, find Susie and tell her dinner's ready."	He should be able to carry out a sequence of two simple directions.
5 yr	Do neighbors and others outside the family understand most of what he says?	His speech should be intelligible, although some sounds may still be mispronounced.
	Can he carry on a conversation with other children or familiar grown-ups?	Most children of this age can carry on a conversation if the vocabulary is within their experience.
	Does he begin a sentence with "I" instead of "me"; "he" instead of "him?"	He should use some pronouns correctly.
	Is his grammar almost as good as his parents'?	Most of the time, it should match the patterns of grammar used by the adults of his family and neighborhood.

*From Asbed et al. *Volta Review*, 72 (No. 1): 23, 1970.

one in every thousand live births in the United States is profoundly deaf, and approximately 25 in every thousand live births have a moderate to severe hearing loss. Detection of hearing loss or impairment is most important in the very young. These hearing losses have to be diagnosed early in order to begin rehabilitative treatment. Hearing losses go hand in hand with speech losses. It sometimes takes special effort to differentiate between the hearing loss and the speech loss. Table 1 gives normative behavior for children being assessed for hearing and speech problems. For very young children, the ability to respond to jangling keys or noisemakers should be observed carefully. Any child who after a screening procedure is suspected of having a hearing loss should be referred for a definitive work-up. The definitive work-up may take the form of intensive behavioral testing, impedance testing, or auditory evoked potentials.

Children with severe hearing losses can be given hearing aids and started on appropriate infant auditory training programs. They will then be able to benefit from exposure to language during the most formative years for language, up to approximately age six. When a child is diagnosed later than 3 or 4 years of age, his chances of optimizing his potential are limited.

Another important aspect of hearing problems concerns those children with serous or mucoid otitis media, which, as mentioned above, is one of the sequelae of otitis media. The persistence of thick, mucoid fluid results in a moderate hearing loss. The child's symptoms may not refer immediately to hearing. Some of these children become very difficult and their parents and teachers consider them to be primary behavior problems. They do poorly in school because they cannot hear all that is said. Studies have shown that these children are significantly poorer in verbal intelligence when tested with normal control groups. It is important to recognize this disease of the middle ear; if it exists, the hearing must be tested. If a conductive loss is shown and has been present for some time, the child should be treated by myringotomy and, if there is no speech problem, by adenoidectomy. In many instances, in addition to the adenoidectomy, small polyethylene tubes are placed through the tympanic membrane to serve as artificial eustachian tubes, until the middle ear mucosa can recover sufficiently to prevent reaccumulation of fluid.

REFERENCES

DEAFNESS: ITS CAUSE AND PATHOLOGY

Frazier, G. R. Profound childhood deafness. J. Medical Genet., 1:118, 1964.

Konigsmark, B. W. Hereditary Deafness in Man. Part 1, New Eng. J. Med., Vol. 281, No. 13, p. 713, Sept. 25, 1969; Part 2, New Eng. J. Med., Vol. 281, No. 14, p. 774, Oct. 2, 1969; Part 3, New Eng. J. Med., Vol. 281, No. 15, p. 827, Oct. 9, 1969.

Marcus, E. B. Ototoxic medication in premature children. Arch. Otolaryng., 77:198, 1963.

Matkin, N. D., and Carhart, R. Auditory profiles associated with Rh incompatibility. Acta Otolaryng., 84:502, 1966.

McConnell, F., and Ward, P. H. Deafness in Childhood. Nashville, Tenn. Vanderbilt University Press, 1967.

Myklebust, H. R. Auditory Disorders in Children. New York, Grune and Stratton, 1954.

Omerod, F. C. Pathology of congenital deafness. J. Laryng., 74:19, 1960.

Robinson, J. C., and Cambon, K. G. Hearing loss in infants with tuberculous mothers treated with streptomycin during pregnancy. New Eng. J. Med., 271: 949, 1964.

DEAFNESS: DIAGNOSIS

Asbed, R. A., Masland, M. W., Sever, J. L., and Weinberg, M. M. Early case finding of children with communication problems, Part I: report of a community screening program. Volta Review, 72(No. 1):23, Jan., 1970.

Ewing, A. W. G. The ascertainment of deafness in infancy and early childhood. J. Laryng., 59:309, 1944.

Rapin, I. Evoked responses in normal, brain-damaged and deaf infants. Neurology, 117:881, 1967.

———— Ruben, R. J., and Lytle, M. Diagnosis of hearing loss in infants using auditory evoked responses. Laryngoscope, 80(No. 5): 712, May, 1970.

Ruben, R. J., and Rozycki, D. Diagnostic screening for the deaf child. Arch. Otolaryng., 91:429, May, 1970.

de Schweinitz, L., Miller, A. C., and Miller, J. B. Delays in the diagnosis of deafness among preschool children. Pediatrics, 24:462, 1959.

DEAFNESS: TRAINING AND INTELLECTUAL DEVELOPMENT

Ewing, A., and Ewing, E. C. Linguistic development and mental growth in hearing-impaired children. Volta Reveiw, 65:180, 1963.

———— and Ewing, E. C. Teaching Deaf Children to Talk. Washington, D.C., The Volta Bureau, 1967.

Wedenberg, E. Auditory training of deaf and hard of hearing children. Acta Otolaryng., Supplement 94, 1951.

chapter 32

GENERAL PEDIATRIC PRACTICES

ARNOLD H. EINHORN

General Care of Healthy Infants and Children

32.1
GENERAL HEALTH SUPERVISION

Responsibility for health care of the child for the purpose of achieving in each infant, child, and adolescent optimal physical, intellectual, and emotional growth and development lies with the parents, the community, and the pediatrician or family physician. The diagnosis of disease and the treatment of children during specific illnesses have been extensively discussed throughout the various sections of this text. The preventive health services which each child should receive from infancy through adolescence have been described in detail in the section on preventive pediatrics (Sec. 1.2). *Standards of Child Health Care,* a publication of the Council on Pediatric Practice of the American Academy of Pediatrics, also constitutes an excellent guide for the development of appropriate standards in the delivery of preventive pediatric care.

Both the preventive pediatric care and the management of the sick child should be delivered on a continuing personalized basis. Whether the health services are rendered in the office of a practicing pediatrician or in the ambulatory care unit of any other medical facility, it is highly desirable that the health supervision of the child be given by his personal "primary physician."

Periodic health supervision should be planned at regular intervals, their frequency depending upon the child's age, health status, and individual needs. The American Academy of Pediatrics recommends that 9 to 12 visits be made during the first year of life (every four to six weeks during the first six months and every two months during the second six months); four during the second year; two during the third year; one or two during the fourth, fifth, and sixth years; and yearly thereafter. This schedule, which provides for adequate supervision, should be applied with flexibility; many pediatricians may opt in favor of a more individualized program.

Health supervision visits should include: a medical and developmental history which should be reviewed and updated at each visit; a complete physical examination with measurements, appraisal of the child's physical, mental, and emotional development and adjustment, and detection of variations from the normal; appropriate immunizations; and, where indi-

cated, tuberculin test and suitable laboratory examinations. Specific instructions should be given to the parents concerning general care, hygiene, diet, accident prevention, and the treatment of any special health problem. Printed instructions or pamphlets prepared in advance may prove useful in covering adequately some of the more straightforward but time-consuming items of parental guidance and counseling. Parents should be apprised of the stage of growth and development that their child has reached and its relation to normal growth. The reasons for any immunizations, tests, or treatment planned or required during health supervision visits should be explained to the parents. The need may arise for the pediatrician's assistance to the parents in the management or the prevention of behavior or personality problems. The pediatrician's anticipatory guidance plays an important role in the establishment and maintenance of good physician-parent rapport. It also helps parents to gain ability and self-confidence, thereby promoting good parent-child relationships.

32.2
HYGIENE AND GENERAL CARE

Parents' questions concerning hygiene and general care of infants and young children engage an increasing proportion of the time of the pediatrician. To a certain extent, the amount of satisfaction he derives from his practice is determined by his interest and proficiency in advising parents about these matters. In this area, more so than in the treatment of the sick child, the pediatrician must refrain from being rigid and dictatorial.

Many factors besides his advice will determine what parents actually do. It is important, therefore, for the pediatrician to inquire into what the parents think they ought to do about specific aspects in the general care of their children and to relate his counsel to this knowledge. In a sense, the best first answer to a parent's question might be, "What do you think?" This attitude is not incompatible with the needs of those parents who, through such questioning, are found to require more authorative guidance.

Books and newspaper and magazine articles on pediatric subjects written for parents are read extensively today in the United States, and the pediatrician probably is well advised to acquaint himself with them. Pediatricians differ in their opinions about how useful such material is and in their advice to parents about reading in this area. Again, however, the physician's advice may have to depend on his assessment of the parents, and he should realize that in most instances popular guides will be read.

The general care of the newborn infant is discussed in the section on the newborn infant. Breast feeding, artificial milk formulas, and other aspects related to feeding of infants and children are discussed in Section 3.3. In this section only a few aspects of hygiene and general care of older infants and children have been selected for consideration.

CARE OF THE SKIN. The skin of a young infant is relatively delicate. Cleanliness must be secured without the use of strongly alkaline soaps, or too much rubbing. Excoriations and intertrigo are much easier to prevent than to cure.

Diapers should be removed as soon as soiled or wet. Excoriations of the skin of the buttocks and groin are associated most commonly with ammoniacal dermatitis (Sec. 26.8). It is therefore essential to keep the diaper area as clean and dry as possible. Soiled buttocks are best cleaned with soft absorbent cotton moistened with water, baby lotion, or mineral oil. Although the practice of covering the diaper of an infant with rubber or plastic material to protect the outer garments has been condemned, it is done almost universally. If wet or soiled diapers are removed promptly most infants apparently tolerate the use of such coverings, and the advantages cannot be denied. However, it should be abandoned if marked irritation of the underlying skin develops. Disposable diapers which are moisture absorbing and convenient to use are now being marketed.

Bathing. Except in the neonatal period before the dried umbilical stump has separated, a daily bath is desirable. It should be given in a warm room (room temperature, 75° to 80° F). For the first few months the temperature of the water should be at about 96° to 98° F. By the sixth month the temperature of the bath for healthy infants may be lowered to about 95° to 92° F, and by the end of the first year to about 90° F. Before placing an infant in the tub the temperature should be tested with the extensor surface of elbow or hand and should feel comfortably warm to the skin.

A folded diaper should be placed in the bottom of the tub to prevent the baby from slipping—the infant should be securely supported during its bath. After the bath, the skin of most infants requires nothing further than careful drying; others, particularly very fat infants, benefit by the application of a small amount of oil or lanolin or of some bland absorbent powder in the folds of the skin. Care must be taken to prevent massive aspiration of powders.

The time of the bath may be varied to suit the convenience of the family routine. Bathing a baby too soon after a feeding may produce regurgitation or vomiting. Therefore it is best to plan an infant's bath before a feeding. During childhood the warm bath is usually given at night, and the temperature of the bath may be regulated by the child's desires.

Once or twice a week during his bath a baby's scalp should be shampooed with mild soap lather. If seborrheic dermatitis of the scalp ("cradle cap") is present, crusts can be softened with petroleum jelly (Vaseline) or mineral oil left on overnight and washed off in the morning.

CARE OF THE EYES, NOSE, MOUTH, AND TEETH. In general, the eyes of infants need no special care. They should be protected from too strong light during early infancy, less on account of the possibility of harm to the eye itself, which is almost negligible, than because strong light appears at times to be a disagreeable stimulus to the infant. Soapy water should be kept out of the eyes when the baby's face is washed or his scalp is soaped during his bath.

The infant's nose does not require attention ordinarily, but if necessary the anterior nares may be cleansed with small cotton swabs moistened with warm water. The mouths of very young infants require no cleansing. Dental care is discussed elsewhere (Sec. 29.3).

CARE OF THE GENITAL ORGANS. The female genital organs need but little attention in young children, except as to cleanliness. This is more often neglected in older children than in infants.

In uncircumcized boys, it is common practice to retract the foreskin in order to break up preputial adhesions and remove smegma. The procedure must be carried out gently if trauma is to be avoided; with sufficient care even the smallest preputial orifices can be dilated. However, we are inclined to question the value of this procedure, having seen more difficulty from paraphimosis and from trauma with subsequent infection than from leaving the foreskin alone. A preputial cavity partially sealed off by adhesions and filled with smegma does no harm even if the condition persists for years. Exceptionally, when the preputial orifice is so small as to impede the flow of urine, some dilation is indicated; it need not be carried beyond the point of bringing the glans into view.

AIRING. In summer, a newborn infant can be allowed out of doors at the end of the first week; the time of first airing at other seasons will depend upon the weather and the attitude of the family. During the outing, his head should be protected from the wind. The time spent outdoors will also vary with seasons, usually limited initially to about one-half hour, but rapidly increasing to two or three hours. There is no reason why a healthy 4- or 5-month-old child should not sleep out of doors in pleasant weather. Infants and very young children should not be out of doors when there are extremes of temperature, high winds, or storms.

EXERCISE. This is no less important in infancy than in later childhood. An infant gets his exercise in crying, kicking his legs about, and waving his arms. By these means pulmonary expansion and muscular development are increased. An infant's clothing should be loose enough not to interfere with exercise. Infants who are old enough to crawl or stand usually take sufficient exercise unless they are restrained. They should be allowed to do what they are eager to do and have the opportunity to use their muscles. Exercise may be encouraged by placing a mattress or a thick pad or quilt on the floor in a warm room and allowing the infant to roll and tumble upon it at will. A large bed may answer the same purpose.

CLOTHING. The clothing of infants should be light, warm, nonirritating, and loose enough to allow free motion of the extremities. The essentials are the diaper and some garment like a shirt with which to hold it in place; for warmth other articles may be added either as actual clothing or as bedding. Since wool is irritating to the skin of many infants, especially when the child is overclothed, the undergarments are best made of cotton. Knitted goods are warmer than woven goods and allow more expansion. Overdressing is a common mistake. The overclothed child is likely to be fretful and to perspire. Evidence of inadequate clothing is less definite. One cannot assume that an infant is underclothed because his hands and feet feel cool, since this is habitual in many normal infants.

CRYING. After the newborn period, crying calls for an inquiry into its cause, even though in the early months of life an adequate cause may not easily be found.

SLEEP. The young infant should have a separate crib which levels and does not rock. The mattress should be quite firm. A pillow should be omitted. Separate beds for older children are desirable for restful sleep and may also prevent the spread of infection.

Training in proper habits of sleep should begin at birth. From the outset, an infant should be accustomed to being put into his crib while awake and going to sleep of his own accord. Infants will from the start tolerate a moderate amount of noise without waking; it is therefore unnecessary to modify the customary noises of the household routine in their favor.

The periods of sleep in young infants are usually from 2 to 4 hours long, with the exception of once or twice in the 24 hours, when a long sleep of 5, 6, or even 8 hours occurs. One purpose of a feeding schedule is to train the child to take this long sleep at night, for the convenience of the rest of the family. The habit of regular sleep is best established by waking the infant for his daytime feedings and allowing him to sleep as long as possible during the night.

By the age of 3 months many infants will sleep 12 hours at night without waking. At 6 months a healthy infant will usually sleep for 16 to 18 hours a day, the waking periods being only from half an hour to 2 hours long. At the age of 1 year most infants sleep for 14 or 15 hours—for 11 or 12 hours at night, and 2 or 3 hours during the day, usually in two naps. At 2 years usually 13 to 14 hours of sleep are taken—11 or 12 hours at night and 1 or 2 hours during the day, generally in a single nap. After the third year the heavy sleep of childhood is commonly seen. At the age of 4 years children usually sleep between 11 and 12 hours. It is desirable, and in most cases possible, to keep up the daily nap until children are 4 years old. From 6 to 10 years the amount of sleep taken is 10 or 11 hours; and from 12 to 16 years, 9 hours on an average. These figures are, however, not to be considered as universally applicable. There is a wide range in individual requirements, which may vary, for example, between 8 and 17 hours a day in healthy children at 2½ years of age. A child, if given suitable opportunity to sleep, will take what he needs, and not necessarily the same amount from day to day.

Young infants will often fall asleep within a few minutes after being put to bed. As they grow older their behavior in this regard soon becomes more variable, so that it is not uncommon for a child to take from half an hour to an hour to go to sleep. Wakefulness of this extent need not occasion concern; indeed, if a child regularly falls asleep the moment he lies down it is possible that his hours of rest need to be lengthened.

Some infants sleep more soundly in the prone than in the supine position. The popular belief that an infant is liable to be smothered if put to bed "on his face" appears unfounded. When carefully investigated, crib deaths (Sec. 13.15) attributed to smothering have almost invariably been found to be due to some other cause.

Disturbances of sleep are discussed in Chapter 6, page 274.

TOILET TRAINING. Present experience would indicate that no single method of toilet training is applicable to all infants or to all parents. The fact that inept attempts at early training have often failed to achieve any practical results, except to build up resentment on the part of the child, has prompted many pediatricians to condemn all efforts in this direction. This attitude has been reinforced by certain untested theoretical considerations. We are inclined to view the matter more optimistically. Certainly early training, properly carried out, can ease greatly the burden of daily care and can add measurably to the mother's enjoyment of her task as a parent, as well as to the child's sense of accomplishment.

Many infants can become accustomed to having bowel movements when placed upon a small chamber as early as the second half of the first year. Such attempts may be started as soon as the infant is able to sit alone and as soon as experience has shown that the child tends to move his bowels at a particular time of the day. Since peristalsis is usually stimulated by the taking of food, the infant should be put on the chamber soon after the feeding which immediately precedes the time when he habitually has a movement; he should be kept there anywhere from a few minutes up to a quarter of an hour—never long enough to make him tired or fretful. Association of a particular posture and a particular piece of bathroom fixture with the act of moving his bowels favors the formation of a habit. Parents should be warned that the training process requires patience, especially in the beginning, and that uniform success is not to be expected even after many days of trial. They should understand that if the chamber is allowed to become associated in the infant's mind with his own fatigue or his parent's irritability, he may react unfavorably to the educational venture by resisting training or by withholding his stools.

The training of the bladder is more difficult than that of the bowels and can seldom be accomplished before the middle of the second year. The procedure is similar to that employed in training of the bowels. By the end of the first year many infants are able to give recognizable warning, by voice or facial expression, of a desire to empty the bladder. When this stage has been reached, often at about the time an infant learns to walk, an attempt at bladder training may be made. The child may be put on the chamber at frequent intervals—every 30 to 60 minutes —for periods during the day. By patience and expressions of approval for successful performance, in the course of a week or 10 days it is often possible to train a child to be dry in the daytime. A child can seldom achieve bladder control at night before the age of 2 years. The subject of nocturnal enuresis is discussed elsewhere (Chap. 6, p. 272).

32.3
IMMUNIZATION AGAINST INFECTIOUS DISEASES

Immunization procedures are an important part of the overall health supervision of all infants and children. For families who do not avail themselves of private medical care, local health agencies have the responsibility to organize and provide such essential services.

The schedule outlined in Table 1 may be used as a flexible guide, which may be modified, *within certain limits,* to fit individual situations. Minor adjustments in timing may be made for the convenience of the parents or the physician. Furthermore, continued development of new biologic products necessitate periodic revisions of the immunization schedule.

No inoculation should be performed when there are signs of acute illness. In most instances interrupted primary series of immunizations need not be started again, but may simply be completed. At the time of an injury no booster tetanus toxoid dose is needed by a fully immunized child for clean, minor wounds, unless 10 years or more have elapsed since the last dose. For contaminated wounds, a booster dose should be given if more than five years have elapsed since the last dose.

In the United States, routine smallpox vaccination is no longer recommended by the United States Public Health Service (see Sec. 14.40). In those children for whom this vaccination is still recommended, it should not be administered when an active skin eruption such as eczema, scabies, poison ivy, or impetigo is present in the child or in unvaccinated members of the family (Sec. 14.40).

Appraisal and Care of the Sick Child

32.4
SYMPTOMATOLOGY AND DIAGNOSIS

In diseases of childhood, age plays a more important part in symptomatology and differential diagnosis than in the diseases of adults. It is not so much that diseases in early life are unique as that the patient's responses to illness are influenced by his age, stage of development, and past experiences. The peculiarities of early life are greatest at birth and diminish with advancing age. In the first two or three

years of a child's life, before speech has developed, the chief and almost sole reliance of the physician must be upon objective signs of disease. In older children the symptoms of disease are much the same as in adults, and similar methods of examination may be employed.

Certain fundamental facts are always to be kept in mind. A sick infant or child, however varied and widespread his symptoms, is likely to be suffering from only one disease or the complications of one disease. The student approaching pediatric problems for the first time is often baffled by the variety and

TABLE 1.   *Recommended Schedule for Active Immunization and Tuberculin Testing of Normal Infants and Children**

Age	Immunization
2-3 months	DTP, trivalent OPV[†][‡], or Type 1 OPV
3-4 months	DTP, trivalent OPV[†], or Type 3 OPV
4-5 months	DTP, trivalent OPV[†], or Type 2 OPV
9-11 months	Tuberculin test[§]
12 months	Measles vaccine (live, attenuated)
15-18 months	DTP, trivalent OPV, (smallpox vaccine[†][‖]), rubella vaccine[#] (live attenuated)
2 years	Tuberculin test[§]
3 years	DTP, tuberculin test[§]
4 and 5 years	Tuberculin Test[§]
6 years	TD, (smallpox vaccine[‖]), tuberculin test[§], trivalent OPV[†]
7, 8, 9, and 10 years	Tuberculin test[§]
12-16 years	TD[**], (smallpox vaccine[‖]), tuberculin test[§][**], mumps vaccine[‡‡] (live attenuated)

DTP   Diphtheria and tetanus toxoids, and pertussis vaccine combined.

OPV   Oral poliovaccine. If trivalent OPV is used, interval should be six weeks or longer.

TD   Tetanus and diphtheria toxoids, *adult type*, for those over 6 years of age, in contrast to diphtheria and tetanus (DT) containing a larger amount of diphtheria antigen.

*From *Report of the Committee on the Control of Infectious Diseases.* American Academy of Pediatrics, 1971.

[†]Some authorities recommend that DTP, OPV, measles, and smallpox immunizations should always be given singly and never in combinations.

[‡]Immunization may be started at any age. The immune response is limited in a proportion of young infants, and the recommended booster doses are designed to insure or maintain immunity. Protection of infants against pertussis should start early. In newborn infants the best protection against pertussis is avoidance of household contacts by adequate immunization of older siblings.

[§] Frequency of repeated tuberculin tests is dependent on risk of exposure of children under care and the prevalence of tuberculosis in the population group. In high risk situations, interval between routine tuberculin testing should not exceed six months. Under normal conditions, where risk of exposure to active tuberculosis is remote, yearly testing should be adequate.

[‖]Routine smallpox vaccination is no longer recommended in the United States. Where indicated, initial smallpox vaccine may be given at any time between 12 and 24 months of age; after age 12, every 3 to 10 years.

[#]Rubella vaccine: Live vaccine is recommended for boys and girls between the age of 1 year and puberty. Children in kindergarten should be given priority because they are the major source of virus dissemination. A history of rubella illness is not reliable enough to exclude children from immunization.

[**]After age 12, tetanus toxoid booster every 10 years as TD.

[‡‡]Mumps Vaccine: It is recommended that all males in preadolescent or in older age groups, who have not experienced mumps, be immunized.

apparent remoteness of symptoms caused by a single disease factor. For example, digestive and neurologic symptoms commonly accompany pathologic processes, particularly inflammations, in practically any part of the body and are not necessarily significant in pointing to the alimentary tract or to the central nervous system as the site of trouble.

The History

Since the patient can seldom tell his own story, information must be obtained from the parent, guardian, or whoever is looking after the child. The initial history should be as complete as possible (Table 2). However, it is desirable to review the history repeatedly. During the course of a specific illness certain parts of the history may assume increased importance and require more detailed inquiry. Also, it should be realized that the initial history of an acutely ill child is usually taken at a time when the mother or other informant is under considerable stress, and reviewing the data at a later occasion may yield important additional information. Certain aspects of the history, particularly those concerning psychologic factors, depend upon a relationship between the physician and the family which takes time to develop. It is apparent that continuity of care, which provides an ongoing relationship, also contributes to better interpretation of the history.

TABLE 2.   *Suggested Outline for History and Physical Examination of a Sick Patient*

The following schematic outline is suggested as a useful guide for the work-up of a sick infant or child.

I **History**

Chief Complaint: (In parent's words.)

Source of History: Mother, father, doctor's note, etc. . . . with estimate of reliability.

Present Illness: Chronologically, where possible, with dates. Initial symptom and date of onset; subsequent symptoms chronologically. Pertinent negative data, obtained by direct questioning.

Past History:

1. *Birth*
   A. Date, hospital where born. Birth weight. Respirations—spontaneous, or after resuscitation. Presentation of fetus.
   B. Parity of mother; term or premature; diet and lab studies obtained during pregnancy; complications of pregnancy (bleeding, toxemic infections, etc.); length, type, and complications of delivery; anesthesia during labor.

2. *Neonatal Period*
   Cyanosis; pallor; convulsions; jaundice; hemorrhage; birth marks or deformities; respiratory or feeding difficulties.

3. *Nutrition*
   Breast or bottle fed—type of formula.
   Vitamins—type, when started, and when stopped. Orange juice.
   Age solids started—any food intolerances.
   Appetite—Weight—at 1 month, 6 months, 1 year, and present.

4. *Development*
   Smiled; head up; rolled over; reached for objects; sat without support; stood, with and without support; walked; first tooth; first words. Toilet training—when began and when successfully completed.
   Age started school—scholastic and social achievement; present grade in school.

5. *Habits and Personality*
   Hours of sleep, dreams, nightmares; exercise; favorite games and hobbies; thumb-sucking; nail-biting; tantrums; breath-holding; tics; enuresis; encopresis; personal habits; masturbation; history of pica; social adjustment—hostile, aggressive, submissive, friendly, etc.

6. *Immunization* (Indicate source of information: Health Department record, mother's verbal information, school record.)

   Date, type of reaction, and boosters (if any).
   Smallpox, diphtheria, pertussis, tetanus, polio (Salk/oral), measles, mumps, rubella; BCG

7. Tuberculin tests: Tine or PPD

8. *General Health*

9. *Previous Illnesses* (Age, severity, complications, and sequelae.)
   A. Contagion—measles, mumps, varicella, rubella, pertussis, etc.
   B. Other medical illnesses—hospitalized?—if so, when, where, and for how long, therapy received, final diagnosis.
   C. Surgical conditions—date and place of operation.
   D. Accidents, fractures, etc.

10. *Allergy*
    Eczema, asthma, hay fever, hives, food or drug sensitivities to penicillin, sulfas, etc.

11. *System Review* (List only positives.)
    A. Head, eyes, ears, nose, and throat
       1. Headache, head trauma.
       2. Eyes—vision, glasses, squint, inflammatory disease.
       3. Ears—hearing, otitis, discharge.
       4. Nose—discharge, epistaxis.
       5. Mouth—gingivitis, condition of teeth, date of last dental visit.
       6. Throat—tonsillitis, recurrent pharyngitis.

    B. Respiratory
       Chronic cough, frequent URI's, previous pneumonia, exposure to tuberculosis, previous chest x-ray, and when.

    C. Cardiac
       History of murmurs, acute rheumatic fever; history of dyspnea, orthopnea, cyanosis.

    D. Gastrointestinal
       Appetite and digestion. Bowel habits, character and frequency of stools. Jaundice, diarrhea, constipation, vomiting, hematemesis; passage of worms.

TABLE 2.   (continued)

   E. Genitourinary
       ? Circumcised; dysuria; hematuria; polydipsia; nocturia, frequency. Onset of menarche in females.

   F. Neuromuscular
       Tremors, convulsions, weakness or paralysis, polio.

   G. Joints
       Arthritis or arthralgia; loss of mobility.

   H. Hematologic Disorders
       Hemorrhages, anemia, bleeding tendency.

   I. Recent Onset of Infection

12. *Family History*
     Parents and Grandparents: Age, occupation, state of physical and emotional health; and, if parents are not
       living, age at death, cause, and nature of symptoms.
     Siblings: Age, state of health, and where living. (If not living, age of death, cause, and nature of symptoms.)
     Familial Illnesses or Anomalies: Tuberculosis, syphilis, diabetes, cancer, epilepsy, rheumatic fever, allergy,
       hereditary blood dyscrasias, mental retardation, dystrophies, congenital anomalies, heredo-degenerative
       diseases.
     Family Pedigree: If existence of a genetic anomaly is suspected.

       Persons Included
       Begin pedigree with the patient (identified by arrow—proband or propositus), then include, as a minimum,
         the following living or dead relatives in this order:
           a. siblings (record in order of birth, with eldest on left)
           b. parents (father, and male ancestors in general, on left)
           c. father's siblings
           d. all descendants of father's siblings
           e. father's parents
           f. mother's siblings
           g. all descendants of mother's siblings
           h. mother's parents
           i. all descendants of case and his siblings

       Information Required
       As each relative, living or dead, is added to pedigree, inquire of informant whether or not relative has had:
           a. same affliction as propositus
           b. any other chronic disorder or defect (Ask this for one person at a time rather than for group.)

       Pedigree Symbols

Symbol		Symbol	
□	Male	□—○	Marriage
○	Female	□═○	Consanguineous marriage
◇	Sex unknown	□⌐¦⌐○	Illegitimacy
◈⑧	8 persons, sex unknown	□⊥○	No offspring
◇	Pregnancy		
(□)	Adopted		Identical twins
■	Examined, affected with trait		Fraternal twins
⊟	Examined, negative for trait		
□	Reported normal for trait	Ⅲ	Reliably reported to have trait
□s	Single	Ⅱ	Questionably reported to have trait

       SMALL SYMBOLS

       ▫ ○ ◇ Lived less than one day   ⊞ ⊕ ◈ Stillbirth   ▫ ⊙ ◇ Miscarriage

TABLE 2.   (continued)

13. *Social History*

Living Circumstances: Place and nature of dwelling; sleeping arrangements; number of persons living in home in addition to parents and children; relation of such persons to family members.

Economic Circumstances: Members of family who work; working hours if unusual; general level of economic independence, support from community agencies if any.

Neighborhood Circumstances:

Available Recreational and Educational outlets in neighborhood.

End of Family History

II Physical Examination:

Temperature   Pulse   Respirations
Blood Pressure   Surface Area in M²
Weight (kg) (%)   Height (cm) (%) percentiles for height and weight

(If less than 3%, indicate also age for which height and weight are in 50% group.)
(See percentile charts in Appendix.)

Head Circumference (%)   Chest Circumference (%)   (Percentiles)

1. *General Appearance*
   Age, sex, state of nutrition, attitude, position, sensorium, type of cry or voice, acutely or chronically ill, distress, gait.

   Personality, intelligence, cooperation, interest in environment; gross developmental status for age.

2. *Head*
   Contour, bossing, texture of hair, scalp, fontanels—with dimensions in cm, if open, and comment on tension sutures.

   Percussion and auscultation—parotid glands.

3. *Eyes*
   Pupils, sclerae, conjunctivae, extraocular movements, nystagmus, ptosis, squint, photophobia, vision, ophthalmoscopic exam.

4. *Ears*
   Hearing, discharge, canals. Examination of drums—color, bulging, light reflex, perforation; mastoid tenderness.

5. *Nose*
   Patency of nares, flaring of alae nasi, discharge, obstruction, mucous membranes, and turbinates—swollen, red pale, boggy. Septum; sinus tenderness (frontal and maxillary).

6. *Mouth and Throat*
   Lips: color, dryness, fissures, sores, herpes. *Tongue:* color, moisture, coating, fissures, ulcers, frenulum protrusion. *Breath. Teeth:* number, arrangement, caries. *Gums:* color, hypertrophy, bleeding, ulcers. *Buccal mucosa:* color, exudate, postnasal discharge, lymphoid tissue, palpation of adenoids in infants. *Epiglottis. Tonsils:* size, signs of inflammation, exudate, membrane. *Pillars.*

7. *Neck*
   Flexibility, swelling, thyroid enlargement, trachea in midline.

8. *Lymph Glands*
   Size in centimeters, consistency, tenderness, mobility, fluctuation, discrete or matted, GGE.

9. *Spine*
   Curvature, tenderness along spinous process, mobility, CVA tenderness.

10. *Thorax*
    Contour, respiration, rate, regularity, abdominal or thoracic adequacy, and symmetry of expansion.

11. *Lungs*
    Percussion, palpation, fremitus, auscultation.

12. *Cardiovascular*
    Heart: Inspection, precordial bulge, apical heave.
    Palpation: PMI—diffuse or circumscribed, thrills, shocks.
    Percussion: Heart borders.
    Auscultation: Rhythm, character, and quality of sounds. M1 vs M2 vs A2.
    Murmurs: Time, duration, location, intensity, transmission, alteration with change of position, with patient's exercise.
    Pulse: Radial and femoral—rate and rhythm, volume.

TABLE 2. (continued)

13. *Abdomen*

    Inspection: Contour, umbilicus, hernia, distension, veins, visible peristalsis.

    Percussion: Fluid wave, shifting dullness, tympanites, bladder, liver, spleen. Also a good method for localizing point of tenderness.

    Palpation: Tone, tenderness, direct or indirect rebound. Diastasis recti, masses, liver, spleen, kidneys, auscultation of bowel sounds.

14. *Genitalia*

    Male: Prepuce or circumcision, meatus; testes—descent, hydrocele.

    Female: External examination only—vulva, clitoris, discharge.

15. *Rectal* (Can be deferred unless this examination is relevant to the child's illness on suspected condition.)

    Fissures, hemorrhoids, prolapse. Sphincter tone—masses, tenderness, stool in ampula.

16. *Skin*

    Texture, color, tissue turgor, temperature, moisture, icterus, cyanosis, eruption, scars, ecchymosis, petechiae, spiders, desquamation, hemangiomata, mongolian spots, nevi.

17. *Extremities*

    Tone, color, warmth; clubbing, cyanosis, mobility of joints, hip abduction in infants, with knees flexed.

    Feet: deformities, decreased ankle movements.

18. *Neurologic*

    A. *Mental State:* intelligence.

    B. *Motor:* gait, stance, Romberg, muscle power, paresis, paralysis, spasticity, rigidity, flaccidity, clonus, carpopedal spasm, tics, tremors, athetosis, etc.

    C. *Tone:* on palpation, ballotement, and stretching; flaccidity, hypotonia, hypertonus, spasticity, rigidity, cogwheel phenomenon.

    D. *Cranial Nerves*

        I. Smell

        II. Sight, visual fields, optic discs—sensory arc of papillary constriction.

        III. Elevation of upper lids. EOM—superior, inferior, medical recti, inferior oblique, motor arc of papillary constriction (dilation if via cervical sympathetics).

        IV. EOM—superior oblique.

        V. Motor—muscles of mastication—jaw jerk. Jaw deviates to side of lesion. Sensory—sensation to face, forehead, lips, tongue buccal mucosa, eyes. Sensory arc of corneal reflex.

        VI. External rectus.

        VII. Peripheral lesion—paralysis of all mimetic muscles, widened palpebral fissure with inability to close eye, often associated with increased tearing. Loss of taste on interior 2/3 of tongue. Loss of motor arc or corneal reflex. Supranuclear lesion—weakness of lower 1/2 of face. No loss of taste. Involuntary expressions of emotion are intact and symmetrical.

        VIII. Auditory—hearing—vesticular nystagmus, vertigo.

        IX. Taste on posterior 1/3 of tongue—elevation of palate, sensory arc of gag reflex.

        X. Swallowing, elevation of epiglottis, movements of vocal cords.

           a. Cranial—deviation of uvula away from side of lesion.

           b. Spinal—innervates sternomastoid and trapezius. Atrophy, drooping, and inability to shrug shoulders. Poor head turning against resistance (away from side of weakness).

        XI. Tongue movements. Tongue atrophy. Tongue moves toward side of lesion.

    E. *Reflexes*

    2+ is normal. Deep tender biceps, triceps, radial, knee, ankle, Chvostek sign.

    Superficial—Abdominal, cremasteric.

    Abnormal—Hoffman, Babinski, Kerning, Brudzinski, "tache cerebrale".

    In infants—grasp, suck, Moro, root tonic neck.

    F. *Sensory system:* superficial and deep sensations; pinprick, touch, sense of position, vibratory sense.

    G. *Cerebellar signs:* incoordination, ataxia, intention tremor, passpointing dysdiadochokinesia, rebound phenomenon, slurred speech, nystagmus, or extreme lateral gaze.

    H. *Special senses:* hearing—response to loud sounds, normal voice, whispers; vision—moving lights or objects, charts in older children.

III Formulation: Should include:

1. A brief summary of pertinent history and physical findings.
2. A discussion of the differential diagnosis, and of the problem as presented by this patient.
3. The diagnosis or diagnoses.
4. Plan for diagnostic work-up in order of importance.

IV Plan:

All diagnostic studies planned, diet, therapeutic regimen.

Family History

It is important to obtain information about the age, physical condition, and state of health of each parent and all members of the family. A listing of the mother's pregnancies in chronologic order may provide important information regarding miscarriages and abortions and, by describing the sibship of which the patient is a member, will fill in the picture of the family group. If any brothers or sisters have died, the date and cause of death should be recorded. Acute illness of recent date in a member of the household may be the source of infection transmitted to the patient. Of equal importance is the history of chronic infection, particularly tuberculosis, in any household contact. When a heritable condition is present or suspected, pertinent information should be gathered regarding its distribution in the family and among the forebears; this applies to a wide spectrum of diseases and syndromes, including allergic manifestations, rheumatic disease, diabetes, renal disease, congenital malformations, inborn errors of metabolism, anomalies of growth and development, degenerative diseases of the nervous system, and mental disorders. Particular attention should in these circumstances be directed to exploring the possibility of consanguineous marriage. A knowledge of the environment in which the patient lives will help the examiner to appreciate the chances of exposure to specific infections, as well as many pertinent psychologic and emotional factors.

Past History

The type of inquiry will depend in large part on the age of the patient. The outline which follows is designed chiefly as a guide in management of problems of the infant.

PREGNANCY. The mother should be questioned regarding the duration of pregnancy, her attitude toward it, her health during that period, and any occurrence which might have had a harmful effect on the development and health of the child, such as infectious disease, hemorrhage, drugs, or x-ray radiation. The mother's blood group and Rh factor status, if known, should be recorded.

BIRTH AND NEONATAL PERIOD. One should inquire about the character of labor—about sedation used during labor and delivery, whether delivery was spontaneous or instrumental, prolonged or precipitate—and about the condition and vigor of the infant at birth—whether there was difficulty of resuscitation, early cyanosis, jaundice, eruptions, hemorrhage, or convulsions. Knowledge about the mother's response to the infant after delivery and on returning home may help in understanding subsequent problems in the mother-child relationships.

FEEDING. The early feeding history should be explored carefully, with questions about the duration of breast feeding and reasons for weaning, formulas used for artificial feeding and reasons for changes, amounts and duration of administration of vitamin supplements, and the time of addition of solid foods and the success or difficulties encountered in their use. In the case of the older child, the early feeding history need not be as complete unless the nature of the complaint is such as to make full information helpful. In any case, the child's approximate daily food intake should be ascertained, together with information as to his approach to meals—whether eager or apathetic, whether he feeds himself or is helped, whether his dietary habits are regular or capricious. One should ascertain the attitude of the parents towards the child's eating, noting whether the child is forced, entreated, cajoled, threatened, or rewarded.

GROWTH AND DEVELOPMENT. The best idea of the child's physical growth may be obtained from a weight and height record if one has been kept. If not available, one must depend upon general statements as to how the child thrived at different periods. A history of dentition, including the patient's age at the time of eruption of the first teeth and the time and order in which subsequent teeth appeared, serves as an index of maturation. So also does the age when the anterior fontanel closed. Other developmental landmarks should be recorded: the age at which the child first smiled, held his head erect, recognized people or objects, sat alone, stood with support and alone, crawled, walked, used words and sentences. The behavior development of a normal child during the first two years is a subject with which the physician should be familiar if he would detect early those differences, often slight at this age, in children whose development is retarded.

Past Illnesses

INFECTIOUS DISEASES. One should record attacks of infectious diseases: measles, rubella, scarlet fever, diphtheria, pertussis, mumps, chickenpox, and poliomyelitis, with details as to duration, severity, and complications.

RESPIRATORY SYSTEM. The past occurrence of respiratory infections should be ascertained along with their severity, manifestations, durations, and complications such as otitis media, bronchitis, pneumonia, cervical adenitis, croup, chronic cough, mouth-breathing, persistent fever.

CARDIOVASCULAR SYSTEM. Inquiry should be made as to the occurrence of cyanosis, dyspnea, excessive sweating during infancy, fatigability, syncope, joint pains, and epistaxis.

GASTROINTESTINAL SYSTEM. One should inquire about the history of early feeding difficulties, diarrhea, constipation, abnormalities of the stools (size, odor, color, presence of blood, mucus, or pus), and vomiting; whether this is associated with infections or emotional upsets related to certain foods; and whether it is occasional or habitual.

GENITOURINARY SYSTEM. Significant items in the past history are infections of the urinary tract, hematuria, dysuria, frequency, urgency, dribbling, enuresis, edema, and oliguria. Repeated bouts of unexplained fever with or without other symptoms may point to abnormality of this system.

NERVOUS SYSTEM. Inquiry should be made concerning convulsions; if they have occurred, considerable detail should be sought regarding the circumstances of their occurrence. A convulsion which takes place at the onset of a febrile illness is of quite different significance from one not associated with infection.

OPERATIONS AND INJURIES. The dates, nature, and complications of all operations and serious injuries should be recorded. In the case of operations it is well to inquire about the indications and the results.

IMMUNIZATIONS. The dates of all immunizations and tests for immunity should be recorded.

Psychologic Investigation

Information about a child's general adjustment and about his reaction to a specific illness should be an integral part of the medical history. In order to ask questions appropriate to the age of the child, the physician must have some knowledge of what constitutes healthy emotional adjustment at different ages. The occurrence of such symptoms as restlessness, irritability, tantrums, night terrors, and tics should be noted, as well as indications of how a child gets along with his peers at play and at school and with his siblings and parents. Some indication of the attitude of the parents toward the child can also be obtained from appropriate questions in the history. Korsch has made an attempt to systematize to some extent the method of obtaining this part of the pediatric history.

Present Illness

It is first of all important to obtain as definite a statement as possible as to when the child was last quite well, whether the onset of the illness was abrupt or gradual, and with what particular symptoms it began. It is then usually advantageous to allow the mother to give her own account of the illness without interruption, going back later for amplification. Attention should be paid to the chronology of the appearance of symptoms and each should be traced up to the time of the visit. The administration of medicines should be noted along with dose and effect. Other questions asked will obviously depend on the nature of the complaint or disease.

The Examination

The success of the examination (Table 2) will depend in large measure upon the approach of the examiner. A frightened child is a difficult subject, and the ability of the physician to gain the patient's confidence in the first few moments helps in obtaining cooperation for the subsequent examination. Instruments not to be used in the examination should not be in evidence, and those actually to be employed are best introduced one at a time. A stethoscope or reflex hammer will lose much of its capacity to inspire fear if the child is allowed to examine and play with it before it is brought into use. While restraint of the child is sometimes necessary, it is best reserved until really needed. The more unpleasant parts of the examination—ears, mouth, throat, and rectum—are usually best left to the last. No rule, however, applies to all situations. The pediatrician must be an opportunist and seize his chance while he may. If the child is quiet at first, he may begin by palpating the abdomen or listening to the heart. Crying may afford an opportunity for listening to breath sounds (and testing for fremitus and hernia). In examining infants, it is helpful to use a sugar pacifier, which may easily be made by using a teaspoonful of sugar tied in gauze and moistened in water.

General Inspection

In acute disease, much of importance can be learned from simple observation. The following features may serve as examples.

The state of physical development in relation to the child's age should be noted: Is he robust or frail? His posture of choice should be observed—whether he lies on the side, back, or face, the state of flexion of the extremities, and whether the head is drawn back. The type and amount of spontaneous activity may disclose a tendency to spare or protect some part of the body and will reveal whether the child is restless and excitable, or drowsy and apathetic. With older children the amount of prostration will usually indicate to the practiced eye whether the condition is grave, but infants not infrequently deceive even the most experienced observer. Children as well as infants offer no objection to being examined completely stripped provided the room is comfortably warm. In these circumstances one may note accurately the color of the skin, whether it is pale or cyanotic or jaundiced, and the presence of rashes or focal lesions, their character and distribution. It is important to observe facial expression, whether it is alert or dull, peaceful or anxious, and whether the features are contracted from time to time as if in pain.

Several features of respiration are better gauged

with the eye than with the stethoscope. Respiratory difficulty may be limited to inspiration, or to expiration, or may involve both phases of respiration. Inspiratory retraction—suprasternal, supracavicular, infrasternal, or intercostal—should be carefully noted. Marked dyspnea, whatever its origin, is usually accompanied by active dilation of the alae nasi. One hemithorax may show an inspiratory lag, or the breathing may be predominantly costal or abdominal in type, suggesting paralysis of one or another group of respiratory muscles. Nasal obstruction is usually accompanied by snorting or mouth-breathing.

It is important, though not always easy, to determine whether a child cries from fright, from general irritability which may come from any acute disease, or from pain. The cry of fright is usually evident because it comes with the physician's approach and ceases when he goes away. Children of indulgent parents will often cry when anything out of the usual routine occurs. The cry of pain may be distinctive; it may be accompanied by some attempt at localization, as when a child puts his hand to an inflamed part; but in infancy the pain of acute inflammation is often indicated only by general restlessness and irritability. The cry of some diseases is quite characteristic; the short, catchy cry of acute pneumonia, the hoarse cry of laryngitis, and, in a child with scurvy or some acute inflammatory process, the sharp cry whenever his bed or body is touched. A child, or even an infant, may actually be too ill to cry.

Measurements

BODY MEASUREMENTS. These are of greatest value in chronic diseases, particularly disturbances of nutrition, but may also be of assistance in acute conditions. They also serve as a point of reference for subsequent progress. The important measurements are the head and chest circumferences, the weight, and the body length or height. The circumference of the abdomen varies so much with the degree of distension that it is of little help as a measure of growth and development.

The techniques of measurement of head circumference, body weight, recumbent length, and standing height, or stature, have been described in detail in Chapter 4 (pp. 245-247). In taking the circumference of the head the largest measurement (over the occipital and frontal eminences) is preferable. The measurement of the chest is usually taken over the nipples. The body length of an infant is best taken on a measuring table or with a portable board as the child lies upon his back upon the table or a firm bed. For older children a measuring rod or a fixed measuring board is convenient.

To estimate properly the significance of measurements they should be compared with the normal averages and with each other. It should be remembered that the head is normally larger than the chest until near the end of the first year; after this time, with normal development, the chest should be larger. Any great disproportion between the size of the head and chest is suggestive of disease. The measurements are important for early recognition of abnormalities such as hydro- or microcephalus, cretinism, and chondrodystrophy, the variations often being marked before other symptoms are prominent. When measurements are taken regularly, the variations from the normal are readily appreciated and great assistance is gained from these data. Such a record made from year to year is of great value in indicating progress. **PULSE, RESPIRATION, AND TEMPERATURE.** The significance of these signs is not to be measured by adult standards, since the susceptible nervous system of infants and very young children greatly exaggerates the reaction to all forms of acute infection.

The rate, regularity, and quality of the pulse should be noted. In young children, the rate of the pulse is of less importance than its force and quality. A slow, irregular pulse is always significant; a slight irregularity of the pulse during sleep has no special significance. Furthermore, the pulse rate varies normally with respiration in many children. The pulse rate is greatly increased by slight disturbances; the approach of a stranger or the examination by the physician may cause it to rise 20 or 30 beats. In acute disease, a pulse rate of 150 is common, and 170 or 180 is often seen when other symptoms are not particularly severe.

The rate, depth, and rhythm of respiration should be noted. The last often cannot be determined except by attentively watching the child for several minutes. In premature and very young infants a rather marked irregularity may be seen, often approaching the Biot type. In the very young, it is not to be taken as indicating a cerebral lesion, since newborn infants frequently present a respiration of this type, but only during the first weeks of life. Irregularity of rhythm at other times should suggest cerebral disease. The respiratory rate is proportionately greater in infants than in adults. In pneumonia and acute bronchiolitis it not infrequently rises to 70 or 80, and occasionally it may be over 100 a minute.

In general, the temperature of infants and very young children should be taken in the rectum. In many hospital nurseries for newborn infants, especially in premature units, axillary temperatures are taken as a routine in order to avoid the stimulus to defecation caused by insertion of a thermometer into the rectum. Under normal conditions the rectal temperature varies between 97.6° and 99.8° F; occasionally the range may be as wide as 97.0° to 100.6° F in apparently perfect health. It has been shown that the rectal temperature may rise as much as 3° F following exercise. Neither oral nor axillary readings are influenced by muscular work to a comparable extent.

Except in young infants, who may have little

or no fever even with severe infections, the increase in body temperature from infections or from any other cause tends to be greater in infants and children than it does in adults. Moreover, high fever may be present in cases which are not serious. In such circumstances the temperature seldom remains at a high point for more than a few hours. A continuous or recurring high temperature has greater significance.

Puzzling and apparently alarming temperatures are seen in infants as a result of the application of artificial heat. In one of our patients, an infant 2 days old, a temperature of 107° F was caused by the proximity of two large hot-water bottles placed in the baby's basket. The younger and feebler the child, the more readily are such temperature produced.

Subnormal temperatures are commonly seen in premature infants, in whom the temperature may fall below 95° F. This phenomenon is also seen after defervescence of fevers of various kinds and in wasting diseases.

BLOOD PRESSURE. The measurement of blood pressure in infants and children is discussed in Chapter 21.

Mental Development

The first examination of every new patient, unless he is acutely or seriously ill, should include an evaluation of his intelligence. In the case of newborn infants, whose brains function chiefly at a subcortical level, one has little to go on except the facial expression and perhaps the measurement of the head. From the second month onward, however, an increasing variety of devices are at hand for determining the stage of mental development at which the patient has arrived for comparison with his chronologic age. Some of these resources are listed in summary form in Chapter 5 and in Section 15.1. They range from the evoking of a smile during the second month to the posing of arithmetic problems and questions on current events in the case of older children. The clinician, who is not primarily concerned with the formal calculation of an intelligence quotient, should nevertheless have at his command a sufficiently detailed understanding of the accomplishments which a normal infant or child of a given age may be expected to perform, so that he may judge whether his patient is unusually bright, average, or retarded, and may thus be in a better position to evaluate the complaints, responses, and general behavior of his patient.

Local Examination

SKIN. The skin should first be inspected for eruptions, and it is important that the entire eruption be examined in order that its distribution as well as the character of individual lesions may be appreciated. Marked wrinkling or loss of elasticity of the skin is one of the best indications of loss in weight. The rapidity with which a fold of skin and subcutaneous tissue pinched up in the thumb and finger resumes its normal contour when released is a convenient measure of dehydration. Edema may be localized or general, increasing or receding. Bed sores are more frequently seen over the occiput than over the sacrum. Any large veins should be noted.

SUPERFICIAL LYMPH NODES. All lymph node areas should be examined, not only the cervical, axillary, and inguinal, but also the occipital, posterior cervical, pre- and retroauricular, submental, supraclavicular, and epitrochlear. Many healthy children will have moderate enlargement of the cervical, axillary, or inguinal nodes due usually to minor infections in the regions which they drain. However, the cause of marked enlargement of any of these groups, or any enlargement of the epitrochlear nodes, should be thoroughly investigated.

HEAD. One should note whether the cranial sutures are ossified or unnaturally open or separated; also whether the fontanel is closed or, if open, whether it is depressed or bulging. Craniotabes should be tested for during the first year.

EYES. The condition of the conjunctivae and lids should be noted, as well as the presence of ptosis, strabismus, or other paralysis, but particularly the condition of the pupils, whether contracted or dilated, and the nature of their response to light. One should look also for the presence of corneal ulcers or opacities. The sclerae should be examined for the discoloration of jaundice. Examination of the eyegrounds and appraisal of usual acuity should not be neglected simply because the patient is young.

EARS. Otoscopic examination of the ears must often be preceded by removal of cerumen. This can usually be accomplished by the use of a curette, care being taken to avoid trauma to the canal wall with resultant hemorrhage, which may obscure the membrane. Small bits of wax may often be easily removed by means of a cotton applicator dipped in mineral oil. When the canal is filled with impacted cerumen, it is sometimes necessary to syringe the canal with warm water. The normal and abnormal tympanic membrane is described in Chapter 31.

Examination of the eardrums should be a part of every routine physical examination; the drums should be carefully followed in all diseases involving the mouth, rhinopharynx, and the lower respiratory tract; in all communicable diseases; and in head trauma. In any acute febrile condition, and particularly when otorrhea already exists, one should look for tenderness or swelling over the mastoid bone.

Screening tests for gross abnormalities of hearing are an important part of the physical examination of infants and children.

NOSE. The appearance of the nasal mucosa should be noted and the character of any nasal discharge determined. Cultures should invariably be made from purulent discharges. In young infants, an abundant discharge tinged with blood should suggest syphilis; in older children, diphtheria. A chronic discharge should suggest paranasal sinusitis; chronic rhinorrhea after head injury, a fracture of the ethmoidal cribiform plate; and a purulent discharge from one side, a foreign body.

MOUTH. The appearance of the mucous membrane of the mouth and gums, as well as the teeth, may often be ascertained by watching the child while he is crying. It should be noted whether the tongue is dry or moist, clear or coated, whether thrush or any other form of stomatitis is present, and whether the gums are congested, swollen, or hemorrhagic. The number, position, and character of the teeth are important. The color of the mucous membrane may be significant. Cyanosis or pallor should be noted. On the mucous membrane of the hard palate may often be found the first local evidence of scarlet fever, in the form of a minute punctate eruption; the cheeks opposite the molar teeth may show the presence of Koplik spots, the earliest reliable sign of measles. The pharynx should be examined for inflammation, exudate, and membrane. The size and appearance of the tonsils should be noted, though size alone is not a reliable index of infection. A thorough though brief inspection of the entire pharynx may be made when the child gags as the tongue depressor is applied to the posterior part of the tongue. However, this maneuver is very dangerous in the presence of respiratory infection accompanied by signs of obstruction, for it may elicit a fatal vagovagal reflex. In children with laryngeal stridor it is possible in many instances to effect a brief inspection of the posterior structures of the mouth and pharynx during the inspiratory phase of crying, which may even bring an inflamed, edematous epiglottis into view.

NECK. One should consider the position in which the head is held and the amount of rigidity of the cervical muscles. Considerable information may be derived in diseases of the nervous system by noting the ease with which the head is raised by the patient when the trunk is lifted from the supine to a sitting position.

CHEST. In young children particular importance should be attached to the shape and symmetry of the chest. Rickets and pulmonary or cardiac disease may produce striking alterations in the configuration of the thorax. One should also notice the recession of the soft parts—intercostal spaces, the suprasternal notch, or the epigastrium; the amount of this is usually the best means of judging the severity of obstructive dyspnea. Details regarding the physical examination of the lungs are discussed in Chapter 26.

HEART. In patients less than 2 years of age loud cardiac murmurs are almost invariably of congenital origin, and soft murmurs heard over the precordium are frequently functional even when transmitted to the axilla. Acquired cardiac disease is rare until after the age of 3 years. Marked sinus arrhythmia is a common finding in children and may lead an inexperienced observer to suspect an abnormality of conduction. Additional detail on the evaluation of the heart is given in Section 20.2.

ABDOMEN. Symmetric distension of the abdomen is usually due to tympanites, which can be readily confirmed by percussion. In very young patients shifting dullness is not infrequently demonstrable when ascites is absent. With free peritoneal fluid in significant amount, a fluid wave can be due to enlargement of an underlying organ, to weakness of overlying parietes, or to some pathologic structure such as a tumor or cyst. The vigor of peristaltic activity in the intestinal tract can be judged to some extent by listening for approximately one minute while the stethoscope bell is applied to the abdominal wall in the region of the umbilicus. In infants whose gain in weight has been delayed for any reason, the pattern of intestinal coils can often be seen through the thin abdominal wall, with the slow writhing characteristic of normal peristaltic activity. Deep waves in the epigastrium, moving always from left to right, are gastric in origin and usually denote pyloric or duodenal obstruction. Abdominal tenderness when present should be carefully evaluated and its distribution localized as soon as possible. The size and position of the liver and spleen are best determined by palpation. The lower border of the right lobe of the liver can usually be made out distinctly in patients less than 2 years of age. If the spleen can easily be felt below the ribs, it is, as a rule, enlarged. If it cannot be felt in a satisfactory examination, it is not sufficiently enlarged to be of diagnostic importance. Umbilical hernia is common in the first year of life.

SPINE. The spine should be carefully examined to detect variations from the normal, which are recognized by decreases or increases of the normal curves, and by the appearance of abnormal curvatures and protrusions. If found, it should be determined whether these are permanent, or reducible by change of posture.

EXTREMITIES. The color of the extremities and the character of the peripheral circulation should be noted, as well as any evidences of edema or hemorrhage in the form of punctuate or larger extravasations. Clubbing of the fingers and toes should be looked for, and any abnormality in the nails or desquamation of palms or soles recorded. In examining the extremities one should note especially the presence of tenderness, flaccidity, or rigidity of muscles, whether the limbs are wasted or plump, and the degree of muscular power. Any abnormal swelling on the shaft or near the ends of the bones should be noted, as well as the contours of the joints and their range of motion. In the patient of suitable age, provided he is not too ill, the gait, and the posture assumed on sitting and standing should be observed. Certain deformities dependent on functional rather than structural abnormality are not easily evaluated in the recumbent child—for example, those resulting from weak feet.

Palpation of the femoral artery pulsation in the inguinal region should be a part of the physical examination of every patient seen for the first time; the most common cause of absent pulsations is congenital coarctation of the aorta.

REFLEXES. The tendon reflexes may be difficult to obtain in an infant at any one examination, and at another they may appear exaggerated. Lively patellar reflexes, unless accompanied by rigidity and ankle clonus, are not often indicative of disease. The plantar cutaneous reflex of Babinski in extension is normally present during the first year but takes on increasing pathologic significance thereafter. The abdominal reflexes can be regularly obtained after the age of 6 months and the cremasterics somewhat later. In children both of these sets of superficial reflexes may be quite lively.

Since satisfactory elicitation of the Chvostek sign is dependent on a certain degree of repose of the features, it is wise to make this test at the beginning of the examination of a patient, before the child has become disturbed.

GENITAL ORGANS. Male children should be examined to determine the presence of hypospadias, phimosis, or of undescended testicles. Hydrocele is a frequent condition and may be mistaken for hernia. In the female, it is important to recognize the existence of hymenal imperforation, labial fusion, vaginal atresia, or clitoral enlargement. Every vaginal discharge is significant, and, if purulent, should be examined bacteriologically. In both girls and boys the presence of sexual hair or abnormal pigmentation should be noted.

Collection of Body Fluids For Laboratory Analysis

The examination is not complete without investigation of the urine and blood and, in infants, of the stools as well. In the collection of samples of urine from male infants, the penis in inserted into a collapsible plastic container. For female infants a similar collecting device may be held against the vulva in the same way. The head of the bed should be raised a few inches. When pyuria is suspected, catheterization under strict aseptic precautions may be justified; not infrequently the infant will void when the tip of the catheter is applied to the urethral meatus. The use of a suprapubic puncture for the aspiration of urine has proved to be a safe procedure, and does not carry with it the potential complications of catheterization. In older children, voided specimens are satisfactory and should be used.

BLOOD. When a small amount of blood is required, as for hemoglobin estimation and cell counts, it is often easier to obtain it from the infant's heel than from the fingertip or ear. Preliminary immersion of the foot in hot water induces a capillary distension that favors a free flow, and it is usually possible to obtain 1 or 2 ml in this manner, enough for serologic or certain chemical tests. If the capillary dilation is adequate, blood so obtained has the characteristics of arterial blood. Amounts larger than 1 to 2 ml are usually better taken by venipuncture.

CEREBROSPINAL FLUID. For all ordinary diagnostic purposes cerebrospinal fluid is withdrawn from the lumbar subarachnoid space. Collections of fluid from the cisterna magna or cerebral ventricles should be considered neurosurgical procedures.

Lumbar puncture. The patient is placed upon his side and held with the neck and thighs strongly flexed to separate the spines and laminae of the vertebrae. A local anesthetic is desirable except in the small infant, where it is probably unnecessary. Under aseptic precautions the needle is inserted in the midline at the level of the crest of the ilium or just above this and pointed straight forward or slightly cephalad. The distance it must be introduced in order to enter the subarachnoid space varies with the age and, to a lesser extent, with the state of nutrition of the patient; as a rule, it is about 1 to 2 cm in infants, increasing to about 3 to 4 cm in children 3 to 5 years of age. An experienced operator can tell from the sudden change of resistance to the needle when its point has pierced the dura, but without this skill the best procedure is to introduce the needle a small distance at a time and remove the obturator to see whether spinal fluid flows out. If by accident the tip traverses the subarachnoid space and meets the plexus of veins on the anterior wall of the spinal canal, contamination of the fluid with blood may occur. A slow flow may result from low pressure, from obstruction of the lumen with tissue, or because the exudate is too thick to flow freely. Raising the patient to a sitting posture usually causes a freer flow, as does flexing the head upon the chest or pinching the skin to make the child cry.

Fluid should be collected in separate tubes, since in this way the needle is washed clear of traumatic blood by the first portion, and the cell count in the last tube is made more reliable. A fairly satisfactory measure of spinal fluid pressure may be obtained by allowing the first fluid obtained to flow through a rubber connecting tube into a vertical glass tube of about 1 mm bore and using this as a water manometer. More accurate methods require special apparatus, but the error of uncontrolled intrathoracic pressure is so large that refined manometric methods ordinarily have no great advantage. When the purpose of the puncture is diagnostic, the withdrawal of from 6 to 10 ml of fluid is usually sufficient. For the reduction of pressure the fluid may be allowed to flow until it emerges at a rate of only one or two drops per minute. In this way one can safely withdraw from infants and children larger amounts in proportion to the body weight than would be possible with adults. When medication or air is injected, the amount should always be at least 5 ml less than the amount of spinal fluid previously withdrawn. After any spinal puncture the patient should be watched for 10 or 15 minutes for symptoms of collapse; this applies particularly when medication has been administered. The information provided by the examination of the cerebrospinal fluid is described in Sections 14.3 and 15.1.

The danger of lumbar puncture in the presence of increased intracranial pressure is explained in Section 15.5. There has been considerable discussion of the possible risk of causing meningitis by performing lumbar puncture in the presence of bacteremia, which has been done experimentally in laboratory animals. However, a clinical survey of the experience of five pediatric hospitals failed to reveal evidence that such induced infection is an important hazard. At any rate, when the consequences of a late diagnosis of meningitis are weighed against the rather remote chance of producing meningitis by means of the procedure, the decision is almost invariably in favor of lumbar puncture.

Strict attention to aseptic technique is essential. When medications are to be injected, their sterility must be beyond question. This is equally true with regard to the syringes and other equipment used. Solutions of antibiotics to be injected intrathecally should be made up expressly for that purpose. It is risky to employ solutions which have been in general use about the ward. Septic meninigitis has been produced in patients who had received intrathecal injections of contaminated penicillin.

PERITONEAL, PLEURAL, AND SUBDURAL FLUIDS. Diagnostic puncture of the peritoneum may be done in infants and children when other signs of purulent peritonitis are equivocal.

Aspiration of the pleural cavity in infants and young chidren is performed when fluid or air collections are suspected.

Aspiration of subdural collections of fluid is described elsewhere (Sec. 15.1).

32.5
GENERAL THERAPEUTIC MEASURES

REST. The importance of rest in the management of acute illness can hardly be doubted. An overzealous therapeutic campaign which deprives the patient of sleep and contributes to fatigue is to be avoided. Sedation may be necessary if there is undue restlessness. The management of convalescence may be a more difficult matter. There has been an increasing tendency toward early ambulation of surgical patients, chiefly to avoid psychologic attitudes of invalidism and to escape the metabolic complications of immobilization —a loss of nitrogen and potassium from the body and decalcification of the bones with hypercalcemia, hypercalciuria, and possible formations of renal calculi. In the case of children it is difficult to lay down rules; one must judge by the response of the individual child, avoiding a degree of exertion apt to cause fatigue while encouraging the patient to do what he

appears to tolerate well. Quiet diversions are helpful to allay the boredom of a stay in bed.

Questions concerning the limitation of activity in children with various chronic illnesses, such as heart or kidney disease, are discussed in the relevant sections.

DIET. The ability of young subjects, particularly infants, to digest food is often impaired in parenteral disease as well as in primary disorders of the gastrointestinal tract. Reduction of food intake may be necessary to avoid vomiting, diarrhea, or distension. Digestion is particularly apt to be disturbed at the onset of an acute disease, often only during the first few hours. Occasionally the digestive incapacity persists for a long period. Digestion and assimilation of fat and carbohydrate may be disturbed to a variable extent; protein usually continues to be well handled in the presence of infections. Although the difficulty is essentially one of gastrointestinal function, the intermediary metabolism of foodstuffs may be affected as well. Carbohydrate tolerance tests in infections often give evidence of impaired liver function, and ketosis may have a similar significance.

The dietary management of acute disease may be guided to a large extent by the child's appetite. Often this serves to limit the intake, particularly for solid foods, and forcing of food should by all means be avoided. Fluids should, however, be freely offered.

In the presence of nausea and vomiting, one is limited in the use of the oral route. A reduction in the fat content of the diet occasionally helps under these circumstances. Skimmed milk may be offered, or fruit juices, broths, and cereals. A predominantly carbohydrate diet is suitable for an acute illness of brief duration but not for a chronic disorder. In the latter case, protein, vitamin, and mineral requirements become major considerations.

ADMINISTRATION OF FLUIDS. The correction of fluid loss is indicated in any acute illness. Fever per se causes increased evaporation from the skin and lungs. Large amounts of water may be lost with vomiting and diarrhea. In infancy the depletion of body fluids may be rapid and of severe degree; dehydration is especially common at this age.

Oral Administration of Fluids. Most infants will readily take water from a bottle, particularly when small amounts are offered at frequent intervals rather than large amounts at one time. Occasionally feeding by spoon or medicine dropper is required. There is no objection to sweetening the water by the addition of 5 percent sugar. The administration of water by mouth in acute illnesses is not apt to be overdone; one should at least aim to overcome the oliguria which accompanies the onset of many infections. Infants with diarrhea should be given electrolyte solutions by mouth (Sec. 3.7).

In older children large amounts of water can be given by mouth with skillful nursing. The variety of disguises in which water may be clothed is great— fruit juices, clear broth, ginger ale, cola beverages, gelatin pudding. Here it is particularly important to keep in mind that small amounts offered frequently will net a larger intake than large amounts at longer intervals. In the presence of vomiting, surprisingly large amounts may be tolerated when given in frequent teaspoonful doses. When there is nausea, fluids are often better borne when given ice-cold.

Gavage and Nasogastric Tube Feeding. When the patient is too ill or too weak to swallow adequate amounts of fluid given by mouth, they may be administered through a plastic or soft rubber tube inserted through a nostril into the stomach. The rate of administration should be steady, and slow enough to avoid over-filling the stomach and thereby inducing vomiting.

The older methods of intermittent gavage have now largely been replaced by the use of indwelling nasogastric tubes made of one of the plastics. This method has proved invaluable in the feeding of premature infants. Soft plastic catheters are available in small size and with rounded ends to minimize the risk of gastric perforation.

Intravenous Infusion. When fluids cannot be taken by mouth they should be given by intravenous infusion. The ease with which this procedure is accomplished depends very largely on the skill of the operator. With suitably sharp needles, those experienced in intravenous technique can enter the superficial veins of the scalp, elbow, or ankle of even small infants. With properly secured needles, the infant's total daily fluid requirement may be supplied by slow intravenous drip.

When the superficial veins are not suitable for infusion, catheterization of the internal saphenous vein at the ankle provides a reliable means of continuous fluid administration. This approach is often used to great advantage for patients undergoing surgery. The technique is not difficult. The foot is first immobilized by taping it to a splint. Procaine is infiltrated into the skin just anterior and proximal to the medial malleolus. A transverse incision is made through the skin and subcutaneous tissue and the vein identified. This is facilitated by the application of a tourniquet above the site of incision. The vein is then freed from the underlying tissue with a small forceps, and a silk ligature is passed underneath the exposed vessel. A small opening is made into the vein with small sharp-pointed scissors, and a plastic catheter is introduced and passed cephalad in the lumen of the vein to a distance of a centimeter or two before being tied in place with the silk ligature.

Intravenous infusion is invaluable not only in the treatment of dehydration, burns, and hypovolemic shock, but also for the administration of medication when other routes are not desirable. When infants and children undergo long or especially traumatic surgical operations, it is valuable to have an intravenous infusion running before the operation is begun. It provides a route for the correction of fluid loss during the operation and makes possible the prompt administration of blood or plasma should hemorrhage or shock supervene during the operation. Once the operation has begun, it becomes at best difficult to establish an infusion without deranging drapes, and the resulting delay may be serious. Since needles are often dislodged from veins during operations, it is more satisfactory to insert and securely fasten into the vein a plastic indwelling catheter, which is introduced into the vessel either through a "cut-down" incision or through the lumen of a specially designed needle (Intracath). Thus, the exigencies of the operation can be met and the fluid, blood, and plasma requirements of the immediate postoperative period can be supplied.

When continuous infusions are used, it is important to maintain a careful hourly tabulation of the amount of fluids administered and of the concomitant urinary output and specific gravity. Relatively small variations in rate of flow, as measured by the number of drops per minute, may in the course of 24 hours result in a large deviation from the amounts of fluid planned for the day's total.

Transfusions. These are employed not only in anemia but to combat shock. When the purpose is to expand blood volume rather than to supply red cells, one may use plasma protein fraction (plasmanate) or human serum albumin instead of whole blood. There is rarely need for employing routes other than the intravenous. A suitable superficial vein can nearly always be found.

The blood of the recipient must be matched with that of the prospective donor to ensure compatibility as to both major types and Rh subgroups. Recipients who have had numerous transfusions over a period of years not infrequently experience febrile reactions following administration of blood which by every conventional test had been shown to be compatible. In such situations the prophylactic administration of adrenocortical steroid preparation tends to suppress unfavorable reactions. A suitable dose is 25 mg of cortisone given by mouth in three doses—one before, one during, and one following transfusion.

Care must be taken to minimize the chances of transmitting disease through the transfusion of blood. The donor's blood is tested serologically for evidence of syphilis and the donor himself examined for any evidence of primary syphilis which may be present before the serologic reaction has become positive. Individuals who have had malaria or who have recently been in an area of malaria epidemicity should be excluded as donors, as should persons with evidence of active infection of any sort.

The prevention of viral hepatitis is more difficult, since individuals may transmit this disease without showing clinical evidence of jaundice. Any unit of whole blood, plasma, or plasma fraction has the potential for transmitting either serum or infectious hepatitis. Detection of hepatitis-associated-antigen (HAA) offers a specific test for the diagnosis of serum hepatitis; there is no way at the present to eliminate the risk of infectious hepatitis. The danger of transmitting serum hepatitis is particularly great when pooled plasma is used, since the plasma of a single carrier may contaminate an entire pool, thereby infecting a large number of recipients. Because of this hazard, the use of pooled plasma should be avoided. Some plasma components, such as plasma protein fraction (plasmanate) and serum albumin, can be rendered safe by heating at 60° C for 10 hours. Other blood fractions have a high-risk potential for hepatitis transmission; these include fibrinogen and concentrates of factors VIII and IX.

When large transfusions are given, especially exchange transfusions in hemolytic disease of the newborn or in the treatment of poisoning, it is important to use blood which has been stored for not more than a few days. Older blood may have dangerously high plasma potassium levels, resulting in disastrous hyperkalemia in the patient.

INHALATIONS. In diseases affecting the larynx, trachea, or bronchioles, inhalations of steam or, preferably, cold mist are given to infants by means of a tent or a small chamber enclosing the head. In the home, as an emergency measure for obtaining high humidity in the treatment of croup or acute bronchiolitis, hot-water taps may be turned on in the bathroom to generate steam; the patient may then be held in the arms until his condition is relieved or until more permanent measures are set up in his own room. Nebulizing devices are also available for the administration of cold steam and the humidification of the ambient air.

OXYGEN ADMINISTRATION. When indicated, humidified oxygen is best administered by mask by means of one or another type of oxygen tent, the sort used depending on the size of the patient. For young infants an incubator offers a convenient device for oxygen therapy. Oxygen should be passed through water into the tent, chamber, or mask to counteract its harmful drying effects on the respiratory mucosa.

GASTRIC LAVAGE. The introduction of a soft catheter or small tube into an infant's stomach causes far less distress than in the case of an adult. For the removal of gas and liquid contents in acute gastric distension the procedure is immediately and often strikingly effective. Gastric lavage is often necessary in the emergency treatment of poisoning. Although little danger exists of the tube's being accidentally introduced into the larynx, it is good policy to pause for a few seconds after the tube is in place to make sure that there is no to-and-fro motion of respired air. On removal the tube should be pinched tightly to prevent accidental leakage of its contents into the trachea.

ENEMAS. Simple enemas of normal saline or of hypertonic phosphate solution are useful for the relief of fecal impaction (see also Sec. 23.7). Oil retention enemas may be used when the fecal mass is hard and dry and expelled with difficulty. Enemas should be given with a soft rubber bulb or through a soft rubber catheter. Because of the danger of water intoxication, tap water enemas must not be used, especially in chronic constipation. A large volume of hypotonic fluid administered per rectum, if retained, removes electrolytes from body fluids and induces symptoms of hypoelectrolytemia ("water intoxication"). Indeed, fatalities have been known to occur in patients with megacolon, following rectal instillation of large quantities of tap water.

ANESTHESIA. Much can be done to avert the severe emotional upsets associated with inhalational anesthesia by a combination of intelligent psychologic preparation, judicious administration of preanesthetic medication, and skillful induction of anesthesia. A preoperative visit to the patient by the anesthesiologist is of value in the psychologic preparation of the child. It is helpful for the child to recognize the anesthesiologist as a friend when the time for surgery arrives. The visit also serves to permit the anesthesiologist to acquaint himself with the child's medical status and to decide upon agents and techniques to be used. A consultation involving anesthesiologist, surgeon, and pediatrician may be helpful.

The use of preanesthetic medication is of importance not only in the induction of the anesthesia but also in lessening the danger of postoperative psychic disturbance. The child should arrive in the induction room well under the influence of his medication. Medications given hurriedly as the child is wheeled from his room serve no good purpose; they should be given about one hour before the start of anesthesia, to allow time to take effect. The choice of drugs and their doses will depend on the age and weight of the patient, his metabolic state, the type of anesthesia to be used, and the presence or absence of pain. The drugs most frequently used are sodium secobarbital (Seconal), and scopolamine or atropine, often in combination with morphine or meperidine (Demerol). Tribromoethanol administered by rectum offers the obvious advantage of permitting the child to be taken from his room unconscious after a relatively pleasant induction. This is particularly helpful for children who must have repeated operations. The method is not without disadvantages, however, because of the prolonged recovery period following its use.

Induction itself should be carried out in a quiet room outside the operating room. As induction agents, open hose cyclopropane or open drop Vinethene are widely used because they are relatively nonirritating and quickly acting. Nevertheless, induction with ethyl ether can be remarkably pleasant if one proceeds slowly and carefully. Intravenous thiopental (Pentothal) may be used to advantage, provided the venipuncture does not start the child crying.

A number of differences between adults and children pose special problems in the conduct of the anesthesia. In general, the margin of safety in dosage is smaller in children than in adults and the risks of overdosage greater, whatever the agent. The greater metabolic activity of the child, relative to body weight, results in greater oxygen need and greater carbon dioxide production. In supplying the former and removing the latter, open drop techniques offer fewer difficulties than are encountered in the use of the various anesthesia machines. The respiratory dead space is small in children and the added dead space of the apparatus is relatively great, especially when designed for adult use. Newly designed anesthesia machines are available for pediatric use only, which do not impose a significant increase in dead space or in resistance to breathing for prematures and infants up to 1 year of age.

The importance of the use of an intravenous cannula or catheter in meeting fluid, electrolyte, and blood requirements during and immediately following surgery has been mentioned.

Local anesthetics are on the whole not as helpful in operations on infants and children as in those on adults. In early infancy, particularly within the first three or four months, it is often possible to perform an abdominal operation such as the Fredet-Ramstedt operation for pyloric stenosis under the combined influence of morphine, sugar pacifiers,* and local anesthesia; success in such cases depends in part, however, on the feebleness of the patient. Robust infants and children up to school age or beyond usually require a general anesthetic when any is called for.

Attention should be paid to heat regulation during surgery, particularly with infants and during hot weather. Infants less than 6 months of age often become hypothermic during anesthesia, while children more than 1 year of age often become hyperthermic. Those in between may change either way. A circulating hot- or cold-water mattress will help to control temperature. Hypothermia may result in depressed respirations or apnea, and in cardiac arrhythmias. Hyperthermia is often associated with convulsions which, under anesthesia, cause death in about one out of five cases. The danger of heat retention is enhanced by extensive draping of the patient during long operations in a small field, particularly in plastic operations. In such cases, supplying adequate amounts of fluid and electrolytes will help offset this danger, and it may be of help to blow compressed air beneath the drapes. When rebreathing systems which employ carbon dioxide absorption canisters are being used, heat generated in the canisters may contribute to heat retention. Frequent changing of canisters or cooling them with ice will help to reduce this difficulty.

Hypothermia. In cardiac survery, lowering the body temperature to the vicinity of 30° C has proved to be of value by permitting brief interruptions in blood circulation. Hypothermia is also applied at times during neurosurgical procedures and in the treatment of acute cerebral edema. The details of the methods used, as well as the dangers such as ventricular fibrillation and diminished resistance to

infection inherent in the procedure, are beyond the scope of this text.

USE OF DRUGS. The major classes of drugs used in the treatment of infants and children are discussed in connection with the conditions in which they have their greatest usefulness. Thus, adrenocorticosteroids are considered in the chapter on the endocrine system (Sec. 16.5), antibiotics under infectious diseases (Sec. 14.1), anticonvulsants under the nervous system (Sec. 15.9), and antihistamines under allergy (Sec. 11.3). Other drugs are discussed elsewhere in relation to specific diseases; fetal pharmacology is considered in detail in a separate section (Sec. 2.7). For a discussion of specific drugs, the reader is referred to the individual sections of the book.

Although various rules have been devised for relating adult doses to children and infants, these have often very limited applications because of considerable variations between different drugs. There is evidence that the correlation of dosage with body surface area is even closer than with body weight, as determined by blood concentrations of the drug—sulfadiazine or acetylsalicylic acid, for example. However, it is in general preferable to know the dosage required for infants for each drug to be employed. With some agents the dosage commonly used is roughly proportional to either the age or the weight of the child, and with others, doses only slightly less than the adult dose are required. Opiates as a rule may be given in doses proportional to the body weight, 0.15 to 0.2 mg of morphine sulfate per kilogram being a safe level. To a few drugs, such as atropine, infants are relatively more sensitive than are adults. Among the drugs to which infants are more tolerant may be mentioned barbiturates, epinephrine, and biologic preparations in general. Roughly half an adult dose may be given to a child of 3 or 4 years, and one-fourth of the adult dose may be given to an infant of 6 months.

REFERENCES

American Academy of Pediatrics. Report of the committee on the control of infectious diseases. Red Book, 16th ed., 1971.

———— Council on pediatric practice. Standards of child health care, 1967.

———— Child health record from infancy to adulthood, 1968.

———— and McKeith, R. The Child and His Symptoms: A Comprehensive Approach, 2nd ed. Oxford, Blackwell Scientific Publications Ltd., 1968.

Barness, L. A., ed. Manual of Pediatric Diagnosis. Chicago, Year Book Medical Publishers, Inc., 1966.

Committee on Child Health, American Public Health Association. Health Supervision of Young Children. New York, American Public Health Association, Inc., 1955.

Illingworth, R. S. The Normal Child. Some Problems of

---

* One or two teaspoons of cane sugar wrapped in gauze and moistened with water. Sometimes a dozen or more are used at a single operation.

the First Five Years and Their Treatment, 4th ed. London, J. & A. Churchill, 1968.

——— Common Symptoms of Diseases in Children, 3rd ed. Oxford, Blackwell Scientific Publications Ltd., 1971.

Korsch, B. M. Practical techniques of observing, interviewing, and advising parents in pediatric practice as demonstrated in an attitude study project. Pediatrics, 18:467, 1956.

Paul, J. R., Jr. (chairman). Committee on School Health, Evanston, Ill., American Academy of Pediatrics, 1966.

Silver, H. K., Kempe, C. H., and Bruyn, H. B. Hand-
book of Pediatrics, 6th ed. Los Altos, Calif., Lange Medical Publications, 1965.

Smith, C. H. Transfusions in pediatric practice: indications and limitations. Pediatrics, 17:596, 1956.

Smith, R. M. Anesthesia for Infants and Children. St. Louis, The C. V. Mosby Co., 1963.

Spock, B. The Common Sense Book of Baby and Child Care, 2nd ed. New York, Duell, Sloan & Pearce, 1957.

United States Children's Bureau, Department of Health, Education, and Welfare. Infant Care. New York, Lancer Books, Inc., 1964.

The Child's Environment

32.6
PEDIATRIC PRACTICE, AN ECOLOGY OF THE FAMILY UNIT

As all living organisms, children differ in their physical, physiologic, and behavioral characteristics. Normal and abnormal individual variations are not only governed by genetic determinants; they are also the product of a myriad of environmental factors and influences (Fig. 1). In a simplified schema of life, Figure 1 portrays in capsule form the subjection of somatic life, behavior and personality, and growth and development to the combined and interacting effects of genetic and environmental factors. Environmental stimuli constantly challenge the host's adjustment and vary both qualitatively and quantitatively with the nature of his surroundings. The host's "terrain" depends upon his genetic makeup; his response to the environmental stimuli is controlled by both inherited and acquired features.

All external conditions and influences in the child's surroundings exert major effects upon his attributes and health status. Apley has emphasized the fact that the child's environment is a *continuum* that is unceasingly modified by nature and by man himself; the child has to adapt to all these modifications. Good health ensues if the adaption is satisfactory, and ill health when it is not. Adaption to the environment may not occur without stress, which may lead ultimately to disease. The environment should not be considered in physical terms only. Equally important are cultural, social, and psychologic factors which interplay and overlap with other influences. Other people are also part of the child's surroundings and contribute to his individuality, his well-being, and his

overall health. Purdom has depicted the following ecologic interacting system:

$$MAN \rightleftharpoons ENVIRONMENT$$

where not only do man and his environment interact, but man is shown to be a vital factor of his own environment.

Ecology, which derives from the Greek οικος meaning "home" or "house," is defined as the relation of plants and animals to their environment and to one another. The term, by no means a neologism, has become in the last decade a quasi-household word since Rachel Carson has alerted mankind to the dangers associated with the uncontrolled and unbridled manipulations of the environment by man. In an earlier and equally remarkable work, *Ecology of Human Disease,* May formulated a dynamic concept of medical ecology in terms of concern with survival of the individual through the study of the "home" or "seat" of illness. In this concept disease is viewed not merely as the impairment of health but as the convergence within the host of environmental stimuli (organic, inorganic, or sociocultural). The bodily reactions actuated by these stimuli result either in ecologic *adaptation* (survival) or in *maladjustment* (illness and/or death). Disease becomes "that alteration of the living tissues that jeopardizes survival in their environment."

The child's environment encompasses all substances, forms of life, forces, conditions, and influences under which he lives (Table 1). As summarized in Table 1, man's surroundings comprise a *natural environment* and a *man-made environment.* The latter includes finite products of varying size, consistency, and mobility; in addition, there are situations, circumstances, conditions, and resources which result from human groupings, associations, interactions, and activities, and which we have termed

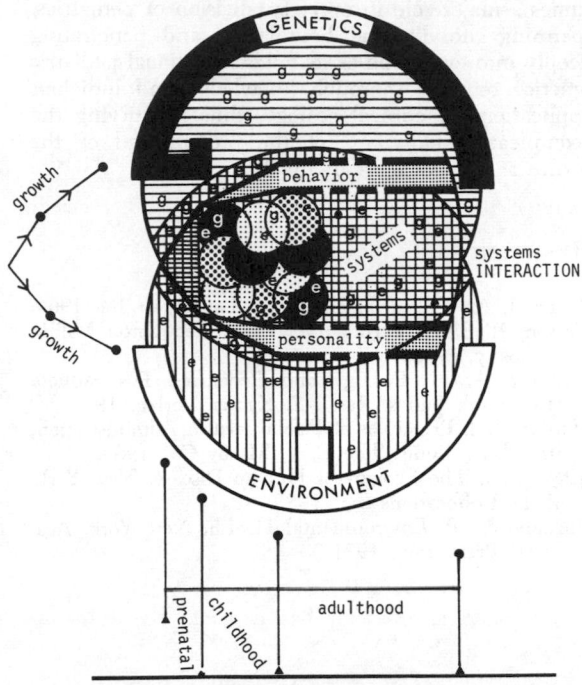

Fig. 1. This figure schematizes human life molded by genetic and environmental determinants (g = genetic factors; e = environmental factors). *Somatic life* is represented in the central core of the "capsule" by the overlapping multishaded circles symbolizing the interaction and interdependence of the various internal biologic systems. *Personality* and *behavior* are featured peripherally. *Growth* and *development* are expressed by the surface increases of the areas depicting prenatal life and childhood. The darkly shaded section pictures the *intrauterine existence* when viability and development of the conceptus are directly effected by the ecology of gestation.

TABLE 3.   *Environment*

I. NATURAL ENVIRONMENT

  A. Physical and Chemical Constituents

air and other gases
water and other liquids
fire
temperature, humidity, atmospheric pressure
light, infra-red, UV, electromagnetic energies; vibration
radiation
solid elements and compounds: organic
                                inorganic

  B. Living Organisms

microorganisms
macroorganisms, including MAN

  C. Geography (direct relationship with A. and B.)

climate, altitude
temperature
humidity
luminosity
flora and fauna

II. MAN-MADE ENVIRONMENT

  A. "Altered" Natural Environment
  (e.g., buildings, transportation, food processing, etc.)

  B. "Situational" Environment

family (or household unit)
community, country, and/or ethnic group
psychosocial environment
socioeconomic environment
nutritional environment
educational environment
recreational environment
religion
health care

"*situational*" *environment*. Certain environmental conditions such as air, water, food, and shelter, are essential requirements for survival. Others merely affect body functions, performance, and comfort without being fundamentally indispensable for the sustenance of life. Still others constitute, become, or are made into ecologic hazards (see also Chap. 13).

Environmental hazards may be *biologic* (infections, parasitism, zoonoses); *chemical* (toxins, poisons, irritants, drugs, air and water pollutants); *physical* (ionizing radiations, vibrations, mechanical injury, noise, humidity, fire, heat); *sociologic* (poverty, overcrowding, social isolation, lawlessness); and *psychologic* (emotional stress, anxiety, insecurity, guilt, boredom, rebellion). However, all manipulations of the environment by man are not necessarily harmful. Although many chemicals are potentially dangerous, the judicious use of some of these may improve the quality of life. Thus, fluoride concentration of drinking water if suitably adjusted prevents tooth decay; similarly, minute amounts of iodide will prevent goiter in areas where this condition is endemic. The specific effects of the environment upon the individual child may depend entirely on the nature, size, or amount of environmental stimuli, as in poisoning. However, a quantitative assessment of the hazard is often difficult. Chemicals, such as pesticides depositing into a stream, may concentrate in certain tissues of plants, animals, or fish; as these are consumed, successive concentrations may result in a manifold increase over the initial content. The consequences of environmental influences may also vary considerably in specific situations, particularly when genetic aberrations exist. Thus, high altitude, without significant effect on most children, may produce thrombotic episodes in individuals with sickle-cell anemia, and during gestation may untowardly affect the unborn fetus; there are familial and ethnic variations in the susceptibility to tuberculosis; and diets which are appropriate for the vast majority of children cause considerable harm in those with inborn errors of metabolism, such as phenylketonuria and galactosemia.

The achievement, maintenance, and restoration, if required, of optimal physical, intellectual, and emotional growth and development, are the objectives laid down for the provision of child health care. "Health," as defined by the World Health Organization "is a state of complete physical, mental, and social well-being and not merely the absence of disease." In a broader ecologic context the health status of a child is a matter of individual physiologic and psychosocial "adaption" or "maladjustment" to his environment. The child develops in surroundings which are being changed more rapidly than ever. The pediatrician's role as the child's primary physician is to ensure for the child on a continuing basis the best possible "adaption"; and to anticipate, prevent, and correct all factors apt to disrupt the complex interactions between the child's internal biologic systems and the total external environmental system. In the preface of the last edition of this text the inevitable trend toward increasing specialization within pediatrics has been stressed. Scientific progress and advances in medicine have made necessary the steadily growing array of subspecialties. However, medical ecology assumes a major role in every subdivision of pediatrics, spanning the dividing boundaries, and penetrating deeply into every one of its fields. A rational pediatric practice requires thorough knowledge and judicious applications of clinical ecology, thus identifying the "compleat pediatrician" of the present and of the future as the ecologist of the family unit.

REFERENCES

Apley, J. An ecology of childhood. Lancet, ii: 1-4, 1964.
Carson, R. Silent Spring. New York, Houghton Mifflin Company, 1962.
Einhorn, A. H. Ecology and Pediatrics. Postgraduate Monograph Series. Basel, S. Karger Verlag, 1972.
Hanlon, J. J. Principles of Public Health Administration, 5th ed. St. Louis, The C. V. Mosby Co., 1969.
May, J. M. The Ecology of Human Disease. New York, M. D. Publications Inc., 1958.
Purdon, W. P. Environmental Health. New York, Academic Press, Inc., 1971.

APPENDIX

Introduction	1915
Normal Values	1916
Hematology (See Table 1, Chap. 17.1, p. 1156)	
Blood Chemistry	1916
Cerebrospinal Fluid	1919
Urine and Renal Function	1919
Amino Acids	1920
Normal Growth	1921
Measurements at Different Ages	1921
Nomograms for Surface Area	1925
Stages of Puberty	1926
Live Births and Infant Mortality Rates	1929

INTRODUCTION

Values in this appendix are represented by a mean and the variation about the mean. Variation is usually expressed either as the standard deviation of the population, or as a range of values from two standard deviations above the mean to two standard deviations below. The range thus represents 95 percent of the values in a normally distributed population.

The limitations of this conventional expression of normal ranges are multiple, but a full discussion of these is beyond the scope of an introduction to the appendix of a clinical textbook. Briefly, there are three types of problems. The first has to do with the representativeness of the sample from which the primary data were obtained. Heights of white middle-class children, for instance, do not provide a relevant standard for many less privileged children. The error introduced by this bias in sampling could be avoided if only data obtained from well-defined populations were presented, but such data are limited. There would also be no sampling error if large numbers of children from all sorts of populations made up the sample, but then the applicability of the normal value to a given child would still be in question.

The second problem is closely related: normality is often only what we say it is. For example, the normal ranges of hemoglobin presented in this appendix do not describe 95 percent of the hemoglobin values found in a population of black urban children. No doubt there is more hemoglobin-lowering pathology in a black population, but 95 percent of the values in a white population includes some pathology as well, so why is the one population "normal" and the other not?

The third problem comes from the assumption of a bell-shaped distribution of values. In fact, many physiologic control mechanisms favor deviations above the mean over those below: body temperature and blood sugar are two examples of this. The error introduced by these differences in the shape of the underlying distribution are usually inconsequential but may become important when data are derived from small or unrepresentative samples.

The introduction to the Biological Handbooks, from which some values in this appendix are taken, makes a point that bears repeating here. "Another estimate of the lower and upper range of variation is based on the judgment of an individual experienced in measuring the quantity in question. The trustworthiness of such limits should not be underestimated."

TABLE 1.   *Blood Chemistry*

Determination	Values
Ammonia (whole blood)	
newborn	90-150 μg/100 ml
later	45-80 μg/100 ml[1]
Amylase (whole blood)	6-33 units/100 ml[2]
Ascorbic acid (serum)	0.5-1.5 mg/100 ml[3]
Base (Na + K + Ca + MG) (serum)	143-150 mEq/L[4]
Bicarbonate (serum)	24-31 mEq/L[5]
Bilirubin (serum)	
cord	up to 1.8 mg/100 ml
1-5 days	mean peak 6 mg/100 ml[6]
	range 2-12
later	< 0.8 mg/100 ml total
Bromsulphalein (BSP)	
newborn	up to 20% retention (up to 30% with respiratory distress)
later	< 5% retention
Calcium (serum)	8.8-10.4 mg/100 ml[7]
Carbon dioxide content (plasma)	
newborn	19.7-27.5 mm/L[8]
later	24.5-30.1 mm/L[9]
Carotene	
newborn	3-15 μg/100 ml
later	40-130 μg/100 ml[10]
Cephalin flocculation	
infancy	erratic
later	0-1 +
Ceruloplasmin (serum)	
newborn	4-15 mg/100 ml
> 6 months	20-50 mg/100 ml[11]
Chloride (serum)	100-107 mEq/L[12]
Cholesterol (serum)	
newborn	80-165 mg/100 ml
later	165-245 mg/100 ml[13]
Cholinesterase	0.56-1.32 pH units/hr/100 ml[14]
Copper (serum)	
newborn	15-50 μg/100 ml
> 6 months	> 0-150 μg/100 ml[15]
Creatinine (serum)	
cord blood	0.6-1.8 mg/100 ml
newborn	0.6-1.5 mg/100 ml
infants	0.8-1.4 mg/100 ml
later	0.7-1.7 mg/100 ml[16]
Fibrinogen (plasma)	200-390 mg/100 ml[17]
Glucose (fasting)	
newborn	20-80 mg/100 ml[18]
later	75-95 mg/100 ml[19]
Hydroxycorticoids (plasma)	
newborn	—
later	10-15 μg/100 ml[20]
Iodine, protein-bound	
2-6 days	7.0-11.7 μg/100 ml[21]
later	4.0-8.0 μg/100 ml
Iron	

	Mean Serum Fe, μg/100 ml	Total Fe, Binding Capacity	Percent Saturation
newborn	148	262	65
1-6 mo	132	412	32
6-12 mo	106	429	25
1-2 yr	95	414	22
2-6 yr	116	395	28
6-12 yr	127	340	38[22]

TABLE 1. (continued)

Determination	Values
Ketones	up to 1.5 mg/100 ml
Lactic acid (fasting)	1.06-1.78 mm/L[23]
Lactic dehydrogenase	200-680 units/ml[24]
Lead (serum)	< 60 μg/100 ml[25]
Lipids (serum)	
total	411-781 mg/100[26]
phospholipids, newborn	125 mg/100 ml mean
phospholipids, later	225 mg/100 ml mean
Magnesium (serum)	1.6-2.6 mEq/L[27]
Nonprotein nitrogen (serum)	
newborn	20-38 mg/100 ml
infants	23-44 mg/100 ml
later	25-40 mg/100 ml[28]
Osmolality (serum)	285-295 mOsm/L
pH (arterial whole blood)	7.38 (0.03 lower in venous blood)[29]
P_{CO_2} (arterial)	32-46 mm Hg
P_{O_2} (arterial)	85-100 mm Hg
Phenylalanine (serum)	0.7-1.3 mg/100 ml[30]
Phosphatase, acid	0.5-5.0 King-Armstrong units[31]
Phosphatase, alkaline	
infants	10-20 King-Armstrong units
adults	4-13 King-Armstrong units
Phosphorous, inorganic (serum)	3.6-5.9 mg/100 ml[32]
Potassium (serum)	
newborn	4-7 mEq/L
later	4.1-5.9 mEq/L[34]

Proteins and immunoglobulins:[33]

	Total proteins g/100 ml mean ± 1 S.D. and range	Albumin (1) g/100 ml mean ± 1 S.D. and range	Alpha-1 (1) g/100 ml mean ± 1 S.D. and range	Alpha-2 (1) g/100 ml mean ± 1 S.D. and range	Beta (1) g/100 ml mean ± 1 S.D. and range	Gamma (1) g/100 ml mean ± 1 S.D. and range
Cord Blood	6.22 ± 1.21 (4.78 − 8.04)	3.23 ± 0.82 (2.17 − 4.04)	0.41 ± 0.10 (0.25 − 0.66)	0.68 ± 0.14 (0.44 − 0.94)	0.74 ± 0.30 (0.42 − 1.56)	1.28 ± 0.23 (0.81 − 1.61)
1-3 mo	5.64 ± 1.04 (3.64 − 7.38)	3.41 ± 0.72 (2.05 − 4.46)	0.24 ± 0.09 (0.08 − 0.43)	0.74 ± 0.24 (0.40 − 1.13)	0.59 ± 0.20 (0.39 − 1.14)	0.66 ± 0.24 (0.25 − 1.05)
4-6 mo	5.43 ± .84 (4.29 − 6.10)	3.46 ± 0.36 (3.17 − 3.88)	0.17 ± 0.04 (0.12 − 0.25)	0.67 ± 0.11 (0.52 − 0.84)	0.61 ± 0.14 (0.44 − 0.76)	0.61 ± 0.26 (0.24 − 0.90)
7-12 mo	6.54 ± .76 (5.10 − 7.31)	3.62 ± 0.60 (3.22 − 4.31)	0.35 ± 0.15 (0.15 − 0.55)	0.99 ± 0.30 (0.78 − 1.46)	0.79 ± 0.16 (0.63 − 0.91)	0.84 ± 0.36 (0.32 − 1.18)
13-24 mo	6.66 ± 0.93 (3.69 − 7.50)	3.63 ± 0.80 (1.89 − 5.03)	0.31 ± 0.15 (0.09 − 0.58)	0.88 ± 0.42 (0.41 − 1.36)	0.77 ± 0.31 (0.36 − 1.41)	1.09 ± 0.32 (0.36 − 1.62)
25-36 mo	6.98 ± 0.66 (6.38 − 8.06)	4.11 ± 0.78 (3.57 − 5.50)	0.23 ± 0.09 (0.19 − 0.26)	0.89 ± 0.14 (0.68 − 1.09)	0.67 ± 0.14 (0.47 − 0.91)	1.08 ± 0.28 (0.73 − 1.46)
3-5 yr	6.65 ± 0.85 (4.88 − 8.06)	3.95 ± 0.57 (2.93 − 5.21)	0.21 ± 0.08 (0.08 − 0.40)	0.70 ± 0.15 (0.43 − 0.99)	0.67 ± 0.11 (0.47 − 1.01)	1.13 ± 0.31 (0.54 − 1.66)
6-8 yr	6.95 ± 0.55 (5.97 − 7.94)	4.03 ± 0.45 (3.26 − 4.95)	0.22 ± 0.09 (0.09 − 0.45)	0.67 ± 0.10 (0.50 − 0.83)	0.72 ± 0.11 (0.45 − 0.93)	1.31 ± 0.32 (0.70 − 1.95)
9-11 yr	7.43 ± 0.84 (6.32 − 9.00)	4.24 ± 0.79 (3.16 − 4.97)	0.30 ± 0.07 (0.12 − 0.38)	0.75 ± 0.27 (0.67 − 0.87)	0.84 ± 0.16 (0.63 − 1.02)	1.46 ± 0.41 (0.79 − 2.03)
12-16 yr	7.25 ± 0.85 (6.25 − 8.75)	4.26 ± 0.64 (3.19 − 5.13)	0.19 ± 0.07 (0.09 − 0.32)	0.71 ± 0.15 (0.50 − 0.97)	0.68 ± 0.15 (0.48 − 0.88)	1.40 ± 0.31 (1.08 − 1.96)

TABLE 1.   (continued)

	IgG (2) mg/100 ml mean ± 1 S.D. and range	IgA (2) mg/100 ml mean ± 1 S.D. and range	IgM (2) mg/100 ml mean ± 1 S.D. and range	IHA titer mean and range
Cord Blood	1086 ± 290 (740 − 1374)	2 ± 2 (0 − 15)	14 ± 6 (0 − 22)	[a]0
1-3 mo	512 ± 152 (280 − 950)	16 ± 10 (4 − 36)	28 ± 14 (15 − 86)	[b]1:5 0-1:10
4-6 mo	520 ± 180 (240 − 884)	22 ± 14 (11 − 52)	36 ± 18 (21 − 74)	[b]1:10 0-1:160
7-12 mo	742 ± 226 (281 − 1280)	54 ± 17 (22 − 112)	76 ± 27 (36 − 150)	[c]1:80 0-1:640
13-24 mo	945 ± 270 (290 − 1300)	67 ± 19 (9 − 143)	88 ± 36 (18 − 210)	[c]1:80 0-1:640
25-36 mo	1030 ± 152 (546 − 1562)	89 ± 34 (21 − 196)	94 ± 23 (43 − 115)	[d]1:160 1:10 −1:640
3-5 yr	1150 ± 244 (546 − 1760)	126 ± 31 (56 − 284)	87 ± 24 (26 − 121)	1:80 1:5 −1:640
6-8 yr	1187 ± 289 (596 − 1744)	147 ± 35 (56 − 330)	108 ± 37 (54 − 260)	1:80 1:5 −1:640
9-11 yr	1217 ± 261 (744 − 1719)	146 ± 38 (44 − 208)	104 ± 46 (27 − 215)	1:160 1:20 −1:640
12-16 yr	1248 ± 221 (796 − 1647)	168 ± 54 (64 − 290)	96 ± 31 (60 − 140)	1:160 1:10 −1:320

Determination	Values
Sodium (serum)	133-148 mEq/L[35]
Thymol turbidity	0-5 units
Transaminases (serum)	

	SGOT, units	SGPT, units
infancy	< 67	< 54
later	< 27	< 30[36]

Urea nitrogen (serum)	
newborn	7-13 mg/100 ml
infants	9-16 mg/100 ml
later	11-18 mg/100 ml[37]
Uric acid (serum)	2-5.7 mg/100 ml[38]
Vitamin A (serum)	> 40 µg/100 ml[39]
Vitamin C	0.5-1.0 mg/100 ml[40]

DATA FROM THE FOLLOWING SOURCES: [1]Dienst and Morris. J. Lab. Clin. Med., 64:495, 1964.   [2]Street and Close. Nature (London), 179:164, 1957.   [3]Tisdall. In Brenneman's Practice of Pediatrics, Vol. 1, Chap. 31, 1948. Hagerstown, Md., W.F. Prior Co.   [4]Sunderman. Amer. J. Clin. Path, 15:219, 1945.   [5]Hald et al. J. Clin. Invest., 26:983, 1947.   [6]Arias et al. Ann. N.Y. Acad. Sci., 111:274, 1963.   [7]Hunter. Nature (London), 182:263, 1958.   [8]Eisenman. J. Biol. Chem, 71:611, 1926.   [9]Goldschmidt and Light. Amer. J. Physiol., 73:127, 1925.   [10]May et al., Amer. J. Dis. Child, 59:1167, 1940.   [11]Sheinberg. Personal communication.   [12]Hald. J. Clin. Invest., 26:983, 1947.   [13]Hodges et al. Amer. J. Dis. Child., 65:858, 1943.   [14]Scudamore. J. Lab. Clin. Med., 37:860, 1951.   [15]Sheinberg. Personal communication.   [16]Josephson et al. Acta. Paediat (Suppl.), 135:11, 1962.   [17]Sunderman and Boerner. In Normal Values in Clinical Medicine, 1949. Philadelphia, W.B. Saunders Co.   [18]Pedersen. Acta Paediat. (Suppl.), 77:201, 1949.   [19]Somogyi. J. Biol. Chem., 179:189, 1948.   [20]O'Brien et al. In Laboratory Manual of Pediatric Micro-Biochemical Techniques, 1968. New York, Harper & Row.   [21]Man et al. Pediatrics, 9:32, 1952.   [22]Smith et al. In Clinical Advances in Pediatrics, Vol. 5, 1952.   [23]Laudahn. Klin. Wschr., 37:850, 1959.   [24]Wroblewski. Ann. N.Y. Acad. Sci., 75:322, 1958.   [25]Kehoe. Ind. Hyg. Tox, 2, 1949.   [26]Boyd. J. Clin. Invest., 13:347, 1934.   [27]Simonson et al. J. Biol. Chem, 169:39, 1947.   [28]Josephson et al. Acta Paediat. (Suppl.), 135:11, 1962.   [29]Kennedy and Sokoloff. J. Clin. Invest., 36:1130, 1957.   [30]Johnson and Bergheim. J. Biol. Chem., 188:883, 1951.   [31]Fishman et al. J. Clin. Invest., 32:1034, 1953.   [32]Bullock. Amer. J. Dis. Child, 40:725, 1930.   [33]Ellis and Robbins. Unpublished data.   [34]Bierman et al. J. Clin. Invest., 32:637, 1953.   [35]Falk et al. Amer. J. Physiol., 153:381, 1948.   [36]O'Brien et al. In Laboratory Manual of Pediatric Micro-Biochemical Techniques, 1968. New York, Harper & Row.   [37]Josephson et al. Acta Paediat (Suppl.), 135:11, 1962.   [38]Cantarow and Trumper. In Clinical Biochemistry, 1955. Philadelphia, W.B. Saunders Co.   [39]O'Brien et al. In Laboratory Manual of Pediatric Micro-Biochemical Techniques, 1968. New York, Harper & Row.   [40]O'Brien et al. In Laboratory Manual of Pediatric Micro-Biochemical Techniques, 1968. New York, Harper & Row.

TABLE 2. *Cerebrospinal Fluid*

Age	Cells/mm^3 *	Protein*,† mg/100 ml	Glucose‡ mg/100 ml
0-2 months	15§	10-123§	30-70‖
2-4 months	5	11-47	55-70
5 months-13 years	3	≤ 30#	55-70

*Concentrations of cells and protein modified from Widell. Acta Paediat. (Suppl.), 115, 1958.

†Upper of limit of normal is 10-15 mg/100 ml lower for cisternal concentration and 15-25 mg/100 ml lower for ventricular concentration.

‡Concentrations of glucose from Geigy Scientific Tables, 1962, p. 597.

§May be high in premature infant.

‖May be lower in young infants.

#Upper limit of normal protein concentration is usually considered to be 40 mg/100 ml. However the value given here has been documented by Widell and confirmed by Abramowicz. Clin. Pediat., 8:300, 1969.

TABLE 3. *Urine* *

Determination	Value
Addis count:	
protein	20 mg/12 hr
RBC	250,000
WBC	1,000,000
Calcium	1000-5000 µg/kg/24 hr
Creatinine	12-25 mg/kg/24 hr†
Glucose	1.4 mg/kg/24 hr
Uric acid	5-12 mg/kg/24 hr

*Modified from Metabolism, prepared under the auspices of the Committee on Biological Handbooks, 1968, Table 113, p. 562, and from Spector, W.S., ed. The Handbook of Biologic Data, 1956, Table 44.

†Excretion of creatinine is constant for an individual but increases with age.

TABLE 4. *Renal Function* *

Function	Method	1-7 days	8-30 days	1-3 mos	6-12 mos	> 2 years
Concentration capacity mOsm/L	After 12-18 hr of water deprivation	—	850 ± 125	—	1070 ± 125	1080 ± 170
Glomerular filtration rate ml/min/1.73 m²	Inulin or mannitol clearance	39 ± 11	50 ± 7	58 ± 14	103 ± 25	127 ± 21
Hydrogen ion excretion µEq/min/1.73 m²	5-8 hr after acute administration of ammonium chloride	3.5 ± 1.5	—	—	62 ± 25	52 ± 10
Renal bicarbonate threshold mM/L serum bicarbonate	During continuous infusion of sodium bicarbonate	—	—	22 ± 0.5		26 ± 1
Renal plasma flow ml/min/1.73 m²	PAH clearance without correction for extraction ratio	—	148	203	480	650 ± 120
Urinary pH	5-8 hr after acute administration of chloride	5.0	—	—	4.8 ± 0.3	4.8 ± 0.3
	Urea clearance	25 ± 5	36 ± 6	45 ± 15	68 ± 16	75 ± 18

*Modified from Metabolism, prepared under the auspices of the Committee on Biological Handbooks, 1968, Table 113, p. 562. Values expressed as mean ± 2 SD.

TABLE 5.   *Amino Acids in Plasma*

Amino Acid	Values (µmoles/L)	
	Infants*	Children†
Taurine	—	57-115
Hydroxyproline	—	25
Aspartic acid	15-23	4-20
Threonine	105-249	42-95
Serine	77-185	79-112
Asparagine and glutamine	—	57-467
Proline	89-297	68-148
Glutamic acid	—	23-250
Glycine	143-283	117-223
Alanine	186-398	137-305
Valine	85-237	128-283
Half cystine	24-60	45-77
Methionine	12-24	11-16
Isoleucine	23-55	28-84
Leucine	35-119	56-178
Phenylalanine	35-75	26-61
Ornithine	28-72	27-86
Lysine	79-191	56-178
Histidine	50-106	24-85
Arginine	44-80	23-86
Tryptophan	—	—
β-Alanine	—	—

*Dickinson et al. Pediatrics, 36:2, 1965.
†Scriver and Davies. Pediatrics, 36:592, 1965.

Normal Growth

The following standards are from Falkner, F. Some physical growth standards for white North American children. Pediatrics, 29:467, 1962. Fourteen sources were used to present useful and reasonably representative standards. A discussion on use of such standards for recording and interpretation of physical growth is in Chapter 4.

Median (50th percentile), 95th, and 5th percentiles of body weight, length, height, and head circumference. Where gains (increments) are shown, the figure at a specific age denotes the gain over the previous period stated.

TABLE 6. *Body Weight (in Pounds) of Children from Birth to Three Years*

Boys: 0-3 Years

Age	Weight			Age	Three-monthly Gains		
	5thP	50thP	95thP		5thP	50thP	95thP
Birth	5.9	7.5	9.1	4 wk	0.4	4.8	8.0
1 mo	7.3	9.4	11.1	3 mo	3.6	5.7	8.2
3 mo	9.8	13.4	16.0	6 mo	2.0	4.6	6.6
6 mo	14.7	18.0	21.3	9 mo	1.5	3.4	5.1
9 mo	16.8	21.4	25.1	1 yr	0.9	2.3	3.9
1 yr	18.7	23.3	27.8	18 mo	0.7	1.5	2.5
2 yr	23.3	28.3	33.3	2 yr	0.6	1.3	2.2
3 yr	27.1	32.5	37.9	3 yr	0.5	1.1	1.7

Girls: 0-3 Years

Age	Weight			Age	Three-monthly Gains		
	5thP	50thP	95thP		5thP	50thP	95thP
Birth	5.3	7.3	8.8	4 wk	0.7	3.5	6.8
1 mo	6.6	8.3	9.8	3 mo	3.2	5.1	7.2
3 mo	10.2	12.4	14.4	6 mo	2.1	4.2	7.2
6 mo	13.4	16.7	19.8	9 mo	1.5	2.8	5.2
9 mo	15.3	19.8	24.1	1 yr	1.1	2.3	3.6
1 yr	17.4	21.7	26.0	18 mo	0.5	1.5	2.6
2 yr	22.3	27.1	31.9	2 yr	0.3	1.3	2.2
3 yr	26.3	32.3	38.3	3 yr	0.4	1.0	1.9

TABLE 7.   *Length (in Inches) of Children from Birth to Three Years*

Boys: 0-3 Years

Age	Length			Age	Three-monthly Gains		
	5thP	50thP	95thP		5thP	50thP	95thP
Birth	18.4	19.8	21.2	3 mo	2.9	3.9	4.9
1 mo	19.9	21.4	22.9	6 mo	1.9	2.7	3.5
3 mo	22.6	24.0	25.4	9 mo	1.2	1.9	2.6
6 mo	25.1	26.7	28.3	1 yr	1.0	1.6	2.3
9 mo	27.2	28.7	30.2	18 mo	0.7	1.3	1.9
1 yr	28.4	30.2	32.0	2 yr	0.5	1.0	1.5
2 yr	32.1	34.6	37.1	3 yr	0.6	0.8	1.0
3 yr	35.3	37.8	40.3				

Girls: 0-3 Years

Age	Length			Age	Three-monthly Gains		
	5thP	50thP	95thP		5thP	50thP	95thP
Birth	18.3	19.5	20.7	3 mo	2.7	3.7	4.7
1 mo	19.5	21.0	22.5	6 mo	1.6	2.6	3.6
3 mo	22.2	23.6	25.0	9 mo	1.1	1.9	2.7
6 mo	24.6	26.1	27.6	1 yr	0.5	1.5	2.5
9 mo	26.3	27.9	29.5	18 mo	0.4	1.25	2.0
1 yr	27.6	29.4	31.2	2 yr	0.6	1.0	1.4
2 yr	31.6	33.8	36.0	3 yr	0.6	0.8	1.0
3 yr	35.3	37.5	39.7				

TABLE 8.   *Head Circumference (in Inches) of Children from Birth to Three Years*

Boys: 0-3 Years

Age	Circumference			Age	Three-monthly Gains		
	5thP	50thP	95thP		5thP	50thP	95thP
Birth	12.8	13.7	14.6	1 mo	1.6	2.4	3.2
3 mo	15.3	16.0	16.7	3 mo	1.4	2.0	2.6
6 mo	16.4	17.2	18.0	6 mo	0.8	1.2	1.6
9 mo	17.2	18.0	18.8	9 mo	0.5	0.8	1.1
1 yr	17.6	18.5	19.3	1 yr	0.2	0.5	0.8
18 mo	18.1	19.0	20.0	18 mo	0.2	0.3	0.4
2 yr	18.5	19.4	20.3	2 yr	0.1	0.2	0.3
3 yr	18.9	19.8	20.7	3 yr	0.0	0.1	0.2

Girls: 0-3 Years

Age	Circumference			Age	Three-monthly Gains		
	5thP	50thP	95thP		5thP	50thP	95thP
Birth	12.6	13.5	14.3	1 mo	1.6	2.4	3.2
3 mo	14.9	15.7	16.4	3 mo	1.3	2.0	2.6
6 mo	16.0	16.8	17.6	6 mo	0.7	1.1	1.5
9 mo	16.7	17.5	18.3	9 mo	0.5	0.7	1.0
1 yr	17.2	18.0	18.8	1 yr	0.2	0.5	0.7
18 mo	17.7	18.5	19.3	18 mo	0.2	0.3	0.6
2 yr	18.1	18.9	19.7	2 yr	0.1	0.2	0.3
3 yr	18.7	19.4	20.2	3 yr	0.0	0.1	0.2

TABLE 9. Height and Body Weight of Children Aged 4-18 Years

Boys

Ages (yr)	Height (in inches)			Weight (in pounds)		
	5thP	50thP	95thP	5thP	50thP	95thP
4	38.3	40.8	43.3	30.0	36.1	42.2
5	40.3	43.4	46.4	33.0	40.3	47.6
6	42.8	45.9	49.0	36.0	44.7	53.4
7	44.8	48.1	51.4	40.3	50.9	61.5
8	46.9	50.5	54.1	44.4	57.4	70.4
9	48.8	52.8	56.8	48.0	64.4	80.4
10	50.6	54.9	59.2	51.4	71.4	91.4
11	51.9	56.4	60.9	53.3	78.9	102.5
12	53.5	58.6	63.7	60.0	86.0	113.5
13	55.2	61.3	67.4	65.3	98.6	131.9
14	57.5	64.1	70.7	75.5	111.8	148.1
15	61.0	66.9	72.8	88.0	124.3	160.6
16	63.8	68.9	74.0	97.8	133.8	169.8
17	65.2	69.8	74.4	106.5	139.8	174.0
18	65.9	70.2	74.5	110.3	144.8	179.3

Girls

Ages (yr)	Height (in inches)			Weight (in pounds)		
	5thP	50thP	95thP	5thP	50thP	95thP
4	38.1	40.7	43.3	28.8	36.1	43.4
5	40.6	43.4	46.2	32.2	40.9	49.6
6	42.8	45.9	49.0	35.5	45.7	55.9
7	44.5	47.8	51.1	38.3	51.0	63.7
8	46.4	50.0	53.6	42.0	57.2	72.4
9	48.2	52.2	56.2	45.1	63.6	82.1
10	49.9	54.5	59.1	48.2	71.0	95.0
11	51.9	57.0	62.1	55.4	82.0	108.6
12	54.1	59.5	64.9	63.9	94.4	124.9
13	57.1	62.2	66.8	72.8	105.5	138.2
14	58.5	63.1	67.7	83.0	113.0	144.0
15	59.5	63.8	68.1	89.5	120.0	150.5
16	59.8	64.1	68.4	95.1	123.0	150.1
17	60.1	64.2	68.3	97.9	125.8	153.7
18	60.1	64.4	68.7	96.0	126.2	156.4

TABLE 9. (continued)

Mean Annual Height Gains (in inches)

Boys	Age (yr)	Girls
2.8	4	2.8
2.6	5	2.7
2.5	6	2.5
2.4	7	2.25
2.4	8	2.3
2.3	9	2.3
2.1	10	2.4
1.7	11	2.5
1.6	11½	—
1.9	12	3.1
2.6	13	2.3
3.0	13½	—
3.2	14	1.4
3.4	14½	—
3.1	15	0.6
2.0	16	0.3
0.9	17	0.1
0.4	18	0.0

Mean Annual Weight Gains (in pounds)

Boys	Age (yr)	Girls
4.4	4	4.4
4.5	5	4.4
4.8	6	4.4
5.5	7	5.3
6.4	8	6.4
7.0	9	7.6
7.0	10	9.4
6.8	11	10.6
7.4	11½	—
8.4	12	12.6
—	12½	13.3
11.8	13	13.2
—	13½	—
15.0	14	8.6
15.4	14½	—
10.8	15	4.4
8.8	16	2.8
6.6	17	0.7
4.4	18	0.0

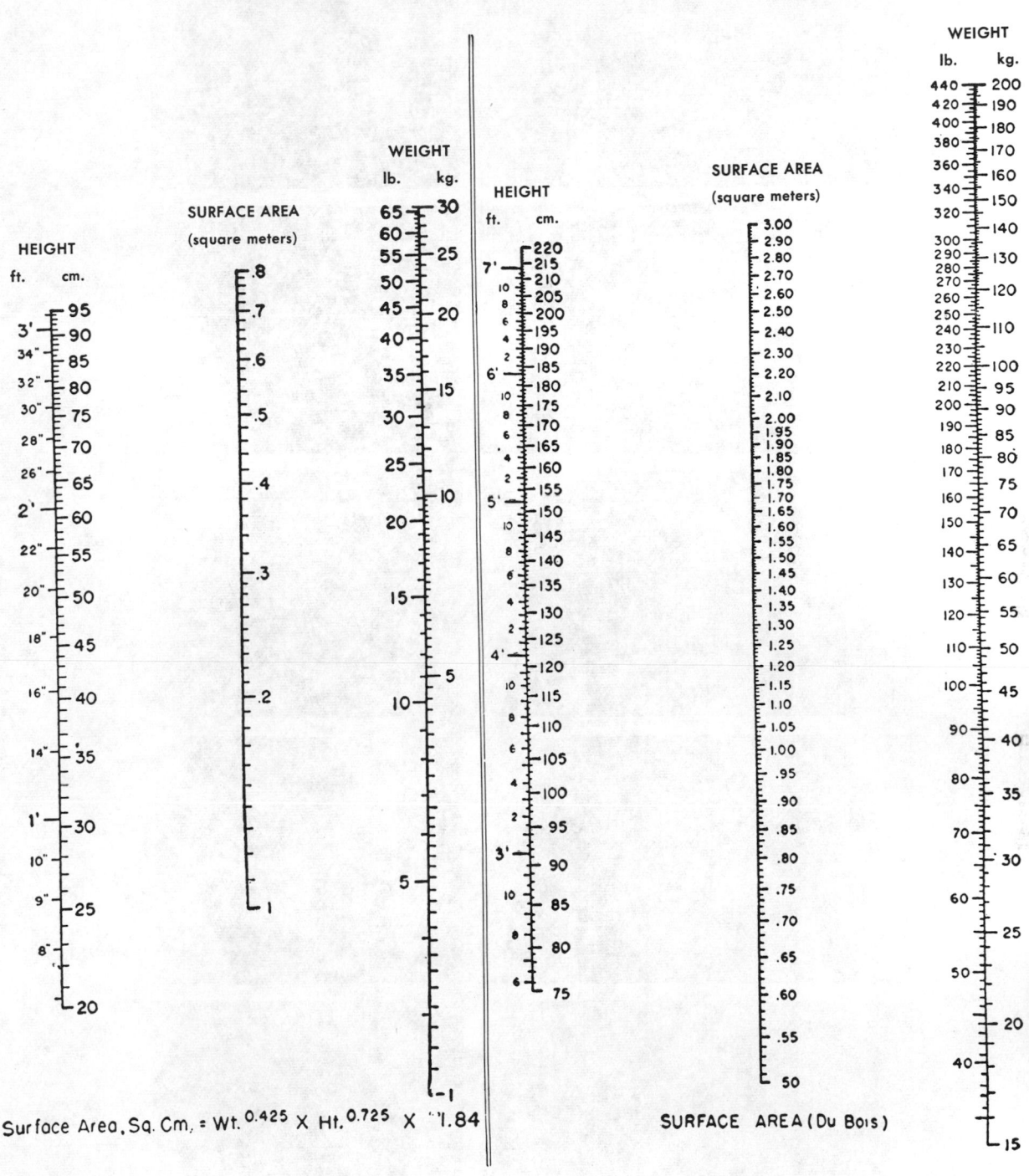

HEIGHT

ft.   cm.

SURFACE AREA
(square meters)

WEIGHT
lb.   kg.

HEIGHT
ft.   cm.

SURFACE AREA
(square meters)

WEIGHT
lb.   kg.

Surface Area, Sq. Cm. = Wt.$^{0.425}$ X Ht.$^{0.725}$ X 71.84

SURFACE AREA (Du Bois)

INFANTS

CHILDREN

Nomograms for estimating surface area of infants and children. A straight line joining the patient's height and weight crosses the center column at the calculated surface area. Based on the Meeh-DuBois formula. (From Crawford, Terry, and Rourke. *Pediatrics.* 5:783, 1950.)

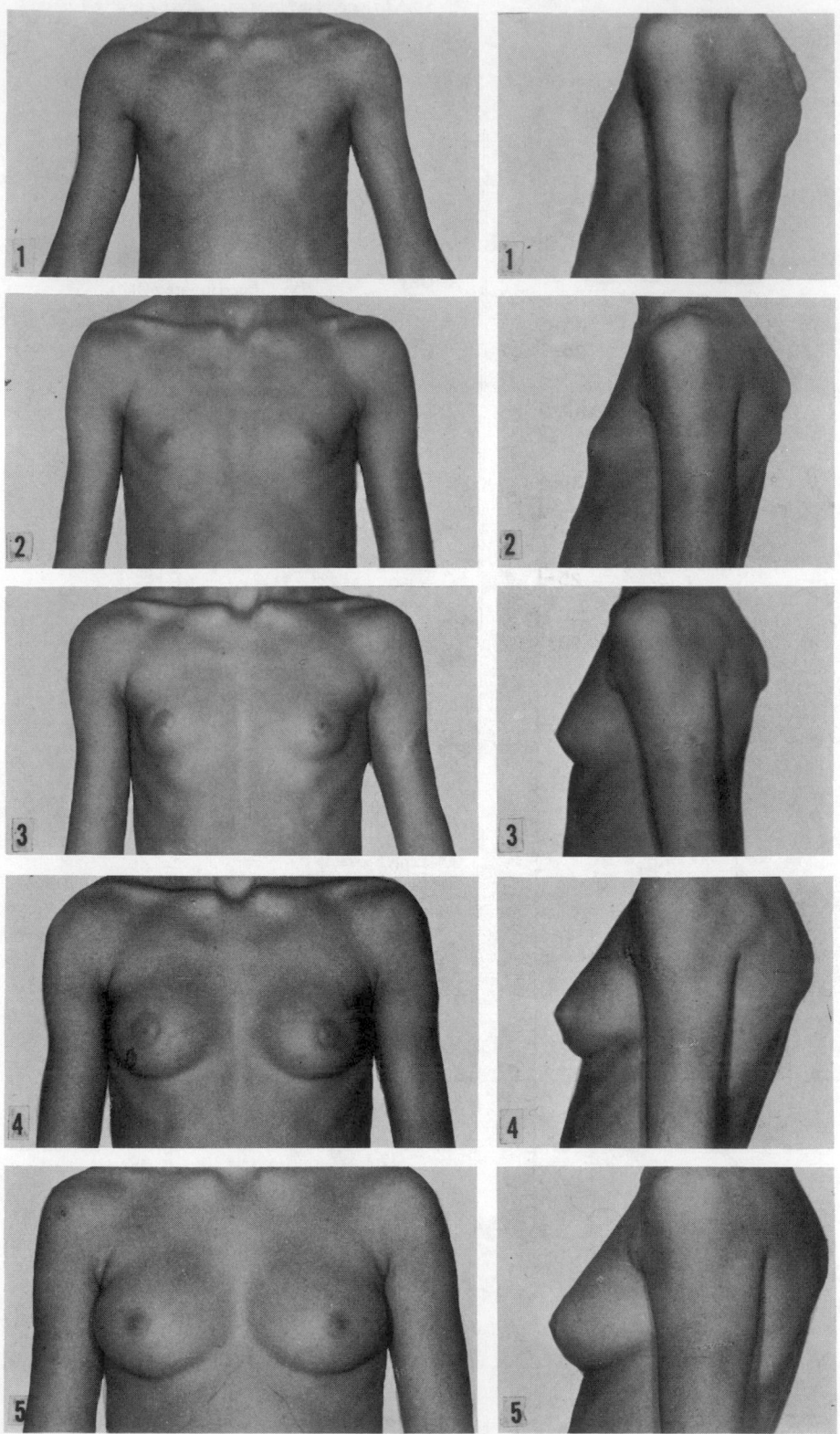

STAGES INDICATING PUBERTY STATUS. Girls: Breasts. 1. Prepubertal. Childhood appearance. Flat. 2. Small raised breast bud. 3. General enlargement and raising of breast and areola. 4. Areola and papilla forming separate contour to breast. 5. Adult breast. Areola now in same contour as breast.

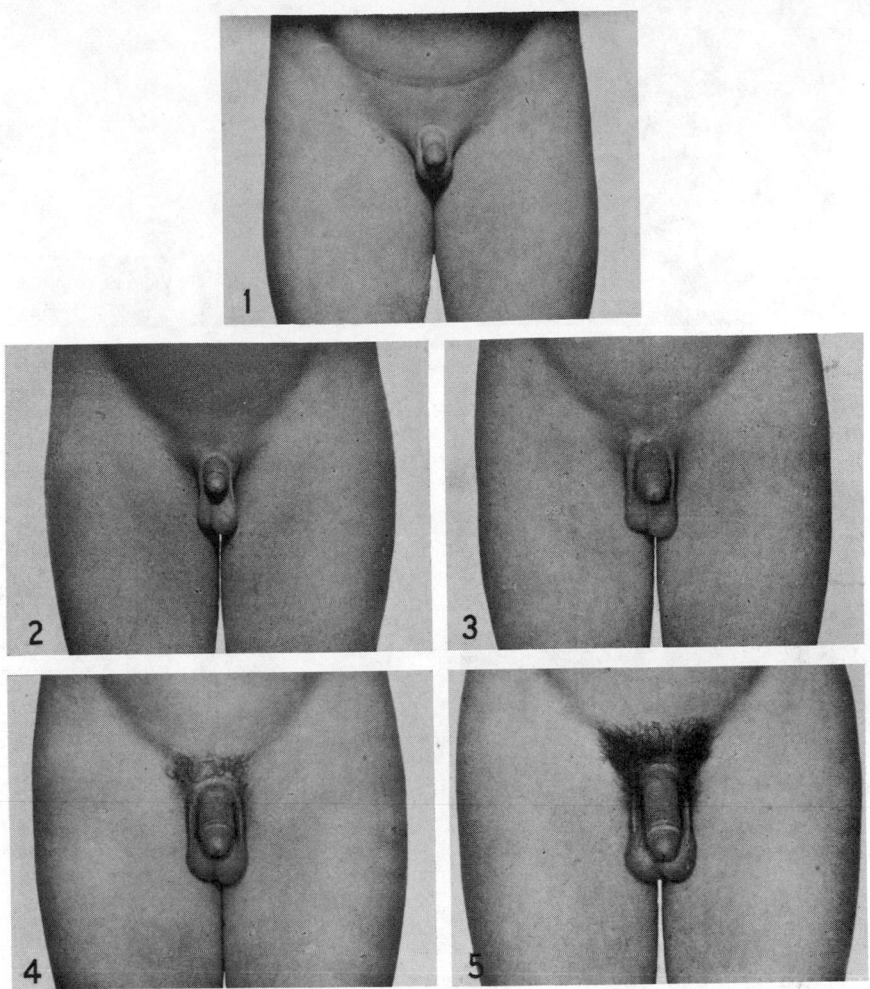

STAGES INDICATING PUBERTY STATUS. Boys: Genitalia. 1. Prepubertal. Testes and penis size similar to early childhood. 2. Testes enlarging. Scrotal skin reddens and coarsens. 3. Continuing stage 2. Penis lengthening. 4. Penis enlarging in general size. Scrotal skin pigmented. 5. Adult genitalia.

The stages illustrated on pages 1926 to 1928 are used as standards by the Centre International de l'Enfance Coordinated Growth Studies (Falkner, F., ed. Child Development: an international method of study, Karger, Basel, 1960). They are originally from Tanner, J. M. Growth at Adolescence, 2nd ed. Springfield, Charles C Thomas, Publisher, 1962. Thus, an individual child will have two ratings. Usually the stage of pubic hair is placed second: Example: Boy Age 12 yrs. 3 mos. Puberty Rating 2:2.

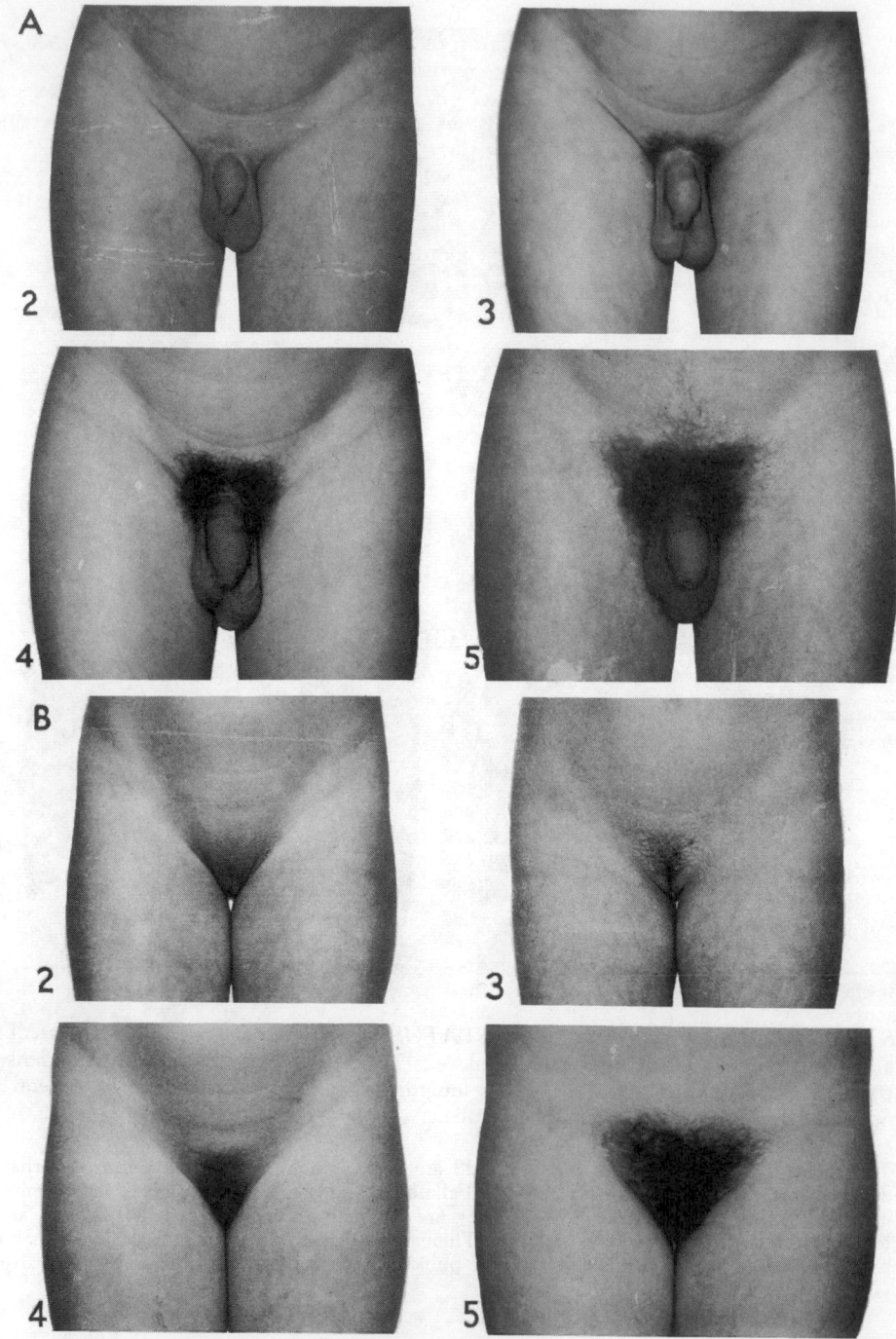

STAGES INDICATING PUBERTY STATUS. Boys and Girls: Pubic Hair. 1. Prepubertal. No true pubic hair. 2. Sparse growth of downy hair mainly at base of penis, or at sides of labia. 3. Pigmentation, coarsening and curling with increase in amount of hair. 4. Adult hair, but limited in area and no spread to thighs. 5. Adult hair with horizontal upper border and spread to thighs.

TABLE 10.   *Live Births and Infant Mortality Rates, by Color, Each State and Selected Cities, 1968*
             (Rate per 1,000 live births. By place of residence)

Division, State and City	Live Births			Infant Mortality Rate		
	Total	White	All Other	Total	White	All Other
UNITED STATES						
Geographic Divisions:						
New England	193,352	182,322	11,030	19.8	19.2	31.8
Middle Atlantic	603,164	507,826	95,338	21.2	18.6	35.0
East North Central	705,654	609,786	95,868	21.5	19.4	35.4
West North Central	267,786	247,644	20,142	19.4	18.5	31.8
South Atlantic	535,334	383,300	152,034	24.3	19.6	36.2
East South Central	233,102	169,436	63,666	26.2	20.9	40.5
West South Central	360,274	284,202	76,072	22.6	19.4	35.0
Mountain	152,766	138,982	13,784	21.1	19.7	36.1
Pacific	450,132	388,726	61,406	19.1	18.5	22.9
New England:						
Maine	16,958	16,728	230	21.5	21.5	26.1
New Hampshire	12,430	12,334	96	18.8	18.9	10.4
Vermont	7,652	7,608	44	19.7	19.8	—
Massachusetts	91,984	87,134	4,850	19.9	19.2	34.2
Rhode Island	15,272	14,438	834	21.3	20.6	33.6
Connecticut	49,056	44,080	4,976	19.0	17.8	30.1
Middle Atlantic:						
New York	302,414	249,686	52,728	20.9	18.3	33.5
New Jersey	114,398	94,614	19,784	21.2	17.9	36.5
Pennsylvania	186,352	163,526	22,826	21.7	19.6	37.2
East North Central:						
Ohio	185,814	163,818	21,996	20.3	18.7	32.5
Indiana	91,718	83,488	8,230	21.9	20.5	36.7
Illinois	193,520	155,924	37,596	23.4	20.0	37.6
Michigan	160,142	136,424	23,718	21.6	19.3	34.8
Wisconsin	74,460	70,132	4,328	19.5	18.8	31.2
West North Central:						
Minnesota	64,716	63,034	1,682	18.4	18.1	26.8
Iowa	46,736	45,650	1,086	19.1	18.8	32.2
Missouri	74,466	63,074	11,392	21.4	19.3	33.4
North Dakota	10,588	9,998	590	16.9	16.9	16.9
South Dakota	11,428	10,130	1,298	20.5	19.0	32.4
Nebraska	24,260	22,898	1,362	18.0	17.1	33.0
Kansas	35,592	32,860	2,732	19.4	18.5	30.7
South Atlantic:						
Delaware	9,846	7,888	1,958	20.2	16.0	37.3
Maryland	68,104	52,710	15,394	21.3	17.9	33.3
District of Columbia	14,928	2,412	12,516	25.9	16.6	27.7
Virginia	81,902	62,964	18,938	22.7	18.7	36.2
West Virginia	29,290	27,872	1,418	23.4	22.4	42.3
North Carolina	92,682	64,938	27,744	26.3	20.9	38.7
South Carolina	49,134	30,214	18,920	27.0	20.5	37.4
Georgia	87,458	58,788	28,670	25.4	19.4	37.6
Florida	101,990	75,514	26,476	24.1	19.8	36.5
East South Central:						
Kentucky	56,458	51,436	5,022	21.9	21.0	31.5
Tennessee	67,294	53,034	14,260	23.2	19.8	35.8
Alabama	63,602	42,016	21,586	26.6	20.9	37.7
Mississippi	45,748	22,950	22,798	35.5	22.9	48.1
West South Central:						
Arkansas	33,128	24,406	8,722	23.2	18.6	36.0
Louisiana	74,178	45,660	28,518	25.3	18.2	36.8
Oklahoma	41,006	34,358	6,648	20.0	19.5	22.6
Texas	211,962	179,778	32,184	22.2	19.8	35.6

TABLE 10.   (continued)

Division, State and City	Live Births			Infant Mortality Rate		
	Total	White	All Other	Total	White	All Other
Mountain:						
Montana	11,998	10,994	994	19.5	18.3	33.2
Idaho	13,120	12,808	312	18.4	18.2	28.8
Wyoming	5,770	5,482	288	21.3	19.5	55.6
Colorado	36,948	35,078	1,870	20.6	20.3	27.3
New Mexico	20,346	17,364	2,982	23.9	22.3	33.5
Arizona	32,716	27,180	5,536	23.0	19.7	38.8
Utah	23,206	22,538	668	17.6	16.6	52.4
Nevada	8,672	7,538	1,134	26.5	25.5	33.5
Pacific:						
Washington	57,200	53,360	3,840	19.7	19.0	28.6
Oregon	32,210	30,932	1,278	19.7	19.3	29.0
California	339,760	295,626	44,134	19.0	18.4	22.6
Alaska	6,430	4,584	1,846	21.8	16.6	34.7
Hawaii	14,532	4,224	10,308	18.2	15.6	19.2
Selected Cities:						
New York	136,302	96,694	39,608	23.2	19.1	33.4
Chicago	66,870	37,926	28,944	28.7	21.9	37.7
Los Angeles	50,488	36,608	13,880	21.3	18.4	27.7
Philadelphia	35,080	20,554	14,526	29.2	24.0	36.6
Detroit	29,172	14,304	14,868	27.1	18.8	35.2
Baltimore	16,598	7,234	9,364	28.8	20.2	35.5
Houston	24,998	17,902	7,096	23.7	19.9	33.5
Cleveland	15,320	9,078	6,242	26.3	23.1	31.1
Washington, D.C.	14,928	2,412	12,516	25.9	16.6	27.7
St. Louis	13,022	6,690	6,332	27.6	21.1	34.6

Sources: 1968—Vital Statistics of the United States, Volume I, Natality, Section 2, Table 2-1.
1968—Vital Statistics of the United States, Volume II, Part A, Section 2, Table 2-6.
1968—Vital Statistics of the United States, Infant Death, Volume II, Mortality, Part B, Section 7, Table 7-1.

INDEX

Abdomen *1900–1906. See also* Abdominal.
  at birth, **75, 82**
  in cystic fibrosis 419
  in general examination *1900,* **1906**
  in marasmus 171
  x-ray, in lead poisoning **544**
Abdominal actinomycosis **786**
Abdominal bruit 1439
Abdominal calcification 677, *678,* 1111, 1561, 1649, 1670
Abdominal cramps 140, 1592
Abdominal distension
  in aganglionic megacolon 1622
  in appendicitis 1640
  in botulism 610
  in gastric paralysis 1652
  in gastric perforation **1652**
  in β-lipoprotein deficiency 377
  in nephrotic syndrome 1500
  in newborn *82*
  in rickets 201
  in sepsis neonatorum 597
  in Tay-Sachs disease 912
Abdominal enlargement
  in cystic fibrosis 419
  in liver tumors 1693
  in β-thalassemia 1181
Abdominal epilepsy **1574**
Abdominal lymph nodes **677, 678**
Abdominal lymphosarcoma **1226**
Abdominal mass
  in neuroblastoma 1111
  in Wilms' tumor **1561**
Abdominal massage, in pheochromocytoma 1109
Abdominal migraine 1574
Abdominal muscles
  congenital absence of 82, **1028,** 1547, 1548, **1559–1560**
  rigidity 1641, **1648–1649**
  spasm
    in black widow spider bite **844**
    in tetanus **659**
  weakness, in poliomyelitis **745**
Abdominal pain **1599–1600**
  in abdominal tuberculosis 677
  in acute glomerulonephritis 1484

Abdominal pain (*cont.*)
  in acute intermittent porphyria **409,** 1008
  in amebiasis **828**
  in anaphylactoid purpura 1233
  in appendicitis **1640–1641**
  in ascariasis **802**
  in Brennemann syndrome 1641
  in Coxsackie virus infections 750
  in cystic fibrosis 420
  in diabetes mellitus 346
  in hemorrhagic fever 847, 848
  in herpangina 751
  in Hodgkin's disease 1223
  in hookworm infection 806
  in hyperchylomicronemia, familial 374, 376
  in hyperparathyroidism 209
  in hyperprebetalipoproteinemia, familial 376
  in leukemia 1209
  in lymphocytic choriomeningitis 729
  in lymphogranuloma inguinale 776
  in lymphosarcoma 1226
  in malaria 832
  in measles 732, 734
  in mercury poisoning 549
  in mixed porphyria 410
  in neurologic disease **850**
  in peptic ulcer **1638**
  in peritonitis **1648–1649**
  in pleurodynia 750
  in poisoning 532
  in polyarteritis nodosa 514
  in psittacosis 776
  in rheumatic fever 494, 496
  in right heart failure **1421**
  in sickle-cell anemia **1177**
  in taeniasis 818
  in ulcerative colitis 1644
  in viral hepatitis 708
Abdominal paracentesis 679
Abdominal parietes, malformations **1630–1635**
Abdominal tenderness
  in amebiasis **828**
  in appendicitis **1640**
Abdominal tuberculosis **677–679**

Abdominal venous distension 1691
Abdominal x-ray, and pica 544
Abdomino-anal pull-through procedure 1628
Abdomino-perineal pull-through procedure *1623*
Abducens nerve palsy
    in brain tumors 942, 945
    in craniospinal focal sepsis 1010–1016
    in Gradenigo syndrome 1888
    in polyneuritis 1008
    in pseudotumor cerebri 958
Aberrant coronary vessels 370, 1395, 1434
Abetalipoproteinemia (ABL) *see* β-Lipoprotein defi-
    ciency
ABL *see* β-Lipoprotein deficiency
ABO erythroblastosis 1189, 1197–1198
Abortion, selective 317
Abrasions, and battered child syndrome 557
Abscess. *See also specific organs and locations.*
    amebic 825, 829
    in aspergillosis 787
    brain 1011–1025
    in brucellosis 611
    cerebellar 1012
    in heroin addicts 561
    due to *H. influenzae* 619
    lung 825, 829, 1306
    mediastinal 1637
    perinephric 1543
    perirectal 1643
    peritoneal 1649
    peritonsillar 1878
    in rat-bite fever 634
    due to salmonellae 636
    spinal 1015–1016
    subphrenic 1649
Absence attacks 982, 988, 999
Absidia 795
Abstinence syndrome 562–563, 564, 569, 573–575
    alcohols 569–570
    barbiturates 565
    glutethimide 564
    heroin 562–563, 573–575
    neonatal 54, 573–575
Abstract thinking, difficulties in, in minimal cerebral
    dysfunction 880
Abuse, child *see* Battered child syndrome
Academic failure 260
Acanthamoeba 830
Acanthocephala 797
Acanthocytosis *see* β-Lipoprotein deficiency
Acantholysis 1780
Acanthosis 1787, 1806
Acanthosis nigricans 1804–1805
"Acapulco gold" 572
Accelerator globulin *see* Factor V
Accelerin *see* Factor VI
Accessory digit 1708
Accessory lung lobes 1304
Accessory spleens 1217
Accidental deaths 517, 519, 524, 527
    and battered child syndrome 557
Accidental ingestions *see* Poisonings
Accident prevention 518–519
Accident proneness 518
Accidents 517–558
    accidents, general 517–519
    burns 519–524

Accidents (*cont.*)
    drowning 524–526
    intentional accidents 556–558. *See also* Child abuse.
    poisonings 526–556
Accommodative strabismus 1833
Acetabular angle
    in congenital hip dislocation 1748
    in Down's syndrome 1718
Acetabular dysplasia 1748
Acetabulum (of fluke) 812
Acetate, incorporation into fetal lipids, 39
Acetoacetic acid 344
Acetominophen 362
Acetone 344, *530*, 347
    determination, serum, in diabetes mellitus 347
Acetozolamide (Diamox) 555, 998–1000, 1035, 1525, 1825
    in epilepsy 998–1000
    in salicylate poisoning 555
Acetylation
    fetal 53
    placental 52
Acetylcholine 139, 454, 551, 559, 609, 610
    in PAT 1364
Acetylcholinesterase 551
Acetyl CoA 136, 140, 179, 218, 344
N-Acetylcysteine 426
N-Acetylgalactosaminidase deficiency 381
Acetyl β-methacholine 464
N-Acetyl-neuraminic acid (sialic acid) 907
N-Acetylneuraminidase 381
Acetylphenylhydrazine 394
Acetyl salicylic acid (ASA) *see* Salicylates
Acetylcystein, irrigation 1616
N-Acyl-sphingosine 907
N-Acetyltyrosine ethyl ester 390
Achalasia
    of distal colon 1624
    of esophagus 1575
Achillean reflex, in hypothyroidism 1076
Achlorhydria *see* Achylia
Acholic stools 1683
Achondroplasia 859, 1695, 1719–1722
Achromobacter 596, 597
    gastric 1567, 1594
Achylia, pancreatic 418, 425
"Acid" 571
Acid-base, metabolism 221–226, 229–230, 1524–1527
    disturbances 229–230, 344–351, 1278, 1466, 1524–1527
    fetal balance 47–48
    and phosphate 144
    postnatal balance 67
    renal regulation 1459
Acid fast bacilli *see* Mycobacteria
Acid glycosaminoglycans 1766
"Acidhead" 571
Acidified milk *see* Cow's milk
Acidity, gastric *see* Stomach, acidity
Acid phosphatase, serum 58, 383, 913, 1663
Acidosis, hyperchloremic 1525
Acidosis, metabolic 93, 223, 229–230, 328, 344–351, 379,
    501, 507, 532, 613, 1278, 1282, 1402, 1466, 1521–
    1527
    in Addison's disease 1094
    in airway obstruction 1278
    in asthma 467
    of birth asphyxia, 66–67
    in chronic renal failure 1466

Acidosis, metabolic (*cont.*)
  in cyanotic congenital heart disease **1402**
  in diabetes mellitus **344–351**
  in distal RTA **1525–1526**
  in *E. coli* infections 642
  in Fanconi syndrome **1521–1524**
  and high-protein feeding 110
  in iron poisoning 537
  maternal 47, 48, 67
  in low-birth-weight infant 93
  in R.D.S. 1262
  renal tubular **1525–1527**
  in shigellosis 640
Acidosis, respiratory **223,** 330
  in airway obstruction **1278**
  in cystic fibrosis 417
Ackee fruit, and hypoglycemia 362
Acne 457, 1127, **1815–1816**
Acoustic neurinoma 943
Acoustic neuroma 1886
Acoustic nerve tumors, and neurofibromatosis 928
Acquired heart disease *see* Cardiovascular diseases; Circulatory system
Acquired metabolic diseases **362**
Acriflavine 810
Acrocentric chromosome 308
Acrocephalopolysyndactyly *see* Carpenter's syndrome
Acrocephalosyndactyly *see* Apert's syndrome
Acrocephaly 1697
Acrocyanosis, of newborn 78
Acrodermatitis enteropathica 1588
Acrodynia ("pink disease") **549–550**
Acromegaly 250, 859, 1049
  in colloid brainstem cyst 946
Acrylic palatine obturator 1843
ACTH **1048,** 1049, **1051,** 1052–1055, 1092–1094, **1099–1100,** 1102, 1104
  and carbohydrate tolerance **1051**
  deficiency 1052–1053, 1055
  function, evaluation of **1051**
  and heroin 559
  and lipolysis 218
  release **1048,** 1051
  stimulation 1094
ACTH therapy 366, 368, 457, **686, 998–1000,** 1102, 1104.
      See also Adrenocorticosteroid therapy.
  in allergic disease 457
  in epilepsy **998–1000**
  in hypoglycemia 368
  in ITP **1234**
  in neonatal hypoglycemia **366**
  in tuberculosis **686**
Actin 511
Actinic keratoses 1799
Actinomyces israelii **785**
Actinomycetes 581, 676
Actinomycin D, in Wilms' tumor 1561
Actinomycosis **785–786, 1308**
  pulmonary **1308**
Activated charcoal USP 535
Activated partial thromboplastin time 1231, **1237–1243**
Activity, physical
  caloric requirements for 128
  and diabetes mellitus 353
  in glycogenosis type I 368
  in kwashiorkor 173
  role in neonatal thermogenesis 30

Activity, physical (*cont.*)
  and water loss 142
Acute bronchitis **1290**
Acute cerebellar ataxia *see* Cerebellar ataxia, acute
Acute conjunctivitis **1820**
Acute glomerulonephritis 389, 490, 514, 1464, **1482–1488**
  and rheumatic fever 1483
Acute illness, and personality disorders 267
Acute infantile hemiplegia **962**
Acute intermittent porphyria (Swedish type) **409–410,** 1008
Acute labyrinthitis **1042**
Acute nephritis *see* Acute glomerulonephritis
Acute phase reactants **497,** 511, 515
Acute radiation nephritis **1511**
Acute respiratory disease (ARD) **725–726**
"Acyanotic tetralogy of Fallot" 1404
Acyl dehydrogenase 379
AD (adenoid degeneration) virus 725
1-Adamantanamine **695**
Adamantine hydrochloride 760
Adaption, ecologic **1912–1914**
Adaptive behavior 851
Addiction, narcotic **558–575**
Addis count **1460**
Addison's disease **1093–1094,** 1163
  and juvenile pernicious anemia 1163
Adenine 294
Adenitis *see* Lymphadenopathy
Adenocarcinoma, thyroid **1087**
Adenohypophysis *see* Pituitary, anterior
Adenoidectomy **1877–1880**
  bleeding after 1230
  contraindications in cleft palate 1846
Adenoids **1877–1880**
Adenoma, adrenocortical **1098–1099**
Adenoma hepatic 1693
Adenoma sebaceum *see* Tuberous sclerosis
Adenomatous polyps, in rectum 1661
Adenopathy *see* Lymphadenopathy
Adenopharyngoconjunctival (APC) viruses **1821**
Adenosine diphosphate 1236
Adenosine phosphates 144, 1236
Adenosine triphosphate *see* ATP
Adenoviral conjunctivitis **1821**
Adenoviral diseases **725–728**
Adenovirus 227, 576, 625, 641, **725–726, 1821**
  in unexplained infant-death 576
Adenyl cyclase **373,** 444
Adenylic acid 144
ADH *see* Antidiuretic hormone
Adiadokokinesis 377
Adipocyte 218
Adipose cell *see* Fat cells
Adipose tissue *see* Fat
Aditus ad antrum 1882
Admission procedures, of low-birth-weight infant 104
Adolescence **262–263**
  behavioral changes 262
  and diabetes mellitus 354
  goiter in **1077–1082**
  health supervision 8
  obesity in, 214
  and school difficulties 283
  suicide in **290–293**
"Adolescent" goiter **1080**
Adolescent growth 240

Adoption 6
ADP *see* Adenosine diphosphate
Adrenal androgens 1093, 1095
Adrenal atrophy, after long-term steroid therapy 1095
Adrenal cortex 1090–1106
  and acid-base homeostasis 223
  fetal, steroid synthesis 40–41
  hormones 1090–1092, **1093**, 1094–1101, **1102–1106**. *See also* Adrenal cortical hormones.
  hyperadrenalism **1093–1101**
    Cushing's syndrome **1099–1100**
    hyperaldosteronism **1101**
    nonvirilizing adrenal hyperplasia, congenital **1097**
    virilizing syndromes **1095–1099**
      acquired adrenal hyperplasia **1098**
      adrenocortical tumors **1098–1099**
      congenital adrenal hyperplasia **1095–1098**
  hypoadrenalism **1093–1095**
    Addison's disease **1093–1094**
    other types of adrenal insufficiency **1094–1095**
  structure and secretory function **1090–1092**
  tumors 13, **1098–1099**, 1127, 1706
Adrenal cortical hormones 1090–1092, **1093**, 1094–1100, 1102–1106
  action 1093, 1104
  disorders responding to pharmacologic actions of 1002
  drug and dosage **1104–1106**
  effect of large doses **1003–1004**
  metabolism **1093**
  relative potency **1004**
  therapeutic uses *see* Adrenal corticosteroid therapy; Adrenal glucocorticoids
  withdrawal **1106**
Adrenal, cortical hyperplasia, 83, 240, 1057, **1095–1098**, **1127, 1134**
  and acanthosis nigricans 1805
Adrenal cortical insufficiency 597, 1055, **1093–1095**, **1097–1098**
  acute **1094–1095**
  in Addison's disease **1093–1094**
  in adrenal hypoplasia, congenital, bilateral **1094–1095**
  chronic *see* Addison's disease
  in congenital adrenal hyperplasia **1095–1098**
  and hypoglycemia 361
  and hypoparathyroidism 211
  and long-term steroid therapy 1095
  with virilization **1097**
  and vomiting 1574
Adrenal corticosteroid therapy 1002, **1104–1106**
  in acne, intralesional 1816
  and adrenal insufficiency **1093–1095, 1098**
  in anaphylactoid purpura, **1233**
  in aplastic anemia **1166–1167**
  and aspergillosis 787
  in asthma 466–467
  in atopic eczema 474
  in autoimmune acquired hemolytic disease **1185**
  in bacterial meningitis **606**
  in Bell's palsy 1008
  in brain tumors **941**
  in bronchiolitis **1282**
  cataracts due to **1826**
  in chemical pneumonitis 1312
  in conjunctivitis **1822**
  in contact dermatitis, 474–475
  during craniopharyngioma neurosurgery **953**
  in cytomegalic inclusion disease 704

Adrenal corticosteroid therapy (*cont.*)
  in dermatomyositis 512
  in drownings 526
  in endobronchial tuberculosis 667–668
  in epiglottitis **1282–1283**
  in epilepsy 998–1000
  and Frei test 776
  during gestation 55
  in glycogenosis 368
  in Hamman Rich syndrome 1319
  in Hand-Schüller-Christian syndrome 1249
  in head trauma **974**
  in hemangiomas 1813, 1839, 1848
  in *Herpesvirus hominis* infection 716
  in hypercalcemia, idiopathic 208
  hyperparathyroidism 209
  in hypoglycemia 366
  in hypophosphatasia 206
  and iatrogenic hypopituitarism 1056
  in infantile cortical hyperostosis 1741
  in ITP **1234**
  in kerosene poisoning 540
  in Letterer-Siwe disease **1247**
  in leukemia **1210, 1212**
  long-term, as cause of adrenal insufficiency **1095**
  in lymphosarcoma **1227**
  in measles 735
    and fetal masculinization 55
  in neonatal thrombocytopenic purpura **1235**
  in nephrotic syndrome **1503–1504**, 1505
  in neural tumor with diarrheal syndrome 1113
  in obstructive airway disease **1282**
  in pleurisy, tuberculous 668
  in polyarteritis nodosa 514
  in polyneuropathies 1008
  in regional enteritis **1643**
  of rheumatic fever **500–501**
  in rheumatoid arthritis **506–507**
  in rickettsioses 785
  in RS viral disease 724
  in rubella thrombocytopenic purpura **762**
  in sarcoidosis 1253
  in scleroderma **513**
  in sepsis neonatorum 598
  in serum sickness 486
  in SLE 510, **1493**
  in snakebites 556
  in Stevens-Johnson syndrome 1778
  in subglottic hemangioma 1285
  topical
    in acne, 1816
    interstitial keratitis, syphilitic 658
    for tuberculin test reaction 681
  in trichinosis 809
  in tuberculosis 667–668, **686**, 1102
  in typhoid fever 638
  and ulcer **1639**
  in ulcerative colitis **1646–1647**
  in uveitis 1828
  and varicella 701
  and viral hepatitis 709
Adrenal crisis **1093**
Adrenalectomy **1100**
Adrenal glucocorticoids **1102**
  in allergic disorders **456–457**
  diabetogenic action 355
  and hyperparathyroidism 209

Adrenal hyperplasia *see* Adrenal cortical hyperplasia
Adrenal hypoplasia, bilateral, congenital **1094–1095**
Adrenalin *see* Epinephrine
Adrenal insufficiency *see* Adrenal cortical insufficiency
Adrenal medulla **1107–1113**
Adrenal necrosis, in cytomegalic inclusion disease 704
Adrenal rests 1127
Adrenal vein catheterization, in hyperaldosteronism 1448
Adrenarche, premature 1129
β-Adrenergic receptor 52, 444
β-Adrenergic stimulants, and fetal myocardium 52
Adrenocortical adenoma and carcinoma **1098–1099**
Adrenocortical tumors **1098–1099**, 1127, 1706
Adrenocorticotropic hormone (ACTH) *see* ACTH
Adrenocorticotropin (ACTH) *see* ACTH
Adrenogenital syndrome 83, 240, 1057, **1095–1098**, 1127,
    1134, 1805
Adsorbents, in poisonings 535
Adult hemoglobin *see* Hemoglobin A
"Adult type" toxoid, against diphtheria 618
Adversive seizures 982, **988**
Adynamia episodica **1034–1035**
Aedes 810
Aedes aegypti **848**
Aerobacter aerogenes 65
    in urinary tract infection 1539
Aerocele 968
Aerosol 426
"A" frame, in cerebral palsy **886**
Afibrinogenemia **1241**
African trypanosomiasis **834–835**
Agammaglobulinemias **387–389**, 437, 508, 645, 704, 734,
    1808
Aganglionic megacolon 1583, **1601**, 1617, **1621–1624**
Agar electrophoresis 373
Age
    bone 240
    developmental 240
    maternal *see* Maternal age
    maturational 240
    and suicide 290
Agenesis
    corpus callosum **862**, 931
    lung **1303**
    tricuspid valve 1382–1383
    upper Mullerian duct 1117
Agglutinins
    in brucellosis 611
    in leptospirosis 621
    in rickettsia 779, 780
    in tularemia 692, 693
Agitation 456
Aglossia-adactylia syndrome 1848
Aglossia congenita **1848**
AGN *see* Acute glomerulonephritis
Agranulocytosis 455, 1163, **1204–1206**, 1224
    and candidiasis 795
    and gingivostomatitis *1854*
Aggression, in suicide 292
Aggressive behavior 280, 468
AH *see* Antihyaluronidase
AHF *see* Factor VIII
AHG *see* Factor VIII
AIP *see* Acute intermittent porphyria (Swedish type)
Air conduction 463, **1881–1882**
Air embolism 1363
Air encephalography **855**, 862

Air flow, resistance to 90
Air hunger 1218
Airing **1895**
Airways **1274–1277**
Airway obstruction **1277–1297**, 1401
    in asthma **464–465**
    in cystic fibrosis 416
    diagnostic procedures **1278–1280**
    diseases causing, **1284–1297**
    signs and symptoms **1277–1278**
    treatment **1280–1283**
        inspiratory obstruction **1284–1287**
        lower airway obstruction **1287–1297**
Airway resistance
    in low-birth-weight infant **90–92**
    in newborn 1256
Airway trauma **1285**
Akinetic attacks **989**, **1000**
ALA *see* Aminolevulinic acid
ALA synthetase 405, 410
β-Alanine, abnormalities 174, 327, **335**, 336
Alastrim (variola minor) **771**
Albers-Schonberg's disease *see* Osteopetrosis
Albinism 318, 323, **326–327**, 1799, **1800**, 1824
Albright's syndrome *see* Polyostotic fibrous dysplasia
Albumin-bilirubin bond 1674
Albumin, serum (or plasma)
    in AGN 1484
    and bilirubin **1678**
    and calcium concentration 196
    hepatitis free 711
    and hypostatic pressure 222
    in hypocaloric dwarfism 170
    in kwashiorkor 173, 174
    in liver disease **1672**
    in marasmus 171
    in nephrotic syndrome **1500–1501**
Albuminuria. *See also* Proteinuria.
    in acute glomerulonephritis **1483–1485**
    in hemorrhagic fever 848
    in lead poisoning 542
    in leptospirosis **621**
    in nephrotic syndrome **1500**, **1507**
    in postural proteinuria **1478–1479**
Albustix (bromophenol blue paper) 1460
Alcohol, **569–570**. *See also* Ethanol, Propanol.
    abstinence syndrome **570**
    abuse **569–570**
    and acute intermittent porphyria 410
    and breast-feeding 152
        in colic 1600
        in renal failure 1465
    and conjugating activity 55
    and fetus 55, *84*
    and hypoglycemia 362
    intoxication 528, *530*, **569–570**
Alcoholism, chronic **569–570**
    effect on fetus 55
Alcopara *see* Bephenium hydroxynaphthoate
Aldehyde oxidase 146
Aldolase 511, 1031
Aldosterone 176, 1093, 1095, **1100**, 1421, 1446, 1527
Aldrich's syndrome **1236**
    and pseudotumor cerebri 958
Alexander's disease **917**
Alimentary disorders, as psychopathology **269–272**
Alkalemia 223

Alkalescens-Dispar 639
Alkali, milk curd modification by 160
Alkali, therapy *see* Bicarbonate
Alkaline phosphatase, serum
  in amebic liver abscess 829
  in Caffey's disease 1741
  in cystic fibrosis 422
  in Fanconi syndrome **1521–1524**
  in hepatocellular disease **1672**
  in hypophosphatasia **206**
  in kwashiorkor 174
  in pregnancy 59
  in primary hypophosphatemia **204**
  in scurvy 189
  in vitamin D deficiency **198**
  in vitamin D-resistant rickets 204, **206**
Alkalosis, maternal, effect on fetus 47, 67
Alkalosis, metabolic, **223**
  in cystic fibrosis 417
  in hyperaldosteronism 1101, 1445
Alkalosis, respiratory **223**
Alkaptonuria 318, **323, 326**
Alleles 300, **377**
Allelic mutations 320
Allelism **300**
Allergen avoidance **450–452**
Allergens, in breast milk 153
Allergic
  conjunctivitis **1820**
  drug reactions 481–483
  gastroenteropathy 1595
  hydrarthrosis 505
  purpura *see* Anaphylactoid purpura
  rhinitis 442, 445, 448, 454, 458, **459–461**, 1807
  "salute" 459
  "shiner" 460
Allergy 442–489, 490
  allergic rhinitis **459–461**
  angioedema **477–478**
  asthma **464–467**
    psychologic aspects of asthma **468–471**
  atopic dermatitis **471–474**, 1806–1808
  contact dermatitis **475–476**
  diagnostic methods in allergy **448–449**
  drug allergy **478–483**
  hypersensitivity reactions to physical factors, **487–489**
  hyposensitization **452–454**
  inhalant, to insect emanations 484
  insect allergy **483–484**
  pathophysiology of allergic disease **442–448**
  serous otitis media **461–463**
  serum sickness **485–486**
  to stinging insects **483–484**
  treatment of allergic disorders, principles of **450**
    allergen avoidance **450–452**
    drug therapy **454–460**
    prophylaxis of atopic disorders 458
  to tuberculin 682
  urticaria **477–478**
Allometric relationship, in relation to fetal body composition 31
"Allometry" 31
Allopurinol (Zyloprim) 339, 1212
Allpyral 454
Alopecia 212, 300, 550, 1032, 1767, 1838
Alopecia mucinosa 1764, *1765*
Alper's disease **915**

Alpha *see* α-*specific terms·*
Alpha chains, in hemoglobin **1175–1176**
Alpha lipoprotein deficiency *see* α-Lipoprotein deficiency
Alpha thalassemia *see* α-Thalassemia
Alport's disease 1514, 1885
Altafur, in Chagas' disease 837
Alternate-day prednisone therapy 457, 467
Altitude, and transplacental oxygen diffusion 46, 47
Alton giant 250
Aluminium 145
Aluminium hydroxide 197, 210, 1467
Alveolar hydatid disease 821, **823**
Alveolar processes **1861**
Alveolar ridge lesions **1838–1840**
Alveolar surface area **1301**
Alveolar ventilation/perfusion ratio **93**, 416, 464, **1262–1264**
Alveolar ventilation, in low-birth-weight infant 92
Amaurosis *see* Blindness
Amaurotic familial idiocy 859, **910, 912**
  congenital (Norman-Wood disease) **910**
Amberlite IRA-400 1595
Ambiguous genitalia *1548*
Ambilhar *see* Niridazole
Amblyopia
  ex anopsia **1832**
  hysterical 284
Amebiasis 638, 640, **825–830**, *826*
Ameboma **828**
Amelia 1707
Ameloblasts 1856
Amelogenesis imperfecta **1863**
Amenorrhea 220, 270, 561, **1116–1120**
  in sarcoidosis 1252
American Heart Association 500
American hookworm *see* Necator americanus
American leishmaniasis **837–838**
American trypanosomiasis *see* Chagas' disease
Amethopterin 185, **1209–1210**
Amino acids 131–135, 170, 171, 296, 344, **1568**
  absorption **132, 1568**
  in breast milk 158
  catabolism 132
  in cow's milk *158*
  "dispensable" 132
  distribution 132
  "essential" **132**
  excretion *see* Amino-acidurias
  in fetus **39**
  and high-protein feedings 110
  in hypocaloric dwarfism 171
  in kwashiorkor 174
  malabsorption **1595**
  metabolism, disorders of **321–338**
    of amino acid metabolism **321–334**
    of amino acid transport 336
    of urea cycle **334–336**. *See also individual diseases* e.g., Albinism; Alkaptonuria.
  in low-birth-weight infant 110
  in nutrition **131–135**
  for parenteral nutrition 135
  in protein synthesis 35
  requirements **133–135**
  sequence 318
  transport, disorders of **336–338**. *See also* Cystinuria; Hartnup disease; Iminoglycinuria.
  in various foods 134

Amino-acidurias 174, 206, **321–341**, 1165, **1517–1519**. *See also specific disorders.*
  in acute cerebellar ataxia **1042**
  in ataxia-telangiectasia 930
  in cystinosis **1522**
  in Fanconi syndrome **1521–1524**
  in lead poisoning 542
  in vitamin D deficiency rickets 198
  in Wilson's disease 1523
p-Aminobenzoic acid (PABA) 582
γ-Aminobutyric acid 335
p-Aminohippurate **1462**
α-Amino-β-imidazolypropionic acid *see* Histidine
β-Aminoisobutyric acid 335
β-Aminoisobutyric aciduria **341**, 1519
δ-Aminolevulinic acid (ALA) 405, 410, 411, 545
Aminophylline **456, 466–467, 1281**, 1293, 1424
Aminopyrin 359, 1204
4-Aminoquinoline *see* Chloroquine
Ammonia 334, 335, 530, 534
  in hepatic failure 1692
Ammoniacal dermatitis **1814–1815**, 1894
Ammoniated mercury 549
Ammonium acetate 535
Ammonium chloride 566, 1462
Ammonium excretion **1459**, 1462
Amnesia, hysterical 284
Amniocentesis 18, **57–59**, 317, 339, 382, **1192–1193**, 1196
Amniography 60, 62
Amnion
  in multiple births 118
  nodosum 65, 1471
  "whole mount" examination **65**
Amnionic sac, in multiple births 118
Amnionitis 65, 596
Amnioscopy 57, **57**
Amniotic fluid 8, 18, 19, 50, **57–59**, 64, 1192, 1270
  and intravascular clotting 1242
Amniotic membranes, premature rupture of 596
Amobarbital 563
Amphetamines 532, 571, **881**
  abuse **565–566**, 571
  in epilepsy 998
  poisoning, acute **565–566**
Amphotericin B **1307–1308**, 581, 787–788, 793, 794, 795–796, 838, 1509, 1791, 1823
Ampicillin **585, 602–606**, 620, 623, 632–633, 637, 638, 640, **1286–1542**
  in bacterial meningitis **602–606**
  in *E. coli* infections of newborn 642
  in epiglottitis **1286**
  H. influenzae infections 620
  in meningococcal infections 623
  in parapertussis 633
  in pertussis 632
  in salmonellosis 637
  in shigellosis 640
  in typhoid fever **638**
  in urinary tract infections **1542**
Amyl nitrate 533
Amylase, serum
  in kwashiorkor 174
  in mumps **739**
Amylo-1,6-glucosidase 371
Amyloidosis 1218
Amylopectin 371, 1688

Amylopectinosis *see* Glycogenosis type IV
Amyotonia congenita (Werdnig-Hoffman disease) **923**, 1027, **1325**. *See also* Arthrogryposis multiplex.
Amyotrophic lateral sclerosis, familial juvenile **923**
Anabolic steroid therapy 370, 428, 1465, 1686
  and hyperbilirubinemia 1686
Anagen alopecia 1760
Anal. *See also* Anus; Anorectal.
  agenesis 1626
  atresia 76
  dimple, in imperforate anus **1625**
  fissures 1601, **1659**
  fistula **1648**
  patency, assessment 77, 104
  ulcer 1659
Analbuminemia 391
Analgesia 20, 54, 68, 409, 477
  and birth asphyxia 68
  during delivery 20
  during labor 54
  in porphyria 409
  and urticaria 477
Analgia, congenital 924
β-Analyl-l-methylhistidine 335
Anamnestic response 435
Anaphylactoid purpura (Henoch-Schönlein's) 613, **1232–1233**, 1307, **1492–1493**
Anaphylatoxins 446
Anaphylaxis **453**, 455, 477, **485**, 585
Anasarca 422, 817, 1189, 1500
Anastomosis, vascular 123, 1405, 1416
  placental 123
Ancylostoma braziliense **807**, 1792
Ancylostoma caninum 807
Ancylostoma duodenale 805
Androgen-induced female pseudohermaphrodism, placental 1134
Androgens 56, 243, 370, 425, 1092–1093, 1119, 1127–1128, 1134, 1465, 1686
  adrenal **1092–1093, 1119**
  and fetal sex differentiation 56
  and growth 243
  ovarian 1119
Androgen-secreting ovarian tumors 1119
Androgenic sexual precocity **1127–1128**
Androgenic steroids, anabolic 428
Androstenedione, fetal synthesis 40
Anemia **1162–1203**
  in acute glomerulonephritis 1484
  and breast feeding 145, 156
  and cardiac hypertrophy 1433
  in cephalhematoma 967
  in Chediak-Higashi syndrome 1802
  and chloramphenicol 588
  due to chronic blood loss 174
  in diphyllobothriasis 821
  erythroblastosis fetalis *see* Erythroblastosis fetalis
  in hookworm infection 174, 806
  neonatorum 1187
  and neuroblastoma 1111
  and pericarditis 1427
  in portal hypertension 1691
  of prematurity 1157
  of protein malnutrition 174
  pyridoxin deficiency 184
  pyridoxin responsive 185
  in regional enteritis 1642

Anemia (cont.)
  in renal failure, chronic **1647**
  in rheumatoid arthritis 505
  in sepsis neonatorum 597
  in SLE 509
  in splenic injury 1218
  in splenomegaly 1206
  in ulcerative colitis 1644
  in whipworm infections 805
  and zinc deficiency 146
Anemias **1161–1203**
  due to blood loss **1201–1202**
  due to bone marrow replacement **1167**
  of chronic infections, uremia, malignancy **1167–1169**
  classification **1160**
  due to destruction of red cells **1169–1201**. *See also*
      Hemolytic anemias.
  hemolytic **1169–1201**. *See also* Hemolytic anemias.
  hypoplastic and aplastic anemias **1165–1167**
  iron-deficiency anemia **1160–1163**. *See also* Iron-defi-
      ciency.
  megaloblastic anemias **1163–1165**. *See also* Megalo-
      blastic anemias.
  production defects of red cells and hemoglobin **1160–
      1169**
Anencephalus 315, 861, **868–870**
  diagnosis in utero 60
Anergy **682**
Anesthesia **1910–1911**
  and ADH release, **1152**
  epidural 20, 54
  and delivery 54, 70
  hysterical 284
  during labor 54, 70
  in pregnancy and labor 68
  spinal 54
  transplacental diffusion 54
ANF *see* Antinuclear factors
Angiitis 513
Angina 370, 376, 1841
Angiocardiography **1357–1363**, 1405, 1407, 1410, 1416
Angioedema **389–390**, **477–478**
Angiofibroma, juvenile **1873**
Angiography 855, 949, 958, 962, 972, **1010–1016**
Angiokeratoma corporis diffusum universalis *see* Fabry's
      disease
Angiomas, of small bowel 1661
Angioneurotic edema 153, **389–390**, 454, 455, 500, 585,
      477–478
  hereditary **389–390**
Angiopathy, systemic 510
Angiotensin 1421, **1442**
Angular conjunctivitis 1820
Angular stomatitis 180–182, 1854
Anhalonidine 569
Anhaptoglobinemia, hereditary 390
Anhidrosis 1817
Anhidrotic ectodermal dysplasias 930
Anicteric hepatitis **708, 1690**
Aniline 529, 532
Animal carriers 621, 671, 691, 698, 728, 755–756, 780, 782,
      783, 789, 791, 802, 808, 812, 818, 821, 835, 838, 839
Animal danders 450, 474
Anions, cellular 222
Aniridia 1561, 1706, 1825, **1827**
Anisocoria 75, 662, 671, 691–692
Anisocytosis 1177, 1184

Ankle swelling
  in rickets 201
  in scurvy 188
Ankyloglossia 1848
Ankylosis
  in alkaptonuria 326
  in rheumatoid arthritis 504, 505
Annular pancreas 426, **1613–1615**
Anocutaneous fistula *1630*
Anodontia **1564–1565**, 1838
Anomalies, congenital *see* Congenital anomalies
Anomalous left coronary artery 1395, 1434
Anomie 292
Anoperineal fistulas 1626
Anopheles 810, 831
Anophthalmos 1817
Anorectal disorders **1621–1624, 1625–1630, 1648**, 1661
  abscesses **1648**
  fistula **1648**
  inflammatory diseases **1648**
  malformations 1556, **1621–1624, 1625–1630**
Anorexia 207, 209, 228, *269*, 454, 509, 621, **1161**, *1421*
  hysterical 284
  in iron deficiency **1161**
  nervosa **270**
Anosmia 379, 459, 924, 1055, 1871
Anovulation 1117
Anovulatory agents 185
Anovulatory bleeding **1116**
Anovulatory cyclic therapy, in acne 1816
Anovulvar fistula 1628
Anoxia, in newborn **67–74, 1258**
Anoxic spells 711, **1402–4103**, 1410
  in tetralogy of Fallot **1402–1403**
  in transposition of great arteries 1410
Anserine 335
Antagonism, between trace elements 146
Antenatal period **15–66**
Antepar *see* Piperazine citrate
Antepartum vaginal bleeding, and respiratory distress
      syndrome 1261
Anterior encephaloceles **872**
Anterior fontanel **1700**
Anterior horn cell disease 851
Anterior pituitary *see* Pituitary, anterior
Anti-A titers, in visceral larva migrans 803
Antibacterial therapy *see* Antimicrobial therapy
Antibiotics *see* Antimicrobial therapy
Antibodies **431–440**
  anti-influenzal 721
  antiplatelets 1233
  antithyroid 1068, 1079, 1085
  in breast milk 148, **152,** 159
  in candidiasis 796
  in coccidioidal granuloma **790**
  in colostrum 150
  in cow's milk 159
  in cystic fibrosis 422
  in cytomegalic inclusion disease 704
  in ECHO virus infections 754
  in poliomyelitis **734**
  to polysaccharide antigens 388
  in Rocky Mountain spotted fever 782
  in salmonella infections 637
  in syphilis, titration, quantitative **654**
7S Antibody 505, 654
19S Antibody 654

Anticholinergic activity 454
Anticholinergic agents 1639
Anticholinesterase medication, overdosage 1036–1037
Anticholinesterase miotics, accommodative strabismus 1833
Anticoagulant(s)
    circulating 1241–1242
    therapy 1242
Anticodon 35
Anticonvulsant therapy 995–1000
    in bacterial meningitis 607
    in cerebral palsy 886
    in lead poisoning 548
    and lymphoma 1223
Anti-D antibody 1187–1189, 1196–1197
Antideoxyribonucleotidase B 497
Antidiarrheal drugs 1646
Antidiuretic effect, of oxytocin 56
Antidiuretic hormone (ADH) 1148–1153
Antidiuretic hormone-deficient diabetes insipidus 1150
Antidiuretic hormone release, excessive 1152–1153
Antidiuretic hormone-resistant (nephrogenic) diabetes insipidus 1150–1151
Antidiuretic hormone secretion 1148–1153
    in bacterial meningitis 606
    and heroin 559
    inappropriate 409
Anti-DNA antibody 509
Anti-DNase B see Antideoxyribonucleotidase B
Antidotes 533–535
Antiemetics 660
    during pergnancy 17
"Anti-Freeze" 572
Antigen 388, 431–432, 444–457, 647–648, 699, 1187–1189, 1196–1197
Antigen-binding capacity 432
Antigenicity 431
Antigenic specificity 431
Antigen-reactive site 431
    in autoimmune acquired hemolytic anemia 1184–1185
    on cord blood 64
    direct 87
    in malaria 831
Antiglomerular basement membrane disease 1489
Antihelix 1882
Antihemophilia factor (AHF) see Factor VIII
Antihemophilia globulin (AHG) see Factor VIII
Antihistamines 454–455, 461, 474, 478, 489, 529
Antihistone antibody 509
Antihyaluronidase 497
Antihypertensive drugs 55, 1447–1448, 1467, 1486
Antiinflammatory action, of corticosteroids 1102
Antiinflammatory agents, in obstructive airway disease 1282
Antiluetic therapy 657–658
Antimalarial chemotherapy 833–834
    in epilepsy 998
    in rheumatoid arthritis 507
    in systemic lupus erythematosus 510
Antimicrobial therapy 579–596
    agents in common use 584–491
        with broad spectrum 580, 584–586
        with intermediate spectrum 586–588
        with narrow spectrum 584–586
    in allergic disorders 458
    antituberculous 684–687
    of bacterial meningitis 602–606

Antimicrobial therapy (cont.)
    of brucellosis 611
    of cholera 613
    in craniospinal focal sepsis 1011–1016
    in cystic fibrosis 427
    in diarrheal disease 228
    of diphtheria 617
    effect on fetus 56
    in heart failure 1424
    of H. influenzae infections 620
    incompatibilities 588–589
    and kidney function impairment 591
    of leptospirosis 622
    and impaired liver function 591
    in low-birth-weight newborn 594–595
    in lymphogranuloma venereum 776
    in measles 734, 735
    mechanism of action 580
    of meningococcal infections 622–623
    of mycoplasma infections 625
    of neonatal pneumonia 1270
    nephrotoxicity 1509
    in newborn infants 594–595
    in otitis media 1887
    of parapertussis 633
    of pertussis 632
    principles of 579
    prophylactic use of 589
    prophylaxis of meningitis contacts 608
    of psittacosis 776
    of pyoderma
        staphylococcal 646
        streptococcal 651
    of rat-bite fever 634
    resistance to 583–584
    RS viral disease 724
    of salmonella infections 637, 638
    of shigellosis 640–641
    of smallpox 772
    of staphylococcal disease 645–646
    of streptococcal infections 650–652
    of syphilis 652–658
    transplacental diffusion 56
    of tuberculosis 685–687
    of tularemia 693
    of urinary tract infections 1542
    in urticaria 477
    and vitamin K deficiency 140
Antimongolism see Monosomy G
Antimongoloid palpebral slant 1144, 1841
Antimonials, pentavalent, in kala-azar 838
Antimony, in schistosomiasis 815
Anti-NADase see Antinicotinamide adenine dinucleotidase
Antinicotinamide adenine dinucleotidase 496
Antinuclear antibodies 505, 511, 514
Antinuclear factors 509
Antinucleoprotein antibody 509
Antipernicious anemia extrinsic factor see Vitamin B$_{12}$
Antiplatelet factor 1233, 1235
Antipyrine, placental clearance of 45
Antiscorpion serum 845
Antiserotonin activity 455
Antisocial behavior 279–281
Antispasmodics 1611, 1646
Antistreptokinase 497

Antistreptolysin O (ASLO) 492, 494, **496–497**, 510, 648, 764, **1483–1484**
"Antitemplates," and growth 239
Antithyroid antibodies 1068, 1075, 1079
Antithyroid drugs **1085**
  during gestation 55
Antithrombin 1229
Antitoxin
  botulism **609–610**
  diphtheria **616–617**
  snake 556
  tetanus **660–661**
  α_1-antitrypsin deficiency **391**, 1689
Antrypol *see* Suramin
Antrum 1882
Ant sting 844
Anuria **621**, **1464**, 1484
Anus 74, 76, 83, 104, **1625–1630**, **1648**
  fistula in ano **1548**
  imperforate 74, 83, **1626–1630**
  of newborn 76, 83, 104
Anxiety **282**, 361, 468, **1277**
  in airway obstruction **1277**
  in asthmatics 468
  in hypoglycemia 361
Aorta (aortic)
  arch anomalies **1416**
  atresia 1377, **1388–1389**
  coarctation **1390–1391**, 1446
  dextroposition 1402
  double arch 1416
  homografting 1415
  hypoplastic arch 1371, 1415
  isthmus aplasia **1391**
  regurgitation murmur **495**, 1343
  right-sided arch **1416–1417**
  stenosis 1371, **1388**
  vascular ring **1417**
Aortography 1391, 1440, 1443, 1446
Aortopulmonary fenestration 1376, **1395**
Aortopulmonary shunt (operative) 1405, 1416
Apathy 229, 671, 852
  in iron deficiency **1161**
  in kwashiorkor 173
APC (adenoidal-pharyngeal-conjunctival) virus 725
Apert's syndrome (acrocephalosyndactyly) 305, 1698, 1705, **1841**, 1872
Apgar score *71*, **72**, 76
  of low-birth-weight-infant 90
  and neonatal morbidity and mortality 115
Aphasia 276
  in cerebral arterial thrombosis 962
  in white matter diseases 916
Aphonia, hysterical 284
Aphthae **1853**
Aphthous stomatitis 1643, 1645, **1853**
Apical abscess 660
Apical systolic murmur 494
Aplastic crises **1167–1168**
  in β-thalassemia 1181
Aplastic kidney 1477
Apnea 70, 360, 597, 1258, 1268, 1270
  in neonatal hypoglycemia 360
  in neonatal pneumonia 1270
  in newborn 70, 1258
  "primary" and "secondary" **70**
  in pulmonary dysmaturity 1268
  in sepsis neonatorum 597

Apneic spells 111, **1402–1403**, 1410
Apocrine sweat 423
Appendiceal abscess 1640
Appendicitis 734, 768, 1600, 1648, **1640–1642**
  in measles 734
Appetite
  as guide to caloric requirements 130
  regulation 216
Appetite, increased 271, 418, 425–428, 574, 1083
  in cystic fibrosis 418, 425, 426, 428
  in Graves' disease 1083
  in neonatal narcotic withdrawal syndrome 574
Appetite depression in amphetamine addict 565
"Apple" shaped heart **1407**
Aqueduct of Sylvius, stenosis 862, **863**
Aqueous humor 344
Aqueous penicillin G *see* Penicillin G
Arabinose 359
Arachidonic acid 135
Arachnidism **844–845**
  necrotic 1793
Arachnodactyly 1708
Arachnoid membrane and villi 862
Aralen *see* Chloroquine
"Arborization" block 1364
Arbovirus encephalitides *see* Arthropod-borne viral encephalitides
Arched palate *see* High-arched palate
Arches 313
Arcus corneae 88
  in hypercholesteremia, familial 375
Arcus juvenilis *see* Arcus corneae
Arcus senilis 1822
Areflexia, tendinous
  in familial dysautonomia 1040
  in Friedreich's ataxia 922
  in Lowe's syndrome 1522
  in organophosphate poisoning 551
  in thiamine deficiency 179
Arginine 219, **336**, **337**
Arginine stimulatory test **1050**
Argininosuccinase 334
Argininosuccinic acid 334
Argininosuccinic acid synthetase 334
Argininosuccinicaciduria 1759
Arhinencephaly *see* Holoprosencephaly
Ariboflavinosis *see* Riboflavin deficiency
Aristocort *see* Adrenocorticosteroid therapy
Arithmetic 260
Arithmetic mean *see* Mean, arithmetic
Armadillos 835
Arnold-Chiari malformation 863, 876, 1702, 1716
Aromatic hydrocarbons **530**
Arrhenoblastoma 1119, 1127
Arrhythmias 82, 494, 1338, **1354**, 1363, 1368, 1408
  in diphtheria **615**
Arsenic 145, 513, **530**, 533, 1686
Arsenicals
  in African trypanosomiasis 834
  in breast milk 152
Arsobal *see* Mel B
Arterial dye curves **1359–1360**
Arterial oxygen saturation **1377**, 1401
Arterial oxygen unsaturation 1401
Arterial systems, fetal 49
Arterial thrombosis
  cerebral **962**
  in periarteritis nodosa 513

Arteriography, cerebral **855**, 958, 962, **1010–1016**
Arterioles, in scleroderma 512
Arteriosclerosis 344, 376, **1841**
  in diabetes mellitus 344
  in progeria **1841**
Arteriovenous fistula 74, 1373, **1396–1397**
  cerebral deep midline 963
  placental 120
  pulmonary 1377
Arthrogram, in congenital hip dislocation **1747–1748**
Arthralgia 503, 1727
  in African trypanosomiasis 834
  in coccidioidomycosis 789
  in hemorrhagic fever 848
  in leukemia 1209
  in malaria 832
  in measles 732
  in murine typhus 780
  in rheumatic fever **496**
  in Rocky Mountain spotted fever 781
  in *Schistosomiasis mansoni* infection 814
  in systemic lupus erythematosus **508–509**
Arthritis 387, **490–512**, **514–516**, 1643, 1645
  acute
    helpful historical and physical findings **515**
    primary differential diagnosis of **514**
    suggested work-up **514–516**
  in brucellosis 611
  due to *H. influenzae* 619, **620**
  in Lesch-Nyhan syndrome 339
  in rat-bite fever 634
  in rheumatic fever **490–502**. See also Rheumatic poly-
    arthritis.
  in rheumatoid arthritis **503–507**
  in rubella **761**
  due to salmonellae 636, 637
  in scleroderma 512
  in systemic lupus erythematosus **508–509**
Arthrogryposis multiplex 78, **1029**
Arthro-onycho-dysplasia *see* Nail-patella syndrome
Arthropod-borne rickettsioses **777–783**
Arthropod-borne viral encephaltides 1016, **1017–1018**
Arthropods, diseases caused by **777–783**, **844–846**, **1017–
    1018**, **1792–1794**
Arthrotomy 505
Articulation defects 276, **277**
Artificial colonization, bacterial 645
Artifical insemination 317
Artificial respiration **72–73**, *103,* 104, 525 **646–647, 1260,
    1265, 1283**
Aryl sulfatase A, deficiency **384**, 911, **916, 917**
Ascariasis 439, 442, 477, **797–802,** *798*
Ascaris lumbricoides 439, 442, 477, **797–802,** *798*
Ascending aorta-right pulmonary artery anastomosis
    (Waterston-Cooley) 1405
Ascending paralysis 745, 718, 756, **1006, 1325**
Aschoff body **493**
Ascites 61, 71, 136, 509, **678–679,** 817, 1128, 1330, 1421,
    1660, 1687, 1691
Ascorbic acid 43, 109, 138, **139,** 143, 155, 157, 162, 166,
    176, 185, **186–191,** 325, 430, 589
Ascorbic acid deficiency *see* Scurvy
Ascorbic acid load test 191
Aseptic meningitis *see* Meningitis, aseptic
Aseptic necrosis, femur and humerus in sickle-cell dis-
    ease 1177
ASK *see* Antistreptokinase
ASLO *see* Antistreptolysin O

Ask-Upmark kidney **1475**
ASO *see* Antistreptolysin O test
Asparaginase, in leukemia 1211
Asparagine 336
Aspartic acid 340, 334
"Aspergilloma" 787
Aspergillosis **786–787,** 1225, **1307,** 1429
Aspergillus niger 786
Aspergillus fumigatus 786, 1307, 1429
Aspermia, "idiopathic" 311
Aspiration **577,** 668, **1270–1271,** 1278, **1288**
  and early feedings 109
  of foreign bodies **577,** 668, 1278, **1288**
  of meconium **1270–1271**
Asphyxia, birth *see* Birth asphyxia
Asphyxiating thoracic dystrophy of Jeune **1327**
Aspirin *see* Salicylates
Assaultiveness 280
Assisted ventilation **72–73,** *103,* 104, 525, **646–647, 1260,
    1265, 1283**
Association, National, of Mothers of Twins 124
Association for the Aid of Crippled Children 897
Asthma 426, 442, 448, 454, 455, 457, 458, **464–471,** 472,
    479, 514, **1292–1294, 1295,** 1807
  and drug allergy *see* Drug allergy
  and fat-free diet 136
  in Klinefelter's syndrome (XXY) 903
Asthmatic bronchitis **1290**
Asthmatic personality **470**
Astiban, in schistosomiasis 815
Astigmatism 1835
Astrocytomas 927, 937, **941–942,** 947, 949, **950–952**
  cerebellar 937–940, **941–942**
  cerebral hemispheres **949**
  and neurofibromatosis 927
  of optic nerve and chiasm **951–952**
  of thalamus **947**
Asymmetry 13, 250, 853, 1099, 1696, **1706,** 1748
  of face 853, 1696
  of skin folds, thigh 1748
Atabrine *see* Quinacrine
Atarax *see* Hydroxyzine
Ataxic cerebral palsy 884
Ataxia 384, 587, 851, **1041–1043,** 1163
  acute, cerebellar **1041–1043**
  in argininosuccinic aciduria 334
  in ataxia-telangiectasia 929
  in barbiturate addict 564
  in basal ganglia degeneration 921
  in beta-lipoprotein deficiency 377
  in brain abscess 1012
  in brainstem gliomas 945
  in brain tumors **940,** 942, 943, 945
  in cerebellar abscess 1012
  in cerebellar astrocytoma 942
  in cerebellar degeneration 921
  in encephalitis **1016–1023**
  in Friedreich's ataxia **922**
  in gray matter diseases **912–915**
  in Hartnup disease 923
  in hypoglycemia 361
  hysterical 284
  in lead poisoning 544
  in mercury poisoning 549
  in Refsum's syndrome 924, **1008**
  in white matter diseases 916, 918
Ataxia-telangiectasia hereditary Louis-Bar syndrome
    389, 437, 851, 922, 929

Atelectasis 415, **420–421**, 1296, 1401
  in asthma 465
  in esophageal atresia 1605
Atheroma 344, 375–376, **1841**
Atherosclerosis 344, 376, **1841**
Athetoid cerebral palsy, due to kernicterus **1192**
Athetosis 116, 671, **851**, **884**, **919–921**, 947, 1192
  in basal ganglia degenerations **919–921**
  in thalamic tumors 947
Atonic diplegia **884**
Atopic dermatitis 47, 442, **471–474**, **1806–1808**
  and fat-free diet 136
  IgE in 436
  and vaccination 773
Atopic diathesis 472
Atopic eczema 47, 442, 458, **471–474**, **1806–1808**
  and fat-free diet 136
  IgE in 436
  and vaccination 773
Atopic state 479
"Atopy" **442–443**
ATP 35, 358, **392–393**, 1170, 1229, 1669
ATP synthesis, and erythrocyte sodium permeability, 1170
Atransferrinemia 390
Atresia
  anal 76, **1872**
  biliary 201, **1682–1684**
    and vitamin K deficiency 140
  choanal 71, 74, 80, 81, **1872**
  duodenal 74, 76, **1613–1615**
  esophageal 75, 81, **1604–1606**
  ileal 420, 426, **1616**
  intestinal 1613
  jejunal **1616**
  nasopharyngeal 1878
  rectal **1628**
  vaginal 1117
Atrial
  ejection murmurs **1342–1343**
  extrasystoles **1368**
  fibrillation **1369–1370**
  flutter 1364, **1369–1370**
  hypertrophy 1381
  pressure at birth 70
  septal defect 1373, 1376, **1398–1401**
  shunt in hydrocephalus **867**
Atrioventricular
  block 495, **1366–1370**
  canal 1398, 1400
  conduction defects **494**, 495, 1071, 1252, **1366–1370**
  node 1421
  valves 1339
  valves obstruction **1380–1384**
Atrophic pelvifemoral dystrophy of Leyden and Mobius 1031
Atropine 273, 532, 1423
  in organophosphate poisoning **551–552**
  in PAT 1364
Atropine methyl nitrate (Eumydrin), in pyloric stenosis **1611**
Attention span, short 880
Atypical lymphocytes see Lymphocytes, atypical
Audiography 463, 1883
Audiometry 463, 1883
Auditory deficit see Deafness
Auerbach's plexus 1621
Aura **481**

Aura (cont.)
  in migraine 1002
Aural polyp 1885
Aureomycin, in tularemia 693
Austin Flint murmur 1374
Australia antigen **707**
Australian X disease see Murray valley encephalitis
Autism, due to congenital rubella **766**
Autistic posturing, and rumination 1578
Autoagglutination, red blood cell 509
Autoclaving, and destruction of bacteria and spores 157
Autoeczematization 475
Autohemolysis 377, **1184–1185**
Autoimmune acquired hemolytic anemia **1184–1185**
Autoimmune lymphopenia 389
Autoimmune thyroiditis see Hashimoto's struma
"Autoimmunity" 387, 490
Automatic walking, in newborn 85, **88**
Automatisms, in newborn *85*, **86–88**
Autonomic epilepsy 982, 988, **991**, **1000**, 1056, 1575
Autonomic nervous system, 409, 1040, 1065
  in acute intermittent porphyria (Swedish type) 409
  and thyroid hormone action 1065
Autonomic pelvic nerves 1550
Autonomic receptor function, of fetal tissue 52
Autoradiographic methods *309*
Autosomal dominant inheritance **298–299, 314**. *See also* Dominant.
Autosomal recessive inheritance and disorders **299**, 390, 399, 404
Autosomal sex-influenced trait **200, 315**
Autosomes 298, 309
A-variant, G6PD deficiency 394
AV block see Atrioventricular
AV node see Atrioventricular
Average **232**
Avidin 140
Avitaminosis see Vitamin deficiency
AVR, AVL, and AVF leads 1348
Axenfeld's syndrome 1826
Axial skeleton **1714–1719**
  pelvis **1718**
  thoracic cage **1714–1715**
  vertebral column **1715–1718**
Axillary hair 241, **1123–1124**
Axillary nerve injury 978
6-Azauridine 340
Azathioprine 1204, 1504, **1643**, **1648**
  in chronic renal insufficiency **1648**
  in nephrotic syndrome 1504
  in regional enteritis **1643**
Azotemia 1514
Azurophilic granules, in granulocytes 911, 913

Babbling 254
Babinski sign **851**
  in Friedreich's ataxia 922
  in spastic paraplegia, familial 922
"Baby talk" 277
Backache **673–674**, 760, 780, 789, **1015–1016**, 1716
  in coccidioidomycosis 789
  in murine typhus 780
  in smallpox 760
  in spinal abscess **1015–1016**
  in spondylolisthesis 1716
  in tuberculosis of spine **673–674**

Bacillary dysentery *see* Shigellosis
Bacillus anthrax 431
Bacillus calmette and Guerin *see* BCG
Bacillus proteus *see* Proteus
Bacillus serratio 1571
Bacillus subtilis 156
  and inhibition of growth by β-2-thienylalanine 325
Bacitracin 581, **586**, 1509
Back tenderness
  in spinal abscess **1015–1016**
  in tuberculosis of spine **673–674**
Bacteremia
  in tuberculosis 664
  in typhoid fever **637–638**
Bacillus thiaminolyticus 179
Bacteria *see* specific organisms; Bacterial disease
  associated with particular infections **589, 590**
  in bottled milk 156
  intestinal **1570–1572**
Bacterial counts **1541**
Bacterial cultures, in newborn 104
Bacterial diseases **596–693**
  botulism **609–610**
  brucellosis **610–611**
  cholera **612–614**
  diphtheria **614–618**
  empyema
    endocarditis 498, 560–561, 1384, 1397, **1429–1431**
    erysipelas 649
  enteropathogenic *Escherichia coli* infections **641–643**
  Haemophilus influenzae infections **618–621**
  impetigo
    staphylococcus 645
    streptococcal 649
  leptospirosis **621–622**
  meningitis **598–609, 619–621, 622–625**
  meningococcal infections **622–625**
  mycobacterial diseases other than tuberculosis **690–691**
  mycoplasma infections **625–626**
  parapertussis **632–633**
  pertussis **627–632**
  pyoderma
    staphylococcal 648
    streptococcal 649
  rat-bite fever **634–635**
  salmonella infections **635–638**
  scarlatina 649
  sepsis neonatorum **696–698**
  shigellosis **638–641**
  staphylococcal enterocolitis **646–647**
  staphylococcal food poisoning **646–647**
  staphylococcal infections **644–647**
  streptococcal infections **647–652**
  syphilis **652–662**
  tetanus **568–662**
  tuberculosis **662–690**
  tularemia **690–693**
  typhoid fever **637–638**
Bacterial endocarditis 498, 560–561, 1384, 1397, **1429–1431**
Bacterial interference 645
Bacterial intermediary metabolism, agents affecting **582**
Bacterial intrauterine infections **18**
Bacterial membrane, agents affecting **581**
Bacterial meningitis *see* Meningitis, bacterial
Bacterial pharyngitis, acute 1878
Bacterial nucleic acid synthesis, agents affecting **581**
Bacterial pneumonias **1305–1307**

Bacterial protein synthesis, agents affecting **581**
Bacterial resistance to antibiotics **583–584**
Bacterial skin infections **1781–1784**
Bacterial wall, agents affecting **580**
Bacteriology 609
  in tuberculosis 661–665, **682–683**
Bacteriophage 645, 646
Bacteriostatic antibiotics **580, 582**
Bacteriuria 1468, **1539–1546**
Bacteroides 587
"Bad Trip" 569
Badger 755
"Bag" 559, 571
Bagassosis **1313**
BAL 391, **546–548**, 549, 835
  in lead poisoning **546–548**
  in mercury poisoning 549
Balanitis 1553
Balanoposthitis **1544**, 1553
Balantidiasis **838–839**
Balantidium coli 227, **838–839**
BAL-CaEDTA therapy, in lead poisoning **546–548**
Baldness *see* Alopecia
Balkan nephropathy **1508**
Ball of fear 270
Ballismus 851
Balloon catheter septostomy 1407, 1412
Balloon-cheeked appearance, of infant of diabetic mothers **126**
Balo's concentric sclerosis 918
"Bamboo joint" defect of hair shafts 1760
Banana sugar 161
Bancroft's filariasis **810–811**
Band forms 1163
Band keratopathy **1824**
"Bang" 571
Banthine *see* Methantheline bromide
Barbiturates 84, 532, **563–564**, 571, 573, 1911
  and acute intermittent porphyria **410**
  and ataxia 1042
  in breast milk 152
  during delivery 20
  and fetus 55
  during labor 52
  and mixed porphyria 410
  poisoning **564–565**
  transplacental diffusion 54
  withdrawal 575
"Barbs" 571
Barium enema 828, **1622, 1645, 1658**
  in amebiasis 828
  in congenital megacolon **1622**
  in intussusception **1658**
  in ulcerative colitis **1645**
Barium sulfate, and gastrolith 1651
Barking 851
Barlow's disease *see* Scurvy
Baroreceptors 69
Barotrauma, to middle ear 1889
Barr body 309, **1132**
Barrel-chested appearance 465
Basal cell nevus syndrome 931, 1696, 1716
Basal cisterns, obstruction of 672
Basal diastolic murmur *see* Diastolic murmur, basal
Basal ganglia, degenerations of **919–921**
Basal metabolism 128
  in cretinism 1071

Basal skull fractures **968, 970, 1055**
Base excess 223
Basement membrane 344, 508, 511, 512, 1451
Basidiobolus 795
Basilar skull fracture **968–970**
Basophilic adenoma **1057, 1100**
Basophilic granules 1203
Basophilic degranulation test 483
Basophilic stippling 542, 545, 1181
Basophils 445, 459, **1204**
Bassen-Kornzweig syndrome *see* β-Lipoprotein deficiency
Bathing **1894**
   of low-birth-weight infant 106
Bathing trunk nevus **1803**
Bats 755, 791
"Bat-wing," radiographic image 862
Batten-Spielmeyer-Vogt disease 910, **912–913**
Battered child syndrome 519, **556–558, 1711–1712**
Battey bacilli 691
Battle's sign *see* Retroauricular ecchymosis
Bazin's disease *see* Erythema induratum
BCG 438, 439, 682, **683–684,** 1211
   in leukemia 1211
Beaked nose 1699, **1841–1842**
Beaten silver appearance, of skull 854
Becker variant of pseudohypertrophic muscular dystrophy
      1030
Beckwith syndrome *see* Wiedemann-Beckwith syndrome
Beckwith's visceral cytomegaly *see* Wiedemann-Beckwith
      syndrome
Bed rest **1908**
   in acute glomerulonephritis **1486**
   in heart failure 1424
Bed-wetting 267
Bedbug 691
Bee sting 555, 844
   and tetanus 659
Bednar's aphthae **1838**
Beef tapeworm *see Taenia saginata*
Behavior
   aggressive 280
   antisocial **277–281**
   normal development 253–263
Behavioral abnormalities **277–281**
   in asthmatic children 468
   in Chagas' disease 836
   due to congenital rubella 767
   in Graves' disease 1083
   in hypoglycemia 361
   in lead poisoning 544
   in mental retardation **895**
   in phenylketonuria 324
   in rumination 1578
   in tuberculous meningitis 671
BEI *see* Butanol extractable iodine
Bell's nerve 978
Bell's palsy 746, 853, **978, 1009**
Benadryl *see* Diphenhydramine hydrochloride
Bender-Gestalt 548
Bender (Visual-Motor Gestalt test) 548, 881
Benedict's solution 351, 601
   screening test for cerebrospinal fluid sugar 601
Benesh Brace Boot **886**
Benign congenital hypotonia (of Walton) 923, 1027
Benign familial pemphigus 1780
Benign febrile convulsions **1001**
Benign mucosal pemphigoid 1779

Benign nonbacterial lymphadenitis *see* Cat scratch disease
Benign paroxysmal vertigo 1002
Benign recurrent hematuria **1507**
"Bennies" 571
Bentonite flocculation
   in echinococcosis 822
   in visceral larva migrans 803
Benzathin penicillin *see* Penicillin
Benzedrine *see* Amphetamine sulfate; Dextroamphetamine
Benzene 1166
Benzene hexachloride (Kwell) 837, 845, 1797
Benzimidazole derivatives **695**
Benzine 530, **538–540**
Benzocaine 641
Benzol 1236
Benzyl penicillin *see* Penicillin G
Benzylpenicillinic acid (BPE) 480
Benzylpenicilloyl (BPO) 480
Bephenium hydroxynaphthoate (Alcopara) **806**
Beriberi *see* Thiamine deficiency
Berkow's table 520, *522*
"Bernice" 571
Berries 529
   and urticaria 477
Berry spot test, for detection of mucopolysaccharidoses
      914
Beryllium 1312
Beta *see* β- *specific terms*
Beta-adrenergic stimulants *see* β-Adrenergic stimulants
Beta-alanine *see* β-Alanine
Beta-aminoisobutyric aciduria *see* β-Aminoisobutyric
Beta chains, in hemoglobin **1175–1176**
Beta-delta thalassemia *see* β-Thalassemia
Beta-galactosidase *see* β-Galactosidase
Beta-globulins *see* Globulins
Beta-glycosidase *see* β-Glycosidase
Beta-hemolytic streptococci *see* Streptococcus, β-hemolytic
Beta$_{IC}$ globulin *see* β$_{IC}$-Globulin
Betaine 330
Beta-lipoprotein deficiency *see* β-Lipoprotein deficiency
Beta-2-phenylalanine *see* β$_2$-Phenylalanine
Beta-thalassemia *see* β-Thalassemia
Bezoars 1651
Bicarbonate
   and acid-base metabolism **222–223, 1459**
   fetal plasma concentration 48
   reabsorption **1455, 1459, 1524–1525**
   sweat in in cystic fibrosis 414
   therapy 340
      in acute renal failure **1464**
      in airway obstruction **1278–1279**
      in asphyxia **1278–1279, 1282**
      in asthma **467**
      at birth 73, **1258–1259**
      in cyanotic heart disease **1379**
      in newborn **1258–1259**
      in salicylate intoxication **553–555**
Bicuspids **1856–1861**
Bielchowsky disease (late infantile amaurotic familial
      idiocy) 910, **912–913**
Bifid scrotum 1134
Bifocal glasses, in accommodative squint 1833
"Big D" 571
Bigeminy **1369**

Big toe, and gout 515
Bile pigments 1671
Bile-salt agar 612
Bile salts 477
Biliary atresia 1682–1686
Biliary cirrhosis 1682, 1683, 1686, 1691
Biliary colic 409
Biliary ducts, in cystic fibrosis 414
Biliary obstruction 1682–1684
  in clonorchiasis 816
Bilirubin 1673–1765. See also Hyperbilirubinemia.
  in amniotic fluid 57, 59
  in cord blood 64
  in cretinism 1071
  encephalopathy 1677
  in kwashiorkor 174
  metabolism 1673–1675
    in newborn 1675–1676
    and sulfonamides 586
  and sulfonamides 56, 586
  in viral hepatitis 708
Bilirubinuria 1686
Binocular fixation 254
Biochemical disorders 58
Biochemical genetics 294
Biochemistry, of amniotic fluid 58
Biometry 232–235
Biopsy
  cerebral 905, 912
  dental nerve 917
  kidney 1463, 1501
  liver 1673, 1683
  lung 1302
  lymphnode 387, 388, 699, 1224, 1228, 1247, 1252
  muscle 370
  peroral, 1587
  rectal 414, 1622
  skin 1247, 1252
Biotin 138, 140
Biovular twin see Twins, fraternal
Biparietal diameter, by ultrasound 60
Biphasic course, in poliomyelitis 744–746
Biplane angiocardiography 1359–1363
Bird handlers 775
Bird-headed dwarfism 115, 249, 1838, 1841–1842
Bird-headed facial appearance 1838, 1841–1842
Birth 64–127
  acid-base balance at 67
  asphyxia 66, 68, 74, 89, 97
  circulatory adjustments at 69–70, 1333–1334
  examination at see Newborn
  examination before 56–66
  eye injuries 1817–1818
  multiple see Multiple births
  rate in U.S. 2
  resuscitation after 70–74, 103, 104, 1260
  size, and mortality in twins 122
  and socioeconomic factors 22
  weight 235, 244
    and Apgar score 76
    in cystic fibrosis, failure to regain 418
    and gestational age 23, 125
    and head circumference 25
    of infants of diabetic mothers 126
    and length 25
    low see Low-birth-weight infants
    of obese children 215

Birth (cont.)
  weight (cont.)
    and parity 125
    relationship to neonatal outcome 111, 112, 113–114
Bismuth subnitrate 532
Bite
  of rabies 756–758
  rat 634
Bitemporal hemianopia
  in brain tumors 939, 952, 940
  in craniopharyngioma 952
Bithionol [2,2′-thiobis (4,6-dichlorophenol)] 476
  in fascioliasis 817
  in paragonimiasis 816
Biting, in rabies 756
Biting, of hands and feet, in acrodynia 550
Bitot's spot 177, 1823
Bjørnstad's syndrome 1760
"Black beauties" 571
"Black dot" ringworm 1790
"Black measles" 733
"Black sickness" see Kala-azar
"Black tabs" 571
Black tongue 181
Black-widow-spider bite 844
Blackfan-Diamond syndrome 1165
Blackfly 811
Blackhead see Comedo
Blackmail, and suicide 292
Bladder 1549–1553
Bladder carcinoma 814
Bladder and bowel dysfunction 973–975, 1007
  in acute polyneuritis 1007
  in craniocerebral trauma 973–975
  in spinal cord injury 975
Bladder injuries 1562
Bladder neck obstruction 1558
Bladder paralysis, in poliomyelitis 745, 747
"Bladder worm" see Cysticercus
Blalock-Taussig anastomosis 1405–1406
Blastocyst 40, 118
Blastomyces dermatitidis 787
Blastomycin skin test 788
Blastomycosis 787–788
  and Addison's disease 1093
  pulmonary 1308
Bleeding see Hemorrhage
  gastrointestinal 1578–1580
  in hemorrhagic disorders 1229–1243
  in infantile kala-azar 837
  in rubella 762
Bleeding time 326, 368, 1230, 1233–1243
  in albinism 326
  in glycogenosis type I 368
Blennorhea see Inclusion conjunctivitis
Bleoresin 475
Belpharoconjunctivitis 1818, 1820
Belpharospasm 1825
Blind pouch, in esophagela atresia 1605
"Blinding filariasis" see Onchocerciasis
Blindness 377, 381, 1251, 1698, 1832
  in cerebral embolism 962
  in congenital toxoplasmosis 840
  due to cytomegalic inclusion disease 703
  in gray matter diseases 912–913
  in Lowe's syndrome 1522
  night see Nyctalopia

Blindness (cont.)
  due to smallpox 771
  secondary to syphilitic keratitis 657
  in white matter diseases 918–919
Blinking 274, 851
Blinking, infrequent, in Graves' disease 1084
Blister beetles 845
Blistering diseases 1770–1781, 1806
Blistering eruptions on palms and soles 1806
Bloch-Sulzberger's syndrome see Incontinentia pigmenti
Block, cardiac see Heart block
Block, paracervical see Paracervical block
β-Blocking agents, in pheochromocytoma 1110
Blocking antibodies 445, 452
Blood and blood-forming organs 1155–1244
  blood-forming-organ disorders 1215–1228. See also
      Bone marrow; Spleen; Lymphnodes.
  fetal erythropoiesis 47–49, 1155–1157. See also Ery-
      thropoiesis.
  hemostasis disorders 1228–1244. See also Hemostasis.
  neonatal erythropoiesis 1157–1167
  in newborn 1157–1158
  red blood cell disorders 1161–1203. See also Anemias;
      Polycythemia; Erythrocytes; Erythrocytosis.
  in sickle-call anemia 1178
  in thalassemia major 1182
  and viral hepatitis 710
  white blood cell disorders 1203–1215. See also Leuco-
      cytes.
Blood-cerebrospinal fluid barrier 862
Blood coagulation 1228–1244. See also Coagulation;
      Hemostasis.
Blood cultures 515
  in sepsis neonatorum 597
  in typhoid fever 637–638
Blood disorders
  and bone lesions 1743, 1744
  and contraindications to vaccination 773
Blood flow
  in fetus, distribution 1333
  in low-birth-weight infant 96
  placental 45
  pulmonary 1377–1378. See also Pulmonary, blood flow.
  renal see Renal, blood flow
  umbilical 44
  uterine 43. See also Uterine blood flow.
Blood-forming organs, disorders of 1215–1228. See also
      Spleen; Lymphnodes.
Blood gases 71, 1258–1260, 1278–1279
  in airway obstruction 1278–1279
  in asthma 465
  in cystic fibrosis 427
  in neonatal narcotic withdrawal 575
  transplacental exchange 66, 67
Blood gases, arterial, of the newborn 1258–1260
Blood glucose cystine agar 693
Blood groups 302
  association with disease 302
  of twins 118
Blood loss 806, 1161, 1201–1202
  anemia(s) due to 1201–1202
  chronic 1161, 1219
  in hookworm infection 806
  in portal hypertension 1219
Blood oxygen saturation, and sickling 1176
Blood, P_{CO_2} see P_{CO_2}, blood
Blood pH see pH, blood

Blood, P_{O_2} see P_{O_2}, blood
Blood pressure, systemic
  in bulbar poliomyelitis 745
  in craniocerebral trauma 967
  in low-birth-weight infants 96, 96, 97
  measurement 1437
  in newborn 82
  in obesity 220
  regulation of 1437
Blood sampling 1907–1908
  arterial 105
  of fetus 64
Blood, in stool, 636, 640, 828, 1579–1580
  in amebiasis 828
  in salmonella infections 636
  in shigellosis 640
Blood transfusions see Transfusions
Blood values, normal, at all ages 1156–1157
Blood vessels
  in diabetes mellitus 343–344
  and hemorrhagic disorders 1230, 1232–1233
  and hemostasis 1228–1229
  of newborn 82
  in systemic lupus erythematosus 509
Blood viscosity, in cyanotic polycythemia 1402
Blood volume 1437
  fetal 49
  in low-birth-weight infant 96
  in term infant 1157
Blount's disease 1739
"Blow" 571
Blow flies 846
Blow-out skull fracture 1705
"Blue acid" 571
"Blue angels" 571
"Bluebirds" 571
"Blue devils" 571
"Blue dots" 571
"Blue heavens" 571
Blue light, and bilirubin 1678
Blue sclerae 1765, 1824
"Blue spells" in tetralogy of Fallot 1402–1403
"Blue-velvets" 571
Blueberry muffin lesion
  in rubella, congenital 765
  in thrombocytopenic purpura 765, 1233–1237
Blurred vision 454, 501
  in botulism 610
  in organophosphate poisoning 551
  in pseudotumor cerebri 958
Boarding schools 266
Bochdalek, formation 1632
Body
  measurements 77, 244–247, 1904
  rocking, and rumination 1578
  size, and infant of diabetic 126
  surface area 245, 521–523, 1911
  temperature 98, 1904–1905
  types 216
  weight 127, 214, 221, 235–236, 245, 1900, 1904. See also
      Weight.
Body build, and obesity 216
Body composition
  changes during growth 237
  fetal 25, 28–34
  fluids 221–222
Body fat 215, 217–219

Body fat (*cont.*)
  growth and 236
Body fluids **221–222**
  collection for laboratory **1907–1908**
Body hair 241
Body lead burden 544
Body louse **845, 1796**
Body mastery 257, 291–292
Boeck's sarcoid *see* Sarcoidosis
Bohn's pearls 1837
Boiling, milk 157
"Bombita" 571
Bone **1695–1753**. *See also* Skeletal.
  and calcium metabolism **195–196**
  in Fanconi syndrome 1521
  and magnesium metabolism 197
  mineralization **1737**
  and phosphate metabolism **196–197**
  in Refsum's disease **379**
Bone age
  in cretinism 1074
  in hypothyrodism 1076
  in obesity 217
  in sexual precocity **1126–1127**
Bone ankylosis, in rheumatoid arthritis 504, 507
Bone atrophy **1713**
Bone conduction 463
Bone contusions **1713**
Bone deformities
  in metaphysial dysostosis 206
  in rickets **200–202**
Bone demineralization 208, 209, 1100
  in Cushing's syndrome 1100
  due to parathyroid excess 208
Bone destruction, in actinomycosis 786
Bone disorders, resembling rickets **206–207**
Bone formation, and calcium 143
Bone growth 236
  disturbances, in rheumatoid arthritis 504
Bone infections, in *Haemophilus influenzae* 619, **620**
Bone lead 541
Bone lesions
  in blood disease **1743, 1744**
  in brucellosis 611
  in chronic renal disease **1467**
  in eosinophilic granuloma 1249
  Gaucher's disease 383–384
  in Hand-Schüller-Christian syndrome 1247, **1248–1249**
  in hypervitaminosis A **1741–1742**
  in Niemann-Pick disease 384
  and reticulum cell sarcoma 1226
  in rheumatoid arthritis 503
  in rickets 199, **200–202**
  in sarcoidosis **1251–1252**
  in syphilis **655**
Bone marrow
  aplasia 388
  in Burkitt's tumor **1227**
  in Chagas' disease 836
  hypoplasia 530, 538–540
  in ITP **1234**
  replacement anemia **1167**
  stimulation, due to glucocorticoids 1093
  and thrombocytopenia **1236**
  transplants, **388**
Bone neoplasms, 209, 673, **1743–1745**

Bone pain **1743–1745**
  in hyperparathyroidism 209
  in leukemia 1209, 1743, **1744**
  in neuroblastoma 1111
  in sickle-cell anemia 1177, **1743**
  in β-thalassemia 1181
Bone rarefaction, occipital, in cerebellar astrocytoma, 942
Bone shaft *see* Diaphysis
Bone structure, disorders of 195
Bone tenderness 1742
Bone tumors 209, 673, **1743–1745**
  metastatic 209, 1110
Bonnevie-Ullrich syndrome *see* Gonadal dysgenesis
"Boo" 572
Boot-shaped heart, tetralogy of Fallot 1404
Borates *530*
Borax *530*
Borborygmi 1653
Bordet medium 630
Bordetella bronchiseptica **627, 630**, 633
Bordetella parapertussis 627, 630, **632–633**
Bordetella pertussis **627–628, 630–633**
Boric acid poisoning 528–529, 532, 533
Bornholm disease *see* Pleurodynia
Boron 145
Bors test 1550
Boston exanthem 754
Bot fly 846
Bothria 820
Botulism **609–611**
Bounding pulse, in patent ductus arteriosus 1394
Bourneville-Pringle's disease *see* Tuberous sclerosis
Bow-leg deformity 1739
  nonrachitic **1709**
Bowing of tubular bones, prenatal **1708–1709**
"Boy" 572
BP *see* Bullous pemphigoid
Braces, in cerebral palsy **886**
Brachial angiography 942
Brachial neuritis, familial, recurrent 924
Brachial plexus injury 83, 124, **977**, 1632, 1817
Brachycephaly 901, 1838
Brachydactyly 212, 1708, 1841
Brachymesophalangia 1708
Brachymetacarpia 1708
Brachyfurricephaly 1841
Bradycardia 19, 54, 64, 82, *97*, *203*, *551*, *569*, 1071, 1278, **1366–1367**
  due to calcium therapy 203
  in cretinism 1071
  fetal 19, 54, 64
  in low-birth-weight infant 97
  in newborn 82
  in organophosphate poisoning 551
Bradykinesia, in basal ganglia degenerations **919–921**
Bradykinin-kallikrein system 413
Brain **857–1006, 1009–1023**. *See also* Cerebral.
  fetal metabolism of 40, 42
Brain abscess 422, 560, 579, 599, 645, 694, 794, 816, 825, 829, **1011–1015**, 1402, **1404**
  amebic abscess of, 825, 829
  in cryptococcosis 694
  in heroin addicts 560
  in paragonimiasis 816
  in tetralogy of Fallot **1404**
Brain damage 64, 74, 879, **882–886**

Brain defects, prenatal and developmental 857–878
  agenesis of corpus callosum 862
  holoprosencephaly (archinencephaly) 860–861
  hydranencephaly 861–862
  median cleft face syndrome 861
  median facial defects 860–861
  megalencephaly 857, 859–860
  megalocephaly 857, 859–860
  micrencephaly 857, 859
  microcephaly 857, 859
Brain scan
  in brain tumors 378, 941, 942, 944, 948
  in pseudotumor cerebri 958
Brain tumors 937–954, 1695
  brainstem tumors 944–945
  cerebellar tumors 941–945
  cerebral hemisphere tumors 947–949
  clinical manifestations 938–941
  craniopharyngioma 952–954
  diagnostic procedures 941
  fourth ventricle tumors 943–944
  hypertension in 1447
  infratenterioral tumors 941–945
  optic nerve and chiasmal tumors 950–952
  posterior fossa tumors 938–940, 941–947
  thalamic tumors 946–947
  third ventricle tumors 945–946
Brainstem
  degenerations 923–924
  glioma 852, 853, 937, 941, 944–955
  tumors 850, 944–945, 1008
Branched-chain amino acids 327
Branched-chain keto-aciduria see Maple syrup urine
Branchial arches 1703, 1844, 1884
Branchial cleft 81
Bran flakes 1602
Brazilian pemphigus 1780
Breast 81, 148–156, 241, 1122, 1123–1124
  in newborn 81
Breast binders 153
Breast care
  during lactation 153
  postpartum 20
Breast development 1122, 1123–1124
  stages of, 241
Breast enlargement 81, 153, 241, 1129
  in boys 241
  during breast feeding 153
  in newborn 81, 1129
Breast feeding 148–156. See also Lactation.
Breast milk 134, 148–156
  amino acids in 150, 158
  antibodies in 159
  buffer, value of 152
  caloric distribution in 137
  caloric value and 149, 160
  carbohydrates in 159
  composition 150, 158
  differences with cow's milk, 137, 157
  enzymes in 152, 159
  factors affecting 152
  fat in 151, 158, 159
  fatty acids in 159
  and heroin 559, 574
  and jaundice 1680
  manual expression of 153, 154, 155, 156
  minerals in 151, 158

Breast milk (cont.)
  protein 150, 158
  secretion of 149, 153–154
  sugar in 151
  vitamin D in 197
  vitamins in 152, 159
Breast pump 153, 154, 156
Breath, first see First breath
Breath-holding spells 281, 853, 991
Breathing see Respiration
Breech extraction, and spinal cord trauma 975
Breech presentation 79, 84
Bremil 162
Brennemann's syndrome 1641
Brill-Zinsser disease 778, 780
British anti-Lewisite see BAL
Broad beta hyperlipoproteinemia 376
"Broad-spectrum" antibiotics see Antimicrobial therapy
"Broad-spectrum" penicillins see Penicillin
Broad thumbs 1841
4-Bromo-3-methyl-isothiozole-5-carboxaldehyde-thiosemi-
      carbazone 771
Bromophenol blue paper (Albustix) 1460
Bronchi 1274
  mucoid impaction of, in cystic fibrosis 422
Bronchial adenoma 1289
Bronchial asthma see Asthma
Bronchial challenge testing, in allergic disease 449
Bronchial compression 1289
Bronchial hypersecretion
  in dysautonomia 1041
  in organophosphate poisoning 551
Bronchial lavage 422
Bronchial mucus, in cystic fibrosis 416, 422
Bronchial obstruction
  in cystic fibrosis 422
  foreign bodies 1278
  in tuberculosis 664
Bronchial tumors 1289
Bronchiectasis 387, 415, 422, 426, 432, 628, 816, 1294–
      1297
  and craniospinal focal sepsis 1010–1016
  in cystic fibrosis 415
  and pertussis 628
Bronchiolar muscle 1277
Bronchioles 1274
Bronchiolitis 426, 466, 626, 668, 720, 723, 724, 726, 761,
      1292
  chronic obliterative 1290–1292
  due to Coxsackie B virus 761
Bronchitis 466, 692, 1290
Bronchoconstriction 551
Bronchodilators 1281
  in asthma 466–467, 1293
Bronchography 1278, 1295–1296
  in bronchiectasis 1295, 1296
  in obstructive airway disease 1278
Broncholytic drugs 426
Bronchopneumonia
  in kerosene poisoning 538–540
  in measles 731, 734
  in pertussis 629
  in psittacosis 775
  in tularemia 692
Bronchopulmonary dysplasia 1265, 1266, 1269
Bronchopulmonary lavage 427
Bronchoscopy 422, 467, 1278

Bronchospasm 577
Brood capsule 821
"Brown" 572
Brown spider 844
"Brownies" 571
Brown fat 99, *99*
Brucella **610, 612**
  abortus **610–612**
  agglutinins, 611, 693
  bronchisepticus *see Bordetella bronchiseptica*
  melitensis **610**
  vaccine 611
Brucellosis 156, 396, **610–612**, 692, 698
Brudzinski's sign 750
  in bacterial meningitis **599**
  in cryptococcosis 794
  in encephalitis 1016–1023
  in lymphocytic choriomeningitis 729
  in poliomyelitis **745**
  in polyneuritis **1007**
  in subarachnoid hemorrhage 963
Bruising
  in hemorrhagic disorders 1229
  in leukemia 1209
Bruit, intracranial 979
Brushfield's spots *899*, 1827
Brussels sprouts 208
"Bu" 572
Bubble ventriculogram, in hydrocephalus *866*
Budd-Chiari syndrome 1691
Budin 101
Buffalo hump, of Cushing's syndrome 1099
Buffy coat, ascorbic acid in 191
Bulbar paralysis 924
  in acute intermittent porphyria 409
  in Krabbe's disease 917
  in poliomyelitis **744–745**, 850
Bulbospinal paralysis, in poliomyelitis 745
Bulging fontanel *see* Fontanel, bulging of
Bull-neck, in diphtheria **615**
Bullae 407, 411, 1753, **1770–81**, 1811
Bullae, plantar and palmar, in syphilis **654**
Bullous CIE *see* Ichthyosiform erythroderma
Bullous congenital ichthyosiform erythroderma 1756–1757
Bullous eruption of hand and feet, recurrent **1771**
Bullous erythema multiforme **1778**
Bullous impetigo (Ritter's disease) 645, 702, 1782
Bullous pemphigoid (BP) **1779**
"Bummer" 569, 571
Bundle branch block 1364
Buphthalmos 1822, 1825
Burkitt's lymphoma 717
Burkitt's tumor **1227**
Burning foot syndrome 140
Burning sensation, and skin 409
Burns **519–524**, 1639
  and battered child syndrome 557
Burow's solution (aluminum acetate) 474, 475, 1809, 1886
Bursa of Fabricius 387, 484
Bursitis 514, 515
Bushy eyebrows 1842
Butanol extractable iodine (BEI) 1501, **1062–1063**
Butler-Albright syndrome **1525–1526**
Butterfly rash, in systemic lupus erythematosus *508*

"Button" 571
B-variant, G6PD deficiency 395

"C" 571
C carbohydrate substance, in streptococcal cell wall **647**
C_3 ($\beta_1 C$) globulin deficiency **389**, 440
C_1, to C_9 complement fraction **389**, **440**, 446
C_2 deficiency **389**
C_1 esterase deficiency **389**, 440
C_2H_5OH *see* Alcohol abuse
C_{11} hydroxylase deficiency 1446
CA (croup-associated) virus 723
Cabbage 208
Cachexia, in diabetes mellitus 344
Caddis fly 484
CaEDTA 544, **546–548**, 950, 955
  lead mobilization test **544**
  in lead poisoning **546–548**
Café-au-lait nevus (spot) 892, 853, 1805
  in neurofibromatosis *927*
  in optic nerve and chiasm tumors 950
  in spinal cord tumors 955
Cafergot, in migraine 1003
Caffeine 1574
Caffey's disease *see* Infantile cortical hyperostosis
Calamine lotion 1809
Calcific tendonitis 514, 515
Calcification
  abdominal 677, 1670
  articular 209, **511, 512**, 1726
  of cartilage, in scurvy 187
  of intervertebral disks 1717
  intracranial
    in brain tumors **946**, 950, 952
    in cytomegalic inclusion disease 703
    of falx cerebri 931
    in toxoplasmosis **840**
    in tuberculous meningitis 672
    in tuberous sclerosis 927
  pulmonary 664, **666**, 789, 791
  of teeth 1858–1859
Calcifications, muscular 511
  subcutaneous 209, **511, 512**
  thyroidal 1070
Calcinosis 510, 513
Calcinosis universalis 1034
Calcitonin *see* Thyrocalcitonin
Calcium 192, **195–197**
  absorption 143
  excretion 143
  extracellular 196
  fetal 32
  in hemostasis 143, *1229*
  homeostasis 208
    in diarrhea **228, 230**
    disturbances of 225, 228
  intestinal malabsorption of 198
  in myotonia 1032
  serum 195, 198, 209, 210
    in hypercalcemia, idiopathic 207
    and parathyroid 208
Calcium carbimide 330
Calcium carbonate 210
Calcium gluconate 535, 587
  in black widow spider bite **844**
Calcium oxalate lithiasis 330

Calculi 330, 336, 338, 340, **1525, 1535–1538,** 1686
in bile ducts 1686
in urinary tract *see* Urolithiasis
Calliphora *see* Blow flies
Callitroga *see* Screw-worms
Calomel 550
Caloric deficiencies **170–176**
Caloric intake in diabetes mellitus **350, 354**
and obesity 216
Caloric requirements 17, **128–131,** *130, 131,* 143, 165
for activity 128
for basal metabolism 128
gestational 17
for growth 130
for loss in excreta 130, 131
of low-birth-weight infant 108
in renal failure 1465
for specific dynamic action of food 130–131
Caloric restriction, in obesity 220
Caloric value
of breast milk 149, *160*
of cow's milk *160*
of evaporated milk 162
of milk formula 161
Calories, percentage distribution of **137**
Calorimetry 128
Calvé's disease **1739–1740**
Calvé's vertebra plana 1716–1717
Camel 821
Camphor 528, 532, *530*
Camphorated oil 528
Camptodactyly 1708, 1732
Canal of Nuck 1631
Canavan's disease *see* Spongy sclerosis
Cancrum oris *see* Noma
Candida albicans 227, 438, **795–796,** 1760, **1790,** 1791, **1854–1855**
Candida guilliermondii 795
Candida krusei 795
Candida parapsilosis 795
Candida tropicalis 795
Candidiasis 211, 329, **795–796**
in Addison's disease 1094
cutaneous 78
oral 81, **1854–1855**
pulmonary **1308**
"Candledripping," on pneumoencephalography in tuberous sclerosis 926
"Candy" 571
Cane sugar 160, 161
Canine distemper 730
"Canker sores" **1853**
Cannabichromine 566
Cannabidial 566
Cannabidiolic acid 566
Cannabinol 566
Cannabirigeral 566
"Cannabis" 572
Cannabis sativa 566
Canton variant, G6PD deficiency 394
Capillary hemangioma 901
Capitate-hamate "fusion" in chondroectodermal dysplasia 1725
Capreomycin 686, 691
Capsular cataract 1826
Capsular swelling test in influenza bacillus infections **618–619**

Caput medusae 1218
Caput quadratum 1695
Caput succedaneum 79
Car sickness **272**
Caramelization of sugar 157
Carbamyl aspartic acid 340
Carbamyl phosphate 334
Carbamyl phosphate synthetase deficiency **334**
Carbarsone in balantidiasis 839
Carbenicillin **585, 598**
in bacterial meningitis *603–605*
Carbohydrate 38–39, 42, **136–137,** *159,* 160, 163, **341–373,** 1568
absorption of **1568**
and birth hypoxia 42
in breast milk *159*
in cow's milk *159,* 160
digestion of **1568**
evaluation of, in diabetes mellitus 352
injury (Mehlnahrschaden) 137
malabsorption of **1590–1594**
mellituria **356–360**
metabolism of 42, **341**
anomalies of **341–373**
in diabetes mellitus *343–356*
in fetus *38–39,* 50
fructose 358–359
galactose 356–358
in glycogenoses 360–373
in hypoglycemia 360–366
pathways of 360
and nitrogen excretion 137
in nutrition **136–137**
pentose metabolism **359–360**
requirements, of low-birth-weight infant 110
and resistance to hypoxia of newborn **42–43**
supplements in infant feeding 160, 163
Carbohydrate-induced hyperlipemia *see* Hyperprebeta-lipoproteinemia, familial
Carbon dioxide (CO_2)
content 230
injection in pericarditis **1426**
in perinatal period 66, 67
snow 1788
tension *see* Pco_2
transplacental transfer 44
Carbonic anhydrase inhibitor *see* Acetozolamide
Carbon monoxide 528, 532
Carbon tetrachloride *530,* 532, 1686
Carbon trichlorethane *530*
Carboxypeptidases 132, 145
Carcinoids **1661**
Carcinoma
adrenocortical **1098–1099**
hepatocellular 1693
Cardiac *see* Heart; Circular system; Cardiovascular disease
Cardiac arrest **1370**
due to calcium therapy 203
in dysautonomia 1041
Cardiac catheterization **1354–1363**
Cardiac conduction 379
Cardiac enlargement *see* Cardiomegaly
Cardiac failure *see* Heart failure, congestive
Cardiac glycosides **1422**

Cardiac hemochromatosis 1432
Cardiac hypertrophy *see* Cardiomegaly
Cardiac massage 525
    at birth 73
Cardiac output 48–49, 1437
    of fetus 48–49
    of newborn **1259**
Cardiac tamponade **1425**
Cardiomegalic glycogenosis *see* Glycogenosis type II
Cardiomegaly 121, 179, 370, 497, 499, 500, 504, 750,
        922, 1031, 1034, 1083, 1177, 1181, **1371–1376,**
        1388, 1394, 1397, 1400, 1410, 1413, 1414, **1420,**
        1425, 1432–1435
    in cardiomuscular glycogen disease 1035
    in Coxsackie virus 750
    in familial periodic paralysis **1034**
    in Friedreich's ataxia 922
    in Graves' disease 1083
    in glygogenosis type II 370, 1035
    in heart failure **1420**
    in muscular dystrophy 1031
    in sickle-cell anemia 1177
    in β-thalassemia 1181
    in thiamine deficiency 179
    in twins 121
Cardiomuscular glycogen disease (Pompe) **1035**
Cardiomyopathies **1432**
Cardiopulmonary failure
    in kyphoscoliosis 1328
    and obesity 1328
Cardiospasm *see* Achalasia
Cardiovascular contour 1345
Cardiovascular diseases **490–502, 504, 509, 511, 513, 514,**
        1363–1435
    signs and symptoms of **1334–1338**
Cardiovascular diseases, acquired
    arrest **1370**
    arrhythmias **1368–1370**
    atrial fibrillation **1370**
    atrial flutter **1369**
    AV dissociation **1366**
    bigeminy **1369**
    cardiomyopathies **1432–1434**
    conduction defects **1366–1370**
    congestive failure **1335, 1414–1425**
    in dermatomyositis 511
    endocarditis **1429–1431**
    extra systoles **1368**
    heartbeat disorders **1369–1370**
    infections of the heart **1425–1431**
    mitral insufficiency 494, 499
    myocardial diseases **1428–1429, 1433–1434**
    myocarditis **1428–1429**
    nodal tachycardia **1366**
    paroxysmal atrial tachycardia **1364–1365**
    in polyarteritis nodosa 514
    rheumatic heart disease *see* Rheumatic
    in rheumatoid arthritis 504
    in scleroderma 513
    in SLE 509
    tachycardias **1364–1366**
    ventricular fibrillation **1370**
    ventricular tachycardia **1366**
Cardiovascular diseases, congenital **1335–1337, 1370–1425**
    acyanotic heart disease **1337, 1371–1376, 1379–1401**
    anomalous left coronary artery origin **1395–1454**

Cardiovascular diseases, congenital (*cont.*)
    anomalous pulmonary venous drainage 1373, 1377,
        1412–1414
    aortic arch anomalies 1371, **1416**
    aortic arch hypoplasia 1371
    aortic atresia 1377, **1388–1389**
    aortic isthmus aplasia 1391
    aortic stenosis 1371, **1387–1388**
    aortopulmonary fenestration 1376, **1395**
    arteriovenous fistula 1373, **1396**
    asymptomatic heart disease **1337**
    atrial septal defects 1373, **1398–1401**
    atrioventricular canal **1398**
    cardiomyopathies **1433–1434**
    coarctation of aorta 1371, **1390–1391,** 1446
    coronary arteriovenous fistula 1373, **1396**
    coronary artery, aberrant origin **1395, 1454**
    corrected transposition **1398**
    cor triatriatum 1371, **1383**
    cyanotic heart disease **1335, 1337, 1376–1379, 1382,**
        1401–1418
    double aortic arch 1416
    Ebstein's disease 1376, **1408–1409**
    endocardial fibroelastosis **1453**
    Fallot's tetralogy **1404–1406**
    Formen ovale, incompetent 1373, **1399**
    heartbeat disorders **1369–1370**
    hypoplastic aortic arch 1371
    hypoplastic left heart complex **1415–1416**
    left-to-right shunts **1373–1376, 1393–1401**
    left ventricular-to-right atrieal shunt **1398**
    mitral atresia 1371, 1377, **1384**
    mitral stenosis **1383–1384**
    obstructive conditions **1337, 1371–1372**
    ostium primus defects 1373, **1399**
    ostium secundum defects **1399**
    patent ductus arteriosus 1373, 1376, **1393–1396**
    ostium secundum defects **1399**
    peripheral pulmonary artery stenosis 1389
    precapillary pulmonary arterial obstruction 1389
    pulmonary atresia or stenosis with intarct ventricularis
        septum 1371, **1407–1408**
    pulmonary arteriovenous fistula 1377
    pulmonary artery stenosis, peripheral **1389**
    pulmonary venous obstruction 1380, 1384
    pulmonary venous return anomalies 1373, 1377, **1412–**
        1414
    pulmonic atresia 1377, **1387–1388**
    pulmonic stenosis 1371, **1386–1387**
    regurgitant lesions **1373–1376**
    renal artery stenosis **1391**
    right aortic arch **1416**
    right-to-left shunts **1376–1379, 1401–1418**
    single atrium 1376
    single ventricle 1376
    tetralogy of Fallot **1402–1406**
    total anomalous pulmonary venous drainage 1373,
        1377, **1412–1414**
    transposition of great arteries 1377, **1409–1412**
    tricuspid atresia 1371, 1376, **1382–1383**
    tricuspid stenosis 1376, **1381–1382**
    truncus arteriosus **1414–1415**
    valsalva sinus fistula 1373, **1395–1396**
    vascular ring **1417**
    ventricular septal defect 1373, **1396–1398**
Cardiovascular function, in-low-birth-weight infant 96

Cardiovascular lesions
  in cystic fibrosis **417**, 420
  in hypercalcemia, idiopathic 207
  in obesity 214
  in rheumatic fever **493**
Cardiovascular radiography *1338–1344*
Cardiovascular sounds *1338–1344*
Cardioversion, in PAT 1365
Carditis, rheumatic *see* Rheumatic carditis
Care
  of low-birth-weight infant *see* Low-birth-weight infant
  of twins 123
Caries, dental 136, **1867–1868**
Carnosine (-ase, -emia, -uria) 335
Carob flour 641
β-Carotene 138, 177
Carotenemia, and cretinism **1070–1071**
Carotenoid pigments, as precursors of vitamin A 138
Carotid angiography **855,** 860, 941, 942–944, 953, 958, 965, 972, **1016**
Carotid artery laceration 979
Carotid body massage in PAT 1364
Carotid-cavernous fistula 979
Carotid ligation 979
Carp-mouth 1841
Carpenter's syndrome (acrocephalopolysyndactyly) 1698, 1708, **1841**
Carpopedal spasm 212
Carriers of salmonella 635
"Carrier" state in amebiasis **829**
  of salmonella 635
"Cartilage-hair" hypoplasia 389, 1760
Cartridge wounds and tetanus 659
"Cartwheels" 571
Casal's necklace 181
Caseation 662, **665,** 673, 677, 791
Casein 150, 157, 357
Caseous necrosis 791
Casoni skin test 822
Castellani's paint 1791
Cat(s) **697–700,** 803
  and leptospirae 621
  and murine typhus 780
Catalase 405
Cataplexy 1003
Cataracts 331, 385, 473, 1725, **1826–1827,** 1838, 1842
  in cerebral cholesterosis 914
  in dystrophia myotonica 1032
  in galactosemia 357
  in gray matter diseases 914
  and hereditary nephritis 1514
  in Lowe's syndrome 1522
  nuclear 358
  posterior subcapsular 504
  in rheumatoid arthritis 504
  in riboflavin deficiency 180
  in rubella, congenital 764, **766**
Catarrhal gingivostomatitis **1852**
Catarrhal stage, pertussis 628
Catatonic attitudes 287
Cat claw disease *see* Cat scratch disease
Cat cry syndrome *see* Cri du chat
Catecholamines 132, 218, 362, 366, 373, 454, 1041, **1107–1113,** 1439, 1445
  deficiency, and hypoglycemia 362
  in dysautonomia 1041

Catecholamines (*cont.*)
  in hypertension 1439
  in pheochromocytoma 1445
Catechol-*o*-methyl transferase 1107
Caterpillars 845
Cat flea 820
  and murine typhus 780
Cathepsins 441, 1567
Cat scratch antigen 698, **699**
Cat scratch disease (fever) 396, 692, **697–700,** 1797
Cattle
  and leptospirae 621
Cauda equina lesion 955
Caudal anesthesia 54
  during delivery 20
Caudal regression syndrome 1707
Cavernous hemangioma 1728, **1813**
Cavernous sinus thrombosis **960**
Cavitation 666
CDC standard rubella HI antibody test **762–763**
CDE (Fisher-Race) nomenclature **1196–1197**
C. diphtheriae see Corynebacterium diphtheriae
Ceasarean sections 596
Celiac axis angiography 1693
Celiac disease, idiopathic 426, **1584–1588**
Celiac syndrome *see* Malabsorption syndromes
β-Cell hyperplasia 363
Cell growth **237**
Cell multiplication, in marasmus 171
Cell nevus **1802**
β-Cells
  in cystic fibrosis 414
  in islets of Langerhans **344**
Cellular immunity **387–389,** 444
Cellulitis 645, 701, **1781–1783**
  due to *H. influenzae* 619
Cellulose acetate electrophoresis 373
Celontin (Methsuximide) **998–1000**
Cementoblasts 1856
Center
  for low-birth-weight infant **101–103**
  for newborn **101–103**
  regional perinatal **101**
Centipedes 845
Central cataract 1826
Central core disease 923, **1028**
Central incisor **1856–1861**
Central nervous system *see* Nervous system
Central sucker 812
Central tendencey **232**
Central ulcers, cornea **1822**
Centrencephalic seizures **982, 987**
Centromere 308, 309
Cephalhematoma 79, **80, 967,** 1695, 1704
Cephalin flocculation test, in infectious mononucleosis 718
Cephalins 907
Cephaloglycin **586**
Cephaloridine **586**
Cephalosporins **586**
Cephalothin **586,** 646
Ceramic containers, lead-glazed and plumbism 543
Ceramide 381, 907
Ceramide dihexoside 911, 913
Ceramide-galactose 907, 917
Ceramide-galactose-sulfate (sufatide) **907,** 909
Ceramide glucose 907, 911, 913
Ceramide-glucose-sulfate 911

Ceramide lactoside 383
Ceramide trihexoside 383, 385, 911, 913
Cercariae 813, 815, 816
Cereals 166
  introduction into diet 155
Cerebellar abscess 1012
Cerebellar astrocytoma 937–940, 941–942
Cerebellar ataxia 379, 389, 745, 754, 851, 955, 1041–1043
  acute 851, 1041–1043
  due to ECHO viruses 754
  and intraspinal tumor 955
  in poliomyelitis 745
Cerebellar degeneration 921–922
Cerebellar tumors 938–940, 941–943
Cerebellopontine angle meningioma 943
Cerebral angiography 855, 860, 941, 942, 944, 953, 958, 965, 972, 1010–1016
  in aneurysm intracranial 965
  in brain tumors 941, 942–944, 949, 953
  in subdural hematoma 972
Cerebral arterial thrombosis 962
Cerebral arteriography 855, 860, 941, 942–944, 953, 958, 965, 972, 1010–1016
Cerebral biopsy, in degenerative diseases 905, 912
Cerebral cholesterosis 909, 914
Cerebral contusion 972–974
Cerebral cysticercosis 818
Cerebral dysfunction
  chronic and nonprogressive 879
  minimal see Minimal cerebral dysfunction
Cerebral edema 859, 957
  and heroin use 560
  in white matter diseases 917
Cerebral embolism 962
Cerebral gigantism 250, 859, 1058, 1695
Cerebral gray matter diseases 907–916. See also specific diseases.
Cerebral gray matter, nonstorage degeneration of 915–916
Cerebral hemiatrophy, in cerebral arterial thrombosis 962
Cerebral hemispheres tumors 947–950
Cerebral hemorrhage 962–965, 970–972
Cerebral hydatid cyst 822–823
Cerebral infarcts 1011–1012
Cerebral laceration 972–974
Cerebral lipids 907
Cerebral malaria 832
Cerebral neoplasm see Brain tumors
Cerebral palsy 12, 339, 879, 882–886
  and enamel hypoplasia 1862–1863
  due to kernicterus 1677
  in twins 121
Cerebral salt-wasting 1152
Cerebral sclerosis, progressive, and pertussis 630
Cerebral thrombosis 962, 1402, 1404
  in tetralogy of Fallot 1404
Cerebral tumors see Brain tumors
Cerebral vascular accidents, 960–965
  in sickle-cell disease 1177
Cerebral vascular malformations 963–964
Cerebral venous thrombosis 960–961
Cerebral white matter diseases 916–919
  basal ganglia degenerations 919–921
  demyelinating scleroses 917–919
  leucodystrophies 916–917
  polymorphous, neuroabiotrophies 921–925

Cerebro-hepato-renal syndrome (Zellweger) 1478, 1693–1694
Cerebromacular degenerations 909–914, 916–917
  Fabry's disease 911, 913–914
  familial amaurotic idiocy 910–913
  gangliosidosis 910–913
  Gaucher's disease 911, 913
  globosidoses 911, 913–914
  Krabbe's disease 911, 916–917
  lactosyl ceramidosis 911
  later forms 912–913
  metachromatic leucodystrophy 911, 916
  Niemann-Pick disease 911, 913
  sphingolipidoses 911, 913, 915–917
Cerebro-oculo-renal dystrophy 1522
Cerebroside 907
Cerebroside sulfate sulfatase deficiency 909
Cerebroside sulfatransferase 917
Cerebrosidose 1829
Cerebrospinal fluid 601–602, 856, 1907–1908
  in acute polyneuritis 1007
  in African trypanosomiasis 834
  antibody measurement 654
  in bacterial meningitis 600–607
  in brain tumors 941, 945, 947, 949
  in cerebral arterial thrombosis 962
  in cerebral vascular malformations 963
  in chorea 494
  circulation 862
  in coccidioidomycosis 790
  in congenital toxoplasmosis 840
  in Coxsackie virus infections 750–752
  in craniospinal focal sepsis 1010–1016
  in cryptococcosis 794
  cultures 597, 600–602
  in ECHO virus infectious 753, 754
  in encephalitis 1016–1023
  enzymes, in brain tumors 941, 949
  examination 601–602, 856, 1097–1908
    in amebic meningoencephalitis 830
    in bacterial meningitis 601–602
  fistula 876
  in head injury 968–975
  in hydrocephalus 865
  in intracranial bleeding 963
  in Krabbe's disease 917
  leakage 874, 967, 970
    in basal skull fractures 970
    in meningomyelocele 874
  in leptospirosis 622
  in leukemia 1211
  in lymphocytic choriomeningitis 729
  in malaria 832
  in measles 731
  in meningococcal meningitis 623
  millipore filtration 941, 943
    tumor cells in 941, 943
  in poliomyelitis 746
  and pseudomotor cerebri 957, 959
  in Refsum's syndrome 924
  in Rocky Mountain spotted fever 782
  in rubella 761
  and sodium 222
  in spinal cord injury 976
  sugar
    in medulloblastoma 940
  in syphilis 655

Cerebrospinal fluid (*cont*.)
  in tuberculous meningitis **671–672**
  in white matter diseases 916–918
Cerebrovascular disease **960–965,** 1177
Ceroid 1689
Ceroid lipofuscinosis 911–912
Ceroid pigment, in cystic fibrosis 416
Ceruloplasmin 145, **390–391,** 422, 1162
  and copper
    in kwashiorkor 174
    in Wilson's disease **920–921**
Cerumen 1881
Cervical adenitis 650, 1222. *See also* Lymphadenopathy.
  tuberculous **676**
Cervical cultures 515
Cervical intervertebral articulations, in rheumatoid arthritis 504, **505**
Cervical intramedullary glioma, in spinal cord tumors 954
Cervical mass, and neuroblastoma 1111
Cervical spine, 504, **505–506,** 673, **1715–1718**
Cervicitis 625
Cervicodorsal scoliosis 1715
Cesarean section, and respiratory distress syndrome **1261**
Cesium chloride 760
Cestodes, diseases caused by **817–823**
CF antibody, in rubella **762–763**
CGD *see* Chronic granulomatous disease
Chagas' disease **835,** 1624
Chagoma **835–836**
Chalasia of the esophagus **1575**
Chalazion **1819**
Chamber and great vessel localization abnormalities **1418–1419**
Chancre 653
Chancroid 1797
Charcoal, activated USP in poisonings 535
Charcot-Marie-Tooth disease *see* Peroneal muscular atrophy
"Charge" 572
"Charlie" 571
Chediak-Higashi syndrome 1008, **1206, 1801–1802**
Cheilosis and pyridoxin deficiency 184
Chelation therapy 337, 391, **546–548,** 549, 835, 950, 955, 1523, 1824
Chemical burns **519**
Chemical composition, fetal **28–34**
Chemical control of respiration, in newborn 1258
Chemical diabetes *see* Latent diabetes
Chemical factors, and urticaria 477
Chemical growth **237**
Chemical homeostasis **222–223**
Chemical "maturation" 133
Chemical neutralizers, in poisonings 535
Chemical pneumonitis **1312**
Chemical toxins, and growth retardation 248
Chemoreceptors (and reflexes), in the newborn 68, 1258
Chemosis, of conjunctivae 188, 809, 1084, 1819, 1821
  in hyperthyroidism 1084
  in trichinosis 809
Chemotaxis bacteriolysis 389
Chemotherapy
  of diarrheal disease 228
  for intracranial tumors **941**
  of rheumatic fever 500
Cherry-red color of skin 528
Cherry-red spot, macular **381–384,** 912, 913
  in Niemann-Pick disease 913

Cherry-red spot, macular (*cont*.)
  in Tay-Sachs disease 912
"Cherubism" 1696, **1846–1847**
Chest **1255–1331**
  in asthma **465**
  at birth **75–81**
  protrusions **1715**
  structural abnormalities of **1325–1329,** 1715
  in trauma 1329
Chest circumference, 88, **1900–1904**
Chest deformity **1714–1715**
  due to bone dysplasia **1327–1328**
  in cystic fibrosis 416
  in rickets 200
Chest pain 750, 791, 1278, 1329, 1430
  in bacterial endocarditis 1430
  due to bronchial and tracheal foreign bodies 1278
  in histoplasmosis 791
  in pleurodynia 750
  in spontaneous penumothorax 1329
Chest wall **1322–1329**
  changes with growth 1324
  diseases of 1324–1329
  function of 1322–1324
Chewing, difficulty in myasthenia 1037
Cheyne-Stokes respiration 1490
Chiasmal gliomas 939, 941, **950–952**
Chickenpox *see* Varicella
Chigger mite 845
Chigger repellant 845
Chiggers 847
Chigoe flea 845
Chikungunya virus infection **847–848**
Child abuse *see* Battered child syndrome
Child population **2**
  growth of 2
  morbidity **4**
Children-and-Youth Projects 10
Child Welfare Law 9
Chilopoda *see* Centipedes
Chimerism 123, 388
Chimpanzee coryza agent 724
Chinese liver fluke *see* Clonorchis sinensis
"Chipping" 571
Chlamydia 581, 586, 588, 1821
Chlamydozoaceae 698
Chloral hydrate 410, 532
Chlorambucil (Leukeran) **1225,** 1504
Chloramphenicol 56, 427, 582, **588,** 591, 602, *603,* **1166**
  in actinomycosis 786
  and aplastic anemia **1166**
  in cholera **612–614**
  effects on newborn and fetus 56
  H. influenzae infections 620
  in meningococcal infections 623
  optic neuritis or atrophy and 416, 422
  in pertussis 632
  in rickettsial diseases **778,** 783, **784**
  in salmonellosis 637
  in shigellosis 640
  and thrombocytopenia 1236
  toxicity in neonates 478
  in tularemia 693
  in typhoid fever **638**
Chloride 29, 32, 143, 237, 414, 422–424
  in fetal body composition 29, 32
  growth patterns of 237

Chloride (cont.)
requirements 143
in sweat 414, 422–424
Chlorinated hydrocarbons 532
Chlorine 1312
Chloroform 532, 1686
in status epilepticus 999
Chlorophyll 405
Chloroquine 816, 999, 1314
in amebic liver abscess **830**
in malaria **833–834,** *833*
in paragonimiasis 816
in rheumatoid arthritis 507
Chloroquine retinopathy 510
Chlorpromazine (thorazine) 20, 562, 566, 569, 661, **882,**
1041, 1575, 1686
and hyperbilirubinemia 1686
in tetanus 661
Chlorpropamide
and drug purpura 1235
in NDI **1529**
Chlortetracycline 594
in leptospirosis **622**
in pertussis 632
Chlorthiazide 55, 338, 355, 1151, 1235, 1423, **1529**
and drug purpura 55, 1235
Choanal atresia 71, 74, 80, **1872**
Chocolate products 391, 477
Choking attacks, in esophageal atresia **1605**
Choking while feeding, in "vascular ring" 1417
Cholangiography 1693
Cholangitis, suppurative, in clonorchiasis 816
Cholcalciferol 197, 201, 204, 213
Cholecystitis 786
in clonorchiasis 816
Cholecystography 1693
Choledochal cyst 1683
Cholelithiasis 709
Cholera **612–614**
Cholestasis 1672, **1686–1687**
Cholesteatoma 1886
Cholesterol 40, 135, 369, **373,** 375, 376, 379, 344
in diabetes mellitus 344
esters 135
fetal synthesis of 40
in kwashiorkor 174
in scurvy 186
Cholesterol acyltransferase 379
Cholesterol desmolase system 1097, 1098
Cholestyramine 376
Choline 132, 138, 139, 330
Cholinergic crisis 1037,
Cholinergic urticaria 477, 489
Cholinesterase, 174, 422, 551–552, 805
in kwashiorkor 174
Cholinesterase inhibition 532, **551–552,** 805
in organic phosphate ester poisoning **551–552**
"Cholly" 571
Chondrodystrophia calcificans congenita 1725
Chondrodystrophy 401
Chondroectodermal dysplasia **1327, 1724–1725,** 1838, 1865
Chondroitic acid 398
Chondroitin sulfate-B 914, 1763
Chondroitin sulfuric acid 144
Chondromyxoid fibroma 1743
Chondroplasia **240**
Chorda tympani 1883

Chordee 1139, **1553**
Chorea 273, 276, 490, 494, **495–496,** 497, 498, 499, 500, **851**
in basal ganglia degenerations **919–921**
and pseudotumor cerebri 958
Chorea, Huntington's *see* Huntington's chorea
Chorea minor *see* Chorea
Choreic hand 496
Choreiform movements 851
Choreoathetosis 399, 852, 921
familial paroxysmal 921
Chorioamnionitis 65, 596
Chorioepithelioma 1126
Chorion 40, 119
Chorionic gonadotropin, in cryptorchidism **1555**
Chorionic sac, in multiple births 119
Chorioretinitis 703, **840,** 892, 1828
in cytomegalic inclusion disease 703
in toxoplasmosis **840,**
Choristomatic cyst of the tongue **1850**
Choroid 1827
Choroidal tubercles 677
Choroideremia 1827
Choroid plexectomy **865–866**
Choroid plexus 677, 862, 863, **868, 943**
papilloma **868, 943**
tumor 863
Christmas factor *see* Factor IX
Chromaffin cells 1046, 1107
Chromatids 308
"Chromatin negativity" 309
Chromatin, prediction of sex from cells, in amniotic
fluid 58
Chromatography, of morphine 559
Chromatolysis 744
Chromium–51
tagged red cells *61,* 1221
Chromophobe adenoma 1055, **1057**
Chromophobe cells 1048
Chromosomal
abnormalities 294, 297, **309–311, 897–905,** 1866
breakage, in measles 731
Chromosomes, human 58, 294, 297, **304, 309–311,** 731,
897–905, 1866
and development **304**
Chronic brain syndrome 879
Chronic bronchitis 692, **1290**
Chronic encephalitides 1023
Chronic granulomatous disease (CGD) **396–398, 1206**
Chronic illness, and personality disorders 267
Chronic nephritis *see* Glomerulonephritis
Chronic nonspecific diarrhea *see* Irritable colon syn-
drome
Chronic polyarthritis *see* Rheumatoid arthritis
Chronic thyroiditis *see* Hashimoto's struma
Chrysops 812
Chubbiness, in glycogenosis type I 368
Chvostek's sign 1035
Chyle 1330
Chylomicrons 374, 377, 1583
Chylothorax 136, 1330
Chylous ascites 136, 677, 1330, **1660**
in abdominal tuberculosis 677
Chyluria, in Bancroft's filariasis **811**
Chymotrypsin 132
"Ciba" 571
Cicatricial pemphigoid 1779

Cigarette burns
  in battered child 558
  in heroin addicts 561
Cilia 1871
Ciliary body 1827
  tuberculosis of 677
Circulating anticoagulants 1241–1242
Circulatory collapse
  in Addison's disease 1093
  in adrenal cortical hyperplasia 1097
  in adrenal insufficiency 1094
  in anorexia nervosa 270
  in black widow spider 844
  in bulbar poliomyelitis 745
  in cholera 613
  in congenital adrenal hyperplasia 1097
  in craniocerebral trauma 967–968
  in cystic fibrosis 422
  in extradural hematoma 971
  in fetal hemorrhage 1159
  in Herpesvirus hominis infection 715
  in hypoplastic left heart complex 1416
  in meningococcemia 606, 623
  in myocarditis, diphtheritic 1428
  in neonatal narcotic withdrawal syndrome 574
  in Rocky Mountain spotted fever 782
  in sepsis neonatorum 597
  in shigellosis 640
  in sickle-cell anemia 1177
  in skull fractures 1704
  in solar urticaria 487
  in splenic injury 1217
  therapy, in bacterial meningitis 606
Circulatory derangements
  in cretinism 1071
  in low-birth-weight infant 96–97
Circulatory system 1333–1435. See also Heart; Cardio-
    vascular; Cardiac.
  adjustments after birth 69–70, 1333–1334
  cardiac catheterization 1354–1363
  diseases 1334–1338, 1363–1435
    acquired 1337–1338, 1425–1435
    aortic arch anomalies 1416–1417
    arrhythmias 1315, 1354, 1368
    asymptomatic 1337
    clinical manifestation 1334–1338
    conduction defects 1366–1367
    congenital heart disease 1335–1337, 1370–1425
    congestive heart failure 1335, 1419–1425
    cyanotic heart disease 1335–1337, 1376–1379, 1381–
      1382, 1401–1418
    endocarditis 1429–1431
    heartbeat disorders 1363–1370
    infections of the heart 1425–1431
    myocardial disorders 1379, 1432–1435
    myocarditis 1428–1429
    obstructive conditions and lesions 1371–1372, 1379–
      1393
    pericarditis 1425–1428
    shunts, left to right 1373–1376, 1393–1401
    shunts, right to left 1376–1379
    tachycardias 1364–1368
  electrocardiography 1346–1354. See also specific dis-
    eases.
  fetal circulation 1333–1334
  feto-maternal, disturbances of 66
  fluoroscopy, cardiac 1344–1346

Circulatory system (cont.)
  heart murmurs 1341–1344
  heart sounds 1338–1344
  left-to-right shunts 1373–1376, 1393–1401
  in low-birth-weight infant 94, 96–97
  myocardial contractility impairment 1329, 1432–1435
  postnatal adjustments 69–70, 1333–1334
  pressure overload effects 1371–1373
  radiography, cardiac 1344–1346
  rectocardiography 1344–1346
  regurgitant lesions 1371–1376
  right-to-left shunts 1376–1377
Circumcision 83, 1229, 1237, 1544, 1553
Circumflex nerve injury 978
Circumoval precipitin test, in schistosomiasis 814
Cirrhosis, liver 259, 362, 371, 391, 414, 420, 422, 920,
      1218, 1687, 1690–1691
  congenital, in Fanconi syndrome and tyrosinuria
      1523
  in cystic fibrosis 414, 420, 422, 1688
  after erythroblastosis fetalis 1192
  in galactosemia 1690
  in glycogenosis type IV 371
  and hypoglycemia 362
  in β-thalassemia 1181
  in Wilson's disease 920, 1688, 1690
Cisterns (basalis, chiasmaticus, and magna) 862
Citrate 143
Citric acid cycle 136, 179
Citrulline 320, 334, 340
Citrullinemia 320, 334
Clam digger's itch see Schistosomal dermatitis
Clamydia oculogenitalis 1819
Class intervals 232
Clavicle, fracture, in newborn 81
Claw hand 399
Cleaning agents 529
Clearance, renal see Renal clearance
Cleft, branchial see Branchial cleft
Cleft lip 81, 315, 861, 1838, 1844–46, 1850, 1866, 1877
Cleft palate 81, 276, 315, 901, 1838, 1842, 1844–1846,
      1850, 1866, 1872, 1877
Cleft tongue 1850
Cleidocranial dysostosis 851, 1669, 1702, 1716, 1731–1732,
      1841, 1865
Climate 1912–1913
  and growth 243
"Climbing up the legs" (Gower's sign), in muscular
      dystrophy 1030
Clinitest tablets 351
Clinodactyly 899, 1708
Clitoris 83, 1095, 1098, 1124
  hypertrophy 1095, 1098
Cloacal exstrophy 1554
Clofibrate 376
Clomiphene citrate 1050
Clonal selection theory 1184
Clonorchiasis 816–817
"Closed" therapy, of burns 523
Clostridium botulinum 531, 609–611
Clostridium perfringens (welchii) 156, 1032
Clostridium tetani 523, 658–662
Clothing 1895
Clot retraction 1229, 1234
Clotting time 1231
"Cloverleaf skull" 1697
Cloxacillin 585, 646

Clubbing, of fingers 420, 426, 465, 1294, 1305, 1314, 1401, 1407, **1742–1743**, 1761
  in bronchietasis 1294
  in cystic fibrosis 420
  in pulmonary A.V. fistulas 1305
  in pulmonary collagen disorders 1314
Clubfoot *see* Talipes
Clubfoot deformity, congenital **1709**
"Cluster of grape" opacifications, in cystic fibrosis 422
Clutton's joints 657, 658
CO₂ *see* Carbon dioxide
Coagulase-negative staphylococcus 645
Coagulase-positive staphylococcus aureus **644–647**
Coagulation, blood **1228–1243**
Coagulation disorders 55, **1237–1243**. *See also individual disorders;* Coagulation factor deficiencies; Intravascular coagulation.
  in newborn 55
  due to salicylates 501
Coagulation factor deficiencies **1237–1243**. *See also Individual factor deficiencies.*
  acquired **1241–1243**
    anticoagulants, circulating **1241–1242**
    factor V deficiency **1241**
    factors VIII and IX, secondary to hypothyroidism **1241**
    fibrinolytic purpura **1242**
    intravascular clotting with factors consumption **1242–1243**
    in open-heart surgery **1243**
    vitamin K dependent factors **1241**
  congenital **1237–1241**
    afibrinogenemia **1240**
    combined deficiencies **1241**
    factors VIII and IX, with hypothyroidism **1241**
    factor XI **1241**
    factor XII **1241**
    factor XIII **1241**
    hemophilias
      factor VIII, 1236, **1237–1240**, 1242
      factor IX, **1240**, 1242
      factor XI, **1240**, 1242
    prothrombin, factors V, VII, and X **1240–1241**
    transient deficiencies in the newborn **1241**
    vitamin K dependent **1241**
Coagulation factors **1229–1231**, **1237–1243**, **1672–1673**
  in liver function evaluation **1672–1673**
Coagulation, intravascular *see* Intravascular coagulation
Coagulation tests **1230–1232**, **1233–1243**
Coal tar 474
Coarctation of the aorta 82, 1371, **1390–1391**, 1446
  in gonadal dysgenesis 1141
Coarse features, 399, 404
Coated tongue **1851**
Cobalamine *see* Vitamin B₁₂
Cobalt 60, 405
  in neuroblastoma 1111
Cobalt deficiency 146
Cocaine 532, 533, **567, 571**, 573, 575
Coccidioidal granuloma **789–790**
Coccidioides immitis **788–789**, 1307
Coccidioidin skin test **790**
Coccidioidomycosis 676, **788–791**, 1797
  pulmonary 1307
Cochlea 1884
Cockayne (Neil) syndrome 249, **1842**

Cockroaches 484
Codeine 446, 515, 573, 1280
  for treatment of migraine 1003
Codon 35
Coenzyme A 140, 144, 179, 328
Coenzyme B₁₂ 329
Coenzymes I 181
Coenzymes II 181
Coeur-en-sabot, in tetralogy of Fallot 1404
Coffee and breast feeding 152
Cognitive development **254–255**
Cohn fraction I 1239
"Coke" 571
Colace *see* Dioctyl sodium sulfosuccinate
Cola drinks 391
Colchicine 308, 339, 515, 516
Cold
  in myotonia 1032
  and urticaria 478
Cold antibodies 1184
Cold hemagglutinins **625–626**
Coldness of hands and feet in familial dysautonomia 1040
Cold sores *see* Herpes simplex
Cold stress
  in depressed newborn 68
  and low-birth-weight infant 99
  and respiratory stimulation 69
Cold test 488
"Cold turkey" 571
Colectomy 1647
Colic, abdominal **1599**
Colistimethate (polymyxin E) 581, 587, 1509
  in *E. coli* infections of newborn 642
  in shigellosis 640
  in urinary tract infections **1542**
Colistin (polymyxin E) *see* Colistimethate
Collagen diseases *see* Connective tissue diseases
Collector's itch *see* Schistosomal dermatitis
Colliquative necrosis 177
Collodion babies 1757, *1758*
Colloid brainstem cyst 941, **946**
Colloid solutions, in burns **522**
Coloboma 1817, 1827
Colon. *See also* Intestines.
  bacteria 156
  duplication of 1618
  fluid exchange **1569–1570**
  neoplasm, in ulcerative colitis 1646
  polypoid adenomatosis of 1662
Colonization, staphylococcal **644–645**
Colony counts **1541**
Color
  at birth **75, 78**
  blindness 300, 1144
  vision 177
Colostomy, in aganglionic megacolon 1623
Colostrum **150**, 386
Coma 327, 329, 334, 361, 363, 379, 532, 780, **853**
  in Addison's disease 1093
  in amebic meningoencephalitis 830
  in black widow spider bite **844**
  after cranial injury **967–975**, **1704**
  in diabetes mellitus 346
  in hypoglycemia of newborn 361
  in rabies 756

Coma (*cont.*)
  in schistosomiasis 814
  in sickle-cell disease 1177
  in skull fractures **1704**
Combined coagulation factor, deficiencies **1241**
Combined Fat- and Carbohydrate-induced hyperlipemia
      see Hyperchylomicronemia; Hyperbetalipopro-
      teinemia, mixed type, familial
Comedo **1815–1816,** *1816*
Comitant strabismus **1832–1833**
"Common atrioventricular valve" 1400
"Common cold viruses" 726
Common wart **1787–1788**
Communicating hydrocephalus **863**
Community aspects of pediatric practice 1
Community services 7
Compazine *see* Prochlorperazine
Compensatory head posture **1834**
Competence, need for 260
Complement fixation (CF) (Complement-fixing anti-
      bodies)
  of adenovirus 725, **726**
  in blastomycosis 788
  in Brill-Zinsser disease 780
  in Chagas' disease 836
  in coccidioidal granuloma **790**
  in coccidioidomycosis 790
  in cytomegalic inclusion disease 704
  in echinococcosis 822
  of herpes virus 712, 716
  in influenza 722
  in leptospirosis **622**
  in lymphogranuloma venereum 776
  in measles **733**
  in mumps 739, 783
  in *mycoplasma pneumoniae* infection 626
  in parainfluenza **723**
  in psittacosis 776
  in rhinoviral disease 727
  rickettsial 779
  in Rocky Mountain spotted fever 782
  of RS virus 724
  in rubella 762–763
  in schistosomiasis 814
  in smallpox 771
  for syphilis **654**
  to thyroid antibodies 1079–1080
  in toxoplasmosis **841**
  in trichinosis **809**
  varicella 700
Complement, synovial **505**
Complement system, serum **389,** 396, **440,** 446, 477, 486,
      497, 508, 509, 1482
  activation mechanisms **1481**
  C_{1q}, C_3, C_4, and C_5 components **389, 440,** 446
  in glomerulonephritis 1481–1482
Complete AV block *1366*
Complete precocious puberty 1123, **1124–1126**
Complete transposition of the great arteries 1377, 1403,
      1409–1412
Compliance, pulmonary 90, **1258**
Compositional homeostasis, fetal 33
Compound F *see* Hydrocortisone
Compound S (11-deoxy-17-hydroxycorticosterone) 1051,
      1097. *See also* 11-Desoxycortisol; Adrenal cor-
      tical hormones.
Comprehensive health care **6, 10**

Compression fractures, vertebral *1730*
Compulsion neurosis 270
Compulsions **286**
Concentrating ability **1454–1459,** 1460–1462
Concentrating inability in sickle-cell anemia 1177–117i
Concussion 972
Condensed milk 162, 175
Conditional vitamins *see* Vitamins
Conduction (AV) defects **1366–1370**
  in cretinism 1071
  in rheumatic carditis 493, **494**
  in sarcoidosis 1252
Conductive hearing loss 1884
Condyloma acuminatum 1787, 1788
Condyloma, perianal in syphilis *655*
Cones, retinal 177
Confusion 287
  in diabetes mellitus 351
Congenital adrenal hyperplasia **1095–1098,** 1432, 1574
Congenital afibrinogenemia **1241**
Congenital amaurotic familial idiocy **910**
Congenital anomalies
  classification 12
  in Down's syndrome 897
  epidemiology 11
  factors determining, and hydramnios in infant of dia-
      betic mother 127
  in low-birth-weight infant **115**
  and maternal rubella **764–768**
  and radiation 12
  and rubella 12, 18, **764–768**
  and single umbilical artery 65
  in small-for-age newborn 115
  in twins 60, 119, 121
Congenital aplasia of thymus 388 (Louis-Bar syndrome)
Congenital cyanotic heart disease, manifestations **of**
      1336–1337
Congenital defects *see* Congenital anomalies
Congenital dislocation of the hip **1746–1750**
Congenital erythropoietic porphyria 407
Congenital facial diplegia *see* Mobius' syndrome
Congenital glaucoma 1822
  in congenital rubella *766*
Congenital heart disease 760, **1370–1425.** *See also* Car-
      diovascular diseases, congenital.
  and imperforate anus 1627
  manifestations of **1335–1337**
  pathophysiology **1370–1379**
  due to rubella 765
Congenital hemihypertrophy 13, 250, 1099, **1706**
Congenital hepatic fibrosis **1691**
Congenital hypofibrinogenemias 1240
Congenital malaria 832
Congenital malformations *see* Congenital anomalies
Congenital megacolon 1583, **1601, 1621–1624**
Congenital myasthenia gravis **1037**
Congenital myotonia **1031–1032**
Congenital nephrosis *see* Nephrotic syndrome, congen-
      ital
Congenital nystagmus **1834–1835**
Congenital rubella *see* Rubella, congenital
Congenital spherocytosis 1679
Congenital spinocerebellar ataxia *see* Spinocerebellar
      degeneration
Congenital torticollis 1695
Congenital toxoplasmosis *see* Toxoplasmosis

Congenital universal muscular hypoplasia of Krabbe 1027–1028
Congenital virilizing adrenal hyperplasia **1095–1098**
Congestive heart failure, *see* Heart failure, congestive
Congestive splenomegaly **1218–1220**
"Congo mataby" 572
Conjugated bilirubin **1673–1674**
Conjugated hyperbilirubinemia
  in newborn **1682–1685**
  in older children **1685–1687**
Conjugated neonatal hyperbilirubinemia **1682–1685**. *See also specific diseases.*
Conjugate eye movements 1832
Conjugate gaze, paresis in brainstem tumors **945**
Conjugating activity 52–54
  and alcohol 55
  fetal 53
  pharmacologic induction 54
  and phenobarbital 54
  placental 52
Conjugation
  interbacterial transfer by 583
  bilirubin **1674–1675**
  defect 1071
Conjunctiva **1819–1822**
  xerosis of 177
Conjunctival edema 460
  in cavernous sinus thrombosis 960
Conjunctival hemorrhage *see* Hemorrhage, conjunctival
Conjunctival scarring in trachoma 777
Conjunctival telangiectasia in ataxia-telangiectasia *930*
Conjunctival tests 449
Conjunctivitis 387, 701, 763, **1819–1822**
  in coccidioidomycosis 789
  due to ECHO viruses 754
  epidemic, *H. influenzae* 619
  in erythema multiforme 1778
  follicular, adenoviral 725
  in leptospirosis 621
  in measles 732
  in mycoplasma infections 625
  unilateral 718
Conn's syndrome *see* Hyperaldosteronism
Connective tissue diseases **490–516**
  affecting chest wall **1328–1329**
  altered resistance in 645
  dermatomyositis 490, 505, 506, **510–512**
  juvenile rheumatoid arthritis **502–508**
  polyarthritis nodosa 490, 505, 506, **513–514**
  pulmonary lesions in **1313–1315**
  rheumatic fever **490–503**, 504, 505, 506
  rheumatoid arthritis 490, 495, 495, 498, **503–507**
  scleroderma 490, 505, 506, **512–513**
  systemic lupus erythematosus 490, 495, 505, 506, **508–510**
Connective tissue nevi 1767
Consanguinity 299, 303, 368, 371
Constant exotropia 1833
Constipation 273, 409, 454, **1600–1602**
  in appendicitis 1640
  in cretinism 1070–1071
  in Fanconi syndrome 1521
  in hypercalcemia, idiopathic 207
  hysterical 284
  in lymphogranuloma inguinale 776
  in pheochromocytoma 1109
  in pyloric stenosis 1609

Constipation (*cont.*)
  in salmonella infections 636
  in viral hepatitis 708
Constrictive pericarditis 679, **1426–1427**
Contactants, and urticaria 477
Contact dermatitis 473, **475–476**, 1814
Continuous murmur **1344**, **1394–1396**
Contractures 178, 504, 507, **1028**, 1036, 1725, 1772
Controlyte 1466
Conus medullaris ($_{21}$-L$_1$ vertebral levels) injury **976**
Convalescent zoster globulin 702, 1231
Convergence 1832
Convergent strabismus (Esotropia) **1832–1833**
Conversion hysteria 270
Convulsions 209, 212, 328, 357, 422, 456, 529, 533, 537, 585, 588, 853, **980–1002**, 1518
  in acute intermittent porphyria (Swedish type) 409
  in Addison's disease 1093
  in argininosuccinic aciduria 334
  in bacterial meningitis **599**, **600**
  in basal ganglia degeneration 919, 920
  in brain tumors **940–941**, 943, 947
  in carnosinemia 335
  in cerebral arterial thrombosis 962
  in cerebral cysticercosis **818**
  in cerebral embolism 962
  in cerebral palsy **885**
  in Chagas' disease 836
  in cholera 613
  in citrullinemia 334
  in congenital toxoplasmosis **840**
  in cranial subdural empyema 1011
  in craniocerebral trauma **968–975**
  in craniospinal focal sepsis **1011–1016**
  in cytomegalic inclusion disease 703
  in dysautonomia 1041
  in encephalitis **1016–1023**
  equivalents 982, **988**
  in exanthem subitum **705**
  in glycogenosis type I 368
  in glycogenosis type O 368
  in gray matter diseases 912, 915
  in hemorrhagic fever 848
  in heroin-withdrawal 562
  in *Herpesvirus hominis* infection 715
  in homocystinuria 331
  in hyper-beta-alaninemia 335
  in hyperlysinemia 335
  and hypernatremia 229
  in hyperprolinemia 330
  hypocalcemic 531
  in hypoglycemia 351
  in hypoglycemia of newborn 361
  in infant of diabetic mother 127
  in infections of nervous system **1011–1024**
  in intracranial bleeding 963
  in kernicterus 1677
  ketotic hypoglycemia **363**
  in low-birth-weight infant 115
  in maple syrup urine disease 327
  in measles 732, **735**
  in methylmalonic acidemia 329
  in neonatal narcotic withdrawal syndrome 574
  in nonketotic hyperglycinemia 329
  in odor-of-sweaty-feet syndrome 379
  in organophosphate poisoning 551
  in paragonimiasis 816

Convulsions (*cont.*)
  in pertussis 628, 630, 632
  in phenylketonuria 324
  due to poisons 532
  in psittacosis 776
  and pyridoxin deficiency 184
  in Rocky Mountain spotted fever 782
  in salicylate intoxication 552
  in scorpion sting 845
  in sepsis neonatorum 597
  in sickle-cell disease 1177
  in smallpox 771
  in systemic lupus erythematosus 509
  in taeniasis 818
  in tetany 200
  in tuberculous meningitis 671
  in white matter diseases 916, 917, 918, 919
  in Wilson's disease 391
Convulsive equivalent 982, **988**
Convulsive seizures *see* Convulsions
Cooing 254
Cooley's anemia **1180–1183**
Coombs' antiglobulin test **1193–1194,** 1676
  in autoimmune acquired hemolytic disease **1185**
Coombs'-positive hemolytic anemia 585
Coordination 252, 256, 260, **851,** 880
  in minimal cerebral dyfunction syndrome 880
Copepod 821
"Copilots" 571
Copper **145,** 390–391
  antagonism with other trace elements 146
  deficiency 195
    in kwashiorkor 174
    in marasmus 172
  in Wilson's disease 920
Copperheads 556
Copper wire screening test 533
Coproporphyrin 57, 405, 410, 543, **545**
Coproporphyrin III 411
Coproporphyrinogen 405
Coproporphyrinuria, estimation of **545**
Coracidium 821
Coral snakes 556
Cordran 475
Cords of Billroth 1216
Cord, spinal *see* Spinal cord
Cords, splenic 1216
Cord, umbilical *see* Umbilical cord
Corectopia 1827
Core, of finger pattern 313
Cornea 337, 379, 391, 1818, **1822–1824**
  in alpha lipoprotein deficiency 377
  congenital anomalies **1822**
  in congenital rubella **766**
  foreign bodies **1822**
  in Hurler's syndrome 399
  inflammations **1822–1824**
  in riboflavin deficiency 180
  in Scheie's syndrome 404
  xerosis of 177
Corneal anesthesia, in familial dysautonomia 1040
Corneal arcus 375
Corneal clouding **399–404,** 766, 1824, 1825
  in mucopolysaccharidoses **399–404,** 1824
Corneal opacities 384
  in Hurler's disease 914
  in Morquio syndrome 404

Corneal opacities (*cont.*)
  in trachoma 777
Corneal ulceration 785
Cornelia de Lange syndrome 1029, **1842,** 1848
Corn oil 135
  of low-birth-weight infant 110
Corn syrup 161
Coronal suture separation *969*
Coronal suture synostosis **1697–1699**
Coronary arteries, aberrant origin **1395, 1434**
Coronary arteriovenous fistula 1373, **1396**
Coronary artery, anomalous left **1395, 1434**
Coronary artery occulsion 370, 376
  in progeria **1841**
Cor pulmonale 1285
Corpus callosum **862**
Corrected transposition 1396, **1398**
Corrosive esophagitis **1636–1637**
Corrosive gastritis 1637
Cortical atrophy
  in maple syrup urine disease 327
  in phenylketonuria 324
Cortical hemisensory loss in cerebral arterial thrombosis 962
Cortical hyperostosis, infantile **1741,** *1742*
Cortical thrombophlebitis 1011
Corticoids *see* Adrenal cortical hormones; Adrenal corticosteroids
Corticosteroids *see* Adrenal corticosteroids
Corticotropin *see* ACTH
Cortisol (hydrocortisone) *see* Hydrocortisone
Cortisone acetate in congenital adrenal hyperplasia **1098,** *1104*
Cortisone *see* Adrenal corticosteroids
Cortisone-stressed glucose tolerance test **345**
Cortriatriatum 1371, **1383**
Corynebacterium acnes 1815–1816
Corynebacterium diphtheriae (Klebs-Loeffler bacillus) **614–618,** 1821
Coryza 648, 726
  due to ECHO viruses 754
  in measles 732
Coryzaviruses 726
"Coseasonal therapy" in allergic disorders 452
Costochondral junction
  in achondroplasia *1720*
  in rickets 200
  in scurvy 189
Cotazyme 428
Cottonmouth moccasins 556
Cough 418, 668, **1277,** 1280
  in heart failure 1421
  hysterical 284
  in measles 732
  medicines 529
  in streptococcal pharyngitis 648
Coughing attacks
  "coupling enzyme" 1061
  in esophageal atresia **1605**
Cow's milk **156–164**
  acidified milk **161**
  in allergic infants 162
  allergy 577
  amino acids in 158
  antibodies in 159
  ascorbic acid in 186
  caloric distribution in 137

Cow's milk (*cont.*)
  caloric value and *160*
  carbohydrates in 159
  chemical composition 157, *158*
  cultured milk 161
  dietary of 161
  differences between breast milk and, 157–160
  directions for preparation of 163–164
  dried 162
  enzymes in 159
  evaporated 162
  fat in 157, *159*, 160
  feeding 156–166
  fermented milk 161
  formula preparation 163–164
    of low-birth-weight infant 106, 118
  half skimmed milk, 161
  homogenized milk, 161
  humanized 162
  and hypoparathyroidism 212
  iced 163
  intolerance, and gastrointestinal blood loss 1161
  microorganisms in 156
  minerals in *158*
  modification of 160
  protein in *158*
  skim milk 161, 177
    and hypertonic dehydration 229
  special products 162
  vitamins in 159
  vitamin D in 201
Coxalgia, idiopathic 1746
Coxa plana 1738
Coxa valga, in progeria 1841
Coxa vara 201, 1718
Coxiella burnetti 625, 783
Coxsackie viruses 695, 726, 733, 749–752, 1337, 1684, 1853
  A9 infections 733
  Group B myocarditis 1429
Coyote 691
CPK *see* Creatine phosphokinase
51Cr Edta 1462
Crab 815, 816
Crab louse 845, *1793*
Cracket-pot sign (Macewen's sign) 1012
"Cradle cap" 1759, 1894
Cramps 371
Cranial
  bossing 1838
  defects 1700–1702
  dermal sinus, 877
  enlargement, in brain tumors 938
  epidural abscess 1010–1012
  molding 1704
  muscles, congenital defects of 1028–1029
  nerve degenerations 924–925
  nerve injuries 979
  nerve palsies 853, 1008–1009
    in brain abscess 1012
    in brain tumors 939, 942–945
    in CNS leukemia 1211
    in Leigh's disease 916
    in polyneuritis 1007
  nerves 1901
  neuropathy, in brain tumor 939–942, 943, 944, 945
  subdural empyema 1010, 1011

Cranial (*Cont.*)
  sutures 1695
    premature fusion of *see* Craniosynosostosis
  tenderness, in craniospinal focal sepsis 1010–1016
Craniocerebral trauma 967–975
  antisocial behavior after 280
  and battered child syndrome 557
  cerebral confusion 972–974
  cerebral laceration 973–974
  concussion 972
  extradural hematoma 970–971
  and pseudomotor cerebri 958
  sequelae 974–975
  skull fractures 967–970
  subdural hematoma 971–972
Craniofacial dysostosis 1841
Craniopharyngioma 941, 952–954, 1051, 1055
Craniospinal abscess 1010
Craniospinal focal sepsis 1009–1016
Craniosynostosis, premature 184, 859, 1695, 1697–1700
  in hypophosphatasia 206
Craniotabes 79, 80, *200*, 1701
Craniotomy
  in brain tumors 942, 943, 944, 947, 949, 952, 954
  in subdural hematoma 971
Cranium bifidum 869–870
"Crashing" 571
Crayfish 815
C-reactive protein 497, 511
Creatine 132
Creatine phosphokinase 511, 1671, 1688
Creatinine 1461–1462
  in amniotic fluid 59
  clearance 1461, 1484
  in kwashiorkor 174
Creatinuria 511
Creeping eruption 807
Cresols *530*
Cretinism 78, 80, 370, 892, 1067, 1075, 1848
Cretinoid facies 1071
Creutzfeldt-Jakob disease 905
Cri du chat syndrome 901, *903*, 1696, 1842
Cribriform plate of ethmoid fracture and pneumococcal
    meningitis 601
Crigler-Najjar syndrome 1680
Crippled children's program 9
Crisis
  adrenal 1093
  in sickle cell 1177
CRM *see* Cross-reacting material
Cromoglycate disodium 458
Cross-agglutination 611
Crossed extension reflex *see* Reflexes
Crossed eyes *see* Strabismus
Crossing-over 297, 300
Cross-reacting material 320, 779
Cross reactions, proteus and rickettsiae 779
Cross-resistance 582
Cross-sectional study 234
Crotamiton cream (Eurax) 1797
Croup 720, 1285
Crouzon's disease 1699–1700, 1831, 1855
Crown-heel length 88, 246–247
Crown-rump length 88, 246–247
CRP *see* C-reactive protein
Cruelty 279
Crush injuries, to the spine 975

Crustacea phylum arthropoda 821
Crusting 472, 473
Cry 84, 85, 92, 1071
  in cretinism 1071
  high-pitched *see* High-pitched cry
  in newborn 84, 85
  volume of 92
Crying 252, 1895
  vital capacity 92
Cryoglobulinemia 488, 509
Cryosurgery 1057, 1100
Cryotherapy 1823
Cryptococcosis **793–795**, 1225, 1252, **1308**
  pulmonary **1308**
Cryptococcus neoformans **793–794**
  in Hodgkin's disease 1225
  meningitis 1252
Cryptorchidism 250, 1097, 1098, 1134, 1144, 1522, **1554–1555,** 1559, 1841
Crypts of Morgagni 1648
Crystalline lens 344
Crystalluria 339, 340
  in gout 338
CS antigen *see* Cat scratch antigen
CSD *see* Cat scratch disease
CSF *see* Cerebrospinal fluid
"Cube" 571
"Cubehead" 571
Cubitus valgus 1141, 1144
Cuddling 268
Culex 810, **1018**
Culex Aedes sollicitans 1018
Culex pipiens 1018
Culex tarsalis 1018
Cultural deprivation *see* Deprivation
Cultural factors, and language development 257
Cultures, bacterial **579**
Curare, in tetanus 661
Curds 160
Curling's ulcer 523, 1638–1639
"Cushingoid facies" 456
Cushing's syndrome 219, **1057, 1099–1100,** 1119, 1202
  and acanthosis nigricans 1805
  hypertension in 1446
Cutaneous anergy to PPD
  in Hodgkin's disease 1225
  in sacroidosis 1252
Cutaneous blastomycosis **788**
Cutaneous fungal infections **1788–1791**
Cutaneous hypersensitivity, in mercury poisoning 549
Cutaneous larva migrans **807**
Cutaneous leishmaniasis **837–838**
Cutaneous lesions
  in congenital erythropoietic porphyria 407
  in erythropoietic protoporphyria 409
  in mixed porphyria 410
  in rheumatoid arthritis 504
  in spinal cord tumors **955**
Cutaneous myiasis 846
Cutaneous porphyria **411**
Cutaneous *see* Skin
Cutaneous tuberculosis *see* Tuberculosis, of skin
"Cutback" procedure 1628
"Cutdown" procedure **1909**
Cutis hyperelastica *see* Ehlers-Danlos syndrome
Cutis laxa **1764,** *1765*
Cutler-Power-Wilder test 1094

Cyanide poisoning 332, 532, 533
Cyanocobalamine *see* Vitamin B_{12a}
Cyanosis 362, 395, 465, 524, 532, 668, 1314, **1336, 1377–1378,** 1906
  in airway obstruction **1277**
  in bacterial meningitis **600**
  at birth 75, 78
  and breath holding spells 281
  in bulbar poliomyelitis 745
  in Coxsackie virus infections 750
  differential, in patent ductus arteriosus 75
  in esophageal atresia **1605**
  in glycogenosis type II 370
  in heart failure 1421
  in histoplasmosis 791
  in hypoglycemia of newborn 360
  in infantile kala-azar 837
  in low-birth-weight infant 96
  in neonatal pneumonia 1270
  in newborn 75, 78
  in penumocystis pneumonia 842
  in pulmonary A.V. fistulas 1305
  in pulmonary dysmaturity 1268
  in rabies 756
  in R.D.S. 1261
  in sepsis neonatorum 597
  due to tuberculous tracheobronchial nodes 667
  in "Vascular ring" 1417
Cyanotic congenital heart disease **1335–1337, 1376–1379, 1381–1382, 1401–1418**
  and brain abscess 1012
3'5'-Cyclic adenosine monophosphate. *See also* Cyclic AMP.
  and thrombocytopenia 1236
Cyclic AMP 208, 212, 218, 373, 444
Cyclic vomiting **1575**
Cyclocryotherapy 1825
Cyclodiatherum 1825
Cyclogyl 1817
Cyclomydril **1817**
Cyclophosphamide (Cytoxan) 1112, **1209–1210,** 1225, **1227,** 1468, 1504
  in Burkitt's tumor 1227
  in chronic renal insufficiency 1468
  in Hodgkin's disease 1225
  in lymphoblastic leukemia **1209–1210**
  in lymphosarcoma **1227**
  in nephrotic syndrome 1504
  in neuroblastoma 1112
Cyclopia 809, 1817
Cyclopia-archinencephaly 1702
Cyclopin 696
Cycloplegics 1817
Cycloserine (Oxamycin) 684–686
Cyclotron irradiation 1057
Cyclotropia **1832–1833**
Cylindruria 509, 514, 1514
  in acute glomerulonephritis **1483–1488**
Cymothoidism 1792
Cyproheptadine 455, 478, 489
Cyst(s)
  in acne 1815
  bone 1743
  enteric **1618**
  hepatic 1694
  jaw 931
  kidney 1474, **1477–1478**

Cyst(s) (cont.)
 lung 1304
 mesentery 1620–1621
 ovarian 82, 1119
 of toxoplasma 840
Cystadenoma, ovarian 1119
Cystathione synthetase 58, 144, 185, 332
Cystathioninase 185
Cystathionine 185, 320, 331, 332
Cystathioninuria 185, 320, 331
Cysteine 144, 331
Cystic adenomatoid malformation of the lung 1304
Cystic cerebellar hemisphere astrocytoma 942
Cystic demineralization 209
Cysticercoid larvae 820
Cysticercosis cellulosae 818–819, 863, 1032
Cystic fibrosis of pancreas 201, 413–430, 466, 645, 720,
  1294, 1584, 1594, 1659, 1702, 1873
 bacteriology 422–423
 clinical picture 418–422
 diagnostic tests 423–425
 differential diagnosis 425–426
 pathogenesis 413–414
 pathologic physiology 416–418
 pathology 414–416
 prognosis 429
 and prolapse of rectum 1659
 treatment 426–429
Cystic hygroma, in subglottic hemangiomas 1285
Cystic tuberculosis of bone 675
Cystine 132, 144, 198, 336–337, 1518, 1522–1523, 1595, 1824
 stones 336
 storage disease see Cystinosis
Cystinosis 198, 336, 1522–1523, 1824
Cystinuria 336–337, 1518, 1595
Cystitis 1543–1549
 due to salmonellae 636
 schistosomal 814
Cystometry 1550
Cystoscopy 1549
Cystourethrography, voiding 1549
Cytarabine see Cytosine arabinoside (cytarabine)
Cytochrome 393, 405, 622
Cytochrome oxidase 622
Cytogenetics, 58, 295, 308–312, 897–903
 of amniotic fluid 58
Cytoid bodies 509
Cytomegalic inclusion disease 18, 703–706, 865
 congenital 115
 in Hodgkin's disease 1225
 intrauterine infection 18
Cytomegalovirus 18, 703–705, 711, 1684
Cytoplasmic inclusions 508, 724, 770, 776, 1820, 1821
 in lymphogranuloma inguinale 776
 in smallpox 770
 in systemic lupus erythematosus 508
Cytosar see Cytosine arabinoside
Cytosine 294
Cytosine arabinoside (cytarabine)
 in herpetic keratitis 716
 in lymphoblastic leukemia 1209–1210
Cytotoxic drugs, 1204, 1504
 in nephrotic syndrome 1504
 and neutropenia 1204
Cytoxan see Cyclophosphamide

"Dabbling 571

Dacryostenosis 1824
Dactylitis
 syphilitic 655
 tuberculous 674, 675
"Dagga" 572
Dairy products, in transmission of diarrhea 228
Dandy-Walker syndrome 863, 865
D antigen 1187–1189, 1196–1197
Darier's disease 930, 1759, 1780
Darier's sign 478, 1811
Dark-field microscopy 622, 653
Darvon see Dextropropoxyphene
Daunomycin 1211
Dawdling 269
Dawson's subacute inclusion body encephalitis see Sub-
  acute sclerosing panencephalitis
Daydreaming 269
o,p'-DDD   (2[2-chlorophenyl]-2-[4-chlorophenyl]-1,1-di-
  chlorethane) 1099
DDT (diphenyltrichloroethane) 532, 535, 837, 845, 1042
 and ataxia 1042
 in pediculosis 845
D/D translocation 901
Deacidite FF (Permutit) 1595
Dead space, respiratory 1275
 of low-birth-weight newborn 92, 92
Deaf mutism 1090
 and familial goiter 1068
Deafness 330, 331, 379, 399, 462, 579, 587, 760, 852, 1161,
  1165, 1802, 1842, 1850, 1884, 1889–1891
 in cerebral palsy 885
 in congenital rubella 765–766
 due to cytomegalic inclusion disease 703
 after erythroblastosis fetalis 1192
 in gonadal dysgenesis 1141
 in gray matter diseases 914, 915
 and hereditary nephritis 1514
 in Hunter's syndrome 399
 in Hurler's disease 914
 hysterical 284
 due to kernicterus 1677
 in low-birth weight infants 116
 in megaloblastic anemia 1165
 after meningitis 608
 in mucopolysaccharidoses 399–404
 due to mumps 738
  encephalitis 1019
 nerve deafness 738, 1068
 in Refsum's syndrome 924, 1008
 in Rocky Mountain spotted fever 782
 in sarcoidosis 1252
 and speech defect 276
 and tuberculous meningitis 672, 673
 in white matter diseases 916
Death rate see Mortality
Death, sudden and unexpected, 376, 525, 575–578, 1337,
  1388
 in aortic stenosis 1337, 1388
 in childhood 577–578
 due to cleaning fluid inhalation 568
 in infancy 575–577
 intrauterine, fetus of diabetic mother 125
 in sickle-cell anemia 1177
Debre-Semelaigne syndrome 1029, 1036
Decarboxylase enzymes 179
Decarboxylation 179, 183
Deceleration 235

Decerebrate rigidity
  in gray matter diseases 912–914
  in maple syrup urine disease 327
  in white matter diseases 916–918
Decongestants 1282
Deep tendon reflexes, in hypothyroidism 1076
Deer 691
Deer fly 691
Deer fly fever see Tularemia
Defecation 1567
Deficiency diseases 170–194
  gingivostomatitis 1854
  tongue in 1851
Deformities 515
  in rheumatoid arthritis 504, 505
  in tuberculosis of the hip 674
Degenerations of basal ganglia 919–921
Degenerative and demyelinating diseases of the nervous
      system 905–932
  gray matter diseases 907–916
    storage disease of gray matter
      cerebromacular degenerations 909–913
      generalized lipidoses 912–913
      glycogen storage diseases 915
      mucopolysaccharidoses 914–915
      non-storage degeneration of gray matter 915–916
  neurocutaneous syndromes 925–931
  therapy 931–932
  white matter diseases 916–919
    basal ganglia degenerations 919–921
    brainstem and spinal cord degeneration 923–924
    cranial and peripheral nerve degeneration 924–925
    cerebellar degeneration 921–923
    demyelinating scleroses 917–919
    leucodystrophies 916–917
    polymorphous neuroabiotrophies 921–925
Degradative enzymes, deficiency of 404
Dehydration 209, 224–231, 344, 379, 613, 640, 642, 1150,
    1278, 1534
  in airway obstruction 1278
  in cholera 613
  in diabetes insipidus 1150
  in diabetes mellitus 344
  in E. coli infections 642
  pathogenesis 224
  physical findings 228
  in renal vein thrombosis 1534
  in shigellosis 640
  hypertonic, and central nervous system 224–225
  hypotonic 229–231
  isotonic 229
7-Dehydrocholesterol 139
Dehydroepiandrosterone 18, 40, 1092, 1093
18-Dehydrogenase 1092, 1095
7-Dehydrotachysterol 197
Dejerine-Sottas syndrome 924, 1008
DeLange (Cornelia) syndrome 1029, 1842, 1848
"Delayed blanch reaction," in atopic eczema 473
Delayed hypersensitivity 444, 446, 459, 475
Delayed speech see Speech retardation
Deletion, in chromosomes 310
Delirium, 182, 501, 532, 549, 552, 599, 733, 770
  in black widow spider bite 844
  in bulbar poliomyelitis 745
  hysterical 284
  in meningococcal infections 623
  in rabies 756

Delivery 66–70
Delivery, preterm, effect on infant 89
Delivery room
  for low-birth-weight-infant 103
  neonatal examination in 74–77
Delphian node 1079
Deltaaminolevulinic acid (ALA). See also δ-aminole-
    vulinic acid.
  dehydrase 405
  synthetase 405, 410
Delta chains, in hemoglobin 1175–1176
Dematobia hominis see Bot fly
Dementia 915
  in brain tumors 946
  in basal ganglia degeneration 919–921
  in Friedreich's ataxia 922
  in gray matter diseases 912, 914–915
Dementia infantilis see Heller's disease
Demerol see Meperidine
Demethylation, in fetus 53
Demineralization of bone 208, 209, 1100
Demyelinating scleroses 917–919
Demyelination, focal, in niacin deficiency 182
Dendritic keratitis, in herpes simplex 1823
Dengue virus infection 847–848
Density flotation rate 376
Dental abnormalities 404. See also Teeth.
  in hypophosphatasia 206
  in incontinentia pigmenti 1804
Dental age 1859–1861
  in hypocaloric dwarfism 170
Dental alveolar sepsis, and craniospinal focal sepsis
    1010–1016
Dental caries 136, 1867–1868
  and carbohydrates 136
Dental changes, in scurvy 188
Dental discoloration 12, 407, 1192, 1863
Dental enamel, hypoplasia, 56, 212
Dental eruption 1859–1861
Dental extraction, bleeding following 1230
Dental fluorescence, and tetracycline 12
Dental lamina dura, loss of, in hyperparathyoridism
    209
Dental loosening, in Hand-Schüller-Christian syndrome
    1248
Dental malocclusion 460, 1868–1869
  in hypercalcemia, idiopathic 207
Dental nerve biopsy, in metachromatic leucodystrophy
    917
Dental occlusion 1861–1862, 1868–1869
Dental papilla 1856
Dental sepsis, in osteopetrosis 1734
Dental tissues 1856–1857
Dentine 1856
Dentistry for handicapped children 1869
Dentition 241
Denver Developmental Screening Examination 892
11-Deoxycorticosterone 1446
Deoxynucleosides 696
Deoxypyridoxin 184
Deoxyribonuclease 441
Deoxyribonucleic acid (DNA) 712, 1665
Deoxyribonucleotides 35
Dependency, in asthmatics 468
Dephosphorylation 144
Depigmentation 123, 511, 925, 1800, 1802

Depigmented nevi, in tuberous sclerosis **926**
Depot fat *see* Fat
Depressants, abuse of **563–565**, 571, 572, 573
Depressed skull fractures **969–970**, *970*
Depression 270, 307
 in amphetamine addict 565
 in asthmatics 468
 at birth 73, *84*
 in marihuana user 566
Deprivation
 cultural, and health care 6
 emotional, and personality difficulties 268
 effect on fetal growth 26
 maternal, and rumination syndrome 1577
 social, and health care 6
Dermacentor andersoni 781
Dermacentor variabilis 781
Dermal fibrosis 512
Dermal ridge *313*
Dermal sarcoid 1251
Dermal sinus 606, **876–877**, 1015, 1702
Dermatitis
 contact 473, **475–476**, 1814
 due to formalin 476
 herpetiformis (DH) 702, 1588, 1775
 and niacin deficiency **181**, 182
 and pyridoxin deficiency 184
 schistosomal 815
Dermatoglyphic
 analysis **313–314**
 anomalies 1841–1842
 patterns **313**
Dermatographia 671
Dermatomyositis 478, 505, **510–512**, 513–516
Dermatophagoides pteronyssinus 461
Dermatophytes 1788
Dermatophytids **1790**
Dermis, diseases of **1763–1770**
 in scleroderma **512**
Dermoid cysts 1831
 of nasopharynx 1878
Dermoids, of cornea 1822
Dermolytic bullous dermatosis **1772–1775**
de Sanctis-Cacchione syndrome *see* Xeroderma pigmentosum
Descemet's membrane 920, 921
Descending aorta-left pulmonary artery anastomosis (Potts-Smith-Gibson) 1405
Desensitization **452**
Desferol *see* Desferroxiamine
Desferroxiamine (Desferol) 533, 575, **576**
Desiccated thyroid (USP) **1073–1074**
Desmolase system 1097, 1098
Desoxycorticosterone acetate (DOCA) 1034, **1094, 1098**, 1445
11-Desoxycortisol (Compound S) 1051, 1097
Desquamation 182, **649, 733**
 in kwashiorkor 173
 in measles 733
 in scarlet fever 649
Desquamative interstitial pneumonitis **1315–1316**
Desulfuration 183
"DET" 572
Detergents, and atopic eczema 474
Determination 307
DeToni-Debré-Fanconi syndrome *see* Fanconi syndrome
Detrusor 1550

Deutan 302
Deuterium 217
DEV *see* Duck embryo vaccine
Development **232, 304**
 and chromosomes **304**
 emotional 116, **116–117**
 mental and intellectual 257, **1908**
  in cerebral palsy 123
  in glycogenosis type I 368
  in high-birth-weight infant 125
  in low-birth-weight infant **115**
  and malnutrition 243
  in twins 123
 physical 302. *See also* Growth, physical.
 psychologic *see* Psychologic development
 single genes affecting **304**
Developmental age 240
Developmental defects, due to congenital rubella **766**
Developmental disorders of teeth **1862**
Developmental history **1898**
Developmental lag, in mental retardation 891
Developmental milestones **850–851, 1898**
 in neurologic diagnosis **850–851**, *851*
Developmental retardation
 mental *see* Development, mental; Retardation, mental
 physical *see* Development, physical
Developmental sequences, and accidents 517
Developmental tests **892**
Deviant behavior 879
 in minimal cerebral dysfunction syndrome **880**
Deviation, standard *see* Standard deviation
Devic's disease *see* Neuromyelitis optica
Dexamethasone *1104. See also* Adrenocortical steroids.
 in brain tumors **941**
Dexamethasone suppression test 1100
Dexedrine *see* Dextroamphetamine sulfate
"Dexies" 571
Dextrimaltose 161
Dextrins 161
Dextroamphetamine (Benzedrine) 529, **881**, 896
Dextrocardia 81
Dextromethorphan 1280
Dextropropoxyphene (Darvon) 532, 533
Dextrostix (paper strips) 351, 631
D. fragilis see Dientamoeba fragilis
DH *see* Dermatitis herpetiformis
Diabetes insipidus 219, 954, 1055, 1057, **1150–1152**
 in craniopharyngioma 952, 954
 in Fabry's disease 914
 in Hand-Schüller-Christian syndrome 1247, **1249**
 nephrogenic 1529
 in sarcoidosis 1252
Diabetes mellitus 18, 315, **343–356**, 374, 456, 1165
 acidosis 338, 344, **346, 347–349**, 553
  and vomiting 1574
 activity 353
 and Addison's disease 1094
 adolescence **354, 355**
 and candidiasis 795
 coma 344, 346, **347–349**
 and cryptococcosis 794
 and cystic fibrosis 422
 diagnosis **346–347**
 diet 349, **350–351**
 drugs in 355
 education of patient and family **350–352**
 etiology **343–344**

Diabetes mellitus (cont.)
  extended care 352–356
  family reaction 351, 354
  fluid therapy 348–349
  gestational 125
  glomerulosclerosis 344, 1509–1510
  glucose administration 348
  home care 351–352
  in infants of diabetic mothers 127
  insulin therapy 347–349, 352–353
  and intercurrent illness 354
  ketoacidosis 338, 344, 346–349
  in Klinefelter's syndrome (XXY) 903
  laboratory diagnosis 346–347
  latent diabetes 345
  maternal 18, 38, 59, 125
    and fetal glucose utilization 38
    and malformations 56
    and necrobiosis lipoidica 1763
    newborn infant of 125–127
    placenta lactogenic hormone in 126, 126
  natural history 344–346
  nephropathy 1509–1510
  overt diabetes 345
  pathology 344
  prediabetes 345
  prognosis 356
  severity of initial illness 346
  stomatitis in 1854
  subclinical diabetes 345
  summer camps 355
  treatment 347–350, 352–353
Diacetyl morphine see Heroin
Diagnosis, general 1896–1908
Dialysis
  in poisonings 535
  in renal failure 1465, 1468–1469
Diamine oxidase, in pregnancy 59
Diaminodiphenyl sulfone 1776
Diamniotic sac 119
Diamox see Acetazolamide
Diaper dermatitis 476, 1814, 1894
Diapers 1894
  aniline dye on 529
Diaphoresis
  in scorpion sting 845
  in trichinosis 809
Diaphragm 1323
  eventration 1326, 1632
  hernia 1632–1634
  paralysis 1325–1326
  weakness 513
Diaphyseal aclasis see Multiple hereditary exotoses
Diaphysis
  in rickets 199–200
  in scurvy 189–190
Diarrhea 166, 174, 226–232, 388, 454, 532, 613–614, 636, 639–640, 1500, 1580–1599, 1639, 1647
  acute 1580–1582
  in Addison's disease 1093
  in aganglionic magacolon 1621
  in amebiasis 828
  in balantidiasis 838
  bloody 639–640, 816, 828, 1644, 1647
  during breast feeding 155
  in candidiasis 796
  of cholera 613–614

Diarrhea (cont.)
  chronic 1582–1599
    amino acid malabsorption syndromes 1595
    carbohydrate malabsorption syndromes 1590–1594
    irritable colon syndrome 1596–1599
    lipid malabsorption syndromes 1583–1590
    and neural tumor 1113
    protein acid malabsorption syndromes 1595
  due to ECHO virus 754
  in fascioliasis 817
  in fasciolopsiasis 817
  in galactosemia 357
  in heroin withdrawal 562
  in histoplasmosis 792
  hysterical 284
  infantile 156–157, 226–232
  in infantile kala-azar 837
  in iron poisoning 537
  in malaria 832
  in mercury poisoning 549
  in niacin deficiency 182
  in paragonimiasis 816
  in phycomycosis 795
  in regional enteritis 1643
  in renal vein thrombosis 1534
  due to salmonella 636
  in sepsis neonatorum 597
  in shigellosis 639–640
  in smallpox 771
  staphylococcal 156–157, 645, 646–647
    starvation 164
  in streptococcal pharyngitis 648
  in strongyloidiasis 808
  in trichinosis 809
  in ulcerative colitis 1644, 1647
  in viral hepatitis 708
Diastasis recti abdominis 82
Diastatic fractures of skull 968, 969
Diastematomyelia 874, 875, 876, 1551, 1716
Diastolic murmurs (and rumble) 495, 1344–1348, 1381
Diastrophic dwarfism 1708, 1715, 1724
Diazepam see Valium
Diazoxide 366, 1102, 1448
Dibasic amino-aciduria 337, 1518
Dibenzyline see Phenoxybenzamine hydrochloride
Dichlorvos 805
Dicloxacillin 585, 646
Dieldrin 837
Diencephalic epilepsy (thalamic-hypothalamic) 982, 988
Diencephalic syndrome 378, 941, 946–947
Dientamoeba fragilis 825
Diet 148–168, 1908. See also Nutrition.
  in acne 1816
  in acute glomerulonephritis 1486
  in celiac disease 1588
  in chronic uremia 1465–1466
Dietary 148–168, 1908
  goitrogens 1079
  iodide 1059
  treatment
    diabetes mellitus 349–350
    epilepsy 1000
Diethylcarbamazine 446, 810, 812
Diethylstilbestrol 1134
  for mumps orchitis 740
Diethyltoluamide 845
Differentiation 307

DiGeorge's syndrome *see* Thymic aplasia
Digestion 1564–1569
 absorption, gastrointestinal 1567–1569
 of proteins 132, 1567–1568
 secretions, gastrointestinal 1567–1569
Digitalis (Digitoxin, Digoxin) 501, 1365, 1370, **1421–1423**
 in atrial fibrillation 1370
 and drug purpura 1235
 intoxication 1369
 in PAT **1365**
 toxicity 1369, **1422–1423**
Digits, anomalies 212, 541, **1707–1708,** 1841
Diglycerides 373
Dihexoside 907
Dihydrotachysterol 205–213
3,4-Dihydroxyphenylalanine 327, 1799
Diiodohydroxyquinoline **829–830, 839**
Diiodotyrosine (DIT) **1061–1062**
Dilantin *see* Diphenylhydantoin
Dimercaprol (BAL) *see* BAL
2,3-Dimercapto-1-propanol(BAL) *see* BAL
2,5-Dimethoxy-4-methyl-amphetamine *see* STP
Dimethylglycine 330
Dimethylphthalate 845
Dinitrobenzene 532
Dinitrochlorobenzene 475
Dinitrofluorbenzene 388
2,4-Dinitrophenylhydrazine 327
Dioctyl sodium sulfosuccinate (colace) 1602
Diodoquin *see* Diiodohydroxyquinoline
Diphenhydramine hydrochloride (Benadryl) 454, 458,
  474, 486, 532, **882,** 1575, 1808
Diphenoxylate (Lomotil) 533, 1646
Diphenylhydantoin (Dilantin) 186, 410, 508, 532, **995,**
  1000, 1042, 1063, 1423, 1851
 and acute intermittent porphyria 410
 and ataxia 1042
 in epilepsy **995–1000**
 and gingival hyperplasia 1851
 and PBI 1063
Diphenylmethane derivatives **882**
Diphosphoglycerate **392–393**
2,3-Diphosphoglycerate, of red cell 94
2,3-Diphosphoglycerate mutase deficiency **1175**
Diphospho pyridine nucleotide *see* DPN, and DPNH
Diphtheria **614–618,** 1428, 1821, 1852
 antitoxin **615, 616–618**
 conjunctivitis 1821
 myocarditis 1428
 paralysis **616, 617**
 toxoid 617, **618,** *1897*
Diphyllobothriasis 820
Diphyllobothrium latum 139, **820,** 1164
 spirometra 821
Diplegia, spastic 115
Diplococcus pneumoniae see Pneumococcus
Diploic space widening, in thalassemia major 1182
Diplopia 454, 531, 1832–1833
 in botulism 610
 in brain tumors **938**
 in craniospinal focal sepsis **1010–1016**
 hysterical 284
 in multiple sclerosis 918
 in pseudotumor cerebri 958
 in taeniasis 818
Diptera 846
Dipterous infestation **846**

Dipylidiasis **820**
Diplylidium caninum **820**
Direct bilirubin *see* Conjugated bilirubin
Direction 254
Direct mucosal challenge test 460
Disaccharidases
 deficiency 160, 231, **1590–1594**
 in kwashiorkor 173
Disaccharides 160, *1590–1594*
 malabsorption **1590–1594**
 tolerance tests 1593
Disadvantaged children 6
Discharge procedures, of low-birth-weight infants 107
Disciform keratitis 715
Discoid lupus erythematosus 1760
Dishing of hands, in chorea 496
Disialic acid 907
Disinfectants 529
Dislocations 1712
 of hip, congenital 1746–1750. *See also* Hip.
 of lens **1827**
 of spine 1716
Disobedience 279
Disodium cromoglycate *see* Cromoglycate disodium
Dispersion, measures of **234**
Disseminated encephalomyelitides, acute *see* Encephalo-
  myelitides
Disseminated hemangiomatosis (Rendu, Osper, and
  Weber) **929, 1234,** 1305, 1824
Disseminated histioreticuloendotheliosis, acute 1245,
  1246–1247
Disseminated intravascular coagulation 624, 733, **1236,**
  1242–1243, 1533
Disseminated lipogranulomatosis *see* Fabry's disease
Disseminated sclerosis *see* Multiple sclerosis
Dissociative feelings 361
Distal renal tubular acidosis **1525–1527**
Distractibility 880
Distribution curve **232**
 of stature for age **232,** *232,* 245
DIT *see* Diiodotyrosine
Diuretics 55, 338, **355,** 501, 1235, 1466, 1504, 1521, **1529**
 in Fanconi syndrome 1521
 in heart failure **1423**
 in nephrotic syndrome **1504**
 in renal insufficiency 1466
Divergent strabismus 1831, **1832–1833**
Diverticula 1765
 of pharynx 1878
"Diverticulitis" 1619
Dizygosity 302
Dizygous twin *see* Twins, fraternal
Dizziness 454
 in pseudotumor cerebri 958
"DMA" 571
"DMDA" 571
"DMT" 572
DNA 21, 35, 237, **294, 296,** 304, 307, 309, 383, 694, 695,
  712, 725
 molecule **294–296**
 replication 309
 tissue 21, 237
 viruses 695, 712, 725
DNBC *see* Dinitrochlorobenzine
DNFB *see* Dinitrofluorbenzene
-D-N-hexosaminidase 912
DOCA *see* Desoxycorticosterone acetate

Doctor-patient relationship, in middle childhood 261
Dog 802
  and leptospirae 621
  rabies in 755
  tapeworm *see Dipylidium caninum; Echinococcus granulosus*
  tick 692, 781
"Dollies" 572
"Dolls" 571
"Dolophine" 572
"DOM" 572
DOM *see* STP
Dominance, intermediate 299
Dominant trait, autosomal **298–299, 314,** 375, 409, 410
Dominant, X-linked trait **299,** 314
"Dominoes" 571
Dopa 1107
Dopamine **1107–1113**
Dopa quinone 1799
"Dope" 572
Doppler effect *see* Radiography
Doriden *see* Glutethimide
Dorsal slit 1553
Double aortic arch **1416**
Double-barreled enterostomy 1616
"Double bubble" radiologic sign **1613**
"Double male" syndrome (YY, XYY, XXYY, and XXXYY) 903
Double refractile spherules, in coccidioidomycosis 790
"Double trouble" 571
Doughy consistency, in hypernatremia 229
Dove 775
"Downs" 571, 582
Down's syndrome 58, 78, 80, 81, 115, 185, 310, 316, 338, 398, 574, **897–900,** 1201, 1613, 1622 1681, 1866
  and aganglionic megacolon 1622
  cytogenetics of amniotic fluid 58
  and duodenal atresia 1613
  and hyperbilirubinemia 1681
  and leukemia 1208
Doxycycline 783
Doxylamine 454
2,3 DPG *see* 2,3-Diphosphoglycerate
DPN 139
DPNH **392–393**
DPNH-methemoglobin reductase 393
  deficiency **395–396**
DPNH oxidase 396
DPT (combined tetanus toxoid, diphtheria toxoid, and pertussis vaccine) 572, **618, 660,** 744, *1897*
Dracontiasis **809–810**
Dracunculus medinensis 809
Draught 153
Dread of inferiority 260
Dream activity, and asthmatic attacks 471
"Dreamer" 571
Dribbling incontinence 1551
Drisdol 203
Drooling 880
"Drop" 572
Dropped beats 1369
Drop seizures 989
Drowning **524–526**
Drowsiness 506
Drug abuse **558–573**
  alcohols **569–570**
  amphetamines **565–566**

Drug abuse (*cont.*)
  cocaine **567**
  depressants **563–565**
  general considerations **570**
  glue sniffing **567–568**
  hallucinogenics **568–569**
  lexicon of terms **571–572**
  marihuana **566–567**
  psychedelics **568–569**
Drug addiction **558–575**
  and malaria transmission **834**
Drug allergy (hypersensitivity, idiosyncrasy, intolerance and reactions), 477, **478–483,** 513
Drug-induced hemolysis 393, 1175
  with positive Coombs' test **1185–1186**
Drug-induced megaloblastic anemia **1164**
Drug-metabolizing enzymes 1667
Drug overdosage **478**
Drug poisoning **527–537**
Drug purpura **1235–1236**
Drug reactions, classification 478
Drug related neutropenias **1204**
Drug resistance **583–584**
Drug sensitivity **500**
  in cretinism 1071
Drug therapy, **1911**
  in allergic disorders **454–458**
  anticonvulsant **995–1000**
  antidiarrheal 1646
  antihistamines **454–455**
  antihypertensive 55
  antithyroid 55
  in breast feeding 152
  in diabetes mellitus 355
  enzyme activity induction 54
  of epilepsy **995–1000**
  expectorants **457**
  fetal effects 51–57
  and hyperbilirubinemia 54
  in intracranial tumors **941**
  in mental retardation **895–896**
  metabolism in fetus 52–56
  methylxanthines **456**
  in minimal brain dysfunction syndrome **881–882**
  photosensitivity-inducing **487–488**
  placental transmission 52
  sedatives **457–458**
  sympathomimetic amines **455–456**
  teratogenicity 12
  and urticaria 477
  and vomiting 1574
"Drumstick" 309
Dry mouth, in botulism 610
Dryness, of mucous membranes 569
DTP vaccination 1897
DT vaccination 1897
Duarte variant, of galactosemia **358**
"Duby" 572
Duchenne's pseudohypertrophic muscular dystrophy 315, 370, **1030**
Duck embryo vaccine (DEV) 759
Duct, pharyngoglossal *see* Pharyngoglossal duct
Ductus arteriosus 48, 70, 94, 95, **1393–1396**
"Dugee" 572
Duhamel's procedure 1623
Duke bleeding time 1237
"Dumbell tumors" 1745

Duodenal
  atresia 1613–1615
  obstruction 1612–1614
  ulcer, in cystic fibrosis 422
Duodenitis, in viral hepatitis 708
Duodenoduodenostomy 1615
Duodenojejunostomy 1615
Duodenum 422, 708, 1612–1615
Duplications (enteric cysts)
  esophagus 1606
  intestinal tract 1606, 1608, 1618
  stomach 1608
Dural sinus thrombosis 960–961
Dural tears 1704
Dura mater 862
"Dust" 571
Dust, and atopic eczema 474
Dwarfism 249, 1052–1056, 1726–1727, 1841–1842. See also
     Short stature; Growth retardation.
  bird-headed 249, 1838, 1841–1842
  hypocaloric 170
  primordial 249
  psychosocial 175, 1056
  zinc deficiency 146
Dwarf, pituitary see Pituitary dwarfism
Dwarf tapeworm see Hymenolepsis nana
Dyclone solution 1779
Dye dilution curves 1357
Dyke-Davidoff-Masson syndrome 854
Dysarthria 920
  in ataxia-telangiectasia 930
  in basal ganglia degeneration 920
  in cerebellar degeneration 921
  in familial dysautonomia 1040
  in Friedreich's ataxia 922
  in white matter diseases 916, 918
Dysautonomia, familial 1040–1041, 1865
Dyschondrosteosis 1729
Dyscoria 1827
Dyscorticism 1095
Dyscrasias, blood see Blood and blood forming organ
     disorders
Dysentery 638, 1579
  amebic see Amebiasis
  bacillary see Shigellosis
  schistosomal 814
Dysesthesia, in Fabry's disease 913
Dysgammaglobulinemia 387
  and contraindications to vaccination 773
Dyshidrotic eczema 1806
Dyskinesia 884
Dyskinetic cerebral palsies 884
Dyskinetic movements, in scorpion sting 845
Dyslexia 880
Dysmaturity 574
Dysmyelinating leucodystrophies see Leucodystrophies
Dysmyelination 916
Dysostosis 1719
Dysostosis craniofacialis see Crouzon's disease
Dysphagia
  in botulism 610
  in esophageal duplication 1606
  in familial periodic paralysis 1034
  in herpangina 751
  in scleroderma 512–513
  in "vascular ring" 1417

Dysplasia
  definition 1719
  generalized 1841
  renal 1471
  skeletal 1719–1735
Dysplasia epiphysealis multiplex 1726
Dysplasia epiphysealis punctata 1715, 1722, 1725–1726
Dyspnea 520, 532, 668, 724, 1314, 1375, 1632
  in asthma 465
  in glycogenosis type II 370
  in heart failure 1420
  in Herpesvirus hominis infection 715
  in H. influenzae infections 620
  hysterical 284
  in "vascular ring" 1417
Dysrhythmias 982, 983–985, 986, 989–991, 993, 994
Dyssynergia cerebellaris myoclonica 921
Dystocia 201
Dystonia 851, 852
  in basal ganglia degenerations 919–921
Dystonia musculorum deformans 852, 920
Dystonic movements 852
Dystrophia myotonica 1032
Dystrophic epidermolysis bullosa 1772–1775
Dystrophic ophthalmoplegia 1031
Dystrophy, skeletal 1719
Dystropia canthorum 1702
Dysuria 454, 679
  in blastomycosis 788
DZ twin see Twins, fraternal

Eagle flocculation test 654
Ear 1881–1892
  deafness 1889–1892
  examination 1882–1883, 1905
  and gestational age 80
  growth and development 1882
  infections 1886–1889
  inherited diseases 1884–1885
  lobule 1882
  malformations 1144, 1884
  of newborn 80, 81
  physiology 1881–1882
  pinnae 80, 388, 1881, 1882
  trauma 1889
  tuberculosis of 677
  tumors 1885–1886
Ear drum 1881–1883
Early feedings, of low-birth-weight infant 109
Eaton's agent see Mycoplasma pneumoniae
East-African kala-azar 837
East-African sleeping sickness see African trypanosomiasis
Eastern equine encephalitis 1016, 1017–1018
EBS see Epidermolysis bullosa simplex
Ebstein's anomaly 1376, 1408–1409
EB virus 717
EB virus antibody 763
Ecchymoses 189, 501, 557, 780, 792, 847, 1111, 1209, 1228–
     1244, 1704
  and battered child syndrome 557
  in hemorrhagic disorders 1228–1244
  in hemorrhagic fever 847
  in histoplasmosis 792
  in leukemia 1209
  and neuroblastoma 1111
  in salicylate toxicity 501

Ecchymoses (*cont.*)
 in scurvy 189
 in skull fractures 1704
 in typhus, epidemic 780
ECF *see* Extracellular fluid
ECG *see* Electrocardiography
Echinococcosis **821–823**
Echinococcus granulosus **821–823**
Echinococcus multilocularis **823**
Echocardiography, in pericarditis **1426**
Echoencephalography **852**, 941, **948**, 949, 958
 in brain tumors 941, **948,** *949*
 in pseudotumor cerebri 958
Echolalia 276
Echoventriculography 857
ECHO virus 227, 576, 641, 695, 726, **752–754**, 1042
 and acute cerebellar ataxia 1042
 in unexplained infant-death 576
E. coli see Escherichia coli
Ecology **1912–1914**
Economic Opportunity Act 9, 10
Ecthyma **1781–1783**
Ectodermal dysplasia (anhidrotic type) 930–*931*, 1865
 sweat electrolytes in 424
Ectodermosis erosiva pluriorificialis 1854
Ectomorphic body types 216
Ectopia cordis 1328
Ectopia lentis 1765
 in homocystinuria 331
 in Marfan's syndrome 1732
Ectopic bowel opening 1625
Ectopic gastric mucosa 1619
Ectopic kidney **1557**
Ectopic pancreatic tissue 1662
Ectopic parathyroid tissue 388
Ectopic perineal anus **1626,** 1629, *1630*
Ectopic testis 1555
Ectopic thyroid tissue 1850
Ectopic ureters 1551, **1558**
Ectothrix 1788
Ectropion 1757, 1818
Eczema 47, 136, 436, 44, **471–474**, 773, **1806–1808.** *See also*
  Atopic eczema.
 herpeticum (Kaposi's disease) 714, 1785
 vaccinatum 771
Eczematoid rash, in phenylketonuria 323–324
Edathamil calcium disodium (EDTA), in band keratopathy **1824**
EDC 17
Edema 173, 270, 366, 410, 512
 in abdominal tuberculosis 677
 in acute glomerulonephritis **1484–1486**
 in celiac disease **1586**
 in Chagas' disease 836
 in cystic fibrosis 428
 in erythroblastosis fetalis 1187, **1189,** 1191
 in exudative gastroenteropathy **1594–1595**
 of face *see* Facial edema
 in fasciolopsiasis 817
 in hypoproteinemia 173, 1586, 1594
 in infectious mononucleosis 718
 in kala-azar 837
 in kwashiorkor 173
 in low-birth-weight infant 96
 in mumps 739
 in nephrotic syndrome **1500**
 protein content of edema fluid 96

Edema (*cont.*)
 of scalp, in anaphylactoid purpura **1233**
 in scurvy 188–189
 and skin 409
 in thiamine deficiency 179
 in trichinosis 809
Edmonston B vaccine 736
Edrophonium chloride (Tensilon) 923, **1036**
 in myasthenia **1036**
EDTA *see* Edathamil
Educational programs
 accident prevention 518
 in mental retardation **895**
 in minimal brain dysfunction syndrome **881**
 poisoning prevention 536
 for prevention of drowning 526
E.E.C. *see* Enteropathogenic *E. coli*
EEG *see* Electroencephalography
Eel fly 846
Eels 1035
Egg 140, **166–167**, 474, 477
 and allergic rash 474, 477
 and biotin deficiency 140
Egg-shaped cardiac silhouette 1410
Eggs, of parasites *see* Ova
Egocentrism 280
 between 3 and 5 years of age 258
E. histolytica see Entamoeba histolytica
Ehlers-Danlos syndrome **1232, 1765,** 1766
Ehrlich's reagent 1671, 1675
Eighth nerve
 deafness **738,** 1019, 1514, 1885
 tumors of 1886
Ejaculation 1123
Ejection click 1342
Ejection murmurs 495, **1341–1343,** 1384
EKG *see* Electrocardiography
Elastin 1763
Elastolysis, generalized *see* Cutis laxa
Elastosis 1799
Elastosis perforans serpiginosa **1766**
Elbow restraints
 for atopic eczema 474
 in rumination 1578
Electrical burns 519, *520, 521*
Electrocardiography (electrocardiogram) **1346–1354,** 140
 abnormalities
  in cardiomegalic glycogenosis (type II) 370
  in cretinism 1071
  in diabetes mellitus 347
  and digitalis 1422–1423
  in heroin user 559–560
  in hypoplastic left heart complex 1416
  in K^+ deficiency 230
  in measles 734
  in pericarditis 1425
  in pulmonary atresia with intact ventricular septum
   1408
  in tetralogy of Fallot 1404–1405
  in transposition of great arteries 1410
  in ventricular hypertrophy **1350–1351**
 arrhythmias **1354**
 electrolyte effects **1351–1352**
 methods **1347–1349**
 normal **1349–1350**
Electrodesiccation 1788

Electrodiagnostic procedures, in neurologic diagnosis 856–857
Electroencephalography (-gram) (EEG) 856, **982–986, 989–991, 993–994**
  of absence attacks **989**
  in brain tumors 941, **948**
  in cat scratch disease 699
  in cerebral palsy 885
  in craniospinal focal sepsis **1010–1016**
  in encephalotrigeminal angiomatosis 929
  in epilepsy **982–986, 989–991, 993, 994**
  in febrile convulsions **1001**
  in galactosemia 357
  in head size abnormalties 859–860
  in homocystinuria 331
  in hyperglycinemia 328
  in hyperprolinemia 330
  in low-birth-weight infant 115, 116
  in migraine 1002
  in minimal brain dysfunction syndrome **880–881**
  in neurocutaneous syndromes **925–931**
  in pseudomotor cerebri 958
  in vitamin B_6 deficiency 184
Electrolytes
  imbalance 1623
  physiology **221–228**
  requirements 143
    in acute renal failure **1464**
    of low-birth-weight infant 108
Electromyography 511, **856–857**
  in dystrophia myotonica 1032
  in myopathies **1025**, *1026*
  in polyneuritis 1007
Electrophoresis 1178, 1179
  of lipoproteins **373**
  starch gel 358
Electroretinography (ERG) 178, 1829
  in Tay-Sachs disease 912
Elephantiasis
  in Bancroft's filariasis **811**
  in Malayan filariasis **811**
  in schistosomiasis 813
Elfin facies 207, 1848
Elimination, disorders of, as psychopathologic symptoms and syndromes **272–273**
Elixophyllin 456, 466
Elliptocytosis, hereditary **1172**
Ellis-van Creveld syndrome *see* Chondroectodermal dysplasia
Ellsworth-Howard test 213
Eltor biotype, of *Vibrio cholerae* 612
EM *see* Erythema multiforme
Emaciation 270
  in diencephalic syndrome 946
Embden-Myerhof pathway 369, 393, **1172**
  of erythrocyte **1172–1174**
Embolism cerebral 962
Embryonal rhabdomyosarcoma metastatic 1745
Embryonal sarcoma, testis 1561
Embryonic growth 21
Embryotoxon 1822
Emesis *see* Vomiting
Emetine hydrochloride
  in amebiasis **829–830**
  in fascioliasis 817
  in paragonimiasis 816
Emmetropia 1835

Emotional deprivation 268
Emotional development *see* Development, emotional
Emotional disturbances 280, 281, 495
  in asthma 468
  in burned children 519
Emotional environment, and growth 243
Emotional lability, in minimal cerebral dysfunction syndrome 880
Emotional reactions **281**
Emphysema, obstructive 720, 724, 1277
  in cystic fibrosis 415, 416, 417
Empyema **1329**
  due to *H. influenzae* 619, **620**
Enamel formation **1856**
  and prematurity; cerebral palsy **1862–1863**
  and tetracycline 56
Enamel hypoplasia **1862–1863**
Enamel organ **1856**
Enanthem
  in measles **732–733**
  in scarlet fever 649
Encephalitis 485, 553, 708, 746, 851, **1016–1023,** 1055
  in cat scratch disease 698
  in chickenpox 701
  chronic and subacute, due to slow viruses 1023
  in ECHO virus 753
  due to herpesvirus **715**
  lethargica *see* Von Economo's disease
  periaxialis diffusa *see* Schilder's disease
  and pertussis 628
  postinfectious **1020–1022**
  primary viral **1016–1020**
  following rabies vaccination **1022**
  in smallpox 771
  in toxoplasmosis 840
Encephalocele 857, 861, **869–870,** 1695, 1702, 1872
Encephalomyelitis
  acute, disseminated **918**
  in measles 731, 735
Encephalomyocarditis, of the newborn, due to Coxsackie virus 750
Encephalopathies, static **879–905**
  cerebral palsy **882–887**
  mental retardation, **887–905**
  minimal cerebral dysfunction syndrome **879–882**
Encephalopathy
  in cat scratch disease 698
  hypertensive, in AGN **1484–1486,** 1490
  lead *see* Lead poisoning
  following pertussis prophylaxis 1022
  in polyarteritis nodosa 514
  toxic, in measles 735
Encephalotrigeminal angiomatosis 853, **928–929,** *928–929,* 960
Enchondromatosis *see* Ollier's syndrome
Encopresis **272, 1603**
Endemic goiter **1077–1079**
Endemic typhus *see* Murine typhus
Endobronchial tuberculosis **667**
Endocardial cushion 1398
Endocardial cushion defect 1396, **1400–1401**
Endocardial fibroelastosis 370, 1337, **1433**
Endocarditis, bacterial 498, 1384, 1397, **1429–1431**
  in brucellosis 611
  and craniospinal focal sepsis **1010–1016**
  and heroin use **560–561**
  with preexisting heart disease **1429–1431**

Endocarditis (*cont.*)
  without preexisting heart disease 1431
  due to salmonellae 636
  due to *Staphylococcus aureus* 645
  in systemic lupus erythematosus 508, **508–509**
  in tetralogy of Fallot 1404
Endocarditis, candida 796
Endocrine dysfunction or disorders **1045–1153**
  and acanthosis nigricans 1805
  in craniopharyngioma 952
  and hypoglycemia 361, 362
  and myocardial disease 1432
  in tumors of the central nervous system 941
Endocrine factors, and growth 243
Endocrine myopathies 1036
Endocrine system **1045–1153.** *See also specific endocrine*
    glands.
  adrenal cortex **1090–1106**
  adrenal medulla **1107–1113**
  anterior pituitary *see* Pituitary, anterior
  diabetes insipidus **1148–1153**
  diabetes mellitus **343–356**
  hypothalamus **1046–1047**
  neuro-endocrine communications **1045–1046**
  ovaries **1115–1120**
  parathyroid 195, **208–213**
  pineal organ **1113–1115**
  pituitary, anterior **1046–1058**
  pituitary, posterior **1148–1153**
  puberty, endocrine changes at **1120–1122**
  sex differentiation abnormalities **1130**
  sexual precocity **1122–1130**
  sympathetic nervous tissue **1107–1113**
  thyroid **1058–1090**
  water homeostasis, primary disturbances **1148–1153**
Endogenous hyperlipemia *see* Hyperprebetalipoprotein-
    emia, familial
Endomorphic body type 216
Endoplasmic reticulum, of hepatocyte **1666–1667**
Endotoxin
  in meningococcemia 624
  in shigellosis 640
Endotracheal intubation *see* Intubation, endotracheal
Enemas 646, 1602, **1910**
Energy balance **128–138**
  and obesity 216
Energy equivalents, of foodstuffs 128
Energy loss, in excreta 130, 131
Energy metabolism **128–131**
Energy requirements 128–131
Enfamil 162
Engelmann's disease **1731–1732**
Enophthalmos 852, 1817
Entamoeba histolytica 227, 638, **825–830**, 826, 1010
Enteric cysts **1618**
Enteric fever due to salmonellae **636**
"Enteric precautions," in shigellosis 640
Enteritis
  in candidiasis 796
  due to enteropathogenic *E. coli* **641–642**
  regional **1642–1643**
Enterobacteriaciae **585–588**
Enterobiasis **803–804**, *798*
Enterobius vermicularis 798, **803–804**
Enterocolic fistula 1646
Enterocolitis 227
  in aganglionic megacolon 1622

Enterocolitis (*cont.*)
  pseudomembranous 1583
  staphylococcal 645, **646–647**
Enterogastrone 417
Enterohepatic circulation 591, 1569
Enterokinase deficiency **1594**
Enteropathogenic *E. coli see Escherichia coli,* enteropath-
    ogenic
Enteropathy
  exudative **1594–1595**
  gluten-induced **1584–1588**
  protein-induced 1592
Enterotoxin 641
  of *Vibrio cholerae* **612–614**
Enteroviruses 711, 726, **742–752**
  Coxsackie viruses **749–752**
  ECHO viruses **752–754**
  poliomyelitis **742–749**
  polioviruses 742–749
Entrombicula alfreddugesi see Chigger mite
Entropion 1818
Enuresis **272–273, 1551–1552**
Envenomization, due to arthropods **844–846**
Environment 1, **1912–1914**
  and growth 240, 243
  and health care 6
  intrauterine 66
  and low-birth-weight infant 89
  and mortality 4
  noise-free, in tetanus 661
  school 8
Environment allergens 450
Environment control measures, in allergic rhinitis 461
Environmental factors
  and atopic eczema 472
  and language development 257
  and rheumatic fever 492
  and tuberculosis **663**
Environmental hazards **517–557**, 1913
  accidents **517–526**
  burns **519–524**
  drowning **524–526**
  child abuse **556–558**
  drug abuse **558–573**
  neonatal drug addiction **573–575**
  poisonings **526–556**
  sudden death **575–578**
Environmental manipulation
  in allergic disorders 450
  in atopic eczema 473
Environmental rejection, in minimal cerebral dysfunc-
    tion syndrome 880
Environmental temperature *see* Thermal environment
Enzootic marasmus, 146
Enzyme(s)
  activity 318, **320–321**
  at birth **42–43**
  in breast milk 159
  in cow's milk 159
  debranching 371
  defects 320
  development, fetal 34–37
  drug-metabolizing 53
  of erythrocytes *see* Erythrocyte enzymes
  in fetal tissues 37–41
  gastrointestinal **1567–1569**
  in high-risk pregnancies 59

Enzyme(s) *(cont.)*
  hydrolytic, fetal 53
    placental 52
  "immaturity" 43
  intestinal, deficiency **1590–1594**
  of leucocytes *see* Leucocyte enzymes
  in muscular dystrophy 1031
  neonatal 42
  pharmacologic induction of 54
  placental 37, 52
  precursors **320, 321**
  product deficit 321
  stimulation, in fetus, by drugs 53
Eosin-methylene blue stain 448
Eosinophil count 448
Eosinophilia 448, 460, 465, 585, 587, 588, 1307, 1775, 1792
  in bronchial mucus 448
  in coccidioidomycosis 790
  in diphyllobothriasis 821
  in dracontiasis 809
  in echinococcosis 822
  in enterobiasis 803
  in fascioliasis 817
  in fasciolopsiasis 817
  in heroin users 562
  in loaiasis 812
  in Malayan filariasis **811**
  in nasal secretions 448
  of peripheral blood 465
  in rheumatoid arthritis 505
  in sarcoidosis 1252
  in *Schistosomiasis mansoni* infection 814
  in strongyloidiasis 808
  in trichinosis **809**
  in trichiuriasis **805**
  in visceral larva migrans 802
Eosinophilic adenoma 250, **1049, 1056**
Eosinophilic granuloma 674, 913, 1245, **1249–1250**, 1717, 1740, 1886
Eosinophilic inclusions, in measles 730, 733
Eosinophils 1203, 1204, 1245
Ependymoma 937, **943–944**
  and neurofibromatosis 927
Ephedrine 275, 455, 456, 532, **1281**
Ephelis (freckles) 1803
Epicanthus (epicanthal fold) 324, *899,* 1145, 1181, 1547, 1702, 1818
  in β-thalassemia 1181
Epidemic conjunctivitis (pink-eye) **1820**
Epidemic encephalitis, type A *see* Von Economo's disease
Epidemic keratoconjunctivitis **1821**
  in adenoviral disease **725**
Epidemic myalgia *see* Pleurodynia
Epidemic parotitis *see* Mumps
Epidemic typhus *see* Typhus, epidemic
Epidemiology, of congenital malformations **11–14.** *See also specific diseases.*
Epidermal keratinocytes **1799–1780**
Epidermal ridges 313
Epidermal scaling disorders **1755–1757**
Epidermis **1753–1755**
Epidermoidomas 1702
Epidermolysis bullosa **1770–1775**
Epidermolysis bullosa hereditaria "letalis" **1771–1772,** *1774*
Epidermolysis bullosa simplex (EBS) **1770,** *1771, 1772*
Epidermolytic hyperkeratosis **1756–1757**

Epidermophyton floccosum 1789
Epidermophyton infections **1789–1790**
Epididymis, in cystic fibrosis 415
Epidural abscess 1009–1011, 1015–1016
  spinal 1010, **1015**
Epidural anesthesia
  during delivery 20
  during labor 54
Epigastric hernia *see* Hernia, epigastric
Epiglottitis 619, **620, 1286**
Epilepsia partialis continua 988
Epilepsy **980–1001**
  classification **981**–986
  definitions **981**
  differential diagnosis **993–994**
  diagnostic evaluation **991**
  drug therapy **995–1000**
  management **995–1001**
  pathogenesis **986–987**
  prognosis **994–995**
  seizure types **987–991**
Epiloia *see* Tuberous sclerosis
Epinephrine 355, 362, 371, 372, 453, 455, 456, 457, 465, 468, 486, 585, **1107–1113,** 1281, **1423,** 1911
  in heart failure **1423**
  in hypoglycemia 366
  and uterine blood flow 44
Epiphora 1824
Epiphyseal dysgenesis, in cretinism **1071–1072**
Epiphyseal dysplasia **1725–1727**
  in Refsum's syndrome 924, **1008**
Epiphyseal fracture, in scurvy 189
Epiphyseal fusion, in growth, physical 1096
Epiphyseal maturation delay, in Cushing's syndrome **1100**
Epiphyseal plate, in rickets 200, *202*
Epiphyseal separations **1712–1713**
Epiphyseal stippling, in cretinism 1070, **1071–1072**
Epiphyses **188–190, 198–200,** 924, 1008, 1070, **1071–1072, 1096, 1100,** 1712–1713, **1725–1727**
  in rickets **198–200,** *202*
  in scurvy **188–190**
Epiphysis *see* Pineal organ
Episcleritis **1824–1825**
Episomes 583
Epispadias *1547,* **1554**
Epispadias-Exstrophy complex **1554**
Epistaxis 368, 1161, 1230, **1876**
  in hemorrhagic fever 848
  in measles 735
  in pertussis 629
  in rubella 762
  in β-thalassemia 1181
  in von Willebrand's disease 1236
Epithelial pearls 81, 1837
Epithelioid cells 791
Epitrochlear lymphadenopathy
  in cat scratch disease 698
  in syphilis 655
Epsilon-amino caproic acid (EACA) 1237, 1240, 1242, 1243
Epstein-Barr virus, and Burkitt's tumor 1227
Epstein's pearls 1837
Epulis, congenital **1839**
Erb's palsy *see* Paralysis, brachial plexus
Erection 278
Ergocalciferol 197, 201, 204, 213
Ergomar, for migraine 1003, 1574

Ergot 532
Ergotamine, for migraine 1003, 1574
Ergothioneine 144
Ergotism 531
Erosions, esophageal see Esophagus
Erosions, pharyngeal see Pharyngeal
Eruption cysts 1838–1839
Eruption of teeth 1859–1861
Eruption, skin
  in acrodynia 550
  in adenoviral disease 726
  in African trypanosomiasis 834
  in alastrim 771
  in anaphylactoid purpura 1233
  in atopic eczema 472–473, 1806–1808
  in Brill-Zinsser disease 780
  in coccidioidomycosis 789
  due to Coxsackie A viruses 751
  in dermatomyositis 511–512
  in ECHO virus infections 753–754
  in erythropoietic porphyria, 407
  in exanthem subitum 705
  in graft versus host disease 388
  in "hand, foot and mouth disease" 751
  in hemorrhagic fever 848
  in herpes 714
  in infectious mononucleosis 718
  in Letterer-Siwe disease 1246
  in lymphogranuloma inguinale 776
  in measles 732–733
  in murine typhus 780
  in nummular eczema 472
  in rat-bite fever 634
  in rheumatoid arthritis 504
  in rickettsialpox 783
  in Rocky Mountain spotted fever 781, 782
  in rubella 761
  in scarlet fever 649
  in scrub typhus 783
  in serum sickness 485
  in SLE 508
  in smallpox 770
  in syphilis 655
  in toxoplasmosis, congenital 840
  in tularemia 692
  in typhus, epidemic 780
  and urticaria 477
  in varicella 700–702
  in zoster 1784–1785
Eruptive gingivitis 1852
Eruptive xanthoma 374
  in hyperchylomicronemia, mixed type, familial 376
  in hyperprebetalipoproteinemia, familial 376
Erysipelas 589, 649–650, 701, 1782
Erysipeloid rash, due to Achromobacter 597
Erythema 407, 409, 410, 471, 472, 487, 508, 529, 1645, 1776
Erythema induratum (Bazin's disease) 676
Erythema marginatum 490, 494, 496, 499, 501
Erythema multiforme 513
Erythema neonatorum 18, 1814
Erythema nodosum 514, 665, 676, 1251, 1643, 1645, 1797
  in coccidioidomycosis 789
  erythema toxicum 78, 1814
  histoplasmosis 792
  in Mycoplasma pneumoniae infections 626
Erythrasma 1784
"Erythroblastic anemia" see β-Thalassemia

Erythroblastosis fetalis 1187–1198, 1679
  ABO erythroblastosis 1197–1198
  amniotic fluid in 57–58
  and conjugated hyperbilirubinemia 1685
  factors other than D (Rho) erythroblastosis 1196–1197
  fetal radiography in 60
  and hypoglycemia 362
  Rh (D) antigen erythroblastosis 1187–1196
    diagnosis 1192–1194
    etiology 1187–1189
    pathogenesis 1189–1190
    pathology 1190–1191
    prevention 1196
    prognosis 1194
    symptoms 1191–1192
    treatment 1194–1196
Erythrocytes
  antibodies 387
  catalase deficiency 396
  in cholesterol acyltransferase deficiency 379
  count 1156
  destruction 1679
  diameter 1156
  disorders 1161–1203. See also Anemias; Erythrocytosis; Polycythemia.
  enzymes 391–396, 1172–1175
    abnormalities of Embden-Myerhof pathway 1172–1174
    abnormalities of hexose monophosphate shunt and glutathione metabolism 1174–1175
  hypoplasia, congenital 1165
  glucose metabolism (enzymatic reactions) 393
  in lipoprotein deficiency 377
  membrane abnormalities 1170–1172
  of newborn, enzymatic activities 393
  osmotic fragility 1180
  sedimentation rate 174, 494, 497, 499, 505, 509, 511, 513, 514
Erythrocytosis 1202
Erythroderma, ichthyosiform, congenital (bullous CIE) 1756–1757
Erythrogenesis imperfecta 1165
Erythrogenic toxin, of scarlet fever 648
Erythroid hyperplasia
  in erythropoietic porphyria 407
  in hemolytic anemias 1169, 1170–1201
  in malaria 831
Erythroleukemia 1208
Erythromycin 502, 583, 585–586, 591, 608
  in diphtheria 617
  in meningococcal infections 623
  in Mycoplasma penumoniae infection 626
  in pertussis 632
  in staphylococcal disease 646
  in streptococcal infections 651
Erythropoiesis, fetal and neonatal 1155–1160
Erythropoietic coproporphyria 409
Erythropoietic porphyrias 407–409
Erythropoietic protoporphyria 407–409
Erythropoietin 1157
Escape, DOCA 1445
Eschar, in scrub typhus 783
Escherichia coli 388, 439, 583–588, 596, 597, 1276, 1429, 1431, 1648
  bacterial endocarditis 1429
  chorioamnionitis 65
  diarrhea 227, 641–642

Escherichia coli (cont.)
   enteropathogenic 175, 227, 641–642
   meningitis 598–608
   urinary tract infection 1539
Esophagitis
   acute **1635–1636**
   corrosive **1636**
Esophagography 1607, 1652
Esophagoscopy 1650, 1652
Esophagus, **1604–1607**, **1635–1637**, **1650**, **1652**
   achalasia **1575–1576**
   atresia **1604–1606**
   bleeding in portal hypertension 422, 1219, 1578, **1652**, 1691
   caustic burns of 531, 1636
   chalasia, **1575**
   duplication, congenital **1606**
   erosions 109
   foreign bodies **1650**
   hiatal hernia **1607**
   hiatus 1632
   inflammatory disease **1635–1637**
   malformations **1604–1607**
   periesophageal mediastinal abscess **1637**
   in schistosomiasis 813
   shortening, congenital 1606
   stenosis, congenital **1606**
   varices 422, 1219, *1220*, 1578, **1652**, 1691
Esotropia **1832–1833**
ESR *see* Erythrocyte sedimentation rate
Essential amino acids *see* Amino acids
Essential familial hyperlipemia *see* Hyperprebetalipoproteinemia, familial
Essential fatty acids *see* Fatty acids
Essential hypertension **1441**
Essential nutrients *see* Nutrients
Essential oils *530*
Esterase, in kwashiorkor 174
Estriol
   in amniotic fluid 57
   in high-risk pregnancy 59
   synthesis by "fetoplacental" unit 40
   urinary, gestational, 18, 126
Estrogen **1115–1120**, 1121, **1128–1129**
   of adrenal cortex 1128
   breakthrough bleeding **1116**
   and breast milk flow 153
   deficiency **1116**, 1119
   and growth 239
   and lipid synthesis **218**
   in medicines 1128
   in skin creams 1128
   therapy 1055
   and uterine blood flow 44
   withdrawal bleeding **1115–1116**
Estrogenic precocious puberty **1128–1129**
Estrogen-producing testicular tumors 1117, 1126
Ethacrynic acid, in heart failure 1424
Ethambutol 686
Ethanol *see* Ethyl alcohol
Ethanolamines 454
Ethionamide 686, 697
Ethmoid sinus 1831, **1871**
Ethyl alcohol 55, **84**, *152*, 362, 410, 528, *530*, **569–570**, 1465, 1600
   in acute renal failure 1465
   and fetus 55

Ethyl chloride, freezing with 807
Ethylenediamine-Tetraacetic acid *see* CaEDTA
Ethylene glycol 1509
Ethylstibamine, in kala-azar 838
17 α-Ethynyl-19-nortestosterone (Norlutin) 1134
17 α-Ethynyltestosterone (Lutocylol, Pranone, Nugestoral) 1134
Eucalyptol poisoning 532
Eumydrin *see* Atropine methyl nitrate
Euphoria 454
   in diencephalic syndrome 946
Eurax *see* Crotamiton cream
Eustachian tube 462, **1881–1882**
Euthyroid 1073
Evans' rule 522
Evans' syndrome 1185
Evaporation 141
Eventration of the diaphragm **1326**, **1632**
Eversion of eyelid 1818
Ewing's tumor **1743**
Examination, physical *1900–1901*, **1905–1908**
   during prenatal care 17
Exanthematous conjunctivitis 1821
Exanthem *see* Eruption, skin
Exanthem subitum (roseola infantum) **705–706**, 733, 763, 958
"Exceptional" twins 123
Excessive appetite *see* Appetite, excessive
Excessive sleep *see* Sleep, excessive
Excessive uterine bleeding *see* Uterine bleeding, excessive
Exchange transfusion, **535**, **1195–1196**
   in cytomegalic inclusion disease 704
   in erythroblastosis fetalis **1195–1196**, 1678
   in hyperbilirubinemia of newborn 1678
   in poisonings **535**
   in salicylate intoxication
   in viral hepatitis 709
Excitability of the nervous system, and calcium 196
Excoriations 573–575, 1894
Excreta, energy loss in 130, 131
Exercise **1895**
   and obesity 216, 220
Exfoliation, of primary teeth **1860**
Exfoliative dermatitis **1759**
   due to Dilantin 998
Exhilaration 528
Exomphalos *see* Omphalocele
Exophthalmos 188, **852**, 979, 1699, **1831**. *See also* Proptosis.
   in cavernous sinus thrombosis 960
   in Graves' disease 1083
   in Hand-Schüller-Christian syndrome 1247, **1248**
   in hyperthyroidism 1084
   in neurofibromatosis 928
   in optic nerve and chiasm tumors **950**
Exostoses **1727–1728**
Exotoxin, of tetanus **658–659**
Expectorants 457
Expiratory grunting, R.D.S. 1261
Expressive language, flow of 880
Expressivity 305, 314
Exstrophy, bladder **1547**, **1554**
Extensor plantar sign **851**, 922
External auditory canal 1881–1883
External ear **1881–1882**
   diseases **1884–1887**

External ear (cont.)
  growth and physiology 1881–1882
  malformations of 1884
  trauma 1889
External secretory tissue (IgA globulins) 436–437
External strabismus 1699
External urinary sphincter 1550
Extracardiac lesions, in rheumatic fever 493
Extracellular fluid 221–222
  fetal 29
Extracorpuscular hemolytic disorders 1169, 1184–1199
Extradural hematoma 970–971
Extrahepatic biliary atresia 1682–1684
Extramedullary leukemia 1211–1212
Extraocular muscles, injury 1818
Extraocular muscles, paresis, in posterior fossa tumors
    939
Extrapulmonary tuberculosis see Tuberculosis, extrapul-
    monary
Extrapyramidal reactions, due to phenothiazines 882
Extrapyramidal signs, in thalamic tumors 947
Extrapyramidal syndromes 919–921
Extrasystoles 1368–1370
Extremities 1706–1714
  in achondroplasia 1719–1724
  acquired conditions 1711–1713
  developmental anomalies 1706–1711
  examination of 1901, 1906
  of newborn 83
Exudate, pharyngeal, in streptococcal pharyngitis 648
Exudation 472, 473, 475
Exudative enteropathy 1594–1595
Eyeballs
  in dehydration 229
  in PAT 1364
Eye color, in phenylketonuria 324
Eyelids 1818–1819
  infections 1818–1819
  injuries 1817
Eyes 1817–1835, 1895, 1905. See also Ocular; Ophthal-
    mic; specific eye structures and diseases.
  birth injuries 1817–1818
  conjunctiva 1819–1822
  cornea 1822–1824
  in cystic fibrosis 422
  in Ehlers-Danlos syndrome 1765
  examination 1817, 1905
  foreign bodies 1822
  glaucoma, congenital 1825
  in Graves' disease 1083, 1084
  herpes simplex 714, 1823
  in hydrocephalus 865
  injuries 1828
  iris 1827
  lacrimal apparatus 1824
  lens 1826–1827
  lids 1818–1819
  of newborn 80
  nystagmus 1834–1835
  optic nerve 1828–1830
  orbit 1830–1831
  phakomatoses 1826
  prophylaxis, in newborn 104
  refractive errors 1835
  retina 1828–1830
  in rheumatoid arthritis 504
  riboflavin deficiency 180–181

Eyes (cont.)
  in rubella, congenital 764, 766
  sclera 1824–1825
  strabismus 1832–1833
  syphilis 1823
  in thiamine deficiency 180
  tuberculosis 677, 1823
  uvea 1827–1828
  in zoster 1785

FA antibody, in rubella 762–763
Fabry's disease (GL$_3$-globosidosis) 384–385, 911, 913–914
Face 78, 80, 207, 399–404, 512, 1100, 1139, 1838, 1841–1845
  in cretinism 1071
  in Cushing's syndrome 1100
  in gonadal dysgenesis 1139
  in Hunter's syndrome 399
  in hypercalcemia, idiopathic 207
  in mucopolysaccharidosis 399–404
  of newborn 78, 80
  in scleroderma 512
Facial actinomycosis 785
Facial asymmetry 1696, 1717
Facial clefts 331
Facial diplegia, congenital 1029
Facial edema
  in African trypanosomiasis 834
  in pertussis 629
  in serum sickness 485
  in trichinosis 809
  due to tuberculous tracheobronchial nodes 667
Facial flush
  in hemorrhagic fever 847
  in neuroblastoma 1111
Facial grimacing
  in dystonia musculorum deformans 920
  in Wilson's disease 920
Facial hair 241
Facial hypoplasia 1841–1842
Facial muscles, atrophy, in dystrophia myotonica 1032
Facial nerve injury 979
Facial paralysis 80, 600, 853, 883, 979, 1007, 1008–1009,
    1887
Facial phycomycosis 795
Facial weakness, in myasthenia 1037
Facioscapulohumeral muscular dystrophy of Landouzy
    1030
Factor I see Fibrinogen
Factor II see Prothrombin
Factor III see Tissue thromboplastin
Factor IV see Calcium
Factor V 1229, 1231, 1240–1241
  in hemorrhagic fever 848
  in Rocky Mountain spotted fever 782
Factor VI 1229
Factor VII 1229, 1231, 1240–1241
Factor VIII 1229, 1231, 1236, 1237–1240, 1241–1242
  concentrate 300, 1238–1239
  in hemorrhagic fever 848
  in viral hepatitis 711
  in von Willebrand's disease 1236
Factor IX 1229, 1231, 1240, 1241
  in Rocky Mountain spotted fever 782
  and viral hepatitis 711
Factor X 1240–1241
Factor XI 1229, 1231, 1240, 1241

Factor XII **1229**, 1231, **1241**
Factor XIII (fibrin-stabilizing factor) **1229–1240**
Factors (coagulation) **1229–1231**
　and deficiencies **1237–1243, 1672–1673**
Factors VIII and IX deficiencies, with congenital hypo-
　　thyroidism **1241**
Failure to thrive 209, 426, 1527, 1731
　in anomalous pulmonary venous drainage 1413
　in Fanconi syndrome 1521
　in heart failure 1420
　in homocystinuria 331
　in idiopathic hypercalcemia 207
　in distal renal tubular acidosis **1525**
　in transposition of great arteries 1410
　in tyrosinosis 326
Fainting 336
Fall, and splenic injury 1217
Fallen arch **1709–1710**
Fallopian tube 1631
Fallot's tetralogy **1402–1406**
False-positive serologic test for syphilis
　in lymphocytic choriomeningitis 729
　in SLE 509
Familial dysautonomia 850, **1040–1041**
　absense of tearing in 1824
　corneal hypesthesia in 1824
　tongue in **1850**
Familial erythrophagocytic lymphohistiocytosis 1246,
　　1250
Familial factor, in rheumatic fever 492
Familial fibrous dysplasia of the jaws 1696
Familial goiter 1070, **1080**
Familial hemophagocytic reticulocytosis 1246, **1250**
Familial hypercholesterolemia *see* Hyperbetalipopro-
　　teinemia
Familial hypoaldosteronism 1095
Familial hypophosphatemia 1519
Familial juvenile nephronophthisis **1515**
Familial male precocious puberty 1124
Familial myoclonus epilepsy of Unverricht **990**
Familial nephrotic syndrome **1499–1500**
Familial neuroblastoma 1110
Familial paroxysmal choreoathetosis 921
Familial periodic paralysis **1034**
Familial spongy degeneration of the neuraxis *see* Spongy
　　sclerosis
Familial thrombocytopenic purpura **1235**
Familial twinning *see* Multiple births
Familial vitamin D-resistant rickets 1520
Familial xanthurenic aciduria *see* Xanthurenic aciduria,
　　familial
Family
　and anorexia nervosa 270
　and asthmatic child **468**
　and diabetes 354
　and suicide 290, 292, 293
Family counseling
　in leukemia **1215**
　in minimal brain dysfunction syndrome **881**
Family evaluation, in mental retardation **894**
Family history *1899*, **1902**
　in epilepsy **992**
Family relationships, in diabetes mellitus **354**
Fanconi syndrome (aplastic anemia) **1165**
Fanconi syndromes (renal) 204, **206**, 326, 340, 356, 536,
　　542, 1517, **1520–1524**

Fanconi syndromes (renal) (*cont.*)
　primary 1521–1522
　　idiopathic Fanconi syndrome 1521
　secondary 1522–1524
　　cirrhosis, congenital with tyrosinemia **1523**
　　cystinosis **1522**
　　fructose intolerance, hereditary **1523**
　　galactosemia **1523**
　　glycogen storage disease **1523**
　　Lowe syndrome **1522**
　　Luder-Sheldon syndrome **1515–1521**
　　toxins 1514
　　Wilson's disease **1523**
Farber's disease **913**
Far-Eastern hemorrhagic fever **847**
"Farmer's lung" 787, **1313**
Farquhar's familial hemophagocytic reticulosis 12
Fasciculations 551
Fasciola hepatica 817
Fascioliasis **817**
Fasciolopsiasis **817**
Fasciolopsis buski **817**
Fat **135–136**, 171, **373–386**, 1569, **1583–1590**. See also
　　Lipids.
　absorption **1583**
　adipose tissue 135, **217**, 373, 377, **378**
　　in dermatomyositis 510–511
　assimilation 136, **1569**
　body composition **217**
　in breast milk 135, 158, **159**
　cells 217, **378**
　in cow's milk 135, 157, 158, *159*, 160
　depot fat 135
　in diabetes 344
　digestion **1569**
　　in cystic fibrosis 417
　emulsification 136
　energy equivalent of 128
　fat-free diet 135, 136
　in fetal body composition **28**
　growth patterns of 237
　high fat diet 136
　indications for reducing 136
　intake, **135–136**
　iodine index 135
　and ketosis 136, 344
　metabolic anomalies **373–386**
　necrosis, subcutaneous **1768**
　and neonatal thermogenesis 29
　in nutrition 128, **135–136**
　in obesity **214–220**
　pad 135
　requirements, of low-birth-weight infant 110
　in stools 136, **1583–1590**
　stores **217**
　synthesis 135
　vitamin A and 138
　vitamin K and 139
Fatigability 371, 459
　in diabetes mellitus 346
　in glycogenosis type I 368
Fatigue, in heart failure 1420
Fatty acids 42, 135, 151, 159, 174, 369, 377, **1566, 1569**
　in breast milk 151, *159*
　essential **135**
　fetal synthesis 42
　free **218**, 344, 366, 373, 1815

Fatty acids (*cont.*)
  in glycogenosis type I 369
  in kwashiorkor 174
  long-chain 218, 377
  medium-chain 427, 1569, 1588, 1590, 1643
  metabolism, anomaly of 136, 379
  in milk 135
  short-chain 158, 1569
  and staphylococci in infant intestine 1570
  unsaturated 110, 135
Fatty liver *see* Liver
Favism **1175**
"Favus" 1790
Fazio-Londes disease 924
Fear reactions **282**
Feathers 450
  and atopic eczema 474
Febrile convulsions **1001–1002**
Febrile nodular nonsuppurative panniculitis **1768–1769**
Febrile relapsing panniculitis **378–379**
Fecal contamination
  and salmonellosis 639
  and viral hepatitis **710**
Fecal incontinence, in acute polyneuritis **1007**
Fecal play, and rumination 1578
Feces *see* Stools
Federal Hazardous Substances Labelling Act 536
Feedback control, absence of 321
Feeding **108–111, 148–170**
  artificial **156–164**
  breast **148–156**
  center 217
  diets **148–168**
  difficulty 269, 370, 850
    in bacterial meningitis 600
    in hypoglycemia of newborn 360
  gavage *see* Gavage
  history *1898*, **1902**
  of low-birth-weight infant 106, **108–111**
  parenteral **168**
  solid foods **164–168**
  techniques **148–168**
Feelings 254
Female pseudohermaphrodism *see* Pseudohermaphrodism, female
Feminization **1128–1129, 1137–1138**
  due to adrenocortical tumor 1128
  due to skin creams 1128
Feminizing syndromes **1128–1129**
Feminizing testes, syndromes 1117, **1137–1138**
Femoral epiphyses, distal, and fetal maturity 59
Femoral hernia 1632
Femur
  aseptic necrosis of 1177
  hypoplasia 1707, 1709, 1915
  lateral torsion of 1710
  Legg-Perthes disease **1739**
  slipped epiphysis **1750**
Fermentative diarrhea **1592**
Fermented milk *see* Cow's milk
Fermi technique 424
Ferric chloride test 326, 327, 533
Ferric iron *see* Iron
Ferrihemoglobin 392
Ferritin 1158, 1674
Ferrochelatase 405
Ferrous gluconate 537

Ferrous iron *see* Iron
Ferrous sulfate USP **537, 1162**
Fertility, and cystic fibrosis 413
Feto-maternal transfusion 84
"Fetoplacental unit," estriol production by 41
Fetus (fetal) **15, 66–70**
  abnormalities, and single umbilical artery 65
  acid-base balance 19, **47**
  amino acid metabolism **38**
  and antihypertensive drugs 55
  and antithyroid drugs 55
  ascites 61, 82
  bicarbonate concentration, plasma 48
  blood volume 49
  bradycardia 54
  carbohydrate metabolism **37, 42**
    and birth hypoxia 42
  chemical composition **28–34**
  chronic deprivation 26–27
  circulation **47, 48–49, 1333–1334**
  cord compression 19
  death, diagnosis 60, *61*
  deprivation and fetal growth 26–27
  distress 26, 27, 64, 71, 89
  drug distribution and metabolism **52–56**
  electrocardiography 62, 63
  endocrine interrelationships with placenta **40–41**
  enzymes **34–40**
  erythropoiesis **1155–1160**
  examination of **56–66**
  fatty acid synthesis 42
  fetus to fetus transfusion syndrome *see* Twins
  glucose metabolism 50, 56
  glycogen **30**
  growth **21–28**
  head compression 19
  heart 60
    monitoring 19, **62**, 71
    rate 19, **63–64**
  hemoglobin *see* Hemoglobin F
  hemorrhage **1158–1159**
  hypoglycemia 50
  hypoxia 63
  I_{131} on, 55
  IgG synthesis by 432, 434
  iron metabolism **1158**
  kidney **49–50, 1453–1454**
  masculinization, and steroid therapy 55
  maturity estimation 59
  measurements **24–25**, 60
  membranes, examination 65
  monitoring 19
  mortality, in rubella 760
  narcotic withdrawal syndrome 574
  organs, growth of 25
  oxygenation 47
  pancreas, 56
  pharmacology **51–56**
  pH, during labor 19
  phenobarbital and, 54, 55
  physiology **43–50**
  pulmonary vessels 1334
  pyruvate utilization rate 38
  radiography 59, 60, *61*
  renal physiology **49–50, 1453–1454**
  and reserpine 55
  respiration **46–47**

Fetus (fetal) (cont.)
  respiratory quotient 39, 42
  sex differentiation 56
  size estimation 60
  steroid synthesis **40**
  and thiouracil 55
  thyroid 55, **1065–1067**
  thyroxine 1066
  transamination **38**
  transition to newborn **66–77**
  tricarboxylic cycle 38
  ultrasound examination 59
  wasting 26, 27
  water and electrolyte balance **49–50**
  weight/placental weight ratio 44
Fever
  in African trypanosomiasis 834
  in amebiasis 828
  in Brill-Zinsser disease 780
  in brucellosis 611
  in Caffey's disease 1741
  and caloric requirements 131
  in Chagas' disease 836
  in coccidioidomycosis **789**
  in hemorrhagic fever 848
  in Hodgkin's disease 1223
  in infantile kala-azar 837
  in measles 732
  in murine typhus 780
  in Q fever 783
  in rheumatic fever **496**
  in rheumatoid arthritis **504,** 506
  in rickettsialpox 783
  in Rocky Mountain spotted fever 781
  in scrub typhus 778
  in sickle-cell anemia 1176
  in systemic lupus erythematosus **508–509**
  in trichinosis 809
  in tularemia 692
  in typhus, epidemic **779–781**
  in viral hepatitis 706, 708
  and water loss 142
"Fever blisters" see Herpes simplex
FFA see Fatty acids, free
FH see Hemoglobin F
Fibrillary neuroglia 868
Fibrin 196, 1229
Fibrin-stabilizing factor deficiency see Factor XII
Fibrinogen 497, **1229, 1240,** 1242
  and viral hepatitis 711
Fibrinolysis **1242**
Fibrinolytic enzyme system alteration 1263
Fibrinolytic purpura **1242**
Fibrinolytic system 1229
Fibrinous pleurisy 494
Fibrinous tenosynovitis 512
Fibroadenomas, of kidney, in tuberous sclerosis 925
Fibro-AHF 1239
Fibroangiomatous nevi, in tuberous sclerosis **925**
Fibroblast cultures, and cystic fibrosis tissue 414, 425
Fibroblasts 329, 334, 340, 370, 379, 382, 383, *403*
Fibrocystic disease of pancreas see Cystic fibrosis of
    pancreas
Fibroelastosis, endocardial **1433**
Fibroma molluscum, in neurofibromatosis 927
Fibroma, scalp, in tuberous sclerosis 925
Fibromatosis of gingivae **1852**

Fibroplasia, retrolental see Retrolental fibroplasia
Fibrous cortical defects **1743**
Fibrous dysplasia
  familial 1676, **1846–1847**
  nasal and paranasal bones **1874**
  of skull bones 1831
Fibula, aplasia 1707
"Fibular sign," in Duchenne type muscular distrophy
    1708
"Fiery serpent" 809
Fièvre boutonneuse **781**
Fighting, in rabies 756
FIGLU see Formanino glutamic acid
"Figure-of-eight" cardiac silhouette 1413, *1414*
Filaments, of hepatocytes 1667–1668
Filaria pneumonitis **1312**
Filariasis **810–812**
  Bancroft's **810–811**
  loaiasis **812**
  Malayan **811**
  onchocerciasis (blinding filariasis) **811–812**
Filariform larvae 805, 808
Filiform warts 1787
Finger patterns **313**
Finger ridge count **313**
Fingers 212, 504, **1707–1708,** 1841. See also Digits.
  in rheumatoid arthritis 504
Finger-sucking **275**
Fire ant 844
First brachial arch 1703, 1844, 1884
First breath 49, 68, 69, **1255–1257**
First-degree AV block 1367
Fish 166, 816
  mercury contamination of 550
Fish liver oils 177
Fish tapeworm see Diphyllobothrium latum
Fissured tongue **1849**
Fissure in ano 1579, **1659**
Fistula
  in ano **1648**
  arteriovenous **1396**
  branchial 81
  coronary arteriovenous **1396**
  rectovesical 76
  from sinus of Valsalva **1395–1396**
  tracheoesophageal 74, 75
Fixed specific gravity, in sickle-cell anemia 1177
Flaccidity 370
  in newborn 85
Flail footdrop 978
Flame burns 519
Flank pain 1537
  in sickle-cell anemia
Flapping of hands, in hepatic failure 1692
Flaring 1305
Flaring, of lower rib cage 1714
"Flashbacks," and marihuana use 566
"Flashing" 572
Flatfoot **1709–1710**
Flat warts 1787
Flavin phosphate 144
Flavobacterium 596
Flavoproteins 138, 181
Fleabite dermatitis 78
Flea (*X. cheopis*) 691, 777, 780, 847
  and murine typhus 780
Fleet's Phospho-Soda 828

Flesh-colored papules 1767
Flesh flies 846
Flexion contractures, 78, 504, 507, **1028**, 1036, 1725, 1772
  in Addison's disease 1036
  in rheumatoid arthritis 504, 507
Flies 228, 749
Flinging movements 991
Flocculation tests **654**, 708, 1672
Flocculonodular lobe, of cerebellum 939
"Floppy infant" syndrome **923, 1027–1028**
Flowers, as poisons 529
Flow murmurs **1343–1344**
Fluid(s), body see Body fluids
Fluid administration **1908–1910**
Fluid compartments **221–222**
Fluid and electrolytes **221–231, 1908–1910**
  losses
    in burns 520–523
    in cholera **612–614**
    in diarrhea **224–228**
  physiology **221–228**
  requirements **224**
    of low-birth-weight infant 108
  therapy **1908–1910**
    of bacterial meningitis **606**
    of burns **520**
    in cholera **613–614**
    and diarrhea **228–231**
    in drownings **526**
    in lead poisoning 547
    in obstructive airway disease **1282**
Flukes see Trematodes
Fluonid 475
Fluoracetate 532
Fluorescence
  dental, in erythropoietic porphyria 407
  dental, and tetracycline 12
  under Wood's ultraviolet light 407
Fluorescent antibody test
  in Chagas' disease 836
  diphtheria 616
  for enteropathogenic *E. coli* identification 642
  in herpes 715
  in malaria 833
  in measles 733
  in rabies 757
  in toxoplasmosis **841**
Fluorescent antinuclear antibody test **509**, 515
Fluorescent Y **1132**
Fluorides 532, 535
Fluorine 146
Fluoroscopy 1374
  in cardiovascular diseases **1344–1346**
  in obstructive airway disease **1278**
9α-Fluoro-hydrocortisone 1094, 1098, *1104. See also* Adrenal cortical hormone.
9α-Fluoro-16α-hydroxyprednisolone *1104. See also* Adrenal cortical hormones.
9α-Fluoro-16α-methyl prednisolone *1104. See also* Adrenal cortical hormones.
Flush method (blood pressure) 1438
"Flush test" (of I$_{131}$) 1059
"Flying saucers" 572
Fly maggots **846**
Foam cells 375, 382, 913, 1245, 1248
Focal glomerulonephritis **1489–1490**

Focal neurologic signs, in brain tumors **938–941**
Focal seizures 853, **982, 987–988, 999**
Foerster's sign **884**
Folic acid **138, 185–186,** 340
  in kwashiorkor 175
Folic acid antagonists 185
Folic acid deficiency **185–186, 1164**
  in marasmus 172
  in kwashiorkor 175
Folinic acid 139, 185
Follicle-stimulating hormone (FSH) 1048, **1049–1050, 1120**
Follicular adenocarcinoma of thyroid **1087**
Follicular conjunctivitis 1820
  in adenoviral disease **725**
Follicular cysts 1128
Follicular keratosis, in Darier's disease 930
Folliculitis **1781–1783**
Follow-up care, of low-birth-weight infant 107
Fontanel **1700**
  bulging of
    in bacterial meningitis **599–600**
    and fever 958
    in hydrocephalus 859
    in hypervitaminosis A 174
    in intracranial bleeding 963
    in meningococcal infections 623
    after nalidixic acid therapy 958
    in newborn neurological examination 84, **853**
    and roseola infantum 958
    in rubella, congenital 765
    in sepsis neonatorum 597
    in subdural effusions 624
    after tetracycline therapy 958
    in tuberculous meningitis 671
  delayed closure, in rickets 200
  depression, in dehydration 229
Food
  allergy (sensitivity) 449, 472, 474
  and botulism **609**
  elimination and provocation trials 449
  forcing 269
  handlers 825
    and typhoid carriers, 635, 638
  poisoning 227, **609, 636, 646–647**
  as source of toxicity 531
  and urticaria 477
Food and Drug Administration 536
"Footballs" 571
Footdrop 514
Foot patterns 314
Foramen magnum, in achondroplasia **1721**
Foramen of Bochdalek 1632
Foramen of Luschka 862
Foramen of Magendie 862
Foramen of Monro 862
Foramen of Morgagni 1632
Foramen ovale 48, 70, 94, **1398–1399**
  closure of 95
Foramen primum 1398
Forceps 75
Forehead wrinkling, absence of, in Graves' disease 1084

Foreign body, **577**, **668**, 1117, 1278, **1288**, **1650–1651**, 1822, 1876
  aspiration 668, **1288**
  in esophagus **1650**
  in intestinal tract **1651**
  in larynx **1278**
  nasal **1876**
  obstruction, laryngotracheal and sudden death **577**
  ocular **1822**
  in throat 1650
  in trachea 1278
  in vagina 1117
Foreign proteins, sensitization to **485**
Foreskin 1894
"Forking" of aqueduct of Sylvius causing hydrocephalus **863**, *864*
Formaldehyde 530, 535
Formaldehyde sulfoxalate 535
Formamino glutamic acid 186
Formiminoglutamic acid 327
Formula, milk *see* Milk formula
Formulas, milk *see* Cow's milk
Fornix 1819
Four X chromosomal constitution 311
Fourteen and six per second positive spike dysrhythmia **982**, *985*
Fourth ventricle 862
  tumors **943–944**
Fox 691, 755
Fractures 1729. *See also particular bone.*
  base of skull **968**, **970**
  clavicle in newborn 81
  in Cushing's syndrome **1100**
  in eosinophilic granuloma 1249
  of extremities 1711
  multiple, and battered child syndrome 557
  through paranasal sinuses 968
  pathologic 1279, **1734**
  of petrous bone 969
  skull *see* Skull fractures
Fragilitas ossium *see* Osteogenesis imperfecta
Framework marrow 188
Franceschetti syndrome *see* Treacher-Collins syndrome
Fraternal twins *see* Twins, fraternal
Freckles *see* Ephelis
Fredet-Ramstedt operation 1611
Free fatty acids 218, 366, 373
  in diabetes mellitus 344
  sebum 1815
Freemartins 123
"Free" thyroxine **1063**
Freezing, of milk 157
Frei test **776**
"French-blues" 571
Frenulum linguae 81, 1851
Frequency 340, 679
Fresh frozen plasma transfusions 1235, 1236, **1238–1240**
Freshwater drownings **525**
Fretfulness 671
Friction rub 512
  in coccidioidomycosis 789
Friction rub, pericardial 494, 499, **1425**
Friedreich's ataxia 377, 851, **922–923**
  and cardiac involvement 1433
"Friedreich's foot" 922
"Frog breathing" 69, 1256
Froin syndrome **956**

Frontal abscess **1011–1015**, 1012, 1014
Frontal bossing **1841–1842**
Frontal lobe epilepsy 982, 988
Frontal meningoencephalocele 861
Frontal sinus **1871**
Frothing 81, 1421
Frostig tests 895
Fructokinase 358
  deficiency 362
Fructose, 356, **358–359**, 372
  intolerance, hereditary 359, **1523**, 1687
  loading test 358
  metabolism **358–359**
Fructose-1-phosphate 358, 1687
  aldolase 359
Fructosuria 356, **358–359**, 362
  in newborn infant 356
Fruits 166
Frustration threshold, low 880
FSF *see* Factor XIII
FSH *see* Follicle-stimulating hormone
Fuadin *see* Stibophen
Fucose 414
Fuel oil 530, **538–540**
"Fugitive swelling" 812
Functional constipation 1601
Functional mental retardation **890**
Functional (innocent) murmur **495**
Functional residual capacity (FRC)
  in asthma **465**
  in low-birth-weight infant 91
  of newborn 1258
Fungal infections *see* Mycotic infections
Fungistatic preparations **1788**
"Fungus balls" 786
Funnel chest *see* Pectus excavatum
Furazolidine
  in cholera **612–614**
  in shigellosis 640
Furniture polishes 538
  pneumonitis **1312**
Furosemide, in nephrotic syndrome 1504
Furuncle 219, 701, **1781–1783**
  and craniospinal focal sepsis **1010–1016**
Furunculosis 219, 387, 645, 701, 734

G6PD *see* Glucose-6-phosphate dehydrogenase
"Gage" 572
Gait disturbance 1731
  in basal ganglia degeneration 919–920
  in cerebellar degeneration 921
  in dystonia musculorum deformans 920
  in Pott's disease 673
  in spinal cord tumors **954**
Gal-1-P *see* Galactose-1-phosphate
Galactitol 358
Galactoceramide 911
Galactocerebroside 383
Galactocerebroside-β-galactosidase 385
Galactokinase, 356–357, 358
  deficiency 356, **358**
Galactolipids 135
Galactorrhea 1076, 1126
Galactose 356–358, 369, 371
"Galactose diabetes" 358
Galactose and fructose intolerance, familial **359**

Galactosemia 35, **356–358,** 357, 396, 1523, 1687
    cataracts in 1826
    genetics of 35
    and vomiting 1574
Galactose-1-phosphate 357, 1687
Galactose-1-phosphate uridyl transferase 58, 356, 357, **357–358**
    genetics of 35
Galactose-6-phosphate 357
β-Galactosidase deficiency **383,** 912, 914
Galactosphingosulfatides 917
Galactosuria, in newborn infant 356
Galactosyl ceramidase deficiency 911
Galea, laceration 966, **967**
Galen, vein of 963
Gallop rhythm 370, **495,** 497
    in Graves' disease 1083
Gallstones, in hereditary spherocytosis 1171
Galton 123
Gambian or Mid-African sleeping sickness *see* African
        trypanosomiasis
Gamblegram 221
Gametes 310
Gametocytes 831
Gametogenesis 297
Gamma chains, in hemoglobin **1175–76**
Gamma globulin *see* γ-Globulins
Ganglioneuroblastoma **1112–1113**
Ganglioneuroma **1113**
Ganglionic blocking agents
    in acute glomerulonephritis 1486
    in hypertension 1448
Gangliosides 399, **907–911,** 1829
Gangliosidoses **382, 910–913**
Gangrene, in Rocky Mountain spotted fever 781, 782
Gangrenous stomatitis *see* Noma
"Ganja" 572
Gargoyle facies **399–404**
Gargoylism *see* Hurler's syndrome
Garland-Moorhouse syndrome *see* Spinocerebellar de-
        generation
Garré's sclerosing osteomyelitis 1743
Gases, blood *see* Blood gases
Gas gangrene 1032
Gasoline 530, **538–540**
Gasping 68, 70, *71,* 1256, 1258
    in birth asphyxia 68, 69
Gasp reflex 1256
"Gassing" 572
Gastric *see* Stomach
Gastritis **1637–1638**
    in viral hepatitis 708
Gastrocnemius-soleus muscle 201
Gastroenteritis, 227, **612–614,** 635–637, 641–642, 646–647,
        703, 796
    in cytomegalic inclusion disease 703
    due to *salmonellae* 635–637
Gastrointestinal complaints
    in hemorrhagic fever 848
    in nephrotic syndrome 1500
    in neurologic disorders **849–850**
Gastrointestinal tract 1564–1662. *See also specific dis-
        orders; organs.*
    abdominal pain **1599–1600**
    absorption **1567–1569**
    aganglionic megacolon **1621–1624**
    anatomy, physiology, and biochemistry **1264–1272**

Gastrointestinal tract (*cont.*)
    anorectal conditions 1621–1624, 1625–1630, 1648
    appendicitis **1640–1641**
    bleeding 1166, 1230, **1570–1580**
        in measles 735
        in rubella 762
        in scorpion sting 845
    celiac disease **1584–1588**
    constipation, 207, 273, 284, 708, 1070–1071, **1600–1602**
    corrosive esophagitis **1636**
    defecation **1567**
    in dermatomyositis **510–511**
    diarrhea **1580–1599**
    digestion **1564**
    enzymes **1567–1569**
    esophagitis **1635–1636**
    exudative enteropathy **1594–1595**
    fetal 60
    foreign bodies **1650–1651**
    gastritis **1637–1638**
    hernias **1630–1634**
    heroin, effect on **559–560**
    infections of 226, **1635–1650**
    inflammatory conditions, **1635–1650**
    intussusception 191, 1226, 1233, 1579, 1600, 1620, **1654–
        1659**
    lye ingestion **1636–1637**
    malabsorption syndrome **1583–1595**
    malformations **1603–1635**
        abdominal parietes **1630–1635**
        aganglionic megacolon 1583, **1601,** 1617, **1621–1624**
        anorectal **1625–1630**
        gastric **1608–1612**
        intestinal **1612–1624**
    meconium ileus **1616–1617**
    motility **1564–1567**
    neoplasms 1559, **661–662**
    omphalocele, 82, 1030, **1615, 1634,** 1848
    peptic ulcer **1638–1639**
    perforation 109, 512, 1233, **1618,** 1652
    peritonitis, **1648–1649**
    pruritis ani 1602
    pyloric stenosis **1608–1612**
    rectal incontinence 1602
    regional enteritis **1642–1643**
    rumination syndrome **1576–1578**
    surgical conditions 1612–1663. *See also individual con-
        ditions.*
    symptomatic conditions **1573–1603**
        abdominal pain **1599–1600**
        bleeding 1166, 1230, **1578–1580**
        constipation **1600–1602**
        diarrhea **1580–1599**
        pruritis ani **1602**
        rectal incontinence **1602**
        rumination **1576–1578**
        vomiting **1573–1576**
    tuberculosis of **677–678**
    ulcerative colitis **1644–1647**
    volvulus 1600, **1615**
    vomiting **1573–1576**
Gastroliths 1651
Gastrophilis 807
Gastroschisis 1613, **1634**
Gastrostomy 1605
    for low-birth-weight-infant feeding 109
"Gaucher cells" 383

Gaucher's disease (GL-globosidosis) **383–384**, 911, **913**, 1218, 1688, 1805, 1829
"Gauge" 572
Gaussian curve **232**
Gavage feeding 1909
    of low-birth-weight-infant 106, 109
Gefüllte fish 820
Gel electrophoresis 374
Gemonil (Methbarbital) **999**
General health care **1893–1896**
Generalized convulsions 982, 987, **998–1000**
Generalized elastolysis *see* Cutis laxa
Generalized visceral hemangiomatosis 1693
General pediatric practices **1893–1914**
General therapeutic measures **1908–1911**
Genes 35, 36, **294–321**
    action, biochemical aspects of **318–321**
    activation 307
    duplication 297
    frequency 302
    functions 35
    inactivation 307
    locus 318, 320
    operator 36
Genetic code 35, 296
Genetic control of differentiation 307
Genetic counseling **314–317**
    in Down's syndrome 899–900
Genetic disease, in families and populations **298–303**
"Genetic drift" 303
Genetic factors
    in drug allergy 479
    and growth 240, 242–243
    in lupus erythematosus 508
    in obesity 215
    and tuberculosis **663**
Genetic heterogeneity 316, 320
Genetic load 297
Genetic markers 302
Genetic principles **294–317**
    cytogenetics **308–312**
    dermatoglyphic analysis **313–314**
    developmental genetics **304–308**
    genetic disease in families and populations **298–304**
    molecular genetics **294–298**
Genetic transmission *see* Inheritance
Geniculate ganglion 979
Genital development *see* Gonadal development
Genitalia 83, **1553–1556**, 1894, 1901, 1907
    of newborn, 83
Genital tract infections **1544–1546**
Genitourinary tumors **1560–1562**
Genotypes 300
Gentamicin 581, **587**, 595, 597, *603–605*, 1542
    in bacterial meningitis **603–605**
    in urinary tract infections **1542**
Gentian violet 1791
Genu valgum 201, 331, 404
Genu varus 201
Geographic tongue **1848–1849**
Geophagy, in visceral larva migrans 803
German measles *see* Rubella
Germinal cell aplasia 1144
Germinal center cells 387
Gesell test 265, 892
Gestational age 21
    and amniotic fluid 58

Gestational age (*cont.*)
    and birth size in twins 122
    and birth weight *23*, 23, 125
    and body length 24
    definition 21
    and ears 80, *81*
    and neonatal mortality 111, *112*, **113**
    and organ weights 25
    and prenatal growth 25
    and skin creases *79*
    by ultrasound technique *60*
Gestational diabetes *see* Diabetes, gestational
Gestation time *see* Gestational age
GFR *see* Glomerular filtration rate
GH *see* Growth hormone
Ghon focus 664, *666*
Gianotti-Crosti syndrome **1810**
Giant cell granuloma 1839
Giant cell hepatitis **1684**
Giant cell pneumonia 388, **733**
Giant cells
    in Bancroft's filariasis 811
    in herpes simplex 713
    in lymphogranuloma inguinale 776
    in zoster 1785
Giant cell tumor **1743**
Giant hairy nevus 868
Giant hemangioma, and thrombocytopenia 1236
Giant urticaria
    in loaiasis 812
    in strongyloidiasis 808
Giardia intestinalis (Giardiasis) 175, *838*, 1588
Giardia lamblia see Giardia intestinalis
Gibbs-Donnan equilibrium 222
Gibbus 399
Giemsa's stain 833
von Gierke's disease 307
Gigantism 250, 363
    and acanthosis nigricans 1805
Gilbert's syndrome **1685–1686**
Gilles de la Tourette's syndrome 851
"Gin" 571
Gingival
    disorders **1851–1855**
    fibromatosis **1851**
    hemorrhage 1854
    hyperplasia 404, 998, **1851–1852**, 1868
    lead lines 544
    pigmentation 1093
    swelling, in scurvy 189
Gingivitis **1852**
Gingivostomatitis 714, **1852–1854**
"Girl" 571
GL$_1$-globosidosis *see* Gaucher's disease
Gland, mammary *see* Mammary gland
Glandular fever *see* Infectious mononucleosis
Glandular hypospadias 1554
Glandular tularemia **692**
Glans penis, of newborn 83
Glaucoma 331, **766**, 1251, 1522, 1822, **1825–1826**
    congenital 331, 1822, **1825–1826**
    due to congenital rubella 764, **766**
    in Lowe's syndrome 1522
    in sarcoidosis 1251
Glenn shunt 1407
Gliadin **1584**
Glioblastoma 947

Glioma
  of brainstem **944–945**
  of cerebral hemispheres *947*
  of hypothalamus **946–947**
  intramedullary **954**
  neurofibromatosis 927
  of optic nerve and chiasm **951–952**
  of optic tract 1057
  of pineal gland **946–947**
Gliosis
  in Alper's disease 915
  in toxoplasmosis **840**
  in tuberos sclerosis 925, *926*
Globe (ocular) and adnexae 1817–1818
Globin, in hemoglobin **1175–76**, 1674
Globoid cell leucodystrophy (Krabbe's disease) **385**, 859,
    911, **917**
Globoside 385
Globosidoses **385, 911, 913–914, 916–917**
Globulins 1672
α-Globulins 497
  fetoprotein 1693
  $α_2$-globulin, 389, 499
  in nephrotic syndrome 1501
β-Globulins 1501, 1672
  in kwashiorkor 174
$β_1$C-Globulin 1492
γ-Globulins **387–388**, 497, 499, 508, 684, 1501, 1672
  in asthma 458
  in CSF, in white matter disease 918, 919
  in *Herpesvirus hominus* infection **716**
  in malaria 832
  and rubella during pregnancy **764**
  vaccinia immune **771–772**
  in varicella 702
  in viral hepatitis **709–710, 711**
$γ_{1A}$-Globulin *see* Immunoglobulin G
$γ_A$-Globulin *see* Immunoglobulin A (IgA)
$γ_D$-Globulin *see* Immunoglobulin D (IgD)
$γ_E$ Globulin *see* Immunoglobulin E (IgE)
$γ_G$-Globulin *see* Immunoglobulin G (IgG)
$γ_M$-Globulin *see* Immunoglobulin M (IgM)
Globus pallidus 919, 920
Glomerular filtration **1454, 1461–1462**
  in diarrhea 229
  in utero 89
Glomerular filtration rate (GFR) **1461–1462**, 1484
  in acute glomerulonephritis 1484
Glomerular function **1454**
Glomerular lesions
  in diabetes mellitus, 344, **1509–1510**
  of systemic lupus erythematosus 500, **1492**
Glomerulonephritis 267, 739, **1480–1498**
  acute 440, 485, 650, 701, 1433, **1483–1488**
  chronic, progressive **1489–1498**
  etiology and pathogenesis **1480–1482**
  and myocardial disease 1433
  rapidly progressive **1489**
  and serum sickness 445
  in systemic disease **1492–1498**
Glomerulosclerosis, in diabetes mellitus 344
Glomerulotubular interrelations **1456**
Glossitis 180
  and pyridoxin deficiency 184
Glossoptosis 81, 1842–1843
Glucagon 218, 219, 355, 363, 368, 369, 371, 372, 373
  in the treatment of hypoglycemia 366

Glucagon deficiency, and hypoglycemia 362
Glucagon tolerance test **365**
Glucocerebrosidase 58, 383
Glucocerebroside 383, 907, 911, 913
Glucocorticoids 1093, **1102–1106**. *See also* Adrenocortical
    hormones.
Gluconeogenesis 218, 343, 344, 362, 363, 368, 371
  due to glucocorticoids 1093
Glucose
  absorption 1558
    in cystic fibrosis 417
  administration
    in acute intermittent porphyria 410
    at birth 73
    in diabetes **348**
    in hyperkalemia 1464
    in hypoglycemia **366**
  blood
    in celiac disease **1585**
    control of **350**
    normal newborn values **360**
    source of **360**
  disappearance curve **347**
  erythrocytic enzyme reactions *393*
  feeding of infants of diabetic mothers 127
  in fetal tissues 38, 50, 56
  gestational 17
  metabolism 37–38, 341, *342*, 1558
  and phosphate metabolism 196
  placental secretion of 37
  tolerance test (GTT) 17, 219, 1051
    and ACTH function 1051
    in celiac disease 426, 1585
    cortisone-stressed **345**
    in Cushing's syndrome 1100
    in cystic fibrosis 417, 422
    in diabetes **345–347**
    gestational 17
    in glycogenosis type I 369
    in hyperchylomicronemia and hyperprebetalipopro-
        teinemia, mixed type, familial 376
    in hyperpituitarism 1057
    in hyperprebetalipoproteinemia, familial 376
    in hypoglycemia **365**
    and STH function 1051, 1053–1054, 1057
Glucose-galactose-N-Acetylgalactosamine 381
Glucose-6-phosphatase 36, 372, 1667
  in fetal tissues 36, 181
  in glycogenosis I, absence of, 368
Glucose-1-phosphate 369, 372
Glucose-6-phosphate 369
  deficiency **368–369**
Glucose-6-phosphate dehydrogenase 58, 300, *357*
  deficiency 299, 307, 320, 393, **394–395, 1175, 1679**
    and malaria **832**
    and primaquine 833
    and sulfonamides 586
    and vitamin K 1679, 1681
  in Down's syndrome 899
Glucose phosphate isomerase deficiency **1175**
α-Glucosidase 58, 1035, 1432, 1568
α-1-Glucosidase (acid maltase) deficiency 1035, 1432, 1568
Glucuronic acid 1674
Glucuronolactone loading test 360
Glucuronyl transferase activity 53, 54, 1677
Glucuronyl transferase deficiency 54, 1666, **1680–1681**
"Glue ears" *see* Otitis media, serous

Glue sniffing **528,** *529,* **567–568,** 572
Glutamic acid 132, 297, 327, 336
Glutamic oxalacetic transaminase (GOT) 560, **1671**
 in muscular dystrophy 1031
Glutamic pyruvic transaminase (GPT) **1671**
Glutamine 336, **1584**
Glutathione peroxidase 398, **1175**
Glutathione reductase 395, **1175**
Glutathione synthetase 395, **1175**
Glutathionine 132, 144, **393**
Gluten enteropathy 387, 417, 426, **1584–1588**
Glutethimide 532, 563, **563–564,** 565
Glycerides 135, **373**
Glycerinetellurite-taurocholate agar 612
Glycerol 218
Glycerol guaiacolate 457, 1236
Glycerophosphates 144, 218
Glycerophosphatides **907**
Glycine 52, 55, 174, **328–330,** 334, 336, 337, 339, 405, 1518–1519
Glycinuria hereditary **1518,** 1519
Glycogen 341, 360, 369
 debranching enzymes **370**
 fetal 30, 37, 40
 hepatic 1669
 myopathies **1035**
 placental 37
 storage diseases *see* Glycogenoses
 stores
  in kwashiorkor 173
  in marasmus 171
 synthetase **368**
Glycogenolysis 344
Glycogenoses **367–373,** 424 **1035,** 1432, 1523, **1687–1688**
 and hypoglycemia 362
 and liver disease 1687–1688
 sweat electrolytes in 424
 type O (glycogen synthetase deficiency) **368**
 type I (G-6-phosphatase deficiency) **369–370**
 type Ia 369
 type Ib 369
 type II (cardiomegalic *or* Pompe's disease) 370, 915, **1035,** 1432
 type IIa 370
 type IIb **370**
 type III (debranching enzyme deficiency) **370–371**
 type IIIa, b, c, and d *371*
 type IV (amylopectinosis *or* long-chain storage disease) **371**
 type V (McArdle's disease, total phosphorylase deficiency **371,** 1035
 type VI (partial phosphorylase deficiency) **372**
 type VII (phosphofructokinase deficiency) **372**
 type VIII **372**
 type IXa and b **372**
 type X **372**
 undefined and mixed types 372
Glycol *530*
Glycolipids 907, 914
Glycolysis
 and birth hypoxia 42
 in erythrocyte 392
 in fetal tissues 36, 38
Glycolytic and related pathways of erythrocyte **1172–1174,** *1173*
Glycopeptide **580–581**
Glycoprotein, in stool of cystic fibrosis 414

β-Glycosidase 1568
 deficiency **383,** 1568
Glycosides 1422
Glycosuria **344–355,** 1516–1517, **1521–1524**
 in acrodynia 550
 in colloid brainstem cyst 946
 in Cushing's syndrome 1100
 in cystinosis 1522
 in diabetes mellitus **344–355**
 in Fanconi syndrome **1521–1524**
 in glucose-galactose malabsorption 1591
 in intracranial bleeding 963
 renal **1516–1517**
 type B 1517
 Wilson's disease 1523
Glycosyl ceramidase defect **911,** 913
Glyoxylic acid 330
Gnathostoma spingerum 807
Gnathostomiasis 1792
Goat 821
Goat's milk 162
Goiter **1077–1082**
 adolescent **1080**
 congenital 55
 and deaf mutism **1068**
 endemic **1077–1079**
 familial **1080**
 due to goitrogenous agents **1079**
 Hashimoto's struma **1080**
 iodine deficiency **1077–1079**
 lingual thyroid **1081–1082**
 of newborn, transient, with hypothyroidism 1077
 simple goiter **1077–1082**
  etiology **1077**
  treatment **1080–1081**
 thyroglossal duct "cysts" **1081–1082**
 thyroiditis, subacute **1082**
Goitrogens 55, 1059, 1079
"Gold dust" 571
Goldenhar syndrome *see* Ocular-auriculo-vertebral dysplasia
Gold therapy
 and aplastic anemia 1166
 in rheumatoid arthritis 507
 and thrombocytopenia 1236
Golgi apparatus 399
Gomori's methenamine silver technique 842
Gonadal agenesis 1842
Gonadal development **241–242**
 stages of 241
Gonadal dysgenesis (Turner's syndrome) 309, 310, 903, 1116, 1130, **1139–1144,** 1150, 1557, 1842
 and horseshoe kidneys 1557
 male pseudohermaphrodism as a variant of **1138–1139**
Gonadal dysplasia *see* Gonadal dysgenesis
Gonadectomy 1142, 1147
Gonadotropin
 in cryptorchidism **1555**
 deficiency 1052, **1055**
 excess and sexual precocity **1126–1127**
 in gonadal dysgenesis 1140, 1142
 in hepatoblastoma 1693
 -producing tumors 1126
 in Silver syndrome **1706**
Gondi 839
Gonioscopic examination 1825
Gonitomy **1825**

Gonococcal arthritis 514, 515
Gonococcal conjuctivitis 1819
Gonococcal urethritis 1544
Gonococcal vaginitis 1117, 1544
Gonorrheal ophthalmia *see* Ophthalmia, gonorrheal
Gonorrheal ophthalmia neonatorum 1819
Goodpasture's syndrome 446, 1464, 1482, **1494**
"Goofballs" 571
"Goose flesh," in heroin withdrawal 562
Gordan-Armstrong incubator 104
GOT *see* Glutamic oxalacetic transaminase
Gout **338**, 368, 370, 514–516, **1508**
  arthritis 338, 514, 515, 516
  in glycogenosis type I 368
  nephropathy **1508**
Gower's sign, in Duchenne pseudohypertrophic muscular dystrophy **1030**, *1031*
Gower's type muscular dystrophy 1031
GPT *see* Glutamic pyruvic transaminase
Gradenigo syndrome **1888**
Graft versus host disease **388**
Gram-negative bacteria 580-581
  IgM in antibodies against 435
Gram-positive bacteria **490–493**, **496–497**, 580–581, 583, **596**, **598–609**, **622–635**, **644–647**, **647–652**
Gram-stained urinary sediment examination 1541
Grand mal epilepsy 982, **987**
Granulocytes *1157, 1203*
Granulocytic leukemia
  acute **1214**
  chronic **1214**
Granulocytopenia, in aplastic anemia 1166. *See also* Leucopenia.
Granuloma annulare **1763**
Granulomas
  in actinomycosis **786**
  amebic of skin, **829–830**
  in blastomycosis *788*
  in brucellosis 611
  in cat scratch disease 698
  in sarcoidosis **1250–1251**
  due to tuberculosis 668
Granulomatosis, military, due to *Vibrio fetus* 597
Granulomatous adenitis, due to mycobacteria 690
Granulomatous arteritis (Takayasu's disease) 960
Granulomatous disease, chronic **396–398**, **1206**
Granulomatous uveitis **1827**, 1828
Granulosa cell tumor **1128**
Grasp reflex 76, *85*, **87**, 854
"Grass" 572
Grass pollen 464
Graves' disease **1082–1087**
"Gray baby" syndrome 588, 594
Gray matter diseases *see* Cerebral gray matter diseases
"Gray syndrome," due to chloramphenicol 1677
Great toe(s)
  in gout 338
  underdevelopment of, in myositis ossificans 1034
Great vein of Galen, arteriovenous fistula 1396
"Greenies" 571
Greulich-Pyle standards 240
Grimacing 671, 851
Griseofulvin **1788**
  and acute intermittent porphyria 410
Ground itch 806
"Growing pains" 494

Growth hormone 170, 176, 218, 219, 241, 249, **343**, **1049**
  deficiency 320
  and growth 239, 243
  and hypoglycemia 361
  peripheral resistance to **1056**
  in treatment of hypoglycemia 366
Growth, physical **232–251**, 399
  abnormal growth **248–251**
  acceleration and 235
  in adolescence 241
  "antitemplates" 239
  arrest *see* Growth retardation; Short stature
  assessment in perinatal period 244
  and biometry **232–235**
  and body fat 217, 236
  and bone 236
  caloric requirements for 130
  "catch-up" **237**, 243
  cellular **237**
  chemical **237**
  clinical appraisal of **244–248**
  control of **237–239**
  control center 239
  deceleration and 235
  distance curves *235*
  disturbances *see* Growth retardation; Abnormal growth; Short stature; Overgrowth
  embryonic 21
  environmental factors and 240
  factors influencing 238, 240, **242–243**
  failure *see* Growth retardation; Short stature
  fetal **21–28**
  of head 236
  history *1898*, **1902**
  illness 243
  inhibition, due to glucocorticoids 1093
  inhibition factors 239
  in kwashiorkor 173
  linear 240
  longitudinal study of 235
  long-term trend, secular 239
  in low-birth-weight infant **105**, **116**
  lymphoid tissue 236
  maturity 240
  of muscle 236
  and nitrogen requirements 133
  nutritional requirements for **128–148**
  of organs **21–28**, 33, **236**
  overgrowth 250
  parental size 245
  patterns **235–244**
  percentiles *234*
  prediction of 241
  prenatal factors 238
  prepubertal 242
  rate of **235–244**
  retardation *see* Growth retardation
  socioeconomic conditions and 240
  standards of 245
  stunting *see* Growth retardation
  techniques of measurements **245**
  in twins **238–239**
  and weight 235
Growth, retardation 26, 219, **248–250**, 340, 404, **1052–1056**, **1841–1842**. *See also* Dwarfism.
  in chronic renal disease **1468**
  in congenital adrenal hyperplasia **1096**

Growth, retardation (cont.)
  in congenital heart disease 1402, **1636**
  constitutional delay and 249
  in craniopharyngioma 952
  in cretinism 1074
  in Cushing's syndrome **1100**
  in cystic fibrosis **419**
  in diabetes mellitus 344
  in familial dysautonomia 1040
  in Fanconi syndrome 1521
  fetal **26–28, 33**
    hematocrit in 65
    hemoglobin in 65
  in glycogenosis type I 368
  in glycogenosis type VI 372
  in histidinemia 327
  in hypercalcemia, idiopathic 207
  in hypocaloric dwarfism 170
  in hypothyroidism juvenile acquired **1075–1076**
  intrauterine see Small-for-age newborn
  and malnutrition 176, 239, 243
  in marasmus 171
  in Maroteaux-Lamy syndrome 404
  in pheochromocytoma 1109
  in renal tubular acidosis, distal **1525**
  skeletal 212
  in tetralogy of Fallot 1403
  in tricuspid atresia 1407
  in twins 121
  in vitamin D resistant rickets 204
Grunt 75
  respiratory 81
Grunting in R.D.S. 1261
GSH (reduced glutathione) see Glutathione
GSH-peroxidase 393
GSSG (oxidized glutathione) see Glutathione
Guaiacolate 457
Guanase 340
Guanethidine 1467
  in Graves' disease 1065
Guanidine **695**
Guanine 294
Guanine phosphoriboryl transferase 58
Guanylic acid 339
Guarnieri bodies **770**
Guillain-Barré syndrome 485, 718, 746, 754, **1006–1008,** 1152, **1325,** 1447
Guinea pig inoculation 691
Guinea worm see Dracunculus medinensis
Gum arabic 1312
Gummas, syphilitic 657
Gums see Gingiva
Gunn rat 1680
Günther's disease see Congenital erythropoietic porphyria
Guthrie test **325**
Gynecomastia 1129, 1136, 1144
  in boys 241
  in Klinefelter's syndrome (XXY) 903

"H" 572
HAA see Hepatitis-associated antigen (HAA)
Habit spasms **851**
Habitual vomiting **1574**
Haemophilus influenzae infections 423, 439, 585, 596, **598–609, 618–620,** 1286, **1292,** 1329, 1887

Haemophilus influenzae infections (cont.)
  bronchiolitis **1292**
  cellulitis **1782**
  conjunctivitis **1820**
  empyema 1329
  epiglottis 1286
  meningitis 439, **598–608**
Haemophilus pertussis see Bordetella pertussis
Haff disease 1035
Hageman factor see Factor XII
Hailey-Hailey disease see Benign familial pemphigus
Hair 241, **1123–1124, 1759–1761.** See also various body areas.
  abnormalities **1759–1761**
    in albinism 326
    in argininosuccinic aciduria 334
    in hypothyroidism 1076
    in incontinentia pigmenti 1804
    in kwashiorkor 173
    in marasmus 171
    in phenylketonuria 324
  axillary **1123–1124**
  follicle disorders 1755
  pubic **1123–1124**
  shaft abnormalities **1759**
"Hair-ball" tumor 271, **1651**
"Hair-on-end" appearance (radiography)
  in sickle-cell disease 1177
  in thalassemia 1182
Half-skimmed milk see Cow's milk
Hallermann-Streiff syndrome 1831, 1838, 1841, 1842
Hallervorden-Spath disease **920**
Hallucinations 287, 501, 522, **566–569,** 571
  and LSD 568
  and marihuana use 566
  and peyote 569
Hallucinogens **568–569,** 571
Halo nevus **1801**
"Halo" sign 60
Halzoun, in fascioliasis 817
Hamartoma 13, 1055, 1125, 1693
Hamman-Rich syndrome see Pulmonary fibrosis, chronic
"Hammered silver" cranial appearance 1699
Hand and wrist, radiography for bone age **240**
Handedness 277
  in minimal cerebral dysfunction syndrome 880
Hand, foot, and mouth disease **751**
Hand-foot syndrome, in sickle-cell disease 1176, 1743
Handicapped children, health services 9
Handicaps
  of low-birth-weight infant 106, *114,* **115–117**
  of small-for-age newborn *114,* **115–117**
Hand, in achondroplasia *1722*
Hand-Schüller-Christian disease 909, 913, 1055, 1245, **1247–1249,** 1702, 1740
Handwashing compulsions 286
Hansel's stain 448, 460
H.A.P. see Heredopathia atactica polyneuritiformis
Haptens 445
Haptoglobin 390
"Hard stuff" 572
Hardy-Weinberg principle 302
Harelip see Cleft palate
Harlequin color change, in low-birth-weight infant 97
"Harlequin fetus" 1757
Harrison's groove 200, 1714

"Harry" 572
Hartmanella 830
Hartnup disease 181, 321, **851**, 923, 1042, **1518**, 1595
Harvester ant 844
"Hash" 572
Hashimoto's struma 211, **1079–1080**
    and Graves' disease 1084
Hashish *see* Marihuana
Hashitoxicosis 1084
Hassall's corpuscles 388
Haverhill fever *see* Rat-bite fever
"Hay" 572
Hay fever *see* Allergic rhinitis
HBB *see* 2-(α-Hydroxybenzyl)-benzimidazole (HBB)
HbG$_{Chesapeake}$ 1179
HbG$_{Kansas}$ 1179
HbG$_{Ranier}$ 1179
HbG$_{Yakima}$ 1179
25-HCC *see* 25-Hydroxycholecalciferol
HCG *see* Human chorionic gonadotropin
Head 75, 79–80, 236, **1695–1705**, **1900**, **1905**. *See also*
        Skull; Cranial.
    circumference 245, 247, *858*
    control, in vertical position 854
    enlargement 500, 624, **851**, 859, **862–864**, **1695**
        in neurologic disease **851**
        sudden, in bacterial meningitis 600
    examination *1900*, 1905
    growth and 236
    in hydrocephalus **862–864**, *865*
    injury *see* Craniocerebral trauma
    of low-birth-weight infant 88, 236
    in mental retardation 892
    of newborn *see* Newborn
    nodding *see* Spasmus nutans
    in relation to birth weight 25, 27
    rolling 274
        rumination 1578
    tilt **852**, **1834**
        in posterior fossa tumor **933–941**, 942–943
    trauma *see* Craniocerebral trauma
    variations in shape **1695–1700**
    variations in size **1695**
Headaches 454, 456, 459, 501, 569, 599, 770, 783, **853**
    in acute glomerulonephritis 1484
    in adenoviral disease 725
    in African trypanosomiasis 834
    in amebic meningoencephalitis 830
    in brain tumors 437, **938**, 942, 943
    in brucellosis 611
    in cerebral cysticercosis 818
    in cerebral embolism 962
    in cerebrovascular malformations 963
    in coarctation of aorta 1337
    in coccidioidomycosis 789
    due to Coxsackie viruses 750
    in craniospinal focal sepsis **1010–1016**
    in cryptococcosis 794
    in encephalitis 1016–1023
    in hemorrhagic fever 847
    in herpangina 751
    in Hurst disease 918
    in lymphocytic choriomeningitis 729
    in measles 732
    in meningococcal infections 623
    in migraine **1002**

Headaches *(cont.)*
    in murine typhus 780
    in mycoplasma infections 625
    in paragonimiasis 816
    in pheochromocytoma **1109–1110**
    in poliomyelitis **744–746**
    in pseudotumor cerebri 958
    in rabies 765
    in rickettsial infection 779
    in rickettsialpox 783
    in Rocky Mountain spotted fever 781, 782
    in schistosomiasis 814
    in scrub typhus 783
    as seizure equivalent 991
    and sinusitis **1876**
    in trichinosis 809
    in tuberculous meningitis 671
    in tularemia 692
    in viral hepatitis 708
Head-banging 273
Head louse **845**, **1796–1797**
Head Start Program 9, 10
Heaf test **680–682**
Health care 1–7, 15–21, **1893–1914**
    comprehensive 6
    deprivation 6
    and environment 6
    periodic evaluation 7
    and prejudice 6
    prenatal 15–21
    and socioeconomic factors 1, 3, 6
Health services
    development of 8
    handicapped children 9
    prenatal **7**, 15–21
Health supervision **1893**
Health visits, frequency of, **1893**
Hearing
    evaluation 1833
    loss *see* Deafness
    in low-birth-weight infant **116**
Heart. *See also* Cardiac; Cardiovascular diseases; Circu-
        latory system.
    abnormalities
        and asplenia 1217
        and brain abscess **1011–1013**
        in Chagas' disease **836**
        in cretinism 1071
        in cystic fibrosis 413
        in Fabry's disease 384–385
        in glycogenosis type II 370, 1432
        in mucopolysaccharidoses 399, 404
        in rheumatic fever 490–495, 497–499, 501
        due to rubella, congenital *765*
        in systemic lupus erythematosus **508–509**
    arrhythmias 111
    at birth 75, **81**
    block 212, 499
        in Chagas' disease 836
        congenital 82
        in sarcoidosis 1252
    murmurs *see* Murmurs
    muscle function and calcium 196
    rate
        fetal 49
        of low-birth-weight infant 96
        of newborn 75, 82

Heart (cont.)
  size, in Addison's disease 1093
  sounds 1338–1341
    abnormalities 1363–1368
    in newborn 71, 82
Heartbeat disorders 1363–1370. See also Arrhythmias;
    AV block; Tachycardia; Bradycardia.
Heart failure, congestive 97, 376, 428, 494, 497, 499–501,
    513, 1336–1337, 1419–1425, 1533
  in acute glomerulonephritis 1484
  in anomalous pulmonary venous drainage 1413
  in aortic stenosis 1388
  in congenital heart diseases 1335
  in cystic fibrosis 420
  in diphtheria 616
  in Friedreich's ataxia 922
  in hypoplastic left heart complex 1416
  in β-thalassemia 1181
  in thiamine deficiency 179
  in transposition of the great arteries 1409–1410
  treatment 501
  in trichinosis 809
"Hearts" 571
Heart valve prostheses, and hemolysis 1186
Heat and urticaria 478
Heat loss, in low-birth-weight infant 97, 105. See also
    Thermoregulation.
Heat production see Thermogenesis
Heat prostration, in cystic fibrosis 422
Heat stress 424
"Heavenly blue" 572
Heavy metal poisoning 356
Heavy metals 1509
Heel to ear maneuver 86, 87
Height 215, 245–247, 1900, 1904
  crown-rump 247
  normal growth 1923–1924
  and obesity 217
  sitting 247
  standing 245, 246
Height-weight tables 215
Heinz bodies 395, 1179, 1217
Hektoen variant, G6PD deficiency 395
Hela cells 724
Helenine 696
Helicopter transportation, for low-birth-weight infant
    102
Heliotrope erythema of eyelids and face 1032
Helium 217
Helium washout curves, in asthma 465
Helix 1882
Heller procedure 1576
Heller's disease 908, 914
Helminthic diseases 797–825
Helminths see Parasites, helminths
Hemadsorption-inhibition, in parainfluenza 723
Hemagglutination-inhibition (HI)
  in adenoviral disease 726
  and measles 733
  in rubella 760, 762–763, 767–768
Hemagglutination test
  in Chagas' disease 836
  in ecchinococcosis 822
  in toxoplasmosis 841
Hemangiectatic hypertrophy of a limb 930
Hemangioblastoma, in Von Hippel-Lindau's disease
    929

Hemangiomas 78, 81, 929, 1236, 1285, 1620, 1693, 1812–
    1814, 1848
  of bowel 1620
  in disseminated hemangiomatosis 929
  and encephalotrigeminal angiomatosis 929
  hepatic 1693
  subglottic 1285
  of tongue 1848
Hemarthrosis 1230, 1238, 1746
  in hemophilia 1238
Hematemesis 189, 456, 514, 1578–1579, 1691
  in hemorrhagic fever 843, 847
  in phycomycosis 795
  in portal hypertension 1219
  in scurvy 191
Hematochezia 1579–1580
Hematocrit 1156
  in asthma 465
  in premature infants 65
Hematoma of scalp 967
Hematopoiesis see Erythropoiesis
Hematoxylin bodies, in systemic lupus erythematosus
    508
Hematuria 207, 330, 340, 509, 514, 1177, 1238, 1490,
    1500, 1509, 1514, 1534, 1885
  in acute glomerulonephritis 1483–1488
  in anaphylactoid purpura 1233
  in bacterial endocarditis 1430
  benign recurrent 1507–1508
  due to menstruation 1136
  in renal vein thrombosis 1534
  in rubella 762
  in sarcoidosis 1252
  in schistosomiasis haematobium infection 814
  in scurvy 188, 189
  in urinary tract infections 1540–1542
Hemazoin 831
Heme 132, 405
  biosynthesis of 542
  in cord blood 64
Hemianopia 1047
  in cerebral arterial thrombosis 962
Hemiatrophy 250, 1706
  facial 853
Hemic cardiac murmurs 1171
Hemiconvulsion 988
Hemicrania 869, 1002
Hemifacial microsomia 1696
Hemihypertrophy 13, 250, 1099, 1706
Hemimelia 1707
Hemiparesis 1012
  in brain tumors 940, 945, 947
  in encephalotrigeminal angiomatosis 929
  in infections of nervous system 1011–1024
Hemiplegia 331, 600, 816, 883, 1002
  in cerebral arterial thrombosis 962
  in measles 735
  due to mumps 738
  in sickle-cell disease 1177
Hemispheric malformation, cerebral 964
Hemivertebra 1715, 1716
Hemizygosity 299, 315
Hemodialysis 385, 1692
  in barbiturate poisoning 565
  in chronic renal failure 1468
  in poisonings 535
  in salicylate poisoning 555

Hemoglobin 144, 308, 405, **1557**
  with altered oxygen affinity 1179–1180
  concentration
    and cyanosis **1377**
    in fetus **1155**
    of newborn 1157–1158
  development of 308
  of fetal blood 66
  heat-stability test 1179
  mean corpuscular concentration *1157*
  structure abnormalities *see* Hemoglobinopathies
  synthesis abnormalities *see* Thalassemias
  variants 318
Hemoglobin A ($a_2\beta_2$ 6 glulys) 94, 297, **1175, 1178**
  in cord blood 64, 65
  in growth-retarded fetus 65
Hemoglobin A, β-chain of 297
Hemoglobin A_2 297, 1175
Hemoglobin A_2, δ-chain of 297
"Hemoglobin Barts" 1183
Hemoglobin, β-chain of 300
Hemoglobin C 300
Hemoglobin C disease 1178–1179
Hemoglobin C-beta thalassemia disease 1184
Hemoglobin $C_{Georgetown}$ 1178
Hemoglobin C_{Harlem} 1178
Hemoglobin D 1180
Hemoglobin E 1180
Hemoglobin electrophoresis **1178,** 1179–1180
Hemoglobinemia 522, 525
Hemoglobin F 94, 297, **1155, 1175**
  hereditary persistence of **1179**
Hemoglobin F, γ-chain of 297
Hemoglobin $gamma_4$ (Barts) 1184
Hemoglobin $G_{Chesapeake}$ 1179
Hemoglobin G_{Kansas} 1179
Hemoglobin Gower-2 ($a_2\epsilon_2$) 308
Hemoglobin G_{Ranier} 1179
Hemoglobin G_{Yakima} 1179
"Hemoglobin H disease" 1184
Hemoglobin Lepore 297
Hemoglobin Lepore disease 297, **1179**
Hemoglobin M disease 1179
Hemoglobin S 300, **1176–1180**
Hemoglobin$_{Zurich}$ 1179
Hemoglobinopathies 1175, **1176–1180.** *See also individual diseases.*
Hemoglobinuria 390, 522, 525, 1175, 1184
  paroxysmal, nocturnal **1187**
Hemolysis 396, 407, **1169–1198.** *See also* Hemolytic anemias.
  by hydrogen peroxide 141
Hemolytic anemia 110, 393–394, 708, 765, **1169–1201,** 1705, 1743
  bone lesions in **1743**
  in congenital erythropoietic porphyria 407
  in congenital rubella 765
  in viral hepatitis 708
Hemolytic anemias 110, 393–394, 708, 765, **1169–1201,** 1705, 1743. *See also specific diseases.*
  ABO erythroblastosis 1187, 1189, **1197–1198**
  autoimmune acquired **1184–1185**
  2,3-diphosphoglycerate mutase deficiency 1174
  drug-induced **1175,** 1185–1186
  elliptocytosis, congenital **1172**
  enzymatic defects of erythrocytes **1172–1175**

Hemolytic anemias (*cont.*)
  erythroblastosis fetalis **1187–1198**
  extracorpuscular hemolytic disorders 1169, **1184–1199**
  favism **1175**
  glucose-6-phosphate dehydrogenase (G6PD) deficiency **1174–1175**
  glucose phosphate isomerase deficiency **1174**
  glutathione peroxidase deficiency **1175**
  glutathione reductase deficiency **1175**
  glutathione synthetase deficiency **1175**
  hemoglobin C disease **1178–1179**
  hemoglobin M disease **1179**
  hemoglobinopathies **1176–1180**
  hemosiderosis, pulmonary idiopathic **1186**
  hexokinase deficiency **1175**
  hypersplenism **1186**
  intracorpuscular hemolytic disorders **1169–1184**
  membrane anomalies of erythrocytes **1170–1172**
  nonspherocytic hemolytic anemia, congenital **1175**
  phosphofructokinase deficiency **1175**
  phosphoglycerate kinase deficiency **1175**
  pyknocytosis, infantile **1187**
  pyruvate kinase deficiency **1175**
  sickle-cell anemia **1176–1178**
  sickle-cell–hemoglobin C disease **1179**
  spherocytosis, hereditary **1170–1172**
  stomatocytosis, congenital **1172**
  thalassemias **1180–1184**
  triosephosphate isomerase deficiency **1175**
  vitamin E deficiency anemia 110, **1187**
β-Hemolytic streptococcus *see* Streptococcus, β-hemolytic
Hemolytic thrombocytopenic-uremic syndrome **1243, 1494–1495**
Hemolytic-uremic syndrome 1464, **1494–1495**
Hemophilia 299, 302
  arthritis 514
  bone lesions in 1743
  hemarthrosis in **1238**
Hemophilias 1237-1240, 1242. *See also* Factors VIII, IX, XI.
  factor VIII deficiency 1236, **1237–1240,** 1242
  factor IX deficiency **1240,** 1242
  factor XI deficiency **1240,** 1242
Hemophilus influenzae see Haemophilus influenzae
Hemoptysis 422, **1277–1278,** 1305
  in aspergillosis 787
  in blastomycosis 787
  in bronchiectasis **1294**
  in coccidioidomycosis 789
  in hemorrhagic fever 847
  in paragonimiasis 816
  in pulmonary ascariasis 801–802
  in *Schistosoma japonicum* infection 814
Hemorrhage
  and battered child syndrome 557
  gastrointestinal 1166, 1230, **1570–1580**
  gingival 1854
  in hypernatremic dehydration 225
  of intestinal mucosa, in shigellosis 639
  intracranial **962–965, 970–972**
  in Letterer-Siwe disease 1247
  in leukemia 1213
  in newborn 75, 80
  in pertussis **629,** 630
  in portal hypertension **1219**
  with salicylate therapy 501

Hemorrhage (cont.)
  subperiosteal 188
  subpleural 188
Hemorrhagic chickenpox 702
Hemorrhagic disorders 1229–1244
  classification 1230
  clinical aspects 1232–1244
    blood vessel anomalies, disorders due to 1229–1233
      anaphylactoid purpura 1232–1233
      cutis hyperelastica 1232
      hereditary hemorrhagic telangiectasia 1232
      infections, severe 1232
      pulmonary hemosiderosis, idiopathic 1232
      secondary vascular purpuras 1232
    coagulation disorders 1237–1243
      acquired 1241–1423
      congenital 1237. See also Hemophilias; Coagulation factor deficiencies.
    platelet disorders 1233–1237
      functional platelet disorders 1236. See also Thrombasthenia; Thrombopathias.
      thrombocytopenias 1233–1236
      von Willebrand's disease 1236–1237
  diagnosis 1229–1231
Hemorrhagic fevers 846–848
Hemorrhagic smallpox 771
Hemorrhoids 1603, 1660
Hemosiderin 145, 831, 1158, 1219
Hemosiderosis, pulmonary, idiopathic 1186, 1232, 1320
Hemostasis
  disorders of 1229–1244. See also specific diseases; Hemorrhagic disorders.
  mechanisms 1228–1229
Hemostatic agents 1238
Hemothorax 1329
"Hemp" 572
Henderson-Hasselbalch equation 222, 1258
Henoch-Schönlein purpura 513, 1232–1233, 1307, 1492–1493
  renal manifestations 1492–1493
Heparin 144, 375, 1229
  in asthma 458
  in intravascular coagulation 624, 1242
Heparinlike anticoagulants 1242
Heparitin sulfate 399, 914, 915
Hepatic see Liver
Hepatic porphyrias 409–411
"Hepatiticomimetic" infections 706
Hepatitis 507, 560, 574, 706–712, 739, 1684, 1688, 1689–1690
  in amphetamine addict 565
  cholestatic
    and erythromycin estolate 585
    and lincomycin 586
  due to Coxsackie viruses 749
  and heroin abuse 560
  and hypoglycemia 362
  and isoniazid 685
  neonatal 198, 391, 711–812, 1684
    in rubella, congenital 765
  viral 201, 706–712
Hepatitis-associated antigen (HAA) 707, 708, 1609, 1909
Hepatoblastoma 1693, 1706
  and sexual precocity in boys 1126
Hepatocellular injury 1671–1672
Heptatocellular neoplasms 1693
Hepatocyte 1663

Hepatolenticular degeneration see Wilson's disease
Hepatomas 326, 370
Hepatomegaly 1312, 1421, 1687–1689. See also Hepatosplenomegaly.
  in argininosuccinic aciduria 334
  in brucellosis 611
  in chronic granulomatous disease 396 ·
  in Coxsackie virus 750
  in cytomegalic inclusion disease 703
  in familial hyperchylomicronemia 374
  in fascioliasis 817
  in galactosemia 357
  in gangliosidosis, generalized 382
  in Gaucher's disease 383
  in glycogenoses 368–372
  in graft versus host disease 388
  in Hand-Schüller-Christian syndrome 1248
  in heart failure 1421
  in hemorrhagic fever 848
  in hepatitis 1690
  in hereditary fructose intolerance 359
  in Hunter's syndrome 399
  in Hurler's syndrome 399
  in infectious mononucleosis 718
  in leptospirosis 621
  in leukemia 1209
  in lipidoses 381–385
  in malaria 832
  in mucopolysaccharidoses 398–404
  in Niemann-Pick disease 384
  in Rocky Mountain spotted fever 782
  in schistosomiasis 813–814
  in sepsis neonatorum 597
  in sickle-cell anemia 1177
  in systemic lupus erythematosus 509
  in β-thalassemia 1180–1181
  in Tay-Sachs disease 381
  in tyrosinemia 1523
  in visceral larva migrans 802
Hepatorenal syndrome 1511
Hepatosplenomegaly. See also Hepatomegaly; Splenomegaly.
  in Chagas' disease 836
  in Chediak-Higashi syndrome 1206, 1802
  in gray matter diseases 913–914
  in histoplasmosis 792
  in Hodgkin's disease 1223
  in Hurler's disease 914
  in hyperchylomicronemia, and hyperprebetalipoproteinemia, mixed type, familial 376
  in hyperprebetalipoproteinemia, familial 376
  in rubella, congenital 765
  in toxoplasmosis, congenital 840
  in Wilson's disease 920
Hep$_2$ cells 724
Herald patch 1809
Herculean appearance, in congenital myotonia 1031
Hereditary angioneurotic edema (Osler-Quincke's disease) 389, 440
Hereditary episodic adynamia 1034–1035
Hereditary fructose intolerance see Fructose intolerance, hereditary
Hereditary hepatic coproporphyria 411
Hereditary hemorrhagic telangiectasia see Telangiectasia
Hereditary lipodystrophy 1514
Hereditary metabolic diseases 318–320

Hereditary methemoglobinemia *see* Methemoglobinemia, hereditary
Hereditary nephritis **1514–1515**
Hereditary nonspherocytic hemolytic anemias *see* Hemolytic anemias
Hereditary osteolysis 1514
Hereditary spherocytosis *see* Spherocytosis
Hereditary thymic dysplasia 388
Hereditary tyrosinemia 1688
Heredity *see* Inheritance
Heredofamilial neuritis 1008
Heredopathia atactica polyneuritiformis *see* Refsum's syndrome
Hering and Breuer inflation reflex 1258
Hermaphrodism 1130, **1133, 1139**
Hernias **1630–1635**
    diaphragmatic 71, 73, 75, 81, 82, **1632–1634**
    epigastric 1632
    femoral 1632
    hiatal 1578, 1607
    in Hurler's syndrome 599, 914
    inguinal 83, **1631–1632**
    intrauterine diagnosis *61*
    of linea alba 1632
    in pertussis 630
    retrosternal 1633
    umbilical 82, 899, **1630–1631**
        in cretinism 1071
Heroin 54, 533, **559–563, 573–575**
    abstinence syndrome **562–563**
    in newborn 54, **573–575**
    toxicity, acute **563**
Herpangina **1853**
    due to Coxsackie viruses **751**
"Herpes gladiatorium" 714
Herpes hominis virus infections 473, 703, 704, 711, **712–717, 1823**
    dermatitis, primary **814**
    encephalitis 1016, **1019**
    gingivostomatitis 714, **1853**
    keratitis **714–715**
    keratoconjunctivitis **714**
    in kwashiorkor 174
    meningitis 715
    in newborns **715**
"Herpes labialis" *see Herpes hominis* virus infections
Herpeslike virus (HLV) and Burkitt's tumor 1227
Herpes simplex *see Herpes hominis* virus infections
Herpes zoster **1784–1786**
    in Hodgkin's disease 1225
    pneumonitis 1785
"Herpetic whitlows" 714
Herxheimer reaction 658
Hess, Julius 101
Heterochromatin 1665
Heterochromia iridum 1802, 1885
Heterophil agglutination test, in infectious mononucleosis **718**
Heterophil antibodies **718–719**
Heterozygosity, genetic **299, 315**
Heterozygote carrier
    of cystic fibrosis 425
    in X-linked inheritance 299, 300, 315
Heterozygous state 299
Hexachlorobenzene, and acquired cutaneous porphyria 411
Hexachlorophene 644, 1783

Hexaethylphosphate 550
Hexapoda *see* Insects
Hexobarbital 54
Hexokinase 358, **1175**
Hexokinase deficiency **1175**
Hexosaminadase deficiency 382, **909,** 911
Hexose monophosphate shunt 393, 396
    of erythrocyte **1172–1174, 1173, 1178**
Hexose phosphates 144
Hexoside 907
Hexylresorcinol
    in fasciolopsiasis 817
    in trichuriasis **805**
HI antibody *see* Hemagglutination-inhibition antibody
Hiatus hernia *see* Hernia, hiatal
Hiatus semilunaris 1871
High-arched palate 1144, 1838, **1841–1842**
    in gonadal dysgenesis 1141
    in newborn 81
High-birth-weight infant 115, **124–129**
    congenital anomalies in 115
High-calcium vegetables 208
High-carbohydrate feeding 368, 370
High frequency hearing loss 1885
High F-thalassemia 1180
High output states 1341
High-pitched cry 85
    in hypoglycemia of newborn 360
    in kernicterus 1677
    in neonatal narcotic withdrawal syndrome 574
High-protein diet, in glycogenosis type III 371
High-risk pregnancies 18–19, 59
Hilar cell tumors 1119
H. influenzae see Haemophilus influenzae infections
HIOMT **1114–1115**
Hip
    abduction, in spina bifida 874
    coxa plana **1738–1739**
    dislocation, congenital 84, 315, 874, **1746–1750,** 1842
    instability in rickets 201
    pain 1738, 1746, 1750
Hippocratic nails 1761
Hirschsprung's disease *82,* 1601, 1617, **1621–1624**
Hirsutism 220, 912, 1119, 1128, *1761*
Hirudinea 797
Histamine 445, 446, 454, 459, 477, 1041
Histamine test, in dysautonomia 1041
Histidase 37, 43, 327
Histidine 132, **327,** 335, 336
Histidinemia **327**
Histiocytes 775, **1245**
    in lymphogranuloma inguinale 776
Histocompatibility antigens **438**
Histoplasmin skin test 79
Histoplasmosis (*Histoplasma capsulatum*) **791–793,** 1093, 1218, 1225, **1307**
History
    in allergic disease 448
    in epilepsy **992**
    in general health appraisal **1897–1903,** *1898–1900*
    low-birth-weight 17
    obstetrical 17
    and prenatal care 17
Hives *see* Urticaria
HLA system 438
HLV *see* Herpeslike virus
HMP shunt *see* Hexose monophosphate shunt

Hoarse cry 720
Hoarseness
  in heart failure 1421
  in histoplasmosis 791
  in streptococcal pharyngitis 648
  of thiamine deficiency 179
Hodgkin's disease 389, 398, 478, 480, 719, 1218, **1223–1226**
  and cryptococcosis 794
Hofnagel syndrome 853
Holoprosencephaly **860–861,** 1702
Holt-Oram syndrome 1707
Home care
  in diabetes mellitus 351
  of low-birth-weight infant 107
Homeostasis, compositional, in fetus 33
Homeothermic responses, in low-birth-weight infant, 98
Homocysteine 332
Homocystinuria 185, **331–332,** 1708, 1734
Homogenized milk *see* Cow's milk
Homogentisic acid 325, 326
Homogentisic acid oxidase 326
Homonymous hemianopsia 883
  in encephalotrigeminal angiomatosis 929
Homosexuality 1130
Homovanillic acid (HVA) **1111,** 1041
Homozygosity 299, 378
Honey 161
"Honeycomb lungs," in Letterer-Siwe disease 1247
"Hooded" penis **1553**
"Hooked" 571, 582
Hooklets 817
Hooks 812, 818
Hookworm infection 174, 477, **805–807**
"Hophead" 571
Hordeolum **1819**
Hormones. *See also specific hormones.*
  of adrenal cortex
  of anterior pituitary **1048–1049**
  control of pigmentation **1799–1800**
  and fetal development 55
  during gestation 55
  and growth 243
  hydrolysis by placenta 56
  in high-risk pregnancies 59
  ovarian 1115–1120
  of parathyroid 208
  thyroid **1061–1065**
  and vitamin B$_6$ 185
Horner's syndrome 84, 852, **1817–1818**
"Horse" 572
Horse fly 691
Horse serum antitoxin 486
Horse serum sensitization **485**
Horses, and leptospirae 621
Horseshoe kidney **1557**
  in gonadal dysgenesis 1141
Hosiery dermatitis 476
Hospitalization 256
  causes and duration **5**
Hot water burns **519**
House dust 450
House fly 484
  and shigella 639
Household contacts of hepatitis, immune globulin and **709–710**
Household products, as poisons 529
Housing, deteriorated, and lead poisoning **543, 548**

Howell-Jolly bodies 1217
H. parapertussis see Bordetella parapertussis
HPL *see* Lactogenic hormone, placental
H type of tracheoesophageal fistula 1605
"Huffing" 572
Human antitoxin, tetanus **660–661**
Human chorionic gonadotropin (HCG) 1120, 1126
Human immune (gamma) globulin, in measles **735–736**
Human milk *see* Breast milk
Humerus, aseptic necrosis 1177
Humoral antibodies 444
Hunger, in hypoglycemia 361
Hunger pains, in taeniasis 818
Hunter's syndrome 320, **399,** *400–402,* **915,** 1824
Huntington's chorea **919–920**
Hurler's syndrome (gargoylism) 195, 320, **399,** *400–402,* 859, 909, **914,** *915,* 1824, 1831
Hurst disease *see* Necrotizing hemorrhagic leucoencephalitis, acute
Hürthle cell adenocarcinoma, of thyroid 1088
Hutchinson's teeth **656**
Hutchinson's triad 656
HVA *see* Homovanillic acid
Hyaline-like membrane **1262**
Hyaline membrane disease 75, 122, 720, **1261–1265,** 1401
  in twins 122
Hyaluronic acid 1763
Hycanthone, in schistosomiasis 815
Hydantoins, and aplastic anemia 1166
Hydatid cysts **821–823**
Hydatid disease *see* Echinococcosis
Hydralazine 509, **1448, 1467**
Hydramnios 17, **1189,** 1616
  in multiple births 120
Hydranencephaly **861–862,** 865
Hydration **228–231, 522–524, 606, 613–614**
  in bacterial meningitis **606**
  in burns **522–524**
  in diarrhea **613–614**
  in sickle-cell anemia 1178
Hydroarthrosis, intermittent 514, 515
Hydroaxines 84
Hydrocarbon products
  pneumonitis **539, 1312**
  poisoning 530, **538–540**
Hydrocele 83, **1556, 1631–1632,** 1907
Hydrocephalus 84, 399, 608, **851,** 859, **862–868,** 970
  in achondroplasia **1721**
  in basal cell nevus syndrome 931
  in basal skull fracture sequella 970
  in brain tumors **938,** 942, 943, 947
  diagnosis in utero 60, *61*
  meningitis sequela **608**
  due to meningomyelocele 876
  in neurocutaneous melanosis **867,** 929
  in occipital encephalocele 871
  due to subarachnoid hemorrhage 963
  in toxoplasmosis **840**
  in tuberous sclerosis 925
Hydrochloric acid, production of, and heroin use 560
Hydrochlorthiazide 1467, 1521
  in nephrotic syndrome 1504
Hydrocolpos 1550, **1556**
Hydrocortisone 176, 218, 219, 340, 363, 1090–1092, **1093,** 1094–1100, **1102–1106**
Hydrocortisone cyclopentylpropionate, in congenital adrenal hyperlasia **1098**

Hydrocortisone secretion 1093, 1102
Hydrogen ions
  at birth 67, 68
  excretion 1462, 1524
  homeostasis disturbances 225, 228, 229–230
  metabolism 222
  transplacental exchange 66, 67
Hydrogen peroxide 395, 396
Hydrolases 1668
Hydrolysis, placental, of hormones 56
Hydrolytic enzymes
  placental 52
  fetal 53
Hydroma, subepicranial 967
Hydronephrosis 1472, 1556–1557
Hydropericardium 1189
Hydrophthalmos 1522
Hydrops fetalis 60, 61, 84, 1187, 1189
  diagnosis in utero 60, 61
Hydrothorax 1189
Hydroureter 1472
25-Hydroxylation 198
2-(α-Hydroxybenzyl)-benzimidazole (HBB) 695
β-Hydroxybutyric acid 344
25-Hydroxycholecalciferol (25-HCC), in uremia 1467
17-Hydroxycorticosteroids (17-OHCS) 126, 220, 1051
18-Hydroxydesoxycorticosterone 1092, 1095
5-Hydroxyindolacetic acid 184
Hydroxyindole-o-methyl transferase (HIOMT) see
  HIOMT
α-Hydroxy-β-ketoadipate 330
5-Hydroxykynureine 184
11β-Hydroxylase 1092, 1095
17α-Hydroxylase 1092, 1095
21-Hydroxylase 1092, 1095
Hydroxylating activity, of fetal tissues 53
Hydroxylation 186
Hydroxylysine 1763
p-Hydroxyphenyllactic acid 191, 326
o-Hydroxy-phenylacetyl glutamine 324
p-Hydroxyphenylpyruvic acid 43, 191, 325
p-Hydroxyphenylpyruvic acid oxidase 325
α-Hydroxyphytanic acid 379
17-Hydroxyprogesterone 1120–1121
Hydroxyproline 186, 336, 337, 1518, 1716
Hydroxyprolinemia 331
Hydroxproline oxidase 331
Hydroxypyrazolopyrimidine see Allopurinal
4-Hydroxypyrazolopyrimidine 370
Δ⁵-3β-Hydroxysteroid 1097, 1099
Δ⁵-3β-Hydroxysteroid dehydrogenase 40, 1092, 1095–1097
Hydroxystilbamide (-ine)
  in blastomycosis, cutaneous 788
  in kala-azar 838
  in Pneumocystis carinii pneumonia 842, 1312
5-Hydroxytryptamine see Serotonin
5-Hydroxytryptophan decarboxylase 324
25-Hydroxy-vitamin D 197, 201, 203
Hydroxyzine 478, 489, 1808
Hygiene 1893–1896
Hymenal polyp 1556
Hymenal tag 83
Hymenolopsiasis 819–820
Hymenolopsis nana 819–820
Hymenopterous disease 844
Hyperactivity 324, 574, 608, 852, 879, 880, 919–921
  after meningitis 608

Hyperactivity (cont.)
  in minimal cerebral dysfunction syndrome 880
  in neonatal narcotic withdrawal syndrome 574
Hyperacusis, in Tay-Sachs disease 912
Hyperadrenalism 1095–1101
Hyperalanemia 1042
Hyper-β-alaninemia 335
Hyperalanuria 1042
Hyperaldosteronism 1101, 1445
Hyperalimentation, intravenous 109, 135, 168, 1582
Hyperaminoacidemia 174
Hyperammonemia 334
Hyperbaric oxygen see Oxygen, hyperbaric
Hyperbilirubinemia 54–55, 357, 359, 597, 708–712, 1169,
    1170–1201, 1271, 1673, 1676–1670
  conjugated 357, 359, 597, 708–712, 1673, 1681–1687,
      1689–1690
    drug-induced 1681, 1684
    in galactosemia 357
    in hepatitis 708–712, 1689–1690
    in hereditary fructose intolerance 359
    in newborn 1682–1685
    in older children 1686–1687
    in sepsis neonatorum 597
  unconjugated 54–55, 1169, 1170–1201, 1271, 1673, 1676–
      1681, 1685–1686
    and alcohol 55
    due to breast milk 1680
    due to erythroblastosis fetalis 1679
    due to glucuronyl transferase deficiency, inherited
        1680
    due to G6PD deficiency 1679
    in hereditary spherocytosis 1170
    and maternal diabetes 1271, 1681
    in newborn 1676–1681
    in older children 1685–1686
    and phenobarbital 54
Hypercalcemia 195, 203, 207, 208, 209, 1462, 1508, 1699
  band keratopathy in 1824
  due to hypervitaminosis D 205, 207
  idiopathic 203, 207–208
  immobilization 209
  in sarcoidosis 1252
Hypercalciuria 205, 208, 209, 1508, 1527
Hypercapnia 66, 68, 91
Hypercholesterolemia, familial 375
Hyperchylomicronemia, familial 374
Hyperglobulinemia 511, 513
  in dermatomyositis 511
  in ecchinococcosis 822
  in kala-azar 837
  in malaria 832
  in polyarteritis nodosa 514
  in sarcoidosis 1542
  in schistosomiasis 814
  in scleroderma 513
  in SLE 508, 509
  in visceral larva migrans 803
Hyperglycemia 219
  in acrodynia 550
  in Cushing's syndrome 1100
  in diabetes mellitus 344–355
  in intracranial bleeding 963
  and LSD 568
  in offspring of diabetic mothers 216
Hyperglyceridemia see Hypertriglyceridemia

Hyperglycinemias 231, **328–330**
  with hypooxaluria 330
  idiopathic 1519
  ketotic hyperglycinemia **328**
  methylmalonic acidemia **329**
  nonketotic hyperglycinemia **329**
  sarcosinemia **330**
Hyperglycinuria 328–330, 337, 1536
Hyperimmune
  human pertussis gamma globulin 632
  serum globulin 739
  vaccinal gamma globulin **771**
Hyperinflation **1277**, 1296
Hyperinsulinemia 1639
Hyperinsulinism 219, 1639
Hyperirritability *see* Irritability
Hyperkalemia **1034**, **1464**, 1466
  in acute renal failure **1464**
Hyperkalemic paralysis **1034**
Hyperkeratosis 189, 930, **1757–1758**, 1787, 1806, 1838
  follicular, in scurvy 189
  in neurocutaneous syndrome 930
  of palms and soles **1757–1758**
  in vitamin A deficiency *177*
Hyperkinesia 324, 574, 608, 852, **879**, **880**, 919–921
  in basal ganglia degenerations 919–921
  in phenylketonuria 324
Hyperkinetic child 879
Hyperlactic acidemia, in glycogenosis type I 369
Hyperlipemia 374–375, 1484, 1500, 1683
  in acute glomerulonephritis 1484
  Burger-Grutz *see* Hyperchylomicronemia, familial
  fat-induced *see* Hyperchylomicronemia, familial
Hyperlipoproteinemia *see* Hypercholesteremia, familial
  Fredrickson type I *see* Hyperchylomicronemia, familial
  Fredrickson type II *see* Hypercholesteremia, familial
  Fredrickson type III *see* Broad beta hyperlipoproteinemia
  Fredrickson type IV *see* Hyperprebetalipoproteinemia, familial
  Fredrickson type V *see* Hyperchylomicronemia *and* Hyperprebetalipoproteinemia, mixed type, familial
Hyperbetalipoproteinemia, familial **375–376**, 410
Hyperlysinemia **335**
Hypernatremia 222, **229**, 525
  in diabetes insipidus 1150
  in hyperaldosteronism 1101, 1445
Hypernatremic dehydration *see* Dehydration, hypertonic
Hyperopia 1835
Hyperosmolarity 348, 1153
  due to angiocardiography **1363**
Hyperostosis 877
  in hypervitaminosis A **1732**
  infantile, cortical **1741**, *1742*
Hyperoxaluria **330**, 1536
Hyperoxia 105
  and uterine blood flow 44
Hyperparathyroidism 207, **208–210**, 1467, 1508, **1525–1526**, 1536
  in chronic renal disease 1467
  in distal RTA **1525–1526**
  neonatal 208
  primary **208–209**
  secondary 209, **210**
Hyperphosphatemia 208, 209, 212
Hyperphosphaturia 1519

Hyperphospholipidemia 374
Hyperpigmentation 410, 411, **1802**
  in kwashiorkor 173
Hyperpituitarism **1056–1058**
Hyperplastic primary vitreous 1829
Hyperpnea 70, 501, 506
  in acidosis 230
Hyperprebetalipoproteinemia, familial **376**
Hyperprolinemia **330–331**
Hyperproteinemia
  in cystic fibrosis, 422, 428
  in hookworm infection 806
Hyperpyrexia. *See also* Fever.
  in Addison's disease 1093
  in craniopharyngioma 952
  in cystic fibrosis 422
  in diabetes insipidus 1150
  in dysautonomia 1040–1041
  in encephalitis 1016–1023
  and LSD 568
  in neonatal narcotic withdrawal syndrome 574
  in salicylate poisoning **552–556**
Hyperpyruvic acidemia 1042
Hyperreflexia 330
  in spinal cord tumors 955
Hypersensitivity reactions 454, **471–489**, 490, **585**, **1313**
  to heat 489
  to inhaled organic material **1313**
  to light **487–488**
  to the penicillins **585**
  to physical factors **487–489**
Hypersomnia 1056
Hypersplenism 422, **1186**, 1219, **1220–1221**
  in sickle-cell disease 1178
  in β-thalassemia 1183
Hypertelorism 901, 931, 1145, 1547, 1697, **1702–1703**, 1831, 1841–1842
Hypertension, systemic arterial 207, 209, 456, 509, 679, 1278, **1437–1449**, 1490, 1533
  in acrodynia 550
  in acute glomerulonephritis **1484–1486**
  in acute intermittent porphyria 409
  in amphetamine addict 565
  in black widow spider bite **844**
  chronic 1448
  in chronic renal disease **1467**
  in coarctation 1390
  in congenital adrenal hyperplasia 1097
  in craniopharyngioma 952
  in Cushing's syndrome **1100**
  in dysautonomia 1040–1041
  in Fabry's disease 914
  in hemorrhagic fever 847
  in heroin withdrawal 562
  in hyperaldosteronism **1101**
  in neuroblastoma 1111
  in organic phosphate ester poisoning 551
  in patent ductus arteriosus **1394**
  in polyarteritis nodosa **1494**
  in primary hyperaldosteronism 1445
  in renal dysplasia 1477
  following x-ray therapy **1511**
Hypertensive emergencies, treatment **1448**
Hypertensive encephalopathy, of acute glomerulonephritis **1484–1486**
Hypertensive form of congenital adrenal hyperplasia **1097**

Hypertensive retinopathy, in pheochromocytoma 1109–1110

Hyperthermia. *See also* Hyperpyrexia; Fever.
  accidental, in low-birth-weight infant 99

Hyperthyroidism 495
  and acanthosis nigricans 1805
  and chronic myopathy 1036
  and myocardial disease 1432
  neonatal 84

Hypertonic dehydration *see* Dehydration, hypertonic

Hypertonicity 330

Hypertrichosis 366
  in congenital erythropoietic porphyria 407
  in mixed porphyria 410

Hypertriglyceridemia 374, 378

Hypertropia 1832–1833

Hypertrophic chondrodystrophy 1721

Hypertrophic osteoarthropathy 1401

Hypertrophic polyneuropathy of Dejerine-Sottas, chronic 924, 1008

Hypertrophic pyloric stenosis, congenital 1608–1612

Hypertussis 632

Hyperuricemia 338–340, 366, 1508
  in glycogenosis type I 369

Hypervalinemia 328

Hyperventilation
  for petit mal absence seizures 988, 993
  in salicylate intoxication 552–554
  and water loss 142

Hypervitaminosis A 177, 178, 1741, 1742

Hypervitaminosis D 203, 204, 205, 207, 209

Hypervolemia, in low-birth-weight infant 97

Hypesthesia, hysterical 284

Hyphae 787

Hypnotics
  obstetric use 55
  transplacental diffusion 55

Hypoactivity in minimal cerebral dysfunction syndrome 880

Hypoadrenalism 1093–1095
  and candidiasis 795

Hypoalbuminemia 1484, 1500, 1692
  in acute glomerulonephritis 1484
  in hepatic failure 1692
  in kwashiorkor, 174
  and iron deficiency anemia 1162
  in nephrotic syndrome 1500

Hypocalcemia 84, 85
  in hypoparathyroidism 208, 210–213
  in infant of diabetic mother 127
  neonatal 84, 85, 211–212
  following parathyroidectomy 209
  in uremia, chronic 1467
  in vitamin D deficiency 198–203
  in vitamin D deficiency rickets 203

Hypocalcemic tetany *see* Tetany

Hypocaloric dwarfism *see* Dwarfism, hypocaloric

Hypochondriacal trends 282, 283–284

Hypochromia 1162, 1181, 1183

Hypocomplementemic glomerulonephritis 389, 1484

Hypocupremia 145

Hypoderma *see* Eel fly

Hypodipsia 1153

Hypoelectrolytemia 1580

Hypofibrinogenemia 1240

Hypogammaglobulinemia 437, 480, 1879

Hypogammaglobulinemia (*cont.*)
  and pneumocystis pneumonia 842
  transient, of infancy 388

Hypogenitalism *see* Hypogonadism

Hypoglossal facial anastomosis 979

Hypoglycemia 84, 219, 360–366, 569, 1049, 1055
  in acquired metabolic diseases 362
  in Addison's disease 1093
  in adrenal insufficiency 361, 1095
  in cholera 613–614
  classification 361–363
  in diabetes mellitus 345, 351–353
  diagnosis 363–366
  fetal 59
  in glycogenoses 368–370
  due to hereditary fructose intolerance 359, 362
  in hereditary metabolic diseases 362
  idiopathic 363
  in infants of diabetic mothers 127, 362
  ketotic 363, 366
  leucine-sensitive 363, 366
  neonatal 127, 307, 363–366
  oral, agents 345
  postprandial 345
  provocative tests in 365
  treatment 366
  unresponsiveness 1051

Hypogonadism 146, 219, 1117, 1123, 1125, 1165, 1117, 1181
  in Fanconi syndrome 1165
  hypogonadotropic 1117, 1125
  in sickle-cell disease 1117
  in thalassemia 1181
  zinc deficiency 146

Hypogonadotropism 1125

Hypokalemia 524, 1423, 1466
  in familial periodic paralysis 1034
  in hyperaldosteronism 1101, 1045
  in kwashiorkor 174
  in nephrotic syndrome 1504

Hypokalemic alkalosis, in Cushing's syndrome 1100

Hypokalemic paralysis 1034, 1445

Hypomagnesemia 84, 174, 853

Hyponatremia 222, 229, 410, 524
  in acute renal failure 1464
  in bacterial meningitis 606
  with central nervous system disorders 1152
  in cystic fibrosis 422
  in diabetes insipidus 1150
  in distal RTA 1525–1526
  in neonate, and pitocin induction 17

Hyponatremic dehydration *see* Dehydration, hypotonic

Hypooxaluria 330

Hypoparathyroidism 195, 210–213, 338, 851
  and Addison's disease 1094
  and adrenal insufficiency 211
  and candidiasis 795
  and juvenile pernicious anemia 1163
  neonatal 210–213
  and pseudotumor cerebri 957

Hypophosphatasia 195, 206, 207, 1699, 1702, 1708, 1734, 1865
  and pseudotumor cerebri 957

Hypophosphatemia 196–198, 203, 204–206, 209, 1520, 1521–1524
  acute 196

Hypophosphatemia (cont.)
 chronic 196–197
 of Fanconi syndrome 1521–1524
 hereditary 1520
 iatrogenic 197
 primary 204–205. See also Vitamin D resistant rickets, familial.
 of renal tubular origin with associated rickets 203
Hypophysiotropic hormones 1046
Hypopigmentation 1800–1802
Hypopituitarism 1052–1056
 and muscle weakness and atrophy 1036
Hypoplastic aortic arch 1371
Hypoplastic left heart complex 1415–1416
Hypoproteinemia 1500, 1586
 in cystic fibrosis 428
Hypoprothrombinemia 174, 357, 685, 1240
Hypopyon 1822
Hypopyon keratitis 715
Hyporeflexia, tendinous, in familial dysautonomia 1040.
  See also Areflexia.
Hyposensitization therapy 452–454, 459, 461, 466, 484
Hyposmia 1055
Hypospadiac phallus 1139
Hypospadias 83, 250, 1097, 1098, 1139, 1547, 1553, 1553–1554
Hyposthenuria, in sickle-cell anemia 1178–2179
Hypotelorism, orbital 861, 1699, 1702
Hypotension 454, 780
 in craniopharyngioma 952
 in low-birth-weight infant 97
 in splenic injury 1218
Hypotension, maternal
 during delivery 20
 during local anesthesia 54
Hypotension, postural, in familial dysautonomia 1040
Hypothalamic-pituitary control, of thyroid secretion 1064
Hypothalamic-pituitary-gonadal interaction 1120, 1123
Hypothalamus 98, 217, 218, 219, 250, 941, 1046–1047
 appetite regulation 217
 dysfunction 1047
  in craniopharyngioma 952
  gigantism 250
  and temperature regulation 98
  in tumors of the central nervous system 941
Hypothermia 965, 1910
 in bacterial meningitis 600
 in craniopharyngioma 952
 in familial dysautonomia 1040
 in hypoglycemia of newborn 361
 in infant of diabetic mother 127
 in neonatal cretinism 1070
 and resuscitation of newborn 74
 in sepsis neonatorum 597
Hypothyroidism 211, 250, 331, 361, 373, 685, 1067–1077
 and acanthosis nigricans 1805
 and Addison's disease 1094
 and candidiasis 795
 constipation in 1601
 cretinism 1067–1075
 with goiter, of newborn, transient 1077
 and hyperbilirubinemia 1681
 juvenile hypothyroidism 1075–1077
 and juvenile pernicious anemia 1163
 and myocardial disease 1432
 and neural maturation 1065

Hypothyroidism (cont.)
 thyroglossal cyst surgery 1082
Hypotonia 335, 1027–1028
 in galactosemia 357
 in Lowe's syndrome 1522
 in Werdnig-Hoffman disease 923
Hypotonic dehydration see Dehydration, hypotonic
Hypotrichosis, in ectodermal dysplasia 931
Hypotropia 1832–1833
Hypouricemia 340
Hypoventilation, alveolar, in low-birth-weight newborn 92
Hypovolemia, in low-birth-weight infant 97
Hypovolemic shock see Circulatory collapse
Hypoxanthine 340
Hypoxanthine guanine phosphoribosyl transferase 321, 339
Hypoxemia 427, 464, 1277, 1402
 at birth 66
 in cystic fibrosis 417
Hypoxia 68, 91, 93
 at birth 42
 in bulbar poliomyelitis 746
 and carbohydrate metabolism 42–43
 fetal 47
 and growth retardation 248
 insensitivity to, in dysautonomia 1041
 maternal, and uterine blood flow 44
Hypsarrhythmia 982, 984, 990–991
Hysteria 276, 284–285, 994

131 I 1059–1090
 during gestation 55
 treatment of hyperthyroidism 1084–1085
 uptake 1053
125 I-iothalamate 1462
131 I-thyroxine 1062
Iatrogenic hypopituitarism 1056
"Ice water" test of Bors 1550
I-cell disease 404
ICF see Intracellular fluid
Ichthyol 474
Ichthyosiform erythroderma, bullous, congenital 1756–1757
Ichthyosiform erythroderma, nonbullous, congenital (nonbullous CIE) 1757
Ichthyosis 379, 1755–1757
 in neurocutaneous syndromes 930
 in Refsum's syndrome 94, 1008
Ichthyosis hystrix 1757
Ichthyosis vulgaris 1755–1756, 1807
Ictal paralysis see Inhibitory seizures
Icteric phase, of viral hepatitis 708
Icterus see Jaundice
Icterus gravis 1187
 infratentorialis 940
 nonepileptic 991
"Id" eruption 1790
Identical twin see Twins, monozygous
Idioglossia 76
Idiolalia see Idioglossia
Idiopathic celiac disease 1584–1588
Idiopathic familial osteoarthropathy 1702
Idiopathic hypercalcemia see Hypercalcemia, idiopathic

Idiopathic hypercalciuria **1527**
Idiopathic nephrotic syndrome *see* Nephrotic syndrome
Idiopathic thrombocytopenic purpura *see* Thrombocyto-
    penic purpura, idiopathic (ITP)
"Idiot pills" 571
IDU (iododesoxyuridine) 696, 716, 760, **1823**
    in dendritic keratitis **1823**
IgA, IgD, IgE, IgG, IgG$_2$, and IgM *see* Immunoglobulins
Ileal atresia **1616**
Ileostomy 1647, 1654
Ileus **1653**
Iliac adenitis 1641
Iliac horn syndrome *see* Nail-patella syndrome
Illinois Test of Psycholinguistic Abilities (ITPA) 895
Imaginative play 258
Imidazoleacetic acid 327
Imidazole amino-aciduria 335
Imidazolepyruvic acid 327
Imino acids 1518
Iminoglycinuria 337, **1518**
Imipramine 532
Imitation, and tic 274
Immune response, heterogeneity of **444–445**
Immunity
    acquired **431–441**
    to coccidioidomycosis 789
    external secretory tissue **436–437**
    to influenza 721
    lymphocyte-mediated **437–438**
    to malaria 832
    in measles 730, 732
    in mumps 738
    "natural" **438–440**
    in rubella **760–761**
    to smallpox 72
    tissue transplantation **438**
    in viral hepatitis 707
Immunizations 8, **1896**, *1897*. *See also* Vaccination.
    cholera **614**
    diphtheria **618**
    DPT **618**, *1897*
    measles **735–736**
    mumps 739
    pertussis 631, *1897*
    poliomyelitis **747–748**
    rabies **758–759**
    rubella **763–764**
    salmonella 637
    smallpox **772–775**, **1896**, 1897
    tetanus **660**, *1897*
    typhoid fever 638
    typhus **780–781**
Immunocompetent cells, development of **431–432**
Immunodiffusion test, in rubella **762–763**
Immunofluorescence (FA), in rubella **762–763**
Immunogenicity 431
Immunogens 431, 435
Immunoglobulin deficiencies **386–389**
    and lymphomas **1226**
    and recurrent pulmonary infections **1310**
Immunoglobulin producing cells 431
Immunoglobulins 318, **386–389**, 396, **431–440**, 442
    IgA **386–389**, **436–437**, 444
        in cystic fibrosis 423
    IgD **386–388**, 432, 435
    IgE **386–388**, **435**, 444, 488, 1806
        and atopic eczema 472
        myeloma protein 435

Immunoglobulins (*cont.*)
    IgG **386–389**, 396, 432, **433–435**, 505, 654, 767
    IgG$_2$ 432
    IgM, **386–388**, 396, **432–433**, 435, 440, 444, 488, 505, 654,
        767
        fluorescent treponemal antibody **654**
        in kwashiorkor 174
        in marasmus 171
        and maternal gestational hepatitis 711
        structure-function relationships of 432
        in viral hepatitis **707–708**, **709–710**, **711**
Immunologic competence **431–432**
    of the fetus 764
Immunologic drug purpura **1235**
Immunologic mechanisms **431–441**
    acquired mechanisms **431–438**
    in allergic disease **445–447**
        external secretory tissue (IgA globulins) **436–437**
        immunocompetent cells, **431–432**, 764
        immunoglobulins, structure-function relationships
            432–436 (IgM, IgA, IgG, IgD, IgE)
        lymphocyte immunity, mediated **437–438** (thymic de-
            pendent)
        tissue transplantation immunity **438**
    "natural" immunity **438**
    nonspecific factors **440–441**
        complement **440**
        lysozyme **440–441**
    in serum sickness **485**
    in syphilis **654**
Immunologic tolerance **452**
Immunology **431–441**
Immunosuppressant drugs
    in chronic renal insufficiency **1468**
    and contraindications to vaccination 773
    and cryptococcosis 794
    in nephrotic syndrome **1504**
    and pneumocystis pneumonia 842
    in regional enteritis **1643**
    in ulcerative colitis **1646–1647**
Immunotherapy 459, 466, 484
Imperforate anus **1625–1630**
Imperforate hymen 1117
Impetigo 645, 707, **1781–1783**
    in newborn 78
    perioral 1776
    streptococcal **649**
Impotence 454
Impulsivity, in minimal cerebral dysfunction syndrome
        880
Inapparent infections, with salmonellae 636
"Inappropriate ADH secretion" syndrome 1152
Inattention, in hypoglycemia 361
Inborn errors of metabolism *see* Metabolism, anomalies
Inbreeding coefficient 303
Incarceration, hernial **1631**
Incisor teeth
    Hutchinson's **656**
    in phenylketonuria 324
Inclusion blenorrhea 80, 1819
Inclusion bodies 80
    in lead poisoning 542
    in measles 733
Inclusion conjunctivitis **777**
Inclusion cyst 81, 1837
Incompatibilities
    of intravenous antibacterial drugs **588–589**
Incontinentia pigmenti 889, 931, **1804**

Incoordination 140, 361, 404, 454, 544, 1040
  in lead poisoning 544
Increased intracranial pressure
  in craniopharyngioma 952
  and craniospinal focal sepsis 1010–1016
  in optic nerve and chiasm tumors 950
Incubators 104
Incus 1881–1882, 1884
Independent genetic assortment 300
Indican 336
Indifference to pain, congenital 924
Indirect bilirubin see Unconjugated bilirubin
Indium 113-M-tagged albumin 62
Indole 336
Indolylacetic acid 336
Indolylacetylglutamine 336
Indolypyruvic acid 336
Indomethacin 515, 516
Indoxyl sulfate see Indican
Inebriation 528
Infant Hercules 1031
Infantile colic 1600
Infantile cortical hyperostoses 191, 1702, 1741, 1742
Infantile eczema 1806
Infantile familial amaurotic idiocy see Tay-Sachs disease
Infantile nephrosis see Nephrotic syndrome, congenital
Infantile paralysis see Poliomyelitis
Infantile polycystic disease 1471, 1477
Infantile pyknocytosis 1187
Infantile spasms see Massive myoclonic spasms
Infant of diabetic mother
  and hypoglycemia 362
  obesity in 216
Infant morbidity 3
Infant mortality 3
Infections 579–848, 1009–1024, 1781–1799
  and anemia 1167
  and diabetes 347
  of heart 1425
  of inner ear 1887
  intrauterine see Intrauterine infections
  and nephrosis 1500
  of nervous system other than bacterial meningitis 1009–1024
    chronic and subacute encephalitides 1023
    craniospinal focal sepsis 1009–1016. See also Craniospinal focal sepsis.
    encephalitis 1016–1023. See also Encephalitis.
  in renal failure 1465
  of skin 1781–1799
  and thrombocytopenia 1236
  of urinary and genital tracts 1539–1546
  and urticaria 477
Infectious diarrhea 226
Infectious diseases 579–848, 1009–1024, 1781–1799
  antimicrobial therapy 579
  bacterial 609–693. See also Bacterial diseases; individual diseases.
  immunization 8
  mycotic 785–796. See also Mycotic infection, disorder.
  parasitic 797–845. See also Parasitic infections.
  unclassified 846–848. See also Hemorrhagic fevers.
  viral 694–784. See also Viral infections and specific diseases.
Infectious hepatitis see Hepatitis, viral
Infectious mononucleosis 654, 709, 717–719, 1218
  encephalitis 1016, 1019–1020
  tonsillar hypertrophy in 1878

Infectious myositis 1032
Infectious polyneuritis 746
Inferior vena cava 48, 1549
Infertility 311
Infestations, of skin 1792–1797
Infiltrative cardiomyopathies 1432–1433
Inflammatory diseases, systemic, and anemia 1167
Influenza bacillus infections see Haemophilus influenzae infections
Influenza viruses and diseases 437, 625, 695, 720–722
Infranuclear cranial nerve palsy 939
Infundibular pulmonic stenosis 1344, 1402
Ingestions, accidental see Poisonings
Inguinal hernia see Hernia, inguinal
INH see Isoniazid
Inhalant abuse 567–568
Inhalant allergens 450, 464
  insect emanations 484
  and urticaria 477
Inhalation, of poisons 528–529
Inheritance
  autosomal dominant 298–299, 314
  autosomal recessive 299, 315
  autosomal sex-influenced 300
  crossing-over 300–302, 301
  independent assortment 300, 301
  linkage 300–302
  multifactorial 302, 345
  X-linked 299
Inhibitory seizures 988
Injuries
  to cornea 1818
  to spleen 1217–1218
  and tetanus 659
Inner ear 1882–1892
  diseases 1884–1891
  physiology 1882
Innocent murmur 495, 1342
Innocent pulmonic ejection murmurs 1341
Inoculation lymphoreticulosis see Cat scratch disease
Inoculations, and poliomyelitis 744
Inosinic acid 339
Inositol 138, 140
Inositol phosphatides 373
Insect allergy 483–484
Insect bites 692, 702, 845, 1792–1793
Insecticides 529, 550, 780, 781
Insect vectors 691, 845
Insecurity 283
Insensible water loss see under Water loss
Insomnia 274, 456, 569
  in heroin withdrawal 562
  in rabies 756
Isotonic enemas, in aganglionic megacolon 1623
Inspiratory obstruction 1284–1287
Inspiratory stridor 1284
Inspissated bile 1683
"Instant zen" 571
Institutional care 5
Institutionalization 452
  of asthmatic children 469
  of retarded children 896–897
Instruments, unsterile, and viral hepatitis 711
Insulin 170, 176, 218, 341, 349, 343–356, 362, 363
  fetal secretion of, 56
  and lipid synthesis 218
  requirements in diabetes mellitus 352
  tolerance test 1051

Insulinlike substances 343, **345,** 359
Intellectual development *see* Development, intellectual
Intelligence 257
  in cerebral palsy 885
  in Down's syndrome **897**
  in twins 123
Intelligence quotient 257, **887**
Intentional accidents *see* Battered child syndrome
Intentionality 254
Intercostal muscles **1323**
Intercostal retractions *see* Retractions
Interference dissociation **1368–1369**
Interferon **697,** 713, 721, 722
Interictal 981
Intermediate dominance 299
Intermittent branched-chain amino-aciduria 327
Intermittent exotropia 1833
Intermittent positive pressure breathing 467
Internal auditory meatus 1886
Internal hemorrhage, in splenic injury 1217
Internal pudendal nerve 1550
Internal saphenous catheterization **1909**
Intersexuality **118–119, 1130–1148**
Interstitial cell tumors, of testes 1127, 1561
Interstitial emphysema, in pertussis 630
Interstitial fluid 222
Interstitial keratitis, syphilitic 653, **656,** 658, **1823**
Intersitial neuritis of Dejerine-Sottas **924, 1008**
Interstitial plasma cell pneumonia, of *pneumocystis carinii* **841–842**
Interstitial pneumonitis
  due to chemical agents **1312**
  chronic, of unknown etiology **1316**
  desquamative **1315–1316**
  in hemorrhagic fever 848
  due to hypersensitivity **1313–1316**
  due to infectious agents **1311**
  in measles **733–734**
Intertrigo 1894
Intervertebral disk **674,** **1739–1741**
Intestinal disaccharidases *see* Disaccharidases, intestinal
Intestinal fluid, IgG in 433
Intestinal fluke *see Fasciolopsis buski*
Intestines **1612–1624, 1640–1647**
  absorption **1567–1570**
  aganglionic megacolon **1621**
  amebiasis *see* Amebiasis
  appendicitis **1640–1642**
  atresia **1613**
  bacteria of **1570, 1570–1572, 1595**
  bleeding, in Meckel's diverticulum 1619
  candidiasis **796**
  in cystic fibrosis **414–417**
  digestion *see* Digestion, intestinal
  enzyme deficiencies **1590–1594**
  inflammatory diseases **1640–1647**
  intussusception 191, 1579, 1600, 1620, **1654–1659**
  lymphangiectasia 389
  lymphatic transport abnormalities **1589–1590**
  malabsorption **1583–1595**
    and folic acid deficiency **1164**
  malformations **1612–1624**
  malrotation 1615
  motility **1566–1567**
  mucosa *see* Mucosa, intestinal
  obstruction 426
    in ascariasis **802**

Intestines (*cont.*)
  obstruction (*cont.*)
    in fasciolopsiasis 817
    and heroin use 560
    and hyperbilirubinemia 1681
    due to meconium ileus 420
    after neonatal period **1654–1659**
    in neonatal period 420, **1612–1618**
  polyps **1661–1662**
  primary infection of **677**
  secretions **1567–1570**
  stenosis **1313**
  tuberculosis of **678**
  ulceration, in shigellosis 639
  volvulus 1600, **1615**
Intoxication *see* Poisonings
Intraabdominal calcifications, in meconium peritonitis **1617**
Intracath 1909
Intracellular fluid **221–222**
Intracellular losses in diarrhea 230
Intracellular parasites, protective role of lymphocytes against 431, 438
Intracellular water *see* Water, intracellular
Intracerebral calcifications, in cytomegalic inclusion disease 703
Intracorpuscular hemolytic disorders 1169, **1170–1184**
Intracranial
  aneurysm **965**
  bruit 853
    in cerebral vascular malformations 963
  calcification 854
    brain tumors 943, 946, 952, *953,* 954
    in encephalotrigeminal angiomatosis *929*
  in tuberous sclerosis 925–927
  hemorrhage **962–965**
    in newborn 82
    in pertussis 629, 630
    in scurvy 188
    in twins 122, 123
  hypertension 854
    in bacterial meningitis **599**
    in brain tumors **938,** 942–947, 950
    in pseudotumor cerebri **957–960**
    in tuberous sclerosis 925–927
  pressure, increased *see* Intracranial hypertension
Intradermal brucella test 611
Intradermal nevus **1802**
Intragluteal injections 978
Intrahepatic atresia 1683
Intramedullary abscess 1010, **1015–1016**
Intramedullary gliomas **954**
Intramuscular injections, iatrogenic trauma secondary to 978
Intranuclear inclusion bodies 700
  in herpes simplex **713**
  in lead poisoning 542
  in zoster 1785
Intraocular hemorrhage 1818
Intraocular pressure increase 1825
Intraperitoneal transfusion 60
Intraspinal ganglioneuroma 955
Intraspinal lipomas 954
Intraspinal tumors **954,** 955
Intrathecal therapy
  of bacterial meningitis 606
  of tuberculous meningitis **671–673**

Intrathoracic pressure, during first breath 69
    in newborn *1256*
Intrauterine amputations 1707
Intrauterine growth retardation, in gonadal dysgenesis
        1140, 1142
Intrauterine-growth retarded newborn *see* Small-for-age
        newborn
Intrauterine infections 18, 84
    and multiple births 122
Intrauterine malnutrition 574
Intrauterine transfusion **1196**
Intravascular coagulation 624, **1236, 1242–1243,** 1533
    and thrombocytopenia **1236**
Intravascular red cell destruction, and hemolysis **1186–
        1187**
Intravenous infusion 1909
Intravenous urography (IVU) 1540–1544, **1549**
    in hypertension 1442
    in neuroblastoma 1111
Intrinsic factor deficiency 139, **1163**
Intubation, endotracheal 72, 526, **1280,** 1283, 1294
Intussusception 191, 1226, 1233, 1579, 1600, 1620, **1654–
        1659**
    in anaphylactoid purpura 1233
    and lymphosarcoma 1226
Inulin clearance **146**
    and diet 90
Invalidism 283
Invert sugar 161
Involuntary movements 851
    in basal ganglia degenerations **919–921**
    in gray matter diseases 915
    in newborn 85
    in white matter diseases 919
Iodide(s) 535, **1059–1061,** 1797
    and goiter 457
    goiter in the newborn **1078**
    placental transport 1065
    "pump" 1059
    sensitivity, in Hashimoto's struma 1080
    suppression test 1080
Iodine 145, 513
    concentrating defect **1070**
    deficiency goiter **1077–1079**
    fixation of, by leucocyte 396
    metabolism **1059–1065**
    protein-bound (PBI) *see* Protein-bound iodine
    radioactive *see* I[131]
    thyroxine **1062**
Iodized salt, in nutrition 145
5-Iodo-2'-deoxyuridine (IDUR) **696,** 716, 760, **1823**
    in *Herpesvirus hominis* infection 716
Iodoproteins 1061, **1070**
Iodothyronine 1061
    formation, defect of **1070**
Iodotyrosine deiodinase **1068**
Iodotyrosines 1060, 1061
Ion concentration, and urolithiasis **1536**
Ioniazid chemoprophylaxis **683**
Ionic constituents, of body fluids **221–222**
Ionizing radiation **12**
Iontophoresis 423
"Iowa Norms" 215
Ipecac fluid extract 534
Ipecac syrup USP, in acute poisoning **534–535**
IPPB *see* Intermittent positive pressure breathing
IQ *see* Intelligence quotient

Iridocyclitis **1827–1828**
    in heysetic keratitis 715
    in rheumatoid arthritis 504, 506
    in sacroidosis 1251
    in zoster 1788
Iris **1827**
    in albinism 326
    bombé 1828
    depigmentation, in Horner's syndrome 1817
    tremor, in Marfan's syndrome 1732
Iris-type skin lesions, erythema multiforme 1778
Iritis **1827–1828**
    in rheumatoid arthritis 504, 506
    in sarcoidosis 1251
    syphilitic 656
Iron **144–145,** 405, 535, 1674
    absorption 144
    in amniotic fluid 57
    binding capacity 1643
    in breast milk 151
    in cow's milk 1161
    deficiency anemia, **1157–1158, 1160–1163**
        and cranial aberrations 1705
        in ulcerative colitis 1644
    deficiency 145
        in kwashiorkor 175
        in marasmus 172
    fetal 30, **1158**
    intramuscular 1162
    metabolism anomaly, in Hallervorden-Spatz disease
        920
    metabolism in fetus and newborn **1158–1159**
    poisoning 145, **537–538**
    preparations **537**
    requirements 145, **1161–1162**
    in typical foods **1161**
Irritability 207, 330, 370, 456, 544, 550, 600, 733, 880
    in acute cerebellar ataxia 1041
    in Caffey's disease 1741
    in hypoglycemia 351, 361
    in infant of diabetic mother 127
    in iron deficiency anemia 1161
    in kwashiorkor 173
    in newborn *84,* 85
    in phenylketonuria 323
    in rabies 756
    in tuberculous meningitis 671
    in viral hepatitis 708
Irritable colon syndrome 1596
Isatin β-thiosemicarbazone 695
Islet cell adenomas 362
Islets of Langerhans 344
    in cystic fibrosis 414
Isochromosome-X (XX[I]) 1142
Isoenzymes 37
Isohemagglutinins 387
Isolette 104
Isoleucine 132, 327, 329, *336*
Isomaltase 1568, **1591, 1593–1594**
    deficiency, congenital **1591, 1593–1594**
Isonatremic dehydration *see* Dehydration, isotonic
Isoniazid 184, 661–679, **685–687**
Isonicotinic acid amide (Pyrazinamide) *see* Pyrazinamide
Isonicotinic acid derivatives **685**
Isonicotinic acid hydrazide (Isoniazid) *see* Isoniazid
Isopropyl alcohol 528

Isoproterenol 426, 455, 465, 466, 1281
    in asthma 1293
    in heart failure 1423
Isosexual feminine maturation 1117
Isosexual precocious puberty 1126
Isotonic dehydration see Dehydration, isotonic
Isotope disappearance curves 1462
Isovaleric acidemia 328, 379
Isoxyl 686
Isthmus of aorta, interruption of 1391
Isuprel see Isoproterenol
Itching see Pruritus
Itch mite 845
ITP see Thrombocytopenic purpura, idiopathic
IUDR 696
Ivemark's syndrome 1478
Ivy bleeding time 1237
IWL (insensible water loss) see Water loss

Jackknife seizures see Massive myoclonic spasms
Jacksonian epilepsy 982, 988
Jactatio capitis nocturna 274
Jadassohn-Lewandowski syndrome 1838
Jamaican vomiting sickness 362
Jansky-Bielchowsky disease see Bielchowsky disease
Japanese encephalitis 1016, 1017–1018
Jargon phase 254
Jaundice. See also Hyperbilirubinemia.
    in bacterial meningitis 600
    in cephalhematoma 967
    in cytomegalic inclusion disease 703
    in fascioliasis 817
    in galactosemia 357–358
    in Hand-Schüller-Christian syndrome 1247, 1248–1249
    in hemolytic anemias 393, 1169–1201, 1679, 1685–1686
    hereditary fructose intolerance 359
    in hereditary spherocytosis 1170
        in Herpesvirus hominis infection 715
    in infectious mononucleosis 718
    in leptospirosis 621
    in Letterer-Siwe disease 1246
    in neonatal cretinism 1070
    in newborn 75, 78, 121, 1676–1685
        of addicted mother 575
        conjugated hyperbilirubinemia 1682–1685
        unconjugated hyperbilirubinemia 1676–1681
    in the older child 1685–1687
        conjugated hyperbilirubinemia 1686–1687
        unconjugated hyperbilirubinemia 1685–1686
    in psittacosis 776
    in rubella, congenital 765
    in sepsis neonatorum 597
    in syphilis 655
    in toxoplasmosis, congenital 840
    in twins 121
    in viral hepatitis 708
Jaw
    in actinomycosis 786
    bone growth 1861
    fibrous dysplasia, familial 1846–1847
    hypoplasia 1713
    in infantile cortical hyperostosis 1741
    malformations of 1842–1843, 1846–1847
    micrognathia 1713, 1842–1843
    prognathism 335, 1145, 1699
    in rheumatoid arthritis 504

Jaw (cont.)
    in tetanus 658–659
    tumors, in Burkitt's lymphoma 1227
"Jaw-winking phenomenon" of Marcus Gunn 1028–1029
JBE see Junctional bullous epidermatosis
Jealousy 267, 281, 282–283
Jejunal atresia 1616
"Jelly babies" 571
Jennerian vesicle 774
Jervell, Lange-Nielsen syndrome 1885
Jet-type nebulizers 426
Jeune's disease (asphyxiating thoracic dystrophy) 1478, 1715, 1725
Jimsonweed 569
Jitteriness 273
    in hypoglycemia of newborn 361
Joints 1746–1751. See also Arthralgia, Arthritis, and Polyarthritis.
    in anaphylactoid purpura 1233
    in connective tissue disorders 494, 504, 509, 511
    coxalgia, idiopathic 1746
    fluid
        examination and cultures 515
        in rheumatoid arthritis 503
    hemarthrosis 1238, 1746
    hip dislocation, congenital 1746–1750
    in Hunter's syndrome 399
    in Hurler's syndrome 399
    infections, H. influenzae 619, 620
    pain 209, 1727
        in renal rickets 210
        in sickle-cell anemia 1177
        in vitamin D resistant rickets, of adolescence 205
    pneumococcal meningitis 601
    in polymyositis 511
    in rheumatoid arthritis 503–505
    in rubella 761
    in sarcoidosis 1252
    in Scheie syndrome 404
    in scurvy 189
    slipped femoral epiphysis 1750
    subluxation, in Ehlers-Danlos syndrome 1765
    in vitamin D resistant rickets 205
"Joints" 566
"Jolly beans" 571
"Jolt" 572
"Jones Criteria," of rheumatic fever 500
Jugular vein compression test 960
Junctional bullous epidermatosis (JBE) 1771–1772, 1774
Junctional nevus 1802
"Junk" 572
"Junkie" 571
Juvenile angiofibroma 1873
Juvenile hypothyroidism, acquired 1075–1077
Juvenile kyphosis see Scheuermann's disease 1715
Juvenile myasthenia gravis 1036, 1037–1038
Juvenile polyps 1662
Juvenile roundback deformity see Scheuermann's disease
Juvenile thyrotoxicosis see Graves' disease
Juvenile xanthogranuloma 1812
Juxtaglomerular cells 1046

40K 217
"Kabure itch" 814
Kahn flocculation test 654
Kala-azar 837–838

Kale 208
Kanamycin 581, 587, 595, 597, 598, 686, 691, 1509
  in bacterial meningitis *603–605*
  in urinary tract infections **1542**
Kaolin 641
Kapok 450
Kaposi's varicelliform eruption (eczema herpeticum) 473, 714, 1785
Karyotype notation **312**
Kassowitz's law 653
Katayama disease 814
Kayexalate (sodium polystyrene sulfonate) **1466–1467**
Kayser-Fleischer ring 120, 391, *821*, 1824
Keloids *1767, 1768*
Kenalog 475, 1779
Keratin 1755
Keratinization, diseases of 1755
Keratinocyte 1806
  of pigmentation **1799–1800**
Keratitis 656, 714–715, 1251, 1821, **1822–1823**
  herpetic **714–715**
  interstitial, in syphilis **656**
  mycotic **1823**
  in sarcoidosis 1251
Keratoconjunctivitis 734, 1785, *1821*
  epidemic adenoviral **725**
  herpetic **714**
Keratoconus 1826
Keratoderma palmaris et plantaris **1757–1758**
Keratolytics 1809
Keratomalacia 177, 1823
Keratoplasty 716
Keratosis 182
Keratosulphate 401
Kerion 1788–1789
Kerion celsi *1789*, 1790
Kernicterus 116, 852, **1192, 1677–1678**
  and cerebral palsy 882
  in twins 123
Kernig sign. *See also* Meningeal signs.
  in bacterial meningitis **599**
  in cryptococcosis 794
  in encephalitis **1016–1023**
  in poliomyelitis **745**
  in polyneuritis **1007**
  in subarachnoid hemorrhage **963**
Kerosene poisoning **538–540**
  pneumonia **1312**
Ketoacidosis **136**, 229, 328, 329, 501, 507
  in cyclic vomiting 1575
  in diabetes mellitus **344–351**
  and fat intake 136
  in glycogenosis type I **368–369**
Ketogenic diet 136
  in epilepsy **1000**
17-Ketogenic steroids (17-KGS) 220, 1051
α-Ketoglutarate 179, 181, 330
α-Ketoisocaproic acid 328
α-Keto-isocaproate decarboxylase 58
Ketones 530
Ketone serum
  in diabetes mellitus 347
  in glycogenoses 369, 371
Ketonuria 328, **344–355**, 368, 553
  in diabetes mellitus **344–355**
  in glycogenosis type I 368
  in salicylate poisoning **553**

Ketosis *see* Ketoacidosis
17-Ketosteroids 241, 599, 1051, 1099, 1119, 1124, 1127
  in adrenal hyperplasia, congenital, virilizing 1097
  in adrenal tumors 1099
  and heroin 599
Ketotic hyperglycinemia **328**
Ketotic hypoglycemia **363, 366**
17-KGS *see* 17-Ketogenic steroids
"Kick" 572
Kidneys and urinary tract **1451–1563**. *See also* Renal; Urology.
  abscess **1495**
    and craniospinal focal sepsis **1010–1016**
  and acid-base homeostasis 223, **1458–1459, 1524**
  agenesis 80, 304, 305, **1476–1477**
  in anaphylactoid purpura 1233, **1492–1493**
  arteriography 1534
  arteriovenous fistula **1534**
  artery occlusion **1391, 1533–1534**
  biopsy, percutaneous **1463**, 1492
  blood flow 49, 89, **1462**
  calcinosis 207, 209
  circulatory disturbances **1533–1534**
  clearance methods **1461–1462**
  clearance, of sodium 108
  colic 336, 409, **1535–1538**
  concentrating capacity 1460, **1484–1485**
  congenital abnormalities **1471–1472, 1474–1478, 1557**
  control of water excretion **1457**
  cortical cysts 1478
  cortical dysplasia 1477
  cortical necrosis 1473, 1509, **1533**
  cystic disorders 1474, **1477–1478**
  developmental abnormalities **1474–1478**
    aplasia **1476–1477**
    dysplasias 1471, **1476–1477**
    hypoplasia 330, **1475**
  in Fabry's disease 384–385
  failure 198, 209, 513, 579, 613, **1463–1470,** 1490
    acute **1463–1465,** 1484
    chronic **1465–1469,** 1510
    in Fabry's disease 914
    in gout 338
    in sarcoidosis 1252
    in sickle-cell disease 1510
    and vomiting 1574
  Fanconi syndrome **1520–1524**
  fetal, development and physiology 49–50, 89, **1451–1454**
  function 89, **1459–1463**
    clinical evaluation **1459–1463**
    tests **1460–1462**
  functional development **1453–1459**
  glomerulonephritis **1480–1498**
    acute **1470–1480**
    chronic **1489–1491**
    rapidly progressive **1489**
    in systemic disease **1491–1498**
  glomerulotubular interrelations 1456
  in glycogenosis type I 369
  glycosuria, renal **1516–1517**
  in gonadal dysgenesis 1141
  Goodpasture syndrome 446, 1464, **1482, 1494**
  hemolytic uremic syndrome 1243, **1494–1495**
  hereditary nephropathies **1514–1516**
  homotransplantation **1469**
  in hypertension 1443

Kidneys and urinary tract (*cont.*)
  hypoplasia 330, **1475–1476**
  immaturity 50
  infarction 1472
  infection **1539–1544**
  insufficiency *see* Renal failure
  in leptospirosis **621**
  leukemic infiltration **1212**
  maturation 89, **1453–1454**
  medullary necrosis 1473, *1474*
  micropuncture 1455
  miscellaneous nephropathies **1506–1514**
  morphologic development **1451–1452**
  neonatal renal abnormalities **1471–1474**
  nephrotic syndrome **1499–1507**
  of newborn 83, **1454, 1471–1474**
  phosphate threshold 1519
  physiology **1453–1459**
  postural proteinuria **1478–1479**
  proximal renal tubular disorders **1520–1527**
  reabsorptive mechanisms **1455**
  secretory mechanism **1455**
  in systemic lupus erythematosus **508–509**
  transplantation 330, 385, **1469**
  trauma 1561–1562
  tuberculosis **1543**
  tubular acidosis **1524–1527**
  tubular disorders 356, **1516–1529**
  tubular function **1455**
  tubular necrosis 1473
  tubular reabsorption
    of amino acids 198
    of calcium 195, 208
    of magnesium 208
    of phosphate 196, 208
    in vitamin D resistant rickets 206
  uremia **1463–1470**
  urolithiasis **1535–1538**
  urology, **1546–1563**
  vein thrombosis 1472, **1534**
    in infant of diabetic mother 127
  and water excretion control **1457–1458**
"Kief" 572
Kiesselbach's area 1876
Kinins 446, 477
"Kinky hair" disease 1760
Kirner's anomaly 1708
Klebsiella 227, 439, 586, 596
  -*Aerobacter* 397
  -*enterobacter* 597
  pneumoniae (Friedländer's bacillus) 641
Klebs-Loeffler bacillus 614
Kleeblattschädel 1697
Kleinhauer technique 64
Klinefelter's syndrome (XXY) 309, 310, 311, **903**, 1708
Klippel-Feil malformation 1716
Klippel-Trenaunay syndrome *see* Hemangiectatic hypertrophy of limb
Knee swelling, in scurvy 188
Knoch knee **1709**
Koch-Weeks bacillus conjunctivitis 1820
Koebner phenomenon 1809
Kohler's disease **1739**
Koilonychia 1761
Kolmer complement fixation test 654
Koplik's spots 730, **732**, 763, **1852**, 1906
Korean hemorrhagic fever **847**

Krabbe's congenital universal muscular hypoplasia 1027–1028
Krabbe's disease *see* Globoid-cell leucodystrophy
Krebs cycle 140
"K$_t$" value for glucose disappearance rate **347, 363**
Kufs disease (adolescent-adult amaurotic familial idiocy) 910, **912–913**
Kugelberg-Welander syndrome 923
Kuru 905
Kveim test **1252–1253**
Kwashiorkor 170, **172–175,** 186
  and growth retardation 248
Kwell *see* Benzene hexachloride
Kynureninase 185
Kynurenine 184, 336
Kyphoscoliosis **1328**
  in Friedreich's ataxia 922
  in Hurler's disease 914
Kyphosis 399, 404, **1715,** 1739–1740
  in cystic fibrosis 419
  in Hurler's disease 399
  in Pott's disease **673–674**

Labial frenulum 1837
Labial fusion 1095
Labia minora adherence **1556**
Labile factor *see* Factor V
Labioscrotal fusion 1134
Labor 54, **66–70**
Laboratory examination, at birth 76
Laboratory, newborn center 103
Labyrinth 1884
Labyrinthitis 1887
Lacerations, and battered child syndrome 557
Lacerations, of scalp **966**
Lacquers 538
Lacrimal apparatus **1824**
Lacrimal duct, nonpatency of 80, 1824
Lacrimal gland enlargement
  in leukemia 1209
  in mumps 739
Lacrimation 459, 1821, 1827. *See also* Tearing.
  in familial dysautonomia, defective 1040
  in heroin withdrawal 562
  in neonatal narcotic withdrawal syndrome 574
  in organic phosphate ester poisoning 551
  in trachoma 777
α-Lactalbumin 150, 157
β-Lactamase 583
β-Lactamase-resistant penicillins **584–585.** *See also* Penicillins.
Lactase deficiency **1591–1592, 1594**
  in cystic fibrosis 417
Lactate 37, 67, 369, 371, 372. *See also* Lactic acid.
  fetal 37
  in glycogenoses 369, 371, 372
  postnatal 67
Lactated Ringer solution 349
Lactation **153–154**
  and hyperbilirubinemia **1680**
Lactescence of plasma 374
Lactic acid 229, 338, 369, 1574
  fetal production of 37, 40, 42
  producing bacteria 156
Lactic acidemia 368, 370, 1574. *See also* Lactate.
Lactic dehydrogenase (LDH) 37, 58, 511, 1164, 1533

Lactobacillus 156
  acidophilus 161
  bifidus **1570–1572**
  bulgaricus 161
Lactogemic hormone, placental *126*
  in diabetic pregnancies 126
Lactoglobulins 150
Lactose 356, 357, 559
  in infant feeding 160
Lactose intolerance 172, **1591–1592**
Lactose malabsorption, congenital **1591–1592**
Lactosuria 356, 1593
Lactosyl ceramidase defect **911**
Lactosyl ceramidosis (GL$_2$-globosidosis) **911**
Lactrodectism 844
Lactrodectus mactans *see* Black widow spider
Lacunar skull **1702**
"Ladd's bands" **1615**
Lafora bodies 913, 990
Lafora progressive familial myoclonus *see* Myoclonic epilepsy, progressive familial
Lagophthalmos 1817
Lakes 862
Lambdoidal sutures, synostosis 1697
Lamellar cataract 1826
Lamellar ichthyosis **1757**, *1758*
Lameness, in tuberculosis of the hip 674
Lamina dura loss, in hyperparathyroidism 209
Laminectomy 876, 877, **976**
  in tumors of spinal cord 956
Lanatoside C 1422
Langhans giant cells 791
Language development 254, **257**
Language difficulties, in minimal cerebral dysfunction syndrome **880**
Language disorders **276–278**
Lanol 476
Lanosterol 40
Lanugo 75, 78
LAP *see* Leucocyte alkaline phosphatase
Lard 138
Large-for-gestational-age newborn *see* High-birth-weight infant
Larsen's syndrome 1716
Larva migrans 846
Larvae, *Ascaris 801*
Larval migration
  of ascariasis 802
  of hookworm **806**
Larval stages, of nematodes **797**
Laryngeal branch of vagus **1274**
Laryngitis 720, **1286**
Laryngomalacia **1284–1285**
Laryngoscopy 71, *72*, **72–73**, 1278
Laryngospasm 212, 281, 551, 577, 756, 1278
Laryngotracheobronchitis ("croup") 615, 620, **720**, 733, **1285–1286**
  in measles 733
Larynx **1284–1287**
  abscess **1285**
  angioedema 477, **478**
  aplasia **1284**
  burns of 519
  compression **1285**
  diphtheria **615**
  edema 390
  fibroleiomyomas 1285

Larynx (*cont.*)
  inflammation **1285–1287**
  obstruction **620, 720, 733, 1284–1285**
    due to *H. influenzae* **620**
    in fascioliasis 817
  papillomas 1285
  paralysis, in poliomyelitis **744, 746**
  stenosis **1284**
  stridor **1277**
    congenital **1284–1285**
  structural defects **1284–1285**
  tuberculosis 677
  tumors **1285**
  web **1284**
    congenital 71, **1284–1285**
Latent diabetes **345**
Lateral incisor **1856–1861**
Lateral sinus thrombosis 58, **960**
Latex flocculation test, in trichinosis **809**
Lathyrism 531
LATS *see* Long-acting thyroid stimulator (LATS)
Laudanum 641
Laughter, uncontrollable, as seizure equivalent 991
Laurence-Moon-Biedl syndrome 219, 1698, 1708, 1828
Lauric acids 151
Lavage, bronchopulmonary 427
Laxatives 1602
  in poisonings **535**
"Lazy leucocyte" syndrome **1206**
"L.B.J. stay away" 571
LBM *see* Lean body mass
LCAT *see* Cholesterol acyltransferase
L. canicola see Leptospirosis
LDH *see* Lactic dehydrogenase
Lead 145, **540–548**, 1509
  and ataxia 1042
  in breast milk 152
  encephalitis 542, **544**, 545–546
  metabolism **541**
  nephropathy 1509
  nipple shields 543
  paint 543
  poisoning 198, 533, **540–548**
    clinical features **544**
    diagnosis **544–546**
    epidemiology **542–544**
    treatment **546–548**
Lead acetate *530*
Lead oxide *530*
Lean body mass 28, 29, 215, 217
  fetal 29, 31–34
Learning disabilities
  after meningitis 608
  in minimal cerebral dysfunction syndrome **880**
  specific 852
Learning process, in middle childhood 260
Leaves, as poisons 529
Leber's optic atrophy **924**
LE cell phenomenon **509**
LE cells 499, 505, 508, **509**, 511, 513
Lecithin 373, 907
Lecithin:cholesterol acyltransferase deficiency, familial 379
Left atrial tumor **1383**
Left atrium, volume load 1372
Left coronary artery, from pulmonary artery 1434
Left heart failure 1373, **1420–1424**

Left-to-right shunt 495, 1374–1375, **1393–1401**
Left ventricle, pressure overload **1371–1372**, 1374
Left ventricular hypertrophy, **1372**
  EKG diagnosis **1350–1351**
Left ventricular-to-right atrial shunt **1398**
Legg-Calvé-Perthes' disease **1738–1739**
Leg tenderness, in scurvy 188
Leg ulcers, in sickle-cell anemia 1177
Leigh's disease *see* Necrotizing encephalopathy
Leiner's disease 1759
Leishmania braziliensis **837–838**
Leishmania donovani **837–838**
Leishmaniasis **837–838**
Leishmania tropica **837–838**
Length **245**, 246
  fetal 24
Lennox syndrome **982**
Lens **1826–1827**
  dislocation **1827**
  and hereditary nephritis 1514
  opacities 212
Lenticonus 1827
Lentigo simplex 1802
Leprechaunism **1842**
Lepromatous leprosy 389, 1797
Leptomeningeal carcinomatosis 943
Leptomeningeal cyst 968, *970*
Leptospira **621–622**, 709
Leptospira **621–622**, 709
Leptospirosis **621–622**, 692
Lesch-Nyhan syndrome 321, **339**, 884
"Letdown" phenomenon 153
Lethal genes **306**
Lethargy 327, 329, 334, 346, 357, 379, 532
  in acute cerebellar ataxia 1041
  in cytomegalic inclusion disease 703
  in hemorrhagic fever 847
  in kernicterus 1677
  in meningococcal infections 623
  in subdural effusions 624
Letterer-Siwe's disease 734, 1218, 1245, **1246–1247**, 1759
Leucine 132, 135, 183, 327, 329, 336, 363, 366
Leucine-sensitive hypoglycemia 363, 366
Leucine tolerance test 365
Leucocyte(s) *1157*, **1203–1204**. *See also* Leucocytosis.
  alkaline phosphatase **398**, 1203
  casts 1541
  in chronic granulomatous disease **396–398**
  diseases of **1203–1215**. *See also individual diseases.*
    leucopenias **1204–1206**
    leukemia **1208–1215**
    lymphocytosis, acute infectious **1206–1207**
  enzyme, and deficiencies of **391–393**, 393–394, **396–398**
  function disorders 1206
  histamine release test 449
  in zinc 145
Leucocytosis 410, 485, 497, 503, 631
  in pertussis 631
  in rheumatoid arthritis 505
  in splenic injury 1217
Leucocyturia **1540**
Leucodystrophies **916–917**
Leucoencephalitis, necrotizing, hemorrhagic, acute **918**
Leuconostoc 439
Leucopenia(s) 340, 485, 611, 705, 770, 1163, **1204–1206**, 1224, 1691, 1802
  drug-induced 1086

Leucopenia(s) *(cont.)*
  in histoplasmosis 792
  in kala-azar 837
  in Rocky Mountain spotted fever 782
  in rubella 763
  in salmonella infections 636
  in sepsis neonatorum 597
  in systemic lupus erythematosus 509
  in typhoid fever 637
Leukemia 209, 341, 506, 510, 676, 734, **1208–1215**
  acute, granulocytic **1214**
  acute, lymphoblastic (stem cell) 514, **1208–1213**
    complications **1211–1213**
    therapy **1209–1211**, 1213
  acute, monocytic 440, **1214**
  bone lesions in 550, **1743–1744**
  and candidiasis 795
  chronic, granulocytic **1214**
  chronic myelogenous, and long-arm deletion 310
  and cryptococcosis 794
  and cytomegalic inclusion disease 704
  gingival hemorrhage **1854**
  neonatal **1213–1214**
  parent information of diagnosis **1215**
  and *Pneumocystis carinii* pneumonia 842
  risk and chromosomal abnormalities 13
Leukemia cutis 1209
  bone pain 505, **1743–1744**
Leukemic transformation of lymphosarcoma 1226
Leukemoid reaction 1203
Leukeran *see* Chlorambucil
Levaditi (silver) stain 653
Levallorphan 54, 533
Levo-epinephrine preparations 1825
Levofuraltadone *see* Altafur
Levophed *see* Norepinephrine
Leydig cells 1120, 1137
L-forms 580
LH *see* Luteinizing hormone
LH-releasing factor **1120**
Liability 315
Libman-Sacks endocarditis, in systemic lupus erythematosus 508
Lice *see* Louse
Lichen nitidis **1810**
Lichen scrofulosorum 676
Lichenification 472, 473, 1806
L. icterohemorrhagiae see Leptospirosis
Liddle's syndrome *see* Pseudohyperaldosteronism
Lidocaine (Xylocaine) 1366
"Lid poppers" 571
Ligamentous laxity, in Marfan's syndrome 1732
Light
  and bilirubin **1678**
  and urticaria 478
Lighter fluid 530, 538–540
Lightning seizures *see* Massive myoclonic spasms
Lightwood's syndrome **1525**
Lignac-Fanconi syndrome 336, **1522–1523**
Limb-girdle muscular dystrophy **1031**
Limp, hysterical 284
Limp infant syndrome 370, **923**, **1027–1028**
Limpness, in hypoglycemia 361
Lincomycin **586**, 591
  in streptococcal infections **651**
Lindane, and ataxia 1042
Linea alba 1814

Linear nevus 1757
Linear nevus sebaceus 889, **931**
Linear verrucous lesions 1804
Lingual cysts, in subglottic hemangiomas 1285
Lingual goiter **1081–1082, 1850**
Linkage **300**
Linoleic acid 135, 377
Lip, cleft *see* Cleft lip
Lipase 218, 417, 441
  in kwashiorkor 174
Lipemia
  in diabetes mellitus 347
  in glycogenosis type I 369
  retinalis 375
Lipid(s). *See also* Fat.
  cerebral *see* Cerebral lipids
  in fat cells 217
  in fetus 39
  malabsorption **1583–1590**
  metabolism, anomalies of **373–385**
    heredopathia atactica polyneuritiformis **379**
    hyperlipoproteinemias **374–377**
    lecithin:cholesterol acyltransferase deficiency **379**
    lipidoses **381–385**, 908–911, **912–914, 916–917**
    lipoprotein deficiencies **377–378**
    progressive lipodystrophy **378**
    relapsing panniculitis **378**
    short-chain fatty acid anomaly **379**
  plasma **373–374**
  solubilization anomalies **1584**
  in stools 1572
  tissue lipids 135
Lipidoses **381–385**, 908–911, **912–914, 916–917**
  cerebral cholesterosis 909, **914**
  Fabry's disease **384–385**, 911, **913–914**
  Farber's disease **913**
  Gaucher's disease **383–384**, 911, **913**, 1218, 1688, 1805, 1829
  generalized **912–913**
  generalized gangliosidosis **382–383**
  globoid leucodystrophy (Krabbe's disease) **385**, 911, **917**
  Heller's disease 909, **914**
  metachromatic leucodystrophy (sulfatide lipidosis) **384**, 904, **916–917**
  Niemann-Pic disease **384**, 911, **913**, 1688
  ocular manifestations in, **1829**
  Tay-Sachs disease **381–382**, 908, 909, 910, **912–913**, 1829
  Unverricht's disease **913**
Lipodystrophic diabetes, and acanthosis nigricans 1805
Lipofuscin 911–912
Lipogranulomas, of viscera, in Farber's disease 913
Lipogranulomatosis subcutanea 1769
Lipoic acid 144, 179
Lipoid nephrosis *see* Nephrotic syndrome
Lipolysis **218**, 343, 344, **584**
Lipolytic hormones **218–219**
Lipomas, of the small bowel 1661
Lipomatosis, congenital 1594
Lipomucopolysaccharidoses **404**
Lipopolysaccharide (LPS) **580–581**
α-Lipoprotein deficiency 374, **377**, 923, 1008, 1589, 1666
β-Lipoprotein deficiency (acanthocytosis) 1588
Lipoprotein lipase 375
Lipoproteins 135, **373–374**
Lips, malformations of **1844–1846**
Lip, sucking 1868

Liquid nitrogen 1788
Lisping 277
Listeria monocytogenes 596, 597
  meningitis 598
Listlessness 363
  in hypoglycemia 361
Liver
  abscess 396
  amebic, abscess **829–830**
  biopsy 332
    in Chagas' disease 836
    in kala-azar 837
  cancer 13
  cell necrosis, in Q fever 784
  cirrhosis *see* Cirrhosis
  in cystic fibrosis 413
  in diphtheria 615
  encephalopathy, and heroin abuse **560**
  failure 1683, 1687, 1692
  fatty 139
  fibrosis **1691**
    in syphilis 653
  function tests 829
    in cytomegalic inclusion disease 703
    in hypoglycemia 365
  and glucose metabolism 341
  in glycogenosis type I **369**
  in glycogenosis type II 370
  herniation into chest 1632
  infarction 514
  of newborn 82
    in kwashiorkor 173
    protein synthesis by 132
  phosphorylase 372
  porphyrias **409–411**
  pulsations, in tricuspid stenosis 1381
  steatosis 135
  toxicity 455
  in tyrosinosis 326
  in ulcerative colitis 1644
Lizards 555
Loaiasis (*Loa loa*) **812**
Lobar emphysema **1288**
Lobectomy 1304
Lobstein's disease *see* Osteogenesis imperfecta
Lockjaw *see* Tetanus
"Locus" **298**
Lofenolac 324
Löffler's medium **616**, 1855
Löffler's syndrome 790, 801, 802, 1792
  in strongyloidiasis 808
Lomotil *see* Diphenoxylate
Lonolac 1466
Long-acting thyroid stimulator (LATS) 1050, **1082–1083**
Long-arm deletions, chromosomal 310, **1841, 1842**
  -18 deletion **1841**
  -21 deletion **1842**
Long-chain fatty acids *see* Fatty acids
Long-chain glycogen storage disease *see* Glycogenosis type IV
Long-chain hydrocarbon pneumonitis **1312**
Longevity, and obesity 215
Longitudinal study of growth 235
Long thoracic nerve 778
Loop of Henle 1451
Loop patterns **313**
Looser-Milkman zones 206

Lophophorine 569
Lordosis 201
  in achondroplasia 1722
  due to spina bifida 874
Loss, and suicide 291
Loss of contact 287
Loss of turgor 229
Louis-Bar syndrome *see* Ataxia-telangiectasia, hereditary
Louse 699, 777, **1793–1797**
  and epidemic typhus 779
Louse-borne typhus *see* Typhus, epidemic
Lovebirds 775
Low-birth-weight infant **88–117**
  and antenatal infections 115
  and antimicrobial therapy 594
  bradycardia in 97
  caloric requirements 108
  carbohydrate requirements 110
  care of **104–108**
  center for **101–103**
  and cerebral palsy 882
  and chloramphenicol 588
  circulation **94–97**
  congenital anomalies in 115
  cyanosis in 96
  definitions 88
  discharge procedures 107
  edema of 96
  EEG abnormalities in 115, 116
  electrolyte requirements 108
  emotional development of **116–117**
  examination of 104
  fat requirements 110
  feeding of **108–111**
  fluid requirements 108
  handicap of 105
  harlequin color change in 97
  hearing in **116**
  hemoglobin 65
  homeothermic responses of 98
  hypervolemia in **96**
  hypotension in 97
  immediate care of 103
  incubators for 104
  intellectual development **115**
  iron stores in 145
  and mental retardation in 115, 116
  milk formula 106, **108**
  morbidity 113–117
  mortality rates **112,** 113
  mothering-in 107
  in multiple births 119
  neurologic sequelae in 115
  outcome **111–117**
  oxygen consumption 93
  oxygen therapy **105**
  parent education 106
  physiology **88–100**
  and prenatal care 17
  prevention of infection in 106
  protein requirements 110
  recommended regimen 110
  respiration **90–94**
  resuscitatoin tray for *103*
  and smoking 22
  supportive care of **100–108**
  teeth anomalies, developmental **1862–1863**

Low-birth-weight infant (*cont.*)
  thermoregulation **97–99,** 105
  transportation **102**
  ventilation-perfusion relationships 93
  vision in **116**
  vitamin K$_1$ in 106
  vitamin K deficiency 140
Low-calcium diet
  in hypercalcemia 208
  in sarcoidosis 1253
Low-copper diet 391
Lower airway obstruction **1287–1297**
Lower motor neuron disease **851**
Lowe's syndrome **1522,** 1826
Low-fat diet 709, 1589, 1590
Low hairline, in gonadal dysgenesis 1139
Lown Cardioverter 1363
Low-set ears 901, 1547, 1842
Low-sodium milk 1466
Loxosceles laeta 1793
Loxosceles reclusa 1793
LSD **568,** 571
LTH *see* Prolactin (mammotropic hormone)
Lubasporin 1549
Lucanthone *see* Miracil D
Lückenschädel **1702**
Luder-Sheldon syndrome **1521–1522**
Lugol's solution 1074, 1078, 1086
Lumbar lordosis, in cystic fibrosis 419
Lumbar puncture 856, **1907–1908**
Lumbar spina bifida 1716
Lumbosacral
  meningomyelocele *873,* **874**
  sinus 955
Luminescence 532
Lundeen Evelyn 101
Lungs **1255–1335.** *See also* Pulmonary; Chest; Respiratory.
  and acid-base homeostasis 223
  biopsy 1302
  compliance in newborn 90, 1258
  diseases *see* Pulmonary diseases
  of fetus 89, **1255**
  inflation, response to **1258**
  of newborn 81, **1258**
  tissue resistance 91
  volumes
    in asthma **465**
    in low-birth-weight infant 91
    in newborn **1258**
  water loss from 142, 224
Lupus erythematosus disseminatus *see* Systemic lupus
    erythematosus
Lupus nephritis **508,** 1493–1494
Lupus vulgaris **676**
Luteal phase 1120
Luteinized follicular cyst, of ovary 1128
Luteinizing hormone (LH) 1048, **1049,** 1120–1121
Lutembacher's syndrome 1383
LVH *see* Left ventricular hypertrophy
Lye ingestion **1636–1637**
Lyell's disease **1776–1778**
Lying 279
Lymphadenitis *see* Lymphadenopathy
Lymphadenoid goiter *see* Hashimoto's struma
Lymphadenopathy 672, 690, **717–719,** 1206, **1221–1222,**
    1248, **1251**
  acute **1221**

Lymphadenopathy (cont.)
  in Bancroft's filariasis 811
  after BCG vaccination 684
  benign, nonbacterial see Cat scratch disease
  in blastomycosis 788
  in brucellosis 611
  in Burkitt's tumor 1227
  in cat scratch disease 698, 699
  cervical 615
  in Chagas' disease 836
  chronic 1222
  due to Coxsackie A viruses 751
  due to ECHO viruses 753
  in exanthem subitum 705
  in Hashimoto's struma 1079
  in histoplasmosis 792
  in infectious mononucleosis 717–719
  in Letterer-Siwe disease 1246
  in leukemia 1209
  in lymphogranuloma inguinale 776
  in measles 733, 734
  mesenteric 1600, 1642
  in Mycoplasma pneumoniae infections 626
  preauricular 1821
  in pyoderma, streptococcal 649
  in rat-bite fever 634
  in rheumatoid arthritis 503–504
  in rubella 760, 761
  in sarcoidosis 1251
  in Schistosomiasis mansoni infection 814
  septic 396
  in serum sickness 487
  in streptococcal infections 648–650
  suboccipital 760, 761
  in syphilis 655
  in systemic lupus erythematosus 509
  in toxoplasmosis 840
  in tuberculosis 662–671, 672
  in tularemia 692–693
  in zoster 1785
Lymphangiectasia 1706
Lymphangiography 1224, 1706
Lymphangioma 81, 1814
  of liver 1693
Lymphangitis 649
  in Bancroft's filariasis 811
  in Malayan filariasis 811
Lymphatic growth 236
Lymphatic obstruction, in Bancroft's filariasis 811
Lymphedema 1330, 1683, 1814
  in Bancroft's filariasis 811
  in gonadal dysgenesis 1141
Lymphnode(s) 386, 1221–1228, 1900, 1905
  adenitis, inflammatory 1221–1222 see Lymphadenopathy
  in agammaglobulinemias 387
  biopsy 387–388, 1224, 1226, 1247, 1252
    in Bancroft's filariasis 811
    in cat scratch disease 698
    in Hodgkin's disease 1224
    in Letterer Siwe's disease 1247
    in lymphomas 1224, 1226
    in sarcoidosis 1252
  enlargement see Lymphadenopathy
  in general examination 1900, 1905
  in Hodgkin's disease 1223–1224
  malignant lymphomas 1222–1227. See also Lymphomas.
  needle aspiration 1224

Lymphnode(s) (cont.)
  rickettsiae in 779
Lymphoblastic leukemia 1209–1210
Lymphoblasts, primitive 1208–1209
Lymphocyte-mediated immunity, thymic dependent 437–438
Lymphocytes 386–389, 437, 442, 446, 1157, 1204, 1216
  atypical 718–719
  in immunologic mechanisms 431–440
  in infectious mononucleosis 718
  transformation test 449
Lymphocytic choriomeningitis 728–729
Lymphocytosis 630, 705, 1206–1207
  acute infectious 1206–1207
  in pertussis 630
  in roseola infantum 705
Lymphogranuloma inguinale 776
Lymphogranuloma venereum 776, 1797
Lymphohistiocytosis, generalized 1246, 1250
Lymphoid cells 386–389
Lymphoid hyperplasia
  due to ECHO viruses 753
  in Hodgkin's disease 1223
  in infectious mononucleosis 718
  in measles 730
Lymphoid tissues, in marasmus 171
Lymphomas 506, 511, 776, 1218, 1222–1228
  Burkitt's tumor 1227
  Hodgkin's disease 1223–1226
  lymphosarcoma 1226–1227
  pneumocystis pneumonia 842
Lymphonodular pharyngitis
  due to Coxsackie A virus 751
  and smallpox vaccination 773
Lymphopenia 388, 734, 1224
Lymphopenic agammaglobulinemia see Hereditary thymic dysplasia
Lymphoreticular malignancy 387–389
"Lymphorrhages" 1038
Lymphosarcoma 510, 676, 1167, 1226–1227
  of bowel 1661
  and cryptococcosis 794
Lyon hypothesis 299–300, 308, 309
Lyphilized AHF concentrate 1239
Lysergic acid diethylamide (LSD) 571
Lysine 132, 151, 335, 336, 337
  in wheat protein 134
Lysine tolerance test 335
Lysolecithin 373, 379, 477
Lysosomal α-glucosidase 370
Lysosomes 166, 177, 370, 1668–1669, 1806
Lysozyme 440

M-8450 696
Macewen's cracked-pot resonance 1012
Machado-Guerreiro test 836
Machinery-type murmur 1393, 1406
Macrocephaly see Megalocephaly
Macroconidia 1788
Macrocranium 1695
Macrocytic anemia 186, 189
Macrogamete 831
Macrogametocyte 831
Macrogenitosomia praecox 946, 1117
Macroglossia 81, 363, 370, 899, 1030, 1035, 1285, 1848

Macrophages 447, 791
Macrosomia 125, **126**, 1848
Macules **1753**
Maculopapular eruption
  in infectious mononucleosis 718
  in rhenumatoid arthritis **504**, 506
MAF (Macrophage aggregation factor) 447
Maffucci's syndrome 1728, 1814
Maggot infestations *see* Myasis
Magnesium 84, **143**, 195, **197**, 208
Magnesium ammonium phosphate stones 1536
Magnesium sulfate 632, **1486**
"Mainlining" 559, 572
Maize diet, and niacin deficiency 181
"Majocchilike" granulomas 1790
Major arteries obstruction **1389–1391**
Major clinical (Jones) criteria, of rheumatic fever **494–496**, 500
Major illness, of poliomyelitis **744–746**
Malabsorption **1583–1595**
  in beta lipoprotein deficiency 377
  and hypocaloric dwarfism 170
  in niacin deficiency 182
  syndromes **1583–1595**
  of vitamin D 201
Maladie de Roger 1397
Maladjustment, ecologic **1912–1914**
Malar bone hypoplasia **1838**
Malaria 830–834, 1218
  and fetal growth retardation 22
"Malarial cachexia" 832
Malassezia furfur 1788
Malathion 551
Malayan filariasis **811**
Mal de Meleda **1758**
Male pseudohermaphrodism *see* Pseudohermaphrodism, male
Male Turner's syndrome **1143**
Malformations, congenital *see* Congenital anomalies
Malignancy, and anemia 1167
Malignant hypertension, in polyarteritis nodosa 514
Malignant tertian malaria 832
Malignant tumors of bone 1743
Malleus 462, 1881–1882, 1884
Malnutrition **170–176**
  and candidiasis 1858
  in celiac disease **1586**
  and growth 243
  and growth retardation 248
  marasmus **171–172**
  and mental development 243
  protein caloric *see* Kwashiorkor
Malocclusion **1868–1869**
  in β-thalassemia 1181
Malpighian corpuscles 1216
Malrotation, intestinal **1615**
Maltose 161
Maltreatment of children *see* Battered child syndrome
Mammary development 153
Mammary gland **81**
  in newborn 81
Mammotropic hormone 1048
Mandible *see* Jaw
Mandibular hypoplasia *see* Micrognathia
Mandibular prognathism 335, 1145, 1699
Mandibulofacial dysotosis *see* Treacher-Collins syndrome
Manganese 145

Mania 501
Maniacal behavior, in rabies **756**
Manic-depressive psychoses 286
Manipulation, environmental 1912–1913
  in suicide 292
Manipulation of the body **275**
Man-made environment **1912–1913**
Mannitol
  in lead poisoning 548
  in renal failure 1464
Mantoux test **680–682**
"Mao" 572
Maple-bark strippers' disease **1313**
Maple syrup urine disease **327–328**, 362, 1595
Marasmic kwashiorkor 173
Marasmus 170, **171–172**
  and cerebral palsy 882
Marble bones *see* Osteoporosis
Marboran *see* N-Methylisatin-beta-thiosemicarbazone
Marcus Gunn phenomenon 852, 1028–1029
Marfan's syndrome 305, 1058, 1708, 1732, 1766
Marginal gingivitis **1852**
Marginal ulcers, cornea **1822**
Marihuana **566–567**, 572
Marinesco-Sjögren syndrome 922. *See also* Spinocerebellar degeneration.
Maroteaux-Lamy syndrome **404**, 1727
Marseille fever **781**
Marshall's type ectodermal dysplasia **1842**
"Maryjane" 572
"Mary Warner" 572
Masculinization, fetal, due to steroid therapy 55. *See also* Virilizing syndromes.
Masern (Ger.) *see* Measles
Massive myoclonic spasms **990–991**, **1000**
  in tubercus sclerosis 925
Massive spasms *see* Massive myoclonic spasms
Mass reflex, in spinal cord injury 975
Mast cells 446
Mastitis 81, 149, 156, 645
Mastocytosis 478
Mastoid cells 1882
Mastoidectomy **1887**, 1888
Mastoid granuloma 1011
Mastoiditis 599, 650, 1887
  and craniospinal focal sepsis **1010–1016**
  and pneumococcal meningitis 601
Masturbation 263, 269, 274, 275, 278
  in enterobiasis 803
Maternal age
  and breast feeding 152
  and Down's syndrome 897, *898*
  and multiple births 118
  and neonatal mortality 111
  and outcome of newborn 111
Maternal deprivation
  and growth retardation 249
  and personality development 254
  and psychosocial dwarfism 175
  and rumination **1576–1578**
Maternal diabetes, and neonatal jaundice 1681
Maternal drugs, fetal effects of **51–57**
Maternal enzymes, in high-risk pregnancy 59
Maternal hyperparathyroidism, in neonatal tetany 212
Maternal nursing *see* Breast feeding
Maternity and Infant Care Projects 10
Matulane *see* Procarbazine

Maturational age 240
Maturational indicators 241, *242*
Maturation, chemical *see* Chemical maturation
Maturation patterns, classification **241**
Maturity
   general **240–241**
   in newborn, assessment of **84–88,** *85, 86, 87*
Mauriac's syndrome 367
Maxilla
   bone growth *1861*
   hypoplasia 1699
Maxillary sinus **1871**
Maxillary sinus fracture **1705**
Maximum tubular reabsorption of phosphate
     (Tm$_{phosphate}$) **1519**
May fly 484
Mazzini flocculation test 654
McArdle's disease *see* Glycogenosis type V
McBride's "Rule of 4" 1859
McCune-Albright disease *see* Polyostotic fibrous dysplasia
Mealworms 819
Mean, arithmetic **232**
Mean corpuscular hemoglobin *1157*
Mean corpuscular erythrocyte volume **1155–1156,** *1157*
Measles 388, 682, 684, **729–737,** 763
   antibodies 434
   appendicitis, 734
   atypical form 736
     after vaccination 736
   clinical picture **732–733**
   complications **733–735**
   diagnosis **733**
   encephalitis **1020**
     sexual precocity after 1126
   immunity 732
   immunization 434, **736–737**
   keratoconjunctivitis **1821**
   laboratory **733**
   myocarditis 1429
   pathogenesis 732
   pathology **730–731**
   prophylaxis **735–737**
   treatment **735**
   virus **729–730**
     and subacute sclerosing panencephalitis **919**
Measurements, body **1904**
   fetal 24
Measuring board *246*
Measuring table 246
Meat 166
Meat-based preparations 357
Meatal stenosis 1559
Meatal ulcer 1550–1551, 1553
Mebaral (Mephobarbital) *995, 996,* **998, 1000**
Mechanical ileus **1653**
Mechanobullous diseases *see* Epidermolysis bullosa
Mecholyl (Acetyl β-methacholine) 1654, 1824
   in PAT 1364
Meckel's cartilage 1861, 1884
Meckel's diverticulum 1161, 1599, **1618–1620,** 1649
Meclizine 17
Meconium 426, **1270,** 1571
   in amniotic fluid 58, 75
   in cystic fibrosis 420
   delay in passing 1622
Meconium aspiration **1270–71**
Meconium ileus 419, **420–421,** 425, **1616**

Meconium peritonitis 420, **1617**
Meconium plug **1617**
Meconium staining, of amniotic fluid 57, 64
Medial longitudinal fasciculus syndrome 1834
Medial torsion of tibia **1710**
Median cleft face syndrome **861, 1702,** 1838
Median facial defects **860–861,** 1838
Median nerve, compression of, in rubella 761
Median nerve injury **978**
Mediastinal emphysema 701, 1312
Mediastinal lymphadenopathy
   in blastomycosis **787**
   in Hodgkin's disease **1223–1224**
Mediastinal lymphosarcoma 1226
Mediastinal mass, and pheochromocytoma 1110
Mediastinal shift 1632
Medicaid program 10
Mediterranean anemia *see* β-Thalassemia
Mediterranean variant, G6PD deficiency 394
Medium-chain tryglycerides 427, 1569, 1588, 1590, 1643
Medroxyprogesterone acetate 1125
Medullary cystic disease **1515**
Medullary plate 872
Medullary stenosis **1735**
Medullary tube 872
Medulloblastoma 937–940, **942–943**
Meeting Street School Test 892
Megacolon, aganglionic **1621–1624**
Megacystis **1557–1558**
Megaesophagus 1576
Megakaryocytes **1234,** 1235–1237
Megalencephaly **1695**
Megaloblastic anemia 340, **1163–1165**
Megalocephaly **857–860,** 917, **1695**
   in Alexander's disease 917
   in Canavan's disease 917
   in cerebral arterial thrombosis 962
   in disseminated hemangiomatosis 929
Meghini needle biopsy 1692
Megalocornea **1822,** 1825
Meglumine diatrozoate 60, 62
Mehlnahrschaden 137
Meiosis 300, 310
Meiotic nondisjuction 1144
Meissner's plexus 1621
Mel B, in African trypanosomiasis **834**
Melanin 132, **326–327,** 1693
Melanocytes 326, **1799–1780,** 1780–1865
Melanocyte-stimulating hormone (MSH) 1048, 1093, **1800**
Melanogenesis 327
Melanoleucoderma 931
Melanoma **1803**
Melanosis "bathing suit" nevus 475, **867–868**
Melarsen oxide 834
Melarsoprol *see* Mel B
Melatonin (5-methoxy-N-acetyltryptamine) 1046, **1113–**
   1123
Melena 514, **1579–1580**
   in anaphylactoid purpura 1233
   in hemorrhagic fever 847, 848
Mellaril *see* Thioridazine
Mellituria **356–360,** 545, 550, **1516–1517,** 1520–1524
Membrane removal in subdural hematoma 607, 973
Membranes
   examination at birth 76
   premature rupture of 18, 65, 76
Membranoproliferative glomerulonephritis 1490

Membranous conjunctivitis 1820–1821
Membranous nephropathy *1501*
Memory 254
"Memory" phenomenon *see* Anamnestic response
Menarche, 241, **1115–1120, 1122**
  age of 240, 241
Ménière's disease 853
Meningeal hemorrhage 963
Meningeal signs **599**, 729, **745**, 794, 832, 836, 918, **932**, 940, 945, 946, **963**, 1016–1023
  in bacterial meningitis **599**
  in brain tumors 940, 945, 946
  in Chagas' disease 836
  in cryptococcosis 794
  in encephalitis 1016–1023
  in Hurst disease 918
  in lymphocytic choriomeningitis 729
  in malaria 832
  in poliomyelitis **745**
  in polyneuritis **1007**
  in subarachnoid hemorrhage 963
Meningioma 954
  and neurofibromatosis 927
Meningismus
  in mycoplasma pneumoniae infections 626
  in rabies 756
Meningitis
  aseptic 672, **745**
    due to Coxsackie viruses **750**
    due to ECHO viruses **753**
    due to herpesvirus **715**
    in infectious mononucleosis 718
    due to leptospirae **621**
    in lymphocytic choriomeningitis **729**
    due to psittacosis 775
  bacterial **598–609**. *See also specific organisms.*
    in basal skull fracture 970
    and brain abscess 1012
    in brucellosis 611
    cerebrospinal fluid examination **601–602**
    clinical features **599–600**
    etiologic diagnosis **600–602**
    due to *H. influenzae* **619–620**
    laboratory findings **601–602**
    due to meningococcus, **622–625**
    neonatal 597, **598–600**
    prognosis **607–609**
    prophylaxis of contacts **608**
    recurrent 1015
      due to dermal sinus **876–877**
    due to Salmonellae **636, 637**
    following splenectomy 1217
    due to *Staphylococcus aureus* **645**
    due to streptococcus 598, 650
    subdural effusions **607**
    treatment **602–607**
    tularemic 692
  circumscripta 1010
  mycotic
    candidal 796
    coccidioidal 790
    cryptococcal 794
  serous **672**. *See also* Tuberculous meningitis.
    in pertussis 630
Meningocele 872, 1695
Meningococcemia *see* Meningococcus infections

Meningococcus infections 576, **598–609, 622–625**, 1232, 1242
Meningoencephalitis **1016–1023**
  in African trypanosomiasis **834**
  amebic **830**
  due to herpesvirus, secondary **715**
  mumps **738**
  in paragonimiasis 816
  after pertussis vaccine 631, **1022**
  phycomycosis 795
  postinfectious **1020–1022**
  primary viral **1016–1020**
  slow viruses **1023**
  subacute **1023**
  due to *Vibrio fetus* 597
Meningomyelocele 84, 863, **873–876**
Menometrorrhagia 561, 1236
  in Von Willebrand's disease 1236
Menses *see* Menstruation
Menstruation 152, 219, 220, 241, 270, 278, 561, 1115–1120, **1121–1122, 1124**, 1236, 1252
  abnormalities 219, 220, 270, 561, **1115–1120**, 1236, 1252
  and acute intermittent porphyria 410
  and breast feeding 152
  dysfunction, in adolescence **1115–1120**
Mental confusion 501
Mental development *see* Development, mental
Mental deficiency *see* Mental retardation
Mental retardation 212, 219, 381, 385, **887–905**, 1804, 1838, 1841
  amino acid metabolism and 322
  in argininosuccinic aciduria 334
  in carnosinemia 335
  in cerebral gray matter diseases 912, 914–915
  in cerebral palsy **885**
  in cerebral white matter diseases 916
  chromosomal disorders associated with **897–905**
  in citrullinemia 334
  classification **887–891**
  in cystathioninuria 331
  due to cytomegalic inclusion disease 703
  definition **887**
  distribution 891
  etiology **887–891**
  in galactosemia **357–358**
  in glycogenosis type O 368
  in Hartnup disease 336
  high-risk predisposing factors *891*
  in histidinemia 327
  in Hunter's syndrome **399**
  in Hurler's syndrome 399, 914
  in homocystinuria 331
  in hydroxyprolinemia 331
  in hyperammonemia 334
  in hypercalcemia, idiopathic 207
  in hyperlysinemia 335
  in hyperprolinemia 330
  in hypervalinemia 328
  incidence **891**
  in isovaleric acidemia 379
  due to kernicterus 1677
  laboratory studies 892
  and lead poisoning **540–548**
  in Lesch-Nyhan syndrome 339
  in lipomucopolysaccharidoses 404
  in low-birth-weight infant 116, 155
  in Lowe's syndrome 1522

Mental retardation (*cont.*)
  after meningitis 608
  in mucopolysaccharidoses 399–404
  in neurocutaneous syndromes 925–931
  in nonketotic hyperglycinemia 330
  in phenylketonuria 323
  physical findings 892
  physician's role 892
  presenting symptoms 891
  psychologic testing 894
  due to rubella, congenital 766
  in Sanfilippo syndrome 399, 915
  social behavioral evaluation 894
  due to toxoplasmosis congenital 840
  treatment 894–897
  and tuberculosis 326
  and tuberculous meningitis 672, 673
  in twins 123
Meperidine (Demerol) 54, 84, 532, 533, 573, 1910
Mephenesin 661
Mephobarbital *see* Mebaral
Meprobamate 661, 999, 1235
  and drug purpura 1235
  in tetanus 661
β-Mercaptoethylamine 140
6-Mercaptopurine 1204, 1209–1210, 1227, 1643
Mercurial diuretics 549, 1423
Mercuric bichloride 810
Mercuric chloride 549
Mercurous chloride (calomel) 549
Mercury 12, 152, 535, 548–550, 1312, 1509
  in breast milk 152
  nephropathy 1509
  poisoning 533, 548–550
    hypertension in 1447
  sources 548–550
  vapors 548–549, 1312
Merozoites 831
Merrill-Palmer test 265
Merycism (Merycasm) *see* Rumination syndrome
Mesantoin (methylphenylethyl hydantoin) 995, 997, 998–1000
Mescaline *see* Peyote
Mesenteric adenitis 1600, 1642
Mesenteric cysts 1620–1621
Mesodermal dysgenesis 1826
Mesoinositol 140
Mesomorphic body type 216
Mesoorchium torsion 1556
Messenger RNA *see* RNA, messenger
Mestinon *see* Pyridostigmine bromide
Metabolic acidosis *see* Acidosis
Metabolic alkalosis *see* Alkalosis
Metabolic "cooperativity" 382
Metabolic liver disorders 1687–1689
Metabolic myopathies 1034–1035
Metabolic rate, basal 128
  and birth weight 29–30, 32–33
  placental 44
  in salicylism 554
Metabolism
  anomalies of 306, 318–413
    of amino acids 321–338
    biochemical aspects of gene action 318–321
    of carbohydrates 341–373
    of erythrocyte enzymes 391–396
    of leucocyte enzymes 397–398

Metabolism (*cont.*)
  anomalies of (*cont.*)
    of lipids and lipoproteins 373–385
    mucopolysaccharidoses 398–404
    porphyrias 405–411
    of protein metabolism 386–398
    purine and pyrimidine metabolism 338–341
    of urea cycle 334–336
  basal 128–131
  inborn error of *see* Metabolism, anomalies of
  in the obese 217–218
Metacarpal bone
  in Hurler's disease 914
  shortening 1708
Metacentric chromosome 308
Metacercariae 815, 816, 817
Metachromasia *403*, 917
Metachromatic granules, in fibroblasts of cystic fibrosis 425
Metachromatic inclusions, leucocytes 399
  in Hurler's disease 914
Metachromatic leucodystrophy (sulfatide lipidosis) 384, 916–917
Metachromatic sulfatides 384, 917
Metal-binding and related proteins, deficiencies 390–391
Metamyelocytes 1163, 1203
Metanephric blastema 1451
Metanephros 1451
Metaphase 308
Metaphyseal dysostosis 195, 206, 1721, 1725
Metaphyseal dysplasia (Pyle's disease) 1732, 1733
Metaphyses
  in rickets 198–200
  in scurvy 189
  in spine deformities 206
  in vitamin D resistant rickets 206
Metastasis
  liver 1694
  of neuroblastoma 1110–1111
Metastatic calcification, subcutaneous 212
Metatropic dwarfism 1721, 1722, *1723, 1724*
Methacholine, hypersensitivity to, in dysautonomia 1041
Methadone 533, 572, 574
  abstinence syndrome, in newborn 574
  in heroin withdrawal 562
  poisoning 563
Methamphetamine abstinence syndrome, in newborn 574
Methanol *see* Methyl alcohol
Methantheline bromide (Banthine) 1643, 1646
Methbarbital *see* Gemonil
Methemoglobinemia 392, 524, 529, 532
  hereditary 392, 395–396
Methenamine 588
Methicillin 585, 598
Methimazole, in thyrotoxicosis 1086
Methionine 132, 135, 139, 144, 326, 328, 329, 331, 332
Methocarbamol 661
  in black widow spider bite 844
Methotrexate 941, 1210–1211, 1504
  in brain tumors 941
  in lymphoblastic leukemia 1210, 1211
  in lymphosarcoma 1227
  in nephrotic syndrome 1504
Methotrexate, intrathecal, in CNS leukemia 1211
3-Methoxy-4-hydroxymandelic acid (VMA) *see* VMA
Methsuximide *see* Celontin
Methyl alcohol 530, 532, 535

Methyl bromide 528
Methyl cellulose 1603, 1817
α-Methyldopa in hypertension 1448, 1467
Methylene blue stain 601
1-Methylhistidine 335
Methylmalonic acid 329
Methylmalonic acidemia 329
Methylmalonyl CoA 329
Methylmalonyl CoA isomerase (Mutase) 329
Methyl octanoic acid 581
Methylphenidate hydrochloride (Ritalin) 163, 881
Methylphenylethyl-hydantoin see Mesantoin
Methylpyrilene 559
Methyl salicylate poisoning 552–556
Methyl scopolamine nitrate (Skopolate) 1612
Methyl testosterone 390
   and PBI 1063
4-Methylumbelliferyl-β-D-N-acetylgalactosaminide   381,
   383
Methylxanthines 456
Metronidazole (Flagyl)
   in amebic liver abscess 830
   in giardiasis 838
Metyrapone (SU-4885) 1051
Meyer-Betz disease 1035
"Mezz" 572
MGK see Neisseria meningitidis
Micrencephaly 857–859, 1695
Microangiopathic hemolytic anemia 1186
Microbial constituents as viral inhibitors 696
Microbodies 1666, 1667
Microcardia 270
Microcephaly 12, 84, 115, 324, 330, 334, 363, 703, 765,
      857–859, 899, 912, 1695
   in Batten-Spielmeyer-Vogt disease 912
   in cytomegalic inclusion disease 703
   and radiation 12
   in rubella, congenital 765
   in toxoplasmosis 840
Microcornea 1822, 1826
Microcrania 861, 1699, 1841
Microcytosis 1162, 1183
Microencephaly 892, 1695, 1699, 1804, 1841
Microfilaria 810–812
   of Onchocerca volvulus 812
Microgamete 831
Microgametocytes 831
Microglossia 1848
Micrognathia (micrognathism) 81, 388, 504, 901, 1547,
      1703, 1838, 1842–1843
Microgyria 1029
Microinfarcts, in Rocky Mountain spotted fever 782
Micromelic dwarfism 1722
Microphthalmia (microphthalmos) 901, 1165, 1817, 1838
Micropolygyria 859
Microsomes, and drug-metabolizing activity 53
Microspherocytes 1179
   in ABO incompatibility 1198
Microsporum infections 1788
   audouini 1788, 1791
   anis 1788
   gypseum 1788, 1791
Microthelia, in gonadal dysgenesis 1141
Microtubules, of hepatocytes 1667–1668
Microvilli, placental 44
Micturition 1550
Middle cerebral artery 964

Midfacial hypoplasia 1841–1842
MIF see Migration inhibition factor
Migraine 852, 1002–1003
Migration inhibition factor 447
Migratory polyarthritis 494
Mikulicz syndrome 1209
Milia 78, 1814
Miliaria 1808–1809
   crystallina 1808
   rubra 1808–1809, 1814
Miliary granulomatosis
   due to Vibrio fetus 597
Miliary tuberculosis 510, 665, 668–670, 1218
Milium 668
Milk
   boiling 157, 160
   breast see Breast milk
   and brucellosis 611
   condensed 162
   cow's see Cow's milk
   differences between cow's milk and breast milk 157–160
   formulas see Cow's milk
   freezing of 157
   and galactosemia 357
   goats' 162
   human see Breast milk
   humanized 162
   and iron deficiency 1161
   light and 157
   microorganisms in 156
   mixtures see Cow's milk
   sterilization of 157
   in transmission of diarrhea 228
Milk-associated gastroenteropathy 1595
Milk-borne disease 156, 228, 1595
Milk-free diet, in galactosemia 357
Miller-Abbott intestinal tube 1649
Miller-Hinton agar 622
Million reagent 191
Milontin, in epilepsy 998–1000
Milroy's disease 1589, 1814
Mimea 596
Mineralization, bone
   in hypophosphatasia 206
   and rickets 200
Mineral oil, in costipation 1602
Minerals
   in breast milk 151, 158
   in colostrum 150
   in cow's milk 158
   growth patterns of 237
   in nutrition 142–147
      macromineral nutrients 142–145
      requirements of low-birth-weight infant 109
      trace elements 145–147
Mineral seal oil 530, 538–540
Mineral spirits 530, 538–540
Minimal bactericidal concentration, of antibiotic 584
Minimal cerebral dysfunction syndrome 115, 116, 879–882
Minimal inhibitory concentration, of antibiotic 584
Minor critical criteria 496
   of rheumatic fever 496, 500
Minor illness, in poliomyelitis 744–746
Minor motor seizures 989–991, 1000
Mintezol see Thiabendazole
Miosis 532, 852, 1817
   and heroin use 559

Miosis (cont.)
  in organophosphate poisoning 551
Miracidium 813, 817
Miracil D, in schistosomiasis 814–815
Mirror writing 880
Missing teeth 1564–1565
"Mist tent" 426
MIT see Monoiodotyrosine
Mites 777, 845, 847, 1797
Miticidal chemicals 783
Mitochondria 581, 1064, 1669
Mitotic index 438
Mitotic nondisjunction 1144
Mitral atresia 1371, 1377, 1383
Mitral flow murmurs 1344
Mitral insufficiency 494, 499
Mitral regurgitation 494, 499
Mitral stenosis 495, 499, 1371, 1383–1384
  congenital 1383–1384
Mitral valvulitis 499
Mixed forms of cerebral palsy 884
Mixed laterality 277
Mixed porphyria (South African Type) 410–411
MLD see Metachromatic leucodystrophy
"Mobile care" vehicle 101
  for low-birth-weight infant 102
Möbius' syndrome 850, 853, 1009, 1029
Mods, retinal 177
Mogadon (nitrazepam) in epilepsy 998
Mohr syndrome 1850
Molars 1856–1861
Molasses 161
Molding, skull 79, 1704
Molds 450
Molecular genetics 294–298
Molluscoid pseudotumors, in Ehlers-Danlos syndrome 1765
Molluscum contagiosum 1786
Moloney test 618
Molts 797, 805
Molybdenum 146
Mongolian spots 78, 79, 1803
Mongolism see Down's syndrome
Mongoloid slant, eyes
  in β-thalassemia 1181
Mongoose 755
Monilethrix 1760
Monilia 388
Moniliasis see Candidiasis
Monitoring, fetal heart 19, 62, 71
Monkey 821
"Monkey on the back" 571
6-Monoacetyl morphine 559
Monoamine oxidase 1107
Monoamnionic sac 119
Monochorial see Monochorionic
Monochorionic twins 302
Monocular strabismus 1832
Monocytes 1157, 1204
Monocytic leukemia, acute 1214
Monoiodotyrosine (MIT) 1061–1062
Mononeuritis multiplex 924
Mononucleosis, infectious see Infectious mononucleosis
Monoplegia 884
Monosaccharide tolerance tests 1593
Monosialic acid 907
Monosialicganglioside trihexomide 907

Monosialoganglioside 383
Monosomy G (22/22 Monosomy, Antimongolism) 901
Monostotic fibrous dysplasia 1886
Monovular twin see Twins, monozygous
Monozygosity 302
Moon face 901, 1105
Moose 821
Morax-Axenfield diplobacillus 1820
Morbidity 3–4
  and gestational age, 111, 113
Morbilli see Measles
"Morgan's lines" 473
Morning glory seed 569, 572
Morning stiffness 515
  in rubella 761
Moro reflex 76, 85, 87, 327, 854, 1192
Morphea see Scleroderma, "focal"
Morphine 515, 559–560, 563, 1911
  addiction in newborn 54, 573–575
Morquio syndrome 400–404, 1726–1727, 1824
Morquio-Ullrich disease 1727
Mortality 2–4, 113–114
  and birth weight 112, 113
  and gestational age 111, 112, 113
  in high-birth-weight infant 124
  infant 3
  leading causes of 4, 5
  perinatal 4, 112, 113
  in preschool years 4
  in school years 4
  in twins 122, 122
Mosaicism 897
Mosher "lifesaver" 620
"Mota" 572
Mother-child interactions 255
Mothering 268
Mothering-in, of low-birth-weight infant 107
Moths 484
Motor cortex 851
Motor development 252, 851
Motor disorders 284, 851
  hysterical 284
  as psychopathologic symptoms and syndromes 274–275
Motor incoordination 140, 260, 361, 404, 454, 544, 851, 1040. See also Ataxia; Incoordination.
  in infancy and toddlerhood 252
  in preschool years 256
Motor retardation, 381, 851, 1040, 1838, 1841–1842
Motor weakness. See also Paralysis.
  in acute polyneuritis 1007
  in brain tumors 940, 945, 947
  in multiple sclerosis 918
  in spinal cord tumors 955
Mottling, circulatory 78, 1070–1071
  in cretinism 1070–1071
  in newborn 78
Mount and Reback syndrome see Familial paroxysmal choreoathetosis
Mouth 1837–1856, 1894, 1900, 1906. See also Oral; Specific structures and disease.
  alveolar ridge lesions 1838–1840
  floor of mouth lesions 1838–1840
  gums and oral mucosa lesions 1851–1855
  lip, palate, and jaw malformations 1841–1848
  of newborn 80, 1837–1838
  tongue 1848–1851

Movements, involuntary *see* Involuntary movements
M protein
  precipitin method 648
  of streptococcal cell wall **648**
mRNA *see* RNA, messenger
M-serotypes 648
MSH *see* Melanocyte-stimulating hormone
Mucha-Habermann disease **1810**
Mucin test 515
Mucocele
  oral 1837, **1839**
  of paranasal sinus 1702
Mucocutaneous leishmaniasis **837–838**
Mucoid impaction, in cystic fibrosis 427
Mucoitin sulfuric acid 144
Mucomyst *see* N-Acetylcysteine
Mucopolysaccharides **398–404**, *403*, 414, 425
Mucopolysaccharidoses **398–404**, 892, **914–915**, 1824, 1875
  types I, II and III **399**, *400, 401, 403*, 404, 909, **914–915**, *915*
  type IV, **400**, 404
  types V, VI, VII and VIII, **404**
Mucoproteins 144, 695
Mucormycosis *see* Phycomycosis
Mucosa, intestinal
  in kwashiorkor 173
  in lipoprotein deficiency 377
  in marasmus 171
Mucosal-cell transport abnormalities **1584–1589**
Mucous cysts *see* Mucoceles
Mucous membrane
  bleeding in leukemia 1209
  in dehydration 229
  herpetic infections of 714
  mutilation in kala-azar 837
  tests in allergic disease **449**
Mucoviscidosis *see* Cystic fibrosis of pancreas
Mucus 144
  in cystic fibrosis 413, 416
Mucus stools in amebiasis 828
"Mud" 572
Mukerjee's choleraphage 612
Mullsoy 162
Multicystic kidney **1471–1472**, 1477
Multifactorial traits **302**, **315**
Multinucleate giant cells, in measles 730, **733**
Multiocular hydatid disease 821, *823*
Multiparity, and iron deficiency anemia 1161
Multiple births **117–124**. *See also* Twin.
  and cerebral palsy 882
  and congenital anomalies 60
  familial 118
  fetal complications **119–122**
  incidence 117–118
  intertwin relationships 123–124
  neonatal complications **122–123**
  and neonatal mortality 113
  perinatal mortality 122
  placentation of twins **118**
  prognosis in **123**
Multiple fractures 315
Multiple hereditary exotoses **1727–1728**
Multiple puncture tests (Heaf and Tine) **680–682**
Multiple sclerosis **918**, 1042
Multiple X chromosome syndromes 309, 310
Mumps 720, **737–740**, 1887
  meningoencephalitis **738**, **1018–1019**

Mumps (*cont.*)
  myocarditis 1429
  orchitis **738–739**
  vaccine *1897*
Muramic acid 440
Murine (endemic) typhus 777, 778, **780–781**
Murmurs 82, 207, **494–495**, 498, 1177, 1181, **1341–1344**
  aortopulmonary fenestration **1395**
  atrial septal defects **1398–1401**
  diastolic, basal 495
  functional (innocent) **495**
  in funnel chest 1714
  innocent 495
  in iron deficiency anemia 1161
  machinery type 1342, **1393–1394**, 1406
  middiastolic, apical **495**, 1374, 1394
  midsystolic 1342
  of mitral regurgitation **494–495**
  patent ductus arteriosus **1394**
  presystolic, apical 495
  in rheumatic carditis **494–495**, 497, 498
  systolic 207, **494–495**, 1161, 1181, **1341–1342**, 1343, **1397–1401**, 1714
  to and fro, 1344
  in β-thalassemia 1181
  in ventricular septal defect 1397
Murray Valley encephalitis (Australian X disease) 1016, **1017–1018**
Muscarine 532
Muscle
  atrophy
    in dermatomyositis 511
    in marasmus 171
    in polyneuritis, acute **1007**
    in scleroderma 512
    in tuberculosis of the hip 674
  biopsy 370, 371, 511, 514, 809
  congenital defects **1028**
  contraction, and calcium 196
  contractures, in myositis fibrosa 1033
  cramps, in heroin withdrawal 562
  in dermatomyositis **510–511**
  diseases **1025–1040**
    arthrogryposis multiplex **1029**
    clubfoot, congenital **1029**
    cranial muscles, congenital defects of **1028–1029**
    endocrine myopathies **1036**
    limp infant (floppy child) syndrome **1027–1028**
    metabolic myopathies **1034–1035**
    muscular dystrophies **1030–1031**
    muscular hypertrophy, congenital **1029–1030**
    myasthenia gravis **1036–1038**
    myositis **1032–1034**
    myotonias **1031–1032**
    skeletal muscles, congenital defects of **1028**
    torticollis, congenital **1029**
  dystrophy *see* Muscular dystrophy
  in glycogenoses **369**, 370
  growth **236**
  hypertrophy **1029–1030**, 1031, 1035, 1097, 1848
  hypoplasia **1027–1028**
  hypotonia, **1027–1028**, 1071
  incoordination 511, 1040
  mass increase
    in congenital adrenal hyperplasia 1035, 1097
  pain. *See also* Myalgia.
    in brucellosis 611

Muscle (*cont.*)
  pain (*cont.*)
    in coccidioidomycosis 789
    in dermatomyositis **511**
    myohemoglobinuria 1035
    in pleurodynia **750**
    in poliomyelitis **744–746**
    in polyarteritis nodosa 514
    in rat-bite fever 634
  phosphorylase 371, 372
  "pseudohypertrophy" 370
  recoil
    in newborn *86,* **86**
  rigidity 287, 1640
  spasm 673, 809, 1217
  sugar 140
  tenderness 809, 1035
  tone **86,** 854
  wasting
    in kwashiorkor 173
    in rheumatoid arthritis 506
  weakness 377, 404, 409, 495, **851**
    in dermatomyositis 511
    in dystrophia myotonica 1032
    in episodic adynamia **1034–1035**
    in familial periodic paralysis **1034**
    in Fanconi syndrome 1521
    in Friedreich's ataxia 922
    in glycogenoses **1035**
    in hyperkalemic paralysis **1034**
    in hyperthyroidism 1084
    in hypokalemic paralysis **1034**
    in hypothyroidism **1035**
    in kwashiorkor 173
    in muscular dystrophies **1028, 1030**
    in myasthenia **1036–1038**
    in potassium deficiency 230, **1034**
    in scleroderma **512**
    in vitamin D resistant rickets 206
Muscular dystrophy 370, 511, **1028, 1030–1031, 1326**
  of Batten and Turner 1027
  and cardiac hypertrophy 1433
Musculoskeletal deformities, in Friedreich's ataxia 922
Musical murmur 495
Muskrat 757
Mustargen *see* Nitrogen mustard
"Muta" 572
Mutations 294, **297,** 318
  single gene **304,** 314
Mutism **276**
  hysterical 284
Myalgia 494
  in hemorrhagic fever 848
  in measles 732
  in murine typhus 780
  in Rocky Mountain spotted fever 781
Myasthenia gravis 325, 511, 852, 923, 1008, **1036–1038,** **1326,** 1818
Mycobacteria (and diseases caused by) **662–691**
  nontuberculous **690–691**
    M. balnei 691
    M. fortuitum 662, 690–691
    M. intracellulare (Battey bacilli) 662, 690–691
    M. kansasii 662, 690
    M. leprae (Hansen's bacillus) 662, 690–691
    M. marinum **690**
    M. paratuberculosis (Johne's bacillus) 662

Mycobacteria (and diseases caused by) (*cont.*)
  scotochromogenic bacilli 690–691
    M. scrofulaceum 690
    M. ulcerans 662, **690**
  tuberculous 662
    M. avium 662, 690
    M. bovis 662, 690
    M. tuberculosis (var. *hominis* **622**) 438, 662–690
Mycolog cream 1814
Mycoplasma infections **625–626**
  arthritidis 625
  fermentans 625
  hominis **625**
  orale 625
  pharynges 625
  pneumoniae 432, 581, 585–586, **625–626,** 726, **1311**
  salivarium 625
Mycostatin, in candidiasis 796
Mycotic diseases **785–796**
  actinomycosis **785–786**
  aspergillosis **786–787**
  blastomycosis **787–788**
  candidiasis **795–796**
  coccidioidomycosis **788–791**
  cryptococcosis **793–795**
  histoplasmosis **791–793**
  keratitis **1823**
  phycomycosis **795**
  pulmonary infections **1307–1308**
  of skin **1788–1791**
Mydriasis 532, 551, **1817**
  in amphetamine addict 565
  in heroin withdrawal 562
  and LSD 568
Myelin degeneration, in thiamine deficiency 179
Myelinoelastic diseases **916, 918–919**
Myelitis 699, 708
  in African trypanosomiasis 834
Myelocytes 1203
Myelodysplasia *see* Spina bifida cystica
Myelography **855,** 868, 876, 955, **956** 1015
Myelomeningocele, and neurogenic bladder dysfunction 1552
Myeloschisis *see* Spina bifida cystica
Myenteric (Auerbach's) plexus 1621
Myiasis **846**
Myocardial Aschoff body 493
Myocardial contractility impairment **1379**
Myocardial disorders **1432–1435**
  anomalous left coronary 1395, 1435
Myocardial fibrosis, in cystic fibrosis 415
Myocardial hemosiderosis, in β-thalassemia 1181
Myocardial infarction 376
Myocardiopathy 511
Myocarditis 485, **1428–1429**
  acute 1337
  in Chagas' disease 836
  due to Coxsackie viruses 749
  in diphtheria 615
  interstitial
    in Friedreich's ataxia 922
  in measles 734
  in mumps 739
  in poliomyelitis 744
  of rheumatic fever **493**
  in systemic lupus erythematosus 509
  in toxoplasmosis 840

Myocarditis (*cont.*)
  in trichinosis 808
Myoclonic epilepsies **989–990, 999–1000**
  progressive familial (Unierricht's disease) 913, **990**
Myoclonic spasms, massive 585, **990–991, 1000**
Myoclonic twitching 921, **989**
Myoclonus **989**
  in Alper's disease 915
Myodystrophia fetalis deformans *see* Arthrogryposis
    multiplex
Myoglobin 144, 1158
Myoglobinuria 371, 1158, 1464
Myohemoglobin 1035
Myohemoglobinuria **1035**
Myomas, of small bowel 1661
Myonecrosis 579
Myopathies 370, 372, 456
Myopia, in low-birth-weight infant 116, 1835
Myosin 511
Myositis 511, **1032–1034**
  fibrosa **1033**
  ossificans **1033–1034,** 1708
  in toxoplasmosis 840
Myotonias **1031–1032**
Myotonic dystrophy 850, 1032
Myriasis 1792
Myringotomy 463, **1887**
Mysoline (Primidone) 186, **999**
Mysterica fragrans 569
Mytelase (ambenonium chloride), in myasthenia 1038
Myxedema 1071, **1072, 1075–1077**
  of vocal cords 1041
Myxovirus group **720–725**
MZ *see* Twins, monozygous

NAD *see* Niacin adenine dinucleotide
NADH$_2$ 218
NADP *see* Niacin adenine dinucleotide phosphate
Naegeli's syndrome 931
Naegleria gruberi 830
Nafcillin **585**
NaHCO$_3$ *see* Bicarbonate
Nail-biting 276
Nail-patella syndrome 1514, 1707, 1734
Nails
  anomalies of 250, 1761
  ectodermal dysplasia of 1707
  in hypoparathyroidism 212
  keratinization of the 1755
  thickening 1838
Naladixic acid 581, **588**
  and bulging fontanel 958
Nalline, nalorphine 54, 533, 559, *563*
  test **563**
NAMRU 2 solution, in cholera treatment **613**
Naphtha 530, **538–540**
Naphthalene *530*
Naphuride *see* Suramin
Narcolepsy **295, 1003–1004**
Narcotics
  addiction **558–575**
  antagonists 84
  in burns 523
  during labor 54, 70
  neonatal **573–575**
  withdrawal 84, **573–575**

Nasal *see* Nose
Nasal bridge, in hypercalcemia 207
Nasal carriers
  of *N. meningitidis*, prophylaxis **608**
  of *S. aureus* 645
Nasal challenge test 449
Nasal clefts 388
Nasal colonization, staphylococcal 644
Nasal decongestants 1877
Nasal diphtheria, primary 615
Nasal discharge 459
Nasal eosinophilia 460
Nasal flaring, R.D.S. 1261
Nasal itching 459
Nasal obstruction 459
Nasal regurgitation, in poliomyelitis **744–746**
Nasal septal hematoma 1875
Nasal septum *1875*
Nasal stuffiness 459
  in neonatal narcotic withdrawal syndrome 574
Nasal swab culture, in pertussis **630–631**
Nasal voice, in poliomyelitis **744–746**
Nasogastric tubes 1909
  for low-birth-weigh infant 109
Nasoorbital encephalocele *871*
Naso-, and oropharynx **1887–1880**
Nasopharyngeal angiofibroma, in subglottic hemangiomas
    1285
Nasopharyngeal swabs, measles virus in 734
Nasopharyngitis 619
Nasopharynx **1877–1880**
Nasotracheal intubation 1280, 1286
Natal teeth **1838**
National Association of Mothers of Twins 124
National Association for the Help of Retarded Children
    897
"Natural detoxification" 583
Natural environment 1912
"Natural" immunity 438
Nature/nurture influences 123
Nausea 209, 361, 454, 456, 301, 519
  in migraine **1002**
  in pseudotumor cerebri 958
  in viral hepatitis **708**
NDI *see* Nephrogenic diabetes insipidus
Nebulizers 426, 467
Necator americanus **805–807**
Neck *1900*, **1906**
  of newborn 75, 81
Neck hyperextension
  in bronchial adenoma 1289
  in vascular ring 1417
Neck pain, and foreign bodies in larynx and trachea
    1278
Neck veins, distension, in right heart failure **1421**
Necrobiosis lipoidica **1763,** *1764*
Necrotic arachnidism **1793**
Necrotic lesions, in typhus, epidemic 780
Necrotizing encephalopathy (Leigh's disease) 915
Necrotizing enterocolitis
  in Hirschsprung's disease 646
  neonatal *1582*
Necrotizing hemorrhagic leucoencephalitis, acute **918**
Needle aspiration, in cat scratch antigen 699
"Needle tracks," in drug addict 559
Negativism 269, 276
Neglected children 558

Negri bodies **756,** 957, 1016
Neisseria meningitidis 576, **584–588, 598–609, 622–625,** 1232, 1242. *See also* Meningococcus.
Nelson's familial lymphohistiocytosis 1246, **1250**
Nemaline myopathy 923, **1028**
Nematodes, diseases caused by **797–812.** *See also* Parasites.
Nematomorpha 797
"Nemmies" 571
Neomycin 476, 581, **587,** 602, 1236, 1509
  in *E. coli* infections of newborn 641
Neonatal **66–127.** *See also* Newborn.
  agranulocytosis 1205
  anoxia **67–74, 1258**
    and hyperbilirubinemia 1681
  breast hyperplasia, 1129
  cephalhematoma 79, **80,** 1695, 1704
  diabetes mellitus 344
  duodenal obstruction **1613–1615**
  erythropoiesis **1155–1160**
  hepatitis 198, **1684**
  herpes 713
  hypocalcemia 84, 85, 127, **211–212,** 1388
  hypoglycemia 127, 307, **361–362,** 363, 368, 574, 1095
  hypoparathyroidism **210–213**
  hypothyroidism, **1067–1068, 1070–1071,** 1077
  intestinal perforation **1618**
  jaundice 75, 78, 121, **1676–1685**
    and cretinism 1070–1071
  ketonuria 368
  kidney 831, **1454, 1471–1474**
  Letterer-Siwe's disease 1246
  leukemia **1213–1214**
  morbidity **113–117,** *115*
  mortality 64, *76,* 111, **112–113**
  myasthenia **1036**
  narcotic addiction **573–575**
  neurologic examination **83–86, 853–854**
  renal abnormalities **1471–1474**
  sclerema 1768
  sepsis **596–598, 645–647**
  subcutaneous fat necrosis 1768
  teeth **1838**
  tetany 212, **388**
  thrombocytopenic purpura 765, **1235**
  thrush 78, **1854–1855**
  thymectomy *see* Thymectomy, neonatal
Neoplasms. *See also* Tumors; *specific organs or systems.*
  alimentary tract **1661–1662**
  genitourinary tract **1560–1562**
  skeletal system **1743–1745**
  thyroid **1087–1088**
Neostibosan *see* Ethylstibamine
Neostigmine 587
Neostigmine bromide (Prostigmine) *see* Prostigmine
Neo-Synephrine 1272, **1282,** 1817, 1876
Nephrectomy 1475, 1534 *1561*
Nephritis *see* Glomerulonephritis
  hereditary **1514–1515**
Nephroblastoma 1561. *See also* Wilms' tumor.
Nephrocalcinosis 207, 330, 1252, 1463, 1508, 1825
  in renal tubular acidosis, distal **1525**
  in sarcoidosis 1252
Nephrogenesis **1451–1452**
Nephrogenic diabetes insipidus (NDI) 424, **1150–1151, 1529**
  sweat electrolytes in 424

Nephrolithiasis, in sarcoidosis 1252
Nephron, fetal 50
Nephronophthisis 1460, **1515,** 1518
Nephropathies. *See also* Kidneys.
  due to drugs 1509
  hereditary **1514–1516**
  lead 542, 1509
  miscellaneous 1506
  toxic **1509**
Nephrotic syndrome 374, 389, **1499–1057**
  congenital **1506–1507**
  in diabetic children 1509
  in Fanconi syndrome 1523
  in sickle-cell disease 1177, **1510–1511**
Nephrotoxic nephropathy **1509**
Nephrotoxicity **586–588, 1509**
  of bacitracin 586
  of gentamicin 588
  of kanamycin 587
  of polymyxins B, E 587
  of sulfonamides 586
  of vancomycin 586
Nephrotoxins 1509
Nerve conduction studies **856–857**
Nerve conduction velocities 1025
Nerve deafness **738,** 1019, 1514, 1885
  in hereditary nephritis **1514**
Nerve root pain, in zoster 1785
Nerve tissue vaccine (NTV) 759
Nervi erigentes 1550
Nervousness, in Graves' disease 1083
Nervous system **849–1042**
  cerebrovascular diseases **960–966**
  degenerative and demyelinating diseases **907–937**
  in dermatomyositis 510–511
  developmental defects **857–878**
  disorders specific to children **1040–1042**
    acute cerebellar ataxia **1041–1042**
    familial dysautonomia **1040–1041**
    spasmus nutans **1040**
  infections other than meningitides **1008–1025**
  mental retardation **887–904**
  muscle diseases **1025–1040**
  neurologic diagnosis **849–878**
  paroxysmal disorders **980,** 1006
  peripheral neuropathies **1006–1008**
  prenatal defects **857–878**
  pseudotumor cerebri **957–960**
  trauma to **966–980**
  tumors of, **937–957**
Nervous system complications
  of infectious mononucleosis **719**
  in kerosene poisoning **539**
  in leukemia **1211**
  in malaria 832
  in measles 731, **733–735**
  in paragonimiasis 816
  in phycomycosis 795
  in Rocky Mountain spotted fever 782
  in thrombocytopenic purpura, idiopathic (ITP) 1234
Nervous system excitation, due to histaminic therapy 454
Nervous system syphilis 655
Neural ectoderm 872
Neural maturion, thyroid deficiency of **1065**
Neural plate closure defects **868**
  cranial anomalies **868–872**

Neural plate closure defects (*cont.*)
  cranial anomalies (*cont.*)
    anencephalus **868–870**
    cranium bifidum **869–872**
    encephaloceles 869–872
  dermal sinus **876–877**
  diastematomyelia **876**
  spina bifida 872–876
  spinal anomalies **872–877**
Neural tumor, and chronic diarrhea **1113**
Neuraminic acid 914
Neuraminidase 721
Neuritis, peripheral, in thiamine deficiency 179. *See also*
      Neuropathies, peripheral.
Neuroabiotrophies, polymorphous 921–925
Neuroblastoma 331, 955, 1042, **1110–1112**, 1167, 1447,
      1693, 1715, 1745, 1831
  exophthalmos in 1831
  hypertension in 1447
  intraspinal extension 1715
  occult, and acute cerebellar ataxia 1042
Neurocutaneous melanosis **929**
Neurocutaneous syndromes 925–931, **1826**
Neuroendocrine communications **1045–1046**
Neuroendocrine transducer cells **1045–1046**
Neurofibromas **927–928**, **954–956**, 1831
Neurofibromatosis 358, 853, **927–928**, **954–956**, 1109, 1696,
      1715, 1745, 1805, 1826, 1848
  and pheochromocytoma 1109
Neurogenic bladder **1552–1553**
Neurogenic nystagmus **1834**
Neurogenic polydipsia 1151
Neurohumors 1047
Neurohypophysis *see* Pituitary, posterior
Neurologic anomalies. *See also* Nervous system.
  in acute intermittent porphyria (Swedish type) 409
  in Chagas' disease 836
  due to congenital rubella 766
  due to Coxsackie viruses 750
  in ECHO virus infections 753
  in mixed porphyria 410
  in niacin deficiency 182
  in phenylketonuria 324
Neurologic deficit, and Apgar score 76
Neurologic diagnosis 849–857
  ancillary procedures 854–857
  history **849**
  neurologic examination 83–86, *850*, 853–854, *1901*
  symptoms and signs 849–854
Neurologic examination 853–854, *1901*
  in epilepsy 922–993
  of the newborn 76, 83–86, *850*, 853–854
  and outcome in low-birth-weight infant 115
Neurologic sequelae,
  of hypernatremic dehydration 231
  in low-birth-weight infant 115
  of meningitis **608**
Neuromotor diseases which impair ventilation **1324–**
      1326
Neuromuscular disorders **1468**
  in triosephosphate isomerase, deficiency 393
Neuromyelitis optica (Devic's disease) **918**
Neuronophagia 744
Neuropathies peripheral 924, **1006–1009**
  in acanthocytosis 1008
  in acute intermittent porphyria **409**, 1008
  acute polyneuritis **1006–1008**

Neuropathies peripheral (*cont.*)
  in brain tumors 943
  in cat scratch disease 699
  in Charcot Marie Tooth disease **924, 1008**
  due to chloramphenicol 588
  chronic and recurrent polyneuropathies **1008**
  cranial nerve palsies 853, **1008–1009**
  Dejerine Sottas polyneuropathy **924, 1008**
  in dermatomyositis 511
  in infectious mononucleosis 718
  and isoniazid 685
  in lead poisoning 544
  in lipomucopolysaccharidoses (type VIII) 404
  in measles 735
  in polyarteritis nodosa 514, 1008
  in pyridoxin deficiency 184
  in Refsum's syndrome **379, 924, 1008**
  in serum sickness 485
  in smallpox 771
  in systemic lupus erythematosus 509, 1008
  in thiamine deficiency 179
  in tri-ortho-cresyl phosphate poisoning 532
  in viral hepatitis 708
"Neurophysins" 1149
Neurosyphilis 658
Neurotic traits, and rumination 1578
Neurotoxicity, of isoniazid 685
Neurovisceral gangliosidosis *see* Tay-Sachs disease
Neutralizing antibodies, and tests
  in adenoviral infections 725, **726**
  in cytomegalic inclusion disease 704
  in *Herpesvirus hominis* infection 716
  in measles 732
  in mumps 738, **739**
  in rhinoviral disease 727
  in rickettsia infections 780
  of RS virus 724
  in rubella **762–763, 767–768**
Neutralizing antigens, of herpesvirus 712
Neutropenia 328, 329, 366, 387, 586, 705, 782, **1204–1206,**
      1594
Neutrophilia, due to glucocorticoids 1093
Neutrophils 1203
Nevoid lentigo *1802*
Nevoxanthoedothelioma **1812**
Nevus (Nevi) **1767–1768**
  araneus 1813
  flammeus **1812–1813**
  vasculosus **1812–1813**
Newborn **66–127**. *See also* Neonatal.
  abdomen 75, **82**
  and antimicrobial therapy 594
  anus 74, 76, 83, 104, **1626–1630**
  Center for 101
  circulatory system **69–70, 1333–1334**
  color 75, 78
  cry *see* Cry
  cyanosis 75, 78, 1261
  diabetic mother 115, **125–127,** 1261
  diarrhea **226–230,** 1582
  ears 80, *81*
  examination 74–78, 83–86, 853–854
  extremities of **83**
  eyes **80**
  face 78, 80, 1071
  genitalia of **83**
  head 75, **79–81**

Newborn (cont.)
  heart 69–70, 75, 81, **1333–1334**
    rate 82
  hemangiomas 78
  hemorrhagic disease of, 106, **140**, **1241**, 1679
  high-birth-weight infant see High-birth-weight infant
  impetigo 78, 645
  incubators for *104*
  iron metabolism **1158**
  kidney 83, **1454**, **1471–1474**
  maturity assessment **84–88**
  meningitis in 597, **599–600**, 645
  molding of head 79
  mouth 81, **1837–1838**
  muscle tone 85, *86, 86, 87*
  neck **75**, **81**
  necrotizing enterocolitis **1582**
  nose 81
  pneumonia **1270**
  pneumothorax **1271**
  pulmonary hemorrhage **1271–1272**
  rectum 76, 83, **1625–1630**
  reflex activity *85*, **87–88**, *850*, **853–854**
  respiratory depression in 54, 55
  resuscitation tray *103*
  righting reactions 87
  skin 75, 78, **1768**, **1814**
  splenic rupture 1218
  *Standards and Recommendations for Hospital Care
    of Newborn Infants* 7, 102
  staphylococcal disease in **644–645**
  stomach 76, 109, **1564–1567**, 1618, **1652**
  thyrotoxicosis **1087**
  transition from fetus to **66–77**
  treatment and initial appraisal of **71–74**
  vaginal discharge in 83
  vomiting **1574–1575**
    blood in vomitus **1578**
Newcastle disease 720
Niacin 138, 139, **181–183**, 336
Niacin adenine dinucleotide phosphate 181
Niacinamide 139
Niacin deficiency (pellagra) 135, 139, **181–183**, 336
Nickel 145
Nickerson-Kveim skin test **1252–1253**
Niclosamide (Yomesan) **819**
  in hymenolepiasis **820**
Nicotinamide 183
Nicotine 532
Nicotinic acid see Niacin
Niemann-Pick disease 911, **913**, 1218, 1688, 1829
  Type D (Nova Scotia variant) 384
Night blindness (nyctalopia) 1823, **1827–1828**
"Night Cry," in tuberculosis of the hip 674
Nightmares **275**
Night-terrors **275**
Nighttime bottle caries syndrome **1867**
Nikolsky's sign 1776, 1780
"Nimby" 571
Nipple, breast **1123–1127**
  care 20, 153
  fissure 153
  shields, lead 543
  supernumerary 81
Nipples, bottle 163
  for low-birth-weight infant 106, 109

Niridazole (Ambilhar)
  in dracontiasis **810**
  in schistosomiasis 815
Nitrates 532
Nitricobalamine see B_{12b}
Nitrites 532
Nitroblue tetrazolium (NBT) 396, 398
  test **396–398**, 1206
Nitrocatechol sulfate 384
Nitrofurantoin **587**
Nitrofurazone 1545
Nitrogen
  balance in marasmus 172
  dioxide pneumonitis 1312
  excretion, and carbohydrate intake 136
  fecal losses 133
  growth patterns of 237
  in marasmus 172
  requirements 131, **133**
  retention, in breast-fed infant 134
Nitrogen mustard (Mustargen) 1204, 1225, 1236
Nitroprusside 332
  test 1537
"Nits" 1796
N-Methylisatin-beta-thiosemicarbazone (Marboran) **771–772**, **773–774**
(NNN) medium 837
N_1-Methyl nicotinamide 182, 184
Nocardia 586
Nocardia minutissima **1784**
Nocardiosis, pulmonary **1308**
  in Hodgkin's disease 1225
Nocturia, in diabetes mellitus 346
"Nod" 572
Nodal escape **1368**
Nodal extrasytoles **1368**
Nodal rhythm **1366**
Nodal tachycardia **1366**
Nodules 508, 1763, 1769
Noma 734, 1855
Nonallelic mutations 320
Nonbullous congenital ichthyosiform erythroderma (non-bullous CIE) **1757**
Noncatecholamine sympathomimetic drugs 456
Nondisjunction, of chromosomes **310**
Nonesterified fatty acids see Free fatty acids
Nonketotic hyperglycinemia **329**
Nonlipid reticuloendothelioses **1245–1250**
Nonmotor brain damage 879
Nonparalytic poliomyelitis **745**
Nonspecific pericarditis **1427**
Nonspherocytic hemolytic anemia, cogenital **1175**
Nonvitamin D deficiency rickets 203
Norepinephrine 456, **1107–1113**
  hypersensitivity to, in dysautonomia 1041
  and thermogenesis 99
  and uterine blood flow 44
Norethandrolone 1465, 1686
Norethynodrel (Enovid) 1134
Norm **232**
Norman-Wood disease see Amaurotic familial idiocy, congenital
Normoblasts 1169, 1181, 1184, 1218
North Queensland tick typhus 781
Nose and paranasal sinuses 1145, **1871–1877**, **1894**, **1900**, **1905–1906**
  epistaxis **1876**

Nose and paranasal sinuses (*cont.*)
  foreign bodies **1876**
  growth **1871–1872**
  infections **1874–1875**
  inherited diseases **1872–1873**
  malformations **1872**
  of newborn 80
  nose drops 461, 529, **1876–1877**
  physiology **1871**
  trauma **1875–1876**
  tumors **1873–1874**
Nose-bleed *see* Epistaxis
Nose-picking 273
Nosopsyllus 819
Novobiocin
  effects on newborn and fetus 56
  and glucuronyl transferase 1681
NPH insulin 349
NTV *see* Nerve tissue vaccine
Nuchal rigidity. *See also* Kernig sign.
  in acute cerebellar ataxia 1041
  in bacterial meningitis **599**
  in brain tumors 940–945, 946
  in cervical adenitis 1222
  in Chagas' disease 836
  in cryptococcosis 794
  in encephalitis 1016–1023
  in lymphocytic choriomeningitis 729
  in meningococcal infections 623
  in malaria 832
  in poliomyelitis **744–745**
  in polyneuritis **1007**
  in subarachnoid hemorrhage 963
  in trichinosis 809
Nuclear cataracts, in congenital rubella *766*
Nuclear-cytoplasmic interactions, in genetics 308
Nuclear palsies, in brainstem gliomas **939**
Nuclear transplantation **307**
Nucleoproteins 144
Numbness 569
  in rubella arthritis 761
Nummular eczema 472
Nurses, for low-birth-weight infant 103
Nursing care, for low-birth-weight infant 103, **106**
Nursing, maternal *see* Breast feeding
Nutmeg **569**
Nutrients, essential *see* Nutrition
Nutrition **128–231**
  artificial feeding *see* Cow's milk
  breast-feeding *see* Breast feeding
  caloric distribution 137
  caloric requirements 137
  deficiencies
    of specific nutrients **170–194**
    of calories and protein **170–176**
    vitamins, diseases **176–194**
  diets **148–168**
    for infants of 6–9 months *167*
    in shigellosis **640–641**
  disorders of nutritional homeostasis **170–231**
  eggs 166–167
  energy requirements **128–131**
  essential nutrients **131–148**
    amino acids *see* Amino acids
    carbohydrate 136
    fat **135–136**. *See also* Lipids.
    minerals **142–147**

Nutrition (*cont.*)
  essential nutrients (*cont.*)
    protein *see* Protein
    vitamins **137–141**, 166
    water **141–142**
  feeding during the second year **167–168**
  feeding techniques **148–168**
  and growth 243
  infant feeding **163–168**
  "junior" foods 166–167
  mistakes in infant feeding **165**
  in obesity 220
  overfeeding of infants 164
  parenteral *see* Parenteral nutrition
  precooked foods 166
  recommended dietary allowances (RDA) **146**
  solid foods, introduction of **166**
Nutritional cataract 1826
Nutritional influences and growth 243
Nuts 391
Nyctalopia 177, 1823, **1827–1828**
Nystagmoid movements 939
Nystagmus 377, 671, **852, 1834**
  in acute cerebellar ataxia 1041
  in albinism 326
  in barbiturate addict 564
  in brain tumors **938, 939**, 942, 943, 945, 946, 950
  in cerebral white matter diseases 916
  in dextropropoxyphere (Darvon) poisoning 532
  in Friedreich's ataxia 922
  in Lowe's syndrome 1522
  rotary 378
  in spasmus nutans 1040
Nystatin 581, 1791

O₂ *see* Oxygen
Oasthouse syndrome 327, 1595
Obesity **214–221**, 237, 250, 271, 338, 1056, 1058
  adipose tissue **217–219**
  and caloric requirements 131
  and cardiopulmonary failure **1328**
  in children of diabetic mothers 127
  in colloid brainstem cyst 946
  in craniopharyngioma 952
  in Cushing's syndrome **1099–1100**
  etiology **215–217**
  experimental obesity **219–220**
  treatment **220**
Obligatory vitamins *see* Vitamins
Obligatory water loss *see* Water loss
Obliterative bronchiolitis, chronic **1290–1292**
Obsessive fear of germs 286
Obstetric management **15–21**
  analgesic during delivery 20
  during labor and delivery **19–20**
  prenatal care **15–19**
  puerperium **20–21**
Obstructive airway diseases **1284–1298**
  lower airways **1287–1298**
  upper airways **1284–1287**
Obstructive circulatory lesions and conditions **1371–1379,
    1379–1393**
Obstructive hydrocephalus **863**
Obstructive megaureter **1557**
Obstructive uropathy 210, **1556**
Occipital dermal sinus *876, 877*

Occipital lobe epilepsy 982, **988**
Occipital lymphadenopathy, in rubella 760, **761**
Occipital neuralgia 673
Occipitofrontal circumference (OFC) 857
  in hydrocephalus **856**
Occipitoposterior presentations 75
Occlusion disorders **1868–1869**
Occlusion of teeth **1861–1862, 1868–1869**
Occlusive cerebrovascular disease **960**
Ochronosis 326
Ochronotic arthritis 326
Octomethyl pyrophosphoramide (OMPA) *see* OMPA
Ocular *see* Eye
Ocular abnormalities (disorders, lesions) 852, 1041–1042, 1817–1832
  in Lowe's syndrome 1522
  in onchocerciasis **811**
  in sarcoidosis **1251**
  in tularemia 692
Ocular dysmetria **1041–1042**
Ocular foreign bodies **1822**
Ocular granuloma, in cat scratch disease 698
Ocular hypertelorism *see* Hypotelorism
Ocular nystagmus **1834**
Ocular pemphigus 1779
Ocular sparganosis 821
Ocular syphilis **1823**
Ocular torticollis 1834
Ocular tuberculosis **1823**
Oculo-auriculo-vertebral syndrome of Goldenhar 1696, 1716, 1831, 1842
Oculoglandular syndrome of Parinaud, in cat scratch disease 698
Oculoglandular tularemia **692**
Oculogyric crises 532
Oculomandibulodyscephaly with hypotrichosis (Haller-mann-Streiff syndrome) 1831, **1838**
Oculomotor nerve injury **979**
Odontoblasts 1856
Odor
  of bitter almonds 532
  in phenylketonuria 323
  urine, in maple syrup urine disease 327
  of violets 532
  of vomitus, in poisoning 532
Odor-of-sweaty-feet syndrome **379**
OFC *see* Occipitofrontal circumference
Ogival palate **1841–1842**. *See also* High-arched palate.
17-OH-corticosteroids *see* 17-hydroxycorticosteroids
17-OHCS *see* 17-hydroxycorticosteroids
Oil of wintergreen *see* Methyl salicylate
Old English furniture polish **1312**
Old tuberculin of Koch (OT) 680
Old World hookworm *see Ancylostoma duodenale*
Olein, in breast milk 151
Olfaction 1871
Oligo-1,4 → 1,4-glucantransferase 371
Oligodactyly 1842
Oligohydramnios 50, 1471
  and renal agenesis 1546
Oligoméganéphronie 1475
Oligomenorrhea 561
Oligosaccharide malabsorption **1590–1594**
Oligospermia 311
Oliguria 209, 409, 525, 559, 780, **1463–1464**, 1514
  in dehydration 229
  in hemorrhagic fever 847

Oliguria (*cont.*)
  in leptospirosis **621**
Olive oil 135
Olivopontocerebellar degenerations 922
Ollier's syndrome **1728**
Olser-Quincke's disease *see* Hereditary angioneurotic edema
OMPA 550–551
Omphalitis 1691
Omphalocele 82, 1030, **1615, 1634**, 1848
Omphalomesenteric duct **1618–1620**
Omphalomesenteric vessels 1618
Onchocerca volvulus **811–812**
Onchocerciasis **811–812**
Oncogenesis 13
Oncotic pressure 386
Oncovin *see* Vincristine
"Onion skin" lesions, of blood vessels, in systemic lupus erythematosus 508
Ontogenesis, of fetal thyroid function **1065–1067**
Onychogryphosis 1761
Onycholysis 1761
Onychophagia *see* Nail-biting
Oocyst 831, 839
Oophorectomy 1128
Open-heart surgery, 1387, 1405
  and coagulation factor deficiencies 1243
  and cytomegalovirus infection 704
"Open" therapy of burns 523
Operant conditioning, in mental retardation **895**
Operations, precipitating personality disorders 268, 287
Operator genes 36
Operculate egg, of fish tapeworm *820*
Operculum 815
"Operon" 36
Ophthalmia, gonorrheal 80, 1819
Ophthalmia neonatorum 80, **1819**
Ophthalmia, sympathetic 1828
Ophthalmic zoster 1785
Ophthalmology **1817–1832**
Ophthalmoplegia
  in acute polyneuritis **1007**
  in hyperthyroidism 1084
  in migraine 1002
  in myasthenia 1037
  in thiamine deficiency 179
Opisthotonos 327, 532, 673, 853
  in congenital toxoplasmosis **840**
  in kernicterus 1677
  in tuberculous meningitis 671
Opium 641
  overdose 563
  poppy 559
  withdrawal log (D.W.L.) score *562*
Opossums 691, 757, 835
Oppenheim's disease *see* Amyotonia congenita
Opsoclonus 852, 955, 1041–1042, 1111
Opsonocytophagic test of Huddleson 611
Optic atrophy
  in basal ganglia degeneration 916, 920
  in brain tumors 938, 939, 946, **950, 952**
  in cerebellar degeneration 922
  and chloramphenicol 416, 422
  in Friedreich's ataxia 922
  in gray matter diseases 912, 913, 915
  in optic nerve and chiasm tumors 950
  in white matter diseases 916

Optic chiasm 1047
Optic disk 1828
Optic nerve **1828–1830**
  astrocytoma, and neurofibromatosis 927
  and chiasm tumors **950–952**
  injury 979
  tumors, in neurofibromatosis 928
Optic neuritis 588, 852, **938**
  and chloramphenicol 416, 422, 588
  in cystic fibrosis 416, 422
  due to mumps 738
  in neuromyelitis optica 918
  varicella complications 701
Opticokinetic nystagmus **939,** 947
Oral actinomycosis **785**
Oral clefts **1866**
Oral-facial-digital syndrome 1478
Oral feedings, in diarrheal disease **1581**
Oral hypoglycemic agents, in juvenile diabetes 355
Oral mucosa, and inflammatory lesions **1852–1855**
Oral smear method, for sex chromatin 1132
Oral thrush **1854–1855**
"Oranges" 571
Orange juice 166, 191
Orbit **1830–1831**
  hemorrhage into, in scurvy 188
Orbital cellulitis 1820
  and phycomycosis 795
Orbital encephalocele 1702
Orbital ecchymoses
  in anterior fossa basilar fracture 969
  in basilar skull fracture 968
Orbital fracture 979
Orbital fractures **1705**
Orbital hypotelorism 860, 1699, **1722**
Orbital swelling, and neuroblastoma 1111
Orchidoblastoma 1561
Orchiopexy 1555
Orchitis, mumps **738–739**
Organ of Corti 1882, 1884
Organelles **1663**
Organic mental syndromes **975**
Organic mercurials 549
Organic phosphate ester poisoning **550–552**
Organification, of iodide **1060–1061**
Organogenesis 764
Oriental lung fluke *see Paragonimus westermani*
Oriental sore **837–838**
Ornamental plants, as poisons 529
Ornithine 334, 336, 337, 340
Ornithine transcarbamylase 334
Ornithine transcarbamylase deficiency 334
Ornithinemia 334
Ornithosis **775**
Orofacial digital syndrome **1850**
Oropharyngeal abscesses, in subglottic hemangiomas 1285
Oropharynx *see* Naso-and oropharynx
Orthopnea, in heart failure 1421
Orthostatic proteinuria *see* Postural proteinuria
Orotic aciduria **340,** 1165
Orotidylic acid 340
Orotidylic pyrophosphorylase 340
Ortolani maneuver 84, 1747, **1749**
Osgood-Schlatter's disease **1739**
Osmolality
  of body fluids 224

Osmolality (*cont.*)
  of body fluids (*cont.*)
    in diarrhea 229
    of fetal and maternal plasma 50
  of urine
    in diabetes insipidus **1150**
    fetal urine 49
Osmosis 222
Osmotic pressure, in fetus 50
Osseous defects, in Letterer-Siwe disease 1247
Osseous maturation
  in hypocaloric dwarfism 170
  in marasmus 171
Ossification, centers of **240**
  in infant of diabetic mother *126*
Osteitis
  deformans (Paget's disease) 1766
  fibrosa 210
    in chronic spinal disease 1467
  of spine 1717
  syphilitic, 655, 657
Osteoarthritis 326
Osteoarthropathy, pulmonary **1742–1743**
Osteoblasts 198
Osteochondritis metaphyseal plates, in syphilis 655
Osteochondroses **1737–1741**
  juvenile **1737–1745**
  of the patella **1739**
  of tarsal navicular **1739**
  of tibial tuberosity **1739**
Osteogenesis **240**
Osteogenesis imperfecta 115, 195, 305, 315, 1696, 1702,
    1722, **1729,** 1885
  tarda **1729**
Osteogenic fibroma 1743
Osteogenic sarcoma **1743–1744**
Osteoid 198, 199, 206, 240
Osteoid osteoma **1743**
Osteomalacia 143, **197, 200**
  in chronic renal disease 1467
  in renal tubular acidosis, distal **1525**
  with rickets and renal tubular acidosis 206
  in vitamin D resistant rickets 206
Osteomyelitis 396, 505, 645, 673, 701
  in cat scratch disease 698
  in coccidioidal granuloma 789
  and craniospinal focal sepsis **1010–1016**
  of mandible 1734
  due to salmonellae 636
  in sepsis neonatorum 597
  in sickle-cell disease 1177
  syphilitic *655*
Osteo-onychodysplasia 1514
Osteopetrosis (Albers-Schönberg disease) 195, 1167, 1734,
    1865
Osteoporosis 328, 329, 331
  in Cushing's syndrome of vertebrae 1100
  in Fanconi syndrome 1521
  due to glucocorticoids 1093
  in rheumatoid arthritis 503, 507
  in sickle-cell disease 1177
Osteopsathyrosis **1729**
Osteosclerosis 1744
Osteotomy 205, 206
Ostial obstruction 459
Ostium abrioventriculare commune (cor biloculare)
    and congenital asplenia 1217

Ostium primum **1398–1399**
Ostium primum defects 1398, **1400–1401**
OT *see* Old tuberculin
Otitic hydrocephalus 957
Otitis externa **1886**
Otitis media 387, 599, 650, **1887**
  antimicrobial therapy **1887**
  and craniospinal focal sepsis **1010–1016**
  in Hand-Schüller-Christian syndrome 1248
  due to *H. influenzae* 619
  in low-birth-weight infant 109
  in measles 731, 734
  in *Mycoplasma pneumonia* infections 626
  in pertussis 629
  serous **461–463,** 1882, 1887
  tuberculous 677
Otoclerosis 305, 1885
Otorrhea, in basilar skull fracture 968, 970, 1704
Ototoxicity
  of gentamicin 588
  of kanamycin 478, 587
  of polymyxin B and E 587
  of vancomycin 586
Outer ear *see* External ear
Ova, parasitic
  Ascaris lumbricoides 801
  Hymenolepsis nana 820
  of pinworm *804*
  Schistosoma mansoni 813
  of trematode 812
  of whipworm *804*
Ovarian agenesis *see* Gonadal dysgenesis
Ovarian androgen secretion 1119
Ovarian cyst *82*, 1119, 1561
Ovarian dysfunction 220, **1115–1120**
Ovarian involvement, in mumps **739**
Ovarian tumors, 1119, 1126, **1561**
  androgen secreting 1119, 1126
  estrogen secreting 1119
Ovarian virilizing syndromes **1127–1128**
Ovary (-ies) **1115–1120**
  growth and 236
  in hernial sac 1631
Overactivity *see* Hyperactivity
Overnutrition (overeating, overfeeding)
  and growth 243
  of infants 164
  and obesity 216
Oversolicitousness (oversolicitude, overprotectiveness)
    268, 269, 283, 518
Overt diabetes **345**
Overweightness *see* Obesity
Ovulation 1124
  multiple 117
Ovum 40
  "splitting" of 118
"Owsleys" 571
OX-2 *Proteus vulgaris* 779
  agglutinins
    in Rocky Mountain spotted fever **782**
    in scrub typhus 783
OX-19 *Proteus vulgaris* **779**
  agglutinins 778
    in Rocky Mountain spotted fever **782**
    in murine typhus 781
    in scrub typhus 783
    in typhus, epidemic 780

OX-K *Proteus vulgaris* **779**
  agglutinins, in scrub typhus 783
Oxacillin **585**, 646
Oxalate 143
Oxalates 143, 532, 533
Oxalic acid 330, 530, 531, 535, 1509
Oxaloacetic acid 136
Oxalosis *330*
Ox cell hemolysin test **718**
Ox eye *see* Buphthalmos
Oxidative activity
  of fetal tissues 53
Oxycel 1238
Oxycephaly 1697, 1830
Oxygen
  hyperbaric 73, 1378
  in sickle-cell anemia 1178
  transplacental diffusion of **46–47**
Oxygen affinity
  of fetal erythrocytes, 66
  of red cell, postnatal 94
Oxygen-carrying capacity
  of fetal blood 66
Oxygen consumption 396
  fetal 33, 46, 47
  of fetal blood 66
  in low-birth-weight newborn **93**
  placenta 33
  uterus 33
Oxygen deficit, in blood of newborn 94
Oxygen pressure
  effect on fetal circulation 49
  and onset of breathing 49
  in umbilical blood 46, 47, 49
Oxygen saturation
  at birth 66
  fetal 49
Oxygenation, fetal 47
Oxygen therapy, **1910**
  in cyanotic heart disease **1378–1379**
  in heart failure 1178
  in low-birth-weight infant **105**
  in obstructive airway disease, 1282
  and retrolental fibroplasia **1829**
Oxymetholone, and aplastic anemia 1167
Oxyphenbutazone 502
Oxytetracycline 608
  in leptospirosis **622**
  in pertussis 632
Oxytocic factor, and breast milk flow 153
Oxytocin
  and fetal water intoxication 56
  induction 20
    and hyponatremia, fetomaternal 17
Oxytocinase 59
Oxyuriasis 1603

PABA *see* p-Aminobenzoic acid
Pachymeningitis spinalis 1010, **1015–1016**
Pachyonychia congenita **1838**
Paco$_2$, in airway obstruction **1278**
Padded sideboards 501
P. aeruginosa see Pseudomonas aeruginosa
PAH clearance **1462**
Pain
  in appendicitis 1640

Pain (*cont.*)
  on defecation 1659
  in extremities 1742
  generalized insensitivity to 1712
  in pericarditis **1425**
  in Pott's disease 673
  in spinal cord tumors **954**
Painful crisis, of sickle-cell anemia **1177**
Paints 538
  and lead poisoning **543**
Pairing, nonhomologous 297
Palatal paralysis, in diphtheria 616
Palate, **1841–1846**
  arched *see* High-arched palate
  cleft *see* Cleft palate
  in hypercalcemia 207
  perforation, syphilitic 657
Palatine tonsil 1877
Palindromic rheumatism 514, 515
Pallidonigral hyperpigmentation 920
Pallor 75, 78, 189, 361, 532, 597, 750, 837, **1160–1203,**
    1208–1209, 1416, 1420
  in anemias **1160–1203**
  at birth 75, 78
  in heart failure 1420
  in hypoglycemia 361
  in hypoplastic left heart complex 1416
  in infantile kala-azar 837
  in iron deficiency **1161**
  in leukemia **1208–1209**
  in scurvy 189
  in sepsis neonatorum 597
  in beta thalassemia 1181
Palmar creases 313, 314
Palmar patterns **313–314**
Palmar xanthomas 376
Palmitin 151
Palpebral edema, unilateral, in Chagas' disease 836
Palpitations 282, 454, 456, 1083
  in Graves' disease 1083
PAM (2-pyridine aldoxime methiodide, Pralidoxime
    iodide) **552**
2-PAM (2-pyridine aldoxime) 533
"Panama red" 572
Pancreas
  annular *see* Annular pancreas
  cystic fibrosis of *see* Cystic fibrosis
  fetal 56
Pancreatic amylase 1568
Pancreatic enzymes
  tests for 424
  in treatment of cystic fibrosis 428
Pancreatic insufficiency 1594
  neutropenia in **1206**
Pancreatic lipase 424
Pancreatic trypsin *see* Trypsin, pancreatic
Pancreatitis 374, 409
  due to ascariasis 802
  in mumps **739**
Pancytopenia 507, 1206
Panencephalitis (Pette and Doring) *see* Subacute scleros-
    ing panencephalitis
Panic reactions. *See also* Anxiety.
  in asthmatics 468
  in marihuana user 566
Panniculitis, febrile, nodular, nonsuppurative **1768–1769**
Panophthalmitis 1820

Panstrongylus 835
Panteric granules 428
Pantothenic acid 138, 140
Pao$_2$, in airway obstruction **1278**
Papanicolaou smear 17, 18, 733
Papaver somniferum 559
Paper electrophoresis 373, 378
Papillae, of tongue 649, 1041, **1840**
  in dysautonomia 1041, **1840**
  in scarlet fever 649
Papillary ependymoma 868
Papilledema 509, **599, 671,** 859, 865, **938,** 958, **1010–1016,**
    1439
  in acute polyneuritis **1007**
  in bacterial meningitis **599**
  in brain tumors **938,** 942, 943, 945, 947
  in craniospinal focal sepsis **1010–1016**
  in cryptococcosis 794
  in hyperaldosteronism 1101
  in hypertension **1439**
  in pseudotumor cerebri 958
  in tuberculous meningitis **671**
Papillitis *see* Optic neuritis
Papilloma 813, **868,** 1806
  choroid plexus **868**
  in schistosomiasis 813
Papillomatosis 1806
Papular urticaria 702
Papules **1753**
  of acne 1815
Papulonecrotic lesions 1645
Papulovesicular eruption, in Rickettsialpox 783
Para-aminosalicylic acid (PAS) 685
Parabens 476
Parabiotic syndrome 84
Paracentesis, pericardial 1426
Paracervical block, during labor 54
Paracolon bacteria 156
Paracolobactrum 65
Paradoxical behavior 258
Paraganglia 1107
Paragonimiasis *799,* 815
Parainfluenza respiratory disease and viruses 625, **722–**
    723
Parakeet 775
Parakeratosis 1787
Paraldehyde 410
  in head injury 973
Paralysis (paresis)
  in botulism 610
  brachial plexus 83, 124, **977,** 1632, 1817
  CNS syphilis 657
  due to Coxsackie viruses **750**
  cranial nerves **1008–1009**
  diaphragm 124, **1325–1326**
  in diphtheria **616, 617**
  in ECHO virus infections **753**
  facial *see* Facial paralysis
  hysterical 284
  laryngeal **744–746**
  in meningomyelocele 874
  in metabolic myopathies 1034
  due to mumps 738
  pharyngeal **744–746**
  phrenic nerve 124, **1325–1326**
  in poliomyelitis **744–745**
  in rabies 756

Paralysis (paresis) (*cont.*)
  in sting of caterpillars 845
  in tick bite 845
  upward gaze 884
Paralytic ileus **1654**
Paralytic poliomyelitis **745–746**
Paralytic squint 852
Paralytic strabismus **1833–1834**
Paramethadione 508
Paramyotonia **1032**
Paramyxovirus 508, 730, 760
Paranasal sinuses. *See also* Nose and paranasal sinuses.
  in cystic fibrosis, clouding of 422
  fractures 968
Paraesophageal hernias **1607**
Paraphimosis *1553*
Paraplegia 699
  in spinal abscess **1015–1016**
  in neuroblastoma 1111
Parasites and parasitic diseases **797–848**, *798–801*
  arthropod caused diseases **844–848**
    arachnidism **844–845**
    centipedes (Chilopoda) 845
    insects (Hexapoda) **845**
    lactrodectism **844**
    mites 845
    scorpions **844–845**
    ticks 845
  helminths **797–825**, *798–801*
    cestodes (tapeworms) *799*, **718–823**
      Cysticercus cellulosae *799*, **818–819**
      Diphyllobothrium latum *799*, **820–821**
        spirometral (sparganosis) *799*, 821
      Dipylidium canium *799*, **820**
      Echinococcus granulosis (hydatid disease) **821–823**
      Hymenolepsis diminuta *799*, **819–820**
      Hymenolepsis nana *799*, **819–820**
      Taenia saginata *799*, **818–819**
      Taenia solium *799*, **817–819**
    flatworms *see* Trematodes; Cestodes
    flukes *see* Trematodes
    nematodes (roundworms) **797–812**, *798–799*
      Ancylostoma braziliense (hookworm disease) *798*, **807**
      Ancylostoma duodenale (hookworm disease) *798*, **805–807**
      Ascaris lumbricoides **797–802**, *798*
      Brugia (Wuchereria) malayi (Malayan filariasis) *798*, **811**
      Dracunculus medinesis (dracontiasis) *799*, **809–810**
      Enterobius vermicularis *798*, **803–804**
      Loa loa loaiasis *799*, **812**
      Necator americanus (hookworm disease) *798*, **805–807**
      Onchocerca volvulus *798*, **811**
      Strongyloides sterocoralis *798*, **807–808**
      Toxicara canis (cutaneous larva migrans), *798*, **802–803**
      Toxicara cati (cutaneous larva migrans) *798*, **802–803**
      Trichinella spiralis (trichinosis), *798*, **808–809**
      Trichuris trichiura *798*, **804–805**
      Wuchereria bancrofti (Bancroft's filariasis) *798*, **810–811**
    tapeworms *see* Cestodes
    trematodes (flukes) *799*, **812–817**
      Clonorchis sinensis *799*, **816–817**

Parasites and parasitic diseases (*cont.*)
  helminths (*cont.*)
      Fasciola hepatice *799*, **817**
      Fasciolopsis buski *799*, **817**
      Paragonimus westermani *799*, **815–816**
      Schistosoma haematobium *799*, **813–815**
      Schistosoma japonicum *799*, **813–815**
      schistosoma mansoni *799*, **813–815**
  hymenopterous disease 844
    myiasis **846**
  protozoa *799*, 800, 801, 825–844. For disease, *see* Protozoan diseases.
      Balantidium coli 827, **838–839**
      Dientamoeba fragilis 825
      Entamoeba histolytica **825–830**, *827*
      Giardia intestinalis 827, **838–839**
      Leishmania braziliensis 828, **837–838**
      Leishmania donovani 828, **837–838**
      Leishmania tropica 828, **837–838**
      Plasmodium falciparum 827, **830–834**
      Plasmodium malariae 827, **830–834**
      Plasmodium ovale 827, **830–834**
      Plasmodium vivax, 827, **830–834**
      Pneumocystic carinii 828, **841–843**
      Toxoplasma gondii 827, **839–841**
      Trypanosoma cruzi 828, **835–837**
      Trypanosoma gambiense 828, **834–835**
      Trypanosoma rhodosiense 828, **834–835**
  worms *see* Helminths
Parasitic infestations, and urticaria 477
Parasitic pneumonias **1311–1312**
Parastic skin diseases **1792**
Paratesticular tumors 1561
Parathion 532, **550–554**
Parathyroid
  adenoma **208, 209**
  diseases **208–213**
  hormone 143, 144, 195, 196, 198, **208–213**
Parathyroidectomy 209, 210
  in chronic renal disease 1467
Paraventricular hypothalamic nuclei 1046
Paravertebral abscess, in Pott's disease 674
Paregoric USP 641
  in neonatal narcotic withdrawal 575
Parent counselling 8, **1893**
  in epilepsy 995
Parent-child relationship 269, 270, 271, 272, 350–352, 1161, 1576–1578
  and adolescent 262–263
Parent deprivation 426, 1586–1578
Parent education and information
  in accident prevention **518**, 520, 526, 536
  in diabetes mellitus **350–352**
  and leukemia **1215**
  and low-birth-weight infant 106
Parental size, and physical growth 245
Parenteral nutrition 109, 135, **168, 1582**
Paresis *see* Paralysis
Paresthesias 761, 1163
  due to antihistaminics 454
  anxiety reaction 292
  in brain tumors 943
  in Fabry's disease 913
  in hyperaldosteronism 1101
  in mercury poisoning 549

Paresthesias (*cont.*)
  in multiple sclerosis 918
  in pantothenic acid deficiency 140
  in pernicious anemia 1163
  in poliomyelitis **744–746**
  in polyneuritis acute **1007**
  in rubella arthritis 761
Parietal bosses, frontal 200
Parietal foramina **1701**
Parinaud's oculoglandular syndrome 698–699, **945**, 1821, 1834
Parity
  and birth weight **125**
  and breast feeding 152
  and high-birth-weight 124
  and neonatal mortality 111
  and outcome of newborn 111
Parkes-Weber syndrome 1814
Parkinsonism 391
Paromomycin (Humatin) **587**, 830
Parotid gland 597
  in cat scratch disease 698
  in cystic fibrosis 422
  in mumps **737–738**
Parotitis
  epidemic *see* Mumps
  in herpangina 751
Paroxysmal atrial tachycardia (PAT) **1364–1366**
Paroxysmal disorders, of the nervous system **980–1005**
  epilepsy **981–1001.** *See* Epilepsy.
  febrile convulsion **1001–1002**
  migraine **1002–1003**
  narcolepsy **1003–1004**
Paroxysmal fussing **1600**
Paroxysmal hypernea attacks, in tetralogy of Fallot **1402–1403**
Paroxysmal nocturnal hemoglobinuria **1187**
Paroxysmal polyspike and wave dysrhythmia **982**, *983*
Paroxysmal supraventricular tachycardia 1408
Paroxysmal tachycardia *see* Tachycardia
Paroxysms
  in malaria 832
  of pertussis **628–633**
  in tetanus **659–660**
Parrot 775
Parrot's pseudoparalysis, in syphilis 655
Pars distalis, of anterior pituitary 1046
Pars flaccida, of anterior pituitary 1883
Pars intermedia, of anterior pituitary 1046
Pars tuberalis 1046
Partial albinism **1800**
Partial anomalous venous connection without atrial septal defect **1401**
Partial thromboplastin time **1231**, 1234–1237
Partial transposition of the great arteries 1377
Partnership for Health Act 10
PAS *see* Para-aminosalicylic acid
Passive immunization *see* Immunization, passive
Passive transfer tests 447, **449**
Passivity 219
Past history, in general health appraisal *1898–1899, 1902–1903*
Past pointing 377, 1833
Pasteur vaccine 1022
Pasteurella tularensis (Bacterium tularense) 611, **691–693**, 1821
Pasteurization **157**

PAT *see* Paroxysmal atrial tachycardia
Patau syndrome *see* 13/15 Tisomy
Patch test (Vollmer) 475, **682**
Patellar, osteochondrosis **1739**
Patent ductus arteriosus 1373, 1376, **1393–1396**
Patent foramen ovale **1399**
Patent urachus 1549
Pathologic fractures 328, **1729**, 1734
Paul and Bunell test 718
PBG urinary 410, 411
PBI *see* Protein-bound iodine
Pco$_2$, arterial 47–48, 64, 68, 92–94, 223, 230, **1258–1259**
  in diarrhea 230
  fetal and perinatal 47, 48, 64, 66–68
  in low-birth-weight infant 92, 94
  maternal 47, 48
  in newborn 66–68, **1258–1259**
PDA *see* Patent ductus arteriosus
Paradichlorobenzene *530*
"Peaches" 571
"Peanuts" 571
"Pearl Pill" 571
"Pearly gates" 572
Pectin 641
Pectoral muscle agenesis 1028
Pectus carinatum 81, 331, **1327**, 1732
Pectus excavatum 71, 331, 1144, **1326–1327**, **1714**, 1732
Pedal syndactyly 1698
Pediatric practice, community aspects 1
Pediculosis 844, **1793–1797**
Pediculus humanus capitis **1796–1797**
Pediculus humanus corporis 1796
Pediculus humanus var. *capitis see* Head louse
Pedigree 14, 299, 316, *1899*
Pegonone (Ethotoin), in epilepsy **998–1000**
PEI *see* Phosphate excretion index
Pel-Ebstein fever 1223
Pelizaeus-Merzbacher's disease **916**
Pellagra *see* Niacin deficiency
Pellets, DOCA **1098**
Pellotine 569
Pelvic ectopia 1557
Pelvic nerve 1550
Pelvic radiotherapy 12
Pelvis **1718**
  in chondroectodermal dysplasia 1725
Pemphigus (P) 702, 1755, **1779–1780**
  foliaceus 1780
  vegetans 1780
Pendred's syndrome **1068**
Pendular nystagmus, and brain tumors **939**
Penetrance **305**
Penicillamine 184, 337, **391**, **547**, 1523
  in cystinuria 337
  in lead poisoning **547**
  in Wilson's disease, **391**, 1523
Penicillin(s) 480–481, **579–581**, **584–585**, 597, 608
  in acute glomerulonephritis 1485
  in actinomycosis 786
  allergy 442, 445
  in bacterial endocarditis **1430**
  in bacterial meningitis **602–606**, 608
  benzathin penicillin 584, 1485
  "broad spectrum" **585**
  dimethoxyphenyl penicillin 1509
  in diphtheria **617**
  in gonococcal conjunctivitis **1819**

Penicillin(s) (cont.)
  hypersensitivity 442, 445, **480–481**
  in lymphogranuloma venereum 776
  in meningococcal infections 623
  Penicillin G (benzyl penicillin)
  Penicillin V 584, 608
  procaine **584**
  prophylaxis **500–502**, 1217, 1397
  in psittacosis 776
  in rat-bite fever 634
  in rheumatic fever **500–502**
  in staphylococcal disease 646
  in streptococcal infection **650–651**
  in syphilis 653, **657–658**
  in tetanus 661
  in ventricular septal defect 1397
Penicillium molds **696**
  cyclopium 696
  funiculosum 696
  stoloniferum 696
Penis **1553–1554**
  injuries **1562**
Pennsylvania Amish 303
Pentamidine isethionate
  in African trypanosomiasis **834**
  in pneumocystis pneumonia 842, 1312
Pentolinium tartrate, in acute glomerulonephritis 1486
Pentose metabolism **359–630**
Pentose phosphate shunt 179
Pentosuria **359**
Pentothal (Thiopental) 1910
Pepsin 132, 1567
Pepsinogen 1567
Peptic esophagitis 1607
Peptic ulcer 456, 1579, 1619, **1638–1639**
Peptidases 132
Percentiles 234
Perch 821
Perchlorate 1059
Perchlorate "flush" tests 1068
Percussion tenderness of skull 1012
Percutaneous needle biopsy
  in biliary atresia **1683**
  kidney biopsy 1463
Percutaneous splenic venography 1692
Perennial allergic rhinitis 459
"Perennial therapy," in allergic disorders 452
Perforation
  intestinal, in anaphylactoid purpura 1233
  intestinal, in newborn **1618**
  stomach 1638, **1652–1653**
Perfumes 529
Periactin (Cyproheptadine) 1648
Perianal abscess 1648
Periarterial fibrosis, in systemic lupus erythematosus 508
Periarteritis nodosa 1008, 1797
  as a complication of rat-bite fever 634
Peribronchial abscesses, in cystic fibrosis 415
Peribronchiolitis, in cystic fibrosis 415
Peribronchitis
  in cystic fibrosis 415
  in *Pneumocystis carinii* pneumonia 1311–1312
Pericardial effusion 494, 499, **1425–1426**
  in cretinism 1071
Pericardial friction rub 494, 499, **1425**
Pericardial paracentesis **1426**

Pericarditis 396, 494, 514, 611, 750, **1425–1431**
  due to Coxsackie viruses 749
  in pleurodynia 750
  purulent, 1427
    due to *H. influenzae* 619, 620, 1427
    in sepsis neonatorum 597
    tularemic 692
  rheumatic *see* Rheumatic pericarditis
  in rheumatoid arthritis 504, 606
  in systemic lupus erythematosus 509
  tuberculous **679**
Pericranium 967
Peridontal membrane 1856, *1857*
Perinatal malaria 832
Perinatal medicine **15–126**
Perinatal mortality *see* Mortality, perinatal
Perinatal period 6
  definition 4
Perinatal physiology **43–50**
Perinatal regional center 101
Perinephric abscess **1543**
  and craniospinal abscess **1010–1016**
Perinephritis 679, 1543
Periodic breathing
  in low-birth-weight infant 93
Periodic health evaluations **7**
Periodic (cyclic) neutropenia **1205**
Periodic paralysis, in hyperaldosteronism 1101
Periodontal disease 1866
Perioral lesions, in syphilis **655**
Periorbital edema 1800
  in *Schistosoma mansoni* infection 814
  in trichinosis **809**
Periosteal hyperostosis, with dysproteinemia **1742**
Periostitis
  in coccidioidal granuloma **789–790**
  syphilitic 657
Peripheral nerve degenerations **924–925**
Peripheral nerve injuries **977–979**
Peripheral neuritis *see* Neuropathies, peripheral
Peripheral neuropathy *see* Neuropathies, peripheral
Peripheral polyneuropathy *see* Neuropathies, peripheral
Peripheral pulmonary arterial stenosis 1376, **1389**
Peripheral resistance **1437**
Periportal fibrosis, in schistosomiasis 813
Perirectal abscess 1643
Perirenal abscess **1543**
  and craniospinal focal sepsis **1010–1016**
Perisplenitis 1219
Peristaltic waves, in pyloric stenosis **1609**
Peritoneal abscess 1649
Peritoneal dialysis 1692
  in chronic renal failure 1468–1469
  in poisonings 535
  in salicylate poisoning **555**
Peritoneal irritation 374
Peritoneal shunt, in hydrocephalus 867
Peritoneum 60, 597, **1648–1649**
  hemorrhage in scurvy 188
  in rheumatic fever 494
Peritonitis 422, 560, 611, 1500, 1640, **1648–1649**
  in aganglionic megacolon 1622
  focal, in rheumatic fever 494
  in phycomycosis 795
  tuberculous **678–679**
Peritonsillar abscess **1878**
Perlèche *see* Stomatitis, angular

Permanent teeth **1856–1857, 1860–1861**
Permease 318
Pernicious anemia 139, 186, **1163**
  and Addison's disease 1094
  in diphyllobothriasis 821
Peroneal muscular atrophy **924, 1008**
Peroneal nerve injury 979
Peroral intestinal biopsy **1587, 1589–1590, 1592**
Peroxidase defect **1061, 1068**
Peroxisomes *see* Microbodies
Peroxyhemoglobin 395
Perphenazine (Trilafon) 1575
Persimmon 1651
Persistent hyperplastic primary vitreous **1829**
Persistent vitelline duct **1618–1620**
Personality change **852**
  in brain tumors **940**, 942, 943
Personality development **253–263**, *1898*
  in adolescence **262**
  in infancy and toddlerhood **254–255**
  in middle childhood **260**
  in preschool years **258**
Personality disorders **267–270**
Perspiration, excessive
  in familial dysautonomia 1040
  in Graves' disease 1083
  in neuroblastoma 1111
Pertussis (whooping cough), 426, **627–632**, 1294
  encephalopathy 631, **1022**
  and tuberculosis 631
  vaccination **631**, *1897*
Perverted appetite 271
Pes cavus 116, 331
  in Friedreich's ataxia 922
  in Refsum's syndrome 924
Pes planus 324
Pes valgus **1709–1710**
Pesticides **529**
Petechiae 1820
  in aplastic anemia 1166
  in bacterial endocarditis 1430
  in bacterial meningitis **599, 601, 623**
  in cytomegalic inclusion disease 703
  in hemorrhagic disorders 1229
  in hemorrhagic fever 847
  in Letterer-Siwe disease 1246
  in leukemia 1209
  in meningococcemia **623–624**, 1232
  in newborn 78
  in Rocky Mountain spotted fever 781
  in scurvy 189
  of soft palate, in streptococcal pharyngitis 648
  in septicemia 1232, 1236
  in streptococcal pharyngitis 648
  in thrombocytopenic purpura, idiopathic 1234
  in typhus epidemic 780
  in unexplained infant-death 576
Petit mal 853, 982, **988–989, 999**
Petit mal "automatism" 988
Petit mal variant **982**
Petroleum distillates 530, **538–540**
Petrositis **1888**
Petrous bond fracture 979
Pette and Doring panencephalitis *see* Subacute sclerosing
      panencephalitis
Petting 263
Peutz-Jeghers syndrome **1661**, 1803

Peyer's patches 431, **637**, 678
Peyote (mescaline) 568
pH
  blood **222–223, 225–226, 553–555, 1258–1259, 1278–1279,
        1462**
    in airway obstruction **1278–1279**
    in asthma 465
    at birth 66–68, **1258–1259**
    correction, at birth **73**
    in cystic fibrosis 427
    in diarrhea **229–231**
    fetal 19, 48, 64
    in salicylate poisoning **553–555**
  urinary **552–555, 1462, 1521–1524, 1524–1527**, 1536
    in Fanconi syndrome **1521–1524**
    in RTA **1524–1527**
    in salicylate poisoning **553–555**
    and urolithiasis **1536**
Phaenicia *see* Blow flies
Phage group *see* Bacteriophage group
Phagocytes 441, 449, 1245, 1302
Phagocytosis (endocytosis) 389, 441, 648, 1248, 1302, 1668
  in chronic granulomatous disease 396
Phakomatoses *see* Neurocutaneous syndromes
Phalangeal anomalies **1708**
Phallus 1134
Pharmaceutical samples, and poisonings **528**
Pharmacologic enzyme induction 54
Pharmacology, fetal **51–56**
Pharyngitis 720, 723, **1878**
  streptococcal **648–649**
Pharyngoconjunctival fever **725, 1821**
Pharyngoglossal duct 81
Pharyngotonsillar tularemia **692**
Pharynx **1877–1880**. *See also* Naso- and Oropharynx.
  abscess, posterior **1878**
  erosions 109
Pheasant 775
Phenacemide *see* Phenurone
Phenacetin 532
Phenergan *see* Promethazine
Phenethicillin **584**
Phenobarbital 54, 55, 501, 575, 1041. *See also* Barbitu-
        rates.
  and enzyme activity 54
  in epilepsy **995–1000**
  and fetal glucozonyl transferase 53
  in glucuronyl transferase deficiency **1678–1681**
  in jaundice of newborn **1678–1681**
  and neonatal bilirubin 54
  and neonatal depression 55
  in obstructive airway disease 1283
  and placental oxidation of drugs 52
Phenocopies **306**
Phenol **530**, 1809
Phenothiazines 455, 458, 488, 532, 660, **881–882**, 896, 852,
        1166, 1236, 1466
Phenotype 296
Phenotypic females with sexual infantilism 1116
Phenoxybenzamine hydrochloride (Dibenzyline) 1110
Phenoxymethyl penicillin *see* Penicillin V
Phenoxy penicillins. *See also* Penicillin.
  in staphylococcal disease 646
Phenoxypropanediol 661
Phentolamine **1110**
Phenurone (phenacemide) 999
Phenylacetic acid 323, 324

Phenylalanine 132, 322, *323*, **324–325** 336
  -free diet 324, 326
  hydroxylase 324
Phenylalaninemia 320, **323–324**
  in low-birth-weight infant 110
Phenylbutazone 507, 516
  and drug purpura 1235
Phenlyephrine (Neo-Synephrine) 455, **1282**
  in PAT 1364
Phenylethanolamine-N-methyl transferase 1107
Phenylketonuria 185, 318, **322–325** 473, 1595, 1800, 1808
  biochemical findings **324**
  clinical findings **323–324**
  diagnostic screening **325**
  genetics **324**
  treatment **324–325**
Phenyllactic acid 191, 324
Phenylpyruvic acid 191, *323*, 324
Pheochromocytoma 550, **1109–1110**, 1432, 1439, **1444–1445**
  and neurofibromatosis 927
Philadelphia chromosome (Ph1) 310, 398
Phimosis 1553
PHLA *see* Postheparin liplytic activity
Phlebitis 509, 585
Phlebotomus *see* Sandfly
Phlebotomy 1202, 1486
Phlyctenular conjunctivitis 665, **677 1823**
Phlyctenular keratoconjunctivitis **1823**
Phlyctenule **1823**
Phocomelia 306, 1707
Phonocardiography **1338–1344**
Phonography, for fetal heart monitoring 62
Phosphate 143, 198, 204, 206, 209, **1519–1520, 1521–1526**
  absorption, in vitamin D resistant rickets 206
  clearance 1519
    in Fanconi syndrome **1521–1524**
    in distal RTA **1525–1526**
  deficiency of 197
  enemas 1602
  excretion index (PET) 1519
  intracellular 196
  metabolism 196–197
  mobilization, and parathyroid 208
  transport disorders **1519–1520**
Phosphatases 145
Phosphatidyl choline *see* Lecithin
Phosphatidyl ethanolamines 373
Phosphatidyl serines 373
Phosphoadenosine 140
Phosphoadenosine-5'-phosphosulfate 399
Phosphocreatine 144
Phosphoethanolamine 206
Phosphofructokinase 372, 393
  deficiency 394, **1175**
6-Phosphogluconate dehydrogenase 395
Phosphogluconic acid 181
6-Phosphogluconic dehydrogenase 58
Phosphoglycerate kinase deficiency 393, **394, 1175**
Phosphohexosisomerase 372
Phospholipids 135, 139, 144, **373**
Phosphoribosyl pyrophosphate 339
Phosphorus **143–144,** 1579, 1686
  absorption 144
  deficiency 144
  in fructose intolerance 359
  poisoning 532
  requirement 144

Phosphorylase 183, 369
Phosphorylase kinase 372
Phosphorylation 144
Phosphoryl choline 907
Photoallergic reaction **487–488**
Photophobia 550, 599, 1206, 1522, 1819, 1823, 1825, 1827
  in acute cerebella ataxia 1041
  in albinism 326
  in erythropoietic protoporphyria 407
  in lymphocytic choriomeningitis 729
  in measles 732
  in rickettsial infection 779
  in Rocky Mountain spotted fever 781
Photosensitivity 410, 1803
  in cutaneous porphyria 411
  in Hartnup disease 336
  in hereditary hepatic coproporphyria 411
  induced by drugs and chemicals 487
  in mixed porphyria 410
Photosensitization 455, 487
Photosensitizing serum factors 487
Phototherapy, in hemolytic disease **1678**
Phototoxic reactions **487–488**
Phrenic nerve palsy 1632
Phrynoderma, in vitamin A deficiency 178
Phthirius humanus var. *corporis see* Body louse
Phthirius pubis **1793–1797**
Phycomycosis **795**
Phylum arthropoda *see* Arthropods
Phylum protozoa 825
Physical activity *see* Activity, physical
Physical examination *see* Examination, physical
Physical exertion, and poliomyelitis 744
Physical factors, and urticaria 478
Physical growth *see* Growth, physical
Physical therapy *see* Physiotherapy
Physician, role in suicide 290, 293
Physiologic anemia, of newborn 1157
Physiologic jaundice of newborn **1676–1685.** *See also* Jaundice.
Physiology
  fetal 43
  of low-birth-weight infant 88
  renal, in fetus **49–50**
Physiotherapy
  of burns **524**
  in cystic fibrosis **426–427**
  in dermatomyositis **512**
  in polyneuritis 1008
  in rheumatoid arthritis 507
  in scleroderma **513**
Phytanic acid 379, 1008
Phytate 143, 144
Phytic acid hydroxylase 58
Phytobezoars 1651
Phytohemagglutinin stimulation 388
Pial membrane 862
Pica 271, 532, **542–546**
Pickwickian syndrome 219, 1003, **1328**
Picornaviruses **726–727, 740–755**
  enteroviruses 740, **742–752**
    Coxsackie viruses **749–752**
    ECHO viruses 740, **752–754**
    polioviruses **742–749**
  rhinoviruses 726–728, 740
  inhibition of 695
P.I.D. 515

Piebaldism 1799
Pierre Robin syndrome 81, 1703, 1826, 1831, **1842–1843**
Pigeon 775
Pigeon breast *see* Pectus carinatum
Pigeon breeders' lung **1313**
Pigmentation **1799–1805**
  in Addison's disease 1093
  in dermatomyositis 512
  disorders **1799–1805**
  in growth, physical 1096
  in neurofibromatosis 927
  in β-thalassemia 1181
Pigmented nevi **1802**
  in gonadal dysgenesis 1140, 1142
Pigs, and leptospirae 621
Pike 821
Pili annulati 1760
Pili torti 1760
Pill-rolling 991
Pilocarpine 532
Pilocarpine iontophoresis 423
Pilo-erection, and LSD 568
Pinealocytes 1115
Pineal organ **1113–1115**
Pineal tumors 1115
Pinealoma **945**, 1123
  aberrant 1055
Pine products 530, 538–540
Ping-pong fractures of skull **968**
Pink-eye *see* Epidemic conjunctivitis
"Pinks" 571
Pink's disease *see* Acrodynia
Pinna 80, 388, 1881, 1882
Pinocytosis 1668
"Pins and needles," in rubella 761
Pinta 652
Pinworm *see* Enterobius vermicularis
Pinworm infection *see* Enterobiasis
Piperazine citrate
  in ascaris infection **802**
  in enterobiasis **804**
"Pithed frog" position, in scurvy 188
Pitocin induction 17, 20, 56
  and fetal water intoxication 56
  and hyponatremia, fetomaternal 20
Pitressin 1654
Pituitary, anterior **1046–1058**
Pituitary dwarfism 239, 250, 1116
Pituitary function, laboratory measurements of **1049–1052**
Pituitary gigantism 859
Pituitary gonadotropins, in Klinefelter's syndrome (XXY) 903
Pituitary growth hormone 196
Pituitary tumors 219, **1056–1057**
Pityriasis
  alba 472, 1800
  lichenoides **1810**
  rubra pilaris 1759, **1809**
Placement of children 266
Placenta 22, 44
  alkaline phosphatase 59
  anesthetics 54
  antithyroid drugs 55
  arteriovenous shunt 120
  and barbiturates 54, 55
  clearance **45–46**

Placenta (*cont.*)
  in diabetic pregnancies 126
  diamine oxidase 59
  diffusing capacity 44
  and drugs 52, **51–52**
  endocrine interrelationships with fetus 40–41
  enzyme activity 37, 52
  examination 65, 76
  exchange unit 43
  and fetal growth **22**
  glucose-6-phosphate 37
  and glucose tranfser 50
  glycogen 37
  and heroin 559, 574
  hypoplasia 22
  and IgG immunoglobulin 432
  infection, rubella **764**
  and insulin 56
  lactogenic hormone *see* Lactogenic hormone
  localization **61**
  membrane 44
  and multiple births **118–119**, *119*
  oxygen consumption 33
  oxytocinase 59
  permeability 45
  previa 61, 84
  progesterone production 40
  and steroid conversion by 123
  and steroid hormones 55–56
  and Thiouracil 55
  and thyroid hormones **1066–1067**
  thyroxine transport **1065–1066**
  transplacental exchange, basic physiology of 43
  TSH transport 1066
  vascular anastomosis 123
Plagiocephaly 1698, 1831
Plant constituents, as poisons 529
Plantar wart 1787
Plaques 1767
Plaque-like lesions 1763
Plasma
  fresh frozen *see* Fresh frozen plasma
  and viral hepatitis **710–711, 1910–1911**
Plasma cell pneumonia, of pneumocystis carinii **841–842, 1311–1312**
Plasma cells 387–388, 432, 437, 442, 775, 1216
Plasma compartment **221–222**
Plasmafibrinogen **1229**
Plasma membrane, of hepatocyte **1663–1665**
Plasma thromboplastin antecedent *see* Factor XI
Plasma thromboplastin component *see* Factor IX
Plasma volume 222
  in kwashiorkor 173
Plasmanate 711, 1910
Plasmids 583, 641
Plasmin 1229
Plasminogen 1229
Plasminogen activator, in R.D.S. 1263
Plasmodium falciparum **830–835**
Plasmodium malariae **830–835**
Plasmodium ovale **830–835**
Plaster, and lead poisoning **543**
Plastic form, of tuberculous peritonitis **678–679**
Platelet adhesiveness, and salicylates 501
Platelet concentrates (PC), in leukemia 1213
Platelet-rich plasma (PRP), in leukemia 1213

Platelets, 1157, **1228–1237**, 1242–1243
  adhesiveness **1228–1229**
    deficiency **1236–1237**
  count **1230**, 1233–1243
    following splenectomy 1218
  disorders **1233–1237**
  in homocystinuria 331
  phospholipid (platelet Factor III) 1229
  in sepsis neonatorum 597
  sequestration 1223, 1236
  smear 1230
Platyspondyly 404
Play, disinclination to, in tuberculous meningitis 671
Play therapy 266
Pleiotropy 305
Plethora
  in infant of diabetic mothers *126*
  in polycythemia 1202
  in twin 120
Pleural diseases **1329–1331**
Pleural effusion **1329–1330**
  in Burkitt's tumor 1227
  in coccidioidomycosis 789
  in gonadal dysgenesis 1140, 1142
  in kerosene poisoning 539
  in nephrotic syndrome 1500
  due to psittacosis 775
  in rheumatic fever 494
  in systemic lupus erythematosus **508–509**
  tuberculous **668**
  in tularemia 692
Pleural shunt, in hydrocephalus **867**
Pleurisy 611, 701, 789
  due to Coxsackie B virus 751
  in *Mycoplasma pneumoniae* infections 626
  in pleurodynia 750
  in polyarteritis nodosa 514
  in systemic lupus erythematosus **508–509**
  tuberculous **668**
Pleuritic pain, in coccidioidomycosis 789
Pleurodynia 750
Pleuroperitoneal canal 1632
Plumbism *see* Lead poisoning
PN *see* Polyarteritis nodosa
Pneumatization of paranasal sinuses 1700
Pneumatosis intestinalis **1582**
Pneumococcemia 576
Pneumococcus 442, 576, 596, **598–608**
  meningitis **598–608**
  pneumonia 442
  post-splenectomy infection 1217
Pneumocystis carinii 388, **841–843**, **1311–1312**
Pneumoencephalocele 968
Pneumoencephalography **855**, 859, 860, 867, 877
  in brain tumors 151, 496 941, 945, 949
  in hydrocephalus **865**
  in incontinentia pigmenti 931
  in neurocutaneous syndromes **925–931**
  in pseudotumor cerebri 958
  in tuberous sclerosis *926*, 927
Pneumomediastinum 75, 81
Pneumonectomy 1304
Pneumonias 387, 508, 645, 1177, 1265, **1305–1312**
  bacterial **1305–1307**
    due to *H. influenzae* 619, **620**
    in pertussis 629
    "pneumonia alba" 653

Pneumonias (*cont.*)
  intrauterine 71, 73
  Mycoplasma pneumoniae **1311**
  mycotic **1307–1308**
    in actinomycosis 785
    in aspergillosis necrotizing 787
  neonatal **1270**
  parasitic **1311–1312**
    ascaris 801
  viral **1311**
    in cat scratch disease 698
    due to Coxsackie virus **751**
    influenza 721
    primary atypical 625, 719, 726
Pneumonitis 514, 726, **1310–1322**
  in cytomegalic inclusion disease 703
  in cystic fibrosis 415
  in kerosene poisoning 538–540
  in phycomycosis 795
  in strongyloidiasis 808
  in zoster 1785
Pneumothorax 75, 81, 422, 666, 1265, **1271**, 1312, **1329–1330**
  in kerosene poisoning 539, *540*
  in Letterer-Siwe disease 1247
  neonatal **1271**
  in pertussis 630
  in staphylococcal penumonia 1329
Pneumo-otoscope **1883**
Pneumoperitoneum, in gastric perforation **1652**
Po$_2$
  fetal and maternal 47, 48
  in newborn **1258–1259**
Podophyllin 1788
Pogonomyronex *see* Harvester ant
p-OH-Phenyllactic acid 186
p-OH-Phenylpyruvic acid 186
Poikilocytosis 1184
  in sickle-cell disease 1177
Poikilothermia 1056
Poison control centers 529
Poisonings **527–556**
  general **527–537**
  prevention **536**
  specific **537–556**
    estrogens 1128
    iron **537–538**
    kerosene **538–540**
    lead **540–548**
    mercury **548–550**
    organic phosphates **550**
    salicylates **552–555**
    snake bites **555–556**
    vitamin A **1741–1742**
  treatment **533–536**
Poison ivy dermatitis 475, **476**
Poison oak dermatitis **476**
"Poison-prone" age **527–528**
Poisons **528–538**
Pokerfaced expression, in chorea 496
Poland's syndactyly 1708
Polaramine 1808
Poliodysplasia *see* Progressive degeneration of cerebral
    gray matter
Poliodystrophy *see* Progressive degeneration of cerebral
    gray matter

Poliomyelitis 726, **732–749**, 1008, 1325
  and acute cerebellar ataxia 1042
  clinical manifestations **744**
  etiology **742**
  laboratory diagnosis 746
  myocarditis **1429**
  prevention **747**, *1897*
  treatment **746**
Pollen, and urticaria 477
Polyarteritis nodosa 505, 511, **513–514**, 1314, 1494
Polyarthralgia 511
  in rubella **761**
Polyarthritis 490, **494–495**, 499, **503–507**, 511, **761**
  chronic *see* Rheumatoid arthritis
  in polymyositis **511**
  rheumatic *see* Rheumatic polyarthritis
  in rheumatoid arthritis **503–507**
  due to subacute bacterial endocarditis 499
Polychromasia 1181, 1184
  in sickle-cell disease 1177
Polycoria 1827
Polycystic disease **1477**, 1691
  infantile **1471**
Polycystic kidney, in tuberous sclerosis 926
Polycythemia 1336, 1407
  in cyanotic heart disease 1336, **1401–1402**, 1407
  in infant of diabetic mother 127
  vera **1202**
Polydactyly (polydactylism), 83, 250, 861, 901, 1698, **1707–1708, 1841**
Polydipsia **1150–1152**
  in diabetes insipidus 1150
  in diabetes mellitus 346
  in Hand-Schüller-Christian syndrome 1249
Polyene antibiotics 581
Polyglutamic acid 431
Polygyria 1029
Polyhydramnios 50
Polymorphism in genetics 303
Polymyoclonia 955, 1111
Polymyositis (dermatomyositis) **511, 1032–1033**
Polymyxin B 423, 446, 581, 587, 598, **603–605**, 606, 1509
  in *E. coli* infections of newborn 642
Polymyxin E (colistimethate) 606
Polyneuritis *see* Neuropathies, peripheral
Polyneuropathy *see* Neuropathies, peripheral
Polyornithine 418
Polyostotic fibrous dysplasia 928, 1126, 1696, **1733, 1734,** 1805, 1874
Polyp(s)
  aural 1885
  intestinal **1661**
  nasal 419, 1873
Polypectomy 460
Polypeptides 132, 296, 300
Polyphagia 346, 946
Polypoid adenomatosis of colon 1661
Polysaccharide antibody, Group A 497
Polysaccharides, starch intolerance **1590–1594**
Polysome 581
Polysyndactyly 1698, **1707–1708**, 1841
Polyuria 209, **346, 1150–1152**, 1473
  in colloid brainstem cyst 946
  in diabetes insipidus **1150–1152**
  in diabetes mellitus 346
  in distal RTA **1525–1526**
  in Fanconi syndrome 1521

Polyuria (*cont.*)
  in Hand-Schüller-Christian syndrome 1249
  in hyperaldosteronism 1101
  in renal tubular acidosis, distal **1525**
Polyvinyl alcohol (PVA) mixture 828
Polyvinylpyrrolidone 1312
Pompe's disease *see* Glycogenosis type II
Popliteal angle *86*, 87
Population differences
  in perinatal mortality 112–113
  and twin 118
Population genetics 294, 302
Poral occlusion *see* Miliaria
Porencephaly 330, 857, 962
Pork products 809
  and trichinosis 808
Pork tapeworm *see* Taenia solium
Porphobilinogen (PBG) 405
Porphyria **405–411**, 850
  in animals **411**
  biosynthesis *406*
  classification **405–307**
  cutanea tarda 1770
  erythropoietic porphyrias **407–409**
    congenital erythropoietic porphyria (Günther's disease) *407*
    erythropoietic coproporphyria **409**
    erythropoietic protoporphyria **407**
  hepatic porphyria **409–411**
    acute intermittent porphyria (Swedish type) **409–410**
    cutaneous porphyria (hereditary and acquired) 411, 1770
    hepatic hereditary coproporphyria 411
    metabolism of **405**
    mixed porphyria ("variegate," South African type) **410–411**
  variegata *see* Mixed porphyria
Porphyrin X 410
Porphyrinogens 405
Porphyrin-peptide conjugates 410
Portal of entry, in neonatal sepsis 596
Portal fibrosis 1682
Portal hypertension 371, 422, **1218–1221**, 1683, 1687, 1688, **1691–1692**
  in abdominal tuberculosis 677
  in schistosomiasis 813
Portal vein 1216, 1218
Porto-caval shunt 1219
Port-wine facial nevus, in encephalotrigeminal angiomatosis 928
Port-wine stain **1812–1813**
Positive pressure ventilation **72–73**
  in R.D.S. **1265**
Postauricular adenopathy, in rubella 761
Postencephalitic asocial behavior 280
Posterior column sensory loss, in Friedreich's ataxia 922
Posterior fontanel **1700**
Posterior fossa 862
Posterior fossa malformations 964
Posterior pharyngeal abscess 1878
Posterior pituitary, and acid-base homeostasis 223
Posterior synechiae 1827, 1828
Posterior urethral valves **1472**, 1550, **1559**
Postgastrectomy anemia 139
Postheparin lipolytic activity 375
Postherpetic neuralgia 1785
Postictal 981

Postinfectious encephalitis **761–762, 1020–1022**
Postinflammatory hypomelanosis 1800
Postkala-azar dermal leishmanoid **837**
Postmaturity 596
Postnecrotic cirrhosis 1691
Postneonatal
  health services 7
  mortality 4
Postpartum 20
Postpericardiotomy syndrome **1427**
Postrenal failure 1464
Postrubella encephalitis 761–762
Poststreptococcal glomerulonephritis **1482–1488**
Postural drainage 427, **467**, 1278, **1280–1281**
  in asthma **467**
  in obstructive airway disease 1278, **1280–1281**
Postural flattening, of skull 1696, *1697,* 1699
Postural hypotension, in familial dysautonomia 1040
Posutral proteinuria **1478–1480**
Posture, of newborn *86*, **86**
Posture disturbance, in spinal cord tumors **954**
Posturing 287, 324
  in thalamic tumors 947
  in Wilson's disease 920
Postvaccinal encephalitis **1021–1022**
"Pot" 572
Potassium **224**
  in acute renal failure 1464
  in Addison's disease 1094
  in diabetes 347
  in distal RTA **1525–1526**
  fetal 32
  growth patterns of 237
Potassium administration, in diarrhea **229–231**
Potassium antimony tartrate *see* Tartar emetic
Potassium chlorate 532
Potassium citrate 1466, **1525–1526**
Potassium deficiency
  in cystic fibrosis 417
  in kwashiorkor 173
  in marasmus 171
  physical signs of 230
Potassium depletion
  in cholera 614
  depletion nephropathy **1508–1509**
Potassium ferricyanide test 533
Potassium intake, in chronic uremia 1467
Potassium intoxication 1464
Potassium iodide 55, 1281
Potassium-losing disorders **1528–1529**
Potassium loss
  in dehydration 226
  in diarrhea 230
Potassium perchlorate 55
Potassium requirements 143
Potassium supplementation, in kwashiorkor 175
Potassium tellurite agar 616
"Potbelly," in cretinism 1071
Potter facies **1547,** *1548*
Potter's syndrome 1472
Pott's disease *see* Tuberculosis, of spine
Potts-Smith-Gibson anastomosis 1405–1406
Pound fractures of skull 968
Poxviruses, inhibition of **695–696**
PPD *see* Purified protein derivative
"P pulmonale" 420
Pralidoxime chloride *see* Protopam chloride

Prausnitz-Kustner (PK) 386, 441
Preauricular fistula *see* Fistula, preauricular
Preauricular lymphadenopathy 698, 1821
Precapillary pulmonary arterial obstruction **1389**
Prechordal mesoderm 860
Precipitation test
  in Chagas' disease 836
  in rubella **762–763**
Precipitous delivery 596
Precocious feminization **1128–1129**
Precocious menstruation 1076
Precocious puberty **1124–1130,** 1734. *See also* Puberty.
  in polyostotic fibrous dysplasia 1734
Precocious sexual development, associated with juvenile,
  hypothyroidism **1076–1077**
Precordial hyperactivity **1394–1396**
Precordial pain 494, 814, **1425**
Precordial thrill, in Graves' disease 1083
Prediabetes 345
Prednisolone *1104. See also* Adrenal cortical hormones.
Prednisone 467, 1104. *See also* Adrenal corticosteroids.
  in lymphoblastic leukemia **1209–1210**
Pregnancy
  drug therapy in 51, **52–56**
  hepatitis in 711
  in heroin users 561
  high risk 59
  in history *1898, 1902*
  and poliomyelitis **744**
Pregnane-3a, 17a, 20a-triol 1097, 1098, 1099
Pregnane-3a, 20 (β)-diol 1677
  and unconjugated hyperbilirubinemia 1677, **1680**
Pregnanediol 41
Pregnanetriol 1127, 1134
Pregnenolone 40
Preictal 981
Preicteric phase, of viral hepatitis 708
Prejudice, and health care 6
Premature adrenarche *see* Adrenarche
Premature aging 1841
Premature closure of sutures 854, 1695
Premature infants *see* Low-birth-weight infant
Premature synostosis 854, 1695
Premature thelarche *see* Thelarche
Premature union of sternal segments 1714
Premature ventricular contractions, in Chagas' disease 836
Premaxilla 1861
Premolars 1859
Prenatal **15–126**
  biochemistry **34–43**
  bowing of tubular bones **1708–1709**
  care **15–18**
  diagnosis **56–66**
  enzymatic development **34–37**
  growth factors 238
  health services **7**
  physiology **43–50**
Prenatal syphilis **652–658**
Prepuce **1553**
Prerenal failure 1464
Preschool
  health services 4
  mortality **4**
"Preseasonal therapy," in allergic disorders 452
Pressure, and urticaria 478
Pressure data, intracardiac **1357,** *1361–1362*
Presystolic murmur, apical (mitral stenosis) **495**

Preterm infant *see* Low-birth-weight infant
Pretibial myxedema, in hyperthyroidism 1084
Preventive pediatrics **1, 1893–1897**
Preventive services 7
Prickly heat **1808–1809**
Primaquine, in malaria **833**
Primary amenorrhea **1116**
Primary atypical pneumonia *see* Pneumonia
Primary constriction, chromosomal 308
Primary granulomatous disease 396
Primary hyperaldosteronism, *see* Hyperaldosteronism
Primary hypophosphatemia *see* Hypophosphatemia, primary
Primary peritonitis **1648**
Primary polycythemia *see* Polycythemia vera
Primary teeth **1856, 1859–1860**
Primary tuberculosis *see* Tuberculosis, pulmonary
Primary viral encephalitis **1016–1020**
Primidone *see* Mysoline
Primitive lymphoblast **1208–1209**
Primordial dwarfism 249
P-R interval 13, 370, **494, 497, 1347, 1354, 1367**
Proaccelerin *see* Factor V
Probanthine *see* Propantheline bromide
Procaine 559
Procaine amide (Pronestyl) 509, 1032, 1366
    in myotonia 1032
    in ventricular tachycardia 1366
Procaine penicillin **584**. *See also* Penicillin.
Procarbazine (Matulane) 1225
Procercoid larva 821
Processus vaginalis 1631
Prochlorperazine (Compazine) 819, 882, 1575
Procidentia **1659**
Proconvertin *see* Factor VII
Proctitis **1644**
Prodome **981, 1002**
Progeria 249, **1841,** 1842
Progestational agents 1125
Progesterone 40, 41, **1116, 1120–1121**
Proglottids 817, 819, 821
Prognathism 335, 1145, 1699, 1842
Progressive degeneration of cerebral gray matter (poliodystrophy, poliodysplasia) **915**
Progressive diaphyseal dysplasia *see* Engelmann's disease
Progressive infantile spinal atrophy *see* Werdnig-Hoffman disease
Progressive lipodystrophy **378**
Progressive muscular dystrophy, Duchenne type 1030
Progressive systemic sclerosis *see* Scleroderma
Proinsulin **343–344**
Prolactin (LTH) 1048
Projectile vomiting, in pyloric stenosis **1609**
Prolactin (mammotropic hormone) 1049
Prolapse, anal or rectal 630, 640, **1659**
Proliferative glomerulonephritis **1489–1491,** 1507
Proline 186, 330, 336, 337, 1518
Proline oxidase 331
Promethazine phenergan 20, 454, 474
Pronator sign, in chorea 496
Pronestyl *see* Procaine amide
Propantheline bromide (Probanthine) 1643, 1646
Prophylaxis of household contacts, in meningitis 608
Prophylaxis, ophthalmic, in newborn 104
Propionic acid 329
Propionyl CoA 329

Propranolol 1423
    in Graves' disease 1065
    and hypoglycemia 362
    in PAT 1365
    in pheochromocytoma 1110
    in thyrotoxicosis **1086**
Proptosis 1697, 1702, 1831. *See also* Exophthalmos.
    in optic nerve and chiasm tumors 950, 952
    and neuroblastoma 1111
Propylene glycol 426, 1509
Propylthiouracil 1061, **1065, 1086**
Prostaglandin 1444
Prostate 1123
    growth and 236
Prostatic abscess **1544,** 1551
Prostatitis **1544**
Prostigmin
    in myasthenia **1036–1038**
    in paralytic ileus **1654**
    in PAT **1364**
Protamine 1243
Protamine zinc insulin 343, **349**
Proteases 132, 441
Protein 131–135, 296, 318
    in amniotic fluid 57
    in breast milk 150, *158*
    caloric ratio of breast milk 134
    in colostrum 150
    in cow's milk *158*
    deficiencies **170–176**
        in cow's milk 135
        hypocaloric dwarfism 170. *See also* Dwarfism.
        kwashiorkor 172. *See also* Kwashiorkor.
        marasmus 171. *See also* Marasmus.
    diet, and renal maturation 90
    digestion, in cystic fibrosis 417
    DNA ratio 248
        in kwashiorkor 173
    in edema fluid 96
    enteropathy 248
    in fetal body composition 29, 32
    growth patterns of 237
    hydrolysates, for parenteral nutrition 135
    hydrolysis **1567–1568**
    intake
        in chronic uremia **1465–1466**
        in cystic fibrosis 428
    loss, and iron deficiency anemia 1162
    malabsorption **1594–1595**
    in meconium of cystic fibrosis 420
    metabolism, anomalies of **386–398, 1688**
        erythrocyte and leukocyte enzyme deficiencies **391–398**
        and liver disease **1688**
        serum and metal-binding protein anomalies **386–391**
    milk 136
    in nutrition **131–135**
        digestibility 132
        requirements **133**
        utilization 133
        in various foods 134
    plasma 171, 222, **386–389,** 1501, 1672
        anomalies of **386–389**
        in hypocaloric dwarfism 171
        in liver disease 1672
    requirements, of low-birth-weight infant 110
    spinal fluid **601–602**

Protein (*cont.*)
  storage **133**
  synthesis 132, 133
  undernutrition 137
Protein-bound iodine (PBI) 219, 370, 410, 1051, **1062–1063**
Protein caloric malnutrition 362
Protein-losing enteropathy 1161, 1592, **1594–1595**
Proteinuria 207, 379, 509, 514, 525, 1478, 1490, 1509, 1514
  in acute glomerulonephritis **1483–1488**
  in Fanconi syndrome **1521–1524**
  in hemorrhagic fever 847
  in hypertension 1439
  in nephrotic syndrome **1500**
  postural **1478**
  in sarcoidosis 1252
  in sickle-cell anemia 1177
  in urinary tract infection 1540–1542
Protein Y and Z, liver **1674**
Proteolytic "cascade" 389
Proteolytic digestion 1567
Proteus vulgaris 227, 427, 585–588, 596, 1539
  meningitis **598–608**
  (OX-19) *see* OX-19 *Proteus vulgaris*
Prothrombin 1229, **1240–1241**
  consumption test 1231
  deficiency 140, 848, 1240–1241
    in hemorrhagic fever 848
  factors V, VII and X deficiencies **1240–1241**
  synthesis 55, 139, 501
    and salicylates 55, 501
  time 140, 1231, **1237–1243**, 1672
Protodiastolic gallop rhythm *see* Gallop rhythm, protodiastolic
Protopam chloride (pralidoxime chloride) **551–552**
Protoporphyrin 410
Protoporphyrin IX 405
Protozoa 581, **825–844**
Protozoan diseases **825–844**
  African sleeping sickness (trypanosomiasis) *827*, *834–835*
  amebiasis **825–830**, *826*
  balantidiasis *826*, **838–839**
  Chagas' disease *827*, **835–837**
  dientamebiasis *825*, 826
  giardiasis *826*, **838**
  hymenopterous disease 844
  leishmaniasis *827*, **837–838**
  malaria *826*, **830–834**
  myiasis 846
  pneumocystis pneumonia *827*, **841–842**
  toxoplasmosis *826*, **839–841**
Provitamin A 177
Proximal renal tubular acidosis **1524–1525**
Proximal renal tubular dysfunction, multiple **1520–1524**
Proximal tubule **1520–1525**
"Prune belly syndrome" 1547, *1548*, **1559–1560**
Prunes 1602
Pruritus 219, 409, 410, 472, 478, 486, 487, 808, 810, 1223, 1779, 1806, 1808, 1811
  in dracontiasis 810
  in pediculosis **845**
  in strongyloidiasis 808
Pruritus ani 803, 1603
  in enterobiasis 803
Pseudarthrosis 1745
Pseudobulbar palsy, in brain tumor **939**

Pseudocholinesterase 551
Pseudocleft of the upper lip 1850
Pseudogout 514
Pseudohemophilia *see* Factor V; Von Willebrand's disease
Pseudohermaphrodism
  female 1130, *1133*, **1134–1136**
  male 1130, *1133*, **1136–1139**
    with adrenal hyperplasia, congenital, nonvirilizing 113
    with ambiguous genitalia or well-developed phallus **1139**
    feminizing testes syndrome (simulant females) **1137–1138**
    as a gonadal dygenesis variant **1138–1139**
Pseudo-Hirschsprung's diseases 1624
Pseudohydrocephalus 1695
Pseudohyperaldosteronism **1528**
Pseudohypertropic dystrophy of Duchenne **1030**
Pseudohyphae 795
Pseudohypoaldosteronism **1527**
Pseudohypoparathyroidism **212**, 213, 1520
Pseudomembrane, diphtheritic **614–618**
Pseudomembranous enterocolitis *see* Enterocolitis, staphylococcal
Pseudomonas aeruginosa (pyocyameus) 227, 388, 423, 523, 585–588, 596, 597, 641, 1429, 1539
  meningitis **598–608**
  septicemia 1212
  in urinary tract infection 1539
Pseudomonas proteus 175
Pseudomucinous cystadenoma 1119
Pseudo-osteochondroses **1739–1741**
Pseudopapilledema 422, **938**
  in disseminated hemangiomatosis 929
Pseudoparalysis
  in scurvy 188
  in syphilis **655**
Pseudopelade 1804
"Pseudorenal diabetes" **1517**
Pseudosexual precocious puberty 1126
Pseudotruncus arteriosus **1387**, 1402
Pseudotubercles, in schistosomiasis 813
Pseudotumor cerebri 588, **957–960**
Pseudo-vitamin D deficient rickets **203**
Pseudoxanthoma elasticum **1765–1766**
Psittacosis **775–776**
  pneumonitis **1311**
Psoas abscess, in Pott's disease **674**
Psoriasis 338, **1758–1759**, 1761
PSS *see* Scleroderma
Psychedelics 263, **568–569**, 571
Psychiatric aberrations, in acute intermittent porphyria 409
Psychogenic vomiting 271
Psychologic aspects, of asthma 468
Psychologic complications, of obesity 219
Psychologic development
  abnormalities of **265–297**
    common psychopathologic symptoms and syndromes **269–290**
    suicide **291–293**
  normal, personality and behavior **253–264**
    in adolescence **262–264**
    in infancy and toddlerhood **253–256**
    in middle childhood **260–262**
    in preschool years **256–260**

Psychologic disturbances, in chronic renal insufficiency 1468
Psychologic dwarfism, simulating idiopathic hypopituitarism 1056
Psychologic factors, and breast feeding 153
Psychologic needs 268
Psychologic tests, in neurologic diagnosis 857
Psychometric testing, in mental retardation 894
Psychomotor disturbances, in congenital toxoplasmosis 840
Psychomotor epilepsy 982, **991**, 999
Psychopathologic symptoms and syndromes 269–290
  alimentary disorders 269–272
  antisocial behavior 279–281
  elimination disorders 272–273
  emotional reactions 281–283
  hypochondrial trends 282, **283–284**
  hysteria **284–285**
  language disorders 269–298
  manipulations of the body **275–276**
  motor disorders 273–274
  school difficulties 283
  sex disorders 278–279
  sleep disturbances 274–275
Psychoses 286–287
  in marihuana user 566
Psychosocial dwarfism see Dwarfism, psychosocial
Psychotherapy
  in asthma 469
  in ulcerative colitis 1646
Psyllium seed 1603
PTA (and deficiency) see Factor XI
PTC (and deficiency) see Factor IX
Pteroylglutamic acid see Folic acid
Pterygia 1803
Pterygoid ulcers 1838
Ptosis 531, 671, **852**, **1036–1038**, 1144, 1817, 1818
  in dystrophia myotonica 1032
  in myasthenia gravis **1036–1038**
  in pinealoma **946**
Puberty
  development, sign 241–242, **1122**
  endocrine changes at **1120–1122**
  first sign of **241–242**
  and mumps **738–739**
  precocious 1124–1130
    androgenic origin **1127–1128**
    complete **1124–1126**
    estrogenic origin 1128–1129
    partial **1129**
    pseudosexual 1126–1127
Pubic hair 241, 1122, **1123–1124**
Public Health 1–14
Pudendal nerves 1550
Puerperium 20
"Puerto Rican syndrome" 291
Pull-through procedure *1623*
Pulmonary see Lung
Pulmonary abscesses 1296
  amebic abscess **825**, **829**
  in coccidioidal granuloma 789
  and craniospinal focal sepsis 1010–1016
  and pulmonary AV fistula 1012
Pulmonary actinomycosis **785**, **1308**
Pulmonary agenesis 1303
Pulmonary alveolar microlithiasis 1320
Pulmonary alveolar proteinosis **1320**

Pulmonary aplasia **1303**
Pulmonary arterial pressure, postnatal 70
Pulmonary arteriovenous fistulas **1304–1305, 1377**
  and brain abscess 1012
Pulmonary artery branch stenosis **1389**
Pulmonary ascariasis 801–802
Pulmonary aspergillosis 787, **1307**
Pulmonary atresia **1371**
  and asplenia 1217
  in tetralogy of Fallot **1402–1404**
Pulmonary atresia or stenosis with intact ventricular septum **1407–1408**
Pulmonary blastomycosis 787, **1308**
Pulmonary blood flow **1301, 1377–1378**
  in newborn 1256
Pulmonary calcification in histoplasmosis 791
Pulmonary candidiasis 796
Pulmonary cavitation in coccidioidomycosis **789**
Pulmonary coccidiodomycosis **1307**
Pulmonary contusion **1329**
Pulmonary cryptococcosis 794
Pulmonary cysts **1304**
  in paragonimiasis 816
  of pneumocystis carinii **841–842**
Pulmonary disease
  due to CFP 413
  in Letterer-Siwe disease 1247
  of the newborn **1261–1273**
  of older infants and children **1284–1329**
  in rheumatic fever 494
  in sarcoidosis **1251–1252**
  in *Schistosomiasis japonicum* infection 814
Pulmonary dysmaturity **1268–1270**
Pulmonary edema 390, 551, 613, **1374**
  in acute glomerulonephritis **1484**
  in heart failure 1421
  in influenza 721
  in kerosene poisoning 538–540
Pulmonary ejection murmurs **1342**
Pulmonary elastic recoil, in newborn **1256**
Pulmonary emboli 564
Pulmonary emphysema 1765
  in pertussis 629
Pulmonary empyema, and craniospinal focal sepsis 1010–1016
Pulmonary fibrosis 426, 1318–1320
Pulmonary fluid, in newborn 1255–1256
Pulmonary function
  in asthma **465**
  of newborn **1255–1261**
  tests 1279, **1302–1303**
Pulmonary hemorrhage **1494**
  in newborn **1271–1272**
Pulmonary hemosiderosis idiopathic see **Hemosiderosis, pulmonary, idiopathic**
Pulmonary histoplasmosis **1307**
Pulmonary hyperinflation **1277**
Pulmonary hypertension 417, 465, 513, 564, 1341, **1373**, 1376, 1413
  in heroin addicts 561
  after shunting procedure 866
Pulmonary hypoperfusion, in RDS **1264**
Pulmonary hypoplasia 73, **1303–1304**, 1633
Pulmonary infarction, in sickle-cell disease 1177
Pulmonary infections **1305–1312**
  in congenital heart disease **1335–1336**
Pulmonary lymphangiectasis congenital **1305**

Pulmonary lymphatics 1305
Pulmonary osteoarthropathy 422, **1742–1743**
Pulmonary parenchyma **1299–1303**
   diagnostic procedures **1302–1303**
   function **1299–1302**
Pulmonary parenchymal diseases **1303–1322**
Pulmonary stenosis
   and asplenia 1217
   in tetralogy of Fallot 1402–1403
Pulmonary surfactant 90, **1256–1257**, 1263–1264
Pulmonary system **1255–1331.** *See also* Lungs; Respiratory; *individual diseases.*
   airways **1274–1277**
   airway obstructive diseases **1277–1279**
   chest wall **1322–1324**
   chest wall diseases **1324–1329**
   parenchyma **1299–1303**
   parenchymal diseases 1299–1309
   pulmonary diseases in the newborn **1261–1273**
   respiratory function
      in newborn **1255–1261**
      in older infants and children **1273–1277, 1299–1300,
         1322–1324**
Pulmonary tuberculosis **665–671.** *See also* Tuberculosis,
   pulmonary.
Pulmonary tumors 1304
Pulmonary valvotomy (Brock) 1408
Pulmonary vascular disease **1375–1376,** 1397
Pulmonary vascular resistance 96, 1374–1376
   and birth asphyxia 69, 70
   in low-birth-weight-infant 95
   in newborn **1256**
Pulmonary veins, congenital stenosis of 1384
Pulmonary veins, pressure load **1372–1380**
Pulmonary venous obstruction **1372, 1380**
Pulmonary ventilation, of newborn **1257**
Pulmonary vessels
   in low-birth-weight-infant 95
   in newborn 70
Pulmonic atresia 1377, **1387–1388**
Pulmonic stenosis *1339,* **1386–1387**
Pulmonic valve 1339, 1377, 1386–1388
Pulsating exophthalmos 1702
Pulse **1904**
   in coarctation 1390
   in patent ductus arteriosus **1394**
Pulse pressure 1071, **1384**
   in cretinism 1071
   narrow **1384**
Pulsus paradoxus 1426
Pupil(s)
   in albinism 326
   dilation in newborn 75
   and marihuana 566
   in Refsum's disease **379, 1008**
   response in newborn 87
   in tuberculous meningitis 671
"Puppy-fat" 236
PPD Battey 682
PPD Gause 682
PPD RT 680
PPD-S 680
Purified protein derivative (PPD) **680**
Purine and Pyrimidine metabolism, disorders of **338–341.**
         See also Beta-aminoisobutyric aciduria; Gout;
         Hyperuricemias; Lesch-Nyhan syndrome; Orotic
         aciduria; Xantinuria

Purines 35, 294, **338–341**
Purkinje cells 921
"Purple flats" 571
Purpura(s) 123, 328, **622–625**
   allergic *see* Anaphylactoid purpura
   anaphylactoid *see* Anaphylactoid purpura
   fibrinolytic purpura **1242**
   hemolytic-thrombocytopenic-uremic syndrome 1495
   in hemorrhagic fever 848
   in *Herpesvirus hominis* infection 715
   in infantile kala-azar 837
   infectious **1232, 1243**
   in ketotic hyperglycinemia 328
   in meningococcal infections **622–625**
   purpura fulminans **1243**
   in rubella 762
   due to salicylate therapy 501
   secondary vascular **1232**
   in SLE 508
   thrombocytopenic **1233–1237**
   thrombotic-thrombocytopenic **1243**
Purulent arthritis 505, 514, 597, 601, **620**
   due to *H. influenzae* 601, 619, **620**
   meningococcal 601
   in neonatal sepsis 597
Purulent meningitis *see* Meningitis, bacterial
Purulent rhinitis *see* Rhinitis, purulent
Pustule
   in acne 1815
   of smallpox **770**
P waves 1347
   in atrial hypertrophy 1381
Pycnodysostosis 1735
Pyelonephritis 170, 210, 422, 636, 786, 796, 1460, **1472,
         1495, 1539–1544**
   candidal 796
   and craniospinal focal sepsis **1010–1016**
Pyknocytosis 1679
Pyle's disease *see* Metaphyseal dysplasia
Pyloric canal ulcers 1638
Pyloric mass, in pyloric stenosis **1609**
Pyloric stenosis 315, 537, **1609**
   and jaundice 1681
Pyloromyotomy, of lower esophagus 1576
Pyloroplasty 1639
Pyocephalus **1015**
Pyocyaneus *see Pseudomonas*
Pyoderma **649,** 1643, 1645, **1781–1784**
Pyoderma gangrenosum 1643, 1645
Pyoderma, streptococcal **649**
Pyogenic arthritis *see* Purulent arthritis
Pyogenic meningitis *see* Meningitis, bacterial
Pyonephrosis 679
Pyopneumothorax 666
Pyramidal deficit, focal in brain tumors **940, 942, 945,**
         946, 947
Pyrazinamide 685, 686
Pyridine carboxylic acid *see* Nicotinic acid
Pyridine nucleotides 144
Pyridium 532
2-Pyridone 184
6-Pyridone 182
Pyridostigmine bromide (Mestinon) in myasthenia **1036,
         1038**
Pyridoxal *see* Pyridoxin
Pyridoxal-ALA imines 410
Pyridoxal-5-phosphate 183, 405

Pyridoxal phosphokinase 185
Pyridoxamin 183, 185
4-Pyridoxic acid 183
Pyridoxin 109, **138**, 139, 145, **183–185**, 331, 332, 391
    deficiency **183–185**, 1084, 1168
    dependency 84, **184–185**, 853
    requirements *184*
    responsive anemia 185
    and sideroblastic anemia 1168
Pyrimethamine (Daraprim) 833
    in toxoplasmosis **841**
Pyrimidines 35, 294, **338–341**
Pyrogallol *530*
Pyrophosphate 140, 1674
Δ'-Pyrroline-5-carboxylic acid dehydrogenase 331
Pyruvate kinase deficiency **393, 1175**
Pyruvic acid 38, 180, 181
Pyrvinium pamoate **804**
Pyuria 1514, **1540–1542**
    in blastomycosis 788
    in sarcoidosis 1252
PZI insulin *see* Protamine zinc insulin

QAC *see* Quaternary ammonium compounds (QAC)
Q fever 777, **783–784**, 1311
QRS complex **1347–1354**
Quadriplegia **883–884**
    in poliomyelitis 745
    in white matter diseases 917–919
Quadruple heart sound rhythm 1408
Quantitative traits 302
Quaternary ammonium compounds (QAC), *530*, 758
Questionable vitamins *see* Vitamins
Quickening 17
Quinacrine (Atabrine)
    in giardiasis 838
    in hymenolepsiasis **820**
    in taeniasis **819**
Quinidine 1370
    and drug purpura 1235
    in PAT 1365
Quinine 532, 559
    and aplastic anemia 1166
    and drug purpura 1235
    in malaria **833**, *833*
    in myotonia 1032
Quinones 139
Quinsy 1878. *See also* Peritonsillar abscess.
"Quint" 571
Quotane ointment 845
Q waves **1347**
    in anomalous left coronary 1395

Rabbit antibody in *H. influenzae* infections 620
Rabbit fever *see* Tularemia
"Rabbit pellets," meconium 1616
Rabies **755–759**
Race, and growth 242
    and suicide 290
Rachitic craniotabes **200**
Rachitic rosary 200
Racoon 755
Radial head dislocation 1734
Radial nerve injury **978**
Radialulnar fusions 1708

Radiation, and growth retardation 248
Radiation nephritis 1112, **1511**
Radiculitis 699
Radioactive iodine *see* I131
Radioactive phosphorus 1202
Radioactive potassium *see* 40K
Radioactive rose bengal excretion 1684
Radioactive scanning, in pericarditis 1426
Radiographic atlas of skeletal development of, the hand
        and wrist 240
Radiography **59–62**
    in anomalous pulmonary venous drainage 1413
    in ascariasis 802
    in asthma 465, *1295*
    in atrioventricular valve obstruction **138**
    for bone age assessment 240
    in cardiovascular disease **1344–1346**
    in celiac disease 1587
    in choanal atresia **1872**
    in cysticercosis 818–819
    in cystic fibrosis 419, *421*, 422
    in cytomegalic inclusion disease 703
    in diaphragmatic hernia **1633**
    in duodenal atresia **1613**
    in erythroblastosis fetalis 60
    of erythroblastotic fetus *60, 61*
    in esophageal atresia **1605**
    for evaluation of subcutaneous fat 217
    for foreign bodies 1650
    in Hunter's syndrome 401
    in hypercalcemia, idiopathic 207
    in hyperparathyroidism 209
    in hypervitaminosis D 209
    in hypophosphatasia *206, 207*
    in imperforate anus **1626**
    in infantile cortical hyperostosis 1741
    in intraspinal tumors **956**
    in juvenile rheumatoid arthritis 505
    of the kidney **1462–1463**
    in lactose malabsorption **1593**
    in lead poisoning **544–545**
    in Legg-Calvé-Perthes disease **1738**
    of mastoids **1887**
    in meconium ileus **1616**
    in meconium peritonitis **1617**
    in microcephaly **859**
    in multiple births 60
    in mycoplasma pneumoniae infections **626**
    obstructive airway disease 1278
    in osteochondroses **1738–1740**
    in osteogenesis imperfecta 1730
    of pericardial effusion 494
    and placental localization 61
    in portal hypertension **1219**
    in pyloric stenosis **1610**
    in regional enteritis **1643**
    in renal rickets 210, **211**
    in rheumatic carditis 494
    in rickets **199–200**
    in scurvy **189–190**
    in sickle-cell anemia 1177
    of skull **854**
    in syphilis **655**
    in tetralogy of Fallot **1404**
    in thalassemia **1181–1182**, *1182*
    in transposition of great arteries **1410**
    in tricuspid atresia 1407

Radiography (*cont.*)
  in truncus arteriosus 1415
  in ulcerative colitis **1645**
  in vitamin D resistant rickets 204, *205*
Radioimmunoassay of insulin 343
Radioiodinated serum albumin (RISA) cisternography 867
Radioisotope
  brain scan **857, 941**
  fetal heart monitoring 62
  placental localization 61, *62*
Radiotherapy
  in brain tumors 942, 943, 944–948, 952
  in chiasmal gliomas 952
  in Hodgkin's disease **1224–1225**
  in lymphosarcoma **1226**
  in neuroblastoma 1111
  and teratogenicity 12
  in tumors of spinal cord 956
  in Wilms' tumor 1561
Radius, aplasia (hypoplasia) 1707
  and thrombocytopenia **1235**
Raffinose 358
Ragweed 447, 450
"Rainbows" 571
Rales 419, 1421
Ramsay-Hunt syndrome 1886
Ranula **1840**
Rapid enzyme-strip, screening test, for spinal fluid sugar 601
Rapoport-Luebering (2,3-DPG cycle) 392
Rash, skin *see* Eruption, skin
Rat(s), and leptospirae 621
Rat bite fever 505, **634**, 692
Rat fleas 780, 819
  and murine typhus 780
Rathke's pouch 1046
Rattlesnakes 556
Raw fish 820
Raynaud's phenomenon 509, 511, **512–513**, 1032
RDS *see* Respiratory distress syndrome
Reading 260, **277–278**, 852, 880
  disability, specific **277**, 880
  retardation 277–278, 852
Reagin 442, 654, **1806**
  antibody (IgE) 442, 447, 448, 459, 472, 477, 479
  mediated hypersensitivity 477
  sensitivity 486
Rebellion 280
Rebound phenomenon, in rheumatic fever 501
Rebound tenderness
  in appendicitis **1640**
  in splenic injury 1217
Recalcification time 1231
Recessive
  autosomal trait **299, 315,** 368, 370, 371, 379
  X-linked front **299, 314,** 315, 387, 399
Recklessness 261
von Recklinghausen's neurofibromatosis 1055
Recoil *see* Muscle recoil
Recreational needs, in mental retardation **895**
Rectal biopsy
  in aganglionic megacolon 1622
  in CNS degenerative diseases 905, 912
  in cystic fibrosis 414
Rectal route, of methylxanthines 456
Rectocloacal fistula *1626*
Rectovaginal fistula 1556, *1626*

Rectovesical fistula **625–1626**
Rectovestibular fistula *1626,* 1629
Rectum (rectal) **1621–1630, 1648, 1659–1660.** *See also* Rectal.
  abscess **1659**
  agenesis 1626
  in anal fissure 1659
  in appendicitis **1640**
  atresia 1628
  bleeding, in cutis laxa 1765
  in cystic fibrosis 422
  examination, incontinence **1603**
  in lymphogranuloma inguinale 776
  malformations **1625–1630**
  in newborn 76, 83
  in niacin deficiency 182
  pain 1601
  perforation 1618
  prolapse 422, 640, 805, **1659,** 1765
  in shigellosis 640
  stricture, in trichuriasis **805**
Recurrent aphthosis **1853**
Recurrent bullous eruption of hands and feet **1771, 1772**
Recurrent familial cholestasis 1686
Recurrent meningitis *1015*
Recurrent typhus fever *see* Brill-Zinsser disease
"Red 88" 571
"Red birds" 571
Red blood cells *see* Erythrocytes
Red bug *see* Chigger mite
Red Cedar, furniture polish 1312
Red cell casts 1460
"Red devils" 571 •
Reduviid bugs 835
Red pulp (splenic) 1216
Red reflex 80
Reduced hemoglobin 1401
Reduced penetrance 305
Reduction, in fetus 53
Reed-Sternberg cells **1223,** 1224
"Reefer" 566, 572
Reflexes *1901,* **1907**
  in acute polyneuritis 1007
  automatic walking *see* Automatic walking
  crossed extension *85,* **88**
  in Friedreich's ataxia 922
  "Moro" *see* Moro reflex
  in newborn *85,* **87–88**
  in poliomyelitis **745**
  in spinal cord tumors **955**
Reflex sympathetic dystrophies 514, 515
Reflux of urine **1560**
Refractive errors **1835**
Refractoriness, of end organ 212
Refsum's syndrome 379, **924–925, 1008**
Regional enteritis 1593, **1642–1643**
Regional ileitis 505, **1642–1643**
  and megaloblastic anemia 1164
Regional medical programs 10
Regitine *see* Phentolamine
Regitine test 1110
Regurgitant murmurs 1343
Regurgitation 850
Reichert's cartilage 1884
Reindeer 821
Reinsch's test 533
Reiter's triad 514, 1544

Rejection 283, 438
  and suicide 292
Religion, and suicide 291
Renal. *See also* Kidney; Urinary tract system.
  clearance 50, 105, 1462
    methods **1461–1462**
    of sodium, 50, 108
  colic 336, 409, **1535–1538**
  diabetes **1516–1517**
  glycosuria 206, 356, **1516–1517**
  hyperphosphatemia 196
  hypertension 331, **1444**
  hypophosphatemia 196
  phosphate threshold 1519
  rickets 337
  tubular acidosis 204, 326, 588, **1524–1527**
  tubular disorders 356, 1516–1529
  tubular function, in utero 89, **1455**
  vein thrombosis 1472, **1534**
    in infant of diabetic mother 127
Rendu-Osler-Weber syndrome 929, **1232**, 1305, 1814
Renin 1421, **1442–1443**, 1567
Rennin 160
Renografin 60
Renovascular hypertension **1442–1443**
Repeatism 518
Replication 35, 296
Reporting, of child battering 558
Repression 307
Resentment 282
Reserpine 532, 1467
  in Graves' disease 1065
  in hypertension 1448
  and neonatal depression 55
  in thyrotoxicosis **1086**
Residential care, long term 5
Residual volume (RV) 465
Residual volume/lung capacity percentage, in asthma 465
Resin uptake tests, indirect **1063**
Resistance, to antimicrobial agents **583–584**
Resorcinol 532
Resource baking mix 1466
Respiration **90–94, 1904.** *See also* Pulmonary system; Respiratory.
  fetal **46–47**
  of low-birth-weight infant 90, **90–94**
  minute volume **92**
  of newborn 81
  onset of breathing 49, **68,** 70
  in utero 90
Respirator therapy
  complications **1265**
  in poliomyelitis **746**
  in tetanus 661
Respiratory
  acidosis 1282, 1633. *See also* Acidosis.
  alkalosis 501. *See also* Alkalosis.
  arrest 456
  dead space **1275**
  depression, in newborn 54, 55
  difficulty
    in dysplasia epiphysealis punctata 1726
    in hypoglycemia of newborn 360
    in Jeune's disease 1725
  distress
    in cytomegalic inclusion disease 703
    and hyperbilirubinemia 1681

Respiratory (*cont.*)
  distress (*cont.*)
    in myasthenia gravis 1036
    in neonatal cretinism 1070
  distress index *see* Retraction scoring
  distress syndrome (RDS) 75, **1261–1265,** 1401
  exercises, in cystic fibrosis 427
  failure
    in organic phosphate ester poisoning 551
    in poliomyelitis **745–747**
  function
    of neonatal blood 94
    in newborn **1255–1262**
    in older infants and children **1273–1277, 1299–1303, 1322–1324**
  illness
    bronchiolitis **1290–1292**
    bronchitis **1290**
    empyema **1329**
    epiglottitis **1286–1287**
    laryngitis **1286**
    influenza **720–722**
    parainfluenza **722–723**
    pneumonias **1305–1307**
    pneumonitis **1311**
  infection
    bacterial **1270, 1285–1287, 1290–1292, 1305–1307, 1329**
    myotic **1307–1308**
    parasitic **1311**
    viral 466, 620, 625, **719–728,** 1285–1287, 1311
      adenoviruses **725–726**
      Coxsackie viruses **751**
      ECHO viruses **754**
      myxoviruses **720–726**
      picornaviruses **726–727**
      respiratory syncytial (RS) virus 628, 646
      rhinoviruses, **726–727**
  mechanics of, in asthma 465
  musculature **1323**
  neurons, birth excitability of 69
  paralysis, in poliomyelitis **745–746**
  quotient (RQ) 39, 42
  rate of newborn 81
  reflexes, in the newborn **1258**
  regulation of, in low-birth-weight newborn **93**
  rhythm, in low-birth-weight newborn 93
  sounds, in airway obstruction **1277**
  system **1258–1331.** *See also* Pulmonary system.
    in cystic fibrosis **416–417**
  tract, burns of **519–520**
Rest, **1908**
  in heart failure 1424
Restlessness 273, 287, 880
  in gray matter diseases 912–914
    in airway obstruction **1277**
  in heroin withdrawal 562
  in lymphocytic choriomeningitis 729
  in rabies 756
Resuscitation of newborn 70–74, *103,* 104, **1260**
Retardation, growth *see* Growth retardation
Retardation, mental *see* Mental retardation
Retardation, speech *see* Speech retardation
Reticulocyte(s) 64, 393, *1157,* **1169,** 1170–1172, 1216
Reticulocytosis 393
  in hemolytic anemias **1169,** 1170–1201
  in malaria 831

Reticuloendothelial system (and cells) 1216, **1245**
  in albinism 326
Reticuloendotheliosis **1245–1250,** 1831
Reticulum cell sarcoma 943, **1226–1227**
Retina 385, 923, **1828–1830**
  in albinism 326
  in cystic fibrosis 416, 422
  degeneration 923, 1842
  detachment 1830
  dysplasia 1829
  edema 385
  in gray matter diseases 912
  hemorrhages *see* Hemorrhages, retinal
  phakoma *926*
  pigmentary degeneration 377, 923, **1828–1829**
  in Tay-Sachs disease 912
  in tuberous sclerosis 925–926
  vessels and oxygen 97
  in viscera larva migrans 802
Retinitis pigmentosa 377, 923, **1828–1829**
  heredopathia atactica polyneuritiformis 379
  in Refsum's syndrome 924, **1008**
Retinitis, in sarcoidosis 1251
Retinoblastoma 1826, **1830,** 1831
Retinol *see* Vitamin A
Retinopathy
  of congenital rubella **766**
  in cystinosis, and diabetes mellitus 344
Retraction, of upper lid, in Graves' disease 1084
Retractions 75, 91, 1261, **1278,** 1305
  intercostal 81, 1305
  in R.D.S. 1261
  score 104
  suprasternal 81
Retraction scoring *104*
Retroauricular ecchymosis (Battle's sign) **968, 969**
Retroauricular lymphadenopathy
  in exanthem subitum 705
  in rubella 761
Retrobulbar glioma 1702
Retrobulbar neuritis
  in measles 735
  in multiple sclerosis 918
Retrograde pyelography 1463
Retrograde urography 1549
Retrolental fibroplasia 97, 105, 116, 1826, **1829–1830**
Retroorbital pain in rickettsial infection 779
Retroperitoneal pneumography, in hyperaldosteronism **1448**
Retropharyngeal abscess 660, 673
Retrosternal hernias 1633
Revaccination 774
Reye's syndrome **1688**
  and hypoglycemia 362
R-factors (resistance factors) 288, 583
R-forms *see* R-factors
Rh antibodies **1187–1189, 1196–1197**
  gestational 18
Rh antigen **1188**
Rh erythroblastosis **1188**
Rh-Hr (Wiener) nomenclature **1196–1197**
Rh system **1187–1189, 1196–1197**
Rhagades, syphilitic **656**
Rhabditoid larvae 805, **807**
  of *Strongyloides stercoralis* **807**
Rhabdomyoma of heart, in tuberous sclerosis 925, *926,* 1433

Rheumatic
  activity 490
  arthritis *see* Rheumatic polyarthritis
  attacks 498, 501
    prevention of initial **501,** 502
  carditis *see* Rheumatic heart disease
Rheumatic fever 190, **490–502,** 505, 506, 510, 514, 515
  clinical features **494–496**
  course **497–499**
  differential diagnosis **499–500**
  epidemiology **492–493**
  etiology **490–492**
  and glomerulonephritis 1483
  incidence **492–493**
  laboratory **496–497**
  pathology **493–494**
  prognosis **497–499**
  prophylaxis **501–502,** 652
  treatment **500–501**
Rheumatic heart disease 267, **490–502,** 1338. *See also* Rheumatic fever.
  carditis, 490, 494–495, 497, **498, 499,** 500–502, **1428**
  course 498
  endocarditis 493
  myocarditis
    acute 493, 494, **499,** 500, 501
    chronic **499**
  pancarditis 493, 499
  pericarditis **494,** 499, **1426–1427**
Rheumatic pneumonitis, 494, 496, 499
Rheumatic polyarthritis 490, **494–495,** 497, 498, 500
Rheumatic recurrences 498
  and streptococcal infections *492*
Rheumatic subcutaneous nodules 490, **493,** 494, **495,** 499, 500
  and neuroblastoma 1111
Rheumatic subject 490
Rheumatoid arthritis, juvenile 490, 495, 499, **503–507**
  band keratopathy in **1824**
  cataracts in 1826
  episcleritis in 1824
  pericarditis in **1427**
Rheumatoid factor 446, 499, 503, 505, 509, 511, 513, 514
  in rubella arthritis 763
Rheumatoid spondylitis 505, **1328**
Rhinitis 461, **566,** 720, 723
  allergic *see* Allergic rhinitis
  medicamentosa 461
  purulent, in low-birth-weight infant 109
  syphilitic **655**
Rhinorrhea 418
  in basilar skull fracture 968, 970
  due to reserpine, in newborn 55
  in skull fractures 1704
Rhinovirus and disease 695, **726–727**
  in unexplained infant death 576
Rhizobium 439
Rhizomelic dwarfism **1720–1722**
Rhizopus 795
Rhodesian or East African sleeping sickness *see* African trypanosomiasis
Rhodhius 836
Rhodopsin 177
RhoGam (Ortho) *see* anti-Rh antibody
Rhonchi 419
Rhubarb 531
Rhus oleoresin **476**

Rhus sensitivity 476
Rhythmic rocking 324
RI (respiratory illness) virus 725
Riboflavin 138, **138**, 157, **181**, 395, 1854
Ribonuclease 441
Ribonucleic acid *see* RNA
Ribonucleic acid polymerase 695
Ribose 359
Ribosome 35, 296, 581
Ribosuria 359
Ribulose 359
Rice and beriberi 138
Rickets 143, **197–206**, 210, 1683
  bone pathology in **198–200**
  in chronic renal disease 1467
  hypophosphatemia, renal, associated with 195, **203–204**
  and laryngeal obstruction 1285
  non-vitamin D deficiency **203**–206
  with osteomalacia and renal tubular acidosis 206
  pseudo-vitamin D deficiency 197, **203**
  renal **210**
  in renal tubular acidosis, distal **1525**
  vitamin D deficiency 146, **197–203**
    and breast feeding 152
  vitamin D dependent 197, **203**
Rickets-like bone disorders **206–207**
  hypophosphatasia **206**
  metaphyseal dysostosis **206–207**
Rickettsiae 581, 585–586, **777–785**
  akari 781, 782
  australis 781
  burneti 1311
  conori 781
  mooseri 780
  orientalis 783
  prowazekii **778**
  rickettsii **781–782**
  siberica 781
  tsutsugamushi 783
Rickettsialpox 702, 781, **782–783**, 1785
Rickettsioses **777–785**
  Q fever 783–784
  scrub typhus **783**
  spotted fevers **781–783**
    Rocky Mountain spotted fever 778, **781–782**
    rickettsialpox **782–783**
  treatment **784–785**
  typhus fevers **779–781**
    Brill-Zinsser disease 778, **780**
    epidemic typhus **779–780**
    murine (endemic) typhus **780–781**
Rickettsiostatic drugs 581, 585–586, **778**, 783, **784**
Righting reactions, of newborn *87*
Right-left confusion, in minimal cerebral dysfunction syndrome 880
Right-to-left shunts 1357, **1376–1379**, **1401–1408**
  in RDS 1262
Right ventricle pressure overload 1372–**1373**, 1394
Right ventricular hypertrophy, EKG diagnosis 1350
Rigidity
  in basal ganglia degenerations **919–921**
  in kernicterus 1677
  in minimal cerebral dysfunction syndrome 880
  in newborn *85*
  in parkinsonism **919**
  in thalamic tumors 947

Riley-Day syndrome *see* Familial dysautonomia
Rinderpest (cattle plague) 730
Ring chromosomes (A, 5, C, D, E, 16, 17, 18, X) **903**
Ring X or Y chromosome 1142
"Ringed hair" 1760
Ring scotoma 1829
Ringer's solution, lactated 349
"Ringworm fungi" **1788–1791**
Rinkel provocation testing method 449
Risk recurrence, determination of, in genetic counseling **315–316**
Risus sardonicus **659**
Ritter's disease **1776–1778**
RLF *see* Retrolental fibroplasia 1829
Ridge count, finger **313**
Ridges, epidermal *see* Epidermal ridges
Riding breeches deformity 1722
Ridley flush-fitting scleral contact lens 1824
Rifampin 608
Rifamycin 581
Right aortic arch 388, **1416**
Right atrium pressure overload 1372
Right coronary artery, from pulmonary artery 1434
Right heart failure **1421–1424**
RNA 21, 35, 694
RNA/DNA ratio, in kwashiorkor 173
RNA, messenger (mRNA) 35, 296, 304, 581, 694, 1665
RNA, molecule **296**
RNA polymerase 581, 695
RNA, transfer (tRNA) 296
RNA viruses 720–725, 741, 755
"Roach" 572
Robaxin *see* Methocarbamol
"Rocket" 572
Rocky Mountain spotted fever 733, 778, **781–782**
Rodents 847
  bites of 757
  and leptospirae 621
Rohrer index 24
Rokitansky-Cushing ulcer 1639
Romaña's sign, in Chagas' disease 836
Romberg's facial hemiatrophy 1696
Rooting reflex *85*, 252, *850*, **854**
"Rope" 572
Rope skipping 260
Rorschach test 266
Rosary
  in rickets 200
  in scurvy 189
Roseola infantum *see* Exanthem subitum
"Roses" 571
Rose spots
  in salmonella infections 636
  in typhoid fever **638**
Rosettes 509
Rotational anomalies, intestine **1615**
Rotheln *see* Rubella
Rothman-Makai disease 1769
Rougeole (Fr.) *see* Measles
Round-back deformity 1740
Roundworms *see* Nematodes
Roussy-Levy syndrome **922**
R protein, of streptococcal cell wall 648
RQ *see* Respiratory, quotient
RS virus *see* Respiratory syncytial virus
RTA *see* Renal tubular acidosis

Rubella 12, 18, 84, 116, 514, 704, 711, 719, 733, **759–769**, 1684, 1884
   antibody **762–763**, **767–768**
   arthritis 514, 515, **761**
   associated disease, neonatal **765**
   embryopathy 12, 18
   encephalitis **1021**
   gestational 18
   glaucoma **766**
   HI antibody test 762
   keratitis 1825
   neutralizing antibody 760
   and patent ductus arteriosus 1393
   rash **761**
   specific IgM **767**
   and thrombocytopenia 1235
   vaccine, live attenuated **763–764**, *1897*
Rubellalike rash, due to ECHO viruses 754
Rubeola *see* Measles
Rubinstein-Taybi syndrome **1841**
Rud's syndrome 390
Rumble, diastolic 495
Rumpel-Leede phenomenon 191, **1231–1234**
   in Rocky Mountain spotted fever 781
Rumination syndrome 850, **1576–1578**
Rupture of membranes, premature 18
"Rush" 572
Russell-Silver dwarfism 1695, **1706**, 1841
Russian spring-summer encephalitis 1016, **1017–1018**
RVH *see* Right ventricular hypertrophy
R wave 1347
Rye, contamination of 531

"Saber shin" 657
Sabin-Feldman dye test **841**
Sabin vaccine (live attenuated) **747–748**, *1897*
Sabouraud's culture medium 791
Sabouraud's dextrose agar media 1791
Sacral meninogomyeloceles **874**
"Sacred mushroom" **569**
Sacrococcygeal teratomas 1718
Sacrococcygeal tumors 83
Sacroiliac abnormalities, in rheumatoid arthritis 505
Sacrum, hypoplasia or aplasia 1718
Saddle nose deformity in syphilis **655**
S-adenosylhomocysteine 332
S-adenosylmethionine 332
Safety glass 518
Safflower oil 135
Sagittal suture synostosis **1697–1699**
Salicylanilides 476
Salicylate(s) 54–55, 462, **500–502**, 515, 529, 532, **552–556**, 1674, 1911
   and coagulation defect in newborn 55
   and hypoglycemia 462
   intoxication **552–556**
     acid base disturbances in **553**
     treatment **553–555**
   obstetric use 54–55
   and PBI 1063
   plasma, following ingestion 554
   renal clearance 555
   teratogenicity 55
   therapy
     of rheumatic fever **500–502**
     in rheumatoid arthritis **506**

Salicylate(s) *(cont.)*
   therapy *(cont.)*
     in SLE 510
   toxicity 501, 507, **552–556**
Salicylazosulfapyridine (Azulfidine) 1646
Salicylic acid ointment 1784, 1788, 1791, 1809, 1816
Salicylism 552
Saline enemas 1602
Salisbury strains 726
Saliva 386, **1567**
Salivary amylase 1567–1568
Salivary glands, 413–414, 422, 457, **737–739**
   in cystic fibrosis 413, 414
   inflammation 457
   in mumps **737–739**
Salivation 550, 1741
   in mumps 738
   in neonatal narcotic withdrawal syndrome 574
   in organic phosphate ester poisoning 551
   in scorpion sting 845
   as seizure equivalent 991
   in Wilson's disease 920
Salk vaccine (formalin inactivated) **747–748**, *1897*
Salmon 821
Salmonellae
   bareilly 635, 637
   choleraesuis 635–637
   derby 635–637
   enteritidis 635–637
   gallinarum 635–637
   hirschfeldii (para C) 635–637
   montevideo 635–637
   oranienburg 635–637
   paratyphi (para A) 635–637
   pullorum 635–637
   schottmuelleri (para B) 635–637
   typhi see Salmonella typhosa
   typhimurium 635–637
   typhosa (S. typhi) 439, 635–637, **637–639**
Salmonella infections 226, 227, 388, 439, 585–588, 596, 609, **635–638**
   "fever" 636
   food poisoning **636**
   meningitis 600
   osteomyelitis **636–637**, 1177–1178
     in sickle-cell anemia 1177–1178
Salmonellosis *see* Salmonella infections
Salol 1651
Salpingitis 786
Salt, and hypertonic dehydration 229
Salt craving, in Addison's disease 1093, 1094–1095
"Salting out" method 1672
Salt losing
   adrenal hyperplasia, congenital virilizing **1095–1098**
   nephropathies **1527–1528**
Salt poisoning 229
Salt-poor human albumin, in nephrotic syndrome 1504
Salt restriction, in heart failure **1424**
Sanatorium 684
Sandbox 803
Sandfly **837**
Sanfilippo syndrome **399**, **915**, 1824
SA node 1421
Sao Paulo typhus 781
Sarampion (Sp) *see* Measles
Sarcoidosis 209, 389, 396, 480, 514, 698, 1245, **1250–1253**, 1797

Sarcomatous degeneration, of exostoses 1728
Sarcophaga *see* Flesh flies
Sarcoptes scabiei **845, 1797**
Sarcosine 330
Sarcosine dehydrogenase 330
Sarcosinemia **330**
Saturated fatty acids, and stomach emptying 1566
S. aureus see Staphylococcus aureus
SBE *see* Bacterial endocarditis
Scabies **845, 1797**
"Scag" 572
Scalded skin syndrome **1776–1778**
Scalene node biopsy, in Hodgkin's disease 1224
Scaling 473, 511, **1755–1759.** *See also* Desquamation.
Scaling disorders **1755–1759**
Scalp edema, in anaphylactoid purpura 1233
Scalp furuncles, in craniospinal focal sepsis **1010–1016**
Scalp hair, loss of **1761**
Scalp injuries **966**
Scalp veins, in hydrocephalus **865**
Scaphocephaly 1697, 1831
Scapular lesions, in Caffey's disease 1741
Scapula, winged 978
Scapulohumeral muscular dystrophy of Erb 1031
Scarf maneuver *86,* **87**
Scarlatina *see* Scarlet fever
Scarlet fever **649,** 733, 763
Scars, and battered child syndrome 557
"Scat" 572
Scheie syndrome **404,** 1824, 1825
Scheuermann's disease 1739, **1740–1741**
Schick test 387, **617–618**
Schilder's leucodystrophy 324, 918
Schilling test **1164**
Schistosoma cercariae 1792
Schistosoma haematobium **813–815**
Schistosoma japonicum **813–815**
Schistosomal dermatitis 815
"Schistosomal fever" 814
Schistosoma mansoni **813–815**
Schistosomiasis **813–815**
  of liver 1691
Schistosomules 813
Schizogony **831**
Schizonts 832, 842
Schizophrenia 286, 914
Schlemm's canal 1825
Schönlein's purpura *see* Anaphylactoid purpura
School 8
  and suicide 290, 293
School age children
  mortality in **4**
  health services 4, **8**
School difficulties 283
  and suicide 292
School performance, poor, in neurologic disease 852
School placement, in cerebral palsy **886**
Schultz-Dale test 449
Schwartzman reaction 1533
Schwartz-Jampel syndrome 1478
Sciatic nerve injury **978–979**
Scintillation scanning 1693
Scintiscanning, hepatic 1673
Sclarlatiniform rash, in streptococcal pharyngitis 648
Sclerae 305, 315, 340, **1824**
Scleral icterus
  in sickle-cell disease 1177

Scleral icterus (*cont.*)
  in β-thalassemia 1181
Sclerema neonatorum 78, 1768
Scleritis 1785, **1824–1825**
Sclerodactyly 513
Scleroderma 505, 512–**513,** 514–516, 1314, **1328–1329**
Scleroderma "focal" (Moyshea) **513,** 1760
Sclerosis, multiple or disseminated *see* Multiple sclerosis
Scolex 817, 818
Scoliosis, 1303, 1715, 1740, 1745
  in familial dysautonomia 1040
  and intraspinal tumor 455
  in neurofibromatosis *928*
  in rickets 200
  due to spina bifida 874
Scorbutic rosary 189
"Score" 572
Scorpions 555, **844–845**
Scorpion venoms **845**
Scotch tape swab technique (NIH swab), for pinworm
  eggs 804
Scotochromogenic bacilli 690, 691
Scotomas 377, 1002
  hysterical 284
Scotometry 178
Screening test
  hearing 189
  for spinal fluid sugar **601**
  vision 7
Screw-worms 846
Scrofuloderma **676**
Scrotal hypospadias 1553
Scrotal stippling, in growth, physical 1096
Scrotal swelling **1631**
Scrotal tongue 1849
Scrotum 1631
Scrub typhus 778, **783**
Scurvy 139, 146, **186–194,** 195, 325, 1232, 1702, 1854
Scurvy line 190
Scutula 1790
SD *see* Standard deviations
Seabathers' eruptions 1792
Seafood, and urticaria 477
Seasonal distribution
  of plumbism **543**
  of unexplained infant death 576
Seasonal influence, on growth 243
Seasonal rhinitis 459
Seat belts 518
Seawater drowning 525
Seaweed dermatitis 1792
Seborrheic dermatitis **473, 1759,** 1814, 1894
  in Letterer-Siwe disease 1246
  in riboflavin deficiency 180
Sebum **1815**
Seckel's bird-headed dwarfism **1814–1842**
Seconal (secobarbital) 20, 563, 1910
Secondary constriction, chromosomal 308
Secondary effects of drugs **478**
Secondary hyperaldosteronism, in distal RTA **1525–1526**
Secondary sexual characteristics *see* Sexual character-
  istics, secondary
Secondary thrombocytopenic purpura **1235–1236**
Secondary vascular purpura 1232
Second branchial arch 1703, 1884
Second heart sound **1339–1341**
Secretin 218

Secretions, in cystic fibrosis 416
Secretions, respiratory **1278, 1280–1281**
Secretory antibody, IgA 732
Secretory otitis media *see* Otitis media, serous
Secundum atrial septal defects **1399–1400**
Sedative(s) 571
  addiction **563–565**
  in allergic disorders 457
  drug toxicity, acute **564–565**
  obstetric use 55
  in obstructive airway disease **1282**
  transplacental diffusion 55
Sedormid, drug purpura 1235
See-saw respirations 81, 1261
Segmental dilation of the colon 1624
Seizure equivalent syndrome 982, **991, 1000**
Seizures *see* Convulsions
Selective angiocardiography 1383
Selenium 141, 146
Self-agression, in suicide 292
Self-blame 269
Self-destructive biting, in Lesch-Nyhan syndrome 339
Self-evaluation 260
Self-rejection 219
Self-replication, of genes 294
Sella turcica
  calcifications, *953*
  in craniopharyngioma 952
  enlargement 1076
  in optic nerve and chiasmal glioma **951**
Semicircular canals 1884
Semilunar valves 1339, **1384–1389**
  obstruction **1384–1389**
Seminiferous tubule dysgenesis (Klinefelter's syndrome)
       309, 310, 311, **903,** 1129, 1130, 1144
Semple vaccine 1022
Sendai virus 723
Senear-Usher syndrome 1780
Sengstaken balloon 1219, 1652
Senile-like appearance **1841–1842**
Sense of identity, in adolescence 262
Sensory deficits **852**
  in brainstem tumors 945
  in encephalitis 1016–1023
  in Friedreich's ataxia 922
Sensory development, in infancy and toddlerhood 252
"Sentinel pile" 1659
Separation
  and suicide 291
  in therapy of asthma **467–471**
  trauma 256
Sepsis 422, 499, 645, 1022, 1679. *See also* Septicemia.
  and adrenal insufficiency 1094
  in aganglionic megacolon 1022
  and breast feeding 152
  and intravascular clotting 1242
  and jaundice **1684–1685**
  and marasmus 172
  neonatorum **596–598**
  renal disease in **1495–1496**
  following splenectomy 1217
  due to *Staphylococcus aureus* 645
  in typhoid fever 637
Septectomy 1407
Septic cerebritis 1011
Septic emboli, in heroin addicts 560
Septicemia *see* Sepsis

Septum pellucidum, rupture of 863
Septum primum 1398
Septum secundum **1398–1399**
  atrial defects **1399–1400**
Sequestered lung 1304
Sequestra 675
Serine 174, 332, 336
Serologic tests
  in Bancroft's filariasis 811
  in blastomycosis 788
  in candidiasis 796
  in Chagas' disease 836
  in coccidioidial granuloma 790
  in poliomyelitis 746
  for rheumatoid factor 505
  for syphilis (STS) 509, **654**
Serology, syphilis (STS) 509, **654**
  false positive **509,** 729
  in heroin addicts 561
Serotonin 132, 183, 186, 324, 452
  in Down's syndrome 899
Serpiginous dermal tunnels, in cutaneous larva migrans
       807
Serotyping of *Salmonella* **637**
Serous meningitis
  pertussis *630*
  tuberculous 672–673
Serous otitis media *see* Otitis media, serous
Serratia 587
Serratia marcescens 397
Serratus anterior palsy 978
Sertoli cells 1144, 1561
Sertoli cell tumors 1561
Serum albumin *see* Albumin, serum
Serum complement *see* Complement, serum
Serum complement system *see* Complement system,
       serum
Serum hepatitis *see* Hepatitis, viral
Serum sickness 442, 445, **485–489,** 511, 513, 514, 515, 585
Serum-sickness-like disease **485**
Setting-sun sign of eyes 854, **865,** 1192
  due to kernicterus 1192
Sewage 749
Sex
  assignment in hermaphrodism **1147**
  chromatin 310, 311, 1116, **1132**
  chromosome abnormalities 903
  chromosomes 298
  differentiation **1130–1132**
  differentiation abnormalities **1130–1148**
  disorders 269
    as psychopathologic symptoms and syndromes 278
  influence on autosomally determined traits 300
  information 278
  and neonatal mortality 113
  prediction 58
  and suicide 290
  of twins 118
Sex-linked ichthyosis **1757**
Sexual characteristics, secondary **241**
Sexual difficulties 269, 278, 293
  and suicide 293
Sexual infantilism 219, 1053, 1139
  in craniopharyngioma 952
  phenotypic females **1116–1117**
Sexual maturation, normal **1122, 1123–1124**
Sexual precocity **1122,** **1124–1130**

Sexual promiscuity, in asthmatics 468
Shohl solution, in distal RTA 1525–1526
"Shooting up" 559, 572
Short attention span 880
Shortchain fatty acids see Fatty acids, shortchain
Short stature 204, 399, 903, 1052–1056, 1142, 1144, 1075–
	1076, 1726–1727, 1804, 1841–1842. See also
	Dwarfism; Growth retardation.
  in achondroplasia 1721–1722
  in familial dysautonomia 1040
  in gonadal dysgenesis 1139
  in Hurler's disease 914
  in Maroteaux-Lamy syndrome 404
  in mucopolysaccharidoses 399–404
  in sickle-cell anemia 1177
  in β-thalassemia 1181
"Shot" 572
Shoulder girdle elevation 465
Shoulder pain, left in splenic injury 1217
Shrubs, as poisons 529
Shrugging of shoulders 851
Shunt, arteriovenous see Arteriovenous shunt
Shunt bilirubin production 1674
Shunt, cardiac
  detection of 1357
  left-to-right 94, 1373–1376, 1393–1401
  right-to-left 94, 1376–1379
Shunt, placental 46
Shunting procedure, in hydrocephalus 865–867
Sialic acid 413, 907
Sia water test, in kala-azar 837
Siberian tick typhus 781
Sibling rivalry 283
Sick child, appraisal and care 1897–1912
Sickle-cell anemia 514, 1176–1178, 1460, 1510–1511, 1879
  bone lesions in 1743
  crisis 1177
  nephropathy 1510–1511
  and pneumococcal meningitis 600
  and salmonella osteomyelitis 636
  trait 299, 1176
Sickle-cell-hemoglobin C disease 300
Sickle-cell β-thalassemia disease 1184
Sickled erythrocytes 1176
  and malaria 832
Sickling 1177–1178
Side-effects of drugs 479
Sideroachrestic anemias 1168
Sideroblastic anemia 1168
Sideroblasts 1168
Sigmoid colostomy 1628
Sigmoidoscopy
  in amebiasis 828
  in ulcerative colitis 1645
Silicon 145
Silverman-Anderson score see Retraction score
Silver nitrate 104, 523–524
  in burns 523–524
Silver syndrome 1706
Simian line 899
Similac 162
"Simon focus" 665
Simple goiter 1077–1081
Simulant females see Feminizing testes syndrome
Simulium 811
Sindig-Larson's disease 1739
Single atrium 1376

Single ventricle 1376
Sinus arrhythmia 1369
Sinus bradycardia 1366, 1423
Sinuses, paranasal see Nose; Paranasal sinuses
Sinuses splenic 1216
Sinusitis 387, 599, 650, 1294, 1876
  and craniospinal focal sepsis 1010–1016
  due to H. influenzae 619
  in measles 731
  and phycomycosis 795
Sinus of Valsalva 1395
Sinus tachycardia 1364
Sinus thrombosis 599
"Situational" environment 1912–1913
Situs inversus, and asplenia 1217
Situs solitus 1419
Sjögren-Larsson syndrome 889, 930, 1757
Sjögren's syndrome 509
Skeletal maturation, in cretinism 1071
Skeletal maturity score 240, 241
Skeletal system 1695–1753. See also Bones; Joints.
  anomalies
    in Fanconi syndrome 1165
    in gonadal dysgenesis 1141
    in infant of diabetic mother 127
  axial skeleton 1714–1719
  and blood diseases 1743, 1744
    acquired diseases 1714–1745
    postnatal conditions 1741
  deformities
    in mucopolysaccharidoses 399–404
    in spinal cord tumors 955
  dysplasias 404, 1719–1735, 1841
  extremities 1706–1714
  joints 1746–1752
  juvenile osteochondroses 1737–1746
  lesions
    in Hand-Schüller-Christian syndrome 1248
    in hypercalcemia, idiopathic 206
    in hypophosphatasia 206–207
    in metaphysial dysostosis 206
    in parathyroid disorders 208–210
  in rickets 198–206
  skull 1695–1706
Skeletal tuberculosis see Tuberculosis, skeletal
Skim milk see Cow's milk
Skin 1753–1816, 1894, 1901, 1905
  abscesses, in brucellosis 611
  abrasions, in neonatal narcotic withdrawal syndrome
    574
  absorption of poisons 528–529
  in acrodynia 550
  in albinism 326
  in atopic eczema 472–473
  atrophy 1838
  bacterial infections of 1781–1784
  and battered child syndrome 557
  at birth 74, 78
  in blastomycosis 788
  blistering diseases 1770–1781
  blotching, in familial dysautonomia 1040
  care 1894
  in contact dermatitis 475–476
  in cutaneous porphyria 411
  definitions 1753
  in dehydration 229
  depigmentation 1206

Skin (cont.)
  in dermamyositis **511–512**
  in dermatomyositis **510–511**
  dermis, diseases of **1763–1769**
  dryness, in hypothyroidism 1076
  eczema **1806–1808**
  erythropoietic porphyria, congenital 407
  in erythropoietic protoporphyria 409
  examination 74, 78, *1901*, 1905
  in Fabry's disease **384**
  fungal infections **1788–1792**
  in Hand-Schüller-Christian syndrome **1248**
  in Hartnup disease 336
  in herpes simplex **713**
  in hookworm infection 806
  hyperkeratosis *177*
  in infantile kala-azar 837
  infections 1781–1798
    and craniospinal focal sepsis **1010–1016**
  in infectious mononucleosis **718**, 719
  infestations **1792–1797**
  keratinization disorders **1755–1763**
  in kwashiorkor 173
  in Letterer-Siwe disease 1246
  leukemia infiltration 1209
  in lupus erythematosus **508**
  in marasmus 171
  mottling 390
  in neurocutaneous syndromes **925–931**
  in neurofibromatosis **927**
  in neurologic diagnosis 853
  in Niemann-Pick disease 384
  in nummular eczema **472**
  parasitic infections of 1792
  phrynoderma *177*
  pigmentation disorders 927, **1799–1805**
  in rickettsialpox 783
  in sarcoidosis **1251**
  in scarlet fever **649**
  in scleroderma **512**
  in smallpox **770**
  in staphylococcal infection of 645
  after subacute fetal distress 27
  in syphilis **655**, 657
  temperature, in Graves' disease 1083
  test
    allergic 448, 460
    candidia 796
    cat scratch 699
    histoplasmin 792
    before horse serum administration **486**
    mumps 739
    schistosomi 814
  tuberculosis of 675–676
  in varicella **701, 702**
  viral infections **1784–1788**
  water loss from 142, 224
Skin biopsy
  in onchocerciasis 812
  in Letterer-Siwe disease **1247**
Skin colonization, staphylococcal **644**
Skin creams, and feminization 1128
Skin creases, and gestational age *79*
Skin-fold thickness 217
"Skin-popping" 559, 562, 572
Skin-sensitizing antibody 446, 452
Skin turgor 229

Skin ulcers
  in dracontiasis 810
  in heroin addicts 561
Skin-window studies 396, 449
Skopolate 1612
Skopyl *see* Methyl scopolamine nitrate
Skull **1695–1706**. *See also* Cranial.
  in achondroplasia **1721**
  acquired anomalies **1704–1706**
  basal fracture, and pneumococcal meningitis 601
  in chronic anemias **1705**
  congenital anomalies **1696–1704**
  defects **1700–1702**
  fractures **601**, **967–970**, **1705**
  in hypophosphatasia 206
  postural flattening 1696, *1697*, 1699
  transillumination *see* Transillumination, of skull
  variations in shape **1695–1700**
Skull radiography 854
  in brain tumors **941–943**, 945, 947, 948
  in craniospinal focal sepsis **1010–1016**
  in epilepsy 993
  in hydrocephalus **865**
  in megalencephaly 860
  in tuberous sclerosis 927
Skunk 691, 755
SLE *see* Systemic lupus erythematosus
Sleep **834, 1895**
  excessive **275**
Sleep disturbances **274–275**, 287
Sleeping sickness *see* African trypanosomiasis
Sleeplessness, in neonatal narcotic withdrawal syndrome
    574
"Sleepwalker" 571
Sleepwalking **274–275**
Sliding hernia 1631
Slipped femoral epiphyses 1713, 1718
Slow-reacting substance of anaphylaxis (SRS-A) 446
Slum areas, and lead poisoning **543**
Slurred speech 671
S.M.A. 162
"Smack" 572
Small-for-age newborn **115–117**
Small for gestational age *see* Small-for-age newborn
Small intestine **1567–1569**, 1631
  absorption **1567–1569**
  duodenal atresia **1613–1615**
  ileal atresia **1615**
  infarction 1631
  intestinal atresia **1613**
  intestinal stenosis **1613**
  jejunal atresia 1615
  "Ladd bands" obstruction **1615**
  malformations **1612–1621**
  midgut volvulus **1615**
  neonatal duodenal obstruction **1613–1615**
  rotational anomalies 1615
  secretions **1567–1569**
  volvulus **1615**
Smallpox 702, **769–775**, 1021
  encephalitis **1021**
  eruption 702, **770–771**
  vaccination **773–775**, **1896,** *1897*
    and atopic eczema 473
    complications **774**
Smears, bacterial **579**
Smegma 1894

Smith-Lemli-Opitz syndrome 1842
Smoke inhalation 519–520
Smoking, and low-birth-weight 22
Smooth muscle spasm
  in asthma 464
  and placental drug oxidation 52
Snail 817
Snake bites 555–556
Sneezing
  in neonatal narcotic withdrawal syndrome 574
  paroxysmal 459
Sniffling 459
"Snorting" 559, 572
"Snow" 571
"Snowman" cardiac silhouette 1413, *1414*
"Snuffles" 655
Soap bubble cranial appearance 1702
Soaps 529
  and atopic eczema 474
Sobee 162
Social adaptation 255, 256
Social behavior, in infancy and toddlerhood 254
Social history *1900*
Social immaturity, in minimal cerebral dysfunction syn-
      drome 880
Social needs, in mental retardation 895
Social Security Act 10
Social Security Amendments 9
Social withdrawal, in asthmatics 468
Society, and suicide 293
Socioeconomic factors
  and birth 22
  and birth weight 22
  on health of children 1
  and language development 257
  and neonatal mortality 113
Sodium
  in Addison's disease 1094
  in cerebrospinal fluid 222
  in diabetes mellitus 347
  in diarrhea 229
  excretion, control of 1458
  in fetal body composition 29, 32
  growth patterns of 237
  intake, in renal disease 1466
  in marasmus 172
  permeability, of erythrocyte, in hereditary spherocy-
      tosis 1170
  requirements 143, 224
  restriction, in nephrotic syndrome 1504
  in sweat 414, 418, 422, 423, 424
Sodium antimony dimercaptosuccinate *see* Astiban
Sodium bicarbonate
  in asthma 1294
  in iron poisoning 537
Sodium chloride supplementation
  in cystic fibrosis 428
  in pseudo hypoaldosteronism 1527
Sodium citrate 1466
  in renal tubular acidosis 1525
Sodium colistimethate *see* Colistimethate
Sodium deoxycholate 760
Sodium metabisulfite 1178
Sodium nitrite 533
Sodium nitroprusside, in hypertension 1448
Sodium perchlorate 1086
Sodium-potassium exchange resin 1466–1467

Sodium sulfate, in sarcoidosis 1253
Sodoku *see* Rat-bite fever
Soft tissue swellings, and battered child syndrome 557
Soil 659
Solar urticaria 487
Solenopsis *see* Fire ant
Solid foods *see* Nutrition
Solvents 538
Somatic sensory seizures 982, 988
Somatotropin (STH) 1048, **1050–1056.** *See also* Growth
      hormone.
Somnolence 229, 455, 532, 733
  in diabetes mellitus 351
Soups 166
South African tick-bite fever 781
Soyalac 162
Soybean formulas 357
  contraindication, in cystic fibrosis 428
Space-form recognition deficit, in gonadal dysgenesis 1141
Spalding-Horner sign 60
Spanking, destructive criticism 266
Sparganosis *799, 821*
Spasm
  of larynx **212,** 281, 551, 577, **756,** 1278
    in rabies **756**
    in tetany **212**
  of muscles of mastication **659–660.** *See also* Trismus.
    in scorpion sting 845
    in tetanus **659–660**
Spasmus nutans 852, **1040,** 1834
Spastic cerebral palsy *883*
Spastic diplegia **884**
  due to congenital rubella **766**
Spastic hemiplegia **883**
Spastic paraplegia **884**
  familial 922
Specific dynamic action of food **130**
Specific learning disabilities 879
Specific reading disability *see* Reading disability, specific
Speech
  development **254**
  disorders **276–278,** 287
    in cerebral gray matter diseases 914, 916
    in cerebral palsy **884, 885**
    in chorea 495
    in metachromatic leucodystrophy 384
    in minimal cerebral dysfunction syndrome **880**
    in neurologic disease 851, *852*
"Speedball" 571
Speed binge 565
Spermatic cord 415, **1556**
  in cystic fibrosis 415
  torsion 1556
Spermatozoa 1123
Spherocytes **1171, 1198**
Spherocytosis, in ABO incompatibility **1198**
Spherocytosis, hereditary **1170–1172**
Sphingolipidoses **911–912**
Sphingolipids **907**
Sphingomyelin 384, 907, 911, **913**
Sphingomyelinase 58, **384,** 911
Sphingomyelinosis (Niemann-Pick disease) **384,** 911, **913,**
      1218, 1688, 1829
Sphingosine 381
Spider bite 555, **844, 1793**
Spider nevus 1813

Spielmeyer-Vogt disease *see* Batten-Spielmeyer-Vogt disease
Spina bifida 315, 863, **872–876**, **1716**
  rehabilitation potential *874*
  varieties of *873*
Spina bifida cystica (meningocele and meningomyelocele) 870, **872–876**, 1551
  and neurogenic bladder dysfunction 1552
Spina bifida occulta 872, **876**
Spina ventosa *see* Tuberculous dactylitis
Spindle fingers, in rheumatoid arthritis 504
Spine (spinal), **1715–1718**, *1900*, **1906**. *See also* Vertebral column.
  anesthesia anomalies (neural plate closure defects) **872–877**
  dermal sinus **876–877**
  atrophy, progressive infantile *see* Werdnig-Hoffman disease
  block, in tuberculous meningitis 672
  compression, in spinal abscess **1015–1016**
  cord, in niacin deficiency 182
  deformity, in Pott's disease **673**
  degenerations **923–924**
  diastematomyelia 876
    spina bifida cystica 872–876, *873*
    spina bifida occulta **872**, *873*
  dysraphism *see* Spina bifida cystica
  epidural abscess 1010, **1015–1016**
  fluid *see* Cerebrospinal fluid
  injuries **975–977**, **1325**
  poliomyelitis **745–746**
  radiography 854
  rigidity of, in Pott's disease 673
  shock **955**
    in spinal cord injury 975
  tumors 250, **954–956**
Spinocerebellar ataxia, congenital *see* Spinocerebellar degeneration
Spinocerebellar degenerations 889, **922–923**
Spinous process, tenderness, in Pott's disease 674
Spirillum minus, rat-bite fever due to **634**
Spirochetal fever *see* Leptospirosis
Spirochetal jaundice *see* Leptospirosis
Spirochetemia 653
Spirochetes 581, **652–656**
Spironolactone therapy 1101, 1423, 1448
  in heart failure 1423
  in hyperaldosteronism **1448**
Spleen, **1215–1221**
  absence of, congenital 1217
  accessory 1217
  circulation **1216**
  diagnostic puncture
    in Chagas' disease 836
    in kala-azar 837
  examination, positions and methods **1215–1216**
  functions **1216–1217**
  hypersplenism **1220–1221**
  and immunoglobulins 386
  injury **1217–1218**
  malformations **1217**
  in marasmus 171
  of newborn 82
  rupture 719
  splenomegally **1218–1220**
  in syphilis 653
  tenderness 375

Spleen (*cont.*)
  transplantation 384
  venography 1692, enlargement *see* Splenomegaly
Splenectomy 393, **402**, 1167, **1171**, 1178–1186, **1216–1217**, 1219–1221, **1234**
  in congenital erythropoietic porphyria **402**
  in hemolytic anemia, hereditary, nospherocytic 393
  in hemolytic anemias **1171**, 1172, 1178–1186
  in hereditary spherocytosis **1171**
  in β-thalassemia 1183
  in thrombocytopenic purpura, idiopathic (ITP) 1233, **1234**
Splenic
  artery 1216
  cords 1216
  neutropenia 1205
  sinuses 1216
  vein 1216
Splenomegaly **1218–1221**. *See also* Hepatosplenomegaly.
  in bacterial endocarditis 1430
  in brucellosis 611
  in congenital erythropoietic porphyria 407
  congestive **1218–1220**
  in cytomegalic inclusion disease 703
  in familial hyperchylomicronemia 374
  in gangliosidosis, generalized 382
  in Gaucher's disease 383, 1218
  in glycogenosis type IV 371
  in graft versus host disease **388**
  in Hand-Schüller-Christian syndrome 1248
  in hemolytic anemia, hereditary, nonspherocytic 393
  in hemolytic anemias **1169**, 1170–1201
  in hereditary spherocytosis 1171
  in infectious mononucleosis **717–719**
  in iron deficiency anemia 1161
  in Letterer-Siwe disease 1246
  in leukemia 1209
  in lipidoses **381**
  in malaria **831–832**
  in mucopolysaccharidoses 399
  in Niemann-Pick disease 384
  due to pleurodynia 750
  in polycythemia 1202
  in rheumatoid arthritis 503–504
  in right heart failure 1421
  in Rocky Mountain spotted fever 782
  in salmonella infections 636
  in schistosomiasis 813–814
    of liver 1691
  in sepsis neonatorum 597
  in sickle-cell disease 1177
  in syphilis 655
  due to systemic lupus erythematosus **509–510**
  in thalassemia **1180–1181**
  with thrombocytopenia 1236
Splenoportography 1219
Splenorenal shunt 1219
Splenosis 1218
Splinter nail hemorrhages, in trichinosis 809
Splints, in cerebral palsy **886**
Spondylitis 1010, 1015
Spondyloepiphyseal dysplasias 1715, 1721, **1725–1727**
Spondylolisthesis 1716
Spongiform encephalopathy 916
Spongy kidneys **1477**
Spongy sclerosis **917**
Spooning, of the hands, in chorea 496

Spoon-shaped nails 1761
Sporangium 790
Sporocysts 813
Sporogony **831**
Sporotrichum schenkii **1790–1791**
Sporozoa 839
Sporozoites 831
Spotted fever group **781–783**
Sprengel's deformity **1715**
Spring catarrh *see* Vernal conjunctivitis
Sprue 417
Spurious strabismus 1832
Sputum
  in actinomycosis 786
  in aspergillosis 787
  in asthma 465
  in bronchiectasis **1294**
  in measles 734
  in paragonimiasis 816
Squalene 40
Squames, anucleated, in amniotic fluid 59
Squamous cell carcinomas 1799
Squatting 1407
  in tetralogy of Fallot **1403**
Squint *see* Strabismus
Squirrel 691, 757
SRS-A *see* Slow-reacting substance of anaphylaxis
SRST syndrome 513
SSLE *see* Subacute sclerosing panencephalitis
SSPE *see* Subacute sclerosing panencephalitis
Stable factor *see* Factor VII
Stachyose 358
Staghorn calculi 336
Standard **232**
Standard deviation 232, **234**
Standards of Child Health Care 1893
Standards of living
  and birth weight 22
  and infant mortality rate 3
Standing height *see* Height, standing
Stapes 1881–1882, 1884
Staphylococcus (staphylococcal)
  albus 1429, 1815
  aureus 156, 423, 427, 523, 560, 583–588, **596, 598–608, 644–647,** 1239, 1270, 1429, 1431, 1580, 1781
  colonization **644–645**
  coagulase negative 645
  empyema **1329**
  enterocolitis **646**
  enterotoxins **647**
  exotoxin in milk 156
  food poisoning **646–647**
  infections **644–647**
  meningitis **598–608**
  pneumonia 645
  epidermis 596
Starch 161, 535, 564, **1590**
Starch granulomata 564
Starch gruels 161
Starch intolerance **1590**
Stare, in Graves' disease 1084
Staring, in hypoglycemia 361
Starvation diarrhea 155, 164
Static encephalopathies **879–905**
Statolon 696
Stature *see* Height, standing
Stature measurement 235

Status asthmaticus 464, **465, 467**
Status demyelinisatus **921**
Status epilepticus **987, 999**
Stealing 279
Stearin, in breast milk 151
Steatocystoma multiplex 1815
Steatopygia 378
Steatorrhea 136, 377, 387, **417–418,** 426, 923, 1572, **1584–1586, 1595,** 1643
  in agammaglobulinemia 387
  in beta lipoprotein deficiency 377, 923
  in carbohydrate malabsorption 1592
  in celiac disease **1584–1586**
  in cystic fibrosis **417–418, 426**
  in vitamin K deficiency 140
Steatosis, hepatic *see* Liver
Stein-Leventhal syndrome 220, 1128
Stem-cell leukemia *see* Leukemia
Stensen's duct, papilla at mouth of, in mumps **738**
Stenver's view 1884
Stercobilins 1675
Sterilization
  human 317
  milk *see* Milk sterilization
  and pyridoxin deficiency 184
Sternal protrusion 404
Sternoclavicular articulation, in rheumatoid arthritis 504
Steroid diabetes 355
Steroids, adrenal *see* Adrenocortical hormones
Stevens-Johnson syndrome 1645, **1778–1779,** 1854
  due to dilantin 998
  and sulfonamides 586
STH *see* Somatotropin; Growth hormone
Stibophen (Fuadin)
  in kala-azar **838**
  in schistosomiasis **815**
Stiff back
  in poliomyelitis **744–746**
  in Pott's disease **673–674**
Stiff neck *see* Nuchal rigidity
Stiffness of fingers, in scleroderma 512
Stigmas, of cogenital syphilis 653
Stilbamidine 788
  in kala-azar **838**
Stilbestrol 1129
  for breast engorgement 156
Stillbirth 64
Still's disease *see* Rheumatoid arthritis
Still's murmur 1342
Stimson's line, in measles 732
Stimulants **571**
  and breast feeding 152
Sting
  caterpillars 845
  wasps 555, 659, 844
Stippled epiphyses **1725–1726**
St. Louis encephalitis 1016, **1017–1018**
Stomach 76, 108, 109, 136, 414, **1564–1567, 1608–1612,** 1618, **1638–1639,** 1652. *See also* Gastric; *specific diseases.*
  achylia 1594
  acidity, 108, **1567**
    in low-birth-weight infant 108
  digestion **1567**
  dilation, acute **1652**
  duplication 1608
  evacuation, in poisoning **533–535**

Stomach (*cont.*)
  lavage, in poisoning **534–535, 1910**
  malformations **1608–1612**
  mucosa in cystic fibrosis 414
  of newborn 76, 109
  paralysis **1652**
  pepsin 1567
  perforation 109, 1618, 1638, **1652**
  proteolysis 1567
  pyloric stenosis **1608–1612**
  retention in pyloric stenosis 1609
  rupture 1618
  secretions 136, **1567**
  varices 1220
Stomatitis 180–181, 550, 715, **1852–1854**
  angular (perleche) 180, 181, 1854
    in B_6 deficiency 181, 1854
    in niacin deficiency 182
Stomatocytosis, congenital **1172**
Stomodeum 1046
Stool cultures, in Salmonella infections **636–637**
Stool pH 229
  in carbohydrate malabsorption **1593**
Stools, 1567, 1570–1572, 1579–1589, 1600–1603
  in celiac disease **1584–1588**
  constipation **1600–1602**
  in cystic fibrosis 417–418, 420
  diarrhea 226–230, **1580–1589**
  in *E. coli* infections **641–642**
  fat in 136. *See also* Steatorrhea.
  hematoschezia **1579–1580**
  and hepatitis virus 707
  impaction 1551
  incontinence (encopresis) 272, **1603**
  lead 541
  in malabsorption syndromes **1583–1593**
  melena **1579–1580**
  poliovirus in 734
  in shigellosis **639–641**
  soiling (encopresis) **272, 1603**
  steatorrhea 136, 377, 387, **417–418,** 426, **1584–1586, 1595**
  water loss in 142, 224
Storage battery casings, and lead poisoning 543
Storage diseases of cerebral gray matter **907–915**
  gangliosidoses 907–909, **910–913**
  generalized lipidoses **913–914**
  globosidoses 911, **913–914**
  glycogen storage disease **915**
  mucopolysaccharidoses **914–915**
Storage, iron **1158**
"STP (Serenity-Tranquility-Peace)" **569,** 572
Strabismus **531,** 671, **852,** 1145, **1832–1835**
  in brain tumors **938,** 939, 950
  in Gaucher's disease 913, 1829
  in hypoglycemia 361
  in low-birth-weight infant 116
  in optic nerve and chiasm tumors 950
  in retinoblastoma 1830
Stramonium *see* Jimsonweed
Stranguria 1561
Strauss syndrome 879
Strawberry appearance, of tongue, in scarlet fever 649
Strawberry hemagioma **1812–1813.** *See also* Hemangioma.
Streak gonads 1138, 1139
Streeter's bands 1707
Strepobacillus moniliformis 505, *634*

Streptococcus (streptococcal) **490–493, 496–497,** 523, 576, 594, 596, 599, 625, **647–652,** 1232, 1270, 1329, **1429,** 1431, **1482–1483, 1781–1782**
  empyema **1329**
  erysipelas **649–650**
  β-hemolytic
    Group A 490, 493–495, 496–497, 499–502, 503, **647–659, 1482–1483,** 1631, **1781–1783**
      and AGN **647–650,** 1431, **1482–1483, 1781–1783**
      antibodies **496–497,** 499–500, 505, 647
      C-carbohydrate 647
      MG agglutinins 625
      M, R, and T proteins **648**
      and rheumatic fever **490–493,** 495, **496,** 499–502, **647–652**
    Group B and C 647
    Group D (enterococci) 584, 596, 647
    Group G 647
  impetigo 649, **1781–1783**
  infections **647–652**
  lactis 156, 161
  meningitis 596, 598, **599–608**
  γ-non-hemolytic **647**
  pharyngitis **648–649**
  pyoderma **649, 1781–1783**
  scarlet fever **649**
  vaccine 652
  α-viridans 599, 1232, **1429**
Streptodornase 672
Streptokinase 388, 672
Streptomyces griseus 685
Streptomycin 581, **586,** 595, 602, 625, **685,** 1509
  in actinomycosis 786
  in *H. influenzae* infections 620
  in shigellosis 640
  in tularemia 693
"Stress" ulcers 1638
Stretching exercises, in cerebral palsy 885
Striae, in Cushing's syndrome **1100**
Striated muscle sarcoidosis 1252
Stridor 520, 720, **1277, 1284–1287**
  in bronchial adenoma 1289
  in inspiratory obstructive diseases **1284–1287**
  in laryngomalacia **1284–1285**
  in "vascular ring" 1417
"String sign"
  in pyloric stenosis **1610**
  in regional enteritis **1643**
Strongyloides 477
Strongyloides stercoralis 477, **807–808**
Strongyloidiasis **807–808**
Strychnine poisoning 532, 660
ST segment **1347–1355**
STS *see* Serodiagnosis of syphilis 654
Stuart-Power factor deficiency *see* Factor X
Stupor 209, 287, 334, 532
  in brain tumors 938, 946
  in lymphocytic choriomeningitis 729
Sturge-Weber-Dimitri syndrome 1812, 1814, 1825, 1826. *See also* Encephalotrigeminal agniomatosis.
Stuttering 276, **277**
St. Vitus' Dance *see* Chorea
Stye *see* Hordeolum
Subacute bacterial endocarditis 505, 510, 514, 1232, **1429–1431**
  and brain abscess **1011–1013**
  and craniospinal focal sepsis **1010–1016**

Subacute bacterial endocarditis (*cont.*)
 caused by *H. influenzae* 619
Subacute encephalitides 1023
Subacute inclusion body encephalitis (Dawson) *see* Subacute sclerosing panencephalitis
Subacute sclerosing leucoencephalitis (van Bogaert) *see* Subacute sclerosing panencephalitis
Subacute sclerosing panencephalitis (SSPE) 731, 919, 990, **1023**
Subarachnoid hemorrhage 960, **963**
Subarachnoid loculations **1015**
Subarachnoid obstruction 672, 863
Subarachnoid space **862**
Subclavian pulmonary anastomosis (Blalock-Taussig) 1405
Subclinical diabetes **345**
Subconjunctival hemorrhage *see* Hemorrhage, subconjunctival
Subcutaneous emphysema, in pertussis 630
Subcutaneous fat loss, in progressive lipodystrophy 378
Subcutaneous fat necrosis 1768
Subcutaneous fungi 1790
Subcutaneous nodules, 1768
 and relapsing panniculitis 378
 in rheumatic fever **493, 495**
 in rheumatoid arthritis 504
Subdural effusions, complicating meningitis 600, 601, **607, 624**
Subdural empyema 599, 1010, **1011**
Subdural hematoma 860, **971**
Subdural taps 607, 860, **971**
 in craniospinal focal sepsis **1010–1016**
Subgaleal hematoma **967**
Subglottic hemangiomas 1285
Subhyaloid hemorrhage **971**
Sublingual gland swelling, in mumps **738**
Subluxation of cervical spine 1717
Subluxation provocation maneuver (Palmén, Coleman) 1747, **1749**
Submaxillary gland swelling, in mumps **738**
Subpericranial hematoma **967**
Subpericranial hydroma **967**
Subperiosteal erosion 209
Subperiosteal hemorrhages *see* Hemorrhage, subperiosteal
Subphrenic abscess 1649
Subsepsis allergica 503
Subungual fibroma 925
Subvalvar aortic stenosis **1388**
Succinyl coenzyme A 328, 329, 405
Suckers 817
Sucking *85*, 87, 854, **1564**
Sucking calluses, of newborn 1837
Sucking corns 81
Sucking difficulty, in neurologic disease **850**
Sucking grooves 820
Sucking lice **1793–1796**
Sucking pad 71
Suckling 153
Sucrase 1568, **1591, 1593–1594**
Sucrase deficiency, congenital **1591, 1593–94**
Sucrose 161, 356, 358
Sucrose-isomaltose malabsorption **1591**
Sucrosuria, in newborn 356
Suction, oropharyngeal 71, 73
Sudanophilic (neutral fat, orthochromic) familial, leucodystrophy **917**
Sudden sniffing death (SSD) **568**

Sudden and unexpected death 376, 525, 568, **575–578,** 1337, 1388. *See also* Death.
"Sugar" 571
Sugar. *See also* Glucose; Carbohydrates.
 in breast milk 151
 in infant feeding 160–161, 163
Sugar, spinal fluid, **601–602**
 in ECHO virus infections 753
 in poliomyelitis 746
 in tuberculous meningitis **671–673**
Suicidal fit 291
Suicide **290–293**
 demography **290–291**
 the family in 291–292, 293
 motives **291–292**
 precipitating events **291–292**
 recommendations **293**
Sulfadiazine 608, 1911. *See also* Sulfonamides.
Sulfamethoxypyridazine 508
Sulfanilamide 532
Sulfapyridine 1776
Sulfatase, placental 56
Sulfatides **384, 907,** 911
Sulfation factor (SF) 1051
Sulfation, fetal 53
Sulfisoxazole *see* Sulfonamides
Sulfobromophthalein (BSP) test 708, **1670**
Sulfolipids 144
Sulfonamides 513, 582, **586,** 608, 624, 686, 1166, 1235, 1542, 1674
 in actinomycosis 786
 and acute intermittent porphyria 410
 and aplastic anemia 1166
 in breast milk 152
 and drug purpura 1235
 and Hartnup disease 336
 in *H. influenzae* infections 620
 in lymphogranuloma venereum 776
 in meningococcal prophylaxis 624
 and mixed porphyria 410
 in newborn 56
 in paragonimiasis 816
 during pregnancy 56
 in psittacosis 776
 resistance meningococci 622
 in shigellosis 640
 in toxoplasmosis **841**
 in trachoma 777
 in urinary tract infections **1542**
Sulfones 1776
Sulfosalicylic acid 1460
Sulfur **144,** 151, 1791
Sulfuric acid 530
Summer camps 266
 for diabetic children 355
Sunburn 1800
Sunlight
 in lupus erythematosus 508
 sensitivity 1803
Sunset sign 854, **865,** 1192
"Superfemale" (XXX and XXXX syndrome) 903
Superior sagittal sinus thrombosis **960**
Superior vena cava 667
 obstruction, in lymphosarcoma 1226
Superior vena cava-right pulmonary artery shunt (Glenn) 1407
Supernumerary nipples *see* Nipples

Suppositories 1602
Suppression amblyopia **1832**
Suppurative arthritis *see* Purulent arthritis
Suppurative complications
   in agammaglobulinemias 387
   in chronic granulomatous disease 1206
Suppurative lymphadenopathy, in cat scratch disease
     698
Supranuclear cranial palsies (VII, and IX) **939**
Suprapubic tap 796, 1541, 1552
Suprasellar undifferentiated carcinoma 1055
Suprasternal retractions *see* Retractions
Supratentorial tumors **947–952**
Supravalvar stenosis
   aortic 1371, **1388**
   pulmonic **1386–1387**
Supraventricular tachycardia *see* Tachycardia
Suramin, in African trypanosomiasis **834–835**
Surface active substances *see* Surfactants
Surface area, body *see* Body surface area
Surface tension, alveolar 90
Surfactant, lung 69, 89, 90, 1256–1257
Sus-phrine 466, 486
Sustagen 271
Suture diastasis, skull 854, 958
Sutures, cranial, in rickets 200
Suxinimides in epilepsy **998–1000**
Swaddling position 1746–1747
Swallowing **1564**
   in dermatomyositis **511–512**
   in familial dysautonomia 1040
   in metachromatic leucodystrophy 384
   in myasthenia 1037
   in neurologic disease **850**
   in poliomyelitis **744–746**
"Swan neck" lesions 1521
S wave **1347**
Sweat
   electrolytes
     in adrenal insufficiency 424
     in cystic fibrosis 414, 418, **425**
     in normal values 423
   glands in cystic fibrosis 414, **417–418**
   test 422, **423–424**
Sweating
   in acrodynia 550
   in brucellosis 611
   in Chediak-Higashi syndrome 1206
   in cystic fibrosis 423
   in familial dysautonomia 1040
   in heart failure **1420–1421**
   in hypoglycemia 361
   in neonatal hypoglycemia 360
   in neonatal narcotic withdrawal syndrome 574
   in organic phosphate poisoning 551
   of palms 512
   in pheochromocytoma **1109–1110**
   in salicylate intoxication 553
   of soles 512
   techniques for inducing 423
Sweaty-feet syndrome **379**
Swenson's modified abdominoperineal pull-through pro-
     cedure **1623**
Swimmer's itch (schistosomal dermatitis) 1792
Swimming 526
   and blennorrhea 777

Syanalar 475
Sydenham's chorea *see* Chorea
Sylvatic rabies 755, 757
Symmer's pipestem cirrhosis 813
Sympathetic-adrenal medullary system 218
Sympathetic ganglion cells 1107
Sympathetic meningitis **601**
Sympathetic nervous system injuries 1817
Sympathetic nervous tissue **1107–1113**
Sympathetic ophthalmia **1828**
Sympathetic overactivity in Graves' disease 1083
Sympathogonia 1107
Sympathomimetic amines 455–456, 461
Sympathomimetic properties of LSD 568
Syncopal episodes as seizure equivalent 991
Syncope **994,** 1278
   in aortic stenosis 1388
Syndactyly (syndactylism) 83, 250, 324, 1698, 1842
Synechiae, posterior 1827
   in sarcoidosis 1251
Synophris 1842
Synovial biopsy 505
Synovial complement 505
Synovial effusions, cytomegalovirus in 704
Synovial membrane, in rheumatoid arthritis 503
Synovial necrosis, focal, in rheumatic fever 493
Synovia of the joints 493, 503, 505, 508, 657, 704
   in systemic lupus erythematosus 508
Synovitis, in rheumatic fever **493**
Syphilis 84, 115, 149, 191, **652–658,** 704, 1218, **1286,** 1684,
     1695, 1797, 1823
   acquired in childhood 657
   clinical features **654**
   early congenital (prenatal) **655–656**
   late congenital **656–657**
   maternal 115, 149
   treatment **657–658**
Syphilitic condyloma *655*
Syphilitic hyperostoses 1695
Syphilitic laryngitis **1286**
Syphilitic osteochondritis 191
Systemic arterial hypertension 1429, 1433, **1437–1449**
Systemic lupus erythematosus (SLE) 389, 440, **446,** 478,
     495, 505, 506, **508–510,** 512–516, 654, 851, 1008,
     1314, **1493–1494**
   due to anticonvulsant therapy 998–999
   and cardiac involvement 1433
   due to dilantin 998
   glomerulonephritis **1493–1494**
   sunlight and 508
Systemic pulmonary anastomosis 1405
Systemic skeletal affections **1719–1737**
Systemic venous drainage **1380**
Systems review **1898–1899**
Systolic ejection clicks 1339
Systolic ejection murmurs **1341–1342**
Systolic heave 1404
Systolic murmur
   apical (mitral regurgitation) **494–495**
   functional **494**
   innocent **494**
   regurgitant **494–495,** 1343

T_3 *see* Triiodothyronine

Tabanid fly 812
Tabes
  juvenile 657
  mesenterica see Abdominal lymph nodes, tuberculosis of
Tache cérébrale 671
Tachycardia 282, 361, 409, 456, 550, 569, 1083, 1278, 1364–1366, 1375, 1420, 1432
  due to anemia 1433
  in bulbar poliomyelitis 745
  in Coxsackie virus infection 750
  in dehydration 229
  in diphtheria 616
  in Graves' disease 1083, 1432
  in heroin withdrawal 562
  in leukemia 1209
  and LSD 568
  in neonatal pneumonia 1270
  in newborn 82
  in neuroblastoma 1111
  paroxysmal atrial 1364
  in pheochromocytoma 1109–1110
  in rheumatic fever 494, 496
  in splenic injury 1218
  supraventricular paroxysmal 82, 1364–1366
  ventricular 1366
Tachypnea 91, 99, 456, 519, 539, 1375, 1420–1421
  in asthma 465
  in neonatal narcotic withdrawal syndrome 574
  in neonatal pneumonia 1270
  of newborn transient 1265–1268
  in pneumocystis pneumonia 842
Taenia saginata 818
Taeniasis 818–819
Taenia solium 818
Tagged albumin 62
T-agglutination technique 648
Takayasu's disease see Granulomatous arteritis
Talipes (Clubfoot, congenital) 1029
Talipes calcaneus 84, 1029
Talipes equinovarus 84, 84, 315, 1029
Talipes equinus 1029
Talipes valgus 1029
Talipes varus 1029
Talking in sleep 274
Tallness 250
  and obesity 217
Tangier disease see α-Lipoprotein deficiency
Tank respirator, in poliomyelitis 746
Tanner-Whitehouse method, for skeletal maturity 241
Tapeworms see Cestodes
Tap-water enemas, and aganglionic megacolon 1623
Target cells 1179, 1217
Tarsal navicular osteochondrosis 1739
Tarsus 1819
Tartar emetic 815
Tartrate 143
Taste buds, absence of, in dysautonomia 1041
Taurine 144, 335
Taussig-Bing malformation 1377, 1403
Tay-Sachs disease 381–382, 908, 909, 910, 912–913, 1829
Tay-Sachs ganglioside 907–911
TB-1 686
TBG see Thyroxin-binding globulin
TBPA see Thyroxin-binding prealbumin
Tea, and breast feeding 152

Teacher
  and the adolescent 263
  and school difficulties 283
  and suicide 293
Tearing 1825. See also Lacrimation.
Tear production, absent, in familial dysautonomia 1040, 1206
Tears 386
  in newborn 80
Technetium, in brain scanning 948
  tagged albumin 62
Tedral 467
Teenage drug abuse, general considerations 570–572
Teeth 1856–1870. See also Disorders of occlusion 1866–1869.
  acquired disorders 1867–1869
  bone growth (jawbones) 1861
  brushing 1868
  buds 81, 1856
  calcification 1858–1859
  in congenital erythropoietic porphyria 407
  decay 1867–1868
  dentistry for handicapped 1869–1870
  developmental disorders 1862–1866
  discoloration by tetracycline 1863
  formation, and calcium 143
  grinding 1865
  growth and development 1856–1862
  Hutchinson's 656
  inherited disorders 1861–1862
  loss, in Hand-Schüller-Christian syndrome 1248
  missing teeth 1864–1865
  natal and neonatal 1838
  occlusion 1861–1863, 1868–1869
  permanent teeth 1860–1861, 1865–1867
  posteruptive conditions 1861–1862
  primary teeth 1856, 1859–1860
  soft tissue disorders 1868
  staining, and tetracyclines 12, 588, 1863
  syphilitic 656
Tegretol (carbamazepine), in epilepsy 998
Telangiectasia 389, 511, 513, 1305, 1803
  hereditary hemorrhagic 1232
  neurocutaneous syndromes 929–930
  in newborn 78
Teleroentgenography 1344–1345
Temperature, body see Body temperature
Temperature, environmental see Thermal environment
Temperature regulation see Thermoregulation
Temper tantrums 258, 281, 324
Temporal bone fracture 1889
Temporal lobe (psychomotor) epilepsy 982, 985, 988
Temporal spike focus 982, 985
Temporomandibular joint 504
TEN see Toxic epidermal necrolysis
Tendinous areflexia see Areflexia
Tendon xanthoma 375, 376
Tenebrio 819
Tenesmus 641, 679, 1644
Tensilon see Edrophonium chloride
Teonanacati see "Sacred mushroom"
TEPP 550–551
Teratogenicity 12
  of rubella 764
  of salicylates 55
  of tolbutamide 56
Teratogens 12

Teratoma
  retroperitoneal 1126
  tonsil, in subglottic hemangiomas 1285
Terminal ileitis 1642
Testcross 300, *301*
Testicular
  atrophy, in dystrophia myotonica 1032
  descent **1555**
  feminization syndrome 310, **1117**
  injuries 1562
  torsion **1555–1556**
  tumors **1561**
  undescended **1554–1555**
Testis (testes) **1554–1556**. *See also* Testicular.
  in cystic fibrosis 415
  ectopy **1555**
  feminizing, syndrome **1117**
  growth and 236
  incarceration 1631–1632
  in inguinal or labial hernia 1138
  interstitial cell tumors 1127
  leukemic infiltration **1212**
  of newborn **83**
Testosterone 1055, 1092, 1093, 1120, 1124, 1166
  fetal synthesis 40
  during gestation 55
  therapy in aplastic anemia 1166
Tests
  coagulation **1230–1231**, *1231*
  Duke bleeding time 1237
  Frostig 895
  for hemorrhagic disorders **1230–1242**, *1231*
  Ivy bleeding time 1237
  nitroblue tetrazolium 1206
  nitroprusside 1537
  renal function **1460–1462**
  Schilling **1164**
  serology, syphilis 509, **604**
  Tober Ayer test **960**
  tourniquet 191, 781, 1231–1234
Tetanolysin 658
Tetanospasmin 658
Tetanus **658–662**, 757, 1716
  in heroin users 562
Tetanus antitoxin 486, **660**
Tetanus-diphtheria toxoid, "adult type" boosters of 660, 1897
Tetanus-toxoid **660**, *1897*
Tetany 196, 200, **209, 212**
  in hyperaldosteronism 1101
  and laryngeal obstruction 1285
  and magnesium deficiency 143
  of newborn *see* Neonatal tetany
  in pertussis 630
  and phosphate excess 144
Tetracycline 502, 536, **588**, 625, 1509
  in acne 1816
  in actinomycosis 786
  in amebiasis **829–830**
  in blennorrhea 777
  in brucellosis 611
  and bulging fontanel 959
  in cholera **612–614**
  in cytomegalic inclusion disease 704
  in *H. influenzae* infections 620
  in lymphogranuloma venereum 776
  in *Mycoplasma pneumoniae* infection 626

Tetracycline (*cont.*)
  in psittacosis 776
  in rat-bite fever 634
  in rickettsial diseases **778, 783**, 784
  in teratogenicity 12
  and tooth discoloration 12, 588, **1863**
  in trachoma 777
  in urinary tract infections **1542**
  and yellow dental fluorescence 12, 588, **1863**
Tetraethyl pyrophosphate (TEPP) *see* TEPP
Tetrachlorethylene
  in fasciolopsiasis 817
  in necator infection **806**
Tetrahexoside 907
Tetrahydrocannabinol 566
Tetrahydrocannabinol-carboxylic acid 566
Tetrahydrofolate methyltransferase 329
Tetrahydrozoline (Tyzine) 529
Tetralogy of Fallot 1387, **1402–1406**
  and occcipital lobe abscess *1013*
3,7,11,15-Tetramethylhexadecanoic acid *see* Phytanic acid
Tetraplegia **883–884**
Tetrapyrrole 405
"Texas tea" 572
T-Globulin 150
Thalamic tumors **947**
Thalamotomy 921
  in dystonia musculorum deformans 920
α-Thalassemia **1183–1184**
β-Thalassemia **1175, 1180–1183**, 1705
  cranial aberrations in 1705
"Thalassemia major" *see* β-Thalassemia
Thalassemia minor **1180**
Thalassemia syndromes **1175, 1180–1186**
Thalidomide 12, 536, 1707
Thallium poisoning 535
  and ataxia 1042
THAM 69, 362, **555, 1379**
  and hypoglycemia 362
  in salicylate poisoning 555
Thanatophoric dwarfism **1327–1328**
THC (Tetrahydrocannabinol) 569
"The chief" 571
"The Establishment" 263
"The hawk" 571
Thelarche, premature **1129**
Theophylline 456, 466, 479
Thermal environment, and newborn body temperature 98
Thermogenesis, in low-birth-weight infant 97, 99, 105
  in newborn, and physical activity 30
  role of adipose tissue 29
Thermoneutral environment, of low-birth-weight infant 98
Thermoregulation, in low-birth-weight infant **97–99, 105**
Thiabendazole
  in ascariasis **802**
  in cutaneous larva migrans **807**
  in strongloidiasis 808
  in swimmer's itch 1792
  in trichinosis 809
  in trichuriasis 805
  in viscera larva migrans **803**
Thiaminase 179
Thiamine 109, **138**, 144, **179–180**
Thiamine deficiency 138, **178–180**
Thiamine phosphate 144

Thiamine pyrophosphate 179
Thiazides 55, 338, 355, 1151, 1235, 1423, **1529**
  and neonatal thrombocytopenia 55
  in NDI **1529**
Thick blood smears, in malaria **833**
Thimerosal (Merthiolate) 549
Thin blood smears, in malaria **833**
Thinners 538
Thiocyanate 1059
6-Thioguanine
  in chronic renal insufficiency **1468**
  in nephrotic syndrome 1504
Thiopental 54, 1910
Thioridazine (Mellaril) **881**
Thiosulfate-citrate-bile-salt-sucrose (CBS) agar 612
Thiosulfate, sodium 533, *534*
Third ventricle
  astrocytomas and neurofibromatosis 928
  tumors **945**
Thirst 456, **1149**, 1218
  in splenic injury 1218
Thompsen's disease *see* Congenital myotonia
Thoracentesis **1329–1330**
Thoracic cage **1714–1715**
Thoracic duct 377, **1330**
Thoracic dystrophy, asphyxiating, of Jeune **1327**
Thoracic motion, mechanics **1323–1324**
Thoracolumbar meningomyelocele **874**
Thoracotomy 1330
Thorax *see* Chest
Thorium dioxide 1013
Thorotrast 1013
"Treadworm" *see Strongyloides stercoralis*
Three-day measles *see* Rubella
Three per second spike, and wave dysrhythmia **982**, *983*, **986**
Threonine 132, 336
Threonine acidemia 329
Thrill 1384, 1404
Throat, in diphtheria **615, 617**
Thrombasthenia 1229, **1236**
Thrombectomy 1534
Thrombin 1229, 1238
Thrombocytopenia(s) 174, 328, 388, 616, 1163, 1166, 1167, 1206, **1233–1236, 1242–1243.** *See also individual diseases.*
  in acute glomerulonephritis 1484
  in cat scratch disease 698
  and congenital absence of radius 1235
  familial thrombocytopenic purpura **1235**
  in Gaucher's disease 383
  in histoplasmosis 792
  idiopathic thrombocytopenic purpura 510 (ITP) **1233–1235**
  in large hemangiomas 1813
  in Letterer-Siwe disease 1246
  in measles 735
  neonatal thrombocytopenic purpura 55, **1235**
  in Rocky Mountain spotted fever 782
  in rubella **762, 765**
  secondary thrombocytopenic purpuras **1235–1236, 1242–1243**
  in SLE 509
  and thiazides 55, 1235
  in toxoplasmosis **840**
  and viral hepatitis 708
Thrombocytopenic purpura *see* Thrombocytopenia(s)

Thromboembolism 331, **962**
Thrombopathias **1236**
Thrombophlebitis of cerebral veins, in measles 735, **962**
Thromboplastin **1229**
  generation test **1231**, 1237–1243
Thrombopoietin deficiency **1236**
Thrombosis
  cerebral, arterial **962**
  cerebral embolism **962**
  of cerebral veins 225, 735, **960–961**
  of dural venous sinuses **960–961**
  in polycythemia 1202
  of portal vein 1691
  of renal vein **1534**
Thrombotic thrombocytopenic purpura (TT) **1432, 1495**
Thrush 81, 1790, **1854–1855**
Thumbs, broad **1841**
Thumb-sucking 273, 275, 1868
Thymectomy, in myasthenia **1038**
Thymine 294
Thymol turbidity 708, 1672
Thymoma, and myasthenia 1038
Thymus (thymic) 386
  aplasia 388
  dependent immunity **437–438**
  dependent "lymphocytes" 387
  dysplasia 438
  due to glucocorticoids 1093
  and immunoglobulins 386
  in marasmus 171
  in mumps 739
  and myasthenia 1038
  in unexplained infant-death 576
Thyrocalcitonin 195, 208, 212
Thyroglobulin (Proloid) 1060, **1061**, 1065, **1073–1074**
Thyroglossal cyst **1850**
Thyroglossal duct "cysts" **1081–1082,** 1285
Thyroid **1058–1090**
  adenoma 1285
  cretinism **1067–1075**
  dysgenesis **1067–1068**
  function
    in fetus **1065–1067**
    in obesity 219
  goiter **1077–1082**
  Graves' disease **1082–1087**
  and growth 243
  Hashimoto's struma **1079–1080**
  hormones 132, **1061–1065**
  hypothyroidism **1067–1077**
  inflammation, in mumps **739**
  iodine metabolism **1059–1065**
  "iodine pump" **1059**
  lesions, in Hand-Schüller-Christian syndrome 1248
  lingual goiter **1081–1082**
  neoplasms **1087–1088**
  palpation of *1083*
  teratoma 1285
  thyrotoxicosis **1082–1087**
Thyroidectomy 1085
Thyroiditis
  autoimmune *see* Hashimoto's struma
  chronic *see* Hashimoto's struma
  subacute **1082**
Thyroid-stimulating hormone (TSH) 1055, **1062–1064, 1065–1066**
Thyrolar 1073

Thyrotoxic myopathy 511
Thyrotoxicosis **1082–1087**
  and hyperbilirubinemia 1686
  and myasthenia gravis 1036
  of newborn **1087**
Thyrotropic hormone (TSH) 218, 1048, **1050**
Thyrotropin-releasing factor (TRF) **1064**
Thyroxin (T_4) 145, 218, 1053, **1058–1090**
  -binding capacity *1062–1064*
  -binding globulin (TBG) **1062**
  -binding prealbumin (TBPA) 1062
  -binding proteins 1062
  iodine, plasma 1062–1063
  synthesis 55
$_1$-Thyroxine (Synthroid) **1073–1074**
Tibia, Blount's disease **1739**
  bowing in rickets 200, 201
  Osgood Schlatter's disease **1739**
  spiral fracture 1712
  torsion 201, **1710**
Tibial nerve injury 979
Tick(s) 691, 777, **781, 845**
  and spotted fever rickettsioses **781**
Tick-borne typhus **781**
Tick vaccine **782**
TICS 273, **851**
Tidal volume 92, 1257, 1275
  of low-birth-weight-infant 92
Tightness, of chest 454
  in asthma 465
Tightness, of hamstrings, in poliomyelitis **744–745**
Tincture of iodine 1791
Tinea pedis 1784
Tinea versicolor 1788, 1791
Tine test **680–682**
Tinnitus 454, 501, 506
Tip-toeing, of newborn 85, 88
Tiredness, in viral hepatitis 708
Tissue factor *1229*
Tissue thromboplastine *1229*
Tissue matching **438**
Tissue transplantation immunity **438**
Title XIX Amendments 9
Titratable acid **1524–1527**
Titubation, in brain tumors 940
To-and-fro murmurs 1344
Tobacco, and breast feeding 152
Tober-Ayer test **960**
α-Tocopherol *see* Vitamin E
Todd's paralysis **988**
Todd units **496**
Toe gait 884
Tofranil (imipramine)
  in enuresis 1551
  in epilepsy **998**
Toilet training 1895
Tolbutamide 363
  and hypoglycemia 362
  teratogenicity 56
  tolerance tests 365
  transplacental diffusion 56
Tolnaftate 1791
Toluene *530*
Toluidine 532
Tone *see* Muscle tone
Tongue 1041, **1848–1851**
  acquired lesions **1850**

Tongue (*cont.*)
  atrophy 1848
  in chorea 496
  in cretinism 1071
  in deficiency diseases 1851
  enlargement *see* Macroglossia
  in familial dysautonomia **1850**
  in glycogenosis type II 370
  in Hurler's disease 914
  malformations **1848–1850**
  in niacin deficiency 182
  in scarlet fever **649**
  in Werdnig-Hoffman disease 923
Tongue-thrusting 1869
Tongue-tie **1848**
Tongue-tie, artificial, in Pierre Robin syndrome 1843
Tonic seizures 987
Tonsil(s) 386, **1877–1881**
  in agammaglobulinemias **387**
  in alpha lipoprotein deficiency 377
  hypertrophy 1878
  in infectious mononucleosis **718**
  and inspiratory obstruction 1285
  of newborn 81
  surgery 1879
  tissue 1878–1879
  and tuberculosis 664, **677**
Tonsillectomy 744, 1230, **1879–1880**
  bleeding after 1230
Tonsillitis 720, **1879–1880**
"Tooies" 571
Tooth *see* Teeth; Dental
Tophi 338, 339
Topical antibiotics 458
Torkildsen shunting procedure **866**
  in pinealoma 946
Torsion, of lower extremities 1710
Torsional strabismus **1832**
Torsion spasm, in thalamic tumors 947
Torticollis 81, 532, 673, 1029, **1717**
  congenital 81, 1029, **1717**
Torulosis *see* Cryptococcosis
Total anomalous pulmonary venous drainage 1377, 1412–1414
Touch preparation, in Letterer-Siwe disease **1247**
Tourniquet test 1231–1234
Tower skull *see* Oxycephaly
Toxemia 55, 59, 119, 185, 596
Toxic agents **528–533.** *See also* Poisonings.
"Toxic arthritis" 1746
Toxic epidermal necrolysis 1755, **1776–1778**
Toxic erythema of the newborn **1814**
Toxic granulations 1203
Toxic megacolon 1646
Toxic nephropathies **1509**
Toxicology **527–556**
  in unexplained infant death 576
Toxin
  botulism **609**
  diphtheria **614–618**
  tetanus **658**
Toxocara canis 802–803, **1312**
Toxocara cati 802–803, **1312**
Toxoid
  botulism **609–610**
  diphtheria **618**, *1897*
  tetanus **660**, *1897*

Toxoplasma gondii 12, **839**, 1032
  and myositis 1032
Toxoplasmosis, congenital 12, 84, 115, 597, 704, 711, **839–841**, 863, 865, 1032, 1684, 1828
  and multiple births 122
  susceptibility to, in Hodgkin's disease 1225
T. pallidum see Treponema pallidum
TPI antibody *see* Treponema immobilizing antibody
TPN 139
TPNH 218, **393**
TPNH-dehydrogenase *see* TPNH-methemoglobin reductase
TPNH-methemoglobin reductase 396
T-protein of streptococcal cell wall **648**
Trachea **1274**
Tracheal aplasia **1284**
Tracheal compression **1289**
  in neonatal thyrotoxicosis 1087
Tracheal intubation 526, 610
Tracheal lavage **1283**
Tracheal leiomyomas 1285
Tracheal obstruction, in fascioliasis 817
Tracheal stenosis 1265, **1284**
Tracheitis 720
Tracheobronchial nodes, tuberculous **667**
Tracheobronchial secretions, excessive, in organic phosphate poisoning 551
Tracheoesophageal fistula *see* Fistula, tracheosophageal
Tracheomalacia **1285**
Tracheo(s)tomy 390, 410, 610, 725, **1280**, 1284, 1285, 1286
  in diphtheria **617**
  in *H. influenzae* infections **620**
  in tetanus 661
Trachoma 777, **1821**
  inclusion conjunctivitis 777
Tragus 1882
Tranquilizers 84, 457, 529, 660
  in asthma **470**
  and urticaria 477
Transaminase 184, 511
Transaminase elevation, in hemorrhagic fever 848
Transamination 39, 183, 368
Transdetermination 307
Transduction 583
Transferrin **390**, 1162
Transfusion(s), blood, 18, 60, 1162, **1166–1167**, 1178, 1180–1183, **1229–1243**, **1909–1910**
  in aplastic anemia **1166–1167**
  in burns **522–523**
  and cytomegalovirus infection 704
  in diarrheal disease 230
  fetal 18, 60
  in hemorrhagic disorders **1229–1243**
  intraperitoneal 18, 60, **1196**
  intrauterine 18, 60, **1196**
  in iron deficiency anemia 1162
  in leukemia **1213**
  and malaria transmission **834**
  in shigellosis 641
  in sickle-cell anemia 1178
  in β-thalassemia **1180–1183**
  and viral hepatitis 707, 710
Transfusion, leucocyte concentrates, in aplastic anemias 1166
Transfusion, plasma 1909–1910
  in burns **522–523**
  ITP 1235
  viral hepatitis **706–711**, **1909–1910**

Transfusion, platelet concentrate (PC)
  in aplastic anemias 1166
  in leukemia 1213
Transfusion, platelet-rich plasma (PRP), in leukemia 1213
Transfusions, exchange *see* Exchange transfusion
Transfusions, fresh frozen plasma 1235, 1236, **1238–1240**
Transfusion syndrome, twin *see* Twins
Transient coagulation factor deficiency, in new born **1241**
Transient familial neonatal hyperbilirubinemia **1679–1680**
Transillumination, of skull 85, 853, **857–859**, *859*, 860
  in encephalocele **871**
  in hydrocephalus **865**
  in subepicranial hydroma 967
Transition milk 150
Transketolase 179, 180
Translocation 310, **897**
Transmethylation 139
Transplacental transmission
  of cytomegalic inclusion disease 703
  of viral hepatitis 711
Transplants
  of bone marrow cells **388**
  of fetal thymus **388**
  of kidney 330, 385, **1469**
Transportation, of low-birth-weight infant 102
Transposition of the great arteries 115, **1409–1412**
Transverse myelitis
  in mumps 738
  in neuromyelitis optica 918
  in schistosomiasis 814
Transvestism 1130
Trauma
  bladder **1561–1562**
  craniocerebral *see* Craniocerebral trauma
  ear **1889**
  kidney **1561–1562**
  nasal **1875**
  to naso-oral pharynx 1879
  to nervous system **966–979**
    craniocerebral trauma **967–975**
    peripheral nerve injuries **977–979**
    scalp injuries **966–967**
    spinal cord injuries **975–977**
  to penis 1562
  and poliomyelitis 744
  to testes 1562
  unrecognized **1711**
  to upper airways **1285**
  to urethra **1562**
  to vertebral column 975
Traumatic arteriovenous fistula, cerebral **964–965**
Traumatic arthritis 514
Traumatic brain abscess 1012
Traumatic herpes **714**
Traumatic pericarditis 1427
Travel, and smallpox vaccination **773**
Treacher-Collins syndrome **1703**, 1831, 1841, 1884, 1885
Trematodes **812–823**. See also Parasites, trematodes.
Tremor(s) 80, 324, 360, 671, 851, **852**
  in ataxia-telangiectasia 930
  in basal ganglia degenerations **919–921**
  in brain tumors 942, 943, 945–947
  essential or familial **921**
  in Friedreich's ataxia 922

Tremor(s) (*cont.*)
  in Graves' disease 1083
  in hepatic failure 1692
  of jaw 80
  in neonatal narcotic withdrawal syndrome 574
  in parkinsonism **919**
  in Wilson's disease 920
Trendlenburg sign 1748
Trephination 1013
Treponema carateum 652
Treponema immobilization test **654**
  in heroin addicts 561
Treponema pallidum 12, 588, **652–658**
Treponema pertenue 652
Triad syndrome *see* Prune belly syndrome
Triamcilone *1104. See also* Adrenal cortical hormones.
  in acne, intralesional 1816
Triatoma 835
TRIC *see* Trachoma inclusion conjunctivitis
Tricarboxylic acid cycle 38, 393
Trichiasis 1818
Trichinella spiralis **808–809**
Trichinosis **808–809**
  and myositis 1032
Trichloroethylene (Trilene) 54
Trichobezoar 271, 1651
Trichophyton infections **1790**
  mentagrophytes **1790**
  rubrum 1790
  schoenleini 1790
  test **1790**
  verrucosum 1790
  violaceum 1790
  tonsurans 1790
Trichorrhexis invaginata 1760
Trichorrhexis nodosa 334, 1759
Trichoschisis 1760
Trichostrongylus 808
  orientalis 806
Trichotillomania **1760**
Trichuriasis *798*, **804–805**
Trichuris trichiura *798*, **804–805**
Tricuspid atresia 1403, **1406–1407**
Tricuspid flow murmurs 1344
Tricuspid insufficiency 499
Tricuspid stenosis 1376, **1381–1382**
Tricuspid valve, in Ebstein's anomaly **1408**
Tridione 508, **995–1000**, 1236
Triethylenemelamine (TEM) 1830
TRF *see* Thyrotropin-releasing factor
Trigeminal nerve 929
Trigeminal zoster 1785
Triggering mechanism of epileptic attacks **986–987**
Triglycerides 218, 369, **373**, 374, 376, 377
Triglycerides, medium chain 110, 377, 428
Trigonitis, in urolithiasis 1537
Trigonocephaly 860, **1699**
Trihexoside 907
Trihexoside-β-galactosidase deficiency 909
Triiodothyronine (T$_3$) 145, **1058–1059**, 1086
  T$_3$ iodine, plasma **1063–1064**
  T$_3$ suppression test 1084
  1-Triiodothyronine (Cytomel) **1073–1074**
Trilene (Trichloroethylene) 54
Trimethadione *see* Tridione
Tri-ortho-cresyl phosphate poisoning **531**
Triosephosphate isomerase deficiency 393, *1175*

Tripelennamine 454
Triphospho pyridine nucleotide *see* TPN
Triplegia **884**
Triplet, of nucleotide 35
Triplets 117, 296. *See also* Multiple births.
Triplex syndromes 309, 310
Triradius **313**
Tris buffer *see* THAM
tris-(hydroxymethyl) aminomethane *see* THAM
Trisialic acid 907
Trismus **659–660**
Trisomy "13/15" (D) (Patau syndrome) 316, 861, **900–901**, 1842, 1866
Trisomy "16–18" 115
Trisomy "18" 1842, 1866
Trisomy "21" (Down's syndrome) *see* Down's syndrome
Trisomy-E (18) 316, **901**, *902*
Trisulfapyrimidines *see* Sulfonamides
Tritiated water, placenta clearance of 45
tRNA *see* RNA, transfer
Tromethamine (THAM), in asthma 1294
Trophoblast 40, 44
Trophozoites 828, 832, 838
Tropical eosinophilia **1312**
Tropical sprue **1588**
Trout 821
TRP *see* Tubular reabsorption of phosphate
Truncus arteriosus 370, 1403, **1414–1415**, 1416
Trypanosomes **834–837**
  lewisi **841**
  rhodesiense **834–835**
  gambiense 834
  cruzi **835–837**
Trypanosomiasis **834–837**
  african **834–835**
  american *see* Chagas' disease
Tryparsamide (Fourneau 270), in african trypanosomiasis **834**
Trypsin 132, 424, 425
Trypsinogen deficiencies 1594
Tryptic activity, in duodenal fluid 424
Tryptophan 132, **135**, 139, 174, 181, 182, 183, 186, 336
L-Tryptophan load test 184
Tryptophan pyrrolase 43
Tse-tse fly **834–835**
TSH *see* Thyrotropic hormone
Tsutsugamushi fever *see* Scrub typhus
TTP *see* Thrombotic thrombocytopenic purpura
Tube dilution method, for antibiotic resistance testing **584**
Tubera, in tuberous sclerosis 925
Tubercle bacillus **662**, 662–689
Tuberculids, papulonecrotic 669, **676**
Tuberculin test 7, 672, 679, **680–682**
  in measles **735**
  products *681*
  in sarcoidosis 1252
  units (TU) **680**
Tuberculoma, of brain 673
Tuberculosis 396, **662–690**, 776, 1797
  acute *670*
  and Addison's disease 1093
  allergy and immunity **664**
  bacteriologic examination **682–683**
  blood picture in **683**
  bovine 156
  chemoprophylaxis **683**

Tuberculosis (*cont.*)
  congenital 665
  clinical forms 665–679
    extrapulmonary 671–679. *See also* Tuberculosis, extra-
      pulmonary and various organs.
    hematogenous dissemination of 668
    pulmonary 665–671. *See also* Tuberculosis, pulmo-
      nary.
  diagnosis 679
  epidemiology 662
  etiology 662
  extrapulmonary 671–679
    abdominal 677–679
    bones 673–675
    ears 677
    eyes 677
    gastrointestinal tract 678–679
    heart 679
    of hip 674
    joints 673–675
    of knee 674
    larynx 677, 1286
    lymph nodes, abdominal 677
    lymph nodes, superficial 677–678, 1222
    meningitis 671–673
    pericardium 679
    peritoneum 678
    renal 679, 1543
    skeletal 673–675
    skin 675–676
    throat 677
    tonsils 677
    urinary tract 679, 1543
  in heroin addicts 561
  immunity and resistance 663, 664
  and kwashiorkor 174
  and marasmus 172
  and measles 735
  and pertussis 631
  prevention of 683
  primary infection 664, 665–666
  pulmonary 665–671
    chronic (reinfection, or adult type) 668, *669*
    endobronchial 667
    hematogenous, protracted 670–671
    miliary 665, 668–670
    pleurisy 668
    primary, locally progressive 666–667
    primary, simple 665–666
    of tracheobronchial nodes 667
  treatment 665–679, 684–687
  tuberculin tests 680–682, *1897*
Tuberculous
  adenitis 677–678, 1222
  dactylitis (spina ventosa) 674, *675*
  enteritis 678
  laryngitis 1286
  meningitis 671–673
    diagnosis 671
    sexual precocity after 1126
    treatment 672, 684–687
  osteitis 1717
  pericarditis 1427
  peritonitis 678–679
  pneumonia 666
  retropharyngeal abscess 677
  spondylitis 673
  synovitis 506

Tuberculous (*cont.*)
  tonsillitis 677
  uveitis 1828
  vaccination 683
  verruca cutis 676
Tuberous sclerosis 853, 892, 925–927, 1055, 1478, 1805,
    1826
Tuberous Xanthomas, in hypercholesteremia, familial
    375
Tubular function 1455
Tubular reabsorption of phosphate (TRP) 1519
Tuft of hair, in spinal cord tumors 955
Tuinal 563
Tularemia 676, 691–693, 776
Tumors
  of bone 1693
  eighth nerve 1886
  of the heart 1432–1433
  hepatic 1693
  nasal 1873–1874
  nervous system 937–957
    brain tumors 937–954. *See also* Brain tumors.
    cerebellum *see* Cerebellar tumors
    craniopharyngioma 952–954
    optic nerve and chiasmal tumors 950–952
    spinal cord tumors 954–950
  ovary 1561
  paranasal 1873–1874
  of respiratory tract 1289
  sacrococcygeal 83
  testis 1561
  of upper airways 1285
  of urogenital sinus 1561
Tunga penetrans see Chigoe flea
Tunica vaginalis 1631
Turgor, loss of, in dehydration 229
Turkey 775
Turner's syndrome *see* Gonadal dysgenesis
Turpentine 530, 538–540
TV programs 258
"Twanging string" murmur 1342
T wave 1347
T wave abnormalities, and electrolyte effects 1351
T wave inversion in acute glomerulonephritis 1484
Tween 80, 477
Twinning *see* Multiple births; Twins
Twins *see* Multiple births
  care of 123
  classification 117
  congenital anomalies in 119, 121
  cerebral palsy in 121
  development, mental 123
  "exceptional" 123
  fetal complication in 119–122
  fetal deprivation in 27
  fraternal 117, 118
  and genetic traits 302
  growth retardation in 121
  hyaline membrane disease in 122
  infections transplacental in 122
  intertwin relationships 123–124
  intracranial hemorrhage in 122, 123
  kernicterus in 123
  monochorionic (monozygous) 117, 118, 302
    growth of *238, 239*
  neonatal complications in 122–123
  perinatal mortality in 122
  placentation of 118

Twins (*cont.*)
  plethora in 119–121
  prenatal problems in 119
  transfusion syndrome **119–121**, *120, 121*
    growth in 239
Twin-to-twin transfusion, growth in twins with 239. *See also* Twins.
Twisting of neck 851
Twitching, in hypoglycemia of newborn 360
Tympanic membrane 1881, **1882–1883**. *See also* Eardrum.
  in basilar skull fracture 968
  in serous otitis media **462**
Tympanomastoiditis **1887**
Typhoid fever 276, 635–637, **637–638**, 692, 1218
  carrier 638
  vaccine 638
Typhoid type tularemia **692**
Typhus fevers 773, **779–781**
  epidemic murine (endemic) **779–780**, **780–781**
Tyrosinase 327, 1799–1800
Tyrosine 132, 174, 322, *323,* 336, 1060, 1110, 1799
Tyrosine hydroxylase 1107
Tyrosinemia 325, **1523**
  in Fanconi syndrome **1523**
  in low-birth-weight infant 110
Tyrosinosis 323, **325–326**, 362
Tyrosinuria 191, 323, **325–326**, 362
  in premature infant 43, 110
Tyzine *see* Tetrahydrozoline

UDPG 357, 1674
UDPGA 1674, 1677
UDPGal 357
UDPGal-4-epimerase 357
UDPGal pyrophosphorylase 357
Ulcerations, of buccal mucosa, in leukemia 1209
Ulcerative colitis 505, 1582, 1599, **1644–1647**, 1797
Ulcer diathesis, and heroin use 560
Ulcer, of frenum of tongue, in pertussis 630
Ulcer(s), gastrointestinal **1638–1639**
  in cytomegalic inclusion disease 704
Ulnar nerve injury **978**
Ulnar polysyndactyly 1698
Ultracentrifugation 378
Ultralente insulin **349**
Ultra-Rubens Venus 378
Ultrasonic nebulizers 426, 1281
Ultrasound techniques *61, 62,* **852,** 941, *948, 949,* 958, 1426
Ultra-superficial skin fungi **1788**
Ultraviolet (UV) radiation 139, 336, 644, **1799**
  in acne **1816**
  for nursery germ control 644
  and photosensitivity 487
  and vitamin D 197
  in vitamin D equivalent 138
Umbilical artery 44, 45, 65, 82, 97, **1262**
  blood flow 44, 45
  catheterization **1262**
  pulsation of 97
  single 65, 82
Umbilical colonization, staphylococcal **644**
Umbilical cord 75, 82
  blood
    examination 64–65
    in growth-retarded 65
    Po_2 and Pco_2 64

Umbilical cord (*cont.*)
  care 106
  clamping, and blood volume 96
  cord compression 19
    fetal 19, 67
  frozen section
  occlusion and first breath 69
  stripping, and blood volume 96
  velamentous insertion of 121, *122*
Umbilical hernia **1630–1631**. *See also* Hernia.
Umbilical venography 1692
Uncinaria stenocephala 807
Uncinate fits 1056
Unconjugated bilirubin **1674**
  in newborn **1676–1677**
Unconjugated neonatal hyperbilirubinemia **1676–1677**
Unconsciousness *see* Coma
Undecylenic acid 1791
Undescended testis **1554–1555**
Undulant fever *see* Brucellosis
Unesterified fatty acids *see* Free fatty acids
Unilocular hydatid cyst **821–822**
Universal albinism **326**
Universal shunting procedures, in hydrocephalus 866
Unsaturated fatty acid *see* Fatty acids
Unstable hemoglobins 1179
Unverricht's disease *see* Myoclonic epilepsy, progressive, familial
Upper motor neuron disease **851**
Upper respiratory infections 720
Uppsala virus **754**
Urachus **1549–1553**
  diverticulum 1550
  sinus 1550
Urea 44, 174, 207, **1461**
  in head trauma **974**
  in kwashiorkor 174
  plasma 207, **1461**
  in porphyria 410
  transplacental transfer 44
Urea clearance **1461**, 1484, 1501
  in acute glomerulonephritis **1484**
Urea cycle
  disorders of 231, **334–336**. *See also* Argininosuccinic aciduria, Citrullinemia, Beta-Alanine abnormalities, Hyperammonemia, Hyperlysinemia.
  enzymes **334**
Uremia 389, 513, 613, *1463–1470*
  and anemia 1167
Uremic osteodystrophy **1467**
Uremic pericarditis 1427
Ureter(s) (ureteral) **1535–1538**, **1557–1558**
  anomalies **1557–1558**
  colic **1535–1538**
    in schistosomiasis haematobium infection 814
  compression by aberrant vessels 1557
  duplication 1558
  ectopia 1558
  fibrosis, in *Schistosomiasis haematobium* infection 814
  obstruction 340, **1557–1558**
Ureteric bud 304, 1451–1452
Ureterocele **1558**
Ureteropelvic obstruction 1556
Ureterovesical junction obstruction **1557–1558**
Urethra (urethral) 1544, 1551, 1556, 1559, **1562**
  calculi 1551
  cultures 515
  diverticuli 1551

Urethra (urethral) (*cont.*)
  hemangiomas 1813
  injuries **1562**
  meatal stenosis 1559
  obstruction 340
  prolapse 1551, 1556
  strictures 1551
Urethritis 625, **1544**
Urethroplasty 1554
Uric acid 338, 340, 369, 372, 515
  nephropathy **1208, 1508**
Uricase 145
Uridine diphosphate galactose (UDPGal) 357
Uridine diphosphoglucose (UDPG) 1674
Uridine diphosphoglucuronic acid (UDPGA) 1674, 1677
Urinalysis **1460**
Urinary tract **1451–1463**. *See also* Kidneys and urinary
    tract.
  anomalies **1476–1563**
    in cryptorchidism **1555**
    in fetus 65
  infection (UTI) 330, **1539–1546**
    candidiasis of **796**
    obstruction 1477
    due to salmonellae 636
Urine (Urinary)
  calculus *see* Urolithiasis
  collections
    in burns **522–523**
    in diabetes mellitus 350
  color
    in acute intermittent porphyria 410
    in alkaptonuria 326
  concentration 1460
  culture **1541**
    in sepsis neonatorum 597
  fetal 50
  frequency 454
  incontinence, in acute polyneuritis **1007**
  infections **1539–1546**
  myiasis 846
  osmolality **1460**
  output
    in burns **522–523**
    in heart failure 1420
    in renal failure 1464
  pH 552–555, **1462, 1521–1524, 1524–1527, 1536**. *See also*
      pH, urinary.
  retention **1550–1551**, 1561
    in botulism 610
  sediment examination **1460**
  water loss in 142, 224
Urobilin 1671
Urobilinogen 407, 1671, 1675
Urocanic acid 327
Urogenital
  pathology, congenital **1546–1549**
  sinus 1095, 1134, 1138, 1098, 1553, 1626
  tumors 1561
Urolithiasis 330, 336, 338, 339, 340, **1525, 1535–1538**
Urology **1546–1563**
Uronic acid 359
Uroporphinuria I 407, 409
Uroporphinuria III 407, 409
Uroporphyrinogen I, synthetase **405**, 407
Uroporphyrinogen III **405**, 407
Uroporphyrin 410

Uroporphyrinuria I and IV 407
Urticaria 454, 455, **477–478**, 487, 500, 515, 585
  in Chagas' disease 836
  cholinergic **489**
  cold **488–489**
  in dracontiasis 810
  in *Schistosoma mansoni* infection 814
  in serum sickness 485
  solar **487**
  in trichinosis 809
Urticaria pigmentosa (Mastocytosis) 478, 1242, **1810–1811**
Ureroplacental insufficiency 19–20
Uterus **43–44**, 236, 569, **1115–1116, 1124**
  aplasia 1117
  bleeding, excessive **1115–1116**
  blood flow 43–44, *44*
  contractions 569
  growth of 236
UTI *see* Urinary tract infection
Utricle 1884
U.V. *see* Ultraviolet
Uvea **1827–1828**
Uveitis 1645, 1824, **1827–1828**
  in rheumatoid arthritis 504
  in sarcoidosis 1251
Uveoparotid fever **1251**

V leads 1347
Vaccination (Vaccines) 387, 388, **1896,** *1897*
  BCG **683–684**
  cholera 614
  herpesvirus 716
  influenza 722
  measles **736–737,** *1897*
  mumps **739,** *1897*
  murine typhus 781
  pertussis **631,** *1897*
  poliomyelitis (Salk and Sabin) **747–748,** *1897*
  Q fever 784
  Rocky Mountain spotted fever 782
  rubella **763–764,** *1897*
  smallpox **772–775, 1896,** *1897*
  streptococcal 652
  tuberculosis **683–684**
  typhoid **638**
  typhus epidemic **780**
  and urticaria 477
Vaccinia 654, **774**
  conjunctivitis 1821
  immune gamma globulin **772**
Vacuolated lymphocyte, in cerebromacular degeneration
    911–913
Vacuum extraction 75
Vagal stimulation, in PAT 1364
Vagina (Vaginal)
  abnormalities **1117**
  atresia 1117
  bleeding 1561
  discharge 83
  mucosa 1124
  prolapse 1765
  septa, congenital, transverse 1117
Vaginitis 625
  in enterobiasis 803
Vago-insulin system 218
Vagotomy 1639

Valine 132, 297, 327, 329, 336
Valine transaminase 58
Valium (diazepam) 562, 973, **998–1000**, 1366
   in epilepsy **998–1000**
   in head injury 973
   in heroin withdrawal 562
   in PAT 1366
Valsalva maneuver, 1342
   in PAT 1364
Valvar aortic stenosis **1388**
Valvar pulmonic stenosis 1371, **1387**
Valvular calcification 498
Valvular insufficiency 498
Valvular sclerosis 498
Valvular stenosis 498
Van Bogaert-Divry syndrome 929
Van Bogaert's leucoencephalitis *see* Subacute sclerosis,
   panencephalitis
Vancomycin 581, **586**, 591, 646, 1509
Van den Bergh reaction **1675**
Van der Hoeve's syndrome 1885
Vanillin mandelic acid (VMA) 1041
   in hypertension 1439
Van't Hoff's rule 98
Vaquez-Osler disease *see* Polycythemia vera
Varicella 388, 602, 654, **700–703**, 1853
   antibody 700
   encephalomyelitis **1021**
   and Hodgkin's disease 1225
   in leukemia 1213
   pneumonia *701*
Varicella-zoster (V-Z) virus **700–703**, 1784
Variola major *see* Smallpox
Variola minor (Alastrim) **771**
Variola sine eruptione 770
Variola virus **769–770**
Varnish 530, 538–540
Vasa previa 121
Vascular collapse *see* Circulatory collapse
Vascular nevi *see* Hemangiomas
Vascular resistance
   peripheral, in low-birth-weight infant 96
   pulmonary *see* Pulmonary, vascular resistance
"Vascular ring" **1417**
Vascular space 222
Vasculitis 511, 513, 585, 1232, 1233
   in Rocky Mountain spotted fever 782
   in rheumatoid arthritis 503
Vas deferens. absence of, in cystic fibrosis 415
Vasomotor reflexes, in low-birth-weight infant 96
Vasopressin
   nasal spray 1152
   tannate, in oil **1151**
VDM 537
VDRL (Venereal Disease Research Laboratories) test **654**
   in heroin addicts 561
Vectorcardiography **1346–1354**
Vegetables 166
   introduction into diet 155
Vegetations, endocardial 1429
Vein of Galen malformation **963**
Velamentous insertion, of umbilical cord 121, *122*
Velban *see* Vinblastine
Velocity curve of growth *235*
"Veneral" wart 1787–1788
Venous distension, scalp and eyelids, in superior sagittal
   sinus thrombosis 960

Venous pressure elevation, in right heart failure **1421**
Venous return obstruction **1380**
Venous stasis, and cerebral palsy 882
Venous thrombosis 97
Ventilation, alveolar, in low-birth-weight newborn 92, *93*
Ventilation, assisted 72–73, *103*, 104, 525, 746–747, **1260,**
   1265, 1283
Ventilation-perfusion imbalance **93**, 416, 464, **1262–1264**
   in asthma 464
   in cystic fibrosis 416
   in low-birth-weight infants **93**
   in RDS **1262–1264**
Ventricular arrhythmias 524, 1252, **1370**
   in sarcoidosis 1252
Ventricular depolarization (QRS) **1347**
Ventricular ejection murmurs **1341–1342**
Ventricular failure **1372**
Ventricular fibrillation 525, **1370**
Ventricular hypertrophy 207, **1372–1373**
   in cystic fibrosis 417–420
   in EKG diagnosis **1350–1353**
Ventricular inversion 1396
Ventricular septal defect 1373, **1396–1398**
Ventricular tap, in tuberculous meningitis 671 672
Ventriculitis 1010
Ventriculocisteronostomy 866
Ventriculography **855,** 859
   in brain tumors 941–947, 949, 951
   in craniospinal focal sepsis **1010–1016**
   in hydrocephalus **865**
Ventriculojugular shunt, in hydrocephalus **867,** 876
Verbal stimulation and language development 257
Verequad 467
Vernal catarrh 1807
Vernal conjunctivitis (spring catarrah) **1820**
Vernix caseosa 78, 1814
   on surface of amnion 65
Verruca(e) **1786–1788**
Verruca accuminata 1787–1788
Verruca cutis, tuberculous 676
Verruca vulgaris **1787–1788**
Verrucous valvulitis, of acute rheumatic fever 493
Vertebrae
   in achondroplasia 1721
   Calvé's disease **1739–1740**
   in Hurler's disease 914
   in hyperparathyroidism 209
   in rickets 200
   in Scheuermann's disease **1715,** 1739, **1740–1741**
Vertebral angiography **942**
Vertebral anomalies, and duplications 1618
Vertebral body collapse, in leukemia 1745
Vertebral column **1715–1718**
   congenital malformations **1715–1718**
   fractures and dislocations **1716–1717**
   infections **1717–1718**
   injury, **975–977**
   Scheuermann's disease **1715,** 1739, **1740–1741**
   scoliosis **1715**
   tuberculosis **673**
Vertical nystagmus 852, **939,** 1834
   and brain tumors **939**
Vertical strabismus 1833
Vertigo **853,** 1833
   in botulism 610
Vesication 845

Vesicles (Vesicular eruption) 407, 409, 508, **701, 713, 751,**
    1770–1781, 1784–1785, 1804, 1811
  in congenital erythropoietic porphyria 407
  in erythropoietic protoporphyria 409
  in herpangina 751
  of herpes simplex **713**
  of varicella **701**
  in zoster **1784–1785**
Vesicular pharyngitis, due to Coxsackie B viruses **751**
Vestibular apparatus 1884
Vestibular neuronitis 851, 853
Vesticoureteral reflux 1560
Via sinistra 48
Vibratory murmur 1342
Vibrio cholerae 227, **612–614**
Vibrio fetus meningoencephalitis 596–597
Vinblastine sulfate (Velban) **1225, 1247**
  in Hodgkin's disease **1225**
  in Letterer-Siwe disease **1247**
Vinca alkaloids 1204, 1247
Vincristine sulfate (Oncovin) 941, **1112, 1209–1210 1225,**
    1227
  in Hodgkin's disease **1225**
  in intracranial tumors 941
  in lymphoblastic leukemia **1209–1210**
  in lymphosarcoma **1227**
  in neuroblastoma **1112**
Vindictive behavior 268
Vinyl ether, in status epilepticus 999
Vioform 476
Viokase 428
Viomycin 686
Viral arthritis 514
Viral cerebellitis 1041
Viral conjunctivitis *see* Inclusion blennorrhea
Viral diseases 18, **694–784, 1016–1023, 1311, 1784–1786.**
    See also specific diseases.
  adenoviral diseases **725–726**
  alastrim 771
  blenorrhea **777**
  cat scratch disease **697–700**
  chickenpox *see* varicella
  coxsackie viruses 726, **749–752**
  cytomegalovirus infection 703
  ECHO viruses 740, **752–754**
  encephalitides **1016–1023**
  entervoviruses 740, **752–754**
  exanthem subitum (roseola) **705–706**
  and growth retardation 248
  hepatitis **706–712,** 1686
  Herpes hominis infections **712–717**
  inclusion conjunctivitis 777
  infectious mononucleosis **717–719**
  influenza **720–722**
  inhibition of viral replication **694–697**
  lymphocytic choriomeningitis **728–729**
  lymphogranuloma venereum 776
  measles **729–737**
  mumps **737–740**
  myxovirus respiratory diseases **720–723**
  ornithosis 775
  parainfluenza respiratory disease **722–723**
  picornaviruses **726–727,** 740, **742–752**
  picornavirus respiratory diseases **726–727**
  pneumonias 1311
  poliomyelitis **742–749**
  polioviruses 740, **742–749**

Viral diseases (*cont.*)
  psittacosis **775**
  rabies **755–759**
  respiratory syncytial (RS) disease **724–725**
  respiratory tract viruses **719–728, 1311**
  rhinoviral diseases **726–727,** 740
  rickettsial **777–785.** *See also* Ricketsioses.
  roseola (exanthem subitum) **705–706**
  rubella **759–769**
  skin infections, viral **1784–1786**
  smallpox **767–775**
  trachoma **777**
  varicella **700–703**
  variola *see* Smallpox
Viral DNA **694–697**
Viral pneumonias **1311**
Viral replication, selective inhibition of **694–697**
Viral RNA **694–697**
Viral skin infections **1784–1786**
Viral structure **694**
Viremia
  in rubella *762*
  in viral hepatitis 707
Virilization 1119, **1127**
Virilizing adrenal tumors 1119
Virilizing syndromes **1095–1099,** 1119, **1127–1128**
  adrenal **1127**
  ovarian **1127–1128**
Virologic studies, in unexplained infant-death 576
Virus elementary bodies, in smallpox lesions 771
Virus excretion, in rubella *762, 767*
Virus inhibitions **694–695**
Visceral cytomegaly *see* Wiedeman-Beckwith syndrome
Visceral larva migrans 439, *798,* **802–803,** 1312
Visceral leishmaniasis *see* Kala-azar
Visceral lesions, of herpes simplex **713**
Vision
  deficit *see* Blindness; Eyes
    in brain tumors **939, 950,** 952
    in cerebral palsy 885
    in craniopharyngioma 952
    hysterical 284
    in optic nerve and chiasm tumors 950
    in sarcoidosis 1251
  in personality development 284
  in gray matter diseases 912
  in hysteria 284
  loss *see* Blindness; Eyes
    in cerebral cysticercosis 818
    in neurologic disease **852**
    in neuromyelitis optica 918
  of low-birth-weight infant **116**
  after meningitis 608
  in paragonimiasis 816
  screening test 7
  in white matter diseases 918, 919
Vistaril *see* Hydroxyrine
Visual field defects
  in brain tumors **939, 950, 952**
  in craniopharyngioma 952
Visual purple 177
Vital statistics 3
Vital capacity **92,** 465, **1257,** 1274
  in asthma **465**
  of newborn 92, **1257**
Vitamin(s) **137–141,** 166, 176–194, 529
  in breast milk 152, *159*

Vitamin(s) (cont.)
  conditional vitamins 138, **139–140**
  cow's milk *159*
  deficiency diseases **176–194**
  estrogen-containing 1128
  obligatory vitamins **138–139**
  questionable vitamins 138, **140–141**
  requirements, of low-birth-weight infant 109
  supplementation in diet 141
Vitamin A 109, 138, **177–178**, 377, 424–428, 1584, 1809, 1824, 1867
  absorption test 424
  alcohol or acetate 425, 426
  in colostrum 150
  deficiency **177–178**
    in kwashiorkor 175
    in marasmus 172
  hypervitaminosis A 177, 178, **1741**, 1742
  intoxication **1741–1742**
    and pseudotumor cerebri 957
  in lipid malabsorption 1583
Vitamin B1 *see* Thiamine
Vitamin B2 *see* Riboflavin
Vitamin B6 *see* Pyridoxin
Vitamin B12 138, 329, 340, 405, **1163–1164**
  in kwashiorkor 174
  in neuroblastoma 1112
Vitamin B12a 138
Vitamin B12b 138
Vitamin C *see* Ascorbic acid
Vitamin D 109, 138, **139**, 141, 143, 144, 155, 161, 166, 195, **197–203**, 204, 207, 208, 210, 213, 428, 1867
  in breast milk 152
  D deficiency **197–203** (see also Rickets)
  in distal RTA **1525–1526**
  in Fanconi syndrome **1521**
  increased requirement for **203**
  intoxication 1508, 1527, 1536
    and cretinism **1070–1071**
  malabsorption **201**
  requirements **201**
  resistance, in chronic renal disease 1467
Vitamin D$_2$ *see* Ergocalciferol
Vitamin D$_3$ *see* Cholecalciferol
Vitamin D resistant rickets 197, **204–206**, 1519, 1699, 1721
  familial (primary hypophosphatemia) **204–205**
  with hyperglycinuria **1519**
  hypophosphatemic, of adolescence **205–206**
Vitamin E 109, 110, 138, **140**, 176, 428
  in beta lipoprotein deficiency **377**
  deficiency
    in cystic fibrosis 416
    and hemolytic anemia 110, **1187**
Vitamin K 106, 138, **139–140**, 201, 533, **1241**, 1672, 1679–1681
  and unconjugated hyperbilirubinemia 1679–1681
  in viral hepatitis 709
Vitelline duct **1618–1620**
Vitiligo 512, 892, 1799, *1800*, **1800–1801**
  in Addison's disease 1093
VKG *see* Vectorcardiography
VMA **1107–1113**
Vocabulary, and preschool child 257
Vocal cord paralysis 1285
Vocalizations 851
Vocational training, of mild retardates **896**

Vogt-Spielmeyer disease *see* Batten-Spielmeyer-Vogt disease
Voice, breaking of 241
Voiding cystourethrography **1549**
Vollmer patch test **682**
"Volume receptor" 1149
Voluntary agencies 9
Volvulus 1600, **1615**, 1621
  of mid-gut 1615
Vomiting 166, 207, 209, 212, 228, 334, 346, 357, 379, 409, 454, 456, 501, 529, 532, 537, 544, 569, 648, 770, 1527, **1573–1576**
  due to achalasia **1575–1576**
  in acute glomerulonephritis 1484
  in acute labyrinthitis 1042
  in amebiasis 828
  in amebic meningoencephalitis 830
  in appendicitis 1640
  in ascaris infection 802
  in bacterial meningitis **599–600**
  in black widow spider bite **844**
  in botulism 610
  in brain tumors **938**, 942, 943, 946, 947
  in candidiasis 796
  in carbohydrate malabsorption 1592
  in cerebral embolism 962
  due to chalasia 1575
  due to CNS disease 1574
  in craniocerebral trauma **968–975**
  in craniospinal focal sepsis **1010–1016**
  in cryptococcosis 794
  in dysautonomia **1040–1041**
  in gastric dilation 1652
  due to gastric distension **1573**
  hereditary fructose intolerance 359
  in herpangina 751
  hysterical 284
  induced, in poisoning **534–535**
  due to infections 1574
  in infections of nervous system **1011–1024**
  in intracranial bleeding 863
  in lymphocytic choriomeningitis 729
  in malaria 832
  in measles 732
  in mercury poisoning 549
  in migraine **1002**
  in neonatal narcotic withdrawal syndrome 574
  in neonatal period **1573**
  in neurologic disease **850, 1574**
  in peptic ulcer 1638
  in peritonitis **1648–1649**
  in phenylketonuria 323
  in poisoning, induced **534–535**
  in pseudo-motor cerebri 958
  psychogenic *see* Psychogenic vomiting
  in pyloric stenosis **1609**
  in renal insufficiency **1466**
  in renal tubular acidosis, distal **1525**
  in renal vein thrombosis 1534
  in Salmonella infections 636
  in scorpion sting 845
  in sepsis neonatorum 597
  in shigellosis 640
  in strongyloidiasis 808
  in subdural effusions 624
  in trichinosis 809
  in tuberculous meningitis 671

Vomiting (*cont.*)
  in tularemia 692
  in viral hepatitis 708
Von Hippel-Lindau's angiomatosis 929, 1814, 1826
  and pheochromocytoma 1109
Von Pirquet 442
Von Willebrand's disease 1229, **1236–1237**
Voracious appetite
  in carbohydrate malabsorption 1592
  in cystic fibrosis 426, 428
  in Graves' disease 1083
Vowel sounds 254
Vrolik's disease 1729
VSD *see* Ventricular septal defect
Vulvovaginitis **1544**, 1556
V-Z virus *see* Varicellazoster (V-Z) virus

Waardenburg's syndrome 1716, 1802, 1884, 1885
Waddling gait, in rickets 201
"Wakeup" 572
"Wakeups" 571
Waldeyer's ring 1877
Walking, automatic *see* Automatic walking
Walking difficulty 201
"Wall eyes" *see* Strabismus 1832
Walton's benign congenital hypotonia 1027
Wandering pacemaker 1367
Warfarin 12
  teratogenicity 12
Warm antibodies 1184
Warts *see* Verrucae
Wasp stings 555, 844
  and tetanus 659
Wassermann complement fixation test 654
  false positive
    in infectious mononucleosis 718
    in rat-bite fever 634
Water 141–142
  absorption, colonic **1569**
  balance **222–223**
    in fetal 49–50
    in renal failure 1464
  basal requirements *142*
  body **221–222**
  in burns **522–523**
    growth patterns of 237
  chemical homeostasis 222–223
  composition of body fluids **221–222**
  control of **1457–1458**
  in cretinism 1071
  deprivation test **1151**
  of diarrhea **228–229**
  diuresis **1149**
  and electrolyte physiology **221–228**
  extracellular 237
  homeostasis **221–222**
    primary disturbances of **1148–1153**
  intake, intoxication
    of fetus, due to oxytocin 56
  intracellular 237
    in diarrhea 229
    fetal 32
    in kwashiorkor 173
    in marasmus 171
  loss 141–142, 224, 522–523
  in nutrition 141–142

Water (*cont.*)
  physiologic expenditures 224
  requirements 141–142
  in transmission
    of diarrhea 228
    of leptospirosis 621
    of *Salmonellae* 636
    of *Vibrio cholerae* 612
Waterborne transmission, of viral hepatitis 710
Watercress 817
Waterhouse-Friderichsen syndrome 599, 606, 608, 624, **664**, 1094
"Waterproofing" recommendations 526
Water rats 692
Waterson-Cooley anastomosis 1405–1406
Waxes 538
Weaning **155–156**
Weasel 757
Webbed neck, in gonadal dysgenesis 1139
Webbed neck, ptosis, and hypogonadism syndrome, associated with congenital heart disease and short stature **1143–1144**
Webbing of the fingers 335
Weber-Christian's febrile relapsing panniculitis 514, **1768–1769**
Weber-Cockayne disease **1771**, *1772*
Wechsler Intelligence Scale for Children 265, 548
"Wedding bells" 572
"Weed" 572
Wegener's granulomatosis 514
Weighing, of newborn 77, 106
Weight **235–236**, 245, *1900*, **1904**
  and dehydration 229
  excess **214, 221**. *See also* Obesity.
  fetal 44
  gain
    in pheochromocytoma 1109
    during pregnancy 17
  loss 506, 514
    in diabetes mellitus 346
    in neuroblastoma 1111
  placental 44
  tables *215*
Weil-Felix reaction, **782–784**
  in Brill-Zinsser disease **782**
  in Q fever **784**
  in rickettsialpox **784**
  in Rocky Mountain spotted fever **782**
  in scrub typhus **783**
Weil's disease *see* Leptospirosis
Weinberg rule 118, 123
Welfare service **8**
Well-child supervision 8
Wenkebach's phenomenon 1369
Werdnig-Hoffman disease 923, **1325**
Wernicke's syndrome, in thiamine deficiency 179
Western equine encephalitis, 1016, **1017–1018**
Wet compresses 474
Wet dressings 475
Wet nursing **155**
Wharton's duct, in mumps **738**
Wheal and erythema reaction 477
Wheal and flare reaction 445, 449
Wheat contamination 531
  and acquired cutaneous porphyria 411
  and lathyrism 531
Wheat gluten 1587

Wheezing 418, 724, 1277
  in asthma **465–466**
  in bronchial adenoma 1289
  due to endobronchial tuberculosis 668
  in heart failure 1421
  in visceral larva migrans 802
Whiplash injuries 975
Whipworm *see Trichuris trichiura;* Trichuriasis
White blood cell casts 1541
White blood cells *see* Leucocytes
White forelock 1802, 1885
"White lightning" 571
White matter diseases *see* Cerebral white matter diseases
White pulp, splenic 1216
White reflex, in retinoblastoma 1830
"Whites" 571
"White stuff" 572
Whitfield's ointment 1791
Whooping cough *see* Pertussis
Whoop, of pertussis **628**
Whorled pigmentation 1804
Whorls, of fingers 313
Widal test **638**
Wiedemann-Beckwith syndrome 13, 115, **363**, 1030, **1848**
Wildervanck's syndrome 1716
"Wild" (nonepidemic), Staphylococci 645
Willis syndrome 219
Wilm's tumor 13, 1447, **1561**, 1693, 1706, 1745, 1827
  and aniridia 1827
  hypertension in 1447
Wilson-Mikity syndrome (pulmonary dysmaturity), 91, **1268–1270**
Wilson's disease 145, 198, 340, 356, **390–391**, 852, **920–921**, 1688, 1824
"Wing-beating" posture holding, in Wilson's disease, 852, 920
Winking 851
"Wired" 571
"Wire Loop" glomerular lesions, in systemic lupus erythematosus 508, **1493**
WISC *see* Wechsler Intelligence Scale for Children
Wiscott-Aldrich syndrome 473, 1807
"Wissler-Fanconi syndrome" 503
Wistar rat 1680
"Witches" milk 81
Withdrawal menses **1115–1116**, 1118
Withdrawal reactions 219, 270
Withdrawal syndrome *see* Abstinence syndrome
Wohlfahrtia 846
Wolf 755
Wolffian-Müllerian duct 1095
Wolff-Parkinson-White syndrome 1338, 1364, 1408
Wolman's disease (familial visceral xanthomatosis) 1688
Woodchuck 691
Wood's U.V. light 407, 1801
Wood tick 691, 781
Wool
  and atopic eczema 474
  and urticaria 477
Word deafness 276
"Works" 559
Worms *see* Parasites, helminths
Wounds, and tetanus 659
Wright's stain 733, 833
Wrist
  radiography for bone age **240**
  in rickets 201

Wristdrop 514
Writing 260
Wryneck *see* Torticollis, congenital
Wyburn-Mason syndrome 929

X-chromosome 204, **308–312**, 1132
  inactivation 299, 308
  monosomy (XO karyotype) 1139–1142
  X polysomy 1132
X and deleted X syndrome 310
X-inactivation hypothesis of Lyon 308
X-linkage 302, 1144
X-linked agammaglobulinemia **387**
X-linked trait **299**, *302*, 314, 372, 384
X or Y chromosome deletion (XXD or XYD) 1142
XO karyotype (gonadal dysgenesis) **1139–1142**
XO/X ring-X karyotype 1142
XO/XX/XXX mosaicism 1142
XO/XY/XYY mosaicism 1137
XX sex chromosomes **308–312**
XXX karyotype 309
XXXY karyotype 311, **1145**
XXY karyotype and variants **1144**
XXYY male **1144**
XY gonadal dysgenesis **1142–1143**
XY sex chromosomes 298, **308–312**
XY/XXY mosaicism 1134, 1144
XYY syndrome **1145**
Xanthelasma 376
Xanthine 340
Xanthine oxidase 146, 340
Xanthine oxidase inhibitor 1212
Xanthinuria **340**
Xanthochromia, of spinal fluid 868
Xanthogranulomatous pyelonephritis **1543**
Xanthomas 374, 375, 376, 1248
  of tendons 914
  tuberosum 1829
Xanthomatosis 1683
Xanthurenic acid 184
Xanthurenic aciduria, familial 185
Xenodiagnosis, in Chagas' disease 836
Xenopsyllus 819
Xeroderma pigmentosum **1803–1804**
Xerophthalmia 177, **1823–1824**
Xerosis *see* Xerophthalmia
Xylene 530
Xylidine 532
Xylocaine 1423
Xylose 359
Xylose tolerance test, in celiac disease **1585**
Xylulose 359

Y chromosome **308**, 312, **1132**
Yawning, in heroin withdrawal 562, 574
Yaws 652
Yellow fever 706
"Yellow jackets" 571
Yomesan *see* Niclosamide
YV plasty 1552

Zarontin (ethosuximide) **998–1000**
ZIG (zoster immune globulin) 702, 1213
Zinc 145

Zinc sulfate 1820
Zollinger-Ellison syndrome 1639
Zona fasciculata 1092
Zona glomerulosa 1092
Zona reticularis 1092

Zonular cataract 1826
Zoster see Herpes zoster
Zoster immune globulin (ZIG) 702, 1213
Zygapophysial arthritis, in rheumatoid arthritis 505, 506
Zygosity 302